2006 STANDARD POSTAGE STAMP CATALOGUE

ONE HUNDRED AND SIXTY-SECOND EDITION IN SIX VOLUMES

VOLUME 2
COUNTRIES OF THE WORLD
C-F

EDITOR	James E. Kloetzel
ASSOCIATE EDITOR	William A. Jones
ASSISTANT EDITOR /NEW ISSUES & VALUING	Martin J. Frankevicz
VALUING ANALYST	Leonard J. Gellman
DESIGN MANAGER	Teresa M. Wenrick
IMAGE COORDINATOR	Nancy S. Martin
MARKETING/SALES DIRECTOR	William Fay
ADVERTISING	Renee Davis
CIRCULATION/PRODUCT PROMOTION MANAGER	Tim Wagner
EDITORIAL DIRECTOR/AMOS PRESS INC.	Michael Laurence

Released May 2005
Includes New Stamp Listings through the June 2005 *Scott Stamp Monthly* Catalogue Update

Scott Publishing Co.

911 Vandemark Road, Sidney, OH 45365-0828
A division of AMOS PRESS, INC., publishers of *Scott Stamp Monthly, Linn's Stamp News, Coin World* and *Coin World's Coin Values.*

Table of Contents

See Volumes 1 for United States, United Nations and Countries of the World A-B
See Volume 3 through 6 for Countries of the World, G-Z.

Volume 3: G-I
Volume 4: J-O
Volume 5: P-Sl
Volume 6: So-Z

Scott Publishing Mission Statement

The Scott Publishing Team exists to serve the recreational, educational and commercial hobby needs of stamp collectors and dealers.

We strive to set the industry standard for philatelic information and products by developing and providing goods that help collectors identify, value, organize and present their collections.

Quality customer service is, and will continue to be, our highest priority. We aspire toward achieving total customer satisfaction.

Copyright Notice

Trademark Notice

ISBN 0-89487-352-0

Library of Congress Card No. 2-3301

Vol. 2 Number Additions, Deletions & Changes

Number in 2005 Catalogue	Number in 2006 Catalogue
Canada	
new	554a
new	554b
new	715b
new	979b
new	1621c
new	1699a
1878a	deleted
new	2001c
new	2004b
2007	1699
new	2011b
Cape of Good Hope	
new	4a
Cape Verde	
new	371
new	371A
new	RA9A
Central African Republic	
633	638
634	633
635	639
636	634
637	640
638	635
639	641
640	636
641	642
642	637
Chad	
515a	deleted
Colombia	
Tolima	
new	2a
Comoro Islands	
962-962	deleted
Costa Rica	
new	538a
Croatia	
116	146A
new	RA20c
new	RA21a
new	RA22a
new	RA23a
new	RA84b
Cyprus	
new	127a
Denmark	
new	357c
1120	1116
1120a	1116a
1121	1117
1121a	1117a
1121b	1117b
1121c	1117c
1122	1119
1122A	1120
1122Ab	1120a
1122Ac	1120b
1123	1121
1123a	1121a
1123B	1123
Ecuador	
new	778A
new	778B
new	780A
new	784A
Ethiopia	
54B	deleted
Falkland Islands	
new	11B
new	15c
new	15d
Finland	
166a	delete
522a	delete
522b	522a
France	
95a	95b
new	95a
new	154a
new	228a
new	333b
French Offices in China	
Port Said	
18	deleted
new	18a
French Offices in Zanzibar	
new	4a
17	deleted
new	17a
French Morocco	
new	135b
new	136b

Scott Publishing Co.

SCOTT 911 VANDEMARK ROAD, SIDNEY, OHIO 45365 937-498-0802

Dear Scott Catalogue User:

Color comes to the Scott Standard catalogues.

As I begin to write this letter for the 2006 Volume 2 *Scott Standard Postage Stamp Catalogue,* copies of the new Volume 1 catalogue have just arrived at our offices. There is no doubt that the color images of stamps that appear for the first time in the 2006 Standard catalogues will be the most striking feature of these new volumes. We hope that catalogue users will be as excited as we are over the improvement that color brings to the catalogues. Many collectors and dealers have already told us that they also like the new coated paper used in this year's catalogues. This new paper stock debuted in last year's U.S. Specialized and Classic Specialized catalogues.

More than 130,000 color stamp images have been scanned for the Standard catalogues. That amounts to approximately 98 percent of the stamp illustrations in these six volumes. We continue to fill in the other two percent of the images that are still in black and white. Our "want list" for scanning is now quite obvious to all who look through these volumes. If the stamp is shown in black and white, we need a nice unused example for scanning purposes. Of course this list will change month-by-month as we make new scans.

Color is only part of the story. There are a huge number of value changes.

There are almost 42,000 value changes in this Volume 2, which covers countries of the world C-F. This number of value changes is less than the 56,000+ changes recorded in the 2006 Volume 1, but it is still a very large number by historical standards. The figure is a full 10,000 more than the number of changes made in last year's Volume 2. As was the case in Volume 1, the changes are well spread throughout most of the countries of the volume, and almost all of the changes are upward value revisions.

One of the main reasons for this enormous quantity of upward value changes is the same phenomenon that we witnessed last year: worldwide currency fluctuations that have seen the U.S. dollar drop against other strong currencies. Once again, the euro, British pound, Australian dollar, New Zealand dollar, Canadian dollar and other currencies have gained significant strength in relation to the U.S. dollar.

As we pointed out in our introductory letter in last year's catalogs, the market for stamps denominated in euros, pounds and the other various strong currencies are largely made in the home countries, and anyone who wants to compete for those stamps must compete with those home-country buyers who are dealing in their own strong currencies. This means that it will take more U.S. dollars to buy those stamps, and it will take more U.S. dollars for U.S. dealers to replenish their stocks.

Being a retail value catalogue, Scott must react to this situation. In short, American collectors and dealers must realize that prices for stamps in U.S. dollars are up, and they must expect to pay more for desirable stamps if they want to be competitive in the worldwide marketplace.

We should also mention that our project of reviewing the more modern stamps from many nations continues. Stamps of a topical nature particularly are rising in price noticeably. This is true even of many quite recent issues. These changes in modern stamp values will help to swell the total number of value changes in this year's catalogues.

Where are the value changes in the 2006 Volume 2?

34,000 of the value changes in Volume 2 are in the non-British countries. The French area leads the way, with 1,925 value changes appearing in the French Offices Abroad section, followed by France itself (1,207), French Polynesia (1,724), Reunion (959), and lesser numbers in the other French areas. The trend in all these areas is toward higher values, often significantly so.

In France, the largest value increases are in the classic period. Typical of the size of the increases is shown by the 1869 5fr gray lilac Napoleon III, Scott 37, which rises in unused condition to $5,000 from $4,300 last year. In French Polynesia, increases are seen throughout, generally in the 10 to 20 percent range. Sometimes the changes are much greater, such as for the 1977 100fr Rubens art stamp, Scott C153, which jumps to $12 mint never hinged and $6.50 used, from just $7.25 mint never hinged and $3.50 used last year.

Other non-British Commonwealth countries with large numbers of changes are Ecuador (2,946), Central African Republic (2,594), People's Republic of Congo (2,211), Cameroun (1,573), Chile (1,379), Dahomey (1,175), Chad (1,116), Cape Verde (1,084) and Dominican Republic (1,035).

In Ecuador, values show a moderate advance in all time periods. Some changes are much more than moderate, such as many early airmails. The 1928 first airmail surcharges, Scott C1-C5, fly to $520 unused and $360 used, from $400 unused and $300 used last year.

Almost all the value changes in the stamps of the other countries showing high numbers of changes are value increases.

How about values for British-area stamps?

There are more than 7,000 value changes in the British areas. Several countries here show large numbers of value changes. Canada and Canadian Provinces show 1,526 changes, followed by Fiji (1,344), Falkland Islands (1,101) and Cayman Islands (902).

In Canada, values for a number of earlier issues are up while there are few changes in the more modern period.

The value changes in the Falkland Islands are spread throughout all periods with substantial increases in the earlier material, especially the 1904-46 issues. The 1933 Centenary set, Scott 65-76, moves to $3,555 unused and $4,508 used, from $3,270 unused and $4,242 used last year.

What's new on the editorial front?

In Canada, a number of new error varieties have been added. Also, the new $5 Moose stamp has had its number changed since its initial listing. It was listed as Scott 2007, but it has now been moved into its more logical position in the Scott 1673-1707 definitive series, and it has been reassigned Scott number 1699.

Three new major numbers have been added to the listings of Cape Verde. Two 4e stamps have been added to the 1976 "Republica / De" and row of stars overprints, and a 1972 30c postal tax stamp with an orange label has been added as Scott RA9A.

Scott numbers 952-962 have been deleted from Comoro Islands, as these stamps have been found to be illegal issues.

Four new surcharged stamps have been added to Ecuador's 1969 surcharge set, Scott 776-786. The new numbers are 778A, 778B, 780A and 784A. In Ethiopia, Scott 54B has been deleted from the listings. It is now believed by experts that this stamp was never an issued stamp but is rather one of the unofficial reproductions known in this country.

A new major number has been added to the Falkland Islands Queen Victoria definitives. Scott 11B is the 1891 1p pale red stamp. It is not an expensive variety. In fact, it is the least expensive of the 1p Victorias from the 1891-99 definitive set.

Happy collecting,

James E Kloetzel

James E. Kloetzel/Catalogue Editor

Acknowledgments

Our appreciation and gratitude go to the following individuals who have assisted us in preparing information included in this year's Scott Catalogues. Some helpers prefer anonymity. These individuals have generously shared their stamp knowledge with others through the medium of the Scott Catalogue.

Those who follow provided information that is in addition to the hundreds of dealer price lists and advertisements and scores of auction catalogues and realizations that were used in producing the catalogue values. It is from those noted here that we have been able to obtain information on items not normally seen in published lists and advertisements. Support from these people goes beyond data leading to catalogue values, for they also are key to editorial changes.

A special acknowledgment to Liane and Sergio Sismondo of The Classic Collector for their extraordinary assistance and knowledge sharing that has aided in the preparation of this year's Standard and Classic Specialized Catalogues.

Roland Austin
Robert Ausubel (Great Britain Collectors Club)
Dr. H.U. Bantz (S. W. Africa Stamp Study Group)
John Barone (Stamptracks)
Jack Hagop Barsoumian (International Stamp Co.)
William Batty-Smith (Sarawak Specialists' Society)
Vladimir Berrio-Lemm (CEFIN_PANAMA)
George G. Birdsall (Northland Auctions)
John Birkinbine II
Keith & Margie Brown
Mike Bush (Joseph V. Bush, Inc.)
John Cardoza
Tina & John Carlson (JET Stamps)
Richard A. Champagne (Richard A.Champagne, Inc.)
Henry Chlanda
Bob Coale
Leroy P. Collins III
Laurie Conrad
Frank D. Correl
Andrew Cronin (Canadian Society of Russian Philately)
Francis J. Crown, Jr.
Tony L. Crumbley (Carolina Coin and Stamp, Inc.)
Stephen R. Datz
Charles Deaton
Tom Derbyshire (University Stamp Co.)
John E. DeStefanis
Kenneth E. Diehl
Bob Dumaine
Mark Eastzer (Markest Stamp Co.)
Esi Ebrani
Paul G. Eckman
George Epstein (Allkor Stamp Co.)
Stephen G. Esrati
Henry Fisher
Joseph E. Foley (Eire Philatelic Association)
Jeffrey M. Forster
Robert S. Freeman
Ernest E. Fricks (France & Colonies Philatelic Society)
Richard Friedberg
Henry L. Gitner (Henry Gitner Philatelists, Inc.)
Michael A. Goldman (Regency Superior, Ltd.)
Daniel E. Grau
Fred F. Gregory
John B. Head
Bruce Hecht (Bruce L. Hecht Co.)
Philip J. Hughes (Croatian Philatelic Society)
Wilson Hulme
Doug Iams
Eric Jackson
Michael Jaffe (Michael Jaffe Stamps, Inc.)
Peter C. Jeannopoulos
Stephen Joe (International Stamp Service)
Richard Juzwin (Richard Juzwin PTY LTD)
Allan Katz (Ventura Stamp Company)
Stanford M. Katz
Lewis Kaufman (The Philatelic Foundation)
Dr. James W. Kerr
Charles F. Kezbers
William V. Kriebel
William Langs
Lester C. Lanphear III
Frederick P. Lawrence
Roberto Liera (AMEXFIL)
Ulf Lindahl (Ethiopian Philatelic Society)
Gary B. Little (Luxembourg Collectors Club)
Pedro Llach (Filatelia Llach S.L.)
Dennis Lynch
Robert L. Markovits (Quality Investors, Ltd.)
Marilyn R. Mattke
William K. McDaniel
Timothy M. McRee
Allen Mintz (United Postal Stationery Society)
Brian Moorhouse
William E. Mooz
Gary M. Morris (Pacific Midwest Co.)
Peter Mosiondz, Jr.
Bruce M. Moyer (Moyer Stamps & Collectibles)
Richard H. Muller (Richard's Stamps)
James Natale
Albert Olejnik
Victor Ostolaza
John E. Pearson (Pittwater Philatelic Service)
John Pedneault
Donald J. Peterson (International Philippine Philatelic Society)
Stanley M. Piller (Stanley M. Piller & Associates)
Virgil Pirvulescu
Todor Drumev Popov
Peter W. W. Powell
Stephen Radin (Albany Stamp Co.)
Ghassan D. Riachi
Eric Roberts
Peter A. Robertson
Omar Rodriguez
Michael Rogers (Michael Rogers, Inc.)
Jon W. Rose
Frans H. A. Rummens (International Bulletin for Netherlands Philately)
Mehrdad Sadri (Persiphila)
Richard H. Salz
Alex Schauss (Schauss Philatelics)
Jacques C. Schiff, Jr. (Jacques C. Schiff, Jr., Inc.)
Bernard Seckler (Fine Arts Philatelists)
Guy Shaw
Charles F. Shreve (Shreves Philatelic Galleries, Inc.)
Jeff Siddiqui (Pakistan Philatelic Study Circle)
Sergio & Liane Sismondo (The Classic Collector)
Jay Smith
Robert M. Spaulding (International Society for Japanese Philately)
Richard Stark
Jerry Summers
Peter Thy (Philatelic Society for Greater Southern Africa)
George P. Wagner
Philip T. Wall
Richard A. Washburn
Giana Wayman (Asociacion Filatélica de Costa Rica)
William R. Weiss, Jr. (Weiss Auctions)
Ed Wener (Indigo)
Ken Whitby
Don White (Dunedin Stamp Centre)
Kirk Wolford (Kirk's Stamp Company)
Urmas Wompa
Robert F. Yacano (K-Line Philippines)
Ralph Yorio
Val Zabijaka
Dr. Michal Zika (Album)
John P. Zuckerman (Siegel Auction Galleries, Inc.)
Alfonso G. Zulueta, Jr.

Addresses, Telephone Numbers, Web Sites, E-Mail Addresses of General & Specialized Philatelic Societies

Collectors can contact the following groups for information about the philately of the areas within the scope of these societies, or inquire about membership in these groups. Aside from the general societies, we limit this list to groups that specialize in particular fields of philately, particular areas covered by the Scott Standard Postage Stamp Catalogue, and topical groups. Many more specialized philatelic society exist than those listed below. These addresses are updated yearly, and they are, to the best of our knowledge, correct and current. Groups should inform the editors of address changes whenever they occur. The editors also want to hear from other such specialized groups not listed.

Unless otherwise noted all website addresses begin with http://

American Philatelic Society
100 Match Factory Place
Bellefonte PA 16823-1367
Ph: (814) 933-3803
www.stamps.org
E-mail: apsinfo@stamps.org

American Stamp Dealers' Association
Joseph Savarese
3 School St.
Glen Cove NY 11542
Ph: (516) 759-7000
www.asdaonline.com
E-mail: asda@erols.com

International Society of Worldwide Stamp Collectors
Anthony Zollo
PO Box 150407
Lufkin TX 75915-0407
www.iswsc.org
E-mail: stamptmf@frontiernet.net

Royal Philatelic Society
41 Devonshire Place
London, United Kingdom W1G 6JY
www.rpsl.org.uk
E-mail: secretary@rpsl.org.uk

Royal Philatelic Society of Canada
PO Box 929, Station Q
Toronto, ON, Canada M4T 2P1
Ph: (888) 285-4143
www.rpsc.org
E-mail: info@rpsc.org

Groups focusing on fields or aspects found in worldwide philately (some may cover U.S. area only)

American Air Mail Society
Stephen Reinhard
PO Box 110
Mineola NY 11501
www.americanairmailsociety.org
E-mail: sr1501@aol.com

American First Day Cover Society
Douglas Kelsey
PO Box 65960
Tucson AZ 85728-5960
Ph: (520) 321-0880
www.afdcs.org
E-mail: afdcs@aol.com

American Revenue Association
Eric Jackson
PO Box 728
Leesport PA 19533-0728
Ph: (610) 926-6200
www.revenuer.org
E-mail: eric@revenuer.com

American Topical Association
Ray E. Cartier
PO Box 57
Arlington TX 76004-0057
Ph: (817) 274-1181
americantopicalassn.org
E-mail: americantopical@msn.com

Errors, Freaks and Oddities Collectors Club
Jim McDevitt
955 S. Grove Blvd #65
Kingsland GA 31548-5263
Ph: (912) 729-1573
www.efoers.org
E-mail: cwouscg@aol.com

Fakes and Forgeries Study Group
Anthony Torres
107 Hoover Rd.
Rochester NY 14617-3611
E-mail: ajtorres@rochester.rr.com

First Issues Collectors Club
Kurt Streepy
P.O. Box 288
Clear Creek IN 47426-0288
www.firstissues.org
E-mail: orders@firstissues.org

International Philatelic Society of Joint Stamp Issues Collectors
Richard Zimmermann
124, Avenue Guy de Coubertin
Saint Remy Les Chevreuse, France F-78470
perso.club-internet.fr/rzimmerm/index.htm
E-mail: rzimmerm@club-internet.fr

National Duck Stamp Collectors Society
Anthony J. Monico
PO Box 43
Harleysville PA 19438-0043
www.hwcn.org/link/ndscs
E-mail: ndscs@hwcn.org

No Value Identified Club
Albert Sauvanet
Le Clos Royal B, Boulevard des Pas Enchantes
St. Sebastien-sur Loire, France 44230
E-mail: alain.vailly@irin.univ_nantes.fr

The Perfins Club
Bob Szymanski
10 Claridge Circle
Milford MA 01757
E-mail: perfinman@comcast.net

Post Mark Collectors Club
David Proulx
7629 Homestead Drive
Baldwinsville NY 13027
E-mail: stampdance@baldcom.net

Postal History Society
Kalman V. Illyefalvi
8207 Daren Court
Pikesville MD 21208-2211
Ph: (410) 653-0665

Precancel Stamp Society
Arthur Damm
176 Bent Pine Hill
North Wales PA 19454
Ph: (215) 368-6082
E-mail: sandamm@enter.net

United Postal Stationery Society
Cora Collins
PO Box 1792
Norfolk VA 23501-1792
www.upss.org
E-mail: poststat@juno.com

Groups focusing on U.S. area philately as covered in the Standard Catalogue

Canal Zone Study Group
Richard H. Salz
60 27th Ave.
San Francisco CA 94121

Carriers and Locals Society
John D. Bowman
232 Leaf Lane
Alabaster AL 35007
Ph: (205) 621-8449
www.pennypost.org
E-mail: johndbowman@charter.net

Confederate Stamp Alliance
Kevin Baker
3015 Fieldview Dr.
Murfreesboro TN 37128
www.csalliance.org
E-mail: kr.baker@comcast.net

Hawaiian Philatelic Society
Kay H. Hoke
PO Box 10115
Honolulu HI 96816-0115
Ph: (808) 521-5721
E-mail: bannan@pixi.com

Plate Number Coil Collectors Club
Frank Covey
16 Grandview Ave.
Macomb IL 61455
www.pnc3.org
president@pnc3.org

United Nations Philatelists
Blanton Clement, Jr.
P.O. Box 146
Morrisvile PA 19067-0146
www.unpi.com
E-mail: bclemjr@yahoo.com

United States Stamp Society
Executive Secretary
PO Box 6634
Katy TX 77491-6631
www.usstamps.org
E-mail: webmaster@usstamps.org

U.S. Cancellation Club
Roger Rhoads
6160 Brownstone Ct.
Mentor OH 44060
www.geocities.com/athens/2088/uscchome.htm
E-mail: rrrhoads@aol.com

U.S. Philatelic Classics Society
Mark D. Rogers
PO Box 80708
Austin TX 78708-0708
www.uspcs.org
E-mail: mrogers23@austin.rr.com

Groups focusing on philately of foreign countries or regions

Aden & Somaliland Study Group
Gary Brown
PO Box 106
Briar Hill, Victoria, Australia 3088
E-mail: garyjohn951@optushome.com.au

Albania Study Circle
Paul Eckman
PO Box 39880
Los Angeles CA 90039
E-mail: peckman797@earthlink.net

American Society of Polar Philatelists (Antarctic areas)
Alan Warren
PO Box 39
Exton PA 19341-0039
www.polarphilatelists.org
E-mail: alanwar@att.net

Andorran Philatelic Study Circle
D. Hope
17 Hawthorn Dr.
Stalybridge, Cheshire, United Kingdom SK15 1UE
www.chy-an-piran.demon.co.uk/
E-mail: apsc@chy-an-piran.demon.co.uk

Australian States Study Circle
Ben Palmer
GPO 1751
Sydney, N.S.W., Australia 1043

Austria Philatelic Society
Ralph Schneider
PO Box 23049
Belleville IL 62223
Ph: (618) 277-6152
www.apsus.esmartweb.com
E-mail: rschneider39@charter.net

American Belgian Philatelic Society
Walter D. Handlin
1303 Bullens Lane.
Woodlin, PA 19094
groups.hamptonroads.com/ABPS
E-mail: wdhandlin1@comcast.net

Bechuanalands and Botswana Society
Neville Midwood
69 Porlock Lane
Furzton, Milton Keynes, United Kingdom MK4 1JY
www.nevsoft.com
E-mail: bbsoc@nevsoft.com

Bermuda Collectors Society
Thomas J. McMahon
PO Box 1949
Stuart FL 34995
www.bermudacollectorssociety.org

Brazil Philatelic Association
William V. Kriebel
1923 ManningSt.
Philadelphia PA 19103-5728
Ph: (215) 735-3697
E-mail: kriebewv@drexel.edu

British Caribbean Philatelic Study Group
Dr. Reuben A. Ramkissoon
3011 White Oak Lane
Oak Brook IL 60523-2513
www.bcpsg.com
E-mail: rramkissoon@juno.com

British North America Philatelic Society (Canada & Provinces)
H. P. Jacobi
150 A St.
Surrey, B.C., Canada V4A 9W4
www.bnaps.org
E-mail: beaver@telus.net

British West Indies Study Circle
W. Clary Holt
PO Drawer 59
Burlington NC 27216
Ph: (336) 227-7461

Burma Philatelic Study Circle
A. Meech
7208 91st Ave.
Edmonton, AB, Canada T6B 0R8
E-mail: ameech@telusplanet.net

Ceylon Study Group
R. W. P. Frost
42 Lonsdale Road, Cannington
Bridgewater, Somerset, United Kingdom TA5 2JS

Channel Islands Specialists Society
Miss S. Marshall
1 Grove Farm Drive, Leeds
West Yorks, LL16 6DD
United Kingdom

China Stamp Society
Paul H. Gault
PO Box 20711
Columbus OH 43220
www.chinastampsociety.org
E-mail: secretary@chinastampsociety.org

Colombia/Panama Philatelic Study Group (CORAPHIL)
PO Box 2245
El Cajon CA 92021
www.copaphil.org
E-mail: jimacross@cts.com

Society for Costa Rica Collectors
Dr. Hector R. Mena
PO Box 14831
Baton Rouge LA 70808
www.socorico.org
E-mail: hrmena@aol.com

Croatian Philatelic Society (Croatia & other Balkan areas)
Ekrem Spahich
502 Romero, PO Box 696
Fritch TX 79036-0696
Ph: (806) 857-0129
www.croatianmall.com/cps/
E-mail: ou812@arn.net

Cuban Philatelic Society of America
Ernesto Cuesta
PO Box 34434
Bethesda MD 20827
www.philat.com/cpsa

Cyprus Study Circle
Jim Wigmore
19 Riversmeet, Appledore
Bideford, N. Devon, United Kingdom EX39 1RE
www.cyprusstudycircle.org/index.htm
E-mail: jameswigmore@aol.com

Society for Czechoslovak Philately
Peter Z. Kleskovic
27 Jay St.
Succasunna NJ 07876-1831
www.czechoslovakphilately.com

Danish West Indies Study Unit of the Scandinavian Collectors Club
John L. Dubois
Thermalogic Corp.
22 Kane Industrial Drive
Hudson MA 01749
Ph: (800) 343-4492
dwi.thlogic.com
E-mail: jld@thlogic.com

East Africa Study Circle
Ken Hewitt
16 Ashleigh Road
Solihull, United Kingdom B91 1AE
E-mail: EASC@ashleigh.me.uk

Egypt Study Circle
Mike Murphy
109 Chadwick Road
London, United Kingdom SE15 4PY
E-mail: egyptstudycircle@hotmail.com

Estonian Philatelic Society
Juri Kirsimagi
29 Clifford Ave.
Pelham NY 10803
Ph: (914) 738-3713

Ethiopian Philatelic Society
Ulf Lindahl
21 Westview Place
Riverside CT 06878
Ph: (203) 866-3540
members.home.net/fbheiser/ethiopia5.htm
E-mail: ulindahl@optonline.net

Falkland Islands Philatelic Study Group
Carl J. Faulkner
Williams Inn, On-the-Green
Williamstown MA 01267-2620
Ph: (413) 458-9371

Faroe Islands Study Circle
Norman Hudson
28 Enfield Road
Ellesmere Port, Cheshire, United Kingdom CH65 8BY
www.faroeislandssc.org.uk
E-mail: jntropics@hotmail.com

Former French Colonies Specialist Society
BP 628
75367 Paris Cedex 08, France
www.ifrance.com/colfra
E-mail: clubcolfra@aol.com

France & Colonies Philatelic Society
Walter Parshall
103 Spruce St.
Bloomfield NJ 07003-3514

Germany Philatelic Society
PO Box 779
Arnold MD 21012-4779
www.gps.nu
E-mail: germanyphilatelic@starpower.net

German Democratic Republic Study Group of the German Philatelic Society
Ken Lawrence
PO Box 210
Bellefonte PA 16823-0210
Ph: (814) 422-0625
E-mail: apsken@aol.com

Gibraltar Study Circle
www.abel.co.uk/~stirrups/GSC.HTM
E-mail: drstirrups@dundee.ac.uk

Great Britain Collectors Club
Parker A. Bailey, Jr.
PO Box 773
Merrimack NH 03054-0773
www.gbstamps.com/gbcc
E-mail: pbaileyjr@worldnet.att.net

Hellenic Philatelic Society of America (Greece and related areas)
Dr. Nicholas Asimakopulos
541 Cedar Hill Ave.
Wyckoff NJ 07481
Ph: (201) 447-6262
E-mail: nick1821@aol.com

International Society of Guatemala Collectors
Mrs. Mae Vignola
105 22nd Ave.
San Francisco CA 94121

Haiti Philatelic Society
Ubaldo Del Toro
5709 Marble Archway
Alexandria VA 22315
www.haitiphilately.org
E-mail: u007ubi@aol.com

Honduras Collectors Club
Jeff Brasor
PO Box 143383
Irving TX 75014

Hong Kong Stamp Society
Dr. An-Min Chung
3300 Darby Rd. Cottage 503
Haverford PA 19041-1064

Society for Hungarian Philately
Robert Morgan
2201 Roscomare Rd.
Los Angeles CA 90077-2222
www.hungarianphilately.org
E-mail: h.alan.hoover@hungarianphilately.org

India Study Circle
John Warren
PO Box 7326
Washington DC 20044
Ph: (202) 564-6876
www.indiastudycircle.org
E-mail: warren.john@epa.gov

Indian Ocean Study Circle
K. B. Fitton
50 Firlands
Weybridge, Surrey, United Kingdom KT13 0HR
www.stampdomain.com/iosc
E-mail: keithfitton@intonet.co.uk

Society of Indo-China Philatelists
Norman S. Davis
PO Box 290406
Brooklyn NY 11229

Iran Philatelic Study Circle
Mehdi Esmaili
PO Box 750096
Forest Hills NY 11375
www.iranphilatelic.org
E-mail: m.esmaili@earthlink.net

Eire Philatelic Association (Ireland)
Myron G. Hill III
PO Box 1210
College Park MD 20741-1210
eirephilatelicassoc.org
E-mail: mhill@radix.net

Society of Israel Philatelists
Paul S. Aufrichtig
300 East 42nd St.
New York NY 10017

Italy and Colonies Study Circle
Andrew D'Anneo
1085 Dunweal Lane
Calistoga CA 94515
www.icsc.pwp.blueyonder.co.uk
E-mail: audanneo@napanet.net

International Society for Japanese Philately
Kenneth Kamholz
PO Box 1283
Haddonfield NJ 08033
www.isjp.org
E-mail: isjp@comcast.net

Korea Stamp Society
John E. Talmage
PO Box 6889
Oak Ridge TN 37831
www.pennfamily.org/KSS-USA
E-mail: jtalmage@usit.net

Latin American Philatelic Society
Jules K. Beck
30 1/2 Street #209
St. Louis Park MN 55426-3551

Latvian Philatelic Society
Aris Birze
569 Rougemount Dr.
Pickering, ON, Canada L1W 2C1

Liberian Philatelic Society
William Thomas Lockard
PO Box 106
Wellston OH 45692
Ph: (740) 384-2020
E-mail: tlockard@zoomnet.net

Liechtenstudy USA (Liechtenstein)
Ralph Schneider
PO Box 23049
Belleville IL 62223
Ph: (618) 277-6152
www.rschneiderstamps.com/Liechtenstudy.htm
E-mail: rsstamps@aol.com

Lithuania Philatelic Society
John Variakojis
3715 W. 68th St.
Chicago IL 60629
Ph: (773) 585-8649
www.filatelija.lt/lps/
E-mail: variakojis@earthlink.net

Luxembourg Collectors Club
Gary B. Little
3304 Plateau Dr.
Belmont CA 94002-1312
www.luxcentral.com/stamps/LCC
E-mail: lcc@luxcentral.com

Malaya Study Group
Keith Elliot
78 Howard Road
Bournemouth, United Kingdom BH8 9ED
home.freeuk.net/johnmorgan/msg.htm

Malta Study Circle
Alec Webster
50 Worcester Road
Sutton, Surrey, United Kingdom SM2 6QB
E-mail: alecwebster50@hotmail.com

Mexico-Elmhurst Philatelic Society International
David Pietsch
PO Box 50997
Irvine CA 92619-0997
E-mail: mepsi@msn.com

Society for Moroccan and Tunisian Philately
206, bld. Pereire
75017 Paris, France
members.aol.com/Jhaik5814
E-mail: splm206@aol.com

Nepal & Tibet Philatelic Study Group
Roger D. Skinner
1020 Covington Road
Los Altos CA 94024-5003
Ph: (650) 968-4163
fuchs-online.com/ntpsc/
E-mail: Hepper@terra.es

American Society of Netherlands Philately
Jan Enthoven
221 Coachlite Ct. S.
Onalaska WI 54650
Ph: (608) 781-8612
www.cs.cornell.edu/Info/People/aswin/NL/neth
E-mail: jenthoven@centurytel.net

New Zealand Society of Great Britain
Keith C. Collins
13 Briton Crescent
Sanderstead, Surrey, United Kingdom CR2 0JN
www.cs.stir.ac.uk/~rgc/nzsgb
E-mail: rgc@cs.stir.ac.uk

Nicaragua Study Group
Erick Rodriguez
11817 S.W. 11th St.
Miami FL 33184-2501
clubs.yahoo.com/clubs/nicaraguastudygroup
E-mail: nsgsec@yahoo.com

Society of Australasian Specialists/Oceania
Henry Bateman
PO Box 4862
Monroe LA 71211-4862
Ph: (800) 571-0293 members.aol.com/stampsho/saso.html
E-mail: hbateman@jam.rr.com

Orange Free State Study Circle
J. R. Stroud
28 Oxford St.
Burnham-on-sea, Somerset, United Kingdom TA8 1LQ
www.ofssc.org
E-mail: jrstroud@classicfm.net

Pacific Islands Study Circle
John Ray
24 Woodvale Avenue
London, United Kingdom SE25 4AE
www.pisc.org.uk
E-mail: info@pisc.org.uk

Pakistan Philatelic Study Circle
Jeff Siddiqui
PO Box 7002
Lynnwood WA 98046
E-mail: jeffsiddiqui@msn.com

Centro de Filatelistas Independientes de Panama
Vladimir Berrio-Lemm
Apartado 0835-348
Panama, 10, Panama
E-mail: filatelia@cwpanama.net

Papuan Philatelic Society
Steven Zirinsky
PO Box 49, Ansonia Station
New York NY 10023
Ph: (718) 706-0616
E-mail: szirinsky@cs.com

International Philippine Philatelic Society
Robert F. Yacano
PO Box 100
Toast NC 27049
Ph: (336) 783-0768
E-mail: ryacano@tria.d.rr.com

Pitcairn Islands Study Group
Nelson A. L. Weller
2940 Wesleyan Lane
Winston-Salem NC 27106
Ph: (336) 724-6384
E-mail: nalweller@aol.com

Plebiscite-Memel-Saar Study Group of the German Philatelic Society
Clay Wallace
100 Lark Court
Alamo CA 94507
E-mail: clayw1@sbcglobal.net

Polonus Philatelic Society (Poland)
Arkadius Walinski
7414 Lincoln Ave. - D
Skokie IL 60076-3898
www.polonus.org

International Society for Portuguese Philately
Clyde Homen
1491 Bonnie View Rd.
Hollister CA 95023-5117
www.portugalstamps.com
E-mail: cjh1491@sbcglobal.net

Rhodesian Study Circle
William R. Wallace
PO Box 16381
San Francisco CA 94116
www.rhodesianstudycircle.org.uk
E-mail: bwall8rscr@earthlink.net

Canadian Society of Russian Philately
Andrew Cronin
PO Box 5722, Station A
Toronto, ON, Canada M5W 1P2
Ph: (905) 764-8968
www3.sympatico.ca/postrider/postrider
E-mail: postrider@sympatico.ca

Rossica Society of Russian Philately
Edward J. Laveroni
P.O. Box 320997
Los Gatos CA 95032-0116
www.rossica.org
E-mail: ed.laveroni@rossica.org

Ryukyu Philatelic Specialist Society
Carmine J. DiVincenzo
PO Box 381
Clayton CA 94517-0381

St. Helena, Ascension & Tristan Da Cunha Philatelic Society
Dr. Everett L. Parker
719 Moosehead Lake Rd.
Greenville ME 04441-9727
Ph: (207) 695-3163
ourworld.compuserve.com/homepages/ ST_HELENA_ASCEN_TDC
E-mail: eparker@midmaine.net

St. Pierre & Miquelon Philatelic Society
Jim Taylor
7704 Birch Bay Dr.
Blaine WA 98230
E-mail: jamestaylor@wavehome.com

Associated Collectors of El Salvador
Jeff Brasor
PO Box 143383
Irving TX 75014

Fellowship of Samoa Specialists
Jack R. Hughes
PO Box 1260
Boston MA 02117-1260
members.aol.com/tongaJan/foss.html

Sarawak Specialists' Society
Stu Leven
4031 Samson Way
San Jose CA 95124-3733
Ph: (408) 978-0193
www.britborneostamps.org.uk
E-mail: stulev@ix.netcom.com

Scandinavian Collectors Club
Donald B. Brent
PO Box 13196
El Cajon CA 92020
www.scc-online.org
E-mail: dbrent47@sprynet.com

Slovakia Stamp Society
Jack Benchik
PO Box 555
Notre Dame IN 46556

Philatelic Society for Greater Southern Africa
William C. Brooks VI
PO Box 4158
Cucamonga CA 91729-4158
Ph: (909) 484-2806
www.homestead.com/psgsa/index.html
E-mail: bbrooks@hss.co.sbcounty.gov

Spanish Philatelic Society
Robert H. Penn
1108 Walnut Drive
Danielsville PA 18038
Ph: (610) 767-6793

Sudan Study Group
Charles Hass
PO Box 3435
Nashua NH 03061-3435
Ph: (603) 888-4160
E-mail: hassstamps@aol.com

American Helvetia Philatelic Society (Switzerland, Liechtenstein)
Richard T. Hall
PO Box 15053
Asheville NC 28813-0053
www.swiss-stamps.org
E-mail: secretary@swiss-stamps.org

Tannu Tuva Collectors Society
Ken Simon
513 Sixth Ave. So.
Lake Worth FL 33460-4507
Ph: (561) 588-5954
www.seflin.org/tuva
E-mail: p003115b@pb.seflin.org

Society for Thai Philately
H. R. Blakeney
PO Box 25644
Oklahoma City OK 73125
E-mail: HRBlakeney@aol.com

Transvaal Study Circle
J. Woolgar
132 Dale Street
Chatham, Kent ME4 6QH, United Kingdom
www.transvaalsc.org

Ottoman and Near East Philatelic Society (Turkey and related areas)
Bob Stuchell
193 Valley Stream Lane
Wayne PA 19087
www.oneps.org
E-mail: president@oneps.org

Ukrainian Philatelic & Numismatic Society
George Slusarczuk
PO Box 303
Southfields NY 10975-0303
www.upns.org
E-mail: Yurko@warwick.net

Vatican Philatelic Society
Sal Quinonez
1 Aldersgate, Apt. 1002
Riverhead NY 11901-1830
Ph: (516) 727-6426

British Virgin Islands Philatelic Society
Roger Downing
PO Box 11156
St. Thomas VI 00801-1156
www.islandsun.com/FEATURES/bviphil9198.html
E-mail: issun@candwbvi.net

West Africa Study Circle
Dr. Peter Newroth
33-520 Marsett Place
Victoria, BC, Canada V8Z 7J1
www.wasc.org.uk/

Western Australia Study Group
Brian Pope
PO Box 423
Claremont, Western Australia, Australia 6910

Yugoslavia Study Group of the Croatian Philatelic Society
Michael Lenard
1514 North 3rd Ave.
Wausau WI 54401
Ph: (715) 675-2833
E-mail: mjlenard@aol.com

Topical Groups

Americana Unit
Dennis Dengel
17 Peckham Rd.
Poughkeepsie NY 12603-2018
www.americanaunit.org
E-mail: membership@americanaunit.org

Astronomy Study Unit

George Young
PO Box 632
Tewksbury MA 01876-0632
Ph: (978) 851-8283
www.fandm.edu/departments/astronomy/miscell/astunit.html
E-mail: george-young@msn.com

Bicycle Stamp Club
Norman Batho
358 Iverson Place
East Windsor NJ 08520
Ph: (609) 448-9547
members.tripod.com/~bicyclestamps
E-mail: normbatho@worldnet.att.net

Biology Unit
Alan Hanks
34 Seaton Dr.
Aurora, ON, Canada L4G 2K1
Ph: (905) 727-6993

Bird Stamp Society
G. P. Horsman
9 Cowley Drive, Worthy Down
Winchester, Hants., United Kingdom SO21 2OW
E-mail: rogerchapman@btinternet.com

Canadiana Study Unit
John Peebles
PO Box 3262, Station "A"
London, ON, Canada N6A 4K3
E-mail: john.peebles@sympatico.ca

Captain Cook Study Unit
Brian P. Sandford
173 Minuteman Dr.
Concord MA 01742-1923
www.captaincooksociety.com
E-mail:
USagent@captaincooksociety.com/

Casey Jones Railroad Unit
Bill Senkus
PO Box 4584
Walnut Creek CA 94596-4584
www.uqp.de/cjr/index.htm
E-mail: cjrru@att.net

Cats on Stamps Study Unit
Mary Ann Brown
3006 Wade Rd.
Durham NC 27705

Chemistry & Physics on Stamps Study Unit
Dr. Roland Hirsch
20458 Water Point Lane
Germantown MD 20874
www.cpossu.org
E-mail: rfhirsch@cpossu.org

Chess on Stamps Study Unit
Anne Kasonic
7625 County Road #153
Interlaken NY 14847
E-mail: akasonic@capital.net

Christmas Philatelic Club
Linda Lawrence
312 Northwood Drive
Lexington KY 40505
Ph: (859) 293-0151
www.hwcn.org/link/cpc
E-mail: stamplinda@aol.com

Christopher Columbus Philatelic Society
Donald R. Ager
PO Box 71
Hillsboro NH 03244-0071
Ph: (603) 464-5379
E-mail: meganddon@tds.net

Collectors of Religion on Stamps
Verna Shackleton
425 North Linwood Avenue #110
Appleton WI 54914
Ph: (920) 734-2417
www://my.vbe.com/~cmfourl/coros1.htm
E mail: corosec@sbcglobal.net

Dogs on Stamps Study Unit
Morris Raskin
202A Newport Rd.
Monroe Township NJ 08831
Ph: (609) 655-7411
www.dossu.org
E-mail: mraskin@cellurian.com

Earth's Physical Features Study Group
Fred Klein
515 Magdalena Ave.
Los Altos CA 94024
www.philately.com/society_news/earths _physical.htm

Ebony Society of Philatelic Events and Reflections (African-American topicals)
Manuel Gilyard
800 Riverside Drive, Ste 4H
New York NY 10032-7412
www.esperstamps.org
E-mail: gilyardmani@aol.com

Embroidery, Stitchery, Textile Unit
Helen N. Cushman
1001 Genter St., Apt. 9H
La Jolla CA 92037
Ph: (619) 459-1194

Europa Study Unit
Donald W. Smith
PO Box 576
Johnstown PA 15907-0576
E-mail: eunity@aol.com or donsmith65@msn.com

Fine & Performing Arts
Rachel S. Smith
8023 Mainsail Drive
Rohnert Park Ca 94928
E-mail: Rachel@nmc.org

Fire Service in Philately
Brian R. Engler, Sr.
726 1/2 W. Tilghman St.
Allentown PA 18102-2324
Ph: (610) 433-2782
E-mail: brenglersr@enter.net

Gay & Lesbian History on Stamps Club
Joe Petronie
PO Box 190842
Dallas TX 75219-0842
www.glhsc.org
E-mail: glhsc@aol.com

Gems, Minerals & Jewelry Study Unit
George Young
PO Box 632
Tewksbury MA 01876-0632
Ph: (978) 851-8283
www.rockhounds.com/rockshop/gmjsuapp.txt
E-mail: george-young@msn.com

Graphics Philately Association
Mark Winnegrad
PO Box 380
Bronx NY 10462-0380

Journalists, Authors & Poets on Stamps
Ms. Lee Straayer
P.O. Box 6808
Champaign IL 61826
E-mail: lstraayer@dcbnet.com

Lighthouse Stamp Society
Dalene Thomas
8612 West Warren Lane
Lakewood CO 80227-2352
Ph: (303) 986-6620
www.lighthousestampsociety.org
E-mail: dalene1@wideopenwest.com

Lions International Stamp Club
John Bargus
304-2777 Barry Rd. RR 2
Mill Bay, BC, Canada V0R 2P0
Ph: (250) 743-5782

Mahatma Gandhi On Stamps Study Circle
Pramod Shivagunde
Pratik Clinic, Akluj
Solapur, Maharashtra, India 413101
E-mail: drnanda@bom6.vsnl.net.in

Mask Study Unit
Carolyn Weber
1220 Johnson Drive, Villa 104
Ventura CA 93003-0540
www.home.prcn.org/~pauld/ata/units/masks.htm
E-mail: kencar@venturalink.net

Masonic Study Unit
Stanley R. Longenecker
930 Wood St.
Mount Joy PA 17552-1926
E-mail: natsco@usa.net

Mathematical Study Unit
Estelle Buccino
5615 Glenwood Rd.
Bethesda MD 20817-6727
Ph: (301) 718-8898
www.math.ttu.edu/msu/
E-mail: m.strauss@ttu.edu

Medical Subjects Unit
Dr. Frederick C. Skvara
PO Box 6228
Bridgewater NJ 08807
E-mail: fcskvara@bellatlantic.net

Mesoamerican Archeology Study Unit
Chris Moser
PO Box 1442
Riverside CA 92502
www.masu.homestead.com/info.html
E-mail:cmoser@ci.riverside.ca.us

Napoleonic Age Philatelists
Ken Berry
7513 Clayton Dr.
Oklahoma City OK 73132-5636
Ph: (405) 721-0044
E-mail: krb2@earthlink.net

Old World Archeological Study Unit
Eileen Meier
PO Box 369
Palmyra VA 22963
Ph: (434) 589-4222
www.owasu.org

Parachute Study Group
Bill Wickert
3348 Clubhouse Road
Virginia Beach VA 23452-5339
Ph: (757) 486-3614
E-mail: bw47psg@worldnet.att.net

Petroleum Philatelic Society International
Linda W. Corwin
5427 Pine Springs Court
Conroe TX 77304
Ph: (936) 441-0216
E-mail: corwin@pdq.net

Philatelic Computing Study Group
Robert de Violini
PO Box 5025
Oxnard CA 93031-5025
www.pcsg.org
E-mail: dviolini@adelphia.net

Philatelic Lepidopterists' Association
Alan Hanks
34 Seaton Dr.
Aurora, ON, Canada L4G 2K1
Ph: (905) 727-6933

Philatelic Music Circle
Cathleen Osborne
PO Box 1781
Sequim WA 98382
Ph: (360) 683-6373
www.stampshows.com/pmc.html

Rotary on Stamps Unit
Richard J. Dickson
PO Box 534
Irvington VA 22480
Ph: (804) 438-1178
E-mail: roshq@kaballero.com

Scouts on Stamps Society International
Carl Schauer
PO Box 526
Belen NM 87002
Ph: (505) 864-0098
www.sossi.org
E-mail: rfrank@sossi.org

Ships on Stamps Unit
Robert Stuckert
2750 Highway 21 East
Paint Lick KY 40461
Ph: (859) 925-4901
www.shipsonstamps.org

Space Unit
Carmine Torrisi
PO Box 780241
Maspeth NY 11378
Ph: (718) 386-7882
stargate.1usa.com/stamps/
E-mail: ctorrisi1@juno.com

Sports Philatelists International
Margaret Jones
5310 Lindenwood Ave.
St. Louis MO 63109-1758
www.sportstamps.org

Stamps on Stamps Collectors Club
Alf Jordan
156 West Elm Street
Yarmouth ME 04096
Ph: (650) 234-1136
www.stampsonstamps.org
E-mail: ajordan1@maine.rr.com

Windmill Study Unit
Walter J. Hollien
PO Box 346
Long Valley NJ 07853-0346
Ph: (908) 876-3672

Wine on Stamps Study Unit
James D. Crum
816 Kingsbury Ct.
Arroyo Grande CA 93420-4517
Ph: (805) 489-3559
E-mail: jdakcrum@aol.com

Women on Stamps Study Unit
Hugh Gottfried
2232 26th St.
Santa Monica CA 90405-1902
E-mail: hgottfried@adelphia.net

Zeppelin Collectors Club
Cheryl Ganz
PO Box A3843
Chicago IL 60690-3843

Expertizing Services

The following organizations will, for a fee, provide expert opinions about stamps submitted to them. Collectors should contact these organizations to find out about their fees andrequirements before submitting philatelic material to them. The listing of these groups here is not intended as an endorsement by Scott Publishing Co.

General Expertizing Services

American Philatelic Expertizing Service (a service of the American Philatelic Society)
100 Match Factory Place
Bellefonte PA 16823-1367
Ph: (814) 237-3803
Fax: (814) 237-6128
www.stamps.org
E-mail: ambristo@stamps.org
Areas of Expertise: Worldwide

B. P. A. Expertising, Ltd.
PO Box 137
Leatherhead, Surrey, United Kingdom KT22 0RG
E-mail: sec.bpa@tcom.co.uk
Areas of Expertise: British Commonwealth, Great Britain, Classics of Europe, South America and the Far East

Philatelic Foundation
70 West 40th St., 15th Floor
New York NY 10018
Ph: (212) 221-6555
Fax: (212) 221-6208
www.philatelicfoundation.org
E-mail:philatelicfoundation@verizon.net
Areas of Expertise: U.S. & Worldwide

Professional Stamp Experts
PO Box 6170
Newport Beach CA 92658
Ph: (877) STAMP-88
Fax: (949) 833-7955
www.collectors.com/pse
E-mail: pseinfo@collectors.com
Areas of Expertise: Stamps and covers of U.S., U.S. Possessions, British Commonwealth

Royal Philatelic Society Expert Committee
41 Devonshire Place
London, United Kingdom W1N 1PE
www.rpsl.org.uk/experts.html
E-mail: experts@rpsl.org.uk
Areas of Expertise: All

Expertizing Services Covering Specific Fields Or Countries

Canadian Society of Russian Philately Expertizing Service
PO Box 5722, Station A
Toronto, ON, Canada M5W 1P2
Fax: (416)932-0853
Areas of Expertise: Russian areas

China Stamp Society Expertizing Service
1050 West Blue Ridge Blvd
Kansas City MO 64145
Ph: (816) 942-6300
E-mail: hjmesq@aol.com
Areas of Expertise: China

Confederate Stamp Alliance Authentication Service
c/o Patricia A. Kaufmann
10194 N. Old State Road
Lincoln DE 19960-9797
Ph: (302) 422-2656
Fax: (302) 424-1990
www.webuystamps.com/csaauth.htm
E-mail: trish@ce.net
Areas of Expertise: Confederate stamps and postal history

Croatian Philatelic Society Expertizing Service
PO Box 696
Fritch TX 79036-0696
Ph: (806) 857-0129
E-mail: ou812@arn.net
Areas of Expertise: Croatia and other Balkan areas

Errors, Freaks and Oddities Collectors Club Expertizing Service
138 East Lakemont Dr.
Kingsland GA 31548
Ph: (912) 729-1573
Areas of Expertise: U.S. errors, freaks and oddities

Estonian Philatelic Society Expertizing Service
39 Clafford Lane
Melville NY 11747
Ph: (516) 421-2078
E-mail: esto4@aol.com
Areas of Expertise: Estonia

Hawaiian Philatelic Society Expertizing Service
PO Box 10115
Honolulu HI 96816-0115
Areas of Expertise: Hawaii

Hong Kong Stamp Society Expertizing Service
PO Box 206
Glenside PA 19038
Fax: (215) 576-6850
Areas of Expertise: Hong Kong

International Association of Philatelics Experts
United States Associate members:

Paul Buchsbayew
119 W. 57th St.
New York NY 10019
Ph: (212) 977-7734
Fax: (212) 977-8653
Areas of Expertise: Russia, Soviet Union

William T.Crowe
(see Professional Stamp Experts)
Areas of Expertise: United States

John Lievsay
(see American Philatelic Expertizing Service and Philatelic Foundation)
Areas of Expertise: France

Robert W. Lyman
P.O. Box 348
Irvington on Hudson NY 10533
Ph and Fax: (914) 591-6937
Areas of Expertise: British North America, New Zealand

Robert Odenweller
P.O. Box 401
Bernardsville, NJ 07924-0401
Ph and Fax: (908) 766-5460
Areas of Expertise: New Zealand, Samoa to 1900

Alex Rendon
P.O. Box 323
Massapequa NY 11762
Ph and Fax: (516) 795-0464
Areas of Expertise: Bolivia, Colombia, Colombian States

Sergio Sismondo
10035 Carousel Center Dr.
Syracuse NY 13290-0001
Ph: (315) 422-2331
Fax: (315) 422-2956
Areas of Expertise: British East Africa, Camerouns, Cape of Good Hope, Canada, British North America

International Society for Japanese Philately Expertizing Committee
32 King James Court
Staten Island NY 10308-2910
Ph: (718) 227-5229
Areas of Expertise: Japan and related areas, except WWII Japanese Occupation issues

International Society for Portuguese Philately Expertizing Service
PO Box 43146
Philadelphia PA 19129-3146
Ph: (215) 843-2106
Fax: (215) 843-2106
E-mail: s.s.washburne@worldnet.att.net
Areas of Expertise: Portugal and colonies

Mexico-Elmhurst Philatelic Society International Expert Committee
PO Box 1133
West Covina CA 91793
Areas of Expertise: Mexico

Philatelic Society for Greater Southern Africa Expert Panel
13955 W. 30th Ave.
Golden CO 80401
Areas of expertise: Entire South and South West Africa area, Bechuanalands, Basutoland, Swaziland

Ukrainian Philatelic & Numismatic Society Expertizing Service
30552 Dell Lane
Warren MI 48092-1862
Ph: (810) 751-5754
Areas of Expertise: Ukraine, Western Ukraine

V. G. Greene Philatelic Research Foundation
P.O. Box 204, Station Q
Toronto, ON, Canada M4T 2M1
Ph: (416) 921-2073
Fax: (416) 921-1282
E-mail: vggfoundation@on.aibn.com
www.greenefoundation.ca
Areas of Expertise: British North America

Information on Catalogue Values, Grade and Condition

Catalogue Value

The Scott Catalogue value is a retail value; that is, an amount you could expect to pay for a stamp in the grade of Very Fine with no faults. Any exceptions to the grade valued will be noted in the text. The general introduction on the following pages and the individual section introductions further explain the type of material that is valued. The value listed for any given stamp is a reference that reflects recent actual dealer selling prices for that item.

Dealer retail price lists, public auction results, published prices in advertising and individual solicitation of retail prices from dealers, collectors and specialty organizations have been used in establishing the values found in this catalogue. Scott Publishing Co. values stamps, but Scott is not a company engaged in the business of buying and selling stamps as a dealer.

Use this catalogue as a guide for buying and selling. The actual price you pay for a stamp may be higher or lower than the catalogue value because of many different factors, including the amount of personal service a dealer offers, or increased or decreased interest in the country or topic represented by a stamp or set. An item may occasionally be offered at a lower price as a "loss leader," or as part of a special sale. You also may obtain an item inexpensively at public auction because of little interest at that time or as part of a large lot.

Stamps that are of a lesser grade than Very Fine, or those with condition problems, generally trade at lower prices than those given in this catalogue. Stamps of exceptional quality in both grade and condition often command higher prices than those listed.

Values for pre-1900 unused issues are for stamps with approximately half or more of their original gum. Stamps with most or all of their original gum may be expected to sell for more, and stamps with less than half of their original gum may be expected to sell for somewhat less than the values listed. On rarer stamps, it may be expected that the original gum will be somewhat more disturbed than it will be on more common issues. Post-1900 unused issues are assumed to have full original gum. From breakpoints in most countries' listings, stamps are valued as never hinged, due to the wide availability of stamps in that condition. These notations are prominently placed in the listings and in the country information preceding the listings. Some countries also feature listings with dual values for hinged and never-hinged stamps.

Grade

A stamp's grade and condition are crucial to its value. The accompanying illustrations show examples of Very Fine stamps from different time periods, along with examples of stamps in Fine to Very Fine and Extremely Fine grades as points of reference. When a stamp seller offers a stamp in any grade from fine to superb without further qualifying statements, that stamp should not only have the centering grade as defined, but it also should be free of faults or other condition problems.

FINE stamps (illustrations not shown) have designs that are quite off center, with the perforations on one or two sides very close to the design but not quite touching it. There is white space between the perforations and the design that is minimal but evident to the unaided eye. Imperforate stamps may have small margins, and earlier issues may show the design just touching one edge of the stamp design. Very early perforated issues normally will have the perforations slightly cutting into the design. Used stamps may have heavier than usual cancellations.

FINE-VERY FINE stamps will be somewhat off center on one side, or slightly off center on two sides. Imperforate stamps will have two margins of at least normal size, and the design will not touch any edge. For perforated stamps, the perfs are well clear of the design, but are still noticeably off center. *However, early issues of a country may be printed in such a way that the design naturally is very close to the edges. In these cases, the perforations may cut into the design very slightly.* Used stamps will not have a cancellation that detracts from the design.

VERY FINE stamps will be just slightly off center on one or two sides, but the design will be well clear of the edge. The stamp will present a nice, balanced appearance. Imperforate stamps will be well centered within normal-sized margins. *However, early issues of many countries may be printed in such a way that the perforations may touch the design on one or more sides. Where this is the case, a boxed note will be found defining the centering and margins of the stamps being valued.* Used stamps will have light or otherwise neat cancellations. This is the grade used to establish Scott Catalogue values.

EXTREMELY FINE stamps are close to being perfectly centered. Imperforate stamps will have even margins that are slightly larger than normal. Even the earliest perforated issues will have perforations clear of the design on all sides.

Scott Publishing Co. recognizes that there is no formally enforced grading scheme for postage stamps, and that the final price you pay or obtain for a stamp will be determined by individual agreement at the time of transaction.

Condition

Grade addresses only centering and (for used stamps) cancellation. *Condition* refers to factors other than grade that affect a stamp's desirability.

Factors that can increase the value of a stamp include exceptionally wide margins, particularly fresh color, the presence of selvage, and plate or die varieties. Unusual cancels on used stamps (particularly those of the 19th century) can greatly enhance their value as well.

Factors other than faults that decrease the value of a stamp include loss of original gum, regumming, a hinge remnant or foreign object adhering to the gum, natural inclusions, straight edges, and markings or notations applied by collectors or dealers.

Faults include missing pieces, tears, pin or other holes, surface scuffs, thin spots, creases, toning, short or pulled perforations, clipped perforations, oxidation or other forms of color changelings, soiling, stains, and such man-made changes as reperforations or the chemical removal or lightening of a cancellation.

Grading Illustrations

On the following two pages are illustrations of various stamps from countries appearing in this volume. These stamps are arranged by country, and they represent early or important issues that are often found in widely different grades in the marketplace. The editors believe the illustrations will prove useful in showing the margin size and centering that will be seen on the various issues.

In addition to the matters of margin size and centering, collectors are reminded that the very fine stamps valued in the Scott catalogues also will possess fresh color and intact perforations, and they will be free from defects.

Most examples shown are computer-manipulated images made from single digitized master illustrations.

Stamp Illustrations Used in the Catalogue

It is important to note that the stamp images used for identification purposes in this catlaogue may not be indicative of the grade of stamp being valued. Refer to the written discussion of grades on this page and to the grading illustrations on the following two pages for grading information.

Fine-Very Fine

SCOTT CATALOGUES VALUE STAMPS IN THIS GRADE

Very Fine

Extremely Fine

Fine-Very Fine

SCOTT CATALOGUES VALUE STAMPS IN THIS GRADE

Very Fine

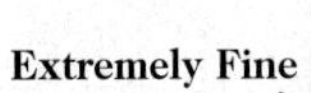

Fine-Very Fine
SCOTT CATALOGUES VALUE STAMPS IN THIS GRADE
Very Fine
Extremely Fine
Fine-Very Fine
SCOTT CATALOGUES VALUE STAMPS IN THIS GRADE
Very Fine
Extremely Fine

For purposes of helping to determine the gum condition and value of an unused stamp, Scott Publishing Co. presents the following chart which details different gum conditions and indicates how the conditions correlate with the Scott values for unused stamps. Used together, the Illustrated Grading Chart on the previous pages and this Illustrated Gum Chart should allow catalogue users to better understand the grade and gum condition of stamps valued in the Scott catalogues.

Gum Categories:	**MINT N.H.**	**ORIGINAL GUM (O.G.)**				**NO GUM**
	 **Mint Never Hinged** *Free from any disturbance*	 **Lightly Hinged** *Faint impression of a removed hinge over a small area*	 **Hinge Mark or Remnant** *Prominent hinged spot with part or all of the hinge remaining*	 **Large part o.g.** *Approximately half or more of the gum intact*	**Small part o.g.** *Approximately less than half of the gum intact*	 **No gum** *Only if issued with gum*
Commonly Used Symbol:	★★	★	★	★	★	(★)
Pre-1900 Issues (Pre-1890 for U.S.)	*Very fine pre-1900 stamps in these categories trade at a premium over Scott value*			Scott Value for "Unused"		Scott "No Gum" listings for selected unused classic stamps
From 1900 to breakpoints for listings of never-hinged stamps	Scott "Never Hinged" listings for selected unused stamps	Scott Value for "Unused" (Actual value will be affected by the degree of hinging of the full o.g.)				
From breakpoints noted for many countries	Scott Value for "Unused"					

Never Hinged (NH; ★★): A never-hinged stamp will have full original gum that will have no hinge mark or disturbance. The presence of an expertizer's mark does not disqualify a stamp from this designation.

Original Gum (OG; ★): Pre-1900 stamps should have approximately half or more of their original gum. On rarer stamps, it may be expected that the original gum will be somewhat more disturbed that it will be on more common issues. Post-1900 stamps should have full original gum. Original gum will show some disturbance caused by a previous hinge(s) which may be present or entirely removed. The actual value of a post-1900 stamp will be affected by the degree of hinging of the full original gum.

Disturbed Original Gum: Gum showing noticeable effects of humidity, climate or hinging over more than half of the gum. The significance of gum disturbance in valuing a stamp in any of the Original Gum categories depends on the degree of disturbance, the rarity and normal gum condition of the issue and other variables affecting quality.

Regummed (RG; (★)): A regummed stamp is a stamp without gum that has had some type of gum privately applied at a time after it was issued. This normally is done to deceive collectors and/or dealers into thinking that the stamp has original gum and therefore has a higher value. A regummed stamp is considered the same as a stamp with none of its original gum for purposes of grading.

Understanding the Listings

On the opposite page is an enlarged "typical" listing from this catalogue. Below are detailed explanations of each of the highlighted parts of the listing.

1 Scott number — Scott catalogue numbers are used to identify specific items when buying, selling or trading stamps. Each listed postage stamp from every country has a unique Scott catalogue number. Therefore, Germany Scott 99, for example, can only refer to a single stamp. Although the Scott catalogue usually lists stamps in chronological order by date of issue, there are exceptions. When a country has issued a set of stamps over a period of time, those stamps within the set are kept together without regard to date of issue. This follows the normal collecting approach of keeping stamps in their natural sets.

When a country issues a set of stamps over a period of time, a group of consecutive catalogue numbers is reserved for the stamps in that set, as issued. If that group of numbers proves to be too few, capital-letter suffixes, such as "A" or "B," may be added to existing numbers to create enough catalogue numbers to cover all items in the set. A capital-letter suffix indicates a major Scott catalogue number listing. Scott uses a suffix letter only once. Therefore, a catalogue number listing with a capital-letter suffix will not also be found with the same letter (lower case) used as a minor-letter listing. If there is a Scott 16A in a set, for example, there will not also be a Scott 16a. However, a minor-letter "a" listing may be added to a major number containing an "A" suffix (Scott 16Aa, for example).

Suffix letters are cumulative. A minor "b" variety of Scott 16A would be Scott 16Ab, not Scott 16b.

There are times when a reserved block of Scott catalogue numbers is too large for a set, leaving some numbers unused. Such gaps in the numbering sequence also occur when the catalogue editors move an item's listing elsewhere or have removed it entirely from the catalogue. Scott does not attempt to account for every possible number, but rather attempts to assure that each stamp is assigned its own number.

Scott numbers designating regular postage normally are only numerals. Scott numbers for other types of stamps, such as air post, semi-postal, postal tax, postage due, occupation and others have a prefix consisting of one or more capital letters or a combination of numerals and capital letters.

2 Illustration number — Illustration or design-type numbers are used to identify each catalogue illustration. For most sets, the lowest face-value stamp is shown. It then serves as an example of the basic design approach for other stamps not illustrated. Where more than one stamp use the same illustration number, but have differences in design, the design paragraph or the description line clearly indicates the design on each stamp not illustrated. Where there are both vertical and horizontal designs in a set, a single illustration may be used, with the exceptions noted in the design paragraph or description line.

When an illustration is followed by a lower-case letter in parentheses, such as "A2(b)," the trailing letter indicates which overprint or surcharge illustration applies.

Illustrations normally are 70 percent of the original size of the stamp. An effort has been made to note all illustrations not illustrated at that percentage. Virtually all souvenir sheet illustrations are reduced even more. Overprints and surcharges are shown at 100 percent of their original size if shown alone, but are 70 percent of original size if shown on stamps. In some cases, the illustration will be placed above the set, between listings or omitted completely. Overprint and surcharge illustrations are not placed in this catalogue for purposes of expertizing stamps.

3 Paper color — The color of a stamp's paper is noted in italic type when the paper used is not white.

4 Listing styles — There are two principal types of catalogue listings: major and minor.

Major listings are in a larger type style than minor listings. The catalogue number is a numeral that can be found with or without a capital-letter suffix, and with or without a prefix.

Minor listings are in a smaller type style and have a small-letter suffix or (if the listing immediately follows that of the major number) may show only the letter. These listings identify a variety of the major item. Examples include perforation, color, watermark or printing method differences, multiples (some souvenir sheets, booklet panes and se-tenant combinations), and singles of multiples.

Examples of major number listings include 16, 28A, B97, C13A, 10N5, and 10N6A. Examples of minor numbers are 16a and C13Ab.

5 Basic information about a stamp or set — Introducing each stamp issue is a small section (usually a line listing) of basic information about a stamp or set. This section normally includes the date of issue, method of printing, perforation, watermark and, sometimes, some additional information of note. *Printing method, perforation and watermark apply to the following sets until a change is noted.* Stamps created by overprinting or surcharging previous issues are assumed to have the same perforation, watermark and printing method as the original. Dates of issue are as precise as Scott is able to confirm and often reflect the dates on first-day covers, rather than the actual date of release.

6 Denomination — This normally refers to the face value of the stamp; that is, the cost of the unused stamp at the post office at the time of issue. When a denomination is shown in parentheses, it does not appear on the stamp. This includes the non-denominated stamps of the United States, Brazil and Great Britain, for example.

7 Color or other description — This area provides information to solidify identification of a stamp. In many recent cases, a description of the stamp design appears in this space, rather than a listing of colors.

8 Year of issue — In stamp sets that have been released in a period that spans more than a year, the number shown in parentheses is the year that stamp first appeared. Stamps without a date appeared during the first year of the issue. Dates are not always given for minor varieties.

9 Value unused and Value used — The Scott catalogue values are based on stamps that are in a grade of Very Fine unless stated otherwise. Unused values refer to items that have not seen postal, revenue or any other duty for which they were intended. Pre-1900 unused stamps that were issued with gum must have at least most of their original gum. Later issues are assumed to have full original gum. From breakpoints specified in most countries' listings, stamps are valued as never hinged. Stamps issued without gum are noted. Modern issues with PVA or other synthetic adhesives may appear ungummed. Self-adhesive stamps are valued as appearing undisturbed on their original backing paper. For a more detailed explanation of these values, please see the "Catalogue Value," "Condition" and "Understanding Valuing Notations" sections elsewhere in this introduction.

In some cases, where used stamps are more valuable than unused stamps, the value is for an example with a contemporaneous cancel, rather than a modern cancel or a smudge or other unclear marking. For those stamps that were released for postal and fiscal purposes, the used value represents a postally used stamp. Stamps with revenue cancels generally sell for less. Scott values for used self-adhesive stamps are for examples either on piece or off piece.

Stamps separated from a complete se-tenant multiple usually will be worth less than a pro-rated portion of the se-tenant multiple, and stamps lacking the attached labels that are noted in the listings will be worth less than the values shown.

10 Changes in basic set information — Bold type is used to show any changes in the basic data given for a set of stamps. This includes perforation differences from one stamp to the next or a different paper, printing method or watermark.

11 Total value of a set — The total value of sets of three or more stamps issued after 1900 are shown. The set line also notes the range of Scott numbers and total number of stamps included in the grouping. The actual value of a set consisting predominantly of stamps having the minimum value of twenty cents may be less than the total value shown. Similary, the actual value or catalogue value of se-tenant pairs or of blocks consisting of stamps having the minimum value of twenty cents may be less than the catalogue values of the component parts.

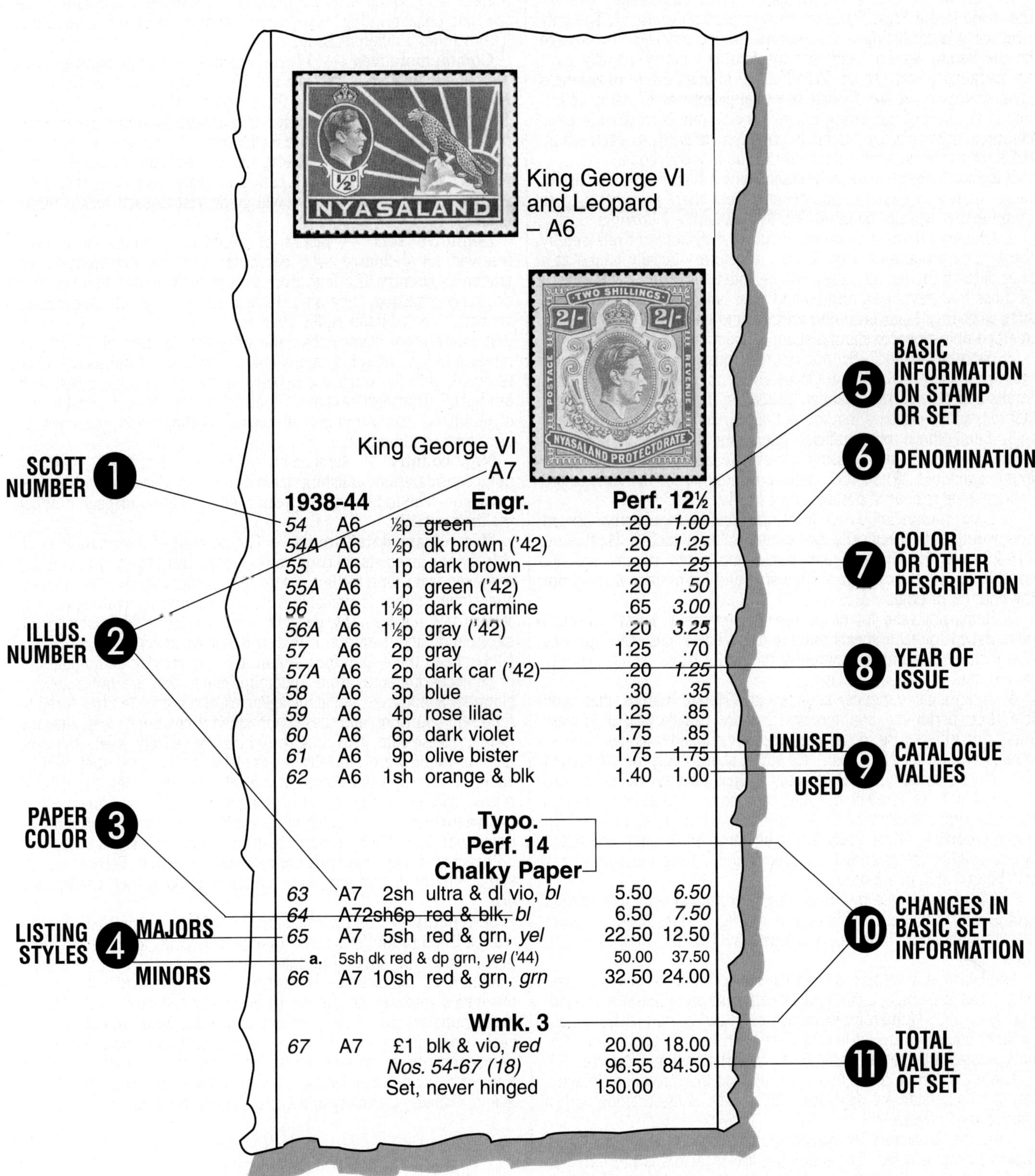
NYASALAND
King George VI
and Leopard
– A6
TWO SHILLINGS
2/- 2/-
POSTAGE
REVENUE
NYASALAND PROTECTORATE
King George VI
A7
1938-44 Engr. Perf. 12½
54 A6 ½p green .20 1.00
54A A6 ½p dk brown ('42) .20 1.25
55 A6 1p dark brown .20 .25
55A A6 1p green ('42) .20 .50
56 A6 1½p dark carmine .65 3.00
56A A6 1½p gray ('42) .20 3.25
57 A6 2p gray 1.25 .70
57A A6 2p dark car ('42) .20 1.25
58 A6 3p blue .30 .35
59 A6 4p rose lilac 1.25 .85
60 A6 6p dark violet 1.75 .85
61 A6 9p olive bister 1.75 1.75
62 A6 1sh orange & blk 1.40 1.00
Typo.
Perf. 14
Chalky Paper
63 A7 2sh ultra & dl vio, bl 5.50 6.50
64 A7 2sh6p red & blk, bl 6.50 7.50
65 A7 5sh red & grn, yel 22.50 12.50
a. 5sh dk red & dp grn, yel ('44) 50.00 37.50
66 A7 10sh red & grn, grn 32.50 24.00
Wmk. 3
67 A7 £1 blk & vio, red 20.00 18.00
Nos. 54-67 (18) 96.55 84.50
Set, never hinged 150.00
SCOTT NUMBER 1
ILLUS. NUMBER 2
PAPER COLOR 3
LISTING STYLES 4
MAJORS
MINORS
5 BASIC INFORMATION ON STAMP OR SET
6 DENOMINATION
7 COLOR OR OTHER DESCRIPTION
8 YEAR OF ISSUE
UNUSED
USED
9 CATALOGUE VALUES
10 CHANGES IN BASIC SET INFORMATION
11 TOTAL VALUE OF SET

Catalogue Listing Policy

It is the intent of Scott Publishing Co. to list all postage stamps of the world in the *Scott Standard Postage Stamp Catalogue*. The only strict criteria for listing is that stamps be decreed legal for postage by the issuing country and that the issuing country actually have an operating postal system. Whether the primary intent of issuing a given stamp or set was for sale to postal patrons or to stamp collectors is not part of our listing criteria. Scott's role is to provide basic comprehensive postage stamp information. It is up to each stamp collector to choose which items to include in a collection.

It is Scott's objective to seek reasons why a stamp should be listed, rather than why it should not. Nevertheless, there are certain types of items that will not be listed. These include the following:

1. Unissued items that are not officially distributed or released by the issuing postal authority. If such items are officially issued at a later date by the country, they will be listed. Unissued items consist of those that have been printed and then held from sale for reasons such as change in government, errors found on stamps or something deemed objectionable about a stamp subject or design.

2. Stamps "issued" by non-existent postal entities or fantasy countries, such as Nagaland, Occusi-Ambeno, Staffa, Sedang, Torres Straits and others. Also, stamps "issued" in the names of legitimate, stamp-issuing countries that are not authorized by those countries.

3. Semi-official or unofficial items not required for postage. Examples include items issued by private agencies for their own express services. When such items are required for delivery, or are valid as prepayment of postage, they are listed.

4. Local stamps issued for local use only. Postage stamps issued by governments specifically for "domestic" use, such as Haiti Scott 219-228, or the United States non-denominated stamps, are not considered to be locals, since they are valid for postage throughout the country of origin.

5. Items not valid for postal use. For example, a few countries have issued souvenir sheets that are not valid for postage. This area also includes a number of worldwide charity labels (some denominated) that do not pay postage.

6. Intentional varieties, such as imperforate stamps that look like their perforated counterparts and are usually issued in very small quantities. Also, other egregiously exploitative issues such as stamps sold for far more than face value, stamps purposefully issued in artificially small quantities or only against advance orders, stamps awarded only to a selected audience such as a philatelic bureau's standing order customers, or stamps sold only in conjunction with other products. All of these kinds of items are usually controlled issues and/or are intended for speculation. These items normally will be included in a footnote.

7. Items distributed by the issuing government only to a limited group, club, philatelic exhibition or a single stamp dealer or other private company. These items normally will be included in a footnote.

The fact that a stamp has been used successfully as postage, even on international mail, is not in itself sufficient proof that it was legitimately issued. Numerous examples of so-called stamps from non-existent countries are known to have been used to post letters that have successfully passed through the international mail system.

There are certain items that are subject to interpretation. When a stamp falls outside our specifications, it may be listed along with a cautionary footnote.

A number of factors are considered in our approach to analyzing how a stamp is listed. The following list of factors is presented to share with you, the catalogue user, the complexity of the listing process.

Additional printings — "Additional printings" of a previously issued stamp may range from an item that is totally different to cases where it is impossible to differentiate from the original. At least a minor number (a small-letter suffix) is assigned if there is a distinct change in stamp shade, noticeably redrawn design, or a significantly different perforation measurement. A major number (numeral or numeral and capital-letter combination) is assigned if the editors feel the "additional printing" is sufficiently different from the original that it constitutes a different issue.

Commemoratives — Where practical, commemoratives with the same theme are placed in a set. For example, the U.S. Civil War Centennial set of 1961-65 and the Constitution Bicentennial series of 1989-90 appear as sets. Countries such as Japan and Korea issue such material on a regular basis, with an announced, or at least predictable, number of stamps known in advance. Occasionally, however, stamp sets that were released over a period of years have been separated. Appropriately placed footnotes will guide you to each set's continuation.

Definitive sets — Blocks of numbers generally have been reserved for definitive sets, based on previous experience with any given country. If a few more stamps were issued in a set than originally expected, they often have been inserted into the original set with a capital-letter suffix, such as U.S. Scott 1059A. If it appears that many more stamps than the originally allotted block will be released before the set is completed, a new block of numbers will be reserved, with the original one being closed off. In some cases, such as the U.S. Transportation and Great Americans series, several blocks of numbers exist. Appropriately placed footnotes will guide you to each set's continuation.

New country — Membership in the Universal Postal Union is not a consideration for listing status or order of placement within the catalogue. The index will tell you in what volume or page number the listings begin.

"No release date" items — The amount of information available for any given stamp issue varies greatly from country to country and even from time to time. Extremely comprehensive information about new stamps is available from some countries well before the stamps are released. By contrast some countries do not provide information about stamps or release dates. Most countries, however, fall between these extremes. A country may provide denominations or subjects of stamps from upcoming issues that are not issued as planned. Sometimes, philatelic agencies, those private firms hired to represent countries, add these later-issued items to sets well after the formal release date. This time period can range from weeks to years. If these items were officially released by the country, they will be added to the appropriate spot in the set. In many cases, the specific release date of a stamp or set of stamps may never be known.

Overprints — The color of an overprint is always noted if it is other than black. Where more than one color of ink has been used on overprints of a single set, the color used is noted. Early overprint and surcharge illustrations were altered to prevent their use by forgers.

Se-tenants — Connected stamps of differing features (se-tenants) will be listed in the format most commonly collected. This includes pairs, blocks or larger multiples. Se-tenant units are not always symmetrical. An example is Australia Scott 508, which is a block of seven stamps. If the stamps are primarily collected as a unit, the major number may be assigned to the multiple, with minors going to each component stamp. In cases where continuous-design or other unit se-tenants will receive significant postal use, each stamp is given a major Scott number listing. This includes issues from the United States, Canada, Germany and Great Britain, for example.

Special Notices

Classification of stamps

The *Scott Standard Postage Stamp Catalogue* lists stamps by country of issue. The next level of organization is a listing by section on the basis of the function of the stamps. The principal sections cover regular postage, semi-postal, air post, special delivery, registration, postage due and other categories. Except for regular postage, catalogue numbers for all sections include a prefix letter (or number-letter combination) denoting the class to which a given stamp belongs. When some countries issue sets containing stamps from more than one category, the catalogue will at times list all of the stamps in one category (such as air post stamps listed as part of a postage set).

The following is a listing of the most commonly used catalogue prefixes.

Prefix... Category

C .... Air Post
M....... Military
P........ Newspaper
N .... Occupation - Regular Issues
O .... Official
Q....... Parcel Post
J......... Postage Due
RA ..... Postal Tax
B........ Semi-Postal
E........ Special Delivery
MR .... War Tax

Other prefixes used by more than one country include the following:
H .... Acknowledgment of Receipt
I......... Late Fee
CO..... Air Post Official
CQ..... Air Post Parcel Post
RAC... Air Post Postal Tax
CF...... Air Post Registration
CB ..... Air Post Semi-Postal
CBO... Air Post Semi-Postal Official
CE ..... Air Post Special Delivery
EY...... Authorized Delivery
S........ Franchise
G .... Insured Letter
GY ..... Marine Insurance
MC .... Military Air Post
MQ.... Military Parcel Post
NC..... Occupation - Air Post
NO .... Occupation - Official
NJ ...... Occupation - Postage Due
NRA... Occupation - Postal Tax
NB ..... Occupation - Semi-Postal
NE ..... Occupation - Special Delivery
QY ..... Parcel Post Authorized Delivery
AR ..... Postal-fiscal
RAJ .... Postal Tax Due
RAB ... Postal Tax Semi-Postal
F........ Registration
EB...... Semi-Postal Special Delivery
EO ..... Special Delivery Official
QE ..... Special Handling

New issue listings

Updates to this catalogue appear each month in the *Scott Stamp Monthly* magazine. Included in this update are additions to the listings of countries found in the *Scott Standard Postage Stamp Catalogue* and the *Specialized Catalogue of United States Stamps*, as well as corrections and updates to current editions of this catalogue.

From time to time there will be changes in the final listings of stamps from the *Scott Stamp Monthly* to the next edition of the catalogue. This occurs as more information about certain stamps or sets becomes available.

The catalogue update section of the *Scott Stamp Monthly* is the most timely presentation of this material available. Annual subscriptions to the *Scott Stamp Monthly* are available from Scott Publishing Co., Box 828, Sidney, OH 45365-0828.

Number additions, deletions & changes

A listing of catalogue number additions, deletions and changes from the previous edition of the catalogue appears in each volume. See Catalogue Number Additions, Deletions & Changes in the table of contents for the location of this list.

Understanding valuing notations

The *minimum catalogue value* of an individual stamp or set is 20 cents. This represents a portion of the cost incurred by a dealer when he prepares an individual stamp for resale. As a point of philatelic-economic fact, the lower the value shown for an item in this catalogue, the greater the percentage of that value is attributed to dealer mark up and profit margin. In many cases, such as the 20-cent minimum value, that price does not cover the labor or other costs involved with stocking it as an individual stamp. The sum of minimum values in a set does not properly represent the value of a complete set primarily composed of a number of minimum-value stamps, nor does the sum represent the actual value of a packet made up of minimum-value stamps. Thus a packet of 1,000 different common stamps — each of which has a catalogue value of 20-cents — normally sells for considerably less than 200 dollars!

The *absence of a retail value* for a stamp does not necessarily suggest that a stamp is scarce or rare. A dash in the value column means that the stamp is known in a stated form or variety, but information is either lacking or insufficient for purposes of establishing a usable catalogue value.

Stamp values in *italics* generally refer to items that are difficult to value accurately. For expensive items, such as those priced at $1,000 or higher, a value in italics indicates that the affected item trades very seldom. For inexpensive items, a value in italics represents a warning. One example is a "blocked" issue where the issuing postal administration may have controlled one stamp in a set in an attempt to make the whole set more valuable. Another example is an item that sold at an extreme multiple of face value in the marketplace at the time of its issue.

One type of warning to collectors that appears in the catalogue is illustrated by a stamp that is valued considerably higher in used condition than it is as unused. In this case, collectors are cautioned to be certain the used version has a genuine and contemporaneous cancellation. The type of cancellation on a stamp can be an important factor in determining its sale price. Catalogue values do not apply to fiscal, telegraph or non-contemporaneous postal cancels, unless otherwise noted.

Some countries have released back issues of stamps in canceled-to-order form, sometimes covering as much as a 10-year period. The Scott Catalogue values for used stamps reflect canceled-to-order material when such stamps are found to predominate in the marketplace for the issue involved. Notes frequently appear in the stamp listings to specify which items are valued as canceled-to-order, or if there is a premium for postally used examples.

Many countries sell canceled-to-order stamps at a marked reduction of face value. Countries that sell or have sold canceled-to-order stamps at *full* face value include United Nations, Australia, Netherlands, France and Switzerland. It may be almost impossible to identify such stamps if the gum has been removed, because official government canceling devices are used. Postally used copies of these items on cover, however, are usually worth more than the canceled-to-order stamps with original gum.

Abbreviations

Scott Publishing Co. uses a consistent set of abbreviations throughout this catalogue to conserve space, while still providing necessary information.

COLOR ABBREVIATIONS

amb .amber
anil ..aniline
ap ....apple
aqua.aquamarine
az.....azure
bis....bister
bl .....blue
bld ...blood
blk ...black
bril ...brilliant
brn...brown
brnshbrownish
brnz .bronze
brt.....bright
brnt..burnt
car ...carmine
cer ...cerise
chlky chalky
cham chamois
chnt .chestnut
choc.chocolate
chr ...chrome
cit ....citron
cl .....claret
cob...cobalt
cop...copper
crim .crimson
cr .....cream
dk ....dark
dl .....dull
dp ....deep
db ....drab
emer emerald
gldn .golden
grysh grayish
grn ...green
grnsh greenish
hel ...heliotrope
hn ....henna
ind ...indigo
int....intense
lav....lavender
lem ..lemon
lil .....lilac
lt......light
mag..magenta
man .manila
mar ..maroon
mv ...mauve
multi multicolored
mlky milky
myr ..myrtle
ol .....olive
olvn olivine
org ...orange
pck...peacock
pnksh pinkish
Prus .Prussian
pur...purple
redsh reddish
res....reseda
ros ...rosine
ryl ....royal
sal ....salmon
saph .sapphire
scar ..scarlet
sep ...sepia
sien ..sienna
sil.....silver
sl......slate
stl ....steel
turq..turquoise
ultra .ultramarine
Ven ..Venetian
ver ...vermilion
vio ...violet
yel....yellow
yelsh yellowish

When no color is given for an overprint or surcharge, black is the color used. Abbreviations for colors used for overprints and surcharges include: "(B)" or "(Blk)," black; "(Bl)," blue; "(R)," red; and "(G)," green.

Additional abbreviations in this catalogue are shown below:

Adm............Administration
AFL.............American Federation of Labor
Anniv. ....Anniversary
APS.............American Philatelic Society
Assoc. ....Association
ASSR...........Autonomous Soviet Socialist Republic
b. ....Born
BEP.............Bureau of Engraving and Printing
Bicent. ....Bicentennial
Bklt. ....Booklet
Brit. ....British
btwn. ....Between
Bur. ....Bureau
c. or ca.........Circa
Cat..............Catalogue
Cent............Centennial, century, centenary
CIO.............Congress of Industrial Organizations
Conf............Conference
Cong............Congress
Cpl..............Corporal
CTO............Canceled to order
d. ....Died
Dbl. ....Double
EKU ....Earliest known use
Engr. ....Engraved
Exhib. ....Exhibition
Expo. ....Exposition
Fed. ....Federation
GB ....Great Britain
Gen.............General
GPO............General post office
Horiz. ....Horizontal
Imperf.........Imperforate
Impt.............Imprint
Intl...............International
Invtd. ....Inverted
L..................Left
Lieut., lt. ....Lieutenant
Litho. ....Lithographed
LL ....Lower left
LR...............Lower right
mm ....Millimeter
Ms. ....Manuscript
Natl. ....National
No. ....Number
NY ....New York
NYC............New York City
Ovpt. ....Overprint
Ovptd. ....Overprinted
P.................Plate number
Perf.............Perforated, perforation
Phil. ....Philatelic
Photo. ....Photogravure
PO ....Post office
Pr. ....Pair
P.R. ....Puerto Rico
Prec. ....Precancel, precanceled
Pres.............President
PTT.............Post, Telephone and Telegraph
Rio ....Rio de Janeiro
Sgt. ....Sergeant
Soc...............Society
Souv............Souvenir
SSR ....Soviet Socialist Republic, see ASSR
St. ....Saint, street
Surch. ....Surcharge
Typo............Typographed
UL ....Upper left
Unwmkd......Unwatermarked
UPU............Universal Postal Union
UR ....Upper Right
US...............United States
USPOD ....United States Post Office Department
USSR...........Union of Soviet Socialist Republics
Vert.............Vertical
VP...............Vice president
Wmk...........Watermark
Wmkd.........Watermarked
WWI...........World War I
WWII..........World War II

Examination

Scott Publishing Co. will not comment upon the genuineness, grade or condition of stamps, because of the time and responsibility involved. Rather, there are several expertizing groups that undertake this work for both collectors and dealers. Neither will Scott Publishing Co. appraise or identify philatelic material. The company cannot take responsibility for unsolicited stamps or covers sent by individuals.

How to order from your dealer

When ordering stamps from a dealer, it is not necessary to write the full description of a stamp as listed in this catalogue. All you need is the name of the country, the Scott catalogue number and whether the desired item is unused or used. For example, "Japan Scott 422 unused" is sufficient to identify the unused stamp of Japan listed as "422 A206 5y brown."

Basic Stamp Information

A stamp collector's knowledge of the combined elements that make a given stamp issue unique determines his or her ability to identify stamps. These elements include paper, watermark, method of separation, printing, design and gum. On the following pages each of these important areas is briefly described.

Paper

Paper is an organic material composed of a compacted weave of cellulose fibers and generally formed into sheets. Paper used to print stamps may be manufactured in sheets, or it may have been part of a large roll (called a web) before being cut to size. The fibers most often used to create paper on which stamps are printed include bark, wood, straw and certain grasses. In many cases, linen or cotton rags have been added for greater strength and durability. Grinding, bleaching, cooking and rinsing these raw fibers reduces them to a slushy pulp, referred to by paper makers as "stuff." Sizing and, sometimes, coloring matter is added to the pulp to make different types of finished paper.

After the stuff is prepared, it is poured onto sieve-like frames that allow the water to run off, while retaining the matted pulp. As fibers fall onto the screen and are held by gravity, they form a natural weave that will later hold the paper together. If the screen has metal bits that are formed into letters or images attached, it leaves slightly thinned areas on the paper. These are called watermarks.

When the stuff is almost dry, it is passed under pressure through smooth or engraved rollers - dandy rolls - or placed between cloth in a press to be flattened and dried.

Stamp paper falls broadly into two types: wove and laid. The nature of the surface of the frame onto which the pulp is first deposited causes the differences in appearance between the two. If the surface is smooth and even, the paper will be of fairly uniform texture throughout. This is known as *wove paper.* Early papermaking machines poured the pulp onto a continuously circulating web of felt, but modern machines feed the pulp onto a cloth-like screen made of closely interwoven fine wires. This paper, when held to a light, will show little dots or points very close together. The proper name for this is "wire wove," but the type is still considered wove. Any U.S. or British stamp printed after 1880 will serve as an example of wire wove paper.

Closely spaced parallel wires, with cross wires at wider intervals, make up the frames used for what is known as *laid paper.* A greater thickness of the pulp will settle between the wires. The paper, when held to a light, will show alternate light and dark lines. The spacing and the thickness of the lines may vary, but on any one sheet of paper they are all alike. See Russia Scott 31-38 for examples of laid paper.

Batonne, from the French word meaning "a staff," is a term used if the lines in the paper are spaced quite far apart, like the printed ruling on a writing tablet. Batonne paper may be either wove or laid. If laid, fine laid lines can be seen between the batons.

Quadrille is the term used when the lines in the paper form little squares. *Oblong quadrille* is the term used when rectangles, rather than squares, are formed. See Mexico-Guadalajara Scott 35-37 for examples of oblong quadrille paper.

Paper also is classified as thick or thin, hard or soft, and by color if dye is added during manufacture. Such colors may include yellowish, greenish, bluish and reddish.

Brief explanations of other types of paper used for printing stamps, as well as examples, follow.

Pelure — Pelure paper is a very thin, hard and often brittle paper that is sometimes bluish or grayish in appearance. See Serbia Scott 169-170.

Native — This is a term applied to handmade papers used to produce some of the early stamps of the Indian states. Stamps printed on native paper may be expected to display various natural inclusions that are normal and do not negatively affect value. Japanese paper, originally made of mulberry fibers and rice flour, is part of this group. See Japan Scott 1-18.

Manila — This type of paper is often used to make stamped envelopes and wrappers. It is a coarse-textured stock, usually smooth on one side and rough on the other. A variety of colors of manila paper exist, but the most common range is yellowish-brown.

Silk — Introduced by the British in 1847 as a safeguard against counterfeiting, silk paper contains bits of colored silk thread scattered throughout. The density of these fibers varies greatly and can include as few as one fiber per stamp or hundreds. U.S. revenue Scott R152 is a good example of an easy-to-identify silk paper stamp.

Silk-thread paper has uninterrupted threads of colored silk arranged so that one or more threads run through the stamp or postal stationery. See Great Britain Scott 5-6 and Switzerland Scott 14-19.

Granite — Filled with minute cloth or colored paper fibers of various colors and lengths, granite paper should not be confused with either type of silk paper. Austria Scott 172-175 and a number of Swiss stamps are examples of granite paper.

Chalky — A chalk-like substance coats the surface of chalky paper to discourage the cleaning and reuse of canceled stamps, as well as to provide a smoother, more acceptable printing surface. Because the designs of stamps printed on chalky paper are imprinted on what is often a water-soluble coating, any attempt to remove a cancellation will destroy the stamp. *Do not soak these stamps in any fluid.* To remove a stamp printed on chalky paper from an envelope, wet the paper from underneath the stamp until the gum dissolves enough to release the stamp from the paper. See St. Kitts-Nevis Scott 89-90 for examples of stamps printed on this type of chalky paper.

India — Another name for this paper, originally introduced from China about 1750, is "China Paper." It is a thin, opaque paper often used for plate and die proofs by many countries.

Double — In philately, the term double paper has two distinct meanings. The first is a two-ply paper, usually a combination of a thick and a thin sheet, joined during manufacture. This type was used experimentally as a means to discourage the reuse of stamps.

The design is printed on the thin paper. Any attempt to remove a cancellation would destroy the design. U.S. Scott 158 and other Banknote-era stamps exist on this form of double paper.

The second type of double paper occurs on a rotary press, when the end of one paper roll, or web, is affixed to the next roll to save time feeding the paper through the press. Stamp designs are printed over the joined paper and, if overlooked by inspectors, may get into post office stocks.

Goldbeater's Skin — This type of paper was used for the 1866 issue of Prussia, and was a tough, translucent paper. The design was printed in reverse on the back of the stamp, and the gum applied over the printing. It is impossible to remove stamps printed on this type of paper from the paper to which they are affixed without destroying the design.

Ribbed — Ribbed paper has an uneven, corrugated surface made by passing the paper through ridged rollers. This type exists on some copies of U.S. Scott 156-165.

Various other substances, or substrates, have been used for stamp manufacture, including wood, aluminum, copper, silver and gold foil, plastic, and silk and cotton fabrics.

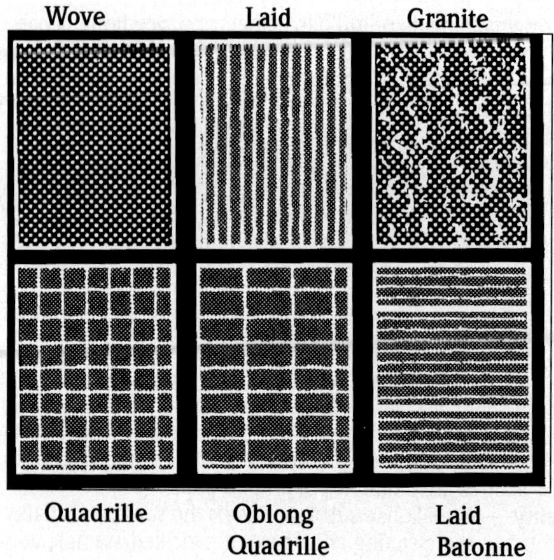

Watermarks

Watermarks are an integral part of some papers. They are formed in the process of paper manufacture. Watermarks consist of small designs, formed of wire or cut from metal and soldered to the surface of the mold or, sometimes, on the dandy roll. The designs may be in the form of crowns, stars, anchors, letters or other characters or symbols. These pieces of metal - known in the paper-making industry as "bits" - impress a design into the paper. The design sometimes may be seen by holding the stamp to the light. Some are more easily seen with a watermark detector. This important tool is a small black tray into which a stamp is placed face down and dampened with a fast-evaporating watermark detection fluid that brings up the watermark image in the form of dark lines against a lighter background. These dark lines are the thinner areas of the paper known as the watermark. Some watermarks are extremely difficult to locate, due to either a faint impression, watermark location or the color of the stamp. There also are electric watermark detectors that come with plastic filter disks of various colors. The disks neutralize the color of the stamp, permitting the watermark to be seen more easily.

Multiple watermarks of Crown Agents and Burma

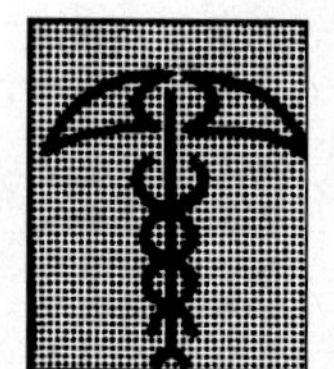

Watermarks of Uruguay, Vatican City and Jamaica

WARNING: Some inks used in the photogravure process dissolve in watermark fluids (Please see the section on Soluble Printing Inks). Also, see "chalky paper."

Watermarks may be found normal, reversed, inverted, reversed and inverted, sideways or diagonal, as seen from the back of the stamp. The relationship of watermark to stamp design depends on the position of the printing plates or how paper is fed through the press. On machine-made paper, watermarks normally are read from right to left. The design is repeated closely throughout the sheet in a "multiple-watermark design." In a "sheet watermark," the design appears only once on the sheet, but extends over many stamps. Individual stamps may carry only a small fraction or none of the watermark.

"Marginal watermarks" occur in the margins of sheets or panes of stamps. They occur on the outside border of paper (ostensibly outside the area where stamps are to be printed). A large row of letters may spell the name of the country or the manufacturer of the paper, or a border of lines may appear. Careless press feeding may cause parts of these letters and/or lines to show on stamps of the outer row of a pane.

Soluble Printing Inks

WARNING: Most stamp colors are permanent; that is, they are not seriously affected by short-term exposure to light or water. Many colors, especially of modern inks, fade from excessive exposure to light. There are stamps printed with inks that dissolve easily in water or in fluids used to detect watermarks. Use of these inks was intentional to prevent the removal of cancellations. Water affects all aniline inks, those on so-called safety paper and some photogravure printings - all such inks are known as *fugitive colors. Removal from paper of such stamps requires care and alternatives to traditional soaking.*

Separation

"Separation" is the general term used to describe methods used to separate stamps. The three standard forms currently in use are perforating, rouletting and die-cutting. These methods are done during the stamp production process, after printing. Sometimes these methods are done on-press or sometimes as a separate step. The earliest issues, such as the 1840 Penny Black of Great Britain (Scott 1), did not have any means provided for separation. It was expected the stamps would be cut apart with scissors or folded and torn. These are examples of imperforate stamps. Many stamps were first issued in imperforate formats and were later issued with perforations. Therefore, care must be observed in buying single imperforate stamps to be certain they were issued imperforate and are not perforated copies that have been altered by having the perforations trimmed away. Stamps issued imperforate usually are valued as singles. However, imperforate varieties of normally perforated stamps should be collected in pairs or larger pieces as indisputable evidence of their imperforate character.

PERFORATION

The chief style of separation of stamps, and the one that is in almost universal use today, is perforating. By this process, paper between the stamps is cut away in a line of holes, usually round, leaving little bridges of paper between the stamps to hold them together. Some types of perforation, such as hyphen-hole perfs, can be confused with roulettes, but a close visual inspection reveals that paper has been removed. The little perforation bridges, which project from the stamp when it is torn from the pane, are called the teeth of the perforation.

As the size of the perforation is sometimes the only way to differentiate between two otherwise identical stamps, it is necessary to be able to accurately measure and describe them. This is done with a perforation gauge, usually a ruler-like device that has dots or graduated lines to show how many perforations may be counted in the space of two centimeters. Two centimeters is the space universally adopted in which to measure perforations.

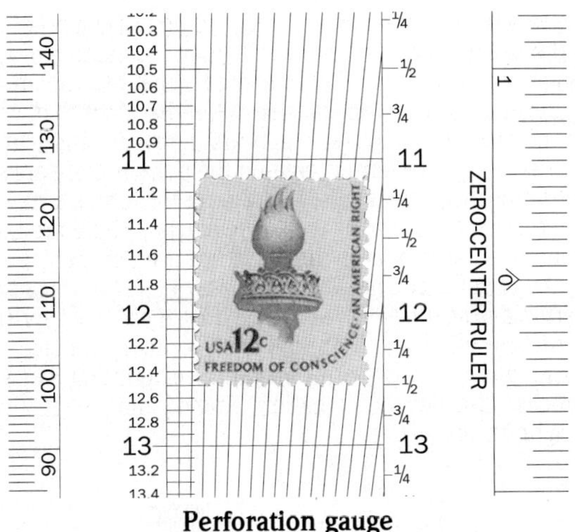

Perforation gauge

To measure a stamp, run it along the gauge until the dots on it fit exactly into the perforations of the stamp. If you are using a graduated-line perforation gauge, simply slide the stamp along the surface until the lines on the gauge perfectly project from the center of the bridges or holes. The number to the side of the line of dots or lines that fit the stamp's perforation is the measurement. For example, an "11" means that 11 perforations fit between two centimeters. The description of the stamp therefore is "perf. 11." If the gauge of the perforations on the top and bottom of a stamp differs from that on the sides, the result is what is known as *compound perforations.* In measuring compound perforations, the gauge at top and bottom is always given first, then the sides. Thus, a stamp that measures 11 at top and bottom and 10 1/2 at the sides is "perf. 11 x 10 1/2." See U.S. Scott 632-642 for examples of compound perforations.

Stamps also are known with perforations different on three or all four sides. Descriptions of such items are clockwise, beginning with the top of the stamp.

A perforation with small holes and teeth close together is a "fine perforation." One with large holes and teeth far apart is a "coarse perforation." Holes that are jagged, rather than clean-cut, are "rough perforations." *Blind perforations* are the slight impressions left by the perforating pins if they fail to puncture the paper. Multiples of stamps showing blind perforations may command a slight premium over normally perforated stamps.

The term *syncopated perfs* describes intentional irregularities in the perforations. The earliest form was used by the Netherlands from 1925-33, where holes were omitted to create distinctive patterns. Beginning in 1992, Great Britain has used an oval perforation to help prevent counterfeiting. Several other countries have started using the oval perfs or other syncopated perf patterns.

A new type of perforation, still primarily used for postal stationery, is known as microperfs. Microperfs are tiny perforations (in some cases hundreds of holes per two centimeters) that allows items to be intentionally separated very easily, while not accidentally breaking apart as easily as standard perforations. These are not currently measured or differentiated by size, as are standard perforations.

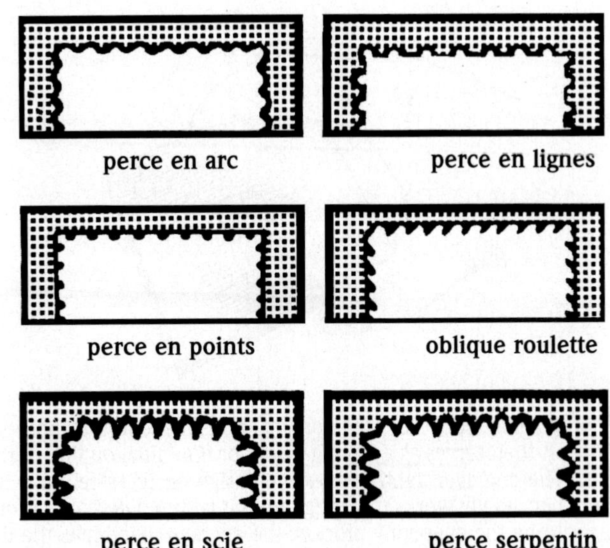

ROULETTING

In rouletting, the stamp paper is cut partly or wholly through, with no paper removed. In perforating, some paper is removed. Rouletting derives its name from the French roulette, a spur-like wheel. As the wheel is rolled over the paper, each point makes a small cut. The number of cuts made in a two-centimeter space determines the gauge of the roulette, just as the number of perforations in two centimeters determines the gauge of the perforation.

The shape and arrangement of the teeth on the wheels varies. Various roulette types generally carry French names:

Perce en lignes - rouletted in lines. The paper receives short, straight cuts in lines. This is the most common type of rouletting. See Mexico Scott 500.

Perce en points - pin-rouletted or pin-perfed. This differs from a small perforation because no paper is removed, although round, equidistant holes are pricked through the paper. See Mexico Scott 242-256.

Perce en arc and *perce en scie* - pierced in an arc or saw-toothed designs, forming half circles or small triangles. See Hanover (German States) Scott 25-29.

Perce en serpentin - serpentine roulettes. The cuts form a serpentine or wavy line. See Brunswick (German States) Scott 13-18.

Once again, no paper is removed by these processes, leaving the stamps easily separated, but closely attached.

DIE-CUTTING

The third major form of stamp separation is die-cutting. This is a method where a die in the pattern of separation is created that later cuts the stamp paper in a stroke motion. Although some standard stamps bear die-cut perforations, this process is primarily used for self-adhesive postage stamps. Die-cutting can appear in straight lines, such as U.S. Scott 2522, shapes, such as U.S. Scott 1551, or imitating the appearance of perforations, such as New Zealand Scott 935A and 935B.

Printing Processes

ENGRAVING (Intaglio, Line-engraving, Etching)

Master die — The initial operation in the process of line engraving is making the master die. The die is a small, flat block of softened steel upon which the stamp design is recess engraved in reverse.

Master die

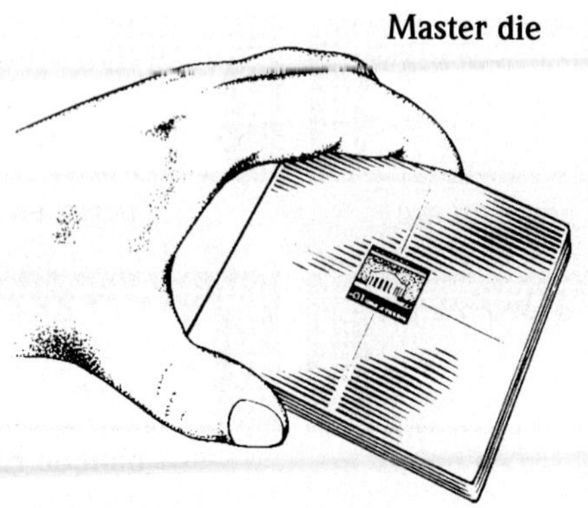

Photographic reduction of the original art is made to the appropriate size. It then serves as a tracing guide for the initial outline of the design. The engraver lightly traces the design on the steel with his graver, then slowly works the design until it is completed. At various points during the engraving process, the engraver hand-inks the die and makes an impression to check his progress. These are known as progressive die proofs. After completion of the engraving, the die is hardened to withstand the stress and pressures of later transfer operations.

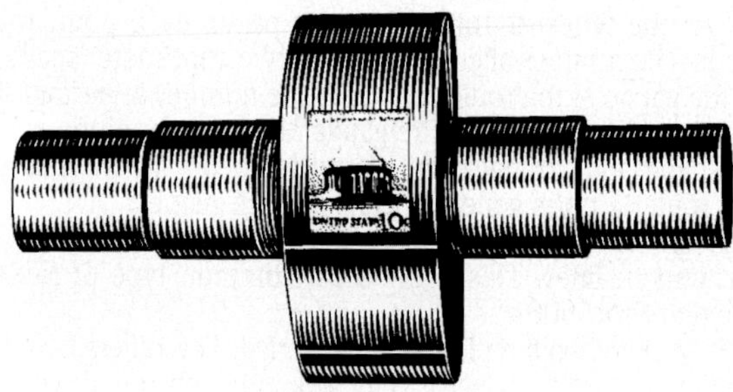

Transfer roll

Transfer roll — Next is production of the transfer roll that, as the name implies, is the medium used to transfer the subject from the master die to the printing plate. A blank roll of soft steel, mounted on a mandrel, is placed under the bearers of the transfer press to allow it to roll freely on its axis. The hardened die is placed on the bed of the press and the face of the transfer roll is applied to the die, under pressure. The bed or the roll is then rocked back and forth under increasing pressure, until the soft steel of the roll is forced into every engraved line of the die. The resulting impression on the roll is known as a "relief" or a "relief transfer." The engraved image is now positive in appearance and stands out from the steel. After the required number of reliefs are "rocked in," the soft steel transfer roll is hardened.

Different flaws may occur during the relief process. A defective relief may occur during the rocking in process because of a minute piece of foreign material lodging on the die, or some other cause. Imperfections in the steel of the transfer roll may result in a breaking away of parts of the design. This is known as a relief break, which will show up on finished stamps as small, unprinted areas. If a damaged relief remains in use, it will transfer a repeating defect to the plate. Deliberate alterations of reliefs sometimes occur. "Altered reliefs" designate these changed conditions.

Plate — The final step in pre-printing production is the making of the printing plate. A flat piece of soft steel replaces the die on the bed of the transfer press. One of the reliefs on the transfer roll is positioned over this soft steel. Position, or layout, dots determine the correct position on the plate. The dots have been lightly marked on the plate in advance. After the correct position of the relief is determined, the design is rocked in by following the same method used in making the transfer roll. The difference is that this time the image is being transferred from the transfer roll, rather than to it. Once the design is entered on the plate, it appears in reverse and is recessed. There are as many transfers entered on the plate as there are subjects printed on the sheet of stamps. It is during this process that double and shifted transfers occur, as well as re-entries. These are the result of improperly entered images that have not been properly burnished out prior to rocking in a new image.

Modern siderography processes, such as those used by the U.S. Bureau of Engraving and Printing, involve an automated form of rocking designs in on preformed cylindrical printing sleeves. The same process also allows for easier removal and re-entry of worn images right on the sleeve.

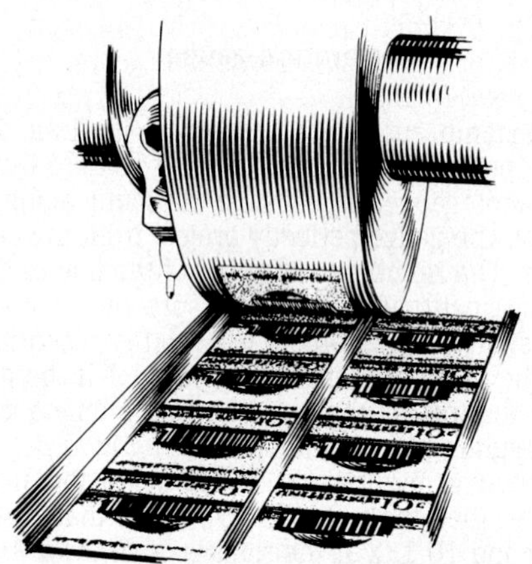

Transferring the design to the plate

Following the entering of the required transfers on the plate, the position dots, layout dots and lines, scratches and other markings generally are burnished out. Added at this time by the siderographer are any required *guide lines, plate numbers* or other *marginal markings.* The plate is then hand-inked and a proof impression is taken. This is known as a plate proof. If the impression is approved, the plate is machined for fitting onto the press, is hardened and sent to the plate vault ready for use.

On press, the plate is inked and the surface is automatically wiped clean, leaving ink only in the recessed lines. Paper is then forced under pressure into the engraved recessed lines, thereby receiving the ink. Thus, the ink lines on engraved stamps are slightly raised, and slight depressions (debossing) occur on the back of the stamp. Prior to the advent of modern high-speed presses and more advanced ink formulations, paper had to be dampened before receiving the ink. This sometimes led to uneven shrinkage by the time the stamps were perforated, resulting in improperly perforated stamps, or misperfs. Newer presses use drier paper, thus both *wet* and *dry printings* exist on some stamps.

Rotary Press — Until 1914, only flat plates were used to print engraved stamps. Rotary press printing was introduced in 1914, and slowly spread. Some countries still use flat-plate printing.

After approval of the plate proof, older *rotary press plates* require additional machining. They are curved to fit the press cylinder. "Gripper slots" are cut into the back of each plate to receive the "grippers," which hold the plate securely on the press. The plate is then hardened. Stamps printed from these bent rotary press plates are longer or wider than the same stamps printed from flat-plate presses. The stretching of the plate during the curving process is what causes this distortion.

Re-entry — To execute a re-entry on a flat plate, the transfer roll is re-applied to the plate, often at some time after its first use on the press. Worn-out designs can be resharpened by carefully burnishing out the original image and re-entering it from the transfer roll. If the original impression has not been sufficiently removed and the transfer roll is not precisely in line with the remaining impression, the resulting double transfer will make the re-entry obvious. If the registration is true, a re-entry may be difficult or impossible to distinguish. Sometimes a stamp printed from a successful re-entry is identified by having a much sharper and clearer impression than its neighbors. With the advent of rotary presses, post-press re-entries were not possible. After a plate was curved for the rotary press, it was impossible to make a re-entry. This is because the plate had already been bent once (with the design distorted).

However, with the introduction of the previously mentioned modern-style siderography machines, entries are made to the preformed cylindrical printing sleeve. Such sleeves are dechromed and softened. This allows individual images to be burnished out and re-entered on the curved sleeve. The sleeve is then rechromed, resulting in longer press life.

Double Transfer — This is a description of the condition of a transfer on a plate that shows evidence of a duplication of all, or a portion of the design. It usually is the result of the changing of the registration between the transfer roll and the plate during the rocking in of the original entry. Double transfers also occur when only a portion of the design has been rocked in and improper positioning is noted. If the worker elected not to burnish out the partial or completed design, a strong double transfer will occur for part or all of the design.

It sometimes is necessary to remove the original transfer from a plate and repeat the process a second time. If the finished re-worked image shows traces of the original impression, attributable to incomplete burnishing, the result is a partial double transfer.

With the modern automatic machines mentioned previously, double transfers are all but impossible to create. Those partially doubled images on stamps printed from such sleeves are more than likely re-entries, rather than true double transfers.

Re-engraved — Alterations to a stamp design are sometimes necessary after some stamps have been printed. In some cases, either the original die or the actual printing plate may have its "temper" drawn (softened), and the design will be re cut. The resulting impressions from such a re-engraved die or plate may differ slightly from the original issue, and are known as "re-engraved." If the alteration was made to the master die, all future printings will be consistently different from the original. If alterations were made to the printing plate, each altered stamp on the plate will be slightly different from each other, allowing specialists to reconstruct a complete printing plate.

Dropped Transfers — If an impression from the transfer roll has not been properly placed, a dropped transfer may occur. The final stamp image will appear obviously out of line with its neighbors.

Short Transfer — Sometimes a transfer roll is not rocked its entire length when entering a transfer onto a plate. As a result, the finished transfer on the plate fails to show the complete design, and the finished stamp will have an incomplete design printed. This is known as a "short transfer." U.S. Scott No. 8 is a good example of a short transfer.

TYPOGRAPHY (Letterpress, Surface Printing, Flexography, Dry Offset, High Etch)

Although the word "Typography" is obsolete as a term describing a printing method, it was the accepted term throughout the first century of postage stamps. Therefore, appropriate Scott listings in this catalogue refer to typographed stamps. The current term for this form of printing, however, is "letterpress."

As it relates to the production of postage stamps, letterpress printing is the reverse of engraving. Rather than having recessed areas trap the ink and deposit it on paper, only the raised areas of the design are inked. This is comparable to the type of printing seen by inking and using an ordinary rubber stamp. Letterpress includes all printing where the design is above the surface area, whether it is wood, metal or, in some instances, hardened rubber or polymer plastic.

For most letterpress-printed stamps, the engraved master is made in much the same manner as for engraved stamps. In this instance, however, an additional step is needed. The design is transferred to another surface before being transferred to the transfer roll. In this way, the transfer roll has a recessed stamp design, rather than one done in relief. This makes the printing areas on the final plate raised, or relief areas.

For less-detailed stamps of the 19th century, the area on the die not used as a printing surface was cut away, leaving the surface area raised. The original die was then reproduced by stereotyping or electrotyping. The resulting electrotypes were assembled in the required number and format of the desired sheet of stamps. The plate used in printing the stamps was an electroplate of these assembled electrotypes.

Once the final letterpress plates are created, ink is applied to the raised surface and the pressure of the press transfers the ink impression to the paper. In contrast to engraving, the fine lines of letterpress are impressed on the surface of the stamp, leaving a debossed surface. When viewed from the back (as on a typewritten page), the corresponding line work on the stamp will be raised slightly (embossed) above the surface.

PHOTOGRAVURE (Gravure, Rotogravure, Heliogravure)

In this process, the basic principles of photography are applied to a chemically sensitized metal plate, rather than photographic paper. The design is transferred photographically to the plate through a halftone, or dot-matrix screen, breaking the reproduction into tiny dots. The plate is treated chemically and the dots form depressions, called cells, of varying depths and diameters, depending on the degrees of shade in the design. Then, like engraving, ink is applied to the plate and the surface is wiped clean. This leaves ink in the tiny cells that is lifted out and deposited on the paper when it is pressed against the plate.

Gravure is most often used for multicolored stamps, generally using the three primary colors (red, yellow and blue) and black. By varying the dot matrix pattern and density of these colors, virtually any color can be reproduced. A typical full-color gravure stamp will be created from four printing cylinders (one for each color). The original multicolored image will have been photographically separated into its component colors.

Modern gravure printing may use computer-generated dot-matrix screens, and modern plates may be of various types including metal-coated plastic. The catalogue designation of Photogravure (or "Photo") covers any of these older and more modern gravure methods of printing.

For examples of the first photogravure stamps printed (1914), see Bavaria Scott 94-114.

LITHOGRAPHY (Offset Lithography, Stone Lithography, Dilitho, Planography, Collotype)

The principle that oil and water do not mix is the basis for lithography. The stamp design is drawn by hand or transferred from engraving to the surface of a lithographic stone or metal plate in a greasy (oily) substance. This oily substance holds the ink, which will later be transferred to the paper. The stone (or plate) is wet with an acid fluid, causing it to repel the printing ink in all areas not covered by the greasy substance.

Transfer paper is used to transfer the design from the original stone or plate. A series of duplicate transfers are grouped and, in turn, transferred to the final printing plate.

Photolithography — The application of photographic processes to lithography. This process allows greater flexibility of design, related to use of halftone screens combined with line work. Unlike photogravure or engraving, this process can allow large, solid areas to be printed.

Offset — A refinement of the lithographic process. A rubber-covered blanket cylinder takes the impression from the inked lithographic plate. From the "blanket" the impression is *offset* or transferred to the paper. Greater flexibility and speed are the principal reasons offset printing has largely displaced lithography. The term "lithography" covers both processes, and results are almost identical.

EMBOSSED (Relief) Printing

Embossing, not considered one of the four main printing types, is a method in which the design first is sunk into the metal of the die. Printing is done against a yielding platen, such as leather or linoleum. The platen is forced into the depression of the die, thus forming the design on the paper in relief. This process is often used for metallic inks.

Embossing may be done without color (see Sardinia Scott 4-6); with color printed around the embossed area (see Great Britain Scott 5 and most U.S. envelopes); and with color in exact registration with the embossed subject (see Canada Scott 656-657).

HOLOGRAMS

For objects to appear as holograms on stamps, a model exactly the same size as it is to appear on the hologram must be created. Rather than using photographic film to capture the image, holography records an image on a photoresist material. In processing, chemicals eat away at certain exposed areas, leaving a pattern of constructive and destructive interference. When the phororesist is developed, the result is a pattern of uneven ridges that acts as a mold. This mold is then coated with metal, and the resulting form is used to press copies in much the same way phonograph records are produced.

A typical reflective hologram used for stamps consists of a reproduction of the uneven patterns on a plastic film that is applied to a reflective background, usually a silver or gold foil. Light is reflected off the background through the film, making the pattern present on the film visible. Because of the uneven pattern of the film, the viewer will perceive the objects in their proper three-dimensional relationships with appropriate brightness.

The first hologram on a stamp was produced by Austria in 1988 (Scott 1441).

FOIL APPLICATION

A modern tecnique of applying color to stamps involves the application of metallic foil to the stamp paper. A pattern of foil is applied to the stamp paper by use of a stamping die. The foil usually is flat, but it may be textured. Canada Scott 1735 has three different foil applications in pearl, bronze and gold. The gold foil was textured using a chemical-etch copper embossing die. The printing of this stamp also involved two-color offset lithography plus embossing.

COMBINATION PRINTINGS

Sometimes two or even three printing methods are combined in producing stamps. In these cases, such as Austria Scott 933 or Canada 1735 (described in the preceding paragraph), the multiple-printing technique can be determined by studying the individual characteristics of each printing type. A few stamps, such as Singapore Scott 684-684A, combine as many as three of the four major printing types (lithography, engraving and typography). When this is done it often indicates the incorporation of security devices against counterfeiting.

INK COLORS

Inks or colored papers used in stamp printing often are of mineral origin, although there are numerous examples of organic-based pigments. As a general rule, organic-based pigments are far more subject to varieties and change than those of mineral-based origin.

The appearance of any given color on a stamp may be affected by many aspects, including printing variations, light, color of paper, aging and chemical alterations.

Numerous printing variations may be observed. Heavier pressure or inking will cause a more intense color, while slight interruptions in the ink feed or lighter impressions will cause a lighter appearance. Stamps printed in the same color by water-based and solvent-based inks can differ significantly in appearance. This affects several stamps in the U.S. Prominent Americans series. Hand-mixed ink formulas (primarily from the 19th century) produced under different conditions (humidity and temperature) account for notable color variations in early printings of the same stamp (see U.S. Scott 248-250, 279B, for example). Different sources of pigment can also result in significant differences in color.

Light exposure and aging are closely related in the way they affect stamp color. Both eventually break down the ink and fade colors, so that a carefully kept stamp may differ significantly in color from an identical copy that has been exposed to light. If stamps are exposed to light either intentionally or accidentally, their colors can be faded or completely changed in some cases.

Papers of different quality and consistency used for the same stamp printing may affect color appearance. Most pelure papers, for example, show a richer color when compared with wove or laid papers. See Russia Scott 181a, for an example of this effect.

The very nature of the printing processes can cause a variety of differences in shades or hues of the same stamp. Some of these shades are scarcer than others, and are of particular interest to the advanced collector.

Luminescence

All forms of tagged stamps fall under the general category of luminescence. Within this broad category is fluorescence, dealing with forms of tagging visible under longwave ultraviolet light, and phosphorescence, which deals with tagging visible only under shortwave light. Phosphorescence leaves an afterglow and fluorescence does not. These treated stamps show up in a range of different colors when exposed to UV light. The differing wavelengths of the light activates the tagging material, making it glow in various colors that usually serve different mail processing purposes.

Intentional tagging is a post-World War II phenomenon, brought about by the increased literacy rate and rapidly growing mail volume. It was one of several answers to the problem of the need for more automated mail processes. Early tagged stamps served the purpose of triggering machines to separate different types of mail. A natural outgrowth was to also use the signal to trigger machines that faced all envelopes the same way and canceled them.

Tagged stamps come in many different forms. Some tagged stamps have luminescent shapes or images imprinted on them as a form of security device. Others have blocks (United States), stripes, frames (South Africa and Canada), overall coatings (United States), bars (Great Britain and Canada) and many other types. Some types of tagging are even mixed in with the pigmented printing ink (Australia Scott 366, Netherlands Scott 478 and U.S. Scott 1359 and 2443).

The means of applying taggant to stamps differs as much as the intended purposes for the stamps. The most common form of tagging is a coating applied to the surface of the printed stamp. Since the taggant ink is frequently invisible except under UV light, it does not interfere with the appearance of the stamp. Another common application is the use of phosphored papers. In this case the paper itself either has a coating of taggant applied before the stamp is printed, has taggant applied during the papermaking process (incorporating it into the fibers), or has the taggant mixed into the coating of the paper. The latter method, among others, is currently in use in the United States.

Many countries now use tagging in various forms to either expedite mail handling or to serve as a printing security device against counterfeiting. Following the introduction of tagged stamps for public use in 1959 by Great Britain, other countries have steadily joined the parade. Among those are Germany (1961); Canada and Denmark (1962); United States, Australia, France and Switzerland (1963); Belgium and Japan (1966); Sweden and Norway (1967); Italy (1968); and Russia (1969). Since then, many other countries have begun using forms of tagging, including Brazil, China, Czechoslovakia, Hong Kong, Guatemala, Indonesia, Israel, Lithuania, Luxembourg, Netherlands, Penrhyn Islands, Portugal, St. Vincent, Singapore, South Africa, Spain and Sweden to name a few.

In some cases, including United States, Canada, Great Britain and Switzerland, stamps were released both with and without tagging. Many of these were released during each country's experimental period. Tagged and untagged versions are listed for the aforementioned countries and are noted in some other countries' listings. For at least a few stamps, the experimentally tagged version is worth far more than its untagged counterpart, such as the 1963 experimental tagged version of France Scott 1024.

In some cases, luminescent varieties of stamps were inadvertently created. Several Russian stamps, for example, sport highly fluorescent ink that was not intended as a form of tagging. Older stamps, such as early U.S. postage dues, can be positively identified by the use of UV light, since the organic ink used has become slightly fluorescent over time. Other stamps, such as Austria Scott 70a-82a (varnish bars) and Obock Scott 46-64 (printed quadrille lines), have become fluorescent over time.

Various fluorescent substances have been added to paper to make it appear brighter. These optical brightners, as they are known, greatly affect the appearance of the stamp under UV light. The brightest of these is known as Hi-Brite paper. These paper varieties are beyond the scope of the Scott Catalogue.

Shortwave UV light also is used extensively in expertizing, since each form of paper has its own fluorescent characteristics that are impossible to perfectly match. It is therefore a simple matter to detect filled thins, added perforation teeth and other alterations that involve the addition of paper. UV light also is used to examine stamps that have had cancels chemically removed and for other purposes as well.

Gum

The Illustrated Gum Chart in the first part of this introduction shows and defines various types of gum condition. Because gum condition has an important impact on the value of unused stamps, we recommend studying this chart and the accompanying text carefully.

The gum on the back of a stamp may be shiny, dull, smooth, rough, dark, white, colored or tinted. Most stamp gumming adhesives use gum arabic or dextrine as a base. Certain polymers such as polyvinyl alcohol (PVA) have been used extensively since World War II.

The *Scott Standard Postage Stamp Catalogue* does not list items by types of gum. The *Scott Specialized Catalogue of United States Stamps* does differentiate among some types of gum for certain issues.

Reprints of stamps may have gum differing from the original issues. In addition, some countries have used different gum formulas for different seasons. These adhesives have different properties that may become more apparent over time.

Many stamps have been issued without gum, and the catalogue will note this fact. See, for example, United States Scott 40-47. Sometimes, gum may have been removed to preserve the stamp. Germany Scott B68, for example, has a highly acidic gum that eventually destroys the stamps. This item is valued in the catalogue with gum removed.

Reprints and Reissues

These are impressions of stamps (usually obsolete) made from the original plates or stones. If they are valid for postage and reproduce obsolete issues (such as U.S. Scott 102-111), the stamps are *reissues.* If they are from current issues, they are designated as *second, third,* etc., *printing.* If designated for a particular purpose, they are called *special printings.*

When special printings are not valid for postage, but are made from original dies and plates by authorized persons, they are *official reprints. Private reprints* are made from the original plates and dies by private hands. An example of a private reprint is that of the 1871-1932 reprints made from the original die of the 1845 New Haven, Conn., postmaster's provisional. *Official reproductions* or imitations are made from new dies and plates by government authorization. Scott will list those reissues that are valid for postage if they differ significantly from the original printing.

The U.S. government made special printings of its first postage stamps in 1875. Produced were official imitations of the first two stamps (listed as Scott 3-4), reprints of the demonetized pre-1861 issues (Scott 40-47) and reissues of the 1861 stamps, the 1869 stamps and the then-current 1875 denominations. Even though the official imitations and the reprints were not valid for postage, Scott lists all of these U.S. special printings.

Most reprints or reissues differ slightly from the original stamp in some characteristic, such as gum, paper, perforation, color or watermark. Sometimes the details are followed so meticulously that only a student of that specific stamp is able to distinguish the reprint or reissue from the original.

Remainders and Canceled to Order

Some countries sell their stock of old stamps when a new issue replaces them. To avoid postal use, the *remainders* usually are canceled with a punch hole, a heavy line or bar, or a more-or-less regular-looking cancellation. The most famous merchant of remainders was Nicholas F. Seebeck. In the 1880s and 1890s, he arranged printing contracts between the Hamilton Bank Note Co., of which he was a director, and several Central and South American countries. The contracts provided that the plates and all remainders of the yearly issues became the property of Hamilton. Seebeck saw to it that ample stock remained. The "Seebecks," both remainders and reprints, were standard packet fillers for decades.

Some countries also issue stamps *canceled-to-order (CTO),* either in sheets with original gum or stuck onto pieces of paper or envelopes and canceled. Such CTO items generally are worth less than postally used stamps. In cases where the CTO material is far more prevalent in the marketplace than postally used examples, the catalogue value relates to the CTO examples, with postally used examples noted as premium items. Most CTOs can be detected by the presence of gum. However, as the CTO practice goes back at least to 1885, the gum inevitably has been soaked off some stamps so they could pass as postally used. The normally applied postmarks usually differ slightly from standard postmarks, and specialists are able to tell the difference. When applied individually to envelopes by philatelically minded persons, CTO material is known as *favor canceled* and generally sells at large discounts.

Cinderellas and Facsimiles

Cinderella is a catch-all term used by stamp collectors to describe phantoms, fantasies, bogus items, municipal issues, exhibition seals, local revenues, transportation stamps, labels, poster stamps and many other types of items. Some cinderella collectors include in their collections local postage issues, telegraph stamps, essays and proofs, forgeries and counterfeits.

A *fantasy* is an adhesive created for a nonexistent stamp-issuing authority. Fantasy items range from imaginary countries (Occusi-Ambeno, Kingdom of Sedang, Principality of Trinidad or Torres Straits), to non-existent locals (Winans City Post), or nonexistent transportation lines (McRobish & Co.'s Acapulco-San Francisco Line).

On the other hand, if the entity exists and could have issued stamps (but did not) or was known to have issued other stamps, the items are considered *bogus* stamps. These would include the Mormon postage stamps of Utah, S. Allan Taylor's Guatemala and Paraguay inventions, the propaganda issues for the South Moluccas and the adhesives of the Page & Keyes local post of Boston.

Phantoms is another term for both fantasy and bogus issues.

Facsimiles are copies or imitations made to represent original stamps, but which do not pretend to be originals. A catalogue illustration is such a facsimile. Illustrations from the Moens catalogue of the last century were occasionally colored and passed off as stamps. Since the beginning of stamp collecting, facsimiles have been made for collectors as space fillers or for reference. They often carry the word "facsimile," "falsch" (German), "sanko" or "mozo" (Japanese), or "faux" (French) overprinted on the face or stamped on the back. Unfortunately, over the years a number of these items have had fake cancels applied over the facsimile notation and have been passed off as genuine.

Forgeries and Counterfeits

Forgeries and counterfeits have been with philately virtually from the beginning of stamp production. Over time, the terminology for the two has been used interchangeably. Although both forgeries and counterfeits are reproductions of stamps, the purposes behind their creation differ considerably.

Among specialists there is an increasing movement to more specifically define such items. Although there is no universally accepted terminology, we feel the following definitions most closely mirror the items and their purposes as they are currently defined.

Forgeries (also often referred to as *Counterfeits*) are reproductions of genuine stamps that have been created to defraud collectors. Such spurious items first appeared on the market around 1860, and most old-time collections contain one or more. Many are crude and easily spotted, but some can deceive experts.

An important supplier of these early philatelic forgeries was the Hamburg printer Gebruder Spiro. Many others with reputations in this craft included S. Allan Taylor, George Hussey, James Chute, George Forune, Benjamin & Sarpy, Julius Goldner, E. Oneglia and L.H. Mercier. Among the noted 20th-century forgers were Francois Fournier, Jean Sperati and the prolific Raoul DeThuin.

Forgeries may be complete replications, or they may be genuine stamps altered to resemble a scarcer (and more valuable) type. Most forgeries, particularly those of rare stamps, are worth only a small fraction of the value of a genuine example, but a few types, created by some of the most notable forgers, such as Sperati, can be worth as much or more than the genuine. Fraudulently produced copies are known of most classic rarities and many medium-priced stamps.

In addition to rare stamps, large numbers of common 19th- and early 20th-century stamps were forged to supply stamps to the early packet trade. Many can still be easily found. Few new philatelic forgeries have appeared in recent decades. Successful imitation of well-engraved work is virtually impossible. It has proven far easier to produce a fake by altering a genuine stamp than to duplicate a stamp completely.

Counterfeit (also often referred to as *Postal Counterfeit* or *Postal Forgery*) is the term generally applied to reproductions of stamps that have been created to defraud the government of revenue. Such items usually are created at the time a stamp is current and, in some cases, are hard to detect. Because most counterfeits are seized when the perpetrator is captured, postal counterfeits, particularly used on cover, are usually worth much more than a genuine example to specialists. The first postal counterfeit was of Spain's 4-cuarto carmine of 1854 (the real one is Scott 25). Apparently, the counterfeiters were not satisfied with their first version, which is now very scarce, and they soon created an engraved counterfeit, which is common. Postal counterfeits quickly followed in Austria, Naples, Sardinia and the Roman States. They have since been created in many other countries as well, including the United States.

An infamous counterfeit to defraud the government is the 1-shilling Great Britain "Stock Exchange" forgery of 1872, used on telegraph forms at the exchange that year. The stamp escaped detection until a stamp dealer noticed it in 1898.

Fakes

Fakes are genuine stamps altered in some way to make them more desirable. One student of this part of stamp collecting has estimated that by the 1950s more than 30,000 varieties of fakes were known. That number has grown greatly since then. The widespread existence of fakes makes it important for stamp collectors to study their philatelic holdings and use relevant literature. Likewise, collectors should buy from reputable dealers who guarantee their stamps and make full and prompt refunds should a purchased item be declared faked or altered by some mutually agreed-upon authority. Because fakes always have some genuine characteristics, it is not always possible to obtain unanimous agreement among experts regarding specific items. These students may change their opinions as philatelic knowledge increases. More than 80 percent of all fakes on the philatelic market today are regummed, reperforated (or perforated for the first time), or bear forged overprints, surcharges or cancellations.

Stamps can be chemically treated to alter or eliminate colors. For example, a pale rose stamp can be re-colored to resemble a blue shade of high market value. In other cases, treated stamps can be made to resemble missing color varieties. Designs may be changed by painting, or a stroke or a dot added or bleached out to turn an ordinary variety into a seemingly scarcer stamp. Part of a stamp can be bleached and reprinted in a different version, achieving an inverted center or frame. Margins can be added or repairs done so deceptively that the stamps move from the "repaired" into the "fake" category.

Fakers have not left the backs of the stamps untouched either. They may create false watermarks, add fake grills or press out genuine grills. A thin India paper proof may be glued onto a thicker backing to create the appearance an issued stamp, or a proof printed on cardboard may be shaved down and perforated to resemble a stamp. Silk threads are impressed into paper and stamps have been split so that a rare paper variety is added to an otherwise inexpensive stamp. The most common treatment to the back of a stamp, however, is regumming.

Some in the business of faking stamps have openly advertised foolproof application of "original gum" to stamps that lack it, although most publications now ban such ads from their pages. It is believed that very few early stamps have survived without being hinged. The large number of never-hinged examples of such earlier material offered for sale thus suggests the widespread extent of regumming activity. Regumming also may be used to hide repairs or thin spots. Dipping the stamp into watermark fluid, or examining it under longwave ultraviolet light often will reveal these flaws.

Fakers also tamper with separations. Ingenious ways to add margins are known. Perforated wide-margin stamps may be falsely represented as imperforate when trimmed. Reperforating is commonly done to create scarce coil or perforation varieties, and to eliminate the naturally occurring straight-edge stamps found in sheet margin positions of many earlier issues. Custom has made straight-edged stamps less desirable. Fakers have obliged by perforating straight-edged stamps so that many are now uncommon, if not rare.

Another fertile field for the faker is that of overprints, surcharges and cancellations. The forging of rare surcharges or overprints began in the 1880s or 1890s. These forgeries are sometimes difficult to detect, but experts have identified almost all. Occasionally, overprints or cancellations are removed to create non-overprinted stamps or seemingly unused items. This is most commonly done by removing a manuscript cancel to make a stamp resemble an unused example. "SPECIMEN" overprints may be removed by scraping and repainting to create non-overprinted varieties. Fakers use inexpensive revenues or pen-canceled stamps to generate unused stamps for further faking by adding other markings. The quartz lamp or UV lamp and a high-powered magnifying glass help to easily detect removed cancellations.

The bigger problem, however, is the addition of overprints, surcharges or cancellations - many with such precision that they are very difficult to ascertain. Plating of the stamps or the overprint can be an important method of detection.

Fake postmarks may range from many spurious fancy cancellations to a host of markings applied to transatlantic covers, to adding normally appearing postmarks to definitives of some countries with stamps that are valued far higher used than unused. With the increased popularity of cover collecting, and the widespread interest in postal history, a fertile new field for fakers has come about. Some have tried to create entire covers. Others specialize in adding stamps, tied by fake cancellations, to genuine stampless covers, or replacing less expensive or damaged stamps with more valuable ones. Detailed study of postal rates in effect at the time a cover in question was mailed, including the analysis of each handstamp used during the period, ink analysis and similar techniques, usually will unmask the fraud.

Restoration and Repairs

Scott Publishing Co. bases its catalogue values on stamps that are free of defects and otherwise meet the standards set forth earlier in this introduction. Most stamp collectors desire to have the finest copy of an item possible. Even within given grading categories there are variances. This leads to a controversial practice that is not defined in any universal manner: stamp *restoration.*

There are broad differences of opinion about what is permissible when it comes to restoration. Carefully applying a soft eraser to a stamp or cover to remove light soiling is one form of restoration, as is washing a stamp in mild soap and water to clean it. These are fairly accepted forms of restoration. More severe forms of restoration include pressing out creases or removing stains caused by tape. To what degree each of these is acceptable is dependent upon the individual situation. Further along the spectrum is the freshening of a stamp's color by removing oxide build-up or the effects of wax paper left next to stamps shipped to the tropics.

At some point in this spectrum the concept of *repair* replaces that of restoration. Repairs include filling thin spots, mending tears by reweaving or adding a missing perforation tooth. Regumming stamps may have been acceptable as a restoration or repair technique many decades ago, but today it is considered a form of fakery.

Restored stamps may or may not sell at a discount, and it is possible that the value of individual restored items may be enhanced over that of their pre-restoration state. Specific situations dictate the resultant value of such an item. Repaired stamps sell at substantial discounts from the value of sound stamps.

Terminology

Booklets — Many countries have issued stamps in small booklets for the convenience of users. This idea continues to become increasingly popular in many countries. Booklets have been issued in many sizes and forms, often with advertising on the covers, the panes of stamps or on the interleaving.

The panes used in booklets may be printed from special plates or made from regular sheets. All panes from booklets issued by the United States and many from those of other countries contain stamps that are straight edged on the sides, but perforated between. Others are distinguished by orientation of watermark or other identifying features. Any stamp-like unit in the pane, either printed or blank, that is not a postage stamp, is considered to be a *label* in the catalogue listings.

Scott lists and values booklet panes. Modern complete booklets also are listed and valued. Individual booklet panes are listed only when they are not fashioned from existing sheet stamps and, therefore, are identifiable from their sheet stamp counterparts.

Panes usually do not have a used value assigned to them because there is little market activity for used booklet panes, even though many exist used and there is some demand for them.

Cancellations — The marks or obliterations put on stamps by postal authorities to show that they have performed service and to prevent their reuse are known as cancellations. If the marking is made with a pen, it is considered a "pen cancel." When the location of the post office appears in the marking, it is a "town cancellation." A "postmark" is technically any postal marking, but in practice the term generally is applied to a town cancellation with a date. When calling attention to a cause or celebration, the marking is known as a "slogan cancellation." Many other types and styles of cancellations exist, such as duplex, numerals, targets, fancy and others. See also "precancels," below.

Coil Stamps — These are stamps that are issued in rolls for use in dispensers, affixing and vending machines. Those coils of the United States, Canada, Sweden and some other countries are perforated horizontally or vertically only, with the outer edges imperforate. Coil stamps of some countries, such as Great Britain and Germany, are perforated on all four sides and may in some cases be distinguished from their sheet stamp counterparts by watermarks, counting numbers on the reverse or other means.

Covers — Entire envelopes, with or without adhesive postage stamps, that have passed through the mail and bear postal or other markings of philatelic interest are known as covers. Before the introduction of envelopes in about 1840, people folded letters and wrote the address on the outside. Some people covered their letters with an extra sheet of paper on the outside for the address, producing the term "cover." Used airletter sheets, stamped envelopes and other items of postal stationery also are considered covers.

Errors — Stamps that have some major, consistent, unintentional deviation from the normal are considered errors. Errors include, but are not limited to, missing or wrong colors, wrong paper, wrong watermarks, inverted centers or frames on multicolor printing, inverted or missing surcharges or overprints, double impressions, missing perforations and others. Factually wrong or misspelled information, if it appears on all examples of a stamp, are not considered errors in the true sense of the word. They are errors of design. Inconsistent or randomly appearing items, such as misperfs or color shifts, are classified as freaks.

Color-Omitted Errors — This term refers to stamps where a missing color is caused by the complete failure of the printing plate to deliver ink to the stamp paper or any other paper. Generally, this is caused by the printing plate not being engaged on the press or the ink station running dry of ink during printing.

Color-Missing Errors — This term refers to stamps where a color or colors were printed somewhere but do not appear on the finished stamp. There are four different classes of color-missing errors, and the catalog indicates with a two-letter code appended to each such listing what caused the color to be missing. These codes are used only for the United States' color-missing error listings.

FO = A *foldover* of the stamp sheet during printing may block ink from appearing on a stamp. Instead, the color will appear on the back of the foldover (where it might fall on the back of the selvage or perhaps on the back of another stamp.)

EP = A piece of *extraneous paper* falling across the plate or stamp paper will receive the printed ink. When the extraneous paper is removed, an unprinted portion of stamp paper remains and shows partially or totally missing colors.

CM = A misregistration of the printing plates during printing will result in a *color misregistration*, and such a misregistraion may result in a color not appearing on the finished stamp.

PS = A *perforation shift* after printing may remove a color from the finished stamp. Normally, this will occur on a row of stamps at the edge of the stamp pane.

Overprints and Surcharges — Overprinting involves applying wording or design elements over an already existing stamp. Overprints can be used to alter the place of use (such as "Canal Zone" on U.S. stamps), to adapt them for a special purpose ("Porto" on Denmark's 1913-20 regular issues for use as postage due stamps, Scott J1-J7) or to commemorate a special occasion (United States Scott 647-648).

A *surcharge* is a form of overprint that changes or restates the face value of a stamp or piece of postal stationery.

Surcharges and overprints may be handstamped, typeset or, occasionally, lithographed or engraved. A few hand-written overprints and surcharges are known.

Personalized Stamps — In 1999, Australia issued stamps with se-tenant labels that could be personalized with pictures of the customer's choice. Other countries quickly followed suit, with some offering to print the selected picture on the stamp itself within a frame that was used exclusively for personalized issues. As the picture used on these stamps or labels vary, listings for such stamps are for *any* picture within the common frame (or any picture on a se-tenant label), be it a "generic" image or one produced especially for a customer, almost invariably at a premium price.

Precancels — Stamps that are canceled before they are placed in the mail are known as precancels. Precanceling usually is done to expedite the handling of large mailings and generally allow the affected mail pieces to skip certain phases of mail handling.

In the United States, precancellations generally identified the point of origin; that is, the city and state. This information appeared across the face of the stamp, usually centered between parallel lines. More recently, bureau precancels retained the parallel lines, but the city and state designations were dropped. Recent coils have a service inscription that is present on the original printing plate. These show the mail service paid for by the stamp. Since these stamps are not intended to receive further cancellations when used as intended, they are considered precancels. Such items often do not have parallel lines as part of the precancellation.

In France, the abbreviation *Affranchts* in a semicircle together with the word *Postes* is the general form of precancel in use. Belgian precancellations usually appear in a box in which the name of the city appears. Netherlands precancels have the name of the city enclosed between concentric circles, sometimes called a "lifesaver." Precancellations of other countries usually follow these patterns, but may be any arrangement of bars, boxes and city names.

Precancels are listed in the Scott catalogues only if the precancel changes the denomination (Belgium Scott 477-478); if the precanceled stamp is different from the non-precanceled version (such as untagged U.S. precancels); or if the stamp exists only precanceled (France Scott 1096-1099, U.S. Scott 2265).

Proofs and Essays — Proofs are impressions taken from an approved die, plate or stone in which the design and color are the same as the stamp issued to the public. Trial color proofs are impressions taken from approved dies, plates or stones in colors that vary from the final version. An essay is the impression of a design that differs in some way from the issued stamp. "Progressive die proofs" generally are considered to be essays.

Provisionals — These are stamps that are issued on short notice and intended for temporary use pending the arrival of regular issues. They usually are issued to meet such contingencies as changes in government or currency, shortage of necessary postage values or military occupation.

During the 1840s, postmasters in certain American cities issued stamps that were valid only at specific post offices. In 1861, postmasters of the Confederate States also issued stamps with limited validity. Both of these examples are known as "postmaster's provisionals."

Se-tenant — This term refers to an unsevered pair, strip or block of stamps that differ in design, denomination or overprint.

Unless the se-tenant item has a continuous design (see U.S. Scott 1451a, 1694a) the stamps do not have to be in the same order as shown in the catalogue (see U.S. Scott 2158a).

Specimens — The Universal Postal Union required member nations to send samples of all stamps they released into service to the International Bureau in Switzerland. Member nations of the UPU received these specimens as samples of what stamps were valid for postage. Many are overprinted, handstamped or initial-perforated "Specimen," "Canceled" or "Muestra." Some are marked with bars across the denominations (China-Taiwan), punched holes (Czechoslovakia) or back inscriptions (Mongolia).

Stamps distributed to government officials or for publicity purposes, and stamps submitted by private security printers for official approval, also may receive such defacements.

The previously described defacement markings prevent postal use, and all such items generally are known as "specimens."

Tete Beche — This term describes a pair of stamps in which one is upside down in relation to the other. Some of these are the result of intentional sheet arrangements, such as Morocco Scott B10-B11. Others occurred when one or more electrotypes accidentally were placed upside down on the plate, such as Colombia Scott 57a. Separation of the tete-beche stamps, of course, destroys the tete beche variety.

Currency Conversion

Country	Dollar	Pound	S Franc	Yen	HK $	Euro	Cdn $	Aus $
Australia	1.3214	2.4694	1.1148	0.0126	0.1697	1.7244	1.0726	-----
Canada	1.2320	2.3024	1.0394	0.0118	0.1582	1.6077	-----	0.9323
European Union	0.7663	1.4321	0.6465	0.0073	0.0984	-----	0.6220	0.5799
Hong Kong	7.7882	14.555	6.5707	0.0743	-----	10.163	6.3216	5.8939
Japan	104.84	195.93	88.454	-----	13.462	136.82	85.101	79.343
Switzerland	1.1853	2.2151	-----	0.0113	0.1522	1.5468	0.9621	0.8970
United Kingdom	0.5351	-----	0.4514	0.0051	0.0687	0.6983	0.4343	0.4050
United States	-----	1.8688	0.8437	0.0095	0.1284	1.3050	0.8117	0.7568

Country	Currency	U.S. $ Equiv.
Cambodia	riel	.0003
Cameroun	Community of French Africa (CFA) franc	.0020
Canada	dollar	.8177
Cape Verde	escudo	.0118
Cayman Islands	dollar	1.220
Central Afica Republic	CFA franc	.0020
Chad	CFA franc	.0020
Chile	peso	.0017
China (Taiwan)	dollar	.0312
China (People's Republic)	yuan	.1208
Christmas Island	Australian dollar	.7568
Cocos Island	Australian dollar	.7568
Columbia	peso	.0004
Comoro Islands	franc	.0027
Congo Republic	CFA franc	.0020
Cook Islands	New Zealand dollar	.6942
Costa Rica	colon	.0022
Croatia	kuna	.1728
Cyprus	pound	2.248
Czech Republic	koruna	.0429
Denmark	krone	.1753
Djibouti	franc	.0057
Dominica	East Caribbean dollar	.3745
Dominican Republic	peso	.0339
Ecuador	US dollar	1.00
Egypt	pound	.1679
Equatorial Guinea	CFA franc	.0020
Eritrea	nakfa	.0741
Estonia	kroon	.0834
Ethiopia	birr	.1163
Falkland Islands	pound	1.8688
Faroe Islands	krone	.1753
Fiji	dollar	.5977
Finland	euro	1.3050
Aland Islands	euro	1.3050
France	euro	1.3050
French Polynesia	Community of French Pacific (CFP) franc	.0110
French So. & Antarctic Terr.	euro	1.3050

Source: ***Wall Street Journal*** *Jan. 10, 2005. Figures reflect values as of Jan. 7, 2005.*

COMMON DESIGN TYPES

Pictured in this section are issues where one illustration has been used for a number of countries in the Catalogue. Not included in this section are overprinted stamps or those issues which are illustrated in each country.

EUROPA

Europa, 1956

The design symbolizing the cooperation among the six countries comprising the Coal and Steel Community is illustrated in each country.

Belgium 496-497
France 805-806
Germany 748-749
Italy 715-716
Luxembourg 318-320
Netherlands 368-369

Europa, 1958

"E" and Dove — CD1

European Postal Union at the service of European integration.

1958, Sept. 13

Belgium 527-528
France 889-890
Germany 790-791
Italy 750-751
Luxembourg 341-343
Netherlands 375-376
Saar 317-318

Europa, 1959

6-Link Enless Chain — CD2

1959, Sept. 19

Belgium 536-537
France 929-930
Germany 805-806
Italy 791-792
Luxembourg 354-355
Netherlands 379-380

Europa, 1960

19-Spoke Wheel CD3

First anniverary of the establishment of C.E.P.T. (Conference Europeenne des Administrations des Postes et des Telecommunications.) The spokes symbolize the 19 founding members of the Conference.

1960, Sept.

Belgium 553-554
Denmark 379
Finland 376-377
France 970-971
Germany 818-820
Great Britain 377-378
Greece 688
Iceland 327-328
Ireland 175-176
Italy 809-810
Luxembourg 374-375
Netherlands 385-386
Norway 387
Portugal 866-867
Spain 941-942
Sweden 562-563
Switzerland 400-401
Turkey 1493-1494

Europa, 1961

19 Doves Flying as One — CD4

The 19 doves represent the 19 members of the Conference of European Postal and Telecommunications Administrations C.E.P.T.

1961-62

Belgium 572-573
Cyprus 201-203
France 1005-1006
Germany 844-845
Great Britain 383-384
Greece 718-719
Iceland 340-341
Italy 845-846
Luxembourg 382-383
Netherlands 387-388
Spain 1010-1011
Switzerland 410-411
Turkey 1518-1520

Europa, 1962

Young Tree with 19 Leaves CD5

The 19 leaves represent the 19 original members of C.E.P.T.

1962-63

Belgium 582-583
Cyprus 219-221
France 1045-1046
Germany 852-853
Greece 739-740
Iceland 348-349
Ireland 184-185
Italy 860-861
Luxembourg 386-387
Netherlands 394-395
Norway 414-415
Switzerland 416-417
Turkey 1553-1555

Europa, 1963

Stylized Links, Symbolizing Unity — CD6

1963, Sept.

Belgium 598-599
Cyprus 229-231
Finland 419
France 1074-1075
Germany 867-868
Greece 768-769
Iceland 357-358
Ireland 188-189
Italy 880-881
Luxembourg 403-404
Netherlands 416-417
Norway 441-442
Switzerland 429
Turkey 1602-1603

Europa, 1964

Symbolic Daisy — CD7

5th anniversary of the establishment of C.E.P.T. The 22 petals of the flower symbolize the 22 members of the Conference.

1964, Sept.

Austria 738
Belgium 614-615
Cyprus 244-246
France 1109-1110
Germany 897-898
Greece 801-802
Iceland 367-368
Ireland 196-197
Italy 894-895
Luxembourg 411-412
Monaco 590-591
Netherlands 428-429
Norway 458
Portugal 931-933
Spain 1262-1263
Switzerland 438-439
Turkey 1628-1629

Europa, 1965

Leaves and "Fruit" CD8

1965

Belgium 636-637
Cyprus 262-264
Finland 437
France 1131-1132
Germany 934-935
Greece 833-834
Iceland 375-376
Ireland 204-205
Italy 915-916
Luxembourg 432-433
Monaco 616-617
Netherlands 438-439
Norway 475-476
Portugal 958-960
Switzerland 469
Turkey 1665-1666

Europa, 1966

Symbolic Sailboat — CD9

1966, Sept.

Andorra, French 172
Belgium 675-676
Cyprus 275-277
France 1163-1164
Germany 963-964
Greece 862-863
Iceland 384-385
Ireland 216-217
Italy 942-943
Liechtenstein 415
Luxembourg 440-441
Monaco 639-640
Netherlands 441-442
Norway 496-497
Portugal 980-982
Switzerland 477-478
Turkey 1718-1719

Europa, 1967

Cogwheels CD10

1967

Andorra, French 174-175
Belgium 688-689
Cyprus 297-299
France 1178-1179
Germany 969-970
Greece 891-892
Iceland 389-390
Ireland 232-233
Italy 951-952
Liechtenstein 420
Luxembourg 449-450
Monaco 669-670
Netherlands 444-447
Norway 504-505
Portugal 994-996
Spain 1465-1466
Switzerland 482
Turkey B120-B121

Europa, 1968

Golden Key with C.E.P.T. Emblem CD11

1968

Andorra, French 182-183
Belgium 705-706
Cyprus 314-316

France 1209-1210
Germany 983-984
Greece 916-917
Iceland 395-396
Ireland 242-243
Italy 979-980
Liechtenstein 442
Luxembourg 466-467
Monaco 689-691
Netherlands 452-453
Portugal 1019-1021
San Marino 687
Spain 1526
Turkey 1775-1776

Europa, 1969

"EUROPA" and "CEPT" CD12

Tenth anniversary of C.E.P.T.

1969

Andorra, French 188-189
Austria 837
Belgium 718-719
Cyprus 326-328
Denmark 458
Finland 483
France 1245-1246
Germany 996-997
Great Britain 585
Greece 947-948
Iceland 406-407
Ireland 270-271
Italy 1000-1001
Liechtenstein 453
Luxembourg 474-475
Monaco 722-724
Netherlands 475-476
Norway 533-534
Portugal 1038-1040
San Marino 701-702
Spain 1567
Sweden 814-816
Switzerland 500-501
Turkey 1799-1800
Vatican 470-472
Yugoslavia 1003-1004

Europa, 1970

Interwoven Threads CD13

1970

Andorra, French 196-197
Belgium 741-742
Cyprus 340-342
France 1271-1272
Germany 1018-1019
Greece 985, 987
Iceland 420-421
Ireland 279-281
Italy 1013-1014
Liechtenstein 470
Luxembourg 489-490
Monaco 768-770
Netherlands 483-484
Portugal 1060-1062
San Marino 729-730
Spain 1607
Switzerland 515-516
Turkey 1848-1849
Yugoslavia 1024-1025

Europa, 1971

"Fraternity, Cooperation, Common Effort" CD14

1971

Andorra, French 205-206
Belgium 803-804
Cyprus 365-367
Finland 504
France 1304
Germany 1064-1065
Greece 1029-1030
Iceland 429-430
Ireland 305-306
Italy 1030-1039
Liechtenstein 485
Luxembourg 500-501
Malta 425-427
Monaco 797-799
Netherlands 488-489
Portugal 1094-1096
San Marino 749-750
Spain 1675-1676
Switzerland 531-532
Turkey 1876-1877
Yugoslavia 1052-1053

Europa, 1972

Sparkles, Symbolic of Communications CD15

1972

Andorra, French 210-211
Andorra, Spanish 62
Belgium 825-826
Cyprus 380-382
Finland 512-513
France 1341
Germany 1089-1090
Greece 1049-1050
Iceland 439-440
Ireland 316-317
Italy 1065-1066
Liechtenstein 504
Luxembourg 512-513
Malta 450-453
Monaco 831-832
Netherlands 494-495
Portugal 1141-1143
San Marino 771-772
Spain 1718
Switzerland 544-545
Turkey 1907-1908
Yugoslavia 1100-1101

Europa, 1973

Post Horn and Arrows CD16

1973

Andorra, French 219-220
Andorra, Spanish 76
Belgium 839-840
Cyprus 396-398
Finland 526
France 1367
Germany 1114-1115
Greece 1090-1092
Iceland 447-448
Ireland 329-330
Italy 1108-1109
Liechtenstein 528-529
Luxembourg 523-524
Malta 469-471
Monaco 866-867
Netherlands 504-505
Norway 604-605
Portugal 1170-1172
San Marino 802-803
Spain 1753
Switzerland 580-581
Turkey 1935-1936
Yugoslavia 1138-1139

Europa, 2000

CD17

2000

Albania 2621-2622
Andorra, French 522
Andorra, Spanish 262
Armenia 610-611
Austria 1814
Azerbaijan 698-699
Belarus 350
Belgium 1818
Bosnia & Herzegovina (Moslem) 358
Bosnia & Herzegovina (Serb) 111-112
Croatia 428-429
Cyprus 959
Czech Republic 3120
Denmark 1189
Estonia 394
Faroe Islands 376
Finland 1129
Aland Islands 166
France 2771
Georgia 228-229
Germany 2086-2087
Gibraltar 837-840
Great Britain (Guernsey) 805-809
Great Britain (Jersey) 935-936
Great Britain (Isle of Man) 883
Greece 1959
Greenland 363
Hungary 3699-3700
Iceland 910
Ireland 1230-1231
Italy 2349
Latvia 504
Liechtenstein 1178
Lithuania 668
Luxembourg 1035
Macedonia 187
Malta 1011-1012
Moldova 355
Monaco 2161-2162
Poland 3519
Portugal 2358
Portugal (Azores) 455
Portugal (Madeira) 208
Romania 4370
Russia 6589
San Marino 1480
Slovakia 355
Slovenia 424
Spain 3036
Sweden 2394
Switzerland 1074
Turkey 2762
Turkish Rep. of Northern Cyprus 500
Ukraine 379
Vatican City 1152

The Gibraltar stamps are similar to the stamp illustrated, but none have the design shown above. All other sets listed above include at least one stamp with the design shown, but some include stamps with entirely different designs. Bulgaria Nos. 4131-4132 and Yugoslavia Nos. 2485-2486 are Europa stamps with completely different designs.

PORTUGAL & COLONIES

Vasco da Gama

Fleet Departing CD20

Fleet Arriving at Calicut — CD21

Embarking at Rastello CD22

Muse of History CD23

San Gabriel, da Gama and Camoens CD24

Archangel Gabriel, the Patron Saint CD25

Flagship San Gabriel — CD26

Vasco da Gama — CD27

Fourth centenary of Vasco da Gama's discovery of the route to India.

1898

Azores 93-100
Macao 67-74
Madeira 37-44
Portugal 147-154
Port. Africa 1-8
Port. Congo 75-98
Port. India 189-196
St. Thomas & Prince Islands 170-193
Timor 45-52

Pombal
POSTAL TAX
POSTAL TAX DUES

Marquis de Pombal — CD28

Planning Reconstruction of Lisbon, 1755 — CD29

Pombal Monument, Lisbon — CD30

Sebastiao Jose de Carvalho e Mello, Marquis de Pombal (1699-1782), statesman, rebuilt Lisbon after earthquake of 1755. Tax was for the erection of Pombal monument. Obligatory on all mail on certain days throughout the year. Postal Tax Dues are inscribed "Multa."

1925

Angola RA1-RA3, RAJ1-RAJ3
Azores RA9-RA11, RAJ2-RAJ4
Cape Verde RA1-RA3, RAJ1-RAJ3
Macao RA1-RA3, RAJ1-RAJ3
Madeira RA1-RA3, RAJ1-RAJ3
Mozambique RA1-RA3, RAJ1-RAJ3

Nyassa RA1-RA3, RAJ1-RAJ3
Portugal RA11-RA13, RAJ2-RAJ4
Port. Guinea RA1-RA3, RAJ1-RAJ3
Port. India RA1-RA3, RAJ1-RAJ3
St. Thomas & Prince
Islands RA1-RA3, RAJ1-RAJ3
Timor RA1-RA3, RAJ1-RAJ3

Vasco da Gama
CD34

Mousinho de Albuquerque
CD35

Dam
CD36

Prince Henry the Navigator
CD37

Affonso de Albuquerque
CD38

Plane over Globe
CD39

1938-39

Angola 274-291, C1-C9
Cape Verde 234-251, C1-C9
Macao 289-305, C7-C15
Mozambique 270-287, C1-C9
Port. Guinea 233-250. C1-C9
Port. India 439-453, C1-C8
St. Thomas & Prince
Islands ... 302-319, 323-340, C1-C18
Timor 223-239, C1-C9

Lady of Fatima

Our Lady of the Rosary, Fatima, Portugal — CD40

1948-49

Angola 315-318
Cape Verde 266
Macao 336
Mozambique 325-328
Port. Guinea 271
Port. India 480
St. Thomas & Prince Islands 351
Timor 254

A souvenir sheet of 9 stamps was issued in 1951 to mark the extension of the 1950 Holy Year. The sheet contains: Angola No. 316, Cape Verde No. 266, Macao No. 336, Mozambique No. 325, Portuguese Guinea No. 271, Portuguese India Nos. 480, 485, St. Thomas & Prince Islands No. 351, Timor No. 254. The sheet also contains a portrait of Pope Pius XII and is inscribed "Encerramento do Ano Santo, Fatima 1951." It was sold for 11 escudos.

Holy Year

Church Bells and Dove
CD41

Angel Holding Candelabra
CD42

Holy Year, 1950.

1950-51

Angola 331-332
Cape Verde 268-269
Macao 339-340
Mozambique 330-331
Port. Guinea 273-274
Port. India 490-491, 496-503
St. Thomas & Prince Islands ...353-354
Timor 258-259

A souvenir sheet of 8 stamps was issued in 1951 to mark the extension of the Holy Year. The sheet contains: Angola No. 331, Cape Verde No. 269, Macao No. 340, Mozambique No. 331, Portuguese Guinea No. 275, Portuguese India No. 490, St. Thomas & Prince Islands No. 354, Timor No. 258, some with colors changed. The sheet contains doves and is inscribed 'Encerramento do Ano Santo, Fatima 1951.' It was sold for 17 escudos.

Holy Year Conclusion

Our Lady of Fatima — CD43

Conclusion of Holy Year. Sheets contain alternate vertical rows of stamps and labels bearing quotation from Pope Pius XII, different for each colony.

1951

Angola 357
Cape Verde 270
Macao 352
Mozambique 356
Port. Guinea 275
Port. India 506
St. Thomas & Prince Islands 355
Timor 270

Medical Congress

CD44

First National Congress of Tropical Medicine, Lisbon, 1952. Each stamp has a different design.

1952

Angola 358
Cape Verde 287
Macao 364
Mozambique 359
Port. Guinea 276
Port. India 516
St. Thomas & Prince Islands 356
Timor 271

Postage Due Stamps

CD45

1952

Angola J37-J42
Cape Verde J31-J36
Macao J53-J58
Mozambique J51-J56
Port. Guinea J40-J45
Port. India J47-J52
St. Thomas & Prince Islands ... J52-J57
Timor J31-J36

Sao Paulo

Father Manuel de Nobrege and View of Sao Paulo — CD46

Founding of Sao Paulo, Brazil, 400th anniv.

1954

Angola 385
Cape Verde 297
Macao 382
Mozambique 395
Port. Guinea 291
Port. India 530
St. Thomas & Prince Islands 369
Timor 279

Tropical Medicine Congress

CD47

Sixth International Congress for Tropical Medicine and Malaria, Lisbon, Sept. 1958. Each stamp shows a different plant.

1958

Angola 409
Cape Verde 303
Macao 392
Mozambique 404
Port. Guinea 295
Port. India 569
St. Thomas & Prince Islands 371
Timor 289

Sports

CD48

Each stamp shows a different sport.

1962

Angola 433-438
Cape Verde 320-325
Macao 394-399
Mozambique 424-429
Port. Guinea 299-304
St. Thomas & Prince Islands ... 374-379
Timor 313-318

Anti-Malaria

Anopheles Funestus and Malaria Eradication Symbol — CD49

World Health Organization drive to eradicate malaria.

1962

Angola 439
Cape Verde 326
Macao 400
Mozambique 430
Port. Guinea 305
St. Thomas & Prince Islands 380
Timor 319

Airline Anniversary

Map of Africa, Super Constellation and Jet Liner — CD50

Tenth anniversary of Transportes Aereos Portugueses (TAP).

1963

Angola 490
Cape Verde 327
Mozambique 434
Port. Guinea 318
St. Thomas & Prince Islands 381

National Overseas Bank

Antonio Teixeira de Sousa — CD51

Centenary of the National Overseas Bank of Portugal.

1964, May 16

Angola 509
Cape Verde 328
Port. Guinea 319
St. Thomas & Prince Islands 382
Timor 320

ITU

ITU Emblem and the Archangel Gabriel — CD52

International Communications Union, Cent.

1965, May 17

Angola 511
Cape Verde 329
Macao 402
Mozambique 464
Port. Guinea 320
St. Thomas & Prince Islands 383
Timor 321

National Revolution

CD53

40th anniv. of the National Revolution. Different buildings on each stamp.

1966, May 28

Angola 525
Cape Verde 338
Macao 403
Mozambique 465
Port. Guinea 329
St. Thomas & Prince Islands 392
Timor 322

Navy Club

CD54

Centenary of Portugal's Navy Club. Each stamp has a different design.

1967, Jan. 31

Angola	527-528
Cape Verde	339-340
Macao	412-413
Mozambique	478-479
Port. Guinea	330-331
St. Thomas & Prince Islands	393-394
Timor	323-324

Admiral Coutinho

CD55

Centenary of the birth of Admiral Carlos Viegas Gago Coutinho (1869-1959), explorer and aviation pioneer. Each stamp has a different design.

1969, Feb. 17

Angola	547
Cape Verde	355
Macao	417
Mozambique	484
Port. Guinea	335
St. Thomas & Prince Islands	397
Timor	335

Administration Reform

Luiz Augusto Rebello da Silva — CD56

Centenary of the administration reforms of the overseas territories.

1969, Sept. 25

Angola	549
Cape Verde	357
Macao	419
Mozambique	491
Port. Guinea	337
St. Thomas & Prince Islands	399
Timor	338

Marshal Carmona

CD57

Birth centenary of Marshal Antonio Oscar Carmona de Fragoso (1869-1951), President of Portugal. Each stamp has a different design.

1970, Nov. 15

Angola	563
Cape Verde	359
Macao	422
Mozambique	493
Port. Guinea	340
St. Thomas & Prince Islands	403
Timor	341

Olympic Games

CD59

20th Olympic Games, Munich, Aug. 26-Sept. 11. Each stamp shows a different sport.

1972, June 20

Angola	569
Cape Verde	361
Macao	426
Mozambique	504
Port. Guinea	342
St. Thomas & Prince Islands	408
Timor	343

Lisbon-Rio de Janeiro Flight

CD60

50th anniversary of the Lisbon to Rio de Janeiro flight by Arturo de Sacadura and Coutinho, March 30-June 5, 1922. Each stamp shows a different stage of the flight.

1972, Sept. 20

Angola	570
Cape Verde	362
Macao	427
Mozambique	505
Port. Guinea	343
St. Thomas & Prince Islands	409
Timor	344

WMO Centenary

WMO Emblem — CD61

Centenary of international meterological cooperation.

1973, Dec. 15

Angola	571
Cape Verde	363
Macao	429
Mozambique	509
Port. Guinea	344
St. Thomas & Prince Islands	410
Timor	345

FRENCH COMMUNITY

Upper Volta can be found under Burkina Faso in Vol. 1

Madagascar can be found under Malagasy in Vol. 3

Colonial Exposition

People of French Empire CD70

Women's Heads CD71

France Showing Way to Civilization CD72

"Colonial Commerce" CD73

International Colonial Exposition, Paris.

1931

Cameroun	213-216
Chad	60-63
Dahomey	97-100
Fr. Guiana	152-155
Fr. Guinea	116-119
Fr. India	100-103
Fr. Polynesia	76-79
Fr. Sudan	102-105
Gabon	120-123
Guadeloupe	138-141
Indo-China	140-142
Ivory Coast	92-95
Madagascar	169-172
Martinique	129-132
Mauritania	65-68
Middle Congo	61-64
New Caledonia	176-179
Niger	73-76
Reunion	122-125
St. Pierre & Miquelon	132-135
Senegal	138-141
Somali Coast	135-138
Togo	254-257
Ubangi-Shari	82-85
Upper Volta	66-69
Wallis & Futuna Isls.	85-88

Paris International Exposition Colonial Arts Exposition

"Colonial Resources" CD74 CD77

Overseas Commerce CD75

Exposition Building and Women CD76

"France and the Empire" CD78

Cultural Treasures of the Colonies CD79

Souvenir sheets contain one imperf. stamp.

1937

Cameroun	217-222A
Dahomey	101-107
Fr. Equatorial Africa	27-32, 73
Fr. Guiana	162-168
Fr. Guinea	120-126
Fr. India	104-110
Fr. Polynesia	117-123
Fr. Sudan	106-112
Guadeloupe	148-154
Indo-China	193-199
Inini	41
Ivory Coast	152-158
Kwangchowan	132
Madagascar	191-197
Martinique	179-185
Mauritania	69-75
New Caledonia	208-214
Niger	72-83
Reunion	167-173
St. Pierre & Miquelon	165-171
Senegal	172-178
Somali Coast	139-145
Togo	258-264
Wallis & Futuna Isls.	89

Curie

Pierre and Marie Curie CD80

40th anniversary of the discovery of radium. The surtax was for the benefit of the Intl. Union for the Control of Cancer.

1938

Cameroun	B1
Cuba	B1-B2
Dahomey	B2
France	B76
Fr. Equatorial Africa	B1
Fr. Guiana	B3
Fr. Guinea	B2
Fr. India	B6
Fr. Polynesia	B5
Fr. Sudan	B1
Guadeloupe	B3
Indo-China	B14
Ivory Coast	B2
Madagascar	B2
Martinique	B2
Mauritania	B3
New Caledonia	B4
Niger	B1
Reunion	B4
St. Pierre & Miquelon	B3
Senegal	B3
Somali Coast	B2
Togo	B1

Caillie

Rene Caille and Map of Northwestern Africa — CD81

Death centenary of Rene Caillie (1799-1838), French explorer. All three denominations exist with colony name omitted.

1939

Dahomey	108-110
Fr. Guinea	161-163
Fr. Sudan	113-115
Ivory Coast	160-162
Mauritania	109-111
Niger	84-86
Senegal	188-190
Togo	265-267

New York World's Fair

Natives and New York Skyline CD82

1939

Cameroun	223-224
Dahomey	111-112
Fr. Equatorial Africa	78-79
Fr. Guiana	169-170
Fr. Guinea	164-165
Fr. India	111-112
Fr. Polynesia	124-125
Fr. Sudan	116-117
Guadeloupe	155-156
Indo-China	203-204
Inini	42-43
Ivory Coast	163-164
Kwangchowan	121-122

Madagascar.....209-210
Martinique.....186-187
Mauritania.....112-113
New Caledonia.....215-216
Niger.....87-88
Reunion.....174-175
St. Pierre & Miquelon.....205-206
Senegal.....191-192
Somali Coast.....179-180
Togo.....268-269
Wallis & Futuna Isls......90-91

French Revolution

Storming of the Bastille CD83

French Revolution, 150th anniv. The surtax was for the defense of the colonies.

1939

Cameroun.....B2-B6
Dahomey.....B3-B7
Fr. Equatorial Africa.....B4-B8, CB1
Fr. Guiana.....B4-B8, CB1
Fr. Guinea.....B3-B7
Fr. India.....B7-B11
Fr. Polynesia.....B6-B10, CB1
Fr. Sudan.....B2-B6
Guadeloupe.....B4-B8
Indo-China.....B15-B19, CB1
Inini.....B1-B5
Ivory Coast.....B3-B7
Kwangchowan.....B1-B5
Madagascar.....B3-B7, CB1
Martinique.....B3-B7
Mauritania.....B4-B8
New Caledonia.....B5-B9, CB1
Niger.....B2-B6
Reunion.....B5-B9, CB1
St. Pierre & Miquelon.....B4-B8
Senegal.....B4-B8, CB1
Somali Coast.....B3-B7
Togo.....B2-B6
Wallis & Futuna Isls......B1-B5

Plane over Coastal Area CD85

All five denominations exist with colony name omitted.

1940

Dahomey.....C1-C5
Fr. Guinea.....C1-C5
Fr. Sudan.....C1-C5
Ivory Coast.....C1-C5
Mauritania.....C1-C5
Niger.....C1-C5
Senegal.....C12-C16
Togo.....C1-C5

Defense of the Empire

Colonial Infantryman — CD86

1941

Cameroun.....B13B
Dahomey.....B13
Fr. Equatorial Africa.....B8B
Fr. Guiana.....B10
Fr. Guinea.....B13
Fr. India.....B13
Fr. Polynesia.....B12
Fr. Sudan.....B12
Guadeloupe.....B10
Indo-China.....B19B
Inini.....B7
Ivory Coast.....B13
Kwangchowan.....B7
Madagascar.....B9
Martinique.....B9
Mauritania.....B14
New Caledonia.....B11
Niger.....B12
Reunion.....B11
St. Pierre & Miquelon.....B8B
Senegal.....B14
Somali Coast.....B9
Togo.....B10B
Wallis & Futuna Isls......B7

Colonial Education Fund

CD86a

1942

Cameroun.....CB3
Dahomey.....CB4
Fr. Equatorial Africa.....CB5
Fr. Guiana.....CB4
Fr. Guinea.....CB4
Fr. India.....CB3
Fr. Polynesia.....CB4
Fr. Sudan.....CB4
Guadeloupe.....CB3
Indo-China.....CB5
Inini.....CB3
Ivory Coast.....CB4
Kwangchowan.....CB4
Malagasy.....CB5
Martinique.....CB3
Mauritania.....CB4
New Caledonia.....CB4
Niger.....CB4
Reunion.....CB4
St. Pierre & Miquelon.....CB3
Senegal.....CB5
Somali Coast.....CB3
Togo.....CB3
Wallis & Futuna.....CB3

Cross of Lorraine & Four-motor Plane CD87

1941-5

Cameroun.....C1-C7
Fr. Equatorial Africa.....C17-C23
Fr. Guiana.....C9-C10
Fr. India.....C1-C6
Fr. Polynesia.....C3-C9
Fr. West Africa.....C1-C3
Guadeloupe.....C1-C2
Madagascar.....C37-C43
Martinique.....C1-C2
New Caledonia.....C7-C13
Reunion.....C18-C24
St. Pierre & Miquelon.....C1-C7
Somali Coast.....C1-C7

Transport Plane CD88

Caravan and Plane CD89

1942

Dahomey.....C6-C13
Fr. Guinea.....C6-C13
Fr. Sudan.....C6-C13
Ivory Coast.....C6-C13
Mauritania.....C6-C13
Niger.....C6-C13
Senegal.....C17-C25
Togo.....C6-C13

Red Cross

Marianne CD90

The surtax was for the French Red Cross and national relief.

1944

Cameroun.....B28
Fr. Equatorial Africa.....B38
Fr. Guiana.....B12
Fr. India.....B14
Fr. Polynesia.....B13
Fr. West Africa.....B1
Guadeloupe.....B12
Madagascar.....B15
Martinique.....B11
New Caledonia.....B13
Reunion.....B15
St. Pierre & Miquelon.....B13
Somali Coast.....B13
Wallis & Futuna Isls......B9

Eboue

CD91

Felix Eboue, first French colonial administrator to proclaim resistance to Germany after French surrender in World War II.

1945

Cameroun.....296-297
Fr. Equatorial Africa.....156-157
Fr. Guiana.....171-172
Fr. India.....210-211
Fr. Polynesia.....150-151
Fr. West Africa.....15-16
Guadeloupe.....187-188
Madagascar.....259-260
Martinique.....196-197
New Caledonia.....274-275
Reunion.....238-239
St. Pierre & Miquelon.....322-323
Somali Coast.....238-239

Victory

Victory — CD92

European victory of the Allied Nations in World War II.

1946, May 8

Cameroun.....C8
Fr. Equatorial Africa.....C24
Fr. Guiana.....C11
Fr. India.....C7
Fr. Polynesia.....C10
Fr. West Africa.....C4
Guadeloupe.....C3
Indo-China.....C19
Madagascar.....C44
Martinique.....C3
New Caledonia.....C14
Reunion.....C25
St. Pierre & Miquelon.....C8
Somali Coast.....C8
Wallis & Futuna Isls......C1

Chad to Rhine

Leclerc's Departure from Chad — CD93

Battle at Cufra Oasis — CD94

Tanks in Action, Mareth — CD95

Normandy Invasion — CD96

Entering Paris — CD97

Liberation of Strasbourg — CD98

"Chad to the Rhine" march, 1942-44, by Gen. Jacques Leclerc's column, later French 2nd Armored Division.

1946, June 6

Cameroun.....C9-C14
Fr. Equatorial Africa.....C25-C30
Fr. Guiana.....C12-C17
Fr. India.....C8-C13
Fr. Polynesia.....C11-C16
Fr. West Africa.....C5-C10
Guadeloupe.....C4-C9
Indo-China.....C20-C25
Madagascar.....C45-C50
Martinique.....C4-C9
New Caledonia.....C15-C20
Reunion.....C26-C31
St. Pierre & Miquelon.....C9-C14
Somali Coast.....C9-C14
Wallis & Futuna Isls......C2-C7

UPU

French Colonials, Globe and Plane — CD99

Universal Postal Union, 75th anniv.

1949, July 4

Cameroun........C29
Fr. Equatorial Africa........C34
Fr. India........C17
Fr. Polynesia........C20
Fr. West Africa........C15
Indo-China........C26
Madagascar........C55
New Caledonia........C24
St. Pierre & Miquelon........C18
Somali Coast........C18
Togo........C18
Wallis & Futuna Isls........C10

Tropical Medicine

Doctor Treating Infant CD100

The surtax was for charitable work.

1950

Cameroun........B29
Fr. Equatorial Africa........B39
Fr. India........B15
Fr. Polynesia........B14
Fr. West Africa........B3
Madagascar........B17
New Caledonia........B14
St. Pierre & Miquelon........B14
Somali Coast........B14
Togo........B11

Military Medal

Medal, Early Marine and Colonial Soldier — CD101

Centenary of the creation of the French Military Medal.

1952

Cameroun........332
Comoro Isls........39
Fr. Equatorial Africa........186
Fr. India........233
Fr. Polynesia........179
Fr. West Africa........57
Madagascar........286
New Caledonia........295
St. Pierre & Miquelon........345
Somali Coast........267
Togo........327
Wallis & Futuna Isls........149

Liberation

Allied Landing, Victory Sign and Cross of Lorraine — CD102

Liberation of France, 10th anniv.

1954, June 6

Cameroun........C32
Comoro Isls........C4
Fr. Equatorial Africa........C38
Fr. India........C18
Fr. Polynesia........C22
Fr. West Africa........C17
Madagascar........C57
New Caledonia........C25
St. Pierre & Miquelon........C19
Somali Coast........C19
Togo........C19
Wallis & Futuna Isls........C11

FIDES

Plowmen CD103

Efforts of FIDES, the Economic and Social Development Fund for Overseas Possessions (Fonds d' Investissement pour le Developpement Economique et Social). Each stamp has a different design.

1956

Cameroun........326-329
Comoro Isls........43
Fr. Polynesia........181
Fr. West Africa........65-72
Madagascar........292-295
New Caledonia........303
Somali Coast........268
Togo........331

Flower

CD104

Each stamp shows a different flower.

1958-9

Cameroun........333
Comoro Isls........45
Fr. Equatorial Africa........200-201
Fr. Polynesia........192
Fr. So. & Antarctic Terr........11
Fr. West Africa........79-83
Madagascar........301-302
New Caledonia........304-305
St. Pierre & Miquelon........357
Somali Coast........270
Togo........348-349
Wallis & Futuna Isls........152

Human Rights

Sun, Dove and U.N. Emblem CD105

10th anniversary of the signing of the Universal Declaration of Human Rights.

1958

Comoro Isls........44
Fr. Equatorial Africa........202
Fr. Polynesia........191
Fr. West Africa........85
Madagascar........300
New Caledonia........306
St. Pierre & Miquelon........356
Somali Coast........274
Wallis & Futuna Isls........153

C.C.T.A.

CD106

Commission for Technical Cooperation in Africa south of the Sahara, 10th anniv.

1960

Cameroun........335
Cent. Africa........3
Chad........66
Congo, P.R........90
Dahomey........138
Gabon........150
Ivory Coast........180
Madagascar........317
Mali........9
Mauritania........117
Niger........104
Upper Volta........89

Air Afrique, 1961

Modern and Ancient Africa, Map and Planes — CD107

Founding of Air Afrique (African Airlines).

1961-62

Cameroun........C37
Cent. Africa........C5
Chad........C7
Congo, P.R........C5
Dahomey........C17
Gabon........C5
Ivory Coast........C18
Mauritania........C17
Niger........C22
Senegal........C31
Upper Volta........C4

Anti-Malaria

CD108

World Health Organization drive to eradicate malaria.

1962, Apr. 7

Cameroun........B36
Cent. Africa........B1
Chad........B1
Comoro Isls........B1
Congo, P.R........B3
Dahomey........B15
Gabon........B4
Ivory Coast........B15
Madagascar........B19
Mali........B1
Mauritania........B16
Niger........B14
Senegal........B16
Somali Coast........B15
Upper Volta........B1

Abidjan Games

CD109

Abidjan Games, Ivory Coast, Dec. 24-31, 1961. Each stamp shows a different sport.

1962

Chad........83-84
Cent. Africa........19-20
Congo, P.R........103-104
Gabon........163-164, C6
Niger........109-111
Upper Volta........103-105

African and Malagasy Union

Flag of Union CD110

First anniversary of the Union.

1962, Sept. 8

Cameroun........373
Cent. Africa........21
Chad........85
Congo, P.R........105
Dahomey........155
Gabon........165
Ivory Coast........198
Madagascar........332
Mauritania........170
Niger........112
Senegal........211
Upper Volta........106

Telstar

Telstar and Globe Showing Andover and Pleumeur-Bodou — CD111

First television connection of the United States and Europe through the Telstar satellite, July 11-12, 1962.

1962-63

Andorra, French........154
Comoro Isls........C7
Fr. Polynesia........C29
Fr. So. & Antarctic Terr........C5
New Caledonia........C33
Somali Coast........C31
St. Pierre & Miquelon........C26
Wallis & Futuna Isls........C17

Freedom From Hunger

World Map and Wheat Emblem CD112

U.N. Food and Agriculture Organization's "Freedom from Hunger" campaign.

1963, Mar. 21

Cameroun........B37-B38
Cent. Africa........B2
Chad........B2
Congo, P.R........B4
Dahomey........B16
Gabon........B5
Ivory Coast........B16
Madagascar........B21
Mauritania........B17
Niger........B15

Senegal B17
Upper Volta B2

Red Cross Centenary

CD113

Centenary of the International Red Cross.

1963, Sept. 2

Comoro Isls. 55
Fr. Polynesia 205
New Caledonia 328
St. Pierre & Miquelon 367
Somali Coast 297
Wallis & Futuna Isls. 165

African Postal Union, 1963

UAMPT Emblem, Radio Masts, Plane and Mail CD114

Establishment of the African and Malagasy Posts and Telecommunications Union.

1963, Sept. 8

Cameroun C47
Cent. Africa C10
Chad C9
Congo, P.R. C13
Dahomey C19
Gabon C13
Ivory Coast C25
Madagascar C75
Mauritania C22
Niger C27
Rwanda 36
Senegal C32
Upper Volta C9

Air Afrique, 1963

Symbols of Flight — CD115

First anniversary of Air Afrique and inauguration of DC-8 service.

1963, Nov. 19

Cameroun C48
Chad C10
Congo, P.R. C14
Gabon C18
Ivory Coast C26
Mauritania C26
Niger C35
Senegal C33

Europafrica

Europe and Africa Linked — CD116

Signing of an economic agreement between the European Economic Community and the African and Malagasy Union, Yaounde, Cameroun, July 20, 1963.

1963-64

Cameroun 402
Chad C11
Cent. Africa C12
Congo, P.R. C16
Gabon C19
Ivory Coast 217
Niger C43
Upper Volta C11

Human Rights

Scales of Justice and Globe CD117

15th anniversary of the Universal Declaration of Human Rights.

1963, Dec. 10

Comoro Isls. 58
Fr. Polynesia 206
New Caledonia 329
St. Pierre & Miquelon 368
Somali Coast 300
Wallis & Futuna Isls. 166

PHILATEC

Stamp Album, Champs Elysees Palace and Horses of Marly CD118

Intl. Philatelic and Postal Techniques Exhibition, Paris, June 5-21, 1964.

1963-64

Comoro Isls. 60
France 1078
Fr. Polynesia 207
New Caledonia 341
St. Pierre & Miquelon 369
Somali Coast 301
Wallis & Futuna Isls. 167

Cooperation

CD119

Cooperation between France and the French-speaking countries of Africa and Madagascar.

1964

Cameroun 409-410
Cent. Africa 39
Chad 103
Congo, P.R. 121
Dahomey 193
France 1111
Gabon 175
Ivory Coast 221
Madagascar 360
Mauritania 181
Niger 143
Senegal 236
Togo 495

ITU

Telegraph, Syncom Satellite and ITU Emblem CD120

Intl. Telecommunication Union, Cent.

1965, May 17

Comoro Isls. C14
Fr. Polynesia C33
Fr. So. & Antarctic Terr. C8
New Caledonia C40
New Hebrides 124-125
St. Pierre & Miquelon C29
Somali Coast C36
Wallis & Futuna Isls. C20

French Satellite A-1

Diamant Rocket and Launching Installation — CD121

Launching of France's first satellite, Nov. 26, 1965.

1965-66

Comoro Isls. C15-C16
France 1137-1138
Fr. Polynesia C40-C41
Fr. So. & Antarctic Terr. C9-C10
New Caledonia C44-C45
St. Pierre & Miquelon C30-C31
Somali Coast C39-C40
Wallis & Futuna Isls. C22-C23

French Satellite D-1

D-1 Satellite in Orbit — CD122

Launching of the D-1 satellite at Hammaguir, Algeria, Feb. 17, 1966.

1966

Comoro Isls. C17
France 1148
Fr. Polynesia C42
Fr. So. & Antarctic Terr. C11
New Caledonia C46
St. Pierre & Miquelon C32
Somali Coast C49
Wallis & Futuna Isls. C24

Air Afrique, 1966

Planes and Air Afrique Emblem — CD123

Introduction of DC-8F planes by Air Afrique.

1966

Cameroun C79
Cent. Africa C35
Chad C26
Congo, P.R. C42
Dahomey C42
Gabon C47
Ivory Coast C32
Mauritania C57
Niger C63
Senegal C47
Togo C54
Upper Volta C31

African Postal Union, 1967

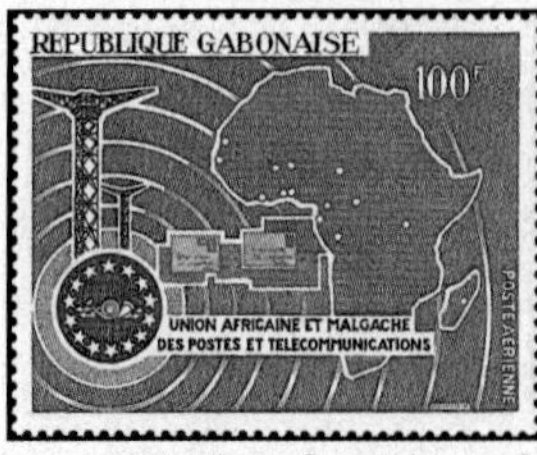

Telecommunications Symbols and Map of Africa — CD124

Fifth anniversary of the establishment of the African and Malagasy Union of Posts and Telecommunications, UAMPT.

1967

Cameroun C90
Cent. Africa C46
Chad C37
Congo, P.R. C57
Dahomey C61
Gabon C58
Ivory Coast C34
Madagascar C85
Mauritania C65
Niger C75
Rwanda C1-C3
Senegal C60
Togo C81
Upper Volta C50

Monetary Union

Gold Token of the Ashantis, 17-18th Centuries — CD125

West African Monetary Union, 5th anniv.

1967, Nov. 4

Dahomey 244
Ivory Coast 259
Mauritania 238
Niger 204
Senegal 294
Togo 623
Upper Volta 181

WHO Anniversary

Sun, Flowers and WHO Emblem CD126

World Health Organization, 20th anniv.

1968, May 4

Afars & Issas....................................317
Comoro Isls......................................73
Fr. Polynesia.............................241-242
Fr. So. & Antarctic Terr....................31
New Caledonia.................................367
St. Pierre & Miquelon.......................377
Wallis & Futuna Isls.........................169

Human Rights Year

Human Rights Flame — CD127

1968, Aug. 10

Afars & Issas............................322-323
Comoro Isls......................................76
Fr. Polynesia.............................243-244
Fr. So. & Antarctic Terr.....................32
New Caledonia.................................369
St. Pierre & Miquelon.......................382
Wallis & Futuna Isls.........................170

2nd PHILEXAFRIQUE

CD128

Opening of PHILEXAFRIQUE, Abidjan, Feb. 14. Each stamp shows a local scene and stamp.

1969, Feb. 14

Cameroun....................................C118
Cent. Africa....................................C65
Chad...C48
Congo, P.R.....................................C77
Dahomey..C94
Gabon...C82
Ivory Coast..............................C38-C40
Madagascar....................................C92
Mali...C65
Mauritania......................................C80
Niger...C104
Senegal...C68
Togo..C104
Upper Volta.....................................C62

Concorde

Concorde in Flight CD129

First flight of the prototype Concorde supersonic plane at Toulouse, Mar. 1, 1969.

1969

Afars & Issas..................................C56
Comoro Isls......................................C29
France...C42
Fr. Polynesia...................................C50
Fr. So. & Antarctic Terr...................C18
New Caledonia.................................C63
St. Pierre & Miquelon.......................C40
Wallis & Futuna Isls.........................C30

Development Bank

Bank Emblem — CD130

African Development Bank, fifth anniv.

1969

Cameroun...499
Chad...217
Congo, P.R................................181-182
Ivory Coast.......................................281
Mali..127-128
Mauritania...267
Niger...220
Senegal.....................................317-318
Upper Volta.......................................201

ILO

ILO Headquarters, Geneva, and Emblem — CD131

Intl. Labor Organization, 50th anniv.

1969-70

Afars & Issas....................................337
Comoro Isls...83
Fr. Polynesia.............................251-252
Fr. So. & Antarctic Terr.......................35
New Caledonia..................................379
St. Pierre & Miquelon........................396
Wallis & Futuna Isls..........................172

ASECNA

Map of Africa, Plane and Airport CD132

10th anniversary of the Agency for the Security of Aerial Navigation in Africa and Madagascar (ASECNA, Agence pour la Securite de la Navigation Aerienne en Afrique et a Madagascar).

1969-70

Cameroun...500
Cent. Africa......................................119
Chad...222
Congo, P.R..197
Dahomey...269
Gabon..260
Ivory Coast.......................................287
Mali...130
Niger...221
Senegal...321
Upper Volta.......................................204

U.P.U. Headquarters

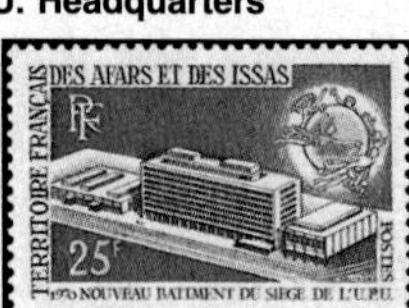

CD133

New Universal Postal Union headquarters, Bern, Switzerland.

1970

Afars & Issas....................................342
Algeria..443
Cameroun...................................503-504
Cent. Africa......................................125
Chad...225
Comoro Isls...84
Congo, P.R..216
Fr. Polynesia.............................261-262
Fr. So. & Antarctic Terr.......................36
Gabon..258
Ivory Coast.......................................295
Madagascar.......................................444
Mali...134-135
Mauritania...283
New Caledonia..................................382
Niger..231-232
St. Pierre & Miquelon...............397-398
Senegal......................................328-329
Tunisia..535
Wallis & Futuna Isls..........................173

De Gaulle

CD134

First anniversary of the death of Charles de Gaulle, (1890-1970), President of France.

1971-72

Afars & Issas............................356-357
Comoro Isls................................104-105
France.....................................1322-1325
Fr. Polynesia.............................270-271
Fr. So. & Antarctic Terr...................52-53
New Caledonia...........................393-394
Reunion.....................................377, 380
St. Pierre & Miquelon................417-418
Wallis & Futuna Isls..................177-178

African Postal Union, 1971

UAMPT Building, Brazzaville, Congo — CD135

10th anniversary of the establishment of the African and Malagasy Posts and Telecommunications Union, UAMPT. Each stamp has a different native design.

1971, Nov. 13

Cameroun.......................................C177
Cent. Africa......................................C89
Chad...C94
Congo, P.R......................................C136
Dahomey...C146
Gabon...C120
Ivory Coast.......................................C47
Mauritania.......................................C113
Niger...C164
Rwanda..C8
Senegal...C105
Togo..C166
Upper Volta.......................................C97

West African Monetary Union

African Couple, City, Village and Commemorative Coin — CD136

West African Monetary Union, 10th anniv.

1972, Nov. 2

Dahomey...300
Ivory Coast.......................................331
Mauritania...299
Niger...258
Senegal...374
Togo..825
Upper Volta.......................................280

African Postal Union, 1973

Telecommunications Symbols and Map of Africa — CD137

11th anniversary of the African and Malagasy Posts and Telecommunications Union (UAMPT).

1973, Sept. 12

Cameroun...574
Cent. Africa......................................194
Chad...294
Congo, P.R..289
Dahomey...311
Gabon..320
Ivory Coast.......................................361
Madagascar.......................................500
Mauritania...304
Niger...287
Rwanda...540
Senegal...393
Togo..849
Upper Volta.......................................297

Philexafrique II — Essen

CD138

CD139

Designs: Indigenous fauna, local and German stamps. Types CD138-CD139 printed horizontally and vertically se-tenant in sheets of 10 (2x5). Label between horizontal pairs alternately commemoratives Philexafrique II, Libreville, Gabon, June 1978, and 2nd International Stamp Fair, Essen, Germany, Nov. 1-5.

1978-1979

Benin.....................................C285-C286
Central Africa........................C200-C201
Chad......................................C238-C239
Congo Republic.....................C245-C246
Djibouti..................................C121-C122
Gabon.....................................C215-C216
Ivory Coast................................C64-C65
Mali..C356-C357
Mauritania..............................C185-C186
Niger......................................C291-C292
Rwanda.....................................C12-C13
Senegal..................................C146-C147

BRITISH COMMONWEALTH OF NATIONS

The listings follow established trade practices when these issues are offered as units by dealers. The Peace issue, for example, includes only one stamp from the Indian state of Hyderabad. The U.P.U. issue includes the Egypt set. Pairs are included for those varieties issues with bilingual designs se-tenant.

Silver Jubilee

Windsor Castle and King George V
CD301

Reign of King George V, 25th anniv.

1935

Antigua ... 77-80
Ascension ... 33-36
Bahamas ... 92-95
Barbados ... 186-189
Basutoland ... 11-14
Bechuanaland Protectorate ... 117-120
Bermuda ... 100-103
British Guiana ... 223-226
British Honduras ... 108-111
Cayman Islands ... 81-84
Ceylon ... 260-263
Cyprus ... 136-139
Dominica ... 90-93
Falkland Islands ... 77-80
Fiji ... 110-113
Gambia ... 125-128
Gibraltar ... 100-103
Gilbert & Ellice Islands ... 33-36
Gold Coast ... 108-111
Grenada ... 124-127
Hong Kong ... 147-150
Jamaica ... 109-112
Kenya, Uganda, Tanganyika ... 42-45
Leeward Islands ... 96-99
Malta ... 184-187
Mauritius ... 204-207
Montserrat ... 85-88
Newfoundland ... 226-229
Nigeria ... 34-37
Northern Rhodesia ... 18-21
Nyasaland Protectorate ... 47-50
St. Helena ... 111-114
St. Kitts-Nevis ... 72-75
St. Lucia ... 91-94
St. Vincent ... 134-137
Seychelles ... 118-121
Sierra Leone ... 166-169
Solomon Islands ... 60-63
Somaliland Protectorate ... 77-80
Straits Settlements ... 213-216
Swaziland ... 20-23
Trinidad & Tobago ... 43-46
Turks & Caicos Islands ... 71-74
Virgin Islands ... 69-72

The following have different designs but are included in the omnibus set:

Great Britain ... 226-229
Offices in Morocco ... 67-70, 226-229, 422-425, 508-510
Australia ... 152-154
Canada ... 211-216
Cook Islands ... 98-100
India ... 142-148
Nauru ... 31-34
New Guinea ... 46-47
New Zealand ... 199-201
Niue ... 67-69
Papua ... 114-117
Samoa ... 163-165
South Africa ... 68-71
Southern Rhodesia ... 33-36
South-West Africa ... 121-124

249 stamps

Coronation

Queen Elizabeth and King George VI
CD302

1937

Aden ... 13-15
Antigua ... 81-83
Ascension ... 37-39
Bahamas ... 97-99
Barbados ... 190-192
Basutoland ... 15-17
Bechuanaland Protectorate ... 121-123
Bermuda ... 115-117
British Guiana ... 227-229
British Honduras ... 112-114
Cayman Islands ... 97-99
Ceylon ... 275-277
Cyprus ... 140-142
Dominica ... 94-96
Falkland Islands ... 81-83
Fiji ... 114-116
Gambia ... 129-131
Gibraltar ... 104-106
Gilbert & Ellice Islands ... 37-39
Gold Coast ... 112-114
Grenada ... 128-130
Hong Kong ... 151-153
Jamaica ... 113-115
Kenya, Uganda, Tanganyika ... 60-62
Leeward Islands ... 100-102
Malta ... 188-190
Mauritius ... 208-210
Montserrat ... 89-91
Newfoundland ... 230-232
Nigeria ... 50-52
Northern Rhodesia ... 22-24
Nyasaland Protectorate ... 51-53
St. Helena ... 115-117
St. Kitts-Nevis ... 76-78
St. Lucia ... 107-109
St. Vincent ... 138-140
Seychelles ... 122-124
Sierra Leone ... 170-172
Solomon Islands ... 64-66
Somaliland Protectorate ... 81-83
Straits Settlements ... 235-237
Swaziland ... 24-26
Trinidad & Tobago ... 47-49
Turks & Caicos Islands ... 75-77
Virgin Islands ... 73-75

The following have different designs but are included in the omnibus set:

Great Britain ... 234
Offices in Morocco ... 82, 439, 514
Canada ... 237
Cook Islands ... 109-111
Nauru ... 35-38
Newfoundland ... 233-243
New Guinea ... 48-51
New Zealand ... 223-225
Niue ... 70-72
Papua ... 118-121
South Africa ... 74-78
Southern Rhodesia ... 38-41
South-West Africa ... 125-132

202 stamps

Peace

King George VI and Parliament Buildings, London
CD303

Return to peace at the close of World War II.

1945-46

Aden ... 28-29
Antigua ... 96-97
Ascension ... 50-51
Bahamas ... 130-131
Barbados ... 207-208
Bermuda ... 131-132
British Guiana ... 242-243
British Honduras ... 127-128
Cayman Islands ... 112-113
Ceylon ... 293-294
Cyprus ... 156-157
Dominica ... 112-113
Falkland Islands ... 97-98
Falkland Islands Dep. ... 1L9-1L10
Fiji ... 137-138
Gambia ... 144-145
Gibraltar ... 119-120
Gilbert & Ellice Islands ... 52-53
Gold Coast ... 128-129
Grenada ... 143-144
Jamaica ... 136-137
Kenya, Uganda, Tanganyika ... 90-91
Leeward Islands ... 116-117
Malta ... 206-207
Mauritius ... 223-224
Montserrat ... 104-105
Nigeria ... 71-72
Northern Rhodesia ... 46-47
Nyasaland Protectorate ... 82-83
Pitcairn Island ... 9-10
St. Helena ... 128-129
St. Kitts-Nevis ... 91-92
St. Lucia ... 127-128
St. Vincent ... 152-153
Seychelles ... 149-150
Sierra Leone ... 186-187
Solomon Islands ... 80-81
Somaliland Protectorate ... 108-109
Trinidad & Tobago ... 62-63
Turks & Caicos Islands ... 90-91
Virgin Islands ... 88-89

The following have different designs but are included in the omnibus set:

Great Britain ... 264-265
  Offices in Morocco ... 523-524
Aden
  Kathiri State of Seiyun ... 12-13
  Qu'aiti State of Shihr and Mukalla ... 12-13
Australia ... 200-202
Basutoland ... 29-31
Bechuanaland Protectorate ... 137-139
Burma ... 66-69
Cook Islands ... 127-130
Hong Kong ... 174-175
India ... 195-198
  Hyderabad ... 51
New Zealand ... 247-257
Niue ... 90-93
Pakistan-Bahawalpur ... O16
Samoa ... 191-194
South Africa ... 100-102
Southern Rhodesia ... 67-70
South-West Africa ... 153-155
Swaziland ... 38-40
Zanzibar ... 222-223

164 stamps

Silver Wedding

King George VI and Queen Elizabeth
CD304 CD305

1948-49

Aden ... 30-31
  Kathiri State of Seiyun ... 14-15
  Qu'aiti State of Shihr and Mukalla ... 14-15
Antigua ... 98-99
Ascension ... 52-53
Bahamas ... 148-149
Barbados ... 210-211
Basutoland ... 39-40
Bechuanaland Protectorate ... 147-148
Bermuda ... 133-134
British Guiana ... 244-245
British Honduras ... 129-130
Cayman Islands ... 116-117
Cyprus ... 158-159
Dominica ... 114-115
Falkland Islands ... 99-100
Falkland Islands Dep. ... 1L11-1L12
Fiji ... 139-140
Gambia ... 146-147
Gibraltar ... 121-122
Gilbert & Ellice Islands ... 54-55
Gold Coast ... 142-143
Grenada ... 145-146
Hong Kong ... 178-179
Jamaica ... 138-139
Kenya, Uganda, Tanganyika ... 92-93
Leeward Islands ... 118-119
Malaya
  Johore ... 128-129
  Kedah ... 55-56
  Kelantan ... 44-45
  Malacca ... 1-2
  Negri Sembilan ... 36-37
  Pahang ... 44-45
  Penang ... 1-2
  Perak ... 99-100
  Perlis ... 1-2
  Selangor ... 74-75
  Trengganu ... 47-48
Malta ... 223-224
Mauritius ... 229-230
Montserrat ... 106-107
Nigeria ... 73-74
North Borneo ... 238-239
Northern Rhodesia ... 48-49
Nyasaland Protectorate ... 85-86
Pitcairn Island ... 11-12
St. Helena ... 130-131
St. Kitts-Nevis ... 93-94
St. Lucia ... 129-130
St. Vincent ... 154-155
Sarawak ... 174-175
Seychelles ... 151-152
Sierra Leone ... 188-189
Singapore ... 21-22
Solomon Islands ... 82-83
Somaliland Protectorate ... 110-111
Swaziland ... 48-49
Trinidad & Tobago ... 64-65
Turks & Caicos Islands ... 92-93
Virgin Islands ... 90-91
Zanzibar ... 224-225

The following have different designs but are included in the omnibus set:

Great Britain ... 267-268
  Offices in Morocco ... 93-94, 525-526
Bahrain ... 62-63
Kuwait ... 82-83
Oman ... 25-26
South Africa ... 106
South-West Africa ... 159

138 stamps

U.P.U.

Mercury and Symbols of Communications — CD306

Plane, Ship and Hemispheres — CD307

Mercury Scattering Letters over Globe
CD308

U.P.U. Monument, Bern
CD309

Universal Postal Union, 75th anniversary.

1949

Aden ... 32-35
  Kathiri State of Seiyun ... 16-19
  Qu'aiti State of Shihr and Mukalla ... 16-19
Antigua ... 100-103
Ascension ... 57-60
Bahamas ... 150-153
Barbados ... 212-215
Basutoland ... 41-44
Bechuanaland Protectorate ... 149-152
Bermuda ... 138-141
British Guiana ... 246-249
British Honduras ... 137-140
Brunei ... 79-82
Cayman Islands ... 118-121
Cyprus ... 160-163
Dominica ... 116-119
Falkland Islands ... 103-106
Falkland Islands Dep. ... 1L14-1L17
Fiji ... 141-144
Gambia ... 148-151
Gibraltar ... 123-126
Gilbert & Ellice Islands ... 56-59
Gold Coast ... 144-147
Grenada ... 147-150

Hong Kong 180-183
Jamaica 142-145
Kenya, Uganda, Tanganyika 94-97
Leeward Islands 126-129
Malaya
  Johore 151-154
  Kedah 57-60
  Kelantan 46-49
  Malacca.......................................18-21
  Negri Sembilan 59-62
  Pahang.......................................46-49
  Penang.......................................23-26
  Perak 101-104
  Perlis 3-6
  Selangor.....................................76-79
  Trengganu 49-52
Malta......................................225-228
Mauritius.................................231-234
Montserrat 108-111
New Hebrides, British 62-65
New Hebrides, French 79-82
Nigeria 75-78
North Borneo...........................240-243
Northern Rhodesia 50-53
Nyasaland Protectorate...............87-90
Pitcairn Islands 13-16
St. Helena 132-135
St. Kitts-Nevis..............................95-98
St. Lucia 131-134
St. Vincent 170-173
Sarawak..................................176-179
Seychelles 153-156
Sierra Leone 190-193
Singapore 23-26
Solomon Islands..........................84-87
Somaliland Protectorate 112-115
Southern Rhodesia 71-72
Swaziland 50-53
Tonga...87-90
Trinidad & Tobago 66-69
Turks & Caicos Islands 101-104
Virgin Islands...............................92-95
Zanzibar..................................226-229

The following have different designs but are included in the omnibus set:

Great Britain 276-279
  Offices in Morocco 546-549
Australia 223
Bahrain 68-71
Burma......................................116-121
Ceylon 304-306
Egypt 281-283
India..223-226
Kuwait 89-92
Oman..31-34
Pakistan-Bahawalpur 26-29, O25-O28
South Africa 109-111
South-West Africa 160-162

319 stamps

University

Arms of University College CD310

Alice, Princess of Athlone CD311

1948 opening of University College of the West Indies at Jamaica.

1951

Antigua 104-105
Barbados 228-229
British Guiana..........................250-251
British Honduras......................141-142
Dominica..................................120-121
Grenada...................................164-165
Jamaica 146-147
Leeward Islands 130-131
Montserrat 112-113
St. Kitts-Nevis..........................105-106
St. Lucia 149-150
St. Vincent 174-175
Trinidad & Tobago 70-71
Virgin Islands...............................96-97

28 stamps

Coronation

Queen Elizabeth II — CD312

1953

Aden 47
  Kathiri State of Seiyun...................28
  Qu'aiti State of Shihr and Mukalla .....
 28
Antigua 106
Ascension 61
Bahamas 157
Barbados 234
Basutoland..45
Bechuanaland Protectorate............153
Bermuda 142
British Guiana.................................252
British Honduras.............................143
Cayman Islands..............................150
Cyprus 167
Dominica... 141
Falkland Islands 121
Falkland Islands Dependencies 1L18
Fiji 145
Gambia 152
Gibraltar.. 131
Gilbert & Ellice Islands.....................60
Gold Coast 160
Grenada.. 170
Hong Kong 184
Jamaica 153
Kenya, Uganda, Tanganyika 101
Leeward Islands 132
Malaya
  Johore 155
  Kedah 82
  Kelantan 71
  Malacca.. 27
  Negri Sembilan 63
  Pahang... 71
  Penang... 27
  Perak 126
  Perlis 28
  Selangor....................................... 101
  Trengganu 74
Malta... 241
Mauritius... 250
Montserrat 127
New Hebrides, British 77
Nigeria 79
North Borneo.................................. 260
Northern Rhodesia 60
Nyasaland Protectorate 96
Pitcairn 19
St. Helena 139
St. Kitts-Nevis................................. 119
St. Lucia 156
St. Vincent 185
Sarawak.. 196
Seychelles 172
Sierra Leone 194
Singapore 27
Solomon Islands............................... 88
Somaliland Protectorate 127
Swaziland 54
Trinidad & Tobago 84
Tristan da Cunha.............................. 13
Turks & Caicos Islands 118
Virgin Islands.................................. 114

The following have different designs but are included in the omnibus set:

Great Britain 313-316
  Offices in Morocco 579-582
Australia 259-261
Bahrain 92-95
Canada 330
Ceylon 317
Cook Islands 145-146
Kuwait.....................................113-116
New Zealand 280-284
Niue 104-105
Oman..52-55
Samoa 214-215
South Africa 192
Southern Rhodesia 80
South-West Africa 244-248
Tokelau Islands....................................4

106 stamps

Royal Visit 1953

Separate designs for each country for the visit of Queen Elizabeth II and the Duke of Edinburgh.

1953

Aden 62
Australia 267-269
Bermuda 163
Ceylon 318
Fiji 146
Gibraltar..146
Jamaica 154
Kenya, Uganda, Tanganyika 102
Malta..242
New Zealand 286-287

13 stamps

West Indies Federation

Map of the Caribbean CD313

Federation of the West Indies, April 22, 1958.

1958

Antigua 122-124
Barbados 248-250
Dominica..................................161-163
Grenada...................................184-186
Jamaica 175-177
Montserrat 143-145
St. Kitts-Nevis..........................136-138
St. Lucia 170-172
St. Vincent 198-200
Trinidad & Tobago 86-88

30 stamps

Freedom from Hunger

Protein Food CD314

U.N. Food and Agricultural Organization's "Freedom from Hunger" campaign.

1963

Aden 65
Antigua 133
Ascension 89
Bahamas 180
Basutoland.. 83
Bechuanaland Protectorate 194
Bermuda.. 192
British Guiana................................. 271
British Honduras............................. 179
Brunei 100
Cayman Islands.............................. 168
Dominica... 181
Falkland Islands 146
Fiji 198
Gambia 172
Gibraltar.. 161
Gilbert & Ellice Islands..................... 76
Grenada.. 190
Hong Kong 218
Malta... 291
Mauritius... 270
Montserrat 150
New Hebrides, British 93
North Borneo.................................. 296
Pitcairn 35
St. Helena 173
St. Lucia 179
St. Vincent...................................... 201
Sarawak.. 212
Seychelles 213
Solomon Islands............................. 109
Swaziland 108
Tonga.. 127
Tristan da Cunha.............................. 68
Turks & Caicos Islands 138
Virgin Islands.................................. 140
Zanzibar.. 280

37 stamps

Red Cross Centenary

Red Cross and Elizabeth II CD315

1963

Antigua 134-135
Ascension 90-91
Bahamas 183-184
Basutoland...................................84-85
Bechuanaland Protectorate......195-196
Bermuda..................................193-194
British Guiana..........................272-273
British Honduras......................180-181
Cayman Islands.......................169-170
Dominica..................................182-183
Falkland Islands 147-148
Fiji 203-204
Gambia 173-174
Gibraltar...................................162-163
Gilbert & Ellice Islands................77-78
Grenada...................................191-192
Hong Kong 219-220
Jamaica 203-204
Malta..292-293
Mauritius..................................271-272
Montserrat 151-152
New Hebrides, British 94-95
Pitcairn Islands 36-37
St. Helena 174-175
St. Kitts-Nevis..........................143-144
St. Lucia 180-181
St. Vincent...............................202-203
Seychelles 214-215
Solomon Islands......................110-111
South Arabia 1-2
Swaziland 109-110
Tonga.......................................134-135
Tristan da Cunha..........................69-70
Turks & Caicos Islands 139-140
Virgin Islands...........................141-142

70 stamps

Shakespeare

Shakespeare Memorial Theatre, Stratford-on-Avon — CD316

400th anniversary of the birth of William Shakespeare.

1964

Antigua 151
Bahamas 201
Bechuanaland Protectorate 197
Cayman Islands.............................. 171
Dominica... 184
Falkland Islands 149
Gambia 192
Gibraltar.. 164
Montserrat 153
St. Lucia 196
Turks & Caicos Islands 141
Virgin Islands.................................. 143

12 stamps

ITU

ITU Emblem CD317

Intl. Telecommunication Union, cent.

1965

Antigua 153-154
Ascension 92-93
Bahamas 219-220
Barbados 265-266
Basutoland...............................101-102
Bechuanaland Protectorate......202-203

Bermuda....196-197
British Guiana....293-294
British Honduras....187-188
Brunei....116-117
Cayman Islands....172-173
Dominica....185-186
Falkland Islands....154-155
Fiji....211-212
Gibraltar....167-168
Gilbert & Ellice Islands....87-88
Grenada....205-206
Hong Kong....221-222
Mauritius....291-292
Montserrat....157-158
New Hebrides, British....108-109
Pitcairn Islands....52-53
St. Helena....180-181
St. Kitts-Nevis....163-164
St. Lucia....197-198
St. Vincent....224-225
Seychelles....218-219
Solomon Islands....126-127
Swaziland....115-116
Tristan da Cunha....85-86
Turks & Caicos Islands....142-143
Virgin Islands....159-160

64 stamps

Intl. Cooperation Year

ICY Emblem CD318

1965

Antigua....155-156
Ascension....94-95
Bahamas....222-223
Basutoland....103-104
Bechuanaland Protectorate....204-205
Bermuda....199-200
British Guiana....295-296
British Honduras....189-190
Brunei....118-119
Cayman Islands....174-175
Dominica....187-188
Falkland Islands....156-157
Fiji....213-214
Gibraltar....169-170
Gilbert & Ellice Islands....104-105
Grenada....207-208
Hong Kong....223-224
Mauritius....293-294
Montserrat....176-177
New Hebrides, British....110-111
New Hebrides, French....126-127
Pitcairn Islands....54-55
St. Helena....182-183
St. Kitts-Nevis....165-166
St. Lucia....199-200
Seychelles....220-221
Solomon Islands....143-144
South Arabia....17-18
Swaziland....117-118
Tristan da Cunha....87-88
Turks & Caicos Islands....144-145
Virgin Islands....161-162

64 stamps

Churchill Memorial

Winston Churchill and St. Paul's, London, During Air Attack CD319

1966

Antigua....157-160
Ascension....96-99
Bahamas....224-227
Barbados....281-284
Basutoland....105-108
Bechuanaland Protectorate....206-209
Bermuda....201-204
British Antarctic Territory....16-19
British Honduras....191-194
Brunei....120-123
Cayman Islands....176-179
Dominica....189-192
Falkland Islands....158-161
Fiji....215-218
Gibraltar....171-174
Gilbert & Ellice Islands....106-109
Grenada....209-212
Hong Kong....225-228
Mauritius....295-298
Montserrat....178-181
New Hebrides, British....112-115
New Hebrides, French....128-131
Pitcairn Islands....56-59
St. Helena....184-187
St. Kitts-Nevis....167-170
St. Lucia....201-204
St. Vincent....241-244
Seychelles....222-225
Solomon Islands....145-148
South Arabia....19-22
Swaziland....119-122
Tristan da Cunha....89-92
Turks & Caicos Islands....146-149
Virgin Islands....163-166

136 stamps

Royal Visit, 1966

Queen Elizabeth II and Prince Philip CD320

Caribbean visit, Feb. 4 - Mar. 6, 1966.

1966

Antigua....161-162
Bahamas....228-229
Barbados....285-286
British Guiana....299-300
Cayman Islands....180-181
Dominica....193-194
Grenada....213-214
Montserrat....182-183
St. Kitts-Nevis....171-172
St. Lucia....205-206
St. Vincent....245-246
Turks & Caicos Islands....150-151
Virgin Islands....167-168

26 stamps

World Cup Soccer

Soccer Player and Jules Rimet Cup CD321

World Cup Soccer Championship, Wembley, England, July 11-30.

1966

Antigua....163-164
Ascension....100-101
Bahamas....245-246
Bermuda....205-206
Brunei....124-125
Cayman Islands....182-183
Dominica....195-196
Fiji....219-220
Gibraltar....175-176
Gilbert & Ellice Islands....125-126
Grenada....230-231
New Hebrides, British....116-117
New Hebrides, French....132-133
Pitcairn Islands....60-61
St. Helena....188-189
St. Kitts-Nevis....173-174
St. Lucia....207-208
Seychelles....226-227
Solomon Islands....167-168
South Arabia....23-24
Tristan da Cunha....93-94

42 stamps

WHO Headquarters

World Health Organization Headquarters, Geneva — CD322

1966

Antigua....165-166
Ascension....102-103
Bahamas....247-248
Brunei....126-127
Cayman Islands....184-185
Dominica....197-198
Fiji....224-225
Gibraltar....180-181
Gilbert & Ellice Islands....127-128
Grenada....232-233
Hong Kong....229-230
Montserrat....184-185
New Hebrides, British....118-119
New Hebrides, French....134-135
Pitcairn Islands....62-63
St. Helena....190-191
St. Kitts-Nevis....177-178
St. Lucia....209-210
St. Vincent....247-248
Seychelles....228-229
Solomon Islands....169-170
South Arabia....25-26
Tristan da Cunha....99-100

46 stamps

UNESCO Anniversary

"Education" — CD323

"Science" (Wheat ears & flask enclosing globe). "Culture" (lyre & columns). 20th anniversary of the UNESCO.

1966-67

Antigua....183-185
Ascension....108-110
Bahamas....249-251
Barbados....287-289
Bermuda....207-209
Brunei....128-130
Cayman Islands....186-188
Dominica....199-201
Gibraltar....183-185
Gilbert & Ellice Islands....129-131
Grenada....234-236
Hong Kong....231-233
Mauritius....299-301
Montserrat....186-188
New Hebrides, British....120-122
New Hebrides, French....136-138
Pitcairn Islands....64-66
St. Helena....192-194
St. Kitts-Nevis....179-181
St. Lucia....211-213
St. Vincent....249-251
Seychelles....230-232
Solomon Islands....171-173
South Arabia....27-29
Swaziland....123-125
Tristan da Cunha....101-103
Turks & Caicos Islands....155-157
Virgin Islands....176-178

84 stamps

Silver Wedding, 1972

Queen Elizabeth II and Prince Philip — CD324

Designs: borders differ for each country.

1972

Anguilla....161-162
Antigua....295-296
Ascension....164-165
Bahamas....344-345
Bermuda....296-297
British Antarctic Territory....43-44
British Honduras....306-307
British Indian Ocean Territory....48-49
Brunei....186-187
Cayman Islands....304-305
Dominica....352-353
Falkland Islands....223-224
Fiji....328-329
Gibraltar....292-293
Gilbert & Ellice Islands....206-207
Grenada....466-467
Hong Kong....271-272
Montserrat....286-287
New Hebrides, British....169-170
Pitcairn Islands....127-128
St. Helena....271-272
St. Kitts-Nevis....257-258
St. Lucia....328-329
St.Vincent....344-345
Seychelles....309-310
Solomon Islands....248-249
South Georgia....35-36
Tristan da Cunha....178-179
Turks & Caicos Islands....257-258
Virgin Islands....241-242

60 stamps

Princess Anne's Wedding

Princess Anne and Mark Phillips — CD325

Wedding of Princess Anne and Mark Phillips, Nov. 14, 1973.

1973

Anguilla....179-180
Ascension....177-178
Belize....325-326
Bermuda....302-303
British Antarctic Territory....60-61
Cayman Islands....320-321
Falkland Islands....225-226
Gibraltar....305-306
Gilbert & Ellice Islands....216-217
Hong Kong....289-290
Montserrat....300-301
Pitcairn Island....135-136
St. Helena....277-278
St. Kitts-Nevis....274-275
St. Lucia....349-350
St. Vincent....358-359
St. Vincent Grenadines....1-2
Seychelles....311-312
Solomon Islands....259-260
South Georgia....37-38
Tristan da Cunha....189-190
Turks & Caicos Islands....286-287
Virgin Islands....260-261

44 stamps

Elizabeth II Coronation Anniv.

CD326

CD327

CD328

Designs: Royal and local beasts in heraldic form and simulated stonework. Portrait of Elizabeth II by Peter Grugeon. 25th anniversary of coronation of Queen Elizabeth II.

1978

Ascension..229
Barbados..474
Belize..397
British Antarctic Territory....................71
Cayman Islands...............................404
Christmas Island...............................87
Falkland Islands..............................275
Fiji..384
Gambia...380
Gilbert Islands................................312
Mauritius...464
New Hebrides, British.......................258
St. Helena.......................................317
St. Kitts-Nevis..................................354
Samoa..472
Solomon Islands...............................368
South Georgia....................................51
Swaziland..302
Tristan da Cunha..............................238
Virgin Islands...................................337

20 sheets

Queen Mother Elizabeth's 80th Birthday

CD330

Designs: Photographs of Queen Mother Elizabeth. Falkland Islands issued in sheets of 50; others in sheets of 9.

1980

Ascension..261
Bermuda..401
Cayman Islands...............................443
Falkland Islands..............................305
Gambia..412
Gibraltar..393
Hong Kong.......................................364
Pitcairn Islands................................193
St. Helena.......................................341
Samoa..532
Solomon Islands...............................426
Tristan da Cunha..............................277

12 stamps

Royal Wedding, 1981

Prince Charles and Lady Diana — CD331

Wedding of Charles, Prince of Wales, and Lady Diana Spencer, St. Paul's Cathedral, London, July 29, 1981.

1981

Antigua...................................623-625
Ascension...............................294-296
Barbados.................................547-549
Barbuda..................................497-499
Bermuda..................................412-414
Brunei.....................................268-270
Cayman Islands........................471-473
Dominica.................................701-703
Falkland Islands.......................324-326
Falkland Islands Dep.............1L59-1L61
Fiji..442-444
Gambia...................................426-428
Ghana.....................................759-761
Grenada...............................1051-1053
Grenada Grenadines.................440-443
Hong Kong...............................373-375
Jamaica...................................500-503
Lesotho...................................335-337
Maldive Islands........................906-908
Mauritius.................................520-522
Norfolk Island..........................280-282
Pitcairn Islands........................206-208
St. Helena...............................353-355
St. Lucia.................................543-545
Samoa.....................................558-560
Sierra Leone............................509-517
Solomon Islands.......................450-452
Swaziland................................382-384
Tristan da Cunha......................294-296
Turks & Caicos Islands.............486-488
Caicos Island................................8-10
Uganda....................................314-316
Vanuatu...................................308-310
Virgin Islands...........................406-408

Princess Diana

CD332

CD333

Designs: Photographs and portrait of Princess Diana, wedding or honeymoon photographs, royal residences, arms of issuing country. Portrait photograph by Clive Friend. Souvenir sheet margins show family tree, various people related to the princess. 21st birthday of Princess Diana of Wales, July 1.

1982

Antigua...................................663-666
Ascension...............................313-316
Bahamas..................................510-513
Barbados.................................585-588
Barbuda..................................544-546
British Antarctic Territory.............92-95
Cayman Islands........................486-489
Dominica.................................773-776
Falkland Islands.......................348-351
Falkland Islands Dep.............1L72-1L75
Fiji..470-473
Gambia...................................447-450
Grenada..............................1101A-1105
Grenada Grenadines.................485-491
Lesotho...................................372-375
Maldive Islands........................952-955
Mauritius.................................548-551
Pitcairn Islands........................213-216
St. Helena...............................372-375
St. Lucia.................................591-594
Sierra Leone............................531-534
Solomon Islands.......................471-474
Swaziland................................406-409
Tristan da Cunha......................310-313
Turks and Caicos Islands.........530A-534
Virgin Islands...........................430-433

250th anniv. of first edition of Lloyd's List (shipping news publication) & of Lloyd's marine insurance.

CD335

Designs: First page of early edition of the list; historical ships, modern transportation or harbor scenes.

1984

Ascension...............................351-354
Bahamas..................................555-558
Barbados.................................627-630
Cayes of Belize...........................10-13
Cayman Islands........................522-525
Falkland Islands.......................404-407
Fiji..509-512
Gambia...................................519-522
Mauritius.................................587-590
Nauru......................................280-283
St. Helena...............................412-415
Samoa.....................................624-627
Seychelles...............................538-541
Solomon Islands.......................521-524
Vanuatu...................................368-371
Virgin Islands...........................466-469

Queen Mother 85th Birthday

CD336

Designs: Photographs tracing the life of the Queen Mother, Elizabeth. The high value in each set pictures the same photograph taken of the Queen Mother holding the infant Prince Henry.

1985

Ascension...............................372-376
Bahamas..................................580-584
Barbados.................................660-664
Bermuda..................................469-473
Falkland Islands.......................420-424
Falkland Islands Dep.............1L92-1L96
Fiji..531-535
Hong Kong...............................447-450
Jamaica...................................599-603
Mauritius.................................604-608
Norfolk Island..........................364-368
Pitcairn Islands........................253-257
St. Helena...............................428-432
Samoa.....................................649-653
Seychelles...............................567-571
Solomon Islands.......................543-547
Swaziland................................476-480
Tristan da Cunha......................372-376
Vanuatu...................................392-396
Zil Elwannyen Sesel.................101-105

Queen Elizabeth II, 60th Birthday

CD337

1986, April 21

Ascension...............................389-393
Bahamas..................................592-596
Barbados.................................675-679
Bermuda..................................499-503
Cayman Islands........................555-559
Falkland Islands.......................441-445
Fiji..544-548
Hong Kong...............................465-469
Jamaica...................................620-624
Kiribati....................................470-474
Mauritius.................................629-633
Papua New Guinea...................640-644
Pitcairn Islands........................270-274
St. Helena...............................451-455
Samoa.....................................670-674
Seychelles...............................592-596
Solomon Islands.......................562-566
South Georgia..........................101-105
Swaziland................................490-494
Tristan da Cunha......................388-392
Vanuatu...................................414-418
Zambia....................................343-347
Zil Elwannyen Sesel.................114-118

Royal Wedding

Marriage of Prince Andrew and Sarah Ferguson CD338

1986, July 23

Ascension...............................399-400
Bahamas..................................602-603
Barbados.................................687-688
Cayman Islands........................560-561
Jamaica...................................629-630
Pitcairn Islands........................275-276
St. Helena...............................460-461
St. Kitts...................................181-182
Seychelles...............................602-603
Solomon Islands.......................567-568
Tristan da Cunha......................397-398
Zambia....................................348-349
Zil Elwannyen Sesel.................119-120

Queen Elizabeth II, 60th Birthday

Queen Elizabeth II & Prince Philip, 1947 Wedding Portrait — CD339

Designs: Photographs tracing the life of Queen Elizabeth II.

1986

Anguilla...................................674-677
Antigua...................................925-928
Barbuda..................................783-786
Dominica.................................950-953
Gambia...................................611-614
Grenada...............................1371-1374
Grenada Grenadines.................749-752
Lesotho...................................531-534
Maldive Islands......................1172-1175
Sierra Leone............................760-763
Uganda....................................495-498

Royal Wedding, 1986

CD340

Designs: Photographs of Prince Andrew and Sarah Ferguson during courtship, engagement and marriage.

1986

Antigua...................................939-942
Barbuda..................................809-812
Dominica.................................970-973
Gambia...................................635-638

Grenada................................1385-1388
Grenada Grenadines................758-761
Lesotho....................................545-548
Maldive Islands.....................1181-1184
Sierra Leone............................769-772
Uganda....................................510-513

Lloyds of London, 300th Anniv.

CD341

Designs: 17th century aspects of Lloyds, representations of each country's individual connections with Lloyds and publicized disasters insured by the organization.

1986

Ascension................................454-457
Bahamas.................................655-658
Barbados.................................731-734
Bermuda..................................541-544
Falkland Islands......................481-484
Liberia..................................1101-1104
Malawi.....................................534-537
Nevis..571-574
St. Helena...............................501-504
St. Lucia..................................923-926
Seychelles...............................649-652
Solomon Islands......................627-630
South Georgia..........................131-134
Trinidad & Tobago...................484-487
Tristan da Cunha.....................439-442
Vanuatu...................................485-488
Zil Elwannyen Sesel................146-149

Moon Landing, 20th Anniv.

CD342

Designs: Equipment, crew photographs, spacecraft, official emblems and report profiles created for the Apollo Missions. Two stamps in each set are square in format rather than like the stamp shown; see individual country listings for more information.

1989

Ascension Is............................468-472
Bahamas.................................674-678
Belize......................................916-920
Kiribati....................................517-521
Liberia..................................1125-1129
Nevis.......................................586-590
St. Kitts...................................248-252
Samoa.....................................760-764
Seychelles...............................676-680
Solomon Islands......................643-647
Vanuatu...................................507-511
Zil Elwannyen Sesel................154-158

Queen Mother, 90th Birthday

CD343

CD344

Designs: Portraits of Queen Elizabeth, the Queen Mother. See individual country listings for more information.

1990

Ascension Is............................491-492
Bahamas.................................698-699
Barbados.................................782-783
British Antarctic Territory..........170-171
British Indian Ocean Territory........106-107
Cayman Islands.......................622-623
Falkland Islands......................524-525
Kenya......................................527-528
Kiribati....................................555-556
Liberia..................................1145-1146
Pitcairn Islands.......................336-337
St. Helena...............................532-533
St. Lucia..................................969-970
Seychelles...............................710-711
Solomon Islands......................671-672
South Georgia..........................143-144
Swaziland................................565-566
Tristan da Cunha.....................480-481
Zil Elwannyen Sesel................171-172

Queen Elizabeth II, 65th Birthday, and Prince Philip, 70th Birthday

CD345

CD346

Designs: Portraits of Queen Elizabeth II and Prince Philip differ for each country. Printed in sheets of 10 + 5 labels (3 different) between. Stamps alternate, producing 5 different triptychs.

1991

Ascension Is............................505-506
Bahamas.................................730-731
Belize......................................969-970
Bermuda..................................617-618
Kiribati....................................571-572
Mauritius.................................733-734
Pitcairn Islands.......................348-349
St. Helena...............................554-555
St. Kitts...................................318-319
Samoa.....................................790-791
Seychelles...............................723-724
Solomon Islands......................688-689
South Georgia..........................149-150
Swaziland................................586-587
Vanuatu...................................540-541
Zil Elwannyen Sesel................177-178

Royal Family Birthday, Anniversary

CD347

Queen Elizabeth II, 65th birthday, Charles and Diana, 10th wedding anniversary: Various photographs of Queen Elizabeth II, Prince Philip, Prince Charles, Princess Diana and their sons William and Henry.

1991

Antigua..................................1446-1455
Barbuda..................................1229-1238
Dominica.................................1328-1337
Gambia...................................1080-1089
Grenada..................................2006-2015
Grenada Grenadines................1331-1340
Guyana...................................2440-2451
Lesotho...................................871-875
Maldive Islands.....................1533-1542
Nevis.......................................666-675
St. Vincent.............................1485-1494
St. Vincent Grenadines............769-778
Sierra Leone..........................1387-1396
Turks & Caicos Islands............913-922
Uganda....................................918-927

Queen Elizabeth II's Accession to the Throne, 40th Anniv.

CD348

CD349

Various photographs of Queen Elizabeth II with local Scenes.

1992 - CD348

Antigua..................................1513-1518
Barbuda..................................1306-1309
Dominica.................................1414-1419
Gambia...................................1172-1177
Grenada..................................2047-2052
Grenada Grenadines................1368-1373
Lesotho...................................881-885
Maldive Islands.....................1637-1642
Nevis.......................................702-707
St. Vincent.............................1582-1587
St. Vincent Grenadines............829-834
Sierra Leone..........................1482-1487
Turks and Caicos Islands.........978-987
Uganda....................................990-995
Virgin Islands..........................742-746

1992 - CD349

Ascension Islands....................531-535
Bahamas.................................744-748
Bermuda..................................623-627
British Indian Ocean Territory........119-123
Cayman Islands.......................648-652
Falkland Islands......................549-553
Gibraltar..................................605-609
Hong Kong..............................619-623
Kenya......................................563-567
Kiribati....................................582-586
Pitcairn Islands.......................362-366
St. Helena...............................570-574
St. Kitts...................................332-336
Samoa.....................................805-809
Seychelles...............................734-738
Solomon Islands......................708-712
South Georgia..........................157-161
Tristan da Cunha.....................508-512
Vanuatu...................................555-559
Zambia....................................561-565
Zil Elwannyen Sesel................183-187

Royal Air Force, 75th Anniversary

CD350

1993

Ascension................................557-561
Bahamas.................................771-775
Barbados.................................842-846
Belize....................................1003-1008
Bermuda..................................648-651
British Indian Ocean Territory........136-140
Falkland Is..............................573-577
Fiji..687-691
Montserrat...............................830-834
St. Kitts...................................351-355

Royal Air Force, 80th Anniv.

Design CD350 Re-inscribed

1998

Ascension................................697-701
Bahamas.................................907-911
British Indian Ocean Terr.........198-202
Cayman Islands.......................754-758
Fiji..814-818
Gibraltar..................................755-759
Samoa.....................................957-961
Turks & Caicos Islands........1258-1265
Tuvalu.....................................763-767
Virgin Islands..........................879-883

End of World War II, 50th Anniv.

CD351

CD352

1995

Ascension................................613-617
Bahamas.................................824-828
Barbados.................................891-895
Belize....................................1047-1050
British Indian Ocean Territory........163-167
Cayman Islands.......................704-708
Falkland Islands......................634-638
Fiji..720-724
Kiribati....................................662-668
Liberia..................................1175-1179
Mauritius.................................803-805
St. Helena...............................646-654
St. Kitts...................................389-393
St. Lucia................................1018-1022
Samoa.....................................890-894
Solomon Islands......................799-803
South Georgia & S. Sandwich Is. 198-200
Tristan da Cunha.....................562-566

UN, 50th Anniv.

CD353

1995

Bahamas.................................839-842
Barbados.................................901-904
Belize....................................1055-1058
Jamaica...................................847-851
Liberia..................................1187-1190
Mauritius.................................813-816
Pitcairn Islands.......................436-439
St. Kitts...................................398-401
St. Lucia................................1023-1026

Samoa 900-903
Tristan da Cunha.......................568-571
Virgin Islands............................807-810

Queen Elizabeth, 70th Birthday

CD354

1996

Ascension.................................632-635
British Antarctic Territory..........240-243
British Indian Ocean Territory........176-180
Falkland Islands 653-657
Pitcairn Islands.........................446-449
St. Helena 672-676
Samoa.......................................912-916
Tokelau 223-227
Tristan da Cunha.......................576-579
Virgin Islands............................824-828

Diana, Princess of Wales (1961-97)

CD355

1998

Ascension...696
Bahamas 901A-902
Barbados 950
Belize...1091
Bermuda...753
Botswana...................................659-663
British Antarctic Territory.................258
British Indian Ocean Terr. 197
Cayman Islands.................... 752A-753
Falkland Islands 694
Fiji..819-820
Gibraltar...754
Kiribati 719A-720
Namibia 909
Niue 706
Norfolk Island 644-645
Papua New Guinea 937
Pitcairn Islands.................................487
St. Helena 711
St. Kitts................................ 437A-438
Samoa 955A-956
Seycelles 802
Solomon Islands.......................866-867
South Georgia & S. Sandwich Islands 220
Tokelau 253
Tonga...980
Niuafo'ou 201
Tristan da Cunha..............................618
Tuvalu 762
Vanuatu 719
Virgin Islands....................................878

Wedding of Prince Edward and Sophie Rhys-Jones

CD356

1999

Ascension.................................729-730
Cayman Islands.........................775-776
Falkland Islands 729-730
Pitcairn Islands.........................505-506
St. Helena 733-734
Samoa.......................................971-972
Tristan da Cunha.......................030-037
Virgin Islands............................908-909

1st Manned Moon Landing, 30th Anniv.

CD357

1999

Ascension.................................731-735
Bahamas 942-946
Barbados 967-971
Bermuda...778
Cayman Islands.........................777-781
Fiji...853-857
Jamaica 889-893
Kirbati 746-750
Nauru...465-469
St. Kitts.....................................460-464
Samoa.......................................973-977
Solomon Islands.......................875-879
Tuvalu 800-804
Virgin Islands............................910-914

Queen Mother's Century

CD358

1999

Ascension.................................736-740
Bahamas 951-955
Cayman Islands.........................782-786
Falkland Islands 734-738
Fiji...858-862
Norfolk Island 688-692
St. Helena 740-744
Samoa.......................................978-982
Solomon Islands.......................880-884
South Georgia & South Sandwich Islands 231-235
Tristan da Cunha.......................638-642
Tuvalu 805-809

Prince William, 18th Birthday

CD359

2000

Ascension.................................755-759
Cayman Islands.........................797-801
Falkland Islands 762-766
Fiji...889-893
South Georgia 257-261
and South Sandwich Islands
Tristan da Cunha.......................664-668
Virgin Islands............................925-929

Reign of Queen Elizabeth II, 50th Anniv.

CD360

2002

Ascension.................................790-794
Bahamas 1033-1037
Barbados 1019-1023
Belize....................................1152-1156
Bermuda....................................822-826
British Antarctic Territory..........307-311
British Indian Ocean Territory........239-243
Cayman Islands.........................844-848
Falkland Islands 804-808
Gibraltar....................................896-900
Jamaica 952-956
Nauru...491-495
Norfolk Island 758-762
Papua New Guinea 1019-1023
Pitcairn Islands.................................552
St. Helena 788-792
St. Lucia 1146-1150
Solomon Islands.......................931-935
South Georgia & So. Sandwich Is. 274-278
Swaziland 706-710
Tokelau 302-306
Tonga...1059
Niuafo'ou 239
Tristan da Cunha.......................706-710
Virgin Islands............................967-971

Queen Mother Elizabeth (1900-2002)

CD361

2002

Ascension.................................799-801
Bahamas 1044-1046
Bermuda....................................834-836
British Antarctic Territory..........312-314
British Indian Ocean Territory........245-247
Cayman Islands.........................857-861
Falkland Islands 812-816
Nauru...499-501
Pitcairn Islands.........................561-565
St. Helena 808-812
St. Lucia 1155-1159
Seychelles 830
Solomon Islands.......................945-947
South Georgia & So. Sandwich Isls. 281-285
Tokelau 312-314
Tristan da Cunha.......................715-717
Virgin Islands............................979-983

Head of Queen Elizabeth II

CD362

2003

Ascension...822
Bermuda...865
British Antarctic Territory.................322
British Indian Ocean Territory 261
Cayman Islands................................878
Falkland Islands 828
St. Helena 820
South Georgia & South Sandwich Islands 294

Tristan da Cunha...............................731
Virgin Islands....................................1003

Coronation of Queen Elizabeth II, 50th Anniv.

CD363

2003

Ascension.................................823-825
Bahamas 1073-1075
Bermuda....................................866-868
British Antarctic Territory..........323-325
British Indian Ocean Territory........262-264
Cayman Islands.........................879-881
Jamaica 970-972
Kiribati 825-827
Pitcairn Islands.........................577-581
St. Helena 821-823
St. Lucia 1171-1173
Tokelau 320-322
Tristan da Cunha.......................732-734
Virgin Islands........................1004-1006

Prince William, 21st Birthday

CD364

2003

Ascension...826
British Indian Ocean Territory 265
Cayman Islands.........................882-884
Falkland Islands 829
South Georgia & South Sandwich Islands 295
Tokelau 323
Tristan da Cunha..............................735
Virgin Islands........................1007-1009

British Commonwealth of Nations

Dominions, Colonies, Territories, Offices and Independent Members

Comprising stamps of the British Commonwealth and associated nations.

A strict observance of technicalities would bar some or all of the stamps listed under Burma, Ireland, Kuwait, Nepal, New Republic, Orange Free State, Samoa, South Africa, South-West Africa, Stellaland, Sudan, Swaziland, the two Transvaal Republics and others but these are included for the convenience of collectors.

1. Great Britain

Great Britain: Including England, Scotland, Wales and Northern Ireland.

2. The Dominions, Present and Past

AUSTRALIA

The Commonwealth of Australia was proclaimed on January 1, 1901. It consists of six former colonies as follows:

New South Wales
Victoria
Queensland
Tasmania
South Australia
Western Australia

Territories belonging to, or administered by Australia: Australian Antarctic Territory, Christmas Island, Cocos (Keeling) Islands, Nauru, New Guinea, Norfolk Island, Papua New Guinea.

CANADA

The Dominion of Canada was created by the British North America Act in 1867. The following provinces were former separate colonies and issued postage stamps:

British Columbia and Vancouver Island
Newfoundland
Nova Scotia
New Brunswick
Prince Edward Island

FIJI

The colony of Fiji became an independent nation with dominion status on Oct. 10, 1970.

GHANA

This state came into existence Mar. 6, 1957, with dominion status. It consists of the former colony of the Gold Coast and the Trusteeship Territory of Togoland. Ghana became a republic July 1, 1960.

INDIA

The Republic of India was inaugurated on January 26, 1950. It succeeded the Dominion of India which was proclaimed August 15, 1947, when the former Empire of India was divided into Pakistan and the Union of India. The Republic is composed of about 40 predominantly Hindu states of three classes: governor's provinces, chief commissioner's provinces and princely states. India also has various territories, such as the Andaman and Nicobar Islands.

The old Empire of India was a federation of British India and the native states. The more important princely states were autonomous. Of the more than 700 Indian states, these 43 are familiar names to philatelists because of their postage stamps.

CONVENTION STATES

Chamba
Faridkot
Gwalior
Jhind
Nabha
Patiala

NATIVE FEUDATORY STATES

Alwar
Bahawalpur
Bamra
Barwani
Bhopal
Bhor
Bijawar
Bundi
Bussahir
Charkhari
Cochin
Dhar
Duttia
Faridkot (1879-85)
Hyderabad
Idar
Indore
Jaipur
Jammu
Jammu and Kashmir
Jasdan
Jhalawar
Jhind (1875-76)
Kashmir
Kishangarh
Las Bela
Morvi
Nandgaon
Nowanuggur
Orchha
Poonch
Rajpeepla
Sirmur
Soruth
Travancore
Wadhwan

NEW ZEALAND

Became a dominion on September 26, 1907. The following islands and territories are, or have been, administered by New Zealand:

Aitutaki
Cook Islands (Rarotonga)
Niue
Penrhyn
Ross Dependency
Samoa (Western Samoa)
Tokelau Islands

PAKISTAN

The Republic of Pakistan was proclaimed March 23, 1956. It succeeded the Dominion which was proclaimed August 15, 1947. It is made up of all or part of several Moslem provinces and various districts of the former Empire of India, including Bahawalpur and Las Bela. Pakistan withdrew from the Commonwealth in 1972.

SOUTH AFRICA

Under the terms of the South African Act (1909) the self-governing colonies of Cape of Good Hope, Natal, Orange River Colony and Transvaal united on May 31, 1910, to form the Union of South Africa. It became an independent republic May 3, 1961.

Under the terms of the Treaty of Versailles, South-West Africa, formerly German South-West Africa, was mandated to the Union of South Africa.

SRI LANKA (CEYLON)

The Dominion of Ceylon was proclaimed February 4, 1948. The island had been a Crown Colony from 1802 until then. On May 22, 1972, Ceylon became the Republic of Sri Lanka.

3. Colonies, Past and Present; ControlledTerritory and Independent Members of the Commonwealth

Aden
Aitutaki
Antigua
Ascension
Bahamas
Bahrain
Bangladesh
Barbados
Barbuda
Basutoland
Batum
Bechuanaland
Bechuanaland Prot.
Belize
Bermuda
Botswana
British Antarctic Territory
British Central Africa
British Columbia and Vancouver Island
British East Africa
British Guiana

British Honduras
British Indian Ocean Territory
British New Guinea
British Solomon Islands
British Somaliland
Brunei
Burma
Bushire
Cameroons
Cape of Good Hope
Cayman Islands
Christmas Island
Cocos (Keeling) Islands
Cook Islands
Crete,
British Administration
Cyprus
Dominica
East Africa & Uganda
Protectorates
Egypt
Falkland Islands
Fiji
Gambia
German East Africa
Gibraltar
Gilbert Islands
Gilbert & Ellice Islands
Gold Coast
Grenada
Griqualand West
Guernsey
Guyana
Heligoland
Hong Kong
Indian Native States
(see India)
Ionian Islands
Jamaica
Jersey
Kenya
Kenya, Uganda & Tanzania
Kuwait
Labuan
Lagos
Leeward Islands
Lesotho
Madagascar
Malawi
Malaya
Federated Malay States
Johore
Kedah
Kelantan
Malacca
Negri Sembilan
Pahang
Penang
Perak
Perlis
Selangor
Singapore
Sungei Ujong
Trengganu
Malaysia
Maldive Islands
Malta
Man, Isle of
Mauritius
Mesopotamia
Montserrat
Muscat
Namibia
Natal
Nauru
Nevis
New Britain
New Brunswick
Newfoundland
New Guinea
New Hebrides
New Republic
New South Wales
Niger Coast Protectorate
Nigeria
Niue
Norfolk Island
North Borneo
Northern Nigeria
Northern Rhodesia
North West Pacific Islands
Nova Scotia
Nyasaland Protectorate
Oman
Orange River Colony
Palestine
Papua New Guinea
Penrhyn Island
Pitcairn Islands
Prince Edward Island
Queensland
Rhodesia
Rhodesia & Nyasaland
Ross Dependency
Sabah
St. Christopher
St. Helena
St. Kitts
St. Kitts-Nevis-Anguilla
St. Lucia
St. Vincent
Samoa
Sarawak
Seychelles
Sierra Leone
Solomon Islands
Somaliland Protectorate
South Arabia
South Australia
South Georgia
Southern Nigeria
Southern Rhodesia
South-West Africa
Stellaland
Straits Settlements
Sudan
Swaziland
Tanganyika
Tanzania
Tasmania
Tobago
Togo
Tokelau Islands
Tonga
Transvaal
Trinidad
Trinidad and Tobago
Tristan da Cunha
Trucial States
Turks and Caicos
Turks Islands
Tuvalu
Uganda
United Arab Emirates
Victoria
Virgin Islands
Western Australia
Zambia
Zanzibar
Zululand

POST OFFICES IN FOREIGN COUNTRIES

Africa
East Africa Forces
Middle East Forces
Bangkok
China
Morocco
Turkish Empire

Colonies, Former Colonies, Offices, Territories Controlled by Parent States

Belgium

Belgian Congo
Ruanda-Urundi

Denmark

Danish West Indies
Faroe Islands
Greenland
Iceland

Finland

Aland Islands

France

COLONIES PAST AND PRESENT, CONTROLLED TERRITORIES

Afars & Issas, Territory of
Alaouites
Alexandretta
Algeria
Alsace & Lorraine
Anjouan
Annam & Tonkin
Benin
Cambodia (Khmer)
Cameroun
Castellorizo
Chad
Cilicia
Cochin China
Comoro Islands
Dahomey
Diego Suarez
Djibouti (Somali Coast)
Fezzan
French Congo
French Equatorial Africa
French Guiana
French Guinea
French India
French Morocco
French Polynesia (Oceania)
French Southern & Antarctic Territories
French Sudan
French West Africa
Gabon
Germany
Ghadames
Grand Comoro
Guadeloupe
Indo-China
Inini
Ivory Coast
Laos
Latakia
Lebanon
Madagascar
Martinique
Mauritania
Mayotte
Memel
Middle Congo
Moheli
New Caledonia
New Hebrides
Niger Territory
Nossi-Be
Obock
Reunion
Rouad, Ile
Ste.-Marie de Madagascar
St. Pierre & Miquelon
Senegal
Senegambia & Niger
Somali Coast
Syria
Tahiti
Togo
Tunisia
Ubangi-Shari
Upper Senegal & Niger
Upper Volta
Viet Nam
Wallis & Futuna Islands

POST OFFICES IN FOREIGN COUNTRIES

China
Crete
Egypt
Turkish Empire
Zanzibar

Germany

EARLY STATES

Baden
Bavaria
Bergedorf
Bremen
Brunswick
Hamburg
Hanover
Lubeck
Mecklenburg-Schwerin
Mecklenburg-Strelitz
Oldenburg
Prussia
Saxony
Schleswig-Holstein
Wurttemberg

FORMER COLONIES

Cameroun (Kamerun)
Caroline Islands
German East Africa
German New Guinea
German South-West Africa
Kiauchau
Mariana Islands
Marshall Islands
Samoa
Togo

Italy

EARLY STATES

Modena
Parma
Romagna
Roman States
Sardinia
Tuscany
Two Sicilies
Naples
Neapolitan Provinces
Sicily

FORMER COLONIES, CONTROLLED TERRITORIES, OCCUPATION AREAS

Aegean Islands
Calimno (Calino)
Caso
Cos (Coo)
Karki (Carchi)
Leros (Lero)
Lipso
Nisiros (Nisiro)
Patmos (Patmo)
Piscopi
Rodi (Rhodes)
Scarpanto
Simi
Stampalia
Castellorizo
Corfu
Cyrenaica
Eritrea
Ethiopia (Abyssinia)
Fiume
Ionian Islands
Cephalonia
Ithaca
Paxos
Italian East Africa
Libya
Oltre Giuba
Saseno
Somalia (Italian Somaliland)
Tripolitania

POST OFFICES IN FOREIGN COUNTRIES

"ESTERO"*
Austria
China
Peking
Tientsin
Crete
Tripoli
Turkish Empire
Constantinople
Durazzo
Janina
Jerusalem
Salonika
Scutari
Smyrna
Valona

*Stamps overprinted "ESTERO" were used in various parts of the world.

Netherlands

Aruba
Netherlands Antilles (Curacao)
Netherlands Indies
Netherlands New Guinea
Surinam (Dutch Guiana)

Portugal

COLONIES PAST AND PRESENT, CONTROLLED TERRITORIES

Angola
Angra
Azores
Cape Verde
Funchal
Horta
Inhambane
Kionga
Lourenco Marques
Macao
Madeira
Mozambique
Mozambique Co.
Nyassa
Ponta Delgada
Portuguese Africa
Portuguese Congo
Portuguese Guinea
Portuguese India
Quelimane
St. Thomas & Prince Islands
Tete
Timor
Zambezia

Russia

ALLIED TERRITORIES AND REPUBLICS, OCCUPATION AREAS

Armenia
Aunus (Olonets)
Azerbaijan
Batum
Estonia
Far Eastern Republic
Georgia
Karelia
Latvia
Lithuania
North Ingermanland
Ostland
Russian Turkestan
Siberia
South Russia
Tannu Tuva
Transcaucasian Fed. Republics
Ukraine
Wenden (Livonia)
Western Ukraine

Spain

COLONIES PAST AND PRESENT, CONTROLLED TERRITORIES

Aguera, La
Cape Juby
Cuba
Elobey, Annobon & Corisco
Fernando Po
Ifni
Mariana Islands
Philippines
Puerto Rico
Rio de Oro
Rio Muni
Spanish Guinea
Spanish Morocco
Spanish Sahara
Spanish West Africa

POST OFFICES IN FOREIGN COUNTRIES

Morocco
Tangier
Tetuan

Dies of British Colonial Stamps

DIE A

DIE B

DIE I

DIE II

DIE A:

1. The lines in the groundwork vary in thickness and are not uniformly straight.

2. The seventh and eighth lines from the top, in the groundwork, converge where they meet the head.

3. There is a small dash in the upper part of the second jewel in the band of the crown.

4. The vertical color line in front of the throat stops at the sixth line of shading on the neck.

DIE B:

1. The lines in the groundwork are all thin and straight.

2. All the lines of the background are parallel.

3. There is no dash in the upper part of the second jewel in the band of the crown.

4. The vertical color line in front of the throat stops at the eighth line of shading on the neck.

DIE I:

1. The base of the crown is well below the level of the inner white line around the vignette.

2. The labels inscribed "POSTAGE" and "REVENUE" are cut square at the top.

3. There is a white "bud" on the outer side of the main stem of the curved ornaments in each lower corner.

4. The second (thick) line below the country name has the ends next to the crown cut diagonally.

DIE Ia.	DIE Ib.
1 as die II.	1 and 3 as die II.
2 and 3 as die I.	2 as die I.

DIE II:

1. The base of the crown is aligned with the underside of the white line around the vignette.

2. The labels curve inward at the top inner corners.

3. The "bud" has been removed from the outer curve of the ornaments in each corner.

4. The second line below the country name has the ends next to the crown cut vertically.

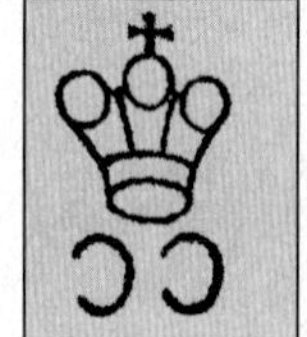

Wmk. 1
Crown and C C

Wmk. 2
Crown and C A

Wmk. 3
Multiple Crown and C A

Wmk. 4
Multiple Crown and Script C A

Wmk. 4a

Wmk. 314
St. Edward's Crown and C A Multiple

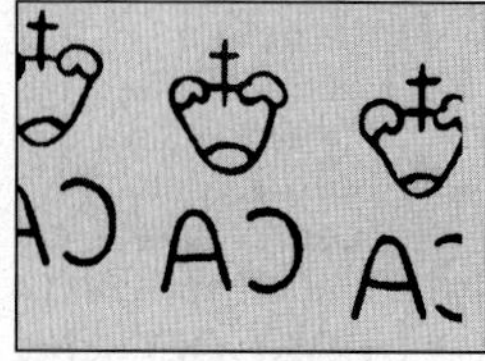

Wmk. 373

Wmk. 384

British Colonial and Crown Agents Watermarks

Watermarks 1 to 4, 314, 373, and 384, common to many British territories, are illustrated here to avoid duplication.

The letters "CC" of Wmk. 1 identify the paper as having been made for the use of the Crown Colonies, while the letters "CA" of the others stand for "Crown Agents." Both Wmks. 1 and 2 were used on stamps printed by De La Rue & Co.

Wmk. 3 was adopted in 1904; Wmk. 4 in 1921; Wmk. 314 in 1957; Wmk. 373 in 1974; and Wmk. 384 in 1985.

In Wmk. 4a, a non-matching crown of the general St. Edwards type (bulging on both sides at top) was substituted for one of the Wmk. 4 crowns which fell off the dandy roll. The non-matching crown occurs in 1950-52 printings in a horizontal row of crowns on certain regular stamps of Johore and Seychelles, and on various postage due stamps of Barbados, Basutoland, British Guiana, Gold Coast, Grenada, Northern Rhodesia, St. Lucia, Swaziland and Trinidad and Tobago. A variation of Wmk. 4a, with the non-matching crown in a horizontal row of crown-CA-crown, occurs on regular stamps of Bahamas, St. Kitts-Nevis and Singapore.

Wmk. 314 was intentionally used sideways, starting in 1966. When a stamp was issued with Wmk. 314 both upright and sideways, the sideways varieties usually are listed also – with minor numbers. In many of the later issues, Wmk. 314 is slightly visible.

Wmk. 373 is usually only faintly visible.

CAMBODIA

kam-'bō-dē-ə

(Kampuchea)

(Khmer Republic)

LOCATION — Southern Indo-China
GOVT. — Republic
AREA — 69,898 sq. mi.
POP. — 11,626,520 (1999 est.)
CAPITAL — Phnom Penh

Before 1951, Cambodia used stamps of Indo-China. In October, 1970, the Kingdom of Cambodia became the Khmer Republic.

From 1978 to 1980 money was abolished.

100 Cents = 1 Piaster
100 Cents = 1 Riel (1955)

Imperforates

Most Cambodia stamps exist imperforate in issued and trial colors, and also in small presentation sheets in issued colors.

Catalogue values for all unused stamps in this country are for Never Hinged items.

Apsaras — A1

King Norodom Sihanouk — A3

Enthronement Hall — A2

1951-52 Unwmk. Engr. *Perf. 13*

No.	Type	Description	Unused	Used
1	A1	10c dk blue green	.90	.70
2	A1	20c cl & org brn	.70	.25
3	A1	30c pur & indigo	.70	.25
4	A1	40c ultra & brt bl grn	.70	.25
5	A2	50c dk grn & dk ol grn	.70	.25
6	A3	80c bl blk & dk bl grn	1.00	.80
7	A2	1pi indigo & purple	1.10	.90
8	A3	1.10pi dp car & brt red	1.25	.80
9	A3	1.50pi blk brn & red brn ('51)	1.60	.90
10	A1	1.50pi dp car & cerise	1.60	.90
11	A2	1.50pi indigo & dp ultra	1.60	.90
12	A3	1.90pi indigo & dp ultra	2.50	1.50
13	A2	2pi dp car & org brn	2.50	1.50
14	A3	3pi dp car & org brn	3.50	1.75
15	A1	5pi indigo & purple	14.00	4.75
a.		Souvenir sheet of 1	35.00	
16	A2	10pi purple & indigo	29.00	13.00
a.		Souvenir sheet of 1	35.00	
17	A3	15pi dk pur & purple	35.00	17.50
a.		Souvenir sheet of 1	35.00	
		Nos. 1-17 (17)	98.35	46.90

Nos. 15a, 16a, 17a sold in a booklet.

Stamps with completely white gum and no toning sell for a premium.

For surcharges see Nos. B1-B4.

Phnom Daun Penh — A4

East Gate, Angkor Thom — A5

Arms of Cambodia — A6

Methods of Mail Transport — A7

1954-55 Unwmk. *Perf. 13*

No.	Type	Description	Unused	Used
18	A4	10c rose carmine	.20	.20
a.		Souvenir sheet of 5 ('55)	45.00	
19	A4	20c dark green	.20	.20
20	A4	30c indigo	.20	.20
21	A4	40c dark purple	.20	.20
22	A4	50c dk violet brn	.20	.20
23	A5	70c chocolate	.35	.25
a.		Souvenir sheet of 5 ('55)	45.00	
24	A5	1pi red violet	.35	.35
25	A5	1.50pi red	.40	.35
26	A6	2pi rose red	.65	.40
a.		Souvenir sheet of 5 ('55)	45.00	
27	A6	2.50pi green	1.00	.50
28	A7	2.50pi blue green	1.40	.60
a.		Souvenir sheet of 5 ('55)	45.00	
29	A6	3pi ultra	1.50	1.25
30	A7	4pi black brown	1.60	1.25
31	A6	4.50pi purple	2.00	1.25
32	A7	5pi rose red	2.00	1.25
33	A6	6pi chocolate	2.50	1.60
34	A7	10pi purple	2.50	1.75
35	A7	15pi deep blue	3.75	2.10
36	A5	20pi ultra	7.50	4.50
37	A5	30pi blue green	10.50	7.25
		Nos. 18-37 (20)	39.00	25.65
		Nos. 18a//28a, Set of 4	180.00	

The 4 souvenir sheets each contain 5 stamps: #18a (10c, 20c, 30c, 40c, 50c); #23a (70c, 1pi, 1.50pi, 20pi, 30pi); #26a (2pi, 2.50pi green, 3pi, 4.50pi, 6pi); #28a (2.50pi blue green, 4pi, 5pi. 10pi, 15pi). Size of #18a, 26a and 28a: 120x120mm. Size of #23a: 160x92mm. Values are for very fine, unblemished sheets. Copies with toning and/or gum bends sell for less.

For overprints see Nos. 99-100.

King Norodom Suramarit — A8

King Norodom Suramarit and Queen Kossamak Nearirat Serey Vathana A9

Portraits: 50c (No. 39), 2.50r, 4r, 6r, 15r, Queen Kossamak Nearirat Serey Vathana.

Perf. 14x13(A8), 13(A9)

1955, Nov. 24 Engr. Unwmk.

No.	Type	Description	Unused	Used
38	A8	50c violet	.40	.40
39	A8	50c indigo	.40	.40
40	A8	1r car lake	.55	.50
41	A9	1.50r dk brown	.65	.50
42	A9	2r black & indigo	.65	.50
43	A8	2r dp ultra	.65	.65
44	A8	2.50r dk vio brn	.65	.65
45	A9	3r brn org & car	.85	.65
46	A8	4r dark green	1.40	1.00
47	A9	5r blk & dk grn	1.60	1.25
48	A8	6r deep plum	1.60	1.25
49	A8	7r dark brown	2.50	1.25
50	A9	10r brn car & vio	2.75	1.40
51	A8	15r purple	3.75	2.50
52	A8	20r deep green	5.50	3.25
		Nos. 38-52 (15)	23.90	16.15

Coronation of King Norodom Suramarit and Queen Kossamak Nearirat Serey Vathana.

See #74-75. For surcharge see #122.

King Norodom Suramarit — A10

Prince Sihanouk, Globe and Flags — A11

Portrait: 3r, 5r, 50r, Queen Kossamak Nearirat Serey Vathana.

1956, Mar. 8 *Perf. 13*

No.	Type	Description	Unused	Used
53	A10	2r dark red	1.50	1.50
54	A10	3r dark blue	2.25	2.25
55	A10	5r yellow green	3.25	3.25
56	A10	10r dark green	9.00	9.00
57	A10	30r dark violet	20.00	20.00
58	A10	50r rose lilac	37.50	37.50
		Nos. 53-58 (6)	73.50	73.50

Coronation of King Norodom Suramarit and Queen Kossamak Nearirat Serey Vathana.

1957, Mar. 1

No.	Type	Description	Unused	Used
59	A11	2r green, ultra & car	1.00	.70
60	A11	4.50r ultra	1.00	.70
61	A11	8.50r carmine	1.00	.70
		Nos. 59-61 (3)	3.00	2.10

Admission to the UN, 1st anniv. (in 1956).

Type of Semi-Postal Stamps, 1957

1957, May 12 Unwmk. *Perf. 13*

No.	Type	Description	Unused	Used
62	SP1	1.50r vermilion	.80	.80
63	SP1	6.50r bluish violet	1.00	1.00
64	SP1	8r dark green	1.00	1.00
		Nos. 62-64 (3)	2.80	2.80

2500th anniv. of the birth of Buddha.

King Ang Duong A12

1958, Mar. 4

No.	Type	Description	Unused	Used
65	A12	1.50r purple & brown	.30	.30
66	A12	5r olive gray & olive	.45	.45
67	A12	10r claret & dull brn	.90	.90
a.		Souvenir sheet of 3, #65-67	4.25	4.50
		Nos. 65-67 (3)	1.65	1.65

King Ang Duong (1795-1860).

No. 67a sold for 25r.

King Norodom I — A13

1958-59 Engr. *Perf. 12½x13*

No.	Type	Description	Unused	Used
68	A13	2r ultra & olive	.35	.35
69	A13	6r orange & sl grn	.55	.55
70	A13	15r green & ol gray	1.00	1.00
a.		Souv. sheet of 3, #68-70 ('59)	4.50	4.50
		Nos. 68-70 (3)	1.90	1.90

King Norodom I (1835-1904).

No. 70a sold for 32r.

Issued: #68-70, 11/3/58; #70a, 1/31/59.

For surcharge see No. 184.

Children of the World — A14

1959, Dec. 9 Unwmk. *Perf. 13*

No.	Type	Description	Unused	Used
71	A14	20c rose violet	.25	.25
72	A14	50c blue	.50	.50
73	A14	80c rose carmine	.75	.75
		Nos. 71-73 (3)	1.50	1.50

Issued to promote friendship among the children of the world.

For surcharges see Nos. 115, B8-B10.

Nos. 49 and 52 with Black Border

1960 *Perf. 14x13*

No.	Type	Description	Unused	Used
74	A8	7r dk brown & blk	3.25	3.25
75	A8	20r dp green & blk	3.25	3.25

Death of King Norodom Suramarit.

Port of Sihanoukville, Prince Sihanouk and Serpent Naga — A15

20r (double size)

1960, Apr. *Perf. 13x12½*

No.	Type	Description	Unused	Used
76	A15	2r carmine & sepia	.40	.40
a.		Cambodian 20r	2.25	2.25
77	A15	5r ultra & dp brown	.40	.40
a.		Cambodian 20r	3.00	3.00
78	A15	20r lilac & dk blue	1.50	1.50
		Nos. 76-78 (3)	2.30	2.30

Opening of the port of Sihanoukville. By error the denomination in Cambodian on the 2r and 5r was engraved as 20r; it was corrected later.

Ceremonial Plow — A16

1960 *Perf. 12*

No.	Type	Description	Unused	Used
79	A16	1r magenta	.40	.40
80	A16	2r brown	.60	.60
81	A16	3r bluish green	1.00	1.00
		Nos. 79-81 (3)	2.00	2.00

Feast of the Sacred Furrow.

Fight Against Illiteracy A17

Water Conservation, Dam at Chhouksar — A18

Dove, Factory and Books
A19

Buddhist Ceremony
A20

Works of Sangkum: 6r, Workman and house. 10r, Woman in rice field.

1960, Sept. 1 Engr. *Perf. 13*

82 A17 2r dk grn, brn & dk bl .40 .35
a. Souvenir sheet of 3 4.00 4.25
83 A18 3r brown & green .55 .35
a. Souvenir sheet of 3 4.00 4.25
84 A19 4r rose car, vio & grn .55 .35
85 A17 6r brown, org & grn .55 .35
86 A17 10r ultra, grn & bis 1.40 .90
87 A20 25r dk car, red & mag 3.00 2.25
Nos. 82-87 (6) 6.45 4.55

No. 82a contains one each of Nos. 82, 85 and 87, and sold for 42r. No. 83a contains one each of Nos. 83, 84 and 86, and sold for 23r. Nos. 82a-83a were issued Dec. 5, 1960.

Cambodian Flag and Dove
A21

Frangipani
A22

1960, Dec. 24 Engr. *Perf. 13*
Flag in Ultramarine and Red

88 A21 1.50r brown & green .40 .25
89 A21 5r orange red .60 .35
90 A21 7r green & ultra 1.25 1.00
a. Souvenir sheet of 3, #88-90 6.50 6.50
b. Souv. sheet of 3 (colors changed) 6.50 6.50
Nos. 88-90 (3) 2.25 1.60

Peace propaganda. No. 90a sold for 16r. No. 90b contains one of each denomination with colors changed to: 1.50r orange red, 5r green & ultramarine, 7r brown & green and sold for 20r.

1961, July 1 Unwmk. *Perf. 13*

91 A22 2r shown .50 .50
92 A22 5r Oleander 1.00 1.00
93 A22 10r Amaryllis 2.10 2.10
a. Souvenir sheet of 3, #91-93 6.00 6.00
Nos. 91-93 (3) 3.60 3.60

No. 93a sold for 20r.

Krishna in Chariot, Khmer Frieze — A23

1961-63 Typo. *Perf. 14x13½*

94 A23 1r lilac .30 .20
94A A23 2r blue ('63) 2.75 1.40
95 A23 3r emerald .80 .40
96 A23 6r orange .80 .40
a. Souvenir sheet of 3 7.50 7.50
Nos. 94-96 (4) 4.65 2.40

Issued to honor Cambodian armed forces.
No. 94A issued in coils. No. 96a contains one each of Nos. 94, 95, 96. Sold for 12r.

Independence Monument — A24

1961, Nov. 9 Engr. *Perf. 13x12½*

97 A24 2r green .50 .50
98 A24 4r gray brown .50 .50
a. Souvenir sheet of 2, #97-98 3.00 3.50
Nos. 97-98,C15-C17 (5) 7.65 4.70

10th anniv. of Independence.
For surcharge see No. 116.

Nos. 27 and 31 Overprinted in Red: "VIe CONFERENCE MONDIALE BOUDDIQUE 12-11-1961"

1961, Nov. 11 *Perf. 13*

99 A6 2.50pi green .45 .40
100 A6 4.50pi purple .75 .70

Sixth World Conference of Buddhism.

Highway (American Aid) — A25

Foreign Aid: 2r, Power station (Czech aid). 4r, Textile factory (Chinese aid). 5r, Hospital (Russian aid). 6r, Airport (French aid).

1961, Dec. Engr. *Perf. 13*

101 A25 2r org & rose car .40 .25
102 A25 3r bl, grn & org brn .40 .25
103 A25 4r dl bl, org brn & mag .40 .25
104 A25 5r dl grn & lil rose .45 .30
105 A25 6r dk bl & org brn .65 .50
a. Souvenir sheet of 5, #101-105 3.25 3.00
Nos. 101-105 (5) 2.30 1.55

Malaria Eradication Emblem — A26

1962, Apr. 7 Unwmk. *Perf. 13*

106 A26 2r magenta & brown .50 .40
107 A26 4r green & dk brown .50 .40
108 A26 6r violet & olive bister .75 .45
Nos. 106-108 (3) 1.75 1.25

WHO drive to eradicate malaria.
For surcharges see Nos. B11-B12.

Fruits
A27

1962, June 4 Engr.

109 A27 2r Turmeric .50 .40
110 A27 4r Cinnamon 1.00 .70
111 A27 6r Mangosteens 1.00 .70
a. Souvenir sheet of 3, #109-111 3.75 3.75
Nos. 109-111 (3) 2.50 1.80

Nos. 111a sold for 15r.

Pineapples — A28

1962 Unwmk. *Perf. 13*

112 A28 2r shown .45 .30
113 A28 5r Sugar cane .65 .50
114 A28 9r Sugar palms .90 .45
Nos. 112-114 (3) 2.00 1.25

No. 73 Surcharged

1962, Nov. 9 *Perf. 13*

115 A14 50c on 80c rose car .50 .35

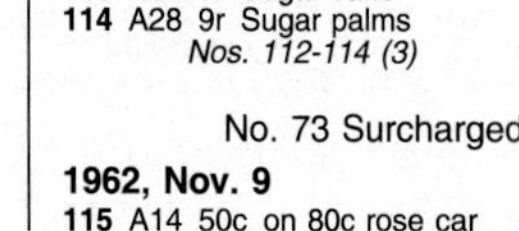

No. 97 Surcharged with New Value in Red and Overprinted in Black with Two Bars and: "INAUGURATION / DU / MONUMENT"

1962

116 A24 3r on 2r green .50 .30

Dedication of Independence Monument.
See No. C18.

Corn, Rice and FAO Emblem
A29

1963, Mar. 21 Engr. *Perf. 13*

117 A29 3r multicolored .70 .45
118 A29 6r org red, vio bl & ocher .70 .45

FAO "Freedom from Hunger" campaign.

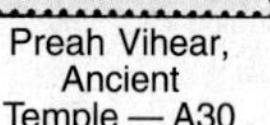

Preah Vihear, Ancient Temple — A30

Tonsay Lake — A31

1963, June 15 *Perf. 12½x13*

119 A30 3r claret, brown & sl grn .40 .25
120 A30 6r org, sl grn & grnsh blk .70 .50
121 A30 15r blue, choc & green 1.25 .80
Nos. 119-121 (3) 2.35 1.55

Return by Thailand of Preah Vihear on the Mekong River.
For overprint see No. 176.

No. 44 Surcharged with New Value and Bars

1963 Engr. *Perf. 14x13*

122 A8 3r on 2½r dk violet brn .50 .35

Perf. 12x12½, 12½x12
1963, Aug. 1 Photo.

7r, Popokvil Falls. 20r, Beach, horiz.

123 A31 3r multicolored .30 .30
124 A31 7r multicolored .60 .50
125 A31 20r multicolored 1.90 1.00
Nos. 123-125 (3) 2.80 1.80

UNESCO Emblem, Scales and Globe
A32

1963, Dec. 10 Engr. *Perf. 13*

126 A32 1r vio bl, rose cl & grn .35 .25
127 A32 3r yel grn, vio bl & rose cl .50 .40
128 A32 12r rose cl, yel grn & vio bl 1.25 1.10
Nos. 126-128 (3) 2.10 1.75

15th anniversary of the Universal Declaration of Human Rights.
For surcharge see No. 183.

Kouprey
A33

1964, Mar. 3 Unwmk. *Perf. 13*

129 A33 50c grn, dk brn & org brn .50 .25
130 A33 3r org, brn, dk brn & grn .80 .50
131 A33 6r blue, dk brn & grn 1.50 .75
Nos. 129-131 (3) 2.80 1.50

Black-billed Magpie — A34

1964, May 2 Engr. *Perf. 13*

132 A34 3r shown 1.10 .65
133 A34 6r Kingfisher 1.75 1.00
134 A34 12r Gray heron 3.25 2.00
Nos. 132-134 (3) 6.10 3.65

For overprint & surcharge see #303, B16.

Emblem of Royal Cambodian Airline
A35

1964 Unwmk. *Perf. 13x12½*

135 A35 1.50r rose car & purple .25 .20
136 A35 3r ver & dk blue .35 .20
137 A35 7.50r ultra & car .80 .50
Nos. 135-137 (3) 1.40 .90

8th anniv. of the Royal Cambodian Airline.

Prince Norodom Sihanouk — A36

1964 Engr. *Perf. 12½x13*

138 A36 2r purple .25 .20
139 A36 3r red brown .50 .35
140 A36 10r dark blue 1.00 .60
Nos. 138-140 (3) 1.75 1.15

10th anniv. of the Sangkum (political party).
For overprints see Nos. 144-145.

A set of three stamps, imperf, showing clasped hands, was prepared for International Cooperation Year but were never issued. Value, $40.

Woman Weaver
A37

Khmer Handicrafts: 3r, Metal worker. 5r, Basket maker.

1965, Feb. 1 *Perf. 13x12½*

141 A37 1r multicolored .30 .25
142 A37 3r red lil, red brn & gray ol .60 .35
143 A37 5r green, dk brn & car 1.10 .70
Nos. 141-143 (3) 2.00 1.30

Nos. 139-140 Overprinted in Black or Red: "CONFERENCE / DES PEUPLES / INDOCHINOIS"

1965, Mar. 1 *Perf. 12½x13*

144 A36 3r red brown .60 .40
145 A36 10r dark blue (R) .90 .50

Conference of the people of Indo-China.

ITU Emblem, Old and New Communication Equipment — A38

1965, May 17 Engr. *Perf. 13*

146 A38 3r green & olive bister .30 .25
147 A38 4r red & blue .50 .30
148 A38 10r violet & rose lilac .70 .60
Nos. 146-148 (3) 1.50 1.15

Centenary of the ITU.

Cotton Plant — A39

3r, Peanut plant. 7.50r, Coconut palm.

1965, Aug. 2 *Perf. 12½x13*

149 A39 1.50r orange, sl grn & pur .35 .30
150 A39 3r blue, yel, grn & brn .65 .55
151 A39 7.50r orange brn & sl grn 1.25 .95
Nos. 149-151 (3) 2.25 1.80

Preah Ko Temple, Rolouoh — A40

Temples at Angkor: 5r, Baksei Chamkrong, Rolouoh. 7r, Banteay Srei (Citadel of Women). 9r, Angkor Wat. 12r, Bayon, Angkor Thom.

1966, Feb. 1 Engr. *Perf. 13*

152 A40 3r gray ol, sal & dl grn 1.25 .80
153 A40 5r lil, dk grn & redsh brn 1.50 .85
154 A40 7r dk grn, redsh brn & bis 2.00 1.60
155 A40 9r vio bl, pur & dk grn 2.50 2.10
156 A40 12r dk grn, rose car & ver 2.75 2.75
Nos. 152-156 (5) 10.00 8.10

For overprints see Nos. 172-175, 177.

WHO Headquarters, Geneva — A41

1966, July 1 Photo. *Perf. 12½x13*
WHO Emblem in Blue and Yellow

157 A41 2r black & pale rose .35 .20
158 A41 3r black & yel grn .45 .30
159 A41 5r black & lt bl .70 .50
Nos. 157-159 (3) 1.50 1.00

Inauguration of WHO Headquarters, Geneva.

Tree Planting — A42

UNESCO Emblem — A43

1966, July 22 Engr. *Perf. 12½x13*

160 A42 1r brn, dull brn & brt grn .25 .20
161 A42 3r org, dull brn & brt grn .50 .30
162 A42 7r gray, dull brn & brt grn .75 .40
Nos. 160-162 (3) 1.50 .90

Issued for Arbor Day.

1966 Photo. *Perf. 13*

163 A43 3r multicolored .45 .25
164 A43 7r multicolored .65 .35

20th anniv. of UNESCO.

Wrestlers and Games' Emblem A44

GANEFO Games (Games Emblem and): 3r, Stadium, Phnom Penh. 7r, Swordsmen. 10r, Indian club swingers. Bas-reliefs from Angkor Wat.

1966, Nov. 25 Engr. *Perf. 13*

165 A44 3r violet blue .35 .20
166 A44 4r green .40 .30
167 A44 7r dk car rose .60 .40
168 A44 10r dark brown .90 .60
Nos. 165-168 (4) 2.25 1.50

Indian Wild Boar A45

Perf. 13x12½, 12½x13

1967, Feb. 20 Engr.

169 A45 3r shown .75 .30
170 A45 5r Muntjac, vert. 1.10 .50
171 A45 7r Elephant 1.60 .75
Nos. 169-171 (3) 3.45 1.55

Nos. 152-153, 155-156 and 121 Overprinted in Red: "ANNEE INTERNATIONALE DU TOURISME 1967"

1967, Apr. 27 Engr. *Perf. 13*

172 A40 3r multicolored .85 .75
173 A40 5r multicolored 1.00 .75
174 A40 9r multicolored 1.40 1.25
175 A40 12r multicolored 1.75 1.50
176 A30 15r multicolored 2.10 1.75
Nos. 172-176 (5) 7.10 6.00

International Tourist Year, 1967.

No. 154 Overprinted in Red: "MILLENAIRE / DE BANTEAY SREI / 967-1967"

1967, Apr. 27

177 A40 7r multicolored 2.00 .75

Banteay Srei Temple at Angkor, millennium.

Royal Ballet Dancer — A46

Various Dancers

1967, June Engr. *Perf. 13*

178 A46 1r orange .60 .60
179 A46 3r Prus blue 1.40 .80
180 A46 5r ultra 1.75 1.10
181 A46 7r carmine rose 2.75 1.50
182 A46 10r multicolored 3.50 2.10
Nos. 178-182 (5) 10.00 6.10

Cambodian Royal Ballet.

Nos. 128 and 70 Surcharged in Red

1967, Sept. 8 Engr.

183 A32 6r on 12r multi .75 .35
184 A13 7r on 15r grn & olive gray 1.00 .55

Intl. Literacy Day, Sept. 8. The surcharge on #184 is adapted to fit the shape of the stamp.

Symbolic Water Cycle — A47

1967, Nov. 1 Typo. *Perf. 13x14*

185 A47 1r black, bl & org .25 .20
186 A47 6r lilac, lt bl & org .55 .30
187 A47 10r dk blue, emer & org .80 .50
Nos. 185-187 (3) 1.60 1.00

Hydrological Decade (UNESCO), 1965-74.

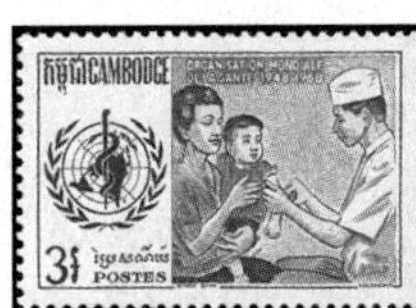

Royal University, Kompong Cham A48

6r, Engineering School, Phnom Penh. 9r, University Center, Sangkum Reastr Niyum.

1968, Mar. 1 Engr. *Perf. 13*

188 A48 4r violet bl & multi .30 .25
189 A48 6r slate & multi .50 .35
190 A48 9r Prus blue & multi .70 .50
Nos. 188-190 (3) 1.50 1.10

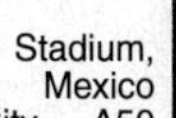
Vaccination and WHO Emblem A49

WHO, 20th Anniv.: 7r, Malaria control and WHO emblem (man spraying DDT).

1968, July 8 Engr. *Perf. 13*

191 A49 3r ultramarine .60 .30
192 A49 7r deep blue .90 .50

Stadium, Mexico City — A50

1968, Oct. 12 Engr. *Perf. 13*

193 A50 1r shown .30 .25
194 A50 2r Wrestling .40 .30
195 A50 3r Bicycling .65 .35
196 A50 5r Boxing, vert. .85 .35
197 A50 7.50r Torch bearer, vert. .95 .45
Nos. 193-197 (5) 3.15 1.70

19th Olympic Games, Mexico City, 12/12-27.

Red Cross Team A51

1968, Nov. 1 Engr. *Perf. 13*

198 A51 3r Prus bl, grn & red .50 .25

Issued to honor the Cambodian Red Cross.

Prince Norodom Sihanouk A52

8r, Soldiers wading through swamp.

1968, Nov. 9

199 A52 7r emer, ultra & pur .50 .30
200 A52 8r bl, grn & dp brn .75 .55

15th anniversary of independence.

Human Rights Flame and Prince Sihanouk A53

1968, Dec. 10 Engr. *Perf. 13*

201 A53 3r blue .40 .20
202 A53 5r bright plum .70 .30
203 A53 7r multicolored .90 .50
Nos. 201-203 (3) 2.00 1.00

International Human Rights Year.

ILO Emblem A54

1969, May 1 Engr. *Perf. 13*

204 A54 3r ultra .35 .20
205 A54 6r dp carmine .60 .30
206 A54 9r blue green .80 .50
Nos. 204-206 (3) 1.75 1.00

ILO, 50th anniversary.

Globe, Red Cross, Crescent, Lion and Sun Emblems A55

1969, May 8

207 A55 1r blue, red & yel .20 .20
208 A55 3r sl grn, red & vio brn .40 .30
209 A55 10r brt lil, red & brn .90 .50
Nos. 207-209 (3) 1.50 1.00

50th anniv. of the League of Red Cross Societies.

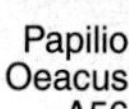
Papilio Oeacus A56

Butterflies: 4r, Papilio agamenon. 8r, Danaus plexippus.

1969, Oct. 10 Engr. *Perf. 13*
210 A56 3r lilac, blk & yel 5.00 1.25
211 A56 4r ver, blk & grn 8.50 2.00
212 A56 8r yel grn, dk brn & org 11.50 3.00
Nos. 210-212 (3) 25.00 6.25

Map of Cambodia and Diesel Engine A57

Various railroad stations and trains.

1969, Nov. 27 Engr. *Perf. 13*
213 A57 3r multicolored 1.00 .75
214 A57 6r slate grn & lt brn 2.00 1.50
215 A57 8r black 3.25 2.25
216 A57 9r dk green & blue 3.75 2.40
Nos. 213-216 (4) 10.00 6.90

Issued to publicize the new rail link between Phnom Penh and Sihanoukville.

Fish — A58

1970, Jan. 29 Photo. *Perf. 13*
217 A58 3r Tripletail 2.40 1.40
218 A58 7r Sleeper goby 4.50 2.40
219 A58 9r Snakehead 5.25 3.00
Nos. 217-219 (3) 12.15 6.80

Wat Maniratanaram — A59

Monasteries: 2r, Wat Tepthidaram, vert. 6r, Wat Patumavati. 8r, Wat Unnalom.

1970, Apr. 29 Photo. *Perf. 13*
220 A59 2r multicolored .30 .25
221 A59 3r multicolored .35 .25
222 A59 6r multicolored .75 .30
223 A59 8r multicolored 1.40 .40
Nos. 220-223 (4) 2.80 1.20

UPU Headquarters and Monument, Bern — A60

1970, May 20
224 A60 1r green & multi .25 .20
225 A60 3r scarlet & multi .35 .20
226 A60 4r dp blue & multi .45 .20
227 A60 10r brown & multi .75 .40
Nos. 224-227 (4) 1.80 1.00

New UPU Headquarters in Bern.

Open Book and Satellite Earth Receiving Station — A61

1970, May 17 Photo. *Perf. 13*
228 A61 3r dk vio bl & multi .25 .20
229 A61 4r sl grn & multi .35 .25
230 A61 9r brn ol & multi .80 .35
Nos. 228-230 (3) 1.40 .80

World Telecommunications Day.

Nelumbium Speciosum A62

Flowers: 4r, Eichhornia crassipes. 13r, Nymphea lotus.

1970, Aug. 17 Photo. *Perf. 13*
231 A62 3r multicolored .50 .25
a. Cambodian and Arabic 3's transposed 15.00 20.00
232 A62 4r multicolored 1.00 .35
233 A62 13r multicolored 2.00 .60
Nos. 231-233 (3) 3.50 1.20

Elephant God, Bas relief at Banteay Srei — A63

1970, Sept. 21 Engr. *Perf. 13*
234 A63 3r lil rose & dp grn .20 .20
235 A63 4r bl grn, grn & lil rose .35 .20
236 A63 7r bl grn, dk brn & grn .55 .30
Nos. 234-236 (3) 1.10 .70

Issued for World Meteorological Day.

Khmer Republic

Globe, Rocket, Dove and UN Emblem A64

1970, Nov. 9 Photo. *Perf. 12½x12*
237 A64 3r black & multi .25 .20
238 A64 5r brown red & multi .35 .25
239 A64 10r dp violet & multi .75 .50
Nos. 237-239 (3) 1.35 .95

25th anniversary of the United Nations.

Education Year Emblem A65

1970, Nov. 9 Engr. *Perf. 13x12½*
240 A65 1r blue .25 .20
241 A65 3r brt rose lilac .30 .20
242 A65 8r blue green .70 .45
Nos. 240-242 (3) 1.25 .85

Issued for International Education Year.

Chuon-Nath — A66

1971, Jan. 27 Photo. *Perf. 13*
243 A66 3r ol grn & multi .20 .20
244 A66 8r purple & multi .45 .30
245 A66 9r violet & multi .65 .50
Nos. 243-245 (3) 1.30 1.00

In memory of Chuon-Nath (1883-1969), Cambodian language expert.
For surcharge see No. 322.

Soldiers in Battle A67

1971, Mar. 18 Photo. *Perf. 13*
246 A67 1r gray & multi .50 .20
247 A67 3r bister & multi .50 .40
248 A67 10r blue & multi 4.00 .75
Nos. 246-248 (3) 5.00 1.35

National territorial defense.
For overprint see No. 321.

UN Emblem, Men of Four Races A68

1971, Mar. 21
249 A68 3r blue & multi .20 .20
250 A68 7r green & multi .30 .25
251 A68 8r brt rose & multi .50 .30
Nos. 249-251 (3) 1.00 .75

Intl. year against racial discrimination.

General Post Office, Phnom Penh — A69

1971, Apr. 19
252 A69 3r blue & multi .20 .20
253 A69 9r lilac rose & multi .55 .35
254 A69 10r black & multi .70 .40
Nos. 252-254 (3) 1.45 .95

Symbolic Globe and Waves A70

Design: 7r, 8r, ITU emblem and waves.

1971, May 17 Photo. *Perf. 13*
255 A70 3r green, blk & bl .20 .20
256 A70 4r yellow & multi .20 .20
257 A70 7r lilac, blk & red .25 .20
258 A70 8r sal pink, blk & red .35 .25
Nos. 255-258 (4) 1.00 .85

3rd World Telecommunications Day.

Erythrina Indica A71

Wild Flowers: 3r, Bauhinia variegata. 6r, Butea frondosa. 10r, Lagerstroemia floribunda, vert.

1971, July 5 *Perf. 13x12½, 12½x13*
259 A71 2r lt ultra & multi .45 .45
260 A71 3r yel grn & multi .55 .55
261 A71 6r blue & multi 1.10 1.10
262 A71 10r brown & multi 1.40 1.40
Nos. 259-262 (4) 3.50 3.50

Khmer Coat of Arms — A72

Flag and Square of the Republic — A73

1971, Oct. 9 Engr. *Perf. 13*
263 A72 3r brt grn & bis .20 .20
264 A73 3r purple & multi .20 .20
265 A73 4r dp claret & multi .25 .20
266 A72 8r orange & bis .45 .25
267 A72 10r lt brn & bis .70 .30
a. Souv. sheet of 3, #263, 266-267 2.25 2.25
268 A73 10r slate grn & multi .70 .35
a. Souv. sheet of 3, #264-265, 268 2.25 2.25
Nos. 263-268 (6) 2.50 1.50

Republic, 1st anniv.
#267a sold for 25r, #268a for 20r.
For overprints and surcharges see Nos. 301-302, B13-B14.

UNICEF Emblem — A74

1971, Dec. 11
269 A74 3r black brown .25 .20
270 A74 5r ultra .35 .20
271 A74 9r dk pur & brn red .55 .35
Nos. 269-271 (3) 1.15 .75

25th anniv. of UNICEF.
This set and others exist with overprint "RPK," both with and without frame. Status has not been determined.

Book Year Emblem A75

1972, Feb. 7
272 A75 3r blue, grn & vio .40 .20
273 A75 8r violet, grn & bl .60 .30
274 A75 9r emerald & multi 1.00 .50
a. Souvenir sheet of 3, #272-274 1.10 1.10
Nos. 272-274 (3) 2.00 1.00

Intl. Book Year. No. 274a sold for 23r.

Lion of St. Mark A76

Designs: 5r, Waves engulfing St. Mark's Basilica. 10r, Bridge of Sighs, vert.

1972, Feb. 7 Engr. *Perf. 13*
275 A76 3r lil rose & org brn .50 .20
276 A76 5r yel grn & org brn .75 .25
277 A76 10r org brn, bl & yel grn 1.25 .45
a. Souvenir sheet of 3, #275-277 1.75 1.75
Nos. 275-277 (3) 2.50 .90

UNESCO campaign to save Venice. No. 277a sold for 23r.

UN Emblem A77

1972, Mar. 28

278 A77 3r deep carmine .20 .20
279 A77 6r deep blue .30 .20
280 A77 9r deep orange .50 .35
a. Souvenir sheet of 3, #278-280 1.50 1.50
Nos. 278-280 (3) 1.00 .75

25th anniv. UN Economic Commission for Asia and the Far East (ECAFE). No. 280a sold for 23r.

Dancing Apsarases — A78

"UIT" A79

1972, May 5 **Engr.** ***Perf. 13***

281 A78 1r golden brn .20 .20
282 A78 3r violet .20 .20
283 A78 7r rose claret .30 .30
284 A78 8r olive brn .40 .30
285 A78 9r blue grn .50 .30
286 A78 10r ultra .65 .30
287 A78 12r purple .85 .30
288 A78 14r Prus blue .90 .45
Nos. 281-288 (8) 4.00 2.35

1972, May 17 **Litho.**

289 A79 3r blk, yel & grnsh bl .25 .20
290 A79 9r blk, dp lil rose & bl grn .50 .25
291 A79 14r blk, brn & bl grn .75 .35
Nos. 289-291 (3) 1.50 .80

4th World Telecommunications Day.

"Human Environment" — A80

1972, June 5 **Engr.**

292 A80 3r org, plum & grn .25 .20
293 A80 12r brt grn & plum .40 .25
294 A80 15r plum & brt grn .60 .35
a. Souvenir sheet of 3, #292-294 2.50 2.50
Nos. 292-294 (3) 1.25 .80

UN Conf. on Human Environment, Stockholm, June 5-16. No. 294a sold for 35r.

For overprints and surcharges see Nos. 304-305, B15, B17.

Javan Rhinoceros A81

1972, Aug. 1 **Engr.** ***Perf. 13***

295 A81 3r shown .45 .20
296 A81 4r Serow .55 .20
297 A81 6r Malayan sambar 1.00 .30
298 A81 7r Banteng 1.50 .30
299 A81 8r Water buffalo 1.75 .50
300 A81 10r Gaur 2.25 .60
Nos. 295-300 (6) 7.50 2.10

Nos. 263, 267, 134, 293, 294 Overprinted in Red

1972, Sept. 9 **Engr.** ***Perf. 13***

301 A72 3r brt grn & bister .75 .30
302 A72 10r orange & bister 1.50 .60
303 A34 12r multicolored 1.50 .75
304 A80 12r brt grn & plum 1.60 .75
305 A80 15r plum & brt grn 2.10 .90
Nos. 301-305 (5) 7.45 3.30

20th Olympic Games, Munich, 8/26-9/11.

Raising Khmer Flag — A82

1972, Oct. 9 **Photo.** ***Perf. 12½x13***

306 A82 3r multicolored .20 .20
307 A82 5r brt rose & multi .25 .30
308 A82 9r yel grn & multi .55 .30
Nos. 306-308 (3) 1.00 .80

2nd anniversary of the establishment of the Khmer Republic.

For surcharge see No. 323.

Stupa and Crest — A83

Apsaras — A84

1973, May 12 **Engr.** ***Perf. 13***

309 A83 3r ocher & multi .30 .20
310 A83 12r yel grn & multi .30 .20
311 A83 14r blue & multi .50 .20
a. Souvenir sheet of 3, #309-311 2.50 2.50
Nos. 309-311 (3) 1.10 .60

New Constitution. No. 311a sold for 34r.

1973, July 23 **Engr.** ***Perf. 13***

Sculptures from Angkor Wat: 8r, 10r, Devata, diff.

312 A84 3r brown black .40 .25
313 A84 8r Prus green .60 .30
314 A84 10r olive bister 1.00 .45
a. Souvenir sheet of 3, #312-314 2.25 2.00
Nos. 312-314 (3) 2.00 1.00

No. 314a sold for 25r.

INTERPOL Emblem — A85

Marshal Lon Nol — A86

1973, Oct. 2 **Engr.** ***Perf. 13***

315 A85 3r green & multi .25 .20
316 A85 7r red brn & multi .35 .20
317 A85 10r olive & multi .50 .30
a. Souvenir sheet of 3, #315-317 1.50 1.25
Nos. 315-317 (3) 1.10 .70

50th anniv. of the Intl. Criminal Police Org. No. 317a sold for 30r.

1973, Oct. 9

318 A86 3r lt grn, blk & brn .20 .20
319 A86 8r brown, ol & blk .40 .30
320 A86 14r black & brn .60 .40
a. Souvenir sheet of 3 2.75 2.75
Nos. 318-320 (3) 1.20 .90

Marshal Lon Nol, 1st pres. of the Republic. No. 320a contains stamps similar to Nos. 318-320 in changed colors. Sold for 50r.

Nos. 248, 243 and 307 Surcharged with New Value, 2 Bars and Overprinted in Red or Silver: "4th ANNIVERSAIRE/DE LA REPUBLIQUE"

1974 **Photo.** ***Perf. 13, 12½x13***

321 A67 10r multi (R) 1.00 .50
322 A66 50r on 3r multi 2.00 1.00
323 A82 100r on 5r multi 7.00 3.50
Nos. 321-323 (3) 10.00 5.00

4th anniversary of the Republic.

Copernicus and "Nerva" — A87

Copernicus, various spacecraft and events.

1974, Sept. 10 **Litho.** ***Perf. 13***

324 A87 1r shown
325 A87 5r Mariner II
326 A87 10r Apollo
327 A87 25r Telstar
328 A87 50r Space walk
329 A87 100r Moon landing
330 A87 150r Separation of spaceship and module
Nos. 324-330 (7) *45.00*
Nos. 324-330, C46-C47 (9) *55.00*

500th anniversary of the birth of Nicolaus Copernicus (1473-1543), Polish astronomer.

Carrier Pigeon and UPU Emblem — A88

Design: 60r, Sailing ship and UPU emblem.

1974, Nov. 2

331 A88 10r multicolored .25 .20
332 A88 60r multicolored .75 .20
Nos. 331-332,C50 (3) 11.00 10.40

Cent. of UPU. A souvenir sheet containing one No. 332 exists.

A set of 9 stamps picturing musical instruments, overprinted and surcharged for use by the Khmer Republic just before the fall of the government in Apr. 1975, exists. Value, $1,100. Value for same set without surcharge, $500.

A89

1976 Summer Olympic Games, Montreal — A90

1r, 18th cent. swordsmen. 5r, Modern fencers. 10r, Ancient Olympic runner. 25r, Modern runner. 50r, Ancient rowers. 100r, Modern kayakers. 150r, Ancient horseman. 200r, Modern equestrian competitor. 250r, Buildings, Olympic flame.

1975, Jan. 2 **Litho.** ***Perf. 13½***

333-341 A89 Set of 9 12.00

Litho. & Embossed

342 A90 1200r gold & multi *35.00*

Souvenir Sheets

343 A89 200r silver & multi *7.50*
344 A89 250r silver & multi *7.50*

Nos. 337-344 are airmail.

A number has been reserved for another souvenir sheet released with this set.

A91

1974 World Cup Soccer Championships — A92

Soccer players and arms of: 1r, Hamburg. 5r, Gelsenkirchen. 10r, Dortmund. 25r, Stuttgart. 50r, Dusseldorf. 100r, Hannover. 150r, Frankfurt. 200r, Munich. 250r, Berlin.

Litho. (#346-354, 356-357)
Litho. & Embossed (#355, 358)

1975, Feb. 13

346-354 A91 Set of 9 7.50
355 A92 1200r gold & multi *37.50*

Souvenir Sheets

356 A91 200r gold & multi *6.00*
357 A91 250r gold & multi *6.00*
358 A92 1200r gold & multi *13.00*

Nos. 350-358 are airmail. Nos. 346-354 exist in imperforate souvenir sheets.

UPU, Cent. — A93

Designs: 15r, Letter carrier, pack mule. 20r, Biplane. 70r, Post coach. 160r, Biplane, Concorde. 180r, Steam-powered wagon. 235r, Postrider, tail of mailplane. 500r, Railway mail car. 1000r, Airship. 2000r, Caravel.

1975, Apr. 12

359-367 A93 Set of 9 8.00
366a Souvenir sheet of 1 *10.00*
367a Souvenir sheet of 1 *10.00*

Nos. 365-367 are airmail.

People's Republic of Kampuchea

Soldiers — A94

Designs, horiz.: 20c, People, flag. 50c, Fishermen. 1r, Soldiers passing flag.

1980, Apr. 10 Litho. *Perf. 11*
368-371 A94 Set of 4 45.00 45.00

Soviet Union, 60th Anniv. — A95

Designs: 50c, Globe, Kremlin. 1r, Buildings, map of USSR.

1982, Dec. 30 *Perf. 12x12½*
372-373 A95 Set of 2 .75 .40

People's Republic of Kampuchea, 4th Anniv. — A96

Designs: 50c, Natl. arms, vert. 1r, shown. 3r, Map, stylized figures, vert. 6r, Temple, vert.

1983, Jan. 7 Litho. *Perf. 13*
374-376 A96 Set of 3 3.50 1.10

Souvenir Sheet

377 A96 6r multicolored 4.75 2.25

1984 Summer Olympic Games, Los Angeles A97

Designs: 20c, Runner with torch. 50c, Javelin. 80c, Pole vault. 1r, Discus. 1.50r, Relay race. 2r, Swimming. 3r, Basketball.
20c-1r, 3r are vert.

1983, Jan. 20 Litho. *Perf. 13*
378-384 A97 Set of 7 7.00 1.50

Souvenir Sheet

385 A97 6r Soccer 5.00 3.00

No. 385 contains one 32x40mm stamp.

Butterflies — A98

20c, Salatura genutia. 50c, Euploea althaea. 80c, Byasa polyeuctes. 1r, Stichophthalma howqua. 1.50r, Kallima inachus. 2r, Precis orithya. 3r, Catopsilia pomona.
20c, 50c, 1.50r, 2r, 3r are vert.

1983, Feb. 18 Litho. *Perf. 13*
386-392 A98 Set of 7 7.00 1.50

Khmer Culture A99

Designs: 20c, Ruins, Srah Srang. 50c, Temple, Bakong. 80c, Ta Son. 1r, North Gate, Angkor Thom. 1.50r, Two winged figures. 2r, Apsara, Angkor. 3r, Statue of Banteai Srei.
80c-3r are vert.

1983, Mar. 15
393-399 A99 Set of 7 5.50 1.50

Folk Dances A100

Various dances. Denominations 50c, 1r, 3r.

1983, Apr. 17 Litho. *Perf. 13*
400-402 A100 Set of 3 3.25 1.00

Souvenir Sheet

403 A100 6r Native, "buffalo" 3.50 1.25

No. 403 contains one 32x40mm stamp.

Raphael (1483-1520) — A101

Parnassus (details): #404, 20c, Dante, Ennius, Homer. #406, 80c, Horace, Ovid, others. #409, 2r, The Muses. #410, 3r, Alcaeus, Petrarch, others.
School at Athens (details): #407, 1r, Euclid, disciples. #408, 1.50r, Telange, Pythagoras.
Details from: #405, 50c, Mass of Bolsena). 6r, Angels from Dispute of the Holy Sacrament, horiz.

1983, May 10 Litho. *Perf. 12½x13*
404-410 A101 Set of 7 6.25 2.00

Souvenir Sheet
Perf. 13

411 A101 6r multicolored 4.50 1.25

No. 411 contains one 40x32mm stamp.

1st Hot Air Balloon Ascension, Bicent. A102

Designs: 20c, Montgolfier. 30c, Ville d'Orleans. 50c, Hydrogen balloon. 1r, Blanchard & Jeffries, 1785. 1.50r, Ascension in Arctic. 2r, Stratosphere balloon. 3r, Balloon race. 6r, Balloons over town.

1983, June 3 *Perf. 12½*
412-418 A102 Set of 7 5.00 1.75

Souvenir Sheet
Perf. 13

419 A102 6r multicolored 5.00 1.25

Reptiles — A103

Designs: 20c, Iguana. 30c, Cobra. 80c, Trionyx turtle. 1r, Chameleon. 1.50r, Boa constrictor. 2r, Crocodile. 3r, Turtle.
30c, 1r, 1.50r are vert.

1983, June 28
420-426 A103 Set of 7 5.00 1.75

Birds A104

Designs: 20c, Lorikeet. 50c, Swallow. 80c, Eagle. 1r, Vulture. 1.50r, Turtle dove. 2r, Magpie. 3r, Hornbill.
20c-50c, 2r-3r are vert.

1983, Sept. 20
427-433 A104 Set of 7 5.50 1.50

Flowers — A105

20c, Sunflower. 50c, Caprifoliacae. 80c, Bougainvillea. 1r, Renonculacae. 1.50r, Nyctaginaceae. 2r, Cockscomb. 3r, Roses.

1983, Oct. 18 *Perf. 13*
434-440 A105 Set of 7 4.25 1.50

1984 Winter Olympic Games, Sarajevo — A106

Designs: 1r, Luge. 2r, Biathlon. 4r, Ski jumping. 5r, Two-man bobsled. 7r, Hockey.

1983, Nov. 10 *Perf. 12½*
441-445 A106 Set of 5 7.50 2.50

Souvenir Sheet

446 A106 6r Cross-country skiing 4.00 1.50

No. 446 contains one 40x32mm stamp.

Fish A107

20c, 1.50r, 2r, 3r, Various Cyprinidae. 50c, Trout. 80c, Catfish. 1r, Moray eel.

1983, Nov. 16 *Perf. 13*
447-453 A107 Set of 7 6.00 1.75

Festival of Rebirth — A108

50c, Factory. 1r, Bull, tractor. 3r, Bridge, ship, train. 6r, Radio antenna. 50c, 3r, 6r vert.

Perf. 12½x13, 13x12½

1983, Dec. 2 Litho.
454-456 A108 Set of 3 3.25 1.00

Souvenir Sheet

457 A108 6r multicolored 3.75 1.25

No. 457 contains one 32x40mm stamp.

People's Republic of Kampuchea, 5th Anniv. — A109

Designs: 50c, Red Cross. 1r, Soldiers. 3r, People celebrating. 6r, Man carrying water.

1984, Jan. 7 Litho. *Perf. 13*
458-460 A109 Set of 3 3.75 1.25

Souvenir Sheet

461 A109 6r multicolored 4.50 1.50

No. 461 contains one 32x40mm stamp.
For surcharges see Nos. 775-776.

1984 Winter Olympics, Sarajevo A110

Designs: 20c, Speed skating. 50c, Hockey. 80c, Slalom skiing. 1r, Ski jumping. 1.50r, Biathlon. 2r, Cross-country skiing. 3r, Pairs figure skating. 6r, Women's figure skating.

1984, Jan. 6 Litho. *Perf. 13*
462-468 A110 Set of 7 5.50 1.75

Souvenir Sheet

469 A110 6r multicolored 4.00 1.25

No. 469 contains one 32x40mm stamp.

Birds — A111

Designs: 10c, Bubulcus ibis. 40c, Lanius schach. 80c, Psittacula himalayana. 1r, Chloropsis aurifrons. 1.20r, Clamator coromandus. 2r, Motacilla cinerea. 2.50r, Dendronanthus indicus.

1984, Feb. 2
470-476 A111 Set of 7 9.00 3.00

Intl. Peace in Southeast Asia Forum — A112

Background color: 50c, Green. 1r, Blue. 3r, Violet.

1984, Feb. 25 *Perf. 13x12½*
477-479 A112 Set of 3 3.75 1.00

Space Exploration — A113

Designs: 10c, Luna 1. 40c, Luna 2. 80c, Luna 3. 1r, Soyuz 6. 1.20r, Soyuz 7. 2r, Soyuz 8. 2.50r, Book, rocket, S.P. Koralev. 6r, Salyut space station.
1r-2.50r are vert.

1984, Mar. 8 *Perf. 12½*
480-486 A113 Set of 7 5.50 1.75

Souvenir Sheet

487 A113 6r multicolored 4.25 1.50

No. 487 contains one 40x32mm stamp.

1984 Summer Olympic Games, Los Angeles A114

Designs: 20c, Discus. 50c, Long jump. 80c, Hurdles. 1r, Relay race. 1.50r, Pole vault. 2r, Javelin. 3r, High jump. 6r, Sprint race.

1984, Apr. 20 *Perf. 13*
488-494 A114 Set of 7 4.00 1.50

Souvenir Sheet

495 A114 6r multicolored 4.00 1.50

No. 495 contains one 32x40mm stamp.

Souvenir Sheet

ESPAÑA '84, Madrid — A115

1984, Apr. 24 *Perf. 12½*
496 A115 5r 1933 Hispano-Suiza K6 5.00 1.50

Wild Animals A116

Designs: 10c, Canis latrans. 40c, Canis dingo. 80c, Lycaon pictus. 1r, Canis aureus. 1.20r, Vulpes vulpes. 2r, Chrysocyon brachyurus, vert. 2.50r, Canis lupus.

1984, May 5 *Perf. 13*
497-503 A116 Set of 7 4.50 1.25

Locomotives — A117

Designs: 10c, BB-1002, France, 1966. 40c, BB-1052, France, 1966. 80c, Franco-Belgian, 1945. 1r, #231-505, Franco-Belgian, 1929. 1.20r, #803, Germany, 1968. 2r, BDE-405, France, 1957. 2.50r, DS-01, France, 1979.

1984, June 15 Litho. *Perf. 12½*
504-510 A117 Set of 7 5.50 1.75

Flowers A118

Designs: 10c, Magnolia. 40c, Plumeria. 80c, Himenoballis. 1r, Peltophorum roxburghii. 1.20r, Couroupita guianensis. 2r, Lagerstroemia. 2.50r, Thevetia perubiana.

1984, July 10 Litho. *Perf. 13*
511-517 A118 Set of 7 4.25 1.50

Classic Automobiles — A119

Designs: 20c, Mercedes-Benz. 50c, Bugatti. 80c, Alfa Romeo. 1r, Franklin. 1.50r, Hispano-Suiza. 2r, Rolls Royce. 3r, Tatra. 6r, Mercedes Benz, diff.

1984, Sept. 15 *Perf. 13x12½*
518-524 A119 Set of 7 5.00 1.25

Souvenir Sheet

Perf. 12½

525 A119 6r multicolored 4.25 1.00

No. 525 contains one 40x32mm stamp.

Musical Instruments — A120

Designs: 10c, Sra Lai. 40c, Skor drum. 80c, Skor thom. 1r, Thro khmer. 1.20r, Raneat ek. 2r, Raneat kong. 2.50r, Thro khe.
10c, 80c are vert.

1984, Oct. 10 *Perf. 13*
526-532 A120 Set of 7 5.25 1.50

Wild Animals A121

Designs: 10c, Gazelle. 40c, Capreolus capreolus. 80c, Lepus. 1r, Cervus elaphus. 1.20r, Elephas maximus. 2r, Genet. 2.50r, Bibos sauveli.
10c-40c, 1r-1.20r are vert.

1984, Nov. 11 *Perf. 13*
533-539 A121 Set of 7 5.25 1.50

Correggio (1489-1534) — A122

Details from paintings: 20c, Rest on Flight into Egypt. 50c, Martyrdom of the Four Saints. 80c, Mystic Marriage of St. Catherine with Saints Francis and Dominic. 1r, Madonna & Child with Saints John the Baptist, Geminian, Peter Martyr and George. 1.50r, Mystic Marriage of St. Catherine. 2r, The Deposition. 2.50r, The Deposition, diff. 6r, Virgin Crowned by Christ.

1984, Dec. 10 *Perf. 12½x13*
540-546 A122 Set of 7 4.25 1.00

Souvenir Sheet

Perf. 12½

547 A122 6r multicolored 4.25 1.00

No. 547 contains one 40x32mm stamp.

Natl. Festival — A123

50c, Oxcart. 1r, Horse-drawn cart. 3r, Elephants. 6r, Oxcart with passengers, vert.

1985, Jan. 5 *Perf. 12½x12*
548-550 A123 Set of 3 4.25 1.00

Souvenir Sheet

Perf. 12½

551 A123 6r multicolored 4.25 1.00

No. 551 contains one 32x40mm stamp.

1986 World Cup Soccer Championships, Mexico — A124

Various soccer players; 20c, vert. 50c, vert. 80c, vert. 1r. 1.50r. 2r, vert. 3r, vert.

1985, Feb. 4 *Perf. 13*
552-558 A124 Set of 7 3.75 1.25

Souvenir Sheet

559 A124 6r multicolored 3.75 1.00

No. 559 contains one 40x32mm stamp.

Motorcycles — A125

20c, 1939 Eska-Mofa. 50c, 1939 Wanderer. 80c, 1929 Premier. 1r, 1939 Ardie. 1.50r, 1932 Jawa. 2r, 1983 Simson. 3r, 1984 CZ-125.

1985, Mar. 8 Litho. *Perf. 13*
560-566 A125 Set of 7 4.00 1.50

Souvenir Sheet

567 A125 6r 1984 MBA 4.00 1.50

No. 567 contains one 40x32mm stamp.

Mushrooms — A126

Designs: 20c, Gymnopilus spectabilis. 50c, Coprinus micaceus. 80c, Amanita panterina. 1r, Hebelona crustuliniforme. 1.50r, Amanita muscaria. 2r, Coprinus comatus. 3r, Amanita caesarea.
Nos. 569-574 are vert.

1985, Apr. 4 *Perf. 13*
568-574 A126 Set of 7 4.75 1.25

Soviet Space Achievements — A127

Designs: 20c, Sputnik. 50c, Yuri Gagarin, rocket. 80c, Valentina Tereshkova, Vostok 6. 1r, Cosmonaut walking in space. 1.50r, Soyuz 4 docked with Soyuz 5. 2r, Lunar rover. 3r, Apollo-Soyuz mission. 6r, Soyuz capsule.

1985, Apr. 12 *Perf. 13*
575-581 A127 Set of 7 4.00 1.25

Souvenir Sheet

582 A127 6r multicolored 4.00 1.00

No. 582 contains one 40x32mm stamp.

Traditional Dances — A128

Designs: 50c, Four dancers. 1r, Three dancers. 3r, One dancer, vert.

1985, Apr. 13 Litho. ***Perf. 12½***
583-585 A128 Set of 3 3.25 1.00

End of World War II, 40th Anniv. A129

Designs: 50c, Soldiers celebrating. 1r, Victory parade, Moscow. 3r, Tank battle.

1985, May 9 Litho. ***Perf. 12x12½***
586-588 A129 Set of 3 4.25 1.50

Cats — A130

Various cats: 20c, 50c, 80c, 1r, 1.50r, 2r, 3r.

1985, May 16 Litho. ***Perf. 12x12½***
589-595 A130 Set of 7 5.00 1.00

Flowers — A131

20c, Lilium Black Dragon. 50c, Iris delavayi. 80c, Crocus aureus. 1r, Cyclamen persicum, wild form. 1.50r, Primula malacoides. 2r, Viola tricolor. 3r, Crocus purpureus.

1985, June 5 Litho. ***Perf. 13***
596-602 A131 Set of 7 3.25 1.00

Intl. Music Year — A132

Paintings: 20c, Mezzetin, by Watteau. 50c, St. Cecilia and the Angel, by Saraceni. 80c, Still Life with Violin, Flute and Guitar, by Oudry, horiz. 1r, Three Musicians, by F. Leger. 1.50r, Opera Orchestra, by Degas. 2r, St. Cecilia, by Schedoni. 3r, Young Harlequin with Violin, by Caillard. 6r, The Fifer, by Manet.

1985, June 13 ***Perf. 13***
603-609 A132 Set of 7 3.50 1.00

Souvenir Sheet

610 A132 6r multicolored 3.25 1.00

No. 610 contains one 32x40mm stamp.

Lenin (1870-1924) A133

1r, Portrait. 3r, Lenin standing, map of Soviet Union.

1985, June 20 Litho. ***Perf. 13***
611-612 A133 Set of 2 3.50 .75

ARGENTINA '85 — A134

Birds: 20c, Xanthopsar flavus. 50c, Sicalis flaveola. 80c, Thraupis bonariensis. 1r, Amblyramphus holosericeus. 1.50r, Chiloroceryle amazona. 2r, Ramphastos toco. 3r, Turdus rufiventris.
20c-80c, 1.50r-2r are vert.

1985, July 5 Litho. ***Perf. 12½***
613-619 A134 Set of 7 4.00 1.00

Ships A135

Designs: 10c, River boat, 1942. 40c, River boat, 1948. 80c, Tugboat, Japan, 1913. 1r, Dredge. 1.20r, Tugboat, US. 2r, Freighter. 2.50r, Tanker, Panama.

1985, Aug. 8
620-626 A135 Set of 7 3.50 1.10

ITALIA 85 — A136

Paintings: 20c, The Flood, by Michelangelo. 50c, Virgin & St. Margaret, by Il Parmigianino (Filippo Mazzola). 80c, Martyrdom of St. Peter Martyr, by Domenichino. 1r, Spring, by Botticelli. 1.50r, Sacrifice of Abraham, by Veronese. 2r, Meeting of St. Joachim and St. Anne, by Giotto. 3r, Bacchus, by Caravaggio.
6r, Early train.

1985, Oct. 25
627-633 A136 Set of 7 3.50 1.00

Souvenir Sheet

634 A136 6r multicolored 3.25 1.00

No. 634 contains one 32x40mm stamp.

Son Ngoc Minh — A137

1985, Dec. 2 Litho. ***Perf. 12x12½***
635-637 A137 Set of 3, 50c, 1r, 3r 3.50 1.25

Fish A138

20c, Barbus tetrazona. 50c, Ophiocephalus micropeltes. 80c, Carassius auratus. 1r, Trichogaster leeri. 1.50r, Puntius hexazona. 2r, Betta splendens. 3r, Datnioides microlepis.

1985, Dec. 28 Litho. ***Perf. 13***
638-644 A138 Set of 7 4.25 1.25

1986 World Cup Soccer Championships, Mexico — A139

Various soccer players: 20c, 50c, 80c, 1r, 1.50r, 2r, 3r.

1986, Jan. 29
645-651 A139 Set of 7 3.50 1.10

Souvenir Sheet

652 A139 6r multicolored 3.00 .90

No. 652 contains one 32x40mm stamp.

Horses A140

Designs: 20c, Cob. 50c, Arabian. 80c, Australian pony. 1r, Appaloosa. 1.50r, Quarter horse. 2r, Vladimir heavy draft. 3r, Andalusian.

1986, Feb. 15
653-659 A140 Set of 7 4.50 1.50

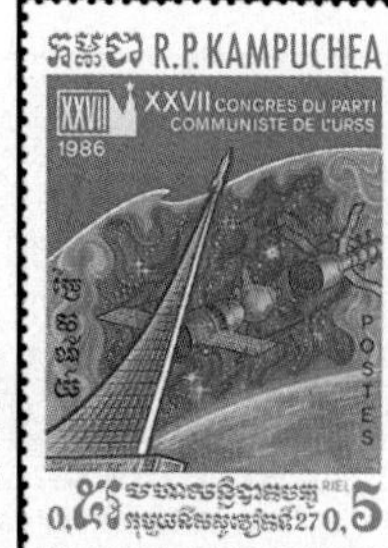

27th Soviet Communist Party Congress A141

Designs: 50c, Space capsules. 1r, Lenin. 5r, Statue, rocket lift-off.

1986, Feb. 25 ***Perf. 12x12½***
660-662 A141 Set of 3 3.25 1.00

Prehistoric Animals — A142

Designs: 20c, Edaphosaurus, horiz. 50c, Sauroctonus, horiz. 80c, Mastodonsaurus, horiz. 1r, Rhamphorhynchus. 1.50r, Brachiosaurus. 2r, Tarbosaurus. 3r, Indricotherium.

1986, Mar. 20 ***Perf. 12½***
663-669 A142 Set of 7 8.00 3.00

Manned Space Flight, 25th Anniv. — A143

10c, Luna 16. 40c, Luna 3. 80c, Vostok. 1r, Alexei Leonov walking in space. 1.20r, Apollo-Soyuz mission. 2r, Soyuz capsule docking with Salyut station. 2.50r, Yuri Gagarin.

1986, Apr. 12 ***Perf. 12½***
670-676 A143 Set of 7 4.00 1.50

Khmer Culture — A144

20c, Temple. 50c, Head of Buddha. 80c, Temple entrance. 1r, 1.50r, 2r, 3r, Various fans.

1986, Apr. 12 ***Perf. 13***
677-683 A144 Set of 7 4.50 1.60

Mercedes-Benz Automobiles — A145

20c, 1885 3-wheel. 50c, 1935 sedan. 80c, 1907 open touring car. 1r, 1920 convertible. 1.50r, 1932 cabriolet. 2r, 1938 2-door. 3r, 1985 sedan.

1986, May 14 ***Perf. 13x12½***
684-690 A145 Set of 7 4.50 1.25

Butterflies A146

Designs: 20c, Danaus genutia. 50c, Graphium amtiphates. 80c, Papilio demoleus. 1r, Danaus sita. 1.50r, Idea blanchardi. 2r, Papilio polytes. 3r, Dabasa payeni.

1986, June 19 ***Perf. 13***
691-697 A146 Set of 7 4.25 1.25

Ships A147

20c, English cog. 50c, Cog. 80c, Nile barge. 1r, Galley. 1.50r, Viking long ship. 2r, Two-masted lateen-rigged ship. 3r, Cog, diff.

1986, July 7 ***Perf. 13***
698-704 A147 Set of 7 4.25 1.50

Halley's Comet — A148

Designs: 10c, Solar system, Copernicus, Galileo, Brahe. 20c, Comet above Adoration of the Magi in painting by Giotto. 50c, Comet, observatory. 80c, Edmond Halley. 1.20r, Giotto probe. 1.50r, Vega probe. 2r, Computer-enhanced images of comet. 6r, Vega probe, diff.

1986, July 21 **Litho.** ***Perf. 12x12½***
705-711 A148 Set of 7 3.50 1.25

Souvenir Sheet

Perf. 13

712 A148 6r multicolored 3.00 1.00

No. 712 contains one 32x40mm stamp.

STOCKHOLMIA 86 — A149

Chess masters: 20c, Ruy Lopez. 50c, Francois Philador. 80c, Adolph Anderssen. 1r, Wilhelm Steinetz. 1.50r, Emanuel Lasker. 2r, José Capablanca. 3r, Alexander Alekhine.
6r, Chess pieces.

1986, Aug. 28 **Litho.** ***Perf. 12½***
713-719 A149 Set of 7 4.00 1.10

Souvenir Sheet

Perf. 13

720 A149 6r multicolored 3.75 1.00

No. 720 contains one 40x32mm stamp.

Cactus — A150

Fruit — A151

20c, Parodia maasii. 50c, Rebutia marsoneri. 80c, Melocactus evae. 1r, Gymnocalycium valnicekianum. 1.50r, Discocactus silichromus. 2r, Neochilenia simulans. 3r, Weingartia chiqichuquensis.

1986, Sept. 25 ***Perf. 13***
721-727 A150 Set of 7 3.75 1.00

1986, Oct. 4 ***Perf. 12½***

Designs: 10c, Bananas. 40c, Papayas. 80c, Mangos. 1r, Breadfruit. 1.20r, Litchi. 2r, Pineapple. 3r, Grapefruit, horiz.

728-734 A151 Set of 7 3.25 1.25

Aircraft — A152

20c, Concorde. 50c, DC-10. 80c, 747. 1r, IL-62. 1.50r, IL-86. 2r, AN-124. 3r, A-300.
Illustration reduced.

1986, Nov. 21
735-741 A152 Set of 7 3.50 1.10

Silverware — A153

Designs: 50c, Elephant, containers. 1r, Covered bowl. 3r, Serving dish.

1986, Dec. 2 ***Perf. 13***
742-744 A153 Set of 3 4.00 1.40

World Wildlife Fund A154

Designs: No. 745, 20c, Kouprey. No. 746, 20c, Gaur. 80c, Banteng. 1.50r, Buffalo.

1986, Dec. 30 **Litho.** ***Perf. 13***
745-748 A154 Set of 4 *12.00* 2.50

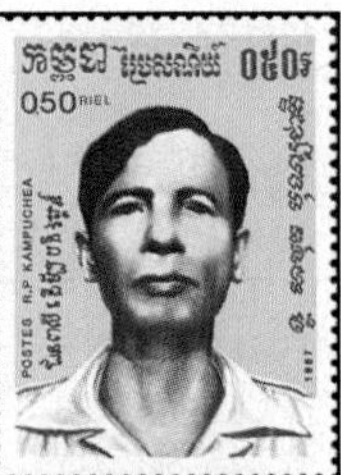

Tou Samouth A155

Denominations and background colors: 50c, green. 1r, blue, 3r, yellow.

1987, Jan. 7 **Litho.** ***Perf. 13***
749-751 A155 Set of 3 3.00 1.00

1988 Winter Olympic Games, Calgary — A156

Designs: 20c, Biathlon. 50c, Women's figure skating. 80c, Speed skating. 1r, Hockey. 1.50r, Luge. 2r, Two-man bobsled. 3r, Cross-country skiing. 6r, Slalom skiing.

1987, Jan. 14 ***Perf. 13x12½***
752-758 A156 Set of 7 3.25 1.10

Souvenir Sheet

Perf. 12½

759 A156 6r multicolored 2.75 .90

No. 759 contains one 40x32mm stamp.

1988 Summer Olympic Games, Seoul — A157

Designs: 20c, Weight lifting, vert. 50c, Archery. 80c, Fencing. 1r, Gymnastics, vert. 1.50r, Discus. 2r, Javelin, vert. 3r, Hurdles. 6r, Wrestling.

1987, Feb. 2 ***Perf. 12½x13, 13x12½***
760-766 A157 Set of 7 3.50 1.25

Souvenir Sheet

Perf. 13

767 A157 6r multicolored 3.00 1.00

No. 767 contains one 40x32mm stamp.

Dogs A158

Designs: 20c, shown. 50c, Greyhound. 80c, Great Dane. 1r, Doberman pinscher. 1.50r, Samoyed. 2r, Borzoi. 3r, Collie.

1987, Mar. 3 ***Perf. 13***
768-774 A158 Set of 7 4.75 1.50

Nos. 458, 463 Surcharged

1987, Mar. **Litho.** ***Perf. 13***
775 A110 35r on 50c #463 5.00
776 A109 50r on 50c #458 5.00

Soviet Spacecraft A159

Designs: 20c, Sputnik. 50c, Weather satellite. 80c, Proton. 1r, Vostok 1. 1.50r, Electron-2. 2r, Kosmos. 3r, Luna 2. 6r, Electron-4.

1987, Apr. 12 **Litho.** ***Perf. 13***
777-783 A159 Set of 7 3.50 1.25

Souvenir Sheet

784 A159 6r multicolored 3.25 1.00

No. 784 contains one 40x32mm stamp.

Silverware — A159a

Designs: 50c, Long-necked pot, vert. 1r, Box. 1.50r, Tea set. 3r, Sword.

1987, Apr. 13 ***Perf. 13***
785-788 A159a Set of 4 2.25 .75

CAPEX 87 — A160

Birds: 20c, Merops nubicus. 50c, Upupa epops. 80c, Balearica pavonina. 1r, Tyto alba. 1.50r, Halcyon leucocephala. 2r, Pycnonotus jocosus. 3r, Ardea purpurea. 6r, Terpsiphone paradisi.
50c-1.50r, 3r are vert.

1987, May 5 ***Perf. 13***
789-795 A160 Set of 7 4.00 1.25

Souvenir Sheet

796 A160 6r multicolored 3.50 1.25

No. 796 contains one 32x40mm stamp.

Early Aircraft Designs A161

Designs by: 20c, Horatio F. Phillips, 1893. 50c, John Stringfellow, 1848. 80c, Thomas Moy, 1875. 1r, Leonardo da Vinci, 1490. 1.50r, Sir George Cayley, 1840. 2r, Sir Hiram Maxim, 1894. 3r, William S. Henson, 1842. 6r, Da Vinci, diff.

1987, Aug. 7 ***Perf. 13***
797-803 A161 Set of 7 3.50 1.25

Souvenir Sheet

Perf. 12½

804 A161 6r multicolored 3.00 1.00

No. 804 contains one 32x40mm stamp.

Reptiles A162

Designs: 20c, Testudo gigantea. 50c, Uromastix acanthinuros. 80c, Cyclura macleayi. 1r, Phrynosoma coronatum. 1.50r, Sauromalus obesus. 2r, Ophisaurus apodus. 3r, Thamnophis sirtalis.

1987, Sept. 9 ***Perf. 13***
805-811 A162 Set of 7 4.25 1.50

HAFNIA 87 — A163

Helicopters: 20c, Kamov KA-15. 50c, Kamov KA-18. 80c, Westland Lynx WG-13. 1r, Sud Aviation Gazelle. 1.50r, Sud Aviation Puma. 2r, Boeing CH-47 Chinook. 3r, Boeing UTTAS. 6r, Fairey Rotodyne.

1987, Oct. 16 ***Perf. 12½x12***
812-818 A163 Set of 7 3.50 1.25

Souvenir Sheet

Perf. 13

819 A163 6r multicolored 3.00 1.00

No. 819 contains one 40x32mm stamp.

Russian October Revolution, 70th Anniv. A164

1987 **Litho.** ***Perf. 12x12¼***
820 A164 2r Soldiers, horse
821 A164 3r Soldiers
822 A164 5r Lenin, aides

Two additional stamps were issued in this set. The editors would like to examine them.

Fire Trucks A165

1987, Nov. 24 **Litho.** ***Perf. 13***
823-829 A165 20c, 50c, 80c, 1r, 1.50r, 2r, 3r, set of 7 6.50 2.00

Telecommunications — A166

50c, Dish antenna, vert. 1r, Broadcast center, vert. 3r, Dish antenna, broadcast center.

Perf. 13x12½, 12x12½, 12½x12

1987, Dec. 2
830-832 A166 Set of 3 3.00 1.00

No. 830 is 29x40mm. No. 831 is 28x44mm. No. 832 printed with se-tenant label.

1988 Winter Olympic Games, Calgary A167

Designs: 20c, Speed skating. 50c, Hockey. 80c, Downhill skiing. 1r, Ski jumping. 1.50r, Biathlon. 2r, Pairs figure skating. 3r, Cross-country skiing. 6r, Four-man bobsled.

1988, Jan. 7 ***Perf. 12½***
833-839 A167 Set of 7 3.00 1.00

Souvenir Sheet

Perf. 13

840 A167 6r multicolored 2.50 .75

No. 840 contains one 32x40mm stamp.

Water Projects A168

Designs: 50c, Canal. 1r, Dam under construction. 3r, Dam, bridge.

1988, Jan. 7 **Litho.** ***Perf. 13***
841-843 A168 Set of 3 4.00 1.25

1988 Summer Olympic Games, Seoul — A169

Designs: 20c, Balance beam, vert. 50c, Uneven bars. 80c, Rhythmic gymnastics ribbon, vert. 1r, Rhythmic gymnastics hoop, vert. 1.50r, Rhythmic gymnastics clubs, vert. 2r, Rhythmic gymnastics ball. 3r, Floor exercise.

Perf. 12½x13, 13x12½

1988, Feb. 2 **Litho.**
844-850 A169 Set of 7 4.00 1.50

Souvenir Sheet

Perf. 12½

851 A169 6r Rhythmic gymnastics, diff. 3.00 1.50

No. 851 contains one 32x40mm stamp.

JUVALUX 88 A170

Various cats. Denominations: 20c, 50c, 80c, 1r, 1.50r, 2r, 3r. Nos. 853-854, 856-858 are vert.

1988, Mar. 15 ***Perf. 12½***
852-858 A170 Set of 7 3.75 1.25

Souvenir Sheet

Perf. 13

859 A170 6r multicolored 3.75 1.25

No. 859 contains one 40x32mm stamp.

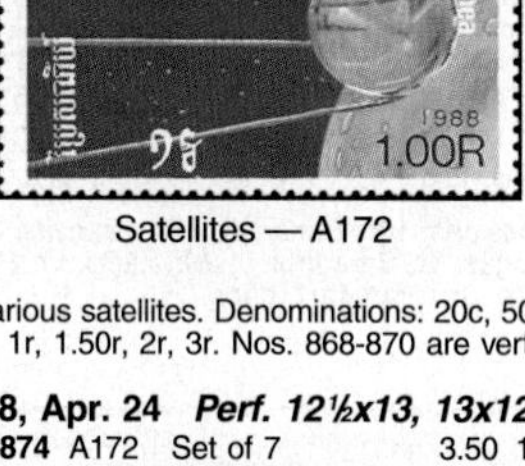

ESSEN 88 — A171

Ships: 20c, Passenger liner. 50c, Passenger liner, diff. 80c, Research ship. 1r, Communications ship. 1.50r, Tanker. 2r, Hydrofoil. 3r, Hovercraft.

1988, Apr. 14 **Litho.** ***Perf. 12½***
860-866 A171 Set of 7 3.50 1.25

Souvenir Sheet

Perf. 13

867 A171 6r Hydrofoil 3.25 1.10

Satellites — A172

Various satellites. Denominations: 20c, 50c, 80c, 1r, 1.50r, 2r, 3r. Nos. 868-870 are vert.

1988, Apr. 24 ***Perf. 12½x13, 13x12½***
868-874 A172 Set of 7 3.50 1.25

Souvenir Sheet

Perf. 13

875 A172 6r multicolored 5.50 1.75

No. 875 contains one 40x32mm stamp.

FINLANDIA 88 — A173

Fish: 20c, Xiphophorus helleri. 50c, Hemigrammus ocellifer. 80c, Macropodus opercularis. 1r, Carassius auratus. 1.50r, Hyphessobrycon inesi. 2r, Corynopoma riisei. 3r, Mollienisia latipinna.
6r, Pterophyllum scalare.

1988, Jun 10 **Litho.** ***Perf. 13x12½***
876-882 A173 Set of 7 3.75 1.25

Souvenir Sheet

Perf. 12½

883 A173 6r multicolored 3.00 1.00

No. 883 contains one 32x40mm stamp.

Shells — A174

Designs: 20c, Helicostyla florida. 50c, Helicostyla marinduquensis. 80c, Helicostyla fulgens. 1r, Helicostyla woodiana. 1.50r, Chloraea sirena. 2r, Helicostyla mirabilis. 3r, Helicostyla limansauensis.

1988, Aug. 5 **Litho.** ***Perf. 13x12½***
884-890 A174 Set of 7 4.25 1.50

Insects — A175

Designs: 20c, Coccinellidae. 50c, Zonabride geminata. 80c, Carabus auronitens. 1r, Apis mellifera. 1.50r, Praying mantis. 2r, Odonata. 3r, Malachius aeneus.

1988, Sept. 6 ***Perf. 13x12½***
891-897 A175 Set of 7 4.25 1.40

Orchids A176

Designs: 20c, Cattleya aclandiae. 50c, Odontoglossum Royal Sovereign. 80c, Cattleya labiata. 1r, Ophrys apifera. 1.50r, Laelia anceps. 2r, Laelia pumila. 3r, Stanhopea tigrina, horiz.

1988, Oct. 10 ***Perf. 12½x13, 13x12½***
898-904 A176 Set of 7 4.25 1.40

Reptiles — A177

Designs: 20c, Naja haje, vert. 50c, Iguana iguana, vert. 80c, Dryophis nasuta. 1r, Terrapene carolina. 1.50r, Cyclura macleayi. 2r, Bothrops bicolor. 3r, Naja naja, with hood spread, vert.

1988, Nov. 7 ***Perf. 12x12½, 12½x12***
905-911 A177 Set of 7 5.50 1.75

Dance of the Peacock A178

50c, 3 dancers, vert. 1r, shown. 3r, 2 dancers.

1988, Dec. 2 ***Perf. 13***
912-914 A178 Set of 3 4.00 1.25

For surcharges see Nos. 1195-1196.

Bridges — A179

1989 ***Perf. 13x12½***
915-917 A179 50c, 1r, 3r, set of 3 3.00 1.00

Decade of Progress — A180

3r, Telecommunications station. 12r, Central Electrical Plant No. 4. 30r, Cement plant, vert.

1989
918-920 A180 Set of 3 3.50 1.25

1990 World Cup Soccer Championships, Italy — A181

Various soccer players. Denominations: 2r, 3r, 5r, 10r, 15r, 20r, 35r.

1989 ***Perf. 12½x13***
921-927 A181 Set of 7 4.50 1.50

Souvenir Sheet
Perf. 13

928 A181 45r multicolored 3.00 1.00

No. 928 contains one 32x40mm stamp.

Trains A182

Various locomotives. Denominations: 2r, 3r, 5r, 10r, 15r, 20r, 35r.

1989 ***Perf. 13***
929-935 A182 Set of 7 4.25 1.50

Souvenir Sheet
Perf. 12½

936 A182 45r multicolored 3.25 1.00

No. 936 contains one 40x32mm stamp.

A183

A184

1989 ***Perf. 13***
937 A183 12r red & black 1.00 .35

Cuban Revolution, 30th anniv.

1989

Birds: 20c, Ara macao. 80c, Kakatoe galerita. 3r, Psittacula krameri. 6r, Ara ararauna. 10r, Poicephalus robustus. 15r, Amazona aestiva. 25r, Pionus senilis, horiz.
45r, Cyanoramphus novaezelandiae.

938-944 A184 Set of 7 3.75 1.25

Souvenir Sheet
Perf. 12½

945 A184 45r multicolored 3.00 1.00

No. 945 contains one 40x32mm stamp.

1992 Winter Olympic Games, Albertville A185

2r, Slalom skiing. 3r, Biathlon. 5r, Cross-country skiing. 10r, Ski jumping. 15r, Speed skating. 20r, Hockey. 35r, Bobsled. 45r, Pairs figure skating.

1989, Mar. 30 ***Perf. 13***
946-952 A185 Set of 7 4.25 1.50

Souvenir Sheet
Perf. 12½

953 A185 45r multicolored 2.75 .90

No. 953 contains one 32x40mm stamp.

Water Lilies A186

20c, Nymphaea capensis (pink). 80c, Nymphaea capensis (purple). 3r, Nymphaea lotus. 6r, Nymphaea Dir. Geo. T. Moore. 10r, Nymphaea Sunrise. 15r, Nymphaea Escarboncie. 25r, Nymphaea Cladstoniana. 45r, Nymphaea Paul Hariot.

1989 ***Perf. 12½x13***
954-960 A186 Set of 7 3.75 1.25

Souvenir Sheet
Perf. 12½

961 A186 45r multicolored 3.00 1.00

No. 961 contains one 32x40mm stamp.

1992 Summer Olympic Games, Barcelona — A187

Designs: 2r, Wrestling. 3r, Pommel horse, vert. 5r, Shot put. 10r, Running, vert. 15r, Fencing. 20r, Canoeing, vert. 35r, Steeplechase, vert. 45r, Weight lifting, vert.

1989 ***Perf. 13***
962-968 A187 Set of 7 4.50 1.50

Souvenir Sheet
Perf. 12½

969 A187 45r multicolored 4.00 1.50

No. 969 contains one 32x40mm stamp.

Mushrooms A188

Designs: 20c, Xerocomus subtomentosus. 80c, Inocybe patouillardii. 3r, Armillaria mellea. 6r, Agaricus campestris. 10r, Paxillus involutus. 15r, Coprinus comatus. 25r, Lepiota procera.

1989 ***Perf. 12½x13***
970-976 A188 Set of 7 3.25 1.10

Horses — A189

Designs: 2r, Shire. 3r, Brabant. 5r, Bolounais. 10r, Breton. 15r, Vladimir heavy draft. 20r, Italian heavy draft. 35r, Freiberger. 45r, Horse-drawn cart.

1989 ***Perf. 12½***
977-983 A189 Set of 7 4.25 1.50

Souvenir Sheet

984 A189 45r multicolored 3.25 1.10

Nos. 977-983 printed with se-tenant label. No. 984 contains one 40x32mm stamp.

Angkor Wat — A190

Denominations: 35r, 50r, 80r, 100r.

1989, May 15 **Litho.** ***Perf. 13¼***
985-988 A190 Set of 4

Cambodia

PHILEXFRANCE 89 — A191

Mail coaches: 2r, 17th cent. 3r, Paris-Lyon, 1720. 5r, 1793. 10r, 1805. 15r, Royal Mail. 20r, 1843. 35r, Paris-Lille, 1837, vert. 45r, 1815, vert.

1989 **Litho.** ***Perf. 13***
989-995 A191 Set of 7 4.50 1.50

Souvenir Sheet
Perf. 12½

996 A191 45r multicolored 3.00 1.50

No. 996 contains one 23x40mm stamp.

BRASILIANA 89 — A192

Butterflies: 2r, Papilio zagreus. 3r, Morpho catenarius. 5r, Morpho aega. 10r, Callithea sapphira. 15r, Catagramma sorana. 20r, Pierella nereis. 35r, Papilio brasiliensis. 45r, Thacia marsyas, horiz.

1989 ***Perf. 13***
997-1003 A192 Set of 7 5.00 1.50

Souvenir Sheet

1004 A192 45r multicolored 4.50 1.50

No. 1004 contains one 40x32mm stamp.

Khmer Boats A193

Various pirogues. Denominations: 3r, 12r, 30r.

1989, Dec. 2 **Litho.** ***Perf. 12½***
1005-1007 A193 Set of 3 3.50 1.25

Natl. Organizations — A194

3r, Youth, vert. 12r, Labor. 30r, Natl. Front.

1990, Jan. 7 **Litho.** ***Perf. 13***
1008-1010 A194 Set of 3 2.40 .90

1990 World Cup Soccer Championships, Italy — A195

Various soccer players. Denominations: 2r, 3r, 5r, 10r, 15r, 20r, 35r.

1990, Jan. 5 **Litho.** ***Perf. 13***
1011-1017 A195 Set of 7 4.00 1.50

Souvenir Sheet

1018 A195 45r multicolored 2.75 1.00

No. 1018 contains one 32x40mm stamp.
For surcharges see Nos. 1072, 1075.

STAMPWORLD LONDON 90 — A196

Various mail coaches. Denominations: 2r, 3r, 5r, 10r, 15r, 20r, 35r.
45r, Single horse van for rural deliveries.

1990 ***Perf. 12½x12***
1019-1025 A196 Set of 7 4.00 1.25

Souvenir Sheet

Perf. 13

1026 A196 45r multicolored 2.50 .90

Nos. 1019-1025 are printed with se-tenant label. No. 1026 contains one 40x32mm stamp.

Rice — A197

Designs: 3r, Woman, rice. 12r, People hauling rice, horiz. 30r, Women threshing rice.

1990, June 19 **Litho.** ***Perf. 13***
1027-1029 A197 Set of 3 3.25 1.25

1992 Winter Olympic Games, Albertville A198

2r, 4-man bobsled. 3r, Speed skating. 5r, Pairs figure skating. 10r, Hockey. 15r, Biathlon. 20r, Luge. 35r, Ski jumping. 45r, Hockey goalie.

1990 **Litho.** ***Perf. 13***
1030-1036 A198 Set of 7 4.50 1.50

Souvenir Sheet

1037 A198 45r multicolored 2.50 .90

No. 1037 contains one 32x40mm stamp.

1992 Summer Olympic Games, Barcelona A199

Designs: 2r, Shooting. 3r, Shot put. 5r, Weight lifting. 10r, Boxing. 15r, Pole vault. 20r, Basketball. 35r, Fencing. 45r, Rhythmic gymnastics.

1990
1038-1044 A199 Set of 7 4.50 1.50

Souvenir Sheet

1045 A199 45r multicolored 2.50 .75

No. 1045 contains one 32x40mm stamp.

Khmer Culture A200

Designs: 3r, Facade, Bantey Srei. 12r, Relief. 30r, Ruins, Banon.

Perf. 12½, 12½x13 (#1048)

1990, Dec. 2 **Litho.**
1046-1048 A200 Set of 3 3.00 1.25

No. 1048 is 36x21mm.

Dogs A201

20c, Poodle. 80c, Shetland. 3r, Samoyed. 6r, Springer spaniel. 10r, Fox terrier. 15r, Afghan. 25r, Dalmatian. 45r, Bernese.

1990 **Litho.** ***Perf. 13***
1049-1055 A201 Set of 7 4.00 1.25

Souvenir Sheet

1056 A201 45r multicolored 3.00 1.00

No. 1056 contains one 40x32mm stamp.

Cacti — A202

Designs: 20c, Cereus hexagonus. 80c, Arthrocereus rondonianus. 3r, Matucana multicolor. 6r, Hildewintera aureispina. 10r, Opuntia retrosa. 15r, Erdisia tenuicula. 25r, Mamillaria yaquensis.

1990
1057-1063 A202 Set of 7 4.00 1.50

NEW ZEALAND 90 — A203

Butterflies: 2r, Zizina oxleyi. 3r, Cupha prosope. 5r, Heteronympha merope. 10r, Dodonidia helmsi. 15r, Argirophenga antipodum. 20r, Tysonotis danis. 35r, Pyrameis gonnarilla. 45r, Pyrameis itea.

1990 ***Perf. 13***
1064-1070 A203 Set of 7 5.00 1.50

Souvenir Sheet

Perf. 12½

1071 A203 45r multicolored 3.25 1.00

No. 1071 contains one 40x32mm stamp.

Nos. 1012, 1013, 1015, 1016 Surcharged in Red

1990 **Litho.** ***Perf. 13***
1072 A195 200r on 3r #1012
1073 A195 300r on 5r multi
1075 A195 800r on 15r multi
1076 A195 1000ron 20r multi

Nos. are reserved for additions to this set.

Intl. Literacy Year — A204

Denominations: 3r, 12r, 30r.

1990 **Litho.** ***Perf. 13***
1077-1079 A204 Set of 3 3.50 1.25

Ships A205

Designs: 20c, English, 1200. 80c, Spanish galleon, 16th cent. 3r, Dutch ship, 1627. 6r, La Couronne, 1638. 10r, L'Astrolabe, 1826. 15r, French packet, Louisiana, 1864. 25r, Clipper ship, 1900, vert. 45r, Merchant ship, 1800.

1990 **Litho.** ***Perf. 13***
1080-1086 A205 Set of 7 4.25 1.50

Souvenir Sheet

Perf. 12½

1087 A205 45r multicolored 3.00 1.00

No. 1087 contains one 32x40mm stamp.

Natl. Building Campaign — A206

3r, Railroad. 12r, Cargo ship, Kampong Som. 30r, Fishing boats, Kampong Som.

1990 **Litho.** ***Perf. 13***
1088-1090 A206 Set of 3 3.25 1.25

PARIS 90 — A207

Chess pieces and: 2r, Sacré Coeur. 3r, Equestrian statue. 5r, Winged Victory of Samothrace. 10r, Chateau, Azay le Riddeau. 15r, Sculpture, "The Dance." 20r, Eiffel Tower. 35r, Arc de Triomphe.
45r, Chess pieces, horiz.

1990, Nov. 15 **Litho.** ***Perf. 13***
1091-1097 A207 Set of 7 6.00 2.00

Souvenir Sheet

1098 A207 45r multicolored 4.25 1.50

No. 1098 contains one 40x32mm stamp.

Space Day — A208

Designs: 2r, Vostok. 3r, Soyuz. 5r, Artificial satellite. 10r, Luna 10. 15r, Mars 1. 20r, Venus 3. 35r, Mir. 45r, Energia, Buran.

1990 **Litho.** ***Perf. 13***
1099-1105 A208 Set of 7 4.75 1.50

Souvenir Sheet

1106 A208 45r multicolored 3.00 1.00

No. 1106 contains one 32x40mm stamp.
For surcharges see Nos. 1145-1151.

Discovery of America, 500th Anniv. (in 1992) — A209

Designs: 2r, Columbus. 3r, Queen Isabella's jewelry chest. 5r, Queen Isabella. 10r, Santa Maria. 15r, Juan de la Cosa. 20r, Columbus Monument. 35r, Pyramid, Yucatan.
45r, Columbus, diff.

1990, Oct. 12 **Litho.** ***Perf. 13***
1107-1113 A209 Set of 7 6.00 2.00

Souvenir Sheet

1114 A209 45r multicolored 3.75 1.25

No. 1114 contains one 32x40mm stamp.

Natl. Festival A210

Designs: 100r, Tire production. 300r, Rural infirmary. 500r, Fisherman, vert.

Perf. 12½, 13 (#1117)

1991, Jan. 7 **Litho.**
1115-1117 A210 Set of 3 3.75 1.25

No. 1117 is 28x40mm.

1994 World Cup Soccer Championships, US — A211

Various soccer players. Denominations: 5r, 25r, 50r, 100r, 200r, 400r, 1000r.

1991, Feb. 15 **Litho.** ***Perf. 13***
1118-1124 A211 Set of 7 5.50 1.75

Souvenir Sheet

1125 A211 900r multicolored 3.00 1.10

No. 1125 contains one 32x40mm stamp.

1992 Winter Olympic Games, Albertville A212

Designs: 5r, Speed skating. 25r, Slalom skiing. 70r, Hockey. 100r, Bobsled. 200r, Freestyle skiing. 400r, Pairs figure skating. 1000r, Downhill skiing.
900r, Ski jumping.

1991, Mar. 30 **Litho.** ***Perf. 12½***
1126-1132 A212 Set of 7 6.00 2.00

Souvenir Sheet

Perf. 13

1133 A212 900r multicolored 3.00 1.00

No. 1133 contains one 32x40mm stamp.

Khmer Culture A213

Statues: 100r, Garuda, 10th cent. 300r, Torso of Vishnu reclining, 11th cent. 500r, Reclining Nandin, 7th cent.

1991, Apr. 13 Litho. *Perf. 12½*
1134-1136 A213 Set of 3 3.25 1.25

1992 Summer Olympic Games, Barcelona A214

Designs: 5r, Pole vault. 25r, Table tennis. 70r, Women's running. 100r, Wrestling. 200r, Women's gymnastics. 400r, Tennis. 1000r, Boxing.
900r, Balance beam.

1991, Apr. 25 Litho. *Perf. 12½x13*
1137-1143 A214 Set of 7 5.00 1.50

Souvenir Sheet
Perf. 13
1144 A214 900r multicolored 3.25 1.00

No. 1144 contains one 32x40mm stamp.

Nos. 1099-1103, 1105 Surcharged in Red

1991 Litho. *Perf. 13*
1145 A208 100r on 2r #1099
1146 A208 150r on 3r #1100
1147 A208 200r on 5r #1101
1148 A208 300r on 10r #1102
1149 A208 500r on 15r #1103
1151 A208 2000r on 35r #1105

Number is reserved for surcharge on No. 1104.

Aircraft — A215

Designs: 5r, DC-10-30. 25r, MD-11. 70r, IL-96-300. 100r, A-310. 200r, YAK-42. 400r, TU-154. 1000r, DC-9

1991, June 15 Litho. *Perf. 13x12½*
1152-1158 A215 Set of 7 5.25 1.75

ESPAMER 91 — A216

Pre-Columbian pottery: 5r, Catamarca. 25r, Catamarca, vert. 70r, Tucuman, vert. 100r, Santiago del Estero. 200r, Santiago del Estero, diff. 400r, Tucuman, diff., vert. 1000r, Catamarca, diff.
900r, Catamarca, diff.

1991, July 10 *Perf. 13*
1159-1165 A216 Set of 7 6.00 2.00

Souvenir Sheet
Perf. 12½
1166 A216 900r multicolored 4.00 1.25

No. 1166 contains one 40x32mm stamp.

Discovery of America, 500th Anniv. (in 1992) — A217

Designs: 5r, Pinta, vert. 25r, Niña, vert. 70r, Santa Maria, vert. 100r, Landing of Columbus. 200r, Encountering new cultures. 400r, First European settlement in Americas. 1000r, Native village.
900r, Columbus.

1991, Oct. 12 *Perf. 12½x13, 13x12½*
1167-1173 A217 Set of 7 6.00 2.00

Souvenir Sheet
Perf. 12½
1174 A217 900r multicolored 3.25 1.10

No. 1174 contains one 40x32mm stamp.

PHILANIPPON 91 — A218

Butterflies: 5r, Neptis pryeri. 25r, Papilio xuthus. 70r, Cyrestis thyodamas. 100r, Argynnis anadiomene. 200r, Lethe marginalis. 400r, Artopoetes pryeri. 1000r, Danaus chrysippus.
900r, Ochlodes subhyalina.

1991, Nov. 16 *Perf. 13*
1175-1181 A218 Set of 7 5.75 2.00

Souvenir Sheet
Perf. 12½
1182 A218 900r multicolored 3.50 1.25

No. 1182 contains one 40x32mm stamp.

Natl. Building Campaign A219

Designs: 100r, Fishing port. 300r, Preparing palm sugar, vert. 500r, Harvesting peppers.

1991, Dec. 2 Litho. *Perf. 12½*
1183-1185 A219 Set of 3 3.50 1.25

Natl. Festival — A220

Traditional costumes: 150r, Chakdomuk. 350r, Longvek. 1000r, Angkor.

1992, Jan. 7 *Perf. 13*
1186-1188 A220 Set of 3 3.75 1.25

1992 Summer Olympic Games, Barcelona A221

5r, Wrestling. 15r, Soccer. 80r, Weight lifting. 400r, Archery. 1500r, Balance beam.
1000r, Equestrian.

1992, Jan. Litho. *Perf. 13*
1189-1193 A221 Set of 5 3.75 1.25

Souvenir Sheet
Perf. 12½
1194 A221 1000r multicolored 2.50 .80

No. 1194 contains one 32x40mm stamp.

Nos. 913-914 Surcharged in Red

1992, Jan. Litho. *Perf. 13*
1195 A178 200r on 3r #914
1196 A178 300r on 1r #913

Fish A222

Designs: 5r, Hyphessobrycon innesi. 15r, Betta splendens. 80r, Nematobrycon palmen. 400r, Colisa lalia. 1500r, Hoplosternum thoracatum.
1000r, Pterophyllum scalare.

1992, Feb. 8 Litho. *Perf. 12½*
1197-1201 A222 Set of 5 4.50 1.50

Souvenir Sheet
1202 A222 1000r multicolored 2.75 1.00

No. 1202 contains one 40x32mm stamp.

1994 World Cup Soccer Championships, US — A223

Various soccer plays. Denominations: 5r, 15r, 80r, 400r, 1500r. Nos. 1203, 1205-1207 are vert.

1992, Mar. 6 Litho. *Perf. 12½*
1203-1207 A223 Set of 5 4.25 1.50

Souvenir Sheet
1208 A223 1000r multicolored 2.75 .90

No. 1208 contains one 40x32mm stamp.

Khmer Culture — A224

19th cent. structures: 150r, Monument. 350r, Stupa. 1000r, Library of Mandapa.

1992, Apr. 13 Litho. *Perf. 12½*
1209-1211 A224 Set of 3 3.50 1.25

Leonardo da Vinci (1452-1519) — A225

Designs: 5r, Automobile. 15r, Container ship. 80r, Helicopter. 400r, Scuba gear. 1500r, Parachute, vert.
1000r, Portrait.

1992, Apr. 15 Litho. *Perf. 12x12½*
1212-1216 A225 Set of 5 4.50 1.50

Souvenir Sheet
Perf. 13
1217 A225 1000r multicolored 2.75 .80

Nos. 1212-1216 each printed with se-tenant labels showing Da Vinci's conceptions of the items shown on the stamps. No. 1217 contains one 32x40mm stamp.

EXPO 92, Seville A226

Inventors, builders: 5r, De la Cierva, autogyro. 15r, Edison, electric light bulb. 80r, Morse, telegraph. 400r, Monturiol, submarine. No. 1222, 1500r, Bell, telephone.
No. 1223, 1500r, Fulton, steamship.

1992, Apr. 23 *Perf. 12½*
1218-1222 A226 Set of 5 4.00 1.25

Souvenir Sheet
Perf. 13
1223 A226 1000r pink & black 2.75 .80

No. 1223 contains one 32x40mm stamp.

1992 Summer Olympic Games, Barcelona — A227

Designs: 5r, Weight lifting. 15r, Boxing. 80r, Basketball. 400r, Sprints. 1500r, Water polo.
1000r, Women's gymnastics.

1992, May 15 *Perf. 13*
1224-1228 A227 Set of 5 5.50 1.75

Souvenir Sheet
Perf. 12½
1229 A227 1000r multicolored 3.75 1.25

No. 1229 contains one 40x32mm stamp.

Environmental Protection — A228

Designs: 5r, Women filling water jars. 15r, Pagoda. 80r, Palm trees. 400r, Boy riding water buffalo. 1500r, Lake, swimmers.
1000r, Angkor Wat.

1992, June 16 Litho. *Perf. 12½*
1230-1234 A228 Set of 5 5.50 1.75

Souvenir Sheet
Perf. 13
1235 A228 1000r multicolored 4.00 1.25

No. 1235 contains one 42x32mm stamp.

GENOA 92 — A229

Explorers, ship: 5r, Bougainville, Boudeuse. 15r, Cook, Endeavour. 80r, Darwin, Beagle. 400r, Cousteau, Calypso. 1500r, Heyerdahl, Kon Tiki.
1000r, Columbus.

1992, Aug. 1 Litho. *Perf. 12x12½*
1236-1240 A229 Set of 5 4.50 1.50

Souvenir Sheet
Perf. 12½

1241 A229 1000r multicolored 2.75 .80

No. 1241 contains one 32x40mm stamp.

Mushrooms A230

Designs: 5r, Albatrellus confluens. 15r, Boletus calopus. 80r, Stropharia aeruginosa. 400r, Telamonia armillata. 1500r, Cortinarius traganus.

1992, Sept. 25 *Perf. 13*
1242-1246 A230 Set of 5 5.00 1.50

Seaplanes — A231

Designs: 5r, Bellanca Pacemaker, 1930. 15r, Canadair CL-215, 1965. 80r, G-21A Goose, 1937. 400r, Sealand SA-6, 1947. 1500r, Short S-23, 1936.
1000r, G-44 Widgeon, 1940.

1992, Oct. 16 *Perf. 12½x12*
1247-1251 A231 Set of 5 4.00 1.25

Souvenir Sheet
Perf. 13

1252 A231 1000r multicolored 2.75 .90

No. 1252 contains one 32x40mm stamp.

Natl. Development A232

Designs: 150r, Dish antenna. 350r, Dish antenna, flags. 1000r, Hotel Cambodiana.

1992, Dec. 2 Litho. *Perf. 12½*
1253-1255 A232 Set of 3 3.25 1.25

Natl. Festival A233

Designs: 50r, Sociological Institute. 450r, Motel Cambodiana. 1000r, Theater.

1993, Jan. 7 Litho. *Perf. 12½*
1256-1258 A233 Set of 3 3.50 1.25

Dolphin, Bathyscaph — A234

Fauna, machine: 150r, shown. 200r, Falcon, jet fighter. 250r, Beaver, dam. 500r, Bat, satellite. 900r, Hummingbird, helicopter.

1993, Feb. 5 Litho. *Perf. 13*
Without Gum
1259-1263 A234 Set of 5 4.00 1.25

Flowers — A235

Designs: 150r, Datura suaveolens. 200r, Convolvulus tricolor. 250r, Hippeastrum hybrid. 500r, Camellia hybrid. 900r, Lilium speciosum.
1000r, Datura suaveolens, camellia, lilium speciosum.

1993, Mar. 15 *Perf. 13*
Without Gum
1264-1268 A235 Set of 5 4.00 1.25

Souvenir Sheet
Perf. 12½

1269 A235 1000r multicolored 2.50 .85

No. 1269 contains one 40x32mm stamp.

Khmer Culture A236

Designs: 50r, Statue of a Nandin. 450r, Temple Vihear. 1000r, Man with offerings.

1993, Apr. 13 Litho. *Perf. 12½*
1270-1272 A236 Set of 3 3.50 1.25

Wildlife — A237

150r, Cynocephalus volans. 200r, Petuarista petuarista. 250r, Ptychozoon homalocephalum. 500r, Rhacophorus nigropalmatus. 900r, Draco volans.

1993, May 4 Litho. *Perf. 12½x12*
Without Gum
1273-1277 A237 Set of 5 4.00 1.25

BRASILIANA 93 — A238

Butterflies: 250r, Symbrenthia hypselis. 350r, Sithon nedymond. 600r, Geitoneura minyas. 800r, Argyreus hyperbius. 1000r, Argyrophenga antipodum.
1500r, Pararge schakra.

1993, June 15 *Perf. 12½x12*
Without Gum
1278-1282 A238 Set of 5 5.25 1.50

Souvenir Sheet
Perf. 12½

1283 A238 1500r multicolored 3.50 1.25

No. 1283 contains one 40x32mm stamp.

UN Transitional Authority in Cambodia (UNTAC) Pacification Program A239

150r, Cambodian soldiers approaching UN base. 200r, Cambodians entering camp. 250r, Cambodians surrendering weapons to UN. 500r, Vocational training. 900r, Cambodians re-entering society.
1000r, Returning to homes and family.

1993, Aug. 4 Litho. *Perf. 12½*
1284-1288 A239 Set of 5 4.00 1.50

Souvenir Sheet
Perf. 13

1289 A239 1000r blue & black 3.75 1.25

No. 1289 contains one 32x40mm stamp.

Ships A240

150r, Venetian caravel. 200r, Phoenician galley. 250r, Egyptian merchantman. 500r, Genoese merchantman. 900r, English merchantman.

1993, Aug. 27 Litho. *Perf. 13*
Without Gum
1290-1294 A240 Set of 5 3.75 1.25

Alberto Santos-Dumont (1873-1932) — A241

Designs: 150r, Portrait, Balloon, Eiffel Tower, vert. 200r, 14-bis, 1906. 250r, Demoiselle. 500r, EMB-201A. 900r, EMB-111.

1993, Sept. 10 *Perf. 13*
Without Gum
1295-1299 A241 Set of 5 4.00 1.25

1994 World Cup Soccer Championships, US — A242

Various soccer plays. Denominations: 250r, 350r, 600r, 800r, 1000r, vert.

1993, Sept. 23 Litho. *Perf. 12½*
1300-1304 A242 Set of 5 5.25 1.75

Souvenir Sheet

1305 A242 1500r multicolored 4.50 1.50

No. 1305 contains one 40x32mm stamp.

BANGKOK 93 — A243

Ducks: 250r, Anas penelope. 350r, Anas formosa. 600r, Aix galericulata. 800r, Aix sponsa. 1000r, Histrionicus histrionicus.
1500r, Head of Air galericulata.

1993, Oct. 1 Litho. *Perf. 13*
Without Gum
1306-1310 A243 Set of 5 5.50 1.75

Souvenir Sheet

1311 A243 1500r multicolored 3.25 1.10

No. 1311 contains one 40x32mm stamp.

Vertical Take-Off Aircraft — A244

Designs: 150r, First helicopter model, France, 1784, vert. 200r, Steam helicopter model, 1863, vert. 250r, New York-Atlanta-Miami autogyro flight, 1927. 500r, Sikorsky helicopter, 1943. 900r, French VTOL jet.
1000r, Juan de la Cierva's autogyro C-4, 1923.

Perf. 12x12½, 12½x12
1993, Nov. 6 Without Gum
1312-1316 A244 Set of 5 3.75 1.25

Souvenir Sheet
Perf. 12½

1317 A244 1000r multicolored 2.50 .90

No. 1317 contains one 40x32mm stamp.

Insects — A245

Designs: 50r, Cnaphalocrosis medinalis. 450r, Cicadelle brune. 500r, Scirpophaga incertulas. No. 1321, 1000r, Diopsis macrophthalma.
No. 1322, Leptocorisa oratorius.

1993, Dec. 2 *Perf. 13*
1318-1321 A245 Set of 4 3.50 1.25

Souvenir Sheet
Perf. 12½

1322 A245 1000r multicolored 2.75 .80

Issued without gum.
No. 1322 contains one 32x40mm stamp.

Independence, 40th Anniv. — A246

Designs: 300r, Ministry of Posts and Telecommunications. 500r, Independence Monument, 1953, vert. 700r, Natl. flag.

1993 Litho. *Perf. 12½*
1323-1325 A246 Set of 3 3.00 1.00

Hummel Figurines A247

Designs: 50r, Boy riding pony. 100r, Girl with baby carriage. 150r, Girl bathing doll. 200r, Girl holding doll. 250r, Boys playing. 300r, Girls pulling boy in cart. 350r, Girls playing ring-around-the-rosie. 600r, Boys with stick and drum.

1993 Litho. *Perf. 12½*
1326-1333 A247 Set of 8 5.00 1.50

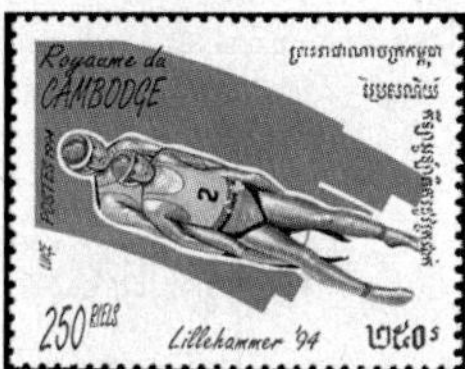

1994 Winter Olympic Games, Lillehammer — A248

150r, Women's figure skating, vert. 250r, Two-man luge. 400r, Downhill skiing. 700r, Biathlon. 1000r, Speed skating, vert. 1500r, Curling, vert.

1994, Jan. 23 *Perf. 13*
1334-1338 A248 Set of 5 5.00 1.50
Souvenir Sheet
1339 A248 1500r multicolored 3.50 1.25
No. 1339 contains one 32x40mm stamp.

Classic Automobiles — A249

Designs: 150r, 1924 Opel. 200r, 1901 Mercedes. 250r, 1927 Model T Ford. 500r, 1907 Rolls Royce. 900r, 1908 Hutton. 1000r, 1931 Duesenberg.

1994, Feb. 20 *Perf. 13*
1340-1344 A249 Set of 5 4.25 1.50
Souvenir Sheet
1345 A249 1000r multicolored 2.75 .90
No. 1345 contains one 32x40mm stamp.

1996 Summer Olympic Games, Atlanta — A250

Designs: 150r, Women's gymnastics. 200r, Soccer. 250r, Javelin. 300r, Canoeing. 600r, Running. 1000r, Diving, horiz. 1500r, Equestrian.

1994, Mar. 20 *Perf. 13*
1346-1351 A250 Set of 6 4.50 1.50
Souvenir Sheet
1352 A250 1500r multicolored 3.50 1.10
No. 1352 contains one 32x40mm stamp.

Khmer Statues — A251

Designs: 300r, Siva and Uma. 500r, Vishnu. 700r, King Jayavarman VII.

1994, Apr. 13
1353-1355 A251 Set of 3 4.50 1.50

Intl. Olympic Committee, Cent. — A252

Designs: 100r, Olympic Flag. 300r, Flag, Torch. 600r, Flag, Baron de Coubertin.

1994, Apr. 23 *Perf. 12½*
1356-1358 A252 Set of 3 3.00 1.00

Prehistoric Animals — A253

150r, Mesonyx. 250r, Doedicurus. 400r, Mylodon. 700r, Uintatherium. 1000r, Hyrachyus.

1994, May 10 *Perf. 12½*
1359-1363 A253 Set of 5 5.00 1.50

1994 World Cup Soccer Championships, U.S. — A254

Various soccer plays. Denominations: 150r, 250r, 400r, 700r, 1000r.

1994, June 17 *Perf. 12½*
1364-1368 A254 Set of 5 5.00 1.50
Souvenir Sheet
1369 A254 1500r multicolored 3.50 1.25
No. 1369 contains one 32x40mm stamp.

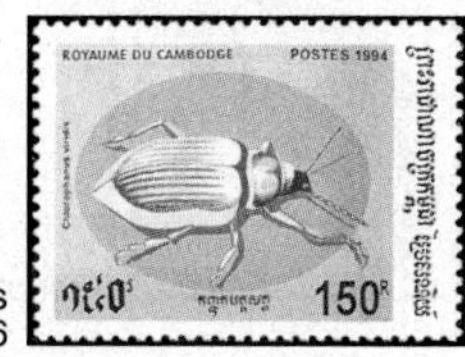

Statues A255

Designs: 300r, shown. 500r, Soldiers in combat, vert. 700r, Lions, vert.

1994 *Perf. 13*
1370-1372 A255 Set of 3 3.75 1.25

Beetles A256

Designs: 150r, Chlorophanus viridis. 200r, Chrysochroa fulgidissima. 250r, Lytta vesicatoria. 500r, Purpuricenus kaehleri. 900r, Dynastes hercules. 1000r, Timarcha tenebricosa.

1994, July 7 *Perf. 12½*
1373-1377 A256 Set of 5 4.00 1.25
Souvenir Sheet
1378 A256 1000r multicolored 2.50 .90
No. 1378 contains one 40x32mm stamp.

Submarines — A257

Designs: 150r, Halley's diving bell, 1690, vert. 200r, Gimnote, 1886. 250r, Peral, 1888. 500r, Nuclear-powered Nautilus, 1954. 900r, Bathyscaphe Trieste, 1953. 1000r, Ictineo, 1885.

1994, Aug. 12 *Perf. 13*
1379-1383 A257 Set of 5 4.50 1.50
Souvenir Sheet
Perf. 12½
1384 A257 1000r multicolored 3.00 1.00
No. 1384 contains one 40x32mm stamp.

Chess Champions — A258

Designs: 150r, Francois-André Philador, 1795. 200r, Louis de la Bourdonnais, 1821. 250r, Adolph Anderssen, 1851. 500r, Paul Morphy, 1858. 900r, Wilhelm Steinitz, 1866. 1000r, Emanuel Lasker, 1894.

1994, Sept. 20 *Perf. 13*
1385-1389 A258 Set of 5 4.50 1.50
Souvenir Sheet
1390 A258 1000r multicolored 3.00 1.00
No. 1390 contains one 32x40mm stamp.

Aircraft A259

Designs: 150r, Sikorsky S-42 flying boat. 200r, Vought-Sikorsky VS-300A helicopter. 250r, Sikorsky S-37 biplane. 500r, Sikorsky S-35 biplane. 900r, Sikorsky S-43 amphibian. 1000r, 1st 4-engine bomber, Ilya Mourometz.

1994, Oct. 6 *Perf. 13*
1391-1395 A259 Set of 5 4.50 1.50
Souvenir Sheet
Perf. 12½
1396 A259 1000r multicolored 3.00 1.00
No. 1396 contains one 40x32mm stamp.

Birds A260

Designs: 150r, Remiz pendulinus, vert. 250r, Panurus biarmicus. 400r, Emberiza rustica. 700r, Emberiza schoeniclus. 1000r, Regulus regulus. 1500r, Pitta angolensis.

1994, Nov. 20 *Perf. 12½*
1397-1401 A260 Set of 5 5.00 1.50
Souvenir Sheet
Perf. 13
1402 A260 1500r multicolored 3.50 1.25
No. 1402 contains one 32x40mm stamp.

Independence Festival — A261

Designs: 300r, Postal Service float. 500r, Soldiers marching. 700r, Army unit marching.

1994, Dec. 9 *Perf. 13*
1403-1405 A261 Set of 3 5.00 1.50

Natl. Development — A262

Designs: 300r, Chruoi Changwar Bridge. 500r, Olympic Commercial Center. 700r, Sakamony Chedei Temple.

1994, Dec. 10
1406-1408 A262 Set of 3 5.00 1.50

Prehistoric Animals — A263

100r, Psittacosaurus. 200r, Protoceratops. 300r, Montanoceraptors. 400r, Centrosaurus. 700r, Styracosaurus. 800r, Triceratops.

1995, Jan. 10
1409-1414 A263 Set of 6 5.00 1.50

Butterflies A264

100r, Anthocharis cardamines. 200r, Iphiclides podalirius. 300r, Mesoacidalia aglaja. 600r, Vanessa atalanta. 800r, Inachis io.

1995, Feb. 12
1415-1419 A264 Set of 5 4.50 1.50

1996 Summer Olympic Games, Atlanta A265

Designs: 100r, Swimming. 200r, Rhythmic gymnastics. 400r, Basketball. 800r, Soccer. 1000r, Cycling. 1500r, Running.
200r-1500r are vert.

1995, Mar. 9
1420-1424 A265 Set of 5 5.00 1.50

Souvenir Sheet

1425 A265 1500r multicolored 3.00 1.00

No. 1425 contains one 32x40mm stamp.

Mushrooms A266

Designs: 100r, Amanita phalloides. 200r, Cantharellus cibarius. 300r, Armillaria mellea. 600r, Agaricus campestris. 800r, Amanita muscaria.

1995, Mar. 23
1426-1430 A266 Set of 5 4.25 1.50

Statues — A267

Designs: 300r, Kneeling ascetic. 500r, Parasurama. 700r, Siva.

1995, Apr. 13 ***Perf. 12½***
1431-1433 A267 Set of 3 3.25 1.10

Protected Wildlife — A268

Designs: 300r, Bos gaurus. 500r, Bos sauveli, vert. 700r, Grus antigone, vert.

1995, May 5 ***Perf. 13***
1434-1436 A268 Set of 3 3.75 1.25

Parrots — A269

Designs: 100r, Lorus lory. 200r, Polytelis alexandrae. 400r, Eclectus voratus. 800r, Ara macao. 1000r, Melopsittacus undulatus.
1500r, Amazona ochrocephala.

1995, May 23 ***Perf. 13***
1437-1441 A269 Set of 5 4.50 1.50

Souvenir Sheet

Perf. 12½

1442 A269 1500r multicolored 4.00 1.50

No. 1442 contains one 32x40mm stamp.

Tourism A270

Public gardens: 300r, Sculpture of Garuda. 500r, Fountain. 700r, Sculpture of mythological figures.

1995, July 15 ***Perf. 12½***
1443-1445 A270 Set of 3 3.25 1.10

Locomotives — A271

100r, Richard Trevithick's steam locomotive, 1804. 200r, George Stephenson's Rocket, 1830. 300r, Stephenson's Locomotion, 1825. 600r, Lafayette, 1837. 800r, Best Friend of Charleston, 1830.
1000r, Stephenson, vert.

1995, Aug. 17
1446-1450 A271 Set of 5 4.25 1.50

Souvenir Sheet

1451 A271 1000r multicolored 2.50 .90

No. 1451 contains one 32x40mm stamp.

World War II Aircraft A272

100r, Bristol Blenheim II, vert. 200r, North American B-25. 300r, Avro Anson. 600r, Avro Manchester. 800r, Consolidated B-24.
1000r, Boeing B-17E.

Perf. 12x12½, 12½x12

1995, Sept. 15
1452-1456 A272 Set of 5 4.25 1.50

Souvenir Sheet

Perf. 12½

1457 A272 1000r multicolored 2.50 .90

No. 1457 contains one 32x40mm stamp.

FAO, 50th Anniv. A273

Designs: 300r, Separating rice plants. 500r, Transplanting rice. 700r, Model rice farm.

1995, Oct. 24 ***Perf. 13***
1458-1460 A273 Set of 3 3.00 1.00

UN, 50th Anniv. A274

Designs: 300r, Bridge. 500r, People on bridge. 700r, Central spans of bridge.

1995, Oct. 24 ***Perf. 12½***
1461-1463 A274 Set of 3 3.75 1.25

Queen Monineath A275

700r, shown. 800r, King Norodom Sihanouk.

1995, Nov. 9 ***Perf. 12½x13***
1464-1465 A275 Set of 2 3.25 1.10

Fish A276

100r, Heniochus acuminatus. 200r, Chelmon rostratus. 400r, Amphiprion percula. 800r, Paracanthurus hepatus. 1000r, Holocanthus ciliaris.
1500r, Coris angulata, vert.

1995, Nov. 19 ***Perf. 12½***
1466-1470 A276 Set of 5 4.50 1.50

Souvenir Sheet

1471 A276 1500r multicolored 3.25 1.00

Main Post Office, Cent. A277

Denominations: 300r, 500r, 700r.

1995, Dec. 2 ***Perf. 12½***
1472-1474 A277 Set of 3 4.00 1.25

Admission to UN, 40th Anniv. — A278

300r, Independence Monument. 400r, Angkor Wat. 800r, Natl. flag, vert.

Perf. 12½x13, 13x12½

1995, Dec. 14 **Litho.**
1475-1477 A278 Set of 3 3.50 1.25

1996 Summer Olympic Games, Atlanta — A279

Designs: 100r, Tennis. 200r, Volleyball. 300r, Soccer. #1480A, 500r, Running. 900r, Baseball. 1000r, Basketball.
1500r, Windsurfing.

1996, Jan. 10 Litho. ***Perf. 12½x13***
1478-1482 A279 Set of 6 4.75 1.50

Souvenir Sheet

Perf. 12½

1483 A279 1500r multicolored 3.00 1.00

No. 1483 contains one 32x40mm stamp.

A280

1996, Jan. 30 ***Perf. 12½***

1484	A280	50r	Kep State Chalet	.20	.20
1485	A280	100r	Power station	.20	.20
1486	A280	200r	Wheelchair	.30	.20
1487	A280	500r	Wheelchair basketball	.60	.20
1488	A280	800r	Making crutches, vert.	.85	.25
1489	A280	1000r	Kep beach	1.00	.35
1490	A280	1500r	Serpent Island	1.75	.45
	Nos. 1484-1490 (7)			4.90	1.85

Wild Cats A281

100r, Felis libyca, vert. 200r, Felis silvestris. 300r, Felis caracal. 500r, Felis geoffroyi. 900r, Felis nigripes. 1000r, Felis planiceps.

1996, Feb. 8 ***Perf. 13***
1491-1496 A281 Set of 6 6.00 2.00

1998 World Cup Soccer Championships, France — A282

Various soccer players. Denominations: 100r, 200r, 300r, 500r, 900r, 1000r. No. 1502 is horiz.

1996, Mar. 15 *Perf. 13*
1497-1502 A282 Set of 6 5.00 1.50

Souvenir Sheet

1503 A282 1500r multicolored 3.00 1.00

No. 1503 contains one 32x40mm stamp.

Khmer Culture — A283

100r, Tusmukh. 500r, Ream Iso. 900r, Isei.

1996, Apr. 13 Litho. *Perf. 12½x13*
1504-1506 A283 Set of 3 2.10 .70

Locomotives — A284

100r, Pacific Type. 200r, Unidentified, 1902. 300r, Unidentified, 1930. 500r, Unidentified, 1914. 900r, LMS #6202, 1930. 1000r, Snake, 1864.
1500r, Canadian Pacific.

1996, Apr. 20
1507-1512 A284 Set of 6 4.50 1.50

Souvenir Sheet

1513 A284 1500r multicolored 2.25 .80

No. 1513 contains one 40x32mm stamp.
CAPEX 96 (#1513).

Birds A285

Designs: 100r, Kittacinela malabarica, vert. 200r, Leiothrix lutea. 300r, Parus varius, vert. 500r, Oriolus chinensis. 900r, Cettia diphone. 1000r, Cyanoptila cyanomelana, vert.

1996, May 7
1514-1519 A285 Set of 6 4.50 1.50

Olymphilex '96 — A286

Designs: 100r, Rhythmic gymnastics. 200r, Judo. 300r, High jump. 500r, Wrestling. 900r, Weight lifting. 1000r, Soccer.
1500r, Diving.

1996, June 14 Litho. *Perf. 13x12½*
1520-1525 A286 Set of 6 3.75 1.25

Souvenir Sheet

Perf. 12½

1526 A286 1500r multicolored 2.10 .75

No. 1526 contains one 32x40mm stamp.

Early Aircraft — A287

100r, Douglas M-2, 1926. 200r, Pitcairn PA-5 Mailwing, 1928. 300r, Boeing 40 B, 1928. 500r, Potez 25, 1925. 900r, Stearman C-3MB, 1927. 1000r, De Havilland DH4, 1918.
1500r, Standard JR-1B, 1918.

1996, July 5 *Perf. 12½x12*
1527-1532 A287 Set of 6 4.50 1.50

Souvenir Sheet

Perf. 13

1533 A287 1500r multicolored 2.75 .90

No. 1533 contains one 40x32mm stamp.

Historic Sites — A288

50r, 100r, 200r, Diff. Apsaras, Tonle Bati. #1537, Statue, Angkor Wat. #1538, Statue of a Goddess. 500r, Carved wall, Tonle Bati. #1540, 1000r, #1543, Various structures, Tonle Bati. #1541, #1544, 1700r, 2500r, 3000r, Various views of Angkor Wat.
Nos. 1539, 1543, 1545-1547 are horiz.

1996-97 Litho. *Perf. 12½*

1534	A288	50r black & yel org	.20	.20
1535	A288	100r black & blue	.20	.20
1536	A288	200r black & tan	.20	.20
1537	A288	300r blk & light bl	.20	.20
1538	A288	300r black & red	.20	.20
1539	A288	500r blk & bright bl	.30	.20
1540	A288	800r black & yel grn	.40	.20
1541	A288	800r black & yel grn	.40	.20
1542	A288	1000r black & green	.50	.20
1543	A288	1500r black & bister	.75	.25
1544	A288	1500r black & brown	.75	.25
1545	A288	1700r black & org brn	.90	.30
1546	A288	2500r black & blue	1.25	.40
1547	A288	3000r black & dk grn	1.50	.50
		Nos. 1534-1547 (14)	7.75	3.50

Issued: 50r, 100r, 200r, 500r, No. 1540, 1000r, No. 1543, 7/30/96; others, 3/26/97.
See Nos. 1686-1692, 1846-1852.

Dinosaurs — A289

No. 1548: a, 50r, Coelophysis. b, 100r, Euparkeria. c, 150r, Plateosaurus. d, 200r, Herrerasaurus.
No. 1549: a, 250r, Dilophosaurus. b, 300r, Tuojiangosaurus. c, 350r, Camarasaurs. d, 400r, Ceratosaurus.
No. 1550: a, 500r, Spinosaurus. b, 700r, Ouranosaurus. c, 800r, Avimimus. d, 1200r, Deinonychus.

1996, Aug. 8 Litho. *Perf. 13*

Sheets of 4

1548 A289 #a.-d. .80 .25
1549 A289 #a.-d. 2.10 .60
1550 A289 #a.-d. 5.25 1.50

Chess Champions A290

100r, José Raul Capablanca. 200r, Alexander Alekhine. 300r, Vassily Smyslov. 500r, Mikhail Tal. 900r, Bobby Fischer. 1000r, Anatoly Karpov.
1500r, Garry Kasparov.

1996, Sept. 10 *Perf. 13*
1551-1556 A290 Set of 6 4.50 1.50

Souvenir Sheet

Perf. 12½

1557 A290 1500r multicolored 2.75 .90

No. 1557 contains one 32x40mm stamp.

Wild Animals A291

Designs: 100r, Ursus arctos. 200r, Panthera leo. 300r, Tapirus indicus. 500r, Camelus ferus. 900r, Capra ibex. 1000r, Zalophus californianus.

1996, Oct. 3 *Perf. 13x12½*
1558-1563 A291 Set of 6 4.25 1.25

Dogs — A292

Designs: 200r, Collie. 300r, Labrador retriever. 500r, Doberman pinscher. 900r, German shepherd. 1000r, Boxer.

1996, Nov. 8 *Perf. 12½x13*
1564-1568 A292 Set of 5 4.00 1.25

Independence — A293

100, 500, 900r, Various water treatment plants.

1996, Nov. 9 *Perf. 13*
1569-1571 A293 Set of 3 2.40 .80

Ships A294

Designs: 200r, Chinese junk. 300r, Galley. 500r, Roman galley. 900r, Clipper ship, 19th cent. 1000r, Paddle steamer Sirius, 1838.
1500r, Great Eastern, 1858.

1996, Dec. 15 *Perf. 12½x13*
1572-1576 A294 Set of 5 4.00 1.25

Souvenir Sheet

Perf. 12½

1577 A294 1500r multicolored 2.75 .90

No. 1577 contains one 40x32mm stamp.

Cambodia's Admission to UPU, 45th Anniv. — A295

Denominations: 200r, 400r, 900r.

1996, Dec. 21 *Perf. 12½*
1578-1580 A295 Set of 3 2.10 .70

New Year 1997 (Year of the Ox) — A296

Paintings of oxen, attributed to Han Huang 723-87): a, Facing left. b, Looking right. c, Brown & white spotted. d, Facing left, head down.

1996, Dec. 28 *Perf. 13x12½*
1581 A296 500r Strip of 4, #a.-d. + label 2.25 .75

UN Intl. Day of Volunteers — A297

Designs: 100r, Phnom Kaun Sat Dam. 900r, Chrey Krem Dam. 1500r, Angkrung Canal.

1996, Dec. 30
1582-1584 A297 Set of 3 2.40 .80

Greenpeace, 25th Anniv. — A298

Helicopter: 200r, Hovering over cargo. 300r, Hovering over ship. 500r, On helipad. 900r, Lifting cargo.
1000r, Close-up of helicopter.

1996, Dec. 30 *Perf. 12½x13*
1585-1588 A298 Set of 4 5.50 1.75

Souvenir Sheet

Perf. 12½

1589 A298 1000r multicolored 3.00 1.00

No. 1589 contains one 32x40mm stamp.

1998 World Cup Soccer Championships, France — A299

Various soccer plays. Denominations: 100r, 200r, 300r, 500r, 900r, 1000r.

1997, Jan. 6 Litho. *Perf. 12½x13*
1590-1595 A299 Set of 6 4.50 1.50

Souvenir Sheet
Perf. 13

1596 A299 2000r multicolored 2.75 .90

No. 1596 contains one 40x32mm stamp.

Elephas Maximus — A300

World Wilflife Fund: a, 300r, Two walking. b, 500r, Three standing. c, 900r, Two fighting. d, 1000r, Adult, calf.

1997, Feb. 12 *Perf. 12½x12*
1597 A300 Strip of 4, #a.-d. *2.50* .85

Birds — A301

600r, Bombycilla garrulus. 900r, Lanius excubitor. 1000r, Passer montanus. 2000r, Phoenicurus phoenicurus. 2500r, Emberiza schoeniclus. 3000r, Emberiza hortulana.

1997, Feb. 20 *Perf. 13x12½*
1598-1603 A301 Set of 6 12.50 4.50

Express mail service.

Fire Fighting Vehicles A302

Designs: 200r, English, 1731. 500r, Putnam, 1863. 900r, Merryweather, 1894. 1000r, Shand Mason Co., 1901. 1500r, Maxim Motor Co., Ford, 1949. 4000r, Merryweather, 1950.
5400r, Mack Truck Co., 1953.

1997, Mar. 11 *Perf. 12½x13*
1604-1609 A302 Set of 6 4.50 1.50

Souvenir Sheet
Perf. 13

1610 A302 5400r multicolored 3.25 1.10

No. 1610 contains one 40x32mm stamp.

Ducks A303

Designs: 200r, Polystieta stelleri. 500r, Alopochen aegyptiacus. 900r, Anas americana. 1000r, Anas falcata. 1500r, Melanitta perspicillata. 4000r, Anas discors.
5400r, Anas formosa, vert.

1997, Apr. 7 *Perf. 12½x13*
1611-1616 A303 Set of 6 4.50 1.50

Souvenir Sheet
Perf. 12½

1617 A303 5400r multicolored 3.25 1.10

No. 1617 contains one 32x40mm stamp.

Heinrich Von Stephan (1831-1897), Founder of UPU — A304

Denominations: 500r, 1500r, 2000r.

1997, Apr. 8 *Perf. 12½x13*
1618-1620 A304 Set of 3 2.50 .85

Khmer Culture — A305

Various views of Bantea Srei Temple. Denominations: 500r, 1500r, 2000r.

1997, Apr. 13 *Perf. 13x12½*
1621-1623 A305 Set of 3 2.50 .85

Cats — A306

Designs: 200r, Birman. 500r, Exotic short-hair. 900r, Persian. 1000r, Turkish. 1500r, American short-hair. 4000r, Scottish fold.
5400r, Sphinx.

1997, May 8 *Perf. 13x12½*
1624-1629 A306 Set of 6 11.00 2.00

Souvenir Sheet
Perf. 13

1630 A306 5400r multicolored 4.00 1.10

No. 1630 contains one 32x40mm stamp.

Trains A307

200r, 4-4-2T, #488. 500r, Frederick Smith 4-6-0. 900r, 0-8-0, #3131. 1000r, Transport #1, London #L44, 0-4-4. 1500r, 0-6-2, #1711. 4000r, 4-6-2, #60523.
5400r, North Yorkshire Moor (K1), 2-6-0, #2005.

1997, Jun 9 *Perf. 12½x12*
1631-1636 A307 Set of 6 4.00 1.25

Souvenir Sheet
Perf. 13

1637 A307 5400r multicolored 2.40 .75

No. 1637 contains one 40x32mm stamp.

Dogs A308

Designs: 200r, Shar-pei. 500r, Tchin-tchin. 900r, Pekinese. 1000r, Chow-chow, vert. 1500r, Pug, vert. 4000r, Akita, vert.
5400r, Tufted Chinese, vert.

1997, July 4 *Perf. 12½x13, 13x12½*
1638-1643 A308 Set of 6 4.50 1.50

Souvenir Sheet
Perf. 12½

1644 A308 5400r multicolored 3.50 1.25

No. 1644 contains one 32x40mm stamp.

ASEAN, 30th Anniv. A309

Designs: 500r, Dunalom Wat. 1500r, Royal Palace. 2000r, Natl. Museum.

1997, Aug. 5 *Perf. 12½x13*
1645-1647 A309 Set of 3 2.25 .75

Ships A310

Designs: 200r, Caravelle, 15th cent. 500r, Spanish galleon, 16th cent. 900r, Galleon "Great Harry," 16th cent. 1000r, Galleon "Le Couronne," 17th cent. 1500r, Cargo ship, 18th cent. 4000r, Clipper ship, 19th cent.
5400r, HMS Victory.

1997, Sept. 10 *Perf. 12½x12*
1648-1653 A310 Set of 6 4.75 1.50

Souvenir Sheet
Perf. 13

1654 A310 5400r multicolored 2.50 .85

No. 1654 contains one 40x32mm stamp.

A311

#1655-1658, Various public gardens. #1659-1661, Various dams. #1657 is vert.

1997, Sept. 30 *Perf. 12½*

1655	A311	300r	black & yel grn	.25	.20
1656	A311	300r	black & red	.25	.20
1657	A311	800r	black & citron	.50	.20
1658	A311	1500r	black & org brn	.85	.30
1659	A311	1700r	blk & red brn	1.10	.35
1660	A311	2500r	blk & grn bl	1.50	.50
1661	A311	3000r	black & blue	1.75	.65
			Nos. 1655-1661 (7)	6.20	2.40

Mushrooms A312

Designs: 200r, Boletus satanas. 500r, Amanita regalis. 900r, Morchella semilibera. 1000r, Gomphus clavatus. 1500r, Hygrophorus hypothejus. 4000r, Albatrellus confluens.
5400r, Boletus chrysenteron.

1997, Oct. 5 *Perf. 12½x13*
1662-1667 A312 Set of 6 4.50 1.50

Souvenir Sheet
Perf. 12½

1668 A312 5400r multicolored 2.75 .85

No. 1668 contains one 32x40mm stamp.

Fish A313

200r, Betta imbellis. 500r, Colisa fasciata. 900r, Puntius conchonius. 1000r, Macropodus concolor. 1500r, Epalzeorhynchos frenatus. 4000r, Capoeta tetrazona.
5400r, Rasbora heteromorpha.

1997, Nov. 8 *Perf. 12½x13*
1669-1674 A313 Set of 6 4.00 1.25

Souvenir Sheet
Perf. 13

1675 A313 5400r multicolored 2.75 .75

No. 1675 contains one 40x32mm stamp.

Independence, 44th Anniv. — A314

Post Offices: 1000r, Kampot. 3000r, Prey Veng.

1997, Nov. 9 *Perf. 13*
1676-1677 A314 Set of 2 2.00 .70

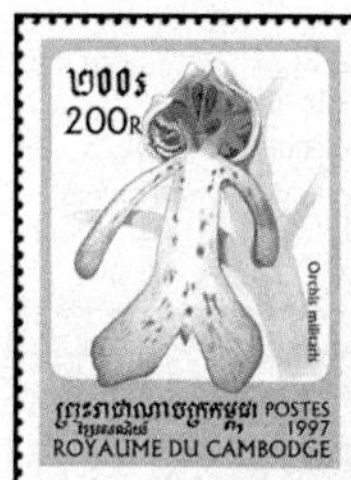

Orchids — A315

200r, Orchis milicaris. 500r, Orchiaceras bivonae. 900r, Orchiaceras spuria. 1000r, Gymnadenia conopsea. 1500r, Serapias neglecta. 4000r, Pseudorhiza bruniana.
5400r, Dactylodenia wintonii.

1997, Dec. 12 *Perf. 13*
1678-1683 A315 Set of 6 10.00 2.00

Souvenir Sheet

1684 A315 5400r multicolored 4.75 1.10

No. 1684 contains one 32x40mm stamp.

Princess Diana (1961-97) A316

Designs: a, 100r, In dark blue jacket. b, 200r, In black dress. c, 300r, Holding hand to throat. d, 500r, Wearing face shield. e, 1000r, Watching mine clearing operation. f, 1500r, With Elizabeth Dole. g, 2000r, Holding land mine. h, 2500r, With members of Mother Teresa's Order.

1997, Dec. 30 *Perf. 12x12½*
1685 A316 Sheet of 8, #a.-h. + label 5.00 1.75

Historic Sites Type of 1996-97

Temples: 300r, Prasat Suorprat. 500r, Preah Kumlung, horiz. 1200r, Prasat Bapuon, horiz. 1500r, Palilai. 1700r, Prasat Prerup, horiz. 2000r, Prasat Preah Khan, horiz. 3000r, Prasat Bayon.

1998 Litho. *Perf. 12½*

1686 A288 300r black & orange .20 .20
1687 A288 500r black & pink .30 .20
1688 A288 1200r black & buff .70 .25
1689 A288 1500r black & buff .85 .30
1690 A288 1700r black & blue 1.00 .35
1691 A288 2000r black & green 1.10 .40
1692 A288 3000r black & violet 1.50 .60
Nos. 1686-1692 (7) 5.65 2.30

New Year 1998 (Year of the Tiger) A317

Various pictures of panthera tigris: 200r, vert., 500r, vert., 900r, vert., 1000r, 1500r, 4000r.
5400r, Tiger, vert.

1998 *Perf. 13*
1693-1698 A317 Set of 6 4.50 1.50

Souvenir Sheet
Perf. 12½
1699 A317 5400r multicolored 2.75 1.00

No. 1699 contains one 32x40mm stamp.

1998 World Cup Soccer Championships, France — A318

Designs showing portion of soccer player at left, various plays at right, stadium: 200r, 500r, 900r, 1000r, 1500r, 4000r.
5400r, Two players kicking ball.

1998 *Perf. 13*
1700-1705 A318 Set of 6 4.50 1.50

Souvenir Sheet
1706 A318 5400r multicolored 2.75 .90

No. 1706 contains one 40x32mm stamp.

Domestic Cats A319

Designs: 200r, Scottish fold. 500r, Ragdoll. 900r, Welsh. 1000r, Devon rex. 1500r, American curl. 4000r, Sphinx.
5400r, Japanese bobtail.

1998
1707-1712 A319 Set of 6 4.50 1.50

Souvenir Sheet
1713 A319 5400r multi 2.75 1.00

No. 1713 contains one 40x32mm stamp.

Italia '98, Intl. Philatelic Exhibition A320

Paintings: 200r, Baptism of Christ from triptych, Jean de Trompes, by Gerard David. 500r, The Virgin of Martin van Niuwenhoven, by Hans Memling. 900r, Baptism of Christ, by Hendrich Goltzius. 1000r, Christ Carrying the Cross, by Luis de Morales. 1500r, Angel in the Desert, by Dirk Bouts. 4000r, The Virgin, by Petrus Christus.
5400r, The Immaculate Conception, by Bartolomé Esteban Murillo.

1998 Litho. *Perf. 12½x13*
1714-1719 A320 Set of 6 4.50 1.50

Souvenir Sheet
Perf. 12½
1720 A320 5400r multicolored 2.75 1.00

No. 1720 contains one 40x32mm stamp.

Butterflies — A321

200r, Phyciodes tharos. 500r, Pararge mergera. 900r, Danaus plexippus. 1000r, Parnassius apollo. 1500r, Papilio machaon. 4000r, Eumenis semele.
5400r, Morpho rhetenor.

1998 *Perf. 12½*
1721-1726 A321 Set of 6 5.00 1.50

Souvenir Sheet
1727 A321 5400r multicolored 3.25 1.00

No. 1727 contains one 40x32mm stamp.

Mail Boxes — A322

Designs: 1000r, 1997. 3000r, 1951.

1998 Litho. *Perf. 13*
1728-1729 A322 Set of 2 2.00 .70

Trains — A323

#1730a, 200r, Oakland, Antioch & Eastern. #1730b, 500r, New York, Westchester & Boston. #1731a, 900r, Spokane & Inland. #1731b, 1000r, International Railway. #1732a, 1500r, British columbia Electric Railway. #1732b, 4000r, Southern Pacific.
5400r, Storage battery locomotive.

1998, Mar. 2 Litho. *Perf. 12½*
1730-1732 A323 Set of 3 pairs, #a.-b. 5.00 1.50

Souvenir Sheet
1733 A323 5400r multicolored 3.50 1.25

Dogs — A324

200r, Rottweiler. 500r, Beauceron. 900r, Boxer. 1000r, Siberian husky. 1500r, Welsh corgi (Pembroke). 4000r, Basset hound.
5400r, Schnauzer.

1998, Mar. 30 Litho. *Perf. 12¼*
1734-1739 A324 Set of 6 4.50 1.50

Souvenir Sheet
Perf. 12½
1740 A324 5400r multicolored 2.75 1.00

Insects A325

200r, Lucanus cervus. 500r, Carabus auronitens. 900r, Rosalia alpina. 1000r, Geotrupes. 1500r, Megasoma elephas. 4000r, Chalcosoma.
5400r, Leptura rubra.

1998, Apr. 10 Litho. *Perf. 12½*
1741-1746 A325 Set of 6 5.00 1.50

Souvenir Sheet
1747 A325 5400r multicolored 3.50 1.25

Khmer Culture A326

Designs: 500r, Prasat Prerup. 1500r, Prasat Bayon. 2000r, Angkor Wat.

1998, Apr. 13 Litho. *Perf. 12¾*
1748-1750 A326 Set of 3 3.25 1.10

Historic Ships A327

200r, Cutter. 500r, Steamship "Britannia." 900r, Viking ship. 1000r, Steamship "Great Britain." 1500r, Coaster. 4000r, Frigate.
5400r, Tartan.

1998, May 7 Litho. *Perf. 12¾*
1751-1756 A327 Set of 6 4.50 1.50

Souvenir Sheet
Perf. 13
1757 A327 5400r multicolored 2.75 1.00

No. 1757 contains one 40x32mm stamp.

Flowers — A328

200r, Petasites japonica. 500r, Gentiana triflora. 900r, Doronicum cordatum. 1000r, Scabiosa japonica. 1500r, Magnolia sieboldii. 4000r, Erythronium japonica.
5400r, Callistephus chinensis.

1998 Litho. *Perf. 12¾*
1758-1763 A328 Set of 6 4.50 1.50

Souvenir Sheet
Perf. 13
1764 A328 5400r multicolored 2.75 1.00

No. 1764 contains one 32x40mm stamp.

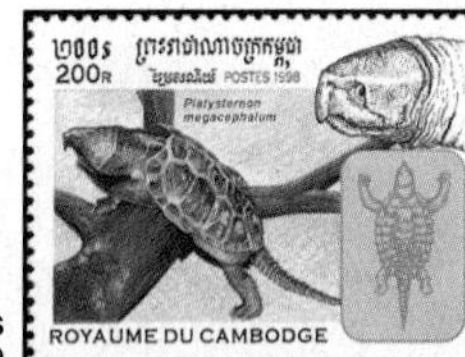

Turtles A329

200r, Platysternon megacephalum. 500r, Chelonia mydas. 900r, Trionyx spiniferus. 1000r, Eretmochelys imbricata. 1500r, Megalochelys gigantea. 4000r, Dermochelys coriacea.

1998, Nov. 8 Litho. *Perf. 12¾*
1765-1770 A329 Set of 6 4.50 1.50

Souvenir Sheet
Perf. 13x13¼
1771 A329 5400r Chelus fimbriatus 2.75 1.00

No. 1771 contains one 40x32mm stamp.

Independence, 45th Anniv. — A330

Various dancers: 500r, 1500r, 2000r.

1998, Nov. 9 Litho. *Perf. 12½x12¼*
1772-1774 A330 Set of 3 2.00 .70

Gemstones A331

Designs: 200r, Aquamarine. 500r, Cat's eye. 900r, Malachite. 1000r, Emerald. 1500r, Turquoise. 4000r, Ruby.
5400r, Diamond, horiz.

1998, Dec. 28 Litho. *Perf. 12¾*
1775-1780 A331 Set of 6 3.00 1.00

Souvenir Sheet
Perf. 13
1781 A331 5400r multi 2.10 .75

No. 1781 contains one 40x32mm stamp.

Wild Cats A332

Designs: 200r, Acinonyx juabatus. 500r, Panthera uncia. 900r, Felis pardalis. 1000r, Panthera pardus. 1500r, Felis serval. 4000r, Panthera onca.
5400r, Panthera tigris.

1998 Litho. *Perf. 12½x12¼*
1782-1787 A332 Set of 6 3.50 1.25

Souvenir Sheet
Perf. 13
1788 A332 5400r multi 2.50 1.00

No. 1788 contains one 32x40mm stamp.

New Year 1999 (Year of the Rabbit) A333

Various rabbits: 200r, 500r, 900r, 1000r, 1500r, 4000r. 4000r is vert.

1999, Jan. 5 Litho. *Perf. 12¾*
1790-1795 A333 Set of 6 4.50 1.50

Souvenir Sheet
Perf. 13

1796 A333 5400r Rabbit, diff. 2.25 .75

No. 1796 contains one 40x32mm stamp.

Trains — A334

Designs: 200r, Stourbridge Lion. 500r, Atlantic. 900r, 035. 100r, Iron Duke. 1500r, 4-6-0. 4000r, 4-4-2.

Perf. 12½x12¼
1999, Nov. 20 Litho.
1797-1802 A334 Set of 6 4.25 1.50

Souvenir Sheet
Perf. 12½

1803 A334 5400r Firefly 2.50 1.00

No. 1803 contains one 40x32mm stamp.

Dogs A335

Designs: 200r, Shiba inu, vert. 500r, Shih tzu. 900r, Tibetan spaniel. 1000r, Ainu, vert. 1500r, Lhasa apso. 4000r, Tibetan terrier.

Perf. 12¼x12½ (200, 1000r), 12¾
1999, Feb. 3 Litho.
1804-1809 A335 Set of 6 4.50 1.50

Souvenir Sheet
Perf. 12½

1810 A335 5400r Tosa inu, vert. 2.75 1.00

Size of Nos. 1804, 1807: 48x30mm. No. 1810 contains one 32x40mm stamp.

Antique Automobiles — A336

Designs: 200r, 1881 La Rapide. 500r, 1895 Duryea. 900r, 1898 Barbarou. 1000r, 1898 Panhard. 1500r, 1901 Mercedes-Benz. 4000r, 1915 Ford.
5400r, 1875 Siegfried Marcus.

1999, Mar. 5 Litho. *Perf. 13x12¾*
1811-1816 A336 Set of 6 3.25 1.10

Souvenir Sheet
Perf. 13

1817 A336 5400r multi 2.25 .75

No. 1817 contains one 40x32mm stamp.

Cats — A337

Designs: 200r, Ragdoll. 500r, Russian blue. 900r, Bombay. 1000r, Snowshoe. 1500r, Oriental. 4000r, Somali.

1999, Mar. 30 Litho. *Perf. 13*
1818-1823 A337 Set of 6 4.50 1.50

Souvenir Sheet

1824 A337 5400r Egyptian mau 2.50 .85

No. 1824 contains one 32x40mm stamp.

Butterflies A338

Designs: 200r, Araschnia levana. 500r, Vanessa cardui, horiz. 900r, Clossiana euphrosyne. 1000r, Coenonympha hero. 1500r, Parnassius apollo, horiz. 4000r, Plebejus argus.
5400r, Palaeochrysophanus hippothoe.

1999, Apr. 25 *Perf. 12¾*
1825-1830 A338 Set of 6 4.50 1.50

Souvenir Sheet
Perf. 12½

1831 A338 5400r multi 2.50 .85

No. 1831 contains one 32x40mm stamp.

Dinosaurs — A339

Designs: 200r, Saurornitholestes. 500r, Prenocephalus. 900r, Wuerhosaurus. 1000r, Muttaburrasaurus. 1500r, Shantungosaurus. 4000r, Microceratops.
5400r, Daspletosaurus.

1999, May 10 Litho. *Perf. 12¾*
1832-1837 A339 Set of 6 3.25 1.00

Souvenir Sheet
Perf. 13

1838 A339 5400r multi 2.25 .75

No. 1838 contains one 40x32mm stamp.

Molluscs A340

Designs: 200r, Flabellina affinis. 500r, Octopus macropus. 900r, Helix hortensis. 1000r, Lima hians. 1500r, Arion empiricorum. 4000r, Anodonta cygnaea.
5400r, Eledone aldrovandii.

1999, May 31 Litho. *Perf. 12¾*
1839-1844 A340 Set of 6 3.25 1.00

Souvenir Sheet
Perf. 12½

1845 A340 5400r multi 2.25 .75

No. 1845 contains one 32x40mm stamp.

Historic Sites Type of 1996-97

Designs: 100r, Prasat Neak Poan, horiz. 300r, Statue, Prasat Neak Poan, horiz. 500r, Prasat Banteay Srey. 1400r, Prasat Banteay Samré, horiz. 1600r, Prasat Banteay Srey, horiz. 1800r, Bas-relief, Angkor Wat. 1900r, Prasat Takeo, horiz.

1999 Litho. *Perf. 12½*
Vignette Colors

1846	A288	100r blue	.20	.20
1847	A288	300r red	.20	.20
1848	A288	500r olive green	.25	.20
1849	A288	1400r bright green	.80	.30
1850	A288	1600r pink	.85	.30
1851	A288	1800r violet	1.00	.35
1852	A288	1900r brown	1.10	.45
		Nos. 1846-1852 (7)	4.40	2.00

Khmer Culture A341

Designs: 500r, Dragon Bridge. 1500r, Temple with 100 columns, Kratie. 2000r, Krapum Chhouk stupa, Kratie.

1999, Apr. 13 *Perf. 13*
1853-1855 A341 Set of 3 2.00 .70

UPU, 125th Anniv. A342

1999 Litho. *Perf. 12½x12¼*
1856 A342 1600r multi 1.00 .30

Independence — A343

People and: 500r, Map. 1500r, Ship, airplane, dove, public works. 2000r, Buildings.

1999, Nov. 9 *Perf. 12½*
1857-1859 A343 Set of 3 1.75 .60

Snakes A344

Designs: 200r, Aspidelaps lubricus. 500r, Epicrates cenchria. 900r, Eunectes notaeus. 1000r, Diadophus punctatus. 1500r, Micrurus fulvius. 4000r, Telescopus semiannulatus.
5400r, Chondropython viridis.

1999, Dec. 6 *Perf. 12¾*
1860-1865 A344 Set of 6 4.50 1.50

Souvenir Sheet
Perf. 13

1866 A344 5400r multi 2.75 1.00

No. 1866 contains one 39x31mm stamp.

Birds of Prey A345

Designs: 200r, Harpia harpyja. 500r, Terthopius ecaudatus, vert. 900r, Neophron pernopterus, vert. 1000r, Falco peregrinus, vert. 1500r, Buteo jamaicensis, vert. 4000r, Haliaetus leucocephalus.
5400r, Milvus milvus.

1999, Oct. 5 Litho. *Perf. 12¾*
1867-1872 A345 Set of 6 4.50 1.50

Souvenir Sheet
Perf. 12½

1873 A345 5400r multi 2.75 1.00

No. 1873 contains one 31x39mm stamp.

Philex France 99 — A346

Still life paintings by: 200r, Henri Fantin-Latour. 500r, Paul Cézanne. 900r, André Derain. 1000r, Henri Matisse. 1500r, Othon Friesz. 4000r, Matisse, diff.
5400r, Cézanne, diff.

1999, June 10 Litho. *Perf. 12½*
1874-1879 A346 Set of 6 3.25 1.10

Souvenir Sheet
Perf. 13

1880 A346 5400r multi 2.25 .75

Souvenir Sheet

China 1999 World Philatleic Exhibition — A347

Pagodas: a, 200r, Tongzhou. b, 500r, Tianing Temple. c, 900r, Summer Palace. d, 900r, Temple of the Clouds. e, 1000r, Bei Hai. f, 1000r, Perfumed Hill. g, 1500r, Yunju. h, 4000r, Miaoying Temple.

Perf. 12¼x12½
1999, Aug. 12 Litho.
1881 A347 Sheet of 8, #a-h, + label 4.50 1.50

Orchids A348

Designs: 200r, Cymbidium insigne. 500r, Papillonanthe teres. 900r, Panisea uniflora. 1000r, Euanthe sanderiana. 1500r, Dendrobium trigonopus. 4000r, Vanda coerulea. 5400r, Paphiopedilum callosum.

1999, Aug. 5 Litho. *Perf. 12¾*
1889-1894 A348 Set of 6 3.25 1.25

Souvenir Sheet
Perf. 12½

1895 A348 5400r multi 2.50 1.00

No. 1895 contains one 32x40mm stamp.

Birds A349

Designs: 200r, Pyrrhula pyrrhula. 500r, Coccothraustes coccothraustes. 900r, Carduelis chloris. 1000r, Dendroica petechia. 1500r, Lanius excubitor. 4000r, Parus caeruleus. 5400r, Erithacus rubecula.

1999, Sept. 5 Litho. *Perf. 12¾*
1896-1901 A349 Set of 6 4.50 1.50

Souvenir Sheet
Perf. 13

1902 A349 5400r multi 2.75 1.00

No. 1902 contains one 40x32mm stamp.

Fish A350

Designs: 200r, Capoeta tetrazona. 500r, Epalzeorhynchus frenatus. 900r, Rasbora kalochroma. 1000r, Etroplus maculatus. 1500r, Betta imbellis. 4000r, Colisa sota. 5400r, Tetraodon biocellatus.

Perf. 12½x12¼
1999, Sept. 20 Litho.
1903-1908 A350 Set of 6 4.50 1.50

Souvenir Sheet
Perf. 13

1909 A350 5400r multi 2.75 1.00

No. 1909 contains one 40x32mm stamp.

Wildlife — A351

Designs: 200r, Ailuropada melanoleuca. 500r, Bos mutus. 900r, Hydropotes inermis. 1000r, Neomys fodiens, horiz. 1500r, Lutra lutra, horiz. 4000r, Panthera tigris, horiz. 5400r, Elaphurus davidianus, vert.

1999, Nov. 20 Litho. *Perf. 12¾*
1910-1915 A351 Set of 6 3.50 1.25

Souvenir Sheet
Perf. 12½

1916 A351 5400r multi 2.50 1.00

No. 1916 contains one 32x40mm stamp.

Bangkok 2000 Stamp Exhibition — A352

Turtle-shaped objects and turtles: 200r, Cuora amboinensis, vert. 500r, Cuora flavomarginata, vert. 900r, Geoemyda spengleri. 1000r, Manouria impressa. 1500r, Chinemys reevesi. 4000r, Heosemys spinosa. 4500r, Hieremys annandalei.

2000, Feb. 27 *Perf. 12¾*
1917-1922 A352 Set of 6 4.50 1.50

Souvenir Sheet
Perf. 13

1923 A352 4500r multi 2.00 .75

No. 1923 contains one 40x32mm stamp.

Dinosaurs — A353

Designs: 200r, Iguanodon. 500r, Euoplocephalus. 900r, Dilophosaurus. 1000r, Diplodocus. 1500r, Stegoceras. 4000r, Stegosaurus. 4500r, Brachiosaurus, vert. Illustration reduced.

2000, Jan. 30 Litho. *Perf. 12½x12¼*
1924-1929 A353 Set of 6 3.00 1.00

Souvenir Sheet
Perf. 12½

1930 A353 4500r multi 2.25 .75

No. 1930 contains one 32x40mm stamp.

Beetles A354

Designs: 200r, Calosoma sycophanta. 500r, Oryctes nasicornis. 900r, Diochrysa fastuosa. 1000r, Blaps gigas. 1500r, Cincindela campestris. 4000r, Cissistes cephalotes. 4500r, Scarabeus aegyptiorum.

2000, Feb. 5 Litho. *Perf. 12¾*
1931-1936 A354 Set of 6 4.50 1.50

Souvenir Sheet
Perf. 13

1937 A354 4500r multi 2.25 .75

No. 1937 contains one 40x32mm stamp.

New Year 2000 (Year of the Dragon) — A355

Various dragons. Denominations: 200r, 500r, 900r, 1000r, 1500r, 4000r.

2000, Jan. 20 Litho. *Perf. 12¼x12½*
1938-1943 A355 Set of 6 4.50 1.50

Souvenir Sheet
Perf. 13

1944 A355 4500r multi 2.25 .75

No. 1944 contains one 32x40mm stamp.

Bettas — A356

Designs: 200r, Unimaculata, Pugnax. 500r, Macrostoma, Taeniata. 900r, Foerschi, Imbellis. 1000r, Tessyae, Picta. 1500r, Edithae, Bellica. 4000r, Smaragdina. 4500r, Splendens. Illustration reduced.

2000, Apr. 10 Litho. *Perf. 12½x12¼*
1945-1950 A356 Set of 6 3.50 1.25

Souvenir Sheet
Perf. 13

1951 A356 4500r multi 2.00 .75

No. 1951 contains one 40x32mm stamp.

Mushrooms A357

Designs: 200r, Amanita muscaria. 500r, Amanita pantherina. 900r, Clitocybe oleana. 1000r, Lactarius scrobiculatus. 1500r, Scleroderma vulgare. 4000r, Amanita verna. 4500r, Amanita phalloides.

2000, Mar. 20 Litho. *Perf. 12¾*
1952-1957 A357 Set of 6 3.50 1.25

Souvenir Sheet
Perf. 13

1958 A357 4500r multi 2.25 .75

No. 1958 contains one 32x40mm stamp.

Khmer Culture — A358

Designs: 500r, Srei Snam. 1500r, Srei Snam, diff. 2000r, Srei Krub Lakhna,

2000, Apr. 13 Litho. *Perf. 13*
1959-1961 A358 Set of 3 2.00 .70

Growing Rice — A359

Designs: 100r, Transporting seedlings. 300r, Harrowing. 500r, Threshing. 1400r, Winnowing. 1600r, Transplanting. 1900r, Plowing. 2200r, Harvesting.

2000 *Perf. 12¼x12½*

Vignette Color

1962	A359	100r brt yel grn		.20	.20
1963	A359	300r brt blue		.20	.20
1964	A359	500r brt pink		.30	.20
1965	A359	1400r brn orange		.80	.25
1966	A359	1600r dull blue		.95	.30
1967	A359	1900r bister brn		1.10	.35
1968	A359	2200r red		1.25	.40
		Nos. 1962-1968 (7)		4.80	1.90

Locomotives — A360

Designs: 200r, Jules Petiet. 500r, Longue Chaudiere. 900r, Les Grand Chocolats. 1000r, Glehn du Bousquet. 1500r, Le Pendule Français. 4000r, TGV 001. 4500r, Le Shuttle.

2000, Mar. 5 Litho. *Perf. 12½x12¼*
1969-1974 A360 Set of 6 4.25 1.40

Souvenir Sheet
Perf. 13

1975 A360 4500r multi 2.00 .75

WIPA 2000 Philatelic Exhibition, Vienna (#1975). No. 1975 contains one 80x32mm stamp.

Birds A361

Designs: 200r, Diomedea irrorata. 500r, Charadrius alexandrinus, vert. 900r, Sula nebouxii. 1000r, Sterna hirundo. 1500r, Larus argentatus, vert. 4000r, Chlidonia hybrida. 4500r, Sula bassana.

2000, May 8 *Perf. 12¾*
1976-1981 A361 Set of 6 4.00 1.25

Souvenir Sheet
Perf. 13

1982 A361 4500r multi 2.00 .75

No. 1982 contains one 40x32mm stamp.

Orchids — A362

Designs: 200r, Cypripedium macranthum. 500r, Vandopsis gigantea. 900r, Calypso bulbosa. 1000r, Vanda luzonica. 1500r, Paphiopedilum villosum. 4000r, Vanda merrillii. 4500r, Paphiopedilum victoria.

2000, May 30 *Perf. 12¾*
1983-1988 A362 Set of 6 4.00 1.25

Souvenir Sheet
Perf. 13

1989 A362 4500r multi 2.00 .75

No. 1989 contains one 32x40mm stamp.

Children's Stories — A363

Designs: 200r, The Courageous Little Tailor, vert. 500r, Tom Thumb, vert. 900r, Thumbelina, vert. 1000r, Pinocchio. 1500r, The Crayfish. 4000r, Peter Pan. 4500r, The Pied Piper, vert.

2000 Litho. *Perf. 12¾*
1990-1995 A363 Set of 6 3.25 3.25

Souvenir Sheet
Perf. 12½

1996 A363 4500r multi 1.75 1.75

No. 1996 contains one 32x40mm stamp.

Water Festival and Tourism A364

Designs: 500r, Men rowing canoe. 1500r, Men at canoe prow. 2000r, Temples, elephant, woman.

2000, June 1 Litho. *Perf. 13*
1997-1999 A364 Set of 3 2.25 2.25

Fire Trucks A365

Designs: 200r, Metz DLK 23-6. 500r, Iveco-Magirus SLF24/100. 900r, Metz SLF 7000 WS. 1000r, Iveco-Magirus TLF 24/50. 1500r, Saval-Kronenburg RFF 11000. 4000r, Metz TLF 24/50.
4500r, Metz TLF 16/25.

2000, July 30 *Perf. 12¾*
2000-2005 A365 Set of 6 4.50 4.50

Souvenir Sheet
Perf. 13

2006 A365 4500r multi 2.40 2.40

No. 2006 contains one 40x32mm stamp.

Independence, 47th Anniv. — A366

Flag, temple and: 500r, Flowers. 1500r, Dove. 2000r, People carrying torch.

2000, Nov. 9 *Perf. 12¾*
2007-2009 A366 Set of 3 2.25 2.25

Antique Automobiles — A367

Designs: 200r, 1912 Rover 12C. 500r, 1907, Austin 30CV. 900r, 1909 Rolls-Royce Silver Ghost. 1000r, 1929 Graham Paige Phaeton DC. 1500r, 1937 Austin 12. 4000r, 1957 Mercedes-Benz 300SL.
4500r, 1936 MG.

2000 *Perf. 12¾*
2010-2015 A367 Set of 6 4.50 4.50

Souvenir Sheet
Perf. 13

2016 A367 4500r multi 2.40 2.40

España 2000 Intl. Philatelic Exhibition (#2016). No. 2016 contains one 40x32mm stamp.

Dachshunds — A368

Designs: 200r, Smooth-haired dachshund. 500r, Wire-haired dachshund. 900r, Long-haired dachshund. 1000r, Two dachshunds. 1500r, Dachshund with pups. 4000r, Dachshunds resting.
4500r, Wire-haired dachshund, vert.

2000 *Perf. 13*
2017-2022 A368 Set of 6 4.50 4.50

Souvenir Sheet
Perf. 12½

2023 A368 4500r multi 2.40 2.40

No. 2023 contains one 32x40mm stamp.

Cats and Art A369

Cat or cats and: 200r, Korean silk painting, 18th cent. 500r, Portuguese tile, 18th cent. 900r, Japanese ceramic cat. 1000r, Egyptian metallic cat. 1500r, Scandinavian engraving. 4000r, Japanese painting.
4500r, Cat on hind legs.

2000 *Perf. 12½x12¼*
2024-2029 A369 Set of 6 4.50 4.50

Souvenir Sheet
Perf. 13x13¼

2030 A369 4500r multi 2.40 2.40

No. 2030 contains one 40x32mm stamp.

Birds A370

Designs: 200r, Creatophora cinerea. 500r, Sturnus vulgaris. 900r, Leiothrix lutea. 1000r, Rupicola rupicola. 1500r, Prunella collaris. 4000r, Panurus biarnicus.
4500r, Muscicapula pallipes, vert.

2000 *Perf. 13*
2031-2036 A370 Set of 6 4.50 4.50

Souvenir Sheet

2037 A370 4500r multi 2.40 2.40

No. 2037 contains one 32x40mm stamp.

Sports — A371

Designs: 200r, Weight lifting. 500r, Rhythmic gymnastics. 900r, Baseball. 1000r, Women's tennis. 1500r, Basketball. 4000r, Women's high jump.

2000 Litho. *Perf. 12¾, 12½ (#2044)*
2038-2043 A371 Set of 6 4.50 4.50

Souvenir Sheet

2044 A371 4500r Runners 2.50 2.50

No. 2044 contains one 32x40mm stamp.

New Year 2001 (Year of the Snake) — A372

Various stylized snakes with background colors of: 200r, Beige. 500r, Dull bister. 900r, Light blue. 1000r, Greenish blue. 1500r, Dull green. 4000r, Blue.
5400r, Blue, horiz.

2001, Jan. 15 Litho. *Perf. 12¼x12½*
2045-2050 A372 Set of 6 4.50 4.50

Souvenir Sheet
Perf. 13x13¼

2051 A372 5400r multi 3.00 3.00

No. 2051 contains one 40x32mm stamp.

Millennium — A373

Designs: 200r, Johannes Gutenberg, printers. 500r, Michael Faraday, electric motor. 900r, Samuel F. B. Morse, telegraph. 1000r, Alexander Graham Bell, telephone. 1500r, Enrico Fermi, nuclear energy. 4000r, Edward Roberts, computer.
No. 2058: a, Christopher Columbus, ships. b, Neil Armstrong, lunar module.

2001 Litho. *Perf. 12¾*
2052-2057 A373 Set of 6 4.50 4.50

Souvenir Sheet
Perf. 12½

2058 A373 5400r Sheet of 2, #a-b + label 6.00 6.00

No. 2058 contains two 40x32mm stamps.

Fire and Rescue Equipment A374

Designs: 200r, 1910 Sandou ladder wagon. 500r, 1899 Gallo cart. 900r, Merryweather pumper, 1950s. 1000r, 1940 Merryweather ambulance. 1500r, 1972 Man-Metz pumper. 4000r, Roman Diesel pumper, 1970s.
5400r, 1898 Metropolitan steam pumper.

2001 *Perf. 12¾*
2059-2064 A374 Set of 6 4.50 4.50

Souvenir Sheet
Perf. 13x13¼

2065 A374 5400r multi 3.00 3.00

No. 2065 contains one 40x32mm stamp.

Mushrooms — A375

Designs: 200r, Lycoperdon perlatum. 500r, Trametes versicolor. 900r, Hipholoma sublateritium. 1000r, Amanita muscaria. 1500r, Lycoperdon umbrinum. 4000r, Cortinarius orellanus.
5400r Amanita phalloides, vert.

2001 *Perf. 12¾*
2066-2071 A375 Set of 6 4.50 4.50

Souvenir Sheet
Perf. 12½

2072 A375 5400r multi 3.00 3.00

No. 2072 contains one 32x40mm stamp.

Belgica 2001 Intl. Stamp Exhibition, Brussels — A376

Butterflies: 200r, Nymphalis polychloros. 500r, Cethosia hypsea. 900r, Papilio palinurus. 1000r, Apatura ilia. 1500r, Parthenos sylvia. 4000r, Morpho grandensis.
5400r, Heliconius melpomene.

2001 *Perf. 12¾*
2073-2078 A376 Set of 6 4.50 4.50

Souvenir Sheet
Perf. 13x13¼

2079 A376 5400r multi 3.00 3.00

Film Personalities A377

Designs: 200r, Gary Cooper. 500r, Marlene Dietrich. 900r, Walt Disney. 1000r, Clark Gable. 1500r, Jeanette MacDonald. 4000r, Melvyn Douglas.
No. 2086: a, Rudolph Valentino. b, Marilyn Monroe.

2001 Litho. *Perf. 12¾*

2080	A377	200r multi		.20	.20
2081	A377	500r multi		.25	.25
2082	A377	900r multi		.45	.45
2083	A377	1000r multi		.50	.50
2084	A377	1500r multi		.80	.80
2085	A377	4000r multi		2.10	2.10
		Nos. 2080-2085 (6)		4.30	4.30

Souvenir Sheet
Perf. 13

2086 A377 5400r Sheet of 2, #a-b 5.75 5.75

Natl. Culture Day A378

Sculptures: 500r, Angkor. 1500r, Bayon. 2000r, Bayon, diff.

2001 Litho. *Perf. 12¾*
2087-2089 A378 Set of 3 2.25 2.25

Temples — A379

Designs: 200r, Preah Vihear. 300r, Thonmanom. 600r, Tasom. 1000r, Kravan. 1500r, Takeo. 1700r, Mebon. 2200r, Banteay Kdei.

2001 *Perf. 12¼x12½*
2090-2096 A397 Set of 7 4.00 4.00

Automobiles — A380

Designs: 200r, 1972 TVR Series M. 500r, 1958 Ferrari 410. 900r, 1995 Peugeot 405. 1000r, 1953 Fiat 8VZ. 1500r, 1997 Citroen Xsara. 4000r, 1997 Renault Espace.
5400r, 1963 Ferrari 250 GT SWB.

2001, June 5 Litho. *Perf. 12¾*
2097-2102 A380 Set of 6 4.50 4.50

Souvenir Sheet
Perf. 13x13¼

2103 A380 5400r multi 3.00 3.00

No. 2103 contains one 40x32mm stamp.

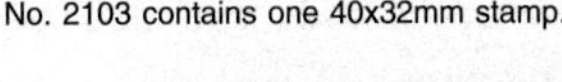

Tourism A381

Designs: 500r, Sourire de Bayon. 1500r, Bayon. 2000r, Bayon, diff.

2001, June 5 *Perf. 12¾*
2104-2106 A381 Set of 3 2.25 2.25

Philanippon '01 — A382

Locomotives: 200r, 4-6-0. 500r, 4-6-4. 900r, 4-4-0. 1000r, 4-6-4, diff. 1500r, 4-6-2. 4000r, 4-8-2.
5400r, Undescribed locomotive.

2001, July 5 *Perf. 12½x12¼*
2107-2112 A382 Set of 6 4.50 4.50

Souvenir Sheet
Perf. 13x13¼

2113 A380 5400r multi 3.00 3.00

No. 2113 contains one 40x32mm stamp.

Penguins A383

Designs: 200r, Aptenodytes forsteri. 500r, Spheniscus demersus. 900r, Spheniscus humboldti. 1000r, Eudypes cristatus. 1500r, Aptenodytes patagonica. 4000r, Pygoscelis antarctica.
5400r, Pygoscelis papua.

2001, Aug. 5 *Perf. 12¾*
2114-2119 A383 Set of 6 4.50 4.50

Souvenir Sheet
Perf. 13x13¼

2120 A383 5400r multi 3.00 3.00

No. 2120 contains one 40x32mm stamp.

Cats A384

Designs: 200r, Singapura. 500r, Cymric. 900r, Exotic shorthair. 1000r, Ragdoll. 1500r, Manx. 4000r, Somali.
5400r, Egyptian Mau.

2001, Aug. 25 *Perf. 12½x12¼*
2121-2126 A384 Set of 6 4.50 4.50

Souvenir Sheet
Perf. 13x13¼

2127 A384 5400r multi 3.00 3.00

No. 2127 contains one 40x32mm stamp.

Kites A385

Designs: 300r, Khleng Chak. 500r, Khleng Kanton. 1000r, Khleng Phnong. 1500r, Khleng Kaun Morn. 3000r, Khleng Me Ambao.

2001, Sept. 7 *Perf. 12¾*
2128-2132 A385 Set of 5 3.50 3.50

Cacti — A386

Designs: 200r, Parodia cintiensis. 500r, Astrophytum astenas. 900r, Parodia faustiana. 1000r, Coryphantha sulcolanata. 1500r, Neochilenia hankena. 4000r, Mammilaria boolii.
5400r, Mammilaria swinglei.

2001, Sept. 15 *Perf. 12¾*
2133-2138 A386 Set of 6 4.50 4.50

Souvenir Sheet
Perf. 12½

2139 A386 5400r multi 3.00 3.00

No. 2139 contains one 32x40mm stamp.

Khmer Culture A387

Designs: 500r, Fish Dance. 1500r, Red Fish Ballet. 2000r, Apsara Ballet.

2001, Oct. 9 *Perf. 12¾*
2140-2142 A387 Set of 3 2.25 2.25

Wolves and Foxes A388

Designs: 200r, Canis lupus occidentalis. 500r, Canis lupus tundrorum, vert. 900r, Vulpes fulvas. 1000r, Canis latrans. 1500r, Vulpes zerda, vert. 4000r, Alopex lagopus.
5400r, Canis lupus signatus, vert.

2001, Oct. 15 *Perf. 12¾*
2143-2148 A388 Set of 6 4.50 4.50

Souvenir Sheet
Perf. 12½

2149 A388 5400r multi 3.00 3.00

No. 2103 contains one 32x40mm stamp.

Human Evolution — A389

Designs: 100r, Australopithecus anamensis. 200r, Australopithecus afarensis. 300r, Australopithecus africanus. No. 2153, 500r, Australopithecus rudolfensis. No. 2154, 500r, Australopithecus boisei. 1000r, Homo habilis. 1500r, Homo erectus. 4000r, Homo sapiens neanderthalensis.
5400r, Homo sapiens sapiens.

2001, Oct. 25 *Perf. 13*
2150-2157 A389 Set of 8 4.50 4.50

Souvenir Sheet

2158 A389 5400r multi 3.00 3.00

No. 2158 contains one 40x32mm stamp.

Chess A390

Designs: 200r, Rook. 500r, Pawn. 900r, King. 1000r, Bishop. 1500r, Queen. 4000r, Knight.
5400r, Pieces of Oriental chess-like game.

2001, Dec. 25 *Perf. 12¾*
2159-2164 A390 Set of 6 4.50 4.50

Souvenir Sheet
Perf. 13

2165 A390 5400r multi 3.00 3.00

No. 2165 contains one 40x32mm stamp.

Italian Soccer A391

Designs: 200r, 1934 World Cup championship team. 500r, 1938 World Cup championship team. 900r, 1968 European Cup championship team. 1000r, 1982 World Cup championship team. 1500r, 2002 World Cup team. 4000r, Italian soccer federation emblem.

2001 *Perf. 12¾*
2166-2171 A391 Set of 6 4.50 4.50

ASEAN Post, 10th Anniv A392

Temples: 500r, Prasat Preah Vihear. 1000r, Prasat Preah Ko. 1500r, Prasat Banteay Srei. 2500r, Prasat Bayon. 3500r, Prasat Angkor Wat.

2002, July 9 *Perf. 13*
2172-2176 A392 Set of 5 5.00 5.00

Sugar Palm — A393

Designs: 300r, Tree. 500r, Female flower. 700r, Male flower. 1500r, Fruit.

2003 Litho.
2177-2180 A393 Set of 4 1.75 1.75

Japanese Grant Aid — A394

Designs: 100r, Drawing of Bridge No. 26, Highway 6A. 200r, Bridge No. 26, Highway 6A. 400r, Chroy Changvar Bridge. 800r, Kizuna Bridge. 3500r, Monument, vert.

2003, Apr. 25
2181-2185 A394 Set of 5 2.75 2.75

Cambodian Red Cross — A395

Designs: 100r, Ox cart. 200r, Woman carrying rice bag, vert. 300r, Queen with Red Cross volunteers. 400r, Queen and women. 500r, Queen and elderly people. 700r, Queen and women, diff. 800r, Queen and Prime Minister's wife giving items to people. 1000r, Like 800r, diff. 1900r, Like 800r, diff., vert. 2100r, Like 800r, diff., vert. 4000r, Queen and Prime Minister's wife with baby.

2003, May 8
2186-2196 A395 Set of 11 6.75 6.75

Cambodia - People's Republic of China Diplomatic Relations, 50th Anniv. — A396

No. 2197: a, Angkor Wat. b, Great Wall of China.
Illustration reduced.

2003, July 19 *Perf. 12¼x12*
2197 A396 2000r Horiz. pair, #a-b 2.25 2.25

Association of South East Asian Nations, 36th Anniv. — A397

Designs: 400r, Conference emblem. 500r, Apsara dancer. 600r, Apsara dancer, diff.

1600r, Apsara dancers. 1900r, Temonorom dancers.

2003, Aug. 8 *Perf. 13*
2198-2202 A397 Set of 5 2.75 2.75

King Norodom Sihanouk — A398

Designs: 200r, Pointing at map. 400r, Meeting rural Cambodians, vert. 500r, Sitting in forest, vert. 800r, Pointing in forest, vert. 1000r, Saluting, vert. 2000r, Saluting, with flag and Independence Monument, vert. 5000r, With handicapped people.

2003, Nov. 9
2203-2209 A398 Set of 7 5.50 5.50

Khmer Culture A399

Sculptures: 100r, Bayon. 200r, Banteay Srei. 400r, Banteay Srei, diff. 800r, Bayon, vert. 3500r, Banteay Srei, vert.
2000r, Unattributed sculpture, vert.

2001, June 5
2210-2214 A399 Set of 5 2.75 2.75

Souvenir Sheet

2215 A399 2000r multi 1.10 1.10

Rural Areas A400

Designs: 600r, Mill. 900r, House, field and cattle. 2000r, House and trees.
2000r, Ox cart and driver.

2004, Apr. 13
2216-2218 A400 Set of 3 2.00 2.00

Souvenir Sheet

2219 A400 2000r multi 1.10 1.10

Tepmonorum Dancers — A401

Dancers with: 400r, Yellow costumes. 1000r, Blue costumes. 2000r, Blue and yellow costumes.
2000r, Blue and yellow costumes, diff.

2004, May 5
2220-2222 A401 Set of 3 2.00 2.00

Souvenir Sheet

2223 A401 2000r multi 1.10 1.100

SEMI-POSTAL STAMPS

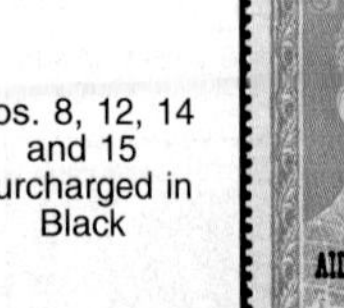

Nos. 8, 12, 14 and 15 Surcharged in Black

1952, Oct. 20 **Unwmk.** *Perf. 13*
B1 A3 1.10pi + 40c 3.50 3.50
B2 A3 1.90pi + 60c 3.50 3.50
B3 A3 3pi + 1pi 3.50 3.50
B4 A1 5pi + 2pi 3.50 3.50
Nos. B1-B4 (4) 14.00 14.00

For students assistance.

Preah Stupa — SP1

1957, Mar. 15 **Engr.** *Perf. 13*
B5 SP1 1.50r + 50c ind, ol & red 1.10 .90
B6 SP1 6.50r + 1.50r red lil, ol & red 1.75 1.50
B7 SP1 8r + 2r bl, ol & red 3.00 2.50
Nos. B5-B7 (3) 5.85 4.90

Birth of Buddha, 1500th anniv. See #62-64.

Type of Regular Issue, 1959, with Red Typographed Surcharge

1959, Dec. 9
B8 A14 20c + 20c rose vio .35 .35
B9 A14 50c + 30c blue .40 .40
B10 A14 80c + 50c rose car .90 .90
Nos. B8-B10 (3) 1.65 1.65

The surtax was for the Red Cross.

Nos. 107-108 Surcharged and Overprinted in Red: "1863-1963 CENTENAIRE DE LA CROIX ROUGE"

1963, Oct. 1 **Unwmk.** *Perf. 13*
B11 A26 4r + 40c grn & dk brn .70 .70
B12 A26 6r + 60c vio & ol bis .90 .90

Centenary of International Red Cross.

Nos. 263, 267, 293-294, 134 Surcharged in Red

1972, Nov. 15 **Engr.** *Perf. 13*
B13 A72 3r + 2r multi .25 .25
B14 A72 10r + 6r multi .40 .35
B15 A80 12r + 7r multi .60 .50
B16 A34 12r + 7r multi .60 .50
B17 A80 15r + 8r multi .90 .75
Nos. B13-B17 (5) 2.75 2.35

Surtax was for war victims. Surcharge arranged differently on Nos. B15-B17.

AIR POST STAMPS

Kinnari — AP1

Unwmk.

1953, Apr. 16 **Engr.** *Perf. 13*
C1 AP1 50c deep green .65 .60
a. Souv. sheet of 4, #C1, C3, C5, C9 50.00 50.00
C2 AP1 3pi red brown .85 .65
a. Souv. sheet of 3, #C2, C4, C8 50.00 50.00
C3 AP1 3.30pi rose violet 1.00 .80
C4 AP1 4pi dk brn & dp bl 1.25 .85
C5 AP1 5.10pi brn, red & org 2.50 2.10
C6 AP1 6.50pi dk brn & lil rose 2.50 2.10
a. Souv. sheet of 2, #C6-C7 50.00 50.00
C7 AP1 9pi lil rose & dp grn 3.75 3.25
C8 AP1 11.50pi multi 7.50 6.25
C9 AP1 30pi dk brn, bl grn & org 15.00 8.25
Nos. C1-C9 (9) 35.00 24.85

#C1a sold for 50pi, #C2a for 25pi, #C6a for 20pi.
Souvenir sheets with completely white gum, no toning and no gum bends sell for a premium.

AP2

1957, Dec. 11
C10 AP2 50c maroon .25 .20
C11 AP2 1r emerald .40 .20
C12 AP2 4r ultra 1.25 .75
C13 AP2 50r carmine rose 5.75 4.00
C14 AP2 100r grn, bl & car 10.00 6.00
a. Souv. sheet of 5, #C10-C14 24.00 24.00
Nos. C10-C14 (5) 17.65 11.15

No. C14a sold for 160r.
See note after #C9.

Independence Type of 1961

1961, Nov. 9 *Perf. 13x12½*
C15 A24 7r multicolored .65 .35
C16 A24 30r grn, car & ultra 2.50 1.10
C17 A24 50r ind, grn & ol 3.50 2.25
a. Souv. sheet of 3, #C15-C17 7.00 7.00
Nos. C15-C17 (3) 6.65 3.70

No. C15 Surcharged with New Value in Red and Overprinted in Black with Two Bars and: "INAUGURATION DU MONUMENT"

1962, Nov. 9
C18 A24 12r on 7r multi 1.75 1.10

Dedication of Independence Monument.

Hanuman, Monkey God — AP3

1964, Sept. 1 **Engr.** *Perf. 13*
C19 AP3 5r multicolored .80 .35
C20 AP3 10r ol bis, lil rose & grn 1.10 .35
C21 AP3 20r vio, bl & ol bis 1.60 .75
C22 AP3 40r bl, ol bis & dk bl 3.50 1.40
C23 AP3 80r multicolored 5.75 3.50
Nos. C19-C23 (5) 12.75 6.35

Nos. C19-C22 Surcharged in Red

1964, Oct.
C24 AP3 3r on 5r multi .60 .55
C25 AP3 6r on 10r multi .95 .85
C26 AP3 9r on 20r multi 1.25 1.10
C27 AP3 12r on 40r multi 1.90 1.60
Nos. C24-C27 (4) 4.70 4.10

18th Olympic Games, Tokyo, Oct. 10-25.

1972 Summer Olympic Games, Munich — AP4

Designs: No. C28, shown. No. C29, Munich churches, Olympic emblem, vert.
Illustration reduced.

Litho. & Embossed

1972, Sept. 28 *Perf. 13½*
C28 AP4 900r gold & multi 19.00 19.00
C29 AP4 900r gold & multi 19.00 19.00
a. Souvenir sheet of 2, #C28-C29 50.00

No. C29a exists imperf.

Apollo 16 AP5

Designs: No. C30, Astronauts in Lunar Rover. No. C31, Astronaut walking on moon.

1972, Sept. 28
C30 AP5 900r gold & multi 19.00 19.00
C31 AP5 900r gold & multi 19.00 19.00
a. Souvenir sheet of 2, #C30-C31 50.00

Pres. Nixon's Visit to the People's Republic of China — AP6

Nixon, Mao Zedong: No. C32, Large portraits (shown). No. C33, Small portraits.

1972, Sept. 28 *Perf. 12½*
C32 AP6 900r gold & multi 60.00 60.00
C33 AP6 900r gold & multi 60.00 60.00

Garuda, 12th Century, Angkor Thom — AP7

1973, Jan. 18 Engr. *Perf. 13*

C34	AP7	3r carmine	.25	.20
C35	AP7	30r violet blue	1.25	.80
C36	AP7	50r dull purple	2.00	1.25
C37	AP7	100r dull green	4.25	2.25
		Nos. C34-C37 (4)	7.75	4.50

1972 Summer Olympic Games, Munich AP8

Gold medalists: No. C38, Heide Rosendahl. No. C39, Mark Spitz.

Litho. & Embossed

1973, May 18 *Perf. 13½*

C38	AP8	900r gold & multi	19.00	19.00
C39	AP8	900r gold & multi	19.00	19.00

A souvenir sheet released with these stamps exists.

Nos. C38-C39 Ovptd. with "MUNICH 1974 / COUPE DE MONDE DE FOOTBALL" and Emblem

1973, Nov. 19

C40	AP8	900r on C38	27.50	27.50
C41	AP8	900r on C39	27.50	27.50

An overprinted souvenir sheet exists.

1974 World Cup Soccer Championships, Munich — AP9

Designs: No. C42, Trophy, players. No. C43, Trophy, players, vert.

1973, Nov. 19 Litho. & Embossed

C42	AP9	900r gold & multi	25.00	25.00
C43	AP9	900r gold & multi	25.00	25.00

A souvenir sheet released with these stamps exists.

John F. Kennedy, Apollo 11 — AP10

#C44, shown. #C45, Kennedy, Apollo 17.

1974, Feb. 18

C44	AP10	1100r gold & multi	30.00	30.00
C45	AP10	1100r gold & multi	30.00	30.00
a.		Souv. sheet of 2, #C44-C45	90.00	

Nos. C44-C45a exist imperf.

Copernicus Type of 1974 and

Copernicus, Sun — AP11

200r, Copernicus and Skylab III. 250r, Copernicus, Concorde and solar eclipse. No. C48, shown. No. C49, Moon, Skylab, hand holding symbol of sun.

1974, Sept. 10 Litho. *Perf. 13*

C46	A87	200r multi	5.00	2.50
C47	A87	250r multi	5.00	2.50

Litho. & Engraved

Perf. 13½

C48	AP11	1200r gold & multi	27.50	27.50

Souvenir Sheet of 1

C49	AP11	1200r gold & multi	27.50	27.50

Nos. C46-C47 exist in perf or imperf souvenir sheets of 1.

UPU Type of 1974 and

AP12

700r, Rocket, globe and UPU emblem. No. C51, UPU Headquarters. No. C52, US #1434-1435.

1974, Nov. 2 Litho. *Perf. 13*

C50	A88	700r gold & multi	10.00	10.00

Litho. & Embossed

Perf. 13½

C51	AP12	1200r gold & multi	25.00	25.00

Souvenir Sheet

C52	AP12	1200r gold & multi	45.00	

Nos. C50-C51 exist in souvenir sheets of one. Nos. C51-C52 exist imperf.

#C53-C54, UPU Centennial, 4/12/75.

Post Aerienne at Right — AP14

Post Aerienne at Left — AP15

Denominations: 5r, 10r, 15r, 25r.

1984, Feb. 1 Litho. *Perf. 12x12½*

C55-C58	AP14	Set of 4	37.50	7.50

1986, Mar. 4 Litho. *Perf. 12x12½*

Denominations: 5r, 10r, 15r, 25r.

C59-C62	AP15	Set of 4	32.50	7.50

POSTAGE DUE STAMPS

D1

Frieze, Angkor Wat — D2

1957 Unwmk. Typo. *Perf. 13½*

Denomination in Black

J1	D1	10c ver & pale blue	.20	.20
J2	D1	50c ver & pale blue	.30	.30
J3	D1	1r ver & pale blue	.70	.70
J4	D1	3r ver & pale blue	.90	.90
J5	D1	5r ver & pale blue	1.40	1.40
		Nos. J1-J5 (5)	3.50	3.50

1974, Feb. 18 Engr. *Perf. 12½x13*

J6	D2	2r ocher	.25	.25
J7	D2	6r green	.30	.30
J8	D2	8r deep carmine	.45	.45
J9	D2	10r violet blue	.55	.55
		Nos. J6-J9 (4)	1.55	1.55

CAMEROONS

ˌka-mə-ˈrün

LOCATION — West coast of Africa, north of equator
GOVT. — British Trust Territory
AREA — 34,081 sq. mi.
POP. — 868,637 (estimated)
CAPITAL — Buea

Prior to World War I, Cameroons (Kamerun) was a German Protectorate. It was occupied during the War by Great Britain and France and in 1922 was mandated to these countries by the League of Nations. Stamps of Nigeria were used in the British part until 1960. The northern section of the British Cameroons became part of the independent state of Nigeria in 1960, and the southern section became a United Kingdom Trust Territory. After a referendum, this U.K.T.T. joined the independent State of Cameroun to form the Federal Republic of Cameroun, Oct. 1, 1961.

Stamps of the German Protectorate, the French Mandate, the independent state and the Cameroun Federal Republic are listed under Cameroun.

Catalogue values for unused stamps in this country are for Never Hinged items.

United Kingdom Trust Territory

Stamps and Type of Nigeria, 1953, Overprinted in Red

Perf. 13½, 14

1960, Oct. 1 Wmk. 4 Engr.

Size: 35½x22½mm

66	A17	½p red org & black	.20	*1.50*
67	A17	1p ol gray & black	.20	*.85*
68	A17	1½p blue green	.20	.25
69	A17	2p gray (II)	.20	*.50*
70	A17	3p purple & black	.20	.20
71	A17	4p ultra & black	.20	*1.50*
72	A18	6p blk & org brn, perf. 14	.35	.25
a.		Perf. 13x13½ ('61)	.25	*2.00*
73	A17	1sh brown vio & blk	.20	.20

Size: 40½x24½mm

74	A17	2sh6p green & black	1.40	.95
75	A17	5sh ver & black	1.90	*4.25*
76	A17	10sh red brn & blk	3.00	*7.75*

Size: 42x31½mm

77	A17	£1 violet & black	10.50	*24.00*
		Nos. 66-77 (12)	18.55	*42.20*

Nos. 66-77 were withdrawn in Northern Cameroons on May 31, 1961, when that territory joined Nigeria and in Southern Cameroons Sept. 30, 1961, when that territory joined the Cameroun Federal Republic.

CAMEROUN

ˌka-mə-ˈrün

(Kamerun)

LOCATION — On the west coast of Africa, north of the equator
GOVT. — Republic
AREA — 183,520 sq. mi.
POP. — 15,456,092 (1999 est.)
CAPITAL — Yaounde

Before World War I, Cameroun (Kamerun) was a German Protectorate. It was occupied during the war by Great Britain and France and in 1922 was mandated to these countries by the League of Nations. The French-mandated part became the independent State of Cameroun on January 1, 1960. The Southern Cameroons, a United Kingdom Trust Territory, joined this state to form the Federal Republic of Cameroun on October 1, 1961. The name was changed to United Republic of Cameroon on May 20, 1972.

Stamps of Southern Cameroons are listed under Cameroons.

100 Pfennig = 1 Mark
12 Pence = 1 Shilling
100 Centimes = 1 Franc

Catalogue values for unused stamps in this country are for Never Hinged items, beginning with Scott 296 in the regular postage section, Scott B29 in the semi-postal section, Scott C8 in the air-post section, Scott J24 in the postage due section, and Scott M1 in the military stamp section.

Watermark

Wmk. 125 — Lozenges

Wmk. 385

Issued under German Dominion

Stamps of Germany Overprinted in Black

1897 Unwmk. *Perf. 13½x14½*

1 A9 3pf yellow brn 11.00 *16.00*
a. 3pf red brown 18.00 *72.50*
b. 3pf dark brown 16.00 *37.50*
2 A9 5pf green 5.00 *8.00*
3 A10 10pf carmine 3.75 *4.50*
4 A10 20pf ultra 4.00 *8.00*
5 A10 25pf orange 20.00 *35.00*
6 A10 50pf red brown 16.00 *29.00*
Nos. 1-6 (6) 59.75 *100.50*

A3

Kaiser's Yacht "Hohenzollern" — A4

1900 Unwmk. Typo. *Perf. 14*

7 A3 3pf brown 1.25 *1.50*
8 A3 5pf green 13.50 1.10
9 A3 10pf carmine 40.00 1.25
10 A3 20pf ultra 25.00 2.25
11 A3 25pf org & blk, *yel* 1.40 *5.50*
12 A3 30pf org & blk, *sal* 1.75 *4.00*
13 A3 40pf lake & blk 1.75 *4.00*
14 A3 50pf pur & blk, *sal* 2.00 *6.00*
15 A3 80pf lake & blk, *rose* 2.75 *11.00*

Engr. *Perf. 14½x14*

16 A4 1m carmine 67.50 *67.50*
17 A4 2m blue 5.00 *65.00*
18 A4 3m black vio 5.50 *100.00*
19 A4 5m slate & car 110.00 *450.00*
Nos. 7-19 (13) 277.40 *719.10*

1905-18 Wmk. 125 Typo.

20 A3 3pf brown ('18) .70
21 A3 5pf green .70 *1.60*
b. Bklt. pane of 6, 2 #21 + 4 #22 62.50
c. Booklet pane of 5 + label 375.00
22 A3 10pf carmine ('06) .75 *1.10*
b. Booklet pane of 5 + label 500.00
23 A3 20pf ultra ('14) 2.50 *125.00*
24 A4 1m carmine ('15) 5.00
25 A4 5m slate & car ('13) 26.00 *4,750.*
Nos. 20-25 (6) 35.65 4,877.

The 3pf and 1m were not placed in use.

Issued under British Occupation

Stamps of German Cameroun Surcharged

C. E. F.

1s.

Wmk. Lozenges (125) (#54-56, 65); Unwmk. (Other Values)

1915 *Perf. 14, 14½*

Blue Surcharge

53 A3 ½p on 3pf brn 15.00 *37.50*
54 A3 ½p on 5pf grn 3.75 *11.00*
a. Double surcharge *1,000.*
b. Black surcharge — —
55 A3 1p on 10pf car 1.50 *11.00*
a. "1" with thin serifs 15.00 *75.00*
b. Double surcharge 325.00
c. Black surcharge 18.00 *65.00*
d. As "c," "1" with thin serifs 190.00

Black Surcharge

56 A3 2p on 20pf ultra 4.00 *24.00*
57 A3 2½p on 25pf org & blk, *yel* 14.00 *55.00*
a. Double surcharge 8,250.
58 A3 3p on 30pf org & blk, *sal* 14.00 *55.00*
59 A3 4p on 40pf lake & blk 14.00 *55.00*
60 A3 6p on 50pf pur & blk, *sal* 14.00 *55.00*
61 A3 8p on 80pf lake & blk, *rose* 14.00 *55.00*
62 A4 1sh on 1m car 190.00 *800.00*
a. "S" inverted 925.00 *3,000.*
63 A4 2sh on 2m bl 190.00 *800.00*
a. "S" inverted 925.00 *3,000.*
64 A4 3sh on 3m blk vio 190.00 *825.00*
a. "S" inverted 925.00 *3,000.*
b. Double surcharge *9,500.*
65 A4 5sh on 5m sl & car 225.00 *875.00*
a. "S" inverted 1,050. *3,250.*
Nos. 53-65 (13) 889.25 *3,658.*

The letters "C. E. F." are the initials of "Cameroons Expeditionary Force."

Numerous overprint varieties exist for #53-65.

Counterfeits exist of Nos. 54a, 54b.

See Cameroons for Nos. 66-77.

Issued under French Occupation

Gabon Nos. 37, 49-52, 54, 57-58, 60, 62-64, 66, 69-71 Overprinted

1915 Unwmk. *Perf. 13½x14*

Inscribed "Congo Français"

101 A10 10c red & car 22.50 15.00

Inscribed "Afrique Equatoriale"

102 A10 1c choc & org 75.00 30.00
103 A10 2c blk & choc 125.00 100.00
104 A10 4c vio & dp bl 125.00 100.00
105 A10 5c ol gray & grn 26.00 15.00
105A A10 10c red & car *16,750.* *18,000.*
106 A10 20c ol brn & dk vio 150.00 150.00
107 A11 25c dp bl & choc 45.00 30.00
108 A11 30c gray blk & red 140.00 140.00
109 A11 35c dk vio & grn 47.50 30.00
a. Double overprint 1,400. —
110 A11 40c choc & ultra 140.00 140.00
111 A11 45c car & vio 160.00 140.00
112 A11 50c bl grn & gray 160.00 140.00
113 A11 75c org & choc 210.00 150.00
114 A12 1fr dk brn & bis 190.00 160.00
115 A12 2fr car & brn 210.00 190.00
Nos. 101-105,106-115 (15) 1,826. 1,530.

The overprint is vertical, reading up, on #101-106, 114-115, horizontal on #107-113.

Stamps of Middle Congo, Issue of 1907, Overprinted

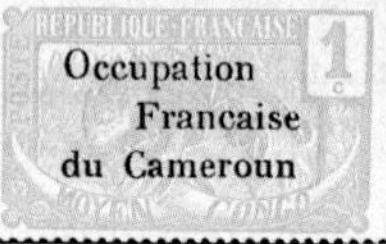

1916 Unwmk.

116 A1 1c ol gray & brn 75.00 75.00
117 A1 2c violet & brn 75.00 75.00
118 A1 4c blue & brown 80.00 75.00
119 A1 5c dk green & blue 22.50 22.50
120 A2 35c violet brn & bl 87.50 60.00
121 A2 45c violet & red 62.50 55.00

The overprint is vert., reading down, on #120-121.

Same Overprint On Stamps of French Congo, 1900

Wmk. Branch of Thistle (122)

122 A4 15c dull vio & ol grn 75.00 75.00
a. Inverted overprint 140.00 110.00

Wmk. Branch of Rose Tree (123)

123 A5 20c yellow grn & org 110.00 65.00
124 A5 30c car rose & org 65.00 55.00
125 A5 40c org brn & brt grn 65.00 60.00
126 A5 50c gray vio & lil 75.00 60.00
127 A5 75c red vio & org 70.00 55.00

Wmk. Branch of Olive (124)

128 A6 1fr gray lilac & ol 92.50 87.50
129 A6 2fr carmine & brn 110.00 92.50
Nos. 116-129 (14) 1,065. 912.50

The overprint is horiz. on No. 122. The overprint is vert., reading down or up, on Nos. 123-129. Values about the same. See the Scott Classic Catalogue.

Values are for copies centered in the grade of fine.

Counterfeits exist of Nos. 101-129.

Stamps of Middle Congo, Issue of 1907 Overprinted

1916-17 Unwmk.

130 A1 1c ol gray & brn .30 .30
131 A1 2c violet & brn .35 .30
132 A1 4c blue & brn .60 .35
133 A1 5c dk green & bl .35 .30
134 A1 10c carmine & bl .70 .50
135 A1 15c brn vio & rose ('17) 1.40 .50
136 A1 20c brown & bl .60 .50
137 A2 25c blue & grn .60 .35
a. Triple overprint *550.00*
138 A2 30c scarlet & grn .70 .50
a. Double overprint *425.00*
139 A2 35c vio brn & bl .60 .50
140 A2 40c dull grn & brn 1.60 .85
141 A2 45c violet & red 1.60 .85
142 A2 50c blue grn & red 1.60 1.00
143 A2 75c brown & blue 1.60 1.00
144 A3 1fr dp grn & vio 1.10 .80
145 A3 2fr vio & gray grn 5.50 4.25
146 A3 5fr blue & rose 7.75 6.50
Nos. 130-146 (17) 26.95 19.35

Nos. 130-146 exist on ordinary paper and, with the exception of No. 135, on chalk surfaced paper. Nos. 137-146 are known with inverted "S" in "Francaise."

On Nos. 137-146 there is 7mm between "Cameroun" and "Occupation."

Provisional French Mandate

Types of Middle Congo, 1907, Overprinted

1921

147 A1 1c ol grn & org .20 .20
148 A1 2c brown & rose .20 .20
149 A1 4c gray & lt grn .35 .30
150 A1 5c dl red & org .35 .30
a. Double overprint 650.00
151 A1 10c bl grn & lt grn .95 .45
152 A1 15c blue & org .35 .30
153 A1 20c red brn & ol .60 .50
154 A2 25c slate & org .80 .50
155 A2 30c rose & ver .95 .45
156 A2 35c gray & ultra .60 .45
157 A2 40c ol grn & org .80 .50
158 A2 45c brown & rose .60 .45
159 A2 50c blue & ultra .70 .45
160 A2 75c red brn & lt grn .80 .50
161 A3 1fr slate & org 1.00 1.10
162 A3 2fr ol grn & rose 4.75 3.25
163 A3 5fr dull red & gray 6.00 4.75
Nos. 147-163 (17) 20.60 14.65

The 2c, 4c, 15c, 25c and 50c exist with overprint omitted. See the Scott Classic Catalogue.

Nos. 152, 162, 163, 158, 160 Surcharged with New Value and Bars

1924-25

164 A1 25c on 15c bl & org ('25) .70 .70
165 A3 25c on 2fr ol grn & rose .95 .95
166 A3 25c on 5fr red & gray .95 .95
a. Pair, one without new value and bars
167 A2 65c on 45c brn & rose ('25) 1.10 1.10
168 A2 85c on 75c red brn & lt grn ('25) 1.60 1.60
Nos. 164-168 (5) 5.30 5.30

French Mandate

Herder and Cattle Crossing Sanaga River — A5

Tapping Rubber Tree — A6

Rope Suspension Bridge A7

1925-38 Typo. *Perf. 14x13½*

170 A5 1c ol grn & brn vio, *lav* .20 .20
171 A5 2c rose & grn, *grnsh* .20 .20
172 A5 4c blue & blk .20 .20
173 A5 5c org & red vio, *lav* .20 .20
174 A5 10c red brn & org, *yel* .35 .30
175 A5 15c sl grn & grn .35 .30
176 A5 15c lilac & red ('27) .70 .50

Perf. 13½x14

177 A6 20c ol brn & red brn .50 .30
178 A6 20c green ('26) .35 .30
179 A6 20c brn red & ol brn ('27) .35 .35
180 A6 25c lt green & blk .60 .35
181 A6 30c bluish grn & ver .35 .20
182 A6 30c dk grn & grn ('27) .60 .35
183 A6 35c brown & black .70 .35
184 A6 35c dl grn & grn ('38) 1.40 .95
185 A6 40c orange & vio 1.40 .85
186 A6 45c dp rose & cer .60 .35
187 A6 45c vio & org brn ('27) 1.60 1.25
188 A6 50c lt green & cer .60 .20
189 A6 55c ultra & car ('38) 1.25 1.10
190 A6 60c red vio & blk .60 .35
191 A6 60c brown red ('26) .60 .35
192 A6 65c indigo & brn .85 .70
193 A6 75c indigo & dp bl .60 .50
194 A6 75c org brn & red vio ('27) 1.00 .80
195 A6 80c carmine & brn ('38) 1.00 .80
196 A6 85c dp rose & bl 1.25 .85
197 A6 90c brn red & cer ('27) 2.00 .85

Perf. 14x13½

198 A7 1fr indigo & brn .80 .70
199 A7 1fr dull bl ('26) .35 .35
200 A7 1fr ol brn & red vio ('27) .80 .50
201 A7 1fr grn & dk brn ('29) 1.75 .80
202 A7 1.10fr rose red & dk brn ('28) 3.50 3.50
203 A7 1.25fr gray & dp bl ('33) 4.00 2.50
204 A7 1.50fr dull bl ('27) .60 .50
205 A7 1.75fr brn & org ('33) 1.10 .95
206 A7 1.75fr dk bl & lt bl ('38) 1.75 .95
207 A7 2fr dl grn & brn org 1.40 .70

208 A7 3fr ol brn & red vio ('27) 5.00 1.25
209 A7 5fr brn & blk, *bluish* 2.50 1.40
a. Cliché of 2fr in plate of 5fr *850.00*
210 A7 10fr org & vio ('27) 9.25 4.25
211 A7 20fr rose & ol grn ('27) 14.00 8.50
Nos. 170-211 (42) 67.20 40.85

Shades exist for several values.
For overprints and surcharge see Nos. 212, 264, 276, 278, 279, B7-B9, B21.

No. 199 Surcharged with New Value and Bars in Red

1926
212 A7 1.25fr on 1fr dull blue .60 .50

Common Design Types pictured following the introduction.

Colonial Exposition Issue
Common Design Types
Name of Country in Black

1931 **Engr.** ***Perf. 12½***
213 CD70 40c deep green 3.50 2.10
214 CD71 50c violet 3.50 2.75
215 CD72 90c red orange 3.50 2.75
216 CD73 1.50fr dull blue 4.00 2.75
Nos. 213-216 (4) 14.50 10.35

Paris International Exposition Issue
Common Design Types

1937 ***Perf. 13***
217 CD74 20c deep violet 1.25 1.25
218 CD75 30c dark green .95 .95
219 CD76 40c carmine rose 1.10 1.10
220 CD77 50c dark brown 1.10 1.10
221 CD78 90c red 1.10 1.10
222 CD79 1.50fr ultramarine 1.10 1.10
Nos. 217-222 (6) 6.60 6.60

French Colonial Art Exhibition
Common Design Type
Souvenir Sheet

1937 ***Imperf.***
222A CD77 3fr org red & blk 5.00 5.75

New York World's Fair Issue
Common Design Type

1939 ***Perf. 12½x12***
223 CD82 1.25fr carmine lake .95 .85
224 CD82 2.25fr ultra .95 .85

For overprints and surcharges see Nos. 280-281, B14-B17, B23, B25.

Mandara Woman — A19

Falls on M'bam River near Banyo — A20

Elephants A21

Man in Yaré — A22

1939-40 **Engr.** ***Perf. 13***
225 A19 2c black brn .20 .20
226 A19 3c magenta .20 .20
227 A19 4c deep ultra .20 .20
228 A19 5c red brown .20 .20
229 A19 10c dp bl grn .20 .20
230 A19 15c rose red .20 .20
231 A19 20c plum .20 .20
232 A20 25c black brn .50 .50
233 A20 30c dk red .50 .35
234 A20 40c ultra .50 .50
235 A20 45c slate green 1.90 1.40
236 A20 50c brown car .60 .35
237 A20 60c pck blue .60 .50
238 A20 70c plum 2.50 2.10
239 A21 80c Prus blue 1.90 1.60
240 A21 90c Prus blue .70 .50
241 A21 1fr car rose 1.40 .70
242 A21 1fr choc ('40) .95 .60
243 A21 1.25fr car rose 3.00 2.10
244 A21 1.40fr org red 1.00 .70
245 A21 1.50fr chocolate .80 .70
246 A21 1.60fr black brn 1.90 1.40
247 A21 1.75fr dk blue 1.10 .70
248 A21 2fr dk green .60 .60
249 A21 2.25fr dk blue 1.10 .70
250 A21 2.50fr brt red vio .95 .80
251 A21 3fr dk violet .80 .50
252 A22 5fr black brn .85 .60
253 A22 10fr brt red vio 1.40 1.10
254 A22 20fr dk green 2.75 1.75
Nos. 225-254 (30) 29.70 22.15

For overprints and surcharges see Nos. 255-263, 265-275, 277, 278A, 279A, B10-B13, B22, B24.

Stamps of 1925-40 Overprinted in Black or Orange
"CAMEROUN FRANCAIS 27.8.40."

1940 ***Perf. 14x13½, 13½x14, 13***
255 A19 2c blk brn (O) .80 .80
256 A19 3c magenta .65 .65
257 A19 4c dp ultra (O) .65 .65
258 A19 5c red brn 2.75 2.50
259 A19 10c dp bl grn (O) .70 .70
260 A19 15c rose red .70 .70
260A A19 20c plum (O) 7.00 7.00
261 A20 25c blk brn .70 .70
b. Inverted overprint 175.00 175.00
261A A20 30c dk red 5.75 5.75
262 A20 40c ultra 3.50 3.50
263 A20 45c slate green 1.60 1.60
264 A6 50c lt grn & cer 1.25 1.00
a. Inverted overprint 160.00
265 A20 60c pck bl 3.50 3.50
266 A20 70c plum 1.10 1.10
267 A21 80c Prus bl (O) 3.50 3.50
268 A21 90c Prus bl (O) .95 .95
269 A21 1.25fr car rose 1.00 .95
270 A21 1.40fr org red 1.40 1.25
271 A21 1.50fr chocolate .70 .60
272 A21 1.60fr blk brn (O) 1.00 .85
273 A21 1.75fr dk bl (O) 1.40 1.25
274 A21 2.25fr dk bl (O) .70 .70
275 A21 2.50fr brt red vio .70 .70
276 A7 5fr brn & blk, *bluish* 14.00 11.00
277 A22 5fr black brn 11.00 10.50
278 A7 10fr org & vio 16.00 13.00
278A A22 10fr brt red vio 32.50 21.00
279 A7 20fr rose & ol grn 35.00 31.00
279A A22 20fr dk green 140.00 140.00

Same Overprint on Stamps of 1939
Perf. 12½x12
280 CD82 1.25fr car lake 3.50 3.50
281 CD82 2.25fr ultra 3.50 3.50
Nos. 255-281 (31) 297.50 274.40

Issued to note Cameroun's affiliation with General de Gaulle's "Free France" movement. Numerous overprint varieties exist.

Cattle Fording Sanaga River and Marshal Petain A22a

1941 **Engr.** ***Perf. 12½x12***
281A A22a 1fr green .60
281B A22a 2.50fr dark blue .60

Nos. 281A-281B were issued by the Vichy government in France, but were not placed on sale in Cameroun.
For surcharges, see Nos. B25A-B25B.

Lorraine Cross and Joan of Arc Shield — A23

1941 **Photo.** ***Perf. 14x14½***
282 A23 5c brown .20 .20
283 A23 10c dk blue .20 .20
284 A23 25c emerald .20 .20
285 A23 30c dp orange .20 .20
286 A23 40c dk slate green .20 .20
287 A23 80c red brown .35 .20
288 A23 1fr dp red lilac .35 .35
289 A23 1.50fr brt red .35 .35
290 A23 2fr gray black .50 .35
291 A23 2.50fr brt ultra .50 .35
292 A23 4fr dull violet .60 .60
293 A23 5fr bister .65 .65
294 A23 10fr dp brown .65 .65
295 A23 20fr dp green 1.40 .85
Nos. 282-295 (14) 6.35 5.35

For surcharges see Nos. 297A-303.

Catalogue values for unused stamps in this section, from this point to the end of the section, are for Never Hinged items.

Eboue Issue
Common Design Type

1945 **Unwmk.** **Engr.** ***Perf. 13***
296 CD91 2fr black .20 .20
297 CD91 25fr Prus green 1.10 .65

Nos. 282, 284, 291 Surcharged with New Values and Bars in Red, Carmine or Black

1946 ***Perf. 14x14½***
297A A23 50c on 5c (R) .25 .25
298 A23 60c on 5c (R) .40 .40
a. Inverted surcharge 92.50
299 A23 70c on 5c (R) .50 .50
300 A23 1.20fr on 5c (C) .50 .50
301 A23 2.40fr on 25c .40 .40
302 A23 3fr on 25c .65 .65
302A A23 4.50fr on 25c .85 .85
303 A23 15fr on 2.50fr (C) .85 .85
Nos. 297A-303 (8) 4.40 4.40

Zebu and Herder A25

Tikar Women — A26

Porters Carrying Bananas — A27

Bowman A28

Lamido Horsemen A29

Farmer — A30

1946 **Engr.** ***Perf. 12½x12, 12x12½***
304 A25 10c blue grn .20 .20
305 A25 30c brown org .20 .20
306 A25 40c brt ultra .20 .20
307 A26 50c olive brn .20 .20
308 A26 60c dp plum .35 .20
309 A26 80c chnt brn .45 .20
310 A27 1fr org red .20 .20
311 A27 1.20fr dp green .50 .20
312 A27 1.50fr dk car 1.40 .75
313 A28 2fr black .20 .20
314 A28 3fr dk carmine .25 .20
314A A28 3.60fr red brn .85 .35
315 A28 4fr dp blue .35 .20
316 A29 5fr brown car .75 .20
317 A29 6fr ultra .75 .20
318 A29 10fr slate green .75 .20
319 A30 15fr grnsh blue 1.10 .35
320 A30 20fr dk green 1.60 .25
321 A30 25fr black 2.00 .60
Nos. 304-321 (19) 12.30 5.10

Shades exist for most values.
For surcharges see Nos. 343-344, 346.

Imperforates
Most Cameroun stamps from 1952 onward exist imperforate in issued and trial colors, and also in small presentation sheets in issued colors.

Military Medal Issue
Common Design Type
Engraved and Typographed

1952 **Unwmk.** ***Perf. 13***
322 CD101 15fr multicolored 4.00 2.00

Porters Carrying Bananas — A32

Picking Coffee Beans — A33

1954 **Engr.**
323 A32 8fr red vio, org brn & vio bl .50 .20
324 A32 15fr brn red, yel & blk brn .90 .30
325 A33 40fr blk brn, org brn & lil rose 1.10 .30
Nos. 323-325 (3) 2.50 .80

FIDES Issue
Common Design Type

Designs: 5fr, Plowmen. 15fr, Wouri bridge. 20fr, Technical instruction. 25fr, Mobile medical station.

1956 **Unwmk.** ***Perf. 13***
326 CD103 5fr org brn & dk brn .65 .30
327 CD103 15fr aqua, slate & blk 1.00 .50
328 CD103 20fr grnsh bl & dp ultra 1.00 .50
329 CD103 25fr dp ultra 1.25 .70
Nos. 326-329 (4) 3.90 2.00

For surcharges see Nos. 345, 347.

Coffee Issue

Coffee A35

1956 **Engr.** ***Perf. 13***
330 A35 15fr car & brt red .90 .25

For surcharge see No. 348.

Autonomous Government

Flag and Woman Holding Child A36

1958
331 A36 20fr multicolored 1.00 .20

Anniv. of the installation of the 1st autonomous government of Cameroun.

Men Looking to the Sun — A37

1958

332 A37 20fr sepia & brn red 1.00 .25

10th anniv. of the signing of the Universal Declaration of Human Rights.

Flower Issue

Common Design Type

Design: 20fr, Randia malleifera.

1959 Photo. *Perf. 12½x12*

333 CD104 20fr dp grn, yel & rose .90 .20

Loading Bananas A38

Harvesting Bananas — A39

1959 Engr. *Perf. 13*

334 A38 20fr dk grn & org .75 .20
335 A39 25fr maroon & slate grn .95 .20

For surcharge see No. 349.

Independent State

Map and Flag of Cameroun — A40

Prime Minister Ahmadou Ahidjo — A41

1960 Unwmk. Engr. *Perf. 13*

336 A40 20fr multicolored .75 .20
337 A41 25fr blk, grn & pale lem .85 .20

Declaration of independence, Jan. 1, 1960. For surcharge see No. 350.

Uprooted Oak Emblem A42

1960

338 A42 30fr red brn, ultra & yel grn 1.10 .40

World Refugee Year, 7/1/59-6/30/60. For surcharge see No. 351.

C.C.T.A. Issue

Common Design Type

1960

339 CD106 50fr dull claret & slate 1.60 .40

UN Headquarters, NYC, and Flag — A43

1961, May 20 *Perf. 13*

Flag in Green, Red and Yellow

340 A43 15fr grn, dk bl & brn .60 .25
341 A43 25fr dk blue & grn .75 .25
342 A43 85fr red, dk bl & vio brn 2.25 .80
Nos. 340-342 (3) 3.60 1.30

Cameroun's admission to the UN, Sept. 20, 1960.

Federal Republic

Stamps of 1946-60 Surcharged in Red or Black:

REPUBLIQUE FEDERALE 2 d

Two types of 2sh6p:
I — Large figures. "2/6" measures 8x3¾mm.
II — Small figures. "2/6" measures 6x2½mm.

Perf. 12x12½, 13

1961, Oct. 1 Engr.

343 A27 ½p on 1fr (#310) .35 .20
344 A28 1p on 2fr (#313) .45 .30
345 CD103 1½p on 5fr (#326) .55 .35
346 A29 2p on 10fr (#318) 1.00 .45
347 CD103 3p on 15fr (#327) 1.25 .60
348 A35 4p on 15fr (Bk) (#330) 1.10 .70
349 A38 6p on 20fr (#334) 2.25 1.00
350 A41 1sh on 25fr (#337) 2.75 1.50
351 A42 2sh6p on 30fr (#338) (I) 5.00 5.00
a. Type II 21.00 21.00
Nos. 343-351 (9) 14.70 10.10

Issued for use in the former United Kingdom Trust Territory of Southern Cameroons.

The "Republique Federale" overprint is in one line on Nos. 345, 347-349, in two vertical lines on No. 350. See Nos. C38-C40.

President Ahidjo and Prime Minister Foncha A45

Unwmk.

1962, Jan. 1 Engr. *Perf. 13*

352 A45 20fr vio & choc 6.50 6.25
353 A45 25fr dk grn & brn 11.00 9.50
354 A45 60fr car & dl grn 32.50 29.00
Nos. 352-354 (3) 50.00 44.75

=

3 d

Same Surcharged for Use in Southern Cameroons

355 A45 3p on 20fr 150.00 150.00
356 A45 6p on 25fr 150.00 150.00
357 A45 2sh6p on 60fr 150.00 150.00
Nos. 355-357 (3) 450.00 450.00

Reunification of the former French and British Sections of Cameroun. It is reported that Nos. 352-357 were withdrawn after a few days and destroyed.

Mustache Monkey A46

Designs: 1fr, 4fr, Elephant, Ntem Falls. 1.50fr, 3fr, Buffon's kob, Dschang. 2fr, 5fr, Hippopotamus. 6fr, 15fr, Mustache monkey. 8fr, 30fr, Manatee, Lake Ossa. 10fr, 25fr, Buffalo, Batouri. 20fr, 40fr, Giraffes, Waza Reservation, vert.

1962 Unwmk. Engr. *Perf. 12*

358 A46 50c brn, brt grn & bl .20 .20
359 A46 1fr gray brn, bl grn & org .20 .20
360 A46 1.50fr brn, lt grn & sl grn .20 .20
361 A46 2fr dk gray, grnsh bl & grn .20 .20
362 A46 3fr brn, org & lil rose .20 .20
363 A46 4fr brn, yel grn & bl grn .25 .20
364 A46 5fr gray brn, grn & sal .25 .20
365 A46 6fr brn, yel & bl .45 .20
366 A46 8fr dk bl, red & grn .90 .20
367 A46 10fr ol blk, org & brt bl .70 .20
368 A46 15fr brn, Prus bl & bl .90 .20
369 A46 20fr brn & gray 1.10 .20
370 A46 25fr red brn, grn & yel 2.75 .20
371 A46 30fr blk, org & bl 3.25 .25
372 A46 40fr dp cl, yel grn & blk 6.25 .40
Nos. 358-372 (15) 17.80 3.25

See Nos. 396-397.

African and Malagasy Union Issue

Common Design Type

1962, Sept. 8 Photo. *Perf. 12½x12*

373 CD110 30fr multicolored 1.50 .45

Village and Map of Cameroun A48

Designs: 20fr, 25fr, Sun rising over city. 50fr, Hands holding scroll.

1962, Oct. 1 Engr. *Perf. 13*

374 A48 9fr pur, olive & dk brn .35 .20
375 A48 18fr grn, org brn & dk bl .45 .20
376 A48 20fr lil rose, ol bis & ind .45 .20
377 A48 25fr bl, red org & sep .55 .20
378 A48 50fr dk red, sepia & bl 1.50 .50
Nos. 374-378 (5) 3.30 1.30

1st anniv. of the reunification of Cameroun.

"School under the Trees" — A49

1962, Nov. 5 Photo. *Perf. 12x12½*

379 A49 20fr ver, emerald & yel 1.00 .20

Literacy and popular education campaign.

Telstar and Globe A50

1963, Feb. 9 Engr. *Perf. 13*

Size: 36x22mm

380 A50 1fr dk bl, olive & pur .20 .20
381 A50 2fr dk bl, claret & grn .20 .20
382 A50 3fr dk grn, ol & dp cl .25 .20
383 A50 25fr grn, dp cl & brt bl 1.00 .40
Nos. 380-383,C45 (5) 4.15 1.65

1st TV connection of the US and Europe through the Telstar satellite, July 11-12, 1962.

High Frequency Transmission Station, Mt. Bankolo — A51

Design: 20fr, Station and wiring plan.

1963, May 18 Photo. *Perf. 12x12½*

384 A51 15fr multicolored .45 .20
385 A51 20fr multicolored .60 .20
Nos. 384-385,C46 (3) 3.55 1.05

Issued to publicize the high frequency telegraph connection Douala-Yaounde.

"Yaoundé-Regional Center of Textbook Production" — A52

1963, Aug. 10 Unwmk. *Perf. 12½*

386 A52 20fr emer, blk & red .45 .20
387 A52 25fr org, blk & red .50 .20
388 A52 100fr gold, blk & red 2.10 .60
Nos. 386-388 (3) 3.05 1.00

UNESCO regional center for the production of school books at Yaounde.

Pres. Ahmadou Ahidjo and Flag — A53

Design: 18fr, Flag and map of Cameroun.

1963, Oct. 1 *Perf. 12x12½*

Flag in Green, Red and Yellow

389 A53 9fr grn, bl & dk brn .45 .20
390 A53 18fr grn, bl & lil .60 .20
391 A53 20fr grn, blk & yel grn .70 .20
Nos. 389-391 (3) 1.75 .60

Second anniversary of reunification.

Scales, Globe, UNESCO Emblem A54

1963, Dec. 10 Photo. *Perf. 12½x12*

392 A54 9fr ultra, blk & sal .35 .20
393 A54 18fr brt yel grn, blk & rose red .45 .20
394 A54 25fr rose red, blk & brt yel grn .60 .20
395 A54 75fr yel, blk & ultra 1.75 .50
Nos. 392-395 (4) 3.15 1.10

Universal Declaration of Human Rights, 15th anniv.

Animal Type of 1962

Design: 10fr, 25fr, Lion, Waza National Park, North Cameroun.

1964, June 20 Engr. *Perf. 13*

396 A46 10fr red brn, bis & grn 1.00 .20
397 A46 25fr green & bister 2.25 .20

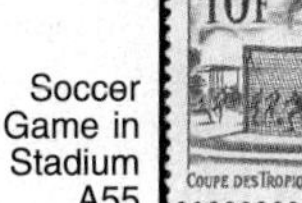

Soccer Game in Stadium A55

18fr, Pile of sports equipment. 30fr, Stadium (outside), flags and map of Africa.

1964, July 11 Engr. *Perf. 13*

398 A55 10fr grn, bl & red brn .55 .20
399 A55 18fr car, grn & vio .65 .20
400 A55 30fr blk, dk bl & org brn 1.00 .20
Nos. 398-400 (3) 2.20 .60

Tropics Cup Games, Yaounde, July 11-19.

Europafrica Issue, 1964

Common Design Type and

Palace of Justice, Yaounde — A56

40fr, Emblems of Science, Agriculture, Industry and Education and two sunbursts.

1964, July 20 Photo. *Perf. 12x13*

401 A56 15fr multicolored 1.10 .25
402 CD116 40fr multicolored 2.00 .60

1st anniv. of the economic agreement between the European Economic Community and the African and Malgache Union.

Hurdling and Olympic Flame — A57

Design: 10fr, Runners, vert.

1964, Oct. 10 Engr. *Perf. 13*

403 A57 9fr red, yel grn & blk 1.25 .40
404 A57 10fr red, vio & ol gray 1.75 .40
Nos. 403-404,C49 (3) 10.50 2.80

18th Olympic Games, Tokyo, Oct. 10-25.

Bamileke Dance Dress — A58

Ntem Falls, Ebolowa Region — A59

Designs: 18fr, Dance mask, Bamenda region. 25fr, Fulani horseman, North Cameroun, horiz.

1964 Unwmk. *Perf. 13*

405 A58 9fr red, yel grn & bl .55 .20
406 A58 18fr bl, red & brn .70 .20
407 A59 20fr dk car, grn & ol .90 .20
408 A58 25fr dk brn, org & car 1.40 .20
Nos. 405-408,C50 (5) 4.45 1.15

Cooperation Issue

Common Design Type

1964, Nov. 7 Engr.

409 CD119 18fr dk bl, yel grn & dk brn .70 .20
410 CD119 30fr red brn, bl grn & dk brn 1.40 .20

Memorial Stone — A60

Diesel Train A61

1965, Jan. 1 Engr. *Perf. 13*

411 A60 12fr bl, indigo & grn .80 .20

Typo. *Perf. 14x13*

412 A61 20fr rose car, yel & grn 2.25 .20

Laying of the 1st rail of the Mbanga-Kumba Railroad, Mar. 28, 1964.

Red Cross Station and Ambulance A62

50fr, Red Cross nurse and infant, vert.

1965, May 8 Engr. *Perf. 13*

413 A62 25fr car, slate grn & ocher .65 .20
414 A62 50fr gray, red & red brn 1.50 .30

Issued for the Cameroun Red Cross.

Coins Inserted in Map of Cameroun, and Bankbook — A63

Savings Bank Building — A64

Design: 20fr, Bankbook and coins inserted in cacao pod-shaped bank, vert.

1965, June 10

Size: 22x37mm

415 A63 9fr grn, red & org .45 .20

Size: 48x27mm, 27x48mm

416 A64 15fr choc, ultra & grn .55 .20
417 A63 20fr ocher, brt grn & brn .65 .20
Nos. 415-417 (3) 1.65 .60

Federal Postal Savings Banks.

Soccer Players and Africa Cup — A65

Unwmk.

1965, June 26 Engr. *Perf. 13*

418 A65 9fr car, brn & yel .55 .20
419 A65 20fr car, slate bl & yel 1.40 .20

Cameroun Oryx Club, winner of the club champions' Africa Cup, February 1965.

Symbolic Map of Europe and Africa — A66

40fr, Delegates around conference table.

1965, July 20 Photo. *Perf. 12x12½*

420 A66 5fr car, blk & lilac .25 .20
421 A66 40fr brn, buff, grn & ultra 1.25 .35

2nd, anniv. of the economic agreement between the European Economic Community and the African and Malgache Union.

UPU Monument, Bern A67

1965, July 26 Engr. *Perf. 13*

422 A67 30fr black & red .80 .25

Cameroun's admission to the UPU, 5th anniv.

ICY Emblem — A68

1965, Sept. 11 Unwmk. *Perf. 13*

423 A68 10fr dk bl & car rose .45 .20

Issued for the International Cooperation Year, 1964-65. See No. C57.

Pres. Ahidjo and Government House — A69

Design: 9fr, 20fr, Pres. Ahidjo and Government House, vert.

Perf. 12x12½, 12½x12

1965, Oct. 1 Photo. Unwmk.

424 A69 9fr multicolored .25 .20
425 A69 18fr multicolored .55 .20
426 A69 20fr multicolored .65 .20
427 A69 25fr multicolored .80 .20
Nos. 424-427 (4) 2.25 .80

Reelection of Pres. Ahmadou Ahidjo.

National Tourist Office, Yaoundé A70

Designs: 9fr, Pouss Musgum houses. 18fr, Great Calao's dance (North Cameroun). 20fr, Gate of Sultan's Palace, Foumban, vert.

1965 Engr. *Perf. 13*

428 A70 9fr brn, rose red & grn .45 .20
429 A70 18fr brt bl, brn & grn .65 .20
430 A70 20fr bl, brn & choc 1.00 .20
431 A70 25fr mar, emer & gray .90 .20
Nos. 428-431 (4) 3.00 .80

See No. C58.

Mountain Hotel, Buea — A71

Designs: 20fr, Hotel of the Deputies, Yaoundé. 35fr, Dschang Health Center.

1966

432 A71 9fr sl grn, rose cl & brn .35 .20
433 A71 20fr brt bl, sl grn & blk .45 .20
434 A71 35fr brn, sl grn & car .80 .30
Nos. 432-434,C63-C69 (10) 14.25 3.45

Bas-relief, Foumban A72

Designs: 18fr, Ekoi mask, vert. 20fr, Mother and child, carving, Bamiléké, vert. 25fr, Ceremonial stool, Bamoun.

1966, Apr. 15 Unwmk.

435 A72 9fr red & blk .55 .20
436 A72 18fr brt grn, org brn & choc .65 .20
437 A72 20fr brt bl, red brn & pur .90 .20
438 A72 25fr pur & dk brn 1.00 .20
Nos. 435-438 (4) 3.10 .80

Intl. Negro Arts Festival, Dakar, Senegal, 4/1-24.

New WHO Headquarters, Geneva — A73

1966, May 3 Photo. *Perf. 12½x13*

439 A73 50fr ultra, red brn & yel 1.25 .35

ITU Headquarters, Geneva — A74

1966, May 3 Photo. *Perf. 12½x13*

440 A74 50fr ultra & yellow 1.25 .35

Phaeomeria Magnifica — A75

"6" and Men Dancing around UN Emblem — A76

Flowers: 18fr, Hibiscus (rose of China). 20fr, Mountain rose.

1966, May 20 *Perf. 12x12½*
Flowers in Natural Colors
Size: 22x36mm

441	A75	9fr red brown	.55	.20
442	A75	18fr green	.70	.20
443	A75	20fr dark green	.70	.20
		Nos. 441-443,C70-C72 (6)	6.80	1.25

See No. 469.

1966, Sept. 20 **Engr.** *Perf. 13*

Design: 50fr, UN General Assembly, horiz.

444	A76	50fr ultra, grn & vio brn	.90	.20
445	A76	100fr red brn, grn & ultra	2.00	.50

6th anniv. of Cameroun's admission to the UN.

Prime Minister's Residence, Buea — A77

Designs (Prime Minister's Residences): 18fr, at Yaoundé, front view. 20fr, at Yaoundé, side view. 25fr, at Buea, front view.

1966, Oct. 1 **Photo.**

446	A77	9fr multicolored	.45	.20
447	A77	18fr multicolored	.65	.20
448	A77	20fr multicolored	.65	.20
449	A77	25fr multicolored	.80	.20
		Nos. 446-449 (4)	2.55	.80

5th anniversary of re-unification.

Learning to Write and UNESCO Emblem A78

#451, Children's heads & UNICEF emblem.

1966, Nov. 24 **Engr.** *Perf. 13*

450	A78	50fr red lil, bl & brn	1.25	.30
451	A78	50fr red lil, blk & brt bl	1.25	.30

20th anniv. of UNESCO, 20th anniv. of UNICEF.

Independence Proclamation — A79

1967, Jan. 1 **Engr.** *Perf. 13*

452	A79	20fr grn, red & yel	2.00	.25

7th anniversary of independence.

Map of Africa and Madagascar, Railroad Tracks and Symbols — A80

25fr, Map of Africa and Madagascar and train.

1967, Feb. 21 **Photo.** *Perf. 13*

453	A80	20fr multicolored	3.50	.20
454	A80	25fr multicolored	5.25	.20

5th Conf. of African and Madagascan Railroad Technicians.

Lions Emblem and Forest — A81

Design: 100fr, Lions emblem and palms.

1967, Mar. 3

455	A81	50fr multicolored	.90	.35
456	A81	100fr multicolored	2.10	.65

Lions International, 50th anniversary.

Jet and I.C.A.O. Emblem — A82

Dove and I.A.E.A. Emblem A83

Perf. 13x12½, 12½x13
1967, Mar. 15 **Photo.**

457	A82	50fr ultra, lt bl, brn & gold	1.25	.35
458	A83	50fr ultra & emer	1.25	.35

UN agencies: No. 457, the ICAO; No. 458, the Intl. Atomic Energy Agency.

Rotary International Emblem — A84

1967, Apr. 17 **Photo.** *Perf. 12½*

459	A84	25fr crim, vio bl & gold	1.00	.20

10th anniversary of the Douala, Cameroun, branch of Rotary International.

Grapefruit — A85

Bird of Paradise Flower — A86

1967, May 10 **Photo.** *Perf. 12x12½*

460	A85	1fr shown	.20	.20
461	A85	2fr Papaya	.20	.20
462	A85	3fr Custard apple	.20	.20
463	A85	4fr Breadfruit	.20	.20
464	A85	5fr Coconut	.35	.20
465	A85	6fr Mango	.45	.20
466	A85	8fr Avacado	.90	.20
467	A85	10fr Pineapple	1.40	.20
468	A85	30fr Bananas	3.50	.20
		Nos. 460-468 (9)	7.40	1.80

For surcharges see Nos. 550, 593.

1967, June 22 **Photo.** *Perf. 12x12½*
Size: 22x36mm

469	A86	15fr lt blue & multi	.90	.20

Sanaga Falls and ITY Emblem — A87

1967, Aug. 14 **Photo.** *Perf. 13x12½*

470	A87	30fr multicolored	.80	.20

Issued for International Tourist Year 1967.

Art of Cameroun: Coconut Harvest A88

Carved Bas-relief: 20fr, Lion hunt. 30fr, Women carrying baskets. 100fr, Carved chest.

1967, Sept. 22 *Perf. 12½x13*

471	A88	10fr brn, bl & car	.35	.20
472	A88	20fr brn, yel & grn	.55	.20
473	A88	30fr emer, brn & car	.90	.20
474	A88	100fr red org, brn & emer	2.25	.40
		Nos. 471-474 (4)	4.05	1.00

Coat of Arms A89

1968, Jan. 1 **Litho.** *Perf. 12½x13*

475	A89	30fr gold & multi	1.00	.20

Spiny Lobster A90

Designs (Fish and Crustaceans): 10fr, River crayfish. 15fr, Nile mouth-breeder. 20fr, Sole. 25fr, Common pike. 30fr, Crab. 40fr, Spadefish, vert. 50fr, Shrimp, vert. 55fr, African snakehead. 60fr, Threadfin.

1968, July 25 **Engr.** *Perf. 13*

476	A90	5fr brn, vio bl & dl grn	.20	.20
477	A90	10fr ultra, brn ol & slate	.20	.20
478	A90	15fr sal, red lil & sepia	.70	.20
479	A90	20fr red brn, dp bl & sep	.80	.20
480	A90	25fr lt brn, emer & slate	.90	.20
481	A90	30fr mag, dk bl & dk brn	1.10	.20
482	A90	40fr slate bl & org	1.60	.20
483	A90	50fr emer, gray & rose car	2.25	.20
484	A90	55fr lt brn, Prus bl & dk brn	3.25	.25
485	A90	60fr brn, bl grn & indigo	5.00	.35
		Nos. 476-485 (10)	16.00	2.20

Tanker, Refinery and Map of Area Served — A91

1968, July 30 **Photo.** *Perf. 12½*

486	A91	30fr multicolored	1.00	.20

Port Gentil (Gabon) Refinery opening, 6/12/68.

Human Rights Flame A92

1968, Sept. 14 **Photo.** *Perf. 12½x13*

487	A92	15fr blue & salmon	.65	.20

Intl. Human Rights Year. See No. C110.

Pres. Ahmadou Ahidjo A93

1969, Apr. 10 **Photo.** *Perf. 12½x12*

488	A93	30fr carmine & multi	.80	.20

Chocolate Vat — A94

Designs: 30fr, Chocolate factory. 50fr, Candy making, vert.

1969, Apr. 24 **Engr.** *Perf. 13*

489	A94	15fr red brn, ind & choc	.45	.20
490	A94	30fr grn, blk & red brn	.70	.20
491	A94	50fr brown & multi	1.00	.20
		Nos. 489-491 (3)	2.15	.60

Cameroun chocolate industry.

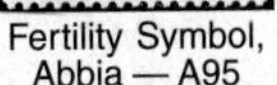

Fertility Symbol, Abbia — A95

Diesel Train on Bridge — A96

Art and Folklore from Abbia: 10fr, Two toucans, horiz. 15fr, Forest symbol. 30fr, Vulture attacking monkey, horiz. 70fr, Oliphant player.

1969, May 30 **Engr.** ***Perf. 13***

492 A95 5fr ultra, Prus bl & brt rose lil .25 .20
493 A95 10fr bl, ol gray & org .35 .20
494 A95 15fr ultra, dk red & blk .45 .20
495 A95 30fr brt bl, lem & grn .80 .20
496 A95 70fr brt bl, dk grn & ver 1.75 .35
Nos. 492-496 (5) 3.60 1.15

Perf. 12½x13, 13x12½

1969, July 11 **Photo.**

Design: 30fr, Kumba Railroad station, horiz.

497 A96 30fr blue & multi 1.00 .20
498 A96 50fr black & multi 2.50 .25

Opening of Mbanga-Kumba Railroad.

Development Bank Issue
Common Design Type

1969, Sept. 10 **Engr.** ***Perf. 13***

499 CD130 30fr vio bl, grn & ocher .80 .20

African Development Bank, 5th anniv.

ASECNA Issue
Common Design Type

1969, Dec. 12 **Engr.** ***Perf. 13***

500 CD132 100fr slate green 2.00 .60

Red Sage — A99

Design: 30fr, Passionflower.

1970, Mar. 24 **Photo.** ***Perf. 12x12½***
Size: 22x36½mm

501 A99 15fr yel grn & multi .45 .20
502 A99 30fr multicolored 1.00 .20
Nos. 501-502,C140-C141 (4) 5.60 1.05

UPU Headquarters Issue
Common Design Type

1970, May 20 **Engr.** ***Perf. 13***

503 CD133 30fr blue, pur & grn 1.00 .20
504 CD133 50fr gray, red & bl 1.50 .20

Brewery A100

Design: 30fr, Cellar with barrels.

1970, July 9 **Engr.** ***Perf. 13***

505 A100 15fr brn, gray & dk grn .45 .20
506 A100 30fr bl grn, dk brn & brn red .90 .20

Cameroun brewing industry.

Ozila Dancers — A101

Cameroun Doll — A102

Design: 50fr, Ozila dancer and drummer.

1970, Oct. 19 **Engr.** ***Perf. 13***

507 A101 30fr multicolored .90 .20
508 A101 50fr red & multi 2.25 .20

1970, Nov. 2

Designs: 15fr, Doll in short skirt. 30fr, Doll with basket on back.

509 A102 10fr car & multi .45 .20
510 A102 15fr dk grn & multi .55 .20
511 A102 30fr brn red & multi 1.50 .20
Nos. 509-511 (3) 2.50 .60

Cogwheels and Grain A103

1970, Feb. 9 **Photo.** ***Perf. 13***

512 A103 30fr multicolored .80 .20

Europafrica Economic Conference.

Federal University, Yaoundé A104

1971, Jan. 19 **Engr.**

513 A104 50fr multicolored 1.00 .20

Inauguration of Federal University at Yaoundé.

Presidents Ahidjo and Pompidou, Flags of Cameroun and France — A105

1971, Feb. 9 **Photo.** ***Perf. 13***

514 A105 30fr multicolored 1.00 .35

Visit of Georges Pompidou, Pres. of France.

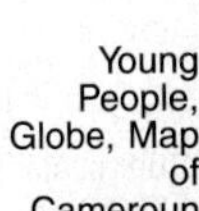
Young People, Globe, Map of Cameroun A106

1971, Feb. 11

515 A106 30fr blue & multi .80 .20

Fifth National Youth Festival, Feb. 11.

Gerbera Hybrida — A107

Men of Four Races — A108

Designs: 40fr, Opuntia polyantha (cactus). 50fr, Hemerocallis hybrida (lily).

1971, Mar. 14 **Photo.**

516 A107 20fr multicolored .55 .20
517 A107 40fr green & multi 1.25 .20
518 A107 50fr blue & multi 1.75 .20
Nos. 516-518 (3) 3.55 .60

1971, Mar. 21 ***Perf. 13x12½***

Design: 30fr, Hands and globe.

519 A108 20fr green & multi .55 .20
520 A108 30fr ultra & multi .70 .20

Intl. year against racial discrimination.

Crowned Cranes at Waza Camp A109

20fr, Canoe on Sanaga River. 30fr, Sanaga River.

1971, Apr. 9. **Engr.** ***Perf. 13***

521 A109 10fr red, grn & blk .70 .20
522 A109 20fr dk grn, brn & red .55 .20
523 A109 30fr red, dk grn & brt bl .70 .20
Nos. 521-523 (3) 1.95 .60

International Court, The Hague — A110

1971, June 14 **Engr.** ***Perf. 13***

524 A110 50fr ultra, org brn & sl grn .90 .20

25th anniversary of the International Court in The Hague, Netherlands.

Liana Bridge — A111

Bamoun Horseman A113

Local Market A112

1971, Aug. 16 **Photo.** ***Perf. 13***

525 A111 40fr multicolored .90 .20
526 A112 45fr multicolored 1.00 .20

1971, Sept. 18

African Art: 15fr, Animal fetish statuette.

527 A113 10fr brown & yellow .20 .20
528 A113 15fr dp brn & org yel .20 .20

Communications Satellite and Globe — A114

1971, Oct. 14 ***Perf. 13x12½***

529 A114 40fr Prus bl, sl grn & org .80 .20

Pan-African telecommunications system.

UNICEF Emblem A115

50fr, UNICEF emblem and grain, vert.

1971, Dec. 11 **Engr.** ***Perf. 13***

530 A115 40fr sl grn, bl grn & plum .90 .20
531 A115 50fr dp bl, dk red & lt grn 1.00 .25

25th anniv. of UNICEF.

Houses from South-Central Region — A116

Design: 15fr, Adamaua round houses.

1972, Jan. 15 **Photo.** ***Perf. 13***

532 A116 10fr dk blue & multi .25 .20
533 A116 15fr black & multi .55 .20

Giraffe — A117

Designs: 5fr, Home industries. 10fr, Smith, horiz. 15fr, Women carrying burdens.

Perf. 13x13½, 13½x13

1972, Feb. 18 **Litho.**

534 A117 2fr multicolored .25 .20
535 A117 5fr black, org & red .25 .20
536 A117 10fr multicolored .25 .20
537 A117 15fr multicolored .25 .20
Nos. 534-537 (4) 1.00 .80

Youth Day 1972.

Soccer Players and Field — A118

Designs: 20fr, African Soccer Cup, vert. 45fr, Team captains shaking hands, vert.

1972, Feb. 22 ***Perf. 13½***

538 A118 20fr gray & multi .55 .20
539 A118 40fr gray & multi .80 .20
540 A118 45fr yellow & multi 1.25 .25
Nos. 538-540 (3) 2.60 .65

African Soccer Cup, Yaoundé, 2/23-3/5.

Government Building, Yaoundé, and Laurel — A119

1972, Apr. 6 **Photo.** ***Perf. 12½x12***

541 A119 40fr multicolored .80 .20

110th session of Inter-Parliamentary Council, Yaoundé, Apr. 1972.

"Fantasia," North Cameroun A120

Bororo Woman — A121

40fr, Boat on Wouri River & Mt. Cameroun.

1972, Apr. 24 ***Perf. 13x12½, 12½x13***

542 A120 15fr dk vio & multi .35 .20
543 A121 20fr multicolored .45 .20
544 A120 40fr multicolored 1.50 .20
Nos. 542-544 (3) 2.30 .60

Chemical Apparatus A122

1972, May 15 **Engr.** ***Perf. 13***

545 A122 40fr lilac, red & green .80 .20

President Ahmadou Ahidjo Prize.

United Republic

Solanum Macranthum A123

Design: 45fr, Wax plant.

1972, July 20 **Photo.** ***Perf. 13***

546 A123 40fr multicolored .90 .20
547 A123 45fr yellow & multi 1.00 .20

Charaxes Ameliae A124

Design: 45fr, Papilio tynderaeus.

1972, Aug. 20 **Photo.** ***Perf. 13***

548 A124 40fr bl, dk bl & gold 2.50 .20
549 A124 45fr lt grn, blk & gold 3.25 .20

No. 468 Surcharged

1972, Aug. 30 **Photo.** ***Perf. 12x12½***

550 A85 40fr on 30fr multicolored 1.00 .20

Resurrection Lily — A125

Great Blue Touraco — A126

Flowers: 45fr, Candlestick cassia. 50fr, Amaryllis.

1972, Sept. 16 ***Perf. 13***

551 A125 40fr lt green & multi 1.00 .20
552 A125 45fr multicolored 1.25 .20
553 A125 50fr lt blue & multi 1.75 .20
Nos. 551-553 (3) 4.00 .60

Perf. 12½x13, 13x12½

1972, Nov. 20 **Litho.**

Design: 45fr, Red-faced lovebirds, horiz.

554 A126 10fr yellow & multi 1.50 .20
555 A126 45fr yellow & multi 3.50 .20

Cotton (North) — A127

10fr, Cacao (south central). 15fr, Logging (southeast & southern coast). 20fr, Coffee (west). 45fr, Tea (northwest & southwest).

1973, Mar. 26 **Photo.** ***Perf. 12½x13***

556 A127 5fr black & multi .25 .20
557 A127 10fr black & multi .25 .20
558 A127 15fr black & multi .65 .20
559 A127 20fr black & multi 1.25 .20
560 A127 45fr black & multi 2.75 .20
Nos. 556-560 (5) 5.15 1.00

Third 5-Year Plan.
For surcharge see No. 568.

Flag and Map of Cameroun, Pres. Ahidjo and No. 331 — A128

Design: 20fr, Proclamation of independence, Pres. Ahidjo and No. 336.

1973, May 20 **Engr.** ***Perf. 13***

561 A128 10fr ultra & multi .65 .20
562 A128 20fr multicolored 1.00 .20
Nos. 561-562,C200-C201 (4) 3.45 .85

United Republic of Cameroun, 1st anniv.

Bamoun Mask — A129

Dr. Hansen — A130

Designs: Various Bamoun masks.

1973, July 10 **Engr.** ***Perf. 13***

563 A129 5fr green, brn & blk .20 .20
564 A129 10fr lilac, brn & blk .25 .20
565 A129 45fr red, brn & blk .70 .20
566 A129 100fr ultra, brn & blk 1.75 .40
Nos. 563-566 (4) 2.90 1.00

1973, July 25 **Engr.** ***Perf. 13***

567 A130 45fr multicolored 1.60 .20

Centenary of the discovery by Dr. Armauer G. Hansen of the Hansen bacillus, the cause of leprosy.

No. 556 Surcharged with New Value, 2 Bars, and Overprinted in Ultramarine: "SECHERESSE/SOLIDARITE AFRICAINE"

1973, Aug. 16 **Photo.** ***Perf. 12½x13***

568 A127 100fr on 5fr multicolored 1.75 .40

African solidarity in drought emergency.

Dancers, South West Africa — A131

WMO Emblem — A132

Designs: Southwest African dances.

1973, Aug. 17 ***Perf. 13***

569 A131 10fr multicolored .20 .20
570 A131 25fr multicolored .55 .20
571 A131 45fr multicolored 1.00 .20
Nos. 569-571 (3) 1.75 .60

1973, Sept. 1 **Engr.** ***Perf. 13***

572 A132 45fr green & ultra 1.60 .20

Cent. of intl. meteorological cooperation.

Garoua Party Headquarters — A133

1973, Sept. 1 **Photo.**

573 A133 40fr multicolored .80 .20

7th anniv. of Cameroun National Union.

African Postal Union Issue, 1973

Common Design Type

1973, Sept. 12 **Engr.**

574 CD137 100fr brt bl, bl & sl grn 1.75 .40

Avocados — A135

1973, Sept. 20

575 A135 10fr shown .65 .20
576 A135 20fr Mangos .70 .20
577 A135 45fr Plums 1.75 .20
578 A135 50fr Custard apple 2.25 .20
Nos. 575-578 (4) 5.35 .80

Kirdi Village A136

45fr, Mabas village. 50fr, Fishing village.

1973, Oct. 25 **Engr.** ***Perf. 13***

579 A136 15fr black, bis & grn .25 .20
580 A136 45fr magenta, brn & org .80 .20
581 A136 50fr green, blk & org 1.00 .20
Nos. 579-581 (3) 2.05 .60

Handshake on Map of Africa — A137

1974, May 15 Engr. *Perf. 12½x13*
582 A137 40fr carmine & multi .55 .20
583 A137 45fr indigo & multi .70 .20

Organization for African Unity, 10th anniv.

Spinning Mill — A138

1974, May 25 Engr. *Perf. 13x12½*
584 A138 45fr multicolored .80 .20

CICAM Industrial Complex.

Carved Panel from Bilinga A139

Cameroun Art (Carvings): 40fr, Detail from Bubinga chair. 45fr, Detail Acajou Ngollon panel.

1974, May 30
585 A139 10fr brt grn & ocher .25 .20
586 A139 40fr red & brown .80 .20
587 A139 45fr blue & rose brn 1.00 .20
Nos. 585-587 (3) 2.05 .60

Zebu — A140

1974, June 1 *Perf. 13½*
588 A140 40fr multicolored 1.40 .20

North Cameroun cattle raising. See No. C210.

Laying Rail Section A141

Designs: 5fr, Map showing line Yaoundé to Ngaoundéré, vert. 40fr, Welding rail joint, vert. 100fr, Train on Djerem River Bridge.

Perf. 12½x13, 13x12½
1974, June 10 Engr.
589 A141 5fr multicolored .55 .20
590 A141 20fr multicolored 1.00 .20
591 A141 40fr multicolored 1.50 .20
592 A141 100fr multicolored 2.75 .40
Nos. 589-592 (4) 5.80 1.00

Opening of Yaoundé-Ngaoundéré railroad line.
For surcharge see No. 596.

No. 466 Surcharged

1974, June 1 Photo. *Perf. 12x12½*
593 A85 40fr on 8fr multi .80 .20

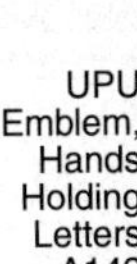

UPU Emblem, Hands Holding Letters A142

1974, Oct. 8 Engr. *Perf. 13*
594 A142 40fr multicolored .90 .20
Nos. 594,C218-C219 (3) 5.90 1.10

Cent. of the UPU.

Presidents and Flags of Cameroun, CAR, Congo, Gabon and Meeting Center — A143

1974, Dec. 8 Photo. *Perf. 13*
595 A143 40fr gold & multi .90 .20

10th anniversary of Central African Customs and Economic Union (Union Douanière et Economique de l'Afrique Centrale, UDEAC). See No. C223.

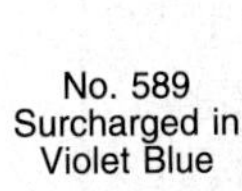

No. 589 Surcharged in Violet Blue

1974, Dec. 10 Engr. *Perf. 12½x13*
596 A141 100fr on 5fr multi 1.75 .45

Virgin of Autun, 15th Century Sculpture A144

Christmas: 45fr, Virgin and Child, by Luis de Morales (c. 1509-1586).

1974, Dec. 20 Photo. *Perf. 13*
597 A144 40fr gold & multi .80 .20
598 A144 45fr gold & multi 1.10 .20

Tropical Plants — A145

1975, Mar. 10 Photo. *Perf. 13*
599 A145 5fr Cockscomb .25 .20
600 A145 40fr Costus spectabilis 1.25 .20
601 A145 45fr Mussaenda erythrophylla 1.75 .20
Nos. 599-601 (3) 3.25 .60

Fishing by Night — A146

1975, Apr. 1 Engr. *Perf. 13*
602 A146 40fr shown 1.40 .20
603 A146 45fr Fishing by day 1.75 .20

Afo Akom Statue and Chief's Stool — A147

Tree Fungus — A148

1975, Apr. 1 Photo.
604 A147 40fr multicolored .55 .20
605 A147 45fr multicolored .70 .20
606 A147 200fr multicolored 2.25 .75
Nos. 604-606 (3) 3.50 1.15

1975, Apr. 14
607 A148 15fr shown *125.00* .20
608 A148 40fr Chrysalis 80.00 .20

Ministry of Posts and Telecommunications — A149

1975, July 21 Engr. *Perf. 13*
609 A149 40fr brn, grn & Prus bl .65 .20
610 A149 45fr Prus bl, brn & grn .90 .20

Presbyterian Church, Elat — A150

Designs: No. 612, Foumban Mosque. 45fr, Catholic Church, Ngaoundere.

1975, Aug. 20 Engr. *Perf. 13*
611 A150 40fr multicolored .45 .20
612 A150 40fr multicolored .45 .20
613 A150 45fr multicolored .65 .20
Nos. 611-613 (3) 1.55 .60

Plowing A151

Design: No. 615, Corn harvest, vert.

Perf. 13x12½, 12½x13
1975, Dec. 15 Photo.
614 A151 40fr deep grn & multi .65 .20
615 A151 40fr deep grn & multi .65 .20

Green revolution.

Zamengoe Satellite Monitoring Station — A152

1976, May 20 Litho. *Perf. 13*
616 A152 40fr shown .45 .20
617 A152 100fr Radar, vert. .90 .40

Porcelain Rose — A153

Design: 50fr, Flower of North Cameroun.

1976, July 20 Litho. *Perf. 12½*
618 A153 40fr multicolored 1.00 .20
619 A153 50fr multicolored 1.40 .20

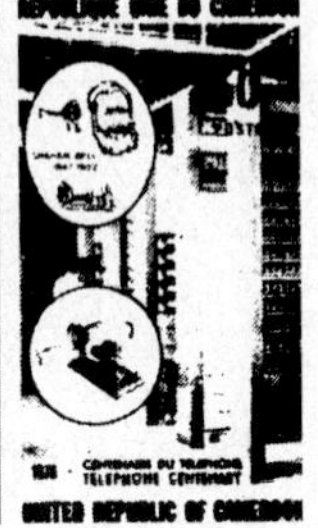

Leopard Dance A154

Telephone Exchange A155

1976, Sept. 15 Litho. *Perf. 12*
620 A154 40fr gray & multi .80 .20
Nos. 620,C233-C234 (3) 2.55 .75

1976, Oct. 5 *Perf. 13*
621 A155 50fr multicolored .80 .20

Centenary of first telephone call by Alexander Graham Bell, Mar. 10, 1876.

Young Men Building House — A156

Design: 45fr, Young women working in field.

1976, Oct. 10 Litho. *Perf. 12*
622 A156 40fr multicolored .35 .20
623 A156 45fr multicolored .55 .20

10th National Youth Day.

Konrad Adenauer (1876-1967), German Chancellor, Cologne Cathedral A157

1976, Oct. 20
624 A157 100fr multicolored .90 .40

Party Headquarters, Douala — A158

No. 626, Party Headquarters, Yaoundé.

1976, Dec. 28 Litho. *Perf. 12*
625 A158 50fr orange & multi .45 .20
626 A158 50fr blue & multi .45 .20

10th anniv. of the Cameroun National Union.

Bamoun Copper Pipe — A159

Ostrich — A160

1977, Feb. 4 Litho. *Perf. 12½*
627 A159 50fr multicolored .70 .20

2nd World Black and African Festival, Lagos, Nigeria, 1/15-2/12. See No. C239.

1977, Mar. 20 Litho. *Perf. 12*
628 A160 30fr shown 2.25 .20
629 A160 50fr Crowned cranes 2.75 .20

Cameroun No. 609 and Switzerland No. 3L1 — A161

1977, June 5 Litho. *Perf. 12*
630 A161 50fr multicolored 1.00 .20
Nos. 630,C252-C253 (3) 4.35 .85

Jufilex Philatelic Exhibition, Bern, Switzerland. See Nos. C252-C253.

Winter Olympics 1976, set of five, 40, 50fr, airmail 140, 200, 350fr, and airmail souv. sheet, 500fr, issued Aug. 10, 1977. Nos. 7701-7706. Value, set $7.50, souvenir sheet $5.

Apollo-Soyuz — A163

Designs: 40fr, Astronaut Thomas P. Stafford, Apollo lifting off. 60fr, Cosmonaut Alexei Leonov, Soyuz lifting off.

1977, Aug. 10 Litho. *Perf. 14x13½*
633 A163 40fr multicolored *.45 .25*
634 A163 60fr multicolored *.70 .50*
Nos. 633-634,C256-C258 (5) *7.55 6.60*

No. 617 Overprinted in French and English in Red: "To the Welfare of the / families of martyrs and / freedom fighters of Palestine."

1977, Aug. 22 Litho. *Perf. 13*
635 A152 100fr multicolored .90 .40

Palestinian fighters and their families.

Chairman Mao and Great Wall A164

1977, Sept. 9 Engr. *Perf. 13*
636 A164 100fr olive & brown 1.60 .40

Mao Tse-tung (1893-1976), Chinese communist leader, first death anniversary.

Nativity, by Albrecht Altdorfer A165

50fr, Madonna of the Grand Duke, by Raphael.

1977, Dec. 15 Litho. *Perf. 12½x12*
637 A165 30fr multicolored .45 .20
638 A165 50fr multicolored 1.00 .20
Nos. 637-638,C264-C265 (4) 7.45 2.40

Christmas 1977.

Gazelle and Rotary Emblem — A166

Pres. Ahidjo, Flag and Map of Cameroun A167

1978, Feb. 11 Litho. *Perf. 12*
639 A166 50fr orange & multi .70 .20

Rotary Club of Yaounde, 20th anniversary.

1978, Apr. 3 Litho. *Perf. 12½*
640 A167 50fr multicolored .90 .20

New flag of Cameroun. See No. C266.

Cardioglossa Escalerae — A168

Design: 60fr, Cardioglossa elegans.

1978, Apr. 5
641 A168 50fr multicolored 1.40 .20
642 A168 60fr multicolored 2.00 .25
Nos. 641-642,C267 (3) 6.15 .85

Jules Verne and "From Earth to Moon" — A169

1978, Oct. 10 Litho. *Perf. 12*
643 A169 250fr multicolored 2.25 1.40

Jules Verne (1828-1905), science fiction writer, birth sesquicentennial. See No. C276.

Hypolimnas Salmacis Drury — A170

Butterflies: 25fr, Euxanthe trajanus ward. 30fr, Euphaedra cyparissa cramer.

1978, Oct. 15
644 A170 20fr multicolored 2.00 .20
645 A170 25fr multicolored 2.25 .20
646 A170 30fr multicolored 3.75 .20
Nos. 644-646 (3) 8.00 .60

Men Planting Seedlings A171

Carved Bamun Drum A172

1978, Oct. 30 *Perf. 12½*
647 A171 10fr multicolored .25 .20
648 A171 15fr multicolored .35 .20

Green barrier against the desert.

1978, Nov. 20 Litho. *Perf. 12½*

60fr, String instrument (Gueguerou), horiz.

649 A172 50fr multicolored .45 .20
650 A172 60fr multicolored .65 .25
Nos. 649-650,C277 (3) 2.20 .85

Pres. Ahidjo, Giscard D'Estaing, Flags of Cameroun and France — A173

1979, Feb. 8 Photo. *Perf. 13*
651 A173 60fr multicolored 1.00 .25

Visit of Pres. Valery Giscard D'Estaing of France to Cameroun.

Human Rights Emblem, Globe, Scroll and African — A174

1979, Feb. 11 Litho. *Perf. 12x12½*
652 A174 5fr multicolored .20 .20

Universal Declaration of Human Rights, 30th anniversary (in 1978). See No. C278. See No. 803.

Boy and Girl Greeting Sun — A175

1979, Aug. 15 Litho. *Perf. 12*
653 A175 50fr multicolored .70 .20

International Year of the Child.

Protected Animals A176

Nos. 655, 658 vert.

1979, Sept. 20 *Perf. 12½*
654 A176 50fr Rhinoceros 1.25 .20
655 A176 60fr Giraffe 1.75 .25
656 A176 60fr Gorilla 1.75 .25
657 A176 100fr Leopard 2.75 .40
658 A176 100fr Elephant 2.75 .40
Nos. 654-658 (5) 10.25 1.50

Eugene Jamot, Map of Cameroun, Tsetse Fly — A177

1979, Nov. 5 Engr. *Perf. 13*
659 A177 50fr multicolored 1.40 .20

Eugene Jamot (1879-1937), discoverer of sleeping sickness cure.

Annunciation, by Fra Filippo Lippi — A178

Paintings; 50fr, Rest During the Flight to Egypt, c. 1620. No. 622, Flight into Egypt, by Jan Joest, No. 663, Nativity, by Joest. 100fr, Nativity, by Botticelli.

1979, Dec. 6 Litho. *Perf. 12½x12*
660 A178 10fr multicolored .20 .20
661 A178 50fr multicolored .45 .25
662 A178 60fr multicolored .60 .30
663 A178 60fr multicolored .60 .30
a. Pair, #662-663 1.25 .65
664 A178 100fr multicolored 1.25 .40
Nos. 660-664 (5) 3.10 1.45

Christmas 1979.

Piper Capense A179

Medicinal Plants: 60fr, Bracken fern.

1979, Dec. 15 Litho. *Perf. 12½*
665 A179 50fr multicolored 1.10 .20
666 A179 60fr multicolored 1.40 .25

Pres. Ahidjo, Cameroun Map, Arms and No. 331 A180

1980, Feb. 12 Litho. *Perf. 12½*
667 A180 50fr multicolored .65 .20

Independence, 20th anniversary.

Congress Building, Bafoussam A181

1980, Feb. 12
668 A181 50fr multicolored .65 .20

Cameroun National Union, 3rd Ordinary Congress, Bafoussam, Feb. 12-17.

Rotary Emblem, Map of Cameroun A182

Rotary Intl., 75th Anniv.: #670, Anniv. emblem.

1980, Mar. 15 Litho. *Perf. 12½*
669 A182 200fr multicolored 2.25 .80
670 A182 200fr multicolored 2.25 .80
a. Souvenir sheet of 2, #669-670 5.00 1.60

Voacanga Medicinal Beans A183

1980, Dec. 3 Litho. *Perf. 12½*
671 A183 50fr shown .90 .20
672 A183 60fr Voacanga tree, vert. 1.00 .25
673 A183 100fr Voacanga flower, vert. 1.60 .40
Nos. 671-673 (3) 3.50 .85

Violet Mellowstone A184

1980, Dec. 5
674 A184 50fr shown .70 .20
675 A184 60fr Patula 1.00 .25
676 A184 100fr Cashmere bouquet 1.60 .40
Nos. 674-676 (3) 3.30 .85

Occupation of Mecca by Mohammed, 1350th Anniversary — A185

1980, Dec. 9
677 A185 50fr multicolored .70 .30

African Slender-snouted Crocodile (Endangered Species) — A186

1980, Dec. 24
678 A186 200fr shown 2.25 .80
679 A186 300fr Buffon's antelope, vert. 3.25 1.20

See Nos. 888-889.

Bororo Girls and Roumsiki Peaks — A187

1980, Dec. 29
680 A187 50fr shown .55 .20
681 A187 60fr Dschang tourist center .55 .25

Banana Tree A188

1981, Feb. 5
682 A188 50fr shown .65 .30
683 A188 60fr Cattle, vert. .80 .40

Girl on Crutches — A189

1981, Feb. 20 Litho. *Perf. 12½*
684 A189 60fr shown .55 .25
685 A189 150fr Boy in motorized wheelchair 1.25 .65

International Year of the Disabled.

Air Terminal, Douala Airport — A190

1981, Apr. 4 Litho. *Perf. 12½*
686 A190 100fr shown .90 .55
687 A190 200fr Boeing 747 2.00 1.10
688 A190 300fr Douala Intl. Airport 2.75 1.60
Nos. 686-688 (3) 5.65 3.25

Cameroun Airlines, 10th anniv.

Pres. Ahidjo Presenting Trophy to Canon Soccer Team — A191

1981, Apr. 20
689 A191 60fr shown .90 .40
690 A191 60fr Union team captain .90 .40

1979 African Soccer Cup champions.

Scaly Anteater A192

Designs: Endangered species.

1981, July 20 Litho. *Perf. 12½*
691 A192 50fr Moutourou 1.00 .20
692 A192 50fr Tortoise 1.00 .20
693 A192 100fr shown 2.10 .40
Nos. 691-693 (3) 4.10 .80

Prince Charles and Lady Diana, St. Paul's Cathedral A193

1981, July 29 Litho. *Perf. 12½*
694 A193 500fr shown 4.50 2.00
695 A193 500fr Couple, royal coach 4.50 2.00
a. Souvenir sheet of 2, #694-695 10.00 4.00

Royal wedding.

Bafoussam-Bamenda Highway — A194

1981, Sept. 10 Litho. *Perf. 12½*
696 A194 50fr multicolored .55 .20

Freighter Cam Iroko (Cameroun Shipping Line) A195

1981, Sept. 25
697 A195 60fr multicolored .70 .40

20th Anniv. of Reunification — A196

1981, Oct. 10 *Perf. 12½x13*
698 A196 50fr multicolored .65 .20

Medicinal Plants — A197

1981, Dec. 31 Litho. *Perf. 12½*

699	A197 60fr Voacanga thouarsii	1.00	.25
700	A197 70fr Cassia alata	1.25	.30

Easter 1982 — A198

Paintings: 100fr, Christ in the Garden of Olives, by Delacroix. 200fr, Descent from the Cross, by Giotto. 250fr, Pieta in the Countryside, by Bellini.

1982, Apr. 10 Litho. *Perf. 13*

701	A198 100fr multicolored	.90	.35
702	A198 200fr multicolored	1.75	.65
703	A198 250fr multicolored	2.25	.90
	Nos. 701-703 (3)	4.90	1.90

PHILEXFRANCE '82 Stamp Exhibition, Paris, June 11-21 — A199

1982, Apr. 25 *Perf. 12*

704	A199 90fr multicolored	1.50	.40

Snakeskin Handbag — A200

1982, Apr. 30 *Perf. 12½*

705	A200 60fr shown	.65	.25
706	A200 70fr Clay water jug	.70	.35

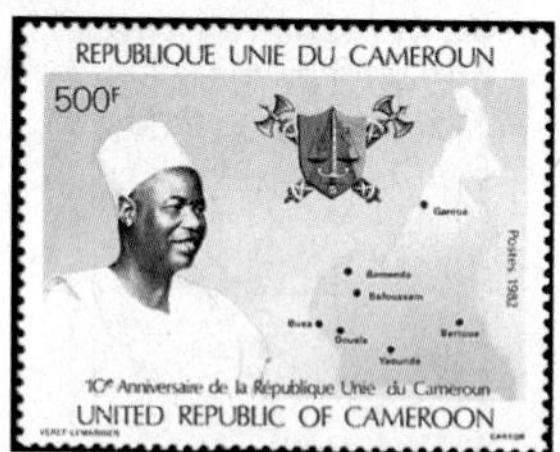

10th Anniv. of Republic — A201

1982, May 20 *Perf. 13*

707	A201 500fr multicolored	5.00	2.00

Town Hall, Douala — A202

1982, June 15 Litho. *Perf. 12½*

708	A202 40fr shown	.45	.20
709	A202 60fr Yaounde	.65	.25

See Nos. 730-731, 757-758, 790-791, 867.

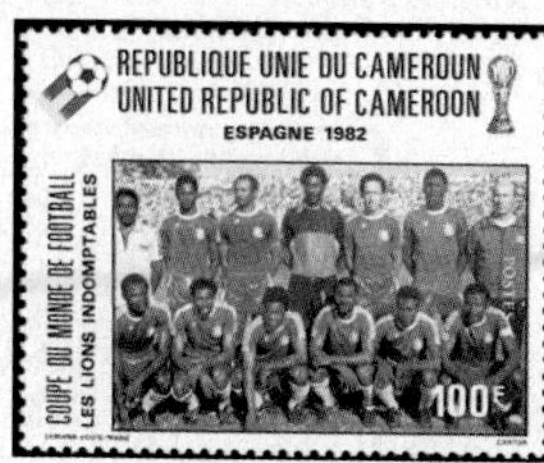

1982 World Cup — A203

1982, July 10 *Perf. 13*

710	A203 100fr Natl. team	1.40	.40
711	A203 200fr Semi-finalists	2.75	.75
712	A203 300fr Players, vert.	4.50	1.25
713	A203 400fr Natl. team 2nd lineup	5.75	1.60
a.	Souvenir sheet of 2, #713	14.50	3.50
	Nos. 710-713 (4)	14.40	4.00

Partridge — A204

1982 *Perf. 12½x13*

714	A204 10fr shown	1.50	.20
715	A204 15fr Turtle dove	1.75	.20
716	A204 20fr Swallow	2.50	.20
717	A204 200fr Bongo antelope	2.25	.80
718	A204 300fr Black colobus	3.50	1.25
	Nos. 714-718 (5)	11.50	2.65

Issued: 200fr, 300fr, July 20; others Aug. 10.

See No. 804.

Scouting Year A205

1982, Sept. 30 Litho. *Perf. 13x12½*

719	A205 200fr Campfire	2.25	.80
720	A205 400fr Baden-Powell	4.00	1.60

25th Anniv. of the Presbyterian Church in Cameroun — A206

1982, Oct. 30 *Perf. 13x12½, 12½x13*

721	A206 45fr Buea Chapel	.55	.20
722	A206 60fr Nyasoso Chapel, vert.	.65	.20

ITU Plenipotentiaries Conference, Nairobi, Sept. — A207

1982, Oct. 5 Litho. *Perf. 12½x13*

723	A207 70fr multicolored	.70	.25

Italy's Victory in 1982 World Cup — A208

1982, Nov. *Perf. 13*

724	A208 500fr multicolored	4.75	2.00
725	A208 1000fr multicolored	9.00	4.00

30th Anniv. of Customs Cooperation Council — A209

1983, Jan. 10 *Perf. 12½x13*

726	A209 250fr Emblem	2.25	.80
727	A209 250fr Headquarters, Brussels	2.25	.80

2nd Yaoundé Medical Conference — A210

1983, Jan. 23 Litho. *Perf. 13*

728	A210 60fr grn & multi	.70	.20
729	A210 70fr brn & multi	.90	.25

City Hall Type of 1982

1983, Feb. 25 Litho. *Perf. 12½*

730	A202 60fr Bafoussam	.55	.25
731	A202 70fr Garoua	.70	.30

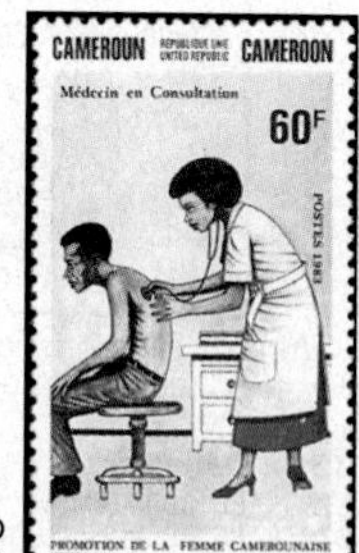

Homage to Women — A211

1983, Apr. 25 Litho. *Perf. 12½*

733	A211 60fr Nurse	.70	.20
734	A211 70fr Lawyer	.70	.25

11th Anniv. of Independence — A212

Flag and Pres. Paul Biya.

1983, May 18 Litho. *Perf. 13*

735	A212 60fr dk grn & multi	.55	.25
736	A212 70fr dk bl & multi	.70	.30

25th Anniv. of Intl. Maritime Org. A213

1983, May 23 *Perf. 13x12½*

737	A213 500fr multicolored	4.50	1.50

Eagle — A214

1983, June 15 Litho. *Perf. 12½x13*

738	A214 25fr shown	1.50	.20
739	A214 30fr Sparrowhawk	2.25	.20
740	A214 50fr Purple heron	4.25	.20
	Nos. 738-740 (3)	8.00	.60

See Nos. 798-800, 873, 882, 886.

A215

A216

1983, July 25 Litho. *Perf. 12*

741	A215 60fr Pearl mask, by Wery-Nwen-Nto, 1899	.70	.25
742	A215 70fr Basket with lid	.90	.30

1983, Aug. 20 Litho. *Perf. 12*

743	A216 90fr Mobile Post Office, horiz	.90	.20
744	A216 150fr Telegraph Operator	1.40	.35
745	A216 250fr Tom-tom	2.75	.55
	Nos. 743-745 (3)	5.05	1.10

World Communications Year.

Endangered Species — A217

1983, Sept. 22 *Perf. 12*

746 A217 200fr Civet Cat 2.25 .40
747 A217 200fr Gorilla, vert 2.25 .40
748 A217 350fr Cobaya, vert 4.25 .80
Nos. 746-748 (3) 8.75 1.60

See No. 887.

Lake Tizon — A218

1983, Nov. 25 **Litho.** *Perf. 13*

749 A218 60fr shown .55 .20
750 A218 70fr Mt. Cameroon .70 .20

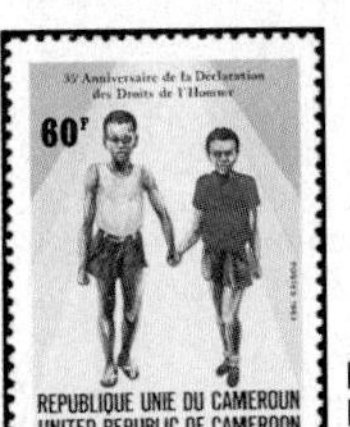

Human Rights Declaration, 35th Anniv — A219

1983, Dec. 20 **Litho.** *Perf. 12½x13*

751 A219 60fr multicolored .55 .20
752 A219 70fr multicolored .70 .20

Christmas 1983 — A220

60fr, Christmas tree. 200fr, Stained glass window, Yaoundé Cathedral. #755, Rest during Flight into Egypt, by Philipp Otto Runge. #756, Angel of the Annunciation. 60fr, 200fr, #756 vert.

1983, Dec. 20 **Litho.** *Perf. 12½*

753 A220 60fr multicolored .45 .20
754 A220 200fr multicolored 1.75 .50
755 A220 500fr multicolored 4.50 1.25
756 A220 500fr multicolored 4.50 1.25
a. Souvenir sheet of 3, #754-756 11.50 3.25
Nos. 753-756 (4) 11.20 3.20

City Hall Type of 1982

1984, Apr. 20 **Litho.** *Perf. 12½*

757 A202 60fr Bamenda .55 .20
758 A202 70fr Mbalmayo .70 .25

Catholic Church, Zoetele — A221

1984, July 25 **Litho.** *Perf. 13*

759 A221 60fr shown .55 .25
760 A221 70fr Protestant Church, Yaounde .70 .25

Endangered Species — A222

1984, Aug. 15

761 A222 250fr Wild pig 3.25 .65
762 A222 250fr Deer 3.25 .65

1984, Oct. 10 **Litho.** *Perf. 13½*

763 A222 60fr Nightingale .20 .20
764 A222 60fr Vultures .20 .20

See No. 883.

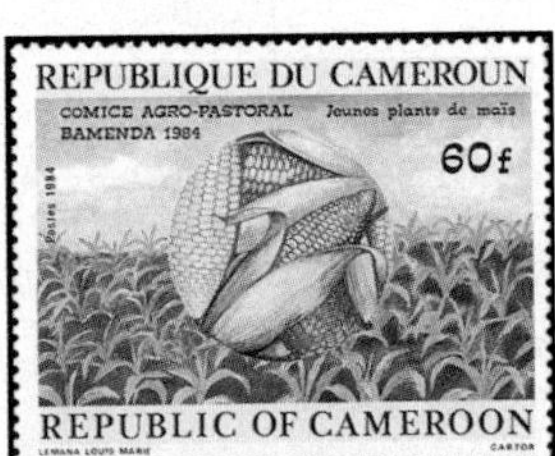

Bamenda Farming Fair — A223

1984, Dec. 10 **Litho.** *Perf. 13*

765 A223 60fr Corn .55 .20
766 A223 70fr Cattle .70 .25
767 A223 300fr Potatoes 2.75 .90
Nos. 765-767 (3) 4.00 1.35

International Civil Aviation Organization, 40th Anniv. — A224

1984, Dec. 20 **Litho.** *Perf. 12½*

768 A224 200fr Icarus 1.75 .60
769 A224 200fr ICAO emblem, vert. 1.75 .60
770 A224 300fr Boeing 747 2.75 .90
771 A224 300fr Solar Princess painting 3.25 .90
Nos. 768-771 (4) 9.50 3.00

Olymphilex '85, Lausanne — A225

Wmk. 385

1985, Apr. 5 **Photo.** *Perf. 13*

772 A225 150fr Wrestlers, exhibition emblem 1.25 .40

Domestic Musical Instruments A226

1985, Apr. 23 *Perf. 13½*

773 A226 60fr Balafons (xylophone) .65 .20
774 A226 70fr Guitar .80 .20
775 A226 100fr Flute 1.10 .30
Nos. 773-775 (3) 2.55 .70

INTELSAT Org., 20th Anniv. — A227

1985, May 8 *Perf. 13*

776 A227 125fr Intelsat V 1.40 .35
777 A227 200fr Intelcam, Yaounde 1.75 .60

New York Headquarters — A228

1985, May 30

778 A228 250fr multicolored 2.25 1.10
779 A228 500fr multicolored 4.50 2.25

UN, 40th anniv.

Pres. Mitterand, Biya — A229

1985, June 20

780 A229 60fr multicolored 1.00 .20
781 A229 70fr multicolored 1.25 .25

Visit of Pres. Mitterand of France.

UNICEF A230

REPUBLIQUE DU CAMEROUN
LA SURVIE DE L'ENFANT
300F
REPUBLIC OF CAMEROON

UN Infant Survival Campaign A231

1985, July 15

782 A230 60fr multicolored .55 .20
783 A231 300fr multicolored 2.75 1.00

Visit of Pope John Paul II, Aug. 10-14 — A232

1985, Aug. 9 *Perf. 13x12½*

784 A232 60fr Pope, papal arms 1.10 .20
785 A232 70fr Pope, crosier 1.40 .25

Size: 55x38mm

786 A232 200fr Pres. Biya, John Paul II 4.00 .70
a. Souv. sheet of 3, #784-786 7.25 4.50
Nos. 784-786 (3) 6.50 1.15

Landscapes — A233

1985, July 25 **Litho.** *Perf. 12½*

787 A233 60fr Lake Barumbi, Kumba .70 .20
788 A233 70fr Bonando Pygmy Village, Doume .70 .20
789 A233 150fr Cameroun River 1.40 .40
Nos. 787-789 (3) 2.80 .80

City Hall Type of 1982

1985, July 30

790 A202 60fr Ngaoundere .55 .20
791 A202 60fr D'Ebolowa .55 .20

Wildlife — A234

Wood Sculptures A235

1985, Aug. 20 *Perf. 13½*

792 A234 125fr Porcupine 1.40 .40
793 A234 200fr Squirrel 2.10 .60
794 A234 350fr Hedgehog 3.50 1.10
Nos. 792-794 (3) 7.00 2.10

1985, Sept. 15

795 A235 60fr Mask .55 .20
796 A235 70fr Mask, diff. .70 .25
797 A235 100fr Wood bas-relief, horiz. 1.00 .30
Nos. 795-797 (3) 2.25 .75

Bird Type of 1983
Inscribed Republic of Cameroon

1985, Nov. 10

798 A214 140fr Toucans 2.10 .50
799 A214 150fr Rooster 2.10 .55
800 A214 200fr Red-throated bee-eater 3.00 .70
Nos. 798-800 (3) 7.20 1.75

See No. 873. For surcharge see No. 871.

American Peace Corps in Cameroun, 25th Anniv. — A237

1986, Jan. 1 Litho. *Perf. 12½*

801	A237	70fr multicolored	.70	.25
802	A237	100fr multicolored	1.00	.30

Stamps of 1979-1982 Redrawn

1986, Mar. *Perf. 13, 13½*

803	A174	5fr multicolored	.20	.20
804	A204	10fr multicolored	.20	.20

Nos. 803-804 inscribed "Republic of Cameroon" instead of "United Republic of Cameroon."

Easter — A238

Insects — A239

Paintings: 210fr, Head of the Virgin, by Pierre-Paul Prud'Hon (1758-1823). 350fr, The Stoning of St. Steven, by Van Scorel (1495-1562).

1986, Apr. 15 *Perf. 13½*

805	A238	210fr multicolored	1.75	.60
806	A238	350fr multicolored	2.75	1.00

1986, Apr. 20

807	A239	70fr Honeybee	1.50	.40
808	A239	70fr Dragonfly	1.50	.40
809	A239	100fr Grasshopper	2.25	.55
		Nos. 807-809 (3)	5.25	1.35

Nos. 808-809 horiz.

Flags, Conference Center — A240

1986, Apr. 25 Litho. *Perf. 13*

810	A240	100fr Map, vert.	1.00	.30
811	A240	175fr shown	1.75	.60

Conference of Ministers of the Economic Commission for Africa, Apr. 9-29.

Statues — A241

1986, July 5 Litho. *Perf. 13½*

812	A241	70fr Bronze earth mother	.65	.25
813	A241	100fr Wood funerary figure	.70	.30
814	A241	130fr Wood equestrian figure	1.25	.40
		Nos. 812-814 (3)	2.60	.95

Queen Elizabeth II, 60th Birthday — A242

1986, July 15 Litho. *Perf. 13*

815	A242	100fr Elizabeth	1.00	.40
816	A242	175fr Elizabeth, Pres. Biya	1.40	.60
817	A242	210fr Elizabeth, diff.	2.00	.75
		Nos. 815-817 (3)	4.40	1.75

Natl. Democratic Party, 1st Anniv. — A243

1986, July 25 *Perf. 12½*

818	A243	70fr Party headquarters, Bamenda	.65	.25
819	A243	70fr Pres. Biya, vert.	.65	.25
820	A243	100fr Presidential address, vert.	.90	.35
		Nos. 818-820 (3)	2.20	.85

Kwem Mask Dancers of the Northeast — A244

1986, Aug. 1 *Perf. 13½*

821	A244	100fr multicolored	1.00	.35
822	A244	130fr multicolored	1.25	.45

Endangered Species — A245

1986, Aug. 20

823	300fr Varanus niloticus	3.00	1.00
824	300fr Panthera pardus	3.00	1.00

For surcharge see No. 872.

A246

A247

Intl. Peace Year: 175fr, 200fr, Desmond Tutu, South Africa, Nobel Peace Prize winner. 250fr, UN and IPY emblems.

1986, Sept. 7 Litho. *Perf. 13½*

825	A246	175fr multicolored	1.40	1.10
826	A246	200fr multicolored	1.75	1.25
827	A246	250fr multicolored	2.25	1.50
		Nos. 825-827 (3)	5.40	3.85

1986, Oct. 30 Litho. *Perf. 13½*

828	A247	70fr multicolored	.65	.25

Natl. Fed. of Associations for the Handicapped.

A248

A249

1986, Nov. 9

829	A248	70fr Family under umbrella	.65	.25
830	A248	100fr Child immunization	.90	.35

African Vaccination Year.

1986, Dec. 20 Litho. *Perf. 13½*

831	A249	70fr Afforestation map	.65	.25
832	A249	100fr Hands, seedling	.90	.35

Arbor Day.

Agricultural Development — A250

1986, Dec. 24

833	A250	70fr ONCPB seminar	.65	.40
834	A250	70fr Coconut farming, Dibombari	.65	.40
835	A250	200fr Pineapple farm	1.75	1.10
		Nos. 833-835 (3)	3.05	1.90

Insects Destructive to Agriculture A251

1987, Sept. 25 Litho. *Perf. 13½*

836	A251	70fr Antestiopsis lineaticollis intricata	1.25	.50
837	A251	100fr Distantiella theobroma	1.75	.70

4th African Games, Nairobi — A252

1987, Oct. 1 *Perf. 12½*

838	A252	100fr Shot put	.90	.70
839	A252	140fr Pole vault	1.25	1.00

Maroua Agricultural Show — A253

1988, Jan. 6

840	A253	70fr Millet field	.65	.50
841	A253	100fr Cotton	.90	.70
842	A253	150fr Cattle	1.25	1.10
		Nos. 840-842 (3)	2.80	2.30

World Wildlife Fund — A254

Baboons, *Papio leucophaeus.*

1988, Apr. 25 Litho. *Perf. 13*

843	A254	30fr Adult	1.75	1.75
844	A254	40fr Adult grooming young	1.75	1.75
845	A254	70fr Baboon on branch	2.75	2.75
846	A254	100fr Adult carrying young	4.50	2.00
		Nos. 843-846 (4)	10.75	8.25

Interparliamentary Union, Cent. — A255

1989 Litho. *Perf. 13½*

847	A255	50fr Natl. Assembly	.45	.30

World Cup Soccer Championships, Italy — A256

1990, Oct. 27 Litho. *Perf. 11½*
Granite Paper

848 A256 200fr shown 1.40 1.00
849 A256 250fr Players, diff. 1.75 1.25
850 A256 250fr Goalkeeper, flags 1.75 1.25
851 A256 300fr Team 2.25 1.50
a. Souv. sheet of 4, #848-851 9.00 6.50
Nos. 848-851 (4) 7.15 5.00

Roger Milla, World Cup Soccer Player A257

1990, July 4 Litho. *Perf. 11½*
Granite Paper

852 A257 500fr multicolored 4.50 3.50
a. Souv. sheet of 1 9.00 6.00

Agriculture A258

70fr, Treating cacao plants. 100fr, Sheep.

1990, Dec. 1 Litho. *Perf. 13½*

853 A258 70fr multicolored .90 .55
854 A258 100fr multicolored 1.25 .80
a. Sheet of 2, #853-854, perf. 12½ 5.25 3.50

For surcharges see Nos. 894-895.

UN Development Program, 40th Anniv. — A259

1990, Dec. 31 Litho. *Perf. 13½*

855 A259 50fr multicolored .45 .40

Intl. Literacy Year A260

1990, Dec. 31

856 A260 200fr bl, blk, & lt bl 1.75 .75

Independence, 30th Anniv. — A261

1991, Jan. 1 *Perf. 13*

857 A261 150fr shown 1.60 1.25
858 A261 1000fr Flag, Palace, #336 9.00 8.00
a. Souv. sheet. of 2, #857-858 11.50 9.25

Fight Against AIDS A262

1991, Jan. 15

859 A262 15fr Hearts, map, vert. .20 .20
860 A262 25fr shown .20 .20

See Nos. 884-885.

Birds A263

Designs: Nos. 861, 864, Pie grieche, vert. Nos. 862, 863, Picathartes chauve.

1991, May 3 Litho. *Perf. 13½*

861 A263 70fr grn & multi .55 .35
862 A263 70fr bl & multi .55 .40
863 A263 300fr blk & multi 2.75 2.00
864 A263 350fr blk & multi 3.00 2.25
a. Souv. sheet of 2, #863-864 6.75 5.00
Nos. 861-864 (4) 6.85 5.00

Wild Animals A264

1991, May 8 *Perf. 13½*

865 A264 125fr Elephant 1.25 1.00
866 A264 250fr Water buffalo 2.50 2.00
a. Souvenir sheet of 2, #865-866, perf. 12½ 5.50 3.00

City Hall Type of 1982 Redrawn

1991 *Perf. 13*

867 A202 40fr multicolored .45 .20

No. 867 inscribed "Republic of Cameroon" instead of "United Republic of Cameroon."

Cameroun Catholic Church, Cent. (in 1990) A265

1991, Dec. 8 Litho. *Perf. 13½*

868 A265 125fr Mvolye church 1.25 .75
869 A265 250fr Akono church 2.25 1.75
a. Souvenir sheet of 2, #868-869 perf. 12½x13 3.50 2.75

Intl. Savings Banks Institute, 7th Meeting of the African Group A266

1991, Dec. 9

870 A266 250fr multicolored 2.25 1.60
a. Souv. sheet of 1, perf. 12½x13 2.40 1.60

Nos. 799 & 824 Surcharged

20 F

1992 *Perf. 13½*

871 A214 20fr on 150fr #799 1.75 .20
872 A245 70fr on 300fr #824 5.75 .55

Bird Type of 1983

1992 Litho. *Perf. 13½*

873 A214 125fr like #800 1.25 .95

Dated 1985.

Cameroun Soccer League A267

125fr, Mbappe Mbappe Samuel (1936-85), soccer player, vert. 250fr, Linafoote League emblem, vert. 400fr, Linafoote emblem, diff. 500fr, Stadium.

1992, Aug. *Perf. 11½*

874 A267 125fr multicolored 1.25 .75
875 A267 250fr multicolored 2.25 1.75
876 A267 400fr multicolored 3.25 2.75
877 A267 500fr multicolored 5.25 3.50
Nos. 874-877 (4) 12.00 8.75

See Nos. 896-896B.

Discovery of America, 500th Anniv. A268

Columbus and: 125fr, Fleet of ships. 250fr, Landing in New World. 400fr, Meeting with natives. 500fr, Map, ships.

1992, Aug.

878 A268 125fr multicolored 1.40 .75
879 A268 250fr multicolored 2.10 1.75
880 A268 400fr multicolored 3.00 2.75
881 A268 500fr multicolored 5.00 3.50
Nos. 878-881 (4) 11.50 8.75

Types of 1983-84 Redrawn and Inscribed "Republic of Cameroon"

1992 Litho. *Perf. 13½*

882 A214 200fr like #739 1.75 1.40
a. Booklet pane of 5
Complete booklet, #882a
883 A222 350fr like #763 2.75 2.50

AIDS Type of 1991

1993 Litho. *Perf. 13½*

884 A262 100fr like #859 .90 .70
885 A262 175fr like #860 1.50 1.25

Types of 1983 Redrawn and Inscribed "Republic of Cameroon"

886 A214 370fr like #738 2.75 2.50

Perf. 13

887 A217 410fr like #746 3.50 2.90

Wild Animal Type of 1980 Inscribed "Republique du Cameroun"

1993 Litho. *Serpentine Die Cut 9½*
Booklet Stamps
Self-Adhesive

888 A186 125fr Crocodile 1.00 .65
a. Booklet pane of 4 4.50
889 A186 250fr Buffon's antelope, vert. 2.10 1.25
a. Booklet pane of 4 9.00

By their nature, Nos. 888a, 889a are complete booklets. The peelable backing serves as a booklet cover.

1994 World Cup Soccer Championships, US — A270

Designs: 125fr, Pres. Paul Biya holding soccer ball, lion. 250fr, Logo, lion, player, map. 450fr, Players, globe, World Cup, flag. 500fr, US eagle, Cameroun lion, soccer ball.

1994, Mar. 28 Litho. *Perf. 13*

890 A270 125fr multicolored .55 .40
891 A270 250fr multicolored 1.00 .75
892 A270 450fr multicolored 2.00 1.50
893 A270 500fr multicolored 2.25 1.75
a. Min. sheet of 4, #890-893 10.50 7.00
Nos. 890-893 (4) 5.80 4.40

Nos. 853-854 Surcharged in Gold and Black

125F

1993 Litho. *Perf. 13½*

894 A258 125fr on 70fr #853
895 A258 125fr on 100fr #854

Cameroun Soccer League Type of 1992

1992-93 Litho. *Perf. 11½*

896 A267 10fr like #876
896A A267 25fr like #875
896B A267 50fr like #874 —

Nos. 896-896A dated 1993.
Issued: 50fr, 8/1/92; others, 1993.

Psittacus Erithacus — A271

1995 Litho. *Perf. 11½*
Granite Paper

897 A271 125fr multicolored .80 .50

Visit of Pope John Paul II A272

1995, Sept. 14 *Perf. 12½*

898 A272 55fr shown .25 .20
a. Souvenir sheet of 1 — —
899 A272 125fr Pope, open text, cross .65 .50
a. Souvenir sheet of 1 — —

UN, 50th Anniv. A273

1995, Oct. 24 *Perf. 11½*

900 A273 200fr shown .80 .60
901 A273 250fr "50," people 1.00 .80

Conf. of Heads of State & Govt., Yaounde A274

Perf. 12½, 14¾x14 (200fr, 250fr)

1996-97 Litho.

902 A274 125fr blue & multi —
902A A274 200fr lt grn & multi ('97) —
902B A274 250fr yel & multi ('97) —
903 A274 410fr pink & multi, vert. —

World Records Set at 1996 Summer Olympic Games, Atlanta
A275

1996 *Perf. 11½*

904 A275 125fr Baily, M. Johnson .55 .45
905 A275 250fr Harrison, Galfione, Perec, vert. 1.00 .90

Universal Declaration of Human Rights, 50th Anniv. — A279

1998 **Litho.** *Perf. 14x14¾*

918 A279 370fr multi — —

Additional stamps may have been released in this set. The editors would like to examine any examples.

1998 World Cup Soccer Championships, France — A280

Design: 125fr, Flag of Cameroun, World Cup trophy, vert.

1998 **Litho.** *Perf. 13*

922 A280 125fr multi
923 A280 250fr multicolored

The editors suspect that additional stamps were released with this stamp, and would like to examine them.

Shrike
A281

1998 **Litho.** *Perf. 13x13¾*

926 A281 125fr multicolored

The editors suspect that additional stamps were released with this stamp, and would like to examine them.

Economic and Monetary Community of Central Africa Week — A281a

1999 ? **Litho.** *Perf. 14½*

928 A281a 225fr multi — —

No. 928 is dated 1999 but the earliest known use of the stamp is 2002. The editors suspect that additional stamps may have been issued in this set and would like to examine any examples. Numbers may change.

Flora & Fauna — A282

1998? **Litho.** *Perf. 14x14½*

929 A282 100fr Pineapple
930 A282 125fr Pineapple
930A A282 150fr Coffee beans
930B A282 175fr Crowned crane
931 A282 200fr Baboon
932 A282 250fr Coffee beans
934 A282 410fr Crowned crane

The editors suspect that additional stamps may have been issued with this set and would like to examine any examples. Nos. 930-931 are dated 1998, but their earliest known use was in 2000.

Peace, Work, Country
A283

2000 **Litho.** *Perf. 11¾*

935 A283 125fr multi — —

The editors suspect that additional stamps may have been issued in this set and would like to examine any examples.

Map and Scenes
A284

Airplane and Wildlife
A285

2000 **Litho.** *Perf. 11¾*

936 A284 200fr multi — —
937 A285 250fr multi — —

The editors suspect that additional stamps may have been issued in this set and would like to examine any examples.

Palais des Congrés, Yaounde
A286

Perf. 11¾x11½

2001, Mar. 26 **Litho.**

938 A286 125fr multi — —

Cameroun - People's Republic of China cooperation, 30th anniv.

Campaign Against AIDS — A287

Design: 125fr, Woman vaccinating child, Chantal Biya Foundation emblem. 250fr, Chantal Biya Foundation emblem, globe, ribbon, woman with fetus.

2001 **Litho.** *Perf. 13¼x13*

939 A287 125fr multi — —
941 A287 250fr multi — —

The editors suspect that additional stamps may have been issued in this set and would like to examine any examples.

2002 World Cup Soccer Championships, Japan and Korea — A287a

2002, June 20 **Litho.** *Perf. 13¾*

943 A287a 125fr multi — —

Two additional stamps exist in this set. The editors would like to examine any examples.

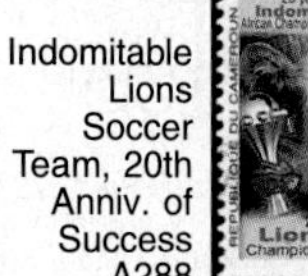

Indomitable Lions Soccer Team, 20th Anniv. of Success
A288

2002 **Litho.** *Perf. 13x13¼*

944 A288 250fr multi — —

The editors suspect that additional stamps may have been issued in this set and would like to examine any examples.

SEMI-POSTAL STAMPS

Curie Issue
Common Design Type

1938 **Unwmk.** *Perf. 13*

B1 CD80 1.75fr + 50c brt ultra 8.00 8.00

French Revolution Issue
Common Design Type

Photogravure; Name and Value Typographed in Black

1939

B2	CD83	45c + 25c green	8.25	8.25
B3	CD83	70c + 30c brown	8.25	8.25
B4	CD83	90c + 35c red org	8.25	8.25
B5	CD83	1.25fr + 1fr rose pink	8.25	8.25
B6	CD83	2.25fr + 2fr blue	10.00	10.00
		Nos. B2-B6 (5)	43.00	43.00

Stamps of 1925-33 Surcharged in Black

1940 *Perf. 14x13½*

B7	A7	1.25fr + 2fr gray & dp bl	12.00	11.00
B8	A7	1.75fr + 3fr brn & org	12.00	11.00
B9	A7	2fr + 5fr dl grn & brn org	12.00	11.00
		Nos. B7-B9 (3)	36.00	33.00

The surtax was used for war relief work.

Regular Stamps of 1939 Surcharged in Black

1940 *Perf. 13*

B10	A20	25c + 5fr blk brn	85.00	70.00
B11	A20	45c + 5fr slate grn	85.00	70.00
B12	A20	60c + 5fr peacock bl	92.50	75.00
B13	A20	70c + 5fr plum	92.50	75.00
		Nos. B10-B13 (4)	355.00	290.00

The surtax was used to purchase Spitfire planes for the Free French army.

Common Design Type and

Military Doctor
SP2

Cameroun Militiaman — SP4

1941 **Photo.** *Perf. 13½*

B13A	SP2	1fr + 1fr red	1.10
B13B	CD86	1.50fr + 3fr maroon	1.10
B13C	SP4	2.50fr + 1fr dk bl	1.10
		Nos. B13A-B13C (3)	3.30

Nos. B13A-B13C were issued by the Vichy government in France, but were not placed on sale in Cameroun.

New York World's Fair Stamps, 1939 Surcharged in Black

1941 *Perf. 12½x12*

B14	CD82	1.25fr + 10fr car lake	77.50	67.50
B15	CD82	2.25fr + 10fr ultra	77.50	67.50

New York World's Fair Stamps, 1939, Surcharged in Black or Blue

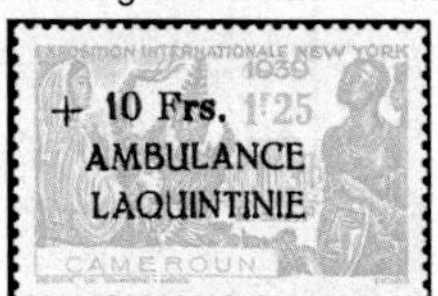

1941

B16	CD82	1.25fr + 10fr car lake (Bl)	17.50	16.00
B17	CD82	2.25fr + 10fr ultra (Bk)	17.50	16.00

The surtax was used to purchase ambulances for the Free French army.

Regular Stamps of 1933-39 Surcharged in Black

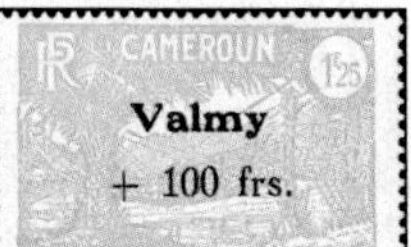

1943 *Perf. 14x13½, 13, 12½x12*

B21	A7	1.25fr + 100 gray & dp bl	8.50	8.50
B22	A21	1.25fr + 100fr car rose	8.50	8.50
B23	CD82	1.25fr + 100fr car lake	8.50	8.50
B24	A21	1.50fr + 100fr choc	8.50	8.50
B25	CD82	2.25fr + 100fr ultra	8.50	8.50
		Nos. B21-B25 (5)	42.50	42.50

Nos. 281A-281B Surcharged in Black or Red

1944 Engr. *Perf. 12½x12*

B25A	50c + 1.50fr on 2.50fr deep blue (R)	.60
B25B	+ 2.50fr on 1fr green	.60

Colonial Development Fund.

Nos. B25A-B25B were issued by the Vichy government in France, but were not placed on sale in Cameroun.

Red Cross Issue

Common Design Type

1944 Photo. *Perf. 14½x14*

B28 CD90 5fr + 20fr rose 1.40 1.10

The surtax was for the French Red Cross and national relief.

Catalogue values for unused stamps in this section, from this point to the end of the section, are for Never Hinged items.

Tropical Medicine Issue

Common Design Type

1950 Engr. *Perf. 13*

B29 CD100 10fr + 2fr dk bl grn & dk grn 3.25 3.25

The surtax was for charitable work.

Independent State

Map and Flag — SP7

Unwmk.

1961, Mar. 25 Engr. *Perf. 13*

B30 SP7	20fr + 5fr grn, car & yel	1.00	1.00
B31 SP7	25fr + 10fr multi	1.25	1.25
B32 SP7	30fr + 15fr car, yel & grn	1.75	1.75
	Nos. B30-B32 (3)	4.00	4.00

The surtax was for the Red Cross.

Federal Republic

Map of Cameroun, Lions Emblem and Physician Helping Leper SP8

1962, Jan. 28

B33 SP8	20fr + 5fr multi	.70	.40
B34 SP8	25fr + 10fr multi	.90	.50
B35 SP8	50fr + 15fr multi	1.75	.85
	Nos. B33-B35 (3)	3.35	1.75

Issued for leprosy relief work.

Anti-Malaria Issue

Common Design Type

1962, Apr. 7 *Perf. 12½x12*

B36 CD108 25fr + 5fr rose lilac 1.00 .45

WHO drive to eradicate malaria.

Freedom from Hunger Issue

Common Design Type

1963, Mar. 21 Engr. *Perf. 13*

B37 CD112	18fr + 5fr multi	1.00	.35
B38 CD112	25fr + 5fr multi	1.25	.40

Antelopes — SP9

Designs: 125fr+10fr, Ourebia ourebi. 250fr+20fr, Kobus defassa.

1991, Apr. 30 Litho. *Perf. 13½x13*

B39 SP9	125fr + 10fr multi	1.60	1.10
B40 SP9	250fr + 20fr multi	2.25	2.25
a.	Souvenir sheet of 2, #B39-B40, perf. 12½	5.25	3.50

AIR POST STAMPS

Common Design Type

1942 Unwmk. Photo. *Perf. 14½x14*

C1	CD87	1fr dk orange	.25	.25
C2	CD87	1.50fr brt red	.25	.25
C3	CD87	5fr brown red	.40	.40
C4	CD87	10fr black	.50	.50
C5	CD87	25fr ultra	.80	.80
C6	CD87	50fr dk green	1.00	1.00
C7	CD87	100fr plum	1.25	1.25
		Nos. C1-C7 (7)	4.45	4.45

Types AP9 and AP10 without "RF" and

Plane Over Coast AP3

1943-44 Photo. *Perf. 13, 13½*

C7A	AP9	25c brown red	.20
C7B	AP9	50c green	.20
C7C	AP10	1fr brt violet	.25
C7D	AP10	5fr red brown	.35
C7E	AP10	10fr black	.45
C7F	AP10	12fr orange	.50
C7G	AP10	20fr crimson	.70
C7H	AP10	50fr blue	.80
C7I	AP3	100fr lilac brown	.80
		Nos. C7A-C7I (9)	4.25

Nos. C7A to C7I were issued by the Vichy Government in France, but were not placed on sale in Cameroun.

For Types AP9 and AP10 inscribed RF, see Nos. C15-C24.

Catalogue values for unused stamps in this section are for Never Hinged items.

Victory Issue

Common Design Type

1946, May 8 Engr. *Perf. 12½*

C8 CD92 8fr dk violet brn .55 .55

European victory of the Allied Nations in WWII.

Chad to Rhine Issue

Common Design Types

1946, June 6

C9	CD93	5fr dk blue grn	.75	.75
C10	CD94	10fr dk rose vio	.95	.95
C11	CD95	15fr red	1.25	1.25
C12	CD96	20fr brt blue	1.25	1.25
C13	CD97	25fr orange red	1.25	1.25
C14	CD98	50fr gray	1.60	1.60
		Nos. C9-C14 (6)	7.05	7.05

Plane and Map — AP9

Seaplane Alighting AP10

Plane and Freighters AP11

1946 Photo. *Perf. 13, 13½*

C15	AP9	25c brown red	.20	.20
C16	AP9	50c green	.20	.20
C17	AP9	1fr brt violet	.25	.25
C18	AP10	2fr olive grn	.40	.40
C19	AP10	3fr chocolate	.40	.40
C20	AP10	4fr deep ultra	.40	.40
C21	AP10	6fr blue grn	.40	.40
C22	AP10	7fr brt violet	.55	.55
C23	AP10	12fr orange	3.00	3.00
C24	AP10	20fr crimson	1.00	1.00
C25	AP11	50fr dk ultra	1.50	1.50
		Nos. C15-C25 (11)	8.30	8.30

Nos. C15 to C25 were issued in 1941 in France by the Vichy Government, but were not sold in Cameroun until 1946.

Birds over Mountains — AP12

Cavalry and Plane — AP13

Warrior, Dance Mask and Nose of Plane — AP14

Perf. 12½

1947, Feb. 10 Unwmk. Engr.

C26	AP12	50fr dk green	2.10	.70
C27	AP13	100fr brn red	3.25	.70
C28	AP14	200fr black	5.50	1.40
		Nos. C26-C28 (3)	10.85	2.80

UPU Issue

Common Design Type

1949, July *Perf. 13*

C29 CD99 25fr multicolored 5.00 3.50

Humsiki Peak — AP16

1953, Feb. 16

C30 AP16 500fr grnsh blk, dk vio & vio bl 14.50 3.00

For surcharge see No. C40.

Edéa Dam and Sacred Ibis — AP17

1953, Nov. 18

C31 AP17 15fr choc, brn lake & ultra 2.75 1.10

Dedication of Edea Dam on the Sanaga River.

Liberation Issue

Common Design Type

1954, June 6

C32 CD102 15fr dk grnsh bl & bl grn 3.75 3.50

Dr. Eugene Jamot, Research Laboratory and Tsetse Flies — AP19

1954, Nov. 29

C33 AP19 15fr dk grn, ind & dk brn 3.50 1.90

75th anniv. of the birth of Dr. Eugene Jamot.

Logging — AP20

100fr, Giraffes. 200fr, Port of Douala.

1955, Jan. 24

C34	AP20	50fr ol grn, brn & vio brn	1.75	.50
C35	AP20	100fr grnsh bl, brn & dk brn	5.00	1.25
C36	AP20	200fr dk grn, choc & dp ultra	6.75	1.60
		Nos. C34-C36 (3)	13.50	3.35

For surcharges see Nos. C38-C39.

Federal Republic

Air Afrique Issue

Common Design Type

Unwmk.

1962, Feb. 17 Engr. *Perf. 13*

C37 CD107 25fr mar, pur & lt grn 1.00 .40

Nos. C35-C36 and C30 Surcharged in Red with New Value, Bars and: "REPUBLIQUE FEDERALE"

Two types of 5sh:
I — "5/-" measures 6½x4mm.
II — "5/" measures 3¾x3mm, No dash after diagonal line.

Three types of 10sh:
I — "10/-" measures 9x3¾mm.
II — "10/-" measures 7x2½-3mm.
III — "1" of "10/" vertically in line with last "E" of "FEDERALE".

Two types of £1:
I — "REPUBLIQUE / FEDERALE" 17¼mm wide.
II — "REPUBLIQUE / FEDERALE" 22mm wide.

1961, Oct. 1 Engr. *Perf. 13*

C38	AP20	5sh on 100fr (I)	10.00	6.00
a.		Type II	32.50	18.00
C39	AP20	10sh on 200fr (I)	20.00	12.50
a.		Type II	75.00	42.50
b.		Type III	30.00	30.00
C40	AP16	£1 on 500fr (I)	32.50	21.00
a.		Type II	57.50	35.00
		Nos. C38-C40 (3)	62.50	39.50

Issued for use in the former United Kingdom Trust Territory of Southern Cameroons.

Kapsikis Mokolo — AP21

Designs: 50fr, Cocotieres Hotel, Douala. 100fr, Cymothoe sangaris butterflies. 200fr, Ostriches, Waza Reservation.

1962, June 15

C41 AP21 50fr sl grn, bl & dl red .90 .25
C42 AP21 100fr multicolored 5.75 .60
C43 AP21 200fr dk grn, blk & bis 8.00 1.40
C44 AP21 500fr vio brn, bl & ocher 9.00 2.25
Nos. C41-C44 (4) 23.65 4.50

Telstar Type of Regular Issue

1963, Feb. 9
Size: 48x27mm

C45 A50 100fr dk grn & red brn 2.50 .65

Edéa Relay Station — AP22

1963, May 18 Photo. ***Perf. 12x12½***
C46 AP22 100fr multicolored 2.50 .65

Issued to publicize the high frequency telegraph connection Douala-Yaoundé.

African Postal Union Issue
Common Design Type

1963, Sept. 8 Unwmk. ***Perf. 12½***
C47 CD114 85fr ultra, ocher & red 2.25 1.00

Air Afrique Issue, 1963
Common Design Type

1963, Nov. 19 ***Perf. 13x12***
C48 CD115 50fr pink, gray, blk & grn 1.25 .40

Olympic Games Type of 1964

300fr, Greco-Roman wrestlers (ancient).

1964, Oct. 10 Engr. ***Perf. 13***
C49 A57 300fr red, dk brn & dl grn 7.50 2.00
a. Sheet of 3, #403-404, C49 13.50 4.25

Kribi Port — AP25

1964, Oct. 26 Unwmk. ***Perf. 13***
C50 AP25 50fr red brn, ultra & grn .90 .35

Black Rhinoceros — AP26

1964, Dec. 15 Engr. ***Perf. 13***
C51 AP26 250fr brn red, grn & dk brn 10.00 1.10

Pres. John F. Kennedy — AP27

1964, Dec. 8 Photo. ***Perf. 12½***
C52 AP27 100fr grn, yel grn & brn 2.50 1.10
a. Souvenir sheet of 4 10.00 4.50

Pres. John F. Kennedy (1917-63).

Abraham Lincoln — AP28

1965, Apr. 20 Unwmk. ***Perf. 13***
C53 AP28 100fr multicolored 2.50 .80

Abraham Lincoln, death centenary.

Syncom Satellite and ITU Emblem — AP29

1965, May 17 Engr.
C54 AP29 70fr red, dk bl, & blk 1.60 .60

Cent. of the ITU.

Sir Winston Spencer Churchill, Statesman and World War II Leader — AP30

Design: 18fr, Churchill, battleship and oak leaves with acorns.

Perf. 13x12½
1965, May 28 Photo. Unwmk.
C55 AP30 12fr multicolored 1.00 .50
C56 AP30 18fr multicolored 1.00 .50
a. Strip of 2, #C55-C56 + label 2.75 1.40

ICY Type of Regular Issue

1965, Sept. 11 Engr. ***Perf. 13***
C57 A68 100fr dk red & dk bl 2.25 .70

Racing Boat, Sanaga River, Edéa — AP31

1965, Oct. 27 Unwmk. ***Perf. 13***
C58 AP31 50fr brn, dk grn & sl 1.75 .35

Edward H. White Floating in Space and Gemini IV — AP32

Designs: 50fr, Vostok 6. 200fr, Gemini V and REP (rendezvous evaluation pod). 500fr, Gemini VI & VII rendezvous.

1966, Mar. 30 Engr. ***Perf. 13***
C59 AP32 50fr car rose & dk sl grn .90 .35
C60 AP32 100fr red lil & vio bl 2.10 .65
C61 AP32 200fr ultra & dk pur 3.75 1.40
C62 AP32 500fr brt bl & indigo 9.00 3.00
Nos. C59-C62 (4) 15.75 5.40

Man's conquest of space.

Hotel Type of Regular Issue

18fr, Mountain Hotel, Buea. 25fr, Hotel Akwa Palace, Douala. 50fr, Terminus Hotel, Yaoundé. 60fr, Imperial Hotel, Yaoundé. 85fr, Independence Hotel, Yaoundé. 100fr, Hunting Lodge, Mora, vert. 150fr, Boukarous (round huts), Waza Camp.

1966
C63 A71 18fr sl grn, brt bl & blk .45 .20
C64 A71 25fr car, ultra & sl .55 .20
C65 A71 50fr choc, grn & ocher 2.25 .35
C66 A71 60fr choc, grn & brt bl 1.40 .35
C67 A71 85fr dk car rose, dl bl & grn 1.75 .50
C68 A71 100fr brn, grn & sl 2.75 .50
C69 A71 150fr brn, dl bl & ocher 3.50 .65
Nos. C63-C69 (7) 12.65 2.75

Issued: #C63-C64, 4/6; #C65-C69, 6/4.

Flower Type of Regular Issue

Flowers: 25fr, Hibiscus mutabilis. 50fr, Delonix regia. 100fr, Bougainvillea.

1966, May 20 Photo. ***Perf. 12½***
Flowers in Natural Colors
Size: 26x45mm

C70 A75 25fr slate green .70 .20
C71 A75 50fr brt grnsh bl 1.40 .20
C72 A75 100fr gold 2.75 .25
Nos. C70-C72 (3) 4.85 .65

Military Police — AP33

25fr, "Army," soldier, tanks & parachutes. 60fr, "Navy," & "Vigilante." 100fr, "Air Force," plane.

1966, June 21 Engr. ***Perf. 13***
C73 AP33 20fr vio bl, org brn & dl pur .55 .20
C74 AP33 25fr dk grn, dl pur & brn .55 .20
C75 AP33 60fr bl grn, bl & ind 1.60 .30
C76 AP33 100fr brn, Prus bl & car rose 2.75 .65
Nos. C73-C76 (4) 5.45 1.35

Issued to honor Cameroun's armed forces.

Wembley Stadium, London — AP34

1966, July 20
C77 AP34 50fr shown 1.40 .25
C78 AP34 200fr Soccer 4.00 1.10

8th World Cup Soccer Championship, Wembley, England, July 11-30.

Air Afrique Issue, 1966
Common Design Type

1966, Aug. 31 Photo. ***Perf. 13***
C79 CD123 25fr red lil, blk & gray .80 .20

Yaoundé Cathedral — AP35

18fr, Buea Cathedral. 30fr, Orthodox Church, Yaoundé. 60fr, Mosque, Garoua.

1966, Dec. 19 Engr. ***Perf. 13***
C80 AP35 18fr choc, bl & grn .45 .20
C81 AP35 25fr brn, grn & brt vio .55 .20
C82 AP35 30fr lil, grn & dl red .70 .20
C83 AP35 60fr mar, brt grn & grn 1.40 .35
Nos. C80-C83 (4) 3.10 .95

Pioneer A and Moon — AP36

1967, Apr. 30 Engr. ***Perf. 13***
C84 AP36 25fr shown .45 .20
C85 AP36 50fr Ranger 6 .90 .35
C86 AP36 100fr Luna 9 2.10 .65
C87 AP36 250fr Luna 10 4.50 2.00
Nos. C84-C87 (4) 7.95 3.20

"Conquest of the Moon."

Flower Type of Regular Issue

1967, June 22 Photo. ***Perf. 12½***
Size: 26x46mm

C88 A86 200fr Thevetia Peruviana 4.50 .90
C89 A86 250fr Amaryllis 5.50 1.10

African Postal Union Issue, 1967
Common Design Type

1967, Sept. 9 Engr. ***Perf. 13***
C90 CD124 100fr red brn, Prus bl & brt lil 2.25 .65

Skis, Ice Skates, Olympic Flame and Emblem — AP38

1967, Oct. 11 Engr. ***Perf. 13***
C91 AP38 30fr ultra & sepia 1.25 .20

Issued to publicize the 10th Winter Olympic Games, Grenoble, Feb. 6-8, 1968.

Cameroun Exhibit, EXPO '67 — AP39

100fr, Bangwa house poles carved with ancestor figures. 200fr, Canadian Pavilions.

1967, Oct. 18

C92	AP39	50fr mag, ol & mar	.90	.25
C93	AP39	100fr dk grn, mar & dk brn	3.00	.55
C94	AP39	200fr brn, lil rose & sl grn	4.00	1.10
		Nos. C92-C94 (3)	7.90	1.90

EXPO '67, International Exhibition, Montreal, Apr. 28-Oct. 27, 1967.

See note after No. C116 regarding 1969 moon overprint.

Konrad Adenauer (1876-1967), Chancellor of West Germany (1949-63) and Cologne Cathedral AP40

70fr, Adenauer and Chancellery, Bonn.

1967, Dec. 1 Photo. *Perf. 12½*

C95	AP40	30fr multi	.90	.20
C96	AP40	70fr multi	1.50	.40
a.		Pair, #C95-C96 + label	3.50	.65

Pres. Ahidjo, King Faisal and View of Mecca — AP41

60fr, Pres. Ahidjo, Pope Paul VI & view of Rome.

1968, Feb. 18 Photo. *Perf. 12½*

C97	AP41	30fr multi	.90	.20
C98	AP41	60fr multi	2.10	.30

Issued to commemorate President Ahidjo's Pilgrimage to Mecca and visit to Rome.

Earth on Television Transmitted by Explorer VI — AP42

30fr, Molniya spacecraft. 40fr, Earth on television screen transmitted by Molniya.

1968, Apr. 20 Engr. *Perf. 13*

C99	AP42	20fr multi	.55	.20
C100	AP42	30fr multi	.80	.20
C101	AP42	40fr multi	1.10	.20
		Nos. C99-C101 (3)	2.45	.60

Telecommunication by satellite.

Forge — AP43

Boxing — AP44

#C103, Tea harvest. #C104, Trans-Cameroun railroad (diesel train emerging from tunnel). 40fr, Rubber harvest. 60fr, Douala Harbor, horiz.

1968, June 5 Engr. *Perf. 13*

C102	AP43	20fr red brn, dk grn & ind	.65	.20
C103	AP43	30fr dk brn, grn & ultra	1.10	.20
C104	AP43	30fr ind, sl grn & bis brn	7.50	.20
C105	AP43	40fr ol bis, dk grn & bl grn	1.10	.20
C106	AP43	60fr ultra, dk brn & sl	3.00	.40
		Nos. C102-C106 (5)	13.35	1.20

Second Economic Development Five-Year Plan.

1968, Aug. 19 Engr. *Perf. 13*

50fr, Long jump. 60fr, Athlete on rings.

C107	AP44	30fr brt grn, dk grn & choc	.65	.20
C108	AP44	50fr brt grn, brn red & choc	1.25	.30
C109	AP44	60fr brt grn, ultra & choc	1.50	.35
a.		Min. sheet of 3, #C107-C109	4.00	1.50
		Nos. C107-C109 (3)	3.40	.85

19th Olympic Games, Mexico City, 10/12-27.

Human Rights Type of Regular Issue

1968, Sept. 14 Photo. *Perf. 12½x13*

C110	A92	30fr grn & brt pink	.80	.20

Martin Luther King, Jr. — AP45

Portraits: No. C112, Mahatma Gandhi and map of India. 40fr, John F. Kennedy. 60fr, Robert F. Kennedy. No. C115, Rev. Martin Luther King, Jr. No. C116, Mahatma Gandhi.

1968, Dec. 5 Photo. *Perf. 12½*

C111	AP45	30fr bl & blk	.45	.20
C112	AP45	30fr multi	.45	.20
C113	AP45	40fr pink & blk	.70	.25
C114	AP45	60fr bluish lil & blk	.90	.40
C115	AP45	70fr yel grn & blk	1.00	.45
a.		Souvenir sheet of 4, #C112-C115	6.25	2.00
C116	AP45	70fr multi	1.00	.50
		Nos. C111-C116 (6)	4.50	2.00

Issued to honor exponents of non-violence. The 2 King stamps (Nos. C111 and C115), the 2 Gandhi stamps (Nos. C112 and C116) and the 2 Kennedy stamps (Nos. C113-C114) are each printed as triptychs with a descriptive label between.

In 1969 Nos. C111-C116 and C94 were overprinted in carmine capitals: "Premier Homme / sur la Lune / 20 Juillet 1969" or "First Man / Landing on Moon / 20 July 1969". Values: on No. C94, $50; on #C111-C116, $275; on No. C115 (2 souvenir sheets, with both overprint types), $300.

PHILEXAFRIQUE Issue

The Letter, by Armand Cambon AP46

1968, Dec. 10

C117	AP46	100fr multi	3.25	.80

PHILEXAFRIQUE, Philatelic Exhibition in Abidjan, Feb. 14-23, 1969. Printed with alternating light green label.

2nd PHILEXAFRIQUE Issue

Common Design Type

Design: Cameroun #199 and Wouri Bridge.

1969, Feb. 14 Engr. *Perf. 13*

C118	CD128	50fr multi	3.25	.55

Caladium Bicolor — AP47

Flowers: 50fr, Aristolochia elegans. 100fr, Gloriosa simplex.

1969, May 14 Photo. *Perf. 12½*

C119	AP47	30fr lil & multi	.70	.20
C120	AP47	50fr grn & multi	1.40	.35
C121	AP47	100fr brn & multi	3.25	.55
		Nos. C119-C121 (3)	5.35	1.10

3rd Intl. Flower Show, Paris, Apr. 23-Oct. 5.

Douala Post Office — AP48

50fr, Buèa P.O. 100fr, Bafoussam P.O.

1969, June 19 Engr. *Perf. 13*

C122	AP48	30fr grn, vio bl & brn	.55	.20
C123	AP48	50fr sl, emer & red brn	.90	.25
C124	AP48	100fr dk brn, brt grn & brn	1.75	.50
		Nos. C122-C124 (3)	3.20	.95

Coronation of Napoleon I, by Jacques Louis David — AP49

Napoleon Crossing Saint Bernard, after J. L. David — AP50

1969, July 4 Photo. *Perf. 12x12½*

C125	AP49	30fr vio bl & multi	1.00	.20

Die-cut Perf. 10

Embossed on Gold Foil

C126	AP50	1000fr gold	40.00	16.00

Bicentenary of birth of Napoleon I.

William E. B. Du Bois (1868-1963), American Writer — AP51

15fr, Dr. Price Mars, Haiti (1876-1969). #C128, Aimé Cesaire, Martinique (1913-). #C130, Langston Hughes, US (1902-67). #C131, Marcus Garvey, Jamaica (1887-1940). 100fr, René Maran, Martinique (1887-1960).

1969, Sept. 25 Photo. *Perf. 12½*

C127	AP51	15fr lt bl & blk	.45	.20
C128	AP51	30fr lem & blk	.55	.20
C129	AP51	30fr rose brn & blk	.55	.20
C130	AP51	50fr gray & blk	.80	.25
C131	AP51	50fr emer & blk	.80	.25
C132	AP51	100fr yel & blk	2.00	.60
a.		Min. sheet of 6, #C127-C132	6.75	2.50
		Nos. C127-C132 (6)	5.15	1.70

Issued to honor Negro writers.

ILO Emblem — AP52

1969, Oct. 29 Photo. *Perf. 13*

C133	AP52	30fr blk, bl grn & gray	.80	.20
C134	AP52	50fr blk, dp lil rose & gray	1.25	.25

50th anniv. of the ILO.

Armstrong, Collins and Aldrin Splashdown in the Pacific — AP53

Design: 500fr, Landing module and Nell A. Armstrong's first step on moon.

1969, Nov. 29 Photo. *Perf. 12½*

C135	AP53	200fr multi	5.00	1.25
C136	AP53	500fr multi	11.50	2.25

See note after Algeria No. 427.

Pres. Ahidjo, Arms and Map of Cameroun — AP54

Embossed on Gold Foil

1970, Jan. 1 ***Die-cut Perf. 10***

C137 AP54 1000fr gold & multi 22.50 8.25

10th anniversary of independence.

Hotel Mont Fébé, Yaoundé — AP55

1970, Jan. 15 **Engr.** ***Perf. 13***

C138 AP55 30fr lt brn, sl grn & gray .80 .20

Lenin — AP56

1970, Jan. 25 **Photo.** ***Perf. 12½***

C139 AP56 50fr org & blk 2.00 .25

Plant Type of Regular Issue

Designs: 50fr, Cleome speciosa (caper). 100fr, Mussaenda erythrophylla (madder).

1970, Mar. 24 **Photo.** ***Perf. 12½***

Size: 26x46mm

C140 A99 50fr blk & multi 1.40 .25
C141 A99 100fr multi 2.75 .40

Map of Africa and Lions Emblem Pinpointing Yaoundé — AP57

1970, May 2 **Photo.** ***Perf. 12½***

C142 AP57 100fr multi 2.25 .50

13th Lions International Congress of District 13, Yaoundé, May 2, 1970.

UN Emblem and Doves — AP58

Design: 50fr, UN emblem and dove, vert.

1970, June 26 **Engr.** ***Perf. 13***

C143 AP58 30fr brn & org 1.00 .20
C144 AP58 50fr Prus bl & sl bl 1.25 .25

25th anniversary of the United Nations.

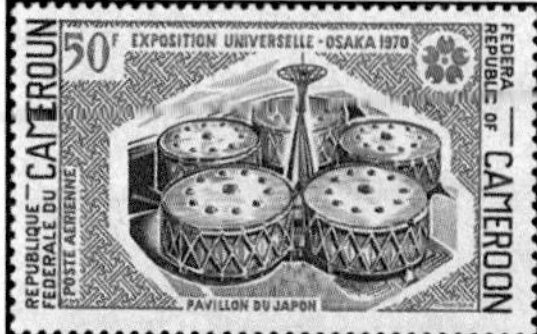

Japanese Pavilion and EXPO Emblem — AP59

Designs (EXPO Emblem and): 100fr, Map of Japan, vert. 150fr, Australian pavilion.

1970, Aug. 1 **Engr.** ***Perf. 13***

C145 AP59 50fr ind, lt grn & ver .90 .25
C146 AP59 100fr bl, lt grn & red 2.00 .40
C147 AP59 150fr choc, bl & gray 3.25 .65
Nos. C145-C147 (3) 6.15 1.30

EXPO '70 International Exhibition, Osaka, Japan, Mar. 15-Sept. 13.

Charles de Gaulle — AP60

Pelé and Team — AP61

Design: 200fr, de Gaulle in unifrom.

1970, Aug. 27

C148 AP60 100fr grn, vio bl & ol brn 2.25 .50
C149 AP60 200fr ol brn, vio bl & grn 4.50 .90
a. Pair, #C148-C149 + label 8.00 1.60

Rallying of the Free French, 30th anniv. For overprints see Nos. C159-C160.

1970, Oct. 14 **Photo.** ***Perf. 12½***

Designs: 50fr, Aztec Stadium, Mexico City, horiz. 100fr, Mexican soccer team, horiz.

C150 AP61 50fr multi .90 .25
C151 AP61 100fr multi 2.00 .50
C152 AP61 200fr multi 3.25 1.00
Nos. C150-C152 (3) 6.15 1.75

9th World Soccer Championships for the Jules Rimet Cup, Mexico City, May 30-June 21, and the final victory of Brazil over Italy.

Ludwig van Beethoven (1770-1827), Composer AP62

1970, Nov. 23 **Engr.** ***Perf. 13***

C153 AP62 250fr multi 5.75 1.00

Christ at Emmaus, by Rembrandt — AP63

150fr, The Anatomy Lesson, by Rembrandt.

1970, Dec. 5 **Photo.** ***Perf. 12x12½***

C154 AP63 70fr grn & multi 1.40 .25
C155 AP63 150fr multi 2.75 .60

Charles Dickens — AP64

Designs: 50fr, Scenes from David Copperfield. 100fr, Dickens holding quill.

1970, Dec. 22 ***Perf. 13***

C156 AP64 40fr blk & rose .65 .20
C157 AP64 50fr bis & multi .70 .20
C158 AP64 100fr rose & multi 1.25 .40
a. Strip of 3, #C156-C158 1.75 1.00

Charles Dickens (1812-1870), English novelist.

De Gaulle Type of 1970 Overprinted with Black Border and: "IN MEMORIAM / 1890-1970"

1971, Jan. 15 **Engr.** ***Perf. 13***

C159 AP60 100fr vio bl, emer & brn red 2.25 .40
C160 AP60 200fr brn red, emer & vio bl 4.50 .80
a. Pair, #C159-C160 + label 7.50 1.40

In memory of Gen. Charles de Gaulle (1890-1970), President of France.

Timber Storage, Douala — AP65

Industrialization: 70fr, ALUCAM aluminum plant, Edea, vert. 100fr, Mbakaou Dam.

1971, Feb. 14 **Engr.** ***Perf. 13***

C161 AP65 40fr dk red, bl grn & ol brn .55 .20
C162 AP65 70fr ol brn, sl grn & brt bl 1.10 .25
C163 AP65 100fr Prus bl, yel grn & red brn 1.75 .40
Nos. C161-C163 (3) 3.40 .85

Relay Race — AP66

50fr, Torch bearer, vert. 100fr, Discus.

1971, Apr. 24 **Engr.** ***Perf. 13***

C164 AP66 30fr dk brn, ver & ind .65 .20
C165 AP66 50fr blk, bl & choc .80 .25
C166 AP66 100fr multi 1.75 .35
Nos. C164-C166 (3) 3.20 .80

75th anniv. of revival of Olympic Games

Fishing Trawler — AP67

Designs: 40fr, Local fishermen, Northern Cameroun. 70fr, Fishing harbor, Douala. 150fr, Shrimp boats, Douala.

1971, May 14 **Engr.** ***Perf. 13***

C167 AP67 30fr lt brn, bl & grn .70 .20
C168 AP67 40fr sl grn, bl & dk brn .90 .20
C169 AP67 70fr dk brn, bl & red org 2.00 .25
C170 AP67 150fr multi 4.25 .60
Nos. C167-C170 (4) 7.85 1.25

Cameroun fishing industry.

Cameroun No. 123 and War Memorial, Yaoundé — AP68

Designs (Cameroun Stamps): 25fr, No. C33 and Jamot memorial. 40fr, No. 431 and government buildings, Yaoundé. 50fr, No. 19 and Imperial German postal emblem. 100fr, No. 101 and World War II memorial.

1971, Aug. 1 **Engr.** ***Perf. 13***

C171 AP68 20fr grn, ocher & dk brn .35 .20
C172 AP68 25fr dk brn, vio bl & sl grn .55 .20
C173 AP68 40fr grn, mar & sl .70 .20
C174 AP68 50fr dk brn, blk & ver 1.00 .20
C175 AP68 100fr mar, sl grn & org 1.75 .40
Nos. C171-C175 (5) 4.35 1.20

PHILATECAM 1971 Philatelic Exhibition.

Cameroun Flag, Pres. Ahidjo and Reunification Highway — AP69

Typographed, Silk Screen, Embossed

1971, Oct. 1 ***Perf. 12½***

C176 AP69 250fr gold & multi 5.75 2.00

PHILATECAM Philatelic Exhibition, Yaoundé-Douala.

African Postal Union Issue, 1971

Common Design Type

1971, Nov. 13 **Photo.** ***Perf. 13x13½***

C177 CD135 100fr bl & multi 2.00 .40

Annunciation, by Fra Angelico — AP71

Christmmas (Paintings): 45fr, Virgin and Child, by Andrea del Sarto. 150fr, Christ Child with Lamb, detail from Holy Family, by Raphael, vert.

1971, Dec. 19 ***Perf. 13x13½, 13½x13***

C178	AP71	40fr multi	.55	.20
C179	AP71	45fr multi	.70	.20
C180	AP71	150fr multi	3.00	.60
		Nos. C178-C180 (3)	4.25	1.00

Cameroun Airlines Emblem AP72

1972, Feb. 2 **Photo.** ***Perf. 12½x12***

C181 AP72 50fr lt bl & multi .80 .20

Inauguration of Cameroun Airlines.

Doge's Palace, by Ippolito Caffi AP73

100fr, 200fr, Details from "Regatta on the Grand Canal," by School of Canaletto.

1972 **Photo.** ***Perf. 13***

C182	AP73	40fr gold & multi	.65	.20
C183	AP73	100fr gold & multi	1.75	.40
C184	AP73	200fr gold & multi	3.50	.80
		Nos. C182-C184 (3)	5.90	1.40

UNESCO campaign to save Venice.

Cosmonauts Patsayev, Dobrovolsky and Volkov — AP74

1972, May 1 **Photo.** ***Perf. 13x13½***

C185 AP74 50fr multi 1.00 .20

Salute-Soyuz 11 space mission, and in memory of the Russian cosmonauts Victor I. Patsayev, Georgi T. Dobrovolsky and Vladislav N. Volkov, who died during Soyuz 11 space mission, June 6-30, 1971.

UN Headquarters, Chinese Flag and Gate of Heavenly Peace — AP75

1972, May 19 ***Perf. 13***

C186 AP75 50fr blk, scar & gold 3.25 .20

Admission of People's Republic of China to UN.

United Republic

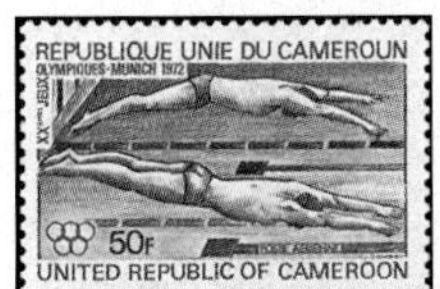

Olympic Rings, Swimming AP76

Designs (Olympic Rings and): No. C188, Boxing, vert. 200fr, Equestrian.

1972, Aug. 1 **Engr.** ***Perf. 13***

C187	AP76	50fr lake & slate grn	.90	.20
C188	AP76	50fr choc & slate	.90	.20
C189	AP76	200fr cl, gray & dk brn	3.50	.70
a.		Min. sheet of 3	5.75	2.25
		Nos. C187-C189 (3)	5.30	1.10

20th Olympic Games, Munich, Aug. 26-Sept. 11. No. C189a contains stamps similar to Nos. C187-C189, but in changed colors. The 50fr (swimming) is Prussian blue, violet & brown; the 50c (boxing) lilac, Prussian blue & brown; the 200fr, Prussian blue & brown.

Nos. C187-C189 Overprinted in Red or Black

a

SUPER WELTER
KOTTYSCH
MEDAILLE D'OR

b

c

1972, Oct. 23 **Engr.** ***Perf. 13***

C190	AP76(a)	50fr (R)	.90	.20
C191	AP76(b)	50fr	.90	.20
C192	AP76(c)	200fr	3.50	.80
		Nos. C190-C192 (3)	5.30	1.20

Gold Medal Winners in 20th Olympic Games: Mark Spitz, US, swimming (#C190); Dieter Kottysch, West Germany, light middleweight boxing (#C191); Richard Meade, Great Britain, 3-day equestrian (#C192).

Madonna with Angels, by Cimabue AP77

Christmas: 140fr, Madonna of the Rose Arbor, by Stefan Lochner.

1972, Dec. 21 **Photo.** ***Perf. 13***

C193	AP77	45fr gold & multi	1.00	.20
C194	AP77	140fr gold & multi	2.75	.45

St. Teresa, the Little Flower — AP78

100fr, Lisieux Cathedral and St. Teresa.

1973, Jan. 2 **Engr.**

C195	AP78	45fr vio bl, pur & mar	.70	.20
C196	AP78	100fr mag, ultra & brn	1.75	.40

Centenary of the birth of St. Teresa of Lisieux (1873-1897), Carmelite nun.

African Unity Hall, Addis Ababa and Emperor Haile Selassie — AP79

1973, Mar. 14 **Photo.** ***Perf. 13***

C197 AP79 45fr yellow & multi 1.00 .20

80th birthday of Emperor Haile Selassie of Ethiopia.

Corn, Grain, Healthy and Starving People — AP80

1973, Apr. 10 **Typo.** ***Perf. 13***

C198 AP80 45fr multi .80 .20

World Food Program, 10th anniversary.

Hearts and Blood Vessels — AP81

Scout Emblem and Flags — AP82

1973, May 5 **Engr.**

C199 AP81 50fr dk car rose & dk vio bl 1.00 .20

"Your Heart is Your Health" and for the 25th anniv. of the WHO.

Type of Regular Issue

Designs: 45fr, Map of Cameroun, Pres. Ahidjo and No. C176. 70fr, National colors and commemorative inscriptions.

1973, May 20 **Engr.** ***Perf. 13***

C200	A128	45fr grn & multi	.80	.20
C201	A128	70fr red & multi	1.00	.25

1973, July 31 **Typo.** ***Perf. 13***

C202	AP82	40fr multi	1.00	.20
C203	AP82	45fr multi	1.25	.20
C204	AP82	100fr multi	3.25	.40
		Nos. C202-C204 (3)	5.50	.80

Cameroun's admission to the World Scout Conference, Mar. 26, 1971.

African Weeks Issue

Head and City Hall, Brussels — AP83

1973, Sept. 17 **Engr.** ***Perf. 13***

C205 AP83 40fr dp brn & rose claret .80 .20

African Weeks, Brussels, Sept. 15-30.

Map of Africa with Cameroun — AP84

1973, Sept. 29 **Engr.** ***Perf. 13***

C206 AP84 40fr blk, red & grn .80 .20

Help for handicapped children.

Zamengoe Radar Station AP85

1973, Dec. 8 **Engr.** ***Perf. 13***

C207 AP85 100fr bl, lt brn & grn 1.50 .40

Chancellor Rolin Madonna, by Van Eyck AP86

Christmas: 140fr, Nativity, by Federigo Barocei.

1973, Dec. 11 **Photo.** ***Perf. 13***

C208	AP86	45fr gold & multi	1.00	.20
C209	AP86	140fr gold & multi	2.75	.70

Zebu Type of 1974

1974, June 1 **Litho.** ***Perf. 13***

C210 A140 45fr Zebu herd 1.40 .20

Churchill and Union Jack AP87

1974, July 10 **Engr.** ***Perf. 13***

C211 AP87 100fr blk, bl & red 1.60 .40

Winston Churchill (1874-1965).

Soccer, Arms of Frankfurt, Dortmund, Gelsenkirchen and Stuttgart — AP88

100fr, Soccer & arms of Berlin, Hamburg, Hanover & Düsseldorf. 200fr, Soccer cup & game.

1974, Aug. 5 Photo. *Perf. 13*

C212 AP88 45fr gray, sl & org .65 .20
C213 AP88 100fr gray, sl & org 1.25 .40
C214 AP88 200fr org, slate & bl 2.25 .65
a. Strip of 3, Nos. C212-C214 5.00 1.40

World Cup Soccer Championship, Munich, June 13-July 7.

Nos. C212-C214 Overprinted in Dark Blue: "7th JULY 1974 / R.F.A. 2 HOLLANDE 1 / 7 JUILLET 1974"

1974, Sept. 16 Photo. *Perf. 13*

C215 AP88 45fr multi .65 .20
C216 AP88 100fr multi 1.25 .40
C217 AP88 200fr multi 2.25 .80
a. Strip of 3, Nos. C215-C217 2.25 1.50

World Cup Soccer Championship, 1974, victory of German Federal Republic.

UPU Type of 1974

100fr, Cameroun #503. 200fr, Cameroun #C29.

1974, Oct. 8 Engr. *Perf. 13*

C218 A142 100fr blue & multi 1.75 .30
C219 A142 200fr red & multi 3.25 .60

Copernicus and Planets Circling Sun — AP89

1974, Oct. 15 Engr. *Perf. 13*

C220 AP89 250fr multi 3.50 1.00

500th anniversary of the birth of Nicolaus Copernicus (1473-1543), Polish astronomer.

21st Chess Olympiad, Nice, France, June 6-30 — AP90

1974, Nov. 3 Photo. *Perf. 13x12½*

C221 AP90 100fr Chess pieces 4.50 .40

Mask and ARPHILA Emblem — AP91

1974, Nov. 30 Engr. *Perf. 13*

C222 AP91 50fr choc & magenta .65 .20

ARPHILA 75, Paris, June 6-16, 1975.

Presidents and Flags of Cameroun, CAR, Gabon and Congo — AP92

1974, Dec. 8 Photo.

C223 AP92 100fr gold & multi 2.25 .40

See note after No. 595.

Man Landing on Moon — AP93

1974, Dec. 15 Engr.

C224 AP93 200fr brn, bl & car 3.25 .80

5th anniv. of man's 1st landing on the moon.

Charles de Gaulle and Félix Eboué — AP94

1975, Feb. 24 Typo. *Perf. 13*

C225 AP94 45fr multi 1.50 .20
C226 AP94 200fr multi 5.00 .80

Felix A. Eboué (1884-1944), Governor of Chad, first colonial governor to join Free French in WWII, 30th death anniversary.

Marquis de Lafayette AP95

American Bicentennial: 140fr, Washington and soldiers. 500fr, Franklin and Independence Hall.

1975, Oct. 20 Engr. *Perf. 13*

C227 AP95 100fr vio bl & multi 2.10 .40
C228 AP95 140fr brn & multi 2.25 .60
C229 AP95 500fr grn & multi 7.25 1.60
Nos. C227-C229 (3) 11.60 2.60

The Burning Bush, by Nicolas Froment AP96

Painting: 500fr, Adoration of the Kings, by Gentile da Fabriano, horiz.

1975, Dec. 25 Photo. *Perf. 13*

C230 AP96 50fr gold & multi .90 .20
C231 AP96 500fr gold & multi 7.25 1.60

Christmas 1975.

Concorde and Route: Paris-Dakar-Rio de Janeiro — AP97

1976, July 20 Litho. *Perf. 13*

C232 AP97 500fr lt bl & multi 5.00 1.60
a. Souvenir sheet of 1 9.00 3.75

1st commercial flight of supersonic jet Concorde from Paris to Rio de Janeiro, Jan. 21. No. C232a sold for 600fr.

For overprint see No. C263.

Dance Type of 1976

50fr, Dancers & drummer. 100fr, Woman dancer.

1976, Sept. 15 Litho. *Perf. 12*

C233 A154 50fr gray & multi .65 .20
C234 A154 100fr gray & multi 1.10 .35

Virgin and Child, by Giovanni Bellini — AP98

Paintings: 30fr, Adoration of the Shepherds, by Le Brun. 60fr, Adoration of the Kings, by Rubens. 500fr, The Newborn, by Georges de la Tour.

1976, Dec. 15 Litho. *Perf. 12½*

C235 AP98 30fr gold & multi .70 .20
C236 AP98 60fr gold & multi .90 .25
C237 AP98 70fr gold & multi 1.25 .25
C238 AP98 500fr gold & multi 9.00 1.60
a. Souv. sheet of 4, #C235-C238 12.50 3.75
Nos. C235-C238 (4) 11.85 2.30

Christmas 1976.

Festival Type of 1977

Traditional Chief on his throne, sculpture.

1977, Feb. 4 Litho. *Perf. 12½*

C239 A159 60fr multi 1.10 .25

Crucifixion, by Matthias Grunewald — AP99

125fr, Christ on the Cross, by Velazquez, vert. 150fr, The Deposition, by Titian.

1977, Apr. 2 Litho. *Perf. 12½*

C240 AP99 50fr gold & multi .90 .20
C241 AP99 125fr gold & multi 1.75 .40
C242 AP99 150fr gold & multi 2.50 .55
a. Souv. sheet of 3, #C240-C242, perf. 12 6.75 1.75
Nos. C240-C242 (3) 5.15 1.15

Easter 1977. No. C242a sold for 350fr.

Lions Emblem, Map of Africa — AP100

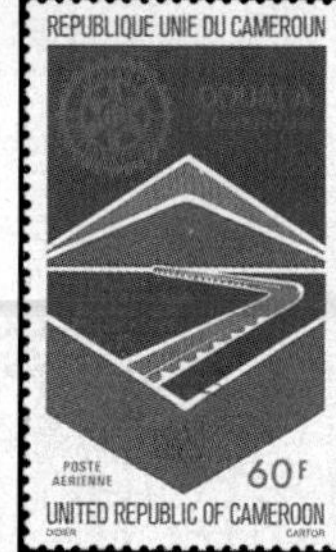

Rotary Emblem AP101

1977, Apr. 29 Litho. *Perf. 12½*

C243 AP100 250fr multi 3.00 1.00

Lions Club of Douala, 19th Cong., 4/29-30.

1977, May 18

C244 AP101 60fr multi .70 .25

Rotary Club of Douala, 20th anniversary.

Antoine de Saint-Exupéry AP102

Charles Lindbergh and Spirit of St. Louis — AP103

Designs: 50fr, Jean Mermoz and his plane. 80fr, Maryse Bastié and her plane. 100fr, Sikorsky S-43. 300fr, Concorde.

1977, May 20 Engr. *Perf. 13*

C245 AP103 50fr org & bl .70 .20
C246 AP102 60fr mag & org .80 .25
C247 AP103 80fr mag & bl 1.00 .30
a. Souv. sheet, #C245-C247 3.00 1.10
C248 AP103 100fr grn & yel 1.10 .40
C249 AP103 300fr multi 4.50 1.25
C250 AP103 500fr multi 6.75 1.75
a. Souv. sheet, #C248-C250 14.50 6.00
Nos. C245-C250 (6) 14.85 4.15

Aviation pioneers and events. No. C247a sold for 200fr. No. C250a sold for 1000fr.

For overprint see No. C262.

Sassenage Castle, Grenoble — AP104

1977, May 21 Litho. *Perf. 12½*
C251 AP104 70fr multi 1.40 .25

10th anniv. of Intl. French Language Council.

Jufilex Type of 1977

Designs: 70fr, Switzerland (Zurich) No. 1L1 and Cameroun No. 16. 100fr, Switzerland (Geneva) No. 2L1 and Cameroun No. 254.

1977, June 5 Litho. *Perf. 12*
C252 A161 70fr multi 1.25 .25
C253 A161 100fr multi 2.10 .40

Apollo-Soyuz Type

100fr, Astronaut Vance Brand, Apollo in orbit. 250fr, Apollo and Soyuz docking. 350fr, Cosmonaut Valery Kubasov, Soyuz in orbit. 500fr, Astronaut Donald Slayton, handshake.

1977, Aug. 10 Litho. *Perf. 14x13½*
C256 A163 100fr multicolored *.90 .75*
C257 A163 250fr multicolored *2.25 2.10*
C258 A163 350fr multicolored *3.25 3.00*
Nos. C256-C258 (3) 6.40 5.85

Souvenir Sheet

C259 A163 500fr multicolored *5.00 4.25*

Diseased Knee, WHO Emblem AP105

1977, Oct. 15 Engr. *Perf. 13*
C260 AP105 70fr multi .70 .25

World Rheumatism Year.

Nos. C249 and C232 Overprinted in Red: "PREMIER VOL PARIS-NEW YORK /FIRST FLIGHT PARIS-NEW YORK / 22 Nov. 1977-22nd Nov. 1977"

Engraved, Lithographed

1977, Nov. 22 *Perf. 13*
C262 AP103 300fr multi 3.25 1.25
C263 AP97 500fr multi 5.00 2.00

Concorde, 1st commercial flight Paris to NY.

Christmas Type of 1977

Paintings: 60fr, Virgin and Child with 4 Saints, by Bellini, horiz. 400fr, Adoration of the Shepherds, by George de la Tour, horiz.

1977, Dec. 15 Litho. *Perf. 12x12½*
C264 A165 60fr multi 1.00 .25
C265 A165 400fr multi 5.00 1.75

Flag Type of 1978

60fr, New flag, Pres. Ahidjo and spear.

1978, Apr. 3 Litho. *Perf. 12½*
C266 A167 60fr multi .55 .20

Frog Type of 1978

Design: 100fr, Cardioglossa trifasciata.

1978, Apr. 5
C267 A168 100fr multi 2.75 .40

L'Arlesienne, by Van Gogh — AP106

#C269, Burial of Christ, by Albrecht Dürer.

1978, May 15 Litho. *Perf. 12½*
C268 AP106 200fr multi 3.00 1.10
C269 AP106 200fr multi 4.00 1.10

Leprosy Distribution on World Map, Raoul Follereau — AP107

1978, June 6 Litho. *Perf. 12*
C270 AP107 100fr multi 1.00 .55

25th World Leprosy Day.

Capt. Cook and Siege of Quebec — AP108

Design: 250fr, Capt. Cook, Adventure and Resolution, map of voyages.

1978, July 26 Engr. *Perf. 13*
C271 AP108 100fr multi 2.10 .55
C272 AP108 250fr multi 5.00 1.40

Capt. James Cook (1728-1779), explorer.

Argentine Soccer Team, Coat of Arms and Rimet Cup — AP109

200fr, Two soccer players, vert. 1000fr, Soccer ball illuminating world map, vert.

1978, Sept. 1 Litho. *Perf. 13*
C273 AP109 100fr multi 1.00 .55
C274 AP109 200fr multi 1.75 1.10
C275 AP109 1000fr multi 10.00 5.50
Nos. C273-C275 (3) 12.75 7.15

11th World Cup Soccer Championship, Argentina, June 1-25.

Jules Verne Type of 1978

Design: 400fr, Jules Verne and "20,000 Leagues Under the Sea," horiz.

1978, Oct. 10 Litho. *Perf. 12*
C276 A169 400fr multi 3.00 2.00

Musical Instrument Type of 1978

Design: 100fr, Man playing Mvet zither.

1978, Nov. 20 Litho. *Perf. 12½*
C277 A172 100fr multi 1.10 .40

Human Rights Type of 1979

1979, Feb. 11 Litho. *Perf. 12x12½*
C278 A174 500fr multi 5.25 2.50

Lions Emblem, Map of District 403 — AP110

1979, Apr. 26 Litho. *Perf. 12½*
C279 AP110 60fr multi .70 .25

21st Congress of Lions Club of Yaoundé.

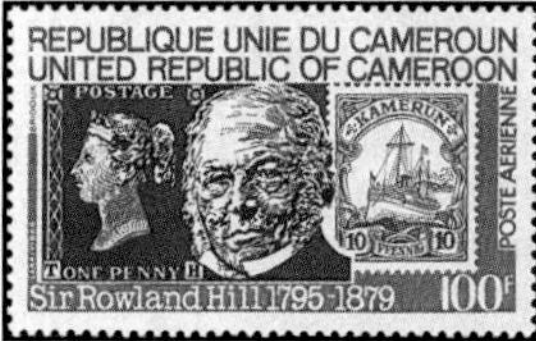

Penny Black, Hill, Cameroun No. 9 — AP111

1979, Oct. 10 Engr. *Perf. 13*
C280 AP111 100fr multi 1.00 .40

Sir Rowland Hill (1795-1879), originator of penny postage.

"TELECOM 79" — AP112

Pope Paul VI — AP113

1979, Sept. 26 Litho. *Perf. 13x12½*
C281 AP112 100fr multi 1.10 .40

3rd World Telecommunications Exhibition, Geneva, Sept. 20-26.

1979, Oct. 23 Engr. *Perf. 12½x13*
C282 AP113 100fr shown 2.25 .40
C283 AP113 100fr John Paul I 2.25 .40
C284 AP113 100fr John Paul II 2.25 .40
Nos. C282-C284 (3) 6.75 1.20

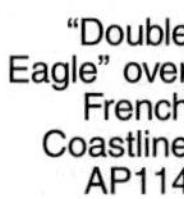

"Double Eagle" over French Coastline AP114

Design: No. C286, Balloonists and balloon.

1979, Dec. 15 Litho. *Perf. 12½*
C285 AP114 500fr multi 5.00 2.25
C286 AP114 500fr multi 5.00 2.25

First Transatlantic balloon crossing.

100-Meter Race — AP115

Designs: 150fr, Figure skating pairs. 200fr, Javelin. 300fr, Wrestling.

1980, Dec. 18 Litho. *Perf. 12½*
C287 AP115 100fr yel brn & brn .90 .50
C288 AP115 150fr bl & brn 1.25 .70
C289 AP115 200fr grn & brn 1.75 1.00
C290 AP115 300fr red & brn 2.50 1.40
Nos. C287-C290 (4) 6.40 3.60

22nd Summer Olympic Games, Moscow, July 19-Aug. 3; 13th Winter Olympic Games, Lake Placid, Feb. 12-24 (150fr).

Alan Shepard and Freedom 7 — AP116

1981, Sept. 15 Litho. *Perf. 12½*
C291 AP116 500fr shown 6.00 4.00
C292 AP116 500fr Yuri Gagarin, Vostok I 6.00 4.00

Manned space flight, 20th anniv.

4th African Scouting Conference, Abidjan, June — AP117

1981, Oct. 5
C293 AP117 100fr Emblem, salute, badge .70 .40
C294 AP117 500fr Scout saluting 4.50 2.00

Guernica (detail), by Pablo Picasso (1881-1973) — AP118

#C296, Landscape, by Paul Cezanne (1839-1906).

1981, Nov. 10 Litho. *Perf. 12½*
C295 AP118 500fr multi 5.00 2.00
C296 AP118 500fr multi 5.00 2.00

Christmas 1981 — AP119

Designs: 50fr, Virgin and Child, by Froment, vert. 60f, San Zeno Altarpiece, by Mantegna, vert. 400fr, Flight into Egypt, by Giotto.

1981, Dec. 1 Litho. *Perf. 12½*
C297 AP119 50fr multi .45 .25
C298 AP119 60fr multi .65 .30
C299 AP119 400fr multi 3.50 2.00
a. Souv. sheet of 3, #C297-C299, perf. 13x13½ 9.00 2.75
Nos. C297-C299 (3) 4.60 2.55

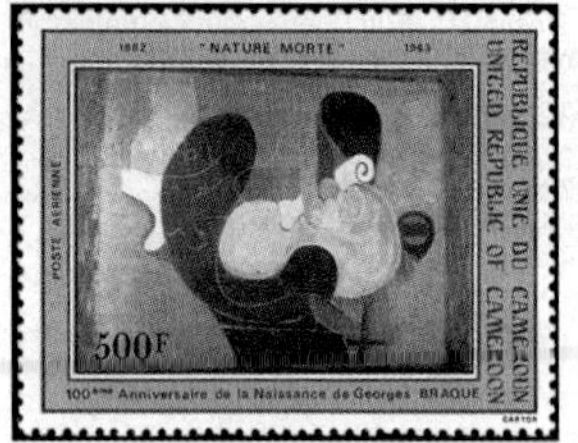

Still Life, by Georges Braque (1882-1963) — AP120

Paintings: No. C301, Olympia, by Edouard Manet (1832-1883).

1982, Dec. 5 Litho. *Perf. 13*

C300 AP120 500fr multi	5.00	2.00
C301 AP120 500fr multi	5.00	2.00

Pres. John F. Kennedy (1917-63) AP121

Lions District 403 (Douala), 2nd Convention, May — AP122

1983, Mar. 15 Litho. *Perf. 13*

C302 AP121 500fr multi	4.50	2.00

1983, May 5 Litho. *Perf. 12½*

C303 AP122 70fr multi	.55	.30
C304 AP122 150fr multi	1.25	.65

Jeanne of Aragon by Raphael AP123

No. C306, Massacre of Scio by Delacroix.

1983, Oct. 15 Litho. *Perf. 13*

C305 AP123 500fr multi	5.00	1.00
C306 AP123 500fr multi	5.00	1.00

Easter 1984 — AP124

200fr, Pieta, by G. Hernandez. 500fr, Martyrdom of St. John the Evangelist, by C. Le Brun.

1984, Mar. 30 Litho. *Perf. 13*

C307 AP124 200fr multi	1.75	.50
C308 AP124 500fr multi	4.50	1.40
a. Souv. sheet of 2, #C307-C308	7.25	2.00

1984 Summer Olympics AP125

European Soccer Championship, June 12-27 — AP126

1984, Apr. 30 *Perf. 12½*

C309 AP125 100fr High jump	.90	.25
C310 AP125 150fr Volleyball	1.25	.30
C311 AP125 250fr Handball	2.25	.55
C312 AP125 500fr Bicycling	4.50	1.10
Nos. C309-C312 (4)	8.90	2.20

See Nos. C321-C324.

1984, June 5 Litho. *Perf. 12½*

C313 AP126 250fr Player in red shorts	2.25	.65
C314 AP126 250fr Yellow shorts	2.25	.65
C315 AP126 500fr Players	4.50	1.25
a. Souvenir sheet of 3	10.00	2.75
Nos. C313-C315 (3)	9.00	2.55

No. C315a contains Nos. C313-C315 in changed panel colors.

Presidential Oath — AP127

1984 Litho. *Perf. 13*

C316 AP127 60fr French inscription	.55	.20
a. English inscription	.55	.20
C317 AP127 70fr French inscription	.55	.20
a. English inscription	.55	.20
C318 AP127 200fr French inscription	1.75	.40
a. English inscription	1.75	.40
Nos. C316-C318 (3)	2.85	.80

Issue dates: French, Sept. 15; English, Nov.

Famous Men — AP128

#C316, Diana in the Bath, by Watteau (1684-1721). #C317, Portrait of Diderot (1713-1784).

1984, Sept. 20 Litho. *Perf. 13*

C319 AP128 500fr Watteau	5.00	1.00
C320 AP128 500fr Diderot, vert.	5.00	1.00

Nos. C309-C312 in Changed Colors with Added Inscriptions
100fr: MOEGENBURG (R.F.A.) 11-08-84
150fr: U.S.A. 11-08-84
250fr: YOUGOSLAVIE 9-08-84
500fr: GORSKI (U.S.A.) 3-08-84

1984, Sept. 26 Litho. *Perf. 12½*

C321 AP125 100fr multi	.90	.20
C322 AP125 150fr multi	1.25	.30
C323 AP125 250fr multi	2.25	.50
C324 AP125 500fr multi	4.50	1.00
Nos. C321-C324 (4)	8.90	2.00

Moon Landing, 15th Anniv. — AP129

1984, Nov. 15 Litho. *Perf. 12½*

C325 AP129 500fr Neil Armstrong	4.50	1.50
C326 AP129 500fr Apollo 12 launching	4.50	1.50

Louis Pasteur (1822-1895), Chemist, Microbiologist — AP130

#328, Mourning Woman (detail), Mausoleum of Henri Claude d'Harcourt, by sculptor Jean Baptiste Pigalle (1714-1785).

1985, Oct. 10 Litho. *Perf. 13*

C327 AP130 500fr multi	5.00	1.75
C328 AP130 500fr multi	5.00	1.75

Christmas AP131

250fr, Children's gifts. 300fr, Akono Church. 400fr, Holy Family & drummer boy. 500fr, The Virgin with the Blue Diadem, by Raphael.

1985, Dec. 20 Litho. *Perf. 13*

C329 AP131 250fr multi	2.25	.90
C330 AP131 300fr multi	2.50	1.10
C331 AP131 400fr multi	3.25	1.50
C332 AP131 500fr multi	4.50	2.00
Nos. C329-C332 (4)	12.50	5.50

1986 World Cup Soccer Championships, Mexico — AP132

1986 *Perf. 13½*

C333 AP132 250fr Argentina, winner	2.75	1.40
C334 AP132 300fr Stadium	2.75	1.60
C335 AP132 400fr Mexican team	3.50	2.25
Nos. C333-C335 (3)	9.00	5.25

Famous Men — AP133

#C336, Pierre Curie (1859-1906), chemist, atom, and elements. #C337, Jean Mermoz (1901-1936), aviator, and aircraft.

1986, Sept. 10 Litho. *Perf. 12½*

C336 AP133 500fr multi	6.25	2.00
C337 AP133 500fr multi	6.25	2.00

AIR POST SEMI-POSTAL STAMPS

Doctor Examining Child — SPAP1

Unwmk.

1942, June 22 Engr. *Perf. 13*

CB1 SPAP1 1.50fr + 50c green	.80
CB2 SPAP1 2fr + 6fr brn & red brn	.80

Native children's welfare fund.

Nos. CB1-CB2 were issued by the Vichy government in France, but were not placed on sale in Cameroun.

Colonial Education Fund

Common Design Type

1942, June 22

CB3 CD86a 1.20fr + 1.80fr blue & red	.80

No. CB3 was issued by the Vichy government in France, but was not placed on sale in Cameroun.

POSTAGE DUE STAMPS

Man Felling Tree — D1

Perf. 14x13½

1925-27 Unwmk. Typo.

J1 D1 2c lt bl & blk	.25	.25
J2 D1 4c ol bis & red vio	.25	.25
J3 D1 5c vio & blk	.50	.50
J4 D1 10c red & blk	.50	.50
J5 D1 15c gray & blk	.60	.60
J6 D1 20c olive grn & blk	.60	.60
J7 D1 25c yel & blk	1.10	1.10
J8 D1 30c blue & org	1.10	1.10
J9 D1 50c brn & blk	1.60	1.60
J10 D1 60c bl grn & rose red	1.60	1.60
J11 D1 1fr dl red & grn, *grnsh*	1.60	1.60
J12 D1 2fr red & vio ('27)	3.25	3.25
J13 D1 3fr org brn & ultra ('27)	5.00	5.00
Nos. J1-J13 (13)	17.95	17.95

Shades occur for several values.

Carved Figures — D2

1939 Engr. *Perf. 14x13*

No.	Type	Value	Color	Unused	Used
J14	D2	5c	brt red vio	.20	.20
J15	D2	10c	Prus blue	.55	.55
J16	D2	15c	car rose	.20	.20
J17	D2	20c	blk brn	.20	.20
J18	D2	30c	ultra	.35	.35
J19	D2	50c	dk grn	.35	.35
J20	D2	60c	brn vio	.65	.65
J21	D2	1fr	dk vio	.80	.80
J22	D2	2fr	org red	1.25	1.25
J23	D2	3fr	dark blue	1.75	1.75
			Nos. J14-J23 (10)	6.30	6.30

Type D2 without "RF"

1944

J23A D2 10c Prussian blue .35

No. J23A was issued by the Vichy government in France, but was not placed on sale in Cameroun.

Catalogue values for unused stamps in this section, from this point to the end of the section, are for Never Hinged items.

D3

1947 Unwmk. *Perf. 13*

No.	Type	Value	Color	Unused	Used
J24	D3	10c	dark red	.20	.20
J25	D3	30c	dp org	.20	.20
J26	D3	50c	grnsh blk	.20	.20
J27	D3	1fr	dark car	.25	.25
J28	D3	2fr	dp yel grn	.40	.40
J29	D3	3fr	dp red lil	.40	.40
J30	D3	4fr	dp ultra	.45	.45
J31	D3	5fr	red brn	.65	.65
J32	D3	10fr	peacock bl	1.10	1.10
J33	D3	20fr	sepia	1.60	1.60
			Nos. J24-J33 (10)	5.45	5.45

Federal Republic

Hibiscus D4

Flowers: No. J35, Erythrina. No. J36, Plumeria lutea. No. J37, Ipomoea. No. J38, Hoodia gordonii. No. J39, Crinum. No. J40, Ochna. No. J41, Gloriosa. No. J42, Costus spectabilis. No. J43, Bougainvillea spectabilis. No. J44, Delonix regia. No. J45, Haemanthus. No. J46, Ophthalmophyllum. No. J47, Titanopsis. No. J48, Amorphophallus. No. J49, Zingiberacee.

Unwmk.

1963, Apr. 10 Engr. *Perf. 11*

No.	Type	Value	Color	Unused	Used
J34	D4	50c	car, bl, grn & yel	.20	.20
J35	D4	50c	car, bl, grn & yel	.20	.20
a.			Pair, #J34-J35	.25	.25
J36	D4	1fr	mag, grn & yel	.20	.20
J37	D4	1fr	mag, grn & yel	.20	.20
a.			Pair, #J36-J37	.25	.25
J38	D4	1.50fr	dk grn, lil & yel	.20	.20
J39	D4	1.50fr	dk grn, lil & yel	.20	.20
a.			Pair, #J38-J39	.25	.25
J40	D4	2fr	org ver, yel & grn	.20	.20
J41	D4	2fr	org ver, yel & grn	.20	.20
a.			Pair, #J40-J41	.25	.25
J42	D4	5fr	mag, grn & yel	.20	.20
J43	D4	5fr	mag, grn & yel	.20	.20
a.			Pair, #J42-J43	.25	.25
J44	D4	10fr	crim, grn & yel	.45	.20
J45	D4	10fr	crim, grn & yel	.45	.20
a.			Pair, #J44-J45	.90	.40
J46	D4	20fr	grn, yel & lil	1.00	.45
J47	D4	20fr	grn, yel & lil	1.00	.45
a.			Pair, #J46-J47	2.00	.90
J48	D4	40fr	lilac & yel	1.75	.80
J49	D4	40fr	lilac & yel	1.75	.80
a.			Pair, #J48-J49	3.50	1.60
			Nos. J34-J49 (16)	8.40	4.90

The pairs are se-tenant at the base.

MILITARY STAMPS

Catalogue values for unused stamps in this section are for Never Hinged items.

M1

Unwmk.

1963, July 1 Typo. *Perf. 13*

M1 M1 rose claret 3.00 3.00

Type of 1963 Inscribed "REPUBLIC UNIE DU CAMEROUN / UNITED REPUBLIC OF CAMEROUN"

1982? Litho. *Perf. 13x13½*

M2 M1 rose claret

CANADIAN PROVINCES

BRITISH COLUMBIA & VANCOUVER IS.

'bri-tish kə-'ləm-bē-ə

and van-'kü-vər 'ī-lənd

LOCATION — On the northwest coast of North America
GOVT. — British Colony
AREA — 355,900 sq. mi.
POP. — 694,300

In 1871 the colony became a part of the Canadian Confederation and the postage stamps of Canada have since been used.

12 Pence = 1 Shilling
20 Shillings = 1 Pound
100 Cents = 1 Dollar (1865)

Values for unused stamps are for examples with original gum as defined in the catalogue introduction. Very fine examples of Nos. 2 and 5-18 will have perforations touching the design on at least one side due to the narrow spacing of the stamps on the plates. Stamps with perfs clear of the design on all four sides are extremely scarce and will command much higher prices.

Queen Victoria — A1

1860 Unwmk. Typo. *Imperf.*

1	A1	2½p dull rose	2,750.	

No. 1 was not placed in use. It is ungummed and may be a proof or reprint.

Perf. 14

2	A1	2½p dull rose	250.00	175.00

VANCOUVER ISLAND

A2

A3

1865 Wmk. 1 *Imperf.*

3	A2	5c rose	*22,500.*	*7,250.*
4	A3	10c blue	1,500.	850.00

Perf. 14

5	A2	5c rose	240.00	175.00
6	A3	10c blue	240.00	170.00

BRITISH COLUMBIA

Seal of British Columbia — A4

1865, Nov. 1

7	A4	3p blue	85.00	80.00

Design A4 of 1865 Surcharged in Various Colors

2c

5c - $1

1867-69 *Perf. 14*

8	2c on 3p brown (Bk)	100.00	100.00
9	5c on 3p brt red (Bk) ('69)	160.00	160.00
10	10c on 3p lil rose (Bl)	1,150.	
11	25c on 3p org (V) ('69)	160.00	160.00
12	50c on 3p violet (R)	700.00	725.00
13	$1 on 3p green (G)	1,000.	

Nos. 10 and 13 were not placed in use.

1869 *Perf. 12½*

14	5c on 3p brt red (Bk)	1,250.	950.00
15	10c on 3p lil rose (Bl)	750.00	750.00
16	25c on 3p orange (V)	550.00	500.00
17	50c on 3p violet (R)	700.00	650.00
18	$1 on 3p green (G)	1,100.	1,200.

NEW BRUNSWICK

'nü 'brənz-ˌwik

LOCATION — Eastern Canada, bordering on the Bay of Fundy and the Gulf of St. Lawrence.
GOVT. — British Province
AREA — 27,985 sq. mi.
POP. — 285,594 (1871)
CAPITAL — Fredericton

At one time a part of Nova Scotia, New Brunswick became a separate province in 1784. Upon joining the Canadian Confederation in 1867 its postage stamps were superseded by those of Canada.

12 Pence = 1 Shilling
100 Cents = 1 Dollar (1860)

Crown of Great Britain and Heraldic Flowers of the United Kingdom A1

1851 Unwmk. Engr. *Imperf.*
Blue Paper

1	A1	3p red	1,900.	425.
a.		3p dark red	1,900.	475.
b.		Half used as 1½p on cover		*4,250.*
2	A1	6p olive yellow	3,750.	750.
a.		6p orange yellow	3,750.	800.
b.		Half used as 3p on cover		*3,000.*
c.		Quarter used as 1½p on cover		*25,000.*
3	A1	1sh brt red violet	*12,500.*	4,500.
a.		Half used as 6p on cover		*20,000.*
b.		Quarter used as 3p on cover		*20,000.*
4	A1	1sh dull violet	*16,000.*	5,000.
a.		Half used as 6p on cover		*20,000.*
b.		Quarter used as 3p on cover		*20,000.*

The reprints are on stout white paper. The 3p is printed in orange and the 6p and 1sh in violet black. Value about $225 per set of 3.

Charles Connell — A2

1860 *Perf. 12*

5	A2	5c brown	*9,500.*

No. 5 was prepared for use but not issued.

Most examples of No. 5 have creases or other faults. Value of an average example is about half that shown here.

Locomotive A3

Victoria A4

A5

A6

Steam and Sailing Ship — A7

Edward VII as Prince of Wales — A8

1860-63 White Paper *Perf. 12*

6	A3	1c red lilac	32.50	32.50
a.		1c brown violet	57.50	45.00
b.		Horiz. pair, imperf. vert.	400.00	
7	A4	2c orange ('63)	10.00	10.00
a.		Vertical pair, imperf. horiz.	500.00	
8	A5	5c yellow green	12.50	12.50
a.		5c blue green	12.50	12.50
b.		5c olive green	110.00	22.50
9	A6	10c vermilion	37.50	37.50
a.		Half used as 5c on cover		675.00
b.		Double impression	*275.00*	140.00
10	A7	12½c blue	57.50	57.50
11	A8	17c black	37.50	37.50
		Nos. 6-11 (6)	187.50	187.50

NEWFOUNDLAND

'nü-fənˌdˌ-lənd

LOCATION — Island in the Atlantic Ocean off the coast of Canada, and Labrador, a part of the mainland
GOVT. — British Dominion
AREA — 42,734 sq. mi.
POP. — 321,177 (1945)
CAPITAL — St. John's

Newfoundland was a self-governing Dominion of the British Empire from 1855 to 1933, when it became a Crown Colony. In 1949 it united with Canada.

12 Pence = 1 Shilling
100 Cents = 1 Dollar (1866)

Values for unused stamps are for examples with original gum as defined in the catalogue introduction. However, very fine examples of Nos. 1-7, 9, 11, 13 and 15 without gum are often traded at values very close to those for examples with original gum.

Watermark

Wmk. 224 — Coat of Arms

As the watermark 224 does not show on every stamp in the sheet, pairs are found one with and one without watermark. This applies to all stamps with watermark 224.

Crown of Great Britain and Heraldic Flowers of the United Kingdom — A1

Rose, Thistle and Shamrock — A3

A2 A4

A5 A6

A7 A8

1857 Unwmk. Engr. *Imperf.*
Thick Porous Wove Paper with Mesh

1	A1	1p brown violet	75.00	*130.00*
a.		Half used as 2p on cover		*9,500.*
2	A2	2p scarlet ver	*12,500.*	4,000.
a.		Vert. half used as 1p on cover		*16,000.*
3	A3	3p green	375.00	375.00
4	A4	4p scarlet ver	*7,500.*	2,850.
a.		Half used as 2p on cover		*17,500.*
5	A1	5p brown violet	225.00	*290.00*
6	A5	6p scarlet ver	*12,500.*	3,500.
7	A6	6½p scarlet ver	3,250.	*2,500.*
8	A7	8p scarlet ver	275.00	*325.00*
a.		Half used as 4p on cover		6,000.
9	A8	1sh scarlet ver	*15,000.*	5,000.
a.		Half used as 6p on cover		*16,000.*

1860
Thin to Thick Wove Paper, No Mesh

11	A2	2p orange	250.00	*325.00*
11A	A3	3p green	65.00	*90.00*
12	A4	4p orange	2,500.	1,000.
b.		Half used as 2p on cover		*12,500.*
12A	A1	5p vio brown	65.00	*125.00*
13	A5	6p orange	3,250.	700.00
15	A8	1sh orange	*21,000.*	8,000.
b.		Half used as 6p on cover		*14,000.*

A 6½p orange exists as a souvenir item.
A 1sh exists in orange on horizontally or vertically laid paper. Most authorities consider these to be proofs. Value, $10,500.

1861-62

15A	A1	1p vio brown	130.00	*190.00*
16	A1	1p reddish brown	*7,500.*	
17	A2	2p rose	130.00	*150.00*
18	A4	4p rose	30.00	*60.00*
a.		Half used as 2p on cover		—
19	A1	5p reddish brown	50.00	*65.00*
a.		5p orange brown	65.00	*80.00*
20	A5	6p rose	15.00	*45.00*
a.		Half used as 3p on cover		*8,500.*
21	A6	6½p rose	65.00	*275.00*
22	A7	8p rose	65.00	*275.00*
23	A8	1sh rose	32.50	*275.00*
a.		Half used as 6p on cover		*17,500.*

Some sheets of Nos. 11-23 are known with the papermaker's watermark "STACEY WISE 1858" in large capitals.
No. 16 was prepared but not issued.
False cancellations are found on Nos. 1, 3, 5, 8, 11, 11A, 12A, 17-23.
Forgeries exist of most or all of Nos. 1-23.

Codfish — A9

Harp Seal — A10

Prince Albert — A11

Victoria — A12

Fishing Ship — A13

Victoria — A14

1865-94 ***Perf. 12***

White Paper(#24, 27, 28)

Thin Yellowish Paper (#25-26, 29-31)

No.	Type	Description	Unused	Used
24	A9	2c green	65.00	25.00
a.		Thin yellowish paper	80.00	32.50
b.		Half used as 1c on cover		*3,750.*
25	A10	5c brown	450.00	300.00
a.		Half used as 2c on cover		—
26	A10	5c black ('68)	250.00	130.00
27	A11	10c black	190.00	50.00
a.		Thin yellowish paper	225.00	95.00
b.		Half used as 5c on cover		*4,000.*
28	A12	12c pale red brn	40.00	40.00
a.		Thin yellowish paper	425.00	160.00
b.		Half used as 6c on cover		*2,250.*
29	A12	12c brn, *white* ('94)	40.00	40.00
30	A13	13c orange	130.00	95.00
31	A14	24c blue, thin transluscent paper	35.00	25.00
a.		Thicker white paper ('70)	175.00	60.00

See Nos. 38, 40.

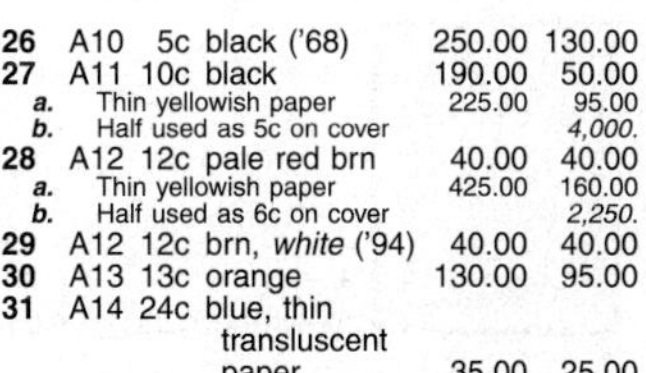

Edward VII as Prince of Wales A15

Queen Victoria A16

1868-94

No.	Type	Description	Unused	Used
32	A15	1c violet	57.50	50.00
32A	A15	1c brown lilac (re-engr. '71)	75.00	65.00
33	A16	3c ver ('70)	325.00	160.00
34	A16	3c blue ('73)	250.00	50.00
35	A16	6c dull rose ('70)	16.00	12.50
36	A16	6c car lake ('94)	25.00	16.00
		Nos. 32-36 (6)	748.50	353.50

In the re-engraved 1c the top of the letters "N" and "F" are about ½mm from the ribbon with "ONE CENT." In No. 32 they are fully 1mm away. There are many small differences in the engraving.

1876-79 ***Rouletted***

No.	Type	Description	Unused	Used
37	A15	1c brn lilac ('77)	125.00	45.00
38	A9	2c green ('79)	140.00	45.00
39	A16	3c blue ('77)	325.00	12.50
40	A10	5c blue	190.00	12.50
		Nos. 37-40 (4)	780.00	115.00

A17

A19

A18

A20

1880-96 ***Perf. 12***

No.	Type	Description	Unused	Used
41	A17	1c violet brown	32.50	10.00
42	A17	1c gray brown	32.50	10.00
43	A17	1c brown ('96)	65.00	37.50
44	A17	1c dp grn ('87)	16.00	3.25
45	A17	1c green ('97)	16.00	5.00
46	A19	2c yellow green	37.50	12.00
47	A19	2c green ('96)	65.00	22.50
48	A19	2c red org ('87)	25.00	8.00
a.		Imperf., pair	250.00	
49	A18	3c blue	37.50	5.00
51	A18	3c umber brn ('87)	32.50	3.75
52	A18	3c vio brown ('96)	80.00	65.00
53	A20	5c pale blue	325.00	8.00
54	A20	5c dark blue ('87)	100.00	6.50
55	A20	5c brt blue ('94)	32.50	6.00
		Nos. 41-55 (14)	897.00	202.50

Newfoundland Dog — A21

Schooner — A22

1887-96

No.	Type	Description	Unused	Used
56	A21	½c rose red	8.00	6.00
57	A21	½c org red ('96)	50.00	40.00
58	A21	½c black ('94)	8.00	6.00
59	A22	10c black	90.00	60.00
		Nos. 56-59 (4)	156.00	112.00

Queen Victoria — A23

1890

No.	Type	Description	Unused	Used
60	A23	3c slate	12.50	2.00
a.		3c gray lilac	16.00	2.00
b.		3c brown lilac	22.50	2.00
c.		3c lilac	16.00	2.00
d.		3c slate violet	30.00	2.50
e.		Vert. pair, imperf. horiz.	600.00	

For surcharges see Nos. 75-77.

Victoria — A24

Cabot (John?) — A25

Cape Bonavista — A26

Caribou Hunting A27

Mining A28

Logging — A29

Fishing — A30

Cabot's Ship "Matthew" A31

Willow Ptarmigan A32

Seals — A33

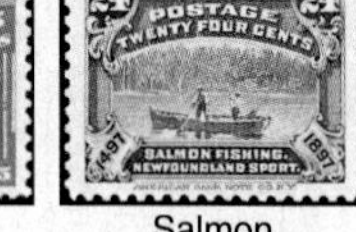
Salmon Fishing — A34

Colony Seal — A35

Iceberg off St. John's — A36

Henry VII — A37

1897, June 24

61	A24	1c deep green	1.50	1.50
62	A25	2c carmine lake	1.75	1.00
63	A26	3c ultramarine	3.25	1.25
64	A27	4c olive green	4.75	2.50
65	A28	5c violet	7.50	2.50
66	A29	6c red brown	5.00	2.90
67	A30	8c red orange	16.00	12.50
68	A31	10c black brown	16.00	6.50
69	A32	12c dark blue	20.00	12.50
70	A33	15c scarlet	20.00	11.50
71	A34	24c gray violet	25.00	10.00
72	A35	30c slate	45.00	45.00
73	A36	35c red	95.00	50.00
74	A37	60c black	16.00	10.00
		Nos. 61-74 (14)	276.75	169.65
		Set, never hinged	475.00	

400th anniv. of John Cabot's discovery of Newfoundland; 60th year of Victoria's reign. The ship on the 10c was previously used by the American Bank Note Co. as the "Flagship of Columbus" on US No. 232. The portrait on the 2c, intended to be of John Cabot, is said to be a Holbein painting of his son, Sebastian.

For surcharges & overprints see #127-130, C2-C4.

No. 60a Surcharged with Bars and

No. 75

ONE CENT
No. 76

No. 77

1897, Oct.

75	A23	1c on 3c gray lilac	50.00	25.00
a.		Double surch., one diag.	*550.00*	
b.		Vert. pair, "ONE CENT" and lower bar omitted on bottom stamp	1,100.	
76	A23	1c on 3c gray lilac	190.00	175.00
77	A23	1c on 3c gray lilac	550.00	550.00
		Nos. 75-77 (3)	790.00	750.00
		Set, never hinged	1,600.	

Most examples of Nos. 75-77 are poorly centered. Fine copies sell for about 70% of the values given. No. 75b is valued in the grade of fine.

Trial surcharges of Nos. 75-77 exist with red surcharge and with double surcharge, one in red and one in black, but these were not issued.

Edward VIII as a Child — A38

Victoria — A39

Edward VII as Prince of Wales — A40

Queen Alexandra as Princess of Wales — A41

Queen Mary as Duchess of York — A42

George V as Duke of York — A43

1897-1901 **Engr.**

78	A38	½c olive green	2.50	2.00
79	A39	1c carmine rose	4.00	4.00
80	A39	1c yel grn ('98)	4.00	.20
b.		Vert. pair, imperf. horiz.	225.00	
81	A40	2c orange	4.25	3.50
82	A40	2c ver ('98)	10.00	.50
b.		Pair, imperf. btwn.	400.00	
83	A41	3c orange ('98)	16.00	.50
a.		Vert. pair, imperf. horiz.	400.00	
84	A42	4c violet ('01)	22.50	3.50
85	A43	5c blue ('99)	25.00	2.25
		Nos. 78-85 (8)	88.25	16.45
		Set, never hinged	132.50	

No. 80b is valued in the grade of fine.

Imperf., Pairs

78a	A38	½c	250.00	
81a	A40	2c	—	*350.00*
82a	A40	2c	250.00	
83b	A41	3c	325.00	
84a	A42	4c	300.00	

Imperf., Pairs

Newfoundland imperforates virtually always are proofs on stamp paper or "postmaster's perquisites." Most part-perforate varieties also are "postmaster's perquisites." These items were not regularly issued, but rather were sold or given to favored persons.

Map of Newfoundland — A44

1908, Sept.

86	A44	2c rose carmine	32.50	1.25
		Never hinged	55.00	

Guy Issue

James I — A45

Arms of the London and Bristol Co. — A46

John Guy — A47

Lord Bacon — A50

Guy's Ship, the "Endeavour" A48

View of Cupids — A49

View of Mosquito — A51

Logging Camp — A52

Edward VII — A54

George V — A55

Paper Mills — A53

SIX CENT TYPES
I — "Z" of "COLONIZATION" reversed.
II — "Z" of normal.

1910, Aug. 15 **Litho.** ***Perf. 12***

87	A45	1c deep green, perf. 12x11	1.60	.90
a.		Perf. 12	3.25	1.75
b.		Perf. 12x14	2.25	2.00
c.		Horiz. pair, imperf. btwn.	200.00	—
d.		Vert. pair, imperf. btwn.	225.00	
88	A46	2c carmine	5.00	1.00
a.		Perf. 12x14	4.50	.75
b.		As "a," horiz. pair, imperf. between	250.00	
c.		Perf. 12x11½	375.00	250.00
89	A47	3c brown olive	9.50	9.50
90	A48	4c dull violet	12.50	9.50
91	A49	5c ultramarine, perf. 14x12	11.00	3.25
a.		Perf. 12	15.00	4.50
92	A50	6c claret, type I	65.00	55.00
92A	A50	6c claret, type II	32.50	32.50
b.		Imperf., pair	260.00	
93	A51	8c pale brown	50.00	45.00
94	A52	9c olive green	50.00	45.00
95	A53	10c vio black	50.00	45.00
96	A54	12c lilac brown	50.00	45.00
a.		Imperf., pair	325.00	
97	A55	15c gray black	65.00	55.00
		Nos. 87-97 (12)	402.10	346.65
		Set, never hinged	750.00	

Tercentenary of the Colonization of Newfoundland.

On No. 87 printing flaws such as "NFW" and "JANES" exist.

1911 **Engr.** ***Perf. 14***

98	A50	6c brown vio	25.00	20.00
99	A51	8c bister brn	65.00	*50.00*
100	A52	9c olive grn	50.00	*45.00*
101	A53	10c violet blk	77.50	*80.00*
102	A54	12c red brown	65.00	60.00
103	A55	15c slate grn	65.00	60.00
b.		Horiz. pair, imperf. btwn.	325.00	
		Nos. 98-103 (6)	347.50	315.00
		Set, never hinged	625.00	

Nos. 100 and 103 are known with papermaker's watermark "E. TOWGOOD FINE."

Imperf., Pairs

98a	A50	6c	250.00
99a	A51	8c	250.00
100a	A52	9c	250.00
101a	A53	10c	250.00
102a	A54	12c	250.00
103a	A55	15c	250.00

Nos. 98a-103a were made with and without gum. Values the same.

Royal Family Issue

Queen Mary — A56

George V — A57

Prince of Wales (Edward VIII) — A58

Prince Albert (George VI) — A59

Princess Mary — A60

Prince Henry — A61

Prince George A62

Prince John A63

Queen Alexandra A64

Duke of Connaught A65

Seal of Colony — A66

1911, June 19 ***Perf. 13½x14, 14***

No.	Type	Description	Unused	Used
104	A56	1c yellow grn	2.50	.20
105	A57	2c carmine	2.25	.20
106	A58	3c red brown	19.00	16.00
107	A59	4c violet	16.00	11.00
108	A60	5c ultra	6.50	1.25
109	A61	6c black	19.00	19.00
110	A62	8c blue (paper colored through)	65.00	55.00
a.		8c peacock blue	70.00	60.00
111	A63	9c bl violet	19.00	17.50
112	A64	10c dark green	35.00	32.50
113	A65	12c plum	32.50	32.50
114	A66	15c magenta	25.00	*32.50*
		Nos. 104-114 (11)	241.75	217.65
		Set, never hinged	410.00	

Coronation of King George V.

Imperf., Pairs
Without Gum

104a	A56	1c	250.00
105a	A57	2c	250.00
108a	A60	5c	250.00
113a	A65	12c	250.00
114a	A66	15c	80.00

Trail of the Caribou Issue

Caribou
A67 A68

1919, Jan. 2 ***Perf. 14***

No.	Type	Description	Unused	Used
115	A67	1c green	1.90	.30
116	A68	2c scarlet	2.25	.40
117	A67	3c red brown	2.50	.20
118	A67	4c violet	4.00	1.00
119	A68	5c ultramarine	5.00	1.00
120	A67	6c gray	19.00	19.00
121	A68	8c magenta	19.00	16.00
122	A67	10c dark green	9.50	4.50
123	A68	12c orange	57.50	40.00
124	A67	15c dark blue	37.50	37.50
125	A67	24c bister	37.50	37.50
126	A67	36c olive green	32.50	32.50
		Nos. 115-126 (12)	228.15	189.90
		Set, never hinged	360.00	

Services of the Newfoundland contingent in WWI.

Each denomination of type A67 is inscribed with the name of a different action in which Newfoundland troops took part.

For overprint & surcharge see #C1, C5.

Imperf., Pairs
Without Gum

115a	A67	1c	200.00
116a	A68	2c	200.00
117a	A67	3c	200.00
118a	A67	4c	200.00
119a	A68	5c	200.00
120a	A67	6c	200.00
121a	A68	8c	200.00
122a	A67	10c	200.00
123a	A68	12c	200.00
124a	A67	15c	200.00
125a	A67	24c	200.00
126a	A67	36c	200.00

No. 72 Surcharged in Black

1920 ***Perf. 12***

No.	Type	Description	Unused	Used
127	A35	2c on 30c slate	4.75	4.75
		Never hinged	7.25	
a.		Inverted surcharge	700.00	

No. 127 with red surcharge is an unissued color trial. 25 examples are known. Value, $1,000.

Nos. 70 and 73 Surcharged in Black

THREE CENTS
Type I — Bars 10½mm apart.
Type II — Bars 13½mm apart.

No.	Type	Description	Unused	Used
128	A33	3c on 15c scar (I)	210.00	190.00
		Never hinged	300.00	
a.		Inverted surcharge	*1,250.*	
129	A33	3c on 15c scar (II)	9.50	9.50
		Never hinged	13.00	13.00
130	A36	3c on 35c red	8.00	8.00
		Never hinged	11.00	
a.		Lower bar omitted	110.00	110.00
b.		Inverted surcharge	—	

The existence of No. 130b has been questioned by specialists. The editor would like to see authenticated evidence of the existence of this stamp.

All copies of the former No. 130c ("THREE" omitted) examined show part of the tops or bottoms of the letters. It is probable that no copies with "THREE" completely omitted exist.

Twin Hills, Tor's Cove — A70

South West Arm, Trinity — A71

War Memorial, St. John's A72

Humber River A73

Coast of Trinity — A74

Upper Steadies, Humber River — A75

Quidi Vidi, near St. John's — A76

Caribou Crossing Lake — A77

Humber River Canyon A78

Shell Bird Island A79

Mt. Moriah, Bay of Islands A80

Humber River near Little Rapids A81

Placentia, from Mt. Pleasant A82

Topsail Falls near St. John's A83

1923-24 **Engr.** ***Perf. 14, 13½x14***

No.	Type	Description	Unused	Used
131	A70	1c gray green	1.50	.20
a.		Booklet pane of 8	400.00	
132	A71	2c carmine	1.50	.20
a.		Booklet pane of 8	250.00	
133	A72	3c brown	1.50	.20
134	A73	4c brn violet	2.00	1.50
135	A74	5c ultramarine	3.25	2.00
136	A75	6c gray black	4.25	4.25
137	A76	8c dull violet	3.25	3.00
138	A77	9c slate green	25.00	20.00
139	A78	10c dark violet	3.50	1.75
140	A79	11c olive green	5.25	5.25
141	A80	12c lake	6.00	6.00
142	A81	15c deep blue	8.00	7.00
143	A82	20c red brn ('24)	11.50	6.50
144	A83	24c blk brn ('24)	50.00	40.00
		Nos. 131-144 (14)	126.50	97.85
		Set, never hinged	205.00	

For surcharge see No. 160.

Imperf., Pairs

131b	A70	1c	160.00
132b	A71	2c	160.00
134a	A73	4c	160.00
135a	A74	5c	160.00
136a	A75	6c	160.00
137a	A76	8c	160.00
138a	A77	9c	160.00
139a	A78	10c	160.00
140a	A79	11c	160.00
141a	A80	12c	160.00
142a	A81	15c	140.00

Nos. 134a-139a, 141a-142a are without gum. Others are either with or without gum.

Map of Newfoundland A84

Steamship "Caribou" A85

Queen Mary, George V — A86

Prince of Wales — A87

Express Train — A88

Newfoundland Hotel, St. John's — A89

Heart's Content — A90

Cabot Tower, St. John's — A91

War Memorial, St. John's — A92

GPO, St. John's — A93

First Nonstop Transatlantic Flight, 1919 — A94

Colonial Building, St. John's — A95

Grand Falls, Labrador — A96

Perf. 14, 13½x13, 13x13½

1928, Jan. 3

No.	Type	Description	Unused	Used
145	A84	1c deep green	1.15	.55
146	A85	2c deep carmine	1.50	.50
a.		Imperf., pair	250.00	
147	A86	3c brown	1.60	.35
148	A87	4c lilac rose	2.00	1.60
149	A88	5c slate green	4.25	3.25
150	A89	6c ultramarine	2.75	2.75
151	A90	8c lt red brown	4.25	3.75
152	A91	9c myrtle green	5.25	4.50
153	A92	10c dark violet	5.00	4.25
154	A93	12c brn carmine	4.00	3.00
155	A91	14c red brown	4.75	4.00
156	A94	15c dark blue	6.50	5.75
157	A95	20c gray black	5.00	4.50
158	A93	28c gray green	20.00	20.00
159	A96	30c olive brown	6.50	6.50
		Nos. 145-159 (15)	74.50	65.25
		Set, never hinged	100.00	

See Nos. 163-182.

No. 136 Surcharged in Red or Black

Type I — 5mm between "CENTS" and bar.
Type II — 3mm between "CENTS" and bar.

1929 ***Perf. 14x13½***

No.	Type	Description	Unused	Used
160	A75	3c on 6c gray black (II) (R)	2.90	2.90
		Never hinged	3.75	
a.		Inverted surcharge (II)	850.00	

The stamps with black surcharge, type I and II, were 1st or trial printings, and were not issued. There were 50 copies of each. Value, each $1,000.

Types of 1928 Issue
Re-engraved

1c — On No. 145 the lines of the engraving are thinner and the impression is clearer than on No. 163. On the former "C. BAULD" is above "C. NORMAN." On the latter these words are transposed.

2c — On the 1928 stamp the "D" of "NEWFOUNDLAND" is 1mm from the scroll at the right; the flag at the stern is lower than the top of the boat davit. On the 1929 stamp the "D" is ½mm from the scroll and the flag rises above the davits.

3c — On the 1928 stamp the pearls at the top of the crown, the jewels of the tiara and the pillars flanking the portraits are all unshaded. On the reengraved stamp there are small curved lines inside the pearls, the jewels of the tiara are in solid color, and the pillars have vertical shading lines. On the 1928 stamps the tablets with "THREE" and "CENTS" have a background of crossed lines (vertical and horizontal). On the 1929 stamp the background is of horizontal lines only.

4c — On the 1928 stamp the figures "4" have shading of horizontal and diagonal crossed lines. There are six circles at each side of the portrait.

On the 1929 stamp the "4s" have shading of horizontal lines only. There are five roses at each side of the portrait.

5c — The crossbars of the telegraph pole touch the frame at the left on the 1929 stamp but just clear it on the 1928 stamp. In the 1928 issue the foliate ornaments beside and below the figures "5" end in small scrolls and a small spur. These spurs are omitted on the 1929 stamp.

6c — On the re-engraved stamp the columns at right and left of the picture have heavy wavy outlines on the inner sides. There is no period after "JOHNS." The numerals in the lower corners are 1½mm wide instead of 1¼mm.

8c — The impression of the 1928 stamp is clear, that of 1931 is slightly blurred. The 1928 stamp has three horizontal lines above "EIGHT CENTS" and four berries on the laurel branch at the right side. On the 1931 stamp there are two horizontal lines and three berries.

10c — On the re-engraved stamp there is no period after "ST. JOHN'S." The letters of "TEN CENTS" are slightly larger and the numerals "10" slightly smaller than in 1928. Inside the "0" of "10" at the right there are two vertical lines instead of three. The clouds are fainter in 1929 and the cross upheld by the figure on the monument is more distinct. On the 1928 stamp the torch at the left side terminates in a single tongue of flame. On the 1929-30 stamp it terminates in two tongues.

15c — On the 1928 stamp the "N" of "NEWFOUNDLAND" is 1½mm from the left frame, the "L" of "LEAVING" is under the first "A" of "AIRPLANE" and the apostrophe in "JOHN'S" breaks the first line above it.

On the 1929 stamp the "N" of "NEWFOUNDLAND" is 1mm from the left frame, the "L" of "LEAVING" is below the "T" of "FIRST" and the apostrophe in "JOHN'S" does not touch the line above it.

20c — On the 1928 stamp the points of the "W" of "NEWFOUNDLAND" are truncated. The "O" is wide and nearly round. The columns that form the sides of the frame have a shading of evenly spaced horizontal lines at their inner sides.

On the 1929-31 stamp the points of the "W" form sharp angles. The "O" is narrow and has a small opening. Many lines have been added to the shading on the inner sides of the columns, making it almost solid.

30c — 1928 stamp. Size: 19¼x24½mm. At the outer side of the right column there are three strong and two faint vertical lines. Faint period after "FALLS."

1931 stamp. Size: 19x25mm. At the outer side of the right column there are two strong vertical lines and a fragment of the lower end of a faint one. Clear period after "FALLS." A great many of the small lines of the design have been deepened making the whole stamp appear darker.

1929-31 Unwmk. *Perf. 13½ to 14*

No.	Type	Description	Unused	Used
163	A84	1c green	1.50	.40
a.		Double impression	*275.00*	
b.		Vert. pair, imperf. btwn.	175.00	
164	A85	2c deep carmine	1.50	.20
165	A86	3c dp red brown	1.50	.20
166	A87	4c magenta	2.25	.90
167	A88	5c slate green	3.00	.90
168	A89	6c ultramarine	7.50	7.50
169	A92	10c dark violet	3.50	1.25
170	A94	15c deep blue ('30)	32.50	32.50
171	A95	20c gray blk ('31)	47.50	22.50
		Nos. 163-171 (9)	100.75	66.35
		Set, never hinged	150.00	

Imperf., Pairs

No.	Type	Denom.	Value
163c	A84	1c	100.00
164a	A85	2c	120.00
165a	A86	3c	100.00
166a	A87	4c	120.00

Types of 1928 Issue

Perf. 13½x14

1931 Re-engraved Wmk. 224

No.	Type	Description	Unused	Used
172	A84	1c green, perf. 13½	1.60	.75
a.		Horiz. pair, imperf. btwn.	375.00	
173	A85	2c red	2.50	.90
174	A86	3c red brown	2.50	.75
175	A87	4c rose	3.25	1.25
176	A88	5c grnsh gray	7.75	5.00
177	A89	6c ultramarine	18.00	12.50
178	A90	8c lt red brn	18.00	12.50
179	A92	10c dk violet	14.50	6.00
180	A94	15c deep blue	42.50	25.00
181	A95	20c gray black	52.50	12.50
182	A96	30c olive brown	35.00	22.50
		Nos. 172-182 (11)	198.10	99.65
		Set, never hinged	300.00	

Codfish — A97

George V — A98

Queen Mary — A99

Prince of Wales — A100

Caribou A101

Princess Elizabeth A102

Salmon Leaping Falls — A103

Newfoundland Dog — A104

Harp Seal Pup — A105

Cape Race — A106

Sealing Fleet — A107

Fishing Fleet Leaving for "The Banks" — A108

FIVE CENT
Die I — Antlers even, or equal in height.
Die II — Antler under "T" higher.

1932-37 Engr. *Perf. 13½, 14*

No.	Type	Description	Unused	Used
183	A97	1c green	1.50	.30
a.		Booklet pane of 4, perf. 13	70.00	
c.		Vert. pair, imperf. btwn.	160.00	
184	A97	1c gray black	.20	.20
a.		Bklt. pane of 4, perf. 13½	50.00	
b.		Booklet pane of 4, perf. 14	65.00	
185	A98	2c rose	1.50	.20
a.		Bklt. pane of 4, perf. 13½	35.00	
b.		Booklet pane of 4, perf. 13	45.00	
186	A98	2c green	.90	.20
a.		Bklt. pane of 4, perf. 13½	25.00	
b.		Booklet pane of 4, perf. 14	32.50	
d.		Horiz. pair, imperf. btwn.	150.00	
187	A99	3c orange brn	.90	.20
a.		Bklt. pane of 4, perf. 13½	52.50	
b.		Booklet pane of 4, perf. 14	65.00	
c.		Booklet pane of 4, perf. 13	70.00	
e.		Vert. pair, imperf. btwn.	130.00	
188	A100	4c deep violet	4.00	1.25
189	A100	4c rose lake	.50	.20
b.		Vert. pair, imperf. btwn.	100.00	
c.		Horiz. pair, imperf. btwn.	100.00	
190	A101	5c vio brn, perf. 13½ (Die I)	6.25	.90
191	A101	5c dp vio, perf. 13½ (Die II)	.90	.20
a.		5c dp vio, perf. 13½ (Die I)	10.00	.80
c.		Horiz. pair, imperf. btwn. (I)	200.00	
g.		Horiz. pair, imperf. btwn. (II)	200.00	
192	A102	6c dull blue	9.00	7.50
193	A103	10c olive black	1.00	.50
194	A104	14c int black	2.75	1.50
195	A105	15c magenta	2.25	1.50
196	A106	20c gray green	2.00	.60
197	A107	25c gray	2.00	1.50
b.		Horiz. pair, imperf. btwn.	225.00	
c.		Vert. pair, imperf. btwn.	325.00	
198	A108	30c ultra	22.50	22.50
b.		Vert. pair, imperf. btwn.	375.00	
199	A108	48c red brn ('37)	9.00	4.00
		Nos. 183-199 (17)	67.15	43.25
		Set, never hinged	95.00	

Two dies were used for 2c green, one for 2c rose.

See Nos. 253-266.

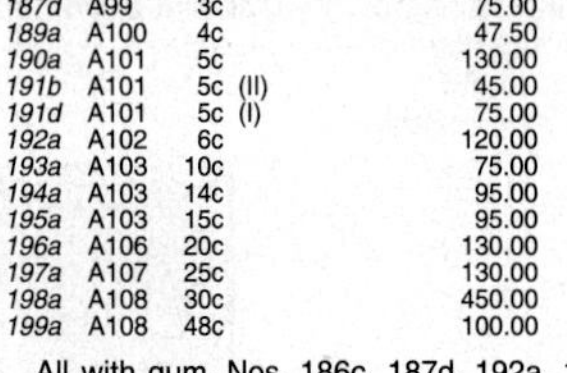

Imperf., Pairs

No.	Type	Denom.	Value
183b	A97	1c	190.00
184c	A97	1c	37.50
185c	A98	2c	130.00
186c	A98	2c	40.00
187d	A99	3c	75.00
189a	A100	4c	47.50
190a	A101	5c	130.00
191b	A101	5c (II)	45.00
191d	A101	5c (I)	75.00
192a	A102	6c	120.00
193a	A103	10c	75.00
194a	A103	14c	95.00
195a	A103	15c	95.00
196a	A106	20c	130.00
197a	A107	25c	130.00
198a	A108	30c	450.00
199a	A108	48c	100.00

All with gum. Nos. 186c, 187d, 192a, 193a and 196a also made without gum; values about 10% less.

Queen Elizabeth when Duchess of York — A109

Corner Brook Paper Mills — A110

Loading Iron Ore at Bell Island — A111

1932

No.	Type	Description	Unused	Used
208	A109	7c red brown	1.00	1.00
a.		Imperf., pair	130.00	
b.		Horiz. pair, imperf. between	400.00	
209	A110	8c orange red	1.00	.80
a.		Imperf., pair	100.00	
210	A111	24c light blue	2.25	2.25
a.		Imperf., pair	175.00	
b.		Double impression	1,100.	
		Nos. 208-210 (3)	4.25	4.05
		Set, never hinged	5.25	

No. 208a was made both with and without gum. Values about the same.

See Nos. 259, 264.

No. C9 Overprinted Bars and

1933, Feb. 9 Wmk. 224 *Perf. 14*

No.	Type	Description	Unused	Used
211	AP6	15c brown	8.25	8.25
		Never hinged	10.50	
a.		Pair, one without overprint	2,500.	
b.		Overprint reading up	2,500.	

"L. & S." stands for "Land and Sea."

Sir Humphrey Gilbert Issue

Sir Humphrey Gilbert — A112

Compton Castle, Home of the Gilbert Family — A113

Gilbert Coat of Arms — A114

Eton College — A115

Token from Queen Elizabeth I — A116

Sir Humphrey Receiving Royal Patents for Colonization A117

Sir Humphrey's Ships Leaving Plymouth, 1583 — A118

The Ships Arriving at St. John's — A119

Annexation of Newfoundland, Aug. 5, 1583 — A120

Coat of Arms of England A121

Sir Humphrey on the Deck of the "Squirrel" A122

Capt. John Mason's Map of Newfoundland, 1626 — A123

Queen Elizabeth I A124

Gilbert Statue at Truro A125

Perf. 13½, 14

1933, Aug. 3 Wmk. 224 Engr.

No.	Type	Description	Unused	Used
212	A112	1c gray black	.80	.55
213	A113	2c green	.95	.55
b.		Double impression	*450.00*	
214	A114	3c yellow brn	1.60	.45
215	A115	4c carmine	1.60	.45
216	A116	5c dull violet	1.90	.95
217	A117	7c blue	16.00	11.50
218	A118	8c orange red	6.50	6.50
219	A119	9c ultramarine	7.00	7.00
220	A120	10c red brown	7.00	5.75
221	A121	14c black	14.00	12.50
222	A122	15c claret	12.50	12.50
223	A123	20c deep green	11.50	9.00
224	A124	24c vio brown	19.00	19.00
225	A125	32c gray	19.00	19.00
		Nos. 212-225 (14)	119.35	105.70
		Set, never hinged	180.00	

350th anniv. of annexation of Newfoundland to England, Aug. 5, 1583, by authority of Letters Patent issued by Queen Elizabeth I to Sir Humphrey Gilbert.

Imperf., Pairs

No.	Type	Denom.	Value
212a	A112	1c	37.50
213a	A113	2c	37.50
214a	A114	3c	200.00
215a	A115	4c	40.00
216a	A116	5c	225.00
219a	A119	9c	200.00
220a	A120	10c	200.00
221a	A120	14c	250.00
222a	A120	15c	160.00
224a	A124	24c	130.00

Common Design Types pictured following the introduction.

Silver Jubilee Issue
Common Design Type

1935, May 6 Wmk. 4 *Perf. 11x12*

226 CD301 4c bright rose 1.25 .45
227 CD301 5c violet 1.25 .60
228 CD301 7c dark blue 3.25 1.75
229 CD301 24c olive green 7.00 4.50
Nos. 226-229 (4) 12.75 7.30
Set, never hinged 17.50

Coronation Issue
Common Design Type

1937, May 12 *Perf. 11x11½*

230 CD302 2c deep green 1.10 .35
231 CD302 4c carmine rose 1.10 .25
232 CD302 5c dark violet 2.50 .60
Nos. 230-232 (3) 4.70 1.20
Set, never hinged 6.00

Codfish
A126

Map of Newfoundland — A127

Caribou
A128

Corner Brook Paper Mills
A129

Salmon
A130

Newfoundland Dog — A131

Harp Seal Pup
A132

Cape Race
A133

Loading Iron Ore at Bell Island
A134

Sealing Fleet
A135

Fishing Fleet Leaving for "The Banks"
A136

Two dies of the 3c
Die I — Fine impression; no lines on bridge of nose.
Die II — Coarse impression; lines on bridge of nose.

Perf. 13, 13½, 14

1937, May 12 Wmk. 224

233 A126 1c gray black .40 .25
234 A127 3c org brn, die I 2.25 .80
a. Die II 1.60 .95
b. Vert. pair, imperf. btwn. (I) 250.00
c. Vert. pair, imperf. btwn. (II) 325.00
d. Horiz. pair, imperf. btwn. (I) 250.00
e. Horiz. pair, imperf. btwn. (II) 325.00
f. Imperf., pair 130.00
235 A128 7c blue 1.75 1.40
236 A129 8c orange red 1.75 1.40
a. Imperf., pair 225.00
b. Vert. pair, imperf. between 550.00
c. Horiz. pair, imperf. between 550.00
237 A130 10c olive gray 3.25 2.75
a. Double impression *225.00*
238 A131 14c black 2.50 2.50
a. Imperf., pair 325.00
239 A132 15c rose lake 3.25 2.50
a. Vert. pair, imperf. between 450.00
240 A133 20c green 2.50 1.60
a. Vert. pair, imperf. between 575.00
241 A134 24c turq blue 3.00 2.75
a. Vert. pair, imperf. between 775.00
242 A135 25c gray 3.00 2.50
a. Imperf., pair 160.00
243 A136 48c dark violet 3.75 3.00
a. Vert. pair, imperf. between 575.00
b. Imperf., pair 190.00
Nos. 233-243 (11) 27.40 21.45
Set, never hinged 35.00

Imperfs are with gum. No. 243b also made without gum; value the same.

Princess Elizabeth — A139

Designs: 2c, King George VI. 3c, Queen Elizabeth. 7c, Queen Mother Mary.

1938, May 12 *Perf. 13½*

245 A139 2c green 1.50 .20
246 A139 3c dark carmine 1.50 .20
247 A139 4c light blue 1.75 .20
248 A139 7c dark ultra 1.25 1.00
Nos. 245-248 (4) 6.00 1.60
Set, never hinged 7.50

See Nos. 254-256, 258, 269.

Imperf., Pairs

245a A139 2c 100.00
246a A139 3c 100.00
247a A139 4c 100.00
248a A139 7c 100.00
Set, never hinged 575.00

George VI and Queen Elizabeth
A141

1939, June 17 Unwmk.

249 A141 5c violet blue .90 .75
Never hinged 1.10

Visit of King George and Queen Elizabeth.

No. 249 Surcharged in Brown or Red

1939, Nov. 20

250 A141 2c on 5c vio blue (Br) .90 .80
251 A141 4c on 5c vio blue (R) .75 .60
Set, never hinged 2.10

There are many varieties of broken letters and figures in the settings of the surcharges.

Sir Wilfred Grenfell and "Strathcona II" — A142

1941, Dec. 1 Engr. *Perf. 12*

252 A142 5c dull blue .30 .20
Never hinged .35

Grenfell Mission, 50th anniv.

Types of 1931-38

1941-44 Wmk. 224 *Perf. 12½*

253 A97 1c dark gray .30 .20
a. Imperf., pair 110.00
254 A139 2c deep green .30 .20
255 A139 3c rose carmine .30 .20
256 A139 4c blue .60 .20
257 A101 5c violet (Die I) .65 .20
a. Imperf., pair 140.00
b. Horiz. pair, imperf. vert. 375.00
c. Double impression 200.00
258 A139 7c vio blue ('42) 1.00 .70
259 A110 8c red .65 .40
260 A103 10c brownish blk .60 .40
261 A104 14c black 1.50 .80
a. Imperf., pair 190.00
c. Vert. pair, imperf. horiz. 200.00
262 A105 15c pale rose vio 1.50 .90
263 A106 20c green 1.25 .80
264 A111 24c deep blue 1.90 1.25
265 A107 25c slate 1.90 1.25
266 A108 48c red brown ('44) 2.50 1.40
Nos. 253-266 (14) 14.95 8.90
Set, never hinged 19.00

Nos. 254 and 255 are re-engraved.

Memorial University College
A143

Unwmk.

1943, Jan. 2 Engr. *Perf. 12*

267 A143 30c carmine 1.00 .80
Never hinged 1.25

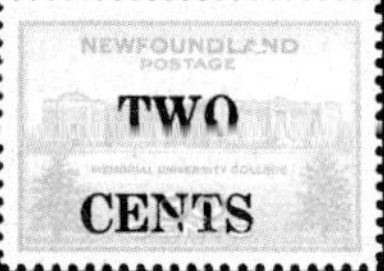

No. 267 Surcharged in Black

1946, Mar. 21

268 A143 2c on 30c carmine .25 .25
Never hinged .30

Princess Elizabeth — A144

Deck of the Matthew
A145

Wmk. 224

1947, Apr. 21 Engr. *Perf. 12½*

269 A144 4c light blue .25 .20
Never hinged .30
a. Imperf., pair 200.00
b. Horiz. pair, imperf. vert. 200.00

Princess Elizabeth's 21st birthday.

1947, June 23

270 A145 5c rose violet .25 .20
Never hinged .30
a. Horiz. pair, imperf. between 650.00
b. Imperf., pair 200.00

Cabot's arrival off Cape Bonavista, 450th anniv.

AIR POST STAMPS

No. 117 Overprinted in Black

1919, Apr. 12 Unwmk. *Perf. 14*

C1 A67 3c red brown *19,000. 14,500.*

No. 70 Surcharged in Black

1919, June 9 *Perf. 12*

C2 A33 $1 on 15c scarlet 190.00 190.00
a. Without comma after "Post" 210.00 *240.00*
b. As "a," without period after "1919" 375.00 375.00

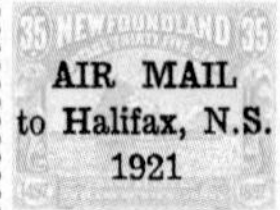

No. 73 Overprinted in Black

1921, Nov. 7

C3 A36 35c red 125.00 *160.00*
a. Inverted overprint *5,000.*
b. With period after "1921" 140.00 *175.00*
c. As "b," inverted *5,250.*

No. C3 was printed in sheets of twenty-five, containing varieties of wide and narrow space between "AIR" and "MAIL," date shifted to right, and with and without period after date.

No. 74 Overprinted in Red

1927, May 21

C4 A37 60c black *32,500. 12,500.*

No. 126 Surcharged in Black

1930, Sept. 25 *Perf. 14*

C5 A67 50c on 36c ol grn *7,500. 7,500.*

Dog Sled and Airplane — AP6

First Transatlantic Mail Airplane and Packet Ship — AP7

Routes of Historic Transatlantic Flights — AP8

1931, Jan. 2 — Engr. — Unwmk.

No.	Type	Description	Unused	Used
C6	AP6	15c brown	9.50	7.00
a.		Horiz. pair, imperf. btwn.	800.00	
b.		Vert. pair, imperf. between	800.00	
c.		Imperf., pair	400.00	
C7	AP7	50c green	32.50	22.50
a.		Horiz. pair, imperf. btwn.	1,100.	700.00
b.		Vert. pair, imperf. between	1,100.	
c.		Imperf., pair	600.00	
C8	AP8	$1 blue	65.00	50.00
a.		Horiz. pair, imperf. btwn.	800.00	
b.		Vert. pair, imperf. between	800.00	
c.		Imperf., pair	600.00	
		Nos. C6-C8 (3)	107.00	79.50
		Set, never hinged	150.00	

1931 — Wmk. 224

No.	Type	Description	Unused	Used
C9	AP6	15c brown	9.50	7.00
a.		Horiz. pair, imperf. between	800.00	
b.		Vert. pair, imperf. between	900.00	
c.		Imperf., pair	475.00	
C10	AP7	50c green	40.00	32.50
a.		Horiz. pair, imperf. between	800.00	
b.		Vert. pair, imperf. between	800.00	
c.		Horiz. pair, Imperf. vert.	800.00	
C11	AP8	$1 blue	95.00	80.00
a.		Vert. pair, imperf. between	850.00	
c.		Horiz. pair, imperf. between	850.00	
d.		Vert. pair, imperf. horiz.	850.00	
e.		Imperf., pair	475.00	
		Nos. C9-C11 (3)	144.50	119.50
		Set, never hinged	210.00	

As the watermark 224 does not show on every stamp in the sheet, pairs are found one with and one without watermark.

For overprint and surcharge see Nos. 211, C12.

No. C11 Surcharged in Red

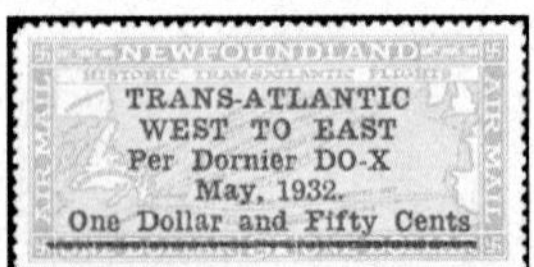

1932, May 19

No.	Type	Description	Unused	Used
C12	AP8	$1.50 on $1 blue	275.00	250.00
		Never hinged	400.00	
a.		Inverted surcharge	*16,000.*	
		Never hinged	*20,000.*	

A stamp of this design was produced in the US in 1932 by a private company under contract with Newfoundland authorities. The government canceled the contract and the stamp was not valid for prepayment of postage. Value, $20.

"Put to Flight" — AP9

"Land of Heart's Delight" AP10

"Spotting the Herd" AP11

"News from Home" AP12

"Labrador, The Land of Gold" AP13

Perf. 11½ (10, 60c), 14 (5, 30, 75c)

1933, June 9 — Engr.

No.	Type	Description	Unused	Used
C13	AP9	5c lt brown	10.00	10.00
b.		Horiz. pair, imperf. btwn.	*1,050.*	
c.		Vert. pair, imperf. btwn.	*1.050.*	
C14	AP10	10c yellow	16.00	15.00
C15	AP11	30c blue	27.50	27.50
C16	AP12	60c green	55.00	52.50
C17	AP13	75c bister	55.00	52.50
b.		Horiz. pair, imperf. btwn.	*1,050.*	
c.		Vert. pair, imperf. btwn.	*1,050.*	
		Nos. C13-C17 (5)	163.50	157.50
		Set, never hinged	240.00	

Beware of clever forgeries of Nos. C13b, C13c, C17b and C17c. Certificates of authenticity are highly recommended.

Imperf., Pairs

No.	Type	Value	Unused
C13a	AP9	5c	225.00
C14a	AP10	10c	160.00
C15a	AP11	30c	475.00
C16a	AP12	60c	525.00
C17a	AP13	75c	500.00

No. C17 Surcharged in Black

1933, July 24 — *Perf. 14*

No.	Type	Description	Unused	Used
C18	AP13	$4.50 on 75c bis	350.00	325.00
		Never hinged	500.00	
a.		Inverted surcharge	*50,000.*	
		Never hinged	—	

Return flight from Chicago to Rome of the squadron of Italian seaplanes under the command of Gen. Italo Balbo.

No. C18a was not regularly issued. The $4.50 on No. C14, 10c yellow, is a proof.

View of St. John's AP14

1943, June 1 — Unwmk. — *Perf. 12*

No.	Type	Description	Unused	Used
C19	AP14	7c bright ultra	.30	.25
		Never hinged	.35	

POSTAGE DUE STAMPS

D1

Perf. 10-10½, Compound

1939-49 — Litho. — Unwmk.

No.	Type	Description	Unused	Used
J1	D1	1c yellow green, perf. 11 ('49)	4.00	5.00
a.		Perf. 10-10½)	5.75	5.00
J2	D1	2c vermilion	6.00	5.00
a.		Perf. 11x9 ('46)	6.00	5.25
J3	D1	3c ultramarine	6.50	5.50
a.		Perf. 11x9 ('49)	7.50	7.50
b.		Perf. 9	400.00	
J4	D1	4c yel org, perf. 11x0 ('10)	8.00	8.00
a.		Perf 10-10½	12.50	12.50
J5	D1	5c pale brown	3.75	3.75
J6	D1	10c dark violet	3.75	3.75
		Nos. J1-J6 (6)	32.00	31.00
		Set, never hinged	50.00	

1949 — Wmk. 224 — *Perf. 11*

No.	Type	Description	Unused	Used
J7	D1	10c dark violet	10.00	12.50
		Never hinged	19.00	
a.		Vert. pair, imperf. between	*650.00*	

NOVA SCOTIA

ˌnō-və-ˈskō-shə

LOCATION — Eastern coast of Canada between the Gulf of St. Lawrence and the Atlantic Ocean
GOVT. — British Crown Colony
AREA — 21,428 sq. mi.
POP. — 386,500 (1871)
CAPITAL — Halifax

Nova Scotia joined the Canadian Confederation in 1867 and is now a province of the Dominion. Postage stamps of Canada are used.

12 Pence = 1 Shilling
100 Cents = 1 Dollar (1860)

Values for unused stamps are for examples with original gum as defined in the catalogue introduction except for Nos. 4-7, which are rarely found with original gum.

Queen Victoria — A1

Crown of Great Britain and Heraldic Flowers of the Empire — A2

1851-57 — Unwmk. — Engr. — *Imperf.*

Blue Paper

No.	Type	Description	Unused	Used
1	A1	1p red brown ('53)	2,500.	500.00
a.		Half used as ½p on cover		—
2	A2	3p bright blue	800.00	160.00
a.		Half used as 1½p on cover		*2,500.*
b.		3p pale blue ('57)	800.00	190.00
c.		As "b," half used as 1½p on cover		*2,500.*
3	A2	3p dark blue	950.00	190.00
a.		Half used as 1½p on cover		*3,500.*
4	A2	6p yellow green	3,500.	500.00
a.		Half used as 3p on cover		*3,500.*
5	A2	6p dark green	6,750.	1,250.
a.		Half used as 3p on cover		*3,500.*
b.		Quarter used as 1½p on cover		*40,000.*
6	A2	1sh reddish pur ('57)	*18,500.*	4,500.
a.		Half used as 6p on cover		*30,000.*
b.		1sh deep purple	*18,500.*	4,500.
7	A2	1sh dull violet	*18,500.*	6,000.
a.		Half used as 6p on cover		*40,000.*
b.		Quarter used as 3p on cover		*55,000.*

Reprints are on thin hard white paper. 1p in brown, 3p in blue, 6p dark green, 1sh violet black. Value about $300 per set.

No. 6 was reproduced by the collotype process in a souvenir sheet distributed at the London International Stamp Exhibition 1950.

Queen Victoria — A3

A5

A6

1860-63 — *Perf. 12*

White or Yellowish Paper

No.	Type	Description	Unused	Used
8	A3	1c black	6.50	5.00
a.		White paper	6.50	5.00
b.		Half used as ½c on cover		*5,000.*
c.		Horiz. pair, imperf. vert.	225.00	
9	A3	2c lilac	7.50	6.50
a.		Yellowish paper	7.50	6.50
b.		Half used as 1c on cover		*2,500.*
10	A3	5c blue	325.00	5.25
a.		Yellowish paper	325.00	5.25
b.		Half used as 2½c on cover		—
11	A5	8½c green	6.50	*12.50*
a.		White paper	6.50	*10.00*
12	A5	10c vermilion	7.50	6.00
a.		Yellowish paper	7.50	6.00
b.		Half used as 5c on cover		*1,000.*
13	A6	12½c black	25.00	25.00
a.		White paper	25.00	25.00
		Nos. 8-13 (6)	378.00	60.25

The stamps of Nova Scotia were replaced by those of Canada.

PRINCE EDWARD ISLAND

ˈprin̩t̩s ˈed-wərd ˈī-ləndz

LOCATION — In the Gulf of St. Lawrence, opposite the provinces of New Brunswick and Nova Scotia
GOVT. — British Crown Colony
AREA — 2,184 sq. mi.
POP. — 92,000 (estimated)
CAPITAL — Charlottetown

Originally annexed to Nova Scotia, Prince Edward Island was a separate colony from 1769 to 1873, when it became a part of the Canadian Confederation. Postage stamps of Canada are now used.

12 Pence = 1 Shilling
100 Cents = 1 Dollar (1872)

A1

A2

Queen Victoria — A3

1861, Jan. 1 — Unwmk. — Typo. — *Perf. 9*

No.	Type	Description	Unused	Used
1	A1	2p dull rose	450.	250.
a.		2p deep rose	525.	300.
b.		Rouletted	*2,500.*	*2,500.*
c.		Horiz. pair, imperf. between	*5,000.*	
d.		Diagonal half used as 1p on cover		*1,500.*
2	A2	3p blue	1,000.	500.
a.		Diagonal half used as 1½p on cover		*1,500.*
b.		Double impression	1,600.	
3	A3	6p yellow green	1,600.	1,000.

A4

A5

Perf. 11, 11½-12 and Compound

1862-65

White or Yellowish Paper

4 A4 1p yellow orange 25.00 25.00
a. 1p brown orange, perf. 11 25.00 25.00
b. Imperf., pair 200.00
c. Half used as ½p on cover *750.00*
5 A1 2p rose 6.50 6.50
a. Yellowish paper 6.50 6.50
b. Imperf., pair 65.00
c. Horiz. pair, imperf. vert. 250.00
d. Vert. pair, imperf. horiz. 160.00
e. Diagonal half used as 1p on cover *1,500.*
f. "TWC" for "TWO" 50.00 25.00
6 A2 3p blue 9.00 *12.50*
a. Yellowish paper 12.50 12.50
b. Imperf., pair 80.00
c. Vert. pair, imperf. horiz. 190.00
d. Horiz. pair, imperf. vert. 190.00
e. Diagonal half used as 1½p on cover 200.00
7 A3 6p yellow green 75.00 75.00
a. 6p blue green 75.00 75.00
b. Imperf. —
c. Diagonal half used as 3p on cover —
8 A5 9p violet 65.00 65.00
a. Imperf., pair 250.00
b. Horiz. pair, imperf. vert. 300.00
c. Diagonal half used as 4½p on cover *1,500.*
Nos. 4-8 (5) 180.50 184.00

Queen Victoria
A6 A7

1868

9 A6 4p black 7.50 17.50
a. Yellowish paper 12.50 20.00
b. Horiz. pair, imperf. vert. 120.00
c. Diagonal half used as 2p on cover *1,000.*
d. Imperf., pair 65.00
e. Horiz. pair, imperf. between 120.00

1870, June 1 Engr. *Perf. 12*

10 A7 4½p brown 50.00 *50.00*

A8

A9

A10

A11

A12

A13

1872, Jan. 1 Typo. *Perf. 12, 12½*

11 A8 1c brown orange 4.50 *6.50*
a. Imperf., pair 190.00
12 A9 2c ultra 12.50 *25.00*
a. Imperf., pair 250.00
b. Diagonal half used as 1c on cover —
13 A10 3c rose 20.00 20.00
a. Imperf., pair 190.00
b. Diagonal half used as 1½c on cover —
c. Horiz. or vert. pair, imperf between 200.00
14 A11 4c green 5.00 *11.50*
a. Imperf, pair 190.00
b. Diagonal half used as 2c on cover *600.*
15 A12 6c black 5.00 *11.50*
a. Horiz. pair, imperf between 190.00
b. Half used as 3c on cover *600.*
16 A13 12c violet 5.00 *20.00*
a. Imperf pair 190.00
b. Half used as 6c on cover —
Nos. 11-16 (6) 52.00 *94.50*

CANADA

ˈka-nə-də

LOCATION — Northern part of North American continent, except for Alaska
GOVT. — Self-governing dominion in the British Commonwealth of Nations
AREA — 3,851,809 sq. mi.
POP. — 28,846,761 (1996)
CAPITAL — Ottawa

Included in the dominion are British Columbia, Vancouver Island, Prince Edward Island, Nova Scotia, New Brunswick and Newfoundland, all of which formerly issued stamps.

12 Pence = 1 Shilling
100 Cents = 1 Dollar (1859)

Catalogue values for unused stamps in this country are for Never Hinged items, beginning with Scott 268 in the regular postage section, Scott B1 in the semi-postal section, Scott C9 in the air post section, Scott CE3 in the air post special delivery section, Scott CO1 in the air post official section, Scott E11 in the special delivery section, Scott EO1 in the special delivery official section, Scott J15 in the postage due section, and Scott O1 in the official section.

Values for unused stamps of #1-33 are for examples with partial original gum. Stamps without gum often trade at prices very close to those of stamps with partial gum. Examples with full original gum and lightly hinged are extremely scarce and generally sell for substantially more than the values listed.

Very fine examples of the perforated issues between Nos. 11-20 will have perforations touching the design or frameline on at least one side due to the narrow spacing of the stamps on the plates. Stamps with perfs clear of the designs on all four sides are extremely scarce and will command much higher prices.

Province of Canada

Beaver — A1

Prince Albert — A2

Queen Victoria — A3

1851 Unwmk. Engr. *Imperf.*

Laid Paper

1 A1 3p red *13,500.* 800.
2 A2 6p slate violet *13,500.* 1,350.
a. Diag. half used as 3p on cover *30,000.*
3 A3 12p black *80,000.* 50,000.

On some stamps the laid lines of Nos. 1-3 are practically invisible.

1852-55

Wove Paper

4 A1 3p red 1,250. 180.
a. 3p brown red ('53) 1,300. 190.
b. Diagonal half used as 1½p on cover *30,000.*
c. Ribbed paper 3,250. 450.
d. Thin paper 1,250. 180.
5 A2 6p slate gray ('55) 9,000. 1,100.
a. 6p brownish gray 10,000. 1,800.
b. 6p greenish gray 9,000. 1,250.
c. Diagonal half used as 3p on cover *15,500.*
d. Thick hard paper (gray vio) 10,000. 2,200.

Re-entries of the 3p are numerous. The main re-entry is distinguishable most easily by the line through "EE" and "PEN."

Most authorities believe the 12p black does not exist on wove paper.

Jacques Cartier — A4

1855

7 A4 10p blue 5,750. 1,350.
a. Thick paper 6,500. 1,650.

Queen Victoria
A5 A6

1857

8 A5 ½p rose 650. 500.
a. Horizontally ribbed paper 8,250. 2,250.
b. Vertically ribbed paper 8,500. 3,250.
9 A6 7½p green 6,500. 2,500.

Very Thick Soft Wove Paper

10 A2 6p reddish pur 13,500. 3,500.
a. Half used as 3p on cover *20,000.*

1858-59 Wove Paper *Perf. 12*

11 A5 ½p rose 2,250. 1,100.
12 A1 3p red 3,500. 650.
13 A2 6p brown vio ('59) 8,250. 4,500.
a. 6p gray violet 8,500. 4,750.
b. Diagonal half used as 3p on cover *15,000*

Nos. 11-13 values are for copies with perfs touching the design.

A7

A8

A9

A10

A11 A12

1859

14 A7 1c rose 275.00 67.50
a. Imperf., pair 3,000.
b. 1c deep rose 450.00 75.00
15 A8 5c vermilion 350.00 27.50
a. Imperf., pair 10,000. —
b. Diagonal half used as 2½c on cover *5,500.*
c. 5c brick red 525.00 25.00
16 A9 10c black brn 8,250. 4,250.
a. Half used as 5c on cover *7,500.*
17 A9 10c red lilac 750.00 95.00
a. 10c violet 800.00 110.00
b. 10c brown 800.00 95.00
c. Imperf., pair 8,250.
d. Diagonal half used as 5c on cover *3,500.*
e. 10c deep red purple 3,000. 600.00
18 A10 12½c yel green 750.00 85.00
a. 12½c blue green 825.00 95.00
b. Imperf., pair 3,000.
19 A11 17c blue 825.00 135.00
a. 17c slate blue 825.00 165.00
b. Imperf., pair 4,000.

No. 15b was used with a 10c for a 12½c rate.

Imperfs. are without gum.

Re-entries of the 5c are numerous. Many of them are slight and have only small premium value. The major re-entry has many lines of the design double, especially the outlines of the ovals and frame at left. Value, used, about $300.

Nos. 14-19 values are for copies with perfs touching the design.

1864

20 A12 2c rose 450.00 225.00
a. 2c deep claret rose 550.00 275.00
b. Imperf., pair 2,500.

Imperfs. are without gum.

Values are for copies with perfs touching the design.

Dominion of Canada

Queen Victoria
A13 A14

A15

A16

A17

A18

A19 A20

1868-76 *Perf. 12, 11½x12 [illegible]*

21 A13 ½c black 70.00 55.00
a. Perf. 11½x12 ('73) 75.00 55.00
b. Watermarked *16,500.* *7,250.*
c. Thin paper 70.00 50.00
22 A14 1c brown red 475.00 80.00
a. Watermarked 2,250. 325.00
b. Thin paper 475.00 80.00
23 A14 1c yellow org 800.00 135.00
a. 1c deep orange 900.00 160.00
24 A15 2c green 475.00 75.00
a. Watermarked 2,250. 275.00
b. Thin paper 625.00 85.00
c. Diag. half used as 1c on cover *3,500.*
25 A16 3c red 800.00 27.50
a. Watermarked 2,750. 275.00
b. Thin paper 850.00 32.50
26 A17 5c ol grn ('75) 1,000. 175.00
a. Perf. 12 *2,500.* 800.00
b. Imperf., pair *11,000.*
27 A18 6c dark brown 1,250. 80.00
a. 6c yellow brown 1,150. 80.00
b. Watermarked *4,500.* *1,350.*
c. Thin paper 1,575. 140.00
d. Diagonal half used as 3c on cover *2,500.*
e. Vert. half used as 3c on cover —
f. 6c black brown, thin paper (Mar. '68, 1st printing) 1,600. 150.00
28 A19 12½c blue 650.00 90.00
a. Watermarked *2,750.* 270.00
b. Thin paper 875.00 110.00
c. Horiz. pair, imperf. vert. —
d. Vert. pair, imperf. horiz. *8,500.*
29 A20 15c gray violet 67.50 32.50
a. Perf. 11½x12 ('74) 850.00 160.00
b. 15c red lilac 725.00 80.00
c. Wmk. (Clutha Mills) 4,000. *800.00*
d. Imperf., pair 1,150.
e. Thin paper 575.00 110.00
30 A20 15c gray 67.50 32.50
a. Perf. 11½x12 ('73) 875.00 160.00
b. 15c blue gray ('75) 100.00 50.00
c. Very thick paper (dp vio) *4,000.* 1,350.

d.	Script wmk., Perf. 11½x12, ('76)		*9,000.*	*3,250.*
e.	15c deep blue		1,400.	225.00

The watermark on Nos. 21b, 22a, 24a, 25a, 27b, 28a and 29c consists of double-lined letters reading: "E. & G. BOTHWELL CLUTHA MILLS." The script watermark on No. 30d reads in full: "Alexr. Pirie & Sons." Values for all these watermarked stamps are for fine examples. **Very fine examples are rare, seldom traded, and generally command premiums of about 100% over the values listed.**

No. 26a unused is valued in the grade of fine. No. 26b is a unique pair.

The existence of No. 28c has been questioned.

1868 — Laid Paper

31	A14	1c brown red	11,000.	4,250.
32	A15	2c green		*175,000.*
33	A16	3c bright red	9,500.	1,050.

Only two examples of No. 32 are known, neither being very fine.

Montreal and Ottawa Printings

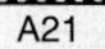
A21

A22

A23

A24

A25

A26

A27

1870-89 — Wove Paper — *Perf. 12*

34	A21	½c black ('82)	11.00	7.50
a.		Imperf., pair	475.00	
b.		Horiz. pair, imperf. between	675.00	
35	A22	1c yellow	32.50	1.10
a.		1c orange ('70)	90.00	8.00
b.		Imperf., pair	300.00	
c.		Diagonal half used as ½c on cover		3,500.
36	A23	2c green ('72)	40.00	1.60
a.		Imperf., pair	550.00	
b.		Diagonal half used as 1c on cover		1,600.
c.		Vert. half used as 1c on cover		1,600.
d.		2c blue green ('89)	75.00	3.75
f.		Double impression	—	—
37	A24	3c orange red ('73)	75.00	2.00
a.		3c rose ('71)	475.00	10.00
b.		3c copper red ('70)	1,000.	50.00
c.		3c dull red ('72)	80.00	1.50
38	A25	5c sl green ('76)	400.00	20.00
39	A26	6c yel brn ('72)	350.00	20.00
a.		Diagonal half used as 3c on cover		500.00
c.		Imperf., pair	*2,250.*	
40	A27	10c dull rose lilac ('77)	550.00	50.00
a.		10c magenta ('80)	600.00	65.00
b.		10c deep lilac rose	550.00	60.00

No. 34a made with and without gum; values the same.

Copies of Nos. 36b and 36c postmarked "Halifax" are a private speculation.

1870 — *Perf. 12½*

37d	A24	3c cop red (Ottawa)	6,250.	1,050.

1873-79 — *Perf. 11½x12*

35d	A22	1c orange	200.00	15.00
36e	A23	2c green	250.00	17.50
37e	A24	3c red	225.00	10.00
38a	A25	5c slate green	525.00	30.00
39b	A26	6c yellow brown	625.00	30.00
40c	A27	10c dull rose lilac	900.00	175.00

The gum on Nos. 35d-40c is always dull and usually blotchy or streaky. It is distinct from the earlier clear, smooth gum and from the bright shiny gums of the later periods.

Nos. 38 and 40 were printed at Montreal. Printings of Nos. 34 to 37, and 39 were made at Ottawa or Montreal and can be separated only by differences in paper and gum.

Ottawa Printing

A28

A29

1888-93 — *Perf. 12*

41	A24	3c brt vermilion	40.00	.80
a.		3c rose carmine	375.00	10.00
42	A25	5c gray	95.00	4.00
43	A26	6c red brown	95.00	10.00
a.		6c chocolate ('90)	175.00	27.50
44	A28	8c violet black ('93)	95.00	4.50
a.		8c blue gray	200.00	4.50
b.		8c slate	130.00	4.50
c.		8c gray	130.00	4.50
45	A27	10c brown red	425.00	30.00
a.		10c dull rose	425.00	30.00
b.		10c pink	425.00	37.50
46	A29	20c ver ('93)	300.00	95.00
47	A29	50c dp blue ('93)	300.00	75.00

Stamps of the 1870-93 issues are found on paper varying from very thin to thick, also occasionally on paper showing a distinctly ribbed surface.

The gum on Nos. 41-47 appears bright and shiny, often with a yellowish tint.

Imperf., Pairs

41b	A24	3c	300.00
42a	A25	5c	550.00
43b	A26	6c	450.00
44d	A28	8c	550.00
45c	A27	10c	450.00
46a	A29	20c	1,000.
47a	A29	50c	1,000.

Nos. 41b-45c made with and without gum. Values the same.

Imperforates and Part-Perforates

From 1859 through 1943 (Nos. 14a/262a), imperforate stamps were printed. These items are listed in this catalogue. The earliest imperforates through perhaps 1917 most likely were from imprimatur sheets (i.e. the first sheets from the approved plates, normally kept in government files) or proof sheets on stamp paper that once were in the post office archives. The imperforates from approximately 1927 to 1943 (often made both with and without gum) were specially created and traded for classic stamps needed for the post office museum, given as gifts to governmental or other dignitaries, or sold or given to favored persons.

The only imperforates from this entire period that were issued to the public were Nos. 90a and 136-138.

Similarly, almost all stamps that are known part-perforate (i.e., horizontal pairs imperforate vertically and vertical pairs imperforate horizontally) were specially made for trading purposes or as presentation items to be given to favored persons. These part-perforates are not listed here, but they are listed in the Scott Classic Specialized Catalogue. Part-perforate error stamps that are believed to have been actually issued to the public are listed in this catalogue.

See the similar imperforates in the air post, Nos. CE1a and CE2a, special delivery, No. F2c (but not No. F1c which was an issued error), postage dues, and Nos. MR4b and MR4c.

Jubilee Issue

Queen Victoria, "1837" and "1897" — A30

1897, June 19 Unwmk. *Perf. 12*

No.	Design	Description	Unused	Used
50	A30	½c black	80.00	75.00
		Never hinged	200.00	
51	A30	1c orange	17.50	8.00
		Never hinged	44.00	
52	A30	2c green	20.00	12.50
		Never hinged	50.00	
53	A30	3c bright rose	13.00	2.00
		Never hinged	31.50	
54	A30	5c deep blue	37.50	22.50
		Never hinged	95.00	
55	A30	6c yellow brown	180.00	150.00
		Never hinged	450.00	
56	A30	8c dark violet	42.50	30.00
		Never hinged	105.00	
57	A30	10c brown violet	90.00	75.00
		Never hinged	225.00	
58	A30	15c steel blue	180.00	150.00
		Never hinged	450.00	
59	A30	20c vermilion	180.00	150.00
		Never hinged	450.00	
60	A30	50c ultra	200.00	150.00
		Never hinged	550.00	
61	A30	$1 lake	600.00	475.00
		Never hinged	1,600.	
62	A30	$2 dk purple	1,000.	500.00
		Never hinged	2,750.	
63	A30	$3 yel bister	1,100.	750.00
		Never hinged	3,000.	
64	A30	$4 purple	1,100.	750.00
		Never hinged	3,000.	
65	A30	$5 olive green	1,100.	750.00
		Never hinged	3,000.	
		Nos. 50-60 (11)	1,040.	825.00
		Nos. 50-60, never hinged	2,651.	

60th year of Queen Victoria's reign.

Roller and smudged cancels on Nos. 61-65 sell for less.

A31

A32

1897-98

No.	Design	Description	Unused	Used
66	A31	½c black	6.50	5.00
		Never hinged	16.00	
67	A31	1c blue green	15.00	1.00
		Never hinged	37.50	
68	A31	2c purple	18.00	1.50
		Never hinged	45.00	
69	A31	3c carmine ('98)	27.50	.35
		Never hinged	70.00	
70	A31	5c dk bl, *bluish*	90.00	5.50
		Never hinged	240.00	
71	A31	6c brown	65.00	25.00
		Never hinged	160.00	
72	A31	8c orange	175.00	8.00
		Never hinged	450.00	
73	A31	10c brown vio ('98)	210.00	65.00
		Never hinged	525.00	
		Nos. 66-73 (8)	607.00	111.35
		Nos. 66-73, never hinged	1,554.	

For surcharge see No. 87.

Imperf., Pairs

No.	Design	Description	Unused
66a	A31	½c	300.
		Never hinged	550.
67a	A31	1c	300.
		Never hinged	550.
68a	A31	2c	300.
		Never hinged	550.
69a	A31	3c	650.
		Never hinged	1,200.
70a	A31	5c	325.
		Never hinged	575.
71a	A31	6c	650.
		Never hinged	1,200.
72a	A31	8c	350.
		Never hinged	650.
73a	A31	10c	450.
		Never hinged	850.

Nos. 66a, 67a, 68a and 70a made with and without gum. Without gum sell for about 95% of the unused hinged price.

1898-1902

TWO CENTS:
Type I — Frame of four very thin lines.
Type II — Frame of a thick line between two thin ones.

No.	Design	Description	Unused	Used
74	A32	½c black	3.25	1.50
		Never hinged	8.50	
75	A32	1c gray green	17.50	.20
		Never hinged	45.00	
76	A32	2c purple (I)	17.50	.20
		Never hinged	45.00	
a.		Thick paper	100.00	10.00
		Never hinged	275.00	
77	A32	2c car (I) ('99)	17.50	.20
		Never hinged	45.00	
a.		2c carmine (II)	20.00	.25
		Never hinged	50.00	
b.		Booklet pane of 6 (II)	1,050.	—
		Never hinged	2,350.	
78	A32	3c carmine	32.50	.60
		Never hinged	82.50	
79	A32	5c blue, *bluish* ('99)	160.00	1.50
		Never hinged	400.00	
80	A32	6c brown	110.00	35.00
		Never hinged	275.00	
81	A32	7c olive yel ('02)	90.00	17.50
		Never hinged	225.00	
82	A32	8c orange	140.00	20.00
		Never hinged	350.00	
83	A32	10c brown vio	225.00	17.50
		Never hinged	575.00	
84	A32	20c olive grn ('00)	350.00	90.00
		Never hinged	925.00	
		Nos. 74-84 (11)	1,163.	184.20
		Nos. 74-84, never hinged	2,976.	

For surcharges see Nos. 88-88C.

Imperf., Pairs

No.	Design	Description	Unused
74a	A32	½c	300.
		Never hinged	550.
75a	A32	1c	750.
		Never hinged	1,350.
77c	A32	2c (I)	300.
		Never hinged	550.
77d	A32	2c (II)	*500.*
e.		As No. 77b, imperf., 2 panes tete beche	*12,000.*
79a	A32	5c	750.
		Never hinged	1,250.
80a	A32	6c	750.
		Never hinged	1,250.
81a	A32	7c	500.
82a	A32	8c	750.
		Never hinged	1,250.
83a	A32	10c	750.
		Never hinged	1,250.
84a	A32	20c	2,500.

Nos. 77d, 77e, 81a and 84a were made only without gum. No. 80a was made only with gum. Others either with or without gum and of these those without gum sell for about ⅔ of the values shown for unused hinged.

Imperial Penny Postage Issue

Map of British Empire on Mercator Projection A33

1898, Dec. 7 Engr. & Typo.

No.	Design	Description	Unused	Used
85	A33	2c black, lav & car	35.00	6.00
		Never hinged	57.50	
a.		Imperf., pair	350.00	
86	A33	2c black, bl & car	30.00	6.00
		Never hinged	50.00	
a.		Imperf., pair	350.00	

Imperfs. are without gum.

Nos. 69 and 78 Surcharged in Black

1899, July

No.	Type	Description	Unused	Used
87	A31	2c on 3c carmine	11.00	6.00
		Never hinged	29.00	
88	A32	2c on 3c carmine	16.00	4.25
		Never hinged	42.50	

No. 78 Surcharged in Blue or Violet

A32a

A32b

1899, Jan. 5

No.	Type	Description	Value
88B	A32a	1(c) on ⅓ of 3c, on cover (Bl)	*6,250.*
88C	A32b	2(c) on ⅔ of 3c, on cover (V)	*6,250.*

Nos. 88B-88C were prepared and used at Port Hood, Nova Scotia, without official authorization.

King Edward VII — A34

1903-08 **Engr.**

No.	Type	Description	Unused	Used
89	A34	1c green	18.00	.20
		Never hinged	37.50	
90	A34	2c carmine	18.00	.20
		Never hinged	37.50	
b.		Booklet pane of 6	950.00	*1,150.*
		Never hinged	*1,500.*	
91	A34	5c blue, *blue*	125.00	3.50
		Never hinged	275.00	
92	A34	7c olive bister	110.00	3.50
		Never hinged	240.00	
93	A34	10c brown lilac	210.00	7.50
		Never hinged	425.00	
94	A34	20c olive green	475.00	40.00
		Never hinged	1,100.	
95	A34	50c purple ('08)	550.00	125.00
		Never hinged	1,300.	
		Nos. 89-95 (7)	1,506.	179.90
		Nos. 89-95, never hinged	3,415.	

Values for Nos. 94 and 95 used are for examples with contemporaneous circular datestamps. Stamps with heavy cancellations or parcel cancellations sell for much less.

Issued: 1c-10c, 7/1/03; 20c, 9/27/04; 50c, 11/19/08.

Imperf., Pairs

No.	Type	Description	Unused	Used
89a	A34	1c	450.00	
90a	A34	2c	27.50	30.00
		Never hinged	42.50	
c.		As No. 90b, imperf, 2 panes tete beche	*12,000.*	
91a	A34	5c	700.00	
92a	A34	7c	450.00	
93a	A34	10c	700.00	

All imperfs except No. 90a made without gum.

No. 90a issued to the public with gum; also made without gum from different plates distinguishable by experts. Value without gum, $350 with certificate of authenticity.

Quebec Tercentenary Issue

Prince and Princess of Wales, 1908 — A35

Jacques Cartier and Samuel de Champlain A36

Queen Alexandra and King Edward A37

Champlain's Home in Quebec A38

Generals Montcalm and Wolfe — A39

View of Quebec in 1700 — A40

Champlain's Departure for the West — A41

Arrival of Cartier at Quebec A42

1908, July 16

No.	Type	Description	Unused	Used
96	A35	½c black brown	3.75	3.50
		Never hinged	8.00	
97	A36	1c blue green	10.00	3.00
		Never hinged	25.00	
98	A37	2c carmine	15.00	1.00
		Never hinged	45.00	
99	A38	5c dark blue	40.00	32.50
		Never hinged	105.00	
100	A39	7c olive green	110.00	62.50
		Never hinged	300.00	
101	A40	10c dark violet	110.00	60.00
		Never hinged	300.00	
102	A41	15c red orange	125.00	75.00
		Never hinged	340.00	
103	A42	20c yel brn	160.00	125.00
		Never hinged	475.00	
		Nos. 96-103 (8)	573.75	362.50
		Nos. 96-103, never hinged	1,548.	

Imperf., Pairs

No.	Type	Description	Value
96a	A35	½c	375.00
		Never hinged	650.00
97a	A36	1c	375.00
		Never hinged	650.00
98a	A37	2c	375.00
		Never hinged	650.00
99a	A38	5c	375.00
		Never hinged	650.00
100a	A39	7c	375.00
		Never hinged	650.00
101a	A40	10c	375.00
		Never hinged	650.00
102a	A41	15c	375.00
		Never hinged	650.00
103a	A42	20c	375.00
		Never hinged	650.00

100 pair of imperfs made, 50 with gum and 50 without. Due to demand, pairs without gum generally sell for 90-95% of the unused hinged price.

King George V — A43

Two dies of 1c.

Die I — The "N" of "ONE" is separated from the oval above it.

Die II — The "N" of "ONE" almost touches the oval above it.

Two dies of 3c carmine.

Die I — The "R" of "THREE" is separated from the oval above it. The bottom line of the vignette does not touch the heavy diagonal stroke at right.

Die II — The "R" of "THREE" almost touches the oval above it. The bottom horizontal line of the vignette touches the heavy diagonal stroke at right.

1911-25

No.	Type	Description	Unused	Used
104	A43	1c green	9.00	.20
		Never hinged	22.50	
a.		Booklet pane of 6	15.00	17.50
		Never hinged	35.00	
105	A43	1c org yel (I) ('22)	9.00	.20
		Never hinged	22.50	
a.		Booklet pane of 4 + 2 labels	40.00	40.00
		Never hinged	90.00	
b.		Booklet pane of 6	32.50	35.00
		Never hinged	70.00	
d.		1c orange yellow (II)	9.00	.20
		Never hinged	22.50	
106	A43	2c carmine	7.50	.20
		Never hinged	21.00	
a.		Booklet pane of 6	25.00	22.50
		Never hinged	55.00	
b.		2c pink	100.00	12.50
		Never hinged	275.00	
c.		2c rose carmine	7.50	.20
		Never hinged	21.00	
d.		As "c," booklet pane of 6	100.00	100.00
		Never hinged	225.00	
107	A43	2c yel green ('22)	6.75	.20
		Never hinged	18.00	
a.		Thin paper ('24)	6.00	2.25
		Never hinged	16.50	
b.		Booklet pane of 4 + 2 labels	47.50	50.00
		Never hinged	105.00	
c.		Booklet pane of 6	225.00	*250.00*
		Never hinged	400.00	
108	A43	3c brown ('18)	10.00	.20
		Never hinged	27.50	
a.		Booklet pane of 4 + 2 labels	60.00	65.00
		Never hinged	120.00	
109	A43	3c car (I) ('23)	6.25	.20
		Never hinged	17.50	
a.		Booklet pane of 4 + 2 labels	47.50	*45.00*
		Never hinged	105.00	
c.		Die II	25.00	.20
		Never hinged	67.50	
110	A43	4c ol bis ('22)	25.00	3.00
		Never hinged	65.00	
111	A43	5c dk bl ('12)	100.00	.50
		Never hinged	250.00	
112	A43	5c violet ('22)	15.00	.50
		Never hinged	40.00	
a.		Thin paper ('24)	12.50	6.00
		Never hinged	32.50	
113	A43	7c yel ocher ('12)	30.00	3.00
		Never hinged	80.00	
114	A43	7c red brown ('24)	14.00	7.50
		Never hinged	37.50	
115	A43	8c blue ('25)	22.50	7.00
		Never hinged	60.00	
116	A43	10c plum ('12)	150.00	1.25
		Never hinged	425.00	
117	A43	10c blue ('22)	30.00	1.50
		Never hinged	80.00	
118	A43	10c bis brn ('25)	27.50	1.50
		Never hinged	75.00	
119	A43	20c olive grn ('12)	65.00	1.25
		Never hinged	170.00	
120	A43	50c blk brn ('25)	60.00	2.25
		Never hinged	160.00	
a.		50c black ('12)	110.00	5.50
		Never hinged	300.00	
122	A43	$1 orange ('23)	75.00	7.50
		Never hinged	200.00	
		Nos. 104-122 (18)	662.50	37.95
		Nos. 104-122, never hinged	1,771.	

For type A43 perforated 12x8 see No. 184.

For surcharges see Nos. 139-140.

Issued: #104, #106, 12/22/11; #105, 6/7/22; #108, 8/6/18; #109, 12/18/23; 4c, 7/7/22; #111, 1/17/12; #112, 2/2/22; #113, 116, 1/12/12; #114, 12/12/24; 8c, 9/1/25; #117, 2/20/22; #118, 8/1/25; 20c, 1/23/12; 50c, 1/26/12; $1, 7/22/23.

Imperf., Panes

No.	Description	Value
105c	As No. 105b, imperf, 2 panes tete beche	*9,500.*
107d	As No. 107c, imperf, 2 panes tete beche	*9,500.*
109b	As No. 109a, imperf, 2 panes tete beche	*9,500.*

Imperf., Pairs

No.	Type	Description	Value
110a	A43	4c	1,250.
		Never hinged	2,250.
112b	A43	5c	1,250.
		Never hinged	2,250.
114a	A43	7c	1,250.
		Never hinged	2,250.
115a	A43	8c	1,250.
		Never hinged	2,250.
118a	A43	10c	1,250.
		Never hinged	2,250.
119a	A43	20c	1,250.
		Never hinged	2,250.
120b	A43	50c	1,500.
		Never hinged	2,500.
122a	A43	$1	1,250.
		Never hinged	2,250.

Nos. 105c and 109b made without gum, others with gum. About half of the No. 120b pairs have creases; value thus $500.

Coil Stamps

1912 ***Perf. 8 Horizontally***

No.	Type	Description	Unused	Used
123	A43	1c dark green	75.00	45.00
		Never hinged	180.00	
124	A43	2c carmine	75.00	45.00
		Never hinged	180.00	

1912-24 ***Perf. 8 Vertically***

No.	Type	Description	Unused	Used
125	A43	1c green	15.00	1.25
		Never hinged	30.00	
126	A43	1c orange yellow (II) ('23)	8.50	5.50
		Never hinged	18.00	
a.		Block of 4 (II)	47.50	47.50
		Never hinged	75.00	
b.		1c orange yellow (I)	8.50	5.50
		Never hinged	18.00	
c.		Block of 4 (I)	350.00	
		Never hinged	525.00	
127	A43	2c carmine	20.00	.90
		Never hinged	40.00	
128	A43	2c green ('22)	11.00	.75
		Never hinged	24.00	
a.		Block of 4	47.50	47.50
		Never hinged	75.00	
129	A43	3c brown ('18)	12.50	.75
		Never hinged	25.00	
130	A43	3c carmine (I) ('24)	55.00	6.00
		Never hinged	120.00	
a.		Block of 4 (I)	550.00	550.00
		Never hinged	825.00	
b.		Die II	70.00	10.00
		Never hinged	150.00	
		Nos. 125-130 (6)	122.00	15.15
		Nos. 125-130, never hinged	257.00	

Nos. 126a and 128a were issued to the public. Nos. 126c and 130a were issued "by favor" as were the various other imperf and part-perfs of this era.

Beware of fakes of No. 130a made from No. 138.

1915-24 ***Perf. 12 Horizontally***

No.	Type	Description	Unused	Used
131	A43	1c dark green	5.75	7.50
		Never hinged	12.00	
132	A43	2c carmine	16.50	8.00
		Never hinged	35.00	
133	A43	2c yellow grn ('24)	60.00	50.00
		Never hinged	130.00	
134	A43	3c brown ('21)	6.50	5.00
		Never hinged	14.00	
		Nos. 131-134 (4)	88.75	70.50
		Nos. 131-134, never hinged	191.00	

"The Fathers of Confederation" — A44

1917, Sept. 15 *Perf. 12*

135 A44 3c brown 32.50 1.00
Never hinged 85.00
a. Imperf., pair 375.00

50th anniv. of the Canadian Confederation. Imperfs. are without gum.

1924 *Imperf.*

136 A43 1c orange yellow 25.00 27.50
Never hinged 45.00
Pair 55.00 60.00
Never hinged 90.00
137 A43 2c green 25.00 27.50
Never hinged 45.00
Pair 55.00 60.00
Never hinged 90.00
138 A43 3c carmine (I) 12.50 12.50
Never hinged 20.00
Pair 27.50 25.00
Never hinged 45.00
Nos. 136-138 (3) 62.50 67.50
Nos. 136-138, never hinged 110.00

No. 109 Surcharged:

a

b

1926 *Perf. 12*

139 A43(a) 2c on 3c car (I) 47.50 45.00
Never hinged 70.00
a. Pair, one without surcharge 275.00
b. Double surcharge 175.00
c. Die II 475.00
140 A43(b) 2c on 3c carmine 22.50 21.00
Never hinged 35.00
a. Double surcharge 175.00
b. Triple surcharge 175.00
c. Double surch., one invtd. 275.00

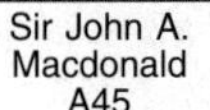

Sir John A. Macdonald A45

Sir Wilfrid Laurier A48

"The Fathers of Confederation" — A46

Parliament Building at Ottawa A47

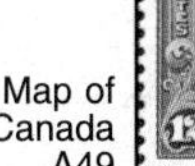

Map of Canada A49

1927, June 29

141 A45 1c orange 2.75 1.00
Never hinged 5.00
142 A46 2c green 1.25 .20
Never hinged 2.50
143 A47 3c brown carmine 6.75 4.50
Never hinged 12.50
144 A48 5c violet 3.50 2.50
Never hinged 6.75
145 A49 12c dark blue 17.50 5.00
Never hinged 30.00
Nos. 141-145 (5) 31.75 13.20
Nos. 141-145, never hinged 57.15

60th year of the Canadian Confederation. Nos. 141-145 exist partly perforated.

Imperf., Pairs

141a A45 1c 90.00
Never hinged 130.00
142a A46 2c 90.00
Never hinged 130.00
143a A47 3c 90.00
Never hinged 130.00
144a A48 5c 90.00
Never hinged 130.00
145a A49 12c 90.00
Never hinged 130.00

Thomas d'Arcy McGee — A50

Laurier and Macdonald A51

Robert Baldwin and Sir Louis Hypolyte Lafontaine A52

1927, June 29

146 A50 5c violet 3.50 2.00
Never hinged 6.50
147 A51 12c green 8.50 4.75
Never hinged 15.00
148 A52 20c brown carmine 20.00 6.00
Never hinged 35.00
Nos. 146-148 (3) 32.00 12.75
Nos. 146-148, never hinged 60.00

Nos. 146-148 were to have been issued in July, 1926, as a commemorative series, but were withheld and issued June 29, 1927. They exist partly perforated.

Imperf., Pairs

146a A50 5c 90.00
Never hinged 130.00
147a A51 12c 90.00
Never hinged 130.00
148a A52 20c 90.00
Never hinged 130.00

King George V — A53

Mt. Hurd from Bell-Smith's Painting "The Ice-crowned Monarch of the Rockies" A54

Quebec Bridge — A55

Harvesting Wheat A56

Schooner "Bluenose" A57

Parliament Building A58

1928-29

149 A53 1c orange 2.50 .35
Never hinged 5.00
a. Booklet pane of 6 17.50 15.00
Never hinged 30.00
150 A53 2c green 1.00 .20
Never hinged 2.00
a. Booklet pane of 6 17.50 18.00
Never hinged 30.00
151 A53 3c dk carmine 20.00 10.00
Never hinged 37.50
152 A53 4c bister ('29) 17.50 4.00
Never hinged 35.00
153 A53 5c dp violet 9.00 2.25
Never hinged 17.50
a. Booklet pane of 6 100.00 100.00
Never hinged 160.00
154 A53 8c blue 12.50 5.50
Never hinged 25.00
155 A54 10c green 12.50 1.00
Never hinged 25.00
156 A55 12c gray ('29) 25.00 5.50
Never hinged 47.50
157 A56 20c dk car ('29) 37.50 10.00
Never hinged 70.00
158 A57 50c dk blue ('29) 150.00 45.00
Never hinged 300.00
159 A58 $1 olive grn ('29) 200.00 55.00
Never hinged 375.00
Nos. 149-159 (11) 487.50 138.80
#149-159, never hinged 937.50

Nos. 149 to 159 exist partly perforated.

Imperf., Panes

149c As No. 149a, imperf, 2 panes tete beche 850.
Never hinged 1,250.
150c As No. 150a, imperf, 2 panes tete beche 850.
Never hinged 1,250.
153c As No. 153a, imperf, 2 panes tete beche 850.
Never hinged 1,250.

Imperf., Pairs

149b A53 1c 60.00
Never hinged 85.00
150b A53 2c 60.00
Never hinged 85.00
151a A53 3c 75.00
Never hinged 105.00
152a A53 4c 75.00
Never hinged 105.00
153b A53 5c 60.00
Never hinged 85.00
154a A53 8c 75.00
Never hinged 105.00
155a A54 10c 125.00
Never hinged 180.00
156a A55 12c 125.00
Never hinged 180.00
157a A56 20c 125.00
Never hinged 180.00
158a A57 50c 550.00
Never hinged 800.00
159a A58 $1 450.00
Never hinged 650.00

Coil Stamps

1929 ***Perf. 8 Vertically***

160 A53 1c orange 25.00 17.50
Never hinged 55.00
Precanceled 10.00
161 A53 2c green 18.00 2.50
Never hinged 40.00

King George V A59

Library of Parliament A60

The Citadel at Quebec A61

Harvesting Wheat A62

Museum at Grand Pré and Monument to Evangeline A63

Mt. Edith Cavell A64

Two dies of 1c.
Die I — 3 thick and one thin colored lines between "P" at right and ornament above it.
Die II — 4 thick colored lines. Curved line in ball of ornament at right is longer than in die I.

Two dies of 2c.
Die I — The top of the letter "P" encloses a tiny dot of color.
Die II — The top of the "P" encloses a larger spot of color than in die I. The "P" appears almost like a "D."

1930-31 *Perf. 11*

162 A59 1c orange 1.00 .50
Never hinged 2.00
163 A59 1c deep green (II) 1.50 .20
Never hinged 2.75
a. Booklet pane of 4 + 2 labels (II) 80.00 80.00
Never hinged 130.00
b. Die I 1.50 .20
Never hinged 2.75
c. Booklet pane of 6 (I) 15.00 15.00
Never hinged 27.50
164 A59 2c dull green (I) .80 .20
Never hinged 1.75
a. Booklet pane of 6 20.00 20.00
Never hinged 35.00
165 A59 2c deep red (I) 1.00 .20
Never hinged 2.00
a. Die II 1.30 .20
Never hinged 2.50
b. Booklet pane of 6 (I) 17.50 17.50
Never hinged 30.00
166 A59 2c dk brn (II) ('31) 1.50 .20
Never hinged 2.75
a. Booklet pane of 4 + 2 labels (II) 90.00 90.00
Never hinged 150.00
b. Die I 2.75 3.75
Never hinged 5.50
c. Booklet pane of 6 (I) 25.00 25.00
Never hinged 40.00
167 A59 3c deep red ('31) 2.00 .20
Never hinged 4.00
a. Booklet pane of 4 + 2 labels 25.00 25.00
Never hinged 40.00
168 A59 4c yel bister 10.00 5.00
Never hinged 18.00
169 A59 5c dull violet 5.00 3.50
Never hinged 10.00
170 A59 5c dull blue 3.00 .20
Never hinged 6.00
171 A59 8c dark blue 15.00 8.50
Never hinged 30.00
172 A59 8c red orange 4.75 3.50
Never hinged 9.50
173 A60 10c olive green 9.00 .90
Never hinged 17.50
174 A61 12c gray black 15.00 4.50
Never hinged 30.00
175 A62 20c brown red 25.00 .45
Never hinged 50.00
176 A63 50c dull blue 150.00 10.00
Never hinged 300.00
177 A64 $1 dk ol green 150.00 17.50
Never hinged 300.00
Nos. 162-177 (16) 394.55 55.55
Nos. 162-177, never hinged 785.85

No. 169 was printed from both flat and rotary press plates.
See No. 201. For surcharge see No. 191. For overprint see No. 203.

Imperf., Pairs

163d A59 1c (II) 1,300.
Never hinged 2,000.
173a A60 10c 1,300.
Never hinged 2,000.
174a A61 12c 500.
Never hinged 750.
175a A62 20c 500.
Never hinged 750.
176a A63 50c 750.
Never hinged 1,125.
177a A64 $1 750.
Never hinged 1,125.

Coil Stamps

1930-31 *Perf. 8½ Vertically*

178 A59 1c orange 11.00 7.50
Never hinged 22.50
179 A59 1c deep green 6.50 5.00
Never hinged 13.00
180 A59 2c dull green 4.50 2.75
Never hinged 9.00
181 A59 2c deep red 17.50 2.25
Never hinged 35.00
182 A59 2c dark brown ('31) 9.00 .60
Never hinged 17.50
183 A59 3c deep red ('31) 13.50 .60
Never hinged 27.50
Nos. 178-183 (6) 62.00 18.70
Nos. 178-183, never hinged 124.50

George V Type of 1912-25

1931, June 24 *Perf. 12x8*

184 A43 3c carmine 4.25 3.50
Never hinged 11.00

Sir Georges Etienne Cartier — A65

1931, Sept. 30 *Perf. 11*

190 A65 10c dark green 7.50 .20
Never hinged 17.50
a. Imperf., pair 425.00
Never hinged 650.00

Nos. 165, 165a Surcharged

1932, June 21

191 A59 3c on 2c dp red (II) 1.00 .20
Never hinged 1.60
a. Die I 2.10 1.50
Never hinged 3.25

King George V — A66

Edward, Prince of Wales — A67

Allegory of British Empire A68

1932, July 12

192 A66 3c deep red .65 .20
Never hinged 1.25
193 A67 5c dull blue 5.00 2.00
Never hinged 10.00
194 A68 13c deep green 5.75 5.00
Never hinged 11.50
Nos. 192-194 (3) 11.40 7.20
Nos. 192-194, never hinged 22.75

Imperial Economic Conference, Ottawa.

Type of 1930 and

King George V — A69

Two dies of 3c.
Die I — Upper left tip of "3" level with horizontal line to its left.
Die II — Raised "3"; upper left tip of "3" is above horizontal line.

1932, Dec. 1

195 A69 1c dark green .75 .20
Never hinged 1.40
a. Booklet pane of 4 + 2 labels 67.50 67.50
Never hinged 105.00
b. Booklet pane of 6 20.00 20.00
Never hinged 30.00
196 A69 2c black brown 1.00 .20
Never hinged 1.80
a. Booklet pane of 4 + 2 labels 62.50 62.50
Never hinged 95.00
b. Booklet pane of 6 17.50 17.50
Never hinged 26.00
197 A69 3c deep red (I) 1.10 .20
Never hinged 2.10
a. Booklet pane of 4 + 2 labels 27.50 27.50
Never hinged 40.00
c. Die II 1.10 .20
Never hinged 2.10
d. As "a," die II 22.50 32.50
Never hinged 35.00
198 A69 4c ocher 32.50 5.50
Never hinged 67.50
199 A69 5c dark blue 7.00 .20
Never hinged 13.00
a. Horiz. pair, imperf. vert. 1,000.
Never hinged 1,500.
200 A69 8c red orange 25.00 3.25
Never hinged 47.50
201 A61 13c dull violet 32.50 2.50
Never hinged 62.50
Nos. 195-201 (7) 99.85 12.05
Nos. 195-201, never hinged 195.80

Type A66 has at the foot of the stamp "OTTAWA-CONFERENCE 1932". This inscription does not appear on the stamps of type A69.

Imperf., Pairs

195c A69 1c 175.00
Never hinged 275.00
196c A69 2c 175.00
Never hinged 275.00
197b A69 3c (I) 175.00
Never hinged 275.00
197e A69 3c (II) —
198a A69 4c 175.00
Never hinged 275.00
199b A69 5c 175.00
Never hinged 275.00
200a A69 8c 175.00
Never hinged 275.00
201a A61 13c 550.00
Never hinged 825.00

No. 197e exists as one unused block of 4.

Government Buildings, Ottawa — A70

1933, May 18 *Perf. 11*

202 A70 5c dark blue 6.00 2.75
Never hinged 12.00
a. Imperf., pair 450.00
Never hinged 725.00

Meeting of the Executive Committee of the UPU at Ottawa, May and June, 1933.

No. 175 Overprinted in Blue

1933, July 24

203 A62 20c brown red 30.00 10.00
Never hinged 50.00
a. Imperf., pair 450.00
Never hinged 725.00

World's Grain Exhibition and Conference at Regina.

Steamship Royal William — A71

1933, Aug. 17

204 A71 5c dark blue 6.00 2.75
Never hinged 12.00
a. Imperf., pair 450.00
Never hinged 725.00

Centenary of the linking by steam of the Dominion, then a colony, with Great Britain, the mother country. The Royal William's 1833 voyage was the first Trans-Atlantic passage under steam all the way.

George V Type of 1932
Coil Stamps

1933 *Perf. 8½ Vertically*

205 A69 1c dark green 11.00 2.25
Never hinged 22.50
206 A69 2c black brown 12.50 .80
Never hinged 25.00
207 A69 3c deep red 11.00 .35
Never hinged 22.50
Nos. 205-207 (3) 34.50 3.40
Nos. 205-207, never hinged 70.00

Cartier's Arrival at Quebec — A72

1934, July 1 *Perf. 11*

208 A72 3c blue 3.00 1.10
Never hinged 6.00
a. Imperf., pair 450.00
Never hinged 725.00

Landing of Jacques Cartier, 400th anniv.

Group from Loyalists Monument, Hamilton, Ontario A73

1934, July 1

209	A73 10c olive green	20.00	6.00
	Never hinged	40.00	
a.	Imperf., pair	1,200.	
	Never hinged	1,800.	

Emigration of the United Empire Loyalists from the US to Canada, 150th anniv.

Seal of New Brunswick — A74

1934, Aug. 16

210	A74 2c red brown	2.00	1.50
	Never hinged	3.75	
a.	Imperf., pair	525.00	
	Never hinged	775.00	

150th anniv. of the founding of the Province of New Brunswick.

Princess Elizabeth A75

Duke of York A76

King George V and Queen Mary — A77

Prince of Wales — A78

Windsor Castle A79

Royal Yacht Britannia A80

1935, May 4 ***Perf. 12***

211	A75 1c green	.50	.30
	Never hinged	.80	
212	A76 2c brown	.55	.20
	Never hinged	1.00	
213	A77 3c carmine	1.75	.20
	Never hinged	3.00	
214	A78 5c blue	5.00	2.50
	Never hinged	8.00	
215	A79 10c green	6.25	2.25
	Never hinged	9.50	
216	A80 13c dark blue	8.00	5.00
	Never hinged	12.75	
	Nos. 211-216 (6)	22.05	10.45
	Nos. 211-216, never hinged	35.05	

25th anniv. of the accession to the throne of George V.

Imperf., Pairs

211a	A75 1c	190.00
	Never hinged	275.00
212a	A76 2c	190.00
	Never hinged	275.00
213a	A77 3c	190.00
	Never hinged	275.00
214a	A78 5c	190.00
	Never hinged	275.00
215a	A79 10c	190.00
	Never hinged	275.00
216b	A80 13c	190.00
	Never hinged	275.00

King George V — A81

Royal Canadian Mounted Police — A82

Confederation Conference at Charlottetown, 1864 — A83

Niagara Falls — A84

Parliament Buildings, Victoria, B.C. — A85

Champlain Monument, Quebec A86

1935, June 1 ***Perf. 12***

217	A81 1c green	.20	.20
	Never hinged	.30	
a.	Booklet pane of 4 + 2 labels	45.00	45.00
	Never hinged	70.00	
b.	Booklet pane of 6	17.50	17.50
	Never hinged	26.00	
218	A81 2c brown	.30	.20
	Never hinged	.50	
a.	Booklet pane of 4 + 2 labels	45.00	45.00
	Never hinged	70.00	
b.	Booklet pane of 6	14.00	14.00
	Never hinged	21.50	
219	A81 3c dk carmine	.50	.20
	Never hinged	.75	
a.	Booklet pane of 4 + 2 labels	15.00	15.00
	Never hinged	22.50	
c.	Printed on gummed side	200.00	
220	A81 4c yel org	2.00	.50
	Never hinged	3.25	
221	A81 5c blue	2.50	.20
	Never hinged	3.75	
a.	Horiz. pair, imperf. vert.	160.00	
	Never hinged	240.00	
222	A81 8c dp orange	2.50	1.75
	Never hinged	4.00	
223	A82 10c car rose	6.00	.20
	Never hinged	9.50	
224	A83 13c violet	7.00	.60
	Never hinged	11.00	
225	A84 20c olive green	17.50	.45
	Never hinged	27.50	
226	A85 50c dull violet	20.00	4.50
	Never hinged	35.00	
227	A86 $1 deep blue	47.50	8.00
	Never hinged	77.50	
	Nos. 217-227 (11)	106.00	16.80
	Nos. 217-227, never hinged	173.05	

Imperf., Pairs

217c	A81 1c	125.00
	Never hinged	175.00
218c	A81 2c	125.00
	Never hinged	175.00
219b	A81 3c	125.00
	Never hinged	175.00
220a	A81 4c	125.00
	Never hinged	175.00
221b	A81 5c	125.00
	Never hinged	175.00
222a	A81 8c	125.00
	Never hinged	175.00
223a	A82 10c	190.00
	Never hinged	275.00
224a	A83 13c	190.00
	Never hinged	275.00
225a	A84 20c	190.00
	Never hinged	275.00
226a	A85 50c	190.00
	Never hinged	275.00
227a	A86 $1	250.00
	Never hinged	350.00

Coil Stamps

1935 ***Perf. 8 Vertically***

228	A81 1c green	11.50	2.50
	Never hinged	17.50	
229	A81 2c brown	12.50	.80
	Never hinged	19.00	
230	A81 3c dark carmine	10.00	.45
	Never hinged	16.00	
	Nos. 228-230 (3)	34.00	3.75
	Nos. 228-230, never hinged	52.50	

George VI — A87

George VI and Queen Elizabeth A88

1937 ***Perf. 12***

231	A87 1c green	.25	.20
	Never hinged	.40	
a.	Booklet pane of 4 + 2 labels	9.00	*10.00*
	Never hinged	15.00	
b.	Booklet pane of 6	1.40	*2.50*
	Never hinged	2.25	
232	A87 2c brown	.40	.20
	Never hinged	.65	
a.	Booklet pane of 4 + 2 labels	10.00	10.00
	Never hinged	16.00	
b.	Booklet pane of 6	4.50	*5.00*
	Never hinged	7.25	
233	A87 3c carmine	.55	.20
	Never hinged	.85	
a.	Booklet pane of 4 + 2 labels	2.00	*2.50*
	Never hinged	3.25	
234	A87 4c yellow	2.25	.20
	Never hinged	3.75	
235	A87 5c blue	2.50	.20
	Never hinged	4.00	
236	A87 8c orange	2.25	.45
	Never hinged	3.75	
	Nos. 231-236 (6)	8.20	1.45
	Nos. 231-236, never hinged	13.40	

Imperf., Pairs

231c	A87 1c	200.00
	Never hinged	300.00
232c	A87 2c	200.00
	Never hinged	300.00
233b	A87 3c	200.00
	Never hinged	300.00
234a	A87 4c	200.00
	Never hinged	300.00
235a	A87 5c	200.00
	Never hinged	300.00
236a	A87 8c	200.00
	Never hinged	300.00

1937, May 10

237	A88 3c carmine	.20	.20
	Never hinged	.25	
a.	Imperf., pair	450.00	
	Never hinged	700.00	

Coronation of King George VI and Queen Elizabeth.

George VI Types of 1937

Coil Stamps

1937 ***Perf. 8 Vertically***

238	A87 1c green	1.50	.90
	Never hinged	2.25	
239	A87 2c brown	2.50	.30
	Never hinged	4.00	
240	A87 3c carmine	4.25	.20
	Never hinged	6.75	
	Nos. 238-240 (3)	8.25	1.40
	Nos. 238-240, never hinged	12.15	

Memorial Chamber, Parliament Building, Ottawa — A89

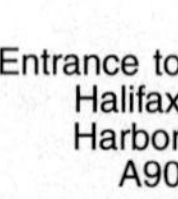

Entrance to Halifax Harbor A90

Fort Garry Gate, Winnipeg A91

Vancouver Harbor A92

Chateau de Ramezay, Montreal A93

1938 *Perf. 12*

241 A89 10c dk carmine 6.00 .20
Never hinged 9.00
a. 10c carmine rose 6.25 .20
Never hinged 9.50
242 A90 13c deep blue 7.50 .45
Never hinged 11.50
243 A91 20c red brown 12.50 .35
Never hinged 19.00
244 A92 50c green 25.00 4.50
Never hinged 37.50
245 A93 $1 dull violet 60.00 6.00
Never hinged 90.00
a. Vert. pair, imperf., horiz. *2,500.*
Nos. 241-245 (5) 111.00 11.50
Nos. 241-245, never hinged 176.50

Imperf., Pairs

241b A89 10c dark carmine 250.00
Never hinged 400.00
241c A89 10c carmine rose 250.00
Never hinged 400.00
242a A90 13c 250.00
Never hinged 400.00
243a A91 20c 250.00
Never hinged 400.00
244a A92 50c 250.00
Never hinged 400.00
245b A93 $1 400.00
Never hinged 600.00

Princess Elizabeth and Princess Margaret Rose — A94

War Memorial, Ottawa — A95

King George VI and Queen Elizabeth A96

Unwmk.

1939, May 15 Engr. *Perf. 12*

246 A94 1c green & black .20 .20
Never hinged .25
247 A95 2c brown & black .20 .20
Never hinged .25
248 A96 3c dk car & black .20 .20
Never hinged .25
Nos. 246-248 (3) .60 .60
Nos. 246-248, never hinged .75

Visit of George VI and Queen Elizabeth to Canada and the US.

Imperf., Pairs

246a A94 1c 275.00
Never hinged 425.00
247a A95 2c 275.00
Never hinged 425.00
248a A96 3c 275.00
Never hinged 425.00

A97

A98

King George VI — A99

Grain Elevators A100

Farm Scene A101

Parliament Buildings — A102

"Ram" Tank — A103

Corvette A104

Munitions Factory A105

Destroyer A106

1942-43 Engr. *Perf. 12*

249 A97 1c green .25 .20
Never hinged .40
a. Booklet pane of 4 + 2 labels 2.75 *3.00*
Never hinged 4.25
b. Booklet pane of 6 1.10 *1.25*
Never hinged 1.75
c. Booklet pane of 3 1.00 1.00
Never hinged 1.60
250 A98 2c brown .35 .20
Never hinged .60
a. Booklet pane of 4 + 2 labels 3.25 *3.50*
Never hinged 5.25
b. Booklet pane of 6 2.75 *3.00*
Never hinged 4.50
d. Vert. strip of 3, imperf. horiz. *3,500.*
251 A99 3c dk carmine .35 .20
Never hinged .60
a. Booklet pane of 4 + 2 labels 1.10 *1.25*
Never hinged 1.75
252 A99 3c rose violet ('43) .35 .20
Never hinged .60
a. Booklet pane of 4 + 2 labels 1.10 *1.25*
Never hinged 1.75
b. Booklet pane of 3 1.60 *1.75*
Never hinged 2.50
c. Booklet pane of 6 2.00 *2.50*
Never hinged 3.25
253 A100 4c greenish black 1.25 .60
Never hinged 1.90
254 A98 4c dk car ('43) .35 .20
Never hinged .60
a. Booklet pane of 6 1.25 2.50
Never hinged 2.00
b. Booklet pane of 3 1.40 2.50
Never hinged 2.10
255 A97 5c deep blue .90 .20
Never hinged 1.50
256 A101 8c red brown 1.25 .45
Never hinged 2.00
257 A102 10c brown 3.25 .20
Never hinged 5.25
258 A103 13c dull green 4.75 3.00
Never hinged 7.50
259 A103 14c dull grn ('43) 5.75 .30
Never hinged 9.00
260 A104 20c chocolate 6.00 .20
Never hinged 10.00
261 A105 50c violet 25.00 1.25
Never hinged 40.00
262 A106 $1 deep blue 57.50 6.00
Never hinged 90.00
Nos. 249-262 (14) 107.30 13.20
Nos. 249-262, never hinged 169.95

Canada's contribution to the war effort of the Allied Nations.

No. 250d totally imperf horiz. is unique. Beware of strips with blind perfs; these sell for much less.

For overprints see Nos. O1-O4.

Imperf., Pairs

249d A97 1c 190.00
Never hinged 275.00
250c A98 2c 190.00
Never hinged 275.00
251b A99 3c 190.00
Never hinged 275.00
252d A99 3c 190.00
Never hinged 275.00
253a A100 4c 190.00
Never hinged 275.00
254c A98 4c 190.00
Never hinged 275.00
255a A97 5c 190.00
Never hinged 275.00
256a A100 8c 190.00
Never hinged 275.00
257a A102 10c 300.00
Never hinged 475.00
258a A103 13c 300.00
Never hinged 475.00
259a A103 14c 300.00
Never hinged 475.00
260a A104 20c 300.00
Never hinged 475.00
261a A105 50c 300.00
Never hinged 475.00
262a A106 $1 300.00
Never hinged 475.00

Types of 1942

Coil Stamps

1942-43 ***Perf. 8 Vertically***

263 A97 1c green ('43) .90 .40
Never hinged 1.50
264 A98 2c brown 1.40 .90
Never hinged 2.25
265 A99 3c dark carmine 1.40 .90
Never hinged 2.25
266 A99 3c rose violet ('43) 2.25 .30
Never hinged 3.75
267 A98 4c dk carmine ('43) 3.75 .25
Never hinged 6.00
Nos. 263-267 (5) 9.70 2.75
Nos. 263-267, never hinged 15.75

See Nos. 278-281.

Catalogue values for unused stamps in this section, from this point to the end of the section, are for Never Hinged items.

Farm Scene, Ontario A107

Great Bear Lake, Mackenzie A108

Hydroelectric Station, Saint Maurice River A109

Combine A110

Logging, British Columbia A111

Train Ferry, Prince Edward Island A112

1946, Sept. 16 Engr. *Perf. 12*

268 A107 8c red brown 1.50 .60
269 A108 10c olive 2.00 .20
270 A109 14c black brown 3.50 .20
271 A110 20c slate black 4.50 .20
272 A111 50c dk blue green 22.50 1.50
273 A112 $1 red violet 45.00 3.00
Nos. 268-273 (6) 79.00 5.70

For overprints see Nos. O6-O10, O21-O23, O25.

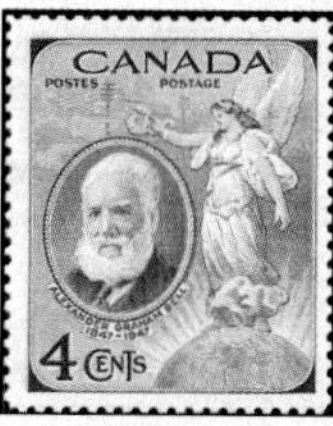

Alexander Graham Bell — A113

1947, Mar. 3

274 A113 4c deep blue .20 .20

Birth centenary of Alexander Graham Bell.

Citizen of Canada — A114

1947, July 1

275 A114 4c deep blue .20 .20

Issued on the 80th anniv. of the Canadian Confederation, to mark the advent of Canadian Citizenship.

Princess Elizabeth — A115

1948, Feb. 16

276 A115 4c deep blue .20 .20

Marriage of Princess Elizabeth to Lieut. Philip Mountbatten, R. N., on Nov. 20, 1947.

Parliament Buildings Ottawa A116

1948, Oct. 1

277 A116 4c gray .20 .20

Centenary of Responsible Government.

George VI Types of 1942
Coil Stamps

1948 ***Perf. 9½ Vertically***

278 A97 1c green 4.50 1.75
279 A98 2c brown 13.00 7.50
280 A99 3c rose violet 8.75 2.00
281 A98 4c dark carmine 11.00 2.25
Nos. 278-281 (4) 37.25 13.50

John Cabot's Ship "Matthew" A117

1949, Apr. 1 **Engr.** ***Perf. 12***

282 A117 4c deep green .20 .20

Entry of Newfoundland into confederation with Canada.

"Founding of Halifax, 1749" A118

1949, June 21 **Unwmk.**

283 A118 4c purple .20 .20

200th anniv. of the founding of Halifax, Nova Scotia.

A119

A120

A121

A122

A123

1949, Nov. 15

284 A119 1c green .20 .20
a. Booklet pane of 3 ('50) .45 .45
285 A120 2c sepia .20 .20
286 A121 3c rose violet .30 .20
a. Booklet pane of 3 ('50) 1.00 1.00
b. Booklet pane of 4 + 2 labels ('50) 1.25 1.25
287 A122 4c dk carmine .45 .20
a. Booklet pane of 3 ('50) 7.50 7.50
b. Booklet pane of 6 ('50) 9.75 9.75
288 A123 5c deep blue 1.10 .20
Nos. 284-288 (5) 2.25 1.00

Stamps from booklet panes of 3 are imperf. on 2 or 3 sides.

"POSTES POSTAGE" Omitted

1950, Jan. 19

289 A119 1c green .20 .20
290 A120 2c sepia .30 .20
291 A121 3c rose violet .20 .20
292 A122 4c dark carmine .25 .20
293 A123 5c deep blue 1.00 .70
Nos. 289-293 (5) 1.95 1.50

See Nos. 295-300, 305-306, 309-310. For overprints see Nos. O12-O20.

Oil Wells, Alberta A124

1950, Mar. 1 **Engr.** ***Perf. 12***

294 A124 50c dull green 10.00 1.00

Development of oil wells in Canada. For overprints see Nos. O11, O24.

Types of 1949
Coil Stamps
"POSTES POSTAGE" Omitted

1950 ***Perf. 9½ Vertically***

295 A119 1c green .65 .25
296 A121 3c rose violet 1.00 .50

With "POSTES POSTAGE"
Perf. 9½ Vertically

297 A119 1c green .40 .20
298 A120 2c sepia 2.50 1.10
299 A121 3c rose violet 1.60 .20
300 A122 4c dark carmine 12.50 .65
Nos. 297-300 (4) 17.00 2.15

See note after No. 288.

Indians Drying Skins on Stretchers A125

1950, Oct. 2 ***Perf. 12***

301 A125 10c black brown .70 .20

Canada's fur resources. For overprint see No. O26.

Fishing A126

1951, Feb. 1 **Unwmk.**

302 A126 $1 bright ultra 55.00 10.00

Canada's fish resources. For overprint see No. O27.

Sir Robert Laird Borden A127

William L. Mackenzie King A128

1951, June 25 ***Perf. 12***

303 A127 3c turquoise green .20 .20
304 A128 4c rose pink .20 .20

George VI Types of 1949

1951 ***Perf. 12***

305 A120 2c olive green .20 .20
306 A122 4c orange vermilion .25 .20
a. Booklet pane of 3 1.50 1.50
b. Booklet pane of 6 2.00 2.00

For overprints see Nos. O28-O29.

Coil Stamps
Perf. 9½ Vertically

309 A120 2c olive green 1.10 .50
310 A122 4c orange vermilion 2.25 .60

Trains of 1851 and 1951 — A129

"Threepenny Beaver" of 1851 — A130

5c, Steamships City of Toronto and Prince George. 7c, Stagecoach and Plane.

1951, Sept. 24 **Unwmk.** ***Perf. 12***

311 A129 4c dark gray .50 .20
312 A129 5c purple 1.50 1.10
313 A129 7c deep blue .90 .25
314 A130 15c bright red .90 .25
Nos. 311-314 (4) 3.80 1.80

Centenary of British North American postal administration.

Princess Elizabeth and Duke of Edinburgh A131

1951, Oct. 26 **Engr.**

315 A131 4c violet .20 .20

Visit of Princess Elizabeth, Duchess of Edinburgh and the Duke of Edinburgh to Canada and the US.

Symbols of Newsprint Paper Production A132

1952, Apr. 1 **Unwmk.** ***Perf. 12***

316 A132 20c gray 1.10 .20

Canada's paper production. For overprint see No. O30.

Red Cross on Sun — A133

1952, July 26 **Engr. and Litho.**

317 A133 4c blue & red .20 .20

18th Intl. Red Cross Conf., Toronto, July 1952.

Sir John J. C. Abbott A134

Alexander Mackenzie A135

1952, Nov. 3 **Engr.**

318 A134 3c rose lilac .20 .20
319 A135 4c orange vermilion .20 .20

Canada Goose A136

1952, Nov. 3

320 A136 7c blue .30 .20

For overprint see No. O31.

Pacific Coast Indian House and Totem Pole — A137

1953, Feb. 2

321 A137 $1 gray 9.50 .60

For overprint see No. O32.

Natl. Wildlife Week — A138

1953, Apr. 1

322 A138 2c Polar bear .20 .20
323 A138 3c Moose .20 .20
324 A138 4c Bighorn sheep .20 .20
Nos. 322-324 (3) .60 .60

Elizabeth II — A139

1953, May 1

325 A139 1c violet brown .20 .20
a. Booklet pane of 3 .80 .60
326 A139 2c green .20 .20
327 A139 3c carmine rose .20 .20
a. Booklet pane of 3 1.25 .80
b. Booklet pane of 4 + 2 labels 1.40 1.40
328 A139 4c violet .20 .20
a. Booklet pane of 3 1.50 1.60
b. Booklet pane of 6 1.50 1.40
329 A139 5c ultramarine .25 .20
Nos. 325-329 (5) 1.05 1.00

Stamps from booklet panes of 3 are imperf. on 2 or 3 sides.
See Nos. 331-333. For overprints see Nos. O33-O37.

Coronation Issue

Queen Elizabeth II — A140

1953, June 1

330 A140 4c violet .20 .20

Coil Stamps

1953 ***Perf. 9½ Vertically***

331 A139 2c green 1.25 .75
332 A139 3c carmine rose 1.25 .75
333 A139 4c violet 3.00 1.25
Nos. 331-333 (3) 5.50 2.75

See note after No. 329.
Issued: 2c, 7/30; 3c, 7/27; 4c, 9/3.

Bobbin, Cloth and Spinning Wheel A141

1953, Nov. 2 ***Perf. 12***

334 A141 50c light green 3.25 .20

For overprint see No. O38.

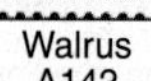

Walrus
A142

Beaver
A143

1954, Apr. 1

335 A142 4c gray .20 .20
336 A143 5c ultramarine .25 .20
a. Booklet pane of 5 + label 1.50 1.50

National Wildlife Week, 1954.

Elizabeth II
A144

Gannet
A145

1954-61

337 A144 1c violet brn .20 .20
a. Booklet pane of 5 + label ('56) 1.00 1.00
338 A144 2c green .20 .20
a. Pane of 25 ('61) 3.75 3.75
339 A144 3c carmine rose .20 .20
a. Horiz. pair, imperf. vert. *1,200.*
340 A144 4c violet .20 .20
a. Booklet pane of 5 + label ('56) 1.25 1.25
b. Booklet pane of 6 ('55) 3.00 3.00
341 A144 5c bright blue .20 .20
a. Booklet pane of 5 + label 1.10 1.10
b. Pane of 20 (5 x 4) ('61) 7.00 7.00
c. Horiz. pair, imperf. vert. *4,000.*
342 A144 6c orange .30 .20
343 A145 15c gray 1.00 .20
Nos. 337-343 (7) 2.30 1.40

Panes of 20 and 25 are imperf. on 4 sides.
Issued: 5c, 15c, 4/1; others, 6/10.
For overprints see Nos. O40-O44.

Luminescence

The overprinting of regular stamps with vertical luminescent bands began experimentally in 1962 when Nos. 337p-341p were released at Winnipeg. The bands are of varying number, position and chemical content.

Tagged varieties of stamps which were issued both untagged and with luminescent overprint are listed with suffix letter "p".

Tagged

1962, Jan. 13

337p A144 1c violet brown .85 .85
338p A144 2c green .85 .85
339p A144 3c carmine rose .85 .85
340p A144 4c violet 2.50 3.00
341p A144 5c bright blue 2.75 2.25
Nos. 337p-341p (5) 7.80 7.80

Coil Stamps

1954 ***Perf. 9½ Vertically***

345 A144 2c green .50 .20
347 A144 4c violet 1.25 .20
348 A144 5c bright blue 2.00 .20
Nos. 345-348 (3) 3.75 .60

Issued: 2c, 9/9; 3c, 8/23; 4c, 7/6.

Sir John Sparrow David Thompson
A146

Sir Mackenzie Bowell
A147

1954, Nov. 1 ***Perf. 12***

349 A146 4c violet .20 .20
350 A147 5c bright blue .20 .20

Eskimo and Kayak
A148

1955, Feb. 21

351 A148 10c violet brown .25 .20

For overprint see No. O39.

Musk Ox — A149

Whooping Cranes
A150

1955, Apr. 4

352 A149 4c purple .20 .20
353 A150 5c blue .25 .20

National Wildlife Week, April 10-16.

Torch, Dove and Maple Leaves — A151

1955, June 1 **Unwmk.**

354 A151 5c light blue .20 .20

ICAO, 10th anniversary.

Pioneer Settlers
A152

1955, June 30 ***Perf. 12***

355 A152 5c ultramarine .20 .20

50th anniv. of the founding of the provinces of Alberta and Saskatchewan.

Globe and Scout Emblem
A153

1955, Aug. 20 **Engr.**

356 A153 5c green & org brown .20 .20

8th Boy Scout World Jamboree, Niagara-on-the-Lake, Ont.

Richard Bedford Bennett
A154

Sir Charles Tupper
A155

1955, Nov. 8

357 A154 4c violet .20 .20
358 A155 5c ultramarine .20 .20

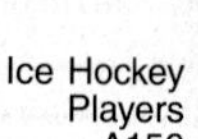

Ice Hockey Players
A156

1956, Jan. 23

359 A156 5c ultramarine .20 .20

Issued to publicize Canada's most popular winter sport.

Caribou
A157

Mountain Goat
A158

1956, Apr. 12

360 A157 4c deep violet .25 .20
361 A158 5c ultramarine .25 .20

National Wildlife Week, 1956.

"Paper Industry"
A159

"Chemical Industry" — A160

1956, June 7 **Engr.**

362 A159 20c green 1.00 .20
363 A160 25c red 1.25 .20

For overprint see No. O45.

House on Fire — A161

1956, Oct. 9 **Unwmk.** ***Perf. 12***

364 A161 5c gray & red .20 .20

Issued to emphasize the needless waste caused by preventable fires.

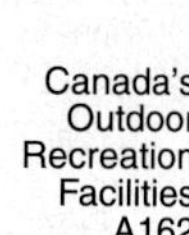

Canada's Outdoor Recreation Facilities
A162

1957, Mar. 7

365 A162 5c Fishing .30 .20
366 A162 5c Swimming .30 .20
367 A162 5c Hunter and dog .30 .20
368 A162 5c Skiing .30 .20
a. Block of 4, #365-368 1.25 1.00

All four designs are printed alternating in sheet of 50, with various combinations possible.

Loon — A163

1957, Apr. 10 ***Perf. 12***

369 A163 5c black .25 .20

David Thompson and Map of Western Canada
A164

1957, June 5 **Unwmk.**

370 A164 5c ultramarine .20 .20

David Thompson (1770-1857), explorer and geographer.

Parliament Building, Ottawa — A165

Post Horn and Globe
A166

1957, Aug. 14 ***Perf. 12***

371 A165 5c dark blue .20 .20
372 A166 15c dark blue 1.90 1.25

UPU, 14th Congress, Ottawa, Aug. 1957.

Miner With Pneumatic Drill — A167

1957, Sept. 5

373 A167 5c black .20 .20

Canada's mining industry; 6th Commonwealth Mining and Metallurgical Congress, Vancouver, Sept. 8-Oct. 8.

Elizabeth II and Prince Philip — A168

1957, Oct. 10 **Unwmk.**

374 A168 5c black .20 .20

Visit of Queen Elizabeth II and Prince Philip to Canada, Oct. 12-16.

Newspapers and Symbols of Industry
A169

1958, Jan. 22 **Engr.**

375 A169 5c black .25 .20

Canadian press; the importance of a free press.

Microscope and Globe — A170

1958, Mar. 5 *Perf. 12*
376 A170 5c blue .25 .20

Intl. Geophysical Year, 1957-1958.

Miner Panning Gold — A171

1958, May 8 **Unwmk.**
377 A171 5c bluish green .20 .20

Province of British Columbia, cent.

La Verendrye A172

1958, June 4 *Perf. 12*
378 A172 5c bright ultra .20 .20

Pierre Gaultier de Varenne, Sieur de la Verendrye, 18th century French explorer of Western Canada.

Champlain and View of Quebec A173

1958, June 26
379 A173 5c dk green & bis brn .20 .20

Founding of Quebec, 350th anniv.

Nurse — A174

1958, July 30 **Engr.**
380 A174 5c rose lilac .20 .20

Importance of health, both to the individual and to the nation.

Kerosene Lamp and Refinery — A175

1958, Sept. 10 *Perf. 12*
381 A175 5c olive & red .20 .20

Centennial of Canada's oil industry.

Speaker's Chair and Mace A176

1958, Oct. 2
382 A176 5c slate blue .20 .20

Bicentennial of the meeting of the first House of Representatives in Canada, Halifax, Oct. 2, 1758.

"Silver Dart" and Delta Wing Planes A177

1959, Feb. 23 *Perf. 12*
383 A177 5c blue & black .20 .20

50th anniv. of the 1st airplane flight in Canada near Baddeck, N. S., with J. A. D. McCurdy as pilot.

Globe and Dove — A178

1959, Apr. 2
384 A178 5c violet blue .20 .20

NATO, 10th anniversary.

Woman Tending Tree — A179

1959, May 13
385 A179 5c apple green & blk .20 .20

Associated Country Women of the World.

Elizabeth II — A180

1959, June 18
386 A180 5c dark carmine .20 .20

Visit of Queen Elizabeth and Prince Philip to Canada, June 18-Aug. 1.

Great Lakes, Maple Leaf and Eagle Emblems A181

1959, June 26 **Engr.**
387 A181 5c red & blue .20 .20
a. Center inverted 8,500. 7,750.

Opening of the St. Lawrence Seaway, June 26, 1959.
See United States No. 1131.

British Lion, Fleur-de-Lis and Maple Leaves A182

1959, Sept. 10 *Perf. 12*
388 A182 5c crim rose & dk green .20 .20

Bicentenary of the Battle of the Plains of Abraham.

Girl Guide Emblem — A183

1960, Apr. 20 **Unwmk.**
389 A183 5c brown org & ultra .20 .20

Canadian Girl Guides Assoc., 50th anniv.

Dollard des Ormeaux and Battle Scene — A184

1960, May 19
390 A184 5c ultra & bis brown .20 .20

Battle of the Long Sault, 300th anniv.

Compass Rose, Earth Mover and Surveyor A185

Emily Pauline Johnson A186

1961, Feb. 8 **Engr.** *Perf. 12*
391 A185 5c green & vermilion .20 .20

Development of Canada's Northland.

1961, Mar. 10
392 A186 5c green & red .20 .20

Emily Pauline Johnson (1861-1913), Mohawk princess and poet.

Arthur Meighen — A187

1961, Apr. 19
393 A187 5c ultramarine .20 .20

Arthur Meighen, Prime Minister of Canada, (1920-21, 1926).

Power Plant and Men Holding Blueprint A188

1961, June 28 **Unwmk.** *Perf. 12*
394 A188 5c lt red brn & blue .20 .20

10th anniv. of the Colombo Plan, initiated to assist underdeveloped countries by providing trained manpower and resources.

Natural Resources and Hands Holding Cogwheel — A189

1961, Oct. 12 **Engr.** *Perf. 12*
395 A189 5c brown & blue grn .20 .20

Canada's "Resources for Tomorrow Program" and to publicize the close link between industry and the country's renewable natural resources.

Young Adults and Education Symbols — A190

1962, Feb. 28 **Unwmk.** *Perf. 12*
396 A190 5c black & lt red brn .20 .20
a. Light red brown (symbols) omitted

Issued to stimulate public awareness of the importance of education.

Scottish Settler and Lord Selkirk A191

1962, May 3 *Perf. 12*
397 A191 5c lt green & vio brn .20 .20

150th anniv. of the Red River Settlement in Western Canada (Prairie Provinces).

Jean Talon Presenting Gifts to Young Farm Couple — A192

1962, June 13 **Unwmk.** *Perf. 12*
398 A192 5c dark blue .20 .20

Jean Talon, administrator of New France (Canada), 1665-1668.

British Columbia Legislative Building and Stamp of 1860 — A193

1962, Aug. 22 **Engr.** *Perf. 12*
399 A193 5c black & rose .20 .20

Centenary of Victoria as incorporated city.

Arms of the Provinces A194

1962, Aug. 31
400 A194 5c brown orange & black .20 .20

Official opening of the Trans-Canada Highway, Rogers Pass, Glacier National Park, Sept. 4.

Queen Elizabeth II and Wheat — A195

Designs (Symbol in upper left corner): 1c, Mineral crystals. 2c, Tree. 3c, Fish. 4c, Electric high tension tower.

1962-63 Engr. *Perf. 12*

401 A195 1c dp brn ('63) .20 .20
a. Booklet pane of 5 + label ('63) 2.50 2.50
402 A195 2c green ('63) .20 .20
a. Pane of 25 ('63) 5.00 5.00
403 A195 3c purple ('63) .20 .20
404 A195 4c carmine ('63) .20 .20
a. Booklet pane of 5 + label ('63) 2.75 2.75
b. Pane of 25 ('63) 7.50 7.50
405 A195 5c violet blue .20 .20
a. Booklet pane of 5 + label ('63) 2.75 2.75
b. Pane of 20 ('63) 8.50 8.50
c. Imperf., pair (#405b) *3,250.*
d. Vert. pair, imperf. horiz. *3,750.* *500.00*
Nos. 401-405 (5) 1.00 1.00

Nos. 402a, 404b, and 405b are imperf. on four sides.

Used examples of No. 405d are canceled "Gonor, MB." Beware of examples with traces of blind perfs; a certificate of authenticity is recommended.

Issued: 5c, 10/3; 1c, 4c, 2/4/63; 2c, 3c, 5/2/63.

For overprints see Nos. O46-O49.

Tagged

1963

401p A195 1c deep brown .20 .20
402p A195 2c green .20 .20
403p A195 3c purple .20 .20
404p A195 4c carmine .75 .50
405p A195 5c violet blue .40 .25
q. Pane of 20 35.00
Nos. 401p-405p (5) 1.75 1.35

See note after No. 343.

Coil Stamps

1962-63 *Perf. 9½ Horiz.*

406 A195 2c green 3.50 1.60
407 A195 3c purple 2.50 1.25
408 A195 4c carmine 3.50 1.75
a. Pair, imperf between *2,500.*
409 A195 5c violet blue 3.50 .75
Nos. 406-409 (4) 13.00 5.35

No. 408a is valued in the grade of fine. Beware of dangerous fakes; a certificate of authenticity is necessary.

Issued: 5c, 10/3; 4c, 2/4/63; 2c, 3c, 5/2/63.

Sir Casimir Stanislaus Gzowski (1813-98), Engineer, Soldier and Educator — A196

1963, Mar. 5 Unwmk. *Perf. 12*

410 A196 5c rose lilac .20 .20

Export Crate and Mercator Map — A197

1963, June 14 Unwmk. *Perf. 12*

411 A197 $1 rose carmine 9.50 1.40

Sir Martin Frobisher (1535-1594), Explorer and Discoverer of Frobisher Bay — A198

1963, Aug. 21 Engr.

412 A198 5c ultramarine .25 .20

Postrider and First Land Mail Routes A199

1963, Sept. 25

413 A199 5c green & red brn .25 .20

Bicentennial of the 1st regular postal service between Quebec, Three Rivers & Montreal.

Jet at Ottawa Airport — A200

Canada Geese — A201

1963-64

414 A200 7c blue ('64) .45 .35
415 A201 15c deep ultra 1.75 .20

See No. 436. For surcharge see No. 430.

"Peace on Earth" — A202

1964, Apr. 8 Engr. & Litho.

416 A202 5c grnsh blue, Prus bl & ocher .20 .20

Issued to promote world peace.

Three-Maple-Leaf Emblem (Canadian Unity) — A203

White Trillium and Arms of Ontario A204

#419, White garden lily and arms of Quebec. #420, Mayflower (trailing arbutus) and arms of Nova Scotia. #421, Purple violet and arms of New Brunswick. #422, Prairie crocus and arms of Manitoba. #423, Dogwood and arms of British Columbia. #424, Lady's slipper and arms of Prince Edward Island. #425, Prairie lily and arms of Saskatchewan. #426, Wild rose and arms of Alberta. #427, Pitcher plant and arms of Newfoundland. #428, Fireweed and arms of Yukon. #429, Mountain avens and arms of Northwest Territories. #429A, Maple leaf and arms of Canada.

1964-66 Engr. & Litho. *Perf. 12*

417 A203 5c lt blue & dk car .20 .20
418 A204 5c red brn, buff & green .20 .20
419 A204 5c grn, yel & org .20 .20
420 A204 5c blue, pink & grn .20 .20
421 A204 5c car, green & vio .20 .20
422 A204 5c red brn, lil & dl grn .20 .20
423 A204 5c lilac, grn & bis .20 .20
424 A204 5c vio, grn & dp rose .20 .20
425 A204 5c sepia, org & grn .20 .20
426 A204 5c dl grn, yel & car .20 .20
427 A204 5c black, grn & car .20 .20
428 A204 5c dk bl, rose & grn .20 .20
429 A204 5c ol, yel & green .20 .20
429A A204 5c dk blue & dp red .20 .20
Nos. 417-429A (14) 2.80 2.80

Issued: #417, 5/14/64; #418-419, 6/30/64; #420-421, 2/3/65; #422-423, 4/28/65; #424, 7/21/65; #425-426, 1/19/66; #427, 2/23/66; #428-429, 3/23/66; #429A, 6/30/66.

No. 414 Surcharged

1964, July 15 Engr.

430 A200 8c on 7c blue .30 .25
a. Pair, one without surcharge *8,000.*
b. Surcharge on reverse, inverted *2,650.*

Nos. 430a and 430b are each unique.

Fathers of Confederation Memorial, Charlottetown — A205

1964, July 29 Engr.

431 A205 5c black .20 .20

Centenary of the Charlottetown, P.E.I., Conference, Sept. 1-9, 1864, which led to the creation of the Canadian nation in 1867.

Maple Leaf and Hand Holding Quill Pen — A206

1964, Sept. 9 Unwmk. *Perf. 12*

432 A206 5c dark brown & rose .20 .20

Centenary of the Quebec Conference, Oct. 10-27, 1864, which led to the creation of the Canadian nation.

Elizabeth II A207

Family and Star of Bethlehem A208

1964, Oct. 5 Engr.

433 A207 5c claret .20 .20

Queen Elizabeth's visit, Oct. 6-13.

1964, Oct. 14 *Perf. 12*

434 A208 3c red .20 .20
a. Pane of 25 6.25 6.25
p. Tagged .40 .25
q. As "a," tagged 10.50 10.00
435 A208 5c blue .20 .20
p. Tagged 1.00 .25

Panes of 25 are imperf. on four sides.

Jet Type of 1964

1964, Nov. 18 Unwmk. *Perf. 12*

436 A200 8c blue .30 .20

Maple Leaf and ICY Emblem A209

1965, Mar. 3 Engr. *Perf. 12*

437 A209 5c slate green .20 .20

International Cooperation Year.

Sir Wilfred Grenfell at Wheel of Hospital Ship Strathcona II A210

1965, June 9 Engr. *Perf. 12*

438 A210 5c Prussian blue .20 .20

Sir Wilfred Grenfell, author, medical missionary and founder of the Grenfell Mission, birth cent.

Canada's Maple Leaf Flag, 1965 A211

1965, June 30 Unwmk.

439 A211 5c blue & red .20 .20

Winston Churchill — A212

1965, Aug. 12 Litho. *Perf. 12*

440 A212 5c brown .20 .20

Sir Winston Spencer Churchill (1874-1965).

Peace Tower, Ottawa — A213

1965, Sept. 8 Engr. *Perf. 12*

441 A213 5c slate green .20 .20

Meeting of the Inter-Parliamentary Union, Ottawa, Sept. 8-17.

Parliament and Ottawa River A214

1965, Sept. 8

442 A214 5c brown .20 .20

Centenary of the selection of Ottawa as national capital.

Gifts of the Wise Men — A215

1965, Oct. 13 Engr.

443 A215 3c olive .20 .20
a. Pane of 25 5.75 5.75
p. Tagged .20 .20
q. As "a," tagged 6.75 6.75
444 A215 5c violet blue .20 .20
p. Tagged .30 .20

Christmas. Panes of 25 are imperf. on four sides.

Alouette II Orbiting Globe — A216

1966, Jan. 5 Unwmk. *Perf. 12*

445 A216 5c dark violet blue .20 .20

Launching (in California) of the Canadian satellite Alouette II, Nov. 28, 1965, as part of the Canadian-American program of space research.

La Salle, Map of 17th Century Canada, Ship, Canoe, Spyglass and Compass — A217

1966, Apr. 13 Engr. *Perf. 12*

446 A217 5c blue green .20 .20

Tercentenary of the arrival in Canada of Rene Robert Cavelier, Sieur de La Salle (1643-1687).

Traffic Signs — A218

1966, May 2

447 A218 5c black, blue & yel .20 .20

Issued to publicize traffic safety.

House of Commons, Thames River and Canadian Delegates A219

1966, May 26

448 A219 5c brown .20 .20

Centenary of the London Conf., Dec. 4, 1866, which resulted in the British North America Act.

Atomic Reactor, Heavy Water Atom Symbol and Microscope A220

1966, July 27 Engr. *Perf. 12*

449 A220 5c deep ultra .20 .20

Peaceful uses of atomic power. The design shows a stylized view of the Douglas Point Nuclear Power Station, Lake Huron, Ontario.

Parliamentary Library, Ottawa — A221

Praying Hands, by Albrecht Dürer — A222

1966, Sept. 8 Engr. *Perf. 12*

450 A221 5c plum .20 .20

12th General Conf. of the Commonwealth Parliamentary Assoc., Ottawa, Sept. 8-Oct. 5.

1966, Oct. 12 Engr. *Perf. 12*

451 A222 3c carmine rose .20 .20
a. Pane of 25 3.25 3.25
p. Tagged .20 .20
q. As "a," tagged 4.00 4.00
452 A222 5c orange .20 .20
p. Tagged .40 .25

Christmas. Panes of 25 are imperf. on four sides.

Canadian Flag over Globe and Centennial Emblem — A223

1967, Jan. 11 Engr. *Perf. 12*

453 A223 5c blue & red .20 .20
p. Tagged .35 .30

Canada's centenary as a nation.

Northern Lights and Dog Team — A224

"Alaska Highway" by A. Y. Jackson A225

Two types of 6c black:

Type I

Type II

Designs: 2c, Totem pole (Pacific Area). 3c, Combine and oil rig (Prairie Region). 4c, Ship in lock (Central Canada). 5c, Lobster traps and boat (Atlantic Provinces). 6c, Transportation means. 10c, "The Jack Pine" by Tom Thomson. 15c, "Bylot Island" by Lawren Harris. 20c, "The Ferry, Quebec" by James Wilson Morrice. 25c, "The Solemn Land" by J. E. H. MacDonald. 50c, "Summer's Stores" by John Ensor (grain elevators). $1, Oilfield near Edmonton, by H. G. Glyde.

1967-72 Engr. *Perf. 12*

454 A224 1c brown .20 .20
a. Booklet pane of 5 + label .40 .40
b. Bklt. pane, 1 #454d, 4 #459 + label, perf. 10 ('68) 2.00 1.75
c. Bklt. pane, 5 #454d + 5 #457d, perf. 10 ('68) 1.50 1.50
d. Perf. 10 ('68) .25 .20
e. Perf. 12½x12 ('71) .20 .20
f. Printed on gummed side 700.00
455 A224 2c green .20 .20
a. Bklt. pane, 4 #455, 4 #456 with gutter btwn. ('70) 1.25 1.25
456 A224 3c dull purple .20 .20
a. Perf. 12½x12 ('71) .50 .25
457 A224 4c car rose .20 .20
a. Booklet pane of 5 + label 1.10 1.10
b. Pane of 25 (5x5) 16.00
c. Booklet pane of 25 + 2 labels, perf. 10 ('68) 6.50
d. Perf. 10 .50 .20
458 A224 5c blue .20 .20
a. Booklet pane of 5 + label 4.50 4.50
b. Pane of 20 25.00
c. Bklt. pane of 20, perf. 10 ('68) 6.50
d. Perf. 10 .50 .20
459 A224 6c org, perf. 10 .25 .20
a. Bklt. pane of 25 + 2 labels, perf. 10 ('68) 6.50
b. Perf. 12½x12 ('69) .25 .20
460 A224 6c black (I), perf. 12½x12 .20 .20
a. Bklt. pane of 25 + 2 labels (I), perf. 10 ('70) 6.50
b. As "a," perf. 12½x12 14.00
c. Type II, perf. 12½x12 .40 .20
d. As "c," booklet pane of 4 3.00 2.75
e. As "d," perf. 10 ('70) 5.00 5.00
f. Type II, perf. 12 ('72) .35 .20
g. Type I, perf. 10 1.30 .30
h. Type II, perf. 10 1.50 .55
i. As "f," printed on gummed side 12.50
461 A225 8c violet brown .20 .20
462 A225 10c olive green .20 .20
463 A225 15c dull purple .35 .20
464 A225 20c dark blue .40 .20
465 A225 25c slate green 1.00 .20
465A A225 50c brown org 3.00 .20
465B A225 $1 carmine rose 6.00 .50
Nos. 454-465B (14) 12.60 3.10

Nos. 454d, 454e, 456a, 457d, 458d, 460c, 460g and 460h are from booklet panes.
Issued: #459, 11/1/68; #460, 1/7/70; others, 2/8/67.
See Nos. 543-544, 549-550.

Tagged

454p A224 1c brown .20 .20
ep. Perf. 12½x12 ('71) .20 .20
455p A224 2c green .20 .20
456p A224 3c dull purple .20 .20
457p A224 4c car rose .45 .20
458p A224 5c blue .45 .20
bp. Pane of 20 45.00 40.00
459p A224 6c org, perf. 10 .50 .20
bp. Perf. 12½x12 ('69) .50 .30
460p A224 6c black (I), perf. 12½x12 .25 .20
cp. Type II ('70) .40 .50
fp. As "cp," perf. 12 ('72) .25 .20
462p A225 10c olive green .65 .25
463p A225 15c dull purple .80 .20
464p A225 20c dark blue 1.30 .50
465p A225 25c slate green 5.00 1.75
Nos. 454p-465p (11) 10.00 4.10

Nos. 454ep and 460cp are from booklet panes Nos. 544q-544s.
Issued: 1c-5c, 2/8/67; #459p, 11/1/68; #460p, 1/7/70; others, 12/9/69.
See note after No. 343.

Coil Stamps

1967-70 *Perf. 9½ Horiz.*

466 A224 3c dull purple 2.50 .85
467 A224 4c carmine rose .75 .50
468 A224 5c blue 1.50 .65

Perf. 10 Horiz.

468A A224 6c orange .30 .20
c. Imperf., pair 225.00
468B A224 6c black, die II .30 .20
d. Imperf., pair 1,250.
Nos. 466-468B (5) 5.35 2.40

Horizontal pairs or blocks of Nos. 468A and 468B may be found with a fine vertical score line between the stamps. These sell for little more than vertical pairs or strips.
Issued: #468A, 1/69; #468B, 8/70; others, 2/8/67.

EXPO '67 Emblem and Canadian Pavilion A226

1967, Apr. 28 Engr. *Perf. 12*

469 A226 5c blue & red .20 .20

EXPO '67, Intl. Exhib., Montreal, Apr. 28-Oct. 27.

Symbolic Woman and Ballot — A227

1967, May 24 Litho. *Perf. 12*

470 A227 5c black & rose lilac .20 .20

50th anniversary of woman suffrage.

Elizabeth II — A228

1967, June 30 Engr. *Perf. 12*

471 A228 5c deep org & purple .20 .20

Centennial Year visit of Queen Elizabeth II and the Duke of Edinburgh.

Runner A229

1967, July 19 Engr. *Perf. 12*

472 A229 5c red .20 .20

Pan-American Games, Winnipeg, Manitoba, July 22-Aug. 7.

Globe and Flash A230

1967, Aug. 31 Unwmk.

473 A230 5c deep ultra .20 .20

50th anniv. of the Canadian Press, news gathering and distributing service.

Georges Philias Vanier A231

Engr. & Litho.

1967, Sept. 15 *Perf. 12*

474 A231 5c black .20 .20

Georges Philias Vanier (1888-1967), Governor General of Canada, 1959-1967.

Toronto in 1967 and Citizens of 1867 — A232

1967, Sept. 28 Engr.

475 A232 5c sl grn & sal pink .20 .20

Centenary of Toronto as capital of Ontario.

Singing Children and Peace Tower, Ottawa — A233

1967, Oct. 11 Engr. *Perf. 12*

476 A233 3c carmine .20 .20
a. Pane of 25 2.50 2.50
p. Tagged .20 .20
q. As "a" tagged 3.50 3.50
477 A233 5c green .20 .20
p. Tagged .25 .20

Christmas. Panes of 25 are imperf. on four sides.

Gray Jays — A234

1968, Feb. 15 Litho.

478 A234 5c green, blk & red .40 .20

Weather Map and Composite of Instruments A235

1968, Mar. 13 ***Perf. 11***

479 A235 5c dk & lt blue, yel & red .20 .20

200th anniv. of Canada's first long-term fixed point weather observations at Fort Prince of Wales, Churchill, by William Wales and Joseph Dymond.

Male Narwhal A236

1968, Apr. 10 **Litho.** ***Perf. 11***

480 A236 5c multicolored .20 .20

Weighing Rain Gauge, World Map and Maple Leaf A237

1968, May 8 **Litho.** ***Perf. 11***

481 A237 5c multicolored .20 .20

Intl. Hydrological Decade, 1965-74.

The Nonsuch A238

Photo. & Engr.

1968, June 5 ***Perf. 10***

482 A238 5c dk blue & multi .20 .20

300th anniv. of the voyage of the Nonsuch which opened the way to Canada's West through the fur trade.

Contemporary and Indian Lacrosse Players — A239

1968, July 3 **Photo. & Engr.**

483 A239 5c yel, black & red .20 .20

George Brown, "Globe" Front Page and Legislature, Prince Edward Island A240

1968, Aug. 21 ***Perf. 10***

484 A240 5c multicolored .20 .20

George Brown (1818-1880), founder of Toronto "Globe" and political leader.

Henri Bourassa and Newspaper Page — A241

Canadian Memorial, Vimy Near France — A242

Litho. & Engr.

1968, Sept. 4 ***Perf. 12***

485 A241 5c ver, buff & black .20 .20

Henri Bourassa (1868-1952), jounalist and statesman.

1968, Oct. 15 **Engr.** ***Perf. 12***

486 A242 15c slate 1.40 1.00

50th anniv. of the Armistice which ended WWI. The stamp shows "The Defenders and the Breaking of the Sword," a detail from the memorial designed by W. S. Allward.

John McCrae and "Flanders Fields" A243

1968, Oct. 15 **Litho. & Engr.**

487 A243 5c multicolored .20 .20

50th death anniv. of Lt. Col. John McCrae (1872-1918), author of "In Flanders Fields."

Eskimo Family, Carving — A244

1968, Nov. **Photo.** ***Perf. 12***

Eskimo soapstone carving: 6c, Mother and infant, by Munamee of Cape Dorset.

488 A244 5c brt blue & black .20 .20
- *a.* Booklet pane of 10 2.75
- *p.* Tagged .20 .20
- *q.* As "a," tagged 3.25

489 A244 6c dp bister & black .20 .20
- *p.* Tagged .25 .20

Christmas. Issued: 5c, Nov. 1; 6c, Nov. 15.

Curling A245

Photo. & Engr.

1969, Jan. 15 ***Perf. 10***

490 A245 6c black, brt blue & car .20 .20

Vincent Massey — A246

Litho. & Engr.

1969, Feb. 20 ***Perf. 12***

491 A246 6c yel olive & dk brn .20 .20

Vincent Massey (1887-1967), 1st Canadian-born Gov. General of Canada, 1952-59.

Return from the Harvest Field, by Aurele de Foy Suzor-Cote A247

1969, Mar. 14 **Photo.**

492 A247 50c multicolored 3.00 2.00

Aurele de Foy Suzor-Cote (1869-1937), painter.

Globe and Tools of Various Trades A248

1969, May 21 **Engr.** ***Perf. 12x12½***

493 A248 6c dk olive green .20 .20

50th anniv. of the ILO.

Vickers Vimy, 1919, and Map of the Atlantic A249

1969, June 13 **Photo. and Engr.**

494 A249 15c red brn, yel grn & lt ultra 1.40 1.25

50th anniv. of the first non-stop Atlantic flight from Newfoundland to Ireland of Capt. John Alcock and Lt. Arthur Whitten Brown.

Sir William Osler — A250

Ipswich Sparrow A251

1969, June 23 ***Perf. 12½x12***

495 A250 6c dk blue & lt red brn .20 .20

Osler (1849-1919), physician, professor of physiology and pathology in Canada, US and England.

1969, July 23 **Litho.** ***Perf. 12***

Birds: 6c, White-throated sparrows, vert. 25c, Hermit thrush.

496 A251 6c multicolored .35 .20

497 A251 10c ultra & multi .60 .40

498 A251 25c black & multi 1.50 1.25

Nos. 496-498 (3) 2.45 1.85

Map of Prince Edward Island A252

Photo. & Engr.

1969, Aug. 15 ***Perf. 12x12½***

499 A252 6c ultra, org brn & black .20 .20

Bicentenary of Charlottetown as capital of Prince Edward Island.

Flags of Summer and Winter Canada Games — A253

Litho. & Engr.

1969, Aug. 15 ***Perf. 12***

500 A253 6c ultra, brt green & red .20 .20

1st Canada Summer Games, Halifax and Dartmouth, N.S., Aug. 16-24.

Sir Isaac Brock and Memorial Queenston Heights — A254

1969, Sept. 12 **Litho. and Engr.**

501 A254 6c yel brown, brn & pale sal .20 .20

Major General Sir Isaac Brock (1769-1812), administrator of Upper Canada and leader in the war of 1812.

Children of Various Races — A255

1969, Oct. 8 **Litho.** ***Perf. 12***

502 A255 5c blue & multi .20 .20
- *a.* Booklet pane of 10 3.25
- *p.* Tagged .20 .20
- *q.* As "a" tagged 3.75

503 A255 6c red & multi .20 .20
- *a.* Black (inscriptions & frame line) omitted 1,750. 1,650.
- *p.* Tagged .25 .20

Christmas.

Stephen Leacock, Comedy Mask and Mariposa View A256

Photo. & Engr.

1969, Nov. 12 ***Perf. 12x12½***

504 A256 6c multicolored .20 .20

Stephen Butler Leacock (1869-1944), humorist, historian and economist.

Manitoba, Crossroads of Canada A257

1970, Jan. 27 **Litho.** ***Perf. 12***

505 A257 6c violet blue & multi .20 .20
- *p.* Tagged .30 .20

Centenary of the province of Manitoba.

Enchanted Owl, by Kenojuak — A258

1970, Jan. 27 Engr. *Perf. 12*
506 A258 6c dark red & black .20 .20

Centenary of Nortwest Territories.

Microscopic View of Inside of Leaf A259

1970, Feb. 18 Photo. & Engr.
507 A259 6c green, lt org & blue .20 .20

Canada's participation in the Intl. Biological Program, 1967-1972.

Emblems of EXPO '67 and '70 — A260

EXPO '70 Emblem and Dogwood, British Columbia A261

Designs: No. 510, EXPO '70 emblem and white garden lily, Quebec. No. 511, EXPO '70 emblem and white trillium, Ontario.

1970, Mar. 18 Litho. *Perf. 12*
508 A260 25c red emblem 1.75 1.75
p. Tagged 2.25 2.25
509 A261 25c violet emblem 1.75 1.75
p. Tagged 2.25 2.25
510 A261 25c green emblem 1.75 1.75
p. Tagged 2.25 2.25
511 A261 25c blue emblem 1.75 1.75
p. Tagged 2.25 2.25
a. Block of 4, #508-511 7.50 7.50
b. As "a," tagged 10.00 10.00
Nos. 508-511 (4) 7.00 7.00

EXPO '70 Intl. Exhibition, Osaka, Japan, Mar. 15-Sept. 13. Nos. 508-511 printed se-tenant in sheets of 50 (5x10), with various combinations possible.

Henry Kelsey A262

Photo. & Engr.
1970, Apr. 15 *Perf. 12x12½*
512 A262 6c multicolored .20 .20

300th birth anniv. of Henry Kelsey, explorer of Canada's western plains.

"A Divided World, with Energy Focused on Unification..." — A263

1970, May 13 Litho. *Perf. 11*
513 A263 10c blue .55 .45
p. Tagged .80 .80
514 A263 15c lilac & dk red .75 .60
p. Tagged 1.25 1.40

25th anniversary of the United Nations.

Louis Riel A264

Mackenzie Rock, Dean Channel A265

1970, June 19 Photo. *Perf. 12½x12*
515 A264 6c red & brt blue .20 .20

Louis Riel (1844-1885), Metis leader who became president of the Council of Assiniboin in 1870.

1970, June 25 Engr. *Perf. 12*
516 A265 6c brown .20 .20

Sir Alexander Mackenzie (1764-1820), Scottish explorer who in 1793 completed the first crossing of the North American continent north of Mexico.

Sir Oliver Mowat and Parliament, Ottawa A266

Photo. & Engr.
1970, Aug. 12 *Perf. 12x12½*
517 A266 6c red & black .20 .20

Sir Oliver Mowat (1820-1903), government leader and a Father of Confederation.

Isle of Spruce, by Arthur Lismer A267

1970, Sept. 18 Litho. *Perf. 11*
518 A267 6c multicolored .20 .20

50th anniv. of "The Group of Seven," Canadian landscape artists.

Santa Claus — A268

Christ Child — A269

Child in the Manger and Star-studded Sky — A270

Christmas: Designs by Canadian School Children.

1970, Oct. 7 Litho. *Perf. 12*
519 A268 5c Santa Claus .25 .20
520 A268 5c Horse-drawn Sleigh .25 .20
521 A268 5c Nativity .25 .20
522 A268 5c Children Skiing .25 .20
523 A268 5c Snowmen and Christmas Tree .25 .20
a. Strip of 5, #519-523 1.75 1.65
524 A269 6c Christ Child .35 .20
525 A269 6c Christmas Tree and Children .35 .20
526 A269 6c Toy Store .35 .20
527 A269 6c Santa Claus .35 .20
528 A269 6c Church .35 .20
a. Strip of 5, #524-528 2.75 2.40
529 A270 10c Christ Child .35 .30
530 A270 15c Snowmobile and Trees .85 .85
Nos. 519-530 (12) 4.20 3.15

Tagged

519p A268 5c multicolored .30 .25
520p A268 5c multicolored .30 .25
521p A268 5c multicolored .30 .25
522p A268 5c multicolored .30 .25
523p A268 5c multicolored .35 .25
ap. Strip of 5, #519p-523p 2.50 2.00
524p A269 6c multicolored .35 .25
525p A269 6c multicolored .35 .25
526p A269 6c multicolored .35 .25
527p A269 6c multicolored .35 .25
528p A269 6c multicolored .40 .25
ap. Strip of 5, #524p-528p 3.00 2.50
529p A270 10c multicolored .40 .45
530p A270 15c multicolored .75 1.10
Nos. 519p-530p (12) 4.50 4.05

Christmas.

The sheets of 100 of both 5c and 6c contain all 5 designs, generally alternating, and arranged to permit vertical and horizontal pairs of each design in the two center vertical and horizontal rows. The center block of 4 is entirely of No. 522 (5c) and 525 (6c). The sheet may also be broken to provide 20 strips of 5, each stamp of different design.

Sir Donald Alexander Smith — A271

1970, Nov. 4 Litho. *Perf. 12*
531 A271 6c dk grn, yel & black .20 .20

Smith (1820-1914), railroad builder and Canadian High Commissioner, 1896-1914.

Big Raven, by Emily Carr — A272

1971, Feb. 12 Litho. *Perf. 12*
532 A272 6c multicolored .20 .20

Emily Carr (1871-1945), painter and writer.

Laboratory Equipment Used for Insulin Discovery — A273

1971, Mar. 3 Litho. *Perf. 11*
533 A273 6c multicolored .20 .20

Discovery of insulin by Dr. Frederick G. Banting and Dr. Charles H. Best, 50th anniversary.

A274

1971, Mar. 24 Litho. *Perf. 11*
534 A274 6c red, org & black .20 .20

Sir Ernest Rutherford (1871-1937), physicist, developer of theory of spontaneous disintegration of the atom.

Spring, Winged Maple Seed A275

Louis Joseph Papineau A276

1971 Litho. *Perf. 11*
535 A275 6c shown .20 .20
a. Imperf., pair *725.00*
536 A275 6c Summer .20 .20
537 A275 7c Autumn .20 .20
538 A275 7c Winter .20 .20
Nos. 535-538 (4) .80 .80

Issue dates: No. 535, Apr. 14; No. 536, June 16; No. 537, Sept. 3; No. 538, Nov. 19.

Litho. & Engr.
1971, May 7 *Perf. 12½x12*
539 A276 6c multicolored .20 .20

Louis Joseph Papineau (1786-1871), member of Legislative Assembly and leader of French Canadian Patriote party.

Map of Copper Mine River Basin A277

1971, May 7 *Perf. 12x12½*
540 A277 6c buff, red & brown .20 .20

Bicentenary of Samuel Hearne's expedition to the Copper Mine River.

Maple Leaves A278

1971, June 1
541 A278 15c blk, red org & yel 1.50 1.25
p. Tagged 2.25 2.25

Inauguration of new transmitters for Radio Canada International.

Computer Tape and Reels — A279

1971, June 1
542 A279 6c black, ultra & red .20 .20

Centenary of measured progress through census.

Migrating Phosphor

Canada's "Ottawa/General" tagging of engraved stamps printed March-October, 1972, used a phosphor which migrates onto or through other stamps, booklet covers and album pages. It fluoresces yellow under ultraviolet light.

This bleeding, contaminating "OP4" phosphor can be somewhat contained in mounts or envelopes of acetate, glassine or polyethylene, but it may leak or penetrate.

The migrating phosphor is found on all copies of Nos. 560p-561p, and on some of Nos. 544p, 544q, 544r, 544s, 562p-565p and 594-598.

Transportation Means — A280

Design: 8c, Library of Parliament.

1971-72 Engr. *Perf. 12½x12*

543 A280 7c slate green .25 .20
- *a.* Booklet pane of 5 + label (#454e, #456a + 3#543) 2.75 1.75
- *b.* Booklet pane of 20 (4 #454e, 4 #456a, 12 #543) 9.25
- *p.* Tagged .50 .25

544 A280 8c slate .20 .20
- *a.* Booklet pane of 6 (3 #454e, 1 #460c, 2 #544) 2.25
- *b.* Booklet pane of 18 (6 #454e, 1 #460c, 11 #544) 7.50
- *c.* Booklet pane of 10 (4 #454e, 1 #460c, 5 #544 ('72) 1.90
- *p.* Tagged .30 .20
- *q.* As "a," tagged 2.00
- *r.* As "b," tagged 6.50
- *s.* As "c," tagged 2.75

Coil Stamps

1971 *Perf. 10 Horiz.*

549 A280 7c slate green .35 .20
- *a.* Imperf, pair 1,000.

550 A280 8c slate .30 .20
- *a.* Imperf, pair 375.00
- *p.* Tagged .30 .20
- *q.* As "p," imperf, pair 550.00

See note below No. 468B.
Issued: 7c, 6/30/71; 8c, 12/30/71.

Abstract "BC" A282

1971, July 20 Litho. *Perf. 12*

552 A282 7c multicolored .20 .20

Centenary of British Columbia's entry into Canadian Confederation.

Indian Encampment on Lake Huron, by Kane — A283

1971, Aug. 11 *Perf. 12½*

553 A283 7c multicolored .30 .20

Paul Kane (1810-1871), painter.

Snowflake A284

Pierre Laporte A285

1971, Oct. 6 Engr. *Perf. 12*

Size: 24x30mm

554 A284 6c dark blue .20 .20
- *p.* Tagged .20 .20
- *a.* All color omitted (from foldover) —
- *b.* Printed on gummed side (from foldover) —

555 A284 7c bright green .20 .20
- *p.* Tagged .25 .20

Litho. and Engr.

Size: 30x30mm

556 A284 10c dp car & silver .30 .30
- *p.* Tagged .35 .30

557 A284 15c lt ultra, dp car & silver .55 .65
- *p.* Tagged .75 .75

Nos. 554-557 (4) 1.25 1.35

Christmas.

1971, Oct. 20 Engr. *Perf. 12½x12*

558 A285 7c black .20 .20

Pierre Laporte (1921-1970), Minister of Labor, kidnapped and killed.

Figuro Skating — A286

1972, Mar. 1 Litho. *Perf. 12*

559 A286 8c deep red lilac .20 .20

World Figure Skating Championships, Calgary, Alberta, Mar. 6-12.

"Your Heart is your Health" A287

1972, Apr. 7 Engr. *Perf. 12x12½*

560 A287 8c red .25 .20
- *p.* Tagged .45 .35

World Health Day, Apr. 7.

Frontenac, by Philippe Hébert and Fort Saint Louis, Quebec A288

Photo. and Engr.

1972, May 17 *Perf. 12x12½*

561 A288 8c red brown & multi .20 .20
- *p.* Tagged .55 .55

Tercentenary of the appointment of Louis de Buade, Count of Frontenac and Palluau (1622-1698), as Governor of New France.

Indians of Canada

Buffalo Chase, by George Catlin A289

Thunderbird, Assiniboin Pattern — A290

In Nos. 562-581, the first two and last two stamps of each annual set are printed checkerwise in same sheet of 50.

1972 Litho. *Perf. 12x12½*

562 A289 8c shown .30 .20
- *p.* Tagged .40 .25

563 A289 8c Plains Indian artifacts .30 .20
- *p.* Tagged .40 .25
- *a.* Pair, #562-563 .60 .50
- *b.* As "a," tagged .80 .60

Perf. 12½x12

Photo. & Engr.

564 A290 8c shown .30 .20
- *p.* Tagged .40 .25

565 A290 8c Ceremonial sun dance costume .30 .20
- *p.* Tagged .40 .25
- *a.* Pair, #564-565 .60 .50
- *b.* As "a," tagged .80 .60

Plains Indians of Canada.
Issued: #562-563, July 6; #564-565, Oct. 4.

Tagged (Nos. 566-581)

1973 Litho. *Perf. 12x12½*

566 A289 8c Algonkian artifacts .30 .20

567 A289 8c "Micmac Indians" .30 .20
- *a.* Pair, #566-567 .60 .50

Perf. 12½x12

Photo. & Engr.

568 A290 8c Thunderbird and belt .30 .20

569 A290 8c Algonkian man and woman .30 .20
- *a.* Pair, #568-569 .60 .50

Algonkian-speaking Indians of Canada (Malecite, Micmac, Montagnais, Algonquin and Ojibwa).
Issued: #566-567, 2/21; #568-569, 11/28.

1974 Litho. *Perf. 12x12½*

570 A289 8c Nootka Sound, house, inside .25 .20

571 A289 8c Artifacts .25 .20
- *a.* Pair, #570-571 .50 .40

Perf. 12½x12

Photo. & Engr.

572 A290 8c Chief wearing Chilkat blanket .25 .20

573 A290 8c Thunderbird from Kwakiutl house .25 .20
- *a.* Pair, #572-573 .50 .40

Pacific Coast Indians of Canada (Haida, Salish, Tsimshian, Chilkat and Kwakiutl).
Issued: #570-571, 1/16; #572-573, 2/22.

1975, Apr. 4 Litho. *Perf. 13½*

574 A289 8c Montagnais-Naskapi artifacts .20 .20

575 A289 8c Dance of the Kutcha-Kutchin .20 .20
- *a.* Pair, #574-575 .40 .40
- *b.* As "a," imperf. between *750.00*

Perf. 12½

576 A290 8c Kutchin ceremonial costume .20 .20

Litho. and Embossed

577 A290 8c Ojibwa thunderbird and Naskapi pattern .20 .20
- *a.* Pair, #576-577 .40 .40

Subarctic Indians.

1976, Sept. 17 Litho. *Perf. 13½*

578 A289 10c Cornhusk mask, artifacts .20 .20

579 A289 10c Iroquoian Encampment, by George Heriot .20 .20
- *a.* Pair, #578-579 .40 .40

Perf. 12½

Litho. & Embossed

580 A290 10c Iroquoian thunderbird .20 .20

Litho.

581 A290 10c Iroquoian man, woman .20 .20
- *a.* Pair, #580-581 .40 .40

Nos. 562-581 (20) 5.00 4.00

Iroquois (Mohawk, Cayuga, Seneca, Oneida, Onondaga and Tuscarora).

Geological Fault — A291

1972, Aug. 2 *Perf. 12*

582 A291 15c shown 1.50 1.25
- *p.* Tagged 2.25 2.25

583 A291 15c Bird's eye view of town 1.50 1.25
- *p.* Tagged 2.25 2.25

584 A291 15c Aerial map photography 1.50 1.25
- *p.* Tagged 2.25 2.25

585 A291 15c Contour lines 1.50 1.25
- *p.* Tagged 2.25 2.25
- *a.* Block of 4, #582-585 6.00 6.00
- *b.* As "a," tagged 9.00 9.00

Nos. 582-585 (4) 6.00 5.00

Earth sciences: 24th Intl. Geological Cong. (#582); 22nd Intl. Geographical Cong. (#583); 12th Cong. of Intl. Soc. of Photogrammetry (#584); 6th Cong. of Intl. Cartographic Assoc. (#585).

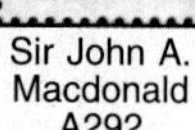
Sir John A. Macdonald A292

Elizabeth II A292a

Forest, Central Canada — A293

Vancouver, B.C. — A294

Designs: 2c, Sir Wilfrid Laurier. 3c, Sir Robert L. Borden. 4c, William Lyon Mackenzie King. 5c Richard Bedford Bennett. 6c, Lester B. Pearson. 7c, Louis St. Laurent. 15c, Mountain sheep, Western Canada. 20c, Grain fields, Prairie. 25c, Polar bears, North. 50c, Seashore. $2, Quebec.

1972-76 Engr. *Perf. 12x12½*

Tagged

586 A292 1c orange ('73) .20 .20
- *a.* Booklet pane, 3 #586, 1 #591, 2 #593 ('74) 1.00
- *b.* Bklt. pane, 6 #586, 1 #591, 11 #593 ('75) 1.40
- *c.* Bklt. pane, 2 #586, 4 #587, 4 #593Ac ('76) 1.00
- *d.* Printed on gummed side 550.00

587 A292 2c green ('73) .20 .20
588 A292 3c brown ('73) .20 .20
589 A292 4c black ('73) .20 .20
590 A292 5c lilac ('73) .20 .20
591 A292 6c dk red ('73) .20 .20
- *a.* Printed on gummed side 150.00

592 A292 7c dk brn ('74) .20 .20
593 A292a 8c ultra ('73) .20 .20
- *b.* Perf. 13x13½ ('76) .50 .20

Perf. 13x13½

593A A292a 10c dk car ('76) .20 .20
- *c.* Perf. 12x12½ .25 .20

Perf. 12½x12

Photo. & Engr.

594 A293 10c multicolored .25 .20
595 A293 15c multicolored .40 .20
596 A293 20c multicolored .45 .20
597 A293 25c multicolored .50 .20
598 A293 50c multicolored 1.00 .20
599 A294 $1 multi ('73) 2.00 .40

Perf. 11

Litho. & Engraved

600 A294 $1 multicolored 4.50 1.50
601 A294 $2 multicolored 3.75 2.00

Nos. 586-601 (17) 14.65 6.70

No. 599 has engraved shading added in some areas.

Plates 1 and 2 of the scenic 10c differ in impression and colors. Plate 1 has distinct crosshatching of "Canada" background. On plate 2, released in 1974, this area appears solidly inked.

A 1976 printing of the 15c shows the blue trees on the hillside as solid color, while the 1972 printing shows clear detail on the trees.

A 1974 printing of the 50c has darker shading and a deeper tone for the dark blue areas of the photogravure impression.

Nos. 600 and 601 are untagged.

1976-77 Photo. & Engr. *Perf. 13½*

594a A293 10c multicolored .25 .20
595a A293 15c multicolored .40 .20
596a A293 20c multicolored .60 .20
597a A293 25c multicolored .60 .20
598a A293 50c multicolored 1.65 .20
599a A294 $1 multi ('77) 2.00 .25

Nos. 594a-599a (6) 5.50 1.25

Coil Stamps

1974-76 Engr. *Perf. 10 Vert.*

604 A292a 8c ultramarine .20 .20
- *a.* Imperf., horiz. pair 125.00

605 A292a 10c dk carmine ('76) .30 .20
- *a.* Imperf., horiz. pair 125.00

See note below No. 468B. No. 604 also exists in vertical multiples without score line.

Candles — A295

Candles and Fruit A296

Christmas: 8c, Like 6c. 15c, Candles, 15th century prayer book, boxes and brass vase.

1972, Nov. 1 Litho. *Perf. 12½x12*

606	A295 6c red & multi	.20	.20
p.	Tagged	.25	.25
607	A295 8c vio blue & multi	.20	.20
p.	Tagged	.30	.25

Perf. 11

608	A296 10c green & multi	.40	.35
p.	Tagged	.60	.60
609	A296 15c yel bister & multi	.60	.65
p.	Tagged	1.10	1.25
	Nos. 606-609 (4)	1.40	1.40

"The Blacksmith's Shop," by Krieghoff — A297

1972, Nov. 29 Litho. *Perf. 12½*

610	A297 8c multicolored	.20	.20
p.	Tagged	.25	.20

Cornelius Krieghoff (1815-1872), painter.

Tagged
From No. 611 onward, all stamps are tagged unless otherwise noted.

Monsignor de Laval — A298

1973, Jan. 31 Litho. *Perf. 11*

611	A298 8c silver, ultra & gold	.20	.20

Francois-Xavier de Montmorency-Laval de Montigny (1623-1708), 1st Bishop of Quebec and founder of many educational institutions; one of the builders of New France.

Commissioner G. A. French and Map of 1874 Trek — A299

10c, Spectrograph. 15c, R.C.M.P. Musical Ride.

1973, Mar. 9 Litho. *Perf. 11*

612	A299 8c dk brn, org & red	.20	.20
613	A299 10c dk blue & multi	.35	.30
614	A299 15c yel grn & multi	.70	.50
a.	Imperf., pair	350.00	
	Nos. 612-614 (3)	1.25	1.00

Royal Canadian Mounted Police, cent.
Imperfs of No. 614 with a double impression and examples with 15c printed on 10c are from printer's waste.

Jeanne Mance A300

1973, Apr. 18

615	A300 8c multicolored	.20	.20

Jeanne Mance (1606-1673), first secular nurse in North America and founder of first hospital, the Hôtel-Dieu in Montreal settlement.

Joseph Howe — A301

1973, May 16

616	A301 8c gold & black	.20	.20

Joseph Howe (1804-1873), journalist, poet and Lieutenant-Governor of Nova Scotia.

Mist Fantasy, by James MacDonald A302

1973, June 8 *Perf. 12½*

617	A302 15c multicolored	.50	.50

Centenary of the birth of James E. H. MacDonald (1873-1932), painter.

Oaks on Shore A303

Photo. & Engr.

1973, June 22 *Perf. 12x12½*

618	A303 8c orange & red brn	.20	.20

Centenary of Prince Edward Island's entry into Confederation.

Scottish Settlers and "Hector" A304

1973, July 20 Litho. *Perf. 12x12½*

619	A304 8c multicolored	.20	.20

Bicentenary of arrival of Scottish settlers at Pictou, N.S.

Queen Elizabeth II — A305

1973, Aug. 2 Photo. and Engr.

620	A305 8c silver & multi	.20	.20
621	A305 15c gold & multi	.55	.50

Visit to Ottawa of Elizabeth II and the Duke of Edinburgh, July 31-Aug. 4, and meeting of Commonwealth Heads of Government, Ottawa, Aug. 2-10.

Nellie McClung — A306

1973, Aug. 29 Litho. *Perf. 10½x11*

622	A306 8c multicolored	.20	.20

Nellie McClung (1873-1951), leader of women's suffrage movement, social reformer and writer.

Montreal Olympic Games — A307

1973, Sept. 20 *Perf. 12x12½*

Size: 26x44mm

623	A307 8c silver & multi	.20	.20
624	A307 15c gold & multi	.55	.45

21st Olympic Games, Montreal, 1976.
See Nos. B1-B3.

Ice Skate — A308

Santa Claus — A309

1973, Nov. 7 Litho. *Perf. 12½x12*

625	A308 6c shown	.20	.20
626	A308 8c Dove	.20	.20

Perf. 10½

627	A309 10c shown	.25	.25
628	A309 15c Shepherd and star	.55	.55
	Nos. 625-628 (4)	1.20	1.20

Christmas.

Children Diving from Dock — A310

1974, Mar. 22 Engr. *Perf. 12*

629	A310 8c shown	.35	.20
630	A310 8c Joggers	.35	.20
631	A310 8c Bicycling family	.35	.20
632	A310 8c Hikers	.35	.20
a.	Block of 4, #629-632	1.40	.85

"Keep Fit." 21st Summer Olympic Games, Montreal, 1976. When stamps are observed at an angle the Montreal Olympic Games' emblem can be seen.

Main St. and Portage Ave., Winnipeg, 1872 — A311

Litho. & Engr.

1974, May 3 *Perf. 12x12½*

633	A311 8c multicolored	.20	.20

Winnipeg's incorporation as a city, cent.

Postmaster A312

1974, June 11 Litho. *Perf. 13½x13*

634	A312 8c shown	.35	.30
635	A312 8c Mail collector and truck	.35	.30
636	A312 8c Mail handler	.35	.30
637	A312 8c Mail sorters	.35	.30
638	A312 8c Mailman	.35	.30
639	A312 8c Rural mail delivery	.35	.30
a.	Block of 6, #634-639	2.25	2.25

Centenary of letter carrier delivery service. Printed in sheets of 50 (5x10).

Agricultural Education A313

1974, July 12 *Perf. 12½x12*

640	A313 8c multicolored	.20	.20

Ontario Agricultural College centenary.

Pedestal, Gallows Frame and Contempra Telephones A314

1974, July 26 *Perf. 12½*

641	A314 8c multicolored	.20	.20
a.	Imperf., pair	*1,250.*	

Centenary of the idea for the telephone by Alexander Graham Bell while visiting Brantford, Canada.

Bicycle Wheel and Cycling Emblem A315

Photo. & Engr.

1974, Aug. 7 *Perf. 12x12½*

642	A315 8c black, red & silver	.20	.20

World Cycling Championships, Montreal, Aug. 14-25.

Mennonite Settlers A316

1974, Aug. 28 Litho. *Perf. 12x12½*

643	A316 8c multicolored	.20	.20

Centenary of arrival of Mennonite settlers in Manitoba.

Snowshoeing
A317

1974, Sept. 23 Engr. *Perf. 13½*

644 A317 8c shown .35 .20
645 A317 8c Skiing .35 .20
646 A317 8c Skating .35 .20
647 A317 8c Curling .35 .20
a. Block of 4, #644-647 1.00 1.00
b. Block or strip of 4, printed on gummed side *1,100.*

"Keep Fit." 1976 Winter Olympic Games. When the stamps are observed at an angle the Montreal Olympic Games' emblem can be seen.

Warning: No. 647b must show each design; blocks exist that contain 2 No. 645 but no example of No. 647.

Mercury with Winged Horses, UPU Emblem
A318

Photo. & Engr.

1974, Oct. 9 *Perf. 12x12½*

648 A318 8c violet, red & blue .20 .20
649 A318 15c violet, red & blue .75 .60

Centenary of Universal Postal Union.

Nativity, by Jean Paul Lemieux
A319

Skaters at Hull, by Henri Masson — A320

Christmas (Paintings): 10c, The Ice Cone, Montmorency Falls, by Robert C. Todd. 15c, Village in the Laurentian Mountains, by Clarence A. Gagnon.

1974, Nov. 1 Litho. *Perf. 13½*

650 A319 6c multicolored .20 .20
651 A320 8c multicolored .20 .20
652 A319 10c multicolored .35 .30
653 A319 15c multicolored .60 .50
Nos. 650-653 (4) 1.35 1.20

Marconi and St. John's, Newfoundland, from Signal Hill — A321

1974, Nov. 15 *Perf. 13*

654 A321 8c multicolored .20 .20

Guglielmo Marconi (1874-1937), Italian electrical engineer and inventor.

Merritt and Welland Canal
A322

Litho. & Engr.

1974, Nov. 29 *Perf. 13x13½*

655 A322 8c multicolored .20 .20

Sesquicentennial of the start of construction of the Welland Canal between Lakes Ontario and Erie, a project conceived and supervised by William Hamilton Merritt (1793-1862). Portrait by Robert Whale.

The Sprinter — A323

The Plunger — A324

Designs: Sculptures by Robert Tait McKenzie, M.D. (1867-1938), and Montreal Olympic Games' emblem.

Perf. 12½x12, 12x12½

1975, Mar. 14 Litho.; Embossed

656 A323 $1 multicolored 1.75 1.60
657 A324 $2 multicolored 3.75 3.75

21st Olympic Games, Montreal, July 17-Aug. 1, 1976.

A325

No. 658, Anne of Green Gables. No. 659, Maria Chapdelaine.

1975, May 15 Litho. *Perf. 13*

658 8c blue & multi .20 .20
659 8c brown & multi .20 .20
a. A325 Pair, #658-659 .30 .30

Birth centenary of Lucy Maud Montgomery (1874-1942), writer and author of "Anne of Green Gables"; Louis Hémon (1880-1913), writer and author of "Maria Chapdelaine." Nos. 658-659 printed checkerwise.

Marguerite Bourgeoys
A327

Alphonse Desjardins
A328

1975, May 30 Litho. *Perf. 12½x12*

660 A327 8c red & multi .20 .20
661 A328 8c red & multi .20 .20

Marguerite Bourgeoys (1620-1700), founder of the Congrégation de Notre-Dame, Montreal, first girls' school in New France; Alphonse Desjardins (1854-1920), journalist, founder of first credit union in North America.

A329

No. 662, Samuel Dwight Chown (1853-1933), Methodist minister, leader of temperance movement, founder of United Church. No. 663, Dr. John Cook (1805-92), 1st Moderator of the United Presbyterian Church in Canada.

Nos. 662-663 printed checkerwise.

Photo. & Engr.

1975, May 30 *Perf. 12x12½*

662 8c dk brown, yel & buff .20 .20
663 8c dk brown, yel & buff .20 .20
a. A329 Pair, #662-663 .60 .60

Pole Vaulting — A331

Hurdling — A332

Design: 25c, Marathon running and Montreal Olympic Games' emblem.

1975, June 11 Litho. *Perf. 12x12½*

664 A331 20c dk blue & multi .55 .45
665 A331 25c maroon & multi .65 .50
666 A332 50c green & multi 1.10 1.00
Nos. 664-666 (3) 2.30 1.95

21st Olympic Games, Montreal, July 17-Aug. 1, 1976.

"Untamed" (Wild Horse Race)
A333

1975, July 3

667 A333 8c gray & multi .20 .20

Centenary of the founding of Calgary.

Female Symbol
A334

"Justice," by Walter S. Allward
A335

Photo. & Engr.

1975, July 14 *Perf. 13*

668 A334 8c dp yel, gray & black .20 .20

International Women's Year.

1975, Sept. 2 Litho. *Perf. 12½*

669 A335 8c multicolored .20 .20

Supreme Court of Canada, centenary.

"Wm. D. Lawrence"
A336

Photo. & Engr.

1975, Sept. 24 *Perf. 13*

670 A336 8c shown .30 .25
671 A336 8c "Beaver" .30 .25
672 A336 8c "Neptune" .30 .25
673 A336 8c "Quadra" .30 .25
a. Block of 4, #670-673 1.20 1.10

Coastal ships.

Santa Claus — A337

Child — A338

Trees — A339

Designs by Canadian School Children: "What Christmas Means to Me."

1975, Oct. 22 Litho. *Perf. 13½*

674 A337 6c shown .20 .20
675 A337 6c Skater .20 .20
a. Pair, #674-675 .25 .25
676 A338 8c shown .20 .20
677 A338 8c Family and Christmas tree .20 .20
a. Pair, #676-677 .30 .30
678 A338 10c Gift box .20 .20
679 A339 15c shown .40 .40
Nos. 674-679 (6) 1.40 1.40

Christmas. Stamps of same denomination printed checkerwise.

Legion Emblem and Bugle
A340

Photo. & Engr.

1975, Nov. 10 *Perf. 13*
680 A340 8c gray & multi .20 .20

Royal Canadian Legion, 50th anniversary.

Olympic Torch Ignited by Satellite in Canada A341

Communication Arts — A342

High-rise Tower, Notre Dame Church, Montreal, and Games' Emblem — A343

Snowflake, Winter Olympics' Emblem — A344

Montreal Olympic Games' Emblem and: 20c, Canadian athletes carrying Olympic flag. 25c, Women athletes receiving Olympic medals.

1976, June 18 Litho. *Perf. 13*
681 A341 8c black & multi .20 .20
682 A341 20c black & multi .50 .40
683 A341 25c black & multi .60 .55
Nos. 681-683 (3) 1.30 1.15

1976 Olympic Games ceremonies.

1976, Feb. 6 Photo. *Perf. 12x12½*

25c, Handicraft tools. 50c, Performing arts.

684 A342 20c gray & multi 1.00 .50
685 A342 25c ocher & multi 1.25 .65
686 A342 50c blue & multi 2.00 1.00
Nos. 684-686 (3) 4.25 2.15

Olympic Fine Arts and Cultural Program.

Photo. & Engr.

1976, Mar. 12 *Perf. 13*

Design: $2, Olympic Stadium, Velodrome, flags and emblem.

687 A343 $1 silver & multi 2.40 1.75
688 A343 $2 gold & multi 4.00 3.25

Nos. 681-688 were issued in commemoration of, or in connection with the 21st Olympic Games, Montreal, July 17-Aug. 1. Nos. 687-688 were issued in panes of 8.

Photo. and Embossed

1976, Feb. 6 *Perf. 12½*
689 A344 20c multicolored .75 .55

12th Winter Olympic Games, Innsbruck, Austria, Feb. 4-15.

Flower Growing from City — A345

1976, May 12 Litho. *Perf. 12x12½*
690 A345 20c multicolored .50 .45

Habitat, UN Conference on Human Settlements, Vancouver, May 31-June 11.

Franklin and Map of North America, 1776 A346

Litho. & Engr.

1976, June 1 *Perf. 13*
691 A346 10c multicolored .20 .20

American Bicentennial; Benjamin Franklin (1706-1790), deputy postmaster general for the colonies (1753-1774).

See US No. 1690.

Royal Military College, Kingston, Ont., Cent. — A347

No. 692, Color Parade, Memorial Arch. No. 693, Wing Parade, Mackenzie Building.

1976, June 1 Litho. *Perf. 12*
692 8c red & multi .20 .20
693 8c red & multi .20 .20
a. A347 Pair, #692-693 .30 .30
b. As "a," imperf. *1,500.*
c. Block of 4, imperf. horiz. *1,000.*
d. As "a," double impression *3,000.*

A few used singles exist of Nos. 692-693 with double impression. Very rare.

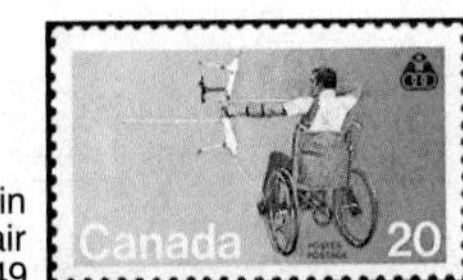

Archer in Wheelchair A349

1976, Aug. 3 *Perf. 12x12½*
694 A349 20c green & multi .45 .40

Olympiad for the Physically Disabled (25th Stoke Mandeville Games), Toronto, Aug. 3-11.

A350

No. 695, The Cremation of Sam McGee. No. 696, The Outlander.

1976, Aug. 17 *Perf. 13½*
695 8c multicolored .20 .20
696 8c multicolored .20 .20
a. A350 Pair, #695-698 .30 .30

Robert W. Service (1874-1958), author of poem "The Cremation of Sam McGee"; Germaine Guevremont, author of "Le Survenant" (The Outlander).

Nativity, St. Michael's, Toronto — A352

Stained-glass windows: 10c, Nativity, St. Jude, London, Ontario. 20c, Nativity, by Yvonne Williams.

1976, Nov. 3 Litho. *Perf. 13½*
697 A352 8c multicolored .20 .20
698 A352 10c multicolored .20 .20
699 A352 20c multicolored .40 .60
Nos. 697-699 (3) .80 1.00

Christmas.

Inland Vessels A353

Litho. & Engr.

1976, Nov. 19 *Perf. 12*
700 A353 10c Northcote .30 .25
701 A353 10c Passport .30 .25
702 A353 10c Chicora .30 .25
703 A353 10c Athabasca .30 .25
a. Block of 4, #700-703 1.25 1.25

Elizabeth II A354

Litho. and Typo.

1977, Feb. 4 *Perf. 12½x12*
704 A354 25c silver & multi .55 .40

25th anniv. of the reign of Elizabeth II.

Bottle Gentian A355

Elizabeth II A356

Parliament, Ottawa A357

Trembling Aspen A358

Main Street, Prairie Town — A359

Fundy National Park — A359a

Designs: 2c, Western columbine. 3c, Canada lily. 4c, Hepatica. 5c, Shooting star. 10c, Franklin's lady's-slipper. No. 712, Jewelweed. No. 715, Parliament, Ottawa. No. 716, Queen Elizabeth II. 20c, Douglas fir. 25c, Maple. 30c, Red oak. 35c, White pine. 60c, Street scene, Ontario City. 75c, Old houses, eastern City Street. 80c, Street leading to the sea, Eastern Maritime Provinces. $2 Kluane National Park.

Litho. & Engr.

1977-82 *Perf. 12x12½*
705 A355 1c multicolored .20 .20
a. Printed on gummed side, precanceled *700.00*
707 A355 2c multicolored .20 .20
a. Printed on gummed side 400.00
708 A355 3c multicolored .20 .20
709 A355 4c multicolored .20 .20
a. Printed on gummed side 175.00
710 A355 5c multicolored .20 .20
711 A355 10c multicolored .20 .20
a. Perf. 13x13½ ('78) .20 .20

Photo. & Engr.

Perf. 13x13½
712 A355 12c multi ('78) .30 .20
713 A356 12c blue & multi .20 .20
a. Perf. 12x12½ .30 .20

Engraved

Perf. 13x13½
714 A357 12c blue .20 .20
a. Printed on gummed side 225.00
715 A357 14c red ('78) .20 .20
a. Printed on gummed side 27.50
b. All color omitted 375.00

Photo. & Engr.

Perf. 13x13½
716 A356 14c red & blk ('78) .20 .20
a. Perf. 12x12½ .25 .20
b. As "a," booklet pane of 25 + 2 labels ('78) 5.00
c. Red omitted *1,200.*

Perf. 13½
717 A358 15c multi .35 .20
718 A358 20c multi .30 .20
719 A358 25c multi .40 .20
720 A358 30c multi ('78) .50 .20
721 A358 35c multi ('79) .50 .20
723 A359 50c multi ('78) 1.00 .20
723A A359 50c multi, litho. & engr. ('78) .90 .20
b. Brown (all inscriptions, etc.) omitted *1,500.*
723C A359 60c multi, litho. ('82) 1.00 .20
724 A359 75c multi ('78) 1.10 .20
725 A359 80c multi ('78) 1.10 .25

Lithographed and Engraved

726 A359a $1 multi ('79) 1.25 .45
a. Untagged 1.90 .60
b. As "a," blk inscriptions omitted 600.00 400.00
727 A359a $2 multi ('79) 2.50 1.10
a. Silver inscriptions omitted 400.00
Nos. 705-727 (23) 13.20 5.80

On No. 715b, a strong embossed impression from the plate, without color, is evident.

On No. 723A license plate on yellow car reads "1978."

See Nos. 781-806, 934-937, 1084.

Coil Stamps

1977-78 Engr. *Perf. 10 Vert.*
729 A357 12c blue .20 .20
a. Imperf., pair 120.00
730 A357 14c red ('78) .25 .20
a. Imperf., pair 120.00

See note below No. 468B.

Eastern Cougar A360

1977, Mar. 30 Litho. *Perf. 12½*
732 A360 12c multicolored .20 .20

Wildlife protection.

April in Algonquin Park, by Thomson — A361

#734, Autumn Birches, by Tom Thomson.

1977, May 26 ***Perf. 12***

733 A361 12c black & multi .20 .20
734 A361 12c ocher & multi .20 .20
a. Pair, #733-734 .40 .40

Tom Thomson (1877-1917), landscape painter, birth centenary. Nos. 733-734 printed checkerwise.

Names of Governors General and Standard A362

1977, June 30 ***Perf. 12½***

735 A362 12c vio blue & multi .20 .20

Honoring Canadian-born Governors General: Vincent Massey, Georges Philias Vanier, Daniel Roland Michener and Jules Léger.

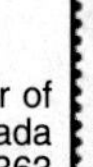

Order of Canada A363

Litho. & Embossed

1977, June 30

736 A363 12c multicolored .20 .20

Order of Canada, 10th anniversary.

Peace Bridge, Canadian, US and UN Flags A364

1977, Aug. 4 **Litho.**

737 A364 12c blue & multi .20 .20

50th anniversary of the Peace Bridge, connecting Fort Erie, Ontario, with Buffalo, N.Y.

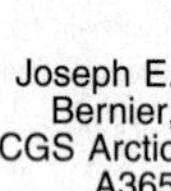

Joseph E. Bernier, CGS Arctic A365

Sandford Fleming, Railroad Bridge A366

1977, Sept. 16 **Engr.** ***Perf. 13***

738 A365 12c dark blue .20 .20
739 A366 12c brown .20 .20
a. Pair, #738-739 .40 .40

Joseph-Elzéar Bernier (1852-1934), explorer; Sandford Fleming (1827-1915), mapped route for Intercolonial Railway and designed Canada's first stamp.

Nos. 738-739 printed checkerwise.

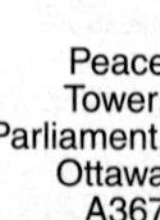

Peace Tower, Parliament, Ottawa A367

1977, Sept. 19 **Litho.** ***Perf. 12½***

740 A367 25c multicolored .60 .55

23rd Commonwealth Parliamentary Conference, Ottawa, Sept. 19-25.

Hunters Following Star — A368

Christmas: 12c, Angelic choir in northern light. 25c, Christ Child in Ring of Glory blessing chiefs from afar. Illustrations for Canada's first Christmas carol, written by Father Brébeuf, 1649.

1977, Oct. 26 ***Perf. 13½***

741 A368 10c multicolored .20 .20
a. Horiz. pair, imperf between *1,000.*
b. Printed on gummed side *550.00*
742 A368 12c multicolored .20 .20
a. Left margin block of 4, left vert. pair imperf, right pair part perf *1,600.*
743 A368 25c multicolored .40 .35
Nos. 741-743 (3) .80 .75

Pinky A369

Designs: Canadian sailing ships.

Litho. and Engr.

1977, Nov. 18 ***Perf. 12x12½***

744 A369 12c shown .20 .20
745 A369 12c Tern schooner .20 .20
746 A369 12c 5-masted schooner .20 .20
747 A369 12c Mackinaw boat .20 .20
a. Block of 4, #744-747 .80 .80
b. As "a," #745, 747 imperf, #744, 746 part perf *2,750.*

See Nos. 776-779.

Seal Hunter, Soapstone Sculpture A370

Disguised Caribou Hunter, Print — A371

Inuit Art: #749, Spear fishing. #751, Walrus hunt. #749-751 are after stonecut prints.

1977, Nov. 18 **Litho.** ***Perf. 12x12½***

748 A370 12c multicolored .20 .20
749 A371 12c multicolored .20 .20
a. Pair, #748-749 .40 .40
b. As "a," gray (inscriptions) omitted on No. 749 *1,750.*
750 A371 12c multicolored .20 .20
751 A371 12c multicolored .20 .20
a. Pair, #750-751 .40 .40
Nos. 748-751 (4) .80 .80

Inuit hunting. Nos. 748-749 and Nos. 750-751 printed se-tenant checkerwise.

Peregrine Falcon A372

1978, Jan. 18

752 A372 12c multicolored .20 .20

Endangered wildlife.

Canada No. 3, 1851 — A373

1978 **Photo. & Engr.** ***Perf. 13½***

753 A373 12c shown .20 .20
754 A373 14c No. 7 .20 .20
755 A373 30c No. 8 .50 .30
756 A373 $1.25 No. 2 1.75 1.00
a. Souvenir sheet of 3 2.75
Nos. 753-756 (4) 2.65 1.70

CAPEX '78, Canadian Intl. Phil. Exhib., Toronto, June 9-18 (cent. of Canada's admission to UPU).

No. 756a contains one each of Nos. 754-756 ($1.25 untagged).

Issue dates: 12c, Jan. 18; others, June 10.

Games' Emblem A374

Stadium A375

Design: 30c, Badminton.

1978, Mar. 31 **Litho.** ***Perf. 12½***

757 A374 14c silver & multi .25 .20
758 A374 30c silver & multi .50 .40

1978, Aug. 3

#760, Running. #761, Alberta Legislature building, Edmonton. #762, Lawn bowling.

759 A375 14c silver & multi .20 .20
760 A375 14c silver & multi .20 .20
a. Pair, #759-760 .40 .40
761 A375 30c silver & multi .50 .40
762 A375 30c silver & multi .50 .40
a. Pair, #761-762 1.00 1.00
Nos. 759-762 (4) 1.40 1.20

Nos. 757-762 commemorate 11th Commonwealth Games, Edmonton, Aug. 3-12.

#760a, 762a printed checkerwise.

A376

No. 763, Capt. Cook, by Nathaniel Dance. No. 764, Nootka Sound, by John Webber.

1978, Apr. 26 ***Perf. 13***

763 14c multicolored .20 .20
764 14c multicolored .20 .20
a. A376 Pair, #763-764 .40 .40

Capt. James Cook (1728-1779), explorer of Canada's East and West Coasts and bicentenary of his anchorage near Anchorage, June 1, 1778. Nos. 763-764 printed checkerwise.

Silver Mine, Cobalt Lake A378

Stripmining, Athabasca Tar Sands A379

1978, May 19 ***Perf. 12½***

765 A378 14c multicolored .20 .20
766 A379 14c multicolored .20 .20
a. Pair, #765-766 .40 .40

Development of national resources. Nos. 765-766 printed checkerwise.

Prince's Gate A380

1978, Aug. 16

767 A380 14c multicolored .20 .20

Canadian National Exhibition, centenary.

Mère d'Youville and Miracle of Food — A381

1978, Sept. 21 ***Perf. 13x13½***

768 A381 14c multicolored .20 .20

Marguerite d'Youville (1701-1771), founder of the Gray Nuns, beatified 1959.

Woman Walking, by Pitseolak A382

Migration, Soapstone by Joe Talurinili A383

Works by Eskimo Artists: No. 771, Plane over village, stonecut and stencil print by Pudlo. No. 772, Dogteam and sled, ivory sculpture by Abraham Kingmeatook.

1978, Sept. 27 ***Perf. 13½***

769 A382 14c multicolored .20 .20
770 A383 14c multicolored .20 .20
a. Pair, #769-770 .40 .40
771 A382 14c multicolored .20 .20
772 A383 14c multicolored .20 .20
a. Pair, #771-772 .40 .40
Nos. 769-772 (4) .80 .80

Travels of the Inuit. Printed checkerwise.

Madonna of the Flowering Pea, Cologne School — A384

Renaissance Paintings in National Gallery of Canada: 14c, Virgin and Child, by Hans Memling. 30c, Virgin and Child, by Jacopo Di Cione.

1978, Oct. 20 ***Perf. 12½***

773 A384 12c multicolored .20 .20
774 A384 14c multicolored .20 .20
a. Black omitted 800.00
775 A384 30c multicolored .45 .25
Nos. 773-775 (3) .85 .65

Christmas.

Sailing Ships Type of 1977

Litho. & Engr.

1978, Nov. 15 ***Perf. 13***

776 A369 14c "Chief Justice Robinson," 1842 .25 .20
777 A369 14c "St. Roch," 1928 .25 .20
778 A369 14c "Northern Light," 1928 .25 .20
779 A369 14c "Labrador," 1954 .25 .20
a. Block of 4, #776-779 1.10 1.10

Ice vessels.

Quebec Carnival — A386

1979, Feb. 1 Litho. *Perf. 13½*
780 A386 14c multicolored .20 .20

Flower, Queen & Parliament Types

1c, Bottle gentian. 2c, Western columbine. 3c, Canada lily. 4c, Hepatica. 5c, Shooting star. 10c, Franklin's lady's-slipper. 15c, Canada violet. No. 789, Elizabeth II. No. 790, Parliament, Ottawa.

Photo. & Engr., Engr. (#790)

1977-83 *Perf. 13x13½*
781 A355 1c multi ('79) .20 .20
a. Perf. 12x12½ ('77) .20 .20
b. Bklt. pane, 2 #781a, 4 #713a .65
782 A355 2c multi ('79) .20 .20
a. Bklt. pane, 4 #782, 3 #716a + label .75
b. Perf. 12x12½ ('78) .20 .20
783 A355 3c multi ('79) .20 .20
784 A355 4c multi ('79) .20 .20
785 A355 5c multi ('79) .20 .20
786 A355 10c multi ('79) .20 .20
787 A355 15c multi ('79) .25 .20
789 A356 17c green & blk ('79) .25 .20
a. Perf. 12x12½ .30 .20
b. Bklt. pane of 25 + 2 labels 7.50
c. Horiz. pair, imperf. btwn. and at left and bottom 1,500.
d. Black inscriptions omitted 750.00
790 A357 17c slate green ('79) .25 .20
a. Printed on gummed side 27.50
791 A356 30c multi ('82) .45 .20
792 A356 32c multi ('83) .50 .20
Nos. 781-792 (11) 2.90 2.20

Nos. 781a, 782b, 789a are from booklet panes. No. 782b has one straight edge, others one or two.
No. 789d also shows the horiz. perfs. shifted.

Parliament Type of 1977

Booklet Stamps

1979, Mar. 28 Engr. *Perf. 12x12½*
797 A357 1c slate blue .45 .20
a. Bklt. pane, 1 #797, 3 #800, 2 #789a 1.25
800 A357 5c violet brown .20 .20

#797 has one straight edge, #800 has one or two.

Coil Stamp

1979, Mar. 8 *Perf. 10 Vert.*
806 A357 17c slate green .25 .20
a. Imperf., pair 120.00

Endangered Wildlife A392

1979, Apr. 10 Litho. *Perf. 12½*
813 A392 17c Soft-shelled turtle .25 .20
814 A392 35c Bowhead whale .60 .35

Ribbon Around Woman's Finger — A393

No. 816, String around man's finger.

1979, Apr. 10
815 A393 17c multicolored .25 .20
816 A393 17c multicolored .25 .20
a. Pair, #815-816 .50 .50

Use postal code. Printed checkerwise.

Fruits of the Earth, by F. P. Grove A394

The Golden Vessel, by Emile Nelligan A395

1979, May 3 *Perf. 13x13½*
817 A394 17c multicolored .25 .20
818 A395 17c multicolored .25 .20
a. Pair, #817-818 .50 .50
c. As "a," left margin block of 4, left vert. pair imperf, right pair part perf 1,600. —

Frederick Philip Grove (1879-1948), teacher and writer; Emile Nelligan (1879-1941), French-Canadian poet. Nos. 817-818 printed checkerwise.
Warning: horizontal pairs exist of No. 818a that appear to be imperforate. These actually are pairs made from No. 818c with normal perforations trimmed off the right edge.

A396

1979, May 11 *Perf. 13½*
819 17c De Salaberry .25 .20
820 17c John By .25 .20
a. A396 Pair, #819-820 .50 .50

Charles-Michel d'Irumberry de Salaberry (1778-1829), and John By (1779-1836), Canadian colonels. Printed checkerwise.

Flag of Ontario A398

Designs: Provincial and Territorial flags.

1979, June 15 Litho. *Perf. 13½*
821 A398 17c shown .25 .20
822 A398 17c Quebec .25 .20
823 A398 17c Nova Scotia .25 .20
824 A398 17c New Brunswick .25 .20
825 A398 17c Manitoba .25 .20
826 A398 17c British Columbia .25 .20
827 A398 17c Prince Edward Island .25 .20
828 A398 17c Saskatchewan .25 .20
829 A398 17c Alberta .25 .20
830 A398 17c Newfoundland .25 .20
831 A398 17c Northwest Territories .25 .20
832 A398 17c Yukon Territory .25 .20
a. Sheet of 12, #821-832 3.25

White Water Kayak Race A399

1979, July 3 *Perf. 12½*
833 A399 17c multicolored .25 .20

Canoe-Kayak (Slalom and Wild Water) World Championships, Jonquière and Desbiens, Quebec, June 30-July 8.

Women's Field Hockey A400

1979, Aug. 16
834 A400 17c multicolored .25 .20

Women's Field Hockey Championship, Vancouver, B.C., Aug. 16-30.

Summer Tent, Print by Kiakshuk A401

Eskimos Building Igloo, by Abraham of Povungnituk A402

Works by Eskimo Artists: No. 837, The Dance, print by Kalvak of Holman Island. No. 838, Two soapstone figures from Repulse Bay, by Madeleine Isserkut and Jean Mapsalak.

1979, Sept. 13 Litho. *Perf. 13½*
835 A401 17c multicolored .25 .20
836 A402 17c multicolored .25 .20
a. Pair, #835-836 .50 .50
837 A401 17c multicolored .25 .20
838 A402 17c multicolored .25 .20
a. Pair, #837-838 .50 .50
Nos. 835-838 (4) 1.00 .80

Inuit shelters and community. Printed checkerwise.

Painted Wooden Train A403

Antique Toys: 17c, Horse, pull toy. 35c, Knitted doll, vert.

1979, Oct. 17 Litho. *Perf. 13*
839 A403 15c multicolored .25 .20
840 A403 17c multicolored .25 .20
841 A403 35c multicolored .50 .30
a. Gold (and tagging) omitted 1,050.
Nos. 839-841 (3) 1.00 .70

Christmas.

Girl Watering Tree of Life — A404

1979, Oct. 24
842 A404 17c multicolored .25 .20

International Year of the Child.

Curtiss HS-2L A405

1979, Nov. 15 Litho. *Perf. 12½*
843 A405 17c shown .25 .20
844 A405 17c Canadair CL-215 .25 .20
a. Pair, #843-844 .50 .50
845 A405 35c Vickers Vedette .55 .50
846 A405 35c Consolidated Canso .55 .50
a. Pair, #845-846 1.10 1.10
Nos. 843-846 (4) 1.60 1.40

Map of Canada Showing Arctic Islands A406

1980, Jan. 23 Litho. *Perf. 13½*
847 A406 17c multicolored .25 .20

Acquisition of the Arctic Islands, centenary.

Downhill Skiing A407

1980, Jan. 23
848 A407 35c multicolored .45 .30

13th Winter Olympic Games, Lake Placid, NY, Feb. 12-24.

Meeting of the School Trustees, by Robert Harris A408

Royal Canadian Academy of Arts Centenary: No. 850, Inspiration, bronze sculpture, by Louis-Philippe Hebert (1850-1917). No. 851, Parliament Buildings, by Thomas Fuller (1822-1919). No. 852, Sunrise on the Saguenay, by Lucius O'Brien (1832-99).

1980, Mar. 6 Litho.
849 A408 17c multicolored .30 .20
850 A408 17c multicolored .30 .20
a. Pair, #849-850 .60 .50
851 A408 35c multicolored .50 .40
852 A408 35c multicolored .50 .40
a. Pair, #851-852 1.10 1.10
Nos. 849-852 (4) 1.60 1.20

Printed checkerwise.

Atlantic Whitefish A409

Endangered wildlife. No. 854, Greater prairie chicken.

1980, May 6 Litho. *Perf. 12½*
853 A409 17c multicolored .25 .20
854 A409 17c multicolored .25 .20

Garden — A410

1980, May 29 Litho. *Perf. 13½*
855 A410 17c multicolored .25 .20

Intl. Flower Show, Montreal, May 17-Sept. 1.

Helping Hands — A411

Litho. & Embossed

1980, May 29 ***Perf. 12½***
856 A411 17c ultra & gold .25 .20

14th World Congress of Rehabilitation International, Winnipeg, June 22-27.

"O Canada" Opening Bars A412

Composers Lavallee, Routhier, Weir A413

1980, June 6 **Litho.** ***Perf. 12½***
857 A412 17c multicolored .25 .20
858 A413 17c multicolored .25 .20
a. Pair, #857-858 .50 .50

"O Canada" centenary. Printed checkerwise in sheets of 16.

John George Diefenbaker (1895-1979), Prime Minister, 1956-63 — A414

1980, June 20 **Engr.** ***Perf. 13½***
859 A414 17c dark blue .25 .20

Emma Albani (1847-1930), Soprano — A415

#861, Healey Willan (1880-1968), organist, composer. Printed checkerwise.

1980, July 4 **Litho.** ***Perf. 13½***
860 A415 17c multicolored .25 .20
861 A415 17c multicolored .25 .20
a. Pair, #860-861 .50 .50

Ned Hanlan (1855-1908), Oarsman A416

1980, July 4 **Litho.**
862 A416 17c multicolored .25 .20

Wheat Fields, Saskatchewan A417

No. 864, Strip mining and town, Alberta.

1980, Aug. 27 **Litho.** ***Perf. 13½***
863 A417 17c multicolored .25 .20
864 A417 17c multicolored .25 .20

75th anniversary of Saskatchewan's and Alberta's creation as Provinces.

Uraninite Molecular Structure A418

1980, Sept. 3
865 A418 35c multicolored .50 .40
a. Printed on gummed side 600.00

Discovery of uranium in Canada, 80th anniversary.

Sedna, by Ashoona Kiawak A419

Return of the Sun, Print by Kenojouak A420

Works by Eskimo Artists: No. 868, Bird Spirit, by Doris Hagiolok. No. 869, Shaman, print by Simon Tookoome.

1980, Sept. 25 **Litho.** ***Perf. 13½***
866 A419 17c multicolored .25 .20
867 A420 17c multicolored .25 .20
a. Pair, #866-867 .50 .50
868 A419 35c multicolored .50 .50
869 A420 35c multicolored .50 .50
a. Pair, #868-869 1.00 1.00
Nos. 866-869 (4) 1.50 1.40

Inuit spirits. Printed checkerwise.

Christmas Morning, by Frank Charles Hennessey — A421

Christmas (Greeting Cards, 1931): 17c, Sleigh Ride, by Joseph Sydney Hallam. 35c, McGill Cab Stand, by Kathleen Morris.

1980, Oct. 22 **Litho.** ***Perf. 12½x12***
870 A421 15c multicolored .25 .20
871 A421 17c multicolored .25 .20
872 A421 35c multicolored .50 .35
Nos. 870-872 (3) 1.00 .75

Avro Canada CF-100, 1950 A422

Military Aircraft: No. 874, Avro Lancaster, 1941. No. 875, Curtiss JN-4 Canuck. No. 876, Hawker Hurricane, 1935.

1980, Nov. 10 ***Perf. 13x13½***
873 A422 17c multicolored .30 .20
874 A422 17c multicolored .30 .20
a. Pair, #873-874 .60 .20
875 A422 35c multicolored .55 .50
876 A422 35c multicolored .55 .50
a. Pair, #875-876 1.10 1.10
Nos. 873-876 (4) 1.70 1.40

Printed checkerwise.

Emmanuel-Persillier Lachapelle, Caduceus — A423

1980, Dec. 5 ***Perf. 13½***
877 A423 17c multicolored .25 .20

Lachapelle (1845-1918), physician, founded Notre Dame Hospital, Montreal, 1880.

Mandora, 18th Century A424

1981, Jan. 19 **Litho.** ***Perf. 12½***
878 A424 17c multicolored .25 .20

"The Look of Music" rare musical instrument exhibition, Vancouver, Nov. 2, 1980-Apr. 5, 1981.

No. 878 exists printed on gummed side with gold color and tagging omitted, from printer's waste.

Emily Stowe (1831-1903) and Toronto General Hospital — A425

Designs: No. 880, Louise McKinney, (1868-1931) Alberta legislative building. No. 881, Idola Saint-Jean, (1875-1945) Quebec legislative building. No. 882, Henrietta Edwards, (1849-1931) clubwomen.

1981, Mar. 4 **Litho.** ***Perf. 13x13½***
879 A425 17c multicolored .30 .20
880 A425 17c multicolored .30 .20
881 A425 17c multicolored .30 .20
882 A425 17c multicolored .30 .20
a. Block of 4, #879-882 1.25 1.25

Vancouver Island Marmot, by Michael Dumas A426

Endangered Wildlife: 35c, Wood bison, by Robert Bateman.

1981, Apr. 6 **Litho.**
883 A426 17c multicolored .30 .20
884 A426 35c multicolored .60 .60

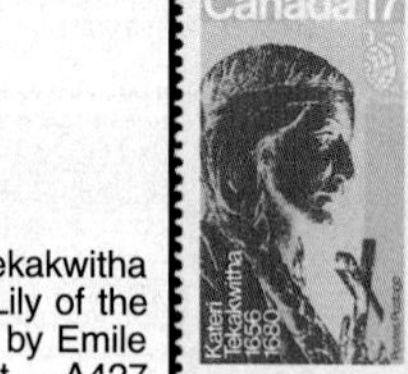
Kateri Tekakwitha ("Lily of the Mohawks"), by Emile Brunet — A427

Brunet Sculpture: #886, Marie de L'Incarnation.

1981, Apr. 24 ***Perf. 12½***
885 A427 17c brown & pale grn .25 .20
886 A427 17c lt blue & ultra .25 .20
a. Pair, #885-886 .50 .50

Beatification of Kateri Tekakwitha (1656-1680), first North American Indian saint, and Marie De L'Incarnation (1599-1672), founder of Ursuline Order.

At Baie Saint-Paul, by Marc-Aurele Fortin (1888-1970) — A428

Paintings: No. 888, Self-portrait, by Frederick H. Varley (1881-1969). 35c, Untitled No. 6, by Paul-Emile Borduas (1905-60).

1981, May 22 **Litho.** ***Perf. 12½***
887 A428 17c multi .25 .20
888 A428 17c multi, vert. .25 .20
a. Imperf, pair *1,100.*

Photo.
Perf. 13
889 A428 35c multi, vert. .40 .40
Nos. 887-889 (3) .90 .80

Map of Canada Showing Provincial Boundaries, 1867 — A429

1981, June 30 **Litho.** ***Perf. 13½***
890 A429 17c shown .30 .20
891 A429 17c 1873 .30 .20
892 A429 17c 1905 .30 .20
893 A429 17c 1949 .30 .20
a. Strip of 4, #890-893 1.20 1.20

Canada Day.

Frere Marie-Victorin (1885-1944) Botanist — A430

Botanists: #895, John Macoun (1831-1920).

1981, July 22 **Litho.** ***Perf. 12½***
894 A430 17c multicolored .25 .20
895 A430 17c multicolored .25 .20
a. Pair, #894-895 .50 .50

Montreal Rose — A431

1981, July 22 ***Perf. 13½***
896 A431 17c multicolored .25 .20

A432

Photo. & Engr.

1981, July 31 ***Perf. 13½***
897 A432 17c multicolored .25 .20

Niagara-on-the-Lake (1st capital of Upper Canada).

A433

1981, Aug. 14 **Litho.**
898 A433 17c multicolored .25 .20

Acadian Congress centenary.

A434

1981, Sept. 8
899 A434 17c multicolored .25 .20

Aaron Mosher (1881-1959), Labor Congress founder.

A435

1981, Nov. 16 **Litho.** ***Perf. 13½***
900 A435 15c 1781 .25 .20
901 A435 15c 1881 .25 .20
902 A435 15c 1981 .25 .20
Nos. 900-902 (3) .75 .60

Christmas; bicentenary of 1st illuminated Christmas tree in Canada.

Canadair CL-41 Tutor A436

1981, Nov. 24 **Litho.** ***Perf. 12½***
903 A436 17c shown .30 .20
904 A436 17c de Havilland Tiger Moth .30 .20
a. Pair, #903-904 .50 .30
905 A436 35c Avro Canada C-102 .55 .45
906 A436 35c de Havilland Canada Dash-7 .55 .45
a. Pair, #905-906 1.10 .80
Nos. 903-906 (4) 1.70 1.30

A437

1981, Dec. 29 **Engr.** ***Perf. 13x13½***
907 A437 (30c) red .55 .20

Coil Stamp
Perf. 10 Vert.

908 A437 (30c) red .85 .20
a. Imperf., pair *300.00*

See Nos. 923-924, 940, 943-946, 950-951.

CANADA '82 Intl. Philatelic Youth Exhibition, Toronto, May 20-24 — A438

1982 **Litho.** ***Perf. 13½***
909 A438 30c No. 1 .45 .20
910 A438 30c No. 102 .45 .20
911 A438 35c No. 223 .50 .35
912 A438 35c No. 155 .50 .35
913 A438 60c No. 158 1.00 .60
a. Souvenir sheet of 5, #909-913 3.25 2.00
Nos. 909-913 (5) 2.90 1.70

Issued: #909, 911, 3/11; others, 5/20.

Jules Leger (1913-1980), 26th Governor General — A439

1982, Apr. 2 **Litho.** ***Perf. 13½***
914 A439 30c multicolored .45 .20

Terry Fox (1958-1981), Marathon of Hope — A440

1982, Apr. 13 ***Perf. 12½***
915 A440 30c multicolored .45 .20

1982 Constitution — A441

1982, Apr. 16 **Litho.** ***Perf. 12x12½***
916 A441 30c multicolored .45 .20

Types of 1979-81 and

Decoy A442

Parliament (Library) A443

Parliament (West Block) — A444

Parliament (East Block) — A445

Elizabeth II — A446

Designs: Artifacts, 18th and 19th cent.

1982-87 **Litho.** ***Perf. 14x13½***
917 A442 1c shown .20 .20
a. Perf. 13x13½ ('85) .20 .20
918 A442 2c Fishing spear .20 .20
a. Perf. 13x13½ ('84) .20 .20
b. Bottom margin block of 4, bottom pair imperf, top pair part perf *1,500.*
c. As "a," printed on gummed side 45.00
919 A442 3c Stable lantern .20 .20
a. Perf. 13x13½ ('85) .20 .20
920 A442 5c Bucket .20 .20
a. Perf. 13x13½ ('84) .20 .20
921 A442 10c Weathercock .20 .20
a. Perf. 13x13½ ('85) .20 .20
922 A442 20c Ice skates .30 .20
a. Brown omitted 300.00

Photo. & Engr.
Perf. 13x13½

923 A437 30c lt blue, bl, & red .45 .20
a. Bklt. pane of 20, perf. 12x12½ 10.00
b. Perf. 12x12½ .60 .20
924 A437 32c beige, red & brn .45 .20
a. Bklt. pane of 25, perf. 12x12½ 11.00
b. Perf. 12x12½ .90 .20
c. As #924, beige (and tagging) omitted 900.00

Litho.
Perf. 13½x13

925 A443 34c multi .50 .20
a. Booklet pane of 25 12.50
b. Perf. 13½x14 ('86) .55 .20
c. Bklt. pane of 25, perf. 13½x14 12.50

Photo. & Engr.
Perf. 13x13½

926 A446 34c lt bl & int bl .50 .20
926A A446 36c plum *3.50 2.00*

Perf. 13½x13

926B A443 36c multi .55 .20
c. Booklet pane of 10 4.75
d. Booklet pane of 25 12.50
e. Perf. 13½x14 ('87) .60 .20
f. Left margin block of 4, left vert. pair imperf, right pair part perf *1,250.*

Litho. ***Perf. 12x12½***
Size A442: 26x20mm

927 A442 37c Wooden plow .55 .20
928 A442 39c Settle-bed .55 .20
929 A442 48c Cradle .65 .30
930 A442 50c Sleigh .70 .25
932 A442 64c Wood stove .90 .40
933 A442 68c Spinning wheel .90 .35

Perf. 13½

934 A359a $1 Glacier Natl. Park 1.40 .45
a. Blue inscriptions omitted *825.00*
b. Imperf., pair *2,000.*
935 A359a $1.50 Waterton Lakes Natl. Park 3.00 .55
a. Black omitted *1,900.*
936 A359a $2 Moraine Lake, Banff Park 3.00 1.00
a. Bluish green inscriptions omitted *900.00*
937 A359a $5 Point Pelee Natl. Park 8.00 2.25
Nos. 917-937 (22) 26.90 10.15

Issued:1c-20c, 10/19; 30c, 5/11; $1.50, 6/18; $5, 1/10/83; 32c, 2/10/83; 37c, 48c, 64c, 4/8/83; $1, 8/15/84; #925, $2, 6/21/85; #926, 7/12/85; 39c, 50c, 68c, 8/1/85; #926B, 3/30/87; #926A, 10/1/87.

For former No. 931, see new No. 723C.

Booklet Stamps
Perf. 12x12½ (A437), 12½x12
Engr.

938 A445 1c sage green ('87) .20 .20
939 A444 2c myrtle grn ('85) .20 .20
a. 2c slate green ('89) .20 .20
940 A437 5c deep claret .20 .20
941 A445 5c dp brown ('85) .25 .20
942 A444 6c henna brn ('87) .20 .20
943 A437 8c dk blue ('83) .40 .20
944 A437 10c dark green .40 .25
945 A437 30c red .70 .30
a. Bklt. pane of 4 + 2 labels (2 #940, 944, 945) .90 *1.25*
946 A437 32c brown ('83) .50 .20
b. Bklt. pane of 4 + 2 labels (2 #940, 943, 946) .90 *1.25*
947 A443 34c dp slate bl ('85) 1.00 .55
a. Bklt. pane of 6 (3 #939, 2 #941, #947) 1.40 *1.25*
948 A443 36c dark lil rose ('87) .85 .55
a. Bklt. pane of 5 + label (2 #938, 2 #942, #948) 1.40 *1.25*

Issued: #940, 10c, 30c, 3/1; 8c, 32c, 2/15/83; #941, 30c, 6/21/85; 1c, 6c, 36c, 3/30/87.

Coil Stamps
Engr. ***Perf. 10 Vert.***

950 A437 30c red .90 .20
a. Imperf., pair 275.00
951 A437 32c brown ('83) .60 .20
a. Imperf., pair 125.00

Perf. 10 Horiz.

952 A443 34c dull red brn ('85) .50 .20
a. Imperf., pair 125.00
953 A443 36c dark red ('87) .55 .20
a. Imperf., pair 225.00

Issued: 30c, 5/11; 32c, 2/10/83; 34c, 8/1/85; 36c, 5/19/87.

See #1080-1083, 1186-1188, 1194-1194A.

Centenary of Salvation Army in Canada A457

1982, June 25 **Litho.** ***Perf. 13***
954 A457 30c multicolored .45 .20

Canada Day A458

Paintings: No. 955, The Highway near Kluana Lake, by A.Y. Jackson. No. 956, Montreal Street Scene, by Adrien Hebert. No. 957, Breakwater, by Christopher Pratt. No. 958, Along Great Slave Lake, by Rene Richard. No. 959, Tea Hill, by Molly Lamb. No. 960, Family and Rainstorm, by Alex Colville. No. 961, Brown Shadows, by Dorothy Knowles. No. 962, The Red Brick House, by David Milne. No. 963, Campus Gates, by Bruno Bobak. No. 964, Prairie Town—Early Morning, by Illingworth Kerr. No. 965, Totems at Ninstints, by Joe Plaskett. No. 966, Doc Snider's House, by Lionel LeMoine FitzGerald.

1982, June 30 ***Perf. 12½x12***
955 A458 30c multicolored .55 .45
956 A458 30c multicolored .55 .45
957 A458 30c multicolored .55 .45
958 A458 30c multicolored .55 .45
959 A458 30c multicolored .55 .45
960 A458 30c multicolored .55 .45
961 A458 30c multicolored .55 .45
962 A458 30c multicolored .55 .45
963 A458 30c multicolored .55 .45
964 A458 30c multicolored .55 .45
965 A458 30c multicolored .55 .45
966 A458 30c multicolored .55 .45
a. Min. sheet of 12, #955-966 6.75

Regina Centenary A459

1982, Aug. 3 ***Perf. 13½x13***
967 A459 30c multicolored .45 .20

Centenary of Royal Canadian Henley Regatta, St. Catharines, Aug. 4-8 — A460

1982, Aug. 4
968 A460 30c multicolored .45 .20

Fairchild FC-2W1 A461

1982, Oct. 5 Litho. *Perf. 12½*

969 A461 30c shown .60 .20
970 A461 30c De Havilland Canada Beaver .60 .20
a. Pair, #969-970 1.20 1.00
971 A461 60c Noorduyn Norseman 1.00 .75
972 A461 60c Fokker Super Universal 1.00 .75
a. Pair, #971-972 2.00 2.00
Nos. 969-972 (4) 3.20 1.90

Christmas A462

Designs: Creche figures.

1982, Nov. 3 *Perf. 13½*

973 A462 30c Holy Family .45 .20
a. All colors except black omitted *10,000.*
b. Printed on gummed side, black omitted *10,000.*
974 A462 35c Shepherds .50 .35
975 A462 60c Three Kings .90 .70
Nos. 973-975 (3) 1.85 1.25

Nos. 973a and 973b are each unique and were caused by a paper foldover.

World Communications Year — A463

1983, Mar. 10 Litho. *Perf. 12x12½*

976 A463 32c multicolored .50 .20

Commonwealth Day — A464

1983, Mar. 14

977 A464 $2 multicolored 8.00 3.50

Scene from Angeline de Montbrun, by Laure Conan (1845-1924), Painted by Rene Milot — A465

Design: No. 979, Sea Gulls, by Edwin John Pratt (1882-1966), woodcut by Claire Pratt.

1983, Apr. 22 Litho. *Perf. 13½*

978 A465 32c multicolored .50 .20
979 A465 32c multicolored .50 .20
a. Pair, #978-979 1.10 1.00
b. As "a," all color missing —

No. 979b resulted from an extraneous piece of paper receiving the colors. After removal, the issued pane shows two vertical pairs without color plus six other stamps with only partial color.

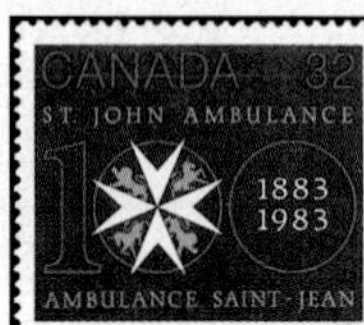

St. John Ambulance Centenary A466

1983, June 3 *Perf. 13½*

980 A466 32c Emblem .50 .20

World University Games, Edmonton, July 1-11 — A467

1983, June 28 *Perf. 13½*

981 A467 32c multicolored .50 .20
a. Printed on gummed side 600.00
982 A467 64c multicolored 1.00 .60

Canada Day — A468

#983, Fort Henry, Ontario. #984, Fort William, Ontario. #985, Fort Rodd Hill, British Columbia. #986, Fort Wellington, Ontario. #987, Fort Prince of Wales, Manitoba. #988, Halifax Citadel, Nova Scotia. #989, Fort Chambly, Quebec. #990, Fort No. 1, Point Levis, Quebec. #991, Fort at Coteau-du-Lac, Quebec. #992, Fort Beausejour, New Brunswick. Sizes: #983, 988: 44x22mm; #984-985, 989-990, 36x22mm; #986-987, 991-992, 28x22mm.

1983, June 30 *Perf. 12½x13*

Booklet Stamps

983 A468 32c multicolored .65 .45
984 A468 32c multicolored .65 .45
985 A468 32c multicolored .65 .45
986 A468 32c multicolored .65 .45
987 A468 32c multicolored .65 .45
988 A468 32c multicolored .65 .45
989 A468 32c multicolored .65 .45
990 A468 32c multicolored .65 .45
991 A468 32c multicolored .65 .45
992 A468 32c multicolored .65 .45
a. Booklet pane of 10, #983-992 7.00

Scouting Year — A469

1983, July 6 *Perf. 13½*

993 A469 32c multicolored .50 .20

Church Council Emblem — A470

1983, July 22 Litho.

994 A470 32c tan & green .50 .20

6th World Council of Churches Assembly, Vancouver, July 24-Aug. 10.

Humphrey Gilbert — A471

1983, Aug. 3 Litho.

995 A471 32c multicolored .50 .20

400th anniv. of discovery of Newfoundland by Sir Humphrey Gilbert (1537-1583).

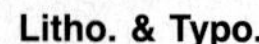

Centenary of Discovery of Nickel, Sudbury, Ontario A472

Litho. & Typo.

1983, Aug. 12 *Perf. 13*

996 A472 32c multicolored .55 .20
a. Silver (and tagging) omitted *650.00*

Beware of forgeries of No. 996a. A certificate of authenticity is mandatory.

Josiah Henson (1789-1883), Preacher — A473

1983, Sept. 16 Litho. *Perf. 13x13½*

997 A473 32c multicolored .50 .20

Antoine Labelle (1833-1891), Deputy Minister for Settlement A474

1983, Sept. 16 *Perf. 13½*

998 A474 32c multicolored .50 .20

Locomotives — A475

1983, Oct. 3 *Perf. 12½x13*

999 A475 32c Toronto 4-4-0, 1853 .50 .30
1000 A475 32c Dorchester 0-4-0, 1836 .50 .30
a. Pair, #999-1000 1.10 .90
1001 A475 37c Samson 0-6-0, 1838 .60 .55
1002 A475 64c Adam Brown 4-4-0, 1860 1.00 .90
Nos. 999-1002 (4) 2.60 2.05

Dalhousie Law School Centenary A476

1983, Oct. 28 *Perf. 13*

1003 A476 32c Arms .50 .20

Christmas A477

1983, Nov. 3 Litho. *Perf. 13½*

1004 A477 32c Urban church .50 .20
1005 A477 37c Family going to church .55 .40
1006 A477 64c Rural church .90 .65
Nos. 1004-1006 (3) 1.95 1.25

Army Regiments, Centenaries A478

19th Cent. Uniforms: No. 1007, Royal Canadian Regiment, British Columbia Regiment. No. 1008, Royal Winnipeg Rifles, Royal Canadian Dragoons.

1983, Nov. 10 *Perf. 13½x13*

1007 A478 32c shown .50 .20
1008 A478 32c multicolored .50 .20
a. Pair, #1007-1008 1.10 1.00

Yellowknife, 50th Anniv. — A479

1984, Mar. 15 Litho. *Perf. 13½*

1009 A479 32c Gold mine .50 .20

50th Anniv. of Montreal Symphony Orchestra A480

1984, Mar. 24 Litho. *Perf. 12½*

1010 A480 32c multicolored .50 .20

450th Anniv. of Cartier's Landing in Quebec A481

1984, Apr. 20 Photo. & Engr.

1011 A481 32c multicolored .50 .20

See France No. 1923.

Voyage of Tall Ships, Saint-Malo, France, to Quebec City — A482

1984, May 18 Litho. *Perf. 12x12½*

1012 A482 32c multicolored .50 .20

450th anniv. of Cartier's landing in Quebec.

Canadian Red Cross Society, 75th Anniv. — A483

1984, May 28 Litho. *Perf. 13*
1013 A483 32c Meritorious Service Medal .50 .20

New Brunswick, Bicentenary A484

Photo. & Engr.
1984, June 18 *Perf. 13*
1014 A484 32c Galleys .50 .20

St. Lawrence Seaway, 25th Anniv. — A485

1984, June 26 Litho. *Perf. 13*
1015 A485 32c Seaway, Lake Superior .50 .20

Canada Day A486

Provincial Landscapes by Jean Paul Lemieux (b. 1904).

1984, June 29 *Perf. 13*
1016 A486 32c New Brunswick .50 .30
1017 A486 32c British Columbia .50 .30
1018 A486 32c Yukon Territory .50 .30
1019 A486 32c Quebec .50 .30
1020 A486 32c Manitoba .50 .30
1021 A486 32c Alberta .50 .30
1022 A486 32c Prince Edward Island .50 .30
1023 A486 32c Saskatchewan .50 .30
1024 A486 32c Nova Scotia, vert. .50 .30
1025 A486 32c Northwest Territories .50 .30
1026 A486 32c Newfoundland .50 .30
1027 A486 32c Ontario, vert. .50 .30
a. Min. sheet of 12, #1016-1027 6.25

Nos. 1018 and 1025 incorrectly inscribed. No. 1018 shows Northwest Territories landscape; No. 1025, Yukon Territory church.

Loyalists, British Flag (1606-1801) — A487

1984, July 3
1028 A487 32c multicolored .50 .20

United Empire Loyalists, American colonists who remained loyal to British throne and emigrated to Canada during American Revolution.

Roman Catholic Church in Newfoundland A488

1984, Aug. 17 Litho. *Perf. 13½*
1029 A488 32c St. John's Basilica .50 .20

Papal Visit A489

1984, Aug. 31 Litho. *Perf. 12½*
1030 A489 32c multicolored .50 .20
1031 A489 64c multicolored 1.00 .60

Lighthouses — A490

1984, Sept. 21 Litho. *Perf. 12½*
1032 A490 32c Louisbourg, 1734 .50 .20
1033 A490 32c Fisgard, 1860 .50 .20
1034 A490 32c Ile Verte, 1809 .50 .20
1035 A490 32c Gibraltar Point, 1808 .50 .20
a. Block of 4, #1032-1035 2.00 1.00

Steam Locomotives — A491

1984, Oct. 25 Litho. *Perf. 12½x13*
1036 A491 32c Scotia .50 .25
1037 A491 32c Countess of Dufferin .50 .25
a. Pair, #1036-1037 1.10 1.00
1038 A491 37c Grand Trunk Class E3 .65 .50
1039 A491 64c Canadian Pacific D10a 1.00 .80
a. Souvenir sheet 2.75 2.00
Nos. 1036-1039 (4) 2.65 1.80

#1039a contains #1036-1039 in changed colors.
See #1071-1074, 1118-1121.

Christmas A492

Paintings: 32c, The Annunciation, by Jean Dallaire. 37c, The Three Kings, by Simone Mary Bouchard. 64c, Snow in Bethlehem, by David Milne.

1984, Nov. 2 Litho. *Perf. 13*
1040 A492 32c multicolored .50 .20
1041 A492 37c multicolored .55 .50
1042 A492 64c multicolored .90 .65
Nos. 1040-1042 (3) 1.95 1.35

Royal Canadian Air Force — A493

1984, Nov. 9 Litho. *Perf. 12x12½*
1043 A493 32c Pilots .50 .20

Cent. of La Presse — A494

1984, Nov. 16 Litho. *Perf. 13x13½*
1044 A494 32c Treffle Berthiaume .50 .20

International Youth Year — A495

1985, Feb. 8 Litho. *Perf. 12½*
1045 A495 32c Heart, arrow, jeans .50 .20

Canadians in Space — A496

1985, Mar. 15 Litho. *Perf. 13½*
1046 A496 32c Astronaut .55 .20

Therese Casgrain (1896-1981), Suffragist A497

Emily Murphy (1868-1933), Writer A498

1985, Apr. 17 Litho.
1047 A497 32c multicolored .50 .20
1048 A498 32c multicolored .50 .20
a. Pair, #1047-1048 1.10 1.00

Gabriel Dumont (1837-1906), Metis Leader — A499

1985, May 6 Litho. *Perf. 13*
1049 A499 32c multicolored .50 .20

Centenary of the Northwest Rebellion.

Canada Day — A500

#1050, Lower Ft. Garry, Manitoba. #1051, Ft. Anne, Nova Scotia. #1052, Ft. York, Ontario. #1053, Castle Hill, Newfoundland. #1054, Ft. Whoop Up, Alberta. #1055, Ft. Erie, Ontario. #1056, Ft. Walsh, Saskatchewan. #1057, Ft. Lennox, Quebec. #1058, York Redoubt, Nova Scotia. #1059, Ft. Frederick, Ontario. Sizes: #1050, 1055: 48x26mm. #1051-1052, 1056-1057: 40x26mm. #1053-1054, 1058-1059, 32x26mm.

1985, June 28 Litho. *Perf. 12½x13*
Booklet Stamps
1050 A500 34c multicolored .70 .60
1051 A500 34c multicolored .70 .60
1052 A500 34c multicolored .70 .60
1053 A500 34c multicolored .70 .60
1054 A500 34c multicolored .70 .60
1055 A500 34c multicolored .70 .60
1056 A500 34c multicolored .70 .60
1057 A500 34c multicolored .70 .60
1058 A500 34c multicolored .70 .60
1059 A500 34c multicolored .70 .60
a. Bklt. pane of 10, #1050-1059 8.00

Intl. Pharmaceutical Federation Congress — A501

Design: Louis Hebert (1575-1627), 1st French Apothecary in North America.

1985, Aug. 30 Litho. *Perf. 12½*
1060 A501 34c multicolored .50 .20

Interparliamentary Union '85, Ottawa — A502

1985, Sept. 3 *Perf. 13½*
1061 A502 34c multicolored .50 .20

A503

1985, Sept. 12 Photo. *Perf. 13½x13*
1062 A503 34c Guide, brownie saluting .50 .20

Natl. Girl Guides movement, cent.

Lighthouses A504

1985, Oct. 3 Litho. *Perf. 13½*
1063 A504 34c Sisters Islets .50 .25
1064 A504 34c Pelee Passage .50 .25
1065 A504 34c Haut-fond Prince .50 .25

1066 A504 34c Rose Blanche .50 .25
a. Block of 4, #1063-1066 2.00 1.75
b. Souv. sheet of 4, #1063-1066 2.25 2.25

Santa Claus Parade A505

Paintings by Barbara Carroll.

1985, Oct. 23 Litho. *Perf. 13½*
1067 A505 34c Santa Claus .50 .20
1068 A505 39c Horse-drawn coach .60 .50
1069 A505 68c Christmas tree 1.00 .70

Perf. 13½ on 3 Sides
1070 A505 32c Polar float .75 .35
a. Booklet pane of 10 7.50
Nos. 1067-1070 (4) 2.85 1.75

No. 1070 printed in booklets only.

Locomotives Type of 1984

1985, Nov. 7 *Perf. 12½x13*
1071 A491 34c Grand Trunk K2 .50 .20
1072 A491 34c Canadian Pacific P2a .50 .20
a. Pair, #1071-1072 1.00 .40
1073 A491 39c Canadian Northern O10a .55 .50
1074 A491 68c Canadian Govt. Railways H4D 1.00 .85
Nos. 1071-1074 (4) 2.55 1.75

1910 Gunner's Mate, World War II Officer, 1985 Woman Recruit — A507

1985, Nov. 8 *Perf. 13½x13*
1075 A507 34c multicolored .50 .20

Royal Canadian Navy, 75th anniv.

Old Holton House, Sherbrooke Street, Montreal, by James Wilson Morrice (1865-1924) A508

1985, Nov. 15 *Perf. 13½*
1076 A508 34c multicolored .50 .20

Montreal Museum of Fine Arts, 120th anniv.

Southwestern Alberta, Computer Design Map — A509

1986, Feb. 13 Litho. *Perf. 12½x13*
1077 A509 34c multicolored .50 .20

1988 Winter Olympics, Calgary, Alberta, Feb. 13-28.

EXPO '86, Vancouver, May 2-Oct. 13 — A510

1986, Mar. 7 Photo. & Engr.
1078 A510 34c Canada Pavilion .50 .20
1079 A510 39c Communications .60 .55

Heritage Artifacts Type of 1982

1987, May 6 Litho. *Perf. 14x13½*
1080 A442 25c Butter stamp .50 .20

Size: 20x26mm

Perf. 12x12½
1081 A442 42c Linen chest 1.10 .20
1082 A442 55c Iron kettle 1.25 .25
1083 A442 72c Hand-drawn cart 1.40 .30
Nos. 1080-1083 (4) 4.25 .95

Park Type of 1979

Litho. & Engr.

1986, Mar. 14 *Perf. 13½*
1084 A359a $5 La Mauricie Natl. Park 7.50 1.75
a. Dark bl inscriptions omitted *1,900. 1,600.*

No. 1084a is valued in the grade of fine as all known examples are centered thus.

Philippe Aubert de Gaspe (1786-1871), Novelist A511

Molly Brant (1736-1796), Iroquois Leader and Loyalist A512

1986, Apr. 14 Litho. *Perf. 12½*
1090 A511 34c multicolored .50 .20

Perf. 13½
1091 A512 34c multicolored .50 .20

EXPO '86 — A513

Photo. & Engr.

1986, Apr. 28 *Perf. 13x13½*
1092 A513 34c Expo Center, Vancouver .50 .20
1093 A513 68c Transportation, horiz. 1.00 .55

Canadian Forces Postal Service, 75th Anniv. A514

1986, May 9 Litho. *Perf. 13½*
1094 A514 34c multicolored .50 .20

Indigenous Birds — A515

1986, May 22
1095 A515 34c Great blue heron .55 .30
1096 A515 34c Snow goose .55 .30
1097 A515 34c Great horned owl .55 .30
1098 A515 34c Spruce grouse .55 .30
a. Block of 4, #1095-1098 2.25 1.75

19th Intl. Ornithological Congress, Ottawa, June 22-29.

Canada Day — A516

Invention blueprints.

1986, June 27 Litho.
1099 A516 34c Rotary snowplow, 1869 .50 .25
1100 A516 34c Canadarm, 1986 .50 .25
1101 A516 34c Anti-gravity flight suit, 1938 .50 .25
1102 A516 34c Variable pitch propeller, 1923 .50 .25
a. Block of 4, #1099-1102 2.00 2.00

Canadian Broadcasting Corp., 50th Anniv. — A517

1986, July 23 Litho. *Perf. 12½*
1103 A517 34c Emblem, map .50 .20

Exploration of Canada A518

#1104, Siberian Indians discover and inhabit America, 10,000 B.C. #1105, Viking settlement, A.D. 1000. #1106, John Cabot lands, 1498. #1107, Henry Hudson pioneers Hudson Strait and Bay, 1610.

1986, Aug. 29 Litho. *Perf. 12½x13*
1104 A518 34c multicolored .50 .25
1105 A518 34c multicolored .50 .25
1106 A518 34c multicolored .50 .25
1107 A518 34c multicolored .50 .25
a. Block of 4, #1104-1107 2.00 2.00
b. Souv. sheet of 4, #1104-1107 2.50 2.50

No. 1107b issued Oct. 1 for CAPEX '87.
See #1126-1129, 1199-1202, 1233-1236.

Peacemakers of the Frontier, 1870s — A519

Designs: No. 1108, Crowfoot (1830-1890), Blackfoot Indian chief. No. 1109, James F. Macleod (1836-1894), asst. commissioner of Northwest Mounted Police.

1986, Sept. 5 *Perf. 13x13½*
1108 A519 34c scar, gray & ind .50 .25
1109 A519 34c ind, gray & scar .50 .25
a. Pair, #1108-1109 1.00 1.00

Intl. Peace Year — A520

Litho. & Embossed

1986, Sept. 16 *Perf. 13½*
1110 A520 34c multicolored .50 .20

1988 Calgary Winter Olympics — A521

1986, Oct. 15 Litho. *Perf. 13½x13*
1111 A521 34c Ice hockey .50 .20
1112 A521 34c Biathlon .50 .20
a. Pair, #1111-1112 1.00 1.00

See #1130-1131, 1152-1153, 1195-1198.

Christmas Angels — A522

1986, Oct. 29 Litho. *Perf. 12½*
1113 A522 34c multicolored .50 .20
1114 A522 39c multicolored .60 .50
1115 A522 68c multicolored 1.00 .65

Booklet Stamps

Size: 72x26mm

Perf. 13½ Horiz.
1116 A522 29c multicolored .90 .65
a. Booklet pane of 10 10.00
b. Perf. 12½ horiz. 7.00
c. Bklt. pane of 10, #1116b 70.00
Nos. 1113-1116 (4) 3.00 2.00

No. 1116 has bar code at left, for use on covers with printed postal code matrix.

John Molson (1763-1836), Entrepreneur — A523

1986, Nov. 4
1117 A523 34c multicolored .50 .20

Locomotives Type of 1985

Locomotives, 1925-1945.

1986, Nov. 21 *Perf. 12½x13*
1118 A506 34c CN V1a .50 .20
1119 A506 34c CP T1a .50 .20
a. Pair, #1118-1119 1.00 1.00
1120 A506 39c CN U2a .60 .60
1121 A506 68c CP H1c 1.00 1.00
Nos. 1118-1121 (4) 2.60 2.00

CAPEX '87 — A524

1987 Litho. & Engr. *Perf. 13x13½*
1122 A524 34c 1st Toronto P.O. .50 .20
1123 A524 36c Nelson-Miramichi P.O. .55 .25
1124 A524 42c Saint Ours P.O. .65 .50
1125 A524 72c Battleford P.O. 1.10 .85
Nos. 1122-1125 (4) 2.80 1.80

Souvenir Sheet

Yellow Green Inscription
1125A Sheet of 4 2.75 2.75
b. A524 36c like #1122 .50 .50
c. A524 36c like #1123 .50 .50
d. A524 42c like #1124 .60 .55
e. A524 72c like #1125 1.00 .90

Issue dates: 34c, Feb. 16; others, June 12.

Exploration Type of 1986

Pioneers of New France: #1126, Etienne Brule (c. 1592-1633), 1st European to see the Great Lakes. #1127, Pierre Esprit Radisson (c. 1636-1710) & Medard Chouart des Groseilliers (1625-98), British expedition to Hudson Bay, 1668. #1128, Louis Jolliet (1645-1700) & Fr. Jacques Marquette (1637-75) discovering the Mississippi River, 1673. #1129, Recollet wilderness mission, 1615.

1987, Mar. 13 Litho. *Perf. 12½x13*

1126 A518 34c multicolored .50 .30
1127 A518 34c multicolored .50 .30
1128 A518 34c multicolored .50 .30
1129 A518 34c multicolored .50 .30
a. Block of 4, #1126-1129 2.00 1.75

Olympics Type of 1986

1987, Apr. 3 *Perf. 13½x13*

1130 A521 36c Speed skating .55 .20
1131 A521 42c Bobsledding .65 .50

Volunteers Week — A525

1987, Apr. 13 *Perf. 12½x13*

1132 A525 36c multicolored .55 .20

Law Day — A526

1987, Apr. 15 *Perf. 14x13½*

1133 A526 36c Coat of arms .55 .20
a. Imperf, pair 1,000.

Canadian Charter of Rights and Freedoms, 5th anniv.

Engineering Institute of Canada, Cent. — A527

1987, May 19 *Perf. 12½x13*

1134 A527 36c multicolored .55 .20

Canada Day — A528

Inventors & communications innovations: #1135, Reginald Aubrey Fessenden (1866-1932), AM radio, 1900. #1136, Charles Fenerty, newsprint, 1838. #1137, Georges-Edouard Desbarats and William Leggo, half-tone engraving, 1869. #1138, Frederick Newton Gisborne, No. America's 1st undersea cable, 1852, New Brunswick-Prince Edward Island.

1987, June 25 Litho. *Perf. 13½*

1135 A528 36c multicolored .55 .25
1136 A528 36c multicolored .55 .25
1137 A528 36c multicolored .55 .25
1138 A528 36c multicolored .55 .25
a. Block of 4, #1135-1138 2.25 2.00

Steamships A529

1987, July 20 *Perf. 13½x13*

1139 A529 36c Segwun, 1887 .55 .30

51x22mm

1140 A529 36c Princess Marguerite, 1948 .55 .30
a. Pair, #1139-1140 1.10 1.10

Shipwrecks A530

1987, Aug. 7

1141 A530 36c Hamilton & Scourge, 1813 .55 .30
1142 A530 36c San Juan, 1565 .55 .30
1143 A530 36c Breadalbane, 1853 .55 .30
1144 A530 36c Ericsson, 1892 .55 .30
a. Block of 4, #1141-1144 2.25 2.25

Air Canada, 50th Anniv. — A531

1987, Sept. 1 *Perf. 13½*

1145 A531 36c multicolored .55 .20

2nd Intl. Francophone Summit, Quebec, 9/2-4 — A532

1987, Sept. 2 *Perf. 13x12½*

1146 A532 36c multicolored .55 .20

9th Commonwealth Meeting, Vancouver, Oct. 13-17 — A533

1987, Oct. 13

1147 A533 36c multicolored .55 .20

Christmas A534

1987, Nov. 2 Litho. *Perf. 13½*

1148 A534 36c Poinsettia .55 .20
1149 A534 42c Holly wreath .65 .50
1150 A534 72c Mistletoe, Christmas tree 1.10 .90

Size: 39x25mm

1151 A534 31c Gifts, Christmas tree .60 .50
a. Booklet pane of 10 5.00
Nos. 1148-1151 (4) 2.90 2.10

No. 1151 has bar code at left, for use on covers with printed postal code matrix. Issued in booklets only.

Olympics Type of 1986

1987, Nov. 13 *Perf. 13½x13*

1152 A521 36c Cross-country skiing .55 .25
1153 A521 36c Ski jumping .55 .25
a. Pair, #1152-1153 1.10 .55

75th Grey Cup, Vancouver, Nov. 29 — A535

1987, Nov. 20 *Perf. 12½*

1154 A535 36c multicolored .55 .20

Types of 1982 and

Elizabeth II A536

Mammals A538

Parliament (Center Block) A537 A539

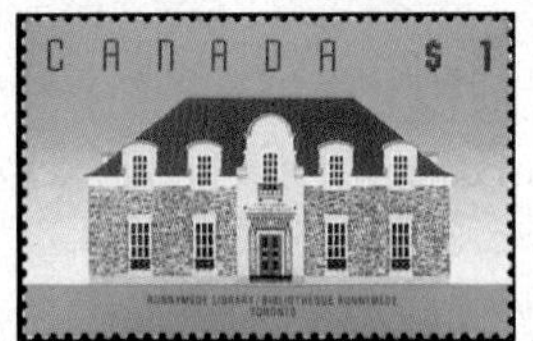

Architecture — A540

Flag and Clouds A541

Flag A542

Natl. Flag, Deciduous Forest A543

Flag and Mountains A544

1987-91 Litho. *Perf. 13x13½*

Sizes Vary on A536, A538

1155 A538 1c Flying squirrel .20 .20
a. Perf. 13x12½ 3.00 .75
1156 A538 2c Prickly porcupine .20 .20
1157 A538 3c Muskrat .20 .20
1158 A538 5c Varying hare .20 .20
a. Imperf, pair 750.00
1159 A538 6c Red fox .20 .20
a. Horiz. pair, imperf 1,700.
1160 A538 10c Skunk .20 .20
a. Perf. 13x12½ 3.50 .35
1161 A538 25c Beaver .35 .20

Perf. 13½x13

1162 A536 37c multicolored .65 .20
1163 A537 37c multicolored .65 .20
a. Bklt. pane of 10, #1163c 6.50
b. Bklt. pane of 25, #1163c 18.00
c. Perf. 13½x14 .70 .20

Perf. 13x12½

1164 A536 38c multicolored .60 .20
a. Perf. 13x13½ .75 .25
b. As "a," bklt. pane of 10+2 labels 5.75
c. Vert. block of 10, middle pair imperf, 2nd and 4th pairs part perf 1,000.
d. Horiz. pair, imperf btwn. 750.00

Perf. 13x13½ on 3 or 4 Sides

1165 A539 38c multicolored .60 .20
a. Bklt. pane of 10+2 labels 6.50
b. Bklt. pane of 25+2 labels 16.50
c. Printed on gummed side 75.00
d. Double impression of all litho colors except black 190.00

Perf. 13½x13

1166 A541 39c multicolored .65 .20
a. Bklt. pane of 10 + 2 labels 6.50
b. Bklt. pane of 25 + 2 labels 20.00
c. Perf. 12½x13 6.00 .35

Perf. 13x13½

1167 A536 39c multicolored .65 .20
a. Bklt. pane of 10 + 2 labels 6.50
b. Perf. 13 6.00 .35
1168 A536 40c multicolored .65 .20
a. Bklt. pane of 10+2 labels 6.50

Perf. 13½x13

1169 A544 40c multicolored .65 .20
a. Bklt. pane of 25+2 labels 20.00
b. Bklt. pane of 10+2 labels 6.50

Perf. 12x12½

1170 A538 43c Lynx 1.00 .35

Perf. 14½x14

1171 A538 44c Walrus 1.00 .20
a. Perf. 12½x13 2.00 .35
b. As "a," bklt. pane of 5 + label 10.00 10.00
c. Perf. 13½x13 260.00 27.50
1172 A538 45c Pronghorn .80 .25
b. As "f," bklt. pane of 5 + label 7.50 4.00
d. Perf. 13 15.00 1.00
f. Perf. 12½x13 1.50 .35
h. Imperf., pair 700.00

Perf. 13

1172A A538 46c Wolverine .80 .25
c. Perf. 12½x13 1.00 .35
e. As "c," bklt. pane of 5 + label 5.00 5.00
g. Perf. 14½x14 4.00 .35

Perf. 12x12½

1173 A538 57c Killer whale 1.00 .30

Perf. 14½x14

1174 A538 59c Musk-ox 1.00 .35
a. Perf. 13 6.00 5.00
1175 A538 61c Timber wolf 1.10 .40
a. Perf. 13 60.00 4.75
1176 A538 63c Harbor porpoise 1.40 .35
a. Perf. 13 6.50 3.50

Perf. 12x12½

1177 A538 74c Wapiti 1.40 .55

Perf. 14½x14

1178 A538 76c Grizzly bear 1.40 .40
a. Perf. 12½x13 2.50 1.50
b. As "a," bklt. pane of 5 + label 12.50 12.50
c. Perf. 13 25.00 10.00
1179 A538 78c Beluga whale 1.40 .60
a. As "c," bklt. pane of 5 12.50 12.50
b. Perf. 13 25.00 4.50
c. Perf. 12½x13 2.50 1.25

Perf. 13

1180 A538 80c Peary caribou 1.40 .60
a. Perf. 12½x13 2.25 .80
b. As "a," bklt. pane of 5 + label 12.50 12.50
c. Perf. 14½x14 4.50 1.75

Perf. 13½

Litho. & Engr.

1181 A540 $1 Runnymede Library, Toronto 1.50 .55
a. Engr. inscriptions inverted 10,000.
b. Imperf, pair 1,200.
1182 A540 $2 McAdam Railway Station 3.50 1.25
a. Imperf., pair 900.00
1183 A540 $5 Bonsecours Market, Montreal 7.50 2.00
Nos. 1155-1183 (30) 32.85 11.40

A later printing of No. 1182 has more intense and clearly defined green shading on the roofline and the deep orange background extends closer to the roofline.

Imperfs exist of Nos. 1155-1157 and 1160, from printer's waste.

Issued: 1c, 2c, 3c, 5c, 6c, 10c, 25c, 10/3/88; 37c, 12/30/87; 38c, 12/29/88; 43c, 57c, 74c, 1/18/88; 44c, 59c, 76c, 1/18/89; $1, $2, 5/5/89; #1166, 12/28/89; 45c, 61c, 78c, #1167, 1/12/90; $5, 5/28/90; 40c, 46c, 63c, 80c, 12/28/90.

Booklet Stamps

Perf. 13½x14 on 3 Sides

Litho.

1184 A542 1c shown .20 .20
a. Perf. 12½x13 15.00 15.00
1185 A542 5c multi .20 .20
a. Perf. 12½x13 15.00 15.00

Perf. 12½x12 on 2 or 3 sides

Engr.

1186 A445 6c dark purple .20 .20
1187 A443 37c dark blue .80 .20
a. Bklt. pane of 4 + 2 labels (#938, 2 #942, #1187) 1.00 1.00
1188 A443 38c dark blue .80 .35
a. Bklt. pane of 5 (3 #939a, #1186, #1188) 1.00 1.00

Perf. 13½x14 on 3 Sides

Litho.

1189 A542 39c multi .80 .25
a. Bklt. pane of 4 (#1184, 2 #1185, #1189) 1.00 1.00
b. Perf. 12½x13 22.50 20.00
c. As "a," perf. 12½x13 50.00 50.00
1190 A542 40c multi .80 .20
a. Bklt. pane of 4 (2 #1184, #1185, #1190) 1.00 1.00

Nos. 1190a, 1190c sold for 50c.

Issued: #1187, 2/3/88; #1188, 1/18/89; #1186, 1989; #1184-1185, 1189, 1/12/90; #1190, 12/28/90.

Self-Adhesives

Die Cut

Booklet Stamps

1191 A543 38c multicolored .90 .50
a. Booklet of 12 11.00
1192 A543 39c Flag, field .90 .50
a. Booklet of 12 11.00
1193 A543 40c Flag, sea-coast .90 .50
a. Booklet of 12 11.00

Issued: 38c, 6/30/89; 39c, 2/8/90; 40c, 1/11/91.

Issued on peelable paper backing serving as booklet cover. Nos. 1191a, 1192a sold for $5, No. 1193a for $5.25.

Coil Stamps

Perf. 10 Horiz.

Engr.

1194 A443 37c dark blue .60 .20
d. Imperf., pair 140.00
1194A A443 38c dark green .65 .20
e. Imperf., pair 300.00
1194B A542 39c violet .65 .20
f. Imperf., pair 140.00
1194C A542 40c blue gray .65 .20
g. Imperf., pair 225.00

Issued: 37c, 2/22/88; 38c, 2/1/89; 39c, 2/8/90; 40c, 12/28/90.

See #1356-1362, 1375-1376, 1388, 1394-1396, 1682-1683, 1687, 1703, 1705.

Olympics Type of 1986

1988, Feb. 12 Litho. *Perf. 12x12½*

1195 A521 37c Alpine skiing .60 .25
1196 A521 37c Curling .60 .25
a. Pair, #1195-1196 1.20 .75
1197 A521 43c Figure skating .70 .60
1198 A521 74c Luge 1.10 .85
Nos. 1195-1198 (4) 3.00 1.95

Exploration Type of 1986

18th Cent. explorers of the western territories: No. 1199, Anthony Henday, who traveled the Prairies in 1754 from the Hayes River to Red Deer, Alberta. No. 1200, George Vancouver (1757-1798), who circumnavigated Vancouver Is. and explored the Pacific Coast, 1792-94. No. 1201, Simon Fraser (1776-1862), fur trader who discovered and navigated the Fraser River. No. 1202, John Palliser (1807-1887), geographer who determined the topographical boundary between Canada and the US from Lake Superior to the Pacific Coast.

1988, Mar. 17 Litho. *Perf. 12½x13*

1199 A518 37c multicolored .55 .30
1200 A518 37c multicolored .55 .30
1201 A518 37c multicolored .55 .30
1202 A518 37c multicolored .55 .30
a. Block of 4, #1199-1202 2.25 2.00

The Young Reader, by Ozias Leduc A546

Photo. & Engr. with Foil Application

1988, May 20 *Perf. 13x13½*

1203 A546 50c multicolored .85 .85

Masterpieces of Canadian art. Printed in sheets of 16.

See Nos. 1241, 1271, 1310, 1419, 1466, 1516, 1545, 1602, 1635, 1754, 1800, 1863, 1916.

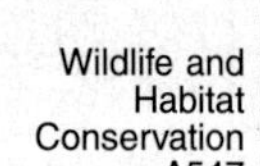

Wildlife and Habitat Conservation A547

1988, June 1 Litho. *Perf. 13x13½*

1204 A547 37c Duck landing .55 .30
1205 A547 37c Moose at water hole .55 .30
a. Pair, #1204-1205 1.10 1.00

Grey Owl, born Archibald Belaney, (b. 1888), conservationist; Ducks Unlimited Canada, 50th anniv.

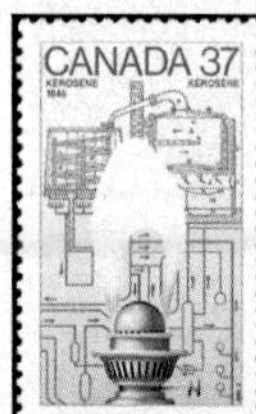

Science and Technology — A548

Inventions: No. 1206, Kerosene, invented by Abraham Gesner (1797-1864), patented in 1854. No. 1207, Marquis wheat, developed in 1908 by Charles Saunders. No. 1208, Electron microscope, developed in 1938 at the University of Toronto by James Hillier and Albert Prebus under the supervision of Eli Burton. No. 1209, Cobalt cancer therapy, introduced by Dr. Harold Johns and Atomic Energy of Canada, Ltd., in 1951.

1988, June 17 *Perf. 12½x13*

1206 A548 37c multicolored .55 .30
1207 A548 37c multicolored .55 .30
1208 A548 37c multicolored .55 .30
1209 A548 37c multicolored .55 .30
a. Block of 4, #1206-1209 2.25 2.00

Intl. Entomology Congress, Vancouver A549

1988, July 4 Litho. *Perf. 12*

1210 A549 37c Short-tailed swallowtail .55 .35
1211 A549 37c Northern blue .55 .35
1212 A549 37c Macoun's Arctic .55 .35
1213 A549 37c Canadian tiger swallowtail .55 .35
a. Block of 4, #1210-1213 2.50 2.00

St. John's, Newfoundland, Cent. of Incorporation — A550

1988, July 22 *Perf. 13½x13*

1214 A550 37c Harbor entrance, skyline .55 .20

Canadian 4-H Council, 75th Anniv. A551

1988, Aug. 5

1215 A551 37c Motto, farm, young scientists .55 .20

Les Forges Du St. Maurice (1738-1883), Canada's 1st Industrial Complex — A552

Litho. & Engr.

1988, Aug. 19 *Perf. 13½*

1216 A552 37c multicolored .55 .20

Canadian Kennel Club, Cent. A553

1988, Aug. 26 *Perf. 12½x12*

1217 A553 37c Tahltan bear dog .65 .35
1218 A553 37c Nova Scotia duck-tolling retriever .65 .35
1219 A553 37c Canadian Eskimo dog .65 .35
1220 A553 37c Newfoundland .65 .35
a. Block of 4, #1217-1220 2.75 2.25

A554

1988, Sept. 14 Litho. *Perf. 13½x13*

1221 A554 37c multicolored .55 .20

Sesquicentennial of the 1st baseball game played in Canada, June 4, 1838 at Beachville, Upper Canada.

A555

1988, Oct. 27 Litho. *Perf. 13½*

Christmas (Icons of the Eastern Church): 32c, Nativity. 37c, Conception. 43c, Virgin and Child. 74c, Virgin and Child, diff.

1222 A555 37c multicolored .60 .20
1223 A555 43c multicolored .70 .50
1224 A555 74c multicolored 1.25 .75

Booklet Stamp

Size: 35½x21mm

Perf. 12½x13½

1225 A555 32c multicolored .70 .70
a. Booklet pane of 10 7.00
Nos. 1222-1225 (4) 3.25 2.15

Millennium of Christianity in the Ukraine. No. 1225 has bar code at left; for use on covers with printed postal code matrix.

Inglis and Anglican Church A556

1988, Nov. 1 *Perf. 12½x12*

1226 A556 37c multicolored .55 .25

Charles Inglis (1734-1816), Canada's 1st Anglican bishop and founder of the Kings-Edgehill School, Nova Scotia, and the University of King's College at Halifax, bicent.

Hopkins and *Canoe Manned by Voyageurs* A557

1988, Nov. 18 *Perf. 13½x13*

1227 A557 37c multicolored .55 .25

Frances Ann Hopkins (1838-1918), painter.

The Bluenose and Capt. Walters — A558

1988, Nov. 18 *Perf. 13½*

1228 A558 37c multicolored .55 .25

Angus Walters (1882-1968), mariner.

Small Craft A559

1989, Feb. 1 Litho. *Perf. 13½x13*

1229 A559 38c Chipewyan canoe .65 .30
1230 A559 38c Haida canoe .65 .30
1231 A559 38c Inuit kayak .65 .30
1232 A559 38c Micmac canoe .65 .30
a. Block of 4, #1229-1232 2.60 2.60

See Nos. 1266-1269, 1317-1320.

Exploration Type of 1986

Explorers of the North: No. 1233, Matonabbee (c. 1737-1782), Indian guide who led 1st overland European expedition to the Arctic Ocean. No. 1234, Relics of expedition led by Sir John Franklin (1786-1847) that proved the existence of the Northwest Passage. No. 1235, Relics of the discovery of the Alberta fossil bed by geologist Joseph Burr Tyrrell (1858-1957). No. 1236, Vilhjalmur Stefansson (1879-1962), American ethnologist who discovered the last uncharted islands in the Arctic Archipelago.

1989, Mar. 22 Litho. *Perf. 12½x13*

1233 A518 38c multicolored .65 .30
1234 A518 38c multicolored .65 .30
1235 A518 38c multicolored .65 .30
1236 A518 38c multicolored .65 .30
a. Block of 4, #1233-1236 2.60 2.60

Photography in Canada, Sesquicentennial — A560

Photographers and their work: No. 1237, William Notman (1826-1891). No. 1238, W. Hanson Boorne (1859-1945). No. 1239, Alexander Henderson (1831-1913). No. 1240, Jules-Ernest Livernois (1851-1933).

1989, June 23 Litho. *Perf. 12½x12*

1237 A560 38c multicolored .65 .30
1238 A560 38c multicolored .65 .30
1239 A560 38c multicolored .65 .30
1240 A560 38c multicolored .65 .30
a. Block of 4, #1237-1240 2.60 2.60

Art Type of 1988

Ceremonial Frontlet (headpiece) Worn by Tsimshian Indian Chiefs, Early 20th Cent.

Litho. with Foil Application

1989, June 29 *Perf. 12½x13*

1241 A546 50c multicolored .90 .80

Masterpieces of Canadian Art and opening of the Museum of Civilization.

Poets — A562

1989, July 7 Litho. *Perf. 13½*
1243 A562 38c Louis Frechette (1839-1908) .60 .30
1244 A562 38c Archibald Lampman (1861-1899) .60 .30
a. Pair, #1243-1244 1.25 1.25

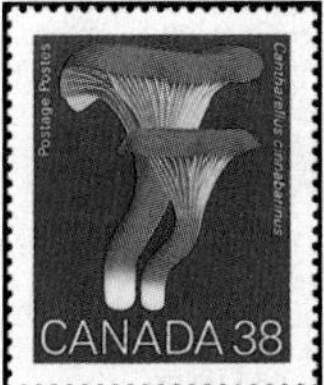
Mushrooms A563

1989, Aug. 4
1245 A563 38c *Clavulinopsis fusiformis* .60 .30
1246 A563 38c *Boletus mirabilis* .60 .30
1247 A563 38c *Cantharellus cinnabarinus* .60 .30
1248 A563 38c *Morchella esculenta* .60 .30
a. Block of 4, #1245-1248 2.50 2.50

Infantry Regiments, 75th Annivs. A564

#1249, Princess Patricia's Canadian Light Infantry. #1250, Royal 22nd Regiment.

Litho. & Engr.
1989, Sept. 8 *Perf. 13*
1249 A564 38c multicolored .70 .35
1250 A564 38c multicolored .70 .35
a. Pair, #1249-1250 1.40 1.30

Intl. Trade A565

1989, Oct. 2 Litho. *Perf. 13½x13*
1251 A565 38c multicolored .65 .30

Performing Arts — A566

1989, Oct. 4 *Perf. 13x13½*
1252 A566 38c Dancers .65 .30
1253 A566 38c Musicians .65 .30
1254 A566 38c Camera, director .65 .30
1255 A566 38c Youth and adult entertainers .65 .30
a. Block of 4, #1252-1255 2.60 2.60

Royal Winnipeg Ballet 50th anniv. (No. 1252), Vancouver Opera 30th anniv. (No. 1253), Natl. Film Board 50th anniv. (No. 1254), and Confederation Center of the Arts, Charlottetown, P.E.I., 25th anniv. (No. 1255).

A566a

A567

Winter landscapes: 33c, *Champ-de-Mars, Winter,* 1892, by William Brymner (1855-1925). 38c, *Bend in the Gosselin River, Arthabaska,* c. 1906, by Marc-Aurele de Foy Suzor-Cote (1869-1937). 44c, *Snow II,* 1915, by Lawren S. Harris (1885-1970). 76c, *Ste. Agnes,* c. 1925-30, by Albert H. Robinson (1881-1956). Nos. 1256-1258 vert.

1989, Oct. 26 Litho. *Perf. 13x13½*
Size of 44c, 76c: 25x31mm
1256 A566a 38c multicolored .65 .30
a. Bklt. pane of 10, #1256b 37.50
b. Perf. 13x12½ 3.75

Perf. 13½
1257 A566a 44c multicolored .75 .55
a. Booklet pane of 5 + label 14.00 14.00
1258 A566a 76c multicolored 1.30 .85
a. Booklet pane of 5 + label 25.00 25.00

Booklet Stamp
Size: 35x21mm
Perf. 12½x13½
1259 A567 33c shown 1.10 1.00
a. Booklet pane of 10 11.00
b. Horiz. pair, imperf btwn. *1,500.*
Nos. 1256-1259 (4) 3.80 2.70

Christmas. No. 1259 has bar code at left; for use on covers with printed postal code matrix. Booklet panes separate easily.

Declaration of War, 1939 — A568

Political and military actions taken by Canada at the outbreak of World War II.

1989, Nov. 10 *Perf. 13½*
1260 A568 38c shown .60 .35
1261 A568 38c Army mobilization .60 .35
1262 A568 38c Navy convoy system .60 .35
1263 A568 38c Commonwealth Air Training Plan .60 .35
a. Block of 4, #1260-1263 2.25 2.00

See Nos. 1298-1301, 1345-1348, 1448-1451, 1503-1506, 1537-1544.

Norman Bethune (1890-1939), Surgeon — A569

Litho. & Engr.
1990, Mar. 2 *Perf. 13x13½*
1264 A569 39c In Canada .70 .30
1265 A569 39c In China .70 .30
a. Pair, #1264-1265 2.25 1.75

See People's Republic of China Nos. 2263-2264.

Small Craft Type of 1989
1990, Mar. 15 Litho. *Perf. 13½x13*
1266 A559 39c Dory .65 .35
1267 A559 39c Pointer .65 .35
1268 A559 39c York boat .65 .35
1269 A559 39c North canoe .65 .35
a. Block of 4, #1266-1269 2.50 2.00

Multicultural Heritage of Canada A570

Litho. & Engr.
1990, Apr. 5 *Perf. 13*
1270 A570 39c multicolored .60 .20
a. Black (inscriptions) omitted *1,000.*

Art Type of 1988
Painting: *The West Wind,* by Tom Thomson.

Litho. with Foil Application
1990, May 3 *Perf. 12½x13*
1271 A546 50c multicolored .85 .75

Masterpieces of Canadian Art.

Mail Trucks
A571 A572

1990, May 3 Litho. *Perf. 13½*
Booklet Stamps
1272 A571 39c multicolored .70 .50
1273 A572 39c multicolored .70 .50
a. Bklt. pane of 8+printed margin (4 each #1272-1273) 6.25
b. Bklt. pane of 9+3 labels, printed margin (5 #1272, 4 #1273) 8.50

Dolls A573

1990, June 8 Litho. *Perf. 12½x12*
1274 A573 39c Native .65 .35
1275 A573 39c Settlers .65 .35
1276 A573 39c 4 Commercial .65 .35
1277 A573 39c 5 Commercial .65 .35
a. Block of 4, #1274-1277 2.75 2.75

Natl. Flag, 25th Anniv. — A574

1990, June 29 *Perf. 13x12½*
1278 A574 39c Flag, fireworks .65 .20
a. Silver (inscriptions) omitted *1,000.*

Printed in sheets of 16.

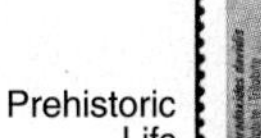

Prehistoric Life A575

Litho. & Engr.
1990, July 12 *Perf. 13x13½*
1279 A575 39c Trilobite .65 .35
1280 A575 39c Sea scorpion .65 .35
1281 A575 39c Fossil algae .65 .35
1282 A575 39c Soft invertebrate .65 .35
a. Block of 4, #1279-1282 2.75 2.75

See Nos. 1306-1309.

Canadian Forests A576

1990, Aug. 7 Litho. *Perf. 12½x13*
1283 A576 39c Acadian .65 .30
a. Sheet of 4 8.50 6.50
1284 A576 39c Great Lakes-St. Lawrence .65 .30
a. Sheet of 4 8.50 6.50
1285 A576 39c Coast .65 .30
a. Sheet of 4 8.50 6.50
1286 A576 39c Boreal .65 .30
a. Block of 4, #1283-1286 2.75 2.25
b. Sheet of 4 8.50 6.50

Sheets of four sold for $1 each through Petro-Canada gas stations, and for full face value through the philatelic bureau. Issue date: Sept. 7.

Weather Observations in Canada, 150th Anniv. — A577

1990, Sept. 5 Litho. *Perf. 12½x13½*
1287 A577 39c multicolored .65 .20

The left and right margin singles of No. 1287 differ slightly in design from stamps from columns 2-4, due to the nature of the continuous cloud design across the pane.

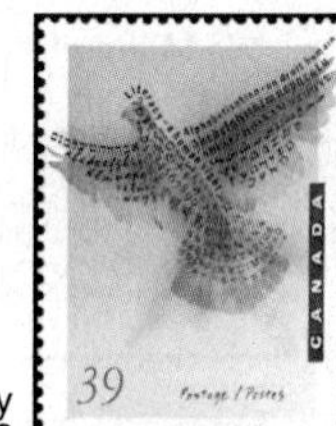
Intl. Literacy Year — A578

1990, Sept. 7 *Perf. 13½x13*
1288 A578 39c multicolored .65 .20

Legendary Creatures A579

1990, Oct. 1 Litho. *Perf. 12½x13½*
1289 A579 39c Sasquatch .60 .60
1290 A579 39c Kraken .60 .60
1291 A579 39c Werewolf .60 .60
1292 A579 39c Ogopogo .60 .60
a. Block of 4, #1289-1292 2.75 2.75
b. As "a," imperf. *1,500.*

Perf. 12½x12
1289a A579 39c 6.50 2.50
1290a A579 39c 6.50 2.50
1291a A579 39c 6.50 2.50
1292c A579 39c 6.50 2.50
d. Block of 4, #1289a-1292c 32.50 11.00

Agnes Campbell Macphail (1890-1954), First Woman Member of Parliament — A580

1990, Oct. 9 Litho. *Perf. 13x13½*

1293 A580 39c multicolored .60 .20

Virgin Mary with Christ Child and St. John the Baptist by Norval Morrisseau A581

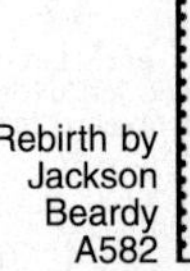

Rebirth by Jackson Beardy A582

Indian Art: 45c, Sculpture of Mother and Child by an Inuit artist. 78c, Children of the Raven by Bill Reid.

1990, Oct. 25 Litho. *Perf. 13½*

1294 A581 39c multicolored .65 .20
a. Booklet pane of 10 6.50
1295 A581 45c multicolored .75 .50
a. Bklt. pane of 5 + label 3.75 3.75
1296 A581 78c multicolored 1.20 .80
a. Bklt. pane of 5 + label 6.00 5.00

Booklet Stamp

Perf. 12½x13 on 2 or 3 Sides

1297 A582 34c multicolored .60 .55
a. Booklet pane of 10 6.00
Nos. 1294-1297 (4) 3.20 2.05

Christmas. No. 1297 has bar code at left; for use on covers with printed postal code matrix.

World War II Type of 1989

1990, Nov. 9 *Perf. 12½x12*

1298 A568 39c Home front .70 .50
1299 A568 39c Communal war efforts .70 .50
1300 A568 39c Food production .70 .50
1301 A568 39c Science and war .70 .50
a. Block of 4, #1298-1301 3.00 2.75

A583

Physicians: No. 1302, Jennie Trout (1841-1921), first licensed Canadian woman physician. No. 1303, Wilder Penfield (1891-1976), neurosurgeon. No. 1304, Sir Frederick Banting (1891-1941), discoverer of insulin. No. 1305, Harold Griffith (1894-1985), anesthesiologist.

1991, Mar. 15 Litho. *Perf. 13½*

1302 A583 40c multicolored .65 .35
1303 A583 40c multicolored .65 .35
1304 A583 40c multicolored .65 .35
1305 A583 40c multicolored .65 .35
a. Block of 4, #1302-1305 2.75 2.75

Prehistoric Life Type of 1990

1991, Apr. 5 Litho. *Perf. 12½x13½*

1306 A575 40c Microfossils .65 .35
1307 A575 40c Early tree .65 .35
1308 A575 40c Early fish .65 .35
1309 A575 40c Land reptile .65 .35
a. Block of 4, #1306-1309 2.75 2.75

Art Type of 1988

Forest, British Columbia by Emily Carr.

Litho. with Foil Application

1991, May 7 *Perf. 12½x13*

1310 A546 50c multicolored .85 .80

Masterpieces of Canadian Art.

A584

1991, May 22 Litho. *Perf. 13x12½*

Public Gardens: #1311, Butchart Gardens, Victoria, B.C. #1312, Intl. Peace Garden, Boissevain, Manitoba. #1313, Royal Botanical Gardens, Hamilton, Ontario. #1314, Montreal Botanical Gardens. #1315, Halifax Public Gardens, Nova Scotia.

Booklet Stamps

1311 A584 40c multicolored .65 .35
1312 A584 40c multicolored .65 .35
1313 A584 40c multicolored .65 .35
1314 A584 40c multicolored .65 .35
1315 A584 40c multicolored .65 .35
a. Strip of 5, #1311-1315 3.25 3.25
b. Bklt. pane, 2 each #1311-1315 6.50

Canada Day — A585

1991, June 28 *Perf. 13½x13*

1316 A585 40c multicolored .60 .20

Small Craft Type of 1989

1991, July 18

1317 A559 40c Verchere rowboat .65 .35
1318 A559 40c Touring kayak .65 .35
1319 A559 40c Sailing dinghy .65 .35
1320 A559 40c Cedar strip canoe .65 .35
a. Block of 4, #1317-1320 2.75 2.75

Canadian Rivers — A586

1991, Aug. 20 *Perf. 13x12½*

Booklet Stamps

1321 A586 40c South Nahanni .70 .35
1322 A586 40c Athabasca .70 .35
1323 A586 40c Boundary Waters-Voyageur Waterway .70 .35
1324 A586 40c Jacques Cartier .70 .35
1325 A586 40c Main .70 .35
a. Strip of 5, #1321-1325 3.50 3.25
b. Bklt. pane, 2 each #1321-1325 7.00

See #1408-1412, 1485-1489, 1511-1515.

Arrival of Ukrainians, Cent. — A587

Paintings by William Kurelek.

1991, Aug. 29 *Perf. 13½x13*

1326 A587 40c Leaving homeland .65 .35
1327 A587 40c Winter in Canada .65 .35
1328 A587 40c Clearing land .65 .35
1329 A587 40c Growing wheat .65 .35
a. Block of 4, #1326-1329 2.75 2.75

Dangerous Public Service Occupations A588

1991, Sept. 23 *Perf. 13½*

1330 A588 40c Ski Patrol .75 .35
1331 A588 40c Police .75 .35
1332 A588 40c Fire fighters .75 .35
1333 A588 40c Search & Rescue .75 .35
a. Block of 4, #1330-1333 3.25 2.75

Folktales A589

1991, Oct. 1 Litho. *Perf. 13½x12½*

1334 A589 40c Witched Canoe .65 .30
1335 A589 40c Orphan Boy .65 .30
1336 A589 40c Chinook Wind .65 .30
1337 A589 40c Buried Treasure .65 .30
a. Block of 4, #1334-1337 2.60 2.25

Queen's University, Kingston, Ont., Sesqui. — A590

1991, Oct. 16 Litho. *Perf. 13x12½*

1338 A590 40c multicolored .65 .30
a. Bklt. pane of 10 + 2 labels 6.50

A591

Santa Claus A592

1991, Oct. 23 *Perf. 13½*

1339 A591 40c At fireplace .70 .20
a. Booklet pane of 10 7.00
1340 A591 46c With white horse, tree .80 .50
a. Bklt. pane of 5 + label 4.00 3.25
1341 A591 80c Sinterklaas, girl 1.25 .70
a. Bklt. pane of 5 + label 6.25 5.75

Booklet Stamp

Perf. 12½x13 on 2 or 3 Sides

1342 A592 35c With punchbowl .60 .20
a. Booklet pane of 10 6.00
Nos. 1339-1342 (4) 3.35 1.60

Christmas. No. 1342 has bar code at left; for use on covers with printed postal code matrix.

Basketball, Cent. — A593

1991, Oct. 25 *Perf. 13x13½*

1343 A593 40c multicolored .65 .20

Souvenir Sheet

1344 Sheet of 3 3.00 2.50
a. A593 40c like #1343 .65 .65
b. A593 46c Player shooting, diff. .90 .90
c. A593 80c Player dribbling 1.40 1.40

No. 1344a has 3-line inscription.

World War II Type of 1989

1991, Nov. 8 *Perf. 13½*

1345 A568 40c Women's Armed Forces .65 .35
1346 A568 40c War industry .65 .35
1347 A568 40c Cadets and veterans .65 .35
1348 A568 40c Defense of Hong Kong .65 .35
a. Block or strip of 4, #1345-1348 2.60 2.25

Types of 1987-91 and

Edible Berries — A594

Hills — A595

Prairie A596

Building A597

Trees — A598

1991-98 Litho. *Perf. 13x13½*

1349 A594 1c Blueberry .20 .20
1350 A594 2c Wild strawberry .20 .20
1351 A594 3c Black crowberry .20 .20
1352 A594 5c Rose hip .20 .20
1353 A594 6c Black raspberry .20 .20
1354 A594 10c Kinnikinnick .20 .20
a. Horiz. pair, imperf at sides and bottom *1,000.*
1355 A594 25c Saskatoon berry .35 .20

Perf. 13½x13

1356 A595 42c multicolored .70 .20
a. Booklet pane of 10 7.00
b. Bklt. pane of 50 + 2 labels 70.00 60.00
c. Bklt. pane of 25 + 2 labels 17.50
d. Vert. pair, imperf between *650.00*

Perf. 13x13½

1357 A536 42c multicolored .70 .20
a. Booklet pane of 10 7.00 6.00
1358 A536 43c multicolored .80 .20
a. Booklet pane of 10 8.00

Perf. 13½x13

1359 A596 43c multicolored .70 .20
a. Booklet pane of 10 7.00
b. Bklt. pane of 25 + 2 labels 20.00
c. Perf. 14½ .90 .20
d. As "c," bklt. pane of 10 9.00
e. As "c," bklt. pane of 25 + 2 labels 22.50 20.00
f. Vert. pair, imperf between (from #1359e) 600.00

Perf. 13x13½

1360 A536 45c multicolored .65 .20
a. Booklet pane of 10 6.50
Complete booklet, #1360a 7.00

Perf. 14½

1361 A597 45c multicolored .65 .20
a. Booklet pane of 10 7.50
Complete booklet, #1361a 8.00

b. Bklt. pane of 25+2 labels 25.00
Complete booklet, #1361b 25.00
c. Perf. 13½x13 .65 .20
d. As "c," bklt. pane of 10 6.50
Complete booklet, #1361d 7.00
e. As "c," bklt. pane of 25 + 2 labels 18.00
Complete booklet, #1361e 18.00

Perf. 13x13½
Size: 16x20mm

1362 A597 45c multicolored .65 .30
a. Booklet pane of 10 6.50
Complete booklet, #1362a 6.50
b. Booklet pane of 30 19.50
Complete booklet, #1362b 19.50

No. 1361 is 17x21mm.

Perf. 13

1363 A598 48c McIntosh apple .80 .25
a. Perf. 14½x14 on 3 sides 1.10 .35
b. As "a," bklt. pane of 5 + label 5.50 3.00
1364 A598 49c Delicious apple .80 .25
a. Perf. 14½x14 1.10 .30
b. As "a," bklt. pane of 5 + 1 label 5.50 3.00
c. Booklet pane of 5 + label 3.75 2.50
1365 A598 50c Snow apple .80 .30
a. Booklet pane of 5 + label 4.00 2.75
b. Perf. 14½x14 1.10 .35
c. As "b," bklt. pane of 5 + label 5.50 3.00
1366 A598 52c Gravenstein apple .85 .25
a. Booklet pane of 5+label 5.00 3.00
Complete booklet, #1366a 5.50
b. Perf. 14½x14 1.00 .35
c. As "b," bklt. pane of 5 + label 5.00 3.00
Complete booklet, #1366c 5.50
1367 A598 65c Black walnut .95 .35
1368 A598 67c Beaked hazelnut .95 .35
1369 A598 69c Shagbark hickory 1.00 .35
1370 A598 71c American chestnut 1.05 .35
a. Perf. 14½x14 2.00 .45
1371 A598 84c Stanley plum 1.30 .40
a. Perf. 14½x14 on 3 sides 1.40 .45
b. As "a," bklt. pane of 5 + label 7.00 5.00
1372 A598 86c Bartlett pear 1.60 .60
a. Perf. 14½x14 2.60 .60
b. As "a," bklt. pane of 5 + 1 label 14.00 10.00
c. Booklet pane of 5 + label 8.00 6.50
1373 A598 88c Westcot apricot 1.40 .50
a. Booklet pane of 5 + label 7.50 5.00
b. Perf. 14½x14 2.75 .65
c. As "b," bklt. pane of 5 + label 14.00 8.00
1374 A598 90c Elberta peach 1.45 .45
a. Booklet pane of 5+label 7.75 5.00
Complete booklet, #1374a 8.00
b. Perf. 14½x14 1.75 .60
c. As "b," bklt. pane of 5+label 8.75 6.50
Complete booklet, #1374c 8.00

Size: 48x40mm
Litho. & Engr.
Perf. 14½x14

1375 A540 $1 Court House, Yorkton 1.50 .55
a. Dk bl (inscriptions) omitted *1,000.*
b. Perf 13½x13 1.75 .55
c. As "b," dk bl (inscriptions) omitted *1,000.*
1376 A540 $2 Provincial Normal School, Truro 3.00 1.00
a. Dk grn (inscriptions) omitted *950.*
b. Engr. inscriptions inverted *6,500.*
c. Perf. 13½x13 3.00 1.00
d. As "c," dk grn (inscriptions) omitted *1,000.*

Perf. 13½x13

1378 A540 $5 Carnegie Public Library, Victoria 7.50 2.50
Nos. 1349-1378 (29) 31.35 11.35

Self-Adhesive
Die Cut
Imperf
Booklet Stamps

1388 A543 42c Flag, mountains .80 .50
a. Booklet of 12 9.75
1389 A543 43c Flag, estuary shore .80 .50
a. Booklet pane of 12 9.75

Nos. 1388a, 1389a issued on peelable paper backing serving as booklet cover and sold for $5.25.

Coil Stamps
Perf. 10 Horiz.
Engr.

1394 A542 42c red .70 .35
a. Imperf., pair 150.00
1395 A542 43c olive green .70 .35
a. Imperf., pair 120.00
1396 A542 45c blue green .65 .30
a. Imperf., pair 110.00
Nos. 1394-1396 (3) 2.05 1.00

Nos. 1349-1363 are known imperf from printer's waste. Items exist imperf in wrong colors and with wrong denominations. These may be essays or printer's waste.

Issued: 1c-25c, 8/5/92; #1356-1357, 1394, 48c, 65c, 84c, 12/27/91; #1388, 1/28/92; #1358-1359, 1364, 1368, 1372, 1395, 12/30/92; #1389, 2/15/93; #1359c-1359e, 1/18/94; #1364c, 1372c, 1/7/94; 50c, 69c, 88c, 2/25/94; $1, $2, 2/21/94; #1375b, 1376c, 2/20/95; #1365c, 1373c, 3/27/95; #1360-1361, 1396, 52c, 71c, 90c, 7/31/95; $5, 2/29/96; #1362, 2/2/98.

1992 Winter Olympics, Albertville A601

1992, Feb. 7 Litho. *Perf. 12½x13*
Booklet Stamps

1399 A601 42c Ski jumping .65 .35
1400 A601 42c Pairs figure skating .65 .35
1401 A601 42c Hockey .65 .35
1402 A601 42c Bobsledding .65 .35
1403 A601 42c Alpine skiing .65 .35
a. Strip of 5, #1399-1403 3.25 3.25
b. Bklt. pane, 2 each #1399-1403 6.50

See Nos. 1414-1418.

City of Montreal, 350th Anniv. — A602

Designs: No. 1404, City of Montreal, modern times. No. 1405, Early settlement of Montreal (Ville-Marie). 48c, Jacques Cartier's chart of Canada, snowshoe, ship's mast. 84c, World map, nocturnal and Aztec calendar stone.

1992, Mar. 25 *Perf. 13½*

1404 A602 42c multicolored .70 .35
1405 A602 42c multicolored .70 .35
a. Pair, #1404-1405 1.40 1.40
1406 A602 48c multicolored .75 .40
1407 A602 84c multicolored 1.30 .80
a. Souvenir sheet of 4, #1404-1407 3.50 3.00
Nos. 1404-1407 (4) 3.45 1.90

Discovery of America, 500th anniv. (#1407).

Nos. 1404-1405 printed checkerwise. No. 1407a with engraved signatures in margin was produced in limited quantities for World Philatelic Youth Exhibition catalogue which sold for $12.

Canadian Rivers Type of 1991
1992, Apr. 22 *Perf. 12½*
Booklet Stamps

1408 A586 42c Margaree .70 .35
1409 A586 42c West (Eliot) .70 .35
1410 A586 42c Ottawa .70 .35
1411 A586 42c Niagara .70 .35
1412 A586 42c South Saskatchewan .70 .35
a. Strip of 5, #1408-1412 3.50 3.50
b. Bklt. pane, 2 each #1408-1412 7.00

Nos. 1408-1412 are horiz.

Alaska Highway, 50th Anniv. — A603

1992, May 15 *Perf. 13½*

1413 A603 42c multicolored .60 .25

1992 Olympic Games Type
1992, June 15 Litho. *Perf. 12½x13*

1414 A601 42c Gymnastics .70 .35
1415 A601 42c Running .70 .35
1416 A601 42c Diving .70 .35
1417 A601 42c Cycling .70 .35
1418 A601 42c Swimming .70 .35
a. Strip of 5, #1414-1418 4.00 4.00
b. Bklt. pane, 2 each #1414-1418 7.00

1992 Summer Olympics, Barcelona.
Stamps in bottom row of #1418b are in different sequence than those in #1418a.

Art Type of 1988

Painting: Red Nasturtiums, by David Milne.

Litho. with Foil Application
1992, June 29 *Perf. 12½x13*

1419 A546 50c multicolored .85 .70

Masterpieces in Canadian Art.

Miniature Sheet

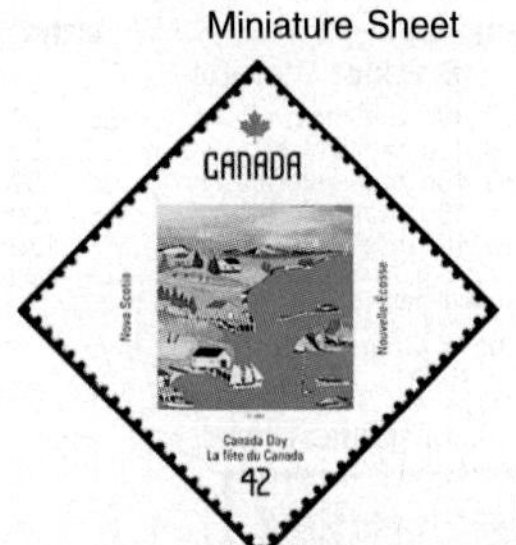

Canada Day A604

1992, June 29 Litho. *Perf. 12½x13*

1420 A604 42c Nova Scotia 1.00 1.00
1421 A604 42c Ontario 1.00 1.00
1422 A604 42c Prince Edward Island 1.00 1.00
1423 A604 42c New Brunswick 1.00 1.00
1424 A604 42c Quebec 1.00 1.00
1425 A604 42c Saskatchewan 1.00 1.00
1426 A604 42c Manitoba 1.00 1.00
1427 A604 42c Northwest Territories 1.00 1.00
1428 A604 42c Alberta 1.00 1.00
1429 A604 42c British Columbia 1.00 1.00
1430 A604 42c Yukon 1.00 1.00
1431 A604 42c Newfoundland 1.00 1.00
a. Sheet of 12, #1420-1431 + 13 labels 15.00 15.00

Canadian Folklore — A605

Legendary heroes: No. 1432, Jerry Potts, guide, interpreter. No. 1433, Captain William Jackman, rescuer. No. 1434, Laura Secord, patriot. No. 1435, Jos Monferrand, lumberjack.

1992, Sept. 8 Litho. *Perf. 12½*

1432 A605 42c multicolored .65 .30
1433 A605 42c multicolored .65 .30
1434 A605 42c multicolored .65 .30
1435 A605 42c multicolored .65 .30
a. Block of 4, #1432-1435 2.75 2.50

Minerals A606

1992, Sept. 21 *Perf. 12½*

1436 A606 42c Copper .80 .35
1437 A606 42c Sodalite .80 .35
1438 A606 42c Gold .80 .35
1439 A606 42c Galena .80 .35
1440 A606 42c Grossular .80 .35
a. Strip of 5, #1436-1440 4.25 4.00
b. Bklt. pane, 2 each #1436-1440 9.00

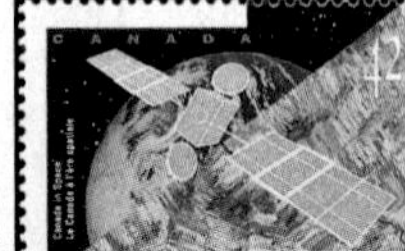

Canada in Space A607

1992, Oct. 1 Litho. *Perf. 13*

1441 A607 42c Anik E2 satellite .70 .70
a. Silver omitted *2,000.* *1,500.*

Size: 32x26mm

1442 A607 42c Earth, space shuttle .70 .70
a. Pair, #1441-1442 1.40 *1.75*
b. As "a," hologram omitted on #1442 *1,500.*

No. 1442 has a holographic image. Soaking in water may affect the hologram.

Natl. Hockey League, 75th Anniv. A608

Designs: No. 1443, Skates, stick, puck, photograph from the early years (1917-1942). No. 1444, Photograph, team emblems from the six-team years (1942-1967). No. 1445, Goalie's mask, gloves, photograph from the expansion years (1967-1992).

1992, Oct. 9 Litho. *Perf. 13x12½*
Booklet Stamps

1443 A608 42c multicolored .65 .20
a. Bklt. pane of 8 + 4 labels 5.25
1444 A608 42c multicolored .65 .20
a. Bklt. pane of 8 + 4 labels 5.25
1445 A608 42c multicolored .65 .20
a. Bklt. pane of 9 + 3 labels 6.00
Nos. 1443-1445 (3) 1.95 .60

A609

No. 1446, Order of Canada, 25th anniv. No. 1447, Daniel Roland Michener (1900-1991), Governor General.

1992, Oct. 21 *Perf. 12½*

1446 42c multicolored .65 .25
1447 42c multicolored .65 .30
a. A609 Pair, #1446-1447 1.40 .75

Nos. 1446-1447 printed in sheets of 25 containing 16 #1446 and 9 #1447.

World War II Type of 1989
1992, Nov. 10 Litho. *Perf. 13½*

1448 A568 42c War reporting .65 .35
1449 A568 42c Newfoundland air bases .65 .35
1450 A568 42c Raid on Dieppe .65 .35
1451 A568 42c U-boats offshore .65 .35
a. Block or strip of 4, #1448-1451 2.75 2.25

A611

Santa Claus A612

1992, Nov. 13 Litho. *Perf. 12½*

1452 A611 42c Jouluvana .70 .20
a. Perf. 13½ .75 .25
b. As "a," booklet pane of 10 7.50 6.75

Perf. 13½

1453 A611 48c La Befana .75 .40
a. Booklet pane of 5 + label 3.75 3.25
1454 A611 84c Weihnachtsmann 1.25 .55
a. Booklet pane of 5 + label 6.25 6.00

Booklet Stamp

Perf. 12½x13

1455 A612 37c Santa Claus .65 .60
a. Booklet pane of 10 6.50
Nos. 1452-1455 (4) 3.35 1.75

Christmas. No. 1455 has bar code at left; for use on covers with printed postal code matrix.

A613

Canadian Women: No. 1456, Adelaide Sophia Hoodless (1857-1910), founder of Victorian Order of Nurses. No. 1457, Marie-Josephine Gerin-Lajoie (1890-1971), founder of Notre-Dame du Bon Conseil Institute. No. 1458, Pitseolak Ashoona (c. 1904-83), Inuit graphic artist. No. 1459, Helen Alice Kinnear (1894-1970), first woman appointed King's Counsel and first federally appointed woman judge.

1993, Mar. 8 Litho. *Perf. 12½*

1456 A613 43c multicolored .65 .30
1457 A613 43c multicolored .65 .30
1458 A613 43c multicolored .65 .30
1459 A613 43c multicolored .65 .30
a. Block or strip of 4, #1456-1459 2.60 2.25

Natl. Council of Women of Canada (NCWC), and Natl. office of YWCA, cent.

Stanley Cup, Cent. — A614

1993, Apr. 16 Litho. *Perf. 13½*

1460 A614 43c multicolored .65 .20

Handcrafted Textiles — A615

#1461, Coverlet, New Brunswick. #1462, Pieced quilt, Ontario. #1463, Doukhobor bedcover, Saskatchewan. #1464, Kwakwaka'wakw ceremonial robe, British Columbia. #1465, Boutonne coverlet, Quebec.

Perf. 13x12½ on 3 Sides

1993, Apr. 30

Booklet Stamps

1461 A615 43c multicolored .65 .30
1462 A615 43c multicolored .65 .30
1463 A615 43c multicolored .65 .30
1464 A615 43c multicolored .65 .30
1465 A615 43c multicolored .65 .30
a. Strip of 5, #1461-1465 3.25 3.00
b. Bklt. pane, 2 ea #1461-1465 7.00

Stamps in bottom row of #1465b are in different sequence than those in #1465a.

Art Type of 1988

Painting: Drawing for The Owl, by Kenojuak Ashevak.

Litho. with Foil Application

1993, May 17 *Perf. 12½x13½*

1466 A546 86c multicolored 1.40 1.00

Intl. Year of Indigenous People.

Historic Canadian Pacific Railway Hotels A616

#1467, Empress, Victoria, B.C. 31468, Banff Springs, Banff, Alberta. #1469, Royal York, Toronto, Ont. #1470, Chateau Frontenac, Quebec. #1471, Algonquin, St. Andrews, N.B.

Perf. 13½ on 3 Sides

1993, June 14 Litho.

Booklet Stamps

1467 A616 43c multicolored .65 .30
1468 A616 43c multicolored .65 .30
1469 A616 43c multicolored .65 .30
1470 A616 43c multicolored .65 .30
1471 A616 43c multicolored .65 .30
a. Strip of 5, #1467-1471 3.25 3.00
b. Booklet pane, 2 #1471a 6.75

Opening of Chateau Frontenac, cent.

Miniature Sheet

Canada Day A617

Provincial and Territorial Parks: No. 1472, Algonquin, Ontario. No. 1473, De la Gaspesie, Quebec. No. 1474, Cedar Dunes, Prince Edward Island. No. 1475, Cape St. Mary's Seabird Ecological Reserve, Newfoundland. No. 1476, Mount Robson, British Columbia. No. 1477, Writing-On-Stone, Alberta. No. 1478, Spruce Woods, Manitoba. No. 1479, Herschel Island, Yukon. No. 1480, Cypress Hills, Saskatchewan. No. 1481, The Rocks, New Brunswick, No. 1482, Blomidon, Nova Scotia. No. 1483, Katannilik, Northwest Territories.

1993, June 30 Litho. *Perf. 13*

1472 A617 43c multicolored .75 .55
1473 A617 43c multicolored .75 .55
1474 A617 43c multicolored .75 .55
1475 A617 43c multicolored .75 .55
1476 A617 43c multicolored .75 .55
1477 A617 43c multicolored .75 .55
1478 A617 43c multicolored .75 .55
1479 A617 43c multicolored .75 .55
1480 A617 43c multicolored .75 .55
1481 A617 43c multicolored .75 .55
1482 A617 43c multicolored .75 .55
1483 A617 43c multicolored .75 .55
a. Sheet of 12, #1472-1483 11.00 10.00

Algonquin Park, centennial.

City of Toronto, Bicent. — A618

1993, Aug. 6 Litho. *Perf. 13½x13*

1484 A618 43c multicolored .65 .20

Canadian Rivers Type of 1991

1993, Aug. 10 *Perf. 13x12½*

Booklet Stamps

1485 A586 43c Fraser .65 .35
1486 A586 43c Yukon .65 .35
1487 A586 43c Red .65 .35
1488 A586 43c St. Lawrence .65 .35
1489 A586 43c St. John .65 .35
a. Strip of 5, #1485-1489 3.25 3.00
b. Bklt. pane, 2 each #1485-1489 7.00

Miniature Sheet

Historic Automobiles — A619

a, 1867 H.S. Taylor Steam Buggy. b, 1908 Russell Model L Touring Car. c, 1914 Ford Model T Open Touring Car. d, 1950 Studebaker Champion Deluxe Starlight Coupe. e, 1928 McLaughlin-Buick Model 28-496 Special Car. f, 1923-24 Gray-Dort 25-SM Luxury Sedan.

1993, Aug. 23 Litho. *Perf. 12½x13*

1490 A619 Sheet of 6 6.25 5.75
a.-b. 43c any single, 35x22mm .70 .70
c.-d. 49c any single, 43x22mm .75 .70
e.-f. 86c any single, 51x22mm 1.30 1.25

See Nos. 1527, 1552, 1604-1605.

Folk Songs A620

Designs: No. 1491, The Alberta Homesteader, Alberta. No. 1492, Les Raftmans, Quebec. No. 1493, I'se the B'y That Builds the Boat, Newfoundland. No. 1494, Onkwa:ri tenhanonniahkwe, Kanien'kehaka (Mohawk).

1993, Sept. 7 Litho. *Perf. 12½*

1491 A620 43c multicolored .65 .30
1492 A620 43c multicolored .65 .30
1493 A620 43c multicolored .65 .30
1494 A620 43c multicolored .65 .30
a. Block of 4, #1491-1494 2.60 2.25

Dinosaurs — A621

1993, Oct. 1 Litho. *Perf. 13½*

1495 A621 43c Massospondylus .65 .30
1496 A621 43c Styracosaurus .65 .30
1497 A621 43c Albertosaurus .65 .30
1498 A621 43c Platecarpus .65 .30
a. Block or strip of 4, #1495-1498 2.60 2.25

See Nos. 1529-1532.

A622

Santa Claus A623

1993, Nov. 4 Litho. *Perf. 13½*

1499 A622 43c Swiety Mikolaj .65 .20
a. Booklet pane of 10 6.50 5.00
b. Horiz. pair, imperf between *950.*
1500 A622 49c Ded Moroz .70 .35
a. Booklet pane of 5 + label 3.50 3.50
1501 A622 86c Father Christmas, Australia 1.10 .40
a. Booklet pane of 5 + label 5.50 5.00

Booklet Stamp

Perf. 13

1502 A623 38c Santa Claus .60 .45
a. Booklet pane of 10 6.00
Nos. 1499-1502 (4) 3.05 1.40

Christmas. No. 1502 has bar code at left; for use on covers with printed postal code matrix.

World War II Type of 1989

1993, Nov. 8 Litho. *Perf. 13½*

1503 A568 43c Aid to Allies .65 .35
1504 A568 43c Bomber forces .65 .35
1505 A568 43c Battle of the Atlantic .65 .35
1506 A568 43c Italian campaign .65 .35
a. Block or strip of 4, #1503-1506 2.75 2.50

Greetings — A624

Design: No. 1508, "Canada" at right.

1994, Jan. 28 Litho. *Die Cut*

1507 A624 43c multicolored .80 .50
1508 A624 43c multicolored .80 .50
a. Bklt pane, 5 ea #1507-1508 8.00

No. 1508a also contains 35 self-adhesive greetings labels in seven designs that complete the design when placed in the central circle of Nos. 1507-1508.
See Nos. 1568-1569, 1600-1601.

Jeanne Sauve (1922-93), Governor General — A625

1994, Mar. 8 Litho. *Perf. 12½x13*

1509 A625 43c + label, multi .65 .25
a. Block or horiz. strip of 4 + 4 labels 2.75 2.50

No. 1509 issued se-tenant with label in sheets of 20 + 20 labels in four designs. In alternating rows, labels appear on left or right side of stamp.

T. Eaton Company, 125th Anniv. — A626

1994, Mar. 17 Litho. *Perf. 13½x13*

1510 A626 43c multicolored .65 .25
a. Booklet pane of 10 + 2 labels 6.50

Canadian Rivers Type of 1991

1994, Apr. 22 *Perf. 13½*

Booklet Stamps

1511 A586 43c Saguenay .65 .30
1512 A586 43c French .65 .30
1513 A586 43c Mackenzie .65 .30
1514 A586 43c Churchill .65 .30
1515 A586 43c Columbia .65 .30
a. Strip of 5, #1511-1515 3.25 3.00
b. Bklt. pane, 2 ea #1511-1515 7.25 6.75

Art Type of 1988

Vera, by Frederick H. Varley (1881-1969).

Litho. with Foil Application

1994, May 6 *Perf. 14x14½*

1516 A546 88c multicolored 1.25 .70

XV Commonwealth Games, Victoria, BC — A627

1994 Litho. *Perf. 14*

1517	A627 43c Lawn bowls	.65	.25
1518	A627 43c Lacrosse	.65	.25
a.	Pair, #1517-1518	1.30	.80
1519	A627 43c Wheelchair marathon	.65	.25
1520	A627 43c High jump	.65	.25
a.	Pair, #1519-1520	1.30	.60
1521	A627 50c Diving	.75	.55
a.	Gold ("CANADA 50") omitted	*1,150.*	
1522	A627 88c Cycling	1.30	.70
a.	Gold ("CANADA 88") omitted	*1,300.*	
	Nos. 1517-1522 (6)	4.65	2.25

Certificates of authenticity recommended for Nos. 1521a and 1522a.

Issued: #1517-1518, 5/20; #1519-1522, 8/5.

Souvenir Sheet

Intl. Year of the Family — A628

Designs: a, Mother and infant. b, Adults, children playing. c, Elderly woman, child. d, Adults, children in class. e, Judge, health care worker, child.

1994, June 2 Litho. *Perf. 14*

1523	A628 Sheet of 5	3.25	3.25
a.-e.	43c any single	.65	.55

Canada Day A629

Maple trees: a, Big leaf. b, Sugar. c, Silver. d, Striped. e, Norway. f, Manitoba. g, Black. h, Douglas. i, Mountain. j, Vine. k, Hedge. l, Red.

1994, June 30 Litho. *Perf. 13x13½*

1524	A629 Sheet of 12	8.00	8.00
a.-l.	43c any single	.65	.50

Billy Bishop (1894-1956), Fighter Ace — A630

Design: No. 1526, Mary Travers, "La Bolduc" (1894-1941), folk singer.

1994, Aug. 12 *Perf. 13*

1525	A630 43c multicolored	.65	.30
1526	A630 43c multicolored	.65	.30
a.	Pair, #1525-1526	1.30	.75

Historic Vehicles Type of 1993

Miniature Sheet

Designs: a, 1942 Ford F60L-AMB military ambulance. b, 1925 REO Speed Wagon Police Wagon. c, 1927 Sicard Snow Remover/Snowblower. d, 1936 Bickle Chieftain Fire Engine. e, 1894 Ottawa Car Company Streetcar. f, 1950 Motor Coach Industries Courier 50 Skyview bus.

1994, Aug. 19 Litho. *Perf. 12½x13*

1527	Sheet of 6	5.50	5.50
a.-b.	A619 43c any single	.65	.60
c.-d.	A619 50c any single	.75	.70
e.-f.	A619 88c any single	1.30	1.20

ICAO, 50th Anniv. A632

1994, Sept. 16 Litho. *Perf. 13*

1528	A632 43c multicolored	.65	.20

Dinosaur Type of 1993

Prehistoric animals: No. 1529, Coryphodon. No. 1530, Megacerops. No. 1531, Short-faced bear. No. 1532, Woolly mammoth.

1994, Sept. 26

1529	A621 43c multicolored	.65	.25
1530	A621 43c multicolored	.65	.25
1531	A621 43c multicolored	.65	.25
1532	A621 43c multicolored	.65	.25
a.	Block or strip of 4, #1529-1532	2.60	2.00

Family Singing Carols A633

Soloist A634

1994, Nov. 3 Litho. *Perf. 13½*

1533	A633 43c multicolored	.65	.20
a.	Booklet pane of 10	6.50	
1534	A633 50c Choir, vert.	.75	.45
a.	Booklet pane of 5 + label	3.75	3.25
1535	A633 88c Caroling, vert.	1.30	.75
a.	Booklet pane of 5 + label	6.50	6.25

Booklet Stamp

Perf. 13

1536	A634 38c multicolored	.65	.60
a.	Booklet pane of 10	6.50	
	Nos. 1533-1536 (4)	3.35	2.00

Christmas. No. 1536 has bar code at left; for use on covers with printed postal code matrix.

Examples exist of 52c and 90c denominations with the same designs as Nos. 1534 (52c) and 1535 (90c). These were prepared in advance in anticipation of a rate increase that was not approved. Virtually all were destroyed, but a small quantity are known in private hands. None were regularly issued or sold at post offices.

World War II Type of 1989

1994, Nov. 7 Litho. *Perf. 13½*

1537	A568 43c D-Day beachhead	.65	.30
1538	A568 43c Artillery-Normandy	.65	.30
1539	A568 43c Tactical Air Forces	.65	.30
1540	A568 43c Walcheren and the Scheldt	.65	.30
a.	Block or strip of 4, #1537-1540	2.75	1.75

1995, Mar. 20 Litho. *Perf. 13½*

1541	A568 43c Veterans return home	.65	.30
1542	A568 43c Freeing the POW	.65	.30
1543	A568 43c Liberation of civilians	.65	.30
1544	A568 43c Crossing the Rhine	.65	.30
a.	Block or strip of 4, #1541-1544	2.75	1.75

Art Type of 1988

Painting: Floraison, by Alfred Pellan (1906-88).

Litho. with Foil Application

1995, Apr. 21 *Perf. 13*

1545	A546 88c multicolored	1.30	.55
a.	Gold foil omitted	—	

Flag Over Lake — A635

1995, May 1 Litho. *Perf. 13½x13*

1546	A635 (43c) multicolored	.65	.25

No. 1546 was valued at the first class domestic letter rate on day of issue.

Fortress of Louisbourg, 275th Anniv. — A636

#1547, Louisbourg Harbor, ships near Dauphin Gate. #1548, Walls, streets, buildings of Louisbourg. #1549, Museum behind King's Bastion. #1550, Drawing of King's Garden, Convent, Hospital and barracks. #1551, Partially eroded fortifications.

1995, May 5 *Perf. 12½x13*

1547	A636 (43c) 48x32mm	.65	.35
1548	A636 (43c) 32x32mm	.65	.35
1549	A636 (43c) 40x32mm	.65	.35
1550	A636 (43c) 56x32mm	.65	.35
1551	A636 (43c) 48x32mm	.65	.35
a.	Strip of 5, #1547-1551	3.25	3.00
b.	Booklet pane, 2 #1551a	6.50	
	Complete booklet, #1551b	6.75	

Nos. 1547-1551 were valued at the first class domestic letter rate on day of issue. No. 1551a is a continuous design.

Historic Vehicles Type of 1993

Miniature Sheet

Farm, frontier vehicles: a, 1950 Cockshutt "30" farm tractor. b, 1970 Bombardier Ski-Doo Olympique 335 snowmobile. c, 1948 Bombardier B-12 CS multi-passenger snowmobile. d, 1924 Gotfredson model 20 farm truck. e, 1962 Robin-Nodwell RN 110 tracked carrier. f, 1942 Massey-Harris No. 21 self-propelled combine.

1995, May 26 Litho. *Perf. 12½x13*

1552	Sheet of 6	5.25	5.25
a.-b.	A619 43c any single, 35x22mm	.65	.65
c.-d.	A619 50c any single, 43x22mm	.70	.70
e.-f.	A619 88c any single, 43x22mm	1.25	1.25

Golf in Canada A637

Designs: No. 1553, Banff Springs Golf Club. No. 1554, Riverside Country Club. No. 1555, Glen Abbey Golf Club. No. 1556, Victoria Golf Club. No. 1557, Royal Montreal Golf Club.

Perf. 13½x13 on 3 Sides

1995, June 6

Booklet Stamps

1553	A637 43c multicolored	.65	.35
1554	A637 43c multicolored	.65	.35
1555	A637 43c multicolored	.65	.35
1556	A637 43c multicolored	.65	.35
1557	A637 43c multicolored	.65	.35
a.	Strip of 5, #1553-1557	3.25	3.25
b.	Booklet pane, 2 #1557a	6.50	
	Complete booklet, #1557b	6.75	

Nat. Golf Week. Canadian Amateur Golf Championship, cent. Royal Canadian Golf Assoc., cent.

Lunenburg Academy, Cent. — A638

1995, June 29 Litho. *Perf. 13*

1558	A638 43c multicolored	.65	.25

Souvenir Sheets

Group of Seven — A639

Painting, original members: No. 1559a, October Gold, by Franklin Carmichael. b, From the North Shore, Lake Superior, by Lawren Harris. c, Evening, Les Eboulements, Quebec, by A.Y. Jackson.

No. 1560a, Serenity, Lake of the Woods, by Frank H. Johnston. b, A September Gale, Georgian Bay, by Arthur Lismer. c, Falls, Montreal River, by J.E.H. MacDonald. d, Open Window, by Frederick Horsman Varley.

Painting, new members: No. 1561a, Mill Houses, by Alfred J. Casson. b, Pembina Valley, by Lionel LeMoine FitzGerald. c, The Lumberjack, by Edwin Headley Holgate.

1995, June 29

1559	A639 Sheet of 3	2.00	2.00
a.-c.	43c any single	.65	.65
1560	A639 Sheet of 4	2.75	2.75
a.-d.	43c any single	.65	.65
1561	A639 Sheet of 3	2.00	2.00
a.-c.	43c any single	.65	.65

Manitoba's Entry Into Confederation, 125th Anniv. — A640

1995, July 14 *Perf. 13½x13*

1562	A640 43c multicolored	.65	.25

Migratory Wildlife — A641

1995, Aug. 15 Litho. *Perf. 13x12½*

1563	A641 45c Monarch butterfly	.65	.30
1564	A641 45c Belted kingfisher	.65	.40
1565	A641 45c Northern pintail	.65	.30
1566	A641 45c Hoary bat	.65	.30
a.	Block or strip of 4, #1563-1566	2.75	2.25

No. 1564 with Revised Inscription

1995, Sept. 26

1567	A641 45c like #1564	.80	.65
a.	Block or strip of 4, #1563, 1565-1567	3.50	3.00

#1564 inscribed "aune," #1567 "Faune." See Mexico #1924.

Greetings Type of 1994

Designs: No. 1568, "Canada" at left. No. 1569, "Canada" at right.

1995, Sept. 1 ***Die Cut***

Self-Adhesive

Size: 46x22mm

1568 A624 45c green & multi .85 .40
1569 A624 45c green & multi .85 .40
a. Bklt. pane, 5 ea #1568-1569 8.50

By its nature, No. 1569a is a complete booklet. The peelable backing serves as a booklet cover.

No. 1569a also contains 15 self-adhesive greetings labels in four designs that complete the design when placed in the central circle of Nos. 1568-1569.

No. 1569a exists with special cover and labels commemorating the Canadian Memorial Chiropractic College, Toronto, 50th anniv.

Bridges A642

#1570, Quebec Bridge, Quebec. #1571, Highway 403-401-410 interchange, Ontario. #1572, Hartland Covered Wooden Bridge, New Brunswick. #1573, Alex Fraser Bridge, British Columbia.

1995, Sept. 1 ***Perf. 12½x13***

1570 A642 45c multicolored .70 .30
1571 A642 45c multicolored .70 .30
1572 A642 45c multicolored .70 .30
1573 A642 45c multicolored .70 .30
a. Block or strip of 4, #1570-1573 2.80 1.60

Canadian Arctic A643

#1574, Polar bear, caribou. #1575, Arctic poppy, cargo canoe. #1576, Inuk man, igloo, sled dogs. #1577, Dog-sled team, ski plane. No. 1578, Children.

1995, Sept. 15 ***Perf. 13x12½***

Booklet Stamps

1574 A643 45c multicolored .70 .30
1575 A643 45c multicolored .70 .30
1576 A643 45c multicolored .70 .30
1577 A643 45c multicolored .70 .30
1578 A643 45c multicolored .70 .30
a. Strip of 5, #1574-1578 3.50 3.50
b. Bklt. pane, 2 #1578a 7.00
Complete booklet, #1578b 7.25

Stamps in bottom row of #1578b are in different sequence.

Comic Book Characters A644

1995, Oct. 2 **Litho.** ***Perf. 13x12½***

Booklet Stamps

1579 A644 45c Superman .70 .30
1580 A644 45c Johnny Canuck .70 .30
1581 A644 45c Nelvana .70 .30
1582 A644 45c Captain Canuck .70 .30
1583 A644 45c Fleur de Lys .70 .30
a. Strip of 5, #1579-1583 3.50 3.25
b. Booklet pane, 2 #1583a 7.00
Complete booklet, #1583b 7.25

Stamps in the bottom row of No. 1583b are in different sequence.

UN, 50th Anniv. A645

1995, Oct. 24 **Litho.** ***Perf. 13½***

1584 A645 45c blue & multi .70 .25

No. 1584 printed in sheets of 10 with top label equal to 10 stamps. Label shows details of Canadian participation in UN activities. UN emblem on No. 1584 is stamped in blue foil.

Capital Sculptures, by Emile Brunet (1893-1977), Sainte-Anne-de-Deaupre Basilica — A646

Holly A647

1995, Nov. 2 **Litho.** ***Perf. 13½***

1585 A646 45c The Nativity .70 .20
a. Booklet pane of 10 7.00
Complete booklet, #1585a 7.25
1586 A646 52c The Annunciation .85 .40
a. Booklet pane of 5 + label 4.25 4.25
Complete booklet, #1586a 4.50
1587 A646 90c Flight to Egypt 1.40 .55
a. Booklet pane of 5 + label 7.00 7.00
Complete booklet, #1587a 7.25

Booklet Stamp

Perf. 12½x13

1588 A647 40c multicolored .65 .60
a. Booklet pane of 10 6.50
Complete booklet, #1588a 6.75
Nos. 1585-1588 (4) 3.60 1.75

Christmas. No. 1588 has bar code at left; for use on covers with printed postal code matrix.

La Francophonie's Agency for Cultural and Technical Cooperation, 25th Anniv. — A648

1995, Nov. 6 ***Perf. 13x13½***

1589 A648 45c multicolored .70 .25

End of the Holocaust, 50th Anniv. — A649

1995, Nov. 9 ***Perf. 12½x13***

1590 A649 45c multicolored .70 .25

Birds A650

#1591, American kestrel. #1592, Atlantic puffin. #1593, Pileated woodpecker. #1594, Ruby-throated hummingbird.

1996, Jan. 9 **Litho.** ***Perf. 13½***

1591 A650 45c multicolored .70 .30
1592 A650 45c multicolored .70 .30
1593 A650 45c multicolored .70 .30
1594 A650 45c multicolored .70 .30
a. Strip of 4, Nos. 1591-1594 2.80 2.75

Issued in panes of 12 stamps, printed checkerwise, and in uncut sheets of 5 panes.

See Nos. 1631-1634, 1710-1713, 1770-1777, 1839-1846, 1886-1889.

High Technology Industries — A651

Designs: No. 1595, Ocean technology. No. 1596, Aerospace technology. No. 1597, Information technology. No. 1598, Biotechnology.

Perf. 13½ on 3 Sides

1996, Feb. 15 **Litho.**

Booklet Stamps

1595 A651 45c multicolored .70 .30
1596 A651 45c multicolored .70 .30
1597 A651 45c multicolored .70 .30
1598 A651 45c multicolored .70 .30
a. Booklet pane of 12, 3 each Nos. 1595-1598 8.50
Complete booklet, No. 1598a 9.00
Nos. 1595-1598 (4) 2.80 1.20

Greetings Type of 1994

"Canada": #1600, at L. #1601, at R.

1996, Jan. 15 **Litho.** ***Die Cut***

Self-Adhesive

Size: 51x25mm

1600 A624 45c green & multi .80 .45
1601 A624 45c green & multi .80 .45
a. Booklet pane, 5 ea #1600-1601 8.00
b. As "a," die cutting omitted —

By its nature No. 1601a is a complete booklet. The peelable backing serves as a booklet cover.

No. 1601a also contains 35 self-adhesive greetings labels in seven designs that complete the design when placed in the central circle of Nos. 1600-1601.

Art Type of 1988

Sculpture: The Spirit of Haida Gwaii, by Bill Reid.

Litho. with Foil Application

1996, Apr. 30 ***Perf. 12½x13***

1602 A546 90c multicolored 1.40 .50

AIDS Awareness — A652

1996, May 8 **Litho.** ***Perf. 13½***

1603 A652 45c multicolored .70 .20

Historic Vehicles Type of 1993

#1604: a, 1899 Still Motor Co. Ltd. Electric Van. b. 1914 Waterous Engine Works Road Roller. c, 1938 International D-35 Delivery Truck. d, 1936 Champion Road Grader. e, 1947 White Model WA 122 Tractor Trailer. f, 1975 Hayes HDX 45-115 Logging Truck.

#1605: a, like #1490a. b, like #1490b. c, like 1527a. d, like #1527b. e, like #1552b. f, like #1604a. g, like #1604b, h, like #1552a. i, like #1604c. j, like 1604d. k, like #1527e. l, like #1527f. m, like #1604e. n, like #1604f. o, like #1490c. p, like #1490d. q, like #1527d. r, like #1490e. s, like #1490f. t, like #1527c. u, like #1552c. v, like #1552d. w, like #1552e. x, like #1552f. y, 1975 Bricklin SV-1 Sports car.

1996 **Litho.** ***Perf. 12½x13***

1604 A619 Sheet of 6 6.00 6.00
a.-b. 45c any single .70 .45
c.-d. 52c any single .80 .50
e.-f. 90c any single 1.40 1.10

1605 A619 Sheet of 25 6.50 6.50
a.-j. 5c any single .20 .20
k.-n. 10c any single .25 .25
o.-x. 20c any single .30 .25
y. 45c multicolored .90 .90

Nos. 1604e-1604f, 1605k-1605n, 1605y are 51x22mm. Nos. 1605o-1605x are 43x21mm.

Yukon Gold Rush, Cent. A653

Designs: a, "Skookum" Jim Mason's discovery on Rabbit (Bonanza) Creek, 1896. b, Miners trekking to gold fields, boats on Lake Laberge. c, Supr. Sam Steele, North West Mounted Police, Alaska-Yukon border. d, Dawson, boom town, city of entertainment. e, Klondike gold fields.

1996, June 13 ***Perf. 13½***

1606 Strip of 5 5.00 4.50
a.-e. A653 45c any single 1.00 .40

CAPEX '96. #1606 was issued in sheets of 10 stamps.

Canada Day — A654

1996, June 28 **Litho.** ***Die Cut***

Self-Adhesive

1607 A654 45c multicolored .70 .25
a. Pane of 12 8.50

Canadian Olympic Gold Medalists A655

#1608, Ethel Catherwood, high jump, 1928. #1609, Etienne Desmarteau, 56 lb. weight throw, 1904. #1610, Fanny Rosenfeld, 100m, 400m relay, 1928. #1611, Gerald Ouellette, smallbore rifle, prone, 1956. #1612, Percy Williams, 100m, 200m, 1928.

Litho. & Typo.

1996, July 8 ***Perf. 13x12½***

Booklet Stamps

1608 A655 45c gold, sep & silver .70 .30
1609 A655 45c gold, sep & silver .70 .30
1610 A655 45c gold, sep & silver .70 .30
1611 A655 45c gold, sep & silver .70 .30
1612 A655 45c gold, sep & silver .70 .30
a. Strip of 5, #1608-1612 3.50 1.50
b. Booklet pane, 2 #1612a 7.00
Complete booklet, #1612b 7.25

British Columbia's Entry Into Confederation, 125th Anniv. — A656

1996, July 19

1613 A656 45c multicolored .70 .25

A657

1996, Aug. 19 Litho. *Perf. 12½x12*

1614 A657 45c Canadian Heraldry .70 .25

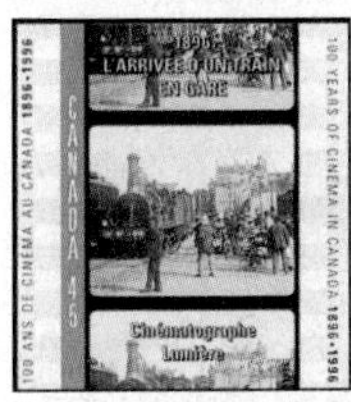

Motion Pictures, Cent. — A658

Film strips from motion pictures: No. 1615a, L'arrivée d'un train en gare, Lumière cinematography, 1896. b, Back to God's Country, Nell & Ernest Shipman, 1919. c, Hen Hop, Norman McLaren, 1942. d, Pour la suite du monde, Pierre Perrault, Michel Brault, 1963. e, Goin' Down the Road, Don Shebib, 1970.

No. 1616a, Mon oncle Antoine, Claude Jutra, 1971. b, The Apprenticeship of Duddy Kravitz, Ted Kotcheff, 1974. c, Les Ordres, Michel Brault, 1974. d, Les Bons Débarras, Francis Mankiewiez, 1980. e, The Grey Fox, Philip Borsos, 1982.

1996, Aug. 22 *Die Cut*

Self-Adhesive

1615 A658 Sheet of 5 3.50
a.-e. 45c Any single .70 .60
1616 A658 Sheet of 5 3.50
a.-e. 45c Any single .70 .60

Edouard Montpetit (1881-1954), Educator A659

1996, Sept. 26 Litho. *Perf. 12½*

1617 A659 45c multicolored .70 .25

Winnie the Pooh A660

Designs: No. 1618, Winnie, Lt. Colebourne, 1914. No. 1619, Winnie, Christopher Robin, 1925. No. 1620, Milne and Shepard's Winnie the Pooh, 1926. No. 1621, Winnie the Pooh at Walt Disney World, 1996.

1996, Oct. 1 Litho. *Perf. 12½x13*

1618 A660 45c multicolored .70 .35
1619 A660 45c multicolored .70 .35
1620 A660 45c multicolored .70 .35
1621 A660 45c multicolored .70 .35
a. Block of 4, #1618-1621 2.80 2.25
b. Souv. sheet of 4, #1618-1621 7.00 6.00
c. Booklet pane of 16, 4 each #1618-1621 11.50
Complete booklet, #1621c 12.00

No. 1621a was issued in booklet panes of 16 stamps (No. 1621c), with the halves of the booklet pane printed tete-beche. The booklet pane of 16 was used as a cover for a souvenir story booklet.

Walt Disney World, 25th anniv.

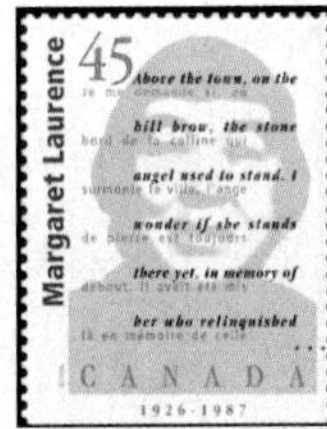

Authors — A661

#1622, Margaret Laurence (1926-87). #1623, Donald G. Creighton (1902-79). #1624, Gabrielle Roy (1909-83). #1625, Felix-Antoine Savard (1896-1982). #1626, Thomas C. Haliburton (1796-1865).

Perf. 13½x13 on 3 Sides

1996, Oct. 10 Litho. & Engr.

Booklet Stamps

1622 A661 45c multicolored .80 .30
1623 A661 45c multicolored .80 .30
1624 A661 45c multicolored .80 .30
1625 A661 45c multicolored .80 .30
1626 A661 45c multicolored .80 .30
a. Strip of 5, #1622-1626 4.00 2.00
b. Booklet pane, 2 #1626a 8.00 4.00
Complete booklet, #1626b 9.50

A662

Christmas: 45c, Children on snowshoes, sled. 52c, Santa Claus skiing. 90c, Children skating.

Perf. 13½ (#1627, 1629a), 12¾x12¼ (#1628, 1629), 13½x13 (#1627a, 1628a)

1996, Nov. 1 Litho.

1627 A662 45c multicolored .70 .20
a. Booklet pane of 10 7.00
Complete booklet, #1627a 8.00
1628 A662 52c multicolored .80 .25
a. Booklet pane of 5 + label 4.00 2.75
Complete booklet, #1628a 4.50
1629 A662 90c multicolored 1.40 .45
a. Booklet pane of 5 + label 7.00 5.50
Complete booklet, #1629a 7.50

UNICEF, 50th anniv.

New Year 1997 (Year of the Ox) — A663

1997, Jan. 7 Litho. *Perf. 13x12½*

1630 A663 45c multicolored .70 .25
a. Souvenir sheet of 2 2.25 2.25
b. As No. 1630, gold omitted *2,750.*

No. 1630a is fan shaped.

No. 1630a with Hong Kong 97 overprint was sold as a limited edition only at the show. Value $6.

Bird Type of 1996

#1631, Mountain bluebird. #1632, Western grebe. #1633, Northern gannet. #1634, Scarlet tanager.

1997, Jan. 10 Litho. *Perf. 12½x13*

1631 A650 45c multicolored .70 .30
1632 A650 45c multicolored .70 .30
1633 A650 45c multicolored .70 .30
1634 A650 45c multicolored .70 .30
a. Block or strip of 4, #1631-1634 2.80 1.90

Nos. 1631-1634 were issued in sheets of 20, 5 each, printed checkerwise to contain 4 complete blocks or 5 strips.

Art Type of 1988

Painting: York Boat on Lake Winnipeg, by Walter J. Phillips.

Litho. with Foil Application

1997, Feb. 17 *Perf. 12½x13*

1635 A546 90c gold & multi 1.40 .55

Canadian Tire, 75th Anniv. A664

1997, Mar. 3 Litho. *Perf. 13x13½*

1636 A664 45c multicolored .70 .25

Father Charles-Emile Gadbois (1906-81), Musicologist A665

1997, Mar. 20 *Perf. 13½x13*

1637 A665 45c multicolored .70 .25

Québec en Fleurs 97, Intl. Horticultural Exhibition A666

Perf. 13x12½ on 3 Sides

1997, Apr. 4 Litho.

Booklet Stamp

1638 A666 45c Blue poppy .70 .25
a. Booklet pane of 12 8.50
Complete booklet, #1638a 9.00

Victorian Order of Nurses for Canada, Cent. A667

1997, May 12 Litho. *Perf. 12½x13*

1639 A667 45c multicolored .70 .25

Law Society of Upper Canada, Bicent. — A668

1997, May 23 *Perf. 13½x13*

1640 A668 45c multicolored .70 .25

Salt Water Fish A669

#1641, Great white shark. #1642, Pacific halibut. #1643, Atlantic sturgeon. #1644, Bluefin tuna.

1997, May 30 Litho. *Perf. 12½x13*

1641 A669 45c multicolored .70 .30
1642 A669 45c multicolored .70 .30
1643 A669 45c multicolored .70 .30
1644 A669 45c multicolored .70 .30
a. Block or strip of 4, #1641-1644 2.80 1.75

Opening of the Confederation Bridge — A670

1997, May 31

1645 A670 45c Lighthouse, bridge .70 .25
1646 A670 45c Bridge, bird .70 .25
a. Pair, #1645-1646 + label 1.40 .75

Gilles Villeneuve (1950-82), Formula One Race Car Driver — A671

45c, Villeneuve winning race in Ferrari T-4. 90c, Close-up, racing in Number 12 Ferrari T-3.

1997, June 12

1647 A671 45c multicolored .70 .25
1648 A671 90c multicolored 1.40 .60
a. Pair, #1647-1648 2.10 1.00
b. Sheet of 4 #1648a 8.50 6.00

John Cabot's Voyage to Canada, 500th Anniv. A672

1997, June 24 Litho. *Perf. 12½x13*

1649 A672 45c multicolored .70 .25

See Italy No. 2162.

Scenic Canadian Highways — A673

Designs: No. 1650, Sea to Sky Highway, British Columbia. No. 1651, The Cabot Trail, Nova Scotia. No. 1652, The Wine Route, starting in Ontario. No. 1653, The Big Muddy, Saskatchewan.

1997, June 30 *Perf. 12½x13*

1650 A673 45c multicolored .70 .50
1651 A673 45c multicolored .70 .50
1652 A673 45c multicolored .70 .50
1653 A673 45c multicolored .70 .50
a. Block or strip of 4, #1650-1653 2.80 2.00

See Nos. 1739-1742, 1780-1783.

Canadian Industrial Design — A674

1997, July 23

1654 A674 45c multicolored .70 .25

No. 1654 was issued with se-tenant label in sheets of 24 + 24 labels. The 12 different labels each appear twice in different colors. In alternating rows, labels appear on left or right side of stamp.

Association of Canadian Industrial Designers, 50th anniv. and 20th Intl. Congress of Intl. Council of Societies of Industrial Design.

Highland Games, Maxville, Ontario — A675

1997, Aug. 1

1655 A675 45c multicolored .70 .25

Knights of Columbus in Canada, Cent. — A676

1997, Aug. 5 *Perf. 13*

1656 A676 45c multicolored .70 .25

28th World Congress of Postal, Telegraph and Telephone Intl. Labor Union, Montreal A677

1997, Aug. 18 Litho. *Perf. 13*

1657 A677 45c multicolored .70 .25

Asia Pacific Year A678

1997, Aug. 25 *Perf. 13½*

1658 A678 45c multicolored .70 .25

Canada-USSR Ice Hockey "Series of the Century," 25th Anniv. — A679

Designs: No. 1659, Canadian players, Paul Henderson, Yvan Cournoyer (No. 12), after scoring winning goal in final game. No. 1660, Canadian team members celebrating victory.

1997, Sept. 20 Litho. *Perf. 14x13*

Booklet Stamps

1659 A679 45c multicolored .70 .30
1660 A679 45c multicolored .70 .30
a. Bklt. pane, 5 ea #1659-1660 7.00
Complete booklet, #1660a 7.50

Famous Politicians A680

#1661, Martha Black (1866-1957). #1662, Lionel Chevrier (1903-87). #1663, Judy LaMarsh (1924-80). #1664, Réal Caouette (1917-76).

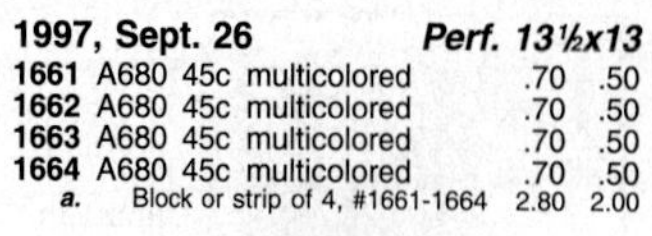

1997, Sept. 26 *Perf. 13½x13*

1661 A680 45c multicolored .70 .50
1662 A680 45c multicolored .70 .50
1663 A680 45c multicolored .70 .50
1664 A680 45c multicolored .70 .50
a. Block or strip of 4, #1661-1664 2.80 2.00

Supernatural — A681

1997, Oct. 1 *Perf. 13x12½*

1665 A681 45c Vampire .70 .25
1666 A681 45c Werewolf .70 .25
1667 A681 45c Ghost .70 .25
1668 A681 45c Goblin .70 .25
a. Block of 4, #1665-1668 2.80 1.50

Christmas — A682

Stained glass windows: 45c, "Our Lady of the Rosary," Holy Rosary Cathedral, Vancouver. 52c, "Nativity Scene," United Church, Leith, Ontario. 90c, Madonna and Child, St. Stephen's Ukrainian Byzantine Rite Roman Catholic Church, Calgary.

1997, Nov. 3 Litho. *Perf. 12½x13*

1669 A682 45c multicolored .70 .20
a. Booklet pane of 10 7.00
Complete booklet, #1669a 7.50
1670 A682 52c multicolored .80 .25
a. Booklet pane of 5 4.00 4.00
Complete booklet, #1670a 4.25
1671 A682 90c multicolored 1.40 .50
a. Booklet pane of 5 7.00 7.00
Complete booklet, #1671a 7.50
Nos. 1669-1671 (3) 2.90 .95

75th Royal Agriculture Winter Fair, Toronto A683

1997, Nov. 6

1672 A683 45c multicolored .70 .25

Types of 1987-98 and:

Traditional Handiwork — A684

Loon A686

Polar Bear — A686a

Moose — A686b

Grizzly Bear — A686c

Flag and Inukshuk — A687

1997-2003 Litho. *Perf. 13x13½*

1673 A684 1c Bookbinding .20 .20
1674 A684 2c Ironwork .20 .20
1675 A684 3c Glass blowing .20 .20
1676 A684 4c Oyster farmer .20 .20
1677 A684 5c Weaving .20 .20
1678 A684 9c Quilting .20 .20
1679 A684 10c Artistic woodworking .20 .20
a. Imperf, single —
b. Block of 4, top two stamps imperf (cut between) —
1680 A684 25c Leatherworking .40 .20

Perf. 13

1682 A536 46c Queen Elizabeth II .70 .30

Perf. 13¼x13

1683 A536 47c multi .75 .30
a. Imperf, pair 600.00

Perf. 13

1687 A541 46c Flag over Icebergs .70 .30
a. Booklet pane of 10 7.00
Complete booklet, #1687a 7.50
1692 A692 55c multicolored .90 .35
a. Booklet pane of 5 + label 4.50 2.50
Complete booklet, #1692a 4.75
1694 A692 73c multicolored 1.10 .50
1696 A692 95c multicolored 1.50 .65
a. Booklet pane of 5 + label 7.50 4.75
Complete booklet, #1696a 8.00

Litho. & Engr.

1697 A686 $1 Loon 1.50 .40
1698 A686a $2 Polar bear 3.00 1.00

Size 63x48mm

Perf. 12½x13

1699 A686b $5 Moose 7.75 2.00
a. Engraved colors (Moose, etc.) omitted —
1700 A686c $8 Grizzly bear 12.00 4.50
Nos. 1673-1700 (18) 31.70 11.90

Coil Stamp

Engr.

Perf. 10 Horiz.

1703 A542 46c red .70 .30
a. Imperf, pair 100.00

Booklet Stamps

Self-Adhesive

Die Cut

1705 A541 46c Flag over Icebergs .70 .30
a. Booklet pane of 30 21.00
b. Imperf, pair 250.00
1706 A692 46c multicolored 2.25 1.10
a. Booklet pane of 18 40.00
1707 A687 47c multi .75 .30
a. Booklet of 10 7.50
b. Booklet of 30 22.50

Nos. 1705a-1706a are complete booklets. The peelable backing serves as a booklet cover.

Issued: #1682, 1687, 1692, 1694, 1696, 1703, 1705-1706, 12/28/98; $8, 10/15/97; $1, $2, 10/27/98; 1c-25c, 4/29/99; 47c, 12/28/00.

See No. 2007.

New Year 1998 (Year of the Tiger) A690

1998, Jan. 8 Litho. *Perf. 13x12½*

1708 A690 45c multicolored .70 .25
a. Souvenir sheet of 2 1.40 1.00

No. 1708a overprinted exists. Value $2.50.

Provincial Leaders A691

Designs: a, John P. Robarts (1917-82), Ontario. b, Jean Lesage (1912-80), Quebec. c, John B. McNair (1889-1968), New Brunswick. d, Tommy Douglas (1904-86), Saskatchewan. e, Joseph R. Smallwood (1900-91), Newfoundland. f, Angus L. MacDonald (1890-1954), Nova Scotia. g, W.A.C. Bennett (1900-79), British Columbia. h, Ernest C. Manning (1908-95), Alberta. i, John Bracken (1883-1969), Manitoba. j, J. Walter Jones (1878-1954), Prince Edward Island.

1998, Feb. 18 Litho. *Perf. 13½*

1709 A691 Sheet of 10 7.00 7.00
a.-j. 45c any single .70 .40

Bird Type of 1996

#1710, Hairy woodpecker. #1711, Great crested flycatcher. #1712, Eastern screech owl. #1713, Gray-crowned rosy-finch.

1998, Mar. 13 Litho. *Perf. 13x13½*

1710 A650 45c multicolored .70 .30
1711 A650 45c multicolored .70 .30
1712 A650 45c multicolored .70 .30
1713 A650 45c multicolored .70 .30
a. Block or strip of 4, #1710-1713 2.80 1.75

Nos. 1710-1713 were issued in sheets of 20, 5 each, printed checkerwise to contain 4 complete blocks or 5 strips.

Maple Leaf — A692

1998, Apr. 14 Litho. *Die Cut*

Self-Adhesive

Booklet Stamp

1714 A692 45c multicolored 1.20 1.30
a. Booklet pane of 18 22.50

Typo. & Embossed

Die Cut Perf. 13

Self-adhesive

1714B A692 45c multicolored 1.00 .30

The peelable paper backing of No. 1714a serves as a booklet cover.

No. 1714B does not have the "POSTAGE / POSTES" and copyright inscriptions found in No. 1714. The gold on No. 1714B is embossed and brighter than that on No. 1714.

See Nos. 1692, 1694, 1696, 1706.

These stamps may be added to the previous definitive set.

Fly Fishing in Canada — A693

Lure, type of fish: No. 1715, Coquihalla orange, steelhead trout. No. 1716, Steelhead bee, steelhead trout. No. 1717, Dark Montreal, brook trout. No. 1718, Lady Amherst, Atlantic salmon. No. 1719, Coho blue, coho salmon. No. 1720, Cosseboom special, Atlantic salmon.

1998, Apr. 16 ***Perf. 12½x13***

1715 A693 45c multicolored .80 .45
1716 A693 45c multicolored .80 .45
1717 A693 45c multicolored .80 .45
1718 A693 45c multicolored .80 .45
1719 A693 45c multicolored .80 .45
1720 A693 45c multicolored .80 .45
a. Vertical strip of 6, #1715-1720 4.75 3.25
b. Bklt. pane, 2 ea #1715-1720 10.00
Complete booklet, #1720a 10.50

Canadian Institute of Mining, Metallurgy and Petroleum, Cent. — A694

1998, May 4 **Litho.** ***Perf. 12½***

1721 A694 45c multicolored .70 .25

Imperial Penny Post, Cent. A695

St. Edward's Crown, #86, Sir William Mulock.

1998, May 29 ***Perf. 12½x13***

1722 A695 45c multicolored .70 .25

#1722 was issued in sheets of 14 + 1 label.

Sumo Wrestling Tournament, Vancouver — A696

Rising sun, mapleleaf and: No. 1723, Two wrestlers. No. 1724, Sumo champion performing bow twirling ceremony.

1998, June 5 **Litho. & Embossed**

1723 A696 45c multicolored .70 .25
1724 A696 45c multicolored .70 .25
a. Horiz. or Vert. Pair, #1723-1724 + 4 labels 1.40 .75
b. Souvenir sheet, #1723-1724 3.00 2.50

Nos. 1723-1724 were printed checkerwise in sheets of 20, 10 each, plus 40 labels.

Canals of Canada — A697

#1725, St. Peters Canal, Nova Scotia. #1726, St. Ours Canal, Quebec. #1727, Port Carling Lock, Ontario. #1728, Locks, Rideau Canal, Ontario. #1729, Peterborough lift lock, Trent-Severn Waterway, Ontario. #1730, Chambly Canal, Quebec. #1731, Lachine Canal, Quebec. #1732, Ice skating on Rideau Canal, Ottawa. #1733, Boat on Big Chute Marine Railway, Trent-Severn Waterway. #1734, Sault Ste. Marie Canal, Ontario.

1998, June 17 **Litho.** ***Perf. 12½***

Booklet Stamps

1725 A697 45c multicolored .75 .60
1726 A697 45c multicolored .75 .60
1727 A697 45c multicolored .75 .60
1728 A697 45c multicolored .75 .60
1729 A697 45c multicolored .75 .60
1730 A697 45c multicolored .75 .60
1731 A697 45c multicolored .75 .60
1732 A697 45c multicolored .75 .60
1733 A697 45c multicolored .75 .60
1734 A697 45c multicolored .75 .60
a. Bklt. pane, #1725-1734 + 10 labels 11.00
Complete booklet, #1734a 12.50

Health Professionals A698

Litho. & Embossed with Foil Application

1998, June 25 ***Perf. 12½***

1735 A698 45c multicolored .70 .25

Royal Canadian Mounted Police, 125th Anniv. — A699

#1736, Male mountie, native, horse. #1737, Female mountie, helicopter, cityscape.

1998, July 3 **Litho.** ***Perf. 12½x13***

1736 A699 45c multicolored .70 .25
1737 A699 45c multicolored .70 .25
a. Pair, #1736-1737 + 2 labels 1.40 .75
b. Souvenir sheet, #1736-1737 + 1 label 1.50 1.50
c. As "b," with signature 2.25 2.25
d. As "b," with Portugal 98 emblem 3.00 3.00
e. As "b," with Italia 98 emblem 3.00 3.00

#1737c-1737e have added inscriptions in gold. Issued: #1737c, 7/3; #1737d, 9/4; #1737e, 10/23.

William James Roué (1879-1970), Naval Architect — A700

Litho. & Engr.

1998, July 24 ***Perf. 13***

1738 A700 45c multicolored .70 .25

Scenic Highway Type of 1997

Designs: No. 1739, Dempster Highway, Yukon. No. 1740, Dinosaur Trail, Alberta. No. 1741, River Valley Scenic Drive, New Brunswick. No. 1742, Blue Heron Route, Prince Edward Island.

1998, July 28 **Litho.** ***Perf. 12½x13***

1739 A673 45c multicolored .70 .30
1740 A673 45c multicolored .70 .30
1741 A673 45c multicolored .70 .30
1742 A673 45c multicolored .70 .30
a. Block or strip of 4, #1739-1742 2.80 1.75

Publication of "Refus Global" by The Automatistes, 50th Anniv. — A701

Painting, artist: No. 1743, "Peinture," Jean-Paul Riopelle. No. 1744, "La dernière campagne de Napoléon," Fernand Leduc. No. 1745, "Jet fuligineux sur noir torturé," Jean-Paul Mousseau. No. 1746, "Le fond du garde-robe," Pierre Gauvreau. No. 1747, "Joie lacustre," Paul-Emile Borduas. No. 1748, "Syndicat des gens de mer," Marcelle Ferron. No. 1749, "Le tumulte á la machoire crispée," Marcel Barbeau.

1998, Aug. 7 ***Die Cut***

Self-Adhesive

Booklet Stamps

1743 A701 45c multicolored .70 .60
1744 A701 45c multicolored .70 .60
1745 A701 45c multicolored .70 .60
1746 A701 45c multicolored .70 .60
1747 A701 45c multicolored .70 .60
1748 A701 45c multicolored .70 .60
1749 A701 45c multicolored .70 .60
a. Booklet pane, #1743-1749 5.50

No. 1746 is 34x48mm. No. 1749a is a complete booklet. The peelable paper backing serves as a booklet cover.

Legendary Canadians A702

#1750, Napoléon-Alexandre Comeau (1848-1923), outdoorsman, "King of the North Shore." #1751, Phyllis Munday (1894-1990), mountaineer, community service worker. #1752, Bill Mason (1929-88), film maker, canoe enthusiast. #1753, Harry "Red" Foster (1905-1985), founder of Canadian Special Olympics, sports enthusiast.

1998, Aug. 15 ***Perf. 13½***

1750 A702 45c multicolored .70 .30
1751 A702 45c multicolored .70 .30
1752 A702 45c multicolored .70 .30
1753 A702 45c multicolored .70 .30
a. Block or strip of 4, #1750-1753 2.80 1.75

Art Type of 1988

Painting: The Farmer's Family (detail), by Bruno Bobak.

Litho. with Foil Application

1998, Sept. 8 ***Perf. 12½x13***

1754 A546 90c gold & multi 1.40 .65

Housing in Canada A703

a, Native peoples. b, Settler. c, Regional. d, Heritage preservation. e, Multiple unit. f, Prefabricated. g, Veterans. h, Planned community. i, Innovative.

1998, Sept. 23

1755 Sheet of 9 7.00 7.00
a.-i. A703 45c Any single .70 .50

University of Ottawa, 150th Anniv. — A704

1998, Sept. 25 ***Perf. 13***

1756 A704 45c multicolored .70 .25

The Circus — A705

Various circus clowns and: No. 1757, Elephant, bear performing tricks. No. 1758, Woman standing on horse, aerial act. No. 1759, Lion tamer. No. 1760, Contortionists, acrobats.

Perf. 13 on 3 Sides

1998, Oct. 1 **Litho.**

Booklet Stamps

1757 A705 45c multicolored .70 .30
1758 A705 45c multicolored .70 .30
1759 A705 45c multicolored .70 .30
1760 A705 45c multicolored .70 .30
a. Bklt. pane, 3 ea #1757-1760 8.50
Complete booklet, #1760a 9.00
b. Souvenir sheet, #1757-1760 3.75 2.25

Stamps in No. 1760b are perforated on all four sides.

John Peters Humphrey (1905-95), Author of Universal Declaration of Human Rights A706

1998, Oct. 7 ***Perf. 13***

1761 A706 45c multicolored .70 .25

Canadian Naval Reserve, 75th Anniv. — A707

1998, Nov. 4 **Litho.** ***Perf. 12½x13***

1762 A707 45c HMCS Sackville .70 .25
1763 A707 45c HMCS Shawinigan .70 .25
a. Pair, #1762-1763 1.40 .65

Christmas — A708

Sculpted wooden angels: 45c, "Angel of Last Judgment" blowing trumpet. 52c, "Adoring Angel" raising hand. 90c, "Adoring Angel, Kneeling," by Thomas Baillairgé.

1998, Nov. 6 ***Perf. 13***

1764 A708 45c multicolored .70 .25
a. Booklet pane of 10 27.50
Complete booklet, #1764a 27.50

b. Perf 13x13½ 225.00 14.00
c. As "b," booklet pane of 10 12.50
Complete booklet, #1764c 13.50

The values for No. 1764b are for singles perfed on all four sides from sheet format. These are extremely scarce. Single stamps from booklet pane No. 1764c have a straight edge on one side. Value, booklet single, unused $1.50, used $2.

Perf. 13x13½

1765 A708 52c multicolored .80 .30
a. Booklet pane of 5 + label 12.50
Complete booklet, #1765a 13.50
b. Perf 13 .90 .45
c. As "b," booklet pane of 5 + label 5.50
Complete booklet, #1765c 5.75
1766 A708 90c multicolored 1.30 .60
a. Booklet pane of 5 + label 15.00
Complete booklet, #1766a 16.00
b. Perf 13 1.40 .60
c. As "b," booklet pane of 5 + label 7.00
Complete booklet, #1766c 7.25
Nos. 1764-1766 (3) 2.80 1.15

New Year 1999 (Year of the Rabbit) A709

1999, Jan. 8 Litho. *Perf. 13½*
1767 A709 46c multicolored .70 .30

Souvenir Sheet

Perf. 12½x13

1768 A709 95c Sheet of 1 1.40 .60
a. Single stamp 1.30 .50

No. 1768 with China 99 overprint was sold only at the show. Value about two-thirds that of unoverprinted sheet.

Le Theatre du Rideau Vert, 50th Anniv. — A710

1999, Feb. 17 Litho. *Perf. 13x12½*
1769 A710 46c multicolored .70 .30

Bird Type of 1996

Designs: No. 1770, Northern goshawk. No. 1771, Red-winged blackbird. No. 1772, American goldfinch. No. 1773, Sandhill crane.

1999, Feb. 24 Litho. *Perf. 12½x13*
1770 A650 46c multicolored .70 .45
1771 A650 46c multicolored .70 .45
1772 A650 46c multicolored .70 .45
1773 A650 46c multicolored .70 .45
a. Block or strip of 4, #1770-1773 2.80 2.20

Booklet Stamps

Self-Adhesive

Serpentine Die Cut Perf. 11½

1774 A650 46c like #1770 .70 .30
1775 A650 46c like #1771 .70 .30
1776 A650 46c like #1772 .70 .30
1777 A650 46c like #1773 .70 .30
a. Booklet pane, 2 each #1774-1775, 1 each #1776-1777 4.25
b. Booklet pane, 2 each #1776-1777, 1 each #1774-1775 4.25
Complete booklet, #1777a, #1777b 8.50

Nos. 1770-1773 were issued in sheets of 20, 5 each, printed checkerwise to contain 4 complete blocks or strips.

The peelable paper backing of Nos. 1777a, 1777b serves as the booklet cover.

Univ. of British Colombia's Museum of Anthropology, 50th Anniv. — A711

1999, Mar. 9 Litho. *Perf. 13½*
1778 A711 46c multicolored .70 .30

Sailing Ship Marco Polo — A712

1999, Mar. 19 Litho. *Perf. 13x12½*
1779 A712 46c multicolored .70 .30
a. Sheet of 2, #1779 perf. 13, Australia #1631 perf. 13½ 2.25 1.25

Australia '99 World Stamp Expo. See Australia #1631a.

Scenic Highway Type of 1997

#1780, Gaspé Peninsula, Highway 132, Quebec. #1781, Yellowhead Highway (PTH 16), Manitoba. #1782, Dempster Highway 8, Northwest Territories. #1783, Discovery Trail, Route 230N, Newfoundland.

1999, Mar. 31 *Perf. 12½x13*
1780 A673 46c multicolored .70 .30
1781 A673 46c multicolored .70 .30
1782 A673 46c multicolored .70 .30
1783 A673 46c multicolored .70 .30
a. Block or strip of 4, #1780-1783 2.80 1.50

Creation of the Nunavut Territory — A713

1999, Apr. 1
1784 A713 46c multicolored .70 .30

Intl. Year of Older Persons — A714

1999, Apr. 12 Litho. *Perf. 13½*
1785 A714 46c multicolored .70 .30

A715

A716

1999, Apr. 19 *Perf. 13*
1786 A715 46c multicolored .70 .45

Baisakhi, Religious Holiday of Sikh Canadians, 300th Anniv.

1999, Apr. 27 *Perf. 13x12½*

Paintings (Canadian Orchids): No. 1787, Arethusa bulbosa, by Poon-Kuen Chow. No. 1788, Amerorchis rotundifolia, by Yakman Lai. No. 1789, Platanthera psycodes, by Lai. No. 1790, Cypripedium pubescens, by Chow.

Booklet Stamps

1787 A716 46c multicolored .70 .30
1788 A716 46c multicolored .70 .30
1789 A716 46c multicolored .70 .30
1790 A716 46c multicolored .70 .30
a. Bklt. pane, 3 ea #1787-1790 8.50
Complete booklet, #1790a 8.50
b. Souvenir sheet, #1787-1790 3.00 2.00

China '99 World Philatelic Exhibition, Beijing. Designs of some stamps contained in No. 1790a extend into selvage of booklet pane.

Issued: No. 1790b, 8/21/99.

Horses A717

#1791, Northern Dancer, thoroughbred race horse. #1792, Kingsway Skoal, bucking horse. #1793, Big Ben, show horse. #1794, Armbro Flight, harness race horse.

1999, June 2 Litho. *Perf. 13x13½*
1791 A717 46c multicolored .70 .45
1792 A717 46c multicolored .70 .45
1793 A717 46c multicolored .70 .45
1794 A717 46c multicolored .70 .45
a. Block or strip of 4, #1791-1794 2.80 2.25

Booklet Stamps

Self-Adhesive

Serpentine Die Cut 11½

1795 A717 46c like #1791 .70 .30
1796 A717 46c like #1792 .70 .30
1797 A717 46c like #1793 .70 .30
1798 A717 46c like #1794 .70 .30
a. Block of 4, #1795-1798 2.50
b. Complete booklet, 3 each #1795-1798 8.50

Nos. 1791-1794 were issued in sheets of 16, 4 each, printed checkerwise to contain 4 complete blocks or strips.

Quebec Bar Assoc., 150th Anniv. — A718

1999, June 3 *Perf. 13½*
1799 A718 46c multicolored .70 .30

Art Type of 1988

Coq Licorne, by Jean Dallaire (1916-65).

Litho. with Foil Application

1999, July 3 *Perf. 12½x13¼*
1800 A546 95c multicolored 1.40 .65
a. Silver omitted *1,100.*

1999 Pan American Games, Winnipeg A719

Designs: No. 1801, Track & field. No. 1802, Cycling, weight lifting, gymnastics. No. 1803, Swimming, sailboarding, kayaking. No. 1804, Soccer, tennis, medal winners.

1999, July 12 *Perf. 13¼*
1801 A719 46c multicolored .70 .30
1802 A719 46c multicolored .70 .30
1803 A719 46c multicolored .70 .30
1804 A719 46c multicolored .70 .30
a. Block of 4, #1801-1804 2.80 1.50

Issued in sheets of 16 stamps.

23rd World Rowing Championships, St. Catherines, Ont. — A720

1999, Aug. 22 Litho. *Perf. 12½x13*
1805 A720 46c multicolored .70 .30

UPU, 125th Anniv. — A721

1999, Aug. 26
1806 A721 46c multicolored .70 .30

Airplanes — A722

No. 1807: a, Fokker DR-1, CT-114 Tutors. b, Tutors, H101 Salto sailplane. c, De Havilland DH100 Vampire MKIII. d, Stearman A-75.

No. 1808: a, De Havilland Mosquito FBVI. b, Sopwith F1 Camel. c, De Havilland Canada DHC-3 Otter. d, De Havilland Canada CC-108 Caribou. e, Canadair CL-28 Argus MK 2. f, North American F-86 Sabre 6. g, McDonnell Douglas CF-18 Hornet. h, Sopwith SF-1 Dolphin. i, Armstrong Whitworth Siskin IIIA. j, Canadian Vickers (Northrop) Delta II. k, Sikorsky CH-124A Sea King helicopter. l, Vickers-Armstrong Wellington MKII. m, Avro Anson MKI. n, Canadair (Lockheed) CF-104G Starfighter. o, Burgess-Dunne seaplane. p, Avro 504K.

Illustration reduced.

1999, Sept. 4 Litho. *Perf. 12½x13*
1807 A722 Sheet of 4 2.80 1.50
a.-d. 46c any single .70 .30
1808 A722 Sheet of 16 11.25 5.50
a.-p. 46c any single .70 .30

Canadian Intl. Air Show, 50th anniv. (#1807). Royal Canadian Air Force, 75th anniv. (#1808). Nos. 1808a-1808p are each 56x28mm.

NATO, 50th Anniv. — A723

1999, Sept. 21 Litho. *Perf. 12½x13*
1809 A723 46c multicolored .70 .30

Frontier College, 100th Anniv. A724

1999, Sept. 24 Litho. *Perf. 13x13½*
1810 A724 46c multicolored .70 .30

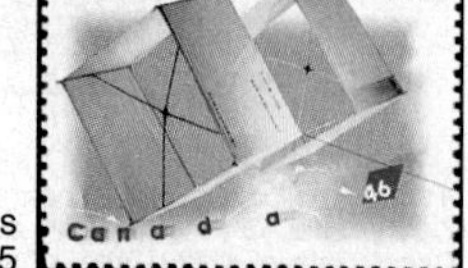
Kites A725

Designs: a, Master Control, sport kite by Lam Hoac (triagular). b, Indian Garden Flying Carpet, edo kite by Skye Morrison (trapezoidal). c, Gibson Girl, manufactured box kite (rectangular). d, Dragon centipede kite by Zhang tian Wei (oval).

Die cut in various patterns

1999, Oct. 1 — Litho.

Self-Adhesive

1811	Complete booklet, 2 each #a.-d.	6.50	
a.-d.	A725 46c any single	.80	.30

A726

A727

Millennium A728

1999, Oct. 12 Holography *Die Cut*

Self-Adhesive (46c)

1812	A726 46c silver	.80	.40
	Pane of 4	3.25	1.75

Litho.

Perf. 13¼

1813	A727 55c multicolored	.80	.70
	Pane of 4	3.25	2.50

Engr.

Perf. 12¾

1814	A728 95c brown	1.50	1.00
	Pane of 4	6.00	5.50
	Nos. 1812-1814 (3)	3.10	2.10

Nos. 1812-1814 each exist in souvenir sheets of 1 with decorative border.

Christmas — A729

1999, Nov. 4 Litho. *Perf. 13¼*

1815	A729 46c Angel, drum	.70	.30
a.	Booklet pane of 10	7.00	—
	Complete booklet	7.00	
1816	A729 55c Angel, toys	.80	.35
a.	Booklet pane of 5 + label	4.00	—
	Complete booklet	4.00	
1817	A729 95c Angel, candle	1.40	.65
a.	Booklet pane of 5 + label	7.00	—
	Complete booklet	7.00	
	Nos. 1815-1817 (3)	2.90	1.30

Souvenir Sheets

Millennium — A730

No. 1818 — Media Technologies: a, IMAX movies. b, Softimage animation software. c, Ted Rogers, Sr. (1900-39) and radio tube. d, Invention of radio facsimile device for transmission of photographs for publishing by Sir William Stephenson (1896-1989) .

No. 1819 — Canadian Entertainment: a, Calgary Stampede. b, Performers from Cirque du Soleil. c, Hockey Night in Canada. d, La Soiree du Hockey.

No. 1820 — Entertainers: a, Portia White (1911-68), singer. b, Glenn Gould (1932-82), pianist. c, Guy Lombardo (1902-77), band leader. d, Félix Leclerc (1914-88), singer, guitarist.

No. 1821 — Fostering Canadian Talent: a, Royal Canadian Academy of Arts (men viewing painting). b, Canada Council (sky, musical staff, "A"). c, National Film Board of Canada. d, Canadian Broadcasting Corporation.

No. 1822 — Medical Innovators: a, Sir Frederick Banting (1891-1941), co-discoverer of insulin, syringe and dog. b, Dr. Armand Frappier (1904-91), microbiologist, holding flask. c, Dr. Hans Selye (1907-82), endocrinologist, and molecular diagram. d, Maude Abbott (1869-1940), pathologist, and roses.

No. 1823 — Social Progress: a, Nun, doctor, hospital. b, Statue of woman holding decree. c, Alphonse Desjardins (1854-1920) and wife Dorimène (1858-1932), credit union founders, and credit union emblem. d, Father Moses Coady (1882-1959), educator of adults.

No. 1824 — Charity: a, Canadian International Development Agency (hands and tools). b, Dr. Lucille Teasdale (1929-96), hospital administrator in Uganda. c, Marathon of Hope inspired by Terry Fox (1958-81). d, Meals on Wheels program.

No. 1825 — Humanitarians and Peacekeepers: a, Raoul Dandurand (1861-1942), b, Pauline Vanier (1898-1991), Red Cross volunteer, and Elizabeth Smellie (1884-1968), head of various nursing services. c, Lester B. Pearson (1897-1972), prime minister, and Nobel Peace Prize winner, and dove. d, Amputee and shadow (Ottawa Convention on Land Mines).

No. 1826 — Canada's First People: a, Chief Pontiac (c. 1720-69). b, Tom Longboat (1887-1949), marathon runner. c, Inuit sculpture of shaman. d, Medicine man.

No. 1827 — Canada's Cultural Fabric: a, Norse boat, L'Anse aux Meadows. b, Immigrants on Halifax's Pier 21. c, Neptune Theater, Halifax (head of Neptune). d, Stratford Festival (actor and theater).

No. 1828 — Literary Legends: a, W. O. Mitchell (1914-98), novelist, and prairie scene. b, Gratien Gélinas (1909-99), actor and playwright, and stars. c, Le Cercle du Livre de France book club. d, Harlequin paperback books.

No. 1829 — Great Thinkers: a, Marshall McLuhan (1911-80), philosopher, and television set. b, Northrop Frye (1912-91), literary critic, and word "code." c, Roger Lemelin (1919-92), novelist, and cast of "The Plouffe Family" TV series. d, Hilda Marion Neatby (1904-75), historian, and farm scene.

No. 1830 — A Tradition of Generosity: a, Hart Massey (1823-96), Hart House, University of Toronto. b, Dorothy (1899-1965) and Izaak Killam (1885-1955), philantropists, and molecular model. c, Eric Lafferty Harvie (1892-1975), philantropist, and mountain scene. d, Macdonald Stewart Foundation.

No. 1831 — Engineering and Technological Marvels: a, Map of Rogers Pass, locomotive, tunnel diggers. b, Manic Dams. c, Canadian satellites, Remote Manipulator Arm. d, CN Tower.

No. 1832 — Fathers of Invention: a, George Klein (1904-92), gearwheels. b, Abraham Gesner (1797-1864), beaker of kerosene and lamp. c, Alexander Graham Bell (1847-1922), passenger-carrying kite, hydrofoil. d, Joseph-Armand Bombardier (1907-64), snowmobile.

No. 1833 — Food: a, Sir Charles Saunders (1867-1937), Marquis wheat. b, Pablum. c, Dr. Archibald Gowanlock Huntsman (1883-1973), marketer of frozen fish. d, Products of McCain Foods, Ltd., tractor.

No. 1834 — Enterprising Giants: a, Hudson's Bay Company (Colonist, Indian, canoe). b, Bell Canada Enterprises (earth, satellite, string of binary digits). c, Vachon Co. snack cakes. d, George Weston Limited (Baked goods, eggs).

1999-2000 Litho. *Perf. 13¼*

1818	A730 Sheet of 4	3.00	3.00
a.-d.	46c any single	.75	.60
1819	A730 Sheet of 4	3.00	3.00
a.-d.	46c any single	.75	.60
1820	A730 Sheet of 4	3.00	3.00
a.-d.	46c any single	.75	.60
1821	A730 Sheet of 4	3.00	3.00
a.-d.	46c any single	.75	.60
1822	A730 Sheet of 4	3.00	3.00
a.-d.	46c any single	.75	.60
1823	A730 Sheet of 4	3.00	3.00
a.-d.	46c any single	.75	.60
1824	A730 Sheet of 4	3.00	3.00
a.-d.	46c any single	.75	.60
1825	A730 Sheet of 4	3.00	3.00
a.-d.	46c any single	.75	.60
1826	A730 Sheet of 4	3.00	3.00
a.-d.	46c any single	.75	.60
1827	A730 Sheet of 4	3.00	3.00
a.-d.	46c any single	.75	.60
1828	A730 Sheet of 4	3.00	3.00
a.-d.	46c any single	.75	.60
1829	A730 Sheet of 4	3.00	3.00
a.-d.	46c any single	.75	.60
1830	A730 Sheet of 4	3.00	3.00
a.-d.	46c any single	.75	.60
1831	A730 Sheet of 4	3.00	3.00
a.-d.	46c any single	.75	.60
1832	A730 Sheet of 4	3.00	3.00
a.-d.	46c any single	.75	.60
1833	A730 Sheet of 4	3.00	3.00
a.-d.	46c any single	.75	.60
1834	A730 Sheet of 4	3.00	3.00
a.-d.	46c any single	.75	.60
	Nos. 1818-1834 (17)	51.00	51.00

Issued: #1818-1821, 12/17; #1822-1825, 1/17/00; #1826-1830, 2/17/00; #1831-1834, 3/17/00.

Stamps similar to these were printed in a hardcover book produced by Canada Post Sept. 15, 1999 that sold for $59.99. Stamps from souvenir sheets show a distinct upward turn of the tails of the nines in the small 1999 date at upper left. The tails of the nines on stamps from the book are flat.

Millennium — A731

2000, Jan. 1 Litho. *Perf. 13x12½*

1835	A731 46c multicolored	.70	.30

New Year 2000 (Year of the Dragon) — A732

Litho. & Embossed

2000, Jan. 5 *Perf. 12½x12¾*

1836	A732 46c multicolored	.70	.25

Souvenir Sheet

Perf. 13¾x13¼

1837	A732 95c multicolored	1.50	.80
a.	Orange and tagging omitted	—	

No. 1837 has rounded corners and contains one 56x29mm stamp.

50th National Hockey League All-Star Game A733

Famous NHL players: a, Wayne Gretzky (Oilers jersey No. 99). b, Gordie Howe (Red Wings jersey No. 9). c, Maurice Richard (red, white and blue Canadiens jersey No. 9). d, Doug Harvey (Canadiens jersey No. 2). e, Bobby Orr (Bruins jersey No. 4). f, Jacques Plante (Canadiens jersey No. 1).

2000, Feb. 5 Litho. *Perf. 12¾*

1838	A733 Sheet of 6	4.25	4.25
a.-f.	46c any single	.70	.60

Bird Type of 1996

Designs: Nos. 1839, 1843, Canada warbler. Nos. 1840, 1844, Osprey. Nos. 1841, 1845, Pacific loon. Nos. 1842, 1846, Blue jay.

2000, Mar. 1 Litho. *Perf. 12½x13¼*

1839	A650 46c multi	.70	.30
1840	A650 46c multi	.70	.30
1841	A650 46c multi	.70	.30
1842	A650 46c multi	.70	.30
a.	Block or strip of 4	2.80	1.50

Booklet Stamps

Self-Adhesive

Die Cut 11½x11¼

1843	A650 46c multi	.70	.30
1844	A650 46c multi	.70	.30
1845	A650 46c multi	.70	.30
1846	A650 46c multi	.70	.30
a.	Booklet pane, 2 each #1843-1844, 1 each #1845-1846	4.25	
b.	Booklet pane, 2 each #1845-1846, 1 each #1843-1844	4.25	
	Complete bklt., #1846a, 1846b	8.50	

Nos. 1839-1842 were issued in sheets of 20, 5 each printed checkerwise to contain 4 complete blocks or strips.

Supreme Court, 125th Anniv. A734

2000, Apr. 10 Litho. *Perf. 12½x13¼*

1847	A734 46c multi	.70	.30

Ritual of the Calling of an Engineer, 75th Anniv. — A735

2000, Apr. 25

1848	A735 46c multi	.70	.30
a.	Tete-beche pair	1.40	.75
b.	Silver ("CANADA 46") omitted	*1,500.*	

Decorated Rural Mailboxes A736

Mailboxes with: No. 1849, Ship, fish, house designs. No. 1850, Flower, cow and church designs. No. 1851, Tractor design. No. 1852, Goose head, house designs.

Perf. 12½x13¼ on 3 sides

2000, Apr. 28

Booklet Stamps

1849	A736 46c multi	.70	.30
1850	A736 46c multi	.70	.30
1851	A736 46c multi	.70	.30
1852	A736 46c multi	.70	.30
a.	Block of 4, #1849-1852	2.50	2.00
b.	Bklt. pane, 3 ea #1849-1852	8.50	
	Complete booklet, #1852a	8.50	

Picture Frame A737

Serpentine Die Cut 11½

2000, Apr. 28 Litho.

Self-Adhesive

1853 A737 46c multi .70 .30
a. Booklet pane of 5 + 5 different labels 3.50
Complete booklet, #1853a 3.50
b. Pane of 25 *35.00*

No. 1853b sold for $24.95 each for one or two sheets, and $22.95 for three to ten sheets. Twenty-five self-adhesive, die cut address labels and reproductions of a photo sent in by the customer are on the reverse of No. 1853b. These panes were not available at post offices or through the philatelic bureau, but special orders from the printer, Ashton-Potter. The front cover of the booklet containing No. 1853a served as the order blank for No. 1853b.

See No. 1882.

A738

A739

A740

A741

A742

A743

A744

A745

A746

Fresh Waters — A747

Serpentine Die Cut 2½ Horiz.

2000, Feb. 23 Litho.

Self-Adhesive

1854 Complete booklet, #a.-e. 4.00
a. A738 55c multi .80 .35
b. A739 55c multi .80 .35
c. A740 55c multi .80 .35
d. A741 55c multi .80 .35
e. A742 55c multi .80 .35
1855 Complete booklet, #a.-e. 7.00
a. A743 95c multi 1.40 .65
b. A744 95c multi 1.40 .65
c. A745 95c multi 1.40 .65
d. A746 95c multi 1.40 .65
e. A747 95c multi 1.40 .65

Queen Mother (b. 1900)
A748

2000, May 23 Litho. ***Perf. 13x13¼***

1856 A748 95c multi 1.40 .65

Boys and Girls Clubs of Canada, Cent. — A749

2000, June 1 ***Perf. 13***

1857 A749 46c multi .70 .30

World Session of Seventh Day Adventist Church, Toronto
A750

2000, June 29 ***Perf. 13½x13¼***

1858 A750 46c multi .70 .30

Stampin' the Future Children's Stamp Design Contest Winners
A751

Designs: No. 1859, Rainbow, space vehicle, astronauts, flag, by Rosalie Anne Nardelli. No. 1860, Three children in space vehicle, three children on ground, by Sarah Lutgen. No. 1861, Children and map of Canada, by Christine Weera. No. 1862, Two astronauts in space vehicle, planets, by Andrew Wright.

2000, July 1 ***Perf. 13¼***

1859 A751 46c multi .70 .30
1860 A751 46c multi .70 .30
1861 A751 46c multi .70 .30
1862 A751 46c multi .70 .30
a. Block or strip, #1859-1862 2.80 1.50
b. Souvenir sheet, #1859-1862 2.80 1.50

Art Type of 1988

The Artist at Niagara, by Cornelius Krieghoff.

Litho. with Foil Application

2000, July 7 ***Perf. 12½x13¼***

1863 A546 95c multi 1.40 .65

Tall Ships in Halifax Harbor — A752

Various ships: No. 1864, Denomination at L. No. 1865, Denomination at R.

Serpentine Die Cut 4¾x5

2000, July 19 Litho.

Booklet Stamps

Self-Adhesive

1864 A752 46c multi .70 .30
1865 A752 46c multi .70 .30
a. Pair, #1864-1865 1.40
b. Booklet, 5 #1864a 7.00

Dept. of Labor, Cent. — A753

2000, Sept. 1 Litho. ***Perf. 12½x13¼***

1866 A753 46c multi .70 .30

Petro-Canada, 25th Anniv. — A754

2000, Sept. 13 Litho. ***Die Cut***

Self-Adhesive

Booklet Stamp

1867 A754 46c multi .70 .30
a. Booklet pane of 12 9.00
Booklet, #1867a 9.00
b. Die cutting inverted (2 points jut at T, L) 6.00 4.50

No. 1867a is the cover of an informational booket about Petro-Canada. No. 1867b was issued in collector packs.

Cetaceans — A755

#1868, Monodon monoceros. #1869, Balaenoptera musculus. #1870, Balaena mysticetus. #1871, Delphinapterus leucas.

2000, Oct. 2 ***Perf. 12½x13***

1868 A755 46c multi .70 .30
1869 A755 46c multi .70 .30
1870 A755 46c multi .70 .30
1871 A755 46c multi .70 .30
a. Block of 4, #1868-1871 2.80 1.50

Christmas
A756

Serpentine Die Cut 11¾

2000, Oct. 5

Booklet Stamp

Self-Adhesive

1872 A756 46c multi .70 .30
a. Booklet pane of 5 + 5 labels 3.50
Booklet, #1872a 3.50

See No. 1882e.

Christmas
A757

Designs: 46c, Adoration of the shepherds. 55c, Creche. 95c Flight into Egypt.

2000, Nov. 3 Litho. ***Perf. 13¼***

1873 A757 46c multi .70 .30
a. Booklet pane of 10 7.00 —
Booklet, #1873a 7.00
1874 A757 55c multi .90 .35
a. Booklet pane of 6 5.50 —
Booklet, #1874a 5.50
1875 A757 95c multi 1.50 .65
a. Booklet pane of 6 9.00 —
Booklet, #1875a 9.00
Nos. 1873-1875 (3) 3.10 1.30

Regiments
A758

No. 1876, Lord Strathcona's Horse Regiment. No. 1877, Les Voltigeurs de Quebec.

2000, Nov. 11 ***Perf. 13¼x13***

1876 A758 46c multi .70 .30
1877 A758 46c multi .70 .30
a. Pair, #1876-1877 1.40 .75

Maple Leaves
A759

Animals
A760

Serpentine Die Cut 8½ Horiz.

2000, Dec. 28 Litho.

Coil Stamps

Self-Adhesive

1878 A759 47c multi .70 .30
1879 A760 60c Red fox 1.40 .40
a. Booklet pane of 6 8.50
1880 A760 75c Gray wolf 1.10 .50
1881 A760 $1.05 White-tailed deer 1.60 .70
a. Booklet pane of 6 9.75
Nos. 1878-1881 (4) 4.80 1.90

Nos. 1879a and 1881a are complete booklets.

Frame Type of 2000

No. 1882: a, Silver. b, Like #1853. c, Mahogany. d, Love (roses). e, Christmas.

Serpentine Die Cut 11¾

2000, Dec. 28 Litho.

Booklet Stamps

Self-Adhesive

1882 Bklt. pane of 5+5 labels 3.50
a.-e. A737 47c Any single .70 .30
Booklet, #1882 3.50

New Year 2001 (Year of the Snake)
A761

Litho. & Embossed

2001, Jan. 5 ***Perf. 13¼***

1883 A761 47c green & multi .70 .30
a. Gold omitted 1,400.

Souvenir Sheet

1884 A761 $1.05 brown & multi 1.60 .70

National Hockey League Stars A762

No. 1885: a, Jean Beliveau (Montreal Canadiens jersey No. 4). b, Terry Sawchuk (goalie in Detroit Red Wings uniform). c, Eddie Shore (Boston Bruins jersey No. 2). d, Denis Potvin (Islanders jersey No. 5). e, Bobby Hull (Chicago Black Hawks jersey No. 9). f, Syl Apps, Sr. (Toronto Maple Leafs jersey).

Perf. 12½x13 on 3 sides

2001, Jan. 18 **Litho.**

1885 Sheet of 6 + 3 labels 4.25 4.25
a.-f. A762 47c Any single .70 .60

Bird Type of 1996

Designs: Nos. 1886, 1890, Golden eagle. Nos. 1887, 1891, Arctic tern. Nos. 1888, 1892, Rock ptarmigan. Nos. 1889, 1893, Lapland longspur.

2001, Feb. 1 **Litho.** ***Perf. 12½x13***

1886 A650 47c multi .70 .30
1887 A650 47c multi .70 .30
1888 A650 47c multi .70 .30
1889 A650 47c multi .70 .30
a. Block or strip of 4, #1886-1889 2.80 1.50

Booklet Stamps

Self-Adhesive

Die Cut 11½x11¼

1890 A650 47c multi .70 .30
1891 A650 47c multi .70 .30
1892 A650 47c multi .70 .30
1893 A650 47c multi .70 .30
a. Booklet pane, 2 each #1890-1891, 1 each #1892-1893 4.25
b. Booklet pane, 2 each #1892-1893, 1 each #1890-1891 4.25
Booklet, #1893a, 1893b 8.50

Nos. 1886-1889 were issued in sheets of 20, 5 each printed checkerwise to contain 4 complete blocks or strips.

Games of La Francophonie, Ottawa and Hull — A763

2001, Feb. 28 ***Perf. 13¼***

1894 A763 47c High jumper .70 .30
1895 A763 47c Dancer .70 .30
a. Horiz. pair, #1894-1895 1.40 .75

World Figure Skating Championships, Vancouver — A764

Designs: No. 1896, Pairs. No. 1897, Ice dancing. No. 1898, Men's singles. No. 1899, Women's singles.

2001, Mar. 19 **Litho.** ***Perf. 13x12½***

1896 A764 47c shown .70 .30
1897 A764 47c multi .70 .30
1898 A764 47c multi .70 .30
1899 A764 47c multi .70 .30
a. Block of 4, #1896-1899 2.80 1.50

First Canadian Postage Stamps, 150th Anniv. — A765

Litho. & Engr.

2001, Apr. 6 ***Perf. 13***

1900 A765 47c multi .70 .30

Toronto Blue Jays Baseball Team, 25th Anniv. A766

2001, Apr. 9 **Litho.** ***Die Cut***

Self-Adhesive

1901 A766 47c multi .70 .30
a. Booklet pane of 8 5.75

No. 1901a is a complete booklet.

Summit of the Americas, Quebec — A767

2001, Apr. 20 ***Perf. 13¼x13***

1902 A767 47c multi .70 .30

Tourist Attractions — A768

No. 1903: a, Butchart Gardens, British Columbia. b, Apple Blossom Festival, Nova Scotia. c, White Pass and Yukon Route. d, Sugar bushes, Quebec. e, Niagara-on-the-Lake, Ontario.

No. 1904: a, The Forks, Manitoba. b, Barkerville, British Columbia. c, Canadian Tulip Festival, Ontario. d, Auyuittuq National Park, Nunavut. e, Signal Hill National Historic Site, Newfoundland.

Die Cut Perf. 11x11¼

2001, May 11 **Litho.**

Self-Adhesive

1903 Booklet of 5 4.50
a.-e. A768 60c Any single .90 .40
1904 Booklet of 5 8.00
a.-e. A768 $1.05 Any single 1.60 .70

Armenian Church, 1,700th Anniv. — A769

2001, May 16 **Litho.** ***Perf. 13x12½***

1905 A769 47c multi .70 .30

Royal Military College of Canada, 125th Anniv. — A770

2001, June 1 ***Perf. 12½x13***

1906 A770 47c multi .70 .30

Eighth Intl. Amateur Athletic Federation World Championships, Edmonton A771

Perf. 12¾x12½

2001, June 25 **Litho.**

1907 A771 47c Pole vault .70 .30
1908 A771 47c Runner .70 .30
a. Pair, #1907-1908 1.40 .75

Pierre Elliott Trudeau (1919-2000), Prime Minister A772

2001, July 1 ***Perf. 13x12½***

1909 A772 47c multi .70 .30
a. Souvenir sheet of 4 2.80 1.50

Roses — A773

Designs: Nos. 1910a, 1911, Morden Centennial. Nos. 1910b, 1912, Agnes. Nos. 1910c, 1913, Champlain. Nos. 1910d, 1914, Canadian White Star.

Illustration reduced.

2001, Aug. 1 **Litho.** ***Perf. 12½x13***

Souvenir Sheet

1910 Sheet of 4 3.50 2.75
a.-d. A773 47c Any single .85 .30

Booklet Stamps

Die Cut

1911 A773 47c multi .70 .30
1912 A773 47c multi .70 .30
1913 A773 47c multi .70 .30
1914 A773 47c multi .70 .30
a. Booklet pane, #1911-1914 2.80
Booklet, 3 #1914a 8.50

Phila Nippon '01, Japan (No. 1910). Die cutting on Nos. 1911-1914 has "thorn" at the center of each side, pointing outward at top and left and toward the design at bottom and right.

Great Peace of Montreal, 300th Anniv. — A774

2001, Aug. 3 ***Perf. 12½x13***

1915 A774 47c multi .70 .30

Art Type of 1988

Design: The Space Between Columns #21 (Italian), by Jack Shadbolt.

Litho. with Foil Application

2001, Aug. 24 ***Perf. 13x13¼***

1916 A546 $1.05 multi 1.60 .70

Shriners — A775

2001, Sept. 19 **Litho.** ***Perf. 13¼x13***

1917 A775 47c multi .70 .30

Frame Type of 2000 Inscribed "Domestic Lettermail / Poste-lettres du régime intérieur"

No. 1918: a, Like #1882a. b, Like #1882b. c, Baby toys and flowers. d, Like #1882d. e, Like #1882e.

Serpentine Die Cut 11¾

2001, Sept. 21

Self-Adhesive

1918 Bklt. pane of 5 + 5 labels 3.50
a.-e. A737 (47c) Any single .70 .30
Booklet, #1918 3.50

Theater Anniversaries — A776

Designs: No. 1919, Théatre du Nouveau Monde, Montreal, 50th anniv. No. 1920, Grand Theater, London, Ont., cent.

2001, Sept. 28 ***Perf. 12½x12¾***

1919 A776 47c multi .70 .30
1920 A776 47c multi .70 .30
a. Horiz. pair, #1919-1920 1.40 .75

Hot Air Balloons A777

Background colors: a, Green. b, Blue violet. c, Red violet. d, Olive.

2001, Oct. 1 ***Die Cut***

Self-Adhesive

1921 Booklet, 2 each #a-d 5.75
a.-d. A777 47c Any single .70 .30

Christmas A778

Illuminated trees and: 47c, Horse-drawn sleigh. 60c, Skaters. $1.05, Children making snowman.

2001, Nov. 1 Litho. *Perf. 12½x13¼*

1922 A778 47c multi .70 .30
a. Booklet pane of 10 7.00
Booklet, #1922a 7.00
1923 A778 60c multi .90 .40
a. Booklet pane of 6 5.50
Booklet, #1923a 5.50
1924 A778 $1.05 multi 1.60 .70
a. Booklet pane of 6 9.75
Booklet, #1924a 9.75

YMCA in Canada, 150th Anniv. — A779

2001, Nov. 8 Litho. *Perf. 13¼*

1925 A779 47c multi .70 .30

Royal Canadian Legion, 75th Anniv. — A780

2001, Nov. 11 *Perf. 12½x13*

1926 A780 47c multi .70 .30

Maple Leaves Type of 2000, Traditional Handiwork Type of 1999 and

Flag and Canada Post Headquarters, Ottawa — A781

Designs: 65c, Jewelry making, horiz. 77c, Basket weaving, horiz. $1.25, Sculpture, horiz.

Serpentine Die Cut 8½ Horiz.

2002, Jan. 2 Litho.

Self-Adhesive

Coil Stamps

1927 A759 48c multi .75 .30
1928 A684 65c multi .95 .40
a. Booklet of 6 6.00
1929 A684 77c multi 1.10 .50
1930 A684 $1.25 multi 1.90 .80
a. Booklet of 6 9.60

Booklet Stamp

Serpentine Die Cut 8½

1931 A781 48c multi .75 .30
a. Booklet of 10 7.50
b. Booklet of 30 22.50
Nos. 1927-1931 (5) 5.45 2.30

By separating the booklet along the columns of rouletting, No. 1931b could be broken up into three separately obtainable examples of No. 1931a.

Reign of Queen Elizabeth II, 50th Anniv. A782

2002, Jan. 2 Litho. *Perf. 13¼x12½*

1932 A782 48c multi .75 .30
a. Imperf, pair —

New Year 2002 (Year of the Horse) — A783

Horse and: 48c, Bamboo leaves. $1.25, Peach blossoms.

Litho. & Embossed With Foil Application

2002, Jan. 3 *Perf. 13¼*

1933 A783 48c multi .75 .30

Souvenir Sheet

1934 A783 $1.25 multi 2.00 .80

National Hockey League Stars A784

No. 1935: a, Tim Horton (Toronto Maple Leafs jersey No. 7). b, Guy Lafleur (Montreal Canadiens jersey No. 10). c, Howie Morenz (Canadiens jersey, with brown gloves). d, Glenn Hall (Chicago Black Hawks jersey No. 1). e, Red Kelly (Maple Leafs jersey No. 4). f, Phil Esposito (Boston Bruins jersey no. 7).

Perf. 12½x13 on 3 Sides

2002, Jan. 12 Litho.

1935 Sheet of 6 + 3 labels 4.50 4.50
a.-f. A784 48c Any single .75 .60

2002 Winter Olympics, Salt Lake City — A785

Designs: No. 1936, Short track speed skating. No. 1937, Curling. No. 1938, Freestyle aerial skiing. No. 1939, Women's hockey.

2002, Jan. 25 Litho. *Perf. 13¼x13*

1936 A785 48c multi .75 .30
1937 A785 48c multi .75 .30
1938 A785 48c multi .75 .30
1939 A785 48c multi .75 .30
a. Block or strip of 4, #1936-1939 3.00 1.75

Appointment of First Canadian Governor General, 50th Anniv. A786

2002, Feb. 1 Litho. *Perf. 13¼x12½*

1940 A786 48c multi .75 .30

Universities — A787

Design: No. 1941, University of Manitoba, 125th anniv. No. 1942, Laval University, 150th anniv. No. 1943, University of Trinity College, 150th anniv. No. 1944, Saint Mary's University, Halifax, 200th anniv.

2002 Litho. *Perf. 13½*

Booklet Stamp

1941 A787 48c multi .75 .30
a. Booklet pane of 8 6.00 —
Booklet, #1941a 6.00
1942 A787 48c multi .75 .30
a. Booklet pane of 8 6.00 —
Booklet, #1942a 6.00
1943 A787 48c multi .75 .30
a. Booklet pane of 8 6.00 —
Booklet, #1943a 6.00
1944 A787 48c multi .75 .30
a. Booklet pane of 8 6.00 —
Booklet, #1944a 6.00
Nos. 1941-1944 (4) 3.00 1.20

Issued: No. 1941, 2/28. No. 1942, 4/4. No. 1943, 4/30. No. 1944, 5/27.

Art Type of 1988

Design: Church and Horse, by Alex Colville.

Litho. with Foil Application

2002, Mar. 22 *Perf. 12½x13*

1945 A546 $1.25 multi 2.00 1.00
a. Foil only (all other colors and tagging omitted) —

Tulips — A788

Tulip varieties: a, City of Vancouver. b, Monte Carlo. c, Ottawa. d, The Bishop.

2002, May 3 *Die Cut*

Self-Adhesive

1946 Booklet pane of 4 3.00
a.-d. A788 48c Any single .75 .30
Booklet, 2 #1946 6.00

Tulips Type of 2002

Souvenir Sheet

No. 1947: a, Like #1946a. b, Like #1946b. c, Like #1946c. d, Like #1946d.

2002, Aug. 30 Litho. *Perf. 13x12½*

1947 Sheet of 4 3.00 1.50
a.-d. A788 48c Any single .75 .30

Dendronepthea Giagantea and Dendronepthea Corals — A789

Tubastrea and Echinogorgia Corals — A790

North Atlantic Pink Tree, Pacific Orange Cup and North Pacific Horn Corals A791

North Atlantic Giant Orange Tree and Black Corals A792

2002, May 19 Litho. *Perf. 12½x13*

1948 A789 48c multi .75 .30
1949 A790 48c multi .75 .30
1950 A791 48c multi .75 .30
1951 A792 48c multi .75 .30
a. Block of 4, #1948-1951 3.00 1.50
b. Souvenir sheet, #1948-1951, perf. 13¼x13 3.00 1.50

See Hong Kong Nos. 979-982.

Tourist Attractions Type of 2001

No. 1952: a, Yukon Quest, Yukon Territory. b, Icefields Parkway, Alberta. c, Agawa Canyon, Ontario. d, Old Port of Montreal, Quebec. e, Kings Landing, New Brunswick.

No. 1953: a, Northern Lights, Northwest Territories. b, Stanley Park, Vancouver, British Columbia. c, Head-Smashed-In Buffalo Jump, Alberta. d, Saguenay Fjord, Quebec. e, Peggy's Cove, Nova Scotia.

2002, June 1 *Die Cut Perf. 11x11¼*

Self-Adhesive

1952 Booklet of 5 5.00
a.-e. A768 65c Any single 1.00 .40
1953 Booklet of 5 10.00
a.-e. A768 $1.25 Any single 2.00 .75

Sculpture — A793

Designs: No. 1954, Embacle, by Charles Daudelin. No. 1955, Lumberjacks, by Leo Mol.

2002, June 10 Litho. *Perf. 13¼*

1954 A793 48c multi .75 .30
1955 A793 48c multi .75 .30
a. Horiz. or vert. pair, #1954-1955 1.50 .60

Canadian Postmasters and Assistants Association, Cent. — A794

2002, July 5 *Perf. 13¼x12½*

1956 A794 48c multi .75 .30

Printed in sheets of 16 stamps + 12 labels.

17th World Youth Day, Toronto — A795

2002, July 23 Litho. *Die Cut*

Booklet Stamp

Self-Adhesive

1957 A795 48c multi .75 .30
a. Booklet of 8 6.00

Public Services International World Congress, Ottawa — A796

2002, Sept. 4 Litho. ***Perf. 12½x13***
1958 A796 48c multi .75 .30

Public Pensions, 75th Anniv. — A797

2002, Sept. 10 ***Perf. 13¼***
1959 A797 48c multi .75 .30

Souvenir Sheet

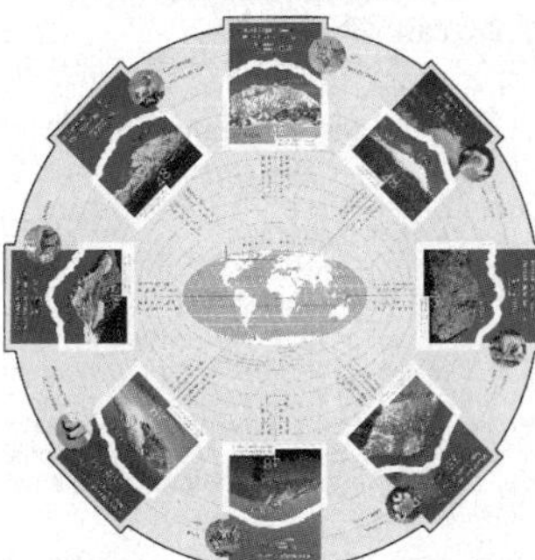

Intl. Year of Mountains — A798

No. 1960: a, Mt. Logan, Canada. b, Mt. Elbrus, Russia. c, Puncak Jaya, Indonesia. d, Mt. Everest, Nepal and China. e, Mt. Kilimanjaro, Tanzania. f, Vinson Massif, Antarctica. g, Mt. Aconcagua, Argentina. h, Mt. McKinley, Alaska.

2002, Oct. 1 Litho. ***Die Cut***
Self-Adhesive
1960 A798 Sheet of 8 + 8 labels 6.00 6.00
a.-h. 48c Any single .75 .30

World Teachers' Day — A799

2002, Oct. 4 Litho. ***Perf. 12½x13***
1961 A799 48c multi .75 .30

Toronto Stock Exchange, 150th Anniv. — A800

2002, Oct. 24 Litho. ***Perf. 12½x13***
1962 A800 48c multi .75 .30

Communication Technology Centenaries — A801

Part of map of North America and: No. 1963, Sir Sandford Fleming (1827-1915), cable-laying ship . No. 1964, Guglielmo Marconi (1874-1937), radio and transmission towers.

2002, Oct. 31 Litho. ***Perf. 13x12½***
1963 48c multi .75 .30
1964 48c multi .75 .30
a. A801 Horiz. pair, #1963-1964 1.50 .75

Cent. of first telegraph message sent over transpacific cable (#1963); first transatlantic radio message (#1964).

Christmas A802

Art by aboriginals: 48c, Genesis, by Daphne Odjig. 65c, Winter Travel, by Cecil Youngfox. $1.25, Mary and Child, sculpture by Irene Katak Angutitaq.

2002, Nov. 4 ***Perf. 12½x13***
1965 A802 48c multi .75 .25
a. Booklet pane of 10 7.50
Booklet, #1965a 7.50
1966 A802 65c multi 1.00 .40
a. Booklet pane of 6 6.00
Booklet, #1966a 6.00
1967 A802 $1.25 multi 2.00 .70
a. Booklet pane of 6 12.00
Booklet, #1967a 12.00
Nos. 1965-1967 (3) 3.75 1.35

Quebec Symphony Orchestra, Cent. A803

2002, Nov. 7
1968 A803 48c multi .75 .30

New Year 2003 (Year of the Ram) — A804

Litho. & Embossed with Foil Application
2003, Jan. 3 ***Perf. 13***
1969 A804 48c shown .75 .30

Souvenir Sheet
Perf. 13¼
1970 A804 $1.25 Ram, diff. 2.00 .80

No. 1970 contains one 33x58mm stamp. Slits replace perforations on the vertical sides of the stamps between the point of the acute angle made with the curving perforations and the point perpendicular to where the perforations on the opposite side form the obtuse angle with the curving perforations.

National Hockey League Stars A805

Designs: Nos. 1971a, 1972a, Frank Mahovlich (orange panel). Nos. 1971b, 1972b, Raymond Bourque (lilac panel). Nos. 1971c, 1972c, Serge Savard (blue panel). Nos. 1971d, 1972d, Stan Mikita (red violet panel). Nos. 1971e, 1972e, Mike Bossy (bright pink panel). Nos. 1971f, 1972f, Bill Durnan (green panel).

Perf. 12½x13¼ on 3 Sides
2003, Jan. 18 Litho.
1971 Sheet of 6 + 3 labels 12.00 2.00
a.-f. A805 48c Any single 2.00 .30

Self-Adhseive
Die Cut
1972 Pane of 6 12.00 2.00
a.-f. A805 48c Any single 2.00 .30

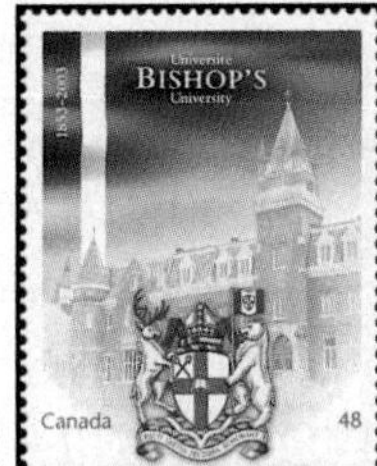

Universities A806

Design: No. 1973, Bishop's University, Lennoxville, Quebec, 150th anniv. No. 1974, University of Western Ontario, London, Ont., 125th anniv. No. 1975, St. Francis Xavier University, Antigonish, N. S., 150th Anniv. No. 1976, Macdonald Institute, Guelph, Ont., cent. No. 1977, University of Montreal, 125th anniv.

2003 Litho. ***Perf. 13¼x13½***
Booklet Stamps
1973 A806 48c multi .75 .30
a. Booklet pane of 8 6.00 —
Booklet, #1973a 6.00
1974 A806 48c multi .75 .30
a. Booklet pane of 8 6.00 —
Booklet, #1974a 6.00
1975 A806 48c multi .70 .30
a. Booklet pane of 8 5.75 —
Complete booklet, #1975a 5.75
1976 A806 48c multi .75 .30
a. Booklet pane of 8 6.00 —
Complete booklet, #1976a 6.00
1977 A806 48c multi .75 .30
a. Booklet pane of 8 6.00 —
Complete booklet, #1977a 6.00

Issued: No. 1973, 1/28. No. 1975, 4/4. No. 1976, 6/20. No. 1977, 9/4. No. 1974, 3/19.
See Nos. 2033-2034.

Bird Paintings by John James Audubon — A807

Designs: No. 1979, Leach's storm petrel. No. 1980, Brant. No. 1981, Great cormorant. No. 1982, Common murre. 65c, Gyrfalcon, vert.

Perf. 13¼x12½
2003, Feb. 21 Litho.
1979 A807 48c multi .75 .30
1980 A807 48c multi .75 .30
1981 A807 48c multi .75 .30
1982 A807 48c multi .75 .30
a. Block of 4, #1979-1982 3.00 1.25

Booklet Stamp
Self-Adhesive
Die Cut
1983 A807 65c multi 1.00 .45
a. Booklet pane of 6 6.00
Nos. 1979-1983 (5) 4.00 1.65

Canadian Rangers — A808

2003, Mar. 3 ***Perf. 12½x13¼***
1984 A808 48c multi .75 .30

American Hellenic Educational Progressive Association In Canada, 75th Anniv. — A809

Perf. 12½x13¼
2003, Mar. 25 Litho.
1985 A809 48c multi .65 .30

Volunteer Firefighters A810

2003, May 30 Litho. ***Perf. 13¼***
1986 A810 48c multi .75 .35

Coronation of Queen Elizabeth II, 50th Anniv. A811

2003, June 2 ***Perf. 13x12½***
1987 A811 48c multi .75 .35

Quebec City, Seal of Sovereign Council of New France, Signature of Pedro da Silva — A812

2003, June 6 ***Perf. 13x12¾***
1988 A812 48c multi .75 .35

Pedro da Silva, first courier in New France, 50th anniv. of Portuguese immigration to Canada.

Tourist Attractions Type of 2001

No. 1989: a, Wilberforce Falls, Nunavut. b, Inside Passage, B. C. c, Royal Canadian Mounted Police Depot Division, Regina, Sask. d, Casa Loma, Toronto, Ont. e, Gatineau Park, Que.

No. 1990: a, Dragon boat races, Vancouver, B. C. b, Polar bear watching, Man. c, Niagara Falls, Ont. d, Magdalen Islands, Que. e, Charlottestown, P. E. I.

2003, June 12 ***Die Cut Perf. 11¼***
Self-Adhesive
1989 Booklet of 5 5.00
a.-e. A768 65c Any single 1.00 .50
1990 Booklet of 5 10.00
a.-e. A768 $1.25 Any single 2.00 .80

Flag and Canada Post Headquarters Type of 2002 With "Vancouver / 2010" Added in Red

Serpentine Die Cut 8½

2003, July 11 Litho.

Booklet Stamp

Self-Adhesive

1991 A781 48c multi 3.00 .35
a. Booklet of 10 00.00
b. Booklet of 30 90.00

Selection of Vancouver as site of 2010 Winter Olympics. By separating the booklet along the columns of rouletting, No. 1991b could be broken up into three separately obtainable examples of No. 1991a.

Canada-Alaska Cruise Scenes — A813

Mountains and: No. 1991C, Totem pole. No. 1991D, Whale's tail.

2003, July 19 Litho. *Die Cut*

Self-Adhesive

1991C A813 ($1.25) multi 4.50 4.50
1991D A813 ($1.25) multi 4.50 4.50
e. Horiz. pair, #1990C-1990D 9.00

Nos. 1991C-1991D were printed in sheets of 10 containing five of each stamp. The blank spaces in each stamp and the three stamp-like vignettes at the left of the sheet that lack die cutting and "Postage Paid / Port Payé" inscription could be personalized on cruise ships. Personalized sheets sold for $19.95 in US currency, while unpersonalized sheets sold for $12.50.

Lutheran World Federation, 10th Assembly, Winnipeg A814

2003, July 21 Litho. *Perf. 12½x13*

1992 A814 48c multi .75 .35

Korean War Armistice Agreement, 50th Anniv. — A815

2003, July 25 *Perf. 12¾*

1993 A815 48c multi .75 .35

Authors A816

Designs: No. 1994, Anne Hébert (1916-2000). No. 1995, Hector de Saint-Denys Garneau (1912-43). No. 1996, Morley Callaghan (1903-90). No. 1997, Susanna Moodie (1803-85), and Catharine Parr Traill (1802-99).

2003, Sept. 8 Litho. *Perf. 13¼x12½*

Booklet Stamps

1994 A816 48c multi .75 .35
1995 A816 48c multi .75 .35
1996 A816 48c multi .75 .35
1997 A816 48c multi .75 .35
a. Block of 4, #1994-1997 3.00 1.40
b. Booklet pane, 2 #1997a 6.00 —
Complete booklet, #1997b 6.00

2003 Road Cycling World Championships, Hamilton, Ont. — A817

2003, Sept. 10 Litho. *Perf. 12½x13*

Booklet Stamp

1998 A817 48c multi .75 .35
a. Booklet pane of 8 6.00 —
Complete booklet, #1998a 6.00

Canadian Astronauts A818

No. 1999: a, Marc Garneau. b, Roberta Bondar. c, Steve MacLean. d, Chris Hadfield. e, Robert Thirsk. f, Bjarni Tryggvason. g, Dave Williams. h, Julie Payette.

Litho. With Foil Application

2003, Oct. 1 *Die Cut*

Self-Adhesive

1999 Sheet of 8 6.00
a.-h. A818 48c Any single .75 .40

Trees of Canada and Thailand — A819

Designs: No. 2000, Acer saccharum leaves (Canada). No. 2001, Cassia fistula (Thailand).

2003, Oct. 4 Litho. *Perf. 12¾x12½*

2000 A819 48c multi .75 .40
2001 A819 48c multi .75 .40
a. Pair, #2000-2001 1.50 .80
b. Souvenir sheet, #2000-2001 1.50 .80
c. As "c," die cutting omitted —

Bangkok 2003 Intl. Philatelic Exhibition (#2001b).

See Thailand No. 2090.

L'Hommage à Rosa Luxemburg, by Jean-Paul Riopelle — A820

Painting details — No. 2002; a, Red and blue dots between birds at LR. b, Bird with yellow beak at center. c, Three birds in circle at R. d, Sun at UR. e, Birds with purple outlines at L. f, Bird with red outline in circle at R. $1.25, Pink bird in red circle at R.

2003, Oct. 7 Litho. *Perf. 12½x13*

2002 A820 Sheet of 6 4.50 2.25
a.-f. 48c Any single .75 .35

Souvenir Sheet

Perf. 12¾

2003 A820 $1.25 multi 2.00 1.00

Christmas A821

Gift boxes and: 48c, Ice skates. 65c, Teddy bear. $1.25, Toy duck.

2003, Nov. 4 *Die Cut*

Booklet Stamps

Self-Adhesive

2004 A821 48c multi .75 .35
a. Booklet pane of 6 4.50
Complete booklet, 2 #2004a 9.00
b. Pair, die cutting omitted —
2005 A821 65c multi 1.00 .50
a. Booklet pane of 6 6.00
2006 A821 $1.25 multi 2.00 .95
a. Booklet pane of 6 12.00
Nos. 2004-2006 (3) 3.75 1.80

Maple Leaf and Samara A822

Maple Leaf on Twig A823

Flag Over Edmonton, Alberta A824

Queen Elizabeth II A825

Litho. & Engr.

2003, Dec. 19 *Perf. 12½x13*

Coil Stamps

Litho.

Self-Adhesive

Serpentine Die Cut 8 Horiz.

2008 A822 49c multi .80 .40

Serpentine Die Cut 8 Vert.

2009 A823 80c red & multi 1.25 .60
2010 A823 $1.40 grn & multi 2.25 1.10

Booklet Stamps

Die Cut

2011 A824 49c multi .80 .40
a. Booklet pane of 10 8.00
b. Pair, die cutting omitted —
2012 A825 49c multi .80 .40
a. Booklet pane of 10 8.00
2013 A823 80c red & multi 1.25 .60
a. Booklet pane of 6 7.50
2014 A823 $1.40 grn & multi 2.25 1.10
a. Booklet pane of 6 13.50
Nos. 2008-2014 (7) 9.40 4.60

New Year 2004 (Year of the Monkey) — A826

Scenes from Chinese story *Journey to the West*: 49c, Monkey King. $1.40, Monkey King, Xuan Zang, Sandy, Pigsy and horse.

Litho. & Embossed with Foil Application

2004, Jan. 8 *Perf. 13x12½*

2015 A826 49c multi .80 .40

Souvenir Sheet

2016 A826 $1.40 multi 2.25 1.10
a. As No. 2016, with 2004 Hong Kong Stamp Expo ovpt. in margin 2.25 1.10

No. 2016 has rouletted tab at right showing bar code.

National Hockey League Stars A827

Designs: Nos. 2017a, 2018a, Larry Robinson (blue background). Nos. 2017b, 2018b, Marcel Dionne (orange background). Nos. 2017c, 2018c, Ted Lindsay (red background). Nos. 2017d, 2018d, Johnny Bower (green background). Nos. 2017e, 2018e, Brad Park (brown background). Nos. 2017f, 2018f, Milt Schmidt (purple background).

Perf. 12½x13¼ on 3 Sides

2004, Jan. 24 Litho.

2017 Sheet of 6 + 3 labels 5.00 2.50
a.-f. A827 49c Any single .80 .40

Self-Adhesive

Die Cut

2018 Pane of 6 5.00 2.50
a.-f. A827 49c Any single .80 .40

Tourist Attractions Type of 2001

Design: No. 2019, Quebec Winter Carnival; No. 2020, St. Joseph's Oratory, Montreal, Quebec; No. 2021, International Jazz Festival, Montreal. No. 2022, Traversée Internationale du Lac St. Jean Swimming Marathon, Quebec; No. 2023, Canadian National Exhibition, Toronto.

2004, Jan. 29 Litho. *Die Cut*

Self-Adhesive

Booklet Stamp

2019 A768 49c multi .75 .40
a. Booklet of 6 4.50
2020 A768 49c multi .75 .40
a. Booklet of 6 4.50
2021 A768 49c multi .75 .40
a. Booklet of 6 4.50
2022 A768 49c multi .75 .40
a. Booklet of 6 4.50
2023 A768 49c multi .75 .40
a. Booklet of 6 4.50

Issued: No. 2019, 1/29; No. 2020, 4/2; No. 2021, 6/1; No. 2022, 6/18; No. 2023, 7/19.

Governor General Ramon John Hnatyshyn (1934-2002) — A828

2004, Mar. 16 Litho. *Perf. 12½x13*

2024 A828 49c multi .75 .40

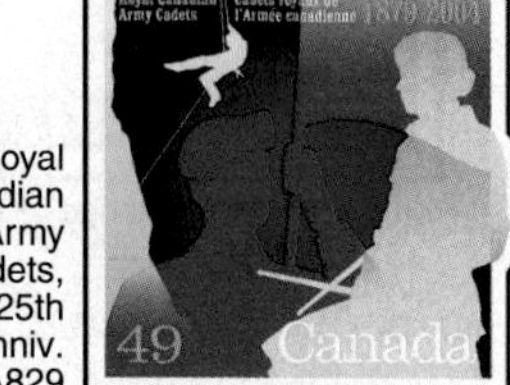

Royal Canadian Army Cadets, 125th Anniv. A829

2004, Mar. 26 Litho. *Die Cut*

Booklet Stamp

Self-Adhesive

2025 A829 49c multi .75 .40
a. Booklet pane of 4 3.00
Complete booklet, 2 #2025a 6.00

The Fram, Ship of Otto Sverdrup (1854-1930), Arctic Explorer — A830

Litho. & Engr.

2004, Mar. 26 ***Perf. 13¼***

2026 A830 49c multi .75 .40

Souvenir Sheet

2027 A830 $1.40 multi + 2 labels 2.10 1.10

See Greenland No. 426, Norway Nos. 1398-1399.

Urban Transit and Light Rail Systems — A831

Train cars, station names and system emblems of: No. 2028, Toronto Transit Commission. No. 2029, TransLink SkyTrain, Vancouver. No. 2030, Société de Transport de Montreal. No. 2031, Calgary Transit Light Rail.

2004, Mar. 30 **Litho.** ***Perf. 12½x13***

2028 A831 49c multi .75 .40
2029 A831 49c multi .75 .40
2030 A831 49c multi .75 .40
2031 A831 49c multi .75 .40
a. Vert. strip of 4, #2028-2031 3.00 1.60

Home Hardware, 40th Anniv. — A832

Die Cut Perf. 11

2004, Apr. 19 **Litho.**

Self-Adhesive

Booklet Stamp

2032 A832 49c multi .75 .40
a. Booklet pane of 10 + label 7.50
Complete booklet, #2032a 7.50

No. 2032a is the inside front cover of the complete booklet. Fifteen self-adhesive seals are on the inside back cover of the complete booklet.

Universities Type of 2003

Designs: No. 2033, Sherbrooke University, Sherbrooke, Quebec, 50th anniv. No. 2034, University of Prince Edward Island, Charlottetown, bicent.

2004 **Litho.** ***Perf. 13¼x13½***

Booklet Stamps

2033 A806 49c multi .75 .40
a. Booklet pane of 8 6.00 —
Complete booklet, #2033a 6.00
2034 A806 49c multi .75 .40
a. Booklet pane of 8 6.00 —
Complete booklet, #2034a 6.00

Issued: No. 2033, 5/4; No. 2034, 5/8.

Montreal Children's Hospital, Cent. — A833

2004, May 6 ***Die Cut Perf. 9½x10¾***

Self-Adhesive

Booklet Stamp

2035 A833 49c multi .75 .40
a. Booklet pane of 4 3.00
Complete booklet, 2 #2035a 6.00

Bird Paintings by John James Audubon A834

Designs: No. 2036, Ruby-crowned kinglet. No. 2037, White-winged crossbill. No. 2038, Bohemian waxwing. No. 2039, Boreal chickadee. 80c, Lincoln's sparrow.

2004, May 14 ***Perf. 12½x13***

2036 A834 49c multi .75 .40
2037 A834 49c multi .75 .40
2038 A834 49c multi .75 .40
2039 A834 49c multi .75 .40
a. Block of 4, #2036-2039 3.00 1.60

Self-Adhesive

Booklet Stamp

Die Cut

2040 A834 80c multi 1.25 .60
a. Booklet pane of 6 7.50
Nos. 2036-2040 (5) 4.25 2.20

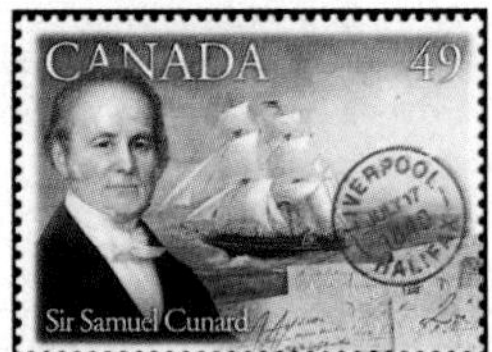

Pioneers of Transatlantic Mail Service — A835

Designs: No. 2041, Sir Samuel Cunard (1787-1865). No. 2042, Sir Hugh Allan (1810-82).

2004, May 28 **Litho.** ***Perf. 13¼x12½***

Self-Adhesive

2041 A835 49c multi .75 .40
2042 A835 49c multi .75 .40
a. Horiz. pair, #2041-2042 1.50 .80

D-Day, 60th Anniv. A836

2004, June 6 **Litho.** ***Perf. 13x12½***

2043 A836 49c multi .75 .40

Pierre Dugua de Mons, Leader of First French Settlement in Acadia, and Ship A837

Litho. & Engr.

2004, June 26 ***Perf. 13x12½***

2044 A837 49c multi .75 .40

See France No. 3032.

Butterfly and Flower A838

Children on Beach A839

Rose A840

Dog A841

Serpentine Die Cut 11¾

2004, June **Litho.**

Self-Adhesive

Booklet Stamps

2045 A838 (49c) multi 3.75 3.75
a. Booklet pane of 2 7.50
Complete booklet, #2045a + phonecard in greeting card 9.25
2046 A839 (49c) multi 3.75 3.75
a. Booklet pane of 2 7.50
Complete booklet, #2046a + phonecard in greeting card 9.25
2047 A840 (49c) multi 3.75 3.75
a. Booklet pane of 2 7.50
Complete booklet, #2047a + phonecard in greeting card 9.25
2048 A841 (49c) multi 3.75 3.75
a. Booklet pane of 2 7.50
Complete booklet, #2048a + phonecard in greeting card 9.25
Nos. 2045-2048 (4) 15.00 15.00

Nos. 2045-2048, have a frame like No. 1918a, and are similarly inscribed "Domestic Lettermail" and "Poste-lettres du régime intérieur," but Nos. 2045-2048 have the vignettes printed on the stamps, while any vignettes found on No. 1918a are affixed stickers. Nos. 2045a-2048a are affixed to the insides of greeting cards that contain detachable phonecards valid for 15 minutes calling time on any touchtone phone in Canada or the United States. The stamps were available only in the greeting card, which sold for $5.99 along with a blank envelope for sending the greeting card.

2004 Summer Olympics, Athens — A842

Olympic rings and: No. 2049, Spyros Louis, 1896 Marathon gold medalist, diagram of track, "Athens" in Greek, and stylized runner. No. 2050, Soccer net inscribed "Canada," girls playing soccer.

2004, July 28 ***Perf. 12½x13¼***

2049 A842 49c multi .75 .40
2050 A842 49c multi .75 .40
a. Horiz. pair, #2049-2050 1.50 .80

Maple Leaf Types of 2003

2004, Aug. 18 **Litho.** ***Die Cut***

Self-Adhesive
Coil Stamps

2053 A822 49c multi .80 .40

Serpentine Die Cut 8¼ Horiz.

2054 A823 80c red & multi 1.25 .60
2055 A823 $1.40 grn & multi 2.25 1.10
Nos. 2053-2055 (3) 4.30 2.10

Montreal Heart Institute, 50th Anniv. — A844

Die Cut Perf. 13½

2004, Sept. 15 Litho.
Self-Adhesive
Booklet Stamp

2056 A844 49c multi .80 .40
a. Booklet pane of 4 3.25
Complete booklet, 2 #2056 6.50

Pets A845

2004, Oct. 1 Litho. *Die Cut*
Self-Adhesive
Booklet Stamps

2057 A845 49c Fish .80 .40
2058 A845 49c Cats .80 .40
2059 A845 49c Rabbit .80 .40
2060 A845 49c Dog .80 .40
a. Booklet pane, #2057-2060 3.20
Complete booklet, 2 #2060a 6.50

Nobel Laureates in Chemistry — A846

Designs: No. 2061, Gerhard Herzberg, 1971 laureate, and molecular structures. No. 2062, Michael Smith, 1993 laureate, and DNA double helix.

2004, Oct. 4 *Perf. 12½x13*

2061 A846 49c multi .80 .40
2062 A846 49c multi .80 .40
a. Pair, #2061-2062 1.60 .80

Queen Type of 2003 and

Red Calla Lilies A852

Flag and Saskatoon, Saskatchewan A853

Flag and Durrell, Newfoundland A854

Flag and Shannon Falls, British Columbia A855

Flag and Mont-Saint-Hilaire, Quebec — A856

Flag and Toronto — A857

Designs: 85c, Yellow calla lily. $1.45, Dutch iris.

Serpentine Die Cut 8 Horiz.

2004, Dec. 20 Litho.
Self-Adhesive
Coil Stamps

2072 A852 50c multi .85 .40
2073 A852 85c multi 1.40 .70
2074 A852 $1.45 multi 2.40 1.25

Booklet Stamps
Die Cut

2075 A825 50c multi .85 .40
a. Booklet pane of 10 8.50
2076 A853 50c multi .85 .40
2077 A854 50c multi .85 .40
2078 A855 50c multi .85 .40
2079 A856 50c multi .85 .40
2080 A857 50c multi .85 .40
a. Booklet pane, 2 each #2076-2080 8.50
2081 A852 85c multi 1.40 .70
a. Booklet pane of 6 8.50
2082 A852 $1.45 multi 2.40 1.25
a. Booklet pane of 6 14.50
Nos. 2072-2082 (11) 13.55 6.70

New Year 2005 (Year of the Cock) — A858

Rooster with: 50c, Red tail feathers. $1.45, Gold tail feathers.

Litho. & Embossed with Foil Application

2005, Jan. 7 *Perf. 13¼*

2083 A858 50c multi .85 .40

Souvenir Sheet
Perf. 12½x13

2084 A858 $1.45 multi 2.40 1.25
a. With dates, Canadian and Chinese flags added in sheet margin 2.40 1.25

Canada — People's Republic of China diplomatic relations, 35th anniv. (#2084a). No. 2084 contains one 40x40mm stamp.

National Hockey League Stars A859

Designs: Nos. 2085a, 2086a, Henri Richard (blue background). Nos. 2085b, 2086b, Grant Fuhr (orange background). Nos. 2085c, 2086c, Allan Stanley (red background). Nos. 2085d, 2086d, Pierre Pilote (green background). Nos. 2085e, 2086e, Bryan Trottier (purple background). Nos. 2085f, 2086f, John Bucyk (yellow background).

Perf. 12½x13¼ on 3 Sides

2005, Jan. 29 Litho.

2085 Sheet of 6 + 3 labels 5.25 5.25
a.-f. A859 50c Any single .85 .40

Self-Adhesive
Die Cut

2086 Pane of 6 5.25
a.-f. A859 50c Any single .85 .40

Fishing Flies — A860

Designs: Nos. 2087a, 2088a, Alevin. Nos. 2087b, 2088b, Jock Scott. Nos. 2087c, 2088d, P. E. I. Fly. Nos. 2087d, 2088c, Mickey Finn.

2005, Feb. 4 *Perf. 12½x13¼*

2087 A860 Sheet of 4 3.50 3.50
a.-d. 50c Any single .85 .40

Self-Adhesive
Serpentine Die Cut 10 Syncopated

2088 A860 Booklet pane of 4 3.50
a.-d. 50c Any single .85 .40
Complete booklet, 2 #2088 7.00

Universities Type of 2003

Design: Nova Scotia Agricultural College, cent.

Die Cut Perf. 12¾x13¼

2005, Feb. 14 Litho.
Booklet Stamp
Self-Adhesive

2089 A806 50c multi .85 .40
a. Booklet pane of 4 3.50
Complete booklet, 2 #2089a 7.00

SEMI-POSTAL STAMPS

Catalogue values for unused stamps in this section are for Never Hinged items.

Olympic Type of 1973 and

SP1

SP2

1974, Apr. 17 Litho. *Perf. 12½*
Size: 20x36mm

B1 A307 8c + 2c multi .30 .30
B2 A307 10c + 5c multi .45 .45
B3 A307 15c + 5c multi .60 .60
Nos. B1-B3 (3) 1.35 1.35

1975, Feb. 5 Litho. *Perf. 13*

B4 SP1 8c + 2c Swimming .30 .30
B5 SP1 10c + 5c Rowing .45 .45
B6 SP1 15c + 5c Sailing .60 .60
Nos. B4-B6 (3) 1.35 1.35

1975, Aug. 6 Litho. *Perf. 13*

B7 SP2 8c + 2c Fencing .30 .30
B8 SP2 10c + 5c Boxing .45 .45
B9 SP2 15c + 5c Judo .60 .60
Nos. B7-B9 (3) 1.35 1.35

1976, Jan. 7

B10 SP2 8c + 2c Basketball .30 .30
B11 SP2 10c + 5c Vaulting .45 .45
B12 SP2 20c + 5c Soccer .70 .70
Nos. B10-B12 (3) 1.45 1.45

21st Olympic Games, Montreal, July 17-Aug. 1. The surtax was for the Canadian Olympic Committee.

Literacy — SP3

1996, Sept. 9 Litho. *Perf. 13x12½*

B13 SP3 45c +5c multi .80 .80
a. Booklet pane of 10 8.00
Complete booklet 8.50

No. B13 has die cut opening in center to represent missing puzzle piece.

Surcharge donated to ABC CANADA literacy organization.

AIR POST STAMPS

Allegory of Flight — AP1

Unwmk.

1928, Sept. 21 Engr. *Perf. 12*

C1 AP1 5c brown olive 10.00 3.50
Never hinged 17.50
a. Imperf., pair 175.00
Never hinged 250.00

No. C1 is known imperforate horizontally and imperforate vertically.

For surcharge see No. C3.

Allegory-Air Mail Circles Globe AP2

1930, Dec. 4 *Perf. 11*

C2 AP2 5c olive brown 52.50 20.00
Never hinged 90.00

For surcharge see No. C4.

No. C1 Surcharged

1932, Feb. 22 *Perf. 12*

C3 AP1 6c on 5c brown olive 8.00 3.25
Never hinged 14.00
a. Inverted surcharge 150.00
Never hinged 210.00
b. Double surcharge 500.00
Never hinged 700.00
c. Triple surcharge 250.00
Never hinged 350.00
d. Pair, one without surcharge 600.00
Never hinged 850.00

Counterfeit surcharges exist.
No. C3b is valued in the grade of fine.

No. C2 Surcharged in Dark Blue

1932, July 12 *Perf. 11*

C4 AP2 6c on 5c olive brown 22.50 10.00
Never hinged 40.00

Daedalus AP3

1935, June 1 Engr. *Perf. 12*

C5 AP3 6c red brown 2.75 1.00
Never hinged 4.00
a. Horiz. pair, imperf. vert. *5,000.*
b. Imperf., pair 500.00
Never hinged 750.00

No. C5a is believed to be unique and is the result of a pre-perforating paper foldover.

For information on imperforate and part-perforate varieties, see note following No. 47a.

Mackenzie River Steamer and Seaplane AP4

1938, June 15

C6 AP4 6c blue 2.75 .35
Never hinged 4.00
a. Imperf., pair 450.00
Never hinged 650.00

Planes and Student Flyers AP5

1942-43

C7 AP5 6c deep blue 4.00 .90
Never hinged 6.00
a. Imperf., pair 450.00
Never hinged 650.00
C8 AP5 7c deep blue ('43) .90 .20
Never hinged 1.30
a. Imperf., pair 450.00
Never hinged 650.00

Canada's contribution to the war effort of the Allied Nations.

Catalogue values for unused stamps in this section, from this point to the end of the section, are for Never Hinged items.

Canada Geese in Flight — AP6

1946, Sept. 16

C9 AP6 7c deep blue 1.00 .20
a. Booklet pane of 4 3.00 3.00

For overprints see Nos. CO1, CO2.

AIR POST SPECIAL DELIVERY STAMPS

Trans-Canada Airplane and Aerial View of a City — APSD1

1942-43 Unwmk. Engr. *Perf. 12*

CE1 APSD1 16c bright ultra 2.00 1.75
Never hinged 3.00
a. Imperf., pair 450.00
Never hinged 650.00
CE2 APSD1 17c brt ultra ('43) 2.50 2.50
Never hinged 3.75
a. Imperf., pair 450.00
Never hinged 650.00

Canada's contribution to the war effort of the Allied Nations.

Catalogue values for unused stamps in this section, from this point to the end of the section, are for Never Hinged items.

DC-4 Transatlantic Mail Plane Over Quebec — APSD2

1946, Sept. 16

CE3 APSD2 17c bright ultra 5.50 4.00

Circumflex accent on second "E" of "EXPRES."

Corrected Die

1946, Dec. 3

CE4 APSD2 17c bright ultra 5.50 4.00

Grave accent on the 2nd "E" of "EXPRES."

AIR POST OFFICIAL STAMPS

Catalogue values for unused stamps in this section are for Never Hinged items.

No. C9 Overprinted in Black

1949 Unwmk. *Perf. 12*

CO1 AP6 7c deep blue 9.00 4.25
a. No period after "S" 75.00 40.00

Same Overprinted

1950

CO2 AP6 7c deep blue 15.00 11.00

SPECIAL DELIVERY STAMPS

SD1

Unwmk.

1898, June 28 Engr. *Perf. 12*

E1 SD1 10c blue green 75.00 10.00
Never hinged 200.00

SD2

1922, Aug. 21

E2 SD2 20c carmine 65.00 8.00
Never hinged 150.00

Five Stages of Mail Transportation SD3

1927, June 29

E3 SD3 20c orange 17.50 12.00
Never hinged 37.50
a. Imperf., pair 150.00
Never hinged 200.00

No. E3 forms part of the Confederation Commemorative issue. It is known imperforate vertically and imperforate horizontally.

SD4

1930, Sept. 2 *Perf. 11*

E4 SD4 20c henna brown 50.00 14.00
Never hinged 100.00

SD5

1933, Dec. 24

E5 SD5 20c henna brown 45.00 15.00
Never hinged 90.00
a. Imperf., pair 450.00
Never hinged 650.00

Allegory of Progress — SD6

1935, June 1 *Perf. 12*

E6 SD6 20c dark carmine 7.50 6.00
Never hinged 11.50
a. Imperf., pair 450.00
Never hinged 650.00

Arms of Canada — SD7

1938-39

E7 SD7 10c dk green ('39) 4.00 2.75
Never hinged 6.00
a. Imperf., pair 450.00
Never hinged 650.00
E8 SD7 20c dark carmine 25.00 25.00
Never hinged 37.50
a. Imperf., pair 450.00
Never hinged 650.00

No. E8 Surcharged in Black

1939, Mar. 1

E9 SD7 10c on 20c dk car 5.00 4.50
Never hinged 7.00

Coat of Arms and Flags SD8

1942, July 1 Engr.

E10 SD8 10c green 2.00 1.75
Never hinged 2.75
a. Imperf., pair 450.00
Never hinged 650.00

Canada's contribution to the war effort of the Allied Nations.

Catalogue values for unused stamps in this section, from this point to the end of the section, are for Never Hinged items.

Arms of Canada — SD9

1946, Sept. 16

E11 SD9 10c green 1.75 1.00

The laurel and olive branches symbolize Victory and Peace.

For overprints see Nos. EO1, EO2.

SPECIAL DELIVERY OFFICIAL STAMPS

Catalogue values for unused stamps in this section are for Never Hinged items.

No. E11 Overprinted in Black

1950 Unwmk. *Perf. 12*

EO1 SD9 10c green 14.00 10.00

Same Overprinted

EO2 SD9 10c green 22.50 14.00

REGISTRATION STAMPS

R1

1875-88 Unwmk. Engr. *Perf. 12*

F1	R1 2c orange	85.00	3.00
a.	2c vermilion	95.00	8.50
b.	2c rose carmine	210.00	90.00
c.	As "a," imperf., pair		—
d.	Perf. 12x11½	350.00	90.00
F2	R1 5c dark green	125.00	4.00
a.	5c blue green ('88)	125.00	4.00
b.	5c yellow green	175.00	6.50
c.	Imperf., pair	*650.00*	
d.	Perf. 12x11½	1,250.	175.00
F3	R1 8c blue	350.00	250.00
	Nos. F1-F3 (3)	560.00	257.00

POSTAGE DUE STAMPS

D1

D2

1906-28 Unwmk. Engr. *Perf. 12*

J1	D1 1c violet	12.50	4.00
	Never hinged	20.00	
a.	Thin paper ('24)	22.50	7.00
	Never hinged	40.00	
b.	Imperf., pair	275.00	
J2	D1 2c violet	12.50	.80
	Never hinged	22.50	
a.	Thin paper ('24)	25.00	9.00
	Never hinged	45.00	
b.	Imperf., pair	275.00	
J3	D1 4c violet ('28)	50.00	17.50
	Never hinged	90.00	
J4	D1 5c violet	12.50	1.50
	Never hinged	22.50	
a.	Thin paper	9.00	6.00
	Never hinged	17.50	
b.	Imperf., pair	275.00	
J5	D1 10c violet ('28)	32.50	12.50
	Never hinged	65.00	
	Nos. J1-J5 (5)	120.00	36.30
	Nos. J1-J5, never hinged	212.50	

In 1924 there was a printing of Nos. J1, J2 and J4 on thin semi-transparent paper. Imperf pairs are without gum.

1930-32 *Perf. 11*

J6	D2 1c dark violet	10.00	3.50
	Never hinged	17.50	
J7	D2 2c dark violet	6.00	.90
	Never hinged	11.00	
J8	D2 4c dark violet	15.00	4.00
	Never hinged	27.50	
J9	D2 5c dark violet	12.50	6.00
	Never hinged	22.50	
J10	D2 10c dark violet ('32)	75.00	9.00
	Never hinged	140.00	
a.	Vert. pair, imperf. horiz.	600.00	—
	Never hinged	900.00	
	Nos. J6-J10 (5)	118.50	23.40
	Nos. J6-J10, never hinged	218.50	

No. J10a is valued in the grade of fine.

D3

D4

1933-34

J11	D3 1c dark violet ('34)	10.00	6.00
	Never hinged	17.50	
a.	Imperf., pair	300.00	
	Never hinged	475.00	
J12	D3 2c dark violet	4.00	1.00
	Never hinged	7.00	
J13	D3 4c dark violet	9.00	6.50
	Never hinged	16.00	
J14	D3 10c dark violet	17.50	5.00
	Never hinged	30.00	
	Nos. J11-J14 (4)	40.50	18.50
	Nos. J11-J14, never hinged	70.50	

Catalogue values for unused stamps in this section, from this point to the end of the section, are for Never Hinged items.

1935-65 *Perf. 12*

J15	D4 1c dark violet	.30	.20
a.	Imperf., pair	175.00	
J16	D4 2c dark violet	.30	.20
a.	Imperf., pair	175.00	
J16B	D4 3c dark vio ('65)	2.50	1.25
J17	D4 4c dark violet	.35	.20
a.	Imperf., pair	175.00	
J18	D4 5c dark vio ('48)	.50	.30
J19	D4 6c dark vio ('57)	2.00	1.00
J20	D4 10c dark violet	.50	.20
a.	Imperf., pair	175.00	
	Nos. J15-J20 (7)	6.45	3.35

D5

1967, Feb. 8 Litho. *Perf. 12*

Size: 20x17mm

J21	D5 1c carmine rose	.20	.20
J22	D5 2c carmine rose	.20	.25
J23	D5 3c carmine rose	.20	.25
J24	D5 4c carmine rose	.25	.25
J25	D5 5c carmine rose	1.25	1.25
J26	D5 6c carmine rose	.25	.25
J27	D5 10c carmine rose	.30	.25
	Nos. J21-J27 (7)	2.65	2.70

1969-78 *Perf. 12*

Size: 20x15¾mm

J28	D5 1c car rose ('70)	.35	.30
a.	Perf. 12½x12 ('77)	.20	.20
J29	D5 2c car rose ('72)	.20	.20
J30	D5 3c car rose ('74)	.25	.20
J31	D5 4c carmine rose	.30	.25
a.	Perf. 12½x12 ('77)	.20	.20
J32	D5 5c car rose, perf. 12½x12 ('77)	.20	.20
a.	Perf. 12	14.00	14.00
J33	D5 6c car rose ('72)	.20	.20
J34	D5 8c carmine rose	.20	.20
a.	Perf. 12½x12 ('78)	.30	.20
J35	D5 10c carmine rose	.40	.20
a.	Perf. 12½x12 ('77)	.20	.20
J36	D5 12c carmine rose	.60	.60
a.	Perf. 12½x12 ('77)	1.25	.60
J37	D5 16c carmine rose ('74)	.30	.25

Perf. 12½x12

J38	D5 20c carmine rose ('77)	.55	.35
J39	D5 24c carmine rose ('77)	.65	.25
J40	D5 50c carmine rose ('77)	.85	.75
	Nos. J28-J40 (13)	5.05	3.95

WAR TAX STAMPS

WT1

WT2

Unwmk.

1915, Mar. 25 Engr. *Perf. 12*

MR1	WT1 1c green	12.50	.20
	Never hinged	27.50	
MR2	WT1 2c carmine	12.50	.25
	Never hinged	27.50	

In 1915 postage stamps of 5, 20 and 50 cents were overprinted "WAR TAX" in two lines. These stamps were intended for fiscal use, the war tax on postal matter being 1 cent. A few of these stamps were used to pay postage.

1916

TWO DIES:

Die I — There is a colored line between two white lines below the large letter "T."

Die II — The right half of the colored line is replaced by two short diagonal lines and five small dots.

MR3	WT2 2c + 1c car (I)	17.50	.20
	Never hinged	30.00	
a.	2c + 1c carmine (II)	100.00	4.50
	Never hinged	175.00	
MR4	WT2 2c + 1c brn (II)	15.00	.20
	Never hinged	27.50	
a.	2c + 1c brown (I)	250.00	10.00
	Never hinged	450.00	
b.	Imperf., pair (I)	130.00	
c.	Imperf., pair (II)	900.00	

#MR4b-MR4c were made without gum.

Perf. 12x8

MR5	WT2 2c + 1c car (I)	35.00	22.50
	Never hinged	65.00	

Coil Stamps

Perf. 8 Vertically

MR6	WT2 2c + 1c car (I)	100.00	7.50
	Never hinged	175.00	
MR7	WT2 2c + 1c brn (II)	22.50	1.00
	Never hinged	40.00	
a.	2c + 1c brown (I)	120.00	7.50
	Never hinged	200.00	

OFFICIAL STAMPS

With Perforated Initials O H M S

On March 28, 1939 the Treasury Board ruled that on and after June 30, 1939 all stamps used by government departments throughout the country should be perforated O H M S (On His Majesty's Service) and that "the Post Office Department is to make arrangements required to provide that all stamps sold to Government Departments are perforated with the letters O H M S." The sale of such perforated stamps was discontinued in 1948.

For listings see the *Scott Classic Specialized Catalogue.*

Catalogue values for unused stamps in this section are for Never Hinged items.

Nos. 249, 250, 252 and 254 Overprinted in Black

1949-50 Unwmk. *Perf. 12*

O1	A97 1c green	1.90	1.75
a.	No period after "S"	45.00	45.00
O2	A98 2c brown	8.75	7.25
a.	No period after "S"	62.50	62.50
O3	A99 3c rose violet	1.90	1.10
O4	A98 4c dark carmine	2.50	.60

Nos. 269 to 273 Overprinted in Black

O6	A108 10c olive	3.00	.50
a.	No period after "S"	50.00	45.00
O7	A109 14c black brown	3.25	2.00
a.	No period after "S"	75.00	67.50
O8	A110 20c slate black	11.00	2.75
a.	No period after "S"	85.00	80.00
O9	A111 50c dk blue grn	190.00	95.00
a.	No period after "S"	500.00	450.00
O10	A112 $1 red violet	65.00	30.00
a.	No period after "S"	*2,000.*	*1,500.*
	Nos. O1-O4,O6-O10 (9)	287.30	140.95

It is recommended that a certificate of authenticity be acquired for O10a.

Same Overprint on No. 294

1950

O11	A124 50c dull green	32.50	20.00

Nos. 284 to 288 Overprinted in Black

1950

O12	A119 1c green	.30	.25
O13	A120 2c sepia	1.00	.60
O14	A121 3c rose violet	1.10	.50
O15	A122 4c dark carmine	1.10	.20
b.	No period after "S"	52.50	45.00
O15A	A123 5c deep blue	2.00	1.10
c.	No period after "S"	47.50	45.00
	Nos. O12-O15A (5)	5.50	2.65

Stamps of 1946-1950 Overprinted in Black

a

b

c

1950

O16	A119(a) 1c grn (#284)	.40	.20
O17	A120(a) 2c sepia (#285)	1.25	.80
O18	A121(a) 3c rose vio (#286)	1.25	.20
O19	A122(a) 4c dk car (#287)	1.25	.20
O20	A123(a) 5c dp bl (#288)	1.50	.85
O21	A108(b) 10c olive	2.25	.45
O22	A109(b) 14c black brn	6.50	2.00
O23	A110(b) 20c slate blk	14.00	1.00
O24	A124(b) 50c dull green	9.00	5.50
O25	A112(b) $1 red violet	100.00	65.00
	Nos. O16-O25 (10)	137.40	76.20

Nos. 301-302 Overprinted Type "b"

1950-51

O26	A125 10c black brown	1.25	.20
a.	Pair, one without "G"	675.00	450.00
O27	A126 $1 brt ultra ('51)	85.00	70.00

It is recommended that a certificate of authenticity be acquired for O26a.

Nos. 305-306 Overprinted Type "a"

1951-52 Unwmk. *Perf. 12*

O28	A120 2c olive green	.50	.20
O29	A122 4c orange ver ('52)	.90	.20

No. 316 Overprinted Type "b"

1952

O30	A132 20c gray	2.00	.20

Nos. 320-321 Overprinted Type "b"

1952-53

O31	A136 7c blue	4.00	1.10
O32	A137 $1 gray ('53)	15.00	10.00

Same Overprints on #325-329, 334

1953-61

O33	A139(a) 1c violet brown	.30	.20
O34	A139(a) 2c green	.30	.20
O35	A139(a) 3c carmine rose	.30	.20
O36	A139(a) 4c violet	.40	.20
O37	A139(a) 5c ultramarine	.40	.20
O38	A141(b) 50c light green	5.00	1.00
a.	Overprinted type "c" ('61)	4.75	2.00
	Nos. O33-O38 (6)	6.70	2.00

No. 351 Overprinted Type "b"

1955-62

O39	A148 10c violet brown	.90	.20
a.	Overprinted type "c" ('62)	1.75	1.25

#337-338, 340-341 Ovptd. Type "a"

1955-56

O40	A144 1c vio brown ('56)	.30	.30
O41	A144 2c green ('56)	.35	.20
O43	A144 4c violet ('56)	1.00	.20
O44	A144 5c bright blue	.60	.20
	Nos. O40-O44 (4)	2.25	.90

No. 362 Overprinted Type "b"

1956-62

O45	A159 20c green	1.75	.20
a.	Overprinted type "c" ('62)	7.00	.50

#401-402, 404-405 Ovptd. Type "a"

1963, May 15 Engr. *Perf. 12*

O46	A195 1c deep brown	.60	.60
a.	Double overprint	700.00	
O47	A195 2c green	.60	.60
a.	Pair, one without "G"	750.00	
O48	A195 4c carmine	.65	.65
O49	A195 5c violet blue	.40	.40
	Nos. O46-O49 (4)	2.25	2.25

CAPE JUBY

'kāp 'jü-bē

LOCATION — Northwest coast of Africa in Spanish Sahara
GOVT. — Spanish administration
AREA — 12,700 sq. mi.
POP. — 9,836
CAPITAL — Villa Bens (Cape Juby)

By agreement with France, Spain's Sahara possessions were extended to include Cape Juby and in 1916 Spanish troops occupied the territory. It was attached for administrative purposes to Spanish Sahara.

100 Centimos = 1 Peseta

CABO JUBI
5
CÉNTIMOS

Stamps of Rio de Oro, 1914 Surcharged in Violet, Red or Green

1916 Unwmk. *Perf. 13*

No.	Type	Description	Unused	Used
1	A6	5c on 4p rose (V)	175.00	19.00
2	A6	10c on 10p dl vio (R)	40.00	19.00
2E	A6	10c on 10p dl vio (V)	125.00	72.50
2G	A6	10c on 10p dl vio (B)	125.00	72.50
3	A6	15c on 50c dk brn (G)	52.50	30.00
4	A6	15c on 50c dk brn (R)	37.50	19.00
5	A6	40c on 1p red vio (G)	77.50	35.00
6	A6	40c on 1p red vio (R)	65.00	26.00
		Nos. 1-6 (8)	697.50	293.00
		Set, never hinged	1,050.	

For type II, inverted and double surcharges, see the *Scott Classic Catalogue.*

Very fine examples of Nos. 1-6 will be somewhat off center. Well centered examples are uncommon and will sell for more.

Stamps of Spain, 1876-1917, Overprinted in Red or Black

1919 *Imperf.*

No.	Type	Description	Unused	Used
7	A21	¼c bl grn (R)	.20	.20

Perf. 13x12½, 14

No.	Type	Description	Unused	Used
8	A46	2c dk brn (Bk)	.20	.20
a.		Double overprint	17.50	15.00
b.		Double overprint (Bk + R)	55.00	50.00
9	A46	5c grn (R)	.45	.45
a.		Double overprint	17.50	15.00
b.		Inverted overprint	27.50	*45.00*
10	A46	10c car (Bk)	.55	.55
a.		Double overprint (Bk + R)	55.00	50.00
11	A46	15c ocher (Bk)	2.50	2.50
b.		Double overprint	17.50	15.00
c.		Red control #	5.50	3.50
d.		As "c," inverted overprint	12.00	
12	A46	20c ol grn (R)	14.50	14.50
13	A46	25c dp bl (R)	2.40	2.40
a.		Double overprint	17.50	15.00
14	A46	30c bl grn (R)	2.40	2.40
15	A46	40c rose (Bk)	2.40	2.40
16	A46	50c sl bl (R)	3.00	3.00
17	A46	1p lake (Bk)	7.50	7.50
18	A46	4p dp vio (R)	29.00	29.00
19	A46	10p org (Bk)	37.50	37.50
		Nos. 7-19 (13)	102.60	102.60
		Set, never hinged	175.00	

Nos. 8-19 have blue control number on back. For imperfs, see the *Scott Classic Catalogue.*

Same on Stamps of Spain, 1920-21

1922 *Imperf.*

No.	Type	Description	Unused	Used
20	A47	1c blue green (R)	20.00	12.50
		Never hinged	32.50	

Engr. *Perf. 13x12½*

Blue Control Number on Back

No.	Type	Description	Unused	Used
23	A46	20c violet	110.00	32.50
		Never hinged	150.00	

A 2c and a 15c exist, values $300 and $7, respectively, for unused, hinged copies, $400 and $10 for never hinged.

Same on Stamps of Spain, 1922-23

1925 *Perf. 13½x13*

No.	Type	Description	Unused	Used
25	A49	5c red vio	4.00	3.00
26	A49	10c bl grn	11.00	3.00
28	A49	20c violet	22.50	9.00
		Nos. 25-28 (3)	37.50	15.00
		Set, never hinged	50.00	

Exists on Spain No. 331, 2c olive green. Value $250 unused hinged and $400 never hinged.

Seville-Barcelona Exposition Issue

CABO JUBY

Stamps of Spain, 1929, Overprinted in Red or Blue

1929 *Perf. 11*

No.	Type	Description	Unused	Used
29	A52	5c rose lake (Bl)	.30	.30
30	A53	10c green (R)	.30	.30
31	A50	15c Prus bl (R)	.30	.30
32	A51	20c pur (R)	.30	.30
33	A50	25c brt rose (Bl)	.30	.30
34	A52	30c blk brn (Bl)	.30	.30
35	A53	40c dk bl (R)	.30	.30
36	A51	50c dp org (Bl)	.60	.60
37	A52	1p bl blk (R)	17.50	17.50
38	A53	4p dp rose (Bl)	22.50	22.50
39	A53	10p brn (Bl)	22.50	22.50
		Nos. 29-39 (11)	65.20	65.20
		Set, never hinged	97.50	

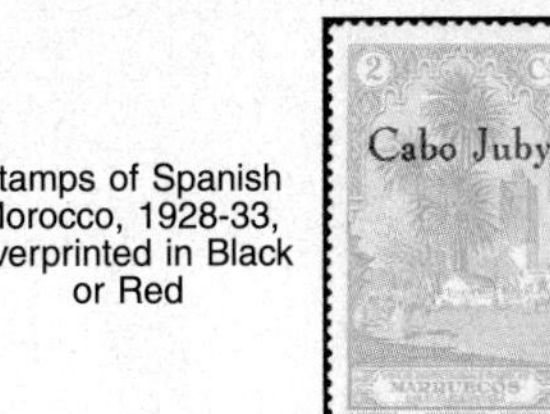

Stamps of Spanish Morocco, 1928-33, Overprinted in Black or Red

1934 *Perf. 14*

No.	Type	Description	Unused	Used
40	A7	1c brt rose (Bk)	.30	.30
41	A2	2c dk vio (R)	3.75	3.75
42	A2	5c dp bl (R)	4.00	4.00
43	A2	10c dk grn (Bk)	8.25	8.25
43A	A10	10c dk grn (R)	2.50	2.50
44	A2	15c org brn (Bk)	20.00	20.00
45	A7	20c sl grn (R)	7.25	7.25
46	A3	25c cop red (Bk)	3.75	3.75
47	A10	30c red brn (Bk)	7.25	7.25
48	A13	40c dp bl (R)	26.00	26.00
49	A13	50c red org (Bk)	50.00	50.00
50	A4	1p yel grn (Bk)	35.00	35.00
51	A5	2.50p red vio (Bk)	75.00	75.00
52	A6	4p ultra (R)	95.00	95.00

No. 43A and 1c, 20c, 30c, 40c, 50c, with control numbers.

Same Overprint in Black on Stamp of Spanish Morocco, 1932

No.	Type	Description	Unused	Used
53	A2	1c car rose ("Ct")	1.60	1.60
		Nos. 40-53 (15)	339.65	339.65
		Set, never hinged	525.00	

Stamps of Spanish Morocco, 1933-35, Overprinted in Black, Blue or Red

1935-36

No.	Type	Description	Unused	Used
54	A8	2c grn (R)	.40	.40
55	A9	5c mag (Bk)	1.60	1.60
55A	A10	10c dk grn (R) ('36)	9.25	9.25
56	A11	15c yel (Bl)	3.50	3.50
57	A12	25c crim (Bk)	37.50	37.50
58	A8	1p sl blk (R)	5.50	5.50
59	A9	2.50p brn (Bl)	22.50	22.50
60	A11	4p yel grn (R)	37.50	37.50
61	A12	5p blk (R)	29.00	29.00
		Nos. 54-61 (9)	146.75	146.75
		Set, never hinged	225.00	

Same Overprint in Black or Red on Stamps of Spanish Morocco, 1935

1935 *Perf. 13½*

No.	Type	Description	Unused	Used
62	A14	25c vio (R)	2.75	2.75
63	A15	30c crim (Bk)	2.75	2.75
64	A14	40c org (Bk)	3.75	3.75
65	A15	50c brt bl (R)	7.00	7.00
66	A14	60c dk bl grn (R)	9.00	9.00
67	A15	2p brn lake (Bk)	47.50	47.50

Same Overprint on Stamps of Spanish Morocco, 1933

Perf. 13½, 14

No.	Type	Description	Unused	Used
68	A7	1c brt rose (Bk)	.20	.20

Perf. 14

No.	Type	Description	Unused	Used
69	A7	20c slate grn (R)	3.50	3.50
		Nos. 62-69 (8)	76.45	76.45
		Set, never hinged	125.00	

Same Overprint on Stamps of Spanish Morocco, 1937

1937 *Perf. 13½*

No.	Type	Description	Unused	Used
70	A21	1c dk bl (Bk)	.30	.30
71	A21	2c org brn (Bk)	.30	.30
72	A21	5c cer (Bk)	.30	.30
73	A21	10c emer (Bk)	.30	.30
74	A21	15c brt bl (Bk)	.30	.30
75	A21	20c red brn (Bk)	.30	.30
76	A21	25c mag (Bk)	.30	.30
77	A21	30c red org (Bk)	.30	.30
78	A21	40c org (Bk)	.85	.85
79	A21	50c ultra (R)	.85	.85
80	A21	60c yel grn (Bk)	.85	.85
81	A21	1p bl vio (Bk)	.85	.85
82	A21	2p Prus bl (Bk)	57.50	57.50
83	A21	2.50p gray blk (R)	57.50	57.50
84	A21	4p dk brn (Bk)	57.50	57.50
85	A22	10p vio blk (R)	57.50	57.50
		Nos. 70-85 (16)	235.80	235.80
		Set, never hinged	350.00	

1st Year of the Revolution.

Same Overprint in Black on Types of Spanish Morocco, 1939

Designs: 5c, Spanish quarter. 10c, Moroccan quarter. 15c, Street scene, Larache. 20c, Tetuan.

1939 Photo. *Perf. 13½*

No.	Type	Description	Unused	Used
86	A25	5c vermilion	.40	.40
87	A25	10c deep green	.40	.40
88	A25	15c brown lake	.40	.40
89	A25	20c bright blue	.40	.40
		Nos. 86-89 (4)	1.60	1.60
		Set, never hinged	1.90	

Same Overprint in Black or Red on Stamps of Spanish Morocco, 1940

1940 *Perf. 11½x11*

No.	Type	Description	Unused	Used
90	A26	1c dk brn (Bk)	.20	.20
91	A27	2c ol grn (R)	.20	.20
92	A28	5c dk bl (R)	.20	.20
93	A29	10c dk red lil (Bk)	.20	.20
94	A30	15c dk grn (R)	.20	.20
95	A31	20c pur (R)	.20	.20
96	A32	25c blk brn (R)	.20	.20
97	A33	30c brt grn (Bk)	.20	.20
98	A34	40c slate grn (R)	.50	.50
99	A35	45c org ver (Bk)	.50	.50
100	A36	50c brn org (Bk)	.55	.55
101	A37	70c saph (R)	1.60	1.60
102	A38	1p ind & brn (Bk)	3.50	3.50
103	A39	2.50p choc & dk grn (Bk)	8.50	8.50
104	A40	5p dk cer & sep (Bk)	8.75	8.75
105	A41	10p dk ol grn & brn org (Bk)	21.00	21.00
		Nos. 90-105 (16)	46.50	46.50
		Set, never hinged	65.00	

Imperfs exist. Value, set $210.

Stamps of Spanish Morocco, 1944, Overprinted in Black or Red

1944, Oct. 2 Unwmk. *Perf. 12½*

No.	Type	Description	Unused	Used
106	A47	1c choc & lt bl	.20	.20
107	A48	2c slate grn & lt grn	.20	.20
108	A49	5c choc & grnsh blk (R)	.20	.20
109	A50	10c brt ultra & red org	.20	.20
110	A51	15c sl grn & lt grn	.20	.20
111	A52	20c dp cl & blk (R)	.20	.20
112	A53	25c lt bl & choc	.20	.20
113	A47	30c yel grn & brt ultra (R)	.20	.20
114	A48	40c choc & red vio	.20	.20
115	A49	50c brt ultra, & red brn	.20	.20
116	A50	75c yel grn & brt ultra (R)	1.00	1.00
117	A51	1p brt ultra & choc	1.00	1.00
118	A52	2.50p blk & brt ultra (R)	2.75	2.75
119	A53	10p sal & gray blk (R)	20.00	20.00
		Nos. 106-119 (14)	26.75	26.75
		Set, never hinged	35.00	

Same Overprint on Stamps of Spanish Morocco, 1946

1946, Mar. *Perf. 10½x10*

No.	Type	Description	Unused	Used
120	A54	1c pur & brn	.20	.20
121	A55	2c dk Prus grn & vio blk (R)	.20	.20
122	A54	10c dp org vio bl	.20	.20
123	A55	15c dk bl & bl grn	.20	.20
124	A54	25c yel grn & ultra	.20	.20
125	A56	40c dk bl & brn (R)	.20	.20
126	A55	45c blk & rose	.30	.30
127	A57	1p dk Prus grn & dp bl	1.25	1.25
128	A58	2.50p dp org & grnsh gray (R)	3.75	3.75
129	A59	10p dk bl & gray (R)	10.50	10.50
		Nos. 120-129 (10)	17.00	17.00
		Set, never hinged	24.00	

Same Overprint in Carmine, Black or Brown on Stamps of Spanish Morocco, 1948

1948, Jan. 1 *Perf. 10, 10x10½*

No.	Type	Description	Unused	Used
130	A64	2c pur & brn	.20	.20
131	A65	5c dp claret & vio	.20	.20
132	A66	15c brt ultra & bl grn (Bk)	.20	.20
133	A67	25c blk & Prus grn	.20	.20
134	A65	35c brt ultra & gray blk	.20	.20
135	A68	50c red & vio (Br)	.20	.20
136	A66	70c dk gray grn & ultra (Bk)	.20	.20
137	A67	90c cer & dk gray grn (Bk)	.20	.20
138	A68	1p brt ultra & vio (Br)	.20	.20
139	A64	2.50p vio brn & sl grn	.70	.70
140	A69	10p blk & dp ultra	2.50	2.50
		Nos. 130-140 (11)	5.00	5.00
		Set, never hinged	8.00	

SEMI-POSTAL STAMPS

Types of Semi-Postal Stamps of Spain, 1926, Overprinted

1926 Unwmk. *Perf. 12½, 13*

No.	Type	Description	Unused	Used
B1	SP1	1c orange	11.00	11.00
B2	SP2	2c rose	11.00	11.00
B3	SP3	5c blk brn	3.00	3.00
B4	SP4	10c dk grn	1.40	1.40
B5	SP1	15c dk vio	.95	.95
B6	SP4	20c vio brn	.95	.95
B7	SP5	25c dp car	.95	.95
B8	SP1	30c ol grn	.95	.95
B9	SP3	40c ultra	.30	.30
B10	SP2	50c red brn	.30	.30
B11	SP4	1p vermilion	.30	.30
B12	SP3	4p bister	1.25	1.25
B13	SP5	10p lt vio	3.00	3.00
		Nos. B1-B13 (13)	35.35	35.35
		Set, never hinged	57.50	

Nos. B12-B13 surcharged "Alfonso XIII" and new value are listed as Spain Nos. B68-B69. See Spain No. B6a.

AIR POST STAMPS

Spanish Morocco, Nos. C1 to C10 Overprinted "CABO JUBY" as on #54-61

1938, June 1 Unwmk. *Perf. 13½*

No.	Type	Description	Unused	Used
C1	AP1	5c brown	.20	.20
C2	AP1	10c brt grn	.20	.20
C3	AP1	25c crimson	.20	.20
C4	AP1	40c light blue	1.75	1.75
C5	AP2	50c brt mag	.20	.20
C6	AP2	75c dk bl	.20	.20
C7	AP1	1p sepia	.20	.20
C8	AP1	1.50p dp vio	1.10	1.10
C9	AP1	2p dp red brn	2.40	2.40
C10	AP1	3p brn blk	6.25	6.25
		Nos. C1-C10 (10)	12.70	12.70
		Set, never hinged	20.00	

Strait of Gibraltar — AP3

Designs: 5c, Ketama landscape. 10c, Mosque, Tangier. 15c, Velez. 90c, Sanjurjo.

1942, Apr. 1 Photo. *Perf. 12½*

No.	Type	Description	Unused	Used
C11	AP3	5c deep blue	.20	.20
C12	AP3	10c org brn	.20	.20
C13	AP3	15c grnsh blk	.20	.20

C14 AP3 90c dk rose .45 .45
C15 AP3 5p black 1.60 1.60
Nos. C11-C15 (5) 2.65 2.65

SPECIAL DELIVERY STAMPS

Special Delivery Stamp of Spain Ovptd. "CABO JUBY" as on #7-28

1919 **Unwmk.** ***Perf. 14***
E1 SD1 20c red (Bk) 1.40 1.40
b. Double overprint 25.00 12.50

Spanish Morocco #E4 Overprinted "CABO JUBY" as on #40-52 in Red

1934
E2 SD2 20c black 9.25 9.25

Spanish Morocco No. E5 Overprinted "CABO JUBY" as on Nos. 54-61

1935
E3 SD3 20c vermilion 2.75 2.75

Same Ovpt. on Spanish Morocco #E6

1937 ***Perf. 13½***
E4 SD4 20c bright carmine 1.00 1.00

1st Year of the Revolution.

Same Ovpt. on Spanish Morocco #E8

1940 ***Perf. 11½x11***
E5 SD5 25c scarlet .35 .35

SEMI-POSTAL SPECIAL DELIVERY STAMP

Type of Semi-Postal Special Delivery Stamp of Spain, 1926, Overprinted "CABO-JUBY" as on Nos. B1-B13

1926 **Unwmk.** ***Perf. 12½, 13***
EB1 SPSD1 20c ultra & black 3.25 3.25

CAPE OF GOOD HOPE

'kāp əv 'gud 'hōp

LOCATION — In the extreme southern part of South Africa
GOVT. — Former British Colony
AREA — 276,995 sq mi. (1911)
POP. — 2,564,965 (1911)
CAPITAL — Cape Town

Cape of Good Hope joined with Natal, the Transvaal and the Orange River Colony in 1910, forming the Union of South Africa.

12 Pence = 1 Shilling

Watermarks

Wmk. 15 — Anchor

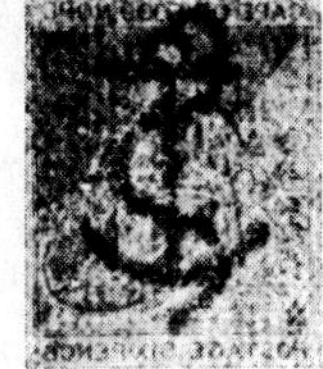
Wmk. 16 — Anchor

"Hope" Seated A1

Printed by Perkins, Bacon & Co.
Wmk. 15

1853, Sept. 1 Engr. *Imperf.*
Bluish Paper

1 A1 1p brick red, bluish paper 3,400. 225.
a. 1p pale brick red, deeply blued paper 4,000. 340.
b. 1p deep brick red, deeply blued paper 5,650. 370.
2 A1 4p deep blue, lightly blued paper 1,450. 125.
a. 4p deep blue, deeply blued paper 2,250. 180.
b. 4p blue, bluish paper 1,575. 165.

Counterfeits exist.

1855-58
White Paper

3 A1 1p rose ('57) 500. 225.
a. 1p dull red 725. 280.
b. 1p brick red 5,650. 1,000.
4 A1 4p blue 475. 50.
a. Half used as 3p on cover 40,000.
b. 4p deep blue 675. 50.
5 A1 6p pale lilac ('58) 850. 225.00
a. 6p rose lilac 1,900. 340.
b. 6p grayish lilac on bluish paper 4,800. 500.00
c. 6p slate purple on bluish paper 4,000. 1,125.
d. Half used as 3p on cover —
6 Al 1sh yellow grn ('58) 2,800. 200.
a. 1sh dark green 280. 550.
b. Half used as 6p on cover —

Nos. 3-6 are known rouletted unofficially.
Counterfeits exist.
No. 4 was reproduced by the collotype process in an unwatermarked souvenir sheet distributed at the London Intl. Stamp Exhib. 1950.

A2

Printed by Saul Solomon & Co.

1861 Laid Paper Unwmk. Typo.

7 A2 1p vermilion 15,750. 2,550.
a. 1p carmine 27,000. 3,400.
b. 1p red 40,000. 4,800.
c. 1p milky blue (error) 31,500.
d. 1p pale blue (error) 34,000.
9 A2 4p milky blue 11,500. 1,800.
a. 4p pale blue 12,500. 2,150.
b. 4p blue 17,000. 3,400.
c. 4p dark blue 110,000. 5,000.
d. Right corner retouched 6,250.
f. 4p vermilion (error) 170,000. 65,000.
g. 4p carmine (error) 110,000.

Nos. 7 and 9 are usually called Wood Blocks. The plates were made locally and composed of clichés mounted on wood. The errors were caused by a cliché of each value being mounted in the plate of the other value.

In 1883 plate proofs of both values on white paper, usually called "reprints," were made. The 1p is in dull orange red; the 4p in dark blue. These are known canceled, as a few were misused as stamps. The proofs do not include the errors.

Counterfeits exist.

Printed by De La Rue & Co.

1863-64 Wmk. 15 Engr.

12 A1 1p dark carmine 160.00 260.00
a. 1p brown red 425.00 280.00
b. 1p deep brown red 425.00 260.00
13 A1 4p dark blue 160.00 57.50
a. 4p slate blue 2,250. 575.00
14 A1 6p purple 200.00 500.00
15 A1 1sh emerald 425.00 500.00
a. 1sh pale emerald 1,150. —

Nos. 12-15 can be distinguished from Nos. 3-6 not only by colors but because Nos. 12-15 often appear in a granular ink or with the background lightly printed in whole or part.

No. 12a, Wmk. 1, is believed to be a proof.
Counterfeits exist.

"Hope" and Symbols of Colony
A3 A6

Frame Line Around Stamp

1864-65 Typo. Wmk. 1 *Perf. 14*

16 A3 1p rose ('65) 90.00 25.00
17 A3 4p blue ('65) 115.00 3.00
a. 4p pale blue 115.00 3.00
b. 4p dull ultramarine 280.00 62.50
c. 4p deep blue ('72) 170.00 4.00
18 A3 6p bright violet 150.00 1.75
a. 6p dull violet 225.00 8.00
b. 6p pale lilac 125.00 24.00
19 A3 1sh yellow green 125.00 3.50
a. 1sh blue green 135.00 4.75
Nos. 16-19 (4) 480.00 33.25

Imperf. stamps are believed to be proofs.
For surcharges see Nos. 20-21, N3.
For types A3 and A6 with manuscript surcharge of 1d or overprints "G. W." or "G," see Griqualand West listings.

Stamps of 1864 Surcharged in Red or Black:

a

b

1868-74 Red Surcharge

20 A3(a) 4p on 6p 260.00 18.00
a. "Peuce" for "Pence" 2,000. 900.00
b. "Fonr" for "Four" 800.00
21 A3(b) 1p on 6p ('74) 550.00 100.00
a. "E" of PENNY omitted 1,150.

Space between words and bars varies from 12½-16mm on #20, and 16½-18mm on #21.

1876 Black Surcharge

22 A3 (b) 1p on 1sh green 80.00 50.00

Without Frame Line Around Stamp

1871-81 *Perf. 14*

23 A6 ½p gray black ('75) 18.00 8.00
24 A6 1p rose ('72) 33.00 .70
25 A6 3p lilac rose ('80) 210.00 26.00
26 A6 3p claret ('81) 135.00 3.00
27 A6 4p blue ('76) 115.00 .85
a. 4p ultramarine 225.00 57.50
28 A6 5sh orange 400.00 18.00
Nos. 23-28 (6) 911.00 56.55

For surcharges see Nos. 29-32, 39, 55.

No. 27 Surcharged in Red

1879

29 A6 3p on 4p blue 115.00 2.25
a. "THE.EE" 2,150. 350.00
b. "PENCB" 1,850. 275.00
c. Double surcharge 8,750. 3,150.
d. As "a," double surcharge — —

Type of 1871 Surcharged in Black THREEPENCE

1880

30 A6 3p on 4p lilac rose 80.00 2.00

No. 25 Surcharged in Black

e

f

31 A6(e) 3p on 3p lil rose 210.00 7.00
a. Inverted surcharge 8,000. 1,050.
32 A6(f) 3p on 3p lil rose 87.50 1.75
a. Inverted surcharge 925.00 45.00

1882-83 Wmk. 2

33 A6 ½p gray black 22.00 2.00
34 A6 1p rose 55.00 1.15
35 A6 2p bister 92.50 .60
36 A6 3p claret 7.50 1.15
37 A3 6p bright violet 105.00 .90
38 A6 5sh orange ('83) 875.00 210.00

For overprint see Rhodesia No. 49.

Nos. 26 and 36 Surcharged in Black

1882 Wmk. 1

39 A6 ½p on 3p claret 3,150. 150.00
a. Hyphen omitted 3,750.

Wmk. 2

40 A6 ½p on 3p claret 29.00 3.75
a. "ENNY" 2,300. 800.00
b. "PENN" 1,150. 700.00
c. Hyphen omitted 750.00 400.00

1884-98 Wmk. 16

41 A6 ½p gray black ('86) 4.50 .20
42 A6 ½p yel grn ('96) 1.75 .55
43 A6 1p rose ('85) 4.50 .20
44 A6 2p bister 7.00 .20
45 A6 2p choc brown ('97) 2.35 .45
46 A6 3p red violet ('98) 8.00 1.00
47 A6 4p blue ('90) 11.00 .55
48 A6 4p pale ol grn ('97) 4.75 1.60
49 A3 6p violet 9.75 .25
50 A3 1sh dull bluish green ('89) 92.50 .45
51 A6 1sh blue grn ('94) 70.00 4.25
52 A6 1sh yel buff ('96) 9.25 1.20
53 A6 5sh orange ('87) 97.50 5.50
54 A6 5sh brown org ('96) 75.00 4.00
Nos. 41-54 (14) 397.85 20.40

For surcharges see Nos. 58, 162, 165-166.
For overprints see Rhodesia Nos. 43, 45-48.

Type of 1871 Surcharged in Black

1891, Mar.

55 A6 2½p on 3p dp mag 3.75 .25
a. "1" of "½" has straight serif 57.50 37.50

Hope Seated — A13

1892-96

56 A13 2½p sage green 9.25 .20
57 A13 2½p ultra ('96) 4.75 .20

For surcharge see No. N4. For overprint see Orange River Colony No. 55.

No. 44 Surcharged in Black

1893, Mar.

58 A6 1p on 2p bister 3.00 .55
a. Double surcharge 450.00
b. No period after "PENNY" 57.50 13.00

Hope Standing A15

Table Mountain and Bay; Coat of Arms A16

1893-1902

59 A15 ½p green ('98) 2.30 .20
60 A15 1p rose 1.45 .20
61 A15 3p red violet ('02) 4.50 1.75
Nos. 59-61 (3) 8.25 2.15

For surcharges see Nos. 163-164, N2. For overprints see Orange River Colony #54, 56, Rhodesia #44, Transvaal #236-236A.

1900, Jan.

62 A16 1p carmine rose 2.90 .25

King Edward VII — A17

Various frames.

1902-04 Wmk. 16

63 A17 ½p emerald 2.60 .20
64 A17 1p car rose 2.35 .20
65 A17 2p brown ('04) 11.00 .95
66 A17 2½p ultra ('04) 3.25 7.50
67 A17 3p red violet ('03) 8.00 .90
68 A17 4p ol green ('03) 9.25 .75
69 A17 6p violet ('03) 17.50 .60
70 A17 1sh bister 14.00 .95
71 A17 5sh brown org ('03) 85.00 15.00
Nos. 63-71 (9) 152.95 27.05

Imperf. stamps are proofs.

ISSUED IN MAFEKING

Excellent forgeries of Nos. 162-180 are known.

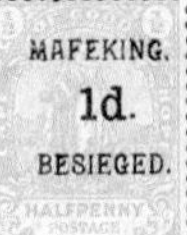

Stamps of Cape of Good Hope Surcharged

1900, Mar. 24

162 A6 1p on ½p grn 210. 75.00
163 A15 1p on ½p grn 260. 85.00
164 A15 3p on 1p rose 230. 57.50
165 A6 6p on 3p red vio 30,000. 290.00
166 A6 1sh on 4p pale ol green 7,000. 375.00

Stamps of Bechuanaland Protectorate Surcharged

1900 **Wmk. 30**
167 A54 1p on ½p ver 210. 70.00
a. Inverted surcharge 4,900.
168 A40 3p on 1p lilac 975. 105.00
a. Double surcharge 18,500.
169 A56 6p on 2p grn & car 2,000. 87.50
170 A58 6p on 3p vio, *yel* 5,500. 325.00
a. Inverted surcharge 25,000.
b. Double surcharge

The lettering of "Mafeking Besieged" shows varying breaks in various letters, and may have either a period or no punctuation after "Mafeking."

On Stamps of Bechuanaland
Wmk. 29
171 A1 6p on 3p violet & black 425. 75.00
Wmk. 30
172 A59 1sh on 4p brn & grn 1,400. 92.50
a. Double surch., one inverted 18,500.
b. Triple surcharge 18,500.
c. Inverted surcharge —
d. Double surcharge 18,500.

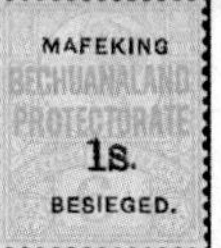

Stamps of Bechuanaland Protectorate Surcharged

173 A40 3p on 1p lilac 1,050. 85.
a. Double surcharge 7,500.
174 A56 6p on 2p grn & car 1,250. 85.
175 A62 1sh on 6p vio, *rose* 5,000. 105.

On Stamps of Bechuanaland
176 A62 1sh on 6p vio, *rose* 16,000. 800.
177 A65 2sh on 1sh green 8,500. 425.

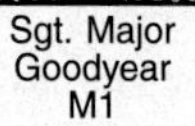

Sgt. Major Goodyear M1

Gen. Robert S. S. Baden-Powell M2

Wmk. OCEANA FINE
Photographic Print
1900, Apr. ***Perf. 12***
Laid Paper
178 M1 1p blue, *blue* 925.00 325.00
179 M2 3p blue, *blue,* 18½mm wide 1,400. 450.00
a. Horiz. pair, imperf btwn. 57,500.
b. Double impression 20,000.
c. Reversed design 57,500. 42,500.
180 M2 3p blue, *blue,* 21mm wide 8,100. 1,500.

The color of the paper varies from pale to deep blue.
OCEANA FINE is a sheet watermark and does not appear on every stamp.
Imperfs of No. 178 are proofs.
There is one used pair of No. 179a privately owned. There are 2 unused and 6 used examples of No. 179c privately owned.
Issued: #179, Apr. 6; #178, 180, Apr. 10.

ISSUED IN VRYBURG

Under Boer Occupation

Cape of Good Hope Stamps of 1884-96 Surcharged

Two Types of Surcharge:
Type I — Surcharge 10mm high. Space between lines 5½mm.
Type II — Surcharge 12mm high. Space between lines 7½mm.

1899, Nov. **Wmk. 16** ***Perf. 14***
N1 A6 ½p on ½p emer (I) 230. 92.50
a. Type II 1,950. 800.
N2 A15 1p on 1p rose (I) 260. 115.
a. Double surcharge
b. Type II 2,200. 925.
N3 A3 2p on 6p vio (II) 2,500. 575.
N4 A13 2½p on 2½p ultra (I) 2,000. 500.
a. Type II 11,500. 5,000.

"Z.A.R." stands for Zuid Afrikaansche Republiek (South African Republic).

Under British Occupation

Transvaal Stamps of 1895-96 Handstamped

1900 **Unwmk.** ***Perf. 12½***
N5 A13 ½p green 2,300.
N6 A13 1p rose & grn 10,000. 4,600.
N7 A13 2p brown & grn
N8 A13 2½p ultra & grn

CAPE VERDE

ˈkāp ˈvərd

LOCATION — A group of 10 islands and five islets in the Atlantic Ocean, about 500 miles due west of Senegal.
GOVT. — Republic
AREA — 1,557 sq. mi.
POP. — 405,748 (1999 est.)
CAPITAL — Praia

The Portuguese territory of Cape Verde became independent on July 5, 1975.

1000 Reis = 1 Milreis
100 Centavos = 1 Escudo (1913)

Catalogue values for unused stamps in this country are for Never Hinged items, beginning with Scott 268 in the regular postage section, Scott J31 in the postage due section, and Scott RA6 in the postal tax section.

Crown of Portugal — A1

King Luiz — A2

Perf. 12½, 13½
1877 **Unwmk.** **Typo.**
1 A1 5r black 2.75 1.25
2 A1 10r yellow 27.50 7.00
3 A1 20r bister 1.75 1.00
4 A1 25r rose 1.40 .85
5 A1 40r blue 67.50 20.00
b. Cliche of Mozambique in Cape Verde plate, in pair with #5 1,100. 1,100.
6 A1 50r green 67.50 20.00
7 A1 100r lilac 5.50 1.90
8 A1 200r orange 3.50 2.25
9 A1 300r brown 4.00 2.75
Nos. 1-9 (9) 181.40 57.00

For expanded treatment of Nos. 1-9, see the *Scott Classic Catalogue.*

1881-85
10 A1 10r green 1.75 1.25
11 A1 20r carmine ('85) 3.50 2.00
12 A1 25r violet ('85) 2.75 1.60
13 A1 40r yellow buff 1.75 1.00
a. Imperf. 1.00
b. Cliche of Mozambique in Cape Verde plate, in pair with #13 70.00 62.50
c. As "b," imperf. 35.00
14 A1 50r blue 4.50 2.50
Nos. 10-14 (5) 14.25 8.35

Reprints of the 1877-85 issues are on smooth white chalky paper, ungummed, and on thin white paper with shiny white gum. They are perf 13½.
For expanded treatment of Nos. 10-14, see the *Scott Classic Catalogue.*

1886 **Embossed** ***Perf. 12½, 13½***
Chalk-Surfaced Paper
15 A2 5r black 3.75 1.60
16 A2 10r green 4.00 1.75
17 A2 20r carmine 5.00 2.75
18 A2 25r violet 4.50 3.25
19 A2 40r chocolate 6.50 2.00
20 A2 50r blue 5.50 2.00
21 A2 100r yel brown 6.50 2.75
22 A2 200r gray lilac 11.00 6.00
23 A2 300r orange 17.00 8.75
Nos. 15-23 (9) 62.75 30.85

The 25r, 50r and 100r have been reprinted in aniline colors with clean-cut Perf. 13½.
For expanded treatment of Nos. 15-19, see the *Scott Classic Catalogue.*
For surcharges see Nos. 59-67, 184-187.

A3

King Carlos — A4

1894-95 **Typo.** ***Perf. 11½, 12½, 13½***
24 A3 5r orange .90 .75
25 A3 10r redsh violet .90 .75
26 A3 15r chocolate 2.25 1.50
a. Perf. 12½ 90.00 67.50
27 A3 20r lavender 2.25 1.50
28 A3 25r dp green 1.90 1.40
a. Perf. 12½ 3.50 2.75
29 A3 50r lt blue 1.90 1.40
a. Perf. 13½ 8.00 3.00
30 A3 75r carmine ('95) 6.50 3.50
a. Perf. 13½ 17.50 10.50
31 A3 80r yel grn ('95) 7.75 4.50
a. Perf. 13½ 25.00 19.00
32 A3 100r brn, *buff* ('95) 5.50 2.75
a. Perf. 12½ 40.00 18.00
33 A3 150r car, *rose* ('95) 18.00 15.00
a. Perf. 12½ 110.00 90.00
b. Perf. 11½ 45.00 30.00
34 A3 200r dk blue, *lt blue* ('95) 18.00 15.00
a. Perf. 12½ 90.00 70.00
35 A3 300r dk blue, *sal* ('95) 20.00 9.50
Nos. 24-35 (12) 85.85 57.55

For surcharges see Nos. 68-78, 137, 189-193, 201-205.

1898-1903 ***Perf. 11½***
Name and Value in Black except 500r
36 A4 2½r gray .25 .20
37 A4 5r orange .30 .20
38 A4 10r lt green .40 .20
39 A4 15r brown 3.25 1.10
40 A4 15r gray grn ('03) 1.00 .75
41 A4 20r gray violet 1.00 .50
42 A4 25r sea green 2.00 .70
a. Perf. 12½ 35.00 20.00
43 A4 25r carmine ('03) .60 .30
44 A4 50r dark blue 2.25 .80
45 A4 50r brown ('03) 2.00 1.40
46 A4 65r slate blue ('03) 30.00 35.00
47 A4 75r rose 4.75 2.00
48 A4 75r lilac ('03) 1.75 1.25
49 A4 80r violet 4.75 2.25
50 A4 100r dk blue, *blue* 1.75 1.00
51 A4 115r org brn, *pink* ('03) 12.00 13.50
52 A4 130r brn, *straw* ('03) 12.00 13.50
53 A4 150r brown, *straw* 8.00 6.75
54 A4 200r red vio, *pnksh* 2.50 1.60
55 A4 300r dk blue, *rose* 8.00 3.00
56 A4 400r dull blue, *straw* ('03) 10.00 6.00
57 A4 500r blk & red, *blue* ('01) 8.00 3.00
58 A4 700r vio, *yelsh* ('01) 16.00 10.00
Nos. 36-58 (23) 132.55 105.00

For overprints and surcharges see Nos. 80-99, 139, 200.

Regular Issues Surcharged in Red or Black

Two spacing types of surcharge. See note above Angola No. 61.

On Issue of 1886
1902, Dec. 1 ***Perf. 12½, 13½***
59 A2 65r on 5r black (R) 4.00 2.50
60 A2 65r on 200r gray lilac 4.00 2.50
61 A2 65r on 300r orange 4.00 2.50
62 A2 115r on 10r green 4.00 2.50
63 A2 115r on 20r rose 4.00 2.50
a. Perf. 13½ 27.50 19.00
64 A2 130r on 50r blue 4.00 2.50
65 A2 130r on 100r brown 4.00 2.50
66 A2 400r on 25r violet 2.00 1.50
67 A2 400r on 40r choc 4.00 2.25
a. Perf. 13½ 27.50 22.50

On Issue of 1894
Perf. 11½, 12½, 13½
68 A3 65r on 10r red violet 4.75 2.75
69 A3 65r on 20r lavender 4.50 2.50
70 A3 65r on 100r brown, *buff* 5.00 3.00
a. Perf 12½ 15.00 13.50
71 A3 115r on 5r orange 2.75 1.90
a. Inverted surcharge 45.00 45.00
72 A3 115r on 25r blue grn 2.75 1.75
a. Perf. 11½ 45.00 25.00
73 A3 115r on 150r car, *rose* 4.75 3.75
a. Perf. 13½ 20.00 12.00
74 A3 130r on 75r car 2.75 2.00
a. Perf. 13½ 45.00 42.50
75 A3 130r on 80r yel grn 2.25 1.75
76 A3 130r on 200r dk blue, *blue* 3.00 1.75
77 A3 400r on 50r lt blue 3.25 2.25
a. Inverted surcharge 65.00 55.00
b. Perf. 13½ 55.00 55.00
78 A3 400r on 300r dk blue, *sal* 1.75 1.10

On Newspaper Stamp of 1893
79 N1 400r on 2½r brown 1.25 1.10
a. Inverted surcharge 27.50
b. Perf. 12½ 45.00 42.50
Nos. 59-79 (21) 72.75 46.85

Reprints of Nos. 59, 66, 67, and 77 have shiny white gum and clean-cut perforation 13½.
For overprint and surcharges see #137, 205-206.

Overprinted in Black On Nos. 39, 42, 44, 47

1902-03 ***Perf. 11½***
80 A4 15r brown 1.50 .80
81 A4 25r sea green 1.50 .80
82 A4 50r blue ('03) 1.75 1.00
83 A4 75r rose ('03) 2.25 1.40
a. Inverted overprint 42.50 42.50
Nos. 80-83 (4) 7.00 4.00

For overprint see No. 139.

No. 46 Surcharged in Black

1905, July 1
84 A4 50r on 65r slate blue 2.50 1.75

Stamps of 1898-1903 Overprinted in Carmine or Green

1911, Aug. 20
85 A4 2½r gray .20 .20
86 A4 5r orange .20 .20
87 A4 10r lt green .60 .50
88 A4 15r gray green .35 .20
89 A4 20r gray violet .65 .65
90 A4 25r carmine (G) .65 .30
91 A4 50r brown 4.00 2.75
92 A4 75r red lilac .85 .50
93 A4 100r dk blue, *blue* .85 .60
94 A4 115r org brn, *pink* .45 1.25
95 A4 130r brown, *straw* .45 1.25
96 A4 200r red vio, *pnksh* 3.25 3.25
97 A4 400r dull bl, *straw* 1.25 1.25
98 A4 500r blk & red, *bl* 1.50 1.00
99 A4 700r violet, *straw* 1.50 1.10
Nos. 85-99 (15) 16.75 15.00

King Manuel II — A5

Overprinted in Carmine or Green

1912 *Perf. 11½x12*

100 A5 2½r violet .20 *1.25*
101 A5 5r black .20 .20
102 A5 10r gray grn .20 .20
103 A5 20r carmine (G) 1.25 .70
104 A5 25r vio brown .25 .20
105 A5 50r dk blue 2.00 1.60
106 A5 75r bister brn .45 .35
107 A5 100r brown, *lt grn* .45 .35
108 A5 200r dk green, *sal* .70 .60
109 A5 300r black, *azure* .70 .60

Perf. 14½x15

110 A5 400r black & blue 2.00 1.60
111 A5 500r ol grn & vio brn 2.00 1.60
Nos. 100-111 (12) 10.40 9.25

Common Design Types pictured following the introduction.

Vasco da Gama Issue of Various Portuguese Colonies

Common Design Types CD20-CD27 Surcharged

On Stamps of Macao

1913, Feb. 13 *Perf. 12½ to 16*

112 CD20 ¼c on ½a blue grn .85 .75
113 CD21 ½c on 1a red .85 .75
114 CD22 1c on 2a red violet .85 .75
115 CD23 2½c on 4a yel grn .85 .75
116 CD24 5c on 8a dk blue 4.00 3.00
117 CD25 7½c on 12a vio brn 3.25 2.00
118 CD26 10c on 16a bister brn 1.40 1.25
119 CD27 15c on 24a bister 3.50 2.50
Nos. 112-119 (8) 15.55 11.75

On Stamps of Portuguese Africa
Perf. 14 to 15

120 CD20 ¼c on 2½r bl grn .65 .55
121 CD21 ½c on 5r red .65 .55
122 CD22 1c on 10r red vio .65 .55
123 CD23 2½c on 25r yel grn .65 .55
124 CD24 5c on 50r dk blue 1.25 .90
125 CD25 7½c on 75r vio brn 1.90 1.60
126 CD26 10c on 100r bis brn 1.25 1.10
127 CD27 15c on 150r bister 1.75 1.50
Nos. 120-127 (8) 8.75 7.30

On Stamps of Timor

128 CD20 ¼c on ½a bl grn .85 .75
129 CD21 ½c on 1a red .85 .75
130 CD22 1c on 2a red vio .85 .75
131 CD23 2½c on 4a yel grn .85 .75
132 CD24 5c on 8a dk blue 4.00 3.00
133 CD25 7½c On 12a vio brn 3.50 2.50
134 CD26 10c on 16a bis brn 1.40 1.25
135 CD27 15c on 24a bister 2.75 1.50
Nos. 128-135 (8) 15.05 11.25
Nos. 112-135 (24) 39.35 30.30

For surcharges see Nos. 197-198.

No. 75 Overprinted in Red

1913 *Perf. 11½, 12½, 13½*

137 A3 130r on 80r yel grn 3.25 2.50

Nos. 73 and 76 overprinted but not issued. Values, $10, $12.

Same Overprint on No. 83 in Green

1914 *Perf. 12*

139 A4 75r rose 3.25 2.50
a. "PROVISORIO" double (G and R) 45.00 40.00

Ceres — A6

Perf. 11½, 12x11½, 15x14

1914-26 **Typo.**

Name and Value in Black

144 A6 ¼c olive brn .20 .20
a. Imperf.
145 A6 ½c black .20 .20
146 A6 1c blue grn .85 .75
147 A6 1c yel grn ('22) .20 .20
148 A6 1½c lilac brown .20 .20
149 A6 2c carmine .20 .20
150 A6 2c gray ('26) .25 *5.00*
151 A6 2½c lt violet .20 .20
152 A6 3c org ('22) .30 .25
153 A6 4c rose ('22) .20 *1.60*
154 A6 4½c gray ('22) .20 *5.00*
155 A6 5c deep blue .75 .45
156 A6 5c brt blue ('22) .20 .20
157 A6 6c lilac ('22) .20 *2.75*
158 A6 7c ultra ('22) .20 *2.75*
159 A6 7½c yel brn .20 *1.00*
160 A6 8c slate .40 .30
161 A6 10c orange brn .20 .20
162 A6 12c blue grn ('22) .35 .25
163 A6 15c plum 4.00 3.00
164 A6 15c brn rose ('22) .25 .20
165 A6 20c yel grn .20 .20
166 A6 24c ultra ('26) 1.50 *1.40*
167 A6 25c choc ('26) 1.50 1.40
168 A6 30c brown, *grn* 3.00 3.00
169 A6 30c gray grn ('22) .75 .25
170 A6 40c brown, *pink* 3.00 3.00
171 A6 40c turq blue ('22) 1.75 .25
172 A6 50c orange, *sal* 3.00 3.00
173 A6 50c violet ('26) 1.75 .30
174 A6 60c dk blue ('22) 1.75 .45
175 A6 60c rose ('26) 1.75 .45
176 A6 80c brt rose ('22) 2.00 1.10
177 A6 1e green, *blue* 3.00 3.00
178 A6 1e rose ('22) 7.00 2.25
179 A6 1e dp blue ('26) 9.00 1.50
180 A6 2e dk violet ('22) 10.00 4.00
181 A6 5e buff ('26) 25.00 12.00
182 A6 10e pink ('26) 50.00 40.00
183 A6 20e pale turq ('26) 75.00 50.00
Nos. 144-183 (40) 210.70 152.45

For surcharge see No. 214.

Provisional Issue of 1902 Overprinted in Carmine

1915 *Perf. 11½, 12½, 13½*

184 A2 115r on 10r green 2.50 2.00
a. Perf. 13½ 15.00 15.00
185 A2 115r on 20r rose 2.00 1.25
a. Perf. 13½ 15.00 15.00
186 A2 130r on 50r blue 2.00 1.10
187 A2 130r on 100r brown 1.50 .70
188 A3 115r on 5r orange 1.25 .40
a. Inverted overprint 30.00
189 A3 115r on 25r blue grn 1.50 .65
a. Perf. 11½ 15.00 15.00
190 A3 115r on 150r car, *rose* 1.00 .40
191 A3 130r on 75r carmine 2.00 .90
192 A3 130r on 80r yel grn 1.50 .70
a. Inverted overprint 30.00
193 A3 130r on 200r bl, *bl* 2.00 .90
a. Perf. 12½ 40.00 32.50
Nos. 184-193 (10) 17.25 9.00

War Tax Stamps of Portuguese Africa Surcharged

1921, Feb. 3 *Perf. 15x14, 11½*

194 WT1 ¼c on 1c green .25 .25
195 WT1 ½c on 1c green .40 .30
a. "1/2" instead of "½" as shown 10.00 10.00
196 WT1 1c green .40 .30

Nos. 127 and 126 Surcharged

Perf. 14 to 15

197 CD27 2c on 15c on 150r 1.00 1.00
198 CD26 4c on 10c on 100r 1.25 1.00
a. On No. 118 (error) 150.00 150.00

The 4c surcharge also exists on No. 134. Value, $500.

No. 50 Surcharged

Perf. 12

200 A4 6c on 100r dk bl, *bl* 1.25 1.25
a. No accent on "U" of surcharge 12.50 8.00
Nos. 194-200 (6) 4.55 4.10

No. 200 has an accent on the "U" of the surcharge.

Stamps of 1913-15 Surcharged

1922, Apr. *Perf. 11½, 12½, 13½*

On No. 137

201 A3 4c on 130r on 80r 1.25 1.25

On Nos. 191-193

202 A3 4c on 130r on 75r 1.60 1.60
203 A3 4c on 130r on 80r 1.25 1.25
204 A3 4c on 130r on 200r .90 .60
a. Perf. 12½ 15.00 15.00
Nos. 201-204 (4) 5.00 4.70

Surcharge of Nos. 201-204 with smaller $ occurs once in sheet of 28. Value eight times normal.

Nos. 78-79 Surcharged

1925 *Perf. 13½, 11½*

205 A3 40c on 400r on 300r .60 .55
206 N1 40c on 400r on 2½r .40 .45

No. 176 Surcharged

1931, Nov. *Perf. 12x11½*

214 A6 70c on 80c brt rose 2.75 1.40

Ceres — A7

1934, May 1 **Wmk. 232**

215 A7 1c bister .20 *.20*
216 A7 5c olive brown .20 .20
217 A7 10c violet .20 .20
218 A7 15c black .20 .20
219 A7 20c gray .20 .20
220 A7 30c dk green .20 .20
221 A7 40c red org .20 .20
222 A7 45c brt blue 1.40 .60
223 A7 50c brown .65 .45
224 A7 60c olive grn .65 .45
225 A7 70c brown org .65 .45
226 A7 80c emerald .65 .45
227 A7 85c deep rose 3.00 1.90
228 A7 1e maroon 2.10 .35
229 A7 1.40e dk blue 2.75 2.40
230 A7 2e dk violet 3.25 1.90
231 A7 5e apple green 14.50 3.75
232 A7 10e olive bister 24.00 14.00
233 A7 20e orange 45.00 18.00
Nos. 215-233 (19) 100.00 46.10

For surcharge see No. 256.

Vasco da Gama Issue
Common Design Types

1938 **Unwmk.** *Perf. 13½x13*

Name and Value in Black

234 CD34 1c gray green .20 *.20*
235 CD34 5c orange brn .20 *.20*
236 CD34 10c dk carmine .20 .20
237 CD34 15c dk vio brn .70 .65
238 CD34 20c slate .35 .20
239 CD35 30c rose vio .35 .20
240 CD35 35c brt green .35 .20
241 CD35 40c brown .35 .20
242 CD35 50c brt red vio .35 .20
243 CD36 60c gray blk .35 .20
244 CD36 70c brown vio .35 .20
245 CD36 80c orange .30 .20
246 CD36 1e red .50 .20
247 CD37 1.75e blue 1.25 .55
248 CD37 2e dk blue grn 2.50 1.50
249 CD37 5e ol grn 5.75 1.50
250 CD38 10e blue vio 9.25 2.00
251 CD38 20e red brown 30.00 4.00
Nos. 234-251 (18) 53.30 12.60

For surcharges see #255, 271-276, 288-292.

Outline Map of Africa — A8

1939, June 23 **Litho.** *Perf. 11½x12*

252 A8 80c vio, *pale rose* 4.00 2.75
253 A8 1.75e blue, *pale bl* 32.50 25.00
254 A8 20e brown, *buff* 70.00 22.50
Nos. 252-254 (3) 106.50 50.25

Visit of the President of Portugal in 1939.

Nos. 239 and 221 Surcharged with New Value and Bars in Black

1948 **Unwmk.** *Perf. 13½x13*

255 CD35 10c on 30c rose violet 1.25 *.70*

Perf. 12x11½
Wmk. 232

256 A7 25c on 40c red orange 1.25 *.70*

Machado Pt., Sao Vicente — A9

Brava Creek, Sao Nicoláo — A10

Designs: 10c, Ribeira Grande. 1e, Harbor, Sao Vicente. 1.75e, Mindelo, distant view. 2e, Joao de Evora Beach. 5e, Mindelo. 10e, Volcano, Fire Island. 20e, Mt. Paul.

Perf. 14½

1948, Oct. 1 **Litho.** **Unwmk.**

257 A9 5c vio brn & bis .25 .20
258 A9 10c ol grn & pale grn .25 .20
259 A10 50c mag & lil rose .45 .20
260 A10 1e brn vio & rose lil 1.60 .70
261 A10 1.75e ultra & grnsh bl 2.00 1.10
262 A10 2e dk brn & buff 4.50 1.25
263 A10 5e ol grn & yel 9.00 2.50
264 A10 10e red & cream 15.00 8.50
265 A10 20e dk vio & bis 37.50 16.00
Nos. 257-265 (9) 70.55 30.65

Lady of Fatima Issue
Common Design Type

1948, Dec.

266 CD40 50c dark blue 6.50 4.50

UPU Symbols — A10a

1949, Oct. ***Perf. 14***
267 A10a 1e red vio & pink 5.00 2.50

UPU, 75th anniversary.

Catalogue values for unused stamps in this section, from this point to the end of the section, are for Never Hinged items.

Holy Year Issue
Common Design Types

1950, May ***Perf. 13x13½***
268 CD41 1e orange brown .90 .45
269 CD42 2e slate 3.50 1.75

Holy Year Conclusion Issue
Common Design Type

1951, Oct. Unwmk. ***Perf. 14***
270 CD43 2e purple & lilac + label 1.40 1.25

Stamps without labels sell for less.

Nos. 240, 244-245, 247, 250 Surcharged with New Value and Bars

Perf. 13½x13

1951, May 21 **Unwmk.**
271 CD35 10c on 35c .65 *.55*
272 CD36 20c on 70c .85 *.65*
273 CD36 40c on 70c 1.00 *.65*
274 CD36 50c on 80c 1.00 *.65*
275 CD37 1e on 1.75e 1.10 *.65*
276 CD38 2e on 10e 5.50 *2.00*
a. 1e on 10e 200.00 125.00
Nos. 271-276 (6) 10.10 *5.15*

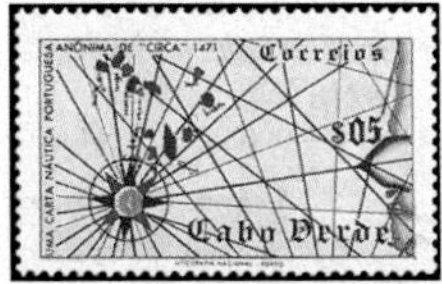

Map of Cape Verde Islands, 1502 A11

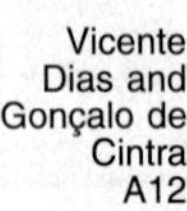

Vicente Dias and Gonçalo de Cintra A12

Portraits: 30c, Diogo Alfonso and Alvaro Fernandes. 50c, Lançarote and Soeiro da Costa. 1e, Diogo Gomes and Antonio da Nola. 2e, Prince Fernando and Prince Henry the Navigator. 3e, Antao Gonçalves and Dinis Dias. 5e, Alfonso Goncalves Baldaia and Joao Fernandes. 10e, Dinis Eanes da Gra and Alvaro de Freitas. 20e, Map of Cape Verde Islands, 1502.

1952, Feb. 24 ***Perf. 14***
277 A11 5c multicolored .20 .20
278 A12 10c multicolored .20 .20
279 A12 30c multicolored .20 .20
280 A12 50c multicolored .20 .20
281 A12 1e multicolored .20 .20
282 A12 2e multicolored 1.25 .20
283 A12 3e multicolored 10.50 1.50
284 A12 5e multicolored 3.50 .70
285 A12 10e multicolored 7.00 1.75
286 A11 20e multicolored 12.50 2.40
Nos. 277-286 (10) 35.75 7.55

Medical Congress Issue
Common Design Type

Design: Hypodermic Injection.

1952, June ***Perf. 13½***
287 CD44 20c ol grn & dk brn .70 .50

No. 247 Surcharged with New Values and "X" in Black

1952, Jan. 25 ***Perf. 13½x13***
288 CD37 10c on 1.75e 1.40 1.10
289 CD37 20c on 1.75e 1.40 1.10
290 CD37 50c on 1.75e 5.75 5.00
291 CD37 1e on 1.75e .70 .25
292 CD37 1.50e on 1.75e .70 .25
Nos. 288-292 (5) 9.95 7.70

Facade of Jeronymos Convent A13

Perf. 13½

1953, Jan. Unwmk. Litho.
293 A13 10c brown & pale olive .20 .20
294 A13 50c purple & fawn .90 .40
295 A13 1e dark green & fawn 2.10 1.10
Nos. 293-295 (3) 3.20 1.70

Exhibition of Sacred Missionary Art held at Lisbon in 1951.

Stamp of Portugal and Arms of Colonies — A13a

1953 **Photo.**
296 A13a 50c multicolored 1.75 1.10

Centenary of Portuguese stamps.

Sao Paulo Issue
Common Design Type

1954 Litho. ***Perf. 13½***
297 CD46 1e green, cream & gray .70 .60

Belem Tower, Lisbon, and Colonial Arms — A14

Arms of Praia — A15

1955, May 15 Litho. ***Perf. 13½***
298 A14 1e multicolored .50 .25
299 A14 1.60e buff & multi .75 .60

Visit of Pres. Francisco H. C. Lopes.

1958, June 14 ***Perf. 12x11½***
300 A15 1e multicolored .65 .45
301 A15 2.50e pink & multi 1.10 .90

Centenary of city of Praia.

Fair Emblem, Globe and Arms — A15a

1958 ***Perf. 12x11½***
302 A15a 2e multicolored .90 .40

World's Fair, Brussels, Apr. 17-Oct. 19.

Tropical Medicine Congress Issue
Common Design Type

1958, Sept. 5 ***Perf. 13½***
303 CD47 3e Aloe vera 5.50 2.10

Prince Henry — A16

Antonio da Nola — A17

1960, June 25 Litho. ***Perf. 13½***
304 A16 2e multicolored .50 .25

500th anniv. of the death of Prince Henry the Navigator.

1960, Oct. Unwmk. ***Perf. 14½***

Design: 2.50e, Diogo Gomes.

305 A17 1e multicolored .75 .45
306 A17 2.50e multicolored 2.50 1.00

Discovery of Cape Verde, 500th anniv.

School Children A18

1960
307 A18 2.50e multicolored 1.25 .65

10th anniv. of the Commission for Technical Cooperation in Africa South of the Sahara (C.C.T.A.).

Arms of Praia — A19

Arms of various cities & towns of Cape Verde.

1961, July Litho. ***Perf. 13½***
308 A19 5c shown .25 .20
309 A19 15c Nova Sintra .25 .20
310 A19 20c Ribeira Brava .25 .20
311 A19 30c Assomada .25 .20
312 A19 1e Maio .65 .20
313 A19 2e Mindelo .65 .20
314 A19 2.50e Santa Maria 1.00 .20
315 A19 3e Pombas 1.60 .50
316 A19 5e Sal-Rei 1.60 .50
317 A19 7.50e Tarrafal 1.75 .90
318 A19 15e Maria Pia 2.40 .90
319 A19 30e San Felipe 6.50 2.50
Nos. 308-319 (12) 17.15 6.70

Sports Issue
Common Design Type

Sports: 50c, Javelin. 1e, Discus. 1.50e, Cricket. 2.50e, Boxing. 4.50e, Hurdling. 12.50e, Golf.

1962, Jan. 18 ***Perf. 13½***
320 CD48 50c lt brown .25 .20
321 CD48 1e lt green .75 .25
322 CD48 1.50e lt blue grn 5.00 2.00
323 CD48 2.50e pale vio bl .75 .35
324 CD48 4.50e orange 1.10 .75
325 CD48 12.50e beige 2.40 1.60
Nos. 320-325 (6) 10.25 5.15

Anti-Malaria Issue
Common Design Type

Design: Anopheles pretoriensis.

1962 Litho. ***Perf. 13½***
326 CD49 2.50e multicolored 1.40 .90

Airline Anniversary Issue
Common Design Type

1963, Oct. Unwmk. ***Perf. 14½***
327 CD50 2.50e gray & multi 1.10 .70

National Overseas Bank Issue
Common Design Type

Design: 1.50e, Jose da Silva Mendes Leal.

1964, May 16 ***Perf. 13½***
328 CD51 1.50e multicolored 1.10 .75

ITU Issue
Common Design Type

1965, May 17 Litho. ***Perf. 14½***
329 CD52 2.50e buff & multi 2.10 1.40

Militia Drummer, 1806 — A20

Designs: 1e, Soldier, Militia, 1806. 1.50e, Grenadier officer, 1833. 2.50e, Grenadier, 1833. 3e, Cavalry officer, 1834. 4e, Grenadier, 1835. 5e, Artillery officer, 1848. 10e, Drum major, infantry, 1856.

1965, Dec. 1 Litho. ***Perf. 14½***
330 A20 50c multicolored .25 .25
331 A20 1e multicolored .45 .25
332 A20 1.50e multicolored .45 .40
333 A20 2.50e multicolored 1.25 .35
334 A20 3e multicolored 2.50 .55
335 A20 4e multicolored 1.10 .55
336 A20 5e multicolored 1.25 .55
337 A20 10e multicolored 2.75 1.75
Nos. 330-337 (8) 10.00 4.65

National Revolution Issue
Common Design Type

1e, Dr. Adriano Moreira School & Health Center.

1966, May 28 Litho. ***Perf. 12***
338 CD53 1e multicolored .60 .45

Navy Club Issue
Common Design Type

Designs: 1e, Capt. Fontoura da Costa and gunboat Mandovy. 1.50e, Capt. Carvalho Araujo and minesweeper Augusto Castilho.

1967, Jan. 31 Litho. ***Perf. 13***
339 CD54 1e multicolored .75 .50
340 CD54 1.50e multicolored 1.25 .90

Virgin Mary Statue — A21

Pres. Rodrigues Thomaz — A22

1967, May 13 Litho. ***Perf. 12½x13***
341 A21 1e multicolored .35 .25

50th anniv. of the apparition of the Virgin Mary to 3 shepherd children at Fatima.

1968, Feb. 9 Litho. ***Perf. 13½***
342 A22 1e multicolored .35 .25

Issued to commemorate the 1968 visit of Pres. Americo de Deus Rodrigues Thomaz.

Cabral Issue

Pedro Alvares Cabral — A23

1e, Cantino's world map, 1502, horiz.

1968, Apr. 22 Litho. ***Perf. 14***
343 A23 1e multicolored .85 .70
344 A23 1.50e multicolored 1.40 .75

See note after Angola No. 545.
For overprint see No. 365.

Sao Vicente Harbor — A24

Physic Nut — A25

Designs: 1.50e, Peanut plant. 2.50e, Castor-oil plant. 3.50e, Yams. 4e, Date palm. 4.50e, Guavas. 5e, Tamarind. 10e, Bitter cassava. 30e, Woman carrying fruit baskets.

1968, Oct. 15 Litho. *Perf. 14*
345 A24 50c multicolored .25 .20
346 A25 1e multicolored .40 .25
347 A25 1.50e multicolored .40 .25
348 A25 2.50e multicolored .40 .25
349 A25 3.50e multicolored .45 .25
350 A25 4e multicolored .45 .25
351 A25 4.50e multicolored .70 .25
352 A25 5 multicolored 1.00 .30
353 A25 10e multicolored 1.25 .60
354 A25 30e multicolored 3.00 2.50
Nos. 345-354 (10) 8.30 5.10

For overprint see No. 372.

Admiral Coutinho Issue
Common Design Type

Adm. Coutinho & map showing route of 1st flight from Lisbon to Rio de Janeiro.

1969, Feb. 17 Litho. *Perf. 14*
355 CD55 30c multi, vert. .35 .25

For surcharge see No. 388.

Vasco da Gama — A26

King Manuel I — A27

Vasco da Gama Issue

1969, Aug. 29 Litho. *Perf. 14*
356 A26 1.50e multicolored .35 .25

Vasco da Gama (1469-1524), navigator.

Administration Reform Issue
Common Design Type

1969, Sept. 25 Litho. *Perf. 14*
357 CD56 2e multicolored .35 .25

King Manuel I Issue

1969, Dec. 1 Litho. *Perf. 14*
358 A27 3e multicolored .55 .35

500th anniv. of the birth of King Manuel I.

Marshal Carmona Issue
Common Design Type

Design: 2.50e, Antonio Oscar Carmona in marshal's uniform.

1970, Nov. 15 Litho. *Perf. 14*
359 CD57 2.50e multi .55 .35

Galleons on Sanaga River — A28

1972, May 25 Litho. *Perf. 13*
360 A28 5e lilac rose & multi .65 .30

4th centenary of the publication of The Lusiads by Luiz Camoens.

Olympic Games Issue
Common Design Type

4e, Basketball & boxing, Olympic emblem.

1972, June 20 *Perf. 14x13½*
361 CD59 4e multicolored .65 .30

For surcharge see No. 371.

Lisbon-Rio de Janeiro Flight Issue
Common Design Type

Design: "Lusitania" landing at San Vicente.

1972, Sept. 20 Litho. *Perf. 13½*
362 CD60 3.50e multi .65 .30

WMO Centenary Issue
Common Design Type

1973, Dec. 15 Litho. *Perf. 13*
363 CD61 2.50e ultra & multi .65 .30

For overprint see No. 387.

Mindelo Desalination Plant — A29

1974 Litho. *Perf. 13½*
364 A29 4e multicolored 1.25 .85

Opening of the Mindelo desalination plant.
For surcharge see No. 371A.

Republic
No. 343 Overprinted: "INDEPENDENCIA / 5-Julho-75"

1975, Dec. 19 Litho. *Perf. 14*
365 A23 1e multicolored .35 .25

Proclamation of Independence.

Amilcar Cabral, Flag and Crowd — A30

1976, Jan. 20
366 A30 5e multicolored .55 .25

3rd anniv. of the assassination of Amilcar Cabral (1924-73), revolutionary leader.

Rising Sun, Coat of Arms, Liberated People — A31

1976, July 5 Litho. *Perf. 14*
367 A31 50c multicolored .25 .20
368 A31 3e multicolored .90 .20
369 A31 15e multicolored 2.00 .35
370 A31 50e multicolored 5.75 1.25
a. Miniature sheet, #367-370 *26.00 26.00*
Nos. 367-370 (4) 8.90 2.00

First anniversary of independence.

Nos. 351, 361, 364 Overprinted with Row of Stars and: "REPUBLICA / DE"

1976 Litho. *Perf. 14*
371 CD59 4e multi —
371A A29 4e multi *37.50 27.50*
372 A25 4.50e multi 4.25 2.25

Amilcar Cabral, Map and Flag of Cape Verde A32

1976, Sept. 19 *Perf. 14*
373 A32 1e multicolored .45 .25

Party of Intl. Action (PAICC), 20th anniv.

Electronic Tree and ITU Emblem — A33

Ashtray — A34

1977, May 17 Litho. *Perf. 13½x13*
374 A33 5.50e multi .45 .25

World Telecommunications Day.

1977, July 5 Litho. *Perf. 14*

Carved Coconut Shells: 30c, Bell on stand. 50c, Lamp with Adam and Eve. 1e, Hollow shell with Nativity. 1.50e, Desk lamp. 5e, Jar. 10e, Jar with hinged cover. 20e, Tobacco jar with palms. 30e, Stringed instrument.

375 A34 20c lilac & multi .25 .20
376 A34 30c rose & multi .25 .20
377 A34 50c salmon & multi .25 .20
378 A34 1e lt green & multi .35 .25
379 A34 1.50e orange yel & multi .35 .25
380 A34 5e gray & multi .70 .35
381 A34 10e lt blue & multi 1.10 .50
382 A34 20e yellow & multi 1.90 1.10
383 A34 30e rose lilac & multi 3.00 1.25
Nos. 375-383 (9) 8.15 4.30

Cape Verde No. 1 and Coat of Arms — A35

Congress Emblem — A36

1977, Sept. 12 Litho. *Perf. 13½*
384 A35 4e blue & multi .35 .25
385 A35 8e lilac & multi .75 .35

Centenary of Cape Verde stamps.

1977, Nov. 15 *Perf. 14*
386 A36 3.50e multi .55 .25

African Party of Independence of Guinea-Bissau and Cape Verde (PAIGC), 3rd cong., Nov. 15-20.

No. 363 Overprinted with Row of Stars and: "REPUBLICA / DE"

1978, May 1 *Perf. 12*
387 CD61 2.50e ultra & multi .55 .25

No. 355 Surcharged with New Value and Bars

1978, May 1 *Perf. 14*
388 CD55 3e on 30c multi 2.25 .35

Antenna and ITU Emblem — A37

1978, May 17 Litho. *Perf. 14*
389 A37 3.50e silver & multi .55 .25

10th World Telecommunications Day.

Freighter Cabo Verde — A38

1978, June 25 Litho. *Perf. 14*
391 A38 1e multicolored .65 .20

First ship of Cape Verde merchant marine.

Map of Africa and Equality Emblem — A39

1978, June 21
392 A39 4.50e multi .55 .25

Anti-Apartheid Year.

Human Rights Emblem — A40

1978, Dec. 10 Litho. *Perf. 14*
393 A40 1.50e multicolored .35 .25
394 A40 2e multicolored .55 .35

Universal Declaration of Human Rights, 30th anniversary.

Children and Balloons, IYC Emblem — A41

IYC Emblem and Child's Drawing: 3.50e, Children and flowers.

1979, June 1 Litho. *Perf. 14*

395 A41 1.50e multi .65 .25
396 A41 3.50e multi 1.10 .35

International Year of the Child.

Pindjiguiti Massacre Monument — A42

Natl. Youth Week — A42a

1979, Aug. 3 *Perf. 13*

397 A42 4.50e multi 2.10 .25

Massacre of Pindjiguiti, 20th anniversary.

1979, Sept. 1 Litho. *Perf. 14*

397A A42a 3.50e Poster 1.10 .25

Centenary of Mindelo — A43

1980, Apr. 23 Litho. *Perf. 12½*

398 A43 4e multicolored .65 .25

Flag of Cape Verde — A44

Stylized Bird, "V" — A45

1980 Litho. *Perf. 12½*

399 A44 4e multicolored 1.25 .25
400 A45 4e multicolored .45 .25
401 A45 7e multicolored .80 .35
402 A45 11e multicolored 1.10 .45
Nos. 399-402 (4) 3.60 1.30

5th anniversary of independence. Issued: No. 399, June 1; others July 5.

A45a

CABO VERDE 1$00 CORREIOS JOGOS OLIMPICOS DE MOSCOVO 1980

A46

1980, May 13

402A A45a 3.50e multi .50 .25
402B A45a 4.50e multi .65 .25

1980 Natl. census.

1980, June 6

403 A46 1e Running .20 .20
404 A46 2.50e Boxing .25 .20
405 A46 3e Basketball .35 .25
406 A46 4e Volleyball .45 .25
407 A46 20e Swimming 1.25 .80
408 A46 50e Tennis 3.75 1.60
Nos. 403-408 (6) 6.25 3.30

Souvenir Sheet

Perf. 13

409 A46 30e Soccer, horiz. *18.00 18.00*

22nd Summer Olympic Games, Moscow, July 19-Aug. 3.

Thunnus Alalunga A47

1980, Nov. 11 Litho. *Perf. 13*

410 A47 50c shown .20 .20
411 A47 4.50e Trachurus trachurus .35 .20
412 A47 8e Muraena helena .60 .25
413 A47 10e Corvina nigra .70 .35
414 A47 12e Katsuwonus pelamis 1.10 .50
415 A47 50e Prionace glauca 3.75 1.75
Nos. 410-415 (6) 6.70 3.25

Lochnera Rosea — A48

1980, Dec. 29

416 A48 50c shown .20 .20
417 A48 4.50e Poinciana regia-bojer .25 .25
418 A48 8e Mirabilis jalapa .70 .35
419 A48 10e Nerium oleander .90 .45
420 A48 12e Bougainvillia litoralis 1.10 .50
421 A48 30e Hibiscus 2.50 1.25
Nos. 416-421 (6) 5.65 3.00

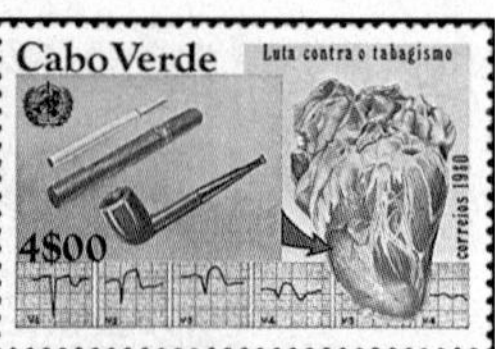

WHO Anti-smoking Campaign — A48a

1980, Sept. 19 *Perf. 12½*

421A A48a 4e multicolored .50 .25
421B A48a 7e multicolored 1.10 .35

Arca Verde A49

1980, Nov. 30 Litho. *Perf. 12½x12*

422 A49 3e shown .25 .20
423 A49 5.50e Ilha do Maio .45 .25
424 A49 7.50e Ilha de Komo .90 .50
425 A49 9e Boa Vista 1.10 .70
426 A49 12e Santo Antao 1.25 .50
427 A49 30e Santiago 3.00 1.25
Nos. 422-427 (6) 6.95 3.40

Hand-woven Bag, Map — A49a

Various hand-woven articles. 10e, vert.

1978, May 21 Litho. *Perf. 14*

427A A49a 50c multi .25 .20
427B A49a 1.50e multi .25 .20
427C A49a 2e multi .50 .25
427D A49a 3e multi .50 .25
427E A49a 10e multi 1.25 .60
Nos. 427A-427E (5) 2.75 1.50

Desert Erosion Prevention Campaign — A50

1981, Mar. 30 Litho. *Perf. 13*

428 A50 4.50e multi .50 .25
429 A50 10.50e multi 1.25 .50

6th Anniv. of Constitution A51

1981, Apr. 15

430 A51 4.50e multicolored .60 .25

Souvenir Sheet

Austria No. B336 A52

1981, May 18

431 A52 50e multicolored 6.25 6.25

WIPA '81 Philatelic Exhibition, Vienna, Austria, May 22-31.

Antenna — A53

1981, Aug. 25 Litho. *Perf. 12½*

432 A53 4.50e shown .60 .25
433 A53 8e Dish antenna .90 .40
434 A53 20e Dish antenna, diff. 1.90 .90
Nos. 432-434 (3) 3.40 1.55

Intl. Year of the Disabled A54

1981, Dec. 25 Litho. *Perf. 12½*

435 A54 4.50e multicolored .65 .35

Purple Gallinule A55

1981, Dec. 30

436 A55 1e Egret, vert. .35 .20
437 A55 4.50e Barn owl, vert. .90 .35
438 A55 8e Passerine, vert. 1.75 .50
439 A55 10e shown 1.90 .60
440 A55 12e Guinea fowl 2.50 .70
Nos. 436-440 (5) 7.40 2.35

Souvenir Sheet

Perf. 13

441 A55 50e Razo Isld. lark 8.50 8.50

No. 441 contains 31x39mm one stamp.

CILSS Congress, Praia, Jan. 17 — A56

1982, Jan. 17 *Perf. 13x12½*

442 A56 11.50e multicolored 1.40 .65

Amilcar Cabral Soccer Championship — A57

Designs: Soccer players and flags.

1982, Feb. 10 Litho. *Perf. 12½*

443	A57	4.50e	multicolored	.50	.25
444	A57	7.50e	multicolored	.80	.35
445	A57	11.50e	multicolored	1.25	.60
			Nos. 443-445 (3)	2.55	1.20

1982 World Cup — A58

Designs: Soccer players and ball.

1982, Apr. 25

446	A58	1.50e	multi	.20	.20
447	A58	4.50e	multi	.45	.25
448	A58	8e	multi	.80	.35
449	A58	10.50e	multi	1.00	.45
450	A58	12e	multi	1.10	.50
451	A58	20e	multi	2.10	.80
			Nos. 446-451 (6)	5.65	2.55

Souvenir Sheet

452	A58	50e	multi	6.25	6.25

First Anniv. of Women's Organization — A59

1982, Apr. 15 Litho. *Perf. 12½x12*

453	A59	4.50e	Marching	.50	.25
454	A59	8e	Farming	1.10	.35
455	A59	12e	Child care	1.50	.60
			Nos. 453-455 (3)	3.10	1.20

Estaleiros Navais Port, St. Vincent - A59a

1982, July 5 Litho. *Perf. 13x12½*

455A	A59a	10.50e	multi	1.60	.60

Natl. independence, 7th anniv.

Return of Barque Morrissey-Ernestina — A60

1982, July 5 Litho. *Perf. 13*

456	A60	12e	multi	1.25	.75

Butterflies — A61

1982, July 27 Litho.

457	A61	2e	Hypolimnas misippus	.35	.20
458	A61	4.50e	Melanitis lede	.70	.25
459	A61	8e	Catopsilia florella	1.10	.25
460	A61	10.50e	Colias electo	1.50	.40
461	A61	11.50e	Danaus chrysippus	1.60	.60
462	A61	12e	Papilio demodecus	2.75	.70
			Nos. 457-462 (6)	8.00	2.40

Francisco Xavier da Cruz (1905-1958), Composer — A62

14e, Eugenio Tavares (1867-1930), poet.

1983, Feb. 20 Litho. *Perf. 13*

463	A62	7e	multi	.40	.25
464	A62	14e	multi	1.75	.80

World Communications Year — A63

1983, Oct. 10 Litho.

465	A63	13e	multicolored	1.50	.75

Local Seashells — A64

1983, Nov. 30 *Perf. 13½*

466	A64	50c	Conus ateralbus	.20	.20
467	A64	1e	Conus decoratus	.25	.20
468	A64	3e	Conus salreiensis	.25	.20
469	A64	10e	Conus verdensis	1.40	.50
470	A64	50e	Conus cuneolus	4.75	2.50
			Nos. 466-470 (5)	6.85	3.60

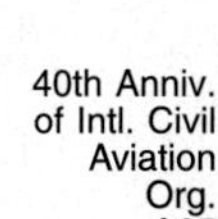

40th Anniv. of Intl. Civil Aviation Org. A65

Airplanes: 50c, Ogma-Auster D5/160, 1966. 2e, De Havilland DH-104 Dove, 1945. 10e, Hawker Siddeley 748-200, 1972. 13e, De Havilland Dragon Rapide, 1945. 20e, De Havilland Twin Otter, 1977. 50e, Britten-Norman Islander, 1971.

1984, Feb. 15 Litho.

471	A65	50c	multicolored	.25	.20
472	A65	2e	multicolored	.25	.25
473	A65	10e	multicolored	1.10	.50
474	A65	13e	multicolored	1.25	.80
475	A65	20e	multicolored	1.75	1.25
476	A65	50e	multicolored	4.25	2.40
			Nos. 471-476 (6)	8.85	5.40

Amilcar Cabral — A66

A67

1983, Jan. 17 Litho. *Perf. 14½*

477	A66	7e	multi	1.00	.50
478	A66	10.50e	multi	1.50	.90
a.			Souvenir sheet of 2, #477-478	30.00	30.00

Amilcar Cabral Symposium, Jan. 17-20. No. 478a sold for 30e.

1983, Dec. 10 Photo. *Perf. 14½*

479	A67	7e	Cross overshadowing islands	1.10	.50

Christianity in Cape Verde, 450th anniv.

Natl. Solidarity Campaign A68

1984, Sept. 12 *Perf. 13½*

480	A68	6.50e	multi	1.00	.25
481	A68	13.50e	multi	2.00	.80

2nd Conference of Natl. Women's Orgs., Mar. 23-27 — A69

1985, Mar. 27 Litho. *Perf. 13½*

482	A69	8e	multicolored	*1.00*	.50

Miniature Sheet

483	A69	30e	multicolored	*30.00*	*30.00*

Natl. Independence, 10th Anniv. — A70

1985, July 5 Litho. *Perf. 14*

484	A70	8c	multicolored	1.10	.50
485	A70	12e	multicolored	1.90	.75

Intl. Youth Year — A71

1985, Sept. 12 Litho. *Perf. 14*

486	A71	12e	multicolored	2.50	.85

Vapor, by Hundertwasser A72

Photogravure and Engraved

1986, Apr. 25 *Perf. 14*

Black Surcharge

487	A72	30e	on 10e multi	20.00	4.00

Souvenir Sheets

Background Color

488	Sheet of 4	100.00	
a.	A72 50e yellow & multi	10.00	10.00
489	Sheet of 4	100.00	
a.	A72 50e red & multi	10.00	10.00
490	Sheet of 4	100.00	
a.	A72 50e green & multi	10.00	10.00

No. 487 exists without surcharge. Value $27.50.

World Wildlife Fund — A73

Perf. 13½x14½

1986, June 15 Litho.

491	A73	8e	Mabuya vaillanti	2.40	1.25
492	A73	10e	Tarentola gigas brancoensis	2.75	1.25
493	A73	15e	Tarentola gigas gigas	4.25	1.25
494	A73	30e	Hemidactylus bouvieri	8.50	2.50
			Nos. 491-494 (4)	17.90	6.25

Souvenir Sheet

495	Sheet of 2	13.50	13.50
a.	A73 50e Mabuya vaillanti	6.00	6.00
b.	A73 50e Hemidactylus bouvieri	6.00	6.00

No. 495 printed with center label picturing progress union emblem. Nos. 495a-495b printed without WWF emblem.

World Food Day — A74

Intl. Peace Year — A75

1986, June 20 *Perf. 14*

496 A74 8e Cauldron .50 .25
497 A74 12e Mortar & pestle .80 .35
498 A74 15e Quern stone 1.40 .50
Nos. 496-498 (3) 2.70 1.10

1986, Dec. 24 Litho. *Perf. 14*

499 A75 12e multicolored .50 .25
500 A75 30e multicolored 2.00 1.25

Natl. Child Survival Campaign A76

1987, Mar. 27 Litho. *Perf. 14*

501 A76 8e multicolored .45 .20
502 A76 10e multicolored .55 .25
503 A76 12e multicolored .60 .35
504 A76 16e multicolored .90 .45
505 A76 100e multicolored 4.25 2.50
Nos. 501-505 (5) 6.75 3.75

Tourism A77

1987, May 17

506 A77 1e Bay, Mindelo .20 .20
507 A77 2.50e Hill country .20 .20
508 A77 5e Mountain peak .25 .25
509 A77 8e Monument .45 .25
510 A77 10e Mountain peaks .60 .25
511 A77 12e Beached boats .80 .35
512 A77 100e Harbor 5.00 2.50
Nos. 506-512 (7) 7.50 4.00

For surcharge see No. 710.

Ships — A78

1987, Aug. 3 *Perf. 13½x14½*

513 A78 12e Carvalho, 1937 .70 .25
514 A78 16e Nauta, 1943 1.10 .25
515 A78 50e Maria Sony, 1911 3.50 1.10
Nos. 513-515 (3) 5.30 1.60

Souvenir Sheet

516 Sheet of 2 9.00 9.00
a. A78 60e Madalan, 1928 4.00 4.00

Crop Protection A80

1988, May 9 Litho. *Perf. 13½*

518 A80 50c Identification of insect plague .20 .20
519 A80 2e Use of insecticides .20 .20
520 A80 9e Import of parasites .50 .25
521 A80 13e Import of predators .60 .25
522 A80 16e Locust 1.00 .40
523 A80 19e Estimation of crop loss 1.25 .60
Nos. 518-523 (6) 3.75 1.90

Souvenir Sheet

524 A80 50e Agricultural Research Institute 5.00 5.00

Maps — A81

1988, July 5 Litho. *Perf. 14*

525 A81 1e Dutch, 17th cent. .20 .20
526 A81 2.50e Belgian, 18th cent. .20 .20
527 A81 4.50e French, 18th cent. .25 .20
528 A81 9.50e English, 18th cent. .55 .25
529 A81 19.50e English, 19th cent. 1.10 .50
530 A81 20e French, 18th cent., vert. 1.25 .60
Nos. 525-530 (6) 3.55 1.95

Churches A82

5e, St. Amaro Abade, Tarrafal, Santiago Is. 8e, Our Lady of the Light, Maio Is. 10e, Nazarene, Praia, Santiago Is. 12e, Our Lady of Rosa'rio, Sao Nicolau Is. 15e, Nazarene, Mindelo, Sao Vicente Is. 20e, Our Lady of Grace, Praia, Santiago Is.

1988, Aug. 15 *Perf. 13½x14½*

531 A82 5e multicolored .20 .20
532 A82 8e multicolored .45 .20
533 A82 10e multicolored .55 .25
534 A82 12e multicolored .60 .25
535 A82 15e multicolored .80 .35
536 A82 20e multicolored 1.10 .40
Nos. 531-536 (6) 3.70 1.65

Water Conservation — A83

1988, Sept. 26 Litho. *Perf. 14*

537 A83 12e multicolored .70 .35

Intl. Red Cross, 125th Anniv. — A84

1988, Oct. 20

538 A84 7e multi .45 .25

3rd Communist Party (PAICV) Congress — A85

Portrait of Pres. Pereira, PAICV secretary-general, and: 7e, S. Jorginho Vocational Training Center. 10.50e, UN Secretary-General Perez de Cuellar. 30e, 100e, Star and text.

Perf. 14½x13½

1988, Nov. 25 Litho.

539 A85 7e multi .40 .25
540 A85 10.50e multi .60 .25
541 A85 30e multi 1.75 .75
Nos. 539-541 (3) 2.75 1.25

Souvenir Sheet

542 A85 100e multi 6.25 6.25

1988 Summer Olympics, Seoul — A86

1988, Dec. 26

543 A86 12e shown .60 .25
544 A86 15e Tennis .90 .35
545 A86 20e Soccer 1.10 .50
546 A86 30e Boxing 1.60 .85
Nos. 543-546 (4) 4.20 1.95

Souvenir Sheet

547 A86 50e Long jump 3.75 3.75

Roberto Duarte Silva (1837-89), Chemist — A86a

1989, May 2 Litho. *Perf. 14¼x14*

547A A86a 12.50e multi .45 .25

2nd JAAC-CV Congress, Sept. 7-12 — A87

1989, Apr. 7 Litho. *Perf. 14*

548 A87 30e Hot air balloon 1.00 .70

Liberty Guiding the People — A88

Relief, Arc de Triomphe — A89

1989, July 7 Litho. *Perf. 14*

549 A88 20e multicolored .80 .40
550 A88 24e multicolored 1.00 .50
551 A88 25e multicolored 1.10 .60
Nos. 549-551 (3) 2.90 1.50

Souvenir Sheet

Perf. 14½x13½

552 A89 100e multicolored 5.00 5.00

French revolution, bicent.

Interparliamentary Union, Cent. — A90

1989, Sept. 18 Litho. *Perf. 14*

553 A90 2e shown .20 .20
554 A90 4e Dove .25 .20
555 A90 13e Natl. Assembly Bldg. .45 .20
Nos. 553-555 (3) .90 .60

Traditional Ceramics A91

1989, Nov. 13 Litho. *Perf. 13½*

Panel Colors

556 A91 13e lilac .50 .25
557 A91 20e red, vert. .70 .40
558 A91 24e brown .90 .50
559 A91 25e orange, vert. .90 .50
Nos. 556-559 (4) 3.00 1.65

Outdoor Toys — A92

1989, Dec. 23

560 A92 1e Yellow truck .20 .20
561 A92 6e Car .20 .20
562 A92 8e White truck .35 .20
563 A92 11.50e Trucks .40 .25
564 A92 18e Scooter .70 .40
565 A92 100e Boat 3.75 2.10
Nos. 560-565 (6) 5.60 3.35

Visit of Pope John Paul II — A93

1990, Jan. 25

566 A93 13e blue & multi .40 .25
567 A93 25e violet & multi .75 .40

Souvenir Sheet

568 A93 200e multi, diff. 10.00 10.00

Turtles A94

1990, May 17 Litho. *Perf. 13½*

569 A94 50c Chelonia mydas .20 .20
570 A94 1e Dermochelys coriacea .20 .20
571 A94 5e Lepidochelys olivacea .25 .20
572 A94 10e Caretta caretta .50 .20
573 A94 42e Eretmochelys imbricata 2.10 .85
Nos. 569-573 (5) 3.25 1.65

Women's Congress A95

1990, Aug. 13

574 A95 9e multicolored .35 .20

A96

A97

Various drawings of soccer players in action.

1990, Aug. 7

575 A96 4e multicolored .20 .20
576 A96 7.50e multicolored .25 .20
577 A96 8e multicolored .25 .20
578 A96 100e multicolored 3.50 2.10
Nos. 575-578 (4) 4.20 2.70

Souvenir Sheet

579 A96 100e multi, diff. 4.50 4.50

World Cup Soccer Championships, Italy. For surcharges see Nos. 711-712.

1990, Oct. 15 ***Perf. 11½***

Vaccinations: 5e, Emile Roux (1853-1933), diphtheria. 13e, Robert Koch (1843-1910), tuberculosis. 20e, Gaston Ramon (1886-1963), tetanus. 24e, Jonas Salk (1914-95), polio.

Granite Paper

580 A97 5e multicolored .35 .20
581 A97 13e multicolored 1.00 .25
582 A97 20e multicolored 1.40 .40
583 A97 24e multicolored 1.75 .50
Nos. 580-583 (4) 4.50 1.35

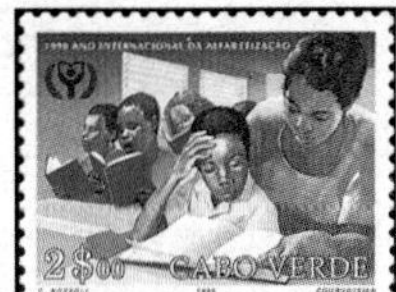

Intl. Literacy Year — A98

Designs: 3e, Adult literacy class. 15e, Teacher holding flash card, children. 19e, Teacher, student at blackboard.

1990, Sept. 28

Granite Paper

584 A98 2e shown .20 .20
585 A98 3e multicolored .20 .20
586 A98 15e multicolored .50 .25
587 A98 19e multicolored .70 .25
Nos. 584-587 (4) 1.60 .90

Traditional Fairy Tales A99

1990, Dec. 20 **Litho.** ***Perf. 12½***

588 A99 50c shown .20 .20
589 A99 2.50e Man catching mermaid .20 .20
590 A99 12e Woman, snake .40 .20
591 A99 25e Man, eggs, woman .90 .40
Nos. 588-591 (4) 1.70 1.00

Fight Against AIDS A100

1991, Feb. 20 **Litho.** ***Perf. 14***

Granite Paper

592 A100 13e multicolored .50 .25
593 A100 24e multi, diff. .90 .60

Fishing — A101

24e, Man removing hook from fish. 25e, Fishing boats. 50e, Two men long-line fishing.

1991, Apr. 23 **Litho.** ***Perf. 11½***

594 A101 10e multicolored .35 .25
595 A101 24e multicolored 1.10 .60
596 A101 25e multicolored 1.10 .60
597 A101 50e multicolored 2.25 1.40
Nos. 594-597 (4) 4.80 2.85

Medicinal Plants — A102

10e, Lavandula rotundifolia. 15e, Micromeria forbesii. 21e, Sarcostemma daltonii. 24e, Periploca chevalieri. 30e, Echium hypertropicum. 35e, Erysimum caboverdeanum.

1991, July 5 **Litho.** ***Perf. 11½***

598 A102 10e multicolored .30 .20
599 A102 15e multicolored .45 .25
600 A102 21e multicolored .65 .25
601 A102 24e multicolored .80 .30
602 A102 30e multicolored 1.00 .40
603 A102 35e multicolored 1.25 .50
Nos. 598-603 (6) 4.45 1.90

Landmarks in Old Ribeira Grande on Santiago Island A103

12.50e, Church of Our Lady of the Rosary, 1495. 15e, Ruins of the Cathedral, 1556. 20e, Fortress of San Felipe, 1587. 30e, Ruins of the Convent of St. Francis, 1642. 100e, Pillory, 1520, vert.

1991, June 25 **Litho.** ***Perf. 11½***

604 A103 12.50e multicolored .45 .25
605 A103 15e multicolored .55 .25
606 A103 20e multicolored .70 .40
607 A103 30e multicolored 1.00 .70
Nos. 604-607 (4) 2.70 1.60

Souvenir Sheet

608 A103 100e multicolored 3.75 3.75

Musical Instruments — A104

1991, Oct. 9 **Litho.** ***Perf. 11½***

609 A104 10e 6-string guitar .35 .20
610 A104 20e Violin .80 .50
611 A104 29e 5-string guitar 1.25 .60
612 A104 47e Cimba 1.90 1.10
Nos. 609-612 (4) 4.30 2.40

Souvenir Sheet

613 A104 60e Accordion, horiz. 2.50 2.50

Christmas A105

1991, Dec. 20 **Litho.** ***Perf. 11½***

614 A105 31e Nativity scene 1.00 .50
615 A105 50e Nativity scene, diff. 1.60 .85

Discovery of America, 500th Anniv. A106

1992, Mar. 31 **Litho.** ***Perf. 11½***

616 A106 40e shown 1.75 1.10
617 A106 40e Columbus on ship 1.75 1.10
a. Pair, #616-617 4.00 4.00

Souvenir Sheet

618 A106 Sheet of 2 7.50 7.50

Stamps in No. 618 are smaller, without white border and "Luis Duran" and "Courvoisier" inscriptions. No. 618 was printed in continuous design and sold for 150e.

Souvenir Sheet

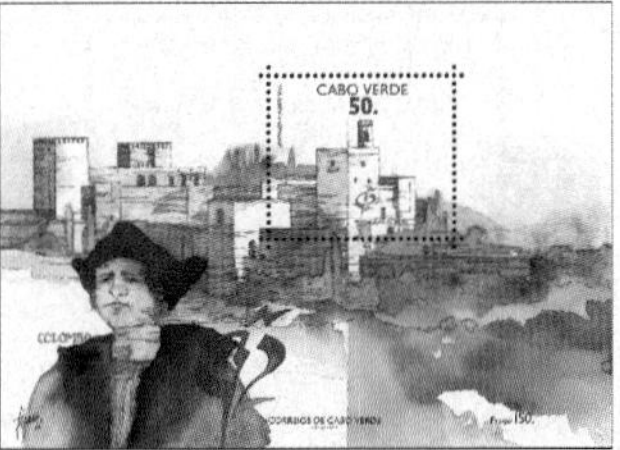

Granada '92 — A107

Illustration reduced.

1992, Apr.24 ***Perf. 11½***

619 A107 50e multicolored 7.50 7.50

No. 619 sold for 150e.

Tropical Fruits A108

1992, Feb. 29 ***Perf. 12x11½***

620 A108 16e Syzygium jambos .65 .30
621 A108 25e Mangifera indica 1.10 .50
622 A108 31e Anacardium occidentale 1.25 .60
623 A108 32e Persea americana 1.50 .70
Nos. 620-623 (4) 4.50 2.10

1992 Summer Olympics, Barcelona A109

1992, June 30 **Litho.** ***Perf. 13½***

624 A109 16e Women's javelin .60 .25
625 A109 20e Weight lifting .75 .30
626 A109 32e Women's pole vault 1.25 .60
627 A109 40e Women's shot put 1.50 .80
Nos. 624-627 (4) 4.10 1.95

Souvenir Sheet

628 A109 100e Women's gymnastics 4.00 4.00

Sugar Cane Production — A110

Designs: 19e, Oxen, sugar cane. 20e, Oxen yoked to press. 37e, Man placing cane inside press. 38e, Refining process.

1992, Nov. **Litho.** ***Perf. 11***

629 A110 19e multicolored .65 .30
630 A110 20e multicolored .65 .30
631 A110 37e multicolored 1.25 .60
632 A110 38e multicolored 1.40 .60
Nos. 629-632 (4) 3.95 1.80

Domestic Animals A111

1992, Nov. ***Perf. 13½***

633 A111 16e Cat .65 .40
634 A111 31e Chickens 1.10 .80
635 A111 32e Dog, vert. 1.25 .90
636 A111 50e Horse 2.00 1.25
Nos. 633-636 (4) 5.00 3.35

Corals A112

1993, Apr. 29 **Litho.** ***Perf. 11½***

637 A112 5e Tubastrea aurea .20 .20
638 A112 31e Corallium rubrum 1.25 .80
639 A112 37e Porites porites 1.50 1.00
640 A112 50e Millepora alcicornis 1.90 1.25
Nos. 637-640 (4) 4.85 3.25

Treaty of Tordesillas, 500th Anniv. (in 1994) A113

Designs: No. 641, King Ferdinand, Queen Isabella of Spain, Pope Alexander VI. No. 642, Pope Julius II, King John II of Portugal. No. 643, Astrolabe, treaty signing. No. 644, Compass rose, map.

1993, Aug. 1 **Litho.** ***Perf. 12x11½***

641 A113 37e multicolored 1.25 .60
642 A113 37e multicolored 1.25 .60
a. Pair, #641-642 3.00 3.00
643 A113 38e multicolored 1.25 .60
644 A113 38e multicolored 1.25 .60
a. Pair, #643-644 3.00 3.00
Nos. 641-644 (4) 5.00 2.40

Souvenir Sheet

Santiago Island, 1806 — A114

1993, July 30 ***Perf. 13½***

645 A114 100e multicolored 4.00 4.00

Brasiliana '93.

Lobsters — A115

1993, Sept. 29 Litho. *Perf. 11½*

646 A115 2e Palinurus charlestoni .20 .20
647 A115 10e Panulirus echinatus .45 .25
648 A115 17e Panulirus regius .90 .40
649 A115 38e Scyllarides latus 1.75 .90
Nos. 646-649 (4) 3.30 1.75

Souvenir Sheet

650 A115 100e Panulirus regius, diff. 4.50 4.50

No. 650 contains one 51x36mm stamp.

Birds A116

1993, Oct. 29 Litho. *Perf. 12x11½*

651 A116 10e Calonectris edwardsii .50 .25
652 A116 30e Sula leucogaster 1.75 .80
653 A116 40e Fregata magnificens 2.25 1.00
a. Souvenir sheet of 1 7.50 7.50
654 A116 41e Phaeton aethereus 2.25 1.00
Nos. 651-654 (4) 6.75 3.05

Hong Kong '94 (#653a).
No. 653a sold for 150e.

Flowers A117

1993, Dec. 16 Litho. *Perf. 12x11½*

655 A117 5e Rosa alexandra .20
656 A117 30e Strelitzia reginae 1.10 .80
657 A117 37e Dianthus barbatus 1.40 1.00
a. Souvenir sheet of 1 5.75 5.75
658 A117 50e Dahlia 1.75 1.25
Nos. 655-658 (4) 4.45 3.05

Singapore '95 (#657a). Issued 9/1/95.
No. 657a sold for 150e.

1994 World Cup Soccer Championships, US — A118

Players, US flag, and: 1e, Giant's Stadium, New Jersey. 20e, Rose Bowl Stadium, Pasadena. 37e, Foxboro Stadium, Boston. 38e, Silverdome, Pontiac. 100e, RFK Stadium, Washington DC.

1994, May 31 Litho. *Perf. 11½*

659 A118 1e multicolored .20 .20
660 A118 20e multicolored .80 .50
661 A118 37e multicolored 1.40 .90
662 A118 38e multicolored 1.50 1.00
Nos. 659-662 (4) 3.90 2.60

Souvenir Sheet

663 A118 100e multicolored 4.00 4.00

Prince Henry the Navigator (1394-1460) — A119

Illustration reduced.

1994, Mar. 4 Litho. *Perf. 12*

664 A119 37e multicolored 1.50 .90

See Brazil #2463, Macao #719, Portugal #1987.

Sharks A120

1994, June 27 Litho. *Perf. 12x11½*

665 A120 21e Eugomphodus taurus .75 .50
666 A120 27e Carcharhinus limbatus 1.00 .65
667 A120 37e Rhiniodon typus 1.25 .90
668 A120 38e Etmopterus spinax 1.50 1.00
Nos. 665-668 (4) 4.50 3.05

Bananas A121

1994, Aug. 16 Litho. *Perf. 11½*

669 A121 12e Prata, vert. .40 .25
670 A121 16e Pao .60 .40
671 A121 30e Ana roberta, vert. 1.10 .75
672 A121 40e Roxa, vert. 1.40 1.00
Nos. 669-672 (4) 3.50 2.40

Souvenir Sheet

673 A121 100e Prata, diff., vert. 7.50 7.50

PHILAKOREA '94, SINGPEX '94 (#673).
No. 673 sold for 150e.

Lighthouses — A122

1994, Oct. 17 *Perf. 12*

674 A122 2e Fontes Pereira de Melo .20 .20
675 A122 37e Morro Negro 1.40 .90
676 A122 38e Amelia, vert. 1.40 1.00
677 A122 50e Maria Pia, vert. 1.90 1.25
Nos. 674-677 (4) 4.90 3.35

Wilhelm Roentgen (1845-1923), Discovery of the X-Ray, Cent. — A123

1995, Mar. 31 Litho. *Perf. 12*

678 A123 20e yellow & multi .75 .50
679 A123 37e blue & multi 1.50 .90
a. Souvenir sheet of 2, #678-679 4.00 4.00

No. 679a sold for 100e.

A124

FAO, 50th Anniv. — A125

1995, May 17 Litho. *Perf. 12*

680 A124 37e multicolored 1.40 .90
681 A125 38e multicolored 1.40 .90

Dogs A126

Dog, scene depicting story of dogs: 1e, Fox terrier, Two foxhounds and fox terrier, by John Emms. 10e, Cavalier King Charles, Shooting over Dogs, by Richard Ansdell. 40e, Rough collie, German shepherd. 50e, Braco, Hounds at Full Cry, by Thomas Blinks.

1995, June 16 Litho. *Perf. 12x11½*

682 A126 1e multicolored .20 .20
683 A126 10e multicolored .45 .25
684 A126 40e multicolored 1.75 1.00
685 A126 50e multicolored 2.10 1.10
Nos. 682-685 (4) 4.50 2.55

Independence, 20th Anniv. — A127

1995, July 20 Litho. *Perf. 12*

686 A127 37e multicolored 1.75 1.10

Traditional Festival A128

Designs: 2e, Horse race. 10e, Horseman leading parade. 37e, People singing, playing drums. 40e, Playing game on horseback.

1995, Oct. 9 *Perf. 12x11½*

687 A128 2e multicolored .20 .20
688 A128 10e multicolored .35 .25
689 A128 37e multicolored 1.25 .80
690 A128 40e multicolored 1.40 .90
Nos. 687-690 (4) 3.20 2.15

Children's Stories A130

Designs: 10e, The cicadas making music, ants. 25e, Cicada being exposed to light. 38e, Cicada with guitar, ants working. 45e, Ants at table making fun of cicada.

1995, Dec. 15 Litho. *Perf. 11½*

692 A130 10e multicolored .35 .25
693 A130 25e multicolored .80 .50
694 A130 38e multicolored 1.25 .80
695 A130 45e multicolored 1.50 1.00
Nos. 692-695 (4) 3.90 2.55

Endangered Plants — A131

20e, Sonchus daltonii. 37e, Echium vulcanorum. 38e, Nauplius smithii. 50e, Campanula jacobaea.

1996, Apr. 24 Litho. *Perf. 11½*

696 A131 20e multicolored .60 .40
697 A131 37e multicolored 1.10 .75
698 A131 38e multicolored 1.10 .75
699 A131 50e multicolored 1.50 1.00
Nos. 696-699 (4) 4.30 2.90

1996 Summer Olympic Games, Atlanta A132

1996, June 30 Litho. *Perf. 11½*

700 A132 1e Tennis .20 .20
701 A132 37e Gymnastics 1.10 .75
702 A132 100e Athletics 3.00 2.00
Nos. 700-702 (3) 4.30 2.95

UNICEF, 50th Anniv. — A133

Water Sports — A134

1996, Aug. 1 Litho. *Perf. 12*

703 A133 20e Young girl .90 .40
704 A133 40e Mother, child 1.75 .85

1996, Oct. 9 Litho. *Perf. 12*

Designs: 2.50e, Fishing. 10e, Windsurfing. 22e, Jet skiing. No. 708, Surfing, horiz. No. 709, Diver's hand, pufferfish, horiz.

705 A134 2.50e multicolored .20 .20
706 A134 10e multicolored .30 .20
707 A134 22e multicolored .65 .40
708 A134 100e multicolored 3.00 2.00
Nos. 705-708 (4) 4.15 2.80

Souvenir Sheet

709 A134 100e multicolored 4.00 4.00

No. 709 contains one 80x61mm stamp.

Nos. 507, 575-576 Surcharged

a

b

1997 **Litho.** ***Perf. 14***
710 A77(a) 3e on 2.50e #507 .20 .20

Perf. 13½
711 A96(b) 37e on 4e #575 1.25 .75
712 A96(a) 38e on 7.50e #576 1.25 .75
Nos. 710-712 (3) 2.70 1.70

Natl. Symbols A135

1997 ***Perf. 12***
713 A135 25e Arms .80 .50
714 A135 37e Anthem 1.10 .75
715 A135 50e Flag 1.60 1.00
Nos. 713-715 (3) 3.50 2.25

World Wildlife Fund A136

Pristis pectinata: a, On seabed. b, Swimming, school of small fish. c, Swimming along seabed, small fish. d, Two near seabed.

1997 **Litho.** ***Perf. 11½***
716 A136 15e Strip of 4, #a.-d. 5.00 5.00

Legends of the Sea — A137

a, Fish, dolphins. b, Merman, mermaid. c, Fish swimming through portal, moray eel.

1997 **Litho.** ***Perf. 11½***
717 A137 45e Strip of 3, #a.-c. 3.50 3.50

Fish A138

Designs: 13e, Thunnus albacares. 21e, Thunnus obesus. 41e, Euthynnus alletteratus. 45e, Katsuwonus pelamis.

1997 **Litho.** ***Perf. 12***
718 A138 13e multicolored .35 .30
719 A138 21e multicolored .60 .60
720 A138 41e multicolored 1.25 1.10
721 A138 45e multicolored 1.40 1.25
Nos. 718-721 (4) 3.60 3.25

1998 World Cup Soccer Championships, France — A139

Designs: 30e, Soccer ball in net, vert. 45e, Soccer player, ball, vert. 50e, Globe, ball, World Cup trophy, fans in stadium.

1998 **Litho.** ***Perf. 12x11½, 11½x12***
722 A139 10e shown .25 .25
723 A139 30e multicolored .80 .80
724 A139 45e multicolored 1.25 1.25
725 A139 50e multicolored 1.40 1.40
Nos. 722-725 (4) 3.70 3.70

Traditional Cuisine A140

5e, Boiled fish. 25e, Xerém com friginato. 35e, Cachupa. 40e, Molho de Saint-Nicholas.

1998 **Litho.** ***Perf. 12x11½***
726 A140 5e multicolored .20 .20
727 A140 25e multicolored .65 .65
728 A140 35e multicolored 1.00 1.00
729 A140 40e multicolored 1.10 1.10
Nos. 726-729 (4) 2.95 2.95

Early Exploration A141

a, Quotation from Lusiadas, two men looking at maps. b, Man with sword, man & woman. c, Compass, map, sailing ship, buildings on cliff.

1998 ***Perf. 11½***
730 A141 50e Strip of 3, #a.-c. 4.00 4.00

Women's Traditional Costumes — A142

1998 **Litho.** ***Perf. 12***
731 A142 10e Brava .25 .25
732 A142 18e Fogo .50 .50
733 A142 30e Boa Vista .80 .80
734 A142 50e Santiago 1.40 1.40
Nos. 731-734 (4) 2.95 2.95

Butterflies and Moths A143

Designs: 5e, Byblia ilithyia. 10e, Aganais speciosa. 20e, Utetheisia pulchella. 30e, Vanessa cardui. 50e, Trichoplusia ni. 100e, Grammodes congenita.

1999, Mar. 16 **Litho.** ***Perf. 11¾***
735 A143 5e multi .20 .20
736 A143 10e multi .25 .25
737 A143 20e multi .50 .50
738 A143 30e multi .75 .75
a. Souvenir sheet, #737-738 2.25 2.25
739 A143 50e multi 1.25 1.25
740 A143 100e multi 2.50 2.50
Nos. 735-740 (6) 5.45 5.45

No. 738a sold for 100e.

First Concorde Flight, 30th Anniv. A144

Concorde: 30e, In flight. 50e, On ground.

1999, June 14 **Litho.** ***Perf. 12***
741-742 A144 Set of 2 2.00 2.00

Famous People — A145

Design: 30e, Alain Gerbault (1893-1941), sailor, boats at dock. 50e, Roberto Duarte Silva (1837-89), chemist, Eiffel Tower.

1999, July 2 **Litho.** ***Perf. 14½***
743 A145 30e multi 2.00 2.00
744 A145 50e multi 3.00 3.00
744a Souvenir sheet, #743-744 6.00 6.00

Philex France 99 (#744a).

A146

UPU, 125th Anniv. A147

1999, Sept. 15 ***Perf. 12x11¾***
745 A146 30e shown .65 .65
746 A147 50e shown 1.10 1.10

With Country Name Added
747 A146 30e multi .65 .65
748 A147 50e multi 1.10 1.10
Nos. 745-748 (4) 3.50 3.50

Dance A148

Designs: 10e, Colá Sanjon, vert. 30e, Contradança, vert. 50e, Desfile de tabanca. 100e, Batuque.

Perf. 11¾x12, 12x11¾
1999, Nov. 5 **Litho.**
749-752 A148 Set of 4 3.75 3.75

Millennium — A149

2000, Jan. 31 **Litho.** ***Perf. 11¾x11½***
753-754 A149 Set of 2 1.90 1.90

SOS Children's Villages A150

Emblem and child: 50e, Seated, vert. 100e, With arms outstretched.

smile ***Perf. 11¾x12, 12x11¾***
2000, Apr. 28 **Litho.**
755-756 A150 Set of 2 2.75 2.75

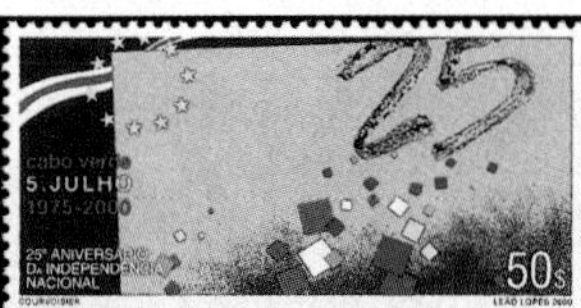

Independence, 25th Anniv. — A151

2000, July 5 ***Perf. 11¾***
757 A151 50e multi .95 .95

2000 Summer Olympics, Sydney A152

Designs: 10e, Women's gymnastics. 40e, Taekwondo. 50e, Women's hurdles.

2000, Sept. 15 **Litho.** ***Perf. 11¾***
758-760 A152 Set of 3 1.60 1.60
760a Souvenir sheet of 3, #758-760 1.60 1.60

Dragoeiro Tree — A153

2000, Oct. 9 **Litho.** ***Perf. 11¾x11½***
761 A153 5e green — —
762 A153 40e red — —
763 A153 60e brown — —

Sao Nicolau Seminary and School — A154

No. 764: a, Seminarians and students (denomination at LR, 27x26mm). b, Seminarians and students (denomination at LL, 29x26mm). c, José Alves Feijo, Dr. Julio Dias and Canon António Bouças (56x26mm).

Illustration reduced.

2000, Dec. 15 **Litho.** ***Perf. 14½***
764 A154 60e Horiz. strip of 3, #a-c 3.00 3.00

Fish A155

Designs: 10e, Diplodus sargus lineatus. 22e, Diplodus prayensis. 28e, Lithognathus mormyrus. 48e, Diplodus fasciatus. 60e, Diplodus puntazzo.

2001, Apr. 24 ***Perf. 12x11¾***
765-769 A155 Set of 5 2.75 2.75

Spiders A156

Designs: 13e, Thomisus onustus. 16e, Scytodes velutina. 40e, Hersiliola simoni. 100e, Loxosceles rufescens.

2001, May 28
770-773 A156 Set of 4 2.75 2.75

Souvenir Sheet

Belgica 2001 Intl. Stamp Exhibition, Brussels — A157

Perf. 11¾x11½

2001, June 9 **Photo.**
774 A157 100e multi 1.75 1.75

Year of Dialogue Among Civilizations — A158

2001, Oct. 9 Litho. ***Perf. 11¾x12***
775 A158 60e multi 1.00 1.00

António Aurélio Gonçalves (1901-84), Writer — A159

2001, Dec. 20 ***Perf. 12¼***
776 A159 100e multi 1.75 1.75

Medicinal Plants A160

Designs: 10e, Euphorbia tuckeyna. 50e, Limonium sunding, vert. 60e, Aeonium gorgoneum, vert. 100e, Polycarpaea gayi, vert.

Perf. 12x11¾, 11¾x12

2002, Apr. 26 **Litho.**
777-780 A160 Set of 4 4.00 4.00

2002 World Cup Soccer Championships, Japan and Korea — A161

Designs: 60e, Player heading ball towards goal. 100e, Player kicking ball towards goal.

2002, July 22 ***Perf. 12x11¾***
781-782 A161 Set of 2 3.00 3.00

Caretta Caretta A162

Designs: 10e, Pair mating. 20e, Female laying eggs, vert. 30e, Eggs hatching. 60e, Hatchlings heading for sea, vert. No. 787, 100e, Turtle swimming underwater.

No. 788, 100e, Turtle on beach.

2002, Sept. 9 ***Perf. 12x11¾, 11¾x12***
783-787 A162 Set of 5 4.00 4.00

Souvenir Sheet

788 A162 100e multi 1.75 1.75

No. 788 contains one 80x60mm stamp.

Basketry A163

Baskets and basket weavers from: 20e, Sao Nicolau Island. 33e, Santo Antao Island. 60e, Santiago Island, 100e, Boa Vista Island.

2002, Oct. 29 ***Perf. 12x11¾***
789-792 A163 Set of 4 4.00 4.00

Composers and Poets A164

Designs: 12e, Katcháss (1951-88), composer. 20e, Jorge Monteiro (1913-98), composer. 32e, Luis Rendall (1898-1986), composer. 47.50e, Jorge Barbosa (1902-71), poet. 60e, Januário Leite (1865-1930), poet. 100e, José Lopes (1872-1962), poet.

2003, Feb. 24
793-798 A164 Set of 6 5.50 5.50

Birds — A165

Designs: 10e, Ardea bournei. 27e, Ardea cinerea. 42e, Bubulcus ibis. 60e, Egretta garzeta.

2003, July 9 ***Perf. 14x13¾***
799-802 A165 Set of 4 2.75 2.75

Cesaria Evora, Singer A166

Designs: 60e, Evora at left. 100e, Evora at right.
200e, Feet of Evora.

2003, May 26 ***Perf. 13¾x14***
803-804 A166 Set of 2 3.00 3.00

Souvenir Sheet

Perf. 12¼x12

805 A166 200e multi + label 3.50 3.50

No. 805 contains one 50x38mm stamp.

Scouting in Cape Verde A167

Emblem and scout of: 60e, Scouts Association of Cape Verde. 100e, Cape Verde Scouts Corps.

2003, Oct. 24 Litho. ***Perf. 13¾x14***
806-807 A167 Set of 2 3.00 3.00

Whales A168

Designs: 10e, Balaenoptera musculus. 20e, Physeter macrocephalus. 50e, Megaptera novaeangliae. 60e, Globicephala macrorhynchus.

2003, Nov. 25 ***Perf. 12***
808-811 A168 Set of 4 2.60 2.60

First Dakar — Praia Seaplane Flight of Europe — Africa — South America Airmail Service, 75th Anniv. — A169

Seaplane and: 10e, Crew. 42e, Pilot Paulin Paris, map of South America - Africa route. 60e, Map of entire route.
100e, Like 10e.

2003, Dec. 11 ***Perf. 14***
812-814 A169 Set of 3 2.10 2.10

Souvenir Sheet

815 A169 100e multi 1.90 1.90

Election of Pope John Paul II, 25th Anniv. — A170

Pope John Paul II and: 30e, Girl. 60e, Boats, horiz.
100e, Censer and crucifix.

2003, Dec. 29 ***Perf. 14x13¾, 13¾x14***
816-817 A170 Set of 2 1.75 1.75

Souvenir Sheet

818 A170 100e multi 1.90 1.90

Trees A171

Windmill A172

Designs: 20e, Khaya senegalensis. 27e, Acacia nilotica. 60e, Ceiba pentandra. 100e, Phoenix atlantica.

2004, Jan. 25 ***Perf. 14x13¾***
819-822 A171 Set of 4 3.75 3.75

2004, June 3 ***Perf. 13¼x13***

Colors: 20e, Blue. 60e, Red. 100e, Green.

823-825 A172 Set of 3 3.50 3.50

2004 Summer Olympics, Athens — A173

Designs: 10e, Taekwondo. 60e, Rhythmic gymnastics. 100e, Boxing, horiz.

Perf. 13¼x13, 13x13¼

2004, Aug. 13 **Litho.**
826-828 A173 Set of 3 3.75 3.75

Lighthouses A174

Designs: 10e, Ponta do Barril Lighthouse, Sao Nicolau Island. 30e, Ponta Jalunga Lighthouse, Brava Island. 40e, D. Luis Lighthouse, Passaros Islands, horiz. 50e, Ponta Preta Lighthouse, Santiago Island, horiz.

2004, Sept. 7
829-832 A174 Set of 4 3.00 3.00

Houses on Fogo Island A175

Various houses: 20e, 40e, 50e, 60e.

2004 ***Perf. 13x13¼***
833-836 A175 Set of 4 4.25 4.25

Telephones — A176

Old telephones and: 10e, Switchboard. 40e, Operator. 60e, Telephone directory. 100e, Truck and telephone poles.

2004
837-840 A176 Set of 4 5.25 5.25

AIR POST STAMPS

Common Design Type
Name and Value in Black

Perf. 13½x13

1938, July 26 **Unwmk.**

C1	CD39	10c red orange	.60	.50
C2	CD39	20c purple	.60	.50
C3	CD39	50c orange	.60	.50
C4	CD39	1e ultra	.60	.50
C5	CD39	2e lilac brown	1.40	.80
C6	CD39	3e dk green	1.75	1.40
C7	CD39	5e red brown	5.50	2.10
C8	CD39	9e rose carmine	9.00	3.75
C9	CD39	10e magenta	9.75	5.00
		Nos. C1-C9 (9)	29.80	15.05
		Set, never hinged	50.00	

No. C7 exists with overprint "Exposicao Internacional de Nova York, 1939-1940" and Trylon and Perisphere.

POSTAGE DUE STAMPS

D1

D2

1904 Unwmk. Typo. *Perf. 12*

No.	Type	Description	Unused	Used
J1	D1	5r yellow grn	.40	*.25*
J2	D1	10r slate	.40	*.25*
J3	D1	20r yellow brn	.50	*.40*
J4	D1	30r red orange	1.25	*.40*
J5	D1	50r gray brown	.50	*.35*
J6	D1	60r red brown	9.25	4.25
J7	D1	100r lilac	1.75	1.25
J8	D1	130r dull blue	1.90	1.25
J9	D1	200r carmine	1.60	1.60
J10	D1	500r dull violet	5.00	*3.00*
		Nos. J1-J10 (10)	22.55	*13.00*

Overprinted in Carmine or Green

1911

No.	Type	Description	Unused	Used
J11	D1	5r yellow grn	.30	.20
J12	D1	10r slate	.30	.20
J13	D1	20r yellow brn	.35	.20
J14	D1	30r orange	.35	.20
J15	D1	50r gray brown	.65	.40
J16	D1	60r red brown	.65	.40
J17	D1	100r lilac	.65	.40
J18	D1	130r dull blue	.75	.65
J19	D1	200r carmine (G)	2.00	1.50
J20	D1	500r dull violet	2.50	1.75
		Nos. J11-J20 (10)	8.50	5.90

1921 *Perf. 11½*

No.	Type	Description	Unused	Used
J21	D2	½c yellow grn	.30	.20
J22	D2	1c slate	.30	.20
J23	D2	2c red brown	.30	.20
J24	D2	3c orange	.30	.20
J25	D2	5c gray brown	.30	.20
J26	D2	6c lt brown	.30	.20
J27	D2	10c red violet	.30	.20
J28	D2	13c dull blue	.55	*.40*
J29	D2	20c carmine	.60	*.50*
J30	D2	50c gray	1.75	*1.10*
		Nos. J21-J30 (10)	5.00	*3.40*

Catalogue values for unused stamps in this section, from this point to the end of the section, are for Never Hinged items.

Common Design Type

Photogravure and Typographed

1952 Unwmk. *Perf. 14*

Numeral in Red, Frame Multicolored

No.	Type	Description	Unused	Used
J31	CD45	10c chocolate	.30	.25
J32	CD45	30c black brown	.30	.25
J33	CD45	50c dark blue	.30	.25
J34	CD45	1e dark blue	.40	.25
J35	CD45	2e red brown	.40	.30
J36	CD45	5e olive green	1.10	1.00
		Nos. J31-J36 (6)	2.80	2.30

NEWSPAPER STAMP

N1

1893 Typo. Unwmk. *Perf. 11½*

No.	Type	Description	Unused	Used
P1	N1	2½r brown	1.50	.60
a.		Perf. 12½	3.00	1.50
b.		Perf. 13½	6.50	3.00

For surcharges see Nos. 79, 206.

POSTAL TAX STAMPS

Pombal Issue

Common Design Types

1925 Unwmk. Engr. *Perf. 12½*

No.	Type	Description	Unused	Used
RA1	CD28	15c dull vio & blk	.75	.70
RA2	CD29	15c dull vio & blk	.75	.70
RA3	CD30	15c dull vio & blk	.75	.70
		Nos. RA1-RA3 (3)	2.25	2.10

St. Isabel — PT1

PT2

1948 Litho. *Perf. 11*

No.	Type	Description	Unused	Used
RA4	PT1	50c dark green	3.75	2.40
RA5	PT1	1e henna brown	7.50	3.00

Catalogue values for unused stamps in this section, from this point to the end of the section, are for Never Hinged items.

No. RA5 Surcharged with New Value and Bars

1959

No.	Type	Description	Unused	Used
RA6	PT1	50c on 1e henna brown	1.40	1.10

Perf. 14

No.	Type	Description	Unused	Used
RA7	PT1	50c carmine rose	2.10	1.00
RA8	PT1	1e blue	2.10	1.00

St. Isabel Type Redrawn

1967-73 Litho. *Perf. 14*

No.	Type	Description	Unused	Used
RA9	PT1	30c (blue panel)	.20	.20
RA9A	PT1	30c (orange panel)	.20	.20
RA10	PT1	50c (lilac rose panel)	.60	.60
RA11	PT1	50c (red panel) ('72)	*.60*	*.60*
RA12	PT1	1e (brn panel)	.85	.85
RA13	PT1	1e (red lilac panel) ('72)	*.85*	*.85*
		Nos. RA9-RA13 (6)	*3.30*	*3.30*

Nos. RA9-RA13 are inscribed "ASSISTENCIA" in large letters in bottom panel and "PORTUGAL" and "CABO VERDE" in small letters in upper left corner.

Revenue Stamps Surcharged in Green, Blue or Black

1967-72 Typo. *Perf. 12*

Black "CABO VERDE" & Value

Pale Green Burelage

No.	Type	Description	Unused	Used
RA14	PT2	50c on 1c org (Bl) ('71)	1.40	.90
a.		Black surcharge ('68?)	*15.00*	*14.50*
RA15	PT2	50c on 2c org (Bk) ('69)	*15.00*	*14.50*
c.		Inverted surcharge	*37.50*	*35.00*
RA16	PT2	50c on 3c org (G) ('72)	1.10	.60
RA17	PT2	50c on 5c org (G) ('72)	1.10	.60
RA18	PT2	50c on 10c org (G) ('71)	1.25	1.00
RA19	PT2	1e on 1c org (Bk)	2.75	2.10
RA20	PT2	1e on 2c org (G) ('71)	1.90	1.75
a.		Blue surcharge ('71)	2.00	1.10
b.		Black surcharge	2.10	2.10
		Nos. RA14-RA20 (7)	*24.50*	*21.45*

POSTAL TAX DUE STAMPS

Pombal Issue

Common Design Types

1925 Unwmk. *Perf. 12½*

No.	Type	Description	Unused	Used
RAJ1	CD28	30c dull vio & blk	.75	.70
RAJ2	CD29	30c dull vio & blk	.75	.70
RAJ3	CD30	30c dull vio & blk	.75	.70
		Nos. RAJ1-RAJ3 (3)	2.25	2.10

CAROLINE ISLANDS

ˈkar-ə-ˌlīn ˈī-ləndz

LOCATION — A group of about 549 small islands in the West Pacific Ocean, north of the Equator.
GOVT. — German colony
AREA — 550 sq. mi.
POP. — 40,000 (approx. 1915)

100 Pfennig = 1 Mark

Watermark

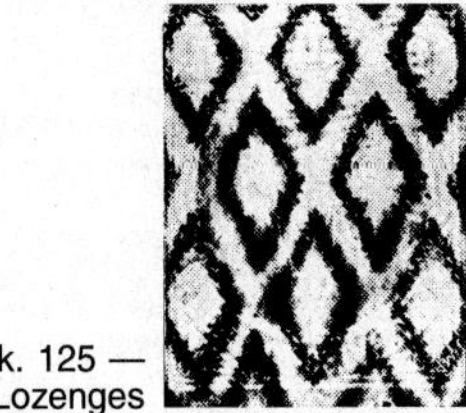
Wmk. 125 — Lozenges

#2

#2a

Stamps of Germany 1889-90 Overprinted in Black

Overprinted at 56 degree Angle

1900 Unwmk. *Perf. 13½x14½*

No.	Type	Description	Unused	Used
1	A9	3pf dk brown	14.00	*16.00*
2	A9	5pf green	16.00	*20.00*
3	A10	10pf carmine	18.00	*22.50*
4	A10	20pf ultra	22.50	*30.00*
5	A10	25pf orange	55.00	*65.00*
6	A10	50pf red brown	55.00	*65.00*
		Nos. 1-6 (6)	180.50	*218.50*

1899

Overprinted at 48 degree Angle

No.	Type	Description	Unused	Used
1a	A9	3pf light brown	525.00	*750.00*
2a	A9	5pf green	650.00	550.00
3a	A10	10pf carmine	75.00	*150.00*
4a	A10	20pf ultra	75.00	*150.00*
5a	A10	25pf orange	*1,500.*	*3,000.*
6a	A10	50pf red brown	*900.00*	*1,750.*

A3

Kaiser's Yacht "Hohenzollern" — A4

1901, Jan. Typo. *Perf. 14*

No.	Type	Description	Unused	Used
7	A3	3pf brown	.90	*1.50*
8	A3	5pf green	.90	*2.00*
9	A3	10pf carmine	.90	*4.75*
a.		Half used as 5pf on cover, back-stamped in Jaluit ('05)		*110.00*
10	A3	20pf ultra	1.25	*7.50*
a.		Half used as 10pf on cover ('10)		*8,000.*
11	A3	25pf org & blk, *yel*	1.50	*15.00*
12	A3	30pf org & blk, *sal*	1.50	*15.00*
13	A3	40pf lake & blk	1.50	*16.00*
14	A3	50pf pur & blk, *sal*	2.00	*20.00*
15	A3	80pf lake & blk, *rose*	3.00	*25.00*

Perf. 14½x14

Engr.

No.	Type	Description	Unused	Used
16	A4	1m carmine	4.00	*60.00*
17	A4	2m blue	6.00	*75.00*
18	A4	3m black violet	10.00	*150.00*
19	A4	5m slate & carmine	150.00	*550.00*
		Nos. 7-19 (13)	183.45	*941.75*

No. 9a is known as the "typhoon provisional" the stock of 5pf stamps having been destroyed during a typhoon. Covers (cards) without backstamp, value about $90.

Forged cancellations are found on #7-19.

No. 7 Handstamp Surcharged **5 Pf**

1910, July 12

No.	Type	Description	Unused	Used
20	A3	5pf on 3pf brown		*5,250.*
a.		Inverted surcharge		*6,000.*
b.		Double surcharge		*5,500.*

Values are for stamps tied to cover. Stamps on piece sell for about 40% less.

1915-19 Wmk. 125 Typo.

No.	Type	Description	Unused	Used
21	A3	3pf brown ('19)	.80	
22	A3	5pf green	10.50	

Engr.

No.	Type	Description	Unused	Used
23	A4	5m slate & carmine	15.00	
		Nos. 21-23 (3)	26.30	

Nos. 21-23 were not placed in use.

CASTELLORIZO

ˌkäs-tə-ˈlor-ə-ˌzō

(Castelrosso)

LOCATION — A Mediterranean island in the Dodecanese group lying close to the coast of Asia Minor and about 60 miles east of Rhodes.
GOVT. — Former Italian Colony
AREA — 4 sq. mi.
POP. — 2,238 (1936)

Formerly a Turkish possession, Castellorizo was occupied by the French in 1915 and ceded to Italy after World War I. In 1945 it became part of Greece.

25 Centimes = 1 Piaster
100 Centimes = 1 Franc

Used values in italics are for postally used copies. Stamps with CTO cancels sell for about the same as hinged, unused stamps.

Issued under French Occupation

Stamps of French Offices in Turkey Overprinted

1920 Unwmk. *Perf. 14x13½*

No.	Type	Description	Unused	Used
1	A2	1c gray	32.50	32.50
a.		Inverted overprint	95.00	95.00
b.		Double overprint	110.00	110.00
2	A2	2c vio brn	32.50	32.50
3	A2	3c red org	32.50	32.50
a.		Inverted overprint	95.00	95.00
4	A2	5c green	37.50	37.50
a.		Inverted overprint	95.00	95.00
5	A3	10c rose	40.00	40.00
6	A3	15c pale red	57.50	57.50
a.		Inverted overprint	175.00	175.00
7	A3	20c brn vio	65.00	65.00
8	A5	1pi on 25c blue	65.00	65.00
a.		Pair, one without overprint	240.00	
9	A3	30c lilac	72.50	72.50

Overprint Reading Down

No.	Type	Description	Unused	Used
10	A4	40c red & pale bl	125.00	125.00
a.		Inverted ovpt (reading up)	500.00	500.00
11	A6	2pi on 50c bis brn & lav	140.00	140.00
a.		Inverted ovpt (reading up)	500.00	500.00
b.		Double overprint	675.00	*675.00*
12	A6	4pi on 1fr cl & ol grn	190.00	190.00
a.		Double overprint	575.00	575.00
b.		Inverted ovpt (reading up)	575.00	575.00
13	A6	20pi on 5fr dk bl & buff	500.00	500.00
a.		Double overprint	1,050.	*1,050.*
		Nos. 1-13 (13)	1,390.	1,390.

No. 1-9 were overprinted in blocks of 25. Position 4 had "CASTELLORIZO" inverted and Positions 8 and 18 had "CASTELLORISO." The later variety also occurred in the setting of the form for Nos. 10-13.

"B. N. F." are the initials of "Base Navale Francaise".

Overprinted in Black or Red

1920

On Stamps of French Offices in Turkey

14 A2 1c gray 18.00 18.00
15 A2 2c vio brn 18.00 18.00
16 A2 3c red org 20.00 20.00
17 A2 5c green (R) 20.00 20.00
19 A3 10c rose 24.00 24.00
20 A3 15c pale red 30.00 30.00
21 A3 20c brn vio 50.00 50.00
22 A5 1pi on 25c bl (R) 47.50 47.50
23 A3 30c lilac (R) 47.50 47.50
24 A4 40c red & pale bl 47.50 47.50
25 A6 2pi on 50c bis brn & lav 47.50 47.50
26 A6 4pi on 1fr claret & ol grn 55.00 55.00
28 A6 20pi on 5fr dk bl & buff 260.00 260.00
Nos. 14-28 (13) 685.00 685.00

On Nos. 25, 26 and 28 the two lines of the overprint are set wider apart than on the lower values.

"O.N.F." are the initials of "Occupation Navale Francaise."

"Casetllorizo" and "astellorizo" varieties are known on Nos. 14-23.

Overprint on 8pi on 2fr (#37), value $900 unused, $1,000 used.

On Stamps of France

30 A22 10c red 30.00 17.50
a. Inverted overprint 150.00
31 A22 25c blue (R) 30.00 16.00
a. Inverted overprint 175.00

This overprint exists on 8 other 1900-1907 denominations of France (5c, 15c, 20c, 30c, 40c, 50c, 1fr, 5fr). These are believed not to have been issued or postally used.

Stamps of France, 1900-1907, Handstamped in Black or Violet

1920

33 A22 5c green 125.00 125.00
34 A22 10c red 125.00 125.00
35 A22 20c vio brn 125.00 125.00
36 A22 25c blue 125.00 125.00
37 A18 50c bis brn & lav 800.00 800.00
38 A18 1fr cl & ol grn (V) 800.00 800.00
Nos. 33-38 (6) 2,100. 2,100.

Nos. 1-38 are considered speculative.

Forgeries of overprints on Nos. 1-38 exist. They abound of Nos. 33-38.

Stamps of French Offices in Turkey handstamped "Occupation Francaise Castellorizo" were made privately.

Issued under Italian Dominion

100 Centesimi = 1 Lira

Italian Stamps of 1906-20 Overprinted

1922 Wmk. 140 *Perf. 14*

51 A48 5c green 2.50 *13.00*
52 A48 10c claret 1.10 *13.00*
53 A48 15c slate 1.90 *13.00*
54 A50 20c brn org 1.10 *13.00*
a. Double overprint 240.00
55 A49 25c blue 1.10 *13.00*
56 A49 40c brown 30.00 16.00
57 A49 50c violet 30.00 16.00
58 A49 60c carmine 30.00 24.00
59 A49 85c chocolate 2.25 *27.50*
Nos. 51-59 (9) 99.95 *148.50*
Set, never hinged 240.00

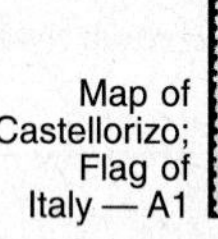

Map of Castellorizo; Flag of Italy — A1

1923

60 A1 5c gray green 2.25 *13.00*
61 A1 10c dull rose 2.25 *13.00*
62 A1 25c dull blue 2.25 *13.00*
63 A1 50c gray lilac 2.25 *13.00*
64 A1 1 l brown 2.25 *13.00*
Nos. 60-64 (5) 11.25 *65.00*
Set, never hinged 27.50

Italian Stamps of 1901-20 Overprinted

1924

65 A48 5c green 1.00 *18.00*
66 A48 10c claret 1.00 *18.00*
67 A48 15c slate 1.00 *22.50*
68 A50 20c brn orange 1.00 *22.50*
a. Double overprint 80.00
69 A49 25c blue 1.00 *18.00*
70 A49 40c brown 1.00 *18.00*
71 A49 50c violet 1.00 *20..00*
72 A49 60c carmine 1.00 *25.00*
a. Double overprint 250.00
73 A49 85c red brown 1.00 *32.50*
74 A46 1 l brn & green 1.00 *32.50*
Nos. 65-74 (10) 10.00 *227.00*
Set, never hinged 25.00

Ferrucci Issue

Types of Italian Stamps of 1930, Overprinted in Red or Blue

1930 Wmk. Crowns (140)

75 A102 20c violet 4.50 *4.50*
76 A103 25c dark green 4.50 *10.00*
77 A103 50c black 4.50 *4.50*
78 A103 1.25 l deep blue 4.50 *11.00*
79 A104 5 l + 2 l dp car (Bl) 19.00 *45.00*
Nos. 75-79 (5) 37.00 *75.00*
Set, never hinged 90.00

Garibaldi Issue

Types of Italian Stamps of 1932, Overprinted like Nos. 75-79 in Red or Blue

1932

80 A138 10c brown 16.00 *32.50*
81 A138 20c red brn (Bl) 16.00 *32.50*
82 A138 25c dp grn 16.00 *32.50*
83 A138 30c bluish slate 16.00 *32.50*
84 A138 50c red vio (Bl) 16.00 *32.50*
85 A141 75c cop red (Bl) 16.00 *32.50*
86 A141 1.25 l dull blue 16.00 *32.50*
87 A141 1.75 l + 25c brn 16.00 *32.50*
88 A144 2.55 l + 50c org (Bl) 16.00 *32.50*
89 A145 5 l + 1 l dl vio 16.00 *32.50*
Nos. 80-89 (10) 160.00 *325.00*
Set, never hinged 400.00

CAYMAN ISLANDS

ˌkā-ˈman ˈī-lənds

LOCATION — Three islands in the Caribbean Sea, about 200 miles northwest of Jamaica
GOVT. — British Crown Colony, formerly a dependency of Jamaica
AREA — 100 sq. mi.
POP. — 39,335 (1999 est.)
CAPITAL — George Town, located on Grand Cayman

12 Pence = 1 Shilling
20 Shilling = 1 Pound
100 Cents = 1 Dollar (1969)

Watermark

Wmk. 362 — Basotho Hat Multiple

Catalogue values for unused stamps in this country are for Never Hinged items, beginning with Scott 112.

Victoria A1 Edward VII A2

1900 Typo. Wmk. 2 *Perf. 14*

1 A1 ½p pale green 5.25 *17.50*
2 A1 1p carmine rose 5.25 2.75

1901-03

3 A2 ½p green ('02) 5.25 *29.00*
4 A2 1p car rose ('03) 11.50 *10.50*
5 A2 2½p ultramarine 11.50 *14.00*
6 A2 6p chocolate 35.00 *70.00*
7 A2 1sh brown orange 70.00 *125.00*
Nos. 3-7 (5) 133.25 *248.50*

1905 Wmk. 3

8 A2 ½p green 8.00 *10.00*
9 A2 1p carmine rose 16.00 *20.00*
10 A2 2½p ultramarine 8.00 3.75
11 A2 6p chocolate 19.00 *45.00*
12 A2 1sh brown orange 37.50 *55.00*
Nos. 8-12 (5) 88.50 *133.75*

For surcharge see No. 17.

1907, Mar. 13

13 A2 4p brown & blue 37.50 *70.00*
14 A2 6p ol green & rose 37.50 *80.00*
15 A2 1sh violet & green 65.00 *92.50*
16 A2 5sh ver & green 210.00 *350.00*
Nos. 13-16 (4) 350.00 *592.50*

Numerals of 4p, 1sh and 5sh of type A2 are in color on colorless tablet.

For surcharges see Nos. 18-20.

Nos. 9, 16, 13 Handstamped

#17

#18

#19

#20

1907-08

17 A2 ½p on 1p 50.00 *80.00*
18 A2 ½p on 5sh 400.00 *450.00*
a. Inverted surcharge *35,000.*
b. Double surcharge *11,000.* *11,000.*
c. Dbl. surch., one inverted
d. Pair, one without surcharge *52,500.*
19 A2 1p on 5sh 290.00 *400.00*
a. Double surcharge *16,000.* *7,500.*
20 A2 2½p on 4p ('08) 1,750. *2,900.*
a. Double surcharge *35,000.* *21,000.*

The 1p on 4p is a revenue stamp not authorized for postal use. Value about $300. Varieties exist.

A3 A4

1907-09 *Perf. 14*

21 A3 ½p green 3.00 4.75
22 A3 1p carmine rose 1.75 .85
23 A3 2½p ultramarine 4.00 4.00

Chalky Paper

24 A3 3p violet, *yellow* 3.75 *7.50*
25 A3 4p blk & red, *yel* 57.50 *80.00*
26 A3 6p violet 11.50 *40.00*
27 A3 1sh black, *grn* 8.75 *26.00*
28 A3 5sh grn & red, *yel* 45.00 *70.00*
Nos. 21-28 (8) 135.25 *233.10*

Issued: ½p, 1p, 12/27; 2½p, 3p, 4p, 5sh, 3/30/08; 6d, 10/2/08; 1sh, 4/5/09.

Forged cancellations are found on No. 28.

1908, Mar. 30 Wmk. 2

29 A3 1sh black, *green* 70.00 *100.00*
30 A3 10sh grn & red, *grn* 190.00 *260.00*

Numerals of 3p, 4p, 1sh and 5sh of type A3 are in color on plain tablet.

Forged cancellations are found on No. 30.

1908 Wmk. 3

Ordinary Paper

31 A4 ¼p brown 2.40 .60

King George V A5 A6

1912-20

32 A5 ¼p brown ('13) 1.25 .50
33 A5 ½p green 3.25 *6.00*
34 A5 1p carmine ('13) 4.00 *3.00*
35 A5 2p gray 1.25 *12.50*
36 A5 2½p ultra ('14) 8.50 *13.50*

Chalky Paper

37 A5 3p vio, *yel* ('13) 3.00 *22.50*
38 A5 4p blk & red, *yel* ('13) 1.25 *12.50*
39 A5 6p vio & red vio ('13) 4.50 *9.00*
40 A5 1sh blk, *grn* ('13) 4.25 *32.50*
41 A5 2sh vio & ultra, *bl* 14.50 *57.50*
42 A5 3sh green & vio 22.50 *77.50*
43 A5 5sh grn & red, *yel* ('14) 90.00 *190.00*
44 A5 10sh grn & red, *bl grn*, olive back ('18) 225.00 *240.00*
a. 10sh green & red, *grn* ('13) 150.00 *240.00*
Nos. 32-44 (13) 383.25 *677.00*

The first printings of the 3p, 1sh and 10sh have a white back.

For surcharges see Nos. MR1-MR7.

1913, Nov. 19

Surface-colored Paper

45 A5 3p violet, *yel* 4.25 *9.50*
46 A5 1sh black, *green* 4.25 *4.25*
47 A5 10sh grn & red, *grn* 100.00 *175.00*
Nos. 45-47 (3) 108.50 *188.75*

Numeral of ¼p, 2p, 3p, 4p, 1sh, 2sh, 3sh and 5sh of type A5 are in color on plain tablet.

1921-26 Wmk. 4 *Perf. 14*

50 A6 ¼p yel brown .60 *1.75*
51 A6 ½p gray green .60 .35
52 A6 1p rose red 1.75 *1.00*
53 A6 1½p orange brn 2.10 .35
54 A6 2p gray 2.10 *4.75*
55 A6 2½p ultramarine .60 .60
56 A6 3p violet, *yel* 1.25 *4.75*
57 A6 4½p olive grn 2.75 *3.75*
58 A6 6p claret 6.50 *37.50*
59 A6 1sh black, *grn* 11.50 *37.50*
60 A6 2sh violet, *blue* 17.00 *29.00*
61 A6 3sh violet 27.50 19.00
62 A6 5sh green, *yel* 29.00 *55.00*
63 A6 10sh car, *green* 72.50 *100.00*
Nos. 50-63 (14) 175.75 *295.30*

Issued: 1½p, 4/4/21; ¼p, ½p, 1p, 2p, 2½p, 6p, 2sh, 3sh, 4/1/22; 3p, 4½p, 6/29/23; 5sh, 2/15/25; 1sh, 5/15/25; 10sh, 9/5/26.

1921-22 **Wmk. 3**

64 A6 3p violet, *org* 1.75 *9.50*
65 A6 4p red, *yel* 1.25 *4.75*
66 A6 1sh black, *green* 1.50 *11.50*
67 A6 5sh green, *yel* 19.00 *85.00*
68 A6 10sh car, *green* 72.50 *125.00*
Nos. 64-68 (5) 96.00 *235.75*

Issued: 4p, 4/1/22; others, 4/4/21.

King William IV, King George V A7

Perf. 12½

1932, Dec. 5 **Wmk. 4** **Engr.**

69 A7 ¼p brown 1.90 1.25
70 A7 ½p green 3.25 *9.50*
71 A7 1p carmine 3.25 *9.50*
72 A7 1½p orange 3.25 3.25
73 A7 2p gray 3.25 *4.25*
74 A7 2½p ultramarine 3.25 1.75
75 A7 3p olive green 4.00 *6.00*
76 A7 6p red violet 11.50 *27.50*
77 A7 1sh brn & black 20.00 *37.50*
78 A7 2sh ultra & blk 55.00 *90.00*
79 A7 5sh green & blk 100.00 *140.00*
80 A7 10sh car & black 300.00 *425.00*
Nos. 69-80 (12) 508.65 *755.50*

Centenary of the formation of the Cayman Islands Assembly.

Common Design Types pictured following the introduction.

Silver Jubilee Issue

Common Design Type

1935, May 6 ***Perf. 13½x14***

81 CD301 ½p green & black .20 *1.10*
82 CD301 2½p blue & brown 1.10 1.10
83 CD301 6p ol grn & lt bl 1.10 *3.75*
84 CD301 1sh brt vio & ind 7.75 7.50
Nos. 81-84 (4) 10.15 13.45
Set, never hinged 14.00

King George V A8

Catboat A9

Red-footed Boobies A10

Conches and Coconut Palms — A11

Hawksbill Turtles A12

1935-36 ***Perf. 12½***

85 A8 ¼p brown & blk .60 *1.25*
86 A9 ½p yel grn & ultra 1.25 1.25
87 A10 1p car & ultra 5.00 2.75
88 A11 1½p org & black 1.75 *2.10*
89 A9 2p brown vio & ultra 4.50 1.40
90 A12 2½p dp blue & blk 4.00 1.50
91 A8 3p ol grn & blk 3.00 *3.50*
92 A12 6p red vio & blk 10.50 5.00
93 A9 1sh org & ultra 7.25 *7.75*
94 A10 2sh black & ultra 55.00 42.50
95 A12 5sh green & blk 60.00 60.00
96 A11 10sh car & black 85.00 *110.00*
Nos. 85-96 (12) 237.85 239.00
Set, never hinged 350.00

Issued: #86, 2½p, 6p, 1sh, 1/1/36; others, 5/1/35.

Coronation Issue

Common Design Type

1937, May 13 ***Perf. 11x11½***

97 CD302 ½p deep green .20 *1.50*
98 CD302 1p dark carmine .25 .25
99 CD302 2½p deep ultra .55 .55
Nos. 97-99 (3) 1.00 2.30
Set, never hinged 2.00

Beach View, Grand Cayman A13

Dolphin — A14

Hawksbill Turtles — A16

Map of the Islands A15

Cayman Schooner A17

Perf. 12½; 11½x13 or 13x11½ (A14, #111); 14 (#104, 107)

1938-43 **Engr.**

100 A13 ¼p red orange .45 *.60*
a. Perf. 13½x12½ ('43) .20 *.70*
101 A14 ½p yel green .70 *.60*
a. Perf. 14 ('43) .90 *1.50*
102 A15 1p carmine .20 *.80*
103 A13 1½p black .20 .20
104 A16 2p dp violet ('43) .40 .30
a. Perf. 11½x13 2.10 .25
105 A17 2½p ultra .25 .20
106 A15 3p orange .25 .20
107 A16 6p dk ol grn ('43) 2.10 2.10
a. Perf. 11½x13 6.00 4.25
108 A14 1sh reddish brown 4.75 1.60
a. Perf. 14 ('43) 3.00 2.10
109 A13 2sh green 20.00 15.00
110 A17 5sh deep rose 22.50 16.00
111 A16 10sh dark brown 16.00 9.75
a. Perf. 14 ('43) 16.00 9.75
Nos. 100-111 (12) 67.80 47.35
Never hinged 125.00

See Nos. 114-115.

Catalogue values for unused stamps in this section, from this point to the end of the section, are for Never Hinged items.

Peace Issue

Common Design Type

1946, Aug. 26 **Wmk. 4** ***Perf. 13½***

112 CD303 1½p black .25 .20
113 CD303 3p orange .25 .20

Types of 1938

1947, Aug. 25 ***Perf. 12½***

114 A17 2½p orange 3.00 .60
115 A15 3p ultramarine 3.50 .35

Silver Wedding Issue

Common Design Types

1948, Nov. 29 **Photo.** ***Perf. 14x14½***

116 CD304 ½p dark green .20 .20

Perf. 11½x11

Engr.; Name Typo.

117 CD305 10sh blue violet 17.50 17.50

UPU Issue

Common Design Types

Engr.; Name Typo. on #119, 120

1949, Oct. 10 ***Perf. 13½, 11x11½***

118 CD306 2½p orange .30 *.70*
119 CD307 3p indigo 1.75 *2.00*
120 CD308 6p olive .70 *2.00*
121 CD309 1sh red brown .70 .40
Nos. 118-121 (4) 3.45 5.10

Catboat A18

Designs: ½p, Coconut grove. 1p, Green turtle. 1½p, Thatch rope industry. 2p, Caymanian seamen. 2½p, Map. 3p, Parrot fish. 6p, Bluff, Cayman Brac. 9p, George Town harbor. 1sh, Turtle "crawl". 2sh, Cayman schooner. 5sh, Boat-building. 10sh, Government offices.

Perf. 11½x11

1950, Oct. 2 **Wmk. 4** **Engr.**

122 A18 ¼p rose red & blue .20 *.60*
123 A18 ½p bl grn & red vio .20 *1.25*
124 A18 1p dp blue & olive .60 *.75*
125 A18 1½p choc & bl grn .30 *.75*
126 A18 2p rose car & vio 1.25 *1.50*
127 A18 2½p sepia & aqua 1.25 .65
128 A18 3p bl & blue grn 1.75 1.50
129 A18 6p dp bl & org brn 2.00 1.25
130 A18 9p dk grn & rose red 5.50 2.00
131 A18 1sh red org & brn 3.50 2.75
132 A18 2sh red vio & vio 8.50 9.50
133 A18 5sh vio & olive 13.50 7.50
134 A18 10sh rose red & blk 18.00 15.00
Nos. 122-134 (13) 56.55 45.00

Types of 1950 with Portrait of Queen Elizabeth II and

Lighthouse, South Sound — A20

Elizabeth II and Turtles — A21

Perf. 11½x11, 11x11½

1953-59 **Engr.**

135 A18 ¼p rose red & bl .95 .60
136 A18 ½p bl grn & red vio .55 .55
137 A18 1p dp bl & olive .65 .50
138 A18 1½p choc & bl grn .50 .20
139 A18 2p rose car & vio 2.75 1.00
140 A18 2½p black & aqua 3.50 .95
141 A18 3p blue & bl grn 4.00 .70
142 A20 4p dp blue & black 2.00 .50
143 A18 6p dp bl & red brn 1.75 .20
144 A18 9p dk green & rose red 5.25 .25
145 A18 1sh red org & brn 3.00 .20
146 A18 2sh red vio & vio 12.50 9.25
147 A18 5sh violet & olive 14.00 8.00
148 A18 10sh rose red & blk 14.50 8.50
149 A21 £1 bright blue 30.00 11.50
Nos. 135-149 (15) 95.90 42.90

Issued: 4p, 3/2; 2p, 2½p, 9p, 6/2/54; ½p, 1p, 1½p, 6p, 7/7/54; ¼p, 3p, 1sh-10sh, 2/21/55; £1, 1/6/59.

Coronation Issue

Common Design Type

1953, June 2 ***Perf. 13½x13***

150 CD312 1p brt green & black .30 *.75*

Arms of Cayman Islands A22

Perf. 12

1959, July 4 **Wmk. 4** **Photo.**

151 A22 2½p dull blue & blk .55 1.00
152 A22 1sh red orange & blk .65 .40

Granting of a new constitution.

Cayman Parrot — A23

Catboat A24

1½p, Orchid. 2p, May of Islands. 2½p, Fisherman casting net. 3p, West Bay Beach. 4p, Green turtle. 6p, Cayman schooner. 9p, Angler with kingfish. 1sh, Iguana. 1sh3p, Swimming pool, Cayman Brac. 1sh9p, Girl and sailboat. 5sh, Fort George. 10sh, Coat of Arms. £1, Queen Elizabeth II.

Perf. 11x11½, 11½x11

1962, Nov. 28 **Wmk. 314** **Engr.**

153 A23 ¼p rose red & emer .50 *1.10*
154 A24 1p olive & black .70 .20
155 A24 1½p purple & yel 2.25 .90
156 A24 2p sepia & blue .90 .35
157 A24 2½p green & vio .70 *1.10*
158 A24 3p car & blue .25 .20
159 A24 4p pur & green 1.10 .65
160 A24 6p sepia & green 2.75 .35
161 A23 9p pur & vio bl 1.90 .45
162 A24 1sh rose & sepia .70 .20
163 A24 1sh3p brn org & lt grn 3.25 2.10
164 A24 1sh9p vio & bl grn 13.50 1.50
165 A24 5sh grn & dl pur 7.75 7.25
166 A23 10sh blue & olive 15.00 9.50
167 A23 £1 blk & car rose 17.00 *19.00*
Revenue cancel .75
Nos. 153-167 (15) 68.25 44.85

Freedom from Hunger Issue

Common Design Type

1963, June 4 **Photo.** ***Perf. 14x14½***

168 CD314 1sh9p car rose .50 .25

Red Cross Centenary Issue

Common Design Type

Wmk. 314

1963, Sept. 2 **Litho.** ***Perf. 13***

169 CD315 1p black & red .20 .20
170 CD315 1sh9p ultra & red 1.10 1.75

Shakespeare Issue

Common Design Type

1964, Apr. 23 **Photo.** ***Perf. 14x14½***

171 CD316 6p deep lilac rose .30 .25

ITU Issue

Common Design Type

1965, May 17 **Litho.** **Wmk. 314**

172 CD317 1p ultra & red lil .20 .20
173 CD317 1sh3p rose lil & grn .90 .75

Intl. Cooperation Year Issue

Common Design Type

1965, Oct. 25 **Wmk. 314** ***Perf. 14½***

174 CD318 1p blue grn & claret .20 .20
175 CD318 1sh lt vio & green .65 .65

Churchill Memorial Issue
Common Design Type

1966, Jan. 24 Photo. ***Perf. 14***
Design in Black, Gold and Carmine Rose

176 CD319 ¼p bright blue .20 .20
177 CD319 1p green .20 .20
178 CD319 1sh brown .60 .60
179 CD319 1sh9p violet 1.00 1.00
Nos. 176-179 (4) 2.00 2.00

Royal Visit Issue
Common Design Type

1966, Feb. 4 Litho. ***Perf. 11x12***
180 CD320 1p violet blue .70 .25
181 CD320 1sh9p dk car rose 2.75 1.25

World Cup Soccer Issue
Common Design Type

1966, July 1 Litho. ***Perf. 14***
182 CD321 1½p multicolored .20 .20
183 CD321 1sh9p multicolored .65 .65

WHO Headquarters Issue
Common Design Type

1966, Sept. 20 Litho. ***Perf. 14***
184 CD322 2p multicolored .50 .20
185 CD322 1sh3p multicolored 1.10 .85

UNESCO Anniversary Issue
Common Design Type

1966, Dec. 1 Litho. ***Perf. 14***
186 CD323 1p "Education" .20 .20
187 CD323 1sh9p "Science" .90 .30
188 CD323 5sh "Culture" 1.90 1.00
Nos. 186-188 (3) 3.00 1.50

Telephone and Map of Caymans — A25

Perf. 14½x14
1966, Dec. 5 Litho. Wmk. 314
189 A25 4p multicolored .20 .20
190 A25 9p multicolored .30 .30

Linking of the Cayman telephone system with the intl. system.

BAC 1-11 Jet Liner over Schooner — A26

1966, Dec. 17
191 A26 1sh blue, ol & black .35 .35
192 A26 1sh9p ultra, grn & sepia .75 .75

Opening of the Grand Cayman Airport jet service.

Water Skiing and ITY Emblem A27

ITY Emblem and: 6p, Skin diving. 1sh, Sport fishing. 1sh9p, Sailing.

Perf. 14½x14
1967, Dec. 1 Photo. Wmk. 314
193 A27 4p multi & gold .40 .20
a. Gold omitted 100.00
194 A27 6p multi & gold .40 .25
195 A27 1sh multi & gold .40 .35
196 A27 1sh9p multi & gold .50 .60
Nos. 193-196 (4) 1.70 1.40

International Tourist Year.

Human Rights Flame and Freed Slaves A28

1968, June 3 Photo. Wmk. 314
197 A28 3p slate bl, grn & gold .20 .20
198 A28 9p lt brn, grn & gold .20 .20
199 A28 5sh ultra, grn & gold .70 .70
Nos. 197-199 (3) 1.10 1.10

International Human Rights Year.

Long Jump A29

1sh3p, High jump. 2sh, Pole vault, vert.

1968, Oct. 1 Litho. ***Perf. 13½***
200 A29 1sh multicolored .20 .20
201 A29 1sh3p multicolored .25 .25
202 A29 2sh yellow & multi .40 .40
Nos. 200-202 (3) .85 .85

19th Olympic Games, Mexico City, 10/12-27.

Adoration of Shepherds, by Carel Fabritius — A30

Christmas: 1p, 8p, 2sh, Adoration of the Shepherds, by Rembrandt.

Perf. 14x14½
1968, Nov. 18 Photo. Wmk. 314
203 A30 ¼p brown & multi .20 .20
a. Gold omitted 190.00
204 A30 1p violet & multi .20 .20
205 A30 6p multicolored .20 .20
206 A30 8p car & multi .20 .20
207 A30 1sh3p multicolored .25 .25
208 A30 2sh gray & multi .40 .40
Nos. 203-208 (6) 1.45 1.45

1969, Jan. 8 Unwmk.
209 A30 ¼p red lilac & multi .20 .20

Grand Cayman Thrush A31

1p, Brahman cattle. 2p, Blowholes on coast. 2½p, Map of Grand Cayman. 3p, Town scene in George Town. 4p, Royal poinciana. 6p, Map of Cayman Brac and Little Cayman. 8p, Motor vessels at berth. 1sh, Basket making. 1sh3p, Beach scene. 1sh6p, Rope making. 2sh, Barracudas. 4sh, Government House. 10sh, Coat of arms. £1, Queen Elizabeth II.

Unwmk.
1969, June 5 Litho. ***Perf. 14***
210 A31 ¼p multi .20 *.90*
211 A31 1p multi .20 .20
212 A31 2p multi .20 .20
213 A31 2½p multi .20 .20
214 A31 3p multi .20 .20
215 A31 4p multi .20 .20
216 A31 6p multi .20 .20
217 A31 8p multi .20 .20
218 A31 1sh multi .25 .20
219 A31 1sh3p multi .30 *1.25*
220 A31 1sh6p multi .40 *1.25*
221 A31 2sh multi 1.25 *1.00*
222 A31 4sh multi .70 *1.00*
223 A31 10sh multi, vert. 1.25 *1.75*
224 A31 £1 multi, vert. 3.00 2.50
Nos. 210-224 (15) 8.75 *11.25*

See #262-276. For surcharges see #227-241.

1969, Aug. 11 Wmk. 314 Sideways
225 A31 ¼p multicolored .40 .30

Type of 1969 Surcharged

1969, Sept. 8 Wmk. 314 ***Perf. 14***
227 A31 ¼c on ¼p multi .20 *.65*
228 A31 1c on 1p multi .20 .20
229 A31 2c on 2p multi .20 .20
230 A31 3c on 4p multi .20 .20
231 A31 4c on 2½p multi .20 .20
232 A31 5c on 6p multi .20 .20
233 A31 7c on 8p multi .20 .20
234 A31 8c on 3p multi .20 .20
235 A31 10c on 1s multi .35 .20
236 A31 12c on 1sh3p multi .50 *1.10*
237 A31 15c on 1sh6p multi .65 *.70*
238 A31 20c on 2sh multi 1.75 1.25
239 A31 40c on 4sh multi .65 *.70*
240 A31 $1 on 10sh multi 1.40 *2.10*
241 A31 $2 on £1 multi 2.10 *2.75*
Nos. 227-241 (15) 9.00 10.85

The surcharge is arranged differently on various denominations.

Madonna and Child, by Alvise Vivarini — A32

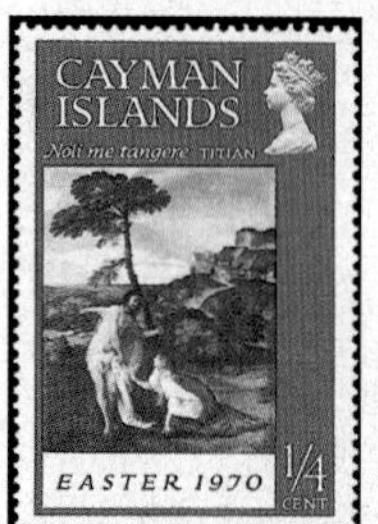

"Noli me Tangere," by Titian — A33

Christmas: 1c, 7c, 20c, The Adoration of the Kings, by Jan Gossaert.

1969, Nov. 4 Photo. ***Perf. 14***
242 A32 ¼c blue & multi .20 .20
243 A32 ¼c emer & multi .20 .20
244 A32 ¼c red org & multi .20 .20
245 A32 ¼c brt pink & multi .20 .20
246 A32 1c vio blue & multi .20 .20
247 A32 5c red org & multi .20 .20
248 A32 7c dk green & multi .20 .20
249 A32 12c emer & multi .20 .20
250 A32 20c multicolored .20 .20
Nos. 242-250 (9) 1.80 1.80

1970, Mar. 23 Litho. Unwmk.
251 A33 ¼c dull grn & multi .20 .20
252 A33 ¼c dk car & multi .20 .20
253 A33 ¼c violet & multi .20 .20
254 A33 ¼c bister & multi .20 .20
255 A33 10c vio blue & multi .20 .20
256 A33 12c red brn & multi .25 .25
257 A33 40c brn vio & multi .60 .60
Nos. 251-257 (7) 1.85 1.85

Easter.

Barnaby from "Barnaby Rudgo" by Dickens (1812-70), English Novelist — A34

Characters from Charles Dickens: 12c, Sairey Gamp, from "Martin Chuzzlewit." 20c, Mr. Micawber and David, from "David Copperfield." 40c, The Marchioness from "The Old Curiosity Shop."

1970, June 17 Photo. ***Perf. 14½x14***
258 A34 1c ol green, yel & blk .20 .20
259 A34 12c red brn, brick red & black .20 .20
260 A34 20c dk ol bister, gold & black .35 .35
261 A34 40c dp ultra, lt bl & blk .75 .75
Nos. 258-261 (4) 1.50 1.50

Type of Regular Issue 1969 Values in Cents and Dollars

Designs: ¼c, Grand Cayman thrush. 1c, Brahman cattle. 2c, Blowholes on coast. 3c, Royal poinciana. 4c, Map of Grand Cayman. 5c, Map of Cayman Brac and Little Cayman. 7c, Motor vessels at berth. 8c, Town scene in George Town. 10c, Basket making. 12c, Beach scene. 15c, Rope making. 20c, Barracudas. 40c, Government House. $1, Coat of arms, vert. $2, Queen Elizabeth II, vert.

Wmk. 314
1970, Sept. 8 Litho. ***Perf. 14***
262 A31 ¼c multicolored .20 .20
263 A31 1c multicolored .20 .20
264 A31 2c multicolored .20 .20
265 A31 3c multicolored .20 .20
266 A31 4c multicolored .20 .20
267 A31 5c multicolored .35 .20
268 A31 7c multicolored .30 .20
269 A31 8c multicolored .30 .20
270 A31 10c multicolored .30 .20
271 A31 12c multicolored .90 .65
272 A31 15c multicolored 1.25 *2.50*
273 A31 20c multicolored 3.00 1.10
274 A31 40c multicolored .85 .65
275 A31 $1 multicolored 1.25 *4.00*
276 A31 $2 multicolored 2.00 *4.00*
Nos. 262-276 (15) 11.50 14.70

The Three Wise Men A35

Christmas: 1c, 10c, 20c, Nativity and globe.

1970, Oct. 8 Litho. ***Perf. 14***
277 A35 ¼c brt grn & yel grn .20 .20
278 A35 1c bl grn, yel grn & blk .20 .20
279 A35 5c dp claret & org .20 .20
280 A35 10c red org, yel & blk .20 .20
281 A35 12c ultra & lt grnsh bl .20 .20
282 A35 20c grn, yel grn & blk .25 .25
Nos. 277-282 (6) 1.25 1.25

Grand Cayman Terrapin A36

Cayman Islands Turtles: 7c, Green turtle. 12c, Hawksbill turtle. 20c, Turtle farm.

1971, Jan. 28 ***Perf. 14x14½***
283 A36 5c multicolored .60 .45
284 A36 7c multicolored .80 .45
285 A36 12c multicolored 1.75 .55
286 A36 20c multicolored 2.75 2.75
Nos. 283-286 (4) 5.90 4.20

Dendrophylax Fawcetii — A37

Adoration of the Kings, 15th Century — A38

Wild Orchids of West Indies: 2c, Schomburgkia thomsoniana. 10c, Vanilla claviculata. 40c, Oncidium variegatum.

1971, Apr. 7 Wmk. 314 *Perf. 14*

287 A37 ¼c brown & multi .20 *.85*
288 A37 2c ol green & multi .55 *.70*
289 A37 10c gray bl & multi 2.00 .55
290 A37 40c lt violet & multi 4.25 *3.25*
Nos. 287-290 (4) 7.00 *5.35*

1971, Sept. 27 *Perf. 14*

Christmas: 1c, 15c, Nativity (detail), Paris, 14th cent. 5c, 20c, Adoration of the Kings (detail), Burgundian, 15th cent.

291 A38 ¼c gold & multi .20 .20
292 A38 1c gold & multi .20 .20
293 A38 5c gold & multi .20 .20
294 A38 12c gold & multi .20 .20
295 A38 15c gold & multi .25 .25
296 A38 20c gold & multi .30 .30
a. Souvenir sheet of 6, #291-296 2.75 2.75
Nos. 291-296 (6) 1.35 1.35

Underwater Cable, Turtle and Telephone — A39

1972, Jan. 10

297 A39 2c multicolored .20 .20
298 A39 10c multicolored .20 .20
299 A39 40c multicolored .80 .80
Nos. 297-299 (3) 1.20 1.20

Coaxial cable for world communications.

Courthouse — A40

Designs: 15c, 40c, Legislative Assembly Building, George Town.

1972, Aug. 15 *Perf. 13½x14*

300 A40 5c dp car & multi *.30 .30*
301 A40 15c lilac rose & multi *.30 .30*
302 A40 25c dull grn & multi *.45 .45*
303 A40 40c dk blue & multi *.70 .70*
a. Souvenir sheet of 4, #300-303 *1.75 1.75*
Nos. 300-303 (4) *1.75 1.75*

New Cayman Islands government buildings.

Silver Wedding Issue, 1972

Common Design Type

Design: Queen Elizabeth II, Prince Philip, hawksbill turtle and conch.

1972, Nov. 20 Photo. *Perf. 14x14½*

304 CD324 12c vio black & multi .20 .20
305 CD324 30c olive & multi .40 .40

$1 Note and 1c Coin A41

6c, $5 note and 5c coin. 15c, $10 note and 10c coin. 25c, $25 note and 25c coin.

1973, Jan. 15

306 A41 3c emerald & multi .20 .20
307 A41 6c yellow & multi .25 .50
308 A41 15c lilac & multi .65 .40
309 A41 25c orange & multi 1.10 .60
a. Souvenir sheet of 4, #306-309 4.25 4.25
Nos. 306-309 (4) 2.20 1.70

First Cayman Islands coinage and bank notes, May 1, 1972.

Last Supper A42

Stained Glass Windows: 10c, Christ Carrying Cross, vert. 12c, Resurrection, vert. 30c, Crucifixion.

Perf. 14½x14, 14x14½

1973, Apr. 11 Litho.

310 A42 10c pink & multi .20 .20
311 A42 12c yel green & multi .20 .20
312 A42 20c lt blue & multi .30 .30
313 A42 30c yellow & multi .40 .40
a. Souvenir sheet of 4 1.60 1.60
Nos. 310-313 (4) 1.10 1.10

Easter. No. 313a contains 4 stamps similar to Nos. 310-313 with simulated perforations.

Nativity — A43

White-winged Dove — A44

Christmas: 5c, 12c, 25c, Adoration of the Magi, from Breviary of Queen Isabella. 9c, 15c, Like 3c, Nativity from Sforza Book of Hours.

1973, Oct. 2 *Perf. 14½*

314 A43 3c dull green & multi .20 .20
315 A43 5c dull pur & multi .20 .20
316 A43 9c sepia & multi .20 .20
317 A43 12c dk blue & multi .20 .20
318 A43 15c dp rose & multi .20 .20
319 A43 25c black & multi .30 .30
Nos. 314-319 (6) 1.30 1.30

Princess Anne's Wedding Issue

Common Design Type

1973, Nov. 14 Wmk. 314 *Perf. 14*

320 CD325 10c brt green & multi .20 .20
321 CD325 30c lilac & multi .30 .30

1974, Jan. 2 Litho. *Perf. 14x14½*

322 A44 3c shown 2.25 .30
323 A44 10c Vitelline warblers 3.00 .30
324 A44 12c Greater Antillean grackles 3.00 .30
325 A44 20c West Indian red-bellied woodpecker 4.75 .80
326 A44 30c Stripe-headed tanagers 6.00 1.50
327 A44 50c Yucatan vireos 8.00 5.00
Nos. 322-327 (6) 27.00 8.20

See Nos. 354-359.

One-room Schoolhouse — A45

Designs: 20c, New comprehensive school. 30c, Creative Arts Center, Mona, Jamaica.

1974, May 1 *Perf. 14*

328 A45 12c multicolored .20 .20
329 A45 20c multicolored .20 .20
330 A45 30c multicolored .30 .30
Nos. 328-330 (3) .70 .70

25th anniv. of the University College of the West Indies.

Hermit Crab and Pirate Gold A46

Coat of Arms — A47

Elizabeth II — A48

Designs: 3c, Pirate, treasure chest and lion's paw. 4c, Spotted scorpionfish and crown. 5c, Flint-lock pistol and brain coral. 6c, Blackbeard on Grand Cayman and green turtle. 8c, 9c, Jeweled pomander and porkfish. 10c, Spiny lobster and gold coins. 12c, Jeweled sword, dagger and sea fan. 15c, Cabrit's murex and jeweled necklace. 20c, Queen conch, pistol and gold cup. 25c, Hogfish and pirate chest. 40c, Gold chalice and sea whip.

Wmk. 314 Upright, Sideways (#331-332, 336, 344-345)

1974-75 Litho. *Perf. 14*

331 A46 1c multi ('75) 4.25 1.50
a. Wmk. upright 3.75 1.50
332 A46 3c multicolored 4.25 .90
a. Wmk. upright 4.75 .90
333 A46 4c multicolored .60 *.85*
334 A46 5c multicolored 3.75 .90
335 A46 6c multicolored .45 *2.75*
336 A46 8c multicolored 3.00 *10.00*
337 A46 9c multicolored 4.50 *11.00*
338 A46 10c multicolored 5.50 .95
339 A46 12c multicolored .45 *1.90*
340 A46 15c multicolored .55 *1.50*
341 A46 20c multicolored 4.25 3.50
342 A46 25c multicolored .55 *.85*
343 A46 40c multicolored 5.00 1.50
344 A47 $1 multicolored 3.50 *4.00*
345 A48 $2 multicolored 9.25 *7.75*
Nos. 331-345 (15) 49.85 *49.85*

Issued: #332, 11/12; 8c, 12/16; #331, 9/29; others, 8/1.

1976-77 Wmk. 373

332b A46 3c multicolored 1.10 *3.50*
333a A46 4c multi ('77) 1.40 *4.00*
334a A46 5c multi ('77) 7.00 5.25
336b A46 8c multicolored 8.25 4.50
338b A46 10c multicolored 3.00 *3.50*
341b A46 20c multicolored 3.75 2.75
344a A47 $1 multi ('77) 7.00 *8.25*
345b A48 $2 multicolored 7.75 5.75
Nos. 332b-345b (8) 39.25 *37.50*

Issued: 3c, 8c, 10c, 20c, $2, 9/3; 4c, 5c, $1, 10/19.

Design Smaller

Size: 40x25mm

Wmk. 373 (Sideways on 1c-40c)

1978-80

346 A46 1c multicolored 1.50 *1.50*
346A A46 3c multicolored 1.25 .50
346B A46 5c multi ('79) 3.25 *3.25*
347 A46 10c multicolored 2.50 .75
347A A46 20c multicolored 5.25 1.50
347B A46 40c multi ('79) 21.00 21.00
347C A47 $1 multi ('80) 26.00 7.50
348 A48 $2 multi ('80) 9.50 *20.00*
Nos. 346-348 (8) 70.25 *56.00*

Issued: 1c, 3c, 3/16; 10c, 20c, 5/25; 5c, 12/11; $2, 4/3; $1, 7/30.

Sea Captain and Ship — A49

1974, Oct. 7 Wmk. 314 *Perf. 14*

349 A49 8c shown .20 .20
350 A49 12c Thatch weaver .25 .20
351 A49 20c Farmer .45 .40
a. Miniature sheet of 3, #349-351 1.50 *2.00*
Nos. 349-351 (3) .90 .80

Arms of Cinque Ports and Lord Warden's Flag — A50

Churchill Coat of Arms — A51

1974, Nov. 30

352 A50 12c multicolored .20 .20
353 A51 50c multicolored .70 .70
a. Souvenir sheet of 2, #352-353 1.10 *1.25*

Sir Winston Churchill (1874-1965).

Bird Type of 1974

Wmk. 314

1975, Jan. 1 Litho. *Perf. 14*

354 A44 3c Yellow-shafted flicker .65 .40
355 A44 10c West Indian tree duck 1.25 .40
356 A44 12c Yellow warblers 1.60 .60
357 A44 20c White-bellied dove 2.75 2.75
358 A44 30c Magnificent frigate bird 4.50 *4.50*
359 A44 50c Cayman amazon 5.25 *10.00*
a. Wmk. 362 (Lesotho) 400.00
Nos. 354-359 (6) 16.00 *18.65*

Ivory Crosier with Crucifixion — A52

Design: 35c, Crucifixion, ivory and gilt. Designs show heads of 14th century French pastoral staffs.

Wmk. 314

1975, Mar. 24 Litho. *Perf. 14*

360 A52 15c plum & multi .20 .20
361 A52 35c gray & multi .65 .65
a. Souvenir sheet of 2, #360-361 1.10 1.10

Easter. No. 361a exists imperf.

See Nos. 366-367.

Israel Hands A53

Designs: Pirates and various scenes.

1975, July 25 Wmk. 314

362 A53 10c shown .50 .20
363 A53 12c John Fenn .50 .20
364 A53 20c Thomas Anstis .80 .40
365 A53 30c Edward Low .95 *1.50*
Nos. 362-365 (4) 2.75 2.30

Easter Type of 1975

Designs after ivory carved pastoral staffs showing Virgin and Child with angels, French, 14th century.

Wmk. 373

1975, Oct. 31 Litho. *Perf. 14*

366 A52 12c dk green & multi .20 .20
367 A52 50c multicolored .70 .70
a. Souvenir sheet of 2, #366-367 1.40 *1.75*

Christmas.

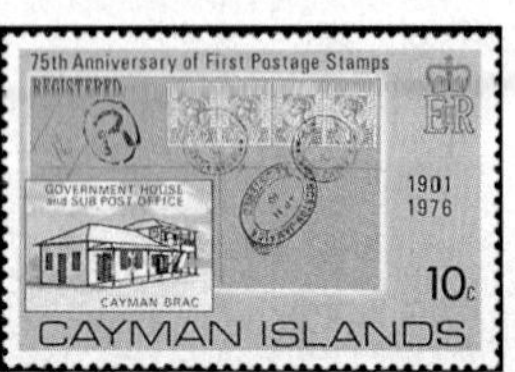

Registered Letter with Nos. 1-2; Cayman Brac Government House and Sub Post Office — A54

Cayman Islands 1st postage stamps, 75th anniv.: 20c, Cayman Islands #1 and cancelation used 1890-94; 30c, #2, 20; 50c, #1-2.

1976, Mar. 12 Litho. *Perf. 13½x14*

368 A54 10c lt blue & multi .20 .20
369 A54 20c pink & multi .25 .25
370 A54 30c multicolored .40 .40
371 A54 50c yellow & multi .60 .60
a. Souvenir sheet of 4, #368-371 3.75 3.75
Nos. 368-371 (4) 1.45 1.45

Seals of Georgia, Delaware and New Hampshire — A55

15c, Seals of SC, NJ, MD. 20c, Seals of VA, RI, MA. 25c, Seals of NY, CT, NC. 30c, Seal of PA, Liberty Bell and Great Seal of the US.

Wmk. 373

1976, May 29 Litho. *Perf. 14*

372 A55 10c olive & multi .35 .20
373 A55 15c blue & multi .45 .20
374 A55 20c multicolored .60 .25
375 A55 25c blue grn & multi .85 .50
376 A55 30c red brn & multi 1.00 .75
a. Souvenir sheet of 5 + label 6.50 *6.50*
Nos. 372-376 (5) 3.25 1.90

American Bicentennial. Nos. 372-376 printed in sheets of 5. No. 376a contains one each of Nos. 372-376 and corner label inscribed "USA 200."

French Class 470 Racing Dinghies — A56

Queen Elizabeth II — A57

Design: 50c, One racing dinghy.

1976, Aug. 16 Litho. *Perf. 14*

377 A56 20c multicolored .65 .40
378 A56 50c multicolored 1.10 1.10

21st Olympic Games, Montreal, Canada, July 17-Aug. 1.

Perf. 14x13½, 13½x14

1977, Feb. 7 Litho. Wmk. 373

8c, Prince Charles, 1973 visit. 50c, Preparation for anointing ceremony, horiz.

379 A57 8c multicolored .20 .20
380 A57 30c multicolored .35 .30
381 A57 50c multicolored .55 .50
Nos. 379-381 (3) 1.10 1.00

25th anniv. of the reign of Elizabeth II.

Scuba Diving A58

10c, Divers examining underwater wreck. 20c, Fairy basslets (fish). 25c, Sergeant majors (fish).

1977, July 25 *Perf. 13½*

382 A58 5c multicolored .20 .20
383 A58 10c multicolored .25 .25
384 A58 20c multicolored .50 .50
385 A58 25c multicolored .70 .65
a. Souvenir sheet of 4 2.50 2.50
Nos. 382-385 (4) 1.65 1.60

Tourist publicity. No. 385a contains one each of Nos. 382-385, perf. 14½.

Composia Fidelissima — A59

Butterflies: 8c, Heliconius charitonius. 10c, Danaus gilippus. 15c, Agraulis vanillae. 20c, Junonia evarete. 30c, Anartia jatrophae.

1977, Dec. 2 Wmk. 373 *Perf. 14x13*

386 A59 5c multicolored 1.10 .20
387 A59 8c multicolored 1.25 .25
388 A59 10c multicolored 1.40 .30
389 A59 15c multicolored 1.75 .50
390 A59 20c multicolored 1.90 .55
391 A59 30c multicolored 2.25 1.00
Nos. 386-391 (6) 9.65 2.80

Cruise Ship "Southward" A60

Designs: 5c, "Renaissance." 30c, New harbor, vert. 50c, "Daphne," vert.

1978, Jan. 23 Litho. *Perf. 14*

392 A60 3c multicolored .35 .20
393 A60 5c multicolored .35 .20
394 A60 30c multicolored 1.10 .50
395 A60 50c multicolored 1.50 .75
Nos. 392-395 (4) 3.30 1.65

New harbor and cruise ships.

Crucifixion, by Dürer — A61

Explorers, Singing Game — A62

Etchings by Dürer: 15c, Christ at Emmaus. 20c, Entry into Jerusalem. 30c, Christ washing Peter's feet.

1978, Mar. 20 Litho. *Perf. 12*

396 A61 10c multicolored .30 .20
397 A61 15c multicolored .40 .25
398 A61 20c multicolored .50 .30
399 A61 30c multicolored .60 .45
a. Souvenir sheet of 4, #396-399 4.75 *4.75*
Nos. 396-399 (4) 1.80 1.20

Easter; Albrecht Dürer (1471-1528). Nos. 396-399 issued in sheets of 6.

1978, Apr. 25 Litho. *Perf. 14*

10c, Girls' Brigade presenting flag. 20c, Guides studying Bible, playing guitar, tennis and volleyball. 50c, Guides setting table.

400 A62 3c multicolored .20 .20
401 A62 10c multicolored .35 .30
402 A62 20c multicolored .60 .55
403 A62 50c multicolored 1.25 1.25
Nos. 400-403 (4) 2.40 2.30

3rd Intl. Council Meeting of Girls' Brigade.

Elizabeth II Coronation Anniversary Issue

Common Design Types

Souvenir Sheet

1978, June 2 Unwmk. *Perf. 15*

404 Sheet of 6 2.50 *3.00*
a. CD326 30c Yale of Beaufort .40 .40
b. CD327 30c Elizabeth II .40 .40
c. CD328 30c Screech owl .40 .40

No. 404 contains 2 se-tenant strips of Nos. 404a-404c, separated by horizontal gutter with commemorative and descriptive inscriptions.

A63

A63a

A63: 1c, Trumpetfish. 3c, Nassau grouper. 5c, French angelfish. 10c, Schoolmaster snappers. 20c, Banded butterflyfish. 50c, Black-bar soldierfish.

A63a: 3c, Four-eyed butterflyfish. 5c, Grey angel fish. 10c, Squirrelfish. 15c, Parrotfish. 20c, Spanish hogfish. 30c, Queen angelfish.

1978-79 Wmk. 373 Litho. *Perf. 14*

405 A63 1c multicolored .20 .20
406 A63 3c multicolored .35 .20
407 A63a 3c multicolored .30 .20
408 A63a 5c multicolored .35 .20
409 A63 5c multicolored .30 .20
412 A63a 10c multicolored .55 .20
413 A63 10c multicolored .55 .20
414 A63a 15c multicolored .65 .30
415 A63a 20c multicolored .90 .40
416 A63 20c multicolored 1.10 .40
417 A63a 30c multicolored 1.75 .60
418 A63 50c multicolored 2.50 1.00
Nos. 405-418 (12) 9.50 4.10

Issued: design A63, 4/20/79; design A63a, 8/28/78.

Lockheed Lodestar — A64

Aircraft: 5c, Consolidated PBY. 10c, Vickers Viking. 15c, BAC1-11. 20c, Piper Cheyenne, HS 125 and Bell 47. 30c, BAC1-11.

1979, Feb. 5 *Perf. 14½*

420 A64 3c multicolored .35 .20
421 A64 5c multicolored .35 .20
422 A64 10c multicolored .50 .20
423 A64 15c multicolored .90 .35
424 A64 20c multicolored 1.10 .40
425 A64 30c multicolored 1.50 .50
Nos. 420-425 (6) 4.70 1.85

Opening of Owen Roberts Airport, 25th anniv.

Rowland Hill and No. 2 — A65

Sir Rowland Hill (1795-1879), originator of penny postage, and: 10c, Great Britain #132. 20c, Cayman Islands #149. 50c,Cayman Islands #20.

Perf. 13½x14½

1979, Aug. 15 Litho.

426 A65 5c multicolored .20 .20
427 A65 10c multicolored .20 .20
428 A65 20c multicolored .45 .45
Nos. 426-428 (3) .85 .85

Souvenir Sheet

429 A65 50c multicolored 1.40 1.40

Flight into Egypt A66

Christmas: 20c, Shepherds, Star of Bethlehem. 30c, Nativity. 40c, Three Kings, Star of Bethlehem.

1979, Nov. 20 Litho. *Perf. 13½*

430 A66 10c multicolored .20 .20
431 A66 20c multicolored .25 .20
432 A66 30c multicolored .40 .25
433 A66 40c multicolored .70 .30
Nos. 430-433 (4) 1.55 .95

Bonaventure House, Rotary Emblem — A67

Perf. 14x13½, 13½x14

1980, Feb. 14 Litho. Wmk. 373

434 A67 20c shown .30 .20
435 A67 30c Paul P. Harris, vert. .50 .25
436 A67 50c Anniversary emblem, vert. .80 .50
Nos. 434-436 (3) 1.60 .95

Rotary International, 75th anniversary.

Mailman, London 1980 Emblem A68

1980, May 6 Litho. *Perf. 14*

437 A68 5c shown .20 .20
438 A68 10c Cat boat .20 .20
439 A68 15c Mounted mailman .25 .25
440 A68 30c Mail wagon .50 .35
441 A68 40c Mailman on bicycle .55 .40
442 A68 $1 Mail truck 1.00 .75
Nos. 437-442 (6) 2.70 2.15

London '80 Intl. Stamp Exhib., May 6-14.

Queen Mother Elizabeth Birthday Issue

Common Design Type

1980, Aug. 4 Litho. *Perf. 14*

443 CD330 20c multicolored .40 .40

Spondylus Americanus A69

1980, Aug. 12 *Perf. 14½x14*

444 A69 5c shown .75 .20
445 A69 10c Murex brevifrons .75 .25
446 A69 30c Cymatium femorale 1.50 .55
447 A69 50c Vasum muricatum 1.75 1.00
Nos. 444-447 (4) 4.75 2.00

See Nos. 502-505, 518-521.

Lantana — A70

1980, Oct. 21 Litho. *Perf. 14*

448 A70 5c shown .20 .20
449 A70 15c Bauhinia .30 .20
450 A70 30c Hibiscus .60 .25
451 A70 $1 Milk and wine lily 1.50 1.25
Nos. 448-451 (4) 2.60 1.90

See Nos. 478-481.

Juvenile Tarpon and Fire Sponges — A71

1980, Dec. 9 Litho. *Perf. 13½x13*

452 A71 3c shown 1.25 *1.75*
453 A71 5c Mangrove root oysters 1.50 *.90*
a. Wmk. 384 2.75 2.50
b. Wmk. 384, perf. 14 2.75 2.50
454 A71 10c Mangrove crab .60 *.95*
a. Wmk. 384, perf. 14 4.00 3.25
455 A71 15c Lizard, crescent spot butterfly 1.25 *1.75*
456 A71 20c Tricolored heron 1.75 *2.40*
457 A71 30c Red mangrove flower .85 *1.10*
458 A71 40c Red mangrove seeds .90 *1.25*
459 A71 50c Waterhouse's leaf-nosed bat 1.50 *1.75*
460 A71 $1 Black-crowned night heron 6.75 *5.75*
461 A71 $2 Cayman Isls. arms 2.50 *4.25*
462 A71 $4 Queen Elizabeth II 5.00 5.50
Nos. 452-462 (11) 23.85 *27.35*

Nos. 452-462 also issued inscribed 1982 (Value, $35); 5c, 1984; 3c-$2, 1985. Other dates probably exist. No. 453a has large imprint date.
Issued: #453a, 4/86; #453b, 454a, 6/86.

Bread and Wine — A72

1981, Mar. 17 Wmk. 373 *Perf. 14*

463 A72 3c shown .20 .20
464 A72 10c Crown of thorns .20 .20
465 A72 20c Crucifix .35 .35
466 A72 $1 Christ 1.00 *1.10*
Nos. 463-466 (4) 1.75 1.85

Easter.

Wood Slave A73

1981, June 16 Litho. *Perf. 13½*

467 A73 20c shown .40 .40
468 A73 30c Cayman iguana .60 .60
469 A73 40c Lion lizard .80 .80
470 A73 50c Freshwater turtle .95 .95
Nos. 467-470 (4) 2.75 2.75

Royal Wedding Issue

Common Design Type

1981, July 22 Litho. *Perf. 14*

471 CD331 20c Bouquet .35 .35
472 CD331 30c Charles .55 .55
473 CD331 $1 Couple 1.25 1.25
Nos. 471-473 (3) 2.15 2.15

Intl. Year of the Disabled A74

1981, Sept. 29 Litho. *Perf. 14*

474 A74 5c Scuba divers .20 .20
475 A74 15c Old School for Handicapped .25 .25
476 A74 20c New School for Handicapped .35 .35
477 A74 $1 Beach scene 1.75 1.75
Nos. 474-477 (4) 2.55 2.55

Flower Type of 1980

1981, Oct. 20 Litho. *Perf. 14*

478 A70 3c Bougainvillea .25 .20
479 A70 10c Morning glory .25 .20
480 A70 20c Wild amaryllis .55 .55
481 A70 $1 Cordia 2.75 2.75
Nos. 478-481 (4) 3.80 3.70

TB Bacillus Centenary — A75

1982, Mar. 24 Litho. *Perf. 14½*

482 A75 15c Koch, horizontal microscope .35 .35
483 A75 30c Koch, vert. .70 .70
484 A75 40c Microscope, vert. .85 .85
485 A75 50c Koch, diff., vert. 1.10 1.10
Nos. 482-485 (4) 3.00 3.00

Princess Diana Issue

Common Design Type

1982, July 1 Litho. *Perf. 13*

486 CD333 20c Arms *.65* .40
487 CD333 30c Diana *1.10* .75
488 CD333 40c Wedding *1.25* .75
489 CD333 50c Portrait *4.00* 1.50
Nos. 486-489 (4) *7.00* 3.40

Scouting Year A76

1982, Aug. 24 Wmk. 373 *Perf. 14*

490 A76 3c Pitching tent .30 .20
491 A76 20c Cooking .75 .75
492 A76 30c Troop 1.10 1.10
493 A76 50c Boating skills 1.50 1.50
Nos. 490-493 (4) 3.65 3.55

Christmas 1982 — A77

Virgin and Child Paintings by Raphael.

1982, Oct. 26 *Perf. 14½*

494 A77 3c multicolored .20 .20
495 A77 10c multicolored .30 .30
496 A77 20c multicolored .60 .60
497 A77 30c multicolored .90 .90
Nos. 494-497 (4) 2.00 2.00

Representative Govt. Sesquicentennial — A78

1982, Nov. 9 Litho. Wmk. 373

498 A78 3c Mace .20 .20
499 A78 10c Old Courthouse .20 .20
500 A78 20c Commonwealth Parliamentary Assoc. arms .40 .40
501 A78 30c Legislative Assembley building .65 .65
Nos. 498-501 (4) 1.45 1.45

Shell Type of 1980

1983, Jan. 11 Litho. *Perf. 13½*

502 A69 5c Natica canrena .20 .20
503 A69 10c Cassis tuberosa .30 .30
504 A69 20c Strombus gallus .75 .75
505 A69 $1 Cypraecassis testiculus 3.75 3.75
Nos. 502-505 (4) 5.00 5.00

Visit of Queen Elizabeth II and Prince Philip A79

1983, Feb. 15 Litho. *Perf. 14*

506 A79 20c Legislative Building, Cayman Brac .50 .50
507 A79 30c Leg. Bldg., Grand Cayman .85 .75
508 A79 50c Prince Philip 1.50 1.25
509 A79 $1 Queen Elizabeth II 2.50 2.50
a. Souvenir sheet of 4, #506-509 6.00 6.00
Nos. 506-509 (4) 5.35 5.00

A80

1983, Mar. 14

510 A80 3c Globe .25 .20
511 A80 15c Flags .60 .50
512 A80 20c Fisherman .70 .60
513 A80 40c Elizabeth II 1.10 .85
Nos. 510-513 (4) 2.65 2.15

Commonwealth Day.

Manned Flight Bicentenary and Mosquito Research and Control Unit — A81

Airplanes.

1983, Oct. 10 Litho. *Perf. 14½*

514 A81 3c MRCU Cessna .95 .65
515 A81 10c Consolidated Catalina PBY 1.00 .65
516 A81 20c Boeing 727 1.90 1.90
517 A81 40c Hawker Siddeley HS-748 2.75 *3.50*
Nos. 514-517 (4) 6.60 6.70

Shell Type of 1980

1984, Jan. 18 *Perf. 14x14½*

518 A69 3c Natica floridana 1.40 .35
519 A69 10c Conus austini 1.60 .35
520 A69 30c Colubrania obscura 4.50 *4.50*
521 A69 50c Turbo cailletii 4.75 *4.75*
Nos. 518-521 (4) 12.25 *9.95*

Lloyd's List Issue

Common Design Type

1984, May 16 Litho. *Perf. 14*

522 CD335 5c Cruise ship .70 .20
523 CD335 10c The Old Harbor .75 .25
524 CD335 25c Ridgefield 1.50 1.50
525 CD335 50c Goldfield 3.00 *3.00*
Nos. 522-525 (4) 5.95 *4.95*

Souvenir Sheet

526 CD335 $1 Goldfield, diff. 3.50 3.50

No. 525 Overprinted: "U.P.U. CONGRESS HAMBURG 1984"

1984, June 18

527 CD335 50c multicolored 1.50 1.60

Local Birds — A82

Perf. 14x14½

1984, Aug. 15 Litho. Wmk. 373

528 A82 5c Snowy egret 1.25 .60
529 A82 10c Bananaquit 1.25 .60
530 A82 35c Kingfisher 4.50 3.00
531 A82 $1 Brown booby 8.00 *9.00*
Nos. 528-531 (4) 15.00 *13.20*

Christmas — A83 Orchids — A84

#532a-532d, evening beach scenes. #533a-533d, daytime boating and beach scenes.

1984, Oct. 17 Litho. *Perf. 14*

532 Strip of 4 4.00 *4.00*
a.-d. A83 5c Any single 1.00 *1.00*
533 Strip of 4 5.00 *4.50*
a.-d. A83 25c Any single 1.25 *1.10*

Souvenir Sheet

534 A83 $1 Bonfire, diff. 5.00 5.00

No. 534 contains one stamp 29x48mm.

1985, Mar. 13 Litho. *Perf. 14x13½*

535 A84 5c Schomburgkia thomsoniana var. 1.60 .50
536 A84 10c Schomburgkia thomsoniana 1.60 .50
537 A84 25c Encyclia plicata 3.75 1.50
538 A84 50c Dendrophylax fawcetti 5.75 3.75
Nos. 535-538 (4) 12.70 6.25

Shipwrecks A85

Unspecified shipwrecks found in Cayman waters.

1985, May 22 *Perf. 14*

539 A85 5c multicolored 1.40 .50
540 A85 25c multicolored 4.50 2.00
541 A85 35c multicolored 5.00 4.00
542 A85 40c multicolored 5.25 5.25
Nos. 539-542 (4) 16.15 11.75

Intl. Youth Year — A86

5c, Natl. Athletic Assoc. track competition. 15c, High school students studying in Grand Cayman Campus Library. 25c, Amateur League Competition Football. 50c, Natl. Netball Assoc. competition.

1985, Aug. 14 *Perf. 14½*

543 A86 5c multicolored .25 .20
544 A86 15c multicolored .45 .35
545 A86 25c multicolored .90 .65
546 A86 50c multicolored 1.75 1.75
Nos. 543-546 (4) 3.35 2.95

Telecommunications, 50th Anniv. — A87

Designs: 5c, Morse Code transmitter, 1935. 10c, Hand-cranked telephone, 1935. 25c, Tropospheric scatter dish, 1966. 50c, Earth dish receiver, 1979.

1985, Oct. 25 *Perf. 14*

547 A87 5c multicolored .60 .60
548 A87 10c multicolored .65 .65
549 A87 25c multicolored 1.75 1.00
550 A87 50c multicolored 3.00 *3.75*
Nos. 547-550 (4) 6.00 6.00

Birds A88

1986, Mar. 20 **Litho.** **Wmk. 384**

551 A88 10c Magnificent frigatebird 2.40 1.00
552 A88 25c West Indian whistling duck 3.00 1.60
553 A88 35c La Sagra's fly-catcher 3.50 3.50
554 A88 40c Yellow-faced grass-quit 4.00 4.00
Nos. 551-554 (4) 12.90 10.10

Nos. 552-553 vert.

Queen Elizabeth II 60th Birthday
Common Design Type

Designs: 5c, As bridesmaid at wedding of Lady Mary Cambridge, 1931. 10c, Royal visit to Norway, 1955. 25c, Inspecting West Indian troop, royal tour, 1985. 50c, Gulf tour, 1979. $1, Visiting Crown Agents' offices, 1983.

1986, Apr. 21 *Perf. 14x14½*

555 CD337 5c scar, blk & sil .20 .20
556 CD337 10c ultra, blk & sil .25 .25
557 CD337 25c grn & multi 1.90 .90
558 CD337 50c vio & multi .95 1.00
559 CD337 $1 rose vio & multi 1.40 *1.75*
Nos. 555-559 (5) 4.70 4.10

Royal Wedding Issue, 1986
Common Design Type

Designs: 5c, Informal portrait. 50c, Andrew in uniform, helicopter.

Perf. 14½x14

1986, July 23 **Litho.** **Wmk. 384**

560 CD338 5c multicolored .25 .20
561 CD338 50c multicolored 1.25 1.25

Marine Life — A89

Perf. 13½x13

1986, Sept. 15 **Wmk. 373**

562 A89 5c Rhynchocinetes rigeus .80 *.55*
563 A89 10c Nemaster rubiginosa .80 *.55*
564 A89 15c Calcinus tibicen .70 *.65*
565 A89 20c Rhodactis sanctithomae .70 *.85*
566 A89 25c Spirobranchus giganatea .45 *2.40*
567 A89 35c Diodon holacanthus .70 *2.75*
568 A89 50c Pseudocorynactis aribbeorum .80 *4.25*
569 A89 60c Astrophyton muricatum 3.50 *8.00*
570 A89 75c Cyphoma gibbosum 9.50 *10.50*
571 A89 $1 Conolylactis gigantea 2.25 *2.75*
572 A89 $2 Malacoctenus boehlkei 5.00 *4.50*
573 A89 $4 Lima scabra 10.00 *7.00*
Nos. 562-573 (12) 35.20 *44.75*

Nos. 562-565, 571-573 exist inscribed "1987," Nos. 562-566, 572 "1990."

Tourism A90

Perf. 13x13½

1987, Jan. 26 **Wmk. 384**

574 A90 10c Golfing 3.00 1.00
575 A90 15c Sailing 3.25 1.00
576 A90 25c Snorkeling 3.25 1.50
577 A90 35c Parasailing 3.25 2.00
578 A90 $1 Fishing 6.50 *9.00*
Nos. 574-578 (5) 19.25 *14.50*

Fruit — A91

1987, May 20 *Perf. 14½*

579 A91 5c Akee .70 .70
580 A91 25c Breadfruit 1.60 .50
581 A91 35c Papaya 1.60 .75
582 A91 $1 Soursop 4.25 *5.00*
Nos. 579-582 (4) 8.15 *6.95*

Lizards — A92

1987, Aug. 26 **Litho.** *Perf. 14*

583 A92 10c Lion lizard 1.75 .45
584 A92 50c Iguana 4.25 3.25
585 A92 $1 Anole 5.25 5.25
Nos. 583-585 (3) 11.25 8.95

Flowers — A93 Herons — A95

Butterflies A94

1987, Nov. 18 *Perf. 14½x14*

586 A93 5c Poinsettia 1.00 .50
587 A93 25c Periwinkle 2.75 .80
588 A93 35c Yellow allamanda 2.75 1.10
589 A93 75c Blood lily 4.75 5.50
Nos. 586-589 (4) 11.25 7.90

1988, Mar. 29 **Wmk. 384** *Perf. 14*

Designs: 5c, Hemiargus ammon erembis and Strymon martialis. 25c, Phocides pigmalion batabano. 50c, Anaea troglodyta cubana. $1, Papilio andraemon andraemon.

590 A94 5c multicolored 1.90 .60
591 A94 25c multicolored 4.00 1.25
592 A94 50c multicolored 6.00 5.00
593 A94 $1 multicolored 7.75 7.75
Nos. 590-593 (4) 19.65 14.60

1988, Jan. 26 **Litho.** *Perf. 14*

594 A95 5c Butorides striatus 2.25 .60
595 A95 25c Egretta tricolor 4.25 .80
596 A95 50c Nycticorax violaceus 5.50 5.50
597 A95 $1 Egretta caerulea 6.00 6.00
Nos. 594-597 (4) 18.00 12.90

1988 Summer Olympics, Seoul — A96

1988, Sept. 21 *Perf. 14½*

598 A96 10c Cycling 2.10 .60
599 A96 50c Natl. team, passenger jet 3.50 2.50
600 A96 $1 Yachting 3.75 3.75
Nos. 598-600 (3) 9.35 6.85

Souvenir Sheet

Wmk. 373

601 A96 $1 Tennis 6.50 6.50

No. 601 commemorates the 75th anniv. of the Intl. Tennis Federation.

Visit of Princess Alexandra A97

1988, Nov. 1 **Wmk. 373** *Perf. 15*

602 A97 5c Portrait 2.40 1.10
603 A97 $1 Seated in garden 8.50 6.50

Cayman Islands P.O., Cent. — A98

Designs: 5c, P.O., Georgetown, 1889, and Jamaica #24, canceled. 25c, S.S. Orinoco and Cayman Isls. #1. 35c, Grand Cayman G.P.O. and #442. $1, Cayman Airways mail plane and #191.

1989, Apr. 12 **Wmk. 384** *Perf. 14½*

604 A98 5c multicolored .95 .95
605 A98 25c multicolored 2.00 1.00
606 A98 35c multicolored 2.25 1.25
607 A98 $1 multicolored 9.25 9.25
Nos. 604-607 (4) 14.45 12.45

A99 A100

Mutiny on the Bounty: a, Capt. Bligh. b, HMS Providence, two crewmen. c, HMS Assistant, transplanted breadfruit. d, Moving breadfruit on land, in longboat. e, Midshipman among casks and crates.

1989, May 24 *Perf. 14*

608 Strip of 5 26.00 26.00
a.-e. A99 50c any single 5.00 5.00

Perf. 14½x14

1989, Oct. 18 **Litho.** **Wmk. 373**

609 A100 5c Panton House .65 .65
610 A100 10c Town Hall .65 .65
611 A100 25c Old Courts House 1.40 .60
612 A100 35c Elmslie Memorial Church 1.50 .85
613 A100 $1 Post office 3.75 4.00
Nos. 609-613 (5) 7.95 6.75

Natl. Trust emblem & architecture, George Town.

Island Surveys A101

Maps or survey ships: 5c, Navigational instruments and George Gauld's map of 1773. 25c, Instruments and map created by surveyors aboard HMS *Vidal*, 1956. 50c, *Mutine*, 1914. $1, HMS *Vidal*.

1989, Nov. 15

614 A101 5c multicolored 1.25 1.00
615 A101 25c multicolored 3.50 1.25
616 A101 50c multicolored 5.25 *4.00*
617 A101 $1 multicolored 8.50 *8.50*
Nos. 614-617 (4) 18.50 *14.75*

Angelfish A102

1990, Apr. 25 **Wmk. 384** *Perf. 14*

618 A102 10c French 1.90 .60
619 A102 25c Gray 3.50 1.25
620 A102 50c Queen 5.25 5.25
621 A102 $1 Rock beauty 8.50 8.50
Nos. 618-621 (4) 19.15 15.60

Queen Mother, 90th Birthday
Common Design Types

1990, Aug. 4 **Wmk. 384** *Perf. 14x15*

622 CD343 50c King, Queen Elizabeth, 1948 1.50 *2.25*

Perf. 14½

623 CD344 $1 King, Queen with Churchill, 1940 3.50 *4.00*

Butterflies
A103

1990, Oct. 24 ***Perf. 14½x14***

624 A103 5c Soldier 1.40 1.00
625 A103 25c Pygmy blue 3.00 2.00
626 A103 35c Cayman crescent spot 3.75 2.25
627 A103 $1 Gulf fritillary 8.25 8.25
Nos. 624-627 (4) 16.40 *13.50*

Expo '90, International Garden and Greenery Exposition, Osaka, Japan.

Hurricane Awareness — A104

Designs: 5c, Goes weather satellite. 30c, Meteorologist tracks storm. 40c, Hurricane damage. $1, Lockheed WP-3D Orion flying in hurricane's eye.

1991, Aug. 8 ***Perf. 14***

628 A104 5c multicolored 1.40 1.25
629 A104 30c multicolored 3.25 1.50
630 A104 40c multicolored 3.50 1.75
631 A104 $1 multicolored 7.75 7.75
Nos. 628-631 (4) 15.90 *12.25*

Christmas
A105

Local flowers and Christmas scenes: 5c, Angel's trumpet, angels with trumpets. 30c, Golden trumpet, Mary on donkey led by Joseph. 40c, Christmas flower, Adoration of the Magi. 60c, Tree of life, nativity scene.

1991, Nov. 6 **Wmk. 373**

632 A105 5c multicolored .75 .75
633 A105 30c multicolored 2.10 .60
634 A105 40c multicolored 2.25 1.00
635 A105 60c multicolored 2.75 *3.50*
Nos. 632-635 (4) 7.85 *5.85*

Island
Scenes
A106

Perf. 12½x13, 13x12½

1991, Dec. 11 **Litho.** **Wmk. 373**

636 A106 5c Coconut tree, vert. .65 .30
637 A106 15c Beach scene 1.40 .35
638 A106 20c Poincianas in bloom .75 .40
639 A106 30c Blowholes 1.40 .55
640 A106 40c Police band 3.25 1.40
641 A106 50c Downtown scene, vert. 2.50 1.40
642 A106 60c The Bluff, Cayman Brac 2.25 *2.00*
643 A106 80c Coat of arms, vert. 1.90 2.25
644 A106 90c View of Hell 1.90 2.25
645 A106 $1 Sportfishing 3.75 2.25
646 A106 $2 Harbor scene, vert. 8.25 6.00
647 A106 $8 Queen Elizabeth II, vert. 19.00 17.00
Nos. 636-647 (12) 47.00 36.15

Queen Elizabeth II's Accession to the Throne, 40th Anniv.

Common Design Type

Wmk. 373, 384 (40c)

1992, Feb. 6 **Litho.** ***Perf. 14***

648 CD349 5c multicolored .40 .40
649 CD349 20c multicolored 1.40 .45
650 CD349 30c multicolored 1.50 .65
651 CD349 40c multicolored 1.50 1.25
652 CD349 $1 multicolored 2.75 *3.50*
Nos. 648-652 (5) 7.55 *6.25*

1992
Summer
Olympics,
Barcelona
A107

1992, Aug. 5 **Wmk. 373**

653 A107 15c Cyclist 2.00 .50
654 A107 40c Two cyclists 3.25 1.40
655 A107 60c Feet, pedals 4.00 4.00
656 A107 $1 Two cyclists, diff. 5.00 5.00
Nos. 653-656 (4) 14.25 *10.90*

Island
Heritage — A108

1992, Oct. 21

657 A108 5c Lady with donkey .70 .70
658 A108 30c Making fish nets 1.75 1.00
659 A108 40c Maypole dancing 3.00 1.60
660 A108 60c Basket making 3.50 *3.50*
661 A108 $1 Cooking on caboose 4.25 *4.25*
Nos. 657-661 (5) 13.20 *11.05*

Rays
A109

Perf. 13½x14

1993, June 16 **Litho.** **Wmk. 373**

662 A109 5c Yellow stingray 1.00 .75
663 A109 30c Southern stingray 2.50 1.50
664 A109 40c Spotted eagle ray 3.00 1.75
665 A109 $1 Manta ray 6.25 6.25
Nos. 662-665 (4) 12.75 *10.25*

A110

A111

Tourism: No. 666a, Turtle, sailboats. b, Diver, coral, boats. c, Golf. d, Beach, tennis. e, Pirates, sailing ship.

No. 667: a, Cruise ship, boat, sailboat. b, City street scene. c, Submarines. d, Cyclist, scooters. e, Jet planes.

Perf. 14x13½

1993, Sept. 30 **Litho.** **Wmk. 373**

666 A110 15c Strip of 5, #a.-e. 9.00 9.00
667 A110 30c Strip of 5, #a.-e. 9.50 9.50
f. Booklet pane of 10, #666-667 24.00

1993, Oct. 29 ***Perf. 14***

Various views of Grand Cayman Parrot.

668 A111 5c green & multi 1.25 1.25
669 A111 5c red & multi 1.25 1.25
670 A111 30c yellow & multi 3.25 3.25
671 A111 30c blue & multi 3.25 3.25
Nos. 668-671 (4) 9.00 *9.00*

Christmas
A112

Christmas scenes, orchids: 5c, Manger, Ionopsis utricularioides. 40c, Shepherd, lamb, Encyclia cochleata. 60c, Magi, Vanilla pompona. $1, Virgin in prayer, Oncidium caymanense.

Perf. 13½x14

1993, Dec. 6 **Litho.** **Wmk. 384**

672 A112 5c multicolored 1.10 .60
673 A112 40c multicolored 3.00 .80
674 A112 60c multicolored 3.75 *3.75*
675 A112 $1 multicolored 5.00 *5.00*
Nos. 672-675 (4) 12.85 *10.15*

Souvenir Sheet

Reef Life — A113

Designs: a, Holocanthus ciliaris. b, Bodianus pulchellus, anisotremus virginicus. c, Holocanthus tricolor, gramma loreto. d, Pomacanthus paru, chaeton striatus.

Perf. 14½x13

1994, Feb. 18 **Litho.** **Wmk. 373**

676 A113 60c Sheet of 4, #a.-d. 14.00 14.00

Hong Kong '94.

Royal
Visit — A114

Designs: 5c, Cayman Islands, United Kingdom flags. 15c, Royal yacht Britannia. 30c, Queen Elizabeth II. $2, Queen, Prince Philip.

1994, Feb. 22 ***Perf. 14½***

677 A114 5c multicolored 1.25 .60
678 A114 15c multicolored 2.75 1.00
679 A114 30c multicolored 2.75 1.10
680 A114 $2 multicolored 7.75 7.75
Nos. 677-680 (4) 14.50 *10.45*

West Indian
Whistling
Duck
A115

5c, One standing. 15c, Landing in water. 20c, Four ducks, various activities. 80c, One raising wings. $1, Adult, chick.

Wmk. 373

1994, Apr. 21 **Litho.** ***Perf. 14***

681 A115 5c multi, vert. 1.25 .65
682 A115 15c multi 1.90 .70
683 A115 20c multi 1.90 .75
684 A115 80c multi, vert. 4.25 *4.50*
685 A115 $1 multi, vert. 4.75 *5.00*
a. Souvenir sheet of 1 12.00 *12.00*
Nos. 681-685 (5) 14.05 *11.60*

No. 685a has a continuous design and contains Cayman Islands Natl. Trust emblem.

Butterflies
A116

No. 686: a, Fulvous hairstreak. b, Atala butterfly.

No. 687: a, Barred sulphur. b, Dorantes skipper.

Wmk. 373

1994, Aug. 16 **Litho.** ***Perf. 13½***

686 A116 10c Pair, #a.-b. 2.50 *2.75*
687 A116 $1 Pair, #a.-b. 12.00 *12.00*

Wreck of the Ten
Sail,
Bicent. — A117

Perf. 13½x14

1994, Oct. 12 **Litho.** **Wmk. 373**

688 A117 10c shown .75 .75
689 A117 10c multicolored .75 .75
690 A117 15c multicolored 1.00 .50
691 A117 20c multicolored 1.25 .60
692 A117 $2 multicolored 7.25 7.25
Nos. 688-692 (5) 11.00 *9.85*

Sea
Turtles
A118

Wmk. 384

1995, Feb. 28 **Litho.** ***Perf. 14***

693 A118 10c Green .80 .40
694 A118 20c Kemp's ridley 1.10 .50
695 A118 25c Hawksbill 1.25 .60
696 A118 30c Leatherback 1.40 .70
697 A118 $1.30 Loggerhead 5.25 5.25
698 A118 $2 Pacific ridley 6.75 6.75
a. Souvenir sheet, #693-698 16.00 16.00
Nos. 693-698 (6) 16.55 14.20

1995
CARIFTA &
IAAF Games
A119

1995, Apr. 15 **Litho.** ***Perf. 14***

699 A119 10c Running .95 .50
700 A119 20c Pole vault 1.40 1.00
701 A119 30c Javelin 1.90 1.10
702 A119 $1.30 Sailing 6.75 6.75
Nos. 699-702 (4) 11.00 *9.35*

Souvenir Sheet

703 A119 $2 Medal winners 8.75 *8.75*

End of World War II, 50th Anniv.

Common Design Type

10c, Two soldiers, Cayman Home Guard. 25c, Freighter Comayagua torpedoed off Caymans, 5/14/42. 40c, Type IXc U-Boat U-125. $1, Navy airship L-3 used for U-boat patrol. $1.30, Reverse of War Medal 1939-45.

Wmk. 373

1995, May 8 **Litho.** ***Perf. 13½***

704 CD351 10c multicolored 1.25 .50
705 CD351 25c multicolored 2.75 .80
706 CD351 40c multicolored 3.25 2.00
707 CD351 $1 multicolored 6.00 *6.00*
Nos. 704-707 (4) 13.25 *9.30*

Souvenir Sheet

Perf. 14

708	CD352	$1.30 multicolored	5.00	5.00

Souvenir Sheet

Queen Mother, 95th Birthday — A120

1995, Aug. 25 *Perf. 14½*

709	A120	$4 multicolored	12.50	12.50

Singapore '95.

A121

A122

Animals of the Nativity.

1995, Nov. 1 *Perf. 14*

710	A121	10c Ox	.90	.25
711	A121	20c Sheep, lamb	1.25	.40
712	A121	30c Donkey	2.10	.50
713	A121	$2 Camels	7.25	*8.50*
a.		Souvenir sheet of 4, #710-713	11.50	*11.50*
		Nos. 710-713 (4)	11.50	*9.65*

Wmk. 384

1996, Mar. 21 Litho. *Perf. 14*

Wild fruit.

714	A122	10c Sea grape	.60	.25
715	A122	25c Guava	1.25	.60
716	A122	40c West Indian cherry	1.90	1.10
717	A122	$1 Tamarind	3.75	3.75
		Nos. 714-717 (4)	7.50	5.70

Modern Olympic Games, Cent. — A123

Perf. 14x13½

1996, June 19 Litho. Wmk. 384

718	A123	10c Sailing	.60	.40
719	A123	20c Sailboarding	1.10	.50
720	A123	30c Sailing, diff.	1.40	.75
721	A123	$2 Running	6.25	*6.25*
		Nos. 718-721 (4)	9.35	7.90

Symbols of National Identity — A124

Designs: 10c, Guitar, music, natl. song. 20c, Boeing 737. 25c, Queen Elizabeth II opening Legislative Assembly. 30c, Seven Mile Beach. 40c, Scuba diver, stingrays. 60c, School children, Cayman Turtle Farm. 80c, Cayman parrot, natl. bird. 90c, Silver thatch palm, natl. tree. $1, Natl. flag. $2, Wild banana orchid, natl. flower. $4, Natl. arms. $6, Natl. currency.

Wmk. 373

1996, Sept. 26 Litho. *Perf. 14*

722	A124	10c multicolored	.45	.40
		Complete booklet, 10 #722	4.75	
723	A124	20c multicolored	.95	.75
724	A124	25c multicolored	1.00	.70
725	A124	30c multicolored	1.00	.75
		Complete booklet, 10 #725	10.50	
726	A124	40c multicolored	1.40	1.00
		Complete booklet, 10 #726	14.00	
727	A124	60c multicolored	1.90	1.50
728	A124	80c multicolored	3.25	2.75
a.		Souvenir sheet of 1	3.25	3.25
729	A124	90c multicolored	2.25	2.75
730	A124	$1 multicolored	3.50	3.00
731	A124	$2 multicolored	6.25	6.50
732	A124	$4 multicolored	11.50	14.50
733	A124	$6 multicolored	14.50	18.00
		Nos. 722-733 (12)	47.95	52.60

No. 728a for Hong Kong '97. Issued 2/3/97.
Nos. 723, 725, 727 exist dated "1999."

Christmas A125

Designs: 10c, Christmas time on North Church Street. 25c, Santa "Gone Fishing." 30c, "Claus Encounters." $2, "Caymanian Christmas."

Wmk. 373

1996, Nov. 12 Litho. *Perf. 14*

734	A125	10c multicolored	.65	.35
735	A125	25c multicolored	1.60	.90
736	A125	30c multicolored	1.90	1.10
737	A125	$2 multicolored	4.00	4.00
		Nos. 734-737 (4)	8.15	6.35

Queen Elizabeth II and Prince Philip, 50th Wedding Anniv. — A126

#738, Queen. #739, Royal Guard. #740, Young Prince riding horse. #741, Queen in blue, Prince in military attire in open carriage. #742 Prince holding horse's reins. #743, Queen looking at horses.
$1, Queen, Prince in open carriage.

Perf. 14x13½

1997, July 10 Litho. Wmk. 373

738	A126	10c multicolored	1.10	1.10
739	A126	10c multicolored	1.10	1.10
a.		Pair, #738-739	2.25	2.25
740	A126	30c multicolored	1.75	1.75
741	A126	30c multicolored	1.75	1.75
a.		Pair, #740-741	3.50	3.50
742	A126	40c multicolored	2.10	2.10
743	A126	40c multicolored	2.10	2.10
a.		Pair, #742-743	4.25	4.25
		Nos. 738-743 (6)	9.90	9.90

Souvenir Sheet

744	A126	$1 multicolored	5.75	5.75

Telecommunications — A127

Designs: 10c, Children using the Internet. 25c, Cable and wireless ship. 30c, Children wearing numbers of new area code, "345." 60c, Cable and wireless satellite communications.

Perf. 14x14½

1997, Oct. 10 Litho. Wmk. 384

745	A127	10c multicolored	.45	.30
746	A127	25c multicolored	1.10	.75
747	A127	30c multicolored	1.25	.90
748	A127	60c multicolored	2.50	2.50
		Nos. 745-748 (4)	5.30	4.45

Christmas A128

Santa Claus: 10c, Relaxing in hammock, Little Cayman. 30c, With children on bluff, Cayman Brac. 40c, Playing golf. $1, Diving with stingrays.

Wmk. 373

1997, Dec. 3 Litho. *Perf. 13*

749	A128	10c multicolored	.40	.25
750	A128	30c multicolored	.85	.45
751	A128	40c multicolored	1.75	.75
752	A128	$1 multicolored	2.75	3.00
		Nos. 749-752 (4)	5.75	4.45

Diana, Princess of Wales (1961-97)

Common Design Type

Portraits: a, 10c. b, 20c. c, 40c. d, $1.

Perf. 14½x14

1998 Litho. Wmk. 373

752A	CD355	10c Like #753a	.25	.25
752B	CD355	20c Like #753b	.50	.50

Sheet of 4

753	CD355	#a.-d.	5.75	5.75

No. 753 sold for $1.70 + 30c, with surtax from international sales being donated to the Princess Diana Memorial Fund and surtax from national sales being donated to designated local charity.

Royal Air Force, 80th Anniv.

Common Design Type of 1993 Re-Inscribed

Designs: 10c, Hawker Horsley. 20c, Fairey Hendon. 25c, Hawker Siddeley Gnat. 30c, Hawker Siddeley Dominie.

No. 758: a, 40c, Airco DH-9. b, 60c, Spad 13 Scout. c, 80c, Airspeed Oxford. d, $1, Martin Baltimore.

Wmk. 373

1998, Apr. 1 Litho. *Perf. 14*

754	CD350	10c multicolored	.85	.85
755	CD350	20c multicolored	1.10	1.10
756	CD350	25c multicolored	1.25	1.25
757	CD350	30c multicolored	1.50	1.50
		Nos. 754-757 (4)	4.70	4.70

Souvenir Sheet

758	CD350	Sheet of 4, #a.-d.	9.00	9.00

Birds — A129

Designs: 10c, West Indian whistling duck. 20c, Magnificent frigatebird. 60c, Red footed booby. $1, Grand Cayman parrot.

1998 Litho. Wmk. 373 *Perf. 13½*

759	A129	10c multicolored	.80	.50
760	A129	20c multicolored	1.40	.50
761	A129	60c multicolored	2.50	2.50
762	A129	$1 multicolored	3.00	3.00
		Nos. 759-762 (4)	7.70	6.50

Christmas A130

Santa at various island locations: 10c, At Blowholes. 30c, Diving on wreck of MV Capt. Keith Tibbetts. 40c, Visiting Pedro Castle. 60c, Arriving at Little Cayman.

1998 *Perf. 14x14½*

763	A130	10c multicolored	.40	.40
764	A130	30c multicolored	1.00	.80
765	A130	40c multicolored	1.25	1.00
766	A130	60c multicolored	2.50	2.50
		Nos. 763-766 (4)	5.15	4.70

Easter A131

Artworks by Miss Lassie (Gladwyn Bush): 10c, "They Rolled the Stone Away." 20c, "Ascension," vert. 30c, "The World Praying for Peace." 40c, "Calvary," vert.

Wmk. 373

1999, Mar. 26 Litho. *Perf. 13*

767	A131	10c multicolored	.40	.40
768	A131	20c multicolored	.75	.75
769	A131	30c multicolored	1.10	1.10
770	A131	40c multicolored	1.25	1.25
		Nos. 767-770 (4)	3.50	3.50

Vision 2008 A132

Children's drawings: 10c, "Cayman House." 30c, "Coral Reef." 40c, "Fisherman on North Sound." $2, "Three Fish and A Turtle."

1999, June *Perf. 13½*

771	A132	10c multicolored	.30	.30
772	A132	30c multicolored	.95	.95
773	A132	40c multicolored	1.10	1.10
774	A132	$2 multicolored	5.75	5.75
		Nos. 771-774 (4)	8.10	8.10

Wedding of Prince Edward and Sophie Rhys-Jones

Common Design Type

Perf. 13¾x14

1999, June 16 Litho. Wmk. 384

775	CD356	10c Separate portraits	.50	.50
776	CD356	$2 Couple	5.25	5.25

1st Manned Moon Landing, 30th Anniv.

Common Design Type

Designs: 10c, Coast Guard during launch. 25c, 3rd stage fires and puts rocket in orbit. 30c, Aldrin descends to lunar surface. 60c, Lander module sent back to moon.
$1.50, Looking at earth from moon.

1999, July 20 *Perf. 14x13¾*

777	CD357	10c multicolored	.40	.40
778	CD357	25c multicolored	.95	.95
779	CD357	30c multicolored	1.10	1.10
780	CD357	60c multicolored	2.25	2.25
		Nos. 777-780 (4)	4.70	4.70

Souvenir Sheet

Perf. 14

781	CD357	$1.50 multicolored	5.25	5.25

No. 781 contains one circular stamp 40mm in diameter.

Queen Mother's Century

Common Design Type

Queen Mother: 10c, Looking at London's defenses, 1940. 20c, At Clarence House, 94th birthday. 30c, With Princes Charles and William. 40c, Reviewing the Chelsea Pensioners, 1986.

$1.50, At her wedding.

Wmk. 384

1999, Aug. 18 Litho. *Perf. 13¼*

782 CD358 10c multicolored .45 .45
783 CD358 20c multicolored .80 .80
784 CD358 30c multicolored 1.25 1.25
785 CD358 40c multicolored 1.50 1.50
Nos. 782-785 (4) 4.00 4.00

Souvenir Sheet

786 CD358 $1.50 multicolored 4.50 4.50

Christmas — A133

Wmk. 373

1999, Nov. 17 Litho. *Perf. 13¼*

787 A133 10c #242, vert. .25 .25
788 A133 30c #532d, vert. .70 .70
789 A133 40c #749, vert. .90 .90
790 A133 $1 #431 2.40 2.40
a. Souv. sheet, #787-790, perf. 12 4.25 4.25
Nos. 787-790 (4) 4.25 4.25

British Monarchs — A134

No. 792: a, Henry VIII. b, Mary I. c, Charles II. d, Anne. e, George IV. f, George V.

Wmk. 373

2000, Feb. 29 Litho. *Perf. 14*

791 A134 10c Henry VII .40 .40

Sheet of 6

792 A134 40c #a.-f. 7.00 7.00

The Stamp Show 2000, London.

Sesame Street — A135

Designs: 10c, Ernie. 30c, Big Bird.

No. 795: a, Grover. b, Zoe. c, Oscar the Grouch. d, The Count. e, Like 30c. f, Cookie Monster. g, Like 10c. h, Bert. i, Elmo in pond.

No. 796, Elmo collecting stamps.

Perf. 14½x14¾

2000, Mar. 15 Litho. Wmk. 373

793 A135 10c multi .25 .25
794 A135 30c multi .75 .75
795 A135 20c Sheet of 9, #a-i 5.75 5.75

Souvenir Sheet

796 A135 20c multi 1.75 1.75

Prince William, 18th Birthday

Common Design Type

10c, In checked shirt and in sweater and checked shirt. 20c, In white shirt and black bow tie. 30c, In blue casual shirt, vert. 40c, As child, with beret, vert. $1, As infant.

Perf. 14¼x13¾, 13¾x14¼

2000, June 21 Litho. Wmk. 373

Stamps With White Border

797 CD359 10c multi .35 .35
798 CD359 20c multi .75 .75
799 CD359 30c multi 1.00 1.00
800 CD359 40c multi 1.40 1.40
Nos. 797-800 (4) 3.50 3.50

Souvenir Sheet

Stamps Without White Border

Perf. 14¼

801 Sheet of 5 7.50 7.50
a. CD359 10c multi .35 .35
b. CD359 20c multi .75 .75
c. CD359 30c multi 1.00 1.00
d. CD359 40c multi 1.40 1.40
e. CD359 $1 multi 3.50 3.50

Marine Life A136

10c, Green turtle. 20c, Queen angelfish. 30c, Parrotfish. $1, Green moray eel.

Wmk. 384

2000, Aug. 25 Litho. *Perf. 14*

802-805 A136 Set of 4 5.50 5.50

National Drug Council A137

Various children's drawings. Denominations, 10c, 15c, 30c, $2.

2000, Aug. 25

806-809 A137 Set of 4 9.50 9.50

Christmas A138

10c, Backing sand. 30c, Christmas dinner. 40c, Yard dance. 60c, Conch shell border.

Perf. 14½x14¼

2000, Nov. 14 Wmk. 373

810-813 A138 Set of 4 7.25 7.25

UN Women's Human Rights Campaign — A139

Wmk. 373

2001, Mar. 8 Litho. *Perf. 14*

814 A139 10c multi .75 .75

Cayman Brac A140

Designs: 15c, Red mangrove. 20c, Peter's Cave, vert. 25c, Bight Road stairway, vert. 30c, Westerly Pond. 40c, Aerial view. 60c, Marshes.

2001, Apr. 21

815-820 A140 Set of 6 6.75 6.75

Non-profit Organizations — A141

Designs: Nos. 821, 826a, 15c, National Council of Voluntary Organizations. Nos. 822, 826b, 20c, Cayman Humane Society. Nos. 823, 826c, 25c, Red Cross/Red Crescent. Nos. 824, 826d, 30c, Cayman Islands Cancer Society, vert. Nos. 825, 826e, 40c, Lions Club of Tropical Gardens, vert.

Wmk. 373

2001, Aug. 15 Litho. *Perf. 14*

Stamps With White Margins

821-825 A141 Set of 5 3.60 3.60

Souvenir Sheet

Stamps With Pink Margins

826 A141 Sheet of 5, #a-e 5.25 5.25

No. 826 sold for $1.80, 50c of which went to the various organizations honored.

Transportation — A142

Designs: No. 827, Walking home. No. 828, Boy on donkey. 20c, Bananas by canoe. 25c, Horse and buggy. 30c, Catboats. 40c, Schooner. 60c, Police bicycle, vert. 80c, Lady drivers. 90c, Launcing Cimboco, vert. $1, Seaplane. $4, Freighter. $10, Boeing 767.

Perf. 14¼x14½, 14½x14¼

2001, Sept. 29 Litho. Wmk. 373

827 A142 15c multi .35 .35
828 A142 15c multi .35 .35
829 A142 20c multi .45 .45
830 A142 25c multi .60 .60
831 A142 30c multi .70 .70
832 A142 40c multi .95 .95
833 A142 60c multi 1.40 1.40
834 A142 80c multi 1.90 1.90
835 A142 90c multi 2.10 2.10
836 A142 $1 multi 2.25 2.25
837 A142 $4 multi 9.25 9.25
838 A142 $10 multi 22.50 22.50
Nos. 827-838 (12) 42.80 42.80

Christmas A143

Santa Claus: 15c, With children on dock. 30c, On eagle ray. 40c, In catboat. 60c, Parasailing.

Perf. 14¼x14½

2001, Nov. 21 Litho. Wmk. 373

839-842 A143 Set of 4 4.75 4.75

In Remembrance of Sept. 11, 2001 Terrorist Attacks — A144

Perf. 14x14¾

2002, Jan. 22 Litho. Wmk. 373

843 A144 $1 multi 4.75 4.75

Reign Of Queen Elizabeth II, 50th Anniv. Issue

Common Design Type

Designs: Nos. 844, 848a, 15c, Princess Elizabeth as child. Nos. 845, 848b, 20c, In 1976. Nos. 846, 848c, 30c, With Princess Margaret, 1942. Nos. 847, 848d, 80c, In 1996. No. 848e, $1, 1955 portrait by Annigoni (38x50mm).

Perf. 14¼x14½, 13¾ (#848e)

2002, Feb. 6 Litho. Wmk. 373

With Gold Frames

844-847 CD360 Set of 4 4.00 4.00

Souvenir Sheet

Without Gold Frames

848 CD360 Sheet of 5, #a-e 9.50 9.50

Peanuts Comic Strip Characters A145

Designs: 15c, Snoopy painting Woodstock at Cayman Brac Bluff. 20c, Charlie Brown and Sally at Hell Post Office. 25c, Peppermint Patty and Marcie at Little Cayman beach. 30c, Snoopy and Boeing 737-200. 40c, Linus and Snoopy at Point of Sand. 60c, Charlie Brown at Links Golf Course.

Wmk. 373

2002, Mar. 9 Litho. *Perf. 14*

849-854 A145 Set of 6 8.00 8.00
854a Souvenir sheet, #849-854 8.00 8.00

2002 World Cup Soccer Championships, Japan and Korea — A146

Denominations: 30c, 40c.

2002, Apr. 30 *Perf. 13¾*

855-856 A146 Set of 2 4.00 4.00

Queen Mother Elizabeth (1900-2002)

Common Design Type

Designs: 15c, Wearing hat (sepia photograph). 30c, Wearing dark blue hat. Nos. 859, 861a, 40c, Wearing hat (black and white photograph). Nos. 860, 861b, $1, Wearing tiara.

Perf. 13¾x14¼, 14¼ (#859-860)

2002, Aug. 5 Litho. Wmk. 373

With Purple Frames

857-860 CD361 Set of 4 7.75 7.75

Souvenir Sheet

Without Purple Frames

Perf. 14½x14¼

861 CD361 Sheet of 2, #a-b 7.75 7.75

Christmas A147

Designs: 15c, Hail Mary. 20c, Journey to Bethlehem. 30c, Her firstborn Son. 40c, I bring good tidings. 60c Star in the east.

Wmk. 373

2002, Oct. 18 Litho. *Perf. 14*

Stamps + labels

862-866 A147 Set of 5 5.00 5.00
866a Souvenir sheet of 5, #862-866 + 5 labels 5.00 5.00

Aviation in the Cayman Islands, 50th Anniv. A148

Designs: 15c, PBY Catalina Flying Boat. 20c, First landing at Grand Cayman Airport, 1952. 25c, Cayman Brac Airways AC 50. 30c, Cayman Airways B-737. 40c, Concorde at original airport, 1984. $1.30, Island Air DHC6.

2002, Nov. 8

867-872 A148 Set of 6 8.75 8.75

Children's Games A149

Designs: 15c, Rope skipping. 20c, Maypole dancing. 25c, Gig. 30c, Hopscotch. $1, Marbles.

Wmk. 373

2003, May 27 Litho. *Perf. 13¾*

873-877 A149 Set of 5 5.75 5.75

Head of Queen Elizabeth II

Common Design Type

Wmk. 373

2003, June 2 Litho. *Perf. 13¾*

878 CD362 $4 multi 13.50 13.50

Coronation of Queen Elizabeth II, 50th Anniv.

Common Design Type

Designs: Nos. 879, 15c, 881a, 20c, Queen wearing crown. Nos. 880, $2, 881b, $4, Queen holding symbols of office.

Perf. 14¼x14½

2003, June 2 Litho. Wmk. 373

Vignettes Framed, Red Background

879-880 CD363 Set of 2 6.50 6.50

Souvenir Sheet

Vignettes Without Frame, Purple Panel

881 CD363 Sheet of 2, #a-b 12.50 12.50

Prince William, 21st Birthday

Common Design Type

Color photographs: 15c, William with backpack at right. 40c, William in suit and tie at left

No. 884: a, William with hand on chin at right. b, William with white bow tie at left.

Wmk. 373

2003, June 21 Litho. *Perf. 14¼*

882 CD364 15c multi .45 .45
883 CD364 40c multi 1.25 1.25
884 Horiz. pair 5.50 5.50
a. CD364 80c multi 2.50 2.50
b. CD364 $1 multi 3.00 3.00
Nos. 882-884 (3) 7.20 7.20

Discovery of the Cayman Islands, 500th Anniv. A150

Designs: 15c, Turtle hatchlings. No. 886, 20c, Old waterfront. No. 887, 20c, Turtle and ship of Christopher Columbus. 25c, Nassau grouper. 30c, Cayman Brac schooner "Kirk-B." 40c, George Town harbor. 60c, Musical instruments. 80c, Smokewood tree. 90c, Little Cayman Baptist Church. $1, Thatch rope. $1.30, Children's dance troupe. $2, Parliament in session.

Wmk. 373

2003, July 24 Litho. *Perf. 13¾*

885-896 A150 Set of 12 24.00 24.00
896a Souvenir sheet, #885-896 24.00 24.00

Holiday Greetings A151

Various Christmas decorations and inscriptions of: 15c, Merry Christmas. 20c, Celebrate With Family. 30c, Happy New Year. 40c, Happy Holidays. 60c, Seasons Greetings.

Wmk. 373

2003, Nov. 4 Litho. *Perf. 13¼*

897-901 A151 Set of 5 4.00 4.00

Worldwide Fund for Nature (WWF) A152

Short-finned pilot whale: 15c, Adult and calf. 20c, Pod of four whales. 30c, Two whales at surface. 40c, One adult.

2003, Nov. 26 *Perf. 14*

902-905 A152 Set of 4 2.60 2.60
905a Sheet, 4 each #902-905 10.50 10.50

Shipping Registry, Cent. — A153

Ships: 15c, Lady Slater. 20c, Seanostrum. 30c, Kirk Pride. $1, Boadicea.

Perf. 14x14¾

2004, Jan. 29 Litho. Wmk. 373

906-909 A153 Set of 4 4.00 4.00

Easter — A154

Designs: 15c, Jesus Carrying His Cross. 30c, The Ascension.

2004, Mar. 16 *Perf. 14¾x14*

910-911 A154 Set of 2 1.10 1.10

2004 Summer Olympics, Athens — A155

Designs: 15c, Swimmer. 40c, Runner. 60c, Long jumper. 80c, Swimmers.

Perf. 13½x13¼

2004, Aug. 23 Litho. Wmk. 373

912-915 A155 Set of 4 4.75 4.75

Blue Iguana A156

Designs: 15c, Adult on rocks. 20c, Eggs. 25c, Four juveniles. 30c, Juvenile on finger. 40c, Adult with open mouth. 90c, Eye.

No. 922: a, 60c, On rock facing right. b, 80c, On rock facing left.

2004, Oct. 26 Litho. *Perf. 13¾*

916-921 A156 Set of 6 5.50 5.50

Souvenir Sheet

922 A156 Sheet of 2, #a-b 4.75 4.75

No. 922 sold for $1.90.

WAR TAX STAMPS

No. 36 Surcharged:

a

b

1917, Feb. 26 Wmk. 3 *Perf. 14*

MR1 A5(a) 1½p on 2½p 11.00 *13.50*
a. Fraction bar omitted 150.00 *210.00*
MR2 A5(b) 1½p on 2½p 2.10 *7.25*
a. Fraction bar omitted 85.00 *150.00*

No. 1 exists with missing period. On No. 1 the distance between "WAR STAMP" and "1½" varies.

Surcharged WAR STAMP 1½d

1917, Sept. 4

MR3 A5 1½p on 2½p ultra 900.00 *2,250.*

Surcharged

1917, Sept. 4

MR4 A5 1½p on 2½p ultra .30 *.65*

No. 33 Overprinted

1919, Feb. 4

MR5 A5 ½p green .70 *3.00*

The "brownish paper" variety comes from the interleaving used for shipment from England.

Type of 1912-16 Surcharged

1919, Feb. 4

MR6 A5 1½p on 2½p orange .95 *1.50*

No. 35 Surcharged

1920, Mar. 10

MR7 A5 1½p on 2p gray 1.75 *8.50*

The "rose-tinted paper" variety comes from the interleaving used for shipment from England.

A surcharge in red was not issued.

CENTRAL AFRICAN REPUBLIC

'sen-trəl 'a-fri-kə

LOCATION — Western Africa, north of equator
GOVT. — Republic
AREA — 241,243 sq. mi.
POP. — 3,444,951 (1999 est.)
CAPITAL — Bangui

The former French colony of Ubangi-Shari, a unit in French Equatorial Africa, proclaimed itself the Central African Republic Dec. 1, 1958. It became the Central African Empire Dec. 4, 1976. It became the Central African Republic again in 1979.

100 Centimes = 1 Franc

Catalogue values for all unused stamps in this country are for Never Hinged items.

Watermark

Wmk. 385

Central African Republic

Premier Barthélemy Boganda and Flag — A1

Design: 25fr, Boganda and flag, horiz.

Unwmk.

1959, Dec. 1 Engr. *Perf. 13*

1 A1 15fr multi .35 .20
2 A1 25fr multi .55 .20

1st anniv. of the Republic and honoring Premier Barthélemy Boganda (1910-59).

For overprints & surcharge see #12, 59, M1-M2.

Imperforates

Many stamps of Central African Republic exist imperforate in issued and trial colors, and also in small presentation sheets in issued colors.

Common Design Types pictured following the introduction.

C.C.T.A. Issue
Common Design Type

1960, May 21 Unwmk. *Perf. 13*

3	CD106 50fr lt grn & dk bl	1.75	.65

Dactyloceras Widenmanni — A2

Designs: Various butterflies.

1960-61

4	A2	50c bl grn & dk red	.20	.20
5	A2	1fr multi	.20	.20
6	A2	2fr dk grn & brn	.20	.20
7	A2	3fr yel grn & dk red	.25	.20
8	A2	5fr multi	.30	.20
9	A2	10fr multi	.70	.35
10	A2	20fr multi	1.50	.50
11	A2	85fr multi	5.75	1.60
		Nos. 4-11 (8)	9.10	3.45

Issued: 50c-3fr, 6/10/61; others, 9/3/60.

No. 2 Overprinted: "FETE NATIONALE 1-12-1960"

1960, Dec. 1

12	A1 25fr multi	1.40	1.40

National Holiday, Dec. 1, 1960.

Louis Pasteur and Pasteur Institute, Bangui A3

1961, Feb. 25 Unwmk. *Perf. 13*

13	A3 20fr multi	1.10	.80

Opening of Pasteur Institute at Bangui.

Flag, Map, and UN Emblem A4

1961, Mar. 4 Engr.

14	A4	15fr multi	.45	.30
15	A4	25fr multi	.55	.30
16	A4	85fr multi	1.50	1.00
		Nos. 14-16 (3)	2.50	1.60

Admission to the UN.

No. 15 Overprinted in Green: "FETE NATIONALE 1-12-61" and Star

1961, Dec. 1

17	A4 25fr multi	2.00	2.00

National Holiday, Dec. 1.

No. 16 Surcharged in Red Brown: "U.A.M. CONFERENCE DE BANGUI 25-27 Mars 1962"

1962, Mar. 25

18	A4 50fr on 85fr multi	1.75	1.75

Conf. of the African and Malgache Union at Bangui, Mar. 25-27.

Abidjan Games Issue
Common Design Type

1962, July 21 Photo. *Perf. 12½x12*

19	CD109 20fr Hurdling	.50	.30
20	CD109 50fr Bicycling	1.25	.80
	Nos. 19-20,C6 (3)	4.00	2.60

African-Malgache Union Issue
Common Design Type

1962, Sept. 8 Unwmk.

21	CD110 30fr multi	1.25	1.25

African and Malgache Union, 1st anniv.

Pres. David Dacko — A5

Soldiers with Flag — A6

1962 *Perf. 12*

22	A5	20fr multi	.35	.20
23	A5	25fr multi	.55	.20

For surcharge see No. 60.

1963, Aug. 13 Photo.

24	A6	20fr blk & multi	.70	.35

National Army, third anniversary.

Waves Around Globe A6a

Design: 100fr, Orbit patterns around globe.

1963, Sept. 19 Unwmk. *Perf. 12½*

25	A6a	25fr plum & grn	.70	.55
26	A6a	100fr org, bl & grn	1.75	1.50

Issued to publicize space communications.

Young Pioneers A7

1963, Oct. 14 Engr. *Perf. 12½*

27	A7	50fr grnsh bl, vio bl & brn	.90	.55

Issued to honor Young Pioneers.

Boali Falls — A8

1963, Oct. 28 *Perf. 13*

28	A8	30fr bl, grn & red brn	.90	.45

Colotis Evippe A9

Designs: Various butterflies.

1963, Nov. 18 Photo. *Perf. 12½x13*

29	A9	1fr multi	.25	.20
30	A9	3fr multi	.55	.30
31	A9	4fr multi	.80	.40
32	A9	60fr multi	5.25	3.00
		Nos. 29-32 (4)	6.85	3.90

For surcharge see No. 58.

UNESCO Emblem, Scales and Tree — A9a

1963, Dec. 10 *Perf. 13*

33	A9a	25fr grn, ol & red brn	.90	.55

15th anniversary of the Universal Declaration of Human Rights.

Leaves and IQSY Emblem A10

1964, Apr. 20 Engr. *Perf. 13*

34	A10	25fr org, Prus grn & bis	1.25	.80

International Quiet Sun Year, 1964-65.

Child — A11

"All Men Are Men" — A12

Designs: Heads of Children.

1964, Aug. 13 Unwmk. *Perf. 13*

35	A11	20fr multi	.35	.20
36	A11	25fr multi	.45	.30
37	A11	40fr multi	.60	.45
38	A11	50fr multi	.80	.45
a.		Miniature sheet of 4, #35-38	3.50	3.50
		Nos. 35-38 (4)	2.20	1.40

Cooperation Issue
Common Design Type

1964, Nov. 7 Engr.

39	CD119 25fr grn, mag & dk brn	.90	.55

1964, Dec. 1 Litho. *Perf. 13x12½*

40	A12	25fr multi	.90	.45

Issued to publicize National Unity.

Putting Yoke on Oxen A13

Designs: 50fr, Ox pulling harrow. 85fr, Team of oxen in field. 100fr, Hay wagon.

1965, Apr. 28 Engr. *Perf. 13*

41	A13	25fr sl grn, sep & rose	.55	.30
42	A13	50fr sl grn, lt bl & brn	.90	.45
43	A13	85fr bl, grn & red brn	1.25	.70
44	A13	100fr multi	1.75	.90
		Nos. 41-44 (4)	4.45	2.35

For surcharges see Nos. 63-64.

Telegraph Receiver by Pouget-Maisonneuve — A14

ITU cent.: 30fr, Chappe telegraph, vert. 50fr, Doignon regulator, vert. 85fr, Pouillet telegraph transcriber.

1965, May 17 Unwmk.

45	A14	25fr red, grn & ultra	.55	.40
46	A14	30fr lake & grn	.60	.40
47	A14	50fr car & vio	.95	.60
48	A14	85fr red lil & slate	1.75	1.00
		Nos. 45-48 (4)	3.85	2.40

"Health" A15

25fr, "Clothes;" shuttle, cloth & women. 60fr, "Teaching;" student & school. 85fr, "Food;" mother feeding child, tractor in wheat field.

1965, June 10 Engr. *Perf. 13*

49	A15	25fr ultra, brt grn & brn	.45	.30
50	A15	50fr ultra, brn & grn	.80	.45
51	A15	60fr grn, ultra & brn	.90	.60
52	A15	85fr multi	1.25	.70
		Nos. 49-52 (4)	3.40	2.05

Issued to publicize the slogans and aims of "M.E.S.A.N." (Mouvement d'Evolution Sociale de l'Afrique Noire). See No. C30.

Caterpillars and Moth on Coffee Branch — A16

Designs: 3fr, Hawk moth and caterpillar on coffee leaves, horiz. 30fr, Platyedra moth and larvae on cotton plant.

1965, Aug. 25 Engr. *Perf. 13*

53	A16	2fr dk pur, dp org & sl grn	.25	.20
54	A16	3fr blk, sl grn & red	.70	.25
55	A16	30fr red lil, red & sl grn	4.00	.90
		Nos. 53-55 (3)	4.95	1.35

Issued to publicize plant protection.

Boy Scout, Tents and Animals A17

Design: 25fr, Campfire and Scout emblem.

1965, Sept. 27 Unwmk. *Perf. 13*

56	A17	25fr red org, bl & red lil	.90	.25
57	A17	50fr brn & Prus bl	1.25	.60

Issued to honor the Boy Scouts.

Nos. 30, 1 and 22 Surcharged in Black or Brown

Engraved; Photogravure
Perf. 13, 12, 12½x13

1965, Aug. 26 Unwmk.

58	A9	2fr on 3fr multi	5.25	5.25
59	A1	5fr on 15fr multi	4.25	4.25
60	A5	10fr on 20fr multi (Br)	5.75	5.75
		Nos. 58-60 (3)	15.25	15.25

The surcharges are adjusted to shape of stamps.

UN Emblem and Wheat A18

1965, Oct. 16 Engr. *Perf. 13*
61 A18 50fr ocher, sl grn & brt bl 1.10 .70

FAO "Freedom from Hunger Campaign."

Diamond Cutter A19

1966, Mar. 14 Engr. *Perf. 13*
62 A19 25fr car rose, dk pur & brn 1.00 .45

Nos. 43-44 Surcharged

1966, Feb.
63 A13 5fr on 85fr multi .35 .30
64 A13 10fr on 100fr multi .55 .45

Issue dates: 5fr, Feb. 17; 10fr, Feb. 15.

Statue of Mbaka Woman Porter — A20

WHO Headquarters, Geneva — A21

1966, Apr. 9 Photo. *Perf. 13x12½*
65 A20 25fr multi .90 .45

Intl. Negro Arts Festival, Dakar, Senegal, Apr. 1-24.

1966, May 3 Photo. Unwmk.
66 A21 25fr pur, bl & yel .90 .45

Inauguration of the WHO Headquarters, Geneva.

Eulophia Cucullata — A22

Orchids: 5fr, Lissochilus horsfalii. 10fr, Tridactyle bicaudata. 15fr, Polystachya. 20fr, Eulophia alta. 25fr, Microcelia macrorrhynchium.

1966, May 16 Photo. *Perf. 12x12½*
Orchids in Natural Colors
67 A22 2fr dk red .35 .20
68 A22 5fr brn org & vio .55 .20
69 A22 10fr bl grn & blk .60 .25
70 A22 15fr lt grn & dk brn 1.00 .45
71 A22 20fr dk grn 1.60 .70
72 A22 25fr lt ultra & brn 2.50 .95
Nos. 67-72 (6) 6.60 2.75

For surcharge see No. 78.

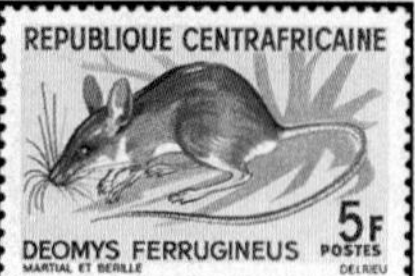
Congo Forest Mouse A23

Rodents: 10fr, One-stripe mouse. 20fr, Dollman's tree mouse, vert.

1966, Sept. 15 Photo. *Perf. 12½x12*
73 A23 5fr yel & multi .65 .30
74 A23 10fr tan & multi 1.10 .45
75 A23 20fr lt grn & multi 2.25 .80
Nos. 73-75 (3) 4.00 1.55

UNESCO Emblem — A24

Pres. Jean Bedel Bokassa — A25

1966, Dec. 5 Photo. *Perf. 13*
76 A24 30fr multi .70 .35

20th anniv. of UNESCO.

1967, Jan. 1 *Perf. 12x12½*
77 A25 30fr yel grn, blk & bis brn .70 .35

No. 72 Surcharged with New Value and "XX"

1967, May 8 Photo. *Perf. 12x12½*
78 A22 10fr on 25fr multi .50 .25

See No. C43.

Central Market, Bangui A26

1967, Aug. 8 Photo. *Perf. 12½x13*
79 A26 30fr multi .90 .40

Safari Hotel, Bangui A27

1967, Sept. 26 Photo. *Perf. 12½x13*
80 A27 30fr multi .90 .40

Leucocoprinus Africanus — A28

Various Mushrooms

1967, Oct. 3 Engr. *Perf. 13*
81 A28 5fr dk brn, ol & ocher *9.00* .80
82 A28 10fr dk brn, ultra & yel *14.00* *1.25*
83 A28 15fr dk brn, sl grn & yel *16.00* *1.40*
84 A28 30fr multi *45.00* *4.00*
85 A28 50fr multi *70.00* *6.00*
Nos. 81-85 (5) *154.00* *13.45*

Map, Radio Tower, Projector and People A29

1967, Oct. 31
86 A29 30fr emer, ocher & indigo .90 .45

Radiovision service.

African Hair Style — A30

Various African Hair Styles.

1967, Nov. 7 Engr. *Perf. 13*
87 A30 5fr ultra, dk brn & bis brn .25 .20
88 A30 10fr car, dk brn & bis brn .45 .25
89 A30 15fr dp grn, dk brn & bis brn .70 .40
90 A30 20fr org, dk brn & bis brn .70 .40
91 A30 30fr red lil, dk brn & bis brn 1.25 .55
Nos. 87-91 (5) 3.35 1.80

Nurse Vaccinating Children A31

1967, Nov. 14
92 A31 30fr dk red brn & brt grn .90 .55

Vaccination campaign, 1967-70.

Douglas DC-3 A32

1967, Nov. 24
93 A32 1fr shown .20 .20
94 A32 2fr Beechcraft Baron .20 .20
95 A32 5fr Douglas DC-4 .20 .20
Nos. 93-95,C47-C49 (6) 18.60 7.40

Pierced Stone, Kwe Tribe — A33

Designs: 30fr, Primitive dwelling at Toulou, horiz. 100fr, Megaliths, Bouar. 130fr, Rock painting (people), Toulou, horiz.

1967, Dec. 26 Engr. *Perf. 13*
96 A33 30fr crim, ind & mar .70 .20
97 A33 50fr ol brn, ocher & dk grn 1.40 .50
98 A33 100fr dk brn, brt bl & brn 2.75 .65
99 A33 130fr dk red, brn & dk grn 3.00 .65
Nos. 96-99 (4) 7.85 2.00

6th Pan-African Prehistoric Cong., Dakar.

Tanker, Refinery and Map of Area Served — A33a

1968, July 30 Photo. *Perf. 12½*
100 A33a 30fr multi .90 .30

Issued to commemorate the opening of the Port Gentil (Gabon) Refinery, June 12, 1968.

Bulldozer Clearing Land — A34

Designs: 10fr, Baoule cattle. 20fr, 15,000-spindle spinning machine. No. 104, Automatic Diederichs looms. No. 105, Bulldozer.

1968, Oct. 1 Engr. *Perf. 13*
101 A34 5fr blk, grn & dk brn .35 .20
102 A34 10fr blk, pale grn & bis brn .50 .30
103 A34 20fr grn, red brn & yel .80 .30
104 A34 30fr brn, ol & ultra 1.25 .55
105 A34 30fr ind, red brn & sl grn 1.25 .55
Nos. 101-105 (5) 4.15 1.90

Issued to publicize "Operation Bokassa."

Bangui Mosque A35

1968, Oct. 14
106 A35 30fr grn, bl & ocher .80 .40

Hunting Knife of Baya and Boufi Tribes A36

20fr, Hunting knife of Nzakara tribe. 30fr, Crossbow of Babinga & Babenzele (pygmy) tribes.

1968, Nov. 19 Engr. *Perf. 13*
107 A36 10fr lem, Prus bl & ultra .50 .25
108 A36 20fr ultra, dk ol & sl grn .60 .30
109 A36 30fr sl grn, ultra & brn org 1.50 .40
Nos. 107-109 (3) 2.60 .95

"Ville de Bangui," 1958 — A37

River Boats: 30fr, "J. B. Gouandjia," 1968. 50fr, "Lamblin," 1944.

1968, Dec. 10 Engr. *Perf. 13*
Size: 36x22mm
110 A37 10fr mag, brt grn & vio bl .60 .40
111 A37 30fr bl, grn & brn 1.00 .45
112 A37 50fr brn, sl & ol grn 1.75 .55
Nos. 110-112,C62-C63 (5) 8.25 3.65

Woman Javelin Thrower — A38

1969, Mar. 18 Photo. *Perf. 13x12½*

113 A38 5fr shown .25 .20
114 A38 10fr Women runners .25 .20
115 A38 15fr Soccer .45 .25
Nos. 113-115,C71-C72 (5) 4.05 1.55

BIT and ILO Emblems and Worker A39

1969, May 20 Photo. *Perf. 12½x13*

116 A39 30fr dp bl, grn & ol brn 1.00 .40
117 A39 50fr dp car, grn & ol brn 1.50 .55

50th anniv. of the ILO.

Pres. Bokassa — A40

Garayah — A41

1969, Dec. 1 Litho. *Perf. 13x13½*

118 A40 30fr vermilion & multi .60 .30

ASECNA Issue

Common Design Type

1969, Dec. 12 Engr. *Perf. 13*

119 CD132 100fr dp bl 2.00 .80

1970, Jan. 6 Engr. *Perf. 13*

Musical Instuments: 15fr, Ngombi (harp) horiz. 30fr, Xylophone, horiz. 50fr, Ndala (lute) horiz. 130fr, Gatta and babyon (drums).

120 A41 10fr yel grn, dk grn & ocher .60 .25
121 A41 15fr bl grn, ocher & dk brn .60 .25
122 A41 30fr mar, ocher & dk brn 1.00 .45
123 A41 50fr rose car & ind 1.40 .55
124 A41 130fr brt bl, brn & ol 4.75 .95
Nos. 120-124 (5) 8.35 2.45

UPU Headquarters Issue

Common Design Type

1970, May 20 Engr. *Perf. 13*

125 CD133 100fr ultra, ver & red brn 1.75 .70

Loading Platform and Flour Storage Bins A42

50fr, Flour milling machinery. 100fr, View of mill.

1970, Feb. 24 Litho. *Perf. 14*

126 A42 25fr sl & multi 10.50 .70
127 A42 50fr lil & multi 22.50 1.50
128 A42 100fr red & multi 32.50 2.50
Nos. 126-128 (3) 65.50 4.70

Inauguration of SICPAD (Société Industrielle Centrafricaine des Produits Alimentaires et Dérivés), a part of Operation Bokassa, 2/22/68.

Pres. Bokassa — A43

1970, Aug. 13 Litho. *Perf. 14*

129 A43 30fr multi 5.25 3.50
130 A43 40fr multi 7.00 4.25

Cheese Factory, Sarki — A44

Silk Worm — A45

10fr, M'Bali Ranch. 20fr, Zebu, vert.

Perf. 13x13½, 13½x13

1970, Sept. 15

131 A44 5fr red & multi .35 .20
132 A44 10fr red & multi 5.25 4.00
133 A44 20fr red & multi .90 .55
134 A45 40fr red & multi 2.25 .95
Nos. 131-134,C83 (5) 11.75 6.80

Issued to publicize Operation Bokassa, a national development plan.

Nos. 131-134 exist perf 10.

Gnathonemus Monteiri — A46

River Fish: 20fr, Mormyrus proboscirostris. 30fr, Marcusenius wilverthi. 40fr, Gnathonemus elephas. 50fr, Gnathonemus curvirostris.

1971, Apr. 6 Photo. *Perf. 12½*

135 A46 10fr multi .35 .25
136 A46 20fr multi .70 .30
137 A46 30fr multi 1.00 .60
138 A46 40fr multi 2.25 .70
139 A46 50fr multi 2.50 1.10
Nos. 135-139 (5) 6.80 2.95

Berberati Cathedral A47

1971, July 20 Litho. *Perf. 13½*

140 A47 5fr grn & multi .50 .25

New Roman Catholic Cathedral at Berberati.

Charles de Gaulle — A48

Gray Galago — A49

1971, Aug. 20 *Perf. 13½x13*

141 A48 100fr brt bl & multi 3.00 1.75

In memory of Gen. Charles de Gaulle (1890-1970), president of France.

1971, Oct. 25 Photo. *Perf. 13*

Designs: 40fr, Elegant galago. 100fr, Calabar potto, horiz. 150fr, Bosman's potto, horiz. 200fr, Oustalet's colobo, horiz.

142 A49 30fr pink & multi .80 .60
143 A49 40fr lt bl & multi 1.00 .70
144 A49 100fr multi 2.75 1.50
145 A49 150fr multi 4.50 2.40
146 A49 200fr multi 5.75 3.00
Nos. 142-146 (5) 14.80 8.20

Alan B. Shepard — A50

#148, Yuri Gagarin. #149, Edwin E. Aldrin, Jr. #150, Alexei Leonov. #151, Neil A. Armstrong on moon. #152, Lunokhod I on moon.

1971, Nov. 19 Litho. *Perf. 14*

147 A50 40fr vio & multi .50 .30
148 A50 40fr vio & multi .50 .30
149 A50 100fr multi 1.25 .45
150 A50 100fr multi 1.25 .45
151 A50 200fr red & multi 2.50 1.10
152 A50 200fr red & multi 2.50 1.10
Nos. 147-152 (6) 8.50 3.70

Space achievements of US and Russia.

"Operation Bokassa" and Pres. Bokassa A51

1971, Dec. 1 Photo. *Perf. 13*

153 A51 40fr red & multi .80 .45

12th anniversary of independence.

Racial Equality Emblem A52

1971, Dec. 6 Litho.

154 A52 50fr multi .80 .45

Intl. Year Against Racial Discrimination.

Bokassa School Emblem and Cadets — A53

Book Year Emblem — A54

1972, Jan. 1 Photo.

155 A53 30fr gold & multi .80 .45

J. B. Bokassa Military School.

1972, Mar. 11 Photo. *Perf. 12½x13*

156 A54 100fr red brn, gold & org 3.25 1.50

International Book Year 1972.

"Your Heart is your Health" A55

1972, Apr. 7 Photo. *Perf. 13x12½*

157 A55 100fr yel, blk & car 1.75 .95

World Health Day.

Red Cross Workers in Village — A56

1972, May 8 *Perf. 13*

158 A56 150fr multi 3.25 1.60

25th World Red Cross Day.

Globe A57

1972, May 17 **Litho.**
159 A57 50fr yel, blk & dp org .80 .55

4th World Telecommunications Day.

Pres. and Mrs. Bokassa and Family — A58

1972, May 28 ***Perf. 14***
160 A58 30fr yel & multi .60 .30

Mother's Day. Mothers' gold medal awarded to Catherine Bokassa.

Pres. Bokassa Planting Cotton, Map of Africa — A59

1972, June 5 **Photo.** ***Perf. 13***
161 A59 40fr yel & multi .60 .40

Operation Bokassa, a natl. development plan.

Postal Checking and Savings Center A60

1972, June 21
162 A60 30fr yel org & multi .60 .40

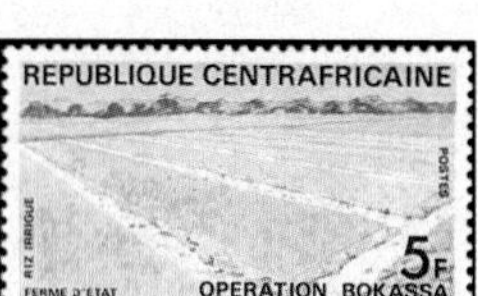

Irrigated Rice Fields — A61

"Le Pacifique" Apartment House A62

25fr, Plowing rice field. #166, Swimming pool, Hotel St. Sylvestre. #167, Entrance, Hotel St. Sylvestre. #168, J. B. Bokassa University.

1972 **Litho.** ***Perf. 13x13½***
163 A61 5fr multi 1.10 .25
164 A61 25fr multi 1.90 .30

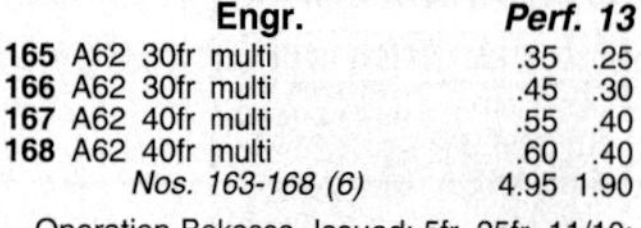

Engr. ***Perf. 13***
165 A62 30fr multi .35 .25
166 A62 30fr multi .45 .30
167 A62 40fr multi .55 .40
168 A62 40fr multi .60 .40
Nos. 163-168 (6) 4.95 1.90

Operation Bokassa. Issued: 5fr, 25fr, 11/10; #165, 6/27; #166-167, 12/9; #168, 8/26.

Bull Chasing Woman on Clock Face — A63

Scenes Painted on Clock Faces: 10fr, Men & open cooking fire. 20fr, Fishermen. 30fr, Palms, monkeys & giraffe. 40fr, Warriors.

1972, July 31 **Photo.** ***Perf. 12½***
169 A63 5fr dk red & multi .25 .25
170 A63 10fr brt bl & multi .25 .25
171 A63 20fr grn & multi .50 .30
172 A63 30fr yel & multi .70 .45
173 A63 40fr vio & multi 1.00 .60
Nos. 169-173 (5) 2.70 1.85

HORCEN Central African clock and watch factory.

Protestant Youth Center — A64

10fr, Postal runner carrying mail in cleft stick.

1972, Aug. 12 ***Perf. 13***
174 A64 10fr multi, vert. .25 .25
175 A64 20fr multi .45 .30
Nos. 174-175,C95-C98 (6) 7.60 5.05

Centraphilex 1972, Central African Philatelic Exhibition, Bangui.

Mail Truck A65

1972, Oct. 23 **Photo.** ***Perf. 13***
176 A65 100fr ocher & multi 1.75 .70

Universal Postal Union Day.

Mother Teaching Child to Write — A66

Central African Mothers: 10fr, Caring for infant. 15fr, Combing child's hair. 20fr, Teaching to read. 180fr, Nursing. 190fr, Teaching to walk.

1972, Dec. 27 ***Perf. 13½x13***
177 A66 5fr multi .20 .20
178 A66 10fr lil & multi .25 .20
179 A66 15fr dl org & multi .25 .20
180 A66 20fr yel grn & multi .45 .25
181 A66 180fr multi 2.50 1.25
182 A66 190fr pink & multi 2.50 1.25
Nos. 177-182 (6) 6.15 3.35

Farmer Carrying Sheaf — A67

1973, May 30 **Photo.** ***Perf. 13***
183 A67 50fr vio bl & multi .80 .45

10th anniv. of the World Food Program.

Garcinia Punctata A68

African Flora: 20fr, Bertiera racemosa. 30fr, Corynanthe pachyceras. 40fr, Combretodendron africanum. 50fr, Xylopia Villosa, vert.

1973, June 8
184 A68 10fr pale bl & multi .50 .25
185 A68 20fr multi .80 .30
186 A68 30fr lt gray & multi 1.00 .45
187 A68 40fr multi 1.60 .60
188 A68 50fr multi 2.00 .80
Nos. 184-188 (5) 5.90 2.40

For surcharge see No. 193.

Pygmy Chameleon A69

1973, June 26 **Photo.** ***Perf. 13***
189 A69 15fr multi 1.40 .40

Caterpillar — A70

Designs: Various caterpillars.

1973, Aug. 6 **Photo.** ***Perf. 13***
190 A70 3fr multi .80 .30
191 A70 5fr multi 1.25 .40
192 A70 25fr multi 2.75 .60
Nos. 190-192 (3) 4.80 1.30

For surcharge see No. 259.

No. 184 Surcharged with New Value, 2 Bars, and Overprinted in Red: "SECHERESSE SOLIDARITE AFRICAINE"

1973, Aug. 16
193 A68 100fr on 10fr multi 1.60 1.00

African solidarity in drought emergency.

African Postal Union Issue
Common Design Type

1973, Sept. 12 **Engr.** ***Perf. 13***
194 CD137 100fr dk brn, red org & ol 1.00 .55

Pres. Bokassa and CAR Flag — A71

1973, Nov. 30 **Photo.** ***Perf. 12½***
195 A71 1fr brn & multi .20 .20
196 A71 2fr pur & multi .20 .20
197 A71 3fr vio bl & multi .20 .20
198 A71 5fr ocher & multi .20 .20
199 A71 10fr multi .35 .20
200 A71 15fr org & multi .35 .25
201 A71 20fr multi .45 .25
202 A71 30fr dk grn & multi .45 .30
203 A71 40fr dk brn & multi .60 .40
Nos. 195-203,C117-C118 (11) 4.95 3.30

INTERPOL Emblem A72

1973, Dec. 20 ***Perf. 13x12½***
204 A72 50fr yellow & multi .80 .45

Intl. Criminal Police Organization, 50th anniv.

Catherine Bokassa Center A73

40fr, Ambulance in front of Catherine Bokassa Center.

1974, Jan. 24 **Engr.** ***Perf. 13***
205 A73 30fr multi .35 .25
206 A73 40fr multi .45 .30

Catherine Bokassa Center for Mothers and Children.

Cigarette-making Machine — A74

10fr, Cigarette in ashtray, & factory. 30fr, Hand lighting cigarette, & Administration Building.

1974, Jan. 29
207 A74 5fr slate grn & multi .20 .20
208 A74 10fr slate grn & multi .35 .25
209 A74 30fr slate grn & multi .45 .25
Nos. 207-209 (3) 1.00 .70

Publicity for Centra cigarettes.

"Communications" A75

1974, June 8 **Photo.** ***Perf. 12½x13***
210 A75 100fr multi 1.60 .85

World Telecommunications Day.
For surcharge see No. 280.

People and WPY Emblem A76

1974, June 20 **Engr.** ***Perf. 13***
211 A76 100fr red, slate grn & brn 1.00 .55

World Population Year.
For surcharge see No. 281.

Mother, Child, WHO Emblem — A77

1974, July 10

212	A77	100fr multi	1.60	.70

26th anniv. of WHO.
For surcharge see No. 282.

Hoeing — A78

Veterans' activities: 10fr, Battle scene ("yesterday"). 15fr, Pastoral scene ("today"). 20fr, Rice planting. 25fr, Storehouse. 40fr, Veterans Headquarters. Borders show tanks and tractors.

1974, Nov. 15 Litho. *Perf. 13*

213	A78	10fr multi	.20	.20
214	A78	15fr multi	.25	.20
215	A78	20fr multi	.25	.20
216	A78	25fr multi	.35	.25
217	A78	30fr multi	.35	.25
218	A78	40fr multi	.55	.25
		Nos. 213-218 (6)	1.95	1.35

For surcharges see Nos. 260, 265, 267.

Presidents and Flags of Cameroun, CAR, Congo, Gabon and Meeting Center — A79

1974, Dec. 8 Photo. *Perf. 13*

219	A79	40fr gold & multi	.60	.40

See #C126 and note after Cameroun #595.
For surcharge see No. 272.

House in OCAM City — A80

Scenes in housing development, OCAM City.

1975, Feb. 1 Photo. *Perf. 13*

220	A80	30fr multi	.35	.25
221	A80	40fr multi	.45	.30
222	A80	50fr multi	.55	.30
223	A80	100fr multi	.90	.55
		Nos. 220-223 (4)	2.25	1.40

For surcharges see Nos. 269, 273.

1975, Feb. 22

Cottage scenes in J. B. Bokassa "pilot village."

224	A80	25fr multi	.25	.20
225	A80	30fr multi	.35	.25
226	A80	40fr multi	.45	.30
		Nos. 224-226 (3)	1.05	.75

For surcharges see Nos. 268, 270, 274.

Foreign Ministry A81

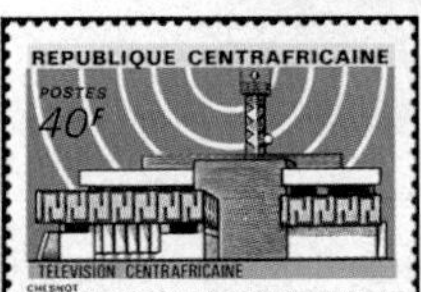

Television Station A82

1975, Feb. 28 *Perf. 13x12½*

227	A81	40fr multi	.60	.40

Perf. 13

228	A82	40fr multi	.60	.40

Public buildings, Bangui.
For surcharges see Nos. 275-276.

Bokassa's Saber — A83

Design: 40fr, Bokassa's baton.

1975, Feb. 22 Photo. *Perf. 13*

229	A83	30fr dp bl & multi	.50	.30
230	A83	40fr vio bl & multi	.50	.30

Jean Bedel Bokassa, President for Life and Marshal of the Republic. See Nos. C127-C128. For surcharge see No. 286.

Traffic Signs A84

1975, Mar. 20

231	A84	5fr Do Not Enter	.20	.20
232	A84	10fr Stop	.20	.20
233	A84	20fr No parking	.25	.20
234	A84	30fr School	.45	.25
235	A84	40fr Intersection	.70	.30
		Nos. 231-235 (5)	1.80	1.15

For surcharges see Nos. 261, 277.

Buffon's Kob — A85

1975, June 24 Photo. *Perf. 13*

236	A85	10fr shown	.35	.30
237	A85	15fr Wart hog	.80	.30
238	A85	20fr Waterbuck	1.10	.30
239	A85	30fr Lion	1.10	.45
		Nos. 236-239 (4)	3.35	1.35

For surcharges see Nos. 262-263, 266, 271.

Crane Lifting Log onto Truck A86

Designs: 10fr, Forest, vert. 15fr, Tree felling, vert. 100fr, Log pile. 150fr, Logs transported by raft. 200fr, Lumberyard.

1975, Nov. 28 Engr. *Perf. 13*

240	A86	10fr multi	.20	.20
241	A86	15fr multi	.25	.20
242	A86	50fr multi	.50	.20
243	A86	100fr multi	1.25	.55
244	A86	150fr multi	1.50	1.00
245	A86	200fr multi	1.90	1.10
		Nos. 240-245 (6)	5.60	3.25

Promotion of Central African wood.
For surcharges see Nos. 264, 279.

Women's Heads and Various Occupations — A87

1975, Dec. 10 Photo.

246	A87	40fr multi	.45	.25
247	A87	100fr multi	1.25	.55

International Women's Year 1975.

Alexander Graham Bell — A88

1976, Mar. 25 Litho. *Perf. 12½x13*

248	A88	100fr yel & blk	2.00	1.00

Centenary of first telephone call by Alexander Graham Bell, Mar. 10, 1876.
For surcharge see No. 283.

Satellite and ITU Emblem — A89

#250, UPU emblem, various forms of mail transport.

1976 Engr. *Perf. 13*

249	A89	100fr vio bl, claret & grn	1.75	1.00
250	A89	100fr car, grn & ocher	1.50	.80

World Telecommunications Day (No. 249); Universal Postal Union Day (No. 250).
For surcharges see Nos. 284-285.

Soyuz on Launching Pad — A90

Design: 50fr, Apollo rocket.

1976, June 14 Litho. *Perf. 14x13½*

251	A90	40fr multi	.60	.25
252	A90	50fr multi	.90	.25
		Nos. 251-252,C135-C137 (5)	7.40	2.25

Apollo Soyuz space test project, Russo-American cooperation, launched July 15, link-up July 17, 1975.
For surcharges see Nos. 287, 290, C161, C168, C173, C177.

Drurya Antimachus — A91

Butterfly: 40fr, Argema mittrei, vert.

1976, Sept. 20 Litho. *Perf. 12½*

253	A91	30fr ocher & multi	6.25	1.10
254	A91	40fr ultra & multi	9.00	1.10
		Nos. 253-254,C145-C146 (4)	34.00	5.05

For surcharge see #278.

Slalom, Piero Gros — A92

60fr, Karl Schnabel and Toni Innauer.

1976, Sept. 23 *Perf. 13½*

255	A92	40fr multi	.60	.25
256	A92	60fr multi	.90	.30
		Nos. 255-256,C147-C149 (5)	6.85	2.45

12th Winter Olympic Games winners, Innsbruck.
For surcharges see Nos. 288, 291, C164, C170, C174, C178.

Viking Components A93

Design: 60fr, Viking take-off.

1976, Dec.

257	A93	40fr multi	.60	.25
258	A93	60fr multi	.90	.30
		Nos. 257-258,C151-C153 (5)	7.15	2.40

Viking Mars project.
For surcharges and overprints see Nos. 289, 292, 391-392, C165, C171, C175, C179.

Central African Empire

Stamps of 1973-76 Overprinted with Bars and "EMPIRE CENTRAFRICAIN" in Black, Green, Violet Blue, Silver, Carmine, Brown or Red

Printing and Perforations as Before

1977, Mar.

259	A70	3fr	(#190; B)	.25	.25
260	A78	10fr	(#213;B)	.25	.25
261	A84	10fr	(#232;VB)	.25	.25
262	A85	10fr	(#236;C)	.25	.25
263	A85	15fr	(#237;C)	.45	.45
264	A86	15fr	(#241;B)	.25	.25
265	A78	20fr	(#215;B)	.35	.35
266	A85	20fr	(#238;C)	.45	.45
267	A78	25fr	(#216;B)	.35	.35
268	A80	25fr	(#224;B)	.35	.35
269	A80	30fr	(#220;VB)	.45	.45
270	A80	30fr	(#225;B)	.45	.45
271	A85	30fr	(#239;C)	.55	.55
272	A79	40fr	(#219;B)	.65	.65
273	A80	40fr	(#221;VB)	.70	.70
274	A80	40fr	(#226;B)	.65	.65
275	A81	40fr	(#227;B & S)	.65	.65
276	A82	40fr	(#228;B)	.70	.70
277	A84	40fr	(#235;VB)	.70	.70
278	A91	40fr	(#254;B)	.70	.70
279	A86	50fr	(#242;Br)	.90	.90
280	A75	100fr	(#210;B)	1.75	1.75
281	A76	100fr	(#211;B)	1.75	1.75
282	A77	100fr	(#212;G)	1.75	1.75
283	A88	100fr	(#248;R)	1.75	1.75
284	A89	100fr	(#249;B)	2.00	2.00
285	A89	100fr	(#250;B)	2.25	2.25
			Nos. 259-285 (27)	21.55	21.55

Stamps of 1975-76 Overprinted "EMPIRE CENTRAFRICAIN" in Black on Silver Panel

1977, Apr. 1

286	A83	40fr multi (#230)	.80	.80
287	A90	40fr multi (#251)	.65	.65
288	A92	40fr multi (#255)	.65	.65
289	A93	40fr multi (#257)	.65	.65
290	A90	50fr multi (#252)	.90	.90
291	A92	60fr multi (#256)	.80	.80
292	A93	60fr multi (#258)	.80	.80
		Nos. 286-292 (7)	5.25	5.25

Pierre and Marie Curie — A94

Design: 60fr, Wilhelm C. Roentgen.

1977, Apr. 1 Litho. *Perf. 13½*

293	A94	40fr multi	.70	.30
294	A94	60fr multi	.70	.40
		Nos. 293-294,C180-C182 (5)	6.85	3.45

Nobel Prize winners.

Italy No. C42 and Faustine Temple, Rome — A95

60fr, Russia #C12 & St. Basil's Cathedral, Moscow.

1977, Apr. 11 Litho. *Perf. 11*

295	A95	40fr multi	.90	.25
296	A95	60fr multi	1.00	.40
		Nos. 295-296,C184-C186 (5)	8.90	2.55

75th anniversary of the Zeppelin.

Lindbergh over Paris — A96

Designs: 60fr, Santos Dumont and "14 bis." 100fr, Bleriot and monoplane. 200fr, Roald Amundsen and "N24." 300fr, Concorde. 500fr, Lindbergh and Spirit of St. Louis.

1977, Sept. 30 Litho. *Perf. 13½*

297	A96	50fr multi	.60	.20
298	A96	60fr multi	.90	.25
299	A96	100fr multi	1.50	.40
300	A96	200fr multi	2.25	.55
301	A96	300fr multi	4.50	1.25
		Nos. 297-301 (5)	9.75	2.65

Souvenir Sheet

302	A96	500fr multi	5.00	2.00

History of aviation, famous fliers.

Shot on Goal A97

Designs: 60fr, Heading ball in net. 100fr, Backfield defense. 200fr, Argentina '78 poster. 300fr, Mario Zagalo and stadium. 500fr, Ferenc Puskas.

1977, Nov. 18 Litho. *Perf. 13½*

303	A97	50fr multi	.50	.20
304	A97	60fr multi	.60	.25
305	A97	100fr multi	1.00	.30
306	A97	200fr multi	1.75	.55
307	A97	300fr multi	3.00	.90
		Nos. 303-307 (5)	6.85	2.20

Souvenir Sheet

308	A97	500fr multi	4.25	1.75

World Soccer Championships, Argentina, June 1-25, 1978.
For overprints see Nos. 370-375.

Emperor Bokassa I, Central African Flag — A98

1977, Dec. 4 Litho. *Perf. 13½*

309	A98	40fr multi	.35	.20
310	A98	60fr multi	.50	.25
311	A98	100fr multi	.90	.45
312	A98	150fr multi	1.25	.60
		Nos. 309-312,C188-C189 (6)	7.25	3.55

Coronation of Emperor Bokassa I, Dec. 4.

Lilium — A99

Electronic Tree, ITU Emblem — A100

1977 Litho. *Perf. 13½x14*

313	A99	5fr shown	.50	.30
314	A99	10fr Hibiscus	1.00	.55

For overprints see Nos. 408-409.

1977

315	A100	100fr blk, org & brn	2.50	1.60

World Telecommunications Day.

Bible and People A101

1977 Litho. *Perf. 14x13½*

316	A101	40fr multi	6.75	1.50

Bible Week.

People and Rotary Emblem A102

1977

317	A102	60fr multi	3.75	2.00

Rotary Club of Bangui, 20th anniversary.

Holy Family, by Rubens A103

Rubens Paintings: 150fr, Marie de Medicis. 200fr, Son of artist. 300fr, Neptune. 500fr, Marie de Medicis, diff.

1978, Jan. 26

318	A103	60fr multi	.60	.20
319	A103	150fr multi	1.25	.40
320	A103	200fr multi	2.00	.60
321	A103	300fr multi	3.00	.80
		Nos. 318-321 (4)	6.85	2.00

Souvenir Sheet

322	A103	500fr gold & multi	5.00	2.00

Peter Paul Rubens (1577-1640).

Rhinoceros — A104

Endangered Animals and Wildlife Fund Emblem: 50fr, Slender-nosed crocodile. 60fr, Leopard, vert. 100fr, Giraffe, vert. 200fr, Elephant. 300fr, Gorilla, vert.

1978, Feb. 21 Litho. *Perf. 13½*

323	A104	40fr multi	*.90*	.25
324	A104	50fr multi	*1.50*	.30
325	A104	60fr multi	*1.60*	.40
326	A104	100fr multi	*2.50*	.60
327	A104	200fr multi	*7.25*	.95
328	A104	300fr multi	*8.75*	1.60
		Nos. 323-328 (6)	*22.50*	4.10

Bokassa Sports Palace A105

Design: 60fr, Sports Palace, side view.

1978 *Perf. 14*

329	A105	40fr multi	.45	.25
330	A105	60fr multi	.60	.40

Automatic Telephone Exchange, Bangui A106

1978

331	A106	40fr multi	.45	.25
332	A106	60fr multi	.60	.40

Diligence and Satellite — A107

Designs (UPU Emblem and): 50fr, Steam locomotive and communications via satellite. 60fr, Paddle-wheel steamer and ship-to-shore communication via satellite. 80fr, Old mail truck and satellite.

1978, May 17 *Perf. 13½*

333	A107	40fr multi	.20	.20
334	A107	50fr multi	2.75	1.25
335	A107	60fr multi	.25	.20
336	A107	80fr multi	.35	.20
		Nos. 333-336,C191-C192 (6)	5.55	2.40

Posts and telecommunications, cent. of progress.

Mask — A108

Capt. Cook on "Endeavour" A109

Designs: 30fr, Mask. 60fr, Women dancers, horiz. 100fr, Men dancers, horiz.

Perf. 13½x14, 14x13½

1978, July 11 Litho.

337	A108	20fr blk & yel	.70	.30
338	A108	30fr blk & brt bl	.70	.30
339	A108	60fr blk & multi	1.75	.60
340	A108	100fr blk & multi	3.00	.95
		Nos. 337-340 (4)	6.15	2.15

Black-African World Arts Festival, Lagos.
For overprints see Nos. 411-412.

1978, Aug. 30 *Perf. 14½*

60fr, Resolution off Hawaii. 200fr, Hawaiians welcoming Capt. Cook. 350fr, Masked rowers in Hawaiian boat.

341	A109	60fr multi, horiz.	.70	.20
342	A109	80fr multi	1.00	.25
343	A109	200fr multi, horiz.	2.25	.70
344	A109	350fr multi, horiz.	3.75	1.25
		Nos. 341-344 (4)	7.70	2.40

Capt. James Cook (1728-1779), explorer.

Dürer, Self-portrait A110

Dürer Paintings: 80fr, The Four Apostles. 200fr, Virgin and Child. 350fr, Emperor Maximilian I.

1978, Oct. 24 Litho. *Perf. 13½*

345	A110	60fr multi	.60	.25
346	A110	80fr multi	.90	.25
347	A110	200fr multi	2.25	.85
348	A110	350fr multi	4.00	1.40
		Nos. 345-348 (4)	7.75	2.75

Albrecht Dürer (1471-1528), German painter.

Tutankhamen's Gold Mask — A111

Treasures of Tutankhamen: 60fr, King and Queen, gold back panel of throne. 80fr, Gilt folding chair. 100fr, King wearing crowns of Upper and Lower Egypt, painted wood sculpture. 120fr, Lion's head. 150fr, Tutankhamen, wood stature. 180fr, Gold throne. 250fr, Gold miniature coffin.

1978, Nov. 22

349 A111 40fr multi .60 .30
350 A111 60fr multi .80 .40
351 A111 80fr multi 1.10 .55
352 A111 100fr multi 1.25 .55
353 A111 120fr multi 1.75 .60
354 A111 150fr multi 2.25 .70
355 A111 180fr multi 2.75 .85
356 A111 250fr multi 3.50 1.10
Nos. 349-356 (8) 14.00 5.05

Tutankhamen, c. 1358 B.C., King of Egypt.

Lenin at Smolny Institute — A112

Soviet Union, 60th anniv.: 60fr, 200fr, 300fr, Various Lenin portraits. 100fr, Ulyanov family, horiz. 150fr, Lenin, Cruiser "Aurora" and flag, horiz. 500fr, "Aurora" and star.

1978, Nov. ***Perf. 14***

357 A112 40fr multi .50 .30
358 A112 60fr multi .60 .40
359 A112 100fr blk & gold 1.00 .45
360 A112 150fr blk, gold & red 1.75 .70
361 A112 200fr multi 2.50 1.00
362 A112 300fr multi 3.25 1.40
Nos. 357-362 (6) 9.60 4.25

Souvenir Sheet

363 A112 500fr multi 5.00 4.00

Catherine Bokassa A113

Design: 60fr, Emperor Bokassa.

1978, Dec. 4 **Litho.** ***Perf. 13***

364 A113 40fr multi .60 .25
365 A113 60fr multi .80 .30

1st anniv. of coronation. See No. C202.

Rowland Hill, Letter Scale and G.B. No. 1 — A114

Rowland Hill and: 50fr, US #1, mailman on bicycle. 60fr, Austria #P4, 19th cent. mailman. 80fr, Switzerland #2L1, postilion and mailcoach.

1978, Dec. 9 **Litho.** ***Perf. 13½***

366 A114 40fr multi .35 .20
367 A114 50fr multi .45 .25
368 A114 60fr multi .45 .30
369 A114 80fr multi .60 .25
Nos. 366-369,C203-C204 (6) 6.60 3.05

Sir Rowland Hill (1795-1879), originator of penny postage.

Nos. 303-307 Overprinted in Silver: "VAINQUEUR: ARGENTINE"

1978, Dec. 27

370 A97 50fr multi .50 .25
371 A97 60fr multi .60 .30
372 A97 100fr multi .90 .55
373 A97 200fr multi 2.00 1.00
374 A97 300fr multi 3.00 1.40
Nos. 370-374 (5) 7.00 3.50

Souvenir Sheet

No. 308 Overprinted in Silver: "ARGENTINE-PAYS BAS 3-1 / 25 juin 1978"

375 A97 500fr multi 4.50 4.50

Argentina's victory in World Cup Soccer Championship 1978.

Children Painting and Dutch Portrait — A115

UNICEF, Eagle Emblems and: 50fr, Eskimo children skiing, ski jump. 60fr, Children with toy racing car, Carl Benz with early car model. 80fr, Children launching rocket, Intelsat.

1979, Mar. 6 **Litho.** ***Perf. 13½***

376 A115 40fr multi .60 .20
377 A115 50fr multi .70 .20
378 A115 60fr multi .80 .20
379 A115 80fr multi 1.10 .30
Nos. 376-379,C206-C207 (6) 6.95 1.95

International Year of the Child.

High Jump, Moscow '80 Emblem and "M" — A116

Designs (Moscow '80 Emblem, Various Sports and): 50fr, Bicycling and "O." 60fr, Weight lifting and "C." 80fr, Judo and "K."

1979, Mar. 16 **Litho.** ***Perf. 13***

380 A116 40fr multi .50 .20
381 A116 50fr multi .60 .20
382 A116 60fr multi .70 .20
383 A116 80fr multi 1.00 .30
Nos. 380-383,C209-C210 (6) 5.80 1.90

22nd Olympic Games, Moscow, July 19-Aug. 3, 1980. Background letters on Nos. 380-383, C209-C210 spell "Mockba." A 1500fr gold embossed stamp showing emblems and Discobolus exists.

Memorial, Bangui, Butterfly, Hibiscus — A117

Design: 150fr, Canoe, truck and letters.

1979, June 8 **Litho.** ***Perf. 12x12½***

384 A117 60fr multi 1.50 .80
385 A117 150fr multi 3.50 2.00

Philexafrique II, Libreville, Gabon, June 8-17. Nos. 384, 385 each printed in sheets of 10 with 5 labels showing exhibition emblem.

Schoolgirl A118

1979, July 25 **Litho.** ***Perf. 12½x12***

386 A118 70fr multi .85 .40

Intl. Bureau of Education, Geneva, 50th anniv.

Chicken A119

1979, Aug. ***Perf. 13***

387 A119 10fr shown 1.75 1.10
388 A119 20fr Bull 1.75 1.10
389 A119 40fr Sheep 3.75 2.10
Nos. 387-389,C211 (4) 12.50 6.30

National Husbandry Assoc.

Souvenir Sheet

Virgin and Child, by Dürer — A120

1979, Aug. ***Perf. 13½***

390 A120 500fr lt grn & dl red 4.75 1.60

Albrecht Dürer (1471-1528), German engraver and printer.

Central African Republic

Nos. 257-258 Overprinted "ALUNISSAGE/APOLLO XI/ JUILLET/1969" and Emblem

1979, Nov. 11 **Litho.** ***Perf. 13½***

391 A93 40fr multi .60 .30
392 A93 60fr multi .70 .40
Nos. 391-392,C212-C214 (5) 6.45 3.35

Apollo 11 moon landing, 10th anniversary.

Girl and Rose A121

1979, Dec. 15

393 A121 30fr Butterfly and girl, vert. .25 .20
394 A121 40fr shown .45 .20
395 A121 60fr Hansel and Gretel, vert. .50 .25
396 A121 200fr Cinderella 2.00 .70
397 A121 250fr Mermaid, vert. 2.50 .80
Nos. 393-397 (5) 5.70 2.15

International Year of the Child.

Locomotive, U.S. Type A27, Hill — A122

Locomotives, Hill and Stamps: 100fr, France #1. 150fr, Germany type A11. 250fr, Great Britain #32. 500fr, CAR #2.

1979, Dec. 20

398 A122 60fr multi .50 .20
399 A122 100fr multi 1.00 .30
400 A122 150fr multi 1.50 .45
401 A122 250fr multi 2.75 .95
Nos. 398-401 (4) 5.75 1.90

Souvenir Sheet

402 A122 500fr multi 5.25 2.00

Sir Rowland Hill (1795-1879), originator of penny postage.

Basketball, Moscow '80 Emblem — A123

Pre-Olympic Year: Men's or women's basketball.

1979, Dec. 28 **Litho.** ***Perf. 14½***

403 A123 50fr multi .45 .20
404 A123 125fr multi 1.00 .35
405 A123 200fr multi 1.75 .55
406 A123 300fr multi 3.00 .80
407 A123 500fr multi 4.50 1.40
Nos. 403-407 (5) 10.70 3.30

For overprints see Nos. 425-429.

Nos. 313-314, 337-338 Overprinted "REPUBLIQUE CENTRAFRICAINE" in Black on Silver Panel and

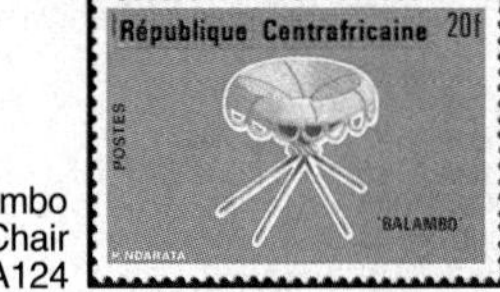

Balambo Chair A124

Perf. 13½x14, 14x13½

1980, Mar. 20 **Litho.**

No.	Type	Description	Unused	Used
408	A99	5fr multi	.20	.20
409	A99	10fr multi	.20	.20
410	A124	20fr multi	.25	.20
411	A108	20fr multi	.25	.20
412	A108	30fr multi	.45	.25
		Nos. 408-412 (5)	1.35	1.05

Viking Satellite — A125

1980, Apr. 8 ***Perf. 13½***

No.	Type	Description	Unused	Used
413	A125	40fr shown	.50	.20
414	A125	50fr Apollo-Soyuz	.60	.20
415	A125	60fr Voyager	.70	.20
416	A125	100fr European Space Agency emblem, flags	1.10	.30
		Nos. 413-416,C221-C222 (6)	6.15	1.85

Walking, Olympic Medal, Moscow '80 Emblem — A126

1980, July 25 **Litho.** ***Perf. 13½***

No.	Type	Description	Unused	Used
417	A126	30fr shown	.45	.20
418	A126	40fr Relay race	.50	.20
419	A126	70fr Running	.70	.20
420	A126	80fr High jump	.80	.25
		Nos. 417-420,C231-C232 (6)	4.85	1.50

For overprints see #462-465, C248-C250.

Fruit — A126a

1980, Aug. 1 **Litho.** ***Perf. 13½***

No.	Type	Description	Unused	Used
420A	A126a	40fr multicolored		
420B	A126a	70fr green & multi	—	—

Agricultural Development A127

1980, Nov. 4 **Litho.** ***Perf. 13½***

No.	Type	Description	Unused	Used
421	A127	30fr shown	.25	.20
422	A127	40fr Telecommunications	.45	.20
423	A127	70fr Engineering	.80	.25
424	A127	100fr Civil engineering	1.00	.40
		Nos. 421-424,C234-C235 (6)	5.65	2.15

Europe-Africa cooperation.

Nos. 403-407 Overprinted with Medal and Country

1980, Nov. 12 ***Perf. 14½***

No.	Type	Description	Unused	Used
425	A123	50fr multi	.50	.20
426	A123	125fr multi	1.00	.40
427	A123	200fr multi	1.75	.55
428	A123	300fr multi	2.75	.90
429	A123	500fr multi	4.50	1.60
		Nos. 425-429 (5)	10.50	3.65

Virgin and Child, by Raphael — A128

African Postal Union, 5th Anniversary A129

Christmas: Virgin & Child paintings by Raphael.

1980, Dec. 20 ***Perf. 12½***

No.	Type	Description	Unused	Used
430	A128	60fr multi	.60	.25
431	A128	150fr multi	1.50	.60
432	A128	250fr multi	2.75	1.10
		Nos. 430-432 (3)	4.85	1.95

1980, Dec. 24 **Photo.** ***Perf. 13½***

No.	Type	Description	Unused	Used
433	A129	70fr multi	.70	.40

Peruvian Soccer Team, Soccer Cup — A130

1981, Jan. 13 **Litho.** ***Perf. 13½***

No.	Type	Description	Unused	Used
434	A130	10fr shown	.20	.20
435	A130	15fr Scotland	.20	.20
436	A130	20fr Mexico	.25	.20
437	A130	25fr Sweden	.25	.20
438	A130	30fr Austria	.35	.20
439	A130	40fr Poland	.45	.20
440	A130	50fr France	.50	.20
441	A130	60fr Italy	.60	.20
442	A130	70fr Germany	.70	.25
443	A130	80fr Brazil	.80	.25
		Nos. 434-443,C237-C238 (12)	6.60	2.90

ESPANA '82 World Cup Soccer Championship.

13th World Telecommunications Day — A131

1981, May 17 **Litho.** ***Perf. 12½***

No.	Type	Description	Unused	Used
444	A131	150fr multi	1.25	.70

Apollo 15 Crew on Moon — A132

Space Exploration: Columbia space shuttle.

1981, June 10 **Litho.** ***Perf. 14***

No.	Type	Description	Unused	Used
445	A132	100fr multi	.90	.30
446	A132	150fr multi	1.25	.40
447	A132	200fr multi	1.75	.60
448	A132	300fr multi	3.00	1.00
		Nos. 445-448 (4)	6.90	2.30

Souvenir Sheet

No.	Type	Description	Unused	Used
449	A132	500fr multi	4.25	1.60

Family of Acrobats with Monkey, by Picasso A133

Picasso Birth Cent.: 50fr, The Balcony. 80fr, The Artist's Son as Pierrot. 100fr, The Three Dancers.

1981, June 30 ***Perf. 13½***

No.	Type	Description	Unused	Used
450	A133	40fr multi	.45	.20
451	A133	50fr multi	.60	.25
452	A133	80fr multi	1.00	.25
453	A133	100fr multi	1.25	.40
		Nos. 450-453,C245-C246 (6)	7.65	2.15

First Anniv. of Zimbabwe's Independence — A134

1981, July 9 **Litho.** ***Perf. 12½***

No.	Type	Description	Unused	Used
454	A134	100fr multi	1.00	.45
455	A134	150fr multi	1.40	.55
456	A134	200fr multi	2.10	.70
		Nos. 454-456 (3)	4.50	1.70

Prince Charles and Lady Diana — A135

1981, July 24 ***Perf. 14***

No.	Type	Description	Unused	Used
457	A135	75fr Charles	.50	.25
458	A135	100fr Diana	.75	.30
459	A135	150fr St. Paul's Cathedral	1.25	.45
460	A135	175fr shown	1.60	.50
		Nos. 457-460 (4)	4.10	1.50

Souvenir Sheet

No.	Type	Description	Unused	Used
461	A135	500fr Couple	4.00	1.40

Royal Wedding.
For overprints see Nos. 529-533.

Nos. 417-420 Overprinted with Event, Winner and Country in Gold

1981 **Litho.** ***Perf. 13½***

No.	Type	Description	Unused	Used
462	A126	30fr multi	.25	.20
463	A126	40fr multi	.35	.20
464	A126	70fr multi	.60	.30
465	A126	80fr multi	.70	.40
		Nos. 462-465,C248-C249 (6)	4.05	1.75

Prince Charles and Lady Diana — A136

1981, Aug. 20 **Litho.** ***Perf. 13½***

No.	Type	Description	Unused	Used
466	A136	40fr shown	.45	.20
467	A136	50fr Crowned Prince of Wales	.45	.25
468	A136	80fr Diana	.80	.30
469	A136	100fr Naval training	1.00	.40
		Nos. 466-469,C251-C252 (6)	6.20	2.10

Royal wedding.

1906 Renault — A137

1981, Sept. 22 **Litho.** ***Perf. 12½***

No.	Type	Description	Unused	Used
470	A137	20fr shown	.25	.20
471	A137	40fr Mercedes-Benz, 1937	.60	.20
472	A137	50fr Matra-Ford, 1969	.70	.20
473	A137	110fr Tazio Nuvolari, 1927	1.40	.40
474	A137	150fr Jackie Stewart, 1965	2.00	.55
		Nos. 470-474 (5)	4.95	1.55

Souvenir Sheet

Perf. 10

No.	Type	Description	Unused	Used
475	A137	450fr Finish line, 1914	5.00	5.00

Grand Prix of France, 75th anniv.

World Food Day A138

1981, Oct. 16

No.	Type	Description	Unused	Used
476	A138	90fr multi	.90	.30
477	A138	110fr multi	1.00	.40

Navigators and their Ships — A139

1981, Sept. 4 **Litho.** ***Perf. 13½***

No.	Type	Description	Unused	Used
478	A139	40fr C.V. Rietschoten	.45	.30
479	A139	50fr M. Pajot	.50	.45
480	A139	60fr K. Jaworski	.70	.55
481	A139	80fr M. Birch	.90	.60
		Nos. 478-481,C254-C255 (6)	5.80	4.00

Downfall of Empire A140

1981, Oct. 6

482	A140	5fr Bayonet through crown	.20	.20
483	A140	10fr like #482	.20	.20
484	A140	25fr Victory holding map	.25	.20
485	A140	60fr like #484	.70	.25
486	A140	90fr Toppled Bokassa statue	1.00	.40
487	A140	500fr like #486	4.25	2.00
		Nos. 482-487 (6)	6.60	3.25

Komba — A141

1981, Nov. 17

488	A141	50fr shown	.65	.20
489	A141	90fr Dodoro, horiz.	1.25	.25
490	A141	140fr Kaya, horiz.	2.10	.40
		Nos. 488-490 (3)	4.00	.85

Central African States Bank A142

1981, Dec. 12 Litho. *Perf. 12½x13*

491	A142	90fr multi	.90	.30
492	A142	110fr multi	1.00	.40

Christmas 1981 — A143

Virgin and Child Paintings.

1981, Dec. 24

493	A143	50fr Fra Angelico, 1430	.90	.30
494	A143	60fr Cosimo Tura, 1484	1.00	.40
495	A143	90fr Bramantino	1.60	.45
496	A143	110fr Memling	2.00	.70
		Nos. 493-496,C260-C261 (6)	11.75	3.00

Scouting Year — A144

1982, Jan. 13 *Perf. 12½*

497	A144	100fr Hiking	1.10	.40
498	A144	150fr Scouts, horiz.	1.75	.55
499	A144	200fr Hiking	2.50	.80
500	A144	300fr Salute, flag, vert.	3.50	1.25
		Nos. 497-500 (4)	8.85	3.00

Souvenir Sheet

Perf. 13

501	A144	500fr Scout, Baden-Powell, vert.	5.75	1.60

Elephant A145

1982, Jan. 22 *Perf. 13½*

502	A145	60fr shown	.80	.20
503	A145	90fr Giraffes	1.00	.30
504	A145	100fr Addaxes	1.10	.30
505	A145	110fr Okapi	1.40	.45
		Nos. 502-505,C263-C264 (6)	12.30	3.30

Norman Rockwell Illustrations A146

1982, Feb. 17 *Perf. 13½x14*

506	A146	30fr Grandfather snowman	.25	.20
507	A146	60fr Croquet players	.50	.25
508	A146	110fr Women talking	1.10	.40
509	A146	150fr Searching	1.60	.55
		Nos. 506-509 (4)	3.45	1.40

AT 16 Dirigible A147

1982, Feb. 27 Litho. *Perf. 13½*

510	A147	5fr shown	.20	.20
511	A147	10fr Beyer-Garrat locomotive	.20	.20
512	A147	20fr Bugatti 24 "Royale," 1924	.25	.20
513	A147	110fr Vickers "Valentia," 1928	1.25	.40
		Nos. 510-513,C266-C267 (6)	10.15	3.05

Bellvue Garden, by Edouard Manet — A148

Anniversaries: 400fr, Goethe, vert. #519-520, Princess Diana, 21st birthday, July 1, vert. 300fr, George Washington, vert.

1982, Apr. 6 Litho. *Perf. 13*

517	A148	200fr multi	2.75	.60
517A	A148	300fr multi	2.75	.95
518	A148	400fr multi	3.75	1.25
519	A148	500fr multi	4.50	2.00
		Nos. 517-519 (4)	13.75	4.80

Souvenir Sheet

520	A148	500fr multi	5.00	1.40

23rd Olympic Games, Los Angeles, 1984 — A149

1982, July 24 Litho. *Perf. 13½*

521	A149	5fr Soccer	.20	.20
522	A149	10fr Boxing	.20	.20
523	A149	20fr Running	.25	.20
524	A149	110fr Long jump	.90	.30
		Nos. 521-524,C269-C270 (6)	8.80	3.10

21st Birthday of Princess Diana — A150

Portraits.

1982, July 20 Litho. *Perf. 13½*

525	A150	5fr multi	.20	.20
526	A150	10fr multi	.20	.20
527	A150	20fr multi	.25	.20
528	A150	110fr multi	1.25	.30
		Nos. 525-528,C272-C273 (6)	9.90	3.10

Nos. 457-461 Overprinted in Blue: "NAISSANCE ROYALE 1982"

1982, Aug. 20 *Perf. 14*

529	A135	75fr multi	.50	.25
530	A135	110fr multi	.70	.40
531	A135	150fr multi	1.25	.55
532	A135	175fr multi	2.00	.80
		Nos. 529-532 (4)	4.45	2.00

Souvenir Sheet

533	A135	500fr multi	3.75	3.00

Birth of Prince William of Wales, June 21.

2nd UN Conference on Peaceful Uses of Outer Space, Vienna, Aug. 9-21 — A151

Various satellites and space scenes.

1982, Aug. 15 Litho. *Perf. 13½*

534	A151	5fr multi	.20	.20
535	A151	10fr multi	.20	.20
536	A151	20fr multi	.25	.20
537	A151	110fr multi	.90	.30
		Nos. 534-537,C277-C278 (6)	8.80	3.10

Sakpa Basket A152

Baskets and bowls.

1982, Sept. 2 *Perf. 13*

538	A152	5fr shown	.20	.20
539	A152	10fr like 5fr	.20	.20
540	A152	25fr Ngbenda gourd, vert.	.25	.20
541	A152	60fr like 25fr	.70	.20
542	A152	120fr Ta ti ngou jugs	1.50	.40
543	A152	175fr Kangu bowls	2.00	.60
544	A152	300fr Kolongo bowls, vert.	4.00	1.25
		Nos. 538-544 (7)	8.85	3.05

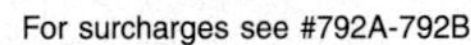

For surcharges see #792A-792B.

1982 World Cup Soccer Championships, Spain — A152a

Various soccer plays.

1982, Sept. Litho. *Perf. 13½x13*

Overprinted in Silver or Gold

545	A152a	60fr Italy, 1st, 2nd	.80	.25
546	A152a	150fr Poland, 3rd	1.60	.55
547	A152a	300fr France, 4th	3.50	1.25
		Nos. 545-547 (3)	5.90	2.05

Souvenir Sheet

548	A152a	500fr Italy, 1st (G)	4.75	1.40

Not issued without overprint.

13th World UPU Day — A153

1982, Oct. 9

549	A153	60fr multi	.50	.25
550	A153	120fr multi	1.10	.45

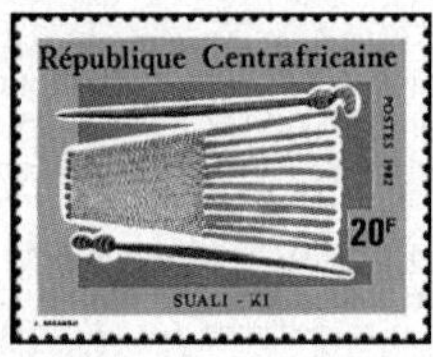

Comb and Hairpins A154

1982, Oct. 20 *Perf. 13x12½*

551	A154	20fr multi	.20	.20
552	A154	30fr multi	.35	.25
553	A154	60fr multi	.70	.30
554	A154	80fr multi	1.00	.40
555	A154	120fr multi	1.40	.45
		Nos. 551-555 (5)	3.65	1.60

Artist Pierre Ndarata and No.69 A155

1982, Oct. *Perf. 13*

556	A155	40fr Jean Tubind at easel, vert.	.20	.20
557	A155	70fr shown	.40	.20
558	A155	90fr like 70fr	.50	.25
559	A155	140fr like 40fr	.90	.35
		Nos. 556-559 (4)	2.00	1.00

TB Bacillus Centenary A156

1982, Nov. 30 *Perf. 13½x13*

560	A156	100fr vio & blk	1.00	.30
561	A156	120fr red org & blk	1.25	.45
562	A156	175fr bl & blk	2.00	.80
		Nos. 560-562 (3)	4.25	1.55

10th Anniv. of UN Conference on Human Environment
A157

1982, Dec. 8

563 A157 120fr multi 1.00 .40
564 A157 150fr multi 1.25 .55
565 A157 300fr multi 2.75 1.00
Nos. 563-565 (3) 5.00 1.95

Granary
A158

1982, Dec. 15 ***Perf. 13***

566 A158 60fr multi .50 .25
567 A158 80fr multi .80 .40
568 A158 120fr multi 1.00 .55
569 A158 200fr multi 2.10 .90
Nos. 566-569 (4) 4.40 2.10

A159 A160

1982, Dec.

570 A159 100fr multi .90 .40
571 A159 120fr multi 1.25 .45

ITU Plenipotentiaries Conf., Nairobi, Sept.

1983, Jan. 31 **Litho.** ***Perf. 13½x13***

572 A160 5fr Modes of communication .20 .20
573 A160 60fr like 5fr .50 .20
574 A160 120fr Map, jet 1.25 .40
575 A160 175fr like 120fr 1.60 .55
Nos. 572-575 (4) 3.55 1.35

UN Decade for African Transportation and Communication, 1978-88.

Chess Champions — A161

Men and Chess Pieces: 5fr, Steinitz, first world champion, 1886. 10fr, Aaron Niemzovitch, castle. 20fr, Alexander Alekhine, knights. 110fr, Botvinnik. 300fr, Boris Spassky, glass pieces. 500fr, Bobby Fischer, king, knight. 600fr, Korchnoi, Karpov, pawn. No. 582A, Bobby Fischer. No. 582B, Reti, Larsen, Petrossian, and Mecking, horiz.

1983, Jan. 15

576 A161 5fr multi .20 .20
577 A161 10fr multi .20 .20
578 A161 20fr multi .20 .20
579 A161 110fr multi 1.25 .20
580 A161 300fr multi 3.00 .55
581 A161 500fr multi 5.00 1.40
Nos. 576-581 (6) 9.85 2.75

Souvenir Sheet

582 A161 600fr multi 5.25 1.60

Litho. & Embossed

Perf. 13½

Size: 35x60mm

582A A161 1500fr gold & multi 13.50 3.50

Souvenir Sheet

582B A161 1500fr gold & multi 9.00 9.00

No. 582 contains one 56x33mm stamp, No. 582B one 35x60mm stamp. 300fr, 500fr, 600fr, Nos. 582A and 582B are airmail.

Marshal Tito (1892-1980)
A162

1983, Jan. 22

583 A162 20fr George Washington .20 .20
a. Souvenir sheet 5.00 —
584 A162 110fr shown 1.10 .30
a. Souvenir sheet 5.00 —

1982 World Cup Soccer Championships, Spain — A162a

Trophy, flags, scores, players: 5fr, Hamilton, Pezzey. 10fr, Borovski, Boniek. 20fr, Littbarski, Zamora. 110fr, Zico, Passarella. 300fr, Rossi, Smolarek. 500fr, Rummenigge, Giresse. 600fr, Rossi, Rummenigge. No. 584I, Platini. No. 584J, Rossi.

1983, Feb. 8 **Litho.** ***Perf. 13½***

584B A162a 5fr multi .20 .20
584C A162a 10fr multi .20 .20
584D A162a 20fr multi .20 .20
584E A162a 110fr multi 1.10 .30
584F A162a 300fr multi 3.00 .70
584G A162a 500fr multi 5.00 1.40
Nos. 584B-584G (6) 9.70 3.00

Souvenir Sheet

584H A162a 600fr multicolored 5.00 4.25

Litho. & Embossed

584I A162a 1500fr gold & multi 22.50 6.50

Souvenir Sheet

584J A162a 1500fr gold & multi 9.00 9.00

Nos. 584F-584J are airmail.

Easter 1983
A163

Rembrandt Paintings.

1983, Apr. 16

585 A163 100fr Entombment .90 .40
586 A163 300fr Crucifixion 2.25 1.25
587 A163 400fr Descent from the Cross 3.25 1.60
Nos. 585-587 (3) 6.40 3.25

Vintage Cars and their Makers
A164

A164a

Designs: 10fr, Emile Levassor, Rene Panhard, 1895 car. 20fr, Henry Ford, 1896 car. 30fr, Louis Renault, 1899 car. 80fr, Ettore Bugatti, type 37, 1925. 400fr, Enzo Ferrari, 815 sport, 1940. 500fr, Ferdinand Porsche, 356 coupe, 1951. 600fr, Karl Benz, velocipede, 1886. No. 594A, F.H. Royce and C.S. Rolls, 1911 Rolls-Royce Silver Ghost. No. 594B, G. Daimler, 1900 Mercedes 35CV.

1983, June 3 **Litho.** ***Perf. 13½***

588 A164 10fr multi .20 .20
589 A164 20fr multi .20 .20
590 A164 30fr multi .25 .20
591 A164 80fr multi .90 .30
592 A164 400fr multi 4.25 1.10
593 A164 500fr multi 5.00 1.40
Nos. 588-593 (6) 10.80 3.40

Souvenir Sheet

594 A164 600fr multi 5.25 1.60

Litho. & Embossed

594A A164a 1500fr gold & multi 13.50 4.00

Souvenir Sheet

594B A164a 1500fr gold & multi 9.00 6.00

Nos. 592-594B are airmail.

25th Anniv. of Intl. Maritime Org. — A165

1983, July 8 **Litho.** ***Perf. 12½x13***

595 A165 40fr multi .45 .20
596 A165 100fr multi .90 .40

World Communications Year — A166

1983, July 22

597 A166 50fr multi .45 .25
598 A166 130fr multi 1.25 .45

Pre-Olympics, Los Angeles
A167

1984 Summer Olympics, Los Angeles
A167a

1983, Aug. 3 **Litho.** ***Perf. 13***

599 A167 5fr Gymnast .20 .20
600 A167 40fr Javelin throwing .35 .20
601 A167 60fr Pole vault .60 .25
602 A167 120fr Fencing 1.25 .30
603 A167 200fr Cycling 2.10 .40
604 A167 300fr Sailing 3.00 .80
Nos. 599-604 (6) 7.50 2.15

Souvenir Sheet

605 A167 600fr Handball 4.50 1.60

Litho. & Embossed

Perf. 13½

605A A167a 1500fr Shot put 13.50 3.50

Souvenir Sheet

605B A167a 1500fr Dressage, horiz. 9.00 9.00

Nos. 603-605B are airmail.

Namibia Day — A168

1983, Sept. 16 **Litho.** ***Perf. 13***

606 A168 100fr multi 1.00 .40
607 A168 200fr multi 1.75 .80

Manned Flight Bicentenary — A169

A169a

Designs: 50fr, J. Montgolfier and his balloon, 1783. 100fr, J.P. Blanchard, English Channel crossing, 1785. 200fr, L.-J. Gay-Lussac, 4000-meter balloon ascent, 1804. 300fr, Giffard and his dirigible, 1852. 400fr, Santos Dumont, dirigible, Eiffel Tower. 500fr, A. Laquot, captive observation balloon, 1914. 600fr, J.A. Charles, first gas balloon; G. Tissandier, dirigible, 1883. No. 614, Marquis d'Arlandes and Jean Francois Pilatre de Rozier, Montgolfier balloon. No. 614B, Ferdinand von Zeppelin, Graf Zeppelin, horiz.

1983, Sept. 30 **Litho.** ***Perf. 13½***

608 A169 50fr multi .45 .20
609 A169 100fr multi 1.00 .40
610 A169 200fr multi 2.25 .80
611 A169 300fr multi 3.00 1.10
612 A169 400fr multi 4.00 1.50
613 A169 500fr multi 5.25 1.90
Nos. 608-613 (6) 15.95 5.90

Souvenir Sheet

614 A169 600fr multi 5.00 1.40

Litho. & Embossed

614A A169a 1500fr gold & multi 13.50 4.00

Souvenir Sheet

614B A169a 1500fr gold & multi 9.00 9.00

Nos. 612-614B are airmail.

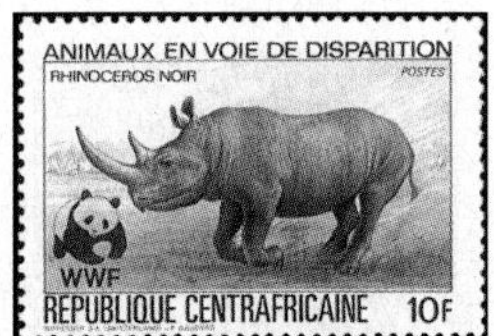

Black Rhinoceros and World Wildlife Emblem — A170

Various black rhinoceroses.

1983, Nov. 14

615 A170 10fr multi .20 .20
616 A170 40fr multi .60 .20
617 A170 70fr multi 1.00 .25
618 A170 180fr multi 3.00 .55
Nos. 615-618 (4) 4.80 1.20

Nos. 615-618 were issued in support of the World Wildlife Fund.
See Nos. C291A-C293.

UPU Day, World Communications Year — A171

1983, Nov. 2 Litho. *Perf. 13*

619 A171 205fr multi 1.75 .90

2nd Anniv. of the Natl. Military Committee A172

Gen. Andre Kolingba, head of state.

1983, Sept. 1 *Perf. 12½*

620 A172 65fr sil & multi .50 .25
621 A172 130fr gold & multi 1.25 .45

Earth Satellite Receiving Station, Bangui M'Poko — A173

1983 *Perf. 13*

622 A173 130fr multi 1.25 .55

Natl. Day of the Handicapped and the Elderly — A174

1983, Dec. 20 Engr. *Perf. 13x12½*

623 A174 65fr vio & org .50 .30
624 A174 130fr ultra & org 1.00 .45
625 A174 205fr dk grn & org 1.60 .80
Nos. 623-625 (3) 3.10 1.55

Fishing Resources A175

1983, Dec. 31 Litho. *Perf. 12½*

626 A175 25fr Breeding tank .20 .20
627 A175 65fr Net fishing .80 .25
628 A175 100fr Dam fishing .90 .40
629 A175 130fr Still life with fish 1.90 .70
630 A175 205fr Basket trap 2.00 .70
Nos. 626-630 (5) 5.80 2.25

Wildlife Protection — A176

1984, Jan. 25 *Perf. 13*

631 A176 30fr Forest fire 1.75 .40
632 A176 130fr Hunters 2.50 1.10

CC-1500 Locomotive — A177

1984, July 16 Litho. *Perf. 12½*

633 A177 110fr CC-1500 locomotive 1.25 .30
634 A177 240fr PLM series 210, 1868 2.75 .85
635 A177 350fr 231-726 locomotive, 1937 4.00 1.10
636 A177 440fr Pacific S3/6, 1908 5.25 1.25
637 A177 500fr Henschel 151 series 45, 1937 6.25 1.60
Nos. 633-637 (5) 19.50 5.10

For overprints see Nos. 702, 704.

Packet Ship Pericles — A177a

1984, July 23 Litho. *Perf. 12½*

638 A177a 65fr shown .80 .30
639 A177a 120fr Three-master Pereire 1.25 .55
640 A177a 250fr Admella 2.75 1.10
641 A177a 400fr Royal William 5.00 1.90
642 A177a 500fr Great Britain 5.75 2.40
Nos. 638-642 (5) 15.55 6.25

For overprints see Nos. 701, 703.

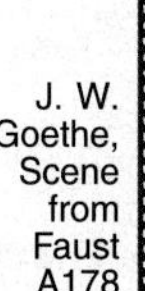

J. W. Goethe, Scene from Faust A178

Designs: 100fr, Henri Dunant, Red Cross Founder, Battle of Solferino, 125th anniv. 200fr, Alfred Nobel, Nobel Foundation headquarters. 300fr, Lord Baden-Powell, World Scouting Jamboree, Alberta, 1983. 400fr, John F. Kennedy, first man on the Moon, 1969. 500fr, 600fr, wedding of Prince and Princess of Wales.

1984, Feb. 25 Litho. *Perf. 13½*

643 A178 50fr multi .50 .20
644 A178 100fr multi 1.00 .40
645 A178 200fr multi 2.25 .55
646 A178 300fr multi 3.00 1.10
647 A178 400fr multi 4.00 1.10
648 A178 500fr multi 5.00 1.10
Nos. 643-648 (6) 15.75 4.45

Souvenir Sheet

649 A178 600fr multi 4.50 1.40

Nos. 647-649 are airmail.

Old Masters A179

Paintings: 50fr, Madonna and Child, by Raphael. 100fr, Madonna with Pear, by Durer. 200fr, Aldobrandini Madonna, by Raphael. 300fr, Madonna with Carnation, by Durer. 400fr, Virgin and Child, by Correggio. 500fr, La Bohemienne, by Modigliani. 600fr, Madonna and Child on the Throne, by Raphael.

1984, Mar. 30 Litho. *Perf. 13½*

650 A179 50fr multi .50 .20
651 A179 100fr multi 1.00 .25
652 A179 200fr multi 2.25 .45
653 A179 300fr multi 3.25 .85
654 A179 400fr multi 4.25 1.90
655 A179 500fr multi 5.25 2.50
Nos. 650-655 (6) 16.50 6.15

Miniature Sheet

656 A179 600fr multi 5.00 1.40

No. 656 contains 1 stamp, size 30x59mm.
Nos. 654-656 are airmail.

Space — A180

1984, Aug. 6 Litho. *Perf. 13½*

657 A180 20fr Galileo, Ariane rocket .25 .20
658 A180 70fr Piccard, X-15, balloon .60 .25
659 A180 150fr Oberth, satellite 1.25 .45
660 A180 205fr Einstein, satellites 1.75 .55
661 A180 300fr Curie, Viking vehicle 3.00 .80
662 A180 500fr Merbold, Spacelab 4.50 1.00
Nos. 657-662 (6) 11.35 3.25

Miniature Sheet

663 A180 600fr Armstrong, Apollo 11, horiz. 4.50 1.40

No. 663 contains 1 stamp, size: 42x36mm.
300fr, 500fr and 600fr are airmail.

Forestry Resources A181

UNICEF — A182

1984, Oct. 9 Litho. *Perf. 13x12½*

664 A181 70fr Forest .90 .30
665 A181 130fr Logging 1.75 .55

1984, Oct. 27 Litho. *Perf. 13x12½*

666 A182 10fr Weighing child .20 .20
667 A182 30fr Vaccinating child .35 .25
668 A182 65fr Giving liquids .50 .30
669 A182 100fr Balancing diet 1.10 .55
Nos. 666-669 (4) 2.15 1.30

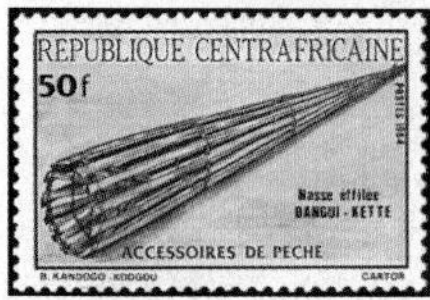

Fishing Traps A183

1984, Nov. 6 Litho. *Perf. 13*

670 A183 50fr Bangui-Kette .70 .30
671 A183 80fr Mbres 1.00 .55
672 A183 150fr Bangui-Kette 1.75 .55
Nos. 670-672 (3) 3.45 1.40

Mushrooms A184

1984, Nov. 15 Litho. *Perf. 13½*

673 A184 5fr Leptoporus lignosus .20 .20
674 A184 10fr Phlebopus sudanicus .20 .20
675 A184 40fr Termitomyces letestui .60 .20
676 A184 130fr Lepiota esculenta 1.50 .30
677 A184 300fr Termitomyces aurantiacus 3.25 .80
678 A184 500fr Termitomyces robustus 5.75 1.25
Nos. 673-678 (6) 11.50 2.95

Souvenir Sheet

679 A184 600fr Tricholoma-lobayensis 5.75 1.40

Nos. 677-679 are airmail.

1984 Winter Olympics, Sarajevo A184a

Gold medalists, communications satellite and events: 30fr, Gaetan Boucher, Canada, 1000 and 1500-meter speed skating. 90fr, W. Hoppe, R. Wetzig, D. Schauerhammer and A. Kirchner, German Democratic Republic, 4-man bobsled. 140fr, Paoletta Magoni, Italy, women's slalom. 200fr, Jayne Torvill and Christopher Dean, Great Britain, ice dancing. 400fr, Matti Nykaenen, Finland, 90-meter ski jumping. 500fr, USSR, ice hockey. 600fr, Bill Johnson, US, men's downhill.

1984, Nov. 30 Litho. *Perf. 13½*

679A A184a 30fr multi .25 .20
679B A184a 90fr multi .90 .30
679C A184a 140fr multi 1.40 .40
679D A184a 200fr multi 2.00 .55
679E A184a 400fr multi 3.75 1.00
679F A184a 500fr multi 4.75 1.25
Nos. 679A-679F (6) 13.05 3.70

Souvenir Sheet

679G A184a 600fr multi 4.50 1.40

Nos. 679E-679G are airmail.

Flowers — A185

1984, Nov. 22 Litho. *Perf. 13½*

680	A185 65fr Hibiscus	.90	.40
681	A185 130fr Canna Indica	1.60	.50
682	A185 205fr Eichlornia Crassipes	2.50	1.00
	Nos. 680-682 (3)	5.00	1.90

Economic Campaign — A186

1984, Dec. 3 Litho. *Perf. 13½*

683	A186 25fr Cotton planting	.35	.25
684	A186 40fr Selling cotton crop	.60	.40
685	A186 130fr Cotton market	1.60	.55
	Nos. 683-685 (3)	2.55	1.20

World Food Day A187

1984, Dec. 10 Litho. *Perf. 13½*

686	A187 205fr Picking corn	2.25	.90

OLYMPHILEX '85 — A188

Publicity posters from previous Games and host city landmarks.

1985, Mar 18 Litho. *Perf. 13½*

687	A188 5fr Stockholm, 1912	.20	.20
688	A188 10fr Paris, 1924	.20	.20
689	A188 20fr London, 1948	.20	.20
690	A188 100fr Tokyo, 1964	4.75	1.00
691	A188 400fr Mexico	2.10	.45
692	A188 500fr Munich, 1972	2.50	.55
	Nos. 687-692 (6)	9.95	2.60

Souvenir Sheet

693	A188 600fr Athens, 1896, Baron Pierre de Coubertin	5.00	1.50

Nos. 691-693 are airmail. No. 693 contains one 60x30mm stamp.

Anniversaries and Events — A189

Queen Mother, 85th Birthday — A189a

Famous men: 50fr, Abraham Lincoln, American Civil War soldiers. 90fr, Auguste Piccard (1884-1962), inventor, bathyscaphe Trieste. 120fr, Gottlieb Daimler (1834-1900), 1938 Mercedes Type 540. 200fr, Louis Bleriot (1872-1936), inventor, plane. 350fr, Anatoly Karpov, world chess champion. 400fr, Jean Henri Dunant (1828-1910), Red Cross founder, worker caring for wounded soldier.

1984, Dec. 22 Litho. *Perf. 13½*

694	A189 50fr multi	.50	.20
695	A189 90fr multi	.90	.30
696	A189 120fr multi	1.50	.40
697	A189 200fr multi	2.25	.55
698	A189 350fr multi	3.50	.80
698A	A189 400fr multi	3.50	.90
	Nos. 694-698A (6)	12.15	3.15

Nos. 698-698A are airmail.

Souvenir Sheet

1984 Litho. *Perf. 13½*

698B	A189a 600fr multi	4.50	1.40

Bangui Rotary Club and Water — A190

1984, Dec. 29

699	A190 130fr multi	1.75	.45
700	A190 205fr multi	2.50	.80

Nos. 635//641, C302A Overprinted with Exhibitions in Red

1985, Mar. 13 Litho. *Perf. 12½*

701	A177 250fr Argentina '85, Buenos Aires (#640)	2.25	1.25
702	A177a 350fr Tsukuba Expo '85 (#635)	3.25	1.60
703	A177 400fr Italia '85, Rome (#641)	4.00	2.00
704	A177a 440fr Mophila '85, Hamburg (#636)	5.00	2.40
	Nos. 701-704 (4)	14.50	7.25

Souvenir Sheet

Perf. 13½x13

705	AP89 500fr Olymphilex '85, Lausanne	4.50	4.50

500fr airmail.

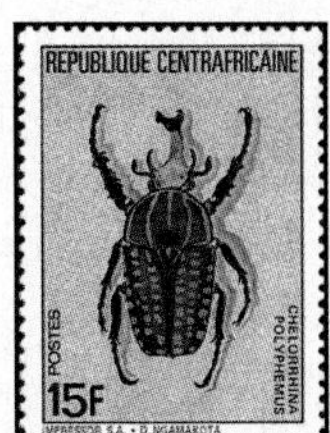

Beetles — A191

1985, Mar. Litho. *Perf. 13½*

706	A191 15fr Chelorrhina polyphemus	.35	.20
707	A191 20fr Fornasinius russus	.45	.20
708	A191 25fr Goliathus giganteus	.50	.20
709	A191 65fr Goliathus meleagris	1.25	.30
	Nos. 706-709 (4)	2.55	.90

Audubon Birth Bicentenary — A192

Illustrations of North American bird species by John Audubon.

1985, Mar. 25 Litho. *Perf. 13½*

710	A192 40fr Cyanocitta cristata	.70	.20
711	A192 80fr Caprimulgus carolinensis	1.00	.20
712	A192 130fr Campephilus principales	1.75	.25
713	A192 250fr Calocitta formosa	2.50	.55
714	A192 300fr Coccizus minor, horiz.	2.75	.60
715	A192 500fr Hirundo rustica, horiz.	4.50	1.10
	Nos. 710-715 (6)	13.20	2.90

Souvenir Sheet

716	A192 600fr Dryocopus pileatus, horiz.	5.25	1.40

Nos. 714-716 are airmail.

Intl. Youth Year A193

Famous children's book authors and scenes from their best-known novels: 100fr, The Jungle Book, 1894, by Kipling, vert. 200fr, Les Cavaliers, 1967, by Joseph Kessel (1898-1979). 300fr, Twenty-Thousand Leagues Under the Sea, 1873, by Verne. 400fr, The Adventures of Tom Sawyer, 1876, by Twain.

1985, Apr. Litho. *Perf. 13*

718	A193 100fr multi	1.00	.45
719	A193 200fr multi	2.00	.85
720	A193 300fr multi	2.50	1.25
721	A193 400fr multi	3.50	2.10
	Nos. 718-721 (4)	9.00	4.65

Philexafrica '85, Lome — A194

#722, UPU emblem, Postmen unloading parcel post van. #723, Exhibition emblem, scout troop.

1985, May 15 *Perf. 13x12½*

722	A194 200fr multi	2.25	.90
723	A194 200fr multi	2.25	.90
a.	Pair, #722-723 + label	5.25	4.50

Rabies Vaccine Cent., Louis Pasteur (1822-95), Chemist, Microbiologist — A195

Anniversaries and events: 200fr, Battle of Solferino, founding of the Red Cross, 125th Anniv., founder Jean-Henri Dunant (1828-1910), horiz. 300fr, Girl Guides, 75th anniv. 450fr, Elizabeth, the Queen Mother, 85th birthday. 500fr, Statue of Liberty, cent.

1985, June *Perf. 13*

724	A195 150fr multi	1.50	.70
725	A195 200fr multi	1.75	.90
726	A195 300fr multi	2.10	1.40
727	A195 450fr multi	3.50	2.25
728	A195 500fr multi	4.50	2.50
	Nos. 724-728 (5)	13.35	7.75

1986 World Cup Soccer Championships, Mexico — A196

Famous soccer players and match scenes.

1985, July 24 Litho. *Perf. 13½*

730	A196 5fr Pele	.20	.20
731	A196 10fr Tony Schumacher	.20	.20
732	A196 20fr Paolo Rossi	.20	.20
733	A196 350fr Kevin Keegan	3.25	.90
734	A196 400fr Michel Platini	3.75	.90
735	A196 500fr Karl Heinz Rummenigge	4.50	1.10
	Nos. 730-735 (6)	12.10	3.50

Souvenir Sheet

736	A196 600fr Diego Armando Maradona	4.50	1.40

Nos. 734-736 are airmail.

Kotto Waterfalls A197

1985, July 27 Litho. *Perf. 13½*

737	A197 65fr multi	.90	.30
738	A197 90fr multi	1.00	.40
739	A197 130fr multi	1.60	.60
	Nos. 737-739 (3)	3.50	1.30

State Visit of Pope John Paul II — A198

Portraits.

1985, Aug. 14

740	A198 65fr multi	1.10	.40
741	A198 130fr multi	2.25	.80

Natl. Economic Development Campaign — A199

Designs: 5fr, Troops plowing. 60fr, Soldier preparing field for planting, vert. 130fr, Planting cotton seeds, vert.

1985, Sept. 1 *Perf. 13*

742 A199 5fr multi .20 .20
743 A199 60fr multi .70 .30
744 A199 130fr multi 1.40 .45
Nos. 742-744 (3) 2.30 .95

Queen Mother, 85th Birthday — A200

1985, Sept. 16 **Litho.** *Perf. 13½*

745 A200 100fr Age 4, with brother .70 .25
746 A200 200fr Duchess of York, 1923 1.60 .35
747 A200 300fr Reviewing Irish Guards, 1928 2.50 .70
748 A200 350fr Family portrait, 1936 2.75 .75
749 A200 400fr George VI coronation, 1937 3.25 .90
750 A200 500fr Wedding anniv., 1948 4.25 1.00
Nos. 745-750 (6) 15.05 3.95

Souvenir Sheet

751 A200 600fr Christening Prince Charles, 1948 4.25 1.40

Nos. 749-751 are airmail.

Dr. Rene Labusquiere (1919-1977), Promoter of Preventive Medicine — A201

1985, Sept. 22 **Litho.** *Perf. 13½*

752 A201 10fr multi .20 .20
753 A201 45fr multi .45 .20
754 A201 110fr multi .70 .45
Nos. 752-754 (3) 1.35 .85

Natl. Postal Service — A202

1985, Oct. 9 *Perf. 12½*

755 A202 15fr Loading mail van .20 .20
756 A202 60fr Bangui P.O., van .60 .25
757 A202 150fr Hdqtrs, Bangui, and vans 1.50 .80
Nos. 755-757 (3) 2.30 1.25

Space Research — A203

Designs: 40fr, Yuri Gagarin and Sergei Korolev, Soviet cosmonauts. 110fr, Nicolaus Copernicus, Cassini probe. 240fr, Galileo, Viking orbiter. 300fr, Theodor von Karman (1881-1963), American aeronautical engineer, and space shuttle recovering Palapa B satellite. 450fr, Percival Lowell (1855-1916), American astronomer, and Viking probe. 500fr, Dr. U. Merbold and orbiting space station project Colombo. 600fr, Apollo 11 Project, first step on Moon by Neil Armstrong.

1985, Oct. 31 **Litho.** *Perf. 13½*

758 A203 40fr multi .25 .20
759 A203 110fr multi 1.00 .30
760 A203 240fr multi 2.25 .55
761 A203 300fr multi 3.00 .80
762 A203 450fr multi 4.50 1.00
763 A203 500fr multi 5.00 1.10
Nos. 758-763 (6) 16.00 3.95

Souvenir Sheet

Imperf

764 A203 600fr multi 4.50 1.40

Nos. 762-764 are airmail.

Solar Energy Apparatus, Damara — A204

1985, Nov. 4 **Litho.** *Perf. 13½*

765 A204 65fr multi .60 .30
766 A204 130fr multi 1.25 .55

Girl Guides Nature Study — A205

1985, Nov. 16 *Perf. 13*

767 A205 250fr shown 3.25 1.40
768 A205 250fr Quaka Sugar Refinery 3.25 1.40
a. Pair, #767-768 + label 9.00 6.00

PHILEXAFRICA '85, Lome, Togo, 11/16-24.

State Visit of Pres. Mitterand of France, Dec. 12-13 — A206

1985-86 **Litho.** *Perf. 13x12½*

769 A206 65fr multi .70 .25
770 A206 130fr multi 1.40 .55
770A A206 160fr multi ('86) 1.90 .80
Nos. 769-770A (3) 4.00 1.60

Issued: #769-770, Dec. 12.

UN 40th Anniv., Central Africa Admission, 25th Anniv. — A207

1985, Dec. 18 *Perf. 13½*

771 A207 140fr multi 1.25 .55

Intl. Youth Year A208

Designs: 40fr, David, by Andrea del Verrocchio; Madonna with the Carnation, 1470, by Leonardo da Vinci. 80fr, Johann Sebastian Bach. 100fr, St. John at Patmos, 1619, by Velazquez. 250fr, The Erl King score, by Franz Schubert. 400fr, Portrait of Vicente Osorio de Moscoso, by Goya. 500fr, The Young Mozart Playing in Paris, 1764. 600fr, Woman in a Plumed Hat, 1901, by Picasso.

1985, Dec. 28

772 A208 40fr multi .35 .20
773 A208 80fr multi .80 .25
774 A208 100fr multi 1.10 .25
775 A208 250fr multi 2.25 .55
776 A208 400fr multi 4.00 .90
777 A208 500fr multi 4.50 1.10
Nos. 772-777 (6) 13.00 3.25

Souvenir Sheet

778 A208 600fr multi 5.25 1.40

Nos. 776-778 are airmail.

Halley's Comet A209

100fr, Edmond Halley, British astronomer. 200fr, Sir Isaac Newton's telescope & comet sighting. 300fr, Halley & Newton observing comet. 350fr, US probe. 400fr, Soviet probe plotting comet's perihelion. 500fr, Isodensity photograph of comet. 600fr, Comet, Earth, Sun & probe.

1985, Dec. 31

779 A209 100fr multi .70 .25
780 A209 200fr multi 1.75 .40
781 A209 300fr multi 2.50 .45
782 A209 350fr multi 3.00 .80
783 A209 400fr multi 3.50 .85
784 A209 500fr multi 4.50 1.00
Nos. 779-784 (6) 15.95 3.75

Souvenir Sheet

785 A209 600fr multi 4.50 1.40

Nos. 783-785 are airmail.

Christopher Columbus — A210

Various events leading to the discovery of America and beyond.

1986

786 A210 90fr Plotting course .80 .25
787 A210 110fr Receiving blessing 1.00 .25
788 A210 240fr Fleet in port 2.25 1.25
789 A210 300fr Trade with natives 3.00 .55
790 A210 400fr Storm at sea 4.00 2.00
791 A210 500fr Fleet at sea 5.00 2.40
Nos. 779-784 (6) 15.95 3.75

Souvenir Sheet

792 A210 600fr Portrait 5.25 1.40

Nos. 790-792 are airmail.

Nos. 543-544 Surcharged

30F ▬

1986, Apr. 1 **Litho.** *Perf. 13*

792A A152 30fr on 175fr Kangu bowls
792B A152 65fr on 300fr Kolongo bowls

Hairstyles A211

France- Central Africa Week — A212

1986, May 21 **Litho.** *Perf. 12½*

793 A211 20fr multi .35 .20
794 A211 30fr multi .45 .25
795 A211 65fr multi .50 .40
796 A211 160fr multi 2.50 .70
Nos. 793-796 (4) 3.80 1.55

1986, May 26

797 A212 40fr Communications, horiz. .35 .20
798 A212 60fr Youth, horiz. .50 .25
799 A212 100fr Basket maker .70 .40
800 A212 130fr Bicycling 1.50 .55
Nos. 797-800 (4) 3.05 1.40

Centrapalm Palm Oil — A213

25fr, 65fr, Refinery, Bossongo, and palm tree. 120fr, 160fr, Refinery and palm tree.

1986, Aug. 12 **Litho.** *Perf. 13½*

801 A213 25fr multi .25 .25
802 A213 65fr multi .70 .40
803 A213 120fr multi, vert. 1.25 .80
804 A213 160fr multi, vert. 1.75 .60
Nos. 801-804 (4) 3.95 2.05

Dogs and Cats A214

1986, Sept. 9

805 A214 10fr Pointer .20 .20
806 A214 20fr Egyptian mau .25 .20
807 A214 200fr Newfoundland 2.25 .55
808 A214 300fr Borzoi 3.00 .60
809 A214 400fr Persian red 4.25 .85
Nos. 805-809 (5) 9.95 2.40

Souvenir Sheet

810 A214 500fr Spaniel, Burmese-Malayan 4.50 1.40

Nos. 808-810 are airmail.

African Coffee Producers Organization, 25th Anniv. — A215

1986, Sept. 25 Litho. *Perf. 13*
811 A215 160fr multi 1.50 .55

1986 World Cup Soccer Championships, Mexico — A216

Satellites, final scores, World Cup and athletes: 30fr, Muller, Socrates. 110fr, Scifo, Ceulemans. 160fr, Stopyra, Platini. 350fr, Brehme, Schumacher. 450fr, Maradona. 500fr, Schumacher, Burruchaga.

1986, Nov. 12 *Perf. 13½*
812 A216 30fr multi .25 .20
813 A216 110fr multi .90 .25
814 A216 160fr multi 1.25 .30
815 A216 350fr multi 3.00 .80
816 A216 450fr multi 4.00 1.10
Nos. 812-816 (5) 9.40 2.65

Souvenir Sheet

817 A216 500fr multi 4.00 1.40

Nos. 816-817 are airmail.

US Anniversaries and Events A217

15fr, Judith Resnik. 25fr, Frederic Auguste Bartholdi. 70fr, Elvis Presley. 300fr, Ronald McNair. 450fr, Christa McAuliffe. 500fr, Challenger Astronauts: McAuliffe, Scobee, Smith, Resnik, Onizuka, McNair, Jarvis.

1986, Nov. 19
818 A217 15fr multi .20 .20
819 A217 25fr multi .35 .20
820 A217 70fr multi 1.25 .20
821 A217 300fr multi 2.75 .60
822 A217 450fr multi 4.00 1.10
Nos. 818-822 (5) 8.55 2.30

Souvenir Sheet

823 A217 500fr multi 4.50 1.40

US space shuttle Challenger explosion; Statue of Liberty, cent. #822-823 are airmail. For surcharges & overprint see #851-851B.

Flora and Fauna A218

1986, May 30 Litho. *Perf. 13½*
824 A218 25fr Allamanda nerifolia .25 .20
825 A218 65fr Taurotragus eurycerus .80 .20
826 A218 160fr Plumieria acuminata 1.75 .30
827 A218 300fr Acinonyx jubatus 3.50 .80
828 A218 400fr Eulophia erthoplata 3.75 .90
829 A218 500fr Leopard 5.00 1.10
Nos. 824-829 (6) 15.05 3.50

Souvenir Sheet

830 A218 600fr Derby's eland, eulophia cucullata 5.00 1.50

#824, 826, 828 vert. #828-830 are airmail. #830 contains one 51x30mm stamp.

Intl. Peace Year — A219

Air Africa, 25th Anniv. — A220

1986, Nov. 29
831 A219 160fr multi 1.50 .55

1986, Dec. 15
832 A220 200fr multi 1.75 .80

UNICEF, 40th Anniv. — A221

1986, Dec. 24
833 A221 15fr shown .20 .20
834 A221 130fr Child immunization 1.00 .55
835 A221 160fr Youth, food, map 1.10 .70
Nos. 833-835 (3) 2.30 1.45

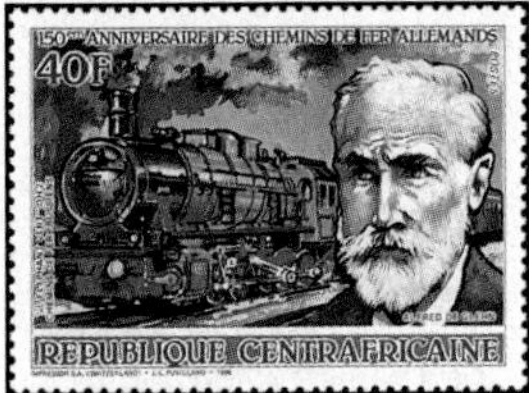

German Railways Sesquicentenary — A222

Inventors and locomotives: 40fr, Alfred de Glehn, Prussian Railways DH2 Green Elephant. 70fr, Rudolf Diesel, S3/6 No. 1829 Rheingold. 160fr, Carl Golsdorf, Trans-Europe Express train Type 103. 300fr, Wilhelm Schmidt, Beyer Garratt locomotive. 400fr, Monsieur de Bousquet, Series 3500 compound locomotive. 500fr, Werner von Siemens, 1980s electric locomotive.

1986, Dec. 31
836 A222 40fr multi .50 .20
837 A222 70fr multi .90 .20
838 A222 160fr multi 2.00 .40
839 A222 300fr multi 3.50 .60
840 A222 400fr multi 4.00 1.10
Nos. 836-840 (5) 10.90 2.50

Souvenir Sheet

841 A222 500fr multi 4.50 1.40

Nos. 840-841 are airmail. No. 841 contains one 42x36mm stamp.

Agriculture Radio Project A223

1986, Dec. 27 Litho. *Perf. 13½*
842 A223 170fr shown 2.00 .90
843 A223 265fr Satellite communication 3.00 1.40

Pan-African Telecommunications Union congress, Dec. 7, 1986.
No. 842 exists in souvenir sheet of one.

Space A224

Scientists and inventions: 25fr, Sir William Herschel (1738-1822), British astronomer, and Miranda satellite. 65fr, Wernher von Braun (1912-1977), American engineer, and Mars rover. 160fr, Rudolf Hanel, Mariner Mark II and Titan. 300fr, Patrick Baudry, Hermes shuttle and Eureka platform. 400fr, U. Keller, Halley's Comet and Giotto probe. 500fr, Wubbo Ockels, Ulf Merbold and Columbus European Space Station. 600fr, Wilhelm Obers (1758-1840) and Mariner Mark II surveying asteroids. No. 850 horiz.

1987, Jan. 27
844 A224 25fr multi .25 .20
845 A224 65fr multi .60 .20
846 A224 160fr multi 1.50 .30
847 A224 300fr multi 2.50 .75
848 A224 400fr multi 2.75 .90
849 A224 500fr multi 3.75 1.25
Nos. 844-849 (6) 11.35 3.60

Souvenir Sheet

850 A224 600fr multi 4.50 1.75

Nos. 848-850 are airmail.

No. 820 Surcharged

1987, Feb. 20 Litho. *Perf. 13½*
851 A217 485fr on 70fr Elvis Presley 6.75 1.10

Nos. 820 and 851 Ovptd. "Elvis PRESLEY / 1977-1987" in Black

1987, Feb. 20 Litho. *Perf. 13½*
851A A217 70fr multi .90 .25
851B A217 485fr on 70fr multi 5.25 1.75

Overprint in red exists.

1992 Barcelona Olympics A225

Athletes and landmarks or sights: 30fr, Soccer player, Lady with Umbrella fountain. 150fr, Judo, Barcelona Cathedral. 265fr, Cyclist, Church of the Holy Family, by Gaudi. 350fr, Gymnast, Tomb of Columbus. 495fr, Runner, human tower. 500fr, Swimmer, Statue of Columbus.

1987, June 4
852 A225 30fr multi .35 .20
853 A225 150fr multi 1.25 .45
854 A225 265fr multi 2.25 .80
855 A225 350fr multi 3.25 1.00
856 A225 495fr multi 5.00 1.40
Nos. 852-856 (5) 12.10 3.85

Souvenir Sheet

857 A225 500fr multi 4.00 1.40

Nos. 855-857 are airmail.

A226

1988 Winter Olympics, Calgary A227

1987, June 26
858 A226 20fr Two-man luge .25 .20
859 A226 140fr Cross-country skiing 1.25 .45
860 A226 250fr Women's figure skating 2.10 .80
861 A226 300fr Hockey 2.75 .90
862 A226 400fr Men's slalom 3.50 1.10
Nos. 858-862 (5) 9.85 3.45

Souvenir Sheet

863 A227 500fr Downhill skiing 4.00 1.40

Nos. 861-863 are airmail.

Intl. Peace Year — A228

1987, July 20
864 A228 50fr dull ultra, sepia & blk .45 .25
865 A228 160fr lt ol grn, sep & blk 1.25 .60

Intl. Decade of Drinkable Water — A228a

Designs: 5fr, Woman at village pump; 10fr, Two women at village pump; 200fr, Three women at village pump.

1987, Sept. 22 Litho. *Perf. 13½*
865A A228a 5fr multi 30.00 —
865B A228a 10fr multi 30.00 —
865C A228a 200fr multicolored 35.00 —
Nos. 865A-865C (3) 95.00 .00

Butterflies A229

1987, Oct. 5 Litho. *Perf. 13½*

866 A229 100fr Charaxes candiope 1.40 .85
867 A229 120fr Graphium leonidas 1.75 .90
868 A229 130fr Charaxes brutus 2.10 .90
869 A229 160fr Salamis aetiops 2.25 1.10
Nos. 866-869 (4) 7.50 3.75

Pygmy Soccer Team from Nola — A230

1987, Nov. 30 Litho. *Perf. 13*

870 A230 90fr multi 1.00 .60
871 A230 160fr multi 1.60 .90

Integration of the pygmy people into Central African society.

Dinosaurs — A231

Perf. 14x13½, 13½x14

1988, Mar. 19 Litho.

872 A231 50fr Brontosaurus .45 .20
873 A231 65fr Triceratops .60 .25
874 A231 100fr Ankylosaurus .90 .40
875 A231 160fr Stegosaurus 1.50 .60
876 A231 200fr Tyrannosaurus rex 1.75 .80
877 A231 240fr Corythosaurus 2.25 .90
878 A231 300fr Allosaurus 2.75 1.25
879 A231 350fr Brachiosaurus 3.25 1.50
Nos. 872-879 (8) 13.45 5.90

Nos. 876-879 vert.

Anniversaries and Events A232

Designs: 40fr, Pres. James Madison and "We the People..." from the US Constitution. 160fr, Elizabeth II and Duke of Edinburgh . 200fr, Steffi Graf, tennis champion. 300fr, Garri Kasparov of Russia, 1985 world chess champion. 400fr, Boris Becker, 1985-86 Wimbledon champion. 500fr, Christoph Willibald Gluck (1714-87), composer. Nos. 880-884 vert.

1988, Feb. 15 *Perf. 13½*

880 A232 40fr multi .35 .20
881 A232 160fr multi 1.40 .25
882 A232 200fr multi 1.75 .45
883 A232 300fr multi 2.75 .80
884 A232 400fr multi 3.25 1.25
Nos. 880-884 (5) 9.50 2.95

Souvenir Sheet

885 A232 500fr multi 4.25 1.40

US Constitution bicentennial (40fr); 40th wedding anniv. of Elizabeth II and Prince Philip (160fr). Nos. 883-885 are airmail.

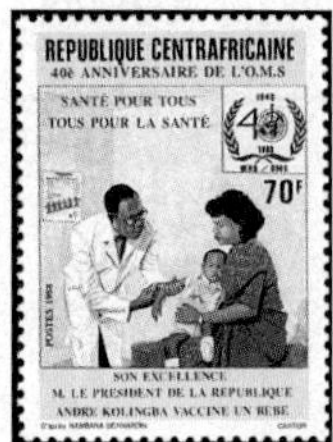

World Health Organization, 40th Anniv. — A233

1988, Apr. 7 Litho. *Perf. 13½*

886 A233 70fr multi .60 .40
887 A233 120fr multi .90 .55

Scout Ornithological Activities A234

Scouts and: 25fr, *Merops nubicus.* 170fr, *Euplectes hordeacea.* 300fr, *Ceryle rudis.* 400fr, *Estrilda bengala.* 450fr, *Kaupifalco monogrammicus.* 500fr, *Lamprotornis splendidus.*

1988, July 1 Litho. *Perf. 13½*

888 A234 25fr multi .20 .20
889 A234 170fr multi 1.25 .70
890 A234 300fr multi 2.25 2.00
891 A234 400fr multi 3.00 2.00
892 A234 450fr multi 3.50 2.40
Nos. 888-892 (5) 10.20 7.30

Souvenir Sheet

893 A234 500fr multi 5.00 1.50

Nos. 891-893 are airmail.
For surcharges see Nos. 921-924.

1988 Summer Olympics, Seoul A235

1988, Sept. 30

894 A235 150fr Running, vert. 1.10 .25
895 A235 300fr Judo, vert. 2.50 .70
896 A235 400fr Soccer, vert. 2.75 1.00
897 A235 450fr Tennis, vert. 3.25 1.10
Nos. 894-897 (4) 9.60 3.05

Souvenir Sheet

898 A235 500fr Boxing 4.00 1.40

Nos. 896-898 are airmail.

1988 Winter Olympics, Calgary — A236

1988, Sept. 30 Litho. *Perf. 13½*

899 A236 170fr Cross-country skiing 1.25 .30
900 A236 350fr Ice hockey 2.00 .60
901 A236 400fr Downhill skiing 2.75 .90
902 A236 450fr Freestyle 3.00 1.00
Nos. 899-902 (4) 9.00 2.80

Souvenir Sheet

903 A236 500fr shown 4.00 1.40

Nos. 899-902 vert. Nos. 901-903 are airmail.

Natl. Arbor Day — A237

1988, July 16 Litho. *Perf. 13½*

904 A237 50fr Students planting trees .45 .25
905 A237 100fr like 50fr .90 .55
906 A237 130fr Forest (before and after) 1.25 .60
Nos. 904-906 (3) 2.60 1.40

L'Amitie Hospital, 1st Anniv. A238

1988, Nov. 30

907 A238 5fr shown .20 .20
908 A238 60fr Aerial view .60 .40
909 A238 160fr Front gate 1.25 .80
Nos. 907-909 (3) 2.05 1.40

Proclamation of Central African Republic, 30th Anniv. A238a

Design: 65fr, Dove, map, flag, people, vert. 240fr, Government buildings, horiz.

1988 (?) Litho. *Perf. 13½*

909A A238a 65fr multi 45.00 —
909C A238a 240fr multicolored 45.00 —

An additional stamp was released in this set. The editors would like to examine it.

A239

A240

Olympic Medalists, Seoul, 1988: 150fr, Kristine Otto, DDR, swimming. 240fr, Matt Biondi, US, swimming. 300fr, Florence Griffith-Joyner, US, running. 450fr, Pierre Durand, France, equestrian. 600fr, Carl Lewis, US, running.

1989, Apr. 1

910 A239 150fr multi 2.10 .55
911 A239 240fr multi 3.25 .80
912 A239 300fr multi 4.00 1.10
913 A239 450fr multi 6.75 1.75
a. Souv. sheet of 4, #910-913 16.00
Nos. 910-913 (4) 16.10 4.20

Souvenir Sheet

914 A239 600fr multi 5.25 2.00

Nos. 913-914 airmail. No. 914 contains one 37x43mm stamp.

1989, Apr. 10 Litho. *Perf. 13½*

Transportation Innovations, Inventors: 20fr, Hebmuller and 1953 Volkswagen Beetle. 205fr, Werner von Siemens (1816-1892) and 1879 Locomotive B. 300fr, Dennis Conner, skipper of *Stars and Stripes,* winner of the 1988 America's Cup. 400fr, Andre Citroen (1878-1935) and 1955 Citroen-15 SIX. 450fr, Marc Seguin (1786-1875) and 1895 Decauville-Mallet 020-020. 750fr, Frederick S. Duesenberg (1876-1932), brother August, US flag and 1929 J Phaeton.

915 A240 20fr multi .20 .20
916 A240 205fr multi 1.75 .55
917 A240 300fr multi 2.25 .60
918 A240 400fr multi 3.25 1.10
919 A240 450fr multi 4.00 1.25
Nos. 915-919 (5) 11.45 3.70

Souvenir Sheet

920 A240 750fr multi 5.75 1.50

Nos. 919-920 airmail. No. 920 contains one 43x37mm stamp.
#915-919 exist in souvenir sheets of 1.

Nos. 889-892 Surcharged in Black or Silver

1988, Oct. 7 Litho. *Perf. 13½*

921 A234 30fr on 170fr (B) .35 .20
922 A234 70fr on 300fr 1.00 .55
923 A234 160fr on 400fr 1.75 .85
924 A234 200fr on 450fr 2.25 1.10
Nos. 921-924 (4) 5.35 2.70

Nos. 923-924 are airmail.

PHILEXFRANCE '89, French Revolution Bicent. — A241

Designs: 200fr, Allegory in Honor of Liberty. 300fr, Declaration of Human Rights and Citizenship. 500fr, The Bastille, horiz.

1989, July 7 Litho. *Perf. 13*

925 A241 200fr multi 1.75 .80
926 A241 300fr multi 3.75 1.25
a. Pair, #925-926 + label 6.00 6.00

Souvenir Sheet

927 A241 500fr multi 4.50 3.50

Souvenir Sheet

Statue of Liberty — A242

Designs: a, Crown and torch observatories lit at night. b, Working on statue's coiffure. c, Face and scaffolding. d, Workman sanding copper sheeting around the crown observatory. e, Re-opening ceremony, 1986. f, Crown observatory at night.

Wmk. 385

1989, July Litho. *Perf. 13*

928 Sheet of 6 9.00 9.00
a.-c. A242 150fr any single 1.40 .60
d.-f. A242 200fr any single 1.60 1.00

Statue of Liberty cent. (in 1986). Photograph of the statue is reversed.

M. Champagnat (1789-1840), Founder of the Marist Order — A243

1989 Litho. *Perf. 13½*

929 A243 15fr Madonna and child, map .20 .20
930 A243 50fr Cross, Earth .40 .25
931 A243 160fr shown 1.25 .80
Nos. 929-931 (3) 1.85 1.25

Nos. 929-930 vert.

Harvest Feast, Bambari A244

1989, Oct. 15

932 A244 100fr Produce .90 .55
933 A244 160fr Ox plow 1.40 .60

World Food Day A245

1989, Oct. 16

934 A245 60fr Domestic animals .50 .30
935 A245 240fr Arresting ivory poachers 2.00 1.00

French Revolution, Bicent. — A246

Battle scenes and leaders: 160fr, Brig.-Gen. Francois-Christophe Kellermann (1735-1820), Battle of Valmy, Sept. 22, 1792. 200fr, Minister of War Charles-Francois du Perier Dumouriez (1739-1823), Battle of Jemappes, Nov. 7, 1792. 500fr, Gen. Jean-Charles Pichegru (1761-1804), capture of the Dutch fleet, Jan. 22, 1795. 600fr, Gen. Louis-Lazare Hoche (1768-97), Battle of Quiberon Bay, July 21, 1795. 1000fr, Napoleon at the Battle of Rivoli Veronese, Jan. 15, 1797.

1989, Dec. 5 Litho. *Perf. 13½*

936 A246 160fr multicolored 1.25 .40
937 A246 200fr multicolored 1.60 .55
938 A246 500fr multicolored 5.00 1.10
939 A246 600fr multicolored 4.50 1.00
a. Souvenir sheet of 4, #936-939 12.00 12.00
Nos. 936-939 (4) 12.35 3.05

Souvenir Sheet

940 A246 1000fr multicolored 8.50 1.75

PHILEXFRANCE '89. Nos. 938-940 are airmail.

No. 936 is incorrectly inscribed "Francois-Etienne." Jemappes is incorrectly spelled on No. 937. No. 940 is incorrectly inscribed "January 14."

1990 World Cup Soccer Championships, Italy — A247

Various athletes and Italian landmarks: 20fr, Bell tower, Palermo Cathedral. 120fr, Trinity of the Mount, Rome. 160fr, St. Francis Church apse, Bologna. 200fr, Palace, Florence. 1000fr, Milan Cathedral.

1989, Dec. 23

941 A247 20fr multicolored .20 .20
942 A247 120fr multicolored 1.10 .40
943 A247 160fr multicolored 1.25 .40
944 A247 200fr multicolored 1.50 .55
Nos. 941-944 (4) 4.05 1.55

Souvenir Sheet

945 A247 1000fr multicolored 7.50 1.50

Nos. 942 and 945 are airmail.

Save the Forests A247a

1989 Litho. *Perf. 13½*

945A A247a 160fr multicolored 1.25 .60

Town of Bangui, Cent. A247b

Designs: 100fr, Governor's Palace, 1906. 160fr, Outpost. 200fr, A. Dolisie, founder of Bangui, vert. 1000fr, Signing of peace treaty between Michel Dolisie and Chief Gbembo, 1889, vert.

1989 Litho. *Perf. 13½*

945B A247b 100fr multi 1.00 .40
945C A247b 160fr multi 1.40 1.00
945D A247b 200fr multi 2.00 .95
945E A247b 1000fr multi 9.00 4.25
Nos. 945B-945E (4) 13.40 6.60

Championship Team from Central Africa, 1987 — A248

1990, Feb. 23 Litho. *Perf. 13½*

946 A248 160fr Flag, players, trophy 1.25 .60
947 A248 240fr shown 2.10 .85
948 A248 500fr like 160fr 4.25 1.75
Nos. 946-948 (3) 7.60 3.20

African Basketball Championships. Dated 1988. Nos. 946 and 948 vert.

A249

A250

1990, Feb. 23 Litho. *Perf. 13½*

949 A249 100fr multicolored .90 .40
950 A249 130fr multicolored 1.00 .55

Central Africa, winner of the 1987 African Basketball Cup Championships, Tunis. Dated 1989.

1990, Mar. 12 Litho. *Perf. 13½*

1992 Winter Olympics, Albertville: No. 955A, Slalom skier. No. 955B, Pairs figure skating.

951 A250 10fr Speed skating .20 .20
952 A250 60fr Cross-country skiing .50 .25
953 A250 500fr Slalom 4.00 1.00
954 A250 750fr Figure skating 5.75 1.40
Nos. 951-954 (4) 10.45 2.85

Souvenir Sheet

955 A250 1000fr Downhill skiing 7.50 1.50

Litho. & Embossed

955A A250 1500fr gold & multi 10.00 3.50

Souvenir Sheet

955B A250 1500fr gold & multi 10.00 10.00

Nos. 953-955B are airmail. No. 955 contains one 36x42mm stamp. Nos. 951-954 exist in souvenir sheets of one.

Scout, *Euphaera eusemoides* — A251

Boy scouts and butterflies: 65fr, *Cymothoe beckeri*. 160fr, *Pseudacraea clarki*. 250fr, *Charaxes castor*.300fr, *Euphaedra gausape*. 500fr, *Graphium ridleyanus*. 1000fr, *Euphaedra edwardsi*. No. 962A, Antanartia delius. No. 962B, Spotted flycatcher. No. 962C, Cymothoe sangaris.

1990, Mar. 26

956 A251 25fr multicolored .25 .20
957 A251 65fr multicolored .50 .20
958 A251 160fr multicolored 1.10 .25
959 A251 250fr multicolored 2.00 .55
960 A251 300fr multicolored 2.50 .60
961 A251 500fr multicolored 4.25 1.00
Nos. 956-961 (6) 10.60 2.80

Souvenir Sheet

962 A251 1000fr multicolored 8.50 2.00

Litho. & Embossed

Perf. 12½

962A A251 1500fr gold & multi 12.50 4.00

Perf. 13½

962B A251 1500fr gold & multi 12.50 4.00

Souvenir Sheet

962C A251 1500fr gold & multi 10.00 10.00

Nos. 962A-962C are airmail. No. 962A exists in a souvenir sheet of 1.

1992 Summer Olympics, Barcelona A252

1990, Apr. 1 Litho. *Perf. 13½*

963 A252 10fr Javelin .20 .20
964 A252 40fr Runner .35 .20
965 A252 130fr Tennis 1.00 .25
966 A252 240fr Hurdles 1.75 .55
967 A252 400fr Yachting 3.25 1.00
968 A252 500fr Soccer 4.00 1.10
Nos. 963-968 (6) 10.55 3.30

Souvenir Sheet

969 A252 1000fr Boxing 7.50 1.50

Nos. 963-965 vert. Nos. 967-969 are airmail.

Pres. Gorbachev, Pres. Bush — A253

Pres. Gorbachev, Pope John Paul II — A254

1990, July 27 Litho. *Perf. 13½*

970 A253 120fr multicolored .85 .25
971 A254 200fr multicolored 1.40 .30

Pope John Paul II-Gorbachev meeting Dec. 2, 1989. Bush-Gorbachev Summit Meeting Dec. 3, 1989. Nos. 970-971 exist in souvenir sheets of 1.

Great Britain No. 1, Sir Rowland Hill (1795-1879) — A255

1990, July 27

972 A255 130fr multicolored .90 .25

No. 972 exists in a souvenir sheet of 1.

Events and Anniversaries — A256

Designs: 160fr, Galileo Probe to Jupiter. 240fr, Neil Armstrong, 1st man on moon. 250fr, Concorde, rapid-transit train, Rotary Intl. emblem.

1990, July 27 Litho. *Perf. 13½*

973	A256	160fr multicolored	1.00	.40
974	A256	240fr multicolored	1.60	.50
975	A256	250fr multicolored	3.50	.50
		Nos. 973-975 (3)	6.10	1.40

Wildlife Protection A258

100fr, Declining elephant population, vert.

1991, Jan. 25 Litho. *Perf. 13½*

976	A258	15fr gold & multi	.45	.20
977	A258	60fr multicolored	1.40	.40
978	A258	100fr multicolored	2.25	.55
		Nos. 976-978 (3)	4.10	1.15

Eutropius A259

Design: 240fr, Distichodus.

1991, Jan. 26

979	A259	50fr multicolored	.45	.25
980	A259	160fr gold & multi	1.75	.75
981	A259	240fr multicolored	3.00	1.50
		Nos. 979-981 (3)	5.20	2.50

Fight Against AIDS A260

Design: 120fr, Class speaker, vert.

1991, Jan. 24

982	A260	5fr gold & multi	.25	.20
983	A260	70fr multicolored	1.00	.55
984	A260	120fr multicolored	1.60	.80
		Nos. 982-984 (3)	2.85	1.55

Central African Diamonds A260a

Designs: 65fr, Woman polishing diamond, 160fr, Map, diamond.

1991, Feb. 14 Litho. *Perf. 11½*
Granite Paper

984A	A260a	65fr multicolored
984B	A260a	160fr multicolored

Assumption of Power by Pres. Andre Kolingba, 10th Anniv. (in 1991) — A261

1992, Sept. 1 Litho. *Perf. 13x13½*

985	A261	160fr multicolored	1.50	.60

Anniversaries and Events — A262

Designs: 80fr, Maybach Zeppelin, zeppelin airship, Count Ferdinand Zeppelin. 140fr, Child being comforted, Jean-Henri Dunant. 160fr, Benetton-Ford B 192, Michael Schumacher. 350fr, Konrad Adenauer signing Constitution of German Republic. 500fr, Pope John Paul II, mother and child, map. 600fr, Wolfgang Amadeus Mozart. 1000fr, Columbus at La Rabida, sailing ship, and building in Seville, Spain.

1992, Sept. 22 Litho. *Perf. 13½*

986	A262	80fr multicolored	.60	.20
987	A262	140fr multicolored	1.50	.25
988	A262	160fr multicolored	1.75	.40
989	A262	350fr multicolored	4.00	1.10
990	A262	500fr multicolored	5.75	1.40
991	A262	600fr multicolored	7.50	1.50
		Nos. 986-991 (6)	21.10	4.85

Souvenir Sheet

992	A262	1000fr multicolored	7.50	2.00

Count Zeppelin, 75th anniv. of death (#986). Jean-Henri Dunant, first recipient of Nobel Peace Prize, 90th anniv. (in 1991) (#987). Grand Prix of Monaco (#988). Brandenburg Gate, bicent (#989). Visit of Pope John Paul II to Africa (#990). Wolfgang Amadeus Mozart, bicent. of death (in 1991) (#991). Discovery of America, 500th anniv. and Expo '92, Seville (#992).

Nos. 990-992 are airmail. Nos. 986-991 exist in souvenir sheets of 1.

For overprint see No. 1073.

A264

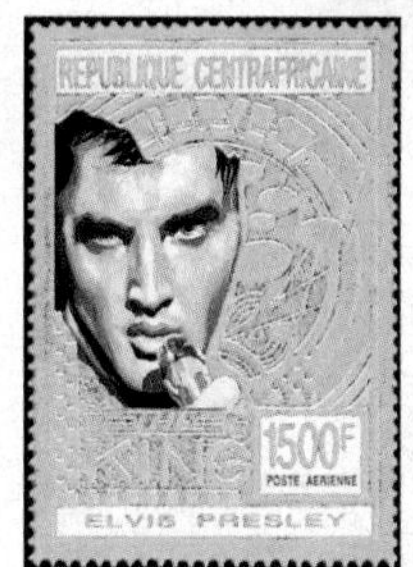

Elvis Presley (1935-1977) A264a

Portrait of Presley, song or movie: 200fr, Heartbreak Hotel, 1956. 300fr, Love Me Tender, 1957. 400fr, Jailhouse Rock, 1957. 600fr, Harem Scarum, 1965.

1000fr, With guitar, at microphone.

No. 1001A, Holding microphone. No. 1001B, Playing guitar.

1993, July 12 Litho. *Perf. 13½*

997	A264	200fr multicolored	2.00	.25
998	A264	300fr multicolored	3.00	.50
999	A264	400fr multicolored	3.50	.60
1000	A264	600fr multicolored	5.00	1.00
		Nos. 997-1000 (4)	13.50	2.35

Souvenir Sheet

1001	A264	1000fr multicolored	8.00	2.40

Litho. & Embossed

1001A	A264a	1500fr gold & multi	11.00	7.50

Souvenir Sheet

1001B	A264a	1500fr gold & multi	11.00	7.50

Nos. 1000-1001B are airmail. Nos. 997-1000, 1001A exist imperf. and in souvenir sheets of one. Nos. 1001, 1001B exist imperf.

Wedding of Japan's Crown Prince Naruhito and Masako Owada — A265

A265a

Designs: 50fr, Princess Masako, parents. 65fr, Crown Prince Naruhito, parents. 160fr, Princess Masako, Harvard University 450fr, Crown Prince Naruhito, Oxford University. 750fr, Crown Prince, Princess.

1993, July 12 Litho. *Perf. 13½*

1002	A265	50fr multi	.25	.20
1003	A265	65fr multi	.60	.25
1004	A265	160fr multi	1.60	.25
1005	A265	450fr multi	4.00	1.00
		Nos. 1002-1005 (4)	6.45	1.70

Souvenir Sheet

1006	A265	750fr multi	6.25	2.00

Litho. & Embossed

1006A	A265a	1500fr gold & multi	11.50	3.50

Nos. 1005-1006A are airmail. Nos. 1002-1005, 1006A exist imperf. and in souvenir sheets of one. No. 1006 exists imperf.

A266

1994 World Cup Soccer Championships, US — A266a

Designs show winning team, scenes from: 40fr, Amsterdam, 1928; Montevideo, 1930. 50fr, Rome, 1934; Paris, 1938. 60fr, Rio, 1950; Berne, 1954. 80fr, Stockholm, 1958; Santiago, 1962. 160fr, London, 1966; Mexico City, 1970. 200fr, Munich, 1974; Buenos Aires, 1978. 400fr, Madrid, 1982; Mexico City, 1986. 500fr, Rome, 1990; emblem for US competition, 1994.

1000fr, 1990 German team; 1994 US team.

No. 1015A, Pele, Brazil. No. 1015B, Gerd Muller, Germany.

1993, Oct. 9 Litho. *Perf. 13½*

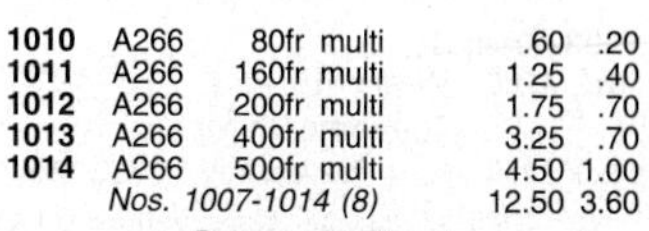

1007	A266	40fr multi	.35	.20
1008	A266	50fr multi	.35	.20
1009	A266	60fr multi	.45	.20
1010	A266	80fr multi	.60	.20
1011	A266	160fr multi	1.25	.40
1012	A266	200fr multi	1.75	.70
1013	A266	400fr multi	3.25	.70
1014	A266	500fr multi	4.50	1.00
		Nos. 1007-1014 (8)	12.50	3.60

Souvenir Sheet

1015	A266	1000fr multi	8.50	2.50

Litho. & Embossed

1015A	A266a	1500fr gold & multi	11.50	

Souvenir Sheet

1015B	A266a	1500fr gold & multi	11.50	

#1015 contains one 60x30mm stamp. #1007-1014 exist in souvenir sheets of one.

Nos. 1015A-1015B are airmail.

Miniature Sheets

Modern Olympic Games, Cent. (in 1996) — A267

No. 1016: a, Ancient olympian. b, Baron de Coubertin, 1896. c, Charles Bennett, 1900. d, Etienne Desmarteau, 1904. e, Harry Porter, 1908. f, Patrick MacDonald, 1912. g, No games, 1916. h, Frank Loomis, 1920. i, Albert White, 1924.

No. 1017: a, El Ouafi, 1928. b, Eddie Tolan, 1932. c, Jesse Owens, 1936. d, No games, 1940. e, No games, 1944. f, Tapio Rautavaara, 1948. g, Jean Boiteux, 1952. h, Petrus Kasterman, 1956. i, Sante Gaiardoni, 1960.

No. 1018: a, Anton Geesink, 1964. b, Bob Beamon, 1968. c, Mark Spitz, 1972. d, Nadia Comaneci, 1976. e, Aleksandre Dityatin, 1980. f, J.F. Lamour, 1984. g, Pierre Durand, 1988. h, Michael Jordan, 1992. i, Soccer player, 1996.

1993 Litho. *Perf. 13½*
Sheets of 9

1016	A267	90fr #a.-i.	6.50	3.25
1017	A267	100fr #a.-i.	7.25	3.75
1018	A267	160fr #a.-i.	11.50	5.75

Miniature Sheet

Dinosaurs — A268

Designs: No. 1019a, 25fr, Saltoposuchus. b, 25fr, Rhamphorhynchus. c, 25fr, Dimorphodon. d, 25fr, Archaeopteryx. e, 30fr, Compsognathus longipes. f, 30fr, Cryptocleidus oxoniensis. g, 30fr, Stegosaurus. h, 30fr, Cetiosaurus. i, 50fr, Brontosaurus. j, 50fr, Corythosaurus casuarius. k, 50fr, Styracosaurus. l, 50fr, Gorgosaurus. m, 500fr, Scolosaurus. n, 500fr, Trachodon. o, 500fr, Struthiomimus. p, 500fr, Tarbosaurus.

No. 1020, Tylosaur.

1993, Dec. 3

1019 A268 Sheet of 16, #a.-p. 19.00 19.00

Souvenir Sheet

1020 A268 1000fr multicolored 7.75 2.25

No. 1020 is airmail and contains one 51x60mm stamp.

Biodiversity A269

Various fauna surrounding: 100fr, Man planting tree. 130fr, Man with local fauna, vert.

1993, Oct. 20 Litho. *Perf. 13½*

1021 A269 100fr multicolored .90 .45

1022 A269 130fr multicolored 1.25 .70

M'Bali Dam — A270

1993, Jan. 14 Litho. *Perf. 13*

1023 A270 160fr shown 1.50 .30

1024 A270 200fr Women, men with fish 2.00 .40

Cooperation Council, 40th Anniv. — A271

1993, Jan. 26

1025 A271 240fr multicolored 2.25 .50

Intl. Conference on Nutrition, Rome — A272

1993, Apr. 1

1026 A272 90fr shown .70 .20

1027 A272 140fr Fresh foods 1.25 .30

University of Bangui A273

1993, Apr. 8

1028 A273 100fr multicolored .90 .25

Dated 1992.

Environmental Development A274

Designs: 160fr, Woman with vegetables, fruit. 240fr, Woman cooking food.

1993, Oct. 27 Litho. *Perf. 13½*

1029 A274 160fr multicolored 1.60 .80

1030 A274 240fr multicolored 2.25 .95

Miniature Sheets

1994 Winter Olympics, Lillehammer A275

Past Winter Olympic champions: 1031a, Th. Haug, Nordic combined skiing, Chamonix, 1924. b, J. Heaton, 1-man sled, St. Moritz, 1928. c, B. Ruud, ski jumping, Lake Placid, 1932. d, I. Ballangrud, speed skating, Garmisch-Partenkirchen, 1936. e, G. Fraser, women's slalom skiing, St. Moritz, 1948. f, German 4-man bobsled, Oslo, 1952. g, USSR hockey team, Cortina D'Ampezzo, 1956. h, J. Vuarnet, downhill skiing, Squaw Valley, 1960.

No. 1032a, M. Goitschel, giant slalom, Innsbruck, 1964. b, Jean-Claude Killy, slalom skiing, Grenoble, 1968. c, U. Wehling, Nordic combined, Sapporo, 1972. d, Rodnina & Zaitsev, pairs figure skating, Innsbruck, 1976. e, E. Heiden, speed skating, Lake Placid, 1980. f, K. Witt, figure skating, Sarajevo, 1984. g, J. Mueller, luge, Calgary, 1988. h, E. Grospiron, freestyle skiing, Albertville, 1992. i, Speed skiing, Lillehammer, 1994.

1994, Jan. 14 Litho. *Perf. 13½*

1031 A275 100fr Sheet of 8, #a.-h. + label 6.00 6.00

1032 A275 200fr Sheet of 9, #a.-i. 14.00 14.00

1994 Winter Olympics, Lillehammer — A276

Design: 1500fr, Women figure skaters.

1994 Litho. & Embossed *Perf. 13½*

1033 A276 1500fr gold & multi 10.50

#1033 is airmail & exists in a souvenir sheet of 1. Value $20.

Flowers, Vegetables, Fruit, & Mushrooms A277

Flowers: No. 1034a, 25fr, Ansellia africana. b, 60fr, Polystachia bella. c, 90fr, Aerangis rhodosticta. d, 500fr, Angraecum eburneum.

Vegetables: No. 1035a, 30r, Yams. b, 65fr, Manioc. c, 100fr, Corn. d, 400fr, Sweet potato.

Fruits: No. 1036a, 40fr, Orange. b, 70fr, Banana. c, 160fr, Mango. d, 300fr, Coffee.

Mushrooms: No. 1037a, 50fr, Termitomyces schimperi. b, 80fr, Sympodia arborescens. c, 200fr, Phlebopus sudanicus. d, 600fr, Leucocoprinus africanus.

1994, Jan. 21 Litho. *Perf. 13½*

1034 A277 Strip of 4, #a.-d. 5.00 2.50

1035 A277 Strip of 4, #a.-d. 4.50 2.25

1036 A277 Strip of 4, #a.-d. 4.25 2.00

1037 A277 Strip of 4, #a.-d. 7.00 3.50

e. Sheet of 16, #1034-1037 21.00 10.50

Catholic Church in Africa, Cent. — A278

Designs: 130fr, Monsignor Augouard, founder of mission, St. Paul of the Rapids. 160fr, Monsignor Grandin, Abbe Boganda, first sacred ordainment, 1938. 240fr, Father Louis Godart, House of Charity, Bangui.

1994, June 2 Litho. *Perf. 13½*

1038 A278 130fr multicolored .50 .25

1039 A278 160fr multicolored .65 .30

1040 A278 240fr multicolored .95 .45

Nos. 1038-1040 (3) 2.10 1.00

Relics from Early Civilizations, Landmarks — A279

Designs: 10fr, Cabin-shaped cinerary urn, Rome. 25fr, Face of the secret denunciation, Venice, vert. 30fr, Statue of the Tetrarchs, Venice, vert. 50fr, Little cube-shaped building, Palermo, vert. 65fr, Frieze, The Alhambra, Granada, vert. 90fr, Grand Chateau, Bellinzona. 100fr, Museum D'Orsay, Paris, vert. 130fr, Granary, Galicia. 140fr, Mural, by Diego Rivera, Mexico, vert. 160fr, Guacamaya mask, Mexico, vert. 200fr, Ivory mask, Western Africa, vert. 240fr, La Sagrada Familia, Barcelona, vert. 260fr, Casbah of Amerhidil. 300fr, Gold aureus of Sulla, Rome, 82 BC. 400fr, Chimborazo volcano.

1994, June 2 *Perf. 13*

1041-1055 A279 Set of 15 9.75 4.50

D-Day, 50th Anniv. — A280

Pegasus Bridge, June 6: No. 1056a, British troops crossing bridge, piper. b, Glider, British and German soldiers. c, German soldiers.

Operation COBRA, July 24: a, Tank, monument, soldiers. b, Bombers, soldiers, gun barrel. c, Tank, soldiers up close.

1994, Oct. 25 Litho. *Perf. 13½*

1056 A280 600fr Strip of 3, #a.-c. 7.50 3.75

1057 A280 600fr Strip of 3, #a.-c. 7.50 3.75

Nos. 1056b, 1057b are 30x46mm. Nos. 1056-1057 are continuous designs. See No. C359.

Anniversaries & Events — A281

Characters from "Star Wars:" a, Han Solo, Chewbaca. b, Darth Vader, Princess Leia, Luke Skywalker, R2D2, C3PO. c, Obi Wan Kenobi.

First manned moon landing, 25th anniv.: No. 1059a, 400fr, Buzz Aldrin. b, 500fr, Neil Armstrong, Apollo 11 liftoff. c, 600fr, Michael Collins.

No. 1060a, 400fr, Theodor von Karman. b, 500fr, Apollo 11 command module, Werner von Braun. c, 600fr, Hermes Rocket, Hermann Oberth.

1994, Oct. 25 Litho. *Perf. 13½*

1058 A281 600fr Strip of 3, #a.-c. 7.25 3.50

1059 A281 Strip of 3, #a.-c. 6.00 3.00

1060 A281 Strip of 3, #a.-c. 6.00 3.00

Motion Pictures, cent. (#1058).

Nos. 1058b, 1059b, 1060b are 60x51mm. Nos. 1058-1060 are continuous design and exist in a souvenir sheet of 1.

Natl. Assembly A282

1994, Dec. 8

1061 A282 65fr blue & multi .30 .20

1062 A282 430fr yel brn & multi 1.75 .90

Antoine de Saint-Exupery (1900-44), Aviator, Author — A283

1994, Dec 16

1063 A283 80fr Airplane .30 .20

1064 A283 235fr Portrait, vert. .95 .50

Inauguration of Pres. Ange-Felix Patasse, 1st Anniv. — A284

1994, Oct. 22

1065 A284 65fr blue & multi .25 .20

1066 A284 300fr yellow & multi 1.25 .60

1067 A284 385fr green & multi 1.50 .75

Nos. 1065-1067 (3) 3.00 1.55

A285

Intl. Olympic Committee, Cent. — A286

1994, Oct. 25

1068 A285 60fr bl grn & multi .25 .20
1069 A285 405fr yel grn & multi 1.60 .80

Souvenir Sheet

1070 A286 675fr Pierre de Coubertin 2.75 1.40

No. 1070 is airmail.

Nos. 1031-1032 Ovptd. with Medalist & Country Name in Gold

Overprints on No. 1031: No. 1071a, "F.B. LUNDBERG / NORVEGE." b, "G. HACKL / ALLEMAGNE." c, "B. DAEHLIE / NORVEGE." d, "J.O. KOSS / NORVEGE." e, "V. SCHNEIDER / SUISSE." f, "MEDAILLE D'OR / ALLEMAGNE." g, "MEDAILLE D'OR / SUEDE." h, "T. MOE / U.S.A."

Overprints on No. 1032: No. 1072a, "M. WASMEIER / ALLEMAGNE." b, "T. STANGASSINGER / AUTRICHE." c, "MEDAILLE D'OR / PAR EQUIPES / JAPON." d, "Y. GORDEYEVA / S. GRINKOV / RUSSIE." e, "D. JANSEN / U.S.A." f, "O. BAYUL / UKRAINE." g, "G. HACKL / ALLEMAGNE." h, "J.-L. BRASSARO / CANADA." i, "K. SEIZINGER / ALLEMAGNE."

1994

1071 A275 100fr Sheet of 8, #a.-h. + label 6.00 3.00
1072 A275 200fr Sheet of 9, #a.-i. 14.00 7.00

No. 988 Overprinted in Silver

MICHAEL SCHUMACHER
CHAMPION DU MONDE
FORMULE I 1994

1994, Dec. 28 Litho. *Perf. 13½*

1073 A262 160fr multicolored 9.00 4.50

No. 1073 also exists in souvenir sheet of 1.

1995 Boy Scout Jamboree, Holland — A287

Scout with mushrooms or butterflies: 300fr, Armillariela mellea. 385fr, Charaxes pleione. 405fr, Charaxes candiope. 430fr, Charaxes pollux. 500fr, Volvaria esculenta. 1000fr, Cortinarius.

2000fr, Euphaedra medon.

1995, May 24

1074-1079 A287 Set of 6 14.00 7.00
1077a Sheet, #1075-1077 5.75 2.75
1079a Sheet, #1074, #1078-1079 8.25 4.00

Souvenir Sheet

1080 A287 2000fr multicolored 8.75 4.25

Nos. 1074-1079 exist in souvenir sheets of 1. No. 1080 is airmail and contains one 39x57mm stamp.

1994 World Cup Soccer Championships, US — A288

Stadium: 300fr, Citrus Bowl, Orlando. 385fr, RFK Stadium, Washington, DC. 405fr, Soldier Field, Chicago. 430fr, Cotton Bowl, Dallas. 500fr, Giants Stadium, East Rutherford, NJ. 1000fr, Foxboro Stadium, Foxboro, MA.

2000fr, Rose Bowl, vert.

1995, July 14 Litho. *Perf. 13½*

1081-1086 A288 Set of 6 13.00 6.50

Souvenir Sheet

1087 A288 2000fr multicolored 11.50 5.75

No. 1087 is airmail.

African Development Bank, 30th Anniv. — A289

1995, June 29

1088 A289 70fr multicolored .30 .20
1089 A289 200fr multicolored .90 .45

Nos. 1088-1089 also exist in souvenir sheet of 1.

Fish A290

Designs, 25fr, 300fr, Auchenoglanis. 30fr, 50fr, Chrisicntys.

1995, June 22

1090-1093 A290 Set of 4 1.75 .90

Entertainers A291

Designs: 300fr, Freddie Mercury (Queen). 385fr, Jimi Hendrix. 430fr, Marilyn Monroe. 500fr, Michael Jackson. 600fr, Jerry Garcia (Grateful Dead). 800fr, Elvis Presley.

1500fr, Charlton Heston in "Planet of the Apes." 2000fr, Marilyn Monroe, diff.

1995, July 21

1094-1099 A291 Set of 6 13.00 6.50

Souvenir Sheets

1099B A291 1500fr multicolored 6.75 3.25
1100 A291 2000fr multicolored 8.75 4.25

Nos. 1094-1099 exist in souvenir sheets of 1. No. 1100 is airmail. No. 1099B contains one 51x60mm airmail stamp.

Volleyball, Cent. — A292

1995, Oct. 3 Litho. *Perf. 13½*

1101 A292 300fr multicolored 1.25 .65

No. 1101 exists in a souvenir sheet of 1.

Sports Figures A293

400fr, Andre Agassi, tennis. 500fr, Boris Becker, tennis. 700fr, Ayrton Senna (1960-94) race car driver. 800fr, Michael Schumacher, F-1 world driving champion.

2000fr, Michael Schumacher, diff.

1996, June 20 Litho. *Perf. 13½*

1102-1105 A293 Set of 4 10.75 5.50

Souvenir Sheet

1106 A293 2000fr multicolored 9.00 4.50

#1102-1105 exist in souvenir sheets of 1.

1996 Summer Olympic Games, Atlanta A294

Olympic athletes, sites in Atlanta: 170fr, Atlanta-Fulton County Stadium. 300fr, Martin Luther King Memorial. 350fr, Alexander H. Stephens Monument. 600fr, High Museum of Art.

2000fr, Pierre de Coubertin, runner.

1996, June 20

1107-1110 A294 Set of 4 6.50 3.25

Souvenir Sheet

1110A A294 2000fr multicolored 7.50 3.75

No. 1110A contains one 42x51mm stamp.

UN, 50th Anniv. (in 1995) A295

1996, July 15 *Perf. 14*

1111 A295 5fr "50," emblem, vert. .20 .20
1112 A295 430fr shown 1.75 .90

#1111-1112 exist in souvenir sheets of 1.

1996 Summer Olympic Games, Atlanta A296

1900 Summer Olympics, Paris: 235fr, Alvin Kraenzlein, vert. 300fr, Paris Stadium. 385fr, Irving Baxter. 430fr, British soccer team.

Past Olympic medalists: No. 1117a, Miruts Yifter, 5,000-meters, 1980. b, Germany, team dressage, 1976. c, Bruce Jenner, decathlon, 1976. d, Mark Gorski, 1000-meter match sprint, 1984. e, Randy Williams, long jump, 1972. f, Shinodu Sekine, judo, 1972. g, Kiyomi Kato, wrestling, 1972. h, Mitsuo Tsukahama, gymnastics, 1976. i, Hartwig Steenken, Germany, 1972.

No. 1118, Betty Cuthbert, 100-meters, 1956. No. 1119, Gerhard Stock, javelin, 1936.

1996, July 19

1113-1116 A296 Set of 4 5.50 2.75
1117 A296 200fr Sheet of 9, #a.-i. 7.25 3.50

Souvenir Sheets

1118-1119 A296 1000fr each 4.00 2.00

Olymphilex '96 (#1113-1116, 1118-1119).

Francophonie, 25th Anniv. (in 1995) — A297

300fr, "25 ANS" surrounded by "1970-1995."

1996, July 22

1120 A297 235fr multicolored .95 .50
1121 A297 300fr multicolored 1.25 .60

#1120-1121 exist in souvenir sheets of 1.

FAO, 50th Anniv. (in 1995) A298

Designs: 10fr, Fish being lifted in net, vert. 385fr, Boy drinking water.

1996

1122 A298 10fr multicolored .20 .20
1123 A298 385fr multicolored 1.50 .75

#1122-1123 exist in souvenir sheets of 1.

Queen Elizabeth II, 70th Birthday A299

a, Formal portrait. b, In blue suit. c, In red hat.

1000fr, Balmoral Castle.

1996, July 24 *Perf. 13½x14*

1124 A299 300fr Strip of 3, #a.-c. 3.50 1.75

Souvenir Sheet

1125 A299 1000fr multicolored 4.00 2.00

Nos. 1124 was issued in sheets of 9 stamps.

Pets — A300

1996 Litho. *Perf. 13½*

1126 A300 250fr Dog 1.10 .60
1127 A300 600fr Cat 2.75 1.40

#1126-1127 exist in souvenir sheets of 1.

1998 World Cup Soccer Championships, France — A301

Winning country, year, player: No. 1128a, Uruguay 1930, Pedro Cea (Argentina), Italy 1934. b, Italy 1938, Piola (Italy), Uruguay 1950. c, Germany 1954, Brazil 1958, Walter, (Germany). d, Amarillo, (Brazil), Brazil 1962, England 1966.

No. 1129: a, Brazil 1970, Pele (Brazil), Germany 1974. b, Kempes (Argentina), Argentina 1978, Italy 1982. c, Argentina 1986, Mattaus (Germany), Germany 1990. d, Platini (France), Brazil 1994.

1996 Litho. *Perf. 13½*
Sheets of 4

1128 A301 375fr #a.-d. 6.50 3.25
1129 A301 425fr #a.-d. 7.50 3.75

Dinosaur Eggs — A302

Denomination at: a, LR. b, LL.

1996, Apr. 28

1130 A302 140fr Pair, #a.-b. 1.25 .65
c. Souv. Sheet, #1130a-1130b 1.25 .65

CHINA '96 (#1130c).

Scouting A303

Raptors, butterflies, mushrooms: 175fr, Buzzard. 200fr, H. misippus. 300fr, Lepiota aspera. 350fr, Raptor with feathers ruffled. 450fr, Amanita caesarea. 500fr, Morpho portis-nymphalidae.

1996 Litho. *Perf. 13½*

1131-1136 A303 Set of 6 9.00 4.50

Nos. 1132-1133, 1135 exist in souvenir sheets of 1.

Horses A304

Great Nebula, Andromeda A305

No. 1137: a, Appaloosa. b, Arabian. c, Quarter horse. d, Belgian. e, Pure blood English. f, Mustang. g, Haflinger. h, Welsh pony.

No. 1138: a, Pinto. b, Palomino. c, Welara. d, Morgan. e, Standard American. f, Norwegian fjord. g, Shetland. h, Shire.

1000fr, Saddlebred.

1996, Nov. 20 *Perf. 14*
Sheets of 8

1137-1138 A304 235fr #a.-h., ea 7.50 3.75

Souvenir Sheet

1139 A304 1000fr multicolored 4.00 2.00

1996, Nov. 22

Designs: b, Halley's Comet. c, Jupiter. d, Saturn. e, Moon. f, Mars.

1140 A305 300fr Sheet of 6, #a.-f. 7.25 3.50

Wildlife — A306

Flowers: a, Bomax costatum. b, Clappertonia flcifolia. c, Canarina abyssinica. d, Kigelia africana. e, Adenium obesum. f, Oncoba spinosa. g, Orinum ornatum. h, Gloriosa simplex. i, Strophanthus gratus.

Bird: 1500fr, Sagittarius serpentarius.

1997, Feb. 6 Litho. *Perf. 14*

1141 A306 205fr Sheet of 9, #a.-i. 7.50 3.75

Souvenir Sheet

1142 A306 1500fr multicolored 6.00 3.00

Intl. Express Mail Service A307

300fr, Globe, international express mail routes. 405fr, Emblem of hand holding letter.

1996 Litho. *Perf. 13½*

1143 A307 300fr multicolored 1.25 .65
1144 A307 405fr multicolored 1.75 .90

No. 1144 exists in a souvenir sheet of 1.

Human Rights Advocates A308

Designs: a, Dalai Lama. b, Martin Luther King. c, John F. Kennedy. d, Nelson Mandela. e, Mother Teresa. f, Mahatma Gandhi.

1996

1145 A308 175fr Sheet of 6, #a.-f. + 2 labels 4.50 2.25

Red Cross and Red Crescent Societies — A309

Designs: a, Doctor with patient. b, Man sifting grain. c, Using stethoscope on patient. d, Wounded man. e, Bandaging patient. f, Aiding infant.

1996

1146 A309 250fr Sheet of 6, #a.-f. + 2 labels 6.50 3.25

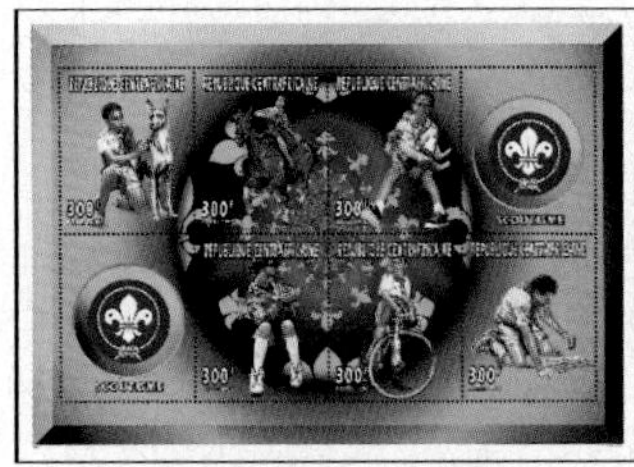
Boy Scouts — A310

Boy scout: a, With dog. b, Riding horse. c, Holding cat. d, Holding butterfly. e, On bicycle. f, Playing game.

Butterfly: 2000fr, Saturnidae, horiz.

1996 Litho. *Perf. 13½*

1147 A310 300fr Sheet of 6, #a.-f. + 2 labels 8.00 4.00

Souvenir Sheet

1148 A310 2000fr multicolored 9.00 4.50

No. 1148 contains one 42x36mm stamp.

Lions Intl., Rotary Intl. — A311

Designs: a, Child drinking from cup. b, Child carrying sack. c, Girl holding sheaves of grain. d, Man breaking bread. e, Woman cooking over fire. f, Boy, corn stalk.

1996

1149 A311 500fr Sheet of 6, #a.-f. + 2 labels 13.00 6.50

Flora and Fauna A312

15fr, Cucumis sativus, vert. 20fr, Phyllochistis citrella. 40fr, Cetonia aurata. 65fr, Nomadacris septemfasciata. 100fr, Crocodilus vulgaris. 140fr, Athyrium filix, vert. 405fr, Rhopalo ceres.

1996

1150-1156 A312 Set of 7 3.50 1.75

#1151, 1156 exist in sourvenir sheets of 1.

UN, UNICEF, 50th Anniv. — A313

Designs: a, Futuristic space vehicle. b, MIR space station. c, US space shuttle, space station. d, Woman carrying food. e, Child receiving vaccination. f, Baby being weighed.

1996

1157 A313 350fr Sheet of 6, #a.-f. + 2 labels 9.00 4.50

Elizabeth Taylor, Actress — A314

Princess Diana — A315

Various portraits.

1997, Apr. 10 Litho. *Perf. 14*
Sheets of 6

1158 A314 300fr #a.-f. 7.25 3.50
1159 A315 300fr #a.-f. 7.25 3.50

Souvenir Sheets

1160 A314 1500fr multicolored 6.00 3.00
1161 A315 1500fr multicolored 6.00 3.00

For overprints see Nos. 1181-1182.

UNESCO, 50th Anniv. A316

No. 1162: a, Fortress ruins, Ethiopia. b, Victoria Falls, Zambia. c, River during dry season, Zimbabwe. d, Nature Reserve, Niger. e, Pelican, Natl. Park, Mauritania. f, Native huts in village, Niokolo-Kobo Natl. Park, Senegal. g, M'Zab Valley, Algeria. h, Mosque, Morocco.

No. 1163: a, c, Ruins of Roman Amphitheater, France. b, Split, Croatia. d, e, Quedlinberg, Germany. f, h, Tower of London, England. g, Olympic Natl. Park, US.

No. 1164: a, Horyu-Ji, Japan. b, Waterfalls, Amazon River, Los Katios Natl. Park, Colombia. c, Abu Mena Church, Egypt. d, Boat on river, Fortress of Suomenlinna, Finland. e, Venice, Italy. f, Mural, Potala Palace, Lhasa, Tibet, China. g, Cathedral, town of Olinda, Brazil. h, Monastery, Mystras, Greece.

No. 1165, Jiuzhaigou Valley, China. No. 1166, Interior, Pilgrimage Church of Wies, Germany. No. 1167, Ruins of Fountains Abbey, Studley Park, England.

1997, Apr. 30 *Perf. 13½x14*
Sheets of 8 + Label

1162-1164 A316 235fr #a.-h., ea 7.50 3.75

Souvenir Sheets

1165-1167 A316 1000fr each 4.00 2.00

UNICEF, 50th Anniv. — A317

No. 1168: a, 200fr, UN headquarters building. b, 250fr, Baby. c, 500fr, Danny Kaye seated inside vehicle.
1500fr, Child.

1997, Apr. 30 *Perf. 14*
1168 A317 Sheet of 3, #a.-c. 3.75 1.90

Souvenir Sheet

1169 A317 1500fr multicolored 6.00 3.00

US Pres. Bill Clinton and His Cat, "Socks" — A318

Designs: a, b, c, e, g, h, i, Socks in various poses. d, f, Clinton, Socks.

1996
1170 A318 200fr Sheet of 9, #a.-i. 7.25 3.50

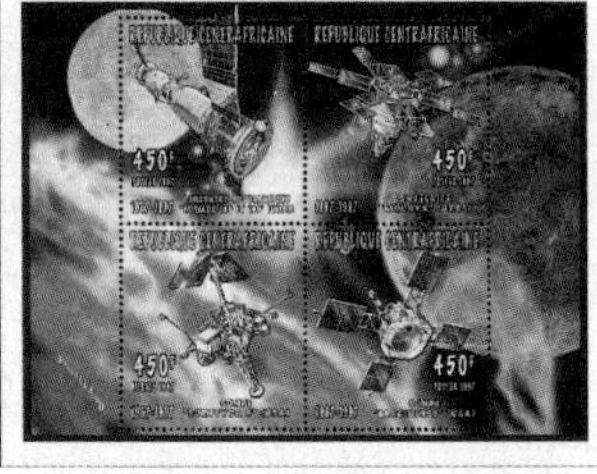
Conquest of Space — A319

Events in 1977: No. 1171: a, Voyager 1, US. b, Space Shuttle Enterprise, US. c, Meteosat 1, US. d, Salyut 6 Space Station, USSR.
Events in 1982: No. 1172: a, Salyut 7 Space Station, USSR. b, Landsat 4 Satellite, US. c, Venera 13, USSR. d, IRAS Infrared Telescope, US.
Events of 1967: No. 1173: a, Cosmos 186 & 188. b, Molnya satellite. c, Surveyor 3. d, Mariner 5.
Events in 1972: No. 1174: a, Copernicus probe, US. b, Pioneer 10, US. c, Apollo 16, US. d, Apollo 17, John F. Kennedy.
Events of 1962: No. 1175: a, Mariner 2, US. b, OSO 1, US. c, John Glenn. d, Mars 1, USSR.
Events of 1957: No. 1176: a, Vostok 1, Yuri Gagarin, USSR. b, Sputnik 2, USSR. c, Sputnik 1, USSR. d, Bell X15, US.
2000fr, Voyager, Pioneer 10, Apollo 11, US.

1997 *Perf. 13½*

Sheets of 4

1171 A319 250fr #a.-d. 4.00 2.00
1172 A319 350fr #a.-d. 5.75 3.00
1173 A319 450fr #a.-d. 7.25 3.75
1174 A319 500fr #a.-d. 8.00 4.00
1175 A319 600fr #a.-d. 9.75 5.00
1176 A319 800fr #a.-d. 13.00 6.50

Souvenir Sheet

1177 A319 2000fr multicolored 8.00 4.00

No. 1177 contains one 60x30mm stamp.
No. 1173 exists imperf.

Marilyn Monroe (1926-62) — A320

Various portraits.

1997
1178 A320 375fr Sheet of 9, #a.-i. 12.75 6.50

John F. Kennedy (1917-63) — A321

Various portraits.

1997
1179 A321 300fr Sheet of 9, #a.-i. 10.00 5.00

Bruce Lee (1940-73), Actor — A322

Various portraits.

1997 **Litho.** *Perf. 13½*
1180 A322 200fr Sheet of 9, #a.-i. 6.75 3.25

Nos. 1159, 1161 Ovptd. "In Memoriam"

1997 *Perf. 14*
1181 A315 300fr Sheet of 6, #a.-f. 7.25 3.50

Souvenir Sheet

1182 A315 1500fr multicolored 6.00 3.00

Nos. 1181-1182 each contain "Diana, Princess of Wales (1961-1997) IN MEMORIAM" in sheet margin and on each stamp in No. 1181.

Dogs & Cats — A323

Dogs: No. 1183: a, Chinese crested. b, King Charles spaniel. c, Dachshund. d, Borzoi. e, Chow chow. f, Welsh springer. g, Rottweiler. h, Keeshond.
Cats: No. 1184: a, Birman. b, Black and white Persian. c, Siamese kitten. d, Red and black. e, American curl. f, Cornish rex. g, Silver shaded. h, White-footed cat.
1500fr, Pekingese. 2000fr, Somali.

1997 **Litho.** *Perf. 13½*

Sheets of 8

1183 A323 175fr #a.-h. 4.00 2.00
1184 A323 250fr #a.-h. 7.50 3.75

Souvenir Sheets

1185 A323 1500fr multicolored 5.50 2.75
1186 A323 2000fr multicolored 7.50 3.75

Nos. 1185-1186 each contain one 42x51mm stamp.

Return of Hong Kong to China — A324

No. 1187: a, Tung Chee-Hwa, taking down British flag. b, Raising Chinese flag, Chris Patten, British flag. c, Jiang Zemin, skyline at night. d, City lights, Queen Elizabeth II.
600fr, Tung Chee-Hwa.

1997
1187 A324 175fr Sheet of 4, #a.-d. 2.60 1.25

Souvenir Sheet

1188 A324 600fr multicolored 2.40 1.25

No. 1188 contains one 38x42mm stamp.

Paintings by Hiroshige (1797-1858) A325

No. 1189: a, Minami-Shinagawa and Samezu Coast. b, Plum Garden, Kamata. c, The Kawaguchi Ferry and Zenkoji Temple. d, Armor-Hanging Pine, Hakkeizaka. e, Robe-Hanging Pine, Senzoku Pond. f, Benten Shrine, Inokashira Pond.
No. 1190: a, A Little Brown Owl on a Pine Branch with a Crescent Moon Behind. b, Sparrows and Camellia in snow. c, Three Wild Geese Flying Downward across the Moon. d, A Blue Bird on a Yellow-flowered Hibiscus. e, Five Swallows in flight.
No. 1191: a, Sparrows and Wild Rose. b, Peonies. c, Morning Glory and Cricket. d, Blossoming Plum Tree. e, Kingfisher above a Yellow-flowered Water Plant.
No. 1192, Haneda Ferry and Benten Shrine. No. 1193, A Bird Clinging to a Tendril of Wisteria. No. 1194, Butterfly and Peony.

1998, Feb. 20 **Litho.** *Perf. 14*

Sheets of 6 & 5

1189 A325 300fr #a.-f. 6.25 3.00
1190 A325 430fr #a.-e. 7.50 3.75
1191 A325 500fr #a.-e. 8.50 4.25

Souvenir Sheets

1192-1194 A325 1500fr each 5.00 2.50

Nos. 1190-1191 each contain five 26x72mm stamps. Nos. 1192-1194 each contain one 26x72mm stamp.

Chinese Lunar New Year A326

Animals representing lunar year: a, Rat. b, Ox. c, Tiger. d, Hare. e, Dragon. f, Snake. g, Horse. h, Sheep. i, Monkey. j, Rooster. k, Dog. l, Boar.
1000fr, Tiger, diff.

1998 **Litho. & Typo.** *Perf. 14*
1195 A326 150fr Sheet of 12, #a.-l. 7.25 3.75

Souvenir Sheet

1196 A326 1000fr gold & multi 3.50 1.75

Intl. Scouting, 90th Anniv. A327

Insects: No. 1196A: b, Apis mellifica. c, Lucanus cervus. d, Oryctes nasicornis. e, Pseudacraea boisduvalii. f, Helictopleurus quadripunctatus, euchroea spininasuta. g, Bombus terrestris. h, Charaxes smaragdalis. i, Euchroea coelestis, mantis religiosa.
Wildlife — No. 1197: a, Coracias caudata, Otocyon megalotis. b, Gnu. c, Milvus aegyptus, pelecanus onocrotalus. d, Panthera leo. e, Loxondonta africana. f, Buffalo. g, Hippopotamus amphibius. h, Acinonyx jubatus.
Raptors — No. 1198: a, Buteo rufinus. b, Circus aeruginosus. c, Aquila verreauxii. d, Circaetus gallicus. e, Terathopius ecaudatus. f, Haliaeetus vocifer. g, Milvus milvus. h, Accipiter badius.

1997(?) **Litho.** *Perf. 13*

Sheets of 8

1196A A327 200fr #b.-i. 5.75 2.75
1197 A327 300fr #a.-h. 8.50 4.25
1198 A327 350fr #a.-h. 10.00 5.00

1998 World Cup Soccer Championships, France — A328

Player, country, vert: No. 1199, Moore, England. No. 1200, Rahn, Germany. No. 1201, Paulao, Angola. No. 1202, Shearer, England.
No. 1203: a, Seaman, England. b, Schillaci, Italy. c, Romario, Brazil. d, McCoist, Scotland. e, Makanaky, Angola. f, Moore, England. g, Muller, Germany. h, Schmeichel, Denmark.
No. 1204, Moore, England, diff. No. 1205, Pele, Brazil.

1998, June 2 *Perf. 13½x14, 14x13½*
1199-1202 A328 300fr Set of 4 4.00 2.00
1203 A328 205fr Sheet of 8 + label 5.50 5.50

Souvenir Sheets

1204-1205 A328 1500fr each 5.00 5.00

Diana, Princess of Wales (1961-97)
A329

Various portraits.

1998 ***Perf. 13½***

Sheets of 9

1206	A329	200fr #a.-i.	6.50	3.25
1207	A329	250fr #a.-i.	8.00	4.00

Diana, Princess of Wales (1961-97) — A330

Diana wearing gowns in one of four seasons: No. 1208, White gown, spring. No. 1209, Blue gown, summer. No. 1210, Bridal gown, fall. No. 1211, High-collared white gown, winter.

1998 **Litho.** ***Perf. 13½***

Souvenir Sheets

1208	A330	1500fr multicolored	5.25	2.50
1209	A330	1500fr multicolored	5.25	2.50
1210	A330	2000fr multicolored	7.25	3.50
1211	A330	2000fr multicolored	7.25	3.50

Nos. 1208-1211 each contain one 50x60mm stamp.

Jacqueline Kennedy Onassis (1929-94)
A331

Various portraits.

1997 **Litho.** ***Perf. 13½***

1212	A331	250fr Sheet of 9, #a.-i.	8.00	4.00

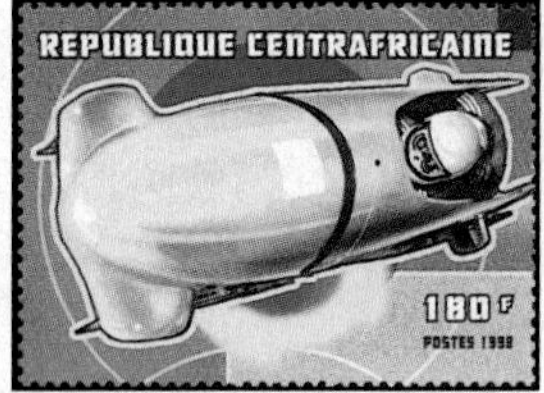

1998 Winter Olympic Games, Nagano — A332

Mirror images of vignette with different backgrounds, denomination at — No. 1213: a, Bobsled, LR. b, Slalom skier, CL. c, Ski jumper, CL. d, Bobsled, LL. e, Slalom skier, CR. f, Ski jumper, CR.

No. 1214: a, Ice hockey, LR. b, Cross-country skier, CR. c, Speed skater, LR. d, Ice hockey, LL. e, Cross-country skier, CL. f, Speed skater, LL.

No. 1215: a, Snow boarding, UR. b, Downhill skier, CR. c, Pairs figure skating, CR. d, Snow boarding, UL. e, Downhill skier, CL. f, Pairs figure skating, CL.

No. 1216, Cross-country, freestyle skiers.

1998

Sheets of 6

1213	A332	180fr #a.-f.	3.75	1.75
1214	A332	300fr #a.-f.	6.25	3.00
1215	A332	350fr #a.-f.	7.50	3.75

Souvenir Sheet

1216	A332	2000fr multicolored	7.00	3.50

Sports
A333

Cyclists — No. 1217: a, Woman wearing helmet. b, Woman in pink, white & black outfit. c, Man in black & white outfit. d, Man in yellow & black outfit.

Female tennis players — No. 1218: a, Holding racket above head. b, Wearing black head band. c, Wearing white head band. d, Wearing dreadlocks.

Male tennis players — No. 1219: a, Holding racket with his right hand. b, In blue shirt, shorts. c, Holding racket behind head. d, Wearing cap backwards.

Golfers — No. 1220: a, Completing swing. b, Hitting ball in sand trap. c, In orange knickers, argyle socks. d, Lining up putt.

1998 **Litho.** ***Perf. 13½***

Sheets of 4

1217	A333	350fr #a.-d.	4.75	2.25
1218	A333	375fr #a.-d.	5.25	2.50
1219	A333	450fr #a.-d.	6.50	3.25
1220	A333	500fr #a.-d.	7.25	3.50

Mickey Mouse, 70th Birthday
A334

Scenes from various Disney films drawn by Floyd Gottfredson.

No. 1221: a, 10/78. b, 11/78. c, 3/79. d, 7/79. e, 9/79.

No. 1222: a, 10/79. b, 2/80. c, 4/80. d, 6/80. e, 7/80.

No. 1223: a, 11/80. b, 3/81. c, 6/81. d, 9/81. e, 3/82.

No. 1224: a, 5/82. b, 7/82. c, 10/82. d, 3/83. e, 5/83.

No. 1225, Mickey with camera, flashlight. No. 1226, Mickey with pearl in box. No. 1227, Mickey and magic lamp. No. 1228, Floyd Gottfredson.

Perf. 13½x14, 14x13½

1999, Feb. 10 **Litho.**

Sheets of 5 + Label

1221	A334	280fr #a.-e.	4.75	2.25
1222	A334	365fr #a.-e.	6.25	3.00
1223	A334	390fr #a.-e.	6.75	3.25
1224	A334	440fr #a.-e.	7.50	3.75

Souvenir Sheets

1225-1226	A334	1500fr each	5.00	2.50
1227-1228	A334	2000fr each	6.75	3.25

Birds of Africa — A335

World Wildlife Fund — A336

#1229, Pandion haliaetus. #1230, Chaetops frenatus. #1231, Tachymarptis melba. #1232, Ceratogymna bucinator. #1233, Laniarius atrococcineus. #1234, Coturnix coturnix.

No. 1235: a, Lamprotornis superbus. b, Agapornis personatus. c, Coracias spatulata. d, Euplectes jacksoni. e, Nectarinia violacea. f, Emberiza schoeniclus. g, Pica pica. h, Tauraco erythrolophus. i, Sitta europaea.

No. 1236: a, Merops apiaster. b, Coracias garrulus. c, Cuculus canorus. d, Hirundo rustica. e, Motacilla flava. f, Ardea cinerea. g, Falco tinnunculus. h, Tyto alba. i, Charadrius hiaticula.

1500fr, Eremophila alpestris. 2000fr, Delichon urbica.

1999, Mar. 10 **Litho.** ***Perf. 14***

1229-1234	A335	500fr Set of 6	10.00	5.00

Sheets of 9

1235	A335	280fr #a.-i.	8.50	4.25
1236	A335	490fr #a.-i.	15.00	7.50

Souvenir Sheets

1237	A335	1500fr multicolored	5.00	2.50
1238	A335	2000fr multicolored	7.00	3.50

1999

Balaeniceps rex: a, Eating fish. b, Up close. c, Standing. d, One in flight, one up close.

1239	A336	200fr Strip of 4, #a.-d.	2.75	1.25

No. 1239 was issued in sheets of 16 stamps.

Trains
A337

No. 1240: a, 40fr, 2-4-0 Steam locomotive. b, 50fr, German Mallat. c, 60fr, Shunting locomotive. d, 260fr, Rhodesian 14A 2-6-2+2-6-2 Garrat. e, 280fr, Steam train. f, 390fr, Engine No. 7, 0-6-0 Baldwin, 1920. g, 440fr, Amtrak passenger train. h, 460fr, German TEE diesel. i, 490fr, "Sir Nigel Gresley."

No. 1241: a, 40fr, Steam train. b, 50fr, 4-4-0, LNWR, 1897. c, 60fr, 2-4-0 locomotive, Midland. d, 260fr, Class XC. e, 280fr, 2-6-0T Sernada and Aveiro, 1910. f, 390fr, East Daggafontein Mines train, Great Britain. g, 440fr, Union Pacific. h, 460fr, Engine No. 6, Baldwin. i, 490fr, 4-4-2 aerodynamic train, Belgium, 1939.

No. 1242, Fairlie, Snake and Auckland, New Zealand, 1874. No. 1243, Steam train arriving at the London-Brighton Depot.

1999, Mar. 11

Sheets of 9

1240-1241	A337	#a.-i., each	8.50	4.25

Souvenir Sheets

1242-1243	A337	2000fr each	6.75	3.25

Prehistoric Animals
A338

No. 1244: a, Archaeopteryx. b, Stegosaurus. c, Placerias. d, Rutiodon. e, Tyrannosaurus rex. f, Lystrosaurus.

No. 1245: a, Spinosaurus. b, Cynognathus. c, Kuehneosaurus. c, Compsognathus. d, Compsognathus. e, Triceratops. f, Euoplocephalus.

2000fr, Desmatosuchus.

1998 **Litho.** ***Perf. 13½***

Sheets of 6

1244	A338	250fr #a.-f.	5.75	2.75
1245	A338	300fr #a.-f.	6.75	3.25

Souvenir Sheet

1246	A338	2000fr multicolored	7.50	3.75

No. 1246 contains one 51x36mm stamp.

Transportation
A339

Antique automobiles — No. 1247: a, 1899 Fiat. b, First Chevrolet. c, Serpolet steam carriage. d, 130HP Fiat.

Cyclists — No. 1248: a, Swiss rider. b, US rider. c, Miguel Indurain (riding to right). d, Jan. Ullrich (riding to left).

Sports cars — No. 1249: a, Porsche Boxster. b, Corvette. c, Jaguar S-type. d, Maserati 3200 GT.

High-speed trains — No. 1250: a, TGV Atlantique. b, Shin Kansen. c, ETR X-500. d, Advanced passenger train.

Trains — No. 1251: a, Cornish Riviera Express. b, Lancashire and Yorkshire Railway. c, Type 230. d, Pacific Mallard.

Fire trucks: No. 1252: a, 1916 Seagrave. b, 1927 Ahrens-Fox Model JS-2. c, 1992 Diesel. d, 1958 Mack Bulldog, Type B-95.

Space flight of John Glenn — No. 1253: a, Portrait in business suit. b, In Project Mercury spacesuit. c, In shuttle launch suit, 1998. d, Orbiting earth, Space Shuttle.

Supersonic airplanes — No. 1254: a, Boeing 2707. b, Transatmospheric prototype. c, Tupolev 144. d, Project of European Supersonic ESRP.

1998

Sheets of 4

1247	A339	300fr #a.-d.	4.50	2.25
1248	A339	350fr #a.-d.	5.25	2.50
1249	A339	400fr #a.-d.	6.25	3.00
1250	A339	450fr #a.-d.	6.75	3.25
1251	A339	500fr #a.-d.	7.50	3.75
1252	A339	600fr #a.-d.	9.00	4.50
1253	A339	800fr #a.-d.	12.00	6.00
1254	A339	1000fr #a.-d.	15.00	7.50

Scouting
A340

Scouts with flowers — No. 1255: a, Vanilla planifolia. b, Flamboyant. c, Angraecum sesquipedale.

Scouts with butterflies or bird — No. 1256: a, Hesperie a bande. b, Philepitte souimanga. c, Dryope.

Scouts with dogs, cats, and their young — No. 1257: a, Basenji. b, Egyptian mau cat. c, White dog.

Scouts with minerals — No. 1258: a, Tourmaline. b, Jasper. c, Madgascar corundum.

Scouts administrering Red Cross aid — No. 1259: a, Girl Scout wiping child's tears. b, Scout bandaging child. c, Scout kneeling to help child.

Scouts in leisure activities — No. 1260: a, Playing table tennis. b, Playing chess. c, Riding horse.

1998 **Litho.** ***Perf. 13½***

Sheets of 3

1255	A340	400fr #a.-c.	4.50	2.25
1256	A340	475fr #a.-c.	5.25	2.50
1257	A340	500fr #a.-c.	5.75	2.75
1258	A340	600fr #a.-c.	6.75	3.25
1259	A340	700fr #a.-c.	7.75	3.75
1260	A340	800fr #a.-c.	9.00	4.50

Minerals
A341

No. 1261: a, Hematite (red). b, Challophyllite. c, Fer natif. d, Sylvanite. e. Hematite (specularite). f, Spodumene.

No. 1262: a, Amber. b, Opal. c, Struvite. d, Rhodochrosite. e, Polybasite. f, Silver.

1998 Litho. *Perf. 13½*

Sheets of 6

1261 A341 400fr #a.-f. 9.00 4.50
1262 A341 600fr #a.-f. 13.50 6.75

A number has been reserved for a souvenir sheet to go with this set.

Mushrooms A342

40fr, Jelly babies. 50fr, Herald of winter. 65fr, Dentate elf cup. 280fr, Pink wax cap. 345fr, Tripe fungus. 465fr, Funnel tooth. 485fr, Common white saddle. 600fr, False morel.

No. 1272: a, Parrot wax cap. b, Orange naval cap. c, Amethyst deceiver. d, Plums and custard. e, Blue legs. f, Tawny funnel cap. g, Goblet. h, Spindle-shank. i, Buttery tough shank.

No. 1273: a, Fetid mummy cap. b, Stainer. c, Lilac bonnet. d, Firm-fleshed brittle gill. e, Fly agaric. f, Arched bonnet. g, King bolete. h, Orange birch bolete. i, Dog stinkhorn.

1500fr, Hedgehog puffball. 2000fr, Striated earth star.

1999, June 11 Litho. *Perf. 14*

1264-1271 A342 Set of 8 8.75 4.25

Sheets of 9

1272 A342 390fr #a.-i. 13.00 6.50
1273 A342 440fr #a.-i. 13.50 6.75

Souvenir Sheets

1274 A342 1500fr multicolored 5.25 2.50
1275 A342 2000fr multicolored 7.50 3.75

Birds A343

No. 1276: a, Psittacula himalayama. b, Anodorhynchus hyacinthinus. c, Trichoglossus haematodus. d, Xipholena punicea. e, Chloebia gouldiae. f, Ramphastos tucanus.

No. 1277: a, Falco sparverius. b, Polyborus plancus. c, Terathopius ecaudatus. d, Tyto alba. e, Claucidium passerinum. f, Speotyto cunicularia.

1999 Litho. *Perf. 13½*

Sheets of 6

1276 A343 350fr #a.-f. 7.50 3.75
1277 A343 500fr #a.-f. 10.50 5.25

Dogs, Cats, & Horses A344

Designs: 60fr, Doberman, vert. 280fr, Domestic cat, vert. No. 1280, 390fr, Korat, vert. No. 1281, 390fr, Hanoverian, vert. 440fr, Ardennais. 490fr, Lhasa apso.

Dogs — No. 1284: a, Alaskan malamute. b, Musterlander. c, German shepherd. d, Borzoi. e, Afghan hound. f, Irish terrier. g, Komondor. h, Finnish spitz.

Cats — No. 1285: a, American bobtail. b, American curl. c, Singapura. d, Burmese. e, Tortoise shell. f, Scottish fold. g, British shorthair blue. h, Turkish van.

Horses — No. 1286: a, Shire. b, Clydesdale. c, Arabian. d, Soviet work horse. e, Finnish work horse. f, Percheron. g, Draco. h, North Swedish.

No. 1287, Beagle. No. 1288, Havana. No. 1289, Hanoverian.

1999, July 9 Litho. *Perf. 14*

1278-1283 A344 Set of 6 7.00 3.50

Sheets of 8

1284 A344 465fr #a.-h. 13.00 6.50
1285 A344 485fr #a.-h. 13.50 6.75
1286 A344 515fr #a.-h. 14.00 7.00

Souvenir Sheets

1287-1289 A344 2000fr each 9.50 3.50

Nos. 1287-1289 each contain one 44x56mm stamp.

Butterflies A345

Designs: 40fr, Heliconius melpomene. 65fr, Large oak blue. 280fr, Danaus chrysippus. 345fr, Aricia agestis. 485fr, Danis danis. 600fr, Plebejus argus.

No. 1296: a, Delias mysis. b, Ornithoptera priamus. c, Phoebis philea. d, Heliconius doris. e, Thecla coronata f, Lycaena dispar. g, Bematistes aganise. h, Pereute leucodrosime.

No. 1297: a, Colotis danae. b, Eueides isabella. c, Papilio cresphontes. d, Mimacraea marshalli. e, Parathyma nefte. f, Appias nero. g, Uraneis ucubis. h, Eurema brigitta.

No. 1298: a, Heliconius melpomene, diff. b, Mylothris chloris. c, Catopsilia florella. d, Hebomoia glaucippe. e, Palla ussheri. f, Papilio glaucus. g, Colias erytheme. h, Euploea corus.

No. 1299, Unnamed. No. 1300, Papilio, glaucus, vert.

1999, Dec. Litho. *Perf. 14*

1290-1295 A345 Set of 6 6.50 3.25

Sheets of 8

1296 A345 280fr #a.-h. 7.75 4.00
1297 A345 390fr #a.-h. 11.00 5.50
1298 A345 465fr #a.-h. 13.00 6.50

Souvenir Sheets

1299-1300 A345 1500fr each 5.25 2.50

Trains A346

Designs: No. 1301, 280fr, Le Capitole, France. No. 1302, 390fr, Montreaux-Bern Line, Switzerland. No. 1303, 485fr, Zugspitzbahn, Switzerland. No. 1304, 485fr, Rhatische Bahn, Swizerland.

No. 1305: a, Schwebebahn, Germany. b, Reichsbahn Class 44, Germany. c, Rembrandt, Germany. d, Trans-Europe Express, Germany. e, Inter-city, Germany. f, Steam locomotive, Germany.

No. 1306: a, ETR300, Italy. b, Mistral, France. c, ER200, Russia. d, Pendoline, Italy. e, Class 1100, Netherlands. f, Rheingold Express, Germany.

No. 1307, TGV, France. No. 1308, Austrian train.

2000, Jan. 25

1301-1304 A346 Set of 4 5.75 3.00

Sheets of 6

1305 A346 280fr #a.-f. 6.00 3.00
1306 A346 390fr #a.-f. 8.25 4.25

Souvenir Sheets

1307-1308 A346 1500fr each 8.00 2.50

Flowers — A347

No. 1309: a, Orchid, b, Water crinum. c, Flame lily. d, Narcissus poeticus. e, Belladonna lily. f, Table Mountain orchid. g, Upland cotton. h, Narcissus jonquilla.

No. 1310: a, Moore's crinum. b, Cyrtanthus brachyscyphus. c, Namaqualand daisy. d, "Narcissus poeticus," diff. e, Painted homeria. f, Helen O'Connor. g, Pink oxalis. h, Pink oxalis and pink arum.

No. 1311: a, Yellow wild iris. b, White arum lily (mountains in background). c, Blue tulip. d, Osteospermum. e, Table Mountain orchid, diff. f, White arum lily (with stems and leaves). g, Daisy. h, Meadow saffron.

No. 1312, Amaryllis belladonna, horiz. No. 1313, African tulip tree, horiz. No. 1314, Bird of paradise, horiz.

2000, Feb. 24 Sheets of 8

1309 A347 280fr #a.-h. 6.75 3.50
1310 A347 390fr #a.-h. 9.25 4.75
1311 A347 515fr #a.-h. 12.00 6.00

Souvenir Sheets

1312-1314 A347 1500fr each 4.50 2.25

Inscription on No. 1310d is incorrect.

Birds A348

Designs: 100fr, Dendrocygna bicolor, vert. 150fr, Tockis flavirostris, vert. 200fr, Treron calva. 300fr, Ardeola ralloides. 450fr, Passer melanus, vert. 750fr, Sturnus vulgaris, vert.

No. 1321, vert.: a, Trachyphonus vaillantii. b, Polyhierax semitorquatus. c, Tockus nasutus. d, Estrilda astrild. e, Merops persicus. f, Amandava subflava. g, Guttera pucherani. h, Oriolus oriolus. i, Bycanistes brevis.

No. 1322: a, Butoides striatus. b, Limnocorax flavirostra. c, Terathopius ecaudatus. d, Mycteria ibis. e, Actophilornis africanus. f, Poicephalus rueppellii. g, Alopochen aegyptiacus. h, Morus capensis. i, Sagittarius serpentarius.

No. 1323: a, Gyps africanus. b, Tyto alba. c, Pelecanus onocrotalus. d, Ephippiorhynchus senegalensis. e, Ardea goliath. f, Sylvia communis. g, Buteo rufofuscus. h, Parus caeruleus. i, Dromas ardeola.

No. 1324, Buphagus africanus. No. 1325, Haliaeetus vocifer. No. 1326, Erythropgia coryphaeus, vert.

2000, Feb. 25

1315-1320 A348 Set of 6 5.75 3.00

Sheets of 9

1321 A348 390fr #a.-i. 10.50 5.25
1322 A348 440fr #a.-i. 12.00 6.00
1323 A348 485fr #a.-i. 13.00 6.50

Souvenir Sheets

1324-1326 A348 2000fr each 6.00 3.00

Aviation A349

Designs: 280fr, Spirit of St. Louis. 345fr, Hindenburg. 465fr, Flight at Kitty Hawk. 485fr, AH-1 Cobra.

No. 1331: a, Fokker triplane. b, Spad XIII. c, Blériot XI. d, Nieuport 12. e, Sopwith Camel. f, 1920s US Mail plane. g, Otto Lilienthal's hang glider. h, Hydrogen-filled balloon of J. A. C. Charles.

No. 1332: a, Mitchell-B25. b, P-38E Lightning. c, Vought F-4U Corsair. d, Mitsubishi Zero. e, B-17 Flying Fortress. f, P-51 Mustang. g, Flying Tiger plane. h, Messerschmitt Bf-109.

No. 1333: a, X-1. b, B-52C. c, Boeing 707. d, F-16C. e, Sabre jet. f, MiG-15. g, F-4 Phantom. h, F-117A Stealth.

No. 1334, Concorde. No. 1335, Space shuttle "Enterprise."

2000, Feb. 28

1327-1330 A349 Set of 4 4.75 2.40

Sheets of 8

1331 A349 345fr #a.-h. 8.25 4.25
1332 A349 390fr #a.-h. 9.25 4.75
1333 A349 515fr #a.-h. 12.50 6.25

Souvenir Sheets

1334-1335 A349 1500fr each 4.50 2.25

Chess Players — A350

No. 1336, 280fr: a, Otto IV of Brandenburg. b, Mme. de Verzu and Chevalier de Bourgogne. c, Chess Players by Estienne Porcher. d, Fresco by F. Pella.

No. 1337, 300fr: a, Two Nobles. b, Depiction from book of Jean Wauquelin. c, Girolamo de Cremona. d, Ashtapada.

No. 1338, 390fr: a, Ulysses and Palamedes. b, Christian cavalier and Muslim. c, Two Moorish women. d, Burzurgmikhr and Kannuja.

No. 1339, 465fr: a, Two men, 18th Cent. b, Napoleon and Cornwallis. c, Adolf Anderssen and Wilhelm Steinitz. d, Queen Victoria.

No. 1340, 485fr: a, Two women. b, Chess on an enlarged board. c, Xerxes. d, King Evil-Merodach.

No. 1341, 515fr: a, King Henry VIII of England. b, Queen Elizabeth I of England. c, King Charles I of England. d, Russian czarevitch.

Illustration reduced.

1999 Litho. *Perf. 13½*

Sheets of 4, #a-d

1336-1341 A350 Set of 6 30.00 15.00

Cosmonauts and Astronauts — A351

No. 1342, 485fr: a, Vladimir Soloviev. b, Georgi Beregovoy. c, Alexei Leonov. d, Pavel Popovich. e, Yuri Gagarin. f, Valentina Tereshkova. g, Helena Kondakova. h, Gherman Titov. i, Alexander Volkov.

No. 1343, 515fr: a, Neil Armstrong. b, Edwin Aldrin. c, Michale Collins. d, Alan Bean. e, James Lovell. f, Alan Shepard. g, David Scott. h, John Young. i, Eugene Cernan.

2000fr, Armstrong and Gagarin, horiz.

Illustration reduced.

1999

Sheets of 9, #a-i

1342-1343 A351 Set of 2 27.50 14.00

Souvenir Sheet

1344 A351 2000fr multi 6.25 3.00

No. 1344 contains one 60x51mm stamp.

Millennium — A352

2000, Mar. 31 *Perf. 14*

1345 A352 515fr multicolored 1.50 .75

Issued in sheets of six.

2000 Summer Olympics, Sydney — A353

No. 1346, 300fr: a, Individual dressage. b, Rhythmic gymnastics. c, Women's 100-meter hurdles. d, Cycling.
No. 1347, 485fr: a, Tennis. b, Diving. c, Soccer. d, Pole vault.
No. 1348, 750fr: a, Long jump. b, Judo. c, Basketball. d, Show jumping.
No. 1349, 800fr: a, Boxing. b, Table tennis. c, Women's 200-meter sprint. d, Individual three-day equestrian event.
Illustration reduced.

2000 ***Perf. 13½***
Sheets of 4, #a-d
1346-1349 A353 Set of 4 30.00 15.00

2002 Winter Olympics, Salt Lake City — A354

No. 1350, 280fr: a, Freestyle skiing. b, Cross-country skiing. c, Bobsled. d, Men's slalom.
No. 1351, 390fr: a, Luge. b, Women's ski relay. c, Downhill skiing. d, Short track skating.
No. 1352, 465fr: a, Women's figure skating. b, Hockey. c, Ski jumping. d, Biathlon.
No. 1353, 515fr, a, Pairs figure skating. b, Women's giant slalom. c, Speed skating. d, Nordic combined.
Illustration reduced.

2000
Sheets of 4, #a-d
1350-1353 A354 Set of 4 21.00 10.50

SEMI-POSTAL STAMPS

Anti-Malaria Issue
Common Design Type
Perf. 12½x12
1962, Apr. 7 Engr. Unwmk.
B1 CD108 25fr + 5fr slate 1.25 1.25

WHO drive to eradicate malaria.

Freedom from Hunger Issue
Common Design Type
1963, Mar. 21 ***Perf. 13***
B2 CD112 25fr + 5fr multi 1.10 1.10

Guinea Fowl and Partridge SP1

Designs: 10fr+5fr, Yellow-backed duiker and snail. 20fr+5fr, Elephant, tortoise and hippopotamus playing tug-of-war. 30fr+10fr, Cuckoo and tortoise. 50fr+20fr, Patas monkey and leopard.

1971, Feb. 9 Photo. ***Perf. 12½x12***

B3	SP1	5fr + 5fr multi	4.00	2.00
B4	SP1	10fr + 5fr multi	5.25	2.50
B5	SP1	20fr + 5fr multi	6.75	2.75
B6	SP1	30fr + 10fr multi	9.00	7.00
B7	SP1	50fr + 20fr multi	15.00	12.00
		Nos. B3-B7 (5)	40.00	26.25

Lengué Dancer — SP2

Dancers: 40fr+10fr, Le Lengué. 100fr+40fr, Teke. 140fr+40fr, Englabolo.

1971 Litho. ***Perf. 13***

B8	SP2	20fr + 5fr multi	.50	.25
B9	SP2	40fr + 10fr multi	.80	.40
B10	SP2	100fr + 40fr multi	2.25	1.25
B11	SP2	140fr + 40fr multi	3.00	1.50
		Nos. B8-B11 (4)	6.55	3.40

AIR POST STAMPS

Central African Republic

Abyssinian Roller — AP1

Birds: 200fr, Gold Coast touraco. 500fr, African fish eagle.

Unwmk.
1960, Sept. 3 Engr. ***Perf. 13***

C1	AP1	100fr vio bl, org brn & emer	2.25	.70
C2	AP1	200fr multi	4.25	2.00
C3	AP1	500fr Prus bl, emer & red brn	13.50	4.75
		Nos. C1-C3 (3)	20.00	7.45

French Equatorial Africa No. C37 Surcharged in Red

1960, Dec. 15 ***Perf. 13***
C4 AP8 250fr on 500fr grnsh blk, blk & slate 7.50 7.50

17th Olympic Games, Rome, 8/25-9/11.

Air Afrique Issue
Common Design Type
1962, Feb. 17 Unwmk. ***Perf. 13***
C5 CD107 50fr vio, lt grn & red brn .90 .55

Founding of Air Afrique airline.

Pole Vault — AP1a

1962, July 21 Photo. ***Perf. 12x12½***
C6 AP1a 100fr grn, yel, brn & blk 2.25 1.50

Abidjan games.

Red-faced Lovebirds — AP2

1962-63 Engr. ***Perf. 13***

C7	AP2	50fr Great blue touraco	2.25	.55
C8	AP2	250fr shown ('63)	6.75	2.50

Issued: 50fr, Nov. 15; 250fr, Mar. 11, 1963.

Runner with Torch and Palm Branch — AP3

1962, Dec. 24
C9 AP3 100fr gray grn, brn & car 2.50 1.50

Tropics Cup Games, Bangui, Dec. 24-31.

African Postal Union Issue
Common Design Type
1963, Sept. 8 Photo. ***Perf. 12½***
C10 CD114 85fr emer, ocher & red 1.75 .85

Sun Shining on Africa — AP4

1963, Nov. 9 ***Perf. 13x12***
C11 AP4 25fr bl, yel & vio bl .70 .40

Issued for African unity.

Europafrica Issue
Common Design Type
1963, Nov. 30 ***Perf. 12x13***
C12 CD116 50fr ultra, yel & dk brn 2.50 2.00

Diesel Engine — AP5

Various Locomotives; 25fr, 50fr, vertical.

1963, Dec. 1 Engr. ***Perf. 13***

C13	AP5	20fr brn, cl & dk grn	.70	.60
C14	AP5	25fr brn, bl & choc	.80	.70
C15	AP5	50r brn, red lil & vio	2.75	2.50
C16	AP5	100fr brn, grn & dl red brn	3.75	3.25
a.		Min. sheet of 4, #C13-C16	12.50	12.50
		Nos. C13-C16 (4)	8.00	7.05

Bangui-Douala railroad project.

Bangui Cathedral — AP6

1964, Jan. 21 Unwmk. ***Perf. 13***
C17 AP6 100fr yel grn, org brn & bl 2.10 1.10

Radar Tracking Station and WMO Emblem — AP7

1964, Mar. 23 Engr. ***Perf. 13***
C18 AP7 50fr org brn, bl & pur 1.10 1.10

World Meteorological Day.

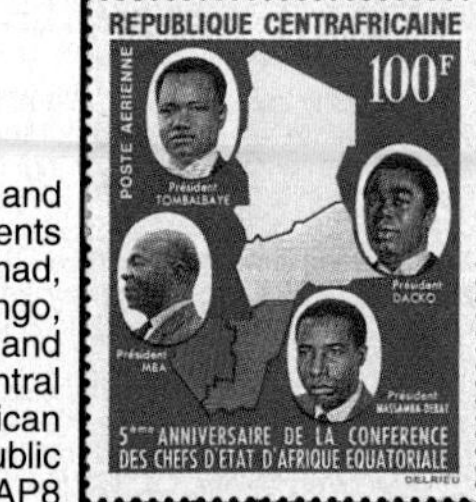

Map and Presidents of Chad, Congo, Gabon and Central African Republic AP8

1964, June 23 Photo. ***Perf. 12½***
C19 AP8 100fr multi 1.60 .80

5th anniversary of the Conference of Chiefs of State of Equatorial Africa.

Javelin Throwers — AP9

Designs: 50fr, Basketball game. 100fr, Four runners. 250fr, Swimmers, one in water.

1964, June 23 Engr. ***Perf. 13***

C20	AP9	25fr grn, dk brn & lt vio bl	.50	.30
C21	AP9	50fr blk, car & grn	1.00	.45
C22	AP9	100fr grn, vio bl & dk brn	2.25	.95
C23	AP9	250fr grn, blk & car	6.25	2.50
a.		Min. sheet of 4, #C20-C23	15.00	15.00
		Nos. C20-C23 (4)	10.00	4.20

18th Olympic Games, Tokyo, 10/10-25/64.

John F. Kennedy — AP10

1964, July 4 Photo. ***Perf. 12½***

C24	AP10	100fr lil, brn & blk	2.50	1.75
a.		Min. sheet of 4	10.50	10.50

Industrial Symbols, Maps of Africa and Europe — AP11

1964, Dec. 19 Unwmk. *Perf. 13x12*
C25 AP11 50fr yel, org & grn 1.40 .85

See note after Cameroun No. 402.

International Cooperation Year Emblem — AP12

1965, Jan. 2 *Perf. 13*
C26 AP12 100fr red brn, yel & bl 1.75 .80

International Cooperation Year.

Nimbus Weather Satellite — AP13

1965, Mar. 23 Engr. *Perf. 13*
C27 AP13 100fr org brn, ultra & blk 1.75 .80

Fifth World Meteorological Day.

Lincoln and Statue of Liberty — AP14

1965, Apr. 15 Photo. *Perf. 13*
C28 AP14 100fr bluish grn, ind & bis 1.75 .80

Centenary of death of Abraham Lincoln.

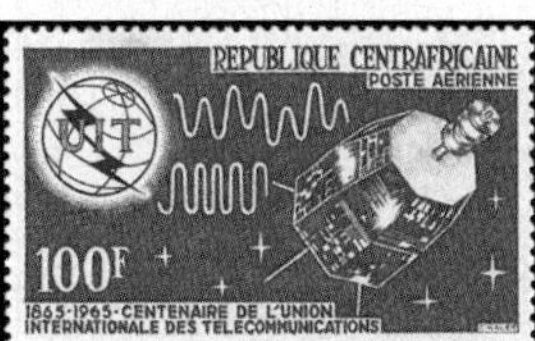
ITU Emblem and Relay Satellite — AP15

1965, May 17 Engr. *Perf. 13*
C29 AP15 100fr dk grn vio bl & brn 1.90 1.25

Centenary of the ITU.

"Housing," New Home in Village — AP16

1965, June 10 Unwmk.
C30 AP16 100fr ultra, brn & sl grn 1.25 .80

See note after No. 52.

Europafrica Issue

Tractor, Cotton Picker, Cotton, Sun and Emblem — AP17

1965, Nov. 7 Photo. *Perf. 12x13*
C31 AP17 50fr multi 1.00 .80

See note after Chad No. C11.

Mercury by Antoine Coysevox AP18

Father Holding Sick Child — AP19

1965, Dec. 5 Engr. *Perf. 13*
C32 AP18 100fr red brn, bl & blk 2.50 1.10

5th anniv. of Central African Republic's admission to the UPU.

1965, Dec. 12

Design: 100fr, Mother and child.

C33 AP19 50fr dk bl, car & blk 1.10 .45
C34 AP19 100fr red brn, red & brt grn 2.50 1.10

Issued to honor the Red Cross.

Air Afrique Issue
Common Design Type

1966, Aug. 31 Photo. *Perf. 13*
C35 CD123 25fr bl, blk & lem .90 .40

For surcharge see No. C43.

Surveyor Spacecraft on Moon — AP20

Designs: No. C37, Luna 9 on Moon and Earth. 200fr, Rocket take-off, Jules Verne's "From the Earth to the Moon."

1966, Oct. 24 Photo. *Perf. 12x12½*
C36 AP20 130fr multi 1.50 .95
C37 AP20 130fr multi 1.50 .95
C38 AP20 200fr multi 2.75 1.75
a. Souv. sheet of 3, #C36-C38 8.00 8.00
Nos. C36-C38 (3) 5.75 3.65

Conquest of the Moon.
For surcharges see Nos. C58, C61.

Eugene A. Cernan, Gemini 9 and Agena Rocket — AP21

No. C40, Pavel R. Popovich and rocket.

1966, Nov. 14 Photo. *Perf. 13*
C39 AP21 50fr multi 1.10 .55
C40 AP21 50fr multi 1.10 .55

American and Russian astronauts.

Diamant Rocket, D-1 Satellite and Globe with Map of Africa — AP22

1966, Nov. 14 Engr.
C41 AP22 100fr brt rose lil & brn 1.75 .95

Issued to commemorate the launching of France's first satellite, Nov. 26, 1965, and the launching of the D-1 satellite, Feb. 17, 1966.

Exchange of Agricultural and Industrial Products between Africa and Europe — AP23

1966, Dec. 5 Photo. *Perf. 12x13*
C42 AP23 50fr multi 1.25 .95

See note after Gabon No. C46.

No. C35 Surcharged

1967, May 8 *Perf. 13*
C43 CD123 5fr on 25fr multi .50 .30

The surcharge obliterates the "2" of the original 25fr denomination.

DC-8F Over M'Poko Airport, Bangui — AP24

1967, July 3 Engr. *Perf. 13*
C44 AP24 100fr sl, dk grn & brn 2.25 1.00

View of EXPO '67, Montreal — AP25

1967, July 17
C45 AP25 100fr vio bl, dk red brn & dk grn 2.10 .80

International Exposition. EXPO '67, Montreal, Apr. 28-Oct. 27.

African Postal Union Issue, 1967
Common Design Type

1967, Sept. 9 Engr. *Perf. 13*
C46 CD124 100fr brt grn, dk car rose & plum 2.10 .85

Potez 25 TOE — AP26

1967, Nov. 24 Engr. *Perf. 13*
C47 AP26 100fr shown 2.00 .80
C48 AP26 200fr Junkers 52 4.50 1.75
C49 AP26 500fr Caravelle 11R 11.50 4.25
Nos. C47-C49 (3) 18.00 6.80

For surcharges see Nos. C59-C60.

Presidents Boganda and Bokassa — AP27

1967, Dec. 1 Photo. *Perf. 12½*
C50 AP27 130fr org, red, lt bl & blk 2.25 1.25

9th anniversary of the republic.

Pres. Jean Bedel Bokassa AP28

1968, Jan. 1 ***Perf. 12½x12***
C51 AP28 30fr multi .90 .45

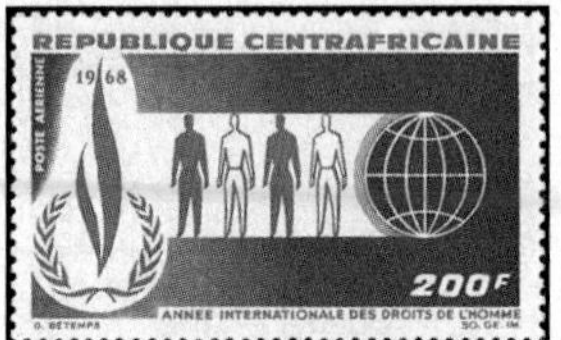

Human Rights Flame, Men and Globe — AP29

1968, Mar. 26 **Photo.** ***Perf. 13***
C52 AP29 200fr brt grn, vio & ver 3.50 1.60

International Human Rights Year.

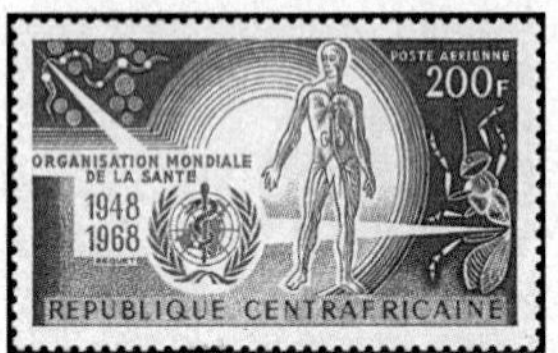

Man, WHO Emblem and Tsetse Fly — AP30

1968, Apr. 8 **Engr.**
C53 AP30 200fr multi 3.75 2.00

20th anniv. of WHO.

Javelin Thrower — AP31

Space Probe Landing on Venus — AP32

1968, Apr. 16 **Engr.** ***Perf. 13***
C54 AP31 200fr shown 5.00 3.25
C55 AP31 200fr Downhill skier 5.00 3.25

The 1968 Olympic Games.

1968, Apr. 23
C56 AP32 100fr ultra, dk & brt grn 1.60 .95

Venus exploration by Venus IV, 10/18/67.

Marie Curie and "Cancer Destroyed" — AP33

1968, Apr. 30
C57 AP33 100fr vio, brt bl & brn 2.50 1.10

Marie Curie (1867-1934), scientist.

Nos. C36-C37 and C47-C48 Surcharged with New Value

Photogravure; Engraved

1968, Sept. 16 ***Perf. 12x12½, 13***
C58 AP20 5fr on 130fr multi .20 .20
C59 AP26 10fr on 100fr multi .25 .20
C60 AP26 20fr on 200fr multi .45 .30
C61 AP20 50fr on 130fr multi 1.00 .55
Nos. C58-C61 (4) 1.90 1.25

On No. C58 the old denomination has been obliterated with "XIX," on No. C61 the obliteration is a rectangular bar. On Nos. C59-C60 the last zero of the old denomination has been obliterated with a black square.

River Boat Type of Regular Issue

Craft: 100fr, "Pie X," Bangui, 1894. 130fr, "Ballay," Bangui, 1891.

1968, Dec. 10 **Engr.** ***Perf. 13***
Size: 48x27mm
C62 A37 100fr bl, dk brn & ol 2.40 1.00
C63 A37 130fr brt pink, sl grn & slate 2.50 1.25

PHILEXAFRIQUE Issue

Mme. de Sévigné, French School, 17th Century AP34

1968, Dec. 17 **Photo.** ***Perf. 12½***
C64 AP34 100fr brn & multi 3.00 2.40

Issued to publicize PHILEXAFRIQUE, Philatelic Exhibition in Abidjan, Feb. 14-23. Printed with alternating brown label.

2nd PHILEXAFRIQUE Issue

Common Design Type

Design: 50fr, Ubangi-Shari No. J16, cotton field and Pres. Bokassa.

1969, Feb. 14 **Engr.** ***Perf. 13***
C65 CD128 50fr bis brn, blk & dk grn 1.75 1.75

Holocerina Angulata Aur. — AP35

Butterflies and Moths: 20fr, Nudaurelia dione fabr. 30fr, Eustera troglophylla hamp., vert. 50fr, Aurivillius aratus west. 100fr, Epiphora albida druce.

1969, Feb. 25 **Photo.**
C66 AP35 10fr yel & multi .70 .30
C67 AP35 20fr vio & multi 1.00 .45
C68 AP35 30fr multi 2.50 .80
C69 AP35 50fr multi 4.25 2.00
C70 AP35 100fr multi 7.00 3.00
Nos. C66-C70 (5) 15.45 6.55

Boxing — AP36

1969, Mar. 18 **Photo.** ***Perf. 13***
C71 AP36 50fr shown 1.00 .30
C72 AP36 100fr Basketball 2.10 .60

Apollo 8 over Moonscape — AP37

1969, May 27 **Photo.** ***Perf. 13***
C73 AP37 200fr dp bl, gray & yel 3.50 1.75

US Apollo 8 mission, the 1st men in orbit around the moon, Dec. 21-27, 1968.
For overprint see No. C81.

Market Cross, Nuremberg, and Toys — AP38

1969, June 3
C74 AP38 100fr blk, brt rose lil & emer 2.00 .95

Intl. Toy Fair in Nuremberg, Germany.

Napoleon as First Consul, by Anne-Louis Girodet-Trioson — AP39

Designs: 130fr, Napoleon meeting Emperor Francis II, by Antoine Jean Gros, horiz. 200fr, The Wedding of Napoleon and Marie-Louise, by Georges Rouget, horiz.

1969, Nov. 4 **Photo.** ***Perf. 12½***
C75 AP39 100fr multi 2.00 1.25
C76 AP39 130fr brn & multi 3.00 1.50
C77 AP39 200fr multi 5.00 2.75
Nos. C75-C77 (3) 10.00 5.50

Napoleon Bonaparte (1769-1821).

Pres. Bokassa, Map of Africa and Flag — AP40

Franklin Delano Roosevelt — AP41

1970, Jan. 1 ***Die-cut; Perf. 10½***
Embossed on Gold Foil
C78 AP40 2000fr gold 32.50 32.50

1970 **Litho.** ***Perf. 13½x14***
C79 AP41 100fr shown 2.00 1.00
C80 AP41 100fr Lenin 3.25 1.25

Roosevelt, 25th death anniv., Lenin, birth cent.
Issue dates: #C79, Apr. 29; #C80. Apr. 22.

No. C73 Overprinted in Red:
ATTERRISSAGE
d'APOLLO 12
19 novembre 1969

1970, June 1 **Photo.** ***Perf. 13***
C81 AP37 200fr multi 14.00 9.50

Moon landing mission of Apollo 12, 11/14-24/69.

AP42

1970, Sept. 15 **Litho.** ***Perf. 10***
C82 AP42 Pair + label 4.00 3.00
a. 100fr Dancer 1.75 .55
b. 100fr Still life 1.75 .55

Knokphila 70, 6th Intl. Phil. Exhib. at Knokke, Belgium, July 4-10. Imperf. between stamps and label.

Sericulture Type of Regular Issue

1970, Sept. 15 ***Perf. 10***
C83 A45 140fr multi 3.00 1.10

C.A.R. Flag, EXPO Emblem and Pavilion AP43

1970, Dec. 18 **Litho.** ***Perf. 13½x13***
C84 AP43 200fr red & multi 3.75 1.75

Intl. Exposition EXPO '70, Osaka, Japan.

Soccer — AP44

1970, Dec. 8 ***Perf. 13x13½***
C85 AP44 200fr multi 3.50 1.60

World Soccer Championships, Mexico, May 30-June 21, 1970.

Dove — AP45

1970, Dec. 31
C86 AP45 200fr bl, yel & blk 3.50 1.60

25th anniversary of the United Nations.

Presidents Mobutu, Bokassa, and Tombalbaye — AP46

1971, Jan. 10
C87 AP46 140fr multi 3.00 1.10

Return of Central African Republic to the United States of Central Africa which also includes Congo Democratic Republic and Chad.

Satellite over Globe — AP47

1971, May 17 Photo. *Perf. 12½*
C88 AP47 100fr multi 2.00 .85

3rd World Telecommunications Day.

African Postal Union Issue, 1971
Common Design Type

Design: 100fr, Carved head and UAMPT building, Brazzaville, Congo.

1971, Nov. 13 Photo. *Perf. 13x13½*
C89 CD135 100fr bl & multi 2.00 .85

Child and Education Year Emblem — AP48

1971, Nov. 11 Litho. *Perf. 13x13½*
C90 AP48 140fr multi 2.00 .80

25th anniv. of UNESCO.

Fight Against Cancer — AP49

Gamal Abdel Nasser — AP50

1971, Nov. 20 Photo. *Perf. 12½*
C91 AP49 100fr grn & multi 2.50 1.10

1972, Jan. 15
C92 AP50 100fr dk red, blk & bister 2.00 .85

In memory of Gamal Abdel Nasser (1918-1970), president of Egypt.

Olympic Rings and Boxing — AP51

No. C94, Track and Olympic rings, vert.

1972, May 26 Engr. *Perf. 13*
C93 AP51 100fr brn org & sepia 1.60 .80
C94 AP51 100fr green & violet 1.60 1.10
a. Miniature sheet of 2 4.50 4.50

20th Olympic Games, Munich, Aug. 26-Sept. 10. No. C94a contains 2 stamps similar to Nos. C93-C94, but in changed colors. The boxing stamp is red lilac and green, the track stamp ocher and red lilac.
For overprints see Nos. C100-C101.

Arrows with Symbols of Agriculture and Industry — AP53

Tiling's Mail Rocket, 1931, and Mailman — AP52

Designs: 50fr, DC-3 and mailman riding camel, vert. 150fr, Sirio satellite and rocket, vert. 200fr, Intelsat 4 and rocket.

1972, Aug. 12
C95 AP52 40fr bl, org & indigo .60 .45
C96 AP52 50fr bl, brn & org .80 .55
C97 AP52 150fr brn, org & gray 2.25 1.25
C98 AP52 200fr brn, bl & org 3.25 2.25
a. Souv. sheet of 4, #C95-C98 8.50 8.50
Nos. C95-C98 (4) 6.90 4.50

Centraphilex 1972, Central African Philatelic Exhibition, Bangui.

Europafrica Issue

1972, Nov. 17 Litho. *Perf. 13*
C99 AP53 100fr multi 1.60 .80

Nos. C93-C94, C94a Overprinted
a. POIDS-MOYEN / LEMECHEV MEDAILLE D'OR
b. LONGUER / WILLIAMS MEDAILLE D'OR

1972, Nov. 24 Engr.
C100 AP51 (a) 100fr 1.60 .95
C101 AP51 (b) 100fr 1.60 .95
a. Miniature sheet of 2 3.50 3.50

Gold Medal Winners in 20th Olympic Games: Viatscheslav Lemechev, USSR, middleweight boxing; Randy Williams, US, broad jump.

Lunar Rover and Module — AP54

1972, Dec. 18 Engr. *Perf. 13*
C102 AP54 100fr slate grn, bl & gray 1.60 .80

Apollo 16 US moon mission, 4/15-27/72.

Virgin and Child, by Francesco Pesellino AP55

Christmas: 150fr, Adoration of the Child with St. John the Baptist and St. Romuald, by Fra Filippo Lippi.

1972, Dec. 25 Photo.
C103 AP55 100fr gold & multi 1.50 .85
C104 AP55 150fr gold & multi 2.50 1.25

Parthenon, Athens, Spyridon Louis, Marathon, 1896 — AP56

Olympic Rings and: 40fr, Arc de Triomphe, Paris, H. Barrelet, single scull, 1900. 50fr, Old Courthouse and Western Arch, St. Louis, Myer Prinstein, triple jump, 1904. 100fr, Tower, London, Henry Taylor, swimming, 1908. 150fr, City Hall, Stockholm, Greco-Roman wrestling, 1912.

1972, Dec. 28 Engr.
C105 AP56 30fr brt grn, mag & brn .35 .25
C106 AP56 40fr vio bl, emer & brn .45 .25
C107 AP56 50fr car rose, vio bl & Prus bl .50 .40
C108 AP56 100fr sl, red lil & brn 1.00 .45
C109 AP56 150fr red lil, blk & Prus bl 1.60 1.10
Nos. C105-C109 (5) 3.90 2.45

Olympic Games 1896-1912.

WHO Emblem, Surgeon and Nurse — AP57

1973, Apr. 7 Photo. *Perf. 13*
C110 AP57 100fr multi 1.60 .80

WHO, 25th anniv.

AP58

AP58a

1973, May 17 Litho. *Perf. 12½*
C111 AP58 200fr World map, arrows, waves 2.50 1.10

5th International Telecommunications Day.

1973, Sept. 17 Engr. *Perf. 13*

Head and City Hall, Brussels.

C112 AP58a 100fr pur, ocher & brn 1.25 .70

African Weeks, Brussels, Sept. 15-30, 1973.

Europafrica Issue

Map of Central African Republic with Industry and Agriculture, Young Man — AP59

1973, Sept. 28 Engr. *Perf. 13*
C113 AP59 100fr sepia, grn & org 1.60 .80

Carrier Pigeon with Letter and UPU Emblem — AP60

1973, Oct. 9 Photo.
C114 AP60 200fr multi 2.25 1.10

Universal Postal Union Day.

WMO Emblem, Weather Map — AP61

1973, Oct. 20 Engr. *Perf. 13*

C115 AP61 150fr brt ultra & sl grn 2.50 1.00

Cent. of intl. meteorological cooperation.

Copernicus, Heliocentric System — AP62

1973, Nov. 2 Photo.

C116 AP62 100fr gold & multi 2.75 1.75

Copernicus (1473-1543), Polish astronomer.

Pres. Bokassa AP63

Pres. Bokassa — AP64

St. Teresa — AP66

UPU Emblem, Letter — AP67

Presidents and Flags of Cameroun, CAR, Gabon and Congo — AP68

Marshal Bokassa AP69

Mask, Map of Africa, Arphila Emblem — AP70

Albert Schweitzer and Dugout, Lambarene AP71

Pres. Bokassa's Houseboat, Bow — AP72

Monument to Franco-CAR Cooperation AP73

Presidents and Flags of France and CAR AP74

1973, Nov. 30 Photo. *Perf. 12½*

C117 AP63 50fr multi .70 .40
C118 AP64 100fr multi 1.25 .70

Rocket Launch and Apollo 17 Badge — AP65

1973, Dec. 15 Engr. *Perf. 13*

65fr, Capsule over moonscape, horiz. 100fr, Moon landing, horiz. 150fr, Astronauts on moon. 200fr, Splashdown with parachutes and badge.

C119 AP65 50fr ver, gray grn & brn .50 .30
C120 AP65 65fr dk brn, brn red & sl grn .70 .40
C121 AP65 100fr ver, slate & choc 1.00 .55
C122 AP65 150fr brn, ol & sl grn 1.60 .80
C123 AP65 200fr red, bl & sl grn 2.00 1.10
Nos. C119-C123 (5) 5.80 3.15

Apollo 17 US moon mission, 12/7-19/72.

1973, Dec. 25

C124 AP66 500fr vio bl & grnsh bl 6.25 3.50

St. Teresa of the Infant Jesus, the Little Flower (1873-1897), Carmelite nun.

1974, Oct. 9 Engr. *Perf. 13*

C125 AP67 500fr multi 6.75 4.00

Centenary of Universal Postal Union.
For surcharge see No. C159.

1974, Dec. 8 Photo. *Perf. 13*

C126 AP68 100fr gold & multi 1.25 .80

See note after Cameroun No. 595.
For surcharge see No. C155.

100fr, Bokassa in Marshal's uniform with cape.

1975, Feb. 22 Photo. *Perf. 13*

C127 AP69 50fr tan & multi .60 .40
C128 AP69 100fr tan & multi 1.25 .45

Jean Bedel Bokassa, President for Life and Marshal of the Republic.

1975, Aug. 25 Engr. *Perf. 13*

C129 AP70 100fr brt bl, red brn & red 1.25 .60

ARPHILA 75 International Philatelic Exhibition, Paris, June 6-16.
For surcharge see No. C156.

1975, Sept. 30 Engr. *Perf. 13*

C130 AP71 200fr blk, ultra & ol 3.25 1.75

Dr. Albert Schweitzer (1875-1965), medical missionary and musician.
For surcharge see No. C158.

40fr, Pres. Bokassa's houseboat, stern.

1976, Feb. 22 Litho. *Perf. 13*

C131 AP72 30fr multi .60 .30
C132 AP72 40fr multi .80 .45

1976, Mar. 5

C133 AP73 100fr multi 1.25 .80
C134 AP74 200fr multi 2.25 1.25

Official visit of Pres. Valery Giscard d'Estaing to Central African Republic, 3/5-8.

For surcharge see No. C157.

Apollo Soyuz Type, 1976

Designs: 100fr, Soyuz space ship. 200fr, Apollo space ship. 300fr, Astronauts and cosmonauts in cabin. 500fr, Apollo and Soyuz after link-up.

1976, June 14 Litho. *Perf. 14x13½*

C135 A90 100fr multi 1.00 .25
C136 A90 200fr multi 1.90 .55
C137 A90 300fr multi 3.00 .95
Nos. C135-C137 (3) 5.90 1.75

Souvenir Sheet

C138 A90 500fr multi 5.00 1.75

For surcharges see #C161, C168, C173, C177.

French Hussar AP75

Uniforms: 125fr, Scottish "Black Watch." 150fr, German dragoon. 200fr, British grenadier. 250fr, American ranger. 450fr, American dragoon.

1976, July 4 *Perf. 13½*

C139 AP75 100fr multi .80 .30
C140 AP75 125fr multi .90 .45
C141 AP75 150fr multi 1.10 .45
C142 AP75 200fr multi 1.75 .55
C143 AP75 250fr multi 2.25 .95
Nos. C139-C143 (5) 6.80 2.70

Souvenir Sheet

C144 AP75 450fr multi 6.75 2.00

American Bicentennial.
For surcharges see Nos. C162, C166-C167, C169, C172, C176.

Acherontia Atropos — AP76

100fr, Papilio nireus & niocha marnois.

1976, Sept. 20 Litho. *Perf. 12½*

C145 AP76 50fr multi 6.25 1.10
C146 AP76 100fr multi 12.50 1.75

For surcharges see Nos. C160, C163.

Olympic Winners Type, 1976

Designs: 100fr, Women's figure skating, Dorothy Hamill, vert. 200fr, Ice skating, Alexander Gorshkov and Ludmilla Pakhomova. 300fr, Men's figure skating, John Curry, vert. 500fr, Downhill skiing, Rosi Mittermaier, vert.

1976, Sept. 23 Litho. *Perf. 13½*

C147 A92 100fr multi .60 .30
C148 A92 200fr multi 2.00 .60
C149 A92 300fr multi 2.75 1.00
Nos. C147-C149 (3) 5.35 1.90

Souvenir Sheet

C150 A92 500fr multi 5.00 1.75

For surcharges see #C164, C170, C174, C178.

Viking Mars Type, 1976

Designs: 100fr, Phases of Mars landing. 200fr, Viking descending on Mars, horiz. 300fr, Viking probe. 500fr, Viking flight to Mars, horiz.

1976, Dec.

C151 A93 100fr multi .90 .30
C152 A93 200fr multi 2.00 .60
C153 A93 300fr multi 2.75 .95
Nos. C151-C153 (3) 5.65 1.85

Souvenir Sheet

C154 A93 500fr multi 5.00 1.75

For surcharges and overprints see Nos. C165, C171, C175, C179, C212-C215.

Central African Empire

Stamps of 1973-76 Overprinted with Bars and "EMPIRE CENTRAFRICAIN" in Black, Violet Blue or Gold

Printing and Perforations as Before

1977, Mar.

C155 AP68 100fr (#C126;B) 1.00 1.00
C156 AP70 100fr (#C129;VB) 1.00 1.00
C157 AP73 100fr (#C133;G) 1.00 1.00
C158 AP71 200fr (#C130;B) 3.00 1.50
C159 AP67 500fr (#C125;B) 9.00 9.00
Nos. C155-C159 (5) 15.00 13.50

No bar on No. C159.

Stamps of 1976 Overprinted "EMPIRE CENTRAFRICAIN" in Black on Silver Panel

1977, Apr. 1

C160 AP76 50fr (#C145) .50 .50
C161 A90 100fr (#C135) 1.00 1.00
C162 AP75 100fr (#C139) 1.00 1.00
C163 AP76 100fr (#C146) 1.00 1.00
C164 A92 100fr (#C147) 1.00 1.00
C165 A93 100fr (#C151) 1.00 1.00
C166 AP75 125fr (#C140) 1.25 1.25
C167 AP75 150fr (#C141) 1.50 1.50
C168 A90 200fr (#C136) 2.50 2.50
C169 AP75 200fr (#C142) 2.25 2.25
C170 A92 200fr (#C148) 2.00 2.00
C171 A93 200fr (#C152) 2.00 2.00
C172 AP75 250fr (#C143) 2.50 2.50
C173 A90 300fr (#C137) 3.25 3.25
C174 A92 300fr (#C149) 3.25 3.25
C175 A93 300fr (#C153) 3.25 3.25
Nos. C160-C175 (16) 29.25 29.25

Souvenir Sheets

C176 AP75 450fr (#C144) 5.00 5.00
C177 A90 500fr (#C138) 7.25 7.25
C178 A92 500fr (#C150) 5.00 5.00
C179 A93 500fr (#C154) 5.00 5.00

Overprint on type AP75 is in upper and lower case letters.

Nobel Prize Type, 1977

Designs: 100fr, Rudyard Kipling. 200fr, Ernest Hemingway. 300fr, Luigi Pirandello. 500fr, Rabindranath Tagore.

1977, Apr. 1 Litho. *Perf. 13½*

C180 A94 100fr multi .95 .40
C181 A94 200fr multi 1.90 .70
C182 A94 300fr multi 2.75 .95
Nos. C180-C182 (3) 5.60 2.05

Souvenir Sheet

C183 A94 500fr multi 5.25 1.75

Zeppelin Type of 1977

100fr, Germany #C42 and North Pole. 200fr, Germany #C44 and Science and Industry Building, Chicago. 300fr, Germany #C35 and Brandenburg Gate, Berlin. 500fr, US #C14 and US Capitol.

1977, Apr. 11 Litho. *Perf. 11*

C184 A95 100fr multi 1.25 .30
C185 A95 200fr multi 2.50 .60
C186 A95 300fr multi 3.25 1.00
Nos. C184-C186 (3) 7.00 1.90

Souvenir Sheet

C187 A95 500fr multi 5.00 2.00

75th anniversary of Zeppelin.

Bokassa Type of 1977

1977, Dec. 4 Litho. *Perf. 13½*

C188 A98 200fr multi 1.75 .80
C189 A98 300fr multi 2.50 1.25
a. Souvenir sheet, 500fr 5.00 2.50

Coronation of Emperor Bokassa I, Dec. 4. No. C189a contains a horizontal stamp in similar design. A 2500fr gold embossed horizontal stamp in similar design exists. Value $20.

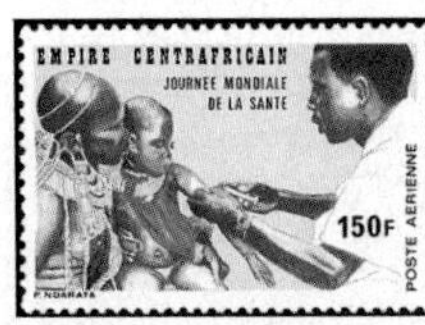

Vaccination AP77

1977 Litho. *Perf. 14x13½*

C190 AP77 150fr multi 3.75 1.25

World Health Day.

Communications Type of 1978

Designs: 100fr, Balloon and spaceships docking in space. 200fr, Hydrofoil and Concorde. 500fr, Tom-tom and Zeppelin. No. C193A, Early postman and rider, UPU emblem, Concorde. No. C193B, Mail coach, dove, satellites.

1978, May 17 Litho. *Perf. 13½*

C191 A107 100fr multi 1.00 .25
C192 A107 200fr multi 1.00 .30

Souvenir Sheet

C193 A107 500fr multi 5.25 2.25

Cent. of progress of posts and telecommunications. No. C193 contains one 53x35mm stamp.

1978, Mar. 21 Litho. & Embossed

Size: 57x39mm

C193A A107 1500fr gold & multi 13.00 4.00

Souvenir Sheet

C193B A107 1500fr gold & multi 13.00 4.75

Nos. C193A-C193B exist imperf. No. C193A exists in a souvenir sheet of one. No. C193B contains one 57x39mm stamp.

Clement Ader and his Plane — AP78

Designs: 50fr, Wilbur and Orville Wright and plane. 60fr, John W. Alcock, Arthur W. Brown and plane. 100fr, Alan Cobham and plane 150fr, Claude Dornier and hydroplane. 500fr, Wilbur and Orville Wright and plane.

1978, Sept. 19 *Perf. 14*

C194 AP78 40fr multi .50 .20
C195 AP78 50fr multi .50 .20
C196 AP78 60fr multi .60 .25
C197 AP78 100fr multi 1.10 .40
C198 AP78 150fr multi 1.75 .60
Nos. C194-C198 (5) 4.45 1.65

Souvenir Sheet

C199 AP78 500fr multi 5.00 1.75

History of aviation.

Philexafrique II-Essen Issue

Common Design Types

#C200, Crocodile, #C3. #C201, Birds, Mecklenburg-Schwerin #1.

1978, Nov. 1 Litho. *Perf. 12½*

C200 CD138 100fr multi 1.75 1.10
C201 CD139 100fr multi 1.75 1.10
a. Pair, #C200-C201 + label 5.75 5.75

Bokassa Type of 1978

150fr, Catherine & Jean Bedel Bokassa.

1978, Dec. 4 Litho. *Perf. 13*

C202 A113 150fr multi, horiz. 1.75 .70

First anniv. of coronation. A 1000fr gold embossed souvenir sheet showing Emperor Bokassa exists. Value $9.

Rowland Hill Type of 1978

Designs (Rowland Hill and): 100fr, Mailman and Tuscany No. 23. 200fr, Balloon and France No. 1. 500fr, Central Africa Nos. 1-2.

1978, Dec. 27

C203 A114 100fr multi 3.25 1.40
C204 A114 200fr multi 1.50 .65

Souvenir Sheet

C205 A114 500fr multi 5.00 1.75

Sir Rowland Hill (1795-1879), originator of penny postage. No. C205 contains one 37½x39mm stamp. 1500fr gold embossed stamp and souvenir sheet exist.

IYC Type of 1979

Designs (UNICEF, Eagle Emblems and): 100fr, Chinese girl flying kites and German Do-X flying boat, 1929. 200fr, Boys playing leapfrog, hurdler and Olympic emblem. 500fr, Child with abacus and Albert Einstein with his equation.

1979, Mar. 6 *Perf. 13½*

C206 A115 100fr multi 1.25 .40
C207 A115 200fr multi 2.50 .65

Souvenir Sheet

C208 A115 500fr multi 5.00 1.75

International Year of the Child. No. C208 contains one 56x33mm stamp. 1500fr gold embossed stamp and souvenir sheet exist.

Olympic Type of 1979

Moscow '80 Emblem, various Sports and: 100fr, Hurdles & "B." 200fr, Broad jump & "A."

1979, Mar. 16 Litho. *Perf. 13*

C209 A116 100fr multi 1.00 .35
C210 A116 200fr multi 2.00 .65

22nd Olympic Games, Moscow, July 19-Aug. 3, 1980. A 1500fr gold embossed souvenir sheet exists showing diver, runner and javelin.

National Husbandry Association Type

1979, Aug. Litho. *Perf. 13*

C211 A119 60fr Horse 5.25 2.00

Central African Republic

Nos. C151-C154 Overprinted "ALUNISSAGE/APOLLO XI/ JUILLET 1969" and Emblem in Black or Silver

1979, Oct. Litho. *Perf. 14x13½*

C212 A93 100fr multi .90 .55
C213 A93 200fr multi 1.75 .85
C214 A93 300fr multi 2.50 1.25
Nos. C212-C214 (3) 5.15 2.65

Souvenir Sheet

C215 A93 500fr multi (S) 5.00 5.00

Apollo 11 moon landing, 10th anniversary.

Ski Jump, Lake Placid '80 Emblem — AP79

1979, Nov. 11 Litho. *Perf. 13½*

C216 AP79 60fr shown .60 .20
C217 AP79 100fr Downhill skiing 1.00 .40
C218 AP79 200fr Hockey 2.10 .85
C219 AP79 300fr Bobsledding 3.00 1.25
Nos. C216-C219 (4) 6.70 2.70

Souvenir Sheet

C220 AP79 500fr multi 5.00 1.75

13th Winter Olympics Games, Lake Placid, NY, Feb. 12-24, 1980.
For overprints see Nos. C224-C228.

Space Type of 1980

1980, Apr. 8 Litho. *Perf. 13½*

C221 A125 150fr Early satellites 1.50 .40
C222 A125 200fr Space shuttle 1.75 .55

Souvenir Sheet

C223 A125 500fr Apollo 11, Armstrong 5.00 1.40

Litho. & Embossed

Size: 51x57mm

C223A A125 1500fr Armstrong, Apollo 11 12.50 3.00

Souvenir Sheet

C223B A125 1500fr Space shuttle, horiz. 9.00

C223A-C223B exist imperf. No. C223A exists in a souvenir sheet of one. Value $40. No. C223B contains one 57x51mm stamp.

Nos. C216-C220 Overprinted:

a — C224ovpt

b. VAINQUEUR / MOSER-PROELL / AUTRICHE
c. VAINQUEUR / ETATS-UNIS
d. VAINQUEUR / STENMARK / SUEDE
e. VAINQUEURS / SCHAERER-BENZ / SUISSE

1980, May 12 Litho. *Perf. 13½*

C224 AP79 (a) 60fr multi .45 .20
C225 AP79 (b) 100fr multi .70 .40
C226 AP79 (c) 200fr multi 1.75 .85
C227 AP79 (d) 300fr multi 2.50 1.25
Nos. C224-C227 (4) 5.40 2.70

Souvenir Sheet

C228 AP79 (e) 500fr multi 4.50 4.50

World Telecommunications Day — AP80

1980, June 26 Litho. *Perf. 12½*

C229 AP80 100fr multi 1.00 .55
C230 AP80 150fr multi, vert. 1.25 .80

Olympic Type of 1980

1980, July 25 Litho. *Perf. 13½*

C231 A126 100fr Boxing .90 .25
C232 A126 150fr Hurdles 1.50 .40

Souvenir Sheet

C233 A126 250fr Long jump 2.75 .65

Litho. & Embossed

C233A A126 1500fr Relay race, diff. 13.50 4.00

Souvenir Sheet

C233B A126 1500fr Basketball, vert. 10.00 4.75

22nd Summer Olympic Games, Moscow, July 19-Aug. 3. #C233 contains one 39x36mm stamp.
For overprints see Nos. C248-C250B.

Europe-Africa Type of 1980

1980, Nov. 4 Litho. *Perf. 13½*

C234 A127 150fr Meteorology 1.40 .50
C235 A127 200fr Aviation 1.75 .60

Souvenir Sheet

C236 A127 500fr Concorde jet 5.00 1.60

No. C236 contains one 41½x29mm stamp.

Litho. & Embossed

Size: 42x39mm

C236A A127 1500fr Boy Scouts 13.00 4.00

Souvenir Sheet

C236B A127 1500fr Concorde 10.50 4.75

Nos. C236A-C236B exist imperf. No. C236A exists in a souvenir sheet of one. No. C236B contains one 42x39mm stamp.

Soccer Type of 1981

1981, Jan. 13 Litho. *Perf. 13½*

C237 A130 100fr Netherlands .90 .25
C238 A130 200fr Spain 1.40 .55

Souvenir Sheet

C239 A130 500fr Argentina 5.75 1.75

Litho. & Embossed

Size: 57x39mm

C239A A130 1500fr Players, trophy 21.00 5.50

Souvenir Sheet

C239B A130 1500fr Players, trophy, diff. 9.00 4.00

No. C239A exists with tabs for either Philexafrique II or Essen 78.

Nos. C239A-C239B exist imperf. No. C239A exists in a souvenir sheet of one. Value $32.50. No. C239B contains one 36x60mm stamp.

Jacob Wrestling with the Angel, by Rembrandt AP81

Rembrandt Paintings: 90fr, Christ during the Storm. 150fr, Jeremiah Mourning the Destruction of Jerusalem. 250fr, Tobit Accusing Anne of Theft of a Goat. 500fr, Belshazzar's Feast, horiz.

1981, Feb. 20 ***Perf. 12½***

C240	AP81	60fr multi	.50	.20
C241	AP81	90fr multi	.80	.25
C242	AP81	150fr multi	1.25	.55
C243	AP81	250fr multi	2.25	.65
		Nos. C240-C243 (4)	4.80	1.65

Souvenir Sheet

C244 AP81 500fr multi 4.50 1.75

Picasso Type of 1981

Paintings: 150fr, Woman in Mirror with Self-portrait. 200fr, Woman Sleeping, The Dream. 500fr, Portrait of Maia (the Artist's Daughter). No. C247A, Two Women and Glasses, Picasso. No. C247B, Woman with Handbag, statue of standing woman, vert.

1981, June 30 Litho. ***Perf. 13½***

C245	A133	150fr multi	2.10	.45
C246	A133	200fr multi	2.25	.60

Souvenir Sheet

C247 A133 500fr multi 5.25 1.40

No. C247 contains one 42x46mm stamp.

Litho. & Embossed

Size: 57x39mm

C247A A133 1500fr gold & multi 13.50 4.00

Souvenir Sheet

C247B A133 1500fr gold & multi 10.50

Nos. C247A-C247B exist imperf. No. C247A exists in a souvenir sheet of one. Value $21. No. C247B contains one 39x58mm stamp.

Nos. C231-C233B Overprinted with Event, Winner and Country in Gold

1981 Litho. ***Perf. 13½***

C248	A126	100fr multi	.90	.25
C249	A126	150fr multi	1.25	.40

Souvenir Sheet

C250 A126 250fr multi 2.25 .65

Litho. & Embossed

C250A A126 1500fr on #C233A 12.50

Souvenir Sheet

C250B A126 1500fr on #C233B 12.00

Royal Wedding Type of 1981

1981, Aug. 20 Litho. ***Perf. 13½***

C251	A136	150fr Prince of Wales arms	1.50	.40
C252	A136	200fr Palace	2.00	.55

Souvenir Sheet

C253 A136 500fr St. Paul's Cathedral 4.50 1.40

No. C253 contains one 60x32mm stamp.

Litho. & Embossed

Size: 51x42mm

C253A A136 1500fr Diana, Charles 13.50 4.00

Souvenir Sheet

C253B A136 1500fr Charles, Diana, ship 9.75

Nos. C253A-C253B exist imperf. No. C253A exists in a souvenir sheet of one. Value $17.50. No. C253B contains one 51x42mm stamp.

Navigator Type of 1981

1981, Sept. 4 Litho. ***Perf. 13½***

C254	A139	100fr O. Kersauson	1.00	.70
C255	A139	200fr Chichester	2.25	1.40

Souvenir Sheet

C256 A139 500fr A. Colas 4.50 1.40

Litho. & Embossed

Size: 51x42mm

C256A A139 1500fr Riguidel 13.50 4.50

Souvenir Sheet

C256B A139 1500fr Tabarly 10.50

Nos. C256A-C256B exist imperf. No. C256A exists in a souvenir sheet of one. Value $20. No. C256B contains one 51x42mm stamp.

Lizard AP82

1981, Oct. 30 ***Perf. 12½x13***

C257	AP82	30fr shown	.80	.25
C258	AP82	60fr Snake	.90	.30
C259	AP82	110fr Crocodile	1.75	.45
		Nos. C257-C259 (3)	3.45	1.00

Christmas Type of 1981

1981, Dec. 24 ***Perf. 13½***

C260	A143	140fr Correggio	2.25	.45
C261	A143	200fr Gentileschi, 1610	4.00	.70

Souvenir Sheet

C262 A143 500fr Holy Family, by Cranach 6.25 1.75

No. C262 contains one 41x50mm stamp.

Litho. & Embossed

Size: 30x60mm

C262A A143 1500fr Hans Memling, c. 1470 13.50 4.50

Souvenir Sheet

C262B A143 1500fr Fra Angelico, 1438 9.75

Nos. C262A-C262B exist imperf. No. C262A exists in a souvenir sheet of one. Value $20. No. C262B contains one 30x60mm stamp.

Animal Type of 1982

1982, Jan. 22 Litho. ***Perf. 13½***

C263	A145	300fr Mandrill	3.00	.65
C264	A145	500fr Lion	5.00	1.40

Souvenir Sheet

C265 A145 600fr Nile crocodiles 6.25 1.60

No. C265 contains one 47x38mm stamp.

Litho. & Embossed

Size: 51x57mm

C265A A145 1500fr Leopard, Rotary emblem 13.50 4.00

Souvenir Sheet

C265B A145 1500fr Emblem, eagle, horiz. 11.50

Nos. C265A-C265B exist imperf. No. C265A exists in a souvenir sheet of one. Value $37.50. No. C265B contains one 57x51mm stamp.

Transportation Type of 1982 and

AP82a

Designs: 300fr, Savannah cargo ship. 500fr, Columbia space shuttle. 600fr, Spirit of Locomotion emblem. No. C268A, Space shuttle launch, horiz. No. C268B, Shuttle, space telescope.

1982, Feb. 27 Litho. ***Perf. 13½***

C266	A147	300fr multicolored	3.25	.65
C267	A147	500fr multicolored	5.00	1.40

Souvenir Sheet

C268 A147 600fr multicolored 5.00 1.60

Litho. & Embossed

C268A AP82a 1500fr gold & multi 13.50 4.50

Souvenir Sheet

C268B AP82a 1500fr gold & multi 10.50

No. C268 contains one 39x43mm stamp. No. C268B contains one 51x42mm stamp.

Olympic Type of 1982

1982, July 24 Litho. ***Perf. 13½***

C269	A149	300fr Diving	2.75	.80
C270	A149	500fr Equestrian	4.50	1.40

Souvenir Sheet

C271 A149 600fr Basketball 5.00 1.60

No. C271 contains one 38x56mm stamp.

Diana Type of 1982

1982, July 20 Litho. ***Perf. 13½***

C272	A150	300fr multi	3.00	.80
C273	A150	500fr multi	5.00	1.40

Souvenir Sheet

C274 A150 600fr multi 5.25 1.60

No. C274 contains one 56x32mm stamp.

Christmas 1982 AP83

Raphael Paintings.

1982, Dec. ***Perf. 13***

C275	AP83	150fr Beautiful Gardener	1.50	.40
C276	AP83	500fr Holy Family	4.50	1.40

Space Type of 1982

Designs: Various satellites and space scenes. No. C279A, European communications satellite, controller. No. C279B, Viking on Mars, vert.

1982, Aug. 15 Litho. ***Perf. 13½***

C277	A151	300fr multi	2.75	.80
C278	A151	500fr multi	4.50	1.40

Souvenir Sheet

C279 A151 600fr multi 4.50 1.60

Litho. & Embossed

Size: 60x36mm

C279A A151 1500fr gold & multi 13.50 4.50

Souvenir Sheet

C279B A151 1500fr gold & multi 10.50

Nos. C279A-C279B exist imperf. No. C279A exists in a souvenir sheet of one. Value $50. No. C279B contains one 36x60mm stamp.

Birth of Prince William of Wales, June 21, 1982 — AP84

Designs: No. C281, Diana, William, Charles. No. 281B, Diana, William, vert.

1983, Jan. 22

C280 AP84 500fr Diana, William 5.00 1.40

Souvenir Sheet

C281 AP84 600fr Family 5.00 4.00

Litho. & Embossed

C281A AP84 1500fr gold & multi 13.50 3.50

Souvenir Sheet

C281B AP84 1500fr gold & multi 9.00

REPUBLIQUE 65F CENTRAFRICAINE

Manned Flight Bicentenary AP85

1983, Apr.

C282	AP85	65fr Robert's & Hullin's balloon	.90	.20
C283	AP85	130fr John Wise's, 1859	1.25	.35
C284	AP85	350fr Mail balloon, 1870	3.00	.90
C285	AP85	400fr Dirigible Underberg	3.50	1.10
		Nos. C282-C285 (4)	8.65	2.55

Souvenir Sheet

C286 AP85 500fr Montgolfiere, 1783 5.25 1.40

République Centrafricaine 100F

Pre-Olympics — AP86

Various equestrian events.

1983, July Litho. ***Perf. 13***

C287	AP86	100fr multi	.90	.40
C288	AP86	200fr multi	2.00	.60
C289	AP86	300fr multi	2.50	.80
C290	AP86	400fr multi	3.25	1.10
		Nos. C287-C290 (4)	8.65	2.90

Souvenir Sheet

C291 AP86 500fr multi 5.25 1.40

Animal Type of 1983

Endangered Animals, Rotary Emblem

1983, Nov. 14 Litho. ***Perf. 13½***

C291A A170 400fr Black rhinoceros, parrot, zebra, scouts 6.25 1.25

C292 A170 500fr shown 7.25 1.40

Souvenir Sheet

C293 A170 600fr Leopard 5.25 1.50

15th World Scout Jamboree, Alberta (400fr). No. C293 contains one 47x32mm stamp.

Christmas 1983 AP88

Paintings: 130fr, Annunciation, by da Vinci. 205fr, Virgin of the Rocks, by da Vinci. 350fr, Adoration of the Shepherds, by Rubens. 500fr, Virgin and Child with Donor, by Rubens.

1984, Jan. 3 Litho. *Perf. 13*

C294 AP88 130fr multi .90 .25
C295 AP88 205fr multi 1.50 .35
C296 AP88 350fr multi 2.50 .80
C297 AP88 500fr multi 4.00 1.00
Nos. C294-C297 (4) 8.90 2.40

1984 Summer Olympics — AP89

Various gymnastic and rhythmic gymnastic events. 65fr, 100fr, 205fr, 350fr vert.

1984, Mar. 13 Litho. *Perf. 13*

C298 AP89 65fr multi .50 .20
C299 AP89 100fr multi 1.00 .25
C300 AP89 130fr multi 1.25 .30
C301 AP89 205fr multi 2.00 .45
C302 AP89 350fr multi 3.25 .85
Nos. C298-C302 (5) 8.00 2.05

Souvenir Sheet

Perf. 13½x13

C302A AP89 500fr Rhythmic formation 4.50 1.25

For overprint see No. 705.

Summer Olympics Winners AP90

1985, Jan. 7 Litho. *Perf. 14*

C303 AP90 60fr 400 meter relay .50 .25
C304 AP90 140fr 400 meter hurdles 1.25 .30
C305 AP90 300fr 5000 meter race 3.00 .80
C306 AP90 440fr Decathlon 4.00 1.00
Nos. C303-C306 (4) 8.75 2.35

Souvenir Sheet

C307 AP90 500fr 800 meter race, horiz. 4.50 4.50

Christmas 1984 — AP91

Paintings by Titian: 130fr, Virgin and Infant Jesus. 350fr, Virgin with Rabbit. 400fr, Virgin and Child.

1985, Jan. 17 Litho. *Perf. 13*

C308 AP91 130fr multi 1.10 .55
C309 AP91 350fr multi 2.50 1.10
C310 AP91 400fr multi 3.50 1.25
Nos. C308-C310 (3) 7.10 2.90

Audubon Bicentenary — AP92

1985, Jan. 25 Litho. *Perf. 13*

C311 AP92 60fr Otus asio .60 .25
C312 AP92 110fr Coccizus minor, vert. 1.00 .45
C313 AP92 200fr Zenaidura macroura, vert. 1.75 1.00
C314 AP92 500fr Aix sponsa 4.50 2.50
Nos. C311-C314 (4) 7.85 4.20

Christmas 1985 AP93

Religious paintings: 100fr, Virgin with Angels, by the Master of Burgo de Osma. 200fr, Nativity, by Louis Le Nain (1593-1648). 400fr, Virgin and Child with Dove, by Piero de Cosimo (1462-1521).

1985, Dec. 24 Litho. *Perf. 13*

C315 AP93 100fr multi 1.00 .40
C316 AP93 200fr multi 2.25 .85
C317 AP93 400fr multi 4.25 1.90
Nos. C315-C317 (3) 7.50 3.15

Halley's Comet — AP94

1986, Mar. 8

C318 AP94 110fr Edmond Halley .90 .25
C319 AP94 130fr Giotto probe 1.25 .25
C320 AP94 200fr Comet, planet 1.75 .45
C321 AP94 300fr Vega probe 2.50 .60
C322 AP94 400fr Space shuttle 4.00 1.00
Nos. C318-C322 (5) 10.40 2.55

Christmas AP95

Painting details: 250fr, Nativity, by Giotto. 440fr, Adoration of the Magi, by Botticelli, vert. 500fr, Nativity, by Giotto, diff.

1986, Dec. 24 Litho. *Perf. 13½*

C323 AP95 250fr multi 2.00 1.10
C324 AP95 440fr multi 3.50 1.75
C325 AP95 500fr multi 4.25 2.10
Nos. C323-C325 (3) 9.75 4.95

Tennis at the 1988 Olympics — AP96

Various plays.

1986, Dec. 31 *Perf. 12½*

C326 AP96 150fr multi 1.50 .60
C327 AP96 250fr multi, vert. 2.75 .70
C328 AP96 440fr multi, vert. 3.50 1.25
C329 AP96 600fr multi 5.75 1.40
Nos. C326-C329 (4) 13.50 3.95

1988 Summer Olympics, Seoul — AP97

1987, June 15 Litho. *Perf. 13*

C330 AP97 100fr Triple jump, vert. .80 .40
C331 AP97 200fr High jump 1.60 .80
C332 AP97 300fr Long jump 2.25 1.10
C333 AP97 400fr Pole vault, vert. 3.00 1.60
Nos. C330-C333 (4) 7.65 3.90

Souvenir Sheet

C334 AP97 500fr High jump, diff. 4.00 3.25

1988 Summer Olympics, Seoul — AP98

Stamps on stamps and gymnasts: 90fr, No. C94, balance beam, vert. 200fr, No. C21, balance beam, diff. 300fr, No. C22, pommel horse. 400fr, No. C23, parallel bars. 500fr, No. C93, rings.

1988, July 26 Litho. *Perf. 13*

C335 AP98 90fr multi .60 .40
C336 AP98 200fr multi 1.25 .80
C337 AP98 300fr multi 1.90 1.10
C338 AP98 400fr multi 2.75 1.60
Nos. C335-C338 (4) 6.50 3.90

Souvenir Sheet

C339 AP98 500fr multi 3.50 2.75

1st Moon Landing, 20th Anniv. AP99

1989, Aug. 4 Litho. *Perf. 13*

C340 AP99 40fr Apollo 11 .30 .25
C341 AP99 80fr Apollo 15 .60 .30
C342 AP99 130fr Apollo 16 1.10 .55
C343 AP99 1000fr Apollo 17 9.00 2.75
Nos. C340-C343 (4) 11.00 3.85

World Cup Soccer Championships, Italy — AP100

1990, July 7 Litho. *Perf. 13*

C344 AP100 5fr multicolored .20 .20
C345 AP100 30fr multi, diff. .25 .20
C346 AP100 500fr multi, diff. 3.75 1.00
C347 AP100 1000fr multi, diff. 8.50 1.60
Nos. C344-C347 (4) 12.70 3.00

Charles de Gaulle (1890-1979) — AP101

1990, July 27 *Perf. 13½*

C348 AP101 500fr multicolored 3.50 .90

No. C348 exists in a souvenir sheet of 1.

For overprint see No. C360.

Don Mattingly, Baseball Player — AP102

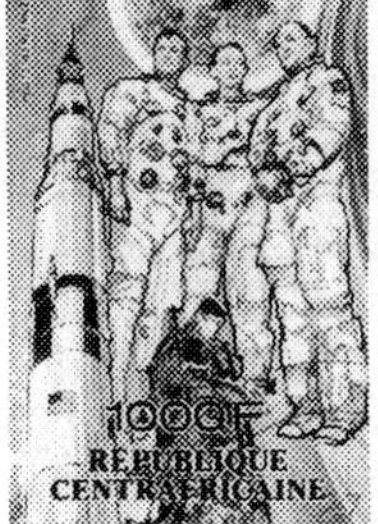

Saturn V Rocket, Apollo 11 Astronauts AP103

Charles de Gaulle, Birth Cent. AP104

No. C352, De Gaulle and Cross of Lorraine.

1990, July 27 Litho. *Perf. 13½*
C349 AP102 300fr multicolored 2.25 .80

Souvenir Sheet

C350 AP103 1000fr multicolored 7.50 1.75

Litho. & Embossed

C351 AP104 1500fr gold & multi 12.50 3.50

Souvenir Sheet

C352 AP104 1500fr gold & multi 10.00

No. C351 exists in souvenir sheet of 1. Value $12.50.
For overprints see Nos. C355-C356.

Visit of Pope John Paul II to Africa AP105

Pope John Paul II and: No. C353, Mother Theresa, portrait. No. C354, Papal arms, globe.

1993 Litho. & Embossed *Perf. 13½*
C353 AP105 1500fr gold & multi 10.50 2.75

Souvenir Sheet

C354 AP105 1500fr gold & multi 17.50

No. C351 Ovptd. "6 JUIN / 1944"
No. C352 Ovptd. in Silver in Sheet Margin

Litho. & Embossed

1994, June 6 *Perf. 13½*
C355 AP104 1500fr gold & multi 10.50 9.00

Souvenir Sheet

C356 AP104 1500fr gold & multi 10.50 9.00

Overprint on No. C356 contains map, soldiers and "50 eme ANNIVERSAIRE DU /DEBARQUEMENT." No. C355 exists in souvenir sheet of 1.

Souvenir Sheets

Japanese Exploration of Antarctica — AP106

1994, Oct. 25
C357 AP106 1200fr Nobu Shirase 3.75 3.75
C358 AP106 1200fr Schooner Kainman Maru, horiz. 3.75 3.75

D-Day, 50th Anniv. (in 1994) — AP107

Designs: a, Gliders over Pegasus Bridge, Sword beach. b, Fighter planes over Juno, Gold and Omaha beaches. c, Planes over Utah beach, St. Mere Eglise.

Litho. & Embossed

1995, Oct. 25 *Perf. 13½*
C359 AP107 1000fr Strip of 3, #a.-c. 11.00 11.00

No. C359b is 60x45mm.

No. C348 Overprinted Souvenir Sheet

IN MEMORIAM
1970-1995

1995, Oct. 10 Litho. *Perf. 13½*
C360 AP101 500fr multicolored 10.50 10.50

AIR POST SEMI-POSTAL STAMPS

Isis of Kalabsha SPAP1

Unwmk.

1964, Mar. 7 Engr. *Perf. 13*
CB1 SPAP1 25fr + 10fr multi 1.25 1.25
CB2 SPAP1 50fr + 10fr multi 2.10 2.10
CB3 SPAP1 100fr + 10fr multi 3.25 3.25
Nos. CB1-CB3 (3) 6.60 6.60

UNESCO world campaign to save historic monuments in Nubia.

African Infants and Globe — SPAP2

1971, Dec. 11 Litho. *Perf. 13x13½*
CB4 SPAP2 140fr + 50fr multi 3.00 1.75

25th anniv. of UNICEF, and Children's Day.

POSTAGE DUE STAMPS

Sternotomis Virescens — D1

Beetles: #J2, Sternotomis gama. #J3, Augosoma centaurus. #J4, Phosphorus virescens, ceroplesis carabarica. #J5, Cetoine scaraboidae. #J6, Ceroplesis S.P. #J7, Macrorhina S.P. #J8, Cetoine scaraboidae. #J9, Phryneta leprosa. #J10, Taurina longiceps. #J11, Monohamus griseoplagiatus. #J12, Jambonus trifasciatus.

Unwmk.

1962, Oct. 15 Engr. *Perf. 11*
J1 D1 50c grn & dp org .20 .20
J2 D1 50c grn & dp org .20 .20
a. Pair, #J1-J2 .25
J3 D1 1fr blk, brn & lt grn .25 .25
J4 D1 1fr blk, brn & lt grn .25 .25
a. Pair, #J3-J4 .50
J5 D1 2fr blk, org & yel grn .35 .35
J6 D1 2fr blk & red org .35 .35
a. Pair, #J5-J6 .70
J7 D1 5fr brn, org & grn .45 .45
J8 D1 5fr brn, org, grn & red .45 .45
a. Pair, #J7-J8 .90
J9 D1 10fr blk, grn & brn .85 .85
J10 D1 10fr blk, grn & grn .85 .85
a. Pair, #J9-J10 1.75
J11 D1 25fr blk, bl grn & brn 2.00 2.00
J12 D1 25fr blk, brn & bl grn 2.00 2.00
a. Pair, #J11-J12 4.00
Nos. J1-J12 (12) 8.20 8.20

Pairs se-tenant at the base.

Giant Anteater — D2

1985, Jan. 25 Litho. *Perf. 12½*
J13 D2 5fr multi .45 .45
J14 D2 20fr multi .80 .80
J15 D2 30fr multi 1.00 1.00
Nos. J13-J15 (3) 2.25 2.25

MILITARY STAMPS

No. 1 Overprinted

Unwmk.

1962, Jan. 1 Engr. *Perf. 13*
M1 A1 bl, car, grn & yel 11.50 —

No. 1 Overprinted

1963
M2 A1 bl, car, grn & yel 13.00 —

OFFICIAL STAMPS

Central African Republic

Coat of Arms — O1

Imprint: "d'après G. RICHER SO.GE.IM."

Perf. 13x12½

1965-69 Litho. Unwmk.

Arms in Original Colors

O1 O1 1fr blk & brn org .20 .20
O2 O1 2fr blk & violet .20 .20
O3 O1 5fr blk & gray .20 .20
O4 O1 10fr blk & green .25 .20
O5 O1 20fr blk & red brn .50 .25
O6 O1 30fr blk & emer ('69) .90 .55
O7 O1 50fr blk & dk bl 1.00 .70
O8 O1 100fr blk & bister 2.25 1.10
O9 O1 130fr blk & ver ('69) 3.50 2.25
O10 O1 200fr blk & claret 5.25 2.75
Nos. O1-O10 (10) 14.25 8.40

Redrawn
Imprint: "d'après G. RICHER DELRIEU"

1971 Photo. *Perf. 12x12½*

Arms in Original Colors

O11 O1 5fr blk & gray .20 .20
O12 O1 30fr blk & emer .45 .25
O13 O1 40fr blk & dp claret .60 .30
O14 O1 100fr blk & bister 1.40 .55
O15 O1 140fr blk & lt bl 2.50 .85
O16 O1 200fr blk & claret 3.00 1.40
Nos. O11-O16 (6) 8.15 3.55

Empire

Nos. O11, O13-O16 Overprinted with Bar and "EMPIRE CENTRAFRICAIN"

1977 Litho. *Perf. 12x12½*
O17 O1 5fr multi .20 .20
O18 O1 40fr multi .35 .20
O19 O1 100fr multi 1.00 .45
O20 O1 140fr multi 1.40 .70
O21 O1 200fr multi 2.25 1.00
Nos. O17-O21 (5) 5.20 2.55

Type of 1965 Inscribed: "EMPIRE CENTRAFRICAIN"

1978, July Litho. *Perf. 12½*
O22 O1 1fr multi .20 .20
O23 O1 2fr multi .20 .20
O24 O1 5fr multi .20 .20
O25 O1 10fr multi .20 .20
O26 O1 15fr multi .20 .20
O27 O1 20fr multi .20 .20
O28 O1 30fr multi .25 .25
O29 O1 40fr multi .35 .25
O30 O1 50fr multi .50 .30
O31 O1 60fr multi .70 .40
O32 O1 100fr multi .90 .55
O33 O1 130fr multi 1.50 .95
O34 O1 140fr multi 1.60 .95
O35 O1 200fr multi 3.25 1.25
Nos. O22-O35 (14) 10.25 6.10

CENTRAL LITHUANIA

'sen-trəl ˌli-thə-'wā-nē-ə

LOCATION — North of Poland and east of Lithuania
CAPITAL — Vilnius

At one time Central Lithuania was a grand duchy of Lithuania but at the end of the 18th Century it fell under Russian rule. After World War I, Lithuania regained her sovereignty but certain areas were occupied by Poland. During the Russo-Polish war this territory was seized by Lithuania whose claim was promptly recognized by the Soviet Government. Under the leadership of the Polish General Zeligowski the territory was recaptured and it was during this occupation the stamps of Central Lithuania came into being. Subsequently the territory became a part of Poland.

100 Fennigi = 1 Markka

Coat of Arms — A1

Perf. 11½, Imperf.

1920-21	**Typo.**	**Unwmk.**	
1	A1 25f red	.25	*.50*
2	A1 25f dark grn ('21)	.25	*.50*
3	A1 1m blue	.25	*.50*
4	A1 1m dark brn ('21)	.25	*.50*
5	A1 2m violet	.25	*.50*
6	A1 2m orange ('21)	.25	*.50*
	Nos. 1-6 (6)	1.50	*3.00*

For surcharges see Nos. B1-B5.

Lithuanian Stamps of 1919 Surcharged in Blue or Black

Perf. 11½x12, 12½x11½, 14

1920, Nov. 23		**Wmk. 145**	
13	A5 2m on 15sk lil	12.50	*30.00*
a.	Inverted surcharge	*125.00*	
14	A5 4m on 10sk red	17.50	*25.00*
a.	Inverted surcharge	*125.00*	
15	A5 4m on 20sk dl bl (Bk)	17.50	*25.00*
a.	Inverted surcharge	*125.00*	
16	A5 4m on 30sk buff	12.00	*20.00*
a.	Inverted surcharge	*125.00*	
17	A6 6m on 50sk lt grn	12.00	*20.00*
a.	4m on 50sk (error)	*125.00*	
b.	10m on 50sk (error)	*125.00*	
18	A6 6m on 60sk vio & red	22.50	*40.00*
a.	4m on 60sk (error)	*125.00*	
b.	10m on 60sk (error)	*125.00*	
19	A6 6m on 75sk bis & red	22.50	*40.00*
a.	4m on 75sk (error)	*125.00*	
b.	10m on 75sk (error)	*125.00*	
20	A8 10m on 1auk gray & red	20.00	35.00
a.	Inverted surcharge	*190.00*	
21	A8 10m on 3auk lt brn & red	*450.00*	*800.00*
22	A8 10m on 5auk bl grn & red	*425.00*	*800.00*
	Nos. 13-20 (8)	136.50	*235.00*
	Nos. 13-22 (10)	*1,011.*	*1,835.*

Reprints of Nos. 17a, 17b, 18a, 18b, 19a, 19b. Value, each $45.

Counterfeits of Nos. 21-22 exist.

Lithuanian Girl — A2

Warrior — A3

Holy Gate of Vilnius — A4

Tower and Cathedral, Vilnius — A5

Rector's Insignia — A6

Gen. Lucien Zeligowski — A7

Perf. 11½, Imperf.

1920	**Litho.**	**Unwmk.**	
23	A2 25f gray	.20	*.75*
24	A3 1m orange	.20	*.75*
25	A4 2m claret	.30	*1.00*
26	A5 4m gray grn & buff	.70	*1.00*
27	A6 6m rose & gray	1.75	*1.00*
28	A7 10m brown & yellow	2.50	*3.25*
	Nos. 23-28 (6)	5.65	*7.75*

For surcharges see Nos. B13-B14, B17-B19.

St. Anne's Church, Vilnius — A8

St. Stanislas Cathedral, Vilnius — A9

White Eagle, White Knight Vytis — A10

Queen Hedwig and King Ladislas II Jagello — A11

Coat of Arms of Vilnius — A12

Poczobut Astronomical Observatory A13

Union of Lithuania and Poland — A14

Tadeusz Kosciuszko and Adam Mickiewicz A15

1921		***Perf. 14, Imperf.***		
35	A8	1m dk gray & yel	.50	*1.00*
36	A9	2m rose & green	.50	*1.00*
37	A10	3m dark green	.60	*1.25*
38	A11	4m brown & buff	.60	*1.25*
39	A12	5m red brown	.60	*1.25*
40	A13	6m slate & buff	.60	*2.50*
41	A14	10m red vio & buff	1.50	*2.50*
42	A15	20m blk brn & buff	1.50	*2.50*
		Nos. 35-42 (8)	6.40	*13.25*

Set, perf. 13½, $150.

Peasant Girl Sowing — A16

White Eagle and Vytis — A17

Great Theater at Vilnius — A18

Allegory: Peace and Industry — A19

Gen. Zeligowski Entering Vilnius — A20

Gen. Zeligowski — A21

1921-22		***Perf. 11½, Imperf.***		
53	A16	10m brown ('22)	6.00	*10.00*
54	A17	25m red & yel ('22)	7.50	*15.00*
55	A18	50m dk blue ('22)	6.00	*10.00*
56	A19	75m violet ('22)	6.00	*10.00*
57	A20	100m bl & bister	2.50	*5.75*
58	A21	150m ol grn & brn	2.50	*5.75*
		Nos. 53-58 (6)	30.50	*56.50*

Opening of the Natl. Parliament, Nos. 53-56; anniv. of the entry of General Zeligowski into Vilnius, Nos. 57-58.

SEMI-POSTAL STAMPS

Nos. 1-6 Surcharged in Black or Red

1921	**Unwmk.**	***Perf. 11½, Imperf.***	
B1	A1 25f + 2m red (Bk)	.50	*1.00*
B2	A1 25f + 2m dk green	.50	*1.00*
B3	A1 1m + 2m blue	1.50	*3.00*
B4	A1 1m + 2m dk brown	1.50	*3.00*
B5	A1 2m + 2m violet	1.00	*2.00*
B6	A1 2m + 2m orange	1.00	*2.50*
	Nos. B1-B6 (6)	6.00	*12.50*

The surcharge means "For Silesia 2 marks." The stamps were intended to provide a fund to assist the plebiscite in Upper Silesia.

Nos. 25, 26 Surcharged:

a

b

Perf. 11½, Imperf.

B13	A4 (a) 2m + 1(m) claret	2.75	10.00
B14	A5 (b) 4m + 1m gray green & buff	2.75	10.00

Nos. 25-26, 28 with inset

Perf. 11½, Imperf.

B17	A4 2m + 1m claret	.50	2.50
B18	A5 4m + 1m gray green & buff	.50	2.00
B19	A7 10m + 2m brn & yel	.90	3.75
	Nos. B13-B19 (5)	7.40	28.25

POSTAGE DUE STAMPS

University, Vilnius D1

Castle Hill, Vilnius D2

Castle Ruins, Troki — D3

Holy Gate, Vilnius — D4

St. Stanislas Cathedral D5

St. Anne's Church, Vilnius D6

1920-21	**Unwmk.**	***Perf. 11½, Imperf.***		
J1	D1	50f red violet	.30	*.60*
J2	D2	1m green	.30	*.60*
J3	D3	2m red violet	.40	*.60*
J4	D4	3m red violet	.60	*1.25*
J5	D5	5m red violet	.90	*2.50*
J6	D6	20m scarlet	2.25	*4.00*
		Nos. J1-J6 (6)	4.75	*9.55*

CEYLON

si-'lăn

LOCATION — An island in the Indian Ocean separated from India by the Gulf of Manaar
GOVT. — Independent republic within the British Commonwealth
AREA — 25,332 sq. mi.
POP. — 12,670,000 (est. 1971)
CAPITAL — Colombo

Ceylon changed its name to Republic of Sri Lanka on May 22, 1972.

12 Pence = 1 Shilling
100 Cents = 1 Rupee (1872)

Values for unused stamps are for examples with original gum as defined in the catalogue introduction except for Nos. 2, 5, 8-9 which seldom have any remaining trace of their original gum. Many unused stamps of Ceylon, especially between Nos. 59 and 274, have toned gum or tropical stains. Values quoted are for stamps with fresh gum. Toned stamps have lower values, and common stamps with toned gum are worth very little.

Very fine examples of Nos. 1-15 will be cut square, will have small margins, but will show an intact design. Inferior examples with the design partly cut away will sell for much less, and examples with large margins will command higher prices. Very fine examples of Nos. 17-58b will have perforations just cutting into the design on one or more sides due to the narrow spacing of the stamps on the plates and to imperfect perforating methods. Stamps with perfs clear on all four sides are extremely scarce and will command substantially higher prices.

Catalogue values for unused stamps in this country are for Never Hinged items, beginning with Scott 290 in the regular postage section and Scott B1 in the semi-postal section.

Watermarks

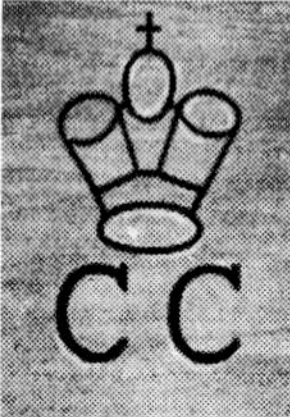

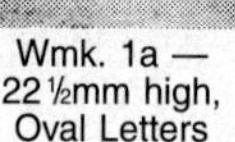

Wmk. 1a — 22½mm high, Oval Letters

Wmk. 1b — 21mm high, Round Letters

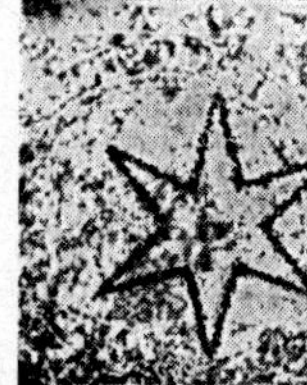

Wmk. 6 — Large Star

Wmk. 290 — Lotus and "Sri" Multiple

Queen Victoria
A1 A2

1857 Engr. Wmk. 6 *Imperf.*

Blued Paper

1	A1	1p blue		225.00
2	A1	6p plum	*10,000.*	525.00

1857-59

White Paper

3	A1	1p deep turq	750.00	35.00
4	A1	2p deep green	175.00	65.00
a.		2p yellow green	575.00	100.00
5	A2	4p dl rose ('59)	*57,500.*	5,250.
6	A1	5p org brown	1,750.	175.00
6A	A1	6p plum	*2,100.*	160.00
7	A1	6p brown	*7,000.*	550.00
8	A2	8p brown ('59)	*25,500.*	*1,750.*
9	A2	9p lil brn ('59)	*37,500.*	1,050.
10	A1	10p vermilion	925.00	350.00
11	A1	1sh violet	5,250.	225.00
12	A2	1sh9p green ('59)	875.00	*925.00*
a.		1sh9p yellow green	*4,750.*	*3,500.*
13	A2	2sh blue ('59)	6,500.	1,400.

Stamps of type A2 frequently have repaired corners.

Nos. 3-4 exist unofficially rouletted.

No. 5 was reproduced by the collotype process in a souvenir sheet distributed at the London International Stamp Exhibition 1950. The paper is unwatermarked.

A3

1857-58 Typo. Unwmk.

14	A3	½p lilac ('58)	200.00	*225.00*
15	A3	½p lilac, *bluish*	3,750.	550.00

No. 14 exists unofficially rouletted.

Nos. 14-15, 38 are printed on surface-glazed paper. Values are for stamps without cracking of the surface, and examples showing cracking should be discounted.

Clean-Cut Perf. 14 to 15½

1861 Wmk. 6 Engr.

17	A1	1p blue	175.00	18.00
18	A1	2p yel green	190.00	27.50
b.		Vert. pair, imperf between		—
19	A2	4p dull rose	2,300.	350.00
20	A1	5p org brown	95.00	10.00
20A	A1	6p brown	2,300.	125.00
b.		6p bister brown		210.00
21	A2	8p brown	2,200.	575.00
22	A2	9p lilac brown	6,500.	275.00
23	A1	1sh violet	110.00	17.50
24	A2	2sh blue	3,250.	750.00

Rough Perf. 14 to 15½

25	A1	1p blue	140.00	8.75
b.		Blued paper	575.00	24.00
26	A1	2p yel green	450.00	92.50
27	A2	4p rose red	450.00	92.50
28	A1	6p olive brown	875.00	100.00
a.		6p deep brown	1,000.	110.00
b.		6p bister brown	1,600.	160.00
29	A2	8p brown	1,600.	650.00
30	A2	8p yel brown	1,600.	400.00
31	A2	9p olive brown	575.00	70.00
32	A2	9p deep brown	87.50	75.00
33	A1	10p vermilion	275.00	25.00
a.		Imperf. vert., pair		—
34	A1	1sh violet	275.00	17.50
35	A2	1sh9p green	750.00	
36	A2	2sh blue	700.00	160.00

The 1sh9p green was never placed in use.

1863 *Perf. 12½*

37	A1	10p vermilion	250.00	18.00

1864 Typo. Unwmk.

38	A3	½p lilac	225.00	200.00

See note following No. 15.

1863 Engr. *Perf. 13*

39	A1	1p blue	140.00	7.00
40	A1	5p car brown	1,600.	175.00
41	A1	6p deep brown	190.00	29.00
42	A2	9p brown	1,400.	110.00
43	A1	1sh grayish violet	2,000.	92.50

Parts of the papermaker's sheet watermark, "T. H. SAUNDERS 1862," may be found on some copies of Nos. 39-43.

Perf. 12

44	A1	1p blue	1,400.	150.00
a.		Horiz. pair, imperf. btwn.		*12,000.*

Two Types of Watermark Crown and CC (1)

1863-67 Typo. Wmk. 1a *Perf. 12½*

45	A3	½p lilac	45.00	35.00
a.		½p reddish lilac	57.50	45.00

Engr.

46	A1	1p blue	125.00	5.75
a.		1p dark blue	125.00	5.75
c.		Perf. 11½	3,000.	375.00
47	A1	2p gray green	80.00	11.50
48	A1	2p emerald	150.00	110.00
48A	A1	2p yel green	10,000.	475.00
48B	A1	2p bottle green		—
49	A1	2p olive	260.00	260.00
50	A2	4p rose	440.00	92.50
a.		4p carmine rose	640.00	160.00
51	A1	5p car brown	200.00	70.00
52	A1	5p olive green	875.00	275.00
e.		5p deep sage green	2,100.	400.00
53	A1	6p choc brown	160.00	7.50
a.		Perf. 13	1,700.	160.00
b.		6p black brown	160.00	10.50
c.		As "b," double impression		3,250.
d.		6p reddish brown	190.00	14.00
54	A2	8p red brown	100.00	52.50
55	A2	9p brown	350.00	50.00
c.		Perf. 13	4,400.	800.00
56	A1	10p vermilion	2,000.	70.00
a.		10p orange	4,600.	475.00
58	A2	2sh blue	290.00	35.00

The ½p, 1p blue, 2p olive, 4p and 5p green exist imperf.

Wmk. 1b

46d	A1	1p blue	175.00	11.50
e.		1p dark blue	160.00	9.25
49d	A1	2p orange yellow	100.00	6.00
e.		2p olive yellow	125.00	11.50
f.		2p olive green	175.00	30.00
50b	A2	4p rose	225.00	65.00
c.		4p carmine rose	125.00	
			usi=y>	40.00
52b	A1	5p myrtle green	100.00	15.00
c.		5p olive green	110.00	15.00
d.		5p bronze green usi=y>	37.50	52.50
53d	A1	6p chocolate brown	37.50	40.00
e.		6p brown	87.50	11.50
54a	A2	8p red brown	70.00	65.00
55a	A2	9p dark brown	52.50	7.00
b.		9p bister brown	500.00	35.00
56b	A1	10p orange	92.50	11.00
c.		10p orange red	55.00	14.00
d.		10p vermilion	3,750.	160.00
57	A1	1sh purple	100.00	8.25
a.		1sh reddish lilac	325.00	32.50
58a	A2	2sh deep blue	140.00	14.00
b.		2sh indigo	210.00	22.50

The 1p blue and 6p brown exist imperf.
For overprints see Nos. O2, O4-O7.

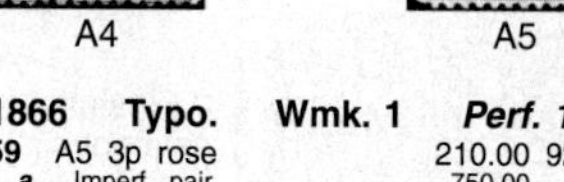

A4 A5

1866 Typo. Wmk. 1 *Perf. 12½*

59	A5	3p rose	210.00	92.50
a.		Imperf., pair	750.00	

For overprint see No. O3.

1868 *Perf. 14*

61	A4	1p blue	30.00	9.25
62	A5	3p rose	82.50	47.50

For overprint see No. O1.

A6 A7

A8 A9

A10

A11

A12 A13

A14

A15

A16

1872-80 *Perf. 14*

63	A6	2c brown	18.00	2.90
64	A7	4c gray	40.00	1.75
65	A7	4c lil rose ('80)	62.50	1.75
66	A8	8c orange	46.00	6.25
a.		8c orange yellow	32.50	7.00
67	A9	16c violet	100.00	3.00
68	A10	24c green	62.50	2.25
69	A11	32c slate bl ('77)	175.00	17.50
70	A12	36c blue	175.00	21.00
71	A13	48c rose	85.00	6.25
72	A14	64c red brn ('77)	300.00	75.00
73	A15	96c olive gray	225.00	30.00
		Nos. 63-73 (11)	*1,289.*	*167.65*

For surcharges see #83-84, 94A-110, 112-114. For types surcharged see #124-129.

1872 *Perf. 12½*

74	A6	2c brown	2,900.	200.00
75	A7	4c gray	1,600.	300.00

1879 *Perf. 14x12½*

77	A6	2c brown	425.00	75.00
78	A7	4c gray	1,600.	40.00
79	A8	8c orange	450.00	55.00

Perf. 12½x14

82	A16	2r50c claret	550.00	350.00

The 32c and 64c are known perf. 14x12½, but were not regularly issued.

No. 82, perf. 12½, was not regularly issued.

See Nos. 142, 158. For surcharges see Nos. 111, 115, 130. For types surcharged see Nos. 160-161.

Nos. 68, 72 Surcharged

1882 *Perf. 14*

83	A10	16c on 24c green	27.50	7.50
84	A14	20c on 64c red brn	11.00	6.50
a.		Double surcharge		1,300.

1883-99 Wmk. 2

85	A6	2c pale brown	65.00	2.00
86	A6	2c green ('84)	3.00	.20
a.		Perf. 12	3,500.	
87	A6	2c org brn ('99)	3.00	.40
88	A7	4c lilac rose	3.50	.35
89	A7	4c rose ('84)	4.50	13.50
a.		Perf. 12	3,500.	
90	A7	4c brt rose ('98)	8.75	9.25
91	A7	4c yellow ('99)	3.50	3.25
92	A8	8c orange	5.00	9.25
93	A9	16c violet	1,750.	175.00
94	A10	24c purple brown	1,250.	
b.		Perf. 12	3,750.	

Nos. 86a, 89a, 94 and 94b were never placed in use. A 48c brown, perf. 12, was prepared but not issued.

For surcharges and overprints see Nos.116-123, 143-151D, 155-156, O8-O9.

Issues of 1872-82 Surcharged:

Postage &

FIVE CENTS

Revenue

a

b

c

d

1885 **Wmk. 1** ***Perf. 14***

94A A9 (a) 5c on 16c 3,250.
95 A10 (a) 5c on 24c 3,250. 110.00
96 A11 (a) 5c on 32c 65.00 20.00
a. Inverted surcharge 1,500.
97 A12 (a) 5c on 36c 300.00 12.00
a. Inverted surcharge 2,250.
98 A13 (a) 5c on 48c 1,250. 65.00
99 A14 (a) 5c on 64c 110.00 7.00
a. Double surcharge 1,150.
100 A15 (a) 5c on 96c 525.00 75.00
101 A9 (b) 10c on 16c 5,750. 2,400.
102 A10 (b) 10c on 24c 500.00 125.00
103 A12 (b) 10c on 36c 450.00 200.00
104 A14 (b) 10c on 64c 475.00 175.00
105 A10 (b) 20c on 24c 65.00 21.00
106 A11 (c) 20c on 32c 75.00 65.00
107 A11 (c) 25c on 32c 18.00 5.25
108 A13 (c) 28c on 48c 45.00 7.00
a. Double surcharge 1,400.
109 A12 (b) 30c on 36c 16.50 10.50
a. Inverted surcharge 240.00 110.00
110 A15 (b) 56c on 96c 30.00 21.00

Perf. 12½

111 A16 (d) 1r12c on 2r50c 550.00 110.00

Perf. 14x12½

112 A11 (a) 5c on 32c 750.00 57.50
113 A14 (a) 5c on 64c 700.00 47.50
114 A14 (b) 10c on 64c 75.00 110.00
a. Vert. pair, imperf. btwn. 3,500.

Perf. 12½x14

115 A16 (d) 1r12c on 2r50c 110.00 50.00

Perf. 14

Wmk. 2

117 A7 (a) 5c on 4c rose 25.00 4.00
a. Inverted surcharge 350.00
118 A8 (a) 5c on 8c org 82.50 8.00
a. Inverted surcharge 2,400.
b. Double surcharge 1,750.
119 A9 (a) 5c on 16c vio 110.00 12.50
a. Inverted surcharge 225.00
120 A10 (a) 5c on 24c pur brn — 600.00
121 A9 (b) 10c on 16c vio *6,000.* 1,250.
122 A10 (b) 10c on 24c pur brn 15.00 7.00
123 A9 (b) 15c on 16c vio 12.50 8.75

A 5c on 4c lilac rose and a 5c on 24c green are known to exist and are considered to be a forgeries.

Types of 1872-80 Surcharged

e

f

g

1885-87

124 A 8 (e) 5c on 8c lilac 18.00 1.60
125 A10 (f) 10c on 24c pur brn 11.00 7.50
126 A 9 (f) 15c on 16c org 62.50 10.00
127 A11 (f) 28c on 32c sl bl 26.00 2.90
128 A12 (f) 30c on 36c ol grn 32.50 16.00
129 A15 (f) 56c on 96c ol gray 57.50 16.00

Wmk. 1 Sideways

130 A16 (g) 1r12c on 2r50c cl 42.50 *100.00*
Nos. 124-130 (7) *250.00 154.00*

A23

A24

FIVE CENTS
Type I — Thin lines in background. Hair and curl clear.
Type II — Thicker lines in background. Heavier shading under chin.

1886 **Wmk. 2**

131 A23 5c lilac, type I 2.60 .20
a. Type II 7.00 .20

For overprint see No. O12.

1886-1900

132 A24 3c org brn & green ('93) 3.75 .50
133 A24 3c green ('00) 2.90 .60
134 A24 6c rose & blk ('99) 1.75 .50
135 A24 12c ol grn & car ('00) 4.50 *8.00*
136 A24 15c olive green 5.75 1.40
137 A24 15c ultra ('00) 6.25 1.50
138 A24 25c brown 4.25 1.10
a. 25c brown, value in ol yel 110.00 80.00
139 A24 28c slate 21.00 1.60
140 A24 30c vio & org brown ('93) 5.00 2.25
141 A24 75c blk & org brown ('00) 5.50 *7.00*
Nos. 132-141 (10) 60.65 *24.45*

Numeral tablet of 3c, 12c and 75c has lined background with colorless value and "c."

For surcharges & overprints see #152-154, 157, 159, O10-O11, O13-O17.

1887 **Wmk. 1**

142 A16 1r12c claret 25.00 22.50

For overprint see No. O18.

Issue of 1883-84 Surcharged

1888-90 **Wmk. 2**

143 A7 2c on 4c lilac rose 1.60 .90
a. Inverted surcharge 22.50 20.00
b. Double surcharge, one invtd. 225.00
144 A7 2c on 4c rose 2.50 .35
a. Inverted surcharge 15.00 *16.00*
b. Double surcharge 250.00

Surcharged

145 A7 2c on 4c lilac rose .85 .35
a. Inverted surcharge 32.50 35.00
b. Double surcharge 75.00 75.00
c. Double surcharge, one invtd. 70.00 62.50
146 A7 2c on 4c rose 5.50 .20
a. Double surcharge, one invtd. 85.00 *92.50*
b. Double surcharge 80.00 *85.00*
c. Inverted surcharge 250.00

Surcharged

147 A7 2c on 4c lilac rose 75.00 32.50
a. Inverted surcharge 110.00 42.50
b. Double surcharge, one inverted 150.00

148 A7 2c on 4c rose 2.50 .85
a. Inverted surcharge 14.00 9.75
b. Double surcharge, one inverted 9.25 *11.50*
c. Double surcharge 150.00 125.00

Surcharged

149 A7 2c on 4c lilac rose 50.00 21.00
a. Inverted surcharge 150.00 35.00
150 A7 2c on 4c rose 3.00 1.25
a. Inverted surcharge 14.00 6.25
b. Double surcharge 110.00 110.00
c. Double surcharge, one inverted 14.00 7.00

Surcharged

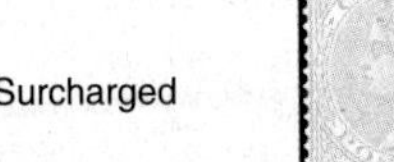

151 A7 2c on 4c rose 11.50 1.10
a. Inverted surcharge 19.00 6.25
b. Double surcharge 100.00 100.00
c. Double surch., one invtd. 21.00 9.75
i. "S" of "Cents" inverted 210.00
151D A7 2c on 4c lilac rose 52.50 30.00
e. Inverted surcharge 80.00 45.00
f. Double surcharge 260.00
g. Double surch., one invtd. 100.00 100.00
h. "S" of "Cents" inverted 450.00

Counterfeit errors of surcharges of Nos. 143 to 151D are prevalent.

No. 136 Surcharged

1890

152 A24 5c on 15c ol green 2.90 2.25
a. "Flve" instead of "Five" 110.00 92.50
b. "REVENUE" omitted 190.00 160.00
c. Inverted surcharge 542.50 *55.00*
d. Double surcharge 110.00 *140.00*
e. As "a," inverted surcharge — 1,100.
f. Inverted "s" in "Cents" 70.00 *80.00*
g. As "f," inverted surcharge 1,250.00
h. As "b," invtd. "s" in "Cents" 1,000.

Nos. 138-139 Surcharged

1891

153 A24 15c on 25c brown 12.50 *14.00*
154 A24 15c on 28c slate 16.00 9.75

Nos. 88, 89 and 139 Surcharged

1892

155 A7 3c on 4c lilac rose 1.10 *3.75*
156 A7 3c on 4c rose 4.25 *8.00*
a. Double surcharge, one invtd.
157 A24 3c on 28c slate 4.50 *4.00*
a. Double surcharge 140.00
Nos. 155-157 (3) 9.85 *15.75*

Type of 1879

1898

158 A16 2r50c violet, *red* 32.50 *62.50*

No. 136 Surcharged in Black

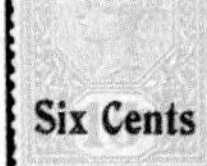

1899

159 A24 6c on 15c olive green .80 .85

Surcharged Type "g" in Black

1899 **Wmk. 1**

160 A16 1r50c on 2r50c gray 22.50 *52.50*
161 A16 2r25c on 2r50c yel 40.00 *92.50*

A35

1900 **Wmk. 1**

162 A35 1r50c car rose 22.50 *40.00*
163 A35 2r25c dull blue 35.00 *40.00*

King Edward VII

A36 A37

A38

A39

A40

1903-05 **Wmk. 2**

166 A36 2c org brown 2.25 .20
167 A37 3c green 2.25 1.10
168 A37 4c yel & blue 2.25 *4.00*
169 A38 5c dull lilac 1.75 .70
170 A39 6c car rose 11.00 1.75
171 A37 12c ol grn & car 5.75 *11.00*
172 A40 15c ultra 7.50 3.50
173 A40 25c bister 4.50 *9.25*
174 A40 30c vio & green 3.75 *4.50*
175 A37 75c bl & org ('05) 3.50 *21.00*
176 A40 1r50c gray ('04) 75.00 62.50
177 A40 2r25c brn & grn ('04) 75.00 57.50
Nos. 166-177 (12) 194.50 177.00

For overprints see Nos. O19-O24.

1904-10 **Wmk. 3**

178 A36 2c orange brown 1.75 .20
a. 2c orange 1.75 .55
179 A37 3c green 1.75 .20
180 A37 4c yel & blue 2.25 1.75
181 A38 5c dull lilac 2.50 1.40
a. Booklet pane of 12
182 A39 6c car rose 1.75 .20
183 A40 10c ol grn & vio ('10) 2.75 2.50
184 A37 12c ol grn & car 1.75 *2.00*
185 A40 15c ultra 2.25 .70
186 A40 25c bister ('05) 7.00 4.25
187 A40 25c slate ('10) 2.75 1.75
188 A40 30c vio & grn ('05) 2.75 *3.00*
189 A40 50c brown ('10) 4.50 *8.50*
190 A37 75c bl & org ('05) 6.00 *9.25*
191 A40 1r vio, *yel* ('10) 8.50 *11.50*
192 A40 1r50c gray ('05) 29.00 11.50
193 A40 2r scar, *yel* ('10) 17.50 *30.00*
194 A40 2r25c brn & grn 25.00 *32.50*
195 A40 5r blk, *grn* ('10) 42.50 *75.00*
196 A40 10r blk, *red* ('10) 100.00 *175.00*
Nos. 178-196 (19) 262.25 *371.20*

No. 181 exists on ordinary and chalky paper.

A41

A42

1908
197 A41 5c deep red violet 2.75 .20
a. Booklet pane of 12
198 A42 6c carmine rose 1.40 .20

1911, July 5
199 A40 3c green 1.10 .85

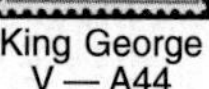
King George V — A44

King George V — A45

3 AND 6 CENTS
Type I — Small "c" after value, 2¼mm wide and 2mm high.
Type II — Large "c" after value, 2½mm wide and 2¼mm high.
1, 5 AND 9 CENTS are Type II, other denominations Type I.

Die I

For description of the dies, see back of this section of the Catalogue.

1912-25 Wmk. 3
200 A44 1c dp brn (Die Ib) ('20) 1.10 .20
201 A44 2c brown org .35 .20
202 A44 3c dp grn (Die Ia, type II) 2.90 .45
a. 3c deep green, die I, type I 5.00 1.25
203 A44 5c red violet 1.10 .70
204 A44 6c car (Die Ib, type II) 1.50 1.00
a. 6c carmine, die I, type I 1.75 .45
b. As "a," bklt. pane of 6
205 A44 10c olive green 3.50 2.00
206 A44 15c ultra 2.00 1.40

Chalky Paper
207 A44 25c yel & ultra 2.00 2.00
208 A44 30c green & vio 4.50 3.75
209 A44 50c black & scar 1.40 *2.00*
210 A44 1r violet, *yel* 3.75 *4.00*
211 A44 2r blk & red, *yel* 3.75 *12.50*
212 A44 5r blk, *green* 19.00 *32.50*
a. 5r black, *bl grn,* olive back 18.00 *40.00*
b. 5r blk, *emer* (Die II) ('20) 50.00 *110.00*
213 A44 10r vio & blk, *red* 70.00 *92.50*
a. Die II ('20) 85.00 *150.00*
214 A44 20r blk & red, *bl* 140.00 *150.00*
215 A45 50r dull violet 400.00
216 A45 100r gray black 1,600.
217 A45 500r gray green *5,250.*
218 A45 1000r vio, *red* ('25) *18,500.*
Nos. 200-214 (15) 256.85 *305.20*

Although Nos. 217 and 218 were theoretically available for postage it is not probable that they were ever used for other than fiscal purposes.

The 1r through 100r with revenue cancellations sell for minimal prices.

For surcharge & overprints see #223, MR1-MR3.

Die I
Surface-colored Paper

1913-14
220 A44 1r violet, *yellow* 3.50 *5.50*
221 A44 2r black & red, *yel* 3.00 *14.00*
222 A44 5r black, *green* 21.00 *37.50*
Nos. 220-222 (3) 27.50 *57.00*

No. 203 Surcharged

1918
223 A44 1c on 5c red violet .20 .25

For overprint see No. MR4.

Die I

1921-33 Wmk. 4
Ordinary Paper
225 A44 1c dp brn (Die Ib) ('27) .85 .40
226 A44 2c brn org (Die II) .70 .25
227 A44 3c green (Die Ia, type II) 3.00 .85
228 A44 3c slate (Die Ia, type II) ('22) .85 .20
229 A44 5c red vio (Die I) .55 .20
230 A44 6c carmine (Die Ib, type II) 2.25 .85
231 A44 6c vio (Die Ib, type II) ('22) 1.10 .20
232 A44 9c red, *yel* (Die II) ('26) .90 .35
233 A44 10c olive green 1.60 .45
a. Die II 2.00 .70
234 A44 12c scarlet, Die II 1.10 *2.50*
a. Die I ('25) 5.00 *6.25*
235 A44 15c ultramarine 3.75 *11.00*
236 A44 15c green, *yel,* Die II 1.75 1.10
a. Die I ('22) 1.75 1.40
237 A44 20c ultra, Die II ('24) 4.00 *.50*
a. Die I ('22) 4.00 7.00
238 A44 25c yel & blue 1.90 *2.10*
a. Die II 3.50 1.40

For surcharges see Nos. 248-249.

Chalky Paper
239 A44 30c green & violet 1.75 *3.00*
a. Die II 3.50 1.40
240 A44 50c blk & scar (Die II) 1.75 .90
a. Die I 62.50 *85.00*
241 A44 1r vio, *yel,* Die II 18.00 *27.50*
a. Die I 18.00 *30.00*
242 A44 2r blk & red, *yel* (Die II) 8.00 *8.50*
243 A44 5r blk, *emer,* (Die II) 32.50 *57.50*
244 A44 20r blk & red, *bl,* (Die II) 160.00 *210.00*
245 A45 50r dull vio 450.00 *800.00*
246 A45 100r gray black 1,750.
247 A45 100r ultra & dl vio ('27) 1,500.
Nos. 225-244 (20) 246.30 328.35

Nos. 228, 231 Surcharged

1926
248 A44 2c on 3c slate .90 1.10
a. Double surcharge 80.00
b. Bar omitted 85.00 *100.00*
249 A44 5c on 6c violet .55 .45
a. Double surcharge

A46

1927-29 Chalky Paper Wmk. 4
254 A46 1r red vio & dl vio ('28) 2.90 1.40
255 A46 2r car & green ('29) 4.25 3.00
256 A46 5r brn vio & grn ('28) 16.00 *22.50*
257 A46 10r org & green 40.00 *92.50*
258 A46 20r ultra & dl vio 110.00 *210.00*
Nos. 254-258 (5) 173.15 *329.40*

Common Design Types pictured following the introduction.

Silver Jubilee Issue
Common Design Type

1935, May 6 Engr. *Perf. 13½x14*
260 CD301 6c gray blk & ultra .40 .25
261 CD301 9c indigo & green .65 .65
262 CD301 20c blue & brown 4.25 2.50
263 CD301 50c brt vio & ind 5.00 5.00
Nos. 260-263 (4) 10.30 8.40

Tapping Rubber Tree — A47

Colombo Harbor — A49

Adam's Peak — A48

Picking Tea — A50

Coconut Palms — A53

Rice Terraces A51

River Scene A52

Temple of the Tooth, Kandy A54

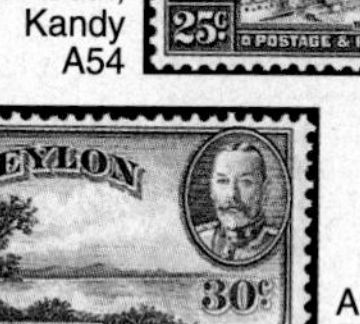
Ancient Reservoir A55

Wild Elephants A56

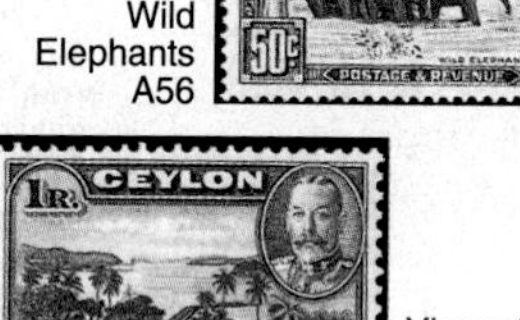
View of Trincomalee A57

Perf. 11x11½, 11½x11; 11½x13, 13x11½ (A47, A48, A53); 14 (A56)

1935-36 Wmk. 4
264 A47 2c car rose & blk .35 *.45*
a. Perf. 14 10.00 .45
265 A48 3c olive & black .40 *.45*
a. Perf. 14 30.00 .40
266 A49 6c blue & black .35 .35
267 A50 9c org red & ol grn 1.10 .75
268 A51 10c dk vio & blk 1.40 *2.50*
269 A52 15c grn & org brn 1.10 .60
270 A53 20c ultra & black 2.00 *2.90*
271 A54 25c choc & dk ultra 1.60 1.40
272 A55 30c green & lake 2.50 *3.00*
273 A56 50c dk vio & blk 9.75 2.00
274 A57 1r brown & vio 21.00 18.00
Nos. 264-274 (11) 41.55 32.40

Issued: 2c, 15c, 25c, 5/1/35; 10c, 6/1/35; 1r, 7/1/35; 30c, 8/1/35; 3c, 10/1/35; 6c, 9c, 20c, 50c, 1/1/36.

Coronation Issue
Common Design Type

1937, May 12 *Perf. 11x11½*
275 CD302 6c dark carmine .35 .20
a. Booklet pane of 10
276 CD302 9c deep green 1.25 *2.50*
a. Booklet pane of 10 150.00
277 CD302 20c deep ultra 1.75 *3.50*
Nos. 275-277 (3) 3.35 6.20
Set, never hinged 7.00

Types of 1935 with "Postage & Revenue Removed" and Picturing George VI and:

Ancient Guard Stone — A68

George VI — A69

Sigiriya (Lion Rock) — A61

Perf. 11x11½, 11½x11; 12 (#286)

1938-52 Engr. Wmk. 4
278 A47 2c car rose & blk ('44) .45 *.95*
a. Perf. 13½x13 ('38) 100.00 2.00
b. Perf. 13½ ('38) 2.00 .20
c. Perf. 12 ('49) 1.25 *4.00*
d. Perf. 11½x13 ('38) 9.00 2.00
279 A48 3c dk grn & blk ('42) .50 .20
a. Perf. 13x13½ ('38) 225.00 10.00
b. Perf. 14 ('41) 100.00 1.10
c. Perf. 13½ ('38) 3.50 .20
d. Perf. 12 ('46) .70 *.95*
e. Perf. 13x11½ 8.00 .50
280 A49 6c blue & black .20 .20
281 A61 10c blue & black 1.60 .20
282 A52 15c red brn & grn 1.25 .20
283 A50 20c dull bl & blk 2.25 .20
284 A54 25c choc & dk ultra 3.25 .25
285 A55 30c dk grn & rose car 8.00 2.25
286 A56 50c dk vio & blk ('46) 2.75 .20
a. Perf. 14 ('42) 90.00 29.00
b. Perf. 13x11½ ('38) 140.00 40.00
c. Perf. 13x13½ ('38) 300.00 3.00
d. Perf. 13½ ('38) 15.00 .35
e. Perf. 11½x11 ('42) 4.00 4.00
287 A57 1r dk brn & bl vio 10.50 1.40
288 A68 2r dark car & blk 9.25 2.90

***Perf. 14* Typo.**
289 A69 5r brn vio & grn 27.50 4.00
289A A69 10r yel org & dl grn ('52) 42.50 25.00
Nos. 278-289A (13) 110.00 37.95

No. 289A differs from type A69 in having "REVENUE" inscribed vertically at either side of the frame. This revenue 10r was valid for postage Dec. 1, 1952-Mar. 14, 1954.

See #292, 295. For surcharges see #290-291.

Catalogue values for unused stamps in this section, from this point to the end of the section, are for Never Hinged items.

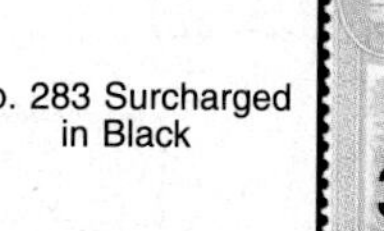

No. 283 Surcharged in Black

1940, Nov. 5 *Perf. 11x11½*
290 A50 3c on 20c dull bl & blk 2.90 .20

No. 280 Surcharged with New Value and Bars

1941, May 10
291 A49 3c on 6c blue & black .20 .20

Coconut Palms — A70

1943-47 Wmk. 4 Engr. *Perf. 12*

292 A70 5c red org & ol grn ('47) 2.00 .35
a. Perf. 13½ ('43) .35 .20

Peace Issue

Common Design Type

1946, Dec. 10 *Perf. 13½x14*

293 CD303 6c deep blue .20 .20
294 CD303 15c brown .20 .20

Guard Stone Type of 1938

1947, Mar. 15 *Perf. 11x11½*

295 A68 2r violet & black 2.25 1.75

Parliament Building, Colombo — A71

Adam's Peak A72

Dagoba at Anuradhapura A74

Temple of the Tooth, Kandy A73

1947, Nov. 25 *Perf. 11x12, 12x11*

296 A71 6c deep ultra & black .20 .20
297 A72 10c car, orange & black .20 .20
298 A73 15c red vio & grnsh blk .20 .20
299 A74 25c brt green & bister .20 .20
Nos. 296-299 (4) .80 .80

New constitution of 1947.

National Flag A75

D. S. Senanayake A76

Engr., Flag Typo. (A75); Engr. (A76)

Perf. 12½x12, 12x12½, 13x12½

1949 Wmk. 4

300 A75 4c org brn, car & yel .20 .20
301 A76 5c dark green & brn .20 .20

Wmk. 290

302 A75 15c red org, car & yel .30 .20
303 A76 25c dp blue & brown .20 .20
Nos. 300-303 (4) .90 .80

Size of No. 302: 28x22¼mm.
1st anniv. of Ceylon's independence.
Issued: #300-301, Feb. 4; #302-303, Apr. 5.

A77

A78

Design: 15c, Lion Rock and UPU symbols.

Wmk. 290

1949, Oct. 10 Engr. *Perf. 12*

304 A77 5c dk green & brown .85 .20
305 A77 15c dark car & black 1.25 1.25
306 A78 25c ultra & black 1.25 1.25
Nos. 304-306 (3) 3.35 2.70

75th anniv. of the UPU.

Kandyan Dancer A79

Kiri Vehera, Polonnaruwa A80

Vesak Orchid — A81

Sigiriya — A82

Ratmalana, Plane — A83

Vatadage Ruins at Madirigiriya A84

1950, Feb. 4 *Perf. 12x12½*

307 A79 4c bright red & choc .20 .20
308 A80 5c green .20 .20
309 A81 15c pur & blue green 1.75 .35
310 A82 30c carmine & yel .35 .35

Perf. 11x11½, 11½x11

311 A83 75c red org & blue 5.50 .20
312 A84 1r red brn & dp blue 2.00 .35
Nos. 307-312 (6) 10.00 1.65

See Nos. 340-345.

Coconut Palms — A85

Star Orchid — A86

1951-52 Unwmk. Photo. *Perf. 11½*

313 A85 10c gray & dark green 1.10 .75
314 A86 35c dk grn & rose brn ('52) 1.75 1.75
a. Corrected inscription ('54) 7.00 .70

On No. 314a a dot has been added above the third character in the second line of the Tamil inscription.

Issue dates: 10c, Aug. 1; 35c, Feb. 1.

See No. 351.

Mace and Symbols of Industry A87

Perf. 12½x14

1952, Feb. 23 Wmk. 290

315 A87 5c green .20 .20
316 A87 15c brt ultramarine .30 .25

Colombo Plan Exhibition, February 1952.

Coronation Issue

Queen Elizabeth II — A88

1953, June 2 Engr. *Perf. 12x12½*

317 A88 5c green 1.00 .20

Royal Procession A89

1954, Apr. 10 *Perf. 13x12½*

318 A89 10c deep blue .35 .20

Visit of Queen Elizabeth II and the Duke of Edinburgh, 1954.

Sambar in Ruhuna National Park — A90

Rubber Trees — A91

Designs: 3c, Ancient guard stone. 6c and 10r, Harvesting rice. 25c, Sigiriya fresco. 50c, Outrigger fishing canoe. 85c, Tea Picker. 2r, Gal Oya dam. 5r, Bas-relief, "The Lovers."

1954 Unwmk. Photo. *Perf. 11½*

Size: 21x25½mm

319 A90 2c green & brown .20 .20
320 A90 3c violet & black .20 .20
321 A90 6c yel grn & blk brn .20 .20
322 A90 25c vio bl, bl & brn orange .20 .20

Size: 25½x21mm

323 A91 40c black brown 5.25 1.00
324 A91 50c indigo .40 .20

Size: 23x32½mm, 32½x23mm

325 A90 85c dk grn & gray .60 .20
326 A91 2r blue & blk brn 7.25 1.25
327 A90 5r dp org & blk brn 5.00 1.40
328 A90 10r brown 42.50 11.00
Nos. 319-328 (10) 61.80 15.85

See Nos. 346-356.

Issued: 25c, 50c, 5r, 10r, 3/15; others, 5/15.

Nos. 327-328 with revenue cancellations sell for minimal prices.

King Coconuts — A92

Symbols of Agriculture A93

1954, Dec. 1

329 A92 10c brown & orange .25 .20

See No. 349.

Perf. 14x14½

1955, Dec. 10 Wmk. 290

330 A93 10c orange & brown .20 .20

Royal Agricultural and Food Exhibition.

House of Representatives — A94

1956, Mar. 26 Unwmk. *Perf. 11½*

Granite Paper

331 A94 10c deep green .20 .20

25th anniv. of Prime Minister Sir John Kotelawala's entry into the Ceylon Legislature.

Arrival of Vijaya in Ceylon — A95

Dharmachakra Encircling Globe — A96

1956, May 23 Granite Paper

332 A95 3c dull vio gray & saph .20 .20
333 A96 15c ultramarine .25 .20

Birth of Buddha, 2500th anniv. See #B1-B2.

Methods of Transportation — A97

35c, 85c, Ceylon's 1st stamp & coat of arms.

1957, Apr. 1 Photo. *Perf. 12½x13*

334 A97 4c blue green & ver .75 .35
335 A97 10c blue & vermilion .75 .20

Perf. 11½

Granite Paper

336 A97 35c blue, yel & brown .40 .40
337 A97 85c dull grn, yel & brn .85 *1.00*
Nos. 334-337 (4) 2.75 1.95

Ceylon's 1st postage stamps, cent.

Nos. B1-B2 Overprinted with Black Bars and Squares

1958, Jan. 15 **Unwmk.**

Granite Paper

338 SP1 4c dp blue & lt yel .20 .20
a. Inverted overprint 12.50
b. Double overprint 12.50
339 SP1 10c dk gray, yel & brt pink .20 .20
a. Inverted overprint 20.00

The overprint obliterates the surtax and inscription at right.

Types of 1950-54 Redrawn

Perf. 12x12½

1958-59 **Engr.** **Wmk. 290**

340 A79 4c brt red & chocolate .20 .20
341 A80 5c green .20 *1.00*
342 A81 15c purple & blue grn 4.50 1.10
343 A82 30c car & yel ('59) .20 *1.50*

Perf. 11½x11

344 A83 75c red org & bl ('59) 11.00 2.75

Perf. 11x11½

345 A84 1r red brn & dp blue .85 .20
Nos. 340-345 (6) 16.95 6.75

Issued: 4c, 5/14; 5c, 15c, 1r, 10/1; 30c, 75c, 5/1.

For surcharge see No. 368.

1958-59 **Unwmk.** **Photo.** ***Perf. 11½***

Granite Paper

346 A90 2c green & brown .20 .40
347 A90 3c violet & black .20 .55
348 A90 6c yel grn & blk brn .20 .50
349 A92 10c brown & orange .20 .20
350 A90 25c vio bl, bl & brn orange .20 .20
351 A86 35c dk grn & rose brn 7.75 .40
352 A91 50c indigo .25 .20
353 A90 85c dark green & gray 4.50 4.50
354 A91 2r blue & blk brn 1.25 .25
355 A90 5r dp org & blk brn 4.75 .40
356 A90 10r brown 11.00 1.40
Nos. 346-356 (11) 30.50 9.00

Designs and sizes of Nos. 340-356 remain as before, but wording has been changed to be predominantly Singhalese. "Ceylon" appears in small letters only in English and Tamil.

Nos. 355-356 with revenue cancellations sell for minimal prices.

Issue dates: 35c, 50c, July 15; 10c, Oct. 1; 85c, May 1, 1959; others, May 14, 1958.

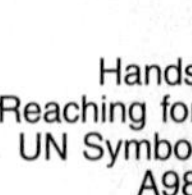

Hands Reaching for UN Symbol A98

Perf. 13x12½

1958, Dec. 10 **Photo.** **Unwmk.**

357 A98 10c red brown & red .20 .20
358 A98 85c Prus green & red .55 .55

10th anniv. of the signing of the Universal Declaration of Human Rights.

Pirivena Universities and Founders A99

1959, Dec. 31

359 A99 10c brt ultra & dp org .20 .20

Institution of Pirivena Universities; founders Hikkaduwe Sri Sumangala Nayaka Thero and Ratmalane Sri Dharmaloka Nayake Thero.

Uprooted Oak Emblem A100

Prime Minister Bandaranaike A101

1960, Apr. 7 **Photo.** ***Perf. 11½***

Granite Paper

360 A100 4c chocolate & gold .20 *.50*
361 A100 25c vio blue & gold .20 .20

World Refugee Year, 7/1/59-6/30/60.

1961, Jan. 8 **Granite Paper**

Two types:
I - Gray hair at temple.
II - Dark hair at temple (redrawn).

362 A101 10c vio bl & gray bl (I) .20 .30
a. Type II .45 .20

Solomon West Ridgeway Dias Bandaranaike, assassinated Sept. 26, 1959.

Badge of Singhalese Scouts — A102

Malaria Eradication Emblem — A103

1962, Feb. 26 **Unwmk.** ***Perf. 11½***

Granite Paper

363 A102 35c dark blue & ocher .25 .20

Boy Scouts of Ceylon, 50th anniv.

Perf. 14½x14

1962, Apr. 7 **Photo.** **Wmk. 290**

364 A103 25c lt sep, red org & brn .20 .20

WHO drive to eradicate malaria.

Monoplane 1938, and De Havilland Comet IV — A104

1963, Feb. 28 **Unwmk.** ***Perf. 11½***

Granite Paper

365 A104 50c lt grnsh blue & blk .45 .45

25th anniv. of Ceylonese airmail service.

Stylized Vase and Wheat Emblem A105

1963, Mar. 21

Granite Paper

366 A105 5c blue & orange ver .30 *1.50*
367 A105 25c olive & brown 1.75 .35

FAO "Freedom from Hunger" campaign.

No. 340 Surcharged

Perf. 12x12½

1963, June 1 **Engr.** **Wmk. 290**

368 A79 2c on 4c brt red & choc .20 .20
a. Inverted surcharge 25.00
b. Double surcharge 17.50

Rural Life — A106

1963, July 5 **Photo.** ***Perf. 14x14½***

369 A106 60c dull red & black .75 .55

50th anniv. of the Cooperative Movement.

Landscape and Elephant A107

1963, Dec. 2 **Wmk. 290**

370 A107 5c blue & black .55 .30

National Conservation Week.

S.W.R.D. Bandaranaike A108

Anagarika Dharmapala A109

Perf. 11½

1963, Sept. 26 **Unwmk.** **Engr.**

Granite Paper

371 A108 10c blue .20 .20

Redrawn

1964, July 1 **Photo.**

Granite Paper

372 A108 10c grnsh gray & bl vio .20 .20

Frame redrawn on No. 372; inscription in bottom panel replaced by ornament.

For surcharge see No. 389.

1964, Sept. 16 **Unwmk.** ***Perf. 11½***

Granite Paper

373 A109 25c gray brn & dull yel .20 .20

Anagarika Dharmapala, Buddhist missionary, birth cent.

Ceylon Jungle Fowl — A110

Vatadage Ruins at Madirigiriya A111

Tea Picker — A112

Designs: 5c, Hill myna. 15c, Blue peafowl. 75c, Asiatic black-headed oriole. 5r, Girls, working in rice field. 10r, Map of Ceylon on scroll, showing agricultural development stations.

Wmk. 290, Unwmkd. (20c)

1964-69 **Photo.** ***Perf. 14, 11½ (20c)***

374 A110 5c brt bl, blk, yel & grn 2.00 1.40
375 A110 15c yel, grn, blk, brt bl & rose 3.00 .25

376 A111 20c dk red brn, *buff* .20 .25
377 A110 60c yel & multi 4.25 1.10
a. Blue omitted 50.00
b. Red omitted 50.00
378 A110 75c ol, blk, org & brn 3.00 .75
a. Souvenir sheet of 4 10.00
b. As "a," overprinted 8.50
379 A112 1r brown & grn 1.00 .25
c. Brown omitted 125.00
379A A111 5r multicolored 5.00 4.00
379B A112 10r brown & multi 20.00 3.50
Nos. 374-379B (8) 38.45 11.50

No. 378a contains four imperf. stamps with simulated perforations similar to Nos. 374-375 and 377-378.

No. 378b is overprinted "First National Stamp Exhibition 1967" in two lines of black capitals.

No. 376 is on granite paper.

Issued: 20c, 1r, 10/1; 5c, 15c, 60c, 75c, 2/5/66; 5r, 8/15/69; 10r, 10/1/69.

See No. 325.

Exhibition Buildings, Cogwheels — A113

1964, Dec. 1 **Unwmk.** ***Perf. 11***

"Industrial Exhibition" in Singhalese and English

380 A113 5c multicolored .20 *.50*

"Industrial Exhibition" in Singhalese and Tamil

381 A113 5c multicolored .20 *.50*
a. Pair, #380-381 .25 *1.00*

1965 Industrial Exhibition.

Railroad Trains, 1864-1964 A114

Wmk. 290

1964, Dec. 21 **Photo.** ***Perf. 14***

"Railway Centenary" in Singhalese and English

382 A114 60c lil rose, bl & yel grn 2.50 .40

"Railway Centenary" in Singhalese and Tamil

383 A114 60c lil rose, bl & yel grn 2.50 .40
a. Vertical pair, #382-383 5.25 5.25

Centenary of Ceylonese railroads.

ITU Emblem, Old and New Communication Equipment — A115

1965, May 17 ***Perf. 14***

384 A115 2c ultra & red 1.40 1.00
385 A115 30c brown & red 3.50 .45

ITU, centenary.

ICY Emblem A116

1965, June 26 **Unwmk.** ***Perf. 11½***

Granite Paper

386 A116 3c rose car & dk bl 1.40 1.00
387 A116 50c gold, rose car & blk 3.50 .45

International Cooperation Year.

Municipal Council Building A117

1965, Oct. 29 Photo. *Perf. 11½*
Granite Paper

388 A117 25c gray & green .20 .20

Centenary of Colombo Municipal Council.

No. 372 Surcharged

1965, Dec. 18 Photo. *Perf. 11½*

389 A108 5c on 10c .20 .25

D. S. Senanayake — A118

View and Arms of Kandy — A119

1966, Mar. 22 Unwmk. *Perf. 11½*
Granite Paper

390 A118 10c bright green .85 .20

D. S. Senanayake, first prime minister of Ceylon, 14th death anniv. See No. 418.

Perf. 14x13½
1966, June 15 Photo. Wmk. 290

391 A119 25c multicolored .20 .20

Centenary of Kandy Municipal Council.

Opening of WHO Headquarters, Geneva A120

Unwmk.
1966, Oct. 8 Litho. *Perf. 14*

392 A120 4c multicolored 2.50 2.50
393 A120 1r multicolored 9.00 1.50

Rice, Map of Ceylon, FAO Emblem — A121

UNESCO Emblem A122

Design: 30c, Rice and globe.

1966, Oct. 25 Photo. *Perf. 11½*
Granite Paper

394 A121 6c dk green, org & brn .20 *.45*
395 A121 30c brt blue, org & brn .45 .20

Intl. Rice Year under sponsorship of the FAO.

1966, Nov. 3 Litho. *Perf. 12*

396 A122 3c tan & multi 2.25 1.90
397 A122 50c brt green & multi 6.75 1.00

20th anniv. of UNESCO.

Map of Ceylon and UNESCO Emblem — A123

Worshippers at Buddhist Shrine A124

1966, Dec. 1 Unwmk. *Perf. 14*

398 A123 2c yel brn, yel & blue .20 *.55*
399 A123 2r multicolored .65 .25

Intl. Hydrological Decade (UNESCO), 1965-74.

1967, Jan. 2 Photo. *Perf. 12*

Designs: 20c, Muhintale Rock. 35c, Sacred Bo Tree. 60c, Adam's Peak.

400 A124 5c multicolored .20 *.40*
401 A124 20c multicolored .20 .20
402 A124 35c multicolored .20 .20
403 A124 60c multicolored .20 .20
Nos. 400-403 (4) .80 1.00

1st anniv. of the Poya Holiday System, Buddhist holiday replacing Sunday.

Dutch Ramparts, Clock Tower and Arms of Galle A125

1967, Jan. 5 Litho. *Perf. 14x13½*

404 A125 25c dk green & multi .55 .20

Centenary of Galle Municipal Council.

Tea Research A126

40c, Tea tasting (cup & loose tea). 50c, Tea picking. 1r, Tea export (crate & freighter).

1967, Aug. 1 Unwmk. *Perf. 13½*

405 A126 4c multicolored .55 .60
406 A126 40c multicolored 1.75 1.40
407 A126 50c multicolored 1.75 .20
408 A126 1r multicolored 1.75 .20
Nos. 405-408 (4) 5.80 2.40

Centenary of the Ceylonese tea industry.

Elephant and ITY Emblem A127

1967, Aug. 15 Litho.

409 A127 45c multicolored 3.25 .85

Intl. Tourist Year.

Girl Guide, Jubilee Emblem and Flag — A128

1967, Sept. 19 *Perf. 12x12½*

410 A128 3c green & multi .45 .20
411 A128 25c org yel & multi .65 .20

Ceylon Girl Guide Assoc., 50th anniv.

Henry S. Olcott and Buddhist Flag A129

Perf. 13½
1967, Dec. 12 Unwmk. Litho.

412 A129 15c multicolored .25 .20

Colonel Henry S. Olcott (1832-1907), an American who reorganized the Buddhist hierarchy and school system in Ceylon and was the first president of the Theosophical Society.

Independence Memorial, Colombo A130

Design: 1r, Flag of Ceylon and mace.

1968, Feb. 4 Wmk. 290 *Perf. 14*

413 A130 5c multicolored .20 .40
414 A130 1r multicolored .45 .20

20th anniversary of independence.

D. B. Jayatilaka — A131

1968, Feb. 14 Photo.

415 A131 25c brown .20 .20

Sir Don Baron Jayatilaka (1868-1944), Buddhist leader and scholar.

Hygiene Institute, Kalutara A132

Perf. 11½x12
1968, Apr. 4 Litho. Wmk. 290

416 A132 50c multicolored .20 .20

WHO, 20th anniversary.

Jet over Colombo Terminal A133

1968, Aug. 5 *Perf. 13½*

417 A133 60c org brn, dk bl & org .45 .20

Opening of Colombo Airport.

D. S. Senanayake — A134

1968, Sept. 23 Photo. *Perf. 14*

418 A134 10c deep green .20 .20

See No. 390.

Open Koran A135

1968, Oct. 14 Photo. *Perf. 14*

419 A135 25c org brn, blk, blue & emerald .20 .20

1,400th anniversary of the Koran.

Human Rights Flame A136

Perf. 12½x13½
1968, Dec. 10 Unwmk.

420 A136 2c multicolored .20 .20
421 A136 20c multicolored .20 .20
422 A136 40c multicolored .20 .20
423 A136 2r multicolored .60 *1.50*
Nos. 420-423 (4) 1.20 2.10

International Human Rights Year.

Ceylon Buddhist Headquarters, Colombo — A137

1968, Dec. 19 Litho. *Perf. 13½*

424 A137 5c multicolored .20 *.30*

All-Ceylon Buddhist Cong., 50th anniv.

A multicolored 50c showing the Sri Padmaya (Sacred Footprint) on Adam's Peak was prepared but the issuance order was countermanded on Dec. 18. Some were sold in ignorance of the withdrawal order.

E. W. Perera — A138

"Strength in Saving" — A139

Wmk. 290
1969, Feb. 17 Photo. *Perf. 14*

425 A138 60c brown .20 .25

E. W. Perera, member of Legislative Council.

1969, Mar. 20

426 A139 3c blue, yel & black .20 .20

National Savings Movement, 25th anniv.

A140

A141

4c, Seat of Enlightenment under Bodhi Tree. 6c, Buduresmala (disk symbolic of six-fold Buddha rays).

Wmk. 290

1969, Apr. 10 Litho. *Perf. 15*

427	A140 4c orange & multi	.20	.25
428	A140 6c gold & multi	.20	.25
429	A140 35c scarlet & multi	.20	.20
	Nos. 427-429 (3)	.60	.70

Vesak Day, which commemorates the birth, enlightenment and death of Buddha.

For surcharges see Nos. 463, 466.

1969, Apr. 29 Photo. *Perf. 14x14½*

430 A141 15c org yel & multi .20 .20

Alexander Ekanayake Goonesingha (1891-1967), trade unionist, political leader and diplomat.

ILO, 50th Anniv. A142

1969, May 4 *Perf. 14½x14*

431	A142 5c grnsh bl & black	.20	.20
432	A142 25c car rose & black	.20	.20

Convocation Hall, University of Ceylon A143

Elephant Lamp (Ath Pana) — A144

35c, "Lamp of Education," globe & flags. 50c, Uranium atom diagram. 60c, Symbols of science education. 1r, Aerial view of Sigiriya rock fortress.

Unwmk.

1969, Aug. 1 Litho. *Perf. 14*

Inscribed: "SIYAWASA"

433	A143 4c yellow & multi	.20	*.50*
434	A144 6c multicolored	.25	*1.00*
435	A143 35c multicolored	.20	.20
436	A144 50c red & multi	.20	.20
437	A143 60c blue & multi	.20	.20
438	A144 1r yel & multi	.30	.20
	Nos. 433-438 (6)	1.35	2.30

Centenary of public education and archaeological research.

For surcharges see Nos. 464-467.

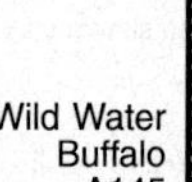

Wild Water Buffalo A145

15c, Slender loris. 50c, Axis deer. 1r, Leopard.

Perf. 14x13½

1970, May 11 Litho. Unwmk.

439	A145 5c lt blue & multi	.55	*1.00*
440	A145 15c buff & multi	1.10	.25
441	A145 50c salmon & multi	1.10	1.00
442	A145 1r gray & multi	1.10	*1.25*
	Nos. 439-442 (4)	3.85	3.50

Symbols of Agriculture and Industry A146

1970, June 17

443 A146 60c multicolored .20 .20

Asian Productivity Year.

Inauguration of UPU Headquarters, Bern — A147

1970, Aug. 14 Litho. Unwmk.

444	A147 50c org, black & blue	.20	.20
445	A147 1.10r red, black & blue	2.75	.25

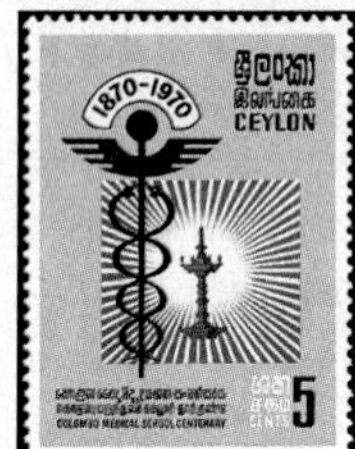

Caduceus and Oil Lamp — A148

1970, Sept. 1 *Perf. 13½x14*

446	A148 5c multicolored	.35	*.40*
447	A148 45c gray & multi	.35	*.40*

Centenary of the Ceylon Medical School.

Victory March and S.W.R.D. Bandaranaike A149

1970, Sept. 25 *Perf. 14*

448 A149 10c red & multi .20 .20

For surcharge see No. 465.

UN Emblem and Dove — A150

Keppetipola Dissawe — A151

1970, Oct. 24 Photo. *Perf. 12½x14*

449 A150 2r dp orange & multi 2.25 2.25

25th anniversary of the United Nations.

1970, Nov. 26 Litho. *Perf. 14x14½*

450 A151 25c multicolored 1.75 1.10

The 152nd anniversary of the execution of Keppetipola Dissawe, leader of the Great Rebellion of 1817-18.

Ola Leaf Manuscript and Education Year Emblem — A152

1970, Dec. 21 Photo. *Perf. 13*

451 A152 15c brown & multi .20 .25

International Education Year.

Charles Henry de Soysa — A153

Edward Henry Pedris — A154

1971, Mar. 3 Litho. *Perf. 14x13½*

452 A153 20c orange & multi .20 .25

de Soysa (1836-90), philanthropist who founded hospitals and schools.

1971, July 8 Litho. *Perf. 14x14½*

453 A154 25c blue & multi .20 .20

Edward Henry Pedris (1888-1925), patriot.

A 5c stamp for the 10th Conf. of World Fellowship of Buddhists, Ceylon, May 9-13, was supposedly not issued without "1972" overprint. See Sri Lanka No. 471.

Lenin (1870-1924) A156

Cumaratunga Munidasa A157

1971, Aug. 31 *Perf. 14½*

455 A156 40c dp car & multi .20 .20

1971, Oct. 29 *Perf. 14*

Poets and Philosophers: #457, Ananda Coomaraswamy (1887-1947). #458, Rev. S. Mahinda Thero (1905-51). #459, Ananda Rajakaruna (1885-1957). #460, Arumuga Navalar (1822-78).

456	A157 5c brown	.20	.20
457	A157 5c slate	.20	.20
458	A157 5c deep orange	.20	.20
459	A157 5c dp vio blue	.20	.20
460	A157 5c brown red	.20	.20
	Nos. 456-460 (5)	1.00	1.00

CARE Package A158

1971, Dec. 28 *Perf. 14x13*

461 A158 50c purple, blue & pink .20 .20

25th anniv. of CARE, a US-Canadian Co-operative for American Relief Everywhere.

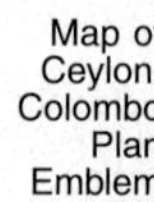

Map of Ceylon, Colombo Plan Emblem A159

1971, Dec. 28 Litho. *Perf. 14x14½*

462 A159 20c multicolored .20 .20

20th anniversary of the Colombo Plan.

Issues of 1969-70 Surcharged

a

b

c

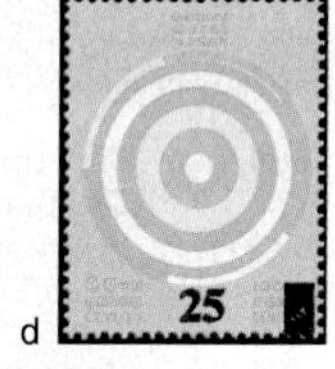

d

e

Wmk. 290, Unwmkd.

1971, Dec. 5 *Perf. 15, 14*

463	A140 (a)	5c on 4c (#427)	.20	.20
464	A143 (b)	5c on 4c (#433)	.20	.20
465	A149 (c)	15c on 10c (#448)	.20	.20
466	A140 (d)	25c on 6c (#428)	.20	.20
467	A144 (e)	25c on 6c (#434)	.20	.20
		Nos. 463-467 (5)	1.00	1.00

Nos. 463-466 exist with surcharge inverted.

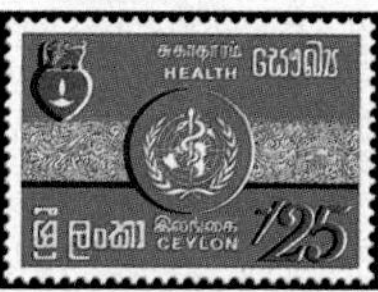

WHO Emblem and Heart — A160

1972, May 2 Unwmk. *Perf. 13x13½*

468 A160 25c multicolored .20 .20

"Your heart is your health," World Health Day.

UN Emblem, Map Showing Asian Highway
A161

1972, May 2 *Perf. 13x12½*
469 A161 85c lt blue & multi 1.00 .25

Economic Commission for Asia and the Far East (ECAFE), 25th anniversary.

SEMI-POSTAL STAMPS

Catalogue values for unused stamps in this section are for Never Hinged items.

Lamp and Dharmachakra
SP1

Design: 10c+5c, Hand of Peace.

Perf. 11½
1956, May 10 **Unwmk.** **Photo.**
Granite Paper
B1 SP1 4c + 2c dp bl & lt yel .35 .30
B2 SP1 10c + 5c dk gray, yel & brt pink .50 .40

2500th anniv. of the birth of Buddha. The surtax went to the Buddha Jayanti Fund. For overprints, see Nos. 338-339.

WAR TAX STAMPS

Nos. 201, 202, 202a and 203 Overprinted

Die I
1918 **Wmk. 3** *Perf. 14*
MR1 A44 2c brown orange .25 *.45*
a. Double overprint 30.00 35.00
b. Inverted overprint 40.00 *45.00*
MR2 A44 3c dp grn (Die Ia, type II) 2.00 .45
a. 3c dp green (Die I, type I) .20 *.55*
b. Double overprint (Die I) 70.00 *75.00*
MR3 A44 5c red violet .55 .35
a. Double overprint 37.50 *42.50*
b. Inverted overprint 92.50

Same Overprint on No. 223
MR4 A44 1c on 5c red violet .20 .30
a. Double overprint 160.00
Nos. MR1-MR4 (4) 3.00 1.55

OFFICIAL STAMPS

Regular Issues Overprinted

1869 **Wmk. 1** *Perf. 12½, 14*
Black Overprint
O1 A4 1p blue 72.50
O2 A1 2p yellow 72.50
O3 A5 3p rose 125.00
O4 A2 8p red brown 72.50
O5 A1 1sh gray lilac 150.00

Red Overprint
O6 A1 6p brown 72.50
O7 A2 2sh blue 125.00
a. Imperf. *1,000.*
Nos. O1-O7 (7) 690.00

Nos. O1-O7 were never placed in use. The overprint measures 15mm on #O1, O3.

Regular Issues Overprinted in Black or Red

1895-1900 **Wmk. 2** *Perf. 14*
O8 A6 2c green 9.75 .50
O9 A6 2c org brn ('00) 8.00 .70
O10 A24 3c org brn & grn 11.50 .90
O11 A24 3c green ('00) 9.25 2.50
O12 A23 5c lilac 4.00 .35
O13 A24 15c olive green 14.00 .55
O14 A24 15c ultra ('00) 18.00 .70
O15 A24 25c brown 11.50 2.00
O16 A24 30c vio & org brn 15.00 .70
O17 A24 75c blk & org brn (R) ('99) 6.25 *7.50*
Wmk. 1
O18 A16 1r12c claret 85.00 62.50
Nos. O8-O18 (11) 192.25 78.90

1903-04 **Wmk. 2**
O19 A36 2c orange brown 15.00 1.10
O20 A37 3c green 8.50 2.25
O21 A38 5c dull lilac 21.00 1.75
O22 A40 15c ultramarine 32.50 3.25
O23 A40 25c bister 25.00 21.00
O24 A40 30c violet & green 14.00 1.75
Nos. O19-O24 (6) 116.00 31.10

CHAD

'chad

(Tchad)

LOCATION — Central Africa, south of Libya
GOVT. — Republic
AREA — 495,572 sq. mi.
POP. — 7,557,436 (1999 est.)
CAPITAL — N'Djamena

A former dependency of Ubangi-Shari, Chad became a separate French colony in 1920. In 1934, the colonies of Chad, Gabon, Middle Congo and Ubangi-Shari were grouped in a single administrative unit known as French Equatorial Africa, with the capital at Brazzaville. The Republic of Chad was proclaimed November 28, 1958.

100 Centimes = 1 Franc

Catalogue values for unused stamps in this country are for Never Hinged items, beginning with Scott 64 in the regular postage section, Scott B1 in the semi-postal section, Scott C1 in the air post section, Scott CB1 in the air post semi-postal section, Scott J23 in the postage due section, Scott M1 in the military stamp section, and Scott O1 in the officials section.

See French Equatorial Africa No. 190 for stamp inscribed "Tchad."

Types of Middle Congo, 1907-17, Overprinted

Perf. 14x13½, 13½x14
1922 **Unwmk.**
1 A1 1c red & violet .25 .25
a. Overprint omitted 150.00
2 A1 2c ol brn & salmon .35 .35
a. Overprint omitted 175.00
3 A1 4c ind & vio .90 .90
4 A1 5c choc & grn 1.00 1.00
5 A1 10c dp grn & gray grn 1.60 1.60
6 A1 15c vio & red 1.75 1.75
7 A1 20c grn & vio 3.00 3.00
8 A2 25c ol brn & brn 6.75 6.75
9 A2 30c rose & pale rose 1.25 1.25
10 A2 35c dl bl & dl rose 2.10 2.10
11 A2 40c choc & grn 2.40 2.40
12 A2 45c vio & grn 1.75 1.75
13 A2 50c dk bl & pale bl 2.10 2.10
14 A2 60c on 75c vio, *pnksh* 3.00 3.00
a. "TCHAD" omitted 200.00
b. "60" omitted 200.00
15 A1 75c red & violet 2.40 2.40
16 A3 1fr indigo & salmon 8.25 8.25
17 A3 2fr indigo & violet 13.50 13.50
18 A3 5fr ind & olive brn 13.50 13.50
Nos. 1-18 (18) 65.85 65.85

See Nos. 26a, 32a, 38a, 55a.

Stamps of 1922 Overprinted in Various Colors:

Nos. 19-28

Nos. 29-50

1924-33
19 A1 1c red & vio .20 .20
a. "TCHAD" omitted 140.00
b. Double overprint 225.00
c. Violet omitted 190.00
20 A1 2c ol brn & sal .20 .20
a. "TCHAD" omitted 125.00
b. Double overprint 160.00
21 A1 4c ind & vio .20 .20
a. "TCHAD" omitted 600.00
22 A1 5c choc & grn (Bl) .80 .60
a. "TCHAD" omitted 125.00
23 A1 5c choc & grn .35 .35
a. "TCHAD" omitted 150.00
24 A1 10c dp grn & gray grn (Bl) .85 .65
25 A1 10c dp grn & gray grn .85 .65
26 A1 10c red org & blk ('25) .35 .35
a. "Afrique Equatoriale Française" omitted 140.00
b. "TCHAD" omitted 140.00
27 A1 15c vio & red .35 .35
28 A1 20c grn & vio .55 .55
a. "TCHAD" omitted 160.00
b. "Afrique Equatoriale Française" doubled 250.00
29 A2 25c ol brn & brn .35 .35
a. "Afrique Equatoriale Française" doubled 100.00
30 A2 30c rose & pale rose .50 .50
31 A2 30c gray & bl (R) ('25) .35 .35
32 A2 30c dk grn & grn ('27) .95 .95
a. "Afrique Equatoriale Française" omitted 250.00
33 A2 35c ind & dl rose .35 .35
34 A2 40c choc & grn .95 .95
a. Dbl. overprint (R + Bk) 190.00
35 A2 45c vio & grn .65 .65
a. Dbl. overprint (R + Bk) 190.00
36 A2 50c dk bl & pale bl 1.10 1.00
a. Inverted overprint 110.00
37 A2 50c grn & vio ('25) .95 .95
38 A2 65c org brn & bl ('28) 1.40 1.40
a. "Afrique Equatoriale Française" omitted 190.00
39 A2 75c red & vio 1.10 1.00
40 A2 75c dp bl & lt bl (R) ('25) .50 .50
a. "TCHAD" omitted 190.00
41 A2 75c rose & dk brn ('28) 1.75 1.75
42 A2 90c brn red & pink ('30) 5.25 5.25
43 A3 1fr ind & salmon 1.25 1.25
44 A3 1.10fr dl grn & bl ('28) 1.90 1.90
45 A3 1.25fr org brn & lt bl ('33) 5.75 5.75
46 A3 1.50fr ultra & bl ('30) 5.25 5.25
47 A3 1.75fr ol brn & vio ('33) 32.50 32.50
48 A3 2fr ind & vio 2.10 1.90
a. Double impression of frame 425.00
49 A3 3fr red vio ('30) 8.50 8.50
50 A3 5fr ind & ol brn 2.50 2.10
Nos. 19-50 (32) 80.60 79.20

See No. 58a.

Types of 1922 Overprinted like Nos. 29-50 and Surcharged with New Values

1924-27
51 A2 60c on 75c dk vio, *pnksh* .65 .65
a. "60" omitted 125.00
52 A3 65c on 1fr brn & ol grn ('25) 1.25 1.25
53 A3 85c on 1fr brn & ol grn ('25) 1.25 1.25
54 A2 90c on 75c brn red & rose red ('27) .95 .95
55 A3 1.25fr on 1fr dk bl & ultra (R) ('26) .35 .35
a. "Afrique Equatoriale Française" omitted 125.00
56 A3 1.50fr on 1fr ultra & bl ('27) 1.10 1.10
57 A3 3fr on 5fr org brn & dl red ('27) 3.25 3.25
58 A3 10fr on 5fr ol grn & cer ('27) 8.50 8.50
a. "10fr" omitted 325.00
59 A3 20fr on 5fr vio & ver ('27) 13.50 13.50
Nos. 51-59 (9) 30.80 30.80

Common Design Types pictured following the introduction.

Colonial Exposition Issue
Common Design Types
1931 **Engr.** *Perf. 12½*
Name of Country in Black
60 CD70 40c deep green 3.50 *3.50*
61 CD71 50c violet 3.50 *3.50*
62 CD72 90c red orange 3.50 *3.50*
63 CD73 1.50fr dull blue 3.50 *3.50*
Nos. 60-63 (4) 14.00 *14.00*

Catalogue values for unused stamps in this section, from this point to the end of the section, are for Never Hinged items.

Republic

"Birth of the Republic"
A1

"Solidarity of the Community"
A2

1959 **Unwmk.** **Engr.** *Perf. 13*
64 A1 15fr ultra, grn & maroon .55 .20
65 A2 25fr dk grn & dp claret .70 .20

1st anniv. of the proclamation of the Republic.

Imperforates
Most Chad stamps from 1959 onward exist imperforate in issued and trial colors, and also in small presentation sheets in issued colors.

C.C.T.A. Issue
Common Design Type
1960
66 CD106 50fr rose lil & dk pur 1.25 .35

Flag and Map of Chad and UN Emblem — A3

Unwmk.

1961, Jan. 11 Engr. *Perf. 13*

Flag in blue, yellow and carmine

67 A3 15fr brn & dk bl .45 .20
68 A3 25fr org brn & dk bl .65 .20
69 A3 85fr slate grn & dk bl 1.75 .40
Nos. 67-69 (3) 2.85 .80

Admission of Chad to United Nations.

Chari Bridge and Hippopotamus — A4

Abtouyoua Mountain and Ox — A5

Designs: 50c, Biltine and dorcas gazelle. 1fr, Logone and elephant. 2fr, Batha and lion. 3fr, Salamat and buffalo. 4fr, Ouaddai and Kudu. 15fr, Bessada and giant eland. 20fr, Tibesti mountains and mouflon. 25fr, Rocherg and antelope. 30fr, Kanem and cheetah. 60fr, Borkou and oryx. 85fr, Gorge of Archet and addax.

Perf. 13½x14, 14x13½

1961-62 Typo.

70 A5 50c yel grn & dk grn ('62) .20 .20
71 A5 1fr bl grn & dk bl grn ('62) .20 .20
72 A5 2fr dk red brn & blk ('62) .20 .20
73 A5 3fr ocher & dl grn ('62) .20 .20
74 A5 4fr dk crim & blk ('62) .20 .20
75 A4 5fr yellow & blk .20 .20
76 A5 10fr pink & blk .25 .20
77 A5 15fr lilac & blk ('62) .55 .20
78 A5 20fr red & blk .65 .20
79 A5 25fr blue & blk ('62) .70 .20
80 A5 30fr ultra & blk ('62) .80 .20
81 A5 60fr yel & ol grn ('62) 1.60 .20
82 A5 85fr org & blk 2.00 .25
Nos. 70-82 (13) 7.75 2.65

First anniversary of Independence.
For overprint see No. M1.

Abidjan Games Issue

Common Design Type

1962, July 21 Photo. *Perf. 12½x12*

83 CD109 20fr Relay race .55 .20
84 CD109 50fr High jump 1.40 .30
Nos. 83-84,C8 (3) 4.45 1.25

African-Malgache Union Issue

Common Design Type

1962, Sept. 8 Unwmk.

85 CD110 30fr dk bl, bluish grn, red & gold .90 .20

Pres. Ngarta Tombalbaye — A7

1963, Apr. 22 *Perf. 12x12½*

86 A7 20fr multi .45 .20
87 A7 85fr multi 1.25 .30

For surcharge, see No. 125.

Space Communciations Issue

Waves Around Globe — A8

Design: 100fr, Orbit patterns around globe.

Perf. 12½

1963, Sept. 19 Unwmk. Photo.

88 A8 25fr grn & pur .65 .20
89 A8 100fr pink & ultra 2.25 .60

Ancestral Mask — A9

Excavated Sao Art: 5fr, Clay weight. 25fr, Ancestral clay statuette. 60fr, Gazelle, bronze. 80fr, Bronze pectoral.

1963, Dec. 2 Engr. *Perf. 13*

90 A9 5fr brt grn & red brn .20 .20
91 A9 15fr gray, dl cl & red .25 .20
92 A9 25fr dk bl & org brn .70 .25
93 A9 60fr org brn & slate grn 2.00 .35
94 A9 80fr org red & olive 2.25 .40
Nos. 90-94 (5) 5.40 1.40

UNESCO Emblem, Scales and Tree — A10

1963, Dec. 10

95 A10 25fr green & maroon .70 .20

15th anniv. of the Universal Declaration of Human Rights.

Potter A11

Perf. 12½

1964, Feb. 5 Unwmk. Engr.

96 A11 10fr shown .25 .20
97 A11 30fr Boatmaker .65 .20
98 A11 50fr Weaver 1.00 .25
99 A11 85fr Smiths 1.60 .35
Nos. 96-99 (4) 3.50 1.00

Barograph and WMO Emblem A12

1964, Mar. 23 *Perf. 13*

100 A12 50fr red lil, pur & ultra 1.00 .25

Fourth World Meteorological Day.

Cotton A13

1964, Apr. 6 Photo. *Perf. 12½x13*

101 A13 20fr shown 1.25 .35
102 A13 25fr Royal poinciana 1.40 .40

Co-operation Issue

Common Design Type

1964, Nov. 7 Engr. *Perf. 13*

103 CD119 25fr ver, dk bl & dk brn .70 .25

National Guard and Map of Chad A14

Design: 25fr, Infantry, flag and map, vert.

Perf. 12½x13, 13x12½

1964, Dec. 11 Photo.

104 A14 20fr multi .65 .20
105 A14 25fr lt bl & multi .80 .20

Issued to honor the army of Chad.

Aoudad or Barbary Sheep A15

10fr, Addax. 20fr, Oryx. 25fr, Derby's eland, vert. 30fr, Giraffe, buffalo & lion, Zakouma Park, vert. 85fr, Great kudu at water hole, vert.

Perf. 12½x12, 12x12½

1965, Jan. 11 Unwmk.

106 A15 5fr dk brn, ultra & yel .45 .20
107 A15 10fr ultra, org & blk .70 .20
108 A15 20fr multi 1.25 .20
109 A15 25fr multi 1.60 .25
110 A15 30fr multi 2.25 .40
111 A15 85fr multi 4.50 .75
Nos. 106-111 (6) 10.75 2.00

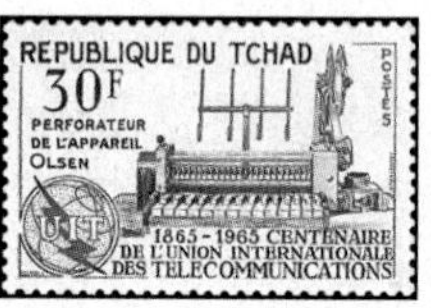

Olsen Perforator A16

Designs: 60fr, Mildé telephone, vert. 100fr, Distributor of Baudot telegraph.

1965, May 17 Engr. *Perf. 13*

112 A16 30fr multi .70 .20
113 A16 60fr multi 1.00 .45
114 A16 100fr multi 1.75 .60
Nos. 112-114 (3) 3.45 1.25

Cent. of the ITU.

Motorized Police A17

Perf. 12½x12

1965, June 22 Photo. Unwmk.

115 A17 25fr ol, dk grn, gold & brn .70 .25

Issued to honor the national police.

Guitar A18

Musical Instruments from National Museum: 1fr, Drum and stool, vert. 3fr, Shoulder drums, vert. 15fr, Viol. 60fr, Harp, vert.

1965, Oct. 26 Engr. *Perf. 13*

Size: 22x36mm, 36x22mm

116 A18 1fr car, emer & brn .20 .20
117 A18 2fr red, brt lil & brn .20 .20
118 A18 3fr red & sepia .20 .20
119 A18 15fr red, ocher & sl grn .70 .20
120 A18 60fr maroon & slate grn 1.60 .60
Nos. 116-120,C23 (6) 5.15 2.25

Head and Bowl — A19

WHO Headquarters, Geneva — A20

Sao Art: 20fr, Head. 60fr, Head with crown. 80fr, Circlet with human head. From excavations at Bouta Kebira and Gawi.

1966, Apr. 1 Engr. *Perf. 13*

121 A19 15fr ol, choc & ultra .35 .20
122 A19 20fr dk red, brn & bl grn .70 .20
123 A19 60fr brt bl, choc & ver 1.60 .50
124 A19 80fr brn org, grn & pur 2.25 .60
Nos. 121-124 (4) 4.90 1.50

Issued to publicize the International Negro Arts Festival, Dakar, Senegal, Apr. 1-24.

No. 86 Surcharged with New Value and Two Bars in Orange

1966, Apr. 15 Photo. *Perf. 12x12½*

125 A7 25fr on 20fr multi .70 .30

1966, May 3

126 A20 25fr car, lt ultra & yel .55 .20
127 A20 32fr emer, ultra & yel .70 .20

New WHO Headquarters, Geneva.

Staff of Mercury and Map of Africa A21

1966, May 24 *Perf. 12½x12*

128 A21 30fr multi .70 .25

Central African Customs and Economic Union (Union Douaniere et Economique de l'Afrique Centrale, UDEAC).

Soccer Player — A22

Design: 60fr, Soccer player facing left.

1966, July 12 Engr. *Perf. 13*

129 A22 30fr grn, bl grn & mar .70 .25
130 A22 60fr dk bl, gray & car 1.25 .30

8th World Cup Soccer Championship, Wembley, England, July 11-30.

Young Men, Flag and Emblem A23

1966, Aug. 11 Photo. *Perf. 12½x13*

131 A23 25fr dk bl & multi .70 .20

Chad Youth Movement.

Greek Columns and UNESCO Emblem — A24

1966, Aug. 23 Engr. *Perf. 13*

132 A24 32fr sl bl, vio & car rose .70 .20

20th anniv. of UNESCO.

Reconstructed Skull of Chadanthropus — A25

1966, Sept. 20 Engr. *Perf. 13*

133 A25 30fr gray, red & ocher 1.75 .50

Yves Coppens' discovery of Lake Chad man.

Stone Axe — A26

Prehistoric Tools: 30fr, Flint arrow head. 85fr, Bone harpoon. 100fr, Sandstone millstone with grinder.

1966, Dec. 11 Engr. *Perf. 13*

134 A26 25fr dp bl, red & dk brn .55 .20
135 A26 30fr brn, dp bl & blk .70 .20
136 A26 85fr dk red, brt bl & brn 2.00 .50
137 A26 100fr Prus grn, dk brn & bis brn 2.25 .65
a. Miniature sheet of 4, #134-137 7.50 5.00
Nos. 134-137 (4) 5.50 1.55

Map of Chad and Various Sports — A27

1967, Apr. 10 Photo. *Perf. 12x12½*

138 A27 25fr multi .70 .30

Issued for Sports Day, Apr. 10, 1967.

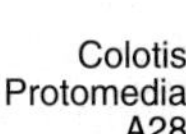

Colotis Protomedia A28

Various Butterflies.

1967, May 23 Photo. *Perf. 12½x12*

139 A28 5fr blue & multi 1.75 .20
140 A28 10fr emerald & multi 3.50 .20
141 A28 20fr orange & multi 7.00 .40
142 A28 130fr red & multi 14.50 .70
Nos. 139-142 (4) 26.75 1.50

WHO Headquarters, Brazzaville — A29

1967, Sept. 23 Photo. *Perf. 12½x13*

143 A29 30fr vio bl & multi .70 .25

Opening of the Regional Office of the WHO, Brazzaville.

Jamboree Emblem and Boy Scouts A30

32fr, Jamboree emblem and Boy Scout.

1967, Oct. 17 Photo. *Perf. 12½x13*

144 A30 25fr multi .65 .20
145 A30 32fr multi .70 .20

12th Boy Scout World Jamboree, Farragut State Park, Idaho, Aug. 1-9.

Great Mills of Chad A31

30fr, Lake reclamation project, grain fields.

1967, Nov. 14 Engr. *Perf. 13*

146 A31 25fr brt bl, ind & sep .55 .20
147 A31 30fr ultra, emer & ol brn .70 .20

Economic development of Chad.

Woman and Harp Player A32

Rock Paintings: 30fr, Giraffes. 50fr, Camel rider hunting ostrich.

1967, Dec. 19 Engr. *Perf. 13*
Size: 36x22mm

148 A32 15fr bl, sal & mar 1.00 .20
149 A32 30fr grnsh bl, sal & mar 2.00 .40
150 A32 50fr emer, sal & mar 2.75 .55
Nos. 148-150,C38-C39 (5) 14.25 3.50

Balloud expedition in the Ennedi Mountains. See Nos. 163-166.

Rotary Emblem — A33

Map of Chad, WHO Emblem, Well, Physicians, Mother and Child — A34

1968, Jan. 9 Photo. *Perf. 13x12½*

151 A33 50fr multi 1.25 .40

Rotary Club of Chad, 10th anniversary.

1968, Apr. 6 *Perf. 13x12½*

152 A34 25fr multi .55 .20
153 A34 32fr multi .70 .20

20th anniv. of WHO.

"Water" Aiding Agriculture and Industry A35

1968, Apr. 23 Engr. *Perf. 13*

154 A35 50fr grnsh bl, brn & brt grn .90 .25

Hydrological Decade (UNESCO), 1965-74.

National Administration School — A36

1968, Aug. 20 Engr. *Perf. 13*

155 A36 25fr slate, brn red & rose vio .55 .20

Boy Learning to Write A37

1968, Sept. 10

156 A37 60fr dk bl, dk brn & blk .90 .30

Issued for National Literacy Day.

Cotton Harvest A38

Loom, Fort Archambault Factory — A39

Tiger Moth — A40

1968, Sept. 24 Engr. *Perf. 13*

157 A38 25fr Prus bl, choc & dk grn .65 .20
158 A39 30fr brt grn, ol & ultra .70 .20

Issued to publicize the cotton industry.

1968, Oct. 1 Photo.

Moths: 30fr, Owlet. 50fr, Saturnid (Gynanisa maja). 100fr, Saturnid (Epiphora bauhiniae).

159 A40 25fr multi 4.50 .45
160 A40 30fr multi 5.25 .50
161 A40 50fr multi 8.00 .60
162 A40 100fr multi 9.00 .75
Nos. 159-162 (4) 26.75 2.30

Rock Paintings Type of 1967

Rock Paintings: 2fr, Archers. 10fr, Costumes (4 women, 1 man). 20fr, Funeral vigil. 25fr, Dispute.

1968, Nov. 19 Engr. *Perf. 13*
Size: 36x22mm

163 A32 2fr scar, salmon & brn .45 .20
164 A32 10fr pur, salmon & dk red 1.25 .20
165 A32 20fr grn, salmon & mar 2.75 .50
166 A32 25fr bl, salmon & maroon 3.00 .60
Nos. 163-166 (4) 7.45 1.50

Man and Human Rights Flame — A41

St. Paul — A42

1968, Dec. 10 Engr. *Perf. 13*

167 A41 32fr grn, brt bl & red .70 .20

International Human Rights Year.

1969, May 6 Litho. *Perf. 12½x13*

Apostles: 1fr, St. Peter. 2fr, St. Thomas. 5fr, St. John the Evangelist. 10fr, St. Bartholomew. 20fr, St. Matthew. 25fr, St. James the Less. 30fr, St. Andrew. 40fr, St. Jude. 50fr, St. James the Greater. 85fr, St. Philip. 100fr, St. Simon.

168 A42 50c multi .20 .20
169 A42 1fr multi .20 .20
170 A42 2fr multi .20 .20
171 A42 5fr multi .20 .20
172 A42 10fr multi .20 .20
173 A42 20fr multi .25 .20
174 A42 25fr multi .35 .20
175 A42 30fr multi .45 .20
176 A42 40fr multi .55 .20
177 A42 50fr multi .65 .20
178 A42 85fr multi 1.00 .40
179 A42 100fr multi 1.10 .40
a. Sheet of 12, #168-179 5.50 1.75

Jubilee Year of the Catholic Church in Chad.

Tractors and Trucks — A43

1969, June 19 Engr. *Perf. 13*

180 A43 32fr grn, red brn & ind .70 .20

50th anniv. of the ILO.

Deborah Meyer, US, 200 Meter Freestyle A44

Woman with Flowers, by Veneto — A45

Winners of 1968 Olympic Games: #182, Roland Matthes, East Germany, 100m backstroke. #183, Klaus DiBiasi, Italy, springboard diving. #184, Bruno Cipolla, Primo Baran and Renzo Sambo, Italy, pair with coxswain. #185, Annemarie Zimmermann and Rosewitha Esser, West Germany, women's kayak tandem. #186, Sailing, G.B. #187, Pierre Trentin, France, 1000 meter bicycling. #188, Pier Franco Vianelli, Italy, 196k bicycle road race. #189, Daniel Morelon and Pierre Trentin, France, tandem.

#190, Daniel R. Rebillard, France, 4000m pursuit (bicycle). #191, Ingrid Becker, West Germany, pentathlon. #192, Jean J. Guyon, France, equestrian. #193, Olympic dressage team, West Germany. #194, Bernd Klinger,

West Germany, small bore rifle. #195, Manfred Wolke, East Germany, welterweight. #196, Randy Matson, US, shot put. #197, Colette Besson, France, 400m run. #198, Mohammed Gammoudi, Tunisia, 5,000m run. #199, Tommie Smith, US, 200m run.

#200, David Hemery, G.B., 200m hurdles. #201, Willie Davenport, US, 110m hurdles. #202, Bob Beamon, US, long jump. #203, Sawao Kato, Japan, all around gymnastics. #204, Dick Fosbury, US, high jump.

Paintings: #206, Holy Family, by Murillo, horiz. #207, Adoration of the Magi, by Rubens. #208, Portrait of an African Woman, by Bezombes. #209, Three Black Men, by Rubens. #210, Mother and Child, by Gauguin.

1969, June 30 Litho. ***Perf. 12½x13***

181-204 A44 1fr set of 24 7.25 7.25

Perf. 12½x13, 13x12½

205-210 A45 1fr set of 6 1.75 1.75

Issued to stress the brotherhood of mankind.

For overprints see Nos. 244A-244F, 245A-245X.

Cochlospermum Tinctorium — A46

Flowers: 4fr, Parkia biglobosa. 10fr, Pancratium trianthum. 15fr, Morning glory.

1969, July 8 Photo. ***Perf. 12½x13***

211 A46 1fr pink, yel & blk .55 .20
212 A46 4fr dk grn, yel & red .80 .20
213 A46 10fr dk grn, yel & gray 1.00 .20
214 A46 15fr vio bl & multi 1.75 .20
Nos. 211-214 (4) 4.10 .80

Meat Freezer, Farcha A47

30fr, Cattle at Farcha slaughterhouse.

1969, Aug. 19 Engr. ***Perf. 13***

215 A47 25fr sl grn, ocher & red brn .55 .20
216 A47 30fr red brn, sl grn & gray .70 .20

Economic development in Chad.

Development Bank Issue

Common Design Type

1969, Sept. 10

217 CD130 30fr dl red, grn & ocher .55 .20

Tilapia Nilotica A48

Fish: 3fr, Citharinus latus. 5fr, Tetraodon fahaka strigosus. 20fr, Hydrocyon forskali.

1969, Nov. 25 Engr. ***Perf. 13***

218 A48 2fr choc, grn & gray .55 .20
219 A48 3fr gray, red & bl .80 .20
220 A48 5fr ocher, blk & yel 1.25 .20
221 A48 20fr blk, red & grn 3.50 .20
Nos. 218-221 (4) 6.10 .80

ASECNA Issue

Common Design Type

1969, Dec. 12 Engr. ***Perf. 13***

222 CD132 30fr orange .70 .25

Pres. François Tombalbaye A49

Lenin — A50

1970, Jan. 11 Litho. ***Perf. 14***

223 A49 25fr multi .55 .20

1970, Apr. 22 Photo. ***Perf. 11½***

224 A50 150fr gold, blk & buff 2.75 1.00

Lenin (1870-1924), Russian communist leader.

UPU Headquarters Issue

Common Design Type

1970, May 20 Engr. ***Perf. 13***

225 CD133 30fr dk red, pur & brn .70 .25

During the 1970-73 period three different agents had entered into contracts to produce stamps with various officials of the Chad government, apparently including Pres. Tombalbaye.

In June 1973, Tombalbaye declared that some of the stamps produced by these agents were not recognized by the Chad government but might be put on sale at a later date, and that other stamps produced and shipped to Chad were refused by the government.

In July 1973, the Chad government announced that the stamps that were not recognized would be put on sale by the end of the year. We have no evidence that this actually happened.

Apollo Program — A50a

Designs: 15fr, Apollo 11 in Lunar orbit. 25fr, Apollo 12 astronaut deploying lunar research equipment. 40fr, Astronaunt, lunar module on moon. 50fr, Astronauts Conrad and Bean in life raft after splashdown, horiz.

1970, June 12 Litho. ***Perf. 12x12½***

225A A50a Strip of 3, #b-d 5.50

Souvenir Sheet

Perf. 13½x13

225E A50a 50fr multicolored 9.00

No. 225E contains one 66x44mm stamp. 15fr, 25fr are airmail.

Expo '70, Japan — A50b

Japanese prints of women: 50c, by Kiyonaga. 1fr, by Utamaro. 2fr, from Heian period.

1970, June 12 Litho. ***Perf. 12x12½***

225F A50b Strip of 3, #a-c 12.50

For overprint see No. 239C.

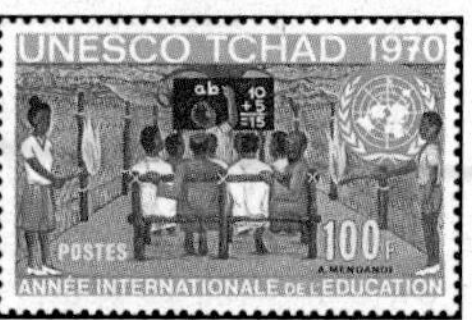

Adult Education Class and UN Emblem — A52

1970, June 16 Litho. ***Perf. 14***

226 A52 100fr blue & multi 1.60 .50

International Education Year.

1970 World Cup Soccer Championships, Mexico City — A53a

Bull's Head, Symbols of Weather and Agriculture — A53

1970, July 22 Engr. ***Perf. 13***

227 A53 50fr org, gray & grn .90 .20

Issued for World Meteorological Day.

Designs: 1fr, Three players, Italian flag. 4fr, Franz Beckenbauer, German flag. Nos. 227C, 227E, English players receiving World Cup trophy, 1966. No. 227D, Three players, Brazilian flag. No. 227F, Four players, "1970."

1970-71 Litho. ***Perf. 12***

227A A53a 1fr multicolored
227B A53a 4fr multicolored
227C A53a 5fr multicolored
227D A53a 5fr multicolored
Nos. 227A-227D(3) 3.50

Embossed

Die Cut Perf 13

227E A53a 5fr gold 16.00

Souvenir Sheet

Litho.

Perf. 13½x13

227F A53a 15fr multicolored 5.75

No. 227F contains one 66x44mm stamp. Nos. 227D, 227F are airmail.

Issued: #227A-227D, 227F, 7/2; #227E, 11/1/71.

For overprints see Nos. 267A-267E.

Christmas A53b

Virgin and Child by: 3fr, Solario. 25fr, Durer. 32fr, Fouquet.

1970, Aug. 19 Litho. ***Perf. 12x12½***

227G A53b 3fr multicolored
227H A53b 25fr multicolored
227I A53b 32fr multicolored
Nos. 227G-227I (3) 12.50

No. 227I is airmail.

Ahmed Mangue, Minister of Education — A54

1970, Sept. 15 Litho. & Engr.

228 A54 100fr gold, car & blk 1.40 .40

1972 Summer Olympics, Munich — A54a

Designs: No. 228A, 3fr, Horses pulling chariot. 8fr, Men running. 10fr, No. 228C, Woman hurdling. No. 228B, 20fr, Equestrian. 35fr, Woman diving. No. 228D, Woman diver in tuck position.

1970 Litho. ***Perf. 12½x12***

228A A54a Strip of 3, #a-c 3.75

Perf. 12x12½

228B A54a Pair, #a-b + label 3.75

Embossed

Die Cut Perf 13

228C A54a 10fr gold 16.00

Souvenir Sheet

Litho.

Perf. 13½x13

228D A54a 40fr multicolored 9.00

10fr, 35fr, Nos. 228C-228D are airmail. No. 228D contains one 66x43mm stamp.

Issued: #228A-228B, 228D, Sept; #228C, 10/14.

For overprints see Nos. 239D-239F.

Tanner A55

Designs: 2fr, Cloth dyer, vert. 3fr, Camel turning oil press. 4fr, Water carrier. 5fr, Copper worker.

1970, Oct. 10 Engr. ***Perf. 13***

229 A55 1fr ol brn, bl & brn .20 .20
229A A55 2fr dk brn, ol & ind .20 .20
229B A55 3fr pur, ol brn & rose car .25 .20

229C A55 4fr choc, lem & bl grn .35 .20
229D A55 5fr red, choc & sl grn .45 .20
Nos. 229-229D (5) 1.45 1.00

UN Emblem, Grain and Dove — A56

1970, Oct. 24 Photo. *Perf. 12x12½*
230 A56 32fr dk bl & multi .70 .25

25th anniversary of United Nations.

OCAM Headquarters, Map of Africa, Stars — A57

1971, Jan. 23 Photo. *Perf. 12½x12*
231 A57 30fr dk grn & multi .70 .20

OCAM (Organisation Commune Africaine, Malgache et Mauricienne) Summit Conference, N'djamena, Jan. 22-30.

Space Exploration — A57a

Illustration reduced.

1971, Feb. 16 Litho. *Perf. 13x13½*
231A A57a 8fr shown .55
231B A57a 10fr Apollo 11 .80
231C A57a 35fr Soviet space station 5.75
Nos. 231A-231C (3) 7.10

Embossed

Die Cut Perf 13

231D A57a 8fr gold, like #231A 7.50
f. Sheet of 1, Imperf.

Souvenir Sheet

Perf. 13½x13

231E A57a 40fr John F. Kennedy, Apollo spacecraft, vert. 9.00

Nos. 231C, 231E are airmail. No. 231Df contains one 73x45mm stamp with same size design as No. 231D. No. 231E contains one 33x50mm stamp.

Nos. 231D, 231Df probably were not available in Chad.

1972 Winter Olympics, Sapporo A57b

Paintings by Kiyonaga: 50c, Cherry Trees in Bloom, Tokyo. 1fr, Snowy Morning. 2fr, Sake Party.

1971 Litho. *Perf. 12x12½*
231G A57b 50c multicolored .75
231H A57b 1fr multicolored 1.25
231I A57b 2fr multicolored 2.00
Nos. 231G-231I (3) 4.00

Embossed

Die Cut Perf 13

231J A57b 2fr gold, like #231I 16.00
k. Sheet of 1, Imperf. 32.50

Issued: #231G-231I, 2/16; #231J-231Jk, 11/1. #231Jk contains one 43x54mm stamp with same size design as #231I.

For overprints see Nos. 246A-246C.

Nos. 231J-231Jk probably were not available in Chad.

Portraits of French Royalty — A57c

Designs: No. 232A, 25fr, The Dauphin (Louis XVII), by J.M. Vien the Younger. 32fr, Marie Antoinette, by E. Vigee-Lebrun. 60fr, Louis XVI, by J.S. Duplessis.

No. 232B, 25fr, Comtesse du Barry, by E. Vigee-Lebrun. 40fr, Louis XV, by M.Q. Delatour.

No. 232C, 40fr, Marie Antoinette, by Charpentier. 50fr, Louis XVI (Dauphin), by Michel Van Loo.

No. 232D, 35fr, Madame de Pompadour (detail), by Delatour. 70fr, Louis XV by Delatour.

No. 232E, 30fr, Madame de Pompadour (entire), by Delatour. 60fr, Marie Leszczynska, by Jean Marc Nattier. 80fr, Louis XV, by Van Loo.

No. 232F, 40fr, Duc D'Orleans as Regent, by 19th cent. French school. 200fr, Louis XIV, by H. Rigaud.

No. 232G, 100fr, Madame de Montespan, by Henry Gascard. 100fr, Madame de Maintenon, by Pierre Mignard.

No. 232H, 50fr, Colbert, by Claude Lefebvre. 200fr, Louis XIV, by J. Garnier.

No. 232J, 50fr, Marie Therese, by Mignard. 200fr, Louis XIV, by Marot.

No. 232K, 50fr, Marie de la Valliere, by English school. 200fr, Louis XIV, by French school.

No. 232L, 100fr, Giulio Cardinal Mazarin, by Mignard. 100fr, Anne of Austria, by Rubens.

No. 232M, 50fr, Vicomte de Turenne, by Champaigne. 200fr, Louis XIV as a Boy, by Mignard.

No. 232N, 100fr, Marquis de Cinq-Mars, by M. le Nain. 150fr, Cardinal Richelieu, by Champaigne.

No. 232P, 150fr, Anne of Austria, by Rubens. 250fr, Louis XIII (detail), by Simon Vouet.

No. 232Q, 150fr, Marriage of Marie de Medicis (looking right), by Rubens. 150fr, Mirror image.

No. 232R, 150fr, Duke of Sully, by Quesnel. 150fr, Mirror image.

No. 232S, 150fr, Henry IV, by Rubens. 150fr, Marie de Medicis, by Rubens.

No. 232T, 200fr, Gabrielle d'Estrees, by unknown artist. 250fr, Henry IV, by French school, c. 1595.

No. 232U, 150fr, Jeanne d'Albret, by Francois Clouet. 200fr, Marie de Medicis as a Girl, by Angelo Bronzino.

No. 232V, 200fr, Henry III, by Clouet. 250fr, Ambroise Pare, by 16th century French school.

No. 232W, 150fr, Catherine de Medicis, by Clouet. 250fr, Henry II, by Clouet.

No. 233A, 200fr, Elizabeth of Austria, by Clouet. 250fr, Charles IX, by Clouet.

No. 233B, 200fr, Mary Stuart, by 16th cent. Scottish school. 300fr, Diane of Poitiers, by Fontainbleu school.

No. 233C, 200fr, Elizabeth of Valois, by Alonso S. Coello. 250fr, Francis, Duke of Alencon, by Clouet.

No. 233D, 150fr, Marguerite d'Angouleme, by Clouet. 300fr, Francis I, by Clouet.

No. 233E, 200fr, Francis I, by Titian. 300fr, Francis I as Dauphin, by Corneille of Lyon.

No. 233F, 100fr, Anne of Austria, by Coello. 250fr, Louis XIII, by Champaigne.

No. 233G, 200fr, Marie de Medicis, by Rubens. 200fr, Marie de Medicis, Louis XIII, by Rubens.

No. 233H, 150fr, The Exchange of Princess Elizabeth of France and Princess Anne of Austria on the Andaye River, by Rubens. 250fr, Louis XIII of France and Navarre, by Vouet.

No. 233J, 250fr, Marie de Medicis, by Rubens. 250fr, Henry IV, by Rubens.

No. 233K, Louis XV and the Dauphin at Battle of Fontenoy. No. 233L, The Grand Dauphin and his Family, by Mignard. No. 233M, Madame de Montespan, horiz. No. 233N, Madame de la Valliere and her Children. No. 233P, The Birth of Louis XIII at Fontainebleau, by Rubens. No. 233Q, Reconciliation of the Queen and Louis XIII, by Rubens. No. 233R, Henry IV Entrusting Regency to Marie de Medici, by Rubens. No. 233S, The Majority of Louis XIII, by Rubens. No. 233T, The Apotheosis of Henry IV and the Proclamation of Regency, by Rubens. No. 233U, Felicity of the Regency, by Rubens.

1971-73 Litho. *Perf. 12½x13*
232A A57c Strip of 3, #aa-ac *2.25*
232B A57c Pair, #aa-ab *1.40*
232C A57c Pair, #aa-ab *1.40*
232D A57c Pair, #aa-ab *1.75*
232E A57c Strip of 3, #aa-ac *3.50*
232F A57c Pair, #aa-ab *3.50*
232G A57c Pair, #aa-ab *2.25*
232H A57c Pair, #aa-ab *3.50*
232J A57c Pair, #aa-ab *3.50*
232K A57c Pair, #aa-ab *3.50*
232L A57c Pair, #aa-ab *2.25*
232M A57c Pair, #aa-ab *3.50*
232N A57c Pair, #aa-ab *3.50*
232P A57c Pair, #aa-ab *5.50*
232Q A57c Pair, #aa-ab *3.75*
232R A57c Pair, #aa-ab *4.00*
232S A57c Pair, #aa-ab *4.00*
232T A57c Pair, #aa-ab *6.75*
232U A57c Pair, #aa-ab *5.00*
232V A57c Pair, #aa-ab *6.75*
232W A57c Pair, #aa-ab *5.75*
233A A57c Pair, #aa-ab *6.75*
233B A57c Pair, #aa-ab *7.25*
233C A57c Pair, #aa-ab *6.00*
233D A57c Pair, #aa-ab *6.75*
233E A57c Pair, #aa-ab *7.25*
233F A57c Pair, #aa-ab *5.50*
233G A57c Pair, #aa-ab *5.50*
233H A57c Pair, #aa-ab *5.50*
233J A57c Pair, #aa-ab *6.75*
Nos. 232A-233J (30) 134.55

Souvenir Sheets

Perf. 13x13½, 13½x13, 13½

233K A57c 75fr multi *5.75*
233L A57c 100fr multi *5.00*
233M A57c 200fr multi *4.50*
233N A57c 300fr multi *4.50*
233P A57c 350fr multi *11.00*
233Q A57c 400fr multi *14.50*
233R A57c 400fr multi *9.00*
233S A57c 400fr multi *9.00*
233T A57c 400fr multi *5.50*
233U A57c 500fr multi *12.50*
Nos. 232K-233U (31) 192.75

Nos. 232A 60fr, 232B 40fr, 232C 50fr, 232D 70fr, 232E 80fr, 232F 200fr, 232G, 232H 200fr, 232J 200fr, 232K, 232L, 232M 200fr, 232N-233U are airmail.

Issued: 1971 — #232A, 2/24; #232B, 3/30; #232C, 3/4; #232D, 233K, 3/15; #232E, 4/12; #232F, 233L, 4/26; #232G, 8/10; #232H, 9/6; #232J, 9/23; #232K, 10/6; #232L, 10/26; #232M, 11/16; #232N, 11/20.

1972 — #232P, 233P, Jan.; #232Q, 233M-233N, Feb.; #233Q-233R, May; #232R, 233S, 6/15; #232S, 233T, 6/26; #232T, 8/8; #232U, 8/17; #232V, 8/30; #232W, 233U, 12/11; #233A, 12/18; #233B, 12/28.

1973 — #233C-233J.

Nos. 233K-233L, 233T-233U each contain one 37x62mm stamp. Nos. 233N, 233P each contain one 32x50mm stamp. No. 233M contains one 45x65mm stamp. Nos. 233Q-233R, 233U each contain one 65x45mm stamp.

Nos. 232Q-232V, 233G, 233J, 233R-233U and possibly 232P, 232W-233F, 233H probably were not available in Chad.

Symbolic Tree — A58

1971, Mar. 21 Engr. *Perf. 13*
236 A58 40fr bl grn, dk red & grn .90 .20

Intl. year against racial discrimination.

Paintings of Flowers A58a

Designs: 1fr, The Three Graces (detail), by Rubens. 4fr, Imperial Bouquet, by Van Os. 5fr, Bouquet, by Jan Brueghel.

1971, Apr. 28 Litho. *Perf. 12x12½*
236A A58a Strip of 3, #a-c 5.00

For overprint see No. 278A.

Summer Olympic Games — A58b

15fr, Swimming. 20fr, Women's relay races. 25fr, Swimming, medals. 50fr, Running.

Perf. 12x12½, 12½x12

1971, Apr. 28 Litho.
236B A58b 15fr multi, vert. 1.60
236C A58b 20fr multi, vert. 2.40
236D A58b 25fr multi 3.25
Nos. 236B-236D (3) 7.25

Embossed

Perf. 13

236E A58b 25fr gold, like No. 236D 16.00

Souvenir Sheet

Litho.

Die Cut Perf 13

236F A58b 50fr multicolored 9.00

Nos. 236D-236F are airmail. No. 236F contains one 62x36mm stamp.

Issued: #236B-236D, 236F, 4/28; #236E, 11/1.

For overprints see Nos. 251A-251D.

No. 236E probably was not available in Chad.

Map of Africa, Radar Antenna A59

Map of Africa and: 40fr, Communications tower. 50fr, Communications satellite.

1971, May 17 Engr. *Perf. 13*
237 A59 5fr ultra, org & dk red .20 .20
238 A59 40fr pur, emer & brn .70 .20
239 A59 50fr dk red, blk & brn .90 .20
Nos. 237-239 (3) 1.80 .60

3rd World Telecommunications Day.

Apollo 11 — A59a

1971, July 5 Embossed *Perf. 13*
239A A59a 10fr gold 20.00
b. Sheet of 1, Imperf. 35.00

No. 239Ab contains one 73x45mm stamp with same size design as No. 239A.

Nos. 239A-239Ab probably were not available in Chad.

No. 225F Overprinted in Gold

1971, July 17 Litho. *Perf. 12x12½*
239C A50b Strip of 3, #a-c 5.50

1972 Winter Olympics, Sapporo.

Nos. 228A-228B, 228D Ovptd. with "MUNICH 72" and Olympic Rings in Gold

Perf. 12½x12, 12x12½
1971, Nov. 1 Litho.
239D A54a Strip of 3, #a-c 9.00
239E A54a Pair, #a-b + label 5.50

Souvenir Sheet
Perf. 13½x13
239F A54a 40fr on #228D 18.00

UNICEF Emblem and Children — A60

1971, Dec. 11 Engr. *Perf. 13*
240 A60 50fr Prus bl, emer & brt pink 1.00 .20

25th anniv. of UNICEF.

Gorane Nangara Dancers A61

Dancers: 15fr, Girls' initiation dance, Yondo. 30fr, Women of M'Boum, vert. 40fr, Men of Sara Kaba, vert.

1971, Dec. 18 Litho. *Perf. 13*
241 A61 10fr blk & multi .70 .20
242 A61 15fr brn org & multi 1.00 .20
243 A61 30fr bl & multi 1.40 .20
244 A61 40fr yel grn & multi 1.75 .20
Nos. 241-244 (4) 4.85 .80

Nos. 205-210 Ovptd. in Gold

1971 Litho. *Perf. 12½x13, 13x12½*
244A-244F A45 1fr on #205-210 4.00

Nos. 244A-244F probably were not available in Chad.

Presidents Pompidou and Tombalbaye, Map with Paris and Fort Lamy — A62

1972, Jan. 25 Photo. *Perf. 13*
245 A62 40fr blue & multi 1.60 .20

Visit of Pres. Georges Pompidou of France, Jan. 1972.

Nos. 181-204 Ovptd. with "MUNICH 72" and Olympic Rings in Gold

1972, Feb. 7 Litho. *Perf. 12½x13*
245A-245X A44 1fr on #181-204 14.50

Nos. 245A-245X probably were not available in Chad.

Nos. 231G-231I Ovptd. in Gold

a

b

1972, Feb. Litho. *Perf. 12x12½*
246A A57b 50c Pair, #d.-e. 1.40
246B A57b 1fr Pair, #f.-g. 2.00
246C A57b 2fr Pair, #h.-i. 2.50

Nos. 246A-246C probably were not available in Chad.

President Tombalbaye — A63

1972, Apr. 13 Litho. *Perf. 13*
247 A63 30fr multi .35 .20
247A A63 40fr multi .55 .20
Nos. 247-247A,C112-C113 (4) 2.70 .80

Downhill Skiing — A64

75fr, Women's figure skating. 150fr, Luge.

1972, Apr. 13 *Perf. 13½*
248 A64 25fr multi .25 .20
249 A64 75fr multi .70 .25
250 A64 150fr multi 1.40 .45
Nos. 248-250,C114-C115 (5) 5.70 1.95

11th Winter Olympic Games, Sapporo, Japan.

Heart — A65

Gorrizia Dubiosa — A66

1972, Apr. 25 Engr. *Perf. 13*
251 A65 100fr purple, bl & car 1.60 .20

"Your heart is your health," World Health Month.

Nos. 236B-236D, 236F Ovptd. with "MUNICH 72" and Olympic Rings in Gold

1972 Litho. *Perf. 12x12½, 12½x12*
251A A58b 15fr multicolored 3.00
251B A58b 20fr multicolored 4.50
251C A58b 25fr multicolored 7.00
Nos. 251A-251C (3) 14.50

Souvenir Sheet
Die Cut Perf 13
251D A58b 50fr multicolored 42.50

Nos. 251C-251D are airmail.

1972, May 6 Photo.

Insects and Spiders: 2fr, Spider (argiope sector). 3fr, Silk spider (nephila senegalense). 4fr, Beetle (oryctes boas). 5fr, Dragonfly (hemistigma albipunctata).

252 A66 1fr green & multi 1.25 .20
253 A66 2fr blue & multi 2.00 .20
254 A66 3fr car rose & multi 2.25 .20
255 A66 4fr yellow grn & multi 4.00 .25
256 A66 5fr dp green & multi 4.50 .30
Nos. 252-256 (5) 14.00 1.15

Trains — A66a

1972 Litho. *Perf. 12*
256A A66a 10fr Orient Express .90
256B A66a 40fr Osaka Express 1.90
256C A66a 50fr St. Germain 2.25
256D A66a 150fr Blue train 4.50
256E A66a 200fr Trans-Europe Express 8.00
Nos. 256A-256E (5) 17.55

Souvenir Sheet
256F A66a 300fr Rogers "Madison," 1855 12.50

No. 256F contains one 60x40mm stamp. See note before No. 225A.

Scout Greeting — A67

70fr, Mountain climbing. 80fr, Canoeing.

1972, May 15 Photo.
257 A67 30fr multi .45 .20
258 A67 70fr multi .80 .20
259 A67 80fr multi 1.00 .20
Nos. 257-259,C118-C119 (5) 4.90 1.30

Scout Jamboree.

Hurdles, Motion and Olympic Emblems A68

Motion and Olympic Emblems and: 130fr, Gymnast on rings. 150fr, Swimming. 300fr, Bicycling.

1972, June 9 Litho. *Perf. 13½*
260 A68 50fr blk & multi .70 .20
261 A68 130fr blk & multi 1.75 .25
262 A68 150fr blk & multi 2.00 .30
Nos. 260-262 (3) 4.45 .75

Souvenir Sheet
263 A68 300fr blk & multi 4.50 2.00

20th Olympic Games, Munich, Aug. 26-Sept. 10.

Ski Jump, Kasaya, Japan — A69

Designs: 75fr, Cross-country skiing, P. Tyldum, Sweden. 100fr, Figure-skating, pairs, L. Rodnina and A. Ulanov, USSR. 130fr, Men's speed skating, A. Schenk, Netherlands.

1972, June 15 *Perf. 14½*
264 A69 25fr gold & multi .35 .20
265 A69 75fr gold & multi .90 .25
266 A69 100fr gold & multi 1.40 .35
267 A69 130fr gold & multi 1.75 .40
Nos. 264-267,C130-C131 (6) 10.65 2.20

11th Winter Olympic Games, gold-medal winners. Nos. 264-267 exist se-tenant with label showing earth satellite.

Nos. 227A-227D, 227F Overprinted With Soccer Ball, "MUNICH 72" and Olympic Rings in Gold

1972 Litho. *Perf. 12*
267A A53a 1fr multicolored .85
267B A53a 4fr multicolored 1.10
267C A53a 5fr multicolored 1.75
267D A53a 5fr multicolored 1.75
Nos. 267A-267D (4) 5.45

Souvenir Sheet
Perf. 13½x13
267E A53a 15fr multicolored 8.00

Nos. 267D-267E are airmail.
Nos. 267A-267E probably were not available in Chad.

TV Tower and Weight-lifting — A70

Designs (TV Tower, Munich and): 40fr, Woman sprinter. 60fr, Soccer goalkeeper.

1972, Aug. 15 Litho. *Perf. 14½*

268 A70 20fr gold & multi .60 .20
269 A70 40fr gold & multi .75 .20
270 A70 60fr gold & multi 1.25 .20
Nos. 268-270,C135-C137 (6) 9.20 1.75

20th Summer Olympic Games, Munich. Nos. 268-270 exist se-tenant with label showing arms of Munich.

Domestic Animals A71

1972, Aug. 29 Engr. *Perf. 13*

271 A71 25fr Dromedary .55 .20
272 A71 30fr Horse .70 .20
273 A71 40fr Dog 1.00 .20
274 A71 45fr Goat 1.25 .20
Nos. 271-274 (4) 3.50 .80

For surcharge see No. 293.

Tobacco Cultivation A72

1972, Oct. 24 Engr. *Perf. 13*

275 A72 40fr shown .70 .20
276 A72 50fr Plowing 1.00 .20

Massa Warrior — A73

Design: 20fr, Moundang warrior.

1972, Nov. 15 Photo. *Perf. 14x13*

277 A73 15fr orange & multi .70 .20
278 A73 20fr yellow & multi .90 .20

No. 236A Overprinted "Noel 1972" in gold

1972 Litho. *Perf. 12x12½*

278A A58a Strip of 3, #a-c

No. 278A probably was not available in Chad.

King Faisal and Pres. Tombalbaye — A74

1972, Nov. 17 Litho. *Perf. 13*

279 A74 100fr gold & multi 2.25 .40

Visit of King Faisal of Saudi Arabia. See No. C143.

Gen. Gowon and Pres. Tombalbaye — A75

1972, Dec. 7

280 A75 70fr multi .90 .20

Visit of Gen. Yakubu Gowon of Nigeria.

Olympic Emblem and 100-meter Sprint, Valeri Borzov, USSR — A76

Designs (Olympic Emblem and): 20fr, Shotput, Komar, Poland. 40fr, Hammer throw, Bondartchuk, USSR. 60fr, Discus, Danek, Czechoslovakia.

1972, Dec. 22 *Perf. 11*

281 A76 10fr multi .50 .20
282 A76 20fr multi .50 .20
283 A76 40fr multi .65 .20
284 A76 60fr multi 1.00 .20
Nos. 281-284,C148-C149 (6) 8.90 2.10

20th Summer Olympic Games, winners.

Olympic Emblem and Fencing, Woyda, Poland — A77

Olympic Emblem and: 30fr, 3-day equestrian event, Richard Meade, Gt. Britain. 50fr, Two-man sculls, Brietzke-Mager, East Germany.

1972, Dec. 22

285 A77 20fr gold & multi .60 .20
286 A77 30fr gold & multi .60 .20
287 A77 50fr gold & multi .90 .20
Nos. 285-287,C151-C152 (5) 9.10 1.85

20th Summer Olympic Games, winners.

1972 Summer Olympics Gold Medalists — A77a

20fr, Teofilo Stevenson, boxing, Cuba. 25fr, Yugoslavia, team handball. 30fr, M. Peters, pentathlon, Great Britain. 40fr, basketball, USSR. No. 287E, W. Ruska, judo, Netherlands. No. 287F, Women's gynmastics, Ludmila Tourischeva, USSR. 75fr, Men's volleyball, Japan. No. 287H, A. Scalzone, shooting, Italy. No. 287I, Soccer, Poland. 130fr, J. Williams, archery, US. No. 287K, A. Nakayama, men's rings, Japan. No. 287L, Field hockey, West Germany. 200fr, Vassily Alexeiev, weight lifting, USSR. 250fr, D. Morelon, cycling, France.

1972, Dec. 22 Litho. *Perf. 11½*

287A A77a 20fr multicolored
287B A77a 25fr multicolored
287C A77a 30fr multicolored
287D A77a 40fr multicolored
287E A77a 50fr multicolored
287F A77a 50fr multicolored
287G A77a 75fr multicolored
287H A77a 100fr multicolored
287I A77a 100fr multicolored
287J A77a 130fr multicolored
287K A77a 150fr multicolored
287L A77a 150fr multicolored
Nos. 287A-287L (12) 17.50

Souvenir Sheets

Perf. 15

287M A77a 200fr multicolored 12.50
287N A77a 250fr multicolored 12.50

Nos. 287G-287N are airmail.

Soviet Flag and Shield — A78

1972, Dec. 30 Litho. *Perf. 12*

288 A78 150fr red & multi 1.75 .40

50th anniversary of the Soviet Union.

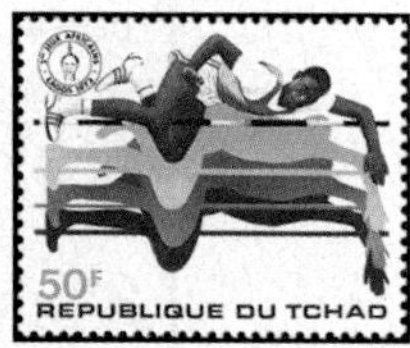

High Jump — A79

Designs (Games Emblem and): 125fr, Running. 200fr, Shot put. 250fr, Discus.

1973, Jan. 17 Litho. *Perf. 13½x13*

289 A79 50fr vio bl & multi .70 .20
290 A79 125fr olive & multi 1.50 .40
291 A79 200fr lilac & multi 2.75 .65
Nos. 289-291 (3) 4.95 1.25

Souvenir Sheet

292 A79 250fr brn & multi 3.50 2.00

2nd African Games, Lagos, Nigeria, 1/7-18.

Paintings with Musical Instruments — A79a

Details from Paintings: 30fr, Madeleine Playing her Lute, by unknown artist. 70fr, A Concert, by Lorenzo Costa. 100fr, Bass and Sheet Music, by Jean-Baptiste Oudry, horiz. 125fr, St. Cecilia and Angel, by Carlo Saraceni. 150fr, Woman Listening to Violinist, by Gabriel Metsu. 300fr, Still Life with Musical Instruments, by Pieter Claesz, horiz.

1973, Apr. Litho. *Perf. 11½*

292A A79a 30fr multicolored
292B A79a 70fr multicolored
292C A79a 100fr multicolored
292D A79a 125fr multicolored
292E A79a 150fr multicolored
Nos. 292A-292E (5) 12.50

Souvenir Sheet

Perf. 15

292F A79a 300fr multicolored 12.50

Nos. 292D-292F are airmail.

No. 271 Surcharged with New Value, 2 Bars, and Overprinted in Red: "SECHERESSE SOLIDARITE AFRICAINE"

1973, Aug. 16 Engr. *Perf. 13*

293 A71 100fr on 25fr multi 2.00 .40

African solidarity in drought emergency.

African Postal Union Issue

Common Design Type

1973, Sept. 17 Engr. *Perf. 13*

294 CD137 100fr multicolored 1.60 .40

Easter A79b

Details from paintings: 40fr, Christ on the Cross, by Lucas Cranach. 60fr, Supper in Emmaus, by Titian, horiz. 120fr, The Crucifixion, by Durer. 150fr, The Tribute, by Titian. 250fr, The Pieta, by Botticelli. 400fr, Entombment of Christ, by Gaspard Isenmann, horiz.

1973 Litho. *Perf. 11½*

294A A79b 40fr multicolored
294B A79b 60fr multicolored
294C A79b 120fr multicolored
294D A79b 150fr multicolored
294E A79b 250fr multicolored
Nos. 294A-294E (5) 12.50

Souvenir Sheet

Perf. 15

294F A79b 400fr multicolored 12.50

Nos. 294A, 294D-294F are airmail.

Animals
A79c

1973 Litho. *Perf. 13½*

294G A79c 20fr Sheep
294H A79c 30fr Camels
294J A79c 100fr Cats
294K A79c 130fr Dogs
294L A79c 150fr Horses
Nos. 294G-294L (5) 12.50

Nos. 294J-294L are airmail.
See note before No. 225A.

Christmas — A79d

30fr, The Virgin & Infant Surrounded by Saints, by Lorenzo Lotto. 40fr, Madonna and Child with St. Peter and a Martyred Saint, by Paolo Veronese (not Tintoretto), vert. 55fr, Nativity Scene, by Martin Schongauer, vert. 60fr, Nativity Scene, by Federico Barocci, vert. 250fr, Adoration of the Magi, by Stephan Lochner, vert. 400fr, Epiphany, by Hans Memling.

1973 Litho. *Perf. 11½*

294M A79d 30fr multicolored
294N A79d 40fr multicolored
294P A79d 55fr multicolored
294Q A79d 60fr multicolored
294R A79d 250fr multicolored
Nos. 294M-294R (5) 12.50

Souvenir Sheet

Perf. 15

294S A79d 400fr multicolored 12.50

Nos. 294Q-294S are airmail.
See note before No. 225A.

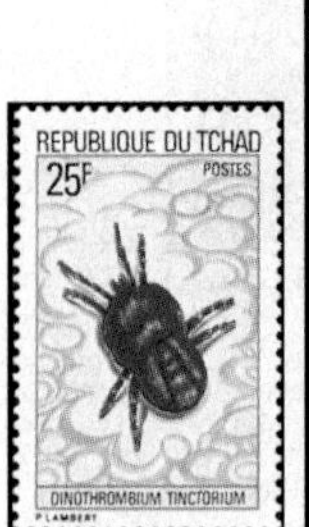

Dinothrombium Tinctorium
A80

Rotary Emblem
A81

1974, Sept. 3 Photo. *Perf. 13*

No.	Type	Value	Description	Unused	Used
295	A80	25fr	*shown*	1.25	.20
296	A80	30fr	*Bupreste sternocera*	1.75	.20
297	A80	40fr	*Diptere hyperechia*	2.25	.20
298	A80	50fr	*Chrysis*	2.75	.25
299	A80	100fr	*Longicorn beetle*	4.00	.40
300	A80	130fr	*Spider*	6.25	.55
			Nos. 295-300 (6)	18.25	1.80

1975, Apr. 11 Typo. *Perf. 13*

301 A81 50fr multi .90 .20

Rotary International, 70th anniversary.

Craterostigma Plantagineum — A82

Flowers: 10fr, Tapinanthus globiferus. 15fr, Commelina forskalaei, vert. 20fr, Adenium obesum. 25fr, Yellow hibiscus. 30fr, Red hibiscus. 40fr, Kigelia africana.

1975, Sept. 25 Photo. *Perf. 13*

No.	Type	Value	Description	Unused	Used
302	A82	5fr	org & multi	.35	.20
303	A82	10fr	gray bl & multi	.55	.20
304	A82	15fr	yel grn & multi	.70	.20
305	A82	20fr	lt brn & multi	.90	.20
306	A82	25fr	lil & multi	1.60	.20
307	A82	30fr	bis & multi	1.75	.20
308	A82	40fr	ultra & multi	2.75	.20
			Nos. 302-308 (7)	8.60	1.40

A. G. Bell, Satellite and Waves — A83

1976, June 10 Litho. *Perf. 12½*

309 A83 100fr bl, brn & ocher 1.25 .20
310 A83 125fr lt grn, brn & ocher 1.75 .25

Centenary of first telephone call by Alexander Graham Bell, Mar. 10, 1876.

Ice Hockey, USSR — A84

90fr, Ski jump, Karl Schnabl, Austria.

1976, June 21 *Perf. 14*

311 A84 60fr multi .70 .20
312 A84 90fr multi 1.10 .20
Nos. 311-312,C178-C179 (4) 7.55 1.65

12th Winter Olympic Games, winners. See No. C180.

High Hurdles
A85

1976, July 12 Litho. *Perf. 13½*

313 A85 45fr multi .65 .20
Nos. 313,C187-C189 (4) 7.10 1.65

21st Summer Olympic Games, Montreal, Canada.
See No. C190.

Mars Landing and Viking Rocket
A86

Mars Landing and: 90fr, Viking trajectory, Earth to Mars.

1976, July 23 *Perf. 14*

314 A86 45fr multi .45 .20
315 A86 90fr multi .90 .25
Nos. 314-315,C191-C193 (5) 6.60 1.90

Viking Mars project.
For overprints see Nos. 379-380.

Robert Koch, Medicine — A87

Design: 90fr, Anatole France, literature.

1976, Dec. 15

316 A87 45fr multi .70 .20
317 A87 90fr multi 1.40 .25
Nos. 316-317,C196-C198 (5) 8.85 2.00

Nobel Prize winners.

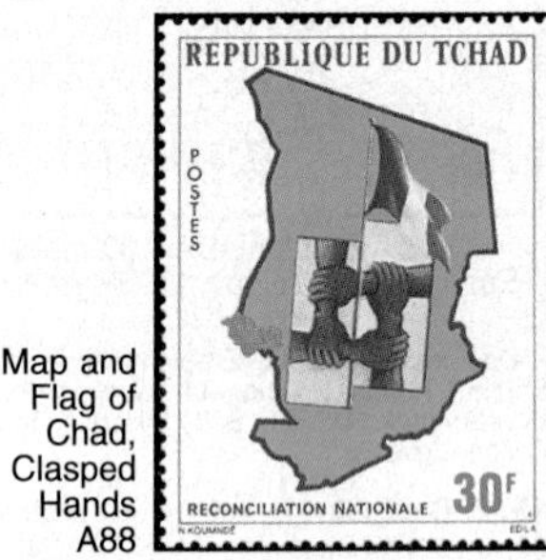

Map and Flag of Chad, Clasped Hands
A88

120fr, Map of Chad, people & occupations.

1976, Sept. 15 Litho. *Perf. 12½x13*

318 A88 30fr multi .55 .20
319 A88 60fr orange & multi 1.00 .20
320 A88 120fr brown & multi 2.00 .25
Nos. 318-320 (3) 3.55 .65

National reconciliation.

Freed Political Prisoners — A89

Designs: 60fr, Parade of cadets.

1976, Sept. 25 Litho. *Perf. 12½*

321 A89 30fr blue & multi .25 .20
322 A89 60fr black & multi .70 .20
323 A89 120fr red & multi 1.25 .25
Nos. 321-323 (3) 2.20 .65

Revolution of Apr. 13, 1975, 1st anniv.

Decorated Calabashes — A90

Designs: Various pyrographed calabashes.

1976, Nov. Litho. *Perf. 12½x13*

324 A90 30fr multi .35 .20
325 A90 60fr multi .80 .20
326 A90 120fr multi 1.60 .25
Nos. 324-326 (3) 2.75 .65

Germany No. C57 and Friedrichshafen, Germany — A91

1977, Mar. 30 *Perf. 14*

327 A91 100fr multi 1.25 .25
Nos. 327,C206-C209 (5) 10.60 1.90

75th anniversary of the Zeppelin.

Elizabeth II in Coronation Regalia and Clergy — A92

Design: 450fr, Elizabeth II and Prince Philip.

1977, June 15 Litho. *Perf. 14x13½*

328 A92 250fr multi 3.00 .45

Souvenir Sheet

329 A92 450fr multi 5.25 1.40

25th anniv. of the reign of Elizabeth II.
For overprints see Nos. 347-348.

Simon Bolivar
A93

Famous Personalities: 175fr, Joseph J. Roberts. No. 332, Queen Wihelmina of Netherlands. No. 333, Charles de Gaulle. 325fr, King Baudouin and Queen Fabiola of Belgium.

1977, June 15 *Perf. 13½x14*

No.	Type	Value	Description	Unused	Used
330	A93	150fr	multi	1.40	.25
331	A93	175fr	multi	2.00	.30
332	A93	200fr	multi	2.75	.35
333	A93	200fr	multi	2.75	.35
334	A93	325fr	multi	3.75	.50
			Nos. 330-334 (5)	12.65	1.75

Post and Telecommunications Emblem — A94

Map of Chad and Waves — A95

Society Emblem — A96

1977, Aug. 15 Litho. *Perf. 13*
335 A94 30fr yel & blk .45 .20
Perf. 12½
336 A95 60fr multi .70 .20
Perf. 13½x13
337 A96 120fr multi 1.50 .40
Nos. 335-337 (3) 2.65 .80

Telecommunications (30fr); Natl. Telecommunications School, 10th anniv. (60fr); Intl. Telecommunication Soc. of Chad (120fr).

WHO Emblem and Man (Back Pain) — A97

World Rheumatism Year (WHO Emblem and): 60fr, Woman's head (neck pain), horiz. 120fr, Leg (knee pain).

Perf. 12½x13, 13x12½
1977, Nov. 10 Engr.
338 A97 30fr multi .45 .20
339 A97 60fr multi .90 .20
340 A97 120fr multi 1.25 .40
Nos. 338-340 (3) 2.60 .80

World Cup Emblems and Saving a Goal — A98

Designs (Argentina '78, World Cup Emblems and): 60fr, Heading the ball. 100fr, Referee whistling a goal. 200fr, World Cup poster. 300fr, Pelé. 500fr, Helmut Schoen and Munich stadium.

1977, Nov. 25 Litho. *Perf. 13½*
341 A98 40fr multi .45 .20
342 A98 60fr multi .70 .20
343 A98 100fr multi 1.00 .25
344 A98 200fr multi 2.25 .50
345 A98 300fr multi 3.50 .75
Nos. 341-345 (5) 7.90 1.90

Souvenir Sheet

346 A98 500fr multi 5.25 1.10

World Cup Soccer Championship, Argentina '78.
For overprints see Nos. 359-364.

Nos. 328-329 Overprinted in Silver: "ANNIVERSAIRE DU COURONNEMENT 1953-1978"

1978, Sept. 13 *Perf. 14x13½*
347 A92 250fr multi 2.75 .60

Souvenir Sheet

348 A92 450fr multi 5.00 1.25

25th anniv. of coronation of Elizabeth II.

Abraham and Melchisedek, by Rubens — A99

Rubens Paintings: 120fr, Helene Fourment, vert. 200fr, David and the Elders of Israel. 300fr, Anne of Austria, vert. 500fr, Marie de Medicis, vert.

1978, Nov. 23 Litho. *Perf. 13½*
349 A99 60fr multi .70 .20
350 A99 120fr multi 1.60 .35
351 A99 200fr multi 2.75 .75
352 A99 300fr multi 4.00 1.10
Nos. 349-352 (4) 9.05 2.40

Souvenir Sheet

353 A99 500fr multi 6.25 2.50

Peter Paul Rubens (1577-1640).

Dürer Portrait A100

Dürer Paintings: 150fr, Jacob Muffel. 250fr, Young Woman. 350fr, Oswolt Krel.

1978, Nov. 23
354 A100 60fr multi .55 .20
355 A100 150fr multi 1.60 .50
356 A100 250fr multi 2.75 .80
357 A100 350fr multi 4.00 1.10
Nos. 354-357 (4) 8.90 2.60

Head, Village and Fly — A101

1978, Nov. 28 *Perf. 13*
358 A101 60f multi .70 .20

National Health Day.

Nos. 341-346 Overprinted in Silver:
a. 1962 BRESIL-TCHECOSLOVAQUIE / 3-1
b. 1966 / GRANDE BRETAGNE / -ALLEMAGNE (RFA) / 4-2
c. 1970 BRESIL-ITALIE 4-1
d. 1974 ALLEMAGNE (RFA)- / PAYS BAS 2-1
e. 1978 / ARGENTINE -/ PAYS BAS / 3-1
f. ARGENTINE -PAYS BAS / 3-1

1978, Dec. 30 Litho. *Perf. 13½*
359 A98(a) 40fr multi .45 .20
360 A98(b) 60fr multi .70 .20
361 A98(c) 100fr multi 1.25 .30
362 A98(d) 200fr multi 2.25 .60
363 A98(e) 300fr multi 3.25 .95
Nos. 359-363 (5) 7.90 2.25

Souvenir Sheet

364 A98(f) 500fr multi 5.25 1.50

World Soccer Championship winners.

UPU Emblems, Camel Caravan, Satellites — A102

Design: 150fr, Obus woman and houses, Massa Territory, hibiscus.

1979, June 8 Litho. *Perf. 12x12½*
365 A102 60fr multi 2.75 .20
366 A102 150fr multi 4.50 .40

Philexafrique II, Libreville, Gabon, June 8-17. Nos. 365, 366 each printed in sheets of 10 with 5 labels showing exhibition emblem.

Wildlife Fund Emblem and Gazelle — A103

Protected Animals.

1979, Sept. 15 Litho. *Perf. 14½*
367 A103 40fr shown 1.40 .20
368 A103 50fr Addax 1.60 .20
369 A103 60fr Oryx antelope 1.75 .35
370 A103 100fr Cheetah 3.25 .75
371 A103 150fr Zebra 4.50 .90
372 A103 300fr Rhinoceros 9.00 1.25
Nos. 367-372 (6) 21.50 3.65

Souvenir Sheet

Holy Family, by Dürer — A104

1979, Sept. 1 *Perf. 13½*
373 A104 500fr brown & dull red 6.25 1.50

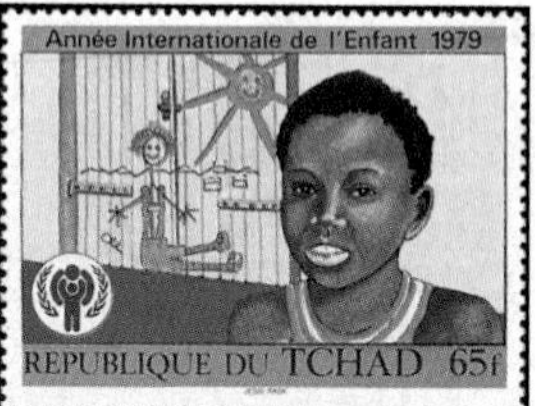

Boy and Handpainted Doors — A105

IYC Emblem and: 75fr, Oriental girl. 100fr, Caucasian girl, doves. 150fr, African boys. 250fr, Pencil and outlines of child's hands.

1979, Sept. 19 Litho. *Perf. 13½*
374 A105 65fr multi .55 .20
375 A105 75fr multi .70 .20
376 A105 100fr multi .90 .20
377 A105 150fr multi 1.40 .30
Nos. 374-377 (4) 3.55 .90

Souvenir Sheet

378 A105 250fr multi 2.75 .50

Nos. 314-315 Overprinted "ALUNISSAGE/APOLLO XI/JUILLET 1969" and Emblem

1979, Nov. 26 Litho. *Perf. 13½x14*
379 A86 45fr multi .55 .20
380 A86 90fr multi .90 .30
Nos. 379-380,C240-C242 (5) 6.70 2.20

Apollo 11 moon landing, 10th anniversary.

Ski Jump, Lake Placid '80 Emblem — A106

Lake Placid '80 Emblem and: 20fr, Slalom, vert. 40fr, Biathlon, vert. 150fr, Women's slalom, vert. 350fr, Cross-country skiing. 500fr, Downhill skiing.

1979, Dec. 18 *Perf. 14½*
381 A106 20fr multi .25 .20
382 A106 40fr multi .55 .20
383 A106 60fr multi .70 .20
384 A106 150fr multi 1.60 .50
385 A106 350fr multi 2.75 1.25
386 A106 500fr multi 4.00 1.75
Nos. 381-386 (6) 9.85 4.10

13th Winter Olympic Games, Lake Placid, NY, Feb. 12-24, 1980.

Jet over Map of Africa A107

1980, Feb. 20 Litho. *Perf. 12½*
387 A107 15fr yellow & multi .20 .20
388 A107 30fr blue & multi .35 .20
389 A107 60fr red & multi .55 .20
Nos. 387-389 (3) 1.10 .60

ASECNA (Air Safety Board), 20th anniv.

1982 World Cup Soccer Championships, Spain — A108

1982 Litho. *Perf. 13½*

390	A108	30fr Hungary	.25	.20
391	A108	40fr Italy	.35	.20
392	A108	50fr Algeria	.45	.20
393	A108	60fr Argentina	.55	.20
		Nos. 390-393,C258-C259 (6)	5.25	1.40

21st Birthday of Princess Diana A109

1982, July 2 Litho. *Perf. 13½*

395	A109	30fr 1961	.25	.20
396	A109	40fr 1965	.35	.20
397	A109	50fr 1967	.45	.20
398	A109	60fr 1975	.55	.20
		Nos. 395-398,C260-C261 (6)	5.25	2.00

For overprints see Nos. 413-419B.

A110

1984 Summer Olympics, Los Angeles — A110a

#405A, Runner. #405B, Long jumper, vert.

1982, Aug. 2 Litho. *Perf. 13½*

399	A110	30fr Gymnast	.25	.20
400	A110	40fr Equestrian	.35	.20
401	A110	50fr Judo	.45	.20
402	A110	60fr High jump	.55	.20
403	A110	80fr Hurdles	.90	.25
404	A110	300fr Woman gymnast	2.75	.95
		Nos. 399-404 (6)	5.25	2.00

Souvenir Sheet

405 A110 500fr Relay race 5.00 1.50

For surcharge see No. C302.

1982, July 31 Litho. & Embossed

405A A110a 1500fr gold & multi 15.00

Souvenir Sheet

405B A110a 1500fr gold & multi 11.00

No. 405 contains one 56x39mm stamp. Nos. 403-405B airmail.

Scouting Year — A111

Boy Scouts, 75th Anniv. A111a

Scouts from various countries. No. 412A, Lord Robert Baden-Powell. No. 412B, Scouts at campsite, Baden-Powell, horiz.

1982, July 15

406	A111	30fr West Germany	.25	.20
407	A111	40fr Upper Volta	.35	.20
408	A111	50fr Mali	.45	.20
409	A111	60fr Scotland	.55	.20
410	A111	80fr Kuwait	.90	.25
411	A111	300fr Chad	2.75	.95
		Nos. 406-411 (6)	5.25	2.00

Souvenir Sheet

412 A111 500fr Chad, diff. 5.00 1.50

Litho. & Embossed

412A A111a 1500fr gold & multi 15.00

Souvenir Sheet

412B A111a 1500fr gold & multi 15.00

No. 412 contains one 53x35mm stamp. Nos. 410-412B airmail.
For overprints see Nos. 466-472B.

Nos. 395-398, C260-C262B Overprinted: "21 JUIN 1982 / WILLIAM ARTHUR PHILIP LOUIS/ PRINCE DE GALLES"

1982, Oct. 4 Litho. *Perf. 13½*

413	A109	30fr multi	.25	.20
414	A109	40fr multi	.35	.20
415	A109	50fr multi	.45	.20
416	A109	60fr multi	.55	.20
417	A109	80fr multi	.90	.25
418	A109	300fr multi	2.75	.95
		Nos. 413-418 (6)	5.25	2.00

Souvenir Sheet

419 A109 500fr multi 5.00 1.50

Litho. & Embossed

419A AP71b 1500fr on #C262A 15.00

Souvenir Sheet

419B AP71b 1500fr on #C262B 12.50

Birth of Prince William of Wales, June 21. Nos. 417-419B airmail.

A112

1982 World Cup Soccer Championships, Spain — A112a

Various players and flags. No. 426A, Dino Zoff, Italy, holding World Cup trophy. No. 426B, Paolo Rossi, Italy, two players, trophy, horiz.

1982, Nov. 30

420	A112	30fr multi	.25	.20
421	A112	40fr multi	.35	.20
422	A112	50fr multi	.45	.20
423	A112	60fr multi	.55	.20
424	A112	80fr multi	.90	.25
425	A112	300fr multi	2.75	.95
		Nos. 420-425 (6)	5.25	2.00

Souvenir Sheet

426 A112 500fr multi 5.00 1.50

Litho. & Embossed

426A A112a 1500fr gold & multi 15.00

Souvenir Sheet

426B A112a 1500fr gold & multi 15.00

No. 426 contains one 56x32mm stamp. Nos. 424-426B airmail. For surcharge see No. C306.

A113

Chess Champions — A113a

#433A, Bobby Fischer. #433B, William Steinitz.

1982, Dec. 24

427	A113	30fr Philidor	.90	.20
428	A113	40fr Paul Morphy	1.00	.20
429	A113	50fr Howard Staunton	1.10	.20
430	A113	60fr Capablanca	1.25	.20
431	A113	80fr Boris Spassky	2.00	.25
432	A113	300fr Anatoly Karpov	3.50	.75
		Nos. 427-432 (6)	9.75	1.80

Souvenir Sheet

433 A113 500fr Victor Korchnoi 8.00 1.50

Litho. & Embossed

433A A113a 1500fr gold & multi 16.00

Souvenir Sheet

433B A113a 1500fr gold & multi 11.00

No. 433 contains one 53x35mm stamp. Nos. 431-433B airmail.
For overprints see Nos. 459-465.

2nd UN Conference on Peaceful Uses of Outer Space, Vienna, Aug. 9-21 — A114

A114a

Inventors and Satellites: 30fr, K.E. Tsiolkovsky, Soyuz. 40fr, R.H. Goddard, space telescope design. 50fr, Korolev, ultraviolet telescope. 60fr, von Braun, Columbia space shuttle. 80fr, Esnault Pelterie, Ariana rocket. 300fr, H. Oberth, orbital space station. 500fr, Pres. Kennedy, Apollo 11 badge, lunar rover. No. 440A, Sir Bernard Lovell, Viking I & II. No. 440B, Sir Isaac Newton, satellite TDF 1.

1983, Feb. 1 Litho. *Perf. 13½*

434	A114	30fr multi	.25	.20
435	A114	40fr multi	.35	.20
406	A114	50fr multi	.45	.20
437	A114	60fr multi	.55	.20
438	A114	80fr multi	.90	.25
439	A114	300fr multi	2.75	.95
		Nos. 434-439 (6)	5.25	2.00

Souvenir Sheet

440 A114 500fr multi 5.00 1.50

Litho. & Embossed

440A A114a 1500fr gold & multi 15.00

Souvenir Sheet

440B A114a 1500fr gold & multi 11.00

No. 440 contains one 42x50mm stamp. Nos. 438-440B airmail.

Bobsledding — A115

Woman Figure Skater A115a

Design: No. 447B, Slalom skier, horiz.

1983, Apr. 25 Litho. *Perf. 13½*

441	A115	30fr shown	.25	.20
442	A115	40fr Speed skating	.35	.20
443	A115	50fr Cross-country skiing	.45	.20
444	A115	60fr Hockey	.55	.25
445	A115	80fr Ski jumping	.90	.30
446	A115	300fr Downhill skiing	2.75	1.00
		Nos. 441-446 (6)	5.25	2.15

Souvenir Sheet

447 A115 500fr Figure skating 5.00 1.50

Litho. & Embossed

447A A115a 1500fr gold & multi 15.00

Souvenir Sheet

447B A115a 1500fr gold & multi 11.00

14th Winter Olympic Games, Sarajevo, Yugoslavia, Feb. 8-19, 1984. Nos. 445-447B airmail. For surcharge see No. C298.

First Manned Balloon Flight, 200th Anniv. A116

Designs: 25fr, Hot air balloon, Montgolfier Brothers. 45fr, Captive balloon, Pilatre De Rozier. 50fr, First parachute descent, Jacques Garnerin. 60fr, Chelsea balloon, J.P. Blanchard.

1983, May 30 Litho. *Perf. 13½*

448	A116	25fr multi	.25	.20
449	A116	45fr multi	.35	.20
450	A116	50fr multi	.45	.20
451	A116	60fr multi	.55	.20
		Nos. 448-451,C268-C269 (6)	5.25	1.45

Automobiles — A116a

Automobiles and their builders: 25fr, 1927 Mercedes Type S, Gottlieb Daimler and Karl Benz. 45fr, 1913 Torpedo Martini Type GC 32-2, 6L, Friedrich Martini. 50fr, 1926 Chrysler "70," Walter P. Chrysler. 60fr, 1929 Alfa Romeo 6C 1750 Grand Sport, Nicola Romeo. 80fr, 1934 Phantom II Continental, Stewart Rolls and Henry Royce. 250fr, 1948 Talbot Lago, Lord Shrewsbury and Talbot.

1983, July 15 Litho. *Perf. 13½*

451A A116a 25fr multicolored
451B A116a 45fr multicolored
451C A116a 50fr multicolored
451D A116a 60fr multicolored
451E A116a 80fr multicolored
451F A116a 250fr multicolored
Nos. 451A-451F (6) 6.25 1.50

Nos. 451E-451F are airmail.

1984 Summer Olympics, Los Angeles A117

A117a

1983, Nov. 15 Litho. *Perf. 13½*

452 A117 25fr Kayak .25 .20
453 A117 45fr Long jump .55 .20
454 A117 50fr Boxing .65 .20
455 A117 60fr Discus .70 .20
456 A117 80fr Running .90 .25
457 A117 350fr Equestrian 3.25 .75
Nos. 452-457 (6) 6.30 1.80

Souvenir Sheet

458 A117 500fr Gymnastics 5.00 .80

Litho. & Embossed

458A A117a 1500fr Hurdles 15.00

Souvenir Sheet

458B A117a 1500fr Equestrian, vert. 11.00

Nos. 456-458B are airmail.

Pres. Hissein Habre — A117b

Designs: Nos. 458D, 458H, Sources of food. Nos. 458E, 458I, Dove of peace, different tribal groups, country map.

1983, Dec. 26 Litho. *Perf. 13½*

458C A117b 50fr multicolored .55 .20
458D A117b 50fr multicolored .55 .20
458E A117b 50fr multicolored .55 .20
458F A117b 60fr multicolored .65 .20
458G A117b 80fr multicolored .80 .25
458H A117b 80fr multicolored .80 .25
458I A117b 80fr multicolored .80 .25
458J A117b 100fr multicolored 1.00 .35

Numbers have been reserved for 4 airmail values in this set. The editors would like to see these stamps.

Nos. 427-433 Overprinted: "60e ANNIVERSAIRE FEDERATION / MONDIALE D'ECHECS 1924-1984"

1983, Dec. 27 Litho. *Perf. 13½*

459 A113 30fr multi .80 .20
460 A113 40fr multi 1.00 .20
461 A113 50fr multi 1.25 .20
462 A113 60fr multi 1.60 .20
463 A113 80fr multi 2.00 .30
464 A113 300fr multi 4.00 .75
Nos. 459-464 (6) 10.65 1.85

Souvenir Sheet

465 A113 500fr multi 4.00 1.10

World Chess Fedn., 60th anniv.

Nos. 406-412B Ovptd. with Emblem for the 15th World Scout Jamboree, Alberta, Canada, 1983

1983, Dec. 27 Litho. *Perf. 13½*

466 A111 30fr multi .25 .20
467 A111 40fr multi .35 .20
468 A111 50fr multi .45 .20
469 A111 60fr multi .55 .20
470 A111 80fr multi .65 .20
471 A111 300fr multi 2.75 .50
Nos. 466-471 (6) 5.00 1.50

Souvenir Sheet

472 A111 500fr multi 5.00 .80

Litho. & Embossed

472A A111a 1500fr on #412A 15.00

Souvenir Sheet

472B A111a 1500fr on #412B 11.00

Locomotive "Lady," 1879 — A118

1984, Mar. 15

473 A118 50fr shown .55 .20
474 A118 200fr Sailboat, Lake Chad 2.00 .30
475 A118 300fr Graf Zeppelin 2.75 .45
476 A118 350fr Renault desert transport, 1930 3.25 .55
477 A118 400fr Bloch 120 monoplane 3.50 .75
478 A118 500fr Air Africa DC-8 4.50 1.00
Nos. 473-478 (6) 16.55 3.25

Souvenir Sheet

479 A118 600fr Intelsat V satellite 5.25 2.50

Nos. 477-479 airmail. For surcharge see No. 579.

Liberation, 2nd Anniv. — A119

Pres. Hissein Habre — A120

1984, June 6 *Perf. 12½*

480 A119 50fr multi .55 .20

1984, June 18 *Perf. 12½x13*

481 A120 125fr multi 1.40 .40

Anniversaries and Events — A121

Designs: 50fr, Pres. Habre, civil war martyrs. 200fr, Paul Harris, Rotary Intl. headquarters, Illinois. 300fr, Alfred Nobel, will establishing fund for Prizes. 350fr, Raphael, detail from Virgin with Child and St. John the Baptist. 400fr, Rembrandt, detail from The Holy Family. 500fr, J.W. Goethe, scene from Faust. 600fr, Rubens, detail from Helene Forement and Her Two Children.

1984, Jan. 16 Litho. *Perf. 13½*

482 A121 50fr multi .45 .20
483 A121 200fr multi 1.75 .30
484 A121 300fr multi 2.75 .45
485 A121 350fr multi 3.50 .55
486 A121 400fr multi 4.00 .60
487 A121 500fr multi 5.25 .70
Nos. 482-487 (6) 17.70 2.80

Souvenir Sheet

488 A121 600fr multi 6.25 1.25

Nos. 486-488 are airmail.

Homage to Our Martyred Dead — A122

1984, Feb. 22 Litho. *Perf. 13½*

500 A122 50fr multi .45 .20
501 A122 80fr multi .70 .20
502 A122 120fr multi 1.00 .20
503 A122 200fr multi 1.75 .25
504 A122 250fr multi 2.25 .40
Nos. 500-504 (5) 6.15 1.25

#503-504 airmail. For surcharge see #C303.

World Communications Year — A123

1984, Feb. 29 Litho. *Perf. 13½*

505 A123 50fr sil & multi .45 .20
506 A123 60fr sil & multi .55 .20
507 A123 70fr sil & multi .70 .20
508 A123 125fr sil & multi 1.00 .20
509 A123 250fr sil & multi 2.25 .40
Nos. 505-509 (5) 4.95 1.20

#508-509 airmail. For surcharge see #C304.

Anniversaries and Events — A123a

50fr, Durer, detail from Madonna of the Rosary. 200fr, Henri Dunant, Red Cross founder, Battle of Solferino. 300fr, Early telephone, Goonhilly Downs Satellite Station, Britain. 350fr, J.F. Kennedy, Neil Armstrong's 1st step on Moon, 1969. 400fr, Europe-Africa Satellite infrared photograph. 500fr, Prince Charles & Lady Diana. 600fr, Wedding photograph of Prince Charles & Lady Diana.

1984

510 A123a 50fr multi .45 .20
511 A123a 200fr multi 2.00 .30
512 A123a 300fr multi 2.75 .45
513 A123a 350fr multi 3.25 .50
514 A123a 400fr multi 3.50 .55
515 A123a 500fr multi 4.50 .80
Nos. 510-515 (6) 16.45 2.80

Souvenir Sheet

516 A121 600fr multicolored 5.25

A souvenir sheet of 6 containing #510-515 exists. Nos. 514-516 are airmail.
For surcharge see No. 578.

Development of Communications — A123b

Ships and locomotives.

1984, Aug. 1 Litho. *Perf. 12½*

517 A123b 90fr Indiaman, East India Co. 1.00 .20
518 A123b 100fr Nord 701, 1885 1.00 .20
519 A123b 125fr Vera Cruz 1.60 .20
520 A123b 150fr Columbia, 1888 1.60 .20
521 A123b 200fr Carlisle Castle 2.25 .25
522 A123b 250fr Rete Mediterranea, 1900 2.75 .30
523 A123b 300fr Britannia 3.00 .35
524 A123b 350fr Mav 114 3.50 .50
Nos. 517-524 (8) 16.70 2.20

Christmas — A124

1984, Dec. 28 Litho. *Perf. 13*

525 A124 50fr lt bl & org brn .45 .20
526 A124 60fr ver & org brn .55 .20
527 A124 80fr emer & org brn .70 .20
528 A124 85fr rose lil & org brn .70 .20
529 A124 100fr org yel & org brn .90 .20
530 A124 135fr dp bl vio & org brn 1.10 .20
Nos. 525-530 (6) 4.40 1.20

European Music Year — A125

Mushrooms A126

Instruments.

1985, Apr. 30 Litho. *Perf. 12x12½*

531 A125 20fr Guitar .20 .20
532 A125 25fr Harp .25 .20
533 A125 30fr Xylophone .35 .20
534 A125 50fr Shoulder drum .45 .20
535 A125 70fr like #534 .65 .20
536 A125 80fr like #532 .70 .20
537 A125 100fr like #531 .90 .20
538 A125 250fr like #533 2.25 .30
Nos. 531-538 (8) 5.75 1.70

1985, May 15 Litho. *Perf. 12½*

539 A126 25fr Chlorophyllum molybdites .55 .20
540 A126 30fr Tulostoma volvulatum .65 .20
541 A126 50fr Lentinus tuberregium .90 .20
542 A126 70fr like #541 1.25 .20
543 A126 80fr Podaxis pistillaris 1.50 .20
544 A126 100fr like #539 2.25 .35
Nos. 539-544 (6) 7.10 1.35

Anniversaries and Events — A127

Designs: 25fr, Abraham Lincoln. 45fr, Henri Dunant, Geneva birthplace and red cross. 50fr, Gottlieb Daimler, 1887 Motor Carriage. 60fr, Louis Bleriot, Bleriot XI monoplane, 1909. 80fr, Paul Harris, Chicago site of Rotary Intl. founding. 350fr, Auguste Piccard, bathyscaphe Trieste, 1953. 600fr, Anatoly Karpov, 1981 world chess champion. 1500fr, Paul Harris.

1985, May 25 Litho. *Perf. 13½*

545 A127 25fr multi .25 .20
546 A127 45fr multi .55 .20
547 A127 50fr multi .70 .20
548 A127 60fr multi .90 .20
549 A127 80fr multi 1.00 .20
550 A127 350fr multi 3.75 .45
Nos. 545-550 (6) 7.15 1.45

Souvenir Sheets

551 A127 600fr multi 6.25 .85

Litho. & Embossed

551A A127 1500fr Paul Harris on Medal 13.50

No. 551A contains one 130x90mm stamp.
Nos. 548-551A are airmail.
Souvenir sheets of 1 exist for #545-551.

Intl. Youth Year — A128

1985, May 30 Litho. *Perf. 13*

552 A128 70fr Development levels, vert. .65 .20
553 A128 200fr Globe 1.60 .25

A129

3rd Anniv. of the Republic A130

Perf. 13, 12½x13

1985, June 7 Litho.

554 A129 70fr Hand, claw .65 .20
555 A129 70fr Hands, map .65 .20
556 A130 70fr Pres. Hissein Habre .65 .20
557 A129 110fr like #554 1.10 .20
558 A129 110fr like #555 1.10 .20
559 A130 110fr like #556 1.10 .20
Nos. 554-559 (6) 5.25 1.20

Audubon Birth Bicent. — A131

Mammals A132

1985, July 20 Engr. *Perf. 13*

560 A131 70fr Stork .90 .20
561 A131 110fr Ostrich 1.25 .20
562 A131 150fr Marabou 1.75 .20
563 A131 200fr Snake eagle 2.25 .25
Nos. 560-563 (4) 6.15 .85

Souvenir Sheet

564 A131 500fr like 200fr 6.25 .70

1985, Aug. 25

565 A132 50fr Waterbuck .70 .20
566 A132 70fr Kudus, horiz. .90 .20
567 A132 250fr Shaggy mouflon 2.75 .40
Nos. 565-567 (3) 4.35 .80

Souvenir Sheet

568 A132 500fr White rhinoceros 5.25 .85

UN, 40th Anniv. — A133

1985, Nov. 24

569 A133 200fr brt bl, red & brn 2.00 .25

Chad Admission to UN, 25th Anniv. — A134

1985, Nov. 24

570 A134 300fr red, brt bl & yel 3.00 .50

President's Visit to the Nation's Interior A135

1986, June 7 Litho. *Perf. 12½x13*

571 A135 100fr multi 1.00 .20
572 A135 170fr multi 2.00 .35
573 A135 200fr multi 2.25 .45
Nos. 571-573 (3) 5.25 1.00

Lions Club Intl. — A135a

1987 Litho. *Perf. 14*

573A A135a 30fr Like #573C
573C A135a 100fr Sick child
573E A135a 170fr Three children, horiz.
573F A135a 200fr Eye exam, horiz.

There are two additional stamps in this. The editors would like to examine them.

World Wildlife Fund — A136

Various mouflons, *Ammotragus lervia.*

1988, Nov. 10 Litho. *Perf. 13*

574 A136 25fr shown 1.75 .30
575 A136 45fr Adult, young 2.10 .50
576 A136 70fr Two adults, diff. 2.75 .80
577 A136 100fr Adults, young 4.25 1.25
Nos. 574-577 (4) 10.85 2.85

Nos. 512 and 475 Surcharged

1989 Litho. *Perf. 13½*

578 A123a 170fr on 300fr #512
579 A118 240fr on 300fr #475

Liberation — A137

World Post Day — A137a

1989 *Perf. 11½x12*

580 A137 20fr multi .20 .20
581 A137 25fr multi .25 .20
582 A137 40fr multi .45 .20
583 A137 100fr multi 1.00 .30
584 A137 170fr multi 1.60 .50
Nos. 580-584 (5) 3.50 1.40

1989, Oct. 9 Photo. *Perf. 12*

Granite Paper

584A A137a 100fr grn bl & multi
584B A137a 120fr red & multi
584C A137a 170fr purple & multi
584D A137a 250fr olive & multi
Nos. 584A-584D (4) 150.00

Visit of Pope John Paul II — A138

Cathedral in Chad and: 20fr, 100fr, Pope holding crosier. 80fr, 170fr, Pope, diff.

1989, Dec. 20 Litho. *Perf. 13*

585 A138 20fr multicolored .30 .20
586 A138 80fr multicolored 1.00 .40
587 A138 100fr multicolored 1.25 .50
588 A138 170fr multicolored 2.00 1.00
Nos. 585-588 (4) 4.55 2.10

Traditional Hair Styles — A139

1989, Oct. 9 Photo. *Perf. 12*

Granite Paper

589 A139 100fr apple grn & multi
590 A139 120fr purple & multi
591 A139 170fr pink & multi
592 A139 250fr org yel & multi
Nos. 589-592 (4) 150.00

Vaccinations A140

1991, Dec. 1 Photo. *Perf. 11½*

Granite Paper

593 A140 30fr brown & multi .25 .20
594 A140 100fr green & multi .90 .45
595 A140 170fr vio & multi 1.50 .75

596 A140 180fr blue & multi 1.60 .80
597 A140 200fr red & multi 1.75 .90
Nos. 593-597 (5) 6.00 3.10

A141

1991, Dec. 1 **Litho.**

598 A141 10fr green & multi .20 .20
599 A141 20fr lilac & multi .20 .20
600 A141 40fr yellow & multi .35 .20
601 A141 70fr blue & multi .60 .30
602 A141 130fr tan & multi 1.10 .60
603 A141 200fr pink & multi 1.75 .90
Nos. 598-603 (6) 4.20 2.40

Liberty and Democracy Day, Dec. 1, 1990.

Fight Against Insect Pests — A141a

1992, Sept. 1 **Photo.** ***Perf. 12***

603A A141a 25fr multicolored — —
603B A141a 45fr multicolored
603C A141a 100fr multicolored
603D A141a 150fr multicolored
603E A141a 170fr multicolored — —
Nos. 603A-603E (5) 150.00

A142

1992, Nov. 15 **Litho.** ***Perf. 11½***

604 A142 20fr bright yel & multi .20 .20
605 A142 45fr golden yel & multi .35 .20
606 A142 85fr pink & multi .70 .35
607 A142 170fr blue & multi 1.40 .70
608 A142 300fr gray & multi 2.75 1.25
Nos. 604-608 (5) 5.40 2.70

Doctors Without Borders, 20th anniv.

Campaign Against Illiteracy A143

1992, Nov. 30

609 A143 25fr yel grn & multi .20 .20
610 A143 40fr golden yel & multi .35 .20
611 A143 70fr pink & multi .55 .30
612 A143 100fr lilac & multi .70 .40
613 A143 180fr blue & multi 1.50 .60
614 A143 200fr gray & multi 1.60 .70
Nos. 609-614 (6) 4.90 2.40

Intl. Conference on Nutrition, Rome — A144

1992, Dec. 15

615 A144 10fr yellow & multi .20 .20
616 A144 60fr pink & multi .70 .25
617 A144 120fr yel grn & multi 1.25 .40
618 A144 500fr blue & multi 3.50 1.50
Nos. 615-618 (4) 5.65 2.35

Palace of the People A145

1993, Apr. 15 **Litho.** ***Perf. 11½***

619 A145 80fr multicolored
620 A145 100fr multicolored
621 A145 130fr multi — —
622 A145 400fr multicolored
Nos. 619-622 (4) 150.00

Natl. Conference A146

OAU, 30th Anniv. A147

1993, Dec. 1 **Litho.** ***Perf. 11¾***

Granite paper

623 A146 55fr multicolored .45 .35
624 A146 70fr multicolored .65 .45
625 A146 110fr multi 1.00 .80
626 A146 125fr multi 1.00 .90
Nos. 623-626 (4) 3.10 2.50

1993, Dec. 4 **Litho.** ***Perf. 11½x11¾***

627 A147 15fr multicolored .20 .20
628 A147 30fr multicolored .25 .20
629 A147 110frmulti 1.00 .80
630 A147 190frmulti 1.75 1.40
Nos. 627-630 (4) 3.20 2.60

Victor Schoelcher (1804-93), Abolitionist A148

Perf. 11¾x11½

1993, Dec. 26 **Litho.**

631 A148 55fr multicolored .35 .35
632 A148 105fr multicolored 1.00 .70
633 A148 125fr multi 1.25 1.00
634 A148 300fr multicolored 2.75 2.00

Tourism A149

Perf. 11¾x11½

1993, Dec. 27 **Litho.**

635 A149 15fr multi 35.00 18.00
636 A149 95fr multi 35.00 18.00
637 A149 100fr multicolored 35.00 18.00

An additional stamp was issued in this set. The editors would like to examine it.

Bank of Central African States A150

1994, June 22 **Litho.** ***Perf. 11½***

639 A150 20fr multicolored .20
640 A150 30fr pink & multi .20
641 A150 105fr blue & multi .65
642 A150 190fr lilac & multi 1.25

Huts for Storing Grain A151

75fr, Arabe, kim. 150fr, Sara, moundang. 300fr, Boulala, kotoko. 450fr, Ouaddai, kenga.

1995, Oct. 15 **Litho.** ***Perf. 14***

643 A151 75fr multicolored .40
644 A151 150fr multicolored .75
645 A151 300fr multicolored 1.40
646 A151 450fr multicolored 2.25

Souvenir Sheet

Chinese Post, Cent. — A151a

1996 **Litho.** ***Perf. 13¼***

646A A151a 270fr multi 1.50 1.00

1996 Olympic Games, Atlanta — A151b

No. 646B: e, Tennis. f, Equestrian. g, Soccer. h, Boxing.

No. 646C: i, Judo. j, Running. k, Cycling. l, Table tennis.

1500fr, Hurdler.

1996 **Litho.** ***Perf. 13¼***

646B A151b 250fr Sheet of 4, #e-h 3.75 3.75
646C A151b 300fr Sheet of 4, #i-l 4.50 4.50

Souvenir Sheet

646D A151b 1500fr multi 5.75 5.75

No. 646D contains one 39x57mm stamp.

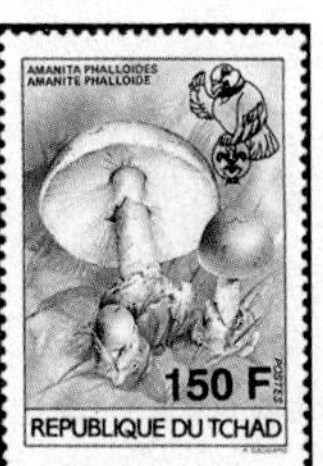

1995 Boy Scout Jamboree, Holland — A152

Mushrooms: 150fr, Amanita phalloides. 170fr, Phallus impudicus. 200fr, Lyloperdon perlatum. 350fr, Hydne commun. 450fr, Agaricus bisporus. 800fr, Cortinarius orellanus.

1500fr, Pleurotus ostreatus.

1996, Apr. 15 **Litho.** ***Perf. 13½***

647-652 A152 Set of 6 8.50 4.25
a. Souvenir sheet, #647-652 8.50 4.25

Souvenir Sheet

653 A152 1500fr multicolored 6.00 3.00

Nos. 647-652 exist in souvenir sheets of 1.

Butterflies, Mushrooms and Minerals — A152a

No. 653A: g, Papilio zalmoxis. h, Anacridium melanorhodon. i, Otidea leporina. j, Haliaetus vocifer.

No. 653B: k, Amanita phalloides, Papilio dardanus. l, Papilio antimachus, Cortinarius praestans. m, Phallus impudicus, Chrysidia croesus. n, Papilio dardanus, Lycoperon perlatum.

No. 653C: o, Charaxes brutus. p, Epiphora albida. q, Euchloron megaera. r, Salamis duprei.

No. 653D: s, Disthene. t, Olivine. u, Sphene. v, Hemimorphite.

No. 653E, Argema mittrei. No. 653F, Zoisite.

1996 **Litho.** ***Perf. 13¼***

653A A152a 350fr Sheet of 4, #g-j 5.25 5.25
653B A152a 400fr Sheet of 4, #k-n 6.00 6.00
653C A152a 650fr Sheet of 4, #o-r 9.75 9.75
653D A152a 800fr Sheet of 4, #s-v 12.00 12.00
Nos. 653B-653D (3) 27.75 27.75

Souvenir Sheets

653E A152a 2000fr multi 7.50 7.50
653F A152a 2000fr multi 7.50 7.50

A number has been reserved for an additional sheet in this set. Nos. 653E-653F each contain one 42x36mm stamp.

Greenpeace, 25th Anniv. — A153

Designs: a, 170fr, Green coral, school of small fish. b, 200fr, Yellow & orange coral. c, 300fr, Red orange coral. d, 350fr, White coral.

1500fr, Diver, coral, vert.

1996, July 16

654 A153 Block of 4, #a.-d. 4.00 4.00

Souvenir Sheet

655 A153 1500fr multicolored 6.00 6.00

Entertainers A154

#656, 170fr, Bob Marley. #657, 170fr, Marilyn Monroe. #658, 200fr, Elvis Presley. #659, 200fr, Monroe. #660, 300fr, Monroe. #661, 350fr, Stevie Wonder. #662, 350fr, Presley. #663, 400fr, John Lennon. #664, 500fr, Presley. #665, 600fr, Lennon. #666, 700fr, Madonna. #667, 800fr, Presley. #668, 1000fr, Monroe.

#669, Tina Turner. #670, Clint Eastwood. #670A, Presley.

1996, May 15

656-668	A154	Set of 13	22.50	11.50
665a		Sheet of 2, #663, 665	4.00	2.00
667a		Sheet of 4, #658, 662, 664, 667	7.25	3.50
668a		Sheet of 4, #657, 659-660, 668	6.50	3.25

Souvenir Sheets

669-670A	A154	1500fr each	6.00	3.00

Nos. 656-668 exist in souvenir sheets of 1. No. 670A contains one 51x90mm stamp.
See No. 674.

Pres. Bill Clinton — A155

#671: b, Elvis Presley in white jumpsuit.
#672: a, Pres. Richard Nixon. b, Presley in white shirt, black jacket.

1996, Dec. 17 Litho. *Perf. 13½*
Sheets of 2

671	A155	1500fr #a.-b.	13.50	6.75
672	A155	1500fr #a.-b.	13.50	6.75

Giant Panda A156

a, Holding branch, left claw out. b, Holding branch. c, Lying on back. d, Holding branch in mouth.

1996, Oct. 15

673	A156	100fr Sheet of 4, #a.-d.	1.75	.90

Entertainers Type of 1996

1996 Litho. *Perf. 13½*

674	A154	500fr Jerry Garcia	2.25	1.10

No. 674 exists in a souvenir sheet of 1.

1998 World Cup Soccer Championships, France — A157

1998 World Cup Soccer Championships, France — A157a

Unidentified players, stadium: No. 675, 150fr, The Beaujoire, Nantes. No. 676, 200fr, Lescure Park, Bordeaux. No. 676A, 300fr, Municipal Stadium, Toulouse. No. 676B, 600fr, Felix Bollaert, Lens. No. 677A: b, Player in white shirt. c, Player in red shirt.

1996, Dec. 17

675-676B	A157	Set of 4	5.50	2.75

Souvenir Sheet

677	A158m	1500fr George Weah	6.75	3.25
677A	A157a	3000fr Sheet of 2, #b-c	—	—

Dinosaurs, Dog & Cats, Butterflies & Insects — A158

Dinosaurs — #678: a, Heterodontosaurus. b, Ornitholestes. c, Dromaeosaurus. d, Pinacosaurus.
#679: a, Corythosaurus. b, Ankylosaurides. c, Ornithomimus. d, Styracosaurus.
Dogs & cats — #680: a, Artois. b, Bengal. c, Persian. d, Vendeen.
Butterflies & insects — #681a, Euphaedra zaddachi. b, Pseudacraea dolomena. c, Cicindela barbara. d, Goliath.

1996, Oct. 15

678	A158	150fr Sheet of 4, #a.-d.	2.75	1.40
679	A158	200fr Sheet of 4, #a.-d.	3.50	1.75
680	A158	250fr Sheet of 4, #a.-d.	4.50	2.25
681	A158	300fr Sheet of 4, #a.-d.	5.50	2.75

Ovptd. in Gold in Sheet Margin

1997 Litho. *Perf. 13½*

678e	Sheet of 4	2.25	1.10
679e	Sheet of 4	3.00	1.50
680e	Sheet of 4	4.25	2.10

Gold overprints on Nos. 678e-680e contain two-line inscription in Chinese and Hong Kong '97 exhibition emblem.

UNICEF, UN, 50th Anniv., Lions Intl. — A159

UNICEF, 50th anniv.: No. 682a, 150fr, Girl, boy turtles. b, 400fr, Feeding small child.
UN, 50th anniv.: No. 683a, 170fr, Huygens probe, starving child. b, 500fr, Man with plant, Marsnet probe.
Lions Intl.: No. 684a, 200fr, Man carrying sack of grain. b, 800fr, Men examining plants, native man stirring kettle over fire.

1996, Oct. 15 Litho. *Perf. 13½*

682	A159	Pair, #a.-b. + label	2.50	1.25
683	A159	Pair, #a.-b. + label	3.00	1.50
684	A159	Pair, #a.-b. + label	4.50	2.25

Nos. 682-684 exist as souvenir sheets with colored margins.

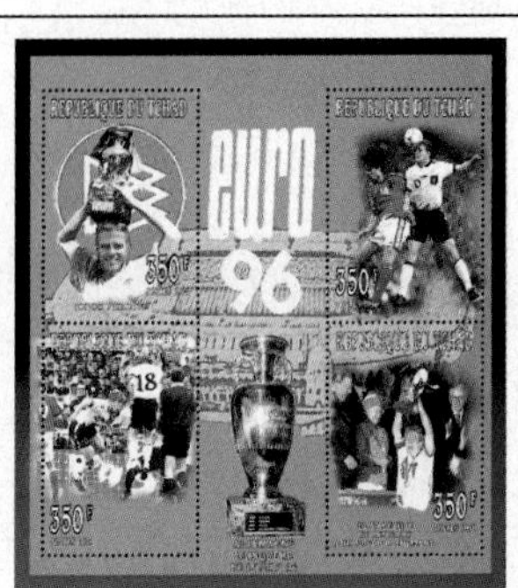

1996 European Soccer Championships — A160

Designs: a, Oliver Bierhoff holding trophy. b, Two players. c, Two players, referee. d, Queen Elizabeth II, player holding trophy.

1996, Dec. 17

685	A160	350fr Sheet of 4, #a.-d.	6.25	3.00

Michael Schumacher, 1995 World Driving Champion — A161

a, Ferrari Formula-1 race car. b, Schumacher close-up. c, Schumacher in Benetton uniform. d, Benetton Formula-1 race car.
#687, Schumacher with arms raised. #687A, Winner of 1996 Italian Grand Prix.

1997, June 16

686	A161	700fr Sheet of 4, #a.-d.	12.50	6.25

Souvenir Sheets

687	A161	2000fr multicolored	9.00	4.50
687A	A161	2000fr multicolored	9.00	4.50

No. 687 contains one 36x51mm stamp.

1998 Winter Olympic Games, Nagano, Japan A162

100fr, Women's figure skating. 170fr, Hockey. 350fr, Downhill skiing. 750fr, Speed skating.
1500fr, Slalom skiing.

1996, Dec. 17

688-691	A162	Set of 4	6.25	3.00

Souvenir Sheet

692	A162	1500fr multicolored	6.75	3.25

World Wildlife Fund — A163

Struthio camelus rothschildi: a, Female. b. Male. c, Chicks. d, Male, female up close.

1996, Dec. 17 Litho. *Perf. 13½*

693	A163	200fr Block of 4, #a.-d.	10.50	2.50

Jacqueline Kennedy Onassis (1929-94) — A164

Various portraits.

1996, Dec. 17

694	A164	200fr Sheet of 9, #a.-i.	8.00	4.00

Intl. Red Cross, Rotary Intl., Scouts — A165

Intl. Red Cross: No. 695: a, 100fr, Woman, airplane. b, 350fr, Man, train.
Rotary Intl.: No. 696: a, 300fr, Boy, water coming through pipes. b, 700fr, Native boy and man, volunteers.
Scouts: No. 697: a, 250fr, Boy scout holding book, hyena. b, 1000fr, Garry Kasparov, chess player, scout.

1996, Oct. 15 Litho. *Perf. 13½*

695	A165	Pair, #a.-b. + label	2.00	1.00
696	A165	Pair, #a.-b. + label	4.50	2.25
697	A165	Pair, #a.-b. + label	5.50	2.75

Nos. 695-697 exist in souvenir sheets with colored margins.

Japanese Sumo Wrestling A166

Various wrestlers in ring.

1996, Dec. 17 Litho. *Perf. 13½*

698	A166	400fr Sheet of 4, #a.-d.	7.25	3.50

China '96 — A168

Various paintings showing mountains and trees.

1996

704	A168	100fr Sheet of 9, #a.-i.	4.00	2.00

Marilyn Monroe — A168a

Various portraits.

1997 Litho. *Perf. 13¼*

704J A168a 500fr Sheet of 9, #k-s 15.00 15.00

History of Space Travel — A169

No. 705: a, Lunar N1 rocket, USSR, Saturn 1, US, Apollo 1 crew, Grissom, White, Chaffee. b, Launch of Soyuz, USSR, V.M. Komarov. c, US Lunar Orbiter 4. d, Neil Armstrong, US, Molnya 1, USSR. e, Venera 4, USSR, Mariner, US. f, Surveyor 3, US.

No. 706: a, Ariane 1, Landsat 4, US. b, Spacelab & space shuttle, NASA, ESA, Thomas Mattingly, US. c, L-Sat Telecom Satelite, ESA. d, J.L. Chretien, Soviet Salyut 7, US Space Shuttle. e, Venera 13, USSR. f, Intelsat 6, US.

No. 707: a, John Glenn, Atlas rocket, Mercury capsule. b, Mariner 2, US. c, Scott Carpenter, US. d, Telstar, Tiros 6, US. e, Vostok capsule, USSR, Bell X15 airplane, US. f, Mars 1, USSR.

No. 708: a, "Sounds of Earth" record, Voyager 1 & 2, US. b, Himawari 1, MU-3H, Japan, Atlas Centaur, US. c, Soviet Salyut 6, Proton rocket, Galileo (1564-1642). d, Meteosat, SMS Geos, Atlas EF, US. e, Boeing 747, space shuttle, US. f, ISEE, US.

No. 709: a, Saturn 5, US, OAO 3 Copernicus. b, Pioneer 10, US. c, Luna 20, USSR, John F. Kennedy. d, Landsat 1, US. e, Apollo 16, US astronauts Mattingly, Duke, Young. f, Lunar Rover, US Apollo 17 astronauts Schmitt, Evans, Cernan.

No. 710: a, RD 107 rocket, USSR, Vanguard rocket, US, Vanguard I, US. b, Aerobee, Goddard rockets, Robert H. Goddard. c, Laika, 1st dog in space, USSR. d, Theodor von Karman, V2A, Gird 09 rockets, USSR. e, Sputnik 1, USSR, Korolev airplane. f, Sanger, Bell X1 airplanes, US, Eugene Sanger.

No. 711, US Astronauts, Neil Armstrong, Michael Collins, Edwin E. Aldrin, Jr., USSR animals in space, Laika, Felix the cat.

Illustration reduced.

1997 Litho. *Perf. 13½*

Sheets of 6

705 A169	150fr #a.-f.	3.25	1.60
706 A169	250fr #a.-f.	5.50	2.75
707 A169	300fr #a.-f.	6.75	3.50
708 A169	450fr #a.-f.	10.00	5.00
709 A169	475fr #a.-f.	10.50	5.25
710 A169	800fr #a.-f.	17.50	9.00

Souvenir Sheet

711 A169 2000fr multicolored 7.50 3.75

No. 711 contains one 80x85mm stamp.

Elvis Presley — A169a

Various portraits.

1997 Litho. *Perf. 13¼*

711A A169a 300fr Sheet of 9, #b-j 9.00 9.00

Jacqueline Kennedy Onassis (1929-94) — A170

Various portraits.

1997, July 15 Litho. *Perf. 13½*

712 A170 150fr Sheet of 9, #a.-i. 5.25 2.50

Pres. John F. Kennedy — A170a

No. 712J: k, Standing, looking right. l, With family. m, Looking left. n, With statue of George Washington. o, Seated, with Great Seal of the United States. p, Facing forward, with stars and arrows. q, In chair. r, With statue of Lincoln. s, Behind podium, with flag and Capitol.

1997 Litho. *Perf. 13¼*

712J A170a 250fr Sheet of 9, #k-s 7.50 7.50

Diana, Princess of Wales (1961-97) — A171

Various portraits.

1997

Sheets of 9

713 A171 300fr #a.-i. 10.00 5.00
714 A171 450fr #a.-i. 15.00 7.50

Souvenir Sheet

715 A171 2000fr multicolored 7.50 3.75

No. 715 contains one 42x60mm stamp.

Deng Xiaoping and Bruce Lee — A171a

No. 715A — Deng and: c, Child. d, Chinese flag. e, Dancer. f, Boats in water. g, Farmers. h, Cityscape.

No. 715B — Lee and movie titles: i, Operation Dragon. j, La Fureur du Dragon. k, La Fureur de Vaincre. l, La Flute Silencieuse. m, Le Jeu de la Mort. n, Le Retour du Dragon.

1997 Litho. *Perf. 13¼*

715A A171a 75fr Sheet of 6, #c-h 1.50 1.50
715B A171a 125fr Sheet of 6, #i-n 2.50 2.50

Souvenir Sheet

Design: 1000fr, Deng and stars.

715O A171a 1000frmulti — —

No. 715O contains one 36x41mm stamp.

Mahatma Gandhi (1869-1948), Mother Teresa (1910-97) — A172

a, Gandhi seated, dendrobium speciosum. b, Mother Teresa with Indian people. c, Bulbophyllum umbellatum, Gandhi with 2 women.

1998, Feb. 5 Litho. *Perf. 13½*

716 A172 150fr Sheet of 3, #a.-c. 1.75 .85

Famous Men — A173

300fr, Nelson Mandela, Pres. of South Africa, diamond. 450fr, Albert Einstein (1879-1955), physicist, satellite. 800fr, Robert Barany (1876-1936), physician, Felix the space cat.

2000fr, Alfred Nobel (1833-96).

1998, Feb. 5

717-719 A173 Set of 3 6.00 3.00

Souvenir Sheet

720 A173 2000fr multicolored 7.50 3.75

Nos. 717-719 exist in souvenir sheets of 1. No. 720 contains one 41x60mm stamp.

See Nos. 729-734.

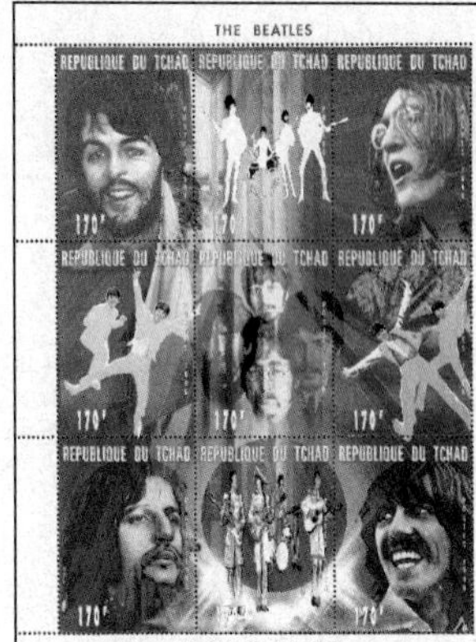

The Beatles — A174

No. 721: a-i, Various portraits of John Lennon.

The Beatles: No. 722: a, Paul McCartney. b, Silhouettes. c, John Lennon. d, George Harrison, Lennon. e, Four faces. f, McCartney, Ringo Starr. g, Starr. h, Four in Sgt. Pepper's costumes. i, Harrison.

Life of John Lennon: No. 723: a, Yoko Ono. b, With McCartney. c, In profile. d, Wearing suit. e, Wearing white shirt, tie. f, With mother. g, Wearing dark glasses. h, With guru. i, In white suit.

No. 724: Various portraits of Lennon, McCartney, Harrison, Starr.

No. 724J, Beatles in suits and ties. No. 724K, Beatles in Sgt. Pepper uniforms.

1996 Litho. *Perf. 13½*

721 A174 100fr Sheet of 9, #a-f 3.00 3.00
722 A174 170fr Sheet of 9, #a.-i. 5.00 2.50
723 A174 200fr Sheet of 9, #a.-i. 6.25 3.25
724 A174 300fr Sheet of 9, #a.-i. 9.50 4.75

Souvenir Sheets

724JA174 1500frmulti 5.00 5.00
724KA174 1500frmulti 5.00 5.00

Rotary Intl. — A175

Antelopes: a, 170fr, Damaliscus dorcas. b, 350fr, Oryx gazella. c, 500fr, Addax nasomaculatus. d, 600fr, Aepyceros melampus.

1996, Dec. 17

725 A175 Block of 4, #a.-d. 6.50 3.25

#725a-725d exist in souvenir sheets of 1.

No. 725 Overprinted in Gold

1996

726 A175 Block of 4, #a.-d. 6.50 3.25

#726a-726d exist in souvenir sheets of 1.

Marilyn Monroe (1926-1962) — A176

Various portraits.

1996

727 A176 250fr Sheet of 9, #a.-i. 8.00 4.00

Souvenir Sheet

728 A176 1500fr multicolored 5.25 2.50

No. 728 contains one 51x90mm stamp.

Famous People Type of 1997

Nobel Prize winners: 100fr, Mother Teresa (1910-97), humanitarian. 150fr, Martin Luther King, Jr. (1929-68), civil rights leader. 475fr, Otto Hahn (1879-1968), chemist, nuclear powered ship. 500fr, Ivan Pavlov (1849-1936), physiologist, Russian space dog, Laika. 600fr, Johannes van der Waals (1837-1923), physicist. 1000fr, Sir Edward Appleton (1892-1965), physicist, Concorde jet.

1998, Feb. 5

729-734 A173 Set of 6 13.00 6.50

Nos. 729-734 exist in souvenir sheets of 1.

Scouting A177

Wild animals: No. 735: a, Hyena. b, Mongoose.
No. 736: a, Wildcat. b, Addax nasomaculatus.
No. 737: a, Fennec. b, Hyena, diff.

1998, Feb. 6

735 A177 150fr Pair, #a.-b. 1.25 .60
736 A177 550fr Pair, #a.-b. 4.25 2.25
737 A177 600fr Pair, #a.-b. 4.75 2.50

Cats and Dogs — A178

No. 738: a, Maine coon. b, Singapore.
No. 739: a, Siberian husky. b, Malamute.
No. 740: a, Spitz. b, Eskimo.
No. 741: a, Siamese. b, Common cat.
No. 742, Abyssinian. No. 743, Samoyed.

1998, Feb. 6

738 A178 300fr Pair, #a.-b. 2.25 1.10
739 A178 450fr Pair, #a.-b. 3.50 1.75
740 A178 475fr Pair, #a.-b. 3.50 1.75
741 A178 500fr Pair, #a.-b. 3.75 1.90

Souvenir Sheets

742-743 A178 1500fr each 5.75 3.00

Nos. 742-743 each contain one 42x60mm stamp.

Airplanes, Ships, & Trains A179

Early aircraft — No. 743A: b, Latecoere 28, France. c, D'Equeuilly, France. d, Liore et Olivier Leo-213, France. e, Louis Bleriot monoplane. f, Graf Zeppelin LZ 127. g, Caproni CA 133, Italy.

Airplanes — No. 744: a, Sikorsky US-44A. b, Short S25/V Sandringham 4. c, Bristol 167 Brabazon 1. d, Savoia S13 Bis. e, Curtiss CR-3. f, Curtiss R3C-2.

Ships — No. 745: a, Normandy, 1935. b, Persia, 1856. c, Queen Elizabeth II, 1968. d, Christian Radich, 1937. e, Amerigo Vespucci, 1933. f, Tovarich, 1933.

Classic sports cars — No. 745G: h, 1963-65 Porsche 356 SC. i, 1961-66 AC Cobra. j, 1960-61 Maserati Tipo 63 Birdcage. k, 1962-63 Austin Healey 3000 MK11. l, 1959-62 Ferrari 250 GT Berlinetta SWB. m, 1958 Aston Martin DB4.

Trains — No. 746: a, BRB cog steam train. b, AE 4/7 10969. c, Crocodile of Saint-Gothard BE 6/8 111. d, RAE 2/4 1001. e, Steam train, Spain. f, RE 6/6 11612 express.

High speed trains — No. 746G: h, ETR 470, Italy. i, TGV Metro, France. j, Hikari, Japan. k, TGV 001 turbotrain, France. l, Eurostar 3203/3204 Metro train, France, Germany, Great Britain. m, 990 ICE train, Germany.

#747, Steam locomotive, C5/6 2978. #748, TGV, France.

1998, Feb. 4

Sheets of 6

743A A179 150fr #b.-g. 3.50 1.75
744 A179 200fr #a.-f. 4.50 2.25
745 A179 250fr #a.-f. 5.75 3.00
745G A179 300fr #h.-m. 6.75 3.50
746 A179 350fr #a.-f. 8.00 4.00
746G A179 400fr #h.-m. 9.00 4.50

Souvenir Sheets

747 A179 1500fr multicolored 5.75 3.00
748 A179 2000fr multicolored 7.50 3.75

Nos. 747-748 contain one 36x42mm stamp.
Swiss rail service, 150th anniv. (#746-747).
Issued: #745G, 2/6.
See No. 758.

Diana, Princess of Wales (1961-97) A180

Various portraits.
2000fr, Portrait wearing high lace collar.

1997 **Litho.** ***Perf. 13½***

749 A180 250fr Sheet of 9, #a.-i. 8.00 4.00

Souvenir Sheet

749J A180 2000fr multicolored 7.75 4.00

Literacy Campaign A181

Kellou Dahalob — A182

1997, June 16

750 A181 150fr olive & multi .50 .25
751 A181 300fr buff & multi 1.00 .50
752 A181 475fr salmon & multi 1.60 .80
Nos. 750-752 (3) 3.10 1.55

1998, Apr. 8

753 A182 50fr pink & multi .20 .20
754 A182 100fr blue & multi .35 .20
755 A182 150fr green & multi .60 .30
756 A182 300fr lilac & multi 1.00 .50
757 A182 400fr yellow & multi 1.40 .70
Nos. 753-757 (5) 3.55 1.90

Transportation Type of 1997

Modern aircraft — No. 758: a, SAT, France, Germany. b, BAC/Aerospatiale Concorde. c, X001, Japan. d, Bell X-2, US. e, Douglas X-3, US. f, Aerospatiale STS 2000, France.

1998, Feb. 4 **Litho.** ***Perf. 13½***

Sheet of 6

758 A179 475fr #a.-f. 11.00 5.75

A183

A184

#759-761, Woman Using Grindstone. #762-764, Woman kneeling.

1997, June 16

759 A183 50fr vio & multi, vert. .20 .20
760 A183 100fr grn & multi, vert. .35 .20
761 A183 150fr yel & multi, vert. .50 .25
762 A183 300fr vio & multi 1.00 .50
763 A183 450fr grn & multi 1.60 .80
764 A183 500fr yel & multi 1.75 .85
Nos. 759-764 (6) 5.40 2.80

1998, June 20 **Litho.** ***Perf. 13½***

765 A184 150fr blue & multi .55 .25
766 A184 300fr green & multi 1.10 .55
767 A184 475fr pink & multi 1.75 .85
768 A184 500fr blue green & multi 1.75 .85
Nos. 765-768 (4) 5.15 2.50

Protect the Ozone Layer.

Fauna — A185

Bats — No. 769: a, Holding mouse, tree branch. b, Drinking. c, One in flight, bottom of mouse. d, One flying left. e, One flying right. f, Mouse on rock, bat landing.

Horses — No. 769G: h, Gray Arabian. i, Brown Arabian. j, Przewalski's. k, Australian brumbies. l, Camargue. m, Zebras.

Sea mammals — No. 769N: o-t, Various portraits of Trichechus senegalensis.

Gorillas & chimpanzees — No. 770: a, Chimpanzee scratching head. b, Gorilla walking on all fours. c, Gorilla seated. d, Chimpanzee swinging from branch. e, Chimpanzee using stick. f, Two gorillas.

Raptors — No. 771: a, Terathopius ecaudatus. b, Buteo buteo. c, Sagittarius serpentarius. d, Polemaetus belligosus. e, Circaetus allicus. f, Aquila chrysaetos.

Reptiles — No. 771G: h, Crocodylus niloticus. i, Drendroaspis angusticeps. j, Bitis nasicornis. k, Chamaeleo johnstoni. l, Naja nigricolis. m, Meroles cuneirostris.

Mushrooms — No. 771N: o, Coprinus atramentarius. p, Romaria botrytis. q, Aleuria aurantia. r, Amanita muscaria. s, Macrolepiota rhacodes. t, Helvella crispa.

Mushrooms — No. 771U: v, Morchella vulgaris. w, Tuber aestiuum. x, Tuber melanosporum. y, Mitrophora hybrida. z, Morchella conica. aa, Choeromyces meandriformis.

Butterflies — No. 772: a, Charaxes jasius. b, Hamanumidia daedalus. c, Charaxes bohemani. d, Hallimoides rumia, denomination LL. e, Hallimoides rumia, denomination LR. f, Pseudacraea boisduuali.

1500fr, Coelogyne ovalis, palla ussheri. 2000fr, Baleniceps, Neurophyllum clauatum.

1998, June 20

Sheets of 6

769 A185 150fr #a.-f. 3.75 1.90
769G A185 250fr #h.-m. 5.00 2.50
769N A185 300fr #o.-t. 6.00 6.00
770 A185 300fr #a.-f. 7.25 3.75
771 A185 350fr #a.-f. 8.50 4.25
771G A185 450fr #h.-m. 9.00 9.00
771N A185 475fr #o.-t. 9.50 9.50
771U A185 500fr #v.-aa. 10.00 10.00
772 A185 600fr #a.-f. 14.50 7.25

Souvenir Sheets

773 A185 1500fr multicolored 6.00 3.00
773A A185 2000fr multicolored 6.75 3.50

Nos. 773-773A contain one 51x42mm stamp.

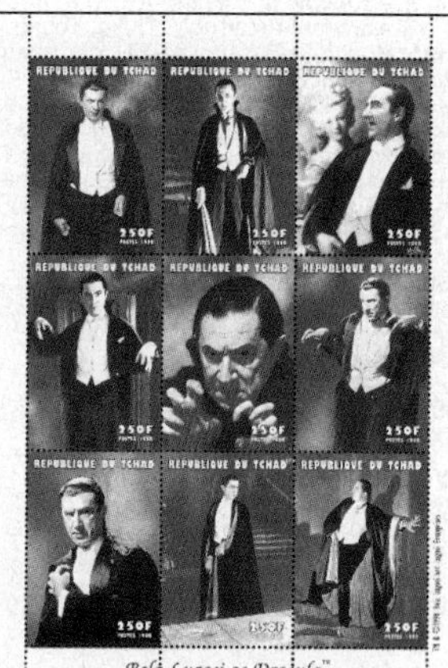

Bela Lugosi as Dracula — A185a

Lugosi in various poses.

1998, Dec. 11 **Litho.** ***Perf. 13½***

773B A185a 250fr Sheet of 9, #d.-l. 7.75 7.75

Souvenir Sheet

773C A185a 1500fr multi, horiz. 5.25 5.25

Diana, Princess of Wales — A186

Various portraits: a, 200fr. b, 250fr. c, 300fr. d, 400fr. e, 475fr. f, 500fr. g, 800fr. h, 900fr. i, 1000fr.

1999, Jan. 10 Litho. *Perf. 12½*
774 A186 Sheet of 9, #a.-i. 16.00 8.00

Birds — A187

Designs: 75fr, Ibis ibis. 150fr, Ephippiorhynchus senegalensis. 200fr, Phoenicopterus ruber. 300fr, Leptoptilus crumeniferus. 400fr, Scopus umbretta. 475fr, Platalea alba.
1000fr, Balaeniceps rex.

1999, Jan. 15 Litho. *Perf. 12¾*
775-780 A187 Set of 6 5.25 2.50

Souvenir Sheet

781 A187 1000fr multicolored 2.25 1.10

No. 781 contains one 32x40mm stamp.

Fire Trucks A188

50fr, 1840 model. 150fr, 1920 Fiat. 200fr, 1915 Mack. 300fr, 1930 Renault. 400fr, Pegaso M 1090. 500fr, 1960 Jet Fire Power.
700fr, 1720 King George III Fire Company.

1998, Dec. 30
782-787 A188 Set of 6 5.25 2.50

Souvenir Sheet

788 A188 700fr multicolored 2.25 1.10

No. 788 contains one 35x28mm stamp.

Minerals — A188a

No. 788A: a, Opal. b, Cyanite. c, Chalcopyrite. d, Apatite. e, Celestite. f, Scorodite.
No. 788B: a, Agate. b, Wulfenite. c, Barytine. d, Tanzanite. e, Amazonite. f, Malachite.

1998, Nov. 12 Litho. *Perf. 13½*

Sheets of 6

788A A188a 475fr #a.-f. 10.00 5.00
788B A188a 500f #a.-f. 10.50 5.25

Dinosaurs — A188b

No. 788C: a, Dilophosaurus. b, Argentinosaurus. c, Kritosaurus. d, Scutellosaurus. e, Ornithomimosaurus. f, Bactrosaurus.
No. 788D: a, Coelophysis. b, Kannemeyeria. c, Apatosaurus. d, Scipionyx. e, Lystrosaurus. f, Kentrosaurus.
No. 788E, Giganotosaurus, vert.

1998, Nov. 12 Litho. *Perf. 13¼*

Sheets of 6

788C A188b 400fr #a.-f. 5.75 3.00
788D A188b 450fr #a.-f. 6.50 3.25

Souvenir Sheet

788E A188b 2000fr multi 4.75 2.40

US Pres. Ronald Reagan — A189

No. 789: a, Family portrait as young boy. b, In front of family home. c, In football uniform, as radio announcer. d, Riding horse. e, Up close portrait. f, With Nancy, greeting Pope John Paul II. g, Making speech at podium. h, Being sworn in as president. i, At desk in Oval Office.
2000fr, At desk, White House.

1999, Feb. 2 Litho. *Perf. 13½*
789 A189 450fr Sheet of 9, #a.-i. 14.50 7.25

Souvenir Sheet

790 A189 2000fr multicolored 7.25 3.50

American Railroads — A190

Train, railroad pioneer: a, "Alco" Santa Fe, 1945, Cyrus Holliday. b, Rio Grande, 1961, J.F. Stevens. c, Amtrak, 1976, Thomas Dehone Judah. d, 250 Gobernador, 1884, Mark Hopkins. e, Meeting of Central Pacific and Union Pacific at Promontory Point, 1869, Leland Stanford, Thomas Durant. f, Great Northern W1, 1947, Jim Hill. g, Union Pacific Railroad, 1951, G.M. Dodge. h, Pennsylvania GG1, 1934, S.M. Vauclain. i, 151 Santa Fe U.P, 1917, S. Barstow Strong.

1999, Feb. 2
791 A190 200fr Sheet of 9, #a.-i. 6.50 3.25

Fossils and Cave Paintings — A191

Fossils: a, Harlania enigmatica. b, Spirophyton. c, Fossils, dunes of Djourab.
Cave paintings: d, Chain of people, oxen, Bardai. e, Man of Gonoa. f, Oxen, Kozen, Borkou.

1998, Dec. 11
792 A191 150fr Sheet of 6, #a.-f. 3.25 1.60

Frank Sinatra — A191a

Sinatra with: h, Blonde actress. i, Green jacket. j, Ava Gardner. k, Striped suit. l, Actor. m, Gun. n, Dark green hat. o, Oscar statuette. p, Military cap.

1998, Dec. 30 Litho. *Perf. 13½*
792G A191a 300fr Sheet of 9, #h.-p. 10.00 5.00

James Dean (1931-55), Actor — A192

Various portraits.

1999, Feb. 2
793 A192 200fr Sheet of 9, #a.-i. 6.50 3.25

Pope John Paul II — A193

Various portraits.

1999, Feb. 2
794 A193 300fr Sheet of 9, #a.-i. 9.50 4.75

Souvenir Sheet

795 A193 1500fr multicolored 5.50 2.75

No. 795 contains one 58x51mm stamp.

John Glenn's Return to Space — A194

Various portraits.

1999, Feb. 11 Litho. *Perf. 13½*

796 A194 500fr Sheet of 9, #a.-i. 16.00 8.00

Souvenir Sheet

797 A194 2000fr multicolored 7.25 3.50

No. 797 contains one 57x51mm stamp.

Kofi Annan, UN Secretary-General — A195

Various portraits.

1999, Feb. 11

798 A195 150fr Sheet of 9, #a.-i. 4.75 2.50

Chess — A196

No. 798J: k, Paul Morphy. l, Chess board, Morphy-Anderssen, 1858. m, Adolf Anderssen. n, Emanuel Lasker. o, Chess board, Lasker-Capablanca, 1914. p, José Raul Capablanca. q, David Bronstein. r, Chess board, Bronstein-Botvinnik, 1951. s, Mikhail Botvinnik.

a, Bobby Fischer. b, Chess board, Fischer-Tal, 1961. c, Mikhail Tal. d, Boris Spassky. e, Chess board, Spassky-Petrosian, 1969. f, Tigran Petrosian. g, Garry Kasparov. h, Chess board, Kasparov-Karpov, 1960. i, Anatoly Karpov.

2000fr, Margrave Othon IV of Brandenburg.

1999, Feb. 20

Sheets of 9

798J A196 375fr #k.-s. 12.00 6.00
799 A196 500fr #a.-i. 16.00 8.00

Souvenir Sheet

800 A196 2000fr multi 7.00 3.50

Dated 1998. No. 800 contains one 58x51mm stamp. Sheets of 3 stamps, containing Nos. 798Jk-798Jm, 798Jn-798Jp, 798Jq-798Js, 799a-799c, 799d-799f, or 799g-799i exist.

Souvenir Sheets

France, 1998 World Cup Champions — A197

No. 801: a, Bikente Lizarazu. b, Christian Karembeu. c, Frank Leboeuf. d, Emmanuel Petit.

No. 802: a, Fabien Barthez. b, Marcel Desailly. c, Didier Deschamps. d, Christophe Dugarry.

No. 803: Youri Djorkaeff. b, Aime Jacquet. c, Lilian Thuram. d, Zinedine Zidane.

2000fr, Deschamps holding World Cup.

1999, Feb. 20 Litho. *Perf. 13½*

Sheets of 4

801 A197 300fr #a.-d. 4.25 2.00
802 A197 400fr #a.-d. 5.75 2.75
803 A197 500fr #a.-d. 7.25 3.50

Perf. 13¼

804 A197 2000fr multicolored 7.25 3.50

No. 804 contains one 57x51mm stamp.

Hokusai Paintings A198

Designs: a, Voyagers Crossing the Oi River. b, Bird. c, On Totomi Mountain. d, Evening at Ueno. e, Higashimachi-matsuri-yatai-tenjou. f, Evening shower at Yoshiwara. g. Woman with Umbrella. h, Cascade. i, Courtesan.

1999, Sept. 10 Litho. *Perf. 13½*

805 A198 475fr Sheet of 9, #a.-i. 16.00 8.00

Japex '99.

Millennium — A199

Highlights of 1000-1899 — No. 806: a, Commercial routes in West Africa. b, Crusades. c, Notre Dame Cathedral. d, Ming dynasty tombs. e, Discovery of America. f, Albrecht Dürer. g, Sir Isaac Newton. h, American Independence. i, Napoleon.

1900-24 — #807: a, Return of Halley's Comet. b, Lord Baden-Powell founds Scouting movement. c, Sinking of the Titanic. d, 1st film in Technicolor. e, Marconi sends 1st message across Atlantic, birth of radio. f, Harry Houdini. g, Capablanca-Lasker chess matches. h, Pierre & Marie Curie win Nobel Prize. i, Theft of the Mona Lisa.

1925-49 — #808: a, Birth of Marilyn Monroe. b, Discovery of Pluto. c, Laurel and Hardy. d, Independence of India. e, Alexander Fleming discovers penicillin. f, Introduction of Volkswagen Beetle & Vespa motor scooter. g, Opening of film "Dracula." h, World War II. i, Discovery of Lascaux cave drawings.

1950-74 — #809: a, 1st flight of the Concorde, 7 original astronauts. b, Death of Buddy Holly. c, 1st Super Bowl. d, Death of Eva Peron. e, Art by Andy Warhol. f, The Beatles. g, Cultural Revolution in China. h, Assassination of Pres. John F. Kennedy. i, Cuban Revolution.

1975-99 — #810: a, Death of Princess Diana. b, Death of Enzo Ferrari. c, Akira. d, Argentina, 1986 World Cup Soccer champions. e, B. Lara breaks cricket records. f, France, 1998 World Cup Soccer champions. g, Explosion of the Space Shuttle Challenger. h, Pope John Paul II meets Lech Walesa. i, Deaths of Frank Sinatra, Freddie Mercury.

1999, Sept. 10

Sheets of 9

806 A199 150fr #a.-i. 4.75 2.40
807 A199 300fr #a.-i. 9.25 4.75
808 A199 450fr #a.-i. 14.00 7.00
809 A199 475fr #a.-i. 14.50 7.25
810 A199 500fr #a.-i. 15.00 7.50
Nos. 806-810 (5) 57.50 28.90

Souvenir Sheet

PhilexFrance '99 — A200

Illustration reduced.

1999, Sept. 10

811 A200 1500fr multi 5.50 2.75

I Love Lucy — A201

No. 812: a, Lucy leaning against tree, Ricky. b, Lucy, Ricky kissing. c, Lucy pointing gun. d, Ricky falling to ground. e, Lucy in apartment. f, Ricky holding animal. g, Ricky drinking from canteen. h, Lucy, Ricky talking. i, Lucy behind bush.

No. 813, Lucy in grape vat. No. 814, Lucy, Ricky in bed.

1999, Feb. 20 Litho. *Perf. 13¼*

812 A201 450fr Sheet of 9, #a.-i. 13.00 6.50

Souvenir Sheets

813 A201 1500fr multi 6.25 3.00
814 A201 2000fr multi 8.25 4.00

Dated 1998.

Betty Boop — A202

No. 815: a, With cat and dog. b, In flowered dress. c, Looking back over shoulder. d, With hammer, dresser. e, As majorette. f, In red dress with fur collar. g, Holding paper. h, Holding blue dress. i, Holding telephone.

No. 816, With feathered hat. No. 817, In leopard-spotted blouse.

1999, Feb. 20 Litho. *Perf. 13¼*

815 A202 450fr Sheet of 9, #a.-i. 13.00 6.50

Souvenir Sheets

816 A202 1500fr multi 6.25 3.00
817 A202 2000fr multi 8.25 4.00

Dated 1998.

Antique Automobiles — A203

150fr, 1900 F.N. 300fr, 1906 Bianchi. 400fr, 1906 Renault. 500fr, 1919 Pierce-Arrow. 700fr, 1919 Citroen 5CV. 900fr, 1928 Ford. 1000fr, 1898 Renault.

1999 Litho. *Perf. 13x12¾*

818-823 A203 Set of 6 5.50 2.75

Souvenir Sheet

Perf. 13x13¼

824 A203 1000fr multi 2.40 1.25

No. 824 contains one 40x31mm stamp.

Locomotives — A204

Designs: 150fr, 0-4-4-0. 300fr, Red 0-4-0. 400fr, Green 0-6-0. 500fr, Brown 0-4-0. 700fr, Blue 0-4-0. 900fr, Blue 0-6-0.

1000fr, Electric locomotive.

1999 *Perf. 12¾*

825-830 A204 Set of 6 5.50 2.75

Souvenir Sheet

Perf. 13x13¼

831 A204 1000fr multi 2.40 1.25

No. 831 contains one 36x28mm stamp.

Wonders of Forgotten Cultures — A205

Designs: 50fr, Easter Island. 150fr, Stonehenge. 300fr, Jericho. 400fr, Machu Picchu. 500fr, Valley of Statues. 700fr, Chichén Itzá. 900fr, Persepolis.

1999 ***Perf. 12¾***
832-838 A205 Set of 7 9.00 4.50

Chad postal officials have declared the following items to be "not authorized:"

Set of six stamps of various denominations: New Year 2000 (Year of the Dragon)

Sheet of nine stamps of various denominations: Orchids

Sheet of nine 150fr stamps: Spanish Impressionist paintings

Sheet of nine 300fr stamps: Millennium (Composers), Van Gogh paintings

Sheet of nine 450fr stamps: Millennium (Marilyn Monroe), French Impressionist paintings

Sheet of nine 475fr stamps: Impressionist paintings

Sheet of nine 500fr stamps: Renoir nudes, Elvis Presley, Olympics

Souvenir sheets of one: Millennium (three 300fr, two 450fr, one 475fr, three 500fr, one 1500fr), New Year 2000 (1000fr), Palace of Versailles (1500fr, 2000fr), Hiroshige paintings (1500fr, 2000fr).

Minerals A206

Designs: 150fr, Wulfenite. 200fr, Argentite. 400fr, Siderite. 500fr, Dolomite and quartz. 700fr, Azurite. 900fr, Spinel and calcite. 1000fr, Cassiterite.

2000, Jan. 15 **Litho.** ***Perf. 12¾***
839-844 A206 Set of 6 8.75 8.75

Souvenir Sheet

845 A206 1000fr multi 3.00 3.00

Dated 1999.

Elvis Presley — A207

No. 846: a, Playing guitar, wearing red jacket. b, Holding microphone and guitar, wearing red jacket. c, Holding guitar, wearing gold jacket. d, Playing guitar wearing black leather jacket. e, Playing guitar, wearing black jacket. f, Playing guitar, wearing blue jacket. g, Holding microphone, wearing blue shirt. h, Singing, wearing brown jacket. i, Holding microphone, wearing striped yellow jacket.

2000, Mar. 10 ***Perf. 13¼***
846 A207 300fr Sheet of 9, #a-i 8.00 8.00

Dated 1999.

Carl Benz and Mercedes-Benz Automobiles — A208

No. 847: a, 1934 W-25. b, 1934 500 K. c, 1964 230 SL. d, 1935 150. e, 1954 300 SL. f, 1971 280 SE.
2000fr, 1934 500 K, diff.

2000, Mar. 10
847 A208 250fr Sheet of 6, #a-f 4.50 4.50

Souvenir Sheet

848 A208 2000fr multi 6.00 6.00

No. 847 contains six 30x30mm stamps. Dated 1999.

Trains — A209

No. 849: a, FES 3228, European Union flag. b, TGV Duplex, French flag. c, 500 Series Unit W1, Japanese flag. d, AVE Class 100, Spanish flag. e, ICE3, German flag. f, ETR 500, Italian flag.
2000fr, TGC 001 V56, TGV Duplex, Etienne Chambron.

2000, Mar. 10
849 A209 600fr Sheet of 6, #a-f 10.50 10.50

Souvenir Sheet

850 A209 2000fr multi 6.00 6.00

No. 849 contains six 30x30mm stamps. Dated 1999.

French Rulers — A210

No. 851, 150fr: a, Charlemagne. b, King Charles VIII. c, King Francis I. d, King Henry II. e, Catherine de Medici. f, King Henry III.

No. 852, 200fr: a, King Louis XII. b, King Louis XIII. c, King Louis XIV. d, King Louis XV. e, King Louis XVI. f, King Louis XVIII.

No. 853, 300fr — Napoleon Bonaparte: a, Standing, wearing red cape. b, On horseback, wearing red cape. c, On horseback, with soldier at right. d, On horseback, with crowd at right. e, Standing with opter people. f, On white horse, leading battle.

2000, Mar. 10

Sheets of 6, #a-f

851-853 A210 Set of 3 11.50 11.50

Dated 1999.

Pope John Paul II — A211

No. 854 — Pope John Paul II and: a, Dalai Lama. b, Fidel Castro. c, King Hassan II of Morocco. d, Grand Rabbi Elio Toaff. e, Patriarch Bartholomew I. f, Mother Teresa.

2000, Mar. 10
854 A211 475fr Sheet of 6, #a-f 8.50 8.50

Dated 1999.

Space — A212

No. 855: a, Sputnik, dog Laika. b, Yuri Gagarin, Vostok 1. c, Konstantin Feoktistov, Vladimir Komarov, Boris Yegorov, Voskhod 1. d, Luna 1, chimpanzee Ham. e, Neil Armstrong, Michael Collis, Edwin Aldrin, Apollo 11. f, Aldrin, splashdown of capsule.

2000, Mar. 10
855 A212 500fr Sheet of 6, #a-f 9.00 9.00

Dated 1999.

Betty Boop Type of 1999

No. 856: a, Wearing red and violet striped leotard, kicking leg up. b, As cheerleader. c, At football field, holding pennant. d, At ice cream shop. e, Wearing yellow and green striped leotard. f, Wearing baseball cap and orange shorts. g, Wearing baseball cap and checked shirt. h, Seated, drinking beverage. i, Wearing cut-off shorts.

No. 857, 1500fr, Riding bicycle. No. 858, 2000fr, Wearing glasses, elbow and knee pads.

2000, Mar. 30
856 A202 250fr Sheet of 9, #a-i 6.75 6.75

Souvenir Sheets

857-858 A202 Set of 2 10.50 10.50

The Three Stooges — A213

No. 859, 250fr, horiz.: a, Larry, in surgeon's gown, and Curly. b, Curly, Moe, Larry around barrel. c, Moe, Larry and Curly on horse. d, Larry attacking man. e, Moe getting hair pulled. f, Moe with mallet. g, Curly, Moe and Larry in western outfits, outdoors. h, Larry, Curly and Moe in white doctor's jackets. i, Man looking at Moe.

No. 860, 300fr, horiz.: a, Larry grabbing Moe's chin. b, Moe and Larry holding scrolls. c, Moe, yellow background. d, Larry, blue background. e, Moe, Shemp and Larry. f, Shemp, blue background. g, Shemp, yellow background. h, Shemp pointing bellows at Larry. i, Moe and Larry in white.

No. 861, 1500fr, Moe in surgeon's gown. No. 862, 1500fr, Moe wearing hat. No. 863, 2000fr, Curly, Moe and Larry in western outfits, outdoors. No. 864, 2000fr, Larry with violin.

2000

Sheets of 9, #a-i

859-860 A213 Set of 2 14.50 14.50

Souvenir Sheets

861-864 A213 Set of 4 21.00 21.00

Issued: Nos. 859, 861, 863, 3/30; Nos. 860, 862, 864, 5/29.

I Love Lucy Type of 1999

No. 865: a, Lucy dancing, man in background. b, Lucy dancing, with knees bent and arms extended. c, Lucy in doorway. d, Lucy dancing behind sofa. e, Lucy kicking out leg. f, Lucy being caught by two men. g, Lucy with one arm extended. h, Lugy being sprayed with seltzer water. i, Lucy with leg on dance rail.

No. 866, 1500fr, Lucy looking at clown, horiz. No. 867, 2000fr, Lucy with clown costume and arms extended.

2000, May 29
865 A201 225fr Sheet of 9, #a-i 6.00 6.00

Souvenir Sheets

866-867 A201 Set of 2 10.50 10.50

N'Djamena, Cent. A213a

Background colors: 150fr, Blue. 300fr, Red. 475fr, Green.

2000, May 29 **Litho.** ***Perf. 13¼***
867A-867C A213a Set of 3 — —

Chadian Political History — A214

No. 868, 150fr: a, Louis Léon César Faidherbe. b, François Joseph Lamy. c, Henri Eugène Gouraud. d, Gustav Nachtigal. e, Head of Rabah on spike. f, Fernand Foureau.

No. 869, 300fr: a, Pierre Savorgnan de Brazza. b, Philippe Marie de Hautecloque Leclerc. c, Emile Gentil. d, Gabriel Lisette. e, Charles de Gaulle. f, Felix Eboué.

2000, May 29 ***Perf. 13½***

Sheets of 6, #a-f

868-869 A214 Set of 2 8.00 8.00

Wildlife, Map of Chad, Scouting Emblem — A215

No. 870, 150fr — Giraffa camelopardalis: a, Pair, one with head lowered. b, Pair, both with heads extended. c, Pair near forest. d, Trio.

No. 871, 200fr: a, Pair of Gazella granti in field. b, Gazella cuiveri. c, Gazella dorcas. d, Pair of Gazella granti at waterhole.

No. 872, 250fr — Addax nasomaculatus: a, View of head. b, Lying in grass. c, Standing. d, Grazing.

No. 873, 300fr — Ammotragus lervia: a, Pair. b, View of head. c, Standing on mountain ledge. d, Standing, with purple mountain in background

No. 874, 375fr — Diceros bicornis: a, View of head. b, Facing right, line of dark green foliage in background. c, Facing left. d, Facing right, with trees in background.

No. 875, 400fr — Panthera pardus: a, On tree branch. b, Lying in grass. c, Standing. d, View of head.

No. 876, 450fr: a, Head of Theropithecus gelada. b, Cercopithecus aethiops. c, Papio anubis. d, Adult and juvenile Thereopithecus gelada.

No. 877, 450fr — Hippopotamus amphibius: a, Pair laying in mud. b, With open mouth. c, Standing. d, Herd.

No. 878, 475fr — Oryx dammah: a, Facing right, green foliage in background. b, View of head. c, Pair. d, Grazing, mountain in background.

No. 879, 500fr — Panthera leo: a, Male on female. b, Females at waterhole. c, Female and cub. d, Female and male.

No. 880, 600fr — Loxodonta africana: a, With tree at right. b, Facing right. c, View of head. With tree and mountain in background.

No. 881, 750fr — Syncerus caffer: a, Juvenile, adult grazing. b, Adult in field. c, Pair lying on ground. d, With grass in mouth.

No. 882, 1000fr, Pair of Diceros bicornis. No. 883, 1000fr, Pair of Hippopotamus amphibius fighting. No. 884, 1500fr, Panthera leo with kill.

Illustration reduced.

2000, Aug. 1 ***Perf. 13¼***

Horiz. Strips of 4, #a-d

870-881 A215 Set of 12 55.00 55.00

Souvenir Sheets

882-884 A215 Set of 3 9.75 9.75

Nos. 882-884 each contain one 36x51mm stamp.

Miniature Sheet

Baseball Player — A216

2000, Oct. 11 **Litho. & Embossed**

885 A216 3000fr gold & multi 8.00 8.00

Exists with silver background.

High-five of Teenagers — A217

No. 886: a, Moon Hee-jun and Lee Jae-won. b, Jang Woo-hyuk and ear of Tony An. c, Tony an and Kang Ta. d, Jang Woo-hyuk. e, Entire group. f, Kang Ta. g, Moon Hee-jun. h, Lee Jae-won. i, Tony An.

2000 **Litho.**

886 A217 150fr Sheet of 9, #a-i 4.00 4.00

Sports and Chess — A218

No. 887, 30fr — Dogs involved in sport activities: a, Sled dogs. b, Dog racing. c, Hunting dogs. d, Dogs and skier.

No. 888, 70fr — Various sports: a, Petanque. b, Rugby. c, Archery. d, Jai alai.

No. 889, 250fr — 2000 Summer Olympics, Sydney: a, Fencing. b, Judo. c, Tennis. d, Boxing.

No. 890, 300fr — 2000 Summer Olympics, Sydney: a, Cycling. b, Basketball. c, Beach volleyball. d, Baseball.

No. 891, 400fr — Soccer players: a, Zinedine Zidane. b, Lilian Thuram. c, Yuri Djorkaeff. d, Nicolas Anelka

No. 892, 475fr — 2000 Summer Olympics, Sydney: a, Table tennis. b, Equestrian. c, Swimming. d, Kayaking.

No. 893, 500fr — Golf: a, Man with white pants swinging club. b, Golfer analyzing putt. c, Man with black pants swinging club. d, Woman golfer.

No. 894, 750fr — Formula I race drivers: a, Michael Schumacher. b, Mikka Hakkinen. c, Ralf Schumacher. d, David Coulthard.

No. 895, 1000fr — Chess: a, Knight with shield. b, Knight on donkey. c, Knight with attendant. d, Horses and wheeled castle.

2000fr, Venus Williams.

2001, Jan. 31 ***Perf. 13¼***

Sheets of 4, #a-d

887-895 A218 Set of 9 42.50 42.50

Souvenir Sheet

896 A218 2000fr multi 5.75 5.75

2000 Summer Olympics, Sydney (No. 896). No. 896 contains one 36x51mm stamp.

Trains — A219

No. 897, 200fr: a, Mallard, 1935. b, P8 Prussian, 1908. c, F2A, 1936. b, 240 P, 1940.

No. 898, 300fr: a, NSB No. 3641. b, New Zealand Railways Sereis EW. c, Series 277, Renfe. d, Series DF4 Vent d'Est IV Co-Co.

No. 899, 400fr: a, SNCF Series 9100 2-D-2, 1950. b, SNCF Series 72000 C-C, 1967. c, CC 21000, 1969. d, VL-80, 1963.

No. 900, 475fr: a, GNER Eurostar. b, Electric EMU ETR 500. c, DER OBB 1016 001. d, GNER train.

No. 901, 500fr: a, OL-49, 1951. b, Pacific Series 16E, 1935. c, Andaluces 030, 1877. d, Franco-Crosti Gr. 743, 1937.

No. 902, 500fr: a, JR West 8-car unit E4. b, TGV KTX. c, 300 Series unit J3. d, E3 Series unit R6.

No. 903, 600fr: a, 2D2 PO, 1926. b, Metropolitan BB Vickers, 1920. c, DB ET 491, 1935. d, Series D, 1925.

No. 904, 600fr: a, Electric EMU 490. b, Acela, 2001. c, CFF-FFS Electric EMU RABe 500. d, ICE-T Bavereihe 41.

No. 905, 750fr: a, Single Driver, 1870. b, Great Western Railway Castle, 1923. c, Schools Class, 1930. d, 230 Besa, 1905.

No. 906, 750fr: a, TGV Thalys. b, TGV Duplex. c, TGV La Poste. d, TGV Atlantique.

1500fr, SAR Series 26 2-D-2. 2000fr, TGV Sud-est.

2001, June 22 **Litho.**

Sheets of 4, #a-d

897-906 A219 Set of 10 55.00 55.00

Souvenir Sheets

907-908 A219 Set of 2 9.25 9.25

Nos. 907-908 each contain one 51x36mm stamp.

British Royalty — A220

No. 909, 300fr — Queen Mother: a, With King George VI. b, With young daughter. c, With Prince Charles. d, Waving. e, Wearing tiara and yellow dress. f, Wearing pink dress and hat. g, Wearing green dress and hat. h, Holding flowers. i, With dogs.

No. 910, 300fr — Prince William wearing: a, Black suit with lapel handkerchief. b, Suit with red and blue vest. c, Suit with gold vest. d, Sweater, looking right. e, Black suit and dark blue tie. f, Sweater, facing forward. g, Blue shirt with button. h, Dark blue shirt without button. i, Light blue suit.

2001, July 22 ***Perf. 13¼***

Sheets of 9, #a-i

909-910 A220 Set of 2 15.00 15.00

No. 910 contains nine 36x51mm stamps.

French Rulers — A221

No. 911, 300fr: a, King Francis I. b, King Louis XIII. c, Elizabeth of Austria, consort of King Charles IX. d, King John II the Good.

No. 912, 375fr: a, King Louis XIV. b, King Francis I, diff. c, King Louis XVI. d, King Louis XVIII.

No. 913, 475fr: a, King Louis XV as child. b, King Louis XV as adult. c, Queen Marie Antoinette. d, King Charles VII.

No. 914, 500fr — Napoleon Bonaparte wearing: a, White tunic. b, Black jacket. c, Emperor's robes. d, Red tunic.

2001, July 22

Sheets of 4, #a-d

911-914 A221 Set of 4 18.50 18.50

Stamps of Nos. 911-913 exist in souvenir sheets of 1.

Pope John Paul II — A222

No. 915, 800fr: a, Standing in room, looking left. b, Waving, c, Holding flowers. d, With blue sky background.

No. 916, 1000fr: a, Wearing red hat. b, Wearing miter, waving. c, Bending to kiss ground. d, Wearing miter, holding crucifix.

4000fr, Wearing zucchetto.

2001 **Litho.** ***Perf. 13¼***

Sheets of 4, #a-d

915-916 A222 Set of 2 20.00 20.00

Miniature Sheet

Litho. & Embossed

917 A222 4000fr gold & multi 11.50 11.50

Issued: Nos. 915-916, 7/22; No. 917, 7/23. No. 917 contains one 60x90mm stamp and exists with a silver background. Stamps of Nos. 915-916 exist in souvenir sheets of 1.

Famous Men — A223

Designs: 200fr, Charles Darwin (1809-82), naturalist. 250fr, Christopher Columbus (1451-1506), explorer. 300fr, Jacques-Yves Cousteau (1910-97), marine scientist. 350fr, Albert Schweitzer (1875-1965), missionary. 400fr, Juan Manuel Fangio (1911-95), race car driver. 450fr, Nicolaus Copernicus (1473-1543), astronomer. 500fr, Robert Stephenson (1803-59), engineer. 550fr, Etienne Chambron, high speed rail pioneer. 600fr, Garry Kasparov, chess player. 750fr, Lord Robert Baden-Powell (1857-1941), founder of scouting. 800fr, Neil Armstrong, astronaut. 1000fr, Sir Alexander Fleming (1881-1955), bacteriologist.

2001, Oct. 30 **Litho.**

918-929 A223 Set of 12 17.00 17.00

Nos. 918-929 exist in souvenir sheets of 1.

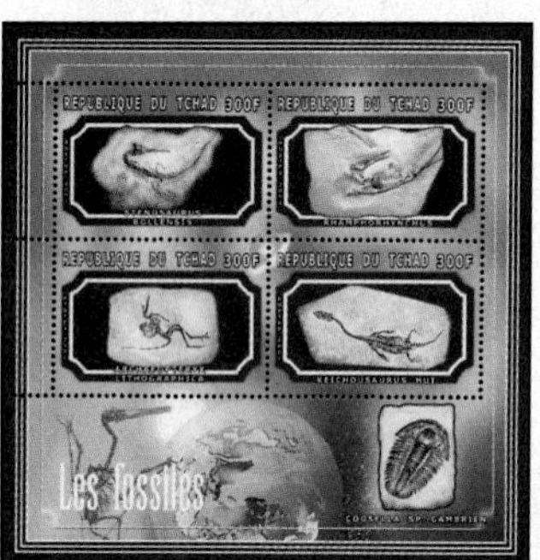

Fossils, Dinosaurs, Meteorites and Minerals — A224

No. 930, 300fr — Fossils: a, Stenosaurus bollensis. b, Rhamphorhynchus. c, Archaeopteryx lithographica. d, Keichousaurus hui.

No. 931, 375fr — Dinosaurs: a, Mesadactylus. b, Pteranodon. c, Tropeognathus. d, Quetzalcoatlus.

No. 932, 400fr — Meteorites found in: a, India. b, Nigeria. c, US. d, Australia.

No. 933, 500fr — Dinosaurs: a, Deinonychus. b, Seismosaurus. c, Pleurocoelus, Acrocanthosaur. d, Styracosaurus.

No. 934, 500fr — Minerals: a, Fluorite. b, Pyrite. c, Wulfenite. d, Merovingian scoria.

No. 935, 550fr — Meteorites found in: a, Antarctica. b, Libya. c, USSR. d, China.

No. 936, 600fr — Minerals: a, Magnetite. b, Kunzite. c, Apophyllite, Stilbite. d, Fluorite, diff.

No. 937, 750fr — Minerals: a, Quartz. b, Merovingian scoria, diff. c, Epidote. d, Amethyst, agate.

3000fr, Tyrannosaurus rex, vert.

2001, Dec. 27 Litho.

Sheets of 4, #a-d

930-937 A224 Set of 8 42.50 42.50

Miniature Sheet

Litho. & Embossed

938 A224 3000fr gold & multi 8.00 8.00

No. 938 contains one 60x90mm stamp and exists with silver background.

French Kings — A225

Designs: No. 939, 3000fr, Louis IX. No. 940, 3000fr, Francis I. No. 941, 3000fr, Henry IV. No. 942, 3000fr, Louis XIII. No. 943, 3000fr, Louis XV.

2002, Apr. 10 Litho. & Embossed

Gold & Multicolored

939-943 A225 Set of 5 40.00 40.00

Nos. 939-943 exist with silver background.

Artists and Their Paintings — A226

On Nos. 944-957, painting titles (in French) and artist's birth and death dates are in margins adjacent to each stamp. On Nos. 958-962 painting titles are not shown, but artist's name is in sheet margin

No. 944, 150fr: a, Berthe Morisot (1841-95). b, Cache-cache. c, Le Berceau. d, Au bal. e, Jeune femme se poudrant. f, Paule Gobillard peignant.

No. 945, 200fr: a, Marc Chagall (1887-1985). b, Nature morte. c, Le violoniste vert. d, La maison bleue. e, Mariage. f, Le soldat ivre.

No. 946, 250fr: a, Camille Pissarro (1830-1903). b, Les chataigniers a Osny. c, Le verger. d, Le repos des glaneuses. e, Jeune paysanne prenant son cafe. f, Le bergére.

No. 947, 300fr: a, Alfred Sisley (1839-99). b, Le pont de Villeneuve la Garenne. c, Allee de jardin a Louveciennes. d, Meule de foin bord du Loing. e, Moret sur Loing. f, Moulin a Moret.

No. 948, 325fr: a, Paul Delvaux (1897-1994). b, La voix publique. c, Nocturnes. d, Balgnade des Nymphes. e, Pygmalion. f, Jeunes femmes revant.

No. 949, 350fr: a, Edouard Manet (1832-83). b, Le Déjeuner sur l'herbe. c, Olympia. d, Le fifre. e, La serveuse de bocks. f, Le balcon.

No. 950, 375fr: a, Vincent van Gogh (1853-90). b, Champ de blé avec cypres. c, Rue a Auvers. d, La sieste. e, Chambre jaune a Arles. f, Rue de village.

No. 951, 400fr: a, Salvador Dali (1904-89). b, Cannibalisme en automne. c, Corpus Hypercubicus. d, Le sommeil. e, Le tentation de St. Antoine. f, Meditation sur harpe.

No. 952, 425fr: a, Paul Cézanne (1839-1906). b, Les baigneurs. c, Les grandes baigneuses (light blue background). d, Les grandes baigneuses, diff. (dark blue background). e, Les baigneueses. f, Les baigneurs au repos.

No. 953, 450fr: a, Pablo Picasso (1881-1973). b, Les demoiselles d'Avignon. c, Femme a l'eventail. d, La danse. e, La vie. f, La mere et son fils.

No. 954, 475fr: a, Amadeo Modigliani (1884-1920). b, Nu souche sur un divan. c, Nu debout. d, Cariatide debout. e, Nu allongé. f, Nu assis de dos.

No. 955, 500fr: a, Auguste Renoir (1841-1919). b, Diane chasseresse. c, Nu allongé. d, Baigneuses. e, Baigneuse assise. f, Nymphe au printemps.

No. 956, 550fr: a, Edgar Degas (1834-1917). b, Femme se coiffant. c, Aprés le bain (view of front of seated woman). d, Femme se peignant. e, Aprés le bain (view of back of woman). f, Aprés le bain (woman dressing).

No. 957, 600fr: a, Henri Matisse (1869-1954). b, Le nu bleu. c, Le genou levé. d, Nu assis sur un fauteuil. e, Odalisques. f, Nu allongé.

No. 958, 1500fr, Gustave Caillebotte. No. 959, 1500fr, Picasso, diff. No. 960, 1500fr, Auguste Renoir, diff. No. 961, 2000fr, Pablo Picasso, diff. No. 962, 2000fr, Van Gogh, diff.

2002, Apr. 10 ***Perf. 12¾x13¼***

Sheets of 6, #a-f

944-957 A226 Set of 14 87.50 87.50

Souvenir Sheets

Perf. 13¼x12¾

958-962 A226 Set of 5 23.00 23.00

Nos. 944a-955a and 957a exist in souvenir sheets of 1 that are perf. 13¼x12¾.

Miniature Sheet

Zeppelin NT — A227

No. 963: a, 475fr, Over Lake Constance. b, 500fr, Over Frankfurt. c, 600fr, Over Nürburgring, Germany. d, 750fr, At 2001 Salon du Bourget.

2002, Oct. 30 ***Perf. 13¼***

963 A227 Sheet of 4, #a-d 7.25 7.25

Nos. 963a-963d exist in souvenir sheets of 1.

Fauna and Mushrooms — A228

No. 964, 150fr: a, Hemichromis lifalili. b, Trichechus senegalensis. c, Synodontis nigriventris. d, Gnathonemus petersii. e, Ctenopoma ansorgii. f, Pseudocrenilabrus multicolor.

No. 965, 300fr, vert.: a, Nectarina venusta. b, Lamprotornis splendidus. c, Poicephalus meyeri. d, Halcyon leucocephala. e, Quelea quelea. f, Merops pusillus.

No. 966, 350fr, vert.: a, Terathopius ecaudatus. b, Gymnogyps californianus. c, Buteo jamaicensis. d, Lophaetus occipitalis. e, Aquila rapax. f, Melierax metabates.

No. 967, 375fr, vert.: a, Elanus caeruleus. b, Harpia harpyja. c, Gyps rueppellii. d, Milvus migrans. e, Torgos tracheliotus. f, Aquila chrysaetos.

No. 968, 550fr: a, Kallimoides rumia. b, Zophopetes dysmephila. c, Megalopalpus zymna. d, Coeliades forestan. e, Catopsilia florella. f, Anaphaesis aurota.

No. 969, 600fr: a, Amanita muscaria. b, Amanita rubescens. c, Cortinarius orellanus. d, Hygrophorus hypothejus. e, Leccinum piceinum. f, Strobilomyces strobilaceus.

2003, June 2 Litho.

Sheets of 6, #a-f

964-969 A228 Set of 6 50.0050.00

Stamps of Nos. 965-969 exist in a set of twelve souvenir sheets of two, with each souvenir sheet of two containing adjacent stamps found in the sheet of six.

Chad - Taiwan Cooperation — A229

Flags and: 50fr, Grain. 100fr, Surgeon's hands, Red Cross. 150fr, Bridge. 300fr, Handshake, maps.

2003, Dec. 1

970-973 A229 Set of 4 2.25 2.25

973a Booklet pane, 2 each #970-973 4.50 —

Complete booklet, #973a 4.50

973b Souvenir sheet, #970-973 2.25 2.25

SEMI-POSTAL STAMPS

Catalogue values for unused stamps in this section are for Never Hinged items.

Anti-Malaria Issue

Common Design Type

Perf. 12½x12

1962, Apr. 7 Engr. Unwmk.

B1 CD108 25fr + 5fr orange .90 .45

Freedom from Hunger Issue

Common Design Type

1963, Mar. 21 ***Perf. 13***

B2 CD112 25fr + 5fr dk grn, dk bl & brn .90 .45

Red Cross, Mother and Children — SP1

1974, Oct. 2 Photo. ***Perf. 12½x13***

B3 SP1 30fr + 10fr multi .90 .20

Red Cross of Chad, first anniversary.

AIR POST STAMPS

Catalogue values for unused stamps in this section are for Never Hinged items.

Olympic Games Issue

French Equatorial Africa No. C37 Surcharged in Red

Unwmk.

1960, Dec. 15 Engr. ***Perf. 13***

C1 AP8 250fr on 500fr grnsh blk, blk & slate 11.00 4.50

17th Olympic Games, Rome, Aug. 25-Sept. 11. Surcharge 46mm wide; illustration reduced.

Red Bishops — AP1 Discus Thrower — AP2

Birds in pairs: 100fr, Scarlet-chested sunbird. 200fr, African paradise flycatcher. 250fr, Malachite kingfisher. 500fr, Nubian carmine bee-eater.

1961-63 Unwmk. Engr. ***Perf. 13***

C2	AP1	50fr dk grn, mag & blk	1.00	.30
C3	AP1	100fr multi	3.50	1.00
C4	AP1	200fr multi	5.25	1.60
C5	AP1	250fr dk bl, grn & dp org ('63)	8.00	2.50
C6	AP1	500fr multi	18.00	5.50
		Nos. C2-C6 (5)	35.75	10.90

Air Afrique Issue

Common Design Type

1962, Feb. 17 Unwmk. ***Perf. 13***

C7 CD107 25fr lt bl, org brn & blk .70 .20

Abidjan Games Issue

1962, July 21 Photo. ***Perf. 12x12½***

C8 AP2 100fr brn, lt grn & blk 2.50 .75

African Postal Union Issue

Common Design Type

1963, Sept. 8 Unwmk. ***Perf. 12½***

C9 CD114 85fr dk bl, ocher & red 1.60 .40

Air Afrique Issue, 1963

Common Design Type

1963, Nov. 19 ***Perf. 13x12***

C10 CD115 50fr multi 1.60 .40

Europafrica Issue

Common Design Type

1963, Nov. 30 Photo. ***Perf. 12x13***

C11 CD116 50fr dp grn, yel & dk brn 1.25 .40

Mail Truck and Broussard Plane — AP4

Unwmk.

1963, Dec. 16 Engr. ***Perf. 13***

C12 AP4 100fr sl grn, ultra & red brn 2.75 .20

Chiefs of State Issue

Map and Presidents of Chad, Congo, Gabon and Central African Republic AP4a

1964, June 23 Photo. ***Perf. 12½***

C13 AP4a 100fr multi 1.60 .20

See note after Central African Republic No. C19.

Europafrica Issue, 1964

Globe and Emblems of Industry and Agriculture — AP5

1964, July 20 ***Perf. 13x12***
C14 AP5 50fr brn, pur & dp org 1.25 .30

See note after Cameroun No. 402.

Soccer — AP6

Designs: 50fr, Javelin throw, vert. 100fr, High jump, vert. 200fr, Runners.

1964, Aug. 12 **Engr.** ***Perf. 13***
C15 AP6 25fr yel grn, sl grn & org brn .70 .20
C16 AP6 50fr org brn, ind & brt bl 1.40 .30
C17 AP6 100fr blk, red & brt grn 2.50 .50
C18 AP6 200fr bis, blk & car 4.25 1.00
a. Min. sheet of 4, #C15-C18 12.50 4.75
Nos. C15-C18 (4) 8.85 2.00

18th Olympic Games, Tokyo, 10/10-25/64.

Communications Symbols — AP7

1964, Nov. 2 **Litho.** ***Perf. 12½x13***
C19 AP7 25fr lil, dk brn & lt red brn .70 .20

Pan-African and Malagasy Posts and Telecommunications Cong., Cairo, Oct. 24-Nov. 6.

President John F. Kennedy (1917-63) — AP8

1964, Nov. 3 **Photo.** ***Perf. 12½***
C20 AP8 100fr multi 2.10 .70
a. Souvenir sheet of 4 9.50 5.00

ICY Emblem — AP9

1965, July 5 **Photo.** ***Perf. 13***
C21 AP9 100fr multi 1.40 .25

International Cooperation Year, 1965.

Abraham Lincoln — AP10

1965, Sept. 7 **Unwmk.** ***Perf. 13***
C22 AP10 100fr multi 2.10 .35

Centenary of death of Abraham Lincoln.

Musical Instrument Type

Design: 100fr, Xylophone (marimba).

1965, Oct. 26 **Engr.** ***Perf. 13***
Size: 48x27mm
C23 A18 100fr ocher, brt bl & vio bl 2.25 .85

Sir Winston Spencer Churchill (1874-1965) AP11

1965, Nov. 23 **Engr.** ***Perf. 13***
C24 AP11 50fr dk grn & blk 1.25 .20

Dr. Albert Schweitzer and Outstretched Hands — AP12

1966, Feb. 15 **Photo.** ***Perf. 12½***
C25 AP12 100fr multi 2.25 .25

Dr. Albert Schweitzer (1875-1965), medical missionary, theologian and musician.

Air Afrique Issue, 1966

Common Design Type

1966, Aug. 31 **Photo.** ***Perf. 13***
C26 CD123 30fr yel grn, blk & gray .70 .20

White-throated Bee-eater — AP13

Birds: 50fr, Blue-eared glossy starling. 200fr, African pygmy kingfisher. 250fr, Red-throated bee-eater. 500fr, Little green bee-eater.

1966-67 **Photo.** ***Perf. 13x12½***
C27 AP13 50fr gold & multi 1.25 .20
C28 AP13 100fr bluish gray & multi 2.75 .30
C29 AP13 200fr grnsh gray & multi 5.25 .65
C30 AP13 250fr pale bl & multi 5.75 .80
C31 AP13 500fr pale sal & multi 11.00 1.60
Nos. C27-C31 (5) 26.00 3.55

Issued: 100fr, 200fr, 500fr, 8/18/66; others, 3/21/67.

For surcharges see Nos. C67-C69.

Congress Hall — AP14

1967, Jan. 5 **Photo.** ***Perf. 12½***
C32 AP14 25fr multi .70 .20

Opening of the new Congress Hall.

Breguet 19 Biplane — AP15

Planes: 30fr, Latécoère 631 hydroplane. 50fr, Douglas DC-3. 100fr, Piper Cherokee 6.

1967, Aug. 1 **Engr.** ***Perf. 13***
C33 AP15 25fr sky bl, sl grn & lt brn .70 .20
C34 AP15 30fr sky bl, indigo & grn .90 .20
C35 AP15 50fr sky bl, ol bis & sl grn 1.60 .25
C36 AP15 100fr dk bl, sl grn & dk red 3.00 .35
Nos. C33-C36 (4) 6.20 1.00

First anniversary of Air Chad.

African Postal Union Issue, 1967

Common Design Type

1967, Sept. 9 **Engr.** ***Perf. 13***
C37 CD124 100fr ol, brt pink & red brn 1.75 .40

Rock Painting Type of Regular Issue

1967, Dec. 19 **Engr.** ***Perf. 13***
Size: 48x27mm
C38 A32 100fr Masked dancers 4.00 .95
C39 A32 125fr Rabbit hunt 4.50 1.40

Downhill Skiing — AP16

1968, Feb. 5 **Engr.** ***Perf. 13***
C40 AP16 30fr shown .90 .20
C41 AP16 100fr Ski jump, vert. 2.75 .50

10th Winter Olympic Games, Grenoble, France, Feb. 6-18.

Konrad Adenauer (1876-1967), Chancellor of West Germany (1949-63) AP17

1968, Mar. 19 **Photo.** ***Perf. 12½***
C42 AP17 52fr grn, dk brn & lt lil 1.25 .30
a. Souvenir sheet of 4 5.00 2.00

The Snake Charmer, by Henri Rousseau — AP18

Design: 130fr, "War" by Henri Rousseau.

1968, May 14 **Photo.** ***Perf. 13½***
Size: 41x41mm
C43 AP18 100fr ultra & multi 2.75 .30
Size: 48x35mm
Perf. 12½
C44 AP18 130fr brn & multi 4.50 .40

Hurdlers — AP19

1968, Oct. 16 **Engr.** ***Perf. 13***
C45 AP19 32fr shown .90 .20
C46 AP19 80fr Relay race 2.25 .20

19th Olympic Games, Mexico City, 10/12-27.

PHILEXAFRIQUE Issue

The Actor Wolf (Bernard), by Jacques L. David AP20

1969, Jan. 15 **Photo.** ***Perf. 12½***
C47 AP20 100fr multi 3.50 .35

PHILEXAFRIQUE, Philatelic Exhib. in Abidjan, Feb. 14-23. Printed with alternating label.

2nd PHILEXAFRIQUE Issue

Common Design Type

50fr, Chad #J12 and Moundang Dancers.

1969, Feb. 14 **Engr.** ***Perf. 13***
C48 CD128 50fr red, brt bl, brn & grn 2.10 .30

Gustav Nachtigal and Tibesti Gorge, 1869 — AP21

#C50, Heinrich Barth & Lake Chad, 1851.

1969, Feb. 17
C49 AP21 100fr vio bl, dk brn & brn 2.10 .25
C50 AP21 100fr grn, pur & bl 2.10 .25

German explorers Gustav Nachtigal (1834-85) and Heinrich Barth (1821-65), and state visit of the Pres. of West Germany Heinrich Lubke.

Apollo 8, Earth and Moon — AP22

1969, Apr. 10 Photo. *Perf. 13*
C51 AP22 100fr multi 2.00 .45

US Apollo 8 mission, the 1st men in orbit around the moon, Dec. 21-27, 1968.

Mahatma Gandhi — AP23

#C53, John F. Kennedy. #C54, Dr. Martin Luther King, Jr. #C55, Robert F. Kennedy.

1969, May 20 Photo. *Perf. 12½*
C52 AP23 50fr blk & lt grn 1.10 .25
C53 AP23 50fr blk & tan 1.10 .25
C54 AP23 50fr blk & pink 1.10 .25
C55 AP23 50fr blk & lt vio bl 1.10 .25
a. Souvenir sheet of 4, #C52-C55 5.25 7.00
Nos. C52-C55 (4) 4.40 1.00

Issued to honor exponents of non-violence.

Presidents Tombalbaye and Mobutu, Map and Flags of Chad and Congo — AP24

Embossed on Gold Foil

1969 *Die-cut; Perf. 13½*
C56 AP24 1000fr gold, dk bl & red 24.00 24.00

1st anniv. of the establishment of the Union of Central African States, comprising Chad, Congo Democratic Republic and Central African Republic.

Napoleon Visiting Hospital, by Alexandre Veron-Bellecourt — AP25

Paintings: 85fr, Battle of Wagram, by Horace Vernet. 130fr, Battle of Austerlitz, by Francois Pascal Gerard.

1969, July 23 Photo. *Perf. 12x12½*
C57 AP25 30fr multi 1.00 .25
C58 AP25 85fr multi 2.25 .65
C59 AP25 130fr multi 4.00 1.10
Nos. C57-C59 (3) 7.25 2.00

Bicentenary of birth of Napoleon I.

Apollo 11 Issue

Astronaut on Moon — AP26

Embossed on Gold Foil

1969, Oct. 17 *Die-cut; Perf. 13½*
C60 AP26 1000fr gold 25.00 17.50

See note after Algeria No. 427.

Village Life, by Goto Narcisse — AP27

#62, Women at the Market, by Iba N'Diaye. #63, Woman with Flowers, by Iba N'Diaye, vert.

1970 Photo. *Perf. 12x12½, 12½x12*
C61 AP27 100fr multi 2.75 .20
C62 AP27 250fr grn & multi 4.50 .35
C63 AP27 250fr brn & multi 4.50 .35
Nos. C61-C63 (3) 11.75 .90

Issued: 100fr, Mar. 17; #C62-C63, Aug. 28.

Napoleon — AP27a

Designs: Nos. C63A, C63E, Napoleon II, Duke of Reichstadt, vert.

No. C63B: g, 10fr, Crossing the Grand St. Bernard, by David. h, 25fr, Emperor Napoleon, by Gerard. i, 32fr, Marriage of Napoleon and Marie Louise, by Rouget.

40fr, Napoleon after return from Elba, vert.

Perf. 12x12½, 12½x12

1970-71 Litho.
C63A AP27a 10fr multicolored 3.75
C63B AP27a Strip of 3, #g.-i. 12.50

Embossed

Perf. 13

C63C AP27a 10fr gold 18.00
f. Sheet of 1, Imperf. 35.00

Souvenir Sheets

Litho.

Perf. 13x13½

C63D AP27a 40fr multicolored 9.00

Embossed

Imperf

C63E AP27a 10fr gold, like #C63A 35.00

#C63A is printed se-tenant with label. #C63D contains one 43x67mm stamp. #C63Cf contains one 53x42mm stamp with same size design as #C63Bg. #C63E contains one 43x104mm stamp with same size design as #C63A.

No. C63E probably was not available in Chad.

Issued: #C63B, 6/12; #C63A, C63D-C63E, 4/1971; #C63C, 11/1/71.

EXPO Emblem and Osaka Print — AP28

EXPO Emblem and: 100fr, Tower of the Sun. 125fr, Osaka print, diff.

1970, June 30 Engr. *Perf. 13*
C64 AP28 50fr bl, red brn & sl grn .65 .20
C65 AP28 100fr red, yel grn & Prus bl 1.25 .20
C66 AP28 125fr blk, dk red & bis 1.75 .25
Nos. C64-C66 (3) 3.65 .65

Issued to publicize EXPO '70 International Exhibition, Osaka, Japan, Mar. 15-Sept. 13.

1968 Summer Olympics, 1970 World Cup Soccer Championships, Mexico - AP28a

1970, July 1 Litho. *Perf. 12½x12*
C66A AP28a 5fr Flags, soccer players 1.25

Souvenir Sheet

Perf. 13½x13

C66C AP28a 15fr Olympic torch, soccer player 5.75

No. C66A printed in sheets of 2 + 2 labels.
No. C66C contains one 66x43mm stamp.
For overprints see Nos. C88A-C88B.

Nos. C28-C30 Surcharged in Carmine with New Value and Bars and Overprinted:

a. "APOLLO XI / 1er débarquement sur la lune/20 juillet 1969"
b. "APOLLO XII / Exploration de la lune / 19 Novembre 1969"
c. "APOLLO XIII / Exploit spatial / 11-17 avril 1970"

1970, July 9 Photo. *Perf. 13x12½*
C67 AP13 (a) 50fr on 100fr 1.00 .25
C68 AP13 (b) 100fr on 200fr 1.75 .35
C69 AP13 (c) 125fr on 250fr 2.50 .50
Nos. C67-C69 (3) 5.25 1.10

Space missions of Apollo 11, 12 and 13.

DC-8 "Fort Lamy" over Airport — AP29

1970, Aug. 5 *Perf. 12½*
C70 AP29 30fr dk sl grn & multi 1.00 .20

Souvenir Sheet

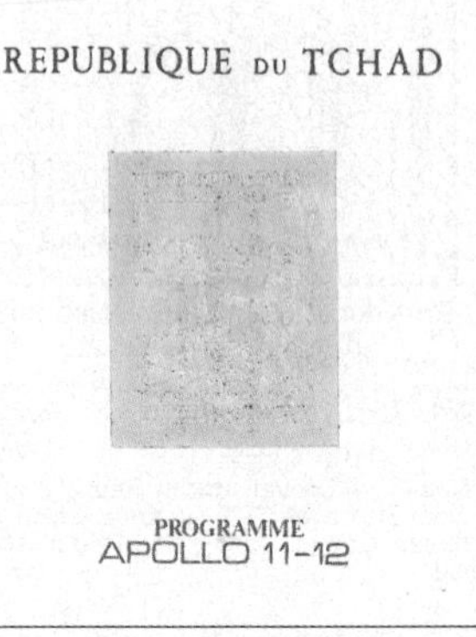

Apollo 12 — AP29a

1970, Sept. Embossed *Imperf.*
C70A AP29a 25fr gold 32.50

No. C70A probably was not available in Chad.

The Visitation, Venetian School, 15th Century AP30

Paintings, Venetian School: 25fr, Nativity, 15th century. 30fr, Virgin and Child, c. 1350.

1970, Dec. 15 Photo. *Perf. 12½x12*
C71 AP30 20fr gold & multi .70 .20
C72 AP30 25fr gold & multi 1.00 .20
C73 AP30 30fr gold & multi 1.10 .20
Nos. C71-C73 (3) 2.80 .60

Christmas 1970. See Nos. C105-C108.

Post Office Mauritius and Emblem AP31

1971, Jan. 23 Engr. *Perf. 13*
C74 AP31 10fr shown .20 .20
C75 AP31 20fr Tuscany #23 .35 .20
C76 AP31 30fr France #8 .55 .20
C77 AP31 60fr US #2 1.00 .20
C78 AP31 80fr Japan #8 1.40 .25
C79 AP31 100fr Saxony #1 1.75 .25
a. Souvenir sheet of 6, #C74-C79 7.25 3.00
Nos. C74-C79 (6) 5.25 1.30

Publicity for PHILEXOCAM, philatelic exhibition, Fort Lamy, Jan. 23-30.

Gamal Abdel Nasser — AP32

1971, Feb. 16 Photo. *Perf. 12½*
C80 AP32 75fr multi 1.00 .20

In memory of Gamal Abdel Nasser (1918-1970), President of Egypt.

Presidents Mobutu, Bokassa and Tombalbaye — AP33

1971, Apr. 28 Photo. *Perf. 13*

C81 AP33 100fr multi 1.60 .20

Return of Central African Republic to the United States of Central Africa which also includes Congo Democratic Republic and Chad.

Map of Africa, Communications Network and Symbols — AP34

1971, May 17 Engr. *Perf. 13*

C82 AP34 125fr ultra, sl grn & brn red 2.10 .20

Pan-African telecommunications system.

Boys Around Campfire, Torii AP35

1971, Aug. 24 Photo. *Perf. 12½*

C83 AP35 250fr multi 5.00 .40

13th Boy Scout World Jamboree, Asagiri Plain, Japan, Aug. 2-10.

White Egret — AP36

1971, Sept. 28 Photo. *Perf. 13x12½*

C84 AP36 1000fr blk, dk bl & ocher 50.00 4.50

Greek Marathon Runners — AP37

45fr, Ancient Olympic Stadium. 75fr, Greek wrestlers. 130fr, Olympic Stadium, Athens, 1896.

1971, Oct. 5 *Perf. 12½*

C85 AP37 40fr multi .70 .20
C86 AP37 45fr multi .90 .20
C87 AP37 75fr multi 1.60 .25
C88 AP37 130fr multi 1.75 .35
Nos. C85-C88 (4) 4.95 1.00

75th anniv. of modern Olympic Games.

Nos. C66A, C66C Ovptd. in Gold

1971 Litho. *Perf. 12½x12*

C88A AP28a 5fr on #C66A 2.25

Souvenir Sheet

Perf. 13½x13

C88B AP28a 15fr on #C66C 5.00

Overprint on No. C88B is 36mm long.

Duke Ellington — AP38

Charles de Gaulle — AP39

50fr, Sidney Bechet. 100fr, Louis Armstrong.

1971, Oct. 20 Litho. *Perf. 13*

C89 AP38 50fr multi 1.75 .20
C90 AP38 75fr lt bl & multi 2.75 .30
C91 AP38 100fr multi 4.50 .40
Nos. C89-C91 (3) 9.00 .90

Famous American jazz musicians.

Lithographed and Embossed

1971, Nov. 9 *Perf. 12½*

Design: No. C93, Félix Eboué.

C92 AP39 200fr grn, yel grn & gold 7.25 2.50
C93 AP39 200fr bl, lt bl & gold 7.25 2.50
a. Souv. sheet, #C92-C93 + label 18.00 5.00

Charles de Gaulle (1890-1970), pres. of France.

African Postal Union Issue, 1971

Common Design Type

Design: 100fr, Sao antelope head and UAMPT building, Brazzaville, Congo.

1971, Nov. 13 Photo. *Perf. 13x13½*

C94 CD135 100fr bl & multi 1.40 .20

Apollo 15 Rocket AP40

80fr, Apollo 15 capsule, horiz. 150fr, Lunar module on Moon, horiz. 250fr, Astronaut making tests. 300fr, Moon-buggy. #C100, Successful splashdown, horiz. #C101, Apollo 15 insignia.

1972, Jan. 5 Litho. *Perf. 13½*

C95 AP40 40fr multi .45 .20
C96 AP40 80fr multi .80 .20
C97 AP40 150fr multi 1.40 .30
C98 AP40 250fr multi 2.25 .45
C99 AP40 300fr multi 2.75 .60
C100 AP40 500fr multi 5.00 1.25
Nos. C95-C100 (6) 12.65 3.00

Souvenir Sheet

C101 AP40 500fr multi 6.25 1.10

Apollo 15 moon landing.

Soyuz 11 Link-up — AP41

Designs: 30fr, Soyuz 11 on launching pad, vert. 50fr, No. C108, Cosmonauts in uniform. 200fr, V. I. Patsayev. No. C106, V. N. Volkov. 400fr, G. L. Dobrovolsky. No. C109, Three cosmonauts.

1972, Jan. 5 *Perf. 13½x13*

C102 AP41 30fr multi .25 .20
C103 AP41 50fr multi .45 .20
C104 AP41 100fr multi .80 .25
C105 AP41 200fr multi 1.75 .50
C106 AP41 300fr multi 2.75 .75
C107 AP41 400fr multi 3.50 1.00
Nos. C102-C107 (6) 9.50 2.90

Souvenir Sheets

C108 AP41 300fr multi 3.00 .95
C109 AP41 400fr multi 3.50 1.25

Soyuz 11 link-up project.

Bobsledding — AP42

Design: 100fr, Slalom.

1972, Feb. 24 Engr. *Perf. 13*

C110 AP42 50fr Prus bl & rose red .90 .20
C111 AP42 100fr red lil & slate grn 1.75 .20

11th Winter Olympic Games, Sapporo, Japan, Feb. 3-13.

Pres. Tombalbaye Type, 1972

1972, Apr. 13 Litho. *Perf. 13*

C112 A63 70fr multi .80 .20
C113 A63 80fr multi 1.00 .20

11th Winter Olympic Type, 1972

130fr, Speed skating. #C115, Ice hockey. #C116, Ski jumping. 250fr, 4-man bobsled.

1972, Apr. 13 *Perf. 13½*

C114 A64 130fr multi 1.25 .45
C115 A64 200fr multi 2.10 .60

Souvenir Sheets

C116 A64 200fr multi 3.00 .75
C117 A64 250fr multi 4.00 1.00

Scout Jamboree Type, 1972

Designs: 100fr, Cooking preparation. 120fr, Lord Baden Powell. 250fr, Hiking.

1972, May 15

C118 A67 100fr multi 1.25 .30
C119 A67 120fr multi 1.40 .40

Souvenir Sheet

C120 A67 250fr multi 5.00 .75

Zebras — AP43

African wild animals: 30fr, Mandrills. 100fr, African elephants. 130fr, Gazelles. 150fr, Hippopotamuses. 200fr, Lion cub.

1972, May 15 Litho. *Perf. 13*

C121 AP43 20fr multi .35 .20
C122 AP43 30fr multi .45 .20
C123 AP43 100fr multi 1.25 .35
C124 AP43 130fr multi 2.00 .50
C125 AP43 150fr multi 3.00 .75
Nos. C121-C125 (5) 7.05 2.00

Souvenir Sheet

C126 AP43 200fr multi 12.50 1.50

View of Venice, by Caffi — AP44

Paintings by Ippolito Caffi: 40fr, Sailing ship and Doge's Palace, vert. 140fr, Grand Canal, vert.

1972, May 23 Photo.

C127 AP44 40fr gold & multi 1.00 .20
C128 AP44 45fr gold & multi 1.60 .20
C129 AP44 140fr gold & multi 3.00 .60
Nos. C127-C129 (3) 5.60 1.00

UNESCO campaign to save Venice.

11th Winter Olympic Winners Type, 1972

Designs: 150fr, Slalom, B. Cochran, US. 200fr, Women's figure skating, B. Schuba, Austria. 250fr, Ice hockey, USSR. 300fr, 2-man bobsled. W. Zimmerer and P. Utzschneider, West Germany.

1972, June 15 *Perf. 14½*

C130 A69 150fr gold & multi 2.75 .45
C131 A69 200fr gold & multi 3.50 .55

Souvenir Sheets

C132 A69 250fr gold & multi 3.00 .80
C133 A69 300fr gold & multi 3.50 1.10

Nos. C130-C131 exist se-tenant with label showing earth satellite.

Daudet, "Tartarin de Tarascon," Book Year Emblem — AP45

1972, July 22 Engr. *Perf. 13*

C134 AP45 100fr dk red, lil & dk brn 1.75 .20

Intl. Book Year, 1972, and to honor Alphonse Daudet (1840-1897), French writer.

20th Summer Olympics Type, 1972

Designs (TV Tower, Munich and): 100fr, Gymnast. 120fr, Pole vault. 150fr, Fencing. 250fr, Hammer throw. 300fr, Boxing.

1972, Aug. 15

C135 A70 100fr gold & multi 1.75 .30
C136 A70 120fr gold & multi 2.10 .35
C137 A70 150fr gold & multi 2.75 .50
Nos. C135-C137 (3) 6.60 1.15

Souvenir Sheets

C138 A70 250fr gold & multi 3.25 .90
C139 A70 300fr gold & multi 3.75 1.00

Nos. C135-C137 exist se-tenant with label showing arms of Munich.

Lunokhod on Moon — AP46

Russian moon missions: 100fr, Luna 16 on moon and rocket in flight, vert.

1972, Sept. 19

C140 AP46 100fr dk bl, pur & bis 1.75 .20
C141 AP46 150fr slate, brn & lil 2.25 .25

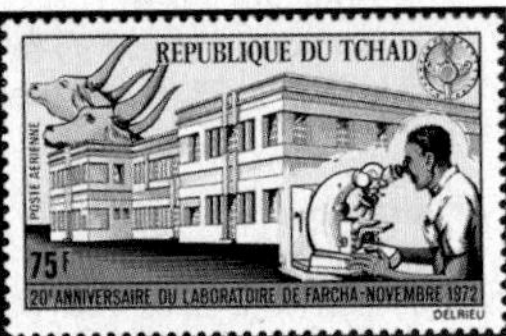

Farcha Laboratory, Cattle, Scientist — AP47

1972, Nov. 11 Photo. *Perf. 13*

C142 AP47 75fr yellow & multi 1.25 .20

20th anniversary of the Farcha Laboratory for veterinary research.

King Faisal and Holy Kaaba, Mecca — AP48

1972, Nov. 17

C143 AP48 75fr multi .50 .25

Visit of King Faisal of Saudi Arabia.

Christmas Type of 1970

Christmas: 40fr, Virgin and Child, by Giovanni Bellini. 75fr, Virgin and Child, by Dall'Occhio. 80fr, Nativity, by Fra Angelico, horiz. 95fr, Adoration of the Kings, by Il Perugino.

1972, Dec. 15 Photo. *Perf. 13*

C144 AP30 40fr gold & multi .20 .20
C145 AP30 75fr gold & multi .40 .20
C146 AP30 80fr gold & multi .45 .20
C147 AP30 95fr gold & multi .45 .25
Nos. C144-C147 (4) 1.50 .85

Summer Olympic Winners Type, 1972

Olympic Emblems and: 150fr, Pole vault, Nordwig, East Germany. 250fr, Hurdles, Milburn, US. 300fr, Javelin, Wolfermann, West Germany.

1972, Dec. 22

C148 A76 150fr multi 2.50 .50
C149 A76 250fr multi 3.75 .80

Souvenir Sheet

C150 A76 300fr multi 12.50 .95

Summer Olympic Winners Type, 1972

Olympic Emblem and: 150fr, Dressage, Mancinelli, Italy. #C152, Finn class sailing, Serge Maury, France. #C153, Swimming, Mark Spitz.

1972, Dec. 22 Litho. *Perf. 11*

C151 A77 150fr gold & multi 2.75 .45
C152 A77 250fr gold & multi 4.25 .80

Souvenir Sheet

C153 A77 250fr multi 12.50 .80

Copernicus and Solar System — AP49

1973, Mar. 31 Engr. *Perf. 13*

C154 AP49 250fr gray, mag & brn 5.00 .70

500th anniversary of the birth of Nicolaus Copernicus (1473-1543), Polish astronomer.

Horses — AP49a

Details from paintings: 20fr, A Horse Frightened by Lightning, by Theordore Gericault. 60fr, The White Horse, by Paul Potter. 100fr, Mares and Foals, by George Stubbs. 150fr, Horse Head, by Theordore Gericault, vert. 500fr, The Carriage, by Vernet.

1973 Litho. *Perf. 11½*

C154A AP49a 20fr multicolored
C154B AP49a 60fr multicolored
C154C AP49a 100fr multicolored
C154D AP49a 150fr multicolored
Nos. C154A-C154D (4) 12.50

Souvenir Sheet

Perf. 15

C154E AP49a 500fr multicolored

See note before No. 225A.

Airplanes — AP49b

1973 Litho. *Perf. 12*

C154F AP49b 5fr Fokker F VII/3M
C154G AP49b 25fr DH 89A Rapide
C154H AP49b 70fr Viscount
C154J AP49b 150fr Boeing 747
C154K AP49b 200fr Concorde
Nos. C154F-C154K (5) 12.50

Souvenir Sheet

Perf. 12

C154L AP49b 350fr Concorde, diff. 12.50

Nos. C154L contains one 60x40mm stamp. See note before No. 225A.

Skylab over Africa — AP50

1974, Aug. 6 Engr. *Perf. 13*

C155 AP50 100fr shown 1.25 .25
C156 AP50 150fr Skylab 2.25 .35

Exploits of Skylab, US manned space station.

Soccer — AP51

125fr, 150fr, Soccer players; 125fr, vert.

1974, Oct. 22 Engr. *Perf. 13*

C157 AP51 50fr dl red & choc .70 .20
C158 AP51 125fr red & dp grn 1.60 .30
C159 AP51 150fr grn & rose red 2.25 .40
Nos. C157-C159 (3) 4.55 .90

World Cup Soccer Championship, Munich, June 13-July 7.

Family and WPY Emblem — AP52

1974, Nov. 11

C160 AP52 250fr multi 3.50 .65

World Population Year.

Mail Delivery by Canoe — AP53

UPU Cent.: 40fr, Diesel train. 100fr, Jet. 150fr, Spacecraft.

1974, Dec. 20 Engr. *Perf. 13*

C161 AP53 30fr car & multi .55 .20
C162 AP53 40fr ultra & blk .90 .20
C163 AP53 100fr brn, ultra & blk 1.75 .30
C164 AP53 150fr grn, lil & ol 2.25 .45
Nos. C161-C164 (4) 5.45 1.15

Women of Different Races, IWY Emblem — AP54

1975, June 25 Photo. *Perf. 13*

C165 AP54 250fr bl & multi 4.25 .35

International Women's Year 1975.

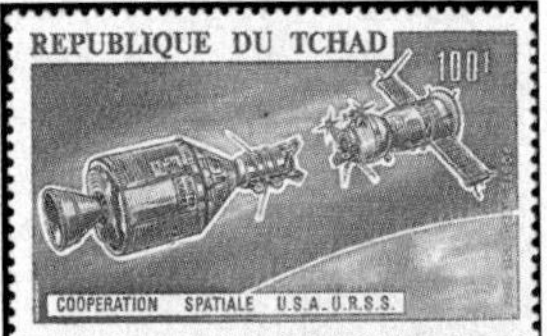

Apollo and Soyuz Before Link-up — AP55

130fr, Apollo and Soyuz after link-up.

1975, July 15 Engr. *Perf. 13*

C166 AP55 100fr ultra, choc & grn 1.25 .25
C167 AP55 130fr vio bl, brn & grn 1.75 .35

Apollo Soyuz space test project (Russo-American space cooperation), launching 7/15; link-up 7/17.

For overprints see Nos. C171-C172.

Soccer Player, View of Montreal — AP56

Olympic Rings, Montreal Skyline: 100fr, Discus thrower. 125fr, Runner.

1975, Oct. 14 Engr. *Perf. 13*

C168 AP56 75fr car & slate grn .90 .25
C169 AP56 100fr car, choc & bl grn 1.25 .35
C170 AP56 125fr brn, bl & car 1.75 .50
Nos. C168-C170 (3) 3.90 1.10

Pre-Olympic Year 1975.

Nos. C166-C167 Overprinted: "JONCTION / 17 JUILLET 1975"

1975, Nov. 4 Engr. *Perf. 13*

C171 AP55 100fr multi 1.60 .25
C172 AP55 130fr multi 2.00 .35

Apollo-Soyuz link-up in space, July 17.

Stylized British and American Flags, "200" — AP57

1975, Dec. 5 Engr. *Perf. 13*

C173 AP57 150fr vio bl, car & ol bis 2.10 .50

American Bicentennial.

Adoration of the Shepherds, by Murillo — AP58

Christmas (Paintings): 75fr, Adoration of the Shepherds, by Georges de La Tour. 80fr, Virgin and Child with Bible, by Rogier van der Weyden, vert. 100fr, Holy Family, by Raphael, vert.

1975, Dec. 15 Litho. *Perf. 13x12½*

C174 AP58 40fr yel & multi .70 .20
C175 AP58 75fr yel & multi 1.25 .25
C176 AP58 80fr yel & multi 1.40 .25
C177 AP58 100fr yel & multi 2.25 .30
Nos. C174-C177 (4) 5.60 1.00

12th Winter Olympic Winners Type, 1976

250fr, 4-man bobsled, West Germany. 300fr, Speed skating, J. E. Storholt, Norway. 500fr, Downhill skiing, F. Klammer, Austria.

1976, June 21 *Perf. 14*

C178 A84 250fr multi 2.50 .55
C179 A84 300fr multi 3.25 .70

Souvenir Sheet

C180 A84 500fr multi 5.25 1.25

Paul Revere's Ride and Portrait by Copley — AP59

American Bicentennial: 125fr, Washington crossing Delaware. 150fr, Lafayette offering his services to America. 200fr, Rochambeau at Yorktown with Washington. 250fr, Franklin presenting Declaration of Independence. 400fr, Count de Grasse's victory at Cape Charles.

1976, July 4 Litho. *Perf. 14*

C181	AP59	100fr multi	1.00	.30
C182	AP59	125fr multi	1.10	.35
C183	AP59	150fr multi	1.40	.40
C184	AP59	200fr multi	2.10	.50
C185	AP59	250fr multi	2.75	.55
		Nos. C181-C185 (5)	8.35	2.10

Souvenir Sheet

C186	AP59	400fr multi	5.25	1.10

Summer Olympics Type, 1976

1976, July 12

C187	A85	100fr Boxing	1.10	.30
C188	A85	200fr Pole vault	2.10	.50
C189	A85	300fr muShot put	3.25	.65
		Nos. C187-C189 (3)	6.45	1.45

Souvenir Sheet

C190	A85	500fr Sprint	5.25	1.10

Viking Mars Project Type, 1976

Mars Lander and: 100fr, Viking landing on Mars. 200fr, Capsule over Mars. 250fr, Lander over Mars. 450fr, Lander and probe.

1976, July 23 Litho. *Perf. 14*

C191	A86	100fr multi	1.00	.30
C192	A86	200fr multi	2.00	.55
C193	A86	250fr multi	2.25	.60
		Nos. C191-C193 (3)	5.25	1.45

Souvenir Sheet

C194	A86	450fr multi	5.00	1.00

For overprints see Nos. C240-C243.

Concorde — AP60

1976, Oct. 15 Litho. *Perf. 12½*

C195	AP60	250fr bl, blk & ver	5.25	.35

First commercial flight of supersonic jet Concorde, Jan. 21.

Nobel Prize Type, 1976

100fr, Albert Einstein, physics. 200fr, Dag Hammarskjold, peace. 300fr, Shinichiro Tomanaga, physics. 500fr, Alexander Fleming, medicine.

1976, Dec. 15

C196	A87	100fr multi	1.25	.30
C197	A87	200fr multi	2.25	.55
C198	A87	300fr multi	3.25	.70
		Nos. C196-C198 (3)	6.75	1.55

Souvenir Sheet

C199	A87	500fr multi	7.25	.90

Adoration of the Shepherds, by Gerard van Honthorst — AP61

Christmas (Paintings): 30fr, Nativity, by Albrecht Altdorfer, vert. 60fr, Nativity, by Hans Holbein, vert. 150fr, Adoration of the Kings, by Gerard David.

1976, Dec. 22 Litho. *Perf. 12½*

C200	AP61	30fr gold & multi	.45	.20
C201	AP61	60fr gold & multi	.70	.20
C202	AP61	120fr gold & blk	1.40	.35
C203	AP61	150fr gold & blk	2.00	.40
		Nos. C200-C203 (4)	4.55	1.15

Lesdiguières Bridge, by Jongkind — AP62

Design: 120fr, Sailing Ship and Boats, by Johan Barthold Jongkind (1819-1891).

1976, Dec. 27 Photo. *Perf. 13*

C204	AP62	100fr multi	1.60	.20
C205	AP62	120fr multi	2.00	.20

Centenary of impressionism.

Zeppelin Type of 1977

125fr, Germany #C40, North Pole. 150fr, Germany #C45, Chicago department store. 175fr, Germany #C38 and scenes of NYC and London. 200fr, 500fr, US #C15, NYC.

1977, Mar. 30 *Perf. 11*

C206	A91	125fr multi	1.75	.30
C207	A91	150fr multi	2.10	.35
C208	A91	175fr multi	2.50	.45
C209	A91	200fr multi	3.00	.55
		Nos. C206-C209 (4)	9.35	1.65

Souvenir Sheet

C210	A91	500fr multi	7.25	1.25

Sassenage Castle, Grenoble — AP63

1977, May 21 Litho. *Perf. 12½*

C211	AP63	100fr multi	.90	.20

Intl. French Language Council, 10th Anniv.

Lafayette and Ships — AP64

American Bicentennial: 120fr, Abraham Lincoln, eagle and flags, vert. 150fr, James Madison and family.

1977, July 30 Engr. *Perf. 13*

C212	AP64	100fr multi	1.25	.25
C213	AP64	120fr multi	1.60	.30
C214	AP64	150fr multi	2.10	.45
		Nos. C212-C214 (3)	4.95	1.00

Lindbergh and Spirit of St. Louis — AP65

100fr, Concorde. 150fr, 200fr, 300fr, Various Lindbergh portraits & Spirit of St. Louis.

1977, Sept. 27

C215	AP65	100fr multi	1.00	.30
C216	AP65	120fr multi	1.00	.35
C217	AP65	150fr multi	1.40	.50
C218	AP65	200fr multi	2.00	.60
C219	AP65	300fr multi	2.75	.75
		Nos. C215-C219 (5)	8.15	2.50

Charles A. Lindbergh's solo transatlantic flight from NY to Paris, 50th anniv., and 1st supersonic transatlantic flight of Concorde.

For overprint see No. C227.

Mariner 10 — AP66

Spacecraft: 200fr, Lunokhod on moon, Luna 21. 300fr, Viking on Mars.

1977, Oct. 10 Engr. *Perf. 13*

C220	AP66	100fr multi	1.00	.25
C221	AP66	200fr multi	1.75	.50
C222	AP66	300fr multi	2.50	.65
		Nos. C220-C222 (3)	5.25	1.40

Running — AP67

1977, Oct. 24 Engr. *Perf. 13*

C223	AP67	30fr shown	.35	.20
C224	AP67	60fr Volleyball	.70	.20
C225	AP67	120fr Soccer	1.25	.25
C226	AP67	125fr Basketball	1.10	.35
		Nos. C223-C226 (4)	3.40	1.00

No. C215 Overprinted: "PARIS NEW-YORK / 22.11.77"

1977, Nov. 22

C227	AP65	100fr multi	2.75	.20

Concorde, 1st commercial flight Paris-NYC.

Virgin and Child, by Rubens AP68

Rubens Paintings: 60fr, Virgin and Child and Two Donors. 100fr, Adoration of the Shepherds. 125fr, Adoration of the Kings.

1977, Dec. 20 Litho. *Perf. 12½x12*

C228	AP68	30fr multi	.70	.20
C229	AP68	60fr multi	1.00	.20
C230	AP68	100fr multi	1.40	.30
C231	AP68	125fr multi	1.75	.40
		Nos. C228-C231 (4)	4.85	1.10

Christmas 1977.

Antoine de Saint-Exupéry — AP69

50fr, Wilbur & Orville Wright & Flyer. 80fr, Hugo Junkers & his plane. 100fr, Gen. Italo Balbo & his plane. 120fr, Concorde. 500fr, Wilbur & Orville Wright & Flyer.

1978, Oct. 25 Litho. *Perf. 13½*

C232	AP69	40fr multi	.55	.20
C233	AP69	50fr multi	.70	.20
C234	AP69	80fr multi	1.00	.25
C235	AP69	100fr multi	1.40	.30
C236	AP69	120fr multi	1.60	.40
		Nos. C232-C236 (5)	5.25	1.35

Souvenir Sheet

C237	AP69	500fr multi	6.25	1.75

History of aviation and 75th anniversary of 1st powered flight.

Philexafrique II-Essen Issue

Common Design Types

#C238, Rhinoceros & Chad #C6. #C239, Kingfisher & Mecklenburg-Strelitz #1.

1978, Nov. 1 *Perf. 12½*

C238	CD138	100fr multi	2.75	.30
C239	CD139	100fr multi	2.75	.30
a.		Pair, #C238-C239 + label	7.25	.75

Nos. C191-C194 Overprinted "ALUNISSAGE/APOLLO XI/ JUILLET 1969"

1979, Nov. 26 Litho. *Perf. 13½x14*

C240	A86	100fr multi	1.00	.30
C241	A86	200fr multi	2.00	.60
C242	A86	250fr multi	2.25	.80
		Nos. C240-C242 (3)	5.25	1.70

Souvenir Sheet

C243	A86	450fr multi	5.00	1.00

Apollo 11 moon landing, 10th anniversary.

Hurdles, Moscow '80 Emblem — AP70

Emblem and: 30fr, Field hockey. 250fr, Swimming. 350fr, Running. 500fr, Yachting.

1979, Nov. 30 *Perf. 13½*

C244	AP70	15fr multi	.20	.20
C245	AP70	30fr multi	.25	.20
C246	AP70	250fr multi	1.75	.60
C247	AP70	350fr multi	2.75	1.00
		Nos. C244-C247 (4)	4.95	2.00

Souvenir Sheet

C248	AP70	500fr multi	5.25	1.50

Pre-Olympic Year.

For overprints see Nos. C254-C255.

Austria Jubilee Issue of 1910, Canoe, Hill — AP71

Hill, Stamps & Vessels: 100fr, US design A97, dhow. 200fr, France #21, Sidewheeler. 300fr, Holstein #16, ocean liner. 500fr, Chad #J13, ocean liner.

1979, Dec. 3 *Perf. 14x13½*

C249	AP71	65fr multi	.55	.20
C250	AP71	100fr multi	1.25	.25
C251	AP71	200fr multi	2.00	.45
C252	AP71	300fr multi	2.50	.70
		Nos. C249-C252 (4)	6.30	1.60

Souvenir Sheet

C253	AP71	500fr multi	5.25	1.50

Sir Rowland Hill (1795-1879), originator of penny postage.

For overprints see Nos. C256-C257.

Nos. C244-C245, C249-C250 Overprinted: "POSTES 1981" in Red or Overprinted and Surcharged Silver on Red

Perf. 13½, 14x13½

1981, Nov. 15 **Litho.**

C254	AP70	30fr on 15fr multi	1.10	.20
C255	AP70	30fr multi	1.10	.20
C256	AP71	60fr on 65fr multi	2.00	.20
C257	AP71	60fr on 100fr multi	2.00	.20
		Nos. C254-C257 (4)	6.20	.80

Soccer Type of 1982 and

1982 World Cup Soccer Championships, Spain — AP71a

#C259C, Soccer players, ball, & trophy, vert.

1982 **Litho.** *Perf. 13½*

C258	A108	80fr Brazil	.90	.20
C259	A108	300fr W. Germany	2.75	.40

Souvenir Sheet

C259A	A108	500fr like 300fr	5.00	.70

Litho. & Embossed

C259B	AP71a	1500fr gold & multi	15.00	

Souvenir Sheet

C259C	AP71a	1500fr gold & multi	12.50	

No. C259A contains one 42x51mm stamp.

For surcharge see No. C305.

Diana Type of 1982 and

Princess Diana, 21st Birthday — AP71b

Design: No. C262A, Portrait, horiz.

1982, July 2 **Litho.** *Perf. 13½*

C260	A109	80fr 1977	.90	.25
C261	A109	300fr 1980	2.75	.95

Souvenir Sheet

C262	A109	500fr 1981	5.00	1.50

Litho. & Embossed

C262A	AP71b	1500fr gold & multi	15.00	

Souvenir Sheet

C262B	AP71b	1500fr gold & multi	15.00	

For overprints see Nos. 419A-419B.

Manned Flight Bicentenary AP72

Balloons: 100fr, Charles' & Roberts', 1783. 200fr, J.P. Blanchard, Berlin, 1788. 300fr, Charles Green, London, 1837. 400fr, Modern blimp. 500fr, Montgolfiere, 1783.

1983, Apr. **Litho.** *Perf. 13*

C263	AP72	100fr multi, vert.	1.00	.25
C264	AP72	200fr multi, vert.	2.25	.40
C265	AP72	300fr multi	3.25	.60
C266	AP72	400fr multi	4.00	.75
		Nos. C263-C266 (4)	10.50	2.00

Souvenir Sheet

C267	AP72	500fr multi, vert.	5.25	1.25

Balloon Type and

First Balloon Ascension, Bicent. — AP72a

80fr, Steam Powered Airship, H. Giffard. 250fr, Graf Zeppelin; Airship L-1, 1st flight. 300fr, 1st Balloon Flight, Montgolfier & Rozier. #C270A, Airship Hindenburg, Count Ferdinand von Zeppelin. #C270B, Jean-Francois Pilatre de Rozier & Marquis d'Arlandes, 1st balloon ascension.

1983, May 30 **Litho.** *Perf. 13*

C268	A116	80fr multi	.90	.25
C269	A116	250fr multi	2.75	.40

Souvenir Sheet

C270	A116	300fr multi	3.50	1.00

Litho. & Embossed

Perf. 13½

C270A	AP72a	1500fr gold & multi	15.00	

Souvenir Sheet

C270B	AP72a	1500fr gold & multi	11.00	

For surcharge see No. C299.

1984 Summer Olympics — AP73

Various kayak scenes.

1984, Mar. 1 **Litho.** *Perf. 13*

C271	AP73	100fr multi	.90	.20
C272	AP73	200fr multi	1.75	.25
C273	AP73	300fr multi	2.75	.50
C274	AP73	400fr multi	3.50	.60
		Nos. C271-C274 (4)	8.90	1.55

Souvenir Sheet

C275	AP73	500fr multi	4.00	.70

Natl. Goals — AP73a

#C276, C278, Peace & reconciliation. #C277, C279, Self-sufficiency in food production.

1983, Dec. 26 **Litho.** *Perf. 13½*

C276	AP73a	150fr multi	1.40	.40
C277	AP73a	150fr multi	1.40	.40
C278	AP73a	200fr multi	2.00	.55
C279	AP73a	200fr multi	2.00	.55
		Nos. C276-C279 (4)	6.80	1.90

For surcharges see Nos. C300-C301.

Souvenir Sheet

Paul P. Harris (1868-1947), Founder of Rotary Intl. — AP73b

Litho. & Embossed

1984, Jan. 16 *Perf. 13½*

C279B	AP73b	1500fr gold & multi	11.00	

IYY, PHILEXAFRICA '85 — AP74

1985, May 2 **Litho.** *Perf. 13*

C280	AP74	200fr Boy scout, tree	2.75	.25
C281	AP74	200fr Air Chad Fokker 27	2.75	.25
a.		Pair, #C280-C281 + label	6.25	.50

IYY, PHILEXAFRICA Type of 1985

1985, Nov. 1 **Litho.** *Perf. 13x12½*

C283	AP74	250fr Girl, Scout ceremony	2.75	.40
C284	AP74	250fr Communications and transportation	2.75	.40
a.		Pair, #C283-C284 + label	6.25	.80

ASCENA Airlines, 25th Anniv. — AP75

1985, Aug. 25 *Perf. 12½*

C285	AP75	70fr bl & multi	.55	.20
C286	AP75	110fr org & multi	.90	.20
C287	AP75	250fr yel & multi	2.10	.35
		Nos. C285-C287 (3)	3.55	.75

Victor Hugo (1802-1885), French Novelist — AP76

Scene from Les Miserables.

1985, Nov. 24 **Engr.** *Perf. 13*

C288	AP76	70fr org brn, chlky bl & dp brn	.70	.20
C289	AP76	110fr lake, dk brn & dk grn	1.00	.20
C290	AP76	250fr brt org, blk & dk red	2.10	.40
C291	AP76	300fr dk red, cl & sl bl	2.25	.50
		Nos. C288-C291 (4)	6.05	1.30

Christmas 1985 — AP77

1985, Dec. 22 **Litho.** *Perf. 13½*

C292	250fr Adoration of the Magi	2.10	.40

1988 Summer Olympics, Seoul — AP78

1988, June 1 **Litho.** *Perf. 13*

C293	AP78	100fr 400-Meter hurdles, vert.	1.00	.30
C294	AP78	170fr 5000-Meter race	1.60	.55
C295	AP78	200fr Long jump	2.00	.65
C296	AP78	600fr Triple jump, vert.	5.25	1.90
		Nos. C293-C296 (4)	9.85	3.40

Souvenir Sheet

C297	AP78	750fr 10,000-Meter race, vert.	7.25	2.50

Stamps of 1982-84 Surcharged

1989 ***Perfs. as Before***

C298	A115	100 on 300fr #446
C299	A116	100 on 250fr #C269
C300	AP73a	100 on 200fr #C278
C301	AP73a	100 on 200fr #C279
C302	A110	170 on 300fr #404
C303	A122	170 on 200fr #503
C304	A123	170 on 250fr #509
C305	A108	170 on 300fr #C259
C306	A112	240 on 300fr #425

AIR POST SEMI-POSTAL STAMPS

Catalogue values for unused stamps in this section are for Never Hinged items.

Ramses II Battling the Hittites (from Abu Simbel) — SPAP1

Unwmk.

1964, Mar. 9 Engr. *Perf. 13*

CB1 SPAP1 10fr + 5fr multi .55 .20
CB2 SPAP1 25fr + 5fr multi 1.00 .20
CB3 SPAP1 50fr + 5fr multi 2.00 .50
Nos. CB1-CB3 (3) 3.55 .90

UNESCO world campaign to save historic monuments in Nubia.

Lions Emblem SPAP2

1967, July 5 Photo. *Perf. 13*

CB4 SPAP2 50fr + 10fr multi 1.40 .20

50th anniv. of Lions Intl. and to publicize the Lions work for the blind.

POSTAGE DUE STAMPS

Postage Due Stamps of France Overprinted

1928 Unwmk. *Perf. 14x13½*

J1 D2 5c light blue .20 .20
J2 D2 10c gray brown .20 .20
J3 D2 20c olive green .35 .35
J4 D2 25c bright rose .55 .55
J5 D2 30c light red .55 .55
J6 D2 45c blue green .95 .95
J7 D2 50c brown violet 1.25 1.25
J8 D2 60c yellow brown 1.25 1.25
J9 D2 1fr red brown 1.40 1.40
J10 D2 2fr orange red 3.25 3.25
J11 D2 3fr bright violet 2.75 2.75
Nos. J1-J11 (11) 12.70 12.70

Huts — D3

Canoe — D4

1930 Typo. *Perf. 14x13½, 13½x14*

J12 D3 5c dp bl & olive .40 .40
J13 D3 10c dk red & brn .40 .40
J14 D3 20c grn & brn .65 .65
J15 D3 25c lt bl & brn .90 .90
J16 D3 30c bis brn & Prus bl .90 .90
J17 D3 45c Prus bl & olive 1.25 1.25
J18 D3 50c red vio & brn 1.90 1.90
J19 D3 60c gray lil & bl blk 2.50 2.50
J20 D4 1fr bis brn & bl blk 2.50 2.50
J21 D4 2fr vio & brn 5.00 5.00
J22 D4 3fr dp red & brn 29.00 29.00
Nos. J12-J22 (11) 45.40 45.40

In 1934 stamps of Chad were superseded by those of French Equatorial Africa.

Catalogue values for unused stamps in this section, from this point to the end of the section, are for Never Hinged items.

Republic

Rhinoceros — D5

Tibesti Pictographs: #J24, Kudu. #J25, 2 antelopes. #J26, 3 antelopes. #J27, Ostrich. #J28, Horned bull. #J29, Bull. #J30, Wild swine. #J31, Elephant. #J32, Rhinoceros. #J33, Warrior with spear and shield. #J34, Masked archer.

Unwmk.

1962, Apr. 20 Engr. *Perf. 13*

J23 D5 50c olive bister .25 .20
J24 D5 50c brown red .25 .20
a. Pair, #J23-J24 .50
J25 D5 1fr blue .35 .20
J26 D5 1fr green .35 .20
a. Pair, #J25-J26 .70
J27 D5 2fr vermilion .45 .20
J28 D5 2fr maroon .45 .20
a. Pair, #J27-J28 .90
J29 D5 5fr slate green .70 .20
J30 D5 5fr violet blue .70 .20
a. Pair, #J29-J30 1.40
J31 D5 10fr brown 1.25 .30
J32 D5 10fr orange brown 1.25 .30
a. Pair, #J31-J32 2.50
J33 D5 25fr carmine rose 3.00 .75
J34 D5 25fr violet 3.00 .75
a. Pair, #J33-J34 6.00
Nos. J23-J34 (12) 12.00 3.70

Dolls — D6

1969, Sept. 19 Engr. *Perf. 14x13*

J35 D6 1fr Kanem .20 .20
J36 D6 2fr Kotoko .20 .20
J37 D6 5fr Leather .20 .20
J38 D6 10fr Kotoko .35 .20
J39 D6 25fr Guera .35 .20
Nos. J35-J39 (5) 1.30 1.00

MILITARY STAMPS

Catalogue values for unused stamps in this section are for Never Hinged items.

No. 78 Overprinted "F.M."

1965 Typo. *Perf. 14x13½*

M1 A5 20fr red & black 275.00 225.00

Flag Bearer and Map of Chad — M1

1st Regiment Emblem — M2

1968 Unwmk. Litho. *Perf. 13x12½*

M2 M1 tan & multi 1.60 .50

1972, Jan. 21 Photo. *Perf. 13*

M3 M2 blue & multi .90 .25

OFFICIAL STAMPS

Catalogue values for unused stamps in this section are for Never Hinged items.

Flag and Map of Chad — O1

Perf. 13½x14

1966-71 Typo. Unwmk.

Flag in blue, yellow and carmine

O1 O1 1fr light blue .20 .20
O2 O1 2fr gray .20 .20
O3 O1 5fr black .20 .20
O4 O1 10fr violet blue .20 .20
O5 O1 25fr orange .25 .20
O6 O1 30fr bright green .45 .20
O7 O1 40fr carmine ('71) .70 .20
O8 O1 50fr red lilac .70 .20
O9 O1 85fr green 1.00 .30
O10 O1 100fr brown 1.60 .35
O11 O1 200fr red 2.75 .50
Nos. O1-O11 (11) 8.25 2.75

Flag and Map Type of 1966-71 Redrawn with "N'Djamena" as Capital on Map

Perf. 13½x13¼, 11¾ (100fr)

2000 ? Litho.

Frame Color

O12 O1 85fr orange — —
O13 O1 100fr brown — —
O14 O1 200fr green — —
O15 O1 250fr lilac — —

No. O14 has central flag stripe in yellow, while others have orange stripe.

Additional stamps may have been issued in this set. The editors would like to examine any examples. Numbers may change.

CHILE

'chi-lē

LOCATION — Southwest corner of South America
GOVT. — Republic
AREA — 284,520 sq. mi.
POP. — 14,973,843 (1999 est.)
CAPITAL — Santiago

100 Centavos = 1 Peso
1000 Milésimos = 100 Centésimos = 1 Escudo (1960)
100 Centavos = 1 Peso (1975)

Catalogue values for unused stamps in this country are for Never Hinged items, beginning with Scott 257 in the regular postage section, Scott B3 in the semi-postal section, Scott C125 in the airpost section, and Scott CB1 in the airpost semi-postal section.

Pen cancellations are common on the 1862-67 issues. Such stamps sell for much less than the quoted values which are for those with handstamped postal cancellations.

Watermarks

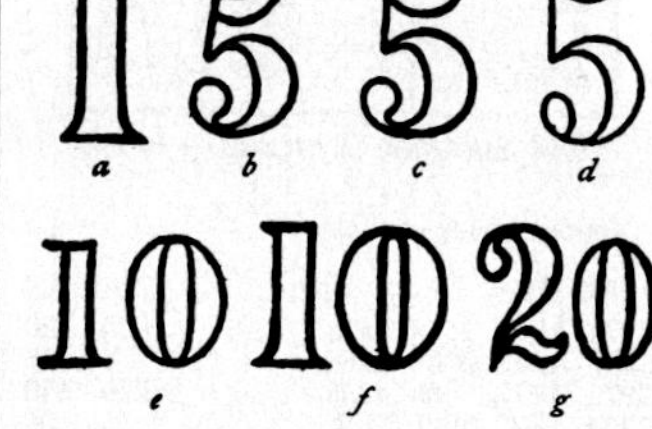

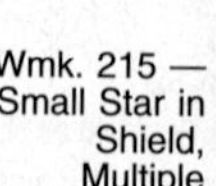

Wmk. 215 — Small Star in Shield, Multiple

Christopher Columbus — A1

London Prints

1853 Wmk. b Engr. *Imperf.*

Blued Paper

1 A1 5c brown red *375.00* 80.00
a. White paper 110.00

Wmk. e

White Paper

2 A1 10c dp brt bl *400.00* 95.00
a. Blued paper *150.00*
b. Diag. half used as 5c on cover *350.00*
c. Horiz. half used as 5c on cover *350.00*
d. Vert. half used as 5c on cover *350.00*

Santiago Prints

Impressions Fine and Clear

1854 Wmk. b and e

White Paper

3 A1 5c pale red brn 325.00 55.00
a. 5c deep red brown *350.00* 55.00
b. 5c chestnut *575.00* 85.00
e. Double impression 225.00
4 A1 5c burnt sienna *1,100.* 175.00
a. 5c dull chocolate *2,000.* 850.00
5 A1 10c deep blue *875.00* 125.00
a. 10c slate blue 125.00
b. 10c greenish blue *375.00*
d. Diag. half used as 5c on cover 450.00
e. Horiz. half used as 5c on cover 450.00
f. Vert. half used as 5c on cover 450.00
6 A1 10c lt dl bl *875.00* 125.00
a. 10c pale blue 125.00
b. Diag. half used as 5c on cover 425.00
c. Horiz. half used as 5c on cover 425.00
d. Vert. half used as 5c on cover 425.00

Litho.

7 A1 5c pale brown *1,000.* 275.00
a. 5c red brown *1,450.* 275.00

London Print

1855 Blued Paper Wmk. c Engr.

8 A1 5c brown red 110.00 9.25
Fiscal cancellation 1.00

Santiago Prints

Impressions Worn and Blurred

1856-62 Wmk. b and e

White Paper

9 A1 5c rose red ('58) 37.50 7.00
Fiscal cancellation 1.00
a. 5c carmine red ('62) 90.00 18.00
b. 5c orange red ('61) 225.00 100.00
c. 5c dull redsh brn ('57) 250.00 22.50
f. Printed on both sides 450.00 *250.00*
g. Double impression 450.00 90.00
10 A1 10c sky blue ('57) 125.00 27.50
Fiscal cancellation 1.75
a. 10c deep blue 125.00 27.50
b. 10c light blue ('59) 150.00 18.50
c. 10c indigo blue ('60) 175.00 50.00
k. Printed on both sides *250.00*
n. Diag. half used as 5c on cover *125.00*
o. Horiz.. half used as 5c on cover *140.00*
p. Vert. half used as 5c on cover *150.00*

London Prints

1862 Wmk. a, f and g

11 A1 1c lemon yellow 22.50 *27.50*
a. Double impression *350.00*
12 A1 10c bright blue 32.50 14.00
Fiscal cancellation 1.50
a. 10c deep blue 32.50 14.00
b. Blued paper — 17.50
c. Wmkd. "20" (error) *5,000.* *2,500.*
d. Diag. half used as 5c on cover 100.00
e. Horiz. half used as 5c on cover 110.00
f. Vert. half used as 5c on cover 125.00
13 A1 20c green 110.00 47.50
Fiscal cancellation 5.00
Nos. 11-13 (3) 165.00 89.00

Santiago Print

1865 **Wmk. d**

14 A1 5c rose red 37.50 9.25
Fiscal cancellation 1.00
a. 5c carmine red 37.50 9.25
b. Printed on both sides 300.00 *200.00*
c. Laid paper — *90.00*
d. Double impression — *160.00*

The 5c rose red (shades) on unwatermaked paper, either wove or ribbed, and on paper watermarked Chilean arms in the sheet are reprints made about 1870.

No. 13 has been reprinted in the color of issue and in fancy colors, both from the original engraved plate and from lithographic transfers. The reprints are on paper without watermark or with watermark CHILE and Star.

A2

A3

1867 **Unwmk.** ***Perf. 12***

15 A2 1c orange 22.50 17.50
Pen cancellation .40
16 A2 2c black 27.50 *35.00*
Pen cancellation .40
17 A2 5c red 19.00 1.75
Pen cancellation .20
18 A2 10c blue 19.00 5.50
Pen cancellation .25
19 A2 20c green 27.50 2.75
Pen cancellation .35
Nos. 15-19 (5) 115.50 62.50

Unused values for Nos. 15-19 are for stamps with original gum.

1877 ***Rouletted***

20 A3 1c gray 2.50 1.40
21 A3 2c orange 13.00 4.25
22 A3 5c dull lake 15.00 .30
23 A3 10c blue 12.50 1.90
a. Diagonal half used as 5c on cover —
24 A3 20c green 14.00 3.25
Nos. 20-24 (5) 57.00 11.10

The panel inscribed "CENTAVO" is straight on No. 22.

A4

A5

Columbus — A6

1878-99 ***Rouletted***

25 A4 1c green ('81) .90 .20
26 A4 2c rose ('81) .90 .20
27 A5 5c dull lake ('78) 7.25 .90
28 A5 5c ultra ('83) 1.90 .20
29 A5 10c orange ('85) 2.75 .35
a. 10c yellow 9.00 1.90
30 A5 15c dk grn ('92) 2.75 .55
31 A5 20c gray ('86) 2.75 .55
32 A5 25c org brn ('92) 2.75 .55
33 A5 30c rose car ('99) 7.25 3.75
34 A5 50c lilac ('78) 45.00 27.50
35 A5 50c violet ('85) 2.75 1.90
36 A6 1p dk brn & blk ('92) 19.00 2.75
a. Imperf. horiz. or vert., pair 75.00
Nos. 25-36 (12) 95.95 39.40

For surcharge and overprint see Nos. 50, O16.

Columbus
A7 A8

1894 **Re-engraved**

37 A7 1c blue green .90 .20
38 A7 2c carmine lake .90 .20

In type A4 there is a small colorless ornament at each side of the base of the numeral, above the "E" and "V" of "CENTAVO." In type A7 these ornaments are missing, the figure "1" is broader than in type A4 and the head of the figure "2" is formed by a curved line instead of a ball.

1900-01

Type I — There is a heavy shading of short horzontal lines below "Chile" and the adjacent ornaments.

Type II — There is practically no shading below "Chile" and the ornaments.

Type I

39 A8 1c yel grn .80 .20
40 A8 2c brn rose 1.00 .20
41 A8 5c dp bl 6.50 .20
42 A8 10c violet 6.50 .55
43 A8 20c gray 6.50 2.50
44 A8 30c dp org ('01) 6.50 2.50
45 A8 50c red brn 6.50 2.50
Nos. 39-45 (7) 34.30 8.65

Type II

46 A8 1c yel grn ('01) .80 .20
47 A8 2c rose ('01) .80 .20
48 A8 5c dull blue ('01) 5.00 .25
a. Printed on both sides —
49 A8 10c vio ('01) 6.00 .65
Nos. 46-49 (4) 12.60 1.30

For surcharge see No. 57.

No. 33 Surcharged in Black

1900

Black Surcharge

50 A5 5c on 30c rose car 1.00 .25
a. Inverted surcharge 30.00 22.50
b. Double surcharge 90.00 60.00
c. Double surcharge, both invtd. 90.00 60.00
d. Double surcharge, one invtd. 90.00 60.00

Columbus — A10

1901-02 ***Perf. 12***

51 A10 1c green .30 .20
52 A10 2c carmine .45 .20
53 A10 5c ultra 1.00 .20
54 A10 10c red & blk 1.75 .35
55 A10 30c vio & blk 5.50 .35
56 A10 50c red org & blk 7.00 2.10
Nos. 51-56 (6) 16.00 3.40

No. 44 Surcharged in Dark Blue

1903 ***Rouletted***

57 A8 10c on 30c orange 1.75 .50
a. Inverted surcharge 17.50 10.50
b. Double surcharge 25.00 15.00
c. Double surch., one inverted 25.00 15.00
d. Double surch., both invtd. 25.00 15.00
e. Stamp design printed on both sides

Pedro de Valdivia — A11

Coat of Arms — A12

A13

Telegraph Stamps Surcharged or Overprinted in Black

Type I — Animal at left has neither mane nor tail.

Type II — Animal at left has mane and tail.

1904 ***Perf. 12***

58 A11 1c on 20c ultra .40 .30
a. Imperf. horiz., pair 40.00 40.00
b. Inverted surcharge 50.00 50.00
59 A13 2c yel brn, I .25 .20
a. Inverted overprint 20.00 20.00
b. Pair, one without overprint 50.00 50.00
60 A13 5c red, I .35 .20
a. Inverted overprint 20.00 20.00
c. Pair, one without overprint 50.00 50.00
61 A13 10c ol grn, I 1.25 .40
a. Inverted overprint 50.00 50.00
Nos. 58-61 (4) 2.25 1.10

Perf. 12½ to 16

62 A13 2c yel, brn, II 4.50 4.50
63 A11 3c on 5c brn red 37.50 32.50
a. Inverted surcharge
64 A12 3c on 1p brn, II .45 .30
a. Double surcharge 50.00 50.00
65 A13 5c red, II 5.50 5.50
a. Inverted overprint
66 A13 10c ol grn, II 14.50 10.00
67 A11 12c on 5c brn red .90 .45
a. No star at left of "Centavos" 3.00 2.50
b. Inverted surcharge 40.00 40.00
c. Double surcharge 50.00 50.00
Nos. 62-67 (6) 63.35 53.25

Counterfeits exist of the overprint and surcharge varieties of Nos. 57-67.

For overprint see No. O12.

A14

A15

Columbus — A16

1905-09 ***Perf. 12***

68 A14 1c green .25 .20
69 A14 2c carmine .30 .20
70 A14 3c yel brn .65 .30
71 A14 5c ultra .70 .20
72 A15 10c gray & blk 1.10 .20
73 A15 12c lake & blk 5.00 1.75
74 A15 15c vio & blk 1.25 .20
75 A15 20c org brn & blk 2.25 .20
76 A15 30c bl grn & blk 3.25 .30
77 A15 50c ultra & blk 3.25 .30
78 A16 1p gold, grn & gray 16.00 11.00
Nos. 68-78 (11) 34.00 14.85

A 20c dull red and black, type A15, was prepared but not issued. Value $125. "Specimen" copies of Nos. 74, 76-78 exist, punched to prevent postal use.

For surcharges and overprints see Nos. 79-82, O9, O11-O15.

Nos. 73, 78 Surcharged in Blue or Red

a

b

1910

79 A15 (a) 5c on 12c (Bl) .45 .20
80 A16 (b) 10c on 1p (R) 1.00 .25
81 A16 (b) 20c on 1p (R) 1.50 .55
82 A16 (b) 1p (R) 2.75 1.00
Nos. 79-82 (4) 5.70 2.00

The 1p is overprinted "ISLAS DE JUAN FERNANDEZ" only. The use of these stamps throughout Chile was authorized.

Independence Centenary Issue

Oath of Independence A17

Monument to O'Higgins — A26

Gen. Manuel Blanco Encalada — A29

Designs: 2c, Battle of Chacabuco. 3c, Battle of Roble. 5c, Battle of Maipu. 10c, Naval Engagement of "Lautaro" and "Esmeralda." 12c, Capturing the "Maria Isabel." 15c, First Sortie of Liberating Forces. 20c, Abdication of O'Higgins. 25c, Chile's First Congress. 50c, Monument to José M. Carrera. 1p, Monument to San Martin. 5p, Gen. José Ignacio Zenteno. 10p, Adm. Lord Thomas Cochrane.

1910

Center in Black

83 A17 1c dk green .20 .25
a. Center inverted *7,000.*
84 A17 2c lake .20 .25
85 A17 3c red brown .80 .45
86 A17 5c dp blue .45 .20
87 A17 10c gray brn .80 .30
88 A17 12c vermilion 1.90 1.00
89 A17 15c slate 1.90 .40
90 A17 20c red orange 2.50 .75
91 A17 25c ultra 3.25 1.50
92 A26 30c violet 2.50 .75
93 A26 50c olive grn 5.50 2.25
94 A26 1p yel org 12.50 5.25
95 A29 2p red 12.50 5.25
96 A29 5p yel grn 35.00 17.50
97 A29 10p dk violet 30.00 16.00
Nos. 83-97 (15) 110.00 52.10

Columbus A32

De Valdivia A33

Mateo de Toro Zambrano A34

Bernardo O'Higgins A35

Ramón Freire — A36

F. A. Pinto — A37

Joaquín Prieto — A38

Manuel Bulnes — A39

Manuel Montt — A40

José Joaquín Pérez — A41

Federico Errázuriz Zanartu — A42

José de Balmaceda — A43

Designs: 1p Aníbal Pinto. 2p, Domingo Santa María. 10p, Federico Errázuriz Echaurren.

Outer backgrounds consist of horizontal and diagonal lines

1911 Engr. *Perf. 12*

98	A32	1c dp green	.25	.20
99	A33	2c scarlet	.25	.20
100	A34	3c sepia	.75	.25
101	A35	5c dk blue	.25	.20
102	A36	10c gray & blk	.75	.20
a.		Center inverted	800.00	600.00
103	A37	12c carmine & blk	1.00	.20
104	A38	15c violet & blk	.90	.20
a.		Center inverted	*1,000.*	
105	A39	20c org red & blk	1.75	.20
a.		Center inverted	50.00	50.00
106	A40	25c lt blue & blk	2.10	.55
107	A41	30c bis brn & blk	3.25	.25
108	A42	50c myr grn & blk	3.75	.25
109	A43	1p green & blk	7.00	.30
110	A43	2p ver & blk	12.50	1.00
111	A43	5p ol grn & blk	45.00	7.00
112	A43	10p org yel & blk	37.50	5.50
		Nos. 98-112 (15)	117.00	16.50

See Nos. 117, 121, 123, 127-128, 133-141, 143, 155A, 157-161, 165-169,171-172 and designs A47-A55, A57. For overprints see Nos. C6, C6B-C6D, C7-C8, C10-C11, C13-C21, O19-O22, O24-O27, O30-O34, O40.

Columbus A47

Toro Zambrano A48

Freire A49

O'Higgins A50

1912-13 Engr. *Perf. 12*

113	A47	2c scarlet	.20	.20
114	A48	4c black brn	.30	.20
115	A49	8c gray	1.00	.20
116	A50	10c blue & blk	1.00	.20
a.		Center inverted	500.00	400.00
b.		Imperf. horiz. or vert., pair	50.00	
117	A37	14c car & blk	1.00	.20
121	A38	40c violet & blk	4.50	.50
123	A40	60c lt blue & blk	10.00	1.25
		Nos. 113-123 (7)	18.00	2.75

See Nos. 125-126, 131, 164, 170, 173. For overprints see Nos. C6E, O18, O23, O28, O29.

Cochrane A52

Columbus A53

1915 Engr. *Perf. 13½x14*

124	A52	5c slate blue	.55	.30
a.		Imperf., pair	11.50	

See Nos. 155, 162-163. For overprints see Nos. O17, O37.

1918

125	A49	8c slate	13.00	.50

No. 125 is from a plate made in Chile to resemble No. 115. The top of the head is further from the oval, the spots of color enclosed in the figures "8" are oval instead of round, and there are many small differences in the design.

1921

Worn Plate

126	A49	8c gray	20.00	5.00

No. 126 differs from No. 125 in not having diagonal lines in the frame and only a few diagonal lines above the shoulders (due to wear), while No. 125 has diagonal lines in the oval up to the level of the forehead.

1915-25 Typo. *Perf. 13½ to 14½*

127	A32	1c gray green	.20	.20
128	A33	2c red	.20	.20
129	A53	4c brown ('18)	.25	.20

Frame Litho.; Head Engr.

131	A50	10c bl & blk	1.25	.20
a.		10c dark blue & black	1.25	.20
b.		Imperf., pair	110.00	
c.		Center inverted	325.00	
133	A38	15c vio & blk	.90	.20
134	A39	20c org red & blk	1.40	.20
a.		20c brown orange & blk	1.75	.20
135	A40	25c dl bl & blk	.55	.20
136	A41	30c bis brn & blk	1.75	.20
137	A42	50c dp grn & blk	1.75	.20

Perf. 14

138	A43	1p grn & blk	8.00	.20
139	A43	2p red & blk	9.75	.20
a.		2p vermilion & black	32.50	.60
140	A43	5p ol grn & blk ('20)	24.00	.60
141	A43	10p org & blk ('25)	25.00	1.75
		Nos. 127-141 (13)	75.00	4.55

The frames have crosshatching on the 15c, 20c, 30c, 2p, 5p and 10p. They have no crosshatching on the 10c, 25c, 50c and 1p.

Nos. 131a and 134a are printed from new head plates which give blacker and heavier impressions. No. 131a exists with; (a) frame litho., head engr.; (b) frame typo., head engr.; (c) frame typo., head litho. No. 134a is with frame typo., head engr.

A 4c stamp with portrait of Balmaceda and a 14c with portrait of Manuel de Salas were prepared but not placed in use. Both stamps were sent to the paper mill at Puente Alto for destruction. They were not all destroyed as some were privately preserved and sold.

Columbus A54

Manuel Rengifo A55

Types of 1915-20 Redrawn

1918-20 *Perf. 13½x14½*

143	A32	1c gray grn ('20)	.30	.20
144	A54	4c brown	.50	.20

No. 143 has all the lines much finer and clearer than No. 127. The white shirt front is also much less shaded.

1921

145	A55	40c dk vio & blk	2.00	.40

For overprints see Nos. C6A, C9.

Pan-American Congress Building — A56

Adm. Juan José Latorre — A57

1923, Apr. 25 Typo. *Perf. 14½x14*

146	A56	2c red	.20	.20
147	A56	4c brown	.20	.20

Typo.; Center Engr.

148	A56	10c blue & blk	.20	.20
149	A56	20c orange & blk	.50	.20
150	A56	40c dl vio & blk	.75	.20
151	A56	1p green & blk	.90	.30
152	A56	2p red & blk	3.25	.40
153	A56	5p dk grn & blk	11.50	3.00
		Nos. 146-153 (8)	17.50	4.70

Fifth Pan-American Congress.

Typographed; Head Engraved

1927 *Perf. 13½x14½*

154	A57	80c dk brn & blk	2.00	.60

Types of 1915-25 Issues Inscribed: "Chile Correos"

Perf. 13½x14½

1928-31 Engr. Wmk. 215

155	A52	5c slate blue	.90	.20

Frame Typo.; Center Engr.

155A	A38	15c violet & blk	*350.00*	
156	A55	40c dk vio & blk	.40	.20
157	A42	50c dp grn & blk	1.75	.20

Perf. 14

158	A43	1p green & blk	.70	.20
159	A43	2p red & blk	3.25	.20
160	A43	5p ol grn & blk	6.50	.25
161	A43	10p orange & blk	6.50	1.10
		Nos. 155,156-161 (7)	20.00	2.35

Paper of #155-161 varies from thin to thick.

Types of 1915-25 Issues Inscribed: "Correos de Chile"

1928 Engr. *Perf. 13½x14½*

162	A52	5c deep blue	.35	.20

1929 Litho.

163	A52	5c light green	.30	.20

Frame Litho.; Center Engr.

164	A50	10c blue & blk	1.25	.20
165	A38	15c violet & blk	1.50	.20
166	A39	20c org red & blk	3.50	.20
167	A40	25c blue & blk	.60	.20
168	A41	30c brown & blk	.45	.20
169	A42	50c dp grn & blk	.40	.20
		Nos. 163-169 (7)	8.00	1.40

Redrawn

1929 Frame Typo.; Center Litho.

170	A50	10c blue & blk	2.00	.20
171	A38	15c violet & blk	1.75	.20
172	A39	20c org red & blk	2.75	.20
		Nos. 170-172 (3)	6.50	.60

1931 Unwmk.

173	A50	10c blue & blk	.70	.20

In the redrawn stamps the lines behind the portraits are heavier and completely fill the ovals. There are strong diagonal lines above the shoulders. On #170 the head is larger than on #164, 173.

A58

Prosperity of Saltpeter Trade A59 A60

Perf. 13½x14

1930, July 21 Litho. Wmk. 215

Size: 20x25mm

175	A58	5c yellow grn	.35	.20
176	A58	10c red brown	.35	.20
177	A58	15c violet	.35	.20
178	A59	25c deep gray	1.40	.40
179	A60	70c dark blue	3.50	1.00

Perf. 14

Size: 24½x30mm

180	A60	1p dk gray grn	2.50	.50
		Nos. 175-180 (6)	8.45	2.50

Cent. of the 1st shipment of saltpeter from Chile, July 21, 1830.

Manuel Bulnes A61

Bernardo O'Higgins A62

1931 *Perf. 13½, 14*

181	A61	20c dark brown	.90	.30

For overprints see Nos. O35, O39.

1932

182	A62	10c deep blue	1.00	.30

For overprints see Nos. O36, O38.

Mariano Egana — A63

Joaquin Tocornal — A64

1934 *Perf. 13½x14*

183	A63	30c magenta	.50	.20

Perf. 14

184	A64	1.20p bright blue	.90	.20

Centenary of the constitution.

José Joaquín Pérez — A65

1934 *Perf. 13½x14*

185	A65	30c bright pink	1.40	.30

Atacama Desert — A66

Designs: 10c, Fishing boats. 20c, Coquito palms. 25c, Sheep. 30c, Mining. 40c, Lonquimay forest. 50c, Colliery at Port Lota. 1p, Shipping at Valparaiso. 1.20p, Puntiagudo volcano. 2p, Diego de Almagro. 5p, Cattle. 10p, Mining saltpeter.

Wmk. 215

1936, Mar. 1 Litho. *Perf. 14*

186 A66 5c vermilion .30 .20
187 A66 10c violet .20 .20
188 A66 20c magenta .20 .20
189 A66 25c grnsh blue 1.60 .40
190 A66 30c lt green .20 .20
191 A66 40c blk, *cream* 1.60 .50
192 A66 50c bl, *bluish* .80 .20

Engr.

193 A66 1p dk green .85 .25
194 A66 1.20p dp blue 1.00 .35
195 A66 2p dk brown 1.00 .40
196 A66 5p copper red 2.75 1.10
197 A66 10p dk violet 6.50 4.00
Nos. 186-197 (12) 17.00 8.00

400th anniv. of the discovery of Chile by Diego de Almagro.

Laja Waterfall — A78 Fishing in Chiloé — A84

Designs: 10c, Agriculture. 15c, Boldo tree. 20c, Nitrate Industry. 30c, Mineral spas. 40c, Copper mine. 50c, Mining. 1.80p, Osorno Volcano. 2p, Mercantile marine. 5p, Lake Villarrica. 10p, State railways.

Perf. 13½x14

1938-40 Litho. Wmk. 215

198 A78 5c brn car ('39) .20 .20
199 A78 10c sal pink ('39) .20 .20
200 A78 15c brn org ('40) .20 .20
201 A78 20c light blue .20 .20
202 A78 30c brt pink .20 .20
203 A78 40c lt grn ('39) .20 .20
204 A78 50c violet .20 .20

Engr. *Perf. 14*

205 A84 1p orange brn .20 .20
206 A84 1.80p deep blue .45 .40
207 A84 2p car lake .20 .20
208 A84 5p dk slate grn .35 .20
209 A84 10p rose vio ('40) .90 .20
Nos. 198-209 (12) 3.50 2.60

See Nos. 217-227. For surcharge and overprints see Nos. 253, O41-O66, O70-O71.

Map of the Americas — A89

Unwmk.

1940, Sept. 11 Litho. *Perf. 14*

210 A89 40c dl grn & yel grn .20 .20

Pan American Union, 50th anniversary.

Camilo Henríquez — A90

Founding of Santiago A93

Designs: 40c, Pedro de Valdivia. 1.10p, Benjamin Vicuna Mackenna. 3.60p, Diego Barros Arana.

Perf. 14½x14, 14½

1941, Jan. 23 Engr. Wmk. 215

211 A90 10c carmine lake .20 .20
212 A90 40c green .25 .20
213 A90 1.10p red .90 .50
214 A93 1.80p blue .90 .50
215 A90 3.60p indigo 2.75 2.00
Nos. 211-215 (5) 5.00 3.40

400th anniversary of Santiago.

Types of 1938

Perf. 13½x14

1942-46 Unwmk. Litho.

217 A78 10c sal pink ('43) .20 .20
218 A78 15c brown org ('43) .20 .20
219 A78 20c lt blue ('43) .20 .20
220 A78 30c brt pink ('43) .20 .20
221 A78 40c yellow grn .70 .20
222 A78 50c violet ('43) .20 .20

Engr. *Perf. 14*

223 A84 1p brown orange 1.40 .20
225 A84 2p car lake ('43) .20 .20
226 A84 5p dk sl grn ('43) .45 .20
227 A84 10p rose violet ('46) .75 .20
Nos. 217-227 (10) 4.50 2.00

Valentin Letelier — A95 University of Chile — A98

Designs: 40c, Andrés Bello. 90c, Manuel Bulnes. 1.80p, Manuel Montt.

1942, Nov. 1 *Perf. 14x14½, 14 (1p)*

228 A95 30c rose red .20 .20
229 A95 40c deep green .20 .20
230 A95 90c rose violet 1.00 .90
231 A98 1p deep brown .60 .50
232 A95 1.80p dark blue 2.00 1.75
Nos. 228-232 (5) 4.00 3.55

University of Chile cent. See No. C89.

Manuel Bulnes — A100

Map Showing Strait of Magellan — A104

Designs: 30c, Juan Williams Wilson. 40c, Diego Duble Almeida. 1p, José Mardones.

1944, Mar. 2 Litho. *Perf. 14*

233 A100 15c black .20 .20
234 A100 30c deep rose .20 .20
235 A100 40c yellow green .20 .20
236 A100 1p brown carmine .85 .20
237 A104 1.80p ultra 1.25 .70
Nos. 233-237 (5) 2.70 1.50

100th anniversary of the occupation of the Strait of Magellan.

Red Cross and Lamp of Life — A105

Serpent and Cup — A106

1944, Oct. 18 Unwmk.

238 A105 40c green, red & blk .25 .20
239 A106 1.80p ultra & red .60 .35

80th anniv. of the Intl. Red Cross Soc.

Bernardo O'Higgins — A107

"Embrace of Maipú" (O'Higgins Joining San Martin) — A108

Designs: 40c, Abdication of O'Higgins. 1.80p, Battle of Rancagua.

1945 Engr. *Perf. 14 (15c), 14½*

Center in Black

240 A107 15c carmine .25 .20
241 A108 30c brown .25 .20
242 A108 40c deep green .25 .20
243 A108 1.80p dark blue 1.25 .80
Nos. 240-243 (4) 2.00 1.40

Death of Bernardo O'Higgins in 1842, cent.

A111

A112

Proposed Columbus lighthouse.

Wmk. 215

1945, Sept. 10 Litho. *Perf. 14*

244 A111 40c light green .35 .20

Issued in honor of the discovery of America by Columbus and the Memorial Lighthouse to be erected in his memory.

1946 Engr.

245 A112 40c dark green .20 .20
246 A112 1.80p dark blue .20 .20

80th anniv. of the death of Andrés Bello, poet and educator.

Map Showing Chile's Claims of Antarctic Territory A113

1947, May 12 Litho. *Perf. 14½*

247 A113 40c carmine .35 .20
248 A113 2.50p deep blue .70 .25

Eusebio Lillo and Ramon Carnicer A114

1947, Sept. 18 Engr.

249 A114 40c dark green .20 .20

Centenary of national anthem.

Miguel de Cervantes Saavedra A115

1947, Oct. 11 Wmk. 215

250 A115 40c dk carmine .20 .20

400th anniv. of the birth of Cervantes, novelist, playwright and poet.

Arturo Prat Chacón and Iquique Naval Battle A116

1948, Dec. 24 *Perf. 14½*

251 A116 40c deep blue .20 .20

Centenary of the birth of Arturo Prat Chacon, Chilean naval hero.

Bernardo O'Higgins — A117

Perf. 13½x14

1948 Wmk. 215 Litho.

252 A117 60c black .20 .20

See #262. For surcharges see #266-267.

No. 203 Surcharged in Black

1948

253 A78 20c on 40c lt grn .20 .20

Chilean Pigeons — A118

FAUNA: a, Chilean Otter. c, Chilean pigeons. d, American skunk. f, Southern sea lions. g, Sugar-cane borer moth. h, Emperor penguins. i, Bat. j, Chinchilla. k, Grant's stag beetle. l, Trevally (fish). m, Chilean slender lizard. o, Crested caracara. q, Red-gartered coot. r, Chilean guemal (deer). s, Spiny rock lobster. u, Tilefish. v, Praying mantis. x, Torrent duck. y, Red conger.
FLORA: b, Araucarian pine (monkey puzzle tree). e, Evening primrose. n, Chilean red bell flower. p, Loxodon (flower). t, Boldo tree. w, Coquito palm trees.

Wmk. 215

1948, Dec. 6 Litho. *Perf. 14*
254 A118 60c Block of 25 10.00
Never hinged 15.00
a.-y. any single .25 .20
255 A118 2.60p Block of 25 15.00
Never hinged 22.50
a.-y. any single .35 .25

Issued in panes of 100.
Cent. (in 1944) of the publication of the 1st volume of Claudio Gay's Natural History of Chile. See No. C124.

Catalogue values for unused stamps in this section, from this point to the end of the section, are for Never Hinged items.

Benjamin Vicuna Mackenna — A121

1949, Mar. 22 Engr. *Perf. 13½x14*
257 A121 60c deep blue .20 .20

See No. C126.

Symbols of Arts and Crafts Education — A122

Heinrich von Stephan — A123

Design: 2.60p, Badge and book.

Unwmk.

1949, Nov. 11 Litho. *Perf. 14*
258 A122 60c lilac rose .20 .20
259 A122 2.60p violet blue .40 .30
Nos. 258-259,C127-C128 (4) 2.20 1.30

Cent. of the foundation of Chile's School of Arts and Crafts.

1950, Jan. 6 Engr.
260 A123 60c deep carmine .20 .20
261 A123 2.50p deep blue .40 .30
Nos. 260-261,C129-C130 (4) 1.45 1.10

UPU, 75th anniv.

O'Higgins Type of 1948

1950 Litho. *Perf. 13x14*
262 A117 60c black .20 .20

For surcharge see No. 266.

San Martín — A124

Isabella I — A125

Wmk. 215

1951, Mar. 16 Engr. *Perf. 14*
263 A124 60c deep blue .30 .20

Cent. of the death of Gen. José de San Martin. See No. C165.

1952, Mar. 20
264 A125 60c brt blue .30 .20

500th anniv. of the birth of Queen Isabella I of Spain. See No. C166.

Bernardo O'Higgins A126

Mateo de Toro Zambrano A127

1952 Unwmk. Litho. *Perf. 13½x14*
265 A126 1p dk blue grn .30 .20

See No. 275. For overprints see Nos. O67-O69.

#262, 252 Surcharged "40 Ctvs." in Red

1952, Sept.
266 A117 40c on 60c black .30 .20

Wmk. 215

267 A117 40c on 60c black .30 .20

1953, Mar. 13 Wmk. 215
268 A127 80c green .20 .20

See No. 285.

Valdivia Arms — A128

Old Fort — A129

3p, Modern Valdivia. 5p, Street in ancient Valdivia.

1953, May *Perf. 14*
269 A128 1p brt ultra .35 .20
270 A129 2p dull rose vio .35 .20
271 A129 3p blue green .45 .20
272 A129 5p deep brown .45 .20
Nos. 269-272,C167 (5) 2.60 1.05

4th centenary of the founding of Valdivia, capital of Valdivia province.

José Toribio Medina (1852-1930), Historian and Bibliographer A130

1953, June Engr. *Perf. 14½*
273 A130 1p brown .30 .20
274 A130 2.50p deep blue .40 .20

O'Higgins Type of 1952

Perf. 13½x14

1953, Oct. Wmk. 215 Litho.
275 A126 1p dk blue green .35 .20

For overprint see No. O69.

A131

A132

1953, Oct. 15 Engr. *Perf. 14½*
276 A131 1p Stamp of 1853 .20 .20

Centenary of Chile's first postage stamps.
Souvenir sheet including No. 276 is noted below No. C168.

1953, Nov. 5 Litho. *Perf. 13½x14*

Census chart and map.

277 A132 1p blue green .30 .20
278 A132 2.50p violet blue .30 .20
279 A132 3p chocolate .50 .20
280 A132 4p carmine .50 .20
Nos. 277-280 (4) 1.60 .80

12th general census of population and housing.

Arms of Angol — A133

Ignacio Domeyko — A134

1954, May 28 Unwmk. *Perf. 14*
281 A133 2p deep carmine .30 .20

400th anniversary of the founding of Angol, capital of Malleco province.

1954, Aug. 16 Engr. *Perf. 13½x14*
282 A134 1p greenish blue .30 .20

150th anniversary of the birth of Ignacio Domeyko (1802-89), mineralogist and educator. See No. C171.

Early Steam Locomotive — A135

1954, Sept. 10 Wmk. 215 *Perf. 14½*
283 A135 1p red .50 .25

Centenary (in 1951) of the first South American railroad. See No. C172.

Adm. Arturo Prat Chacón — A136

Arms of Viña del Mar — A137

1954 Unwmk. Litho. *Perf. 14*
284 A136 2p dk violet blue .30 .20

75th anniv. of the naval Battle of Iquique.

Toro Zambrano Type of 1953

1954, Nov. 6 *Perf. 13½x14*
285 A127 80c green .30 .20

1955, Mar. 5 Wmk. 215 *Perf. 14*

Design: 2p, Arms of Valparaiso.

286 A137 1p violet blue .30 .20
287 A137 2p carmine .30 .20

1st Intl. Phil. Exhib., Valparaiso, Mar. 1955.

Dr. Alejandro del Rio — A138

1955, May 24 *Perf. 13½x14*
288 A138 2p violet blue .35 .20

14th Pan-American Sanitary Conference.

Christ of the Andes, Emblems of Chile, Argentina A139

1955, Aug. 31 Unwmk. *Perf. 14½*
289 A139 1p violet blue .30 .20

Reciprocal visits of Presidents Juan D. Peron and Carlos Ibanez del Campo. See No. C173.

Manuel Rengifo — A140

5p, Mariano Egana. 50p, Diego Portales.

1955-56 Unwmk. *Perf. 14x14½*

290 A140 3p violet blue .30 .20
291 A140 5p dk car rose .30 .20
292 A140 50p rose lilac ('56) 1.75 .40
Nos. 290-292 (3) 2.35 .80

Joaquin Prieto (1786-1854), soldier and political leader; president, 1831-41. See No. QRA1.

Jose M. Carrera A141

Ramón Freire A142

Portraits: 5p, Manuel Bulnes. 10p, Pres. Francisco A. Pinto. 50p, Manuel Montt.

Perf. 14x14½

1956-58 Unwmk. Litho.

293 A141 2p purple .30 .20
293A A142 3p lt violet blue .25 .20
294 A141 5p redsh brn (19½x23mm) .30 .20
a. Size 19x22mm .30 .20
295 A142 10p vio (19x22¼mm) .30 .20
a. Perf. 13½x14 (19¼x22½mm) ('58) .55 .25
296 A141 50p rose red .50 .20
Nos. 293-296 (5) 1.65 1.00

Wmk. 215

297 A141 2p dull purple .30 .20
298 A142 3p violet blue .30 .20

#294 has yellow gum; #294a, white gum.
For overprints see Nos. O72-O76.

Federico Santa Maria — A143

Gabriela Mistral — A144

Unwmk.

1957, Jan. 31 Engr. *Perf. 14*

299 A143 5p dk red brown .30 .20

25th anniv. of the Federico Santa Maria Technical University. See Nos. C190-C191.
Souvenir sheet including No. 299 is noted below No. C191.

1958, Jan. 10

300 A144 10p red brown .40 .20

Issued in honor of Gabriela Mistral, poet and educator. See No. C192.

Arms of Osorno — A145

Arms of Santiago — A146

Design: 50p, Garcia Hdo. de Mendoza.

1958, Mar. 23 Litho. *Perf. 14*

301 A145 10p carmine .20 .20

Engr.

302 A145 50p green .40 .20

400th anniversary of the founding of the city of Osorno, capital of Osorno province.
Souvenir sheet including No. 302 in red brown is noted below No. C193.

1958, Oct. 18 Unwmk. *Perf. 14*

303 A146 10p dark violet .20 .20

Natl. Philatelic Exposition, Santiago, Oct. 18-26.
Souvenir sheet including No. 303 in deep red is noted below No. C194.

Symbolical Savings Bank — A147

Modern Map of Antarctica — A148

1958, Dec. 18

304 A147 10p dark blue .40 .20

Savings Bank for Public Employees, cent.
Souvenir sheet including No. 304 in violet is noted below No. C195.

1958, Aug. 28 Unwmk. *Perf. 14*

305 A148 40p rose carmine .20 .20

IGY, 1957-1958. See No. C214.

Antarctic Map and "La Araucana" A149

Map of Strait of Magellan, 1588 — A150

1958 Litho. *Perf. 14*

310 A149 10p violet blue .40 .20

Engr.

311 A150 200p dull purple 1.50 1.10
Nos. 310-311,C199-C200 (4) 4.20 2.35

For overprint see No. O77.

Valdivia River Bridge — A153

1959, Feb. 9 Engr. *Perf. 14*

319 A153 40p green .40 .20

Cent. of the German School in Valdivia and to publicize the Valdivia Phil. Exhib., 2/9-18.
Souvenir sheet including No. 319 is noted below No. C213.

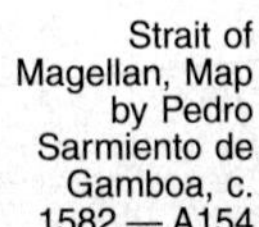

Strait of Magellan, Map by Pedro Sarmiento de Gamboa, c. 1582 — A154

1959, Aug. 27 Litho.

320 A154 10p dull purple .40 .20

Juan Ladrillero expedition to explore the Strait of Magellan, 1557-58, 400th anniv. See #C215.

Diego Barros Arana — A155

Henri Dunant — A156

1959, Aug. 27

321 A155 40p ultra .40 .20

50th anniv. of the death of Diego Barros Arana (1830-1907), historian. See No. C216.

1959, Oct. 6 Unwmk. *Perf. 14*

322 A156 20p red & red brn .40 .20

Cent. of the Red Cross idea. See No. C217.

Manuel Bulnes — A157

Francisco A. Pinto — A158

Choshuenco Volcano A159

#326, Choshuenco volcano, redrawn. 5c, Manuel Montt. 10c, Maule River Valley. 20c, 1e, Inca Lake.

1960-67 Litho. *Perf. 13x14*

323 A157 5m bluish grn .20 .20
324 A158 1c carmine .20 .20

Perf. 14

Size: 29x25mm

325 A159 2c ultra ('61) .20 .20

Perf. 14x13

Size: 23½x18mm

326 A159 2c ultra ('62) .20 .20

Perf. 13x14

327 A157 5c blue .20 .20

Perf. 14

Size: 29x25mm

328 A159 10c green ('62) .20 .20
329 A159 20c Prus blue ('62) .35 .20
329A A159 1e bluish grn ('67) .60 .25
Nos. 323-329A (8) 2.15 1.65

On No. 325 "Volcan Choshuenco" is at upper left, below "Correos." On No. 326, it is at bottom, above "Centesimos."
For overprint and surcharge see #O79, RA1.

Refugee Family A160

1960, Apr. 7 *Perf. 14½*

330 A160 1c green .20 .20

WRY, July 1, 1959-June 30, 1960. A souvenir sheet is noted below No. C218.

Type of Air Post Issue, 1962, and

Arms of Chile A161

José M. Carrera A162

#332, Palace of Justice. 5c, Natl. Memorial. 10c, Manuel de Toro y Zambrano and Martinez de Rozas. 20c, Manuel de Salas and Juan Egana. 50c, Manuel Rodriguez and Juan Mackenna.

Wmk. 215 (#331, 1e); Unwmk.

1960-65 Engr. *Perf. 14½*

331 A161 1c maroon & sepia .20 .20
332 A161 1c brn & claret ('62) .20 .20
333 A162 5c grn & Prus grn ('61) .20 .20
334 AP54 10c brn & vio brn ('64) .40 .25
334A AP54 20c ind & bl grn ('65) .40 .25
335 AP54 50c red brn & mar ('65) .60 .25
336 A162 1e gray ol & brn 1.00 .40
Nos. 331-336,C218A-C220D (14) 6.25 3.45

150th anniv. of the formation of the 1st Natl. Government. A souvenir sheet is noted below No. C220B. See No. C285.

Family — A163

Design: 10c, Various buildings.

Unwmk.

1960, Jan. 18 Litho. *Perf. 14*

337 A163 5c green .20 .20
338 A163 10c brt violet .20 .20

13th population census (No. 337) and 2nd housing census (No. 338).

Chamber of Deputies A164

1961, Aug. 14 Unwmk. *Perf. 14½*

339 A164 2c red brown .60 .20

150th anniv. of the 1st National Congress. See No. C245.

Soccer Players and Globe A165

Design: 5c, Goalkeeper and stadium, vert.

1962, May 30 Engr. *Perf. 14½*

340 A165 2c blue .40 .20
341 A165 5c green .50 .20

World Soccer Championship, Chile, May 30-June 17. Note on souvenir sheet follows No. C247.

Mother and Child — A166

Centenary Emblem — A167

1963, Mar. 21 Litho. *Perf. 14*

342 A166 3c maroon .30 .20

FAO "Freedom from Hunger" campaign. See No. C248.

1963, Aug. 23 Unwmk. *Perf. 14*

343 A167 3c red & gray .30 .20

Cent. of the Intl. Red Cross. See #C249.

Fireman Carrying Woman — A168

Enrique Molina — A169

1963, Dec. 20 Unwmk. *Perf. 14*

344 A168 3c violet .40 .20

Centenary of the Santiago Fire Brigade. See No. C250.

1964, Nov. 14 Litho. *Perf. 14*

Design: No. 346, Magr. Carlos Casanueva.

345 A169 4c bister brown .30 .20
346 A169 4c rose claret .30 .20
Nos. 345-346,C257-C258 (4) 1.00 .80

Enrique Molina, founder of the University of Concepcion, and Msgr. Carlos Casanueva, rector of the Catholic University, 1920-53.

Easter Island Statue — A170

Copihue, National Flower — A171

Design: 30c, Robinson Crusoe.

1965-69 Litho. *Perf. 14x14½*

347 A170 6c rose lilac .55 .20
347A A170 10c rose pink ('68) .20 .20

Perf. 14

348 A171 15c yel grn & rose red .55 .20
348A A171 20c yel grn & rose red ('69) .20 .20

Perf. 14x14½

349 A170 30c rose claret .45 .20
Nos. 347-349 (5) 1.95 1.00

For surcharge see No. RA2.

Skier — A172

Lorenzo Sazie — A173

1965, Aug. 30 *Perf. 14*

350 A172 4c blue green .35 .20

World Skiing Championships, Chile, 1966.

1966, Feb. 9 Litho. *Perf. 14x14½*

351 A173 1e green .90 .20

Cent. of the death of Dr. Lorenzo Sazie, dean of the Faculty of Medicine, University of Santiago.

German Riesco, President in 1901-1906 — A174

Portrait: 30c, Jorge Montt (1847-1922), president in 1891-1896.

1966 Unwmk. *Perf. 13x14*

354 A174 30c violet .25 .20
355 A174 50c dull brown .30 .20

For surcharge see No. 450.

William Wheelwright and S.S. Chile — A175

1966, Aug. 2 *Perf. 14½*

358 A175 10c ultra & lt bl .30 .20

125th anniv. (in 1965) of the arrival of the paddle steamers "Chile" and "Peru." See No. C268.

Learning to Read — A176

1966, Aug. 13 Litho. *Perf. 14*

359 A176 10c red brown .30 .20

Literacy campaign

UN and ICY Emblems A177

1966, Oct. 28 Unwmk. *Perf. 14½*

360 A177 1e green & brown 1.25 .25

Intl. Cooperation Year, 1965. See No. C269.

Capt. Luis Pardo and Ship in Antarctica — A178

1967, Jan. Litho. *Perf. 14½*

361 A178 20c turquoise blue .40 .25

Rescue of the Shackleton South Pole expedition by Capt. Luis Pardo of Chile, 50th anniv. See #C271.

Family — A179

Trees and Mountains A180

1967, Apr. 13 Unwmk. *Perf. 14*

362 A179 10c magenta & blk .35 .20

8th Intl. Conf. for Family Planning, Santiago, Apr. 1967. See No. C272.

1967, June 9 Litho. *Perf. 14½*

363 A180 10c blue grn & lt bl .35 .20

Reforestation Campaign. See No. C274.

Lions Emblem — A181

1967, July 12 Litho. *Perf. 14*

364 A181 20c Prus blue & yel .35 .25
Nos. 364,C275-C276 (3) 1.60 .80

50th anniv. of Lions Intl.

Chilean Flag A182

1967, Oct. 20 Unwmk. *Perf. 14½*

365 A182 80c crimson & ultra .50 .25

Natl, flag, 150th anniv. See No. C277.

José Maria Cardinal Caro — A183

1967, Dec. 4 Engr. *Perf. 14½*

366 A183 20c deep carmine .70 .35

Cent. of the birth of José Maria Cardinal Caro, the first Chilean cardinal. See #C279.

San Martin and O'Higgins — A184

1968, Apr. 23 Litho. Unwmk.

367 A184 3e blue .60 .25

Sesquicentennial of the Battles of Chacabuco and Maipu. See No. C280.

Farm Couple — A185

1968, June 18 *Perf. 14½*

368 A185 20c black, org & grn .35 .25

Agrarian reforms. See No. C281.

Juan I. Molina A186

1968, Aug. 27 Litho. *Perf. 14½*

369 A186 2e red lilac .50 .25

Issued to honor Juan I. Molina, educator and scientist. See No. C282.

Hand Holding Cogwheel — A187

1968, Sept. ***Perf. 14x14½***
370 A187 30c deep carmine .30 .25

Fourth census of manufacturers.

Map of Chiloé Province, Sailing Ship and Coastal Vessel A188

1968, Oct. 7 ***Perf. 14½***
371 A188 30c ultra .40 .25

Anniversaries of the founding of five towns in Chiloé Province. See No. C283.

Automobile Club Emblem A189

1968, Nov. 10 **Engr.** ***Perf. 14½x14***
372 A189 1e carmine rose .35 .25

40th anniversary of the Automobile Club of Chile. See No. C284.

Francisco Garcia Huidobro A190

Design: 5e, King Philip V of Spain.

1968, Dec. 31 **Litho.** ***Perf. 14½***
373 A190 2e pale rose & ultra .40 .20
374 A190 5e brown & yel grn .40 .20
Nos. 373-374,C288-C289 (4) 1.20 .80

225th anniv. of the founding of the State Mint (Casa de Moneda de Chile).

Satellite and Radar Station A191

1969, May 20 **Litho.** ***Perf. 14½***
375 A191 30c blue .30 .25

Inauguration of ENTEL-Chile, the 1st commercial satellite communications ground station, Longovilo.
See #C290. For surcharges see #397, C308.

Red Cross, Crescent and Lion and Sun Emblems A192

1969, Sept. **Litho.** ***Perf. 14½***
376 A192 2e violet blue & red .40 .25

50th anniversary of the League of Red Cross Societies. See No. C291.

Rapel Hydroelectric Plant — A193

1969, Nov. 18 **Litho.** ***Perf. 14½***
377 A193 40c green .30 .25

See No. C292.

Col. Rodriguez Monument — A194

1969, Nov. 24
378 A194 2e rose claret .40 .25

150th anniversary of the death of Col. Manuel Rodriguez. See No. C293.

EXPO '70 Emblem — A195

1969, Dec. 2 **Litho.** ***Perf. 14***
379 A195 3e blue .50 .25

EXPO '70 Intl. Exhibition, Osaka, Japan, Mar. 15-Sept. 13, 1970. See No. C294.

Open Book A196

1969, Dec. 3 ***Perf. 14½***
380 A196 40c red brown .35 .25

Translation of the Bible into Spanish by Casiodoro de Reina, 400th anniv. See No. C295.

Globes and ILO Emblem A197

1969, Dec. 17 ***Perf. 14½***
381 A197 1e green & blk .35 .25

ILO, 50th anniv. See No. C296.

Human Rights Flame A198

1969, Dec. 18
382 A198 4e blue & red .60 .25

Human Rights Year, 1968. See No. C297.

Policarpo Toro and Easter Island A199

1970, Jan. 26 ***Perf. 14½***
383 A199 5e lilac .60 .25

80th anniversary of the acquisition of Easter Island. See No. C298.

Sailing Ship and Arms of Valdivia A200

1970, Feb. 4 **Litho.** ***Perf. 14½***
384 A200 40c dk carmine .50 .25

150th anniv. of the capture of Valdivia during Chile's war of independence by Thomas Cochrane (1775-1860), naval commander. See No. C299.

Paul Harris and Rotary Emblem — A201

1970, Mar. 18 **Litho.** ***Perf. 14***
385 A201 10e violet blue 1.00 .25

Cent. of the birth of Paul Harris (1868-1947), founder of Rotary Intl. See No. C300.

Mahatma Gandhi — A202

1970, Apr. 1 **Litho.** ***Perf. 14½***
386 A202 40c blue green 3.25 .30

Mohandas K. Gandhi (1869-1948), leader in India's fight for independence, birth cent. See #C301. For surcharge see #449.

Santo Domingo Church, Santiago, Chile — A203

1970, Apr. 30 **Engr.**

Designs: 2e, Casa de Moneda de Chile, horiz. 3e, Pedro de Valdivia. 5e, Bridge, horiz. 10e, Ambrosio O'Higgins.

387 A203 2e violet brown .40 .20
388 A203 3e dark red .40 .20
389 A203 4e dark blue .30 .20
390 A203 5e brown .30 .20
391 A203 10e green .30 .20
Nos. 387-391 (5) 1.70 1.00

Exploration and development of Chile by Spanish explorers.
A sheet containing imperf examples of Nos. 388, 390 and 391 exists. It was not valid for postage.

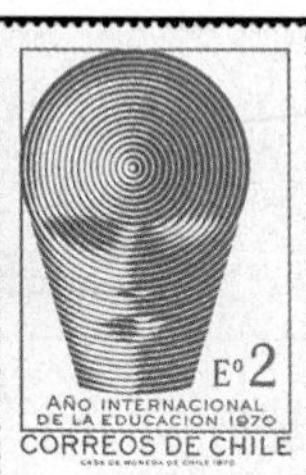

Education Year Emblem — A204

Virgin and Child — A205

1970, July 17 **Litho.** ***Perf. 14½***
392 A204 2e claret .35 .25

International Education Year. See No. C302.

1970, July 28
393 A205 40c green .30 .25

O'Higgins National Shrine at Maipu. See No. C303. For surcharge see No. 454.

Torch and Snake — A206

Copper Symbol, Chile Arms — A207

1970, Aug. 11
394 A206 40c claret & light blue .50 .25

International Cancer Congress, Houston, Texas, May 22-29. See No. C304.

1970, Oct. 21 **Litho.** ***Perf. 14½***
395 A207 40c car & lt red brn .35 .25

Nationalization of the copper industry. See No. C305. For surcharge see No. 459.

Dove and World Map A208

1970, Oct. 22
396 A208 3e rose magenta & pur .40 .25

25th anniv. of the UN. See No. C306.

No. 375 Surcharged in Red

1970, Dec. 24 **Litho.** ***Perf. 14½***
397 A191 52c on 30c blue .45 .25

Freighter and Ship's Wheel — A209

1971, Jan. 18 Litho. *Perf. 14*

398 A209 52c deep carmine .30 .20

Natl. Maritime Commission. See #C307.

Bernardo O'Higgins and Ship A210

1971, Feb. 3 *Perf. 14½*

399 A210 5e grnsh bl & grn .50 .20

150th anniv. of the expedition to liberate Peru from Spanish rule. See No. C309.

Youth, Girl and UN Emblem A211

1971, Feb. 11 Litho. *Perf. 14½*

400 A211 52c dk blue & brn .35 .20

1st meeting in Latin America of the Executive Council of UNICEF, Santiago, May 20-31, 1969. See No. C310.

Chilean Boy Scout Emblem — A212

1971, Feb. 10 *Perf. 14*

401 A212 1e green & brn .35 .20

Founding of Chilean Boy Scouts, 60th anniversary. See No. C311.

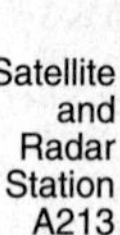

Satellite and Radar Station A213

1971, May 25 Litho. *Perf. 14½*

402 A213 40c dull green .50 .20

First commercial Chilean satellite communications ground station, Longovilo. See No. C312.

Diver with Harpoon Gun A214

1971, Sept. 1

403 A214 1.15e lt & dk green 1.00 .25

404 A214 2.35e vio bl & dp vio bl .30 .25

10th World Championship of Underwater Fishing.

Ferdinand Magellan and Sailing Ship — A215

1971, Nov. 3

405 A215 35c lt vio & brn vio .30 .25

450th anniv. of 1st trip through and discovery of the Strait of Magellan, Oct. 21-Nov. 28, 1520.

Dagoberto Godoy and Plane over Andes — A216

1971, Nov. 4

406 A216 1.15e blue & grn .40 .20

First trans-Andean flight, Dec. 12, 1918.

Virgin of San Cristobal — A217

Chilean Flag and Congress Emblem A218

Congress Emblem and: 4.35e, Church of San Francisco. 9.35e, Central post office, horiz. 18.35e, La Posada (Inn) del Corregidor, horiz.

1971

407 A217 1.15e dk blue .60 .30

408 A218 2.35e ultra & car .60 .30

409 A217 4.35e brown red .60 .30

410 A217 9.35e violet .60 .30

411 A217 18.35e lilac rose 1.25 .30

Nos. 407-411 (5) 3.65 1.50

10th Cong. of the Postal Union of the Americas and Spain, Santiago.

An imperf souvenir sheet containing #407-411 was not valid for postage. Value $11.

Issued: 2.35e, 4.35e, Nov. 5; 1.15e, Nov. 11; 9.35e, Nov. 18; 18.35e, Nov. 19.

Observation Dome, Cerro el Tololo Observatory — A219

1971, Dec. 18

412 A219 1.95e lt & dk blue .35 .20

Boeing 707 over Easter Island A220

1971, Dec. 18

413 A220 2.35e dk brn & yel .40 .20

Inauguration of regular flights: Santiago, Easter Island, Tahiti.

Alonso de Ercilla y Zuniga — A221

1972, Mar. 20 Engr. *Perf. 14*

414 A221 1e dark red .40 .20

4th centenary (in 1969) of "La Araucana," by Alonso de Ercilla y Zuniga (1533-1596), Spanish author. See No. C313.

Map of Antarctica and Dog Sled — A222

1972, Mar. 20 Litho. *Perf. 14½x15*

415 A222 1.15e vio bl & blk .60 .25

416 A222 3.50e blue grn & grn 1.00 .25

10th anniversary (in 1971) of the Antarctic Treaty pledging peaceful uses of and scientific cooperation in Antarctica.

For surcharge see No. 630.

"Your Heart is your Health" — A223

1972, Apr. 2 Litho. *Perf. 14½*

417 A223 1.15e black & car .40 .25

World Health Month.

For surcharge see No. 631.

People and Statement by Pres. Allende — A224

Conference Hall and UN Emblem — A225

1972, Apr. 13 Litho. *Perf. 14½*

418 A224 35c dl grn & buff .35 .25

419 A225 1.15e ultra & pur .40 .20

420 A224 4e dk pur & pale rose .60 .35

421 A225 6e orange & vio bl .50 .20

Nos. 418-421 (4) 1.85 1.00

3rd UN Conf. on Trade and Development (UNCTAD III), Santiago, Apr.-May 1972. Design A224 is perf. horiz. in the middle.

Soldier, 1822, Andes, Military College Emblem A226

1972, June 9

422 A226 1.15e blue & yel .35 .25

Sesquicentennial of Bernardo O'Higgins Military College.

Miner Holding Copper Ingot, Chilean Flag — A227

Sailing Ship — A228

1972, July 11 Litho. *Perf. 15x14½*

423 A227 1.15e blue & rose red .35 .20

424 A227 5e blue, blk & rose red .45 .20

Nationalization of copper industry.

1972, Aug. 4

425 A228 1.15e violet brown .50 .25

Arturo Pratt Naval Training School, sesqui.

Mt. Calan Observatory — A229

1972, Aug. 31 Litho. *Perf. 14½*

426 A229 50c ultra .40 .25

University of Chile Mt. Calan Observatory.

Carrier Pigeon — A230

1972, Oct. 9 Litho. *Perf. 14½*

427	A230	1.15e red lilac & vio	.35	.25

Intl. Letter Writing Week, Oct. 9-15.

René Schneider and Army Flag — A231

1972, Oct. 25 *Perf. 14*

428	A231	2.30e multi	.40	.30

2nd anniv. of the death of Gen. René Schneider. No. 428 is perforated vertically in the middle.

Book and Young People A232

1972, Oct. 31 *Perf. 14½*

429	A232	50c black & dp org	.40	.25

International Book Year 1972.

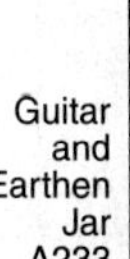

Guitar and Earthen Jar A233

Designs: 2.65e, Fish and produce. 3.50e, Stove, pots and rug, vert.

1972, Nov. 20 Litho. *Perf. 14½*

430	A233	1.15e red & blk	.30	.20
431	A233	2.65e ultra & rose lake	.40	.20
432	A233	3.50e red & red brn	.40	.20
		Nos. 430-432 (3)	1.10	.60

Tourism Year of the Americas.

José M. Carrera Before Execution A234

Map of Antarctica, Flag at Base — A235

1973, Feb. 1 Litho. *Perf. 14½*

433	A234	2.30e lt ultra	.40	.25

Sesquicentennial of the death of José Miguel Carrera (1785-1821), Chilean revolutionist and dictator.

1973, Feb. 8

434	A235	10e ultra & red	.50	.20

Bernardo O'Higgins Antarctic Base, 25th anniv.

Naval Air Service Emblem, Destroyer A236

La Silla Observatory A237

1973, Mar. 16 Litho. *Perf. 14½*

435	A236	20e brt bl & ocher	.45	.25

Chilean Naval Aviation, 50th anniversary.

1973, Apr. 25 Litho. *Perf. 14½*

436	A237	2.30e ultra & blk	.40	.25

INTERPOL Emblem A238

Designs: 50e, Fingerprint over globe.

1973, Sept. 23 Litho. *Perf. 14½*

437	A238	30e bister & ultra	.65	.30
438	A238	50e black & red	.85	.30

50th anniversary of International Criminal Police Organization.

Grapes — A239

Chilean wine export: 100e, Globe inscribed "Chile Exporta Vino."

1973, Dec. 10 Litho. *Perf. 14½*

439	A239	20e buff & lilac	.40	.20
440	A239	100e blue & claret	1.00	.25

UPU Headquarters, Bern — A240

1974, Apr. 4

441	A240	500e on 45c green	.75	.25

UPU cent. No. 441 was not issued without dark green surcharge and overprint.

Bernardo O'Higgins, Armed Forces Emblems — A241

1974, Apr. 11 Litho. *Perf. 14½*

442	A241	30e shown	.30	.20
443	A241	30e Soldiers with mortar	.30	.20
444	A241	30e Navy anti-aircraft gunners	.30	.20
445	A241	30e Pilot in cockpit	.30	.20
446	A241	30e Mounted policeman	.30	.20
		Nos. 442-446 (5)	1.50	1.00

Honoring the Armed Forces.

Soccer Ball and Globe — A242

Traffic Police — A243

1000e, Soccer ball and stadium, horiz.

1974 Litho. *Perf. 14*

447	A242	500e dk red & org	.60	.25
448	A242	1000e bl & indigo	1.25	.30

World Cup Soccer Championship, Munich, June 13-July 7.

A souvenir sheet contains 2 imperf. stamps similar to Nos. 447-448, with blue marginal inscription. Printed on thin card. Size: 90x119mm. Value, $12.

Nos. 386, 355 Surcharged

1974, June Litho. *Perf. 14½*

449	A202	100e on 40c bl grn	.35	.25

Perf. 13x14

450	A174	300e on 50c dl brn	.40	.20

1974, June 20 *Perf. 14½*

451	A243	30e red brn & grn	.40	.20

Traffic safety.

Santiago-Australia Air Service — A244

1974, Sept. 5 Litho. *Perf. 14½x14*

452	A244	Block of 4	4.00	2.50
a.		200e Easter Island turtle	.60	.25
b.		200e Polynesian dancer	.60	.25
c.		200e Map of Fiji Islands	.60	.25
d.		200e Kangaroo	.60	.25

Inauguration of air service by LAN (Chile's national airline) from Santiago to Easter Island, Tahiti, Fiji, Australia.

Globe Cut to Show Mantle and Core — A245

1974, Sept. 9 *Perf. 14x14½*

453	A245	500e red brn & org	.90	.20

International Volcanology Congress, Santiago, Sept. 9-14.

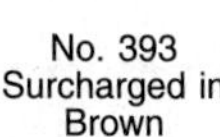

No. 393 Surcharged in Brown

1974, Oct. 24 Litho. *Perf. 14½*

454	A205	100e on 40c green	.40	.25

Inauguration of the O'Higgins National Shrine at Maipu, Oct. 24, 1974.

Juan Fernandez Archipelago — A246

1974, Nov. 22 Litho. *Perf. 14½x14*

455	A246	Block of 4	3.00	2.00
a.		200e Robinson Crusoe Island	.60	.35
b.		200e Chonta palms	.60	.35
c.		200e Mountain goat	.60	.35
d.		200e Spiny rock lobster	.60	.35

400th anniversary of discovery of Juan Fernandez Archipelago.

O'Higgins and Bolivar A247

1974, Dec. 9 *Perf. 14½*

456	A247	100e red brn & buff	.30	.25

Sesquicentennial of the Battles of Junin and Ayacucho.

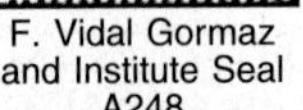

F. Vidal Gormaz and Institute Seal A248

Albert Schweitzer A249

1975, Jan. 22 Litho. *Perf. 14½*

457 A248 100e rose claret & bl .35 .25

Centenary of the Naval Hydrographic Institute; F. Vidal Gormaz was first commandant.

1975, Apr. 7 Litho. *Perf. 14x14½*

458 A249 500e yel & red brn .70 .25

Dr. Albert Schweitzer (1875-1965), medical missionary, birth centenary.

No. 395 Surcharged in Red

1975, Apr. 7 *Perf. 14½*

459 A207 70e on 40c car & lt red brn .35 .25

Volunteer Lifeboat Service — A250

1975, Apr. 15 Litho. *Perf. 14½x14*

460 A250 Block of 4 5.50 3.50
a. 150e Lighthouse .80 .25
b. 150e Shipwreck .80 .25
c. 150e Lifeboat .80 .25
d. 150e Sailor reaching for life preserver .80 .25

Valparaiso Volunteer Lifeboat service, 50th anniversary.

Note: souvenir cards were issued by Chile starting in 1975 for various issues. They were printed on thin card. These are not souvenir sheets.

Frigate Lautaro A251

1975, May 21 Photo. & Engr.

461 A251 500e shown .65 .25
462 A251 500e Corvette Baquedano .65 .25
463 A251 500e Cruiser Chacabuco .65 .25
464 A251 500e Brigantine Goleta Esmeralda .65 .25
a. Block of 4, #461-464 5.25 5.25
465 A251 800e like #461 .85 .30
466 A251 800e like #462 .85 .30
467 A251 800e like #463 .85 .30
468 A251 800e like #464 .85 .30
a. Block of 4, #465-468 7.00 7.00
469 A251 1000e like #461 1.25 .40
470 A251 1000e like #462 1.25 .40
471 A251 1000e like #463 1.25 .40
472 A251 1000e like #464 1.25 .40
a. Block of 4, #469-472 9.25 9.25
Nos. 461-472 (12) 11.00 3.80

Shipwreck of training frigate Lautaro, 30th anniversary. Se-tenant in sheets of 25 (5x5) with 7 Lautaro stamps and 6 each of the others.

Happy Mother, by Alfredo Valenzuela P. — A252

Diego Portales, Finance Minister — A253

Paintings: No. 474, Young Girl, by Francisco Javier Mandiola. No. 475, Lucia Guzman, by Pedro Lira Rencoret. No. 476, Woman, by Magdalena Mira Mena.

1975, Oct. 13 Litho. *Perf. 14½*

473 A252 50c multicolored .80 .25
474 A252 50c multicolored .80 .25
475 A252 50c multicolored .80 .25
476 A252 50c multicolored .80 .25
Nos. 473-476 (4) 3.20 1.00

International Women's Year 1975. Gray inscription on back, printed beneath gum, gives details about painting shown.

Inscribed D. Portales

1975-78 Litho. *Perf. 13x14*

477 A253 10c gray grn .30 .20
478 A253 20c violet ('76) .30 .20
479 A253 30c orange ('76) .30 .20
480 A253 50c lt brown .30 .20
481 A253 1p blue .30 .20
482 A253 1.50p ocher ('76) .30 .20
483 A253 2p gray ('77) .30 .20
483A A253 2.50p citron ('78) .30 .20
483B A253 3.50p pnksh rose ('78) .35 .20
484 A253 5p rose claret .35 .20
Nos. 477-484 (10) 3.10 2.00

See #635-639. For surcharge see #533.

Cochrane and Liberating Squadron, 1820 — A254

#486, Capture of Valdivia, 1820. #487, Capture of Three-master Esmeralda, 1820. #488, Cruiser Cochrane, 1874. #489, Destroyer Cochrane, 1962.

1976, Jan. 6 *Perf. 14½*

485 A254 1p multicolored .70 .25
486 A254 1p multicolored .70 .25
487 A254 1p multicolored .70 .25
488 A254 1p multicolored .70 .25
489 A254 1p multicolored .70 .25
a. Strip of 5, #485-489 3.50 3.50

Lord Thomas Cochrane, first commander of Chilean Navy, birth bicentenary.

Flags of Chile and Bolivia A255

1976, May 25 Litho. *Perf. 14½*

490 A255 1.50p multicolored 1.50 .25

Sesquicentennial of Bolivia's independence.

Lake of the Inca, OAS Emblem A256

1976, June 11

491 A256 1.50p multicolored 1.25 .25

6th General Assembly of the Organization of American States.

George Washington A257

1976, July 3

492 A257 5p multicolored .80 .25

American Bicentennial.

Minerva and Academy Emblem A258

1976, July

493 A258 2.50p multicolored .80 .25

Polytechnic Military Academy, 50th anniv.

Araucan Indian — A259

Designs: 2p, Condor with broken chain. 3p, Winged woman, symbolizing rebirth.

1976, Sept. 20 Litho. *Perf. 14½*

494 A259 1p blue & multi .30 .20
495 A259 2p blue & multi 1.50 .75
496 A259 3p yellow & multi .60 .20
a. Strip of 3, #494-496 2.50 2.00

3rd anniversary of the Military Junta.

View, Antarctica — A260

1977, Feb. 10 Litho. *Perf. 14½*

497 A260 2p multicolored 8.00 .45

Visit of President Augusto Pinochet to Antarctica.

School Emblem, Planted Field — A261

Justice — A262

1977, Mar. 10 *Perf. 14½*

498 A261 2p multicolored 1.40 .30

Cent. of advanced agricultural education.

1977, Mar. 30 Litho. *Perf. 14½*

499 A262 2p brown & slate 1.40 .30

Supreme Court of Justice, sesquicentennial.

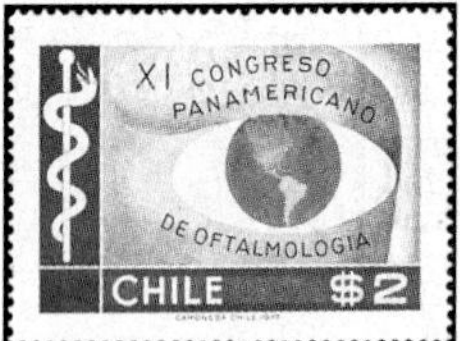

Eye with Globe, Caduceus — A263

1977, Mar. 30 Litho. *Perf. 14½*

500 A263 2p multicolored 1.60 .45

11th Pan-American Ophthalmological Cong.

Mounted Policeman A264

Designs: No. 502, Policewoman with children. No. 503, Paine Peaks and Osorno Volcano, crossed rifle emblem. No. 504, Crossed rifle emblem, mounted and motorcycle policemen, helicopter and automobile, horiz.

1977, Apr. 27

501 A264 2p multicolored .45 .25
502 A264 2p multicolored .45 .25
503 A264 2p multicolored .45 .25
504 A264 2p multicolored .45 .25
Nos. 501-504 (4) 1.80 1.00

Chilean police organization, 50th anniv.

Intelsat Satellite over Globe — A265

1977, May 17 Litho. *Perf. 14½*

505 A265 2p multi .60 .25

World Telecommunications Day.

El Mercurio's First Front Page, Press and Ship — A266

1977, July 5 Litho. *Perf. 14½*

506 A266 2p multi .40 .20

El Mercurio de Valparaiso, first Chilean newspaper, 150th anniversary.

St. Francis, Birds and Cross — A267

Science and Technology A268

1977, July 26 Litho. *Perf. 14½*

507 A267 5p multi 1.40 .25

St. Francis of Assisi, 750th death anniv.

1977, Aug. 26 Litho. *Perf. 14½*

508 A268 4p multi .55 .25

Young Mother Weaving — A269

Diego de Almagro — A270

#510, Handicapped boy in wheelchair & nurse. #511, Children dancing in circle. #512, Old man & home.

1977, Sept. 13 Litho. *Perf. 14½*

509 A269 5p multi .60 .20
510 A269 5p multi .60 .20
511 A269 10p multi, horiz. 1.25 .25
512 A269 10p multi, horiz. 1.25 .25
Nos. 509-512 (4) 3.70 .90

4th anniversary of Government Junta and social services of armed forces.

1977, Oct. 31 Engr. *Perf. 14½*

513 A270 5p rose & carmine .40 .25

Diego de Almagro (1475-1538), leader of Spanish expedition to Chile.

Bell, Letters, Dove and Child A271

1977, Dec. 12 Litho. *Perf. 14½*

514 A271 2.50p multi .40 .20

Christmas 1977.

Loading Timber A272

1978 Litho. *Perf. 15*

515 A272 10p multi 1.25 .25
516 A272 20p multi 1.50 .35

No. 516 inscribed "CORREOS," ship is flying Chilean flag.

Papal Arms and Globe A273

University — A274

1978 Litho. *Perf. 14½*

521 A273 10p multi .85 .25
522 A274 25p multi 1.75 .60

World Peace Day (10p); Catholic University of Valparaiso, 50th anniversary (25p). Issue dates: 10p, July 28; 25p, July 31.

O'Higgins, by Gil de Castro — A275

1978, Aug. 20 Litho. *Perf. 15*

523 A275 10p multi .90 .30

Bernardo O'Higgins (1778-1842), soldier and statesman.

Chacabuco Victory Monument A276

1978, Sept. 11

524 A276 10p multi .90 .30

160th anniv. of O'Higgins victory at Chacabuco, and 5th anniv. of military government.

Teacher Writing on Blackboard — A277

1978, Sept. 21

525 A277 15p multi .85 .25

10th anniversary and 9th Reunion of Inter-american Council for Education, Science and Culture (C.I.E.C.C.), Sept. 21-29.

First National Fleet, by Thomas Somerscales — A278

Design: 30p, Last Moments of Rancagua Battle, by Pedro Subercaseaux.

1978 Litho. *Perf. 15*

526 A278 20p multi 1.90 .45
527 A278 30p multi 2.10 .70

Bernardo O'Higgins (1778-1842), soldier and statesman.

Issue dates: 20p, Oct. 9; 30p, Oct. 2.

San Martin-O'Higgins Medal, by Rene Thenot, 1942 — A279

1978, Oct. 20

528 A279 7p multi .50 .25

José de San Martin and Bernardo O'Higgins, 200th birth anniversaries.

Council Emblem — A280

1978, Nov. 27 Litho. *Perf. 14½*

529 A280 50p multi 3.75 1.50

Intl. Council of Military Sports, 30th anniv.

Three Kings — A281

Virgin and Child — A282

1978, Dec. 14 Litho. *Perf. 14½*

530 A281 3p multi .75 .20
531 A282 11p multi 1.40.40

Christmas 1978.

Philippi Brothers A283

1978, Dec. 29 Litho. *Perf. 14½x15*

532 A283 3.50p multi .40 .20

Bernardo E. Philippi (1811-1852) and Rodulfo A. Philippi (1808-1904), scientists and travelers.

No. 477 Surcharged in Bright Green

1979 Litho. *Perf. 13x14*

533 A253 3.50p on 10c gray grn .25 .20

Flags of Chile and Salvation Army — A284

1979, Mar. 17 Litho. *Perf. 14½*

534 A284 10p multi 1.25 .65

Salvation Army in Chile, 70th anniversary.

Pope Paul VI (1897-1978) — A285

1979, Mar. 30

535 A285 11p multi 1.25 .75

Battle of Maipu Monument — A286

1979, Apr. 17 Litho. *Perf. 14½*

536 A286 8.50p multi 1.40 .50

Bernardo O'Higgins (1778-1842), Liberator of Chile.

Naval Battles A287

1979, May 21 Litho. *Perf. 14½*

537 A287 3.50p Angamos .70 .25
538 A287 3.50p Iquique .70 .25
539 A287 3.50p Punta Gruesa .70 .25
Nos. 537-539 (3) 2.10 .75

Centenary of victorious naval battles against Peru.

1903 Ambulance and Red Cross — A288

1979, June 29 Litho. *Perf. 14½*

540 A288 25p multi 3.50 1.00

75th anniversary of Chilean Red Cross.

Diego Portales — A289

1979-86 Litho. *Perf. 13½*

542 A289 1.50p ocher .25 .20
543 A289 2p gray ('81) .25 .20
544 A289 3.50p red .30 .20
545 A289 4.50p bl grn ('81) .40 .20
546 A289 5p rose claret .50 .20
547 A289 6p emerald .60 .30
548 A289 7p yellow ('82) .55 .30
549 A289 10p blue ('82) .80 .30
550 A289 12p orange ('86) .35 .20
Nos. 542-550 (9) 4.00 2.10

1.50p, 3.50p, 5p and 6p inscribed "D. Portales."

People and Flag — A290

1979, Aug. 28 Litho. *Perf. 14½*

551 A290 10p multi .90 .60

Yugoslavian immigration, centenary.

Coat of Arms and Mt. Castillo A290a

1979, Oct. 12 Litho. *Perf. 14½*

552 A290a 20p multi 2.00 1.00

Coyhaique 50th anniv.

IYC Emblem, Playground — A291

IYC Emblem, Children's Drawings: 11p, Girl and shadow, vert. 12p, Dancing.

1979, Oct. 9 *Perf. 14½*

553 A291 9.50p multi .80 .55
554 A291 11p multi 1.00 .60
555 A291 12p multi 1.50 .65
Nos. 553-555 (3) 3.30 1.80

International Year of the Child.

Telecom 79 A292

1979, Oct. 26 Litho. *Perf. 14½*

556 A292 15p multi 1.50 .75

3rd World Telecommunications Exhibition, Geneva, Sept. 20-26.

Puerto Williams, 25th Anniversary — A293

1979, Nov. 21

557 A293 3.50p multi .60 .20

Adoration of the Kings A294

1979, Dec. 4 Litho. *Perf. 15*

558 A294 3.50p multi .60 .25

Christmas 1979.

Rafael Sotomayor, Minister of War — A295

Military heroes.

1979, Dec. 29 *Perf. 13½*

559 A295 3.50p ocher & brn .50 .25
560 A295 3.50p Erasmo Escala .50 .25
561 A295 3.50p Emilio Sotomayor .50 .25
562 A295 3.50p Eleuterio Ramirez .50 .25
a. Block of 4, #559-562 2.00 2.00

Bell UH-1 Rescue Helicopter at Tinguiririca Volcano, by S.O. Mococain — A296

Air Force, 50th Anniversary: No. 564, Flying boat Catalina Skua over Antarctic, by E.F. Alvarez. No. 565, F5-E Tiger II over Andes, by M.M. Barria.

1980, Mar. 21 Litho. *Perf. 13½*

563 A296 3.50p shown .50 .25
564 A296 3.50p Jet .50 .25
565 A296 3.50p Sea plane .50 .25
Nos. 563-565 (3) 1.50 .75

The Death of Bueras, by Pedro Leon Carmona — A297

1980, Apr. 14 Litho. *Perf. 13½*

566 A297 12p multi 1.00 .50

Charge of Bueras, Battle of Maipo, 1818.

Rotary International, 75th Anniversary — A298

1980, Apr. 15

567 A298 10p multi 1.00 .45

Gen. Manuel Baquedano, by Pedro Subercaseaux A299

Gen. Pedro Lagos, Battle Scene, by Subercaseaux — A300

Battle of Morro de Arica Centenary (Subercaseaux Paintings): No. 570, Commander Juan J. San Martin, battle scene.

1980, June 7 Litho. *Perf. 13½*

568 A299 3.50p multi .40 .20
569 A300 3.50p multi .40 .20
570 A300 3.50p multi .40 .20
Nos. 568-570 (3) 1.20 .60

Score and Perez's Silhouette — A301

1980, June 27 Litho. *Perf. 13½*

571 A301 6p multi .60 .30

Osman Perez Freire (1880-1930), composer, and fragment from his song "Ay, Ay, Ay."

Mt. Gasherbrum II, Chilean Flag, Ice Pick — A302

1980, July 9

572 A302 15p multi 1.40 .60

Chilean Himalayan expedition, June 1979.

"Charity," Stained-glass Window A303

1980, July 18

573 A303 10p multi 1.50 .35

Daughters of Charity, 125th anniv. in Chile.

Condor, Colors of Chile — A304

1980, Sept. 11 Litho. *Perf. 13½*

574 A304 3.50p multi .40 .25

17th anniversary of constitution.

Inca Child Mummy A305

Pablo Burchard, by Pedro Lira A306

1980, Sept. 14
575 A305 5p shown .60 .20
576 A305 5p Claudio Gay .60 .20
a. Pair, #575-576 + label 1.40 1.25

Natl. Museum of Natural History (founded by Claudio Gay, 1800-73) sesqui.

1980, Sept. 27 Litho. *Perf. 13½*
577 A306 3.50p multi .40 .20

Museum of Fine Art centenary (directed by Burchard, 1932).

Santiago International Fair — A307

1980, Oct. 30
578 A307 3.50p multi .40 .20

Nativity — A308

Christmas 1980: 3.50p, Family, vert.

1980, Nov. 25 Litho. *Perf. 13½*
579 A308 3.50p multi .60 .25
580 A308 10.50p multi 1.25 .45

Infantryman 1879 — A309

Congress Emblem — A310

Pacific War period uniforms, 1879.

1980, Nov. 27
581 A309 3.50p shown .60 .20
582 A309 3.50p Cavalry officer .60 .20
583 A309 3.50p Artillery officer .60 .20
584 A309 3.50p Engineer colonel .60 .20
a. Block of 4, #581-584 3.50 3.50

See Nos. 606-609.

1980, Dec. 1
585 A310 11.50p multi 1.25 .60

23rd Intl. Cong. of Military Medicine & Pharmacy.

Eradication of Hoof and Mouth Disease A311

1981, Jan. 16 Litho. *Perf. 13½*
586 A311 9.50p multi .90 .25

Moai Statues, Easter Island — A312

1981, Jan. 28 Litho. *Perf. 13½*
587 A312 3.50p shown .30 .25
588 A312 3.50p Robinson Crusoe Island .50 .25
589 A312 10.50p Penguins, Antarctic Territory 2.40 .60
Nos. 587-589 (3) 3.20 1.10

National Heroine Javiera Carrera, by O.M. Pizarro, Birth Bicentenary — A313

1981, Mar. 20
590 A313 3.50p multi .40 .20

UPU Membership Centenary A314

1981, Apr. 1
591 A314 3.50p multi .40 .25

C130 Hercules Air Force Transport Plane Unloading Cargo — A315

1981, Apr. 21
592 A315 3.50p multi 1.00 .40

Lieutenant Marsh Air Force Base, 1st anniv.

13th World Telecommunications Day — A316

1981, May 17 Litho. *Perf. 13½*
593 A316 3.50p multi .40 .20

Arturo Prat Naval Base A317

1981, June 23 Litho. *Perf. 13½*
594 A317 3.50p multi .75 .25

Capt. Jose Luis Araneda A318

1981, June 26
595 A318 3.50p multi .40 .20

Battle of Sangrar centenary.

Philatelic Society of Chile, 90th Anniv. A319

1981, July 29 Litho. *Perf. 13½*
596 A319 4.50p multi .40 .20

Minister Recabarren and Chief Conuepan Giving Speeches, by Hector Robles Acuna — A320

1981, Aug. 7
597 A320 4.50p multi .90 .25

Temuco city centenary.

Exports A321

1981, Aug. 31 Litho. *Perf. 13½*
598 A321 14p multi .80 .35

Presidential Palace — A322

1981, Sept. 11
599 A322 4.50p multi .80 .20

Natl. liberation, 8th anniv.

St. Vincent de Paul, 400th Birth Anniv. A323

1981, Sept. 27 Litho. *Perf. 13½*
600 A323 4.50p multi .50 .25

Andres Bello, Poet and Sholar, Birth Bicentenary A324

1981, Sept. 29
601 A324 4.50p Coin .40 .25
602 A324 9.50p Bust, books .60 .30
603 A324 11.50p Statue, arms 1.00 .40
Nos. 601-603 (3) 2.00 .95

2nd Congress of South American Uniformed Police A325

1981, Oct. 15
604 A325 4.50p multi .50 .20

World Food Day A326

1981, Oct. 16
605 A326 5.50p multi .50 .25

Uniform Type of 1980

1879 Parade Uniforms.

1981, Nov. 6 *Perf. 13½*
606 A309 5.50p Infantry private .80 .25
607 A309 5.50p Cadet .80 .25
608 A309 5.50p Cavalryman .80 .25
609 A309 5.50p Artilleryman .80 .25
a. Block of 4, #606-609 4.00 3.00

Intl. Year of the Disabled A327

1981, Nov. 11
610 A327 5.50p multi 1.00 .30

Christmas 1981 — A328

1981, Nov. 25
611 A328 5.50p Nativity .50 .25
612 A328 11.50p Three Kings 1.00 .40

50th Anniv. of Federico Santa Maria Technical University — A329

1981, Dec 1 Litho. *Perf. 13½*
613 A329 5.50p multi .40 .25

Dario Salas (1881-1941), Educator — A330

1981, Dec. 4
614 A330 5.50p multi .45 .25

FIDA '82, 2nd Natl. Air Force Fair — A331

1982, Mar. 6 Litho. *Perf. 13½*
615 A331 4.50p multi .50 .20

1980 Constitution — A332

1982, Mar. 11
616 A332 4.50p Cardinal Caro, family .50 .25
617 A332 11p Diego Portales 1.50 .40
618 A332 30p Bernardo O'Higgins 2.50 .90
Nos. 616-618 (3) 4.50 1.55

Panamerican Institute of Geography and History, 12th General Assembly A333

1982, Mar. 22 Litho. *Perf. 13½*
619 A333 4.50p multi .50 .25

American Air Forces Cooperation System — A334

1982, Apr. 12
620 A334 4.50p multi .45 .20

Pedro Montt — A335

Fish Exports — A336

1982, Mar. 27
621 A335 4.50p light vio .50 .20

1982, May 3 Litho. *Perf. 13½*
622 A336 20p multi 2.00 .75

Scouting Year — A337

#623b, Robert Baden-Powell.

1982, May 21 Litho. *Perf. 13*
623 Pair *37.50 27.50*
a.-b. A337 4.50p, either single *10.00 3.50*

Battle of Concepcion Centenary A338

Chacabuco Regiment officers killed in battle.

1982, June 18 Litho. *Perf. 13½*
624 Block of 4 2.50 2.50
a. A338 4.50p I. Carrera Pinto .50 .20
b. A338 4.50p A. Perez Canto .50 .20
c. A338 4.50p J. Montt Salamanca .50 .20
d. A338 4.50p L. Cruz Martinez .50 .20

UN World Assembly on Aging, July 26-Aug. 6 — A339

1982, Aug. 5
625 A339 4.50p multi .40 .25

TB Bacillus Centenary A340

1982, Aug. 31
626 A340 4.50p multi .40 .20

9th Anniv. of National Liberation — A341

1982, Sept. 11 Litho. *Perf. 13½*
627 A341 4.50p multi .40 .20

Christmas 1982 — A342

Children's drawings.

1982, Nov. 2
628 A342 10p multi 1.00 .25
629 A342 25p multi, vert. 1.50 .60

Nos. 416-417 Surcharged in Green or Black

1982, Nov. *Perf. 14½x15, 14½*
630 A222 1p on 3.50p bl grn & grn (G) .20 .20
631 A223 2p on 1.15p blk & car .20 .20

Marist Alumni, 9th World Congress A342a

Virgin Mary & Marcellus Champagnat (founder of Marist Brotherhood), stained glass window, Church of the Sacred Heart of Jesus, Barcelona.

1982, Nov. 11 Litho. *Perf. 13½*
631A A342a 7p multi 1.40 .40

El Sur Newspaper Centenary A342b

1982, Nov. 15
631B A342b 7p Wooden hand-press, mast-head .50 .25

110th Anniv. of South American Steamship Co. — A342c

1982, Dec. 20
631C A342c 7p Steamer Copiapo .75 .30

60th Anniv. of Radio Club of Chile — A342d

1982, Dec. 29
631D A342d 7p multi .50 .25

First Anniv. of Postal Agreement with Order of Malta — A343

1983, Mar. 30 Litho. *Perf. 13½*
632 25p Arms of Order of Malta 2.00 .40
633 50p Chile 4.00 .80
a. Pair, #632-633 6.00 5.00

D.D. No. 20
This and similar inscriptions indicate that the stamps would be sold at a discount if purchased in large quantities.

D. Portales Type of 1975 Inscribed Diego Portales and:

Ramon Barros Luco A344

Juan Luis Sanfuentes A344a

1983-88 Litho. *Perf. 13½*

634	A344	1p	grnsh bl	.20	.20
635	A253	1p	chalky bl	.20	.20
636	A253	1.50p	ocher	.20	.20
637	A344	2p	dl vio ('84)	.20	.20
638	A253	2p	ol gray	.20	.20
639	A253	2.50p	lemon	.20	.20
640	A253	5p	red lilac	.35	.25
641	A344	5p	crim rose	.20	.20
642	A344a	5p	red ('84)	.20	.20
643	A344	7p	ultra	.30	.20
644	A344a	9p	brn ('84)	.25	.20

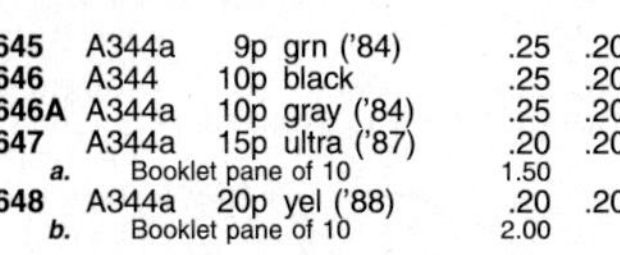

645 A344a 9p grn ('84) .25 .20
646 A344 10p black .25 .20
646A A344a 10p gray ('84) .25 .20
647 A344a 15p ultra ('87) .20 .20
a. Booklet pane of 10 1.50
648 A344a 20p yel ('88) .20 .20
b. Booklet pane of 10 2.00

Nos. 644, 647, 648 inscribed "D.S. No. 20."
Issued: No. 640, 8/85.
For surcharge see No. 779.

50th Anniv. of Bureau of Investigation
A345

1983, June 19 Litho. *Perf. 13½*
649 A345 20p multi 1.25 .50

Antonio Cardinal Samore (1905-1983) — A346

1983, June 26
650 A346 30p multi 2.00 .60

Centenary of Cliff Elevators in Valparaiso
A347

1983, Aug. 19 Litho. *Perf. 13½*
651 A347 40p multi 4.00 .45

Pucara de Quitor Settlement Ruins, San Pedro de Atacama — A348

No. 653, Llamas, rock painting, Rio Ibanez, Aisen. No. 654, Duck-shaped jug with human head, Diaguita cultures. No. 655, Puoko Tangata carved stone head, Easter Isld.

1983, Aug. 26
652 A348 7p multi .75 .30
653 A348 7p multi .75 .30
654 A348 7p multi .75 .30
655 A348 7p multi, vert. .20 .20
Nos. 652-655 (4) 2.45 1.10

10th Anniv. of National Liberation — A349

1983, Sept. 11 Litho. *Perf. 13½*
656 A349 7p Angel with broken chains .60 .25
657 A349 7p Couple, flag .60 .25
658 A349 10p Family, torch .60 .25
659 A349 40p Coat of arms, "10" 2.00 .75
a. Strip of 4, #656-659 5.00 3.50

For surcharges see Nos. 669-670.

Famous Hondurans
A350

#660, Francisco Morazan (1792-1842), Advocate of United Central America. #661, Jose Cecilio Del Valle (1777-1834), Scholar and Leader of Pan Americanism.

1983, Oct. 3 Litho. *Perf. 13½*
660 A350 7p multi .40 .20
661 A350 7p multi .40 .20
a. Pair, #660-661 .80 .80

World Communications Year — A351

1983, Oct. 13 Litho. *Perf. 13½*
662 7p Central P.O. .85 .25
663 7p Challenger spaceship .85 .25
a. A351 Pair, #662-663 1.75 1.75

Christmas 1983 — A353

Childrens' Drawings: 10p Chilean Peasant, Hanny Chacon. 30p, Holy Family. Lucrecia Cardenas, vert.

1983, Nov. 14 Litho. *Perf. 13*
664 A353 10p multi .50 .20
665 A353 30p multi 1.50 .40

Design descriptions printed on back on top of gum.

State Railways Centenary — A354

Train Cars: a, Presidential coach, 1911. b, Service coach, 1910; tender, 1929. c, Locomotive Type 80, 1929.

1984, Jan. 4 Litho. *Perf. 13½*
666 Strip of 3 8.50 7.50
a.-c. A354 9p, any single 2.00 .40

3rd Intl. Air Fair, Santiago, Mar. 3-11 — A355

1984, Jan. 31 Litho. *Perf. 13½*
667 A355 9p Flags, plane .90 .20

20th Anniv. of Nuclear Energy Commission — A356

1984, Apr. 16 Litho. *Perf. 13*
668 A356 9p multi .50 .25

Nos. 656-657 Surcharged in Purple

1984, June 11 Litho. *Perf. 13½*
669 A349 9p on 7p #656 .45 .25
670 A349 9p on 7p #657 .45 .25
a. Pair, #669-670 1.00 .75

Antarctic Colonization — A357

1984, June 18
671 A357 15p Women's expedition .60 .35
672 A357 15p Villa las Estrellas Station .60 .35
673 A357 15p Scouts, flag, Air Force base .60 .35
a. Strip of 3, #671-673 4.75 4.50

10th Anniv. of Regionalization — A358

Designs: a, Parinacota Church, Tarapaca. b, El Tatio geyser, Antofagasta. c, Copper mining, Atacama. d, Tololo Observatory, Coquimbo. e, Valparaiso Harbor, Valparaiso. f, Ahu Akivi head sculptures, Easter Isld. g, St. Francis Church, Santiago. h, El Hunique House, O'Higgins. i, Colburn Machicura Dam and Hydroelectric Power Station, Maule. j, Sta. Juana de Guadalcazar Fort, Bio-Bio. k, Indian woman, Araucania. l, Guar Isld. Church, Los Lagos. m, Main road, Gen. del Campo. n, Shepherds' Monument, Magellanes and Antarctic. o, Family, Villa las Estrellas Station, Antarctic.

1984, July 11
674 Sheet of 15 13.00 13.00
a.-o. A358 9p multi, any single .45 .35

Capt. Pedro Sarmiento de Gamboa, Map, 1584 — A359

1984, July 31 Litho. *Perf. 13*
675 A359 100p multi 4.50 1.00

400th anniv. of Spanish presence in Straits of Magellan.

State Bank of Chile Centenary — A360

1984, Sept. 6 Litho. *Perf. 13½*
676 A360 35p Founder Antonio Varas de la Barra, coin 1.00 .45

11th Anniv. of Liberation — A361

1984, Sept. 11
677 A361 20p Monument to O'Higgins 1.10 .30

Circus Centenary — A362

1984, Sept. 28 Litho. *Perf. 13½*
678 A362 45p Clown 1.50 .70

Endangered Species, World Wildlife Emblem — A363

1985, July Litho. *Perf. 13½*
679 A363 9p Chinchilla *5.50* .25
680 A363 9p Blue whale *5.50* .25
681 A363 9p Sea lions *5.50* .25
682 A363 9p Chilean huemuls *5.50* .25
a. Block of 4, #679-682 *22.50* 9.00

Christmas 1984 — A364

Children's drawings.

1984, Nov. 20 Litho. *Perf. 13½*
683 A364 9p Shepherds .40 .20
684 A364 40p Bethlehem 1.50 .40

Santiago University Planetarium Opening — A365

1984, Dec. 29
685 A365 10p multi .70 .20

Flora and Fauna — A366

Wildlife: a, Conepatus chinga. b, Leucocoryne purpurea. c, Himantopus himantopus. d, Lutra felina. e, Balbisia peduncularis. f, Psittacus cyanalysias. g, Pudu pudu. h, Fuschia magellanica. i, Diuca diuca. j, Dusicyon griseus. k, Alstroemeria sierrae. l, Glaucidium nanum.

1985, Feb.
686 Block of 12 13.00 9.00
a.-l. A366 10p, Any single .65 .35

American Airforces Cooperation System, 25th Anniv. A367

1985, Mar. 26
687 A367 45p Emblem, flags 2.00 1.10

Chile-Argentina Peace Treaty — A368

1985, May 2 Litho. *Perf. 13½*
688 A368 20p Papal arms, flags 2.50 .50

Fr. Joseph Kentenich (1885-1968), Founder, Intl. Schonstatt Movement of Catholic Laymen A369

1985, May 19 Litho. *Perf. 13½*
689 A369 40p Portrait, La Florida Sanctuary, Santiago .70 .40

Antarctic Treaty, 25th Anniv. — A370

Resources, research: 15p, Krill, pack ice, map. 20p, Seismological Station, O'Higgins' Base. 35p, Georeception Station, dish receiver.

1985, June 21
690 A370 15p multi .65 .35
691 A370 20p multi .85 .50
692 A370 35p multi 1.50 .75
Nos. 690-692 (3) 3.00 1.60

Canis Fulvipes — A371

Endangered wildlife: b, Phoenicoparrus jamesi. c, Fulica gigantea. d, Lutra provocax.

1985, Aug. 9 Litho. *Perf. 13½*
693 Block of 4 10.00 3.50
a.-d. A371 20p, any single 1.40 .30

Intl. Youth Year A372

UN, 40th Anniv. A373

1985, Aug. 31
694 A372 15p multi .50 .25
695 A373 15p multi .50 .25
a. Pair, #694-695 1.50 1.50

Gen. Jose Miguel Carrera Verdugo (1785-1821) — A374

1985, Oct. 8 Litho. *Perf. 13½*
696 A374 40p multi .90 .55

Farmer and Ox-drawn Hay Cart — A375

Folklore: b, Street photographer, wet plate camera. c, One-man band. d, Basket maker.

1985, Oct.
697 Block of 4 1.25 .90
a.-d. A375 10p, any single .25 .20

For surcharges see Nos. 770-771.

Christmas 1985 — A376

Holy Family — A376a

Winning children's drawings, 7th natl. design contest.

1985, Nov. 4
698 A376 15p Nativity .55 .20
699 A376 100p Father Christmas, vert. 3.75 1.00

Nos. 698-699 inscribed in black on gummed side with child's name, age, school and region.

1985 Litho. *Perf. 13½*
699A A376a 10p buff & brn .30 .20

For surcharge see No. 768.

16th Armed Forces Conference — A377

20p, Cavalryman, Directorial Escort, 1818. 35p, Officer, Grand Guard, 1813.

1985, Nov. 15 Litho. *Perf. 13½*
700 A377 20p multicolored .75 .25
701 A377 35p multicolored 1.00 .35

Halley's Comet — A378

1985, Nov. 29 Litho. *Perf. 13½*
702 A378 45p multicolored .75 .25
a. Souvenir sheet 17.50 17.50

No. 702a exists imperf. Value $27.50.

Natl. Solidarity Campaign — A379

1985
703 A379 5p red & blue .50 .50

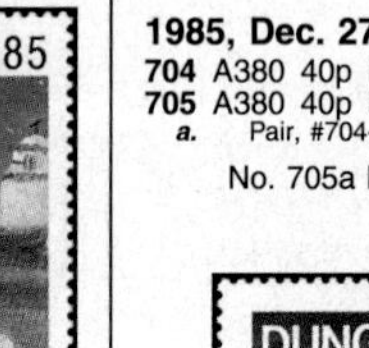

Campaign for Prevention of Forest Fires — A380

1985, Dec. 27
704 A380 40p Forest .75 .40
705 A380 40p Fire destruction .75 .40
a. Pair, #704-705 2.75 1.50

No. 705a has continuous design.

Dungeness Point Lighthouse, Straits of Magellan — A381

1986, Jan. 26
706 A381 45p shown 1.40 .45
707 A381 45p Evangelistas Lighthouse 1.40 .45
a. Pair, #706-707 3.50 2.25

No. 707a continuous design.

View of Santiago, Mackenna — A382

1986, Jan. 28
708 A382 30p multi .45 .20

Benjamin Vicuna Mackenna (d. 1886), municipal superintendent of Santiago, 1872-1875.

Diego Portales, Natl. Crest, Text — A382a

1986, Feb. Litho. *Perf. 13½*
708A A382a 12p on 3.50p multi .45 .20

No. 708A not issued without surcharge.

1986 World Cup Soccer Championships, Mexico — A383

Host stadiums: 15p, Natl. Stadium, Chile, 1962. 20p, Aztec Stadium, Mexico, 1970. 35p, Maracana Stadium, Brazil, 1950. 50p, Wembley Stadium, Great Britain, 1966.

1986, Feb. 18
709 A383 15p multi .40 .25
710 A383 20p multi .55 .25
711 A383 35p multi .80 .35
712 A383 50p multi 1.25 .50
Nos. 709-712 (4) 3.00 1.35

Environmental Conservation — A384

1986, Feb. 28

713 A384 20p Water .65 .20
714 A384 20p Air .65 .20
715 A384 20p Soil .65 .20
Nos. 713-715 (3) 1.95 .60

Sailing Ship Santiaguillo, Flags — A385

1986, Mar. 20

716 A385 40p multi .80 .45

Discovery of Valparaiso Bay, 450th anniv.

A386

A387

1986, Apr. 9

717 A386 45p multi 1.00 .45

Interamerican Development Bank, 25th anniv.

1986, Apr. 30 Litho. *Perf. 13½*

718 A387 15p multi .65 .25

St. Rosa de Lima (1586-1617), sanctuary at Pelequen.

Moai Statues, Easter Is. — A388

1986, May 15

719 A388 60p Raraku Volcano 1.50 .50
a. Souvenir sheet *10.50 10.50*
720 A388 100p Tongariki Ruins 2.75 .85
a. Souvenir sheet *16.00 16.00*

AMERIPEX '86 — A389

1986, May 23

721 A389 100p multi 2.50 1.10

Historic Naval Ships — A390

1986, May 30

722 A390 35p Schooner Ancud, 1843 .70 .35
723 A390 35p Armed merchantman Aguilar, 1830 .70 .35
724 A390 35p Corvette Esmeralda, 1856 .70 .35
725 A390 35p Frigate O'Higgins, 1834 .70 .35
a. Block of 4, #722-725 5.00 5.00

See Nos. 752-753.

Paintings by Juan Francisco Gonzalez (1853-1933) A391

1986, June 24

726 A391 30p Rush and Chrysanthemums .75 .30
727 A391 30p Gate of La Serena .75 .30
a. Pair, #726-727 2.00 1.50

Exports — A392

Designs: a, Saltpeter. b, Iron. c, Copper. d, Molybdenum.

1986 Litho. *Perf. 13½*

728 A392 Block of 4 1.60 1.25
a.-d. 12p, any single .25 .20

Antarctic Fauna — A393

a, Sterna vittata. b, Phalacrocorax atriceps. c, Aptenodytes forsteri. d, Catharacta lonnberg.

1986, July 16 Litho. *Perf. 13½*

729 Block of 4 6.50 4.00
a.-d. A393 40p, any single 1.00 .40

Writers — A394

No. 730, Pedro de Ona (1570-1643). No. 731, Vicente Huidobro (1893-1948).

1986, Aug. 19

730 A394 20p multi .40 .25
731 A394 20p multi .40 .25
a. Pair, #730-731 1.50 .90

Has continuous design.

Military Academy, Cent. — A395

1986, Sept. 8 Litho. *Perf. 13½*

732 A395 45p Major-General, 1878 .75 .40
733 A395 45p Major, 1950 .75 .40
a. Pair, #732-733 1.75 1.10

Art A396

1986, Oct. 17 *Perf. 13½*

734 A396 30p Diaguita urn, duck jug .50 .25
735 A396 30p Mapuche silver ornament, embroidery .50 .25
a. Pair, #734-735 2.00 1.50

Christmas — A397

8th Natl. design contest-winning children's drawings.

1986, Nov. 19 Litho. *Perf. 13½*

736 A397 15p multi .60 .20
737 A397 105p multi 2.40 .55

Nos. 736-737 inscribed in black on gummed side with child's name, age, school and region.

Christmas A397a

Design: Shepherds see star, Bethlehem.

1986, Nov. Litho. *Perf. 13½*

737A A397a 12p multi .35 .20

Intl. Peace Year — A398

1986, Nov. 26

738 A398 85p multi 1.50 .60

Natl. Women Volunteers — A399

1986, Dec. 15 Litho. *Perf. 13½*

739 A399 15p multi .35 .20

Crowning of Our Lady of Mt. Carmel, Patron of Chile, by Pius XI, 60th Anniv. — A400

1986, Dec. 19

740 A400 25p multi .70 .25

Andean Railways Kitson-Meyer No. 59, 1907, Designed by Robert Sterling — A401

1987, Jan. 27 Litho. *Perf. 13½*

741 A401 95p multi 2.75 1.10

Arturo Prat Naval Base, Greenwich Island, the Antarctic, 40th Anniv. — A402

Illustration reduced.

1987, Feb. 6

742 100p Storage and power supplies 4.50 2.00
743 100p Working and living quarters 4.50 2.00
a. A402 Pair, #742-743 9.00 7.00

State Visit of Pope John Paul II, Apr. 1-6, 1987 A403

Pope John Paul II and: 20p, Christ the Redeemer statue. 25p, Votive Church, Maipu. 90p, Cross of the Seas, Straits of Magellan. 115p, Virgin of the Hill.

1987 Litho. *Perf. 13½*

744 A403 20p multi .30 .20
745 A403 25p multi .40 .20
746 A403 90p multi 1.40 .60
747 A403 115p multi 1.90 .95
a. Souv. sheet of one 4.75 4.75
747B A403 115p multi 2.00 1.00
Nos. 744-747B (5) 6.00 2.95

No. 747a sold for 250p.

No. 747B differs from No. 747 in that the Statue of the Virgin has a halo and Pope John Paul II is smiling.

Issue date: Nos. 744-747a, Apr. 6.

Los Carabineros (Natl. Guard), 60th Anniv. — A404

World Youth Soccer Championships A405

1987, Apr. 21

748 A404 50p Cavalry showmanship .80 .35
749 A404 50p Air-sea rescue .80 .35
a. Pair, #748-749 2.40 2.00

1987, May 28

b, Concepcion Stadium, kick play. c, Antofagasta Stadium, dribbling the ball. d, Valparaiso Stadium, heading the ball.

750 Block of 4 3.50 3.50
a.-d. A405 45p any single .70 .50

Souvenir Sheet

751 A405 45p Four players 3.00 3.00

No. 751 sold for 150p.

Naval Ships Type of 1986

1987, May 29

752 A390 60p Battleship Almirante Latorre, 1913 1.00 .60
753 A390 60p Cruiser O'Higgins, 1936 1.00 .60
a. Pair, #752-753 3.00 2.00

Diego Portales (1793-1837), Finance Minister — A406

1987, June 16

754 A406 30p multi .50 .25

Public Works Ministry, Cent. — A407

1987, June 26

755 A407 25p multi .55 .30

Infantry School, Cent. — A408

1987, July 9

756 A408 50p Entrance .50 .25
757 A408 100p Soldiers, natl. flag 1.00 .50

Miniature Sheet

Flora and Fauna — A409

Designs: a, Chiasognathus granti. b, Calidris alba. c, Hippocamelus antisensis. d, Jubaea chilensis. e, Colias vauthieri. f, Pandion haliaetus. g, Cephalorhynchus commersonii. h, Austrocedrus chilensis. i, Jasus frontalis. j, Stephanoides fernandensis. k, Vicugna vicugna. l, Thyrsopteris elegans. m, Lithodes antarctica. n, Pterocnemia pennata. o, Lagidium viscacia. p, Cereus atacamensis.

1987, July 30

758 Sheet of 16 13.00 13.00
a.-p. A409 25p any single .45 .25

Intl. Year of Shelter for the Homeless A410

The Guitarist of Quinchamali A411

1987, Aug. 6

759 A410 40p multi .60 .30

1987, July Litho. *Perf. 13½*

Legends and folk tales: b, El Caleuche. c, El Pihuychen. d, La Lola.

760 Block of 4 1.60 1.00
a.-d. A411 15p any single .20 .20

Nos. 760a-760d exist ovptd. "D.S. No 20." in golden brown on back. Value $2.50.

For surcharges see Nos. 812, 1104.

FISA '87, Santiago — A412

1987, Oct. 16 Litho. *Perf. 13½*

761 A412 20p multi .25 .20

25th Intl. agriculture and exports exhibition.

Rear Admiral Carlos Condell de la Haza (1813-1887), Naval Hero at the Battle of the Pacific — A413

1987, Nov. 7

762 A413 50p multi 1.10 .65

Christmas 1987 — A414

COBRE '87, Intl. Conf. on Copper — A415

Children's drawings: 30p, Holy Family. 100p, Star Over Bethlehem, horiz.

1987, Nov. 13

763 A414 30p multi .60 .25
764 A414 100p multi 2.40 .75

1987, Nov. 23

765 A415 40p Foundry .60 .30
a. Souv. sheet of one 2.50 2.50

No. 765 sold for 150p.

Natl. Antarctic Exploration Commission, 25th Anniv. — A415a

1987, Dec. 11 Litho. *Perf. 13½*

765B A415a 45p multi 1.10 .50

Ramon Freire Serrano (1787-1851), Chief of State A416

To Smoke Is To Contaminate A417

1987, Dec. 29 *Perf. 13x13½*

766 A416 20p pale lil & rose claret .40 .30

1987, Dec. Litho. *Perf. 13½*

767 A417 15p blue & ver .30 .20

Natl. Commission for the Control of Smoking.

No. 699A Surcharged in Green

1987 Litho. *Perf. 13½*

768 A376a 12p on 10p buff & brn .30 .20

Christmas 1987 — A418

1987, Dec.

769 A418 15p ultra, org yel & blk .30 .20
a. Bklt. pane of 10 4.00

No. 769a exists ovptd. "D.S. No 20." on back.

No. 697 Surcharged with New Value and 6 Bars in Rose Red and Black

1987, Dec.

770 Block of 4 1.10 .80
a.-d. A375 12p on 10p, #697a-697d .25 .20
771 Block of 4 1.10 .80
a.-d. A375 15p on 10p, #697a-697d .25 .20

St. John Bosco (1815-1888), Educator Canonized in 1934 — A419

1988, Jan. 29

772 A419 40p multi .75 .30

20th Music Week, Frutillar — A420

1988, Jan. 27

773 A420 30p multi .50 .25

FIDA '88, 5th Intl. Aviation Fair — A421

1988, Mar. 4 Litho. *Perf. 13½*

774 A421 60p dark blue & blue .90 .60

1988 Summer Olympics, Seoul — A422

Flags of Chile and Korea, events: 50p, Shot put, pole vault, javelin. 100p, Swimming, cycling, running.

1988, Mar. 18 *Perf. 13½*

775 A422	50p multi	1.00	.50
776 A422	100p multi	2.25	.90
a.	Souv. sheet of 2, #775-776	4.50	4.50

No. 776a sold for 250p.

Natl. Agricultural Soc., 150th Anniv. — A423

1988, Apr. 8

777 A423	45p multi	1.40	.35

Intl. Red Cross and Red Crescent Organizations, 125th Annivs. — A424

1988, May 10

778 A424	150p multi	2.10	.65

No. 645 Surcharged

1988 **Litho.** *Perf. 13½*

779 A344a	20p on 9p green	.25	.20

Easter Island Folk Art — A425

Designs: Nos. 780, 782, Carved wooden head from Kava Kava. Nos. 781, 783, Bird man stone carving from Tangata Manu.

1988, Apr. 1 **Litho.** *Perf. 13½*

780 A425	20p brick red & blk	.30	.20
781 A425	20p brick red & blk	.30	.20
a.	Bklt. pane, 6 #780, 4 #781	2.00	
b.	Pair, #780-781	.65	.65
782 A425	20p yel & blk	.30	.20
783 A425	20p yel & blk	.30	.20
a.	Bklt. pane, 6 #782, 4 #783	2.00	
b.	Pair, #782-783	.65	.65
	Nos. 780-783 (4)	1.20	.80

Nos. 782-783 inscribed "D.S. No 20."
For surcharges see Nos. 813-816, 955-956.

Merino, Biplane, Jet Passenger Plane and Supersonic Fighter Plane — A426

1988, May 17 **Litho.** *Perf. 13½*

784 A426	35p multi	.90	.25

Commodore Arturo Merino Benitez (b. 1888), aviation pioneer.

Naval Tradition — A427

Designs: No. 785, Training ship *Esmeralda.* No. 786, Capt. Arturo Pratt, a stained-glass window in the Naval Museum, Valparaiso.

1988, May 23

785	50p multi	.90	.50
786	50p multi	.90	.50
a.	A427 Pair, #785-786	2.25	1.75

Pontifical Catholic University of Chile, Santiago, Cent. — A429

1988, June 21

787 A429	40p Papal & university arms	.90	.25

Locomotives — A430

1988, July 22 **Litho.** *Perf. 13½*

788 A430	60p Esslingen No. 3331	.55	.40
789 A430	60p North British No. 45	.55	.40
a.	Souv. sheet, #788-789, imperf	6.50	6.50
b.	Pair, #788-789	1.60	1.60

Arica-La Paz Railway, 75th anniv. (#788); Antofagasta Bolivia Railway, cent. (#789).

Jose Miguel Carrera Natl. Institute, 175th Anniv. — A431

1988, Aug. 10 **Litho.** *Perf. 13½*

790 A431	45p multi	.60	.30

Annexation of Easter Is., Cent. — A432

1988, Sept. 9

791 A432	50p Ship, officer	1.00	.40
792 A432	50p Map, globe	1.00	.40
a.	Pair, #791-792	2.50	1.50
793 A432	100p Easter Is. folk dancers	1.50	.75
794 A432	100p Stone ruins	1.50	.75
a.	Souv. sheet of 4, #791-794, imperf.	7.00	6.50
b.	Pair, #793-794	5.00	3.00
	Nos. 791-794 (4)	5.00	2.30

Miniature Sheet

Flowers — A433

Designs: a, *Chloraea chrysantha.* b, *Lapageria rosea.* c, *Nolana paradoxa.* d, *Rhodophiala advena.* e, *Schizanthus hookeri.* f, *Acacia caven.* g, *Cordia decandra.* h, *Leontochir ovallei.* i, *Alstroemeria pelegrina.* j, *Copiapoa cinerea.* k, *Salpiglossis sinuata.* l, *Leucocoryne coquimbensis.* m, *Eucryphia glutinosa.* n, *Calandrinia longiscapa.* o, *Desfontainia spinosa.* p, *Sophora macrocarpa.*

1988, Aug. 23 **Litho.** *Perf. 13½*

795	Sheet of 16	15.00	15.00
a.-p.	A433 30p any single	.45	.25

First Domestic Airmail Route, 1919 — A434

1988, Oct. 11

796 A434	150p Clodomiro Figueroa Ponce's aircraft	1.90	1.00

Christmas 1988

A435 A436

Children's drawings: 35p, Nativity, by Paulette Thiers, age 8. 100p, Going to church, by Jose M. Lamas, age 9, horiz.

1988, Nov. 17

797 A435	20p rose lake & org yel	.40	.20
a.	Bklt. pane of 10	6.00	
798 A435	20p rose lake & org yel	.40	.20
a.	Bklt. pane of 10	6.00	
799 A436	35p multi	.60	.20
800 A436	100p multi	1.00	.40
	Nos. 797-800 (4)	2.40	1.00

No. 798 inscribed "D.S. No 20."

Artisans — A437

1988, Oct. 25 **Litho.** *Perf. 13½*

801 A437	25p Potter	.40	.20
802 A437	25p Weaver	.40	.20
a.	Pair, #801-802	1.00	.75

No. 802a has continuous design.

Natl. Philatelic Soc., Cent. — A438

1988, Nov. 24

803 A438	40p No. 38, cancellation	.60	.20

School Crossing Guards — A439

1988, Oct. 26

804 A439	45p multi	.60	.25

A440

Battle scenes and: #805, 807, Commanders. #806, 808, Servicemen.

1989, Jan. 12 **Litho.** *Perf. 13½*

805	50p Manuel Bulnes (1799-1866)	.50	.25
806	50p Cavalryman	.50	.25
a.	A440 Pair, #805-806	1.75	.60
807	100p Roberto Simpson	.95	.50
808	100p Seaman	.95	.50
a.	A440 Pair, #807-808	3.25	1.25
	Nos. 805-808 (4)	2.90	1.50

Battles of 1839: Yungay (50p) and Casma (100p). Nos. 806a, 808a have continuous designs.

Municipal Annivs. A442

Municipal coats of arms and: 30p, San Ambrosio Church. 35p, Craftsman sculpting marble. 45p, Laja Spring and falls.

1989, Jan. 20

809 A442	30p multi	.25	.20
810 A442	35p multi	.35	.20
811 A442	45p multi	.40	.20
	Nos. 809-811 (3)	1.00	.60

Founding of Vallenar, 200th anniv. (30p); founding of Combarbala, 200th anniv. (35p); founding of Los Angeles, 250th anniv. (45p).

Nos. 760a-760d and 780-783 Surcharged

a

b

1989, Mar. 20 Litho. *Perf. 13½*

812 Block of 4 1.25 .75
a.-d. A411(a) 25p on 15p #760a-760d, any single .25 .20
813 A425(b) 25p on 20p #780 .25 .20
814 A425(b) 25p on 20p #781 .25 .20
815 A425(b) 25p on 20p #782 .20 .20
816 A425(b) 25p on 20p #783 .20 .20
Nos. 812-816 (5) 2.15 1.55

Surcharge differs on Nos. 814, 816.
Issued: #812-814, 3/20. #815-816, 11/30.

Women Beatified — A443

A444

1989, Mar. 21 Litho. *Perf. 13½*

818 A443 40p Sr. Teresa de Los Andes .50 .25
819 A443 40p Laura Vicuna .50 .25
a. Pair, #818-819 1.50 1.00

No. 819a has continuous design.

1989, Mar. 31

820 A444 100p Christopher Columbus 1.25 .60
821 A444 100p Galleons 1.25 .60
a. Pair, #820-821 2.75 1.75
b. Souvenir sheet of 2, #820-821 5.00 3.75
c. Souvenir sheet of 2, #820-821 5.00 3.75

EXFINA '89, Santiago. No. 821a has continuous design. No. 821b margin pictures Columbus's coat of arms and the Order of the Great Admiralty, No. 821c margin Nos. 55, 69, 18, 76, 37, 1, 20 and 98.

CORFO Development Corp., 50th Anniv. — A445

1989, Apr. 4

822 A445 60p Shipping .60 .30
823 A445 60p Lumber .60 .30
824 A445 60p Communication .60 .30
825 A445 60p Coal .60 .30
a. Block of 4, #822-825 3.00 2.50

Gabriela Mistral (1889-1957), Poet — A446

1989, Apr. 7 Litho. *Perf. 13½*

826 A446 30p Poet, steeple .40 .20
827 A446 30p Poet, children .40 .20
828 A446 30p Poet working .40 .20
829 A446 30p Receiving Nobel Prize, 1945 .40 .20
a. Block of 4, #826-829 1.75 1.00

Exports — A447

#830, 832, Grapes. #831, 833, Apple.

1989, Apr. 19

830 A447 25p indigo & brt yel grn .25 .20
831 A447 25p ver & brt yel grn .25 .20
a. Bklt. pane, 5 each #830-831 2.20
b. Pair, #830-831 1.40 .75
832 A447 25p indigo & pale yel org .25 .20
833 A447 25p ver & pale yel org .25 .20
a. Bklt. pane, 5 each #832-833 2.50
b. Pair, #832-833 1.40 .75
Nos. 830-833 (4) 1.00 .80

Nos. 832-833 inscribed "D.S. No 20."
See Nos. 861-864, 943-946. For surcharges see Nos. 956B-956C, 1085-1088.

Military Justice Department, 150th Anniv. — A448

1989, Apr. 24 Litho. *Perf. 13½*

834 A448 50p multicolored .60 .25

Monument to the Martyrs of Carabineros de Chile — A449

1989, Apr. 26

835 A449 35p multicolored .50 .20

Surveyor and Penguins — A450

1989, May 29

836 A450 150p multi 2.00 .85

Antarctic Research Institute expeditions, 25th anniv.

Naval Engineers, Cent. — A451

#837, Naval school. #838, Seamen in boiler room. #839, Ship, helicopter, submarine. #840, *Aquiles* launch, Asmar-Talcahuano.

1989, May 31

837 A451 45p multicolored .75 .25
838 A451 45p multicolored .75 .25
839 A451 45p multicolored .75 .25
840 A451 45p multicolored .75 .25
a. Block of 4, #837-840 3.00 3.00

Horse-drawn Carriage (Victoria), Vina del Mar — A452

Early transportation: 35p, Launch off Chiloe Is., vert. 40p, Cart, Cautin. 45p, Ferry, Rio Palena. 50p, Car transport, Lake Gral, Carretta. 60p, Incline railroad, Valparaiso. 100p, Cable car (funicular), Santiago.

1989-92 Litho. *Perf. 13½*

841 A452 30p black & orange .30 .20
842 A452 60p black & lemon .55 .25
842A A452 60p like No. 842 .45 .20
843 A452 100p black & brt yel grn .90 .45

1989-91

844 A452 35p black & brt blue .30 .20
845 A452 40p black & olive .35 .20
846 A452 45p blk & pale blue grn .35 .20
846A A452 45p black & lt ol grn .35 .20
847 A452 50p black & scarlet .45 .20
Nos. 841-847 (9) 4.00 2.10

Nos. 842A, 846A inscribed DS No. 20.
Issued: #841-842, 843, 4/22/89; #846A, 2/1/91; #842A, 1992; others, 8/1989.
#846 exists dated 1991, #847 dated 1992.
For surcharge see No. 1002.
This is an expanding set. Numbers will change if necessary.

Export Type of 1989

#861, 863, Grapes. #862, 864, Apple.

1989, May 22

861 A447 5p dark blue & gray .20 .20
862 A447 5p brt red, dark blue & gray .20 .20
a. Pair, #861-862 .50 .50
863 A447 10p dark blue & gray .20 .20
864 A447 10p brt red, dark blue & gray .20 .20
a. Pair, #863-864 .50 .50

A453

A454

1989, Aug. 25 Litho. *Perf. 13½*

865 A453 250p multicolored 3.00 1.25
a. Souvenir sheet of 1 8.00 8.00

World Stamp Expo '89.

1989, Oct. 12

UPAE emblem and pre-Columbian peoples: 30p, Atacamena potter. 150p, Selk'nam-onas bow hunter.

866 A454 30p multicolored .40 .20
867 A454 150p multicolored 2.10 .75

Drawing by Christina Lopez — A455

1989, Nov. 20 Litho. *Perf. 13½*

868 A455 100p multicolored 1.25 .40

Christmas.

Christmas Ornaments — A456

Nos. 869, 871, Balls. Nos. 870, 872, Bells.

1989

869 A456 25p dull green & org .25 .20
870 A456 25p dull green & org .25 .20
a. Bklt. pane, 5 each Nos. 869-870 2.00
b. Pair, #869-870 .55 .40
871 A456 25p dull green & ver .25 .20
872 A456 25p dull green & ver .25 .20
a. Bklt. pane, 5 each Nos. 871-872 2.00
b. Pair, #871-872 .55 .40
Nos. 869-872 (4) 1.00 .80

Nos. 871-872 inscribed "D.S. No 20."

Miniature Sheet

Wildlife, Natl. Parks — A457

Designs: a, Vicuna, Lauca Park. b, Chilean flamingos, Salar de Surire. c, Cactus, La Chimba Reserve. d, Guanaco, Pan de Azucar Park. e, Song bird, Father Jorge Park. f, Terns, Rapa Nui Park. g, Ferret, La Campana Park. h, Duck, Rio Clarillo Park. i, Cypress tree, Rio de Los Cipreses Reserve. j, Black-headed swan, Laguna de Torca Reserve. k, Puma, Laguna del Laja Park. l, Araucaria tree, Villarrica Park. m, Flower, Vicente Perez Rosales Park. n, Lenga tree, Dos Lagunas. o, Sea lion, Laguna San Rafael Park. p, Rhea, Torres del Paine Park.

1990, Jan. 25

873 Sheet of 16 10.50 7.50
a.-p. A457 35p any single .50 .20

1990 World Cup Soccer Championships, Italy — A458

1990, Feb. 23

874 A458 50p Cleated shoe .60 .25
875 A458 50p Hand .60 .25
876 A458 50p Soccer ball .60 .25
877 A458 50p Athlete .60 .25
a. Block of 4, #874-877 2.50 2.00

Natl. Air Force A459

Various aircraft: No. 878, Vickers Wibault. No. 879, Curtiss O1E Falcon. No. 880, Pitts S2A. No. 881, Extra 300.

1990, Mar. 16 Litho. *Perf. 13½*

878 A459 40p multicolored .50 .20
879 A459 40p multicolored .50 .20
880 A459 40p multicolored .50 .20
881 A459 40p multicolored .50 .20
a. Souvenir sheet of 4, #878-881 2.10 1.50
Nos. 878-881 (4) 2.00 .80

FIDAE '90.

Discovery of America 500th Anniv. (in 1992) — A460

Maps and 16th cent. men: No. 882, Incan. No. 883, Spanish infantryman.

1990, Apr. 20 Litho. *Perf. 13½*

882 60p multicolored .50 .20
883 60p multicolored .50 .20
a. A460 Pair, #882-883 1.50 1.00

Port Cities A462

1990, Apr. 27

884 A462 40p Valparaiso .50 .20
885 A462 40p San Vicente .50 .20
a. Pair, #884-885 1.25 1.00

Democracy — A463

1990, June 8 Litho. *Perf. 13½*

886 A463 20p Sunrise .20 .20
887 A463 30p Peace dove .30 .20
888 A463 60p Pleasure .50 .25
889 A463 100p Star .90 .45
a. Souvenir sheet of 4, #886-889 3.00 3.00
Nos. 886-889 (4) 1.90 1.10

Equality — A464

1990, June 8

890 A464 45p multicolored .50 .25
a. Souvenir sheet 1.00 1.00

No. 890a margin continues the design.

Naval Tradition — A465

#891, Transport ship Piloto Pardo. #892, Oceanographic research ship Yelcho.

1990, May 30 Litho. *Perf. 13½*

891 A465 50p multicolored .60 .20
892 A465 50p multicolored .60 .20
a. Pair, #891-892 1.40 1.00

A466

A467

1990, June 12

893 A466 250p Sir Rowland Hill 3.00 1.40
a. Souvenir sheet of 1 5.00 4.00

Penny Black, 150th anniv.
No. 893a margin continues the design.

1990, June 21

894 A467 150p multicolored 1.50 .65

Organization of American States, cent.

Marine Resources — A468

Designs: a, Scallop. b, Clam. c, Swordfish. d, Crab. e, Fish. f, Baiting, processing.

1990, July 27 Litho. *Perf. 13½*

895 Block of 6 3.00 2.00
a.-f. A468 40p any single .30 .20

Curimon Convent A469

1990, Aug. 1

896 A469 50p multicolored .50 .20

250th anniversary of San Felipe.

Environmental Protection — A470

1990, Sept. 1 Litho. *Perf. 13½*

897 A470 35p Aerosol propellants .25 .20
898 A470 35p Deforestation .25 .20
899 A470 35p Smokestacks .25 .20
900 A470 35p Oil slick, shore .25 .20
901 A470 35p Forest fire .25 .20
a. Strip of 5, #897-901 1.50 .90
b. Bklt. pane, 2 each #897-901 5.25

Inscribed "D.S. No 20"

902 A470 35p Aerosol propellants .25 .20
903 A470 35p Deforestation .25 .20
904 A470 35p Smokestacks .25 .20
905 A470 35p Oil slick, shore .25 .20
906 A470 35p Forest fire .25 .20
a. Strip of 5, #902-906 1.50 .90
b. Bklt. pane, 2 each #902-906 5.25
Nos. 897-906 (10) 2.50 2.00

See Nos. 988-997.

Presidents of Chile — A471

1990, Sept. 4

912 A471 35p Salvador Allende .25 .20
913 A471 35p Eduardo Frei .25 .20
914 A471 40p Jorge Alessandri .35 .20
915 A471 45p Gabriel Gonzalez V .40 .20
916 A471 50p Juan Antonio Rios .45 .25
917 A471 60p Pedro Aguirre Cerda .50 .30
918 A471 70p Juan E. Montero .60 .30
919 A471 80p Carlos Ibanez .70 .35
920 A471 90p Emiliano Figueroa .80 .40
921 A471 100p Arturo Alessandri .85 .45
Nos. 912-921 (10) 5.15 2.85

Nos. 914, 918, 920-921 exist dated 1992.

Rodeos — A472

Designs: a, Rodeo ring. b, Men on horses. c, Man stopping horse. d, Men, horses, bull.

1990, Sept. 24

926 Block of 4 2.40 1.75
a.-d. A472 45p any single .40 .20

Discovery of America, 500th Anniv. (in 1992) — A473

1990, Oct. 12 Litho. *Perf. 13½*

927 A473 30p Phoenicopterus chilensis .50 .20
928 A473 150p Arctocephalus australis 2.10 .60

King and Queen of Spain's Visit — A474

#930, Arms of King Juan Carlos I, Chilean Arms.

1990, Oct. 18

929 A474 100p shown .90 .45
930 A474 100p Denomination at LR .90 .45
a. Pair, #929-930 2.10 1.50

Malleco Bridge, Cent. — A475

Design: #932, Boy waving at train on bridge.

1990, Oct. 26 Litho. *Perf. 13½*

931 A475 60p multicolored 1.00 .45
932 A475 60p multicolored 1.00 .45
a. Pair, #931-932 2.40 1.50

Chilean Antarctic Territorial Claims, 50th Anniv. — A476

Design: #934, Penguins, helicopter, camp.

1990, Nov. 6 *Perf. 13½*

933 A476 250p multicolored 2.25 1.10
934 A476 250p multicolored 2.25 1.10
a. Souvenir sheet of 2, #933-934 8.00 8.00

A477

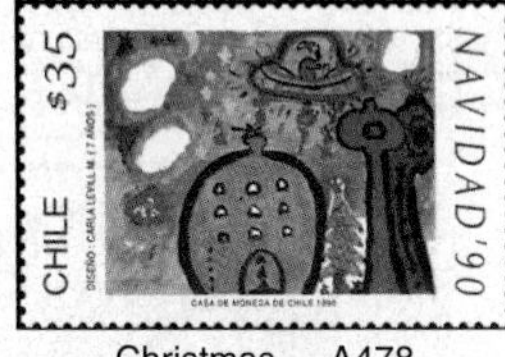

Christmas — A478

1990, Nov. 20 Litho. *Perf. 13½*

935 A477 35p lt green & bl grn .40 .20
a. Booklet pane of 10 3.00
936 A477 35p dull org & bl grn .25 .20
a. Booklet pane of 10 2.50
937 A478 35p shown .25 .20
938 A478 150p Underwater dwelling 1.25 .65
Nos. 935-938 (4) 2.15 1.25

No. 936 inscribed "D.S. No.20."

National Congress — A479

1990, Dec. 21 Litho. *Perf. 13½*

939 A479 100p Congress chamber .90 .40
940 A479 100p Early congressional session .90 .40
a. Pair, #939-940 1.90 1.25

City of Santiago, 450th Anniv. — A480

1991, Feb. 7

941 A480 100p Colorado House .85 .40
942 A480 100p Skyline .85 .40
a. Pair, #941-942 1.90 1.25
b. Souvenir sheet of 2, #941-942 2.50 2.50

Exports Type of 1989

Nos. 943, 945, Grapes. Nos. 944, 946, Apple.

1991, Feb. 8 *Perf. 13½ on 3 Sides*

943 A447 45p indigo & brt pink .35 .20
944 A447 45p ver & brt pink .35 .20
a. Bklt. pane, 5 each #943-944 6.00
945 A447 45p indigo & yel .35 .20
946 A447 45p ver & yel .35 .20
a. Bklt. pane, 5 each #945-946 6.00
Nos. 943-946 (4) 1.40 .80

Nos. 945-946 inscribed "D.S. No.20."
For surcharges see Nos. 1085-1088.

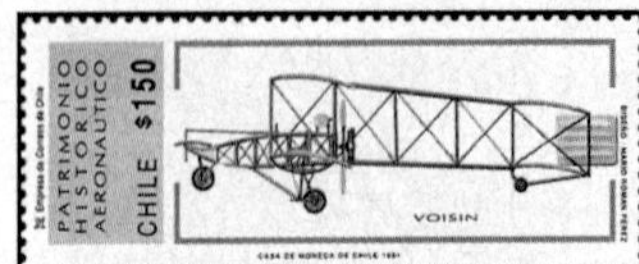

Historical Aircraft — A481

Designs: a, Voisin. b, S.E. 5a. c, Morane Saulnier MS 35. d, Consolidated PBY-5A/OA-10 Catalina. Illustration reduced.

1991, Mar. 21 **Litho.** ***Perf. 13½***

947 A481 150p Block of 4, #a.-d. 6.50 4.00

American Soccer Cup, Chile — A482

1991, Apr. 12 **Litho.** ***Perf. 13½***

948 A482 100p shown 1.00 .35
949 A482 100p Ball, goalie 1.00 .35
a. Pair, #948-949 2.00 .90

Coal Mining A483

Design: #951, Miners dumping cart of coal.

1991, Apr. 18

950 A483 200p shown 1.40 .70
951 A483 200p multicolored 1.40 .70
a. Pair, #950-951 4.00 2.75

Cultural Art — A484

Design: #953, Small sculptures, spurs, dish.

1991, Apr. 29

952 A484 90p shown .65 .35
953 A484 90p multicolored .65 .35
a. Pair, #952-953 2.00 1.25

Chilean Scientific Society, Cent. — A485

1991, Apr. 29

954 A485 45p blue grn & blk .50 .20

Nos. 782-783 Surcharged

a

b

1991, Apr. 30

955 A425(a) 45p on 20p, #782 .30 .20
956 A425(b) 45p on 20p, #783 .30 .20
a. Pair, #955-956 1.00 .75

Nos. 832-833 Surcharged

1991, May 6 **Litho.** ***Perf. 13½***

956B A447 45p on 25p, #832 .25 .20
956C A447 45p on 25p, #833 .25 .20
d. Pair, #956B-956C 1.00 .75

Santiago Cathedral A486

1991, May 9 **Litho & Engr.**

957 A486 300p red brn, sal & blk 2.10 1.00

World Telecommunications Day — A487

1991, May 17 **Litho.**

958 A487 90p multicolored 1.00 .30

A488

A489

1991, May 23

959 A488 100p Pope Leo XIII .70 .30

Rerum Novarum Encyclical, cent.

1991, May 28 **Litho.** ***Perf. 13½***

Rescue of Shackleton Expedition, 75th anniv.: a, Lt. Luis Pardo, Sir Ernest Shackleton. b, Rescue ship, Yelcho. c, Sailor pointing to survivors. d, Shackleton's ship, Endurance.

960 A489 50p Block of 4, #a.-d. 2.00 1.50
e. Miniature sheet, #960 2.50 2.50

21st General Assembly of Organization of American States, Santiago — A490

1991, June 5

961 A490 70p multicolored .70 .25

New Carabinero School — A491

1991, Juno 12

962 A491 50p multicolored .60 .20

Natl. Merchant Marine Day — A492

1991, June 26

963 A492 45p black & red .50 .20

11th Pan American Games, Havana — A493

1991, July 23

964 A493 100p Runners, torch, flags .90 .35
965 A493 100p Cycling, running, basketball .90 .35
a. Pair, #964-965 2.00 1.50

Founding of the City of Los Andes, Bicent. — A494

1991, July 29

966 A494 100p multicolored 1.00 .35

Miniature Sheet

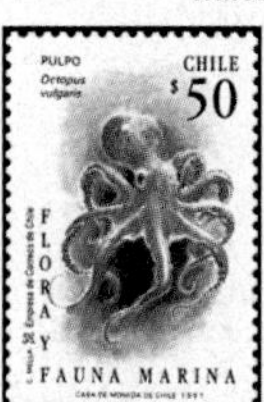

Marine Life — A495

Designs: No. 967a, Octopus vulgaris. b, Durvillaea antarctica. c, Paralichthys adspersus. d, Austromegabalanus psittacus. e, Concholepas concholepas. f, Cancer setosus. g, Lessonia nigrescens. h, Loxechinus albus. i, Homalaspis plana. j, Porphyra columbina. k, Oplegnathus insignis. l, Chorus giganteus. m, Rhynchocinetes typus. n, Engraulis ringens. o, Gracilaria spp. p, Pyura chilensis.

1991, Aug. 20 **Litho.** ***Perf. 13½***

967 Sheet of 16 10.50 5.00
a.-p. A495 50p any single .35 .20

1891 Revolution, Cent. — A496

Jose M. Balmaceda (1840-1891) and: No. 968, Machinery. No. 969, Teacher, students at Valentin Letelier School of Medicine.

1991, Aug. 29

968 A496 100p multicolored .70 .35
969 A496 100p multicolored .70 .35
a. Pair, #968-969 1.50 .90

Chilean Art — A497

Paintings: 50p, Woman in Red, by Pedro Reszka. 70p, The Traveler, by Camilo Mori. 200p, Head of Child, by Benito Rebolledo. 300p, Boy Wearing a Fez, by A. Valenzuela Puelma.

1991, Sept. 26

970 A497 50p multicolored .50 .20
971 A497 70p multicolored .50 .25
972 A497 200p multicolored 2.00 .70
973 A497 300p multicolored 3.00 1.00
Nos. 970-973 (4) 6.00 2.15

Antarctic Treaty, 30th Anniv. — A498

1991, Oct. 7 **Litho.** ***Perf. 13½***

974 A498 80p shown 1.10 .45
975 A498 80p Birds, sea life 1.10 .45
a. Pair, #974-975 3.50 1.25

Intl. Letter Writing Week A499

1991, Oct. 9

976 A499 45p shown .35 .20
977 A499 70p Envelope filled with people .50 .25

America Issue — A500

UPAEP emblem, sailing ships and: 150p, Navigator.

1991, Oct. 14

978 A500 50p multicolored .50 .20
979 A500 150p multicolored 1.50 .50

A501

A502

1991, Oct. 21

980 A501 45p blue hat .30 .20
981 A501 45p red hat .30 .20
a. Pair, #980-981 1.00 .50
b. Souvenir sheet of 2, #980-981 2.00 2.00

Pablo Neruda, (1904-1973), Nobel Prize winner for literature, 1971. Nos. 981a has a continuous design.

1991, Nov. 4

982 A502 45p Boy with stars .35 .20
983 A502 100p Girl with stars .70 .35

Christmas.

Christmas
A503 A504

1991, Nov. 18 Litho. *Perf. 13½*

984 A503 45p violet & brt pink .30 .20
985 A504 45p violet & brt pink .30 .20
a. Pair, #984-985 .60 .20
b. Bklt. pane of 5 #985a 6.00
986 A503 45p violet & brt pink .30 .20
987 A504 45p violet & brt pink .30 .20
a. Pair, #986-987 .60 .20
b. Bklt. pane of 5 #987a 6.00
Nos. 984-987 (4) 1.20 .80

Nos. 986-987 inscribed "D.S. No. 20."
For surcharges see Nos. 1016-1019.

Environmental Protection Type of 1990

1992, Jan. 28 Litho. *Perf. 13½*

Lemon & Black

988 A470 60p like #897 .40 .20
989 A470 60p like #898 .40 .20
990 A470 60p like #899 .40 .20
991 A470 60p like #900 .40 .20
992 A470 60p like #901 .40 .20
a. Strip of 5, #988-992 2.25 1.50
b. Bklt. pane, 2 each #988-992 4.50

Inscribed "D.S. No. 20"

Orange & Dark Green

993 A470 60p like #902 .40 .20
994 A470 60p like #903 .40 .20
995 A470 60p like #904 .40 .20
996 A470 60p like #905 .40 .20
997 A470 60p like #906 .40 .20
a. Strip of 5, #993-997 2.25 1.50
b. Bklt. pane, 2 each #993-997 4.50
Nos. 988-997 (10) 4.00 2.00

Wolfgang Amadeus Mozart, Death Bicent. (in 1991) — A505

1992, Jan. 31

998 A505 60p shown .35 .20
999 A505 200p Hands at piano 1.25 .65
a. Sheet of 2, #998-999 2.40 2.40

FIDAE '92, Intl. Air and Space Fair — A506

1992, Mar. 5 Litho. *Perf. 13½*

1000 A506 60p multicolored .60 .20

16th Population and Housing Census
A507

1992, Mar.

1001 A507 60p multicolored .60 .20

No. 846 Surcharged in Red Brown

1992, Mar.

1002 A452 60p on 45p .60 .20

Chilean Cities — A508

Cities' coat of arms and: 80p, Church of San Jose de Maipo. 90p, People making pottery. 100p, Lircunlauta House. 150p, Wine and lumber industries. 250p, Huilquilemu cultural center. Illustration reduced.

1992, Apr. 10 Litho. *Perf. 13½*

1003 A508 80p multicolored .65 .25
1004 A508 90p multicolored .75 .25
1005 A508 100p multicolored .80 .30
1006 A508 150p multicolored 1.25 .45
1007 A508 250p multicolored 2.00 .75
Nos. 1003-1007 (5) 5.45 2.00

80p, San Jose de Maipo, 200th anniv. 90p, Melipilla, 250th anniv. 100p, San Fernando, 250th anniv. 150p, Cauquenes, 250th anniv. 250p, Talca, 250th anniv.

Expo '92, Seville
A509

1992, Apr. 23

1008 A509 150p Pavilion 1.25 .45
1009 A509 200p Iceberg 1.75 .60
a. Sheet of 2, #1008-1009 *3.25 3.25*

A510

Easter Island
A511

Marine life: No. 1010a, Morula praecipua, Strombus maculatus, Cypraea caputdraconis. b, Codium pocockiae. c, Myripristis tiki. d, Sargassum skottsbergii. e, Pseudolabrus fuentesi. f, Pocillopora danae. g, Panulirus pascuensis. h, Tripneustes gratilla.

No. 1011b, Natives, airplane, petroglyph.

1992, June 9 Litho. *Perf. 13½*

1010 A510 60p Sheet of 8, #a.-h. 4.00 2.50
1011 A511 200p Pair, #a.-b. 3.00 1.40

Natl. Council of the Disabled — A512

Military Chiefs of Staff, 50th Anniv. — A513

1992, June 23

1012 A512 60p multicolored .60 .20

1992, July 3

1013 A513 60p multicolored .60 .20

Submarine Forces, 75th Anniv. — A514

Coat of arms and: 250p, Officer using periscope, control room.

1992, July 4

1014 A514 150p multicolored 1.50 .50
1015 A514 250p multicolored 2.00 .80

Nos. 984-987 Surcharged

1992, Aug. 11 Litho. *Perf. 13½*

1016 A503 60p on 45p No. 984 .35 .20
1017 A504 60p on 45p No. 985 .35 .20
a. Pair, #1016-1017 1.40 .70
1018 A503 60p on 45p No. 986 .35 .20
1019 A504 60p on 45p No. 987 .35 .20
a. Pair, #1018-1019 1.40 .70
Nos. 1016-1019 (4) 1.40 .80

Nos. 1018-1019 inscribed "D.S. No. 20."

Emperor Penguins — A515

1992, Sept. 28 Litho. *Perf. 13½*

1020 A515 200p shown 1.25 .55
1021 A515 250p Adults with young 1.50 .70
a. Souv. sheet of 2, #1020-1021 4.75 4.75

Central Post Office, Santiago, 1772 — A516

1992, Oct. 9

1022 A516 200p multicolored 1.50 .60

Discovery of America, 500th Anniv. — A517

UPAEP emblem and: 200p, Calendar stone, astrolabe, Columbus. 250p, Church, map of Central and South America, sailing ship.

1992, Oct. 20

1023 A517 200p multicolored 1.50 .60
1024 A517 250p multicolored 2.00 .70

Radio Chile, 75th Anniv. — A518

Bernardo O'Higgins (1778-1842)
A519

1992, Oct. 22

1025 A518 250p multicolored 1.75 .70

1992, Oct. 23

1026 A519 60p multicolored .50 .20

Claudio Arrau, Pianist — A520

1992, Nov. 12 Litho. *Perf. 13½*

1027 A520 150p As child .90 .45
1028 A520 200p As adult 1.25 .60
a. Souv. sheet of 2, #1027-1028 3.00 3.00

Natl. Human Rights Day — A521

1992, Dec. 10

1029 A521 100p multicolored .60 .30
a. Souvenir sheet of 1 1.10 1.10

Christmas — A522

Designs: Nos. 1030, 1032, Denomination at LR. Nos. 1031, 1033, Denomination at LL.

1992, Dec. 12 Litho. *Perf. 13½*

1030 A522 60p buff & brown .30 .20
1031 A522 60p buff & brown .30 .20
a. Pair, #1030-1031 .65 .30
b. Booklet pane of 5 #1031a 3.25
1032 A522 60p buff & red .30 .20
1033 A522 60p buff & red .30 .20
a. Pair, #1032-1033 .65 .30
b. Booklet pane of 5 #1033a 3.25
Nos. 1030-1033 (4) 1.20 .80

Nos. 1032-1033 inscribed "DS/20."

A523

A524

University of Chile, 150th Anniv.: a, Statue. b, Coat of arms, facade of building.

1992, Nov. 19 Litho. *Perf. 13½*

1034 A523 200p Pair, #a.-b. 3.00 1.25
c. Souvenir sheet of 1, #1034 4.00 4.00

Nos. 1034a-1034b have a continuous design.

1992, Dec. 12

1035 A524 70p black & yellow .60 .25

23rd meeting of Latin American Energy Ministers.

Churches of Chile — A525

#1036, 1038, Achao #1037, 1039, Castro.

1993, Mar. 1 Litho. *Perf. 13½*

1036 A525 70p black & pink .45 .25
1037 A525 70p black & pink .45 .25
a. Pair #1036-1037 .90 .90
b. Booklet pane of 5 #1037a 6.50

Inscribed "DS/20"

1038 A525 70p black & yellow .45 .25
1039 A525 70p black & yellow .45 .25
a. Pair, #1038-1039 .90 .90
b. Booklet pane of 5 #1039a 6.50
Nos. 1036-1039 (4) 1.80 1.00

See Nos. 1053-1060, 1093-1098.
For surcharges see Nos. 1129-1130.

Arrival of the Jesuits, 400th Anniv. — A526

Canonization of St. Teresa of the Andes, 1993 — A527

1993 Litho. *Perf. 13½*

1040 A526 200p St. Ignatius of Loyola 1.50 .60
a. Souvenir sheet of 1 2.00 2.00
1041 A527 300p St. Teresa of the Andes 2.50 1.00

Issue dates: 200p, Mar. 15; 300p, Mar. 31. No. 1040a sold for 250p.

World Festival of Theatre of the Nations — A528

Clotario Blest (1899-1990), Syndicalist A530

Second Space Conference of the Americas — A529

1993, Apr. 22

1042 A528 250p multicolored 2.00 .75

1993, Apr. 26

1043 A529 150p multicolored .90 .45
a. Souvenir sheet of 1 2.10 2.10

No. 1043a sold for 350p.

1993, Apr. 30

1044 A530 70p multicolored .50 .20

Intl. Labor Day.

Vicente Huidobro, Poet (1893-1948) A531

1993, May 19 Litho. *Perf. 13½*

1045 A531 100p shown .60 .30
1046 A531 100p Portrait, seated .60 .30
a. Pair, #1045-1046 1.50 1.00

Antique Fire Engines — A532

#1047, 1902 Watterous Engineering Co. Ltd., Canada. #1048, 1872 Merryweather, England.

1993, June 30 Litho. *Perf. 13½*

1047 A532 100p multicolored .80 .30
1048 A532 100p multicolored .80 .30
a. Souv. sheet of 2, #1047-1048 2.50 2.50

No. 1048a sold for 400p.

Aircraft — A533

Designs: No. 1049, Douglas B-26 Invader. No. 1050, Mirage M50 Panther. No. 1051, Sanchez Besa. No. 1052, Bell 47D1 helicopter.

1993, July 13

1049 A533 100p multicolored .55 .30
1050 A533 100p multicolored .55 .30
1051 A533 100p multicolored .55 .30
1052 A533 100p multicolored .55 .30
a. Block of 4, #1049-1052 3.00 2.50

Church Type of 1993

Designs: 10p, Chonchi. 20p, Vilupulli. 30p, Llau-llao. 40p, Dalcahue. 50p, Tenaun. 80p, Quinchao. 90p, Quehui. 100p, Nercon.

1993, July Litho. *Perf. 13½*

1053 A525 10p green & black .20 .20
1054 A525 20p black & brown .20 .20
1055 A525 30p black & vermilion .20 .20
1056 A525 40p black & blue .25 .25
1057 A525 50p black & green blue .30 .30
1058 A525 80p black & buff .45 .45
a. Booklet pane of 10 7.00
1059 A525 90p olive & black .50 .50
a. Booklet pane of 10 7.50
Complete booklet, #1059a 7.50
1060 A525 100p gray vio & blk .55 .55
a. Booklet pane of 10 7.50
Nos. 1053-1060 (8) 2.65 2.65

Issued: #1058a, 1/1/94; #1059a, 1995; #1060a, 2/1/96.
No. 1058 exists dated 1994.
See No. 1093 for 80p black & violet.

Natl. Dance, "La Cueca" — A534

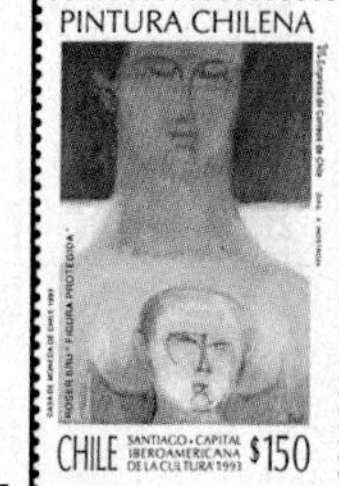

Paintings — A535

1993, Sept. 15 Litho. *Perf. 13½*

1061 A534 70p Cueca chilota .60 .20
1062 A534 70p Cueca central .60 .20
1063 A534 70p Cueca nortina .60 .20
Nos. 1061-1063 (3) 1.80 .60

1993, Sept. 28

Designs: 80p, Tarde Amanecer, by Mario Carreno, horiz. 90p, Summer, by Gracia Barrios, horiz. 150p, Figura Protegida, by Roser Bru. 200p, Tangueria-Valparaiso, by Nemesio Antunez, horiz.

1064 A535 80p multicolored .55 .25
1065 A535 90p multicolored .60 .25
1066 A535 150p multicolored 1.00 .40
1067 A535 200p multicolored 1.40 .55
Nos. 1064-1067 (4) 3.55 1.45

Chilean Mint, 250th Anniv. A536

1993, Oct. 7 Litho. & Engr.

1068 A536 250p multicolored 1.75 .70
a. Souvenir sheet of 1 2.50 2.50

A537

A538

1993, Oct. 19 **Litho.**
1069 A537 80p multicolored .70 .25

Urban transportation system, 25th anniv.

1993, Oct. 12 **Litho.** ***Perf. 13½***
1070 A538 150p Cyanoliseus patagonus 1.00 .40
1071 A538 200p Hippocamelus bisulcus 1.50 .55

America issue.

Chilean Possession of Straits of Magellan, 150th Anniv. — A539

1993, Oct. 21
1072 A539 100p multicolored .80 .30

Naval Anniversaries — A540

1993, Oct. 27
1073 A540 80p Sailing ships .65 .25
1074 A540 80p Schooner .65 .25
1075 A540 80p Assault ship .65 .25
1076 A540 80p Patrol boat .65 .25
Nos. 1073-1076 (4) 2.60 1.00

Sailing of first naval squadron (#1073), Arturo Prat Naval Academy (#1074), Marine Corps (#1075), 175th anniversaries. Alejandro Navarette School for Cadets (#1076), 125th anniv.

Intl. Year of Indigenous Peoples — A541

1993, Nov. 24
1077 A541 100p multicolored .70 .30

Christmas A542

Pygoscelis Adelie A543

1993, Dec. 1 **Litho.** ***Perf. 13½***
1078 A542 70p tan & violet .50 .20
a. Booklet pane of 10 6.00
1079 A542 70p green & blue .50 .20
a. Booklet pane of 10 6.00

No. 1079 inscribed "DS/20."
For surcharge see No. 1131.

1993, Dec. 3
1080 A543 200p Nesting 1.40 .50
1081 A543 250p Adult, chicks 1.60 .65
a. Souv. sheet of 2, #1080-1081, imperf. 3.50 3.50

Chilean Antarctica.
No. 1081a has simulated perfs.

Chilean Cities — A544

1993, Dec. 15
1082 A544 80p Rancagua .60 .20
1083 A544 80p Curico .60 .20
1084 A544 80p Ancud .60 .20
Nos. 1082-1084 (3) 1.80 .60

Rancagua and Curico, 250th anniv. Ancud, 225th anniv.

Nos. 943-946 Surcharged

1993 **Litho.** ***Perf. 13½ on 3 Sides***
1085 A447 60p on 45p, #943 .35 .20
1086 A447 60p on 45p, #944 .35 .20
a. Bklt. pane, 5 each #1085-1086 3.50
1087 A447 60p on 45p, #945 .35 .20
1088 A447 60p on 45p, #946 .35 .20
a. Bklt. pane, 5 each #1087-1088 3.50
Nos. 1085-1088 (4) 1.40 .80

Nos. 1087-1088 inscribed "D.S. No. 20."

Intl. Year of the Family — A545

1994, Jan. 17 **Litho.** ***Perf. 13½***
1089 A545 100p multicolored .70 .25

Musical Instruments — A546

Designs: a, Violin. b, Cello.

1994, Jan. 27 **Litho.** ***Perf. 13½***
1091 A546 150p Pair, #a.-b. 2.50 2.50

No. 1091 has a continuous design.

Church Type of 1993

Designs: 80p, Quinchao. 90p, Quehui. #1097, 1098, Nercon.

1994-96 **Litho.** ***Perf. 13½***
1093 A525 80p black & violet .50 .25
1095 A525 90p red & black .50 .25
a. Booklet pane of 10 4.75
Complete booklet, #1095a 4.75
1097 A525 100p yellow & black .55 .30
a. Booklet pane of 10 6.00
Complete booklet, #1097a 6.00
1098 A525 100p gray vio & blk .60 .30
a. Booklet pane of 10 6.50
Complete booklet, #1098a 6.50
Nos. 1093-1098 (4) 2.15 1.10

Issued: 80p, 1/1/94; 90p, 1995; #1097-1098, 2/1/96.
Nos. 1093, 1095, 1097 inscribed "DS/20."
This is an expanding set. Numbers may change.

Souvenir Sheet

Natl. Aviation Museum, 50th Anniv. — A547

Aircraft: a, Sukhoi SU-30 Flanker. b, Vought-Sikorsky OS-2U3 Kingfisher. c, Lockheed F-117A Nighthawk. d, Northrop F-5E Tiger III.

1994, Mar. 17 **Litho.** ***Perf. 13***
1102 A547 300p Sheet of 4, #a.-d. + 2 labels 7.00 4.25

Intl. Air and Space Fair, FIDAE '94.
See No. 1159.

College of Agronomy, 50th Anniv. — A548

1994, Apr. 28 **Litho.** ***Perf. 13***
1103 A548 220p multicolored 1.10 .55

No. 760 Surcharged

1994, May 1 **Litho.** ***Perf. 13½***
1104 Block of 4 1.75 1.00
a.-d. A411 80p on 15p any single .35 .20

Concepcion University, 75th Anniv. — A549

Sections of mural, by Jorge Gonzalez Camarena: No. 1105, Cactus plant, skeletons. No. 1106, Flags, pillars, nude woman, faces. No. 1107, Flags, bodies, woman, soldier in armor. No. 1108, Women's faces, pipelines.

1994, May 14 **Litho.** ***Perf. 13***
1105 A549 250p multicolored 1.25 .60
1106 A549 250p multicolored 1.25 .60
1107 A549 250p multicolored 1.25 .60
1108 A549 250p multicolored 1.25 .60
a. Strip of 4, #1105-1108 + label 5.50 3.50

No. 1108a is a continuous design.

Chilean Antarctic Institute, 30th Anniv. — A550

Designs: No. 1109, Penguins, buildings. No. 1110, Buildings, coastal waters.

1994, May 31 ***Perf. 13***
1109 A550 300p multicolored 1.50 .85
1110 A550 300p multicolored 1.50 .85
a. Pair, #1109-1110 3.50 2.00

No. 1110a is a continuous design.

Antique Fire Engines — A551

#1111, Merryweather steam pumper, England, 1869. #1112, Western lever pumper, US, 1863. #1113, Mieusset steam pumper, France, 1905. #1114, Merryweather pumper, England, 1903.

1994, July 19 **Litho.** ***Perf. 13***
1111 A551 150p multicolored .75 .35
1112 A551 150p multicolored .75 .35
1113 A551 150p multicolored .75 .35
1114 A551 150p multicolored .75 .35
a. Block of 4, #1111-1114 3.75 3.00

Javiera Carrera Girls' School, Cent. — A552

1994, Aug. 10
1115 A552 200p multicolored 1.00 .50

Arms, Sights from Chilean Cities — A553

Designs: 90p, Porvenir, cent. 100p, Villa Alemana, cent. 150p, Constitucion, bicent. 200p, Linares, bicent. 250p, Copiapo, 250th anniv. 300p, La Serena, 450th anniv.

1994, Aug. 26
1116 A553 90p multicolored .45 .20
1117 A553 100p multicolored .55 .25
1118 A553 150p multicolored .85 .35
1119 A553 200p multicolored 1.25 .50
1120 A553 250p multicolored 1.60 .60
1121 A553 300p multicolored 1.75 .75
Nos. 1116-1121 (6) 6.45 2.65

Miniature Sheet of 8

Butterflies — A554

Designs: a, Vanessa terpsichore. b, Hypsochila wagenknechti. c, Battus polydamas. d, Polythysana apollina. e, Satyridae. f,

Tetraphloebia stellygera. g, Eroessa chilensis. h, Phoebis sennae.

1994, June 24 Litho. *Perf. 13*
1122 A554 100p #a.-h. 5.00 5.00

20th Intl. Conference on Data Bases — A555

1994, Sept. 21 Litho. *Perf. 13½*
1123 A555 100p multicolored .60 .30

America Issue — A556

Early postal transport vehicles: 80p, Van. 220p, DH-60-G, Gypsy Moth.

1994, Oct. 12
1124 A556 80p multicolored .50 .25
1125 A556 220p multicolored 1.50 .65

A557

A558

1994, Oct. 31 Litho. & Engr.
1126 A557 300p multicolored 1.60 .80

Beatification of Father Alberto Hurtado.

1994 Litho. *Perf. 13½*
1127 A558 80p multicolored .60 .25
a. Booklet pane of 10 6.00
Complete booklet, #1127a 6.00

Inscribed "DS/20"

1128 A558 80p multicolored .60 .25
a. Booklet pane of 10 7.00
Complete booklet, #1128a 7.00

Christmas.

Nos. 1036-1037, 1079 Surcharged

Perf. 13½ on 3 Sides

1994, Nov. 4 Litho.
1129 A525 80p on 70p #1036 .45 .25
1130 A525 80p on 70p #1037 .45 .25
a. Pair, #1129-1130 .90 .50
b. Booklet pane, 5 #1130a 7.00
Complete booklet, #1130b 7.00

1131 A542 80p on 70p #1079 .45 .25
a. Booklet pane, 10 #1131 7.00
Complete booklet, #1131a 7.00

Size and location of surcharge varies.

Miniature Sheet

Intl. Women's Day — A559

Designs: a, Star, "Women enriching the future." b, Moon, sun, "Women bringing harmony." c, Bird, "Women bringing peace." d, Earth, "Women changing the world."

1995, Mar. 8 Litho. *Perf. 13½*
1132 A559 90p Sheet of 4, #a.-d. 3.75 2.00

Ancud Seminary of Conciliation, 150th Anniv. — A560

1995, Apr. 27
1133 A560 200p multicolored 1.10 .55

Destroyer Admiral Williams A561

1995, Apr. 21
1134 A561 100p multicolored .70 .30

World Conference on Social Development A562

1995, Apr. 25
1135 A562 150p multicolored .85 .40

Order of St. Augustine in Chile, 400th Anniv. — A563

Stained glass, Cathedral of Santiago.

1995, Apr. 28
1136 A563 250p multicolored 1.40 .70

Petroglyphs — A564

Designs: a, Ceremonial mask, Buitre, Limari Province. b, Lamas, Taira Sector, El Loa Province. c, Harpooned whale, El Medano, Taltal Province. d, Two masks, Encanto, Ovalle.

1995, June 16 Litho. *Perf. 13½*
1137 A564 150p Block of 4, #a.-d. 3.25 3.25

Miniature Sheet

Motion Pictures, Cent. — A565

Posters: a, Director's chair, camera. b, Charlie Chaplin in "The Kid." c, Lumiere brothers' 1895 Cinematographe. d, "Valparaiso, My Love", with Aldo Francia.

1995, June 21
1138 A565 100p Sheet of 4, #a.-d. 4.50 2.25

City of Parral, Bicent. A566

1995, June 30 Litho. *Perf. 13½*
1139 A566 200p multicolored 1.10 .60

Miniature Sheet

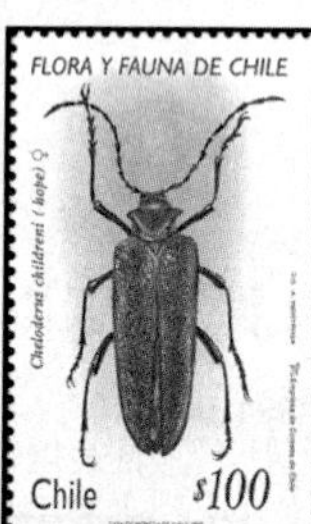

Insects and Cacti — A567

a, Cheloderus childreni. b, Eulychnia acida. c, Chiasognathus grantii. d, Browningia candelaris. e, Copiapoa dealbata. f, Acanthinodera cummingi. g, Neoporteria subgibbosa. h, Semiotus luteipennis.

1995, Aug. 10 Litho. *Perf. 13½*
1140 A567 100p Sheet of 8, #a.-h. 5.00 2.50

2nd World Congress of Police, Santiago — A568

1995, Oct. 2
1141 A568 200p multicolored 1.10 .55

Ministry of Housing and Urban Development, 30th Anniv. — A569

Design: Tower of Babel V, by Mario Toral.

1995, Oct. 5 Litho. *Perf. 13½*
1142 A569 200p multicolored 1.10 .60

Andres Bello (1781-1865), Scholar, Author A570

1995, Oct. 9 Litho. & Engr.
1143 A570 250p dk brn & blk 1.40 .70

Andres Bello Convenant, 25th anniv.

UNESCO, UN, FAO, 50th Anniv. — A571

Designs: a, Hands holding book, UNESCO emblem. b, Hands clasped between two globes, UN emblem. c, Hand holding seedling, FAO emblem.

1995, Oct. 10 Litho. *Perf. 13½*
1144 A571 100p Strip of 3, #a.-c. 1.75 .90

No. 1144 is a continuous design.

America Issue — A572

Children's drawings of environmental protection: 100p, Family in garden, trees, vert. 250p, Three people working with trees.

1995, Oct. 12 Litho. *Perf. 13½*
1145 A572 100p multicolored .60 .30
1146 A572 250p multicolored 1.50 .75

A573

A574

Chilean Soccer, Cent.: a, Carlos Dittborn. b, Hugo Lepe. c, Eladio Rojas. d, Honorino Landa.

1995, Nov. 13 Litho. *Perf. 13½*

1147 A573 100p Sheet of 4, #a.-d. 2.25 1.10

1995, Oct. 24 Litho. *Perf. 13½*

1148 A574 250p multicolored 1.25 .75

51st World Congress of Cape Horn captains.

Gabriela Mistral (1889-1957), 50th Anniv. of Receiving Nobel Prize for Literature A575

Litho. & Engr.

1995, Nov. 15 *Perf. 13½*

1149 A575 300p blue black & blk 1.60 .80

Eudyptes Chrysolophus A576

1995, Nov. 22 Litho. *Perf. 13½*

1150 A576 100p shown .65 .25

1151 A576 250p Penguins, diff. 1.50 .70

a. Souv. sheet, #1150-1151 3.50 3.50

No. 1151a sold for 600p.

Chilean Export Assoc., 60th Anniv. — A577

Cargo ship and: a, Kiwi fruit. b, Grapes. c, Peaches. d, Apples.
Jet plane and: e, Various berries.

1995, Dec. 1

1152 A577 100p Strip of 5, #a.-e. 2.75 2.75

Christmas

A578 A579

1995, Nov. 13

Booklet Stamps

1153 A578 90p brt blue & blue .50 .25

1154 A579 90p brt blue & blue .50 .25

a. Bklt. pane, 5 ea #1153-1154 5.00

Complete booklet, #1154a 5.00

1155 A578 90p brt grn & brown .50 .25

1156 A579 90p brt grn & brown .50 .25

a. Bklt. pane, 5 ea #1155-1156 5.00

Complete booklet, #1156a 5.00

Nos. 1155-1156 inscribed "DS/20."

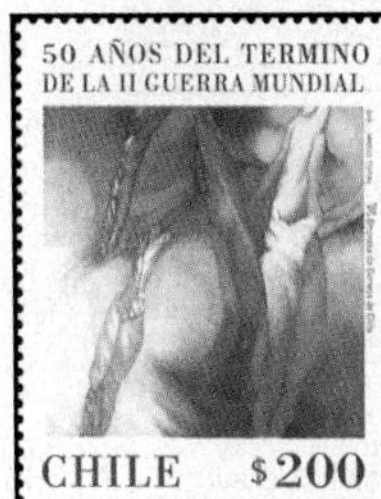

End of World War II, 50th Anniv. A580

1995, Dec. 20 Litho. *Perf. 13½*

1157 A580 200p multicolored 1.10 .55

Petroleum Production in Chile, 50th Anniv. — A581

Designs: a, Off-shore oil derrick, one main tower. b, Refinery, road trees, building. c, Refinery, up close. d, Off-shore oil derrick, four towers.

1995, Dec. 29

1158 A581 100p Block of 4, #a.-d. 2.25 2.25

Aviation Type of 1994

Designs: a, Embraer EMB-145. b, Mirage M5M Elkan. c, DHC-6 Twin Otter Series 300. d, SAAB JAS 39, Gripen.

1996, Mar. 9 Litho. *Perf. 13½*

1159 A547 400p Sheet of 4, #a.-d. 9.00 7.50

Intl. Air and Space Fair, FIDAE '96.

Men's High School, La Serena, 175th Anniv. — A582

1996, Apr. 12

1160 A582 100p multicolored .55 .30

Espamer '96, World Philatelic Exhibition — A583

Designs: No. 1161, Old Train Station, Cordoba. No. 1162, Lope de Vega Theater.

1996, Apr. 25

1161 A583 200p multicolored 1.10 .60

1162 A583 200p multicolored 1.10 .60

a. Pair, #1161-1162 2.25 2.25

Accident Prevention A584

Traffic safety: No. 1163a, Cross street at crosswalk. b, Respect traffic police. c, Obey traffic signals. d, Wait for ride on sidewalk. e, Don't cross street between parked cars. f, Never ride on side of bus. g, Walk beside road facing oncoming traffic. h, Pay attention to where you are walking. i, Don't play on streets. j, Obey traffic rules while riding a bicycle.

Safety in the home: No. 1164a, Extinguish matches after using. b, Be careful with boiling water. c, Curb sharp objects. d, Protect electrical outlets. e, Don't improvise electrical connections. f, Don't play radio or TV too loudly. g, Check all gas connections. h, Don't overload electrical outlets. i, Keep flammable materials away from furnace. j, Keep toys off floor.

Recreational safety: No. 1165a, Swim only in designated areas. b, Keep hands, head inside the car. c, Don't get a sunburn. d, Don't contaminate water with detergents. e, Don't litter. f, Extinguish camp fires. g, Don't bother others when swimming. h, Check car safety features. i, Keep kites away from electrical wires. j, Don't run in swimming pool area.

Safety in the workplace: No. 1166a, Use protective gear. b, Use only safe tools. c, Keep you mind on your work. d, Use proper tools. e, Avoid work accidents. f, Keep stairs free of objects. g, Don't carry objects that obstruct your view. h, Check ladder before using. i, Keep area clean, organized. j, Be aware of protruding nails.

Proper use of drugs and alcohol: No. 1167a, Don't drink and drive. b, Don't drink if you are pregnant. c, Don't encourage friends to drink. d, Alcohol and work don't mix. e, Drinking could destroy your family. f, Drugs can't make you happy. g, Drugs don't make you successful. h, Be happy without drugs. i, For your family say "no" to drugs. j, Drug free, happy and confident.

Safety in schools: No. 1168a, Keep calm in case of fire. b, Don't run along sides of buildings. c, Don't play dangerous jokes. d, Don't sit or stand in high dangerous places. e, Don't run on stairs. f, Don't walk and drink at the same time. g, Don't rock on chairs. h, Don't play with sharp objects. i, Don't open doors abruptly. j, Don't talk to strangers outside the school.

1996, May 2

1163 A584 50p Block of 10, #a.-j. 3.50 1.75

1164 A584 50p Block of 10, #a.-j. 3.50 1.75

1165 A584 50p Block of 10, #a.-j. 3.50 1.75

1166 A584 50p Block of 10, #a.-j. 3.50 1.75

1167 A584 50p Block of 10, #a.-j. 3.50 1.75

1168 A584 50p Block of 10, #a.-j. 3.50 1.75

No. 1 Dry Dock, Talcahuano, Cent. — A585

1996, May 20

1169 A585 200p multicolored 1.10 .55

Sculptures — A586

#1170, Mariner's Compass, by Ricardo Mesa, vert. #1171, Friendship, by Francisca Cerda, vert. #1172, Andes Winds, by Benito Rojo. #1173, Memory, by Fernando Undurraga.

1996, June 20 Litho. *Perf. 13½*

1170 A586 150p multicolored .85 .40

1171 A586 150p multicolored .85 .40

a. Pair, #1170-1171 3.50 3.50

1172 A586 200p multicolored 1.10 .55

1173 A586 200p multicolored 1.10 .55

a. Pair, #1172-1173 4.00 4.00

Nos. 1170-1173 (4) 3.90 1.90

Intl. Day Against Use of Illegal Drugs and Drug Trafficking — A587

1996, June 26

1174 A587 250p multicolored 1.40 .70

1996 Summer Olympic Games, Atlanta — A588

Designs: a, Boxer's glove. b, Runner's shoe. c, Roller blade. d, Ball.

1996, July 3

1175 A588 450p Block of 4, #a.-d. 9.00 7.50

Order of Mother of God, 50th Anniv. of Presence in Chile — A589

1996, Aug. Litho. *Perf. 13½*

1176 A589 200p multicolored 1.10 .55

Lyceum of San Fernando, 150th Anniv. — A590

1996, Aug. 2

1177 A590 200p multicolored 1.10 .55

4th Intl. Congress of Earth Sciences — A591

Globe showing portions of continents, and: a, Forest fire. b, Smoke stacks creating air pollution. c, Cutting down trees. d, Surveying equipment, desert.

1996, Aug. 5 Litho. *Perf. 13½*

1178 A591 200p Block of 4, #a.-d. 4.50 4.50

Minerals — A592

a, Kroehnkita. b, Lapis lazuli. c, Bornite. d, Azurite.

1996, Aug. 9

1179 A592 150p Block of 4, #a.-d. 3.25 3.25

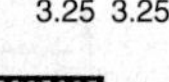

German Immigration, 150th Anniv. — A593

Designs: 250p, House, lake, mountain. 300p, Monument showing arrival on boat.

1996, Aug. 22

1180 A593 250p multicolored 1.40 .70
1181 A593 300p multicolored 1.60 .80

Aptenodytes Patagonica A594

1996, Sept. 9 Litho. *Perf. 13½*

1182 A594 250p shown 1.40 .70
1183 A594 300p Molting 1.60 .80
a. Souvenir sheet, #1182-1183 4.25 4.25

Castro Fire Dept., Cent. A595

Designs: a, 1937 Italian pumper. b, 1940 Ford fire truck. c, Gorlitz G.A. Fischer manual 4-speed pumper. d, 1907 pumper.

1996, Sept. 14

1184 A595 200p Block of 4, #a.-d. 3.50 3.50

Ecotourism in National Parks — A596

Designs: a, River rafting. b, Horseback riding. c, Snow skiing. d, Hiking around cacti.

1996, Sept. 27

1185 A596 100p Sheet of 4, #a.-d. 2.25 2.25

Juan José Latorre Benavonte (1846-1912), Admiral — A597

1996, Oct. 8

1186 A597 200p multicolored 1.10 .55

Historical Costumes — A598

America issue: No. 1187, Two women, child, dog, vert. No. 1188, Two men with horse, vert. 250p, Two men on horseback.

1996, Oct. 23

1187 A598 100p multicolored .55 .30
1188 A598 100p multicolored .55 .30
a. Pair, #1187-1188 1.40 1.40
1189 A598 250p multicolored 1.40 .70

Church, City of Arica — A599

150p, Fauna, mountains, Parinacota Park.

1996, Nov. 18 Litho. *Perf. 13½*

1190 A599 100p multicolored .55 .30
1191 A599 150p multicolored .80 .40

Christmas — A600

1996, Nov. 25

1192 A600 100p black & multi .55 .25
a. Booklet pane of 10 5.50
Complete booklet, #1192a 5.50
1193 A600 100p orange & multi .55 .25
a. Booklet pane of 10 5.50
Complete booklet, #1193a 5.50

No. 1193 is inscribed DS/20.

Mythology
A601 A602

1997, Feb. 12 Litho. *Perf. 13½*

1194 A601 40p black & blue .20 .20
1195 A602 110p black & green .60 .30
a Booklet pane of 10 6.00
Complete booklet, #1195a 6.00
1196 A602 110p black & orange .60 .30
a. Booklet pane of 10 6.00
Complete booklet, #1196a 6.00

No. 1195 inscribed DS/20.

Sixth Summit of Spanish-Americana Heads of State and Government — A603

Mural, Visual Memory of the Nation, by Mario Toral: No. 1198, Left half. No. 1199, Right half.

1996, Nov. 6

1198 A603 110p multicolored .60 .30
1199 A603 110p multicolored .60 .30
a. Pair, #1198-1199 1.25 .60

No. 1199a is a continuous design.

State Visit of King Carl XVI Gustaf, Queen Silvia of Sweden — A604

Design: Nobel Laureates Pablo Neruda, Gabriela Mistral, Nobel medal.

1996, Dec. 3

1200 A604 300p multicolored 1.60 .80

UNICEF, 50th Anniv. — A605

1996, Dec. 11

1201 A605 200p multicolored 1.10 .55

Frontier Region, Cent. — A606

#1202, Christian Alliance & Missionary Church, cent. #1203, Lonquimay municipality, cent.

1997

1202 A606 110p multicolored .60 .30
1203 A606 110p multicolored .60 .30

Issued: #1202, 1/19; #1203, 1/25.

Arturo Prat Antarctic Naval Base, 50th Anniv. — A607

1997, Feb. 6 Litho. *Perf. 13½*

1204 A607 250p Aerial view, vert. 1.40 .70
1205 A607 300p shown 1.75 .85

Controller General of the Republic, 70th Anniv. — A608

1997, Mar. 26

1206 A608 110p multicolored 1.60 .35

Opening of Metro Line 5 — A609

1997, Apr. 2

1207 A609 200p multicolored 1.10 .55

Interamerican Masonic Confederation, 50th Anniv. — A610

1200p, Emblems, compass, square, book.

1997, Apr. 8

1208 A610 250p shown 1.40 .70

Souvenir Sheet

1209 A610 1200p multicolored 6.75 6.75

No. 1209 contains one 48x60mm stamp.

Heinrich von Stephan (1831-97) A611

1997, Apr. 15

1210 A611 250p multicolored 1.40 .70

World Book and Copyright Day — A612

1997, Apr. 23

1211 A612 110p multicolored .60 .35

Details from "Death to the Invader," by David Alfaro Siqueiros (1896-1974), Muralist — A613

1997, June 26 Litho. *Perf. 13½*

1212 A613 150p shown 1.25 .35
1213 A613 200p Detail, diff. 1.50 .50

Souvenir Sheets

1214 A613 1000p like #1212 5.25 5.25
1215 A613 1000p like #1213 5.25 5.25

#1214-1215 each contain one 48x36mm stamp.

Providencia, Cent. — A614

1997, July 17

1216 A614 250p multicolored 1.25 .70

A615 A616

1997, Sept. 1

1217 A615 300p multicolored 1.60 .90

Diplomatic relations between Chile and Japan, cent. See Japan No. 2578.

1997, Oct. 1 Litho. *Perf. 13½*

1218 A616 110p Quality .60 .30

1st Radio Broadcast in Chile, 75th Anniv. — A617

1997 Litho. *Perf. 13½*

1219 A617 110p multicolored .60 .40

Chilean Opera Singers A618

Singer, opera: 120p, Carlo Morelli, "Rigoletto." 200p, Pedro Navia, "La Bohéme." 250p, Renato Zanelli, "Faust." 300p, Rayèn Quitral, "The Magic Flute." 500p, Ramón Vinay, "Othello."

1997, Oct. 15

1220 A618 120p multicolored .65 .35
1221 A618 200p multicolored 1.10 .55
1222 A618 250p multicolored 1.40 .70
1223 A618 300p multicolored 1.60 .80
1224 A618 500p multicolored 2.75 1.40
Nos. 1220-1224 (5) 7.50 3.80

America Issue — A619

Life of a postman: 110p, Delivering mail on bicycle. 250p, Delivering mail on horseback.

1997, Oct. 12 Litho. *Perf. 13½*

1225 A619 110p multicolored .60 .30
1226 A619 250p multicolored 1.40 .70

Christmas — A620

1997 Litho. *Perf. 13½*

1227 A620 110p multicolored .60 .30
a. Booklet pane of 10 6.00
Complete booklet, #1227a 6.00
1228 A620 110p multicolored .60 .30
a. Booklet pane of 10 6.00
Complete booklet, #1228a 6.00

No. 1228 is inscribed D/S20 and was only issued in booklets.

Chilean Post, 250th Anniv. A621

Designs: 120p, Postman canceling letters. 300p, Man depositing letter into postbox.

1997, Dec. 22

1229 A621 120p multicolored .65 .35
1230 A621 300p multicolored 1.60 .80

Dogs
A622 A623

1998 Litho. *Perf. 13½*

1231 A622 120p Great Dane .60 .20
1232 A623 120p Dalmatian .60 .20
a. Pair, #1231-1232 1.25 1.00
b. Booklet pane, 5 #1232a 7.00
Complete booklet, #1232b 7.00
1233 A622 120p Great Dane .60 .20
1234 A623 120p Dalmatian .60 .20
a. Pair, #1233-1234 1.25 1.00
b. Booklet pane, 5 #1234a 7.00
Complete booklet, #1234b 7.00

Nos. 1233-1234 are inscribed DS/20.

2nd Summit of the Americas, Santiago — A624

1998, Apr. 17 Litho. *Perf. 13½*

1235 A624 150p multicolored .75 .40

Souvenir Sheet

1236 A624 1000p Logo, diff. 5.00 5.00

No. 1236 contains one 26x42mm stamp.

Paintings — A625

350p, "Los Zambos de Calama," by Mauricio Moran. 400p, "Sandia Calada," by Roser Bru.

1998, May 14 Litho. *Perf. 13½*

1237 A625 350p multicolored 1.75 1.00
1238 A625 400p multicolored 2.00 1.25

Capuchin Order in Chile, 150th Anniv. — A626

Designs: 150p, Native village, friar writing in book. 250p, Friar aiding injured man.

1998, May 18

1239 A626 150p multicolored .75 .40
1240 A626 250p multicolored 1.25 .60

1998 World Cup Soccer Championships, France — A627

Players and: 250p, Crowd. 350p, World Cup Trophy. 500p, Map of France. 700p, Chilean flag.
1500p, Player, vert.

1998, May 23

1241 A627 250p multicolored 1.25 .60
1242 A627 350p multicolored 1.75 .85
1243 A627 500p multicolored 2.50 1.25
1244 A627 700p multicolored 3.50 1.75
Nos. 1241-1244 (4) 9.00 4.45

Souvenir Sheet

1245 A627 1500p multicolored 7.50 7.50

A628

A629

Antarctic Research: 250p, Scientific Committee on Antarctic Research, 25th meeting. 350p, Natl. Administrators of Antarctic Programs, 10th meeting.

1998, July 22

1246 A628 250p Logo, penguin 1.25 .60
1247 A628 350p Penguins, map, logo 1.75 .85

1998, Apr. 3

1248 A629 120p multicolored .60 .30

Captain Arturo Prat Chacon, 150th birth anniv.

Army Veterinarian Service, Cent. — A630

350p, Veterinarian listening to horse's heartbeat.

1998, Apr. 20

1249 A630 250p multicolored 1.25 .60
1250 A630 350p multicolored 1.75 .85

Merchant Marine's Director General of Maritime Territory, 150th Anniv. — A631

1998, Aug. 31 Litho. *Perf. 13½*

1251 A631 500p multicolored 3.00 1.25

Intl. Year of the Ocean.

Intl. Year of the Ocean A632

#1252, Nautical cartography. #1253, Iceberg. 500p, Silhouette of stone head, Easter Island.

1998, Sept. 10

1252 A632 400p multicolored 2.25 1.00
1253 A632 400p multicolored 2.25 1.00
1254 A632 500p multicolored 2.75 1.25
Nos. 1252-1254 (3) 7.25 3.25

Folk Singers and Composers — A633

Designs: 200p, Clara Solovera Cortes (1909-92). 250p, Francisco Flores del Campo (1908-93). 300p, Victor Jara Martinez (1932-73). 350p, Violeta Parra Sandoval (1917-67).

1998, Sept. 14

1255 A633 200p multicolored .95 .45
1256 A633 250p multicolored 1.25 .55
1257 A633 300p multicolored 1.40 .65
1258 A633 350p multicolored 1.75 .75
Nos. 1255-1258 (4) 5.35 2.40

World Stamp Day A634

1998, Oct. 9 Litho. *Perf. 13½*

1259 A634 250p multicolored 1.10 .55

Francisco Bilbao (1823-65), Writer A635

Litho. & Engr.

1998, Oct. 29 *Perf. 13½*

1260 A635 250p multicolored 1.40 .70

Chilean Painters — A636

Designs: 300p, Self-portrait, by Augusto Eguiluz (1894-1969), vert. 450p, Landscape, by Agustin Abarca (1882-1953).

1500p, "Two Nudes," by Henriette Petit (1894-1983).

1998, Nov. 3 Litho.

1261 A636 300p multi 1.40 .75
1262 A636 450p multi 2.25 1.10

Souvenir Sheet

1262A A636 1500p multicolored 7.00 7.00

No. 1262A contains one 36x47mm stamp.

Catholic University of Valparaiso, 70th Anniv. — A637

1998, Nov. 18 Litho. *Perf. 13½*

1263 A637 130p multicolored .60 .30

Prominent Women from the University of Chile — A638

America Issue: 120p, Amanda Labarca, edcuator. 250p, Marta Brunet, writer.

1998, Nov. 19 Litho. *Perf. 13½*

1264 A638 120p multicolored .60 .35
1265 A638 250p multicolored 1.25 .65

1999 World Scout Jamboree, Chile — A639

Scouting emblems and: 120p, Children of two races, stylized tents. 200p, Robert Baden-Powell. 250p, Stylized doves. 300p, Scout, stylized tents. 1000p, Scouts, leaders seated in semi-circle, vert.

3000p, Jamboree emblem over drawing of Jamboree site at Picarquin, emblems of past jamborees, Intl. Scouting Emblem.

1998, Dec. 27

1266 A639 120p multicolored .55 .30
1267 A639 200p multicolored .90 .45
1268 A639 250p multicolored 1.10 .55
1269 A639 300p multicolored 1.25 .65
1270 A639 1000p multicolored 4.50 2.25
Nos. 1266-1270 (5) 8.30 4.20

Imperf

Size: 126x104mm

1270A A639 3000p multicolored 13.00 13.00

Birds — A640

Designs: 10p, Zonotrichia capensis. 20p, Curaeus curaeus.

1998, Nov. 29

1271 A640 10p multicolored .50 .20
1272 A640 20p multicolored .50 .20

Exist dated "2000."

See Nos. 1313-1314, 1385-1386.

World Equestrian High Jump Record, 50th Anniv. — A641

Captain Alberto Larraguibel and Huaso.

1999, Feb. 5 Litho. *Perf. 13½*

1273 A641 200p multicolored .85 .50

Temuco Fire Dept., Cent. — A642

Designs: 140p, 1900 pumper. 200p, 1929 Ford. 300p, 1955 Ford K tanker. 350p, 1967 Mercedes Benz hook and ladder truck.

1500p, Firefighter rescuing victim, vert.

1999, Feb. 18 Litho. *Perf. 13½*

1274 A642 140p multicolored .65 .30
1275 A642 200p multicolored .95 .40
1276 A642 300p multicolored 1.50 .60
1277 A642 350p multicolored 1.75 .70
Nos. 1274-1277 (4) 4.85 2.00

Souvenir Sheet

1278 A642 1500p multicolored 7.00 7.00

Chilean Chamber of Deputies, 1000th Session — A643

1999, Mar. 3 *Perf. 13½*

1279 A643 140p multicolored .60 .40

Sacred Heart College, 150th Anniv. — A644

1999, Mar. 15

1280 A644 250p multicolored 1.10 .75

Economic Development Corporation (CORFO), 60th Anniv. — A645

Pedro Aguirre Cerda, former president of Chile.

1999, Apr. 29 *Perf. 13½*

1281 A645 140p multicolored .65 .40

Chilean Insurance Assoc., Cent. — A646

1999, May 18 Litho. *Perf. 13½*

1282 A646 140p multicolored .55 .45

Chilean Antarctica A647

Designs: 360p, Leptonychotes weddellii. 450p, Pygoscelis antarctica.

1500p, Arctocephalus gazella, penguins.

1999, June 15

1283 A647 360p multicolored 1.50 .70
1284 A647 450p multicolored 2.50 .85

Souvenir Sheet

1285 A647 1500p multicolored 7.50 7.50

No. 1285 contains one 35x48mm stamp.

Easter Island A648

1999, June 25

1286 A648 360p multicolored 1.50 1.50

Souvenir Sheet

Barcelona Soccer Club, Cent. — A649

Illustration reduced.

1999

1287 A649 1000p multicolored 5.00 5.00

University of Santiago, 150th Anniv. — A650

Designs: 140p, Monument, students in training room, School of Arts and Sciences, 1849. 250p, Technical equipment, building on campus, State Technical University, 1947. 300p, Student looking into microscope, computer, modern building, 1999.

1999, July 6 Litho. *Perf. 13½*

1288 A650 140p multicolored .60 .30
1289 A650 250p multicolored 1.00 .50
1290 A650 300p multicolored 1.40 .60
Nos. 1288-1290 (3) 3.00 1.40

Alexander von Humboldt (1769-1859), 200th Anniv. of Scientific Research in Latin America — A651

Face from monument and: 300p, Bust of Humboldt, wildlife, mountains. 360p, Portrait of Humboldt, penguins, sea.

1999, July 16

1291 A651 300p multicolored 1.25 .60
1292 A651 360p multicolored 1.50 .75

China '99, World Philatelic Exhibition, Beijing — A652

Chinese, Chilean flags and: 140p, Pagoda. 450p, Chinese junk.
1500p, Great Wall of China, Gate of Heavenly Peace.

1999, Aug. 10

1293 A652 140p multicolored .60 .30
1294 A652 450p multicolored 1.75 .90

Souvenir Sheet

1295 A652 1500p multicolored 6.25 3.00

No. 1295 contains one 60x48mm stamp.

City of Quilpue, Cent. — A653

1999, Aug. 20

1296 A653 250p multicolored 1.00 .50

A654 A655

140p, Raúl Cardinal Silva Henriquz (1907-99). 200p, Walking in street clothes, administering sacrament, face of Christ.

1999, Aug. 9

1297 A654 140p shown .60 .30
1298 A654 200p multicolored .80 .40

Holy Year 2000.

1999, Sept. 23 Litho. *Perf. 13½*

1299 A655 140p multicolored .60 .30

Red Cross blood donation campaign.

2000 World Congress of Authors & Composers, Santiago — A656

1999, Oct. 5

1300 A656 170p multicolored .70 .35

Intl. Year of Older Persons — A657

1999, Oct. 6

1301 A657 250p multicolored 1.00 .50

UPU, 125th Anniv. A658

1999, Oct. 9

1302 A658 300p Red mailbox 1.75 .60
1303 A658 360p Gold mailbox 1.75 .75
a. Pair, #1302-1303 + label 3.50 2.75

Nos. 1302-1303 printed in sheets of 16 pairs, with label in central column.

America Issue, A New Millennium Without Arms — A659

1999, Oct. 12

1304 A659 140p shown 1.00 .30
1305 A659 320p Broken bomb 1.50 .65

Labor Management, 75th Anniv. — A660

1999, Aug. 23

1306 A660 320p multicolored 1.25 .65

Interamerican Development Bank, 40th Anniv. — A661

1999, Oct. 29 Litho. *Perf. 13½*

1307 A661 360p multicolored 1.50 .75

A662

A663

1999, Dec. 1

1308 A662 450p multicolored 1.75 .90

Holy Year 2000.

1999, Dec. 1

1309 A663 170p multicolored .70 .35

Inscribed "D.S. 20"

1310 A663 170p multicolored .70 .35
a. Booklet pane of 10 7.00
Complete booklet, #1310a 7.00
b. Booklet pane of 5 3.50
Complete booklet, #1310b 3.50

Nos. 1309-1310 each were issued se-tenant with two labels that served as a lottery ticket and stub.

Union Leaders — A664

#1311, Luis Emilio Recabarren Serrano (1876-1924), Clotario Leopoldo Blest Riffo (1899-1990). #1312, Tucapel Jiménez Alfaro (1921-82), Manuel Bustos Huerta (1943-99).

1999, Dec. 29 Litho. *Perf. 13½*

1311 A664 200p multi .80 .40
1312 A664 200p multi .80 .40
a. Pair, #1311-1312 + label 1.60 .80

Bird Type of 1998

Designs: 50p, Campephilus magellanicus, vert. 100p, Falco peregrinus cassini, vert.

2000, Feb. *Perf. 13½*

1313 A640 50p multi .20 .20
1314 A640 100p multi .40 .20

Discovery of Juan Fernández, Archipelago, 425th Anniv. — A665

a, Más Afuera (Alejandro Selkirk) Island, Santa Clara Island, tip of Más a Tierra (Robinson Crusoe) Island. b, Más a Tierra Island. c, Dendroseris litoralis. d, Rhaphythamnus venustus. e, Lobster. f, Lobster's antenna, boat. g, Boat, Gavilea insularis. h, Gavilea insularis.

2000, Feb. 29 *Perf. 13¼*

1315 A665 360p Sheet of 8, #a.-h. 16.00 16.00

Condorito, Cartoon Character by Rene Rios Boettiger Pepo — A666

Condorito: 150p, Celebrating millennium. 260p, As soccer player. 480p, As fire fighter. 980p, On horse.
2000p, With people.

2000, Mar. 20 *Perf. 13½*

1316 A666 150p multi .75 .30
1317 A666 260p multi 1.50 .50
1318 A666 480p multi 2.50 .95
1319 A666 980p multi 5.25 2.00
Nos. 1316-1319 (4) 10.00 3.75

Souvenir Sheet

1320 A666 2000p multi 8.00 8.00

Easter Island — A667

Designs: 200p, Dancer, stone weapon. 260p, Stone statue and carvings. 340p, Island native, stone statue. 480p, Female dancer, inscribed tablet, map of island.

2000, Apr. 27 Litho. *Perf. 13¼*

1321 A667 200p multi 1.00 .50
1322 A667 260p multi 1.25 .60
1323 A667 340p multi 1.75 .90
1324 A667 480p multi 2.40 1.25
Nos. 1321-1324 (4) 6.40 3.25

Town of Carahue, Cent. (in 1998) — A668

Bridge and: No. 1325, Locomotive, pottery. No. 1326, Potatoes.

2000, May 5

1325 A668 220p multi 1.10 .55
1326 A668 220p multi 1.10 .55
a. Pair, #1325-1326 2.50 2.00

El Mercurio Newspaper, Cent. — A669

2000, June 1

1327 A669 370p multi 2.00 1.00

4th Natl. Masonic Convention — A670

2000, June 23

1328 A670 460p multi 2.50 1.25

Medicinal Plants — A671

Designs: 200p, Quillaja saponaria. 360p, Fabiana imbricata.

2000, July 3

1329 A671 200p multi 1.00 .50
1330 A671 360p multi 2.75 1.40

Discovery of Brazil, 500th Anniv. — A672

Designs: 260p, Map of Brazil, butterfly, girl. 1500p, Monkey, parrots, boy.

2000, July 10

1331 A672 260p multi 1.50 .75

Souvenir Sheet

1332 A672 1500p multi 8.50 8.50

No. 1332 contains one 48x36mm stamp.

Folklore A673

Religious festivals: 150p, Dancer in devil costume, La Tirana. 200p, Festival of San Pedro de Atacama. 370p, Candlemas Festival, Copiapo. 460p, Chinese dancers, Andacollo.

2000, July 13

1333 A673 150p multi .80 .40
1334 A673 200p multi 1.10 .55
1335 A673 370p multi 2.00 1.00
1336 A673 460p multi 2.50 1.25
Nos. 1333-1336 (4) 6.40 3.20

Prehistoric Animals — A674

No. 1337: a, Milodon. b, Titanosaurus. c, Plesiosaurus. d, Iguanodon.
Illustration reduced.

2000

1337 A674 150p Block of 4, #a-d 2.25 1.10

José de San Martín (1778-1850) — A675

2000, Aug. 25 Litho. *Perf. 13½*

1338 A675 320p multi 1.40 .70

World Meteorological Organization, 50th Anniv. — A676

2000, Aug. 28

1339 A676 320p multi 1.40 .70

Antarctic Fauna — A677

450p, Sphenis magellanicus, vert. 650p, Megaptera novaeangliae. 940p, Orcinus orca.

2000, Sept. 15

1340-1342 A677 Set of 3 8.75 4.50

Souvenir Sheet

1343 A677 2000p Mirounga leonina, vert. 10.00 10.00

No. 1343 contains one 36x48mm stamp.

2000 Summer Olympics, Sydney — A678

Sydney Opera House, Olympic flag and: a, 290p, Chilean flag, tennis player, soccer player, sprinter. b, 290p, Australian flag, archer, high jumper, cyclist.
Illustration reduced.

2000, Sept. 20

1344 A678 Pair, #a-b 3.00 1.50

City of Concepcion, 450th Anniv. — A679

Mural by Gregorio De la Fuente: a, Indian holding stick. b, Soldier on white horse. c, Finger pointing upward. d, Seated figure, arms, horse-drawn carriage. e, Horse, statue, train. f, People and rainbow.

2000, Oct. 2

1345 Horiz. strip of 6 7.50 7.50
a.-f. A679 250p Any single 1.25 .65

America Issue, World AIDS Day — A680

Designs: 150p, Heart, clasped hands of adult and child. 220p, Clasped hands.

2000, Oct. 12

1346-1347 A680 Set of 2 2.00 1.00

Penal Reform — A681

Designs: 150p, Flag, court proceedings. 2000p, People, doors of Justice Ministry.

2000, Nov. 16

1348 A681 150p multi .70 .35

Souvenir Sheet

1349 A681 2000p multi 10.50 10.50

Christmas — A682

Designs: a, Star of Bethlehem. b, Santa Claus flying over town. c, Three Magi on camels. d, Star on top of Christmas tree. e, Boy at mailbox. f, Sleeping child. g, Two Magi, cow. h, Baby Jesus, cow. i, Mary, Joseph. j, Girl putting ornaments on tree.

2000, Nov. 20 *Perf. 13½*

1350 Block of 10 7.50 7.50
a.-j. A682 150p Any single .75 .40

Inscribed "DS/20"

Perf. 13½ on 3 sides

1351 Booklet pane of 10 9.00
a.-j. A682 150p Any single .90 .45
Booklet, #1351 9.00

National Zoo, 75th Anniv. — A683

Various animals and birds, denomination in: a, LL. b, LR. c, UL. d, UR
Illustration reduced.

2001, Jan. 13 Litho. *Perf. 13½*

1352 A683 160p Block of 4, #a-d 3.50 3.50

San Sebastian Festival, Yumbel — A684

2001, Jan. 18

1353 A684 210p multi 1.00 .50

Father Alberto Hurtado (1901-52) A685

Hurtado and: 160p, Truck. 340p, Children.

2001, Jan. 20

1354-1355 A685 Set of 2 2.50 1.25

Bird Type of 1998

No. 1356, vert.: a, Sephanoides fernandensis. b, Mimus thenca. c, Pteroptochos megapodius. d, Enicognathus leptorhynchus. Size of Nos. 1356a-1356d: 24x29mm.

2001, Jan. 29

1356 A640 160p Block of 4, #a-d 3.50 3.50

Assembly of Governors of Inter-American Development Bank and Investment Corporation — A686

2001, Mar. 16

1357 A686 230p multi 1.00 .50

Souvenir Sheet

Air Force Anniversaries — A687

No. 1358: a, Lockheed C-130 Hercules, map of Antarctica. b, Flugzeugbau Extra-300, acrobatic squadron. c, North American AT-6 Texan. d, Consolidated PBY-5A/OA-10 Catalina, map of Easter Island.

2001, Mar. 29

1358 A687 260p Sheet of 4, #a-d 5.50 5.50

Air Force presence in Antarctica, 50th anniv. (No. 1358a); Halcones acrobatic squadron, 20th anniv. (No. 1358b); Aviation Group No. 1, 75th anniv. (No. 1358c); First flight of Easter Island, 50th anniv. (No. 1358d).

Nationalization of Copper Industry, 30th Anniv. — A688

Design: 2000p, Miner and equipment.

2001, Apr. 26 Litho. *Perf. 13¼*

1359 A688 400p multi 2.00 1.00

Souvenir Sheet

1359A A688 2000p multi 10.00 10.00

Organ Donation — A689

2001, May 3

1360 A689 160p multi .80 .40

Easter Island — A690

Designs: No. 1361, Stone carvings, map of island and: a, Compass rose. b, Bird and native. No. 1361C, Artifact and map of island. Illustration reduced.

2001, June 25

1361 A690 260p Horiz. pair, #a-b 2.50 2.50

Souvenir Sheet

1361C A690 2000pmulti 10.00 10.00

Lynchailurus Colocolo — A691

2001

1362 A691 100p multi .50 .25

Endangered species.

Valparaiso Firefighting Corps, 150th Anniv. — A692

Firefighters and: 160p, Manuel Blanco Encalada. 260p, Old pumper, building on fire, modern fire truck. 350p, Flags, building. 490p, Helicopter, rail tank car.
2000p, Helicopter, modern fire truck.

2001, June 28 Litho. *Perf. 13¼*

1363-1366 A692 Set of 4 6.00 3.00

Souvenir Sheet

1367 A692 2000p multi 10.00 10.00

Mushrooms A693

Designs: 300p, Macrolepiota rhacodes. 400p, Laccata ohiensis.

2001, July 25 Litho. *Perf. 13¼*

1368-1369 A693 Set of 2 3.25 1.60

24th Conference of American Armies, Santiago — A694

2001, Aug. 13

1370 A694 350p multi 1.75 .85

Bernardo O'Higgins (1778-1842), Soldier and Statesman — A695

2001, Aug. 17

1371 A695 260p multi 1.25 .60

Chilean Antarctic Research — A696

Designs: 350p, Researcher, Leptonychotes weddellii. 700p, Researchers, Macronectes giganteus. 2000p, Chionis alba.

2001, Aug. 29

1372-1373 A696 Set of 2 4.75 2.40

Souvenir Sheet

1374 A696 2000p multicolored 9.00 9.00

America Issue — UNESCO World Heritage — A697

World Heritage Sites and stamps: 160p, Quinchao Church, #1058. 230p, Tenaun Church, #1057.

2001, Oct. 9 Litho. *Perf. 13¼*

1375-1376 A697 Set of 2 1.90 .95

Cape Horn A698

2001, Nov. 22

1377 A698 220p multi 1.00 .50

El Indice del Indice, by Roberto Matta (1911-2002) — A699

2001, Nov. 5 Litho. *Perf. 13¼*

1378 A699 300p multi 1.40 .70

Railroads in Chile, 150th Anniv. — A700

No. 1397 (50x29mm): a, Caldera Station, train cars. b, Locomotive and Copiapó Station. 220p, Train on bridge.

2001, Nov. 20

1379 A700 200p Horiz. pair, #a-b 2.00 1.00

1380 A700 220p multi 1.00 .50

Christmas — A701

Designs: a, Heads of three shepherds. b, Shepherd and cow. c, Joseph and Mary. d, Donkey and Magus. e, Cow and two Magi. f, Head of shepherd. g, Two sheep. h, Infant Jesus. i, Shepherd with staff. j, One sheep. Illustration reduced.

2001, Nov.

1381 A701 160p Block of 10, #a-j 8.00 8.00

Inscribed "DS/20"

1382 A701 160p Block of 10, #a-j 8.00 8.00

k. Booklet pane, #1382 with straight edge at right 9.50 —

Complete booklet, #1382k 9.50

Rotary Intl. Emblem, Map of Chile, Globe, Tropic of Capricorn Monument — A702

2001, Dec. 21

1383 A702 240p multi 1.25 .65

Antofagasta Rotary Club, 75th anniv.

Taxation Department, Cent. — A703

2002, Jan. 14

1384 A703 180p multi .80 .40

Bird Type of 1998

Designs: 10p, Turdus falcklandii. 20p, Sturnella loyca.

2002, Jan. 25

1385 A640 10p multi .25 .20

1386 A640 20p multi .25 .20

City of Valdivia, 450th Anniv. — A704

2002, Feb. 9

1387 A704 260p multi 1.25 .65

Carabinero Force, 75th Anniv. — A705

2002, Apr. 8

1388 A705 250p multi 1.25 .65

Ignacy Domeyko (1802-89), Mineralogist — A706

2002, Apr. 11

1389 A706 290p multi 1.40 .70

City of Villarrica, 450th Anniv. — A707

2002, Apr. 26

1390 A707 290p multi 1.25 .65

Town of Calbuco, 400th Anniv. — A708

2002, May 2

1391 A708 230p multi 1.10 .55

Barros Arana Natl. Boarding School — A709

2002, May 20
1392 A709 250p multi 1.25 .65

Abolition of Death Penalty, 1st Anniv. — A710

2002, May 29
1393 A710 240p multi 1.25 .65

Endangered Species Type of 2001

Designs: 10p, Oreailurus jacobita. 20p, Oncifelis geoffrovi.

2002, June 5
1394 A691 10p multi .25 .20
1395 A691 20p multi .25 .20

Easter Island A711

Map of Easter Island and: 250p, Toromiro sophora, moai. 450p, Bird, row of moai statues, native in traditional costume.
2000p, Toromiro sophora and bird.

2002, July 1
1396-1397 A711 Set of 2 3.00 1.50
Souvenir Sheet
1398 A711 2000p multi 9.00 9.00

No. 1398 contains one 47x47mm stamp.

World Heritage Sites — A712

Churches and stamps: 230p, Achao, #1036. 290p, Dalcahue, #1056.

2002, July 27
1399-1400 A712 Set of 2 2.25 1.10

America Issue — Youth, Education, and Literacy — A713

Designs: 230p, Adult students. 450p, Woman reading to child, teacher, boy at computer.

2002, Sept. 9
1401-1402 A713 Set of 2 3.00 1.50

Children's Toys — A714

Designs: 290p, Pinwheel. 380p, Kite, vert.

2002, Sept. 16
1403-1404 A714 Set of 2 3.00 1.50

Observatories — A715

Designs: 450p, Cerro-Tololo. 550p, Paranal. 2000p, Cerro-Tololo, diff.

2002, Sept. 27
1405-1406 A715 Set of 2 4.00 2.00
Souvenir Sheet
1407 A715 2000p multi 8.50 8.50

No. 1407 contains one 47x47mm stamp.

University of Chile Clinical Hospital, 50th Anniv. — A716

2002, Oct. 17
1408 A716 250p multi 1.10 .55

Forestry Education, 50th Anniv. — A717

2002, Oct. 22
1409 A717 250p multi 1.10 .55

12th Convention on International Trade in Endangered Species Conference — A718

Designs: 300p, Phoenicoparrus andinus. 450p, Vicugna vicugna.
2000p, Chinchilla lanigera.

2002, Oct. 29
1410-1411 A718 Set of 2 3.50 1.75
Souvenir Sheet
1412 A718 2000p multi 9.00 9.00

No. 1412 contains one 47x47mm stamp.

Protected Whales — A719

Designs: 250p, Eubalaena australis. 500p, Balaenoptera acutorostrata.
2000p, Physeter macrocephalus.

2002, Nov. 2
1413-1414 A719 Set of 2 3.00 1.50
Souvenir Sheet
1415 A719 2000p multi 9.00 9.00

Violence Against Women Prevention Day — A720

2002, Nov. 22
1416 A720 230p multi 1.00 .50

Town of Puerto Varas, 150th Anniv. A721

2002, Nov. 29
1417 A721 190p multi .80 .40

Bird Type of 1998

Designs: 500p, Campephilus magellanicus, vert. 1000p, Falco peregrinus cassini, vert.

2003, Jan. 15 **Litho.** ***Perf. 13¼***
1418 A640 500p multi 1.50 .75
1419 A640 1000p multi 3.50 1.75

Puerto Montt, 150th Anniv. A722

2003, Feb. 13
1420 A722 240p multi .90 .45

Claudio Arrau (1903-91), Pianist — A723

2003, June 9 **Litho.** ***Perf. 13¼***
1421 A723 200p multi .60 .30

First Chilean Postage Stamps, 150th Anniv. — A724

No. 1422 — Mailbox, building and: a, #1. b, #2.
2000p, Building, #1 and various other stamps.
Illustration reduced.

2003, July 1
1422 A724 300p Horiz. pair, #a-b 1.75 .85
Souvenir Sheet
1423 A724 2000p multi 5.75 3.00

SEMI-POSTAL STAMPS

S. S. Abtao and Captain Policarpo Toro SP1

S. S. Abtao and Brother Eugenio Eyraud SP2

Perf. 14½x15

1940, Mar. 1 **Engr.** **Unwmk.**
B1 SP1 80c + 2.20p dk grn & lake 1.40 1.25
B2 SP2 3.60p + 6.40p lake & dk grn 1.40 1.25
a. Pair, #B1-B2 3.50 3.50

50th anniv. of Chilean ownership of Easter Is. Surtax used for charitable institutions.
Sheets containing 15 of each value, with 9 se-tenant pairs.

Catalogue values for unused stamps in this section, from this point to the end of the section, are for Never Hinged items.

Pedro de Valdivia — SP3

Portraits: 10c+10c, Jose Toribio Medina.

1961, Apr. 29 **Photo.** ***Perf. 13x12½***
B3 SP3 5c + 5c pale brn & sl grn 1.25 .40
B4 SP3 10c + 10c buff & vio blk .90 .30

Printed without charge by the Spanish Mint as a gift to Chile. The surtax was to aid the 1960 earthquake victims and to increase teachers' salaries. See Nos. CB1-CB2.

No. 402 Surcharged in Dark Green

1974, Mar. 25 Litho. *Perf. 14½*
B5 A213 27e + 3e on 40c dl grn .40 .25

Cent. of intl. meteorological cooperation. The 3e surtax of Nos. B5-B10 was for modernization of the postal system.

No. 412 Surcharged in Dark Blue

1974, Apr. 25 Litho. *Perf. 14½*
B6 A219 27e + 3e on 1.95e .40 .25

500th anniversary of the birth of Nicolaus Copernicus (1473-1534), Polish astronomer.

No. 329A Surcharged

1974, May 2 Litho. *Perf. 14*
B7 A159 27e + 3e on 1e bluish grn .35 .25

Centenary of the city of Vina del Mar.

#377 Surcharged in Blk, #395, 380 in Red

1974 Litho. *Perf. 14½*
B8 A193 47e + 3e on 40c grn .35 .25
B9 A207 67e + 3e on 40c multi .40 .25
B10 A196 97e + 3e on 40c red brn .35 .25
Nos. B8-B10 (3) 1.10 .75

Issued: #B8, 6/7; #B9, 7/9; #B10, 6/20.

AIR POST STAMPS

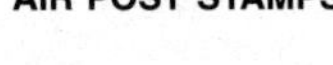

Black Surcharge

Lithographed; Center Engraved
1927 Unwmk. *Perf. 13½x14*
Black Brown & Blue
C1 40c on 10c 250.00 27.50
C2 80c on 10c 250.00 37.50
C3 1.20p on 10c 250.00 45.00
C4 1.60p on 10c 250.00 45.00
C5 2p on 10c 250.00 45.00
Nos. C1-C5 (5) 1,250. 200.00

Issued for air post service between Santiago and Valparaiso. The stamps picture Bernardo O'Higgins and are not known without surcharge.

Regular Issues of 1915-28 Overprinted or Surcharged in Black, Red or Blue

Inscribed: "Chile Correos"

1928-29 *Perf. 13½x14, 14*
C6 A39 20c brn org & blk (Bk) .30 .25
C6A A55 40c dk vio & blk (R) .30 .20
C6B A43 1p grn & blk (Bl) 1.00 .50
C6C A43 2p red & blk (Bl) 1.50 .30
f. 2p ver & blk (Bl) 65.00 15.00
C6D A43 5p ol grn & blk (Bl) 2.40 .75
C6E A50 6p on 10c dp bl & blk (R) 40.00 22.50
C7 A43 10p org & blk (Bk) ('29) 9.50 3.00
C8 A43 10p org & blk (Bl) 35.00 22.50
Nos. C6-C8 (8) 90.00 50.00

On Nos. C6B to C6D, C7 and C8 the overprint is larger than on the other stamps of the issue.

Same Overprint or Surcharge on Nos. 155, 156, 158-161
Inscribed: "Chile Correos"

1928-32 Wmk. 215
C9 A55 40c vio & blk (R) .40 .30
C10 A43 1p grn & blk (Bl) 1.10 .45
C11 A43 2p red & blk (Bl) 5.75 1.50
C12 A52 3p on 5c sl bl (R) 21.00 20.00
C13 A43 5p ol grn & blk (Bl) 4.25 1.50
C14 A43 10p org & blk (Bk) 22.50 7.25
Nos. C9-C14 (6) 55.00 31.00

Same Overprint on Nos. 166-169, 172 and 158 in Black or Red
Inscribed: "Correos de Chile"

1928-30
C15 A39 20c (#166) ('29) .75 .50
C16 A39 20c (#172) ('30) .35 .20
C17 A40 25c bl & blk (R) .45 .20
C18 A41 30c brn & blk .20 .20
a. Double ovpt., one inverted 250.00 250.00
C19 A42 50c dp grn & blk (R) .25 .20
Nos. C15-C19 (5) 2.00 1.30

Inscribed: "Chile Correos"

1932 *Perf. 13½x14, 14*
C21 A43 1p yel grn & blk (Bk) 2.75 1.50

Condor on Andes — AP1a

Airplane Crossing Andes — AP3

Los Cerrillos Airport — AP2

1931 Litho. *Perf. 13½x14, 14½x14*
C22 AP1a 5c yellow grn .25 .20
C23 AP1a 10c yellow brn .25 .20
C24 AP1a 20c rose .25 .20
C25 AP2 50c dark blue 1.00 .40
C26 AP3 50c black brn .60 .20
C27 AP3 1p purple .50 .20
C28 AP3 2p blue blk .75 .25
a. 2p bluish slate .90 .40
C29 AP2 5p lt red 2.25 .25
Nos. C22-C29 (8) 5.85 1.90

For surcharges see Nos. C51-C53.

Airplane over City — AP4

Two Airplanes over Globe — AP9

Designs: 30c, 40c, 50c, Wings over Chile. 60c, Condor. 70c, Airplane and Star of Chile. 80c, Condor and Statue of Canpolican. 3p, 4p, 5p, Seaplane. 6p, 8p, 10p, Airplane. 20p, 30p, Airplane and Southern Cross. 40p, 50p, Airplane and symbols of space.

Perf. 13½x14
1934-39 Engr. Wmk. 215
C30 AP4 10c yel grn ('35) .25 .20
C31 AP4 15c dk grn ('35) .35 .20
C32 AP4 20c dp bl ('36) .20 .20
C33 AP4 30c blk brn ('35) .20 .20
C34 AP4 40c indigo ('38) .20 .20
C35 AP4 50c dk brn ('36) .20 .20
C36 AP4 60c vio blk ('35) .20 .20
C37 AP4 70c blue ('35) .35 .20
C38 AP4 80c ol blk ('35) .20 .20

Perf. 14
C39 AP9 1p slate blk .20 .20
C40 AP9 2p grnsh bl .20 .20
C41 AP9 3p org brn ('35) .25 .20
C42 AP9 4p brn ('35) .25 .20
C43 AP9 5p org red .25 .20
C44 AP9 6p yel brn ('35) .35 .20
a. 6p brown ('39) 2.50 1.75
C45 AP9 8p grn ('35) .30 .20
C46 AP9 10p brn lake .35 .20
C47 AP9 20p olive .35 .20
C48 AP9 30p gray blk .40 .20
C49 AP9 40p gray vio 1.00 .60
C50 AP9 50p brn vio 1.25 .60
Nos. C30-C50 (21) 7.30 5.00

Nos. C30-C50 have been re-issued in slightly different colors, with white gum. The first printings are considerably scarcer.
See Nos. C90-C107B, C148-C154.

Types of 1931 Surcharged in Black or Red

Perf. 13½x14, 14½x14
1940 Wmk. 215
C51 AP1a 80c on 20c lt rose .40 .20
C52 AP2 1.60p on 5p lt red 2.25 .70
C53 AP3 5.10p on 2p sl bl (R) 1.60 1.10
Nos. C51-C53 (3) 4.25 2.00

The surcharge on #C52 measures 21½mm.

Plane and Weather Vane — AP14

Plane and Caravel — AP23

Designs (Plane and): 20c, Globe. 30c, Chilean flag. 40c, Star of Chile and Southern Cross. 50c, Mountains. 60c, Tree. 70c, Lakes. 80c, Shore. 90c, Sunrise. 2p, Compass. 3p, Telegraph lines. 4p, Rainbow. 5p, Factory. 10p, Snow-capped mountain.

1941-42 Wmk. 215 Litho. *Perf. 14*
C54 AP14 10c ol gray .20 .20
C55 AP14 20c dp rose .20 .20
C56 AP14 30c blue vio .20 .20
C57 AP14 40c dl red brn .20 .20
C58 AP14 50c red org ('42) .35 .20
C59 AP14 60c dp green .20 .20
C60 AP14 70c rose .30 .25
C61 AP14 80c ultra ('42) 1.50 .45
C62 AP14 90c dk brown .45 .25
C63 AP23 1p brt blue .30 .20
C64 AP23 2p rose lake .45 .30
C65 AP23 3p dk bl grn & yel grn .65 .50
C66 AP23 4p bl vio & buff 1.00 .65
C67 AP23 5p dk rose red ('42) 9.00 4.50
C68 AP23 10p gray grn & bl grn 5.00 3.50
Nos. C54-C68 (15) 20.00 11.80

The 1p, dated "1541-1941", commemorates the 400th anniversary of Santiago.

1942-46 Unwmk.
C69 AP14 10c ultra ('43) .20 .20
C70 AP14 10c rose lil ('45) .20 .20
C71 AP14 20c dull grn ('43) .20 .20
C72 AP14 20c cop brn ('45) .20 .20
C73 AP14 30c dull vio ('44) .20 .20
C74 AP14 30c ol blk ('45) .20 .20
C75 AP14 40c red brn ('44) .30 .20
C76 AP14 40c ultra ('45) .20 .20
C77 AP14 50c rose ('43) .20 .20
C78 AP14 50c org red ('45) .20 .20
C79 AP14 60c orange .20 .20
C79B AP14 60c dp grn ('46) .20 .20
C80 AP14 70c rose ('45) .45 .35
C81 AP14 80c slate grn .20 .20
C82 AP14 90c brown ('45) .45 .35
C83 AP23 1p gray grn & lt bl ('43) .25 .20
C84 AP23 2p org red ('43) .45 .20
C85 AP23 3p dk pur & pale org ('43) .45 .20
C86 AP23 4p bl grn & yel grn .45 .35
C87 AP23 5p dk rose car ('43) .35 .20
a. 5p dk car rose ('44) .20 .20
C88 AP23 10p sapphire ('43) .45 .35
Nos. C69-C88 (21) 6.00 4.80

No. C83 is without dates "1541-1941."
See Nos. C109-C123. For surcharges see Nos. C145-C147

Coat of Arms and Plane AP29

1942, Nov. 5 Engr. *Perf. 14½*
C89 AP29 100p car lake 25.00 20.00

University of Chile centenary.

Types of 1934-39
Perf. 13½x14
1944-55 Unwmk. Engr.
C90 AP4 10c yel grn ('55) .25 .20
C92 AP4 20c deep blue .20 .20
C93 AP4 30c black brn .20 .20
C94 AP4 40c indigo .20 .20
C95 AP4 50c dk brn ('47) .20 .20
C96 AP4 60c slate vio .20 .20
C97 AP4 70c blue ('48) .20 .20
C98 AP4 80c olive blk .20 .20

Perf. 14
C99 AP9 1p slate blk .20 .20
C100 AP9 2p grnsh bl .25 .20
C101 AP9 3p org brn ('45) .20 .20
C102 AP9 4p brown .20 .20
C103 AP9 5p org red .35 .20
C104 AP9 6p yel brn ('46) .40 .20
C105 AP9 8p green .40 .20
C106 AP9 10p brn lake 1.10 .20
C107 AP9 20p ol gray ('45) .75 .20
a. Imperf., pair 70.00
C107B AP9 50p rose vio ('50) 17.50 2.50
Nos. C90-C107B (18) 23.00 5.90

Plane and Radio Tower — AP30

1945 Unwmk. Litho. *Perf. 14*
C108 AP30 1.60p brt violet .55 .25

See Nos. C118-C119.

Types of 1941-45
1946-48 Wmk. 215
C109 AP14 10c rose lil ('47) .20 .20
C110 AP14 20c dk red brn ('48) .20 .20
C111 AP14 20c dull grn ('48) 1.50 .30
C112 AP14 30c black ('48) .20 .20
C113 AP14 40c ultra ('48) .20 .20
C114 AP14 60c ol grn ('48) .20 .20
C115 AP14 80c ol blk ('48) .20 .20
C116 AP14 90c choc ('48) .20 .20
C117 AP23 1p gray grn & lt bl ('48) .20 .20
C118 AP30 1.60p brt violet .20 .20
C119 AP30 1.80p brt vio ('48) .20 .20
C119A AP23 2p org red .40 .20
C120 AP23 3p dk pur & pale org ('47) 1.50 .30
C121 AP23 4p bl grn & yel grn ('48) 1.10 .45
C122 AP23 5p rose car ('47) .80 .20

C123 AP23 10p sapphire ('47) 1.00 .20
Nos. C109-C123 (16) 8.30 3.65

No. C117 is without dates "1541-1941."
For surcharges see Nos. C145, C147.

Flora and Fauna Type of 1948

1948
C124 A118 3p Block of 25 35.00
Never hinged 50.00
a.-y. any single 1.00 1.00

Catalogue values for unused stamps in this section, from this point to the end of the section, are for Never Hinged items.

Air Line Emblem and Planes — AP32

1949 Wmk. 215 Litho. *Perf. 14*
C125 AP32 2p ultra .40 .25

20th anniversary of the establishment of Chile's National Air Line.

Benjamin Vicuna Mackenna AP33

Factory, Badge and Book AP34

1949, Mar. 22 Engr. *Perf. 13½x14*
C126 AP33 3p dk car rose .25 .20

Unwmk.
1949, Nov. 11 Litho. *Perf. 14*

Design: 10p, Column and cogwheel.

C127 AP34 5p green .60 .35
C128 AP34 10p red brown 1.00 .45

Centenary of the founding of Chile's School of Arts and Crafts.

Plane and Globe — AP35

1950, Jan. Engr.
C129 AP35 5p green .25 .20
C130 AP35 10p red brown .60 .40

75th anniv. of the UPU.

Plane over Snow-capped Mountain AP36

Araucarian Pine and Plane — AP38

Plane and: 40c, Coast and Sunrise. 60c, Over fishing boat. 2p, Chilean flag. 3p, Dock crane. 4p, Above river. 5p, Blast furnace. 10p, Mountain lake. 20p, Cable cars.

Imprint: "Especies Valoradas-Chile"

1950-54 Wmk. 215 Litho. *Perf. 14*
C135 AP36 20c yel brn ('54) .20 .20
C136 AP36 40c purple ('52) .20 .20
C137 AP36 60c lt bl ('53) 1.25 .70
C138 AP38 1p dull green .20 .20
C139 AP38 2p brown red .20 .20
C140 AP38 3p violet bl .20 .20
C141 AP38 4p red org ('54) .20 .20
C142 AP38 5p violet .20 .20
C143 AP38 10p yel grn ('53) .20 .20
C144 AP38 20p red brn ('54) .35 .20
Nos. C135-C144 (10) 3.20 2.50

See Nos. C155-C164, C207-C212.

Nos. C115, C81 and C116 Surcharged with New Value in Carmine or Black

1951-52 Wmk. 215
C145 AP14 40c on 80c ol blk (C) ('52) .20 .20

Unwmk.
C146 AP14 40c on 80c sl grn (C) ('52) 5.00 3.50

Wmk. 215
C147 AP14 1p on 90c choc .20 .20
Nos. C145-C147 (3) 5.40 3.90

Types of 1934-39

1951-53 Unwmk. Engr. *Perf. 14*
C148 AP9 1p deep blue .20 .20
C149 AP9 2p blue .35 .20
C150 AP9 6p bis brn ('52) .45 .20
C151 AP9 30p dk gray ('53) 4.00 .60
C152 AP9 40p dk pur brn 12.00 1.60
C153 AP9 50p dark purple 20.00 6.50
Nos. C148-C153 (6) 37.00 9.30

Wmk. 215
C154 AP9 50p dk pur ('52) .80 .40

Types of 1950-54
Designs as Before
Imprint: "Especies Valoradas-Chile"

1951-55 Unwmk. Litho. *Perf. 14*
C155 AP36 20c yel brn ('54) .20 .20
C156 AP36 40c purple .20 .20
C157 AP36 60c lt blue ('53) .25 .20
C158 AP38 1p dk bl grn ('55) .20 .20
C159 AP38 2p brown red .20 .20
C160 AP38 3p violet bl .20 .20
C161 AP38 4p red org ('52) .30 .20
C162 AP38 5p violet .30 .20
C163 AP38 10p emerald .30 .20
C164 AP38 20p brown .40 .20
Nos. C155-C164 (10) 2.55 2.00

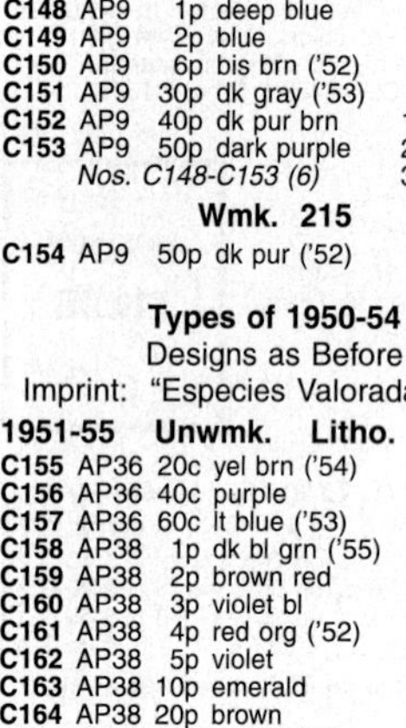

San Martin Crossing Andes AP40

Wmk. 215
1951, Mar. 16 Engr. *Perf. 14½*
C165 AP40 5p red violet .40 .25

Gen. José de San Martín, death cent.

Isabella Type of Regular Issue, 1952.

1952, Mar. 21 *Perf. 14*
C166 A125 10p carmine .50 .30

A souvenir card without franking value was issued for the Hispano-Chilean Philatelic Exhibition at Santiago, Oct. 12, 1969. It contains 2 imperf. stamps similar to Nos. 264 and C166- 60c green and 10p rose red. Size: 115x137½mm.

Ancient Fortress AP42

1953, Apr. 28
C167 AP42 10p brown car 1.00 .25

4th centenary of the founding of Valdivia.

Stamp Centenary Type of 1953

1953, Oct. 15 Engr. *Perf. 14½*
C168 A131 100p dp grnsh bl 1.25 .75

An imperf. souvenir sheet contains one each of Nos. 276 and C168, with inscriptions in black at top and bottom center. Sheet measures 178x229mm. It is stated that this sheet was not valid for postage.

Early Plane and Stylized Modern Version — AP44

Unwmk.
1954, May 26 Engr. *Perf. 14*
C170 AP44 3p deep blue .20 .20

25th anniversary of the founding of Chile's National Air Line.

Domeyko Type of Regular Issue, 1954.

1954, Aug. 16 *Perf. 13½x14*
C171 A134 5p orange brown .20 .20

Railroad Type of Regular Issue, 1954

1954, Sept. 10 Wmk. 215 *Perf. 14½*
C172 A135 10p dk purple .40 .20

An imperforate souvenir sheet contains one each of Nos. 283 and C172. Size: 174x232mm. Value, $200.

Presidential Visits Type of 1955

1955, May 24
C173 A139 100p red 1.50 1.25

Jet Plane in Clouds — AP48

Comet Air Liner — AP49

Designs: 2p, Helicopter over bridge. 10p, Oil derricks and plane. 50p, Control tower and plane. 200p, Beechcraft monoplane. 500p, Douglas DC-6.

Perf. 14½x14, 14x13½ (AP49)
1955-56 Engr. Wmk. 215
C174 AP48 1p dp red lil ('56) .20 .20
C175 AP48 2p pale brn ('56) .20 .20
C176 AP48 10p bluish grn ('56) .20 .20
C177 AP48 50p rose ('56) .60 .25
C178 AP49 100p green .80 .20
C179 AP49 200p dp ultra 5.00 .70
C180 AP49 500p dk carmine 6.00 .70
Nos. C174-C180 (7) 13.00 2.45

Stamps similar to type AP49, but inscribed in escudo currency, are listed as type AP58.

1956-58 Unwmk.

Designs: 5p, Train and plane. 20p, Jet plane and Easter Island statue.

C183 AP48 5p violet .20 .20
C184 AP48 10p grn ('57) .20 .20
C185 AP48 20p ultra .20 .20
C186 AP48 50p rose ('57) .20 .20
C187 AP49 100p bl grn ('57) .40 .20
a. Lithographed ('60) .40 .20
C188 AP49 200p dp ultra ('57) .50 .20
C189 AP49 500p car ('58) .65 .20
Nos. C183-C189 (7) 2.35 1.40

Symbols of University Departments — AP50

Design: 100p, View of the University.

1956, Dec. 15 Unwmk. *Perf. 14½*
C190 AP50 20p green .25 .20
C191 AP50 100p dk vio bl 1.00 .60

25th anniversary of the Federico Santa Maria Technical University, Valparaiso.
A souvenir sheet contains one each of Nos. 299, C190-C191, imperf. It was not issued for postal use, though some served postally. Size: 127x160mm. Value, $50.

Mistral Type of Regular Issue, 1958

1958, Jan. 10 Engr. *Perf. 14*
C192 A144 100p green .20 .20

Ambrosio O'Higgins — AP51

1958, Mar. 23
C193 AP51 100p lt blue .25 .20

Founding of the city of Osorno, 500th anniv.
A souvenir sheet contains one each of Nos. 302 and C193, imperf. and printed in red brown. It was not issued for postal use, though some served postally. Size: 155x138mm. Value, $27.50.

Exhibition Type of Regular Issue

1958, Oct. 18 Unwmk.
C194 A146 50p dull green .20 .20

A souvenir sheet contains one each of Nos. 303 and C194, imperf. and printed in deep red. It was not issued for postal use, though some served postally. Size: 188x220mm. Value, $27.50.

Bank Type of Regular Issue, 1958.

1958, Dec. 18 Engr. *Perf. 14*
C195 A147 50p redsh brown .20 .20

A souvenir sheet contains one each of Nos. 304 and C195, printed in dull violet, imperf. It was not issued for postal use, though some served postally. Value, $150.

Antarctic Types of Regular Issue

1958 Litho. *Perf. 14*
C199 A149 20p violet .20 .20

Engr.
C200 A150 500p dark blue 2.10 .85

Symbols of Various Religions AP52

Perf. 14½
1959, Jan. 23 Unwmk. Engr.
C206 AP52 50p dk car rose .20 .20

10th anniversary of the Universal Declaration of Human Rights.

Types of 1950-54.
Imprint: "Casa de Moneda de Chile."

Designs: 50p, Plane silhouette over shore. 100p, Plane over map of Antarctica. 200p, Plane over natural arch rock.

1959 Litho. *Perf. 14*

C207	AP38	1p dk blue grn	.60	.35
a.	Wmk. 215		30.00	
C208	AP38	10p emerald	.40	.20
C209	AP38	20p red brown	.25	.20
C210	AP38	50p yellow grn	.25	.20
C211	AP38	100p car rose	.25	.20
C212	AP38	200p brt blue	.40	.20
	Nos. C207-C212 (6)		2.15	1.35

Carlos Anwandter AP53

1959, June 18 Engr. *Perf. 14*

C213 AP53 20p rose carmine .20 .20

Centenary of the German School in Valdivia, founded by Carlos Anwandter.

A souvenir sheet contains one each of Nos. 319 and C213, imperf. It was not issued for postal use, though some served postally. Value, $32.50.

IGY Type of Regular Issue, 1958.

1959, Aug. 28 Unwmk. *Perf. 14*

C214 A148 50p green .20 .20

Ladrillero Type of Regular Issue

1959, Aug. 28 Litho.

C215 A154 50p green .20 .20

Barros Arana Type of Regular Issue

1959, Aug. 28

C216 A155 100p purple .40 .20

Red Cross Type of Regular Issue

1959, Oct. 6

C217 A156 50p red & blk .25 .20

WRY Type of Regular Issue, 1960.

1960, Apr. 7 Unwmk. *Perf. 14½*

C218 A160 10c violet .25 .20

A souvenir sheet contains two stamps similar to Nos. 330 and C218, the 1c printed in blue, the 10c airmail in maroon. The sheet is imperf., printed on thin cardboard. Size: 160x204mm. Value, $110.

Type of Regular Issue, 1960-62, and

José Agustin Eyzaguirre and José Miguel Infante — AP54

Designs: 2c, Palace of Justice. 5c, National memorial. No. C220, Arms of Chile. No. C220A, José Gaspar Marin and J. Gregorio Argomedo. 50c, Archbishop J. I. Cienfuegos and Brother Camilo Henriquez. 1e, Bernardo O'Higgins.

1960-65 Unwmk. Engr. *Perf. 14½*

C218A	AP54	2c mar & gray vio ('62)	.20	.20
C219	A162	5c vio bl & dl pur ('61)	.20	.20
		Wmk. 215		
C220	A161	10c dk brn & red brn	.20	.20
		Unwmk.		
C220A	AP54	10c vio brn & brn ('64)	.40	.25
C220B	AP54	20c dk bl & dl pur ('64)	.25	.20
C220C	AP54	50c bl grn & ind ('65)	1.00	.25
C220D	A162	1e dk red & red brn ('63)	1.00	.40
		Nos. C218A-C220D (7)	3.25	1.70

150th anniv. of the formation of the 1st Natl. Government.

A souvenir sheet contains two airmail stamps: a 5c brown similar to No. C219 (National Memorial) and a 10c green, type A161. The sheet is imperf., printed on heavy paper with papermaker's watermark. Size: 120x168mm. Value, $30.

Map and Rotary Emblem — AP55

Unwmk.

1960, Dec. 1 Litho. *Perf. 14*

C221 AP55 10c blue .45 .20

South American Rotary Regional Conference, Santiago, 1960.

A souvenir sheet contains one 10c maroon, type AP55, with brown marginal inscription. Size: 118x158mm. Value, $60.

The souvenir sheet was overprinted in green "El Mundo Unida Contra la Malaria" and the outline of a mosquito, and released in October, 1962. Value, $27.50.

Plane over Mountain Lake — AP56

Designs: 1m, Araucarian pine and plane. 2m, Chilean flag and plane. 3m, Plane and dock crane. 4m, Plane above river (vignette like AP39). 5m, Blast furnace. 2c, Plane over cable cars. 5c, Plane silhouette over shore. 10c, Plane over map of Antarctica. 20c, Plane over natural arch rock.

Imprint: "Casa de Moneda de Chile."

1960-62 Litho. *Perf. 14*

C222	AP56	1m orange	.20	.20
C223	AP56	2m yellow grn	.20	.20
C224	AP56	3m violet	.20	.20
C225	AP56	4m gray olive	.20	.20
C226	AP56	5m brt bl grn	.20	.20
C227	AP56	1c ultra	.20	.20
C228	AP56	2c red brn ('61)	.25	.20
C229	AP56	5c yel grn ('61)	1.25	.20
C230	AP56	10c car rose ('62)	.30	.20
C231	AP56	20c brt bl ('62)	.35	.20
		Nos. C222-C231 (10)	3.35	2.00

Oil Derricks and Douglas DC-6 — AP57

Beechcraft Monoplane AP58

5m, Train and plane. 2c, Jet plane & Easter Island statue. 5c, Control tower & plane. 10c, Comet airliner. 50c, Douglas DC-6.

Perf. 14x13½

1960-67 Unwmk. Litho.

C234	AP57	5m red brown	.20	.20
C235	AP57	1c dull blue	.20	.20
C236	AP57	2c ultra ('62)	.20	.20
C237	AP57	5c rose red ('64)	.20	.20
C238	AP58	10c ultra ('67)	.20	.20
C239	AP58	20c car ('62)	.20	.20
C240	AP58	50c green ('63)	.20	.20
		Nos. C234-C240 (7)	1.40	1.40

Stamps similar to type AP58, but inscribed in peso ($) currency, are listed as type AP49.

Congress Type of Regular Issue.

1961, Oct. 5 *Perf. 14½*

C245 A164 10c gray green .95 .60

Soccer Type of Regular Issue, 1962.

Designs: 5c, Goalkeeper and stadium, vert. 10c, Soccer players and globe.

1962, May 30 Unwmk. Engr.

C246 A165 5c rose lilac .20 .20
C247 A165 10c dk carmine .25 .20

A souvenir sheet of four contains one each of Nos. 340-341, C246-C247, imperf., with light brown marginal inscriptions. Size: 123x194mm. Sold for 7.50 escudos (face value, 22 centavos). Value, $7.50.

Hunger Type of Regular Issue.

20c, Mother with empty bowl, horiz.

1963, Mar. 21 Litho. *Perf. 14*

C248 A166 20c green .20 .20

Red Cross Type of Regular Issue.

Design: 20c, Centenary emblem and plane silhouette, horiz.

1963, Sept. 6 Unwmk. *Perf. 14*

C249 A167 20c gray & red .20 .20

Fire Engine of 1860's AP59

1963, Dec. 20 Litho. *Perf. 14½*

C250 AP59 30c red .20 .20

Centenary of the Santiago Fire Brigade.

Western Hemisphere AP60

1964, Apr. 9 Unwmk. *Perf. 14½*

C254 AP60 4c ultra .20 .20

Issued in memory of President John F. Kennedy and to honor the Alliance for Progress.

Battle of Rancagua — AP61

1965, May 7 Engr. *Perf. 14½*

C255 AP61 5c dull grn & sepia .20 .20

Battle of Rancagua, 10/7/14, 150th anniv.

ITU Emblem, Old and New Communication Equipment AP62

1965, May 7 Litho. *Perf. 14½x14*

C256 AP62 40c red & maroon .20 .20

ITU centenary.

Portrait Type of 1964

Portraits: No. C257, Enrique Molina. No. C258, Msgr. Carlos Casanueva.

1965, June Litho. *Perf. 14*

C257 A169 60c brt violet .20 .20
C258 A169 60c green .20 .20

See note after No. 346.

Skier Type of Regular Issue 1965

Design: 20c, Skier, horiz.

1965, Aug. 30 Unwmk. *Perf. 14*

C259 A172 20c ultra .25 .20

Fishing Boats, Angelmo Harbor AP63

Aviators' Monument AP64

1965

C260 AP63 40c brown .20 .20

Perf. 14x14½

C262 AP64 1e car rose .20 .20

Andrés Bello (1780?-1865), Venezuela-born Writer and Educator — AP65

1965, Nov. 29 Engr. Unwmk.

C263 AP65 10c dk car rose .20 .20

Skiers — AP66

Basketball AP67

1966, Apr. 6 Litho. *Perf. 14*

C264 AP66 4e dk bl & red brn .60 .20

World Skiing Championships, Partillo, Aug. 1966.

1966, Apr. 28

C265 AP67 13c rose carmine .20 .20

International Basketball Championships.

Slalom AP68

Perf. 14½x15

1966, July 20 Litho. Unwmk.

C266 AP68 75c rose car & lil .20 .20
C267 AP68 3e ultra & lt bl .20 .20

Intl. Skiing Championships, Partillo, August 1966. A souvenir sheet of 2 contains imperf. stamps similar to Nos. C266-C267. No gum. Size: 109x140mm. Value $5.

Ship Type of Regular Issue

1966 Litho. *Perf. 14½*

C268 A175 70c Prus grn & yel grn .25 .20

See note below No. 358.

ICY Type of Regular Issue

1966, Oct. 28 Unwmk. *Perf. 14½*

C269 A177 3e blue & carmine .50 .25

A souvenir sheet of 2 contains imperf. stamps similar to Nos. 360 and C269. No gum. Size: 111x140mm. Value $7.50.

Chilean Flag and Ships — AP69

1966, Nov. 21 Litho. *Perf. 14*
C270 AP69 13c dull red brn .25 .20

Centenary of the city of Antofagasta.

Pardo Type of Regular Issue

40c, Pardo & map of Chile's claim to Antarctica.

1967, Jan. 6 Unwmk. *Perf. 14½*
C271 A178 40c ultra .25 .20

See note below No. 361.

Family Type of Regular Issue

1967, Apr. 13 Litho. *Perf. 14*
C272 A179 80c brt bl & blk .25 .20

Ruben Dario and Title Page of "Azul" AP70

1967, May 15 Engr. *Perf. 14½*
C273 AP70 10c dark blue .25 .20

Ruben Dario (pen name of Felix Ruben Garcia Sarmiento, 1867-1916), Nicaraguan poet, newspaper correspondent and diplomat.

Tree Type of Regular Issue

1967, June 9 Litho.
C274 A180 75c grn & pale rose .25 .20

Lions Type of Regular Issue

1967 Litho. *Perf. 14*
C275 A181 1e purple & yel .35 .25
C276 A181 5e blue & yel .90 .30

A souvenir sheet without franking value contains 3 imperf. stamps, 20c, 1e and 5e, in violet blue and yellow. Size: 110x140mm. Value, $13.50.

Issue dates: 1e, July 12; 5e, Aug. 11.

Flag Type of Regular Issue

1967, Oct. 20 Unwmk. *Perf. 14½*
C277 A182 50c ultra & crimson .20 .20

ITY Emblem AP71

1967, Nov. 22 Litho. *Perf. 14½*
C278 AP71 30c lt vio bl & blk .20 .20

Issued for International Tourist Year, 1967.

Caro Type of Regular Issue, 1967.

1967, Dec. 4 Engr. *Perf. 14½*
C279 A183 40c violet .50 .25

Type of Regular Issue, 1968

1968, Apr. 23 Litho. *Perf. 14½*
C280 A184 2e brt violet .60 .25

Sesquicentennial of the Battles of Chacabuco and Maipu. A souvenir sheet of 2 contains imperf. stamps similar to Nos. 367 and C280. Value, $12. A second sheet exists with the 2e in green and the 3e in brown. Size: 139½x100mm. Value, $12.

Farm Type of Regular Issue

1968, June 18 Unwmk.
C281 A185 50c blk, org & grn .25 .20

Juan I. Molina, Educator and Scientist AP72

1968, Aug. 27 Litho. *Perf. 14½*
C282 AP72 1e bright green .25 .20

Map of Chiloé Province — AP73

British Crown and Map of Chile — AP74

Perf. 14½

1968, Oct. 7 Unwmk. Litho.
C283 AP73 1e rose claret .20 .20

Anniversaries of the founding of five towns in Chiloé Province.

Auto Club Type of Regular Issue

1968, Nov. 10 Engr. *Perf. 14½x14*
C284 A189 5e ultra .25 .20

1968, Nov. 12 Litho. *Perf. 14½*

50c, Chilean coat of arms (horiz.; similar to type A161). 3e, British coat of arms, horiz.

C285 AP74 50c green & brn .20 .20
C286 AP74 3e bl & org brn .25 .20

Engr.

C287 AP74 5e purple & mag .30 .20
Nos. C285-C287 (3) .75 .60

Visit of Queen Elizabeth II of Great Britain, Nov. 11-18. A souvenir sheet of 3 contains imperf., lithographed stamps similar to Nos. C285-C287. Size: 124½x190mm. The souvenir sheet also publicizes the British-Chilean Philatelic Exhibition. Value, $10.

First Coin Minted in Chile and Coin Press AP75

Design: 1e, Chile No. 128.

1968, Dec. 31 Litho. *Perf. 14½*
C288 AP75 50c ocher & vio brn .20 .20
C289 AP75 1e lt bl & dp org .20 .20

225th anniversary of the founding of the State Mint (Casa de Moneda de Chile).

A souvenir sheet of 4 contains imperf. stamps similar to Nos. 373-374, C288-C289. Size: 150x119mm. Value, $10.

Satellite Type of Regular Issue

1969, May 20 Litho. *Perf. 14½*
C290 A191 2e rose lilac .25 .20

Red Cross Type of Regular Issue

1969, Sept. Litho. *Perf. 14½*
C291 A192 5e black & red .25 .20

A souvenir card contains 2 imperf. stamps similar to Nos. 376 and C291, with red marginal inscription. Size: 109x140mm. Value $4.50.

Dam Type of Regular Issue

1969, Nov. 18 Litho. *Perf. 14½*
C292 A193 3e blue .25 .20

Rodriguez Type of Regular Issue

1969, Nov. 24
C293 A194 30c brown .25 .20

EXPO '70 Type of Regular Issue

1969, Dec. 1 Litho. *Perf. 14*
C294 A195 5e red .25 .20

Bible Type of 1969

1969, Dec. 2 *Perf. 14½*
C295 A196 1e green .25 .20

ILO Type of Regular Issue

1969, Dec. 17 *Perf. 14½*
C296 A197 2e rose lil & blk .25 .20

Human Rights Year Type of 1969

1969, Dec. 18
C297 A198 4e brown & red .25 .25

A souvenir sheet of 2 contains imperf. stamps similar to Nos. 382 and C297. Size: 110x140mm. Value, $9.

Easter Island Type of 1970

1970, Jan. 26
C298 A199 50c dull grnsh bl .30 .20

Ship Type of Regular Issue

1970, Feb. 4 Litho. *Perf. 14½*
C299 A200 2e deep ultra .30 .20

Rotary Type of Regular Issue

1970, Mar. 18 Litho. *Perf. 14*
C300 A201 1e rose claret .35 .25

Gandhi Type of Regular Issue

1970, Apr. 1 Litho. *Perf. 14½*
C301 A202 1e red brown .30 .20

Education Year Type of 1970

1970, July 17 Litho. *Perf. 14½*
C302 A204 4e red brown .30 .25

National Shrine Type of 1970

1970, July 28 Litho. *Perf. 14½*
C303 A205 1e ultra .25 .20

Cancer Type of Regular Issue

1970, Aug. 11
C304 A206 2e brn & lt olive .25 .20

A few copies are known inscribed "Correos de Chile" instead of "Correos Aereo Chile."

Copper Type of Regular Issue

1970, Oct. 21 Litho. *Perf. 14½*
C305 A207 3e grn & lt red brn .25 .20

United Nations Type of 1970

1970, Oct. 22
C306 A208 5e dk car & grn .30 .20

Freighter Type of Regular Issue

1971, Jan. 18 Litho. *Perf. 14*
C307 A209 5e lt red brown .35 .20

No. C290 Surcharged in Red

1971, Jan. 21 Litho. *Perf. 14½*
C308 A191 52c on 2e rose lil .25 .20

Liberation Type of Regular Issue

1971, Feb. 3 *Perf. 14½*
C309 A210 1e gray bl & brn .25 .20

UNICEF Type of Regular Issue

1971, Feb. 11 Litho. *Perf. 14½*
C310 A211 2e blue & grn .25 .20

Boy Scout Type of Regular Issue

1971, Feb. 10 *Perf. 14*
C311 A212 5c dk car & ol .25 .20

Satellite Type of Regular Issue

1971, May 25 Litho. *Perf. 14½*
C312 A213 2e brown .25 .20

De Ercilla Type of Regular Issue

1972, Mar. 20 Engr. *Perf. 14*
C313 A221 2e Prussian blue .25 .20

A souvenir card contains impressions of Nos. 414 and C313 with black marginal inscription commemorating España 75 Philatelic Exhibition. Size: 165x220mm.

AIR POST SEMI-POSTAL STAMPS

Catalogue values for unused stamps in this section are for Never Hinged items.

Type of Semi-Postal Stamps, 1961

Portraits: 10c+10c, Alonso de Ercilla. 20c+20c, Gabriela Mistral.

Perf. 13x12½

1961, Apr. 29 Photo. Unwmk.
CB1 SP3 10c + 10c salmon & choc .95 .30
CB2 SP3 20c + 20c gray & dp cl .95 .30

Printed without charge by the Spanish Mint as a gift to Chile. The surtax was to aid the 1960 earthquake victims and to increase teachers' salaries.

ACKNOWLEDGMENT OF RECEIPT STAMPS

AR1

1894 Unwmk. *Perf. 11½*
H1 AR1 5c brown .75 .50
a. Imperf., pair 3.00

The black stamp of design similar to AR1 inscribed "Avis de Paiement" was prepared for use on notices of payment of funds but was not regularly issued.

POSTAGE DUE STAMPS

D1

D2

Handstamped

1894 Unwmk. *Perf. 13*

J1	D1	2c black, *straw*	11.00	5.00
J2	D1	4c black, *straw*	11.00	5.00
J3	D1	6c black, *straw*	11.00	5.00
J4	D1	8c black, *straw*	11.00	5.00
J5	D2	10c black, *straw*	11.00	5.00
J6	D1	16c black, *straw*	11.00	5.00
J7	D1	20c black, *straw*	11.00	5.00
J8	D1	30c black, *straw*	11.00	5.00
J9	D1	40c black, *straw*	11.00	5.00
		Nos. J1-J9 (9)	99.00	45.00
J1a	D1	2c black, *yellow*	45.00	42.50
J2a	D1	4c black, *yellow*	37.50	30.00
J3a	D1	6c black, *yellow*	27.50	25.00
J4a	D1	8c black, *yellow*	11.00	9.00
J5a	D2	10c black, *yellow*	11.00	9.00
J6a	D1	16c black, *yellow*	11.00	9.00
J7a	D1	20c black, *yellow*	11.00	9.00
J8a	D1	30c black, *yellow*	11.00	9.00
J9a	D1	40c black, *yellow*	11.00	9.00
		Nos. J1a-J9a (9)	176.00	151.50

Counterfeits exist.

D3

1895 Litho. *Perf. 11*

J19	D3	1c red, *yellow*	5.00	2.00
J20	D3	2c red, *yellow*	5.00	2.00
J21	D3	4c red, *yellow*	4.25	2.00

J22 D3 6c red, *yellow* 5.00 2.00
J23 D3 8c red, *yellow* 3.25 2.00
J24 D3 10c red, *yellow* 3.25 3.00
J25 D3 20c red, *yellow* 3.25 1.50
J26 D3 40c red, *yellow* 3.25 2.00
J27 D3 50c red, *yellow* 3.25 2.00
J28 D3 60c red, *yellow* 6.50 3.00
J29 D3 80c red, *yellow* 6.50 4.25
J30 D3 1p red, *yellow* 6.50 4.25
Nos. J19-J30 (12) 55.00 30.00

Nos. J19-J30 were printed in sheets of 100 (10x10) containing all 12 denominations.
Counterfeits of Nos. J19-J42 exist.

1896 ***Perf. 13½***
J31 D3 1c red, *straw* .75 .35
J32 D3 2c red, *straw* .75 .35
J33 D3 4c red, *straw* 1.00 .35
J34 D3 6c red, *straw* 2.00 .75
J35 D3 8c red, *straw* 1.00 .40
J36 D3 10c red, *straw* .75 .40
J37 D3 20c red, *straw* .75 .40
J38 D3 40c red, *straw* 12.00 10.00
J39 D3 50c red, *straw* 12.00 10.00
J40 D3 60c red, *straw* 12.00 10.00
J41 D3 80c red, *straw* 12.00 10.00
J42 D3 100c red, *straw* 25.00 21.00
Nos. J31-J42 (12) 80.00 64.00

D4

D5

1898 ***Perf. 13***
J43 D4 1c scarlet .35 .30
J44 D4 2c scarlet .90 .60
J45 D4 4c scarlet .35 .30
J46 D4 10c scarlet .35 .30
J47 D4 20c scarlet .35 .30
Nos. J43-J47 (5) 2.30 1.80

1924 ***Perf. 11½, 12½***
J48 D5 2c blue & red .75 .60
J49 D5 4c blue & red .75 .60
J50 D5 8c blue & red .75 .60
J51 D5 10c blue & red .75 .60
J52 D5 20c blue & red .75 .35
J53 D5 40c blue & red .75 .60
J54 D5 60c blue & red .75 .60
J55 D5 80c blue & red .75 .60
J56 D5 1p blue & red 1.00 .75
J57 D5 2p blue & red 1.75 1.25
J58 D5 5p blue & red 1.75 1.25
Nos. J48-J58 (11) 10.50 7.80

Nos. J48-J58 were printed in sheets of 150 containing all 11 denominations, and in sheets of 50 containing the five lower denominations, providing various se-tenants.

All values of this issue exist imperforate, also with center inverted, but are not believed to have been regularly issued. Those with inverted centers sell for about 10 times normal stamps.

OFFICIAL STAMPS

For Domestic Postage

O1

Single-lined frame
Control number in violet

1907 **Unwmk.** ***Imperf.***
O1 O1 dl bl, "CARTA" org 22.50 17.50
O2 O1 red, "OFICIO" bl 22.50 17.50
O3 O1 vio, "PAQUETE" red 22.50 17.50
O4 O1 org, *bl*, "EP" vio 22.50 17.50
Nos. O1-O4 (4) 90.00 70.00

The diagonal inscription in differing color indicates type of usage: CARTA for letters of ordinary weight; OFICIO, heavy letters to 100 grams; PAQUETE, parcels to 100 grams; E P (Encomienda Postal), heavier parcels; C (Certificado), as on No. O8, registration including postage.

Varieties include CARTA, PAQUETE and E P inverted, OFICIO omitted, etc.

Double-lined frame
Large control number in black
Perf. 11

O5 O1 bl, "CARTA" yel 8.00 7.00
O6 O1 red, "OFICIO" bl 8.00 5.25
O7 O1 brn, "PAQUETE" grn 8.00 5.25
O8 O1 grn, "C" red 110.00 82.50
Nos. O5-O8 (4) 134.00 100.00

Nos. O5-O8 exist in tête bêche pairs; with CARTA, OFICIO or PAQUETE double or inverted, and other varieties.
Counterfeits of Nos. O1-O8 exist.

For Foreign Postage

Regular Issues of 1892-1909 — a Overprinted in Red

On Stamps of 1904-09

1907 ***Perf. 12***
O9 A14 1c green 7.50 7.50
a. Inverted overprint 17.50
O10 A12 3c on lp brn 14.00 13.00
a. Inverted overprint 52.50
O11 A14 5c ultra 10.00 9.50
a. Inverted overprint 35.00
12 A15 10c gray & blk 10.50 10.50
O13 A15 15c vio & blk 14.00 13.00
O14 A15 20c org brn & blk 14.00 14.00
O15 A15 50c ultra & blk 45.00 45.00

On Stamp of 1892
Rouletted

O16 A6 1p dk brn & blk 110.00 87.50
Nos. O9-O16 (8) 225.00 200.00

Counterfeits of Nos. O9-O16 exist.

Regular Issues of 1915-25 Overprinted — b in Red or Blue

1926 ***Perf. 13½x14, 14***
O17 A52 5c slate bl (R) 2.50 .50
O18 A50 10c bl & blk (R) 4.00 .75
O19 A39 20c org red & blk (Bl) 2.00 .40
O20 A42 50c dp grn & blk (Bl) 2.00 .40
O21 A43 1p grn & blk (R) 2.75 .70
O22 A43 2p ver & blk (Bl) 4.00 1.00
Nos. O17-O22 (6) 17.25 3.75

Nos. O21 and O22 are overprinted vertically at each side.

Nos. O17 to O22 were for the use of the Biblioteca Nacional.

Regular Issue of 1915-25 Overprinted in Red — c

1928 ***Perf. 13½x14, 14***
O23 A50 10c bl & blk 6.50 2.00
O24 A39 20c brn org & blk 3.00 1.00
O25 A40 25c dl bl & blk 7.50 1.00
O26 A42 50c dp grn & blk 4.00 1.00
O27 A43 1p grn & blk 5.00 1.50
Nos. O23-O27 (5) 26.00 6.50

The overprint on Nos. O23 to O26 is 16½mm high; on No. O27 it is 20mm.

Regular Issues of 1928-30 Overprinted in Red — d

On Stamp Inscribed: "Correos de Chile"

1930-31
O28 A50 10c bl & blk 3.00 1.50

Wmk. 215
On Stamps Inscribed: "Correos de Chile"

O29 A50 10c bl & blk 6.00 3.00
O30 A39 20c org red & blk .75 .50
O31 A40 25c bl & blk .75 .50
O32 A42 50c dp grn & blk 1.50 .75

On Stamps Inscribed: "Chile Correos"

O33 A42 50c dp grn & blk 1.50 .75
O34 A43 1p grn & blk 1.50 .75
Nos. O28-O34 (7) 15.00 7.75

Same Overprint on No. 181

1933 ***Perf. 13½x14***
O35 A61 20c dk brn .75 .25

Same Overprint in Red on No. 182

1935 **Wmk. 215**
O36 A62 10c deep blue .75 .50

No. 163 Ovptd. Type "b" in Red Inscribed: "Correos de Chile"

1934
O37 A52 5c lt grn .60 .50

Overprint "b" on No. 182

1935
O38 A62 10c dp bl .50 .50

Same Overprint in Black on No. 181

1936 **Wmk. 215** ***Perf. 13½x14***
O39 A61 20c dk brn 10.00 .50

Overprint "b" in Red on No. 158

1938 ***Perf. 14***
O40 A43 1p grn & blk 2.50 1.00

Nos. 204 and 205 Overprinted Type "d" in Black

1939 ***Perf. 13½x14, 14***
O41 A78 50c violet 4.00 2.50
O42 A84 1p org brn 5.00 4.00

Stamps of 1938-40 Overprinted Type "b" in Black, Red or Blue

1940-46 ***Perf. 13½x14, 14***
O43 A78 10c sal pink ('45) 2.00 1.75
O44 A78 15c brn org 1.00 .40
O45 A78 20c lt bl (R) ('42) 1.50 .60
O46 A78 30c brn pink (Bl) .75 .40
O47 A78 40c lt grn .75 .40
O48 A78 50c vio ('45) 4.00 .75
O49 A84 1p org brn ('42) 2.50 .75
O50 A84 1.80p dp bl (R) ('45) 10.00 6.00
O51 A84 2p car lake ('42) 2.00 1.25
Nos. O43-O51 (9) 24.50 12.30

Overprint "b" in Black on Nos. 223, 225
Unwmk.

O58 A84 1p brn org 2.50 1.50
O59 A84 2p car lake ('46) 5.00 2.00

Regular Issues of 1938-43 Overprinted Diagonally in Carmine, Black or Blue — e

Wmk. 215, Unwmkd.

1948-54 ***Perf. 13½x14, 14***
O60 A78 20c lt bl, #219 (C) .75 .35
O61 A78 30c brt pink, #202 (Bl) ('54) 1.50 .50
O62 A78 40c brt grn, #203 ('54) 2.50 1.25
O63 A78 50c vio #222 ('49) .75 .40
O64 A84 1p org brn, #205 2.50 1.00
O65 A84 2p car lake, #207 ('54) 1.00 .50
O66 A84 5p dk sl grn, #208 (C) ('51) 1.75 1.00
Nos. O60-O66 (7) 10.75 5.00

Overprint "e" Diagonally on Nos. 265 and 275 in Red or Black

Wmk. 215, Unwmkd.

1953-55 ***Perf. 13½x14, 13x14***
O67 A126 1p dk bl grn, #265 (R) 1.00 .50
O68 A126 1p dk bl grn, #265 (Bk) ('55) .75 .50
O69 A126 1p dk bl grn, #275 (R) ('55) .75 .50
Nos. O67-O69 (3) 2.50 1.50

Overprint "e" Horizontally on Nos. 207, 209 in Black or Blue

1955-56 **Wmk. 215** ***Perf. 14***
O70 A84 2p car lake ('56) 1.75 .75
O71 A84 10p rose vio (Bl) 2.75 1.75

Overprint "e" Horizontally on Nos. 293-295 and Types of 1956 Regular Issue in Black or Red

1956 **Unwmk.** ***Perf. 14x14½***
O72 A141 2p purple 1.00 .60
O73 A142 3p lt vio bl (R) 3.00 2.00
O74 A141 5p redsh brn .75 .35
O75 A142 10p vio (19x22¼mm) (R) 3.00 1.75
a. Perf. 13½x14 (19½x22½mm) ('58) .50 .40
O76 A141 50p rose red 2.50 1.00

No. 310 Overprinted in Red Vertically, Reading Down, Similar to Type "e"
Size of Overprint: 21x2½mm

1958 **Litho.** ***Perf. 14***
O77 A149 10p vio blue *200.00 30.00*

Overprint "e" Horizontally on No. 327 in Red

1960 **Unwmk.** ***Perf. 13x14***
O79 A157 5c blue 1.75 .70

POSTAL TAX STAMPS

Talca Issue.
A 10c blue postal tax stamp, inscribed "Bicentenario de Talca" and picturing a coat of arms, was issued in 1942. It was sold only in Talca and was required for a time on all domestic letters sent from that city. The tax helped pay for Talca's bicentenary celebration. Value 20 cents.

Nos. 326 and 347 Surcharged

1970 **Unwmk.** **Litho.** ***Perf. 14x13***
RA1 A159 10c on 2c ultra .20 .20
Perf. 14x14½
RA2 A170 10c on 6c rose lil .20 .20

Chilean Arms — PT1

Perf. 14½x14
1970, Apr. 23 **Litho.** **Unwmk.**
RA3 PT1 10c blue .20 .20

See No. RA6.

No. RA3 Surcharged in Red

a

b

1971-72
RA4 PT1 (a) 15c on 10c bl .20 .20
RA5 PT1 (b) 15c on 10c bl ('72) .20 .20

Type of 1970

1972, July **Litho.** ***Perf. 14½x14***
RA6 PT1 15c rose red .20 .20

No. RA6 Surcharged in Ultramarine

1972-73

RA7 PT1 20c on 15c rose red .20 .20
RA8 PT1 50c on 15c rose red ('73) .20 .20

No. RA8 has 9 bars instead of 8.

The surtax on Nos. RA1-RA8 was for modernization of postal system. Compulsory on all inland mail.

PARCEL POST POSTAL TAX STAMP

Pres. J. J. Prieto V. — PPT1

Unwmk.

1957, Apr. 8 **Litho.** ***Perf. 14***

QRA1 PPT1 15p green .30 .30

The surtax aided the Prieto Foundation. No. QRA1 was required on parcel post entering or leaving Chile.

CHINA

'chī-nə

LOCATION — Eastern Asia
GOVT. — Republic
AREA — 2,903,475 sq. mi.
POP. — 462,798,093 (1948)

10 Candareen = 1 Mace
10 Mace = 1 Tael
100 Cents = 1 Dollar (Yuan) (1897)

Watermarks

Wmk. 103 — Yin-Yang Symbol

Wmk. 261 — Character Yu (Post) Multiple

Issues of the Imperial Maritime Customs Post

Imperial Dragon — A1

1878 Unwmk. Typo. *Perf. 12½*
Thin Paper
Stamps printed 2½-3¼mm apart

1	A1	1c green	175.00	100.00
a.		1c dark green	300.00	150.00
2	A1	3c brown red	300.00	100.00
a.		3c vermilion	375.00	125.00
3	A1	5c orange	400.00	100.00
a.		5c bister orange	725.00	250.00

Imperforate essays of Nos. 1-3 have an extra circle near the dragon's lower left foot. Copies with the circle completely or mostly removed are proofs or unfinished stamps.

1882
Thin or Pelure Paper
Stamps printed 4½mm apart

4	A1	1c green	250.00	150.00
a.		1c dark green	275.00	160.00
5	A1	3c brown red	475.00	110.00
6	A1	5c orange yellow	9,000.	600.00

1883 *Rough to smooth Perf. 12½*
Medium to Thick Opaque Paper
Stamps printed 2½ to 3¼mm apart

7	A1	1c green	200.00	150.00
a.		1c dark green	325.00	175.00
b.		1c light green	300.00	200.00
c.		Vert. pair, imperf. between	*25,000.*	
8	A1	3c brown red	350.00	72.50
a.		3c vermilion	625.00	77.50
b.		Vert. pair, imperf. between		*25,000.*
9	A1	5c yellow	600.00	82.50
a.		5c chrome yellow	725.00	100.00
b.		Horiz. pair, imperf. btwn.		*25,000.*

Nos. 1-9 were printed from plates of 25, 20 or 15 individual copper dies, but only No. 5 exists in the 15-die setting. Many different printings and plate settings exist. All values occur in a wide variety of shades and papers. The effect of climate on certain papers has produced the varieties on so-called toned papers in Nos. 1-15.

Value for No. 8b is for a damaged copy.

Counterfeits, frequently with forged cancellations, occur in all early Chinese issues.

Imperial Dragon — A2

1885 Wmk. 103 *Perf. 12½*

10	A2	1c green	62.50	11.50
a.		Vert. pair, imperf. btwn.	*13,000.*	*13,000.*
b.		Horiz. pair, imperf. btwn.		
11	A2	3c lilac	100.00	17.00
a.		Horiz. pair, imperf. btwn.	*16,000.*	*16,000.*
b.		Vert. pair, imperf. btwn.		*18,000.*
12	A2	5c grnsh yellow	100.00	18.00
a.		5c bister brown	140.00	24.00
b.		Vert. pair, imperf. btwn.	*18,000.*	*18,000.*
c.		Horiz. pair, imperf. btwn.		*18,000.*
		Nos. 10-12 (3)	262.50	46.50

1888 *Perf. 11½-12*

13	A2	1c green	17.00	11.00
14	A2	3c lilac	67.50	7.50
b.		Double impression		*900.00*
15	A2	5c grnsh yellow	125.00	25.00
b.		Horiz. pair, imperf. vert.		—
c.		Double impression	600.00	600.00
		Nos. 13-15 (3)	209.50	43.50

Nos. 10-15 were printed from plates made of 40 individual copper dies, arranged in two panes of 20 each. Several different settings exist of all values.

Imperforates of Nos. 13-15 are considered proofs by most authorities.

Stamps overprinted "Formosa" in English or Chinese are proofs.

For surcharges see Nos. 25-27, 75-77.

"Shou" and "Wu Fu" — A3

Dragon and Hydrangea Leaves — A4

"Pa Kua" Signs in Corners — A5

Dragon and Peony — A6

Carp, the Messenger Fish — A7

Dragon, "Pa Kua" and Immortelle A8

Dragons and "Shou" A9

Dragons and Giant Peony — A10

Junk on the Yangtse A11

1894 Lithographed in Shanghai

16	A3	1c orange red	9.00	*11.00*
a.		Vert. pair, imperf. btwn.	*1,750.*	*1,500.*
b.		Horiz. pair, imperf. btwn.	*3,500.*	*3,500.*
c.		Vert. pair, imperf. horiz.	*2,400.*	*2,400.*
17	A4	2c green	15.00	7.50
a.		Horiz. pair, imperf. btwn.	*2,500.*	*2,500.*
18	A5	3c orange	11.00	4.50
a.		Vert. pair, imperf. btwn.	*2,500.*	*2,500.*
b.		Horiz. pair, imperf. btwn.	*3,000.*	*3,000.*
19	A6	4c rose pink	52.50	55.00
a.		Horiz. pair, imperf. btwn.	*2,750.*	
20	A7	5c dull orange	87.50	100.00
a.		Horiz. pair, imperf. btwn.	*3,000.*	*3,000.*
21	A8	6c dark brown	17.50	8.00
a.		Vert. pair, imperf. btwn.	*5,500.*	
b.		Horiz. pair, imperf. btwn.	*5,500.*	
22	A9	9c dark green	60.00	16.00
a.		Imperf., pair	*1,500.*	
b.		Horiz. pair, imperf. vert.	*3,000.*	*3,000.*
c.		Vert. pair, imperf. horiz.	*3,000.*	
d.		Vert. pair, imperf. btwn.	*3,500.*	*3,500.*
e.		Tete beche pair, vert.	*850.00*	*900.00*
f.		Tete beche pair, imperf. horiz.	*4,000.*	
g.		Tete beche pair, imperf. vert.	*4,000.*	*4,000.*
h.		Vert. strip of 3, imperf. btwn.	*4,000.*	
i.		Tete beche pair, horiz.	*1,000.*	*1,050.*
23	A10	12c orange	150.00	80.00
24	A11	24c carmine	200.00	70.00
a.		Vert. pair, imperf. btwn.	*6,000.*	
		Nos. 16-24 (9)	602.50	352.00

60th birthday of Tsz'e Hsi, the Empress Dowager. All values exist in several distinct shades.

On Mar. 20, 1896, the Customs Post was changed, by Imperial Edict, effective Jan. 1, 1897, to a National Post and the dollar was adopted as the unit of currency.

Time was required to work out details of the Imperial Post and design new stamps. As a provisional measure, stocks of Nos. 16-24 were ordered surcharged with new values in dollars and cents. It is believed that only the Shanghai office stock of Nos. 16-24 (plus any reserve stock at the printers) was surcharged with small figures of value. Other post offices throughout China were instructed to return all unoverprinted stocks on receipt of the new surcharges.

Early in the year it was apparent that all stamps would be exhausted before the new issues were ready (Nos. 86-97), and since the stones from which Nos. 16-24 had been printed no longer existed, new stones were made from the original transfers. A printing from the new stones was made early in 1897 and surcharged with large figures of value spaced 2½mm below the Chinese characters. During the surcharging, sheets from the 1894 (original) printing were received from outlying post offices and surcharged as they arrived. A small quantity of the 1897 printing reached the public without surcharge (Nos. 16n-24n).

Additional stamps were still required and another printing was made from the new stones and surcharged with large figures, but in a new setting with 1½mm between the Chinese characters and the value. Additional sheets of the 1894 printing were received from the most distant post offices and were also surcharged with the 1½mm setting. Thus there are four different sets of the large-figure surcharges. All these stamps were regularly issued but no attempt was made by the post office to separate printings. Some values are difficult to distinguish as to printing, particularly in used condition.

See No. 73. For surcharges see Nos. 28-72, 74.

1897 Lithographed in Shanghai

16n	A3	1c pink	*500.*
17n	A4	2c olive green	*700.*
18n	A5	3c chrome yellow	*475.*
p.		3c yellow buff	*850.*
19n	A6	4c pale rose	*550.*
20n	A7	5c yellow	*550.*
21n	A8	6c red brown	*750.*
22n	A9	9c yellowish green	*2,750.*
p.		9c emerald green	
23n	A10	12c yellowish orange	*2,750.*
24n	A11	24c purplish red	*1,300.*

The colors of the 1897 printings are pale or dull; the gum is thin and white. The 1894 printing has a thicker, yellowish gum.

The set of 9 values on thick unwatermarked paper is a special printing of 5,000 sets ordered by P. G. von Mollendorf, a Customs official, for presentation purposes. Value, set $1,500.

For surcharges see Nos. 47-55, 65-72.

Issues of the Chinese Government Post

Preceding Issues Surcharged in Black

Small Numerals 2½mm Below Chinese Characters Surcharged on Nos. 13-15

1897, Jan. 2 *Perf. 11½-12*

25	A2	1c on 1c	17.50	24.00
26	A2	2c on 3c	125.00	60.00
27	A2	5c on 5c	47.50	16.00
		Nos. 25-27 (3)	190.00	100.00

Surcharged on Nos. 16-24

28	A5	½c on 3c	9.50	7.50
a.		"1" instead of "½"	350.00	350.00
b.		Horiz. pair, imperf. btwn.	*3,000.*	
c.		Vert. pair, imperf. horiz.	*3,000.*	*2,250.*
d.		Double surcharge	*10,000.*	*10,000.*
e.		Vert. pair, imperf. btwn.	*3,000.*	
29	A3	1c on 1c	7.50	8.00
a.		Inverted surcharge	*9,000.*	*3,500.*
30	A4	2c on 2c	10.00	5.50
a.		Horiz. pair, imperf. vert.	*2,000.*	
b.		Vert. pair, imperf. btwn.	*2,000.*	
c.		Double surcharge	*7,500.*	
d.		Inverted surcharge	—	*15,000.*
e.		Horiz. pair, imperf. btwn.	*2,000.*	
31	A6	4c on 4c	8.25	5.50
a.		Double surcharge	*14,000.*	*14,000.*
b.		Vert. pair, imperf. btwn.	*3,000.*	*3,000.*
c.		Horiz. pair, imperf. btwn.	*3,000.*	*3,000.*
32	A7	5c on 5c	10.00	5.50
a.		Vert. pair, imperf. btwn.	*3,000.*	*3,000.*
33	A8	8c on 6c	13.00	6.75
a.		Vert. pair, imperf. btwn.	*2,100.*	*2,100.*
b.		Vert. strip of 3, imperf. btwn.	*2,000.*	*2,000.*
c.		Horiz. pair, imperf. btwn.	*2,250.*	*2,250.*
34	A8	10c on 6c	40.00	45.00
b.		Vert. pair, imperf. btwn.	*2,100.*	*2,100.*
c.		Horiz. pair, imperf. vert.	*2,400.*	*2,400.*
35	A9	10c on 9c	210.00	75.00
a.		Double surcharge	*40,000.*	*40,000.*
b.		Inverted surcharge	*15,000.*	*15,000.*
36	A10	10c on 12c	175.00	110.00
a.		Vert. pair, imperf. horiz.	*1,500.*	
b.		Vert. pair, imperf. btwn.	*1,500.*	*1,800.*
37	A11	30c on 24c	225.00	125.00
a.		Vert. pair, imperf. btwn.	*7,500.*	
		Nos. 28-37 (10)	708.25	393.75

Small Numerals 4mm Below Chinese Characters

25a	A2	1c on 1c green	45.00	45.00
28f	A4	½c on 3c orange	35.00	35.00
29b	A3	1c on 1c vermilion	50.00	50.00
30f	A4	2c on 2c dark green	30.00	30.00
31d	A6	4c on 4c dark pink	30.00	30.00
32b	A7	5c on 5c dull orange	30.00	30.00
33d	A8	8c on 6c brown	20.00	20.00
35c	A9	10c on 9c dark green	250.00	250.00
37b	A11	30c on 24c dark red	350.00	200.00

Preceding Issues Surcharged in Black

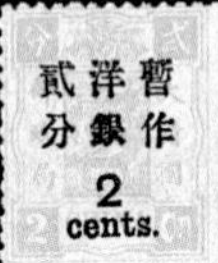

Large Numerals
Numerals 2½mm below Chinese characters

1897, Mar.

Surcharged on Nos. 16-24

38 A5 ½c on 3c 2,000. 750.
b. Inverted surcharge *4,500.*
39 A3 1c on 1c 550. 150.
40 A4 2c on 2c 275. 225.
41 A6 4c on 4c 325. 275.
b. Horiz. pair, imperf. btwn. *11,000.*
42 A7 5c on 5c 150. 150.
43 A8 8c on 6c 1,200. 1,200.
44 A9 10c on 9c 450. 275.
45 A10 10c on 12c *35,000.* 2,500.
46 A11 30c on 24c 950. 1,000.
b. 2mm spacing between "30" and "cents." *15,000.*

Same Surcharge on Nos. 16n-24n

47 A5 ½c on 3c 9.75 22.50
a. "cen" for "cent" 850.00 850.00
b. Vert. pair, imperf. btwn. *1,500.* *1,500.*
c. Vert. pair, imperf. horiz. 1,100. 1,100.
d. As "a" and "c" *9,500.* *9,500.*
e. As "a" and "b" *7,500.* *7,500.*
f. Horiz. pair, imperf. btwn. *1,900.* *1,900.*
48 A3 1c on 1c 7.50 7.00
a. Horiz. pair, imperf. btwn. *2,500.*
49 A4 2c on 2c 6.25 5.00
50 A6 4c on 4c 9.00 8.00
a. Horiz. pair, imperf. btwn. *3,250.* *3,250.*
b. Vert. pair, imperf. btwn. *4,000.*
51 A7 5c on 5c 16.00 8.00
52 A8 8c on 6c 225.00 175.00
53 A9 10c on 9c 77.50 45.00
a. 10c on 9c emerald 80.00 50.00
b. Pair, one without surcharge 825.00
54 A10 10c on 12c 150.00 35.00
55 A11 30c on 24c 250.00 125.00
a. 2mm spacing btwn "30" and "cents" *1,000.* 400.00
b. Vert. pair, imperf. btwn. *6,250.*

All recorded unused copies of #45 are flawed.

Numerals 1½mm below Chinese characters

1897, May

Surcharged on Nos. 16-24

56 A5 ½c on 3c org yel 300. 250.
57 A3 1c on 1c 200. 175.
58 A4 2c on 2c — *1,250.*
59 A6 4c on 4c 160. 150.
60 A7 5c on 5c 100. 92.50
61 A8 8c on 6c 900. 675.
62 A9 10c on 9c 200. 150.
63 A10 10c on 12c 850. 650.
64 A11 30c on 24c *27,500.* —

Same Surcharge on Nos. 16n-24n

65 A5 ½c on 3c 7.00 *8.00*
a. Inverted surcharge *3,000.* 3,000.
b. ½mm spacing *1,500.* *1,200.*
66 A3 1c on 1c 8.00 5.00
67 A4 2c on 2c 9.50 6.50
a. Inverted surcharge *8,750.* *8,750.*
b. Vert. pair, imperf. btwn. *8,500.*
68 A6 4c on 4c 160.00 100.00
a. Inverted surcharge 1,300. 1,300.
69 A7 5c on 5c 160.00 90.00
70 A9 10c on 9c 100.00 27.50
a. Inverted surcharge 1,000. 1,000.
71 A10 10c on 12c 200.00 55.00
72 A11 30c on 24c *13,000.* 2,600.

Same Surcharge (1½mm Spacing) on Type A12, and

A12

A12a

Redrawn Designs
Printed from New Stones

1897

73 A12 ½c on 3c yel 150.00 140.00
a. ½mm spacing *7,000.* *7,000.*
74 A12a 2c on 2c yel grn 32.50 14.00
a. Horiz. pair, imperf. btwn. *6,000.*

Nos. 73 and 74 were surcharged on stamps printed from new stones, which differ slightly from the originals. On No. 73 the numeral "3" and symbols in the four corner panels have been enlarged and strengthened. On No. 74, the numeral "2" has a thick, flat base.

Surcharged on Nos. 13-15

75 A2 1c on 1c green 300.00 *400.00*
76 A2 2c on 3c lilac 725.00 *700.00*
77 A2 5c on 5c grnsh yel 160.00 *275.00*

Type A13 Surcharged in Black:

A13

a

b

c

d

e

f

g

1897 Unwmk. *Perf. 12 to 15*

78 A13 (a) 1c on 3c red 175.00 100.00
a. No period after "cent" 200.00 150.00
b. Central character with large "box" 200.00 150.00
79 A13 (b) 2c on 3c red 500.00 150.00
a. Inverted surcharge *7,500.* *5,000.*
b. Inverted "S" in "CENTS" 625.00 400.00
c. No period after "CENTS" 625.00 400.00
d. Comma after "CENTS" 500.00 250.00
e. Double surcharge *25,000.* *25,000.*
f. Dbl. surch., both inverted *50,000.*
g. Double surch. (blk & grn) *52,500.*
80 A13 (c) 2c on 3c red 175.00 175.00
81 A13 (d) 4c on 3c red *8,750.* *5,500.*
a. Double surcharge (blk & vio) *45,000.* *35,000.*
82 A13 (e) 4c on 3c red 275.00 125.00
83 A13 (f) $1 on 3c red *225,000.*
a. No period after "r" —
84 A13 (g) $1 on 3c red 1,250. 750.00
85 A13 (g) $5 on 3c red 7,250. 7,000.
a. Inverted surcharge *15,000.* *12,500.*

A few copies of the 3c red exist without surcharge; one canceled. No. 79 with green surcharge is a trial printing. Value for faulty upper left corner block, $190,000.

No. 79g is unique. The only canceled copy of #83 is in a museum.

Dragon — A14

Carp — A15

Wild Goose — A16

"Imperial Chinese Post"
Lithographed in Japan
Perf. 11, 11½, 12

1897, Aug. 16 Wmk. 103

86 A14 ½c purple brn 2.50 2.00
a. Horiz. pair, imperf. btwn. 475.00
87 A14 1c yellow 2.75 1.75
88 A14 2c orange 2.75 1.10
a. Vert. pair, imperf. horiz. 450.00
89 A14 4c brown 5.50 1.60
a. Horiz. pair, imperf. btwn. 750.00
90 A14 5c rose red 5.75 1.90
91 A14 10c dk green 15.00 1.50
92 A15 20c maroon 35.00 8.00
93 A15 30c red 60.00 18.00
94 A15 50c yellow grn 40.00 26.00
a. 50c black green 325.00
b. 50c blue green 675.00
95 A16 $1 car & rose 140.00 110.00
a. Horiz. pair, imperf. vert. —
96 A16 $2 orange & yel 900.00 800.00
a. Horiz. pair, imperf. vert. —
97 A16 $5 yel grn & pink 600.00 575.00

The inner circular frames and outer frames of Nos. 86-91 differ for each denomination.

No. 97 imperforate was not regularly issued. **Copies have been privately perforated and offered as No. 97**. Shades occur in most values of this issue.

A17

A18

A19

"Chinese Imperial Post"
Engraved in London

1898 Wmk. 103 *Perf. 12 to 16*

98 A17 ½c chocolate 1.75 1.00
a. Vert. pair, imperf. btwn. 675.00 400.00
b. Vert. pair, imperf. horiz. 675.00 400.00
99 A17 1c ocher 2.00 1.00
a. Vert. pair, imperf. btwn. 190.00 190.00
b. Horiz. pair, imperf. btwn. 300.00 300.00
100 A17 2c scarlet 3.25 1.00
a. Vert. pair, imperf. btwn. 150.00 150.00
b. Horiz. pair, imperf. vert. 150.00 150.00
101 A17 4c orange brn 3.50 1.00
a. Vert. pair, imperf. btwn. 300.00
b. Horiz. pair, imperf. vert. 210.00 210.00
c. Horiz. pair, imperf. btwn. 525.00 525.00
d. Horiz. strip of 3, imperf. btwn. 700.00 700.00
102 A17 5c salmon 5.25 1.10
a. Vert. pair, imperf. btwn. 240.00 240.00
b. Horiz. pair, imperf. btwn. 275.00 275.00
c. Vert. pair, imperf. horiz. 275.00 275.00
d. 5c pale reddish orange 8.75 2.25
e. As "d," vert pair, imperf. btwn. 300.00 300.00
103 A17 10c dk blue grn 6.50 1.00
a. Vert. or horiz. pair, imperf. btwn — —
104 A18 20c claret 35.00 4.75
a. Horiz. pair, imperf. btwn. 600.00 600.00
b. Vert. pair, imperf. horiz. 000.00 000.00
c. Vert. pair, imperf. btwn. 675.00 675.00
105 A18 30c dull rose 22.50 6.50
a. Horiz. pair, imperf. btwn. 675.00
b. Vert. pair, imperf. horiz. 675.00
c. Vert. pair, imperf. btwn. 675.00
106 A18 50c lt green 37.50 7.00
a. Vert. pair, imperf. btwn. 600.00
107 A19 $1 red & pale rose 150.00 18.00
108 A19 $2 brn, red & yel 250.00 45.00
109 A19 $5 dp grn & sal 450.00 150.00
a. Horiz. pair, imperf. btwn. *7,500.*
b. Vert. pair, imperf. btwn. *7,750.*
Nos. 98-109 (12) 967.25 237.35

No. 98 surcharged "B. R. A.-5-Five Cents" in three lines in black or green, was surcharged by British military authorities shortly after the Boxer riots for use from military posts in an occupied area along the Peking-Mukden railway. Usually canceled in violet.

See note following No. 122.

1900(?)-06 Unwmk. *Perf. 12 to 16*

110 A17 ½c brown 1.25 1.00
a. Horiz. pair, imperf. btwn. 275.00 275.00
b. Vert. pair, imperf. btwn. 275.00 275.00
111 A17 1c ocher 1.25 1.00
a. Horiz. pair, imperf. btwn. 190.00 190.00
b. Vert. pair, imperf. btwn. 190.00 190.00
c. Vert. pair, imperf. horiz. 190.00 190.00
112 A17 2c scarlet 2.25 1.00
a. Horiz. pair, imperf. btwn. 160.00 160.00
b. Vert. pair, imperf. btwn. 160.00 160.00
c. Vert. pair, imperf. horiz. 160.00 160.00
d. Horiz. pair, imperf. vert. 160.00 160.00
e. Vert. strip of 3, imperf. btwn. 160.00 160.00
113 A17 4c orange brn 2.75 1.00
a. Horiz. pair, imperf. btwn. 275.00 275.00
b. Vert. pair, imperf. btwn. 275.00 275.00
114 A17 5c rose red 16.00 1.75
a. Vert. pair, imperf. btwn. 260.00 260.00
b. Vert. pair, imperf. horiz. 225.00 225.00
115 A17 5c orange 13.50 2.25
a. 5c yellow 150.00 18.00
b. Vert. pair, imperf. btwn. 300.00 300.00
c. Horiz. pair, imperf. btwn. 300.00 300.00
116 A17 10c green 10.50 1.00
a. Vert. pair, imperf. btwn. 225.00
b. Horiz. pair, imperf. btwn. 225.00
c. Vert. pair, imperf. horiz. 225.00
d. Vert. strip of 3, imperf. btwn. 400.00
117 A18 20c red brown 16.00 1.10
a. Horiz. pair, imperf. btwn. 375.00
b. Vert. pair, imperf. btwn. 325.00
c. Vert. pair, imperf. horiz. 325.00
118 A18 30c dull red 16.00 1.00
a. Vert. pair, imperf. btwn. 675.00
119 A18 50c yellow grn 27.50 1.60
a. Horiz. pair, imperf. btwn. 850.00
120 A19 $1 red & pale rose ('06) 82.50 10.00
121 A19 $2 brn red & yel ('06) 200.00 22.50
122 A19 $5 dp grn & sal 300.00 100.00
Nos. 110-122 (13) 689.50 145.20

See #124-130. For surcharges and overprints see #123, 134-177, J1-J6, Offices in Tibet 1-11.

Diagonal Half of No. 112 Surcharged on Stamp and Envelope

Postage
1 Cent
Paid

1903

123 A17 1c on half of 2c scarlet, on cover *1,250.*

Used Oct. 22 to Oct. 24. Value is for cover mailed to post office other than sending office (Foochow) and bearing backstamp showing arrival date. Locally addressed or unaddressed covers without backstamps properly used are worth approximately $1,000. Others are worth less.

Forgeries are plentiful, particularly on pieces of cover. Certificates of authenticity are mandatory.

1905-10

124 A17 2c green ('08) 1.10 1.00
a. Horiz. pair, imperf. btwn. 300.00 300.00
b. Vert. pair, imperf. btwn. 300.00 300.00
c. Horiz. pair, imperf. vert. 300.00 300.00
d. Horiz. strip of 4, imperf. btwn. 675.00 675.00

125 A17 3c slate grn ('10) 2.25 1.00
a. Horiz. pair, imperf. btwn. 225.00
b. Vert. pair, imperf. btwn. 225.00
126 A17 4c vermilion ('09) 2.75 1.00
127 A17 5c violet 4.50 1.00
a. 5c lilac 5.25 1.00
b. Horiz. pair, imperf. btwn. 325.00
c. Vert. pair, imperf. btwn. 325.00
d. Vert. pair, imperf. horiz. 275.00
128 A17 7c maroon ('10) 8.00 4.50
129 A17 10c ultra ('08) 10.00 1.00
a. Horiz. pair, imperf. btwn. 325.00
b. Vert. pair, imperf. btwn. 325.00
c. Vert. pair, imperf. horiz. 30.00 300.00
130 A18 16c olive grn ('07) 32.50 8.00
Nos. 124-130 (7) 61.10 17.50

Temple of Heaven, Peking — A20

1909 ***Perf. 14***

131 A20 2c orange & green 3.25 *4.25*
132 A20 3c orange & blue 4.75 *10.00*
133 A20 7c orange & brn vio 7.00 *5.00*
Nos. 131-133 (3) 15.00 *19.25*

1st year of the reign of Hsuan T'ung, who later became Henry Pu-yi and then Emperor Kang Teh of Manchukuo.

Stamps of 1902-10 Overprinted with Chinese Characters

Foochow Issue

Overprinted in Red or Black

1912 ***Perf. 12 to 16***

134 A17 3c slate grn (R) 175. 75.
135 A19 $1 red & pale rose 1,500. 1,400.
136 A19 $2 brn red & yel 2,000. 1,700.
137 A19 $5 dp grn & sal 3,000. 2,500.

The overprint "Ling Shih Chung Li" or "Provisional Neutrality," signified that the P.O. was conducted neutrally by agreement between the Manchu and opposing forces.

Nanking Issue

Overprinted in Red or Black

138 A17 1c ocher (R) 165. 100.
139 A17 3c slate grn (R) 150. 90.
140 A17 7c maroon 350. 225.
141 A18 16c olive grn (R) 1,500. 1,500.
142 A18 50c yellow grn (R) 1,500. 1,200.
143 A19 $1 red & pale rose 1,400. 1,100.
144 A19 $2 brn red & yel 2,750. 2,750.
145 A19 $5 dp green & sal 5,500. 5,500.

Vertical overprint reads: "Chung Hwa Min Kuo" (Republic of China).

Stamps of this issue were also used in Shanghai and Hankow.

Additional values were overprinted but not issued. Excellent forgeries of the overprints of Nos. 134-145 exist.

Issues of the Republic

Overprinted in Black or Red

Overprinted by the Maritime Customs Statistical Department, Shanghai

146 A17 ½c brown .70 .50
a. Inverted overprint 37.50 37.50
b. Double overprint 95.00
147 A17 1c ocher (R) 1.10 .50
a. Vert. pair, imperf. horiz. 190.00 190.00
b. Inverted overprint 150.00 95.00
c. Double overprint 190.00 150.00
d. Horiz. pair, imperf. btwn. 275.00 240.00
e. Horiz. pair, imperf. vert. 140.00
f. Pair, one without overprint 140.00
148 A17 2c green (R) .95 .50
a. Vert. pair, imperf. btwn. 190.00 190.00
149 A17 3c slate grn (R) 1.40 .35
a. Inverted overprint 100.00 60.00
b. Horiz. or vert. pair, imperf. btwn 275.00 275.00
d. Horiz. pair, imperf. vert. 110.00
150 A17 4c vermilion 2.50 .35
a. Vert. pair, imperf. btwn. 750.00
151 A17 5c violet (R) 3.00 .35
a. Horiz. pair, imperf. btwn.
152 A17 7c maroon 4.50 1.10
153 A17 10c ultra (R) 4.75 .55
a. Double overprint 190.00
b. Pair, one without overprint 700.00
c. Brownish red overprint 12.00 6.75
d. Inverted overprint 240.00 240.00
154 A18 16c olive grn (R) 11.00 4.00
155 A18 20c red brown 9.00 2.75
156 A18 30c rose red 11.50 2.75
157 A18 50c yel grn (R) 20.00 2.75
158 A19 $1 red & pale rose 140.00 11.50
a. Inverted overprint *8,250.*
159 A19 $2 brn red & yel 100.00 30.00
a. Inverted overprint 260.00 260.00
160 A19 $5 dp grn & sal 275.00 190.00
Nos. 146-160 (15) 585.40 247.95

Stamps with blue overprint similar to the preceding were not an official issue but were privately made by a printer in Tientsin.

Overprinted in Red

Overprinted by the Commercial Press, Shanghai

This type differs in that the top character is shifted slightly to right and the bottom character is larger and has small "legs".

161 A17 1c ocher 3.25 .55
a. Inverted overprint 375.00 375.00
b. Vert. pair, imperf. btwn. 450.00
c. Double overprint 450.00
162 A17 2c green 22.50 1.65
a. Inverted overprint 1,100. 900.00
b. Vert. pair, imperf. btwn. 260.00
c. Horiz. pair, imperf. btwn. 300.00
d. Horiz. strip of 3, imperf. btwn. 475.00

Overprinted in Blue, Carmine or Black

Overprinted by Waterlow & Sons, London

163 A17 ½c brown (Bl) .75 .45
a. Vert. pair, imperf. btwn. 1,050. 1,050.
164 A17 1c ocher (C) .75 .45
a. Horiz. pair, imperf. btwn. 190.00
165 A17 2c green (C) 1.40 .55
166 A17 3c slate grn (C) 1.60 .65
a. Inverted overprint 1,600.
167 A17 4c vermilion (Bk) 3.00 .90
168 A17 5c violet (C) 3.25 .80
169 A17 7c maroon (Bk) 20.00 12.50
170 A17 10c ultra (C) 8.00 1.40
a. Vert. pair, imperf. btwn. 525.00 525.00
171 A18 16c olive grn (R) 26.00 7.75
172 A18 20c red brn (Bk) 17.50 2.10
173 A18 30c dull red (Bk) 55.00 4.00
174 A18 50c yellow grn (R) 77.50 8.00
175 A19 $1 red & pale rose (Bk) 110.00 10.50
176 A19 $2 brn red & yel (Bk) 225.00 110.00
177 A19 $5 dp grn & sal (C) 325.00 250.00
Nos. 163-177 (15) 874.75 410.05

Due to instructions issued to postmasters throughout China at the time of the Revolution, a number of them prepared unauthorized overprints using the same characters as the overprints prepared by the government. While many were made in good faith, some, like the blue overprints from Tientsin, were bogus, and the status of certain others is extremely dubious.

Dr. Sun Yat-sen — A21

1912, Dec. 14 ***Perf. 14½***

178 A21 1c orange 1.75 *2.50*
179 A21 2c yellow grn 1.75 *2.50*
180 A21 3c slate grn 1.75 *2.50*
181 A21 5c rose lilac 3.25 2.25
182 A21 8c dp brown 3.25 3.00
183 A21 10c dull blue 3.25 3.00
184 A21 16c olive grn 7.25 6.75
185 A21 20c maroon 15.00 5.50
186 A21 50c dk green 26.00 20.00
187 A21 $1 brown red 100.00 30.00
188 A21 $2 yellow brn 210.00 175.00
189 A21 $5 gray 85.00 100.00
Nos. 178-189 (12) 458.25 353.00

Honoring the leader of the Revolution.

President Yuan Shih-kai — A22

1912, Dec. 14

190 A22 1c orange .90 .90
191 A22 2c yellow green .90 .90
192 A22 3c slate green .90 .90
193 A22 5c rose lilac 1.00 1.00
194 A22 8c deep brown 3.50 2.25
195 A22 10c dull blue 2.50 1.40
196 A22 16c olive green 3.75 *4.00*
197 A22 20c maroon 3.00 *2.50*
198 A22 50c dark green 18.00 11.00
199 A22 $1 brown red 60.00 30.00
200 A22 $2 yellow brown 67.50 30.00
201 A22 $5 gray 210.00 190.00
Nos. 190-201 (12) 371.95 274.85

Honoring the 1st pres. of the Republic.

Junk — A24

Reaping Rice — A25

Gateway, Hall of Classics, Peking — A26

DESIGN A24

London Printing: Vertical shading lines under top panel fine, junk with clear diagonal shading lines on sails, right pennant of junk usually long, lines in water weak except directly under junk.

Peking Printing: Vertical shading lines under top panel and inner vertical frame line much heavier, water and sails of junk more evenly and strongly colored, white wave over "H" of "CHINA" pointed upward, touching the junk.

DESIGN A25

London: Front hat brim thick and nearly straight, left foot touches shadow.

Peking: Front hat brim thin and strongly upturned, left foot and sickle clearly outlined in white, shadow of middle tree lighter than those of the right and left trees.

DESIGN A26

London: Light colored walk clearly defined almost to the doorway, figure in right doorway "T" shaped with strong horizontal cross-bar, white panel in base of central tower rectangular, vertical stroke in top left character uniformly thick at its base, tree to right of doorway ends in minute dots.

Peking: Walk more heavily shaded near doorway, especially at right; figure in right doorway more like a "Y", white panel at base of central tower is a long oval, right vertical stroke in top left character incurved near its base, tree at right has five prominent dots at top.

London Printing: By Waterlow & Sons, London, perf. 14 to 15.

Peking Printing: By the Chinese Bureau of Engraving and Printing, Peking, perf. 14.

London Printing

1913, May 5 ***Perf. 14-15***

202 A24 ½c black brn .45 .20
a. Horiz. or vert. pair, imperf. btwn. 190.00
203 A24 1c orange .45 .20
a. Horiz. pair, imperf. btwn. 225.00
b. Vert. pair, imperf. btwn. 150.00
c. Horiz. strip of 5, imperf. btwn 600.00
204 A24 2c yellow grn 1.50 .20
a. Horiz. pair, imperf. btwn. 375.00
205 A24 3c blue grn 3.75 .20
a. Horiz. pair, imperf. btwn. 190.00
b. Vert. pair, imperf. btwn. 375.00
206 A24 4c scarlet 5.50 .40
207 A24 5c rose lilac 15.00 .40
208 A24 6c gray 2.50 .55
209 A24 7c violet 12.00 5.50
210 A24 8c brown org 22.50 1.40
211 A24 10c dk blue 19.00 .60
a. Horiz. pair, imperf. btwn. 350.00 350.00
b. Vert. pair, imperf. btwn. 375.00 275.00
212 A25 15c brown 17.50 3.75
213 A25 16c olive grn 9.00 1.10
214 A25 20c brown red 15.00 1.60
215 A25 30c brown vio 17.50 1.10
a. Horiz. pair, imperf. btwn. 375.00 375.00
216 A25 50c green 32.50 2.25
217 A26 $1 ocher & blk 82.50 2.50
218 A26 $2 blue & blk 140.00 10.00
219 A26 $5 scarlet & blk 225.00 75.00
220 A26 $10 yel grn & blk 700.00 575.00
Nos. 202-220 (19) 1,321. 681.95

First Peking Printing

1915 ***Perf. 14***

221 A24 ½c black brn .45 .20
222 A24 1c orange .45 .20
223 A24 2c yellow grn .85 .20
224 A24 3c blue grn .85 .20
225 A24 4c scarlet 9.25 .20
226 A24 5c rose lilac 3.75 .20
a. Booklet pane of 4 110.00
227 A24 6c gray 9.25 .25
228 A24 7c violet 11.00 3.25
229 A24 8c brown org 6.25 .25
230 A24 10c dk blue 7.25 .45
a. Booklet pane of 4 110.00
231 A25 15c brown 20.00 3.00
232 A25 16c olive grn 7.75 .45
233 A25 20c brown red 8.75 .45
234 A25 30c brown vio 7.75 .45
235 A25 50c green 19.00 .45
236 A26 $1 ocher & blk 62.50 .55
237 A26 $2 blue & blk 140.00 2.25
a. Center inverted *20,000.*
238 A26 $5 scarlet & blk 350.00 22.50
239 A26 $10 yel grn & blk 525.00 150.00
Nos. 221-239 (19) 1,190. 185.50

1919

240	A24	1½c violet	1.65	.40
241	A25	13c brown	4.00	.45
242	A26	$20 yellow & blk	2,250.	1,800.

Nos. 226 and 230 overprinted in red with five characters in vertical column were for postal savings use.

The higher values of the 1913-19 issues are often overprinted with Chinese characters, which are the names of various postal districts. Stamps were frequently stolen while in transit to post offices. The overprints served to protect them, since the stamps could only be used in the districts for which they were overprinted.

Compare designs A24-A26 with designs A29-A31. For surcharges and overprints see Nos. 247, 288, B1-B3, Sinkiang 1-38.

Yeh Kung-cho, Hsu Shi-chang and Chin Yun-peng A27

1921, Oct. 10

243	A27	1c orange	4.75	1.25
244	A27	3c blue green	4.75	1.25
245	A27	6c gray	4.75	1.25
246	A27	10c blue	4.75	1.25
		Nos. 243-246 (4)	19.00	5.00

National Post Office, 25th anniversary. For overprints see Sinkiang Nos. 39-42.

No. 224 Surcharged in Red

1922

247	A24	2c on 3c blue green	2.10	.40
a.		Inverted surcharge	*19,000.*	

Second Peking Printing

A29

A30

A31

Types of 1913-19 Issues Re-engraved

Type A29: Most of the whitecaps in front of the junk have been removed and the water made darker. The shading lines have been removed from the arabesques and pearls above the top inscription. The inner shadings at the top and sides of the picture have been cut away.

Type A30: The heads of rice in the side panels have a background of crossed lines instead of horizontal lines. The Temple of Heaven is strongly shaded and has a door. There are rows of pearls below the Chinese characters in the upper corners. The arabesques above the top inscription have been altered and are without shading lines.

Type A31: The curved line under the inscription at top is single instead of double. There are four vertical lines, instead of eight, at each side of the picture. The trees at the sides of the temple had foliage in the 1913-19 issues, but now the branches are bare. There are numerous other alterations in the design.

1923 ***Perf. 14***

248	A29	½c black brown	.75	.20
a.		Horiz. pair, imperf. btwn.	165.00	165.00
b.		Horiz. pair, imperf. vert.	140.00	140.00
249	A29	1c orange	.45	.20
a.		Imperf., pair	110.00	
b.		Horiz. pair, imperf. vert.	110.00	
c.		Booklet pane of 6	90.00	
d.		Booklet pane of 4	45.00	
250	A29	1½c violet	1.40	.70
251	A29	2c yellow grn	.75	.20
252	A29	3c blue green	2.25	.20
a.		Booklet pane of 6	75.00	
253	A29	4c gray	10.00	.60
254	A29	5c claret	1.60	.35
a.		Booklet pane of 4	90.00	
255	A29	6c scarlet	3.25	.35
256	A29	7c violet	3.25	.35
257	A29	8c orange	6.50	.35
258	A29	10c blue	5.00	.25
a.		Booklet pane of 6	110.00	
b.		Booklet pane of 2	140.00	
259	A30	13c brown	11.50	.45
260	A30	15c dp blue	3.75	.45
261	A30	16c olive grn	4.50	.45
262	A30	20c brown red	3.75	.00
263	A30	30c purple	12.00	.30
264	A30	50c dp green	21.00	.45
265	A31	$1 org brn & sep	22.50	.45
266	A31	$2 blue & red brn	30.00	.60
267	A31	$5 red & slate	50.00	2.50
268	A31	$10 green & claret	275.00	30.00
269	A31	$20 plum & blue	475.00	100.00
		Nos. 248-269 (22)	944.20	139.70

Nos. 249 and 275 exist with webbing watermark from experimental printing.

To prevent speculation and theft, the dollar denominations were overprinted with single characters in red for use in Kwangsi ($1-$20) and Kweichow ($1-$5).

See Nos. 275, 324. For surcharges and overprints see Nos. 274, 289, 311, 325, 330, 339-340, Szechwan 1-3, Yunnan 1-20, Manchuria 1-20, Sinkiang 47-69, 114, C1-C4.

Temple of Heaven, Peking — A32

1923, Oct. 17 ***Perf. 14***

270	A32	1c orange	3.50	.85
271	A32	3c blue green	3.50	1.75
272	A32	4c red	7.50	1.75
273	A32	10c blue	11.00	2.25
		Nos. 270-273 (4)	25.50	6.60

Adoption of Constitution, October, 1923. For overprints see Sinkiang Nos. 43-46.

No. 253 Surcharged in Red

1925

274	A29	3c on 4c gray	1.90	.20
a.		Inverted surcharge	*22,500.*	*10,000.*
b.		Vert. pair, imperf. btwn.		

Junk Type of 1923

1926

275	A29	4c olive green	1.25	.20
a.		Horiz. pair, imperf. vert.	175.00	
b.		Horiz. pair, imperf. btwn.	175.00	
c.		Horiz. strip of 3, imperf. btwn.	225.00	

Marshal Chang Tso-lin — A34

President Chiang Kai-shek — A35

1928, Mar. 1 ***Perf. 14***

276	A34	1c brown orange	1.00	1.00
277	A34	4c olive green	2.75	2.75
278	A34	10c dull blue	6.75	3.75
279	A34	$1 red	37.50	*45.00*
		Nos. 276-279 (4)	48.00	52.50

Assumption of office by Marshal Chang Tso-lin. The stamps of this issue were only available for postage in the Provinces of Chihli and Shantung and at the Offices in Manchuria and Sinkiang.

For overprints see Manchuria Nos. 21-24, Sinkiang 70-73.

1929, May

280	A35	1c brown orange	.85	.35
281	A35	4c olive green	1.25	.65
282	A35	10c dark blue	10.00	1.00
283	A35	$1 dark red	55.00	40.00
		Nos. 280-283 (4)	67.10	42.00

Unification of China.

For overprints see Yunnan Nos. 21-24, Manchuria 25-28, Sinkiang 74-77.

Sun Yat-sen Mausoleum, Nanking — A36

1929, May 30 ***Perf. 14***

284	A36	1c brown orange	.90	.65
285	A36	4c olive green	.75	1.10
286	A36	10c dark blue	5.50	1.90
287	A36	$1 dark red	52.50	22.50
		Nos. 284-287 (4)	59.65	26.15

The transfer of Dr. Sun Yat-sen's remains from Peiping to the mausoleum at Nanking.

For overprints see Yunnan Nos. 25-28, Manchuria 29-32, Sinkiang 78-81.

Nos. 224 and 252 Surcharged in Red

1930

288	A24	1c on 3c blue green	1.10	2.00
289	A29	1c on 3c blue green	.85	.35
a.		No period after "Ct"	17.50	17.50

See Nos. 311, 325, 330.

Dr. Sun Yat-sen — A37

Type I — Double-lined circle in the sun.
Type II — Heavy, single-lined circle in the sun.

Printed by De la Rue & Co., Ltd., London

Perf. 11½x12½, 12½x13, 12½, 13½

1931, Nov. 12 **Engr.**

Type I

290	A37	1c orange	.45	.20
291	A37	2c olive green	.55	.30
292	A37	4c green	.85	.20
293	A37	20c ultra	1.10	.20
294	A37	$1 org brn & dk brn	8.25	.35
295	A37	$2 blue & org brn	22.50	2.25
296	A37	$5 dull red & blk	32.50	3.50
		Nos. 290-296 (7)	66.20	7.00

1931-37

Type II

297	A37	2c olive grn	.35	.20
298	A37	4c green	.60	.20
299	A37	5c green ('33)	.35	.20
300	A37	15c dk green	3.75	.85
301	A37	15c scarlet ('34)	.40	.20
302	A37	20c ultra ('37)	.75	.20
303	A37	25c ultra	.40	.60
304	A37	$1 org brn & dk brn	9.25	.35
305	A37	$2 blue & org brn	17.00	.75
306	A37	$5 dull red & blk	32.50	3.50
		Nos. 297-306 (10)	65.35	7.05

Stamps issued prior to 1933 were printed by a wet-paper process, and owing to shrinkage such stamps are 1-1½mm narrower than the later dry-printed stamps.

Early printings are perf. 12½x13. Nos. 304, 305 and 306 were later perf. 11½x12½.

See #631-635. For surcharges and overprints see #341, 343, 678, 682, 684-685, 689-691, 768, 843, 1N1, 2N1-2N5, 2N57-2N59, 2N83-2N84, 2N101-2N106, 2N116, 2N124-2N126, 3N1-3N5, 4N1-4N5, 5N1-5N4, 6N1-6N5, 7N1-7N4, 7N54, 8N2-8N3, 8N43-8N44, 8N54, 8N57, 8N69-8N71, 8N85, 9N1-9N5, Taiwan 19, 21-22, Northeastern Provinces 44, Szechwan 4-11, Yunnan 29-44, Sinkiang 82-97.

"Nomads in the Desert" — A38

1932 **Unwmk.** ***Perf. 14***

307	A38	1c deep orange	22.50	19.00
308	A38	4c olive green	22.50	19.00
309	A38	5c claret	22.50	19.00
310	A38	10c deep blue	22.50	19.00
		Nos. 307-310 (4)	90.00	76.00

Northwest Scientific Expedition of Sven Hedin. A small quantity of this issue was sold at face at Peking and several other cities. The bulk of the issue was furnished to Hedin and sold at $5 (Chinese) a set for funds to finance the expedition.

#252 Surcharged in Black Like #288

1932

311	A29	1c on 3c blue green	2.00	1.10

Martyrs Issue

Teng Keng A39

Ch'en Ying-shih A40

Chu Chih-hsin A45

Sung Chiao-jen A46

Huang Hsing A47

Liao Chung-kai A48

1932-34 ***Perf. 14***

312	A39	½c black brown	.20	.20
313	A40	1c orange ('34)	.20	.20
314	A39	2½c rose lilac ('33)	.20	.20
315	A48	3c dp brown ('33)	.20	.20
316	A45	8c brown orange	.35	.20
317	A46	10c dull violet	.40	.20
318	A45	13c blue green	.50	.20
319	A46	17c brown olive	.40	.20
320	A47	20c brown red	.80	.20
321	A48	30c brown violet	1.10	.20
322	A47	40c orange	.95	.25
323	A40	50c green ('34)	3.50	.25
		Nos. 312-323 (12)	8.80	2.50

Perfs. 12 to 13 and compound and with secret marks are listed as Nos. 402-439. No. 316 re-drawn is No. 485.

For overprints and surcharge see Nos. 342, 472, 474, 478-479, 486-487, 490, 531-536, 539-541, 544-549, 616, 619, 622-624, 647-659, 662-663, 665, 669, 672, 698, 704, 711, 713-715, 720-721, 831, 846-847, 867, 870, 872, 881-882, J120-J121, 1N14-1N15, 1N59, 2N6-2N9, 2N32-2N56, 2N60, 2N76-2N82, 2N85, 2N87-2N90, 2N107-2N115, 2N118, 2N121-2N123, 3N6-3N10, 3N34-3N55, 3N59, 4N6-4N9, 4N39-4N64, 4N69, 5N5-5N8, 5N34-5N60, 5N65, 6N6-6N8, 6N35-6N61, 6N66, 7N5-7N7, 7N30-7N53, 7N55, 7N59, 8N1, 8N4, 8N28-8N42, 8N45, 8N47-8N50, 8N60-8N61, 8N68, 8N73, 8N76-8N79, 8N89, 8N97, 8N99-8N100, 8N103-8N104, 9N72-9N77, Taiwan 14-17, 20, 28A, 74, Northeastern Provinces 6-8, 11, Szechwan 12-23, Yunnan 49-60, Sinkiang 102-113, 140-161, 197.

Junk Type of 1923 Issue

1933 ***Perf. 14***

324	A29	6c brown	18.00	1.10

#275 Surcharged in Red Like #288

1933

325 A29 1c on 4c olive green 1.40 .30
a. No period after "Ct" 17.50 17.50

Tan Yuan-chang — A49

1933, Jan. 9

326 A49 2c olive green 2.25 .35
327 A49 5c green 2.25 .35
328 A49 25c ultra 7.00 1.25
329 A49 $1 red 55.00 17.50
Nos. 326-329 (4) 66.50 19.45

Tan Yuan-chang, more commonly known as Tan Yen-kai, a prominent statesman in China since the revolution of 1912 and Pres. of the Executive Dept. of the Natl. Government. Placed on sale Jan. 9, 1933, the date of the ceremony in celebration of the completion of the Tan Yuan-chang Memorial Hall and Tomb at Mukden.

For overprints see Yunnan Nos. 45-48, Sinkiang 98-101.

#251 Surcharged in Red Like #288

1935 ***Perf. 14***

330 A29 1c on 2c yellow grn 2.25 .20

Emblem of New Life Movement A50

Four Virtues of New Life A51

Lighthouse — A52

1936, Jan. 1

331 A50 2c olive green .65 .40
332 A50 5c green 1.00 .20
333 A51 20c dark blue 5.00 .70
334 A52 $1 rose red 24.00 4.00
Nos. 331-334 (4) 30.65 5.30

"New Life" movement.

Methods of Mail Transportation A53

Maritime Scene — A54

Shanghai General Post Office — A55

Ministry of Communications, Nanking — A56

1936, Oct. 10

335 A53 2c orange .40 .40
336 A54 5c green .50 .20
337 A55 25c blue 3.75 .40
338 A56 $1 dk carmine 22.50 4.00
Nos. 335-338 (4) 27.15 5.00

Founding of the Chinese PO, 40th anniv.

Nos. 260 and 261 Surcharged in Red

1936, Oct. 11

339 A30 5c on 15c dp blue 1.00 .35
340 A30 5c on 16c olive grn 3.00 .85

No. 298 Surcharged in Red

1937

341 A37 1c on 4c green, type II 1.00 .25
a. Upper left character missing

Nos. 322 and 303 Surcharged in Black or Red

1938 ***Perf. 12½, 14***

342 A47 8c on 40c orange (Bk) 1.50 .50
343 A37 10c on 25c ultra (R) 1.00 .20

Dr. Sun Yat-sen — A57

Type I - Coat button half circle. Six lines of shading above head. Top frame partially shaded with vertical lines.

Type II - Coat button complete circle. Nine lines of shading above head. Top frame partially shaded with vertical lines.

Type III - Coat button complete circle. Nine lines of shading above head. Top frame line fully shaded with vertical lines.

Printed by the Chung Hwa Book Co.

1938 **Unwmk.** **Engr.** ***Perf. 12½***

Type I

344 A57 $1 henna & dk brn 67.50 9.50
345 A57 $2 dp blue & org brn 13.00 3.25
346 A57 $5 red & grnsh blk 100.00 14.00
Nos. 344-346 (3) 180.50 26.75

1939

Type II

347 A57 $1 henna & dk brn 13.00 .65
348 A57 $2 dp blue & org brn 16.00 3.00

1939-43

Type III

349 A57 2c olive green .20 .20
350 A57 3c dull claret .20 .20
351 A57 5c green .20 .20
352 A57 5c olive green .20 .20
353 A57 8c olive green .20 .20
354 A57 10c green .20 .20
355 A57 15c scarlet 1.10 2.00
356 A57 15c dk vio brn ('43) 15.00 *27.50*
357 A57 16c olive gray 1.50 .40
358 A57 25c dk blue .35 .60
359 A57 $1 henna & dk brn 1.75 .60
360 A57 $2 dp blue & org brn 3.25 .50
a. Imperf., pair 275.00
361 A57 $5 red & grnsh blk 2.25 .50
362 A57 $10 dk green & dull pur 13.00 1.75
363 A57 $20 rose lake & dk blue 45.00 40.00
Nos. 349-363 (15) 84.40 *75.05*

Several values exist imperforate, but these were not regularly issued. No. 361 imperforate is printer's waste.

See Nos. 368-401, 506-524. For surcharges and overprints see Nos. 440-448, 473, 475-477, 480-481, 482-484, 489, 537-538, 615, 618, 620, 660-661, 664, 666-668, 673-676, 680-681, 686, 688, 699-703, 707-709, 717, 719, 830, J67-J68, M2, M11-M12, 1N2-1N13, 1N23-1N42, 1N57-1N58, 2N10-2N31, 2N61-2N75, 2N86, 2N91-2N93, 2N117, 2N119-2N120, 3N11-3N33, 3N56-3N58, 3N60-3N61, 4N10-4N38, 4N65-4N68, 4N70-4N71, 5N9-5N33, 5N61-5N64, 5N66-5N68, 6N9-6N34, 6N62-6N65, 6N67-6N69, 7N8-7N29, 7N56-7N58, 7N60-7N61, 8N5-8N27, 8N46, 8N51-8N53, 8N55-8N56, 8N58-8N59, 8N62-8N67, 8N72, 8N74-8N75, 8N80-8N84, 8N86-8N88, 8N90, 8N95-8N96, 8N98, 8N101-8N102, 8N105-8N106, 9N6-9N71, 9N97, 9N99, Taiwan 78, 84, Northeastern Provinces 9-10, Sinkiang 115-139, 174-188, 196, 198.

Chinese and American Flags and Map of China — A58

Printed by American Bank Note Co.

Frame Engr., Center Litho.

1939, July 4 **Unwmk.** ***Perf. 12***

Flag in Deep Rose and Ultramarine

364 A58 5c dark green 1.50 .50
365 A58 25c deep blue 1.50 .75
366 A58 50c brown 3.50 1.00
367 A58 $1 rose carmine 5.50 2.00
Nos. 364-367 (4) 12.00 4.25

150th anniv. of the US Constitution.

Type of 1939-41 Issue
Re-engraved

2c, 1939-41

Re-engraved

8c, 1939-41

Re-engraved

1940 ***Perf. 12½***

368 A57 2c olive green .20 .20
369 A57 8c olive green .20 .20

Type of 1938-41 Issue

1940 **Unwmk.** ***Perf. 14***

Type III

370 A57 2c olive green 2.10 .80
371 A57 5c green 4.25 2.10
372 A57 $1 henna & dk brn 70.00 15.00
373 A57 $2 dp blue & org brn 16.00 4.25
374 A57 $5 red & grnsh blk 21.00 14.00
375 A57 $10 dk grn & dull pur 62.50 10.00
Nos. 370-375 (6) 175.85 46.15

See surcharge note following No. 363.

Type of 1939-41

1940 **Wmk. 261** ***Perf. 12½***

Type III

376 A57 $1 henna & dk brn 6.00 *7.50*
377 A57 $2 dp blue & org brn 8.00 *7.50*
378 A57 $5 red & grnsh blk 8.00 *15.00*
379 A57 $10 dk green & dull pur 12.00 *25.00*
380 A57 $20 rose lake & dp blue 16.00 *25.00*
Nos. 376-380 (5) 50.00 *80.00*

See surcharge note following No. 363.

Printed by the Dah Tung Book Co.

Type III with Secret Marks

Five Cent

Type III — Characters joined

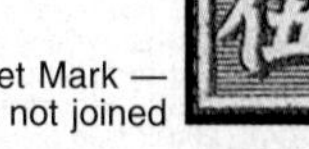

Secret Mark — Characters not joined

Eight Cent

Type III — Characters not joined

Secret Mark — Characters joined

Ten Cent

Type III — Characters sharp and well shaped

Secret Mark — Characters coarse and varying in thickness

Dollar Values

Type III

Secret Mark

1940 **Unwmk.** ***Perf. 14***

381 A57 5c green .20 .20
382 A57 5c olive green .20 .20
383 A57 8c olive green .40 .20
a. Without "star" in uniform button 1.50 *2.50*
384 A57 10c green .20 .20
385 A57 30c scarlet .35 .20
386 A57 50c dk blue .45 .20
387 A57 $1 org brn & sepia 2.25 .20
388 A57 $2 dp blue & yel brn .90 .35
389 A57 $5 red & slate grn .90 .45
390 A57 $10 dk grn & dull pur 3.75 2.10
391 A57 $20 rose lake & dk blue 11.00 3.25
Nos. 381-391 (11) 20.60 7.55

Type III with Secret Marks

1940 **Wmk. 261** ***Perf. 14***

392 A57 5c green .20 .20
393 A57 5c olive green .20 .20
394 A57 10c green .35 .20
395 A57 30c scarlet .20 .20
396 A57 50c dk blue .55 .20
397 A57 $1 org brn & sepia 3.75 2.25
398 A57 $2 dp blue & yel brn 10.50 10.50
399 A57 $5 red & slate grn 8.75 *8.75*
400 A57 $10 dk grn & dull pur 12.50 13.00
401 A57 $20 rose lake & dk blue 20.00 18.00
Nos. 392-401 (10) 57.00 53.50

Nos. 383, 384, 385, 397, 400 and 401 exist perf. 12½, but were not issued with this perforation.

See surcharge note following No. 363.

Types of 1932-34
Martyrs Issue with Secret Mark

1932-34 Issue. In the left Chinese character in bottom row, the two parts are not joined.

Secret Mark, 1940-41 Issue. The two parts are joined.

Perf. 12½, 13 and Compound

1940-41 **Wmk. 261**

402 A39 ½c olive blk .25 .20
403 A40 1c orange .25 .20
404 A46 2c dp blue ('41) .25 .20
405 A39 2½c rose lilac .25 .20
406 A48 3c dp yellow brn .25 .20
407 A39 4c pale vio ('41) .25 .20
408 A48 5c dull red org ('41) .25 .20
409 A45 8c dp orange .25 .20
410 A46 10c dull violet .25 .20
411 A45 13c dp yellow grn .25 .20
412 A48 15c brown car .25 .20
413 A46 17c brown olive .25 .20
414 A47 20c lt blue .25 .20
415 A45 21c olive brn ('41) 1.00 1.00
416 A40 25c red vio ('41) .25 .20
417 A46 28c olive ('41) .25 .20
418 A48 30c brown car .25 .20
a. Vert. pair, imperf. btwn. 125.00
419 A47 40c orange .25 .20
420 A40 50c green .25 .20

Unwmk.

421 A39 ½c olive black .20 .20
422 A40 1c orange .20 .20
a. Without secret mark 2.25 2.25
b. Horiz. pair, imperf. vert. 110.00
423 A46 2c dp blue .20 .20
a. Vert. pair, imperf. horiz. 100.00
b. Horiz. pair, imperf. between 160.00
424 A39 2½c rose lilac .20 .20
425 A48 3c dp yellow brn .20 .20
426 A39 4c pale violet .20 .20
427 A48 5c dull red org .20 .20
428 A45 8c dp orange .20 .20
429 A46 10c dull violet 2.75 .35
430 A45 13c dp yel grn .20 .20
431 A48 15c brown car .20 .20
432 A46 17c brn olive .20 .20
433 A47 20c lt blue .20 .20
a. Vert. pair, imperf. horiz. 125.00
b. Horiz. pair, imperf. vert. 125.00
434 A45 21c olive brn .20 .20
435 A40 25c rose vio .20 .20
436 A46 28c olive .20 .20
437 A48 30c brown car 2.25 2.25
438 A47 40c orange .20 .20
439 A40 50c green 3.00 .30
Nos. 402-439 (38) 16.70 10.70

Several values exist imperforate, but they were not regularly issued.

Used values are for favor cancels. Postally used copies sell for more.

See surcharge note following No. 323.

Regional Surcharges.

The regional surcharges, Nos. 440-448, 482-484, 486-491, 525-549, have been listed according to the basic stamps, with black or red surcharges. The surcharges of the individual provinces, plus Hong Kong and Shanghai, are noted in small type. The numeral following each letter is the surcharge denomination. These surcharges are identified by the following letters:

a — Hong Kong
b — Shanghai
bx — Anhwei
c — Hunan
d — Kansu
e — Kiangsi
f — Eastern Szechwan
g — Chekiang
h — Fukien
i — Kwangsi
j — Kwangtung
k — Western Szechwan
l — Yunnan
m — Honan
n — Shensi
o — Kweichow
p — Hupeh

Regional Surcharges on Stamps of 1939-40:

Hong Kong — a4

Shanghai — b3

Hunan — c3

Kansu — d3

Kiangsi — e3

Eastern Szechwan — f3

Chekiang — g3

1940-41 **Unwmk.** ***Perf. 12½, 14***

Carmine Surcharge

440 A57 4c on 5c ol grn (#382) .55 .55
r. Lower right character duplicated at left 30.00 32.50

Black Surcharge

441 A57 3c on 5c grn (#351) (b3) 1.10 1.25
442 A57 3c on 5c ol grn (#352) (c3, d3) .60 1.60
443 A57 3c on 5c grn (#381) (b3) .55 1.10
444 A57 3c on 5c ol grn (#382) (e3) .65 .85
r. Lower left character duplicated at right (Kiangsi) 42.50 42.50
(b3) Shanghai .65 1.40
(f3) Eastern Szechwan .65 1.60

The Kansu surcharges of #442 are of 6 types. Differences include formation of top part of fen character (at left of "3"), fen with low right hook, height of "3" (5-4mm), space between upper and lower characters (6-9mm), etc.

1940-41 **Wmk. 261** ***Perf. 14***

445 A57 3c on 5c grn (#392) (e3) .55 1.25
r. Lower left character duplicated at right (Kiangsi) 35.00 35.00
(b3, c3) Shanghai, Hunan .55 1.40
446 A57 3c on 5c ol grn (#393) (f3) .65 1.60
(b3) Shanghai .85 1.60
r. Lower left character duplicated at right (f3) 60.00 65.00

Red Surcharge

447 A57 3c on 5c grn (#392) (g3) 1.10 3.00
448 A57 3c on 5c ol grn (#393) (g3) 5.00 5.00

Dr. Sun Yat-sen — A59

Printed by American Bank Note Co.

1941 **Unwmk.** **Engr.** ***Perf. 12***

449 A59 ½c sepia .20 .30
450 A59 1c orange .20 .20
451 A59 2c brt ultra .20 .20
452 A59 5c green .20 .20
453 A59 8c red orange .20 .25
454 A59 8c turq green .20 .20
455 A59 10c brt green .20 .20
456 A59 17c olive 3.50 11.00
457 A59 25c rose violet .20 1.00
458 A59 30c scarlet .20 .25
459 A59 50c dk blue .20 .20
460 A59 $1 brown & blk .30 .20
461 A59 $2 blue & blk .30 .20
a. Center inverted *12,500.*
462 A59 $5 scarlet & blk .50 .20
463 A59 $10 green & blk 3.75 1.00
464 A59 $20 rose vio & blk 2.10 *5.00*
Nos. 449-464 (16) 12.45 20.60

For surcharges see Nos. 488, 491, 542-543, 617, 621, 670, 677, 687, 705-706, 712, 716, 718, M1, M3-M4, 1N16-1N22, 1N43-1N56, 9N78-9N96, 9N98, 9N100.

Industry and Agriculture — A60

1941, June 21 ***Perf. 12½***

465 A60 8c green .20 .20
466 A60 21c red brown .20 .20
467 A60 28c dk olive grn .20 .20
468 A60 33c vermilion .90 1.50
469 A60 50c dp ultra 1.10 .85
470 A60 $1 dk violet 1.40 .85
Nos. 465-470 (6) 4.00 3.80

Souvenir Sheet

Imperf

Typo.

471 Sheet of 6 35.00 35.00
a. A60 8c dull green 2.00 2.00
b. A60 21c dark orange brown 2.00 2.00
c. A60 28c dull yellow green 2.00 2.00
d. A60 33c red 2.00 2.00
e. A60 50c dull blue 2.00 2.00
f. A60 $1 dark violet 2.00 2.00

The Thrift Movement and its aim to "Save for Reconstruction."

Issued in sheets measuring 155x171mm, without gum.

This sheet exists with additional blue marginal overprints in Russia, French and Chinese reading "Souvenir of the Exhibition of the Russian Philatelic Society in China, Shanghai, China, Feb. 28, 1943."

The overprinting was applied by the society, and when so overprinted this sheet had no franking power.

Stamps of 1939-41 Overprinted in Carmine or Blue

1941, Oct. 10 ***Perf. 12½, 14, 13***

472 A40 1c dull orange .20 *.60*
473 A57 2c olive grn (C) .20 *.60*
474 A39 4c pale violet (C) .20 *.60*
475 A57 8c ol grn (#369) (C) .20 *.60*
476 A57 10c green (#354) (C) .20 *.60*
477 A57 16c ol gray (#357) (C) .20 *.60*
478 A45 21c olive brn (C) .20 *.60*
479 A46 28c olive (C) .55 *1.65*
480 A57 30c scarlet .65 *3.25*
481 A57 $1 hn & dk brn (#359) 3.25 3.25
Nos. 472-481 (10) 5.85 *12.35*

Chinese Republic, 30th anniversary.

Kiangsi — e7

Eastern Szechwan — f7

Chekiang — g7

Fukien — h7

1941 **Unwmk.** ***Perf. 12½, 14***

482 A57 7c on 8c (#353) (g7, h7) .55 1.10
483 A57 7c on 8c (#369) (f7) .45 .55
484 A57 7c on 8c (#383) (h7) .55 .90
(e7) Kiangsi .65 .90
(g7) Chekiang .65 1.10
r. Without "star" in uniform button 65.00

Type of 1932-34 Re-engraved

1941 **Unwmk.** ***Perf. 14***

485 A45 8c deep orange 11.00 55.00

The original stamps are 19½mm wide, the re-engraved 21mm.

Eleven other values of the Martyrs Issue and types A37 and A57 exist re-engraved, but were not issued.

Hunan — c1

Kiangsi — e1

Fukien — h1

Kwangsi — i1

Kwangtung — j1

1942

Red Surcharge

486 A39 1c on ½c blk brn (#312) (i1) .85 *1.75*
(c1) Hunan 1.60 *2.75*
487 A39 1c on ½c ol blk (#421) (e1) .45 1.60
(c1) Hunan .55 *2.00*
(i1) Kwangsi 1.65 *2.50*
(h1) Fukien 5.00 *8.00*
488 A59 1c on ½c sepia (#449) (j1) .85 *1.60*
(c1) Hunan 1.10 *2.50*

Hunan — c40

Eastern Szechwan — f40

Western Szechwan — k40

Yunnan — l40

Red Surcharge

489 A57 40c on 50c dk bl (#386) (f40) .65 1.10
(k40) Western Szechwan 3.75 *5.00*
(l40) Yunnan 3.25 *3.25*
r. Inverted surcharge (Yunnan) 110.00

Wmk. 261

490 A40 40c on 50c grn (#420) (c40) 1.60 *5.50*

Unwmk.

491 A59 40c on 50c dk bl (#459) (c40) 2.75 *7.50*

Dr. Sun Yat-sen — A62

Central Trust Printing

Perf. 10½-11, 11½-12½, 13 and Compounds

1942-43 **Typo.**

Without Gum

492 A62 10c dp green ('43) .20 .35
493 A62 16c dull ol brn 12.50 *40.00*
a. Perf 10½ 475.00 325.00
494 A62 20c dk ol grn ('43) .20 .20
a. Perf. 11 10.00 10.00
495 A62 25c brown vio .20 .20
496 A62 30c dull ver .20 .20
a. Perf. 11 2.75 2.75
497 A62 40c dk red brn ('43) .20 .25
a. Perf. 11x13 85.00
b. Perf. 11 12.00 12.00

498	A62	50c sage green	.20	.20
a.		Perf. 11	6.00	*12.00*
499	A62	$1 rose lake	.30	.20
a.		Perf. 11	35.00	35.00
500	A62	$1 dull grn ('43)	.30	.30
501	A62	$1.50 dp blue ('43)	.30	.30
a.		Perf. 11	250.00	250.00
502	A62	$2 dk blue grn	.30	.30
503	A62	$3 dk yel ('43)	.30	.30
504	A62	$4 red brown	.30	.30
505	A62	$5 cerise ('43)	.30	.30
		Nos. 492-505 (14)	15.80	43.40

Many shades and part-perforate varieties exist.

See Nos. 550 to 563 for other stamps of type A62 with secret mark and new values and colors. For surcharges and overprints see Nos. 525-530, 671, 683, 692-694, 696, 771, 773, 807-809, 811-820, 824-827, 832, 834-834A, 836, 848-850, 852-854, 857, 860-863, 876, 879, M5-M10, Taiwan 55, 86, 99, Kwangsi 6-7, Sinkiang 162-173, 194-195.

Type of 1938
Thin Paper Without Gum

1942-44 Unwmk. Engr. *Imperf.*

506	A57	$10 red brown	.35	.20
507	A57	$20 blue grn	.35	.30
508	A57	$20 rose red ('44)	4.75	1.50
509	A57	$30 dull vio ('43)	.35	.35
510	A57	$40 rose red ('43)	.45	.35
511	A57	$50 blue	1.00	.55
512	A57	$100 org brn ('43)	1.75	1.75

Rouletted

513	A57	$5 lilac gray ('44)	5.00	6.00
a.		Rouletted x perf. 12½	25.00	30.00
514	A57	$10 red brown	3.00	2.50
515	A57	$50 blue	3.00	2.50
a.		Rouletted x imperf.	2.50	—
		Nos. 506-515 (10)	20.00	16.00

1942-45 *Perf. 12½ to 15*

516	A57	$4 dp blue ('43)	.30	.20
517	A57	$5 lil gray ('43)	.40	.30
518	A57	$10 red brown	.40	.30
519	A57	$20 blue grn ('43)	.40	.30
520	A57	$20 rose red ('45)	75.00	60.00
521	A57	$30 dull vio ('43)	.50	.35
522	A57	$40 rose ('43)	.50	.40
523	A57	$50 blue	.50	.40
524	A57	$100 org brn ('45)	80.00	65.00
		Nos. 516-524 (9)	158.00	127.25

Beware of Nos. 508 and 512 with faked perforations that are offered as Nos. 520 and 524.

See surcharge note following No. 363.

No. 493 Overprinted in Black or Red

附加已付 國內平信

1942

525	A62 (i) 16c (Bk)	75.00	85.00
	(c) Hunan	450.00	
	(k) Western Szechwan	175.00	175.00
	(m) Honan	725.00	750.00
r.	Perf. 10½ (Kwangsi)	500.00	
	(n) Shensi	225.00	240.00
s.	Inverted ovpt. (Shensi)	225.00	
526	A62 (d) 16c (R)	45.00	20.00
	(bx) Anhwei	475.00	475.00
	(e) Kiangsi	55.00	40.00
	(f) Eastern Szechwan	110.00	50.00
r.	Perf. 10½ (E. Szechwan)	475.00	
	(h) Fukien	275.00	200.00
	(j) Kwangtung	575.00	600.00
	(l) Yunnan	55.00	35.00
s.	Horiz. pair, imperf. btwn (Yunnan)	600.00	
	(o) Kweichow	250.00	175.00
	(p) Hupeh, perf. 10½	825.00	725.00
t.	Perf. 13 (Hupeh)		

This overprint means "Domestic Ordinary Letter Surcharge Paid." It was applied in various sizes and types by 14 districts, 9 using red ink, 5 using black. (The Anhwei overprint comes in two types.) These overprinted stamps were briefly sold for $1.16 before the government ordered their sale suspended. The vertical bars and 50c surcharge of Nos. 527-528 were then applied.

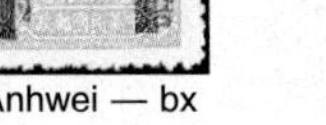
Anhwei — bx

Hunan — c

Kansu — d

Kiangsi — e

Eastern Szechwan — f

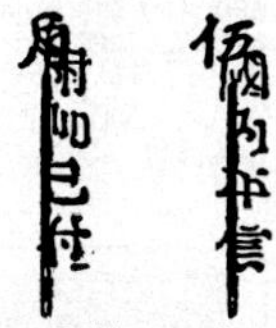
Fukien — h

Kwangsi — i

Kwangtung — j

Western Szechwan — k

Yunnan — l

Honan — m

Shensi — n

Kweichow — o

Hupeh — p

Nos. 525-526 Surcharged "50 cents" and 2 Vertical Bars in Black or Red

1942 Unwmk.

527	A62 50c on 16c (Bk) (c,f)	2.40	2.50
	(i) Kwangsi	4.75	4.75
	(k) Western Szechwan	6.50	6.00
r.	Inverted surch. (W. Szech.)	225.00	
s.	"k" surcharge on #493	325.00	
	(m) Honan	6.50	6.50
	(n) Shensi	3.50	3.50
528	A62 50c on 16c (R) (p)	4.25	4.25
	(bx) Anhwei	85.00	*250.00*
	(d) Kansu	3.25	5.00
	(e) Kiangsi	5.00	9.50
	(h) Fukien	6.00	6.50
	(j) Kwangtung	6.00	5.50
	(l) Yunnan	6.00	7.50
	(o) Kweichow	3.25	6.00
r.	"o" surcharge inverted	250.00	
s.	"p" surch. on #526(f)	80.00	*45.00*

Many varieties of Nos. 527-528 exist, including narrow or wide spacing between the two top characters, or between the vertical bars, or both.

Surcharges on stamps perf. 10½ (basic No. 493a) usually sell at much higher prices.

General Issue

Hunan — c50

Eastern Szechwan — f50

Chekiang — g50

Kwangsi — i50

Kwangtung — j50

Western Szechwan — k50

Honan — m50

Shensi — n50

Kweichow — o50

No. 493 Surcharged in Black, Red or Carmine

1943 Unwmk.

529	A62 50c on 16c (Bk) (m50)	10.00	10.00
	(n50) Shensi	10.00	10.00
r.	Perf. 11x13 (Shensi)	80.00	
530	A62 50c on 16c (C)	.90	1.60
	(c50) Hunan	2.75	5.50
r.	Inverted surch. (Hunan)	50.00	
	(f50) Eastern Szechwan	3.25	2.50
	(g50) Chekiang	37.50	40.00
	(i50) Kwangsi	6.00	7.00
	(j50) Kwangtung	4.50	6.50
	(k50) Western Szechwan	4.50	6.00
	(m50) Honan	7.50	8.00
	(o50) Kweichow	10.00	12.00
s.	"05" instead of "50" (Kweichow)	450.00	

Many varieties of Nos. 529-530 exist, such as narrow or wide spacing horizontally or vertically between the overprinted Chinese characters.

Surcharges on No. 493a (perf. 10½) usually sell at much higher prices.

The General Issue type, No. 530, was distributed to all head offices, which in turn supplied the post offices under their direction. It is surcharged in carmine; the other stamps listed under No. 530 are surcharged in red or carmine.

Hunan — c20

Kansu — d20

Kiangsi — e20

Eastern Szechwan — f20

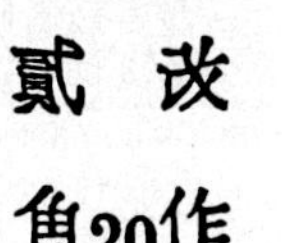
Fukien — h20

Kwangsi — i20

Kwangtung — j20

Western Szechwan — k20

Yunnan — l20

Honan — m20

Shensi — n20

Kweichow — o20

Hupeh — p20

1943 Wmk. 261, Unwmkd.

On No. 318

531	A45 20c on 13c (k20)	2.00	*2.10*
	(d20) Kansu	2.00	*4.50*
	(n20) Shensi	3.00	*3.50*
532	A45 20c on 13c (i20;R)	.70	2.40
	(c20) Hunan	1,000.	
	(e20) Kiangsi	250.00	
	(j20) Kwangtung	75.00	82.50
	(p20) Hupeh	1.75	*3.50*

On No. 411

533	A45 20c on 13c (n20)	2.00	*3.75*
	(d20) Kansu	1.50	*6.75*
	(k20) Western Szechwan	1.40	*6.75*
	(l20) Yunnan	18.00	12.00
	(m20) Honan	300.00	
534	A45 20c on 13c (p20;R)	1.50	*4.75*
	(c20) Hunan	2.25	1.60
	(e20) Kiangsi	7.00	1.90
	(f20) Eastern Szechwan	2.00	*2.40*
	(h20) Fukien	8.00	*8.25*
	(i20) Kwangsi	1.00	*2.40*
	(j20) Kwangtung	16.00	15.00
	(o20) Kweichow	3.00	*3.00*

On No. 430

535	A45 20c on 13c (l20)	2.00	*4.25*
	(d20) Kansu	2.00	*2.40*
	(k20) Western Szechwan	30.00	*37.50*
	(m20) Honan	8.50	*8.25*
	(n20) Shensi	3.00	*4.75*
536	A45 20c on 13c (f20;i20;R)	2.00	*3.00*
	(c20) Hunan	10.00	*8.75*
	(e20) Kiangsi	3.00	*3.50*
	(j20) Kwangtung	2.00	*2.40*
	(o20) Kweichow	2.00	*9.00*
	(p20) Hupeh	2.00	*3.50*

On No. 357

537	A57 20c on 16c (k20)	2.00	*2.40*
	(c20) Hunan	3.00	*12.00*
	(d20) Kansu	3.00	*12.00*
	(m20) Honan	10.00	*16.00*
	(n20) Shensi	3.00	*12.00*
538	A57 20c on 16c (e20, o20; R)	2.00	*12.00*
	(c20) Hunan	10.00	*16.00*
	(i20) Kwangsi	10.00	*12.00*
	(j20) Kwangtung	50.00	*50.00*

On No. 413

539	A46 20c on 17c (c20;R)	2.00	*3.75*
	(i20) Kwangsi	2.00	*2.40*
	(j20) Kwangtung	30.00	40.00

On No. 432

540	A46 20c on 17c (k20)	3.00	5.00
	(d20) Kansu	3.00	5.75
	(m20) Honan	35.00	45.00
541	A46 20c on 17c (e20;R)	2.00	*5.00*
	(j20) Kwangtung	2.25	*11.00*
	(o20) Kweichow	2.00	*6.00*

On No. 456

542	A59 20c on 17c (m20)	175.00	250.00
543	A59 20c on 17c (c20;R)	15.00	22.50

On No. 415

544	A45 20c on 21c (e20;R)	9.50	11.00

On No. 434

545	A45 20c on 21c (c20, k20)	1.00	*3.50*
	(d20) Kansu	1.40	*6.00*
	(l20) Yunnan	1.10	*3.50*
	(m20) Honan	2.25	*8.25*
546	A45 20c on 21c (f20;R)	1.00	*3.75*
	(e20) Kiangsi	1.00	*5.00*
	(h20) Fukien	1.10	*4.25*
	(i20) Kwangsi	1.40	*3.50*

(j20) Kwangtung 2.00 *4.50*
(o20) Kweichow 1.40 *2.40*
(p20) Hupeh 1.00 *5.00*

On No. 417

547 A46 20c on 28c (e20;R) 525.00 *650.00*

On No. 436

548 A46 20c on 28c (l20) 1.10 *5.75*
(d20) Kansu 15.00 21.00
(k20) Western Szechwan 22.50 50.00
(m20) Honan 35.00 40.00
549 A46 20c on 20c (c20;R) 1.00 *3.00*
(c20) Hunan 1.10 *4.25*
(h20) Fukien 1.10 *4.25*
(i20) Kwangsi 1.00 *4.25*
(j20) Kwangtung 1.00 *5.75*
(o20) Kweichow 2.50 *4.25*

Many varieties of Nos. 531-549 exist, such as narrow or wide spacing between the overprinted Chinese characters, and "20" higher or lower than illustrated.

Type of 1942-43
Pacheng Printing

1944-46 **Unwmk.** ***Perf. 12***
Without Gum

550 A62 30c chocolate .35 *10.00*
551 A62 $1 green 3.00 3.00
552 A62 $2 dk vio brn .20 .20
a. Imperf., pair 12.00 12.00
553 A62 $2 dk bl grn .20 .20
a. Perf. 10½ 35.00 26.00
554 A62 $2 deep blue 1.25 1.25
555 A62 $3 lt yellow 1.25 .60
556 A62 $4 violet brn .20 .20
a. Imperf., pair 60.00
557 A62 $5 car ('46) .20 .20
a. Perf. 10½ 60.00 60.00
558 A62 $6 gray vio ('45) .20 .20
559 A62 $10 red brn ('45) .20 .20
a. Imperf., pair 60.00
560 A62 $20 dp ultra ('46) .20 .20
561 A62 $50 dk green ('46) 3.00 .20
562 A62 $70 lilac ('46) 4.00 .20
563 A62 $100 lt brown ('46) .20 .20
Nos. 550-563 (14) 14.45 *16.85*

In the Pacheng printing of the Central Trust type stamps, the secret mark "C" has been added below the lower left foliate ornament beneath the sun emblem. On the $3, it is below the right ornament. New values also include a "P" at right of sun emblem on the $6 and $10, and at right of necktie on the $20. Some values of Pacheng printing exist on paper with elephant watermark in sheet.
See surcharge note following No. 505.

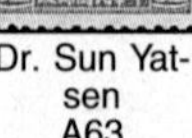

Dr. Sun Yat-sen
A63

Allegory of Savings
A64

1944-46 **Unwmk.** **Typo.** ***Perf. 12½***
Without Gum

565 A63 40c brown red .25 .25
566 A63 $2 gray brown .25 .25
567 A63 $3 red .25 .25
a. $3 orange red 2.50 3.00
568 A63 $3 lt red brown ('45) .60 .50
569 A63 $6 pale lilac gray ('45) .25 .25
570 A63 $10 dull lake ('45) .25 .25
571 A63 $20 rose ('45) .25 .25
a. Perf. 16 325.00 325.00
572 A63 $50 lt brown ('46) .40 .40
573 A63 $70 rose violet ('46) .40 .40
Nos. 565-573 (9) 2.90 2.80

For surcharges see Nos. 772, 774, 828, 833, 835, 836A, 839, 842, 851, 864, 868, 873-875, 877, 880. Taiwan 81, 98, Sinkiang 200-201.

1944-45 **Engr.** ***Perf. 13***
Without Gum

574 A64 $40 indigo ('45) .20 .20
575 A64 $50 yellow grn ('45) .20 .20
576 A64 $100 yellow brn .20 .20
577 A64 $200 dk green ('45) .20 .20
Nos. 574-577 (4) .80 .80

All four values were printed on thick paper; the first three were also printed on thin paper.
For surcharges see Szechwan Nos. F1, F3.

A65

Dr. Sun Yat-sen — A66

1944, Dec. 25 **Litho.**
Without Gum

578 A65 $2 deep green .50 .80
579 A65 $5 fawn .50 .80
580 A65 $6 dull rose vio .95 1.50
581 A65 $10 violet blue 1.90 2.50
582 A65 $20 carmine 4.00 6.00
Nos. 578-582 (5) 7.85 11.60

50th anniversary of the Kuomintang.

1945, Mar. 12
Without Gum

583 A66 $2 gray green .30 .80
584 A66 $5 red brown .40 .80
585 A66 $6 dk vio blue .45 1.25
586 A66 $10 lt blue .70 1.10
587 A66 $20 rose .95 1.50
588 A66 $30 buff 1.50 2.00
Nos. 583-588 (6) 4.30 7.45

Death of Dr. Sun Yat-sen, 20th anniv.

Dr. Sun Yat-sen — A67

1945-46 **Without Gum** ***Perf. 12½***

589 A67 $2 green .25 .35
590 A67 $5 dull green .25 .35
591 A67 $10 dk blue .25 .35
a. Imperf., pair 70.00
592 A67 $20 carmine ('46) .25 .35
a. Imperf., pair 70.00
Nos. 589-592 (4) 1.00 1.40

For surcharges see Nos. 695, 697, 837, 855, Taiwan 58, 82, 87-88.

Statue of Liberty, Map of China, Flags of Great Britain, China and United States, and Chiang Kai-shek
A68

Unwmk.
1945, July 7 **Engr.** ***Perf. 12***
Flags in Dark Blue and Red

593 A68 $1 deep blue .30 .20
594 A68 $2 dull green .40 .35
595 A68 $5 olive gray .40 .35
596 A68 $6 brown .95 .80
597 A68 $10 rose lilac 4.50 *5.00*
598 A68 $20 carmine rose 4.00 *5.00*
Nos. 593-598 (6) 10.55 *11.70*

Signing of a Treaty in 1943 between Great Britain, the US and China.

Pres. Lin Sen (1864-1943)
A69

Pres. Chiang Kai-shek
A70

1945, Aug. **Unwmk.** ***Perf. 12***

599 A69 $1 dp ultra & blk .25 *.75*
600 A69 $2 myrtle grn & blk .25 *.75*
601 A69 $5 red & blk .25 *.75*
602 A69 $6 purple & blk .90 1.25
603 A69 $10 choc & blk 3.25 *1.90*
604 A69 $20 olive grn & blk 4.00 2.75
Nos. 599-604 (6) 8.90 *8.15*

1945, Oct. 10
Flag in Rose Red and Violet Blue

605 A70 $2 green .45 .50
606 A70 $4 dark blue .45 .50
607 A70 $5 olive gray .45 .50
608 A70 $6 bister brown 1.40 2.00
609 A70 $10 gray 3.50 2.00
610 A70 $20 red violet 4.00 3.00
Nos. 605-610 (6) 10.25 8.50

Inauguration of Chiang Kai-shek as president, Oct. 10, 1943.

President Chiang Kai-shek — A71

1945, Oct. 10 **Typo.** ***Perf. 13***
Without Gum
Flag in Carmine and Blue

611 A71 $20 green & blue .25 .20
612 A71 $50 bister brn & bl .50 .35
613 A71 $100 blue .45 .35
614 A71 $300 rose red & blue .45 .35
Nos. 611-614 (4) 1.65 1.25

Victory of the Allied Nations over Japan.

C. N. C. Surcharges

The green surcharges on Nos. 615 to 621, and the surcharges on Nos. 647 to 721, and 768 to 774 represent Chinese National Currency and were applied at Shanghai.

Stamps of 1938-41 Surcharged in Black with Chinese Characters and New Value in Checkered Rectangle at Bottom, Resurcharged in Green

1945 ***Perf. 12, 12½***

615 A57 10c on $20 on 3c (#350) .20 .20
616 A46 15c on $30 on 2c (#423) .20 .35
a. Horiz. pair, imperf. between 90.00
b. Vert. pair, imperf. between 85.00
617 A59 25c on $50 on 1c (#450) .20 .20
618 A57 50c on $100 on 3c (#350) .20 .20
619 A40 $1 on $200 on 1c (#422) .20 .20
a. Horiz. pair, imperf. between 90.00
620 A57 $2 on $400 on 3c (#350) .20 .20
621 A59 $5 on $1000 on 1c (#450) .20 .20
Nos. 615-621 (7) 1.40 1.55

The black (first) surcharges on Nos. 615 to 621 represent Nanking puppet government currency.
In the green surcharge, the characters at the left express the new value and are either two or four in number.

Types of 1932-34, Re-engraved, and Surcharged in Green with Horizontal Bar and Four or Five Chinese Characters and Overprinted in Black:

Perf. 14

622 A47 $10 on 20c brown red 4.00 5.50
623 A47 $20 on 40c orange 21.00 24.00
a. Green surcharge inverted 60.00
624 A48 $50 on 30c violet brn 14.00 18.00
Nos. 622-624 (3) 39.00 47.50

These provisional surcharges were applied in Honan in National currency to stamps of the Hwa Pei (North China) government. The black overprint reads: "Hwa Pei."
The two-character "Hwa Pei" overprint was applied to various stamps in 1941-43 by the North China puppet government. See Nos. 8N1-8N53, 8N60-8N84.

Dr. Sun Yat-sen
A72 A73

1945, Dec. **Typo.** ***Perf. 12***
Without Gum

625 A72 $20 dp carmine .25 .25
626 A72 $30 dp blue .25 .25
627 A72 $40 orange .25 .25
628 A72 $50 green .25 .25
629 A72 $100 dk brown .25 .25
630 A72 $200 brown violet .25 .25
Nos. 625-630 (6) 1.50 1.50

For surcharges see Nos. 810, 829, 838, 865, J110-J119, Taiwan 75, Kwangsi F2, Szechwan F2, F4, Yunnan 66-67, 71.

Type of 1931-37
Perf. 12½, 13x12½, 13½
1946 **Unwmk.**

631 A37 $1 dk violet .30 .20
632 A37 $2 olive green .30 .20
633 A37 $20 brt yellow grn .30 .25
634 A37 $30 chocolate .30 .25
635 A37 $50 red orange .30 .20
Nos. 631-635 (5) 1.50 1.10

$4 blue and $5 red values were prepared but not issued. Value $400.
For surcharges see Nos. 678, 684, 689-690, 768, 843.

1946-47 **Engr.** ***Perf. 14***
Without Gum

636 A73 $20 carmine .75 .25
637 A73 $30 dk blue ('47) .20 .20
638 A73 $50 purple .20 .20
639 A73 $70 red org ('47) 16.00 1.40
640 A73 $100 dk carmine .20 .20
641 A73 $200 olive grn ('47) .20 .20
642 A73 $500 brt bl grn ('47) .20 .20
643 A73 $700 red brown ('47) .20 .20
644 A73 $1000 rose lake .35 .35
645 A73 $3000 blue 1.00 .35
646 A73 $5000 dp green & ver 1.00 .35
Nos. 636-646 (11) 20.30 3.90

For surcharges see Nos. 679, 769, 775, 823, 837A, 844-845, 856, 866, 875A, 878, Taiwan 18, 23-28, 54, 76-77, 100, Northeastern Provinces 41-43, Fukien 5-6, Hunan 1, E1, F1, Kwangsi 11, F2, Szechwan F5-F8, Sinkiang 202-204, People's Republic of China 3L53, 3L67-3L68, 6L28.

Stamps of 1932-41 Surcharged in Black

Perf. 12½, 13, 13x12, 14
Wmk. 261

647 A45 $20 on 8c (#409) .20 *.65*
648 A39 $30 on ½c (#402) 2,000.
649 A45 $50 on 21c (#415) .20 *.20*
650 A45 $70 on 13c (#411) .20 .20
651 A46 $100 on 28c (#417) .20 *.65*

Unwmk.

652 A39 $3 on 2½c (#424) 5.75 5.75
653 A48 $10 on 15c (#431) .20 .20
654 A45 $20 on 8c (#428) .20 .20
655 A47 $20 on 20c (#433) .35 .35
656 A39 $30 on ½c (#421) .20 .20
657 A45 $50 on 21c (#434) .35 .45
657A A45 $70 on 13c (#318) 125.00 125.00
658 A45 $70 on 13c (#430) .35 *.45*
659 A46 $100 on 28c (#436) .35 .35

Forgeries of No. 648 exist.

Stamps and Types of 1931-1946 Surcharged in Black or Carmine

Perf. 12½, 13, 14

1946-47 Wmk. 261

660 A57 $50 on 5c green (#392) .35 .85
661 A57 $50 on 5c ol grn (#393) 21.00 17.50
662 A48 $50 on 5c dl red org (#408) .20 1.10
663 A40 $100 on 1c org (#403) .20 1.10

Perf. 12, 12½, 12½x13, 13, 14

1946-47 Unwmk.

664 A57 $20 on 3c (#350) .20 .35
665 A45 $20 on 8c (#428) .20 .20
666 A57 $50 on 3c (#350) .20 .20
667 A57 $50 on 5c (#352) .20 .20
668 A57 $50 on 5c (#382) .85 1.60
669 A48 $50 on 5c (#427) .20 .20
670 A59 $50 on 5c (#452) .20 .20
671 A62 $50 on $1 (#500) .20 .20
672 A40 $100 on 1c (#422) .20 .20
a. Without secret mark (#422a) 65.00 65.00
673 A57 $100 on 3c (#350) .20 .20
674 A57 $100 on 8c (#353) 12.00 11.00
675 A57 $100 on 8c (#369) 2.00 .35
676 A57 $100 on 8c (#383) .35 .35
a. Without "star" in uniform button (No. 383a) 25.00 16.00
677 A59 $100 on 8c (#454) .20 .20
678 A37 $100 on $1 (#631) .20 .20
679 A73 $100 on $20 (#636) .35 .35
680 A57 $200 on 10c (#354) .75 .25
681 A57 $200 on 10c (#384) .25 1.10
682 A37 $200 on $4 dl bl .50 .20
a. Double surcharge 16.00
683 A62 $250 on $1.50 (#501) .20 .20
a. Perf. 11 250.00 250.00
684 A37 $250 on $2 (#632) .50 .20
685 A37 $250 on $5 car .50 .20
686 A57 $300 on 10c (#354) .20 .20
687 A59 $300 on 10c (#455) .20 .20
688 A57 $500 on 3c (#350) .50 .20
689 A37 $500 on $20 (#633) .20 .20
690 A37 $800 on $30 (#634) .20 .20
691 A37 $1000 on 2c (#297) .55 .35
692 A62 $1000 on $2 (#552) .20 .20
a. Imperf., pair 16.00 16.00
693 A62 $1000 on $2 (#553) .20 .25
694 A62 $1000 on $2 (#554) .25 .55
695 A67 $1000 on $2 (#589) .20 .20
696 A62 $2000 on $5 (#557) .20 .20
697 A67 $2000 on $5 dl grn (C) (#590) .20 .20
Nos. 664-697 (34) 23.55 21.10

Nos. 682 and 685 were not issued without surcharge. No. 682 is perf. 13x13½; No. 685, perf. 12x12½.

The characters at the left express the new value and vary in number.

Stamps of 1938-41 Surcharged in Black

Perf. 12, 12½, 13, 14

1946 Wmk. 261

698 A45 $20 on 8c (#409) 140.00 140.00
699 A57 $50 on 5c (#392) .20 .55
700 A57 $50 on 5c (#393) .50 1.10

1946-48 Unwmk.

700A A57 $20 on 5c (#381) 625.00
701 A57 $20 on 8c (#353) .20 .35
702 A57 $20 on 8c (#369) .35 .35
703 A57 $20 on 8c (#383) .20 .50
a. Without "star" in uniform button (No. 383a) 4.50 4.50
b. Inverted surcharge 20.00
c. Dbl. surch., one on back 32.50 32.50
d. Double surcharge 32.50
704 A45 $20 on 8c (#428) .20 .20
a. Double surcharge 22.50
705 A59 $20 on 8c (#453) .20 .20
706 A59 $20 on 8c (#454) .20 .20
a. Inverted surcharge 13.00
b. Double surcharge 13.00
707 A57 $50 on 5c (#351) 6.75 6.25
708 A57 $50 on 5c (#352) .20 .20
a. Inverted surcharge 27.50
709 A57 $50 on 5c (#381) .70 .70
710 A57 $50 on 5c (#382) .50 .35

711 A48 $50 on 5c (#427) .20 .20
a. Inverted surcharge 27.50
712 A59 $50 on 5c (#452) .50 .20
a. Double surcharge 16.00

Stamps of 1939-41 Surcharged in Blue or Red

1946 Wmk. 261 *Perf. 12½*

713 A40 $10 on 1c org (#403) .20 .20
a. Inverted surcharge 40.00
714 A48 $20 on 3c dp yel brn (#406) 500.00 500.00

Forgeries of No. 714 exist.

1946 Unwmk. *Perf. 12, 12½, 13*

715 A40 $10 on 1c org (#422) .20 .20
a. Without secret mark (#422a) 10.00 12.00
b. Inverted surcharge 8.00 10.00
716 A59 $10 on 1c org (#450) .20 .20
a. Double surcharge 27.50
717 A57 $20 on 2c ol grn (R) (#368) .20 .20
718 A59 $20 on 2c brt ultra (R) (#451) .20 .20
a. Inverted surcharge 20.00
b. Double surcharge 16.00
719 A57 $20 on 3c dl cl (#350) .20 .20
a. Double surcharge 22.50
720 A48 $20 on 3c dp yel brn (#425) .20 .35
721 A39 $30 on 4c pale vio (R) (#426) .20 .25
a. Inverted surcharge 9.00
Nos. 715-721 (7) 1.40 1.60

President Chiang Kai-shek — A74

Perf. 10½-11½

1946, Oct. 31 Engr. Unwmk.

722 A74 $20 carmine .45 .50
723 A74 $30 green .45 .50
724 A74 $50 vermilion .45 .50
725 A74 $100 yellow grn .45 .50
726 A74 $200 yellow org .45 .50
727 A74 $300 magenta .45 .50
Nos. 722-727 (6) 2.70 3.00

60th birthday of Chiang Kai-shek.

Printed by Dah Yeh Printing Co.; the earlier ones are gumless, the later ones gummed.

See Taiwan Nos. 29-34, Northeastern Provinces 30-35.

Printed by Dah Tung Book Co.
Without Gum
Perf. 14

722a A74 $20 carmine 1.00 1.40
723a A74 $30 green 1.00 1.40
724a A74 $50 vermilion 1.00 1.40
725a A74 $100 yellow green 1.00 1.40
726a A74 $200 yellow orange 1.00 1.40
727a A74 $300 magenta 1.00 1.40
Nos. 722a-727a (6) 6.00 8.40

Assembly House, Nanking A75

1946, Nov. 15 Litho. *Perf. 14*
Without Gum

728 A75 $20 green .60 .25
729 A75 $30 blue .60 .25
730 A75 $50 dk brown .60 .25
a. Horiz. pair, imperf. between 55.00 60.00
731 A75 $100 carmine .60 .25
Nos. 728-731 (4) 2.40 1.00

Convening of National Assembly.

For surcharges see Taiwan Nos. 10-13, Northeastern Provinces 26-29.

Entrance to Dr. Sun Yat-sen Mausoleum — A76

Dr. Sun Yat-sen — A77

1947, May 5 Engr.

732 A76 $100 dp green .35 .20
733 A76 $200 deep blue .35 .20
734 A76 $250 carmine .35 .20
735 A76 $350 lt brown .35 .20
736 A76 $400 dp claret .35 .20
Nos. 732-736 (5) 1.75 1.00

First anniversary of return of Chinese National Government to Nanking.

See Taiwan Nos. 35-39, Northeastern Provinces 36-40.

1947 *Perf. 12½, 11½x12½*

737 A77 $500 olive green .25 .20
738 A77 $1000 green & car .25 .20
739 A77 $2000 dp blue & red brn .25 .20
740 A77 $5000 org red & blk .25 .20
Nos. 737-740 (4) 1.00 .80

For surcharge see Szechwan No. 50.

Confucius A78

Confucius' Lecturing School A79

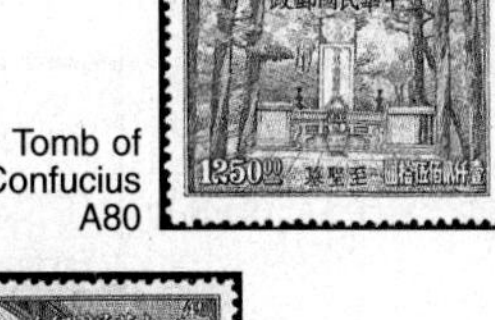

Tomb of Confucius A80

Temple of Confucius A81

1947, Aug. 27 Litho. *Perf. 14*
Without Gum

741 A78 $500 carmine rose .40 .25

Engr.

742 A79 $800 yellow brown .40 .25
743 A80 $1250 blue green .40 .25
744 A81 $1800 blue .40 .25
Nos. 741-744 (4) 1.60 1.00

Sun Yat-sen and Plum Blossoms A82

Chinese Flag and Map of Taiwan A83

1947-48 Engr. *Perf. 14*
Without Gum

745 A82 $150 dk blue .20 .25
746 A82 $250 dp lilac .25 .20
747 A82 $500 blue grn .20 .20
748 A82 $1000 red .20 .20
749 A82 $2000 vermilion .20 .20
750 A82 $3000 blue .20 .20
751 A82 $4000 gray ('48) .20 .20
752 A82 $5000 dk brown .20 .20
753 A82 $6000 rose lilac ('48) .20 .20
754 A82 $7000 lt red brn ('48) .20 .20
755 A82 $10,000 dp blue & car .85 .20
756 A82 $20,000 car & yel grn .25 .20
757 A82 $50,000 grn & dk bl .85 .20
758 A82 $100,000 dl yel & ol grn ('48) 1.40 .20
759 A82 $200,000 vio brn & dp bl ('48) 1.60 .45
760 A82 $300,000 sep & org brn ('48) 1.60 .45
761 A82 $500,000 dk Prus grn & sep ('48) 2.25 .45
Nos. 745-761 (17) 10.85 4.20

See Nos. 788-799. For similar type see Formosa A1. For surcharges see Nos. 770, 804-806, 821-822, 840-841, 858-859, 869, 871, 880A-880B, 885A-885E, 1025-1036, Taiwan 56-57, 59, 89, Fukien 1-4, 7-12, 19-23, Hunan 2-5, C1, Kiangsi 1-3, C1, E1, F1-F2, Kwangsi 8-10, 12-17, Shensi 1-2, C1, E1, Szechwan 24-49, Yunnan 61-62, 69, 205-207, People's Republic of China 3L69-3L70, 3L76, 4L63-4L64, 6L22, 6L27, 6L29, 6L32.

1947, Oct. 25
With Gum

762 A83 $500 carmine .25 .25
763 A83 $1250 deep green .25 .25

Restoration of Taiwan to China, 2nd anniv.

Mobile Post Office — A84

Street-Corner Branch Post Office — A85

1947, Nov. 5

764 A84 $500 carmine .25 .20
765 A85 $1000 lilac .25 .20
766 A85 $1250 green .25 .20
767 A84 $1800 deep blue .25 .20
Nos. 764-767 (4) 1.00 .80

Stamps and Type of 1943-47 Surcharged in Black or Green

1947-48 Unwmk. *Perf. 12½, 13, 14*

768 A37 $500 on $20 brt yel grn (#633) .20 .20
769 A73 $1250 on $70 red org (#639) .20 .20
770 A82 $1800 on $350 yel org .20 .20
771 A62 $2000 on $3 dk yel ('48) (#503) .20 .20
772 A63 $2000 on $3 red (#567) .20 .20
a. On #567a 5.00 2.25
773 A62 $3000 on $3 lt yel ('48) (#555) .20 .20
774 A63 $3000 on $3 lt red brn (G) ('48) (#568) .20 .20
Nos. 768-774 (7) 1.40 1.40

The characters at the left express the new value and vary in number.

No. 640 Surcharged

1948, Aug. *Perf. 14*

775 A73 $5000 on $100 dk car 4.50 35.00

No. 775 received its surcharge in Kwangsi for use in that province.

Map of China and Mail-carrying Vehicles A86

Rural Mail Delivery — A87

Early and Modern Mail Transportation A88

1947, Dec. 16 **Engr.** ***Perf. 12***

776 A86 $100 violet .25 .20
777 A87 $200 brt green .25 .20
778 A87 $300 red brown .25 .20
779 A88 $400 scarlet .25 .20
780 A88 $500 brt vio blue .25 .20
Nos. 776-780 (5) 1.25 1.00

Chinese Postal Administration, 50th anniv.

National Assembly Building and New Constitution A89

1947, Dec. 25 ***Perf. 14***

Without Gum

781 A89 $2000 brt red .25 .20
782 A89 $3000 blue .25 .20
783 A89 $5000 deep green .25 .20
Nos. 781-783 (3) .75 .60

1st anniv. of the adoption of China's new constitution, Dec. 25, 1946.

Chinese Stamps of 1947 and 1912 — A90

Perf. 14, Imperf.

1948, Mar. 20 **Litho.**

Without Gum

784 A90 $5000 dk car rose .50 1.00
a. Vert. pair, imperf. btwn 35.00
785 A90 $5000 dk green .50 1.00
a. Vert. pair, imperf. btwn 35.00

Stamp exhibitions at Nanking, Mar. 20 (No. 784), and at Shanghai, May 19 (No. 785).

Sun Yat-sen Memorial Hall, Taipei — A91

1948, Apr. 28 **Engr.** ***Perf. 14***

786 A91 $5000 violet .20 *1.00*
787 A91 $10000 red .20 *1.00*

Restoration of Formosa to China, 3rd anniv.

Sun Yat-sen Type of 1947-48

1948

Without Gum

788 A82 $20000 rose pink .35 .20
789 A82 $30000 chocolate .20 .20
790 A82 $40000 green .20 .20
791 A82 $50000 dp blue .20 .20
792 A82 $100000 dull grn .20 .20
793 A82 $200000 brn vio .55 .20
794 A82 $300000 yel grn .85 .20
795 A82 $500000 lil rose .85 .20
796 A82 $1000000 claret .55 .20
797 A82 $2000000 vermilion 1.10 .20
798 A82 $3000000 ol bis 2.25 .25
799 A82 $5000000 ultra 4.00 .55
Nos. 788-799 (12) 11.30 2.80

Zeros for "cents" omitted.

For surcharges see Nos. 841, 871, 880A-880B, 885A-885E, 1025-1028, 1031-1036.

Early Ship and Modern Hai Tien — A92

Passenger Ship Kiang Ya — A93

1948, Aug. 16

Without Gum

800 A92 $20000 blue .20 .20
801 A92 $30000 rose lilac .20 .20
802 A93 $40000 yel brown .20 .20
803 A93 $60000 vermilion .20 .20
Nos. 800-803 (4) .80 .80

75th anniversary of the China Merchants' Steam Navigation Company.

Type of 1947-48 Surcharged in Black

1948 **Unwmk.** ***Perf. 14***

804 A82 $4000 on $100 car .20 .65
805 A82 $5000 on $100 car .20 .20
806 A82 $8000 on $700 red brn .20 .20
Nos. 804-806 (3) .60 1.05

Stamps of 1942-46 Surcharged in Black or Red

1948 ***Perf. 12½, 13***

807 A62 $5000 on $1 (#500) .20 .20
808 A62 $5000 on $1 (#551) 15.00 15.00
809 A62 $5000 on $2 (#502) .20 .20
810 A72 $10000 on $20 (#625) .20 .20
811 A62 $20000 on 10c (#492) .20 .20
812 A62 $20000 on 50c (#498;R) .20 .20
813 A62 $30000 on 30c (#496) .20 .20
a. Perf. 10½ 16.00 16.00
Nos. 807-813 (7) 16.20 16.20

Nos. 492, 556 and 558 Surcharged in Black or Carmine

1948

814 A62 $15,000 on 10c dp grn .20 .20
815 A62 $15,000 on $4 vio brn .20 .20
816 A62 $15,000 on $6 gray vio (C) .20 .20
Nos. 814-816 (3) .60 .60

No. 498, 494 and 504 Surcharged in Black

1948 **Unwmk.** ***Perf. 11½, 13***

817 A62 $15,000 on 50c, perf. 13 .20 .20
a. Perf. 11½ 10.00 10.00
818 A62 $40,000 on 20c dk ol grn .20 .20
a. Perf. 11 10.00 7.50
819 A62 $60,000 on $4 red brn .20 .20
Nos. 817-819 (3) .60 .60

Gold Yuan Surcharges
(Nos. 820-885E)

Stamps of 1942-47 Surcharged in Black, Carmine or Red

1948 ***Perf. 14, 13, 11***

820 A62 ½c on 30c (#496) .20 .20
821 A82 ½c on $500 (Bk) (#747) .20 .20
822 A82 ½c on $500 (C) (#747) .20 .20
823 A73 1c on $20 (#636) .20 .20
824 A62 2c on $1.50 (R) (#501) .20 .20
825 A62 3c on $5 (#505) .20 .20
826 A62 4c on $1 (#499) .20 .20
827 A62 5c on 50c (#498) .20 .20
a. Perf. 11 5.00 5.00
Nos. 820-827 (8) 1.60 1.60

On No. 820-827, the position of the surcharged denomination and "Gold Yuan" characters varies, the aim being to obliterate the original denomination.

Stamps of 1940-48 Surcharged in Black, Violet, Carmine, Blue or Green

Perf. 12, 12½, 13, 14, 12½x13

1948-49

828 A63 5c on $20 (#571) .20 .20
829 A72 5c on $30 (C) (#626) .20 .20
a. Double surcharge 16.00
830 A57 10c on 2c (#368) .20 .20
831 A39 10c on 2½c (#424) .20 .20
832 A62 10c on 25c (V) (#495) .20 .20
833 A63 10c on 40c (#565) .20 .20
834 A62 10c on $1 (#500) .20 .20
834A A62 10c on $1 (#551) 160.00 160.00
835 A63 10c on $2 (#566) .20 .20
836 A62 10c on $20 (C) (#560) .20 .20
836A A63 10c on $20 (#571) 110.00 110.00
837 A67 10c on $20 (#592) .20 .20
837A A73 10c on $20 (#636) .65 *2.00*
838 A72 10c on $30 (C) (#626) .20 *.30*
839 A63 10c on $70 (#573) .20 .20
a. Double surcharge 13.00
840 A82 10c on $7000 (#754) .20 .20
841 A82 10c on $20,000 (#788) .20 .20
842 A63 20c on $6 (#569) .20 .20
843 A37 20c on $30 (#634) .35 *1.10*
844 A73 20c on $30 (C) (#637) .20 .20
845 A73 20c on $100 (#640) .20 .20
a. Inverted surcharge 19.00
b. Double surcharge 14.00
846 A39 50c on ½c (#312) 50.00 50.00
847 A39 50c on ½c (#421) .20 .20
a. Inverted surcharge 27.50
848 A62 50c on 20c (#494) .20 .20
849 A62 50c on 30c (Bl) (#496) .20 .20
850 A62 50c on 40c (V) (#497) .20 .20
a. Perf. 11 6.50 7.25
851 A63 50c on 40c (V) (#565) .20 .20
852 A62 50c on $4 (#556) .20 .20
853 A62 50c on $4 (Bl) (#556) .20 .20
854 A62 50c on $20 (C) (#560) .20 .20
855 A67 50c on $20 (V) (#592) .20 *.20*
856 A73 50c on $20 (#636) .20 .20
857 A62 50c on $70 (C) (#562) .20 .20
858 A82 50c on $6000 (#753) .20 .20
859 A82 50c on $6000 (Bl) (#753) .20 .20
860 A62 $1 on 30c (#550) .20 .20
a. Perf. 11 20.00 20.00
861 A62 $1 on 40c (#497) .20 .20
a. Perf. 11 2.75 2.75
862 A62 $1 on $1 (#499) .20 .20
863 A62 $1 on $5 (#557) .20 .20
864 A63 $2 on $2 (R) (#566) .20 .20
865 A72 $2 on $20 (#625) .20 .20
866 A73 $2 on $100 (#640) .20 .20
867 A46 $5 on 17c (#432) .20 .20
868 A63 $5 on $2 (#566) .20 .20
869 A82 $5 on $3000 (C) (#750) .20 .20
870 A47 $8 on 20c (#433) .20 .20
871 A82 $8 on $30,000 (C) (#789) .20 .20
872 A47 $10 on 40c (#438) .20 .20
873 A63 $10 on $2 (G) (#566) .20 .20
874 A63 $10 on $2 (C) (#566) .20 .20
875 A63 $20 on $2 (C) (#566) .20 .20
875A A73 $20 on $20 (#636) 1.40 1.65
876 A62 $50 on 30c (#496) .20 .20
877 A63 $50 on $2 (Bl) (#566) .20 .20
878 A73 $80 on $20 (#636) .20 .20
879 A62 $100 on $1 (#551) .20 .20
a. Perf. 11 *40.00* *40.00*
880 A63 $100 on $2 (C) (#566) .20 .20
880A A82 $50,000 on $20,000 (#788) .80 .35
880B A82 $100,000 on $30,000 (V) (#789) 2.00 .65

Wmk. 261

881 A39 10c on 2½c (#405) .40 *4.00*
882 A39 50c on ½c (#402) .20 *.85*
Nos. 828-882 (61) 336.00 340.90

Characters at left express the new value. Style of characters and numerals varies.

Nos. Q7 to Q9 Surcharged in Black or Carmine

1948 **Unwmk.** ***Perf. 12½***

883 PP2 $200 on $3000 red org .20 .20
884 PP2 $500 on $5000 dk bl (C) .20 .20
885 PP2 $1000 on $10,000 vio .20 .20
Nos. 883-885 (3) .60 .60

Nos. 788-791 Surcharged in Gold Yuan in Red (Nos. 885A, 885D-885E) or Black (Nos. 885B-885C) at Foochow

1949, Apr. 30 **Unwmk.** ***Perf. 14***

885A $20,000 on $40,000 11.00 13.00
885B $50,000 on $30,000 11.00 13.00
885C $100,000 on $20,000 11.00 13.00
885D $200,000 on $40,000 11.00 13.00
885E $200,000 on $50,000 11.00 13.00
Nos. 885A-885E (5) 55.00 65.00

Issued in Fukien Postal District.

Dr. Sun Yat-sen — A94

1949 **Unwmk.** **Engr.** ***Perf. 14***

Without Gum

886 A94 $1 orange .35 .35
887 A94 $10 green .35 .35
888 A94 $20 vio brown .35 .35
889 A94 $50 dk Prus grn .35 .35

890 A94 $100 org brn .35 .35
891 A94 $200 red org .35 .35
892 A94 $500 rose lilac .35 .35
893 A94 $800 car rose .35 *.45*
894 A94 $1000 blue .35 .35

Redrawn

Engr.

Perf. 12½

895 A94 $10 green .35 *2.25*
a. Perf. 14 2.50 *3.50*
896 A94 $20 violet brn .35 .35
a. Perf. 14 .65 *1.60*
Nos. 886-896 (11) 3.85 *5.85*

Small "T" at left of necktie on #895-896a.

Redrawn

1949 Litho. *Perf. 12½*

Without Gum

897 A94 $50 grnsh gray .20 *1.40*
898 A94 $100 dk org brn .20 *.20*
899 A94 $200 orange red .20 *1.40*
900 A94 $500 rose lilac .20 .20
901 A94 $1000 deep blue .20 *.25*
902 A94 $2000 violet .20 .20
903 A94 $5000 light blue .20 .20
904 A94 $10,000 sepia .20 .20
905 A94 $20,000 apple grn .20 .25
906 A94 $50,000 rose pink .20 .20
907 A94 $80,000 brn red .45 .65
908 A94 $100,000 bl grn .20 .20
Nos. 897-908 (12) 2.65 *5.35*

Diagonal lines have been added to the background of the redrawn design.

Zeros for "cents" omitted on No. 908.

See Nos. 973-981. For surcharges see Nos. 991-1006, 1057-1060, Fukien 13-17, Szechwan 51, Tsingtau 1-4, Yunnan 63-65, 68, 70, People's Republic of China 4L34-4L44, 4L48-4L60, 5L43-5L50, 5L54-5L59, 5L91-5L95, 6L1-6L16, 6L23-6L26, 6L30-6L31, 7L6-7L8, 7L13-7L16, 8L12-8L13, 8L48-8L51.

Gold Yuan Surcharge in Black or Other Colors on Revenue Stamps

Plane, Train and Ship — A95

Two types, 50c on $20:
I — Thick numerals in "20." Vertical stroke in lower right corner of vignette. (Dah Tung Book Co.)
II — Thin "20." No vertical stroke in corner. (Central Trust.)

Two types, $2 on $50, $10 on $30, $100 on $50 and $300 on $50:
III — "Y" in lower right corner of vignette. (Dah Yeh Printing Co.)
IV — No "Y" in corner. (Dah Tung, Central Trust or Chung Ming.)

Two types, $50 on $300 and $1000 on $100:
V — Projection on left frame column below foliate ornament. (Dah Yeh Printing Co.)
VI — No projection. (Dah Tung Book Co.)

Litho.; Nos. 923, 933, 935-936 Engr.

1949 *Perf. 12½, 13, 14*

Without Gum

913 A95 50c on $20 red brn, I .20 .20
a. 50c on $20 brown, II .20 .20
914 A95 $1 on $15 red org .20 .20
915 A95 $2 on $50 dk bl, IV (C) .20 .20
a. Type III .25 .25
916 A95 $3 on $50 dk bl (Bl) .20 .20
917 A95 $3 on $50 dk bl .20 .20
918 A95 $5 on $500 brn .20 .20
919 A95 $10 on $30 dk vio, III (Bl) .20 .20
a. Type IV .45 .45
b. Double surcharge, IV
920 A95 $15 on $20 org brn (Bl) .20 .20
921 A95 $25 on $20 org brn (G) .20 .20
922 A95 $50 on $50 dk bl (R O) .20 .20
923 A95 $50 on $300 grn, VI (C) .20 .20
a. $50 on $300 yel grn, V (C) .20 .20
924 A95 $80 on $50 dk bl (Dk Br) .20 .20
925 A95 $100 on $50 dk bl, IV 1.00 .20
a. Type III 2.25 *7.50*
926 A95 $200 on $50 dk bl .20 .20
927 A95 $200 on $500 brn (Bl) .20 .20
928 A95 $300 on $50 dk bl, III (C) .20 .20
a. Type IV .65 1.10
929 A95 $300 on $50 dk bl (Br) 2.00 .60
930 A95 $500 on $15 red org (Bl) .25 .25
931 A95 $500 on $30 dk vio .25 .25
932 A95 $1000 on $50 dk bl (C) 8.00 5.00
933 A95 $1000 on $100 ol grn, V 1.00 .30
a. Type VI 2.75 5.00
934 A95 $1500 on $50 dk bl (Bl) 2.50 1.50
935 A95 $2000 on $300 grn (Bl) .30 .30
a. Horiz. pair, imperf. between
936 A95 $5000 on $100 ol grn (C) 300.00
Nos. 913-936 (24) 318.30
Nos. 913-935 (23) 18.30 11.40

No. 936 was officially authorized, but never issued.

Key pattern of overprinted border inverted and in 2 or 3 detached sections at top and bottom in Blue, Black or Green

1949 Hankow Prints Litho.

Without Gum

Type A95

937 A95 $50 on $10 (Bk) 6.50 6.50
938 A95 $100 on $10 7.75 7.75
939 A95 $500 on $10 (Bk) 5.50 4.50
940 A95 $1000 on $10 4.50 4.50
941 A95 $5000 on $20 11.00 11.00
942 A95 $10,000 on $20 (Bk) 11.00 6.50
943 A95 $50,000 on $20 14.00 11.00
944 A95 $100,000 on $20 (Bk) 16.00 11.00
945 A95 $500,000 on $20 225.00 110.00
946 A95 $2,000,000 on $20 (G) 550.00 165.00
947 A95 $5,000,000 on $20 1,000. 325.00
Nos. 937-944 (8) 76.25 62.75

The $10 stamp is slate green, the $20 red brown.

The basic revenue stamps of Nos. 915-947 were the work of several printers. There are three main types, differing in the bottom label. Nos. 922 and 925 are in a second type: Nos. 923 and 930 in a third. Varieties of paper, color and overprint exist.

Counterfeits exist of Nos. 945-947.

For surcharges and overprints see Nos. 960-970, C63, E13, F3, J122-J126, Hupeh 1-2, People's Republic of China 5L51-5L53, 6L17-6L21.

Redrawn Coarse Impression

1949 Litho.

Without Gum

Size: 18¼x20¾mm

951 A94 $50 green .35 *21.00*
952 A94 $1000 dp blue .40 *2.00*
953 A94 $5000 carmine .40 *2.00*
954 A94 $10,000 brown 3.00 *5.00*
955 A94 $20,000 orange .90 *2.00*
956 A94 $50,000 blue 3.00 3.00
957 A94 $200,000 violet 5.00 3.00
958 A94 $500,000 vio brn 5.00 3.00
Nos. 951-958 (8) 18.05 *41.00*

Zeros for "cents" omitted on Nos. 957-958.

See surcharge note following No. 900.

Locomotive and Ship — A96

1949, May 1 Litho. *Perf. 12½*

Without Gum

959 A96 orange 1.60 1.10
a. Rouletted 8.75 4.00

Nos. 959, C62, E12 and F2 were printed without denomination and sold at the daily rate of the yuan. This was necessitated by the gold yuan inflation.

For surcharges and overprints see Nos. 1130, 1213, Taiwan 97, Fukien 18, Kansu 1, People's Republic of China 24-29, 101-104, 4L31-4L33, 4L45-4L47, 4L61-4L62, 7L9-7L12, 8L52-8L54.

Revenue Stamps Overprinted in Black

1949, May *Perf. 12½, 13, 14*

Without Gum

960 A95 $30 dark violet 70.00 50.00

Engr.

961 A95 $200 violet brown 9.00 5.50
962 A95 $500 dark green 12.00 9.00
Nos. 960-962 (3) 91.00 64.50

A similar overprint appears on #C63, E13, F3, differing in 2nd and 3rd characters of bottom row.

Silver Yuan Surcharge in Black or Other Colors

1949 Litho.

963 A95 1c on $5000 brn (G) 5.00 6.00
964 A95 4c on $100 ol grn (Bl) 2.25 2.00
965 A95 4c on $3000 org) 2.25 2.00
966 A95 10c on $50 dk bl (RV) 3.50 2.00
967 A95 10c on $1000 car 4.50 2.00
a. Inverted surcharge 60.00
968 A95 20c on $1000 red (V) 5.00 3.00
b. Inverted surcharge 27.50
968A A95 50c on $30 dk vio (C) 27.50 6.00
969 A95 50c on $50 dk bl (C) 6.00 2.00
970 A95 $1 on $50 dk bl 15.00 20.00
Nos. 963-970 (9) 71.00 45.00

Nos. 963-965 and 967 are engraved.

Sun Type of 1949 Redrawn Coarse Impression

1949 *Perf. 12½, 13 or Compound*

973 A94 1c apple green 16.00 *6.00*
974 A94 2c orange 3.50 *4.00*
975 A94 4c blue green .20 *2.00*
976 A94 10c deep lilac .20 *2.00*
977 A94 16c orange red .45 *3.00*
978 A94 20c blue .25 *2.00*
979 A94 50c dk brown 1.40 *6.00*
980 A94 100c deep blue 300.00 250.00
981 A94 500c scarlet 400.00 300.00
Nos. 973-981 (9) 722.00 575.00

For surcharges see Nos. 1057-1060.

Flying Geese Over Globe — A97

Pigeons, Globe and Wreath — A98

1949, May Litho. *Perf. 12½*

Without Gum

984 A97 $1 brown org 4.25 8.00
985 A97 $2 blue 35.00 12.00
986 A97 $5 car rose 35.00 15.00
987 A97 $10 blue grn 35.00 30.00
Nos. 984-987 (4) 109.25 65.00

Five other denominations — 10c, 16c, 50c, $20 and $50 — were also printed at Shanghai, but were not issued.

For surcharges see Nos. 1007-1011, 1042-1045, 1061-1063, People's Republic of China 49-56, 5LQ17-5LQ26, 7L17-7L18, 8L14-8L16.

Engraved and Typographed

1949, Aug. 1 Without Gum *Imperf.*

988 A98 $1 org red & blk 6.75 7.50

75th anniv. of the UPU.
Exists with black denomination omitted.

Summer Palace, Peiping — A99

Bronze Bull and Kunming Lake — A100

Engraved and Typographed

1949, Aug. *Rouletted*

Without Gum

989 A99 15c org brn & grn 3.00 *3.00*
990 A100 40c dl grn & car 3.00 *3.00*
a. 2nd and 3rd characters at top transposed 160.00 200.00

Silver Yuan Surcharge in Black on 1949 Sun Yat-sen Issues

1949 *Perf. 12½, 14*

991 A94 1c on $100 org brn (890) 9.25 10.00
992 A94 1c on $100 dk org brn (898) 9.25 10.00
993 A94 2½c on $500 rose lil (892) 11.00 11.00
a. Inverted surcharge 35.00
994 A94 2½c on $500 rose lil (900) 12.50 12.00
995 A94 15c on $10 grn (887) 17.50 25.00
a. Inverted surcharge 40.00
996 A94 15c on $20 vio brn (896) 25.00 32.50
Nos. 991-996 (6) 84.50 100.50

Silver Yuan Surcharge in Black or Carmine

997 A94 2½c on $50 grn (951) 1.60 2.00
998 A94 2½c on $50,000 bl (956) 4.50 2.00
999 A94 5c on $1000 dp bl (952) (C) 3.50 2.00
1000 A94 5c on $20,000 org (955) 2.25 1.75
1001 A94 5c on $200,000 vio (957) (C) 3.50 1.75
1002 A94 5c on $500,000 vio brn (958) 2.25 1.75
1003 A94 10c on $5000 car (953) 6.50 4.25
1004 A94 10c on $10,000 brn (954) 6.50 4.25
1005 A94 15c on $200 red org (891) 8.25 6.50
1006 A94 25c on $100 dk org brn (896) 16.00 16.00
Nos. 997-1006 (10) 54.85 42.25

REPUBLIC OF CHINA

ri-ˈpə-blik of ˈchī-nə

(Taiwan)

LOCATION — Taiwan (since 1949) (Formosa)
GOVT. — Republic
AREA — 13,970 sq. mi.
POP. — 22,113,250 (1999 est.)
CAPITAL — Taipei

Stamps issued and used in Taiwan after Communist forces occupied the Chinese mainland include Taiwan Nos. 91-96, 101-103, J10-J17.

Catalogue values for unused stamps in this country are for Never Hinged items, beginning with Scott 1124 in the regular postage section, Scott B17 in the semi-postal section, Scott C69 in the airpost section, and Scott J142 in the postage due section.

Watermarks

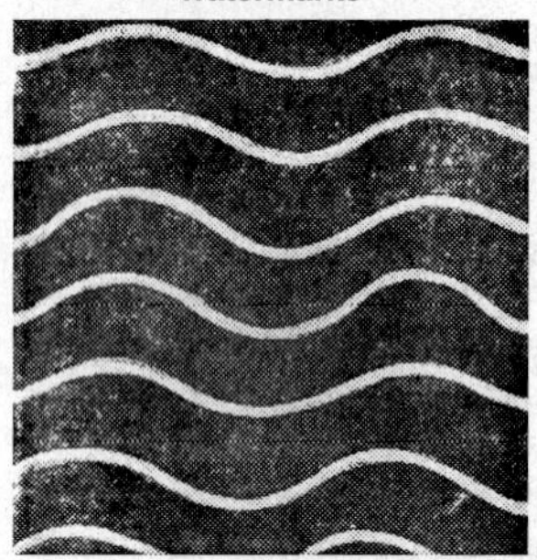

Wmk. 281 — Wavy Lines

Wmk. 323 — Seal Character (found with "Yu" in various arrangements)

Wmk. 368 — JEZ Multiple

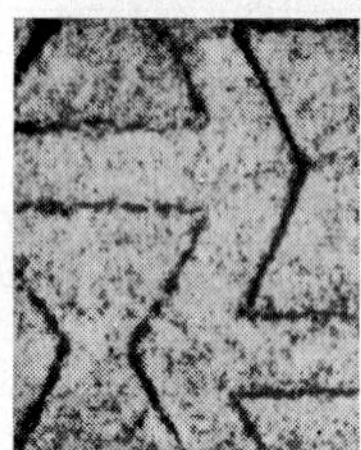

Wmk. 370 — Geometrical Design

Type of 1949 with Value Omitted Surcharged in Various Colors

1950, Jan. 1 Unwmk. *Perf. 12½*

1007 A97 $1 green (Bk) 150.00 5.00
1008 A97 $2 green (C) 150.00 10.00
1009 A97 $5 green (V) 1,400. 55.00
1010 A97 $10 green (Br) 1,000. 95.00
1011 A97 $20 green (Dk Bl) 2,750. 400.00
Nos. 1007-1011 (5) 5,450. 565.00

Two printings of the $1 and $2 show minor differences.

Cheng Ch'eng-kung (Koxinga) — A101

1950, June 26 Typo. *Rouletted*
Without Gum

1012 A101 3c dk gray grn 3.50 .85
1013 A101 10c orange brn 2.50 .25
1014 A101 15c orange yel 12.00 2.00
1015 A101 20c emerald 2.50 .20
1016 A101 30c claret 45.00 11.00
1017 A101 40c red orange 2.50 .25
1018 A101 50c chocolate 8.00 1.00
1019 A101 80c carmine 5.50 2.00
1020 A101 $1 ultra 2.50 1.00
1021 A101 $1.50 green 32.50 2.00
1022 A101 $1.60 blue 15.00 1.00
1023 A101 $2 red violet 20.00 .30
1024 A101 $5 aqua 125.00 20.00
Nos. 1012-1024 (13) 276.50 41.85

Part perf pairs exist of the 10c, 20c, 80c.
The 10c and 20c were reprinted from new plates. There are slight differences.
For surcharges see Nos. 1070-1072, 1105-1108, 1118-1119.

Nos. 751, 753, 788-791, 793, 795-799 Surcharged in Carmine or Black

1950 Engr. *Perf. 14*

1025 A82 3c on $30,000 3.75 2.25
1026 A82 3c on $40,000 (C) 3.25 2.25
1027 A82 3c on $50,000 (C) 3.25 3.00
1028 A82 5c on $200,000 3.75 2.50
1029 A82 10c on $4000 32.50 4.00
1030 A82 10c on $6000 24.00 4.00
1031 A82 10c on $20,000 24.00 4.00
1032 A82 10c on $2,000,000 24.00 4.00
1033 A82 20c on $500,000 35.00 4.00
1034 A82 20c on $1,000,000 42.50 7.50
1035 A82 30c on $3,000,000 52.50 10.00
1036 A82 50c on $5,000,000 (C) 85.00 10.00
Nos. 1025-1036 (12) 333.50 57.50

Issued: #1025-1027, 3/6; #1028, 3/25; #1031, 6/10:#1029-1030, 1032, 1035-1036 , 8/1; #1033-1034, 8/25.
Forgeries exist.

Inverted Surcharge

1029a A82 10c on $4000 125.00
1030a A82 10c on $6000 300.00
1031a A82 10c on $20,000 160.00
1032a A82 10c on $2,000,000 175.00
1033a A82 20c on $500,000 225.00
1034a A82 20c on $1,000,000 225.00

Allegory of Election A102

Perf. 12x12½, Imperf.
1951, Mar. 20 Engr. Unwmk.
Without Gum

1037 A102 40c carmine 14.00 .75
a. Horiz. pair, imperf. btwn. 85.00
1038 A102 $1 dp blue 26.00 2.10
1039 A102 $1.60 purple 30.00 3.25
1040 A102 $2 brown 35.00 4.00
Nos. 1037-1040 (4) 105.00 10.10

Souvenir Sheet
Imperf

1041 A102 $2 dp blue grn *325.00 325.00*

Adoption of local self-government in Taiwan.

Design A97 Surcharged A103

Farmer and Scroll Announcing Tax Reduction A104

Surcharge in Various Colors

1951, July 19 *Perf. 12½*
Without Gum

1042 A103 $5 green (R Br) 52.50 10.00
1043 A103 $10 green (Bk) 110.00 10.00
1044 A103 $20 green (R) 325.00 19.00
1045 A103 $50 green (P) 675.00 82.50
Nos. 1042-1045 (4) 1,162. 121.50

1952, Jan. 1 *Perf. 14*
Without Gum

1046 A104 20c red orange 7.00 1.50
1047 A104 40c dk green 10.00 1.75
1048 A104 $1 brown 13.50 2.75
1049 A104 $1.40 dp blue 19.00 2.50
1050 A104 $2 dk gray 67.50 21.00
1051 A104 $5 brown car 72.50 16.00
Nos. 1046-1051 (6) 189.50 45.50

Land tax reduction of 37.5% in Taiwan.
Value, imperf. set, $425.

Pres. Chiang Kai-shek, Flag and Followers A105

1952, Mar. 1 Unwmk. *Perf. 14*
Without Gum
Flag in Violet Blue and Carmine

1052 A105 40c rose car 7.75 .50
a. Vert. pair, imperf. btwn. 75.00
1053 A105 $1 dp green 15.00 1.75
1054 A105 $1.60 brown org 30.00 1.10
a. Horiz. pair, imperf. btwn. 160.00
1055 A105 $2 brt blue 35.00 14.50
1056 A105 $5 violet brn 50.00 5.00
Nos. 1052-1056 (5) 137.75 22.85

2nd anniv. of Chiang Kai-shek's return to the presidency.
Value, imperf. set, $300.
See Nos. 1064-1069.

Nos. 975-976, 978-979 Surcharged in Black

1952, Aug. 1 *Perf. 12½*

1057 A94 3c on 4c bl grn 4.50 3.00
1058 A94 3c on 10c dp lil 4.50 3.00
a. Inverted surcharge
1059 A94 3c on 20c blue 6.25 4.25
1060 A94 3c on 50c dk brn 7.25 5.00
Nos. 1057-1060 (4) 22.50 15.25

Forgeries exist.

Geese Type of 1949 with Value Omitted Surcharged

1952, Dec. 8

1061 A97 $10 green (P) 75.00 10.00
1062 A97 $20 green (R) 200.00 24.00
1063 A97 $50 green (Bk) 1,500. 675.00
Nos. 1061-1063 (3) 1,775. 709.00

Chiang Type of 1952 Redrawn

Perf. 12½
1953, Mar. 1 Engr. Unwmk.
Without Gum
Flag in Dark Blue & Carmine

1064 A105 10c red orange 4.00 1.50
1065 A105 20c green 8.50 1.50
1066 A105 40c rose pink 12.00 2.00
1067 A105 $1.40 blue 35.00 3.25
1068 A105 $2 brown 77.50 5.75
1069 A105 $5 rose violet 125.00 15.00
Nos. 1064-1069 (6) 262.00 29.00

Chiang Kai-shek's return to presidency, 3rd anniv.
Many differences in redrawn design. Value, imperf. set, $350.

Nos. 1020, 1014, 1016 and 1022 Surcharged in Various Colors

1953 *Rouletted*

1070 A101 3c on $1 ultra (C) 1.60 .35
1070A A101 10c on 15c org yel (G) ('54) 5.75 .75
1071 A101 10c on 30c cl (Bl) 3.00 1.00
1072 A101 20c on $1.60 bl (Bk) 3.50 1.10
Nos. 1070-1072 (4) 13.85 3.20

Chinese characters and ornamental device at bottom differ on each value.
Issued: #1071, 2/1; #1070, 5/25; #1072, 6/13; #1070A, 7/16.

Nurse & Patients — A106

Chiang Kai-shek — A107

1953, July 1 Litho. *Perf. 12½*
Without Gum
Cross in Red, Burelage Color in Italics

1073 A106 40c brown, *buff* 9.00 1.40
1074 A106 $1.60 blue, *bl* 20.00 1.25
1075 A106 $2 green, *yel* 40.00 1.90
1076 A106 $5 red org, *org* 75.00 6.75
Nos. 1073-1076 (4) 144.00 11.30

Chinese Anti-Tuberculosis Association.

1953, Oct. 31 Engr.
Without Gum

1077 A107 10c dk brown 4.75 .25
1078 A107 20c lilac 4.75 .25
1079 A107 40c dp green 4.75 .25
1080 A107 50c dp pink 6.50 .45
1081 A107 80c brown bis 15.00 1.10
1082 A107 $1 dp olive grn 8.25 .25
1083 A107 $1.40 dp blue 8.25 .25
1084 A107 $1.60 dp carmine 8.25 .25
1085 A107 $1.70 apple grn 8.25 1.10
1086 A107 $2 brown 9.75 .25
1087 A107 $3 dark blue 97.50 1.10
1088 A107 $4 aqua 9.75 .70
1089 A107 $5 red orange 15.00 .70
1090 A107 $10 dk green 65.00 3.25
1091 A107 $20 dk brn lake 82.50 9.00
a. Souvenir folder *350.00*
Nos. 1077-1091 (15) 348.25 19.15

67th birthday of Pres. Chiang Kai-shek.
#1091a contains #1077-1091 imperf, arranged in 3 sheets of 5 stamps each.

Silo Highway Bridge — A108

Forest of Evergreens — A109

$1.60 and $5, Silo bridge, side view.

1954, Jan. 28 Unwmk. *Perf. 12½*
Without Gum
Various Frames

1092 A108 40c vermilion 15.00 .70
1093 A108 $1.60 blue violet 67.50 1.40
1094 A108 $3.60 sepia 37.50 1.40
1095 A108 $5 magenta 110.00 8.00
a. Souvenir folder *900.00*
Nos. 1092-1095 (4) 230.00 11.50

Opening of Silo bridge, 1st anniversary.
No. 1095a contains one sheet of 4 containing Nos. 1092-1095 imperforate.

1954, Mar. 12 *Perf. 12x12½*
Without Gum

1096 A109 40c shown 9.25 .80
1097 A109 $10 Nursery 75.00 2.75

Issued to publicize forest conservation.

Runner — A110

Globe, Bridge and Ship — A111

1954, Mar. 29
Without Gum

1098 A110 40c dp ultra 20.00 1.25
1099 A110 $5 carmine 60.00 7.75

11th Youth Day, Mar. 29, 1954.

1954, Oct. 21 *Perf. 12*
Without Gum

1100 A111 40c red orange 12.00 .75
1101 A111 $5 deep blue 15.00 3.00

2nd Overseas Chinese Day, Oct. 21, 1954.

Ex-Prisoner with Broken Chains — A112

Designs: $1, Ex-prisoner with torch and flag, UN emblem. $1.60, Torch and date.

1955, Jan. 23

1102 A112 40c blue green 2.00 .65
a. Vert. pair, imperf. btwn. 140.00
1103 A112 $1 sepia 14.50 5.00
1104 A112 $1.60 lake 14.50 3.25
Nos. 1102-1104 (3) 31.00 8.90

Honoring Chinese who fought on the side of the North Korean army, who, when released January 23, 1954, chose to return to the Republic of China.

Nos. 1019-1021, 1017 Surcharged in Brown, Blue or Green:

a

b

c

1955 *Rouletted*

1105 A101(a) 3c on $1 (Br) 2.00 .50
1106 A101(b) 10c on 80c (Bl) 2.75 .50
1107 A101(b) 10c on $1.50 (Bl) 2.75 .50
1108 A101(c) 20c on 40c (G) 3.25 .85
Nos. 1105-1108 (4) 10.75 2.35

Issued: #1105, 1108, 2/18; #1106-1107, 8/1.

Hand Planting Evergreen Tree — A113

Chiang Kai-shek, Flags, Building A114

Design: $50, Seedling and map of Taiwan.

1955, Apr. 1 *Perf. 12*
Without Gum

1109 A113 $20 dp carmine 27.50 1.00
1110 A113 $50 blue 72.50 5.50

Issued to publicize forest conservation.

1955, May 20 Engr. *Perf. 12*
Without Gum

1111 A114 20c olive 3.25 .30
1112 A114 40c blue green 3.00 .30
1113 A114 $2 car rose 8.00 .90
1114 A114 $7 dp ultra 12.50 1.40
a. Souv. sheet of 4, #1111-1114, imperf. *150.00 150.00*
Nos. 1111-1114 (4) 26.75 2.90

First anniversary of Pres. Chiang Kai-shek's re-election.
No. 1114a is perf. 12 at right edge of sheet. Value is for sheet with right selvage.

Armed Forces Emblem — A115

1955, Sept. 3
Without Gum

1115 A115 40c dk blue 3.50 .50
1116 A115 $2 org ver 12.50 1.25
1117 A115 $7 bl grn 20.00 1.75
a. Sheet of 3, #1115-1117, imperf. *325.00 325.00*
Nos. 1115-1117 (3) 36.00 3.50

Armed Forces Day, Sept. 3.
No. 1117a is perf. 12 at right edge of sheet. Value is for sheet with right selvage.

Nos. 1017, 1018 and C64 Surcharged in Magenta

1955, Sept. 16 Typo. *Rouletted*

1118 A101 20c on 40c red org 4.00 .40
1119 A101 20c on 50c choc 4.00 .40
1120 AP6 20c on 60c dp blue 5.00 .50
Nos. 1118-1120 (3) 13.00 1.30

Flags of UN and China A116

1955, Oct. 24 Engr. *Perf. 11½*
Without Gum

1121 A116 40c dk blue 2.25 .40
1122 A116 $2 dk car rose 4.50 .80
1123 A116 $7 slate green 7.75 1.60
Nos. 1121-1123 (3) 14.50 2.80

10th anniv. of the UN, Oct. 24, 1955.

Catalogue values for unused stamps in this section, from this point to the end of the section, are for Never Hinged items.

Pres. Chiang Kai-shek A117

Birthplace of Sun Yat-sen A118

1955, Oct. 31 Photo. *Perf. 13½*

1124 A117 40c dk bl, red & brn 4.25 .50
1125 A117 $2 grn, red & dk bl 10.50 1.10
1126 A117 $7 brn, red & grn 14.00 2.25
a. Souv. sheet of 3, #1124-1126, imperf. *125.00 125.00*
Nos. 1124-1126 (3) 28.75 3.85

69th birthday of Pres. Chiang Kai-shek.
No. 1126a is perf. 12 at right edge of sheet. Value is for sheet with right selvage.

1955, Nov. 12 Engr. *Perf. 12*
Without Gum

1127 A118 40c blue 1.75 .35
1128 A118 $2 red brown 6.00 .90
1129 A118 $7 rose lake 10.00 1.75
Nos. 1127-1129 (3) 17.75 3.00

90th anniversary, birth of Sun Yat-sen.

No. 959a Surcharged in Bright Green

1956, Feb. 10 Litho. *Rouletted*

1130 A96 20c on orange .45 .20

See No. 1213.

China Map and Transportation Methods — A119

Wmk. 281
1956, Mar. 20 Engr. *Perf. 12*
Without Gum

1131 A119 40c dk carmine 1.75 .25
1132 A119 $1 intense blk 3.50 .50
1133 A119 $1.60 chocolate 4.50 .35
1134 A119 $2 dk green 5.50 .70
Nos. 1131-1134 (4) 15.25 1.80

60th anniv. of the founding of the modern Chinese postal system.

Souvenir Sheets
Imperf

1135 A119 $2 magenta *40.00 20.00*
1136 A119 $2 red *40.00 20.00*

Exhib. for the 60th anniv. of the modern Chinese postal system, Mar. 20, 1956.

Children at Play — A120

Early and Modern Locomotives A121

1956, Apr. 4 Unwmk. *Perf. 12*
Without Gum

1137 A120 40c emerald 1.40 .20
1138 A120 $1.60 dk blue 3.00 .40
1139 A120 $2 dk carmine 3.50 .75
Nos. 1137-1139 (3) 7.90 1.35

Children's Day, Apr. 4, 1956.

1956, June 9 Wmk. 281 Vert.
Without Gum

1140 A121 40c rose car 2.50 .20
1141 A121 $2 blue 6.00 .55
1142 A121 $8 green 7.50 1.25
Nos. 1140-1142 (3) 16.00 2.00

75th anniversary of Chinese Railroads.

Pres. Chiang Kai-shek
A122 A123

A124

Various Portraits of Chiang
Perf. 14½x13½, 14½ (A123), 13½x14½

1956, Oct. 31 Photo. Unwmk.

1143 A122 20c red orange 4.00 .20
1144 A122 40c carmine rose 6.25 .20
1145 A123 $1 brt ultra 8.25 .25
1146 A123 $1.60 red lilac 10.50 .20
1147 A124 $2 red brown 12.50 .30
1148 A124 $8 brt grnsh blue 21.00 .60
Nos. 1143-1148 (6) 62.50 1.75

70th birthday of Pres. Chiang Kai-shek.

Types of Special Delivery, Air Post and Registration Stamps of 1949 Surcharged in Black or Maroon

a

b

c

1956 Unwmk. Litho. *Rouletted*
Without Gum

1150 SD2(a) 3c red violet .90 .20
a. Perf. 12½ 2.75 .30
1151 AP5(b) 3c blue green (M) .90 .20
1152 R2(c) 10c bright red .90 .20
Nos. 1150-1152 (3) 2.70 .60

Issued: #1150, 4/25; #1151, 11/11; #1152, 12/25.

Telecommunications Emblem and Radio Tower — A125

Wmk. 281
1956, Dec. 28 Engr. *Perf. 12*
Without Gum

1153 A125 40c deep ultra 1.00 .20
1154 A125 $1.40 carmine 1.40 .20
1155 A125 $1.60 dark green 2.50 .20
1156 A125 $2 chocolate 3.25 .40
Nos. 1153-1156 (4) 8.15 1.00

Chinese telegraph service, 75th anniv.

Map of China A126

Mother Instructing Mencius A127

Pin Perf., Perf. 12x12½
1957 Litho. Wmk. 281
Without Gum

1157 A126 3c brt blue .65 .20
1158 A126 10c violet 1.10 .20
1159 A126 20c red orange .65 .20
1160 A126 40c rose red 1.25 .20

Unwmk.

1161 A126 $1 orange brown 2.00 .20
1162 A126 $1.60 green 3.00 .25
Nos. 1157-1162 (6) 8.65 1.25

Map inscription reads: "Recovery of Mainland."
See Nos. 1177-1182.

Unwmk.
1957, May 12 Engr. *Perf. 12*

Design: $3, Mother tattooing Yueh Fei.

Without Gum

1163 A127 40c green .95 .20
1164 A127 $3 redsh brown 1.75 .40

Issued to honor Mother's Day, 1957.

Badge of Chinese Boy Scouts — A128

1957, Aug. 11
Without Gum

1165 A128 40c lilac .60 .20
1166 A128 $1 green 1.25 .35
1167 A128 $1.60 dk blue 1.75 .25
Nos. 1165-1167 (3) 3.60 .80

Cent. of the birth of Lord Baden-Powell and to publicize the World Scout Jubilee Jamboree, England, Aug. 1-12.

Globe, Radio Tower and Microphone A129

1957, Sept. 16
Without Gum

1168 A129 40c vermilion .40 .20
1169 A129 50c brt rose lilac .75 .20
1170 A129 $3.50 dark blue 1.00 .50
Nos. 1168-1170 (3) 2.15 .90

30th anniv. of Chinese broadcasting.

Map of Taiwan — A130

1957, Oct. 26
Without Gum

1171 A130 40c blue green 2.75 .35
1172 A130 $1.40 lt ultra 4.50 1.00
1173 A130 $2 gray 6.25 1.50
Nos. 1171-1173 (3) 13.50 2.85

Start of construction on the Cross Island Highway, Taiwan.

Freighter "Hai Min" and River Boat "Kiang Foo" — A131

1957, Dec. 16 Engr. *Perf. 12*
Without Gum

1174 A131 40c deep ultra .40 .25
1175 A131 80c rose lake 1.00 .95
1176 A131 $2.80 vermilion 1.40 1.40
Nos. 1174-1176 (3) 2.80 2.60

85th anniv. of the establishment of the China Merchants Steam Navigation Co.

Type of 1957
Pin Perf., Perf. 12x12½
1957, Dec. 25 Typo. Unwmk.
Without Gum
Dark Blue Frames

1177 A126 3c brt blue .20 .20
1178 A126 10c violet .45 .20
1179 A126 20c brick red .65 .20
1180 A126 40c rose red .80 .20
1181 A126 $1 dp org brn 2.75 .25
1182 A126 $1.60 dp green 3.00 .30
Nos. 1177-1182 (6) 7.85 1.35

Stamps with bars obliterating the face value are specimens.

Butterfly A132

Mme. Chiang Kai-shek Orchid A133

Perf. 13½
1958, Mar. 20 Unwmk. Photo.
Various Insects in Natural Colors

1183 A132 10c pale grn, grn & blk 1.00 .25
1184 A132 40c lem, pink, grn & blk 1.00 .25
1185 A132 $1 yel grn & mar 2.00 .30
1186 A132 $1.40 yel, org & blk 2.75 .45
1187 A132 $1.60 pale brn & dk pur 4.00 .50
1188 A132 $2 brt yel, org & blk 4.25 .75
Nos. 1183-1188 (6) 15.00 2.50

1958, Mar. 20

Orchids: 20c, Formosan Wilson, horiz. $1.40, Klotzsch. $3, Fitzgerald, horiz.

Orchids in Natural Colors

1189 A133 20c chocolate 2.00 .20
1190 A133 40c purple 2.25 .20
1191 A133 $1.40 dk vio brn 3.00 .30
1192 A133 $3 dark blue 3.75 .65
Nos. 1189-1192 (4) 11.00 1.35

World Health Organization Emblem — A134

1958, May 28 Engr. *Perf. 12*
Without Gum

1193 A134 40c dark blue .50 .20
1194 A134 $1.60 brick red .65 .20
1195 A134 $2 deep red lilac .85 .40
Nos. 1193-1195 (3) 2.00 .80

10th anniv. of the WHO.

President's Mansion, Taipei — A135

Wmk. 323
1958, Sept. 20 Engr. *Perf. 12*
Without Gum

1196 A135 $10 blue green 4.00 .20
a. Granite paper 6.00 .20
1197 A135 $20 car rose 14.00 .40
a. Granite paper 14.00 .30
1198 A135 $50 red brown 37.50 1.40
1199 A135 $100 dk blue 77.50 3.50
Nos. 1196-1199 (4) 133.00 5.50

Issued: #1196a, 1197a, 5/24/63.
See #1349-1351. For surcharge see #J131.

Taiwan Farm Scene A136

1958, Oct. 1 Unwmk.
Without Gum

1200 A136 20c emerald 1.00 .20
1201 A136 40c black 1.40 .20
1202 A136 $1.40 brt magenta 1.75 .25
1203 A136 $3 ultra 3.25 .50
Nos. 1200-1203 (4) 7.40 1.15

10th anniversary of the Joint Commission on Rural Reconstruction.

Pres. Chiang Kai-shek A137

1958, Oct. 31 Photo. *Perf. 13½*

1204 A137 40c multicolored .90 .30

Pres. Chiang Kai-shek on his 72nd birthday.

UNESCO Building, Paris A138

1958, Nov. 3 Engr. *Perf. 12*
Without Gum

1205 A138 20c dark blue .30 .20
1206 A138 40c green .40 .20
1207 A138 $1.40 orange ver .60 .35
1208 A138 $3 red lilac 1.00 .50
Nos. 1205-1208 (4) 2.30 1.25

UNESCO Headquarters in Paris opening, Nov. 3.

Flame from Liberty Torch Encircling Globe — A139

1958, Dec. 10 Unwmk.
Without Gum

1209 A139 40c green .20 .20
1210 A139 60c gray brown .30 .20
1211 A139 $1 carmine .50 .20
1212 A139 $3 ultra .75 .40
Nos. 1209-1212 (4) 1.75 1.00

10th anniversary of the signing of the Universal Declaration of Human Rights.

No. 959a Surcharged in Bright Green

Rouletted
1958, Dec. 11 Litho. Unwmk.
Without Gum

1213 A96 20c on orange .55 .20

Ballot Box, Scales and Constitution — A140

1958, Dec. 25 Engr. *Perf. 12*
Without Gum

1214 A140 40c green .90 .20
1215 A140 50c dull purple 1.25 .20
1216 A140 $1.40 car rose 1.50 .25
1217 A140 $3.50 dk blue 2.50 .75
Nos. 1214-1217 (4) 6.15 1.40

Adoption of the constitution, 10th anniv.

Chu Kwang Tower, Quemoy — A141

1959-60 Wmk. 323 Litho. *Perf. 12*

Without Gum

1218 A141 3c orange .35 .20
1218A A141 5c lt yel grn ('60) .40 .20
1219 A141 10c lilac .50 .20
1220 A141 20c ultra .65 .20
1221 A141 40c brown .80 .20
1222 A141 50c bluish grn 1.00 .20
1223 A141 $1 rose red 1.10 .20
1224 A141 $1.40 yel grn 1.50 .20
1225 A141 $2 gray grn 2.00 .20
1226 A141 $2.80 rose pink 2.75 .25
1227 A141 $3 slate blue 3.00 .25
Nos. 1218-1227 (11) 14.05 2.30

See Nos. 1270-1283.

ILO Emblem and Headquarters, Geneva — A142

1959, June 15 Engr. *Perf. 12*

Without Gum

1228 A142 40c blue .30 .20
1229 A142 $1.60 dk brown .40 .20
1230 A142 $3 brt blue grn .50 .20
1231 A142 $5 orange ver 1.00 .50
Nos. 1228-1231 (4) 2.20 1.10

40th anniversary of the ILO.

Bugler and Tents A143

1959, July 8 Unwmk.

Without Gum

1232 A143 40c carmine .85 .20
1233 A143 50c dark blue .90 .25
1234 A143 $5 green 1.75 .55
Nos. 1232-1234 (3) 3.50 1.00

10th World Boy Scout Jamboree, Makiling National Park, Philippines, July 17-26.

Inscribed Stone, Mt. Tai-wu, Quemoy — A144

Map of Taiwan Straits A145

1959, Sept. 3 Engr. *Perf. 12*

Without Gum

1235 A144 40c brown .60 .20
1236 A145 $1.40 ultra .75 .20
1237 A145 $2 green 1.40 .20
1238 A144 $3 dark blue 1.50 .30
Nos. 1235-1238 (4) 4.25 .90

Defense of Quemoy and Matsu islands. For overprints see Nos. 1258-1259.

Pigeons Circling Globe A146

1959, Oct. 4

Without Gum

1239 A146 40c blue .35 .20
1240 A146 $1 rose carmine .60 .20
1241 A146 $2 gray brown .85 .20
1242 A146 $3.50 red orange 1.00 .50
Nos. 1239-1242 (4) 2.80 1.10

Intl. Letter Writing Week, Oct. 4-10.

National Taiwan Science Hall, Taipei — A147

1959, Nov. 12 Photo. *Perf. 13x13½*

1243 A147 40c shown 1.10 .20
1244 A147 $3 Front view 2.40 .70

Emblem A148

1959, Dec. 7 Engr. *Perf. 12*

Without Gum

1245 A148 40c blue green .40 .20
1246 A148 $1.60 red lilac .50 .20
1247 A148 $3 orange .95 .50
Nos. 1245-1247 (3) 1.85 .90

Intl. Confederation of Free Trade Unions, 10th anniv.

Sun Yat-sen, Lincoln and Flags A149

Perf. 13½, 12

1959, Dec. 25 Photo. Unwmk.

1248 A149 40c multicolored .25 .20
1249 A149 $3 multicolored 1.00 .50

Issued to honor Sun Yat-sen and Abraham Lincoln as "Leaders of Democracy."

Mailman on Motorcycle Delivering Night Mail — A150

Postal Launch A151

1960, Mar. 20 Engr. *Perf. 11½*

Without Gum

1250 A150 $1.40 dk violet brn 1.10 .25
1251 A151 $1.60 ultra 1.10 .25

Issued to publicize the Prompt Delivery Service.

WRY Uprooted Oak Emblem — A152

1960, Apr. 7 Photo. *Perf. 13*

1252 A152 40c blk, red brn & emer .50 .20
1253 A152 $3 blk, red org & grn .90 .35

World Refugee Year, 7/1/59-6/30/60.

Cross Island Highway, Taiwan — A153

Design: $1, $2, Road through tunnel, vert.

Perf. 11½

1960, May 9 Engr. Unwmk.

Without Gum

1254 A153 40c green .90 .20
1255 A153 $1 dk blue 1.60 .25
1256 A153 $2 brown vio 1.75 .30
1257 A153 $3 brown 2.25 .35
a. Souv. sheet of 2, #1255, 1257, wmk. 323, imperf. *175.00* *65.00*
Nos. 1254-1257 (4) 6.50 1.10

Opening of the Cross Island Highway, Taiwan.

Red Overprint on Nos. 1237-1238 Chinese and English: "Welcome U.S. President Dwight D. Eisenhower 1960"

1960, June 18 Unwmk. *Perf. 12*

1258 A145 $2 green .90 .30
a. Inverted overprint 2,250. 2,250.
1259 A144 $3 dk blue 1.40 .45

Eisenhower's visit to China, June 18, 1960.

Phonopost — A154

1960, June 27

Without Gum

1260 A154 $2 red orange 1.40 .30

Phonopost Service of the Chinese armed forces.

Two Horses and Groom, by Han Kan — A155

Paintings from Palace Museum, Taichung: $1, Two Riders, by Wei Yen. $1.60, Flowers and Birds by Hsiao Yung, vert. $2, Pair of Mandarin Ducks by Monk Hui Ch'ung.

1960, Aug. 4 Photo. *Perf. 13*

1261 A155 $1 ol gray, blk & brn 3.25 .55
1262 A155 $1.40 bis brn, blk & fawn 5.75 .75
1263 A155 $1.60 multicolored 7.50 1.10
1264 A155 $2 beige, blk & gray grn 13.50 2.00
Nos. 1261-1264 (4) 30.00 4.40

Chinese paintings, 7th-11th centuries.

For other painting types with large straight numerals in the upper corners and large Chinese characters on the side see A186, A241 and A285.

Youth Corps Flag and Summer Activities A156

Reforestation A157

Design: $3, similar to 50c, horiz.

1960, Aug. 20 Engr. *Perf. 12*

Without Gum

1265 A156 50c slate green .50 .20
1266 A156 $3 copper brown 1.10 .45

Summer activities of China Youth Corps.

1960, Aug. 29 Photo. *Perf. 13½x13*

$2, Protection of forest. $3, Timber industry.

1267 A157 $1 multicolored 1.25 .20
1268 A157 $2 multicolored 1.75 .25
1269 A157 $3 multicolored 2.50 .60
a. Souvenir sheet of 3 20.00 14.50
Nos. 1267-1269 (3) 5.50 1.05

Fifth World Forestry Congress, Seattle, Washington, Aug. 29-Sept. 10.

No. 1269a contains Nos. 1267-1269 assembled as a triptych, 65½x40mm and imperf., but with simulated black perforations.

Chu Kwang Tower, Quemoy — A158

Sports — A159

1960-61 Wmk. 323 Litho. *Perf. 12*

Without Gum

1270 A158 3c lt red brown .50 .20
1271 A158 40c pale violet .50 .20
1272 A158 50c orange ('61) .80 .20
1273 A158 60c rose lilac 1.00 .20
1274 A158 80c pale green 1.10 .20
1275 A158 $1 gray grn ('61) 1.25 .20
1276 A158 $1.20 gray olive 1.25 .20
1277 A158 $1.50 ultra 1.50 .25
1278 A158 $2 car rose ('61) 1.75 .20
1279 A158 $2.50 pale blue 1.90 .25
1280 A158 $3 bluish green 2.00 .25
1281 A158 $3.20 lt red brown 1.75 .20
1282 A158 $3.60 vio blue ('61) 3.75 .30
1283 A158 $4.50 vermilion 7.00 .35
Nos. 1270-1283 (14) 26.05 3.20

For surcharges see Nos. J132-J134.

1962-64

Granite Paper

Without Gum

1270a A158 3c light red brown .50 .20
1270B A158 10c emerald ('63) 1.50 .20
1271a A158 40c pale violet .50 .20
1274a A158 80c pale green .50 .20
1275a A158 $1 gray grn ('63) 8.00 .20
1278a A158 $2 carmine rose 4.00 .20
1281a A158 $3.20 red brn ('64) 10.00 .20
1282A A158 $4 brt blue grn 10.00 .20
1283a A158 $4.50 vermilion 15.00 .50
Nos. 1270a-1283a (9) 50.00 2.10

Two types of No. 1271a: I. Seven lines in "0" of "40." II. Eight lines in "0."

Perf. 12½

1960, Oct. 25 Photo. Unwmk.

1284 A159 50c Diving 1.25 .20
1285 A159 80c Discus thrower 1.00 .20
1286 A159 $2 Basketball 2.50 .20
1287 A159 $2.50 Soccer 2.50 .40

1288 A159 $3 Hurdling 3.00 .40
1289 A159 $3.20 Runner 3.25 .60
Nos. 1284-1289 (6) 13.50 2.00

Bronze Wine Container, 1751-1111 B.C. — A160

Flat Bowl, 1111-771 B.C. — A161

Ancient Chinese Art Treasures: $1, Cauldron, 1111-771 B.C. $1.20, Porcelain vase, 960-1126 A.D. $1.50, Perforated tube, 1111-771 B.C. $2, Jug in shape of monk's cap, 1368-1661 A.D. $2.50, Jade flower vase, 1368-1661, A.D.

1961 Photo. *Perf. 13*

1290 A160 80c lt ol, blk & dk vio 1.50 .20
1291 A160 $1 sal, bl & blk 1.90 .25
1292 A160 $1.20 yel, brn & ultra 2.75 .35
1293 A160 $1.50 lil, bl & sep 3.75 .60
1294 A160 $2 pale grn, dk grn & red brn 5.50 .70
1295 A160 $2.50 grnsh bl & dk vio 9.25 1.00
Nos. 1290-1295 (6) 24.65 3.10

Issue dates: Nos. 1290, 1292, 1295, Feb. 1. Nos. 1291, 1293-1294, May 1.

1961

80c, Palace perfumer, 1662-1911. $1, Corn vase, 770-221 B.C. $2, Jade tankard, 960-1126 A.D. $4, Glazed washer, 1127-1279 A.D. $4.50, Jade chimera, 8 B.C.-206 A.D.

1296 A160 80c pink, brn, bl & yel 1.50 .30
1297 A160 $1 cit, blk & brn 2.00 .60
1298 A161 $1.50 sal & ind 4.00 .70
1299 A160 $2 bl, blk & rose 4.00 .60
1300 A161 $4 red, blk & blu-ish gray 6.00 1.25
1301 A161 $4.50 grnsh bl, blk & brn 22.50 2.50
Nos. 1296-1301 (6) 40.00 5.95

Issued: #1296-1298, 8/15; #1299-1301, 9/15.

1962

Designs: 80c, Topaz twin wine vessels, 1662-1911 A.D. $1, Squat pouring vase, 1751-1111 B.C. $2.40, Vase, 1368-1661 A.D. $3, Wine vase, 1751-1111 B.C. $3.20, Covered porcelain jar, 1662-1911 A.D. $3.60, Perforated disc, 206 B.C.-8 A.D.

1302 A160 80c crim, blk & ocher 1.00 .20
1303 A160 $1 blue & vio blk 1.25 .25
1304 A160 $2.40 hn brn, blk & bl 13.50 .75
1305 A160 $3 blue, blk & pink 15.00 .60
1306 A160 $3.20 ultra, lt grn & red 13.00 .60
1307 A160 $3.60 yel, blk & brn 21.00 .80
Nos. 1302-1307 (6) 64.75 3.20

Issue dates: Nos. 1303-1304, 1307, Jan. 15. Nos. 1302, 1305-1306, Feb. 15.

Farmer with Mechanized Plow — A162

Madame Chiang Kai-shek and League Emblem — A163

1961, Feb. 4 Engr. *Perf. 12*
Without Gum

1308 A162 80c rose violet 1.40 .20
1309 A162 $2 green 2.50 .30
1310 A162 $3.20 vermilion 4.00 .30
Nos. 1308-1310 (3) 7.90 .80

1961 agricultural census.

Unwmk.
1961, Mar. 8 Photo. *Perf. 13*
Portrait in Black

1311 A163 80c lt grn & car rose 2.10 .20
1312 A163 $1 yel grn & car rose 2.75 .60
1313 A163 $2 org brn & car rose 3.50 .70
1314 A163 $3.20 lil & car rose 4.25 1.00
Nos. 1311-1314 (4) 12.60 2.50

10th anniversary of the Chinese Women's Anti-Aggression League.

Spiny Lobster and Mail Order Service Emblem — A164

Jeme Tien-yow and Pataling Tunnel — A165

1961, Mar. 20 Engr. *Perf. 11½*
Without Gum

1315 A164 $3 slate green 3.50 .35

Issued to publicize the mail order service for consumer goods.

1961, Apr. 26 *Perf. 11½*
Without Gum

$2, Jeme Tien-yow & 1909 locomotive.

1316 A165 80c lilac 1.40 .20
1317 A165 $2 black, horiz. 2.10 .50

Centenary of the birth of Jeme Tien-yow, builder of the Peking-Kalgan railroad.

Map of China inscribed: "Recovery of the Mainland" — A166

Pres. Chiang Kai-shek — A167

1961, May 20 Photo. *Perf. 13½*

1318 A166 80c multicolored 2.50 .25
1319 A167 $2 multicolored 4.00 1.10
a. Souvenir sheet of 2 14.00 *12.50*

1st anniversary of Pres. Chiang Kai-shek's 3rd term inauguration.

No. 1319a contains one each of Nos. 1318-1319, imperf. with simulated perforations. Without gum.

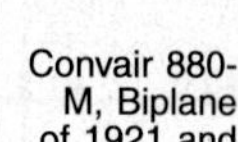

Convair 880-M, Biplane of 1921 and Flag — A168

1961, July 1 *Perf. 13x12½*

1320 A168 $10 multicolored 3.00 1.10

40th anniversary of civil air service.

Sun Yat-sen and Chiang Kai-shek — A169

Flag and Map of China — A170

Perf. 13½
1961, Oct. 10 Unwmk. Photo.

1321 A169 80c gray, lt brn & sl 1.60 .20
1322 A170 $5 gray, ultra, red & beige 3.25 1.40
a. Souvenir sheet of 2 11.50 10.00

50th anniv. of the Republic of China. No. 1322a contains one each of Nos. 1321-1322, imperf. with simulated perforations. No gum.

Green Lake A171

Oil Refinery A173

Lotus Pond A172

Taiwan Scenery: $2, Sun-Moon Lake. $3.20, Wulai waterfalls.

Perf. 13½x14, 14x13½
1961, Oct. 31 Unwmk.

1323 A171 80c multicolored 4.00 .20
1324 A172 $1 multicolored 9.00 .50
1325 A172 $2 multicolored 9.00 .70
1326 A171 $3.20 multicolored 12.00 .90
Nos. 1323-1326 (4) 34.00 2.30

1961, Nov. 14 *Perf. 11½*

Designs: $1.50, Steel works. $2.50, Aluminum plant. $3.20, Fertilizer plant, horiz.

1327 A173 80c multicolored 1.60 .20
1328 A173 $1.50 multicolored 3.25 .50
1329 A173 $2.50 multicolored 4.25 .55
1330 A173 $3.20 multicolored 5.00 .65
Nos. 1327-1330 (4) 14.10 1.90

Chinese industrial development and the Golden Jubilee Convention of the Chinese Institute of Engineers, Nov. 13-16.

Atomic Reactor, Tsing-Hwa University A174

Atomic Reactor in Operation A175

Design: $3.20, Atomic symbol and laboratory, Tsing-Hwa, horiz.

1961-62 Photo. *Perf. 12½*

1331 A174 80c multicolored 2.25 .20
1332 A175 $2 multicolored 4.50 1.40
1333 A175 $3.20 multicolored 4.25 .85
Nos. 1331-1333 (3) 11.00 2.45

Inauguration on Apr. 13, 1961, of the 1st Chinese atomic reactor at the National Tsing-Hwa University Institute of Nuclear Science. Issued: 80c, 12/2; $2, $3.20, 3/20/62.

Microwave Reflector and Telegraph Wires — A176

Design: $3.20, Microwave parabolic antenna and mountains, horiz.

1961, Dec. 28 *Perf. 12½*

1334 A176 80c multicolored 1.25 .20
1335 A176 $3.20 multicolored 2.00 .80

80th anniv. of Chinese telecommunications.

Mechanical Postal Equipment and Twine Tying Machine — A176a

Wmk. 323
1962, Mar. 20 Engr. *Perf. 11½*
Without Gum

1336 A176a 80c chocolate 1.10 .30

Yu Shan Observatory A177

Observation Balloon, Earth and Cumulus Clouds A178

Design: $1, Map showing route of typhoon Pamela, Sept. 1961, horiz.

1962
Without Gum

1337 A177 80c brown .70 .20
1338 A178 $1 bluish black 1.40 .30
1339 A178 $2 green 1.90 .65
Nos. 1337-1339 (3) 4.00 1.15

Issue dates: 80c, $2, Mar. 23; $1, May 7. World Meteorological Day, Mar. 23.

Child Receiving Milk, UN Emblem A179

1962, Apr. 4

Without Gum

1340 A179 80c rose red .85 .20
1341 A179 $3.20 green 1.75 .50
a. Souvenir sheet of 2 11.50 3.50

15th anniv. of UNICEF. No. 1341a contains one each of Nos. 1340-1341 imperf. with simulated perforations.

Malaria Eradication Emblem — A180

Unwmk.

1962, Apr. 7 Photo. *Perf. 13*

1342 A180 80c dk bl, red & lt grn .60 .20
1343 A180 $3.60 brn, pink & grn 1.10 1.00

WHO drive to eradicate malaria.

Yu Yu-jen — A181

Cheng Ch'eng-kung (Koxinga) — A182

1962, Apr. 24 *Perf. 13*

1344 A181 80c gray, blk & pink 1.60 .25

Issued to honor Yu Yu-jen, newspaper reporter, revolutionary leader and co-worker of Sun Yat-sen, on his 84th birthday.

1962, Apr. 29

1345 A182 80c deep claret 1.50 .20
1346 A182 $2 dark green 2.50 .55

300th anniversary (in 1961) of the recovery of Taiwan from the Dutch by Koxinga.

Emblem of Intl. Cooperative Alliance — A183

Clasped Hands Across Globe — A184

Wmk. 323

1962, July 7 Engr. *Perf. 12*

Without Gum

1347 A183 80c brown .70 .20
1348 A184 $2 violet 1.10 .45

Intl. Cooperative Movement and 40th Intl. Cooperative Day, July 7, 1962.

Mansion Type of 1958

1962, July 20

Without Gum

1349 A135 $5 gray green 2.00 .20
1350 A135 $5.60 violet 2.75 .20
1351 A135 $6 orange 2.40 .20
Nos. 1349-1351 (3) 7.15 .60

1963

Granite Paper

1349a A135 $5 gray green 2.50 .20
1350a A135 $5.60 violet 3.00 .20
1351a A135 $6 orange 4.00 .20
Nos. 1349a-1351a (3) 9.50 .60

"Art and Science" — A185

$2, "Education," book and UNESCO emblem, horiz. $3.20, "Communications," globes, horiz.

1962, Aug. 28 Wmk. 323 *Perf. 12*

Without Gum

1352 A185 80c lilac rose .60 .20
1353 A185 $2 rose claret .95 .40
1354 A185 $3.20 yellow green 1.10 .30
Nos. 1352-1354 (3) 2.65 .90

UNESCO activities in China.

Emperor T'ai Tsung, T'ang Dynasty, 627-649 A186

Emperors: $2, T'ai Tsu, Sung dynasty, 960-975. $3.20, T'ai Tsu, Yuan dynasty (Genghis Khan), 1206-27. $4, T'ai Tsu, Ming dynasty, 1368-98.

1962, Sept. 20 Photo. Unwmk.

1355 A186 80c multicolored 7.50 2.00
1356 A186 $2 multicolored 25.00 4.50
1357 A186 $3.20 multicolored 35.00 5.50
1358 A186 $4 multicolored 42.50 14.00
Nos. 1355-1358 (4) 110.00 26.00

Lions International Emblem A187

1962, Oct. 8 *Perf. 13½*

1359 A187 80c multicolored 1.10 .20
1360 A187 $3.60 multicolored 2.10 .80
a. Souvenir sheet of 2 13.50 6.25

45th anniv. of Lions Intl. No. 1360a contains one each of Nos. 1359-1360, imperf. with simulated perforations.

Pole Vaulting — A188

Shooting A189

1962, Oct. 25 Unwmk. *Perf. 13*

1361 A188 80c multicolored .90 .20
1362 A189 $3.20 multicolored 2.10 .40

Sports meet.

Young Farmers and 4-H Emblem — A190

Flag, Liner of China Merchants' Steam Navigation Co. — A191

Design: $3.20, 4-H emblem and rice.

Wmk. 323

1962, Dec. 7 Engr. *Perf. 12*

Without Gum

1363 A190 80c carmine .60 .20
1364 A190 $3.20 green 1.90 .55
a. Souvenir sheet of 2 13.00 8.00

10th anniv. of the 4-H Club in China. No. 1364a contains one each of Nos. 1363-1364, imperf. with simulated perforations.

Perf. 13½

1962, Dec. 16 Unwmk. Photo.

Design: $3.60, Company's Pacific navigation chart and freighter, horiz.

1365 A191 80c multicolored 1.60 .20
1366 A191 $3.60 multicolored 2.50 .80

90th anniversary of the China Merchants' Steam Navigation Co., Ltd.

Farm Woman, Tractor and Plane Dropping Food over Mainland — A192

Perf. 12½

1963, Mar. 21 Unwmk. Photo.

1367 A192 $10 multicolored 4.00 .70

FAO "Freedom from Hunger" campaign.

Torch, Young Couple and Martyrs' Monument, Canton A193

Wmk. 323

1963, Mar. 29 Engr. *Perf. 11½*

Without Gum

1368 A193 80c purple .75 .20
1369 A193 $3.20 green 1.50 .40

Issued for the 20th Youth Day.

Swallows, Pagoda and AOPU Emblem — A194

Designs: $2, Northern gannet, horiz. $6, Japanese crane and pine.

Unwmk.

1963, Apr. 1 Photo. *Perf. 13*

1370 A194 80c multicolored 4.00 .55
1371 A194 $2 multicolored 5.50 .65
1372 A194 $6 multicolored 8.25 2.10
Nos. 1370-1372 (3) 17.75 3.30

1st anniversary of the formation of the Asian-Oceanic Postal Union, AOPU.

Refugee Girl (Li Ying) and Map of China — A195

Refugees Fleeing Mainland A196

Wmk. 323

1963, June 27 Engr. *Perf. 11½*

Without Gum

1373 A195 80c bluish black 1.00 .20
1374 A196 $3.20 dp claret 2.25 .30

1st anniv. of the evacuation of Chinese mainland refugees from Hong Kong to Taiwan. Designs from photographs of refugees.

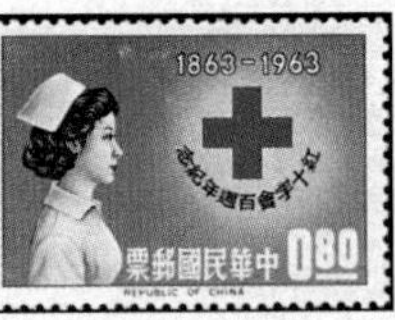

Nurse and Red Cross A197

Design: $10, Globe and Red Cross.

Perf. 12½

1963, Sept. 1 Unwmk. Photo.

1375 A197 80c black & carmine 5.25 .25
1376 A197 $10 slate, gray & car 6.25 2.25

Centenary of International Red Cross.

Basketball Player, Stadium and Asian Cup — A198

$2, Hands reaching for ball and Asian cup.

Wmk. 323

1963, Nov. 20 Engr. *Perf. 12*

Without Gum

1377 A198 80c lilac rose .90 .20
1378 A198 $2 violet 1.75 .60

The 2nd Asian Basketball Championship, Taipei, Nov. 20.

UN Emblem, Torch and Men — A199

Scales and Men of Various Races A200

1963, Dec. 10 Wmk. 323 *Perf. 11½*

Without Gum

1379 A199 80c brt green .70 .30
1380 A200 $3.20 maroon 1.40 .65

Universal Declaration of Human Rights, 15th anniversary.

Village and Orchids
A201

"Kindle the Fire of Conscience"
A202

Perf. 13½x13

1963, Dec. 17 Photo. Unwmk.

1381 A201 40c multicolored 2.50 .35
1382 A202 $4.50 multicolored 4.00 1.60

Contribution of the Good-People-Good-Deeds campaign to improve ethical standards.

Sun Yat-sen and Book, "Three Principles of the People"
A203

1963, Dec. 25 ***Perf. 13***

1383 A203 $5 blue & multi 6.75 1.00

"Land-to-the-Tillers" program, 10th anniv. An 80c was prepared but not issued.

Torch — A204

Hands Unchained — A205

Wmk. 323

1964, Jan. 23 Engr. ***Perf. 11½***
Without Gum

1384 A204 80c red orange .60 .20
1385 A205 $3.20 indigo 1.90 .35

Liberty Day, 10th anniversary.

Broadleaf Cactus
A206

Wu Chih-hwei
A207

Designs: $1, Crab cactus. $3.20, Nopalxochia. $5, Grizzly bear cactus.

Perf. 12½

1964, Feb. 27 Unwmk. Photo.
Plants in Original Colors

1386 A206 80c dp plum & fawn 2.50 .20
1387 A206 $1 dk blue & car 4.25 .90
1388 A206 $3.20 green 6.25 .20
1389 A206 $5 lilac & yellow 6.75 1.10
Nos. 1386-1389 (4) 19.75 2.40

Wmk. 323

1964, Mar. 25 Engr. ***Perf. 11½***
Without Gum

1390 A207 80c black brown 1.40 .20

Centenary of the birth of Wu Chih-hwei (1865-1953), politician and leader of the Kuomintang.

Chu Kwang Tower, Quemoy — A208

Perf. 13x12½

1964-66 Wmk. 323 Litho.
Granite Paper; Without Gum

1391 A208 3c sepia .25 .20
1392 A208 5c brt yel grn ('65) .25 .20
1393 A208 10c yellow grn .25 .20
1394 A208 20c slate grn ('65) .25 .20
1395 A208 40c rose red .25 .20
1396 A208 50c brown .25 .20
1397 A208 80c orange ('65) .25 .20
1398 A208 $1 violet ('65) .25 .20
1399 A208 $1.50 brt lilac ('66) 2.25 .25
1400 A208 $2 lilac rose .25 .20
1401 A208 $2.50 ultra ('65) 2.25 .25
1402 A208 $3 slate 2.25 .30
1403 A208 $3.20 brt blue 4.00 .20
1404 A208 $4 brt green 4.50 .25
Nos. 1391-1404 (14) 17.50 3.05

Nurses Holding Candles
A209

Florence Nightingale and Student Nurse — A210

1964, May 12 Engr. ***Perf. 11½***
Without Gum

1406 A209 80c violet blue 1.40 .25
1407 A210 $4 red 2.25 .50

Issued for Nurses Day.

Shihmen Reservoir
A211

Designs: $1, Irrigation system. $3.20, Main dam and power plant. $5, Spillway.

Perf. 12½

1964, June 14 Unwmk. Photo.

1408 A211 80c multicolored 1.75 .25
1409 A211 $1 multicolored 2.25 .45
1410 A211 $3.20 multicolored 6.25 .55
1411 A211 $5 multicolored 7.00 1.40
Nos. 1408-1411 (4) 17.25 2.65

Completion of Shihmen Reservoir.

15th Century Ship, Modern Liner — A212

Wmk. 323

1964, July 11 Engr. ***Perf. 11½***
Without Gum

1412 A212 $2 orange .80 .20
1413 A212 $3.60 brt green 1.25 .35

China's 10th Navigation Day.

Bananas
A213

Unwmk.

1964, July 25 Photo. ***Perf. 14***

1414 A213 80c shown 8.25 .20
1415 A213 $1 Oranges 14.00 .70
1416 A213 $3.20 Pineapple 17.00 .70
1417 A213 $4 Watermelon 25.00 2.40
Nos. 1414-1417 (4) 64.25 4.00

Artillery, Warships, Jet Fighters
A214

Wmk. 323

1964, Sept. 3 Engr. ***Perf. 11½***
Without Gum

1418 A214 80c dk blue 1.10 .20
1419 A214 $6 violet brown 2.75 .50

Issued for the 10th Armed Forces Day.

Unisphere, Flags of China and U.S. — A215

Chinese Pavilion, NY World's Fair — A216

1964, Sept. 10 Photo. Unwmk.

1420 A215 80c violet & multi 1.25 .25
1421 A216 $5 blue & multi 2.75 .90

NY World's Fair, 1964-65. See #1450-1451.

Cowboy Carrying Calf, and Ranch — A217

Bicycling — A218

Wmk. 323

1964, Sept. 24 Engr. ***Perf. 11½***
Without Gum

1422 A217 $2 brown lake 1.10 .20
1423 A217 $4 dark violet blue 2.25 .80

Animal Protection Week, Sept. 24-30.

1964, Oct. 10 Without Gum

Sports: $1, Runner. $3.20, Gymnast on rings. $10, High jump.

1424 A218 80c violet blue .80 .20
1425 A218 $1 rose red 1.40 .20
1426 A218 $3.20 dull blue grn 1.75 .25
1427 A218 $10 lilac 3.00 1.50
Nos. 1424-1427 (4) 6.95 2.15

18th Olympic Games, Tokyo, Oct. 10-25.

Hsü Kuang-chi
A219

Pharmaceutical Industry
A220

Textile Industry
A221

1964, Nov. 8 Engr. ***Perf. 11½***
Without Gum

1428 A219 80c indigo 2.00 .20

Issued to honor Hsü Kuang-chi (1562-1633), scholar and statesman.

1964, Nov. 11 Photo. Unwmk.

$2, Chemical industry. $3.60, Cement industry.

1429 A220 40c multi 2.25 .20
1430 A221 $1.50 multi 3.00 .70
1431 A220 $2 multi 4.50 .50
1432 A221 $3.60 multi 5.25 1.10
Nos. 1429-1432 (4) 15.00 2.50

Dr. Sun Yat-sen — A222

Eleanor Roosevelt and Scales of Justice — A223

1964, Nov. 24 Engr. Wmk. 323
Without Gum

1433 A222 80c green 1.40 .30
1434 A222 $3.60 purple 3.75 .65

Founding of the Kuomintang by Sun Yat-sen, 70th anniversary.

Unwmk.

1964, Dec. 10 Photo. ***Perf. 13***

1435 A223 $10 violet & brown 1.60 .40

Issued to honor Eleanor Roosevelt (1884-1962) on the 16th anniversary of the Universal Declaration of Human Rights.

Scales, Code Book and Plum Blossom
A224

Rotary Emblem and Mainspring
A225

Wmk. 323

1965, Jan. 11 Engr. ***Perf. 11½***
Without Gum

1436 A224 80c carmine rose .45 .20
1437 A224 $3.20 dull slate grn .70 .40

The 20th Judicial Day.

1965, Feb. 23 Wmk. 323 ***Perf. 11½***
Without Gum

1438 A225 $1.50 vermilion .60 .20
1439 A225 $2 emerald .70 .20
1440 A225 $2.50 blue .90 .30
Nos. 1438-1440 (3) 2.20 .70

Rotary International, 60th anniversary.

Double Carp Design A226

Madame Chiang Kai-shek A227

Wmk. 323
1965, Mar. 29 Engr. ***Perf. 11½***
Granite Paper; Without Gum

1441 A226 $5 purple 9.00 .95
1442 A226 $5.60 dp blue 15.00 1.60
1443 A226 $6 brown 13.50 .95
1444 A226 $10 lilac rose 22.50 .95
1445 A226 $20 rose car 26.00 1.60
1446 A226 $50 green 30.00 3.50
1447 A226 $100 crim rose 37.50 5.75
Nos. 1441-1447 (7) 153.50 15.30

New dies used to reprint #1444-1447, 8/20/67. Remainders of #1441-1447 issued with gum, 11/1/71.

1965, Apr. 17 Photo. Unwmk.

1448 A227 $2 multicolored 12.50 .50
1449 A227 $6 salmon & multi 22.50 3.00

Chinese Women's Anti-Aggression League, 15th anniversary.

Unisphere and Chinese Pavilion — A228

"100 Birds Paying Homage to Queen Phoenix" and Unisphere — A229

1965, May 8

1450 A228 $2 blue & multi 10.50 .75
1451 A229 $10 red, ocher & bis 12.50 1.75

New York World's Fair, 1964-65.

ITU Emblem, Old and New Communication Equipment A230

Design: $5, similar to 80c, vert.

Perf. 13½x13, 13x13½
1965, May 17 Photo. Unwmk.

1452 A230 80c multicolored .60 .20
1453 A230 $5 multicolored 1.75 .55

Centenary of the ITU.

Red Sea Bream A231

Fish: 80c, White pomfret. $2, Skipjack, vert. $4, Moonfish.

1965, July 1 ***Perf. 13***

1454 A231 40c multicolored 1.60 .20
1455 A231 80c multicolored 2.50 .30
1456 A231 $2 multicolored 5.75 1.00
1457 A231 $4 multicolored 10.00 1.50
Nos. 1454-1457 (4) 19.85 3.00

Issued for Fishermen's Day.

Confucius A232

ICY Emblem A233

Portraits: $2.50, Yueh Fei. $3.50, Wen Tien-hsiang. $3.60, Mencius.

Wmk. 323
1965-66 Engr. ***Perf. 11½***
Without Gum

1458 A232 $1 deep carmine 3.00 .35
1459 A232 $2.50 black brown 2.00 .35
1460 A232 $3.50 dark red 4.50 .50
1461 A232 $3.60 dark blue 5.25 .60
Nos. 1458-1461 (4) 14.75 1.80

The $2.50 and $3.50 have colored background.
Forgeries of #1461 exist.
Issued: #1458, 1461, 9/28/65; #1459-1460, 9/3/66.
See Nos. 1507-1508, design A251.

Unwmk.
1965, Oct. 24 Photo. ***Perf. 13***

Design: $6, ICY emblem, horiz.

1462 A233 $2 brn, blk & gold 1.25 .20
1463 A233 $6 brt grn, red & gold 2.75 1.00

International Cooperation Year, 1965.

Street Crossing, Traffic Light A234

Sun Yat-sen A235

Wmk. 323
1965, Nov. 1 Engr. ***Perf. 11½***
Without Gum

1464 A234 $1 brown violet 1.25 .25
1465 A234 $4 crimson rose 2.40 .80

Issued to publicize traffic safety.

Perf. 13½
1965, Nov. 12 Unwmk. Photo.

Designs: $4, Dr. Sun Yat-sen, portrait at right. $5, Sun Yat-sen and flags, horiz.

1466 A235 $1 multicolored 2.50 .20
1467 A235 $4 multicolored 7.75 .60
1468 A235 $5 multicolored 9.25 1.75
Nos. 1466-1468 (3) 19.50 2.55

Children with New Year's Firecrackers A236

Dragon Dance, "Dragon Playing Ball" A237

1965, Dec. 1 Photo. ***Perf. 13***

1469 A236 $1 multi 3.50 .30
1470 A237 $4.50 multi 8.00 1.10

Lien Po from "Marshal and Prime Minister Reconciled" — A238

Facial Paintings for Chinese Operas: $3, Kuan Yü from "Reunion at Ku City." $4, Gen. Chang Fei from "The Battle of Chang Pan Hill." $6, Buddha from "The Flower-Scattering Angel."

1966, Feb. 15 Unwmk. ***Perf. 11½***

1471 A238 $1 olive & multi 8.00 .25
1472 A238 $3 multicolored 13.50 .75
1473 A238 $4 multicolored 22.50 1.00
1474 A238 $6 ver & multi 27.50 2.00
Nos. 1471-1474 (4) 71.50 4.00

Labels with a similar appearance to these stamps exist. These labels have the numbers 1 to 20 in the upper right corner, but lack the "00."

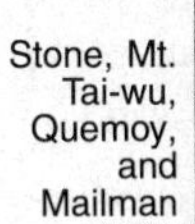

Postal Service Emblem Held by Carrier Pigeon — A239

Stone, Mt. Tai-wu, Quemoy, and Mailman A240

postal service emblem and: $3, Postal Museum. $4, Mailman climbing symbolic slope.

1966, Mar. 20 Photo. ***Perf. 12½***

1475 A239 $1 green & multi 1.25 .20
1476 A240 $2 multicolored 2.50 .30
1477 A240 $3 multicolored 3.00 .40
1478 A239 $4 multicolored 6.25 1.25
Nos. 1475-1478 (4) 13.00 2.15

China postal service, 70th anniversary.

Fishing on a Snowy Day, "Five Dynasties" (907-960) A241

Paintings from Palace Museum: $3.50, Calves on the Plain, Sung artist (960-1126). $4.50, Winter landscape, Sung artist (960-1126). $5, Magpies, by Lin Ch'un, Southern Sung dynasty (1127-1279).

1966, May 20 Photo. ***Perf. 13***

1479 A241 $2.50 blk, brn & red 2.50 .35
1480 A241 $3.50 bis brn, blk & gray 6.50 .50
1481 A241 $4.50 blk, buff & sl 9.00 1.25
1482 A241 $5 multicolored 12.00 1.40
Nos. 1479-1482 (4) 30.00 3.50

Inauguration of Pres. Chiang Kai-shek for a 4th term.

Dragon Boat Race A242

Lion Dance — A243

$4, Lady Chang O flying to the Moon.

1966 Unwmk.

1483 A242 $2.50 multi 1.75 .30
1484 A242 $4 multi 3.50 .40
1485 A243 $6 multi 5.75 .75
Nos. 1483-1485 (3) 11.00 1.45

Dragon Boat, Mid-Autumn and Lunar New Year Festivals. Issued: $2.50, 6/23; $4, 9/29; $6, 11/26.

Flags of China and Argentina A244

1966, July 9 Photo. ***Perf. 13***

1486 A244 $10 multicolored 3.00 .50

Argentina's Independence. 150th anniv.

Lin Sen — A245

Flying Geese — A246

Wmk. 323
1966, Aug. 1 Engr. ***Perf. 11½***
Without Gum

1487 A245 $1 dk brown 1.60 .20

Centenary of the birth of Lin Sen (1867-1943), Chairman of the Nationalist Government of China (1931-43).

1966-67 ***Perf. 11½ Rough***
Granite Paper; Without Gum

1496 A246 $3.50 brown .85 .20
1497 A246 $4 vermilion .80 .20
1498 A246 $4.50 brt green 1.40 .25
1499 A246 $5 rose lilac .85 .20
1500 A246 $5.50 yel grn ('67) 1.60 .20
1501 A246 $6 brt blue 1.90 .30
1502 A246 $6.50 violet 1.60 .25
1503 A246 $7 black .95 .20
1504 A246 $8 car rose ('67) 1.40 .20
Nos. 1496-1504 (9) 11.35 2.00

The $4.50, $5, $6, $7 and $8 were reissued with gum in 1970-71.

Pres. Chiang Kai-shek in Chung San Robe — A247

$5, Chiang Kai-shek in marshal's uniform.

Unwmk.
1966, Oct. 31 Photo. ***Perf. 13***

1505 A247 $1 multicolored 1.50 .25
1506 A247 $5 multicolored 4.75 1.25

Chiang Kai-shek's inauguration for a fourth term as president, May 20, 1966.

Famous Men Type of 1965-66 with Frame Line

Portraits: No. 1507, Tsai Yuan-pei (1868-1940), educator. No. 1508, Chiu Ching (1875-1907), woman educator and revolutionist.

1967 Wmk. 323 Engr. *Perf. 11½*
Without Gum

1507 A232 $1 violet blue 1.60 .25
1508 A232 $1 black 1.60 .25

Issue dates: #1507, Jan. 11. #1508, July 15. No. 1507 is on granite paper.

Motorized Mailman and Microwave Station — A248

"Transportation" and Radar Weather Station — A249

Unwmk.
1967, Mar. 15 Photo. *Perf. 13*

1511 A248 $1 multicolored 1.00 .25
1512 A249 $5 multicolored 1.75 .60

Issued to publicize the progress in communication and transportation services.

Pres. Chiang Kai-shek and Chinese Flag — A250

Chu Yuan, 332-295 B.C. — A251

Design: $4, Different frame.

1967, May 20 Litho. *Perf. 13*

1513 A250 $1 multicolored 1.25 .20
1514 A250 $4 multicolored 2.25 .60

First anniversary of President Chiang Kai-shek's 4th-term inauguration.

Wmk. 323
1967, June 12 Engr. *Perf. 11½*

Portraits: $2, Li Po (705-760). $2.50, Tu Fu (712-770). $3, Po Chu-i (772-846).

Granite Paper; Without Gum

1515 A251 $1 black .85 .20
1516 A251 $2 brown 2.50 .25
1517 A251 $2.50 brown blk 3.50 .45
1518 A251 $3 grnsh black 5.25 .45
Nos. 1515-1518 (4) 12.10 1.35

Issued for Poets' Day.
See design A232.

Hotei, Wood Carving — A252

World Map — A253

Handicrafts: $2.50, Vase and plate. $3, Dolls. $5, Palace lanterns.

Perf. 11½
1967, Aug. 12 Unwmk. Photo.

1519 A252 $1 gray & multi 2.25 .40
1520 A252 $2.50 multi 3.00 .60
1521 A252 $3 multi 3.75 1.00
1522 A252 $5 multi 5.00 2.00
Nos. 1519-1522 (4) 14.00 4.00

Taiwan handicraft industry.

Wmk. 323
1967, Sept. 25 Engr. *Perf. 11½*
Granite Paper; Without Gum

1523 A253 $1 vermilion .45 .20
1524 A253 $5 blue 1.10 .50

1st Conference of the World Anti-Communist League, WACL, Taipei, Sept. 25-29.

Players on Stilts: "The Fisherman and the Woodcutter" A254

Unwmk.
1967, Oct. 10 Photo. *Perf. 13*

1525 A254 $4.50 multi 1.25 .35

Issued for the 56th National Day.

Maroon Oriole — A255

Formosan Birds: $1, Formosan barbet, vert. $2.50, Formosan green pigeon. $3, Formosan blue magpie. $5, Crested serpent eagle, vert. $8, Mikado pheasants.

1967, Nov. 25 Photo. *Perf. 11*
Granite Paper

1526 A255 $1 multi 3.00 .20
1527 A255 $2 multi 4.00 .25
1528 A255 $2.50 multi 5.00 .30
1529 A255 $3 multi 6.00 .40
1530 A255 $5 multi 7.00 .45
1531 A255 $8 multi 8.50 .90
Nos. 1526-1531 (6) 33.50 2.50

Chung Hsing Pagoda — A256

Buddha, Changhua A257

Designs: $2.50, Seashore, Yeh Liu Park. $5, National Palace Museum, Taipei.

Unwmk.
1967, Dec. 10 Photo. *Perf. 13*

1532 A256 $1 multi 1.10 .20
1533 A257 $2.50 multi 2.75 .40
1534 A257 $4 multi 3.50 .50
1535 A257 $5 multi 4.00 .75
Nos. 1532-1535 (4) 11.35 1.85

Issued for International Tourist Year 1967.

China Park, Manila, and Flags — A258

1967, Dec. 30 *Perf. 13½*

1536 A258 $1 multicolored .50 .20
1537 A258 $5 multicolored 1.75 .40

Sino-Philippine Friendship Year 1966-67.

Sun Yat-sen Building, Yangmingshan
A259 A259a

Perf. 13x12½
1968-75 Litho. Wmk. 323
Granite Paper

1538 A259 5c lt brown .45 .20
1539 A259 10c grnsh black .45 .20
1540 A259 50c brt rose lilac .45 .20
1541 A259 $1 vermilion .45 .20
1542 A259 $1.50 emerald .85 .25
1543 A259 $2 plum .80 .20
1544 A259 $2.50 blue .95 .20
1545 A259 $3 grnsh blue 1.00 .25
Nos. 1538-1545 (8) 5.40 1.70

See Nos. 1702-1709. For overprints see Nos. 1723-1725.

Coil Stamps
Perf. 13 Horiz.
Photo. Unwmk.

1546 A259a $1 carmine rose .30 .25
1547 A259a $1 vermilion .30 .25

Issued: 50c, $1, $2.50, 1/23/68; #1546, 3/20/70; #1547, 1/28/75; others 7/11/68.
Inscription on No. 1546 is in color with white background. On No. 1547 it is white with colored background.

Harvesting Sugar Cane A260

Jade Cabbage, 1662-1911 A261

Unwmk.
1968, Mar. 1 Photo. *Perf. 13*

1548 A260 $1 olive & multi 1.40 .20
1549 A260 $4 multicolored 2.40 .45

1968, Mar. 29 Unwmk. *Perf. 13*

Ancient Art Treasures: $1.50, Jade battle axe. $2, Porcelain flower bowl, 960-1126 A.D., horiz. $2.50, Cloisonné enamel vase, 1723-1736 A.D. $4, Agate flower holder in shape of finger citrus, 1662-1911 A.D., horiz. $5, Sacrificial kettle, 1111-771 B.C.

1550 A261 $1 rose & multi 1.50 .20
1551 A261 $1.50 blue & multi 2.25 .50
1552 A261 $2 blue & multi 2.40 .20
1553 A261 $2.50 dull rose & multi 3.00 .50
1554 A261 $4 pink & multi 3.75 .60
1555 A261 $5 blue & multi 4.50 .70
Nos. 1550-1555 (6) 17.40 2.70

For similar artifact designs inscribed "Republic of China," with single-color denominations in slanted numerals and the cents underlined, see types A276, A291, A323, A336, A372, A384, A395, A411.
Artifact designs with denominations in outlined numerals begin with type A439.

View of City in Cathay (1) — A262

Views: No. 1557, City and wall of Forbidden City (2). No. 1558, Wall at right, bridge at left (3). No. 1559, Queen's ship landing at left (4) No. 1560, Palace (5). $5, City wall and gate. $8, Suburb around Great Bridge. Design from scroll "A City in Cathay," painted 1736.

1968, June 18 Photo. *Perf. 13½*
Size: 50x29mm

1556 A262 $1 multicolored 1.60 .30
1557 A262 $1 multicolored 1.60 .30
1558 A262 $1 multicolored 1.60 .30
1559 A262 $1 multicolored 1.60 .30
1560 A262 $1 multicolored 1.60 .30
a. Strip of 5, #1556-1560 8.00 8.00

Size: 60x31mm
Perf. 13x13½

1561 A262 $5 multicolored 8.25 1.60
1562 A262 $8 multicolored 15.00 2.00
Nos. 1556-1562 (7) 31.25 5.10

See Nos. 1610-1614. For similar designs see types A281, A299, A326, A343.

Entrance Gate, Taroko Gorge A263

$8, Sun Yat-sen Building, Yangmingshan.

1968, Feb. 12 Photo. *Perf. 13*

1563 A263 $5 multicolored 1.25 .25
1564 A263 $8 multicolored 2.40 .30

The 17th Annual Conference of the Pacific Area Travel Association.

Vice President Chen Cheng — A264

Flying Geese — A265

1968, Mar. 5

1565 A264 $1 brown & multi 1.25 .20

Vice President Chen Cheng (1898-1965).

Wmk. 323
1968, Mar. 20 Litho. *Perf. 12*
Granite Paper

1566 A265 $1 vermilion 9.00 .20

Souvenir Sheet
Imperf

1567 A265 $3 green 11.00 3.50

90th anniv. of Chinese postage stamps. No. 1567 contains one stamp with simulated perforations.

WHO Emblem and "20" — A266

Symbolic Water Cycle — A267

1968, Apr. 7 Engr. *Perf. 12*
Granite Paper

1568 A266 $1 green .35 .20
1569 A266 $5 scarlet .85 .45

20th anniv. of WHO.

Wmk. 323
1968, June 6 Litho. *Perf. 11½*
Granite Paper

1570 A267 $1 green & org .45 .20
1571 A267 $4 brt blue & org .90 .20

Hydrological Decade (UNESCO) 1965-74.

Broadcasting to Mainland China — A268

Dual Carriers for FM Broadcasting A269

Wmk. 323
1968, Aug. 1 Litho. *Perf. 12*
Granite Paper

1572 A268 $1 bl, vio bl & gray .40 .20
1573 A269 $4 lt ultra & ver .95 .25

40th anniv. of the Broadcasting Corp. of China, and the inauguration of frequency modulation broadcasting.

Human Rights Flame — A270

Crop Improvement and Extension Work — A271

1968, Sept. 3
Granite Paper

1574 A270 $1 multicolored .45 .20
1575 A270 $5 multicolored 1.10 .20

International Human Rights Year 1968.

Wmk. 323
1968, Sept. 30 Litho. *Perf. 12*
Granite Paper

1576 A271 $1 yel, bister & dk brn .30 .20
1577 A271 $5 yel, emer & dk grn 1.10 .50

Joint Commission on Rural Reconstruction, 20th anniversary.

Javelin — A272

Designs: $2.50, Weight lifting. $5, Pole vault, horiz. $8, Woman hurdling, horiz.

Unwmk.
1968, Oct. 12 Photo. *Perf. 13*

1578 A272 $1 multi .40 .20
1579 A272 $2.50 multi .60 .20
1580 A272 $5 multi .90 .25
1581 A272 $8 pink & multi 1.40 .35
Nos. 1578-1581 (4) 3.30 1.00

19th Olympic Games, Mexico City, 10/12-27.

Pres. Chiang Kai-shek and Whampoa Military Academy — A273

Designs: $2, Pres. Chiang Kai-shek reviewing forces of the Northern Expedition. $2.50, Suppression of bandits, reconstruction work and New Life Movement emblem. $3.50, Marco Polo Bridge near Peking and victory parade, Nanking. $4, Original copy of Constitution of Republic of China. $5, Nationalist Chinese flag flying over mainland China.

1968, Oct. 31 *Perf. 11½x12*

1582 A273 $1 multi .55 .20
1583 A273 $2 multi .75 .20
1584 A273 $2.50 multi 1.00 .30
1585 A273 $3.50 multi 1.25 .40
1586 A273 $4 multi 1.60 .65
1587 A273 $5 multi 2.75 .85
Nos. 1582-1587 (6) 7.90 2.60

Chiang Kai-shek's achievements for China.

Cock — A274

Flag — A275

1968, Nov. 12 Litho. *Perf. 12*
Granite Paper

1588 A274 $1 pink & multi 13.00 1.00
1589 A274 $4.50 lilac & multi 27.50 3.50

Issued for use on New Year's greetings.

1968, Dec. 25 Wmk. 323 *Perf. 12½*
Granite Paper

1590 A275 $1 multicolored .40 .20
1591 A275 $5 lt blue & multi .85 .45

Constitution of the Republic of China, 20th anniversary.

Jade Belt Buckle, 1662-1911 A276

Ancient Art Treasures: $1.50, Yellow jade vase, 960-1126 A.D., vert. $2, Cloisonne enamel square teapot, 1662-1911 A.D. $2.50, Kuei, sacrificial bronze vessel, 722-481 B.C. $4, Heavenly ball vase, 1368-1661 A.D., vert. $5, Gourd-shaped vase, 1662-1911 A.D., vert.

Unwmk.
1969, Jan. 15 Photo. *Perf. 13*

1592 A276 $1 dl rose & multi .95 .20
1593 A276 $1.50 rose & multi 1.60 .25
1594 A276 $2 brt rose & multi 2.00 .20
1595 A276 $2.50 lt blue & multi 2.25 .25
1596 A276 $4 tan & multi 2.40 .40
1597 A276 $5 pale blue & multi 2.50 .75
Nos. 1592-1597 (6) 11.70 2.05

Servicemen and Savings Emblem A277

Wmk. 323
1969, Feb. 1 Engr. *Perf. 12*
Granite Paper

1598 A277 $1 dull red brown .20 .20
1599 A277 $4 deep blue .80 .35

Military Savings Program, 10th anniv.

Ti (Flute) A278

Musical Instruments: $2.50, Sheng (13 bamboo pipes connected at the base). $4, P'i p'a (lute). $5, Cheng (zither).

Unwmk.
1969, Mar. 16 Photo. *Perf. 13*

1600 A278 $1 buff & multi .40 .20
1601 A278 $2.50 lt ap grn & multi 1.00 .25
1602 A278 $4 pink & multi 1.25 .30
1603 A278 $5 lt grnsh bl & multi 1.75 .40
Nos. 1600-1603 (4) 4.40 1.15

Sun Yat-sen Building and Kuomintang Emblem A279

Double Carp Design — A280

1969, Mar. 29 Litho. *Perf. 13½*

1604 A279 $1 multicolored .50 .20

10th Natl. Cong. of the Chinese Nationalist Party (Kuomintang), Mar. 29. A $2.50 stamp portraying Sun Yat-sen and Chiang Kai-shek was prepared but not issued.

Perf. 13½x12½
1974 Engr. Wmk. 323
Granite Paper

1606 A280 $10 dark blue 1.40 .20
1607 A280 $20 dark brown 2.75 .20
1608 A280 $50 green 4.50 .40
1609 A280 $100 bright red 5.75 .60
Nos. 1606-1609 (4) 14.40 1.40

1969
Perf. 11½

1606a A280 $10 1.75 .20
1607a A280 $20 2.40 .20
1608a A280 $50 6.25 .25
1609a A280 $100 9.50 .50
Nos. 1606a-1609a (4) 19.90 1.15

The 1969 issue is 27mm high; 1974, 28mm. See No. 1980.

Bridal Procession — A281

Designs: No. 1610, Musicians and standard bearer from bridal procession. $2.50, Emigrant farm family in oxcart. $5, Art gallery. $8, Roadside food stands. Designs from scroll "A City in Cathay," painted in 1736.

Perf. 13½
1969, May 20 Unwmk. Photo.

1610 A281 $1 multi .90 .20
1611 A281 $1 multi .90 .20
a. Pair, #1610-1611 2.00 1.75
1612 A281 $2.50 multi 3.00 .40
1613 A281 $5 multi 3.25 .60
1614 A281 $8 multi 5.25 .95
Nos. 1610-1614 (5) 13.30 2.35

ILO Emblem A282

Wmk. 323
1969, June 15 Engr. *Perf. 11½*
Granite Paper

1615 A282 $1 dark blue .35 .20
1616 A282 $8 dark carmine 1.25 .35

ILO, 50th anniversary.

Family at Dinner Table and Dressing A283

Pupils in Laboratory and Playing — A284

Designs: $2.50, Housecleaning and obeying traffic rules. $4, Recreation (music, fishing, basketball) and education.

Wmk. 323
1969, July 15 Engr. *Perf. 11½*

1617 A283 $1 brick red .20 .20
1618 A283 $2.50 blue .45 .25
1619 A283 $4 green .60 .25
Nos. 1617-1619 (3) 1.25 .70

Model Citizen's Life Movement.

1969, Sept. 1 Wmk. 323 *Perf. 11½*

Design: $1, $5, Pupils with book and various school activities, horiz.

Granite Paper

1620 A284 $1 brt red .20 .20
1621 A284 $2.50 brt green .55 .20
1622 A284 $4 dk blue .75 .30
1623 A284 $5 brown 1.00 .40
Nos. 1620-1623 (4) 2.50 1.10

Free 9-year education system, 1st anniv.

Wild Flowers and Pheasants, by Lu Chih (Ming) A285

Paintings: $2.50, Bamboo and birds, Sung dynasty. $5, Flowers and Birds, Sung dynasty. $8, Cranes and Flowers, by G. Castiglione, S.J. (1688-1766).

1969, Oct. 9 Photo. *Perf. 13½*

1624 A285 $1 multi 1.00 .20
1625 A285 $2.50 multi 2.40 .30
1626 A285 $5 multi 5.75 .50
1627 A285 $8 multi 7.75 .85
Nos. 1624-1627 (4) 16.90 1.85

Golden Scepter Rose — A286

Rocket and Radar Station — A287

Roses: $1, "Charles Mollerin," called black rose. $5, Peace. $8, Josephine Bruce.

1969, Oct. 31 Litho. *Perf. 14*

1628	A286	$1 lt vio & multi	.75	.20
1629	A286	$2.50 lt bl & multi	2.40	.20
1630	A286	$5 dl org & multi	3.00	.25
1631	A286	$8 ap grn & multi	2.75	.55
		Nos. 1628-1631 (4)	8.90	1.20

Wmk. 323

1969, Nov. 21 Engr. *Perf. 11½*

1632	A287	$1 rose claret	1.10	.20

The 30th Air Defense Day.

Symbol of International Cooperation A288

Pekingese — A289

1969, Nov. 25

1633	A288	$1 rose claret	.25	.20
1634	A288	$5 green	.85	.25

5th General Assembly of the Asian Parliamentary Union, Taipei, Nov. 24-28.

1969, Dec. 1 Litho. *Perf. 12*
Granite Paper

1635	A289	50c red & multi	1.25	.25
1636	A289	$4.50 green & multi	6.00	1.50

Issued for use on New Year's greetings.

Satellite, Earth Station and Map of Taiwan A290

Unwmk.

1969, Dec. 28 Photo. *Perf. 13*

1637	A290	$1 brown & multi	.35	.20
1638	A290	$5 vio blue & multi	1.25	.25
1639	A290	$8 purple & multi	1.60	.40
		Nos. 1637-1639 (3)	3.20	.85

Inauguration of the Communication Satellite Earth Station at Chin-Shan-Li, Dec. 28.

Agate Grinding Stone, 1662-1911 A291

Ancient Art Treasures: $1, Carved lacquer ware vase, 1662-1911, vert. $2, White jade Chin-li-chih melons, 1662-1911. $2.50, Black jade shepherd and ram, 206 B.C.-220 A.D. $4, Chien-lung twin porcelain vase, 1736-1796, vert. $5, Ju porcelain vase with 3 bulls, 960-1126, vert.

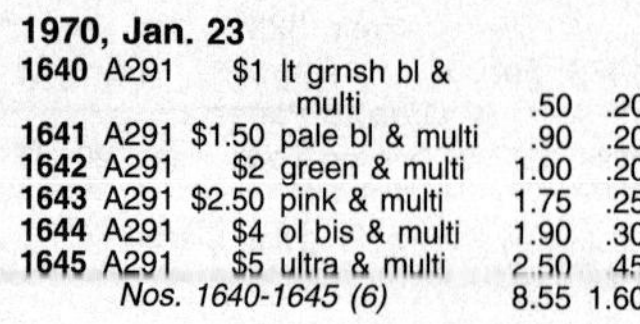

1970, Jan. 23

1640	A291	$1 lt grnsh bl & multi	.50	.20
1641	A291	$1.50 pale bl & multi	.90	.20
1642	A291	$2 green & multi	1.00	.20
1643	A291	$2.50 pink & multi	1.75	.25
1644	A291	$4 ol bis & multi	1.90	.30
1645	A291	$5 ultra & multi	2.50	.45
		Nos. 1640-1645 (6)	8.55	1.60

Hsuan Chuang — A292

Chu Hsi — A293

Design: $2.50, Hua To.

1970 Wmk. 323 Engr. *Perf. 11½*
Granite Paper

1646	A292	$1 car rose	.55	.20
1647	A293	$2.50 blue grn	.80	.25
1648	A293	$4 blue	1.40	.30
		Nos. 1646-1648 (3)	2.75	.75

Issued in memory of Hsuan Chuang (602-664), who propagated Buddhism in China; Chu Hsi (1130-1200), who developed Neo-Confucianism, and Hua To (3rd century A.D.) physician and surgeon.
Issued: $2.50, 3/17; others, 2/20.

EXPO '70 Pavilion, Emblem and Flags of Participants A294

Design: $5, Chinese pavilion, EXPO '70 emblem, exhibition and Chinese flags.

Unwmk.

1970, Mar. 13 Photo. *Perf. 13*

1649	A294	$5 org red & multi	.60	.25
1650	A294	$8 lt blue & multi	1.25	.40

EXPO '70 International Exhibition, Osaka, Japan, Mar. 15-Sept. 13.

Nimbus III and WMO Emblem A295

Design: $1, Agricultural meteorological station and tropical landscape, vert.

Perf. 14x13½, 13½x14

1970, Mar. 23 Litho. Wmk. 323
Granite Paper

1651	A295	$1 green & multi	.25	.20
1652	A295	$8 blue & multi	.85	.40

10th Annual World Meteorological Day.

Martyrs' Shrine, Taipei A296

Shrine's Gate A297

Unwmk.

1970, Mar. 29 Photo. *Perf. 13*

1653	A296	$1 multicolored	.45	.20
1654	A297	$8 multicolored	1.50	.45

Completion of the Martyrs' Shrine in Northern Taipei, dedicated to the memory of 72 young revolutionaries who died Mar. 29, 1911.

Yueh Fei Fighting for Lost Territories A298

Characters from Chinese Operas: $2.50, Emperor Shun and stepmother. $5, The Lady Warrior Chin Liang-yu. $8, Kuan Yu and groom.

1970, May 4 Unwmk. *Perf. 13½*

1655	A298	$1 multi	.80	.20
1656	A298	$2.50 multi	2.00	.30
1657	A298	$5 multi	2.75	.50
1658	A298	$8 multi	4.25	.65
		Nos. 1655-1658 (4)	9.80	1.65

— A299

Three Horses Playing — A300

Horses: #1659, Barren tree at right. #1660, Horse standing in river. #1661, Tree trunk in lower left corner. #1662, Trees in left background. #1663, shown. $8, Groom roping horses. Designs from scroll "One Hundred Horses" by Lang Shih-ning (Giuseppe Castiglione, 1688-1766).

Perf. 13½

1970, June 18 Unwmk. Photo.

1659	A299	$1 multi	.60	.20
1660	A299	$1 multi	.60	.20
1661	A299	$1 multi	.60	.20
1662	A299	$1 multi	.60	.20
1663	A299	$1 multi	.60	.20
a.		Strip of 5, #1659-1663	4.50	4.50
1664	A300	$5 bister & multi	5.75	.70
1665	A300	$8 dl yel & multi	6.75	.90
		Nos. 1659-1665 (7)	15.50	2.60

Lai-tsu Amusing his Old Parents — A301

Chinese Fairy Tales: #1667, Man disguised as deer, and hunters. #1668, Boy cooling his father's bed. #1669, Boy fishing through ice. #1670, Son reunited with old mother. #1671, Emperor tasting mother's medicine. #1672, Boy saving oranges for mother. #1673, Boy saving father from tiger.

Wmk. 323

1970, July 10 Litho. *Perf. 13½*
Granite Paper

1666	A301	10c red & multi	.20	.20
1667	A301	10c car rose & multi	.20	.20
1668	A301	10c lt vio & multi	.20	.20
1669	A301	10c gray & multi	.20	.20
1670	A301	10c emerald & multi	.20	.20
1671	A301	50c bister & multi	.20	.20
1672	A301	$1 sky blue & multi	.40	.20
1673	A301	$1 dp blue & multi	.40	.20
		Nos. 1666-1673 (8)	2.00	1.60

See Nos. 1726-1733.

Man's First Step onto Moon — A302

$1, Pres. Chiang Kai-shek's message brought to the moon. $5, Neil A. Armstrong, Michael Collins, Edwin E. Aldrin, Jr., and moon, horiz.

Perf. 13½x13, 13x13½

1970, July 21 Photo. Unwmk.

1674	A302	$1 yellow & multi	.50	.20
1675	A302	$5 lt yel grn & multi	.85	.30
1676	A302	$8 blue & multi	1.40	.55
		Nos. 1674-1676 (3)	2.75	1.05

1st anniv. of man's 1st landing on the moon.

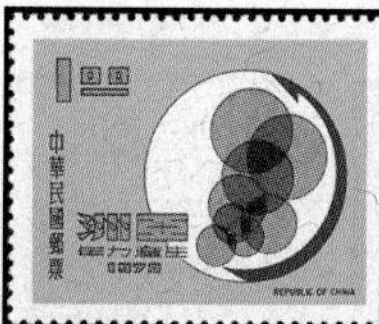

Asian Productivity Year Symbol A303

Wmk. 323

1970, Aug. 18 Litho. *Perf. 13½*
Granite Paper

1677	A303	$1 emerald & multi	.30	.20
1678	A303	$5 blue & multi	1.00	.30

Issued to publicize Asian Productivity Year.

Flags of China and UN — A304

1970, Sept. 19 Wmk. 323 *Perf. 12*
Granite Paper

1679	A304	$5 blue, car & blk	1.40	.45

25th anniversary of the United Nations.

Postal Zone Map — A305

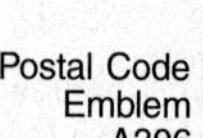

Postal Code Emblem A306

1970, Oct. 8 **Litho.**
1680 A305 $1 lt blue & multi .35 .20
1681 A306 $2.50 green & multi 1.10 .30

Issued to publicize the postal code system.

Eleventh Month Scroll — A307

Designs: A scroll series, "Activities of the 12 Months," painted on silk by a group of painters of the Ch'ien Lung court (1736-1796). Chinese number in parenthesis at right of denomination tells month.

Jan., Feb., Mar.

(一) (二) (三)

Perf. 13½x13
1970-71 **Photo.** **Unwmk.**
1682 A307 $1 multi 1.60 .30
1683 A307 $2.50 multi 3.50 .70
1684 A307 $5 multi 5.25 .80

Apr., May, June

(四) (五) (六)

1685 A307 $1 multi 1.60 .30
1686 A307 $2.50 multi 3.50 .70
1687 A307 $5 multi 5.25 .80

July, Aug., Sept.

(七) (八) (九)

1688 A307 $1 multi 1.60 .30
1689 A307 $2.50 multi 3.50 .70
1690 A307 $5 multi 5.25 .80

Oct., Nov., Dec.

(十) (一十) (二十)

1691 A307 $1 multi 2.40 .45
1692 A307 $2.50 multi 5.25 1.00
1693 A307 $5 multi 9.25 1.25
Nos. 1682-1693 (12) 47.95 8.10

Issued: 31691-1693, 10/21/70; #1682-1684, 1/14/71; #1685-1687, 4/26/71; #1688-1690, 8/27/71.

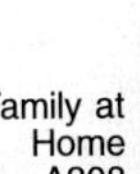

Family at Home A308

Piggy Bank — A309

$4, Family of 5 going on an excursion, vert.

Perf. 13½x14, 14x13½
1970, Nov. 11 **Litho.** **Wmk. 323**
Granite Paper
1694 A308 $1 multicolored .40 .20
1695 A308 $4 yel grn & multi 1.40 .35

Issued to publicize family planning.

1970, Dec. 1 *Perf. 12½x12*
Granite Paper
1696 A309 50c multi 1.00 .25
1697 A309 $4.50 blue & multi 4.00 .60

Issued for use on New Year's greetings.

Tibia Fusus Shells A310

Rare Taiwan Shells: $2.50, Harpeola kurodai. $5, Conus stupa kuroda. $8, Entemnotrochus rumphii.

1971, Feb. 25 *Perf. 13x13½*
1698 A310 $1 vio & multi .25 .20
1699 A310 $2.50 multi 1.00 .25
1700 A310 $5 org & multi 1.25 .45
1701 A310 $8 grn & multi 1.75 .65
Nos. 1698-1701 (4) 4.25 1.55

Sun Yat-sen Building, Yangmingshan A311

Passbook and Postal Savings Certificate A312

Perf. 13½x12½
1971 **Litho.** **Wmk. 323**
Granite Paper
1702 A311 5c brown .25 .20
1703 A311 10c dk gray .25 .20
1704 A311 50c brt rose lilac .70 .20
1705 A311 $1 vermilion .75 .20
1706 A311 $1.50 ultra .80 .25
1707 A311 $2 plum .90 .20
1708 A311 $2.50 emerald 1.00 .20
1709 A311 $3 aqua 1.40 .30
Nos. 1702-1709 (8) 6.05 1.75

Perf. 13½x14
1971, Mar. 20 **Litho.** **Wmk. 323**

$4, People and hand dropping coin into bank.

1712 A312 $1 yel grn & multi .35 .20
1713 A312 $4 ver & multi 1.40 .30

Publicizing Chinese Postal Savings Service.

Cooperation Emblem, Farmers — A313

Rock Monkey — A314

Design: $8, Chinese teaching rice farming to Africans, horiz.

Unwmk.
1971, May 20 **Photo.** *Perf. 13*
1714 A313 $1 multicolored .20 .20
1715 A313 $8 multicolored 1.25 .45

Sino-African Technical Cooperation Committee, 10th anniversary.

1971, June 25 *Perf. 11½*

Taiwan Animals: $2, White-face flying squirrel. $3, Chinese pangolin. $5, Formosan sika deer. $2, $3, $5 are horiz.

1716 A314 $1 gold & multi .35 .20
1717 A314 $2 gold & multi 1.00 .20
1718 A314 $3 gold & multi 1.40 .30
1719 A314 $5 gold & multi 1.60 .50
Nos. 1716-1719 (4) 4.35 1.20

Pitcher — A315

Designs: $2.50, Players at base, horiz. $4, Batter and catcher.

1971, July 29 **Photo.** *Perf. 13*
1720 A315 $1 multi .20 .20
1721 A315 $2.50 multi .40 .20
1722 A315 $4 multi .70 .25
Nos. 1720-1722 (3) 1.30 .65

Pacific Regional competition for the 1971 Little League World Series.

Nos. 1541, 1544-1545 Overprinted in Magenta or Red

Perf. 13x12½
1971, Sept. 9 **Litho.** **Wmk. 323**
Granite Paper
1723 A259 $1 vermilion (M) .20 .20
1724 A259 $2.50 blue (R) .40 .20
1725 A259 $3 grnsh blue (R) .40 .25
Nos. 1723-1725 (3) 1.00 .65

Chinese victory in 1971 Little League World Series, Williamsport, Pa., Aug. 24.

Fairy Tale Type of 1970

Chinese Fairy Tales (Filial Piety): No. 1726, Birds and elephant helping in rice field. No. 1727, Son gathering mulberries for mother. No. 1728, Son gathering firewood. No. 1729, Son, mother and bandits. No. 1730, Son carrying heavy burden. 50c, Son digging for bamboo shoots in winter. No. 1732, Man and wife working as slaves. No. 1733, Father, son and carriage.

1971, Sept. 22 *Perf. 13½*
Granite Paper
1726 A301 10c dp org & multi .20 .20
1727 A301 10c lilac & multi .20 .20
1728 A301 10c ocher & multi .20 .20
1729 A301 10c dp car & multi .20 .20
1730 A301 10c lt ultra & multi .20 .20
1731 A301 50c multicolored .25 .20
1732 A301 $1 emerald & multi .50 .20
1733 A301 $1 lt red brn & multi .50 .20
Nos. 1726-1733 (8) 2.25 1.60

Flag of China, "Double Ten" and Anniversary Emblems A316

Designs (Flag of China and): $2.50, National anthem. $5, Gen. Chiang Kai-shek. $8, Sun Yat-sen.

1971, Oct. 10 **Photo.** *Perf. 13*
1734 A316 $1 orange & multi .30 .20
1735 A316 $2.50 multi .75 .20
1736 A316 $5 green & multi .90 .30
1737 A316 $8 olive & multi .95 .35
Nos. 1734-1737 (4) 2.90 1.05

60th National Day.

Bird in Flight (AOPU Emblem) A317

Perf. 13½x14
1971, Nov. 8 **Litho.** **Wmk. 323**
1738 A317 $2.50 yellow & multi .35 .20
1739 A317 $5 orange & multi .80 .20

Asian-Oceanic Postal Union Executive Committee Session, Taipei, Nov. 8-15.

"White Frost Hawk," by Lang Shih-ning A318

Dog Series I

Designs: $2, "Star-Glancing Wolf." $2.50, "Golden-Winged Face." $5, "Young Black Dragon." $8, "Young Gray Dragon."

Designs from painting series "Ten Prized Dogs," by Lang Shih-ning (Giuseppe Castiglione, 1688-1766).

Perf. 13½x13
1971, Nov. 16 **Litho.** **Unwmk.**
1740 A318 $1 Facing left .40 .20
1741 A318 $2 Lying down .70 .20
1742 A318 $2.50 Scratching 1.00 .30
1743 A318 $5 Facing right 2.50 .50
1744 A318 $8 Looking back 3.50 1.00
Nos. 1740-1744 (5) 8.10 2.20

Dog Series II

Designs: $1, "Black with Snow-white Paws." $2, "Yellow Leopard." $2.50, "Flying Magpie." $5, "Heavenly Lion." $8, "Mottled Tiger."

1972, Jan. 12
1745 A318 $1 Facing right 1.10 .20
1746 A318 $2 Walking 2.10 .20
1747 A318 $2.50 Sleeping 2.75 .30
1748 A318 $5 Facing left 7.50 .50
1749 A318 $8 Sitting 10.00 1.00
Nos. 1745-1749 (5) 23.45 2.20

Squirrels — A319

Perf. 13½x12½
1971, Dec. 1 **Wmk. 323**
1750 A319 Block of 4 4.00 3.50
a. 50c in UL corner .70 .25
b. 50c in UR corner .70 .25
c. 50c in LL corner .70 .25
d. 50c in LR corner .70 .25
1751 A319 Block of 4 17.00 5.00
a. $4.50 in UL corner 4.00 .60
b. $4.50 in UR corner 4.00 .60
c. $4.50 in LL corner 4.00 .60
d. $4.50 in LR corner 4.00 .60

New Year 1972.

Flags of China and Jordan A320

1971, Dec. 16 ***Perf. 13½***

Granite Paper

1752 A320 $5 multicolored 1.25 .25

50th anniversary of the founding of the Hashemite Kingdom of Jordan.

Cargo Ship "Hai King" — A321

$7, Ocean liner & map of Pacific Ocean, vert.

1971, Dec. 16 ***Perf. 12½***

1753 A321 $4 grn, dk bl & red .50 .25
1754 A321 $7 ocher & multi .85 .40

China Merchants Steam Navigation Co., cent.

Downhill Skiing, Olympic Rings A322

$5, Cross-country skiing. $8, Giant slalom.

1972, Feb. 3 ***Perf. 13½***

1755 A322 $1 org, blk & bl .20 .20
1756 A322 $5 yel grn, dp org & blk .40 .20
1757 A322 $8 red, gray & blk .75 .25
Nos. 1755-1757 (3) 1.35 .65

11th Winter Olympic Games, Sapporo, Japan, Feb. 3-13.

Vase, 18th Century — A323

Porcelain Series I

Porcelain Masterworks of Ching Dynasty: $2, Covered jar. $2.50, Pitcher. $5, Vase with 5 openings and dragon design. $8, Covered jar with children design.

Perf. 11½

1972, Mar. 20 **Photo.** **Unwmk.**

1758 A323 $1 violet & multi .50 .20
1759 A323 $2 plum & blue 1.00 .20
1760 A323 $2.50 org ver & bl 1.40 .25
1761 A323 $5 bis brn & bl 1.60 .45
1762 A323 $8 sl grn & multi 2.50 .45
Nos. 1758-1762 (5) 7.00 1.55

See Nos. 1812-1821, 1864-1868.

Nine Flying Doves A324

Perf. 13½x14

1972, Apr. 1 **Litho.** **Wmk. 323**

1763 A324 $1 lt blue & blk .35 .20
1764 A324 $5 lt violet & blk 1.00 .30

Asian-Oceanic Postal Union, 10th anniv.

"Dignity with Self-reliance" — A325

Perf. 13½x12½

1972-75 **Litho.** **Wmk. 323**

1765 A325 5c brown & yel .20 .20
1766 A325 10c blue & org .20 .20
1767 A325 20c cl & yel grn ('75) .20 .20
1768 A325 50c lil & lil rose .20 .20
1769 A325 $1 red & brt bl .30 .20
1770 A325 $1.50 yel & dk bl .40 .20
1771 A325 $2 maroon & org .60 .20
1772 A325 $2.50 emer & ver .40 .20
1773 A325 $3 red & lt grn .75 .20
Nos. 1765-1773 (9) 3.25 1.80

Souvenir Sheet

Imperf

1775 A325 Sheet of 2 5.00 2.25

No. 1775 commemorates ROCPEX '72 Philatelic Exhibition, Taipei, Oct. 24-Nov. 2. It contains 2 stamps similar to Nos. 1771 and 1773 with simulated perforations.

Issued: $1, $1.50, $2, $3, 5/20/72; 5c, 10c, 50c, $2.50, #1775, 10/24/72; 20c, 1975.

For overprints see Nos. 1787-1790.

Emperor Shih-tsung's Procession — A326

Messengers on Horseback — A327

Designs from scrolls depicting Emperor Shih-tsung's (reigned 1522-1566) journey to and from tombs at Cheng-tien. No. 1776 shows land journey departure and is designed from right to left. No. 1779 shows return trip by boat and is designed from left to right. The 5 stamps of Nos. 1776 and 1780 are numbered 1 to 5 in Chinese (see illustrations with Nos. 1682-1686 for numerals).

1972 **Photo.** **Unwmk.** ***Perf. 13½***

1776 Strip of 5 3.25 3.00
a. A326 $1 shown (1) .50 .20
b. A326 $1 Seven carriages (2) .50 .20
c. A326 $1 Carriage drawn by 23 horses (3) .50 .20
d. A326 $1 Procession (4) .50 .20
e. A326 $1 Emperor under 2 canopies (5) .50 .20
1777 A327 $2.50 shown 1.90 .20
1778 A327 $5 Guards with flags, fans & spears 2.75 .20
1779 A327 $8 Sedan chair carried by 28 men 5.50 .40
1780 Strip of 5 3.25 3.00
a. A326 $1 Three barges (1) .50 .20
b. A326 $1 Procession, sedan chairs (2) .50 .20
c. A326 $1 Two barges with trunks (3) .50 .20
d. A326 $1 Procession on land (4) .50 .20
e. A326 $1 Procession, 2 sedan chairs (5) .50 .20
1781 A327 $2.50 Courtiers at city welcoming Emperor 1.90 .20
1782 A327 $5 Orchestra on horseback 2.75 .20
1783 A327 $8 Barges 2.75 .40
Nos. 1776-1783 (8) 24.05 7.60

Issue dates: No. 1776-1779, June 14; Nos. 1780-1783, July 12.

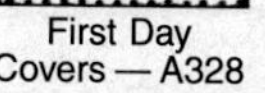

First Day Covers — A328

Magnifying Glass, Tongs, Gauge — A329

Design: $2.50, Sun Yat-sen stamp of 1971 (type A311) under magnifying glass.

Wmk. 323

1972, Aug. 9 **Engr.** ***Perf. 12***

1784 A328 $1 dk vio blue .20 .20
1785 A328 $2.50 brt green .25 .20
1786 A329 $8 scarlet .55 .25
Nos. 1784-1786 (3) 1.00 .65

Promotion of philately. Printed in sheets of 40. Each sheet contains 4 blocks of 10 stamps surrounded by margins with inscriptions.

Nos. 1768-1770, 1772 Overprinted in Dark Blue or Red

Perf. 13½x12½

1972, Sept. 9 **Litho.** **Wmk. 323**

1787 A325 $1 red & brt bl (DB) .20 .20
1788 A325 $1.50 yel & dk bl (R) .25 .20
1789 A325 $2 mar & org (R) .40 .20
1790 A325 $3 red & lt grn (DB) .45 .20
Nos. 1787-1790 (4) 1.30 .80

China's championship victories in the Little League World Series, Gary, Ind., and in the Senior League World Series, Williamsport, Pa., Aug. 1972.

Emperor Yao (2357-2258 B.C.) — A330

Mountain Climbing — A331

Rulers: $4, Emperor Shun (ruled 2255-2208 B.C.). $4.50, Yu, the Great (ruled 2205-2198 B.C.). $5, King T'ang (ruled 1783-1754 B.C.). $5.50, King Wen (ruled 1171-1122 B.C.). $6, King Wu (ruled 1121-1114 B.C.). $7, Chou Kung (died 1105 B.C.). $8, Confucius (551-479 B.C.).

1972-73 **Engr.** ***Perf. 12***

Granite Paper

1791 A330 $3.50 dk blue .40 .20
1792 A330 $4 rose red .60 .20
1793 A330 $4.50 bluish lil .80 .20
1794 A330 $5 brt green .40 .20
1795 A330 $5.50 dp org ('73) 1.25 .25
1796 A330 $6 dp claret ('73) 1.10 .20
a. Perf. 13½x12½ ('76) 1.10 .30
1797 A330 $7 sepia ('73) 1.10 .20
a. Perf. 13½x12½ ('76) 1.10 .30
1798 A330 $8 indigo ('73) 1.25 .20
a. gray, perf. 13½x12½ ('76) 1.75 .35
Nos. 1791-1798 (8) 6.90 1.65

In the first printing, Nos. 1791-1794, 1796-1798 measure 32mm high. In a 1974 reissue they are 33mm.

Unwmk.

1972, Oct. 31 **Photo.** ***Perf. 12***

Designs (China Youth Corps emblem and): $2.50, Skiing (skiers forming circle). $4, Diving. $8, Parachute jumping.

1800 A331 $1 green & multi .20 .20
1801 A331 $2.50 blue & multi .40 .20
1802 A331 $4 orange & multi .60 .20
1803 A331 $8 multicolored 1.00 .25
Nos. 1800-1803 (4) 2.20 .85

China Youth Corps, 20th anniversary.

JCI Emblem A332

1972, Nov. 12 **Litho.** **Wmk. 323**

1804 A332 $1 multicolored .20 .20
1805 A332 $5 orange & multi .35 .20
1806 A332 $8 multicolored .65 .40
Nos. 1804-1806 (3) 1.20 .80

27th Junior Chamber International (JCI) World Congress, Taipei, Nov. 12-19.

Electronic Mail Sorter — A333

Plane, Ship and Pier — A334

Progress of Communications System on Taiwan: $5, Highway overpass over railroad.

Wmk. 323

1972, Nov. 12 **Engr.** ***Perf. 11½***

1807 A333 $1 red .20 .20
1808 A334 $2.50 blue .50 .20
1809 A334 $5 dk violet brn .55 .35
Nos. 1807-1809 (3) 1.25 .75

Cow and Calf (Parental Love) — A335

1972, Dec. 1 **Litho.** ***Perf. 12***

1810 A335 50c red & blk .75 .30
1811 A335 $4.50 yel, red & brn 4.25 .90

New Year 1973. Printed in sheets of 80, divided into 4 panes of 20, separated by vertical and horizontal gutters 2 rows wide. 20 red chops meaning "Happy New Year" are printed in the gutters.

Porcelain Type of 1972 and

Stem Bowl with Dragons A336

Porcelain Series II

Porcelain Masterworks of Ming Dynasty: $1, Covered vase with fruits and flowers. $2, Vase with ornamental and floral design. $2.50, Vase imitating ancient bronze. $5, Flask with flowers of 4 seasons. $8, Garlic head vase.

1973 **Photo.** ***Perf. 11½***

1812 A323 $1 gray & multi .70 .20
1813 A323 $2 lt brn & multi 1.00 .20
1814 A323 $2.50 brt grn & multi 1.40 .20
1815 A323 $5 ultra & multi 1.50 .35
1816 A323 $8 olive & multi 2.25 .60
Nos. 1812-1816 (5) 6.85 1.55

Porcelain Series III

Ming Porcelain: $2, Refuse container with dragons. $2.50, Covered jar with lotus. $5, Covered jar with horses. $8, Bowl with figures of immortals.

1817 A336 $1 gray & multi .70 .20
1818 A336 $2 lt vio & multi 1.00 .20
1819 A336 $2.50 dk red & multi 1.40 .20
1820 A336 $5 blue & multi 1.50 .35
1821 A336 $8 dp org & multi 2.25 .60
Nos. 1817-1821 (5) 6.85 1.55

Issued: #1812-1816, 1/10; #1817-1821, 3/24.

See Nos. 1864-1868.

Oyster Fairy and Fisherman's Dance — A337

1973, Feb. 7 Photo. *Perf. 11½*
Granite Paper

1822	A337	$1 Kicking shuttlecock, vert.	.50	.20
1823	A337	$4 Shown	.80	.20
1824	A337	$5 Rowing boat over land	.90	.25
1825	A337	$8 Old man carrying young lady, vert.	1.00	.40
		Nos. 1822-1825 (4)	3.20	1.05

Chinese folklore popular entertainment.

Bamboo Boat A338

Taiwanese Handicrafts: $2.50, Painted marble vase, vert. $5, Painted glass plate. $8, Doll, bridegroom carrying bride on back, vert.

Perf. 13½x14½, 14½x13½
1973, Mar. 9 Photo.

1826	A338	$1 multi	.20	.20
1827	A338	$2.50 multi	.60	.20
1828	A338	$5 multi	.85	.25
1829	A338	$8 multi	1.25	.40
		Nos. 1826-1829 (4)	2.90	1.05

Federation Emblem, Cargo Hook, Crane — A339

Emblem, Tractor, New Buildings A340

Wmk. 323
1973, Apr. 2 Litho. *Perf. 12½*

1830	A339	$1 salmon & multi	.20	.20
1831	A340	$5 blue & blk	.70	.25

12th convention of International Federation of Asian and Western Pacific Contractors Association, Taipei, Apr. 2-10.

Pres. Chiang Kai-shek, Flag of China — A341

Lin Tse-hsü — A342

Design: $4, like $1 with different border.

Unwmk.
1973, May 20 Photo. *Perf. 12*

1832	A341	$1 yellow & multi	.30	.25
1833	A341	$4 dk grn & multi	1.10	.50

First anniversary of Pres. Chiang Kai-shek's inauguration for a fifth term.

Wmk. 323
1973, June 3 Engr. *Perf. 12*

1834	A342	$1 sepia	.50	.20

Lin Tse-hsü (1785-1850), Governor of Hunan and Kwantung, who destroyed large quantity of opium at Humen, Kwantung, June 3, 1839.

Willows and Palace Gate in the Morning — A343

Lady Watering Peonies, Stone Ornament A344

Design from scroll "Spring Morning in the Han Palace," by Chiu Ying. The five stamps of No. 1835 are numbered 1 to 5 and the five stamps of No. 1838 are numbered 6-10 in Chinese (see illustrations with Nos. 1682-1691 for numerals). The stamps are numbered and listed from right to left.

1973 Photo. Unwmk. *Perf. 11½*
Granite Paper

1835		Strip of 5	3.00	3.00
a.		A343 $1 shown (1)	.40	.20
b.		A343 $1 Ladies feeding peacocks (2)	.40	.20
c.		A343 $1 Lady watering peonies (3)	.40	.20
d.		A343 $1 Pear tree in bloom (4)	.40	.20
e.		A343 $1 Lady musicians (5)	.40	.20
1836	A344	$5 shown	2.25	.60
1837	A344	$8 Lady musicians	3.50	1.00
1838		Strip of 5	3.00	3.00
a.		A343 $1 Ladies playing go (6)	.40	.20
b.		A343 $1 Various games (7)	.40	.20
c.		A343 $1 Talking and playing music (8)	.40	.20
d.		A343 $1 Artist painting portrait (9)	.40	.20
e.		A343 $1 Sentries guarding wall (10)	.40	.20
1839	A344	$5 Ladies playing go	2.25	.60
1840	A344	$8 Girl chasing butterfly	3.50	1.00
		Nos. 1835-1840 (6)	17.50	9.20

Issued: #1835-1837, 6/20; #1838-1840, 7/18.

Fan, Bamboo Design, by Hsiang Tehsin — A345

Designs: Painted fans, Ming dynasty.

Perf. 12½x13
1973, Aug. 15 Photo. Wmk. 368

1841	A345	$1 bister & multi	.35	.20
1842	A345	$2.50 bister & multi	.70	.25
1843	A345	$5 bister & multi	1.25	.35
1844	A345	$8 bister & multi	1.90	.50
		Nos. 1841-1844 (4)	4.20	1.30

See Nos. 1934-1937.

Little League Emblem — A346

INTERPOL Emblem — A347

Wmk. 370
1973, Sept. 9 Litho. *Perf. 13½*

1845	A346	$1 yel, car & dk bl	.40	.20
1846	A346	$4 yel, grn & dk bl	1.40	.35

Chinese victory in Little League Twin Championships, Gary, Ind., and Williamsport, Pa.

Wmk. 370
1973, Sept. 11 Litho. *Perf. 12*

1847	A347	$1 blue & org	.20	.20
1848	A347	$5 green & org	.50	.25
1849	A347	$8 magenta & org	.75	.40
		Nos. 1847-1849 (3)	1.45	.85

Intl. Criminal Police Organization, 50th anniv.

Ch'iu Feng-chia — A348

Wmk. 323
1973, Oct. 5 Engr. *Perf. 11½*

1850	A348	$1 violet black	.70	.25

2nd meeting of overseas Hakkas, Taipei, Oct. 5-7, and to honor Ch'iu Feng-chia (1864-1912), Hakka scholar, poet and revolutionist.

Tsengwen Reservoir A349

Tsengwen Dam — A350

Perf. 13½
1973, Oct. 31 Photo. Unwmk.

1851		Strip of 3	.90	.70
a.		A349 $1 Upper shore	.25	.20
b.		A349 $1 shown	.25	.20
c.		A349 $1 Lower shore	.25	.20

Perf. 12x11½

1852	A350	$5 shown	.65	.30
1853	A350	$8 Spillway	1.00	.60
		Nos. 1851-1853 (3)	2.55	1.60

Inauguration of Tsengwen Reservoir. No. 1851 printed in sheets of 15.

Tiger — A351

Wmk. 370
1973, Dec. 1 Litho. *Perf. 12½*

1854	A351	50c multi	.60	.20
1855	A351	$4.50 multi	1.75	.50

New Year 1974.

"Snow-dotted Eagle," by Lang Shih-ning — A352

#1857, "Comfortable Ride." #1858, "Red Flower Eagle." #1859, "Cloud-running Steed." #1860, "Sky-running steed." $2.50, "Red Jade Seat." $5, "Thunderclap Steed." $8, "Arabian Champion." Designs from painting series "Ten Prized Horses," by Lang Shih-ning (Giuseppe Castiglione, 1688-1766).

1973 Litho. Unwmk. *Perf. 13*

1856	A352	50c shown	.75	.20
1857	A352	$1 Pinto, blk tail	1.00	.20
1858	A352	$1 Facing left	1.00	.20
1859	A352	$1 Facing right	1.00	.20
1860	A352	$1 Pinto, white tail	1.00	.20
a.		Block of 4, #1857-1860	4.50	3.50
1861	A352	$2.50 Palomino	2.25	.40
1862	A352	$5 Grazing	3.75	.75
a.		Souvenir sheet of 4	29.00	11.00
1863	A352	$8 Brown stallion	6.00	.90
		Nos. 1856-1863 (8)	16.75	3.05

#1862a contains 4 stamps with simulated perforations similar to #1856-1857, 1861-1862.

Issued: 50c, $2.50, $5, 11/21; others 12/21.

Porcelain Types of 1972-73
Porcelain Series IV

Porcelain Masterworks of Sung Dynasty: $1, Vase. $2, Three-tiered vase. $2.50, Lotus-shaped bowl. $5, Incense burner. $8, Incense burner on stand.

1974, Jan. 16 Photo. *Perf. 11½*

1864	A323	$1 ultra & multi	.40	.20
1865	A336	$2 multicolored	.80	.20
1866	A336	$2.50 red & multi	1.00	.20
1867	A336	$5 lilac & multi	1.10	.25
1868	A336	$8 green & multi	1.10	.50
		Nos. 1864-1868 (5)	4.40	1.35

Juggler — A353

Taroko Gorge, Hualien — A354

Design: $8, Magician producing dishes from his robe, horiz.

1974, Feb. 6 Photo. *Perf. 11½*

1869	A353	$1 yellow & multi	.20	.20
1870	A353	$8 yellow & multi	1.25	.20

1974, Mar. 22 Photo. *Perf. 12*

Designs: $2.50, Luce Chapel, Tunghai University. $5, Tzu En Pagoda, Sun Moon Lake. $8, Goddess of Mercy, Keelung.

1871	A354	$1 multi	.30	.20
1872	A354	$2.50 multi	.70	.20
1873	A354	$5 multi	.90	.20
1874	A354	$8 multi	1.25	.25
		Nos. 1871-1874 (4)	3.15	.85

Taiwan landmarks.

Fighting Cocks (Brass) A355

Designs: $2.50, Grapes and bowl with fruit (imitation jade). $5, Fisherman (wood carving), vert. $8, Basket with plastic roses, vert.

Perf. 13½x14½, 14½x13½

1974, Apr. 10

1875 A355 $1 bl grn & multi .20 .20
1876 A355 $2.50 brown & multi .50 .20
1877 A355 $5 crimson & multi .70 .25
1878 A355 $8 multicolored 1.50 .40
Nos. 1875-1878 (4) 2.90 1.05

Taiwanese handicraft products.

Sun Yat-sen Memorial Hall — A356

Taiwan landmarks: $2.50, Reaching-moon Tower, Cheng Ching Lake. $5, Orchid Island (boats). $8, Penghu Interisland Bridge.

1974, May 15 Photo. *Perf. 11½*

Granite Paper

1879 A356 $1 blue & multi .30 .20
1880 A356 $2.50 blue & multi .70 .20
1881 A356 $5 blue & multi .90 .20
1882 A356 $8 blue & multi 1.25 .25
Nos. 1879-1882 (4) 3.15 .85

Pres. Chiang and Gate of Whampoa Military Academy A357

Marching Cadets and Entrance Gate — A358

Wmk. 323

1974, June 16 Engr. *Perf. 11½*

1883 A357 $1 carmine rose .20 .20
1884 A358 $14 violet blue .70 .40

50th anniversary of the founding of the Whampoa Military Academy.

Long-distance Runner and Olympic Rings — A359

The Boy Wang Ch'i Fighting Invaders — A360

$8, Women's relay race, Olympic rings.

1974, June 23 Litho. *Perf. 12½*

1885 A359 $1 blue, blk & red .20 .20
1886 A359 $8 pink, blk & red .80 .40

80th anniv. of Intl. Olympic Committee.

1974, July 15 Wmk. 370 *Perf. 13½*

Folk Tales: No. 1888, T'i Ying pleading for her father before the Emperor. No. 1889, Wen Yen-po flushing out ball caught in tree. No. 1890, Boy Wang Hua returning gold piece he found. No. 1891, Pu Shih, a rich sheep raiser and benefactor. No. 1892, K'ung Yung as a child choosing smallest pear. No. 1893, Tung Yu studying. No. 1894, Szu Ma-kuang saving playmate from drowning in water jar.

1887 A360 50c olive & multi .20 .20
1888 A360 50c ultra & multi .20 .20
1889 A360 50c ocher & multi .20 .20
1890 A360 50c red brn & multi .20 .20
a. Block of 4, #1887-1890 .60 .60
1891 A360 $1 green & multi .40 .40
1892 A360 $1 lilac & multi .40 .40
1893 A360 $1 blue & multi .40 .40
1894 A360 $1 car & multi .40 .40
a. Block of 4, #1891-1894 1.60 1.60
Nos. 1887-1894 (8) 2.40 2.40

For similar designs see A380, A427, A456, A495.

Myrtle, by Wei Sheng — A361

Silk Fan Paintings, Sung Dynasty (960-1279 A.D.): $2.50, Cabbage and Insects, by Hsu Ti. $5, Hibiscus, Cat and Dog, by Li Ti. $8, Pomegranate and Birds, by Wu Ping. Fans from National Palace Museum.

Perf. 13x12½

1974, Aug. 14 Photo. Wmk. 368

1895 A361 $1 multi .20 .20
1896 A361 $2.50 multi .60 .20
1897 A361 $5 multi 1.00 .20
1898 A361 $8 multi 1.40 .50
Nos. 1895-1898 (4) 3.20 1.10

See Nos. 1950-1953.

Battle at Marco Polo Bridge, July 7, 1937 A362

Wmk. 370

1974, Sept. 3 Litho. *Perf. 13½*

1899 A362 $1 multicolored .25 .20

Souvenir Sheet

Wmk. 323

Without Gum; Granite Paper

1900 Sheet of 8 6.25 5.00
a. A362 $1, single stamp .55 .50

20th Armed Forces Day. No. 1900 commemorates Armed Forces Stamp Exhibition, Sun Yat-sen Memorial Hall, Sept. 3-9.

Chrysanthemum A363

Designs: Various chrysanthemums.

Unwmk.

1974, Sept. 30 Photo. *Perf. 12*

Granite Paper

1901 A363 $1 lilac & multi .20 .20
1902 A363 $2.50 multi .50 .20
1903 A363 $5 orange & multi .70 .25
1904 A363 $8 multi 1.25 .35
Nos. 1901-1904 (4) 2.65 1.00

Rep. of China Pavilion, EXPO Emblem A364

Map of Fair Grounds, Chinese Flag A364a

Wmk. 370

1974, Oct. 10 Litho. *Perf. 13*

1905 A364 $1 multi .20 .20
1906 A364a $8 multi .70 .40

EXPO '74, Spokane, Wash., May 4-Nov. 4. Theme, "Preserve the Environment."

Steel Mill, Kaohsiung A365

Taichung Harbor A366

Designs: $1, Taiwan North Link Railroad and map. $2, Oil refinery. $2.50, Electric train. $3.50, Taoyuan International Airport. $4, Taiwan North-South Highway and map. $4.50, Kaohsiung shipyard. $5, Su-ao Port.

Perf. 13x12½, 12½x13

1974, Oct. 31 Wmk. 323

1907 A365 50c lilac, yel & brn .20 .20
1908 A365 $1 green & org .20 .20
1909 A365 $2 blue & yel .20 .20
1910 A365 $2.50 emer & org .20 .20
1911 A366 $3 ocher & ultra .20 .20
1912 A366 $3.50 sl grn & yel .20 .20
1913 A366 $4 brown & yel .20 .20
1914 A366 $4.50 ver & bl .35 .20
1915 A366 $5 sepia & dk bl .35 .20
Nos. 1907-1915 (9) 2.10 1.80

Major construction projects.

See Nos. 2009-2017, 2068-2076. For overprints see Nos. 2064-2065, 2112-2113.

Agaricus Bisporus A367

Edible Mushrooms: $2.50, Pleurotus ostreatus. $5, Dictyophora indusiata. $8, Flammulina velutipes.

Perf. 11½

1974, Nov. 15 Unwmk. Photo.

1916 A367 $1 multi .20 .20
1917 A367 $2.50 multi .20 .20
1918 A367 $5 multi 1.00 .20
1919 A367 $8 multi 1.25 .30
Nos. 1916-1919 (4) 2.65 .90

9th Intl. Scientific Congress on the Cultivation of Edible Fungi, Taipei, Nov. 1974.

Batters and World Map — A368

Pitcher and Championship Banners — A369

Wmk. 323

1974, Nov. 24 Litho. *Perf. 13½*

1920 A368 $1 multicolored .20 .20
1921 A369 $8 multicolored .65 .35

China's victory in 1974 Little League Baseball World Series Triple Championships.

Rabbit — A370

Acrobat with Iron Rod — A371

Wmk. 323

1974, Dec. 10 Photo. *Perf. 12½*

1922 A370 50c orange & multi .30 .20
1923 A370 $4.50 brown & multi 1.60 .30

New Year 1975.

1975, Jan. 15 Unwmk. *Perf. 11½*

$5, Two acrobats spinning tops, horiz.

Granite Paper

1924 A371 $4 yellow & multi .60 .40
1925 A371 $5 yellow & multi 1.00 .45

Children Watching Puppet Show — A372

Ceremonial New Year Greetings — A373

Designs from scroll "Festivals for the New Year," by Ting Kuan-p'eng. Nos. 1926a-1926e are numbered 1-5 in Chinese.

1975, Feb. 25 Photo. *Perf. 11½*

Granite Paper

1926 Strip of 5 3.00 2.50
a. A372 $1 Ceremonial New Year Greetings (1) .45 .20
b. A372 $1 Man with trained monkey (2) .45 .20
c. A372 $1 Crowd and musicians (3) .45 .20
d. A372 $1 Picnic under a tree (4) .45 .20
e. A372 $1 shown (5) .45 .20
1927 A373 $2.50 shown 2.00 .30
1928 A373 $5 Children buying firecrackers 2.50 .55
1929 A373 $8 Children and man with trained monkey 4.25 .90
Nos. 1926-1929 (4) 11.75 4.25

Sun Yat-sen Memorial Hall, Taipei A374

Sun Yat-sen's Handwriting — A375

Sun Yat-sen, Bronze Statue in Memorial Hall — A376

Sun Yat-sen Memorial Hall, St. John's University, NY A377

Perf. 13½x14, 14x13½

1975, Mar. 12 Litho.

1930	A374	$1 green & multi	.20	.20
1931	A375	$4 yel grn & multi	.40	.20
1932	A376	$5 yellow & multi	.60	.20
1933	A377	$8 gray & multi	.80	.30
		Nos. 1930-1933 (4)	2.00	.90

Dr. Sun Yat-sen (1866-1925), statesman and revolutionary leader.

Fan Type of 1973 Inscribed "Landscape" (1st Character, 2nd Row)

水山

Painted fans, Ming Dynasty. Second row of inscription gives design description.

Perf. 12½x13

1975, Apr. 16 Photo. Wmk. 368

1934	A345	$1 bister & multi	.20	.20
1935	A345	$2.50 bister & multi	.60	.20
1936	A345	$5 bister & multi	1.25	.35
1937	A345	$8 bister & multi	1.40	.55
		Nos. 1934-1937 (4)	3.45	1.30

Yuan-chin coin, 1122-221 B.C. — A378

Ancient Chinese Coins: $4, Pan-liang, 221-207 B.C. $5, Five chu, 206 B.C.-220 A.D. $8, Five chu, 502-557 A.D.

Wmk. 323

1975, May 20 Litho. *Perf. 13*

1938	A378	$1 salmon & multi	.20	.20
1939	A378	$4 yellow & multi	.70	.20
1940	A378	$5 dl yel & multi	.80	.20
1941	A378	$8 lt vio & multi	1.25	.25
		Nos. 1938-1941 (4)	2.95	.85

The Cloth-bag Monk, by Chang Hung (1577-1668) A379

Chinese Paintings: $4, Lao-tzu Riding Buffalo, by Chao Pu-chih (1053-1110). $5, Portrait of Shih-te, by Wang Wen (1497-1576). $8, Splashed-ink Immortal, by Liang K'ai (early 13th century).

Perf. 11½

1975, June 18 Photo. Unwmk.

Granite Paper

1942	A379	$2 blk, buff & ver	.50	.20
1943	A379	$4 blk, gray & red	1.10	.20
1944	A379	$5 blk, yel & ver	2.10	.30
1945	A379	$8 tan, red & blk	2.75	.50
		Nos. 1942-1945 (4)	6.45	1.20

Chu Yin Reading by the Light of Fireflies — A380

Folk Tales: No. 1947, Hua Mu-lan going to war for her father. No. 1948, King Kou Chien tasting gall. $5, Chou Ch'u killing tiger.

Perf. 14x13½

1975, July 16 Litho. Wmk. 368

1946	A380	$1 olive & multi	.20	.20
1947	A380	$2 bis brn & multi	.25	.20
1948	A380	$2 lt grn & multi	.25	.20
1949	A380	$5 blue & multi	.60	.30
		Nos. 1946-1949 (4)	1.30	.90

See Nos. 2108-2111.

Cherry-Apple Blossoms, by Lin Ch'un — A381

Silk Fan Paintings, Sung Dynasty: $2, Spring Blossoms and Butterfly, by Ma K'uei. $5, Monkeys and Deer, by I Yüan-chih. $8, Tame Sparrow among Bamboo.

Perf. 13x12½

1975, Aug. 15 Litho. Wmk. 323

1950	A381	$1 multicolored	.20	.20
1951	A381	$2 multicolored	.70	.20
1952	A381	$5 multicolored	.90	.25
1953	A381	$8 multicolored	1.75	.50
		Nos. 1950-1953 (4)	3.55	1.15

See Nos. 2001-2004.

Gen. Chang Tzu-chung (1891-1940) A382

#1955, Maj. Gen. Kao Chih-hong (1908-37). #1956, Capt. Sha Shih-chiun (1896-1938). #1957, Maj. Gen. Hsieh Chin-yuan (1905-41). #1958, Lt. Yen Hai-wen (1916-37). #1959, Lt. Gen. Tai An-lan (1905-42).

Wmk. 323

1975, Sept. 3 Engr. *Perf. 12*

1954	A382	$2 carmine	.20	.20
1955	A382	$2 sepia	.20	.20
1956	A382	$2 dull green	.20	.20
1957	A382	$5 violet black	.30	.20
1958	A382	$5 violet blue	.30	.20
1959	A382	$5 dark blue	.30	.20
		Nos. 1954-1959 (6)	1.50	1.20

Martyrs of the resistance fight against Japan.

Lotus Pond with Willows, by Madame Chiang — A383

Paintings by Madame Chiang Kai-shek: $5, Sun Breaks through Mountain Clouds. $8, A Pair of Pine Trees. $10, Fishing and Farming.

Perf. 13½

1975, Oct. 31 Litho. Unwmk.

1960	A383	$2 multicolored	.75	.20
1961	A383	$5 multicolored	1.60	.30
1962	A383	$8 multicolored	2.40	.40
1963	A383	$10 multicolored	3.25	.75
		Nos. 1960-1963 (4)	8.00	1.65

For similar design see type A404.

Cauldron with Phoenix Handles, 481-221 B.C. A384

Ancient Bronzes: $2, Rectangular cauldron, 1122-722 B.C., vert. $8, Flat jar, 481-221 B.C. $10, 3-legged wine vessel, 1766-1122 B.C., vert.

1975, Nov. 12 Photo. *Perf. 12*

1964	A384	$2 pink & multi	.20	.20
1965	A384	$5 lt blue & multi	.65	.20
1966	A384	$8 yellow & multi	.85	.20
1967	A384	$10 lilac & multi	1.00	.30
		Nos. 1964-1967 (4)	2.70	.90

For similar design see type A395. No. 1964 has 7 Chinese characters at left, No. 2005 has 4. No. 1967 has 4 characters at left, No. 2008 has 5.

Dragon, Nine-Dragon Wall, Peihai — A385

Techi Dam — A386

Wmk. 323

1975, Dec. 1 Litho. *Perf. 12½*

1968	A385	$1 orange & multi	.25	.20
1969	A385	$5 green & multi	1.25	.60

New Year 1976.

1975, Dec. 17 Unwmk. *Perf. 13½*

Design: $10, Panoramic view of Techi Dam.

1970	A386	$2 green & multi	.20	.20
1971	A386	$10 blue & multi	.55	.45

Completion of Techi Dam, Tachia River.

Biathlon and Olympic Rings — A387

Olympic Rings and: $5, Luge. $8, Skiing.

1976, Jan. 15 Litho. *Perf. 13½*

1972	A387	$2 blue & multi	.20	.20
1973	A387	$5 blue & multi	.35	.20
1974	A387	$8 blue & multi	.55	.25
		Nos. 1972-1974 (3)	1.10	.65

12th Winter Olympic Games, Innsbruck, Austria, Feb. 4-15.

Chin, Oldest Chinese Instrument A388

Musical Instruments: $5, Se, c. 2900 B.C. $8, Standing kong-ho (harp). $10, Sleeping kong-ho.

1976, Feb. 11 Unwmk. *Perf. 14*

1975	A388	$2 yellow & multi	.25	.20
1976	A388	$5 orange & multi	.40	.20
1977	A388	$8 grnsh bl & multi	.55	.20
1978	A388	$10 multicolored	.80	.30
		Nos. 1975-1978 (4)	2.00	.90

For similar design see Type A407.

Double Carp Type of 1969

Perf. 13½x12½

1976, Dec. 15 Engr. Unwmk.

1980	A280	$14 carmine rose	2.25	.30

Mail Collecting A389

Mail Sorting — A390

Postal Service, 80th Anniv.: $8, Mail transport. $10, Mail delivery.

Wmk. 323

1976, Mar. 20 Litho. *Perf. 13½*

1984	A389	$2 yellow & multi	.20	.20
1985	A390	$5 green & multi	.35	.20
1986	A390	$8 blue & multi	.50	.20
1987	A389	$10 orange & multi	.60	.30
a.		Souv. sheet of 4, #1984-1987	9.00	6.50
		Nos. 1984-1987 (4)	1.65	.90

Pres. Chiang Kai-shek A391

People Paying Homage — A392

#1990, Pres. Chiang lying in state. #1991, Hearse leaving funeral chapel. $5, People along funeral route. $8, Spirit tablet in Tzuhu Guest House. $10, Tzuhu Guest House, Pres. Chiang's burial place.

1976, Apr. 4

1988	A391	$2 gray & multi	.20	.20
1989	A392	$2 gray & multi	.20	.20
1990	A392	$2 gray & multi	.20	.20
1991	A392	$2 gray & multi	.20	.20
1992	A392	$5 gray & multi	.40	.20

1993 A392 $8 gray & multi .40 .25
1994 A392 $10 gray & multi .50 .35
Nos. 1988-1994 (7) 2.10 1.60

Pres. Chiang Kai-shek (1887-1975), first death anniversary.

Flags of China and US — A393

Wmk. 323

1976, May 29 Litho. *Perf. 13½*
1995 A393 $2 multicolored .20 .20
1996 A393 $10 yellow & multi .60 .40

American Bicentennial.

Coin, 12th Century B.C. — A394

Cauldron, Shang Dynasty — A395

Bronze Shovel Coins (pu): $5, Pointed-feet coin, 481-221 B.C. $8, Round-feet coin, 722-481 B.C. $10, Square-feet coin, 3rd-2nd centuries B.C.

1976, June 16
1997 A394 $2 salmon & multi .20 .20
1998 A394 $5 lt blue & multi .50 .20
1999 A394 $8 gray & multi .80 .20
2000 A394 $10 multicolored 1.25 .30
Nos. 1997-2000 (4) 2.75 .90

Fan Painting Type of 1975

Silk Fan Paintings, Sung Dynasty: $2, Hibiscus, by Li Tung. $5, Lilies, by Lin Ch'un. $8, Deer and Pine, by Mou Chung-fu. $10, Quail and Wild Flowers, by Li An-chung.

Perf. 13x12½

1976, July 14 Litho. Wmk. 323
2001 A381 $2 multicolored .45 .20
2002 A381 $5 multicolored 1.10 .20
2003 A381 $8 multicolored 1.40 .30
2004 A381 $10 multicolored 2.25 .40
Nos. 2001-2004 (4) 5.20 1.10

1976, Aug. 25 Photo. *Perf. 11½*
Granite Paper

Ancient Bronzes: $5, 3-legged cauldron, Chou Dynasty (1122-722 B.C.). $8, Wine container, Chou Dynasty. $10, Wine vessel with spout, Shang Dynasty (1766-1122 B.C.).

2005 A395 $2 rose & multi .20 .20
2006 A395 $5 lt blue & multi .70 .20
2007 A395 $8 yellow & multi 1.00 .20
2008 A395 $10 lilac & multi 1.10 .30
Nos. 2005-2008 (4) 3.00 .90

Construction Types of 1974

Designs: $1, Taiwan North Link railroad and map. $2, Railroad electrification. $3, Taichung Harbor. $4, Taiwan North-South Highway and map. $5, Steel Mill, Kaohsiung. $6, Taoyuan International Airport. $7, Kao-hsiung shipyard. $8, Oil refinery. $9, Su-ao Port.

Perf. 13½x12½, 12½x13½

1976 Litho. Wmk. 323
2009 A365 $1 carmine & grn .20 .20
2010 A365 $2 orange & multi .20 .20
2011 A366 $3 violet & multi .20 .20
2012 A366 $4 carmine & multi .20 .20
2013 A365 $5 green & brn .20 .20
2014 A366 $6 brown & multi .30 .20
2015 A366 $7 brown & multi .35 .20
2016 A365 $8 carmine & grn .45 .20
2017 A366 $9 olive & blue .50 .20
Nos. 2009-2017 (9) 2.60 1.80

Chiang Kai-shek and Mother A396

Sun Yat-sen and Chiang Kai-shek at Canton Station — A397

Design: $5, Chiang Kai-shek, portrait.

1976, Oct. 31 Litho. *Perf. 13½*
2023 A396 $2 multicolored .20 .20
2024 A396 $5 multicolored .75 .20
2025 A397 $10 multicolored .90 .40
Nos. 2023-2025 (3) 1.85 .80

Pres. Chiang Kai-shek, 90th anniv. of birth.

Flags of Kuomintang and China A398

Sun Yat-sen and Chiang Kai-shek A399

1976, Nov. 12 *Perf. 13½x14*
2026 A398 $2 multicolored .20 .20
2027 A399 $10 multicolored .65 .45
a. Souv. sheet of 2, #2026-2027 4.50 4.50

11th National Kuomintang Cong., Taipei.

Brazen Serpent — A400

1976, Dec. 15 Wmk. 323 *Perf. 12½*
2028 A400 $1 red, lilac & gold .30 .20
2029 A400 $5 plum, yel & gold 1.50 .25

New Year 1977.

Bird and Plum Blossoms, by Ch'en Hung-shou A401

Chinese Paintings: $8, "Wintry Days" (pine), by Yang Wei-chen. $10, Rock and Bamboo, by Hsia Ch'ang.

Perf. 11½

1977, Jan. 12 Photo. Unwmk.
Granite Paper
2030 A401 $2 multicolored .60 .20
2031 A401 $8 multicolored 1.75 .25
2032 A401 $10 multicolored 2.25 .40
Nos. 2030-2032 (3) 4.60 .85

Black-naped Orioles — A402

Birds of Taiwan: $8, Common Kingfisher. $10, Chinese pheasant-tailed jacana.

1977, Feb. 16 Litho.
2033 A402 $2 multicolored .40 .20
2034 A402 $8 multicolored 1.00 .20
2035 A402 $10 multicolored 1.40 .35
Nos. 2033-2035 (3) 2.80 .75

See Nos. 2163-2165.

Census Emblem, Industry and Commerce A403

Perf. 13½

1977, Mar. 16 Litho. Unwmk.
2036 A403 $2 red & multi .20 .20
2037 A403 $10 purple & multi .60 .40

Industry and Commerce Census.

Green Mountains Rising into Clouds, by Madame Chiang — A404

Landscapes, by Madame Chiang Kai-shek: $5, Boat in the Beauty of Spring. $8, Scholar beside Waterfall. $10, Water Rises to Meet the Bridge.

Perf. 11½

1977, Mar. 31 Unwmk. Photo.
Granite Paper
2038 A404 $2 multi .40 .20
2039 A404 $5 multi 1.60 .25
2040 A404 $8 multi 2.00 .50
2041 A404 $10 multi 2.25 .60
Nos. 2038-2041 (4) 6.25 1.55

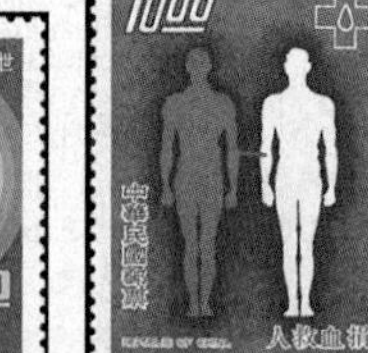

League Emblem — A405

Blood Donation — A406

1977, Apr. 18 Litho. *Perf. 12½*
2042 A405 $2 carmine & multi .20 .20
2043 A405 $10 green & multi .50 .40

10th World Anti-Communist League Conference.

1977, May 5 Wmk. 323 *Perf. 13½*

Design: $2, Donating blood, horiz.

2044 A406 $2 red & black .20 .20
2045 A406 $10 red & black .60 .40

Blood donation movement.

San-hsien A407

Musical Instruments: $5, Tung-hsiao (bamboo flute). $8, Yang-chin (butterfly harpsichord). $10, Pai-hsiao (pipes). Background shows musician playing instrument.

Unwmk.

1977, June 21 Photo. *Perf. 14*
2046 A407 $2 multicolored .20 .20
2047 A407 $5 multicolored .35 .20
2048 A407 $8 multicolored .45 .20
2049 A407 $10 multicolored .60 .30
Nos. 2046-2049 (4) 1.60 .90

Idea Leuconoe — A408

Protected Butterflies: $4, Hebomoia glaucippe formosana. $6, Stichophthalma howqua formosana. $10, Atrophaneura horishana.

1977, July 20 Litho. *Perf. 13½*
2050 A408 $2 ver & multi .30 .20
2051 A408 $4 lt grn & multi .70 .20
2052 A408 $6 lt bl & multi 1.00 .30
2053 A408 $10 yellow & multi 1.25 .45
Nos. 2050-2053 (4) 3.25 1.15

National Palace Museum A409

Temple — A410

Children's Drawings: $2, Sea Goddess Festival. $4, Boats on Shore of Lan-yu.

Wmk. 323

1977, Aug. 27 Litho. *Perf. 13½*
2054 A409 $1 multicolored .20 .20
2055 A409 $2 multicolored .25 .20
2056 A409 $4 multicolored .40 .20
2057 A410 $5 multicolored .50 .25
Nos. 2054-2057 (4) 1.35 .85

8th Exhib. of World School Children's Art.

Carved Lacquer Plate, Wan-li Ware A411

Ancient Carved Lacquer Ware: $5, Bowl, Ching dynasty. $8, Round box, Ming dynasty. $10, Four-tiered box, Ching dynasty.

Perf. 13x14

1977, Sept. 28 Photo. Wmk. 368
2058 A411 $2 multicolored .30 .20
2059 A411 $5 multicolored .60 .20
2060 A411 $8 multicolored 1.25 .20
2061 A411 $10 multicolored 1.10 .30
Nos. 2058-2061 (4) 3.25 .90

Lions International, Emblem and Activities — A412

Unwmk.

1977, Oct. 8 Litho. *Perf. 13*

2062	A412	$2 multicolored	.20	.20
2063	A412	$10 multicolored	.55	.35

Intl. Association of Lions Clubs, 60th anniv.

Nos. 2069 and 2075 Overprinted in Claret

Perf. 13½x12½

1977, Sept. 9 Litho. Unwmk.

2064	A365	$2 orange & multi	.20	.20
2065	A365	$8 carmine & grn	.60	.30

Little League baseball championship.

Chinese Quality Mark — A413

Perf. 13x12½

1977, Oct. 14 Litho. Unwmk.

2066	A413	$2 red & multi	.50	.20
2067	A413	$10 blue & multi	1.50	.30

International Standardization Day.

Construction Types of 1974 Redrawn: Numerals Outlined

Designs as 1976 Issue.

Perf. 13½x12½, 12½x13½

1977 Litho. Unwmk.

Granite Paper

2068	A365	$1 car & dp grn	.20	.20
2069	A365	$2 ver & multi	.20	.20
2070	A366	$3 violet & multi	.20	.20
2071	A366	$4 carmine & multi	.20	.20
2072	A365	$5 green & multi	.30	.20
2073	A366	$6 sepia & multi	.30	.20
2074	A366	$7 sepia & multi	.35	.20
2075	A365	$8 red lil & multi	.40	.20
2076	A366	$9 olive & multi	.40	.20
		Nos. 2068-2076 (9)	2.55	1.80

Numerals are in solid color on #1907-1915, 2009-2017; in outline on #2068-2076.

For overprints see #2064-2065, 2112-2113.

Man and Heart — A414

White Stallion — A415

Perf. 13½x12½

1977, Nov. 12 Litho. Wmk. 323

2077	A414	$2 multicolored	.20	.20
2078	A414	$10 multicolored	.55	.40

Physical health, cardiac care.

Perf. 12½

1977, Dec. 1 Unwmk. Litho.

New Year 1978: $5, Two horses, horiz. Designs from painting "100 Horses," by Lang Shih-ning.

2079	A415	$1 red & multi	.35	.20
2080	A415	$5 emerald & multi	1.25	.30

First Page of Constitution A416

Pres. Chiang Accepting Constitution, 1946 — A417

1977, Dec. 25 Litho. *Perf. 13½*

2081	A416	$2 multicolored	.20	.20
2082	A417	$10 multicolored	.55	.30

30th anniversary of the Constitution.

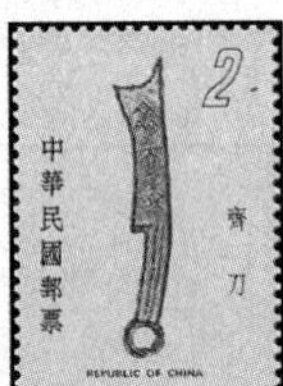

Knife Coin with 3 Characters, 403-221 B.C. — A418

Designs: Ancient knife coins.

1978, Jan. 18 Wmk. 323 *Perf. 13½*

2083	A418	$2 salmon & multi	.30	.20
2084	A418	$5 lt blue & blk	.70	.20
2085	A418	$8 lt gray & multi	.80	.20
2086	A418	$10 tan & multi	1.00	.30
		Nos. 2083-2086 (4)	2.80	.90

China No. 1 and Flag of China — A419

Designs: $5, No. 464 (Sun Yat-sen). $10, No. 1204 (Chiang Kai-shek).

1978, Feb. 21 Litho. *Perf. 13½*

2087	A419	$2 brown & multi	.20	.20
2088	A419	$5 blue & multi	.40	.25
2089	A419	$10 orange & multi	.70	.40
a.		Souv. sheet of 3, #2087-2089	7.75	3.50
		Nos. 2087-2089 (3)	1.30	.85

Centenary of Chinese postage stamps.

Sun Yat-Sen Memorial Hall A420

China Nos. 2079 and 2 — A421

Perf. 14x12½, 12½x14

1978, Mar. 20 Wmk. 323

2090	A420	$2 multicolored	.20	.20
2091	A421	$10 multicolored	.50	.35

ROCPEX '78 Phil. Exhib., Taipei, Mar. 20-29.

Chiang Kai-shek with Revolutionary Army — A422

Pres. Chiang Kai-shek (1887-1975); $2, as young man, 1912, vert. $8, Making speech at Mt. Lu, July 17, 1937. $10, Reviewing Armed Forces on National Day, 1956, and Chinese flags, vert.

1978, Apr. 5 Wmk. 323 *Perf. 13½*

2092	A422	$2 violet & multi	.20	.20
2093	A422	$5 green & multi	.35	.20
2094	A422	$8 blue & multi	.55	.40
2095	A422	$10 vio blue & multi	.70	.50
		Nos. 2092-2095 (4)	1.80	1.30

Nuclear Reactor and Plant — A423

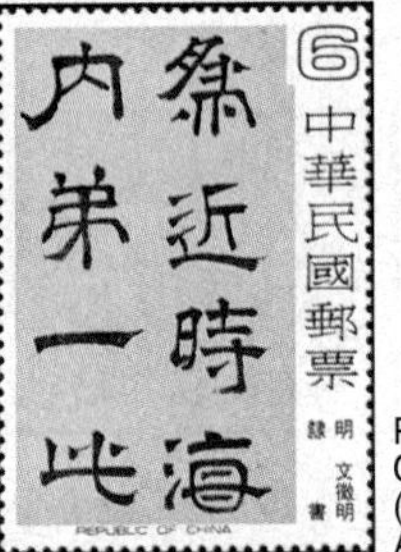

Poem by Wen Cheng-ming (1470-1559) A424

Perf. 13½x12½

1978, Apr. 26 Unwmk.

2096	A423	$10 multicolored	.70	.20

First nuclear power plant on Taiwan.

1978, May 20 Wmk. 323 *Perf. 13½*

Chinese Calligraphy: $2, Letter by Wang Hsi-chih (307-365). $4, Eulogy by Chu Sui-liang (596-658). $8, From Autobiography of Huai-su, Tang Dynasty. $10, Poem by Ch'ang Piao, Sung Dynasty.

2097	A424	$2 multicolored	*.60*	.20
2098	A424	$4 multicolored	*2.40*	.20
2099	A424	$6 multicolored	*2.40*	.50
2100	A424	$8 multicolored	*2.75*	.30
2101	A424	$10 multicolored	*3.50*	.55
		Nos. 2097-2101 (5)	*11.65*	1.75

Head and Dao Cancer Fund Emblem A425

Carved Lacquer Vase, Ming Dynasty A426

1978, June 15 Litho. *Perf. 13½*

2102	A425	$2 red, org & ol	.20	.20
2103	A425	$10 dk & lt bl & grn	.55	.35

Cancer prevention.

1978, July 12

Ancient Carved Lacquer Ware: $2, Box with dragon and cloud design, Ch'ing dynasty, horiz. $5, Double box on legs, Ch'ing dynasty, horiz. $8, Round box with peonies, Ming dynasty, horiz.

2104	A426	$2 gray olive & multi	.25	.20
2105	A426	$5 gray olive & multi	.35	.20
2106	A426	$8 gray olive & multi	.50	.20
2107	A426	$10 gray olive & multi	.70	.30
		Nos. 2104-2107 (4)	1.80	.90

Tsu Ti Practicing with his Sword — A427

Folk Tales: No. 2109, Pan Ch'ao, diplomat and governor. No. 2110, Tien Tan's "Fire Bull Battle." $5, Liang Hung-yu, a general's wife, who served as drummer in battle.

Wmk. 323

1978, Aug. 16 Litho. *Perf. 13½*

2108	A427	$1 multicolored	.25	.20
2109	A427	$2 bister & multi	.55	.20
2110	A427	$2 gray & multi	.55	.20
2111	A427	$5 multicolored	.85	.25
		Nos. 2108-2111 (4)	2.20	.85

For similar designs see types A456, A495.

Nos. 2071 and 2073 Overprinted in Red

1978, Sept. 9 *Perf. 12½x13*

2112	A366	$4 multicolored	.20	.20
2113	A366	$6 multicolored	.40	.30

Triple championships won by Chinese teams in Little League World Series. "1978" overprint on $4 at left, on $6 at right.

Ixias Pyrene A428

Protected Butterflies: $4, Euploea sylvestor swinhoei. $6, Cyrestis thyodamas formosana. $10, Byasa polyeuctes termessus.

1978, Sept. 20

2114	A428	$2 multicolored	.40	.20
2115	A428	$4 multicolored	.50	.20
2116	A428	$6 multicolored	.75	.30
2117	A428	$10 multicolored	1.90	.45
		Nos. 2114-2117 (4)	3.55	1.15

Scout Symbols — A429

Tropical Tomatoes — A430

1978, Oct. 5 Litho. *Perf. 13½*

2118 A429 $2 multicolored .20 .20
2119 A429 $10 multicolored .35 .30

5th Chinese Boy Scout Jamboree, Cheng Ching Lake, Oct. 5-12.

1978, Oct. 23 Wmk. 323

Design: $10, Tropical tomatoes, horiz.

2120 A430 $2 multicolored .30 .20
2121 A430 $10 multicolored 1.25 .40

International Symposium on Tropical Tomatoes, Taiwan, Oct. 23-28.

Sino-Saudi Bridge A431

Design: $6, Buttresses of bridge, flags of Taiwan and Saudi Arabia, horiz.

1978, Oct. 31

2122 A431 $2 multicolored .35 .20
2123 A431 $6 multicolored 1.00 .30

Completion of Sino-Saudi Bridge over Cho-Shui River.

National Flag — A432

1978-80 *Perf. 13½*

2124 A432 $1 red & dk bl, I .20 .20
a. Bklt. pane of 16 ($5, $6, $8, $10, 3 $1, 9 $2) 7.75
b. Type II .20 .20
2125 A432 $2 red & dk bl, I .20 .20
a. Bklt. pane of 15 + label 11.50
b. Type II .20 .20
2126 A432 $3 yel grn & multi ('80) .30 .20
2127 A432 $4 bis & multi ('80) .35 .20
2128 A432 $5 dk grn & multi, I .25 .20
a. Type II .25 .20
2129 A432 $6 brn org & multi .30 .20
2130 A432 $7 dk brn & multi ('80) .35 .20
2131 A432 $8 dk grn & multi, I .45 .20
a. Type II .45 .20
2132 A432 $10 brt bl & multi ('79) .60 .20
2133 A432 $12 brt rose lil & multi ('80) .60 .25
Nos. 2124-2133 (10) 3.60 2.05

Two types exist: I. Second line (red) below flag is same width as blue line. II. Second line is a hairline, notably thinner. The $3, $4, $7 and $12 were issued only in type II; $6, $10, Nos. 2134, 2124a, only in type I.

Nos. 2129-2133 have colorless inscriptions and denomination in a panel of solid color.

Nos. 2124a, 2125a have selvage inscribed in blue. 1980 printings are in green or red.

Coil Stamp

1980, Jan. 15 *Perf. 12 Horiz.*

2134 A432 $2 multicolored .25 .20

See Nos. 2288-2300. For overprints see Nos. 2540-2541.

Three Rams, by Emperor Hsuan-tsung A433

Taoyuan International Airport A434

Wmk. 323

1978, Dec. 1 Litho. *Perf. 12½*

2135 A433 $1 multicolored .25 .20
2136 A433 $5 multicolored 1.40 .40

New Year 1979.

1978, Dec. 31 *Perf. 13½*

$10, Passenger terminal, control tower.

2137 A434 $2 multi .20 .20
2138 A434 $10 multi,horiz. .70 .40

Completion of Taoyuan Intl. Airport.

Oracle Bones and Inscription, 1766-1123 B.C. — A435

Antiquities and Inscriptions: $5, Lehchi cauldron, 722-481 B.C. $8, Small seal (turtle), 206 B.C.-8 A.D. $10, Inscribed stone tablet, 175-183 A.D.

1979, Jan. 17

2139 A435 $2 multicolored .50 .20
2140 A435 $5 multicolored 1.00 .30
2141 A435 $8 multicolored 1.90 .50
2142 A435 $10 multicolored 1.90 .65
Nos. 2139-2142 (4) 5.30 1.65

Origin and development of Chinese characters.

Chihkan Tower, 1653 A436

Taiwan Scenery: $5, Shrine of Confucius, 1665. $8, Shrine of Koxinga, 1661. $10, Eternal Castle and moat.

1979, Feb. 11 Litho. *Perf. 13½*

2143 A436 $2 multicolored .20 .20
2144 A436 $5 multicolored .40 .20
2145 A436 $8 multicolored .50 .20
2146 A436 $10 multicolored 1.00 .25
Nos. 2143-2146 (4) 2.10 .85

Children Playing on Winter Day, Sung Dynasty — A437

1979, Mar. 8

2147 A437 Block of 4 9.50 6.50
a. $5 in UL corner 2.40 .40
b. $5 in UR corner 2.40 .40
c. $5 in LL corner 2.40 .40
d. $5 in LR corner 2.40 .40
e. Souvenir sheet of 4, #2147, imperf. *20.00* 11.00

No. 2147e has simulated perforations.

Lu Hao-tung — A438

Yellow Jade Brush Holder — A439

Perf. 13x12½

1979, Mar. 29 Engr. Wmk. 323

2148 A438 $2 blue .50 .20

Lu Hao-tung (1868-1895), revolutionist.

Unwmk.

1979, Apr. 12 Photo. *Perf. 12*

Ancient Brush Washers: $5, White jade, Ming Dynasty. $8, Dark green jade, Ch'ing Dynasty. $10, Bluish jade, Ch'ing Dynasty. All horiz.

Granite Paper

2149 A439 $2 multicolored .20 .20
2150 A439 $5 multicolored .80 .25
2151 A439 $8 multicolored 1.10 .35
2152 A439 $10 multicolored 1.50 .50
Nos. 2149-2152 (4) 3.60 1.30

For similar artifacts designs with single-color background and denominations in outlined numerals with the cents, see types A453, A469, A489, A523, A547, A582.

Plum Blossoms, Natl. Flower
A440 A440a

Perf. 13½x12½

1979-92 Engr. Wmk. 323

Granite Paper

2153 A440 $10 dk blue 1.60 .20
a. Plain paper ('88) 2.50 .30
2154 A440 $20 brown 2.00 .20
b. Plain paper ('87) 3.50 .60
2154A A440 $40 brt car, plain paper ('85) 2.00 .20
2155 A440 $50 dull green 4.25 .25
a. Plain paper ('87) 5.00 .55
2156 A440 $100 vermilion 6.00 .90
e. Plain paper ('92) 6.00 3.25

Perf. 14x13½

2156A A440a $300 pur & red org ('83) 16.00 3.25
c. Plain paper ('91) 18.00 3.25
2156B A440a $500 vor & brn ('82) 24.00 5.50
d. Plain paper ('91) 26.00 5.50
Nos. 2153-2156B (7) 55.85 10.50

Issued: #2156Ac, 2156Bd, May 1; #2156e, Jan. 7

City Houses and Garden — A441

Design: $10, Rural landscape, horiz.

Perf. 13x12½, 12½x13

1979, June 5 Litho.

2157 A441 $2 multicolored .20 .20
2158 A441 $10 multicolored .75 .35

Protection of the Environment.

Bankbook and Computer Department A442

Designs: $2, Children at counter, vert. $5, People standing in line, vert. $10, Hand putting coin in savings bank, symbolic tree.

1979, July 1 Wmk. 323 *Perf. 13½*

2159 A442 $2 multicolored .20 .20
2160 A442 $5 multicolored .30 .20
2161 A442 $8 multicolored .45 .20
2162 A442 $10 multicolored .55 .25
Nos. 2159-2162 (4) 1.50 .85

Postal savings, 60th anniversary.

Bird Type of 1977

Birds of Taiwan: $2, Swinoe's pheasant. $8, Steere's babbler. $10, Formosan yuhina.

1979, Aug. 8 *Perf. 11½*

2163 A402 $2 multicolored .40 .20
2164 A402 $8 multicolored 1.00 .20
2165 A402 $10 multicolored 1.10 .35
Nos. 2163-2165 (3) 2.50 .75

Rowland Hill, Penny Black A443

Perf. 13½x13

1979, Aug. 27 Litho. Wmk. 323

2166 A443 $10 multicolored .90 .25

Sir Rowland Hill (1795-1879), originator of penny postage.

Jar with Rope Design, Shang Dynasty — A444

Ancient Chinese Pottery: $5, Two-handled jar, Shang dynasty. $8, Red jar with "ears," Han dynasty. $10, Green glazed jar, Han dynasty.

1979, Sept. 12 *Perf. 13½*

2167 A444 $2 multicolored .45 .20
2168 A444 $5 multicolored .90 .20
2169 A444 $8 multicolored 1.50 .20
2170 A444 $10 multicolored 1.75 .30
Nos. 2167-2170 (4) 4.60 .90

Children and IYC Emblem — A445

1979, Sept. 28 **Litho.** *Perf. 13½*

2171 A445 $2 multicolored .20 .20
2172 A445 $10 multicolored .55 .35

International Year of the Child.

Trade Symbols, Competition Emblem A446

1979, Dec. 9 **Litho.** *Perf. 13½*

2173 A446 $2 blue & multi .20 .20
2174 A446 $10 green & multi .55 .35

10th National Vocational Training Competition, Taichung, Dec. 9.

Trees on a Winter Plain, by Li Ch'eng A447

Paintings: $5, Bamboo, Wen T'ung. $8, Old tree, bamboo and rock, by Chao Meng-fu. $10, Twin Pines, by Li K'an.

1979, Nov. 21

2175 A447 $2 multicolored .45 .20
2176 A447 $5 multicolored .90 .25
2177 A447 $8 multicolored 2.10 .40
2178 A447 $10 multicolored 3.00 .50
Nos. 2175-2178 (4) 6.45 1.35

Monkey — A448

1979, Dec. 1 *Perf. 12½*

2179 A448 $1 yellow & multi .45 .20
2180 A448 $6 tan & multi 2.75 .50

New Year 1980.

Rotary Emblem and "75" — A449

Rotary Intl., 75th Anniv.: $12, Anniv. emblem.

1980, Feb. 23 **Litho.** *Perf. 13½*

2181 A449 $2 multicolored .20 .20
2182 A449 $12 multi, vert. .75 .35

Mt. Hohuan A450

Taiwan Landscapes (East-West Cross-Island Highway): $2, Tunnel of Nine Turns, vert. $12, Bridge, Tien Hsiang, vert.

1980, Mar. 1 **Wmk. 323**

2183 A450 $2 multicolored .20 .20
2184 A450 $8 multicolored .70 .20
2185 A450 $12 multicolored 1.10 .35
Nos. 2183-2185 (3) 2.00 .75

A451

A452

1980, Mar. 29 **Engr.** *Perf. 13½x12½*
Granite Paper

2186 A451 $2 red brown .25 .20

Shih Chien-Ju (1879-1900), revolutionist.

1980, Apr. 4 **Litho.** *Perf. 13½*

2187 A452 $2 Chung-cheng Memorial Hall .20 .20
2188 A452 $8 Quotation .35 .20
2189 A452 $12 Bronze statue .45 .50
Nos. 2187-2189 (3) 1.00 .90

Chiang Kai-shek (1887-1975).

Melon-shaped Jade Brush Washer, Ming Dynasty — A453

Jade Pottery: $2, Jar with dragons, Sung dynasty, vert. $8, Monk's alms bowl, Ch'ing dynasty. $10, Yellow jade brush washer, Ch'ing dynasty.

1980, May 20 **Photo.** *Perf. 12*
Granite Paper

2190 A453 $2 multicolored .25 .20
2191 A453 $5 multicolored .50 .20
2192 A453 $8 multicolored .90 .20
2193 A453 $10 multicolored 1.10 .30
Nos. 2190-2193 (4) 2.75 .90

Energy Conservation A454

1980, July 15 **Litho.** *Perf. 13½*

2194 A454 $2 multicolored .20 .20
2195 A454 $12 multicolored .60 .40

A455

A456

T'ang Dynasty pottery.

1980, Aug. 18 **Litho.** *Perf. 13½*

2196 A455 $2 Soldier .30 .20
2197 A455 $5 Roosters .90 .20
2198 A455 $8 Horse 1.25 .20
2199 A455 $10 Camel 1.40 .30
Nos. 2196-2199 (4) 3.85 .90

Perf. 14x13½
1980, Sept. 23 **Litho.** **Wmk. 323**

Folk Tales: $1, Grinding mortar into a needle. No. 2201, Confucius Returning Lost Article (shown). No. 2202, Wen Tien-hsiang in jail. $5, Sending coal in snow.

2200 A456 $1 multicolored .20 .20
2201 A456 $2 multicolored .30 .20
2202 A456 $2 multicolored .30 .20
2203 A456 $5 multicolored 1.00 .30
Nos. 2200-2203 (4) 1.80 .90

Railroad Electrification A457

1980, Oct. 10 *Perf. 13½x14*

2204 A457 $2 shown .35 .20
2205 A457 $2 Taichung Harbor .35 .20
2206 A457 $2 Chiang Kai-shek Airport .35 .20
2207 A457 $2 Steel Mill .35 .20
2208 A457 $2 Sun Yat-sen Freeway .35 .20
2209 A457 $2 Nuclear power plant .35 .20
2210 A457 $2 Petrochemical plants .35 .20
2211 A457 $2 Su-ao Harbor .35 .20
2212 A457 $2 Kaohsiung shipyard .35 .20
2213 A457 $2 North link railroad .35 .20
a. Souv. sheet of 10, #2204-2213 9.00 9.00
b. Block of 10, #2204-2213 3.50 3.50
Nos. 2204-2213 (10) 3.50 2.00

Completion of major construction projects.

10th National Savings Day — A458

Wmk. 323
1980, Oct. 25 **Litho.** *Perf. 13½*

2214 A458 $2 Ancient coin and coin banks .20 .20
2215 A458 $12 shown 1.00 .40

Landscape, by Ch'iu Ying, Ming Dynasty — A459

1980, Nov. 12 **Litho.** *Perf. 13½*

2216 A459 Block of 4 8.00 5.25
a. $5 in UL corner 1.75 .40
b. $5 in UR corner 1.75 .40
c. $5 in LL corner 1.75 .40
d. $5 in LR corner 1.75 .40
e. Souvenir sheet, imperf. 14.50 14.50

No. 2216e has simulated perforations.

Cock — A460

Faces, Flag, Census Form — A461

1980, Dec. 1 *Perf. 12½*

2217 A460 $1 multicolored .50 .20
2218 A460 $6 multicolored 2.10 .35
a. Souv. sheet, 2 each #2217-2218 8.50 8.50

New Year 1981.

1980, Dec. 13 *Perf. 13½*

2219 A461 $2 shown .20 .20
2220 A461 $12 Buildings, horiz. .80 .40

1980 population and housing census.

TIROS-N Satellite — A462

Design: $10, Central weather bureau, horiz.

1981, Jan. 28 **Litho.** *Perf. 13½*

2221 A462 $2 multicolored .20 .20
2222 A462 $10 multicolored .80 .40

Completion of meteorological satellite ground station, Taipei.

"Happiness" A463

New Year 1981 (Calligraphy): No. 2224, Wealth. No. 2225, Longevity. No. 2226, Joy.

1981, Feb. 3 *Perf. 13½x12½*

2223 A463 $5 multi, 5 at B 1.00 .20
2224 A463 $5 multi, 5 at R 1.00 .20
2225 A463 $5 multi, 5 at L 1.00 .20
2226 A463 $5 multi, 5 at T 1.00 .20
a. Block of 4, #2223-2226 4.50 1.75

International Year of the Disabled — A464

1981, Feb. 19 **Litho.** *Perf. 13½*

2227 A464 $2 multicolored .20 .20
2228 A464 $12 multicolored .60 .25

Mt. Ali — A465

1981, Mar. 1

2229 A465 $2 shown .20 .20
2230 A465 $7 Oluanpi Beach .70 .20
2231 A465 $12 Sun Moon Lake 1.10 .30
Nos. 2229-2231 (3) 2.00 .70

A $2 multicolored stamp for the 12th National Kuomintang Congress at Taipei was prepared for release Mar. 29, 1981, but not issued. It showed Sun Yat-sen, Chiang Kai-shek, flags of China and the Kuomintang and a map of China.

Children in Forest A467

Children's Day: Drawings.

1981, Apr. 4

2233 A467 $1 multicolored .20 .20
2234 A467 $2 multicolored .20 .20
2235 A467 $5 multicolored .25 .20
2236 A467 $7 multicolored .30 .25
Nos. 2233-2236 (4) .95 .85

Chiang Kai-shek Memorial Hall — A468

1981, Apr. 5 *Perf. 12½x13½*

2237 A468 20c bluish lilac .20 .20
a. Photo. ('87) .20 .20
2238 A468 40c crim rose .20 .20
a. Photo. ('87) .20 .20
2239 A468 50c dull red brn .20 .20
a. Photo. ('88) .20 .20
Nos. 2237-2239 (3) .60 .60

Chiang Kai-shek (1887-1975).
See Nos. 2601-2603.

Cloisonne Enamel Brush Washer, 15th Cent. A469

Cloisonne Enamel: $5, Ritual vessel, 15th cent., vert. $8, Plate, 17th cent. $10, Vase, Ming Dynasty, vert.

1981, May 20 **Photo.** *Perf. 12*
Granite Paper

2240 A469 $2 multicolored .30 .20
2241 A469 $5 multicolored .65 .20
2242 A469 $8 multicolored .80 .25
2243 A469 $10 multicolored 1.00 .30
Nos. 2240-2243 (4) 2.75 .95

For similar enamelware stamps see Nos. 2318-2321, 2348-2351, 2410-2413.

Early & Modern Locomotives A470

Linnaeus Crab A471

Wmk. 323

1981, June 9 **Litho.** *Perf. 12½*

2244 A470 $2 shown .20 .20
2245 A470 $14 Trains, horiz. .80 .40

Railroad service centenary.

1981, June 14 *Perf. 13½*

2246 A471 $2 De Haan crab, horiz. .20 .20
2247 A471 $5 shown .40 .20
2248 A471 $8 Miers crab, horiz. .60 .20
2249 A471 $14 Rathbun crab 1.10 .30
Nos. 2246-2249 (4) 2.30 .90

Central Weather Bureau, 40th Anniv. — A472

1981, July 1 **Litho.** *Perf. 13½*

2250 A472 $2 multicolored .30 .20
2251 A472 $14 multicolored .80 .40

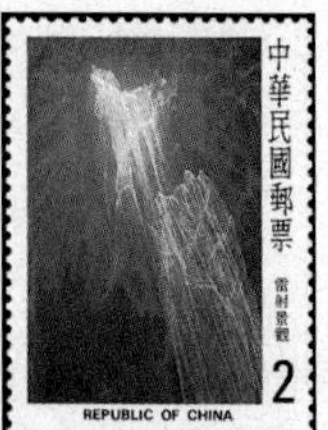

Scene from The Cowherd and the Weaving Maid — A473

Designs: Scenes from the Cowherd and the Weaving Maid.

1981, Aug. 6 **Litho.** *Perf. 13½x14*

2252 A473 $2 multicolored .35 .20
2253 A473 $4 multicolored .60 .20
2254 A473 $8 multicolored 1.10 .20
2255 A473 $14 multicolored 1.60 .50
Nos. 2252-2255 (4) 3.65 1.10

First Lasography Exhibition — A474

Lasography Designs.

1981, Aug. 15 *Perf. 13½*

2256 A474 $2 multicolored .20 .20
2257 A474 $5 multicolored .25 .20
2258 A474 $8 multicolored .50 .20
2259 A474 $14 multicolored .85 .50
Nos. 2256-2259 (4) 1.80 1.10

Soccer Players — A475

1981, Sept. 9 **Litho.** *Perf. 13½*

2260 $5 multicolored .50 .20
2261 $5 multicolored .50 .20
a. A475 Pair, #2260-2261 1.10 .65

Sports Day.

A477

70th Anniv. of Republic: No. 2263, Eastward Expedition (soldiers on Hill). No. 2264, Northward Expedition (Chiang on horse). No. 2265, Resistance War with Japan (Chiang, fist raised). No. 2266, Suppression of Communist Rebels (Battle scene). No. 2267, Counter-offensive and unification. $8, Chiang Kai-shek. $14, Sun Yat-sen.

1981, Oct. 10 *Perf. 13½*

2262 A477 $2 multicolored .20 .20
2263 A477 $2 multicolored .20 .20
2264 A477 $2 multicolored .20 .20
2265 A477 $2 multicolored .20 .20
2266 A477 $3 multicolored .20 .20
2267 A477 $3 multicolored .20 .20
2268 A477 $8 multicolored .45 .25
2269 A477 $14 multicolored 1.00 .45
a. Souv. sheet of 8, #2262-2269 6.50 2.50
Nos. 2262-2269 (8) 2.65 1.90

No. 2269a issued Oct. 25.

ROCPEX TAIPEI '81 Intl. Philatelic Exhibition, Taipei, Oct. 25-Nov. 2 A478

1981, Oct. 25

2270 A478 $2 multicolored .20 .20
2271 A478 $14 multicolored .50 .25

Nos. 2269a, 2270-2271 overprinted with four characters meaning "Best of Show" were not valid for postage. They were inserted in a special "ROCPEX" book, edition of 10,000.

Boys Playing Games (#2272a) — A479

Designs: a.-j. "One Hundred Boys," Sung Dynasty scroll (each stamp is numbered from 1 to 10 in Chinese. See illustrations with Nos. 1682-1691 for numerals.) Two strips of 5 each in continuous design.

1981, Nov. 12

2272 Block of 10 14.50 14.50
a.-e. A479 $2 single (top row) 1.25 .25
f.-j. A479 $2 single (bottom row) 1.25 .25

New Year 1982 (Year of the Dog) — A480

Information Week, Dec. 6-12 — A481

Wmk. 323

1981, Dec. 1 **Litho.** *Perf. 12½*

2273 A480 $1 multicolored .40 .20
2274 A480 $10 multicolored 2.00 .40
a. Souv. sheet, 2 ea #2273-2274 8.00 5.00

1981, Dec. 7 *Perf. 14x13½*

2275 A481 $2 multicolored .30 .20

Telecommunications Centenary — A482

1981, Dec. 28 *Perf. 14x13½, 13½x14*

2276 A482 $2 Telephone, vert. .20 .20
2277 A482 $3 Old, new phones .25 .20
2278 A482 $8 Submarine cable .40 .20
2279 A482 $18 Computers, vert. .55 .30
Nos. 2276-2279 (4) 1.40 .90

Floral Arrangement A483

Various floral arrangements in Ming vases.

Wmk. 323

1982, Jan. 23 **Litho.** *Perf. 13½*

2280 A483 $2 multicolored .20 .20
2281 A483 $3 multicolored .25 .20
2282 A483 $8 multicolored .55 .20
2283 A483 $18 multicolored 1.25 .50
Nos. 2280-2283 (4) 2.25 1.10

Compare with designs A559, A584.

The Ku Cheng Reunion — A484

Designs: Opera scenes.

Wmk. 323

1982, Feb. 15 **Litho.** *Perf. 13½*

2284 A484 $2 multicolored .40 .20
2285 A484 $3 multicolored 1.25 .20
2286 A484 $4 multicolored 1.40 .25
2287 A484 $18 multicolored 2.50 .60
Nos. 2284-2287 (4) 5.55 1.25

Flag Type of 1978
Value Colorless in Colored Panel

1981 **Litho.** *Perf. 13½*
Panel Color

2288 A432 $1 dk blue .20 .20
2289 A432 $1.50 lt olive .20 .20
2290 A432 $2 dk olive bis .20 .20
2291 A432 $3 red .20 .20
2292 A432 $4 blue .20 .20
2293 A432 $5 sepia .20 .20
2294 A432 $6 orange .25 .20
2295 A432 $7 green .40 .20

2296 A432 $8 magenta .50 .20
2297 A432 $9 olive grn .60 .20
2298 A432 $10 dk purple .70 .20
2299 A432 $12 lilac .80 .25
2300 A432 $14 dk green .75 .30
Nos. 2288-2300 (13) 5.20 2.75

Second line (red) below flag is a hairline, notably thinner.
For overprints see Nos. 2540-2541.

Robert Koch A485

Cheng Shih-liang, Revolutionary A486

Wmk. 323

1982, Mar. 24 Litho. *Perf. 13½*
2309 A485 $2 multicolored .25 .20

Tubercle Bacillus centenary.

1982, Mar. 29 Engr. *Perf. 13½x12½*
Granite Paper
2310 A486 $2 carmine rose .25 .20

Children's Day A487

Designs: Various children's drawings.

1982, Apr. 4 Litho.
2311 A487 $2 multi, vert. .40 .20
2312 A487 $3 multicolored .60 .20
2313 A487 $5 multicolored .80 .20
2314 A487 $8 multicolored .80 .20
Nos. 2311-2314 (4) 2.60 .80

Dentists' Day A488

1982, May 4 Litho. *Perf. 13½*
2315 A488 $2 Tooth, boy .30 .20
2316 A488 $3 Flossing, brushing .60 .20
2317 A488 $10 Examination 1.10 .30
Nos. 2315-2317 (3) 2.00 .70

Champleve Enamel Cup and Saucer, 18th Cent. A489

Painted Enamelware: $5, Cloisonne gold-plated duck Ch'ien-lung period (1736-1795), vert. $8, Incense burner, K'ang-hsi period (1662-1722). $12, Cloisonne pitcher, Ch'ien-lung period, vert.

1982, May 20 Photo. *Perf. 12*
Granite Paper
2318 A489 $2 multicolored .40 .20
2319 A489 $5 multicolored .80 .20
2320 A489 $8 multicolored 1.25 .20
2321 A489 $12 multicolored 2.10 .25
Nos. 2318-2321 (4) 4.55 .85

See Nos. 2348-2351.

Poets' Day — A490

Tang Dynasty Poetry Illustrations (618-906): $2, Spring Dawn, by Meng Hao-Jan. $3, On Looking for a Hermit and Not Finding Him, by Chia Tao. $5, Summer Dying, by Liu Yu-Hsi. $18, Looking at the Snow Drifts on South Mountain, by Tsu Yung. Chinese characters are to the left of the denominations on Nos. 2322-2325, Nos. 2396-2399 have no characters to the left of the denominations.

Wmk. 323

1982, June 25 Litho. *Perf. 13½*
2322 A490 $2 multicolored *1.50* .20
2323 A490 $3 multicolored *3.00* .25
2324 A490 $5 multicolored *4.50* .40
2325 A490 $18 multicolored *9.50* 1.00
Nos. 2322-2325 (4) *18.50* 1.85

See Nos. 2352-2355.

5th World Women's Softball Championship, Taipei, July 1-12 — A491

1982, July 2
2326 A491 $2 lt grn & multi .25 .20
2327 A491 $18 tan & multi 1.25 .40

Scouting Year A492

1982, July 18
2328 A492 $2 Crossing bridge, Baden-Powell .20 .20
2329 A492 $18 Emblem, camp .70 .40

Stamp in Tongs A493

1982, Aug. 9
2330 A493 $2 shown .25 .20
2331 A493 $18 Album stamps magnified 1.10 .40

Carved Lion, Tsu Shih Temple — A494

Hsun Kuan Saving Hsiang-cheng City — A495

Tsu Shih Temple of Sanhsia Architecture: $3, Lion brackets, horiz. $5, Sub-lintels. $18, Tiled roof, horiz.

1982, Sept. 1 Litho. *Perf. 13½*
2332 A494 $2 multicolored .25 .20
2333 A494 $3 multicolored .35 .20
2334 A494 $5 multicolored .75 .20
2335 A494 $18 multicolored 1.10 .40
Nos. 2332-2335 (4) 2.45 1.00

1982, Oct. 15 *Perf. 14x13½*

Designs: Scenes from The Thirty-Six Examples of Filial Piety, Folk Tale collection by Wu Yen-huan.

2336 A495 $1 multicolored .20 .20
2337 A495 $2 multicolored .50 .20
2338 A495 $3 multicolored .70 .20
2339 A495 $5 multicolored .80 .25
Nos. 2336-2339 (4) 2.20 .85

30th Anniv. of China Youth Corps A496

1982, Oct. 31
2340 A496 $2 Riding .20 .20
2341 A496 $3 Raising flag, vert. .20 .20
2342 A496 $18 Mountain climbing .60 .40
Nos. 2340-2342 (3) 1.00 .80

Seated Lohan (Buddhist Saint) — A497

New Year 1983 (Year of the Boar) — A498

Paintings of Lohan, Hanging Scrolls by Liu Sung-nien, 13th cent.

Perf. 13x12½
1982, Nov. 12 Litho. Wmk. 323
2343 A497 $2 multicolored .85 .20
2344 A497 $3 multicolored 2.00 .20
2345 A497 $18 multicolored 5.25 .85
a. Souv. sheet, #2343-2345 *19.00* 13.00
Nos. 2343-2345 (3) 8.10 1.25

No. 2345a comes overprinted in red in the sheet margins. Value, unused $18, Used $12.

1982, Dec. 1 *Perf. 12½*
2346 A498 $1 multicolored .60 .20
2347 A498 $10 multicolored 2.75 .45
a. Souv. sheet, 2 ea #2346-2347 *10.00* 5.00

Enamelware Type of 1982

Designs: $2, Square basin, Ch'ing Dynasty (1644-1911). $3, Vase, Ch'ien-lung period (1736-1795). $4, Tea pot, Ch'ien-lung period. $18, Elephant vase, Ch'ing Dynasty.

1983, Jan. 5 Photo. *Perf. 12*
Granite Paper
2348 A489 $2 multi .35 .20
2349 A489 $3 multi, vert. .50 .20
2350 A489 $4 multi .90 .20
2351 A489 $18 multi, vert. 1.40 .50
Nos. 2348-2351 (4) 3.15 1.10

Poetry Illustration Type of 1982

Sung Dynasty Poetry: $2, Seeing the Flowers Fade Away. $3, River. $5, Freckled with Clouds is the Azure Sky. $11, Yielding Fine Fragrance in the Snow. Nos. 2352-2355 vert.

Wmk. 323

1983, Feb. 10 Litho. *Perf. 13½*
2352 A490 $2 multicolored *1.00* .25
2353 A490 $3 multicolored *3.75* .35
2354 A490 $5 multicolored *5.25* .50
2355 A490 $11 multicolored *7.75* .60
Nos. 2352-2355 (4) *17.75* 1.70

Mt. Jade, Taiwan — A499

1983, Mar. 1
2356 A499 $2 Wawa Valley, vert. .50 .20
2357 A499 $3 University Pond, vert. .75 .20
2358 A499 $18 shown 1.25 .50
Nos. 2356-2358 (3) 2.50 .90

400th Anniv. of Arrival of Matteo Ricci (1552-1610), Italian Missionary A500

Perf. 14x13½
1983, Apr. 3 Litho. Wmk. 323
2359 A500 $2 Globe .30 .20
2360 A500 $18 Great Wall 1.00 .35

Mandarin Phonetic Symbols, 70th Anniv. — A501

Scenes from Lady White Snake Fairytale — A502

Wmk. 323

1983, May 22 Litho. *Perf. 13½*
2361 A501 $2 Wu Ching-heng, inventor .30 .20
2362 A501 $18 Children writing 1.00 .30

1983, June 15 *Perf. 14x13½*
2363 A502 $2 multicolored .40 .20
2364 A502 $3 lt blue & multi .75 .20
2365 A502 $3 orange & multi .75 .20
2366 A502 $18 multicolored .90 .50
Nos. 2363-2366 (4) 2.80 1.10

A503

A504

Various bamboo carved objects. Nos. 2367-2369 Ch'ing dynasty.

Wmk. 323

1983, July 14 Litho. *Perf. 13½*

2367	A503	$2	Bamboo jug	.55	.20
2368	A503	$3	Tao-t'ieh motif vase	.70	.20
2369	A503	$4	Landscape sculpture	.80	.20
2370	A503	$18	Brush holder, Ming dynasty	1.75	.40
			Nos. 2367-2370 (4)	3.80	1.00

Wmk. 323

1983, Aug. 5 Litho. *Perf. 13½*

2371	A504	$2	Globe	.20	.20
2372	A504	$18	Emblem	.80	.35

World Communications Year.

Fishing Industry (Local Fish) A505

1983, Aug. 20

2373	A505	$2	Epinephelus tauvina	.20	.20
2374	A505	$18	Saurida undosquamis	.90	.35

40th Journalists' Day — A506

1983, Sept. 1

2375	A506	$2	multicolored	.25	.20

Views of Mongolia and Tibet — A507

1983, Sept. 15

2376	A507	$2	Village	.35	.20
2377	A507	$3	Potala Palace	.60	.20
2378	A507	$5	Sheep grazing	.70	.20
2379	A507	$11	Camel caravan	1.10	.40
			Nos. 2376-2379 (4)	2.75	1.00

2nd East Asian Bird Protection Conference, Oct. — A508

1983, Oct. 8 Litho. *Perf. 13½*

2380	A508	$2	Lanius cristatus, vert.	.40	.20
2381	A508	$18	Butastur indicus	1.60	.40

A509

A510

Plum Blossoms, photography by Hu Ch'ung-hsien.

1983, Oct. 31 Litho. *Perf. 14x13½*

2382	A509	$2	multicolored	.25	.20
2383	A509	$3	multi, diff.	.45	.20
2384	A509	$5	multi, diff.	.50	.20
2385	A509	$11	multi, diff.	.70	.30
			Nos. 2382-2385 (4)	1.90	.90

1983, Nov. 6 *Perf. 13x13½, 13½x13*

2386	A510	$2	JCI and Congress emblems	.25	.20
2387	A510	$18	Globe and emblems, horiz	.90	.40

Jaycees Intl., 38th World Congress, Taipei.

8th Asian-Pacific Cardiology Congress — A511

1983, Nov. 27 Litho. *Perf. 13½*

2388	A511	$2	shown	.25	.20
2389	A511	$18	Electrocardiogram	.90	.40

New Year 1984 (Year of the Rat) — A512

1983, Dec. 1 Litho. *Perf. 12½*

2390	A512	$1	multicolored	.90	.20
2391	A512	$10	multicolored	3.50	.45
a.			Souv. sheet, 2 each #2390-2391	*21.00*	6.00

Literacy Week A513

1983, Dec. 17 Litho. *Perf. 13½*

2392	A513	$2	shown	.25	.20
2393	A513	$18	Modern family, vert.	.90	.35

World Freedom Day A514

1984, Jan. 23 Litho. *Perf. 13½*

2394	A514	$2	Korean War Patriots	.25	.20
2395	A514	$18	Intl. support	1.00	.35

Drama Day — A515

Yuan Dynasty Poetry Illustrations by Tien-shih Lin (Poems by): $2, Kuan Yun-shih. $3, Po Pu. $5, Chang Ko-chiu. $18, Shang Cheng-shu. (See note with Nos. 2322-2325.)

1984, Feb. 15 Litho. *Perf. 13½*

2396	A515	$2	multicolored	*1.40*	.20
2397	A515	$3	multicolored	*2.50*	.25
2398	A515	$5	multicolored	*4.50*	.30
2399	A515	$18	multicolored	*7.00*	1.00
			Nos. 2396-2399 (4)	*15.40*	1.75

A516

A517

A518

Arbor Day — A519

1984, Mar. 12 Litho. *Perf. 13½x14*

2400	A516	$2	multicolored	.70	.20
2401	A517	$2	multicolored	.70	.20
2402	A518	$2	multicolored	.70	.20
2403	A519	$2	multicolored	.70	.20
a.			Block of 4, #2400-2403	3.50	2.25

Lin Chueh-min A520

Central News Agency, 60th Anniv. A521

1984, Mar. 29 Engr. *Perf. 13x12½*

Granite Paper

2404	A520	$2	dark green	.25	.20

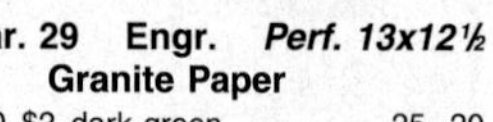

Perf. 14x13½

1984, Apr. 1 Litho. Wmk.

2405	A521	$2	Emblem	.20	.20
2406	A521	$10	Emblem, satellite, dish antenna	.60	.30

God of Longevity — A522

Ch'ing Dynasty Enamelware A523

Paintings by Chang Ta-chien (1899-1983): $2, Five Auspicious Tokens. $18, Lotus Blossoms in Ink Splash.

Wmk. 323

1984, Apr. 20 Litho. *Perf. 11½*

2407	A522	$2	multicolored	.95	.20
2408	A522	$5	multicolored	2.50	.20
2409	A522	$18	multicolored	3.75	.50
			Nos. 2407-2409 (3)	7.20	.90

1984, May 20 Photo. *Perf. 12*

Granite Paper

2410	A523	$2	Cup, pot, plate, horiz.	.30	.20
2411	A523	$3	Wine jug	.60	.20
2412	A523	$4	Teapot	.90	.20
2413	A523	$18	Candle holder	1.25	.45
			Nos. 2410-2413 (4)	3.05	1.05

China Airlines World-wide Service Inauguration A524

1984, May 31 Litho. *Perf. 13½x14*

2414	A524	$2	Jet circling globe	.20	.20
2415	A524	$7	Globe, jet	.35	.20
2416	A524	$11	New York City	.45	.30
2417	A524	$18	Amsterdam	.60	.45
			Nos. 2414-2417 (4)	1.60	1.15

30th Navigation Day A525

Perf. 13½x13

1984, July 11 Litho. Wmk. 323

2418	A525	$2	Container ship	.30	.20
2419	A525	$18	Oil tanker	2.10	.35

1984 Summer Olympics — A526

Alpine Plants — A527

Perf. 13½x14, 14x13½

1984, June 23

2420	A526	$2	Judo, horiz.	.20	.20
2421	A526	$5	Archery	.35	.20
2422	A526	$18	Swimming, horiz.	.70	.60
			Nos. 2420-2422 (3)	1.25	1.00

1984, Aug. 8 ***Perf. 13***

$2, Gentiana arisanensis. $3, Epilobium nankotaizanense. $5, Adenophora uehatae. $18, Aconitum fukutomei.

2423 A527 $2 multi .35 .20
2424 A527 $3 multi .70 .20
2425 A527 $5 multi .95 .20
2426 A527 $18 multi 1.50 .50
Nos. 2423-2426 (4) 3.50 1.10

The Eighteen Scholars, Sung Dynasty Hanging Scroll — A528

Details.

Wmk. 323

1984, Aug. 20 Litho. ***Perf. 13***

2427 A528 $2 Playing instruments *1.25* .20
2428 A528 $3 Playing chess *2.50* .20
2429 A528 $5 Practicing calligraphy *4.00* .25
2430 A528 $18 Painting *9.50* .50
Nos. 2427-2430 (4) *17.25* 1.15

Athletics Day — A529

1984, Sept. 9

2431 $5 Two players .60 .20
2432 $5 One player .60 .20
a. 'A529 Pair, #2431-2432 1.25 .90

A531

A532

1984, Sept. 9

2433 A531 $10 "20," map of Asia .50 .20

Asian-Pacific Parliamentarians' Union, 20th anniv.

1984, Oct. 10 Litho. ***Perf. 12½***

2434 A532 $2 No. 1458 .20 .20
2435 A532 $5 No. 296 .45 .20
2436 A532 $18 Museum .65 .50
a. Souv. sheet of 3, #2434-2436 7.25 2.25
Nos. 2434-2436 (3) 1.30 .90

Postal Museum opening.

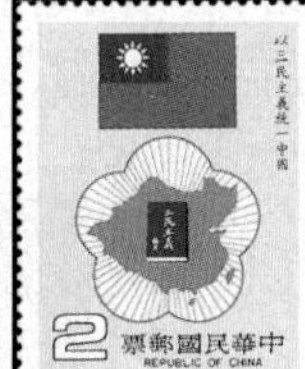

Flag, Alliance Emblem — A533

Veteran's Assistance A534

1984, Oct. 16 ***Perf. 13½***

2437 A533 $2 multicolored .30 .20

Grand Alliance for China's Reunification Under the Three Principles of the People Convention, Taipei, Oct. 16-17.

1984, Nov. 1 Litho. ***Perf. 13½***

2438 A534 $2 Vignettes .30 .20

Pine Tree A535

Bamboo A535a

Plum Tree — A535b

1984-88

2439 A535 $2 multicolored .20 .20
2440 A535a $8 multicolored .55 .20
2441 A535b $10 pale yellow bister background .65 .20
a. Grayish tan background .45 .20
Nos. 2439-2441 (3) 1.40 .60

Issued: #2439-2440, 2441a, 11/12; #2441,1/12/88.

See #2495-2503, 3303.

A536

A537

1984, Dec. 1 ***Perf. 12x12½***

2442 A536 $1 multicolored .50 .20
2443 A536 $10 multicolored 2.50 .30
a. Min. sheet, 2 ea #2442-2443 *6.25* 2.50

New Year 1985 (Year of the Ox).

1985, Jan. 11 Litho. ***Perf. 13½***

2444 A537 $5 Scales, legal codes .45 .20

Judicial Day 1985.

Quemoy and Matsu Scenes A538

1985, Jan. 23 Litho. ***Perf. 13½x14***

2445 A538 $2 Ku-kang Lake, Quemoy .20 .20
2446 A538 $5 Kuang-hai Stone, Quemoy .50 .20
2447 A538 $8 Sheng-li Reservoir, Matsu .65 .20
2448 A538 $10 Tung-chu Lighthouse, Matsu .85 .25
Nos. 2445-2448 (4) 2.20 .85

Sir Robert Hart (1835-1911) A539

1985, Feb. 15 Litho. ***Perf. 14x13½***

2449 A539 $2 No. 1 .30 .20

Inspector General of Chinese Customs, 1863-1908, and founder of the Chinese Postal Service.

Lo Fu-hsing (1886-1914) A540

Tsou Jung (1882-1905) A541

1985, Feb. 24 ***Perf. 13x13½***

2450 A540 $2 multicolored .30 .20

1985, Mar. 29 Engr. ***Perf. 13½x12½***
Granite Paper

2451 A541 $3 green .30 .20

Chung-cheng Memorial Hall Main Gate — A542

1985, Apr. 5 Litho. ***Perf. 13***

2452 A542 $2 shown .20 .20
2453 A542 $8 Tzuhu Memorial .75 .25
2454 A542 $10 Chiang Kai-shek, vert. .90 .30
Nos. 2452-2454 (3) 1.85 .75

Tenth death anniv. of Chiang Kai-shek.

A543

A544

1985, May 8 Litho. ***Perf. 13½***

2455 A543 $2 Carnation .50 .20
2456 A543 $2 Day lily .50 .20
a. Pair, #2455-2456 1.60 .80

Mother's Day.

1985, May 18

2457 A544 $5 Tunnel to Chi-chin Island .45 .20

Kaohsiung Cross-Harbor Tunnel, 1st anniv.

Girl Scouts, 75th Anniv. — A545

Wmk. 323

1985, June 1 Litho. ***Perf. 13½***

2458 A545 $2 multicolored .25 .20
2459 A545 $18 multicolored .90 .30

The Book of Odes, Confucius A545a

1985, June 22 Litho. Wmk. 323

2460 A545a $2 Spring .90 .20
2461 A545a $5 Summer 1.75 .20
2462 A545a $8 Fall 3.50 .30
2463 A545a $10 Winter 4.25 .50
Nos. 2460-2463 (4) *10.40* 1.20

Fruit — A546

Perf. 13½x14

1985, July 5 Litho. Wmk. 323

2464 A546 $2 Wax Jambo .50 .20
2465 A546 $3 Guava .85 .20
2466 A546 $5 Carambola 1.00 .20
2467 A546 $8 Litchi nut 1.10 .30
Nos. 2464-2467 (4) 3.45 .90

Ch'ing Dynasty (1644-1911) Ivory Carvings — A547

1985, July 18 Wmk. 323 ***Perf. 13½***

2468 A547 $2 Dragon Boat .20 .20
2469 A547 $3 Landscape .45 .20
2470 A547 $5 Melon, water container .65 .20
2471 A547 $18 Brush holder, vert. .85 .35
Nos. 2468-2471 (4) 2.15 .95

T'ang Dynasty (618-907) Aristocrat — A548

Designs: $5, Sung Dynasty (960-1280) palace woman. $8, Yuan Dynasty (1280-1368) aristocrat. $11, Ming Dynasty (1368-1644) aristocrat.

1985, Aug. 1 Wmk. 323 *Perf. 13½*

2472 A548 $2 multicolored .40 .20
2473 A548 $5 multicolored 1.25 .20
2474 A548 $8 multicolored 1.75 .20
2475 A548 $11 multicolored 2.25 .30
Nos. 2472-2475 (4) 5.65 .90

4th Asian Conf. on Costume, Aug. 3.

In the 2 rows of Chinese characters above the denomination, the right row has 3 characters and a dot on #2472-2475, 4 characters and a dot on #2549-2552. #2605-2608, 2660-2663 have solid black numerals.

See #2549-2552, 2605-2608, 2660-2663, 2721-2724, 2794-2797.

Social Welfare Program A549

Perf. 13½x14

1985, Aug. 15 Wmk. 323

2476 A549 $2 Heart, bird feeding young .30 .20

Historic Sites A550

Wmk. 323

1985, Sept. 3 Litho. *Perf. 13½*

2477 A550 $2 Taipei North Gate .20 .20
2478 A550 $5 San Domingo Fort, Tamsui .50 .20
2479 A550 $8 Lung Shun Temple, Lukang .65 .20
2480 A550 $10 Confucius Temple, Changhua .85 .25
Nos. 2477-2480 (4) 2.20 .85

Bonsai — A551

Trade Shows — A552

Perf. 13½x14

1985, Sept. 22 Wmk. 323

2481 A551 $2 Oak .20 .20
2482 A551 $5 Five-leaf pine .45 .20
2483 A551 $8 Lohan pine .60 .25
2484 A551 $18 Banyan .90 .50
Nos. 2481-2484 (4) 2.15 1.15

1985, Oct. 5 *Perf. 13½*

Taipei World Trade Center and show emblems: a, Sporting goods. b, Toys and gifts. c, Electronics. d, Machinery. Se-tenant in continuous design.

2485 Strip of 4 2.75 1.25
a.-d. A552 $2 any single .60 .20

Scenes of Modern Taiwan, Map, Flag A553

1985, Oct. 25

2486 A553 $2 shown .50 .20
2487 A553 $18 Chiang Kai-shek, Triumphal Arch 1.75 .40

Defeat of Japanese army, end of World War II, and return of Taiwan to control of the Republic, 40th anniv.

7th Asian Conference on Mental Retardation A554

Sun Yat-sen and Birthplace A555

1985, Nov. 8 *Perf. 14x13½*

2488 A554 $2 multicolored .40 .20
2489 A554 $11 multicolored .90 .30

1985, Nov. 12 *Perf. 13½*

2490 A555 $2 multicolored .40 .20
2491 A555 $18 multicolored 1.00 .40

Postal Life Insurance, 50th Anniv. — A556

New Year 1986 (Year of the Tiger) — A557

1985, Dec. 1

2492 A556 $2 multicolored .30 .20

1985, Dec. 1 *Perf. 12½*

2493 A557 $1 multicolored .60 .20
2494 A557 $10 multicolored 1.60 .35
a. Min. sheet, 2 ea #2493-2494 *8.00* 3.25

Flora Types of 1984

1986, Jan. 10 Litho. *Perf. 13½*

2495 A535 $1 multicolored .20 .20
2496 A535a $11 multicolored .45 .20
2497 A535b $18 multicolored .65 .20

1988, Feb. 12

2498 A535 $1.50 multicolored .20 .20
2499 A535a $7.50 multicolored .40 .20
2500 A535b $16 multicolored 1.00 .30

#2500 has value expressed in dollars and cents.

1989, Feb. 24

2501 A535 $3 multicolored .20 .20
2502 A535a $16.50 multicolored 1.00 .30
2503 A535b $21 multicolored 1.10 .35
Nos. 2495-2503 (9) 5.20 2.15

Cultural Renaissance Movement — A558

Painting: Hermit Anglers on a Mountain Stream, Ming Dynasty, 1386-1644. Continuous design. (Each stamp is numbered from 1 to 5 in Chinese. See illustrations with Nos. 1682-1691 for numerals.)

1986, Jan. 28 Litho. *Perf. 13½*

2507 Strip of 5 8.00 7.00
a.-e. A558 $2 any single *1.40* .25

See No. 2604.

Floral Arrangements A559

Wmk. 323

1986, Feb. 20 Litho. *Perf. 13½*

2517 A559 $2 denom. UL .20 .20
2518 A559 $5 denom. UR .45 .20
2519 A559 $8 shown .50 .20
2520 A559 $10 denom. UL .75 .25
Nos. 2517-2520 (4) 1.90 .85

Compare with designs A483, A584.

Natl. Postal Service, 90th Anniv. A560

$2, Unloading express mail at airport. $5, Motorcycle delivery. $8, Technological innovations. $10, Electronic sorting machine.

1986, Mar. 20

2521 A560 $2 multi .20 .20
2522 A560 $5 multi, vert. .25 .20
2523 A560 $8 multi, vert. .40 .20
2524 A560 $10 multi .50 .25
a. Souv. sheet of 4, #2521-2524 4.25 2.55
Nos. 2521-2524 (4) 1.35 .85

Chen Tien-hua (1875-1905), Revolutionary A561

1986, Mar. 29 Engr. *Perf. 13½x12½*

Granite Paper

2525 A561 $2 violet .20 .20

Yushan Natl. Park A562

1986, Apr. 10 Litho. *Perf. 13½*

2526 A562 $2 multicolored .40 .20
2527 A562 $5 multi, diff. 1.00 .20
2528 A562 $8 multi, diff. 1.25 .20
2529 A562 $10 multi, diff. 1.50 .30
Nos. 2526-2529 (4) 4.15 .90

Power Plants A563

1986, Apr. 29

2530 A563 $2 Hydro-electric .20 .20
2531 A563 $8 Thermo-electric .50 .20
2532 A563 $10 Nuclear .70 .25
Nos. 2530-2532 (3) 1.40 .65

Economic prosperity through energy development.

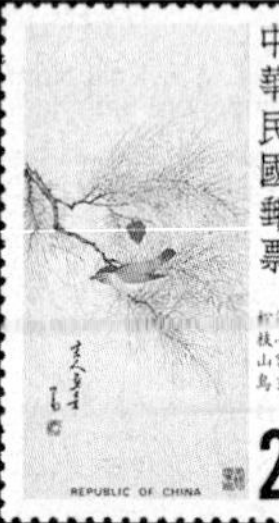

Paintings by P'u Hsin-yu (1896-1963) A564

1986, May 22 *Perf. 11½*

2533 A564 $2 Bird 1.25 .20
2534 A564 $8 Landscape 2.50 .30
2535 A564 $10 Woman in forest 3.75 .35
Nos. 2533-2535 (3) 7.50 .85

Asian Productivity Org., 25th Anniv. — A565

1986, June 3 *Perf. 13x13½*

2536 A565 $2 multicolored .20 .20
2537 A565 $11 multicolored .75 .30

Natl. Productivity Center, 30th anniv.

Coral-reef Fish A566

Designs: a, Chrysiptera starcki. b, Chelmon rostratus. c, Chaetodon xanthurus. d, Chaetodon quadrimaculatus. e, Chaetodon meyeri. f, Genicanthus semifasciatus. g, Genicanthus semifasciatus. h, Pomacanthus annularis. i, Lienardella fasciata. j, Balistapus undulatus.

1986, June 27 *Perf. 13½*

2538 Block of 10 4.50 4.00
a.-j. A566 $2 any single .40 .20

Protection of Intellectual Property Rights — A567

1986, June 12

2539 A567 $2 Macaw .75 .20

Nos. 2294, 2297 Surcharged

1986, July 9 Litho. *Perf. 13½*

2540 A432 $2 on $6 multi .20 .20
2541 A432 $8 on $9 multi .45 .25

60th Anniv. of northward expedition by the national revolutionary army.

Bridges A568

1986, July 30

2542	A568	$2 Tzu Mu, 1965	.30	.20
2543	A568	$5 Chang Hung, 1968	.75	.20
2544	A568	$8 Kuan Fu, 1977	1.00	.20
2545	A568	$10 Kuan Tu, 1983	1.40	.25
		Nos. 2542-2545 (4)	3.45	.85

Love between Liang Shanpo and Chu Yingtai, Folk Tale — A569

Cartoons by Huang Mu-ts'un: a, Yingtai disguised to go to school. b, Yingtai and Shanpo meet in class. c, The friends at pond. d, Yingtai summoned home for arranged marriage. e, Yingtai and Shanpo ascend to heaven as butterflies (each stamp is numbered from 1 to 5 in Chinese. See illustrations with Nos. 1682-1691 for numerals.)

1986, Aug. 12 ***Perf. 12½***

2546	Strip of 5	3.50	2.00
a.-e.	A569 $5 any single	.50	.20

Social Awareness Campaign A570

1986, Sept. 12 Litho. ***Perf. 13½***

2547	A570	$2 Rainbow, children	.30	.20
2548	A570	$8 Children, adults	.60	.25

Folk Costumes — A571

Designs: $2, Shang Dynasty (1766-1122 B.C.) aristocrat. $5, Warring States (403-221 B.C.) aristocrat. $8, Later Han Dynasty (A.D. 25-221) empress. $10, Flying ribbons gown, Wei and Tsin Dynasties (A.D. 221-420) aristocrat.

1986, Sept. 23 Litho. ***Perf. 13½***

2549	A571	$2 multicolored	.60	.20
2550	A571	$5 multicolored	1.00	.20
2551	A571	$8 multicolored	1.25	.20
2552	A571	$10 multicolored	1.90	.20
		Nos. 2549-2552 (4)	4.75	.80

Ch'ing Dynasty Ju-i Scepters A572

1986, Oct. 10 Photo. ***Perf. 14x14½***

2553	A572	$2 White jade	.20	.20
2554	A572	$3 Red coral	.35	.20
2555	A572	$4 Redwood and gems	.45	.20
2556	A572	$18 Gilded wood	1.25	.40
		Nos. 2553-2556 (4)	2.25	1.00

See Nos. 2582-2585.

Chiang Kai-shek A573

Portrait and: $5, Map and flag. $8, Emblem. $10, Flags on globe.

1986, Oct. 31 Litho. ***Perf. 13½***

2557	A573	$2 multicolored	.20	.20
2558	A573	$5 multicolored	.60	.20
2559	A573	$8 multicolored	.80	.20
2560	A573	$8 multicolored	1.00	.25
a.		Souv. sheet of 4, #2557-2560	5.75	2.50
		Nos. 2557-2560 (4)	2.60	.85

Cultural Heritage A574

Architecture: $2, Chin-Kuang Fu land development and defense fund building, 1826. $5, Erh-sha-wan Gun Emplacement, Keelung, 1841, restored 1979. $8, Fort Hsi T'ai, 1886. $10, Matsu Temple, Peng-hu, renovated 1563-1624.

1986, Nov. 14 Litho. ***Perf. 13½***

2561	A574	$2 multicolored	.30	.20
2562	A574	$5 multicolored	.70	.20
2563	A574	$8 multicolored	.80	.25
2564	A574	$10 multicolored	1.00	.30
		Nos. 2561-2564 (4)	2.80	.95

New Year 1987 (Year of the Hare) — A575

1986, Dec. 1 ***Perf. 12½***

2565	A575	$1 dl pink & multi	.50	.20
2566	A575	$10 pale grn & multi	1.75	.30
a.		Souv. sheet, 2 each #2565-2566	*10.50*	3.50

Kenting, 1st Natl. Park A576

1987, Jan. 8 Litho. ***Perf. 13½***

2567	A576	$2 Garden	.30	.20
2568	A576	$5 Shore rocks	.70	.20
2569	A576	$8 Shore and hill	.90	.20
2570	A576	$10 Shore and rocks, diff.	1.25	.30
		Nos. 2567-2570 (4)	3.15	.90

Folk Art — A577

Puppets: $2, Hand puppet. $5, Marionette. $18, Shadow puppet.

1987, Feb. 12 Litho. ***Perf. 14x13½***

2571	A577	$2 multicolored	.30	.20
2572	A577	$5 multicolored	.80	.20
2573	A577	$18 multicolored	1.40	.40
		Nos. 2571-2573 (3)	2.50	.80

Speedpost A578

Wu Yueh (1878-1905), Revolutionary A579

1987, Mar. 20 Litho. ***Perf. 14x13½***

2574	A578	$2 multicolored	.25	.20
2575	A578	$18 multicolored	.90	.40

Stamp Day.

1987, Mar. 29 Engr. ***Perf. 13½x12½***

2576	A579	$2 orange	.50	.20

Landscapes Painted by Madame Chiang Kai-shek — A580

$2, Singing Creek with Bamboo Orchestra. $5, Mountains Draped in Clouds. $8, Vista of Tranquility. $10, Mountains after a Snowfall.

1987, Apr. 10 Litho. ***Perf. 13½***

2577	A580	$2 blk, buff & ver	.30	.20
2578	A580	$5 blk, buff & ver	.75	.20
2579	A580	$8 blk, buff & ver	1.75	.30
2580	A580	$10 blk, buff & ver	2.40	.45
		Nos. 2577-2580 (4)	5.20	1.15

Stone Sculptures — A581

Designs: a, Head of a Bodhisattva, sandstone, Northern Wei Dynasty (386-534). b, Standing Buddha, limestone, Northern Ch'i Dynasty (550-577). c, Head of a Bodhisattva, sandstone, T'ang Dynasty (618-907). d, Seated Buddha, alabaster, T'ang Dynasty.

1987, Apr. 23

2581	Strip of 4	2.75	2.25
a.-d.	A581 $5 any single	.55	.30

No. 2581a shows seven Chinese characters at left; No. 2581c shows five.

Ju-i Scepters, Ch'ing Dynasty A582

1987, May 7 Photo. ***Perf. 14x14½***

2582	A582	$2 Silver and gems	.40	.20
2583	A582	$3 Gold and gems	1.00	.20
2584	A582	$4 Gilded, jade and inlaid gems	1.50	.20
2585	A582	$18 Gilded, inlaid malachite	2.10	.45
		Nos. 2582-2585 (4)	5.00	1.05

Feitsui Reservoir Inauguration A583

1987, June 6 Litho. ***Perf. 13½x14***

2586	A583	$2 Reservoir	.35	.20
2587	A583	$18 Hsintien Stream, reservoir	1.25	.45

Flower Arrangements by Huang Yung-ch'uan A584

Lions Club Intl. 70th Annual Convention, Taipei — A585

1987, June 19 ***Perf. 13½***

2588	A584	$2 denom. LL	.20	.20
2589	A584	$5 denom. LL	.50	.20
2590	A584	$8 Flowers in brown vase	.65	.20
2591	A584	$10 denom. UR	.75	.25
		Nos. 2588-2591 (4)	2.10	.85

Compare with designs A483, A559.

1987, July 1

2592	A585	$2 multicolored	.30	.20
2593	A585	$18 multicolored	1.00	.50

Sino-Japanese War, 50th Anniv. — A586

1987, July 7 ***Perf. 14x13½***

2594	A586	$1 Battle front	.20	.20
2595	A586	$2 Chiang Kai-shek giving speech	.30	.20
2596	A586	$5 Public donating funds	.35	.20
2597	A586	$6 Troops marching	.45	.20
2598	A586	$8 Signing of peace treaty	.65	.25
2599	A586	$18 Parade	.80	.40
		Nos. 2594-2599 (6)	2.75	1.45

Wang Yun-wu (1888-1979), Lexicographer A587

1987, Aug. 14 ***Perf. 13½***

2600	A587	$2 gray black	.25	.20

Memorial Hall Type of 1981

Perf. 12½x13½

1987, Sept. 24 **Photo.**

2601	A468	10c lake	.20	.20
2602	A468	30c brt green	.20	.20
2603	A468	60c brt blue	.20	.20
		Nos. 2601-2603 (3)	.60	.60

A588

Cultural Renaissance Movement — A589

Scroll, 1543, by Weng Chen-ming (1470-1559), a copy of Chao Po-su's *Red Cliff.* Nos. 2604a-2604e and 2604f-2604j are printed in continuous designs. (Each stamp is numbered from 1 to 10 in Chinese. See illustrations with Nos. 1682-1691 for numerals.)

1987, Sept. 22 Engr. *Perf. 13½*

No.	Type	Description	Unused	Used
2604		Block of 10	9.00	9.00
a.-e.	A588	$3 any single	.70	.25
f.-j.	A589	$3 any single	.70	.25

Folk Costumes — A590

$1.50, Han woman, early Ch'ing Dynasty (1644-1911). $3, Wife of a Ch'ing Dynasty Manchu Bannerman. $7.50, Urban woman wearing Manchu ch'i-p'ao dress, c. 1912. $18, Short jacket over long skirt, c. 1920.

1987, Oct. 2 Litho.

No.	Type	Description	Unused	Used
2605	A590	$1.50 multicolored	*.85*	.20
2606	A590	$3 multicolored	*1.10*	.20
2607	A590	$7.50 multicolored	*1.25*	.20
2608	A590	$18 multicolored	*1.50*	.50
		Nos. 2605-2608 (4)	*4.70*	1.10

Nos. 2605-2608 have 3 groups of 2 smaller Chinese characters above denomination. Nos. 2660-2663 have 2 groups of 2 and 4 characters.

A591

A592

1987, Nov. 12 *Perf. 13½x14*

No.	Type	Description	Unused	Used
2609	A591	$3 Ta Chen Tian temple, Taichung	.30	.20
2610	A591	$18 Confucius	1.10	.55

Intl. Symposium on Confucianism, Taipei, Nov. 12-17.

1987, Dec. 1 *Perf. 12½*

No.	Type	Description	Unused	Used
2611	A592	$1.50 multicolored	.60	.20
2612	A592	$12 multicolored	1.60	.30
a.		Souv. sheet, 2 ea #2611-2612	8.00	2.50

New Year 1988 (Year of the Dragon).

Constitution, 40th Anniv. — A593

1987, Dec. 25 Litho. *Perf. 13½*

No.	Type	Description	Unused	Used
2613	A593	$3 multicolored	.20	.20
2614	A593	$16 multi, diff.	.85	.55

Prevent Hypertension Campaign A594

1988, Jan. 8 *Perf. 12½x13½*

No.	Type	Description	Unused	Used
2615	A594	$3 multicolored	.25	.20

Fruit Tree Blossoms — A595

Wmk. 323

1988, Feb. 4 Litho. *Perf. 13½*

No.	Type	Description	Unused	Used
2616	A595	$3 Prunus mume	1.10	.20
2617	A595	$7.50 Prunus armeniaca	1.25	.30
2618	A595	$12 Prunus persica	1.60	.50
a.		Min. sheet of 3, #2616-2618	*17.00*	*17.00*

Wmk. 323

1988, May 5 Litho. *Perf. 13½*

No.	Type	Description	Unused	Used
2619	A595	$3 Paeonia suffruticosa	.30	.20
2620	A595	$7.50 Punica granatum	.90	.30
2621	A595	$12 Nelumbo nucifera	1.10	.50
a.		Min. sheet of 3, #2619-2621	*9.00*	*9.00*

Wmk. 323

1988, Aug. 9 Litho. *Perf. 13½*

No.	Type	Description	Unused	Used
2622	A595	$3 Impatiens balsamina	.30	.20
2623	A595	$7.50 Osmanthus fragrans	.90	.30
2624	A595	$12 Chrysanthemum morifolium	1.10	.50
a.		Min. sheet of 3, #2622-2624	*8.50*	*8.50*

Wmk. 323

1988, Nov. 7 Litho. *Perf. 13½*

No.	Type	Description	Unused	Used
2625	A595	$3 Hibiscus mutabilis	.30	.20
2626	A595	$7.50 Camellia japonica	1.25	.30
2627	A595	$12 Narcissus tazetta	1.50	.50
a.		Min. sheet of 3, #2625-2627	*9.00*	*9.00*
		Nos. 2616-2627 (12)	11.60	4.00

Tourism Day — A596

Folk art: $3, Modeled dough figurines. $7.50, Blown sweet-malt sugar candy. $16, Sugar paintings.

Perf. 13½x14

1988, Mar. 2 Litho. Wmk. 323

No.	Type	Description	Unused	Used
2628	A596	$3 multicolored	.55	.20
2629	A596	$7.50 multicolored	1.10	.30
2630	A596	$16 multicolored	2.00	.70
		Nos. 2628-2630 (3)	3.65	1.20

A597

A598

Perf. 13½x12½

1988, Mar. 29 Engr. Wmk. 323

No.	Type	Description	Unused	Used
2631	A597	$3 brown	.40	.20

Hsu Hsi-lin (1873-1907), hero of the revolution.

1988 Litho. *Perf. 13½*

No.	Type	Description	Unused	Used
2632	A598	$1.50 Biotechnology	.20	.20
2633	A598	$3 Energy resources	.25	.20
2634	A598	$7 Immunization	.35	.25
2635	A598	$7.50 Automation	.35	.25
2636	A598	$10 Telecommunications	.45	.40
2637	A598	$12 Laser technology	.50	.40
2638	A598	$16 Micro-optics	.75	.65
2639	A598	$16.50 Agricultural research	1.00	.65
		Nos. 2632-2639 (8)	3.85	3.00

Industrialization by technological development. Issued: $3, $7.50, $10, $16, Apr. 22; others, May 9.

Police Day A599

Wmk. 323

1988, June 15 Litho. *Perf. 13½*

No.	Type	Description	Unused	Used
2640	A599	$3 Traffic control	.20	.20
2641	A599	$12 Rescue operations	.50	.40

Amphibians A600

1988, July 8 *Perf. 13½x14*

No.	Type	Description	Unused	Used
2642	A600	$1.50 Microhyla butleri	*.80*	.20
2643	A600	$3 Rana taipehensis	*1.25*	.20
2644	A600	$7.50 Microhyla inornata	*1.60*	.35
2645	A600	$16 Rhacophorus smaragdinus	*2.10*	.75
		Nos. 2642-2645 (4)	*5.75*	1.50

China Broadcasting Corp. (BBC), 60th Anniv. — A601

Wmk. 323

1988, Aug. 1 Litho. *Perf. 13½*

No.	Type	Description	Unused	Used
2646	A601	$3 multicolored	.20	.20

Victory at the Battle of Kinmen, 30th Anniv. A602

Designs: $1.50, Chiang Kai-shek and artillery commander. $3, With troops. $7.50, Cannon. $12, Tanks.

1988, Aug. 23

No.	Type	Description	Unused	Used
2647	A602	$1.50 multicolored	.25	.20
2648	A602	$3 multicolored	.30	.20
2649	A602	$7.50 multicolored	.35	.25
2650	A602	$12 multicolored	.50	.40
		Nos. 2647-2650 (4)	1.40	1.05

Sports Promotion — A603

#2651-2652, Basketball. #2653-2654, Baseball.

1988, Sept. 9

No.	Type	Description	Unused	Used
2651		$5 Players	.70	.25
2652		$5 Players	.70	.25
a.		A603 Pair, #2651-2652	1.40	1.10
2653		$5 Batter	.70	.25
2654		$5 Catcher	.70	.25
a.		A603 Pair, #2653-2654	1.40	1.10
		Nos. 2651-2654 (4)	2.80	1.00

#2652a, 2654a have continuous designs.

Yangmingshan Natl. Park — A604

1988, Sept. 16

No.	Type	Description	Unused	Used
2655	A604	$1.50 Volcanic crater	*.20*	.20
2656	A604	$3 Lake	*.35*	.20
2657	A604	$7.50 Tatun Volcanic Range	*.65*	.25
2658	A604	$16 Dormant volcano	*1.25*	.55
		Nos. 2655-2658 (4)	*2.45*	1.20

Lofty Mount Lu, a Hanging Scroll, 1467, By Shen Chou (1427-1509) — A605

Painting details: a, UL. b, UR. c, LL. d, LR.

Wmk. 323

1988, Oct. 19 Litho. *Perf. 11½*

No.	Type	Description	Unused	Used
2659	A605	Block of 4	*5.50*	3.50
a.-d.		$5 any single	*1.25*	.25

Folk Costumes — A606

Designs: $2, Shang Dynasty (1766-1122 B.C.) nobleman. $3, Warring States (403-221 B.C.) ruler. $7.50, Wei-Chin Period (221-420) official. $12, Northern Dynasties (502-581) official.

Perf. 13½x14

1988, Nov. 23 Litho. Wmk. 323

2660 A606 $2 multicolored *.40* .20
2661 A606 $3 multicolored *.70* .20
2662 A606 $7.50 multicolored *1.40* .35
2663 A606 $12 multicolored *2.00* .55
Nos. 2660-2663 (4) *4.50* 1.30

Nos. 2721-2724 have groups of 2 and 6 Chinese characters above denomination; Nos. 2660-2663 groups of 2 and 4; #2794-2797 groups of 1 and 5.

A607

A608

1988, Dec. 1 ***Perf. 12½***

2664 A607 $2 multicolored *.55* .20
2665 A607 $13 multicolored *4.25* .60
a. Souv. sheet, 2 each #2664-2665 *10.50* 10.50

New Year 1989 (Year of the Snake).

Wmk. 323

1989, Jan. 4 Litho. ***Perf. 13½***

2666 A608 $3 black .40 .20

Tai Ch'uan-hsien (1890-1949), party leader.

Pres. Chiang Ching-kuo (1910-88) A609

1989, Jan. 13

2667 A609 $3 shown .20 .20
2668 A609 $6 Suffrage .30 .20
2669 A609 $7.50 Industry .45 .30
2670 A609 $16 Children .70 .65
Nos. 2667-2670 (4) 1.65 1.35

Ni Ying-tien (1884-1910), Revolution Leader — A610

Perf. 13½x12½

1989, Mar. 28 Engr. Wmk. 323

2671 A610 $3 black .20 .20

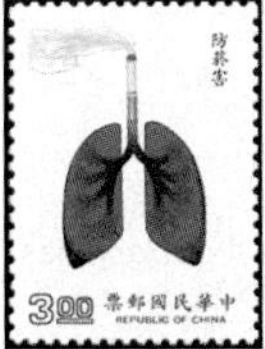

Stop Smoking A611

Lighthouses A612

Perf. 13½x12½

1989, Apr. 7 Litho. Wmk. 323

2672 A611 $3 multicolored .20 .20

1989-91 ***Perf. 13½***

2673 A612 75c Mu Tou Yu .20 .20
2674 A612 $2 Lu Tao .20 .20
2675 A612 $2.25 Pen Chia Yu .20 .20
2676 A612 $3 Pitou Chiao .25 .20
2677 A612 $4.50 Tungyin Tao .30 .20
2678 A612 $6 Chilai Pi .50 .25
2679 A612 $7 Fukwei Chiao .60 .35
2680 A612 $7.50 Hua Yu .65 .35
2681 A612 $9 Oluan Pi .70 .25
2682 A612 $10 Kaohsiung .80 .45
2683 A612 $10.50 Yuweng Tao .85 .35
2683A A612 $12 Tungchu Tao 1.00 .55
2683B A612 $13 Yeh Liu 1.10 .45
2683C A612 $15 Tungchi Yu 1.25 .80
2684 A612 $16.50 Chimei Yu 1.40 .75
Nos. 2673-2684 (15) 10.00 5.55

Issued: $7, $15, 5/19/90; $6, $12, 1/9/91; $2, $3, $7.50, $10, $16.50, 5/20/91; others, 1989.

See Nos. 2811-2823.

1st Natl. Wealth Survey A613

1989, May 18 Litho. ***Perf. 13½***

2685 A613 $3 multicolored .30 .20

Ch'u Ts'u Collection of Poems, 722-481 B.C. — A614

Excerpts: $3, "I once tended nine fields of orchids; Also I had planted a hundred rods of melilotus" (Li Sao). $7.50, "No grief is greater than parting of the living; No joy is more than making new friends" (Chiu Ko, shao ssu ming). $12, "Since my heart is straight and good, Why should I be chagrined at living remote and neglected?" (Chiu Chang, she chiang). $16, "The steed will not gallop itself into servitude; The phoenix has no appetite for slave food." (Chiu Pien).

1989, June 7 Photo. ***Perf. 11½x12***

Granite Paper

2686 A614 $3 Man overlooking fields .35 .20
2687 A614 $7.50 Man, woman on path .90 .45
2688 A614 $12 Man holding staff 1.60 .70
2689 A614 $16 Man, stallion, stone gate 2.00 1.00
Nos. 2686-2689 (4) 4.85 2.35

Compare with types A629, A663. Nos. 2686-2689 have two Chinese characters near denomination. Nos. 2725-2728 have groups of 3 and 4 characters.

Taipei Subway Inauguration — A615

1989, June 27 Litho. ***Perf. 13½***

2690 A615 $3 Subway tunnel .40 .20
2691 A615 $16 Entering underground 1.10 .90

A616

A616a

A616b

Butterflies A616c

$2, *Graphium sarpedon connectens.* $3, *Papilo memnon heronus.* $7.50, *Princeps demoleus libanius.* $9, *Pachliopa aristolochiae interpositas.*

Wmk. 323

1989, July 14 Litho. ***Perf. 13½***

2692 A616 $2 multicolored .20 .20
2693 A616a $3 multicolored .55 .20
2694 A616b $7.50 multicolored 1.40 .30
2695 A616c $9 multicolored 1.75 .35
Nos. 2692-2695 (4) 3.90 1.05

Compare with design A627.

Ch'ing Dynasty Teapots from I-Hsing of Kiangsu, 1644-1911 A617

1989, July 28 ***Perf. 13½x14***

2696 A617 $2 multicolored .25 .20
2697 A617 $3 multi, diff. .70 .20
2698 A617 $12 multi, diff. 1.75 .50
2699 A617 $16 multi, diff. 1.75 .70
Nos. 2696-2699 (4) 4.45 1.60

For stamps with teapot designs and solid black denominations see Nos. 2760-2764.

Intl. Seminar on Fan Chung-yen (989-1052), Military Leader and Civil Service Reformer — A618

Perf. 14x13½

1989, Sept. 1 Litho. Wmk. 323

2700 A618 $12 multicolored .90 .55

Autumn Colors on the Ch'iao and Hua Mountains, 14th Cent., by Ch'iao Meng-fu A619

a, Right side of mountain, trees. b, Trees, left side of mountain. c, House, trees. d, shown.

Wmk. 323

1989, Oct. 5 Litho. ***Perf. 13½***

2701 Strip of 4 7.75 4.50
a.-d. A619 $7.50 any single 1.75 .50

Social Welfare A619a

1989, Nov. 3 Litho. ***Perf. 13½***

2701E A619a $3 multicolored .25 .20

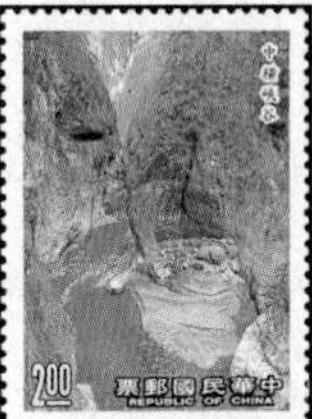

Taroko Natl. Park — A620

New Year 1990 (Year of the Horse) — A621

Designs: $2, Marble gorge, Liwu River. $3, Hohuan Mountain. $12, Waterfall, Cirque of Nanhu. $16, Chingshui Cliff.

Wmk. 323

1989, Nov. 28 Litho. ***Perf. 13½***

2702 A620 $2 multicolored .20 .20
2703 A620 $3 multicolored .25 .20
2704 A620 $12 multicolored .55 .45
2705 A620 $16 multicolored .70 .60
Nos. 2702-2705 (4) 1.70 1.45

1989, Dec. 1 ***Perf. 12½***

2706 A621 $2 multicolored .45 .20
2707 A621 $13 multicolored 1.25 .60
a. Souv. sheet, 2 ea #2706-2707 6.50 2.50

Yu Lu — A622

Men Shen, "guardian spirits" (likenesses of legendary beings placed on residence doors at the new year): No. 2708, Yu Lu. No. 2709, Shen Shu. No. 2710, Wei-ch'ih Ching-te. No. 2711, Ch'in Shu-pao.

Wmk. 323

1990, Jan. 19 Litho. ***Perf. 13½***

2708 A622 $3 shown 1.10 .20
2709 A622 $3 "$3" at LR 1.10 .20
a. Pair, #2708-2709 2.25 2.00
2710 A622 $7.50 "$7.50" at LL 2.75 .50
2711 A622 $7.50 "$7.50" at LR 2.75 .50
a. Pair, #2710-2711 5.50 5.00
Nos. 2708-2711 (4) 7.70 1.40

Nos. 2709a, 2711a have continuous designs.

A623

Scenery — A624

Designs: $2, Lishan House, Pear Mountain. $18, Tayu Pass, Tayuling, vert.

Wmk. 323

1990, Feb. 10 Litho. *Perf. 13½*

2712 A623 $2 multicolored .20 .20
2713 A624 $18 multicolored 1.50 1.00

Labor Insurance System, 40th Anniv. — A625

1990, Mar. 1

2714 A625 $3 multicolored .35 .20

Liquefied Natural Gas A626

$3, Terminal, Yung-an Hsiang of Kaohsiung. $16, Container ship, map, refinery.

1990, Mar. 31 Litho. *Perf. 13½*

2715 A626 $3 multi .20 .20
2716 A626 $16 multi, vert. .90 .65

A627

A627a

A627b

Butterflies A627c

1990, Apr. 20

2717 A627 $2 *Salatura genutia* .20 .20
2718 A627a $3 *Hypolimnas misippus* .20 .20
2719 A627b $7.50 *Pieris canidia* .60 .35
2720 A627c $9 *Precis almana* .80 .45
Nos. 2717-2720 (4) 1.80 1.20

Compare with design A616.

Folk Costumes — A628

$2, Official, Sui & T'ang Dynasties (589-907). $3, Official, T'ang & Sung Dynasties (618-1280). $7.50, Royal guardsman, Chin & Yuan Dynasties (1115-1368). $12, Highest ranking civil official, Ming Dynasty (1368-1644).

1990, May 10 Litho. *Perf. 13½*

2721 A628 $2 multicolored .25 .20
2722 A628 $3 multicolored .50 .20
2723 A628 $7.50 multicolored 1.00 .30
2724 A628 $12 multicolored 1.10 .55
Nos. 2721-2724 (4) 2.85 1.25

See note after No. 2663.

Yueh Fu Classical Poetry A629

Lyrics from Tzu-yeh folk songs, Six Dynasties (222-589): $3, Spring Song at Midnight. $7.50, Summer Song at Midnight. $12, Autumn Song at Midnight. $16, Winter Song at Midnight.

Wmk. 323

1990, June 27 Litho. *Perf. 11½*

Granite Paper

2725 A629 $3 shown .30 .20
2726 A629 $7.50 Couple, river .75 .35
2727 A629 $12 Washing clothes, river 1.75 .55
2728 A629 $16 River in winter 2.50 .80
Nos. 2725-2728 (4) 5.30 1.90

Compare with designs A614 and A663.

Bonsai A630

Designs: $3, *Pinus thunbergii parl.* $6.50, *Ehretia microphylla lamk.* $12, *Buxus harlandii hance.* $16, *Celtis sinensis pers.*

1990, July 20 Litho. *Perf. 13½*

2729 A630 $3 multicolored .20 .20
2730 A630 $6.50 multicolored .45 .30
2731 A630 $12 multicolored .65 .70
2732 A630 $16 multicolored 1.00 .80
Nos. 2729-2732 (4) 2.30 2.00

Snuff Bottles — A631

1990, Aug. 9

2733 A631 $3 Bamboo stem shaped .20 .20
2734 A631 $6 Peony motif .35 .30
2735 A631 $9 Amber .50 .45
2736 A631 $16 White jade 1.00 .80
Nos. 2733-2736 (4) 2.05 1.75

Formosan Firecrest A632

1990, Aug. 20 Litho. *Perf. 13½*

2737 A632 $2 shown .20 .20
2738 A632 $3 Laughing thrush .20 .20
2739 A632 $7.50 White-eared sibia .50 .25
2740 A632 $16 Yellow tit 1.10 .60
Nos. 2737-2740 (4) 2.00 1.25

Sports — A633

1990, Sept. 8 Litho. *Perf. 13½*

2741 A633 $2 Sprint .20 .20
2742 A633 $3 Long jump .20 .20
2743 A633 $7 Pole vault .40 .30
2744 A633 $16 High hurdle 1.00 .60
Nos. 2741-2744 (4) 1.80 1.30

Flying Tigers, 50th Anniv. A634

1990, Sept. 26 Litho. *Perf. 13½*

2745 A634 $3 multicolored .65 .20

Children's Drawings A635

1990, Oct. 9

2746 A635 $2 Cat .20 .20
2747 A635 $3 Peacocks .20 .20
2748 A635 $7.50 Chickens .50 .30
2749 A635 $12 Cattle .80 .50
Nos. 2746-2749 (4) 1.70 1.20

National Theater A636

Photo. & Engr.

1990, Oct. 30 *Perf. 13½*

2750 A636 $3 shown .20 .20
2751 A636 $12 Natl. concert hall .85 .40

A637

A638

Ancient money.

1990, Nov. 5 Litho. *Perf. 13x13½*

2752 A637 $2 Shell .20 .20
2753 A637 $3 Oyster .20 .20
2754 A637 $6.50 Bone .35 .35
2755 A637 $7.50 Jade .40 .40
2756 A637 $9 Bronze .50 .50
Nos. 2752-2756 (5) 1.65 1.65

1990, Dec. 1 *Perf. 12½*

2757 A638 $2 multicolored .45 .20
2758 A638 $13 multicolored 1.75 .50
a. Souv. sheet, 2 ea #2757-2758 *6.25* 2.25

New Year 1991 (Year of the Sheep).

Hu Shih (1891-1962), Educator — A639

Wmk. 323

1990, Dec. 17 Engr. *Perf. 13½*

2759 A639 $3 purple .20 .20

Teapots, Natl. Palace Museum A640

Teapots: $2, Blue phoenix, Ming Dynasty. $3, Dragon handle and spout, Ming Dynasty. $9, Blue landscape, flowered top, Ch'ing Dynasty. $12, Rectangular, passion flower motif, Ch'ing Dynasty. $16, Rectangular, flower motif, Ch'ing Dynasty.

1991, Jan. 18 Photo. *Perf. 12*

Granite Paper

2760 A640 $2 yel, blk & blue .20 .20
2761 A640 $3 brt yel grn & blk .25 .20
2762 A640 $9 pink & multi .65 .40
2763 A640 $12 violet & multi .90 .55
2764 A640 $16 lt blue & multi 1.25 .85
Nos. 2760-2764 (5) 3.25 2.20

God of Happiness A641

God of Joy — A642

1991, Feb. 7 Litho. Perf. 13½
2765 A641 $3 shown .40 .20
2766 A641 $3 God of Wealth .40 .20
2767 A642 $7.50 shown .90 .30
2768 A642 $7.50 God of Longevity .90 .30
Nos. 2765-2768 (4) 2.60 1.00

Perf. 13½ Vert.
2765a A641 $3 *.70* .20
2766a A641 $3 *.70* .20
2767a A642 $7.50 *.70* .20
2768a A642 $7.50 *.70* .20
b. Bklt. pane of 8, 2 each #2765a-2768a + label *8.50*

Native Plants A643

Designs: $2, Petasites formosanus. $3, Heloniopsis acutifolia. $7.50, Disporum shimadai. $9, Viola nagasawai.

1991, Mar. 12 Litho. Perf. 13½
2769 A643 $2 multicolored .20 .20
2770 A643 $3 multicolored .20 .20
2771 A643 $7.50 multicolored .50 .30
2772 A643 $9 multicolored .60 .35

1991, June 12

Designs: $2, Gaultheria itoana. $3, Lysionotus montanus. $7.50, Leontopodium microphyllum. $9, Gentiana flavo-maculata.

2773 A643 $2 multicolored .20 .20
2774 A643 $3 multicolored .25 .20
2775 A643 $7.50 multicolored .80 .30
2776 A643 $9 multicolored 1.00 .35

1991, Sept. 12

Designs: $3.50, Rosa transmorrisonensis. $5, Impatiens devolii. $9, Impatiens uniflora. $12, Impatiens tayemonii.

2777 A643 $3.50 multicolored .25 .20
2778 A643 $5 multicolored .45 .20
2779 A643 $9 multicolored .80 .35
2780 A643 $12 multicolored 1.00 .45

1991, Dec. 12

Designs: $3.50, Kalanchoe garambiensis. $5, Pieris taiwanensis. $9, Pleione formosana. $12, Elaeagnus oldhamii.

2781 A643 $3.50 multicolored .20 .20
2782 A643 $5 multicolored .30 .20
2783 A643 $9 multicolored .65 .40
2784 A643 $12 multicolored .80 .45
Nos. 2769-2784 (16) 8.20 4.55

Hsiung Cheng-Chi (1887-1910), Revolutionary A644

1991, Mar. 28 Engr. Perf. 13½x12½
2785 A644 $3 blue .20 .20

Republic of China, 80th Anniv. A645

1991, Mar. 28 Litho. Perf. 13½
2786 A645 $3 Agriculture .20 .20
2787 A645 $7.50 Science & technology .40 .30
2788 A645 $12 Cultural activities .60 .40
2789 A645 $16 Transportation .90 .55
Nos. 2786-2789 (4) 2.10 1.45

Children's Toys A646

Folk Costumes A647

1991, Apr. 20 Litho. Perf. 13½
2790 A646 $3 Bamboo pony .25 .20
2791 A646 $3 Woven-grass grasshopper .25 .20
2792 A646 $3 Top .25 .20
2793 A646 $3 Pinwheels .25 .20
a. Souv. sheet of 4, #2790-2793 *4.50* 2.00
Nos. 2790-2793 (4) 1.00 .80

See Nos. 2840-2843. Compare with designs A676, A696.

Perf. 13½ Vert.
2790a A646 $3 *.75* .20
2791a A646 $3 *.75* .20
2792a A646 $3 *.75* .20
2793b A646 $3 *.75* .20
c. Bklt. pane, 2 each #2790a-2793b + label *7.00*
Nos. 2790a-2793b (4) *3.00* .80

1991, June 29 Litho. Perf. 13½

Ch'ing Dynasty (1644-1911): $2, Winter court hat, Mang robe. $3, Summer court hat, surcoat. $7.50, Winter overcoat. $12, Common hat, traveling robe.

2794 A647 $2 multicolored .30 .20
2795 A647 $3 multicolored .40 .20
2796 A647 $7.50 multicolored 1.00 .30
2797 A647 $12 multicolored 1.40 .45
Nos. 2794-2797 (4) 3.10 1.15

See note after No. 2663.
Nos. 2794-2797 have groups of one and five Chinese characters.

Traffic Safety Year A648

1991, July 17 Litho. Perf. 13½
2798 A648 $3 shown .30 .20
2799 A648 $7.50 Don't drink & drive .90 .35

Cloisonne Enamel Lions, Ch'ing Dynasty (1644-1911)
A649 A649a

1991, July 20 Litho. Perf. 12½
2800 A649 yel grn & multi .50 .25
2801 A649a violet & multi 2.00 .75
Nos. 2800-2801 (2) 2.50 2.00

#2800 paid basic domestic rate, #2801 paid basic express mail rate on date of issue.

Fruits — A650

Birds — A651

1991, Aug. 10 Litho. Perf. 14x13½
2802 A650 $3 Strawberry .20 .20
2803 A650 $7.50 Grapes .35 .30
2804 A650 $9 Mango .45 .35
2805 A650 $16 Sugar apple .80 .60
Nos. 2802-2805 (4) 1.80 1.45

1991, Aug. 24 Perf. 13½

Designs: a, Myiophoneus insularis. b, Cinclus pallasii. c, Aix galericulata. d, Nycticorax nycticorax. e, Egretta garzetta. f, Rhyacornis fuliginosus. g, Enicurus scouleri. h, Motacilla cinerea. i, Alcedo atthis. j, Motacilla alba.

2806 Block of 10 3.50 2.40
a.-j. A651 $5 any single .30 .20

Outdoor Activities A652

Wmk. 323
1991, Sept. 27 Litho. Perf. 13½
2807 A652 $2 Rock climbing .20 .20
2808 A652 $3 Fishing .25 .20
2809 A652 $7.50 Bird watching .55 .35
2810 A652 $10 Playing in water .80 .50
Nos. 2807-2810 (4) 1.80 1.25

Intl. Federation of Camping and Caravaning, 1991 Rally.

Lighthouse Type of 1989
Inscription Panel in Blue

1991-92 Perf. 13½
2811 A612 50c like #2683C .20 .20
2812 A612 $1 like #2674 .20 .20
2813 A612 $3.50 like #2678 .20 .20
2814 A612 $5 like #2679 .30 .20
a. Booklet pane of 10 4.00
2815 A612 $7 like #2676 .40 .25
2816 A612 $9 like #2681 .55 .35
2817 A612 $10 like #2682 .60 .40
2818 A612 $12 like #2683A .75 .50
a. $12 Bklt. pane of 5 + label 4.00
2819 A612 $13 like #2675 .75 .50
2820 A612 $19 like #2680 1.10 .80
2821 A612 $20 like #2683B 1.25 .80
2822 A612 $26 like #2683 1.60 1.10
2823 A612 $28 like #2684 1.60 1.10
Nos. 2811-2823 (13) 9.50 6.60

Issued: 50c, $3.50, $5, $12, 10/2; #2818a, 9/26/92; $1, $19, $20, 3/2/92; $26, $28, 5/20/92; $7, $9, $10, $13, 8/21/92.

Peacocks by Lan Shih-ning (Giuseppe Castiglione, 1688-1768) A653

$20, Peacock spreading tail feathers.

Perf. 12x11½
1991, Oct. 30 Photo. Unwmk.
Granite Paper
2826 A653 $5 multicolored .40 .20
2827 A653 $20 multicolored 1.60 .85
a. Souvenir sheet of 1 3.25 1.40

New Year 1992 (Year of the Monkey) — A654

Wmk. 323
1991, Nov. 30 Litho. Perf. 12½
2828 A654 $3.50 orange & multi .25 .20
2829 A654 $13 tan & multi .90 .60
a. Souv. sheet, 2 ea #2828-2829 3.75 2.00

Chinese Books A655

Wmk. 323
1992, Jan. 17 Litho. Perf. 13½
2830 A655 $3.50 Scroll .20 .20
2831 A655 $5 Fold bindings .35 .20
2832 A655 $9 Butterfly bindings .60 .35
2833 A655 $15 String bindings 1.00 .65
Nos. 2830-2833 (4) 2.15 1.40

Good Fortune and Satisfaction A656

Five Blessings Upon the House — A657

Nienhwa paintings: No. 2835, Peace in the Wake of Firecrackers. No. 2837, An Abundance for Every Year.

1992, Jan. 27 Litho. Perf. 13½
2834 A656 $5 multicolored .25 .25
2835 A656 $5 multicolored .25 .25
2836 A657 $12 multicolored .75 .60
2837 A657 $12 multicolored .75 .60
a. Bklt. pane, 2 each #2834-2837 + label *6.75*
Nos. 2834-2837 (4) 2.00 1.70

Lunar New Year.

A658

A659

Lunar New Year: a, like #2664. b, like #2611. c, like #2565. d, like #2493. e, like #2442. f, like #2390. g, like #2346. h, like #2273. i, like #2217. j, like #2828. k, like #2757. l, like #2706.

Wmk. 323
1992, Feb. 18 Litho. Perf. 12½
2838 A658 $5 Block of 12, #a.-l., ver & multi 4.25 2.40
m. Sheet of 12, #2838a-2838 l 4.50 2.50

1992, Mar. 12 *Perf. 13½*

Trees: a, Chamaecyparis formosensis. b, Chamaecyparis taiwanensis. c, Calocedrus formosana. d, Cunninghamia konishii. e. Taiwania crypto- merioides.

2839 A659 $5 Strip of 5, #a.-e. 1.75 .55

Children's Toys Type of 1991

1992, Apr. 29 **Litho.** *Perf. 13½*

2840 A646 $5 Walking on iron pots .40 .25
2841 A646 $5 Chopstick gun .40 .25
2842 A646 $5 Hoop rolling .40 .25
2843 A646 $5 Grass fighting .40 .25
a. Sheet of 4, #2840-2843 *3.25 3.25*
b. As "a," imperf. (simulated perfs), red inscription in sheet margin *10.50 10.50*
c. Bklt. pane, 2 each #2840-2843 + label 5.25
Nos. 2840-2843 (4) 1.60 1.00

Issue date: No. 2843b, May 15.

A660

A661

Mother and son in: $3.50, Spring. $5, Summer. $9, Autumn. $10, Winter.

Wmk. 323

1992, May 9 **Litho.** *Perf. 13½*

2844 A660 $3.50 multicolored .20 .20
2845 A660 $5 multicolored .40 .20
2846 A660 $9 multicolored .70 .40
2847 A660 $10 multicolored .80 .45
Nos. 2844-2847 (4) 2.10 1.25

Parent-child relationships.

Wmk. 323

1992, June 25 **Litho.** *Perf. 13½*

Glassware Decorated with Enamel - Vases: $3.50, Faceted, decorated with bats and longevity characters. $5, Double-lobed, with children at play. $7, Flowered. $17, Tutoring scene.

Background colors

2848 A661 $3.50 pink .20 .20
2849 A661 $5 green .30 .20
2850 A661 $7 bister .45 .30
2851 A661 $17 blue 1.25 .70
Nos. 2848-2851 (4) 2.20 1.40

Stone Lion of Lugouqiao A662

Various stone lions.

Wmk. 323

1992, July 7 **Engr.** *Perf. 13½*

2852 A662 $5 olive grn & pur .40 .20
2853 A662 $5 blue & brown .40 .20
2854 A662 $12 org & olive grn .90 .50
2855 A662 $12 purple & black .90 .50
Nos. 2852-2855 (4) 2.60 1.40

Compare with designs A614, A629, A663.

Ku Shih Classical Poetry — A663

Excerpts: $3.50, "Flesh and body are as closely linked as leaves to a tree." $5, "Once a man and woman get married, conjugal love will last forever without doubt." $9, "Man takes pains to uphold virtue." $15, "Tartar horses lean toward the northern wind."

1992, Aug. 8 **Litho.**

2856 A663 $3.50 Children playing near tree .20 .20
2857 A663 $5 Man & woman .45 .20
2858 A663 $9 Couple near stream .75 .35
2859 A663 $15 Horse, tree 1.15 .60
Nos. 2856-2859 (4) 2.55 1.35

Life in the Countryside A664

Scenes of temple fair: a, Two women, man beating drum, crowd. b, Vendor with basket. c, People playing musical instruments. d, Man with food cart. e, Women with umbrella, basket.

Wmk. 323

1992, Sept. 22 **Litho.** *Perf. 11½*

2860 A664 $5 Strip of 5, #a.-e. 3.25 2.25

Silk Tapestries A665

Ming Dynasty Silk Tapestry Drawing on Life: $5, Two Birds Perched on a Red Camellia Branch. $12, Two Birds Playing on a Peach Branch.

1992, Oct. 9 **Litho.** *Perf. 11½*

Granite Paper

2861 A665 $5 multicolored .35 .20
2862 A665 $12 multicolored 1.00 .55
a. Sheet of 2, #2861-2862 1.60 .75

Chinese Opera A666

Actors, props: $3.50, Nin Hsiang-ju's carting to a party from "The General and Premier." $5, Hsao En rowing a boat from "The Lucky Pearl." $9, Wang Chao-chun making peace with the frontier from "Chao-chun Serves as an Envoy." $12, Scene with red sedan chair from "Escort to the Wedding."

Wmk. 323

1992, Oct. 21 **Litho.** *Perf. 13½*

2863 A666 $3.50 multicolored .20 .20
2864 A666 $5 multicolored .40 .20
2865 A666 $9 multicolored .65 .40
2866 A666 $12 multicolored .90 .55
Nos. 2863-2866 (4) 2.15 1.35

Alishan Forest Railway — A667

1992, Nov. 5 *Perf. 11½*

2867 A667 $5 Steam engine .30 .20
2868 A667 $15 Diesel engine 1.00 .60

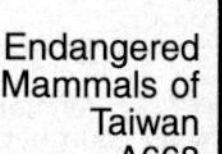

Endangered Mammals of Taiwan A668

Designs: a, Lutra lutra chinensis. b, Pteropus dasymallus formosus. c, Neofelis nebulosa brachyurus. d, Selenarctos thibetanus formosanus.

Perf. 11½x12

1992, Nov. 25 **Photo.** **Unwmk.**

Granite Paper

2869 A668 $5 Block of 4, #a.-d. 1.75 1.00

New Year 1993 (Year of the Rooster) — A669

Design: $13, Rooster facing left.

Wmk. 323

1992, Dec. 1 **Litho.** *Perf. 12½*

2870 A669 $3.50 red & multi .25 .20
a. Perf. 13½ vert. .25 .20
2871 A669 $13 pur & multi .70 .45
a. Souv. sheet, 2 ea #2870-2871 2.25 2.25
b. As "a" with added inscription in border 2.25 2.25
c. Bklt. pane, 5 ea #2870-2871 5.25
d. Perf. 13½ vert. .70 .50
e. Booklet pane, 6 each #2870a, 2871d + label 5.75

Inscription on No. 2871b reads "Philippine Stamp Exhibition 1992-Taipei" in English and Chinese.

Johann Adam Schall von Bell (1592-1666), Astronomer and Missionary — A670

1992 Dec. 10 *Perf. 11½*

2872 A670 $5 multicolored .25 .20

Traditional Nienhwas of Window Frames — A671

Wmk. 323

1993, Jan. 7 **Litho.** *Perf. 11½*

Background Color

2873 A671 $5 brt green .25 .20
2874 A671 $5 red lilac .25 .20
2875 A671 $12 yellow .65 .40
2876 A671 $12 red .65 .40
Nos. 2873-2876 (4) 1.80 1.20

Lunar New Year.

Perf. 13½ Vert.

2873a A671 $5 *1.00* .45
2874a A671 $5 *1.00* .45
2875a A671 $12 *1.00* .45
2876a A671 $12 *1.00* .45
b. Booklet pane, 2 each #2873a-2876a + label *9.00*

Nos. 2873a-2876a are 29x43mm.

Traditional Crafts A672

1993, Jan. 16

2877 A672 $3.50 Clip & paste moldings .20 .20
2878 A672 $5 Lanterns .25 .20
2879 A672 $9 Pottery jars .50 .40
2880 A672 $15 Oil paper umbrella .80 .65
Nos. 2877-2880 (4) 1.75 1.45

Chinese Creation Story — A673

Designs: $3.50, Pan Gu's creation of the universe, vert. $5, Pan Gu transmitted himself into all creatures. $9, Nu Wa created human beings with pestled earth. $19, Nu Wa mended sky with smelted stone, vert.

1993, Feb. 6 *Perf. 12x11½, 11½x12*

2881 A673 $3.50 multicolored .20 .20
2882 A673 $5 multicolored .30 .20
2883 A673 $9 multicolored .55 .40
2884 A673 $19 multicolored 1.10 .90
Nos. 2881-2884 (4) 2.15 1.70

Lucky Animals A674

Water Plants A675

Wmk. 323

1993, Mar. 2 **Litho.** *Perf. 13½*

2885 A674 $3.50 Mandarin duck .20 .20
2886 A674 $5 Chinese unicorn .30 .25
2887 A674 $10 Deer .60 .45
2888 A674 $15 Crane .90 .70
Nos. 2885-2888 (4) 2.00 1.60

See Nos. 2920-2923.

1993, Mar. 12 *Perf. 11½*

2889 A675 $5 Nymphaea x hybrida .35 .20
2890 A675 $9 Nuphar shimadai .65 .40
2891 A675 $12 Eichhornia crassipes .85 .50
Nos. 2889-2891 (3) 1.85 1.10

A676

1993 Litho. Wmk. 323 *Perf. 11½*

2892 A676 $5 Sandbag tossing .35 .20
2893 A676 $5 Bamboo dragonfly twisting .35 .20
2894 A676 $5 Rubber band skipping .35 .20
2895 A676 $5 Waist-strength dueling .35 .20
a. Souv. sheet, #2892-2895 2.25 2.25
b. As "a," with green & black inscriptions in border 2.25 2.25
c. As "a," with red inscription in border 2.25 2.25
Nos. 2892-2895 (4) 1.40 .80

Inscriptions on No. 2895b read "AUSTRALIAN STAMP EXHIBITION 1993-TAIPEI" in Chinese and English.

Inscription on No. 2895c reads "Chinese Stamp Exhibition-Thailand" in Chinese.

Nos. 2895b-2895c each have perforations extending into the margin at top (#2895c) or bottom (#2895b).

Issue dates: Nos. 2892-2895, 2895a, Apr. 20; No. 2895b, Apr. 23; No. 2895c, Apr. 30.

Perf. 13½ Vert.

2892a A676 $5 .65 .25
2893a A676 $5 .65 .25
2894a A676 $5 .65 .25
2895d A676 $5 .65 .25
e. Bklt. pane, 2 each #2892a-2894a, 2895d + label *5.50*

A677

Yangtze River A678

Designs: No. 2896, Source on Ching-Kang-Chang Plateau. No. 2897, Abrupt bend, Chinsha River. No. 2898, Narrow waterway, Roaring Tiger Gorge, Chinsha River. No. 2899, Sheer cliffs, Chuntang Gorge. $9, Three Small Gorges (Dragon Gate, Pawu, and Titsui).

Perf. 13x13½

1993, May 15 Litho. Wmk. 323

2896 A677 $3.50 shown .20 .20
2897 A677 $3.50 multicolored .20 .20
2898 A678 $5 shown .35 .20
2899 A677 $5 multicolored .35 .20
2900 A677 $9 multicolored .65 .40
Nos. 2896-2900 (5) 1.75 1.20

Environmental Protection
A679 A680

Children's paintings: $5, No More Noise Pollution, by Yen Chao-min. $17, Clothing My Hometown with Green, by Hu Hui-chun.

Perf. 12½x13½, 13½x12½

1993, June 5

2901 A679 $5 multicolored .30 .20
2902 A680 $17 multicolored 1.00 .80

Ch'eng-hua Porcelain, Natl. Palace Museum A681

Cups decorated in tou-ts'ai: $3.50, Human figures. $5, Chickens. $7, Flowers and fruits. $9, Dragon.

1993, June 30 *Perf. 12*

2903 A681 $3.50 multicolored .20 .20
2904 A681 $5 multicolored .35 .20
2905 A681 $7 multicolored .50 .35
2906 A681 $9 multicolored .60 .45
Nos. 2903-2906 (4) 1.65 1.20

Vocational Training A682

Wmk. 323

1993, July 24 Litho. *Perf. 12½*

2907 A682 $3.50 Graphic artist .20 .20
2908 A682 $5 Computer operator .25 .20
2909 A682 $9 Carpenter .50 .40
2910 A682 $12 Welder .70 .60
Nos. 2907-2910 (4) 1.65 1.40

Parent-Child Relationship A683

Silhouettes: $3.50, Adult carrying child on shoulders. $5, Father playing flute for daughter. $9, Father teaching daughter. $10, Father, adult son enjoying wildlife.

Wmk. 323

1993, Aug. 4 Litho. *Perf. 11½*

Background Color

2911 A683 $3.50 tan .20 .20
2912 A683 $5 green .30 .20
2913 A683 $9 lilac .60 .45
2914 A683 $10 red brown .70 .55
Nos. 2911-2914 (4) 1.80 1.40

Souvenir Sheet

Taipei '93, Asian Intl. Philatelic Exhibition — A684

Enjoying Antiques, by Tu Chin, 15th cent: a, Man carrying stick. b, Man selecting antiques from table. c, Man seated in chair. d, Two people at table.

Perf. 12x11½

1993, Aug. 14 Photo. Unwmk.

Granite Paper

2915 A684 $5 Sheet of 4, #a.-d. 2.25 1.40

Persimmon A685

Loquat A686

1993, Sept. 10 Litho. *Perf. 12½*

2916 A685 $5 shown .25 .20
2917 A685 $5 Peach .25 .20
2918 A686 $12 shown .80 .60
2919 A686 $12 Papaya .80 .60
Nos. 2916-2919 (4) 2.10 1.60

Lucky Animals Type of 1993

Wmk. 323

1993, Sept. 29 Litho. *Perf. 13½*

2920 A674 $1 Blue dragon .20 .20
2921 A674 $2.50 White tiger .20 .20
2922 A674 $9 Linnet .60 .35
2923 A674 $19 Black tortoise 1.25 .80
Nos. 2920-2923 (4) 2.25 1.55

Taiwan Area Games, Taoyuan — A687

Stone Lions — A688

Designs: a, Taekwondo. b, Pommel horse.

Wmk. 323

1993, Oct. 20 Litho. *Perf. 12½*

2924 A687 $5 Pair, #a.-b. .65 .60

1993, Oct. 30

Stone lions from: $3.50, Taipei New Park. $5, Hsinchu City Council. $9, Hsinchu City God Temple. $12, Fort Providentia, Tainan.

2925 A688 $3.50 multicolored .20 .20
2926 A688 $5 multicolored .30 .20
2927 A688 $9 multicolored .55 .35
2928 A688 $12 multicolored .75 .50
Nos. 2925-2928 (4) 1.80 1.25

Syrmaticus Mikado A689

Designs: a, Hatchling. b, Mother with chicks. c, Immature female, male. d, Adult female, male (profile, showing plumage).

Perf. 11½

1993, Nov. 17 Photo. Unwmk.

Granite Paper

2929 A689 $5 Strip of 4, #a.-d. 1.40 1.25

New Year 1994 (Year of the Dog) — A690

Design: $13, Dog facing left.

Wmk. 323

1993, Dec. 1 Litho. *Perf. 12½*

2930 A690 $3.50 red & multi .20 .20
a. Perf. 13½ vert. .20 .20
b. As "a," bklt. pane of 12 + label 2.75
2931 A690 $13 green & multi .90 .55
a. Souv. sheet, 2 ea #2930-2931 1.10 .75
b. As "a," overprinted in red 1.10 .75

No. 2931b is inscribed in Chinese for Kaohsiung Kuo-kuang Stamp Exhibition-1993, and has additional perforations extending into top and bottom margins.

Asian Vegetable Research and Development Center, 20th Anniv. — A691

1993, Dec. 7

2932 A691 $5 shown .30 .20
2933 A691 $13 Researchers in field .90 .60

Formation of Constitutional Court — A692

Wmk. 323

1994, Jan. 11 Litho. *Perf. 12½*

2934 A692 $5 multicolored .30 .20

Paper Making — A693

Flowers — A694

Designs: No. 2935, Cutting bamboo. No. 2936, Cooking bamboo. No. 2937, Pouring syrup into wooden panel. No. 2938, Stacking panel. No. 2939, Drying paper.

1994, Jan. 24 *Perf. 12x12½*

2935 A693 $3.50 multicolored .20 .20
2936 A693 $3.50 multicolored .20 .20
2937 A693 $5 multicolored .35 .20
2938 A693 $5 multicolored .35 .20
2939 A693 $12 multicolored .80 .50
Nos. 2935-2939 (5) 1.90 1.30

See Nos. 2993-2997, 3071-3075, 3098-3102, 3174-3177.

1994, Feb. 17 *Perf. 12½*

2940 A694 $5 Clivia miniata .30 .20
2941 A694 $12 Cymbidium sinense .80 .50
2942 A694 $19 Primula malacoides 1.10 .85
Nos. 2940-2942 (3) 2.20 1.55

Kinmen Wind Lion Lords — A695

Various Wind Lion Lords.

1994, Mar. 18 Litho. *Perf. 12½*

2943 A695 $5 green & multi .35 .20
2944 A695 $9 yellow & multi .60 .35
2945 A695 $12 org yel & multi .75 .50
2946 A695 $17 blue & multi 1.00 .65
Nos. 2943-2946 (4) 2.70 1.70

Children at Play — A696

#2947, Playing with paper boat. #2948, Fighting with water gun. #2949, Throwing paper airplane. #2950, Playing "train" with rope.

Wmk. 323

1994, Apr. 2 Litho. *Perf. 12½*

2947 A696 $5 multicolored .30 .20
2948 A696 $5 multicolored .30 .20
2949 A696 $5 multicolored .30 .20

2950 A696 $5 multicolored .30 .20
a. Souv. sheet, #2947-2950 1.40 .90
Nos. 2947-2950 (4) 1.20 .80

Perf. 13½ Vert.

2947a A696 $5 .30 .20
2948a A696 $5 .30 .20
2949a A696 $5 .30 .20
2950b A696 $5 .30 .20
c. Bklt. pane, 2 ea #2947a-2949a, 2950b + label 3.00
Nos. 2947a-2950b (4) 1.20 .80

A697

A698

Life in the countryside: $5, Playing chess. $10, Playing musical instruments. $12, Telling stories. $19, Drinking tea.

Wmk. 323

1994, Apr. 25 Litho. *Perf. 12½*

2951 A697 $5 multicolored .25 .20
2952 A697 $10 multicolored .60 .35
2953 A697 $12 multicolored .75 .50
2954 A697 $19 multicolored 1.10 .75
Nos. 2951-2954 (4) 2.70 1.80

1994, May 7

Mother, baby birds: $5, Malay bittern. $7, Little tern, horiz. $10, Common noddy, horiz. $12, Muller's barbet.

2955 A698 $5 multicolored .25 .20
2956 A698 $7 multicolored .40 .25
2957 A698 $10 multicolored .65 .40
2958 A698 $12 multicolored .75 .45
Nos. 2955-2958 (4) 2.05 1.30

A699

A700

Protection of Intellectual Property Rights: $5, Palm-shaped book. $15, Human head, computer disk.

Wmk. 323

1994, May 28 Litho. *Perf. 12½*

2959 A699 $5 multicolored .35 .25
2960 A699 $15 multicolored 1.00 .65

1994, June 11

Designs: $5, Care for Lost Children. $17, Care for the aged.

2961 A700 $5 multicolored .30 .25
2962 A700 $17 multicolored 1.10 .75

Intl. Olympic Committee, Cent. — A701

1994, June 23

2963 A701 $5 shown .35 .25
2964 A701 $15 Sporting events 1.00 .65

A702

A703

Shei-pa Natl. Park: $5, Tapachienshan. $7, Shei-san Landslide Scar. $10, Holy Ridge. $17, Shiah-tsuei Lake.

Wmk. 323

1994, July 1 Litho. *Perf. 12½*

2965 A702 $5 multicolored .35 .20
2966 A702 $7 multicolored .45 .30
2967 A702 $10 multicolored .70 .40
2968 A702 $17 multicolored 1.10 .75
Nos. 2965-2968 (4) 2.60 1.65

1994, July 30 *Perf. 11½x12*

$5, Portrait of Chien Mu (b. 1895), educator.

2969 A703 $5 multicolored .35 .20

Intl. Year of the Family A704

$5, Rainbow, window. $15, Globe, house.

1994, Aug. 25 *Perf. 11½*

2970 A704 $5 multicolored .35 .25
2971 A704 $15 yel & multi 1.00 .65

Invention Myths — A705

Designs: $5, Sueirenjy digging wood to obtain fire. $10, Fushijy drawing Pa-Kua. $12, Shennungjy making agricultural tools. $15, Tsang-jier creating written characters.

1994, Sept. 17 Photo. *Perf. 11½*
Granite Paper

2972 A705 $5 multicolored .30 .20
2973 A705 $10 multicolored .65 .40
2974 A705 $12 multicolored .80 .55
2975 A705 $15 multicolored 1.00 .65
Nos. 2972-2975 (4) 2.75 1.80

A706

A707

Design: $5, Dr. Lin Yutang, linguist, writer, 100th birthday.

Wmk. 323

1994, Oct. 8 Litho. *Perf. 12½*

2976 A706 $5 multicolored .35 .20

1994, Oct. 17

$5, Cheng Ho's ship. $17, Chart, ship, Cheng Ho.

2977 A707 $5 multicolored .35 .25
2978 A707 $17 multicolored 1.00 .70

World Trade Week.

Sun Yat-sen, Founding of Kuomintang, Cent. — A708

Design: $19, Democratic elections, factories, economic development.

Wmk. 323

1994, Nov. 24 Litho. *Perf. 12½*

2979 A708 $5 multicolored .30 .20
2980 A708 $19 multicolored 1.10 .75

A709

A710

1994, Nov. 29

2981 A709 $3.50 Facing right .25 .20
a. Perf. 13½ vert. .25 .20
b. As "a," booklet pane of 6 1.60
Complete booklet, 2 #2981b + label 3.25
2982 A709 $13 Facing left .90 .60
a. Souv. sheet, 2 ea #2981-2982 2.25 1.50

New Year 1995 (Year of the Boar).

1994, Dec. 24 Litho. *Perf. 12½*

2983 A710 $5 Portrait .35 .25
2984 A710 $15 Greeting farm family 1.00 .65

Pres. Yen Chia-kan, 1st death anniv.

Traditional Architecture A711

Roof lines: #2985, Horse's back (shown). #2986, Swallow's tail. $12, Talisman (stove & bowl). $19, Cylinder-shaped brick.

Perf. 12½x12

1995, Jan. 10 Litho. Wmk. 323

2985 A711 $5 multicolored .30 .20
2986 A711 $5 multicolored .30 .20
2987 A711 $12 multicolored .80 .50
2988 A711 $19 multicolored 1.25 .85
Nos. 2985-2988 (4) 2.65 1.75

See Nos. 3079-3082, 3113-3116, 3187-3190, 3235-3238.

Ancient Chinese Engravings — A712

Various floral designs.

1995, Jan. 24 *Perf. 13½*
Denomination in Black

2989 A712 $3.50 multicolored .20 .20
2990 A712 $5 multicolored .30 .20
2991 A712 $19 multicolored 1.25 .85
2992 A712 $26 multicolored 1.75 1.25
Nos. 2989-2992 (4) 3.50 2.50

See Nos. 3018-3021, 3044-3047, 3076-3078, 3178-3181, 3221-3226, 3254-3256, 3299-3300.

Ancient Skills Type of 1994

Methods of irrigation: No. 2993, Water wheel. No. 2994, Gear-driven bucket lift. $5, Pedal-powered hoist. $12, Hand-cranked hoist. $13, Using pole with counter-weight to raise bucket.

Perf. 12x11½

1994, Feb. 14 Litho. Wmk. 323

2993 A693 $3.50 multicolored .20 .20
2994 A693 $3.50 multicolored .20 .20
2995 A693 $5 multicolored .30 .20
2996 A693 $12 multicolored .80 .55
2997 A693 $13 multicolored .90 .60
Nos. 2993-2997 (5) 2.40 1.75

Beauties on an Outing, by Lee Gong-lin — A713

a, Two riders. b, Rider on black horse, woman with child on horse. c, Three riders. d, One rider.

Unwmk.

1995, Mar. 3 Photo. *Perf. 12*
Granite Paper

2998 A713 $9 Strip of 4, #a.-d. 2.50 1.75
e. Souv. sheet, #2998b-2998c 1.25 .80

No. 2998 is a continuous design.

Natl. Health Insurance Plan — A714

Flowers — A715

Perf. 11½x12½

1995, Mar. 1 Litho. Wmk. 323

2999 A714 $12 multicolored .80 .50

1995, Mar. 20 Litho. *Perf. 12½*

3000 A715 $5 Lilium speciosum .25 .20
3001 A715 $12 Haemanthus multiflorus .60 .50
3002 A715 $19 Hyacinthus orientalis 1.25 .85
Nos. 3000-3002 (3) 2.10 1.55

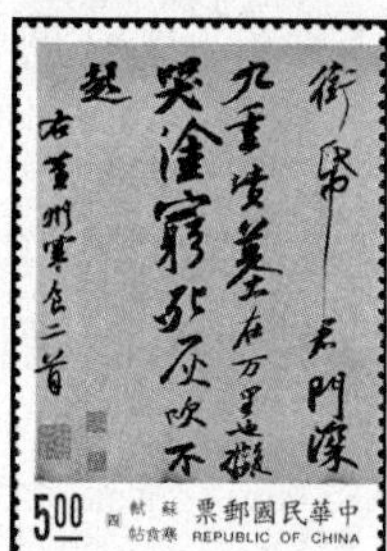
Chinese Calligraphy A716

Cold Food Observance, poem by Su Shih, red inscriptions at: a, Lower left. b, Middle. c, Upper right. d, Right half of design.

1995, Apr. 6 *Perf. 13½*

3003 Strip of 4 2.75 1.75
a.-d. A716 $5 any single .35 .20

Paintings by Tsou I Kuei's — A717

1995, May 5 Photo. *Die Cut*
Self-Adhesive

3004 A717 $5 Red peony .45 .25
3005 A717 $5 Pink peony .45 .25
a. Bklt. pane, 9 ea #3004-3005 8.00

By its nature, No. 3005a is a complete booklet. The peelable backing serves as a booklet cover.

Campaign Against Illegal Drugs — A718

Wmk. 323
1995, June 1 Litho. *Perf. 12½*
3006 A718 $5 shown .30 .20
3007 A718 $15 Arm, hypodermic needle .90 .60

Natl. Taiwan University Hospital, Cent. — A719

Designs: $5, Medical treatment, old hospital. $19, Medical research, new hospital.

1995, June 20
3008 A719 $5 multicolored .30 .25
3009 A719 $19 multicolored 1.25 .85

East Coast Scenes A720

Designs: No. 3010, Green hills above Chichi Bay. No. 3011, Rocky promontory, Shihyuesan. $12, Hsiaoyehlieu. $15, Changhong Bridge.

Wmk. 323
1995, July 1 Litho. *Perf. 12½*
3010 A720 $5 multicolored .30 .20
3011 A720 $5 multicolored .30 .20
3012 A720 $12 multicolored .90 .50
3013 A720 $15 multicolored 1.10 .65
Nos. 3010-3013 (4) 2.60 1.55

Oncorhynchus Masou Formosanus A721

Designs: $5, Mating. $7, Female digging a spot to lay eggs. $10, Hatching of fry. $17, Fry swimming in river.

Perf. 14x14½
1995, July 27 Litho. Unwmk.
3014 A721 $5 multicolored .30 .20
3015 A721 $7 multicolored .45 .30
3016 A721 $10 multicolored .60 .45
3017 A721 $17 multicolored 1.10 .75
Nos. 3014-3017 (4) 2.45 1.70

Ancient Chinese Engraving Type

Various pictures of birds on tree branches.

Wmk. 323
1995, Aug. 18 Litho. *Perf. 13½*
Denomination in Black
3018 A712 $2.50 multicolored .20 .20
3019 A712 $7 multicolored .45 .25
3020 A712 $13 multicolored .80 .55
3021 A712 $28 multicolored 1.90 1.10
Nos. 3018-3021 (4) 3.35 2.10

Marine Life — A722

Louis Pasteur (1822-95) — A723

#3022, Tubastraea aurea. #3023, Chromodoris elizabethina. $5, Spirobranchus gigateus. $17, Himerometra magnipinna.

Wmk. 323
1995, Sept. 7 Litho. *Perf. 12½*
3022 A722 $3.50 multicolored .20 .20
3023 A722 $3.50 multicolored .20 .20
3024 A722 $5 multicolored .35 .20
3025 A722 $17 multicolored 1.00 .65
Nos. 3022-3025 (4) 1.75 1.25

1995, Sept. 20
3026 A723 $17 multicolored 1.40 .65

Natl. Palace Museum, 70th Anniv. A724

Designs: No. 3027, Painting, "Strange Peaks and Myriad Trees." No. 3028, Greenish blue porcelain vase, vert. $5, Bronze X Fu-K'uei Ting vessel, vert. $26, Calligraphy of quatrain in seven-character verse, "The Fragrance of Flowers."

Perf. 12x11½, 11½x12
1995, Oct. 9 Photo. Unwmk.
3027 A724 $3.50 multicolored .20 .20
3028 A724 $3.50 multicolored .20 .20
3029 A724 $5 multicolored .30 .20
3030 A724 $26 multicolored 1.75 1.00
Nos. 3027-3030 (4) 2.45 1.60

A725 A726

End of World War II, 50th Anniv.: $5, Chinese soldiers in battle. $19, Flag, outline map of Taiwan, presidential mansion.

Perf. 11½x12
1995, Oct. 24 Litho. Wmk. 323
3031 A725 $5 multicolored .30 .20
3032 A725 $19 multicolored 1.25 .65
a. Souvenir sheet, #3031-3032 1.75 .90

Wmk. 323
1995, Nov. 10 Litho. *Perf. 12½*

Sea Turtles: No. 3033, Chelonia mydas. No. 3034, Caretta caretta. No. 3035, Lepidochelys olivacea. No. 3036, Eretmochelys imbricata.

3033 A726 $5 multicolored .35 .20
3034 A726 $5 multicolored .35 .20
3035 A726 $5 multicolored .35 .20
3036 A726 $5 multicolored .35 .20
Nos. 3033-3036 (4) 1.40 .80

Taiwan Agricultural Research Institute, Cent. — A727

Perf. 12x11½
1995, Nov. 22 Litho. Wmk. 323
3037 A727 $5 In rice field .35 .20
3038 A727 $28 In anthurium field 1.75 .90

New Year 1996 (Year of the Rat) — A728

Designs: $3.50, $13, Different stylized rats.

Wmk. 323
1995, Dec. 1 Litho. *Perf. 12½*
3039 A728 $3.50 pink & multi .20 .20
a. Perf. 13½ vert. .20 .20
b. As "a," booklet pane of 6 1.40
Complete booklet, 2 #3039b + gutter 2.75
3040 A728 $13 olive & multi .90 .45
a. Souv. sheet, 2 ea #3039-3040 2.25 1.10

Traditional Wedding Ceremony A729

Designs: $5, Escorting bride. $12, Kowtowing Heaven, Earth, and ancestors. $19, Seated in bridal chamber.

1996, Jan. 10
3041 A729 $5 multicolored .35 .20
3042 A729 $12 multicolored .95 .50
3043 A729 $19 multicolored 1.40 .75
Nos. 3041-3043 (3) 2.70 1.45

Ancient Chinese Engraving Type of 1995

Various pictures of fruit.

Wmk. 323
1996, Jan. 25 Litho. *Perf. 13½*
Denomination in Black
3044 A712 $9 multicolored .65 .30
3045 A712 $12 multicolored .90 .45
3046 A712 $15 multicolored 1.10 .55
3047 A712 $17 multicolored 1.25 .60
Nos. 3044-3047 (4) 3.90 1.90

Scenic Dwelling at Chü-Ch'ü, by Wang Meng, Yüan Dynasty — A730

Denominations: a, UL. b, UR. c, LL. d, LR. Illustration reduced.

Perf. 12½x12
1996, Feb. 15 Litho. Unwmk.
3048 A730 Block of 4, #a.-d. 3.00 2.00
a.-d. $5 any single .40 .20

A731

A732

Flowers: $5, Bougainvillea spectabilis. $12, Wisteria sinensis. $19, Merremia tuberosa.

1996, Mar. 8 Unwmk. *Perf. 12½*
3049 A731 $5 multicolored .40 .20
3050 A731 $12 multicolored .85 .45

Wmk. 323
3051 A731 $19 multicolored 1.25 .75
Nos. 3049-3051 (3) 2.50 1.40

Wmk. 323
1996, Mar. 20 Litho. *Perf. 13½*

Chinese Postal Service, Cent.: $5, Mailboxes. $9, Instruments of measurement. $12, Methods of mail transport. $13, Computers, plastic card.

3052 A732 $5 multicolored .30 .20
3053 A732 $9 multicolored .60 .30
3054 A732 $12 multicolored .75 .45
3055 A732 $13 multicolored .85 .50
a. Souvenir sheet, #3052-3055 2.50 1.40
Nos. 3052-3055 (4) 2.50 1.45

Natl. Chiao Tung University, Cent. — A733

Wmk. 323
1996, Apr. 8 Litho. *Perf. 12½*
3056 A733 $19 multicolored 1.25 .70

Penghu Natl. Scenic Areas — A734

#3057, Chimei Giant Lion. #3058, Chipei Beach. $12, Tungpan Yu. $17, Tingkou Yu.

1996, May 1
3057 A734 $5 multicolored .35 .20
3058 A734 $5 multicolored .35 .20
3059 A734 $12 multicolored .80 .45
3060 A734 $17 multicolored 1.10 .65
Nos. 3057-3060 (4) 2.60 1.50

Tzu-Chi Buddhist Compassionate Relief Foundation — A735

Wmk. 323
1996, May 11 Litho. *Perf. 13*
3061 A735 $5 Hand holding people .30 .20
3062 A735 $19 Lotus blossom, sick person 1.25 .70

First Democratic Presidential Election A736

New Pres., Vice Pres. and: $3.50, Natl. flag. $5, Presidential office building. $13, Development of Asia-Pacific Operations Hub project. $15, Greeting people at fair.

1996, May 20 Wmk. 323 *Perf. 12½*
3063 A736 $3.50 multicolored .25 .20
3064 A736 $5 multicolored .35 .20
3065 A736 $13 multicolored .90 .50
3066 A736 $15 multicolored 1.00 .55
a. Souvenir sheet, #3063-3066 2.50 1.40
Nos. 3063-3066 (4) 2.50 1.45

South China Sea Archipelago A737

Outline map of region, Interior Dept. monuments on: $5, Pratas Isl. $17, Itu Aba Isl.

1996, June 5 Wmk. 323 *Perf. 12½*

3067 A737 $5 multicolored .40 .20
3068 A737 $17 multicolored 1.25 .65
a. Souvenir sheet, #3067-3068 1.65 .85

Modern Olympic Games, Cent. — A738

Perf. 12½x12

1996, June 22 Litho. Wmk. 323

3069 A738 $5 Gymnast, cyclist .40 .20
3070 A738 $15 Early Greek athletes 1.10 .55

Ancient Skills Type of 1994

Manufacturing silk: #3071, Feeding silkworms. #3072, Picking out cocoons. $7, Reeling raw silk. $10, Degumming raw silk. $13, Weaving silk.

1996, July 5 *Perf. 12*

3071 A693 $5 multicolored .35 .20
3072 A693 $5 multicolored .35 .20
3073 A693 $7 multicolored .45 .25
3074 A693 $10 multicolored .70 .40
3075 A693 $13 multicolored .90 .50
Nos. 3071-3075 (5) 2.75 1.55

Ancient Chinese Engraving Type of 1995

1996, Aug. 5 *Perf. 13½*

Denomination in Black

3076 A712 $1 Bamboo .20 .20
3077 A712 $10 Orchid .75 .40
3078 A712 $20 Plum tree branch 1.50 .75
Nos. 3076-3078 (3) 2.45 1.35

Traditional Architecture Type of 1995

Parts of column and beam construction.

Perf. 12x11½

1996, Aug. 22 Litho. Wmk. 323

3079 A711 $5 Tou-kung (lion) .40 .20
3080 A711 $5 Chiue-ti .40 .20
3081 A711 $10 Bu-tong .75 .40
3082 A711 $19 Dye-tou 1.40 .70
Nos. 3079-3082 (4) 2.95 1.50

Motion Pictures, Cent. — A739

Chinese movies: No. 3083, Princess Iron Fan, first full-length animated film, 1941. No. 3084, Chin Shan Bi Xie, 1957. $5, Oyster Girl, 1964. $19, City of Sadness, 1989.

1996, Sept. 17 Litho. *Perf. 12½x12*

3083 A739 $3.50 multicolored .25 .20
3084 A739 $3.50 multicolored .25 .20
3085 A739 $5 multicolored .40 .20
3086 A739 $19 multicolored 1.40 .70
Nos. 3083-3086 (4) 2.30 1.30

Winning Pictures from Children's Stamp Design Contest A740

Denomination triangle color, location: a, Red, LR. b, Red, LL. c, Green, LR. d, Green, LL. e, Pink, LL. f, Red, UR. g, Red, UL. h, Green, UR. i, Green, UL. j, Pink, UL. k, Purple, LR. l, Purple, LL. m, Tan, LR. n, Tan, LL. o, Pink, LR. p, Purple, UR. q, Purple, UL. r, Tan, UR. s, Tan, UL. t, Pink, UR.

Perf. 12½x12

1996, Oct. 9 Litho. Unwmk.

3087 A740 $5 Sheet of 20, #a.-t. 8.00 4.00

A741

A742

Ancient Chinese paintings: $5, Autumn Scene with Wild Geese. $7, Reeds and Wild Geese. $13, Wild Geese Gathering on a Shore of Reeds. $15, Wild Geese on a Bank in Autumn.

1996, Oct. 21 Photo. *Perf. 12*

Granite Paper

3088 A741 $5 multicolored .40 .20
3089 A741 $7 multicolored .50 .25
3090 A741 $13 multicolored 1.00 .50
3091 A741 $15 multicolored 1.10 .55
a. Souv. sheet, #3088-3091 3.00 1.50
Nos. 3088-3091 (4) 3.00 1.50

10th Asian Intl. Philatelic Exhib., Taipei '96.

Perf. 12½x12

1996, Nov. 1 Litho. Wmk. 323

Designs: $5, Computerized letters, numbers, bar coding. $26, Globe, graph line.

3092 A742 $5 multicolored .40 .20
3093 A742 $26 multicolored 2.00 1.00

Merchant's Day, 50th Anniv.

A743

A744

Caring for the Handicapped: $5, Woman in wheelchair working at computer. $19, Handicapped child painting picture.

Wmk. 323

1996, Nov. 15 Litho. *Perf. 12½*

3094 A743 $5 multicolored .40 .20
3095 A743 $19 multicolored 1.40 .75

1996, Dec. 2

3096 A744 $3.50 gray & multi .30 .20
a. Perf. 13½ vert. .30 .20
b. As "a," booklet pane of 6 1.80
Complete booklet, 2 #3096b + gutter 3.60
3097 A744 $13 blue & multi 1.10 .55
a. Souv. sheet, 2 ea #3096-3097 3.00 1.50
b. As "a," overprinted 3.00 1.50

New Year 1997 (Year of the Ox).

No. 3097b overprinted in red lilac in sheet margin with Chinese inscription for Kaohsiung Intl. Stamp Exhibition for Chinese Postal Service cent.

Ancient Skills Type of 1994

Making porcelain: No. 3098, Pounding stone, looking at bottom of bowl. No. 3099, Painting, shaping. $7, Painting. $10, Glazing. $13, Firing.

Perf. 11½x12

1997, Jan. 15 Litho. Wmk. 323

3098 A693 $5 multicolored .40 .20
3099 A693 $5 multicolored .40 .20
3100 A693 $7 multicolored .50 .25
3101 A693 $10 multicolored .75 .40
3102 A693 $13 multicolored 1.00 .50
Nos. 3098-3102 (5) 3.05 1.55

A745

A746

Carp encircled by dragons.

Perf. 13x12½

1997, Feb. 14 Engr. Wmk. 323

3103 A745 $50 carmine 3.75 1.90
3104 A745 $60 dark blue 4.50 2.25
3105 A745 $70 red orange 5.25 2.75
3106 A745 $100 olive green 7.50 3.75
Nos. 3103-3106 (4) 21.00 10.65

See Nos. 3131-3132, 3252-3253.

Perf. 12x11½

1997, Feb. 28 Litho. Wmk. 323

3107 A746 $19 Memorial 1.40 .70

Feb. 28, 1947 Rebellion, 50th anniv.

Woody Plants — A747

$5, Rhododendron x mucronatum. $12, Hibiscus rosa-sinensis. $19, Hydrangea macrophylla.

Wmk. 323

1997, Mar. 12 Litho. *Perf. 12½*

3108 A747 $5 multicolored .40 .20
3109 A747 $12 multicolored .85 .45
3110 A747 $19 multicolored 1.25 .70
Nos. 3108-3110 (3) 2.50 1.35

Water Resource Protection
A748 A749

1997, Mar. 22 *Perf. 12½*

3111 A748 $5 multicolored .35 .20
3112 A749 $19 multicolored 1.25 .70

Architecture Type of 1995

Perf. 12x12½

1997, Apr. 9 Litho. Wmk. 323

3113 A711 $5 Door, vert. .40 .20
3114 A711 $5 Gable wall, vert. .40 .20
3115 A711 $10 Carved brick, vert. .80 .40
3116 A711 $19 Column dragon, vert. 1.40 .70
Nos. 3113-3116 (4) 3.00 1.50

Insects — A750

Designs: $5, Dorcus formosanus. $7, Phyllophorina kotoshoensis. $10, Troides magellanus. $17, Megacrania tsudai.

1997, Apr. 25 Photo. *Perf. 11½*

Granite Paper

3117 A750 $5 multicolored .35 .20
3118 A750 $7 multicolored .50 .30
3119 A750 $10 multicolored .75 .40
3120 A750 $17 multicolored 1.25 .70
Nos. 3117-3120 (4) 2.85 1.60

Minerals A751

Wmk. 323

1997, May 8 Litho. *Perf. 13*

3121 A751 $5 Aragonite .30 .20
3122 A751 $5 Alunite .30 .20
3123 A751 $12 Enargite .80 .40
3124 A751 $19 Hokutolite 1.10 .65
Nos. 3121-3124 (4) 2.50 1.45

Nanyashan Outlook A752

1997, May 31 *Perf. 12½*

3125 A752 $5 shown .40 .20
3126 A752 $5 Pitou coastline .40 .20
3127 A752 $12 Stone pillars, Nanya .90 .45
3128 A752 $19 Tsaoling trail .90 .45
Nos. 3125-3128 (4) 2.60 1.30

A753

Around-The-Island Railway System: $5, Cliffs at Chingshuei, Northern Loop Line. $28, Southbound train passing through tunnel, Central Mountain area.

Wmk. 323

1997, June 12 Litho. *Perf. 13½*

3129 A753 $5 multicolored .35 .20
3130 A753 $28 multicolored 1.25 .65

Carp Type

1997, July 3 Engr. *Perf. 13*

3131 A745 $300 vio & dark blue 21.00 11.00
3132 A745 $500 dk red & mag 35.00 18.00

Electronic Industry's Use of Integrated Circuits A754

$5, Integrated circuit for computer & telecommunications industry. $26, Wafer linked to portable computer, cellular phone, electronic synthesizer.

1997, July 16 Litho. *Perf. 12½x12*

3133 A754 $5 multicolored .35 .20
3134 A754 $26 multicolored 1.90 .95

Chinese Martial Arts — A755

Various stances in martial arts.

Wmk. 323

1997, Aug. 8 Litho. *Perf. 13*

3135 A755 $5 shown .35 .20
3136 A755 $5 multi, vert. .35 .20
3137 A755 $9 multicolored .65 .30
3138 A755 $19 multi, vert. 1.25 .65
Nos. 3135-3138 (4) 2.60 1.35

Chinese Classical (Yuan) Opera — A756

Designs: No. 3139, Chang Shen playing musical instrument, Tsuei Ying-ying listening outside, from "Hsi Hsiang Chi." No. 3140, Kuan Gung standing on ferry and holding large knife, enemies in distance, from "Dan Daw Huei." $12, Abduction of Wang Chao-juin on horseback, from "Han Guong Chiou." $15, Emperor Tang Ming Huang envisioning concubine, Makueibo, from "Wu Tong Yu."

1997, Aug. 22

3139 A756 $5 multicolored .35 .20
3140 A756 $5 multicolored .35 .20
3141 A756 $12 multicolored .85 .40
3142 A756 $15 multicolored 1.00 .50
Nos. 3139-3142 (4) 2.55 1.30

Sports — A757

1997, Sept. 9 ***Perf. 12½***

3143 A757 $5 Badminton .35 .20
3144 A757 $12 Bowling .85 .40
3145 A757 $19 Tennis 1.25 .65
Nos. 3143-3145 (3) 2.45 1.25

Ming Dynasty Novel "Journey to the West" — A758

Episodes from novel: No. 3146, "Palm of Buddha," man making inscription while holding pole. No. 3147, "The pilgrimage of T'ang Monk," characters traveling west, one on horse. $5, "The Flaming Mountain," people fighting, fire in background. $20, "The Cobweb Cave," man using pole to fight, spider in cobweb.

1997, Sept. 24 Photo. ***Perf. 11½x12***
Granite Paper

3146 A758 $3.50 multicolored .25 .20
3147 A758 $3.50 multicolored .25 .20
3148 A758 $5 multicolored .35 .20
3149 A758 $20 multicolored 1.40 .70
Nos. 3146-3149 (4) 2.25 1.30

Opening of Second Northern Freeway A759

Designs: $5, Bitan Bridge crossing, Shindian River. $19, Hsinchu interchange.

Wmk. 323

1997, Aug. 26 Litho. ***Perf. 13***

3150 A759 $5 multicolored .35 .20
3151 A759 $19 multicolored 1.25 .65

Illustrations from Ching Dynasty Bird Manual A760

Various birds.

1997, Oct. 9 Photo. ***Perf. 11½***
Granite Paper

3152 A760 $5 Sheet of 20, #a.-t. 7.00 7.00

Compare with Nos. 3268-3269.

New Year 1998 (Year of the Tiger) — A761

Wmk. 323

1997, Dec. 1 Litho. ***Perf. 12½***

3153 A761 $3.50 pink & multi .20 .20
a. Perf. 14 vert. .20 .20
b. As "a," booklet pane of 6 1.50
Complete booklet, 2 #3153b + gutter 3.00
3154 A761 $13 yellow & multi .80 .45
a. Souv. sheet, 2 ea #3153-3154 2.00 1.10

Pres. Chiang Ching-kuo (1910-88) A762

1998, Jan. 13 Engr. ***Perf. 13½***

3155 A762 $5 Portrait, vert. .25 .20

Perf. 11½

3156 A762 $19 shown 1.00 .60

A763

A764

Common Chinese Expressions of Good Fortune, designs: No. 3157, "Happy Occasion of Abundance," fish, vase with pictures of sun and sea. No. 3158, "Harmonious Union as One," flower with two blooms. No. 3159, "Honor and Wealth," flowers growing in pot, vase of flowers. No. 3160, "All is Lucky," bowl of fruit, vase with branch of fruit blossoms.

Perf. 11½x12

1998, Jan. 23 Litho. Wmk. 323
Background Color

3157 A763 $5 pink .30 .20
3158 A763 $5 beige .30 .20
a. Pair, 3157-3158 .60 .30
3159 A763 $12 light yellow .70 .35
3160 A763 $12 tan .70 .35
a. Pair, #3159-3160 1.40 .70
Nos. 3157-3160 (4) 2.00 1.10

Wmk. 323

1998, Mar. 1 Litho. ***Perf. 12½***

Herbaceous Flowers: $5, Gaillardia pulchella. $12, Kalanchoe blossfeldiana. $19, Portulaca oleracea.

3161 A764 $5 multicolored .30 .20
3162 A764 $12 multicolored .70 .40
3163 A764 $19 multicolored 1.25 .60
Nos. 3161-3163 (3) 2.25 1.20

Emperor Shih-tzu, on Hunting Expedition, by Liu Kuan-tao A765

$5, Horseman drawing bow. $19, Emperor Shih-tzu leading hunting party on horseback.

1998, Mar. 20 Photo. ***Perf. 12***
Granite Paper

3164 A765 $5 multicolored .25 .20

Size: 64x40mm

3165 A765 $19 multicolored 1.25 .60
a. Souvenir sheet, #3164-3165 1.50 .75

No. 3165a is a continuous design.

Children's Folk Rhymes A766

#3166, "A Frog Has One Mouth." #3167, "A Little Mouse Climbs an Oil Lamp." $12, "Fireflies." $19, "Egrets."

Wmk. 323

1998, Apr. 4 Litho. ***Perf. 11½***

3166 A766 $5 multicolored .30 .20
3167 A766 $5 multicolored .30 .20
3168 A766 $12 multicolored .70 .40
3169 A766 $19 multicolored 1.25 .60
Nos. 3166-3169 (4) 2.55 1.40

Copyright Law in Taiwan, 70th Anniv. A767

1998, Apr. 30

3170 A767 $19 multicolored 1.25 .60

A768

A769

Portraits of Mythological Character, Chung K'uei: $5, Making ghosts work for him, from Kung Kai's "Chung K'uei Moving," Song Dynasty. $20, Dancing beside small ghost, from "An Auspicious Occasion," Ming Dynasty.

1998, May 15 Photo. ***Perf. 11½***
Granite Paper

3171 A768 $5 multicolored .25 .20
3172 A768 $20 multicolored 1.25 .60

Wmk. 323

1998, May 25 Litho. ***Perf. 11½***

3173 A769 $15 multicolored .90 .45

Intl. Law Assoc., 125th anniv.

Ancient Skills Type of 1994

Ships and methods of transport, horiz.: $5, Grain barge. $7, Six-oared boat. $10, One-wheeled carriage. $13, Southern Chinese one-man push cart.

1998, June 10 ***Perf. 12x11½***

3174 A693 $5 multicolored .30 .20
3175 A693 $7 multicolored .40 .20
3176 A693 $10 multicolored .60 .30
3177 A693 $13 multicolored .80 .40
Nos. 3174-3177 (4) 2.10 1.10

Ancient Chinese Engravings Type of 1995

Redrawn With Chinese Inscription Reading Left to Right

Various floral designs. Denominations do not include two zeros.

Wmk. 323

1998, July 8 Litho. ***Perf. 13½***
Denomination in Red

3178 A712 $7 like #2989 .40 .20
3179 A712 $19 like #2990 1.10 .55
3180 A712 $20 like #2991 1.25 .60
3181 A712 $26 like #2992 1.50 .75
Nos. 3178-3181 (4) 4.25 2.10

Novel, "Red Chamber Dream," by Tsao Hsueh-chin A770

Scenes from love story: No. 3182, Chia Pao-yu visits the garden (with group of women). No. 3183, Lin Tai-yu buries flowers (with hoe). $5, Hsueh Pao-chai plays with butterflies. $20, Shih Hsiang-yun in a drunken sleep (on bench).

1998, July 16 ***Perf. 11x11½***

3182 A770 $3.50 multicolored .20 .20
3183 A770 $3.50 multicolored .20 .20
3184 A770 $5 multicolored .30 .20
3185 A770 $20 multicolored 1.25 .60
Nos. 3182-3185 (4) 1.95 1.20

20th Asia Pacific Jamboree, 8th Taiwan Jamboree — A771

1998, Aug. 5 Litho. ***Perf. 11***

3186 A771 $5 Emblem .30 .20
3186A A771 $5 Tents .30 .20
b. Pair, #3186-3186A .60 .30

Traditional Architecture Type of 1995

Terraces set on raised platforms: #3187, Spirit way (carved stone ramp between two staricases). #3188, Octagonal base of a column. $10, Carved cornerstone. $19, Carved stone drainage spout.

Perf. 11½x12

1998, Aug. 26 Litho. Wmk. 323

3187 A711 $5 multi, vert. .30 .20
3188 A711 $5 multi, vert. .30 .20
3189 A711 $10 multi, vert. .60 .30
3190 A711 $19 multi, vert. 1.10 .55
Nos. 3187-3190 (4) 2.30 1.25

Sports Stamps — A772

Table tennis: No. 3191, Player awaiting serve. No. 3192, Player serving.

Rugby: No. 3193, Two players. No. 3194, Three players.

Wmk. 323

1998, Sept. 9 Litho. ***Perf. 11½***
Denomination Color

3191 $5 green .30 .20
3192 $5 red .30 .20
a. A772 Pair, #3191-3192 .60 .30
3193 $7 red .40 .20
3194 $7 blue .40 .20
a. A772 Pair, #3193-3194 .80 .40
Nos. 3191-3194 (4) 1.40 .80

Chinese Fables A773

Designs: No. 3195, "A Frog in a Well." No. 3196, "The Fox Borrows the Tiger's Ferocity." $12, "Adding Legs to a Drawing of a Snake." $19, "The Snipe and the Clam are at a Deadlock."

Wmk. 323

1998, Sept. 25 Litho. *Perf. 11½*
3195 A773 $5 multicolored .30 .20
3196 A773 $5 multicolored .30 .20
3197 A773 $12 multicolored .70 .35
3198 A773 $19 multicolored 1.10 .55
Nos. 3195-3198 (4) 2.40 1.30

Kinmen National Park A774

#3199, Taiwushan mountain area. #3200, Kunningtou Cliff, beach. $12, Teyueh Tower, Huang Hui-huang's house, Shuitou village. $19, Putou Beach, Liehyu Coast.

1998, Oct. 16
3199 A774 $5 multicolored .30 .20
3200 A774 $5 multicolored .30 .20
3201 A774 $12 multicolored .70 .35
3202 A774 $19 multicolored 1.10 .55
Nos. 3199-3202 (4) 2.40 1.30

Birds — A775

Spizaetus nipalensis: No. 3203, On tree branch. No. 3204, In flight.

Spilornis cheela: No. 3205, On tree branch. No. 3206, In flight.

Ictinaetus malayensis: No. 3207, On tree branch. No. 3208, In flight.

Milvus migrans: No. 3209, Perched on rock. No. 3210, In flight.

1998, Oct. 30 Litho. *Perf. 11½*
3203 $5 multicolored .30 .20
3204 $5 multicolored .30 .20
a. A775 Pair, #3203-3204 .60 .30
3205 $5 multicolored .30 .20
3206 $5 multicolored .30 .20
a. A775 Pair, #3205-3206 .60 .30
3207 $10 multicolored .60 .30
3208 $10 multicolored .60 .30
a. A775 Pair, #3207-3208 1.20 .60
3209 $10 multicolored .60 .30
3210 $10 multicolored .60 .30
a. A775 Pair, #3209-3210 1.20 .60
Nos. 3203-3210 (8) 3.60 2.00

Ancient Jade Carvings A776

#3211, 2 men mining jade on a mountain. #3212, Mountain with 2 pavilions, stream. $7, Figures washing an elephant. $26, Mountain, trees, men.

Perf. 11½x12, 12x11½

1998, Nov. 13 Photo.

Granite Paper
3211 A776 $5 multi .30 .20
3212 A776 $5 multi, vert. .30 .20
3213 A776 $7 multi .45 .20
3214 A776 $26 multi, vert. 1.60 .80
a. Souvenir sheet, #3211-3214 2.75 1.40

New Year 1999 (Year of the Rabbit)
A777 A778

Wmk. 323

1998, Dec. 2 Litho. *Perf. 12½*
3215 A777 $3.50 multicolored .20 .20
a. Perf. 14 vert. .20 .20
b. As "a," booklet pane of 6 1.25
Complete bklt., 2 #3215b + gutter 2.50
3216 A778 $13 multicolored .80 .40
a. Souv. sheet, 2 ea #3215-3216 2.00 1.00
b. As "a," ovptd. in margin, perf. 12½x11¾ 2.00 1.00

No. 3216b was issued 1/30/99 and is inscribed in sheet margin, "ALLIANCE '99 INT'L. FAIR OF PRODUCTS & TRAVEL / Jan. 30-Feb. 1, 1999" and four lines of Chinese text.

Common Expressions of Good Fortune — A779

Expressions, designs: No. 3217, "To have prosperous descendants," gourd on a vine. No. 3218, "A good marriage that soon brings sons," pair of Mandarin ducks, lotus flowers, seeds. No. 3219, "Prosperity from start to finish," egret, flowers. No. 3220, "Reunion and abundance," fish surrounded by flowers.

Perf. 11½x12

1999, Jan. 6 Litho. Wmk. 323
3217 A779 $5 multicolored .30 .20
3218 A779 $5 multicolored .30 .20
3219 A779 $12 multicolored .75 .35
3220 A779 $12 multicolored .75 .35
Nos. 3217-3220 (4) 2.10 1.10

Ancient Chinese Engravings Type
Redrawn With Chinese Inscription
No Zeros
Reading Left to Right

Various pictures of birds on tree branches, bamboo and orchid.

1999, Jan. 20 *Perf. 13½*

Denomination in Red
3221 A712 $1 like #3018 .20 .20
3222 A712 $3.50 like #3019 .20 .20
3223 A712 $5 like #3020 .30 .20
3224 A712 $10 like #3021 .60 .30
3225 A712 $12 like #3076 .75 .35
3226 A712 $28 like #3077 1.75 .90
Nos. 3221-3226 (6) 3.80 2.15

Indoor Potted Plants — A781

$5, Sinningia speciosa. $12, Saintpaulia x hybrida. $19, Anthurium scherzerianum.

Perf. 12½

1999, Feb. 10 Litho. Unwmk.
3228 A781 $5 multicolored .30 .20
3229 A781 $12 multicolored .75 .40
3230 A781 $19 multicolored 1.25 .60
Nos. 3228-3230 (3) 2.30 1.20

Ancient Chinese Painting, "Joy in Peacetime" A782

#3231, Woman holding child, boy with small elephant. #3232, Boy carrying lantern, crane on leash, people under tree. $7, Family, children playing with toy animals on wheels. $26, Women in front of steps, children playing with toys, boy on edge of balcony.

1999, Mar. 2 Photo. *Perf. 12*

Granite Paper
3231 A782 $5 multicolored .30 .20
3232 A782 $5 multicolored .30 .20
3233 A782 $7 multicolored .45 .20
3234 A782 $26 multicolored 1.60 .80
a. Souvenir sheet, #3231-3234 2.75 1.40
Nos. 3231-3234 (4) 2.65 1.40

Traditional Architecture Type of 1995

Decorative features, vert.: No. 3235, Hanging cylinder with carving of woman and deer. No. 3236, Taishi screen. $10, Xuanyu (decorative element on gable). $19, Wood carving.

1999, Mar. 20 Litho. Wmk. 323
3235 A711 $5 multicolored .30 .20
3236 A711 $5 multicolored .30 .20
3237 A711 $10 multicolored .60 .30
3238 A711 $19 multicolored 1.25 .60
Nos. 3235-3238 (4) 2.45 1.30

Children's Folk Rhymes A783

Titles: No. 3239, "Baby Sleep." No. 3240, "Be Brave." $12, "Rock, Rock, Rock." $19, "Buggie Flies."

Perf. 11½x11

1999, Apr. 2 Litho. Unwmk.
3239 A783 $5 multicolored .30 .20
3240 A783 $5 multicolored .30 .20
3241 A783 $12 multicolored .75 .35
3242 A783 $19 multicolored 1.10 .55
Nos. 3239-3242 (4) 2.45 1.30

Taiwan's Aboriginal Culture A784

Celebrations wearing traditional costumes: a, Dancing in row, mountain in background, Atayal Ancestor Festival. b, People wearing hip bells, Saisiat Festival of the Dwarfs. c, Standing arm in arm in circle, Bunun eight-part contrapuntal vocals. d, Row of people standing inside building, Tsou Victory Festival. e, Group outside before large display board, Rukai Harvest Festival. f, Holding bamboo poles in air, Paiwan "Maleveq" Bamboo Festival. g, Men walking while holding millet leaves in air, Puyuma Harvest Ceremony. h, Women dancing in row, tree in background, Ami Harvest Ceremony. i, Holding boat in air, Yami Boat Ceremony.

1999, Apr. 22 *Perf. 13*

Block of 9
3243 A784 $5 #a.-i. + label 3.25 3.25

No. 3243 was issued in sheets of 2 blocks + 2 labels. The labels contain the upper and lower halves of Taiwan. The lower block of 9 is in reverse order.

Intl. Council of Nurses, Cent. A785

1999, May 12 Litho. *Perf. 11½*
3244 A785 $5 shown .30 .20
3245 A785 $17 Nurse, world map 1.00 .50

Chinese Classical Opera — A786

Legends of the Ming Dynasty: No. 3246, Fan Li watching Hsi-shih wash yarn, "Wuan Sha Chi." No. 3247, Tsai Pochieh, Niu looking at moon, Chao Waniang with pipa (stringed instrument) on her back, "The Story of a Pipa." $12, Hung Funu surprising Li Ching, "The Story of Hung Fu." $15, Jueilan setting up incense table, "Paiyueh Pavilion."

1999, May 27 *Perf. 13*
3246 A786 $5 multicolored .30 .20
3247 A786 $5 multicolored .30 .20
3248 A786 $12 multicolored .75 .35
3249 A786 $15 multicolored .90 .45
a. Souvenir sheet, #3246-3249 2.25 1.10
b. As "a," imperf., with added inscription 2.25 1.10
Nos. 3246-3249 (4) 2.25 1.20

No. 3249b was issued 7/23 and is inscribed in sheet margin with exhibition emblem, two lines of Chinese text and "TAIPEI INTERNATIONAL STAMP EXHIBITION 1999 (INVITATIONAL)."

New Taiwan Dollar, 50th Anniv. A787

1999, June 15 *Perf. 11½*
3250 A787 $5 Coins .30 .20
3251 A787 $25 Currency 1.50 .75

Carp Encircled by Dragons Type of 1997 Redrawn With Denominations at Right

1999, July 1 Engr. *Perf. 13½x12½*
3252 A745 $50 green 3.25 1.60
3253 A745 $100 brown 6.25 3.25

Ancient Chinese Engravings Type of 1995
Redrawn With Chinese Inscription
Reading Left to Right

Perf. 13½

1999, July 15 Litho. Unwmk.

Denomination in Red
3254 A712 50c like #3044 .20 .20
3255 A712 $6 like #3045 .40 .20
3256 A712 $25 like #3046 1.50 .75
Nos. 3254-3256 (3) 2.10 1.15

Father's Day A788

Designs: $5, Children with large present, silhouette of their father. $25, Father teaching son how to ride bicycle, girl.

1999, Aug. 8 *Perf. 11½*
3257 A788 $5 multicolored .30 .20
3258 A788 $25 multicolored 1.50 .75

Chinese Gourmet Food A789

Dish, region: a, Peony lobster, Taiwan. b, "Buddha Jumps the Wall" steamed seafood (with blue & white teapot, bowl), Fukien. c, Hors d'oeuvres shaped as star, Canton. d, "Dongpo Pork" (on yellow plate, bowl), Kiangsu and Chekiang. e, "Stewed Fish Jaws" (surrounded by strawberries, pineapple), Shanghai. f, "Beggar's Chicken" (with napkin), Hunan. g, "Carp Jumping over Dragon's Gate," Szechwan. h, "Peking Duck" (in footed dish), Beijing.

Perf. 11½x11¼

1999, Aug 20 Litho. Unwmk.
3259 A789 $5 Block of 8, #a.-h. 2.50 1.25

Outdoor Activities — A790

1999, Sept. 9 *Perf. 11¼x11½*

3260 A790 $5 Diving .30 .20
3261 A790 $6 Rafting .40 .20
3262 A790 $10 Surfing .65 .30
3263 A790 $25 Windsurfing 1.60 .80
Nos. 3260-3263 (4) 2.95 1.50

Taiwanese Opera A791

1999, Oct. 15 Litho. *Perf. 11½x11¼*

3264 A791 $5 Stage, audience .30 .20
3265 A791 $6 Dressing room .40 .20
3266 A791 $10 Actress, tents .65 .30
3267 A791 $25 Actress as clown 1.60 .80
Nos. 3264-3267 (4) 2.95 1.50

Illustrations from Ching Dynasty Bird Manual A792

#3268, Yellow-headed parrot. #3269, Blue-winged parrotlet (4 characters at LL). $12, African gray parrot (5 characters at UL). $25, King parrot (5 characters at UL).

1999, Nov. 11 Litho. *Perf. 11½*

3268 A792 $5 multicolored .30 .20
3269 A792 $5 multicolored .30 .20
3270 A792 $12 multicolored .80 .40
3271 A792 $25 multicolored 1.60 .80
Nos. 3268-3271 (4) 3.00 1.60

Compare with No. 3152.

New Year 2000 (Year of the Dragon)
A793 A794

1999, Dec. 1 Litho. *Perf. 12½*

3272 A793 $3.50 multicolored .25 .20
a. Perf. 13¼ vert. .25 .20
b. As "a," booklet pane of 6 1.50
Complete booklet, 2 #3272b + gutter 3.00
3273 A794 $13 multicolored .80 .40
a. Souv. sheet, 2 ea #3272-3273 2.10 1.10

Millennium A795

#3274, ROCSAT-1. #3275, Deer. $12, Train. $15, Dove, St. Peter's Basilica.

1999, Dec. 31 Litho. *Perf. 11½*

3274 A795 $5 multicolored .30 .20
3275 A795 $5 multicolored .30 .20
3276 A795 $12 multicolored .80 .40
3277 A795 $15 multicolored 1.00 .50
a. Souvenir sheet of 4, #3274-3277, perf. 12 2.40 1.40
b. Souvenir sheet of 4, #3274-3277, imperf. 2.40 1.40
Nos. 3274-3277 (4) 2.40 1.30

Taipei 2000 Stamp Exhibition (No. 3277b). No. 3277b has simulated perforations.

Calligraphy Tools A796

Designs: No. 3278, "Colored Cloud Dragon" writing brushes of Ming Emperor Chia-Ching. No. 3279, "Imperial Dragon Fragrance" ink stick of Ming Emperor Lung-Ching, vert. $7, "Clear Heart House" calligraphic work by Tsai Hsiang, Sung Dynasty, vert. $26, Celadon toad inkstone, Sung Dynasty.

2000, Jan. 12 Photo. *Perf. 11¾*
Granite Paper

3278 A796 $5 multicolored .30 .20
3279 A796 $5 multicolored .30 .20
3280 A796 $7 multicolored .45 .25
3281 A796 $26 multicolored 1.75 .85
Nos. 3278-3281 (4) 2.80 1.50

Opening of Second Southern Freeway A797

Designs: $5, $25, Kaoping River bridge. $12, Interchange.

2000, Feb. 2 Litho. *Perf. 13x13¼*

3282 A797 $5 multi .35 .20
3283 A797 $12 multi .80 .40

Souvenir Sheet
Perf. 12

3284 A797 $25 multi 1.60 .80

No. 3284 contains one 80x30mm stamp.

Seasons A798

Spring — No. 3285: a, Buds on tree. b, Farmer plowing. c, Cranes. d, Farmers planting. e, Basket of offerings to dead ancestors. f, Farmer's clothing.

Summer — No. 3286: a, Rice seedlings. b, Water wheel. c, Ripened rice. d, Cicada on tree. e, Palm leaf fan. f, Watermelons.

Autumn — No. 3287: a, Farmers in field. b, Granary. c, Dew on grass. d, Reddened maple leaves. e, Leafless tree. f, Hoarfrost on leaves.

Winter — No. 3288: a, Jar on table. b, Snow-covered pine trees. c, Snow-covered mountains. d, Bowl of rice balls. e, Snow-covered plum blossoms. f, House and village.

2000, Feb. 3 *Perf. 11¾*

3285 A798 $5 Strip of 6, #a-f 2.00 1.00
3286 A798 $5 Strip of 6, #a-f 2.00 1.00
3287 A798 $5 Strip of 6, #a-f 2.00 1.00
3288 A798 $5 Strip of 6, #a-f 1.90 .95
Nos. 3285-3288 (4) 7.90 3.95

Issued: #3285, 2/3; #3286, 5/5; #3287, 8/4; #3288, 11/3.

Soochow University, Cent. A799

Designs: $5 School gate. $25, Justice statue at Law School.

2000, Mar. 16 *Perf. 13x13¼*

3289 A799 $5 multi .35 .20
3290 A799 $25 multi 1.60 .80

Novel "The Romance of the Three Kingdoms" A800

#3291, Gathering of Liu Bei, Guan Yu and Chang Fei. #3292, Guan Yu reading. $5, Three visits to the thatched cottage. $20, Filling boats with straw for making arrows.

2000, Apr. 12 Litho. *Perf. 11½*

3291 A800 $3.50 multi .25 .20
3292 A800 $3.50 multi .25 .20
3293 A800 $5 multi .35 .20
3294 A800 $20 multi 1.25 .65
a. Souv. sheet, #3291-3294, perf. 12 2.10 1.10
Nos. 3291-3294 (4) 2.10 1.25

Inauguration of New President and Vice-president — A801

a, Pres. Chen Shui-bian, Vice-pres. Lu Hsiu-lien. b, Presidential Office Building. Illustration reduced.

2000, May 20 Litho. *Perf. 11¾*

3295 A801 $5 Pair, #a-b .65 .30
c. Souvenir sheet, 2 #3295 1.40 .65

Tropic of Cancer Monuments A802

2000, June 21 *Perf. 13*

3296 A802 $5 Hsialiao .35 .20
3297 A802 $12 Wuho .80 .40
3298 A802 $25 Chingpu 1.60 .80
Nos. 3296-3298 (3) 2.75 1.40

Ancient Chinese Engravings Type of 1995 Redrawn with Chinese Inscription Reading Left to Right

2000, July 5 Litho. *Perf. 13½*
Denomination in Red

3299 A712 $32 like #3046 2.10 1.10
3300 A712 $34 like #3078 2.25 1.10

Sacred Trees — A803

Designs: $5, Taiwan Giant, Miaoli County. $39, Sleeping Moon, Chiayi County.

2000, July 20 Litho. *Perf. 11¼x11½*

3301 A803 $5 multi .35 .20
3302 A803 $39 multi 2.50 1.25

No. 2499 Surcharged in Red

2000, Aug. 24 Litho. *Perf. 13½*

3303 A535a $3.50 on $7.50 multi .25 .20

Poisonous Plants — A804

Designs: No. 3304, $5, Lycoris radiata. No. 3305, $5, Cerbera manghas. $12, Abrus precatorius. $20, Nerium indicum.

2000, Sept. 8 Litho. *Perf. 13*

3304-3307 A804 Set of 4 2.60 1.40

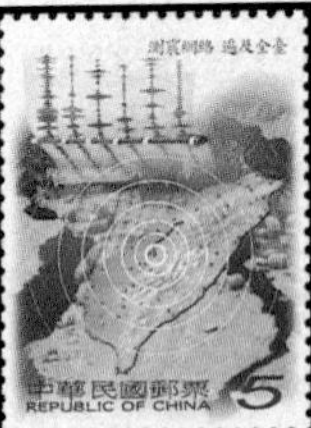

Sept. 21, 1999 Earthquake, 1st Anniv. — A805

Designs: $5, Map, seismograph reading. $12, Rescue workers. $25, Earthquake preparedness.

2000, Sept. 21 *Perf. 11¼x11½*

3308-3310 A805 Set of 3 2.60 1.40

Dragonflies A806

Designs: Nos. 3311, 3315a, $5, Lamelligomphus formosanus. Nos. 3312, 3315b, $5, Anotogaster sieboldii, vert. Nos. 3313, 3315c, $12, Trithemis festiva, vert. Nos. 3314, 3315d, $12, Neurothemis ramburii.

2000, Oct. 11 *Perf. 13*

3311-3314 A806 Set of 4 2.10 1.10

Souvenir Sheet
Stamps Without White Margins
Perf. 11¾

3315 A806 Sheet of 4, #a-d 2.10 1.10

Bird Manual Type of 1999

#3316, $5, Corn bunting (2 characters at UR). #3317, $5, Brambling (3 characters at UL). $12, Bali mynah (3 characters at LR). $25, Indian grackle (2 characters at LR).

2000, Oct. 26 *Perf. 11½*

3316-3319 A792 Set of 4 3.00 1.50

Compare No. 3317 with No. 3378.

Tamkang University, 50th Anniv. A807

$5, Palace Lamp Boulevard, classroom buildings. $25, Maritime Museum, Scroll Plaza.

2000, Nov. 8 *Perf. 13*

3320-3321 A807 Set of 2 1.90 .95

A808

New Year 2001 (Year of the Snake) — A809

2000, Dec. 1 ***Perf. 12½***

3322 A808 $3.50 multi .25 .20
a. Perf. 13¼ vert. .25 .20
b. As "a," booklet pane of 6 1.50
Booklet, 2 #3322b + gutter 3.00
3323 A809 $13 multi .80 .40
a. Souv. sheet, 2 ea #3322-3323 2.10 1.10
b. As "a," with added marginal inscription in red 2.10 1.10

Added marginal inscription of No. 3323b reads in Chinese "Turn-of-the-Century Intl. Stamp Exhibition, Kaohsiung / Dec. 25, 2000-Jan. 3, 2001" in red

Issued: No. 3323b, 12/25/00.

Establishment of Trade Links with People's Republic of China — A810

Ships in Taiwan Strait and: $9, Building. $25, Obelisk.

2001, Jan. 1 **Litho.** ***Perf. 11½***

3324-3325 A810 Set of 2 2.10 1.10

A811

Common Chinese expressions of good fortune: No. 3326, $5, "Marital bliss," twin lotus blossoms on one stalk (pink background). No. 3327, $5, "Success in one's career," longan, lichee and walnuts (light green background). No. 3328, $12, "Producing many offspring," split pomegranates (buff background). No. 3329, $12, "Growing old together with wealth and high position," bulbuls flying around peonies (light orange background).

2001, Jan. 2 ***Perf. 11¾x12¼***

3326-3329 A811 Set of 4 2.10 1.10

Zodiac Signs A812

Designs: No. 3330, $5, Aquarius. No. 3331, $12, Gemini. No. 3332, $25, Libra. No. 3333, $5, Capricorn. No. 3334, $12, Taurus. No. 3335, $25, Virgo. No. 3336, $5, Aries. No. 3337, $12, Leo. No. 3338, $25, Sagittarius. No. 3339, $5, Pisces. No. 3340, $12, Cancer. No. 3341, $25, Scorpio.

2001 ***Perf. 12***

3330-3341 A812 Set of 12 10.00 5.00

Values are for copies with surrounding selvage.

Issued: Nos. 3330-3332, 2/14. Nos. 3333-3335, 4/20. Nos. 3336-3338, 7/25. Nos. 3339-3341, 11/8.

Fruit — A813

2001 **Litho.** ***Perf. 12½x13¼***

3342 A813 $1 Plums .20 .20
3343 A813 $3.50 Tangerines .20 .20
3344 A813 $5 Apples .30 .20
3345 A813 $7 Pears .40 .20
3346 A813 $12 Guavas .70 .35
3347 A813 $20 Longans 1.10 .55
3348 A813 $25 Cantaloupes 1.40 .70
3349 A813 $40 Grapefruit 2.40 2.40
Nos. 3342-3349 (8) 6.70 4.80

Issued: $5, $7, $12, $25, 2/23. $1, $3.50, $20, $40, 8/23.

See Nos. 3408-3411.

Mount Jade A814

Designs: No. 3350, $5, Main peak (shown). No. 3351, $5, Western peak, flowers in foreground. $12, Northern peak. $25, Eastern peak.

2001, Mar. 8 **Litho.** ***Perf. 11½x11¼***

3350-3353 A814 Set of 4 2.75 1.40

Compare Type A814 with Types A834-A837, A855-A858.

Children's Rhymes A815

Designs: No. 3354, $5, Little Ball (blue background). No. 3355, $5, Point to the Water Vat (pink background). $12, Pangolin. $25, Shake and Stamp.

2001, Apr. 4

3354-3357 A815 Set of 4 2.75 1.40

Buddhist Statues — A816

Designs: $5, Sakyamuni Buddha, Northern Wei Dynasty. $9, Seated Buddha, Tang Dynasty. $12, Mahavairocana Buddha, Sung Dynasty.

2001, May 11 ***Perf. 11¼x11½***

3358-3360 A816 Set of 3 1.50 .75
3360a Souvenir sheet, #3358-3360, perf. 12 1.50 .75

Agricultural Implements — A817

Designs: $5, Rice wind drum. $7, Plow. $10, Bamboo rice baskets. $25, Coir rainwear.

2001, May 25 ***Perf. 11½x11¼***

3361-3364 A817 Set of 4 2.75 1.40

Dr. George Leslie Mackay (1844-1901) A818

2001, June 1 ***Perf. 11¼x11½***

3365 A818 $25 multi 1.40 .70

2001 Kiwanis International Convention A819

Designs: $5, Girl, Earth. $25, Mother and child, map.

2001, June 22 ***Perf. 13***

3366-3367 A819 Set of 2 1.75 .85

Kites — A820

No. 3368: a, Dragon. b, Phoenix. c, Tiger. d, Fish.

2001, July 13 ***Perf. 11¼x11½***

3368 Horiz. strip of 4 1.25 .55
a.-d. A820 $5 Any single .30 .20

Carp Encircled by Dragons Type of 1997 With Denominations at Right

2001, Aug. 3 **Engr.** ***Perf. 13***

Size: 25x33mm

3369 A745 $300 red vio & dk bl 17.50 8.75
3370 A745 $500 red & brown 30.00 15.00

Rapid Transit A821

Designs: $5, Train, transit system emblem. $12, Passengers in station, fare card. $25, Chientan Station.

2001, Aug. 14 **Litho.** ***Perf. 13***

3371-3372 A821 Set of 2 1.00 .50

Souvenir Sheet

Perf. 11¾

3373 A821 $25 multi 1.50 .75

No. 3373 contains one 85x42mm stamp.

Fables — A822

Designs: No. 3374, $5, Now Three, Now Four (man and monkeys). No. 3375, $5, Selling the All-Penetrating Sword and Unyielding Shield (men watching man with sword and shield). $12, Waiting by the Tree for the Rabbit. $25, An Old Fool Moves Mountains.

2001, Sept. 6 **Litho.** ***Perf. 11½***

3374-3377 A822 Set of 4 2.75 1.40

Bird Manual Type of 1999 and

Siberian Rubythroat A823

Designs: No. 3379, Waxwing (3 characters at UR). $12, White-rumped munia (2 characters at R). $25, Great barbet (3 characters at LL).

2001, Sept. 28 **Litho.** ***Perf. 11½***

3378 A823 $5 shown .30 .20
3379 A792 $5 multi .30 .20
3380 A792 $12 multi .70 .35
3381 A792 $25 multi 1.50 .75
Nos. 3378-3381 (4) 2.80 1.50

Republic of China, 90th Anniv. A824

Designs: No. 3382, $5, Terminal, Chiang Kai-shek Intl. Airport. No. 3383, $5, Electronic products made in Republic of China. $12, Dancers at National Theater. $15, Dolphins.

2001, Oct. 9 **Litho.** ***Perf. 11½***

3382-3385 A824 Set of 4 2.25 1.10

2001 National Games — A825

Athletes and: $5, Torch. $25, Map.

2001, Oct. 18 **Litho.** ***Perf. 12½***

3386-3387 A825 Set of 2 1.75 .85

34th Baseball World Cup A826

Emblem, map and: No. 3388, $5, Pitcher. No. 3389, $5, Batter. $12, Catcher. $20, Runner sliding.

2001, Oct. 30 ***Perf. 11½***

3388-3391 A826 Set of 4 2.40 1.25
3391a Souvenir sheet, #3388-3391, perf. 12 2.40 1.25

Puppet Theater A827

Designs: $5, Mozhaonu, from "Thunder Storm." $6, Taiyangnu, from "Rising Winds, Surging Clouds." $10, Kuangdao, from "Thunder Crazy Sword." $25, Chin Chia-chien, from "Thunder Golden Light."

2001, Nov. 16 **Litho.** ***Perf. 11½***

3392-3395 A827 Set of 4 2.75 1.40

National Defense Medical Center, Cent. — A828

Designs: $5, Medical students, old medical school building. $25, Doctors, new medical school building.

2001, Nov. 23 ***Perf. 13***

3396-3397 A828 Set of 2 1.75 .85

New Year 2002 (Year of the Horse) — A829

Horse and: $3.50, Clouds. $13, Flowers.

2001, Dec. 3 Litho. *Perf. 12½*

3398 A829 $3.50 multi		.20	.20
a.	Perf. 13¾ vert.	.20	.20
b.	Booklet pane, 12 #3398a	2.40	—
	Booklet, #3398b	2.40	
3399 A829 $13 multi		.75	.35
a.	Souvenir sheet, 2 each #3398-3399	1.90	.95

Paul Cardinal Yu Pin (1901-78) — A830

2001, Dec. 7 *Perf. 11½*

3400 A830 $25 multi		1.40	.70
a.	Souvenir sheet of 1, perf. 12	1.40	.70

Greetings A831

No. 3401: a, Pink chrysanthemums, red background. b, White lilies, red background. c, Pink flowers, yellow background. d, Red orange flowers, yellow background. e, Pink flowers, green background. f, Coral roses, blue green background. g, Star and wreath, blue background. h, Poinsettias, blue background. i, Red violet flowers, purple background. j, Yellow flowers, purple background.

2001, Dec. 12 *Perf. 12½*

3401	Sheet of 10 + 10 labels	3.00	1.50
a.-j.	A831 $5 Any single	.30	.20

Labels could be personalized for an additional fee.

Sheets with blank (unprinted) labels were not released.

Fu Hsing Kang College, 50th Anniv. A832

Designs: $5, Students with flags. $25, Tower, administration building, statue of students.

2002, Jan. 4 *Perf. 11½*

3402-3403 A832	Set of 2	1.75	.85

Expressions of Good Fortune Type of 2001

Designs: No. 3404, $5, "Continuously produce good offspring," lotus and sweet osmanthus flowers in a vase (gradiated pink background). No. 3405, $5, "A high, moral gentleman," orchid and sweet osmanthus in containers (gradiated green background). No. 3406, $12, "A hall full of the rich and famous," flowering crabapple in a vase (gradiated orange background). No. 3407, $12, "Safe and peaceful in all seasons," roses in vase (gradiated purple background).

2002, Jan. 16 *Perf. 11¾x12¼*

3404-3407 A811	Set of 4	2.00	1.00

Fruit Type of 2001

2002, Feb. 8 Litho. *Perf. 12½x13¼*

3408 A813 $6 Avocados	.35	.20
3409 A813 $10 Lichees	.60	.30
3410 A813 $17 Dates	1.00	.50
3411 A813 $32 Passion fruit	1.90	.90
Nos. 3408-3411 (4)	3.85	1.90

Folk Traditions A833

Designs: No. 3412, $5, Release of sky lanterns (orange background). No. 3413, $5, Fireworks display (blue background). $10, Matsu procession (lilac background). $20, Dragon boat race (pink background).

2002, Feb. 26 Litho. *Perf. 12½*

3412-3415 A833	Set of 4	2.25	1.10

See Nos. 3440-3443.

Winter, Mount Hsueh A834

North Ridge, Mount Hsueh A835

Autumn, Mount Hsueh A836

Glacial Cirques, Mount Hsueh A837

2002, Mar. 20 *Perf. 11½*

3416 A834 $5 multi	.30	.20
3417 A835 $5 multi	.30	.20
3418 A836 $12 multi	.70	.35
3419 A837 $25 multi	1.40	.70
Nos. 3416-3419 (4)	2.70	1.45

Compare with Types A814, A855-A858.

Novel "The Romance of the Three Kingdoms" A838

Designs: No. 3420, $3.50, Three heroes battling Lu Bu (warriors on horseback). No. 3421, $3.50, To the rescue of his master's family (one warrior on horseback). $5, Scraping away the poison from the bone (medicinal bleeding). $20, Playing a lute to make the enemy retreat (horseman and gate).

2002, Apr. 4

3420-3423 A838	Set of 4	1.90	.95
a.	Souvenir sheet, #3420-3423, perf. 12	1.90	1.90

Endangered Bird Thalasseus Bernsteini — A839

No. 3424: a, Two birds in flight. b, Bird in flight heading left. c, Bird landing on rock carrying fish. d, Bird on rock with beak open. e, Adult feeding chick. f, Bird diving. g, Bird landing with bill open. h, Bird standing on rock, looking left. i, Adult with chick. j, Adult on nest.

$25, Bird in flight.

2002, May 15 Litho. *Perf. 11½*

3424 A839 $5 Sheet of 10, #a-j	3.00	1.50

Souvenir Sheet

Perf. 12

3425 A839 $25 multi	1.50	.75

No. 3424 contains ten 40x30mm stamps.

Dragon & Carp Type of 1997 Redrawn With Denomination at Right

2002, June 5 Engr. *Perf. 13¼x12½*

3426 A745 $80 brown	4.75	2.50

Porcelain Bowls A840

Ching Dynasty bowls depicting: No. 3427, $5, Peacock (salmon background). No. 3428, $5, Lotus flowers (blue green background). $7, Peonies. $32, Sparrows and bamboo.

2002, June 21 Litho. *Perf. 11½*

3427-3430 A840	Set of 4	3.00	1.50

Flowers — A841

Designs: $5, Matthiola incana. $12, Gardenia jasminoides. $25, Michelia figo.

2002, July 5 *Perf. 13*

3431-3433 A841	Set of 3	2.50	1.25

Cetaceans A842

Designs: No. 3434, $5, Megaptera novaeangliae, whaling ship. No. 3435, $5, Tursiops truncatus, people on shore attracting cetacean. $10, Orcinus orca, boat following cetaceans. $25, Grampus griseus, people rescuing beached dolphin.

2002, July 25 Litho. *Perf. 11½x11¼*

3434-3437 A842	Set of 4	2.75	1.40
a.	Souvenir sheet, #3434-3437, perf. 12	2.75	1.40

Intl. Paralympic Committee World Table Tennis Championships — A843

Player: No. 3438, $5, On crutches. No. 3439, $5, In wheelchair.

2002, Aug. 13 *Perf. 11½x11¼*

3438-3439 A843	Set of 2	.60	.30

Folk Traditions Type of 2002

Designs: No. 3440, $5, Launching of water lanterns (green background). No. 3441, $5, Snatching flags for good luck (yellow background). $10, Worship of the just (blue background). $20, Burning the Prince's boat (red orange background).

2002, Aug. 22 *Perf. 12½*

3440-3443 A833	Set of 4	2.40	1.25

Republic of China - Vatican City Diplomatic Relations, 60th Anniv. A844

Designs: $5, Chinese and Vatican flags, Chinese Presidential building, St. Peter's Basilica. $17, Flags, doves, Celso Cardinal Costantini.

2002, Sept. 20 *Perf. 11½x11¼*

3444-3445 A844	Set of 2	1.25	.65

Bird Manual Type of 1999 and

White-rumped Munia — A845

Designs: No. 3446, $5, Vernal hanging parrot (3 characters at LL). $12, White-headed greenfinch (4 characters at LL). $25, Yunnan greenfinch (2 characters at UL).

2002, Oct. 9

3446 A792 $5 multi	.30	.20
3447 A845 $5 multi	.30	.20
3448 A792 $12 multi	.70	.35
3449 A792 $25 multi	1.40	.70
Nos. 3446-3449 (4)	2.70	1.45

Taiwanese Opera A846

Designs: $5, Liang Shan-po and Chu Ying-tai. $6, Hsueh Ting-shan and Fan Li-hua. $10, Hsueh Ping-kuei and Wang Pao-chuan. $25, The Living Buddha Chikung.

2002, Oct. 25

3450-3453 A846	Set of 4	2.75	1.40

Koalas — A847

Designs: No. 3454, $5, Adult with cub. No. 3455, $5, Adult on branch. $9, Adult with head on branch. $21, Adult with cub, diff.

2002, Nov. 15 *Perf. 11¼x11½*

3454-3457 A847	Set of 4	2.40	1.25
a.	Souvenir sheet, #3454-3457, perf. 12	2.40	1.25

Knots A848

Nos. 3458-3459 — Various knots (Denomination location, denomination color and background color): a, UL, orange, light orange. b, UL, purple, yellow. c, UL, green, light green. d, UL, yellow, light blue. e, UL, blue, pink. f, UR, orange, light orange. g, UR, red violet, yellow. h, UR, blue, light green. i, UR, yellow, light blue. j, UR, red violet, pink.

No. 3460 (yellow denominations, olive green background): a, Like #3458a. b, Like #3458b. c, Like #3458c, d, #3458d, e, Like #3458e. f, Like #3458f. g, Like #3458g. h, Like #3458h. i, Like #3458i. j, Like #3458j.

2002, Nov. 22 Litho. *Perf. 12½*

3458	Block of 10	2.00	1.00
a.-j.	A848 $3.50 Any single	.20	.20
k.	Sheet of 10 #3458f + 10 attached labels	11.00	11.00
l.	Sheet of 10 #3458g + 10 attached labels	11.00	11.00
m.	Sheet of 10 #3458h + 10 attached labels	11.00	11.00
n.	Sheet of 10 #3458i + 10 attached labels	11.00	11.00
o.	Sheet of 10 #3458j + 10 attached labels	11.00	11.00
p.	Sheet , #3458a-3458j + 10 attached labels	11.00	11.00
3459	Block of 10	3.00	1.50
a.-j.	A848 $5 Any single	.30	.20
k.	Sheet of 10 #3459a + 10 attached labels	11.50	11.50
l.	*Sheet of 10 #3459b + 10 attached labels	11.50	11.50
m.	Sheet of 10 #3459c + 10 attached labels	11.50	11.50
n.	Sheet of 10 #3459d + 10 attached labels	11.50	11.50
o.	Sheet of 10 #3459e + 10 attached labels	11.50	11.50
p.	Sheet of 10 #3459f + 10 attached labels	11.50	11.50
q.	Sheet of 10 #3459g + 10 attached labels	11.50	11.50
r.	Sheet of 10 #3459h + 10 attached labels	11.50	11.50
s.	Sheet of 10 #3459i + 10 attached labels	11.50	11.50
t.	Sheet of 10 #3459j + 10 attached labels	11.50	11.50
3460	Block of 10	15.00	7.50
a.-j.	A848 $25 Any single	1.50	.75
k.	Sheet of 10 #3460a + 10 attached labels	23.00	23.00
l.	Sheet of 10 #3460b + 10 attached labels	23.00	23.00
m.	Sheet of 10 #3460c + 10 attached labels	23.00	23.00
n.	Sheet of 10 #3460d + 10 attached labels	23.00	23.00
o.	Sheet of 10 #3460e + 10 attached labels	23.00	23.00
p.	Sheet, #3460a-3460j + 10 attached labels	23.00	23.00
	Nos. 3458-3460 (3)	20.00	10.00

Nos. 3458k-3458p sold for $185 each; Nos. 3459k-3459u for $200 each; Nos. 3460k-3460p for $400 each. Labels, which were personalized, were separated from stamps on Nos. 3458k-3458p, 3459k-3459u, 3460k-3460p by vertical rows of simulated perforations.

New Year 2003 (Year of the Ram) — A849

Designs: $3.50, Yellow ram. $13, Red ram.

2002, Dec. 2 Litho. *Perf. 12¼*

3461	A849 $3.50 multi	.20	.20
a.	Perf. 12¼ Vert.	.20	.20
b.	As "a," booklet pane of 6	1.25	—
	Booklet, 2 #3461b	2.50	
3462	A849 $13 multi	.75	.40
a.	Souvenir sheet, 2 each #3461-3462	1.90	.95
b.	As "a," with Chinese text in red in L & R sheet margins	1.90	.95

Issued: No. 3462b, 1/1/03. Chinese text in left and right sheet margins on No. 3462b commemorates the establishment of Chunghwa Post Co., Ltd.

Street Scene on a Summer Day, by Chen Cheng-po A850

Girl in the White Dress, by Li Mei-shu — A851

Courtyard with Banana Trees, by Liao Chi-chun — A852

Sunrise, by Kuo Po-chuan A853

Perf. 11½x11¼, 11¼x11½

2002, Dec. 6

3463	A850	$5 multi	.30	.20
3464	A851	$5 multi	.30	.20
3465	A852	$10 multi	.60	.30
3466	A853	$20 multi	1.10	.55
		Nos. 3463-3466 (4)	2.30	1.25

Admission to World Trade Organization, 1st Anniv. — A854

2003, Jan. 1 Litho. *Perf. 11½x11¼*

3467	A854 $17 multi	1.00	.50

Spring on Wuyen Peak A855

Glacial Cirques, Mt. Nanhu A856

Mt. Nanhu A857

Snow on Mt. Chungyang Chien A858

2003, Jan. 23

3468	A855	$5 multi	.30	.20
3469	A856	$5 multi	.30	.20
3470	A857	$12 multi	.70	.35
3471	A858	$25 multi	1.40	.70
		Nos. 3468-3471 (4)	2.70	1.45

Compare with Types A814, A834-A837.

Fruit Type of 2001

Perf. 12½x13¼

2003, Feb. 14 Litho.

3472	A813	$9 Rose apples	.50	.25
3473	A813	$13 Kumquats	.75	.40
3474	A813	$15 Lemons	.85	.45
3475	A813	$34 Coconuts	2.00	1.00

Love — A859

Hearts and: No. 3476, $5, Woman tending to man in wheelchair. No. 3477, $5, Family. $10, Landscape. $25, Girl and dogs.

2003, Mar. 20 *Perf. 11¼x11½*

3476-3479	A859	Set of 4	2.60	1.25

Puppet Theater A860

Designs: No. 3480, $5, *Journey to the West* performed on outdoor stage. No. 3481, $5, Puppets on television. $10, *Mysteries of the Wolf Castle* performed at the National Opera House. $25, Screening of movie, *Legend of the Sacred Stone.*

2003, Apr. 3 *Perf. 11½x11¼*

3480-3483	A860	Set of 4	2.60	1.25

Merops Philippinus A861

Designs: Nos. 3484, 3488a, $5, Foraging. Nos. 3485, 3488b, $5, Roosting. Nos. 3486, 3488c, $10, Bathing. Nos. 3487, 3488d, $20, Feeding chick.

2003, May 8 *Perf. 12½*

With White Frame

3484-3487	A861	Set of 4	2.40	1.25

Souvenir Sheet

Without White Frame

3488	A861	Sheet of 4, #a-d	2.40	1.25

No. 3488 contains four 33x25mm stamps.

Furniture — A862

Designs: No. 3489, $5, Wash basin stand. No. 3490, $5, Canopy bed. $12, Taishi chair. $20, Pahsien table.

2003, May 22 *Perf. 11¼x11½*

3489-3492	A862	Set of 4	2.50	1.25

Folktale "Eight Immortals Cross the Sea" — A863

Immortal: No. 3493, $5, Riding catfish. No. 3494, $5, On donkey. $10, Holding fan. $25, In brown robe.

2003, June 12

3493-3496	A863	Set of 4	2.60	1.25

Moths A864

Designs: No. 3497, $5, Antitrygodes divisaria perturbata. No. 3498, $5, Vamuna virilis. $12, Sinna extrema. $20, Thyas juno.

2003, June 26 *Perf. 11½x11¼*

3497-3500	A864	Set of 4	2.50	1.25

Dragonflies A865

Designs: Nos. 3501, 3505a, $5, Acisoma panorpoides panorpoides. Nos. 3502, 3505b, $5, Sympetrum eroticu ardens, vert. Nos. 3503, 3505c, $10, Anax parthenope julius. Nos. 3504, 3505d, $17, Rhyothemis variegata arria, vert.

2003, July 25 *Perf. 12½*

With White Frames

3501-3504	A865	Set of 4	2.25	1.10

Souvenir Sheet

Without White Frames

3505	A865	Sheet of 4, #a-d	2.25	1.10

Stamp size: Nos. 3505a, 3505c, 33x25mm; Nos. 3505b, 3505d, 25x33mm.

Greetings A866

No. 3506: a, Cranes. b, Wood carving and red plate. c, Fish and coin. d, Bamboo. e, Wood carving of bird.

No. 3507: a, Vase with tasseled rope. b, Like #3506a. c, Like #3506b. d, Three brown containers. e, Like #3508. f, Dragon. g, Like #3506c. h, Like #3506d. i, Horse and rider. j, Like #3506e.

No. 3508, Vase with flowers.

2003, Aug. 9 *Perf. 12½*

3506	Horiz. strip of 5	1.00	.50
a.-e.	A866 $3.50 Any single	.20	.20
f.	Sheet of 10 #3506a+ 10 attached labels	11.00	11.00
g.	Sheet of 10 #3506b+ 10 attached labels	11.00	11.00
h.	Sheet of 10 #3506c + 10 attached labels	11.00	11.00
i.	Sheet of 10 #3506d + 10 attached labels	11.00	11.00
j.	Sheet of 10 #3506e + 10 attached labels	11.00	11.00
k.	Sheet , 2 each #3506a-3506e + 10 attached labels	11.00	11.00

3507 Block of 10 3.00 1.50
a.-j. A866 $5 Any single .30 .20
k. Sheet of 10 #3507a + 10 attached labels 11.50 11.50
l. Sheet of 10 #3507b + 10 attached labels 11.50 11.50
m. Sheet of 10 #3507c + 10 attached labels 11.50 11.50
n. Sheet of 10 #3507d + 10 attached labels 11.50 11.50
o Sheet of 10 #3507e + 10 attached labels 11.50 11.50
p. Sheet of 10 #3507f + 10 attached labels 11.50 11.50
q. Sheet of 10 #3507g + 10 attached labels 11.50 11.50
r. Sheet of 10 #3507h + 10 attached labels 11.50 11.50
s. Sheet of 10 #3507i + 10 attached labels 11.50 11.50
t. Sheet of 10 #3507j + 10 attached labels 11.50 11.50
u. Sheet, #3507a-3507j + 10 attached labels 11.50 11.50
3508 A866 $12 multi .70 .35
a. Sheet of 10 #3508 + 10 attached labels 16.00 16.00
Nos. 3506-3508 (3) 4.70 2.35

Nos. 3506f-3506k sold for $185 each; Nos. 3507k-3507u for $200 each; No. 3508a for $270 each. Labels, which were personalized, were separated from stamps on Nos. 3506f-3506k, 3507k-3507u, 3508a by vertical rows of simulated perforations.

Bird Manual Type of 1999 and

White-throated Laughing Thrush — A867

Designs: No. 3510, Great mynah (2 characters at LR). $12, Yellow-legged buttonquail (3 characters at UL). $25, Crested lark (4 characters at L).

Perf. 11½x11¼

2003, Sept. 10 **Litho.**

3509 A867 $5 multi .30 .20
3510 A792 $5 multi .30 .20
3511 A792 $12 multi .70 .35
3512 A792 $25 multi 1.50 .75
Nos. 3509-3512 (4) 2.80 1.50

Chungshan Park, Taichung A868

Tourist attractions: No. 3514, $5, Dongshan River Bridge, Ilan. $11, Badlands, Tianliao. $20, Sansiantai, Chenggong.

2003, Oct. 28 **Litho.** ***Perf. 11½***

3513-3516 A868 Set of 4 2.40 1.25

Chungshan Park, cent. (#3513).

Veterans Day, 25th Anniv. A869

Veterans Affairs Commission insignia and: $5, Veterans building Central Cross-Island Highway. $25, Veterans, homes and hospital for veterans.

2003, Oct. 31

3517-3518 A869 Set of 2 1.75 .90

The Back Yard, by Lu Tie-jhou — A870

A Gold Mine Tower: Jioufen, by Lin Ke-gong — A871

Leisurely, by Chen Jin — A872

East Gate, by Li Ze-fan A873

2003, Nov. 20

3519 A870 $5 multi .30 .20
3520 A871 $5 multi .30 .20
3521 A872 $10 multi .60 .30
3522 A873 $20 multi 1.25 .60
Nos. 3519-3522 (4) 2.45 1.30

New Year 2004 (Year of the Monkey) — A874

Monkey holding fruit: $3.50, With tail. $13, In hand.

2003, Dec. 1 ***Perf. 12¼***

3523-3524 A874 Set of 2 1.00 .50
3523a Perf. 12¼ vert. .20 .20
3524a Sheet, 2 each #3523-3524 2.00 1.00
3523b Booklet pane, 12 #3523a 2.40 —
Complete booklet, #3523b 2.40

Springs A875

Designs: No. 3525, $5, Yangmingshan Hot Springs, fumaroles (light orange background). No. 3526, $5, Suao Cold Springs, Nanfangao Bridge (light blue background). $10, Guanziling Murky Hot Spring, Shuei Huo Tong Yuan. $25, Green Island Seabed Hot Springs, Green Island Lighthouse.

2003, Dec. 14 ***Perf. 13***

3525-3528 A875 Set of 4 2.75 1.40
3528a Souvenir sheet, #3525-3528 2.75 1.40

Completion of Highway 3 — A876

Designs: $5, Jhonggang Interchange. $25, Cingshuei Service Area.
$20, Cingshuei Service Area, diff.

2004, Jan. 8 **Litho.** ***Perf. 12½***

3529-3530 A876 Set of 2 1.75 .90

Souvenir Sheet

Perf. 11½x11¼

3531 A876 $20 multi 1.25 .60

No. 3531 contains one 80x30mm stamp.

Flowers — A877

Designs: No. 3532, $5, Lilium formosanum. No. 3533, $5, Hippeastrum x hybridum. $12, Fressia x hybrida.

2004, Jan. 17 ***Perf. 12¼***

3532-3534 A877 Set of 3 1.40 .70
3534a Souvenir sheet, #3532-3534, perf. 13 1.40 .70
3534b As "a," with Taiwan Flower Expo emblem and text added in margin 1.40 .70

Eight Immortals Cross the Sea Type of 2003

Immortal: No. 3535, $5, With crane and flute. No. 3536, $5, With lotus flower. $10, Holding stick, wearing red robe. $25, Carrying flower basket.

2004, Feb. 25 ***Perf. 11¼x11½***

3535-3538 A863 Set of 4 2.75 1.40

Red Cross Society, Cent. — A878

No. 3539: a, Heart, stylized people with arms raised. b, Heart, stylized people doing Red Cross activities.
Illustration reduced.

2004, Mar. 9 ***Perf. 11¼x11½***

3539 A878 $5 Horiz. pair, #a-b .60 .30

A Young Girl From Lu Kai, by Yan Shui-long A879

Old Street in Taipei, by Yang San-lang A880

Happy Farmers, by Lee Shih-chiao A881

Fish Shop, by Liu Chi-hsiang A882

Perf. 11¼x11½, 11½x11¼

2004, Mar. 25

3540 A879 $5 multi .30 .20
3541 A880 $5 multi .30 .20
3542 A881 $10 multi .60 .30
3543 A882 $20 multi 1.25 .60
Nos. 3540-3543 (4) 2.45 1.30

Butterflies A883

Designs: No. 3544, $5, Parantica sita niphonica. No. 3545, $5, Choaspes benjaminii formosanus. $17, Junonia almana. $20, Artipe eryx horiella.

2004, Apr. 21 ***Perf. 11½x11¼***

3544-3547 A883 Set of 4 3.00 1.50

Yijhen Folk Art Performers A884

Designs: No. 3548, $5, Eight Generals (buff background). No. 3549, $5, Song Jiang Battle Array (grayish blue background). $11, Drum Dance. $25, Stilt walkers.

2004, May 11

3548-3551 A884 Set of 4 2.75 1.40

Inauguration of Pres. Chen Shiu-bian and Vice-President Hsiu-lien Annette Lu — A885

No. 3552 — President, Vice-President and: a, Map of Taiwan, flag, crowd. b, Map of People's Republic of China and Taiwan, handshake, flowers. c, Buildings, crowd. d, Train, highway, buildings.
$12, President, Vice-President, buildings, train, highway.

2004, May 20 ***Perf. 12½***

3552 Horiz. strip of 4 1.25 .60
a.-d. A885 $5 Any single .30 .20

Souvenir Sheet

Perf. 12

3553 A885 $12 multi .75 .35

No. 3553 contains one 80x30mm stamp.

Opening of Movie, *Harry Potter and the Prisoner of Azkaban* — A886

No. 3554: a, $5, Harry, messenger owl, Hedwig, with letter. b, $5, Hedwig, rose background. c, $5, Harry riding Hippogriff. d, $5, Hippogriff, green background. e, $5, Harry, Monster Book of Monsters. f, $25, Crookshanks the Cat.
No. 3555: a, $5, Harry playing quidditch. b, $5, Harry playing quidditch, Dementors. c, $5, Harry and Hermoine riding Hippogriff. d, $5, Harry holding wand, Hogwarts. e, $5, Harry practicing Patronus Charm to repel Dementors. f, $25, Harry thrusting wand.

2004, June 4 ***Perf. 12***

Sheets of 6, #a-f

3554-3555 A886 Set of 2 6.00 3.00

Nos. 3554-3555 were not sold directly to customers at foreign addresses but were made available abroad through Canada Post's philatelic agency.

Old Train Stations A887

Designs: No. 3556, $5, Keelung Station, rickshaws. No. 3557, $5, Taipei Station, automobile. $15, Hsinchu Station, ox and cart. $25, Taichung Station, wagons.

2004, June 9 ***Perf. 13½x13¾***

3556-3559 A887 Set of 4 3.00 1.50

Iron Fort, Nangan Island A888

Cinbi, Beigan Island A889

Fujheng, Tungchu Island A890

Lienyuyikeng, Tungyin Island — A891

2004, July 1 Litho. ***Perf. 11½x11¼***

3560 A888 $5 multi .30 .20
3561 A889 $5 multi .30 .20
3562 A890 $9 multi .55 .25
3563 A891 $25 multi 1.50 .75
Nos. 3560-3563 (4) 2.65 1.40

Matsu National Scenic Area.

Crabs A892

Designs: No. 3564, $3.50, Uca formosensis. No. 3565, $3.50, Uca borealis. $5, Uca arcuata. $25, Uca lactea.

2004, July 21

3564-3567 A892 Set of 4 2.25 1.10

Souvenir Sheet

Listening to the Lute, Attributed to Li Sung — A893

No. 3568: a, $5, Lute player. b, $25, Scholar and woman.

2004, Aug. 6 ***Perf. 12***

3568 A893 Sheet of 2, #a-b 1.75 .90

Souvenir Sheet

Taipei 2005 Intl. Stamp Exhibition — A894

No. 3569: a, $5, Sun Moon Lake. b, $25, Mt. Ali.

2004, Aug. 27 ***Perf. 11½x11¼***

3569 A894 Sheet of 2, #a-b 1.75 .90

Intl. Day of Peace A895

2004, Sept. 21 ***Perf. 12¼x11¾***

3570 A895 $15 multi .90 .45

Souvenir Sheets

Hello Kitty — A896

No. 3571, oval stamps: a, $5, Dear Daniel, donuts. b, $15, Hello Kitty, Taipei 101 Building.

No. 3572, rectangular stamps: a, $5, Hello Kitty, bird, horiz. b, $15, Dear Daniel, Fisherman's Wharf, Danshuei.

2004, Sept. 24 ***Perf.***

3571 A896 Sheet of 2, #a-b 1.25 .60

Perf. 12

3572 A896 Sheet of 2, #a-b 1.25 .60

Sayings With Numbers Greeting Stamps

One Sea of Smooth Sailing A897

Two Lions Bring Good Fortune A898

Three Goats of Auspiciousness — A899

Safety in All Four Seasons A900

Five Blessings at the Door A901

Six is Silky Smooth A902

Married for Seven Lives A903

Eight Immortals Wish for Your Perfection A904

Nine Means Success A905

Ten is All Around Perfection A906

2004, Oct. 10 ***Perf. 12½***

3573 Block of 10 2.10 1.10
a. A897 $3.50 multi .20 .20
b. A898 $3.50 multi .20 .20
c. A899 $3.50 multi .20 .20
d. A900 $3.50 multi .20 .20
e. A901 $3.50 multi .20 .20
f. A902 $3.50 multi .20 .20
g. A903 $3.50 multi .20 .20
h. A904 $3.50 multi .20 .20
i. A905 $3.50 multi .20 .20
j. A906 $3.50 multi .20 .20

Changed Colors

3574 Block of 10 3.00 1.50
a. A897 $5 multi .30 .20
b. A898 $5 multi .30 .20
c. A899 $5 multi .30 .20
d. A900 $5 multi .30 .20
e. A901 $5 multi .30 .20
f. A902 $5 multi .30 .20
g. A903 $5 multi .30 .20
h. A904 $5 multi .30 .20
i. A905 $5 multi .30 .20
j. A906 $5 multi .30 .20

Kaohsiung Medical University, 50th Anniv. A907

Designs: No. 3575, $5, University gate and buildings. No. 3576, $5, Building, researcher, beaker, mosquito and snake.

2004, Oct. 16 ***Perf. 12½***

3575-3576 A907 Set of 2 .60 .30

Main Peak, Mt. Cilai A908

North Peak, Mt. Cilai A909

South Peak, Mt. Cilai A910

Grasslands, Mt. Cilai — A911

2004, Oct. 16 ***Perf. 11½x11¼***

3577 A908 $5 multi .30 .20
3578 A909 $5 multi .30 .20
3579 A910 $12 multi .75 .35
3580 A911 $25 multi 1.50 .75
Nos. 3577-3580 (4) 2.85 1.50

Sports In Which Taiwanese Athletes Won Medals At 2004 Summer Olympics A912

Designs: No. 3581, $5, Women's Taekwondo. No. 3582, $5, Men's Taekwondo, vert. $9, Archery. $12, Athletes on winner's platform, vert.

Perf. 11¼x11½, 11½x11¼

2004, Oct. 22

3581-3584 A912 Set of 4 1.90 .95

Platalea Minor A913

Designs: No. 3585, $2.50, Pair in flight. No. 3586, $2.50, Pair standing on one leg. $15, With wings spread. $25, Foraging for food. $20, Birds in water.

2004, Oct. 30 ***Perf. 13½x13¼***

3585-3588 A913 Set of 4 2.75 1.40

Souvenir Sheet

3589 A913 $20 multi 1.25 .60

No. 3589 contains one 80x30mm stamp.

Pres. Yen Chia-kan (1905-93) A914

2004, Nov. 5 ***Perf. 13¼x13½***

3590 A914 $12 multi .75 .35

New Year 2005 (Year of the Cock) — A915

Designs: $3.50, Cock on lantern. $13, Lanterns, cock
$5, Cock, hen and chick, horiz.

2004, Nov. 10 ***Perf. 12¼x11¾***

3591-3592 A915 Set of 2 1.00 .50

Souvenir Sheet

Perf. 11¾x11¼

3593 A915 $5 multi .30 .20

No. 3593 contains one 46x26mm stamp.

Prefectural Hall, Chiayi A916

East Gate, Chiayi A917

2004, Nov. 20 ***Perf. 13½x13¼***

3594 A916 $5 multi .30 .20
3595 A917 $5 multi .30 .20

Chiayi, 300th anniv.

SEMI-POSTAL STAMPS

SP1

Red or Blue Surcharge

1920, Dec. 1 **Unwmk.** ***Perf. 14, 15***

B1 SP1 1c on 2c green 4.25 1.25
B2 SP1 3c on 4c scar (B) 5.75 2.25
B3 SP1 5c on 6c gray 8.25 2.75
Nos. B1-B3 (3) 18.25 6.25

The surcharge represents the actual franking value. The extra cent helped victims of the 1919 Yellow River flood.

War Refugees SP2

Black Surcharge

1944, Oct. 10 **Engr.** ***Perf. 12***

B4 $2 +$2 on 50c + 50c .75 .75
B5 $4 +$4 on 8c + 8c .75 .75
B6 $5 +$5 on 21c + 21c 1.00 1.00
B7 $6 +$6 on 28c + 28c 1.50 1.50
B8 $10 +$10 on 33c + 33c 2.50 2.50
B9 $20 +$20 on $1 + $1 4.00 4.00
a. Sheet of 6, #B4-B9 32.50 20.00
Nos. B4-B9 (6) 10.50 10.50

The borders of each stamp differ slightly in design. The surtax was for war refugees.

Nos. B4-B8 exist without surcharge, but were not regularly issued.

Great Wall of China — SP4

Chinese Refugee Family — SP5

1948, July 5 **Litho.** ***Perf. 14, Imperf.***

Without Gum

Cross in Carmine

B11 SP4 $5000 + $2000 vio .20 *1.00*
B12 SP4 $10,000 + $2000 brn .20 *1.00*
B13 SP4 $15,000 + $2000 gray .20 *1.00*
a. Cross omitted
Nos. B11-B13 (3) .60 *3.00*

The surtax was for anti-tuberculosis work.

Fakes of B13a exist with cross chemically removed. No genuine used copies are known.

Republic of China (Taiwan)

1954, Oct. 1 **Engr.** ***Perf. 12***

Without Gum

B14 SP5 40c + 10c dp bl 19.00 1.75
B15 SP5 $1.60 + 40c lil rose 45.00 17.00
B16 SP5 $5 + $1 red 100.00 92.50
Nos. B14-B16 (3) 164.00 111.25

The surtax was used to aid in the evacuation of Chinese from North Viet Nam.

Catalogue values for unused stamps in this section, from this point to the end of the section, are for Never Hinged items.

Sept. 21, 1999 Earthquake Relief SP6

a, Damaged buildings, map, rescue workers. b, Hands, heart, earthquake fault.

1999, Nov. 1 **Litho.** ***Imperf.***

Sheet of 2

B17 SP6 $25 +$25, #a.-b. 8.50 8.50

No. B17 has simulated perforations.

AIR POST STAMPS

Curtiss "Jenny" over Great Wall (Bars of Republic flag on tail) — AP1

Unwmk.

1921, July 1 **Engr.** ***Perf. 14***

C1 AP1 15c bl grn & blk 27.50 26.00
C2 AP1 30c scar & blk 27.50 26.00
C3 AP1 45c dull vio & blk 27.50 26.00
C4 AP1 60c dk blue & blk 32.50 30.00
C5 AP1 90c ol grn & blk 45.00 42.50
Nos. C1-C5 (5) 160.00 150.50

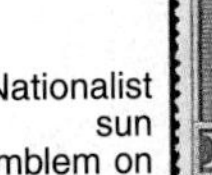

(Nationalist sun emblem on tail) — AP2

1929, July 5

C6 AP2 15c blue grn & blk 3.25 .60
C7 AP2 30c dk red & blk 6.75 2.25
C8 AP2 45c dk vio & blk 13.50 6.50
C9 AP2 60c dk blue & blk 16.00 8.00
C10 AP2 90c ol grn & blk 13.50 14.00
Nos. C6-C10 (5) 53.00 31.35

Junkers F-13 over Great Wall AP3

1932-37

C11 AP3 15c gray grn .40 .40
C12 AP3 25c orange ('33) .40 .40
C13 AP3 30c red 6.25 .40
C14 AP3 45c brown vio .40 .40
C15 AP3 50c dk brown ('33) .40 .40
C16 AP3 60c dk blue .40 .40
C17 AP3 90c olive grn .40 .40
C18 AP3 $1 yellow grn ('33) .40 .40
C19 AP3 $2 brown ('37) 1.10 .40
C20 AP3 $5 brown car ('37) 2.75 3.25
Nos. C11-C20 (10) 12.90 6.85

See #C21-C40. For surcharges and overprints see #C41-C52, C54-C60, 9N111-9N114, 9NC1-9NC7, Szechwan C1, C3-C6, Sinkiang C5-C19.

Type of 1932-37, with secret mark

1932-37 Issue. Lower part of left character joined

Secret Mark, 1940-41 Issue. Separated.

Perf. 12, 12½, 12½x13, 13

1940-41 **Wmk. 261**

C21 AP3 15c gray green .45 .45
C22 AP3 25c yellow org .45 .45
C23 AP3 30c red .45 .45
a. Vert. pair, imperf. between 200.00
C24 AP3 45c dull rose vio ('41) .45 .45
C25 AP3 50c brown .45 .45
C26 AP3 60c dp blue ('41) .45 .45
C27 AP3 90c olive ('41) .45 .45
C28 AP3 $1 apple grn ('41) .45 .45
C29 AP3 $2 lt brown ('41) .45 .45
C30 AP3 $5 lake 1.10 1.10
Nos. C21-C30 (10) 5.15 5.15

Unwmk.

Perf. 12½, 13, 13½

C31 AP3 15c gray green ('41) .40 .30
C32 AP3 25c lt orange ('41) .40 .30
C33 AP3 30c lt red ('41) .40 .30
C34 AP3 45c dl rose vio ('41) .40 .30
C35 AP3 50c brown .40 .30
C36 AP3 60c blue ('41) .40 .30
C37 AP3 90c lt olive ('41) .40 .30
C38 AP3 $1 apple grn ('41) .55 .55
C39 AP3 $2 lt brown ('41) 1.40 1.40
C40 AP3 $5 lake ('41) 1.10 1.10
Nos. C31-C40 (10) 5.85 5.15

For surcharges see note following No. C20.

Nos. C11 and C12 Surcharged

1946, May 2 **Unwmk.** ***Perf. 14***

C41 AP3 $53 on 15c .40 *.90*
C42 AP3 $73 on 25c 1,300. 1,300.

Forgeries of No. C42 exist.

On Nos. C23, C21, C22, C29 and C30

Perf. 13, 13x12, 12½

Wmk. 261

C43 AP3 $23 on 30c red .50 *.35*
C44 AP3 $53 on 15c gray grn 14.00 *17.50*
C45 AP3 $73 on 25c yel org .50 *.35*
C46 AP3 $100 on $2 lt brown 1.00 *.50*
C47 AP3 $200 on $5 lake .50 *.50*
Nos. C43-C47 (5) 16.50 19.20

On Nos. C33, C31, C32, C39 and C40

Perf. 13, 13x12, 13x12½, 12½

Unwmk.

C48 AP3 $23 on 30c lt red .20 .25
a. Inverted surcharge 100.00
b. "2300" omitted 50.00
c. Last character (kuo) of surch. omitted 65.00
C49 AP3 $53 on 15c gray grn .20 .25
a. Horiz. pair, imperf. btwn. 675.00
C50 AP3 $73 on 25c lt org .20 .25
a. Inverted surcharge 525.00

C51 AP3 $100 on $2 lt brn .20 .20
C52 AP3 $200 on $5 lake .20 .20
a. Inverted surcharge 80.00
Nos. C48-C52 (5) 1.00 1.15

The surcharges on #C41-C52 represent Chinese natl. currency and were applied at Shanghai.

Douglas DC-4 over Sun Yat-sen Mausoleum, Nanking — AP4

1946, Sept. 10 Litho. *Perf. 14*
Without Gum

C53 AP4 $27 blue .20 .35

For surcharges see #C61, Szechwan C2.

No. C23 Surcharged in Black

Perf. 13x12

1948, May 18 Wmk. 261

C54 AP3 $10,000 on 30c red .20 .35

Same, in Black or Carmine, on Nos. C33, C32, C37, C36, C18 and C38

Perf. 12½, 13x12½, 14
Unwmk.

C55 AP3 $10,000 on 30c lt red .20 .20
C56 AP3 $20,000 on 25c lt org .20 .20
C57 AP3 $30,000 on 90c lt ol (C) .20 .20
C58 AP3 $50,000 on 60c blue (C) (#C18) .20 .20
C59 AP3 $50,000 on $1 yel grn (C) (#C38) 75.00 70.00
C60 AP3 $50,000 on $1 ap grn (C) .20 .20

No. C53 Surcharged in Black

Perf. 14

C61 AP4 $10,000 on $27 bl .20 .55
Nos. C54-C61 (8) 76.40 71.90

Douglas DC-4 and Arrow — AP5

Perf. 12½

1949, May 2 Unwmk. Litho.
Without Gum

C62 AP5 blue green 3.50 4.00
a. Rouletted 4.50 5.75

See note after No. 959.

For overprints see Taiwan #C1, Fukien #C1, Kansu #C1, PRC #102.

Revenue Stamp Overprinted in Blue

1949, May Engr. *Perf. 14*

C63 A95 $100 olive green 30.00 35.00

See note after No. 962.

Republic of China (Taiwan)

Cheng Ch'eng-kung (Koxinga) — AP6

Rouletted

1950, Sept. 26 Unwmk. Typo.
Without Gum

C64 AP6 60c deep blue 11.00 5.00

For surcharge see No. 1120.

Plane over City Gate, Taipei — AP7

Jet Planes above Chung Shan Bridge — AP8

Two Doves Near Koxinga Shrine — AP9

1954 Engr. *Perf. 11½*
Without Gum

C65 AP7 $1 dk brown 10.00 .70
a. Vert. pair, imperf. btwn. 200.00
C66 AP8 $1.60 olive blk 12.50 .45
a. Vert. pair, imperf. btwn. 140.00
b. Horiz. pair, imperf. btwn. 100.00 110.00
C67 AP9 $5 grnsh blue 17.50 1.10
Nos. C65-C67 (3) 40.00 2.25

Issued: #C66, 8/14; #C65, C67, 9/1.

No. C67 Surcharged in Red

1958, Dec. 11
Without Gum

C68 AP9 $3.50 on $5 grnsh bl 3.50 1.40

Catalogue values for unused stamps in this section, from this point to the end of the section, are for Never Hinged items.

Sea Gull AP10

Sabre Jets in Bomb Burst Formation AP11

1959, Mar. 20 Photo. *Perf. 13*

C69 AP10 $8 blue, gray & blk 4.00 .30

1960, Feb. 29 Unwmk. *Perf. 13*

Plane Formations: $2, Loop, horiz. $5, Diamond formation passing over grounded plane, horiz.

C70 AP11 $1 multicolored 3.50 .30
C71 AP11 $2 multicolored 4.75 .40
C72 AP11 $5 multicolored 6.00 .50
Nos. C70-C72 (3) 14.25 1.20

Issued to honor the Chinese Air Force and the "Thunder Tiger" aerobatic team.

Jet Airliner over Pitan Bridge AP12

Designs: $6, Jet over Tropic of Cancer monument, Kiai, vert. $10, Jet over Lion Head mountain, Sinchu, vert.

1963, Aug. 14 Photo. *Perf. 13*

C73 AP12 $2.50 multi 4.25 .20
C74 AP12 $6 multi 6.50 .25
C75 AP12 $10 multi 8.25 .60
Nos. C73-C75 (3) 19.00 1.05

Boeing 727 over Chilin Pavilion, Grand Hotel AP13

Wild Geese Flying over Mountains AP14

Design: $8, Boeing 727 over National Palace Museum, Taipei.

1967, Apr. 1 Unwmk. *Perf. 13*

C76 AP13 $5 multicolored 2.50 .20
C77 AP13 $8 multicolored 4.00 .45

1969, Aug. 14 Photo. *Perf. 13*

Wild Geese flying over: $5, The sea. $8, The land, horiz.

C78 AP14 $2.50 multicolored 1.75 .20
C79 AP14 $5 multicolored 3.25 .45
C80 AP14 $8 multicolored 4.75 .60
Nos. C78-C80 (3) 9.75 1.25

Presidential Palace and Tzu-Ch'iang Squadron AP15

1980, June 18 Litho. *Perf. 13½*

C81 AP15 $5 shown .25 .20
C82 AP15 $7 China Airlines jet .40 .25
C83 AP15 $12 China flag, jet .70 .40
Nos. C81-C83 (3) 1.35 .85

Civil Aeronautics Administration, 37th Anniv. — AP16

Jet Airliners over: $7, Chiang Kai-shek Intl. Airport, vert. $11, Chung Cheng Memorial Hall. $18, Sun Yat-sen Memorial Hall.

Perf. 14x13½, 13½x14

1984, Jan. 20 Litho.

C84 AP16 $7 multicolored .45 .20
C85 AP16 $11 multicolored .60 .20
C86 AP16 $18 multicolored .90 .35
Nos. C84-C86 (3) 1.95 .75

Airplane AP17

1987, Aug. 4 Litho. *Perf. 13½*

C87 AP17 $9 multicolored .50 .25
C88 AP17 $14 multicolored .75 .50
C89 AP17 $18 multicolored 1.00 .60
Nos. C87-C89 (3) 2.25 1.35

SPECIAL DELIVERY STAMPS

Design: Dragon in irregular oval.

Stamp 8x2½ inches, divided into four parts by perforation or serrate rouletting.

Values of Nos. E1-E8 are for used mailer's receipts. Complete unused strips of four are exceptionally scarce because the first section (#1) was to remain in the P.O. booklet.

The mailer received the righthand section (#4), usually canceled, as a receipt. The middle two sections were canceled and attached to the letter. Upon arrival at the destination P.O. they were canceled again, usually on the back, with the righthand copy (#3) retained by that P.O. The lefthand copy (#2) was signed by the recipient and returned to the original P.O. as evidence of delivery. Sections 2 and 3 usually are thin or badly damaged.

Unused strips of three (#2-4) can be found of Nos. E3-E8.

"Chinese Imperial Post Office" in lines, repeated to form the background which is usually lighter in color than the rest of the design.

Dragon's head facing downward
Background with period after "POSTOFFICE."
No Date

1905 Unwmk. *Perf. 11*

E1 10c grass green 425.00

Serrate Roulette in Black

E2 10c deep green 300.00

1907-10

Dragon's head facing forward
Background with no period after "POSTOFFICE"
No Date

E3 10c light bluish green 175.00

1909-11

Background with date at bottom

E4 10c green (Feby 1909) 125.00
E5 10c bl grn (Jan. 1911) 125.00

1912

"IMPERIAL POST OFFICE" in serifed letters repeated to form the background.
No Date, No Border
Background of 30 or 28 lines

E6 10c green (30 lines) 65.00
a. 28 lines 65.00

Background of 35 lines of sans-serif letters
Colored Border

E8 10c green 125.00

On No. E8 the medallion in the third section has Chinese characters in the background instead of the usual English inscriptions. E6 and E8 occur with many types of four-character overprints reading "Republic of China," applied locally but unofficially at various post offices.

1913

Design: Wild Goose. Stamp 7½x2¾ inches, divided into five parts.
"CHINESE POST OFFICE" in sans-serif letters, repeated to form the background of 28 lines. With border.
Serrate Roulette in Black

E9 10c green 350.00 24.00

Unused values for Nos. E9-E10 are for complete strips of five parts. Used values are for single parts.

1914

"CHINESE POST OFFICE" in antique letters, forming a background of 29 or 30 lines. No border.

Serrate Roulette in Green

E10	10c green	90.00	3.00

On No. E9 the background is in sans-serif capitals, the Chinese and English inscriptions are on white tablets and the serial numbers are in black.

On No. E10 the background is in antique capitals and extends under the inscriptions. The serial numbers are in green.

NOTE:

In February, 1916, the Special Delivery Stamps were demonetized and became merely receipts without franking value. To mark this, four of the five sections of the stamp had the letters A, B, C, D either handstamped or printed on them.

SD1

1941 Unwmk. Typo. *Rouletted*

Without Gum

E11	SD1 ($2) car & yel	26.00	22.50

Motorcycle Messenger — SD2

1949, July Litho. *Perf. 12½*

Without Gum

E12	SD2 red violet	5.00	*11.00*
a.	Rouletted	6.00	*11.00*

See note after No. 959.

For surcharge and overprints see Nos. 1150, Taiwan E1, Fukien E1.

Revenue Stamp Overprinted in Purple Brown

1949

Without Gum

E13	A95 $10 grnsh gray	16.00	16.00

See note after No. 962.

REGISTRATION STAMPS

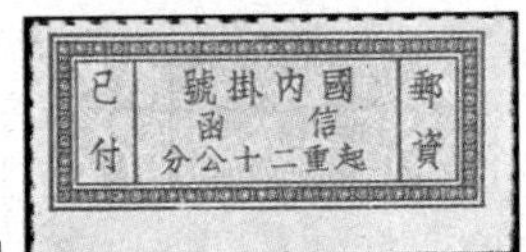

R1

1941 Unwmk. Typo. *Rouletted*

Without Gum

F1	R1 ($1.50) green & buff	18.00	12.00

Mountain Scene — R2

1949, July Litho. *Perf. 12½*

Without Gum

F2	R2 carmine	5.50	*8.00*
a.	Rouletted	6.50	*11.00*

See note after No. 959.

For surcharge and overprints see Nos. 1152, Taiwan F1, Fukien F1, PRC 103.

Revenue Stamp Overprinted in Carmine

1949

F3	A95 $50 dark blue	18.00	14.00

See note after No. 962.

POSTAGE DUE STAMPS

Regular Issue of 1902-03 Overprinted in Black

1904 Unwmk. *Perf. 14 to 15*

J1	A17	½c chocolate	6.00	1.90
J2	A17	1c ocher	6.75	2.50
J3	A17	2c scarlet	7.50	3.50
J4	A17	4c red brn	8.00	4.00
J5	A17	5c salmon	16.00	7.25
J6	A17	10c dk blue grn	26.00	11.00
a.		Vert. pair, imperf. btwn.		475.00
		Nos. J1-J6 (6)	70.25	30.15

D1

1904 Engr.

J7	D1	½c blue	2.25	.50
a.		Horiz. pair, imperf. btwn.	350.00	325.00
J8	D1	1c blue	4.25	.50
J9	D1	2c blue	3.00	.50
a.		Horiz. pair, imperf. btwn.	400.00	350.00
J10	D1	4c blue	5.50	.60
J11	D1	5c blue	7.25	.60
J12	D1	10c blue	7.25	1.50
J13	D1	20c blue	21.00	3.00
J14	D1	30c blue	27.50	20.00
		Nos. J7-J14 (8)	78.00	27.20

Arabic numeral of value at left on #J12-J14.

1911

J15	D1	1c brown	6.25	1.50
J16	D1	2c brown	13.00	13.00

The ½c, 4c, 5c and 20c in brown exist but were not issued as they arrived in China after the downfall of the Ching dynasty.

Issue of 1904 Overprinted in Red

1912

J19	D1	½c blue	425.	325.
J20	D1	4c blue	475.	400.
J21	D1	5c blue	550.	575.
J22	D1	10c blue	850.	650.
J23	D1	20c blue	1,800.	1,500.
J24	D1	30c blue	1,800.	1,500.

Nos. J15-J16 exist with this overprint, but were not regularly issued.

Nos. J25-J33

Nos. J34-J42

1912

Overprinted in Red

J25	D1	½c blue	.20	.20
J26	D1	1c brown	.30	.30
a.		Horiz. pair, imperf. btwn.	550.00	
b.		Inverted overprint	225.00	
J27	D1	2c brown	.35	.30
J28	D1	4c blue	2.75	3.00
J29	D1	5c blue	95.00	90.00
J30	D1	5c brown	1.25	.85
a.		Inverted overprint	200.00	175.00
J31	D1	10c blue	5.00	1.10
J32	D1	20c blue	8.00	5.25
J33	D1	30c blue	11.50	10.00
		Nos. J25-J33 (9)	124.35	111.00

1912

Overprinted in Black

J34	D1	½c blue	6.00	1.40
J35	D1	½c brown	.70	.30
J36	D1	1c brown	.65	.55
a.		Inverted overprint	200.00	175.00
J37	D1	2c brown	3.00	4.25
J38	D1	4c blue	5.00	5.50
J39	D1	5c brown	9.50	7.00
a.		Horiz. pair, imperf. btwn.	700.00	
J40	D1	10c blue	11.50	16.00
J41	D1	20c brown	27.50	30.00
J42	D1	30c blue	57.50	35.00
		Nos. J34-J42 (9)	121.35	100.00

D4 D5 D6

Printed by Waterlow & Sons

1913, May *Perf. 14, 15*

J43	D4	½c blue	.60	.20
a.		Horiz. pair, imperf. btwn.	200.00	
J44	D4	1c blue	1.10	.20
J45	D4	2c blue	2.50	1.75
J46	D4	4c blue	2.00	.20
J47	D4	5c blue	3.00	.20
J48	D4	10c blue	6.00	4.25
J49	D4	20c blue	14.00	7.75
J50	D4	30c blue	18.00	3.50
		Nos. J43-J50 (8)	47.20	18.05

Printed by the Chinese Bureau of Engraving & Printing

1915 Re-engraved *Perf. 14*

J51	D4	½c blue	.50	.55
J52	D4	1c blue	1.25	.20
J53	D4	2c blue	1.25	.20
J54	D4	4c blue	1.25	.20
J55	D4	5c blue	2.50	.50
J56	D4	10c blue	3.00	.70
J57	D4	20c blue	8.00	1.25
J58	D4	30c blue	30.00	3.00
		Nos. J51-J58 (8)	47.75	6.60

In the upper part of the stamps of type D4 there is an ornament of five marks like the letter "V". Below this is a curved label with an inscription in Chinese characters. On the 1913 stamps there are two complete background lines between the ornament and the label. The 1915 stamps show only one unbroken line at this place. There are other minute differences in the engraving of the stamps of the two issues.

1932 *Perf. 14*

J59	D5	½c orange	.20	.20
J60	D5	1c orange	.20	.20
J61	D5	2c orange	.20	.20
J62	D5	4c orange	.40	.20
J63	D5	5c orange	.40	.20
J64	D5	10c orange	.85	.45
J65	D5	20c orange	1.10	.55
J66	D5	30c orange	1.75	.55
		Nos. J59-J66 (8)	5.10	2.55

See Nos. J69-J79. For surcharges see Nos. 1NJ1, 9NJ1-9NJ4.

Regular Stamps of 1939 Overprinted in Black or Red

1940

J67	A57	$1 henna & dk brn (Bk)	1.75	*5.00*
J68	A57	$2 dl bl & org brn (R)	1.75	*5.50*

Type of 1932

Printed by The Commercial Press, Ltd.

Perf. 12½, 12½x13, 13

1940-41 Engr.

J69	D5	½c yellow orange	.20	.30
J70	D5	1c yellow orange	.20	.30
J71	D5	2c yellow orange ('41)	.20	.30
J72	D5	4c yellow orange	.20	.30
J73	D5	5c yellow orange ('41)	.55	.30
J74	D5	10c yellow orange ('41)	.20	.30
J75	D5	20c yellow orange ('41)	.20	.30
J76	D5	30c yellow orange	.20	.30
J77	D5	50c yellow orange	.35	.40
J78	D5	$1 yellow orange	.35	.60
J79	D5	$2 yellow orange	.60	.60
		Nos. J69-J79 (11)	3.25	4.00

For surcharge see No. 1NJ1.

Thin Paper Without Gum

1944 Typo. *Perf. 13*

J80	D6	10c bluish green	.20	*.45*
J81	D6	20c light chalky blue	.20	*.45*
J82	D6	40c dull rose	.20	*.45*
J83	D6	50c bluish green	.20	*.40*
J84	D6	60c dull blue	.20	*.70*
J85	D6	$1 dull rose	.20	*.35*
J86	D6	$2 lilac brown	.20	*.35*
		Nos. J80-J86 (7)	1.40	*3.15*

D7 D8

1945 Without Gum Unwmk.

J87	D7	$2 rose carmine	.20	*.85*
J88	D7	$6 rose carmine	.20	*.85*
J89	D7	$8 rose carmine	.20	*.85*
J90	D7	$10 rose carmine	.20	*1.10*
J91	D7	$20 rose carmine	.20	*1.10*
J92	D7	$30 rose carmine	.40	*1.10*
		Nos. J87-J92 (6)	1.40	*5.85*

For surcharges see Nos. J102-J109.

Thin Paper Without Gum

1947 Litho. *Perf. 14*

J93	D8	$50 plum	.20	*.35*
J94	D8	$80 plum	.20	*.35*
J95	D8	$100 plum	.20	*.35*
J96	D8	$160 plum	.20	*.35*
J97	D8	$200 plum	.20	*.35*
J98	D8	$400 violet brown	.20	*.35*
J99	D8	$500 violet brown	.20	*.35*
a.		Vert. pair, imperf. between	20.00	
J100	D8	$800 violet brown	.20	*.35*
J101	D8	$2000 violet brown	.20	*.35*
		Nos. J93-J101 (9)	1.80	*3.15*

Type of 1945, Redrawn

Surcharged with New Value in Black

1948 Engr. *Perf. 13½x14*

Without Gum

Deep claret

J102	D7	$1000 on $20	.20	*.50*
J103	D7	$2000 on $30	.20	*.50*
J104	D7	$3000 on $50	.20	*.50*
J105	D7	$4000 on $100	.20	*.50*
J106	D7	$5000 on $200	.20	*.50*
J107	D7	$10,000 on $300	.20	*.55*
J108	D7	$20,000 on $500	.20	*.55*
J109	D7	$30,000 on $1000	.20	*.70*
		Nos. J102-J109 (8)	1.60	*4.30*

There are many differences in the redrawn design.

No. 627 Surcharged in Black

1949 *Perf. 12*

J110	A72	1 (c) on $40 orange	.20	*.45*
J111	A72	2 (c) on $40 orange	.20	*.45*
J112	A72	5 (c) on $40 orange	.20	*.45*
J113	A72	10 (c) on $40 orange	.20	*.45*
J114	A72	20 (c) on $40 orange	.20	*.45*
J115	A72	50 (c) on $40 orange	.20	*.50*
J116	A72	$1 on $40 orange	.20	*.50*
J117	A72	$2 on $40 orange	.20	*.50*
J118	A72	$5 on $40 orange	.20	*.75*
J119	A72	$10 on $40 orange	.20	*.50*
		Nos. J110-J119 (10)	2.00	*5.00*

Republic of China (Taiwan)

No. 438 Surcharged in Green or Black

1951 Unwmk. Perf. 12½

J120 A47 40c on 40c org (G) 14.00 *20.00*
J121 A47 80c on 40c org (Bk) 14.00 *20.00*

Revenue Stamps Surcharged in Various Colors

1953 Unwmk. Perf. 12½, 14
Without Gum

J122 A95 10c on $50 dk bl (O) 17.00 3.25
J123 A95 20c on $100 ol grn (Dk Br) 17.00 3.25
J124 A95 40c on $20 org brn 17.00 1.00
J125 A95 80c on $500 sl grn (Dk Bl) 25.00 2.00
J126 A95 $1 on $30 dk vio (G) 25.00 6.75
Nos. J122-J126 (5) 101.00 16.25

D9

D10

D11

1956 Unwmk. Litho. Perf. 12½
Without Gum

J127 D9 20c rose car, & lt bl .80 .20
J128 D9 40c green & buff 1.60 .20
J129 D9 80c brown & gray 3.25 .20
J130 D9 $1 ultra & pink 3.25 .20
Nos. J127-J130 (4) 8.90 .80

No. 1197 Surcharged in Dark Violet

Wmk. 323
1961, Dec. 28 Engr. Perf. 12
Without Gum

J131 A135 $5 on $20 car rose 1.75 .50

Nos. 1274, 1282-1283 Surcharged in Black, Carmine Rose or Blue

1964-65 Litho.

J132 A158 10c on 80c pale grn .20 .20
J133 A158 20c on $3.60 vio bl (CR) ('65) .30 .20
J134 A158 40c on $4.50 ver (B) ('65) .65 .20
Nos. J132-J134 (3) 1.15 .60

1966-76 Wmk. 323 Perf. 12½
Granite Paper; Without Gum

J135 D10 10c dk brn & lil .20 .20
J136 D10 20c blue & yel .40 .20
J137 D10 50c vio bl & lt bl ('70) .65 .20
J138 D10 $1 purple & sal .50 .20
J139 D10 $2 grn & lt bl .65 .20
J140 D10 $5 red & sal 1.25 .30
a. $5 org red & pale yel 1.25 .30
J141 D10 $10 lil rose & pink ('76) 22.50 .75
Nos. J135-J141 (7) 26.15 2.05

The 50c, $10 and No. J140a are gummed. The $1 and $2 were reissued with gum in 1968 and 1973 respectively. No. J140a and the $10 are on ordinary paper.

Catalogue values for unused stamps in this section, from this point to the end of the section, are for Never Hinged items.

1984-88 Litho. Perf. 12½

J142 D11 $1 rose & violet .20 .20
J143 D11 $2 yellow & blue .20 .20
J144 D11 $3 pale grn & brt rose lil .25 .20
J145 D11 $5 blue & yellow .25 .20
J146 D11 $5.50 rose lil & brt blue .40 .35
J147 D11 $7.50 bister yel & dp violet .60 .45
J148 D11 $10 yel & lil rose .50 .30
J149 D11 $20 sky blue & citron 1.60 1.25
Nos. J142-J149 (8) 4.00 3.15

Issued: $3, $5.50, $7.50, $20, Apr. 1, 1988; others, Mar. 15, 1984.

D12

1998, Sept. 30 Litho. Perf. 12½
Background Color

J150 D12 50c orange yellow .20 .20
J151 D12 $1 pink .20 .20
J152 D12 $2 deep pink .20 .20
J153 D12 $5 yellow green .30 .20
J154 D12 $10 blue .60 .30
J155 D12 $20 green 1.25 .60
Nos. J150-J155 (6) 2.75 1.70

PARCEL POST STAMPS

PP1

PP2

PP3

1945-48 Unwmk. Engr. Perf. 13
Without Gum

Q1 PP1 $500 green 10.00 .20
Q2 PP1 $1000 blue 10.00 .20
Q3 PP1 $3000 rose red 20.00 .20
Q4 PP1 $5000 brown 100.00 5.00
Q5 PP1 $10,000 lil gray 160.00 6.00
Q6 PP1 $20,000 red org *2,000.*
Nos. Q1-Q5 (5) 300.00 11.60

No. Q6 was prepared but not issued.
For surcharges see People's Republic of China Nos. 5LQ1-5LQ2, 5LQ27-5LQ28.

Perf. 12½

Q7 PP2 $3000 red org 17.50 .55
Q8 PP2 $5000 dk blue 27.50 .55
Q9 PP2 $10,000 violet 27.50 .55
Q10 PP2 $20,000 dk red 27.50 .55

Perf. 13½

Q11 PP3 $1000 org yel 5.00 .85
Q12 PP3 $3000 bl grn 5.50 .85
Q13 PP3 $5000 org red 5.50 .85
Q14 PP3 $7000 dl blue 5.50 .85
Q15 PP3 $10,000 car rose 6.25 .85
Q16 PP3 $30,000 olive 6.25 .85
Q17 PP3 $50,000 indigo 6.25 .85
Q18 PP3 $70,000 org brn 9.00 .85
Q19 PP3 $100,000 dp plum 9.00 .85

Denomination Tablet Without Inner Frame

Q20 PP3 $200,000 dk grn 12.00 1.60
Q21 PP3 $300,000 pink 12.00 1.60
Q22 PP3 $500,000 vio brn 12.00 1.90
Q23 PP3 $3,000,000 sl bl 13.00 2.75
Q24 PP3 $5,000,000 lilac 13.00 2.75
Q25 PP3 $6,000,000 ol gray 14.00 3.50
Q26 PP3 $8,000,000 scar 14.00 3.75
Q27 PP3 $10,000,000 sage grn 17.50 4.50
Nos. Q11-Q27 (17) 165.75 30.00

Zeros for "cents" omitted on Nos. Q23-Q27.
See Taiwan Nos. Q1-Q5. For surcharges see Nos. 883-885, Northeastern Provinces Q1, Szechwan Q1, People's Republic of China 3LQ1-3LQ9, 5LQ3-5LQ16, 5LQ29-5LQ30.

#Q11-Q15, Q23-Q24 Surcharged in Black or Carmine (#Q35)

1949 Unwmk. Perf. 13½

Q32 PP3 $10 on $3000 4.50 .20
Q33 PP3 $20 on $5000 4.50 .20
Q34 PP3 $50 on $10,000 4.50 .20
Q35 PP3 $100 on $3,000,000 5.50 .20
Q36 PP3 $200 on $5,000,000 10.00 .20
Q37 PP3 $500 on $1000 20.00 .20
Q38 PP3 $1000 on $7000 20.00 .25
Nos. Q32-Q38 (7) 69.00 1.45

5 characters in each line on Nos. Q33-Q38.

MILITARY STAMPS

No. 454 Overprinted in Dull Red

1943-44 Unwmk. Perf. 12

M1 A59 8c turquoise green 2.25 4.00

Nos. 383, 453-454 Overprinted in Red or Black

6mm between characters
Perf. 14, 12½

M2 A57 8c olive green 2.75 4.50
a. 8mm between characters 2.75 4.25
M3 A59 8c red orange (B) 275.00
M4 A59 8c turquoise green 5.50 5.00

Forgeries of No. M3 abound.

No. 493 Overprinted in Red

Perf. 13

M5 A62 16c dull olive brn 5.00 3.25
a. Perf. 10½-11 110.00

No. M5 overprinted in black is a proof.

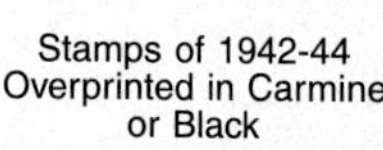

Stamps of 1942-44 Overprinted in Carmine or Black

M6 A62 50c sage green (C) 2.00 3.50
M7 A62 $1 rose lake 3.00 4.25
M8 A62 $1 dull green 3.00 4.25
M9 A62 $2 dk blue grn (C) 4.75 7.00
M10 A62 $2 dk vio brn ('44) 75.00 75.00
Nos. M6-M10 (5) 87.75 94.00

Nos. 383 and 357 Overprinted in Red

1944 Perf. 12, 14

M11 A57 8c olive green 2.75 4.00
a. Right character inverted 160.00
M12 A57 16c olive gray 42.50 42.50

Anti-Aircraft Guns — M1

1945, Jan. 1 Typo. Perf. 12½
Thin Paper Without Gum

M13 M1 rose .60 *4.00*

For overprints see Northeastern Provinces Nos. M2-M3.

TAIWAN

(Formosa)

100 Sen = 1 Yen
100 Cents = 1 Dollar

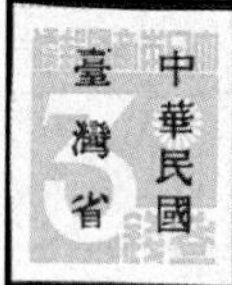

Stamps and Types of Japan (Taiwan) Overprinted in Black

Values in Sen and Yen
Black Overprint

1945 Unwmk. Litho. Imperf.
Stamps Divided by Lines of Colored Dashes

1 A1 3s carmine .60 .75
2 A1 5s blue grn .65 .55
3 A1 10s pale blue 1.10 .55
a. Inverted overprint 100.00
b. Double overprint 110.00
4 A1 30s dk blue 3.25 4.25
5 A1 40s violet 3.00 3.25
6 A1 50s gray brn 3.25 3.00
7 A1 1y olive grn 4.00 4.00

Same Overprint on Types of Japan

8 A99 5y gray grn 16.00 16.00
9 A100 10y brown vio 22.50 22.50
a. Inverted overprint 250.00
Nos. 1-9 (9) 54.35 54.85

The basic stamps of this issue were prepared by Japanese authorities for Taiwan use before the end of World War II when the island reverted to Chinese control. They are printed on crude buff or white wove paper. The overprint translates: "For Use in Taiwan, Chinese Republic."
A second overprinting of Nos. 2-3 was made with a different font.

China, Nos. 728-731, Surcharged in Black

1946 Perf. 14
Without Gum

10 A75 70s on $20 green 1.75 *3.75*
a. Inverted surcharge *800.00*
11 A75 1y on $30 blue 2.40 *4.00*
12 A75 2y on $50 dk brn 1.75 *4.00*
13 A75 3y on $100 car 2.40 *4.00*
Nos. 10-13 (4) 8.30 *15.75*

Convening of the Chinese Natl. Assembly.

China Issues and Types of 1940-1946 Surcharged in Black

a

Perf. 12½, 12½x13, 13, 13x12½, 14

1946-47

14 A46 2s on 2c dp bl .20 .50
15 A48 5s on 5c dl red org .20 .50
16 A39 10s on 4c pale vio .20 .35
17 A48 30s on 15c brn car .20 .30
18 A73 50s on $20 car .30 .25
19 A37 65s on $20 brt yel grn .35 *1.60*
20 A47 1y on 20c lt bl .20 *1.10*
a. Inverted surcharge *375.00*
21 A37 1y on $30 choc .35 *1.10*
22 A37 2y on $50 red org .40 .45
23 A73 3y on $100 dk car .20 .25
24 A73 5y on $200 ol grn .20 .25
25 A73 10y on $500 brt bl grn .25 .35
26 A73 20y on $700 red brn .70 .60
27 A73 50y on $1000 rose lake 1.25 1.25
28 A73 100y on $3000 blue 2.75 .90
Nos. 14-28 (15) 7.75 *9.75*

The bottom line of the surcharge expresses the new value and consists of 2, 3 or 4 characters.

Nos. 14, 18-19, 21-28 issued in 1947.

Same Surcharge on China No. 412

1947 Wmk. 261 *Perf. 13*
28A A48 30s on 15c brn car 70.00 100.00

Type of China, 1946, with additional inscription on both sides of head

1947 Unwmk. Engr. *Perf. 11, 11½*
29 A74 70c carmine 1.75 *2.50*
30 A74 $1 green 1.75 *2.50*
31 A74 $2 vermilion 1.75 *2.50*
32 A74 $3 yel grn 1.75 *2.50*
33 A74 $7 yel org 1.75 *2.50*
34 A74 $10 magenta 1.75 *2.50*
Nos. 29-34 (6) 10.50 *15.00*

60th birthday of Chiang Kai-shek.

Type of China, 1947, with additional inscription above value

1947 *Perf. 14*
35 A76 50c deep green 1.90 2.50
36 A76 $3 deep blue 1.90 2.50
37 A76 $7.50 carmine 1.90 2.50
38 A76 $10 light brown 1.90 2.50
39 A76 $20 deep claret 1.90 2.50
Nos. 35-39 (5) 9.50 12.50

First anniversary of return of Chinese National Government to Nanking.

Dr. Sun Yat-sen — A3

1947, July 10
Without Gum
40 A3 $1 dk brown 2.25 .25
41 A3 $2 org brn .60 .25
42 A3 $3 blue grn .60 .25
43 A3 $5 vermilion .60 .25
44 A3 $9 deep blue .60 .25
45 A3 $10 brt rose car .60 .25
46 A3 $20 deep green .60 .30
47 A3 $50 rose lilac .60 .25
48 A3 $100 blue .60 .60
49 A3 $200 dark red .60 .60
Nos. 40-49 (10) 7.65 3.25

The 30c gray and $7.50 orange were not regularly issued without surcharge. Value for the two stamps, $450.

See #63-68. For overprint and surcharges see #51-53, 69-73, 101-103, J10-J17.

Type of 1947 Surcharged in Black

b

1948 Unwmk. *Perf. 14*
51 A3 $25 on $100 blue 1.10 1.65
52 A3 $500 on $7.50 org 1.10 .55
53 A3 $1000 on 30c gray 4.75 3.50
Nos. 51-53 (3) 6.95 5.70

Stamps of China, 1943-48, Surcharged Type "a" in Black or Carmine

1948-49 *Perf. 12½, 14*
54 A73 $5 on $70 red org .65 *2.50*
55 A62 $10 on $3 dk yel 1.75 *2.75*
56 A82 $10 on $150 dk bl (C) .45 *.70*
57 A82 $20 on $250 dp lil (C) 1.10 .85
58 A67 $100 on $20 car 600.00 600.00
59 A82 $1000 on $20,000 rose pink ('49) 2.25 1.75
Nos. 54-59 (6) 606.20 608.55

The bottom line of the surcharge expresses the new value and consists of 2 or 3 characters.

Forgeries of No. 58 abound.

Type of 1947

1949 Engr. *Perf. 14*
63 A3 $25 olive grn .70 .30
64 A3 $5000 ocher 7.25 .50
65 A3 $10,000 apple grn 8.50 2.00
66 A3 $20,000 ol bister 8.50 3.50
67 A3 $30,000 indigo 9.50 .70
68 A3 $40,000 violet brn 8.50 .60
Nos. 63-68 (6) 42.95 7.60

For overprint and surcharges see #101, 103, J12.

No. 42 and Type of 1947 Surcharged Type "b" in Black, Carmine Violet or Red Violet

1949
69 A3 $300 on $3 bl grn .65 .30
70 A3 $1000 on $3 bl grn (C) 3.00 .55
71 A3 $2000 on $3 bl grn (V) 5.00 .55
72 A3 $3000 on $3 bl grn (RV) 3.75 1.10
73 A3 $3000 on $7.50 org 57.50 1.90
Nos. 69-73 (5) 69.90 4.40

For overprints see Nos. J10-J11.

Stamps of China, 1940-47, Surcharged Type "a" in Black or Carmine
Perf. 12½, 13x13½, 14
74 A39 $2 on 2½c rose lil (#424) .55 *2.00*
75 A72 $5 on $40 org (#627) .70 *1.10*
76 A73 $5 on $50 pur (C) (#638) .70 .25
77 A73 $5 on $100 dk car (#640) .70 .50
78 A57 $20 on 2c ol grn (#368) .75 .75
81 A63 $100 on $20 rose (#571) 1.10 .50
82 A67 $200 on $10 dk bl (C) (#591) 1.75 1.10
84 A57 $500 on $30 dl vio (#521) 6.00 2.10
86 A62 $800 on $4 red brn (#504) 5.25 *4.25*
87 A67 $5000 on $10 dk bl (#591) 6.00 4.00
88 A67 $10,000 on $20 car (#592) 9.50 3.25
89 A82 $200,000 on $3000 bl (C) (#750) 350.00 24.00
Nos. 74-89 (12) 383.00 43.80

Northeastern Provinces No. 47, Surcharged in Green, Red Violet, Black or Blue

1949-50
91 A2 2c on $44 (G) 35.00 6.00
92 A2 5c on $44 (RV) ('50) 32.50 7.00
a. Violet surcharge 57.50 11.50
93 A2 10c on $44 (RV) ('50) 42.50 6.00
94 A2 20c on $44 (Bk) ('50) 55.00 7.00
a. Double surcharge 100.00
95 A2 30c on $44 (Bl) ('50) 62.50 14.00
96 A2 50c on $44 (Bl) ('50) 75.00 17.00
Nos. 91-96 (6) 302.50 57.00

There were two printings of Nos. 91-93, with minor differences.

China 959a, Overprinted in Black

Overprint 15mm Wide

1949 Unwmk. *Rouletted 9½*
97 A96 orange 1.10 .20

China Nos. 567, 498 and 640 Surcharged Type "a" in Black

1948-49 Unwmk. *Perf. 12½, 13, 14*
98 A63 $20 on $3 red 2.25 1.40
99 A62 $50 on 50c sage grn 2.50 1.10
a. Perf. 11 22.50 26.00
100 A73 $600 on $100 dk car 10.00 2.75
Nos. 98-100 (3) 14.75 5.25

Botton line of surcharge consists of 3 characters.

No. 99 has two settings of surcharge: I. Spacing 10mm between rows of characters. II. Spacing 12mm.

#67, 47 and 68 Surcharged in Violet (#101) or Black

1949 *Perf. 14*
101 A3 2c on $30,000 ind 35.00 20.00
102 A3 10c on $50 rose lil 35.00 4.50
103 A3 10c on $40,000 vio brn 80.00 20.00
Nos. 101-103 (3) 150.00 44.50

Numerals slightly larger on Nos. 101-103.

For similar surcharges on China type A82 see China Nos. 1025-1036.

AIR POST STAMP

China No. C62a, Overprinted in Black

Overprint 15mm Wide

1949 Unwmk. *Rouletted 9½*
C1 AP5 blue green 4.50 4.50

SPECIAL DELIVERY STAMP

China No. E12a, Overprinted in Black

Overprint 12½mm Wide

1950 Unwmk. *Rouletted 9½*
E1 SD2 red violet 3.00 4.50

REGISTRATION STAMP

China No. F2a Overprinted in Black

Overprint 12mm Wide

1950 Unwmk. *Rouletted 9½*
F1 R2 carmine 2.25 4.50

TAIWAN POSTAGE DUE STAMPS

D1

Unwmk.
1948, Feb. 10 Litho. *Perf. 14*
Without Gum
J1 D1 $1 blue 1.10 *3.75*
J2 D1 $3 blue 1.10 *4.50*
J3 D1 $5 blue 1.10 *4.50*
J4 D1 $10 blue 1.10 *5.75*
J5 D1 $20 blue 1.10 *3.50*
Nos. J1-J5 (5) 5.50 *22.00*

Nos. J1-J4 Surcharged in Carmine

1948, Dec. 4
J6 D1 $50 on $1 blue 7.75 *10.50*
J7 D1 $100 on $3 blue 7.75 *10.50*
J8 D1 $300 on $5 blue 7.75 *10.50*
J9 D1 $500 on $10 blue 7.75 *10.50*
Nos. J6-J9 (4) 31.00 *42.00*

Nos. 70, 72 and 64 Handstamped in Violet

1949, Aug. 5
J10 A3 $1000 on $3 bl grn 17.50 17.50
J11 A3 $3000 on $3 bl grn 26.00 26.00
J12 A3 $5000 ocher 40.00 40.00
Nos. J10-J12 (3) 83.50 83.50

No. 48 Surcharged in Various Colors

1950
J13 A3 4c on $100 bl (Br) 12.00 9.00
J14 A3 10c on $100 bl (RV) 22.50 *25.00*
J15 A3 20c on $100 bl (Bk) 10.00 *20.00*
J16 A3 40c on $100 bl (C) 47.50 *80.00*
J17 A3 $1 on $100 bl (Bl) 35.00 *45.00*
Nos. J13-J17 (5) 127.00 *179.00*

TAIWAN PARCEL POST STAMPS

Type of China, Parcel Post Stamps of 1945-48 With Added Inscription

1949 Unwmk. Engr. *Perf. 14*
Q1 PP1 $100 bluish grn *225.00* .50
Q2 PP1 $300 rose car *225.00* .50
Q3 PP1 $500 olive green *225.00* .50
Q4 PP1 $1000 slate *225.00* .50
Q5 PP1 $3000 deep plum *225.00* .50
Nos. Q1-Q5 (5) *1,125.* 2.50

Chinese characters in lower corners have colorless background; denomination tablet in color.

OCCUPATION STAMPS

Issued Under Japanese Occupation

Canceled Stamps

Postally used stamps of the Japanese occupation generally have heavy, smudgy cancels.

Kwangtung

China No. 297 Overprinted in Black

1942 Unwmk. *Perf. 12½*

No.	Type	Description	Unused	Used
1N1	A37	2c olive green	6.00	6.00
a.		Inverted overprint	110.00	

Same Overprint in Red or Black on Stamps of China, 1939-41

Perf. 12½, 14

No.	Type	Description	Unused	Used
1N2	A57	3c dl cl (#350)	2.75	2.75
1N3	A57	8c ol grn (#383)	2.75	2.75
1N4	A57	10c grn (#354) (R)	2.50	2.75
1N5	A57	10c grn (#384) (R)	3.50	3.50
1N6	A57	16c ol gray (#357)	4.75	7.25
1N7	A57	30c scar (#385)	4.00	2.75
1N8	A57	50c dk bl (#386) (R)	4.00	8.00
1N9	A57	$1 org brn & sep (#387)	7.25	9.25
1N10	A57	$2 dp bl & yel brn (#388)	8.00	9.50
1N11	A57	$5 red & sl grn (#389)	7.00	8.75
1N12	A57	$10 dk grn & dl pur (#390)	16.00	20.00
1N13	A57	$20 rose lake & dk bl (#391)	7.00	9.50

Same Overprint on China Nos. 422 and 433

Perf. 12½

No.	Type	Description	Unused	Used
1N14	A40	1c orange	1.90	2.40
a.		Inverted overprint	80.00	80.00
1N15	A47	20c lt blue	3.50	4.00

Same Overprint on Stamps of China, 1941

Perf. 12

No.	Type	Description	Unused	Used
1N16	A59	1c orange	2.50	3.75
1N17	A59	5c green	2.50	3.75
1N18	A59	8c turq green	2.75	3.75
1N19	A59	10c brt green	3.25	3.75
1N20	A59	17c olive	3.25	3.75
1N21	A59	30c scarlet	3.25	3.75
1N22	A59	50c dark blue	3.25	3.75
		Nos. 1N1-1N22 (22)	101.65	125.40

Stamps of China, 1939-41 Overprinted in Black

1942 *Perf. 12½, 14*

No.	Type	Description	Unused	Used
1N23	A57	2c olive grn (#368)	.65	.80
1N24	A57	3c dl claret (#350)	.65	.95
1N25	A57	5c olive grn (#352)	.65	1.25
1N26	A57	8c olive grn (#353)	300.00	—
1N27	A57	8c olive grn (#369)	.80	1.00
1N28	A57	10c green (#354)	1.00	1.25
1N29	A57	16c ol gray (#357)	1.25	1.25
1N30	A57	25c dk bl (#358)	1.25	2.75
1N31	A57	30c scarlet (#385)	.80	2.40
1N32	A57	50c dk blue (#386)	2.25	2.75
1N33	A57	$1 org brn & sep (#387)	6.50	8.00
1N34	A57	$2 dp bl & yel brn (#388)	8.00	9.50
1N35	A57	$5 red & sl grn (#389)	10.00	12.00
1N36	A57	$10 dk grn & dl pur (#390)	16.00	20.00
1N37	A57	$20 rose lake & dk bl (#391)	14.00	20.00
		Nos. 1N23-1N25,1N27-1N37 (14)	63.80	83.90

No. 1N26 is valued in fine condition.

Same Overprint on China Nos. 397-401

1942 Wmk. 261 *Perf. 14*

No.	Type	Description	Unused	Used
1N38	A57	$1 org brn & sep	8.00	8.75
1N39	A57	$2 dp bl & yel brn	7.25	8.00
1N40	A57	$5 red & sl grn	9.50	12.00
1N41	A57	$10 dk grn & dl pur	16.00	20.00
1N42	A57	$20 rose lake & dk bl	20.00	24.00
		Nos. 1N38-1N42 (5)	60.75	72.75

Same Overprint on Stamps of China, 1941

1942 Unwmk. *Perf. 12*

No.	Type	Description	Unused	Used
1N43	A59	2c brt ultra	.30	.50
1N44	A59	5c green	.30	.50
1N45	A59	8c red org	.35	.50
1N46	A59	8c turq grn	.35	.90
1N47	A59	10c brt green	.60	.65
1N48	A59	17c olive	.65	1.00
1N49	A59	25c rose vio	.65	1.00
1N50	A59	30c scarlet	.65	1.10
1N51	A59	50c dk blue	.65	1.10
1N52	A59	$1 brn & blk	4.75	8.00
1N53	A59	$2 bl & blk	6.00	8.75
1N54	A59	$5 scar & blk	4.75	4.75
1N55	A59	$10 grn & blk	8.75	13.00
1N56	A59	$20 rose vio & blk	10.50	20.00
		Nos. 1N43-1N56 (14)	39.25	61.75

貼 粵

用 省

圓佰貳售暫

China Nos. 354 and 369 Surcharged in Black

1945 Unwmk. *Perf. 12½*

No.	Type	Description	Unused	Used
1N57	A57	$200 on 10c grn	110.00	50.00
1N58	A57	$400 on 8c ol grn	110.00	60.00

肆 暫

佰

圓 售

China No. 422 Surcharged in Black

1945

No.	Type	Description	Unused	Used
1N59	A40	$400 on 1c org	750.00	600.00

Forgeries exist.

OCCUPATION POSTAGE DUE STAMPS

China, No. J79 Surcharged Diagonally with New Value Between Parallel Lines in Black

1945 Unwmk. *Perf. 12½*

No.	Type	Description	Unused	Used
1NJ1	D5	$100 on $2 yel org	750.00	700.00
a.		Inverted surcharge	1,100.	1,100.

MENG CHIANG (Inner Mongolia)

Nos. 297-298, 301-303 Overprinted

Characters 4mm High — I

Characters 5mm High — II

1941 Engr. Unwmk.

No.	Type	Description	Unused	Used
2N1	A37	2c #297, I	1.25	2.00
a.		Type II	1.60	2.00
2N2	A37	4c #298, II	45.00	—
a.		Type I	60.00	55.00
2N3	A37	15c #301, I	4.75	5.50
a.		Type II	4.50	6.00
2N4	A37	20c #302, II	8.75	8.75
a.		Type I	12.00	16.00
2N5	A37	25c #303, II	12.00	14.00
a.		Type I	92.50	92.50
		Nos. 2N1-2N5 (5)	71.75	30.25

For surcharge see No. 2N116.

On Nos. 312, 314, 318, 321

1941 *Perf. 14*

No.	Type	Description	Unused	Used
2N6	A39	½c #312, I	14.00	17.50
a.		Type II	20.00	—
2N7	A39	2½c #314, II	3.75	3.75
a.		Type I	7.25	8.75
2N8	A45	13c #318, II	1.25	1.10
a.		Type I	110.00	110.00
2N9	A48	30c #321, II	72.50	72.50
		Nos. 2N6-2N9 (4)	91.50	94.85

On Stamps of 1939-41

1941 *Perf. 12½*

No.	Type	Description	Unused	Used
2N10	A57	2c #368, II	2.40	3.00
2N11	A57	3c #350, II	1.00	1.00
a.		Type I	1.25	1.25
2N12	A57	5c #352, II	2.10	2.50
a.		Type I	2.75	6.00
2N13	A57	8c #353, I	1.25	.85
a.		Type II	2.00	2.00
2N14	A57	8c #369, II	8.00	8.00
2N15	A57	10c #354, II	2.25	2.25
2N16	A57	16c #357, II	4.00	4.00
2N17	A57	$1 #359, II	9.50	9.50
a.		Type I	325.00	325.00
b.		#347, I	87.50	80.00
2N18	A57	$5 #361, II	65.00	65.00
		Nos. 2N10-2N18 (9)	95.50	96.10

For surcharges see Nos. 2N117, 2N119.

On Stamps of 1940 with Secret Marks

1941 Unwmk. *Perf. 14*

No.	Type	Description	Unused	Used
2N19	A57	5c #382, II	1.60	1.75
2N20	A57	8c #383, I	3.25	3.25
a.		Type II	55.00	—
2N21	A57	10c #384, II	2.25	2.00
a.		Type I	4.00	4.00
2N22	A57	30c #385, II	2.75	2.75
a.		Type I	4.75	5.00
2N23	A57	50c #386, I	7.25	7.25
a.		Type II	7.25	7.25
2N24	A57	$1 #387, I	11.00	12.00
a.		Type II	20.00	20.00
2N25	A57	$2 #388, I	12.00	14.00
a.		Type II	27.50	27.50
2N26	A57	$5 #389, I	30.00	30.00
a.		Type II	67.50	—
2N27	A57	$10 #390, II	60.00	60.00
a.		Type I	70.00	70.00
2N28	A57	$20 #391, II	100.00	110.00
a.		Type I	100.00	110.00
		Nos. 2N19-2N28 (10)	230.10	243.00

For surcharge see No. 2N120.

On Stamps of 1940 with Secret Marks

1941 Wmk. 261 *Perf. 14*

No.	Type	Description	Unused	Used
2N29	A57	10c #394, II	4.50	4.50
2N30	A57	30c #395, II	4.75	6.00
a.		Type I	65.00	65.00
2N31	A57	50c #396, II	4.00	4.75
		Nos. 2N29-2N31 (3)	13.25	15.25

On Stamps of 1940-41 (Martyrs) with Secret Marks

Perf. 12½, 13 & Compound

1941 Wmk. 261

No.	Type	Description	Unused	Used
2N32	A39	½c #402, II	12.00	14.00
2N33	A40	1c #403, II	1.00	1.00
a.		Type I	3.50	3.50
2N34	A39	2½c #405, I	60.00	60.00
a.		Type II	80.00	80.00
2N35	A48	3c #406, II	3.50	3.50
2N36	A46	10c #410, I	12.50	12.50
a.		Type II	16.00	—
2N37	A46	17c #413, II	47.50	—
a.		Type I	80.00	80.00
2N38	A40	25c #416, II	3.50	3.50
2N39	A48	30c #418, II	60.00	60.00
a.		Type I	72.50	72.50
2N40	A47	40c #419, II	6.00	6.00
a.		Type I	8.00	8.00
2N41	A40	50c #420, I	12.00	12.00
a.		Type II	60.00	—

Unwmk.

No.	Type	Description	Unused	Used
2N42	A39	½c #421, II	1.60	2.25
a.		Type I	5.00	5.00
2N43	A40	1c #422, I	1.60	1.40
a.		Type II	4.25	3.50
2N44	A46	2c #423, I	6.00	6.00
2N45	A48	3c #425, II	3.50	3.50
a.		Type I	4.00	4.00
2N46	A39	4c #426, II	2.00	1.75
2N47	A45	8c #428, II	16.00	—
a.		Type I	80.00	—
2N48	A46	10c #429, I	24.00	24.00
a.		Type II	72.50	—
2N49	A45	13c #430, I	6.50	7.25
a.		Type II	24.00	—
2N50	A48	15c #431, II	4.00	4.00
2N51	A46	17c #432, II	3.75	3.75
a.		Type I	4.75	4.75
2N52	A47	20c #433, II	2.25	3.00
a.		Type I	3.25	3.75
2N53	A45	21c #434, II	4.00	4.00
2N54	A40	25c #435, I	4.75	4.75
2N55	A46	28c #436, II	4.25	4.25
2N56	A40	50c #439, I	4.75	2.40
a.		Type II	7.75	7.75
		Nos. 2N42-2N56 (15)	88.95	72.30

For surcharges see Nos. 2N114-2N115, 2N118, 2N121-2N122.

China Nos. 297-298, 302 Surcharged in Black

1942 Unwmk. *Perf. 12½, 13*

No.	Type	Description	Unused	Used
2N57	A37	1c on 2c ol grn	20.00	20.00
2N58	A37	2c on 4c grn	12.00	12.00
2N59	A37	10c on 20c ultra	32.50	32.50
		Nos. 2N57-2N59 (3)	64.50	64.50

Same, on China No. 313

Perf. 14

No.	Type	Description	Unused	Used
2N60	A40	½c on 1c org	20.00	20.00

Same, on Stamps of China, 1938-41

Perf. 12½

No.	Type	Description	Unused	Used
2N61	A57	1c on 2c (#368)	2.00	1.25
2N62	A57	4c on 8c (#353)	9.50	12.00
a.		Inverted surcharge	47.50	—
2N63	A57	4c on 8c (#369)	1.25	1.25
2N64	A57	5c on 10c (#354)	1.00	.65
2N65	A57	8c on 16c (#357)	4.00	3.00
2N66	A57	50c on $1 (#359)	9.50	9.50
a.		On No. 347	47.50	47.50
b.		On No. 344	400.00	—
2N67	A57	$1 on $2 (#360)	60.00	60.00
		Nos. 2N61-2N67 (7)	87.25	87.65

No. 2N66b was issued without gum.

Same, on Stamps of China, 1940

Perf. 14

No.	Type	Description	Unused	Used
2N68	A57	4c on 8c (#383)	.65	.65
2N69	A57	15c on 30c (#385)	7.25	10.00
a.		Inverted surcharge	55.00	55.00
2N70	A57	25c on 50c (#386)	7.00	8.00
2N71	A57	50c on $1 (#387)	6.00	7.25
2N72	A57	$1 on $2 (#388)	12.00	12.00
2N73	A57	$5 on $10 (#390)	45.00	45.00
2N74	A57	$10 on $20 (#391)	72.50	80.00
		Nos. 2N68-2N74 (7)	150.40	162.90

Same, on China No. 395

1942 Wmk. 261 *Perf. 14*

No.	Type	Description	Unused	Used
2N75	A57	15c on 30c scar	80.00	80.00

Same, on China Nos. 418 and 419

Perf. 12½, 13

No.	Type	Description	Unused	Used
2N76	A48	15c on 30c brn car	47.50	47.50
2N77	A47	20c on 40c org	9.50	11.00
		Nos. 2N75-2N77 (3)	137.00	138.50

Same, on Stamps of China, 1940-41

1942 Unwmk.

No.	Type	Description	Unused	Used
2N78	A40	½c on 1c org	.25	.35
2N79	A39	2c on 4c pale vio	6.00	6.00
2N80	A47	10c on 20c lt bl	6.00	6.00
2N81	A47	20c on 40c org	14.50	14.50
2N82	A40	25c on 50c grn	24.00	24.00
		Nos. 2N78-2N82 (5)	50.75	50.85

Same Surcharge on "New Peking" Prints

Perf. 14

No.	Type	Description	Unused	Used
2N83	A37	1c on 2c ol grn	12.00	20.00
2N84	A37	2c on 4c dl grn	.55	.65
2N85	A46	5c on 10c dl vio	4.00	7.25
2N86	A57	8c on 16c ol gray	1.60	2.40
2N87	A47	10c on 20c red brn	4.75	7.25
2N88	A48	15c on 30c brn car	1.75	2.75
2N89	A47	20c on 40c org	7.25	8.00
2N90	A40	25c on 50c grn	2.00	4.00
2N91	A57	50c on $1 org brn & sep	12.00	12.00
2N92	A57	$1 on $2 dp bl & org brn	30.00	35.00
2N93	A57	$5 on $10 dk grn & dl pur	65.00	65.00
		Nos. 2N83-2N93 (11)	140.90	164.30

The "New Peking" printings were made by the Chinese Bureau of Engraving and Printing for use in Japanese controlled areas of North China. They are on thin, poor quality paper, with dull gum or without gum and there are slight alterations in the designs.

Dragon-Carved Pillar and Doves — A1

Mining Coal — A2

Wmk. Characters in Circle in Sheet

1943 Engr. ***Perf. 12xPin-perf. 12***

2N94	A1	4f deep orange	.25	*.80*
2N95	A1	8f dark blue	.30	*1.00*

5th anniv. of the Inner Mongolia post and telegraph service.

The watermark, which is 40mm in diameter and covers four stamps, occurs three times in the sheet.

1943 Unwmk. Photo. ***Perf. 12***

2N96	A2	4f Prus green	.25	*1.00*
2N97	A2	8f brown red	.30	*1.25*

2nd anniv. of the "Greater East Asia War."

Flying Horse — A3

Yun Wang — A4

1944 ***Perf. 12½x12, 12x12½***

2N98	A3	4f rose	.20	*1.00*
2N99	A4	8f dull blue	.25	*1.00*

5th anniv. of the founding of the Federal Autonomous Government of Mongolia, Sept. 1, 1939.

Industrial Plant — A5

1944, Dec. 8 Photo. ***Perf. 12x12½***

2N100	A5	8f red brown	.25	*1.75*

3rd anniv. of the "Greater East Asia War" and to encourage production increase.

New Peking Printings of 1942 Overprinted in Black

1945 Unwmk. Engr. ***Perf. 14***

Without Gum

2N101	A37	2c olive grn	9.50	—
2N102	A37	4c dull grn	16.00	—
2N103	A37	5c green	17.50	*22.50*
2N104	A57	$1 org brn & sep	2.75	3.50
2N105	A57	$2 dp bl & org brn	12.00	12.00
2N106	A57	$5 red & grnsh blk	40.00	40.00

Same Overprint on New Peking Printings of Martyrs Issue

2N107	A40	1c orange	.80	*.80*
2N108	A45	8c dp orange	.75	*.75*
2N109	A46	10c dl violet	.25	*.35*
2N110	A47	20c red brown	1.75	*2.40*
2N111	A48	30c brown car	.35	*1.25*
2N112	A47	40c orange	.40	*.40*
2N113	A40	50c green	7.25	*8.00*

For surcharges see Nos. 2N123-2N127.

Stamps of Meng Chiang, 1941, Surcharged in Red or Black

50c

10c

$1

1945

2N114	A39	10c on ½c ol blk (#2N42, II, R)	2.00	*2.25*
a.		On #2N42a, I	6.00	*7.25*
2N115	A40	10c on 1c org (#2N43a, II, R)	1.00	*1.25*
a.		Without secret mark (China #422a)	40.00	*40.00*
b.		On #2N43, I	2.50	*2.75*
2N116	A37	50c on 2c ol grn (#2N1a, II, B)	24.00	*30.00*
b.		On #2N1, I	24.00	*30.00*
2N117	A57	50c on 2c ol grn (#2N10, II, B))	.80	*1.50*
2N118	A39	50c on 4c pale vio (#2N46, II, R)	.80	*1.00*
2N119	A57	50c on 5c ol grn (#2N12, II, R)	.55	*1.25*
a.		On #2N12a, I	10.50	*10.50*
2N120	A57	50c on 5c ol grn (#2N19, II, R)	1.00	*1.75*
		Nos. 2N114-2N120 (7)	30.15	*39.00*

Same Surcharge on #2N32, 2N33

1945 **Wmk. 261**

2N121	A39	10c on ½c ol blk, II (R)	20.00	*24.00*
2N122	A40	10c on 1c orange, II (R)	1.00	*1.25*
a.		On #2N33a, I	24.00	—

Same Surcharge on Nos. 2N107, 2N101-2N103 and 2N108

1945 **Unwmk.**

2N123	A40	10c on 1c org (R)	.30	*.60*
2N124	A37	50c on 2c ol grn (Bk)	2.75	*2.75*
2N125	A37	50c on 4c dl grn (R)	4.00	*4.00*
2N126	A37	50c on 5c green	.40	*.40*
2N127	A45	$1 on 8c dp org (R)	.60	*.60*
		Nos. 2N123-2N127 (5)	8.05	*8.35*

NORTH CHINA

Honan

Nos. 297-298, 301-303 Overprinted

I

II

1941 Engr. Unwmk.

3N1	A37	2c #297, II	7.25	7.25
a.		Type I	17.50	17.50
3N2	A37	4c #298, I	7.25	6.00
a.		Type II	27.50	27.50
3N3	A37	15c #301, I	1.75	*2.00*
a.		Type II	2.25	2.00
3N4	A37	20c #302, I	6.50	6.50
3N5	A37	25c #303, II	20.00	20.00
		Nos. 3N1-3N5 (5)	42.75	41.75

1941 ***Perf. 14***

3N6	A39	½c #312, I	2.00	*3.00*
a.		Type II	32.50	—
3N7	A39	2½c #314, I	1.25	*1.75*
a.		Type II	1.75	2.40
3N8	A45	13c #318, II	1.25	1.25
a.		Type I	80.00	80.00
3N9	A48	30c #321, II	14.50	*14.50*
3N10	A47	40c #322, II	80.00	80.00
		Nos. 3N6-3N10 (5)	99.00	100.50

On Stamps of 1939-41

1941 ***Perf. 12½***

3N11	A57	2c #368, II	1.25	1.25
3N12	A57	3c #350, I	.60	.60
a.		Type II	1.00	1.00
3N13	A57	5c #352, II	1.25	.65
a.		Type I	1.90	1.90
3N14	A57	8c #353, II	1.25	1.25
a.		Type I	1.25	1.25
3N15	A57	10c #354, II	2.40	*3.50*
3N16	A57	16c #357, II	1.40	*2.40*
3N17	A57	$1 #359, II	12.00	12.00
a.		Type I	250.00	250.00
b.		On #347, I	47.50	47.50
3N18	A57	$5 #361, II	65.00	65.00
		Nos. 3N11-3N18 (8)	85.15	86.65

For overprints see Nos. 3N56, 3N58, 3N61.

On Stamps of 1940 with Secret Marks

1941 Unwmk. ***Perf. 14***

3N20	A57	5c #382, II	2.00	1.60
3N21	A57	8c #383, II	.50	*.50*
3N22	A57	10c #384, II	1.60	1.25
3N23	A57	30c #385, I	6.50	7.25
a.		Type II	9.00	9.00
3N24	A57	50c #386, I	3.25	*3.00*
a.		Type II	14.00	*14.00*
3N25	A57	$1 #387, I	6.50	*6.50*
a.		Type II	60.00	60.00
3N26	A57	$2 #388, I	12.00	*14.00*
a.		Type II	20.00	*20.00*
3N27	A57	$5 #389, I	32.50	24.00
a.		Type II	47.50	47.50
3N28	A57	$10 #390, II	40.00	40.00
a.		Type I	125.00	125.00
3N29	A57	$20 #391, II	100.00	*110.00*
a.		Type I	100.00	*110.00*
		Nos. 3N20-3N29 (10)	204.85	*208.10*

On Stamps of 1940 with Secret Marks

1941 Wmk. 261 ***Perf. 14***

3N30	A57	5c #392, II	20.00	12.00
3N31	A57	5c #393, II	9.50	6.00
3N32	A57	30c #395, I	20.00	20.00
a.		Type II	32.50	32.50
3N33	A57	50c #396, II	15.00	*20.00*
		Nos. 3N30-3N33 (4)	64.50	58.00

On Stamps of 1940-41 (Martyrs) with Secret Marks

Perf. 12½, 13 & Compound

1941 **Wmk. 261**

3N34	A39	½c #402, II	2.40	*3.00*
3N35	A40	1c #403, II	.60	.40
a.		Type I	1.60	1.60
3N36	A39	2½c #405, II	11.00	*14.00*
3N37	A46	10c #410, II	12.00	*15.00*
a.		Type I	27.50	27.50
3N38	A45	13c #411, II	3.50	3.50
3N39	A46	17c #413, II	3.50	3.50
a.		Type I	8.00	8.00
3N40	A40	25c #416, II	2.60	2.60
3N41	A47	40c #419, II	4.00	4.00
a.		Type I	14.50	14.50
		Nos. 3N34-3N41 (8)	39.60	*46.00*

Unwmk.

3N42	A39	½c #421, II	1.60	1.60
a.		Type I	3.50	3.50
3N43	A40	1c #422, I	2.00	2.00
a.		Type II	3.50	3.50
3N44	A46	2c #423, I	12.00	12.00
3N45	A48	3c #425, I	1.25	*2.00*
3N46	A39	4c #426, II	.70	.70
3N47	A46	10c #429, I	35.00	35.00
3N48	A45	13c #430, II	2.75	2.75
a.		Type I	16.00	16.00
3N49	A48	15c #431, II	3.50	3.50
3N50	A46	17c #432, II	3.50	3.50
a.		Type I	14.00	14.00
3N51	A47	20c #433, II	1.60	1.60
a.		Type I	50.00	40.00
3N52	A45	21c #434, II	3.50	3.50
3N53	A40	25c #435, I	4.00	4.00
3N54	A46	28c #436, II	3.50	3.50
		Nos. 3N42-3N54 (13)	74.90	75.65

For overprints see Nos. 3N55, 3N59.

Overprinted in Red

1942

3N55	A39	4c #3N46	2.75	*3.75*
3N56	A57	8c #3N14	20.00	*27.50*
3N57	A57	8c #369, II	4.75	*8.00*
		Nos. 3N55-3N57 (3)	27.50	*39.25*

The fall of Singapore.

Overprinted in Red

1942

3N58	A57	2c #3N11	8.00	*12.00*
3N59	A39	4c #3N46	14.00	*20.00*
3N60	A57	8c #369, II	35.00	*40.00*
3N61	A57	8c #3N14	27.50	*30.00*
		Nos. 3N58-3N61 (4)	84.50	102.00

Formation of Manchukuo, 10th anniv.

Hopei

Nos. 297-298, 301-303 Overprinted

I

II

1941 Engr. Unwmk.

4N1	A37	2c #297, II	1.10	.70
a.		Type I	3.50	2.75
4N2	A37	4c #298, I	3.75	3.75
a.		Type II	70.00	—
4N3	A37	15c #301, II	2.40	2.40
a.		Type I	3.50	3.25
4N4	A37	20c #302, II	1.50	1.25
4N5	A37	25c #303, II	9.00	7.25
a.		Type I	80.00	75.00
		Nos. 4N1-4N5 (5)	17.75	*15.35*

On Nos. 312, 314, 318, 321

1941 ***Perf. 14***

4N6	A39	½c #312, II	.35	*.60*
a.		Type I	.90	.90
4N7	A39	2½c #314, II	.50	.35
a.		Type I	.50	*.60*
4N8	A45	13c #318, II	1.25	1.10
a.		Type I	2.25	2.25
4N9	A48	30c #321, II	4.75	*6.00*
		Nos. 4N6-4N9 (4)	6.85	*8.05*

On Stamps of 1939-41

1941 ***Perf. 12½***

4N10	A57	2c #368, II	1.00	.50
4N11	A57	2c #349, II	.65	*.80*
4N12	A57	3c #350, II	.35	.35
a.		Type I	1.60	1.60
4N13	A57	5c #352, II	.65	.50
a.		Type I	1.75	1.60
4N14	A57	8c #353, II	.35	.35
a.		Type I	1.40	1.25
4N15	A57	8c #369, II	3.00	3.00
4N16	A57	10c #354, II	.80	.65
4N17	A57	16c #357, II	2.00	.80
4N18	A57	$1 #359, II	8.00	8.00
a.		On #347, I	200.00	—
4N19	A57	$2 #360, II	10.00	10.00
a.		Type I	40.00	40.00
4N20	A57	$5 #361, I	40.00	40.00
a.		Type II	60.00	60.00
4N21	A57	$10 #362, II	160.00	160.00
4N22	A57	$20 #363, II	350.00	350.00
		Nos. 4N10-4N22 (13)	576.80	574.95

For overprints see Nos. 4N66-4N68, 4N70.

On Stamps of 1940 with Secret Marks

1941 Unwmk. ***Perf. 14***

Type II

4N24	A57	5c #382	.60	.50
4N25	A57	8c #383	1.25	1.25
4N26	A57	10c #384	1.00	.30
4N27	A57	30c #385	1.00	1.00
4N28	A57	50c #386	2.00	2.00
4N29	A57	$1 #387	4.00	3.50
4N30	A57	$2 #388	14.00	9.50
4N31	A57	$5 #389	35.00	35.00
4N32	A57	$10 #390	40.00	40.00
4N33	A57	$20 #391	60.00	*72.50*
		Nos. 4N24-4N33 (10)	158.85	165.55

For overprints see Nos. 4N65, 4N71.

Type I

4N24a	A57	5c	1.10	1.10
4N25a	A57	8c	52.50	52.50
4N26a	A57	10c	1.75	.80
4N28a	A57	50c	2.00	2.00
4N29a	A57	$1	6.00	4.00
4N30a	A57	$2	24.00	24.00
4N31a	A57	$5	40.00	40.00
4N32a	A57	$10	55.00	47.50
4N33a	A57	$20	80.00	80.00
		Nos. 4N24a-4N33a (9)	262.35	251.90

On Stamps of 1940 with Secret Marks

1941 Wmk. 261 ***Perf. 14***

4N34	A57	5c #392, II	.40	.40
4N35	A57	5c #393, II	1.25	1.25
4N36	A57	10c #394, II	1.00	.50
4N37	A57	30c #395, II	1.25	1.25
a.		Type I	4.00	4.00
4N38	A57	50c #396, II	4.75	4.75
		Nos. 4N34-4N38 (5)	8.65	8.15

On Stamps of 1940-41 (Martyrs) with Secret Marks

Perf. 12½, 13 & Compound

1941 **Wmk. 261**

4N39	A39	½c #402, II	1.25	1.25
4N40	A40	1c #403, I	1.00	.70
a.		Type II	1.25	1.25
4N41	A46	2c #404, II	.80	*.80*
4N42	A39	2½c #405, II	1.00	*1.40*
4N43	A48	3c #406, II	1.60	*2.40*
4N44	A46	10c #410, II	2.40	*2.40*
a.		Type I	1.50	4.00

4N45 A45 13c #411, II 2.00 2.00
4N46 A46 17c #413, II 2.75 2.75
a. Type I 3.50 3.50
4N47 A40 25c #416, II 2.60 2.60
4N48 A48 30c #418, II 10.00 10.00
a. Type I 27.50 27.50
4N49 A47 40c #419, II 2.75 1.25
a. Type I 4.75 4.75
Nos. 4N39-4N49 (11) 28.15 27.55

Unwmk.

4N50 A39 ½c #421, II 1.25 1.25
a. Type I 1.75 1.75
4N51 A40 1c #422, II 1.75 1.25
a. Type I 2.25 1.60
4N52 A46 2c #423 .40 .40
4N53 A48 3c #425, I 1.25 1.25
a. Type II 2.75 3.50
4N54 A39 4c #426, II 1.00 1.00
4N55 A45 8c #428, II 1.25 1.50
a. Type I 2.75 2.75
4N56 A46 10c #429, II 2.75 2.40
4N57 A45 13c #430, I 2.75 2.75
a. Type II 3.75 3.75
4N58 A48 15c #431, II 4.75 4.75
4N59 A46 17c #432, II 2.75 2.75
a. Type I 4.25 4.75
4N60 A47 20c #433, II 2.60 2.60
a. Type I 3.25 3.25
4N61 A45 21c #434, II 4.00 4.00
4N62 A40 25c #435, I 4.00 4.00
a. Type II 4.00 4.00
4N63 A46 28c #436, II 3.50 3.25
Nos. 4N50-4N63 (14) 34.00 33.15

For overprints see Nos. 4N64, 4N69.

Honan Singapore Overprint in Red

1942
4N64 A39 4c #4N54 1.25 2.75
4N65 A57 8c #4N25 3.25 3.25
4N66 A57 8c #4N14 2.50 4.00
4N67 A57 8c #4N15 8.00 12.00
Nos. 4N64-4N67 (4) 15.00 22.00

Honan Anniv. of Manchukuo Overprint in Red

1942
4N68 A57 2c #4N10 5.50 8.00
4N69 A39 4c #4N54 5.50 6.75
4N70 A57 8c #4N14 72.50 72.50
4N71 A57 8c #4N25 8.00 9.50
Nos. 4N68-4N71 (4) 91.50 96.75

Shansi

Nos. 297-298, 301, 303 Overprinted

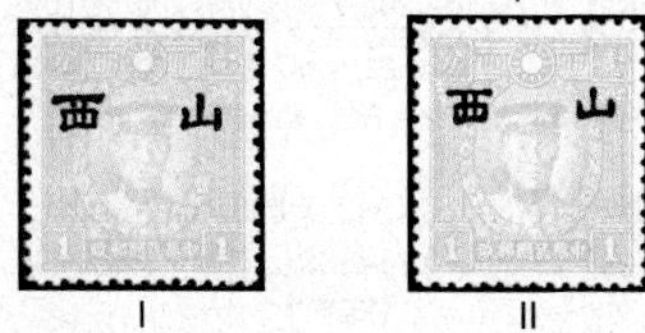

I II

1941 Engr. Unwmk.
5N1 A37 2c #297, II 6.00 6.00
a. Type I 6.00 6.00
5N2 A37 4c #298, I 55.00 55.00
a. Type II 110.00 —
5N3 A37 15c #301, II 4.75 6.00
a. Type I 8.00 9.50
5N4 A37 25c #303, II 8.00 12.00
a. Type I 55.00 60.00
Nos. 5N1-5N4 (4) 73.75 79.00

On Nos. 312, 314, 318, 321

1941 Perf. 14
5N5 A39 ½c #312, II 1.00 1.25
a. Type I 1.75 3.00
5N6 A39 2½c #314, II 1.25 1.40
a. Type I 1.75 1.60
5N7 A45 13c #318, II 2.00 2.00
a. Type I 190.00 190.00
5N8 A48 30c #321, II 8.00 9.50
Nos. 5N5-5N8 (4) 12.25 14.15

On Stamps of 1939-41

1941 Perf. 12½
5N9 A57 2c #368, II .65 .65
5N10 A57 3c #350, II 1.00 1.00
a. Type I 12.00 12.00
5N11 A57 5c #352, II 2.75 2.75
a. Type I 4.00 4.00
5N12 A57 8c #353, II 1.25 1.25
a. Type I 2.75 2.75
5N13 A57 8c #369, II 35.00 20.00
5N14 A57 10c #354, II 3.00 4.00
5N15 A57 16c #357, II 4.00 4.00
5N16 A57 $1 #359, II 10.00 10.00
5N17 A57 $2 #360, II 40.00 40.00
5N18 A57 $5 #361, II 47.50 47.50
Nos. 5N9-5N18 (10) 145.15 131.15

For overprints see Nos. 5N62-5N64, 5N66-5N67.

On Stamps of 1940 with Secret Marks

1941 Unwmk. Perf. 14
5N19 A57 5c #382, II .65 .60
5N20 A57 8c #383, II 1.40 1.40
5N21 A57 10c #384, I 1.00 1.40
a. Type II 4.00 4.00
5N22 A57 30c #385, II 1.75 1.75
a. Type I 2.40 2.40
5N23 A57 50c #386, I 3.50 3.50
a. Type II 4.75 4.75
5N24 A57 $1 #387, I 9.25 9.25
a. Type II 30.00 30.00
5N25 A57 $2 #388, II 14.00 20.00
a. Type I 16.00 20.00
5N26 A57 $5 #389, II 26.00 20.00
a. Type I 80.00 80.00
5N27 A57 $10 #390, II 57.50 57.50
a. Type I 60.00 60.00
5N28 A57 $20 #391, II 57.50 57.50
a. Type I 100.00 110.00
Nos. 5N19-5N28 (10) 172.55 178.90

For overprints see Nos. 5N61, 5N68.

On Stamps of 1940 with Secret Marks

1941 Wmk. 261 Perf. 14
5N29 A57 5c #392, II 1.25 1.25
5N30 A57 5c #393, II 1.00 1.00
5N31 A57 10c #394, II 2.40 2.40
5N32 A57 30c #395, I 65.00 65.00
5N33 A57 50c #396, I 6.00 6.75
Nos. 5N29-5N33 (5) 75.65 76.40

On Stamps of 1940-41 (Martyrs) with Secret Marks

Perf. 12½, 13 & Compound

1941 Wmk. 261
5N34 A39 ½c #402, II 1.25 1.25
5N35 A40 1c #403, II .80 .80
a. Type I 1.25 1.25
5N36 A46 2c #404, II 2.50 2.50
5N37 A39 2½c #405, I 7.25 9.50
5N38 A46 10c #410, I 8.00 8.00
5N39 A45 13c #411, II 3.75 3.75
5N40 A46 17c #413, I 27.50 27.50
5N41 A40 25c #416, II 3.25 3.25
5N42 A48 30c #418, I 125.00 125.00
a. Type II 125.00 125.00
5N43 A47 40c #419, II 4.50 4.50
a. Type I 30.00 30.00
5N44 A40 50c #420, II 6.00 6.00
a. Type I 35.00 35.00
Nos. 5N34-5N44 (11) 189.80 192.05

Unwmk.

5N45 A39 ½c #421, II 2.40 3.00
a. Type I 4.25 4.75
5N46 A40 1c #422, I 2.40 2.40
a. Type II 2.40 2.40
5N47 A46 2c #423, II .60 .60
5N48 A48 3c #425, II 7.25 7.25
5N49 A39 4c #426, II 1.00 1.00
5N50 A45 8c #428, I 12.00 12.00
a. Type II 14.00 14.00
5N51 A46 10c #429, I 40.00 40.00
a. Type II 47.50 47.50
5N52 A45 13c #430, I 16.00 16.00
a. Type II 16.00 16.00
5N53 A48 15c #431, II 5.50 5.50
5N54 A46 17c #432, II 3.50 3.50
a. Type I 4.50 4.50
5N55 A47 20c #433, II 2.60 2.60
a. Type I 3.25 3.25
5N56 A45 21c #434, II 3.50 3.50
5N57 A40 25c #435, I 2.60 2.75
5N58 A46 28c #436, II 4.75 4.75
5N59 A40 50c #439, II 12.00 12.00
Nos. 5N45-5N59 (15) 116.10 116.85

For overprints see Nos. 5N60, 5N65.

Honan Singapore Overprint in Red

1942
5N60 A39 4c #5N49 2.25 2.75
5N61 A57 8c #5N20 3.75 3.75
5N62 A57 8c #5N12 5.50 8.75
5N63 A57 8c #5N13 11.50 16.00
Nos. 5N60-5N63 (4) 23.00 31.25

Honan Anniv. of Manchukuo Overprint in Red

1942
5N64 A57 2c #5N9 9.50 14.00
5N65 A39 4c #5N49 11.00 14.00
5N66 A57 8c #5N12 40.00 47.50
5N67 A57 8c #5N13 60.00 67.50
5N68 A57 8c #5N20 32.50 32.50
Nos. 5N64-5N68 (5) 153.00 175.50

Shantung

Nos. 297-298, 301-303 Overprinted

I

II

1941 Engr. Unwmk.
6N1 A37 2c #297, II 1.25 1.25
a. Type I 3.25 3.25
6N2 A37 4c #298, II 6.00 5.50
a. Type I 7.00 6.00
6N3 A37 15c #301, II 2.00 2.00
a. Type I 2.75 2.75
6N4 A37 20c #302, II 3.75 3.75
6N5 A37 25c #303, II 5.50 5.50
a. Type I 175.00 175.00
Nos. 6N1-6N5 (5) 18.50 18.00

On Nos. 312, 314, 318

1941 Perf. 14
6N6 A39 ½c #312, II 1.00 1.00
a. Type I 2.00 1.25
6N7 A39 2½c #314, II 1.25 1.75
a. Type I 1.25 1.60
6N8 A45 13c #318, II 1.25 1.10
a. Type I 19.00 19.00
Nos. 6N6-6N8 (3) 3.50 3.85

On Stamps of 1939-41

1941 Perf. 12½
6N9 A57 2c #349, II .65 1.25
6N10 A57 2c #368, II 1.10 1.00
6N11 A57 3c #350, II .60 .60
a. Type I 1.25 1.25
6N12 A57 5c #352, II 1.10 1.10
a. Type I 1.25 1.25
6N13 A57 8c #353, II .65 .40
a. Type I .55 .55
6N14 A57 8c #369, II .90 .65
6N15 A57 10c #354, II .75 .65
6N16 A57 16c #357, II 4.50 6.00
6N17 A57 $1 #359, II 11.00 10.00
a. Type I 350.00 350.00
b. On No. 347, I 47.50 47.50
6N18 A57 $5 #361, II 40.00 40.00
Nos. 6N9-6N18 (10) 61.25 61.65

For overprints see Nos. 6N62, 6N64-6N65, 6N67-6N68.

On Stamps of 1940 with Secret Marks

1941 Unwmk. Perf. 14
6N20 A57 5c #382, II 1.25 1.00
6N21 A57 8c #383, II .30 .30
a. Type I 1.25 1.25
6N22 A57 10c #384, II 1.25 1.00
6N23 A57 30c #385, II 1.60 1.25
a. Type I 5.50 6.00
6N24 A57 50c #386, I 6.00 6.00
a. Type II 7.25 6.50
6N25 A57 $1 #387, II 6.00 4.00
a. Type I 14.00 14.00
6N26 A57 $2 #388, II 12.00 12.00
a. Type I 20.00 20.00
6N27 A57 $5 #389, II 24.00 24.00
a. Type I 32.50 32.50
6N28 A57 $10 #390, II 55.00 55.00
a. Type I 60.00 60.00
6N29 A57 $20 #391, II 80.00 80.00
a. Type I 80.00 90.00
Nos. 6N20-6N29 (10) 187.40 184.55

For overprints see Nos. 6N63, 6N69.

On Stamps of 1940 with Secret Marks

1941 Wmk. 261 Perf. 14
6N30 A57 5c #392, II 1.00 1.00
6N31 A57 5c #393, II 1.00 1.00
6N32 A57 10c #394, II 6.50 6.50
6N33 A57 30c #395, II 4.00 3.25
a. Type I 20.00 20.00
6N34 A57 50c #396, II 3.50 3.50
a. Type I 8.00 9.50
Nos. 6N30-6N34 (5) 16.00 15.25

On Stamps of 1940-41 (Martyrs) with Secret Marks

Perf. 12½, 13 & Compound

1941 Wmk. 261
6N35 A39 ½c #402, II 2.40 2.40
6N36 A40 1c #403, II 1.75 1.60
a. Type I 2.25 1.60
6N37 A39 2½c #405, II 7.25 9.50
6N38 A46 10c #410, I 3.25 3.25
6N39 A45 13c #411, II 3.25 3.25
6N40 A46 17c #413, II 3.50 3.50
a. Type I 8.00 8.75
6N41 A40 25c #416, II 3.50 3.50
6N42 A48 30c #418, I 27.50 27.50
6N43 A47 40c #419, II 3.50 3.50
a. Type I 27.50 27.50
6N44 A40 50c #420, II 7.25 7.25
Nos. 6N35-6N44 (10) 63.15 65.25

Unwmk.

6N45 A39 ½c #421, II 1.60 1.60
a. Type I 3.50 3.50
6N46 A40 1c #422, II 1.60 1.25
a. Type I 2.60 2.60
b. On No. 422a, II 80.00 80.00
6N48 A46 2c #423, II 1.60 1.60
6N49 A48 3c #425, I 3.50 4.00
a. Type II 4.00 5.50
6N50 A39 4c #426, II 1.00 .50
6N51 A45 8c #428, II 2.75 2.75
a. Type I 32.50 32.50
6N52 A46 10c #429, I 12.00 12.00
6N53 A45 13c #430, I 3.75 3.75
a. Type II 3.75 3.75
6N54 A48 15c #431, II 4.00 4.00
6N55 A46 17c #432, II 2.75 2.75
a. Type I 4.00 4.00
6N56 A47 20c #433, II 3.75 3.75
a. Type I 5.50 5.50
6N57 A45 21c #434, II 4.00 4.00
6N58 A40 25c #435, I 4.75 4.75
6N59 A46 28c #436, II 4.00 3.25
6N60 A40 50c #439, II 9.50 9.50
Nos. 6N45-6N60 (15) 60.55 59.45

For overprints see Nos. 6N61, 6N66.

Honan Singapore Overprint in Red

1942
6N61 A39 4c #6N50 2.00 2.75
6N62 A57 8c #6N13 20.00 24.00
6N63 A57 8c #6N21 20.00 20.00
6N64 A57 8c #6N14 3.25 5.50
Nos. 6N61-6N64 (4) 45.25 52.25

Honan Anniv. of Manchukuo Overprint in Red

1942
6N65 A57 2c #6N10 2.75 4.00
6N66 A39 4c #6N50 4.00 4.25
6N67 A57 8c #6N13 16.00 20.00
6N68 A57 8c #6N14 40.00 47.50
6N69 A57 8c #6N21 3.25 4.00
Nos. 6N65-6N69 (5) 66.00 79.75

Supeh

Nos. 297-298, 301-302 Overprinted

I

II

1941 Engr. Unwmk.
7N1 A37 2c #297, I 9.50 9.50
a. Type II 12.50 12.50
7N2 A37 4c #298, I 47.50 47.50
a. Type II 90.00
7N3 A37 15c #301, II 2.75 2.75
a. Type I 3.50 3.50
7N4 A37 20c #302, II 3.25 3.25
Nos. 7N1-7N4 (4) 63.00 63.00

On Nos. 312, 314, 318

1941 Perf. 14
7N5 A39 ½c #312, I 3.50 3.50
7N6 A39 2½c #314, II 1.25 1.25
a. Type I 1.25 1.25
7N7 A45 13c #318, II 1.25 1.25
a. Type I 95.00 95.00
Nos. 7N5-7N7 (3) 6.00 6.00

On Stamps of 1939-41

1941 Perf. 12½
7N8 A57 2c #368, II 1.25 2.00
7N9 A57 3c #350, II 1.40 1.40
a. Type I 20.00 20.00
7N10 A57 5c #352, II 1.25 1.75
a. Type I 3.25 3.00
7N11 A57 8c #353, I 2.00 2.00
a. Type II 2.75 2.75
7N12 A57 8c #369, II 32.50 27.50
7N13 A57 10c #354, II 3.00 4.00
7N14 A57 16c #357, II 1.25 2.00
7N15 A57 $1 #359, II 13.00 13.00
a. On No. 347, I 160.00 160.00
Nos. 7N8-7N15 (8) 55.65 53.65

For overprints see Nos. 7N56-7N58, 7N60-7N61.

On Stamps of 1940 with Secret Marks

1941 Unwmk. Perf. 14
7N17 A57 5c #382, II 1.25 1.25
7N18 A57 8c #383, II 1.25 1.25
7N19 A57 10c #384, I 3.50 3.50
a. Type II 3.50 3.50
7N20 A57 30c #385, I 2.75 3.25
a. Type II 6.50 7.25
7N21 A57 50c #386, II 3.75 4.50
a. Type I 4.00 4.00
7N22 A57 $1 #387, I 20.00 24.00
a. Type II 32.50 32.50
7N23 A57 $2 #388, I 20.00 20.00
a. Type II 27.50 32.50
7N24 A57 $5 #389, I 24.00 24.00
a. Type II 65.00 65.00
7N25 A57 $10 #390, I 65.00 65.00
a. Type II 72.50 72.50
7N26 A57 $20 #391, II 80.00 80.00
a. Type I 80.00 90.00
Nos. 7N17-7N26 (10) 221.50 226.75

On Stamps of 1940 with Secret Marks

1941 Wmk. 261 Perf. 14
7N27 A57 10c #394, II 4.00 4.00
7N28 A57 30c #395, I 13.00 14.00
7N29 A57 50c #396, I 14.00 15.00
Nos. 7N27-7N29 (3) 31.00 33.00

On Stamps of 1940-41 (Martyrs) with Secret Marks

Perf. 12½, 13 & Compound

1941 **Wmk. 261**

7N30 A39 ½c #402, II 4.75 4.75
7N31 A40 1c #403, I 1.75 1.75
a. Type II 2.75 2.75
7N32 A46 2c #404, II 1.60 1.60
7N33 A39 2½c #405, I 24.00 24.00
7N34 A46 10c #410, I 16.00 16.00
7N35 A45 13c #411, II 5.50 5.50
7N36 A46 17c #413, II 4.75 4.75
a. Type I 80.00 80.00
7N37 A40 25c #416, II 4.75 4.75
7N38 A48 30c #418, I 12.00 12.00
7N39 A47 40c #419, II 4.75 4.75
a. Type I 7.25 7.25
7N40 A40 50c #420, I 80.00 80.00
Nos. 7N30-7N40 (11) 159.85 159.85

Unwmk.

7N41 A39 ½c #421, II 3.50 3.50
a. Type I 4.75 4.75
7N42 A40 1c #422, II 1.60 1.60
7N43 A46 2c #423, I 12.00 12.00
7N44 A48 3c #425, I 3.50 3.50
7N45 A39 4c #426, II 1.00 1.00
7N46 A46 10c #429, I 40.00 40.00
7N47 A45 13c #430, I 5.50 *6.00*
7N48 A48 15c #431, II 6.00 6.00
7N49 A46 17c #432, II 3.75 3.75
a. Type I 5.50 5.50
7N50 A47 20c #433, II 3.75 3.75
a. Type I 5.50 5.50
7N51 A45 21c #434, II 4.00 4.00
7N52 A40 25c #435, I 5.25 5.25
a. Type II 14.00 14.00
7N53 A46 28c #436, II 5.50 5.50
Nos. 7N41-7N53 (13) 95.35 95.85

For overprints see Nos. 7N55, 7N59.

Honan Singapore Overprint in Red

1942

7N54 A37 4c #298, II 40.00 *47.50*
7N55 A39 4c #7N45 5.00 *5.50*
7N56 A57 8c #7N11a 13.00 *17.50*
7N57 A57 8c #7N12 12.00 *16.00*
Nos. 7N54-7N57 (4) 70.00 *86.50*

Honan Anniv. of Manchukuo Overprint in Red

1942

7N58 A57 2c #7N8 14.00 *20.00*
7N59 A39 4c #7N45 12.00 *14.00*
7N60 A57 8c #7N11a 60.00 *67.50*
7N61 A57 8c #7N12 72.50 *80.00*
Nos. 7N58-7N61 (4) 158.50 *181.50*

North China

For use in Honan, Hopei, Shansi, Shantung and Supeh (Northern Kiangsu)

Stamps of China, 1931-37 Surcharged North China (Hwa Pei) and Half of Original Value

1942 **Unwmk.** ***Perf. 14, 12½***

8N1 A40 ½c on 1c (#313) 1.60 *2.00*
8N2 A37 1c on 2c (#297) .60 .35
8N3 A37 2c on 4c (#298) 1.25 1.00
8N4 A45 4c on 8c (#316) 125.00

Same Surcharge on Stamps of 1938-41

Perf. 12½

8N5 A57 1c on 2c (#349) 4.00 *6.00*
8N6 A57 1c on 2c (#368) .40 .25
8N7 A57 4c on 8c (#353) 1.75 1.00
8N8 A57 4c on 8c (#369) .50 .30
8N9 A57 5c on 10c grn .55 .40
8N10 A57 8c on 16c ol gray 1.60 .65
8N11 A57 50c on $1 (#359) 6.50 6.50
8N12 A57 50c on $1 (#344) 475.00 475.00
8N13 A57 50c on $1 (#347) 95.00 95.00
8N14 A57 $1 on $2 (#360) 10.00 10.00
8N15 A57 $1 on $2 (#345) 27.50 27.50
8N16 A57 $1 on $2 (#348) 125.00 125.00

No. 8N12 was issued without gum.
For overprint see No. 8N58.

Same Surcharge on China Nos. 383-388, 390-391

Perf. 14

8N17 A57 4c on 8c ol grn .55 .55
8N18 A57 5c on 10c grn 1.00 1.60
8N19 A57 15c on 30c scar 1.25 1.00
a. Inverted surcharge 65.00 65.00
8N20 A57 25c on 50c dk bl 1.60 1.40
8N21 A57 50c on $1 org brn & sep 3.75 3.75
8N22 A57 $1 on $2 dp bl & yel brn 4.75 4.75
8N23 A57 $5 on $10 dk grn & dl pur 40.00 40.00
8N24 A57 $10 on $20 rose lake & dk bl 40.00 50.00
Nos. 8N17-8N24 (8) 92.90 103.05

For overprint see No. 8N55.

Same Surcharge on China Nos. 394-396

Wmk. 261

8N25 A57 5c on 10c grn .70 *1.25*
8N26 A57 15c on 30c scar 2.75 *4.00*
8N27 A57 25c on 50c dk bl 1.25 1.25
Nos. 8N25-8N27 (3) 4.70 *6.50*

Same Surcharge on Stamps of 1940-41

1942 **Wmk. 261** ***Perf. 12½, 13***

8N28 A40 ½c on 1c org .25 .20
8N29 A46 1c on 2c dp bl 2.00 2.00
8N30 A45 4c on 8c dp org 16.00 *20.00*
8N31 A46 5c on 10c dl vio 2.00 *2.40*
8N32 A48 15c on 30c brn car 8.00 8.00
8N33 A47 20c on 40c org 4.75 1.75
8N34 A40 25c on 50c grn 4.00 4.00
Nos. 8N28-8N34 (7) 37.00 38.35

Unwmk.

8N35 A40 ½c on 1c org (#422) .25 .20
a. ½c on 1c org (#422a) 30.00 30.00
8N36 A46 1c on 2c dp bl 1.10 1.10
8N37 A39 2c on 4c pale vio .80 .70
8N38 A45 4c on 8c dp org 1.00 1.60
8N39 A46 5c on 10c dl vio 2.40 2.40
8N40 A47 10c on 20c lt bl 3.00 .60
8N41 A47 20c on 40c org 3.25 .80
8N42 A40 25c on 50c grn 2.75 2.75
Nos. 8N35-8N42 (8) 14.55 10.15

Same Surcharge on "New Peking" Prints

Perf. 14

8N43 A37 1c on 2c ol grn .30 .20
8N44 A37 2c on 4c dl grn .75 .20
a. Inverted surcharge 35.00
8N45 A45 4c on 8c dp org .55 .20
8N46 A57 8c on 16c ol gray .30 .20
8N47 A47 10c on 20c red brn 1.40 1.25
8N48 A48 15c on 30c brn car .70 .70
8N49 A47 20c on 40c org 1.75 .25
a. Inverted surcharge 45.00
8N50 A40 25c on 50c grn 1.50 1.25
8N51 A57 50c on $1 org brn & sep 2.75 2.75
8N52 A57 $1 on $2 dp bl & org brn 4.75 2.75
8N53 A57 $5 on $10 dk grn & dl pur 20.00 20.00
Nos. 8N43-8N53 (11) 34.75 *29.75*

See note after No. 2N93. For overprints see #8N54, 8N56-8N57, 8N59.

Nos. 8N44, 8N17 and 8N46 with Additional Overprint in Red

1943 **Unwmk.** ***Perf. 14***

8N54 A37 2c on 4c dl grn .25 *.85*
8N55 A57 4c on 8c ol grn 1.25 *1.40*
8N56 A57 8c on 16c ol gray 1.25 *1.60*
Nos. 8N54-8N56 (3) 2.75 *3.85*

Return of the Foreign Concessions to China.

Nos. 8N44, 8N8 and 8N46 with Additional Overprint in Red

1943, Aug. 15 ***Perf. 14, 12½***

8N57 A37 2c on 4c dl grn .35 *.70*
8N58 A57 4c on 8c ol grn .35 *.80*
8N59 A57 8c on 16c ol gray .40 *.70*
Nos. 8N57-8N59 (3) 1.10 *2.20*

North China Postal Service, 5th anniv.

Stamps of China, 1934-41, Overprinted in Black

1943, Nov. 1

8N60 A40 1c org (#313) .70 .70
8N61 A40 1c org (#422) .70 .60
8N62 A57 10c grn (#354) .40 .35
8N63 A57 $2 dp bl & yel brn (#388) 24.00 24.00
8N64 A57 $5 red & grnsh blk (#361) 16.00 16.00
8N65 A57 $5 red & sl grn (#389) 8.00 8.00
8N66 A57 $10 dk grn & dl pur (#390) 12.00 12.00
8N67 A57 $20 rose lake & dk bl (#391) 72.50 *87.50*
Nos. 8N60-8N67 (8) 134.30 *149.15*

Same Overprint on "New Peking" Prints

8N68 A40 1c orange .25 .20
8N69 A37 2c olive grn .25 *.60*
8N70 A37 4c dull green .25 *1.25*
8N71 A37 5c green .50 *.60*
8N72 A57 9c olive grn .30 *.50*
8N73 A46 10c dl violet .30 *.60*
8N74 A57 16c olive gray .25 *.35*
8N75 A57 18c olive gray .25 *.35*
8N76 A47 20c henna .40 *.50*
8N77 A48 30c brown car .35 .35
8N78 A47 40c brt orange .35 *.60*
a. Inverted overprint 35.00 35.00
8N79 A40 50c green 2.00 2.00
8N80 A57 $1 org brn & sep 3.50 1.00
8N81 A57 $2 bl & org brn 2.00 .85
8N82 A57 $5 red & sl grn 4.00 *6.00*
8N83 A57 $10 dk grn & dl pur 7.25 7.25
8N84 A57 $20 rose lake & dk bl 8.50 *10.00*
Nos. 8N68-8N84 (17) 30.70 *33.00*

See note after No. 2N93. For overprints see Nos. 8N85-8N90, 8N95-8N106.

Nos. 8N70 and 8N62 with Additional Overprint in Red

1944, Jan. 9

8N85 A37 4c dull green .30 *.85*
8N86 A57 10c green .30 *.60*

1st anniv. of the declaration of war against the Allies by North China.

Nos. 8N72, 8N75, 8N79 and 8N80 with Additional Overprint in Red

1944, Mar. 30

8N87 A57 9c olive green .45 *1.25*
8N88 A57 18c olive gray .80 *2.40*
8N89 A40 50c green 4.75 *6.00*
8N90 A57 $1 org brn & sepia 1.75 *2.40*
a. Red overprint inverted 30.00 30.00
Nos. 8N87-8N90 (4) 7.75 *12.05*

North China Political Council, 4th anniv.

Shanghai-Nanking Nos. 9N101-9N104 Surcharged North China (Hwa Pei) and New Value in Red or Black

a

b

c

d

1944 ***Perf. 12½x12, 12x12½***

8N91 OS1 (a) 9c on 50c org 1.10 1.40
8N92 OS1 (b) 18c on $1 grn (R) 1.25 1.75
a. Double surcharge 30.00 30.00
8N93 OS2 (c) 36c on $2 dp bl (R) 1.40 1.75
8N94 OS2 (d) 90c on $5 car rose 1.75 2.00
Nos. 8N91-8N94 (4) 5.50 6.90

Nos. 8N72, 8N75, 8N79 and 8N80 Overprinted in Red or Blue

1944, Aug. 15

8N95 A57 9c olive grn .75 *1.25*
8N96 A57 18c olive gray .75 *2.40*
8N97 A40 50c green 1.25 *1.75*
8N98 A57 $1 org brn & sep (Bl) 2.75 *3.25*
Nos. 8N95-8N98 (4) 5.50 *8.65*

6th anniv. of the General P.O. Dept. of North China.

North China Nos. 8N76, 8N79-8N81 Overprinted in Blue or Black

1944, Dec. 5

8N99 A47 20c henna (Bl) 2.40 *2.75*
8N100 A40 50c green (Bl) 2.40 *2.75*
8N101 A57 $1 org brn & sep (Bl) 4.75 *5.50*
8N102 A57 $2 bl & org brn 1.40 *1.40*
Nos. 8N99-8N102 (4) 10.95 *12.40*

Death of Wang Ching-wei, puppet ruler of China.

North China Nos. 8N76, 8N79-8N81 Overprinted in Red or Black

1945

8N103 A47 20c henna 2.40 *3.25*
8N104 A40 50c green (R) 7.25 7.25
8N105 A57 $1 org brn & sep 2.60 *2.75*
8N106 A57 $2 bl & org brn 1.75 1.60
Nos. 8N103-8N106 (4) 14.00 *14.85*

2nd anniv. of the declaration of war.

Shanghai-Nanking Nos. 9N105-9N106 Surcharged in Red

1945 ***Perf. 12x12½***

8N107 OS3 50c on $3 lt org .55 .70
8N108 OS3 $1 on $6 blue .55 .70

Return of the foreign concessions in Shanghai.

Dragon Pillar
OS1

Dr. Sun Yat-sen
OS2

Designs: $2, Long Bridge and White Pagoda. $5, Tower in Imperial City. $10, Marble Boat, Summer Palace.

1945 Unwmk. Litho. *Perf. 14*
Various Papers

8N109 OS1 $1 dull yellow 1.25 1.25
8N110 OS1 $2 deep blue .25 1.25
8N111 OS1 $5 carmine .85 .60
8N112 OS1 $10 dull green .40 .90
Nos. 8N109-8N112 (4) 2.75 4.00

North China Political Council, 5th anniv.

1945
Without Gum; Various Papers

8N113 OS2 $1 bister .25 .20
8N114 OS2 $2 dark blue .90 .20
8N115 OS2 $5 fawn 2.00 2.00
8N116 OS2 $10 sage green 2.00 .60
8N117 OS2 $20 dull violet 2.00 1.40
8N118 OS2 $50 brown 40.00 47.50
Nos. 8N113-8N118 (6) 47.15 51.90

Nos. 8N113-8N118 without "Hwa Pei" overprint are proofs.

Wutai Mountain, Shansi — OS3

Designs: $10, Kaifeng Iron Pagoda. $20, International Bridge, Tientsin. $30, Taishan Mountain, Shantung. $50, General Post Office, Peking.

1945, Aug. 15
Without Gum; Various Papers

8N119 OS3 $5 gray green .25 .85
8N120 OS3 $10 dull brown .60 .85
8N121 OS3 $20 dull purple .45 1.25
8N122 OS3 $30 slate blue .90 1.25
8N123 OS3 $50 carmine 2.00 2.40
Nos. 8N119-8N123 (5) 4.20 6.60

North China Postal Directorate, 7th anniv.

Shanghai and Nanking

China Nos. 299-303 Surcharged

a

b

Overprinted Type "b"

1942-45 Unwmk. *Perf. 12½, 13½*

9N1 A37 $6 on 5c green .75 1.00
9N2 A37 $20 on 15c scar .35 .75
9N3 A37 $500 on 15c dk grn .25 1.00
9N4 A37 $1000 on 20c ultra 2.75 2.75
9N5 A37 $1000 on 25c ultra 2.75 2.75
Nos. 9N1-9N5 (5) 6.85 8.25

A $1000 on 20c ultramarine, No. 293, exists.

Surcharged Type "a" (Nos. 9N6-9N10) or Type "b" (Nos. 9N11-9N40) on Type A57 Stamps of 1939-41
Perf. 12½

9N6 25c on 5c (#352) 2.00 3.25
9N7 30c on 2c (#368) .20 .25
9N8 50c on 3c (#350) .25 .30
9N9 50c on 5c (#352) .25 .25
9N10 50c on 8c (#353) .25 .35
9N11 $1 on 8c (#353) .25 .20
9N12 $1 on 8c (#369) 12.00 12.00
9N13 $1 on 15c (#356) .25 .20
9N14 $1.30 on 16c (#357) .25 .40
9N15 $1.50 on 3c (#350) .25 .40
9N16 $2 on 5c (#352) 1.10 1.10
9N17 $2 on 10c (#354) .25 .30
9N18 $3 on 15c (#356) .25 .30
9N19 $4 on 16c (#357) .40 .25
9N20 $5 on 15c (#356) .25 .25
9N21 $6 on 5c (#351) .60 1.40
a. Perf. 14 (#371) 50.00 50.00
9N22 $6 on 5c (#352) .25 .35
9N23 $6 on 8c (#353) .40 1.00
9N24 $6 on 8c (#369) 800.00 800.00
9N25 $6 on 10c (#354) .25 .25
9N26 $10 on 10c (#354) .25 .30
9N27 $10 on 16c (#357) .50 .25
9N28 $20 on 3c (#350) .25 .40
9N29 $20 on 15c (#355) 1.10 2.40
9N30 $20 on 15c (#356) .40 .40
9N31 $20 on $2 (#360) 1.40 2.75
9N32 $100 on 3c (#350) .50 .40
9N33 $500 on 8c (#353) 2.40 4.50
9N34 $500 on 8c (#369) 35.00 47.50
9N35 $500 on 10c (#354) 2.40 3.50
9N36 $500 on 15c (#355) 1.25 2.40
9N37 $500 on 15c (#356) 1.00 2.00
9N38 $500 on 16c (#357) 1.25 4.00
9N39 $1000 on 25c (#358) 1.25 2.40
9N40 $2000 on $5 (#361) 1.40 2.40
Nos. 9N1-9N23,9N25-9N40 (39) 76.90 106.65

Nos. 381-391 (Type A57) Surcharged with Type "b"
Perf. 14

9N41 $1 on 8c ol grn .25 .30
9N42 $1.70 on 30c scar .30 .60
a. Perf. 12½ 3.25 3.25
9N43 $2 on 5c ol grn .40 1.25
9N44 $2 on $1 org brn & sep 1.00 2.40
9N45 $3 on 8c ol grn .60 .60
a. $3 on 8c olive green (#383a) 35.00 35.00
b. "3" with flat top .40 .40
9N46 $6 on 5c grn .40 .50
9N47 $6 on 5c ol grn .40 .80
9N48 $6 on 8c ol grn .35 .70
9N49 $10 on 10c grn .40 2.00
a. Perf. 12½ 2.00 6.00
9N50 $20 on $2 dp bl & yel brn 1.25 1.25
9N51 $50 on 30c scar .75 .80
9N52 $50 on 50c dk bl .65 .65
9N53 $50 on $5 red & sl grn .95 .95
9N54 $50 on $20 rose lake & dk bl 2.00 2.40
9N55 $100 on $10 dk grn & dl pur 1.60 1.60
9N56 $200 on $20 rose lake & dk bl .60 1.00
9N57 $500 on 8c ol grn 11.00 13.00
a. $500 on 8c ol grn (#383a) 25.00 24.00
9N58 $500 on 10c grn 2.40 3.50
9N59 $1000 on 30c scar 2.00 2.75
9N60 $1000 on 50c dk bl 1.00 1.40
9N61 $1000 on $2 dp bl & yel brn 2.40 8.00
9N62 $2000 on $5 red & sl grn 1.25 1.60

China Nos. 392-395 and 399-401 (Type A57) Surcharged with Type "b"

1942-45 Wmk. 261 *Perf. 14*

9N63 $2 on $1 org brn & sep, perf. 12½ .80 1.40
9N64 $6 on 5c grn .40 .85
9N65 $6 on 5c ol grn 1.10 1.60
9N66 $50 on $5 red & sl grn .70 1.00
a. Numeral tablet violet .80 1.00
9N67 $100 on $10 dk grn & dl pur .40 .60
9N68 $200 on $20 rose lake & dk bl .50 .60
9N69 $500 on 10c grn 2.00 2.40
9N70 $1000 on 30c scar 2.75 3.25
9N71 $5000 on $10 dk grn & dl pur, perf. 12½ 6.50 8.00
a. Perf. 14 100.00 100.00
Nos. 9N41-9N71 (31) 47.10 67.75

Nos. 9N63 and 9N71 were not issued without surcharge. A $50 on 30c scarlet exists.

Same Surch. on Stamps of 1940-41
Perf. 12½, 13
Wmk. 261

9N72 A46 $30 on 2c dp bl 125.00 125.00

A $7.50 on ½c and a $15 on 1c are known.

Unwmk.

9N73 A39 $7.50 on ½c ol blk 1.25 2.40
9N74 A40 $15 on 1c org .30 1.25
a. Without secret mark 50.00 50.00
9N75 A46 $30 on 2c dp bl 1.10 1.60
9N76 A40 $200 on 1c org .25 .30
9N77 A45 $200 on 8c dp org .70 1.00
Nos. 9N73-9N77 (5) 3.60 6.55

Surcharged Type "a" (Nos. 9N78-9N81) or Type "b" (Nos. 9N82-9N96) on Type A59 Stamps of 1941
Perf. 12

9N78 5c on ½c sepia .20 .30
9N79 10c on 1c orange .20 .30
9N80 20c on 1c orange .20 .40
9N81 40c on 5c green .20 .40
9N82 $5 on 5c green .20 .30
9N83 $10 on 10c brt grn .20 .30
9N84 $50 on ½c sepia .20 .30
9N85 $50 on 1c orange .35 .40
9N86 $50 on 17c olive .35 .50
9N87 $200 on 5c green .35 .40
9N88 $200 on 8c turq grn .20 .25
9N89 $200 on 8c red org .35 .60
9N90 $500 on $5 scar & blk .40 .40
9N91 $1000 on 1c orange .35 .55
9N92 $1000 on 25c rose vio .40 .55
9N93 $1000 on 30c scarlet 1.00 .55
9N94 $1000 on $2 bl & blk 1.00 1.00
9N95 $1000 on $10 grn & blk .40 .55
9N96 $2000 on $5 scar & blk 1.00 1.00
Nos. 9N78-9N96 (19) 7.55 9.05

Stamps of China 1939-41 Surcharged in Red or Blue

1943 Unwmk. *Perf. 12, 12½*

9N97 A57 25c on 5c grn .20 1.25
9N98 A59 50c on 8c red org (Bl) .20 .50
9N99 A57 $1 on 16c ol gray .20 1.40
9N100 A59 $2 on 50c dk bl .20 .50
Nos. 9N97-9N100 (4) .80 3.65

Return of the foreign concessions in Shanghai.

Wheat and Cotton — OS1

Purple Mountain, Nanking OS2

Perf. 12½x12, 12x12½
1944 Engr. Unwmk.

9N101 OS1 50c orange .20 .35
9N102 OS1 $1 green .20 .35
9N103 OS2 $2 deep blue .20 .40
9N104 OS2 $5 carmine rose .20 .40
Nos. 9N101-9N104 (4) .80 1.50

Puppet government at Nanking, 4th anniv.
For surcharges see Nos. 8N91-8N94, 9N107-9N110.

Map of Foreign Concessions in Shanghai — OS3

1944 *Perf. 12x12½*

9N105 OS3 $3 lt orange .20 .35
9N106 OS3 $6 blue .20 .35

1st anniversary of the return of the foreign concessions in Shanghai.
For surcharges see Nos. 8N107-8N108.

Nos. 9N101-9N104 Surcharged in Black with Type "b"

1945, Mar. 30

9N107 OS1 $15 on 50c orange .20 .35
9N108 OS1 $30 on $1 green .20 .35
9N109 OS2 $60 on $2 dp blue .20 .35
9N110 OS2 $200 on $5 car rose .20 .55
Nos. 9N107-9N110 (4) .80 1.60

China Nos. C31, C32, C36 and C38 Surcharged in Red, Green, Orange or Carmine

1945 *Perf. 12½, 13*

9N111 AP3 $150 on 15c (R) .20 .20
9N112 AP3 $250 on 25c (G) .20 .35
9N113 AP3 $600 on 60c (O) .20 .35
9N114 AP3 $1,000 on $1 (C) .20 .35
Nos. 9N111-9N114 (4) .80 1.25

Issue as air raid precaution propaganda.

SHANGHAI AND NANKING AIR POST STAMPS

China Nos. C35 and C38 Surcharged in Black

The surcharges on Nos. 9NC1-9NC7 were in Japanese currency because all air mail then was carried by Japanese planes.

The surcharges translate: (10c) "Airmail fee for postcard within the nation has been paid." (20c) "Airmail fee for letter within the nation has been paid."

1941 Unwmk. *Perf. 12½*

9NC1 AP3 10(s) on 50c brown .40 .40
9NC2 AP3 20(s) on $1 apple grn .20 .35

Two types of surcharge exist on No. 9NC1.

Similar Surcharge on No. C28

1941 Wmk. 261 *Perf. 13*

9NC3 AP3 20(s) on $1 ap grn 16.00 16.00

Nos. C37 and C39 Surcharged

The surcharges translate: (18c and 25c) "Airmail fee for postcard to Japan has been paid." (35c) "Airmail fee for letter to Japan has been paid."

1941 Unwmk. *Perf. 12½, 13*

9NC4 AP3 18(s) on 90c lt olive .20 .60
9NC5 AP3 25(s) on 90c lt olive .20 .60
9NC6 AP3 35(s) on $2 lt brown .20 .60
Nos. 9NC4-9NC6 (3) .60 1.80

No. 9NC6 with Additional Surcharge in Red
Perf. 12½

9NC7 AP3 60(s) on 35(s) on $2 .20 .35

SHANGHAI AND NANKING POSTAGE DUE STAMPS

Postage Due Stamps of China 1932 Surcharged in Black

1945 Unwmk. *Perf. 14*

9NJ1 D5 $1 on 2c org .20 1.25
9NJ2 D5 $2 on 5c org .20 1.25
9NJ3 D5 $5 on 10c org .20 1.25
9NJ4 D5 $10 on 20c org .60 1.75
Nos. 9NJ1-9NJ4 (4) 1.20 5.50

Northeastern Provinces

民 中

國 華

With the end of World War II and the collapse of Manchukuo, the Northeastern Provinces reverted to China. In many Manchurian towns and cities, the Manchukuo stamps were locally handstamped in ideograms: "Republic of China," "China Postal Service" or "Temporary Use for China." A typical example is shown above.

Dr. Sun Yat-sen
A1 A2
Black Surcharge

1946, Feb. Unwmk. Typo. *Perf. 14*

No.	Type	Description	Unused	Used
1	A1	50c on $5 red	.20	*.80*
2	A1	50c on $10 green	.50	*1.25*
3	A1	$1 on $10 green	.20	*1.00*
4	A1	$2 on $20 brown vio	.20	*.80*
5	A1	$4 on $50 brown	.20	*.65*
		Nos. 1-5 (5)	1.30	*4.50*

The two characters at left express the new value.

Stamps of China, 1938-41 Overprinted

1946, Apr. *Perf. 12½, 13, 13½, 14*

No.	Type	Description	Unused	Used
6	A40	1c org (#422)	.20	*1.75*
7	A48	3c dp yel brn (#425)	.20	*1.75*
8	A48	5c dl red org (#427)	.20	*2.25*
9	A57	10c grn (#354)	.20	*1.75*
10	A57	10c grn (#384)	.20	*1.75*
11	A47	20c lt bl (#433)	.20	*1.75*
a.		Horiz. pair, imperf. btwn	90.00	
		Nos. 6-11 (6)	1.20	*11.00*

1946, July Engr. *Perf. 14*
Without Gum

No.	Type	Description	Unused	Used
12	A2	5c lake	.20	*1.25*
13	A2	10c orange	.20	*.90*
14	A2	20c yel grn	.20	*2.50*
15	A2	25c blk brn	.20	*1.25*
16	A2	50c red org	.20	*.85*
17	A2	$1 blue	.20	*.60*
18	A2	$2 dk vio	.20	*.60*
19	A2	$2.50 indigo	.20	*1.25*
20	A2	$3 brown	.20	*.60*
21	A2	$4 org brn	.20	*.90*
22	A2	$5 dk grn	.20	*.60*
23	A2	$10 crimson	.20	*.60*
24	A2	$20 olive	.20	*.60*
25	A2	$50 blue vio	.30	*.60*
		Nos. 12-25 (14)	2.90	*13.10*

Two types of $4, $10, $20 and $50: I- Character *kuo* directly left of sun emblem is open at upper and lower left corners of "box." Diagonal stroke from top center to lower right has no hook at bottom. II- Character is closed at left corners. Diagonal stroke has hook at bottom.

See Nos. 47-52, 61-63. For surcharges see Nos. M1, Taiwan 91-96, People's Republic of China 35-48, 3L37-3L52, 3L55-3L66, 3L71-3L75.

China Nos. 728-731 Surcharged in Black

1946

No.	Type	Description	Unused	Used
26	A75	$2 on $20 green	.20	*.80*
27	A75	$3 on $30 blue	.20	*1.75*
28	A75	$5 on $50 dark brown	.20	*.85*
29	A75	$10 on $100 carmine	.20	*1.10*
		Nos. 26-29 (4)	.80	*4.50*

Convening of Chinese National Assembly.

Type of China, 1946, with added inscriptions on both sides of head:

1947 Engr. *Perf. 11, 11½*

No.	Type	Description	Unused	Used
30	A74	$2 carmine	.35	*1.10*
31	A74	$3 green	.45	*1.25*
32	A74	$5 vermilion	.45	*1.40*
33	A74	$10 yel grn	.60	*1.25*
34	A74	$20 yel org	.70	*1.25*
35	A74	$30 magenta	.70	*1.10*
		Nos. 30-35 (6)	3.25	*7.35*

60th birthday of Chiang Kai-shek.

Type of China, 1947, with additional inscription above value:

1947 Unwmk. Engr. *Perf. 14*

No.	Type	Description	Unused	Used
36	A76	$2 deep green	.20	*.50*
37	A76	$4 deep blue	.20	*.50*
38	A76	$6 carmine	.20	*.50*
39	A76	$10 lt brown	.20	*.60*
40	A76	$20 deep claret	.20	*.65*
		Nos. 36-40 (5)	1.00	*2.75*

First anniversary of return of Chinese National Government to Nanking.

China Nos. 644 to 646 and 634 Surcharged in Black

1947 *Perf. 12½, 14*

No.	Type	Description	Unused	Used
41	A73	$100 on $1000 rose lake	.35	*1.25*
42	A73	$300 on $3000 bl	.35	*1.40*
43	A73	$500 on $5000 dp grn & ver	.35	*1.60*
44	A37	$500 on $30 choc	1.10	*1.75*
		Nos. 41-44 (4)	2.15	*6.00*

Type of 1946

1947 Engr. *Perf. 14*
Without Gum

No.	Type	Description	Unused	Used
47	A2	$44 dk car rose	*25.00*	*35.00*
48	A2	$100 dp grn	.20	*.35*
49	A2	$200 rose brn	.20	*.55*
50	A2	$300 bluish grn	.20	*1.25*
51	A2	$500 rose car	.20	*.35*
52	A2	$1000 dp orange	.25	*.35*
		Nos. 47-52 (6)	*26.05*	*37.85*

For surcharges see note following No. 25.

Stamps and Types of 1946-47 Surcharged in Black or Red

1948 Unwmk. *Perf. 14*

No.	Type	Description	Unused	Used
53	A2	$1500 on 20c yel grn	.55	*2.60*
54	A2	$3000 on $1 blue	.25	*.55*
55	A2	$4000 on 25c blk brn (R)	.25	*.55*
56	A2	$8000 on 50c red org	.25	*.85*
57	A2	$10,000 on 10c org	.30	*.55*
58	A2	$50,000 on $109 dk grn (R)	.60	*3.75*
59	A2	$100,000 on $65 dl grn	.55	*3.75*
60	A2	$500,000 on $22 gray (R)	.90	*3.75*
		Nos. 53-60 (8)	3.65	*16.35*

Type of 1946

1947, Nov. 5
Without Gum

No.	Type	Description	Unused	Used
61	A2	$22 gray	40.00	
62	A2	$65 dull green	45.00	
63	A2	$109 dark green	55.00	
		Nos. 61-63 (3)	140.00	

For surcharges see note following No. 25.

POSTAGE DUE STAMPS

D1

1947 Unwmk. Engr. *Perf. 14*
Without Gum

No.	Type	Description	Unused	Used
J1	D1	10c dark blue	.20	*4.50*
J2	D1	20c dark blue	.20	*4.50*
J3	D1	50c dark blue	.20	*3.50*
J4	D1	$1 dark blue	.20	*2.25*
J5	D1	$2 dark blue	.20	*3.50*
J6	D1	$5 dark blue	.20	*2.25*
		Nos. J1-J6 (6)	1.20	*20.50*

Nos. J4-J6 are known on paper with the papermaker's watermark, "COSMOS BOND."

Nos. J1 to J3 Surcharged in Red

1948

No.	Type	Description	Unused	Used
J7	D1	$10 on 10c dark blue	.20	*3.75*
J8	D1	$20 on 20c dark blue	.20	*3.75*
J9	D1	$50 on 50c dark blue	.20	*3.75*
		Nos. J7-J9 (3)	.60	*11.25*

The surcharge reads "Changed to . . . dollars." Characters at the left express the new value and vary on each denomination.

MILITARY STAMPS

No. 16 Surcharged in Black

1947 Unwmk. *Perf. 14*

No.	Type	Description	Unused	Used
M1	A2	$44 on 50c red org	5.00	*10.00*

The surcharge reads: "Army Post. Temporarily for 44 dollars."

China No. M13 Overprinted in Black

Thin Paper Without Gum
Perf. 12½

No.	Type	Description	Unused	Used
M2	M1	rose	.90	*.90*

China No. M13 Overprinted in Black

No.	Type	Description	Unused	Used
M3	M1	rose	45.00	45.00

PARCEL POST STAMP

China No. Q25 Surcharged in Black

1948 Unwmk. Engr. *Perf. 13½*
Without Gum

No.	Type	Description	Unused	Used
Q1	PP3	$500,000 on $5,000,000 lil		85.00

Used value is for CTO.

The use of this handstamp from Anhwei has not been verified.

Fukien Province

Stamps of China, 1945-49, Surcharged

1949 Engr. *Perf. 14*
Without Gum

No.	Type	Description	Unused	Used
1	A82	1c on $500 bl grn	6.25	*7.00*
2	A82	1c on $7000 lt red brn	15.00	*22.50*
3	A82	2c on $2,000,000 ver	3.75	*4.50*
4	A82	2½c on $50,000 dp bl	22.50	22.50
5	A73	4c on $100 dk car	3.00	3.00
6	A73	10c on $200 ol grn	4.00	4.00
7	A82	10c on $3000 bl	2.50	*3.00*
8	A82	10c on $4000 gray	3.75	*4.50*
9	A82	10c on $6000 rose lil	3.75	*4.25*
10	A82	10c on $100,000 dl grn	3.75	*4.50*
11	A82	10c on $1,000,000 cl	3.75	*4.25*
12	A82	40c on $200,000 brn vio	5.00	*5.50*
		Nos. 1-12 (12)	77.00	*89.50*

The surcharge on No. 2 is handstamped and in slightly larger characters.

Issue dates: No. 2, May 10; others, June.

China Nos. 973, 975-978 Overprinted

1949, June Litho. *Perf. 12½, 13*

No.	Type	Description	Unused	Used
13	A94	1c apple grn	12.00	6.00
14	A94	4c blue green	6.00	1.25
15	A94	10c deep lilac	35.00	18.00
16	A94	16c orange red	7.00	*18.00*
17	A94	20c blue	35.00	18.00
		Nos. 13-17 (5)	95.00	61.25

Same Overprint on China No. 959

1949, July Litho. *Perf. 12½*

No.	Type	Description	Unused	Used
18	A96	orange	47.50	47.50

Same Overprint on Fukien Nos. 1, 3-4, 8, 11 in Black or Red

1949, June Engr. *Perf. 14*

No.	Type	Description	Unused	Used
19	A82	1c on $500 bl grn	100.00	100.00
20	A82	2c on $2,000,000 ver	35.00	35.00
21	A82	2½c on $50,000 dp bl	57.50	57.50
22	A82	10c on $4000 gray	25.00	25.00
23	A82	10c on $1,000,000 cl	92.50	87.50
		Nos. 19-23 (5)	310.00	305.00

AIR POST STAMP

China #C62 Overprinted as #13-17

1949, July Litho. *Perf. 12½*

No.	Type	Description	Unused	Used
C1	AP5	blue green	47.50	25.00

SPECIAL DELIVERY STAMP

China #E12 Overprinted as #13-17

1949, July	Litho.	*Perf. 12½*	
E1 SD2	red violet	32.50	22.50

REGISTRATION STAMP

China #F2 Overprinted as #13-17

1949, July	Litho.	*Perf. 12½*	
F1 R2	carmine	32.50	22.50

Hunan Province

China No. 640 Surcharged

1949, May	Engr.	*Perf. 14*	
1 A73	on $100 dk car	9.00	5.50

The first printing of surcharge on No. 1 is in smaller characters.

China Nos. 797, 788, 750, 747 Surcharged

1949, May	Engr.	*Perf. 14*	
2 A82	1c on $2,000,000 ver	18.00	18.00
3 A82	2c on $20,000 rose pink	18.00	18.00
4 A82	5c on $3000 blue	24.00	*26.00*
5 A82	10c on $500 blue grn	18.00	18.00
	Nos. 2-5 (4)	78.00	80.00

AIR POST STAMP

China No. 790 Surcharged

湘 國內航空 郵資已付

1949, May	Engr.	*Perf. 14*	
C1 A82	On $40,000 green	14.00	*16.00*

SPECIAL DELIVERY STAMP

China No. 637 Surcharged as No. F1 in Red

1949, May	Engr.	*Perf. 14*	
E1 A73	On $30 dark blue	18.00	18.00

REGISTRATION STAMP

China No. 754 Surcharged

1949, May	Engr.	*Perf. 14*	
F1 A73	On $7000 lt red brn	18.00	18.00

Hupeh Province

China Type A95 Surcharged

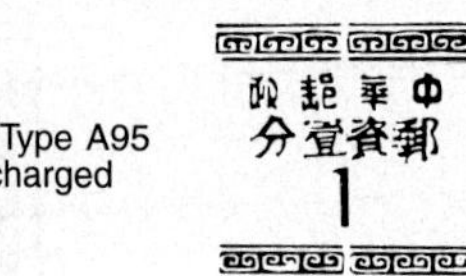

1949, May		Litho.	
1 A95	1c on $20 red brn	45.00	45.00
2 A95	10c on $20 red brn	45.00	45.00

Kansu Province

China No. 959 Handstamped in Purple

1949, Aug.	Litho.	*Perf. 12½*	
1 A96	orange	*1,100.*	

AIR POST STAMP

Same Handstamp Overprinted on China No. C62 in Red

1949, Aug.	Litho.	*Perf. 12½*	
C1 AP5	blue green	*1,100.*	

Counterfeits exist.

Kiangsi Province

China Nos. 789-791 Surcharged

1949	Engr.	*Perf. 14*	
1 A82	On $30,000 choc	37.50	35.00
2 A82	On $40,000 green	37.50	35.00
3 A82	On $50,000 dp bl	37.50	35.00
	Nos. 1-3 (3)	112.50	105.00

AIR POST STAMP

Similar Surcharge on China No. 754

1949	Engr.	*Perf. 14*	
C1 A82	On $7000 lt red brn	40.00	40.00

Third and fourth characters in right column of surcharge read "Air Mail" in Chinese on No. C1, "Registered" on Nos. F1-F2.

SPECIAL DELIVERY STAMP

Similar Surcharge on China No. 750

1949	Engr.	*Perf. 14*	
E1 A82	On $3000 blue	45.00	30.00

See note below No. C1.

REGISTRATION STAMPS

Similar Surcharge on China Nos. 747 and 754

1949	Engr.	*Perf. 14*	
F1 A82	On $500 bl grn	45.00	30.00
F2 A82	On $7000 lt red brn	45.00	30.00

Kwangsi Province

China Nos. 811 and 818 Also Surcharged in Red

1949, May 21		Typo.	
6 A62	5c on $20,000 on 10c dp grn	20.00	20.00
7 A62	5c on $40,000 on 20c dk ol grn	45.00	27.50

China Stamps of 1946-48 Surcharged in Black or Red

桂區 分2圓銀

a

桂 銀圓壹角貳分 區

b

1949	Engr.	*Perf. 14*	
	Type "a" Surcharge		
8 A82	½c on $500,000 lil rose	26.00	19.00
9 A82	1c on $200,000 brn vio	22.50	7.75
10 A82	2c on $300,000 yel grn	77.50	47.50
11 A73	5c on $3000 blue	14.00	7.00
12 A82	5c on $3000 blue	11.50	7.00
13 A82	5c on $40,000 grn	22.50	13.00
	Type "b" Surcharge		
14 A82	13c on $50,000 dp bl (R)	17.00	9.50
15 A82	13c on $50,000 dp bl	62.50	17.00
16 A82	17c on $7000 lt red brn	17.50	11.50
17 A82	21c on $100,000 dl grn	21.00	14.00
	Nos. 8-17 (10)	292.00	153.25

Shensi Province

China Nos. 747, 750 Surcharged

1949, May	Engr.	*Perf. 14*	
1 A82	On $500 bl grn	30.00	30.00
2 A82	On $3000 blue	30.00	30.00

AIR POST STAMP

Similar Surcharge on China No. 754

1949, May	Engr.	*Perf. 14*	
C1 A82	On $7000 lt red brn	35.00	35.00

SPECIAL DELIVERY STAMP

Similar Surcharge on China No. 746 in Red

1949, May	Engr.	*Perf. 14*	
E1 A82	On $250 dp lil	40.00	40.00

REGISTRATION STAMPS

Similar Surcharge on China Nos. 626, 637 in Red

1949, May	Typo.	*Perf. 12*	
F1 A72	on $30 dp bl	40.00	40.00
F2 A73	on $30 dk bl	35.00	35.00

Szechwan Province

Re-engraved Issue of China, 1923, Overprinted

1933	Unwmk.	*Perf. 14*	
1 A29	1c orange	6.25	.60
2 A29	5c claret	6.25	.85
3 A30	50c deep green	19.00	4.00
	Nos. 1-3 (3)	31.50	5.45

The overprint reads "For use in Szechwan Province exclusively."

Same on Sun Yat-sen Issue of 1931-37 Type II

1933-34		*Perf. 12½*	
4 A37	2c olive grn	.60	.60
5 A37	5c green	14.00	1.40
6 A37	15c dk green	4.50	1.75
7 A37	15c scar ('34)	4.00	7.00
8 A37	25c ultra	3.50	1.10
9 A37	$1 org brn & dk brn	12.00	2.40
10 A37	$2 bl & org brn	30.00	4.00
11 A37	$5 dl red & blk	77.50	22.50
	Nos. 4-11 (8)	146.10	40.75

Same on Martyrs Issue of 1932-34

1933		*Perf. 14*	
12 A39	½c black brn	.50	.50
13 A40	1c orange	.75	.30
14 A39	2½c rose lilac	1.75	2.25
15 A48	3c deep brown	1.75	1.75
16 A45	8c brown org	1.10	.90
17 A46	10c dull violet	2.75	.30
18 A45	13c blue green	3.00	.60
19 A46	17c brown olive	3.25	.85
20 A47	20c brown red	5.00	.60
21 A48	30c brown violet	4.00	.60
22 A47	40c orange	8.25	.60
23 A40	50c green	22.50	1.25
	Nos. 12-23 (12)	54.60	10.50

Stamps of China, 1947-48, Surcharged

每重貳拾公分 蓉 國內平信郵資

1949	Engr.	*Perf. 14*	
24 A82	on $150 dk bl	47.50	35.00
25 A82	on $250 dp lil	47.50	35.00
26 A82	on $500 bl grn	14.00	8.50
27 A82	on $1000 red	35.00	27.50
28 A82	on $2000 ver	14.00	10.50
29 A82	on $3000 blue	14.00	10.50
30 A82	on $4000 gray	14.00	10.50
31 A82	on $5000 dk brn	35.00	*40.00*
32 A82	on $6000 rose lil	14.00	14.00
33 A82	on $7000 lt red brn	35.00	30.00
34 A82	on $10,000 dk bl & car	14.00	10.50
35 A82	on $20,000 rose pink	14.00	10.50
36 A82	on $30,000 choc	19.00	14.00
37 A82	on $50,000 grn & dk bl	19.00	17.00
38 A82	on $50,000 dp bl	19.00	14.00
39 A82	on $100,000 dl yel & ol	19.00	14.00
40 A82	on $100,000 dl grn	19.00	17.00
41 A82	on $200,000 vio brn & dp bl	19.00	14.00
42 A82	on $200,000 brn vio	19.00	14.00
43 A82	on $300,000 sep & org brn	26.00	18.00
44 A82	on $300,000 yel grn	26.00	18.00
45 A82	on $500,000 dk Prus grn & sep	19.00	14.00
46 A82	on $1,000,000 claret	35.00	18.00
47 A82	on $2,000,000 ver	19.00	17.00
48 A82	on $3,000,000 ol bis	19.00	17.00
49 A82	on $5,000,000 ultra	70.00	45.00
	Nos. 24-49 (26)	645.00	493.50

Several of Nos. 24-49 exist with inverted surcharge and a few with bottom character of left row repeated in right row, same position.

Counterfeits exist.

China No. 737 Surcharged in Black

1949		*Perf. 12½*	
50 A77	2c on $500 ol grn	26.00	*35.00*

China No. 975 Handstamp Surcharged in Purple

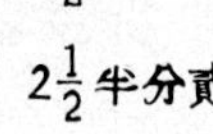

1949		Litho.	
51 A94	2½c on 4c bl grn	22.50	*27.50*

SZECHWAN AIR POST STAMPS

China Nos. C55-C58, C60-C61 Surcharged

Perf. 12½, 13x12½, 14

1949, July **Unwmk.**

No.	Type	Description	Unused	Used
C1	AP3	On $10,000 on 30c	6.00	6.00
a.		On #C54		500.00
C2	AP4	On $10,000 on $27	9.25	*12.50*
a.		Second surcharge inverted	250.00	
b.		On #C53	125.00	
C3	AP3	On $20,000 on 25c	9.25	*10.50*
C4	AP3	On $30,000 on 90c	7.25	*10.50*
C5	AP3	On $50,000 on 60c	85.00	*100.00*
C6	AP3	On $50,000 on $1	11.00	*15.00*
		Nos. C1-C6 (6)	127.75	*154.50*

On No. C2 characters of overprint are arranged in two horizontal rows, and two of four lines are vertical.

SZECHWAN REGISTRATION STAMPS

Stamps of China, 1944-47, Surcharged

Engraved; Typographed (A72)

1949 ***Perf. 12, 13, 14***

No.	Type	Description	Unused
F1	A64	On $100 yel brn	50.00
F2	A72	On $100 dk brn	50.00
F3	A64	On $200 dk grn	100.00
F4	A72	On $200 brn vio	50.00
F5	A73	On $200 ol grn	35.00
F6	A73	On $500 brt bl grn	100.00
F7	A73	On $700 red brn	175.00
F8	A73	On $5000 dp grn & ver	75.00
		Nos. F1-F8 (8)	635.00

PARCEL POST STAMP

China No. Q10 Surcharged

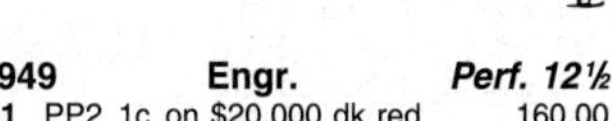

1949 **Engr.** ***Perf. 12½***

No.	Type	Description	Unused
Q1	PP2	1c on $20,000 dk red	160.00

No. Q1 is also found with surcharged value repeated in 5 characters at top of stamp.

Tsingtau Province

China Nos. 890, 903, 945, 894 Handstamp Surcharged in Purple (#1-2), Blue (#3) or Red (#4)

Engraved; Lithographed

1949, May ***Perf. 14, 12½***

No.	Type	Description	Unused	Used
1	A94	1c on $100 org brn	67.50	60.00
2	A94	4c on $5000 lt bl	67.50	60.00
3	A94	6c on $500 rose lil	67.50	60.00
4	A94	10c on $1000 bl	67.50	60.00
		Nos. 1-4 (4)	270.00	240.00

Yunnan Province

Stamps of China, 1923-26, Overprinted

The overprint reads "For exclusive use in the Province of Yunnan." It was applied to prevent stamps being purchased in the depreciated currency of Yunnan and used elsewhere.

1926 **Unwmk.** ***Perf. 14***

No.	Type	Description	Unused	Used
1	A29	½c blk brn	1.10	.20
2	A29	1c orange	1.10	.20
3	A29	1½c violet	2.40	2.40
4	A29	2c yellow grn	1.75	.30
5	A29	3c blue green	1.75	.20
6	A29	4c olive grn	2.25	.30
7	A29	5c claret	2.25	.30
8	A29	6c red	3.25	.70
9	A29	7c violet	3.50	1.10
10	A29	8c brown org	3.00	.80
11	A29	10c dark blue	1.90	.20
12	A30	13c brown	1.10	1.10
13	A30	15c dark blue	1.10	1.10
14	A30	16c olive grn	2.25	1.10
15	A30	20c brown red	5.25	1.90
16	A30	30c brown vio	3.25	3.25
17	A30	50c deep green	3.50	3.25
18	A31	$1 org brn & sep	13.00	8.00
19	A31	$2 blue & red brn	22.50	8.00
20	A31	$5 red & slate	150.00	150.00
		Nos. 1-20 (20)	226.20	184.40

Unification Issue of China, 1929, Overprinted in Red

1929 ***Perf. 14***

No.	Type	Description	Unused	Used
21	A35	1c brown org	1.10	1.10
22	A35	4c olive grn	2.25	*3.50*
23	A35	10c dark blue	4.00	*5.50*
24	A35	$1 dark red	70.00	55.00
		Nos. 21-24 (4)	77.35	65.10

Similar Overprint in Black on Sun Yat-sen Mausoleum Issue

Characters 15½-16mm apart

No.	Type	Description	Unused	Used
25	A36	1c brown orange	1.10	.85
26	A36	4c olive green	1.10	*2.25*
27	A36	10c dark blue	3.25	5.00
28	A36	$1 dark red	45.00	*40.00*
		Nos. 25-28 (4)	50.45	*48.10*

London Print Issue of China, 1931-37, Overprinted

1932-34 **Unwmk.** ***Perf. 12½***

Type I (double circle)

No.	Type	Description	Unused	Used
29	A37	1c orange	2.50	1.75
30	A37	2c olive grn	3.00	*3.50*
31	A37	4c green	2.00	*3.50*
32	A37	20c ultra	2.00	*2.00*
33	A37	$1 org brn & dk brn	30.00	*35.00*
34	A37	$2 bl & org brn	50.00	*55.00*
35	A37	$5 dl red & blk	150.00	*190.00*
		Nos. 29-35 (7)	239.50	*290.75*

Type II (single circle)

No.	Type	Description	Unused	Used
36	A37	2c olive grn	17.00	17.00
37	A37	4c green	11.00	7.00
38	A37	5c green	10.00	6.75
39	A37	15c dk green	5.25	*5.75*
40	A37	15c scar ('34)	5.25	*6.50*
41	A37	25c ultra	7.00	*7.50*
42	A37	$1 org brn & dk brn	45.00	45.00
43	A37	$2 bl & org brn	77.50	77.50
44	A37	$5 dl red & blk	175.00	175.00
		Nos. 36-44 (9)	353.00	348.00

Nos. 36-39, 41-44 were overprinted in London as well as in Peking. The London overprints are 11mm in length; the Peking overprints are 12mm in length. There are other minor differences. Value of London overprints is significantly more than the Peking overprints, which are valued above.

Tan Yuan-chang Issue of China, 1933, Overprinted

1933 ***Perf. 14***

No.	Type	Description	Unused	Used
45	A49	2c olive green	1.10	1.10
46	A49	5c green	1.90	1.50
47	A49	25c ultra	3.25	*3.50*
48	A49	$1 red	50.00	40.00
		Nos. 45-48 (4)	56.25	46.10

Martyrs Issue of China, 1932-34, Overprinted

1933

No.	Type	Description	Unused	Used
49	A39	½c blk brown	1.00	.90
50	A40	1c orange	2.00	1.50
51	A39	2½c rose lilac	2.25	2.50
52	A48	3c deep brown	3.50	1.25
53	A45	8c brown org	1.50	1.50
54	A46	10c dull vio	2.25	2.50
55	A45	13c blue grn	1.40	.60
56	A46	17c brn olive	7.00	7.00
57	A47	20c brown red	1.75	1.75
58	A48	30c brown vio	5.50	5.50
59	A47	40c orange	26.00	26.00
60	A40	50c green	26.00	26.00
		Nos. 49-60 (12)	80.15	77.00

China No. 324 was overprinted with characters arranged vertically, like Sinkiang No. 114, but was not issued.

China Stamps of 1945-49 Surcharged in Black or Blue

Engraved; Lithographed; Typographed

1949 ***Perf. 12, 12½, 14***

No.	Type	Description	Unused	Used
61	A82	1c on $200,000 brn vio	12.50	12.50
62	A82	1.2c on $40,000 grn	12.50	14.00
63	A94	6c on $200 red org	12.50	12.50
64	A94	10c on $20,000 org	12.50	14.00
65	A94	12c on $50 dk Prus grn (Bl)	12.50	12.50
66	A72	12c on $50 grnsh gray (Bl)	12.50	12.50
67	A72	12c on $200 brn vio (Bl)	12.50	14.00
68	A94	30c on $20 vio brn	12.50	12.50
69	A82	$1.20 on $100,000 dl grn	20.00	22.50
		Nos. 61-69 (9)	120.00	127.00

China No. 888 and 630 Surcharged

1949 **Engr.** ***Perf. 14***

No.	Type	Description	Unused
70	A94	4c on $20 vio brn	225.00

Typo. ***Perf. 12***

No.	Type	Description	Unused
71	A72	12c on $200 brn vio	225.00

Manchuria

Kirin and Heilungkiang Issue

Stamps of China, 1923-26, Overprinted

The overprint reads: "For use in Ki-Hei District" the two names being abbreviated.

The intention of the overprint was to prevent the purchase of stamps in Manchuria, where the currency was depreciated, and their resale elsewhere.

1927 **Unwmk.** ***Perf. 14***

No.	Type	Description	Unused	Used
1	A29	½c black brn	1.10	.20
2	A29	1c orange	1.10	.20
3	A29	1½c violet	1.50	1.10
4	A29	2c yellow grn	1.50	.20
5	A29	3c blue grn	1.00	.45
6	A29	4c olive grn	.50	.20
7	A29	5c claret	1.00	.20
8	A29	6c red	1.50	1.10
9	A29	7c violet	3.00	1.10
10	A29	8c brown org	2.00	1.10
11	A29	10c dk blue	1.10	.30
12	A30	13c brown	2.25	1.75
13	A30	15c dk blue	2.25	1.75
14	A30	16c olive grn	2.25	1.60
15	A30	20c brown red	3.50	1.90
16	A30	30c brown vio	5.00	2.00
17	A30	50c dp green	7.00	2.40
18	A31	$1 org brn & sep	15.00	5.00
19	A31	$2 bl & red brn	40.00	11.00
20	A31	$5 red & slate	190.00	190.00
		Nos. 1-20 (20)	282.55	223.55

Several values of this issue exist with inverted overprint, double overprint and in pairs with one overprint omitted. These "errors" were not regularly issued. Forgeries also exist.

Chang Tso-lin Stamps of 1928 Overprinted in Red or Blue

1928 ***Perf. 14***

No.	Type	Description	Unused	Used
21	A34	1c brown org (R)	1.75	1.10
22	A34	4c olive grn (R)	1.10	1.10
23	A34	10c dull blue (R)	3.00	2.25
24	A34	$1 red (Bl)	30.00	27.50
		Nos. 21-24 (4)	35.85	31.95

Unification Issue of China, 1929, Overprinted in Red as in 1928

1929

No.	Type	Description	Unused	Used
25	A35	1c brown orange	1.25	1.25
26	A35	14c olive green	2.25	2.00
27	A35	10c dark blue	8.00	7.50
28	A35	$1 dark red	65.00	*60.00*
		Nos. 25-28 (4)	76.50	*70.75*

Similar Overprint in Black on Sun Yat-sen Mausoleum Issue of China

Characters 15-16mm apart

1929 ***Perf. 14***

No.	Type	Description	Unused	Used
29	A36	1c brown orange	1.40	*1.60*
30	A36	4c olive green	1.75	*1.90*
31	A36	10c dark blue	5.25	3.25
32	A36	$1 dark red	52.50	40.00
		Nos. 29-32 (4)	60.90	46.75

Sinkiang

Stamps of China, 1913-19, Overprinted in Black or Red

The first character of overprint is ½mm out of alignment, to the left, and the overprint measures 16mm.

1915 **Unwmk.** ***Perf. 14***

No.	Type	Description	Unused	Used
1	A24	½c black brn	1.10	.60
2	A24	1c orange	1.10	.45
3	A24	2c yellow grn	1.50	.80
4	A24	3c slate grn	1.50	.40
5	A24	4c scarlet	3.00	.70
6	A24	5c rose lilac	2.25	.60
7	A24	6c gray	4.00	1.75
8	A24	7c violet	4.00	*5.25*
9	A24	8c brown orange	3.50	3.50
10	A24	10c dark blue	3.50	1.75
11	A25	15c brown	4.00	2.25
12	A25	16c olive grn	8.00	5.75
13	A25	20c brown red	8.00	4.50
14	A25	30c brown violet	9.00	7.00
15	A25	50c deep green	25.00	11.50

16 A26 $1 ocher & blk (R) 90.00 40.00
a. Second & third characters of overprint transposed 7,500.
Nos. 1-16 (16) 169.45 86.80

Stamps of China, 1913-19, Overprinted in Black or Red

The five characters of overprint are correctly aligned and measure 15½mm.

1916-19

17 A24 ½c black brn 1.25 1.50
18 A24 1c orange 2.00 1.10
19 A24 1½c violet 2.75 2.50
20 A24 2c yellow grn 2.00 1.10
21 A24 3c slate grn 3.50 .45
22 A24 4c scarlet 3.50 .75
23 A24 5c rose lilac 3.50 .55
24 A24 6c gray 5.00 .75
25 A24 7c violet 5.00 7.00
26 A24 8c brown org 5.50 5.25
27 A24 10c dark blue 5.50 .75
28 A25 13c brown 3.00 5.00
29 A25 15c brown 3.75 5.25
30 A25 16c olive grn 3.50 2.50
31 A25 20c brown red 2.75 1.90
32 A25 30c brown vio 4.25 3.75
33 A25 50c deep green 5.75 3.50
34 A26 $1 ocher & blk (R) 18.00 6.75
35 A26 $2 dk bl & blk (R) 17.50 7.50
36 A26 $5 scar & blk (R) 67.50 24.00
37 A26 $10 yel grn & blk (R) 175.00 110.00
38 A26 $20 yel & blk (R) 900.00 550.00
Nos. 17-38 (22) 1,240. 741.85

For overprint see No. C4.

China Nos. 243-246 Overprinted

1921 *Perf. 14*

39 A27 1c orange 1.10 1.10
40 A27 3c blue green 2.25 2.25
41 A27 6c gray 8.50 6.00
42 A27 10c blue 50.00 50.00
Nos. 39-42 (4) 61.85 59.35

Constitution Issue of China, 1923, Overprinted

1923

43 A32 1c orange 3.75 3.75
44 A32 3c blue green 4.25 4.25
45 A32 4c red 6.25 6.25
46 A32 10c blue 17.50 17.50
Nos. 43-46 (4) 31.75 31.75

Stamps of China, 1923-26, Overprinted as in 1916-19, in Black or Red

1924

Re-engraved

47 A29 ½c black brn .90 1.75
48 A29 1c orange .90 .70
49 A29 1½c violet 1.60 3.00
50 A29 2c yellow grn 2.50 .85
51 A29 3c blue grn 2.50 .75
52 A29 4c gray 2.50 4.00
53 A29 5c claret .85 .60
54 A29 6c red 4.50 1.60
55 A29 7c violet 5.00 4.50
56 A29 8c org brn 10.00 9.00
57 A29 10c dark blue 4.00 1.10
58 A30 13c red brown 3.50 5.00
59 A30 15c deep blue 5.25 4.00
60 A30 16c olive grn 6.00 5.75
61 A30 20c brown red 5.00 3.75
62 A30 30c brown vio 5.75 4.00
63 A30 50c deep green 6.00 4.00
64 A31 $1 org brn & sep (R) 10.50 5.00
65 A31 $2 bl & red brn (R) 22.50 7.25
66 A31 $5 red & slate (R) 57.50 19.00
67 A31 $10 grn & claret (R) 175.00 100.00
68 A31 $20 plum & bl (R) 250.00 190.00
Nos. 47-68 (22) 582.25 375.60

See #69, 114. For overprints see #C1-C3.

Same Overprint on China No. 275

1926

69 A29 4c olive green 2.50 2.50

Chang Tso-lin Stamps of China, 1928, Overprinted in Red or Blue

1928 *Perf. 14*

70 A34 1c brn org (R) 1.10 1.10
71 A34 4c ol grn (R) 1.75 1.75
72 A34 10c dull bl (R) 4.00 4.00
73 A34 $1 red (Bl) 35.00 30.00
Nos. 70-73 (4) 41.85 36.85

Unification Issue of China, 1929, Overprinted in Red as in 1928

1929

74 A35 1c brown org 1.75 1.75
75 A35 4c olive grn 3.00 3.00
76 A35 10c dk blue 7.00 7.00
77 A35 $1 dk red 55.00 45.00
Nos. 74-77 (4) 66.75 56.75

Similar Overprint in Black on Sun Yat-sen Mausoleum Issue of China Characters 15mm apart

1929 *Perf. 14*

78 A36 1c brown org 1.10 1.10
79 A36 4c olive grn 1.65 1.75
80 A36 10c dark blue 3.75 4.00
81 A36 $1 dark red 47.50 37.50
Nos. 78-81 (4) 54.00 44.35

Stamps of Sun Yat-sen Issue of 1931-37 Overprinted

1932 **Type I** *Perf. 12½*

82 A37 1c orange 1.00 2.25
83 A37 2c olive grn 2.50 3.50
84 A37 4c green 1.50 3.75
85 A37 20c ultra 2.25 4.75
86 A37 $1 org brn & dk brn 7.00 11.50
87 A37 $2 bl & org brn 20.00 24.00
88 A37 $5 dl red & blk 22.50 35.00
Nos. 82-88 (7) 56.75 84.75

No. 83 was overprinted in Shanghai in 1938. The overprint differs in minor details.

1932-38

Type II

89 A37 2c olive grn .25 1.10
90 A37 4c green .70 2.25
91 A37 5c green .45 2.25
92 A37 15c dk green .60 2.25
93 A37 15c scar ('34) .60 2.25
93A A37 20c ultra ('38) .45 1.50
94 A37 25c ultra .70 2.25
95 A37 $1 org brn & dk brn 5.25 6.00
96 A37 $2 bl & org brn 11.00 17.50
97 A37 $5 dl red & blk 22.50 35.00
Nos. 89-97 (10) 42.50 72.35

Nos. 89, 90 and 94 were overprinted in London, Peking and Shanghai. Nos. 92, 95-97 exist with London and Peking overprints. Nos. 91 and 93 exist with Peking and Shanghai overprints. No. 93A is a Shanghai overprint. The overprints differ in minor details.

Tan Yuan-chang Issue of China, 1933, Overprinted as in 1928

1933 *Perf. 14*

98 A49 2c olive grn 2.40 2.40
99 A49 5c green 3.00 3.00
100 A49 25c ultra 9.50 9.50
101 A49 $1 red 47.50 40.00
Nos. 98-101 (4) 62.40 54.90

Stamps of China Martyrs Issue of 1932-34 Overprinted

1933-34

102 A39 ½c black brown .20 1.25
103 A40 1c orange 1.10 1.50
104 A39 2½c rose lilac .25 1.10
105 A48 3c deep brown .25 1.10
106 A45 8c brown orange .75 1.25
107 A46 10c dull violet .25 1.10
108 A45 13c blue green .25 1.60
109 A46 17c brown olive .25 .90
110 A47 20c brown red 1.10 2.25
111 A48 30c brown violet .40 1.60
112 A47 40c orange .60 1.10
113 A40 50c green .70 2.25
Nos. 102-113 (12) 6.10 17.00

Nos. 102-113 were originally overprinted in Peking. In 1938, Nos. 103-105, 108-112 were overprinted in Shanghai. The two overprints differ in minor details. No. 105, Shanghai overprint, is scarce. Value $35.

China No. 324 Overprinted as in 1916-19

1936 *Perf. 14*

114 A29 6c brown 11.50 12.00

Stamps of China, 1939-40 Overprinted in Black

1940-45 **Unwmk.** *Perf. 12½*

Type III

115 A57 2c olive green .85 1.00
116 A57 3c dull claret ('41) .20 1.50
117 A57 5c green .20 1.50
118 A57 5c olive green .20 1.50
119 A57 8c olive green ('41) .20 .75
120 A57 10c green ('41) .20 1.10
121 A57 15c scarlet .55 2.50
122 A57 16c olive gray ('41) .40 1.00
123 A57 25c dark blue .55 2.75
124 A57 $1 hn & dk brn (type II) 6.25 11.00
125 A57 $2 dp bl & org brn (type I) 4.50 11.00
126 A57 $5 red & grnsh blk 26.00 32.50
Nos. 115-126 (12) 40.10 68.10

Perf. 14

With Secret Marks

127 A57 8c ol grn (#383a) 1.10 1.65
a. On #383 19.00 22.50
128 A57 10c green ('41) 10.00 13.00
129 A57 30c scarlet ('45) .30 1.10
130 A57 50c dk blue ('45) .55 1.75
131 A57 $1 org brn & sep .55 2.25
132 A57 $2 dp bl & org brn .55 2.25
133 A57 $5 red & sl grn .65 3.75
134 A57 $10 dk grn & dl pur 1.90 2.75
135 A57 $20 rose lake & dk bl 3.50 5.50
Nos. 127-135 (9) 19.10 34.00

Wmk. Character Yu (Post) (261)

Perf. 14

136 A57 5c olive green .20 1.10
137 A57 10c green .25 1.75
138 A57 30c scarlet .25 2.25
139 A57 50c dark blue .30 1.10
Nos. 136-139 (4) 1.00 6.20

Martyrs Issue, 1940-41, Overprinted in Black

Perf. 12, 12½, 13, 13x12, 13½x13

1941-45 **Wmk. 261**

140 A40 1c orange .20 .65
141 A39 2½c rose lilac .20 1.25
142 A45 8c dp org ('45) 3.25 3.25
143 A46 10c dull vio .25 .85
144 A45 13c dp yel grn .55 1.50
145 A46 17c brown olive .55 1.40
146 A40 25c red vio ('45) 1.10 2.00
147 A47 40c orange ('45) 1.90 2.50
Nos. 140-147 (8) 8.00 13.40

Unwmk.

148 A39 ½c olive blk .20 .85
149 A40 1c orange ('45) .20 .65
150 A46 2c dp blue ('45) 1.75 1.00
151 A48 3c dp yel brn .20 1.25
152 A39 4c pale vio ('45) .20 1.25
153 A45 8c dp orange .20 1.50
154 A45 13c dp yel grn ('45) .35 1.10
155 A48 15c brn car ('45) .20 1.10
156 A46 17c brn ol ('45) .20 1.25
157 A47 20c lt blue ('45) .20 .90
158 A45 21c ol brn ('45) .65 1.25
159 A46 28c olive ('45) .80 1.50
160 A47 40c orange ('45) 1.65 3.75
161 A40 50c green ('45) 1.10 1.90
Nos. 148-161 (14) 8.25 19.25

Stamps of China, 1942-43 Overprinted in Carmine, Black or Red

1944 *Perf. 12½, 13*

Without Gum

162 A62 10c dp grn (C) 1.10 2.75
163 A62 20c dk ol grn (C) 1.25 2.75
164 A62 25c violet brn .20 3.00
165 A62 30c dk orange .60 3.25
166 A62 40c red brown .20 3.00
167 A62 50c sage green .20 1.75
a. Perf. 11 10.00 8.50
168 A62 $1 rose lake 2.25 1.75
169 A62 $1 dull green .20 3.00
170 A62 $1.50 dp bl (C) .20 3.25
171 A62 $2 dk bl grn (R) 1.50 2.50
172 A62 $3 yellow .20 4.25
173 A62 $5 cerise 1.50 4.00
Nos. 162-173 (12) 9.40 35.25

For surcharges see Nos. 194-195.

Same Overprint on Stamps of China, 1942-43, in Black

1944-46 *Imperf.*

174 A57 $10 red brown 50.00 67.50
175 A57 $20 rose red 1.90 7.25
176 A57 $30 dull vio 1.25 7.25
177 A57 $40 rose red 1.90 8.00
178 A57 $50 blue ('46) 625.00 675.00
179 A57 $100 orange brn 2.50 8.00

Perf. 13½

180 A57 $4 dp blue .20 4.00
181 A57 $5 lilac gray .30 4.50
182 A57 $10 red brn .30 4.50
183 A57 $20 blue grn .90 5.00
184 A57 $20 rose red 85.00 80.00
185 A57 $30 dull vio 1.25 5.50
186 A57 $40 rose 1.25 6.00
187 A57 $50 blue 1.60 5.00
188 A57 $100 orange brn 67.50 67.50
Nos. 174-177,179-188 (14) 215.85 280.00

Beware of trimmed copies of Nos. 182 and 187 offered as Nos, 174 and 178.

Nos. 162 and 164 Surcharged in Black

1944, Aug. 1

194 A62 12c on 10c dp grn 1.40 3.50
195 A62 24c on 25c brn vio 2.00 3.25

Stamps of China, 1940-41, Overprinted in Black at Chengtu, Szechwan 用貼省新限

1943

196 A57 10c green (#354) 15.00 30.00
197 A47 20c lt blue (#433) 15.00 30.00

Wmk. 261 *Perf. 14*

198 A57 50c dk blue (#396) 15.00 30.00

China Nos. 565 and 567 Overprinted in Black

1945 **Unwmk.** *Perf. 12½*

200 A63 40c brown red .30 .65
201 A63 $3 red .30 .65

China Nos. 640-642, 788, 751, 753 Surcharged in Black or Red

1949 **Engr.** *Perf. 14*

202 A73 1c on $100 dk car 19.00 22.50
203 A73 3c on $200 ol grn (R) 19.00 22.50

204	A73	5c on $500 brt bl grn (R)	19.00	*22.50*
205	A82	10c on $20,000 rose pink	16.00	*20.00*
206	A82	50c on $4000 gray (R)	62.50	62.50
207	A82	$1 on $6000 rose lil	72.50	72.50
		Nos. 202-207 (6)	208.00	*222.50*

AIR POST STAMPS

Sinkiang Nos. 53, 57, 59, 32 Overprinted in Red

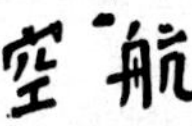

1932-33 Unwmk. *Perf. 14*

C1	A29	5c claret ('33)	150.	85.
C2	A29	10c dark blue ('33)	150.	70.
C3	A30	15c deep blue	1,000.	250.
C4	A25	30c brown violet	375.	300.

Counterfeits exist of Nos. C1-C19.

Air Post Stamps of China, 1932-37 Handstamped in Dull Red

1942

C5	AP3	15c gray green	4.25	*5.50*
C6	AP3	25c orange	250.00	225.00
C7	AP3	30c red	10.00	*16.00*
C8	AP3	45c brown vio	6.25	*10.50*
C9	AP3	50c dk brown	26.00	*30.00*
C10	AP3	60c dk blue	6.25	*13.00*
C11	AP3	90c olive grn	35.00	*47.50*
C12	AP3	$1 yellow grn	7.25	*11.50*
		Nos. C5-C12 (8)	345.00	*359.00*

Same Handstamped Overprint on Air Post Stamps of China, 1940-41 in Dull Red

1942 Wmk. 261 *Perf. 12½, 13, 13½*

C13	AP3	15c gray green	3.25	*4.00*
C14	AP3	25c yellow orange	3.25	*4.00*

1942 Unwmk.

C15	AP3	25c light orange	2.75	2.75
C16	AP3	30c light red	4.00	4.00
C17	AP3	50c brown	5.50	5.50
C18	AP3	$2 light brown	26.00	26.00
C19	AP3	$5 lake	26.00	26.00
		Nos. C15-C19 (5)	64.25	64.25

Twelve values exist with this overprint in black. Their status has not been determined. Inverted overprints exist in both red and black.

Official Perforated Characters

For use on official mail, various Sinkiang stamps were perforated with an arrangement of four Chinese characters ("For Official Business Only"). These include Nos. 1-38, 47-69, 114.

OFFICES IN TIBET

12 Pies = 1 Anna
16 Annas = 1 Rupee

Stamps of China, Issues of 1902-10, Surcharged

1911 Unwmk. *Perf. 12 to 16*

1	A17	3p on 1c ocher	15.00	*27.50*
a.		Inverted surcharge	*3,500.*	
2	A17	½a on 2c grn	15.00	*27.50*
3	A17	1a on 4c ver	15.00	*27.50*
4	A17	2a on 7c mar	15.00	*27.50*
5	A17	2½a on 10c ultra	20.00	*32.50*
6	A18	3a on 16c ol grn	40.00	*50.00*
a.		Large "S" in "Annas"	*1,250.*	
7	A18	4a on 20c red brn	40.00	*50.00*
8	A18	6a on 30c rose red	60.00	*72.50*
9	A18	12a on 50c yel grn	175.00	*250.00*
10	A19	1r on $1 red & pale rose	475.00	*600.00*
11	A19	2r on $2 red & yel	900.00	*1,200.*
		Nos. 1-11 (11)	1,770.	2,365.

CHINA, PEOPLE'S REPUBLIC OF

ˈpē-pəls ri-ˈpə-blik of ˈchī-nə

LOCATION — Eastern Asia
GOVT. — Communist Republic
POP. — 1,246,871,951 (1999 est.)
CAPITAL — Beijing (Peking)

The communists completed their conquest of all mainland China in 1949. They established the Central Government and General Postal Administration in Peking. They ordered all but two regions to stop selling regional issues by June 30, 1950, extending validity one year from that date. The Northeast and Port Arthur-Dairen regions were exempted because their currency had a different value. These two regions stopped using separate issues at the end of 1950. Thereafter unified issues were used throughout mainland China.

On July 1, 1997 Hong Kong returned to Chinese control as an administrative district. Hong Kong stamps issued under Chinese rule will continue to be listed under "Hong Kong."

Reprints

After currency revaluation Mar. 1, 1955, reprints were prepared and put on sale by the Philatelic Agency in order to supply stocks of exhausted issues for collectors. Minor differences in design or paper distinguish the reprints. They are of commemorative and special issues up to the gymnastics set of 1952. Reprints are less expensive. Values are for original issues. Reprint distinctions are footnoted.

Used Stamps

Most used stamps before 1970 exist primarily canceled to order. Postally used copies generally sell for ½ the unused value.

Beginning in 1987 the PRC stopped furnishing quantities of used stamps to the philatelic market. When available, used stamps of these issues sell for the same or more than unused copies.

PRC Issue Numbers

Commemorative issues, beginning in 1949, and special issues, beginning in 1951, bear 4 numbers in lower margin: 1. Issue number. 2. Total of stamps in set. 3. Position of stamp in set. 4. Cumulative number of stamp (usually in parenthesis). A fifth number, the year of issue, was added in 1952.

The numbering system varies at times, with all numbers omitted on Scott 938-1046.

In certain sets listings include parenthetically the position-in-set number. During some periods these parentheses in listings hold the stamp's cumulative number. Issue numbers are noted when one or more designs are not illustrated.

Gum

All stamps to the beginning of 1960 were issued without gum, except as noted. After that date, most stamps have gum, which is translucent and almost invisible. All issues are unwatermarked, unless otherwise noted.

100 fen = 1 yuan ($)

Catalogue values for unused stamps in this country are for Never Hinged items, beginning with Scott 487 in the regular postage section, Scott B1 in the semi-postal section.

Syncopated Perforations

Type A (1st stamp #2880): On the two shorter sides, an oval hole equal in width to three holes is centered.

Lantern and Gate of Heavenly Peace — A1

Globe and Hand Holding Hammer — A2

1949, Oct. 8 Litho. *Perf. 12½*

No.	Type	Value	Color	Unused	Used
1	A1	$30	blue	1.75	1.50
2	A1	$50	rose red	1.75	1.50
3	A1	$100	green	1.75	1.50
4	A1	$200	maroon	1.75	1.50
			Nos. 1-4 (4)	7.00	6.00

1st session of Chinese People's Consultative Political Conference. See #1L121-1L124.

Original

Reprint

Reprints have altered ornament on lantern base. On originals, it is a full oval; in reprints, only a partial circle. Value, set, $1.25 used or unused.

1949, Nov. 16

No.	Type	Value	Color	Unused	Used
5	A2	$100	carmine	5.50	2.50
6	A2	$300	slate green	5.50	2.50
7	A2	$500	dark blue	5.50	2.50
			Nos. 5-7 (3)	16.50	7.50

Asiatic and Australasian Congress of the World Federation of Trade Unions, Peking.

The $100, imperf., is of dubious status.

See Nos. 1L133-1L135.

Original

Reprint

Reprints show heavier shading on index finger and thumb. Value, set $5.00 unused or $2.40 used.

Conference Hall, Peking — A3

Mao Tse-tung on Rostrum A4

1950, Feb. 1 Engr. *Perf. 14*

No.	Type	Value	Color	Unused	Used
8	A3	$50	red	3.25	3.00
9	A3	$100	blue	3.25	3.00
10	A4	$300	red brown	3.25	2.75
11	A4	$500	green	3.25	2.75
			Nos. 8-11 (4)	13.00	11.50

Chinese People's Consultative Political Conference. See Nos. 1L136-1L139.

Original

Reprint

Nos. 8-9: First character in top inscription shows a square, reprints an oblong.

Nos. 10-11: Originals have heavy cross-hatching and lines which touch back of head and top of rostrum. Reprints have lighter lines which do not touch head or top of rostrum. Reprints, value set $4.75.

Gate of Heavenly Peace (actual size) — A5

First Issue: Top line of shading broken at right.

1950, Feb. 10 Litho. *Perf. 12½*

No.	Type	Value	Color	Unused	Used
12	A5	$200	green	5.25	1.10
13	A5	$300	brown red	.20	.90
14	A5	$500	red	.20	.20
15	A5	$800	orange	65.00	.75
16	A5	$1000	dull violet	1.25	.35
17	A5	$2000	olive	7.00	.90
18	A5	$5000	brt pink	.20	.90
19	A5	$8000	blue	.20	2.75
20	A5	$10,000	brown	.60	1.10
			Nos. 12-20 (9)	79.90	8.95

1950, June 9 Typo.

Second Issue: Top line of shading extends to frame line at right.

No.	Type	Value	Color	Unused	Used
21	A5	$1000	dull violet	1.10	.20
22	A5	$3000	red brown	1.10	.20
23	A5	$10,000	brown	1.10	.20
			Nos. 21-23 (3)	3.30	.60

Other Gate of Heavenly Peace issues are illustrated where they are listed. See A10, A13, A14 and A42 for similar designs.

For similar types with Chinese characters in upper right corner see Northeast China A28, A29, Port Arthur & Darien A11, North China A8.

China Nos. 959, C62, E12, F2 Surcharged in Blue, Black, Green or Red

Rouletted, Perf. 12½ (#27, 29)

1950, Mar. Litho.

No.	Type	Value	Description	Unused	Used
24	SD2	$100	on red vio (Bl)	.25	.85
a.			Perf. 12½	6.75	3.00
25	R2	$200	on red (Bk)	2.50	.60
a.			Perf. 12½	35.00	3.50
26	AP5	$300	on bl grn (Bk)	.25	.85
a.			Perf. 12½	.65	1.00
27	A96	$500	on org (Bk)	.20	.30
a.			Perf. 14	65.00	55.00
28	A96	$800	on org (R)	2.50	.20
a.			Perf. 12½	22.50	2.50
b.			Perf. 14	*800.00*	67.50
29	A96	$1000	on org (Bk)	.20	.20
a.			Perf. 14	.20	.20
			Nos. 24-29 (6)	5.90	3.00

No. 27 exists with green surcharge.

Harvesters with Ox — A6

1950, May

No.	Type	Value	Description	Unused	Used
30	A6	$20,000	on $10,000 red	475.00	42.50

No. 30 is surcharged on an unissued stamp of East China.

Flag, Mao Tse-tung, Gate of Heavenly Peace — A7

1950, July 1 *Perf. 14*

Yellow Stars

No.	Type	Value	Color	Unused	Used
31	A7	$800	green & red	16.00	6.50
32	A7	$1000	brn & red	18.00	6.50
33	A7	$2000	dk brn & red	25.00	6.00
34	A7	$3000	dk blue & red	32.50	8.00
			Nos. 31-34 (4)	91.50	27.00

Inauguration of the People's Republic, Oct. 1, 1949. See Nos. 1L150-1L153.

Original

Reprint

Originals have a single curved line in jacket button, reprints have an extra dot in button. Value, set $4.50.

Sun Yat-sen Stamps of Northeastern Provinces Surcharged in Red, Black or Blue

1950, July 1 Engr.

No.	Type	Value	Description	Unused	Used
35	A2	$50	on 20c yel grn	3.50	*6.00*
36	A2	$50	on 25c blk brn	6.50	2.00
37	A2	$50	on 50c red org (Bk)	.55	1.00
38	A2	$100	on $2.50 ind	1.75	1.00
39	A2	$100	on $3 brn (Bk)	2.10	1.00
40	A2	$100	on $4 org brn, Type II (Bl)	1.40	*4.50*
a.			Type I	*800.00*	125.00

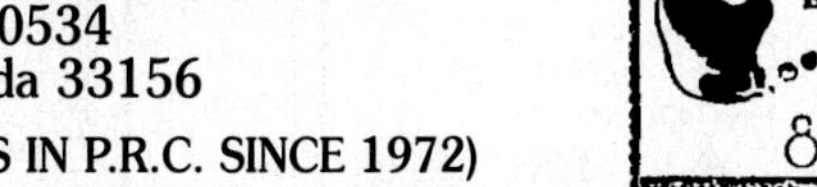

No.	Type	Description	Unused	Used
41	A2	$100 on $5 dk grn (Bk)	2.10	1.00
42	A2	$100 on $10 crim, Type II (Bl)	27.50	6.00
a.		Type I	*7,500.*	
43	A2	$400 on $20 ol, Type II (Bl)	57.50	6.00
a.		Type I	*900.00*	100.00
44	A2	$400 on $44 dk car rose (Bl)	1.10	3.00
45	A2	$400 on $65 dl grn	100.00	15.00
46	A2	$400 on $100 dp grn	24.00	3.00
47	A2	$400 on $200 rose brn (Bk)	110.00	4.00
48	A2	$400 on $300 bluish grn	110.00	4.00
		Nos. 35-48 (14)	448.00	57.50

Flying Geese Type of China Surcharged in Red, Blue, Green, Brown or Black

1950, Aug. 1 ***Perf. 12½, Imperf.***

No.	Type	Description	Unused	Used
49	A97	$50 on 10c dk bl (R)	.20	.35
50	A97	$100 on 16c ol, imperf. (Bl)	.20	.35
51	A97	$100 on 50c dl grn, imperf. (Bl)	.20	.20
52	A97	$200 on $1 org (G)	.20	.20
53	A97	$200 on $2 bl (Br)	6.00	.80
54	A97	$400 on $5 car rose (Bk)	.20	.35
55	A97	$400 on $10 bl grn (Bk)	.20	1.00
56	A97	$400 on $20 pur (Bk)	.20	*2.75*
		Nos. 49-56 (8)	7.40	6.00

Dove of Peace, by Picasso — A8

Chinese Flag and "1" — A9

1950, Aug. 1 **Engr.** ***Perf. 14***

No.	Type	Description	Unused	Used
57	A8	$400 brown	9.50	4.00
58	A8	$800 green	9.50	4.00
59	A8	$2000 blue	9.50	4.00
		Nos. 57-59 (3)	28.50	12.00

World Peace Campaign. See #1L154-1L156.

Paper of originals appears bright under ultraviolet lamp. That of reprints looks dull. Value, set $2.75.

1950 **Engr. & Litho.**

Flag in Red & Yellow

No.	Type	Description	Unused	Used
60	A9	$100 purple	11.00	3.25
61	A9	$400 red brown	17.00	3.25
62	A9	$800 green	17.00	3.25
63	A9	$1000 lt olive	22.50	6.75
64	A9	$2000 blue	32.50	8.25
		Nos. 60-64 (5)	100.00	24.75

1st anniv. of the Chinese People's Republic. Size of $800: 38x46mm; others 26x32mm.

Issue dates: No. 62, Oct. 1; others Oct. 31. See Nos. 1L157-1L161.

$800

Original

Reprint

Reprints are a brighter red, leaves beside "1" are gray brown instead of reddish brown. On the $800 the arrangement of dots in background differs in relationship to large star. Value, set $4.

Gate of Heavenly Peace (actual size) — A10

Third Issue: Cloud almost touches character at upper left. Cloud breaks inner frame line at top.

1950 **Litho.**

No.	Type	Description	Unused	Used
65	A10	$100 lt grnsh bl	32.50	7.00
66	A10	$200 green	350.00	8.75
67	A10	$300 dk carmine	2.50	*3.00*
68	A10	$400 grnsh gray	.90	*3.00*
69	A10	$500 carmine	.60	*3.25*
70	A10	$800 orange	5.00	.25
71	A10	$2000 gray olive	1.40	.40
		Nos. 65-71 (7)	392.90	*25.65*

Issued: $800, 10/8; $500, $2000, 12/1; others, 10/6.

"Communication" and Map of China — A11

1950, Nov. 1 **Litho.**

No.	Type	Description	Unused	Used
72	A11	$400 green & brn	9.50	3.75
73	A11	$800 carmine & grn	9.50	3.75

First All-China Postal Conference, Peking. See Nos. 1L162-1L163.

Original

Reprint

Originals have 3 lines below horizontal bar (2nd character); reprints have four. Value, set $1.25.

Stalin and Mao Tse-tung — A12

1950, Dec. 1 **Engr.** ***Perf. 14***

No.	Type	Description	Unused	Used
74	A12	$400 red	10.00	4.25
75	A12	$800 dp green	10.00	3.25
76	A12	$2000 dk blue	14.00	4.25
		Nos. 74-76 (3)	34.00	11.75

Signing of Sino-Soviet Treaty of Friendship, Alliance and Mutual Assistance. See Nos. 1L176-1L178.

Paper of originals appears bright under ultraviolet lamp. That of reprints looks dull. Value, set $2.75.

East China Issue of 1949 Surcharged in Red, Black, Brown or Blue

Train and Postal Runner — A12a

1950, Dec. **Litho.** ***Perf. 12½***

No.	Type	Description	Unused	Used
77	A12a	$50 on $10 dp ultra (R)	.20	.20
78	A12a	$100 on $15 org ver (Bk)	.20	.20
a.		$100 on $15 red (Bk), perf. 14	.20	.20
79	A12a	$300 on $50 car (Bk)	.20	.20
80	A12a	$400 on $1600 vio bl (Br)	2.00	.20
81	A12a	$400 on $2000 brn vio (Bl)	.85	.20
		Nos. 77-81 (5)	3.45	1.00

East China Issue of 1949 Surcharged in Red or Black

Chairman Mao — A12b

1950, Dec.

No.	Type	Description	Unused	Used
82	A12b	$50 on $10 ultra (R)	.25	.20
83	A12b	$400 on $15 ver (Bk)	.25	.20
84	A12b	$400 on $2000 grn (Bk)	1.75	.20
		Nos. 82-84 (3)	2.25	.60

(actual size) — A13

(actual size) — A14

Fourth Issue: Similar to 3rd issue, but large cloud does not break inner frame line at top.

1950-51 **Litho.**

No.	Type	Description	Unused	Used
85	A13	$100 lt blue	1.60	.75
86	A13	$200 dull green	1.75	.75
87	A13	$300 dull lilac	.40	*5.25*
88	A13	$400 gray grn	.40	*1.00*
89	A13	$500 carmine	.20	*1.10*
90	A13	$800 orange	80.00	1.00
a.		Imperf., pair	—	
91	A13	$1000 violet	.50	*.75*
92	A13	$2000 olive	300.00	3.50
93	A13	$3000 brown	.20	*6.00*
94	A13	$5000 pink	.20	*6.00*
		Nos. 85-94 (10)	385.25	*26.10*

Issued: $200, $300, $500, $800, $2000, $5000, 12/22/50; others 6/8/51.

1951, Jan. 18 **Engr.** ***Perf. 14***

Fifth Issue: Colored network on surface in salmon.

No.	Type	Description	Unused	Used
95	A14	$10,000 brown	1.40	*10.00*
96	A14	$20,000 olive	1.40	*8.25*
97	A14	$30,000 green	27.50	*40.00*
98	A14	$50,000 violet	90.00	17.00
99	A14	$100,000 scarlet	2,000.	175.00
100	A14	$200,000 blue	2,000.	175.00
		Nos. 95-100 (6)	4,120.	425.25

Unit Issue of China Surcharged

1951, May 2 **Litho.** ***Perf. 12½***

No.	Type	Description	Unused	Used
101	SD2	$5 on rose lilac	3.50	.50
102	AP5	$10 on brt grn	.25	.25
103	R2	$15 on red	.20	.25
104	A96	$25 on orange	.70	.25
		Nos. 101-104 (4)	4.65	1.25

Issued for use in Northeast China, but available for use throughout China. Nos. 101-104 rouletted were sold for philatelic purposes only. Value, set $2.75.

Chairman Mao Tse-tung — A15

1951, July 1 **Engr.** ***Perf. 14***

No.	Type	Description	Unused	Used
105	A15	$400 chestnut	4.50	1.25
106	A15	$500 deep green	4.50	1.25
107	A15	$800 crimson	4.50	1.25
		Nos. 105-107 (3)	13.50	3.75

Chinese Communist Party, 30th anniv.

Reprints are on whiter, thinner and harder paper. Value, set $2.50.

Picasso Dove — A16

1951, Aug. 15 ***Perf. 12½***

No.	Type	Description	Unused	Used
108	A16	$400 orange brn	12.00	4.50
109	A16	$800 blue grn	12.00	4.00
110	A16	$1000 dull vio	12.00	4.50
		Nos. 108-110 (3)	36.00	13.00

Reprints are perf 14. Value, set $9.

Remittance Stamp of China Surcharged in Carmine or Black

(same size) — A17

Engraved, Commercial Press

1951, Sept. ***Perf. 12½***

111	A17	$50 on $2 bl grn (C)	.30	*1.00*

Typo., Kang Hwa Printing Co.

Rouletted 9½

112	A17	$50 on $2 gray bl (C)	.85	*7.00*
113	A17	$50 on $5 red org (Bk)	.20	*1.00*
114	A17	$50 on $50 gray (C)	8.00	*4.00*

Lithographed, Central Trust Co.

Perf. 13

115	A17	$50 on $50 gray blk (C)	.20	*.40*

Lithographed, Chung Hwa Book Co.

Perf. 11½x10

116	A17	$50 on $50 gray (C)	2.00	.75
a.		Perf. 11½	1.00	1.00
		Nos. 111-116 (6)	11.55	*14.15*

National Emblem — A18

Engraved; Background Network Lithographed in Yellow

1951, Oct. 1 ***Perf. 14***

117	A18	$100 Prus blue	5.00	3.00
118	A18	$200 brown	5.00	3.00
119	A18	$400 orange	5.00	4.00
120	A18	$500 green	5.00	1.50
121	A18	$800 carmine	5.00	1.50
		Nos. 117-121 (5)	25.00	13.00

Reprints exist but are difficult to distinguish; paper whiter, and colors slightly brighter. Value, set $4.

Rough Perfs

Rough perforations are normal on many early issues. These include Nos. 122-123, 136-140, 155-176, 239-240, 299-300, 453-456, 467-482, 629-634, 684-707, 737-745 and probably others.

Lu Hsun and Quotation — A19

1951, Oct. 19 **Litho.** ***Perf. 12½***

122	A19	$400 lilac	3.75	3.00
123	A19	$800 green	5.25	1.50

15th anniversary of the death of Lu Hsun (1881-1936), writer.

Original / Reprint

Reprints have dot in triangle at lower right; no dot in original. Value, set 75 cents.

Peasant Uprising, Chintien — A20

Design: Nos. 126-127, Coin of Taiping Regime and decrees of peasant government.

1951, Dec. 15 **Engr.** ***Perf. 14***

124	A20	$400 green	5.75	5.00
125	A20	$800 scarlet	5.75	3.00
126	A20	$800 orange	5.75	4.00
127	A20	$1000 deep blue	5.75	3.00
		Nos. 124-127 (4)	23.00	15.00

Centenary of Taiping Peasant Rebellion.

Original

Reprint

Reprints of Nos. 124-125 have additional short stroke at upper left.

Original

Reprint

Reprints of Nos. 126-127 have two short strokes on scale near tail of right dragon on coin. Value, Nos. 124-127, $1.40.

Old and New Methods of Agriculture — A21

1952, Jan. 1

128	A21	$100 scarlet	4.00	2.50
129	A21	$200 bright blue	4.00	2.50
130	A21	$400 deep brown	4.00	1.65
131	A21	$800 green	4.00	1.65
		Nos. 128-131 (4)	16.00	8.30

Agrarian reform.

Original

Reprint

One short horizontal line between legs of plower; 2 lines in reprints. Value, set $1.10.

Potala Monastery, Lhasa — A22

Nos. 134-135, Farmer plowing with yaks.

1952, Mar. 15 ***Perf. 12½***

132	A22	$400 vermilion	5.00	2.50
133	A22	$800 claret	5.00	2.50
134	A22	$800 blue grn	5.00	1.60
135	A22	$1000 dull vio	5.00	1.60
		Nos. 132-135 (4)	20.00	8.20

Liberation of Tibet.

Reprints, perf 14, have a small Chinese character at lower left of the vignette which is missing in the original. Value, set $1.40.

Children of Four Races A23

Hammer and Sickle on Numeral 1 A24

1952, Apr. 12 **Litho.**

136 A23 $400 dull grn .45 .30
137 A23 $800 vio blue .45 .30

Intl. Child Protection Conf., Vienna.

1952, May 1

Labor Day: #139, Dove rising from worker's hand. #140, Dove, hammer, wheat & chimneys.

138 A24 $800 scarlet .20 .20
139 A24 $800 blue grn .20 .20
140 A24 $800 orange brn .50 .20
Nos. 138-140 (3) .90 .60

Physical Exercises — A25

Stamps printed in blocks of four for each color, each block representing a specific setting-up exercise; exercises coincided with a national radio program. Where exercise positions are identical within the block, the serial number (in parenthesis) is the only means of differentiation.

1952, June 20

141 A25 Block of 4 25.00 25.00
a. $400 vermilion (1) 3.50 1.00
b. $400 vermilion (2) 3.50 1.00
c. $400 vermilion (3) 3.50 1.00
d. $400 vermilion (4) 3.50 1.00
142 A25 Block of 4 25.00 25.00
a. $400 blue (5) 3.50 1.00
b. $400 blue (6) 3.50 1.00
c. $400 blue (7) 3.50 1.00
d. $400 blue (8) 3.50 1.00
143 A25 Block of 4 25.00 25.00
a. $400 brown red (9) 3.50 1.00
b. $400 brown red (10) 3.50 1.00
c. $400 brown red (11) 3.50 1.00
d. $400 brown red (12) 3.50 1.00
144 A25 Block of 4 25.00 25.00
a. $400 yellow green (13) 3.50 1.00
b. $400 yellow green (14) 3.50 1.00
c. $400 yellow green (15) 3.50 1.00
d. $400 yellow green (16) 3.50 1.00
145 A25 Block of 4 25.00 25.00
a. $400 red orange (17) 3.50 1.00
b. $400 red orange (18) 3.50 1.00
c. $400 red orange (19) 3.50 1.00
d. $400 red orange (20) 3.50 1.00
146 A25 Block of 4 25.00 25.00
a. $400 dull blue (21) 3.50 1.00
b. $400 dull blue (22) 3.50 1.00
c. $400 dull blue (23) 3.50 1.00
d. $400 dull blue (24) 3.50 1.00
147 A25 Block of 4 25.00 25.00
a. $400 orange (25) 3.50 1.00
b. $400 orange (26) 3.50 1.00
c. $400 orange (27) 3.50 1.00
d. $400 orange (28) 3.50 1.00
148 A25 Block of 4 25.00 25.00
a. $400 dull purple (29) 3.50 1.00
b. $400 dull purple (30) 3.50 1.00
c. $400 dull purple (31) 3.50 1.00
d. $400 dull purple (32) 3.50 1.00
149 A25 Block of 4 25.00 25.00
a. $400 yellow bister (33) 3.50 1.00
b. $400 yellow bister (34) 3.50 1.00
c. $400 yellow bister (35) 3.50 1.00
d. $400 yellow bister (36) 3.50 1.00
150 A25 Block of 4 25.00 25.00
a. $400 sky blue (37) 3.50 1.00
b. $400 sky blue (38) 3.50 1.00
c. $400 sky blue (39) 3.50 1.00
d. $400 sky blue (40) 3.50 1.00
Nos. 141-150 (10) 250.00 250.00

Originals are on thin gray paper, colors darker. Reprints on thicker white paper, colors brighter. Value, set $11.50.

Hunting, Wei Dynasty, A.D. 386-580 A26

Designs from Murals in Cave Temples at Tunhuang, Kansu Province: No. 152, Lady attendants, Sui Dynasty, 581-617 A.D. No. 153, Gandharvas (mythology), Tang Dynasty, 618-906. No. 154, Dragon, Tang Dynasty.

1952, July 1 **Engr.**

151 A26 $800 slate green (1) .35 .25
152 A26 $800 chocolate (2) .35 .25
153 A26 $800 indigo (3) .35 .25
154 A26 $800 dk vio (4) .35 .25
Nos. 151-154 (4) 1.40 1.00

"Glorious Mother Country," 1st series.

Marco Polo Bridge, near Peking A27

Designs: No. 156, Cavalry passing through Great Wall. No. 157, Departure of New Fourth Army. No. 158, Mao Tse-tung and Gen. Chu Teh planning counter-attack.

1952, July 7 **Litho.** ***Perf. 14***

155 A27 $800 brt blue .45 .30
156 A27 $800 blue grn 1.00 .70
157 A27 $800 plum .45 .30
158 A27 $800 scarlet .20 .20
Nos. 155-158 (4) 2.10 1.50

15th anniversary of war against Japan.

Soldier and Tanks — A28

#159, Soldier, sailor & airman, vert. #161, Sailor & warships. #162, Airman & planes.

1952, Aug. 1 **Engr.** ***Perf. 12½***

159 A28 $800 carmine .25 .20
160 A28 $800 deep green .50 .30
161 A28 $800 purple .25 .20
162 A28 $800 orange brown .25 .20
Nos. 159-162 (4) 1.25 .90

25th anniv. of People's Liberation Army.

Huai River Sluice Dam A29

#164, Train on the Chengtu-Chungking Railway. #165, Oil refinery and derricks in the Northwest. #166, Mechanized state farm.

1952, Oct. 1 ***Perf. 14***

163 A29 $800 dk violet .25 .20
164 A29 $800 red .25 .20
165 A29 $800 dk vio brn .25 .20
166 A29 $800 dp green .25 .20
Nos. 163-166 (4) 1.00 .80

"Glorious Mother Country," 2nd series.

Doves and Globe A30

Designs: Nos. 167-168, Picasso dove over Pacific, vert. $2500, as No. 169.

1952, Oct. 2 ***Perf. 14***

167 A30 $400 maroon .25 .25
168 A30 $800 red .25 .25
169 A30 $800 brown orange .25 .25
170 A30 $2500 deep green .50 .50
Nos. 167-170 (4) 1.25 1.25

Peace Conf. of the Asian and Pacific Regions.

Volunteers on the March — A31

#172, Chinese peasants loading supplies. #173, Volunteers attacking across river. #174, Meeting of Chinese & Korean troops.

1952, Oct. 25

171 A31 $800 blue green (1) .25 .20
172 A31 $800 vermilion (2) .25 .20
173 A31 $800 violet (3) .35 .20
174 A31 $800 lake brown (4) .50 .25
Nos. 171-174 (4) 1.35 .85

2nd anniv. of Chinese Volunteers in Korea.

Woman Textile Worker A32

Design: No. 176, Farm woman with sickle.

1953, Mar. 10

175 A32 $800 carmine .40 .20
176 A32 $800 emerald .40 .20

International Women's Day.

Textile Worker — A33

Karl Marx — A34

$200, Shepherdess. $250, Stone lion. $800, Lathe operator. $1600, Coal miners. $2000, Corner tower of Forbidden City, Peking.

1953 **Litho.** ***Perf. 14, 12½ ($250)***

177 A33 $50 magenta .70 .20
178 A33 $200 emerald .35 .20
179 A33 $250 ultra 7.00 1.25
180 A33 $800 blue grn .20 .20
181 A33 $1600 gray .70 .30
182 A33 $2000 red org .20 .20
Nos. 177-182 (6) 9.15 2.35

Issued: #177-181, Mar. 25; #182, May 23.

1953, May 20 **Engr.** ***Perf. 14***

183 A34 $400 dk brown .30 .20
184 A34 $800 slate grn .60 .25

135th anniv. of the birth of Karl Marx.

Workers and Banners — A35

1953, June 25

185 A35 $400 Prus blue .55 .20
186 A35 $800 carmine .35 .20

7th All-China Trade Union Congress.

Picasso Dove — A36

1953, July 25

187 A36 $250 blue grn .80 .20
188 A36 $400 orange brn .40 .20
189 A36 $800 purple .60 .20
Nos. 187-189 (3) 1.80 .60

World Peace.

Groom, Wei Dynasty, 386-580 A37

Scenes from Tunhuang Murals: No. 191, Court Players, Wei Dynasty. No. 192, Battle Scene, Sui Dynasty, 581-617. No. 193, Ox-drawn palanquin, Tang Dynasty, 618-906.

1953, Sept. 1

190 A37 $800 dp green (1) 1.00 .20
191 A37 $800 red org (2) .20 .20
192 A37 $800 Prus blue (3) .45 .20
193 A37 $800 carmine (4) .20 .20
Nos. 190-193 (4) 1.85 .80

"Glorious Mother Country," 3rd series.

Stalin and Mao on Kremlin Terrace A38

Statue of Stalin at Volga-Don Canal — A39

Designs: No. 195, Lenin proclaiming Soviet power. No. 197, Stalin as orator.

1953, Oct. 5

194 A38 $800 green (1) 1.00 .45
195 A38 $800 carmine (2) .45 .20
196 A39 $800 brt blue (3) .40 .20
197 A39 $800 org brn (4) .30 .20
Nos. 194-197 (4) 2.15 1.05

Russian October Revolution, 35th anniv.

Stamps in same designs with two additional characters meaning "Soviet" in the single-line Chinese inscription, and in different colors, were unofficially released at several small post offices in Hunan, Fukien and Canton areas in February, 1953, but were withdrawn after only a small number had been sold. Value, set $7,250 unused, $2,000 canceled.

Compass, 3rd Century B.C. A40

#199, Seismoscope, later Han Dynasty. #200, Drum cart to measure distance, Chin Dynasty. #201, Armillary sphere, Ming Dynasty.

1953, Dec. 1

198 A40 $800 indigo (1) .55 .20
199 A40 $800 dk green (2) .20 .20
200 A40 $800 dk blue (3) .30 .20
201 A40 $800 choc (4) .30 .20
Nos. 198-201 (4) 1.35 .80

Major inventions by ancient and medieval Chinese scientists.

"Glorious Mother Country," 4th series.

Francois Rabelais — A41

(same size) Gate of Heavenly Peace — A42

Designs: $400, Jose Marti, Cuban revolutionary. $800, Chu Yuan (350-275 B.C.), philosopher. $2200, Nicolaus Copernicus, astronomer.

1953, Dec. 30

202 A41 $250 slate grn (3) .45 .25
203 A41 $400 brown blk (4) .45 .25
204 A41 $800 indigo (1) .45 .25
205 A41 $2200 choc (2) .45 .25
Nos. 202-205 (4) 1.80 1.00

1954, Apr. 16 **Litho.**

Sixth Issue: Inscription at upper right.

206 A42 $50 carmine .20 .20
207 A42 $100 lt blue .20 .20
208 A42 $200 green .20 .20
209 A42 $250 ultra 3.00 .30
210 A42 $400 gray grn .20 .20
211 A42 $800 orange .20 .20
212 A42 $1600 gray .20 *.65*
213 A42 $2000 olive .20 *.30*
Nos. 206-213 (8) 4.40 2.25

Textile Plant, Harbin — A43

Lenin — A44

Designs: $200, Tangku Harbor. $250, Tienshui-Lanchow railroad bridge, Kansu Province. $400, Heavy machine-building plant, Taiyuan, Shansi. No. 218, Automatic blast, furnace, Anshan, Manchuria. No. 219, Fushun open-cut coal mine. $2000, Automatic power plant, Northeast. $3200, Prospecting in Tayeh district, Hupeh.

1954, May 1 **Engr.**

214 A43 $100 brown olive .25 .20
215 A43 $200 blue green .25 .20
216 A43 $250 violet .20 .20
217 A43 $400 black .25 .20
218 A43 $800 claret .20 .20
219 A43 $800 indigo .20 .20
220 A43 $2000 red .20 .20
221 A43 $3200 dark brown .45 .30
Nos. 214-221 (8) 2.00 1.70

Economic progress.

1954, June 30 **Engr.**

$400, Lenin and Stalin Monument, Gorki, horiz. $2000, Lenin proclaiming Soviet power.

222 A44 $400 deep green .55 .20
223 A44 $800 dark brown .30 .20
224 A44 $2000 deep carmine 2.25 .30
Nos. 222-224 (3) 3.10 .70

30th anniversary of the death of Lenin.

Pottery Vessels, Neolithic Period, 2000 B. C. — A45

Archeological Treasures: No. 226, Stone clime, Shang Dynasty, c. 1200 B.C. No. 227, Kuo Chi Tsu-pai bronze basin, Middle Chou Dynasty, 816 B.C. No. 228, Lacquered box and wine cup, Warring States Period, 403-221 B.C.

1954, Aug. 25

225 A45 $800 brown .45 .20
226 A45 $800 indigo .45 .20
227 A45 $800 Prus bl .45 .20
228 A45 $800 dk car .45 .20
Nos. 225-228 (4) 1.80 .80

"Glorious Mother Country," 5th series.

Pipe Production, Anshan Steel Mill — A46

Stalin Statue, by Tomsky — A47

Design: $800, Rolling mill, Anshan.

1954, Oct. 1

229 A46 $400 Prus green .45 .30
230 A46 $800 vio brown .45 .30

1954, Oct. 15

Designs: $800, Stalin portrait. $2000, Stalin viewing hydroelectric plant.

Size: 21x45mm

231 A47 $400 black 1.60 .30

Size: 26x37mm

232 A47 $800 black brown .35 .20

Size: 42x26mm

233 A47 $2000 deep red .35 .20
Nos. 231-233 (3) 2.30 .70

First anniversary of the death of Stalin.

Exhibition Building, Peking — A48

1954, Nov. 7

234 A48 $800 brown, *cream* 9.00 3.50
a. Size: 53½x24mm 17.50 3.50

Russian Economic and Cultural Exhibition, Peking. No. 234 measures 52½x24½mm.

Apprentices and Lathe — A49

Progress in Technology: $800, Heavy machinery and workers.

1954, Dec. 15

235 A49 $400 dk olive grn .40 .20
236 A49 $800 bright red .25 .20

Woman Worker Voting — A50

People Celebrating Opening of Congress — A51

1954, Dec. 30

237 A50 $400 deep claret .20 .20
238 A51 $800 bright red .70 .20

First National Congress.

Flags, Worker and Woman Holding Constitution — A52

1954, Dec. 30

239 A52 $400 brown, *buff* .45 .20
240 A52 $800 brt red, *yel* .45 .20

Adoption of Constitution.

High-tension Pylon — A53

1955, Feb. 25

241 A53 $800 dk Prus bl .75 .25

Development of electric power.

Factory Health Workers and Red Cross A54

1955, June 25 **Engr.; Cross Typo.**

242 A54 8f dp grn & red 7.25 2.00

50th anniversary of Chinese Red Cross.

Stalin and Mao in Kremlin A55

Soviet Specialist and Chinese Worker — A56

1955, July 25 **Engr.**

243 A55 8f brown red 6.75 .50
244 A56 20f olive blk 6.75 1.50

5th anniv. of Sino-Soviet Friendship Treaty.

Chang Heng (78-139), Astronomer — A57

Portraits of Scientists: No. 246, Tsu Chung-chih (429-500), mathematician. No. 247, Chang Sui (683-727), astronomer. No. 248, Li Shih-chen (1518-1593), physician and pharmacologist.

1955, Aug. 25 ***Perf. 14***

245 A57 8f sepia, *buff* 2.00 .30
a. Min. sheet, sepia, *white* 22.50 6.75
246 A57 8f dp grn, *buff* 2.00 .30
a. Min. sheet, deep green, *white* 22.50 6.75
247 A57 8f black, *buff* 2.00 .30
a. Min. sheet, blk, *white* 22.50 6.75
248 A57 8f claret, *buff* 2.00 .30
a. Min. sheet, claret, *white* 22.50 6.75
Nos. 245-248 (4) 8.00 1.20

Miniature sheets contain one imperf. stamp.

Steel Pouring Ladle A58

1955-56 **Litho.**

Position-in-set number in ( )

249 A58 8f shown (1) .65 .20
250 A58 8f High tension line (2) .65 .20
251 A58 8f Mechanized coal mining (3) .65 .20
252 A58 8f Tank cars and derricks (4) .65 .20
253 A58 8f Heavy machine shop (5) .65 .20
254 A58 8f Soldier on guard (6) .65 .20
255 A58 8f Spinning machine (7) .65 .20
256 A58 8f Workers discussing 5-year plan (8) .65 .20
257 A58 8f Combine harvester (9) .65 .20
258 A58 8f Milk production (10) .65 .20
259 A58 8f Dam (11) .65 .20
260 A58 8f Pottery industry (12) ('56) .65 .20
261 A58 8f Truck (13) .65 .20
262 A58 8f Ship at dock (14) .65 .20
263 A58 8f Geological survey (15) .65 .20
264 A58 8f Higher education (16) .65 .20
265 A58 8f Family (17) .65 .20
266 A58 8f Workers' rest home (18) ('56) .65 .20
Nos. 249-266 (18) 11.70 3.60

1st 5 Year Plan. Issued: #249-257, 10/1; #258-259, 261-265, 12/15; #260, 266, 2/24/56.

Lenin — A59

Engels — A60

1955, Dec. 15 Engr. *Perf. 14*
267 A59 8f dk blue grn 6.75 .25
268 A59 20f dk rose car 6.75 1.75

85th anniversary of the birth of Lenin.

1955, Dec. 15
269 A60 8f deep orange 6.75 .25
270 A60 20f brown 6.75 1.75

135th anniversary of the birth of Friedrich Engels (1820-1895), German socialist.

Storming Lu Ting Bridge — A61

Crossing Great Snow Mountains A62

1955, Dec. 30
271 A61 8f dark red 6.75 .35
272 A62 8f dark blue 6.75 1.60

Long March of Chinese Communist army, 20th anniversary.

Miner — A63

Gate of Heavenly Peace — A64

Designs: 1f, Machinist. 2f, Airman. 2½f, Nurse. 4f, Soldier. 8f, Steel worker. 10f, Scientist. 20f, Farm woman. 50f, Sailor.

1955-56 Litho. *Perf. 14*
273 A63 ½f orange brn 1.90 .20
274 A63 1f purple 1.90 .20
275 A63 2f green 1.90 .20
276 A63 2½f blue ('56) 1.90 .20
277 A63 4f gray olive 1.90 .45
278 A63 8f red org (Peking printing) 1.90 .65
a. Perf. 12½ (Shanghai printing) 350.00 10.00
279 A63 10f claret ('56) 26.00 .20
280 A63 20f dp blue 6.75 .20
281 A63 50f gray 6.75 .20
Nos. 273-281 (9) 50.90 2.50

Engr.
282 A64 $1 claret ('56) .65 .25
283 A64 $2 sepia ('55) 1.10 .25
284 A64 $5 indigo ('56) 1.75 .40
285 A64 $10 dp org ('56) 5.50 4.25
286 A64 $20 gray vio ('56) 9.00 *17.00*
Nos. 282-286 (5) 18.00 22.15

Nos. 282-286 are the 7th Gate Issue.

Trucks, Mountains, Highway Map — A65

Suspension Bridge over Tatu River — A66

#289, 1st truck arriving in Lhasa, & the Potala.

1956, Mar. 10 Engr.
287 A65 4f dp blue .30 .20
288 A66 8f dk brown .30 .20
289 A65 8f carmine .30 .20
Nos. 287-289 (3) .90 .60

Completion of Sikang-Tibet and Chinghai-Tibet Highways.

Summer Palace and Marble Boat A67

Famous Views of Imperial Peking: No. 291, Peihai Park with Jade Belt Marble Bridge. No. 292, Gate of Heavenly Peace. No. 293, Temple of Heaven. No. 294, Great Throne Hall, Forbidden City.

1956-57
290 A67 4f car rose (1) 2.10 .25
291 A67 4f blue grn (2) 2.10 .25
292 A67 8f red org (3) ('57) 2.10 .25
293 A67 8f Prus blue (4) 2.10 .25
294 A67 8f yellow brn (5) 2.10 .25
Nos. 290-294 (5) 10.50 1.25

Issued: #292, 2/20/57; others, 6/15/56. No. 292 exists with sun rays in background.

Salt Making A68

Designs: No. 296, Dwelling of the Eastern Han period. No. 297, Duck hunting and harvesting. No. 298, Carriage crossing bridge.

1956, Oct. 1
295 A68 4f gray olive .25 .20
296 A68 4f slate blue .25 .20
297 A68 8f gray brown .25 .20
298 A68 8f sepia .25 .20
Nos. 295-298 (4) 1.00 .80

Murals, Tung Han Dynasty, 250 B.C.-220 A.D., found near Chengtu.

Ancient Coins and "Save" A69

1956, Oct. 1
299 A69 4f yellow brown 5.25 .60
300 A69 8f rose red 5.25 .60

Promotion of saving.

Gate of Heavenly Peace — A70

Sun Yat-sen — A71

1956, Nov. 10
301 A70 4f dk green 4.25 .40
302 A70 8f brt red 4.25 .40
303 A70 16f dk carmine 4.25 .80
Nos. 301-303 (3) 12.75 1.60

8th National Congress of the Communist Party of China.

1956, Nov. 12
304 A71 4f brown, *cream* 6.75 .20
305 A71 8f dp blue, *cream* 6.75 1.25

90th anniversary of birth of Sun Yat-sen.

Weight Lifting — A72

1957, Mar. 20 Litho. *Perf. 12½*
Hibiscus red and green; inscription brown
306 A72 4f Shot put (2) 1.10 .20
307 A72 4f shown (5) 1.10 .20
308 A72 8f Track (1) 1.10 .20
309 A72 8f Soccer (3) 1.10 .20
310 A72 8f Bicycling (4) 1.10 .20
Nos. 306-310 (5) 5.50 1.00

First National Workers' Sports Meeting.

Truck Factory No. 1, Changchun — A73

China's truck industry: 8f, Trucks rolling off assembly line.

1957, May 1 Engr. *Perf. 14*
311 A73 4f light brown .45 .25
312 A73 8f slate green .45 .25

Nanchang Uprising — A74

#314, Mao and Chu Teh at Chingkanshan. #315, Crossing Yellow River. #316, Liberation of Nanking, 4/23/49.

1957
313 A74 4f blk vio (1) 8.00 .70
314 A74 4f slate grn (2) 8.00 1.10
315 A74 8f red brn (3) 8.00 .45
316 A74 8f dp blue (4) 8.00 .45
Nos. 313-316 (4) 32.00 2.70

People's Liberation Army, 30th anniv. Issued: #313, 315, 8/10; #314, 8/30; #316, 12/30.

Congress Emblem — A75

1957, Sept. 30
317 A75 8f chocolate 3.50 .40
318 A75 22f indigo 3.50 .60

4th Intl. Trade Union Cong., Leipzig, 10/4-15.

Yangtze River Bridge A76

20f, Road leading to and over bridge.

1957, Oct. 1
319 A76 8f scarlet .45 .25
320 A76 20f slate blue .45 .20

Completion of Yangtze River Bridge at Wuhan.

Fireworks over Kremlin — A77

Designs: 8f, Hammer and sickle over globe and broken chain. 20f, Stylized dove and olive branch. 22f, Hands of three races holding book with Marx and Lenin. 32f, Star and pylon.

1957, Nov. 7
321 A77 4f brt red 6.25 .35
322 A77 8f chocolate 6.25 .35
323 A77 20f dp green 6.25 .35
324 A77 22f red brown 6.25 .35
325 A77 32f dp blue 6.25 2.00
Nos. 321-325 (5) 31.25 3.40

40th anniv. of Russian October Revolution.

Map of Yellow River Basin A78

#327, Sanmen Gorge dam & powerhouse. #328, ocean liner on Yellow River. #329, Dam, irrigation canals & tree-bordered fields.

1957, Dec. 30
326 A78 4f deep orange (1) 8.00 1.25
327 A78 4f deep blue (2) 8.00 1.65
328 A78 8f deep lake (3) 8.00 .60
329 A78 8f blue green (4) 8.00 .60
Nos. 326-329 (4) 32.00 4.10

Yellow River control plan.

Old Man and Young Drummer A79

Crane, Dove and Flowers A80

1957, Dec. 30 **Litho.**

330 A79 8f shown (1) .45 .20
331 A79 8f Plowman (2) .45 .20
332 A79 8f Woman planting tree (3) .45 .20
333 A79 8f Harvest (4) .45 .20
Nos. 330-333 (4) 1.80 .80

Agricultural cooperation.

1958, Jan. 30 **Engr.**

Designs (Congratulatory Banner and): 8f, Crane with hot ingots, cotton bolls and wheat. 16f, Train on bridge, ship and plane.

334 A80 4f emer, *cream* .30 .20
335 A80 8f red, *cream* .30 .25
336 A80 16f ultra, *cream* .30 .20
Nos. 334-336 (3) .90 .65

Fulfillment of First Five-Year Plan.

Sungyu Pagoda, Honan — A81

Trilobite, Kaoli — A82

Ancient Pagodas: No. 338, Chienhsun Pagoda, Yunnan. No. 339, Sakyamuni Pagoda, Shansi. No. 340, Flying Rainbow Pagoda, Shansi.

1958, Mar. 15 **Engr.**

337 A81 8f sepia (1) .90 .20
338 A81 8f Prus blue (2) .90 .20
339 A81 8f maroon (3) .90 .20
340 A81 8f dp green (4) .90 .25
Nos. 337-340 (4) 3.60 .85

1958, Apr. 15

Designs: 8f, Lufeng dinosaur. 16f, Choukoutien sino-megaceros.

341 A82 4f black .65 .20
342 A82 8f sepia .65 .25
343 A82 16f slate green .65 .20
Nos. 341-343 (3) 1.95 .65

Prehistoric animals of China.

Heroes Monument A83

1958, May 1

344 A83 8f scarlet 14.00 1.10
a. Souvenir sheet, imperf. 100.00 45.00

Unveiling of People's Heroes Monument, Peking. No. 344a issued May 30.

Karl Marx — A84

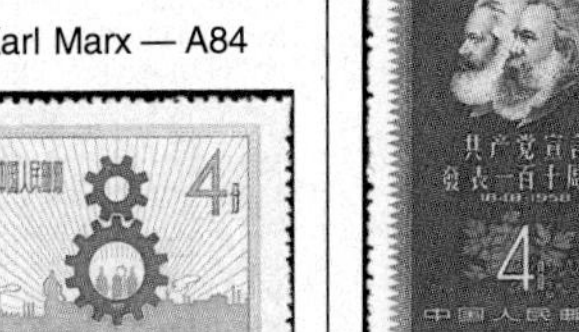

Cogwheels and Factories — A85

Design: 22f, Marx Speaking to German Workers' Educational Association, London, painting by Zhukow.

1958, May 5

345 A84 8f chocolate 7.00 1.00
346 A84 22f dk green 7.00 2.00

Karl Marx (1818-83), 140th birth anniv.

1958, May 25

347 A85 4f brt grnsh bl 6.75 2.50
348 A85 8f red lilac 6.75 .60

8th All-China Trade Union Cong., Peking.

Dove over Globe — A86

Mother and Child — A87

1958, June 1

349 A86 8f violet blue 6.25 .25
350 A86 20f blue green 6.25 3.25

4th Congress of the Intl. Democratic Women's Federation, Vienna, June 1958.

1958, June 1 **Litho.**

Children's Day: No. 352, Watering sunflowers. No. 353, Playing hide-and-seek. No. 354, Sailing toy boat.

351 A87 8f green & multi (1) 10.00 1.60
352 A87 8f green & multi (2) 10.00 1.60
353 A87 8f green & multi (3) 10.00 1.60
354 A87 8f green & multi (4) 10.00 1.60
Nos. 351-354 (4) 40.00 6.40

Kuan Han-ching A88

Designs (Operas): 4f, "Dream of Butterflies." 20f, "The Riverside Pavilion."

1958, June 20 **Engr.**

355 A88 4f indigo, *cr* 7.50 3.50
356 A88 8f brown, *cr* 7.50 .60
357 A88 20f black, *cr* 7.50 .90
a. Souvenir sheet of 3, *ivory* 175.00 60.00
Nos. 355-357 (3) 22.50 *5.00*

700th anniversary of publication of works of Kuan Han-ching (1210-1280), dramatist. No. 357a contains 3 imperf. stamps similar to Nos. 355-357. Size: 130x100mm. Issued June 28.

Planetarium A89

20f, Telescope and stars over Peking.

1958, June 25

358 A89 8f dk green 4.00 .80
359 A89 20fr indigo 4.00 1.60

First Chinese planetarium, Peking.

Marx and Engels — A90

Wild Goose and Broadcasting Tower — A91

8f, Cover of 1st edition of the Communist Manifesto.

1958, July 1

360 A90 4f dk red vio 6.75 3.25
361 A90 8f Prus blue 6.75 .25

110th anniversary of publication of the Communist Manifesto.

1958, July 10

362 A91 4f ultra 5.50 .75
363 A91 8f deep green 5.50 2.25

1st Conference of the Ministers of Posts and Telecommunications of Socialist Countries, Moscow, Dec. 3-17, 1957.

Peony and Doves — A92

Bronze Weather Vane — A93

8f, Olive branch with ribbon & clouds. 22f, Atomic energy symbol over factories.

1958, July 20

364 A92 4f red 8.50 .80
365 A92 8f green 8.50 5.50
366 A92 22f red brown 8.50 2.50
Nos. 364-366 (3) 25.50 8.80

Congress for Disarmament and International Cooperation, Stockholm, July 17-22.

1958, Aug. 25

Designs: No. 368, Weather balloon. No. 369, Typhoon tower and weather map of Asia.

367 A93 8f yel bis & blk (1) .55 .20
368 A93 8f blue & blk (2) .55 .20
369 A93 8f brt grn & blk (3) .55 .20
Nos. 367-369 (3) 1.65 .60

Meteorological services in ancient and modern China.

"5" Encircling IUS Emblem — A94

1958, Sept. 4

370 A94 8f rose lilac 5.50 .30
371 A94 22f dp blue grn 5.50 .90

Intl. Union of Students, 5th Cong., Peking, 9/4-13.
Copies exist with incorrect inscription.

Telegraph Building, Peking A95

1958, Sept. 29

372 A95 4f greenish black 1.75 .20
373 A95 8f rose red 1.75 .20

Opening of Telegraph Building, Peking.

Exhibition Emblem and Exhortation A96

Designs: No. 375, Dragon over clouds signifying "aiming high." No. 376, Flying horses, signifying "great leap forward" in production.

1958, Oct. 1

374 A96 8f slate grn (1) 5.00 .65
375 A96 8f rose car (2) 5.00 .65
376 A96 8f red brown (3) 5.00 2.50
Nos. 374-376 (3) 15.00 3.80

National Exhibition of Industry and Communications, Peking.

Worker and Excavator A97

Design: 8f, Completed dam and pylon.

1958, Oct. 25

377 A97 4f dark brown .50 .20
378 A97 8f deep Prussian blue .60 .20

13 Ming Tombs Reservoir completion.

Sputnik over Armillary Sphere — A98

Designs: 8f, Sputnik 3 in orbit. 10f, Trajectories of 3 Sputniks over earth.

1958, Oct. 30

379 A98 4f scarlet 2.50 .25
380 A98 8f dp violet bl 2.50 .25
381 A98 10f dp green 2.50 1.60
Nos. 379-381 (3) 7.50 2.10

Anniversary of first earth satellite launched by the USSR.

Chinese and North Korean Soldiers A99

Designs: No. 383, Chinese soldier embracing Korean woman. No. 384, Chinese girl presenting flowers to returning soldier.

1958, Nov. 20

382 A99 8f brt purple (1) .90 .25
383 A99 8f chestnut (2) .90 .20
384 A99 8f rose car (3) .90 .20
Nos. 382-384 (3) 2.70 .65

Return of the Chinese Volunteers from Korea.

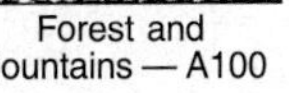

Forest and Mountains — A100

Peony — A101

Afforestation: No. 386, Mounted forest patrol. No. 387, Mechanized lumbering, horiz. No. 388, Tree-planting: "Turning the Country Green," horiz.

1958, Dec. 15

385 A100 8f dp blue grn (1) 2.00 1.10
386 A100 8f slate grn (2) 2.00 .40
387 A100 8f dk purple (3) 2.00 .40
388 A100 8f indigo (4) 2.00 .70
Nos. 385-388 (4) 8.00 2.60

1958, Sept. 25 Litho.

Designs: 3f, Lotus. 5f, Chrysanthemums.

389 A101 1½f lilac rose 5.75 .60
390 A101 3f blue grn 5.75 1.75
391 A101 5f dp orange 5.75 .40
Nos. 389-391 (3) 17.25 2.75

Atomic Reactor A102

1958, Dec. 30 Engr.

392 A102 8f shown 5.75 2.50
393 A102 20f Cyclotron 5.75 .40

Inauguration of China's first atomic reactor and cyclotron, Peking.

Children Launching Model Planes — A103

Camel Carrying Load — A104

8f, Gliders over trees. 10f, Parachutists descending. 20f, Small monoplanes in mid-air.

1958, Dec. 30

394 A103 4f carmine .80 .20
395 A103 8f dp slate grn .80 .20
396 A103 10f dk brown .80 .20
397 A103 20f Prus blue .80 .20
Nos. 394-397 (4) 3.20 .80

Sports-aviation publicity.

1959, Jan. 1

Designs: No. 399, Pomegranates. No. 400, Rooster. No. 401, Theatrical figure.

398 A104 8f vio & blk (1) 6.00 .20
399 A104 8f dp bl grn & blk (2) 6.00 .50
400 A104 8f red & blk (3) 6.00 1.25
401 A104 8f dp bl & blk (4) 6.00 .50
Nos. 398-401 (4) 24.00 2.45

Paper cut-outs (folk art).

Red Flag, Mao and Workers — A105

Women Workers and Atomic Model — A106

Designs: 8f, Traditional and modern blast furnaces. 10f, Steel works and workers.

1959

402 A105 4f brt red 4.50 1.40
403 A105 8f lake 4.50 1.40
404 A105 10f deep red 4.50 1.40
Nos. 402-404 (3) 13.50 4.20

"Great Leap Forward" in steel production. Issue dates: 4f, 8f, Feb. 19; 10f, May 25.

1959, Mar. 8

Design: 22f, Chinese and Soviet women holding banners dated "3.8."

405 A106 8f emerald, *cr* .70 .30
406 A106 22f magenta, *cr* .70 .20

International Women's Day.

Natural History Museum A107

1959, Apr. 1

407 A107 4f greenish blue .45 .20
408 A107 8f olive brown .45 .20

Opening of Museum of Natural History, Peking.

Wheat — A108

Designs on Chinese Flag: No. 410, Rice. No. 411, Cotton bolls. No. 412, Soybeans, rapeseed and peanuts.

1959, Apr. 25

409 A108 8f red (1) 1.40 .30
410 A108 8f red (2) 1.40 .30
411 A108 8f red (3) 1.40 .30
412 A108 8f red (4) 1.40 .30
a. Block of 4, #409-412 11.00 2.40

Successful harvest, 1958.

A109

A110

Designs: 4f, Marx, Lenin and workers. 8f, Black, yellow and white fists holding banner. 22f, Steel workers parading with banners dated "5.1."

1959, May 1

413 A109 4f ultra 4.50 1.40
414 A109 8f red 4.50 1.40
415 A109 22f emerald 4.50 1.40
Nos. 413-415 (3) 13.50 4.20

International Labor Day.

1959, June 20

8f, Peking airport. 10f, Plane loading on runway.

416 A110 8f lilac & blk 8.00 1.00
417 A110 10f ol gray & blk 8.00 .40

Opening of new Peking Airport.

Students with Marx-Lenin Banners A111

Design: 8f, Workers with banners of Mao.

1959, July 1 Photo. *Perf. 11x11½*

418 A111 4f gray, red & dk brn 17.50 5.00
419 A111 8f bis, red & dk brn 17.50 5.00

40th anniv. of the May 4th students' uprising.

Frederick Joliot-Curie — A112

22f, Three races, dove and olive branch.

1959, July 25 Engr. *Perf. 11½*

420 A112 8f violet brn 6.00 3.00
421 A112 22f dk violet 6.00 .20

10th anniv. of the World Peace Movement.

Stamp Printing Plant, Peking A113

1959, Aug. 15 *Perf. 11x11½*

422 A113 8f dp blue grn 7.25 2.00

Sino-Czechoslovak cooperation in stamp production.

Table Tennis — A114

1959, Aug. 30 Litho. *Perf. 14*

423 A114 4f black & blue 2.25 .45
424 A114 8f black & red 2.25 .30

25th World Table Tennis Championships, Dortmund, German Democratic Republic.

Soviet Space Rocket A115

Backyard Steel Production A116

1959, Sept. 10 Photo. *Perf. 11½*

425 A115 8f Prus bl, red & blk 10.00 2.40

Launching of first Russian space rocket, Jan. 2, 1959.

1959, Sept. 25 Engr.

Designs: #426, Sun rising over "industry and agriculture." #428, Farming. #429, Trade. #430, Education. #431, Militia. #432, Communal dining. #433, Nursery. #434, Care for the aged. #435, Health services. #436, Flutist; culture and sports. #437, Flower symbolizing unity of industry, agriculture, trade, education and armed forces.

Position-in-set number in ( ).

426 A116 8f rose (1) .65 .20
427 A116 8f violet brn (2) .65 .20
428 A116 8f dp orange (3) .65 .20
429 A116 8f slate grn (4) .65 .20
430 A116 8f dp blue (5) .65 .20
431 A116 8f olive (6) .65 .20
432 A116 8f indigo (7) .65 .20
433 A116 8f lilac rose (8) .65 .20
434 A116 8f gray blk (9) .65 .20
435 A116 8f emerald (10) .65 .20
436 A116 8f dk violet (11) .65 .20
437 A116 8f red (12) .65 .20
Nos. 426-437 (12) 7.80 2.40

First anniversary of Peoples' Communes.

Mao and Gate of Heavenly Peace — A117

National Emblem A118

Blast Furnaces — A119

Celebration at Gate of Heavenly Peace — A120

Mao Proclaiming Republic — A121

Designs: #439, Marx, Lenin and Kremlin. 22f, Dove over globe.

1959, Sept. 28 Photo. *Perf. 11½x11*

With Gum

438 A117 8f lt brown & red 10.50 5.50
439 A117 8f dull blue & red 10.50 1.75
440 A117 22f blue grn & red 10.50 1.00
Nos. 438-440 (3) 31.50 8.25

1959, Oct. 1 Litho. *Perf. 14*

441 A118 4f pale grn, red & gold 8.00 4.25
442 A118 8f gray, red & gold 8.00 .40
443 A118 10f lt blue, red & gold 8.00 .40
444 A118 20f pale brn, red & gold 8.00 2.50
Nos. 441-444 (4) 32.00 7.55

Engraved and Photogravure

1959, Oct. 1 *Perf. 11½x11*

#446, Large coal mine. #447, Planer, Wuhan heavy machinery plant. #448, Wuhan Yangtze River Bridge. #449, Combine harvester. #450, Hsinankiang hydroelectric station. #451, Spinning machine. #452, Kirin chemical fertilizer plant.

With Gum

445 A119 8f brown & rose red (1) .90 .50
446 A119 8f brown & gray (2) .90 .50
447 A119 8f brown & yel brn (3) .90 .50
448 A119 8f brown & stl bl (4) .90 .50
449 A119 8f brown & org (5) .90 .50
450 A119 8f brown & ol (6) .90 .50

451 A119 8f brown & bl grn (7) .90 .50
452 A119 8f brown & vio (8) .90 .50
Nos. 445-452 (8) 7.20 4.00

1959, Oct. 1 Litho. *Perf. 14*

Designs: 10f, Workers and factory, vert. 20f, People rejoicing, vert.

453 A120 8f cream & multi 4.50 1.60
454 A120 10f cream & multi 4.50 1.60
455 A120 20f cream & multi 4.50 1.60
Nos. 453-455 (3) 13.50 4.80

1959, Oct. 1 Engr.

456 A121 20f deep carmine 22.50 11.00

Nos. 438-456 commemorate 10th anniversary of the Proclamation of the People's Republic of China.

A122

A123

Designs: No. 457, Pioneers' emblem. No. 458, Pioneer Bugler. No. 459, Schoolgirl. No. 460, Girl using rain gauge. No. 461, Boy planting tree. No. 462, Girl figure skater.

1959, Nov. 10 Photo. *Perf. 11½*

457 A122 4f red yel & blk (1) 3.00 .50
458 A122 4f Prus bl & red (2) 3.00 .50
459 A122 8f brn & red (3) 3.00 .50
460 A122 8f dk bl & red (4) 3.00 .50
461 A122 8f red & grn (5) 3.00 .50
462 A122 8f mag & red (6) 3.00 .50
Nos. 457-462 (6) 18.00 3.00

10th anniversary of the Young Pioneers. Black inscription on No. 457 engraved.

1959, Dec. 1 Engr.

4f, Exhibition emblem, communications symbols. 8f, Exhibition emblem & chimneys.

463 A123 4f dark blue .45 .20
464 A123 8f red .45 .20

Exhibition of Industry and Communications, Peking.

Palace of Nationalities
A124

Engraved, Frame Lithographed

1959, Dec. 10 *Perf. 14*

465 A124 4f red & blk 3.50 .50
466 A124 8f brt grn & blk 3.50 .80

Inauguration of the Cultural Palace of Nationalities, Peking.

Athletes' Monument and Track — A125

#468, Parachuting. #469, Marksmanship. #470, Diving. #471, Table tennis. #472, Weight lifting. #473, High jump. #474, Rowing. #475, Track. #476, Basketball. #477, Traditional Chinese fencing. #478, Motorcycling. #479, Gymnastics. #480, Bicycling. #481, Horsemanship. #482, Soccer.

1959, Dec. 28 Litho.

467 A125 8f bis, blk & gray (1) 1.50 .25
468 A125 8f dl bl, blk & gray (2) 1.50 .25
469 A125 8f red brn & blk (3) 1.50 .25
470 A125 8f grn, blk & brn (4) 1.50 .25
471 A125 8f brt grn, blk, brn & gray (5) 1.50 .25
472 A125 8f gray, blk & brn (6) 1.50 .25
473 A125 8f dl bl, blk & brn (7) 1.50 .25
474 A125 8f Prus grn, blk & brn (8) 1.50 .25
475 A125 8f org, blk & brn (9) 1.50 .25
476 A125 8f dl vio, blk & brn (10) 1.50 .25
477 A125 8f lt ol, blk & brn (11) 1.50 .25
478 A125 8f bl, blk & gray (12) 1.50 .25
479 A125 8f gray bl, blk, grn, & bl (13) 1.50 .25
480 A125 8f gray, blk, brn, & vio (14) 1.50 .25
481 A125 8f red org, blk, brn, & gray (15) 1.50 .25
482 A125 8f lt gray, blk, brn, & red (16) 1.50 .25
Nos. 467-482 (16) 24.00 4.00

First National Sports Meeting, Peking.

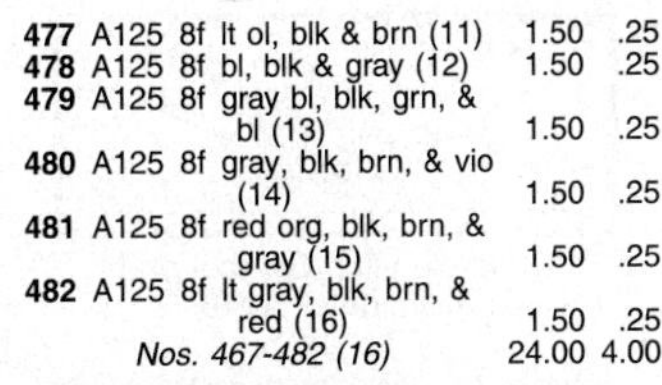
Wheat and Main Pavilion
A126

Designs (Pavilion and): 8f, Meteorological symbols. 10f, Domestic animals. 20f, Fish.

1960, Jan. 20 Engr. & Litho.
Cream Background

483 A126 4f black & org .60 .20
484 A126 8f black & dull bl .60 .20
485 A126 10f black & org brn .60 .20
486 A126 20f black & grnsh bl .60 .30
Nos. 483-486 (4) 2.40 .90

Opening of the National Agricultural Exhibition Halls, Peking.

With Gum
From No. 487 onward all stamps were issued with gum except as noted.

Catalogue values for unused stamps in this section, from this point to the end of the section, are for Never Hinged items.

Conference Hall, Tsunyi
A127

Designs: 8f, Mao addressing conference. 10f, Crossing Chinsha River.

Engraved (4f, 10f); Photogravure (8f)

1960, Jan. 25 *Perf. 11x11½*

487 A127 4f violet & blue 8.00 .95
488 A127 8f red & multi 8.00 2.25
489 A127 10f slate green 16.00 .95
Nos. 487-489 (3) 32.00 4.15

25th anniversary of the Communist Party Conference at Tsunyi.

Clara Zetkin (1857-1933)
A128

Chinese and Russian Workers — A129

8f, Mother, child and dove. 10f, Woman tractor driver. 22f, Women of three races.

1960, Mar. 8 Photo. *Perf. 11½x11*

490 A128 4f black & multi 1.40 .25
491 A128 8f black & multi 1.40 .55
492 A128 10f black & multi 1.40 .55
493 A128 22f black & multi 3.00 .25
Nos. 490-493 (4) 7.20 1.60

50th anniv. of International Women's Day.

1960, Mar. 10

Designs: 8f, Chinese and Russian flags. 10f, Chinese and Russian soldiers.

494 A129 4f dk brown 5.00 2.25
495 A129 8f red, yel & blk 5.00 2.25
496 A129 10f dp blue 8.25 2.25
Nos. 494-496 (3) 18.25 6.75

10th anniv. of Sino-Soviet Treaty of Friendship. Black inscription engraved on No. 495.

Flags of Hungary and China
A130

Design: 8f, Parliament Building, Budapest.

1960, Apr. 4 *Perf. 11x11½*

497 A130 8f yel, blk, red & grn 10.00 2.10
498 A130 8f blue, red & blk 10.00 4.25

15th anniv. of the liberation of Hungary.

Lenin Speaking — A131

Lunik 2, Earth and Russian Arms — A132

Designs: 8f, Portrait of Lenin. 20f, Lenin talking with Smolny Palace guard.

Engraved (4f, 20f); Engraved and Photogravure (8f)

1960, Apr. 22 *Perf. 11½x11*

499 A131 4f violet brn 5.00 1.00
500 A131 8f org red & blk 9.00 4.00
501 A131 20f dk brown 17.50 2.00
Nos. 499-501 (3) 31.50 7.00

90th anniversary of the birth of Lenin.

1960, Apr. 30 Engr. *Perf. 11½*

Design: 10f, Lunik 3 over earth.

502 A132 8f red 2.75 .90
503 A132 10f green 3.50 .90

Russian space flights.

Pioneers and Flags of Czechoslovakia and China — A133

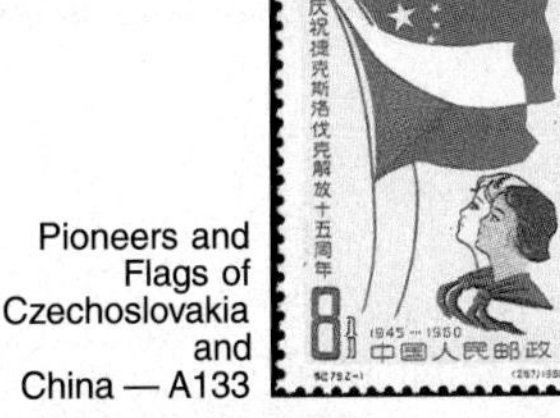
View of Prague with Charles Bridge
A134

Perf. 11½x11; 11x11½

1960, May 9 Photo.

504 A133 8f yellow & multi 8.00 1.40
505 A134 8f deep green 8.00 2.75

Liberation of Czechoslovakia, 15th anniv.

Nostril Bouquet
A135

Designs: Various goldfish.

1960, June 1 *Perf. 11x11½*

506 A135 4f shown (1) 22.50 3.25
507 A135 4f Black-back dragon eye (2) 26.00 3.25
508 A135 4f Bubble eye (3) 26.00 3.50
509 A135 4f Red tiger head (4) 7.50 2.50
510 A135 8f Pearl scale (5) 37.50 4.25
511 A135 8f Blue dragon eye (6) 37.50 4.25
512 A135 8f Skyward eye (7) 7.50 2.00
513 A135 8f Red cap (8) 7.50 2.00
514 A135 8f Purple cap (9) 7.50 2.00
515 A135 8f Red head (10) 7.50 2.00
516 A135 8f Red and white dragon eye (11) 26.00 4.25
517 A135 8f Red dragon eye (12) 26.00 4.25
Nos. 506-517 (12) 239.00 37.50

Sow with Litter
A136

#519, Pig being inoculated. #520, Pigs. #521, Pig and mechanized feeding. #522, Pig and bales.

1960, June 15

518 A136 8f red & blk (1) 13.50 1.40
519 A136 8f dp grn & blk (2) 13.50 1.40
520 A136 8f lil rose & blk (3) 13.50 1.40
521 A136 8f lt yel grn & blk (4) 13.50 1.40
522 A136 8f org & blk (5) 18.00 4.25
Nos. 518-522 (5) 72.00 9.85

Flag Inscribed "Serving the Workers" — A137

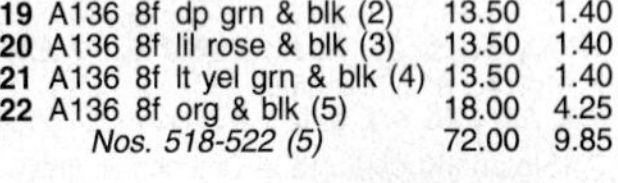

Flowers, Flags of North Korea and China — A138

Design: 8f, Inscribed stone seal.

1960, July 30 Photo. *Perf. 11½x11*

523 A137 4f lt grn, red, pink & brn 5.75 1.50

Photogravure & Engraved

524 A137 8f pale bl, red & bis 8.50 3.00

3rd Natl. Cong. for Literature and Arts, Peking.

1960, Aug. 15 Photo.

Design: 8f, Flying horse of Korea.

525 A138 8f red & multi 11.00 2.50
526 A138 8f ultra, red & indigo 11.00 4.50

15th anniversary of the liberation of Korea.

Railroad Station, Peking — A139

Design: 10f, Train arriving at station.

1960, Aug. 30 *Perf. 11½*

527 A139 8f blue, cream & brn 9.00 3.25
528 A139 10f bluish grn, cr & ind 13.50 4.00

Opening of new Peking Railroad Station.

Girls and Flags of North Viet Nam and China A140

Lake of the Returning Sword, Hanoi A141

Worker and Fresh-air Installation A142

1960, Sept. 2 *Perf. 11x11½, 11½x11*

529 A140 8f red & multi 3.50 .95
530 A141 8f red, gray grn & gray 3.50 2.40

15th anniversary of the Democratic Republic of North Viet Nam.

1960, Sept. 10 *Perf. 11½*

Designs: No. 532, Exterminator. No. 533, Window cleaning. No. 534, Medical examination of child. No. 535, Physical exercise.

531 A142 8f black & orange (1) 1.40 .25
532 A142 8f indigo & slate (2) 1.40 .25
533 A142 8f brown & blue (3) 1.40 .25
534 A142 8f maroon & ocher (4) 1.40 .25
535 A142 8f indigo & brt grn (5) 1.40 .45
Nos. 531-535 (5) 7.00 1.45

National health campaign.

Great Hall of the People — A143

Design: 10f, Inside view.

1960, Oct. 1

536 A143 8f yellow & multi 9.25 2.50
537 A143 10f brown & multi 14.00 3.00

Completion of the Great Hall of the People, Peking.

Dr. Norman Bethune — A144

Engels Addressing Congress at The Hague — A145

No. 539, Dr. Bethune operating on a soldier.

Photo. (No. 538); Engr. (No. 539)

1960, Nov. 20 *Perf. 11½x11*

538 A144 8f red & multi 3.00 .90
539 A144 8f sepia 3.00 .30

Dr. Norman Bethune (1890-1939), Canadian surgeon with 8th Army.

1960, Nov. 28 **Engr.**

540 A145 8f shown 5.75 1.25

Photo.

541 A145 10f Portrait of Engels 8.50 3.00

140th anniversary of the birth of Friedrich Engels (1820-1895), German Socialist.

"Hwang Shi Ba" A146

Freighter A147

1960-61 **Photo.**

Various Chrysanthemums in Natural Colors

542 A146 4f bl gray (1) 12.00 1.10
543 A146 4f pink (2) 22.50 1.10
544 A146 8f dk gray (3) 11.50 1.10
545 A146 8f dp blue (4) 11.50 1.10
546 A146 8f green (5) 11.50 1.10
547 A146 8f magenta (6) 11.50 1.10
548 A146 8f olive (7) 11.50 1.10
549 A146 8f grnsh bl (8) 40.00 1.10
550 A146 10f gray (9) 11.50 1.10
551 A146 10f choc (10) 11.50 1.10
552 A146 20f dp blue (11) 11.50 1.10
553 A146 20f brt red (12) 30.00 3.25
554 A146 22f olive bis (13) 20.00 7.00
555 A146 22f carmine (14) 40.00 11.00
556 A146 30f grnsh gray (15) 12.00 4.50
557 A146 30f brt pink (16) 12.00 4.50
558 A146 35f dp green (17) 16.00 4.50
559 A146 52f brt lilac rose (18) 17.00 8.75
Nos. 542-559 (18) 313.50 55.60

Issued: #548-550, 557-559, 12/10/60; #545-547, 554-556, 1/18/61; #542-544, 2/24/61.

1960, Dec. 15 *Perf. 11½*

Without Gum

560 A147 8f deep blue 3.50 1.40

1st 10,000-ton Chinese-built freighter, launching.

Pantheon, Paris — A148

Design: 8f, Proclamation of the Commune.

Engraved and Photogravure

1961, Mar. 18 *Perf. 11½x11*

561 A148 8f gray blk & red 6.25 1.10
562 A148 8f brown & red 6.25 1.10

90th anniversary of the Paris Commune.

Championship Symbol and Jasmine — A149

Designs: 10f, Table tennis racket and ball; Temple of Heaven. 20f, Table tennis match. 22f, Peking workers' gymnasium.

1961, Apr. 5 **Photo.** *Perf. 11*

563 A149 8f multicolored .80 .50
564 A149 10f multicolored 1.10 1.25
565 A149 20f multicolored 1.60 1.25
566 A149 22f multicolored 2.75 .50
a. Souv. sheet, #563-566 *450.00 250.00*
Nos. 563-566 (4) 6.25 3.50

26th World Table Tennis Championships, Peking.

Jeme Tien-yow — A150

Design: 10f, Train and tunnel, Peking-Changchow Railroad.

1961, June 20 *Perf. 11½x11*

567 A150 8f ol grn & blk 2.25 .65
568 A150 10f org brn & brn 4.00 2.00

Centenary of the birth of Jeme Tien-yow, railroad construction engineer.

Congress Building, Shanghai — A151

Designs: 8f, August 1st Building, Nanchang. 10f, Provisional Central Government Office, Juikin. 20f, Pagoda Hill, Yenan. 30f, Gate of Heavenly Peace, Peking.

1961, July 1 *Perf. 11½*

569 A151 4f gold, red & cl 9.75 .65
570 A151 8f gold, red & bl grn 9.75 2.00
571 A151 10f gold, red & yel brn 9.75 4.50
572 A151 20f gold, red & ultra 18.00 .65
573 A151 30f gold, red & org red 25.00 2.00
Nos. 569-573 (5) 72.25 9.80

40th anniv. of the Chinese Communist Party.

August 1 Building, Nanchang — A152

3f, 4f, 5f, Trees & Sha Cho Pa Building, Juikin. 8f, 10f, 20f, Pagoda Hill, Yenan. 22f, 30f, 50f, Gate of Heavenly Peace, Peking.

1961-62 **Engr.** *Perf. 11*

Without Gum

Size: 24x16mm

574 A152 1f vio blue 6.50 .25
575 A152 1½f maroon 12.00 .25
576 A152 2f indigo 6.50 .95
577 A152 3f dull vio 24.00 1.40
578 A152 4f green 2.40 .20
579 A152 5f gray 1.60 .25
580 A152 8f sepia 1.60 .20
581 A152 10f brt lil rose 4.00 .20
582 A152 20f grnsh bl 1.60 .20
583 A152 22f brown .80 .20
584 A152 30f blue 1.60 .20
585 A152 50f vermilion 1.60 .20
Nos. 574-585 (12) 64.20 4.50

Issued: 1f, 1½f, 5f, 7/20/62; others 7/20/61.

See Nos. 647-654, 1059-1064.

Flowers, Flags of Mongolia and China A153

Design: 10f, Parliament, Ulan Bator, and statue of Sukhe Bator.

1961, July 11 **Photo.** *Perf. 11x11½*

586 A153 8f crim, ultra & yel 10.00 1.60
587 A153 10f orange, blk & yel 17.00 7.25

40th anniv. of the Mongolian People's Republic.

Military Museum — A154

Photo. & Engr.

1961, Aug. 1 *Perf. 11½*

588 A154 8f gray bl, brn & grn 17.00 .85
589 A154 10f gray, blk & grn 14.50 1.40

Opening of the People's Revolutionary Military Museum.

Uprising at Wuchang A155

Sun Yat-sen — A156

Perf. 11x11½, 11½x11

1961, Oct. 10 **Photo.**

590 A155 8f gray & blk 8.00 1.75
591 A156 10f tan & black 12.00 .90

50th anniversary of the 1911 Revolution.

Donkey — A157

Rejoicing Tibetans — A158

Designs: 8f, 10f, 20f, 22f, Horses; 30f, 50f, Camels. Ceramic statuettes from Tang Dynasty (618-906) graves.

1961, Nov. 10 ***Perf. 11½x11***

Statuettes in Original Colors

592	A157	4f dull blue	4.00	.65
593	A157	8f gray green	4.00	.65
594	A157	8f dp purple	4.00	.65
595	A157	10f dp blue	4.00	.65
596	A157	20f olive	8.00	2.00
597	A157	22f blue grn	12.00	2.75
598	A157	30f red brown	16.00	8.00
599	A157	50f slate	16.00	4.50
		Nos. 592-599 (8)	68.00	19.85

1961, Nov. 25

Designs: 8f, Woman sower. 10f, Celebration of bumper crop. 20f, People's representatives. 30f, Tibetan children.

600	A158	4f brn & ocher	3.50	.80
601	A158	8f brn & lt bl grn	3.50	.80
602	A158	10f brn & yel	17.50	1.60
603	A158	20f brn & rose	26.00	2.40
604	A158	30f brn & bluish gray	42.50	3.25
		Nos. 600-604 (5)	93.00	8.85

Rebirth of the Tibetan people.

Lu Hsun — A159

1962, Feb. 26

605	A159	8f red brown & blk	1.60	.30

80th anniv. of the birth of Lu Hsun, writer.

An Chi Bridge, Chao Hsien — A160

Bridges of Ancient China: 8f, Pao Tai, Soochow. 10f, Chu Pu, Kwan Hsien. 20f, Chen Yang, San Kiang.

1962, May 15 ***Perf. 11***

606	A160	4f dk gray blue	1.25	.20
607	A160	8f dp green	1.25	.20
608	A160	10f brown	2.00	.35
609	A160	20f grnsh blue	3.50	.70
		Nos. 606-609 (4)	8.00	1.45

Tu Fu — A161

Cranes and Bamboo — A162

4f, Tu Fu memorial pavilion, Chengtu.

1962, May 25 ***Perf. 11½x11***

610	A161	4f ol bis & blk	11.50	.80
611	A161	8f grnsh bl & blk	11.50	1.90

Poet Tu Fu, 1,250th anniversary of birth.

1962, June 10

10f, Two cranes in flight. 20f, Crane on rock.

612	A162	8f tan & multi	8.75	2.00
613	A162	10f blue & multi	13.00	3.00
614	A162	20f bister & multi	26.00	4.00
		Nos. 612-614 (3)	47.75	9.00

"The Sacred Crane," from paintings by Chen Chi-fo.

Cuban Soldier and Flag A163

Designs: 10f, Sugar cane worker. 22f, Militiaman and woman.

1962, July 10 ***Perf. 11x11½***

615	A163	8f car, rose & blk	18.00	6.50
616	A163	10f green & blk	27.50	2.00
617	A163	22f ultra & blk	62.50	14.00
		Nos. 615-617 (3)	108.00	22.50

Support of Cuba.

Torch and Map of Algeria — A164

Mei Lan-fang — A165

Design: 22f, Algerian soldiers and flag.

1962, July 10 ***Perf. 11½x11***

618	A164	8f dp brown & red org	.30	.25
619	A164	22f ocher & dp brn	1.50	.75

Support of Algeria.

1962 ***Perf. 11½x11, 11x11½***

Designs (Mei Lan-fang in Women's Roles): No. 621, Beating drum. No. 622, With fan. 10f, Lady Yu with swords. 20f, With bag. 22f, Heavenly Maiden, horiz. 30f, With spinning wheel, horiz. 50f, Kneeling, horiz. $3, Scene from opera "Drunken Beauty."

620	A165	4f tan & multi	100.00	4.50
621	A165	8f tan & multi	15.00	2.75
622	A165	8f gray & multi	15.00	2.75
623	A165	10f gray & multi	15.00	5.50
624	A165	20f lt grn & multi	15.00	7.25
625	A165	22f cream & multi	30.00	9.00
626	A165	30f lt blue & multi	60.00	27.50
627	A165	50f buff & multi	50.00	22.50
		Nos. 620-627 (8)	300.00	81.75

Souvenir Sheet

Perf. 11

628	A165	$3 brown & multi	*2,400.*	*950.00*

Stage art of Mei Lan-fang, actor.

Issued: 4f, 8f, 10f, 8/8; $3, 9/15; others 9/1.

Nos. 620-627 exist imperf. Value, set $2,250.

No. 628 contains one 48x58mm stamp and almost always has some faults. Value above is for fault-free examples. Value for No. 628 with small faults, unused $1,500. Excellent forgeries exist.

Flower Drum Dance, Han — A166

Folk Dances: 8f, Ordos, Mongolia. 10f, Catching shrimp, Chuang. 20f, Friend, Yi. 30f, Fiddle dance, Tibet. 50f, Tambourine dance, Uighur.

Cumulative numbers 246-251 at lower right.

1962, Oct. 15 **Litho.** ***Perf. 12½***

Without Gum

629	A166	4f cream & multi	.60	.35
630	A166	8f cream & multi	.60	.35
631	A166	10f cream & multi	.85	.35
632	A166	20f cream & multi	.85	.35
633	A166	30f cream & multi	1.75	.70
634	A166	50f cream & multi	3.50	1.40
		Nos. 629-634 (6)	8.15	3.50

See Nos. 696-707.

Soldiers Storming Winter Palace — A167

Design: 8f, Lenin leading soldiers, vert.

1962, Nov. 7 **Photo.** ***Perf. 11½***

635	A167	8f black & red	12.00	.85
636	A167	20f slate grn & red	27.50	1.50

45th anniversary of the Russian Revolution.

Monument and Map of Albania — A168

Tsai Lun, Inventor of Papermaking A169

Design: 10f, Albanian flag and Girl Pioneer.

1962, Nov. 28 ***Perf. 11½x11***

637	A168	8f Prus blue & sepia	1.40	.35
638	A168	10f red, yel, & blk	2.25	1.00

50th anniversary of Albanian independence.

1962, Dec. 1 ***Perf. 11½x11***

Designs: No. 640, Paper making. No. 641, Sun Szu-miao, physician. No. 642, Writing medical treatise. No. 643, Shen Ko, geologist. No. 644, Making field notes. No. 645, Kuo Shou-chin, astronomer. No. 646, Astronomical instrument.

Cumulative numbers 297-304 at lower right.

639	A169	4f multicolored	5.75	.20
640	A169	4f multicolored	2.75	.30
641	A169	8f multicolored	2.75	.30
642	A169	8f multicolored	2.75	.30
643	A169	10f multicolored	2.75	.30
644	A169	10f multicolored	3.50	.30
645	A169	20f multicolored	7.25	.90
646	A169	20f multicolored	7.25	.90
		Nos. 639-646 (8)	34.75	3.50

Scientists of ancient China.

Building Type of 1961

Designs: 1f, 2f, Building, Nanchang. 3f, 4f, Trees and Sha Cho Pa Building. 8f, 10f, 20f, Pagoda Hill, Yenan. 30f, Gate of Heavenly Peace, Peking.

1962, Jan. **Litho.** ***Rough Perf. 12½***

Size: 21x16mm

Without Gum

647	A152	1f ultra	.45	.20
648	A152	2f greenish gray	.45	.20
649	A152	3f violet gray	.45	.20
650	A152	4f green	.45	.20
651	A152	8f dk olive, perf. 14	.80	.20
b.		Perf. 11x11½	5.00	
652	A152	10f brt rose lilac	1.25	.20
653	A152	20f slate blue	1.25	.20
654	A152	30f dull blue	1.75	.25
		Nos. 647-654 (8)	6.85	1.65

Tank Monument, Havana A170

Crowd in Havana — A171

Designs: No. 656, Cuban revolutionaries. No. 658, Crowd in Peking. No. 659, Cuban soldier. No. 660, Castro and Cuban flag.

Perf. 11½, 11x11½

1963, Jan. 1 **Photo.**

655	A170	4f red & blk brn	27.50	1.90
656	A170	4f green & blk	18.00	1.90
657	A171	8f dull red & brn	18.00	1.90
658	A171	8f dull red & brn	55.00	11.00
659	A170	10f ocher & blk	55.00	5.50
660	A170	10f red, blue & blk	55.00	*15.00*
		Nos. 655-660 (6)	228.50	*37.20*

4th anniversary of the Cuban revolution.

Green Dragontail — A172

Karl Marx — A173

1963 **Without Gum** ***Perf. 11***

661	A172	4f Tibetan clouded yellow (1)	10.00	3.50
662	A172	4f Tritailed glory (2)	10.00	.50
663	A172	4f Neumogeni jungle queen (3)	10.00	.50
664	A172	4f Washan swordtail (4)	10.00	.50
665	A172	4f Striped ringlet (5)	10.00	.50
666	A172	8f shown (6)	10.00	.50
667	A172	8f Dilunulated peacock (7)	10.00	.50
668	A172	8f Yamfly (8)	10.00	.50
669	A172	8f Golden kaiser-i-hind (9)	10.00	.50
670	A172	8f Mushaell hairstreak (10)	10.00	.50

671 A172 10f Yellow orange-tip (11) 10.00 .50
672 A172 10f Great jay (12) 10.00 .50
673 A172 10f Striped punch (13) 10.00 .50
674 A172 10f Hainan violet-beak (14) 10.00 .50
675 A172 10f Omeiskipper (15) 10.00 2.50
676 A172 20f Philippines birdwing (16) 10.00 2.50
677 A172 20f Richtofenis red apollo (17) 10.00 3.25
678 A172 22f Blue-banded king crow (18) 10.00 3.25
679 A172 30f Solskyi copper (19) 10.00 3.25
680 A172 50f Yunnan clipper (20) 10.00 4.50
Nos. 661-680 (20) 200.00 29.25

Issued: #666-675, July 15; others Apr. 5.

1963, May 5 ***Perf. 11½***

Designs: No. 682, "Workers of the World, Unite" on cover of first edition of Communist Manifesto. No. 683, Marx and Engels.

Without Gum

681 A173 8f black, gold & sal (1) 5.00 2.00
682 A173 8f gold & red (2) 5.00 2.00
683 A173 8f gold & choc (3) 5.00 2.00
Nos. 681-683 (3) 15.00 6.00

145th anniversary of birth of Karl Marx (1818-1883), German political philosopher.

Child with Top — A174

Child: #685, eating berries. #686, as traffic policeman. #687, with windmill. #688, listening to caged cricket. #689, with sword. #690, embroidering. #691, with umbrella. #692, playing with sand. #693, playing table tennis. #694, learning to add. #695, with kite.

1963, June 1 **Litho.** ***Perf. 12½***

Without Gum

Multicolored Designs

684 A174 4f grnsh gray (1) .65 .20
685 A174 4f tan (2) .65 .20
686 A174 8f gray (3) .65 .20
687 A174 8f blue (4) .65 .20
688 A174 8f tan (5) .65 .20
689 A174 8f dp gray (6) .65 .20
690 A174 8f citron (7) .65 .20
691 A174 8f gray (8) .65 .20
692 A174 10f green (9) 1.40 .45
693 A174 10f violet (10) 1.40 .45
694 A174 20f bister (11) 2.75 1.00
695 A174 20f green (12) 2.75 1.00
Nos. 684-695 (12) 13.50 4.50

Children's Day. Value, imperf set $125.

Dance Type of 1962

Folk Dances: 4f, Weavers' dance, Puyi. 8f, Kazakh. 10f, Olunchun. 20f, Labor dance, Kaochan. 30f, Reed pipe dance, Miao. 50f, Fan dance, Korea.

Cumulative numbers 261-266 at lower right.

1963, June 15 ***Perf. 12½***

Without Gum

696 A166 4f cream & multi .60 .35
697 A166 8f cream & multi .60 .35
698 A166 10f cream & multi .90 .35
699 A166 20f cream & multi .90 .35
700 A166 30f cream & multi 1.75 .70
701 A166 50f cream & multi 1.75 .70
Nos. 696-701 (6) 6.50 2.80

1963, June 30 **Without Gum**

Folk Dances: 4f, "Wedding Ceremony," Yu. 8f, "Encircling Mountain Forest," Pai. 10f, Long drum dance, Yao. 20f, Third day of the third month dance, Li. 30f, Knife dance, Kawa. 50f, Peacock dance, Thai.

Cumulative numbers 279-284 at lower right.

702 A166 4f cream & multi .75 .35
703 A166 8f cream & multi .75 .35
704 A166 10f cream & multi 1.10 .35
705 A166 20f cream & multi 1.10 .35
706 A166 30f cream & multi 2.25 .60
707 A166 50f cream & multi 3.75 1.00
Nos. 702-707 (6) 9.70 3.00

Giant Panda Eating Apples — A175

Table Tennis Player — A176

Designs: No. 709, Giant panda eating bamboo shoots. 10f, Two pandas, horiz.

1963, Aug. 5 **Photo.** ***Perf. 11½x11***

Size: 28x38mm

708 A175 8f pale blue & blk 27.50 1.75
709 A175 8f pale blue & blk 27.50 6.25

Size: 50x29mm

Perf. 11½

710 A175 10f olive & blk 27.50 3.75
Nos. 708-710 (3) 82.50 11.75

Value, imperf set $225.

1963, Sept. 10 **Engr.** ***Perf. 11½***

No. 712, Trophies won by Chinese team.

711 A176 8f dk olive grn 10.50 .80
712 A176 8f brown 10.50 1.75

27th World Table Tennis Championships.

Snub-nosed Langur — A177

Jade-green Screen Mountain — A178

Designs: 10f, Two monkeys playing. 22f, Two monkeys grooming.

1963, Sept. 23 **Photo.** ***Perf. 11½x11***

713 A177 8f gray & multi 7.75 1.10
714 A177 10f gray & multi 7.75 1.10
715 A177 22f gray & multi 11.50 4.50
Nos. 713-715 (3) 27.00 6.70

Value, imperf set $190.

Engraved and Photogravure

1963, Oct. 15 ***Perf. 11½***

Hwang Shan Landscapes (Yellow Mountains), Anhwei Province. #724-731 horiz.

Design A178

716 4f shown (1) 10.00 1.25
717 4f "Guests Welcoming Pines" (2) 10.00 1.25
718 4f Pines and Rock Behind the Sea (3) 10.00 1.75
719 4f Terrace of Keeping Cool (4) 13.00 1.75
720 8f Mount of Heavenly Capital (5) 13.00 1.75
721 8f Mount of Scissors (6) 13.00 1.75
722 8f Forest of Ten Thousand Pines (7) 13.00 1.75
723 8f "Brush Blooming in Dream" (8) 16.00 1.75
724 10f Mount of Lotus Flower (9) 16.00 1.75
725 10f Cumulus Cloud over West Sea (10) 22.50 1.75
726 10f Old Pines of Hwang Shan (11) 26.00 1.75
727 10f "Watching the Clouds over West Sea" (12) 32.50 1.75
728 20f Mount of Stalagmites (13) 40.00 6.00
729 22f "Stone Monkey Watching the Sea" (14) 40.00 9.50
730 30f Forest of Lions (15) 65.00 35.00
731 50f Three Fairy Tales of Pen Lai (16) 52.50 17.50
Nos. 716-731 (16) 392.50 88.00

Soccer Player — A179

Athletes and Banners — A180

#733, Discus, women's. #734, Diving, men's. #735, Gymnastics, women's.

Engraved and Photogravure

1963, Nov. 17 ***Perf. 11***

732 A179 8f gray, red & blk (1) 11.00 .80
733 A179 8f gray, ultra & blk (2) 11.00 .80
734 A179 8f lt grn, brn & blk (3) 11.00 .80
735 A179 8f gray, lil rose & blk (4) 11.00 .80

Photo. ***Perf. 11½***

736 A180 10f red & multi (5) 11.00 3.25
Nos. 732-736 (5) 55.00 6.45

Games of the Newly Emerging Forces, Djakarta.

Clay Rooster and Goat — A181

Chinese Folk Toys: No. 738, Cloth camel. No. 739, Cloth tigers. No. 740, Clay ox and rider. No. 741, Cloth rabbit, wooden doll, clay roosters. No. 742, Straw rooster. No. 743, Cloth donkey and bird. No. 744, Clay lion. No. 745, Cloth tiger and tumbler doll.

1963, Dec. 10 **Litho.** ***Perf. 11½***

Toys Multicolored; Without Gum

737 A181 4f bister (1) .65 .20
738 A181 4f gray (4) .65 .20
739 A181 4f lt blue (7) .65 .20
740 A181 8f bister (2) .65 .20
741 A181 8f gray (5) .65 .20
742 A181 8f lt blue (8) .65 .25
743 A181 10f bister (3) .65 .25
744 A181 10f gray (6) .65 .25
745 A181 10f lt blue (9) .65 .25
Nos. 737-745 (9) 5.85 2.00

Armed Vietnamese Family — A182

Flags of Cuba and China — A183

Liberation of South Viet Nam: No. 747, Militia with Vietnamese flag.

1963, Dec. 20 **Photo.** ***Perf. 11½x11***

746 A182 8f tan, blk & red 2.75 .80
747 A182 8f red & multi 2.75 1.60

1964, Jan. 1

Design: No. 749, Boy waving Cuban flag.

748 A183 8f red, yel, bl & ind 6.50 .55
749 A183 8f multicolored 17.00 4.00

5th anniversary of the liberation of Cuba.

Woman Driving Tractor — A184

Woman of the People's Commune: No. 751, harvesting. No. 752, picking cotton. No. 753, picking fruit. No. 754, reading book. No. 755, on guard duty.

1964, Mar. 8

750 A184 8f ol, pink & brn (1) .70 .20
751 A184 8f brn yel & org (2) .70 .20
752 A184 8f gray & multi (3) .70 .20
753 A184 8f black, org & bl (4) .75 .20
754 A184 8f green & multi (5) .75 .20
755 A184 8f lilac & multi (6) .75 .30
Nos. 750-755 (6) 4.35 1.30

Chinese and African Men A185

Design: No. 757, African drummer.

1964, Apr. 12 **Photo.** ***Perf. 11***

756 A185 8f red & multi .90 .25
757 A185 8f black & dk brn .90 .25

African Freedom Day.

Marx, Engels, Lenin and Stalin — A186

Design: No. 759, Banners and workers.

1964, May 1 ***Perf. 11½***

758 A186 8f gold, red & blk 16.00 *5.00*
759 A186 8f gold, red & blk 5.50 *1.25*

Labor Day.

Orchard, Yenan A187

Yenan, Shrine of the Chinese Revolution: No. 761, Central Auditorium, Yang Chia Ling. No. 762, Mao's office and residence. No. 763, Auditorium, Wang Chia Ping. No. 764, Border Region Assembly Hall. No. 765, Pagoda Hill and Bridge.

1964, July 1 Photo. *Perf. 11x11½*
760 A187 8f multicolored (1) 17.00 .85
761 A187 8f multicolored (2) 3.25 .40
762 A187 8f multicolored (3) 3.25 .40
763 A187 8f multicolored (4) 3.25 .40
764 A187 8f multicolored (5) 10.50 .85
765 A187 52f multicolored (6) 17.00 3.25
Nos. 760-765 (6) 54.25 6.15

Map and Flag of Viet Nam — A188

Alchemist's Glowing Crucible — A189

1964, July 20 *Perf. 11½*
766 A188 8f multicolored 12.50 3.50

Victory in South Viet Nam.

1964, Aug. 5 *Perf. 11½x11*
767 A189 4f shown (1) 5.25 1.00
768 A189 4f Night-shining jade (2) 5.25 1.00
769 A189 8f Purple Kuo's cap (3) 8.75 1.00
770 A189 8f Chao pink (4) 8.75 1.00
771 A189 8f Yao yellow (5) 8.75 1.00
772 A189 8f Twin beauty (6) 8.75 1.00
773 A189 8f Ice-veiled ruby (7) 8.75 1.40
774 A189 10f Gold-sprinkled Chinese ink (8) 10.50 1.40
775 A189 10f Cinnabar jar (9) 10.50 1.40
776 A189 10f Lan Tien jade (10) 12.50 2.10
777 A189 10f Imperial robe yellow (11) 13.00 2.10
778 A189 10f Hu red (12) 13.00 2.10
779 A189 20f Pea green (13) 26.00 *4.25*
780 A189 43f Wei purple (14) 35.00 *14.00*
781 A189 52f Intoxicated celestial peach (15) 52.50 *17.50*
Nos. 767-781 (15) 227.25 *52.25*

Souvenir Sheet

Perf. 11½

Without Gum

782 A189 $2 Glorious crimson & great gold pink *850.00 400.00*

No. 782 contains one 48x59mm stamp.

Wine Cup — A190

Grain Harvest — A191

Designs: Sacrificial bronze vessels of Yin dynasty, prior to 1050 B.C.

Engraved and Photogravure

1964, Aug. 25 *Perf. 11½x11*
783 A190 4f shown (1) 4.00 .90
784 A190 4f Ku beaker (2) 4.00 .90
785 A190 8f Kuang wine urn (3) 6.75 .90
786 A190 8f Chia wine cup (4) 7.50 .90
787 A190 10f Tsun wine vessel (5) 7.50 .90
788 A190 10f Yu wine urn (6) 7.50 .90
789 A190 20f Tsun wine vessel (7) 8.25 3.50
790 A190 20f Ceremonial cauldron (8) 8.25 3.50
Nos. 783-790 (8) 53.75 12.40

1964, Sept. 26 Photo.

Designs: #792, Students planting trees. #793, Study period. #794, Scientific experimentation.

791 A191 8f multicolored (1) 1.40 .25
792 A191 8f multicolored (2) 1.40 .25
793 A191 8f multicolored (3) 1.40 .25
794 A191 8f multicolored (4) 1.40 .25
Nos. 791-794 (4) 5.60 1.00

Youth helping in agriculture.

Marx, Engels, Trafalgar Square, London — A192

People with Banners — A193

1964, Sept. 28 *Perf. 11½*
795 A192 8f red, gold & red brn 35.00 16.00

Centenary of the First International.

Gold Ink

Stamps with gold ink often show some tarnishing. Values are for untarnished gold color. Tarnished stamps will sell for less.

1964, Oct. 1

No. 797, Gate of Heavenly Peace and Chinese flag. No. 798, People with banners, facing left.

796 A193 8f cream & multi (1) 20.00 1.90
797 A193 8f cream & multi (2) 20.00 2.75
798 A193 8f cream & multi (3) 20.00 2.75
a. Souvenir sheet of 3 *2,000. 600.00*
b. Strip of 3, #796-798 100.00 13.50
Nos. 796-798 (3) 60.00 7.40

15th anniv. of the People's Republic.

No. 798a contains No. 798b in continuous design without separating perfs. No. 798a almost always has disturbed gum, with interleaving paper sticking to it, or tarnished gilt. Such copies sell for considerably less than the very fine example valued above.

Values for No. 798b are for an unfolded strip.

Oil Derricks — A194

Oil industry: 4f, Geological surveyors and truck, horiz. 8f, "Christmas tree" and extraction accessories. 10f, Oil refinery. 20f, Tank cars, horiz.

1964, Oct. 1
799 A194 4f lt blue & multi 47.50 3.00
800 A194 8f lt blue & multi 19.00 1.50
801 A194 8f lilac & multi 19.00 1.50
802 A194 10f slate & multi 47.50 1.50
803 A194 20f brown & multi 92.50 *8.00*
Nos. 799-803 (5) 225.50 *15.50*

Albanian and Chinese Flags A195

10f, Enver Hoxha and Albanian coat of arms.

1964, Nov. 29 *Perf. 11x11½*
804 A195 8f red & multi 9.00 *2.00*
805 A195 10f red, yel & blk 13.50 8.00

20th anniv. of the liberation of Albania.

Power Dam Construction A196

No. 807, Installation of turbogenerator rotor. No. 808, Main dam. 20f, Pylon.

1964, Dec. 15 *Perf. 11½*
806 A196 4f multicolored 55.00 2.25
807 A196 8f multicolored 18.00 .85
808 A196 8f multicolored 35.00 1.40
809 A196 20f multicolored 90.00 6.50
Nos. 806-809 (4) 198.00 11.00

Hsin An Kiang Dam and hydroelectric power station.

Fertilizer Industry — A197

Chemical Industry: #811, Plastics. #812, Medicines. #813, Rubber. #814, Insecticides. #815, Industrial acids. #816, Industrial alkaloids. #817, Synthetic fibers.

1964, Dec. 30 Photo. & Engr.
810 A197 8f red & blk (1) 2.00 .25
811 A197 8f yel grn & blk (2) 2.00 .25
812 A197 8f brown & blk (3) 2.00 .25
813 A197 8f lilac rose & blk (4) 2.00 .25
814 A197 8f blue & blk (5) 2.00 .25
815 A197 8f orange & blk (6) 2.00 .25
816 A197 8f violet & blk (7) 2.00 .25
817 A197 8f brt green & blk (8) 2.00 .25
Nos. 810-817 (8) 16.00 2.00

Mao Studying Map — A198

Mao Tse-tung — A199

Design: No. 819, Victory at Lushan Pass.

1965, Jan. 31 Photo. *Perf. 11*
818 A198 8f red & multi 32.50 4.00
819 A198 8f red & multi 14.00 4.00

Perf. 11½x11
820 A199 8f gold & multi 27.50 5.50
Nos. 818-820 (3) 74.00 13.50

Tsunyi Conference, 30th anniversary.

Conference Hall, Bandung — A200

Lenin — A201

#822, Asians and Africans applauding.

1965, Apr. 18 *Perf. 11½x11*
821 A200 8f cream & multi .90 .20
822 A200 8f cream & multi .90 .20

10th anniversary of the Bandung, Indonesia, Conference, Apr. 1955.

1965, Apr. 25 *Perf. 11½*
823 A201 8f red, choc & salmon 12.50 5.00

95th anniversary of the birth of Lenin.

Chinese Player — A202

1965, Apr. 25 *Perf. 11½*
824 A202 8f shown (1) .50 .20
825 A202 8f European woman (2) .50 .20

826 A202 8f Chinese woman (3) .50 .20
827 A202 8f European man (4) .50 .20
a. Block of 4, #824-827 2.75 .80

28th World Table Tennis Championships, Ljubljana, Yugoslavia, Apr. 15-25.

Climbers on Mt. Minya Konka — A203

Marx and Lenin — A204

Mountain Climbers: No. 829, on Muztagh Ata. No. 830, on Mt. Jolmo Lungma (Mt. Everest). No. 831, Women camping on Kongur Tiubie Tagh. No. 832, on Shisha Pangma.

1965, May 25 **Photo. & Engr.**

828 A203 8f blue, blk & ol (1) 3.50 .70
829 A203 8f blue, blk & ol (2) 4.25 .70
830 A203 8f ultra, blk & gray (3) 4.25 .70
831 A203 8f lt bl, blk & yel gray (4) 4.25 .70
832 A203 8f ultra, blk & gray (5) 5.00 2.75
Nos. 828-832 (5) 21.25 5.55

Chinese mountaineering achievements, 1957-64.

1965, June 21 **Photo.** ***Perf. 11½x11***

833 A204 8f red, yel & blk 11.50 5.00

Postal Ministers' Congress, Peking.

Tseping Valley A205

Chingkang Mountains, Cradle of the Chinese Revolution.

1965, July 1 ***Perf. 11x11½***

834 A205 4f shown (1) 7.25 .65
835 A205 8f San Wan Tsun (2) 7.25 .65
836 A205 8f Octagon Bldg., Mao Ping (3) 29.00 .65
837 A205 8f River and Bridge at Lung Shih (4) 21.00 1.25
838 A205 8f Ta Ching Tsun (5) 14.50 1.25
839 A205 10f Bridge across the Lung Yuan (6) 14.50 .65
840 A205 10f Hwang Yang Mountain (7) 11.00 1.25
841 A205 52f Chingkang peaks (8) 11.00 6.25
Nos. 834-841 (8) 115.50 12.60

Soldiers with Books — A206

1965, Aug. 1 ***Perf. 11½***

Without Gum

842 A206 8f shown (1) 21.00 4.00
843 A206 8f Soldiers reading Little Red Books (2) 21.00 4.00
844 A206 8f With shell and artillery (3) 21.00 2.00
845 A206 8f Rifle instruction (4) 21.00 2.00
846 A206 8f Sewing jacket (5) 10.50 2.00
847 A206 8f Bayonet charge (6) 10.50 2.00
848 A206 8f With Banner (7) 10.50 6.00
849 A206 8f Military band (8) 10.50 3.00
Nos. 842-849 (8) 126.00 25.00

People's Liberation Army. Nos. 846-849 vertical.

"Welcome to Peking" — A207

#851, Chinese and Japanese young men. #852, Chinese and Japanese girls. #853, Musical entertainment. #854, Emblem of meeting.

1965, Aug. 25 ***Perf. 11½x11***

850 A207 4f yellow & multi 1.10 .25
851 A207 8f pink & multi 1.10 .25
852 A207 8f multicolored 1.10 .25
853 A207 10f multicolored 1.60 .25
854 A207 22f lt blue & multi 2.75 .50
Nos. 850-854 (5) 7.65 1.50

Chinese-Japanese Youth Meeting, Peking.

North Vietnamese Soldier — A208

Peoples of the World — A209

Designs: No. 856, Soldier with guns. No. 857, Soldier giving victory salute.

1965, Sept. 2 ***Perf. 11½x11***

855 A208 8f red & red brn (1) 1.10 .20
856 A208 8f red & blk (2) 1.10 .20
857 A208 8f red & vio brn (3) 1.10 .20

Perf. 11½

858 A209 8f black & red (4) 1.10 .20
Nos. 855-858 (4) 4.40 .80

Struggle of the people of Viet Nam.

Mao Tse-tung at His Desk — A210

Crossing Yellow River A211

Victory Monument A212

Design: No. 862, Recruits in cart.

1965, Sept. 3 ***Perf. 11***

859 A210 8f red & multi (1) 21.00 6.50

Perf. 11x11½, 11½x11

860 A211 8f red & dk grn (2) 4.50 .90
861 A212 8f red & dk brn (3) 4.50 .90
862 A211 8f red & dk grn (4) 4.50 .90
Nos. 859-862 (4) 34.50 9.20

20th anniversary of victory over Japan.

2nd National Games — A213

National Games Opening Ceremonies — A214

Perf. 11½x11, 11 (A214)

1965, Sept. 28

863 A213 4f Soccer (1) 8.50 .50
864 A213 4f Archery (2) 8.50 .50
865 A213 8f Javelin (3) 8.50 .50
866 A213 8f Gymnastics (4) 8.50 .50
867 A213 8f Volleyball (5) 8.50 .50
868 A214 10f shown (6) 35.00 .50
869 A213 10f Bicyling (7) 60.00 .50
870 A213 20f Diving (8) 50.00 1.50
871 A213 22f Hurdles (9) 8.50 1.50
872 A213 30f Weight lifting (10) 8.50 4.50
873 A213 43f Basketball (11) 17.00 7.00
Nos. 863-873 (11) 221.50 18.00

Government Building A215

Textile Workers A216

1½f, 5f, 22f, Gate of Heavenly Peace. 2f, 8f, 30f, People's Hall. 3f, 10f, 50f, Military Museum.

1965-66 ***Perf. 11½x11***

Without Gum

874 A215 1f brown .20 .20
875 A215 1½f red lilac .20 *.50*
876 A215 2f green .20 .20
877 A215 3f blue grn .20 .20
878 A215 4f brt blue .20 .20
879 A215 5f vio brn ('66) .40 .20
880 A215 8f rose red .40 .20
881 A215 10f gray olive .80 .20
882 A215 20f violet .80 .20
883 A215 22f orange 1.60 .25
884 A215 30f yellow grn 2.50 .30
885 A215 50f dp blue ('66) 7.50 *1.50*
Nos. 874-885 (12) 15.00 *4.15*

1965, Nov. 30

886 A216 8f shown (1) 6.75 .80
887 A216 8f Machine shop (2) 6.75 .80
888 A216 8f Welder (3) 6.75 .80
889 A216 8f Students (4) 6.75 .80
890 A216 8f Militia (5) 6.75 2.40
Nos. 886-890 (5) 33.75 5.60

Women workers.

Soccer — A217

Children's Sports: No. 892, Racing. No. 893, Tobogganing and skating. No. 894, Gymnastics. No. 895, Swimming. No. 896, Rifle practice. No. 897, Jumping rope. No. 898, Table tennis.

1966, Feb. 25 ***Perf. 11***

891 A217 4f emerald & multi (1) .30 .20
892 A217 4f yel brown & multi (2) .30 .20
893 A217 8f blue & multi (3) .30 .20
894 A217 8f yellow & multi (4) .30 .20
895 A217 8f grnsh bl & multi (5) .55 .20
896 A217 8f green & multi (6) .55 .20
897 A217 10f orange & multi (7) 1.10 .40
898 A217 52f grnsh gray & multi (8) 1.60 1.10
Nos. 891-898 (8) 5.00 2.70

Mobile Transformer A218

New Industrial Machinery: No. 900, Electron microscope, vert. No. 901, Lathe. No. 902, Vertical boring and turning machine, vert. No. 903, Gear-grinding machine. No. 904, Hydraulic press. No. 905, Milling machine. No. 906, Electron accelerator, vert.

Perf. 11x11½, 11½x11

1966, Mar. 30 **Photo. & Engr.**

899 A218 4f yellow & blk (1) 7.25 .90
900 A218 8f blk & lt ultra (2) 11.00 .90
901 A218 8f sal pink & blk (3) 11.00 .90
902 A218 8f olive & blk (4) 11.00 .90
903 A218 8f rose lil & blk (5) 11.00 .90
904 A218 10f gray & blk (6) 14.50 .90
905 A218 10f bl grn & blk (7) 14.50 3.50
906 A218 22f lilac & blk (8) 29.00 5.50
Nos. 899-906 (8) 109.25 14.40

Military and Civilian Workers A219

Women in Various Occupations: No. 908, Train conductor. No. 909, Red Cross worker. No. 910, Kindergarten teacher. No. 911, Road sweeper. No. 912, Hairdresser. No. 913, Bus conductor. No. 914, Traveling saleswoman. No. 915, Canteen worker. No. 916, Rural mail carrier.

1966, May 10 ***Perf. 11x11½***

907 A219 8f red & multi (1) .60 .25
908 A219 8f pale grn & multi (2) .60 .25
909 A219 8f yellow & multi (3) .60 .25
910 A219 8f green & multi (4) .60 .25
911 A219 8f salmon & multi (5) .60 .25
912 A219 8f pale bl & bl (6) .60 .25
913 A219 8f yellow & multi (7) .60 .25
914 A219 8f tan & multi (8) .60 .25
915 A219 8f yel grn & multi (9) .60 .25
916 A219 8f green & multi (10) .60 .25
Nos. 907-916 (10) 6.00 2.50

Statue "Thunderstorm" — A220

22f, Open book and association emblem.

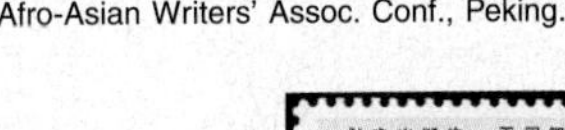

1966, June 27 ***Perf. 11***

917	A220 8f red & black	2.00	.35
918	A220 22f red, gold & yel	6.00	.75

Afro-Asian Writers' Assoc. Conf., Peking.

Sun Yat-sen — A221

1966, Nov. 12 ***Perf. 11½x11***

919	A221 8f sepia & lt buff	24.00	9.00

Birth centenary of Sun Yat-sen.

Athletes Holding Portrait of Mao — A222

Two Women Athletes with Little Red Book A223

#921, Athletes holding Little Red Books. #923, Athletes reading Mao texts.

1966, Dec. 31 ***Perf. 11***

920	A222 8f red & multi (1)	22.50	6.50
921	A222 8f red & multi (2)	22.50	6.50

Perf. 11x11½

922	A223 8f blue & multi (3)	22.50	5.00
923	A223 8f blue & multi (4)	22.50	5.00
	Nos. 920-923 (4)	90.00	23.00

1st Athletic Games of the New Emerging Nations.

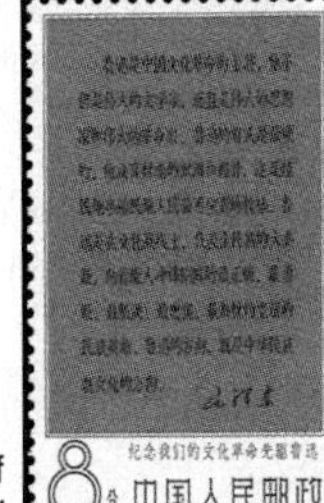

Appreciation of Lu Hsun by Mao — A224

"Be Resolute ...," by Mao Tse-tung — A225

Designs: No. 925, Portrait of Lu Hsun. No. 926, Lu Hsun's handwriting (3 vert. rows).

Engr. & Photo.; Photo. (#925)

1966, Dec. 31 ***Perf. 11½***

924	A224 8f red & black (1)	57.50	7.00
925	A224 8f red & multi (2)	19.00	11.50
926	A224 8f red & black (3)	37.50	11.50
	Nos. 924-926 (3)	114.00	30.00

Lu Hsun, Revolutionary writer (1881-1936).

Perf. 11½x11, 11½ (No. 928)

1967, Mar. 10 **Photo.**

Designs: No. 928, Drilling crew fighting natural gas fire, horiz. No. 929, Attempt to close fire-engulfed valve.

Sizes: Nos. 927, 929, 26x38mm; No. 928, 49x29mm

927	A225 8f red, gold & blk	22.50	8.00
928	A225 8f brick red & blk	26.00	6.00
929	A225 8f brick red & blk	26.00	6.00
	Nos. 927-929 (3)	74.50	20.00

Heroic oil well firefighters.

Liu Ying-chun A226

1967, Mar. 25 ***Perf. 11½x11***

930	A226 8f shown (1)	20.00	6.75
931	A226 8f With book by Mao (2)	20.00	5.25
932	A226 8f Holding bridle of horse (3)	24.00	6.75
933	A226 8f With film slide (4)	24.00	5.25
934	A226 8f Lecturing (5)	24.00	5.25
935	A226 8f Fatal attempt to stop runaway horse (6)	24.00	5.25
	Nos. 930-935 (6)	136.00	34.50

In memory of soldier Liu Ying-chun, hero.

Industrial Growth — A227

Design: No. 937, Banners and people facing left: agricultural growth.

1967, Apr. 15 ***Perf. 11***

936	A227 8f red & multi	32.50	7.25
937	A227 8f red & multi	32.50	7.25

Third Five-Year Plan.

Mao Tse-tung — A228

Thoughts of Mao — A229

1967, Apr. 20 ***Perf. 11½***

938	A228 8f red & multi	70.00	15.00

Red & Gold

939	A229 8f 39 characters	60.00	12.00
940	A229 8f 50 characters	60.00	12.00
941	A229 8f 39 characters in 6 lines	60.00	12.00
942	A229 8f 53 characters	60.00	12.00
943	A229 8f 46 characters	60.00	12.00
a.	Strip of 5, #939-943	1,000.	140.00

Gold & Red

944	A229 8f 41 characters	75.00	15.00
945	A229 8f 49 characters	75.00	15.00
946	A229 8f 35 characters	75.00	15.00
947	A229 8f 22 characters	75.00	15.00
948	A229 8f 29 characters	75.00	15.00
a.	Strip of 5, #944-948	1,000.	140.00
	Nos. 938-948 (11)	745.00	150.00

Thoughts of Mao Tse-tung.

Values for Nos. 943a and 948a are for unfolded strips without tarnishing.

No numbers appear below design on Nos. 938-1046.

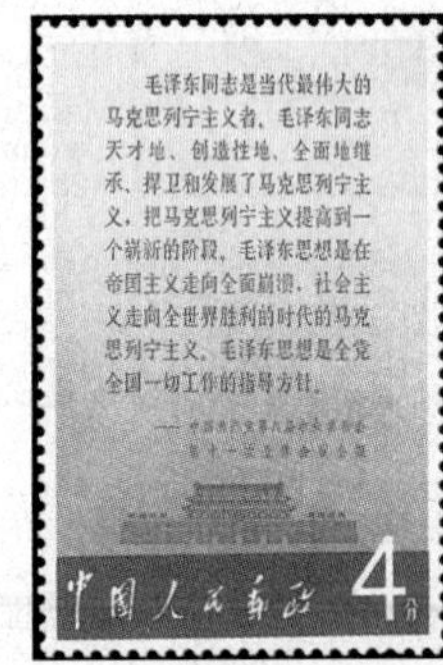

Gate of Heavenly Peace and Text from C. C. P. Communique Praising Mao — A230

Mao and Lin Piao A231

#950, Mao and poem. #951, Mao among people of various races. #952, Mao facing left and Red Guards with books. #953, Mao with upraised right hand. #954, Mao leaning on rail, horiz. 10f, Mao and Lin Piao in discussion, horiz.

Engraved and Photogravure

1967 ***Perf. 11x11½***

Size: 36x56mm

No.	Type	Denom.	Description	Unused	Used
949	A230	4f	yel, red & mar	70.00	12.50

Photo.

No.	Type	Denom.	Description	Unused	Used
950	A230	8f	yel, brn, & red	55.00	12.50
951	A230	8f	yel, red & multi	70.00	12.50
952	A230	8f	yel, red & multi	55.00	12.50

Size: 36x50mm, 50x36mm

Perf. 11

No.	Type	Denom.	Description	Unused	Used
953	A231	8f	black & multi	55.00	12.50
954	A231	8f	black & multi	140.00	24.00
955	A231	8f	lt blue & multi	35.00	8.00
956	A231	10f	black & multi	160.00	24.00
			Nos. 949-956 (8)	640.00	118.50

"Mao Tse-tung Our Great Teacher." Issued: #949-953, 5/1; #954-956, 9/20.

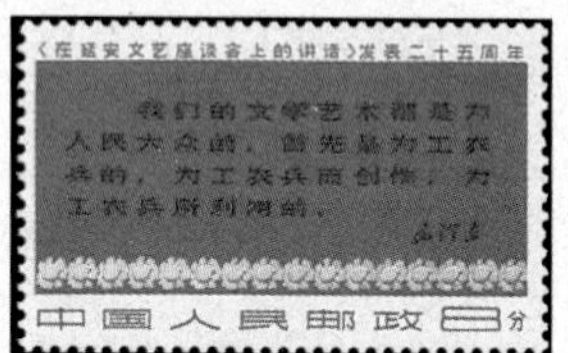

Mao Text (4 lines) — A232

Parade of Supporters — A233

Design: No. 958, Mao text (5 lines).

Engraved and Photogravure

1967, May 23 ***Perf. 11½***

No.	Type	Denom.	Description	Unused	Used
957	A232	8f	black, red & yel	110.00	20.00
958	A232	8f	black, red & yel	160.00	32.50

Photo. ***Perf. 11***

No.	Type	Denom.	Description	Unused	Used
959	A233	8f	multicolored	160.00	32.50
			Nos. 957-959 (3)	430.00	85.00

25th anniversary of Mao Tse-tung's "Talks on Literature and Art" in Yenan.

Mao Tse-tung — A234

1967 **Engr.** ***Perf. 11***

No.	Type	Denom.	Description	Unused	Used
960	A234	4f	brown	27.50	10.00
961	A234	8f	carmine	160.00	8.00
962	A234	35f	dk brown	8.50	15.00
963	A234	43f	vermilion	9.25	15.00
964	A234	52f	carmine	10.50	12.00
			Nos. 960-964 (5)	215.75	60.00

46th anniv. of Chinese Communist Party. Issue dates: 8f, July 1; others Sept.

Mao, "Sun of the Revolution" — A235

No. 966, Mao and people of various races.

1967, Oct. 1 ***Perf. 11½x11***

No.	Type	Denom.	Description	Unused	Used
965	A235	8f	multicolored	45.00	13.00
966	A235	8f	multicolored	27.50	8.50

People's Republic of China, 18th anniv.

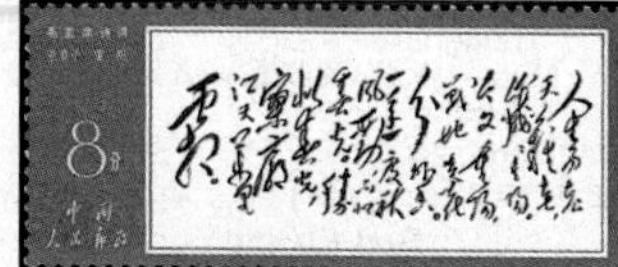

"September 9" — A236

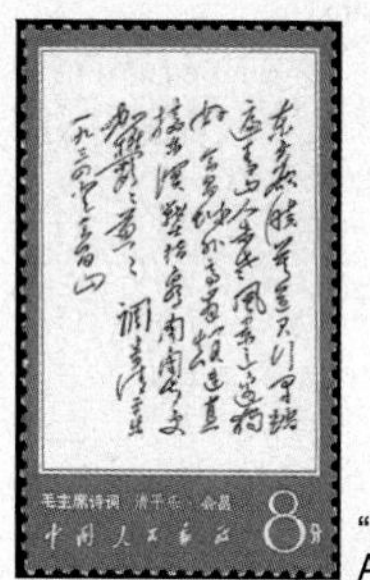

"Huichang" A237

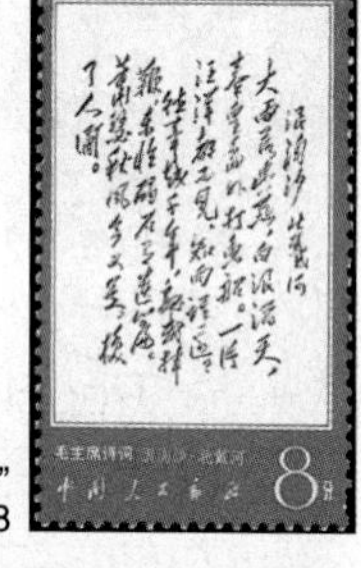

"Peitaiho" A238

Reply to Comrade Kuo Mo-jo — A239

Mao Tse-tung Writing Poems — A240

Poems by Mao: #967, "The Long March." #968, "Liupanshan." #969, shown. #970, "The Cave of the Fairies." #971, "Snow." #972, "Lushan Pass." #975, "Conquest of Nanking." #976, "The Yellow Crane Pavilion." #977, "Swimming." #979, "Changsha."

1967-68 **Photo.** ***Perf. 11***

Size: 79x18½mm

No.	Type	Denom.	Description	Unused	Used
967	A236	4f	9 characters, UL panel	50.00	14.00
968	A236	4f	11 characters, UL panel	17.00	19.00

Size: 60x24mm

Perf. 11½

No.	Type	Denom.	Description	Unused	Used
969	A236	8f	shown, 10 characters in UL panel	50.00	9.50
970	A236	8f	21 characters in UL panel	40.00	14.00
971	A236	8f	11 characters in UL panel	50.00	19.00
972	A236	8f	9 characters in UL panel	50.00	19.00

Size: 29x50mm

No.	Type	Denom.	Description	Unused	Used
973	A237	8f	shown	190.00	19.00
974	A238	8f	shown	425.00	19.00
975	A238	8f	3 rows in bottom panel	140.00	19.00
976	A238	8f	2 rows in bottom panel	60.00	19.00

Size: 52x38mm

Perf. 11

No.	Type	Denom.	Description	Unused	Used
977	A239	8f	3 short vert. rows, at left of poem	160.00	19.00
978	A239	10f	shown	17.00	19.00
979	A239	10f	undivided text	21.00	14.00
980	A240	10f	red, yel & multi	30.00	14.00
			Nos. 967-980 (14)	1,300.	236.50

Issued: #969-970, 980, 10/1; #973-974, 977, 5/20/68; others 7/20/68.

Lin Piao's Epigram on Mao Tse-tung A241

1967, Dec. 26 **Photo.** ***Perf. 11x11½***

No.	Type	Denom.	Description	Unused	Used
981	A241	8f	red & gold	32.50	6.50

Mao and Parade of Artists — A242

"Raid on White Tiger Regiment" — A243

"Red Detachment of Women" — A244

1968 ***Perf. 11½x11; 11 (983, 990)***

No.	Type	Denom.	Description	Unused	Used
982	A242	8f	shown (56x36mm)	42.50	8.00
983	A242	8f	"The Red Lantern," vert.	24.00	7.00
984	A243	8f	shown	42.50	8.00
985	A243	8f	"Shachiapang" (women & soldier)	24.00	7.00
986	A243	8f	"On the Dock"	21.00	7.00
987	A243	8f	"Taking Bandits' Fort"	21.00	7.00
988	A244	8f	shown	35.00	8.00
989	A244	8f	"The White-haired Girl"	35.00	8.00
990	A242	8f	Mao with Orchestra & Chorus (50x36mm)	70.00	10.00
			Nos. 982-990 (9)	315.00	70.00

Mao's direction for revolutionary literature and art. Issued: #982-987, Jan. 30; #988-990, May 1.

"Unite still more closely . . ." — A245

1968, May 31 **Photo.** ***Perf. 11***

No.	Type	Denom.	Description	Unused	Used
991	A245	8f	red, gold & red brn	45.00	10.50

Mao Tse-tung's statement of support of Afro-Americans.

Statement about Cultural Revolution A246

Directives of Chairman Mao: No. 993, Experiences of Revolutionary Committee. No. 994, Leadership role of Revolutionary Committee. No. 995, Basic principle of reform. No. 996, Purpose of Cultural Revolution.

1968, July 20 **Photo.** ***Perf. 11½***

No. of Lines Over Signature

No.	Type	Denom.	Description	Unused	Used
992	A246	8f	shown	72.50	35.00
993	A246	8f	5	72.50	35.00
994	A246	8f	4½	72.50	35.00
995	A246	8f	4	72.50	35.00
996	A246	8f	8	72.50	35.00
a.			Strip of 5, #992-996	*2,250.*	400.00
			Nos. 992-996 (5)	362.50	175.00

Value for No. 996a is for an unfolded strip.

Lin Piao's Statement, July 26, 1965 — A247

1968, Aug. 1 **Engr. & Photo.**

No.	Type	Denom.	Description	Unused	Used
997	A247	8f	red, gold & blk	10.50	5.50

Chinese People's Liberation Army, 41st anniv.

Mao Tse-tung Going to An Yuan, 1921 A248

1968, Aug. 1 *Perf. 11x11½*

No.	Type	Description	Unused	Used
998	A248	8f multicolored	25.00	6.75

Shade varieties include varying amount of red in clouds.

Directive of Chairman Mao — A249

1968, Nov. 30 *Perf. 11½*

No.	Type	Description	Unused	Used
999	A249	8f red & blk brn	50.00	18.00

China Map, Worker, Farmer and Soldier A249a

1968, Nov. Photo. *Perf. 11½x11*

No.	Type	Description	Unused	Used
999A	A249a	8f red, bl & bis	*15,000.*	*5,000.*

Map inscribed: "The entire nation is red." Issued in Canton and quickly withdrawn because Taiwan appears white instead of red.

No. 999A most often is found repaired. Values are for sound, unrepaired examples.

Counterfeits exist.

Woman, Miner and Soldier Holding Little Red Book A250

1968, Dec. 26 *Perf. 11x11½*

No.	Type	Description	Unused	Used
1000	A250	8f multicolored	16.00	3.25

Canceled-to-order

From about this point on stamps are valued postally used.

Yangtze Bridge, Nanking A251

Road across Bridge — A252

No. 1003, Side view. 10f, Aerial view.

Lithographed, *Perf. 11½x11 (A251);* **Photogravure,** *Perf. 11½ (A252)*

1969

Without Gum

No.	Type	Description	Unused	Used
1001	A251	4f multicolored	4.50	2.25
1002	A252	8f multicolored	18.00	6.75
1003	A252	8f multicolored	12.50	6.75
1004	A251	10f multicolored	4.50	2.25
		Nos. 1001-1004 (4)	39.50	18.00

Inauguration of Yangtze Bridge at Nanking on Dec. 29, 1968.

Singer and Pianist A253

(Piano Music from the Opera, "The Red Lantern"): #1006, Woman singer and pianist.

1969, Aug. Photo. *Perf. 11x11½*

Without Gum

No.	Type	Description	Unused	Used
1005	A253	8f multicolored	7.75	7.50
1006	A253	8f multicolored	45.00	11.00

Harvest A254

1969, Oct.

Without Gum

No.	Type	Description	Unused	Used
1007	A254	4f shown	4.00	2.10
a.		Brown omitted	20.00	20.00
1008	A254	8f Two harvesters	8.00	1.40
1009	A254	8f Harvesters with Little Red Books	50.00	8.25
1010	A254	10f Red Cross Worker examining baby	4.00	2.10
		Nos. 1007-1010 (4)	66.00	13.85

Agriculture students.

Armed Forces and Slogan — A255

Guarding the Coast — A256

Designs: No. 1013, 43f, Snow patrol, vert.

1969, Oct. *Perf. 11½*

Without Gum

No.	Type	Description	Unused	Used
1011	A255	8f red & multi	27.50	*10.00*
a.		Bayonets omitted	80.00	40.00
1012	A256	8f blue & multi	4.50	*3.50*
1013	A256	8f blue & multi	4.50	*3.50*
1014	A256	35f black & multi	4.50	*3.50*
1015	A256	43f black & multi	4.50	*3.50*
		Nos. 1011-1015 (5)	45.50	*24.00*

Defense of Chen Pao-tao (Damansky Islands) in Ussuri River.

Farm Woman A257

Designs: 8f, Foundry worker. 10f, Soldier.

1969, Dec. *Perf. 10; 11½*

Without Gum

No.	Type	Description	Unused	Used
1016	A257	4f ver & dk pur	.50	*.40*
a.		Perf 11½	1.75	1.10
1017	A257	8f ver & dk brn	1.00	*.60*
a.		Perf 11½	1.75	1.10
1018	A257	10f ver & blk	2.00	*1.10*
a.		Perf 11½	—	
		Nos. 1016-1018 (3)	3.50	*2.10*

Perforation

Nos. 1016-1018 and some succeeding issues bear two kinds of perforation: clean (Peking) and rough (Shanghai).

Building — A258

Communist Party Building, Shanghai A259

Agriculture Building, Canton — A260

Foundry Worker — A261

Two types of 8f Gate of Heavenly Peace:
I — Strong, definite halo around sun.
II — Halo missing, white shades gradually into red.

1969-72 Photo. *Perf. 10, 11½*

Without Gum

No.	Type	Description	Unused	Used
1019	A258	1f shown	.20	*.20*
1020	A259	1½f shown	.65	.70
a.		Perf. 11½	5.50	4.00
1021	A260	2f shown	.20	*.20*
1022	A260	3f 1929 Party Day House, Pu Tien	.20	.20
1023	A260	4f Mao's Home and Office, Yunnan	.20	*.20*
1024	A261	5f Woman Tractor Driver	1.60	.75
1025	A260	8f Gate of Heavenly Peace, type II	.65	.35
a.		Type I	2.50	1.25
1026	A259	8f Heroes Monument	1.25	.70
a.		Perf. 11½	4.50	3.00
1027	A260	8f Pagoda Hill, Yenan	1.25	*3.50*
1028	A260	8f Gate of Heavenly Peace (no sun)	.20	.20
1029	A260	10f Monument, Tsu Ping	.30	.20
1030	A259	20f Conference Hall, Tsunyi	1.90	1.40
a.		Perf. 11½	6.00	4.50
1031	A260	20f Highway ('72)	.40	.20
1032	A260	22f Shao Shan Village, Birthplace of Mao	.65	.35
1033	A260	35f Conference Hall	.95	.35
1034	A260	43f Chingkang Peaks	1.25	.35
1035	A259	50f as 4f, different view	1.25	1.40
1036	A260	52f People's Hall, Peking	1.90	.35
1037	A261	$1 shown ('70)	4.00	2.75
		Nos. 1019-1037 (19)	19.00	14.35

Kin Hsün-hua A262

Mounted Patrol — A263

1970, Jan. Without Gum *Perf. 11½*

No.	Type	Description	Unused	Used
1045	A262	8f red & black	18.00	*14.50*
a.		8f red & gray brown	20.00	10.00

Death of Kin Hsün-hua in Kirin border flood.

1970, Aug. 1

Without Gum

No.	Type	Description	Unused	Used
1046	A263	8f yel grn & multi	6.75	5.00

People's Liberation Army, 43rd anniv.

Commemorative stamps from Nos. 1047 to 1142 and 1211-1214, carry a cumulative number in parenthesis at lower left and the year at lower right. Where such numbers help to identify, they are quoted in parenthesis.

Cpl. Yang Tse-jung — A264

Ensemble A265

1970, Aug. 1 *Perf. 11½x11, 11x11½*

Without Gum

No.	Type	Description	Unused	Used
1047	A264	8f shown (1)	32.50	8.00
1048	A264	8f Armed guards (2)	3.50	2.50
1049	A264	8f Yang leaping through forest (3)	3.50	2.50
1050	A265	8f shown (4)	27.50	8.00
1051	A265	8f Yang in folk costume (5)	3.50	2.50
1052	A265	8f Four actors (6)	21.00	8.00
		Nos. 1047-1052 (6)	91.50	31.50

Scenes from opera "Taking Tiger Mountain by Strategy." Nos. 1048, 1052, horizontal.

Frontier Guard A266

1971, Jan. Litho. *Perf. 10*

Without Gum

1053 A266 4f multicolored 2.00 1.50
- *a.* Perf. 11½ 2.10 1.10
- *b.* Perf. 11½x10 3.00
- *c.* Perf. 10x11½ 4.00

Banner of the Commune A267

Street Battle, Paris, 1871 A268

10f, Proclamation of the Commune. 22f, Rally.

Perf. 11½x11, 11x11½

1971, Mar. 18 Litho. & Engr.

Without Gum

1054 A267 4f sal & multi 5.00 5.00
1055 A268 8f ver, pink & brn 85.00 9.00
1056 A267 10f ver, pink & dk brn 5.00 6.00
1057 A268 22f ver, pink & dk brn 5.00 6.00
Nos. 1054-1057 (4) 100.00 26.00

Centenary of the Paris Commune.

Redrawn Building Type of 1961

Designs: 2f, 3f, August 1 building, Nanchang. 4f, 52f, Gate of Heavenly Peace, Peking. 10f, 20f, Pagoda Hill, Yenan.

1971, July 1 Litho. *Perf. 11x11½*

Size: 21x16mm

Without Gum

1059 A152 2f slate green 1.00 .50
1060 A152 3f sepia 1.50 1.00
1061 A152 4f brt pink 1.50 1.00
1062 A152 10f brt rose lil 3.75 1.00
1063 A152 20f dk blue grn 2.00 1.00
1064 A152 52f orange 1.00 1.00
Nos. 1059-1064 (6) 10.75 5.50

Paper of Nos. 1059-1064 is white. That of Nos. 647-654 is toned.

Communist Party Building, Shanghai — A269

People and Factories — A270

Designs: No. 1068, Peasant Movement Training Institute. No. 1069, Ching Kang Peaks. No. 1070, Conference Building, Tsunyi. No. 1071, Pagoda Hill, Yenan. No. 1073, People and People's Hall, Peking. No. 1074, People and Pagoda Hill, Yenan. 22f, Gate of Heavenly Peace, Peking.

1971, July 1 Photo. *Perf. 11½*

Red and Gold Frame

Without Gum

1067 A269 4f vermilion (12) 4.00 1.00
1068 A269 4f brt grn (13) 4.00 1.00
1069 A269 8f grnsh bl & red (14) 3.25 1.00
1070 A269 8f ol blk (15) 3.25 1.00
1071 A269 8f bis, grn & red (16) 13.50 2.50
1072 A270 8f yel, red & multi (18) 13.50 2.50
1073 A270 8f yel, red & multi (19) 13.50 2.50
1074 A270 8f yel, red & multi (20) 13.50 2.50
- *a.* Strip of 3, #1072-1074 70.00 35.00

1075 A269 22f red, gold & brn (17) 27.50 2.50
Nos. 1067-1075 (9) 96.00 16.50

50th anniv. of the Chinese Communist Party. No. 1074a has a continuous design and is valued as an unfolded strip.

Chinese Welcome A271

Enver Hoxha — A272

#1077, Chinese & African players. #1078, Chinese & African girl players. 43f, Games' emblem.

1971, Nov. 3 Litho. *Perf. 11½*

Without Gum

1076 A271 8f lil rose & multi 5.75 1.50
1077 A271 8f lt yellow & multi 5.75 1.50
1078 A271 8f dk grn & multi 5.75 1.50
1079 A271 43f grn, gold & org 2.75 1.50
Nos. 1076-1079 (4) 20.00 6.00

Afro-Asian Table Tennis Games, Peking.

1971, Nov. 3 Photo. *Perf. 11*

#1081, Party's birthplace. #1082, Albanian flag. 52f, Albanian partisans, horiz.

Without Gum

1080 A272 8f Prus blue & multi 8.50 5.00
1081 A272 8f buff & multi 6.75 3.00
1082 A272 8f red, yel & multi 6.75 3.00
1083 A272 52f lt blue & multi 7.75 5.00
Nos. 1080-1083 (4) 29.75 16.00

30th anniversary of the founding of Albanian Communist Party.

Yenan Pagoda and 1942 Meeting House A273

1972, May 23 Photo. *Perf. 11*

Without Gum

1084 A273 8f shown (33) 3.75 1.75
1085 A273 8f Uniformed choir (34) 3.75 1.75
1086 A273 8f "Brother & Sister" (35) 4.50 1.75
1087 A273 8f Outdoor performance (36) 4.50 1.75
1088 A273 8f "The Red Signal Lantern" (37) 4.50 1.75
1089 A273 8f Dancer from "The Red Company of Women" (38) 4.50 1.75
Nos. 1084-1089 (6) 25.50 10.50

30th anniversary of the publication of the Discussions on Literature and Art at the Yenan Forum.

Various Ball Games — A274

Workers' Gymnastics A275

1972, June 10

1090 A274 8f shown (39) 6.50 1.00
1091 A275 8f shown (40) 6.50 1.00
1092 A275 8f Tug of war (41) 6.50 1.00
1093 A275 8f Mountain climbers and tents (42) 6.50 1.00
1094 A275 8f Children diving & swimming (43) 6.50 1.00
Nos. 1090-1094 (5) 32.50 5.00

10th anniversary of Mao Tse-tung's edict on physical culture.

Ocean Freighter Fenglei — A276

1972, July 10 Photo. *Perf. 11½*

Without Gum

1095 A276 8f shown (29) 8.00 2.25
1096 A276 8f Tanker Taching No. 30 (30) 8.00 2.25
1097 A276 8f Cargo-passenger ship Changzeng (31) 8.00 2.25
1098 A276 8f Dredger Xienfeng (32) 8.00 2.25
Nos. 1095-1098 (4) 32.00 9.00

Table Tennis Players' Welcome A277

1972, Sept. 2 *Perf. 11½x11, 11x11½*

Without Gum

1099 A277 8f Championship emblem, vert. (45) 1.75 .80
1100 A277 8f shown (46) 1.75 .80
1101 A277 8f Table tennis (47) 1.10 .80
1102 A277 22f Women from different countries, vert. (48) 1.25 1.60
Nos. 1099-1102 (4) 5.85 4.00

First Asian table tennis championships.

Wang Chin-hsi — A278

Workers on Cliffs along Canal — A279

Engraved and Photogravure

1972, Dec. 25 *Perf. 11½x11*

1103 A278 8f multicolored (44) 3.25 1.60

Wang Chin-hsi, the Iron Man, fighter for the working class.

1972, Dec. 30

#1105, Canal flowing through tunnel. #1106, Bridge. #1107, Canal along cliffs.

1104 A279 8f multicolored (49) 1.25 .80
1105 A279 8f multicolored (50) 1.25 .80
1106 A279 8f multicolored (51) 1.25 .80
1107 A279 8f multicolored (52) 1.25 .80
Nos. 1104-1107 (4) 5.00 3.20

Construction of Red Flag Canal, Linhsien county, Honan.

Giant Panda — A280

Woman Coal Miner — A281

Designs: Pandas in various positions. The 8f stamps are horizontal.

Perf. 11½x11, 11x11½

1973, Jan. 15 Photo.

Designs in Black and Red

1108 A280 4f lt yel grn (61) .90 1.60
1109 A280 8f buff (59) .90 1.60
1110 A280 8f lt tan (60) .90 1.60
1111 A280 10f pale green (58) 45.00 15.00
1112 A280 20f pale bl gray (57) 37.50 15.00
1113 A280 43f pale lilac (62) 4.00 5.00
Nos. 1108-1113 (6) 89.20 39.80

1973, Mar. 8 Photo. *Perf. 11½x11*

1114 A281 8f shown (63) 2.25 1.50
1115 A281 8f Committee member (64) 2.25 1.50
1116 A281 8f Telephone line worker (65) 2.25 1.50
Nos. 1114-1116 (3) 6.75 4.50

Intl. Working Women's Day. Designs are after paintings from an exhib. for 30th anniv. of the Yenan Forum on Literature and Art.

Dancing Girl — A282

1973, June 1 Photo. *Perf. 11*

1117 A282 8f shown (86) 1.50 1.25
1118 A282 8f Musician, boy (87) 1.50 1.25
1119 A282 8f Girl with scarf (88) 1.50 1.25
1120 A282 8f Boy with tambourine (89) 1.50 1.25
1121 A282 8f Girl with drum (90) 1.50 1.25
a. Strip of 5, #1117-1121 9.50 7.50
Nos. 1117-1121 (5) 7.50 6.25

Values for No. 1121a are for an unfolded strip.

Tournament Emblem — A283

1973, Aug. 25 Photo. *Perf. 11½*

#1123, Visitors from Asia, Africa and Latin America arriving by plane. #1124, Woman player. 22f, African, Asian & Latin American women.

1122 A283 8f multicolored (91) 2.25 .90
1123 A283 8f multicolored (92) 2.25 .90
1124 A283 8f multicolored (93) 2.25 .90
1125 A283 22f multicolored (94) 1.10 .90
Nos. 1122-1125 (4) 7.85 3.60

Asian, African and Latin American Table Tennis Friendship Invitational Tournament.

The White-haired Girl — A284

Designs: Scenes from the ballet "The White-haired Girl." Nos. 1126, 1129 vert.

1973, Sept. 25 Photo. *Perf. 11½*

1126 A284 8f multicolored (53) 3.00 1.10
1127 A284 8f multicolored (54) 3.00 1.10
1128 A284 8f multicolored (55) 3.00 1.10
1129 A284 8f multicolored (56) 3.00 1.10
Nos. 1126-1129 (4) 12.00 4.40

Fair Building, Canton — A285

1973, Oct. 15 Photo. *Perf. 11*

1130 A285 8f multicolored (95) 3.25 2.25

Export Commodities Fall Fair, Canton.

Teapot with Blue Phoenix Design — A286

Excavated Works of Art: No. 1132, Silver pot with horse design. No. 1133, Black pottery horse. No. 1134, Woman, clay figurine. No. 1135, Carved stone pillar base. No. 1136, Galloping bronze horse. No. 1137, Bronze inkwell (toad). No. 1138, Bronze lamp, Chang Hsin Palace. No. 1139, Bronze tripod. No. 1140, Square bronze pot. 20f, Bronze wine vessel. 52f, Painted red clay tripod.

1973, Nov. 20 *Perf. 11½*

1131 A286 4f ol bis & multi (66) 1.50 1.00
1132 A286 4f ver & multi (67) 1.50 1.00
1133 A286 8f yel grn & multi (68) 1.10 .50
1134 A286 8f brt rose & multi (69) 1.10 .50
1135 A286 8f lt vio & multi (70) .80 .50
1136 A286 8f yel bis & multi (71) .80 .50
1137 A286 8f lt bl & multi (72) .80 .50
1138 A286 8f gray & multi (73) .80 .50
1139 A286 10f yel bis & multi (74) .35 *.50*
1140 A286 10f dp org & multi (75) .35 *.50*
1141 A286 20f lil & multi (76) 1.50 1.25
1142 A286 52f grn & multi (77) 1.50 *2.00*
Nos. 1131-1142 (12) 12.10 9.25

Marginal Markings

Marginal inscriptions on stamps of 1974-91 start at lower loft with "J" for commemoratives and "T" for "special issues," followed by three numbers indicating (a) set sequence for the year, (b) total of stamps in set, and (c) number of stamp within set. At right appears the year date. Listings include the "c" number parenthetically. The "a" number is included only when it will help identify stamps not illustrated.

Example: T26 (6-3), the 3rd stamp of 6 from the 26th special set. Set numbers and or positions will be shown only when they help identify a stamp. An illustrated single stamp set will not have these numbers in the listings.

Woman Gymnast — A287

Designs: No. 1144, Gymnast on rings. No. 1145, Aerial split over balance beam, woman. No. 1146, Gymnast on parallel bars. No. 1147, Uneven bars, woman. No. 1148, Gymnast on horse. T.1.

1974, Jan. 1 Photo. *Perf. 11½x11*

1143 A287 8f lt grn & multi (1) 5.75 2.75
1144 A287 8f lt vio & multi (2) 5.75 2.75
1145 A287 8f lt blue & multi (3) 5.75 2.75
1146 A287 8f sal & multi (4) 5.75 2.75
1147 A287 8f yel & multi (5) 6.50 3.75
1148 A287 8f lil rose & multi (6) 6.50 3.75
Nos. 1143-1148 (6) 36.00 18.50

Girls Twirling Bamboo Diabolos — A288

Designs: No. 1149, Lion Dance, vert. No. 1150, Handstand on chairs, vert. No. 1152, Men balancing jar. No. 1153, Plate spinning, vert. No. 1154, Twirling umbrella, vert. T.2.

1974, Jan. 21 *Perf. 11*

1149 A288 8f brn & multi (1) 5.50 2.50
1150 A288 8f Prus bl & multi (2) 5.50 2.50
1151 A288 8f lilac & multi (3) 5.50 2.50
1152 A288 8f dull bl & multi (4) 6.50 2.50
1153 A288 8f ol grn & multi (5) 6.50 2.50
1154 A288 8f gray & multi (6) 6.50 2.50
Nos. 1149-1154 (6) 36.00 15.00

Traditional acrobatics.

Shao Shan — A289

Transportation by Railroad — A290

1½f, Site of 1st National Communist Party Congress. 2f, Peasant Movement Institute, Kwangchow. 3f, Headquarters of Nanchang Uprising. 4f, Great Hall of the People, Peking. 5f, View of Wen Chia Shih. 8f, Tien An Men. 10f, Tzeping in Chingkang Mountains. 20f, Site of Kutien Meeting. 22f, Tsunyi Conference site. 35f, Yenan (bridge). 43f, Hsi Pai Ho, Communist Party meeting site. 50f, Fairy Cave, Lushan. 52f, Monument to People's Heroes. $2, Trucks on mountain road.

1974 Litho. *Perf. 11*
Without Gum

1163 A289 1f sl grn & pale grn .50 .20
1164 A289 1½f car & buff .50 .20
1165 A289 2f dk blue & pale grn .50 .20
1166 A289 3f dk ol & yel .50 .20
1167 A289 4f red & yel .50 .20
1168 A289 5f brn & lt yel .50 .20
1169 A289 8f dull mag & buff .50 .20
a. Perf. 11½x12 8.00
1170 A289 10f blue & pink .50 .20
1171 A289 20f dk red & buff 1.25 .20
1172 A289 22f vio & lt yel 1.90 .25
1173 A289 35f mar & lt yel 2.50 .75
1174 A289 43f red brn & buff 3.25 *1.25*
1175 A289 50f dk blue & pink *3.75* *2.00*
1176 A289 52f sepia & buff 5.00 2.50

Photogravure & Engraved

1177 A290 $1 multicolored 1.25 .20
1178 A290 $2 multicolored 2.50 .40
Nos. 1163-1178 (16) 25.40 9.15

Capital Stadium — A290a

Design: 8f, Hotel Peking.

1974, Dec. 1 Photo. *Perf. 11*
Without Gum

1179 A290a 4f black & yel grn .20 .20
1180 A290a 8f black & ultra .30 .20

"Veteran Secretary" — A291 Well Diggers — A292

Designs: Nos. 1183-1186 horizontal. T.3.

1974, Apr. 20 Photo. *Perf. 11*

1181 A291 8f shown (1) 1.60 1.10
1182 A292 8f shown (2) 1.60 1.10
1183 A291 8f Spring hoeing (3) 1.60 1.10
1184 A291 8f Farmers (4) 1.60 1.10
1185 A292 8f Farm (5) 2.40 1.10
1186 A291 8f Bumper crops (6) 2.40 1.10
Nos. 1181-1186 (6) 11.20 6.60

Paintings by farmers of Huhsien County, shown at exhibition in Peking.

Mailman on Motorcycle — A293

1974, May 15 Photo. *Perf. 11*

1187 A293 8f shown (1) 6.25 3.50
1188 A293 8f People of the world (2) 6.25 3.50
1189 A293 8f Great Wall (3) 6.25 3.50
Nos. 1187-1189 (3) 18.75 10.50

Centenary of the UPU. J.1.

Barefoot Doctor Inoculating Children — A294

Designs (Barefoot Doctors): No. 1191, Crossing stream at night to reach patient, vert. No. 1192, Gathering herbs, vert. No. 1193, Acupuncture treatment for farmer in the field.

Perf. 11x11½, 11½x11
1974, June 26 Photo.

1190 A294 8f multicolored (82) 1.40 1.00
1191 A294 8f multicolored (83) 1.40 1.00
1192 A294 8f multicolored (84) 1.40 1.00
1193 A294 8f multicolored (85) 1.40 1.00
Nos. 1190-1193 (4) 5.60 4.00

Steel Worker Wang Chin-hsi — A295

#1195, Workers studying Mao's writings around campfire. #1196, Drilling for oil in winter. #1197, Scientific industrial management. #1198, Oil derricks and farms. T.4.

1974, Sept. 30 Photo. *Perf. 11*

1194 A295 8f multicolored (5-1) 1.25 .90
1195 A295 8f multicolored (5-2) 1.25 .90
1196 A295 8f multicolored (5-3) 1.25 .90
1197 A295 8f multicolored (5-4) 1.25 .90
1198 A295 8f multicolored (5-5) 1.25 .90
Nos. 1194-1198 (5) 6.25 4.50

Workers of Taching as examples of achievement.

Members of Tachai Commune — A296

#1200, Farmers leveling mountains and fields in winter. #1201, Scientific farming. #1202, Trucks carrying surplus harvest. #1203, Young workers with banner. T.5.

1974, Sept. 30

1199 A296 8f multi (5-1) 1.75 .80
1200 A296 8f multi (5-2) .90 .80
1201 A296 8f multi (5-3) 1.75 .80
1202 A296 8f multi (5-4) .90 .80
1203 A296 8f multi (5-5) .90 .80
Nos. 1199-1203 (5) 6.20 4.00

Farmers of Tachai as examples of achievement.

Arms of Republic and Members of Ethnic Groups — A297

1974, Oct. 1

1204 A297 8f multi (1-1) 5.50 3.25

Taching Steel Worker — A298

Designs: No. 1206, Tachai farm woman. No. 1207, Soldier, planes and ships. J.3.

1974, Oct. 1

1205 A298 8f multi (3-1) 1.75 1.50
1206 A298 8f multi (3-2) 1.75 1.50
1207 A298 8f multi (3-3) 1.75 1.50
a. Strip of 3, #1205-1207 6.00 5.25

People's Republic of China, 25th anniv.

Values for No. 1207a are for an unfolded strip.

Export Commodities Fair Building, Canton — A299

1974, Oct. 15

1208 A299 8f multicolored 3.50 1.50

Chinese Export Commodities Fair, Canton.

Guerrillas' Monument, Permet, Albania — A300

Albanian Patriots and Coat of Arms — A301

1974, Nov. 29 Photo. *Perf. 11½x11*

1209 A300 8f multicolored 3.50 1.50
1210 A301 8f multicolored 3.50 1.50

Albania's liberation, 30th anniversary.

Water-cooled Generator — A302

Industrial Products: No. 1212, Motorized rice sprouts transplanter. No. 1213, Universal cylindrical grinding machine. No. 1214, Open-air rock drill, vert. All dated 1973.

Photogravure and Engraved

1974, Dec. 23 *Perf. 11*

1211 A302 8f vio & multi (78) 18.00 3.50
1212 A302 8f yel grn & multi (79) 18.00 3.50
1213 A302 8f ver & multi (80) 18.00 3.50
1214 A302 8f blue & multi (81) 18.00 3.50
Nos. 1211-1214 (4) 72.00 14.00

Congress Delegates — A303

Designs: No. 1216, Red flags, constitution and flowers. No. 1217, Worker, farmer and soldier, agriculture and industry.

1975, Jan. 25 Photo. *Perf. 11½*

1215 A303 8f gold & multi (3-1) 3.50 1.40
1216 A303 8f gold & multi (3-2) 3.50 1.40
1217 A303 8f gold & multi (3-3) 3.50 1.40
Nos. 1215-1217 (3) 10.50 4.20

Fourth National People's Congress, Peking.

Teacher Studying Revolutionary Works — A304

#1219, Teacher, children and horse. #1220, Outdoors class. #1221, Class held in boat. T.9.

1975, Mar. 8 Photo. *Perf. 11*

1218 A304 8f multi (4-1) 8.50 2.75
1219 A304 8f multi (4-2) 8.50 2.75
1220 A304 8f multi (4-3) 8.50 2.75
1221 A304 8f multi (4-4) 8.50 2.75
Nos. 1218-1221 (4) 34.00 11.00

Rural women teachers and for International Working Women's Day.

"Broadsword," Encounter Position — A305

#1223, Exercise with 2 swords (woman). #1224, Graceful boxing (woman). #1225, Man leaping with spear. #1226, Woman holding fighting staff. 43f, 2 women with spears against man with 3-section staff.

1975, June 10 Photo. *Perf. 11x11½*

Size: 39x29mm

1222 A305 8f (6-1) 4.50 3.00
1223 A305 8f (6-2) 4.50 3.00
1224 A305 8f (6-3) 4.50 3.00
1225 A305 8f (6-4) 4.50 3.00
1226 A305 8f (6-5) 4.50 3.00

Size: 59x29mm

1227 A305 43f red & multi (6-6) 4.50 6.00
Nos. 1222-1227 (6) 27.00 21.00

Wushu ("Kung Fu"), self-defense exercises. Tête bêche in sheets of 50 (5x10).

Mass Judgment and Criticisms — A306

No. 1229, Brigade leader writing wall newspaper. No. 1230, Study and criticism on battlefield, horiz. No. 1231, Former "slave" led into battle by criticism of Lin Piao and Confucius, horiz. T.8.

Perf. 11½x11, 11x11½

1975, Aug. 20 Photo.

1228 A306 8f red & multi (4-1) 6.50 2.50
1229 A306 8f red & multi (4-2) 6.50 2.50
1230 A306 8f red & multi (4-3) 6.50 2.50
1231 A306 8f red & multi (4-4) 6.50 2.50
Nos. 1228-1231 (4) 26.00 10.00

Campaign to encourage criticism of Lin Piao and Confucius.

Athletes Studying Theory of Dictatorship of Proletariat — A307

3rd National Sports Meet: No. 1232, Women athletes leading parade, vert. No. 1234, Women volleyball players. No. 1235, Runner, soldier, farmer and worker, vert. No. 1236, Young athlete and various sports. No. 1237, Athletes of various races and horse race. 35f, Children and diving tower, vert. J.6.

1975, Sept. 12 Photo. *Perf. 11½*

1232 A307 8f multi (7-1) 1.25 .75
1233 A307 8f multi (7-2) 1.25 .75
1234 A307 8f multi (7-3) 1.25 .75
1235 A307 8f multi (7-4) 1.25 .75
1236 A307 8f multi (7-5) 1.25 .75
1237 A307 8f multi (7-6) 1.25 .75
1238 A307 35f multi (7-7) 3.50 3.00
Nos. 1232-1238 (7) 11.00 7.50

Mountaineers A308

Mt. Everest A309

Design: No. 1240, Mountaineers raising Chinese flag on summit, horiz. T.15.

1975 Photo. *Perf. 11½x11, 11x11½*

1239 A308 8f multi (3-2) .65 .35
1240 A308 8f multi (3-3) .65 .35
1241 A309 43f multi (3-1) .95 .75
Nos. 1239-1241 (3) 2.25 1.45

Chinese Mt. Everest expedition.

Agricultural Workers with Book — A310

#1243, Workers carrying load. #1244, Woman driving harvester combine. J.7.

1975, Oct. 1 *Perf. 11½*

1242 A310 8f multi (3-1) 3.25 1.10
1243 A310 8f multi (3-2) 3.25 1.10
1244 A310 8f multi (3-3) 3.25 1.10
Nos. 1242-1244 (3) 9.75 3.30

National Conference to promote learning from Tachai's achievements in agriculture.

Girl Giving Boy Red Scarf — A311

Designs (Children): No. 1246, Putting up wall posters criticizing Lin Piao and Confucius. No. 1247, Studying. No. 1248, Harvesting. 52f, Physical training. T.14.

1975, Dec. 1 Photo. *Perf. 11½*

1245 A311 8f multi (5-1) 1.25 1.00
1246 A311 8f multi (5-2) 1.25 1.00
1247 A311 8f multi (5-3) 1.25 1.00
1248 A311 8f multi (5-4) 1.25 1.00
1249 A311 52f multi (5-5) 5.75 3.50
Nos. 1245-1249 (5) 10.75 7.50

Moral, intellectual and physical progress of Chinese children.

Woman Plowing Rice Field A312

#1251, Mechanized rice planting. #1252, Drainage and irrigation. #1253, Woman spraying insecticide over cotton field. #1254, Combine. T.13.

1975, Dec. 15 *Perf. 11*

1250 A312 8f multi (5-1) 2.10 1.25
1251 A312 8f multi (5-2) 2.10 1.25
1252 A312 8f multi (5-3) 2.10 1.25
1253 A312 8f multi (5-4) 2.10 1.25
1254 A312 8f multi (5-5) 2.10 1.25
Nos. 1250-1254 (5) 10.50 6.25

Priority program of farm mechanization.

Farmland and Irrigation Canal — A313

Designs of Nos. 1255-1270 numbered J.8.

1976, Feb. 20 Photo. *Perf. 11½*

1255 A313 8f shown (16-1) 3.00 1.75
1256 A313 8f Irrigation canal (16-2) 3.00 1.75
1257 A313 8f Fertilizer plant (16-3) 3.00 1.75
1258 A313 8f Textile plant (16-4) 3.00 1.75
1259 A313 8f Anshan Iron and Steel Co. (16-5) 3.00 1.75

Nos. 1255-1270 commemorate fulfillment of 4th Five-year Plan.

1976, Apr. 9

1260 A313 8f Coal freight trains (16-6) 3.00 1.75
1261 A313 8f Hydroelectric station (16-7) 3.00 1.75
1262 A313 8f Ship building (16-8) 3.00 1.75
1263 A313 8f Oil industry (16-9) 3.00 1.75
1264 A313 8f Pipe line and port (16-10) 3.00 1.75

1976, June 12

1265 A313 8f Train on viaduct (16-11) 4.50 1.75
1266 A313 8f Scientific research (16-12) 4.50 1.75
1267 A313 8f Classroom (16-13) 4.50 1.75

1268 A313 8f Health Center (16-14) 4.50 1.75
1269 A313 8f Apartment houses (16-15) 4.50 1.75
1270 A313 8f Department store (16-16) 4.50 1.75
Nos. 1255-1270 (16) 57.00 28.00

Heart Surgery with Acupuncture Anesthesia — A314

Operating Room and: #1272, Man driving tractor with severed arm restored. #1273, Man exercising broken arm in cast. #1274, Patient threading needle after cataract operation. T.12.

1976, Apr. 9 Photo. *Perf. 11½*
1271 A314 8f brn & multi (4-1) 2.75 1.00
1272 A314 8f yel grn & multi (4-2) 2.75 1.00
1273 A314 8f bl grn & multi (4-3) 2.75 1.00
1274 A314 8f vio bl & multi (4-4) 2.75 1.00
Nos. 1271-1274 (4) 11.00 4.00

Achievements in medical and health services.

Students in May 7 School — A315

Designs: No. 1276, Students as farm workers. No. 1277, Production brigade. J.9.

1976, May 7 Photo. *Perf. 11½*
1275 A315 8f multi (3-1) 1.75 1.40
1276 A315 8f multi (3-2) 1.75 1.40
1277 A315 8f multi (3-3) 1.75 1.40
Nos. 1275-1277 (3) 5.25 4.20

Chairman Mao's May 7 Directive, 10th anniv.

Mass Training in Swimming — A316

No. 1279, Swimmers crossing Yangtze River. No. 1280, Swimmers walking into the surf. J.10.

1976, July 16 Photo. *Perf. 11½*
Size: 47x27mm
1278 A316 8f multi (3-1) 1.75 1.10
Size: 35x27mm
1279 A316 8f multi (3-2) 1.75 1.10
1280 A316 8f multi (3-3) 1.75 1.10
Nos. 1278-1280 (3) 5.25 3.30

Chairman Mao's swim in Yangtze River, 10th anniversary.

Workers, Peasants and Soldiers Going to College — A317

#1282, Classroom. #1283, Instruction on construction site. #1284, Computer room. #1285, Graduates returning home. T.18.

1976, Sept. 6 Photo. *Perf. 11½*
1281 A317 8f multi (5-1) 2.10 1.10
1282 A317 8f multi (5-2) 2.10 1.10
1283 A317 8f multi (5-3) 2.10 1.10
1284 A317 8f multi (5-4) 2.10 1.10
1285 A317 8f multi (5-5) 2.10 1.10
Nos. 1281-1285 (5) 10.50 5.50

Success of proletarian education system.

Power Line Repair by Woman — A318

#1287, Insulator repair. #1288, Cherry picker. #1289, Transformer repair. T.16.

1976, Sept. 15
1286 A318 8f multi (4-1) 1.50 1.40
1287 A318 8f multi (4-2) 1.50 1.40
1288 A318 8f multi (4-3) 3.00 1.40
1289 A318 8f multi (4-4) 3.00 1.40
Nos. 1286-1289 (4) 9.00 5.60

Maintenance of high power lines.

Lu Hsun A319

#1291, Lu Hsun sick, writing in bed. #1292, Lu Hsun with worker, soldier and peasant. J.11.

Photo. & Engr.
1976, Oct. 19 *Perf. 11x11½*
1290 A319 8f multi (3-1) 4.50 1.75
Photo.
1291 A319 8f multi (3-2) 4.50 1.75
1292 A319 8f multi (3-3) 4.50 1.75
Nos. 1290-1292 (3) 13.50 5.25

Lu Hsun (1881-1936), writer and revolutionary leader.

Old Farmer Tying Towel on Student's Head — A320

Designs: No. 1294, Student teaching farm woman, horiz. No. 1295, Students climbing mountain for new water resources. No. 1296, Student testing wheat, horiz. 10f, Student feeding lamb. 20f, Frontier guards, horiz. T.17.

1976, Dec. 22 Photo. *Perf. 11½*
1293 A320 4f multi (6-1) .75 .45
1294 A320 8f multi (6-2) .75 .45
1295 A320 8f multi (6-3) .75 .45
1296 A320 8f multi (6-4) .75 .45
1297 A320 10f multi (6-5) 2.25 1.00
1298 A320 20f multi (6-6) 4.50 2.00
Nos. 1293-1298 (6) 9.75 4.80

Students' efforts to help poor country people.

Mao's Home, Shaoshan — A321

Shaoshan, Mao's birthplace: No. 1300, School building. No. 1301, Farmers' Association building. 10f, Railroad station. T.11.

1976, Dec. 26 *Perf. 11*
1299 A321 4f multi (4-1) .80 .75
1300 A321 8f multi (4-2) 1.25 .75
1301 A321 8f multi (4-3) 1.25 .75
1302 A321 10f multi (4-4) 2.00 1.75
Nos. 1299-1302 (4) 5.30 4.00

Chou En-lai — A322

#1304, Chou giving report at 10th Party Congress. #1305, Chou with Wang Chin-hsi, famous oil worker, horiz. #1306, Chou with people of Tachai, 1973, horiz. J.13.

1977, Jan. 8 Photo. *Perf. 11½*
1303 A322 8f multi (4-1) .70 .70
1304 A322 8f multi (4-2) .70 .70
1305 A322 8f multi (4-3) .70 .70
1306 A322 8f multi (4-4) 5.00 .70
Nos. 1303-1306 (4) 7.10 2.80

Premier Chou En-lai (1898-1976), a founder of Chinese Communist Party, 1st death anniversary.

Liu Hu-lan, an Inspiration A323

Liu Hu-lan, Chinese heroine: No. 1307, Liu Hu-lan monument. No. 1308, Mao Tse-tung quotation: "A great life-a glorious death." J.12.

1977, Jan. 31
1307 A323 8f multi (3-1) 6.00 2.50
1308 A323 8f multi (3-2) 2.25 1.75
1309 A323 8f multi (3-3) 2.25 1.75
Nos. 1307-1309 (3) 10.50 6.00

Uprising in Taiwan A324

Design: 10f, Gate of Heavenly Peace, Peking; Sun Moon Lake, Taiwan, Taiwanese people holding PRC flag. J.14.

1977, Feb. 28 Photo. *Perf. 11*
1310 A324 8f multi (2-1) .90 .70
1311 A324 10f multi (2-2) 2.25 1.40

Uprising of the people of Taiwan, 2/28/47.

Sharpshooters — A325

Militia Women: No. 1313, Women horseback riders. No. 1314, Underground defense tunnel. T.10.

1977, Mar. 8 *Perf. 11½*
1312 A325 8f multi (3-1) 4.25 2.75
1313 A325 8f multi (3-2) 4.25 2.75
1314 A325 8f multi (3-3) 4.25 2.75
Nos. 1312-1314 (3) 12.75 8.25

Forestry — A326

Designs: 1f, Coal mining. 1½f, Sheepherding. 2f, Export (loading railroad car onto ship). 4f, Hydroelectric station. 5f, Fishery. 8f, Combine in field. 10f, Radio tower and mail truck. 20f, Steel production. 30f, Trucks on mountain road. 40f, Textiles. 50f, Tractor assembly line. 60f, Offshore oil rigs and birds, setting sun. 70f, Railroad bridge, Yangtze Gorge. No numbers.

1977 Photo. *Perf. 11½*
1315 A326 1f yel grn, red & blk .20 .20
1316 A326 1½f bl grn, yel grn & brn .20 *.20*
1317 A326 2f org, bl & blk .20 .20
1318 A326 3f ol & dk grn .20 .20
1319 A326 4f lil, org & blk .20 .20
1320 A326 5f lt ol & ultra .20 .20
1321 A326 8f red & yel .20 .20
1322 A326 10f lt grn, org & bl .25 .20
1323 A326 20f org, yel & brn .30 .20
1324 A326 30f bl, lt grn & blk .30 .20
1325 A326 40f multicolored .40 .20
1326 A326 50f cit, red & blk .50 .20
1327 A326 60f pur, yel & org .60 .25
1328 A326 70f blue & multi .90 .30
Nos. 1315-1328 (14) 4.65 2.95

Address by Party Committee A327

Designs: No. 1330, Planting new rice fields. No. 1331, Farmers reading wall newspaper. No. 1332, Land reclamation. T.22.

1977, Apr. 9 *Perf. 11x11½*
1329 A327 8f multi (4-1) .90 .75
1330 A327 8f multi (4-2) .90 .75
1331 A327 8f multi (4-3) .90 .75
1332 A327 8f multi (4-4) .90 .75
Nos. 1329-1332 (4) 3.60 3.00

Building Tachai-type communities throughout China.

Worker at Microphone — A328

Designs: No. 1334, Drilling for oil during snowstorm. No. 1335, Crowd advancing under Red banner. No. 1336, Workers, industrial complex, rocket blast-off. J.15.

1977, Apr. 25 *Perf. 11*
1333 A328 8f multi (4-1) 1.40 1.00
1334 A328 8f multi (4-2) 1.40 1.00
1335 A328 8f multi (4-3) 1.40 1.00
1336 A328 8f multi (4-4) 1.40 1.00
Nos. 1333-1336 (4) 5.60 4.00

Conference on learning from Taching workers in industry.

Mongolians Hailing Anniversary A329

10f, Iron and steel complex, iron ore train. 20f, Cattle grazing in improved pasture. J.16.

1977, May 1 *Perf. 11x11½*
1337 A329 8f multi (3-1) .40 .20
1338 A329 10f multi (3-2) .40 .30
1339 A329 20f multi (3-3) 1.50 .95
Nos. 1337-1339 (3) 2.30 1.45

30th anniversary of Inner Mongolian Autonomous Region.

1877 Flag of Romania and Oak Leaves — A330

Mihai Viteazu Memorial (16th Century Hero) — A331

10f, Battle of Smirdan, by N. Grigorescu. J.17.

1977, May 9 Photo. *Perf. 11*

1340	A330 8f multi (3-1)		.75	.60
1341	A331 10f multi (3-2)		.75	.60
1342	A331 20f multi (3-3)		2.10	1.75
	Nos. 1340-1342 (3)		3.60	2.95

Centenary of Romanian independence.

Yenan "Let 100 Flowers Bloom" A332

#1344, Hammer, sickle, gun & flowers; "Proletarian revolutionary literature will prosper." J.18.

1977, May, 23

1343	A332 8f grn, red & gold	.90	.55
1344	A332 8f lt brn, red & gold	.90	.55

Yenan Forum on Literature & Art, 35th anniv.

Zhu De — A333

Designs: No. 1346, Zhu De, last address to Congress. No. 1347, Zhu De at his desk, horiz. No. 1348, Zhu De on horseback as commander of Red Army. J.19.

1977, July 6 Photo. *Perf. 11½*

1345	A333 8f multi (4-1)	.65	.35
1346	A333 8f multi (4-2)	.65	.35
1347	A333 8f multi (4-3)	.65	.35
1348	A333 8f multi (4-4)	.65	.35
	Nos. 1345-1348 (4)	2.60	1.40

Zhu De (1886-1976), Commander of Red Army, Chairman of National People's Congress.

Military under Mao's Banner — A334

#1350, Red Flag, Soldiers, Chingkang Mountains. #1351, Guerrilla fighters returning to base. #1352, Guerrillas crossing Yangtze. #1353, National defense. J.20.

1977, Aug. 1

1349	A334 8f multi (5-1)	1.50	1.00
1350	A334 8f multi (5-2)	1.50	1.00
1351	A334 8f multi (5-3)	1.50	1.00
1352	A334 8f multi (5-4)	1.50	1.00
1353	A334 8f multi (5-5)	1.50	1.00
	Nos. 1349-1353 (5)	7.50	5.00

Liberation Army Day, 50th anniversary of People's Army.

Gate of Heavenly Peace, People and Red Flags — A335

Designs: No. 1355, People marching under Red Flag with Mao's portrait. No. 1356, People marching under Red Flag with hammer and sickle. J.23.

1977, Aug. 22 Photo. *Perf. 11½x11*

1354	A335 8f multi (3-1)	3.50	2.50
1355	A335 8f multi (3-2)	3.50	2.50
1356	A335 8f multi (3-3)	3.50	2.50
	Nos. 1354-1356 (3)	10.50	7.50

11th National Congress of the Communist Party of China.

Chairman Mao — A336

Designs (Mao Portraits): No. 1358, as young man in Shansi. No. 1359, addressing Communist Party in Plenary Session. No. 1360, Proclaiming People's Republic at Gate of Heavenly Peace. No. 1361, at airport with Chou En-lai and Zhu De, horiz. No. 1362, Reviewing Army as old man. J.21.

1977, Sept. 9 Photo. *Perf. 11½*

1357	A336 8f multi (6-1)	1.00	.80
1358	A336 8f multi (6-2)	1.00	.80
1359	A336 8f multi (6-3)	1.00	.80
1360	A336 8f multi (6-4)	1.00	.80
1361	A336 8f multi (6-5)	1.00	.80
1362	A336 8f multi (6-6)	1.00	.80
	Nos. 1357-1362 (6)	6.00	4.80

Mao-Tse-tung (1893-1976), first death anniversary.

Mao Memorial Hall — A337

Completion of Mao Memorial Hall: No. 1364, Chairman Hua's inscription. J.22.

1977, Sept. 9

1363	A337 8f lt ultra & multi	2.25	1.50
1364	A337 8f lt grn, tan & gold	2.25	1.50

Tractors Moving Drilling Tower — A338

#1366, Shui Pow Tsi oil well and women workers. #1367, Construction of oil pipe line, Taching, and silos. #1368, Tung Fang Hung oil refinery, Peking. #1369, Taching oil loaded into tanker in harbor. 20f, Off-shore drilling platform "Pohai No. 1." T.19.

1978, Jan. 31 Photo. *Perf. 11*

1365	A338 8f multi (6-1)	.35	.40
1366	A338 8f multi (6-2)	.35	.40
1367	A338 8f multi (6-3)	.35	.40
1368	A338 8f multi (6-4)	.35	.40
1369	A338 8f multi (6-5)	.35	.40
1370	A338 20f multi (6-6)	1.90	.90
	Nos. 1365-1370 (6)	3.65	2.90

Development of Chinese oil industry.

"Army Teaching Militia" — A339

#1372, "Army helping with rice planting." T.23.

1978, Feb. 5 Photo. *Perf. 11*

1371	A339 8f multi (2-1)	1.40	1.10
1372	A339 8f multi (2-2)	1.40	1.10

Army and people working as a family.

Red Flags, Mao Tse-tung — A340

Constitution and Red Flags — A341

#1375, Atom symbol over symbols of agriculture & industry. All designs include Great Hall of the People, Peking, & flowers. J.24.

1978, Feb. 26

1373	A340 8f multi (3-1)	.90	.75
1374	A341 8f multi (3-2)	.90	.75
1375	A340 8f multi (3-3)	.90	.75
	Nos. 1373-1375 (3)	2.70	2.25

5th National People's Congress.

Mao's Eulogy for Lei Feng — A342

Lei Feng, Studying Mao's Works — A343

#1377, Chairman Hua's thoughts (5 lines). J.26.

1978, Mar. 5

1376	A342 8f gold & red (3-1)	1.40	1.10
1377	A342 8f gold & red (3-2)	1.40	1.10
1378	A343 8f multicolored (3-3)	1.40	1.10
	Nos. 1376-1378 (3)	4.20	3.30

Lei Feng (1940-1962), communist fighter; 15th anniversary of Chairman Mao's eulogy "Learn from Comrade Lei Feng."

Hsiang Ching-yu — A344

Yang Kai-hui — A345

1978, Mar. 8

1379	A344 8f multi (2-1)	.80	.70
1380	A345 8f multi (2-2)	.80	.70

Hsiang Ching-yu, pioneer of Women's Movement, executed 1928; Yang Kai-hui, communist fighter, executed 1930. J.27.

A346

A346a

A346b

#1381, Conference emblem. #1382, Banners symbolizing industry, agriculture, defense & science. #1383, Red flag, atom symbol & globe. J.25.

1978, Mar. 18 Litho. *Perf. 11½x11*

1381	A346 8f gold & red (3-1)	.90	.70
1382	A346a 8f multi (3-2)	.90	.70
1383	A346b 8f multi (3-3)	.90	.70
a.	Souvenir sheet of 3	*300.00*	200.00
	Nos. 1381-1383 (3)	2.70	2.10

Natl. Science Conf. #1383a contains #1381-1383 with simulated perforations. Sold for 50f.

Release of Weather Balloon A347

Weather Observations: No. 1385, Radar station, typhoon watch. No. 1386, Computer, weather maps. No. 1387, Local weather observers. No. 1388, Rockets intercepting hail clouds. T.24.

1978, Apr. 25 Photo. *Perf. 11x11½*

1384 A347 8f multi (5-1)	.60	.50
1385 A347 8f multi (5-2)	.60	.50
1386 A347 8f multi (5-3)	.60	.50
1387 A347 8f multi (5-4)	.60	.50
1388 A347 8f multi (5-5)	.60	.50
Nos. 1384-1388 (5)	3.00	2.50

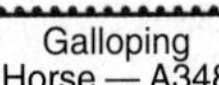

Galloping Horse — A348

Children Playing Soccer — A349

Designs: Galloping Horses, by Hsu Peihung (1895-1953). 40f, 50f, 60f, 70f, $5, horiz. T.28.

1978, May 5 *Perf. 11½x11, 11x11½*

1389 A348 4f multi (10-1)	.85	.75
1390 A348 8f multi (10-2)	.85	.75
1391 A348 8f multi (10-3)	.85	.75
1392 A348 10f multi (10-4)	.85	.75
1393 A348 20f multi (10-5)	3.50	.75
1394 A348 30f multi (10-6)	2.50	.75
1395 A348 40f multi (10-7)	2.50	1.50
1396 A348 50f multi (10-8)	3.50	1.50
1397 A348 60f multi (10-9)	2.50	3.00
1398 A348 70f multi (10-10)	3.50	4.25
Nos. 1389-1398 (10)	21.40	14.75

Souvenir Sheet

1399 A348 $5 multicolored	*175.00*	125.00

No. 1399 contains one stamp showing 4 horses, size: 89x39mm.

1978, June 1 *Perf. 11½*

Designs: No. 1401, Children on the beach. No. 1402, Little girls dancing. No. 1403, Children taking long walks. 20f, Children exercising for good health. T.21.

Size: 22x27mm

1400 A349 8f multi (5-2)	.45	.40
1401 A349 8f multi (5-3)	.45	.40
1402 A349 8f multi (5-4)	.45	.40
1403 A349 8f multi (5-5)	.45	.40

Size: 48x28mm

1404 A349 20f multi (5-1)	.90	.70
Nos. 1400-1404 (5)	2.70	2.30

Build up your health while young.

Synthetic Fiber Feeder A350

Designs: No. 1406, Drawing out threads. No. 1407, Weaving. No. 1408, Dyeing and printing. No. 1409, Finished products. T.25.

1978, June 15 Photo. *Perf. 11½*

1405 A350 8f multi (5-1)	.60	.50
1406 A350 8f multi (5-2)	.60	.50
1407 A350 8f multi (5-3)	.60	.50
1408 A350 8f multi (5-4)	.60	.50
1409 A350 8f multi (5-5)	.60	.50
a. Strip of 5, #1405-1409	3.50	3.00
Nos. 1405-1409 (5)	3.00	2.50

Chemical fiber industry. No. 1409a has continuous design.

Conference Emblem A351

"Develop Economy and Ensure Supplies" A352

1978, June 20 *Perf. 13*

1410 A351 8f multi (2-1)	.40	.30
1411 A352 8f multi (2-2)	.40	.30

Natl. Conf. on Learning from Taching and Tachai in Finance and Trade. J.28.

New Pastures, Mongolia — A353

Designs: No. 1413, Kazakh shepherds selecting sheep for breeding. No. 1414, Mechanized shearing of sheep, Tibet, T.27.

1978, June 30 Photo. *Perf. 11½*

1412 A353 8f multi (3-1)	1.10	.55
1413 A353 8f multi (3-2)	1.10	.55
1414 A353 8f multi (3-3)	1.10	.55
Nos. 1412-1414 (3)	3.30	1.65

Learning from Tachai in developing animal husbandry and new pastoral areas.

Coke Oven — A354

Iron and Steel Industry: No. 1416, Iron furnace. No. 1417, Pouring steel. No. 1418, Steel rolling. No. 1419, Finished iron and steel products. T.26.

1978, July 22

1415 A354 8f multi (5-1)	.70	.45
1416 A354 8f multi (5-2)	.70	.45
1417 A354 8f multi (5-3)	.70	.45
1418 A354 8f multi (5-4)	.70	.45
1419 A354 8f multi (5-5)	.70	.45
Nos. 1415-1419 (5)	3.50	2.25

Iron Fist to Prevent Revisionism A355

Jug in Shape of Sheep — A356

#1421, "Carrying forward revolutionary tradition." #1422, "Strenuous training in military skills to wipe out enemy." T.32.

1978, Aug. 1 Photo. *Perf. 11½*

1420 A355 8f multi (3-1)	.90	.45
1421 A355 8f multi (3-2)	.90	.45
1422 A355 8f multi (3-3)	.90	.45
Nos. 1420-1422 (3)	2.70	1.35

"Learn from Hard-boned 6th Company." (A military unit since 1939).

1978, Aug. 26

Arts and Crafts: 4f, Giant lion (toy; horiz.). No. 1425, Rhinoceros (lacquer ware; horiz). 10f, Cat (embroidery). 20f, Bag (weaving; horiz.). 30f, Teapot in shape of peacock (cloisonné). 40f, Plate with lotus, and swan-shaped box (lacquer ware; horiz.). 50f, Dragon flying in sky (ivory). 60f, Sun rising (jade; horiz.). 70f, Flight to human world (ivory). $3, Flying fairies (arts and crafts; horiz.). T.29.

1423 A356 4f multi (10-1)	.45	.25
1424 A356 8f multi (10-2)	.45	.25
1425 A356 8f multi (10-3)	.45	.25
1426 A356 10f multi (10-4)	.45	.40
1427 A356 20f multi (10-5)	.45	.40
1428 A356 30f multi (10-6)	.45	.40
1429 A356 40f multi (10-7)	.90	.75
1430 A356 50f multi (10-8)	1.75	1.00
1431 A356 60f multi (10-9)	1.75	1.00
1432 A356 70f multi (10-10)	1.75	1.25
Nos. 1423-1432 (10)	8.85	5.95

Souvenir Sheet

1433 A356 $3 multi	*225.00*	150.00

No. 1433 contains one 85x36mm stamp.

Women, Atom Symbol, Rocket and Wheat A357

1978, Sept. 8 Photo. *Perf. 11*

1434 A357 8f multicolored	1.40	.90

4th National Women's Congress.

Ginseng — A358

Flag, Wheat, Cogwheel, Plane, Atom Symbols — A359

Medicinal Plants: No. 1436, Horn of plenty. No. 1437, Blackberry lily. No. 1438, Balloonflower. 55f, Rhododendron dauricum. T.30.

1978, Sept. 15

1435 A358 8f multi (5-1)	.45	.25
1436 A358 8f multi (5-2)	.45	.25
1437 A358 8f multi (5-3)	.45	.25
1438 A358 8f multi (5-4)	.45	.25
1439 A358 55f multi (5-5)	1.75	.80
Nos. 1435-1439 (5)	3.55	1.80

1978, Oct. 11 Photo. *Perf. 11*

1440 A359 8f multicolored	2.25	1.75

9th National Trade Union Congress.

Youth League Emblem A360

1978, Oct. 16

1441 A360 8f multicolored	1.75	1.10

10th Natl. Communist Youth League Cong.

Chinese and Japanese Girls Exchanging Gifts A361

Great Wall and Mt. Fuji A362

1978, Oct. 22

1442 A361 8f multicolored	.65	.40
1443 A362 55f multicolored	1.75	1.50

Signing of Sino-Japanese Peace and Friendship Treaty.

Moslem, Chinese and Mongolian People — A363

Chinsha River Bridge, West Szechuan A364

#1445, Loading coal at Holan Mountain. 10f, Irrigated rice fields & boxthorn. J.29.

1978, Oct. 25

1444 A363 8f multi (3-1)	.90	.75
1445 A363 8f multi (3-2)	.90	.75
1446 A363 10f multi (3-3)	.90	.75
Nos. 1444-1446 (3)	2.70	2.25

20th anniversary of founding of Ningsia Moslem Autonomous Region.

1978, Nov. 1 Photo. *Perf. 11½x11*

Highway Bridges: No. 1448, Hsinhong bridge, Wuhsi. No. 1449, Chiuhsikou bridge, Fengdu. No. 1450, Chinsha River bridge, West Szechuan. 60f, Shangyeh bridge, Sanmen. $2, Hsiang-kiang River bridge. T.31.

1447 A364 8f multi (5-1)	.45	.30
1448 A364 8f multi (5-2)	.45	.30
1449 A364 8f multi (5-3)	.45	.30
1450 A364 8f multi (5-4)	.45	.30
1451 A364 60f multi (5-5)	2.50	1.25
Nos. 1447-1451 (5)	4.30	2.45

Souvenir Sheet

1452 A364 $2 multi	*225.00*	125.00

No. 1452 contains one 86x37mm stamp.

Mechanical Transplanting of Rice Seedlings A365

Paintings: No. 1454, Spraying fields. No. 1455, Seed selection. No. 1456, Trade. No. 1457, Delivery of public grain in city. T.34.

1978, Nov. 30 *Perf. 11½*

1453 A365 8f multi (5-1)	5.00	2.50
1454 A365 8f multi (5-2)	5.00	2.50
1455 A365 8f multi (5-3)	5.00	2.50
1456 A365 8f multi (5-4)	5.00	2.50
1457 A365 8f multi (5-5)	5.00	2.50
a. Strip of 5, #1453-1457	29.00	15.00

Agricultural progress. No. 1457a has a continuous design.

Dancers and Fireworks — A366

Designs: No. 1459, Industry, vert. 10f, Agriculture, vert. J.33.

1978, Dec. 11 Photo. *Perf. 11*

1458	A366	8f multi (3-1)	2.00	.60
1459	A366	8f multi (3-2)	2.00	.60
1460	A366	10f multi (3-3)	1.00	1.00
		Nos. 1458-1460 (3)	5.00	2.20

20th anniversary of Kwangsi Chuang Autonomous Region.

Miners with Pneumatic Drill A367

Mine Development: 4f, Old Tibetan peasant reporting to surveyor. 10f, Open-cut mining with power shovel. 20f, Loaded electric train in pit. T.20.

1978, Dec. 29 Photo. & Engr.

1461	A367	4f multi (4-1)	.55	.30
1462	A367	8f multi (4-2)	.55	.30
1463	A367	10f multi (4-3)	1.25	1.00
1464	A367	20f multi (4-4)	1.25	1.10
		Nos. 1461-1464 (4)	3.60	2.70

A368

A369

Golden Pheasants: 4f, Roosting on rock. 8f, In flight. 45f, Seeking food. T.35.

1979, Jan. 25 Photo. *Perf. 11½*

1465	A368	4f multi (3-1)	1.10	1.00
1466	A368	8f multi (3-2)	3.25	1.00
1467	A368	45f multi (3-3)	2.25	2.00
		Nos. 1465-1467 (3)	6.60	4.00

1979, Mar. 14 Photo. *Perf. 11½x11*

1468	A369	8f Albert Einstein, equation	2.25	1.75

Phoenix Battling Monster, Praying Woman A370

60f, Man riding dragon to heaven. Designs from silk paintings found in Changsha tomb, Warring States Period (475-221 B.C.). T.33.

1979, Mar. 29 *Perf. 11*

1469	A370	8f multi (2-1)	2.40	.75
1470	A370	60f multi (2-2)	1.60	1.50

Summer Palace — A371

Photo., Photo. & Engr. ($5)

1979-80 *Perf. 13*

1471	A371	$1 Pagoda ('80)	.60	.20
1472	A371	$2 Shown	1.25	.50
1473	A371	$5 Temple, Beihai Park	4.00	1.10
		Nos. 1471-1473 (3)	5.85	1.80

Issued: $3, June 16, 1979.

Hammer and Sickle "51" and Bars from "International" — A372

1979, May 1 Photo. *Perf. 11*

1474	A372	8f multicolored	.90	.75

International Labor Day, 90th anniv.

"Tradition of May 4th Movement" A373

Young Woman, Rocket, Antenna, Nuclear Reactor A374

1979, May 4

1475	A373	8f multicolored	.65	.50
1476	A374	8f multicolored	.65	.50

60th anniversary of May 4th Movement.

IYC Emblem, Children Holding Balloons — A375

Children of Three Races, IYC Emblem — A376

1979, May 25 *Perf. 11½*

1477	A375	8f multicolored	1.00	.65
1478	A376	60f multicolored	7.00	5.25

International Year of the Child.

Great Wall in Spring A377

Designs (The Great Wall): No. 1480, in summer. No. 1481, in autumn. 60f, in winter. $2, Guard tower. T.38.

1979, June 25 Photo. *Perf. 11*

1479	A377	8f multi (4-1)	1.00	.80
1480	A377	8f multi (4-2)	1.00	.80
1481	A377	8f multi (4-3)	1.00	.80
1482	A377	60f multi (4-4)	5.75	4.75
		Nos. 1479-1482 (4)	8.75	7.15

Souvenir Sheet

1483	A377	$2 multi	*90.00*	60.00

For overprint see No. 1492.

Roaring Tiger — A379

Manchurian Tiger: 8f, Two young tigers. 60f, Tiger at rest. T.40.

1979, July 20 *Perf. 11½x11*

1484	A379	4f multi (3-1)	1.10	.85
1485	A379	8f multi (3-2)	1.10	.85
1486	A379	60f multi (3-3)	3.50	1.75
		Nos. 1484-1486 (3)	5.70	3.45

Mechanical Harvesting — A380

Work of the Communes: No. 1488, Forestry. No. 1489, Raising ducks. No. 1490, Women weaving baskets. 10f, Fishing. T.39.

1979, Aug. 10 *Perf. 11½*

1487	A380	4f multi (5-1)	.50	.40
1488	A380	8f multi (5-2)	1.00	.90
1489	A380	8f multi (5-3)	1.00	.90
1490	A380	8f multi (5-4)	1.00	.90
1491	A380	10f multi (5-5)	2.00	1.25
		Nos. 1487-1491 (5)	5.50	4.35

No. 1483 Overprinted with Gold Inscription and "1979"

Souvenir Sheet

1979, Aug. 25 Photo. *Perf. 11*

1492	A377	$2 multicolored	*350.00*

31st International Stamp Exhibition, Riccione, Italy. J41 (1-1).

Forged overprints exist.

Games Emblem, Sports — A381

#1494, Soccer, badminton, high jump, speed skating. #1495, Fencing, skiing, gymnastics, diving. #1496, Motorcycling, table tennis, basketball, archery. #1497, Emblem only. J.43.

1979, Sept. 15 *Perf. 11½x11*

1493	A381	8f multi (4-1)	.50	.40
1494	A381	8f multi (4-2)	.50	.40
1495	A381	8f multi (4-3)	.50	.40
1496	A381	8f multi (4-4)	.50	.40
a.		Block of 4, #1493-1496	2.75	2.50

Souvenir Sheet

Perf. 11½

1497	A381	$2 multi, vert.	*40.00*	25.00

4th National Games. Size of stamp in No. 1497: 22x26mm.

Flag and Rainbow — A382

Design: No. 1499, Flag and mountains.

1979, Oct. 1 Photo. *Perf. 11½*

1498	A382	8f multicolored	1.60	1.25
1499	A382	8f multicolored	1.60	1.25

National Emblem — A383

Dancers — A384

1979, Oct. 1 Photo. *Perf. 11½*

1500	A383	8f multicolored	2.00	1.00

Souvenir Sheet

1501	A383	$1 multicolored	*40.00*	25.00

1979, Oct. 1 Photo. *Perf. 11½*

Designs: #1503-1505, various dances. J.47.

1502	A384	8f multi (4-1)	.60	.30
1503	A384	8f multi (4-2)	.60	.30
1504	A384	8f multi (4-3)	.60	.30
1505	A384	8f multi (4-4)	.60	.30
a.		Block of 4, #1502-1505	2.75	2.25

Tractor, Aerial Crop Spraying, Irrigation — A385

#1507, Gear, computers. #1508, Rocket, submarine, jets. #1509, Atom symbol. J.48.

1979, Oct. 1 Photo. *Perf. 11½*

1506	A385	8f multi (4-1)	.65	.55
1507	A385	8f multi (4-2)	.65	.55
1508	A385	8f multi (4-3)	.65	.55
1509	A385	8f multi (4-4)	.65	.55
		Nos. 1506-1509 (4)	2.60	2.20

National Anthem A386

1979, Oct. 1 Engr. *Perf. 11*
1510 A386 8f multicolored 2.75 2.75

Exhibition Emblem — A387

Children Flying Model Planes — A388

1979, Oct. 3
1511 A387 8f multicolored .90 .55

Junior National Scientific and Technological Exhibition.

1979, Oct. 3

#1513, Girls and microscope. #1514, Children and telescope. #1515, Boy catching butterflies. #1516, Girl taking meteorological readings. #1517, Boys sailing model boat. #1518, Girl with book. T.41.

1512 A388 8f multi (6-1) .50 .40
1513 A388 8f multi (6-2) .50 .40
1514 A388 8f multi (6-3) .50 .40
1515 A388 8f multi (6-4) .50 .40
1516 A388 8f multi (6-5) .50 .40
1517 A388 60f multi (6-6) 2.75 1.75
Nos. 1512-1517 (6) 5.25 3.75

Souvenir Sheet
Perf. 11

1518 A388 $2 multi *550.00* 400.00

Study Science from Childhood. No. 1518 contains one stamp, size: 90x40mm.

Yu Shan Mountain A389

Taiwan Landscapes: No. 1520, Sun and Moon Lake. No. 1521, Chihkan Tower. No. 1522, Suao-Hualien Highway. 55f, Tian Xiang Falls. 60f, Banping Mountain. T.42.

1979, Oct. 20 Photo. *Perf. 11x11½*
1519 A389 8f multi (6-1) .80 .65
1520 A389 8f multi (6-2) .80 .65
1521 A389 8f multi (6-3) .80 .65
1522 A389 8f multi (6-4) .80 .65
1523 A389 55f multi (6-5) 2.40 1.40
1524 A389 60f multi (6-6) 3.25 2.75
Nos. 1519-1524 (6) 8.85 6.75

Arts Symbols A390

8f, Seals and modernization symbols. J.39.

1979, Oct. 30
1525 A390 4f multicolored .55 .45
1526 A390 8f multicolored 1.25 .70

4th Natl. Cong. of Literary and Art Workers.

Train in Tunnel A391

Railroads: No. 1528, Mountain bridge. No. 1529, Freight train. T.36.

1979, Oct. 30 Photo. & Engr.
1527 A391 8f multi (3-1) .90 .75
1528 A391 8f multi (3-2) .90 .75
1529 A391 8f multi (3-3) .90 .75
Nos. 1527-1529 (3) 2.70 2.25

Chrysanthemum Petal — A392

Camellias: No. 1531, Lion head. No. 1532, Camellia chryantha. 10f, Small osmanthus leaf. 20f, Baby face. 30f, Cornelian. 40f, Peony camellia. 50f, Purple gown. 60f, Dwarf rose. 70f, Willow leaf spinel pink. $2, Red jewelry. T.37.

1979, Nov. 10 Photo. *Perf. 11x11½*
1530 A392 4f multi (10-1) .80 .50
1531 A392 8f multi (10-2) .80 .50
1532 A392 8f multi (10-3) .80 .50
1533 A392 10f multi (10-4) .80 .50
1534 A392 20f multi (10-5) 1.60 1.00
1535 A392 30f multi (10-6) 3.25 1.00
1536 A392 40f multi (10-7) 2.40 1.00
1537 A392 50f multi (10-8) 2.40 1.00
1538 A392 60f multi (10-9) 1.60 1.00
1539 A392 70f multi (10-10) 1.60 1.00
Nos. 1530-1539 (10) 16.05 8.00

Souvenir Sheet
Perf. 11½x11

1540 A392 $2 multi *110.00* 75.00

No. 1540 contains one 86x36mm stamp.

No. 1540 Overprinted and Numbered in Gold in Margin
Souvenir Sheet

1979, Nov. 10
1541 A392 $2 multicolored *200.00*

People's Republic of China Phil. Exhib., Hong Kong, 1979. J.42 (1-1).
Forged overprints exist.

Norman Bethune Treating Soldier — A393

Design: 70f, Bethune statue.

1979, Nov. 12
1542 A393 8f multi (2-2) 2.25 1.50
1543 A393 70f multi (2-1) .45 .30

Dr. Norman Bethune, 40th death anniv. J.50.

Central Archives Hall A394

Intl. Archives Weeks: No. 1545, Gold archive cabinet, vert. 60f, Pavilion. J.51.

Perf. 11x11½, 11½x11
1979, Nov. 26 Photo.
1544 A394 8f multi (3-1) .40 .35
1545 A394 8f multi (3-2) .40 .35
1546 A394 60f multi (3-3) 5.25 2.00
Nos. 1544-1546 (3) 6.05 2.70

Monkey King in Waterfall Cave — A395

Monkey King, Scenes from Pilgrimage to the West (Novel): No. 1548, Fighting Necha, son of Prince Li. No. 1549, In Mother Queen's peach orchard. No. 1550, In the alchemy furnace. 10f, Subduing the white bone demon. 20f, With palm leaf fan. 60f, In cobweb cave. 70f, Walking on scripture-seeking route. T.43.

1979, Dec. 1 *Perf. 11½x11*
1547 A395 8f multi (8-1) 1.40 1.25
1548 A395 8f multi (8-2) 1.40 1.25
1549 A395 8f multi (8-3) 1.40 1.25
1550 A395 8f multi (8-4) 1.40 1.25
1551 A395 10f multi (8-5) 4.00 1.25
1552 A395 20f multi (8-6) 4.00 1.25
1553 A395 60f multi (8-7) 6.75 3.75
1554 A395 70f multi (8-8) 6.75 3.75
Nos. 1547-1554 (8) 27.10 15.00

Stalin Delivering Speech A396

Joseph Stalin (1879-1953): No. 1555, Portrait of Stalin, vert. J.49.

Perf. 11x11½, 11½x11
1979, Dec. 21 Engr.
1555 A396 8f brown (2-1) 1.10 .90
1556 A396 8f black (2-2) 1.10 .90

A397

A398

1980 Photo. *Perf. 11½*
1557 A397 4f Peony (16-1) .75 .65
1558 A397 4f Squirrels and grapes (16-2) .75 .65
1559 A397 8f Crabs candle and wine (16-3) .75 .65
1560 A397 8f Tadpoles in mountain spring (16-4) .75 .65
1561 A397 8f Chicks (16-5) .75 .65
1562 A397 8f Lotus (16-6) .75 .65
1563 A397 8f Red plum (16-7) .75 .65
1564 A397 8f Kingfisher (16-8) .75 .65
1565 A397 10f Bottle gourd (16-9) 1.50 .65
1566 A397 20f Voice of autumn (16-10) 1.50 .65
1567 A397 30f Wisteria (16-11) 1.50 1.10
1568 A397 40f Chrysanthemums (16-12) 1.50 1.10
1569 A397 50f Shrimp (16-13) 3.00 1.50
1570 A397 55f Litchi (16-14) 3.75 1.90
1571 A397 60f Cabbages, mushrooms (16-15) 5.25 3.75
1572 A397 70f Peaches (16-16) 6.00 5.50
Nos. 1557-1572 (16) 30.00 21.35

Souvenir Sheet

1573 A397 $2 Hyacynth *100.00* 50.00

Qi Baishi paintings. Issued: #1557-1560, 1569-1572, 1/15; others, 5/20. #1573 contains one 37½x61mm stamp. T. 44.

1980, Jan. 25 *Perf. 11½x11*

Opera Masks: No. 1574, Meng Liang Mask from Hongyang Cave Opera. No. 1575, Li Kui, from Black Whirlwind. No. 1576, Huang Gai, from Meeting of Heroes. No. 1577, 10f, Lu Zhishen, from Wild Boar Forest. 20f, Lian Po, from Reconciliation between the General and Minister. 60f, Zhang Fei, from Reed Marsh. 70f, Dou Erdun, from Stealing the Emperor's Horse, T. 45.

1574 A398 4f multi (8-1) .90 .75
1575 A398 4f multi (8-2) 3.50 .75
1576 A398 8f multi (8-3) 1.75 .75
1577 A398 8f multi (8-4) 1.75 .75
1578 A398 10f multi (8-5) 3.50 1.75
1579 A398 20f multi (8-6) 3.50 1.75
1580 A398 60f multi (8-7) 7.25 3.50
1581 A398 70f multi (8-8) 9.00 5.25
Nos. 1574-1581 (8) 31.15 15.25

Speed Skating, Olympic Rings — A399

Monkey, New Year — A400

Olympic Rings and: No. 1582, Chinese flag. No. 1584, Figure skating. 60f, Downhill skiing. J.54.

1980, Feb. 13
1582 A399 8f multi (4-1) .45 .30
1583 A399 8f multi (4-2) .45 .30
1584 A399 8f multi (4-3) .45 .30
1585 A399 60f multi (4-4) 4.75 1.75
Nos. 1582-1585 (4) 6.10 2.65

13th Winter Olympic Games, Lake Placid, NY, Feb. 12-24.

Engraved and Photogravure
1980, Feb. 15 *Perf. 11½*
1586 A400 8f multicolored *225.00 85.00*

Clara Zetkin — A401

Photogravure & Engraved
1980, Mar. 8 *Perf. 11½x11*
1587 A401 8f black & yellow 1.10 .90

International Working Women's Day, 70th anniv., founded by Clara Zetkin (1857-1933).

Orchard A402

Afforestation: 8f, Trees lining highway. 10f, Aerial seeding. 20f, Trees surrounding factory. T.48.

1980, Mar. 12 *Perf. 11x11½*
1588 A402 4f multi (4-1) .45 .25
1589 A402 8f multi (4-2) .45 .25
1590 A402 10f multi (4-3) .90 .50
1591 A402 20f multi (4-4) .90 .50
Nos. 1588-1591 (4) 2.70 1.50

Apsaras, Symbols of Modernization — A403

1980, Mar. 15 Photo. *Perf. 11½*

1592 A403 8f multicolored 1.75 1.25

2nd National Conference of the Scientific and Technical Association of China.

Mail Transport (T.49) — A404

1980, Mar. 20 *Perf. 11x11½*

1593 A404 2f Ship (4-1) 1.00 1.00
1594 A404 4f Bus (4-2) 1.00 1.00
1595 A404 8f Train (4-3) 2.00 1.00
1596 A404 10f Jet (4-4) 3.00 2.00
Nos. 1593-1596 (4) 7.00 5.00

Forgeries exist.

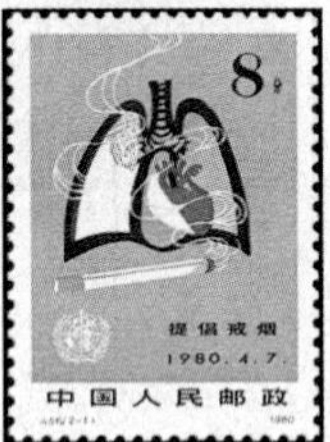

Lungs, Heart, Cigarette, WHO Emblem — A405

Statue of Chien Chen (688-763) — A406

1980, Apr. 7 *Perf. 11½x11*

1597 A405 8f shown (2-1) .80 .45
1598 A405 60f Faces (2-2) 5.00 2.75

Fight against cigarette smoking. J.56.

1980, Apr. 13 *Perf. 11x11½, 11½x11*

Loan to China by Japan of statue of Chien Chen (Jian Zhen), Buddhist missionary to Japan (754-763): No. 1600, Chien Chen Memorial Hall, Yangchou, horiz. 60f, Chien Chen's ship, horiz. His name in Japan is Ganjin. J.55.

1599 A406 8f multi (3-1) 2.40 .85
1600 A406 8f multi (3-2) 2.40 .85
1601 A406 60f multi (3-3) 15.00 6.75
Nos. 1599-1601 (3) 19.80 8.45

Lenin's 110th Birthday — A407

Swallow Chick Kite — A408

Photogravure and Engraved

1980, Apr. 22 *Perf. 11½x11*

1602 A407 8f multicolored 1.40 .90

1980, May 10 Photo. *Perf. 11½*

Designs: Kites. T.50.

1603 A408 8f shown (4-1) 2.50 1.10
1604 A408 8f Slender-swallow (4-2) 2.50 1.10
1605 A408 8f Semi-slender swallow (4-3) 2.50 1.10
1606 A408 70f Dual swallows (4-4) 10.00 4.50
Nos. 1603-1606 (4) 17.50 7.80

Hare Running from Fallen Papaya A409

1980, June 1 Photo. *Perf. 11x11½*

1607 Strip of 4 + label 7.25 6.00
a. A409 8f shown (4-1) 1.40 1.25
b. A409 8f Hare fox, monkey running away (4-2) 1.40 1.25
c. A409 8f Lion instructing animals (4-3) 1.40 1.25
d. A409 8f Discovery of fallen papaya (4-4) 1.40 1.25

Gu Dong fairy tale. T.51.

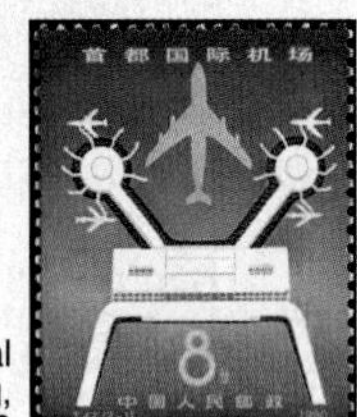

Terminal Building, Jets — A410

1980, June 20 *Perf. 11½*

1608 A410 8f Shown (2-1) 1.10 1.00
1609 A410 10f Runways, jets (2-2) 1.60 1.00

Peking Intl. Airport opening. T.47.

Sika Stag — A411

White Lotus — A412

1980, July 18 Photo. *Perf. 11½*

1610 A411 4f Shown (3-1) 1.00 1.00
1611 A411 8f Doe and fawn (3-2) 1.00 1.00
1612 A411 60f Herd (3-3) 5.25 4.00
Nos. 1610-1612 (3) 7.25 6.00

T.52.

1980, Aug. 4

1613 A412 8f Shown (4-1) 2.00 1.00
1614 A412 8f Rose-tipped snow (4-2) 2.00 1.00
1615 A412 8f Buddha's seat (4-3) 2.00 1.00
1616 A412 70f Variable charming face (4-4) 16.00 7.00
Nos. 1613-1616 (4) 22.00 10.00

Souvenir Sheet

1617 A412 $1 Fresh lotus on rippling water 110.00

#1617 contains one 48x88mm stamp. T.54.

Pearl Cave, Sword-cut Stone Sculptures — A413

Guilin Landscapes: No. 1619, Three mountains, distant views. No. 1620, Nine-horse fresco hill. No. 1621, Egrets around aged banyan. No. 1622, Western hills at sunset, vert. No. 1623, Moonlight on Lijiang River, vert. 60f, Springhead, ancient ferry, vert. 70f, Scenic path, Yangshue, vert. T.53.

1980, Aug. 30 Photo. *Perf. 11½*

1618 A413 8f multi (8-1) 1.25 .60
1619 A413 8f multi (8-2) 1.25 .60
1620 A413 8f multi (8-3) 1.25 .60
1621 A413 8f multi (8-4) 1.25 .60
1622 A413 8f multi (8-5) 1.25 .60
1623 A413 8f multi (8-6) 1.25 .60
1624 A413 60f multi (8-7) 9.00 3.50
1625 A413 70f multi (8-8) 10.00 4.75
Nos. 1618-1625 (8) 26.50 11.85

Entrance Gate and Good Fairies A414

Great Wall, Symbols of Chicago, San Francisco and New York A415

1980, Sept. 13 Photo. *Perf. 11x11½*

1626 A414 8f multicolored .80 .70
1627 A415 70f multicolored 5.50 2.75

Exhibitions of the People's Republic of China in San Francisco, Chicago and New York, Sept.-Dec. Sheets of 12 were sold only at the US exhibitions at increasing prices. Retail value of set of two sheets of 12, approximately $360.

Romanian Flag, Warrior and Scroll — A416

1980, Sept. 20 Photo. *Perf. 11½x11*

1628 A416 8f multicolored 1.75 1.25

2050th anniv. of Dacia, 1st independent Romanian state.

UNESCO Exhibition of Drawings and Paintings (J.60) — A417

1980, Oct. 8 *Perf. 11½*

1629 A417 8f Sea of Clouds, by Liu Haisu (3-1) 1.25 .55
1630 A417 8f Oriole and Magnolia, by Yu Feian, vert., (3-2) 1.25 .55
1631 A417 8f Camels, by Wu Zuoren (3-3) 1.25 .55
Nos. 1629-1631 (3) 3.75 1.65

Scenes from Tarrying Garden (T.56) — A418

1980, Oct. 25 Photo. *Perf. 11½*

1632 A418 8f Quxi Tower (4-1) *3.50* 2.25
1633 A418 8f Yuancui Pavilion (4-2) *3.50* 2.25
1634 A418 10f Hanbi Shanfang (4-3) *3.50* 2.25
1635 A418 60f Guanyun Peak (4-4) *35.00* 14.00
Nos. 1632-1635 (4) *45.50* 20.75

Xu Guangpi (1562-1633), Agronomist A419

Shooting, Olympic Rings — A420

Scientists of Ancient China: No. 1637, Li Bing, hydraulic engineer, 3rd century B.C. No. 1638, Jia Sixie, agronomist, 5th century. 60f, Huang Daopo, textile expert, 13th century. J.58.

Photogravure and Engraved

1980, Nov. 20 *Perf. 11½x11*

1636 A419 8f multi (4-1) 1.75 .85
1637 A419 8f multi (4-2) 1.75 .85
1638 A419 8f multi (4-3) 1.75 .85
1639 A419 60f multi (4-4) 11.00 5.00
Nos. 1636-1639 (4) 16.25 7.55

1980, Nov. 26 Photo.

1640 A420 4f shown (5-1) .45 .20
1641 A420 8f Gymnastics (5-2) .90 .25
1642 A420 8f Diving (5-3) .90 .25
1643 A420 10f Volleyball (5-4) 1.40 .60
1644 A420 60f Archery (5-5) 3.50 1.75
Nos. 1640-1644 (5) 7.15 3.05

Return to International Olympic Committee, 1st anniversary. J.62.

Chinese River Dolphin A421

Photogravure & Engraved

1980, Dec. 25 *Perf. 11x11½*

1645 A421 8f shown (2-1) 1.25 .50
a. Booklet pane of 6 16.00
1646 A421 60f Dolphins (2-2) 5.00 1.50
a. Booklet pane of 1 16.00

Stamps from No. 1645a have straight edges on top or bottom.

Cock — A422

Photogravure & Engraved

1981, Jan. 5 *Perf. 11½*

1647 A422 8f multicolored 5.50 2.75
a. Booklet pane of 12 35.00

New Year 1981.

Stamps from booklet pane have straight edges on top or bottom.

Early Morning in Xishuang Bana (T.55) A423

Perf. 11x11½, 11½x11

1981, Jan. 20 **Photo.**

1648 A423 4f shown (6-1) .70 .55
1649 A423 4f Dai mountain village (6-2) .70 .55
1650 A423 8f Rainbow over Lanchang River (6-3) 1.40 .55
1651 A423 8f Ancient temple vert. (6-4) 1.40 .55
1652 A423 8f Moonlit night, vert. (6-5) 1.40 .55
1653 A423 60f Phoenix tree, vert. (6-6) 5.50 3.25
Nos. 1648-1653 (6) 11.10 6.00

Flower Basket Palace Lantern — A424

Designs: Palace lanterns. T.60.

1981, Feb. 19 **Photo.** *Perf. 11½*

1654 A424 4f multi (6-1) 1.60 .90
1655 A424 8f multi (6-2) 1.60 .90
1656 A424 8f multi (6-3) 1.60 .90
1657 A424 8f multi (6-4) 1.60 .90
1658 A424 20f multi (6-5) 4.00 3.50
1659 A424 60f multi (6-6) 9.50 7.00
Nos. 1654-1659 (6) 19.90 14.10

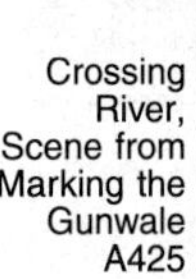

Crossing River, Scene from Marking the Gunwale A425

Scenes from Marking the Gunwale fable. T.59.

1981, Mar. 10 **Photo.** *Perf. 11x11½*

1660 A425 8f Text (5-1) 1.25 1.00
1661 A425 8f shown (5-2) 1.25 1.00
1662 A425 8f Dropping sword in water (5-3) 1.25 1.00
1663 A425 8f Marking gunwale (5-4) 1.25 1.00
1664 A425 8f Searching for sword (5-5) 1.25 1.00
a. Bklt. pane, 2 each #1660-1664 21.00
b. Strip of 5, #1660-1664 8.00 6.50

Chinese Juniper A426

Designs: Miniature landscapes. T.61.

1981, Mar. 31 *Perf. 11½*

1665 A426 4f Chinese elm, vert. (6-1) .75 .65
1666 A426 8f Juniper, vert. (6-2) .75 .65
1667 A426 8f Maidenhair tree, vert. (6-3) .75 .65
1668 A426 10f shown (6-4) .75 .65
1669 A426 20f Persimmon (6-5) 1.50 1.25
1670 A426 60f Juniper (6-6) 4.50 3.00
Nos. 1665-1670 (6) 9.00 6.85

Vase with Tiger-shaped Handles — A427

Cizhou Kiln Ceramic Pottery: 4f, Vase with 2 tigers, Song Dynasty. #1672, Black glazed jar, Jin Dynasty. #1673, Amphora. #1674, Jar with 2 phoenixes (Yuan Dynasty). 10f, Flat flask, Yuan Dynasty. T.62.

1981, Apr. 15 **Photo.** *Perf. 11½x11*

1671 A427 4f multi, vert. (6-1) .35 .30
1672 A427 8f multi (6-2) .75 .70
1673 A427 8f multi, vert. (6-3) .75 .70
1674 A427 8f multi (6-4) .75 .70
1675 A427 10f multi (6-5) 1.50 .70
1676 A427 60f multi (6-6) 3.25 2.75
Nos. 1671-1676 (6) 7.35 5.85

Panda and Colored Stamps — A428

1981, Apr. 29 **Photo.** *Perf. 11½x11*

1677 A428 8f shown (2-1) .25 .25
1678 A428 60f Boat, bird (2-2) 2.50 1.40
a. Booklet pane (8 #1677, souv. sheet with 1677-1678) 9.00

Qinchuan Steer A429

Cattle Breeds: #1680, Binhu buffalo. #1681, Yak. #1682, Black and white dairy cows. 10f, Pasture red cow. 55f, Simmental cross-breed. T.63.

1981, May 5 *Perf. 11x11½*

1679 A429 4f multi (6-1) .35 .30
1680 A429 8f multi (6-2) .35 .55
1681 A429 8f multi (6-3) .35 .55
1682 A429 8f multi (6-4) .35 .55
1683 A429 10f multi (6-5) .75 .55
1684 A429 55f multi (6-6) 4.50 2.10
Nos. 1679-1684 (6) 6.65 4.60

Mail Delivery Slogan — A430

13th World Telecommunications Day — A431

1981, May 9 *Perf. 11*

1685 A430 8f multicolored .70 .20

1981, May 17 *Perf. 11½x11*

1686 A431 8f multicolored .70 .20

Construction Worker — A432

Telephone Building, Peking — A433

1981, May 20 *Perf. 11½*

1687 A432 8f shown (4-1) .55 .45
1688 A432 8f Miner (4-2) .55 .45
1689 A432 8f Children crossing street (4-3) .55 .45
1690 A432 8f Farm worker (4-4) .55 .45
Nos. 1687-1690 (4) 2.20 1.80

National Safety Month. J.65.

1981, June 5 **Engr.** *Perf. 11½x11*

1691 A433 8f violet brown .90 .55

Swaythling Cup, Men's Team Table Tennis — A434

36th World Table Tennis Championships Victory - #1692: a, St. Bride Vase, men's singles (7-3). b, Iran Cup, men's doubles (7-4). c, G. Geist Prize, women's singles (7-5). d, W.J. Pope Trophy, women's doubles (7-6). e, Heydusek Prize, mixed doubles (7-7). #1694, Marcel Corbillon Cup, women's team. #1693-1694 printed in sheets of 16 (8 each) + 2 labels. J.71.

1981, June 30 **Photo.** *Perf. 11½x11*

1692 Strip of 5 1.60 1.50
a.-e. A434 8f multi .20 .20
1693 A434 20f multi (7-1) .80 .75
1694 A434 20f multi (7-2) .80 .75

Chinese Communist Party, 60th Anniv. A435

1981, July 1 **Photo.** *Perf. 11x11½*

1695 A435 8f multicolored .55 .30

Hanpo Pass, Lushan Mountains (T.67) A436

Photogravure & Engraved

1981, July 20 *Perf. 12½x12*

1696 8f Five-veteran Peak, vert. (7-1) .70 .50
1697 8f shown (7-2) .70 .50
1698 8f Yellow Dragon Pool, vert. (7-3) .70 .50
1699 8f Sunlit Peak (7-4) .70 .50
1700 8f Three-layer Spring, vert. (7-5) .70 .50
1701 8f Stone and pines (7-6) .70 .50
1702 60f Dragon-head Cliff, vert. (7-7) 6.25 3.75
Nos. 1696-1702 (7) 10.45 6.75

Tremella Fuciformis A437

Designs: Edible mushrooms. T.66.

1981, Aug. 6 **Photo.** *Perf. 11½*

1703 A437 4f shown (6-1) .30 .25
1704 A437 8f Dictyophora indusiata (6-2) .60 .40
1705 A437 8f Hericium erinaceus (6-3) .60 .40
1706 A437 8f Russula rubra (6-4) .60 .40
1707 A437 10f Lentinus edodes (6-5) .90 .40
1708 A437 70f Agaricus bisporus (6-6) 2.50 1.60
Nos. 1703-1708 (6) 5.50 3.45

Quality Month (J.66) — A438

Lunan Stone Forest, Yunn — A439

1981, Sept. 1 **Photo.** *Perf. 11½x11*

1709 A438 8f Silver medal (2-1) .45 .40
1710 A438 8f Gold medal (2-2) .45 .40

1981, Sept. 18 *Perf. 11½*

Designs: Views of limestone formations, Lunan Stone Forest. #1711-1713 horiz. T.64.

1711 A439 8f multi (5-1) .75 .50
1712 A439 8f multi (5-2) .75 .50
1713 A439 8f multi (5-3) .75 .50
1714 A439 10f multi (5-4) .75 .50
1715 A439 70f multi (5-5) 3.75 4.00
Nos. 1711-1715 (5) 6.75 6.00

Lu Xun, Writer, Birth Centenary (J.67) A440

1981, Sept. 25
1716 A440 8f shown (2-1) .70 .40
1717 A440 20f Portrait (diff.) (2-2) 1.10 1.00

Sun Yat-sen and Text A441

70th Anniv. of 1911 Revolution: No. 1719, 72 Martyrs Grave, Huang Hua Gang. No. 1720, Hubei Provincial Government Headquarters, 1911. J.68.

1981, Oct. 10 Photo. *Perf. 11x11½*
1718 A441 8f multi (3-1) .55 .35
1719 A441 8f multi (3-2) .55 .35
1720 A441 8f multi (3-3) .55 .35
Nos. 1718-1720 (3) 1.65 1.05

Asian Conference of Parliamentarians on Population and Development, Peking, Oct. 27 (J.73) — A442

1981, Oct. 27 *Perf. 11½x11, 11x11½*
1721 A442 8f Tree, vert. (2-1) .20 .20
1722 A442 70f shown (2-2) .70 .60

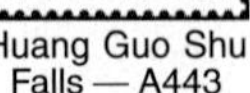
Huang Guo Shu Falls — A443

Cowrie Shell and Shell-shaped Coin — A444

Nos. 1731-1739 are horizontal.

1981-83 Engr. *Perf. 13x13½*
1723 A443 1f Xishuang Banna .20 .20
1724 A443 1½f Mt. Hua .20 .20
1725 A443 2f Mt. Tai .20 .20
1726 A443 3f shown .20 .20
1727 A443 4f Hainan Isld. .20 .20
1728 A443 5f Tiger Hill, Suzhou .20 .20
1729 A443 8f Great Wall .20 .20
1730 A443 10f Immense Forest .20 .20
1731 A443 20f Mt. Tian .25 .20
1732 A443 30f Grassland, Inner Mongolia .25 .20
1733 A443 40f Stone Forest .35 .20
1734 A443 50f Banping Mountain .45 .25
1735 A443 70f Mt. Qomolangma .55 .40
1736 A443 80f Seven-Star Crag .55 .50
1737 A443 $1 Three Gorges, Changjiang River .75 .55
1738 A443 $2 Guilin landscape .90 1.10
1739 A443 $5 Mt. Huangshan 2.40 2.00
Nos. 1723-1739 (17) 8.05 7.00

Issued: #1737-1739, 10/9/82; #1732, 1734-1736 4/1/83.

Photo.
Perf. 11½

1726a A443 3f .20 .20
1727a A443 4f .20 .20
1729a A443 8f .30 .25
1730a A443 10f .40 .35
1731a A443 20f .80 .70
Nos. 1726a-1731a (5) 1.90 1.70

Nos. 1727a, 1729a, 1730a exist tagged. Values 10-15% higher.

Photogravure and Engraved
1981, Oct. 29 *Perf. 11½x11*

Ancient Coins. T.65.

1740 A444 4f shown (8-1) .30 .25
1741 A444 4f Shovel (8-2) .30 .25
1742 A444 8f Shovel, diff. (8-3) .60 .25
1743 A444 8f Shovel, diff. (8-4) .60 .25
1744 A444 8f Knife (8-5) .60 .25
1745 A444 8f Knife (8-6) .60 .25
1746 A444 60f Knife, diff. (8-7) 1.90 1.10
1747 A444 70f Gong (8-8) 3.00 1.90
Nos. 1740-1747 (8) 7.90 4.50

See Nos. 1765-1772.

A445

A446

1981, Nov. 10 Photo. *Perf. 11½x11*
1748 A445 8f multicolored .35 .20

Intl. Year of the Disabled.

1981-82 Photo. *Perf. 11*

Twelve Beauties, from The Dream of Red Mansions, by Cao Xueqin.

1749 A446 4f Daiyu (12-1) .85 .60
1750 A446 4f Baochai (12-2) .85 .60
1751 A446 8f Yuanchun (12-3) .85 .60
1752 A446 8f Yingchun (12-4) .85 .60
1753 A446 8f Tanchun (12-5) .85 .60
1754 A446 8f Xichun (12-6) .85 .60
1755 A446 8f Xiangyuh (12-7) .85 .60
1756 A446 10f Liwan (12-8) 1.60 .60
1757 A446 20f Xifeng (12-9) 1.60 .60
1758 A446 30f Sister Qiao (12-10) 2.50 .60
1759 A446 40f Keqing (12-11) 3.25 2.50
1760 A446 80f Miaoyu (12-12) 6.50 3.75
Nos. 1749-1760 (12) 21.40 12.25

Souvenir Sheet
1761 A446 $2 Baoyu, Daiyu 60.00 42.50

No. 1761 contains one 59x39mm stamp. Issued: #1749, 1751, 1753, 1755, 1757, 1759, 1761, 11/20/81; others, 4/24/82. T.69.

A447

A448

1981, Dec. 21 Photo.
1762 A447 8f Girl playing (2-1) .20 .20
1763 A447 20f Girl holding trophy (2-2) .60 .45

Women's team victory in 3rd World Cup Volleyball Championship (J.76).

Photogravure & Engraved
1982, Jan. 5 *Perf. 11½*
1764 A448 8f multicolored 3.50 2.10
a. Booklet pane of 10 + label 13.50

New Year 1982 (Year of the Dog).
Stamps from No. 1764a have straight edges at top or bottom.

Coin Type of 1981
1982, Feb. 12
1765 A444 4f Guilian mask (8-1) .60 .45
1766 A444 4f Shu shovel (8-2) .60 .45
1767 A444 8f Xia zhuan shovel (8-3) .60 .45
1768 A444 8f Han Dan shovel (8-4) .60 .45
1769 A444 8f Knife (8-5) .60 .45
1770 A444 8f Ming knife (8-6) .60 .60
1771 A444 70f Jin hua knife (8-7) 1.10 .90
1772 A444 80f Yi Liu Hua coin (8-8) 2.25 2.00
Nos. 1765-1772 (8) 6.95 5.75

T.71.

Nie Er (1912-1935), Natl. Anthem Composer — A449

1982, Feb. 15 *Perf. 11x11½*
1773 A449 8f multicolored .30 .20

Intl. Drinking Water and Sanitation Decade, 1981-1990 A450

1982, Mar. 1 *Perf. 11½x11*
1774 A450 8f multicolored .30 .20

TB Bacillus Centenary A451

1982, Mar. 24 *Perf. 11x11½*
1775 A451 8f multicolored .30 .20

Fire Control (T.76) — A452

1982, May 8 Photo. *Perf. 11½x11*
1776 A452 8f Water hoses (2-1) .45 .20
1777 A452 8f Chemical extinguisher (2-2) .45 .20

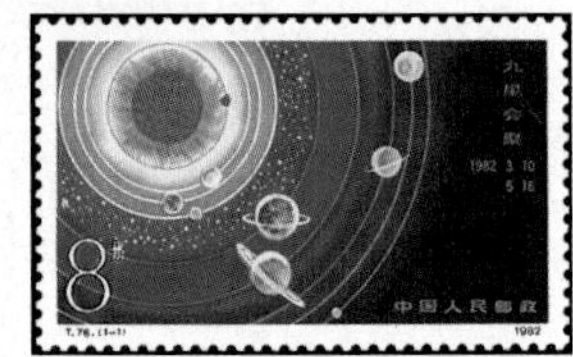
Syzygy of the Nine Planets, Mar. 10 and May 16 — A453

1982, May 16 *Perf. 11½*
1778 A453 8f multicolored .60 .25

Medicinal Herbs A454

Soong Ching Ling (1893-1981), Sun Yat-sen's Widow — A455

1982, May 20 *Perf. 11½x11*
1779 A454 4f Hemerocallis flava (6-1) .40 .35
1780 A454 8f Fritillaria unibracteata (6-2) .40 .35
1781 A454 8f Aconitum carmichaeli (6-3) .40 .35
1782 A454 10f Lilium brownii (6-4) .40 .35
1783 A454 20f Arisaema (6-5) .75 .50
1784 A454 70f Paeonia lactiflora (6-6) 2.25 1.00
Nos. 1779-1784 (6) 4.60 2.90

Souvenir Sheet
1785 A454 $2 Iris tectorum maxim 11.00 8.50

No. 1785 contains one 89x39mm stamp. Nos. 1779-1784 numbered T.72.

1982, May 29 *Perf. 11½*
1786 A455 8f Addressing Consultative Conf. (2-1) .40 .35
1787 A455 20f Portrait (2-2) 1.25 1.10

J.82.

Sable (T.68) A456

1982, June 20 Photo. *Perf. 11½*
1788 A456 8f shown (2-1) .65 .45
1789 A456 80f Sable, diff. (2-2) 3.75 3.00
a. Bklt. pane of 8, 6 8f plus sheetlet of 2 (8f, 80f) 10.50

A457

A458

1982, June 30 ***Perf. 11½x11***

1790	A457	8f multicolored	.20	.20

Natl. census, July 1.

1982, July 25 Photo. ***Perf. 11½x11***

1791	A458	8f multicolored	.20	.20

2nd UN Conference on Peaceful Uses of Outer Space, Vienna, Aug. 9-21.

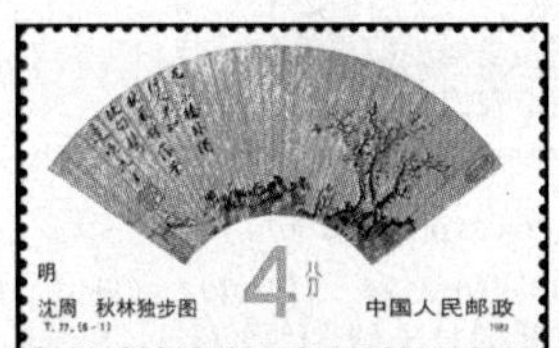

Strolling in Autumn Woods, by Shen Zhou, Ming Dynasty — A459

Fan Paintings (Ming or Qing Dynasty): No. 1793, Jackdaw on Withered Tree, by Tang Yin. No. 1794 Bamboo and Sparrows, by Zhou Zhimian. 10f, Writing Poem under Pine, by Chen Hongshou and Bai Han. 20f, Chrysanthemums, by Yun Shouping, Qing. 70f, Birds, Crape Myrtle and Chinese Parasol, by Wang Wu, Qing. T.77.

1982, July 31 ***Perf. 11½***

1792	A459	4f multi (6-1)	.40	.30
1793	A459	8f multi (6-2)	.80	.60
1794	A459	8f multi (6-3)	.80	.60
1795	A459	10f multi (6-4)	.80	.60
1796	A459	20f multi (6-5)	1.10	.60
1797	A459	70f multi (6-6)	2.25	1.75
		Nos. 1792-1797 (6)	6.15	4.45

A460

A461

1982, Aug. 25 ***Perf. 11½x11***

1798	A460	8f multicolored	.20	.20

60th anniv. of Chinese Geological Society.

1982, Aug. 25 Photo. ***Perf. 11½x11***

1799	A461	4f Orpiment (4-1)	.20	.20
1800	A461	8f Stibnite (4-2)	.20	.20
1801	A461	10f Cinnabar (4-3)	.40	.20
1802	A461	20f Wolframite (4-4)	.65	.45
		Nos. 1799-1802 (4)	1.45	1.05

T.73.

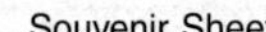

Souvenir Sheet

Messenger, Tomb Mural, Jiayu Pass, Wei-Jin Period — A462

1982, Aug. 25

1803	A462	$1 multicolored	8.00	6.00

All-China Philatelic Federation, 1st Cong.

12th Natl. Communist Party Congress A463

Hoopoe — A464

1982, Sept. 1 ***Perf. 11½***

1804	A463	8f multicolored	.20	.20

1982, Sept. 10 ***Perf. 11½x11***

1805	A464	8f shown (5-1)	.65	.30
1806	A464	8f Swallows (5-2)	.65	.30
1807	A464	8f Oriole (5-3)	.65	.30
1808	A464	20f Chickadees (5-4)	1.00	.50
1809	A464	70f Woodpecker (5-5)	2.75	2.50
		Nos. 1805-1809 (5)	5.70	3.90

Souvenir Sheet

1810	A464	$2 Cuckoos	22.50

#1810 contains one 56x36mm stamp. T.79.

Japan-China Relations Normalization, 10th Anniv. — A465

World Food Day — A466

Flower Paintings: 8f, Plum blossoms, by Guan Shanyue. 70f, Hibiscus, by Xiao Shufang. J.84.

1982, Sept. 29 ***Perf. 11***

1811	A465	8f multi (2-1)	.35	.20
1812	A465	70f multi (2-2)	.65	.55

1982, Oct. 16 ***Perf. 11½***

1813	A466	8f multicolored	.20	.20

Guo Morou (1892-1978), Acad. of Sciences Pres. A467

Bodhisattva, 11th Cent. Sculpture A468

Designs: Portraits. J.87.

1982, Nov. 16 Photo. ***Perf. 11½x11***

1814	A467	8f multi (2-1)	.20	.20
1815	A467	20f multi (2-2)	.30	.25

1982, Nov. 19 ***Perf. 11***

Liao Dynasty Buddha Sculptures, Lower Huayan Monastery. T.74.

1816	A468	8f multi (4-1)	.40	.30
1817	A468	8f multi (4-2)	.40	.30
1818	A468	8f multi (4-3)	.40	.30
1819	A468	70f multi (4-4)	3.25	2.25
		Nos. 1816-1819 (4)	4.45	3.15

Souvenir Sheet

Perf. 11x11½

1820	A468	$2 multicolored	20.00	9.00

No. 1820 contains one 36x55mm stamp.

Dr. D.S. Kotnis, Indian Physician in 8th Army (J.83) A469

Perf. 11½x11, 11x11½

1982, Dec. 9 **Photo.**

1821	A469	8f Portrait, vert. (2-1)	.45	.20
1822	A469	70f Riding horse (2-2)	1.75	1.25

11th Communist Youth League Natl. Congress A470

1982, Dec. 20 ***Perf. 11x11½***

1823	A470	8f multicolored	.20	.20

Bronze Wine Container — A471

Western Zhou Dynasty Bronze (1200-771 B.C.): No. 1825, Three-legged cooking pot. No. 1826, Food bowl. No. 1827, Three-legged cooking pot (diff.). No. 1828, Animal-shaped wine container. 10f, Wine container with lid. 20f, Round food bowl. 70f, Square wine container. T.75.

Photogravure & Engraved

1982, Dec. 25 ***Perf. 11***

1824	A471	4f multi (8-1)	.85	.55
1825	A471	4f multi (8-2)	.85	.55
1826	A471	8f multi (8-3)	.85	.55
1827	A471	8f multi (8-4)	.85	.55
1828	A471	8f multi (8-5)	.85	.55
1829	A471	10f multi (8-6)	1.75	.55
1830	A471	20f multi (8-7)	1.75	1.10
1831	A471	70f multi (8-8)	6.00	2.10
		Nos. 1824-1831 (8)	13.75	6.50

A472

1983, Jan. 5 ***Perf. 11½***

1832	A472	8f multicolored	4.00	3.50
a.		Booklet pane of 12	18.00	

New Year 1983 (Year of the Pig).

Stamps from No. 1832a have straight edges at top or bottom.

A473

A474

Stringed Instruments (T.81).

1983, Jan. 20 ***Perf. 11½x11, 11x11½***

1833	A473	4f Konghou (5-1)	*1.40*	.70
1834	A473	8f Ruan (5-2)	*1.40*	.70
1835	A473	8f Qin, horiz. (5-3)	*1.40*	.70
1836	A473	10f Piba (5-4)	*1.40*	.70
1837	A473	70f Sanxian (5-5)	*12.00*	3.50
		Nos. 1833-1837 (5)	*17.60*	6.30

1983, Feb. 7 Photo. ***Perf. 11½x11***

1838	A474	8f Memorial Tower, Zhengzhou (2-1)	.40	.30
1839	A474	8f Monument, Jiangan (2-2)	.40	.30

60th Anniv. of Peking-Hankow Railroad Workers' Strike (J.89).

The Western Chamber, Traditional Opera, by Wang Shifu (1271-1368) A475

Scenes from the opera.

1983, Feb. 21 Photo. ***Perf. 11x11½***

1840	A475	8f multi (4-1)	1.50	.80
1841	A475	8f multi (4-2)	1.50	.80
1842	A475	10f multi (4-3)	3.00	1.60
1843	A475	80f multi (4-4)	12.00	4.50
		Nos. 1840-1843 (4)	18.00	7.70

Souvenir Sheet
Photogravure and Engraved
Perf. 12

1844 A475 $2 multicolored 55.00 27.50

#1844 contains one 27x48mm stamp. T.82.

Karl Marx (1818-1883) (J.90) — A476

Photogravure & Engraved

1983, Mar. 14 ***Perf. 11½x11***

1845 A476 8f Portrait (2-1) .20 .20
1846 A476 20f Making speech (2-2) .50 .25

Tomb of the Yellow Emperor (T.84) A477

Photogravure & Engraved

1983, Apr. 5 ***Perf. 11½***

1847 A477 8f Tomb, vert. (3-1) .90 .40
1848 A477 10f Hall of Founder of Chinese Culture (3-2) 1.40 .40
1849 A477 20f Cypress tree, vert. (3-3) 2.25 .80
Nos. 1847-1849 (3) 4.55 1.60

World Communications Year — A478

1983, Apr. 28 **Photo.** ***Perf. 11½***

1850 A478 8f multicolored .45 .20

Male Chinese Alligator (T.85) — A479

Photogravure & Engraved

1983, May 24 ***Perf. 11***

1851 A479 8f shown (2-1) .80 .40
1852 A479 20f Female, hatching eggs (2-2) 1.60 .70

Kitten, by Tan Arxi — A480

Various children's drawings. T.86.

1983, June 1 ***Perf. 11½x11***

1853 A480 8f multi (4-1) .25 .20
1854 A480 8f multi (4-2) .25 .20
1855 A480 8f multi (4-3) .25 .20
1856 A480 8f multi (4-4) .25 .20
Nos. 1853-1856 (4) 1.00 .80

6th Natl. People's Congress (J.94) A481

1983, June 6 ***Perf. 11x11½***

1857 A481 8f Hall (2-1) .20 .20
1858 A481 20f Natl. anthem score (2-2) .75 .35

Terra Cotta Figures, Qin Dynasty (221-207 BC) A482

1983, June 30

1859 A482 8f Soldiers (4-1) .80 .60
1860 A482 8f Heads (4-2) .80 .60
1861 A482 10f Soldiers, horses (4-3) .80 .60
1862 A482 70f Excavation site (4-4) 4.75 2.75
a. Bklt. pane of 8 (#1859, 3 #1860, 3 #1861, #1862) 57.50 27.50
Nos. 1859-1862 (4) 7.15 4.55

Souvenir Sheet

1863 A482 $2 Soldier leading horse 55.00 21.00
a. Booklet pane 55.00

#1863 contains one 59x39mm stamp. T.88.

A483

A484

Female roles in Peking opera (T.87).

1983, July 20 **Photo.** ***Perf. 11***
Design A483

1864 4f Sun Yujiao (8-1) .75 .35
1865 8f Chen Miaochang (8-2) .75 .35
1866 8f Bai Suzhen (8-3) .75 .35
1867 8f Sister Thirteen (8-4) .75 .35
1868 10f Qin Xianglian (8-5) .75 .35
1869 20f Yang Yuhuan (8-6) 2.25 .75
1870 50f Cui Yingying (8-7) 4.50 1.60
1871 80f Mu Guiying (8-8) 5.75 2.00
Nos. 1864-1871 (8) 16.25 6.10

1983, Aug. 10 **Photo.** ***Perf. 11½***

Paintings by Liu Lingcang.

1872 A484 8f Li Bai (4-1) .55 .25
1873 A484 8f Du Fu (4-2) .55 .25
1874 A484 8f Han Yu (4-3) .55 .25
1875 A484 70f Liu Zongyuan (4-4) 3.25 2.25
Nos. 1872-1875 (4) 4.90 3.00

Poets and philosophers of ancient China (J.92).

5th Natl. Women's Congress — A485

1983, Sept. 1 **Photo.** ***Perf. 11½***

1876 A485 8f multicolored .20 .20

5th National Games (J.93) — A486

1983, Sept. 16 **Photo.** ***Perf. 11½***

1877 A486 4f Emblem (6-1) .45 .25
1878 A486 8f Gymnast (6-2) .45 .25
1879 A486 8f Badminton (6-3) .45 .25
1880 A486 8f Diving (6-4) .45 .25
1881 A486 20f High jump (6-5) .80 .70
1882 A486 70f Wind surfing (6-6) 2.00 1.75
Nos. 1877-1882 (6) 4.60 3.45

Family Planning (T.91) A487

1983, Sept. 19 ***Perf. 11x11½***

1883 A487 8f One child (2-1) .20 .20
1884 A487 8f Cultivated land (2-2) .20 .20

10th Intl. Trade Union Congress — A488

1983, Oct. 18 **Litho.** ***Perf. 11½***

1885 A488 8f multicolored .20 .20

Swans (T.83) A489

Perf. 11x11½ on 3 sides

1983, Nov. 18 **Photo.**

1886 A489 8f (4-1) .30 .30
1887 A489 8f (4-2) .30 .30
1888 A489 10f (4-3) .55 .30
1889 A489 80f (4-4) 2.00 1.50
a. Booklet pane, 7 #1886, 1 each #1887-1889 10.00
Nos. 1886-1889 (4) 3.15 2.40

A490

A491

Various photos. J.96.

1983, Nov. 24 **Photo.** ***Perf. 11½***

1890 A490 8f multi (4-1) .40 .35
1891 A490 8f multi (4-2) .40 .35
1892 A490 8f multi (4-3) .40 .35
1893 A490 8f multi (4-4) .40 .35
Nos. 1890-1893 (4) 1.60 1.40

85th birth anniv. of Liu Shaoqi, political leader.

1983, Nov. 29 **Photo.** ***Perf. 11½***

1894 A491 8f No. 117 (2-1) .20 .20
1895 A491 20f No. 4L1 (2-2) .50 .25

CHINAPEX '83 Natl. Philatelic Exhibition (J.99).

A492 A493

Various portraits. J.97.

1983, Dec. 26 **Photo.** ***Perf. 11½***

1896 A492 8f 1925 (4-1) .20 .20
1897 A492 8f 1945 (4-2) .20 .20
1898 A492 10f 1952 (4-3) .45 .25
1899 A492 20f 1961 (4-4) 1.00 .90
Nos. 1896-1899 (4) 1.85 1.55

90th birth anniv. of Mao Tse-tung.

Photogravure and Engraved

1984, Jan. 5 ***Perf. 11½***

1900 A493 8f multicolored 2.50 1.10
a. Booklet pane of 12 16.00

New Year 1984 (Year of the Rat).

Stamps from No. 1900a have straight edge at top or bottom.

Beauties Wearing Flowers — A494

Portions of painting by Zhou Fang (Tang Dynasty). T.89.

1984, Mar. 24 Photo. *Perf. 11*

1901 A494 8f multi (3-1) .80 .30
1902 A494 10f multi (3-2) .80 .30
1903 A494 70f multi (3-3) 4.00 2.25
Nos. 1901-1903 (3) 5.60 2.85

Souvenir Sheet

1904 A494 $2 Entire painting 70.00 45.00

No. 1904 contains one 162x40mm stamp.

Chinese Roses (T.93) — A495

Ren Bishi (1904-50), Statesman A496

1984, Apr. 20 Photo. *Perf. 11½*

1905 A495 4f Spring of Shanghai (6-1) .35 .20
1906 A495 8f Rosy Dawn of Pujiang River (6-2) .35 .20
1907 A495 8f Pearl (6-3) .35 .20
1908 A495 10f Black whirlwind (6-4) .35 .25
1909 A495 20f Yellow flower in battlefield (6-5) .65 .35
1910 A495 70f Blue Phoenix (6-6) 1.75 1.10
Nos. 1905-1910 (6) 3.80 2.30

1984, Apr. 30 *Perf. 11½x11*

1911 A496 8f multicolored .20 .20

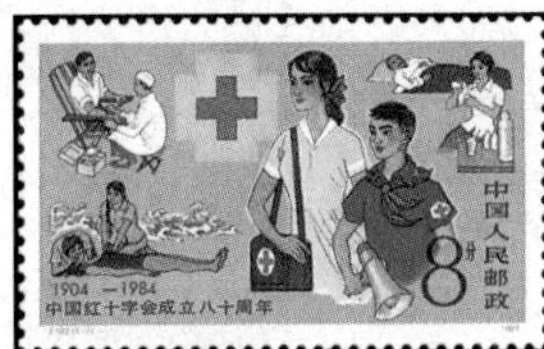

Crested Ibis (T.94) A497

1984, May 15 Photo. *Perf. 11x11½*

1912 A497 8f Flying (3-1) .50 .20
1913 A497 8f Wading (3-2) .50 .20
1914 A497 80f Perching (3-3) 1.50 1.25
Nos. 1912-1914 (3) 2.50 1.65

Chinese Red Cross Society, 80th Anniv. — A498

1984, May 29 *Perf. 11½*

1915 A498 8f multicolored .20 .20

Gezhou Dam, Yangtze River (T.95) — A499

1984, June 15 Photo.

1916 A499 8f Dam (3-1) .25 .25
1917 A499 10f Bridge, vert. (3-2) .30 .25
1918 A499 20f Lock Gate #2 (3-3) .60 .50
Nos. 1916-1918 (3) 1.15 1.00

Zhuo Zheng Garden, Suzhou (T.96) — A500

Photogravure & Engraved

1984, June 30 *Perf. 11½x11*

1919 A500 8f Inverted Image Tower (4-1) .60 .35
1920 A500 8f Loquat Garden (4-2) .60 .35
1921 A500 10f Water Court, Xiao Cang Lang (4-3) .60 .35
1922 A500 70f Yuanxiang Hall, Yiyu Study (4-4) 1.75 1.40
Nos. 1919-1922 (4) 3.55 2.45

1984 Summer Olympics A501

1984, July 28 Photo. *Perf. 11½*

1923 A501 4f Shooting (6-1) .20 .20
1924 A501 8f High jump (6-2) .20 .20
1925 A501 8f Weight lifting (6-3) .20 .20
1926 A501 10f Gymnastics (6-4) .25 .20
1927 A501 20f Volleyball (6-5) .25 .25
1928 A501 80f Diving (6-6) 1.00 .35
Nos. 1923-1928 (6) 2.10 1.40

Souvenir Sheet

1929 A501 $2 Athletes, rings 4.50

#1929 contains one 61x38mm stamp. J.103.

Calligraphy A502

Luanhe River Water Diversion Project (T.97) A503

Artworks by Wu Changshuo. T.98.

1984, Aug. 27 Photo. *Perf. 11½*

1930 A502 4f shown (8-1) .40 .25
1931 A502 4f A Pair of Peaches (8-2) .40 .25
1932 A502 8f Lotus (8-3) .40 .25
1933 A502 8f Wisteria (8-4) .40 .25
1934 A502 8f Peony (8-5) .40 .25
1935 A502 10f Chrysanthemum (8-6) .80 .45
1936 A502 20f Plum Blossom (8-7) .80 .45
1937 A502 70f Seal Cutting (8-8) 2.00 1.60
Nos. 1930-1937 (8) 5.60 3.75

Perf. 11½x11, 11 (#1939)

1984, Sept. 11 Photo.

1938 A503 8f multi (3-1) .20 .20
1939 A503 10f multi, horiz. (3-2) .20 .20
1940 A503 20f multi (3-3) .30 .25
Nos. 1938-1940 (3) .70 .65

Chinese-Japanese Youth (J.104) — A504

1984, Sept. 24 Photo. *Perf. 11½*

1941 A504 8f Neighbors (3-1) .20 .20
1942 A504 20f Planting tree (3-2) .20 .20
1943 A504 80f Dancing (3-3) .60 .50
Nos. 1941-1943 (3) 1.00 .90

People's Republic, 35th Anniv. (J.105) — A505

1984, Oct. 1 Photo. *Perf. 11½x11*

Size: 26x35mm

1944 A505 8f Engineer (5-1) .20 .20
1945 A505 8f Farm woman (5-2) .20 .20
1946 A505 8f Scientist (5-4) .20 .20
1947 A505 8f Soldier (5-5) .20 .20

Size: 36x48mm

Perf. 11

1948 A505 20f Cranes (5-3) .30 .25
Nos. 1944-1948 (5) 1.10 1.05

110th Birth Anniv. of Chen Jiageng (J.106) A506

1984, Oct. 21 Photo. *Perf. 12½x12*

1949 A506 8f Chen Jiageng (2-1) .20 .20
1950 A506 80f Jimei School (2-2) .45 .30

The Maiden's Study A507

Scenes from The Peony Pavilion, by Tang Xianzu. T.99.

Photogravure & Engraved

1984, Oct. 30 *Perf. 11*

1951 A507 8f shown (4-1) .45 .35
1952 A507 8f In the dream-land (4-2) .45 .35
1953 A507 20f Du Liniang drawing self-portrait (4-3) .80 .65
1954 A507 70f Married to Liu Mengmai (4-4) 2.50 2.50
Nos. 1951-1954 (4) 4.20 3.85

Souvenir Sheet

Perf. 11½

1955 A507 $2 Playing in the garden 24.00 12.00

No. 1955 contains one 90x60mm stamp.

Emei Shan Mountain Scenery (T.100) — A508

1984, Nov. 16 *Perf. 11*

1956 A508 4f Baoguo Temple (6-1) .35 .20
1957 A508 8f Leiyin Temple (6-2) .35 .25
1958 A508 8f Hongchun Lawn (6-3) .35 .25
1959 A508 10f Elephant bath (6-4) .35 .35
1960 A508 20f Woyun Temple (6-5) .75 .70
1961 A508 80f Shining Cloud Sea at Jinding (6-6) 3.00 2.25
Nos. 1956-1961 (6) 5.15 4.00

A509

A510

Portraits.

1984, Dec. 15 Photo. *Perf. 11½x11*

1962 A509 8f During the Long March (3-1) .20 .20
1963 A509 10f At 7th Natl. Party Congress (3-2) .20 .20
1964 A509 20f In motorcade (3-3) .25 .20
Nos. 1962-1964 (3) .65 .60

Former party secretary Ren Bishi (1904-50).

1984, Dec. 25 *Perf. 11*

1965 A510 8f Flower arrangement .20 .20

Chinese insurance industry.

New Year 1985 (Year of the Ox) — A511

Photogravure & Engraved

1985, Jan. 5 *Perf. 11½*

1966 A511 8f T.102 .40 .30
a. Bklt. pane of 4 + 8 plus label 13.50

Stamps from No. 1966a have straight edge at top or bottom.

Zunyi Meeting, 50th Anniv. — A512

Paintings: 8f, The Zunyi Meeting, by Liu Xiangping. 20f, The Red Army Successfully Arrived in Northern Shaanxi, by Zhao Yu. J.107.

1985, Jan. 15 Photo. *Perf. 11x11½*

1967 A512 8f multi (2-1) .25 .25
1968 A512 20f multi (2-2) .60 .50

A513

A514

Lantern Folk Festival: No. 1969, Lotus of Good Luck. No. 1970, Auspicious dragon and phoenix. No. 1971, A hundred flowers blossoming. 70f, Prosperity and affluence. T.104.

1985, Feb. 28 *Perf. 11½*

1969	A513	8f multi (4-1)	.40	.20
1970	A513	8f multi (4-2)	.40	.20
1971	A513	8f multi (4-3)	.40	.20
1972	A513	70f multi (4-4)	2.10	1.10
		Nos. 1969-1972 (4)	3.30	1.70

1985, Mar. 8

1973 A514 20f multicolored .20 .20

UN Decade for Women (1976-85).

Mei (Prunus mume) (T.103) — A515

1985, Apr. 5 *Perf. 11*

1974	A515	8f Green calyx (6-1)	.20	.20
1975	A515	8f Pendant mei (6-2)	.20	.20
1976	A515	8f Contorted dragon (6-3)	.20	.20
1977	A515	10f Cinnabar (6-4)	.30	.20
1978	A515	20f Versicolor mei (6-5)	.45	.25
1979	A515	80f Apricot mei (6-6)	2.00	.90
		Nos. 1974-1979 (6)	3.35	1.95

Souvenir Sheet

Perf. 11½

1980 A515 $2 Duplicate and condensed fragrance mei 16.00

No. 1980 contains one 93x52mm stamp.

A516

A518

A517

1985, May 1 **Photo.** *Perf. 11*

1981 A516 8f Huizo Guild Hall, Guangzhou .20 .20

All-China Fed. of Trade Unions.

1985, May 4 **Photo.**

1982 A517 20f multicolored .20 .20

Intl. Youth Year.

1985, May 24 *Perf. 11½*

Paintings of giant pandas: 8f, 20f, 50f, 80f, by Han Meilin; $3, by Wu Zuoren. T.106.

1983	A518	8f multi (4-1), vert.	.20	.20
1984	A518	20f multi (4-2)	.20	.20
1985	A518	50f multi (4-3), vert.	.30	.25
1986	A518	80f multi (4-4)	.45	.40
		Nos. 1983-1986 (4)	1.15	1.05

Souvenir Sheet

Perf. 11x11½

1987 A518 $3 multi, vert. 2.75
a. Ovptd. in sheet margin 5.00

No. 1987 contains one 39x59mm stamp.

No. 1987a ovptd. in sheet margin with panda hologram, PJZ-4 and horizontal Chinese inscription in gold. Issued 10/9/96.

No. 1987a was sold in a mount affixed to a small card.

Xian Xinghai (1905-1945), Composer A519

Agnes Smedley, 1892-1950 (3-1) — A520

Design: Bust, by Cao Chongen and music from The Yellow River Cantata.

1985, June 13 **Photo.** *Perf. 11½x11*

1988 A519 8f multicolored .20 .20

1985, June 25

American journalists: 20f, Anna Louise Strong, 1885-1970 (3-2). 80f, Edgar Snow, 1905-1972 (3-3). J.112.

1989	A520	8f multicolored	.20	.20
1990	A520	20f multicolored	.20	.20
1991	A520	80f multicolored	.55	.35
		Nos. 1989-1991 (3)	.95	.75

Zheng He's West Seas Expedition, 580th Anniv. — A521

#1992, Portrait of the navigator. #1993, Peace envoy. 20f, Trade, cultural exchange. 80f, Honored for navigational feats. J.113.

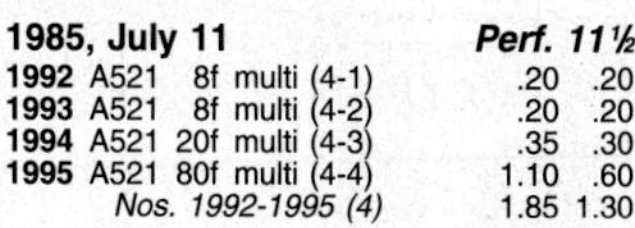

1985, July 11 *Perf. 11½*

1992	A521	8f multi (4-1)	.20	.20
1993	A521	8f multi (4-2)	.20	.20
1994	A521	20f multi (4-3)	.35	.30
1995	A521	80f multi (4-4)	1.10	.60
		Nos. 1992-1995 (4)	1.85	1.30

Xu Beihong, 1895-1953, Painter (J.114) A522

1985, July 19 *Perf. 11½x11, 11x11½*

1996 A522 8f Self-portrait (2-1), vert. .20 .20
1997 A522 20f shown (2-2) .55 .20

A523

A524

Designs: 8f, Lin Zexu, 1785-1850, statesman, patriot. 80f, Burning opium at Humen, bas-relief.

1985, Aug. 30 *Perf. 11*

1998 A523 8f multi (2-1) .20 .20

Size: 51x22mm

1999 A523 80f multi (2-2) .35 .25

Lin Zexu's ban of the opium trade catalyzed the Anglo-Chinese Opium Wars. J.115.

1985, Sept. 1 *Perf. 11½x11*

2000	A524	8f Prosperity (3-1)	.20	.20
2001	A524	10f Celebration (3-2)	.20	.20
2002	A524	20f Abundant Harvest (3-3)	.45	.45
		Nos. 2000-2002 (3)	.85	.85

Tibet Autonomous Region, 20th anniv. (J.116).

End of World War II, 40th Anniv. A525

Woodcuts by Wu Biduan: 8f, The Chinese Army Rose Against the Japanese Agressors at Logouqiao (2-1). 80f, The Eighth Route Army and Militia Fought Around the Great Wall (2-2). J.117.

1985, Sept. 3 *Perf. 11*

2003 A525 8f multi .20 .20
2004 A525 80f multi .25 .20

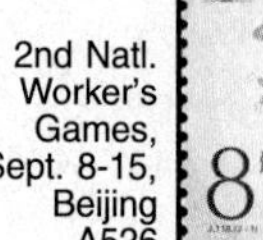

2nd Natl. Worker's Games, Sept. 8-15, Beijing A526

Competitors from various events and: 8f, Men's bicycling (2-1). 20f, Women hurdlers (2-2). J.118.

1985, Sept. 8 *Perf. 11x11½*

2005 A526 8f multi .20 .20
2006 A526 20f multi .25 .25

Xinjiang Uygur Autonomous Region, 30th Anniv. (J.119) A527

1985, Oct. 1 **Photo.** *Perf. 11½*

2007	A527	8f Oasis in the Gobi, woman (3-1)	.20	.20
2008	A527	10f Oil field, Lake Tianchi (3-2)	.20	.20
2009	A527	20f Tianshan pasture, woman (3-3)	.20	.20
		Nos. 2007-2009 (3)	.60	.60

Size of No. 2008, 60x30mm.

1st Natl. Youth Games, Oct. 6-15, Zhengzhou (J.121) — A528

1985, Oct. 6 *Perf. 11½x11*

2010 A528 8f Girls' track & field (2-1) .20 .20
2011 A528 20f Boys' basketball (2-2) .30 .30

Forbidden City Main Buildings — A529

1985, Oct. 10 *Perf. 11½*

2012	A529	8f multi (4-1)	.20	.20
2013	A529	8f multi (4-2)	.20	.20
2014	A529	20f multi (4-3)	.20	.20
2015	A529	80f multi (4-4)	.45	.45
a.		Vert. strip of 4, #2012-2015	.90	.90

Palace Museum, 60th anniv. J.120.

Zou Taofen (1895-1935), Journalist (J.122) — A530

1985, Nov. 5 *Perf. 11½x11*

2016	A530	8f Portrait (2-1)	.20	.20
2017	A530	20f Epitaph by Zhou Enlai (2-2)	.20	.20
a.		Pair, #2016-2017	.30	.30

December 9th Revolution, 50th Anniv. — A531

1985, Dec. 9 *Perf. 11½*

2018 A531 8f Memorial Pavilion .20 .20

New Year 1986 — A532

Natl. Space Industry — A533

Photogravure & Engraved

1986, Jan. 5 *Perf. 11½*

2019 A532 8f multicolored .40 .40
a. Bklt. pane of 4 + 8 with label btwn *5.50*

1986, Feb. 1 **Photo.**

4f, 1st experimental satellite. #2021, Recoverable satellite. #2022, Underwater rocket launch. 10f, Rocket launch. 20f,Earth satellite receiver. 70f, Satellite trajectory diagram. T.108.

2020 A533 4f multi (6-1) .20 .20
2021 A533 8f multi (6-2) .20 .20
2022 A533 8f multi (6-3) .20 .20
2023 A533 10f multi (6-4) .20 .20
2024 A533 20f multi (6-5) .20 .20
2025 A533 70f multi (6-6) .60 .30
Nos. 2020-2025 (6) 1.60 1.30

Dong Biwu (1886-1975), Party Founder (J.123) — A534

Lin Boqu (1886-1960), Party Leader (J.124) — A535

Photogravure and Engraved

1986, Mar. 5 ***Perf. 11½x11***
2026 A534 8f 1975 (2-1) .20 .20
2027 A534 20f 1945 (2-2) .20 .20

1986, Mar. 20
2028 A535 8f shown (2-1) .20 .20
2029 A535 20f Lin standing (2-2) .20 .20

Marshal He Long (1896-1969), Revolution Leader (J.126) — A536

1986, Mar. 22 ***Perf. 11x11½***
2030 A536 8f shown (2-1) .20 .20
2031 A536 20f On horseback (2-2) .20 .20

Halley's Comet — A537

1986, Apr. 11 **Photo.** ***Perf. 11½***
2032 A537 20f dk bl & gray .20 .20

White Crane (T.110) A538

1986, May 22 ***Perf. 11x11½, 11½x11***
2033 A538 8f Two cranes (3-1) .20 .20
2034 A538 10f One flying (3-2), vert. .20 .20
2035 A538 70f Four cranes (3-3), vert. .45 .20
Nos. 2033-2035 (3) .85 .60

Souvenir Sheet

2036 A538 $2 Flock *5.50*

No. 2036 contains one 116x25mm stamp.

Li Weihan (1896-1984), Party Leader (J.127) — A539

1986, June 2 ***Perf. 11x11½***
2037 A539 8f Portrait (2-1) .20 .20
2038 A539 20f Writing (2-2) .20 .20

Intl. Peace Year A540

1986, June 16 ***Perf. 11***
2039 A540 8f multi .20 .20

Mao Dun (1896-1981), Writer (J.129) — A541

1986, July 4 ***Perf. 11x11½***
2040 A541 8f Portrait (2-1) .20 .20
2041 A541 20f Portrait, diff. (2-2) .20 .20

Wang Jiaxiang (1906-1974), Party Leader (J.130) — A542

1986, Aug. 15
2042 A542 8f Portrait (2-1) .20 .20
2043 A542 20f Portrait, diff. (2-2) .20 .20

Teacher's Day A543

1986, Sept. 10 ***Perf. 11***
2044 A543 8f multi .20 .20

Magnolia Liliflora (T.111) A544

1986, Sept. 23 ***Perf. 11x11½***
2045 A544 8f Blossom (3-1) .30 .30
2046 A544 8f Two blossoms (3-2) .30 .30
2047 A544 70f Blossom, diff. (3-3) 2.10 2.10
Nos. 2045-2047 (3) 2.70 2.70

Souvenir Sheet

2048 A544 $2 Three blossoms *9.00*

No. 2048 contains one 132x70mm stamp.

Folk Houses — A545

Perf. 13x13½, 11x11½, (1½f, 3f, #2057-2062)

1986, Apr. 1 **Photo.**
2049 A545 1f Inner Mongolia .20 .20
2050 A545 1½f Tibet .20 .20
2051 A545 2f Northeastern China .20 .20
2052 A545 3f Hunan .20 .20
2053 A545 4f So. Yangtze River .20 .20
2054 A545 8f Beijing .20 .20
2055 A545 10f Yunnan .20 .20
2056 A545 20f Shanghai .20 .20
2057 A545 30f Anhui .25 .20
2058 A545 40f No. Shaanxi .35 .25
2059 A545 50f Sichuan .40 .35
2060 A545 90f Taiwan .70 .50
2061 A545 $1 Fujian .75 .60
2062 A545 $1.10 Zhejiang .80 .70
Nos. 2049-2062 (14) 4.85 4.20

Issue dates: 3f, Dec. 25; 4f, $1, Oct. 15; 20f, 50f, Sept. 10; 40f, Nov. 15; others, Apr. 1.

Postal forgeries of No. 2056 exist.

See Nos. 2198-2207.

1989-90 **Photo.**
2055a Perf. 11x11½ ('89) .20 .20
2056a Perf. 11x11½ ('89) .30 .20
2057a Perf. 13x13½ ('90) .60 .30
2058a Perf. 13x13½ .80 .40
2059a Perf. 13x13½ ('89) 1.00 .55
2061a Perf. 13x13½ ('90) 2.00 1.10
Nos. 2055a-2061a (6) 4.90 2.75

Souvenir Sheet

All-China Philatelic Federation, 2nd Congress — A546

1986, Oct. 17 **Litho.** ***Perf. 11½***
2063 A546 $2 Jade lion *3.25*

Leaders of the 1911 Revolution (J.132) A547

1986, Oct. 10 **Photo.** ***Perf. 11x11½***
2064 A547 8f Sun Yat-sen (3-1) .20 .20
2065 A547 10f Huang Xing (3-2) .20 .20
2066 A547 40f Zhang Taiyan (3-3) .90 .90
Nos. 2064-2066 (3) 1.30 1.30

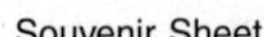

Souvenir Sheet

Sun Yat-sen (1866-1925) — A548

1986, Nov. 12 ***Perf. 11½***
2067 A548 $2 multicolored *6.25*

Marshal Zhu De (1886-1976) (J.134) — A549

Designs: 20f, Orating.

1986, Dec. 1 **Engr.** ***Perf. 11½x11***
2068 A549 8f sepia (2-1) .20 .20
2069 A549 20f myrtle grn (2-2) .30 .20

Sports of Ancient China A550

Stone carvings. T.113.

Perf. 11½x11, 11x11½

1986, Dec. 20 **Photo.**
2070 A550 8f Archery (4-1), vert. .25 .20
2071 A550 8f Weiqi (4-2) .25 .20
2072 A550 10f Golf (4-3) .35 .25
2073 A550 50f Soccer (4-4), vert. 2.75 1.75
Nos. 2070-2073 (4) 3.60 2.40

A551

A552

Photogravure & Engraved

1987, Jan. 5 ***Perf. 11½***
2074 A551 8f blk, dk pink & yel grn .20 .20
a. Bklt. pane of 4 + 8 + label *4.50*

New Year 1987 (Year of the Hare).

1987, Feb. 20 Photo. *Perf. 11½*

2075 A552 8f Traveling (3-1) .35
2076 A552 20f Cave writing (3-2) 1.60
2077 A552 40f Mountain climbing (3-3) 3.25
Nos. 2075-2077 (3) 5.20

Xu Xiake (1587-1621), Ming Dynasty geographer (J.136).

Birds of Prey (T.114) — A553

1987, Mar. 20

2078 A553 8f Kite (4-1) .25 .20
2079 A553 8f Sea eagle (4-2), vert. .25 .20
2080 A553 10f Vulture (4-3), vert. .35 .20
2081 A553 90f Buzzard (4-4) 4.50 1.00
Nos. 2078-2081 (4) 5.35 1.60

Liao Zhongkai (1877-1925), National Party Leader (J.137) — A554

1987, Apr. 23 *Perf. 11½x11*

2082 A554 8f shown (2-1) .20
2083 A554 20f Liao, He Xiangning (2-2) .25

Kites (T.115) — A555

A556

1987, Apr. 1

2084 A555 8f Hawk (4-1) .40
2085 A555 8f Dragon (4-2) .40
a. Pair, #2084-2085 .80
2086 A555 30f Symbolic octagon (4-3) 1.50
2087 A555 30f Phoenix (4-4) 1.50
a. Pair, #2086-2087 3.00
Nos. 2084-2087 (4) 3.80

Nos. 2085a, 2087a have continuous designs.

1987, Apr. 28

Portraits of Ye Jianying (1897-1986), central committee vice chairman (J.138).

2088 A556 8f multi (3-3) .25 .25
2089 A556 10f multi (3-2) .35 .35
2090 A556 30f multi (3-1) 1.60 1.60
Nos. 2088-2090 (3) 2.20 2.20

Caves of the Thousand Buddhas, Dunhuang, Gansu Province — A557

Wall Paintings: 8f, Worshipping Bodhisattvas, Northern Liang Dynasty. 10f, Deer King Jatka, Northern Wei Dynasty. 20f, Heavenly Musicians, Northern Wei Dynasty. 40f, Flying Devata, Northern Wei Dynasty. $2, Mahasattva Jataka. T.116.

1987, May 20 *Perf. 11½*

2091 A557 8f multi (4-1) .35 .20
2092 A557 10f multi (4-2) .40 .25
2093 A557 20f multi (4-3) 1.10 .60
2094 A557 40f multi (4-4) 2.25 1.10
Nos. 2091-2094 (4) 4.10 2.15

Souvenir Sheet

2095 A557 $2 multi *20.00*

No. 2095 contains one 92x73mm stamp.
See Nos. 2149-2152, 2283-2286, 2407-2411, 2505-2508, 2704-2707.

Children's Day Festival A558

Children's drawings: No. 2096, Happy Holiday, by Yan Qinghui, age 7. No. 2097, Peace and Happiness, by Liu Yuan, age 7. T.117.

1987, June 1 *Perf. 12½x12*

2096 A558 8f shown (2-1) .20 .20
2097 A558 8f multi, vert. (2-2) .20 .20

Rural Development A559

Postal Savings Bank Inauguration A560

1987, June 25 *Perf. 11½*

2098 A559 8f Village, southeast China (4-1) .35 .35
2099 A559 8f Market (4-2) .35 .35
2100 A559 10f Dairy industry (4-3) .50 .50
2101 A559 20f Theater (4-4) 1.00 1.00
Nos. 2098-2101 (4) 2.20 2.20

Nos. 2099-2100 horiz. T.118.

1987, July 1

2102 A560 8f multicolored .20 .20

Esperanto Language Movement, Cent. — A561

1987, July 26

2103 A561 8f lt olive grn, blk & brt blue .20

People's Liberation Army, 60th Anniv. (J.140) A562

1987, Aug. 1 *Perf. 11*

2104 A562 8f Flag, Great Wall (4-1) .30
2105 A562 8f Rocket launch, soldier, village (4-2) .30
2106 A562 10f Submarine, sailor (4-3) .40
2107 A562 30f Aircraft, pilot (4-4) 1.10
Nos. 2104-2107 (4) 2.10

Intl. Year of Shelter for the Homeless A563

1987, Aug. 20 *Perf. 11*

2108 A563 8f gray, dk car rose & blk .20

Chinese Art Festival, Sept. 5-25, Beijing — A564

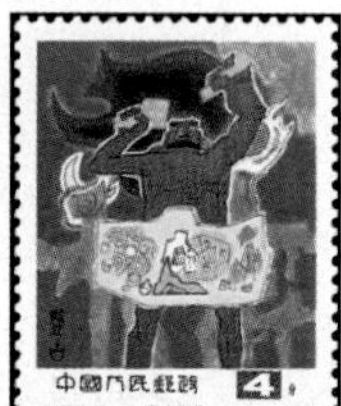

Fairy Tales — A565

1987, Sept. 5 *Perf. 11*

2109 A564 8f brt red, gold & blk .20

1987, Sept. 25 *Perf. 11½*

4f, Pan Gu inventing the universe. #2111, Nu Wa creating man. #2112, Yi shooting nine suns. 10f, Chang'e flying to the moon. 20f, Kua Fu pursuing the sun. 90f, Jing Wei filling the sea. T.120.

2110 A565 4f multi (6-1) .20 .20
2111 A565 8f multi (6-2) .25 .20
2112 A565 8f multi (6-3) .25 .20
2113 A565 10f multi (6-4) .35 .20
2114 A565 20f multi (6-5) .60 .30
2115 A565 90f multi (6-6) 2.50 1.10
Nos. 2110-2115 (6) 4.15 2.20

Communist Party of China, 13th Natl. Congress A566

1987, Oct. 25 *Perf. 11*

2116 A566 8f multicolored .20

Yellow Crane Tower (T.121) A567

1987, Oct. 30

2117 A567 8f shown (4-1) .30 .20
2118 A567 8f Yue Yang Tower (4-2) .30 .30
2119 A567 10f Teng Wang Pavilion (4-3) .35 .35
2120 A567 90f Peng Lai Pavilion (4-4) 3.25 3.25
a. Min. sheet of 4, #2117-2120 *12.00*
Nos. 2117-2120 (4) 4.20 4.10

No. 2120a sold for $1.50.

6th Natl. Games (J.144) — A568

1987, Nov. 20 *Perf. 11½x11*

2121 A568 8f Pole vault (4-1) .20
2122 A568 8f Softball (4-2) .20
2123 A568 30f Weight lifting (4-3) .50
2124 A568 50f Diving (4-4) .90
Nos. 2121-2124 (4) 1.80

Souvenir Sheet

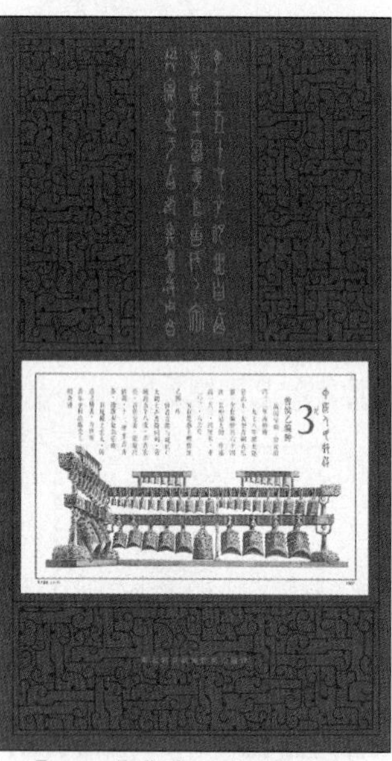

Bronze Bells from the Tomb of Marquis Yi of the Zeng State (c. 433 B.C.), Hubei Province — A569

1987, Dec. 10 Litho. *Imperf.*

2125 A569 $3 multicolored *6.25*

Classic Literature — A570

Outlaws of the Marsh: 8f, Shi Jin practicing martial arts. 10f, Sagacious Lu, the "Tattooed Monk," uprooting a willow tree. 30f, Lin Chong seeking shelter from snow storm at the Mountain Spirit Temple. 50f, Song Jiang helps Ward Chief Chao Gai flee. $2, Outlaws of the Marsh capture treasures. T.123.

1987, Dec. 20 Photo. *Perf. 11*

2126 A570 8f multi (4-1) .35
2127 A570 10f multi (4-2) .45
2128 A570 30f multi (4-3) 1.50
2129 A570 50f multi (4-4) 2.00
Nos. 2126-2129 (4) 4.30

Souvenir Sheet

Perf. 11½x11

2130 A570 $2 multi *16.00*

No. 2130 contains one 90x60mm stamp.
See Nos. 2216-2219, 2373-2377, 2449-2452, 2822-2826, 2889-2893.

New Year 1988 (Year of the Dragon) — A571

Cai Yuanpei (1868-1940), Education Reformer ((J.145) — A572

Photo. & Engr.

1988, Jan. 5 ***Perf. 11½***
2131 A571 8f multicolored *.20*
a. Bklt. pane of 4 + 8 with label between *5.50*

1988, Jan. 11 Photo. ***Perf. 11½x11***
2132 A572 8f shown (2-1) .20
2133 A572 20f Seated (2-2) .20

Tao Zhu (1908-1969), Party Leader (J.146) — A573

1988, Jan. 16 ***Perf. 11x11½***
2134 A573 8f shown (2-1) .20
2135 A573 20f Tao, diff. (2-2) .20

Folklore (T.125) A574

1988, Feb. 10
2136 A574 8f shown (4-1) .20
2137 A574 10f multi, diff. (4-2) .20
2138 A574 20f multi, diff. (4-3) .40
2139 A574 30f multi, diff. (4-4) .65
Nos. 2136-2139 (4) 1.45

A575

A576

1988, Mar. 25 Photo. ***Perf. 11½***
2140 A575 8f multicolored .20

7th Natl. People's Congress.

1988, Apr. 20 Photo. ***Perf. 11½***
2141 A576 8f Wuzhi Mountain (4-1) .20
2142 A576 10f Wanquan River (4-2) .20
2143 A576 30f "End of the Earth" (4-3) .20
2144 A576 $1.10 "Deer Turning Its Head" (4-4) .50
Nos. 2141-2144 (4) 1.10

Establishment of Hainan Province (J.148).

Modern Scientists A577

Designs: 8f, Li Siguang, geologist. 10f, Zhu Kezhen, meteorologist and geographer. 20f, Wu Youxun, physicist. 30f, Hua Luogeng, mathematician. J.149.

1988, Apr. 28 ***Perf. 11x11½***
2145 A577 8f multi (4-1) .20
2146 A577 10f multi (4-2) .20
2147 A577 20f multi (4-3) .20
2148 A577 30f multi (4-4) .25
Nos. 2145-2148 (4) .85

Wall Paintings Type of 1987

Caves of the Thousand Buddhas, Dunhuang, Gansu Province: No. 2149, Hunting, Western Wei Dynasty. No. 2150, Fishing, Western Wei Dynasty. 10f, Farming, Northern Zhou Dynasty. 90f, Building a Pagoda, Northern Zhou Dynasty. T.126.

1988, May 25 ***Perf. 11½x11***
2149 A557 8f multi (4-1) *.20*
2150 A557 8f multi (4-2) *.20*
2151 A557 10f multi (4-3) *.25*
2152 A557 90f multi (4-4) *2.00*
Nos. 2149-2152 (4) *2.65*

Environmental Protection — A578

1988, June 5 Photo. ***Perf. 11***
2153 A578 8f Soil (4-1) .20
2154 A578 8f Air (4-2) .20
2155 A578 8f Water (4-3) .20
2156 A578 8f Prevent noise pollution (4-4) .20
a. Block of 4, #2153-2156 .55

Souvenir Sheet

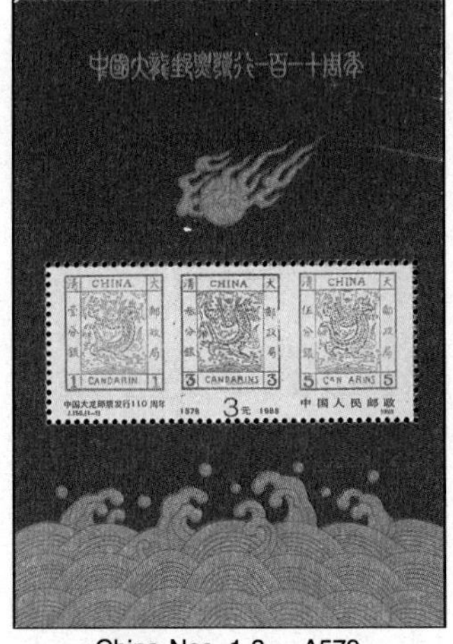
China Nos. 1-3 — A579

Photo. & Engr.

1988, July 2 ***Perf. 13***
2157 A579 $3 multicolored *4.25*

Postage stamps of China, 110th anniv.

11th Asian Games (in 1990), Beijing (J.151) A580

1988, July 20 Photo. ***Perf. 11x11½***
2158 A580 8f Emblem (2-1) .20 .20
2159 A580 30f Character trademark (2-2) .20 .20

See No. 2300a.

Signing of the Sino-Japanese Peace Treaty, 10th Anniv. (J.152) — A581

1988, Aug. 12 Photo. ***Perf. 11***
2160 A581 8f Peony (2-1) .20
2161 A581 $1.60 Sakura (2-2) .80
a. Pair, #2160-2161 .90

Achievements in Construction — A582

Designs: 8f, Coal-loading wharf, Ch'in-huang-tao Port. 10f, Ethylene refinery, Qilu. 20f, Pao-shan steel plant, Shanghai. 30f, Central Television Broadcasting Station. T.128.

1988, Sept. 2 Photo. ***Perf. 11***
2162 A582 8f multi (4-1) .20
2163 A582 10f multi (4-2) .20
2164 A582 20f multi (4-3) .20
2165 A582 30f multi (4-4) .20
Nos. 2162-2165 (4) .80

See #2221-2224, 2279-2282, 2354-2357.

Mt. T'ai Shan, Shantung Province (T.130) — A583

1988, Sept. 14 Photo. & Engr.
2166 A583 8f T'ai Shan Temple (4-1) .25
2167 A583 10f Ladder to Heaven (4-2) .35
2168 A583 20f Daguang peak (4-3) .65
2169 A583 90f Sun-watching peak (4-4) 2.75
Nos. 2166-2169 (4) 4.00

Liao Chengzhi (1908-1983), Party Leader (J.153) — A584

1988, Sept. 25 Photo. ***Perf. 11½x11***
2170 A584 8f shown (2-1) .20
2171 A584 20f Writing (2-2) .20

Marshal Peng Dehuai (1898-1974), Party Leader (J.155) — A585

1988, Oct. 24 Photo. ***Perf. 11x11½***
2172 A585 8f shown (2-1) .20
2173 A585 20f Peng in uniform (2-2) .20

1st Natl. Farmers' Games (J.154) A586

1988, Oct. 9 Photo. ***Perf. 11½***
2174 A586 8f Cycling (2-1) .20
2175 A586 20f Javelin (2-2) .20

Literary Masterpieces — A587

The Romance of the Three Kingdoms, by Luo Guanzhong, 14th cent.: No. 2176, Three heroes' sworn brotherhood (4-1). No. 2177, Battle between Lu Bu and the heroes, vert. (4-2). No. 2178, Struggle between man and woman at Fengyi Pavilion (4-3). No. 2179, Two noblemen, vert. (4-4). No. 2180, Guan Yu's battle through five passes. T.131.

Perf. 11½x11, 11x11½

1988, Nov. 25 Photo.
2176 A587 8f multicolored .30
2177 A587 8f multicolored .30
2178 A587 30f multicolored .80
2179 A587 50f multicolored 1.40
Nos. 2176-2179 (4) 2.80

Souvenir Sheet

Perf. 11

2180 A587 $3 multicolored *16.00*

See #2310-2313, 2403-2406, 2539-2543.

A588

A589

1988, Dec. 5 Photo. ***Perf. 11***
2181 A588 20f multicolored .20

Intl Volunteers' Day.

1988, Dec. 20 Photo. ***Perf. 11½x11***

Milu, *Elaphurus davidianus* (T.132).

2182 A589 8f Buck (2-1) .25
2183 A589 40f Herd (2-2) 1.10

Exist imperf. Value, pairs each $5.50.

Orchids (T.129) — A590

1988, Dec. 25 ***Perf. 12***
2184 A590 8f Da yi pin (4-1) .20
2185 A590 10f Dragon (4-2) .25
2186 A590 20f Large phoenix tail (4-3) .40
2187 A590 50f Silver-edged black (4-4) 1.00
a. Strip of 4, #2184-2187 1.90
Nos. 2184-2187 (4) 1.85

Souvenir Sheet

Perf. 11½x11

2188 A590 $2 Red lotus petal *13.00*

No. 2188 contains one 55x37mm stamp.

A591

A592

Grotto Statuary: $2, Buddha. $5, Warrior, Longmen Grotto, Henan. $10, Goddess. $20, Woman and birds.

Photo & Engr.

1988-89 ***Perf. 11½x11***

2189 A591 $2 buff & reddish blk .45 .25
2190 A591 $5 buff & grnh blk 1.10 .55
2191 A591 $10 buff & brn blk 2.40 1.10
a. Souv. sheet of 1, buff & sep *17.00*
2192 A591 $20 buff & indigo 5.00 2.25
Nos. 2189-2192 (4) 8.95 4.15

Issued: $2, 11/30; $5, 8/10; $10, 10/15; $20, 10/20.

No. 2191a released on Oct. 12, 1989, for the China Natl. Philatelic Exhibition and the 40th anniv. of the People's Republic.

Nos. 2189-2192, 2191a are almost always found with small ink spots on the stamps. Values are for stamps in this condition.

Photo. & Engr.

1989, Jan. 5 ***Perf. 11½***

2193 A592 8f multicolored .25
a. Bklt. pane of 4+8 with label between *4.50*

New Year 1989 (Year of the Snake).

Qu Qiubai (1899-1935), Party Leader (J.157) — A593

1989, Jan. 29 Photo. ***Perf. 11x11½***

2194 A593 8f multi (2-1) .20
2195 A593 20f multi, diff. (2-2) .20

Brown-eared Pheasant, *Crossoptilon mantchuricum* (T.134) — A594

1989, Feb. 21 ***Perf. 11½***

2196 A594 8f multi (2-1) .20
2197 A594 50f multi, diff. (2-2) .30

Folk Houses Type of 1986

1989-91 Photo. ***Perf. 13x13½***

2198 A545 5f Shandong .20 .20
2199 A545 15f Guangxi .20 .20
2200 A545 25f Ningxia .20 .20
2201 A545 80f Shanxi .40 .25
2204 A545 $1.30 Qinghai .50 .30
2206 A545 $1.60 Guizhou .65 .35
2207 A545 $2 Jiangxi .65 .35
Nos. 2198-2207 (7) 2.80 1.85

Issued: 5f, 6/10/91; 15f, 11/25/90; 25f, 11/10/90; 80f, 9/20/90; $1.30, $1.60, 3/10/89; $2, 4/25/91.

This is an expanding set. Numbers will change again if necessary.

Silk Painting Excavated from Han Tomb No. 1 at Mawangdui, Changsha (T.135) A595

1989, Mar. 25 Photo. ***Perf. 11½***

2208 A595 8f In the Heavens (3-1) .20
2209 A595 20f On the Earth, vert. (3-2) .20
2210 A595 30f In the Netherworld, vert. (3-3) .20
Nos. 2208-2210 (3) .60

Textured Paper, Without Gum

Size: 90x165mm

Imperf

2211 A595 $5 Entire painting *4.00*

Prevention and Resistance of Cancer (T.136) — A596

1989, Apr. 7 Litho. ***Perf. 12***

2212 A596 8f shown (2-1) .20
2213 A596 20f Woman's thermogram (2-2) .20

May Fourth Movement, 70th Anniv. (J.158) A597

1989, May 4 Photo. ***Perf. 11***

2214 A597 8f Bas-relief .20

Interparliamentary Union, Cent. — A598

1989, June 29 Photo. ***Perf. 11x11½***

2215 A598 20f multi .20

Literature Type of 1987

Outlaws of the Marsh: 8f, Wu Song slaying a tiger on Jingyang Ridge. 10f, Qin Ming dodging arrows. 20f, Hua Rong shooting a wild goose on Mt. Liangshan. $1.30, Li Kui fighting Zhang Shun from a junk. T.138.

1989, July 25 Photo. ***Perf. 11***

2216 A570 8f multi (4-1) .20
2217 A570 10f multi (4-2) .20
2218 A570 20f multi (4-3) .25
2219 A570 $1.30 multi (4-4) 1.50
Nos. 2216-2219 (4) 2.15

Asia-Pacific Telecommunity, 10th Anniv. — A599

1989, Aug. 4 Litho. ***Perf. 12***

2220 A599 8f multi .20

Type of 1988

Achievements in Engineering and Construction: 8f, Beijing Intl. Telecommunications Building, vert. 10f, Xi Qu Coal Mine, Gu Jiao, Shanxi Province. 20f, Long Yang Gorge Hydroelectric Power Station, Qinghai Province. 30f, Da Yao Shan Tunnel of the Guangzhou-Heng Yang Railway. T.139.

1989, Aug. 10 Photo. ***Perf. 11***

2221 A582 8f multi (4-1) .20
2222 A582 10f multi (4-2) .20
2223 A582 20f multi (4-3) .20
2224 A582 30f multi (4-4) .20
Nos. 2221-2224 (4) .80

Mt. Huashan — A601

Designs: 8f, Five prominent peaks. 10f, View from atop Huashan. 20f, 1000-foot precipice. 90f, Blue Dragon Ridge. T.140.

1989, Aug. 25 Photo. & Engr.

2225 A601 8f multi (4-1) .20
2226 A601 10f multi (4-2) .20
2227 A601 20f multi (4-3) .30
2228 A601 90f multi (4-4) .90
Nos. 2225-2228 (4) 1.60

Modern Art — A602

Paintings: 8f, *The Fable of the White Snake,* by Ye Qianyu. 20f, *Li River in Fine Rain,* by Li Keran. 50f, *Marching Together,* by Wu Zuoren. T.141

1989, Sept. 1 Photo.

2229 A602 8f multi (3-1) .20
2230 A602 20f multi (3-2) .25
2231 A602 50f multi (3-3) .55
Nos. 2229-2231 (3) 1.00

People's Political Conference A603

1989, Sept. 21 ***Perf. 12***

2232 A603 8f No. 2 .20

A604

Confucius (551-479 B.C.) — A605

Designs: 8f, The lecture in the Apricot Temple, Qufu. $1.60, Confucius riding in an ox cart. J.162.

1989, Sept. 28 Photo. ***Perf. 11***

2233 A604 8f shown (2-1) .20
2234 A604 $1.60 multi (2-2) .70

Souvenir Sheet

Litho. ***Imperf.***

Without Gum

2235 A605 $3 multicolored *3.25*

A606

Gate of Heavenly Peace — A607

1989, Oct. 1 Photo. ***Perf. 11x11½***

2236 A606 8f shown (4-1) .20
2237 A606 10f Flowers (4-2) .20
2238 A606 20f Five stars (4-3) .20
2239 A606 40f Construction (4-4) .25
Nos. 2236-2239 (4) .85

Souvenir Sheet

Litho. ***Imperf.***

Without Gum

2240 A607 $3 shown *1.75*

PRC, 40th anniv. J.163.

Photography, Sesquicentennial — A608

1989, Oct. 15 Photo. ***Perf. 11***

2241 A608 8f multicolored .20

Li Dazhao (1889-1927), Party Leader (J.164) — A609

1989, Oct. 29 Photo. *Perf. 11½*

2242 A609 8f Li, soldiers (2-1) .20
2243 A609 20f Li, text (2-2) .20

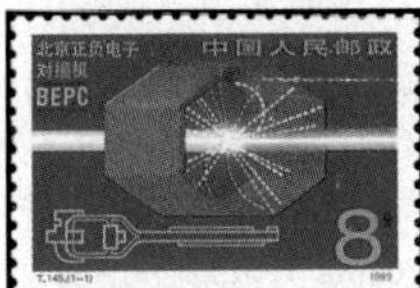

Positron Collider Produced in Beijing A610

1989, Nov. 1 *Perf. 11*

2244 A610 8f multicolored .20

Rocket Defense A611

Designs: 4f, Transporting 3 rockets. 8f, Disassembled rocket on transport. 10f, Launch, vert. 20f, Stage separation in space. T.143.

1989, Nov. 15 Litho. *Perf. 12*

2245 A611 4f multicolored (4-1) .20
2246 A611 8f multicolored (4-2) .20
2247 A611 10f multicolored (4-3) .20
2248 A611 20f multicolored (4-4) .20
Nos. 2245-2248 (4) .80

A612

Views of West Lake (T.144) — A613

1989, Nov. 25 Photo. *Perf. 11x11½*

2249 A612 8f multi (4-1) .20
2250 A612 10f multi, diff. (4-2) .20
2251 A612 30f multi, diff. (4-3) .25
2252 A612 40f multi, diff. (4-4) .35
Nos. 2249-2252 (4) 1.00

Souvenir Sheet

Perf. 11½x11

2253 A613 $5 multicolored *3.50*

11th Asian Games A614

Various stadiums. J.165.

1989, Dec. 15 *Perf. 11x11½*

2254 A614 8f multi (4-1) .20
2255 A614 10f multi (4-2) .20
2256 A614 30f multi (4-3) .20
2257 A614 $1.60 multi (4-4) .30
Nos. 2254-2257 (4) .90

See Nos. 2295-2300.

A615

Narcissus (T.147) — A616

Photo & Engr.

1990, Jan. 5 *Perf. 11½*

2258 A615 8f multicolored .40 .20
a. Bklt. pane of 12 + 4 labels 8.00

New Year 1990 (Year of the Horse).

1990, Feb. 10 Photo. *Perf. 11x11½*

2259 A616 8f multi (4-1) .20
2260 A616 20f multi, diff. (4-2) .20
2261 A616 30f multi, diff. (4-3) .20
2262 A616 $1.60 multi, diff. (4-4) .40
Nos. 2259-2262 (4) 1.00

Norman Bethune (1890-1939), Surgeon (J.166) — A617

Litho. & Engr.

1990, Mar. 3 *Perf. 11x11½*

2263 A617 8f In Canada (2-2) .20
2264 A617 $1.60 In China (2-1) .50
a. Pair, #2263-2264 .65

See Canada #1264-1265.

Intl. Women's Day — A618

1990, Mar. 8 Photo. *Perf. 11½x11*

2265 A618 20f multicolored .20

Afforestation (T.148) — A619

1990, Mar. 12 *Perf. 11*

2266 A619 8f Bird, flora (4-1) .20
2267 A619 10f Buildings (4-2) .20
2268 A619 20f Great Wall, forest, (4-3) .20
2269 A619 30f Bushes, evergreens (4-4) .20
Nos. 2266-2269 (4) .80

Pottery (T.149) — A620

1990, Apr. 10 Litho. *Perf. 12*

2270 A620 8f multi (4-1) .20
2271 A620 20f multi (4-2) .20
2272 A620 30f multi (4-3) .20
2273 A620 50f multi (4-4) .20
Nos. 2270-2273 (4) .80

Li Fuchun (1900-1975), Party Leader (J.168) — A621

1990, May 22 Photo. *Perf. 11x11½*

2274 A621 8f shown .20
2275 A621 20f In uniform (2-2) .20

Bronze Head — A622

Bronze treasures from Emperor Qin Shi Huang Mausoleum: 50f, Horse head. $5, Chariots. T.151.

1990, June 20 Photo. *Perf. 11½x11*

2276 A622 8f shown (2-1) .20
2277 A622 50f multicolored (2-2) .35

Miniature Sheet

Size: 141x79mm

2278 A622 $5 multicolored *4.75*

Achievements Type of 1988

Designs: 8f, 2nd automobile factory. 10f, Yizheng Joint Corporation of Chemical Fiber Industry. 20f, Shengli Oil Field. 30f, Qinshan Nuclear Power Station. T.152.

1990, June 30 Litho. *Perf. 12*

2279 A582 8f shown (4-1) .20
2280 A582 10f multicolored (4-2) .20
2281 A582 20f multicolored (4-3) .20
2282 A582 30f multicolored (4-4) .20
Nos. 2279-2282 (4) .80

Wall Paintings Type of 1987

8f, Flying Devatas. 10f, Worshipping Bodhisatva. 30f, Savior Avolokitesvara. 50f, Indra. T.150.

1990, July 10 *Perf. 11½x11*

2283 A557 8f multi (4-1) .20
2284 A557 10f multi, vert. (4-2) .20
2285 A557 30f multi, vert. (4-3) .40
2286 A557 50f multi (4-4) .70
Nos. 2283-2286 (4) 1.50

Snow Leopard (Uncia Uncia) (T.153) A624

1990, July 20 Photo. *Perf. 11½*

2287 A624 8f multicolored (2-1) .20
2288 A624 50f multicolored (2-2) .25

Chinese Soviet Post Stamp of 1931 A625

Design: 20f, Chinese Red Post issue of West Fukien, 1929. J.169.

1990, Aug. 1 Litho. *Perf. 12*

2289 A625 8f multi (2-1) .20
2290 A625 20f multi, diff. (2-2) .20

Zhang Wentian (1900-1990) (J.170) — A626

1990, Aug. 30 *Perf. 11x11½*

2291 A626 8f shown (2-1) .20
2292 A626 20f multi, diff. (2-2) .20

Intl. Literacy Year — A627

Chinese Films — A628

1990, Sept. 8 *Perf. 11½x11*

2293 A627 20f multicolored .20

1990, Sept. 21 Litho. *Perf. 11*

2294 A628 20f multicolored .20

11th Asian Games, Beijing (J.172) A629

1990, Sept. 22 *Perf. 11x11½*

2295 A629 4f Running (6-1) .20
2296 A629 8f Gymnastics (6-2) .20
2297 A629 10f Karate (6-3) .20
2298 A629 20f Volleyball (6-4) .20
2299 A629 30f Swimming (6-5) .20
2300 A629 $1.60 Shooting (6-6) .60
a. Souv. sheet of 12, #2158-2159, 2254-2257, 2295-2300 *8.00*
Nos. 2295-2300 (6) 1.60

Souvenir Sheet

Sportphilex '90, Beijing — A629a

1990, Sept. 21 Litho. *Perf. 11½*

2300B A629a $10 multicolored *14.50*

Modern Scientists A630

Designs: 8f, Lin Qiaozhi, obstetrician. 10f, Zhang Yuzhe, astronomer. 20f, Hou Debang, chemist. 30f, Ding Ying, agronomist. J.173.

1990, Oct. 10 Litho. *Perf. 12*

2301 A630 8f multicolored (4-1) .20
2302 A630 10f multicolored (4-2) .20
2303 A630 20f multicolored (4-3) .20
2304 A630 30f multicolored (4-4) .25
Nos. 2301-2304 (4) .85

Mt. Hengshan — A631

Designs: 8f, Towering Temple. 10f, South Sacred Mountain. 20f, Forested mountainside. 50f, Imposing Zhurong Peak. T.155.

Photo. & Engr.

1990, Nov. 5 *Perf. 11*

2305 A631 8f multicolored (4-1) .20
2306 A631 10f multicolored (4-2) .20
2307 A631 20f multicolored (4-3) .20
2308 A631 50f multicolored (4-4) .40
Nos. 2305-2308 (4) 1.00

See Nos. 2342-2345. 2628-2631.

Souvenir Sheet

China Philatelic Federation, 3rd Congress — A632

1990, Nov. 28 *Perf. 11½x11*

2309 A632 $2 multicolored *4.75*

Two types of No. 2309 exist. Either two or three of the horizontal bars in seventh character from top right are connected at left side.

Literature Type of 1988

Romance of the Three Kingdoms by Luo Guanzhong: No. 2310, Night Attack on Wuchao. No. 2311, Making Three Calls at the Thatched Cottage. 30f, Rescuing the Master Single-handedly. 50f, Turning the Changban Bridge Upside Down. T.157.

1990, Dec. 10 Photo. *Perf. 11½x11*

2310 A587 20f multicolored (4-1) .20
2311 A587 20f multi, vert. (4-2) .20
2312 A587 30f multicolored (4-3) .25
2313 A587 50f multi, vert. (4-4) .45
Nos. 2310-2313 (4) 1.10

Han Xizai's Night Revels by Gu Hongzhong — A633

Designs: a, Guests enjoying food, music (5-1). b, Music and dance (5-2). c, Hand washing (5-3). d, Musicians (5-4). e, Guests departing (5-5). T.158. (Illustration reduced).

1990, Dec. 20 Litho. *Perf. 12*

2314 Strip of 5 2.75
a.-e. A633 50f any single .55

New Year 1991 (Year of the Sheep) — A634

Photo. & Engr.

1991, Jan. 5 *Perf. 11½*

2315 A634 20f multicolored .35
a. Bklt. pane of 12 + label 4.50

Dujiangyan Irrigation Project — A635

Designs: 20f, Yuzui, flood control. 50f, Feishayan, drainage. 80f, Baopingkou, water volume control. T.156.

1991, Feb. 20 Photo. *Perf. 11½x11*

2316 A635 20f multicolored .20
2317 A635 50f multicolored .30
2318 A635 80f multicolored .50
Nos. 2316-2318 (3) 1.00

A636

A637

1991, Mar. 18

2319 A636 20f multicolored .20

Paris Commune, 120th anniv.

1991, Apr. 20 Photo. *Perf. 10*

2320 A637 20f multi (2-1) .20
a. Perf. 11½x11 1.40

Perf. 11½x11

2321 A637 50f Child & adult hands (2-2) .20

Family planning (T.160).

Horned Animals (T.161) A638

1991, May 10 *Perf. 11x11½*

2322 A638 20f Saiga tatarica (4-1) .20
2323 A638 20f Budorcas taxicolor (4-2) .20
2324 A638 50f Ovis ammon (4-3) .20
2325 A638 $2 Capra ibex (4-4) .50
Nos. 2322-2325 (4) 1.10

A639

A640

1991, May 23 Photo. *Perf. 11*

2326 A639 25f Song and dance (2-1) .20
2327 A639 50f Golden bridge (2-2) .20

Souvenir Sheet

2328 A639 $2 No. 132, cranes 4.50

Occupation of Tibet, 40th anniv. (J.176).

1991, June 22 *Perf. 11½x11*

2329 A640 20f multicolored .20

Antarctic Treaty, 30th anniv.

Rhododendrons — A641

Varieties of rhododendrons. T.162.

1991, June 25 Litho. *Perf. 12*

2330 A641 10f Delavayi (8-1) .20
2331 A641 15f Molle (8-2) .20
2332 A641 20f Simsii (8-3) .20
2333 A641 20f Fictolacteum (8-4) .20
2334 A641 50f Agglutinatum, vert. (8-5) .40
2335 A641 80f Fortunei, vert. (8-6) .65
2336 A641 90f Giganteum, vert. (8-7) .75
2337 A641 $1.60 Rex, vert. (8-8) 1.25
Nos. 2330-2337 (8) 3.85

Souvenir Sheet

Perf. 11½

2338 A641 $5 Wardii *9.50*

No. 2338 contains one 80x40mm stamp.

Chinese Communist Party, 70th Anniv. (J.178) A642

1991, July 1 Photo. *Perf. 11x11½*

2339 A642 20f shown (2-1) .20
2340 A642 50f Hammer and sickle (2-2) .20

Peasant Uprising, 209B.C. A643

1991, July 7

2341 A643 20f brown .20

Mt. Hengshan Type of 1990

Designs: No. 2342, Monastery on mountainside. No. 2343, Snow-covered mountain top. 55f, Inscription carved into mountainside. 80f, Hidden monastery. T.163.

Photo. & Engr.

1991, July 20 *Perf. 11*

2342 A631 20f multi (4-1) .20
2343 A631 20f multi (4-2) .20
2344 A631 55f multi (4-3) .45
2345 A631 80f multi (4-4) .65
Nos. 2342-2345 (4) 1.50

Intl. Union for Quaternary Research, 13th Conf. A644

1991, Aug. 2 Photo. *Perf. 11x11½*

2346 A644 20f multicolored .20

Chengde Mountain Resort — A645

Ch'ing Dynasty Royal Gardens: 15f, Pine valleys. 20f, Mid-lake pavilion. 90f, Islet, maple trees. $2, Chengde Royal Summer Resort. T.164.

1991 *Perf. 11½x11*

2347 A645 15f multi (3-1) .20
2348 A645 20f multi (3-2) .20
2349 A645 90f multi (3-3) .60
Nos. 2347-2349 (3) 1.00

Souvenir Sheet

2350 A645 $2 multicolored *5.75*

No. 2350 contains one 90x40mm stamp. Issue dates: $2, Aug. 19; others, Aug. 10.

A646

A647

Chen Yi, (b. 1901), party leader (J.181).

1991, Aug. 26 Photo. *Perf. 11½x11*

2351 A646 20f shown (2-1) .20
2352 A646 50f Verse (2-2) .20

1991, Sept. 14

2353 A647 80f Disaster relief .30

Achievements Type of 1988

20f, Luoyang glassworks. 25f, Urumchi chemical fertilizer project. 55f, Dalian expressway, Shenyang. 80f, Xichang satellite launching center. T.165.

1991, Sept. 20 Litho. *Perf. 12*

2354 A582 20f multi (4-1) .20
2355 A582 25f multi (4-2) .20
2356 A582 55f multi (4-3) .20
2357 A582 80f multi (4-4) .20
Nos. 2354-2357 (4) .80

Revolutionary Heroes — A648

Designs: No. 2358, Xu Xilin (1873-1907). No. 2359, Qiu Jin (1879-1907). No. 2360, Song Jiaoren (1882-1913). J.182.

1991, Oct. 10 Photo. *Perf. 10*
2358 A648 20f multi (3-1) .20
a. Perf. 11x11½ 1.50

Perf. 11x11½
2359 A648 20f multi (3-2) .20
2360 A648 20f multi (3-3) .20

Jingdezhen Chinaware A649

Designs: 15f, Glazed wine pot and warming bowl, Song Dynasty, vert. No. 2362, Porcelain vase, Yuan Dynasty, vert. No. 2363, Jar, Ming Dynasty. 25f, Porcelain vase, Ch'ing Dynasty, vert. 50f, Modern underglazed plate, vert. $2, Modern octagonal eggshell bowl, T.166.

Perf. 11¼x11½, 11½x11¼ (#2363, 2366)

1991, Oct. 11 Photo.
2361 A649 15f multi (6-1) .20
2362 A649 20f multi (6-2) .20
2363 A649 20f multi (6-3) .20
2364 A649 25f multi (6-4) .20
2365 A649 50f multi (6-5) .20
2366 A649 $2 multi (6-6) .50
Nos. 2361-2366 (6) 1.50

Perf. 11¼x11, 11x11¼ (#2363a, 2366a)

1991
2361a 15f multi .20
2362a 20f multi .20
2363a 20f multi .20
2364a 25f multi .20
2365a 50f multi .20
2366a $2 multi .50
Nos. 2361a-2366a (6) 1.50

Tao Xingzhi, Educator, Birth Cent. (J.183) — A650

1991, Oct. 18 Litho. *Perf. 12*
2367 A650 20f shown (2-1) .20
2368 A650 50f Wearing robe (2-2) .20

Xu Xiangqian, Revolutionary Leader, 90th Birth Anniv. (J.184) — A651

1991, Nov. 8 *Perf. 11x11½*
2369 A651 20f shown (2-1) .20
2370 A651 50f In uniform (2-2) .20

1st Women's Soccer World Championships, Guangdong Province (J.185) — A652

Designs: 50f, Woman kicking soccer ball.

1991, Nov. 16 *Perf. 11½x11*
2371 A652 20f red & multi (2-1) .20
2372 A652 50f grn & multi (2-2) .20

Literature Type of 1987

Outlaws of the Marsh: 20f, Dai Zong sends a false letter from Liangshan Marsh. No. 2374, Ten feet of steel alone captures Stumpy Tiger Wang. No. 2375, Mistress Gu breaks open the jail in Dengzhou to rescue the Xie Brothers. 90f, Sun Li offers a plan to attack Zhu Family manor. $3, Mount Liangshan gallants raid the execution grounds. T.167.

1991, Nov. 19 *Perf. 11*
2373 A570 20f multi (4-1) .20
2374 A570 25f multi (4-2) .20
2375 A570 25f multi (4-3) .20
2376 A570 90f multi (4-4) .90
Nos. 2373-2376 (4) 1.50

Souvenir Sheet
Perf. 11x11½
2377 A570 $3 multicolored *6.75*

No. 2377 contains one 60x90mm stamp.

Beginning with No. 2378 stamps are inscribed "CHINA" and are numbered chronologically with the year followed by the number of the set. Additional numbers in parentheses indicate the number and position of each stamp in a set. We will note these only when helpful in identifying stamps.

New Year 1992, Year of the Monkey
A653 A654

Photo. & Engr.
1992, Jan. 25 *Perf. 11½*
2378 A653 20f Monkey, peach .20
2379 A654 50f Magpies, plum branches .20

Storks — A655

Conifers — A656

1992, Feb. 20 Photo. *Perf. 11x11½*
2380 A655 20f Ciconia nigra .20
2381 A655 $1.60 Ciconia ciconia .70

1992, Mar. 10 Litho. *Perf. 12½*

Designs: 20f, Metasequoia glyptostroboides. 30f, Cathaya argyrophylla. 50f, Taiwania flousiana. 80f, Abies beshanzuensis.

2382 A656 20f multicolored .20
2383 A656 30f multicolored .20
2384 A656 50f multicolored .20
2385 A656 80f multicolored .30
Nos. 2382-2385 (4) .90

Marine Life A660

1992, Apr. 15 Photo. *Perf. 11*
2386 A660 20f Pagrosomus major .20
2387 A660 25f Penaeus chinesis .20
2388 A660 50f Chlamys farreri .20
2389 A660 80f Laminaria japonica .20
Nos. 2386-2389 (4) .80

Publication of "Discussions on Literature and Art at the Yenan Forum," 50th Anniv. — A661

1992, May 23 Photo. *Perf. 11½x11*
2390 A661 20f org, blk & red .20

A662

A663

1992, June 5 Litho. *Perf. 12*
2392 A662 20f multicolored .20

UN Conf. on Human Development, 20th anniv.

1992, June 28

Insects: 20f, Coccinella septempunctata. 30f, Sympetrum croceolum. 50f, Chrysopa septempunctata. $2, Tenodera aridifolia sinensis.

2393 A663 20f multicolored .20
2394 A663 30f multicolored .20
2395 A663 50f multicolored .25
2396 A663 $2 multicolored .80
Nos. 2393-2396 (4) 1.45

1992 Summer Olympics, Barcelona A664

1992, July 25 Photo. *Perf. 11*
2397 A664 20f Basketball, vert. .20
2398 A664 25f Women's gymnastics .20
2399 A664 50f Women's diving .20
2400 A664 80f Weight lifting, vert. .30
Nos. 2397-2400 (4) .90

Souvenir Sheet
2401 A664 $5 Runners *2.50*

No. 2401 contains one 54x40mm stamp.

Intl. Space Year — A665

1992, Aug. 18 Litho. *Perf. 12*
2402 A665 20f multicolored .20

Literature Type of 1988

Romance of the Three Kingdoms by Luo Guanzhong: 20f, Verbal battle with scholars. 30f, Goading Sun Quan with sarcasm, vert. 50f, Jiang Gan stealing the letter. $1.60, Gathering arrows with straw-covered boats, vert.

Perf. 11½x11, 11x11½
1992, Aug. 25 Photo.
2403 A587 20f multi .20
2404 A587 30f multi .20
2405 A587 50f multi .20
2406 A587 $1.60 multi .40
Nos. 2403-2406 (4) 1.00

Wall Paintings Type of 1987

20f, Bodhisattva, vert. 25f, Musical performance, vert. 55f, Flight of a dragon. 80f, Envoy to the western regions. $5, Avalokitesvara-Bodhisattva, vert.

1992, Sept. 15 *Perf. 11*
2407 A557 20f multicolored .20
2408 A557 25f multicolored .20
2409 A557 55f multicolored .25
2410 A557 80f multicolored .35
Nos. 2407-2410 (4) 1.00

Souvenir Sheet
Perf. 11½
2411 A557 $5 multicolored *3.00*

No. 2411 contains one 52x70mm stamp.

Normalization of Diplomatic Relations Between China and Japan, 20th Anniv. — A666

20f, Cranes, Great Wall of China, Mt. Fuji. $2, Japanese, Chinese children, dove.

1992, Sept. 29 Photo. *Perf. 11x11½*
2412 A666 20f multicolored .20
2413 A666 $2 multicolored .75

A667

A667a

Statue of Mazu, Chinese Goddess of the Sea.

1992, Oct. 4 Litho. *Perf. 12*
2414 A667 20f multicolored .20

1992, Oct. 12 Photo. *Perf. 11½x11*
2414A A667a 20f multicolored .20

14th Chinese Communist Party Congress.

Jiao Yulu (1922-1964), Communist Party Leader — A668

1992, Oct. 28 Litho. *Perf. 12*
2415 A668 20f multicolored .20

Famous Men A669

Designs: 20f, Xiong Qinglai, mathematician. 30f, Tang Feifan, microbiologist. 50f, Zhang Xiaoqian, physician. $1, Liang Sicheng, architect.

1992, Nov. 20
2416 A669 20f multicolored .20
2417 A669 30f multicolored .20
2418 A669 50f multicolored .20
2419 A669 $1 multicolored .20
Nos. 2416-2419 (4) .80

Luo Ronghuan, Leader of People's Army, 90th Anniv. of Birth A670

1992, Nov. 26 Photo. *Perf. 11x11½*
2420 A670 20f In dress uniform .20
2421 A670 50f In field uniform .20

Constitution of the People's Republic of China, 10th Anniv. — A671

1992, Dec. 4 *Perf. 11½x11*
2422 A671 20f multicolored .20

Liu Bocheng, Leader of People's Army, Birth Cent. A672

Designs: 20f, In dress uniform. 50f, During period of Long March, vert.

1992, Dec. 4 *Perf. 11x11½, 11½x11*
2423 A672 20f multicolored .20
2424 A672 50f multicolored .20

Quingtian Stone Carvings — A673

1992, Dec. 15 Litho. *Perf. 12*
2425 A673 10f Spring .20
2426 A673 20f Chinese sorghum .20
2427 A673 40f Harvest .20
2428 A673 $2 Blooming flowers, full moon .40
Nos. 2425-2428 (4) 1.00

New Year 1993 (Year of the Rooster)

A674 A675

Photo. & Engr.

1993, Jan. 5 *Perf. 11½*
2429 A674 20f red & black .25
2430 A675 50f red, white & blk .25

Madam Song Quingling, Chinese Communist Leader, Birth Cent. A676

1993, Jan. 20 Photo. *Perf. 11x11½*
2431 A676 20f Portrait .20
2432 A676 $1 With children .30

Camelus Bactrianus Ferus A677

1993, Feb. 20 Litho. *Perf. 12*
2433 A677 20f shown .20
2434 A677 $1.60 Adult, young .45

8th Natl. People's Congress A678

1993, Mar. 15 Litho. *Perf. 12*
2435 A678 20f multicolored .20

A679

A680

Game of Weiqi (Go): 20f, Painting of players of ancient times. $1.60, Game board showing Chinese-style position.

1993, Apr. 30 Litho. *Perf. 12*
2436 A679 20f multi .20
2437 A679 $1.60 multi .40

1993, May 15 Litho. *Perf. 12*

20th Cent. Revolutionaries: 20f, Li Jishen (1885-1959), horiz. 30f, Zhang Lan (1872-1955). 50f, Shen Junru (1875-1963). $1, Huang Yanpei (1878-1965), horiz.

2438 A680 20f multi .20
2439 A680 30f multi .20
2440 A680 50f multi .20
2441 A680 $1 multi .20
Nos. 2438-2441 (4) .80

See Nos. 2483-2486.

A681

A682

1993, May 9 Photo. *Perf. 12*
2442 A681 50f Runner (2-1) .20
2443 A681 50f Mascot (2-2) .20
a. Pair, #2442-2443 .40

First East Asian Games. No. 2443a printed in continuous design.

1993, June 15 Litho. *Perf. 12½*

Bamboo: 20f, Phyllostachys nigra. 30f, Phyllostachys aureosulcata spectabilis. 40f, Bambusa ventricosa. $1, Pseudosasa amabilis. $5, Phyllostachys heterocycla pubescens, horiz.

2444 A682 20f multi .20
2445 A682 30f multi .20
2446 A682 40f multi .20
2447 A682 $1 multi .20
Nos. 2444-2447 (4) .80

Souvenir Sheet

Photo.

Perf. 11

2448 A682 $5 multicolored *2.75*
a. As #2448, added inscription *4.00*

No. 2448 contains one 54x40mm stamp.

No. 2448a is inscribed in sheet margin with hologram of panda at left, Chinese inscription for CHINA '96 and PJZ-3 at bottom, and flag and tagged security emblem at right. Soaking in water may affect the hologram. Issued: May 10, 1996.

Literature Type of 1987

Outlaws of the Marsh: 20f, Chai Jin is trapped in Gaotang. 30f, Shi Qian steals armor. 50f, Xu Ning teaches how to use barbed lance. $2, Shi Xiu leaps from building to rescue condemned man from execution.

1993, Aug. 20 Photo. *Perf. 11*
2449 A570 20f multi .20
2450 A570 30f multi .20
2451 A570 50f multi .20
2452 A570 $2 multi .60
Nos. 2449-2452 (4) 1.20

Changbai Mountains — A683

1993, Sept. 3 *Perf. 11½x11*
2453 A683 20f Tianchi .20
2454 A683 30f Alpine tundra .20
2455 A683 50f Waterfall .20
2456 A683 $1 Mixed forest .20
Nos. 2453-2456 (4) .80

Seventh Natl. Games — A684

Longmen Grottoes — A685

1993, Sept. 4
2457 A684 20f multicolored .20

1993, Sept. 5 Litho. *Perf. 12*

Designs: 20f, Rocana, Ancestor Worshipping Temple. 30f, Sakyamuni, Middle Binyang Cave, Northern Wei. 50f, Maharaja, devas treading on Yaksha. $1, Bodhisattva at the left side of Rocana, Guyang Cave, Northern Wei. $5, Ancestor Worshipping Temple.

2458 A685 20f multi .20
2459 A685 30f multi .20
2460 A685 50f multi .20
2461 A685 $1 multi .20
Nos. 2458-2461 (4) .80

Souvenir Sheets

2462 A685 $5 multicolored *2.75*
a. Overprinted in gold *9.00*
b. Overprinted in silver *5.00*

No. 2462 contains one 120x40mm stamp.

Overprint in margin of No. 2462a includes Chinese characters and "PJZ-1." Bangkok '95 (#2462a). No. 2462a sold for $6.

No. 2462a exists with serial number inscribed in sheet margin. The same number is inscribed on Thailand No. 1615b. These were sold as a set. Value for the two sheets with matching numbers, $26.50.

Sheet margin of No. 2462b contains silver lettering in Chinese for Thailand stamp exhibition and "PJZ-7." No. 2462b exists with serial number inscribed in sheet margin. Value: *$11.50.*

Issued: No. 2462a, 8/95.

Honey Bees A686

1993, Sept. 21 Photo. *Perf. 11½*
2463 A686 10f Queen and two bees .20
2464 A686 15f Extracting nectar .20
2465 A686 20f Two Zhonghua bees .20
2466 A686 $2 Two bees in flight .35
Nos. 2463-2466 (4) .95

Lacquerware — A687

1993, Oct. 20 Photo. *Perf. 12*
2467 A687 20f Bowl .20
2468 A687 30f Duck .20
2469 A687 50f Round tray .20
2470 A687 $1 Lidded box .20
Nos. 2467-2470 (4) .80

Paintings, by Zheng Banqiao — A688

Designs: 10f, Bamboo, rock on fan. No. 2472, Orchard. No. 2473, Orchard, bamboo, rock on scroll, vert. 30f, Bamboo, rock on scroll, vert. 50f, Vase and chrysanthemums. $1.60, Chinese calligraphy on fan.

1993, Nov. 22 Litho. *Perf. 12½*

2471 A688 10f multi (6-1) .20
2472 A688 20f multi (6-2) .20
2473 A688 20f multi (6-3) .20
2474 A688 30f multi (6-4) .20
2475 A688 50f multi (6-5) .20
2476 A688 $1.60 multi (6-6) .50
Nos. 2471-2476 (6) 1.50

A689

A690

1993, Nov. 26 *Perf. 12*

2477 A689 20f multicolored .20

Yang Hucheng, birth cent.

1993 Photo. *Perf. 11½*

Mao Tse-tung (1893-1976).

2478 A690 20f shown .20
2479 A690 $1 Portrait, seated .20

Souvenir Sheet

2480 A690 $5 Standing by Great Wall *2.00*
a. Overprinted in gold in margin 2.00 2.00

No. 2480 contains one 48x58mm stamp. No. 2480a sold for $8.

Issued: $5, 11/16; 20f, $1, 12/26; #2480a, 4/9/99.

New Year 1994 (Year of the Dog)
A691 A692

1994, Jan. 5 Photo. *Perf. 11½*

2481 A691 20f multi .20
2482 A692 50f yel, red & blk .20

20th Cent. Revolutionaries Type

Designs: No. 2483, Chen Qiyou, horiz. No. 2484, Chen Shutong. No. 2485, Ma Xulun. No. 2486, Xu Deheng, horiz.

1994, Feb. 25 Litho. *Perf. 12*

2483 A680 20f blk & brn (4-1) .20
2484 A680 20f blk & brn (4-2) .20
2485 A680 50f blk & brn (4-3) .20
2486 A680 50f blk & brn (4-4) .20
Nos. 2483-2486 (4) .80

Sturgeon — A693

20f, Huso dauricus. 40f, Acipenser sinensis. 50f, Psephurus gladius. $1, Acipenser dabryanus.

1994, Mar. 18 Litho. *Perf. 12½*

2487 A693 20f multi .20
2488 A693 40f multi .20
2489 A693 50f multi .20
2490 A693 $1 multi .20
Nos. 2487-2490 (4) .80

Afforestation Campaign — A694

Designs: 15f, Sand dunes. 20f, Flowers on sand dune. 40f, Forest of poplars. 50f, Oasis.

1994, Apr. 21 Litho. *Perf. 12*

2491 A694 15f multi .20
2492 A694 20f multi .20
2493 A694 40f multi .20
2494 A694 50f multi .20
Nos. 2491-2494 (4) .80

Teapots — A695

Style of teapot: 20f, Round, three-legged. 30f, Square, four-legged. 50f, Eight diagrams. $1, Round-eared.

1994, May 5 Litho. *Perf. 12*

2495 A695 20f multi .20
2496 A695 30f multi .20
2497 A695 50f multi .20
2498 A695 $1 multi .20
Nos. 2495-2498 (4) .80

Huangpu Military School, 70th Anniv. A696

1994, June 16 Litho. *Perf. 12*

2499 A696 20f multicolored .20

Intl. Olympic Committee, Cent. A697

1994, June 23

2500 A697 20f multicolored .20

Ancient Chinese Writers — A698

Designs: 20f, Tao Yuanming holding basket of flowers. 30f, Cao Zhi holding sword at side. 50f, Si Maqian writing on scroll. $1, Qu Yuan walking away with sword under arm.

1994, June 25

2501 A698 20f multi .20
2502 A698 30f multi .20
2503 A698 50f multi .20
2504 A698 $1 multi .20
Nos. 2501-2504 (4) .80

Wall paintings Type of 1987

10f, Flying Devata. 20f, Vimalakirti. 50f, Z. Yichao on the march. $1.60, Sorceresses.

1994, July 16 Photo. *Perf. 11*

2505 A557 10f multi .20
2506 A557 20f multi .20
2507 A557 50f multi .20
2508 A557 $1.60 multi .40
Nos. 2505-2508 (4) 1.00

Zhaojun's Marriage to Xiongnu — A699

1994, Aug. 25 Photo. *Perf. 11½x11*

2509 A699 20f Zhaojun .20 .20
2510 A699 50f Leaving home .20 .20

Souvenir Sheet

Perf. 11½

2511 A699 $3 Wedding *3.00 3.00*

No. 2511 contains one 85x46mm stamp.

Sixth Far East and South Pacific Games for the Disabled, Beijing — A700

1994, Sept. 4 Litho. *Perf. 12*

2512 A700 20f multicolored .20 .20

Wulingyuan State Forest Park — A701

20f, South Gate to Heaven. 30f, Shentangwan. 50f, No. One Bridge. $1, Writing-brush Peak. $3, Picturesque corridor.

1994, Sept. 25 Litho. *Perf. 12*

2513 A701 20f multi, vert. .20
2514 A701 30f multi, vert. .20
2515 A701 50f multi .20
2516 A701 $1 multi .20
Nos. 2513-2516 (4) .80

Souvenir Sheet

Perf. 11½x12

2517 A701 $3 multicolored *3.00*

No. 2517 contains one 50x36mm stamp.

Wuyi Mountains — A702

Designs: a, Jade-girl Peak (4-1). b, Nine-bend Brook (4-2). c, Guadun Village (4-3). d, Alpine Grassland (4-4).

1994, Sept. 30 *Perf. 12*

2518 Strip of 4 1.00
a.-d. A702 50f any single .25

Listening to the Rapids, by Fu Baoshi (1904-65) A703

Paintings: No. 2520, Appreciating a Painting. No. 2521, Dadi's Thatched Hut. 40f, Playing the Ruan. 50f, At Hupao. $1, The Road to Shanyin.

1994, Oct. 5

2519 A703 10f multi (6-1) .20
2520 A703 20f multi (6-2) .20
2521 A703 20f multi (6-3) .20
2522 A703 40f multi (6-4) .20
2523 A703 50f multi (6-5) .20
2524 A703 $1 multi (6-6) .20
Nos. 2519-2524 (6) 1.20

Cranes — A704

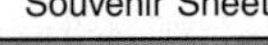

Photo. & Engr.

1994, Oct. 9 *Perf. 11x11½*

2528 A704 20f Whooping crane .20 .20
2529 A704 $2 Black-necked crane .45 .45

See US Nos. 2867-2868.

Souvenir Sheet

UPU, 120th Anniv. — A705

Illustration reduced.

1994, Oct. 9 Litho. *Perf. 12*
2530 A705 $3 multicolored 3.00
a. Ovptd. in sheet margin 3.00

No. 2530a ovptd. in sheet margin with UPU hologram, vertical Chinese inscription in gold. Issued: July 18, 1996.

Gorges of Yangtze River — A706

Designs: 10f, Baidicheng. No. 2532, Qutang Gorge. No. 2533, Wuxia Gorge. 30f, Goddess Peak. 50f, Xiling Gorge. $1, Qu Yuan Memorial Temple.
$5, The Three Gorges.

1994, Nov. 4 Photo. *Perf. 12*
2531 A706 10f multi (6-1) .20
2532 A706 20f multi (6-2) .20
2533 A706 20f multi (6-3) .20
2534 A706 30f multi (6-4) .20
2535 A706 50f multi (6-5) .20
2536 A706 $1 multi (6-6) .20
Nos. 2531-2536 (6) 1.20

Souvenir Sheet

Perf. 11½x11

2537 A706 $5 multicolored 3.25

No. 2537 contains one 116x35mm stamp.

Souvenir Sheet

All-China Philatelic Federation, 4th Congress — A707

Illustration reduced.

1994, Nov. 17 Litho. *Perf. 11*
2538 A707 $3 multicolored 2.00

Literature Type of 1988

Romance of the Three Kingdoms by Luo Guanzhong: 20f, Composing a poem with a lance in hands. 30f, Liu Bei's marriage, vert. 50f, Overwhelming Xiaoyaojin with prowess. $1, Campsites burned, vert.
$5, Fierce battle at Chibi.

Perf. 11½x11, 11x11½

1994, Nov. 24 Photo.
2539 A587 20f multicolored .20
2540 A587 30f multicolored .20
2541 A587 50f multicolored .20
2542 A587 $1 multicolored .20
Nos. 2539-2542 (4) .80

Souvenir Sheet

Perf. 11

2543 A587 $5 multicolored 5.00

No. 2543 contains one 158x36mm stamp.

Special Economic Zones A708

Designs: a, Shenzhen (5-1). b, Zhuhai (5-2). c, Shantou (5-3). d, Xiamen (5-4). e, Hainan (5-4).

1994, Dec. 10 Litho. *Perf. 12*
2544 A708 50f Strip of 5, #a.-e. .60

Pagodas of Ancient China — A709

Designs: No. 2545, Dayan Pagoda, Cien Temple. No. 2546, Zhenguo Pagoda, Kaiyuan Temple. 50f, Liuhe Pagoda, Kaihua Temple. $2, Youguo Temple.

Photo. & Engr.

1994, Dec. 15 *Perf. 11½x11*
2545 20f tan, brn & blk (4-1) .20
2546 20f tan, brn & blk (4-2) .20
2547 50f tan, brn & blk (4-3) .20
2548 $2 tan, brn & blk (4-4) .20
a. Souvenir sheet of 4, #2545-2548 7.00
Nos. 2545-2548 (4) .80

No. 2548a sold for $5.

New Year 1995 (Year of the Boar)
A711 A712

Photo. & Engr.

1995, Jan. 5 *Perf. 11½*
2550 A711 20f multicolored .20
2551 A712 50f multicolored .20

Winter Scenes A713

Designs: 20f, Snow willows, Cold River. 50f, Ice & snow on jade trees, vert.

1995, Jan. 12 Litho. *Perf. 12*
2552 A713 20f multicolored .20
2553 A713 50f multicolored .20

Mt. Dinghushan — A714

Designs: 15f, Topographical map. No. 2555, Stream flowing down from mountain. No. 2556, Buildings on mountain side. $2.30, Peacocks.

1995, Feb. 15 Litho. *Perf. 12½*
2554 A714 15f multi (4-1) .20
2555 A714 20f multi (4-2) .20
2556 A714 20f multi (4-3) .20
2557 A714 $2.30 multi (4-4) .20
Nos. 2554-2557 (4) .80

World Summit for Social Development, Copenhagen — A715

1995, Mar. 6 Photo. *Perf. 11x11½*
2558 A715 20f multicolored .20

Owls — A716

1995, Mar. 22 Photo. *Perf. 11½*
2559 A716 10f Eagle owl .20
2560 A716 20f Long-eared owl .20
2561 A716 50f Snowy owl .20
2562 A716 $1 Grass owl .20
Nos. 2559-2562 (4) .80

Sweet Osmanthus A717

1995, Apr. 14 Litho. *Perf. 12*
2563 A717 20f Thunbergii (4-1) .20
2564 A717 20f Latifolius (4-2) .20
2565 A717 50f Aurantiacus (4-3) .20
2566 A717 $1 Semperflorens (4-4) .20
Nos. 2563-2566 (4) .80

A souvenir sheet of 4, #2563-2566, exists, both perf and imperf. Value, perf $5., imperf. $65.

43rd World Table Tennis Championships, Tianjin — A718

1995, May 1 Litho. *Perf. 12*
2567 A718 20f Athlete .20
2568 A718 50f Arena .20
a. Souv. sheet of 2, #2567-2568 22.50

No. 2568a sold for $7. Issued 8/14/95.

Spring Outing — A719

Designs: No. 2569, Group riding horses. No. 2570, Three riding horses.

1995, May 23 Litho. *Perf. 12*
2569 A719 50f multi (2-1) .25
2570 A719 50f multi (2-2) .25
a. Pair, #2569-2570 .50

No. 2570a is a continuous design.

Shadow Play — A720

Various costumed characters.

1995, June 8 Photo. *Perf. 12x12½*
2571 A720 20f multi (4-1) .20
2572 A720 40f multi (4-2) .20
2573 A720 50f multi (4-3) .20
2574 A720 50f multi (4-4) .20
Nos. 2571-2574 (4) .80

Highway Interchanges, Beijing — A721

1995, June 20 Photo. *Perf. 11½x11*
2575 A721 20f Siyuan .20
2576 A721 30f Tianningsi .20
2577 A721 50f Yuting .20
2578 A721 $1 Anhui .20
Nos. 2575-2578 (4) .80

Diplomatic Relations Between China & Thailand, 20th Anniv. — A722

#2579, Elephants walking right into water. #2580, Elephants walking left into water.

1995, July 1
2579 A722 $1 multi (2-1) .25
2580 A722 $1 multi (2-2) .25
a. Pair, #2579-2580 .50

No. 2580a is a continuous design.

Taihu Lake A723

Lake scenes: No. 2581, Yellow trees. No. 2582, Structures on bank, boats, hills. No. 2583, Structures across inlet. No. 2584, Red trees, home. 230f, Winter scene. 500f, Houses on cliff, lighthouse.

1995, July 20 Photo. *Perf. 11½*
2581 A723 20f multi (5-1) .20
2582 A723 20f multi (5-2) .20
2583 A723 50f multi (5-3) .20
2584 A723 50f multi (5-4) .20
2585 A723 230f multi (5-5) .20
Nos. 2581-2585 (5) 1.00

Souvenir Sheet

Perf. 11

2586 A723 500f multicolored 3.25
a. Ovptd. in sheet margin 8.00

No. 2586 contains one 90x60mm stamp with continuing design.
No. 2586a issued 3/24/97. Gold overprint in sheet margin contains an emblem, Chinese inscription saying "Hong Kong Returns to China" and "PJZ-5."

Posts of Ancient China A724

1995, Aug. 17 Photo. *Perf. 12*
2587 A724 20f Yucheng .20
2588 A724 50f Jimingshan .20

Shaolin Temple, 1500th Anniv.
A725

1995, Aug. 30

2589 A725 20f Entrance (4-1) .20
2590 A725 20f Pagoda Forest (4-2) .20
2591 A725 50f Martial arts (4-3) .20
2592 A725 100f Historical rescue (4-4) .20
Nos. 2589-2592 (4) .80

Cultural Relics of Tibet — A726

1995, Sept. 1

2593 A726 20f Jar .20
2594 A726 30f Casque .20
2595 A726 50f Celestial motion chart .20
2596 A726 100f Pearl mandala .20
Nos. 2593-2596 (4) .80

Wildlife
A727

1995, Sept. 1 ***Perf. 11x11½***

2597 A727 20f Koalas .20
2598 A727 $2.90 Pandas .60

See Australia No. 1459.

End of World War II, 50th Anniv.
A728

10f, July 7th event. #2600, Victory at Taier village. #2601, Soldier, hundred-regiment battle. #2602, Guerrilla war. #2603, Troops on parade, joining forces at Mangyo. 60f, Aircraft donated by Chinese living abroad. #2605, Taiwan recovered. #2606, Japanese surrender aboard USS Missouri.

1995, Sept. 3

2599 A728 10f multi (8-1) .20
2600 A728 20f multi (8-2) .20
2601 A728 20f multi (8-3) .20
2602 A728 50f multi (8-4) .20
2603 A728 50f multi (8-5) .20
2604 A728 60f multi (8-6) .20
2605 A728 100f multi (8-7) .20
2606 A728 100f multi (8-8) .20
Nos. 2599-2606 (8) 1.60

4th World Conference on Women, Beijing
A729

Symbols of: 15f, Equality. 20f, Development. 50f, Peace. 60f, Friendship.

1995, Sept. 4 ***Perf. 12***

2607 A729 15f multi .20
2608 A729 20f multi .20
2609 A729 50f multi .20
2610 A729 60f multi .20
Nos. 2607-2610 (4) .80

The Great Wall — A730

Jiuhua Mountains — A731

1995, Oct. 5 **Photo.** ***Perf. 12½***

2611 A730 60f shown .20
2612 A730 230f Shanhaiguan Pass .60
2613 A730 290f Jinshanling .80
Nos. 2611-2613 (3) 1.60

See Nos. 2755, 2792-2795, 2907-2910, 2934-2941, 2952-2955.

1995, Oct. 9 ***Perf. 12***

10f, Sunrise at Peak Terrace, horiz. #2615, Hall of Meditation. #2616, Temple of Bodhisattva, horiz. #2617, Sunset at Zhiyuan, horiz. #2618, Great Roc. #2619, Phoenix Pine, horiz.

2614 A731 10f multi (6-1) .20
2615 A731 20f multi (6-2) .20
2616 A731 20f multi (6-3) .20
2617 A731 50f multi (6-4) .20
2618 A731 50f multi (6-5) .20
2619 A731 290f multi (6-6) .50
Nos. 2614-2619 (6) 1.50

Motion Pictures, Cent.
A732

Projector and: 20f, Black and white film. 50f, Color film.

1995, Oct. 13

2620 A732 20f blue & black .20
2621 A732 50f multicolored .20

UN, 50th Anniv.
A733

Designs: 20f, UN flag, Headquarters. 50f, Stylized flags, UN emblem, "50."

1995, Oct. 24 **Litho.**

2622 A733 20f multi .20
2623 A733 50f multi .20

Sanqing Mountains — A734

#2624, Good Fortune Land. #2625, Sichun Goddess. 50f, Bodhisattva Enjoys Music. 100f, Huge Boa out of Mountain.

1995, Nov. 1 **Photo.** ***Perf. 12***

2624 A734 20f multi (4-1) .20
2625 A734 20f multi (4-2) .20
2626 A734 50f multi, vert. (4-3) .20
2627 A734 100f multi, vert. (4-4) .20
Nos. 2624-2627 (4) .80

Mt. Hengshan Type of 1990

Songshan Mountains: 20f, Ancient Temple of Mount Song. 50f, Moon waiting at Songmen Gate. 60f, Shaolin Temple. $1, Panorama view of Mt. Song.

Photo. & Engr.

1995, Nov. 10 ***Perf. 11***

2628 A631 20f multi .20
2629 A631 50f multi .20
2630 A631 60f multi .20
2631 A631 $1 multi .20
Nos. 2628-2631 (4) .80

Scenic Views of Hong Kong — A735

Designs: 20f, Victoria Harbor. 50f, Central Plaza at night. 60f, Hong Kong Cultural Center. 290f, Repulse Bay.

1995, Nov. 28 **Photo.** ***Perf. 12***

2632 A735 20f multi .20
2633 A735 50f multi .20
2634 A735 60f multi .20
2635 A735 290f multi .50
Nos. 2632-2635 (4) 1.10

Sun Zi's Art of War — A736

Drawings depicting: No. 2637, Discussing strategy. 30f, Capturing Ying. 50f, Battle at Ailing. 100f, Meeting of sovereigns, Huangchi.

1995, Dec. 4 ***Perf. 11x11½***

2636 A736 20f multi (5-1) .20
2637 A736 20f multi (5-2) .20
2638 A736 30f multi (5-3) .20
2639 A736 50f multi (5-4) .20
2640 A736 100f multi (5-5) .20
Nos. 2636-2640 (5) 1.00

New Year 1996 (Year of the Rat)
A737 A738

Photo. & Engr.

1996, Jan. 5 ***Perf. 11½***

2641 A737 20f multi .20
2642 A738 50f multi .20

3rd Asian Winter Games
A739

#2643, Speed skating. #2644, Ice hockey. #2645, Figure skating. #2646, Skiing.

1996, Feb. 4 **Litho.** ***Perf. 12***

2643 A739 50f multi (4-1) .20
2644 A739 50f multi (4-2) .20
2645 A739 50f multi (4-3) .20
2646 A739 50f multi (4-4) .20
a. Block of 4, #2643-2646 .50

China/Korea Submarine Fiber Optic Cable System — A740

1996, Feb. 8 **Litho.** ***Perf. 12***

2647 A740 20f multicolored .20

First day covers are dated 12/15/95.
See Korea No. 1863.

Shenyang Imperial Palace — A741

Designs: No. 2648, Buildings, denomination UL. No. 2649, Buildings, denomination LR.

1996, Mar. 18 **Photo.** ***Perf. 12***

2648 A741 50f multi (2-1) .20
2649 A741 50f multi (2-2) .20
a. Pair, Nos. 2648-2649 .30

China Post, Cent.
A742

Post Office buildings: 10f, Tianjin Posts Bureau. 20f, Beijing Postal Administration. 50f, Directorate of Posts of China. 100f, Beijing postal hub.
500f, China #78-85.

1996, Mar. 20 ***Perf. 11½***

2650 A742 10f multi .20
2651 A742 20f multi .20
2652 A742 50f multi .20
2653 A742 100f multi .20
Nos. 2650-2653 (4) .80

Souvenir Sheet

Perf. 11

2654 A742 500f multicolored *5.00*

No. 2654 contains one 89x59mm stamp.

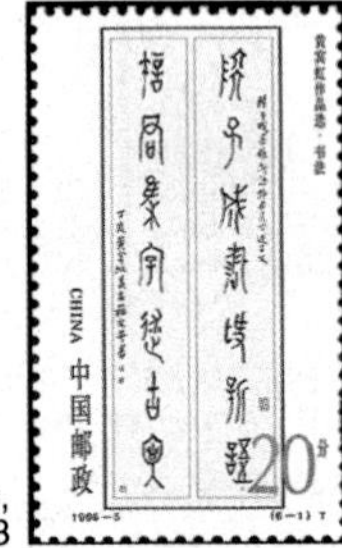

Huang Binhong, Artist — A743

#2655, Calligraphy. #2656, Landscape. 40f, Qingcheng Mts. #2658, View from Xiing. #2659, Colored landscape. 230f, Flowers.

1996, Apr. 5 ***Perf. 11½***

2655 A743 20f multi (6-1) *.20*
2656 A743 20f multi (6-2) *.20*
2657 A743 40f multi (6-3) *.40*
2658 A743 50f multi (6-4) *.50*
2659 A743 50f multi (6-5) *.50*
2660 A743 230f multi (6-6) *2.25*
Nos. 2655-2660 (6) *4.05*

Aircraft — A744

1996, Apr. 17 ***Perf. 12***

2661 A744 20f F-8 (4-1) .20
2662 A744 50f A-5 (4-2) .20
2663 A744 50f Yun-7 (4-3) .20
2664 A744 100f Yun-12 (4-4) .20
Nos. 2661-2664 (4) .80

Potted Landscapes — A745

#2665-2666, Lijing & Divine Peak. #2667-2668, Melting Snow & Eagle Rock. #2668-2669, Manch & Rosy Clouds.

1996, Apr. 18

2665 A745 20f multi (6-1) .20
2666 A745 20f multi (6-2) .20
a. Pair, #2665-2666 .40
2667 A745 50f multi (6-3) .20
2668 A745 50f multi (6-4) .20
a. Pair, #2667-2668 .60
2669 A745 100f multi (6-5) .20
2670 A745 100f multi (6-6) .20
a. Pair, #2669-2670 1.25
Nos. 2665-2670 (6) 1.20

Iron Trees — A746

#2671, Cycas revoluta. #2672, Cycas panzhihuaensis. 50f, Cycas pectinata. 230f, Cycas multipinnata.

1996, May 2 **Litho.** ***Perf. 12***

2671 A746 20f multi (4-1) .20
2672 A746 20f multi (4-2) .20
2673 A746 50f multi (4-3) .20
2674 A746 230f multi (4-4) .35
Nos. 2671-2674 (4) .95

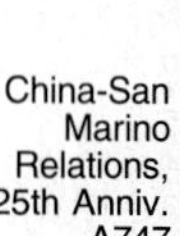

China-San Marino Relations, 25th Anniv. A747

1996, May 6 **Photo.** ***Perf. 12***

2675 A747 100f Great Wall of China (2-1) .30
2676 A747 100f Mt. Titano (2-2) .30
a. Pair, #2675-2676 .60

See San Marino Nos. 1356-1357.

Artifacts from Hemudu Ruins — A748

Designs: 20f, Agricultural tool. 50f, Pile to support building. 100f, Paddles for boats. 230f, Bird and sun carved in wood.

1996, May 12 **Litho.** ***Perf. 12***

2677 A748 20f multi .20
2678 A748 50f multi .20
2679 A748 100f multi .20
2680 A748 230f multi .50
Nos. 2677-2680 (4) 1.10

Souvenir Sheet

CHINA '96, 9th Asian Intl. Philatelic Exhibition — A749

1996, May 18 ***Perf. 11½x12***

2681 A749 500f multicolored *6.00*
a. Overprinted in gold *7.75*

No. 2681 exists imperf.

Overprint in margin of No. 2681a includes Chinese characters, Shanghai '97 exhibition emblem, and "PJZ-6." Issued in 1998.

Children's Activities A750

Designs: 20f, Singing, playing musical instruments. 30f, Pushing child in wheelchair, holding umbrella. 50f, Placing flag on South Pole, penguins. 100f, Planting tree.

1996, June 1 ***Perf. 12***

2682 A750 20f multi .20
2683 A750 30f multi .20
2684 A750 50f multi .20
2685 A750 100f multi .20
Nos. 2682-2685 (4) .80

Modern Olympic Games, Cent. — A751

1996, June 23 **Photo.** ***Perf. 12***

2686 A751 20f multicolored .20

Protection of Land A752

Stylized designs representing: 20f, Making use of land. 50f, Protection of farmland.

1996, June 25 ***Perf. 11x11½***

2687 A752 20f multi .20
2688 A752 50f multi .20

A753

Military Terraces — A754

1996, July 9 **Litho.** ***Perf. 12***

2689 A753 20f multi .20
2690 A754 50f multi .20

Vehicles — A755

#2691, Red Flag, 4-door limousine. #2692, Dongfeng, stake truck. 50f, Jiefang, 4-door truck. 100f, Beijing, canvas-topped jeep.

1996, July 15 **Photo.** ***Perf. 12***

2691 A755 20f multi (4-1) .20
2692 A755 20f multi (4-2) .20
2693 A755 50f multi (4-3) .25
2694 A755 100f multi (4-4) .40
Nos. 2691-2694 (4) 1.05

New Tangshan Built Following 1976 Earthquake — A756

1996, July 28 ***Perf. 11½***

2695 A756 20f Farm cottages (4-1) .20
2696 A756 50f Factory (4-2) .20
2697 A756 50f Street (4-3) .20
2698 A756 100f Port (4-4) .20
Nos. 2695-2698 (4) .80

30th Intl. Geological Conference — A757

1996, Aug. 4 **Litho.** ***Perf. 12***

2699 A757 20f multicolored .20

Tianchi Lake, Tianshan Mountains — A758

20f, High mountain lake. #2701, Splendid Waterfalls. #2702, Snow-capped peaks. 100f, Lakeside scenery.

1996, Aug. 8

2700 A758 20f multi (4-1) .20
2701 A758 50f multi, vert. (4-2) .20
2702 A758 50f multi, vert. (4-3) .20
2703 A758 100f multi (4-4) .40
Nos. 2700-2703 (4) 1.00

Wall Paintings Type of 1987

10f, Illustration of Mount Wutai. 20f, King of Khotan, vert. 50f, Savior Avalokitesvara. 100f, Worshipping Bodhisattvas.

$5, Thousand Arm Avalokitesvara.

1996, Aug. 15 **Photo.** ***Perf. 11***

2704 A557 10f multi, vert. .20
2705 A557 20f multi .20
2706 A557 50f multi .20
2707 A557 100f multi .20
Nos. 2704-2707 (4) .80

Souvenir Sheet

2708 A557 500f multicolored *6.00*

No. 2708 contains one 46x102mm stamp.

Mausoleums of Western Xia — A759

Designs: No. 2709: Mausoleum terrace. No. 2710, Ornament on Divine Gate. 50f, Stele. 100f, Stele remnant, Shouling.

1996, Aug. 22 **Photo.** ***Perf. 11½***

2709 A759 20f multi (4-1) .20
2710 A759 20f multi (4-2) .20
2711 A759 50f multi (4-3) .20
2712 A759 100f multi (4-4) .40
Nos. 2709-2712 (4) 1.00

Railways in China — A760

Designs: 15f, Datong-Quinhuangdao Railway. 20f, Lanzhou-Xinjiang Two-Track Railway. 50f, Beijing-Kowloon Railway. 100f, Beijing Western Railway Station

1996, Sept. 1

2713 A760 15f multi .20
2714 A760 20f multi .20
2715 A760 50f multi .20
2716 A760 100f multi .20
Nos. 2713-2716 (4) .80

A761

A762

Chinese Archives: No. 2717, Archives on tortoise shells, Shang Dynasty. No. 2718, Archives on wood slips, Han Dynasty. 50f, Iron scrolls, Ming Dynasty. 100f, Books of Ch'ing Dynasty.

1996, Sept. 2 Litho. *Perf. 12*

2717 A761 20f multi (4-1) .20
2718 A761 20f multi (4-2) .20
2719 A761 50f multi (4-3) .20
2720 A761 100f multi (4-4) .20
Nos. 2717-2720 (4) .80

1996, Sept. 10 *Perf. 12*

2721 A762 20f Portrait .20
2722 A762 50f In uniform .20

Ye Ting (1896-1946), co-founder of Chinese People's Liberation Army.

96th Conference of Inter-Parliamentary Union — A763

1996, Sept. 16 *Perf. 11½*

2723 A763 20f multi .30

Shanghai — A764

Photo. & Engr.

1996, Sept. 21 *Perf. 11½*

2724 A764 10f Communication (6-1) .20
2725 A764 20f Lujiazui (6-2) .20
2726 A764 20f Jinqiao (6-3) .20
2727 A764 50f Zhanghiang (6-4) .20
2728 A764 60f Waigaoqiao (6-5) .20
2729 A764 100f Residential (6-6) .20
Nos. 2724-2729 (6) 1.20

Souvenir Sheet

Perf. 11

2730 A764 500f Panoramic view 6.00
a. Margin ovptd. 12.00 —

No. 2730 contains one 90x45mm stamp.
No. 2730a issued 10/20/01. It is inscribed in margin with multicolored emblems and gold "PJZ-14," "APEC CHINA 2001," and Chinese characters.

Space Navigation — A765

1996, Oct. 7 Litho. *Perf. 12*

2731 A765 20f Rocket lift-off .20
2732 A765 100f Satellite in orbit .35

Singapore Waterfront — A766

Design: 290f, Panmen, Suzhou, China.

1996, Oct. 9 Photo. *Perf. 11½*

2733 A766 20f multi .20
2734 A766 290f multi .75

See Singapore Nos. 768-769.

Victory of Long March, 60th Anniv. — A767

Designs: 20f, Red Army through Marshland. 50f, Reunion of Three Armies.

1996, Oct. 22 Litho. *Perf. 12*

2735 A767 20f multi .30 .20
2736 A767 50f multi .70 .20

Colored Sculpture of Tianjin A768

Designs: 20f, The Two Immortals. No. 2738, Making Candy. No. 2739, Returning from Fishing. 100f, Xi Chun in Painting.

1996, Nov. 5 Photo. *Perf. 11½*

2737 A768 20f multi (4-1) .20
2738 A768 50f multi (4-2) .20
2739 A768 50f multi (4-3) .20
2740 A768 100f multi (4-4) .20
Nos. 2737-2740 (4) .80

Hong Kong A769

20f, Bank of China. 40f, Container Terminal. 60f, Kai Tak Airport. 290f, Stock Exchange.

1996, Dec. 19 Litho. *Perf. 12*

2741 A769 20f multi (4-1) .20
2742 A769 40f multi (4-2) .20
2743 A769 60f multi (4-3) .20
2744 A769 290f multi (4-4) .45
Nos. 2741-2744 (4) 1.05

A770

A771

1997, Jan. 1

2745 A770 50f Visit China .20

1997, Jan. 1

2746 A771 50f multicolored .20

First natl. agricultural census.

New Year 1997 (Year of the Ox)
A772 A773

Photo. & Engr.

1997, Jan. 5 *Perf. 11½*

2747 A772 50f multi (2-2) .20
2748 A773 150f multi (2-1) .40

Paintings by Pan Tianshou (1897-1971) A774

#2749, Pines on the Yellow Mountain. #2750, Rosy Clouds of Dawn. #2751, Clearing Up after Mould Rains. #2752, Chrysanthemum and Bamboo. #2753, Sleeping Cat. #2754, A Corner of Lingyan Brook.

1997, Mar. 14 Photo. *Perf. 11½*

2749 A774 50f multi (6-1) .30
2750 A774 50f multi (6-2) .30
2751 A774 100f multi (6-3) .65
2752 A774 100f multi (6-4) .65
2753 A774 150f multi (6-5) 1.00
2754 A774 150f multi (6-6) 1.00
Nos. 2749-2754 (6) 3.90

Great Wall Type of 1995

1997, Apr. 1 Photo. *Perf. 13x12*

2755 A730 50f multicolored .20

A776

A777

Tea: No. 2756, People forming circle beside tea tree. No. 2757, Statue of tea sage. No. 2758, Tea utensils, horiz. No. 2759, Painting of tea party, horiz.

1997, Apr. 8 Litho. *Perf. 12*

2756 A776 50f multi (4-1) .20
2757 A776 50f multi (4-2) .20
2758 A776 150f multi (4-3) .45
2759 A776 150f multi (4-4) .45
Nos. 2756-2759 (4) 1.30

1997, May 1 Photo. *Perf. 11½*

Stylized designs depicting: No. 2760, Celebration. No. 2761, Unity (group of people), horiz. 200f, Advance (horses running), horiz.

2760 A777 50f multi (3-1) .20
2761 A777 50f multi (3-2) .20
2762 A777 200f multi (3-3) .80
Nos. 2760-2762 (3) 1.20

Inner Mongolia Autonomous Region, 50th anniv.

Pheasants A778

Designs: 50f, Chinese copper pheasant. 540f, Common pheasant.

Litho. & Engr.

1997, May 9 *Perf. 11½x11*

2763 A778 50f multi (2-1) .20
2764 A778 540f multi (2-2) 1.10

See Sweden Nos. 2225-2226.

Dong Architecture A779

Maiji Grottoes — A780

#2765, Zengchong Drum Tower. #2766, Bai'er Drum Tower. #2767, Wind and Rain Bridge over the River, horiz. #2768, Wind and Rain Bridge in the Field, horiz.

1997, June 2 Litho. *Perf. 12*

2765 A779 50f multi (4-1) .20
2766 A779 50f multi (4-2) .20
a. Pair, #2765-2766 .30
2767 A779 150f multi (4-3) .45
2768 A779 150f multi (4-4) .45
a. Pair, #2767-2768 .90
Nos. 2765-2768 (4) 1.30

1997, June 13

Statues: No. 2769, Buddha and Xieshi Bodhisattva. No. 2770, Xieshi Bodhisattva and his disciple. 100f, Maid. No. 2772, Buddha. No. 2773, Xieshi Bodhisattva. 200f, Provider.

2769 A780 50f multi (6-1) .20
2770 A780 50f multi (6-2) .20
2771 A780 100f multi (6-3) .25
2772 A780 150f multi (6-4) .35
2773 A780 150f multi (6-5) .35
2774 A780 200f multi (6-6) .45
Nos. 2769-2774 (6) 1.80

A780a

A781

Texts surrounded by flowers: 50f, Sino-British Joint Declaration. 150f, Basic Law of the Hong Kong Special Adminstrative Region. 800f, Deng Xiaoping.

1997, July 1 Litho. *Perf. 12*

2774A A780a 50f multi (2-1) .30
2774B A780a 150f multi (2-2) .80

Souvenir Sheets

2774C A781 800f multi 2.50
d. Overprinted in sheet margin 3.00

Litho. (stamp) & Embossed (margin)

Perf. 13½

2775 A781 $50 gold & multi 35.00
a. Overprinted in margin 35.00 35.00

Deng Xiaoping (1904-97), return of Hong Kong to China.

No. 2775 was released in special souvenir folder.

No. 2774d contains gold Chinese inscription for Hong Kong's Return Exhibition Tour, emblem, and "PJZ-8" in sheet margin. Issued: 6/19/98.

Overprint in margin on No. 2775a is Chinese inscription, "2000-1" and "(2-1)J." Issued: 1/1/00.

Ancient Temples of Wutai Mountain — A782

Designs: 40f, Taihuai Township. No. 2777, Nanchan Temple. No. 2778, Foguang Temple. No. 2779, Xiantong Temple. No. 2780, Bodhisattva Summit. 200f, Zhenhai Temple.

1997, July 26 Litho. *Perf. 12*

2776	A782	40f multi (6-1)	.20
2777	A782	50f multi (6-2)	.20
2778	A782	50f multi (6-3)	.20
2779	A782	150f multi (6-4)	.35
2780	A782	150f multi (6-5)	.35
2781	A782	200f multi (6-6)	.45
		Nos. 2776-2781 (6)	1.75

Chinese People's Liberation Army, 70th Anniv. — A783

#2782, Land Force. #2783, Naval Force. #2784, Air Force. #2785, Strategic Missile Troops. 200f, Joint military maneuvers.

1997, Aug. 1

2782	A783	50f multi (5-1)	.20
2783	A783	50f multi (5-2)	.20
2784	A783	50f multi (5-3)	.20
2785	A783	50f multi (5-4)	.20
2786	A783	200f multi (5-5)	.50
		Nos. 2782-2786 (5)	1.30

Shoushan Stone Carvings A784

Designs: No. 2787, "Rhythm of Autumn," vert. No. 2788, "Rhinoceros under Sunshine,", vert. No. 2789, "Jade's Fragrance," (basket of fruit). No. 2790, "Drunken Joy."

800f, Qianlong's Chain Seals.

1997, Aug. 17 Litho. *Perf. 12*

2787	A784	50f multi (4-1)	.20
2788	A784	50f multi (4-2)	.20
2789	A784	150f multi (4-3)	.45
2790	A784	150f multi (4-4)	.45
		Nos. 2787-2790 (4)	1.30

Souvenir Sheet

2791	A784	800f multi	5.00

No. 2791 contains one 60x60mm stamp.

Great Wall Type of 1995

Gates: 30f, Huangyaguan. 100f, Badaling. 150f, Joyongguan. 200f, Zijingguan.

1997, Sept. 1 Photo. *Perf. 13x12*

2792	A730	30f yellow & black	.20
2793	A730	100f vermilion & black	.25
2794	A730	150f green & black	.40
2795	A730	200f red & black	.50
		Nos. 2792-2795 (4)	1.35

Communist Party of China, 15th Natl. Congress A785

1997, Sept. 12 Litho. *Perf. 12*

2796	A785	50f multicolored	.50

A786

#2797, China Rose. #2798, New Zealand Monthly Rose.

1997, Oct. 9 Photo. *Perf. 11½*

2797		150f multi (2-1)	.50
2798		150f multi (2-2)	.50
a.	A786	Pair, #2797-2798	1.00

See New Zealand Nos. 1469-1470.

Eighth Natl. Games A788

1997, Oct. 12 Litho. *Perf. 12*

2799	A788	50f Athletes (2-1)	.20
2800	A788	150f Stadium)2-2)	.45
a.		Souv. sheet, #2799-2800	*5.00*

No. 2800a sold for 300f.

Temple of Heaven, Beijing — A789

#2801, Hall of Prayers for Bumper Harvests. #2802, Imperial Vault of Heaven. #2803, Circular Mound Altar. #2804, Fasting Palace.

1997, Oct. 16 Litho. *Perf. 12*

2801	A789	50f multi (4-1)	.20
2802	A789	50f multi (4-2)	.20
a.		Pair, #2801-2802	.25
2803	A789	150f multi (4-3)	.40
2804	A789	150f multi (4-4)	.40
a.		Pair, #2803-2804	.80
		Nos. 2801-2804 (4)	1.20

Mt. Huangshan — A790

a, Mt. Huangshan at sunrise (8-1). b, Xihai Peaks (8-2). c, Flying Rock in surging clouds (8-3). d, Beihai in drifting clouds (8-4). e, Yuping Peak (8-5). f, Mystical stone (8-6). g, Tiandu Peak over clouds (8-7). h, Fabled Abode of Immortals (8-8).

1997, Oct. 20 Photo. *Perf. 11½*

Sheet of 8 + Label

2805	A790	200f #a.-h.	*10.00*

Nos. 2805d, 2805e are each 36x46mm. 22nd UPU Congress, Beijing, 1999.

City Wall of Xi'an A791

Designs: No. 2806, Surrounding tower. No. 2807, Arrow Tower. No. 2808, Watch Tower. No. 2009, Corner Tower.

1997, Oct. 24 Litho. *Perf. 12*

2806	A791	50f multi (4-1)	.20
2807	A791	50f multi (4-2)	.20
2808	A791	150f multi (4-3)	.40
2809	A791	150f multi (4-4)	.40
		Nos. 2806-2809 (4)	1.20

Three Gorges Dam Project on Yangtze River — A792

#2810, New channel being opened to navigation. #2811, Damming Yangtze River.

1997, Nov. 8 Photo. *Perf. 11½*

2810	A792	50f multi (2-1)	.20
2811	A792	50f multi (2-2)	.20
a.		Pair, #2810-2811	.25

Macao Landmarks — A793

50f, Ma Kok Temple. 100f, Lin Fong Temple. 150f, St. Paul's Ruins. 200f, Guia Lighthouse.

1997, Nov. 11 Litho. *Perf. 12*

2812	A793	50f multi (4-1)	.20
2813	A793	100f multi (4-2)	.25
2814	A793	150f multi (4-3)	.35
2815	A793	200f multi (4-4)	.50
		Nos. 2812-2815 (4)	1.30

Steel Production Exceeds 100 Million Tons in 1996 A794

50f, Ancient method of producing steel. 150f, Modern mill, pouring steel from smelter.

1997, Nov. 25

2816	A794	50f multi (2-1)	.20
2817	A794	150f multi (2-2)	.45

Telecommunications — A795

Stylized designs: #2818, Digital transmissions. #2819, Computer, "X-changing" data. #2820, Computer receiving signals, Chinese landmarks. #2821, Cellular phone transmission, man's head.

1997, Dec. 10

2818	A795	50f multi (4-1)	.20
2819	A795	50f multi (4-2)	.20
2820	A795	150f multi (4-3)	.35
2821	A795	150f multi (4-4)	.35
		Nos. 2818-2821 (4)	1.10

Literature Type of 1987

Outlaws of the Marsh: 40f, Huyan Zhuo coaxes Guan Sheng in a moonlit night. No. 2823, Lu Junyi captures Shi Wengong. No. 2824, Yan Qing defeats sky supporting pillar. 150f, Thunderbolt defeats Imperial Army.

800f, Heroes of Mount Liangshan take seats in order of rank.

1997, Dec. 22 Photo. *Perf. 11*

2822	A570	40f multi (4-1)	.20
2823	A570	50f multi (4-2)	.20
2824	A570	50f multi (4-3)	.20
2825	A570	150f multi (4-4)	.60
		Nos. 2822-2825 (4)	1.20

Souvenir Sheet

2826	A570	800f multicolored	3.25

No. 2826 contains one 60x90mm stamp.

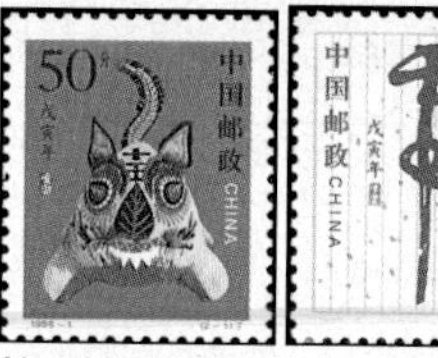

New Year 1998 (Year of the Tiger) A796 A797

Photo. & Engr.

1998, Jan. 5 *Perf. 11½*

2827	A796	50f multi (2-1)	.20
2828	A797	150f multi (2-2)	.35

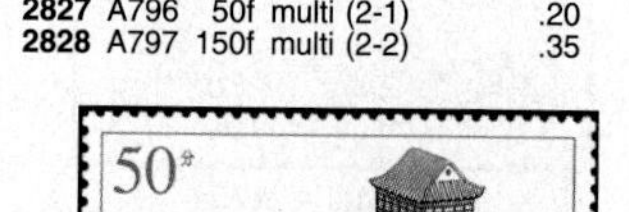

Gardens of Lingnan — A798

1998, Jan. 18 Litho. *Perf. 12*

2829	A798	50f Keyaun (4-1)	.20
2830	A798	50f Liangyuan (4-2)	.20
2831	A798	100f Qinghui (4-3)	.25
2832	A798	200f Yuyin Villa (4-4)	.50
		Nos. 2829-2832 (4)	1.15

Deng Xiaoping (1904-97) — A799

#2833, At middle age. #2834, During Liberation War. #2835, With Mao Tse-tung. 100f, As Chairman of Central Military Commission. 150f, Making speech on 35th anniversary of People's Republic. 200f, Making speech, hand raised, 1992.

1998, Feb. 19 Photo. *Perf. 11½*

2833	A799	50f multi (6-1)	.20
2834	A799	50f multi (6-2)	.20
2835	A799	50f multi (6-3)	.20
2836	A799	100f multi (6-4)	.25
2837	A799	150f multi (6-5)	.35
2838	A799	200f multi (6-6)	.50
		Nos. 2833-2838 (6)	1.70

Chinese People's Police — A800

Designs: 40f, Golden shield. No. 2840, Blitz operation. No. 2841, Cooperation between police and people. 100f, Traffic control. 150f, Fire police. 200f, Border guards.

1998, Feb. 28 **Litho.** ***Perf. 12***

2839	A800	40f multi (6-1)	.20
2840	A800	50f multi (6-2)	.20
2841	A800	50f multi (6-3)	.20
2842	A800	100f multi (6-4)	.25
2843	A800	150f multi (6-5)	.35
2844	A800	200f multi (6-6)	.50
		Nos. 2839-2844 (6)	1.70

A801

A802

1998, Mar. 5

2845 A801 50f multi (1-1) .20 .20

Ninth Natl. People's Congress, Beijing.

1998, Mar. 5 **Photo.** ***Perf. 11½***

Chou En-lai (1898-1976), Communist Party leader: No. 2846, In military uniform on horse. No. 2847, As First Premier, walking. No. 2848, As diplomat wearing lei. No. 2849, Standing and applauding.

2846	A802	50f multi (4-1)	.20
2847	A802	50f multi (4-2)	.20
2848	A802	150f multi (4-3)	.30
2849	A802	150f multi (4-4)	.30
		Nos. 2846-2849 (4)	1.00

Nine-Village Valley — A803

Designs: No. 2850, Fangcao Lake. No. 2851, Wuhua Lake. No. 2852, Shuzheng Waterfalls. No. 2853, Nuorilang Waterfalls.

1998, Mar. 26 **Litho.** ***Perf. 12***

2850	A803	50f multi (4-1)	.20
2851	A803	50f multi (4-2)	.20
2852	A803	150f multi (4-3)	.30
2853	A803	150f multi (4-4)	.30
		Nos. 2850-2853 (4)	1.00

Souvenir Sheet

2854 A803 800f Long Lake 3.00

No. 2854 contains one 93x52mm stamp.

Dai Architecture — A804

#2855, Building on stilts. #2856, Well. #2857, Pavilion. #2858, Pagoda.

1998, Apr. 12 **Photo.** ***Perf. 11½***

2855	A804	50f multi (4-1)	.20
2856	A804	50f multi (4-2)	.20
2857	A804	150f multi (4-3)	.30
2858	A804	150f multi (4-4)	.30
		Nos. 2855-2858 (4)	1.00

Construction, Hainan Special Economic Zone — A805

#2859, Urban construction, Haikou. #2860, Economic development zone, Yangpu. #2861, Phoenix Intl. Airport, Sanya. #2862, Natl. tourism and resort zone, Yalongwan.

1998, Apr. 13 **Litho.** ***Perf. 12***

2859	A805	50f multi (4-1)	.20
2860	A805	50f multi (4-2)	.20
a.		Pair, #2859-2860	.40
2861	A805	150f multi (4-3)	.30
2862	A805	150f multi (4-4)	.30
a.		Pair, #2861-2862	.60
		Nos. 2859-2862 (4)	1.00

Ancient Academies — A806

Designs: No. 2863, Yingtian. No. 2864, Songyang. No. 2865, Yuelu. No. 2866, Bailu.

1998, Apr. 29

2863	A806	50f multi (4-1)	.20
2864	A806	50f multi (4-2)	.20
2865	A806	150f multi (4-3)	.30
2866	A806	150f multi (4-4)	.30
		Nos. 2863-2866 (4)	1.00

Beijing University, Cent. A807

1998, May 4 **Litho.** ***Perf. 12***

2867 A807 50f multicolored .20

22nd UPU Congress, Beijing A808

1998, May 15 **Litho.** ***Perf. 12***

2868	A808	50f Emblem (2-1)	.20
2869	A808	540f Emblem, vert. (2-2)	1.50

Shennongjia Nature Reserve — A809

#2870, Mountain peaks. #2871, River, gorge. #2872, Primitive forest. #2873, Grasslands.

1998, June 6

2870	A809	50f multi (4-1)	.20
2871	A809	50f multi (4-2)	.20
2872	A809	150f multi (4-3)	.40
2873	A809	150f multi (4-4)	.40
		Nos. 2870-2873 (4)	1.20

Chongqing — A810

1998, June 18 **Litho.** ***Perf. 12***

2874	A810	50f Great Hall (2-1)	.20
2875	A810	150f Port (2-2)	.40

Xilinguole Grassland — A811

Designs: No. 2876, Sheep grazing, sheep herders. No. 2877, Cattle grazing, flowers. 150f, Poplar and birch forest, deer. 800f, Xilinguole River Bend.

1998, June 24

2876	A811	50f multi (3-1)	.20
2877	A811	50f multi (3-2)	.20
2878	A811	150f multi (3-3)	.40
		Nos. 2876-2878 (3)	.80

Souvenir Sheet

2879 A811 800f multicolored 2.75

No. 2879 contains one 56x36mm stamp.

Paintings, by He Xiangning (1878-1972) — A812

Perf. 12½ Syncopated Type A (2 Sides)

1998, June 27 **Photo.**

2880	A812	50f Tiger (3-1)	.25
2881	A812	100f Lion, vert. (3-2)	.30
2882	A812	150f Plum blossom, vert. (3-3)	.45
		Nos. 2880-2882 (3)	1.00

Jingpo Lake — A813

Views of lake: No. 2883, Bridge, houses on cliff, boat. No. 2884, Islands, boats at shore. No. 2885, Boat, island. No. 2886, Waterfalls.

1998, Aug. 15 **Litho.** ***Perf. 12***

2883	A813	50f multi (4-1)	.20
2884	A813	50f multi (4-2)	.20
2885	A813	50f multi (4-3)	.20
2886	A813	50f multi (4-4)	.20
a.		Strip of 4, #2883-2886	.55

Würzburg Palace — A814

Puning Temple, Chengde — A815

1998, Aug. 20 **Litho.** ***Perf. 12***

2887	A814	50f multi (2-1)	.20	.20
2888	A815	540f multi (2-2)	1.25	1.25

See Germany Nos. 2012-2013.

Literature Type of 1987

Romance of the Three Kingdoms: No. 2889, Liu Bei finds a guardian for his heir at Baidi City. No. 2890, Zhuge Liang leads his army home, vert. 100f, Death of Zhuge Liang. 150f, Three Kingdoms united under the reign of Jin, vert.

800f, The Stratagem of Empty City.

1998, Aug. 26 **Photo.** ***Perf. 11½***

2889	A570	50f multi (4-1)	.20	.20
2890	A570	50f multi (4-2)	.20	.20
2891	A570	100f multi (4-3)	.25	.25
2892	A570	150f multi (4-4)	.45	.45
		Nos. 2889-2892 (4)	1.10	1.10

Souvenir Sheet

2893 A570 800f multicolored 4.00 3.50

No. 2893 contains one 158x37mm stamp.

Flood Victims Relief — A816

1998, Sept. 10 **Photo.** ***Perf. 13x13½***

2894 A816 50f + 50f label .30 .30

The Louvre, France A817

Design: 200f, Hall of Heavenly Peace, Imperial Palace, China.

1998, Sept. 12 **Photo.** ***Perf. 13x13½***

2895	A817	50f multi (2-1)	.20	.20
2896	A817	200f multi (2-2)	.50	.50

See France Nos. 2669-2670.

Cliff Paintings of Helan Mountains — A818

1998, Sept. 23 **Litho.** ***Perf. 12***

2897	A818	50f Human face (3-1)	.20	.20
2898	A818	100f Hunting (3-2)	.25	.25
2899	A818	150f Ox (3-3)	.35	.35
		Nos. 2897-2899 (3)	.80	.80

Longquan Pottery and Porcelain — A819

Designs: No. 2900, Vase with five spouts. No. 2901, Vase with phoenix ears. No. 2902, Double gourd vase. 150f, Ewer.

1998, Oct. 13

2900 A819 50f multi (4-1) .20 .20
2901 A819 50f multi (4-2) .20 .20
2902 A819 50f multi (4-3) .20 .20
2903 A819 150f multi (4-4) .40 .40
Nos. 2900-2903 (4) 1.00 1.00

Mausoleum of Yandi A820

Designs: 50f, Meridian Gate. 100f, Saluting Pavilion. 150f, Tomb.

1998, Oct. 28 Litho. *Perf. 12*

2904 A820 50f multi (3-1) .20 .20
2905 A820 100f multi (3-2) .25 .25
2906 A820 150f multi (3-3) .35 .35
a. Souvenir sheet, #2904-2906 1.75 1.50
Nos. 2904-2906 (3) .80 .80

Great Wall Type of 1995

10f, Jiumenko Pass. 300f, Niagziguan Pass. 420f, Pianguan Pass. 500f, Bianjing Tower.

1998, Nov. 1 Photo. *Perf. 13x12*

2907 A730 10f apple green & black .20 .20
2908 A730 300f olive & black .75 .75
2909 A730 420f brn org & blk 1.00 1.00
2910 A730 500f blue, black & brown 1.25 1.25
Nos. 2907-2910 (4) 3.20 3.20

Major Campaigns in Liberation War — A821

#2911, Making plans. #2912, Conquering Jinzhou. #2913, Battle in Huaihai. #2914, Liberating Beijing. 150f, People moving supplies.

1998, Nov. 14 Litho. *Perf. 12*

2911 A821 50f red & multi (5-1) .20 .20
2912 A821 50f gray & multi (5-2) .20 .20
2913 A821 50f org yel & multi (5-3) .20 .20
2914 A821 50f orange & multi (5-4) .20 .20
2915 A821 150f brn org & multi (5-5) .35 .35
Nos. 2911-2915 (5) 1.15 1.15

Liu Shaoqi (1898-1969), Communist Party Leader — A822

Various portraits.

1998, Nov. 24 Photo. *Perf. 11½*

2916 A822 50f multi (4-1), vert. .20 .20
2917 A822 50f multi (4-2), vert. .20 .20
2918 A822 50f shown (4-3) .20 .20
2919 A822 150f multi (4-4) .35 .35
Nos. 2916-2919 (4) .95 .95

Chillon Castle, Lake Geneva A823

Bridge 24, Slender West Lake, Yangzhou A824

1998, Nov. 25 *Perf. 11x11½*

2920 A823 50f multi (2-1) .20 .20
2921 A824 540f multi (2-2) 1.30 1.30

See Switzerland Nos. 1037-1039.

Lingqu Canal — A825

#2922, Dam. #2923, Bridge over canal, vert. 150f, Boat approaching lock, vert.

1998, Dec. 1 Litho. *Perf. 12*

2922 A825 50f multi (3-1) .20 .20
2923 A825 50f multi (3-2) .20 .20
2924 A825 150f multi (3-3) .35 .35
Nos. 2922-2924 (3) .75 .75

Buildings in Macao — A826

Designs: 50f, Building complex, Nanwan. 100f, Friendship Bridge. 150f, Macao Stadium. 200f, Macao Intl. Airport.

1998, Dec. 12 Litho. *Perf. 12*

2925 A826 50f multi (4-1) .20 .20
2926 A826 100f multi (4-2) .25 .25
2927 A826 150f multi (4-3) .35 .35
2928 A826 200f multi (4-4) .55 .55
Nos. 2925-2928 (4) 1.35 1.35

11th Communist Party Congress, 20th Anniv. — A827

1998, Dec. 18

2929 A827 50f Deng Xiaoping (2-1) .20 .20
2930 A827 150f Handbill, buildings (2-2) .35 .35

Fish of the Coral Reef A828

a, Pomacanthus imperator (8-1). b, Plectropomus maculatus (8-2). c, Chaetodon plebeius (8-3). d, Chaetodon chrysurus (8-4), vert. e, Heniochus acuminatus (8-5), vert. f, Lutjanus sebae (8-6). g, Balistoides conspicillum (8-7). h, Pygoplites diancanthus (8-8).

1998, Dec. 22 Photo. *Perf. 11½*

Sheet of 8

2931 A828 200f #a.-h. + label 5.00 5.00
i. As No. 2931, with margin ovptd. in gold *5.00 5.00*

UPU, 22nd Congress, Beijing '99 World Philatelic Exhibition.

Nos. 2931d-2931e are each 40x49mm.

No.2931i issued 7/15/00. No. 2931i inscribed in margin in gold "PJZ-12" , "1997-1999" and Chinese characters. Inscription for best philatelic item from 1997-99.

New Year 1999 (Year of the Rabbit)

A829 A830

Photo. & Engr.

1999, Jan. 5 *Perf. 11½*

2932 A829 50f Stylized rabbit (2-1) .20 .20
2933 A830 150f Symbol for rabbit (2-2) .35 .35

Great Wall Type of 1995

5f, Hushan Section. 20f, Shanhaiguan Pass. 40f, Jinshanling Section. 80f, Mutianyu Section. 270f, Pingxingguan Pass. 320f, Desheng Pass. 440f, Yanmen Pass. 540f, Zhenbei Tower.

1999, Mar. 1 Photo. *Perf. 13x12*

2934 A730 5f bl, blk & bl grn .20 .20
2935 A730 20f vio & blk .20 .20
2936 A730 40f pink & blk .20 .20
2937 A730 80f grn, blk & ol .20 .20
2938 A730 270f grn, blk & brn .65 .65
2939 A730 320f vio, blk & bwn .75 .75
2940 A730 440f red brn, blk & bwn 1.10 1.10
2941 A730 540f blue & black 1.25 1.25
Nos. 2934-2941 (8) 4.55 4.55

Stone Carvings of the Han Dynasty A831

#2942, Plowing fields with oxen. #2943, Group weaving. #2944, Three figures dancing in front of fire. #2945, Horses, carriage. #2946, Group in assassination attempt. #2947, Goddess Chang'e.

1999, Mar. 16 *Perf. 12*

2942 A831 50f dark green & blk .20 .20
2943 A831 50f brown & blk .20 .20
2944 A831 50f dark blue & blk .20 .20
2945 A831 150f dark brown & blk .35 .35
2946 A831 150f brown olive & blk .35 .35
2947 A831 150f dark purple & blk .35 .35
Nos. 2942-2947 (6) 1.65 1.65

A832

A833

Chinese Ceramics (Porcelain from the Jun Kiln): 80f, Halberd-shaped cup. 100f, Cup. 150f, Dual-handled stove. 200f, Dual-handled vase with base.

1999, Apr. 8 Photo. *Perf. 11½*

2948 A832 80f multi (4-1) .20 .20
2949 A832 100f multi (4-2) .25 .25
2950 A832 150f multi (4-3) .35 .35
2951 A832 200f multi (4-4) .50 .50
Nos. 2948-2951 (4) 1.30 1.30

Great Wall Type of 1995

Designs: 60f, Huanghua Tower. $10, Huama section. $20, Sanguankou Pass. $50 Jiayuguan Pass.

1999, May 1 Photo. *Perf. 13x12*

2952 A730 60f multicolored .20 .20

Size: 28x22mm

Perf. 11½

Photo. & Engr.

2953 A730 $10 multicolored 2.50 2.50
2954 A730 $20 multicolored 5.25 5.25
2955 A730 $50 multicolored 13.00 13.00
Nos. 2952-2955 (4) 20.95 20.95

1999, May 1 Litho. *Perf. 12*

2956 A833 80f shown (2-1) .20 .20
2957 A833 200f Tree (2-2) .50 .50

Kunming World Horticultural Fair.

Red Deer A834

1999, May 18 Litho. *Perf. 11x11½*

2958 A834 80f Bucks .20 .20
2959 A834 80f Does .20 .20
a. Pair, #2958-2959 .45 .45

See Russia No. 6514.

Beauty of Putuo Mountain — A835

1999, June 3 Litho. *Perf. 12*

2960 A835 30f Puji Temple (6-1) .20 .20
2961 A835 60f Nantian Gate, vert. (6-2) .20 .20
2962 A835 60f 100-step Sand (6-3) .20 .20
2963 A835 80f Pantuo Rock (6-4) .20 .20
2964 A835 80f Fanyin Cave, vert. (6-5) .20 .20
2965 A835 280f Fayu Temple (6-6) .65 .65
Nos. 2960-2965 (6) 1.65 1.65

Fang Zhimin (1899-1935), Revolutionary A836

1999, Aug. 21 Photo. *Perf. 11¼*

2966 A836 80f Close-up (2-1) .30 .30
2967 A836 80f Standing (2-2) .30 .30

Souvenir Sheet

China 1999 World Philatelic Exhibition — A837

Illustration reduced.

1999, Aug. 21 *Perf. 11½x11¼*

2968 A837 800f multicolored 3.25 3.25

Exists overprinted in upper corners in gold.

A838

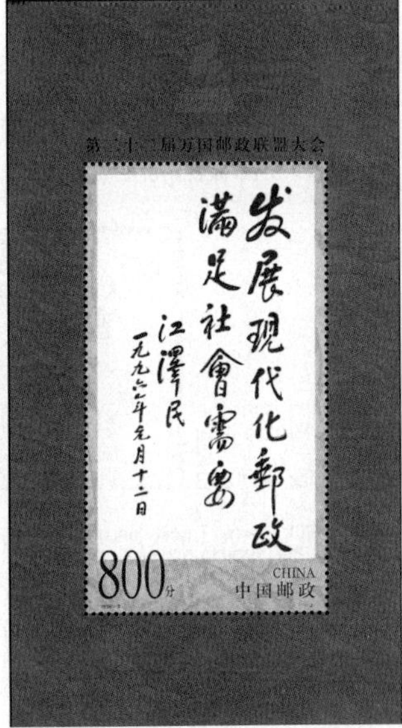

22nd UPU Congress — A839

Congress sites: 80f, 1st, Bern. 540f, 22nd, Beijing.
800f, Inscription by Pres. Jiang Zemin.
A839 illustration reduced.

1999, Aug. 23 **Litho.** *Perf. 12*

2969 A838 80f multi (2-1) .20 .20
2970 A838 540f multi (2-2) 1.25 1.25

Souvenir Sheet

Perf. 12¼

2971 A839 800f multicolored 2.75 2.75

UPU, 125th Anniv. — A840

Intl. Year of the Elderly — A841

1999, Sept. 7 **Litho.** *Perf. 12*

2972 A840 80f multicolored .20 .20

1999, Sept. 9

2973 A841 80f multicolored .20 .20

Chinese People's Political Consultative Conference, 50th Anniv. — A842

1999, Sept. 21

2974 A842 60f Building (2-1) .20 .20
2975 A842 80f Mao Zedong, vert. (2-2) .20 .20

Ethnic Groups in China — A843

Designs (stamp number following "56-" at LR): a, Han (1). b, Mongols (2). c, Hui (3). d, Tibetans (4). e, Uygurs (5) f, Miao (6). g, Yi (7). h, Zhuang (8). i, Bouyei (9). j, Koreans (10). k, Manchu (11). l, Dongs (12). m, Yao (13). n, Bai (14). o, Tujia (15). p, Hani (16). q, Kazak (17). r, Dai (18). s, Li (19). t, Lisu (20). u, Va (21). v, She (22). w, Gaoshan (23). x, Lahu (24). y, Shui (25). z, Dongxiang (26). aa, Naxi (27). ab, Jingpo (28). ac, Kirgiz (29). ad, Tu (30). ae, Daur (31). af, Mulam (32). ag, Qiang (33). ah, Blang (34). ai, Salas (35). aj, Maonan (36). ak, Gelao (37). al, Xibe (38). am, Achang (39). an, Pumi (40). ao, Tajiks (41). ap, Nu (42). aq, Uzbeks (43). ar, Russians (44). as, Ewenki (45). at, De'ang (46). au, Bonan (47). av, Yugur (48). aw, Jing (49). ax, Tartars (50). ay, Drung (51). az, Oroqen (52). ba, Hezhe (53). bb, Moiba (54). bc, Lhoba (55). bd, Jino (56).

1999, Oct. 7 **Photo.** *Perf. 13¼*

2976 A843 80f Sheet of 56, #a.-bd. 15.00 15.00

Mountains — A844

1999, Oct. 5 *Perf. 11½x11¼*

2977 A844 80f Lushan (2-1) .20 .20
2978 A844 80f Kuryongyon (2-2) .20 .20

Project Hope, 10th Anniv. — A845

Li Lisan (1899-1967), Minister of Labor — A847

Scientific and Technological Achievements — A846

1999, Oct. 30 **Photo.** *Perf. 11½*

2979 A845 80f multi .20 .20

1999, Nov. 1 **Litho.** *Perf. 12*

Designs: No. 2980, Cambrian era fossil. No. 2981, Underwater robot. No. 2982, Best result of Goldbach conjecture, vert. No. 2983, 2.16m telescope, vert.

2980 A846 80f multi (4-1) .20 .20
2981 A846 80f multi (4-2) .20 .20
a. Pair, #2980-2981 .45 .45
2982 A846 80f multi (4-3) .20 .20
2983 A846 80f multi (4-4) .20 .20
a. Pair, #2982-2983 .45 .45
Nos. 2980-2983 (4) .80 .80

1999, Nov. 19 **Photo.** *Perf. 11½*

2984 A847 80f As young man (2-1) .20 .20
2985 A847 80f Wearing glasses (2-2) .20 .20

Return of Macao to China — A848

Designs: 80f, Sino-Portuguese declaration, flower. 150f, Basic Law of Macao Special Administrative Region, Great Wall.
800f, $50, Deng Xiaoping.

1999-2000 **Photo.** *Perf. 11¾x11½*

2986 A848 80f multi (2-1) .20 .20
2987 A848 150f multi (2-2) .35 .35

Souvenir Sheets

Perf. 13

2988 A848 800f multi 3.50 3.50

Litho. (stamp) & Embossed (margin)

Perf. 12

2989 A848 $50 multi *20.00 20.00*
a. Overprinted in margin *35.00 35.00*

No. 2988 contains one 60x50mm stamp with star-shaped perforations in the corners.
Overprint in margin on No. 2989a is Chinese inscription, "2000-1" and "(2-2)J."
Issued: No. 2989a, 1/1/00; others, 12/20/99.

Nie Rongzhen (1899-1992), Military Leader — A849

New Year 2000 (Year of the Dragon) — A851

Millennium — A850

1999, Dec. 29 **Litho.** *Perf. 12*

2990 A849 80f In uniform (2-1) .20 .20
2991 A849 80f Seated (2-2) .20 .20

1999, Dec. 31 **Litho.** *Perf. 12*

No. 2992, Sun Yat-sen, #590. No. 2993, #2214. No. 2994, #2339. No. 2995, #2601. No. 2996, Mao Zedong, #456. 200f, #2248. 260f, #2730. 280f, Deng Xiaoping, #2774C.

2992 A850 60f multi (8-1) .20 .20
2993 A850 60f multi (8-2) .20 .20
2994 A850 80f multi (8-3) .20 .20
2995 A850 80f multi (8-4) .20 .20
2996 A850 80f multi (8-5) .20 .20
2997 A850 200f multi (8-6) .45 .45
2998 A850 260f multi (8-7) .60 .60
2999 A850 280f multi (8-8) .65 .65
Nos. 2992-2999 (8) 2.70 2.70

Photo. & Engr.

2000, Jan. 5 *Perf. 11½x11¾*

3000 A851 80f Dragon (2-1) .20 .20
3001 A851 $2.80 Rising sun (2-2) .60 .60

A852

Spring Festival: No. 3002, Welcoming the Spring Festival. No. 3003, Bidding farewell to outgoing year. $2.80, Offering sacrifices to god of land.
$8, Family reunion, horiz.

2000, Jan. 29 **Photo.** *Perf. 11¼*

3002 A852 80f multi (3-1) .20 .20
3003 A852 80f multi (3-2) .20 .20
3004 A852 $2.80 multi (3-3) .65 .65
Nos. 3002-3004 (3) 1.05 1.05

Souvenir Sheet

Perf. 11¼x11

3005 A852 $8 multi *5.00 5.00*
a. Ovptd. in sheet margin *7.50 7.50*

No. 3005 contains one 90x60mm stamp.
No. 3005a contains gold Chinese inscription for New Century Philatelic Exhibition, "2000," and "PJZ-11" in sheet margin. Issued: 4/28.

A853

2000, Feb. 25 **Photo.** *Perf. 13¼x13*

Wildlife.

3006 Sheet of 10 + 2 labels *6.00 6.00*
a. A853 30f Nipponia nippon .20 .20
b. A853 60f Teinopalpus aureus .20 .20
c. A853 80f Ailuropoda melanoleuca .20 .20
d. A853 $1 Crossoptilon manichuricum .20 .20
e. A853 $1.50 Acipenser sinensis .30 .30
f. A853 $2 Rhinopithecus roxellanae .40 .40
g. A853 $2.60 Lipotes vexillifer .55 .55
h. A853 $2.80 Grus japonensis .60 .60
i. A853 $3.70 Panthera tigris .80 .80
j. A853 $5.40 Alligator sinensis 1.25 1.25

Cultural Relics — A854

Designs; 60f, Neolithic Age jade dragon. No. 3008, Dragon-shaped ornament. No. 3009, Carved tile with dragon. No. 3010, Copper mirror with dragon. No. 3011, Bronze dragon. $2.80, Dragon on sandalwood throne.

2000, Mar. 7 Litho. *Perf. 12*

3007 A854 60f multi (6-1) .20 .20
3008 A854 80f multi (6-2) .20 .20
3009 A854 80f multi (6-3) .20 .20
3010 A854 80f multi (6-4) .20 .20
3011 A854 80f multi (6-5) .20 .20
3012 A854 $2.80 multi (6-6) .60 .60
Nos. 3007-3012 (6) 1.60 1.60

Yangtze River Highway Bridges — A855

2000, Mar. 26 Litho. *Perf. 12*

3013 A855 80f Wanxian (4-1) .20 .20
3014 A855 80f Huangshi (4-2) .20 .20
3015 A855 80f Tongling (4-3) .20 .20
3016 A855 $2.80 Jiangyin (4-4) .60 .60
Nos. 3013-3016 (4) 1.20 1.20

Landscapes in Dali — A856

Designs: No. 3017, Cangshan Mountain and Erhai Lake. No. 3018, Pagodas at Chongsheng Temple. No. 3019, Jizu Mountain. $2.80, Shibao Mountain.

Perf. 11¾x11½

2000, Apr. 19 Photo.

3017 A856 80f multi (4-1) .20 .20
3018 A856 80f multi (4-2) .20 .20
3019 A856 80f multi (4-3) .20 .20
3020 A856 $2.80 multi (4-4) .65 .65
Nos. 3017-3020 (4) 1.25 1.25

Legend of Mulan — A857

Mulan: No. 3021, Weaving cloth. No. 3022, Joining army. No. 3023, On expedition. No. 3024, Returning home.

2000, Apr. 30 Litho. *Perf. 12*

3021 A857 80f multi (4-1) .20 .20
3022 A857 80f multi (4-2) .20 .20
3023 A857 80f multi (4-3) .20 .20
3024 A857 80f multi (4-4) .20 .20
a. Strip, #3021-3024 *2.00 2.00*

Taer Lamasery A858

#3025, Good Luck Treasure Pagoda. #3026, Big Golden Tile Palace. #3027, Big Scripture Hall. $2.80, Banqen residence.

2000, May 5

3025 A858 80f multi (4-1) .20 .20
3026 A858 80f multi (4-2) .20 .20
3027 A858 80f multi (4-3) .20 .20
3028 A858 $2.80 multi (4-4) .65 .65
Nos. 3025-3028 (4) 1.25 1.25

Cai Chang and Li Fuchun A859

2000, May 22

3029 A859 80f multi .20 .20

Stampin' the Future Children's Stamp Design Contest Winners — A860

Various children's drawings: #3030, 30f, (8-1). #3031, 60f, (8-2). #3032, 60f, (8-3). #3033, 80f, (8-4). #3034, 80f, (8-5). #3035, 80f, (8-6). $2.60, (8-7). $2.80, (8-8).

Perf. 11½x11¼

2000, June 1 Photo.

3030-3037 A860 Set of 8 2.25 2.25

Chen Yun (1905-95), Statesman A861

#3038, 80f, As a young man (4-1). #3039, 80f, In uniform, vert. (4-2). #3040, 80f, In black jacket, vert. (4-3). $2.80, As old man (4-4).

Perf. 13x13¼, 13¼x13

2000, June 13

3038-3041 A861 Set of 4 1.25 1.25

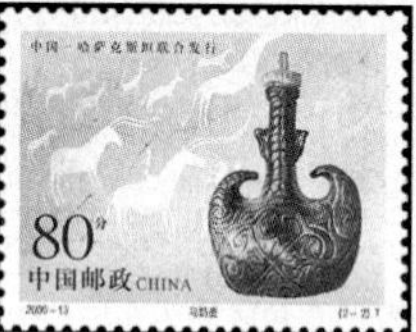

Pots A862

Designs: No. 3042, 80f, Wine vessel (2-1). No. 3042, 80f, Horse milk pot (2-2).

2000, June 28 Litho. *Perf. 12*

3042-3043 A862 Set of 2 .40 .40

Laoshan Mountain — A863

#3044, 80f, Huge Peak (4-1). #3045, 80f, Yangkou Bay (4-2). #3046, 80f, Beijiu Lake (4-3). $2.80, Taiqing Palace (4-4).

Perf. 11½x11¼

2000, July 15 Photo.

3044-3047 A863 Set of 4 1.25 1.25
3047a Souvenir sheet, #3044-3047 *5.00 5.00*

Souvenir Sheet

All-China Philatelic Federation, Fifth Congress — A864

Illustration reduced.

2000, July 18 Litho. *Perf. 12*

3048 A864 $8 multi *5.00 5.00*
a. Margin ovptd. in gold *4.50* —

No. 3048a issued 9/21/01. It is inscribed in margin in gold "PJZ-13," "2001," with Chinese characters and Nanjing 2001 Philatelic Exhibition mascot.

Small Carp Leap Through Dragon Gate Legend — A865

No. 3049: a, Grandma Carp tells a story (5-1). b, Small Carp look for Dragon Gate (5-2). c, Help from Uncle Crab (5-3). d, Small Carp leap through Dragon Gate (5-4). e, Aunt Swallow passes on a letter (5-5).

2000, Aug. 8 Photo. *Perf. 11½*

3049 A865 80f Horiz. strip of 5, #a-e *2.00 2.00*
f. Booklet pane, #3049 + 2 labels, perf. 12 *10.00*
Booklet, #3049f 1.00

Shenzhen Special Eonomic Zone — A866

No. 3050: a, 80f, Financial Center district (5-1). b, 80f, China Intl. Exhibition Center (5-2). c, 80f, Yantian Harbor area (5-3). d, 80f, Shenzhen Bay tourist area (5-4). e, $2.80, Shekou industrial district (5-5).

2000, Aug. 26 Litho. *Perf. 12*

3050 A866 Horiz. strip of 5, #a-e 1.50 1.50

2000 Summer Olympics, Sydney — A867

Illustration reduced.

2000, Sept. 15 Photo. *Perf. 13¼x13*

3051 A867 $8 multi *3.75 3.75*
a. Sheet of 2 *20.00 20.00*

No. 3051a issued 10/31/00.

Beaches — A868

a, Coconuts Bay, PRC (2-1). b, Varadero Beach, Cuba (2-2).

2000, Sept. 26 Litho. *Perf. 12*

3052 A868 Pair .40 .40
a.-b. 80f Any single .20 .20

See Cuba Nos. 4108-4109.

Masks and Puppets A869

No. 3053, Tan background (2-1). No. 3054, Violet blue background (2-2).

2000, Oct. 9 Photo. *Perf. 13x13½*

3053-3054 A869 80f Set of 2 .40 .40

See Brazil Nos. 2767-2768.

Relics from the Tomb of Prince Jing of Zhongshan — A870

#3055, 80f, Eternal Fidelity palace lamp (4-1). #3056, 80f, Bronze pot (4-2). #3057, 80f, Boshan incense burner (4-3). $2.80, Cup (4-4).

2000, Oct. 20 *Perf. 13½x13¼*

3055-3058 A870 Set of 4 1.25 1.25

Ancient Thinkers — A871

#3059, 60f, Confucius (6-1). #3060, 80f, Mencius (6-2). #3061, 80f, Lao Zi (6-3). #3062, 80f, Zhuang Zi (6-4). #3063, 80f, Mo Zi (6-5). $2.80, Xun Zi (6-6).

Photo. & Engr.

2000, Nov. 11 *Perf. 11¼x11*

3059-3064 A871 Set of 6 1.60 1.60

Test of Shenzhou Spacecraft, 1st Anniv. — A872

No. 3065: a, Launch (2-1). b, In orbit (2-2). Illustration reduced.

2000, Nov. 20 Photo. *Perf. 11½*

3065 A872 Pair *1.75 1.75*
a.-b. 80f Any single .20 .20
c. Sheet, 6 #3065 *15.00 15.00*

World Meteorological Organization, 50th Anniv. — A873

Designs: No. 3066, 80f, Weather satellite (4-1). No. 3067, 80f, Weather measuring equipment on Qinghai-Tibetan Plateau (4-2). No. 3068, 80f, Weather-predicting computer (4-3). $2.80, Airplane for cloud seeding (4-4).

2000, Nov. 22 Litho. *Perf. 12*
3066-3069 A873 Set of 4 1.25 1.25

Flowers — A874

#3070, 80f, Scarlet kaffir lily (4-1). #3071, 80f, Noble clivia (4-2). #3072, 80f, Golden striated lily (4-3). $2.80, White kaffir lily (4-4).

Perf. 11¼x11½

2000, Dec. 12 Photo.
3070-3073 A874 Set of 4 1.25 1.25
3073a Souv. sheet, #3070-3073 *6.00 6.00*

Ancient Bells — A875

#3074, 80f, Jingshu bell (4-1). #3075, 80f, Su chime bell (4-2). #3076, 80f, Jingyun bell (4-3). $2.80, Qianlong bell (4-4).

2000, Dec. 31 *Perf. 11¼x11½*
3074-3077 A875 Set of 4 1.25 1.25

Advent of New Millennium A876

Designs: 60f, Sun, moon, date, time, building (5-1). No. 3079, 80f, Dove, Earth (5-2). No. 3080, 80f, Map, leaf, infant's hands (5-3). No. 3081, 80f, Circuitboard, head, Earth, horiz. (5-4). $2.80, Moon, stars, sundial (5-5).

2001, Jan. 1 Litho. *Perf. 12*
3078-3082 A876 Set of 5 1.40 1.40

New Year 2001 (Year of the Snake) — A877

Snake and: 80f, Flower (2-1). $2.80, Chinese character for snake (2-2).

Photo. & Engr.

2001, Jan. 5 *Perf. 11½x11¾*
3083 A877 80f multi .20 .20
a. Sheet of 6 *6.00 6.00*
3084 A877 $2.80 multi .70 .70
a. Sheet of 6 *20.00 20.00*

Clown Roles in Peking Opera — A878

Designs: No. 3085, 80f, Tang Qin (6-1). No. 3086, 80f, Lin Lihua (6-2). No. 3087, 80f, Gao Lishi (6-3). No. 3088, 80f, Jiang Gan (6-4). No. 3089, 80f, Yang Xiangwu (6-5). $2.80, Shi Qian (6-6).

2001, Feb. 15 Photo. *Perf. 11½x11*
3085-3090 A878 Set of 6 1.60 1.60

Wildlife — A879

2001, Mar. 16 *Perf. 13¼x13*
3091 Sheet of 10 + 2 labels *9.00 9.00*
a. A879 30f Budorcas taxicolor *.20 .20*
b. A879 60f Psephurus gladius *.40 .40*
c. A879 60f Elaphurus davidianus *.40 .40*
d. A879 80f Acipenser dabryanus *.50 .50*
e. A879 80f Capra ibex *.50 .50*
f. A879 80f Haliaeetus pelagicus *.50 .50*
g. A879 80f Camelus bactrianus *.50 .50*
h. A879 $1 Uncia uncia *.65 .65*
i. A879 $2.60 Martes zibellina *1.75 1.75*
j. A879 $5.40 Saiga tatarica *3.50 3.50*

Ancient Towns — A880

Designs: No. 3092, 80f, Zhouzhuang, Kunshan (6-1). No. 3093, 80f, Tongli, Wujiang (6-2). No. 3094, 80f, Wuzhen, Tongxiang (6-3). No. 3095, 80f, Nanxun, Huzhou (6-4). No. 3096, 80f, Luzhi, Wuxian (6-5). $2.80, Xitang, Jiashan (6-6).

2001, Apr. 7 Photo. *Perf. 11½x11¼*
3092-3097 A880 Set of 6 2.10 2.10
3097a Booklet pane, #3092-3097 + 6 labels *8.75*
Booklet, #3097a *8.75*

Strange Stories From a Chinese Studio, by Pu Songling A881

Designs: 60f, Ying Ning (4-1). No. 3099, 80f, A Bao (4-2). No. 3100, 80f, Mask of Evildoer (4-3). $2.80, Stealing Peach (4-4). $8, Taoist Priest from Laoshan.

2001, Apr. 21 *Perf. 11½*
3098-3101 A881 Set of 4 1.60 1.60

Souvenir Sheet

Perf. 13½x13

3102 A881 $8 multi *10.00 10.00*

No. 3102 contains one 90x60mm stamp.

Yongle Temple Murals A882

No. 3103: a, Lady Queen Mother (4-1). b, Jade Lady Presenting Treasure (4-2). c, Celestial Worthy of the East (4-3). d, Venus and Mercury (4-4).

2001, May 5 Litho. *Perf. 12*
3103 Horiz. strip of 4 1.60 1.60
a. A882 60f multi .20 .20
b.-c. A882 80f Any single .25 .25
d. A882 $2.80 multi .90 .90

Mount Wudang — A883

Designs: 60f, Nanyan Hall (3-1). No. 3105, 80f, Zixiao Temple (3-2). No. 3106, 80f, Taizi Slope (3-3).
$8, Golden Crown in spring.

Perf. 11¼x11½

2001, May 26 Photo.
3104-3106 A883 Set of 3 .65 .65

Souvenir Sheet

Perf. 12¼x12½

3107 A883 $8 multi + label *7.00 7.00*

No. 3107 contains one 47x71mm stamp.

Ancient Chinese Receptacles A884

Designs: No. 3108, 80f, Earthenware vase. No. 3109, 80f, Porcelain coffee pot.

2001, June 12 *Perf. 11¼x11½*
3108-3109 A884 Set of 2 .40 .40

See Belgium Nos. 1858-1859.

Dragon Boat Festival A885

Designs: No. 3110, Dragon boat race (3-1). No. 3111, Making Zongzi (3-2). $2.80, Expelling five poisons (3-3).

2001, June 25 Photo. *Perf. 13x13½*
3110 A885 80f multi .20 .20
a. Sheet of 9 *8.00*
3111 A885 80f multi .20 .20
a. Sheet of 9 *8.00*
3112 A885 $2.80 multi .70 .70
a. Sheet of 9 *30.00*
Nos. 3110-3112 (3) 1.10 1.10

Nos. 3110-3112 each issued in sheets of 40.

Early Leaders of the Communist Party — A886

Designs: No. 3113, 80f, Wang Jinmei (5-1). No. 3114, 80f, Zhao Shiyan (5-2). No. 3115, 80f, Deng Enming (5-3). No. 3116, 80f, Cai Hesen (5-4). No. 3117, 80f, He Shuheng (5-5).

2001, June 28 *Perf. 11¼x11*
3113-3117 A886 Set of 5 1.00 1.00

Communist Party, 80th Anniv. A887

2001, July 1 Photo. *Perf. 13x13¼*
3118 A887 80f multi .25 .25
a. Sheet of 8 *14.00*

No. 3118 issued in sheets of 40.

Emblem of 2008 Summer Olympics, Beijing — A888

2001, July 14 *Perf. 13x13¼*
3119 A888 80f multi + label .25 .25
a. Sheet of 36 + 39 labels *40.00* —

No. 3119 printed in sheets of 12 stamp + label pairs with one large central label. See Hong Kong No. 940, Macao No. 1067.

No. 3119a contains 12 each of No. 3119, Hong Kong No. 940 (with different adjacent label), and Macao No. 1067 (with different adjacent label).

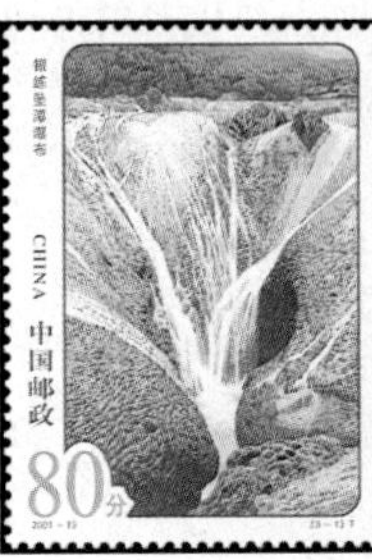

Waterfalls A889

Designs: No. 3120, 80f, Yinlianzhuitan (3-1). No. 3121, 80f, Doupotang, horiz. (3-2). No. 3122, 80f, Dishuitan (3-3).
$8, Huangguoshu.

Perf. 12¼x12, 12x12¼

2001, July 22 Litho.
3120-3122 A889 Set of 3 .60 .60

Souvenir Sheet

Perf. 12

3123 A889 $8 multi *5.00 5.00*

No. 3123 contains one 40x60mm stamp.

Beidaihe Beach — A890

Designs: 60f, Pigeon Nest (4-1). No. 3125, 80f, Zhonghai Beach (4-2). No. 3126, 80f, Lianfeng Hill (4-3). $2.80, Tiger Stone (4-4).

2001, Aug. 5 **Litho.** ***Perf. 12***
3124-3127 A890 Set of 4 1.40 1.40

21st Universiade A891

Emblem, "2001" and: 60f, Concentric circles (3-1). 80f, Runners (3-2). $2.80, Hemispheres of globe (3-3).

2001, Aug. 22 **Litho.**
3128-3130 A891 Set of 3 1.10 1.10
3129a Sheet of 20 +20 labels *20.00*

No. 3129a exists with different margin designs.

Sheets of four No. 3129 plus four labels were not placed on sale but were included with 2001 year sets. Uncut sheets containing two of these sheets also exist.

Datong River Diversion Project — A892

Designs: No. 3131, 80f, Sluice gates (4-1). No. 3132, 80f, Xianming Gorge water pipeline (4-2). No. 3133, 80f, Tunnel (4-3). $2.80, Zhuanglang River Aqueduct (4-4).

2001, Aug. 26
3131-3134 A892 Set of 4 1.40 1.40

Wuhu Bridge — A893

View from: 80f, Shore (2-1). $2.80, Roadway (2-2).

Photo. & Engr.

2001, Sept. 20 ***Perf. 11½x11¼***
3135-3136 A893 Set of 2 1.00 1.00

Orchids A894

Designs: No. 3137, 80f, Paphiopedilum malipoense (4-1). No. 3138, 80f, Paphiopedilum dianthum (4-2). No. 3139, 80f, Paphiopedilum markianum (4-3). $2.80, Paphiopedilum appletonianum (4-4).

2001, Sept. 28 **Photo.** ***Perf. 12½***
3137-3140 A894 Set of 4 1.40 1.40
3140a Souvenir sheet, #3137-3140 *5.75*

Ancient Gold Masks — A895

Designs: No. 3141, 80f, Mask of San Xing Dui (2-1). No. 3142, 80f, Funerary mask of King Tutankhamun, Egypt (2-2).

2001, Oct. 12 ***Perf. 11¾x11½***
3141-3142 A895 Set of 2 .60 .60

See Egypt Nos. 1807-1808.

People's Republic of China as 2001 Asia-Pacific Economic Cooperation Head A896

2001, Oct. 20 **Litho.** ***Perf. 12***
3143 A896 80f multi .25 .25

Souvenir Sheet

Ertan Hydroelectric Plant — A897

2001, Oct. 20 **Litho.** ***Perf. 12¼***
3144 A897 $8 multi *3.00 3.00*

Horses, Zhaoling Mausoleum A898

Horse: a, Facing right, galloping (6-1). b, Facing right, galloping, diff. (6-2). c, Facing right, walking (6-3). d, With attendant (6-4). e, Facing left, walking (6-5). f, Facing left, galloping (6-6).

2001, Oct. 28 **Photo.** ***Perf. 12***

Fawn Background

3145 Horiz. strip of 6 1.75 1.75
a. A898 60f multi .20 .20
b.-e. A898 80f multi .20 .20
f. A898 $2.80 multi .75 .75
g. Sheet, 2 each #3145a-3145c, white background, photo. & embossed *16.00* —
h. Sheet, 2 each #3145d-3145f, white background, photo. & embossed *16.00* —

Sailing Ships — A899

No. 3146: a, Chinese junk, 13th cent. (2-1). b, Portuguese caravel, 15th cent. (2-2).
Illustration reduced.

2001, Nov. 8 ***Perf. 13x13¼***
3146 A899 80f Horiz. pair, #a-b .45 .45

See Portugal No. 2454.

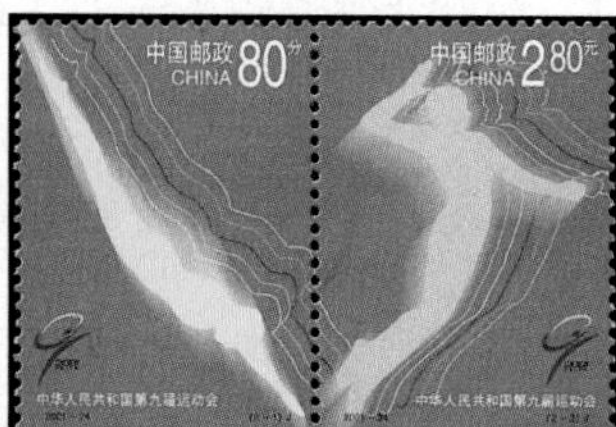

9th Natl. Games — A900

No. 3147: a, 80f, Diving (2-1). b, $2.80, Volleyball (2-2).

2001, Nov. 11 **Litho.** ***Perf. 12***
3147 A900 Horiz. pair, #a-b 1.00 1.00
c. Souvenir sheet, #3147 *3.75 3.75*

Liupan Shan Mountains — A901

Various landscapes: No. 3148, 80f (4-1). No. 3149, 80f (4-2). No. 3150, 80f (4-3). $2.80, (4-4).

Photo. & Engr.

2001, Nov. 24 ***Perf. 11¼x11½***
3148-3151 A901 Set of 4 1.60 1.60

Xiu Xian and the White Snake — A902

Designs: No. 3152, Women, umbrella (4-1). No. 3153, Three men (4-2). No. 3154, Man with sword, man with bowl (4-3). $2.80, Women on bridge (4-4).

Perf. 11½, 11½x11 (#3153-3154)

2001, Dec. 5 **Photo.**
3152 A902 80f multi .20 .20
a. Booklet pane of 1 *1.00* —
3153 A902 80f multi .20 .20
a. Booklet pane of 1 *1.00* —
3154 A902 80f multi .20 .20
a. Booklet pane of 1 *1.00* —
3155 A902 $2.80 multi .75 .75
a. Booklet pane of 1 *3.75* —
Booklet, #3152a-3155a *6.75*
Nos. 3152-3155 (4) 1.35 1.35

Admission to World Trade Organization A903

2001, Dec. 11 **Photo.** ***Perf. 13¼x13***
3156 A903 80f multi 1.25 1.25

Koxinga's Recovery of Taiwan from the Dutch, 340th Anniv. — A904

Koxinga and: No. 3157, 80f, Warriors, ships (3-1). No. 3158, 80f, Warriors, horse (3-2). $2.80, People, trees (3-3).

Perf. 11½x11¼

2001, Dec. 13 **Photo.**
3157-3159 A904 Set of 3 1.50 1.50

Souvenir Sheet

Qinhai - Tibet Railway — A905

2001, Dec. 29 ***Perf. 13¼***
3160 A905 $8 multi *5.00 5.00*

New Year 2002 (Year of the Horse) — A906

Designs: 80f, Ceramic horse (2-1). $2.80, Flowers, Chinese symbol for horse (2-2).

Photo. & Engr.

2002, Jan. 5 ***Perf. 11½***
3161-3162 A906 Set of 2 .90 .90

Nos. 3161-3162 each exist in a miniature sheet of six.

Art of Badashanren (1626-1705) A907

Designs: 60f, Two Eagles (6-1). No. 3164, 80f, Pine Tree (6-2). No. 3165, 80f, Lotus Flowers (6-3). No. 3166, 80f, Chysanthemum in Vase (6-4). $2.60, Two Magpies on a Rock (6-5). $2.80, Landscape After Dong Yuan (6-6).

Perf. 11¼x11½

2002, Jan. 20 **Photo.**
3163-3168 A907 Set of 6 2.10 2.10

Environmental Protection — A908

Designs: 5f, Keeping birth rate low. 10f, Forest conservation. 30f, Conservation of mineral resources. 60f, Preventing air pollution. 80f, Conservation of water. $1.50, Conservation of ocean resources.

Perf. 12¾x13¼ Syncopated

2002 **Photo.**
3169 A908 5f multi .20 .20
3170 A908 10f multi .20 .20
3171 A908 30f multi .20 .20
3172 A908 60f multi .20 .20
3173 A908 80f multi .20 .20
3174 A908 $1.50 multi .35 .35
Nos. 3169-3174 (6) 1.35 1.35

Issued: 10f, 60f, 2/1; others, 4/1.

Birds — A909

Designs: 80f, Yellow-bellied tragopan. $1, Biddulph's ground jay. $2, Taiwan blue magpies. $4.20, Alashan redstart. $5.40, Kozlov's bunting.

2002 ***Perf. 13¼***

3175 A909 80f multi .20 .20
a. Booklet pane of 10 +2 labels 2.00
Booklet, #3175a 2.00
3176 A909 $1 multi .25 .25
3177 A909 $2 multi .50 .50
3178 A909 $4.20 multi 1.00 1.00
3179 A909 $5.40 multi 1.25 1.25
Nos. 3175-3179 (5) 3.20 3.20

Issued: 80f, $1, $2, 2/1; Nos. 3178, 3179, 4/1. No. 3175a, 12/7.

Flowers — A910

No. 3180: a, Camellia nitidissima (2-1). b, Couroupita guianensis (2-2).

2002, Feb. 5 ***Perf. 13¼x13***

3180 A910 80f Horiz. pair, #a-b .40 .40

See Malaysia Nos. 861-864.

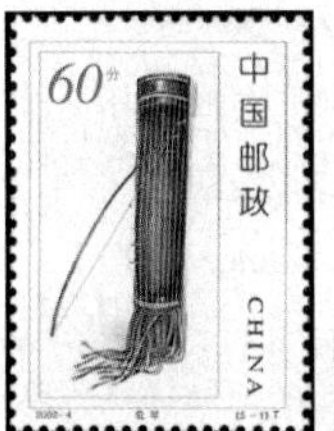

Musical Instruments A911

Designs: 60f, Yaqin (5-1). No. 3182, 80f, Erhu (5-2). No. 3183, 80f, Banhu (5-3). No. 3184, 80f, Satar (5-4). $2.80, Matouqin (5-5).

2002, Feb. 23 **Litho.** ***Perf. 12***

3181-3185 A911 Set of 5 1.40 1.40

Souvenir Sheet

The Royal Carriage, by Yan Liben — A912

2002, Mar. 16 **Photo.**

3186 A912 $8 multi 1.90 1.90

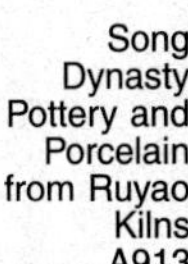

Song Dynasty Pottery and Porcelain from Ruyao Kilns A913

Designs: 60f, Wine vessel (4-1). No. 3188, 80f, Three-legged basin (4-2). No. 3189, 80f, Bowl (4-3). $2.80, Dish (4-4).

2002, Mar. 30 **Litho.**

3187-3190 A913 Set of 4 1.25 1.25

Strange Stories from a Chinese Studio, by Pu Songling A914

No. 3191: a, 60f, Xi Fangping (4-1). b, 80f, Pianpian (4-2).
No. 3192: a, 80f, Tian Qilang (4-3). b, $2.80, Bai Qiulian (4-4).

2002, Apr. 21 **Photo.** ***Perf. 11½***

3191 A914 Vert. pair, #a-b .35 .35
3192 A914 Horiz. pair, #a-b .90 .90

Qianshan Mountain — A915

No. 3193: a, Wuliang Taoist Temple (4-1). b, Maitreya Peak (4-2). c, Longquan Temple (4-3). d, Terrace of Immortals (4-4).

2002, Apr. 26 ***Perf. 12***

3193 Horiz. strip of 4 1.25 1.25
a.-c. A915 80f Any single .20 .20
d. A915 $2.80 multi .65 .65

Ancient City of Lijiang — A916

Designs: No. 3194, 80f, Sifang Street (3-1). No. 3195, 80f, Stream, vert. (3-2). $2.80, House of Naxi people (3-3).

2002, May 1 ***Perf. 11½***

3194-3196 A916 Set of 3 1.10 1.10
a. Souvenir sheet, #3194-3196 1.60 1.60

No. 3196a sold for $6.60.

Ruyi (Good Luck Symbol) — A917

2002, May 10 **Litho.** ***Perf. 12***

3197 A917 80f multi + label .20 .20

Exists in miniature sheet of 4 + 4 vert. labels and in sheet of 16 + 16 horiz. labels.

2002 World Cup Soccer Championships, Japan and Korea — A918

No. 3198: a, 80f, Player (2-1). b, $2.80, Players (2-2).
Illustration reduced.
A souvenir sheet containing People's Republic of China No. 3198, Hong Kong Nos. 978a-978b and Macao 1091a-1091b exists, and sold for premium over face value.

2002, May 16 **Photo.** ***Perf. 12¼***

3198 A918 Horiz. pair, #a-b .65 .65

A souvenir sheet containing No. 3198, Hong Kong Nos. 978a-978b and Macao Nos. 1091a-1091b exists.

Lighthouses A919

Nautical charts and: No. 3199, 80f, Maota Pagoda Lighthouse (5-1). No. 3200, 80f, Jiangxin Pagoda Lighthouses (5-2). No. 3201, 80f, Huaniaoshan Lighthouse (5-3). No. 3202, 80f, Laotieshan Lighthouse (5-4). No. 3203, 80f, Lin'gao Lighthouse (5-5).

Photo. & Engr.

2002, May 18 ***Perf. 11½x11***

3199-3203 A919 Set of 5 1.00 1.00

Yellow River Dams A920

Designs: No. 3204, 80f, Lijia Gorge (4-1). No. 3205, 80f, Liujia Gorge (4-2). No. 3206, 80f, Qingtong Gorge (4-3). No. 3207, 80f, Sanmen Gorge (4-4).
$8, Xiaolangdi, vert.

2002, June 8 **Photo.** ***Perf. 12***

3204-3207 A920 Set of 4 .80 .80

Souvenir Sheet

Perf. 13x13¼

3208 A920 $8 multi 1.90 1.90

No. 3208 contains one 40x60mm stamp.

Dazu Stone Carvings — A921

Designs: No. 3209, 80f, Avalokitesvara of the Sun and Moon, North Mountain (4-1). No. 3210, 80f, Samantabhadra, North Mountain (4-2). No. 3211, 80f, Three Avatamasaka Sages, Holy Summit Mountain (4-3). No. 3212, 80f, Statue in Cave of the Three Emperors, Stone Gate Mountain (4-4).
$8, Avalokitesvara of a Thousand Hands, Holy Summit Mountain.

2002, June 18 **Litho.** ***Perf. 12***

3209-3212 A921 Set of 4 .80 .80

Souvenir Sheet

Photo.

Perf. 13x13¼

3213 A921 $8 multi 1.90 1.90

No. 3213 contains one 40x60mm stamp.

Desert Flowers A922

No. 3214: a, Ammopiptanthus mongolicus (4-1). b, Calligonum rubicandum (4-2). c, Hedysarum scoparium (4-3). d, Tamarix leptostachys (4-4).

2002, June 29 **Photo.** ***Perf. 13x13¼***

3214 Vert. strip of 4 1.25 1.25
a.-c. A922 80f Any single .20 .20
d. A922 $2 multi .50 .50

Antarctic Scenes A923

Designs: No. 3215, 80f, Penguins (3-1). No. 3216, 80f, Aurora Australis (3-2). $2, Bird, Grove Mountains (3-3).

2002, July 15 **Litho.** ***Perf. 12***

3215-3217 A923 Set of 3 .90 .90

Qinghai Lake — A924

Designs: No. 3218, 80f, Lake shore (3-1). No. 3219, 80f, Birds on rock (3-2). $2.80, View of lake and birds (3-3).

2002, July 20

3218-3220 A924 Set of 3 1.10 1.10

Early Communist Party Leaders — A925

Designs: No. 3221, 80f, Huang Gonglue (1898-1931) (5-1). No. 3222, 80f, Xu Jishen (1901-31) (5-2). No. 3223, 80f, Cai Shengxi (1906-32) (5-3). No. 3224, 80f, Wei Baqun (1894-1932) (5-4). No. 3225, 80f, Liu Zhidan (1903-36) (5-5).

2002, Aug. 1 **Photo.**

3221-3225 A925 Set of 5 1.00 1.00

Scientists of Ancient China — A926

Designs: No. 3226, 80f, Bian Que (4-1). No. 3227, 80f, Liu Hui (4-2). No. 3228, 80f, Su Song (4-3). No. 3229, 80f, Song Yingxing (4-4).

Photo. & Engr.

2002, Aug. 20 ***Perf. 11¼x11***
3226-3229 A926 Set of 4 .80 .80

Yandangshan Mountain — A927

Designs: No. 3230, 80f, Xianshengmen Gate (4-1). No. 3231, 80f, Dalongqui Pond (4-2). No. 3232, 80f, Beidou Cave, horiz. (4-3). No. 3233, 80f, Guanyin Peak, horiz. (4-4).

2002, Sept. 7 **Litho.** ***Perf. 12¾***
3230-3233 A927 Set of 4 .80 .80

Mid-Autumn Festival — A928

Designs: No. 3234, 80f, Family reunion (3-1). No. 3235, 80f, People looking at Moon (3-2). $2, The Moon as a matchmaker (3-3).

2002, Sept. 21 ***Perf. 12***
3234-3236 A928 Set of 3 .90 .90

Each printed in sheets of 20. Sheets of nine containing three of each stamp exist with a decorative border and a border with Chinese text for the Beijing 2002 Stamp Exhibition.

Peng Zhen (1902-97) — A929

Designs: No. 3237, 80f, Head of Peng Zhen (2-1). No. 3238, 80f, Peng Zhen standing (2-2).

2002, Oct. 12 ***Perf. 11¾x12***
3237-3238 A929 Set of 2 .40 .40

Architecture in Slovakia and China — A930

No. 3239: a, Bojnice Castle, Slovakia (2-1). b, Handan Congtai Pavilion, China (2-2).

Photo. & Engr.

2002, Oct. 12 ***Perf. 11¼x11***
3239 A930 80f Horiz. pair, #a-b .40 .40

See Slovakia No. 410.

Dong Yong and Lady — A931

No. 3240: a, Dong Yong's filial love moves immortals (5-1). b, Dong Yong marries seventh immortal maiden (5-2). c, Immortal maiden weaving brocade (5-3). d, Dong Yong returns home (5-4). e, Everlasting love (5-5).

2002, Oct. 26 **Litho.** ***Perf. 13¼x13***
3240 Horiz. strip of 5 1.25 1.25
a.-d. A931 80f Any single .20 .20
e. A931 $2 multi .45 .45

Nos. 3240a-3240e exist in booklet panes of one that made up a booklet that had limited distribution to people with standing order accounts.

Flower — A932

2002, Nov. 8 **Litho.** ***Perf. 12***
3241 A932 80f multi + label .20 .20

Exists in a miniature sheet of 4 + 4 labels.

Souvenir Sheet

Hukou Waterfall — A933

Photo. (Margin Photo. & Embossed)

2002, Nov. 8 ***Perf. 13¼x13***
3242 A933 $8 multi 1.90 1.90

Museums — A934

Designs: No. 3243, 80f, Shanxi History Museum (5-1). No. 3244, 80f, Shanghai Museum (5-2). No. 3245, 80f, Henan Museum (5-3). No. 3246, 80f, Tibet Museum (5-4). No. 3247, 80f, Tianjin Natural Museum.

2002, Nov. 9 **Photo.** ***Perf. 12¾***
3243-3247 A934 Set of 5 1.00 1.00

Martial Arts A935

No. 3248: a, Kung Fu (2-1). b, Taekwondo (2-2)

2002, Nov. 20 **Photo.** ***Perf. 12***
3248 A935 80f Vert. pair, #a-b .40 .40

No. 3248 is a joint issue with South Korea No. 2109.

Gibbons — A936

Designs: No. 3249, 80f, Hylobates lar (4-1). No. 3250, 80f, Hylobates leucogenys (4-2). No. 3251, 80f, Hylobates concolor (4-3). $2, Hylobates hoolock (4-4).

Photo. & Engr.

2002, Dec. 7 ***Perf. 11¼x11***
3249-3252 A936 Set of 4 1.10 1.10

New Year 2003 (Year of the Ram) — A937

Designs: 80f, Ram (2-1). $2, Chinese symbol (2-2).

Photo. & Engr.

2003, Jan. 5 ***Perf. 11½***
3253-3254 A937 Set of 2 .70 .70

Sheets of 8 + central label of Nos. 3253-3254 exist.

Yangliuqing New Year Woodprints A938

Designs: No. 3255, 80f, Five boys wrestling for a lotus (4-1). No. 3256, 80f, Zhong Kui, vert. (4-2). No. 3257, 80f, Steaing the herb of immortality (4-3). $2, Wealth in a jade hall (4-4).

2003, Jan. 25 **Photo.** ***Perf. 12***
3255-3258 A938 Set of 4 1.10 1.10

A sheetlet containing two each #3255-3258 exists.

Seal Characters A939

Designs: No. 3259, 80f, 24 characters (2-1). No. 3260, 80f, 12 characters (2-2).

2003, Feb. 22 **Litho.**
3259-3260 A939 Set of 2 .40 .40

A sheetlet exists containg four each Nos. 3259-3260.

Knot A940

2003, Mar. 3
3261 A940 80f multi + label .20 .20

Exists in sheets of 4 stamps + 4 labels.

Lilies A941

Designs: 60f, Lilium taliense (4-1). No. 3263, 80f, Lilium lankongense (4-2). No. 3264, 80f, Lilium distichum (4-3). $2, Lilium lophophorum (4-4).

$8, Lilium leucanthum.

2003, Mar. 5 **Photo.** ***Perf. 13x13¼***
3262-3265 A941 Set of 4 1.00 1.00

Souvenir Sheet

Perf. 13¼

3266 A941 $8 multi 2.00 2.00

Nos. 3262-3265 each exist in sheetlets of 10.

No. 3266 contains one 75x53mm stamp.

Arch Bridges — A942

Designs: No. 3267, 80f, Maple Bridge (4-1). No. 3268, 80f, Xiaoshang Bridge (4-2). No. 3269, 80f, Lugouqiao Bridge (4-3). No. 3270, 80f, Double Dragon Bridge (4-4).

Photo. & Engr.

2003, Mar. 29 ***Perf. 11½***
3267-3270 A942 Set of 4 .80 .80

A sheetlet of 8 exists for each of Nos. 3267-3270.

Chinese and Iranian Buildings A943

Designs: No. 3271, 80f, Bell Tower, Xian, China (2-1). No. 3272, 80f, Mosque, Isfahan, Iran (2-2).

2003, Apr. 15 **Photo.** ***Perf. 13x13¼***
3271-3272 A943 Set of 2 .40 .40

See Iran No. 2856.

A sheetlet exists containing 4 each Nos. 3271-3272.

Souvenir Sheet

Leshan Giant Buddha — A944

Photo. & Engr.

2003, Apr. 28 ***Perf. 12***
3273 A944 $8 multi 2.00 2.00

Gulangyu Island — A945

No. 3274: a, Eight Diagram Building (3-1). b, Sunlight Rock (3-2). c, Shuzhuang Park (3-3)

2003, May 2 Photo. *Perf. 12*

3274	Horiz. strip of 3	.90	.90
a.-b.	A945 80f Either single	.20	.20
c.	A945 $2 multi	.50	.50
d.	Souvenir sheet, #3274	1.25	1.25

A souvenir sheet exists containing three No. 3274.

Campaign to Combat Epidemic of Severe Acute Respiratory Syndrome — A946

2003, May 19 *Perf. 13¼x13*

3275 A946 80f multi .20 .20

Strange Stories from a Chinese Studio, by Pu Songling A947

Designs: 10f, Xiang Yu (6-1). 30f, Tiger of Zhaocheng (6-2). 60f, Huanniang (6-3). 80f, Ah Xiu (6-4). $1.50, Wang Gui'an (6-5). $2, Goddess (6-6).

$8, Princess of Dongting Lake, horiz.

2003, May 16 *Perf. 12*

3276-3281 A947 Set of 6 1.40 1.40

Souvenir Sheet

Perf. 13¼x13

3282 A947 $8 multi 2.00 2.00

No. 3282 contains one 90x60mm stamp.

Sheetlets exist containing 4 each of Nos. 3276-3277, 3278-3279 and 3280-3281.

1976 Meteorite Shower Over Jilin — A948

Designs: No. 3283, 80f, Meteorites falling (3-1). No. 3284, 80f, Dispersal of meteorites (3-2). $2, Meteorite (3-3).

2003, June 21 Litho.

3283-3285 A948 Set of 3 .90 .90

A sheetlet exists containing 3 each of Nos. 3283-3285.

Master-of-Nets Garden, Suzhou — A949

No. 3286: a, 80f, Late Spring Cottage (4-1). b, 80f, Pavilion Greeting the Moon and Breeze (4-2). c, 80f, Veranda of Bamboo (4-3). d, $2, Hall of Ten Thousand Volumes (4-4).

Illustration reduced.

2003, June 29 Photo. *Perf. 12¾*

3286 A949 Horiz. strip of 4, #a-d 1.10 1.10

Tibetan Antelopes A950

Designs: 80f, Antelopes and mountain (2-1). $2, Antelope's head, adult with young (2-2).

Photo. & Engr.

2003, July 20 *Perf. 11x11¼*

3287-3288 A950 Set of 2 .70 .70

Kongtong Mountain — A951

No. 3289: a, 80f, Town of Huangcheng (4-1). b, 80f, Gorge of Playing the Zither (4-2). c, 80f, Pagoda Courtyard (4-3). d, $2, Peak of Thunder (4-4).

Illustration reduced.

2003, July 26 Litho. *Perf. 12*

3289 A951 Block of 4, #a-d 1.10 1.10

Sailing Ship — A952

2003, Aug. 5

3290 A952 80f multi + label .20 .20

Exists in sheets of 4 stamps + 4 labels.

Powered Flight, Cent. — A953

Designs: 80f, Foreign airplanes (2-1). $2, Chinese airplanes (2-2).

2003, Aug. 9 Photo. *Perf. 12¾*

3291-3292 A953 Set of 2 .70 .70

Jinci Temple Painted Statues — A954

Designs: No. 3293, 80f, Ruyi maid (4-1). No. 3294, 80f, Maid holding a towel (4-2). No. 3295, 80f, Maid carrying a royal seal (4-3). $2, Maid singing and dancing (4-4).

2003, Aug. 16 *Perf. 11¾x12*

3293-3296 A954 Set of 4 1.10 1.10

Sheetlets exist containing four each of Nos. 3293-3294 and 3295-3296.

Three Gorges Project — A955

Designs: No. 3297, 80f, Dam and reservoir (3-1). No. 3298, 80f, Ship locks (3-2). $2, Power plant and high tension wire towers (3-3).

2003, Aug. 20 Litho. *Perf. 12*

3297-3299 A955 Set of 3 .90 .90

Traditional Sports of Ethnic Minorities A956

Designs: No. 3300, 80f, Wrestling (4-1). b, No. 3301, 80f, Archery (4-2). No. 3302, 80f, Horse racing (4-3). No. 3303, 80f, Swinging (4-4).

2003, Sept. 5 Photo. *Perf. 13x13½*

3300-3303	A956 Set of 4	.80	.80
3303a	Souvenir sheet, #3300-3303	1.25	1.25

No. 3303a sold for $5. Sheets exist containing four each of No. 3300-3301 and 3302-3303.

Tienanmen Gate, Beijing — A957

2003, Sept. 10 Litho. *Perf. 12*

3304 A957 80f multi + label .20 .20

General Yue Fei (1103-42) — A958

Designs: No. 3305, 80f, Mother tattooing "Loyalty to the Country" on Yue Fei's back (3-1). No. 3306, 80f, Yue Fei standing with sword (3-2). $2, Yue Fei seated (3-3).

2003, Sept. 25

3305-3307 A958 Set of 3 .90 .90

Souvenir Sheet

Water Diversion Projects — A959

2003, Sept. 26 Photo. *Perf. 12¾*

3308 A959 $8 multi 2.00 2.00

Book Printing — A960

Designs: No. 3309, 80f, Ritual of Zhou, China (2-1). No. 3310, 80f, Hungarian Illuminated Chronicle, 1473 (2-2).

2003, Sept. 30 Litho. *Perf. 12*

3309-3310 A960 Set of 2 .40 .40

Nos. 3309-3310 have large perforation holes at the stamp corners. See Hungary Nos. 3863-3864.

Double Ninth Festival — A961

Designs: No. 3311, 80f, Climbing mountain (3-1). No. 3312, 80f, Enjoying the beauty of chrysanthemums (3-2). $2, Playing chess and drinking wine (3-3).

2003, Oct. 4 Photo. *Perf. 11½*

3311-3313 A961 Set of 3 .90 .90

Launch of First Manned Chinese Spacecraft A962

No. 3314: a, 80f, Astronaut, Shenzhou spacecraft (2-1). b, $2, Yang Liwei, flag (2-2).

2003, Oct. 16 *Perf. 13x13¼*

3314 A962 Pair, #a-b .70 .70

A booklet containing No. 3314, Hong Kong No. 1062 and Macao Nos. 1128a-1128b exists. The booklet sold for a premium over face value.

Folktale of Liang Shanbo and Zhu Yingtai — A963

Designs: No. 3315, 80f, Zhu Yingtai, disguised as a man, and Liang Shanbo become sworn brothers at Caoqiao (5-1). No. 3316, 80f, Classmates for three years (5-2). No. 3317, 80f, Bidding farewell (5-3). No. 3318, 80f, Sad parting on the terrace (5-4). $2, Turning into butterflies (5-5).

2003, Oct. 18 *Perf. 12*

3315-3319 A963 Set of 5 1.25 1.25

A booklet containing booklet panes of one of each of Nos. 3315-3319 exists.

China 2003 Intl. Stamp Exhibition, Mianyang A964

2003, Nov. 20 Photo. *Perf. 13¼*
3320 A964 80f multi .20 .20

World AIDS Day — A965

2003, Dec. 1 *Perf. 11¼x11*
3321 A965 80f multi .20 .20

Mao Zedong (1893-1976) — A966

Mao: No. 3322, 80f, Seated in folding chair (4-1). No. 3323, 80f, Standing (4-2). No. 3324, 80f, Seated on bench (4-3). No. 3325, 80f, Seated at desk (4-4).

Litho. & Engr.

2003, Dec. 6 *Perf. 12*
3322-3325 A966 Set of 4 .80 .80

Bronze Objects of Eastern Zhou Dyansty — A967

Designs: No. 3326, 60f, Square plate with turtle and fish patterns (8-1). No. 3327, 60f, Gui of the Duke of Qin (handled bowl with lid) (8-2). No. 3328, 80f, Iron-footed tripod of the King of Zhongshan (8-3). No. 3329, 80f, Gourd-shaped ladle of Yi, the Marquis of Zeng (8-4). No. 3330, 80f, Divine animal wine vessel, vert. (8-5). No. 3331, 80f, Wine vessel with phoenix pattern, vert. (8-6). $1, Square pot with lotus and cranes design, vert. (8-7). $2, Tripod with a dragon-shaped handle, vert. (8-8).

Perf. 11½x11¼, 11¼x11½

2003, Dec. 13 Photo. & Engr.
3326-3333 A967 Set of 8 1.90 1.90

Environmental Protection Type of 2002

Designs: 50f, Prevention and control of desertification. $4.50, Protection of biodiversity.

Perf. 12¾x13¼ Syncopated

2004, Jan. 1 Photo.
3334 A908 50f multi .20 .20
3335 A908 $4.50 multi 1.10 1.10

Bird Type of 2002

Designs: $5, Yellow-bellied tit. $6, Yunnan nuthatch.

2004, Jan. 1 *Perf. 13¼*
3336 A909 $5 multi 1.25 1.25
3337 A909 $6 multi 1.40 1.40

New Year 2004 (Year of the Monkey) A968

2004, Jan. 5 *Perf. 13 Syncopated*
3338 A968 80f multi .20 .20
a. Booklet pane of 10 2.00 —
Complete booklet, #3338a 2.00

Sheets of 4 and sheets of 6 exist.

Taohuawu New Year Pictures — A969

Designs: No. 3339, 80f, Feelings of Pipa (4-1). No. 3340, 80f, Kylin Bringing a Son (4-2). No. 3341, 80f, Liu Hai Playing with the Golden Toad (4-3). $2, Ten Beauties Playing Football (4-4).

2004, Jan. 14 Litho. *Perf. 12*
3339-3342 A969 Set of 4 1.10 1.10
3342a Souvenir sheet, #3339-3342 1.10 1.10

Deng Yingchao (1904-92), Communist Party Leader — A970

No. 3343: a, Holding book. b, Portrait.

2004, Feb. 4 Litho. & Engr.
3343 A970 80f Vert. pair, #a-b .40 .40

Suzhou Industrial Park, 10th Anniv. A971

2004, Mar. 1 Photo. *Perf. 13x13¼*
3344 A971 80f multi .20 .20

See Singapore No. 1084.

Red Cross Society, Cent. — A972

2004, Mar. 10 *Perf. 11¼x11*
3345 A972 80f multi .20 .20

Stories Explaining Chinese Idioms A973

Idioms: No. 3346, 80f, Trying to learn the Handan walk (4-1). No. 3347, 80f, Lord Ye's love for dragon (4-2). No. 3348, 80f, Filling a position in a Yu band (4-3). No. 3349, 80f, When the snipe and the clam grapple (4-4).

Perf. 12½x13¼ Syncopated

2004, Apr. 2
3346-3349 A973 Set of 4 .80 .80

Peacocks — A974

Designs: No. 3350, 80f, Blue peacock (2-1). No. 3351, 80f, Albino peacock, vert. (2-2). $6, Green peacocks.

2004, Apr. 13 *Perf. 12¾*
3350-3351 A974 Set of 2 .40 .40

Souvenir Sheet

Perf. 13¼x13

3352 A974 $6 multi 1.50 1.50

No. 3352 contains one 60x40mm stamp

Nanxi River — A975

No. 3353: a, River and mountain (4-1). b, Tree and boat in foreground, mountains in background (4-2). c, Rocks, boat in river (4-3). d, Boat, spit of land with trees (4-4).

2004, Apr. 24 Photo. *Perf. 12¾*
3353 Horiz. strip of 4 1.00 1.00
a. A975 60f multi .20 .20
b.-c. A975 80f Either single .20 .20
d. A975 $2 multi .45 .45

Danxia Mountain — A976

Designs: 60f, Sengmao Peak (4-1). No. 3355, 80f, Xianlong Lake (4-2). No. 3356, 80f, Chahu Peak (4-3). $2, Jinjiang River (4-4).

2004, May 1 Litho. & Engr. *Perf. 12*
3354-3357 A976 Set of 4 1.00 1.00

Economic and Technological Development Zones, 20th Anniv. — A977

2004, May 4 Litho.
3358 A977 80f multi .20 .20

Hometowns of Returned Chinese — A978

Designs: No. 3359, 80f, Xinglong Overseas Chinese Farm (4-1). No. 3360, 80f, Jinan University (4-2). No. 3361, 80f, Fuqing Rongqiao Development Zone (4-3). No. 3362, 80f, Kaiping (4-4).

2004, May 15 Photo. *Perf. 11x11¼*
3359-3362 A978 Set of 4 .80 .80

Sima Guang Breaking the Vat — A979

Designs: No. 3363, 80f, Sima Guang falling into water (3-1). No. 3362, 80f, Breaking vat (3-2). No. 3363, $2, Rescued (3-3).

2004, June 1 *Perf. 12*
3363-3365 A979 Set of 3 .90 .90

Scenes of Villages of Southern Anhui Province A980

Designs: No. 3366, 80f, Archway (4-1). No. 3367, 80f, Old buildings (4-2). No. 3368, 80f, Buildings on South Lake (4-3). No. 3369, 80f, Moon Pond (4-4).

Photo. & Engr.

2004, June 25 ***Perf. 11x11¼***
3366-3369 A980 Set of 4 .80 .80

Liu Yi Delivering a Letter — A981

Designs: No. 3370, 80f, Dragon Princess asking Liu Yi to deliver a letter (4-1). No. 3371, 80f, Delivering letter to Dongting Lake (4-2). No. 3372, 80f, Family reunion (4-3). $2, Couple embracing (4-4).

2004, July 17 Photo. ***Perf. 13¼x13***

3370 A981 80f multi		.20	.20
a.	Booklet pane of 1	.25	—
3371 A981 80f multi		.20	.20
a.	Booklet pane of 1	.25	—
3372 A981 80f multi		.20	.20
a.	Booklet pane of 1	.25	—
3373 A981 $2 multi		.50	.50
a.	Booklet pane of 1	.70	—
	Complete booklet, #3370a-3373a	1.50	
	Nos. 3370-3373 (4)	1.10	1.10

Complete booklet sold for $6.

Souvenir Sheet

Eight Immortals Crossing the Sea — A982

2004, July 30 ***Perf. 12 Syncopated***
3374 A982 $6 multi 1.50 1.50

Peony — A983

2004, July 31 Litho. ***Perf. 12¾***
3375 A983 80f multi + label .20 .20

2004 Summer Olympics, Athens — A984

Olympic rings and: No. 3376, 80f, Parthenon, Athens (2-1). No. 3377, 80f, Hall of Good Harvest, Temple of Heaven, Beijing.

2004, Aug. 13 Photo. ***Perf. 12¾***
3376-3377 A984 Set of 2 .40 .40

See Greece Nos. 2124-2125.

Deng Xiaoping (1904-97), Chinese Leader — A985

Designs: No. 3378, 80f, Walking (2-1). No. 3379, 80f, Saluting, horiz. (2-2). $6, Seated.

2004, Aug. 22 ***Perf. 12 Syncopated***
3378-3379 A985 Set of 2 .40 .40

Souvenir Sheet

Perf. 13 Syncopated

3380 A985 $6 multi 1.50 1.50

No. 3380 contains one 47x57mm stamp.

South China Tiger A986

Designs: 80f, Head (2-1). $2, Adult and young (2-2).

2004, Aug. 23 Litho. ***Perf. 12***
3381-3382 A986 Set of 2 .70 .70

People's Congress, 50th Anniv. — A987

Designs: No. 3383, 80f, Congress members arriving at Huairentang Hall of Zhongnanhai (2-1). No. 3384, 80f, Interior of Great Hall of the People (2-2).

2004, Sept. 15 ***Perf. 13¼***
3383-3384 A987 Set of 2 .40 .40

Bloodstone Seals A988

No. 3385: a, 80f, Seal of Emperor Qianlong (2-1). b, $2, Seal of Emperor Jiaqing (2-2).

Litho. & Embossed

2004, Sept. 17 ***Perf. 13x13¼***
3385 A988 Vert. pair, #a-b .70 .70

Celery Wormwood A989

Designs: No. 3386, 80f, Purple flowers (4-1). No. 3387, 80f, Blue flowers (4-2). No. 3388, 80f, Red flowers (4-3). $2, Yellow flowers (4-4).

2004, Sept. 19 Photo. ***Perf. 13¼x13***
3386-3389 A989 Set of 4 1.10 1.10

Chinese and Romanian Handicrafts A990

Designs: No. 3390, 80f, Drum with tigers and birds, China (2-1). No. 3391, 80f, Cucuteni pottery jar, Romania (2-2).

2004, Sept. 22 ***Perf. 13 Syncopated***
3390-3391 A990 Set of 2 .40 .40

See Romania No. 4668.

National Symbols A991

Designs: No. 3392, 80f, Flag (2-1). No. 3393, 80f, Arms, vert. (2-2).

Perf. 13¼x13 Syncopated, 13x13¼ Syncopated

2004, Sept. 30
3392-3393 A991 Set of 2 .40 .40

Landscapes of Chinese Borderlands — A992

Designs: No. 3394, 80f, Forest, Xing'an Mountains (12-1). No. 3395, 80f, Lake in Yalu River Basin (12-2). No. 3396, 80f, Reefs in Yellow Sea (12-3). No. 3397, 80f, Zhoushan Archipelago (12-4). No. 3398, 80f, Coast of Taiwan (12-5). No. 3399, 80f, Xisha Islands (12-6). No. 3400, 80f, Karst landscape, Southern Guangxi (12-7). No. 3401, 80f, Rain forest, Southern Yunnan (12-8). No. 3402, 80f, Mt. Qomolangma (12-9). No. 3403, 80f, Pamirs (12-10). No. 3404, 80f, Badain Jaran Desert (12-11). No. 3405, 80f, Hulun Buir Steppe (12-12).

2004, Oct. 1 ***Perf. 12¾***
3394-3405 A992 Set of 12 2.40 2.40
3405a Sheet of 12, #3394-3405 + central label 2.40 2.40

Buildings in China and Spain — A993

Designs: No. 3406, 80f, Jinmao Tower, China (2-1). No. 3407, 80f, Park Guell, Spain.

2004, Oct. 8 ***Perf. 13¼x13***
3406-3407 A993 Set of 2 .40 .40

See Spain Nos.

SEMI-POSTAL STAMPS

Catalogue values for unused stamps in this section are for Never Hinged items.

Girl Holding Ball — SP1

Hands Reading Braille — SP2

1984, Feb. 16 Photo. ***Perf. 11½***
B1 SP1 8f + 2f shown (2-1) .25 .20
B2 SP1 8f + 2f Boy, panda (2-2) .25 .20

Surtax for China Children's Fund. T.92.

1985, Mar. 15 Photo. ***Perf. 11½***

B3	SP2	8f + 2f shown (4-1)	1.00	.60
B4	SP2	8f + 2f Sign language, lip reading (4-2)	1.00	.60
B5	SP2	8f + 2f Artificial limb (4-3)	1.00	.60
B6	SP2	8f + 2f Handicapped person in wheelchair (4-4)	1.00	.60
		Nos. B3-B6 (4)	4.00	2.40

Surtax for China Welfare Fund. T.105.

Children (T.137) SP3

1989, June 1 Litho. ***Perf. 12***

B7	SP3 8f +4f Friends (4-1)	.20	.20
B8	SP3 8f +4f Penguins (4-2)	.20	.20
B9	SP3 8f +4f Bird, Moon, Sun (4-3)	.20	.20
B10	SP3 8f +4f Girl, boy playing ball (4-4)	.20	.20
a.	Strip of 4, #B7-B10	.50	.50

Intl Children's Day, 40th anniv., and 10th Intl. Year of the Child. Surtax for China Children's Fund.

AIR POST STAMPS

Mail Plane and Temple of Heaven — AP1

1951, May 1 Engr. ***Perf. 12½***

Without Gum

C1	AP1	$1000 carmine	.20	.20
C2	AP1	$3000 green	.30	.20
C3	AP1	$5000 orange	.20	.20
C4	AP1	$10,000 vio brn & grn	.25	.25
C5	AP1	$30,000 dk bl & brn	8.00	.75
		Nos. C1-C5 (5)	8.95	1.60

Planes at Airport — AP2

Designs: 28f, Plane over winding mountain highway. 35f, Plane over railroad yard. 52f, Plane over ship.

1957-58 *Perf. 14*

Without Gum

C6	AP2 16f indigo		10.00	.25
C7	AP2 28f olive black		10.00	.25
C8	AP2 35f slate		10.00	5.00
C9	AP2 52f Prus blue ('58)		10.00	.75
	Nos. C6-C9 (4)		40.00	6.25

POSTAGE DUE STAMPS

Grain and Cogwheel — D1

D2

1950, Sept. 1 Typo. *Perf. 12½*

Without Gum

J1	D1	$100 steel blue	.20	.20
J2	D1	$200 steel blue	.20	.20
J3	D1	$500 steel blue	.20	.20
J4	D1	$800 steel blue	27.50	.20
J5	D1	$1000 steel blue	.45	.40
J6	D1	$2000 steel blue	.45	.40
J7	D1	$5000 steel blue	.30	.60
J8	D1	$8000 steel blue	.30	1.00
J9	D1	$10,000 steel blue	.60	2.00
		Nos. J1-J9 (9)	30.20	5.20

1954, Aug. 18 Litho. *Perf. 14*

Without Gum

J10	D2	$100 red	2.00	.20
J11	D2	$200 red	.60	.20
J12	D2	$500 red	2.00	.20
J13	D2	$800 red	.20	.20
J14	D2	$1600 red	.20	.20
		Nos. J10-J14 (5)	5.00	1.00

MILITARY STAMP

Red Star, 8-1 in Center — M1

1953, Aug. Litho. *Perf. 14*

Without Gum

M1	M1 $800 yel, org & red	85.00	27.50

This stamp also was printed in deep purple, orange & red, and blue, orange & red. These were not issued.

While it has been assumed for many years that each color was for a separate branch of the armed forces (army, air force and navy), there is no documentation to support that theory. Quantities printed also do not correspond to the number of servicemen in each branch.

M2

1995 Litho. *Perf 12*

M4	M2 20f multicolored	8.00

NORTHEAST CHINA

The Northeast Liberation Area included the provinces of Liaoning, Kirin, Jehol and Heilungkiang, the area generally known as Manchuria under the Japanese. The first post war issues were local overprints on stamps of Manchukuo. In early 1946, a Ministry of Posts and Telegraphs served the areas already liberated, and in August, 1946, a Communications Committee of the Political Council was established. In June, 1947, these postal services were subordinated to the Harbin General Post Office, and this was extended to Changchun on Oct. 22, 1948, and to Mukden on Nov. 4, 1948. It was rapidly extended to cover all Manchuria.

Rough Perfs

Rough perforations are normal on most regional issues.

All Stamps Issued without Gum

Mao Tse-tung

A1 A2

1946, Feb. Unwmk. Litho. *Perf. 11*

1L1	A1 $1 violet	20.00	9.00
1L2	A2 $2 vermilion	1.40	1.00
1L3	A2 $5 orange	1.40	1.00
a.	Booklet pane of 6	250.00	
1L4	A2 $10 blue	1.40	1.00
a.	Booklet pane of 6	250.00	
	Nos. 1L1-1L4 (4)	24.20	12.00

Value, imperf set $125.

For surcharges see Nos. 1L20-1L23, 1L49-1L50, 1L89, 1L91, 1L93.

Map of China, Lion, Hyena and Chiang Kai-shek — A3

1946, Dec. 12 *Perf. 10½*

1L5	A3 $1 violet	1.50	1.50
1L6	A3 $2 orange	1.50	1.50
1L7	A3 $5 org brn	7.00	7.00
1L8	A3 $10 lt grn	10.00	10.00
a.	Imperf., pair	60.00	
	Nos. 1L5-1L8 (4)	20.00	20.00

10th anniversary of the capture of Chiang Kai-shek at Sian.

Railroad Workers, Chengchow — A4

1947, Feb. 7 *Perf. 10½*

1L9	A4 $1 pink	.75	*1.00*
1L10	A4 $2 dull grn	.75	*1.00*
1L11	A4 $5 pink	1.50	1.50
1L12	A4 $10 dull grn	3.50	3.50
	Nos. 1L9-1L12 (4)	6.50	7.00

24th anniversary of the Chengchow railroad workers' strike and massacre.

Women (Worker, Soldier and Farmer) — A5

Wmk. Chinese Characters in Sheet

1947, Mar. 8 *Perf. 10½x11*

1L13	A5 $5 brick red	.85	.85
1L14	A5 $10 brown	.85	.85

International Women's Day, March 8. Exists imperf.

Same Overprinted in Green ("Northeast Postal Service")

1947, Mar. 18

1L15	A5 $5 brick red	3.00	4.50
1L16	A5 $10 brown	3.00	4.50

Exists imperf.

Children Carrying Banner — A6

1947, Apr. 4 *Perf. 11x10½*

Granite Paper

1L17	A6 $5 rose red	1.50	2.25
1L18	A6 $10 lt green	3.25	3.00
1L19	A6 $30 orange	5.00	4.00
	Nos. 1L17-1L19 (3)	9.75	9.25

Children's Day.

Nos. 1L1-1L2 Surcharged in Red, Brown, Black, Blue or Green

伍拾圓 5000 改作

1947, Apr. Unwmk. *Perf. 11*

1L20	A1 $50 on $1 vio (R)	24.00	25.00
a.	Brown surcharge	24.00	25.00
1L21	A2 $50 on $2 ver	24.00	25.00
a.	Brown surcharge	24.00	25.00
1L22	A1 $100 on $1 vio	24.00	25.00
a.	Green surcharge	24.00	25.00
1L23	A2 $100 on $2 ver (Bl)	24.00	25.00
a.	Green surcharge	24.00	25.00
	Nos. 1L20-1L23 (4)	96.00	100.00

Farmer and Worker — A7

Ax Severing Chain — A8

Wmk. Chinese Characters in Sheet

1947, May 1 *Perf. 10½x11*

Granite Paper

1L24	A7 $10 orange red	1.50	1.50
1L25	A7 $30 ultra	2.00	2.00
1L26	A7 $50 gray green	3.50	3.50
	Nos. 1L24-1L26 (3)	7.00	7.00

Labor Day. Value, imperf. pairs, set $425.

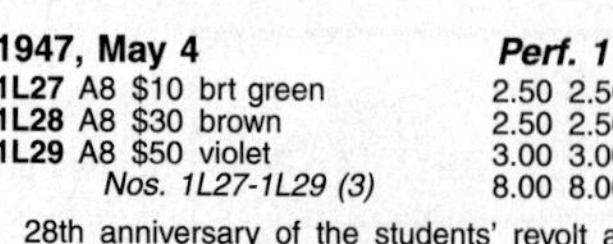

1947, May 4 *Perf. 11*

1L27	A8 $10 brt green	2.50	2.50
1L28	A8 $30 brown	2.50	2.50
1L29	A8 $50 violet	3.00	3.00
	Nos. 1L27-1L29 (3)	8.00	8.00

28th anniversary of the students' revolt at Peking University against the 1918 peace treaty. Value, imperf. pairs, set $525.

Workers with Banner: "Oppose Imperialist Aggression" — A9

1947, May 30 *Perf. 10½x11*

Banner in Red

1L30	A9 $2 brt lilac	1.10	3.00
1L31	A9 $5 brt green	1.10	3.00
1L32	A9 $10 yellow	1.90	3.00
1L33	A9 $20 violet	1.90	3.00
1L34	A9 $30 red brown	1.90	3.00
1L35	A9 $50 dk blue	3.75	3.00
1L36	A9 $100 brown	5.75	3.00
a.	Souvenir sheet of 7	125.00	
	Nos. 1L30-1L36 (7)	17.40	21.00

22nd anniversary of the Shanghai-Nanking Road incident. No. 1L36a is on granite paper and contains 7 imperf. stamps similar to Nos. 1L30-1L36. Size: 215x158mm. Value, imperf. pairs, ordinary paper, set $1,300.

Mao and Communist Flag — A10

1947, July 1 *Perf. 10½x11*

1L37	A10 $10 red	7.25	*9.50*
1L38	A10 $30 brt lilac	7.25	*9.50*
1L39	A10 $50 rose brn	18.00	*25.00*
1L40	A10 $100 vermilion	24.00	*27.50*
	Nos. 1L37-1L40 (4)	56.50	*71.50*

26th anniversary of the founding of the Chinese Communist Party.

Hand Holding Rifle — A11

1947, July 7 *Perf. 10½*

1L41	A11 $10 orange	3.00	4.75
1L42	A11 $30 green	3.00	4.75
1L43	A11 $50 dull blue	4.50	4.75
1L44	A11 $100 brown	6.00	4.75
a.	Souvenir sheet of 4	125.00	*150.00*
	Nos. 1L41-1L44 (4)	16.50	19.00

10th anniversary of the start of Sino-Japanese War. No. 1L44a contains 4 imperf. stamps similar to Nos. 1L41-1L44. Size: 149x107mm.

Exist imperf. Value, set of pairs $1,100.

White Mountain and Black Water, Northeast China — A12

Wmk. Zigzag Lines (141)

1947, Aug. 15 **Perf. 10½**

1L45 A12 $10 brown org 4.50 10.50
1L46 A12 $30 lt ol grn 4.50 10.50
1L47 A12 $50 blue grn 9.00 10.50
1L48 A12 $100 sepia 12.00 10.50
Nos. 1L45-1L48 (4) 30.00 42.00

2nd anniversary of the reoccupation of Northeast China and the surrender of Japan.
Exist imperf. Value, set of pairs $700.

Nos. 1L1-1L2 Surcharged in Black, Red, Green or Blue

拾 改
圓 作
1000

1947, Aug. 29 **Unwmk.** **Perf. 11**

1L49 A1 $5 on $1 vio 22.50 22.50
a. Red surcharge 22.50 22.50
b. Green surcharge 22.50 22.50
1L50 A2 $10 on $2 ver 22.50 22.50
a. Blue surcharge 22.50 22.50
b. Green surcharge 22.50 22.50

Map of Manchuria — A13

1947, Sept. 18 **Unwmk.**

White Paper

1L51 A13 $10 gray green 4.50 8.75
1L52 A13 $20 rose lilac 4.50 8.75
1L53 A13 $30 black brown 8.75 8.75
1L54 A13 $50 carmine 8.75 8.75
Nos. 1L51-1L54 (4) 26.50 35.00

16th anniversary of Japanese attack on Mukden, Sept. 18, 1931.

Northeast Political Council Offices — A14

Mao Tse-tung (Value figures repeated) — A15

1947, Oct. 10 **Perf. 10½**

1L55 A14 $10 yel orange 26.00 26.00
1L56 A14 $20 rose red 26.00 26.00
1L57 A14 $100 brown 72.50 72.50
Nos. 1L55-1L57 (3) 124.50 124.50

35th anniversary of the founding of the Chinese Republic.

1947, Oct. 10 **White Paper** **Perf. 11**

1L58 A15 $1 brown .20 1.50
1L59 A15 $5 gray green 2.00 1.50
1L60 A15 $10 brt green 8.00 8.00
1L61 A15 $15 bluish lilac 8.00 8.00
1L62 A15 $20 brt rose .80 1.50
1L63 A15 $30 green .80 2.00
1L64 A15 $50 black brown 15.00 12.00
1L65 A15 $90 blue 4.50 4.00
Nos. 1L58-1L65 (8) 39.30 38.50

Newsprint

1L66 A15 $100 red .60
a. White paper 4.50 4.00
1L67 A15 $500 red orange 20.00 16.00
a. White paper 27.50 25.00

Type A22 resembles A15, but has "YUAN" at upper right.
The $1, $90 were also printed on newsprint. See footnote following No. 1L72.
See Nos. 1L68-1L72. For surcharges see Nos. 1L84-1L88, 1L90, 1L92, 1L94.

1947, Nov. **Redrawn**

White Paper

1L68 A15 $50 lt grn .75 1.50
1L69 A15 $150 red org, wmkd. Chinese characters 2.00 1.50
a. Unwatermarked 2.75
1L70 A15 $250 bluish lil .60 1.50
a. Wmkd. Chinese characters .90 1.50

Nos. 1L69 and 1L69a exist in same sheet.

1947, Dec. **Unwmk.**

Newsprint

1L71 A15 $300 green 50.00 27.50
1L72 A15 $1000 yellow 1.00 1.00
a. White paper 1.00 1.00
Nos. 1L68-1L72 (5) 54.35 33.00

Panel below portrait 8½x3mm on Nos. 1L68-1L70; 7x3mm on No. 1L58-1L67. Nos. 1L68-1L70 have different ornamental border. Nos. 1L71-1L72 without zeros for cents.
For surcharges see Nos. 1L90, 1L92, 1L94.

Hand Holding Torch — A16

1947, Dec. 12 **Unwmk.** **Perf. 11**

White Paper

1L73 A16 $30 rose red 5.00 7.50
1L74 A16 $90 dk bl 7.00 7.50
1L75 A16 $150 green 10.50 7.50
Nos. 1L73-1L75 (3) 22.50 22.50

11th anniversary of the capture of Chiang Kai-shek at Sian.

Tomb of Gen. Li Chao-lin — A17

Globe and Banner — A18

1948, Mar. 9 **Unwmk.** **Perf. 10½x11**

1L76 A17 $30 green 10.00 10.00
a. Granite paper, wmkd. 10.00 10.00
1L77 A17 $150 vio gray 10.00 10.00
a. Granite paper, wmkd. 10.00 10.00

2nd anniversary of the assassination of Gen. Li Chao-lin, Commander of 3rd Army.

Wmk. Chinese Characters in Sheet

1948, May 1 **Perf. 11x10½**

1L78 A18 $50 red 7.50 12.00
1L79 A18 $150 green 2.75 18.00
1L80 A18 $250 lilac 2.75 35.00
Nos. 1L78-1L80 (3) 13.00 65.00

Labor Day.

Student, Torch and Banner — A19

1948, May 4 **Unwmk.** **Perf. 10½x11**

Granite paper

1L81 A19 $50 green 8.00 7.00
1L82 A19 $150 brown 8.00 11.00
1L83 A19 $250 red 15.00 17.00
Nos. 1L81-1L83 (3) 31.00 35.00

Youth Day, May 4.

Nos. 1L58, 1L61, 1L59, 1L63, 1L65, 1L2-1L4, 1L68-1L69, 1L71 Surcharged in Black, Blue, Red or Green

1948-49 **Perf. 11**

1L84 A15 $100 on $1 75.00 90.00
a. Blue surcharge 50.00 50.00
1L85 A15 $100 on $15 18.00 17.50
a. Blue surcharge 50.00 50.00
1L86 A15 $300 on $5 (R) 55.00 25.00
1L87 A15 $300 on $30 (R) 6.00 10.00
1L88 A15 $300 on $90 (R) 6.00 10.00
1L89 A2 $500 on $2 6.00 6.00
1L90 A15 $500 on $50 (R, '49) 27.50 20.00
1L91 A2 $1500 on $5 (Bl) 6.00 7.50
1L92 A15 $1500 on $150 (G; '49) 22.50 15.00
1L93 A2 $2500 on $10 (R) 7.50 9.00
1L94 A15 $2500 on $300 ('49) 9.00 12.00
Nos. 1L84-1L94 (11) 238.50 222.00

Crane Operator — A20

Wmk. Chinese Characters in Sheet

1948, May **Perf. 11**

1L95 A20 $100 red & pink .75 .45
1L96 A20 $300 vio brn & yel 1.50 1.50
1L97 A20 $500 bl & grn 1.50 1.50
Nos. 1L95-1L97 (3) 3.75 3.45

6th All-China Labor Conference, Harbin.

Farmer, Worker and Soldier Saluting — A21

Mao Tse-tung ("YUAN" at upper right) — A22

1948, Dec. 3 **Unwmk.** **Perf. 11x10½**

White paper

1L98 A21 $500 vermilion 6.00 6.00
1L99 A21 $1500 brt grn 9.00 9.00
1L100 A21 $2500 brown 16.00 16.00
Nos. 1L98-1L100 (3) 31.00 31.00

Liberation of Northeast China.
Values for Nos. 1L98-1L100 are for fine stamps.

1949, Feb. **Perf. 11**

1L101 A22 $300 olive .45 .90
1L102 A22 $500 orange 1.25 1.50
1L103 A22 $1500 bl grn .45 .90
1L104 A22 $4500 brown .45 .90
1L105 A22 $6500 dk bl .45 .90
Nos. 1L101-1L105 (5) 3.05 5.10

See type A15. For surcharges see Nos. 1L126-1L129, 1L131-1L132.

Workers, Globe and Flag — A23

Fields and Factories — A24

1949, May 1 **Perf. 11½**

1L106 A23 $1000 red & dl bl .30 .60
1L107 A23 $1500 red & pale bl .30 .60
1L108 A23 $4500 rose & ol brn .45 .90
1L109 A23 $6500 dl org & grn .45 .90
1L110 A23 $10,000 mar & ultra .55 1.25
Nos. 1L106-1L110 (5) 2.05 4.25

Labor Day.

1949 **Perf. 10, 11**

1L111 A24 $5000 Prus bl 4.00 3.00
1L112 A24 $10,000 org brn .30 1.50
1L113 A24 $50,000 green .40 2.25
1L114 A24 $100,000 violet .80 12.00
Nos. 1L111-1L114 (4) 5.50 18.75

Production in agriculture and industry.

Workers with Flags — A25

Heroes' Monument, Harbin — A26

1949, July 1 **Perf. 11**

1L115 A25 $1500 vio, lt bl & red .40 .60
1L116 A25 $4500 dk brn, lt bl & ver .40 .60
1L117 A25 $6500 gray, lt bl & rose red .80 1.25
Nos. 1L115-1L117 (3) 1.60 2.45

28th anniversary of the founding of the Chinese Communist Party.

1949, Aug. 15 **Perf. 11½x11**

1L118 A26 $1500 brick red .80 1.10
1L119 A26 $4500 yel grn .80 1.10
1L120 A26 $6500 lt blue .80 1.10
Nos. 1L118-1L120 (3) 2.40 3.30

4th anniversary of the Reoccupation, and the surrender of Japan.

"Northeast Postal Service"

The following commemorative issues are similar to those of the People's Republic of China, with the 4 characters shown added in different sizes and various arrangements. Reprints were also issued similar to those of the PRC.

Chinese Lantern Type of PRC, 1949

1949, Sept. 12 **Litho.** **Perf. 12½**

1L121 A1 $1000 dp blue 3.00 5.00
1L122 A1 $1500 scarlet 4.00 5.00
1L123 A1 $3000 green 6.00 6.50
1L124 A1 $4500 maroon 7.00 7.50
Nos. 1L121-1L124 (4) 20.00 24.00

Reprints exist. Value, set $1.10.

Factory — A27

1949, Oct. **Perf. 11x10½**

1L125 A27 $1500 orange .75 1.25

For surcharge see No. 1L130.

Nos. 1L101, 1L103-1L105, 1L125 Surcharged in Black or Green

1949, Nov. 20

1L126 A22 $2000 on $300 20.00 4.25
1L127 A22 $2000 on $4500 (G) 45.00 32.50
1L128 A22 $2500 on $1500 .50 5.00
1L129 A22 $2500 on $6500 22.50 32.50

1L130	A27	$5000 on $1500	.40	*1.75*
1L131	A22	$20,000 on $4500	.25	*5.00*
1L132	A22	$35,000 on $300	.35	*6.75*
		Nos. 1L126-1L132 (7)	89.00	*87.75*

Globe and Hammer Type of PRC

1949, Nov. 15 ***Perf. 12½***

1L133	A2	$5000 crimson	150.00	60.00
1L134	A2	$20,000 dp green	250.00	70.00
1L135	A2	$35,000 vio blue	350.00	90.00
		Nos. 1L133-1L135 (3)	750.00	220.00

Reprints, value; #1L133-1L134, each $1.50; #1L135, $175.

Mao and Conference Hall Types of PRC

1950, Feb. 1 ***Perf. 14***

1L136	A3	$1000 vermilion	10.00	13.00
1L137	A3	$1500 dp blue	10.00	13.00
1L138	A4	$5000 dk vio brn	20.00	14.00
1L139	A4	$20,000 green	20.00	*20.00*
		Nos. 1L136-1L139 (4)	60.00	60.00

Reprints exist. Value, set $4.

Gate of Heavenly Peace — A28

1950 ***Perf. 10½***

Narrow horizontal shading

1L140	A28	$500 olive	1.50	.55
1L141	A28	$1000 orange	1.75	.55
1L142	A28	$1000 lil rose	4.00	.55
1L143	A28	$2000 gray grn	1.10	.20
1L144	A28	$2500 yellow	4.50	.20
1L145	A28	$5000 dp org	20.00	.20
1L146	A28	$10,000 brn org	2.10	.55
1L147	A28	$20,000 vio brn	1.10	.20
1L148	A28	$35,000 dp blue	1.10	.40
1L149	A28	$50,000 brt grn	20.00	.80
		Nos. 1L140-1L149 (10)	57.15	4.20

See A29.

Flag and Mao Type of PRC

1950, July 1 ***Perf. 14***

Yellow Stars

1L150	A7	$5000 grn & red	57.50	52.50
1L151	A7	$10,000 brn & red	72.50	52.50
1L152	A7	$20,000 dk brn & red	80.00	52.50
1L153	A7	$30,000 dk vio bl & red	110.00	72.50
		Nos. 1L150-1L153 (4)	320.00	230.00

Reprints exist. Value, set $7.

Picasso Dove Type of PRC

1950, Aug. 1 **Engr.** ***Perf. 14***

1L154	A8	$2500 brown	10.00	18.00
1L155	A8	$5000 green	15.00	18.00
1L156	A8	$20,000 blue	20.00	18.00
		Nos. 1L154-1L156 (3)	45.00	54.00

Reprints exist. Value, set $4.75.

Flag Type of PRC

1950, Oct. 1 **Engr. & Litho.**

Flag in Red & Yellow

1L157	A9	$1000 purple	35.00	27.50
1L158	A9	$2500 org brn	52.50	35.00
1L159	A9	$5000 dp grn	60.00	45.00
1L160	A9	$10,000 olive	80.00	45.00
1L161	A9	$20,000 blue	125.00	72.50
		Nos. 1L157-1L161 (5)	352.50	225.00

Size of #1L159: 38x47mm, others 26x33mm.
Reprints exist. Value, set $7.

Postal Conference Type of PRC

1950, Nov. 1 **Litho.**

1L162	A11	$2500 grn & dp org	12.00	9.50
1L163	A11	$5000 car & grn	12.00	9.50

Reprints exist. Value, set, $5.

Gate of Heavenly Peace — A29

1950-51 ***Perf. 10½***

Wide horizontal shading

1L164	A29	$5000 orange	6.00	*6.25*
1L165	A29	$30,000 scarlet	2.25	*15.00*
1L166	A29	$100,000 violet	10.00	*16.00*

Wmk. Zigzag Lines (141)

1L167	A29	$250 brown	.90	*1.50*
1L168	A29	$500 olive	.90	*1.50*
1L169	A29	$1000 lil rose	1.25	*2.50*
1L170	A29	$2000 dl grn ('51)	2.00	*2.50*
1L171	A29	$2500 yellow	.00	*2.50*
1L172	A29	$5000 orange	2.25	*2.50*
1L173	A29	$10,000 brn org ('51)	1.60	*2.50*
1L174	A29	$12,500 maroon	.90	*2.50*
1L175	A29	$20,000 dp brn ('51)	1.75	*5.00*
		Nos. 1L164-1L175 (12)	30.70	*60.25*

A $50,000 green was prepared, but not issued. Value $150.

Stalin and Mao Tse-tung Type of PRC

Unwmk.

1950, Dec. 1 **Engr.** ***Perf. 14***

1L176	A12	$2500 red	20.00	10.00
1L177	A12	$5000 dp green	25.00	10.00
1L178	A12	$20,000 dk blue	25.00	10.00
		Nos. 1L176-1L178 (3)	70.00	30.00

Reprints exist. Value, set $2.75.

NORTHEAST CHINA PARCEL POST STAMPS

Locomotive — PP1

1951 **Litho.** ***Perf. 10½***

1LQ1	$100,000 purple	100.00
	Imperf	
1LQ2	$300,000 brown	300.00
1LQ3	$500,000 grnsh bl	500.00
1LQ4	$1,000,000 ver	800.00

Value, Nos. 1LQ2-1LQ4 perf. 10½, $2,250.
For similar type see North China PP1.

PORT ARTHUR AND DAIREN

The Liaoning Postal Administration was established on April 1, 1946, in accordance with the Sino-Soviet Treaty, but was renamed one week later the Port Arthur and Dairen Postal Administration. On Apr. 3, 1947, it was combined with telecommunications and renamed the Kwantung Post and Telegraph General Administration.

On May 1, 1949, the name was again changed to Port Arthur and Dairen Post and Telegraph Administration. Postal tariffs were based on local currency and both Manchukuo and Japanese stamps were overprinted for use.

Gum
#2L1-2L55 were issued with gum.

Manchukuo Nos. 162 and 94 Handstamp Surcharged in Violet ("Liaoning Post")

五 暫
圓 作

1946, Mar. 15

2L1	A19	20f on 30f buff	60.00	60.00
2L2	A18	1y on 12f org	35.00	35.00

Same Surcharge on Japan Nos. 260, 337, 195, 244, 263, 342 in Violet, Red or Black

1946, Apr. 1

2L3	A85	20f on 3s grn (V)	18.00	21.00
2L4	A151	1y on 17s gray vio (R)	15.00	18.00
2L5	A57	5y on 6s car	27.50	27.50
2L6	A57	5y on 6s crim	27.50	27.50
2L7	A88	5y on 6s org	20.00	20.00
2L8	A154	15y on 40s dk vio	100.00	125.00
		Nos. 2L1-2L8 (8)	303.00	334.00

Surcharge sideways on Nos. 2L5-2L6.

Japan Nos. 260 and 263 Surcharged

伍 暫
圓 作

1946, Apr.

2L9	A85	1y on 3s grn		—
2L10	A88	5y on 6s org		—

Sha Ho Kow (suburb of Dairen) issue. The status of this issue is in question.

Manchukuo Nos. 84, 88 and 98 Handstamp Surcharged in Green, Red or Black

1946, May 1

2L11	A16	1y on 1f red brn (G)	17.00	*24.00*
2L12	A18	5y on 4f lt ol grn (R)	22.50	*32.50*
2L13	A19	15y on 30f chnt brn	50.00	*62.50*
		Nos. 2L11-2L13 (3)	89.50	*119.00*

Transfer of postal administration and Labor Day.

Manchukuo Nos. 159, 86 and 94 Surcharged in Green, Red or Black

1946, July 7

2L14	A17	1y on 6f crim rose (G)	10.00	20.00
2L15	A17	5y on 2f lt grn (R)	50.00	85.00
2L16	A18	15y on 12f dp org	110.00	110.00
		Nos. 2L14-2L16 (3)	170.00	215.00

Outbreak of war with Japan, 9th anniv.

Manchukuo Nos. 94, 84 and 158 Surcharged in Black, Green or Red

1946, Aug. 15

2L17	A18	1y on 12f dp org	20.00	27.50
2L18	A16	5y on 1f red brn (G)	50.00	50.00
2L19	A10	15y on 5f gray blk (R)	100.00	100.00
		Nos. 2L17-2L19 (3)	170.00	177.50

Surrender of Japan, first anniversary.

Manchukuo Nos. 159, 94 and 86 Surcharged in Green, Black or Red

1946, Oct. 10

2L20	A17	1y on 6f crim rose (G)	30.00	30.00
2L21	A18	5y on 12f dp org	55.00	55.00
2L22	A17	15y on 2f lt grn (R)	100.00	100.00
		Nos. 2L20-2L22 (3)	185.00	185.00

35th anniversary of Chinese revolution.

Manchukuo Nos. 84, 159 and 94 Surcharged in Black, Green or Blue

1946, Oct. 19

2L23	A16	1y on 1f red brn	45.00	45.00
2L24	A17	5y on 6f crim rose (G)	85.00	85.00
2L25	A18	15y on 12f dp org (Bl)	125.00	125.00
		Nos. 2L23-2L25 (3)	255.00	255.00

10th anniversary of the death of Lu Hsun (1881-1936), writer.

Manchukuo Nos. 86, 159 and 95 Surcharged in Red, Green or Black

1947, Feb. 20

2L26	A17	1y on 2f lt grn (R)	77.50	77.50
2L27	A17	5y on 6f crim rose (G)	150.00	150.00
2L28	A18	15y on 13f dk red brn	300.00	300.00
		Nos. 2L26-2L28 (3)	527.50	527.50

29th anniversary of the Red (USSR) Army.

Manchukuo Nos. 86, 159 and 162 Surcharged in Red, Green or Black

1947, May 1

2L29	A17	1y on 2f lt grn (R)	22.50	22.50
2L30	A17	5y on 6f crim rose (G)	65.00	65.00
2L31	A19	15y on 30f buff	100.00	100.00
		Nos. 2L29-2L31 (3)	187.50	187.50

Labor Day.

Manchukuo Nos. 86, 88, 98 and 162 Surcharged ("Kwantung Postal Service, China")

中國關東郵政

五 暫
圓 作

1947, Sept. 15

2L32	A17	5y on 2f lt grn	37.50	37.50
2L33	A18	15y on 4f lt ol grn	62.50	62.50
2L34	A19	20y on 30f red brn	95.00	95.00
2L35	A19	20y on 30f buff	100.00	100.00
		Nos. 2L32-2L35 (4)	295.00	295.00

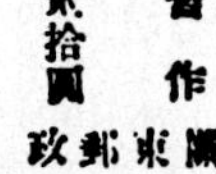

Manchukuo Nos. 86 and 159 Surcharged in Red and Green

Sacred Golden Kite (same size) — A1

1948, Feb. 20

2L36	A17	10y on 2f lt grn (R)	140.00	140.00
2L37	A17	20y on 6f crim rose (G)	175.00	175.00
2L38	A1	100y on bl & red brn	725.00	725.00

30th anniversary of the Red (USSR) Army. No. 2L38 is on an ungummed label for the 2600th anniv. of the Japanese Empire.

Japan No. 260 and Manchukuo Nos. 84, 86 and 88 Surcharged in Red, Blue or Black

1948, July

2L39 A85 5y on 3s grn (R) 110.00 110.00
2L40 A16 10y on 1f red brn (Bl) 225.00 250.00
2L41 A17 50y on 2f lt grn 500.00 475.00
2L42 A18 100y on 4f lt ol grn (R) 875.00 900.00

Smaller Characters on Bottom Line

2L43 A17 10y on 2f lt grn (R) 300.00 225.00
2L44 A16 50y on 1f red brn 350.00 300.00

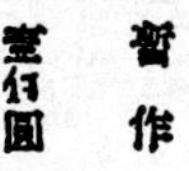

Stamps of Manchukuo Nos. 84, 86 and 88 Surcharged in Blue, Red or Black

1948, Nov. 1

2L45 A16 10y on 1f red brn (Bl) 275.00 600.00
2L46 A17 50y on 2f lt grn (R) 450.00 600.00
2L47 A18 100y on 4f lt ol grn 1,100. 600.00

31st anniversary of the Russian Revolution.

Manchukuo Nos. 86 and 161 Surcharged in Red or Green

1948, Nov. 15

2L48 A17 10y on 2f lt grn 1,050. 1,050.
2L49 A17 50y on 20f brn (G) 1,200. 1,200.

Kwantung Agricultural and Industrial Exhibition.

Manchukuo Nos. 86, 88 and 161 Surcharged in Red, Black or Green

1949, Jan.

2L50 A17 20y on 2f lt grn (R) 500.00
2L51 A18 50y on 4f lt ol grn 700.00
2L52 A17 100y on 20f brn (G) 700.00

Without Gum

From No. 2L56 onward all stamps were issued without gum except as noted.

Farmer and Worker — A2

Train and Ship — A3

Ship at Dock (No. 2L55) — A4

(No. 2L56)

1949 Litho. *Perf. 11, 11½*

2L53 A2 5y pale grn 1.50 *3.75*
2L54 A3 10y orange 11.00 10.50
2L55 A4 50y vermilion 16.00 15.00
2L56 A4 50y red (redrawn) 22.50 22.50
Nos. 2L53-2L56 (4) 51.00 51.75

Issue dates: #2L56, July 7; others Apr. 1.
For surcharges see Nos. 2L62-2L66.

Worker, Flag and Means of Transport A5

1949, May 1 *Perf. 11*

2L57 A5 10y rose pink 15.00 *18.00*
a. 10y vermilion 75.00 75.00

Labor Day. #2L57a is from a worn plate.

Mao Tse-tung and Red Flag — A6

Heroes Monument, Dairen — A7

1949, July 1

2L59 A6 50y red 32.50 35.00

28th anniversary of the founding of the Chinese Communist Party.

1949, Sept.

2L60 A7 10y red, bl & olive 15.00 13.00
a. 10y red, blue & pale blue 100.00 85.00

4th anniversary of victory over Japan and opening of the Dairen Industrial Fair.

Nos. 2L53-2L54 Surcharged in Red or Black

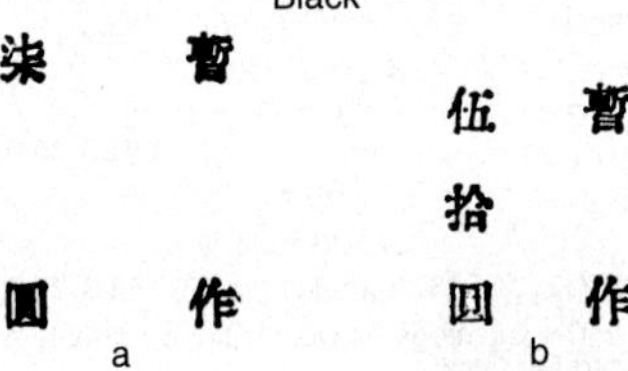

a b

c

1949, Sept. With Gum

2L62 A2(a) 7y on 5y (R) 35.00 27.50
2L63 A2(a) 7y on 5y 30.00 27.50
2L64 A2(b) 50y on 5y (R) 85.00 75.00
2L65 A3(b) 100y on 10y 450.00 350.00
2L66 A3(c) 500y on 10y (R) 600.00 400.00
Nos. 2L62-2L66 (5) 1,200. 880.00

Size of surcharge on No. 2L63: 16x19mm.
A 500y on 5y, red surcharge "c," and a 500y on 10y orange, surcharge "b" were prepared but not issued.

Stalin and Lenin — A8

1949, Nov. 7 *Perf. 11x11½*

2L68 A8 10y dl bl grn (shades) 12.00 13.00

32nd anniversary of the Russian Revolution.

Workers Saluting Mao, Star and Flag — A9

1949, Nov. 16 *Perf. 11*

2L69 A9 35y dk bl, red, & yel 18.00 18.00

Founding of the People's Republic of China.

Stalin — A10

(same size) Gate of Heavenly Peace — A11

1949, Dec. 20 *Perf. 11½*

2L70 A10 20y dull magenta 37.50 *40.00*
2L71 A10 35y rose red 37.50 *40.00*

70th birthday of Stalin.

1950, Mar. 10 Typo. *Perf. 10½*

2L72 A11 10y Prus blue *200.00* *80.00*
2L73 A11 20y dull grn *100.00* *100.00*
2L74 A11 35y red *20.00* *20.00*
2L75 A11 50y deep pur *15.00* *15.00*
2L76 A11 100y lilac rose *20.00* *20.00*
Nos. 2L72-2L76 (5) *355.00* *235.00*

NORTH CHINA

The North China Liberation Area included the provinces of Hopeh, Chahar, Shansi and Suiyuan. The original postal service, begun in the Shansi-Hopeh-Chahar Border Area in December, 1937, became the North China Postal and Telegraph Administration in May, 1949.

All Stamps Issued without Gum Except as Noted

Large Victory Issue

Cavalry Man Holding Nationalist Flag — A1

Wmk. Wavy Lines

1946, Mar. *Perf. 10½*

Granite Paper

Size: 34½x42mm

3L1 A1 $1 red brown 1.00 1.40
a. Newsprint 10.00 12.00
3L2 A1 $2 gray grn 1.00 1.25
3L3 A1 $4 vermilion 1.10 1.25
3L4 A1 $5 vio brn 4.00 1.25
3L5 A1 $8 vio bl 4.00 1.25
3L6 A1 $10 dp car 1.10 1.25
3L7 A1 $12 yellow 3.75 4.50
3L8 A1 $20 lt green 8.00 8.00
Nos. 3L1-3L8 (8) 23.95 20.15

Defeat of Japan.

Small Victory Issue

Perf. 10½x10, 9½ rough

1946, May Unwmk.

Granite paper

Size: 20x21mm

3L9 A1 $1 red org 1.40 *2.00*
3L10 A1 $2 green 2.25 2.00
3L11 A1 $3 lt lilac 4.25 *8.00*
3L12 A1 $5 dull pur 5.75 .25
3L13 A1 $8 dk blue 12.00 *16.00*
3L14 A1 $10 rose red 2.25 *4.00*
3L15 A1 $15 purple *47.50* *40.00*
3L16 A1 $20 green 4.25 *6.00*
3L17 A1 $30 brt grnsh bl 3.50 *7.00*
3L18 A1 $40 brt rose lilac 4.25 3.00
3L19 A1 $50 brown *24.00* .50
3L20 A1 $60 myrtle green *47.50* 1.50

Wmk. Wavy Lines

3L21 A1 $100 orange 1.40 *4.00*
3L22 A1 $200 dull blue 1.40 *4.00*
3L23 A1 $500 rose 45.00 *50.00*
Nos. 3L9-3L23 (15) *206.70* *148.25*

North China Postal and Telegraph Administration

Charging Infantrymen A2

Agriculture and Industry A3

1949, Jan. Unwmk. *Imperf.*

White Paper

3L24 A2 50c brown lake 1.00 1.00
3L25 A2 $1 Prussian blue 1.00 1.00

Newsprint

3L26 A2 $2 apple green 1.00 1.00
3L27 A2 $3 dull violet 1.00 1.00
3L28 A2 $5 brown 1.00 1.00
3L29 A3 $6 deep rose 1.00 1.00
a. White paper 1.00 1.00
3L30 A2 $10 blue grn .20 *.20*
3L31 A2 $12 dp car 1.00 1.00
Nos. 3L24-3L31 (8) 7.20 7.20

No. 3L29 issued in Peking, others in Tientsin.

Remittance Stamps of China Surcharged

A4

壹
$1

叁
$3

1949, Jan. Engr. *Perf. 13*

Small Central Characters

3L32 A4 50c on $50 brn blk 3.00 3.25
3L33 A4 $1 on $50 gray blk 2.10 2.50
3L34 A4 $3 on $50 gray 2.50 2.50

Large Central Characters

3L35 A4 50c on $50 blk 1.50 1.50
3L36 A4 $6 on $20 dk vio brn 1.50 1.50
Nos. 3L32-3L36 (5) 10.60 11.25

Issued in Tientsin.
For surcharges see Nos. 3LQ10-3LQ21.

Sun Yat-sen Type A2 of Northeastern Provinces and China No. 640 Surcharged in Black, Red, Green or Blue

#3L37-3L45, 3L47-3L50, 3L52

#3L46, 3L51, 3L53

c

Type "b," bottom character of left vertical row (yuan) differs. Type "c," top character of right vertical row differs.

1949, Mar. 7 ***Perf. 14***

3L37 A2 50c on 5c lake .20 *2.40*
3L38 A2 $1 on 10c org .20 *1.90*
3L39 A2 $2 on 20c yel grn 42.50 22.50
3L40 A2 $3 on 50c red org .20 *1.40*
3L41 A2 $4 on $5 dk grn 4.75 1.90
3L42 A2 $6 on $10 crim 1.10 *1.90*
3L43 A2 $10 on $300 bluish grn 1.25 *3.75*
3L44 A2 $12 on $1 bl 1.25 *2.75*
3L45 A2 $18 on $3 brn 1.25 *1.40*
3L46 A2 $20 on 50c red org (Bl) 1.25 .95
3L47 A2 $20 on $20 ol, II 1.25 *3.75*
a. Type I 10.00 9.00
3L48 A2 $30 on $2.50 ind (R) 1.25 *3.75*
3L49 A2 $40 on 25c blk brn (R) 4.25 *5.75*
3L50 A2 $50 on $109 dk grn (R) 9.50 7.75
3L51 A2 $80 on $1 bl (R) 15.00 2.75
3L52 A2 $100 on $65 dl grn (R) 19.00 7.75
3L53 A73 $100 on $100 dk car, surch. 16mm wide (Bl) 25.00 2.75
a. Surcharge 14mm wide 25.00 12.00

1949, Apr.

3L55 A2 (c) $2 on 20c yel grn 1.25 *2.75*
3L56 A2 (c) $3 on 50c red org .20 *1.90*
3L57 A2 (c) $4 on $5 dk grn 9.50 3.75
3L58 A2 (c) $6 on $10 crim, II 4.25 3.75
a. Type I 15.00 10.00
3L59 A2 (c) $12 on $1 blue .70 *1.25*

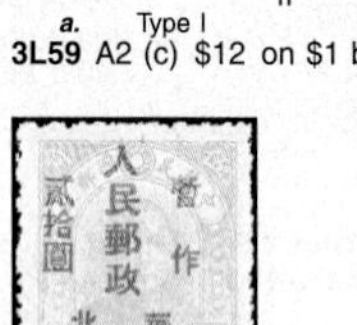
d

e

1949, Apr.

Type "d"

3L60 A2 $1 on 25c blk grn (G) .20 *1.10*
3L61 A2 $10 on $300 bluish grn (R) 9.50 5.25
3L62 A2 $20 on 50c red org (G) 13.00 *22.50*
3L63 A2 $20 on $20 ol (R) 6.50 3.75
3L64 A2 $40 on 25c blk brn (R) 6.50 4.25
3L65 A2 $50 on $109 dk grn, surch. 15mm wide (R) 9.50 *11.50*
a. Surcharge 13mm wide 30.00 11.50
3L66 A2 $80 on $1 bl (R) 6.50 5.75

Type "d" On Stamps on China

3L67 A73 $100 on $100 dk car (G) 52.50 30.00
3L68 A73 $300 on $700 red brn (Bl) 11.00 11.00
3L69 A82 $500 on $500 bl grn (R) 8.00 3.75
3L70 A82 $3000 on $3000 bl (R) 11.00 3.75

Type "e" On Stamps of Northeastern Provinces

1949, Aug.

3L71 A2 $10 on $10 crim, II (Bl) 6.50 3.00
a. Type I 12.50 12.00
3L72 A2 $30 on 20c yel grn (R) 6.50 1.90
3L73 A2 $50 on $44 dk car rose (Bl) 6.50 1.00
3L74 A2 $100 on $3 brn (Bl) 11.00 5.75
3L75 A2 $200 on $4 org brn, II (Bl) 19.00 19.00
a. Type I 1,000. 400.00

On China No. 754 in Blue

3L76 A82 $10 on $7000 lt red brn 11.00 7.75
Nos. 3L37-3L76 (39) 339.80 229.50

Overprints on Nos. 3L71 and 3L76 have 2 characters in center row.

Farmer and Worker on Globe — A5

1949, May 1 **Engr.** ***Perf. 14***

3L77 A5 $20 crimson 1.65 .65
3L78 A5 $40 dark blue 1.65 .80
3L79 A5 $60 brown org 1.65 .65
3L80 A5 $80 dk green 1.65 1.00
3L81 A5 $100 purple 1.65 1.00
Nos. 3L77-3L81 (5) 8.25 4.10

Labor day. Exists imperf. Value, set $12.50. Also issued in blocks of 4, imperf between.

Mao Tse-tung (Chinese Numeral) — A6

Mao Tse-tung (Arabic Numeral) — A7

1949, July 1 ***Perf. 14***

3L82 A6 $10 red .75 *.60*
3L83 A7 $20 dk blue .75 *.60*
3L84 A6 $50 orange 4.00 .60
3L85 A7 $80 dk green .90 *1.00*
3L86 A6 $100 purple 4.00 1.00
3L87 A7 $120 olive .60 *1.00*
3L88 A6 $140 vio brn 4.00 1.00
Nos. 3L82-3L88 (7) 15.00 5.80

28th anniv. of the founding of the Chinese Communist Party. Value, imperf, set $40.

Gate of Heavenly Peace — A8

Farmers and Factory — A9

1949, Nov. 26 **Litho.** ***Perf. 12½***

3L89 A8 $50 orange .20 *3.50*
3L90 A8 $100 crimson .20 *1.00*
3L91 A8 $200 green .55 *1.00*
3L92 A8 $300 rose brn 8.75 2.25
3L93 A8 $400 blue 8.75 2.25
3L94 A8 $500 brown 8.75 1.25
3L95 A8 $700 violet 3.00 3.50
Nos. 3L89-3L95 (7) 30.20 14.75

1949, Dec. **Engr.** ***Perf. 14***

3L96 A9 $1000 orange 2.60 1.50
3L97 A9 $3000 dark blue .20 *1.25*
3L98 A9 $5000 crimson .20 *2.40*
3L99 A9 $10,000 red brown .20 *4.75*
Nos. 3L96-3L99 (4) 3.20 *9.90*

NORTH CHINA PARCEL POST STAMPS

Parcel Post Stamps of China Nos. Q23-Q27 (Type PP3) Surcharged in Red, Black (#3LQ6-3LQ9) or Blue (#3LQ2)

政郵民人
元百捌
北 華
a

作圓佰伍暫
電郵北華
作 暫
500
b

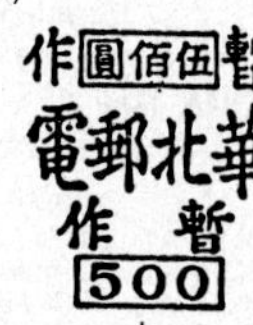

1949, June

Surcharged Type "a"

3LQ1 $300 on $6,000,000 55.00
3LQ2 $400 on $8,000,000 55.00
3LQ3 $500 on $10,000,000 55.00
3LQ4 $800 on $5,000,000 55.00
3LQ5 $1000 on $3,000,000 75.00

Surcharged Type "b"

3LQ6 $500 on $3,000,000 75.00
3LQ7 $1000 on $5,000,000 90.00
3LQ8 $3000 on $8,000,000 225.00
3LQ9 $5000 on $10,000,000 300.00
Nos. 3LQ1-3LQ9 (9) 985.00

Nos. 3LQ8-3LQ9 have large numerals unboxed.

Remittance Stamps of China (like North China Type A4) Surcharged in Black or Red

政郵民人
紙印裹包
元 六
北 華
a

北 華
圓拾貳
紙印裹包
圓拾貳
北 華
b

Peking Surcharge "a"

1949, June **Litho.** ***Perf. 13***

3LQ10 $6 on $5 ver 10.50 3.25
3LQ11 $20 on $50 gray 10.50 3.25
3LQ12 $50 on $20 dk vio brn 10.50 3.25
3LQ13 $100 on $10 ol grn 10.50 6.50

Tientsin Surcharge "b"

Engr. ***Perf. 14***

3LQ14 $20 on $1 brn org 12.00 5.25
a. Perf. 12½ 20.00 7.00
3LQ15 $30 on $2 dk grn 12.00 3.75
a. Red surcharge 20.00 7.00
3LQ16 $30 on $10 ol grn *90.00 40.00*
3LQ17 $100 on $10 gray grn (R) 12.00 5.25

Litho.

Perf. 13

3LQ18 $50 on $5 red 12.00 5.25

Engr.

Perf. 14

3LQ19 $20 on $1 org brn 35.00 16.00

Perf. 12½

3LQ20 $100 on $10 yel grn (R) 60.00 30.00

Typo.

Roulette 9½

3LQ21 $30 on $2 bl grn (R) 45.00 20.00

The surcharge on No. 3LQ19 is without first and last lines.

Nos. 3LQ14, 3LQ14a, 3LQ15, 3LQ15a, 3LQ16-3LQ17, 3LQ19-3LQ20 issued with gum.

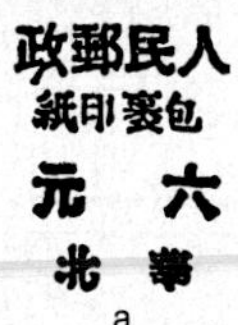

Locomotive — PP1

1949, Nov. **Engr.** ***Perf. 14***

3LQ22 PP1 $500 crimn 8.00 12.50
3LQ23 PP1 $1000 dp bl *60.00* 21.00
3LQ24 PP1 $2000 green *60.00* 30.00
3LQ25 PP1 $5000 dp ol *90.00* 67.50
3LQ26 PP1 $10,000 orange *175.00* 125.00
3LQ27 PP1 $20,000 red brn *350.00* 325.00
3LQ28 PP1 $50,000 brn pur *750.00* 625.00
Nos. 3LQ22-3LQ28 (7) *1,493.* 1,206.

NORTHWEST CHINA

The Northwest China Liberation Area consisted of the provinces of Sinkiang, Tsinghai, Ningsia and the western part of Shensi. The area was first established as the Shensi-Kansu-Ningsia Border Area in October, 1936, after the Long March to Yenan. Remote Sinkiang was not included until late 1949.

All Stamps Issued without Gum

Pagoda on Yenan Hill — A1

1945, Mar. **Litho.** ***Imperf.***

4L1 A1 $1 green 22.50
4L2 A1 $5 dk blue 125.00
4L3 A1 $10 rose red 18.00
4L4 A1 $50 dull pur 14.00
4L5 A1 $100 yel org 18.00
Nos. 4L1-4L5 (5) 197.50

Rouletted 9

4L1a A1 $1 82.50
4L2a A1 $5 125.00
4L3a A1 $10 82.50

First issue; denomination in Chinese and Arabic. Heavy shading at top of vignette. Columns at sides.

See types A2, A3 and A4. For surcharges see Nos. 4L6-4L10, 4L23.

Nos. 4L1-4L2 Surcharged in Red:

a

三暫
十
圓作
b

c

九暫
十
元作
d

1946, Nov.

4L6 A1 (a) $30 on $1 grn 20.00
4L7 A1 (b) $30 on $1 grn *100.00*
a. Rectangular lower left character *1,000.*
4L8 A1 (c) $30 on $1 grn 15.00
4L9 A1 (b) $60 on $1 grn 2,500.
4L10 A1 (d) $90 on $5 dk bl 20.00

Surcharge on Nos. 4L7a is type "b" as illustrated. Surcharge on No. 4L7 differs from "b," having lower left character as in type "a."

Surcharge on No. 4L9 the upper left surcharge character differs from that shown in "b."

A2

Pagoda on Yenan Hill (same size) — A3

1948, June

4L11 A2 $100 buff 160.00
4L12 A2 $300 rose pink 1.10
4L13 A2 $500 red 4.00
4L14 A2 $1000 blue 4.00
4L15 A2 $2000 yel grn 27.50
4L16 A2 $5000 dull pur 11.50
Nos. 4L11-4L16 (6) 208.10

Second issue; denominations in Chinese only. Many shades and proofs exist.

For surcharge see No. 4L24.

1948, Dec.
4L17 A3 10c yel org 1.50
4L18 A3 20c lemon 1.50
4L19 A3 $1 dk blue 1.50
4L20 A3 $2 vermilion 1.50
4L21 A3 $5 pale bl grn 9.00
4L22 A3 $10 violet 13.50
Nos. 4L17-4L22 (6) 28.50

Third issue; ornamental border at sides. Many shades exist.

Nos. 4L2 and 4L13 Surcharged in Red or Black

1949, Jan.
4L23 A1 $1 on $5 dk bl 35.00
4L24 A2 $2 on $500 red 21.00

Pagoda on Yenan Hill — A4

1949, May 1
4L25 A4 50c yel to olive .20 .20
4L26 A4 $1 dl bl to indigo .20 .20
4L27 A4 $3 ol yel to org yel .20 .20
4L28 A4 $5 blue green 1.25 .20
a. Upper left character as on #4L25
4L29 A4 $10 vio to dp vio 4.25 3.50
4L30 A4 $20 pink to rose red 5.75 8.00
Nos. 4L25-4L30 (6) 11.85 12.30

Fourth issue; light shading at top of vignette, columns without ornaments at sides. Many shades exist.

人民郵政(陝)

China Nos. 959, F2 and E12 Overprinted ("People's Post, Shensi")

1949, June 13 Engr. *Perf. 12½*
4L31 A96 orange 15.00 15.00
4L32 R2 carmine 27.50 27.50
4L33 SD2 red vio 27.50 27.50
Nos. 4L31-4L33 (3) 70.00 70.00

Stamps of China, Sun Yat-sen Type A94 of 1949, Overprinted in Black or Red ("People's Post, Shensi")

Lithographed; Engraved
1949, July 1 *Perf. 14, 12½*
4L34 $10 green (887) 1.00 1.00
4L35 $20 vio brn (888) 1.00 2.00
4L36 $20 vio brn (896) 1.00 1.00
4L37 $50 dk Prus grn (889; R) 5.75 5.00
4L38 $50 grn (951) 5.75 5.00
4L39 $100 org brn (890) 14.00 6.00
4L40 $500 ros lil (892) 20.00 6.00
4L41 $1000 dp bl (952; R) 27.50 10.00
4L42 $2000 vio (902;R) 27.50 12.00
4L43 $5000 car (953) 40.00 25.00
4L44 $10,000 brn (954) 75.00 50.00
Nos. 4L34-4L44 (11) 218.50 123.00

Kansu-Ningsia-Tsinghai Area, Lanchow Overprints

China Nos. 959a, F2 and E12 Overprinted ("People's Post, Kansu")

1949, Oct. Engr. *Rouletted*
4L45 A96 orange 12.00 18.00
Perf. 12½
4L46 R2 carmine 20.00 25.00
4L47 SD2 red vio 20.00 25.00
Nos. 4L45-4L47 (3) 52.00 68.00

Stamps of China, Sun Yat-sen Type A94 of 1949, Overprinted ("People's Post, Kansu")

Engraved; Lithographed
1949, Oct. *Perf. 14, 12½*
4L48 $10 grn (887) 2.00 2.00
4L49 $20 vio brn (888) 2.00 3.00
4L50 $50 dk Prus grn (889) 5.00 8.00
4L51 $100 org brn (890) 3.25 3.00
4L52 $100 dk org brn (898) 5.00 4.00
4L53 $200 red org (891) 6.50 5.00
4L54 $500 rose lil (892) 6.50 5.00
4L55 $1000 blue (894) 3.25 3.00
4L56 $1000 dp bl (901) 6.50 5.00
4L57 $2000 vio (902) 11.00 9.00
4L58 $5000 lt bl (903) 22.00 18.00
4L59 $10,000 sepia (904) 30.00 25.00
4L60 $20,000 ap grn (905) 60.00 50.00
Nos. 4L48-4L60 (13) 163.00 140.00

No. 4L54-4L60 exist with wider spaced overprints.

China Nos. 959, F2 and 791-792 Surcharged in Black or Red ("People's Post, Sinkiang")

1949, Oct.
4L61 A96 $1 on org 27.50 25.00
4L62 R2 $3 on car 27.50 25.00
4L63 A82 10c on $50,000 dp bl (R) 27.50 25.00
4L64 A82 $1.50 on $100,000 dl grn (R) 27.50 30.00
Nos. 4L61-4L64 (4) 110.00 105.00

Northwest People's Post

Mao Tse-tung — A5

Great Wall — A6

1949, Oct. 15 Litho. *Imperf.*
4L65 A5 $50 rose 1.75 2.40
a. $200 cliche in $50 plate 200.00
4L66 A6 $100 dark blue .90 *.95*
4L67 A5 $200 orange .90 *4.00*
4L68 A6 $400 sepia 3.50 4.00
Nos. 4L65-4L68 (4) 7.05 *11.35*

EAST CHINA

The East China Liberation Area included the provinces of Shantung, Kiangsu, Chekiang, Anhwei and Fukien. The original postal service established in Shantung in 1941, became the East China Posts and Telegraph General Office in July, 1948.

All Stamps Issued without Gum

Mao Tse-tung — A1

Transportation and Tower — A2

1948, Mar. Litho. *Perf. 10½*
5L1 A1 $50 yel org 1.50 1.00
5L2 A1 $100 dp rose 4.00 3.50
5L3 A1 $200 dk vio bl 4.00 3.50
5L4 A1 $300 brt grn 5.00 3.50
5L5 A1 $500 dp blue 1.90 1.50
5L6 A1 $800 vermilion 5.00 4.00
5L7 A1 $1000 dk blue 10.00 8.00
5L8 A1 $5000 rose 20.00 15.00
5L9 A1 $10,000 dp car 35.00 30.00
Nos. 5L1-5L9 (9) 86.40 70.00

Many varieties, including unissued imperforates exist.

Perf. 9 to 11 and compound
1949, Apr. Litho.
5L10 A2 $1 yel grn .20 .20
5L11 A2 $2 blue grn .20 .20
5L12 A2 $3 dull red .20 .20
5L13 A2 $5 pale brn (ovpt. 4x4mm) .20 .20
a. Without overprint 65.00 65.00
b. Overprint 3x3mm 1.00 1.00
5L14 A2 $10 ultra .20 .20
5L15 A2 $13 brt vio .20 .20
5L16 A2 $18 brt blue .20 .20
5L17 A2 $21 vermilion .20 .20
5L18 A2 $30 gray .20 .20
5L19 A2 $50 crimson .25 *.35*
5L20 A2 $100 olive 10.50 9.00
Nos. 5L10-5L20 (11) 12.55 11.15

Seventh anniv. of Shantung Communist Postal Administration. The overprint on the $5, character "yu" meaning "Posts," obliterates Japanese flag on tower, erroneously included in design. Value, imperfs. of Nos. 5L10-5L12, 5L13a, 5L14-5L20 on different paper, set $125.

Train and Postal Runner (1949.2.7) — A3

Mao, Soldiers, Map — A4

1949, Apr. Litho. *Perf. 8 to 11*
5L21 A3 $1 brt emer .20 .20
5L22 A3 $2 blue grn .20 .20
5L23 A3 $3 dk red .20 .20
5L24 A3 $5 brown .20 .20
5L25 A3 $10 ultra .40 .20
5L26 A3 $13 brt vio .20 .20
5L27 A3 $18 brt blue .20 .20
5L28 A3 $21 vermilion .20 .20
5L29 A3 $30 slate .20 .30
5L30 A3 $50 crimson .30 .30
5L31 A3 $100 olive .60 .60
Nos. 5L21-5L31 (11) 2.90 2.80

7th anniv. of Shantung P. O., Feb. 7. Imperf. sets were sold by the Philatelic Dept., Tientsin P.O. Value $40. See Nos. 5L69-5L76. For surcharges see People's Republic of China Nos. 77-81.

Perf. 9½ to 11 and comp.
1949, Apr.
5L32 A4 $1 brt emer .20 .20
5L33 A4 $2 blue grn .20 .20
5L34 A4 $3 dull red .20 .20
5L35 A4 $5 brown .20 .20
5L36 A4 $10 ultra .20 .20
5L37 A4 $13 brt vio .20 .20
5L38 A4 $18 brt blue .20 .20
5L39 A4 $21 vermilion .20 .20
5L40 A4 $30 gray .20 .20
5L41 A4 $50 crimson .20 .20
5L42 A4 $100 olive 2.00 2.00
Nos. 5L32-5L42 (11) 4.00 4.00

Victory of Hwai-Hai (Hwaiying and Haichow). Imperf. sets were sold by the Philatelic Dept., Tientsin P.O. Value, set $100.

Stamps of China, Sun Yat-sen Type of 1949, Surcharged in Red or Black

(Nanking) — a

(Wuhu) — b

1949, May 4 Engr. *Perf. 12½*
5L43 A94 (a) $1 on $10 grn (895, R) .50 .50
a. Perf. 13 3.00 3.00
5L44 A94 (a) $3 on $20 vio brn (896) .50 .50
a. Perf. 13 .75 2.00
b. Perf. 14 5.50 5.50
c. Surcharge inverted 200.00

Sun Yat-sen Type A94 Surcharged Type "b"

Lithographed, Engraved
1949, May *Perf. 12½, 14*
5L45 $30 on $1000 dp bl (901 7.50 5.00
5L46 $30 on $1000 bl (894) 7.50 5.00
5L47 $50 on $200 org red (899) 7.50 5.00
5L48 $100 on $5000 lt bl (903, R) 16.00 13.00
5L49 $300 on $10,000 sep (904, R) 50.00 40.00
5L50 $500 on $200 org red (899) 75.00 60.00
Nos. 5L45-5L50 (6) 163.50 128.00

Many varieties exist.

China Nos. 913a and 913 Surcharged in Blue, Green, Black or Red

(East China)

1949, May Litho. *Perf. 12½*
5L51 A95 $5 on 50c on $20 brn, II (B) 14.00 10.00
a. Green surcharge 100.00 *50.00*
5L52 A95 $10 on 50c on $20 brn, II 14.00 10.00
5L53 A95 $20 on 50c on $20 red brn, II (R) 14.00 10.00
a. Type I (R) 21.00 21.00
Nos. 5L51-5L53 (3) 42.00 30.00

Stamps of China, Sun Yat-sen Type of 1949, Surcharged in Black or Red

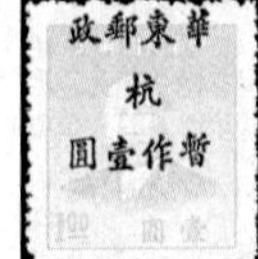
(Hangchow)

Engr., Litho. (No. 5L57)
1949, June 25 *Perf. 14, 12½*
5L54 A94 $1 on $1 org (886) 1.40 1.25
5L55 A94 $3 on $20 vio brn (896, R) .75 .70
5L56 A94 $5 on $100 org brn (890) 3.75 1.65
5L57 A94 $5 on $100 dk org brn (898) 1.75 .50
5L58 A94 $10 on $50 dk Prus grn (889, R) 13.00 10.50
5L59 A94 $13 on $10 grn (895) .30 *.60*
Nos. 5L54-5L59 (6) 20.95 15.20

East China Liberation Area

Maps of Shanghai and Nanking — A5

1949, May 30 Litho. *Perf. 8½ to 11*
5L60 A5 $1 orange ver .20 *.25*
5L61 A5 $2 blue green .20 *.25*
5L62 A5 $3 brt violet .20 *.20*
5L63 A5 $5 violet brn .20 *.20*
5L64 A5 $10 ultra .20 *.20*
5L65 A5 $30 slate .20 *.25*
5L66 A5 $50 carmine .20 *.50*

5L67 A5 $100 olive .20 *.40*
5L68 A5 $500 orange 3.75 2.00
Nos. 5L60-5L68 (9) 5.35 *4.25*

Liberation of Shanghai and Nanking. Many shades, paper and perforation varieties and imperfs. exist.

Train and Postal Runner Type Dated "1949"

1949, July-1950, Feb. ***Perf. 12½, 14***
5L69 A3 $10 dp ultra .20 *.20*
5L70 A3 $15 orange ver .20 *.40*
a. $15 red, perf. 14 .35 .20
5L71 A3 $30 slate green .20 .20
a. Perf. 12½ .35 .20
5L72 A3 $50 carmine .20 *.40*
5L73 A3 $60 bl grn, perf. 14 .20 *.60*
5L74 A3 $100 ol, perf. 14 2.25 .40
5L75 A3 $1600 vio bl ('50) .55 *2.00*
5L76 A3 $2000 brn vio ('50) .70 *2.00*
Nos. 5L69-5L76 (8) 4.50 *6.20*

Chu Teh, Mao, Troops with Flags — A7

Mao Tse-tung — A8

1949, Aug. 17 ***Perf. 12½***
5L77 A7 $70 orange .20 *.20*
5L78 A7 $270 crimson .20 *.20*
5L79 A7 $370 emerald .30 .30
5L80 A7 $470 vio brn .50 .40
5L81 A7 $570 blue .20 *.30*
Nos. 5L77-5L81 (5) 1.40 1.40

22nd anniv. of the People's Liberation Army.
For similar type see Southwest China A1.

1949, Oct.
5L82 A8 $10 dk blue 2.25 *3.00*
5L83 A8 $15 vermilion 2.75 *3.25*
5L84 A8 $70 brown .20 .20
5L85 A8 $100 vio brn .20 .20
5L86 A8 $150 orange .20 .20
5L87 A8 $200 grnsh gray .20 .20
5L88 A8 $500 gray bl .20 .20
5L89 A8 $1000 rose .20 .20
5L90 A8 $2000 emerald .20 .20
Nos. 5L82-5L90 (9) 6.40 *7.65*

For surcharges see People's Republic of China Nos. 82-84.

Stamps of China, Sun Yat-sen Type of 1949 Surcharged in Black or Red

1949, Nov. **Litho.** ***Perf. 12½***
5L91 A94 $400 on $200 org red (899) 22.50 1.00
5L92 A94 $1000 on $50 grnsh gray (897, R) 2.00 .65
5L93 A94 $1200 on $100 dk org brn (898) .20 *1.00*
5L94 A94 $1600 on $20,000 ap grn (905) .20 *2.00*
5L95 A94 $2000 on $1000 dp bl (952,R) .20 *.65*
a. Perf. 14 75.00 25.00
Nos. 5L91-5L95 (5) 25.10 *5.30*

EAST CHINA PARCEL POST STAMPS

Parcel Post Stamps of China 1945-48 Surcharged

(Shantung)

1949, Aug. 1 **Engr.** ***Perf. 13***
5LQ1 PP1 $200 on $500 grn 8.00 8.00
5LQ2 PP1 $500 on $1000 bl 18.00 18.00

Type PP3 ***Perf. 13½***
5LQ3 $200 on $200,000 dk grn 16.00 16.00
5LQ4 $200 on $10,000,000 sage grn 14.00 14.00
5LQ5 $500 on $7000 dl bl 40.00 40.00
5LQ6 $500 on $50,000 indigo 10.00 10.00
5LQ7 $1000 on $10,000 car rose 10.00 10.00
5LQ8 $1000 on $100,000 dk rose brn 18.00 18.00
5LQ9 $1000 on $300,000 pink 10.00 10.00
5LQ10 $1000 on $500,000 vio brn 52.50 45.00
5LQ11 $1000 on $8,000,000 org ver 12.00 12.00
5LQ12 $2000 on $5,000,000 dl vio 30.00 30.00
5LQ13 $2000 on $6,000,000 brn blk 35.00 35.00
5LQ14 $3000 on $30,000 ol 35.00 35.00
5LQ15 $3000 on $70,000 org brn 24.00 24.00
5LQ16 $5000 on $3,000,000 dl bl 52.50 52.50
Nos. 5LQ1-5LQ16 (16) 385.00 377.50

China Type A97, No. 987 Surcharged

政郵東華
$200 $500
$1000 $2000
$5000 $10,000

1949, Sept. 7 **Litho.** ***Perf. 12½***
5LQ17 $200 on $10 57.50 30.00
5LQ18 $500 on $10 57.50 30.00
5LQ19 $1000 on $10 57.50 30.00
5LQ20 $2000 on $10 57.50 30.00
5LQ21 $5000 on $10 57.50 30.00
5LQ22 $10,000 on $10 150.00 30.00
Nos. 5LQ17-5LQ22 (6) 437.50 180.00

Flying Geese Type of China, 1949, and China Nos. 984-986 Surcharged in Red or Black

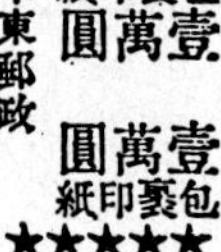

1950, Jan. 28
5LQ23 A97 $5000 on 10c bl vio (R) 97.50 65.00
5LQ24 A97 $10,000 on $1 brn org 97.50 65.00
5LQ25 A97 $20,000 on $2 bl 97.50 65.00
5LQ26 A97 $50,000 on $5 car rose 97.50 65.00
Nos. 5L23-5L26 (4) 390.00 260.00

Parcel Post Stamps of China Type PP3, Nos. Q1-Q2, Q12-Q13 Surcharged in Red or Black

1950, Jan. 28 **Engr.** ***Perf. 13, 13½***
5LQ27 $5000 on $500 grn (R) .50 *55.00*
5LQ28 $10,000 on $1000 bl (R) 125.00 55.00
5LQ29 $20,000 on $3000 bl grn 125.00 85.00
5LQ30 $50,000 on $5000 org red 9.50 55.00
Nos. 5L27-5L30 (4) 260.00 250.00

CENTRAL CHINA

The Central Chinese Liberation Area included the provinces of Honan, Hupeh, Hunan and Kiangsi. The area was established between August and September, 1949, following the occupation of Hankow by Red Army forces.

All Stamps Issued without Gum

Hupeh Postal and Telegraph Administration

Stamps of China, Sun Yat-sen Type A94 of 1949, Surcharged ("Chinese P.O., Temporary Use")

Engraved; Lithographed

1949, June 4 ***Perf. 14, 12½***

Thin parallel lines

6L1 $1 on $200 red org (891) .75 .75
6L2 $6 on $10,000 sep (904) .75 .75
6L3 $15 on $1 org (886) .75 .75
6L4 $30 on $100 org brn (890) 3.75 1.50
6L5 $30 on $100 dk org brn (898) .75 .75
6L6 $50 on $20 vio brn (896) 18.00 7.00
6L7 $80 on $1000 dp bl (901) 2.25 1.00

Thick parallel lines

6L8 $1 on $200 red org (891) 3.75 3.50
6L9 $3 on $5000 lt bl (903) .50 .50
6L10 $10 on $500 rose lil (892) .50 .50
6L11 $10 on $500 rose lil (900) 3.75 3.50
6L12 $50 on $20 vio brn (888) 3.75 3.50
6L13 $50 on $20 vio brn (896) 1.00 1.00
6L14 $80 on $1000 bl (894) 3.75 3.50
6L15 $80 on $1000 dp bl (901) 12.50 8.00
6L16 $100 on $50 dk Prus grn (903) 1.50 2.50
Nos. 6L1-6L16 (16) 58.00 39.00

Kiangsi Postal and Telegraph Administration.

Central Trust Revenue Stamps of China Surcharged ("People's Post, Kiangsi")

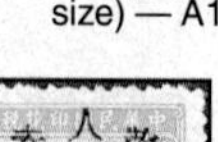
(same size) — A1

$30

$60

1949, June 20 **Engr.** ***Perf. 12½***
6L17 A1 $3 on $30 pur 1.00 1.00
6L18 A1 $15 on $15 red org 1.00 1.00
6L19 A1 $30 on $50 dk bl 1.00 1.00
6L20 A1 $60 on $50 dk bl 1.00 1.00
6L21 A1 $130 on $15 red org 1.00 1.00

The $15 surcharge has 3 characters in left vertical row, the $130 surcharge has 5.

Same Surcharge on Sun Yat-sen Issues of China, 1945-49

Engraved, Lithographed
Perf. 14, 12½
6L22 A82 $1 on $250 dp lil (746) 3.00 3.00
6L23 A94 $5 on $1000 dp bl (901) 3.00 3.00
6L24 A94 $5 on $2000 vio (902) 3.00 3.00
6L25 A94 $5 on $5000 lt bl (903) 1.00 1.00
6L26 A94 $10 on $1000 bl (894) 3.00 3.00
6L27 A82 $20 on $4000 gray 1.00 1.00
6L28 A73 $30 on $100 dk car 3.00 3.00
6L29 A82 $30 on $20,000 rose pink 1.00 1.00
6L30 A94 $80 on $500 rose lil (900) 1.00 1.00
6L31 A94 $100 on $1000 dp bl (901) 1.00 1.00
6L32 A82 $200 on $250 dp lil 2.00 2.00
Nos. 6L17-6L32 (16) 27.00 27.00

Central China Posts and Telegraph Administration

Farmer, Soldier and Worker
A2 A3

I — Top white line of square character (yuan) at upper left does not touch left vertical stroke. No gap in shading between soldier's feet.
II — Top line connects with left vertical stroke. Gap in shading between feet.

Perf. 10 to 11½ & Comp.

1949 **Litho.**
6L33 A2 $1 orange 6.00 1.50
6L34 A2 $3 brn org 2.50 1.50
6L35 A2 $6 emerald 2.50 1.50
6L36 A3 $7 yel brn .40 1.50
6L37 A2 $10 bl grn .20 .30
6L38 A3 $14 org brn 14.00 9.00
6L39 A2 $15 ultra .30 .40
6L40 A2 $30 grn, type I .20 .30
a. Type II .20 .20
6L41 A3 $35 gray bl 9.50 10.00
6L42 A2 $50 rose vio 8.00 4.75
6L43 A3 $70 dp grn .20 .20
6L44 A2 $80 pink .40 .80
6L45 A3 $100 bl grn .25 .30
6L46 A3 $220 rose red 3.25 .60
Nos. 6L33-6L46 (14) 47.70 32.65

For surcharges & overprints see #6L63-6L65, 6L66-6L73, 6L75, 6L90-6L98, 6L100-6L108.

Star Enclosing Map of Hankow Area — A4

Two types of $500:
I — Thick numerals of "500." No period after "500."
II — Thin numerals and period.

Two types of $1000:
I — No period after "1000."
II — Period after "1000."

1949, July
6L48 A4 $110 org brn .25 .80
6L49 A4 $130 violet 3.75 1.25
6L50 A4 $200 dp org .20 .25
6L51 A4 $290 brown 1.50 .20
6L52 A4 $370 dk bl 1.50 .80
6L53 A4 $500 lt bl, I 3.75 .50
a. $500 blue, II 18.00 4.00
6L54 A4 $1000 dull red, II 18.00 1.00
a. $1000 dark red, I 25.00 5.00
6L55 A4 $5000 brown .75 2.00
6L56 A4 $10,000 brt pink 1.50 4.00
Nos. 6L48-6L56 (9) 31.20 10.80

For surcharges and overprints see Nos. 6L74, 6L76-6L81, 6L99, 6L109.

Hankow River Customs Building A5

River Wall, Wuchang — A6

Design: $290, $370, River scene, Hanyang.

1949, Aug. 16 ***Perf. 11***
6L57 A5 $70 green 1.25 .85
6L58 A5 $220 crimson 1.25 1.25
6L59 A5 $290 brown 1.25 1.25
6L60 A5 $370 brt blue 1.25 1.25

6L61 A6 $500 purple 1.25 *1.50*
6L62 A6 $1000 vermilion 1.00 *1.50*
Nos. 6L57-6L62 (6) 7.25 *7.60*

Liberation of Hankow, Wuchang and Hanyang.
Exist imperf. About the same value.
For overprints see Nos. 6L82-6L87.

Nos. 6L35, 6L39 and 6L40 Surcharged in Red ("Honan Renminbi Currency")

1949, July

6L63 A2 $7 on $6 emer 3.00 4.00
6L64 A2 $14 on $15 ultra 4.50 4.50
6L65 A2 $70 on $30 grn 7.50 6.50
Nos. 6L63-6L65 (3) 15.00 15.00

Surcharge shown is for $70. The $7 has 5 characters in left column and no bottom line.

Issues of 1949 Overprinted ("Honan Renminbi Currency")

1949, Aug.

6L66 A2 $3 brn org .85 .85
6L67 A3 $7 yel brn .85 .85
6L68 A2 $10 bl grn 1.75 1.75
6L69 A3 $14 org brn 1.75 1.75
6L70 A2 $30 yel grn (6L40a) 1.75 1.75
6L71 A3 $35 gray bl .85 .85
6L72 A2 $50 rose vio 6.25 6.25
6L73 A3 $70 dp grn 1.75 1.75
6L74 A4 $110 org brn 10.00 10.00
6L75 A3 $220 rose red 3.50 3.50
6L76 A4 $290 brown 12.00 12.00
6L77 A4 $370 blue 14.00 14.00
6L78 A4 $500 bl, II 20.00 20.00
6L79 A4 $1000 dk red, I 30.00 30.00
6L80 A4 $5000 brown 77.50 77.50
6L81 A4 $10,000 brt pink 175.00 175.00
Nos. 6L66-6L81 (16) 357.80 357.80

Width of the overprint varies slightly.

Nos. 6L57-6L62 Overprinted ("Honan Renminbi Currency")

1949, Aug. ***Perf. 11***

6L82 A5 $70 green 4.50 1.25
6L83 A5 $220 crimson 4.50 2.50
6L84 A5 $290 brown 4.50 2.50
6L85 A5 $370 brt bl 4.50 3.50
6L86 A6 $500 purple 4.50 3.50
6L87 A6 $1000 vermilion 4.50 5.00
Nos. 6L82-6L87 (6) 27.00 18.25

Width of overprint on Nos. 6L82-6L85, 7mm; on Nos. 6L86-6L87, 12mm.
Exist imperf. About the same value.

Changchow Issue Surcharged in Red ("Honan Renminbi Currency")

(same size) Mao Tse-tung — A7

1949, Sept. ***Perf. 10***

6L88 A7 $290 on $30 yel grn 35.00 30.00
6L89 A7 $370 on $30 yel grn 52.50 40.00

Issues of 1949 Surcharged

1950, Jan.

6L90 A2 $200 on $1 .45 *1.50*
6L91 A2 $200 on $3 2.75 1.50
6L92 A2 $200 on $6 .45 *1.50*
6L93 A3 $200 on $7 2.75 1.50
6L94 A3 $200 on $14 2.75 1.50
6L95 A3 $200 on $35 2.75 2.25
6L96 A3 $200 on $70 2.75 1.50
6L97 A2 $200 on $80 2.75 1.50
6L98 A3 $200 on $220 2.75 1.50
6L99 A4 $200 on $370 .45 *1.50*
6L100 A3 $300 on $70 .45 *2.25*
6L101 A2 $300 on $80 .45 *1.50*
6L102 A3 $300 on $220 .20 *1.50*
6L103 A2 $1200 on $3 27.50 22.50
6L104 A3 $1200 on $7 5.50 4.50
6L105 A3 $1500 on $14 8.00 6.25
6L106 A2 $2100 on $1 37.50 22.50
6L107 A2 $2100 on $6 37.50 22.50
6L108 A3 $2100 on $35 11.50 9.25
6L109 A4 $5000 on $370 4.50 4.50
Nos. 6L90-6L109 (20) 153.70 113.00

Two types of surcharge exist, differing in spacing of characters in top row.

CENTRAL CHINA PARCEL POST STAMPS

Star and Map of Hankow — PP1

1949, Nov. **Litho.** ***Perf. 11, 11½***

6LQ1 PP1 $5000 brown 1.40 *3.00*
6LQ2 PP1 $10,000 scarlet 9.50 7.50
6LQ3 PP1 $20,000 dk sl grn 3.75 *10.50*
6LQ4 PP1 $50,000 vermilion 1.40 *30.00*
Nos. 6LQ1-6LQ4 (4) 16.05 *51.00*

SOUTH CHINA

The South China Liberation Area included the provinces of Kwangtung and Kwangsi and Hainan Island. The South China Postal and Telegraph Administration was organized on or about Nov. 4, 1949.

All Stamps Issued without Gum

Pearl River Bridge, Canton — A1

1949, Nov. 4 **Litho.** ***Imperf.***

7L1 A1 $10 green .25 .20
7L2 A1 $20 sepia .25 .20
7L3 A1 $30 violet .25 .20
7L4 A1 $50 carmine .25 .20
7L5 A1 $100 ultramarine .40 .20
Nos. 7L1-7L5 (5) 1.40 1.00

For surcharges see Nos. 7L19-7L23.

China Nos. 993-995 With Additional Overprint in Red ("Liberation of Swatow")

1949, Nov. 9

7L6 A94 2½c on $500 rose lil (993) 16.00 16.00
a. Handstamped 52.50 52.50
7L7 A94 2½c on $500 rose lil (994) 25.00 25.00
a. Handstamped 52.50 52.50
7L8 A94 15c on $10 grn (995) 18.00 19.00
a. Handstamped 90.00 70.00

On Unit Issues of China, 1949

7L9 A96 org (959) 18.00 19.00
7L10 AP5 bl grn (C62) 22.50 19.00
7L11 SD2 red vio (E12) 22.50 19.00
7L12 R2 car (F2) 19.00 22.50

On Sun Yat-sen and Flying Geese Issues of China

7L13 A94 2c org (974) 150.00 125.00
7L14 A94 4c bl grn (975) 300.00 450.00
7L15 A94 10c dp lil (976) 13.50 22.50
7L16 A94 20c bl (978) 22.50 22.50
7L17 A97 $1 brn org (984) 37.50 37.50
7L18 A97 $10 bl grn (987) 375.00 375.00
Nos. 7L6-7L18 (13) 1,039. 1,172.

Forgeries exist of #7L13-7L14, 7L18.

Nos. 7L1-7L3 Surcharged in Red or Green

1950, Jan.

7L19 A1 $300 on $30 vio (R) 3.00 1.00
7L20 A1 $500 on $20 brn (R) 3.00 1.00
7L21 A1 $800 on $30 vio (G) 3.50 1.25
7L22 A1 $1000 on $10 gray grn (R) 4.25 1.00
7L23 A1 $1000 on $20 brn (R) 4.25 1.00
Nos. 7L19-7L23 (5) 18.00 5.25

SOUTHWEST CHINA

The Southwest China Liberation Area included the provinces of Kweichow, Szechwan, Yunnan, Sikang and Tibet. The Southwest Postal and Telegraph Administration was organized on or about Nov. 15, 1949 after the liberation of Kweiyang, capital of Kweichow Province.

All Stamps Issued without Gum

Chu Teh, Mao and Troops — A1

1949, Dec. **Litho.** ***Perf. 12½***

8L1 A1 $10 deep blue 2.25 2.50
8L2 A1 $20 rose claret .30 .80
8L3 A1 $30 dp org .45 .80
8L4 A1 $50 gray grn .45 .80
8L5 A1 $100 carmine .30 .50
8L6 A1 $200 blue .45 .60
8L7 A1 $300 bl vio .90 .90
8L8 A1 $500 dk gray 1.50 1.25
8L9 A1 $1000 pale pur 4.50 4.00
8L10 A1 $2000 green 15.00 13.00
8L11 A1 $5000 orange 45.00 40.00
Nos. 8L1-8L11 (11) 71.10 65.15

For surcharges and overprints see Nos. 8L21-8L29, 8L40-8L47, 8L55.

China Nos. 974-975, 984, 986-987 Surcharged ("Kweichow People's Post")

1949, Dec. 1 ***Perf. 12½***

8L12 A94 $20 on 2c org 3.00 4.50
8L13 A94 $50 on 4c bl grn 4.50 4.50
8L14 A97 $100 on $1 brn org 9.00 7.25
8L15 A97 $400 on $5 car rose 15.00 22.50
8L16 A97 $2000 on $10 bl grn 60.00 57.50
Nos. 8L12-8L16 (5) 91.50 96.25

Map of China, Flag Planted in Southwest A2

1950, Jan. **Litho.** ***Perf. 9 to 11½***

8L17 A2 $20 dark blue .35 *.60*
8L18 A2 $30 green .35 .60
8L19 A2 $50 red .35 *.90*
8L20 A2 $100 brown .35 *.90*
Nos. 8L17-8L20 (4) 1.40 *3.00*

Liberation of the Southwest.
For surcharges see #8L30-8L39, 8L56-8L59.

Nos. 8L5-8L6 Surcharged

Perf. 12½

8L21 A1 $300 on $100 car 3.25 2.50
8L22 A1 $500 on $100 car 3.25 2.50
8L23 A1 $1200 on $100 car 6.50 5.00
8L24 A1 $1500 on $200 bl 6.50 5.00
8L25 A1 $2000 on $200 bl 10.00 7.00
Nos. 8L21-8L25 (5) 29.50 22.00

Nos. 8L5-8L6 Overprinted ("East Szechwan")

1950, Jan.

8L26 A1 $100 carmine 6.00 7.50
8L27 A1 $200 blue 6.00 7.50

Nos. 8L5-8L6 Handstamp Surcharged

1950, Jan.

8L28 A1 $1200 on $100 car 15.00 *27.50*
8L29 A1 $1500 on $200 bl 40.00 *27.50*

Many varieties, including wide and narrow settings, exist.

Nos. 8L17-8L20 Surcharged in Black or Red

叁仟圓 改作 伍仟圓

$3000 **$5000**

壹萬圓 貳萬圓 伍萬圓

$10,000 **$20,000** **$50,000**

$60

$300

1950 *Perf. 9 to 11½*

No.	Type	Description	Unused	Used
8L30	A2	$60 on $30	17.50	0.00
8L31	A2	$150 on $30	17.50	6.00
8L32	A2	$300 on $20 (R)	1.75	3.00
8L33	A2	$300 on $100	17.50	6.00
8L34	A2	$1500 on $100	30.00	15.00
8L35	A2	$3000 on $50	7.50	15.00
8L36	A2	$5000 on $50	3.25	15.00
8L37	A2	$10,000 on $50	60.00	30.00
8L38	A2	$20,000 on $50	3.75	30.00
8L39	A2	$50,000 on $50	5.50	40.00
		Nos. 8L30-8L39 (10)	164.25	166.00

Nos. 8L5-8L7 Overprinted ("West Szechwan") 川 西

1950, Jan. *Perf. 12½*

No.	Type	Description	Unused	Used
8L40	A1	$100 carmine	10.50	7.00
8L41	A1	$200 pale blue	17.00	12.00
8L42	A1	$300 blue violet	26.00	18.00
		Nos. 8L40-8L42 (3)	53.50	37.00

Nos. 8L4-8L7 Surcharged

蓉

圓百伍作改

蓉

圓仟貳作改

$2000

1950, Jan.

No.	Type	Description	Unused	Used
8L43	A1	$500 on $100	8.75	8.75
a.		Narrow spacing	70.00	60.00
8L44	A1	$800 on $100	8.75	8.75
8L45	A1	$1000 on $50	11.00	11.00
8L46	A1	$2000 on $200	19.00	19.00
8L47	A1	$3000 on $300	35.00	35.00
		Nos. 8L43-8L47 (5)	82.50	82.50

Two lines of surcharge 7mm apart on No. 8L43, 4mm on No. 8L43a.

China Nos. 975 and 977 Surcharged

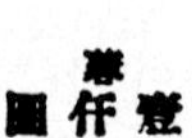

蓉

圓仟壹

$1000

Perf. 12½, 13 or Compound

1950, Jan.

No.	Type	Description	Unused	Used
8L48	A94	$100 on 4c	13.00	13.00
8L49	A94	$200 on 4c	22.50	22.50
8L50	A94	$800 on 16c	65.00	65.00
8L51	A94	$1000 on 16c	300.00	275.00
		Nos. 8L48-8L51 (4)	400.50	375.50

Unit Issue of China Overprinted ("Southwest People's Post")

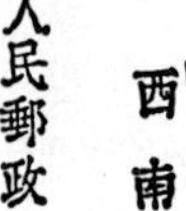

1950, Jan. Engr. ***Rouletted***

No.	Type	Description	Unused	Used
8L52	A96	orange	150.00	175.00
a.		Perf. 12½	225.00	250.00

Perf. 12½

No.	Type	Description	Unused	Used
8L53	SD2	red violet	225.00	250.00
8L54	R2	carmine	225.00	250.00
		Nos. 8L52-8L54 (3)	600.00	675.00

On No. 8L54, space between overprint columns is 3mm and right column is raised to height of left.

Nos. 8L3, 8L17-8L20 Surcharged in Black or Red

1950, Mar. *Perf. 12½, 9 to 11½*

No.	Type	Description	Unused	Used
8L55	A1	$800 on $30	42.50	35.00
8L56	A2	$1000 on $50	9.00	8.00
8L57	A2	$2000 on $100	12.50	12.50
8L58	A2	$4000 on $20 (R)	35.00	25.00
8L59	A2	$5000 on $30	55.00	37.50
		Nos. 8L55-8L59 (5)	154.00	118.00

CHRISTMAS ISLAND

'kris-məs 'ī-lənd

LOCATION — In the Indian Ocean, 230 miles south of Java

GOVT. — A territory of Australia

AREA — 52 sq. mi.

POP. — 2,373 (1999 est.)

Australia took over Christmas Island from Singapore in 1958.

Catalogue values for all unused stamps in this country are for Never Hinged items.

Queen Elizabeth II — A1

Engr.; Name and Value Typo. in Black

1958, Oct. 15 Unwmk. *Perf. 14½*

No.	Type	Description	Unused	Used
1	A1	2c yellow orange	.90	1.90
2	A1	4c brown	.95	.75
3	A1	5c lilac	.95	.75
4	A1	6c dull blue	2.50	.75
5	A1	8c gray brown	5.00	1.25
6	A1	10c violet	3.50	.75
7	A1	12c carmine rose	5.25	4.25
8	A1	20c ultramarine	3.50	4.25
9	A1	50c yellow green	6.00	4.25
10	A1	$1 greenish blue	6.25	4.25
		Nos. 1-10 (10)	34.80	23.15

Map of Island — A2

Island Scene — A3

4c, Moonflower. 5c, Robber crab. 8c, Phosphate train. 10c, Crane loading phosphate. 12c, Flying fish cove. 20c, Loading ship. 50c, Frigate bird. $1, Yellow-billed tropic bird.

Perf. 14x14½, 14½x14

1963, Aug. 28 Engr.

No.	Type	Description	Unused	Used
11	A2	2c orange	.80	.70
12	A2	4c red brown	.45	.30
13	A2	5c rose lilac	.45	.40
14	A3	6c slate	.40	*.70*
15	A2	8c black	2.50	.70
16	A2	10c violet	.40	.30
17	A3	12c dull red	.40	.50
18	A3	20c dark blue	.95	.40
19	A3	50c green	1.25	.40

Size: 35x21mm

No.	Type	Description	Unused	Used
20	A3	$1 orange yellow	2.40	.70
		Nos. 11-20 (10)	10.00	5.10

"Simpson and His Donkey" by Wallace Anderson — A3a

1965, Apr. 14 Photo. *Perf. 13½x13*

No.	Type	Description	Unused	Used
21	A3a	10c brt grn, sepia & blk	.75	*1.00*

ANZAC issue. See note after Australia No. 387.

Moorish Goddess A4

Fish: 1c, Golden striped grouper. 3c, Forceps fish. 4c, Queen triggerfish. 5c, Regal angelfish. 9c, Surgeonfish. 10c, Turkeyfish. 15c, Saddleback butterflyfish. 20c, Clown butterflyfish. 30c, Ghost pipefish. 50c, Lined surgeonfish. $1, Meyer's butterflyfish.

1968-70 Photo. *Perf. 13½*

No.	Type	Description	Unused	Used
22	A4	1c multicolored	.75	1.25
23	A4	2c multicolored	1.00	.55
24	A4	3c multicolored	1.00	.85
25	A4	4c multicolored	1.00	.55
26	A4	5c multicolored	1.00	.55
27	A4	9c multicolored	1.00	1.10
28	A4	10c multicolored	1.00	.55
29	A4	15c multicolored	14.50	7.00
30	A4	20c multicolored	2.75	1.50
31	A4	30c multicolored	14.50	7.00
32	A4	50c multicolored	3.50	*4.25*
33	A4	$1 multicolored	3.50	*5.50*
		Nos. 22-33 (12)	45.50	30.65

Issued: 15c, 30c, 12/14/70; others, 5/6/68.

Christmas Issues

"Hark the Herald Angels Sing" — A5

1969, Nov. 10 Photo. *Perf. 13½*

No.	Type	Description	Unused	Used
34	A5	5c dk blue, gold, buff & red	.25	.25

A6

A7

3c, The Ansidei Madonna, by Raphael. 5c, Virgin and Child, by Morando.

1970, Oct. 26 Photo. *Perf. 14x14½*

No.	Type	Description	Unused	Used
35	A6	3c gold & multi	.20	.20
36	A6	5c silver & multi	.25	.25

1971, Oct. 4

5c, Adoration of the Shepherds, Seville School. 20c, Adoration of the Shepherds, by Guido Reni.

No.	Type	Description	Unused	Used
37	A7	6c black & multi	.75	.50
38	A7	20c dark blue & multi	1.60	1.25

"Flying Fish," 1887 — A8

Ships and Map of Christmas Island: 1c, "Eagle," 1714. 2c, "Redpole," 1890. 3c, "Hoi Houw," 1959. 4c, "Pigot," 1771. 5c, "Valetta," 1968. 7c, "Asia," 1805. 8c, "Islander," 1929-60. 9c, "Imperieuse," 1888 (incorrectly inscribed "Imperious"). 10c, "Egeria," 1887. 20c, "Thomas," 1615. 25c, "Gordon," 1864. 30c, "Cygnet," 1688. 35c, "Triadic," 1958. 50c, "Amethyst," 1857. $1, "Royal Mary," 1643.

1972-73 Photo. *Perf. 14½x13½*

No.	Type	Description	Unused	Used
39	A8	1c yel green & multi	.25	.50
40	A8	2c lt red brn & multi	.30	.60
41	A8	3c dp rose & multi	.30	.60
42	A8	4c multicolored	.40	.65
43	A8	5c multicolored	.40	.65
44	A8	6c lilac & multi	.40	.65
45	A8	7c lt green & multi	.40	.65
46	A8	8c blue & multi	.45	.65
47	A8	9c org & multi	.65	.50
48	A8	10c lem & multi	.55	.60
49	A8	20c tan & multi	.70	.75
50	A8	25c multicolored	.75	1.25
51	A8	30c multicolored	.75	.75
52	A8	35c tan & multi	.75	.75
53	A8	50c ultra & multi	.75	1.25
54	A8	$1 yellow & multi	1.00	1.50
		Nos. 39-54 (16)	8.80	12.30

Issued: 6c, 7c, 8c, 20c, 2/5/72; 1c, 2c, 3c, $1, 6/5/72; 4c, 5c, 9c, 50c, 2/6/73; 10c, 25c, 30c, 35c, 6/4/73.

A9 "Peace"

A9a "Joy"

1972, Oct. 2 Litho. *Perf. 14½*

No.	Type	Description	Unused	Used
55	A9	3c black & multi	.65	.40
56	A9a	3c black & multi	.65	.40
a.		Pair, #55-56	1.40	1.40
57	A9	7c black & multi	.85	.75
58	A9a	7c black & multi	.85	.75
a.		Pair, #57-58	1.75	1.75
		Nos. 55-58 (4)	3.00	2.30

Mother and Child, Christmas Island Map — A10

1973, Oct. 2 Photo. *Perf. 14½x13½*

No.	Type	Description	Unused	Used
59	A10	7c blue & multi	1.00	.60
60	A10	25c brt green & multi	3.00	2.25

Christmas.

Mother and Child with Star and Cross — A11

1974, Oct. 2 Photo. *Perf. 13½x14½*

No.	Type	Description	Unused	Used
61	A11	7c black & lilac rose	.75	.60
62	A11	30c black & yellow	2.25	2.25

Christmas.

Flight into Egypt — A12

1975, Oct. 2 Photo. *Perf. 14½x13½*

No.	Type	Description	Unused	Used
63	A12	10c gold, black & yel	.70	.40
64	A12	35c gold, vio blk & rose	1.40	1.60

Christmas.

Star of Bethlehem and Dove
A13 A14

1976, Oct. 2 Photo. *Perf. 13½*

65 A13 10c red & multi .65 .40
66 A14 10c red & multi .65 .40
a. Pair, #65-66 1.40 1.40
67 A13 35c blue & multi .85 .75
68 A14 35c blue & multi .85 .75
a. Pair, #67-68 1.75 1.75
Nos. 65-68 (4) 3.00 2.30

Christmas.

Andrew Clunies-Ross (first settler) A15

Famous Visitors: 1c, William Dampier, explorer, buccaneer. 2c, Capt. Willem de Vlamingh, Dutch explorer. 3c, Vice Adm. John F. L. P. Maclear, Royal Navy. 4c, John Murray, oceanographer, scientist. 5c, Adm. Pelham Aldrich and crew collecting specimen. 7c, Joseph Jackson Lister, naturalist, and arenga listeri plant. 8c, Adm. William Henry May. 9c, Henry Nicholas Ridley, botanist. 10c, George Clunies-Ross, pioneer phosphate miner. 20c, Capt. Joshua Slocum. 45c, Charles William Andrews, zoologist, and frigate birds. 50c, Karl Richard Hanitsch, zoologist, and fruit pigeon. 75c, Victor W. W. Saunders Purcell, Sinologist. $1, Fam Choo Beng, educator. $2, Harold Spencer-Jones, astronomer.

1977-78 Photo. *Perf. 14x13½*

69 A15 1c multicolored .20 .70
70 A15 2c multicolored .20 .70
71 A15 3c multicolored .25 .70
72 A15 4c multicolored .25 .80
73 A15 5c multicolored .25 .35
74 A15 6c multicolored .25 .55
75 A15 7c multicolored .25 .35
76 A15 8c multicolored .30 .60
77 A15 9c multicolored .35 1.40
78 A15 10c multicolored .30 .50
79 A15 20c multicolored .40 .65
80 A15 45c multicolored .75 .40
81 A15 50c multicolored .90 1.40
82 A15 75c multicolored .80 1.10
83 A15 $1 multicolored .80 1.10
84 A15 $2 multicolored 1.25 1.75
Nos. 69-84 (16) 7.50 13.05

Issued: 1c, 6c, 9c, $1, 4/30/77; 2c, 3c, 4c, $2, 2/22/78; 5c, 7c, 45c, 50c, 5/31/78; 8c, 10c, 20c, 75c, 9/1/78.

Australian Arms, Map of Christmas Island — A16

1977, June 2 Litho. *Perf. 14½x13½*

85 A16 45c multicolored .80 .80

25th anniv. of reign of Elizabeth II.

Souvenir Sheet

Partridge in a Pear Tree — A17

Twelve Days of Christmas: a, Partridge in a pear tree. b, 2 turtle doves. c, 3 French hens. d, 4 calling birds. e, 5 gold rings. f, 6 geese. g, 7 swans. h, 8 maids a-milking. i, 9 ladies dancing. j, 10 lords a-leaping. k, 11 pipers piping. l, 12 drummers drumming.

Unwmk.

1977, Oct. 20 Litho. *Perf. 14*

86 Sheet of 12 1.90 2.25
a.-l. A17 10c, single stamp .20 .20
m. Wmk. 373 ('78) 2.50 3.50

Christmas.

Common Design Types pictured following the introduction.

Elizabeth II Coronation Anniversary
Common Design Types
Souvenir Sheet

1978, Apr. 21 Litho. *Perf. 15*

87 Sheet of 6 3.75 3.75
a. CD326 45c White swan of Bohun .65 *.85*
b. CD327 45c Elizabeth II .65 *.85*
c. CD328 45c Abbott's booby .65 *.85*

No. 87 contains 2 se-tenant strips of Nos. 87a-87c, separated by horizontal gutter with commemorative and descriptive inscriptions.

Souvenir Sheet

Christ Child — A18

Song of Christmas: a, Christ Child. b, Herald angels. c, Redeemer. d, Israel. e, Star. f, Three Wise Men. g, Manger. h. "All He stands for." i, "Shepherds came."

1978, Oct. 2 Litho. *Perf. 14*

88 A18 Sheet of 9 1.50 1.75
a.-i. 10c single stamp .20 .20

Christmas. Each stamp design incorporates one letter of "Christmas."

IYC Emblem, Oriental Children — A19

Design: IYC emblem and children of different races holding hands, continuous design.

1979, Apr. 20 Litho. *Perf. 14*

89 Strip of 5 1.90 2.00
a. A19 20c single stamp .35 .50

International Year of the Child.

Rowland Hill and No. 25 A20

Sir Rowland Hill (1795-1879), originator of penny postage, and Christmas Island stamps: a, #1. b, #11. c, #21. d, #25. e, #34.

1979, Aug. 27 Litho. *Perf. 13x13½*

90 Strip of 5 1.10 1.25
a.-e. A20 20c any single .20 .30

Three Kings Bearing Gifts — A21

Christmas: 55c, Virgin and Child, globe.

1979, Oct. 22 Litho. *Perf. 14x14½*

91 A21 20c multicolored .25 .25
92 A21 55c multicolored .60 .50

25 Years of Golf — A22

1980, Feb. 12 Litho. *Perf. 14½x14*

93 A22 20c shown .30 .35
94 A22 55c Clubhouse .80 1.00

Surveyor, Phosphate Industry A23

1980, May 5 Litho. *Perf. 14x14½*

95 A23 15c shown .30 .40
96 A23 22c Drilling for samples .30 .40
97 A23 40c Sample analysis .35 .45
98 A23 55c Mine planning .55 .65

1980, July 14

99 A23 15c Jungle clearing .30 .30
100 A23 22c Overburden removal .30 .30
101 A23 40c Open cut mining .35 .35
102 A23 55c Restoration .55 .55

1981, Feb. 9

103 A23 22c Screening and stockpiling .30 .30
104 A23 28c Loading train .40 .40
105 A23 40c Rail transport .50 .50
106 A23 60c Drying .60 .60

1981, May 4

107 A23 22c Crushing .30 .35
108 A23 28c Pipeline .40 .45
109 A23 40c Bulk storage .50 .55
110 A23 60c Loading ship .60 .65
Nos. 95-110 (16) 6.60 7.20

Souvenir Sheet

Virgin and Child — A24

1980, Oct. 6 Litho. *Perf. 13½x13*

111 Sheet of 6 2.25 2.40
a. A24 15c Angel .20 .20
b. A24 22c shown .25 .30
c. A24 60c Angel .35 .35
d. A24 15c Angel holding soldier .20 .20
e. A24 22c Kneeling woman and man .25 .30
f. A24 60c Chinese, Indian, European children .35 .35

Christmas. No. 111 contains 2 strips of 3 (Nos. 111a-111c and 111d-111f) with gutter between.

Cryptoblepharus Egeriae — A25

Designs: Reptiles.

1981, Aug. 10 Litho. *Perf. 13x13½*

112 A25 24c shown .30 .30
113 A25 30c Emoia nativitata .50 .50
114 A25 40c Lepidodactylus listeri .60 .60
115 A25 60c Cyrtodactylus nov. .75 .75
Nos. 112-115 (4) 2.15 2.15

Souvenir Sheet

Nativity A26

1981, Oct. 19 Litho. *Perf. 14½x14*

116 Sheet of 4 1.60 1.75
a. A26 18c Angels, star .20 *.25*
b. A26 24c shown .25 *.30*
c. A26 40c Children praying to Jesus .50 *.55*
d. A26 60c Children praying .60 *.70*

Christmas.

Reef Heron A27

1982-83 Litho. *Perf. 14*

117 A27 1c shown .60 .20
118 A27 2c Noddies .60 .20
119 A27 3c Glossy swiftlet .60 .60
120 A27 4c Imperial pigeon .60 .60
121 A27 5c Christmas Isld. silvereyes .70 .60
122 A27 10c Thrush .60 .60
123 A27 25c Silver bosunbird 1.00 .50
124 A27 30c Christmas Isld. emerald doves .65 .60
125 A27 40c Brown boobies .65 .45
126 A27 50c Red-footed boobies .65 .45
127 A27 65c Christmas Isld. frigatebird .65 .45
128 A27 75c Golden bosunbirds .75 .55
129 A27 80c Nankeen kestrel, vert. 1.00 1.50
130 A27 $1 Christmas Isld. hawk owl, vert. 2.10 1.50
131 A27 $2 Goshawk, vert. 1.50 3.25
132 A27 $4 Abbott's boobies, vert. 2.50 2.75
Nos. 117-132 (16) 15.15 14.80

Issued: 1c, 2c, 25c $4, 3/8; 3c, 4c, 10c, $2, 6/14; 40c, 50c, 65c, 75c, 8/23; 5c, 30c, 80c, $1, 2/21/83.

Christmas — A28

25th Anniv. of Boat Club — A29

Paper sculptures.

1982, Oct. 18 Litho. & Embossed

135 A28 27c Joseph .40 .40
136 A28 50c Angel .55 .55
137 A28 75c Mary, Baby Jesus .80 .80
a. Strip of 3, #135-137 1.75 1.75

Perf. 14x14½, 14½x14

1983, May 2 Litho.

Designs: Various boating activities.

138 A29 27c multicolored .50 .50
139 A29 35c multicolored .50 .50
140 A29 50c multi, horiz. .60 .75
141 A29 75c multi, horiz. .65 .75
Nos. 138-141 (4) 2.25 2.50

25th Anniv. of Australian Territory A30

1983, Oct. 1 Litho. *Perf. 14*

142 A30 24c Maps. golden bosun bird, kangaroo .35 .35
143 A30 30c Map, flag .40 .40
144 A30 85c Boeing 727, maps 1.00 1.00
Nos. 142-144 (3) 1.75 1.75

Christmas — A31

Designs: Christmas candles.

1983, Oct. 31 Litho. *Perf. 13½x13*

145 A31 24c multicolored .30 .30
146 A31 30c multicolored .45 .50
147 A31 85c multicolored 1.10 1.40
Nos. 145-147 (3) 1.85 *2.20*

Red Land Crab — A32

1984, Feb. 20 Litho. *Perf. 14x14½*

148 A32 30c Feeding .60 .60
149 A32 40c Migration .70 .70
150 A32 55c Developmental stages .70 .70
151 A32 85c Adult female, young 1.00 1.00
Nos. 148-151 (4) 3.00 3.00

Local Fungi — A33

1984, Apr. 30 *Perf. 13½x14½*

152 A33 30c Leucocoprinus fragilissimus .55 .60
153 A33 40c Microporus xanthopus .65 .75
154 A33 45c Trogia anthidepas .75 .90
155 A33 55c Haddowia longipes .80 1.00
156 A33 85c Phillipsia domingensis 1.00 1.25
Nos. 152-156 (5) 3.75 4.50

Cricket on Christmas Isld., 25th Anniv. A34

1984, July 23 Litho. *Perf. 14*

157 A34 30c Runout .60 .60
158 A34 40c Catch at point .65 .65
159 A34 55c Batsman .70 .70
160 A34 85c Batsman hitting .80 .80
Nos. 157-160 (4) 2.75 *2.75*

Souvenir Sheet

Christmas; Ausipex '84 A35

1984, Sept. 21 Litho. *Perf. 13½*

161 Sheet of 3 + 3 labels 2.50 2.50
a. A35 30c Father Christmas arriving .40 .40
b. A35 55c Distributing gifts .85 .85
c. A35 85c Waving good-bye 1.25 1.25

Crabs A36

1985 Litho. *Perf. 13x13½*

162 A36 30c Birgus latro .80 .80
163 A36 33c Cardiosoma hirtipes .80 .80
164 A36 33c Gecarcoidea natalis .90 .90
165 A36 40c Ocypode ceratophthalma .90 .90
166 A36 45c Ceonobita rugosa .90 .90
167 A36 45c Metasesarma rousseauxi 1.25 1.25
168 A36 55c Coenobita brevimana 1.25 1.25
169 A36 60c Geograpsus stormi 1.25 1.25
170 A36 60c Grapsus tenuicrustatus 1.75 1.75
171 A36 85c Geograpsus grayi 1.90 1.90
172 A36 90c Ocypode cordimana 1.90 1.90
173 A36 90c Geograpsus crinipes 2.40 2.40
Nos. 162-173 (12) 16.00 16.00

Issued: 30c, 40c, 55c, 85c, 1/30; #163, 166, 169, 172, 4/29; #164, 167, 170, 173, 7/22.

Once in Royal David's City — A37

Songs: 33c, While Shepherds Watched Their Flocks by Night. 45c, Away in a Manger. 60c, We Three Kings of Orient Are. 90c, Hark! The Herald Angels Sing.

1985, Oct. 28 Litho. *Perf. 14x14½*

174 A37 27c multicolored .90 *1.10*
175 A37 33c multicolored 1.00 *1.25*
176 A37 45c multicolored 1.25 *1.40*
177 A37 60c multicolored 1.40 *1.50*
178 A37 90c multicolored 1.50 *1.60*
a. Strip of 5, #174-178 6.00 *6.75*

Christmas.

Halley's Comet A38

1986, Apr. 30 Litho. *Perf. 14*

179 A38 33c Over island .60 *.65*
180 A38 45c Edmond Halley .80 *1.00*
181 A38 60c Over phosphate shipping 1.00 *1.75*
182 A38 90c Over Flying Fish Cove 1.50 *2.00*
Nos. 179-182 (4) 3.90 *5.40*

Indigenous Flowers — A39

1986, June 30 Litho. *Perf. 14*

183 A39 33c Ridley's orchid 1.40 .50
184 A39 45c Hanging flower .90 *.85*
185 A39 60c Hoya .90 *1.50*
186 A39 90c Sea hibiscus 1.10 *2.00*
Nos. 183-186 (4) 4.30 *4.85*

Royal Wedding Issue, 1986

Common Design Type

Designs: 33c, Couple in Buckingham Palace garden. 90c, Andrew operating helicopter.

1986, July 23 Litho. *Perf. 14½x14*

187 CD338 33c multicolored .60 *.50*
188 CD338 90c multicolored 1.40 *1.60*

Christmas A40

Santa Claus at Christmas Island.

1986, Sept. 30 Litho. *Perf. 13x13½*

189 A40 30c Speedboating .50 .50
190 A40 36c At the beach .60 .50
191 A40 55c Fishing .90 1.10
192 A40 70c Golfing 1.60 2.50
193 A40 $1 Sleeping in hammock 1.60 3.00
Nos. 189-193 (5) 5.20 7.60

Visiting Ships, Cent. A41

1987, Jan. 21 *Perf. 14½*

194 A41 36c Flying Fish 1.25 .75
195 A41 90c Egeria 2.25 2.25

Wildlife A42

1987-89 Litho. *Perf. 14*

196 A42 1c Blind snake .40 .80
197 A42 2c Blue-tailed skink .40 .80
198 A42 3c Insectivorous bat .80 .80
199 A42 5c Green cricket .80 .80
200 A42 10c Christmas Is. fruit bat .80 .80
201 A42 25c Gecko 1.00 .90
202 A42 30c Praying mantis 1.25 1.10
203 A42 36c Hawk owl 2.75 1.50
204 A42 40c Bull-mouth helmet shell 1.75 1.50
204A A42 41c Nudibranch ('89) 1.25 .60
205 A42 50c Textile cone shell 1.75 1.50
206 A42 65c Brittle-stars 1.25 1.10
207 A42 75c Royal angelfish 1.25 1.50
208 A42 90c Christmas Is. white butterfly 3.75 3.00
209 A42 $1 Mimic butterfly 3.75 3.00
210 A42 $2 Shrew 3.75 6.00
211 A42 $5 Green turtle 4.50 6.00
a. Sheet of 16, #196-204, 205-211 45.00 45.00
Nos. 196-211 (17) 31.20 31.70

Issued: 1c, 2c, 25c, $5, 3/25; 3c, 10c, 36c, $2, 6/24; 40c, 50c, 65c, 75c, 8/26; 5c, 30c, 90c, $1, 3/1/88; 41c, 9/1/89.

Stamps contained in No. 211a inscribed "1988" at bottom.

For overprint see Nos. 246-247.

Souvenir Sheet

Santa Claus Delivering Presents — A43

Illustration reduced.

1987, Oct. 7 Litho. *Perf. 13½*

212 A43 Sheet of 4 5.25 5.25
a. 30c multicolored .60 .60
b. 37c multicolored .65 .65
c. 90c multicolored 1.75 1.75
d. $1 multicolored 1.90 1.90

Christmas. Nos. 212a-212d printed in a continuous design.

Australia Bicentennial A44

Designs: a, First Fleet sighted by 5 Aborginals on land. b, Four Aboriginals on land, one in canoe. c, Ships entering bay, kangaroos. d, Europeans land. e, Flag raising.

1988, Jan. 26 Litho. *Perf. 13*

213 Strip of 5 5.25 *5.25*
a.-e. A44 37c any single 1.00 *1.00*

Nos. 213a-213e printed in a continuous design. See Cocos Islands No. 172.

Annexation of the Island, Cent. — A45

1988, June 8 Litho. *Perf. 14½*

214 A45 37c Capt William Henry May .50 .50
215 A45 53c Annexation ceremony .85 .85
216 A45 95c HMS Imperieuse 1.40 1.40
217 A45 $1.50 Building cairn of stones 1.75 1.75
Nos. 214-217 (4) 4.50 4.50

Settlement of Christmas Is., Cent. — A46

Transportation: 37c, Horse and cart, 1910. 55c, Phosphate mining, 1910. 70c, Steam locomotive, 1914. $1, Arrival of first aircraft, 1957.

1988, Aug. 24 Litho. *Perf. 14½*

218 A46 37c multicolored .75 .40
219 A46 55c multicolored 1.10 .60
220 A46 70c multicolored 1.60 .90
221 A46 $1 multicolored 1.90 1.40
Nos. 218-221 (4) 5.35 3.30

Christmas Presents — A47

1988, Nov. 15 *Perf. 14x14½*

222 A47 32c Bucket, shovel, boat .65 .65
223 A47 39c Snorkeling equipment .80 .80
224 A47 90c Toy soldier, doll, stuffed animals 1.75 1.75
225 A47 $1 Race car, truck, plane 2.00 2.00
Nos. 222-225 (4) 5.20 5.20

Chinese New Year — A48

1989, Jan. 31 *Perf. 14½*
226 A48 39c Good harvest .75 .65
227 A48 70c Prosperity 1.40 1.25
228 A48 90c Good fortune 1.90 1.50
229 A48 $1 Progress 2.10 1.75
Nos. 226-229 (4) 6.15 5.15

Sir John Murray (1841-1914), Oceanographer — A49

1989, Mar. 16 *Perf. 14½x14*
230 A49 39c Portrait .65 .65
231 A49 80c Murray Hill (map) 1.25 1.10
232 A49 $1 Murray's equipment 1.60 1.50
233 A49 $1.10 HMS Challenger 1.75 1.60
Nos. 230-233 (4) 5.25 4.85

Malay-Hari Raya Folk Celebration — A50

1989, May 31 *Perf. 14*
234 A50 39c Children .65 .60
235 A50 55c Tambourine player 1.00 .85
236 A50 80c Girl 1.50 1.25
237 A50 $1.10 Minaret 2.10 1.90
Nos. 234-237 (4) 5.25 4.60

Ferns A51

Christmas A52

1989, Aug. 16
238 A51 41c *Huperzia phlegmaria* .85 .60
239 A51 65c *Asplenium polydon* 1.25 1.00
240 A51 80c *Davallia denticulata* 1.40 1.25
241 A51 $1.10 *Asplenium nidus* 1.75 1.60
Nos. 238-241 (4) 5.25 4.45

1989, Oct. 4 **Litho.** *Perf. 14½x15*

Biblical scenes: 36c, Joseph. 41c, Manger. 80c, Shepherds see star. $1.10, Magi riding camels.

242 A52 36c multi .70 .50
243 A52 41c multi .75 .55
244 A52 80c multi 1.90 .80
245 A52 $1.10 multi 2.00 1.10
Nos. 242-245 (4) 5.35 2.95

Nos. 204A and 209 Overprinted

1989, Oct. 18 **Litho.** *Perf. 14*
246 A42 41c multicolored .75 .50
247 A42 $1 multicolored 2.25 1.00

STAMPSHOW '89, Melbourne.
No. 247 is dated "1989."

1st Sighting of Christmas Is., 375th Anniv. — A53

Sightings of the island: 41c, John Milward, master of the British East India ship *Thomas,* 1615. $1.10, William Mynors, captain of *Royal Mary,* 1643.

1990, Jan. 31 **Litho.** *Perf. 14x15*
248 A53 41c multicolored 2.00 .60
249 A53 $1.10 multicolored 2.50 1.60

Transport Through the Ages — A55

Perf. 14x13½, 13½x14
1990 **Litho.** **Unwmk.**
254 A55 1c Phosphate transport .20 .20
255 A55 2c Phosphate train .45 .40
256 A55 3c Rail car, vert. .25 .20
257 A55 5c Road train .45 .40
258 A55 10c Trishaw, vert. .35 .30
259 A55 15c Terex .75 .65
260 A55 25c Long bus .35 .30
261 A55 30c Passenger rake, vert. .35 .35
262 A55 40c Passenger barge, vert. .40 .40
263 A55 50c Kolek canoe .60 .55
264 A55 65c Flying doctor, ambulance 4.25 1.50
265 A55 75c Tradestore van 1.75 1.50
266 A55 90c Vintage truck 1.75 1.75
267 A55 $1 Water tanker 1.75 1.75
268 A55 $2 Traction engine 2.75 3.25
269 A55 $5 Steam locomotive, flat car 3.75 4.75
Nos. 254-269 (16) 20.15 18.25

Issued: 1c, 3c, 10c, 25c, 30c, 40c, 50c, $5, Apr. 18; others, Aug. 22.

World Wildlife Fund — A56

Abbott's boobies *(Sula abbotti):* 20c, Adult (facing left). 29c, Adult (facing right). No. 273, Adults, nest, hatchling. No. 274a, Adult landing on tree branch. No. 274b, Adult resting on branch. No. 274c, Adult, young in nest.

Perf. 14x14½
1990, June 6 **Litho.** **Unwmk.**
270 A56 10c shown 1.10 .35
271 A56 20c multicolored 1.50 .55
272 A56 29c multicolored 1.75 .60
273 A56 41c multicolored 2.50 .75
Nos. 270-273 (4) 6.85 2.25

Souvenir Sheet
Perf. 14½
274 Sheet of 3 9.00 10.00
a.-c. A56 41c any single 3.00 3.00
d. Overprinted in purple *11.50 11.50*
e. Overprinted in green *15.00 15.00*

No. 274d overprint reads "WORLD STAMP EXHIBITION / AUCKLAND, NEW ZEALAND, 24 AUGUST-2 SEPTEMBER 1990."

No. 274e overprint reads "BIRDPEX '90 National Philatelic Exhibition / University of Canterbury Christchurch NZ 6-9 Dec 1990 / In Conjunction / With The 20th International Ornithological Congress" and Bird's head.

Issued: #274d, Aug. 24; #274e, Dec. 6.

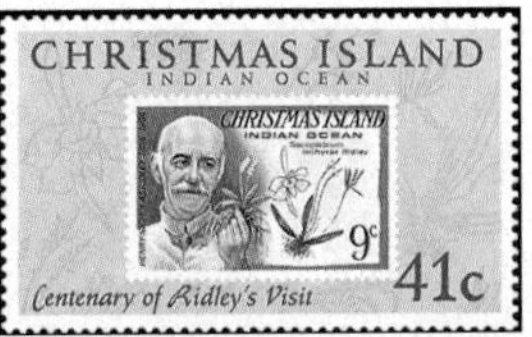
Centenary of Visit by Botanist Henry Ridley — A57

1990, July 11 **Litho.** *Perf. 14½*
275 A57 41c No. 77 1.50 *.80*
276 A57 75c Ridley, vert. 2.25 *2.00*

Christmas A58

Flowers.

1990, Oct. 3 **Litho.** *Perf. 14½*
294 A58 38c Corymborkus veratrifolia .80 .60
295 A58 43c Hoya aldrichii .90 .70
296 A58 80c Quisqualis indica 1.60 2.00
297 A58 $1.20 Barringtonia racemosa 2.00 3.00
Nos. 294-297 (4) 5.30 6.30

1st Phosphate Mining Lease, Cent. — A59

1991, Feb. 13 **Litho.** *Perf. 14½*
298 A59 43c Freighter .90 .90
299 A59 43c Loading rail cars .90 .90
300 A59 85c Shay locomotive 1.25 1.25
301 A59 $1.20 Bucket shovel 1.60 1.60
302 A59 $1.70 Reforestation 1.90 1.90
a. Strip of 5, #298-302 6.50 6.50

Island Police Force — A60

1991, Apr. 17 **Litho.** *Perf. 14½*
303 A60 43c Community relations .90 .65
304 A60 43c Traffic control .90 .65
305 A60 90c Customs and quarantine 1.40 1.60
306 A60 $1.20 Search and rescue 1.90 1.90
a. Souvenir sheet of 4, #303-306 5.25 4.75
Nos. 303-306 (4) 5.10 4.80

Maps — A61

1991, June 19 **Litho.** *Perf. 14*
307 A61 43c 1991 .70 .70
308 A61 75c Goos Atlas, 1666 1.25 1.25
309 A61 $1.10 Apres De Manevillette, 1745 1.60 1.60
310 A61 $1.20 Comberford, 1667 1.90 1.90
Nos. 307-310 (4) 5.45 5.45

Trees A62

1991, Aug. 21 **Litho.** *Perf. 14*
311 A62 43c Bruguiera gymnorrhiza .75 .75
312 A62 70c Syzygium operculatum 1.25 1.25
313 A62 85c Ficus microcarpa 1.40 1.40
314 A62 $1.20 Arenga listeri 2.00 2.00
Nos. 311-314 (4) 5.40 5.40

Christmas A63

Drawings of "What Christmas Means to Me" by: No. 315a, S'ng Yen Luiw. b, Liew Ann Nee. c, Foo Pang Chuan. d, Too Lai Peng. e, Jesamine Wheeler. 43c, Ho Puay Ha. $1, Ng Hooi Hua. $1.20, Yani Kawi.

1991, Oct. 2 **Litho.** *Perf. 14½*
315 Strip of 5 3.00 3.00
a.-e. A63 38c any single .60 .60
316 A63 43c multicolored .75 .65
317 A63 $1 multicolored 1.75 1.75
318 A63 $1.20 multicolored 2.00 2.00
Nos. 315-318 (4) 7.50 7.40

A64

Shells — A65

War Time Evacuation, 50th Anniv.: No. 319, Conference to decide upon evacuation. No. 320, Europeans awaiting barge. $1.05, Barge approaching waiting ship. $1.20, Remaining population waving to TSS Islander.

1992, Feb. 19 **Litho.** *Perf. 14½*
319 A64 45c multicolored .75 .75
320 A64 45c multicolored .75 .75
321 A64 $1.05 multicolored 1.90 1.90
322 A64 $1.20 multicolored 2.10 2.10
Nos. 319-322 (4) 5.50 5.50

1992 **Litho.** *Perf. 15x14½*
327 A65 5c Cypraea tigris .50 .75
328 A65 10c Cypraea caputserpentis .75 .75
329 A65 15c Lambis scorpius 1.00 .75
330 A65 20c Chlamys pallium 1.00 .75
330A A65 25c Engina mendicaria 1.00 .75
331 A65 30c Drupa ricinus 1.00 .75
332 A65 40c Distorsio reticulata 1.00 .80
333 A65 45c Turbo petholatus 1.25 .80
334 A65 50c Cantharus pulcher 1.25 .80
335 A65 60c Conus capitaneus 1.50 .85
336 A65 70c Turbo lajonkairii 1.50 1.00
337 A65 80c Lambis chiragra 2.00 1.10
338 A65 90c Angaria delphinus 2.00 1.25
339 A65 $1 Vasum ceramicum 2.00 1.50
340 A65 $2 Tonna perdix 1.40 2.25
342 A65 $5 Drupa rubusidaea 4.00 4.00
Nos. 327-342 (16) 23.15 18.85

Issued: 10c, 20c, 30c, 45c, 60c, 80c, $1, $2, 4/15; 5c, 15c, 25c, 40c, 50c, 70c, 90c, $5, 8/19.

For overprint see No. 348.

This is an expanding set. Numbers may change.

Sinking of Eidsvold and Nissa Maru, 50th Anniv. A66

Designs: 45c, Eidsvold hit by torpedo. 80c, Eidsvold sinking. $1.05, Nissa Maru hit by torpedo. $1.20, Nissa Maru sinking.

1992, June 17 Litho. ***Perf. 14x13½***

343 A66 45c multicolored .90 .65
344 A66 80c multicolored 1.50 1.50
345 A66 $1.05 multicolored 1.90 2.25
346 A66 $1.20 multicolored 1.90 2.50
Nos. 343-346 (4) 6.20 6.90

Christmas — A67

Coastline, booby birds: a, 40c, Plants on shore, birds. b, 40c, Birds, rocks offshore. c, 45c, Birds on shore. d, $1.05, Birds in flight, coastline. e, $1.20, Forest, rocky coastline.

1992, Oct. 7 Litho. ***Perf. 14½***

347 A67 Strip of 5, #a.-e. 6.00 7.00

No. 342 Ovptd. in Red Violet

1992, Sept. 1 Litho. ***Perf. 15x14½***

348 A65 $5 on #342 9.00 *7.25*

Kuala Lumpur Philatelic Exhibition.

Starting with No. 349, Christmas Island stamps are valid for postage on items mailed in Australia and Australian stamps are valid on items posted on Christmas Island.

Seabirds — A68

Designs: a, Abbott's booby. b, Christmas Island frigatebird. c, Common noddy. d, Golden bosunbird. e, Brown booby.

1993, Mar. 4 Litho. ***Perf. 14½x14***

349 A68 45c Strip of 5, #a.-e. 3.25 3.25
f. Souvenir sheet of 5, #a.-e. 3.50 3.50
g. As "f," overprinted *7.50 7.50*
h. As "f," overprinted *5.25 5.25*

No. 349g Ovptd. in Gold in sheet margin with Taipei '93 emblem and: "ASIAN INTERNATIONAL INVITATION STAMP EXHIBITION / TAIPEI '93" in Chinese and English.

No. 349h Ovptd. in Gold in Sheet Margin with "INDOPEX '93 / 6TH ASIAN INTERNATIONAL PHILATELIC EXHIBITION 1993 / PAMERAN INTERNASIONAL PENGUMPULAN / KEENAM DI ASIA TAHUN 1993" and show emblem.

Issued: #349g, 4/93; #349h, 5/29/93.

Scenic Views — A69

1993, June 1 ***Perf. 14x14½***

350 A69 85c Dolly Beach 1.25 1.25
351 A69 95c Blow holes 1.40 1.40
352 A69 $1.05 Merrial Beach 1.50 1.50
353 A69 $1.20 Rain forest 1.75 1.75
Nos. 350-353 (4) 5.90 5.90

Christmas — A70

1993, Sept. 2 Litho. ***Perf. 14½x14***

354 A70 40c Turtle on beach .55 .55
355 A70 45c Crabs, wave .65 .65
356 A70 $1 Frigatebird, rainforest 1.50 1.50
Nos. 354-356 (3) 2.70 2.70

Naming of Christmas Island, 350th Anniv. — A71

1993, Dec. 1 Litho. ***Perf. 14x14½***

357 A71 $2 multicolored 2.75 2.75

New Year 1994 (Year of the Dog) — A72

1994, Jan. 20 Litho. ***Perf. 14x14½***

358 A72 45c shown .60 .60
359 A72 45c Pekingese .60 .60
a. Pair, #358-359 1.90 1.90
b. Souvenir sheet of 1, #359a 2.25 2.25
c. As "b," overprinted *3.00 3.00*
d. As "b," overprinted *3.00 3.00*
e. As "b," overprinted *3.00 3.00*
f. As "b," overprinted *3.00 3.00*

No. 359c Ovptd. in gold in sheet margin with dog and "Melbourne / STAMP & COIN SHOW / 11-13 February 1994;" No. 359d with "HONG KONG '94 STAMP EXHIBITION" and show emblem; No. 359e with "Canberra /Stamp Show '94 / 19-21 March / 1994" and show emblem; No. 359f with "QUEENSLAND STAMP & COIN SHOW 1994 / JUNE 11, 12, 13."

Issued: #359c, 2/11/94; #359d, 2/18/94; #359e, 3/19/94; #359f, 1995.

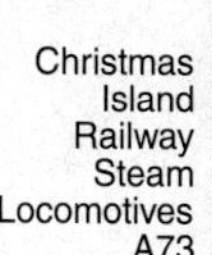

Christmas Island Railway Steam Locomotives A73

1994, May 19 Litho. ***Perf. 14x14½***

360 A73 85c Locomotive No. 4 1.25 1.25
361 A73 95c Locomotive No. 9 1.40 1.40
362 A73 $1.20 Locomotive No. 1 1.75 1.75
Nos. 360-362 (3) 4.40 4.40

Orchids — A74

a, Brachypeza archytas. b, Thelasis capitata. c, Corymborkis veratrifolia. d, Flickingeria nativitatis. e, Dendrobium crumenatum.

1994, Aug. 16 Litho. ***Perf. 14½x14***

363 A74 45c Strip of 5, #a.-e. 3.25 3.25

Christmas A75

1994, Sept. 8 Litho. ***Perf. 14x14½***

364 A75 40c Angel .60 .60
365 A75 45c Wise man .70 .70
366 A75 80c Bethlehem 1.25 1.25
Nos. 364-366 (3) 2.55 2.55

New Year 1995 (Year of the Boar) — A76

Design: 85c, Stylized boar, diff.

1995, Jan. 12 Litho. ***Perf. 14x14½***

367 A76 45c shown .70 .70
368 A76 85c multicolored 1.25 1.25
a. Souvenir sheet, #367-368 2.25 2.25
b. As "a," overprinted *3.50 3.50*

No. 368b ovptd. in gold in sheet margin with outline of boar and: "STAMP & COIN FAIR / ROYAL EXHIBITION BUILDING / MELBOURNE VIC. 3000 . 10-12 FEB 1995."

Christmas Island Golf Course, 40th Anniv. — A77

1995, May 11 Litho. ***Perf. 14***

369 A77 $2.50 multicolored 3.75 3.75

Christmas A78

Santa Claus riding great frigatebird: 40c, Reading map. 45c, Dropping presents. 80c, Waving.

1995, Sept. 14 Litho. ***Perf. 14x14½***

370 A78 40c multicolored .60 .60
371 A78 45c multicolored .70 .70
372 A78 80c multicolored 1.25 1.25
Nos. 370-372 (3) 2.55 2.55

End of World War II, 50th Anniv. — A79

#373a, RAAF reconnaissance flight, 1945. #373b, Arrival of HMS Rother, 1945.

Litho. & Engr.

1995, Oct. 12 ***Perf. 14x14½***

373 Pair 1.75 1.75
a.-b. A79 45c any single .85 .85

Angelfish A80

1995, Oct. 12 Litho.

374 A80 75c Lemonpeel 1.10 1.10
375 A80 $1 Emperor 1.50 1.50

New Year 1996 (Year of the Rat) A81

1996, Jan. 9 Litho. ***Perf. 14x14½***

376 A81 45c Facing right .70 .70
377 A81 45c Facing left .70 .70
a. Pair, #376-377 1.40 1.40
b. Souvenir sheet, #377a 1.90 1.90
c. As "b," overprinted 3.00 3.00

No. 377c overprinted in gold in sheet margin "STAMP AND COIN FAIR / MELBOURNE / 23-25 February 1996."

Fish — A82

1996-97 Litho. ***Perf. 14x14½***

381 A82 20c Pinktail triggerfish .30 .30
383 A82 30c Longnose filefish .45 .45
386 A82 45c Princess anthias .70 .70
390 A82 85c Green moon wrasse 1.25 1.25
391 A82 90c Spotted boxfish 1.40 1.40
392 A82 95c Moorish idol 1.40 1.40
394 A82 $1.20 Glass bigeye 1.75 1.75
Nos. 381-394 (7) 7.25 7.25

Issued: 20c, 30c, 45c, 90c, 4/18/96; 85c, 95c, $1.20, 7/17/97. This is an expanding set. Numbers may change.

Birds — A83

1996, July 11 Litho. ***Perf. 14½x14***

399 A83 45c White-eye .70 .70
400 A83 85c Hawk-owl 1.25 1.25

Christmas A84

Sailing ships, words from Christmas carol: 40c, "I Saw Three Ships." 45c, "Come sailing in." 80c, "On Christmas day in the morning."

1996, Sept. 12 Litho. ***Perf. 14***

401 A84 40c multicolored .65 .65
402 A84 45c multicolored .70 .70
403 A84 80c multicolored 1.25 1.25
Nos. 401-403 (3) 2.60 2.60

Exploration of Australian Coast & Christmas Island by Willem de Vlamingh, 300th Anniv. — A85

"Portrait of a Dutch Navigator," by Jan Verkolje.

1996, Oct. 27 Litho. *Perf. 14*

404 A85 45c multicolored 1.00 1.00

No. 404 was issued se-tenant with Australia No. 1571 (No. 1571a).

New Year 1997 (Year of the Ox) — A86

Constellation and: No. 405, Ox facing right. No. 406, Ox facing left.

1997, Jan. 6 Litho. *Perf. 14x14½*

405 A86 45c multicolored .90 .90
406 A86 45c multicolored .90 .90
a. Pair, #405-406 1.90 1.90
b. Souvenir sheet, #405-406 1.90 2.25

Christmas A87

Santa on Christmas Island: 40c, Reading letters. 45c, Making toys. 80c, In sleigh.

1997, Sept. 11 Litho. *Perf. 14x14½*

407 A87 40c multicolored .60 .60
408 A87 45c multicolored .65 .65
409 A87 80c multicolored 1.25 1.25
Nos. 407-409 (3) 2.50 2.50

New Year 1998 (Year of the Tiger) — A88

1998, Jan. 5 Litho. *Perf. 14x14½*

410 A88 45c shown .65 .65
411 A88 45c Looking backward .65 .65
a. Pair, #410-411 1.50 1.50
b. Souvenir sheet of 2, #410-411 1.50 1.60

Marine Life — A89

Designs: a, 5c, Frigatebird. b, 5c, Ambon chromis, denomination LR. c, 5c, Ambon chromis, denomination LL. d, 5c, Pink anemonefish, denominatiion, UR. e, 5c, Pink anemonefish, denomination LL. f, 10c, Eastern reef egret. g, 10c, Whitelined cod. h, 10c, Pyramid butterfly fish. i, 10c, Dusky parrotfish. j, 10c, Spotted garden eel. k, 25c, Sooty tern. l, 25c, Scissortail sergeant. m, 25c, Thicklip wrasse. n, 25c, Blackaxil chromis. o, 25c, Orange anthias. p, 45c, Brown booby. q, 45c, Green turtle. r, 45c, Pink anemonefish. s, 45c, Blue sea star. t, 45c, Kunie's chromodoris.

1998, Mar. 12 Litho. *Perf. 14*

412 A89 Sheet of 20, #a.-t. 5.50 5.50

Tree Flowers of Christmas — A90

1998, Sept. 3 Litho. *Perf. 14½x14*

413 A90 40c Orchid tree .50 .50
414 A90 80c Flame tree .95 .95
415 A90 95c Sea hibiscus 1.10 1.10
Nos. 413-415 (3) 2.55 2.55

New Year 1999 (Year of the Rabbit) A91

1999, Jan. 14 Litho. *Perf. 14x14½*

416 A91 45c shown .60 .70
417 A91 45c Rabbit looking left .60 .70
a. Pair, #416-417 1.25 1.40
b. Souvenir sheet, #417a 1.50 1.75

Festivals on Christmas Island — A92

Children's drawings: No. 418, Carrying balloons in parade, by Fong Jason. No. 419, Giant crab, by Siti Zanariah Zainal. 85c, Children at night, by Tan Diana, vert. $1.20, Green mosque, tree, by Anwar Ramian, vert.

1999, July 15 Litho. *Perf. 14x14½*

418 A92 45c multicolored .60 .60
419 A92 45c multicolored .60 .60
a. Pair, #418-419 1.25 1.25

Perf. 14½x14

420 A92 85c multicolored 1.10 1.10
421 A92 $1.20 multicolored 1.50 1.50
Nos. 418-421 (4) 3.80 3.80

Christmas A93

Designs: 40c, Santa Claus in hammock. 45c, Santa, birds, crab, lizard, cake. 95c, Santa, booby-drawn sleigh.

1999, Sept. 9 Litho. *Perf. 14x14½*

422 A93 40c multicolored .50 .50
423 A93 45c multicolored .60 .60
424 A93 95c multicolored 1.25 1.25
Nos. 422-424 (3) 2.35 2.35

New Year 2000 (Year of the Dragon) A94

2000, Jan. 13 Litho. *Perf. 14x14½*

425 A94 45c shown .55 .55
426 A94 45c Dragon facing left .55 .55
a. Pair, #425-426 1.10 1.10
b. Souvenir sheet, #426a 1.50 1.75

Faces of Christmas Island — A95

Ordinary people: a, Yeow Jian Min, without shirt. b, Ida Chin, with blue shirt. c, Ho Tak Wah, old man. d, Thomas Faul and James Neill. e, Siti Sanniah Kawi, with striped blouse.

2000, Apr. 13 Litho. *Perf. 14½x14*

427 A95 45c Strip of 5, #a.-e. 3.25 3.75

Christmas — A96

No. 428: a, We three kings of Orient are. b, Bearing gifts we traverse afar. 45c, Star of wonder, star of night.

2000, Sept. 5 Litho. *Perf. 14½x14*

428 Pair 1.25 1.25
a.-b. A96 40c Any single .60 .60
429 A96 45c multi .60 .60

New Year 2001 (Year of the Snake) A97

Snake color: 45c, Green. $1.35, Silver.

Litho. with Foil Application

2001, Jan. 8 *Perf. 14x14½*

430-431 A97 Set of 2 2.25 2.25
a. Souvenir sheet, #430-431 2.25 2.50

Fungi — A98

Designs: $1, Chaetocalathus semisupinus. $1.50, Pycnoporus sanguineus.

2001, Oct. 25 Litho. *Perf. 14x14½*

432-433 A98 Set of 2 3.50 3.75

New Year 2002 (Year of the Horse) — A99

Zodiac Animals and Their Chinese Characters A100

Designs: 45c, Purple horse. $1.35, Gold horse.

No. 436: a, Rat. b, Ox. c, Tiger. d, Rabbit. e, Dragon. f, Snake. g, Horse. h, Sheep. i, Monkey. j, Cock. k, Dog. l, Boar.

Litho. With Foil Application

2002, Jan. 8 *Perf. 14x14½*

434-435 A99 Set of 2 3.25 2.25
a. Souvenir sheet, #434-435 2.25 2.25
436 Sheet of 14, #a-l, #435a 5.00 5.00
a.-d. A100 5c Any single .20 .20
e.-h. A100 15c Any single, orange background .25 .25
i.-l. A100 25c Any single, orange background .35 .35

See No. 442.

Worldwide Fund for Nature (WWF) — A101

Christmas Island birds - No. 437: a, Imperial pigeon. b, Hawk owl.

$1, Goshawk. $1.50, Thrush.

2002, May 1 Litho. *Perf. 14½x14*

437 A101 45c Horiz. pair, #a-b 1.40 1.40
438 A101 $1 multi 1.40 1.40
439 A101 $1.50 multi 2.25 2.25
Nos. 437-439 (3) 5.05 5.05

Zodiac Animals Type of 2002 and

New Year 2003 (Year of the Ram) A102

Designs: 50c, Yellow and orange ram. $1.50, Blue ram.

No. 442: a, Rat. b, Ox. c, Tiger. d, Rabbit. e, Dragon. f, Snake. g, Horse. h, Sheep. i, Monkey. j, Cock. k, Dog. l, Boar.

Litho. With Foil Application

2003, Jan. 7 *Perf. 14x14½*

440-441 A102 Set of 2 2.40 2.40
a. Souvenir sheet, #440-441 2.40 2.40
442 Sheet of 14, #a-l, #441a 4.75 4.75
a.-d. A100 10c Any single, red violet background .20 .20
e.-h. A100 15c Any single, red violet background .20 .20
i.-l. A100 25c Any single, red violet background .30 .30

Christmas — A103

Designs: 45c, Arrival of Santa Claus on whale shark. 50c, Santa giving gifts to red crabs.

2003, Oct. 31 Litho. *Perf. 14½x14*

443-444 A103 Set of 2 1.40 1.40

Zodiac Animals Type of 2002 and

New Year 2004 (Year of the Monkey) A104

Designs: 50c, Yellow and orange monkey. $1.45, Red orange monkey, lotus flower.

No. 447: a, Rat. b, Ox. c, Tiger. d, Rabbit. e, Dragon. f, Snake. g, Horse. h, Sheep. i, Monkey. j, Cock. k, Dog. l, Boar.

Litho. With Foil Application

2004, Jan. 6 *Perf. 14x14½*

445-446 A104 Set of 2 3.00 3.00
446a Souvenir sheet, #445-446 3.00 3.00
447 Sheet of 14, #a-l, #446a 6.25 6.25
a.-d. A100 10c Any single, light and dark blue background .20 .20
e.-h. A100 15c Any single, light and dark blue background .20 .20
i.-l. A100 25c Any single, light and dark blue background .40 .40

No. 446a exists with a 2004 Hong Kong Stamp Expo overprint in sheet margin in red. This sheet was sold at the show, but not on Christmas Island.

Marine Life — A105

No. 448: a, Two butterflyfish, rear of whale shark. b, Three striped fish, front of whale shark. c, Four fish. d, Two fish. e, Two green turtles. f, Two triggerfish (polka dots), red coral at LL. g, Two fish with thin horizontal stripes with yellow tails. h, Two fish with thick vertical stripes. i, Black and white fish. j, Three fish. k, Yellow fish with black spot, blue fish, red coral, yellow coral. l, Striped fish, clam. m, Black fish, small red fish. n Red fish, divers. o, Two striped fish, red coral under denomination. p, Blue and yellow fish, red and white spotted fish, yellow coral. q, Blue and yellow fish, yellow coral, sea anemones. r, Three blue fish with orange spots. s, Sea anemone and two anemonefish. t, Nudibranch, red coral and starfish.

2004, July 13 Litho. *Perf. 14½x14*

448	A105	Sheet of 20	8.25	8.25
a.-e.		10c Any single	.20	.20
f.-o.		25c Any single	.35	.35
p.-t.		50c Any single	.75	.75

CILICIA

sə-'li-shˌē-ˌə

LOCATION — A territory of Turkey, in Southeastern Asia Minor
GOVT. — Former French occupation
AREA — 6,238 sq. mi.
POP. — 383,645
CAPITAL — Adana

British and French forces occupied Cilicia in 1918 and in 1919 its control was transferred to the French. Eventually part of Cilicia was assigned to the French Mandated Territory of Syria but by the Lausanne Treaty of 1923 which fixed the boundary between Syria and Turkey, Cilicia reverted to Turkey.

40 Paras = 1 Piaster

Issued under French Occupation

The overprint on Nos. 2-93 is often found inverted, double, etc.
Numbers in parentheses are those of basic Turkish stamps.

Turkish Stamps of 1913-19 Handstamped

Perf. 11½, 12, 12½, 13½

1919 **Unwmk.**

On Pictorial Issue of 1913

2 A24 2pa red lil (254) 1.40 1.40
3 A25 4pa dk brn (255) 1.10 1.10
4 A27 6pa dk bl (257) 12.50 8.00
5 A32 1¾pi sl & red brn (262) 1.90 1.50

On Issue of 1915

6 A17 1pi bl (300) .75 .75
7 A21 20pa car rose (318) .75 .75
9 A22 20pa car rose (330) 1.90 1.90

On Commemorative Issue of 1916

9A A41 5pa green (345) 100.00 45.00
10 A41 20pa ultra (347) 1.00 .80
11 A41 1pi vio & blk (348) 1.10 1.10
12 A41 5pi yel brn & blk (349) 1.10 1.10

On Issue of 1916-18

13 A44 10pa grn (424) 1.10 1.10
14 A47 50pa ultra (428) 6.75 3.50
15 A51 25pi car, *straw* (434) 1.50 1.50
16 A52 50pi car (437) 1.10 1.00
17 A52 50pi ind (438) 12.50 12.50

On Issue of 1917

18 A53 5pi on 2pa Prus bl (547) 6.00 4.00

On Issue of 1919

19 A47 50pa ultra (555) 9.00 3.00
20 A48 2pi org brn & ind (556) 9.00 4.00
21 A49 5pi pale bl & blk (557) 12.00 3.00

On Newspaper Stamp of 1916

22 N3 5pa on 10pa gray grn (P137) 1.50 1.10

On Semi-Postal Stamps of 1915

22A A21 20pa car rose (B8) 55.00 55.00
22B A21 1pi ultra (B9) 1,500. 1,100.
22C A21 1pi ultra (B13) 1,100. 750.00

On Semi-Postal Stamps of 1916

23 A17 1pi bl (B19) 1.00 .80
24 A21 20pa car rose (B28) 1.25 1.00
25 A21 1pi ultra (B29) 4.50 *5.00*

Turkish Stamps of 1913-18 Handstamped

1919

On Pictorial Issue of 1913

31 A24 2pa red lil (254) 1.00 .80
32 A25 4pa dk brn (255) 1.50 1.50

On Issue of 1915

33 A17 1pi blue (300) 1.25 1.10
34 A22 20pa car rose (330) 1.25 .80

On Commemorative Issue of 1916

35 A41 20pa ultra (347) 1.25 1.10
36 A41 1pi vio & blk (348) .80 .80

On Issue of 1917

40 A53 5pi on 2pa Prus bl (547) 2.50 1.10

On Newspaper Stamp of 1916

41 N3 5pa on 10pa gray grn (P137) 2.50 1.50

On Semi-Postal Stamp of 1915

41A A21 20pa car rose (B8) 150.00 110.00

On Semi-Postal Stamps of 1916

42 A17 1pi blue (B19) 1.50 1.50
43 A21 20pa car rose (B28) 1.50 .80

Turkish Stamps of 1913-19 Handstamped

1919

On Pictorial Issue of 1913

51 A24 2pa red lil (254) 1.50 1.10
52 A25 4pa dk brn (255) 1.50 1.10

On Issue of 1915

53 A17 1pi blue (300) 1.50 .75
55 A22 5pa ocher (328) 5.00 2.25
56 A22 20pa car rose (330) 1.50 1.10

On Commemorative Issue of 1916

57 A41 20pa ultra (347) 1.10 1.10
58 A41 1pi vio & blk (348) 1.10 1.10
59 A41 5pi yel brn & blk (349) 1.25 1.10

On Issue of 1916

59A A17 1pi blue (372) 60.00 50.00

On Issue of 1916-18

60 A43 5pa org (421) 6.00 4.50
61 A46 1pi dl vio (426) 3.00 1.50
63 A52 50pi grn, *straw* (439) 24.00 12.00

On Issue of 1917

64 A53 5pi on 2pa Prus bl (547) 7.00 3.75

On Newspaper Stamp of 1916

65 N3 5pa on 10pa gray grn (P137) 1.50 1.10

On Semi-Postal Stamp of 1915

65A A21 20pa car rose (B8) 825.00 500.00

On Semi-Postal Stamps of 1916

66 A17 1pi blue (B19) 6.00 2.00
67 A19 20pa car (B26) 8.50 3.75
68 A21 20pa car rose (B28) 110.00 60.00
69 A21 20pa car rose (B31) 5.00 2.25

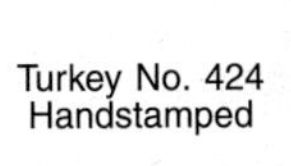

Turkey No. 424 Handstamped

1919

71 A44 10pa green 1.50 1.50

"T.E.O." stands for "Territoires Ennemis Occupés."

Turkish Stamps of 1913-19 Overprinted in Black, Red or Blue

In this setting there are various broken and wrong font letters and the letter "i" is sometimes replaced by a "t."

1919 **On Pictorial Issue of 1913**

75 A30 1pi blue (R) (260) 1.50 .50

On Issue of 1915

76 A21 20pa car rose (318) 3.50 2.00

On Commemorative Issue of 1916

77 A41 20pa ultra (347) 1.50 1.00
78 A41 1pi vio & blk (348) 1.50 .60

On Issue of 1916-18

79 A43 5pa org (Bl) (421) 1.00 .50
80 A44 10pa green (424) 1.00 .50
81 A45 20pa dp rose (Bk) (425) 6.00 5.00
82 A45 20pa dp rose (Bl) (425) .75 .50
83 A48 2pi org brn & ind (429) 1.50 1.00
83C A49 5pi pale bl & blk (R) (430) 1.50 .85
84 A51 25pi car, *straw* (434) 6.00 4.50
85 A52 50pi grn, *straw* (439) 95.00 55.00

On Issue of 1917

85A A53 5pi on 2pa Prus bl (547)
86 A53 5pi on 2pa Prus bl (548) 5.00 3.75

On Newspaper Stamps of 1916-19

87 N3 5pa on 10p gray grn (P137) 2.00 1.75
88 N4 5pa on 2pa ol grn (P173) .75 .50

On Semi-Postal Stamps of 1915-17

90 A21 20pa car rose (B28) 2.00 1.50
91 A41 10pa car (B42) 1.00 .50
92 A11 10pa on 20pa vio brn (B38) 1.10 .75
93 SP1 10pa red vio (B46) 1.75 1.00

It is understood that the newspaper and semi-postal stamps overprinted "Cilicie" were used as ordinary postage stamps.

A1

1920 **Blue Surcharge** ***Perf. 11½***

98 A1 70pa on 5pa red 2.00 .50
99 A1 3½pi on 5pa red 3.00 1.75

Nos. 98-99 exist with surcharge double, inverted, double with one inverted, "OCCUPTTION," etc.

French Offices in Turkey No. 26 Surcharged

1920 ***Perf. 14x13½***

100 A3 20pa on 10c rose red 2.00 .75
a. "PARAS" omitted 25.00 25.00
b. Surcharged on back 22.50 22.50

Three types of "20" exist on No. 100.

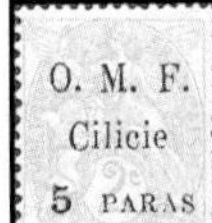

Stamps of France, 1900-17, Surcharged

1920

101 A16 5pa on 2c vio brn .75 .55
102 A22 10pa on 5c green 1.00 .55
103 A22 20pa on 10c red 1.25 1.10
104 A22 1pi on 25c blue 1.50 1.50
105 A20 2pi on 15c gray grn 5.00 4.00
106 A18 5pi on 40c red & gray bl 8.00 6.00
107 A18 10pi on 50c bis brn & lav 7.00 5.50
108 A18 50pi on 1fr cl & ol grn 90.00 90.00
109 A18 100pi on 5fr dk bl & buff 600.00 600.00
Nos. 101-109 (9) 714.50 709.20

Nos. 106 to 109 surcharged in four lines.
"O.M.F." stands for "Occupation Militaire Francaise."

Stamps of France, 1917, Surcharged

1920

110 A16 5pa on 2c vio brn 6.00
111 A22 10pa on 5c green 6.00
112 A22 20pa on 10c red 5.00
113 A22 1pi on 25c blue 5.00
114 A20 2pi on 15c gray grn 15.00
115 A18 5pi on 40c red & gray bl 50.00
116 A18 20pi on 1fr cl & ol grn 70.00
Nos. 110-116 (7) 157.00

On Nos. 115 and 116 "SAND. EST" is placed vertically. "Sand. Est" is an abbreviation of Sandjak de l'Est (Eastern County).
Nos. 110-116 were prepared for use, but never issued.

Stamps of France, 1900-17, Surcharged

1920

117 A16 5pa on 2c vio brn 1.00 .25
a. Inverted surcharge 12.50 12.50
b. Double surcharge 20.00 *21.00*
c. "Cililie" *10.00* *10.00*
d. Surcharge 5pi (error) 25.00 *26.00*
119 A22 10pa on 5c green 1.00 .40
a. Inverted surcharge 12.50 12.50
b. Surch. 5pa (error), invtd. 37.50 30.00
121 A22 20pa on 10c red 1.00 .40
a. Inverted surcharge 12.50 12.50
b. Surch. 10pa (error), invtd. 37.50 30.00
122 A22 1pi on 25c blue .75 .40
a. Double surcharge 47.50 47.50
b. Inverted surcharge 12.50 12.50
123 A20 2pi on 15c gray grn 1.00 .50
a. Double surcharge 17.50 17.50
b. Inverted surcharge 12.50 12.50
124 A18 5pi on 40c red & gray bl 1.50 .75
a. Double surcharge 37.50 37.50
b. Inverted surcharge 12.50 12.50
c. "PIASRTES" 27.50 27.50
125 A18 10pi on 50c bis brn & lavender 2.25 1.25
a. "PIASRTES" 27.50 27.50
126 A18 50pi on 1fr claret & ol grn 6.00 3.00
a. "PIASRTES" 37.50 37.50
b. Inverted surcharge 32.50 26.00
127 A18 100pi on 5fr dk bl & buff 12.00 12.00
a. "PIASRTES" 72.50 72.50
Nos. 117-127 (9) 26.50 18.95

This surcharge has "O.M.F." in thicker letters than the preceding issues.
There were two printings of this surcharge which may be distinguished by the space of 1 or 2mm between "Cilicie" and the numeral.
For overprints see Nos. C1-C2.

AIR POST STAMPS

Nos. 123 and 124 Handstamped

Perf. 14x13½

1920, July 15 **Unwmk.**

No.	Type	Description	Unused	Used
C1	A20	2pi on 15c gray grn	*4,750.*	
C2	A18	5pi on 40c red & gray bl	*4,750.*	
a.		"PIASRTES"		

A very limited number of Nos. C1 and C2 were used on two air mail flights between Adana and Aleppo. At a later date impressions from a new handstamp were struck "to oblige" on stamps of the regular issue of 1920 (Nos. 123, 124, 125 and 126) that were in stock at the Adana Post Office.

Counterfeits exist.

POSTAGE DUE STAMPS

Turkish Postage Due Stamps of 1914 Handstamped

Handstamped

1919 **Unwmk.** *Perf. 12*

No.	Type	Description	Unused	Used
J1	D1	5pa claret	5.00	1.75
J2	D2	20pa red	5.00	1.75
J3	D3	1pi dark blue	7.00	3.25
J4	D4	2pi slate	7.00	3.25
		Nos. J1-J4 (4)	24.00	10.00

Handstamped

No.	Type	Description	Unused	Used
J5	D1	5pa claret	5.00	1.50
J6	D2	20pa red	5.00	1.50
J7	D3	1pi dark blue	8.00	4.00
J8	D4	2pi slate	8.00	3.25
		Nos. J5-J8 (4)	26.00	10.25

Handstamped

No.	Type	Description	Unused	Used
J9	D1	5pa claret	5.00	1.60
J10	D2	20pa red	5.00	1.60
J11	D3	1pi dark blue	7.00	3.25
J12	D4	2pi slate	9.00	4.00
		Nos. J9-J12 (4)	26.00	10.45

Postage Due Stamps of France Surcharged

1921

No.	Type	Description	Unused	Used
J13	D2	1pi on 10c choc	6.00	3.25
J14	D2	2pi on 20c olive grn	6.00	3.50
J15	D2	3pi on 30c red	8.00	4.00
J16	D2	4pi on 50c vio brn	8.00	3.25
		Nos. J13-J16 (4)	28.00	14.00

COCHIN CHINA

ˈkō-chən ˈchī-nə

LOCATION — The southernmost state of French Indo-China in the Cambodian Peninsula.
GOVT. — French Colony
AREA — 26,476 sq. mi.
POP. — 4,615,968
CAPITAL — Saigon

100 Centimes = 1 Franc

Values for unused stamps are for examples without gum, as most stamps were issued in that condition.

Surcharged in Black on Stamps of French Colonies:

a

b

c

1886-87 **Unwmk.** *Perf. 14x13½*

No.	Type	Description	Unused	Used
1	A9(a)	5c on 25c yel, *straw*	140.00	100.00
2	A9(b)	5c on 2c brn, *buff*	18.00	*18.00*
3	A9(b)	5c on 25c yel, *straw*	18.00	18.00
4	A9(c)	5c on 25c blk, *rose* ('87)	37.50	37.50
a.		Dbl. surch., one of type b	*3,100.*	*1,800.*
b.		Triple surch., two of type b	—	—
c.		Inverted surcharge	—	—
		Nos. 1-4 (4)	213.50	173.50

1888

No.	Type	Description	Unused	Used
5	A9	15c on half of 30c brn, *bis*	45.00	

No. 5 was prepared but not issued.

The so-called Postage Due stamps were never issued.

Stamps of Cochin China were superseded by those of Indo-China in 1892.

COCOS ISLANDS

ˈkō-kəs ˈī-ləndz

(Keeling Islands)

LOCATION — Indian Ocean, 1,330 miles northwest of Australia, 580 miles southwest of Java
GOVT. — A territory of Australia
AREA — 6 sq. mi.
POP. — 670 (1994)

Of 27 small coral islands making up two atolls, two islands are inhabited. Cocos Islands stamps are also valid within Australia.

12 Pence = 1 Shilling
100 Cents = 1 Dollar (1969)

Catalogue values for all unused stamps in this country are for Never Hinged items.

Copra Industry — A1

Super Constellation A2

Map of Islands — A3

Designs: 1sh, Coco palms. 2sh, Sailboat (dukong). 2sh3p, Fairy tern.

Perf. 14½

1963, June 11 **Unwmk.** **Engr.**

No.	Type	Description	Unused	Used
1	A1	3p dk red brown	1.50	1.50
2	A2	5p vio blue	2.25	1.40
3	A3	8p red	1.50	2.10
4	A1	1sh green	1.50	1.40
5	A3	2sh dull purple	17.00	4.00
6	A2	2sh3p green	21.00	4.00
		Nos. 1-6 (6)	44.75	14.40

"Simpson and His Donkey" by Wallace Anderson — A3a

1965, Apr. 14 **Photo.** *Perf. 13½x13*

No.	Type	Description	Unused	Used
7	A3a	5p brt grn, sepia & blk	1.00	.85

ANZAC issue. See note after Australia No. 387.

Turbo Lajonkairii — A4

Blenny — A5

Designs: 2c, Tridacna crocea (shell). 3c, Tridacna derasa (shell). 5c, Porites cocosensis (coral). 6c, Flyingfish. 10c, Banded rail (bird). 15c, Java sparrow. 20c, Red-tailed tropic bird. 30c, Sooty tern. 50c, Eastern reef heron. $1, Great frigate bird.

Perf. 13½

1969, July 9 **Unwmk.** **Photo.**

Size: 21½x27mm, 26½x22mm

No.	Type	Description	Unused	Used
8	A4	1c multicolored	.25	*.50*
9	A4	2c multicolored	.90	.65
10	A5	3c multicolored	.35	.20
11	A5	4c multicolored	.25	*.40*
12	A5	5c multicolored	.30	.25
13	A5	6c multicolored	.75	.70
14	A5	10c multicolored	1.00	.70
15	A5	15c multicolored	1.00	.50
16	A5	20c multicolored	1.00	.35
17	A5	30c multicolored	1.00	.40
18	A5	50c multicolored	1.00	.40

Size: 21½x34mm

No.	Type	Description	Unused	Used
19	A4	$1 multicolored	2.75	1.25
		Nos. 8-19 (12)	10.55	6.30

"Dragon" — A6

"Juno" — A7

Perf. 13½x13, 13x13½

1976, Mar. 29 **Photo.**

No.	Type	Description	Unused	Used
20	A6	1c shown	.40	.40
21	A7	2c shown	.40	.40
22	A7	5c "Beagle"	.40	.40
23	A7	10c "Sydney"	.45	.45
24	A7	15c "Emden"	.80	.80
25	A7	20c "Ayesha"	.80	.80
26	A6	25c "Islander"	.80	.80
27	A6	30c "Cheshire"	.80	.80
28	A7	35c "Jukung"	.80	.80
29	A7	40c "Scotia"	.80	.80
30	A6	50c "Orontes"	.80	.80
31	A6	$1 Royal Yacht "Gothic"	1.25	1.25
		Nos. 20-31 (12)	8.50	8.50

Historic ships.

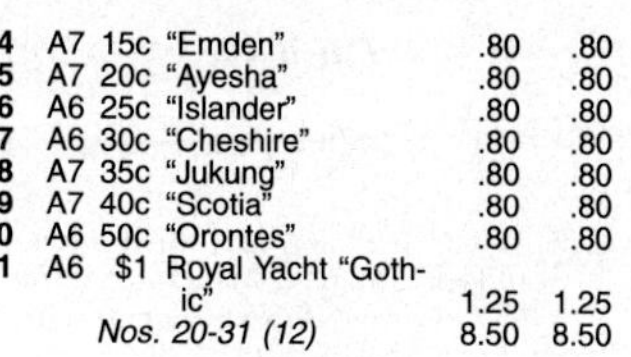

Flag, Southern Cross, Islands' Map — A8

Council Emblem, Sailboat A9

1979, Sept. 3 **Litho.** *Perf. 15½*

No.	Type	Description	Unused	Used
32	A8	20c multicolored	.35	*.30*
33	A9	50c multicolored	.55	*.70*

Inauguration of Cocos Islands' postal service (20c), and establishment of Cocos Islands Council (50c).

Forcipiger Flavissimus A10

Fish: 2c, Chaetodon ornatissimus. 5c, Anthias. 10c, Meyer's coralfish. 15c, Halichoeres. 20c, Amphiprion clarkii. 22c, Balistapus undulatus. 25c, Maori wrasse. 28c, Macropharyngodon meleagris. 30c, Chaetodon madagascariensis. 35c, Centropyge colini. 40c, Bodianus axillaris. 50c, Coris gaimardi. 55c, Spotted wrasse. 60c, Epinepnelus tauvina. $1, Paracanthurus hepatus. $2, Striped butterflyfish.

1979-80 **Litho.** *Perf. 15½*

No.	Type	Description	Unused	Used
34	A10	1c multicolored	.20	*.80*
35	A10	2c multicolored	.20	*.25*
36	A10	5c multicolored	.35	*.85*
37	A10	10c multi ('80)	.20	*.80*
38	A10	15c multicolored	.30	.25
39	A10	20c multicolored	.40	.25
40	A10	22c multi ('80)	.35	.25
41	A10	25c multi ('80)	.40	*.80*
42	A10	28c multi ('80)	.35	.25
43	A10	30c multicolored	.50	.35
44	A10	35c multicolored	.55	*1.25*
45	A10	40c multicolored	.60	.45
46	A10	50c multicolored	.85	.60
47	A10	55c multi ('80)	.75	*1.00*
48	A10	60c multi ('80)	.65	.60
49	A10	$1 multicolored	1.00	*2.50*
50	A10	$2 multi ('80)	2.00	*2.75*
		Nos. 34-50 (17)	9.65	*14.00*

Sailboats in Lagoon A11

Christmas: 25c, Yachts and seagulls, vert.

1979, Oct. 22 **Litho.** *Perf. 15½*

No.	Type	Description	Unused	Used
51	A11	25c multicolored	.35	.25
52	A11	55c multicolored	.55	*.65*

Star of Bethlehem, Map of Cocos Islands A12

Christmas (Map of Cocos Islands and): 28c, Three kings. 60c, Nativity.

1980, Oct. 22 Litho. *Perf. 13½x13*

53 A12 15c multicolored .20 .20
54 A12 28c multicolored .25 .25
55 A12 60c multicolored .80 .80
Nos. 53-55 (3) 1.25 1.25

Flag and Arms of Great Britain — A13

Australian Territory Status, 25th Anniv. (British Flag and Arms of Past Administrators): No. 57, Ceylon, 1878, 1942-1946. No. 58, Straits Settlements, 1886. No. 59, Singapore, 1946. No. 60, Australia (flag), 1955.

1980, Nov. 24 Litho. *Perf. 13½x13*

56 A13 22c multicolored .30 .30
57 A13 22c multicolored .30 .30
58 A13 22c multicolored .30 .30
59 A13 22c multicolored .30 .30
60 A13 22c multicolored .30 .30
a. Strip of 5, Nos. 56-60 1.75 1.75

Eye of the Wind, Map of Cocos Islands — A14

1980, Dec. 18 *Perf. 13x13½, 13½x13*

61 A14 22c shown .45 .45
62 A14 28c Expedition routes, horiz. .45 .45
63 A14 35c Francis Drake, Golden Hinde .45 .45
64 A14 60c Prince Charles, Eye of the Wind .75 .75
Nos. 61-64 (4) 2.10 2.10

Operation Drake circumnavigation.

Livestock in Quarantine A15

1981, May 12 Litho. *Perf. 13½x13*

65 A15 22c Aerial view of station .35 .35
66 A15 45c shown .50 .50
67 A15 60c Livestock, diff. .85 .85
Nos. 65-67 (3) 1.70 1.70

West Island Quarantine Station opening.

Catalina Guba II A16

Inauguration of Air Service to Indian Ocean: No. 69, Avro Lancastrian. No. 70, Douglas DC4 Skymaster, Lockheed Constellation. No. 71, Lockheed Electra. No. 72, Boeing 727.

1981, June 23 Litho. *Perf. 13½x13*

68 A16 22c multicolored .35 .35
69 A16 22c multicolored .35 .35
70 A16 22c multicolored .35 .35
71 A16 22c multicolored .35 .35
72 A16 22c multicolored .35 .35
a. Strip of 5, #68-72 2.00 2.00

Prince Charles and Lady Diana — A17

1981, July 29 Litho. *Perf. 13½x13*

73 A17 24c multicolored .35 .35
74 A17 60c multicolored .90 .90

Royal Wedding.

Angels We Have Heard on High — A18

Christmas: Carols.

1981, Oct. 22 Photo. *Perf. 13½x13*

75 A18 18c shown .35 .35
76 A18 30c Shepherds Why this Jubilee .50 .50
77 A18 60c Come to Bethlehem and See Him .70 .70
Nos. 75-77 (3) 1.55 1.55

Sesquicentennial of Charles Darwin's Visit — A19

1981, Dec. 28 Litho. *Perf. 13½x13*

78 A19 24c Coral .35 .35
79 A19 45c Darwin, coral .50 .50
80 A19 60c Beagle, coral .75 .75
Nos. 78-80 (3) 1.60 1.60

Souvenir Sheet

81 Sheet of 2 1.25 1.25
a. A19 24c Atoll .60 .60
b. A19 24c Atoll, diff. .60 .60

125th Anniv. of Annexation to the British Dominions A20

1982, Mar. 31 Litho. *Perf. 13½x14*

82 A20 24c Queen Victoria .40 .40
83 A20 45c British flag .75 .75
84 A20 60c Capt. Fremantle .85 .85
Nos. 82-84 (3) 2.00 2.00

Scouting Year — A21

Perf. 13½x14, 14x13½

1982, July 21 Litho.

85 A21 27c Baden-Powell .55 .55
86 A21 75c Emblem, map, vert. 1.10 1.10

Macroglossum Corythus — A22

1982, Sept. 6

87 A22 1c Presic villida, vert. 1.10 .70
88 A22 2c Cephonodes picus .45 .45
89 A22 5c shown 1.75 .80
90 A22 10c Chasmina candida, vert. .45 .45
91 A22 20c Nagia linteola .45 *.55*
92 A22 25c Eublemma rivula, vert. .45 *.65*
93 A22 30c Eurrhyparodes tricoloralis, vert. .45 *.55*
94 A22 35c Hippotion boerhaviae 1.75 .85
95 A22 40c Euploea core corinna, vert. .45 *.70*
96 A22 45c Psara hipponalis .60 *.70*
97 A22 50c Danaus chrysippus .70 *1.10*
98 A22 55c Hypolimas misippus, vert. .70 *.60*
99 A22 60c Spodoptera litura, vert. .75 *1.50*
100 A22 $1 Achaea janata, vert. 3.25 3.25
101 A22 $2 Hippotion velox 2.25 *2.40*
102 A22 $3 Utetheisa pulchelloides 3.25 3.25
Nos. 87-102 (16) 18.80 18.50

Christmas A23

1982, Oct. 25 *Perf. 13x13½*

104 A23 21c Holy Family .30 .20
105 A23 35c Angel .45 .30
106 A23 75c Flight into Egypt 1.25 1.25
Nos. 104-106 (3) 2.00 1.75

Christmas A24

Cocos-Malay Culture A25

The Birth of Christ: a, God Will Look After Us; b, Our Baby King Jesus; c, Your Saviour is Born; d, Wise Men Followed the Star; e, And Worship the Lord.

1983, Oct. 31 Litho. *Perf. 14x13½*

107 Strip of 5 1.60 1.60
a.-e. A24 24c any single .30 .30

1984, Jan. 27 Litho. *Perf. 14x13½*

Festive Occasions.

108 A25 45c Hari Raya .65 .45
109 A25 75c Melenggok dance 1.00 .65
110 A25 85c Wedding 1.25 .75
Nos. 108-110 (3) 2.90 1.85

75th Anniv. of Barrel Mail (1909-1955) A26

Designs: 35c, Mail distribution, Direction Isld. 55c, Jukongs retrieving barrels from ocean liner. 70c, Morea receiving outgoing barrel mail, 1909. $1, Barrel mail recovery.

1984, Apr. 20 Litho. *Perf. 13½x14*

111 A26 35c multicolored .50 .50
112 A26 55c multicolored .95 .95
113 A26 70c multicolored 1.00 1.00
Nos. 111-113 (3) 2.45 2.45

Souvenir Sheet

114 A26 $1 multicolored 2.50 *2.50*

375th Anniv. of Islands' Discovery — A27

1984, July 10 Litho. *Perf. 14x13½*

115 A27 30c Capt. William Keeling .70 .45
116 A27 65c The Hector 1.40 1.00
117 A27 95c Astrolabe 1.75 1.40
118 A27 $1.10 Map, 1666 2.00 1.60
Nos. 115-118 (4) 5.85 4.45

AUSIPEX '84 — A28

45c, Malay Settlement, Home Island. 55c, West Island Air Strip, settlement. $2, Jukong ships racing, Melbourne Exhibition Center.

1984, Sept. 21 Litho. *Perf. 13½*

119 A28 45c multicolored .70 .50
120 A28 55c multicolored .80 .65

Souvenir Sheet

121 A28 $2 multicolored 3.25 3.25

Christmas A29

1984, Oct. 31 Litho. *Perf. 13½*

122 A29 24c Fish .45 .45
123 A29 35c Butterfly .70 .70
124 A29 55c Bird 1.10 1.10
Nos. 122-124 (3) 2.25 2.25

Souvenir Sheet

Act of Self-Determination — A30

Integration with Australia: a, Australians welcoming Cocos islanders. b, Australian flag over the islands.

1984, Nov. 30 Litho. *Perf. 13½x14*

125 Sheet of 2 3.00 3.00
a.-b. A30 30c any single 1.25 1.25

Crafts — A31

1985, Jan. 30 *Perf. 14x13½*

126 A31 30c Boat building .60 .30
127 A31 45c Blacksmith .90 .45
128 A31 55c Woodcarving 1.25 .75
Nos. 126-128 (3) 2.75 1.50

Cable-laying Ships — A32

1985, Apr. 24 *Perf. 13½x14*

129 A32 33c Scotia 1.60 .90
130 A32 65c Anglia 2.50 1.50
131 A32 80c Patrol 2.50 2.50
Nos. 129-131 (3) 6.60 4.90

Birds A33

1985, July 17 *Perf. 13½*

132 A33 33c Redfooted booby, vert. 2.00 2.00
133 A33 60c Nankeen night heron 2.25 2.25
134 A33 $1 Buff-banded rail 2.50 2.50
a. "Block" of 3, #132-134 8.75 8.75

Nos. 132-134 printed in a continuous design.

Seashells A34

1985-86 Litho. *Perf. 13½x14*

135 A34 1c Trochus maculatus .55 *.40*
136 A34 2c Smaragdia rangiana .55 *.45*
137 A34 3c Chama .55 *.55*
138 A34 4c Cypraea moneta 1.00 *.55*
139 A34 5c Drupa morum .55 *.55*
140 A34 10c Conus miles .65 *.65*
141 A34 15c Terebra maculata 1.90 1.25
142 A34 20c Fragum fragum 1.90 1.50
143 A34 30c Turbo lajonkairii 1.90 1.50
144 A34 33c Mitra fissurata 2.10 1.50
145 A34 40c Lambis lambis 2.10 1.50
146 A34 50c Tridacna squamosa 2.10 1.75
147 A34 60c Cypraea histrio 2.10 *2.00*
148 A34 $1 Phillidia varicosa 3.00 3.00
149 A34 $2 Halgerda tessellata 3.25 3.25
150 A34 $3 Harminoea cymbalum 4.00 4.00
Nos. 135-150 (16) 28.20 24.40

Issue dates: 1c, 5c, 33c, $1, Sept. 18. 2c, 3c, 10c, $3, Jan. 29, 1986. 15c-30c, 40c, Apr. 30, 1986. 4c, 50c, 60c, $2, July 30, 1986.

For surcharges see #225, 228-229, 231-233.

Souvenir Sheet

Christmas
A35

a, Star LR. b, Star LL. c, Star UR. d, Star UL.

1985, Oct. 30 *Perf. 13½x14*

151 Sheet of 4 2.75 2.75
a.-d. A35 27c any single .65 .65

Darwin's Visit to the Islands — A36

1986, Apr. 1 Litho. *Perf. 14x13½*

152 A36 33c Charles Darwin .85 .40
153 A36 60c Map of voyage 1.50 *1.60*
154 A36 $1 HMS Beagle 2.10 *2.00*
Nos. 152-154 (3) 4.45 *4.00*

Christmas
A37

1986, Oct. 20 Litho. *Perf. 13½x14*

155 A37 30c Coconut palm, holly .60 .60
156 A37 90c Shell, ornament 2.25 *2.25*
157 A37 $1 Tropical fish, bell 2.25 *2.25*
Nos. 155-157 (3) 5.10 *5.10*

Sailboats
A38

a, Jukong. b, Ocean racers. c, Sarimanok. d, Ayesha. #158 has a continuous design.

1987, Jan. 28

158 Strip of 4 5.00 5.00
a.-d. A38 36c any single 1.00 1.00

Island Views — A39

1987, Apr. 8

159 A39 70c Direction Is. 1.00 1.00
160 A39 90c West Is. 1.40 1.40
161 A39 $1 Golf course, Cocos 2.25 *2.50*
Nos. 159-161 (3) 4.65 4.90

Communications — A40

1987, July 29 Litho. *Perf. 13½x14*

162 A40 70c Radio 1.00 1.00
163 A40 75c Air service 1.10 1.10
164 A40 90c Satellite 1.40 1.40
165 A40 $1 Airmail 1.50 1.50
Nos. 162-165 (4) 5.00 5.00

Industries
A41

1987, Sept. 16

166 A41 45c Batik printing 1.00 1.00
167 A41 65c Boat building 1.25 1.25
168 A41 75c Copra production 1.75 1.75
Nos. 166-168 (3) 4.00 4.00

Industrial activities of the Cocos Malay people.

Christmas — A42

1987, Oct. 28 *Perf. 14x13½*

169 A42 30c Peace on Earth .35 .35
170 A42 90c Unity 1.25 1.25
171 A42 $1 Goodwill Towards All 1.40 1.40
Nos. 169-171 (3) 3.00 3.00

Australia Bicentennial
A43

Arrival of the First Fleet, Sydney Cove, Jan. 1788: a, Five aboriginals on shore. b, Four aboriginals on shore, one in canoe. c, Ships entering bay, kangaroos. d, Europeans land, white cranes. e, Flag raising.

1988, Jan. 26 Litho. *Perf. 13*

172 Strip of 5 5.25 5.25
a.-e. A43 37c any single 1.00 1.00

No. 172 has a continuous design. See Christmas Is. No. 213.

Life Cycle of the Coconut — A44

1988, Apr. 13 Litho. *Perf. 14x13½*

173 A44 37c Flower .70 .70
174 A44 65c Small nut stage 1.25 1.25
175 A44 90c Mature nuts 1.50 1.50
176 A44 $1 Seedlings 1.75 1.75
a. Souvenir sheet of 4, #173-176 6.75 6.75
Nos. 173-176 (4) 5.20 5.20

For surcharge see No. O1.

Cocos Postage Stamps, 25th Anniv.
A45

Litho. & Engr.

1988, June 15 *Perf. 15x14*

177 A45 37c No. 1 .85 .60
178 A45 55c No. 4 1.25 1.10
179 A45 65c No. 2 1.40 1.40
180 A45 70c No. 3 1.40 1.40
181 A45 90c No. 5 1.60 1.50
182 A45 $1 No. 6 1.60 1.50
Nos. 177-182 (6) 8.10 7.50

For overprint and surcharge see #216, 236.

Flowering Plants — A46

1988-89 Litho. *Perf. 14x13½*

183 A46 1c Pisonia grandis .55 .45
184 A46 2c Cocos nucifera .55 .45
185 A46 5c Morinda citrifolia 1.10 .55
186 A46 10c Cordia subcordata .75 .55
189 A46 30c Argusia argentea 1.10 .80
190 A46 37c Calophyllum inophyllum 1.60 .80
191 A46 40c Barringtonia asiatica 1.10 *1.00*
192 A46 50c Caesalpinia bonduc 1.40 *2.00*
194 A46 90c Terminalia catappa 1.90 *2.40*
195 A46 $1 Pemphis acidula 1.90 *2.00*
197 A46 $2 Scaevola sericea 2.50 2.00
198 A46 $3 Hibiscus tiliaceus 3.75 3.00
Nos. 183-198 (12) 18.20 16.00

Issued: 1c, 5c, 37c, $3, 7/29; 2c, 10c, 30c, $2, 1/18/89; 40c, 50c, 90c, $1, 4/19/89.

For self-adhesive sheet of 3 see No. 217.

Souvenir Sheet

1988, July 30

199 A46 $3 like No. 198 *7.50 7.50*

SYDPEX '88.

Christmas
A47

1988, Oct. 12 Litho. *Perf. 13½x14*

200 A47 32c multicolored .85 .85
201 A47 90c multicolored 2.10 2.10
202 A47 $1 multicolored 2.25 2.25
Nos. 200-202 (3) 5.20 5.20

1st Aerial Survey of the Indian Ocean Air Route, 50th Anniv. — A48

40c, P.G. Taylor, pilot. 70c, *Guba II* seaplane and crew. $1, *Guba II* landing off Direction Island. $1.10, Unissued 5sh stamp of Australia, 1939.

1989, July 19 Litho. *Perf. 14x13½*

203 A48 40c multicolored .65 .65
204 A48 70c multicolored 1.10 1.10
205 A48 $1 multicolored 1.60 1.60
206 A48 $1.10 multicolored 1.75 1.75
Nos. 203-206 (4) 5.10 5.10

Jukong, Traditional Sailing Vessel of the Cocos Malay People — A49

1989, Oct. 18 Litho. *Perf. 14x13½*

207 A49 35c multicolored .65 .65
208 A49 80c multicolored 1.60 1.60
209 A49 $1.10 multicolored 2.25 2.25
Nos. 207-209 (3) 4.50 4.50

Christmas.

Naval Engagement of the HMAS *Sydney* and the German Raider SMS *Emden*, 75th Anniv. — A50

Designs: 40c, HMAS *Sydney*. 70c, SMS *Emden*. $1, Steam launch belonging to the *Emden*. $1.10, HMAS *Sydney* and naval crest.

1989, Nov. 9 Litho. *Perf. 13½x14*

210 Strip of 4 + label 6.00 6.00
a. A50 40c multicolored .65 .65
b. A50 70c multicolored 1.25 1.25
c. A50 $1 multicolored 1.75 1.75
d. A50 $1.10 multicolored 1.90 1.90
e. Souvenir sheet of 4, #210a-210d 8.00 8.00

Crabs — A52

1990, May 31 Litho. *Perf. 14½*

212 A52 45c Xanthid .90 .90
213 A52 75c Ghost 1.50 1.50
214 A52 $1 Red-backed mud crab 1.90 1.90
215 A52 $1.30 Coconut, vert. 2.40 2.40
Nos. 212-215 (4) 6.70 6.70

No. 180 Overprinted in Red

Litho. & Engr.

1990, Aug. 24 *Perf. 15x14*

216 A45 70c gray, black & red 7.50 7.50

Flowering Plants Type of 1988

1990, Aug. 24 Photo. *Rouletted 9½*

Self-Adhesive

217 Sheet of 3 10.50 10.50
a. A46 10c like No. 186 .40 .40
b. A46 90c like No. 194 2.75 2.75
c. A46 $2 like No. 197 6.25 6.25

World Stamp Exhibition, New Zealand 1990. Nos. 217a-217c inscribed 1990.

Explorers and Their Ships A54

45c, Capt. Keeling, Hector, 1609. 75c, Capt. Fitzroy, Beagle, 1836. $1, Capt. Belcher, Samarang, 1846. $1.30, Capt. Fremantle, Juno, 1857.

1990, Aug. 24 Litho. *Perf. 14½*

218 A54 45c violet brown .80 .80
219 A54 75c pale bl & vio brn 1.40 1.40
220 A54 $1 pale yel & vio brn 1.75 1.75
221 A54 $1.30 buff & vio brn 2.25 2.25
a. Souv. sheet of 4, #218-221, imperf. 6.75 6.75
Nos. 218-221 (4) 6.20 6.20

Christmas — A55

1990, Dec. 12 Litho. *Rouletted 5*

222 A55 40c Star at left .95 .95
a. Bklt. pane of 10 + 2 labels 11.00
223 A55 70c Star in center 1.75 1.75
a. Bklt. pane, 4 #222, 2 #223 + 6 labels 7.00
224 A55 $1.30 Star at right 3.25 3.25
Nos. 222-224 (3) 5.95 5.95

Nos. 140, 141, 143, 146-147, 179 Surcharged in Blue or Black

Litho., Litho. & Engr.

1990-91 *Perf. 13½x14, 15x14*

225 A34 (1c) on 30c #143 *8.00 7.00*
228 A34 (43c) on 10c #140 *45.00 40.00*
229 A34 (43c) on 10c #140 *16.00 14.00*
231 A34 70c on 60c #147 (bk) *8.00 7.00*
232 A34 80c on 50c #146 (bk) *8.00 7.00*
233 A34 $1.20 on 15c #141 (bk) *8.00 7.00*
236 A45 $5 on 65c #179 *70.00 50.00*
Nos. 225-236 (7) 163.00 132.00

Obliterator consists of diagonal lines on No. 228, crosshatched lines on No. 229.

Additional text in surcharges reads: "MAINLAND / POSTAGE PAID" (Nos. 228-229), "ZONE 1 / POSTAGE PAID" (No. 231), "ZONE 2 / POSTAGE PAID" (No. 232), "ZONE 5 / POSTAGE PAID" (No. 233).

Issued: #236, 11/11; #228, 12/18; #225, 229, 231-233, 1/1991.

Beaded Sea Star — A56

1991, Feb. 28 Litho. *Perf. 14½*

237 A56 45c shown .85 .85
238 A56 75c Feather star 1.40 1.40
239 A56 $1 Slate pencil urchin 1.90 1.90
240 A56 $1.30 Globose sea urchin 2.50 2.50
Nos. 237-240 (4) 6.65 6.65

Hari Raya — A57

1991, Mar. Litho. *Perf. 14½*

241 A57 45c multicolored .75 .75
242 A57 75c multi, diff. 1.25 1.25
243 A57 $1.30 multi, diff. 2.25 2.25
Nos. 241-243 (3) 4.25 4.25

Christmas — A58

1991, Nov. 6 Litho. *Perf. 15½*

244 A58 38c Child praying .55 .55
245 A58 43c Child sleeping .70 .70
246 A58 $1 Child singing 1.60 1.60
247 A58 $1.20 Child in wonder 1.90 1.90
Nos. 244-247 (4) 4.75 4.75

Souvenir Sheet

248 Sheet of 4 5.25 5.25
a. A58 38c Two children .60 .60
b. A58 43c Three girls .75 .75
c. A58 $1 Boy, two girls 1.75 1.75
d. A58 $1.20 Boy, girl 2.10 2.10

Nos. 248a-248d are in a continuous design depicting a children's choir.

Crustaceans A59

Designs: 5c, Lybia tessellata. 10c, Pilodius areolatus. 20c, Trizopagurus strigatus. 30c, Lophozozymus pulchellus. 40c, Thalamitoides quadridens. 45c, Calcinus elegans, vert. 50c, Clibarius humilis. 60c, Trapezia rufopunctata, vert. 80c, Pylopaguropsis magnimanus, vert. $1, Trapezia ferruginea, vert. $2, Trapezia guttata, vert. $3, Trapezia cymodoce, vert.

1992 Litho. *Perf. 14½*

249 A59 5c multicolored .25 .25
250 A59 10c multicolored .25 .25
251 A59 20c multicolored .35 .35
252 A59 30c multicolored .55 .55
253 A59 40c multicolored .70 .70
254 A59 45c multicolored .75 .75
255 A59 50c multicolored .80 .80
256 A59 60c multicolored 1.00 1.00
257 A59 80c multicolored 1.25 1.25
258 A59 $1 multicolored 1.60 1.60
259 A59 $2 multicolored 3.25 3.25
260 A59 $3 multicolored 5.00 5.00
Nos. 249-260 (12) 15.75 15.75

Issued: 10c, 30c, 50c, 80c, $1, $2, 8/11; others, 2/28.

Discovery of America, 500th Anniv. — A60

1992, May 22 Litho. *Perf. 14½*

261 A60 $1.05 multicolored 3.00 3.00

Buff-banded Rail — A61

No. 262: a, 10c, Bird looking for food. b, 15c, Adult with chick. c, 30c, Two adults eating. d, 45c, Adult with eggs, hatchling.

No. 263: a, 45c, Two birds, one in water. b, 85c, Chick in nest. c, $1.20, Bird's head.

1992, June 18 Litho. *Perf. 14*

262 A61 Strip of 4, #a.-d. 2.00 2.00

Souvenir Sheet

263 A61 Sheet of 3, #a.-c. 4.00 4.00

World Wildlife Fund (#262).

World War II, 50th Anniv. — A62

45c, Royal Air Force Spitfire fighters. 85c, Japanese bombing of Kampong. $1.20, Sunderland reconnaissance flying boat.

1992, Oct. 13 Litho. *Perf. 14½*

264 A62 45c multicolored .85 .85
265 A62 85c multicolored 1.75 1.75
266 A62 $1.20 multicolored 2.40 2.40
Nos. 264-266 (3) 5.00 5.00

Festive Season — A63 Corals — A64

40c, Storm waves on reef edge. 80c, Direction Island. $1, Moorish idols among coral.

1992, Nov. 10 Litho. *Perf. 15x14½*

267 A63 40c multicolored .60 .60
268 A63 80c multicolored 1.25 1.25
269 A63 $1 multicolored 1.60 1.60
Nos. 267-269 (3) 3.45 3.45

1993, Jan. 28 Litho. *Perf. 14½*

270 A64 45c Lobophyllia hemprichii .70 .70
271 A64 85c Pocillopora eydouxi 1.25 1.25
272 A64 $1.05 Fungia scutaria 1.60 1.60
273 A64 $1.20 Sarcophyton sp. 1.75 1.75
Nos. 270-273 (4) 5.30 5.30

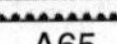

A65 A66

Island Currency Tokens: 45c, 5r token, 1968. 85c, Island scene token, 1968. $1.05, 150r token, 1977. $1.20, Token, 1910.

1993, Mar. 30 Litho. *Perf. 15x14½*

274 A65 45c multicolored .60 .60
275 A65 85c multicolored 1.25 1.25
276 A65 $1.05 multicolored 1.40 1.40
277 A65 $1.20 multicolored 1.75 1.75
Nos. 274-277 (4) 5.00 5.00

1993, June 1 Litho. *Perf. 14½*

Education: 5c, Primary classroom activities. 45c, Secondary studies. 85c, Crafts, traditional basket weaving. $1.05, Office staff, higher education. $1.20, Marine officers, coxswain's training.

278 A66 5c multicolored .20 .20
279 A66 45c multicolored .60 .60
280 A66 85c multicolored 1.25 1.25
281 A66 $1.05 multicolored 1.40 1.40
282 A66 $1.20 multicolored 1.60 1.60
Nos. 278-282 (5) 5.05 5.05

Air-Sea Rescue Service A67

45c, Men in lifeboat. 85c, Westwind Seascan. $1.05, R.J. Hawke inter-island ferry.

1993, Aug. 17 Litho. *Perf. 14½*

283 A67 45c multicolored .70 .70
284 A67 85c multicolored 1.25 1.25
285 A67 $1.05 multicolored 1.75 1.75
a. Souvenir sheet of 3, #283-285 4.50 4.50
Nos. 283-285 (3) 3.70 3.70

A limited printing exists of No. 285a with Taipei '95 overprint. Value, $60.

Festive Season — A68

1993, Oct. 24 Litho. *Perf. 14½*

286 A68 40c pink & multi .50 .50
287 A68 80c blue & multi 1.00 1.00
288 A68 $1 yellow & multi 1.25 1.25
Nos. 286-288 (3) 2.75 2.75

Map and Reef Life — A69 Puppets — A70

Reef triggerfish — No. 289: a, Two fish, purple coral (b). b, Three fish. c, Two fish. d, Two fish, red coral (e). e, One fish.

Green turtles — No. 290: a, Eggs, turtles. b, Two turtles (c). c, Group of baby turtles. d, Baby turtle. e, Fish, large turtle.

Pyramid butterflyfish — No. 291: a, Three fish. b, Two small, one large fish, coral (c). c, One small, one large fish, coral (d). d, Three fish, coral (e). e, Coral, one fish.

Junkongs sailing craft — No. 292: a, One boat, red sail. b, Two boats, one blue & white sail, one red sail. c, One boat, yellow sail. d, Two boats sailing away. e, Two boats, one red sail, one white & blue sail.

1994, Feb. 17 Litho. *Perf. 14½x14*

289 A69 5c Strip of 5, #a.-e. .30 .30
290 A69 10c Strip of 5, #a.-e. .65 .65
291 A69 20c Strip of 5, #a.-e. 1.25 1.25
292 A69 45c Strip of 5, #a.-e. 3.00 3.00
f. Sheet of 20, #289-292 5.25 5.25

No. 292 also produced in sheets of 20.

1994, June 16 Litho. *Perf. 14½x14*

293 A70 45c Prabu Abjasa .60 .60
294 A70 90c Prabu Pandu 1.25 1.25
295 A70 $1 Judistra 1.40 1.40
296 A70 $1.35 Abimanju 1.90 1.90
Nos. 293-296 (4) 5.15 5.15

Christmas A71

1994, Oct. 31 Litho. *Perf. 14x14½*

297 A71 40c Angel .60 .60
298 A71 45c Wise man .65 .65
299 A71 80c Bethlehem 1.25 1.25
Nos. 297-299 (3) 2.50 2.50

Seabirds A72

45c, White-tailed tropicbird, masked booby. 85c, Great frigatebird, white tern.

1995, Mar. 16 Litho. *Perf. 14x14½*

300	A72 45c multicolored		.65	.65
301	A72 85c multicolored		1.25	1.25
a.	Souvenir sheet of 2, #300-301		1.90	1.90
b.	As "a," overprinted		4.50	4.50

No. 301b ovptd. in gold in sheet margin with Jakarta '95 exhibition emblem and: "8th Asian International Philatelic Exhibition / PAMERAN FILATELI INTERNASIONAL ASIA VIII."

No. 301b issued 8/19/95.

Insects — A73

#302a, Yellow crazy ant. b, Aedes mosquito. c, Hawk moth. d, Scarab beetle. e, Lauxaniid fly.

$1.20, Common eggfly butterfly.

1995, July 13 Litho. *Perf. 14½x14*

302	A73	45c Strip of 5, #a.-e.	3.25	3.25
303	A73	$1.20 multicolored	1.75	1.75

Fish — A74

Designs: 5c, Redspot wrasse. 30c, Gilded triggerfish. 40c, Saddled butterflyfish. 45c, Ringeyed hawkfish. 75c, Orangespine unicornfish. 80c, Blue tang. 85c, Humpback wrasse. 90c, Threadfin butterflyfish. $1, Bluestripe snapper. $1.05, Longnosed butterflyfish. $1.20, Freckled hawkfish. $2, Powder blue surgeonfish.

1995-97 Litho. *Perf. 14x14½*

304	A74	5c multicolored	.25	.25
305	A74	30c multicolored	.40	.40
306	A74	40c multicolored	.65	.65
307	A74	45c multicolored	.75	.75
308	A74	75c multicolored	1.10	1.10
309	A74	80c multicolored	1.25	1.25
310	A74	85c multicolored	1.25	1.25
311	A74	90c multicolored	1.40	1.40
312	A74	$1 multicolored	1.60	1.60
313	A74	$1.05 multicolored	1.60	1.60
314	A74	$1.20 multicolored	2.00	2.00
315	A74	$2 multicolored	3.50	3.50
		Nos. 304-315 (12)	15.75	15.75

Issued: 40c, 80c, $1.05, 11/1/95; 30c, 45c, 85c, $2, 8/8/96; 5c, 75c, 90c, $1, $1.20, 8/14/97.

See Nos. 327-329.

Festive Season — A75

Designs: 45c, Greeting others, asking forgiveness. 75c, Drum beaters celebrate Hari Raya Puasa. 85c, Sharing food with friends.

1996, Feb. 19 Litho. *Perf. 14*

316	A75 45c multicolored	.65	.65
317	A75 75c multicolored	1.10	1.10
318	A75 85c multicolored	1.25	1.25
	Nos. 316-318 (3)	3.00	3.00

Animals Imported Into Australia Through Cocos Islands Quarantine Station — A76

1996, June 13 Litho. *Perf. 14½x14*

319	A76	45c Black rhinoceros	.70	.70
320	A76	50c Alpacas	.80	.80
321	A76	$1.05 Boran cattle	1.60	1.60
322	A76	$1.20 Ostrich	1.90	1.90
		Nos. 319-322 (4)	5.00	5.00

A77

A78

Festive Season: 45c, Tambourine, dancing on shore, bird. 75c, Woman clapping, sailboats racing. 85c, Fish, night scene on beach.

1997, Jan. 6 Litho. *Perf. 14x14½*

323	A77 45c multicolored	.65	.65
324	A77 75c multicolored	1.10	1.10
325	A77 85c multicolored	1.25	1.25
	Nos. 323-325 (3)	3.00	3.00

1998, Jan. 22 Litho. *Perf. 14*

Children's drawings: a, Gift package. b, Mosque. c, Cocos Malay woman. d, Island scene. e, Two dancers.

326	A78	45c Strip of 5, #a.-e.	3.25	3.25

Festive Season.

Marine Life Type of 1995

Designs: 70c, Crowned squirrelfish. 95c, Sixstripe wrasse. $5, Goldback anthias.

1998, Aug. 13 Litho. *Perf. 14x14½*

327	A74 70c multicolored	1.10	1.10
328	A74 95c multicolored	1.40	1.40
329	A74 $5 multicolored	7.50	7.50
	Nos. 327-329 (3)	10.00	10.00

Jukong Boats, Hari Raya Festival — A79

a, Women placing items in leaves, people along beach. b, Two women, boats along beach. c, Flowers, man in boat. d, Palm trees, two men, man in boat. e, Two people in boat.

1999, Feb. 11 Litho. *Perf. 14½x14*

330	A79	45c Strip of 5, #a.-e.	3.25	3.25

Flora and Fauna — A80

a, 45c, Two birds on tree branch. b, 25c, Bird in flight. c, 10c, Sailboat with sail down. d, 5c, Sailboat with red sails. e, 45c, Two birds in flight. f, 25c, Butterflies. g, 10c, School of fish. h, 5c, School of fish swimming left, coral. i, 45c, Red hibiscus flower. j, 25c, Three birds in flight. k, 10c, Two moorish idols. l, 5c, Turtles. m, 45c, Butterfly, flowers. n, 25c, Moth with wings folded, flowers. o, 10c, Two gold fish. p, 5c, Various fish swimming right. q, 45c, Yellow hibiscus. r, 25c, Butterfly on flowers. s, 10c, Two birds in flight. t, 5c, Large fish, coral.

1999, June 17 Litho. *Perf. 14x14½*

331	A80	Sheet of 20, #a.-t.	8.50	8.50

Faces of Cocos Islands A81

Ordinary people: a, Ratma Anthoney, with white shirt. b, Nakia Haji Dolman, with multicolored head covering. c, Muller Eymin, with white head covering. d, Courtney Press, with flowered outfit. e, Mhd Abu-Yazid, with blue shirt with stripes.

2000, Apr. 13 Litho. *Perf. 14x14½*

332	A81	45c Strip of 5, #a.-e.	3.50	3.50

Worldwide Fund for Nature — A82

#333: a, Purple crab. b, Little nipper crab.
#334: a, Horn-eyed ghost crab. b, Smooth-banded ghost crab.

Illustration reduced.

2000, June 20 Litho. *Perf. 14x14¾*

333	A82	5c Pair, #a-b	.25	.25
334	A82	45c Pair, #a-b	1.40	1.40

Fish Type of 1995

No. 335: a, Wideband fusilier. b, Striped surgeonfish. c, Orangeband surgeonfish. d, Indo-Pacific sergeant.

2001, Feb. 8 Litho. *Perf. 14x14½*

335	Block of 4	2.75	2.75
a.-d.	A74 45c Any single	.65	.65

Turtles — A83

No. 336: a, Loggerhead. b, Hawksbill. c, Leatherback. d, Green.

Illustration reduced.

2002, Oct. 1 Litho. *Perf. 14x14½*

336	A83 Block of 4	2.75	2.75
a.-d.	45c Any single	.65	.65

Shore Birds — A84

No. 337: a, Eastern reef egret. b, Sooty tern. c, Ruddy turnstone. d, Whimbrel.

2003, June 17 Litho. *Perf. 14x14½*

337	Horiz. strip of 4	2.60	2.60
a.-d.	A84 50c Any single	.65	.65

Royal Visit, 50th Anniv. — A85

Queen Elizabeth II and: No. 338a, Cocos Malay musicians. No. 338b, Royal Yacht Gothic. $1, Clunies Ross (Oceania) House. $1.45, Dignitary presenting model of Malay jukong.

2004, Mar. 16 Litho. *Perf. 14x14½*

338	A85 50c Horiz. pair, #a-b	1.50	1.50
339	A85 $1 multi	1.50	1.50
340	A85 $1.45 multi	2.25	2.25
a.	Souvenir sheet, #338a, 338b, 339, 340	5.25	5.25
b.	As "a," with 2004 World Stamp Championship emblem ovptd. in gold in margin	5.00	5.00
	Nos. 338-340 (3)	5.25	5.25

No. 340b issued 8/28.

OFFICIAL STAMP

No. 175 Ovptd. and Surcharged in Dark Blue

1991, Jan. 25 Litho. *Perf. 14x13½*

O1	A44 (43c) on 90c multi	*150.00*

No. O1 was not sold to the public unused. Used value is for a canceled-to-order copy.

COLOMBIA

kə-'ləm-bē-ə

LOCATION — On the northwest coast of South America, bordering on the Caribbean Sea and the Pacific Ocean
GOVT. — Republic
AREA — 456,535 sq. mi.
POP. — 39,309,422 (1999 est.)
CAPITAL — Bogota

In 1810 the Spanish Viceroyalty of New Granada gained its independence and with Venezuela and Ecuador formed the State of Greater Colombia. In 1832 this state split into three independent units as Venezuela, Ecuador and the Republic of New Granada. The name of the country has been, successively, Granadine Confederation (1858-61), United States of New Granada (1861), United States of Colombia (1861-65), and the Republic of Colombia (1885 to date).

100 Centavos = 1 Peso

Catalogue values for unused stamps in this country are for Never Hinged items, beginning with Scott 594 in the regular postage section, Scott B1 in the semi-postal section, Scott C200 in the airpost section, Scott CE1 in the airpost special delivery section, Scott E2 in the special delivery section, and Scott RA33 in the postal tax section.

In the earlier days many towns did not have handstamps for canceling and stamps were canceled with pen and ink. Pen cancellations, therefore, do not indicate fiscal use. (Postage stamps were not used for revenue purposes.) Used values for Nos. 1-128 are for stamps with illegible manuscript cancels or handstamp cancels of Bogota or Medellin. Stamps with legible manuscript or other handstamped town-name cancels sell for more.

Fractions of many Colombian stamps of both early and late issues are found canceled, their use to pay postage having been tolerated even though forbidden by the postal laws and regulations. Many are known to have been made for philatelic purposes.

Watermarks

Wmk. 116 — Crosses and Circles

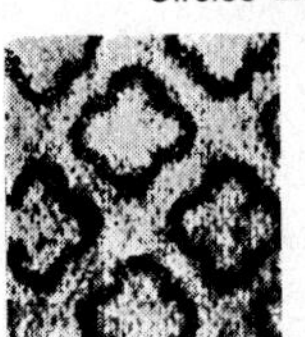

Wmk. 127 — Quatrefoils

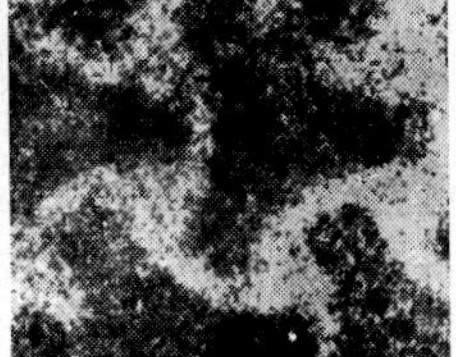

Wmk. 194 — Multiple Curvilinear Triangles

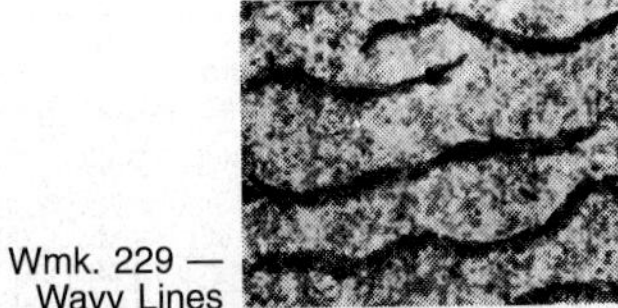

Wmk. 229 — Wavy Lines

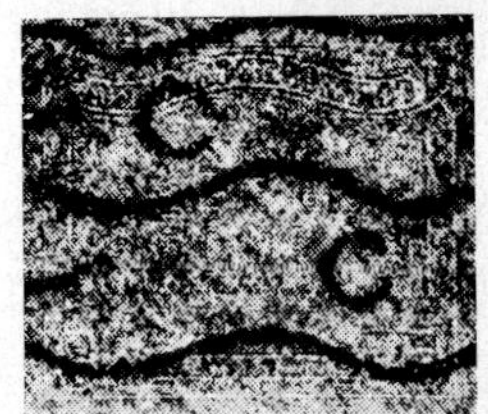

Wmk. 255 — Wavy Lines and C Multiple

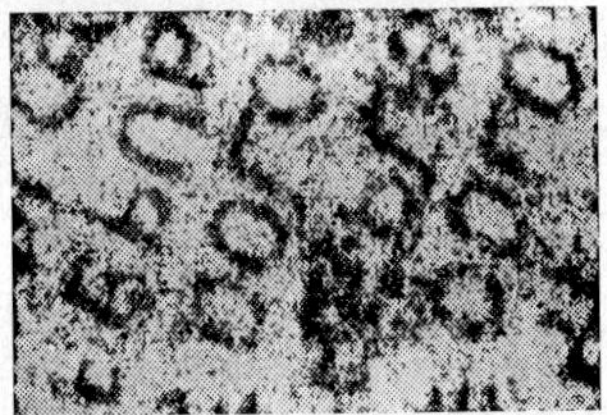

Wmk. 331 — REPUBLICA DE COLOMBIA

Wmk. 334 — Rectangles

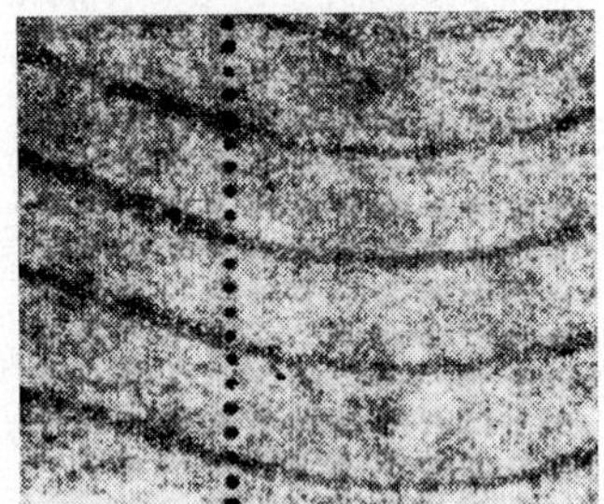

Wmk. 346 — Parallel Curved Lines

Stamps inscribed "Colombia" that show the Panama Canal area were used in Panama and can be found in Vol. 5.

Granadine Confederation

A1

A2 Coat of Arms

Type A1 — Asterisks in frame. Wavy lines in background.

Type A2 — Diamond-shaped ornaments in frame. Straight lines in background. Numerals larger.

1859 Unwmk. Litho. *Imperf.*

Wove Paper

1 A1 2½c green 90.00 90.00
a. 2½c yellow green 90.00 90.00
2 A1 5c blue 110.00 75.00
a. Tête bêche pair 3,500. 5,750.
b. "50" instead of "5" 7,500.
3 A1 5c violet 225.00 90.00
a. Tête bêche pair 5,000. 6,000.
b. "50" instead of "5" 7,500.
4 A1 10c red brown 100.00 62.50
a. 10c buff 100.00 62.50
6 A1 20c blue 90.00 55.00
a. 20c gray blue 90.00 55.00
b. Se-tenant with 5c —
c. Tête bêche pair 25,000. 25,000.
7 A1 1p carmine 60.00 *100.00*
a. 1p rose 75.00 125.00
8 A1 1p rose, *bluish* 350.00

The 10c green is an essay.

Reprints of No. 7 are in brown rose or brown red. Wavy lines of background are much broken; no dividing lines between stamps.

1860

Laid Paper

9 A2 5c lilac 250.00 175.00

Wove Paper

10 A2 5c gray lilac 62.50 50.00
a. 5c lilac 62.50 50.00
11 A2 10c yellow buff 62.50 45.00
a. Tête bêche pair *7,000.*
12 A2 20c blue 160.00 110.00

United States of New Granada

Arms of New Granada — A3

1861

13 A3 2½c black 1,100. 275.00
14 A3 5c yellow 325.00 140.00
a. 5c buff 325.00 140.00
16 A3 10c blue 950.00 140.00
17 A3 20c red 400.00 190.00
18 A3 1p pink 950.00 300.00

There are 54 varieties of the 5c, 20c, and 1 peso.

Forgeries exist of Nos. 13-18.

United States of Colombia

Coat of Arms
A4 A5 A6

1862

19 A4 10c blue 190. 95.
20 A4 20c red *3,500.* 550.
21 A4 50c green 190. 125.
22 A4 1p red lilac 450. 125.
23 A4 1p red lil, *bluish* *4,000.* *1,450.*

No. 23 is on a thinner, coarser wove paper than Nos. 19-22.

1863

24 A5 5c orange 75.00 50.00
a. Star after "Cent" 87.50 57.50
25 A5 10c blue 160.00 19.00
a. Period after "10" 175.00 22.50
26 A5 20c red 175.00 60.00
a. Star after "Cent" 190.00 67.50
b. Transfer of 50c in stone of 20c *14,000.* *4,500.*

Bluish Paper

28 A5 10c blue 125.00 27.50
a. Period after "10" 140.00 29.00
29 A5 50c green 160.00 60.00
a. Star after "Cent" 160.00 67.50

Ten varieties of each.

1864

Wove Paper

30 A6 5c orange 57.50 30.00
a. Tête bêche pair 350.00 325.00
31 A6 10c blue 42.50 12.00
a. Period after 10 42.50 12.00
32 A6 20c scarlet 75.00 45.00
33 A6 50c green 62.50 45.00
34 A6 1p red violet 275.00 140.00

Two varieties of each.

Arms of Colombia
A7 A9

A8

1865

35 A7 1c rose 8.00 8.00
a. bluish pelure paper 22.50 17.50
36 A8 2½c black, *lilac* 15.00 10.00
37 A9 5c yellow 35.00 16.00
a. 5c orange 35.00 16.00
38 A9 10c violet 50.00 3.50
39 A9 20c blue 50.00 16.00
40 A9 50c green 87.50 42.50
41 A9 50c grn (small figures) 87.50 42.50
42 A9 1p vermilion 95.00 14.00
a. 1p rose red 95.00 14.00
b. Period after "PESO" 110.00 16.00

Ten varieties of each of the 5c, 10c, 20c, and 50c, and six varieties of the 1 peso. No. 36 was used as a carrier stamp.

A10 A11 A12

A13

A14

A15

A16

1866

White Wove Paper

45 A10 5c orange 55.00 22.50
46 A11 10c lilac 12.50 4.00
a. Pelure paper 17.50 10.00
47 A12 20c light blue 32.50 17.50
a. Pelure paper 50.00 42.50
48 A13 50c green 13.00 10.00
49 A14 1p rose red, *bluish* 72.50 25.00
a. 1p vermilion 72.50 25.00
51 A15 5p blk, *green* 375.00 175.00
52 A16 10p blk, *vermilion* 275.00 160.00

There are several varieties of the 1 peso having the letters "U," "N," "S" and "O" smaller.

A17

A18

A19 A20

A21

TEN CENTAVOS:

Type I — "B" of "COLOMBIA" over "V" of "CENTAVOS".

Type II — "B" of "COLOMBIA" over "VO" of "CENTAVOS."

ONE PESO:

Type I — Long thin spear heads. Diagonal lines in lower part of shield.

Type II — Short thick spear heads. Horizontal and a few diagonal lines in lower part of shield.

Type III — Short thick spear heads. Crossed lines in lower part of shield. Ornaments at each side of circle are broken. (See No. 97.)

1868

53 A17 5c orange 55.00 42.50
54 A18 10c lilac (I) 3.25 .90
a. 10c red violet (I) 3.25 .90
b. 10c lilac (II) 3.25 .90
c. 10c red violet (II) 3.25 .90
d. Printed on both sides 6.25 2.00
55 A19 20c blue 2.25 1.00
56 A20 50c yellow green 2.50 1.60
57 A21 1p ver (II) 3.25 1.75
a. Tête bêche pair 100.00 85.00
b. 1p rose red (I) 45.00 22.50
c. 1p rose red (II) 3.00 1.75
Nos. 53-57 (5) 66.25 47.75

See Nos. 83-84, 90-97.

Counterfeits or reprints.

10c — There is a large white dot at the upper left between the circle enclosing the "X" and the ornament below.

50c — There is a shading of dots instead of dashes below the ribbon with motto. There are crossed lines in the lowest section of the shield instead of diagonal or horizontal ones.

1p — The ornaments in the lettered circle are broken. There are crossed lines in the lowest section of the shield. These counterfeits, or reprints, are on white paper, wove and laid, on colored wove paper and in fancy colors.

A22

Two varieties

1869-70

Wove Paper

59 A22 2½c black, *violet* 3.50 2.00
a. Laid paper ('70) 250.00 210.00
b. Laid batonné paper ('70) 22.50 19.00

#59, 59a, 59b were used as carrier stamps.

Counterfeits, or reprints, are on magenta paper wove or ribbed.

A23

A24

1870

Wove Paper

62 A23 5c orange 1.60 1.10
a. 5c yellow 1.60 1.10
63 A24 25c black, *blue* 12.50 11.00

See No. 89.

In the counterfeits, or reprints, of No. 63, the top of the "2" of "25" does not touch the down stroke. The counterfeits are on paper of various colors.

A25

A26

5 pesos — The ornament at the left of the "C" of "Cinco" cuts into the "C," and the shading of the flag is formed of diagonal lines.

10 pesos — The stars have extra rays between the points, and the central part of the shield has some horizontal lines of shading at each end.

1870

Surface Colored, Chalky Paper

64 A25 5p blk, *green* 75.00 52.50
65 A26 10p blk, *vermilion* 87.50 52.50

See Nos. 77-79, 125-126.

A27

A28

A29

TEN CENTAVOS:

Type I — "S" of "CORREOS" 2½mm high. First "N" of "NACIONALES" small.

Type II — "S" of "CORREOS" 2mm high. First "N" of "NACIONALES" wide.

1871-74

Thin Porous Paper

66 A27 1c green ('72) 2.75 2.75
67 A27 1c rose ('73) 2.75 2.75
a. 1c carmine ('73) 2.75 2.75
68 A28 2c brown 1.25 1.25
a. 2c red brown 1.25 1.25
69 A29 10c vio (I) ('74) 1.90 1.60
a. 10c lilac (I) ('74) 1.90 1.60
b. 10c violet (II) ('74) 1.90 1.60
c. 10c lilac (II) ('74) 1.90 1.60
d. Laid paper, as #69 ('72) 110.00 110.00
e. Laid paper, as "b" ('72) 110.00 110.00
Nos. 66-69 (4) 8.65 8.35

Counterfeits or reprints

1c — The outer frame of the shield is broken near the upper left corner and the "A" of "Colombia" has no cross-bar.

2c — There are scratches across "DOS" and many white marks around the letters on the large "2." The counterfeits, or reprints, are on white wove and bluish white laid paper.

Condor — A30

Liberty Head
A31 A32

5 pesos, redrawn — The ornament at the left of the "C" only touches the "C," and the shading of the flag is formed of vertical and diagonal lines.

10 pesos, redrawn — The stars are distinctly five pointed, and there is no shading in the central part of the shield.

1877

Wove Paper

73 A30 5c purple 5.25 1.75
a. 5c lilac 5.25 1.75
74 A31 10c bister brown 2.50 .70
a. 10c red brown 2.50 .70
b. 10c violet brown 2.50 .70
75 A32 20c blue 3.25 1.10
a. 20c violet blue 6.50 2.75
77 A26 10p blk, *rose* 87.50 55.00
78 A25 5p blk, *lt grn*, redrawn 32.50 27.50
79 A26 10p blk, *rose*, redrawn 12.50 2.25
a. 10p blk, *dark rose*, redrawn 12.50 2.25
Nos. 73-79 (6) 143.50 88.30

Stamps of the issues of 1871-77 are known with private perforations of various gauges, also with sewing machine perforation.

In the counterfeits, or reprints, of the 5 pesos the ornament at the left of the "C" of "Cinco" is separated from the "C" by a black line.

In the counterfeits, or reprints, of the 10 pesos the outer line of the double circle containing "10" is broken at the top, below "OS" of "Unidos," and the vertical lines of shading contained in the double circle are very indistinct. There is a colorless dash below the loop of the "P" of "Pesos."

1876-79

Laid Paper

80 A30 5c lilac 62.50 50.00
81 A31 10c brown 35.00 2.25
82 A32 20c blue 75.00 55.00
83 A20 50c green ('79) 77.50 52.50
84 A21 1p pale red (II) ('79) 50.00 12.50
Nos. 80-84 (5) 300.00 172.25

1879

Wove Paper

89 A24 25c green 25.00 25.00

1881

Blue Wove Paper

93 A30 5c violet 15.00 10.00
a. 5c lilac 15.00 10.00
94 A31 10c brown 8.75 2.00
95 A32 20c blue 8.75 3.00
96 A20 50c yellow green 9.50 6.00
97 A21 1p ver (III) 13.00 6.00
Nos. 93-97 (5) 55.00 27.00

For types of 1p, see note over No. 53.

Reprints of the 10c and 20c are much worn. On the 10c the letters "TAVOS" of "CENTAVOS" often touch. On the 20c the letters "NT" of "VEINTE" touch and the left arm of the "T" is too long. Reprints of the 25c, 50c and 1p have the characteristics previously described. The reprints are on white wove or laid paper, on colored papers, and in fancy colors. Stamps on green paper exist only as reprints.

A34

A35

A36

1 centavo — The period before "UNION" is round and there are rays between the stars and the condors.

2 centavos — The "2's" and "C's" in the corners are placed upright.

5 centavos — The last star at the right almost touches the frame.

10 centavos — The letters of the inscription are thin; there are rays between the stars and the condor.

1881 ***Imperf.***

White Wove Paper

103 A34 1c green 3.75 3.25
104 A35 2c vermilion 1.60 1.25
a. 2c rose 1.90 1.25
106 A34 5c blue 4.50 1.40
a. Printed on both sides
107 A36 10c violet 3.25 1.00
108 A34 20c black 3.50 1.60
Nos. 103-108 (5) 16.60 8.50

The stamps of this issue are found with perforations of various gauges, also sewing machine perforation, all of which are unofficial. See Nos. 112, 114-115.

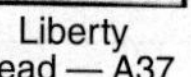
Liberty Head — A37

A37a

1881 ***Imperf.***

109 A37 1c blk, *green* 2.50 *3.75*
110 A37 2c blk, *lilac rose* 2.50 *3.75*
111 A37 5c blk, *lilac* 6.25 1.40
Nos. 109-111 (3) 11.25 *8.90*

Nos. 109 to 111 are found with regular or sewing machine perforation, unofficial.

Reprints:

1c — The top line of the stamp and the top frame extend to the left. 2c — There is a curved line over the scroll below the "AV" of "CENTAVOS."

5c — There are scratches across the "5" in the upper left corner. All three values were reprinted on the three colors of paper of the originals.

Redrawn

1 centavo — The period before "UNION" is square and the rays between the stars and the condor have been wholly or partly erased.

2 centavos — The "2's" and "C's" in the corners are placed diagonally.

5 centavos — The last star at the right touches the wing of the condor.

10 centavos — The letters of the inscription are thick; there are no rays under the stars; the last star at the right touches the wing of the condor and this wing touches the frame.

1883 ***Imperf.***

112 A34 1c green 4.75 4.25
113 A37a 2c rose 1.50 1.40
114 A34 5c blue 3.75 .95
a. 5c ultramarine 3.75 1.00
b. Printed on both sides, reverse ultra 25.00 20.00
115 A36 10c violet 5.00 1.40
Nos. 112-115 (4) 15.00 8.00

The stamps of this issue are found with regular or sewing machine perforation, privately applied.

A38

A39

1883 ***Perf. 10½, 12, 13½***

116 A38 1c gray grn, *grn* .75 .75
a. Imperf., pair 3.75 3.75
117 A39 2c red, *rose* .75 *1.00*
a. 2c org red, *rose* .75 *1.00*
b. 2c red, *buff* 5.50 5.50
c. Imperf., pair (#117 or 117a) 3.75 3.75
d. "DE LOS" in very small caps 11.00 11.00
118 A38 5c blue, *bluish* 1.90 1.25
a. 5c dk bl, *bluish* 1.90 .90
b. 5c blue 2.75 1.90
c. Imperf., pair (#118 or 118a) 6.50 6.50
d. As "b," imperf., pair 9.50 9.50
119 A39 10c org, *yel* .95 *1.10*
a. "DE LOS" in large caps 45.00 20.00
b. Imperf., pair 5.75 5.75
120 A39 20c vio, *lilac* 1.10 1.10
a. Imperf., pair 3.75 3.75
122 A38 50c brn, *buff* 2.25 2.50
a. Perf. 12 2.25 2.50
123 A38 1p claret, *bluish* 4.00 1.50
a. Imperf., pair 12.50 12.50
Nos. 116-123 (7) 11.70 9.20

Redrawn Types of 1877

1883 (?) ***Perf. 10½, 12***

125 A25 5p orange brown 8.00 4.50
126 A26 10p black, *gray* 8.00 4.50

1886 ***Perf. 10½, 11½, 12***

127 A38 5p brown, *straw* 5.75 5.75
a. Imperf., pair 25.00 25.00
128 A38 10p black, *rose* 7.00 7.00
a. Imperf., pair 25.00 25.00

Republic of Colombia

A40

Simón Bolívar — A41

Pres. Rafael Núñez — A42

1886 ***Perf. 10½ and 13½***

129 A40 1c grn, *grn* 1.25 .60
a. Imperf., pair 5.00 5.00
130 A41 5c blue, *bl* 1.25 .35
a. 5c ultra, *blue* 1.25 .35
b. Imperf., pair (#130) 5.00 5.00
131 A42 10c orange 2.75 .60
a. Imperf., pair 7.00 7.00
b. Pelure paper 3.50 .85
Nos. 129-131 (3) 5.25 1.55

Gen. Antonio Jose de Sucre y Alcala — A43

Gen. Antonio Nariño — A44

1887

133 A43 2c org red, *rose* 1.75 .85
a. 2c orange red, *yellowish* 4.50 4.50
b. 2c orange red 5.25 5.25
c. Imperf., pair (#133) 7.75 7.75

134 A44 20c pur, *grysh* 2.25 .85
a. Imperf., pair 6.25 6.25
b. Pelure paper 2.75 1.75

Impressions of No. 134 on white, blue or greenish blue paper were not regularly issued.

Arms — A45

Nariño — A46

1888

135 A45 50c brn, *buff* 1.25 *1.40*
a. Imperf., pair 4.50 4.50
136 A45 1p claret, *bluish* 6.00 1.75
137 A45 1p claret 2.50 1.25
138 A45 5p org brn 6.25 4.25
139 A45 5p black 11.00 7.00
140 A45 10p black, *rose* 13.00 5.25
Nos. 135-140 (6) 40.00 20.90

See Nos. 154, 156-157.

1889

141 A46 20c pur, *grayish* 1.40 1.00
a. Imperf., pair 6.75 6.75

Impressions on white, blue or greenish blue paper were not regularly issued.

A47

A48

A49

A50

A51

1890-91 ***Perf. 10½, 13½, 11***

142 A47 1c grn, *grn* 1.40 1.25
143 A48 2c org red, *rose* .60 *.70*
144 A49 5c bl, *grnsh bl* 1.00 .35
a. 5c deep blue, *blue* 1.00 .35
b. Imperf., pair 4.00 4.00
146 A50 10c brn, *yel* .60 .35
a. 10c brown, *buff* .60 .35
147 A51 20c vio, pelure paper 2.75 *3.50*
Nos. 142-147 (5) 6.35 *6.15*

A52

A52a

A53

A53a

A54

Perf. 10½, 12, 13½, 14 to 15½

1892-99

Ordinary Paper

148 A47 1c red, *yel* .65 .35
149 A52 2c red, *rose* 32.50 32.50
150 A52 2c green .40 .25
a. 2c yellow green .40 .25
151 A49 5c blk, *buff* 5.50 .30
152 A52a 5c org brn, *pale buff* .85 .25
a. 5c red brown, *salmon* ('97) .85 .25
153 A50 10c bis brn, *rose* .60 .35
a. 10c brown, *brownish* .60 .35
154 A53 20c brn, *bl* .60 .35
a. 20c red brown, *blue* .60 .35
b. 20c yel brn, *grnsh bl* ('97) 4.00 *10.00*
c. 20c brown, *buff* ('97) 14.00 10.00
155 A45 50c vio, *vio* .95 .60
156 A53a 50c red vio, *vio* ('99) 1.25
157 A54 1p bl, *grnsh* 1.60 .70
a. 1p blue, *buff* 1.60 .70
158 A45 5p red, *pale rose* 6.25 2.50
159 A45 10p blue 12.00 2.75
a. Thin, pale rose paper 22.50 6.00
Nos. 148-159 (12) 63.15
Nos. 148-155,157-159 (11) 40.90

Type A53a is a redrawing of type A45. The letters of the inscriptions are slightly larger and the numerals "50" slightly smaller than in type A45.

The 20c brown on white paper is believed to be a chemical changeling.

Nos. 148, 150-152a, 153-155, 157, 159 exist imperf. Value per pair, $5-$7.50.

A56

1899

162 A56 1c red, *yellow* .50 .30
163 A56 5c red brn, *sal* .50 .30
164 A56 10c brn, *lil rose* 1.50 .75
165 A56 50c blue, *lilac* 1.00 .95
Nos. 162-165 (4) 3.50 2.30

Cartagena Issues

A57

1899 **Blue Overprint** ***Imperf.***

167 A57 5c red, *buff* 24.00 24.00
a. Sewing machine perf. 24.00 24.00
168 A57 10c ultra, *buff* 24.00 24.00
a. Sewing machine perf. 24.00 24.00

Nos. 168 and 168a differ slightly from the illustration.

Bolivar No. 55 Overprinted with 7 Parallel Wavy Lines and:

A58

A59

A60

A61

Perf. 14 (#169), Sewing Machine Perf.

1899 **Purple Overprint**

169 A18 1c black 50.00 50.00
170 A58 1c brn, *buff* 17.00 17.00
a. Altered from 10c 25.00 25.00
171 A59 2c blk, *buff* 17.00 17.00
a. Altered from 10c 25.00 25.00
172 A60 5c mar, *grnsh bl* 14.00 14.00
a. Perf. 12 14.00 14.00
b. Without overprint 8.75 8.75
173 A61 10c red, *sal* 14.00 14.00
a. Perf. 12 14.00 14.00
Nos. 169-173 (5) 112.00 112.00

Types A58 and A59 illustrate Nos. 170a and 171a, which were made from altered plates of the 10c (No. 168). Nos. 170 and 171 were made from altered plate of the 5c denomination (No. 167), show part of the top flag of the "5" and differ slightly from the illustrations.

Nos. 170-173 exist imperf. Values about same as perf.

A62

1900 ***Imperf.***

Purple Overprint

174 A62 5c red 20.00 20.00
a. Perf. 12 27.50 27.50

A63

A64

"Gobierno Provisorio" at Top

1900 **Litho.** ***Perf. 12 Vertically***

175 A63 1c (ctvo) blk, *bl grn* 35.00 6.00
a. "cvo." 90.00 12.00
b. "cvos." 35.00 6.00
c. "centavo" 42.50 6.00
176 A63 2c black 25.00 3.50
177 A63 5c blk, *pink* 25.00 3.50
a. Name at side (V) 50.00 6.50
178 A63 10c blk, *pink* 25.00 4.00
a. Name at side (V) 50.00 7.50
179 A63 20c blk, *yellow* 35.00 6.00
a. Name at side (G) 70.00 10.00
Nos. 175-179 (5) 145.00 23.00

"Gobierno Provisional" at Top

Name at Side in Black or Green

180 A64 1c (ctvo.) blk, *bl grn* 35.00 5.00
a. "centavo" 100.00 15.00
181 A64 2c blk, *bl grn* 20.00 4.00
182 A64 5c blk (G) 20.00 4.00
a. "ctvos." smaller 40.00 6.00
183 A64 10c blk, *pink* 20.00 4.00
184 A64 20c blk, *yel* (G) 35.00 6.00
Nos. 180-184 (5) 130.00 23.00

Issues of the rebel provisional government in Cucuta.

A65

A66

1901 ***Sewing Machine Perf.***

Purple Overprint

185 A65 1c black .85 .85
a. Without overprint 1.90 1.90
b. Double overprint 2.00 2.00
c. Imperf., pair 2.00 2.00
d. Inverted overprint 1.00 1.00
186 A66 2c blk, *rose* .85 .85
a. Imperf., pair 2.00 2.00
b. Without overprint 1.90 1.90
c. Double overprint 2.00 2.00

A67

A68

1901

Rose Overprint

187 A67 1c blue .85 .85
a. Imperf., pair 3.00 3.00

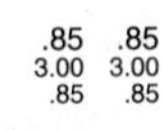

188 A68 2c brown .85 .85
a. Imperf., pair 3.00 3.00
b. Without overprint .85 .85

A69

A70

Sewing Machine or Regular Perf. 12, 12½

1902

Magenta Overprint

189 A69 5c violet 1.75 1.75
a. Without overprint 1.75 1.75
b. Double overprint 1.75 1.75
c. Imperf., pair 3.75 3.75
190 A70 10c yel brn 1.75 1.75
a. Double overprint 1.75 1.75
b. Imperf., pair 3.75 3.75
c. Without overprint 1.75 1.75
d. Printed on both sides 2.50 2.50

A71

A72

1902

Magenta Overprint

191 A71 5c yel brn 1.75 1.75
a. Without overprint 1.60 1.60
b. Imperf., pair 5.00 5.00
192 A71 10c black 1.25 1.25
a. Without overprint 1.00 1.00
b. Imperf., pair 7.50 7.50
193 A72 20c maroon 4.00 2.50
b. Imperf., pair 12.50 12.50
Nos. 191-193 (3) 7.00 5.50

Nos. 191-193 exist tête bêche. Value of 10c and 20c, each $12.50.

Washed copies of Nos. 167-174, 185-193 are offered as "without overprint."

Barranquilla Issues

Magdalena River — A75

Iron Quay at Sabanilla — A76

La Popa Hill — A77

1902-03 ***Imperf.***

194 A75 2c green 1.25 1.25
195 A75 2c dk bl 1.25 1.25
196 A75 2c rose 17.50 17.50
197 A76 10c scarlet .85 .70
198 A76 10c orange 10.00 10.00
199 A76 10c rose .85 .70
200 A76 10c maroon 1.40 1.40
201 A76 10c claret 1.40 1.40
202 A77 20c violet 2.75 2.75
a. Laid paper
203 A77 20c dl bl 7.50 7.50
204 A77 20c dl bl, *pink* *110.00* *110.00*
205 A77 20c car rose 16.00 16.00
Nos. 194-205 (12) *170.75* *170.45*

Sewing Machine Perf. and Perf. 12

194a A75 2c green 7.50 7.50
195a A75 2c dark blue 7.50 7.50
196a A75 2c carmine *35.00* *35.00*
197a A76 10c scarlet 3.50 3.50
198a A76 10c orange *27.50* *27.50*
199a A76 10c rose 5.50 5.50
200a A76 10c maroon 5.50 5.50
201a A76 10c claret 5.00 5.00
202b A77 20c purple .50 .50
c. 20c lilac .55 .55
203a A77 20c dull blue 7.50 7.50
204a A77 20c dull blue, *rose* *140.00* *140.00*
205b A77 20c carmine rose *55.00* *55.00*
Nos. 194a-205b (12) *300.00* *300.00*

See Nos. 240-245.

Cruiser "Cartagena" — A78

Bolívar — A79

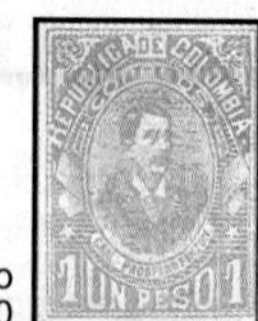
General Próspero Pinzón — A80

A81

A82

1903-04 *Imperf.*

209 A78 5c blue 2.00 2.00
210 A78 5c bister 2.75 2.75
211 A79 50c yellow 3.00 3.00
212 A79 50c green 3.50 3.50
213 A79 50c scarlet 3.50 3.50
214 A79 50c carmine 3.50 3.50
a. 50c rose 3.50 3.50
215 A79 50c pale brown 3.50 3.50
216 A80 1p yellow brn 1.25 1.25
217 A80 1p rose 2.00 2.00
218 A80 1p blue 2.00 2.00
219 A80 1p violet 20.00 20.00
220 A81 5p claret 4.25 4.25
221 A81 5p pale brown 6.50 6.50
222 A81 5p blue green 6.00 6.00
223 A82 10p pale green 6.25 6.25
224 A82 10p claret 20.00 20.00
Nos. 209-224 (16) 90.00 90.00

Nos. 216 and 217 measure 20½x26½mm and No. 218, 18x24mm. Stamps of this issue exist with forged perforations.

Perf. 12

209a A78 5c blue 7.00 7.00
210a A78 5c bister 7.50 7.50
211a A79 50c yellow 12.50 12.50
b. 50c orange 12.50 12.50
212a A79 50c green 20.00 20.00
213a A79 50c scarlet 9.00 9.00
214b A79 50c rose 9.00 9.00
215a A79 50c pale brown 9.00 9.00
216a A80 1p yellow brown 4.00 4.00
217a A80 1p rose 6.00 6.00
218a A80 1p blue 6.00 6.00
219a A80 1p violet 50.00 50.00
220a A81 5p claret 16.00 16.00
221a A81 5p pale brown 18.00 18.00
222a A81 5p blue green 15.00 15.00
223a A82 10p pale green 25.00 25.00
224a A82 10p claret 60.00 60.00
Nos. 209a-224a (16) 274.00 274.00

Laid Paper *Imperf.*

240 A76 10c dk bl, *lil* 5.00 5.00
241 A76 10c dk bl, *bluish* 3.00 3.00
242 A76 10c dk bl, *brn* 3.00 3.00
243 A76 10c dk bl, *sal* 7.00 7.00
244 A76 10c dk bl, *grnsh bl* 4.00 4.00
245 A76 10c dk bl, *dp rose* 3.00 3.00
Nos. 240-245 (6) 25.00 25.00

Perf. 12

240a A76 10c dk bl, *lilac* 10.50 10.50
241a A76 10c dk bl, *bluish* 7.50 7.50
242a A76 10c dk bl, *brn* 7.50 7.50
243a A76 10c dk bl, *salmon* 55.00 55.00
244a A76 10c dk bl, *grnsh bl* 16.00 16.00
245a A76 10c dk bl, *deep rose* 7.50 7.50
Nos. 240a-245a (6) 104.00 104.00

A82a

Imperf., Sewing Machine Perf.

1902 **Typeset**

255 A82a 10c black, *rose* 3.50 3.50
256 A82a 20c blk, *orange* 2.50 2.50

This issue was printed in either Cali or Popayan.

Medellin Issue

A83

1902

257 A83 1c grn, *straw* .25 *.40*
258 A83 2c salmon, *rose* .25 *.40*
259 A83 5c dp bl, *grnsh* .25 *.40*
260 A83 10c pale brn, *straw* .25 *.40*
261 A83 20c pur, *rose* .35 *.40*
262 A83 50c dl rose, *grnsh* 1.75 *2.50*
263 A83 1p blk, *yellow* 3.50 *5.25*
264 A83 5p slate, *blue* 27.50 27.50
265 A83 10p dk brn, *rose* 17.50 17.50
Nos. 257-265 (9) 51.60 54.75

For overprint see No. L8.

Imperf., Pairs

257a A83 1c 8.50 8.50
258a A83 2c 8.50 8.50
259a A83 5c 8.50 8.50
260a A83 10c 8.50 8.50
261a A83 20c 8.50 8.50
262a A83 50c 8.50 8.50
263a A83 1p 22.50 22.50
264a A83 5p 62.50 62.50
265a A83 10p 50.00 50.00

Regular Issue

A84

A85

A86

A87

A88 A89

A90

A91

A92

1902 *Imperf.*

266 A84 2c blk, *rose* .20 .20
267 A85 4c red, *grn* .20 .20
268 A86 5c grn, *bl* .20 .20
269 A87 10c blk, *pink* .20 .20
c. 10c blk, *rose* .75 .50
270 A88 20c brn, *buff* .20 .20
271 A89 50c dk grn, *rose* 1.10 1.10
272 A90 1p pur, *buff* .45 .45
273 A91 5p grn, *bl* 3.25 3.25
274 A92 10p grn, *pale grn* 10.00 5.00
Nos. 266-274 (9) 15.80 10.80

For overprint see No. H13.

Sewing Machine Perf.

266a A84 2c blk, *rose* 1.50 1.50
267a A85 4c red, *grn* 1.25 1.25
268a A86 5c grn, *blue* 1.50 1.50
269a A87 10c blk, *pink* 1.50 1.50
270a A88 20c brn, *buff* 2.50 2.00
271a A89 50c dk grn, *rose* 5.00 4.00
272a A90 1p pur, *buff* 6.00 5.00
273a A91 5p grn, *blue* 27.50 27.50
274a A92 10p grn, *pale grn* 50.00 50.00
Nos. 266a-274a (9) 96.75 94.25

1903 ***Perf. 12***

266b A84 2c blk, *rose* 1.10 1.10
269b A87 10c blk, *pink* 1.25 1.25
270b A88 20c brn, *buff* 1.25 1.25
272b A90 1p pur, *buff* 2.50 2.50
273b A91 5p grn, *blue* 22.50 22.50
274b A92 10p grn, *pale grn* 40.00 35.00
Nos. 266b-274b (6) 68.60 63.60

1903 ***Imperf.***

284 A85 4c blue, *grn* .25 .25
285 A86 5c blue, *blue* .25 .25
286 A88 20c blue,*buff* .25 .25
288 A89 50c blue, *rose* 1.40 1.40
Nos. 284-288 (4) 2.15 2.15

Sewing Machine Perf.

284a A85 4c blue, *grn* 1.75 1.40
285a A86 5c blue, *blue* 1.75 1.40
286a A88 20c blue, *buff* 2.50 2.00
288a A89 50c blue, *rose* 5.00 4.50
Nos. 284a-288a (4) 11.00 9.30

Perf. 12

284b A85 4c blue, *grn* 2.00 2.00
285b A86 5c blue, *blue* 2.00 2.00
286b A88 20c blue, *buff* 2.75 2.75
288b A89 50c blue, *rose* 7.50 7.50
Nos. 284b-288b (4) 14.25 14.25

A93

1904 **Pelure Paper** ***Imperf.***

303 A93 ½c yellow brn 1.00 1.00
304 A90 1c blue green 1.00 1.00
a. 1c yellow green 1.00 1.00
306 A84 2c blue .90 .60
307 A86 5c carmine 1.00 1.00
308 A87 10c violet 1.00 .90
Nos. 303-308 (5) 4.90 4.50

For overprint see No. H13.

1904 ***Perf. 13***

303a A93 ½c yellow brown 3.00 3.00
304b A90 1c blue green 4.00 3.50
c. 1c yellow green 5.00 4.50
306a A84 2c blue 2.50 2.50

Perf. 12

307a A86 5c carmine 2.25 2.25
308a A87 10c violet 2.25 2.25
Nos. 303a-308a (5) 14.00 13.50

A94

A95

Pres. José Manuel Marroquín — A96

Imprint: "Lit. J.L.Arango Medellin. Col."

1904 **Wove Paper** ***Perf. 12***

314 A94 ½c yellow .65 .20
315 A94 1c green .65 .20
316 A94 2c rose .65 .20
317 A94 5c blue 1.00 .20
318 A94 10c violet 1.40 .20
319 A94 20c black 1.40 .25
320 A95 1p brown 15.00 2.50
321 A96 5p red & blk, *yel* 45.00 45.00
322 A96 10p bl & blk, *grnsh* 45.00 45.00
Nos. 314-322 (9) 110.75 93.75

Redrawn

314a A94 ½c .65 .20
315a A94 1c .65 .20
316a A94 2c .65 .20
317a A94 5c 1.00 .20
319a A94 20c 1.40 .20
Nos. 314a-319a (5) 4.35 1.00

Imperf., Pairs

314b A94 ½c 2.50 2.50
315b A94 1c 2.00 2.00
316b A94 2c 2.50 2.50
317b A94 5c 2.50 2.50
318a A94 10c 3.25 3.25
319b A94 20c 6.00 6.00
320a A95 1p 50.00 50.00
Nos. 314b-320a (7) 68.75 68.75

On the redrawn types, the imprint is close to the base of the design instead of being spaced from it. On the redrawn 2c and 5c, the lower end of the vertical white line below "OR" of "CORREOS" forms a hook which turns to the right instead of to the left as in the originals.

See Nos. 325-330. For surcharges see Nos. 351-354, L1-L7, L9-L13, L15-L25.

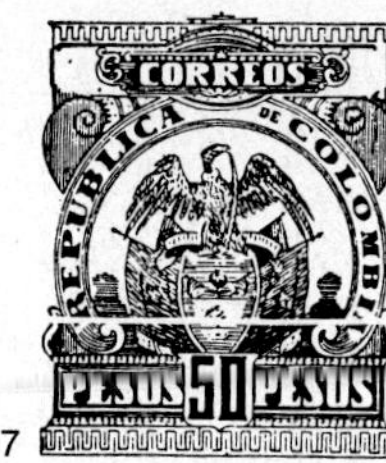

A97

100p has different frame.

1903 ***Imperf.***

323 A97 50p org yel, *pale pink* 70.00 70.00
324 A97 100p dk bl, *dk rose* 60.00 60.00

Imprint: "Lit. Nacional"

Perf. 10, 13, 13½ and Compound

1908

325 A94 ½c orange .60 .20
a. ½c yellow .60 .20
b. Imperf., pair 2.00 1.50
c. Without imprint 4.00 4.00
326 A94 1c yel grn .60 .20
a. Without imprint .60 .20
d. Imperf., pair 3.00 2.50
327 A94 2c red .60 .20
a. 2c carmine .60 .20
b. Imperf., pair 3.00 2.50
328 A94 5c blue .50 .20
a. Imperf., pair 5.00 4.00
329 A94 10c violet *40.00* .70
330 A94 20c gray blk *40.00* .50
Nos. 325-330 (6) *82.30* 2.00

The above stamps may be easily distinguished from those of 1904 by the perforation, by the height of the design, 24mm instead of 23mm, and by the "Lit. Nacional" imprint.

Camilo Torres A99

Policarpa Salavarrieta A100

Bolívar Demanding Liberation of Slaves — A105

Designs: 2c, Nariño. 5c, Bolívar. 10c, Francisco José de Caldas. 20c, Francisco de Paula Santander. 10p, Bolívar Resigning.

1910, Aug. **Engr.** ***Perf. 12***

331 A99 ½c violet & blk .50 .40
a. Center inverted 425.00 425.00
332 A100 1c deep green .40 .40
333 A100 2c scarlet .35 .25
334 A100 5c deep blue 1.25 .45
335 A100 10c plum 10.00 5.00
336 A100 20c black brn 15.00 5.50
337 A105 1p dk violet 50.00 18.00
338 A105 10p claret 200.00 140.00
Nos. 331-338 (8) 277.50 170.00

Colombian independence centenary.

Caldas A107

Monument to Battle of Boyacá A113

View of Cartagena A114

Coat of Arms A118

Designs: 1c, Torres. 2c, Narino. 4c, Santander. 5c, Bolivar. 10c, Jose Maria Cordoba. 1p, Sucre. 2p, Rufino Cuervo. 5p, Antonio Ricaurte y Lozano.

1917	Engr.	Perf. 14	
339 A107	½c bister	.35	.20
340 A107	1c green	.30	.20
341 A107	2c car rose	.30	.20
342 A107	4c violet	.90	.30
343 A107	5c dull blue	1.40	.20
344 A107	10c gray	1.25	.20
345 A113	20c red	3.00	.20
346 A114	50c carmine	1.50	.20
347 A107	1p brt blue	11.00	.40
348 A107	2p orange	10.00	.45
349 A107	5p gray	17.50	6.00
350 A118	10p dk brown	32.50	12.00
	Nos. 339-350 (12)	80.00	20.55

The 1c, 5c, 10c, 50c, 2p, 5p and 10p also exist perf. 11½ and 11½ compounded with 14.

Litho. varieties of Nos. 343, 345 and 346 are counterfeits made to defraud the government.

Imperforate copies of Nos. 339-350 are not known to have been regularly issued.

See Nos. 373-374, 400-405. For overprints and surcharges see Nos. 369-370, 377, 409-410, 440, C1, O3, O5-O9.

Nos. 318-319, 329-330 Surcharged in Red

1918

On Issue of 1904

351 A94	½c on 20c black	1.00	.25
352 A94	3c on 10c violet	2.50	.50

On Issue of 1908

353 A94	½c on 20c gray blk	8.00	5.00
354 A94	3c on 10c violet	12.00	4.25
	Nos. 351-354 (4)	23.50	10.00

Nos. 351-354 inclusive exist with surcharge reading up or down. On one stamp in each sheet the letter "S" in "Especie" is omitted. All denominations exist with a small zero before the decimal in the surcharge.

A119

A120

1918	Litho.	Perf. 13½	
358 A119	3c red	.50	.20
a.	Imperf., pair	4.00	4.00

1920	Engr.	Perf. 14	
359 A120	3c red, *org*	.30	.20
a.	Imperf., pair	3.00	3.00

See #371-372. For surcharge see #453.

A121

A122

A123

Perf. 10, 13½ and Compound

1920-21		Litho.	
360 A121	½c yellow	.50	.25
361 A121	1c green	.85	.20
362 A121	2c red	.65	.20
363 A122	3c green	.65	.20
a.	3c yellow green	.65	.20
364 A121	5c blue	.95	.25
365 A121	10c violet	3.00	1.50
366 A121	20c deep green	8.00	3.50
367 A123	50c dark red	8.00	3.50
	Nos. 360-367 (8)	22.60	9.60

The tablet with "PROVISIONAL" was added separately to each design on the various lithographic stones and its position varies slightly on different stamps in the sheet. For some values there were two or more stones, on which the tablet was placed at various angles.

Nos. 360-366 exist imperf.

See No. 375.

No. 342 Surcharged in Red

a

(15mm wide) — b

1921

369 A107 (a)	3c on 4c violet	.80	.25
a.	Double surcharge	13.00	
370 A107 (b)	3c on 4c violet	3.50	2.00

See No. 377.

Types of 1917-21

1923-24	Engr.	Perf. 13½	
371 A120	1½c chocolate	1.00	.50
372 A120	3c blue	.50	.20
373 A107	5c claret ('24)	2.00	.20
374 A107	10c blue	7.50	.40
	Litho.		
375 A121	10c dark blue	10.00	6.00
	Nos. 371-375 (5)	21.00	7.30

No. 342 Surcharged in Red

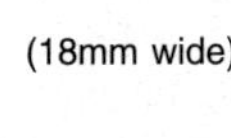

(18mm wide)

1924

377 A107	3c on 4c vio	3.00	1.25
a.	Double surcharge	12.00	
b.	Double surch., one invtd.	12.00	
c.	With added surch. "3cs." in red		

A124

1924-25	Litho.	Perf. 10, 10x13½	
379 A124	1c red	.70	.20
380 A124	3c dp blue ('25)	.70	.20

Exist imperf. Value, each pair $5.

A125 A126

Black, Red or Green Surch. & Ovpt.

Imprint of Waterlow & Sons

1925		Perf. 14, 14½	
382 A125	1c on 3c bis brn	.30	.20
383 A126	4c violet (R)	.40	.20
a.	Inverted surcharge	7.00	7.00

Imprint of American Bank Note Co.

Perf. 12

384 A125	1c on 3c bis brn	6.00	5.00
a.	Inverted surcharge	15.00	15.00
385 A126	4c violet (G)	.40	.30
a.	Inverted overprint	7.50	7.50
	Nos. 382-385 (4)	7.10	5.70

Correos

Provisional

Revenue stamps of basic types A125 and A126 were handstamped as above in violet or blue by the Cali post office in 1925, but were not authorized by the government. Denominations so overprinted are 1c, 2c, 3c, 4c and 5c.

A127

A128

Perf. 10, 13½x10

1926	Litho.	Wmk. 194	
395 A127	1c gray green	.35	.20
396 A128	4c deep blue	.35	.20

Exist imperf. Value, each pair $4.

Types of 1917 and

Sabana Station — A129

1926-29	Unwmk. Engr.	Perf. 14	
400 A107	4c deep blue	.40	.20
401 A118	8c dark blue	.50	.20
402 A107	30c olive bister	4.75	.60
403 A129	40c brn & yel brn	7.50	1.00
404 A107	5p violet	7.50	.70
a.	Perf. 11 ('29)	12.00	1.00
405 A118	10p green	12.00	2.00
a.	Perf. 11 ('29)	25.00	4.00
	Nos. 400-405 (6)	32.65	4.70

For surcharges & overprint see #09-410, O4.

Death of Bolívar A130

1930, Dec. 17		Perf. 12½	
408 A130	4c dk blue & blk	.30	.25

Cent. of the death of Simón Bolívar. See Nos. C80-C82.

Nos. 400 and 402 Surcharged in Red or Dark Blue

1932, Jan. 20		Perf. 14	
409 A107	1c on 4c dp bl (R)	.30	.20
a.	Inverted surcharge	5.25	5.25
410 A107	20c on 30c ol bis	8.00	.70
a.	Inverted surcharge	17.50	
b.	Double surcharge	17.50	

Emerald Mine — A131

Oil Wells — A132

Coffee Cultivation A133

Platinum Mine — A134

Gold Mining — A135

Christopher Columbus — A136

Imprint: "Waterlow & Sons Ltd. Londres"

1932	Wmk. 229	Perf. 12½	
411 A131	1c green	.50	.20
412 A132	2c red	.50	.20
413 A133	5c brown	.55	.20
414 A134	8c blue blk	3.50	.50
415 A135	10c yellow	2.75	.20
416 A136	20c dk blue	8.00	.35
	Nos. 411-416 (6)	15.80	1.65

See #441-442, 464-466a, 517. For surcharges see #455, 527, O1, O10-O11, O13, RA30.

Pedro de Heredia — A137

Coffee Picking — A138

Perf. 11½

1934, Jan. 10	Unwmk.	Litho.	
417 A137	1c dark green	2.25	.65
418 A137	5c chocolate	3.00	.55
419 A137	8c dark blue	2.25	.65
	Nos. 417-419 (3)	7.50	1.85

Cartagena, 400th anniv. See #C111-C114.

1934, Dec.	Engr.	Perf. 12	
420 A138	5c brown	2.25	.20

Discus Thrower — A139

Post and Telegraph Building — A145

Allegory of Olympic Games at Barranquilla — A140

Foot Race A141

Tennis A142

Pier at Puerto Colombia A143

View of the Bay A144

Designs: 2c, Soccer. 10c, Hurdling. 15c, Athlete in stadium. 18c, Baseball. 24c, Swimming. 50c, View of Barranquilla. 2p, Monument to Flag. 5p, Coat of Arms. 10p, Condor.

1935, Jan. 26 Litho. *Perf. 11½*

421	A139	2c bluish grn & buff	1.25	.40
422	A139	4c deep green	1.25	.40
423	A140	5c dk brn & yel	1.25	.40
a.		Horiz. pair, imperf. btwn.	200.00	
424	A141	7c dk carmine	2.50	1.50
425	A142	8c blk & pink	2.00	1.90
426	A141	10c brown & bl	2.75	1.50
427	A143	12c indigo	3.25	2.50
428	A141	15c bl & red brn	5.50	4.25
429	A141	18c dk vio & buff	7.50	6.50
430	A144	20c purple & grn	6.50	5.50
431	A144	24c bluish grn & ultra	6.50	5.25
432	A144	50c ultra & buff	10.00	8.50
433	A145	1p drab & blue	90.00	50.00
434	A145	2p dull grn & gray	110.00	90.00
435	A145	5p pur blk & bl	350.00	275.00
436	A145	10p black & gray	425.00	400.00
		Nos. 421-436 (16)	1,025.	853.60

3rd Natl. Olympic Games, Barranquilla. Counterfeits of 10p exist.

Oil Wells — A155

Gold Mining — A157

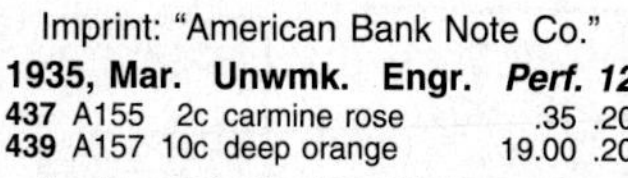

Imprint: "American Bank Note Co."

1935, Mar. Unwmk. Engr. *Perf. 12*

437	A155	2c carmine rose	.35	.20
439	A157	10c deep orange	19.00	.20

See Nos. 468, 470, 498, 516. For surcharge and overprints see Nos. 496, 596, O2.

No. 347 Surcharged in Black

1935, Aug. *Perf. 14*

440	A107	12c on 1p brt bl	3.00	1.40

Types of 1932

Imprint: "Lit. Nacional Bogotá"

1935-36 Litho. *Perf. 11, 11½, 12½*

441	A131	1c lt green	.20	.20
a.		Imperf., pair	3.50	
442	A133	5c brown ('36)	.55	.20
a.		Imperf., pair	4.00	4.00

For surcharge see No. 527.

Bolívar A159

Tequendama Falls A160

Wmk. Wavy Lines. (229)

1937 Engr. *Perf. 12½*

443	A159	1c deep green	.20	.20
a.		Perf. 14		
444	A160	12c deep blue	2.50	.95

See No. 570. For surcharges and overprints see Nos. 454, 456, C231, C326, O12.

Soccer Player — A161

Runner — A163

Discus Thrower — A162

1937, Jan. 4 Photo. Unwmk.

445	A161	3c lt green	1.40	.85
446	A162	10c carmine rose	2.75	1.75
447	A163	1p black	27.50	24.00
		Nos. 445-447 (3)	31.65	26.60

National Olympic Games, Manizales. For surcharge see No. 452.

Exposition Palace — A164

Stadium at Barranquilla A165

Monument to the Colors A166

1937, Jan. 4

448	A164	5c violet brown	.50	.30
449	A165	15c blue	3.75	3.50
450	A166	50c orange brn	9.75	7.50
		Nos. 448-450 (3)	14.00	11.30

Barranquilla National Exposition.

Stamps of 1926-37 Surcharged in Black

1937-38 Unwmk. *Perf. 12½*

452	A161	1c on 3c lt grn	.75	.75
a.		Inverted surcharge	1.75	1.75
453	A118	5c on 8c dk bl	.40	.35
a.		Inverted surcharge	1.75	1.75

Wmk. 229

454	A160	2c on 12c dp bl	.40	.35
455	A134	5c on 8c bl blk	.45	*.55*
a.		Invtd. surcharge	1.50	1.50
456	A160	10c on 12c dp bl ('38)	4.25	.85
a.		Dbl. surcharge	8.50	8.50
		Nos. 452-456 (5)	6.25	2.85

Calle del Arco — A168

Entrance to Church of the Rosary — A169

Arms of Bogotá A170

Gonzálo Jiménez de Quesada A171

Bochica A172

Santo Domingo Convent A173

Mass of the Conquistadors — A174

1938, July 27 Unwmk. *Perf. 12½*

457	A168	1c yellow green	.20	.20
458	A169	2c scarlet	.20	.20
459	A170	5c brown blk	.25	.20
460	A171	10c brown	.60	.30
461	A172	15c brt blue	2.50	1.25
462	A173	20c brt red vio	2.50	1.25
463	A174	1p red brown	37.50	22.50
		Nos. 457-463 (7)	43.75	25.90

Bogotá, 400th anniversary.

Types of 1932

Imprint: "Litografia Nacional Bogotá"

1938, Dec. 5 Litho. *Perf. 10½, 11*

464	A132	2c rose	.80	.30
465	A135	10c yellow	2.00	.30
466	A136	20c dull blue	7.50	1.00
a.		20c dark blue, perf. 12½ ('44)	50.00	5.00
		Nos. 464-466 (3)	10.30	1.60

Types of 1935 and

Bolívar A175

Coffee Picking A176

Arms of Colombia A177

Christopher Columbus A178

Caldas A179

Sabana Station A180

Imprint: "American Bank Note Co."

Wmk. 255

1939, Mar. 3 Engr. *Perf. 12*

467	A175	1c green	.20	.20
468	A155	2c car rose	.20	.20
469	A176	5c dull brown	.20	.20
470	A157	10c deep orange	.85	.20
471	A177	15c dull blue	2.50	.20
472	A178	20c violet blk	6.00	.20
473	A179	30c olive bister	3.50	.30
474	A180	40c bister brn	10.00	2.75
		Nos. 467-474 (8)	23.45	4.25

See Nos. 497-499, 515, 518, 574. For surcharges and overprints see Nos. 506-507, 520-522, 596, RA26, RA47.

Gen. Santander A181

Allegory A182

Gen. Santander A183

Statue at Cúcuta A184

Birthplace of Santander A185

Church at Rosario A186

Paya — A187

Bridge at Boyacá — A188

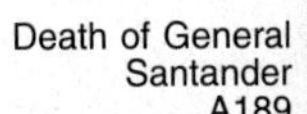

Death of General Santander A189

Invasion of the Liberators A190

Perf. 13x13½, 13½x13

1940, May 6 Engr. Wmk. 229

475	A181	1c olive green	.20	.20
476	A182	2c dk carmine	.40	.25
477	A183	5c sepia	.20	.20
478	A184	8c carmine	1.50	1.50
479	A185	10c orange yel	.65	.50
480	A186	15c dark blue	1.75	1.10
481	A187	20c green	2.25	1.75
482	A188	50c violet	5.25	5.00
483	A189	1p deep rose	17.00	17.00
484	A190	2p orange	52.50	52.50
		Nos. 475-484 (10)	81.70	80.00

Death of General Francisco Santander, cent.

Tobacco Plant — A194

Gen. Santander A195

Garcia Rovira A196

R. Galan — A197

Antonio Sucre — A198

1940-43 Engr. Wmk. 255 *Perf. 12*

488	A194	8c rose car & grn	1.00	.55
489	A195	15c dp blue ('43)	1.10	.25
490	A196	20c gray blk ('41)	2.75	.35
491	A197	40c brown bis ('41)	1.90	.35
492	A198	1p black	6.75	.50
		Nos. 488-492 (5)	13.50	2.00

See #500, 554. For overprint see #RA28.

Arms of Palmira — A199

Unwmk.

1942, July 4 Litho. *Perf. 11*

493 A199 30c claret 1.70 .60

8th Natl. Agricultural Exposition, held at Palmira.

Paradise of Isaacs, Palmira — A200

Signing Treaty of the Wisconsin A201

1942, July 4

494 A200 50c lt blue grn 2.25 .85

Issued in honor of the writer, Jorge Isaacs.

1942, Nov. 21 *Perf. 10½*

495	A201	10c dull orange	1.10	.50
a.		"2. XI.1902" instead of "21. XI. 1902"	14.00	15.00
b.		Perf. 12	3.00	3.00

40th anniv. of the signing of the Treaty of the Wisconsin, Nov. 21, 1902.

No. 470 Surcharged in Black

1944 Wmk. 255 *Perf. 12*

496 A157 5c on 10c dp org .20 .20

Counterfeits exist of No. 496 with inverted or double surcharge.

Types of 1935-41 and

National Shrine — A202

San Pedro Alejandrino A203

Imprint: "Columbian Bank Note Co."

1944-45 Unwmk. Engr. *Perf. 11*

497	A175	1c green	.20	.20
498	A155	2c rose	.20	.20
499	A176	5c dull brown	.20	.20
500	A196	20c gray black	2.50	.75
501	A202	30c dl ol grn ('45)	1.40	.95
502	A203	50c rose	1.75	.95
		Nos. 497-502 (6)	6.25	3.25

No. 499 Surcharged in Black

1944, Oct.

506	A176	1c on 5c dull brn	.20	.20
507	A176	2c on 5c dull brn	.20	.20

Nos. 506 and 507 exist with inverted or double surcharge, created by favor.

Flag — A204

Arms — A205

Murillo Toro — A206

Hospital of St. John of God A207

Virrey Solis A208

1944, Oct. 10 Litho.

508	A204	2c ultra & bis	.20	.20
a.		Sheet of 18	10.00	
b.		Imperf., pair	10.00	
509	A205	5c ultra & bis	.30	.30
a.		Sheet of 22	12.00	
b.		Imperf., pair	10.00	
510	A206	20c blk & bluish grn	1.00	1.00
a.		Sheet of 8	11.00	
b.		Imperf., pair	15.00	
511	A207	40c blk & red	4.25	4.25
a.		Sheet of 4	17.50	
512	A208	1p blk & red	9.25	9.25
a.		Sheet of 2	20.00	
		Nos. 508-512 (5)	15.00	15.00

Souvenir Sheet

Perf. 11x11½ All Around, Stamps Imperf.

513 Sheet of 5, #508-512 12.00 12.00

75th anniv. of Gen. Benevolent Assoc. of Cundinamarca.

Nos. 508-513 were printed in composite sheets containing one each of Nos. 508a, 509a, 510a, 511a and 512a, and two of 513. Fifty of these were presented to government officials.

Murillo Toro — A210

San Pedro Alejandrino — A211

1944, Nov. 10 *Perf. 11*

514 A210 5c lt brown .30 .20

Types of 1932-39 and A211

Imprint: "Litografia Nacional Bogota"

1944 Litho. *Perf. 12½*

515	A175	1c dp green	.35	.20
a.		1c olive green	.35	.20
b.		Imperf., pair	1.75	1.75
516	A155	2c dk carmine	.40	.20
a.		Imperf., pair	1.75	1.75
517	A135	10c yellow org	2.75	.45
518	A179	30c gray olive	7.50	3.50
a.		Imperf., pair	27.50	
519	A211	50c rose	8.00	3.75
		Nos. 515-519 (5)	19.00	8.10

No. 469 Overprinted in Green, Blue or Red

Wmk. 255

1945, July 19 Engr. *Perf. 12*

520	A176	5c dull brn (G)	.20	.20
521	A176	5c dull brn (R)	.20	.20
522	A176	5c dull brn (Bl)	.20	.20
		Nos. 520-522 (3)	.60	.60

Portraits are Joseph Stalin, Franklin D. Roosevelt and Winston Churchill.

Clock Tower, Cartagena — A212

1945, Nov. 15

523 A212 50c olive black 3.75 1.25

For overprints see Nos. 543-544.

Sierra Nevada of Santa Marta A213

Designs: 30c, Seaplane Tolima. 50c, San Sebastian Fort, Cartagena.

Unwmk.

1945, Dec. 14 Litho. *Perf. 11*

524	A213	20c light green	1.50	1.00
525	A213	30c pale blue	1.50	1.00
526	A213	50c salmon pink	1.50	1.00
		Nos. 524-526 (3)	4.50	3.00

25th anniv. of the 1st airmail service in America, according to the inscription, but earlier services are known to have existed.

No. 442 Surcharged in Black

1946, Mar. 8 *Perf. 11x11½, 12½*

527	A133	1c on 5c brown	.20	.20
a.		Inverted surcharge	.90	

Gen. Antonio Jose de Sucre — A216

Wmk. 255

1946, Apr. 16 Engr. *Perf. 12*

Size: 19x26½mm

528	A216	1c brn & turq grn	.20	.20
529	A216	2c vio & rose car	.20	.20

Size: 23x31mm

530	A216	5c sepia & blue	.20	.20
531	A216	9c dk grn & red	.60	.60
532	A216	10c ultra & org	.45	.40
533	A216	20c blk & dp org	.45	.30
534	A216	30c brn red & grn	.70	.30
535	A216	40c ol blk & red vio	.70	.35
536	A216	50c dp brn & vio	.70	.35
		Nos. 528-536 (9)	4.20	2.90

Map of South America A217

National Observatory A218

Unwmk.

1946, June 7 Litho. *Perf. 11*

537	A217	15c ultra	.50	.30
a.		Imperf., pair	4.00	

1946, Aug.

538	A218	5c fawn	.30	.20
a.		Imperf., pair	4.00	

See No. 565.

Andrés Bello — A219

Joaquín de Cayzedo y Cuero — A220

Wmk. 255

1946, Sept. 3 Engr. *Perf. 12*

539 A219	3c sepia	.20	.20
540 A219	10c orange	.55	.30
541 A219	15c slate black	.60	.35
	Nos. 539-541,C145 (4)	1.55	1.05

Bello (1781-1865), poet and educator.

1946, Sept. 20 Wmk. 229 *Perf. 12½*

542 A220	2p bluish green	4.50	1.25

See No. 568. For surcharge see No. 613.

Type of 1945, Overprinted in Black or Green

1946, Dec. 6 Wmk. 255 *Perf. 12*

543 A212	50c red (Bk)	4.00	2.25
a.	Double overprint	25.00	
544 A212	50c red (G)	4.00	2.25
a.	Double overprint	25.00	

5th Central American and Caribbean Championship Games.

Coffee — A221

Engraved and Lithographed

1947, Jan. 10 Wmk. 229 *Perf. 12½*

545 A221	5c multicolored	.40	.20

Colombian Orchid: Masdevallia Nycterina A222

Designs (Orchids): 2c, Miltonia vexillaria. No. 548, Cattleya chocoensis. No. 549, Odontoglossum crispum. No. 550, Cattleya dowiana aurea. 10c, Cattleya labiata trianae.

1947, Feb. 7 Wmk. 255 *Perf. 12*

546 A222	1c multicolored	.35	.20
547 A222	2c multicolored	.35	.20
548 A222	5c multicolored	.75	.20
549 A222	5c multicolored	.75	.20
550 A222	5c multicolored	.75	.20
551 A222	10c multicolored	1.25	.35
	Nos. 546-551 (6)	4.20	1.35

Antonio Nariño — A228

Alberto Urdaneta y Urdaneta — A229

Perf. 12½

1947, May 9 Litho. Unwmk.

552 A228	5c blue, *grnsh*	.25	.20
553 A229	10c red brn, *grnsh*	.30	.20
	Nos. 552-553,C146-C147 (4)	1.40	1.05

4th Pan-American Press Congress, 1946.

Sucre Type of 1940

1947 Wmk. 255 Engr. *Perf. 12*

554 A198	1p violet	2.50	1.00

José Celestino Mutis and José Jerónimo Triana A230

Miguel A. Caro and Rufino J. Cuervo — A231

1947 Wmk. 229 *Perf. 12½*

555 A230	25c olive green	.65	.25
556 A231	3p dark purple	4.00	3.25

See #567, 569. For surcharge see #610.

Metropolitan Cathedral, Plaza Bolívar, Bogotá — A232

National Capitol A233

Ministry of Foreign Affairs A234

A235

1948, Apr. 2

557 A232	5c black brown	.20	.20
558 A233	10c orange	.55	.55
559 A234	15c dark blue	.55	.55
	Nos. 557-559,C148-C149 (5)	2.40	2.40

Miniature Sheet

Imperf

560 A235	50c slate	1.50	1.50

9th Pan-American Conf., Bogotá.

No. RA5A Overprinted in Black

1948 Unwmk. *Perf. 12½*

Without Gum

561 PT3	1c yellow orange	.20	.20

The letter "C" is the initial of "CORREOS."

Nos. RA33, RA24 and RA25 Overprinted in Black

1948 Wmk. 255 *Perf. 12.*

562 PT6	1c olive	.20	.20
563 PT6	2c green	.20	.20
564 PT6	20c brown	.20	.20
	Nos. 562-564 (3)	.60	.60

Nos. 561-564 exist with inverted and double overprints.

Observatory Type of 1946

Unwmk.

1948, June 30 Litho. *Perf. 11*

565 A218	5c blue	.20	.20

Simón Bolívar — A236

Carlos Martinez Silva — A237

Wmk. 255

1948, May 29 Engr. *Perf. 12*

566 A236	15c green	.40	.20

Types of 1946-47

1948 Unwmk. *Perf. 12½*

567 A230	25c green	.30	.20
568 A220	2p dp green	.55	.20
569 A231	3p dp red violet	.70	.20
	Nos. 567-569 (3)	1.55	.60

Falls Type of 1937

1948 Wmk. 229

570 A160	10c red	.20	.20

For overprints see Nos. C231, C326.

Perf. 13½

1948, Dec. 21 Unwmk. Litho.

571 A237	40c carmine	.40	.25

Juan de Dios Carrasquilla A238

1949, May 20 Wmk. 229 *Perf. 12½*

572 A238	5c bister	.20	.20

75th anniv. of the foundation of the Colombian Soc. of Agriculture.

Julio Garavito Armero A239

Arms of Colombia A240

Wmk. 229

1949, Apr. 24 Engr. *Perf. 12*

573 A239	4c green	.30	.20

Issued to honor Julio Garavito Armero (1865-1920), mathematician.

Coffee Type of 1939.

Imprint: "American Bank Note Co."

1949, Aug. 4 Wmk. 255

574 A176	5c blue	.20	.20

1949, Oct. 7 Unwmk. *Perf. 13*

575 A240	15c blue	.20	.20

Issued to honor the new Constitution. See Nos. C164-C165.

Shield and Tree — A241

Francisco Javier Cisneros — A242

1949, Oct. 13 Wmk. 229 *Perf. 12½*

576 A241	5c olive	.20	.20

4th anniv. of Colombia's 1st Forestry Cong. and propaganda for the government's reforestation program.

1949, Dec. 15 Photo. Unwmk.

577 A242	50c red vio & yel	1.00	.60
578 A242	50c green & vio	1.00	.60
579 A242	50c brown & lt bl	1.00	.60
	Nos. 577-579 (3)	3.00	1.80

50th anniv. (in 1948) of the death of Francisco Javier Cisneros.

Masdevallia Chimaera A243

Odontoglossum Crispum — A244

Eastern Hemisphere — A245

Designs: 3c, Cattleya labiata trianae. 4c, Masdevallia nycterina. 5c, Cattleya dowiana aurea. 11c, Miltonia vexillaria. 18c, Santo Domingo post office.

1950, Aug. 22 Photo. *Perf. 13*

580 A243	1c brown	.20	.20
581 A244	2c violet	.20	.20
582 A243	3c rose lilac	.20	.20
583 A243	4c emerald	.25	.20
584 A243	5c red orange	.65	.20
585 A244	11c red	1.50	1.50
586 A244	18c ultra	1.25	.50
	Nos. 580-586 (7)	4.25	3.00

Miniature Sheet

Imperf

587 A245 50c orange yel 1.25 1.25

75th anniv. (in 1949) of the UPU. See No. C199. For surcharge see No. C232.

Antonio Baraya — A246

Perf. 12½

1950, Nov. 27 Unwmk. Engr.

588 A246 2c red .20 .20

Colombian Farm A247

1950, Dec. 28 Photo. *Perf. 11½*

589 A247	5c dp car & buff	.20	.20
590 A247	5c bl grn & gray	.20	.20
591 A247	5c vio bl & gray	.20	.20
	Nos. 589-591 (3)	.60	.60

Issued to publicize rural life.

Arms of Bogotá A248

Arms of Colombia A249

Perf. 12x12½

1950, Dec. 28 Engr. Wmk. 255

592 A248	5p deep green	2.50	.40
593 A249	10p red orange	7.50	.65

Catalogue values for unused stamps in this section, from this point to the end of the section, are for Never Hinged items.

Map and Badge A250

Guillermo Valencia A251

Perf. 12½x13

1951, Jan. 30 Photo. Unwmk.

594 A250 20c red, yel & bl .40 .25

60th anniversary (in 1947) of the formation of the Colombian Society of Engineers.

1951, Oct. 20 Engr. *Perf. 13x13½*

595 A251 25c black .90 .25

Issued to honor Guillermo Valencia (1873-1943), newspaper founder, governor of Cauca, presidential candidate, author.

No. 468 Overprinted in Black

1951, Dec. 11 Wmk. 255 *Perf. 12*

596 A155 2c carmine rose .30 .20

Issued to publicize the reversion of the Mares oil concession to Colombia.

Nicolas Osorio — A252

#598, Pompilio Martinez. #599, Ezequiel Uriocoechea. #600, Jose M. Lombana.

Perf. 11½

1952, Aug. 6 Unwmk. Engr.

Various Frames

597 A252	1c deep blue	.25	.20
598 A252	1c deep blue	.25	.20
599 A252	1c deep blue	.25	.20
600 A252	1c deep blue	.25	.20
	Nos. 597-600 (4)	1.00	.80

Nos. 597-600 were printed in a single sheet containing four panes of twenty-five each, separated by double rows of ornamental tabs. Although inscribed "sobretasa," the stamps were for ordinary postage.

Types of Postal Tax Stamps of 1945-50 and

Communications Building A253 A253a

1952 *Perf. 12*

601 A253 5c ultra .30 .25

Wmk. 255

602 PT10	20c brown	8.00	4.00
603 PT6	25c dk gray	*32.50*	*32.50*
604 PT10	25c blue green	.85	.25
605 A253a	50c orange yel	21.00	12.50
606 A253a	1p rose carmine	2.00	.30
607 A253a	2p lilac rose	21.00	8.50
608 A253a	2p violet	2.25	.60
	Nos. 601-608 (8)	87.90	58.90

Although inscribed "sobretasa," Nos. 601-608 were issued for ordinary postage.
For surcharges see Nos. 612, RA48.

Cathedral of Manizales — A254

Perf. 11½

1952, Oct. 10 Photo. Unwmk.

609 A254 23c blue & gray blk .35 .20

Centenary of city of Manizales.
For surcharge see No. 619.

No. 555 Surcharged in Blue

1952, Oct. 30 Wmk. 229 *Perf. 12½*

610 A230 15c on 25c olive green .45 .25

Latin American Siderurgical Conf., 1952. See No. C226.

Queen Isabella I and Monument A255

Perf. 12½

1953, Mar. 10 Unwmk. Engr.

611 A255 23c blue & black .75 .55

5th cent. of the birth of Queen Isabella I of Spain.
For surcharge see No. 693.

Nos. 606 and 568 Surcharged with New Values in Dark Blue

1953, Oct. 19 Wmk. 255

612 A253a	40c on 1p rose car	1.40	.25
613 A220	50c on 2p dp green	1.40	.25

Manuel Ancizar A256

Portraits: 23c, José Jeronimo Triana. 30c, Manuel Ponce de Leon. 1p, Agustin Codazzi.

Perf. 12½x13

1953, Nov. Engr. Unwmk.

Frames in Black

614 A256	14c rose red	.50	.50
615 A256	23c ultra	.40	.25
616 A256	30c chocolate	.35	.25
617 A256	1p emerald	.35	.25
	Nos. 614-617 (4)	1.60	1.25

Cent. (in 1950) of the establishment of the Chorographic Commission. For surcharges and overprint see Nos. 620, 687, 690, 692, C284.

Murillo Toro and Map — A257

Engraved and Lithographed

1953, Dec. 12 Wmk. 255 *Perf. 12*

Black Surcharge

618 A257 5c on 5p multi .35 .20

2nd Natl. Phil. Exhib., Bogotá, Dec. 1953. See No. C237.

Nos. 609 and 614 Surcharged with New Value or New Value and Ornaments

1953 Unwmk. *Perf. 11½, 12½x13*

619 A254	5c on 23c (C)	.35	.20
620 A256	5c on 14c (Bk)	.35	.25

No. 614 surcharged "CINCO" in blue is listed as No. 687.

Symbolical of St. Francis Receiving Christ's Wounds — A258

1954, Apr. 23 Photo. *Perf. 11½*

621 A258 5c sepia & green .35 .20

400th anniversary of the establishment of Colombia's first Franciscan community.

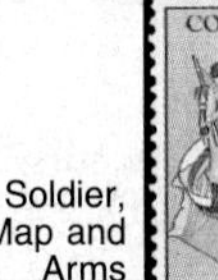

Soldier, Map and Arms A259

1954, June 13 Engr. *Perf. 13*

622 A259 5c dull blue .25 .20

1st anniv. of the assumption of the presidency by Gen. Gustavo Rojas Pinilla. See Nos. C255, 637a.

Sports Emblem — A260

Design: 10c, Stadium and athlete holding arms of Colombia.

1954, July 18 Unwmk.

623 A260	5c deep blue	.40	.20
624 A260	10c red	.75	.20
	Nos. 623-624,C256-C257 (4)	3.05	.95

7th Natl. Athletic Games, Cali, July 1954.

History Academy Seal — A261

1954, July 24

625 A261 5c ultra & green .25 .20

50th anniversary (in 1952) of the Colombian Academy of History.

Convent and Cell of St. Peter Claver — A262

1954, Sept. 9

627 A262	5c dark green	.25	.20
a.	Souvenir sheet	4.50	4.50

300th anniv. of the death of St. Peter Claver.
No. 627a contains one stamp similar to No. 627, but printed in greenish black. Sheet size: 121x129½mm. See Nos. C258-C258a.

Mercury — A263

1954, Oct. 29

628	A263	5c orange	.50	.25
		Nos. 628,C259-C260 (3)	1.20	.65

1st Intl. Fair and Exhibition, Bogota, 1954.

Tapestry Madonna A264

College Cloister A265

Designs: 10c, Brother Cristobal de Torres. 20c, College chapel and arms.

Perf. 12½x11½, 11½x12½

1954, Dec. 6

629	A264	5c orange & blk	.35	.20
630	A264	10c blue	.35	.20
631	A265	15c violet brn	.40	.20
632	A265	20c black & brn	.80	.35
a.		Souvenir sheet	7.50	7.50
		Nos. 629-632,C263-C266 (8)	4.25	2.15

Founding of the Senior College of Our Lady of the Rosary, Bogota, 300th anniv. (in 1953).
No. 632a contains four stamps similar to Nos. 629-632, but printed in different colors: 5c yellow and black, 10c green, 15c dull violet, 20c black and light-blue.

Steel Mill — A266

José Marti — A267

1954, Dec. 12 ***Perf. 12½x13***

633	A266	5c ultra & blk	.25	.20

Issued to mark the opening of the Paz del Rio steel mill, October 1954. See No. C267.

1955, Jan. 28 ***Perf. 13½x13***

634	A267	5c deep carmine	.25	.20

Centenary of the birth of José Marti (1853-1895), Cuban patriot. See No. C268.

Arms, Flags and Soldiers Building Bridge A268

1955, Mar. 23 ***Perf. 12½***

635	A268	10c claret	.25	.20

Issued to honor Colombian soldiers who served in Korea, 1951-53. See Nos. 637a, C269.

Fleet Emblem — A269

M. S. City of Manizales and New York Skyline A270

1955, Apr. 12 **Unwmk.**

636	A269	15c deep green	.20	.20
637	A270	20c violet	.40	.20
a.		Souvenir sheet	7.50	7.50
		Nos. 636-637,C270-C271 (4)	1.45	.90

Grand-Colombian Merchant Fleet.
No. 637a contains four stamps similar to Nos. 622, 635-637, but printed in different colors: 5c blue, 10c dark carmine, 15c green, 20c purple.

Hotel Tequendama and Church of San Diego — A271

1955, May 16 **Photo.** ***Perf. 11½x12***

638	A271	5c blue	.25	.20

See No. C273.

Bolivar's Country Estate, Bogotá A272

1955, Sept. 28 **Engr.** ***Perf. 12½***

639	A272	5c deep ultra	.25	.20

50th anniv. of Rotrary Intl. See No. C274.

Belalcazar, Jiménez de Quesada and Balboa A273

Caravels and Columbus A274

5c, San Martin, Bolivar and Washington.

Engraved and Photogravure

1955, Oct. 29 ***Perf. 13x12½***

640	A273	2c yel grn & brn	.40	.25
641	A273	5c brt bl & brn	.40	.25
642	A274	23c lt ultra & blk	.45	.25
a.		Souvenir sheet	17.50	17.50
		Nos. 640-642,C275-C280 (9)	18.50	12.30

7th Cong. of the Postal Union of the Americas and Spain, Bogota, Oct. 12-Nov. 9, 1955.
No. 642a contains one each of Nos. 640-642, printed in slightly different shades.

José Eusebio Caro — A275

1955, Nov. 29 **Engr.** ***Perf. 13½x13***

643	A275	5c brown	.25	.20

José Eusebio Caro (1817-53), poet. See #C281.

Departmental Issue

Map — A276

View of San Andres Harbor — A277

Cattle at Waterhole A278

Designs: 2c, Docks, Atlantico. 3c, "Industry," Antioquia. 4c, Cartagena Harbor, Bolivar. #647, Steel Mill, Boyaca. #648, Cattle, Cordoba. #649, Map. #650, San Andres Harbor. #651, Cacao picker, Cauca. 10c, Coffee picker, Caldas. 15c, Salt Mine Chapel, Zipaquira, Cundinamarca. 20c, Tropical plants and map, Choco. 23c, Harvester, Huila. 25c, Banana Plantation, Magdalena. 30c, Gold mining, Narifio. 40c, Tobacco plantation, Santander. 50c, Oil wells, North Santander. 60c, Cotton plantation, Tolima. 1p, Sugar industry, Cauca. 3p, Amazon river at Leticia, Amazonas. 5p, Windmills and panoramic view, La Guajira. 10p, Rubber plantation, Vaupes.

Perf. 13½x13, 13x13½, 13
Engr.; Engr. & Litho.

1956 **Unwmk.**

Various Frames

644	A277	2c car & grn	.20	.20
645	A276	3c brn vio & blk	.20	.20
646	A277	4c grn & blk	.20	.20
647	A276	5c dk brn & bl	.20	.20
648	A277	5c ol & dk vio brn	.30	.20
649	A276	5c bl & blk	.25	.20
650	A277	5c car & grnsh bl	.20	.20
651	A277	5c ol grn & red brn	.20	.20
652	A276	10c org & blk	.45	.20
653	A276	15c ultra & blk	.25	.20
654	A276	20c dk brn & bl	.25	.20
655	A277	23c ultra & ver	.30	.20
656	A277	25c ol grn & blk	.30	.20
657	A277	30c ultra & brn	.25	.20
658	A277	40c dl pur & red brn	.25	.20
659	A277	50c dk grn & blk	.25	.20
660	A277	60c pale brn & grn	.25	.20
661	A278	1p mag & grnsh bl	1.50	.20
662	A278	2p grn & red brn	2.25	.25
663	A278	3p car & blk	2.50	.45
664	A278	5p brn & lt ultra	4.75	1.00
665	A276	10p red brn & grn	14.00	6.00
		Nos. 644-665 (22)	29.30	11.30

Nos. 645, 647, 649, 652-654 measure 27x32mm, No. 665 27x37mm. See Nos. 681-684, 685, 688-689. For surcharges and overprints see Nos. 685, 688-689, C289, C312.

Columbus and Proposed Lighthouse A279

1956, Oct. 12 **Photo.** ***Perf. 12***

666	A279	3c gray black	.50	.25

Issued in honor of Christopher Columbus. See Nos. C285, C306.

Altar of St. Elizabeth and Tomb of Jimenez de Quesada A280

1956, Nov. 19 **Unwmk.**

667	A280	5c red lilac	.25	.20

7th cent. of St. Elizabeth of Hungary, patron saint of Sante Fé de Bogotá. See No. C286.

St. Ignatius of Loyola — A281

Javier Pereira — A282

1956, Nov. 26 **Engr.** ***Perf. 12½x13***

668	A281	5c blue	.25	.20

400th anniv. of the death of St. Ignatius of Loyola. See No. C287. For overprint see No. C324.

1956, Dec. 28 **Unwmk.** ***Perf. 12***

669	A282	5c blue	.25	.20

Issued to honor 167-year-old Javier Pereira. See No. C288.

Emblem and Dairy Farm A283

Designs: 2c, Emblem and tractor. 5c, Emblem, coffee and corn.

1957, Mar. 5 **Photo.** ***Perf. 14x13½***

670	A283	1c lt ol grn	.20	.20
671	A283	2c lt brn	.20	.20
672	A283	5c lt bl	.20	.20
		Nos. 670-672,C292-C296 (8)	2.70	1.80

Agrarian Savings Bank of Colombia, 25th anniv.
For overprint see No. C322.

Arms of Military Academy and Gen. Rafael Reyes A284

Design: 10c, Arms and Academy.

1957, July 20 Engr. *Perf. 12½*
673 A284 5c blue .20 .20
674 A284 10c orange .25 .20
a. Souv. sheet of 2 16.00 16.00
Nos. 673-674,C299-C300 (4) .90 .80

50th anniv. of the Colombian Military Academy.
No. 674a contains one each of Nos. 673-674 in slightly different shades.
For overprints see Nos. C328, C312.

Statue of José Matias Delgado — A285

1957, Sept. 16 Photo. *Perf. 12*
675 A285 2c rose brn .25 .20

Issued in honor of Jose Matias Delgado, liberator of El Salvador. See No. C301.

Santo Michelena, Marcos V. Crespo, P. Alcantara Herran and UPU Monument A286

1957, Oct. 10 Unwmk.
676 A286 5c green .20 .20
677 A286 10c gray .30 .20
Nos. 676-677,C302-C303 (4) .90 .80

Intl. Letter Writing Week and 14th UPU Cong.

St. Vincent de Paul and Children — A287

1957, Oct. 18
678 A287 1c dark olive green .25 .20

Colombian Society of St. Vincent de Paul, cent. See No. C304. For overprint see No. C323.

Fencer A288

1957, Nov. 22 Photo. *Perf. 12*
679 A288 4c lilac .25 .20

3rd South American Fencing Championship. See No. C305. For overprint see No. C332.

Francisco José de Caldas and Hypsometer — A289

1958, May 12 Unwmk. *Perf. 12*
680 A289 10c black .25 .20
Nos. 680,C309-C310 (3) 1.00 .60

International Geophysical Year, 1957-58.

Departmental Issue
Type of 1956
Designs as before.

1958 Engr. *Perf. 13*
681 A276 3c ultra & brn .20 .20
682 A276 3c ol grn & pur .20 .20
683 A276 10c grn & brn .20 .20
684 A276 10c dk bl & brn .20 .20
Nos. 681-684 (4) .80 .80

Nos. 646, C291, 614, 653, 655, 616, C308, 615 and 611 Surcharged with New Value, and Old Value Obliterated, or Overprinted in Dark Blue or Green
Perf. 12½, 12½x13, 13

1958-59 Unwmk.
685 A277 2c on 4c grn & blk .25 .20
686 AP48 5c dp plum & multi ('59) .25 .20
687 A256 5c on 14c blk & rose red ("CINCO") ('59) .30 .30
688 A276 5c on 15c ultra & blk .25 .20
689 A277 5c on 23c ultra & ver (G) .25 .20
690 A256 5c on 30c blk & choc .25 .20
691 AP40 10c on 25c rose vio .25 .20
692 A256 20c on 23c blk & ultra (G) ('59) .30 .20
693 A255 20c on 23c bl & blk ('59) .30 .20
Nos. 685-693 (9) 2.40 1.90

On No. 686 the words "Correo Extra Rapido" are obliterated in dark blue.

Father Rafael Almanza and Church of San Diego, Bogota A290

1958, Oct. 23 Photo. *Perf. 14x13*
695 A290 10c purple .25 .20
Nos. 695,C313-C314 (3) .70 .60

For overprint see #C336.

Msgr. R. M. Carrasquilla and Church A291

1959, Jan. 22 *Perf. 14x13*
696 A291 10c dk red brn .25 .20
Nos. 696,C315-C316 (3) 1.05 .60

Cent. of the birth of Msgr. R. M. Carrasquilla (1857-1930), rector of Our Lady of the Rosary Seminary, Bogotá. For overprints see #C335, C341.

Miss Universe 1959 — A292

Jorge Eliecer Gaitan — A293

1959, June 26 Photo. *Perf. 11½*
697 A292 10c multi .70 .25
Nos. 697,C317-C318 (3) 42.10 38.85

Luz Marina Zuluaga, Miss Universe, 1959.
For overprint see No. C342.

1959, July 28 Engr. *Perf. 12x13½*
698 A293 10c on 3c gray bl (Bl) .25 .20
699 A293 30c rose vio .45 .25
Nos. 698-699,C319-C320 (4) 3.50 2.95

Issued in honor of Jorge Eliecer Gaitan (1898-1948), lawyer and politician.
No. 698 exists without blue surcharge.

Gen. Francisco de Paula Santander — A294

Designs: Nos. 701, 703, Simon Bolivar.

1959 Litho. Wmk. 331 *Perf. 12½*
700 A294 5c brown & yel .25 .20
701 A294 5c ultra & bl .25 .20
702 A294 10c gray & grn .25 .20
703 A294 10c gray & red .25 .20
Nos. 700-703,C389 (5) 4.00 1.20

Capitol, Bogota A295

1959
704 A295 2c dk bl & red brn .20 .20
705 A295 3c blk brn & lilac .20 .20

Stamp of 1859 and Mail Transport by Mule — A296

Two-Toed Sloth — A297

Designs (various stamps of 1859 and): 10c, Mail boat on the Magdalena river. 15c, as 5c. 25c, Train.

Unwmk.
1959, Dec. 1 Photo. *Perf. 12*
709 A296 5c org & grn .20 .20
710 A296 10c rose cl & bl .20 .20
711 A296 15c car rose & grn .40 .40
712 A296 25c bl & red brn .50 .50
Nos. 709-712,C351-C354 (8) 5.00 3.30

Centenary of Colombian postage stamps.

1960, Feb. 12 *Perf. 12*

Designs: 10c, Alexander von Humboldt. 20c, Spider monkey.

713 A297 5c grnsh bl & brn .30 .20
714 A297 10c blk & dp car .40 .20
715 A297 20c cit & gray brn .30 .20
Nos. 713-715,C357-C359 (6) 5.75 3.45

Cent. of the death of Alexander von Humboldt (1769-1859), German naturalist and geographer.
For overprint and surcharge see #C411, C413.

Anthurium Andreanum A298

Lincoln Statue, Washington A299

Flower: 20c, Espeletia grandiflora.

1960, May 10
716 A298 5c multi .60 .25
717 A298 20c brn, yel & gray ol .60 .25
Nos. 716-717,C360-C370 (13) 13.95 15.20

See #C420-C425. For overprint see #C412.

Wmk. 331
1960, June 10 Litho. *Perf. 10½*
718 A299 20c rose lil & blk .30 .25
Nos. 718,C375-C376 (3) 1.40 1.05

Florero House, Cradle of the Republic A300

Arms of Santa Cruz de Mompox — A301

Design: 5c, First coins of Republic.

Unwmk.
1960, July 19 Photo. *Perf. 12*
719 A301 5c grn & ocher .25 .20
720 A300 20c ol bis & mar .25 .20
721 A301 20c multi .25 .20
Nos. 719-721,C377-C385 (12) 6.25 4.90

Colombia's independence, 150th anniv.

St. Isidore and Farm Animals — A302

Design: 20c, Nativity by Gregorio de Arce Vasquez y Ceballos.

1960, Sept. 26 *Perf. 12*
722 A302 10c multi .20 .20
723 A302 20c multi .25 .20
Nos. 722-723,C387 (3) .65 .60

St. Isidore the Farmer, patron saint of the rural people.
See Nos. 747, C388, C439-C440.

UN Headquarters and Emblem A303

Wmk. 331
1960, Oct. 24 Litho. *Perf. 11*
724 A303 20c blk & pink .25 .20

Souvenir Sheet

Imperf

725 A303 50c dk brn, brt grn & blk 3.50 3.50

15th anniversary of the United Nations.

Pan-American Highway through Colombia — A304

Alfonso Lopez — A305

1961, Mar. 7 Unwmk. *Perf. 10½x11*

726 A304 20c brn & grnsh bl .70 .65
Nos. 726,C390-C393 (5) 2.70 2.65

8th Pan-American Highway Congress, Bogota, May 20-29, 1960.

1961, Mar. 22 Photo. *Perf. 12½*

727 A305 10c brt rose & brn .25 .20
728 A305 20c vio & brn .25 .20
Nos. 727-728,C394-C395 (4) 1.20 .80

Alfonso Lopez (1886-1959), President of Colombia. See No. C396.

Cauca River Bridge, Cali A306

Page from Resolutions of Confederated Cities — A307

1961-62 *Perf. 12½x13, 13½x13*

729 A306 10c red brn, bl, grn & red ('62) .25 .20
730 A307 20c pale brn & blk .25 .20
Nos. 729-730,C397-C401 (7) 3.00 2.05

50th anniversary (in 1960) of the Department of Valle del Cauca.

View of Cucuta and Arms A308

#732, Arms of Ocana and Pamplona.

1961, Aug. 29 *Perf. 13x13½*

731 A308 20c bl, blk, yel & red .25 .20
732 A308 20c ocher, ultra & red .25 .20
Nos. 731-732,C402-C403 (4) 1.30 .80

50th anniv. (in 1960) of the Department of North Santander.

Arms of Popayan A309

Basketball A310

Designs: No. 734, Arms of Barranquilla. No. 735, Arms of Bucaramanga.

Perf. 12½x13

1961, Oct. 10 Unwmk.

Arms in Multicolor

733 A309 10c blue & silver .25 .20
734 A309 20c blue & yellow .25 .20
735 A309 20c blue & gold .25 .20
Nos. 733-735,C404-C408 (8) 2.75 1.60

Issued to honor Atlantico Department.

1961, Dec. 16 Litho. *Perf. 13½x14*

736 A310 20c shown .25 .20
737 A310 20c Runners .25 .20
738 A310 20c Boxers .40 .25
739 A310 25c Soccer .25 .20
Nos. 736-739,C414-C418 (9) 3.60 2.20

4th Bolivarian Games, Barranquilla, 1961.

Colombian Anti-Malaria Emblem — A311

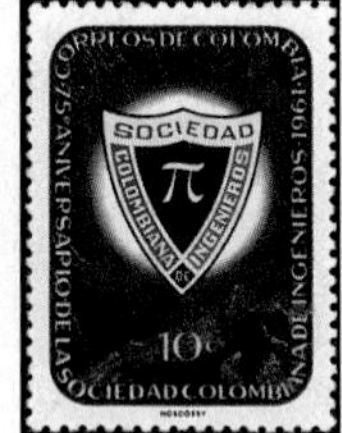

Engineers Society Emblem — A312

Design: 50c, Malaria eradication emblem and mosquito in swamp.

1962, Apr. 12 Unwmk. *Perf. 12*

740 A311 20c lt bis & red .25 .20
741 A311 50c bis & ultra .30 .20
Nos. 740-741,C426-C428 (5) 4.80 4.50

1962, June 12 Photo. *Perf. 11½x12*

742 A312 10c multi .25 .25
Nos. 742,C429-C432 (5) 2.40 2.35

Colombian Society of Engineers, 75th anniv.

Flags of American Nations A313

Woman Casting Ballot and Statue of Policarpa Salavarrieta A314

1962, June 28 *Perf. 13*

Flags in National Colors

743 A313 25c blk & org ver .25 .20

Souvenir Sheet

744 A313 2.50p blk & yel 5.00 5.00

70th anniv. of the founding of the Organization of American States.
See No. C433.

Perf. 12x12½

1962, July 20 Litho. Wmk. 229

745 A314 10c lt bl, gray & blk .25 .20

Issued to publicize women's political rights. See Nos. 752, C434, C448-C450.

Scouts at Campfire and Tents A315

Railroad Map of Colombia A316

Perf. 11½x12

1962, July 28 Photo. Unwmk.

746 A315 10c brt grnsh bl & brn .35 .30
Nos. 746,C435-C438 (5) 5.35 4.80

Colombian Boy Scouts, 30th anniv.

St. Isidore Type of 1960 Redrawn

1962, Aug. 28 *Perf. 12*

747 A302 10c pink & multi .25 .20
Nos. 747,C439-C440 (3) 3.95 3.90

The frame on No. 747 is solid color with white inscription similar to type AP82.

1962, Sept. 28 *Perf. 12½*

748 A316 10c blk, gray, grn & red .20 .20
Nos. 748,C441-C444 (5) 5.75 4.55

Progress of Colombian railroads and the completion of the Atlantic Line from Santa Marta to Bogota.

Post Horn — A317

Perf. 13½x14

1962, Oct. 18 Litho. Wmk. 346

749 A317 20c gold, dl gray vio & blk .25 .20
Nos. 749,C445-C446 (3) .80 .60

50th anniv. of the founding of the Postal Union of the Americas and Spain, UPAE.

"Virgin of the Rock" A318

Red Cross Centenary Emblem A319

1963, Mar. 11 Wmk. 346

750 A318 60c multi .25 .20

Vatican II, the 21st Ecumenical Council of the Roman Catholic Church. See No. C447.

1963, May 1 *Perf. 12x12½*

751 A319 5c olive bister & red .25 .20

Centenary of International Red Cross.

Women's Rights Type of 1962

1963, July 11 Wmk. 346

752 A314 5c org, gray & blk .25 .20
Nos. 752,C448-C450 (4) .95 .80

Manuel Mejia J. and Flag of National Coffee Growers Assn. A320

Perf. 12½x13

1965, Feb. 10 Engr. Unwmk.

753 A320 25c rose & blk .25 .20
Nos. 753,C464-C466 (4) 4.45 .95

Manuel Mejia J. (1887-1958), banker and manager of the National Coffee Growers Association.

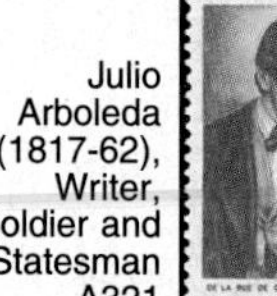

Julio Arboleda (1817-62), Writer, Soldier and Statesman A321

1966, Mar. 9 Litho. *Perf. 14x13½*

754 A321 5c lt brn, lt yel grn & blk .30 .20

Spanish Galleon, 16th Century A322

History of Maritime Mail: 15c, Rio Hacha brigantine, 1850. 20c, Uraba canoe. 40c, Magdalena River steamship and barge, 1900. 50c, Modern motor ship and sea gull.

1966, June 16 Photo. Unwmk.

755 A322 5c org & multi .35 .20
756 A322 15c car rose, blk & brn .35 .20
757 A322 20c brt grn, org & blk .35 .20
758 A322 40c dp bl & multi .50 .20
759 A322 50c pale bl & multi 1.00 .40
Nos. 755-759 (5) 2.55 1.20

Plumed Hogfish A323

Design: 10p, Bat ray and brittle starfish.

1966, Aug. 25 Photo. *Perf. 12½x13*

760 A323 80c multi .25 .20
761 A323 10p multi 7.50 5.00
Nos. 760-761,C481-C483 (5) 23.35 17.30

Arms of Venezuela, Colombia and Chile A324

1966, Oct. 11 Litho. *Perf. 14x13½*

762 A324 40c yel & multi .25 .20
Nos. 762,C484-C485 (3) .70 .60

Visits of Eduardo Frei and Raul Leoni, presidents of Chile and Venezuela.

Camilo Torres, 1766-1816, Lawyer — A325

Portraits: 60c, Jorge Tadeo Lozano (1771-1816), naturalist. 1p, Francisco Antonio Zea (1776-1822), naturalist and politician.

Perf. 13½x14

1967, Jan. 18 Litho. Unwmk.

763 A325 25c vio & bis .25 .20
764 A325 60c dk red brn & bis .25 .20
765 A325 1p grn & bis .35 .25
Nos. 763-765,C486-C487 (5) 1.30 1.05

Issued to honor famous men of Colombia.

Map of South America and Arms A326

1967, Feb. 2 Litho. *Perf. 14x13½*

766 A326 40c multi .25 .20
767 A326 60c multi .25 .20
Nos. 766-767,C488 (3) .85 .60

Declaration of Bogota for cooperation and world peace, signed by Colombia, Chile, Ecuador, Peru and Venezuela.

Monochaetum Orchid and Bee — A327

Orchid: 2p, Passiflora vitifolia and butterfly.

1967, May 23 Litho. *Perf. 14*

768 A327 25c multi .25 .20
769 A327 2p multi 4.25 2.75
Nos. 768-769,C489-C491 (5) 14.70 4.40

1st Natl. Orchid Exhib. and the Topical Phil. Flora and Fauna Exhib., Medellin, Apr. 1967.

Lions Emblem — A328

SENA Emblem — A329

1967, July 12 Litho. *Perf. 13½x14*

770 A328 10p multi 3.00 2.00

50th anniv. of Lions Intl. See No. C492.

Lithographed and Embossed

1967, Sept. 20 Unwmk.

771 A329 5p gold, brt grn & blk 1.40 .25

10th anniv. of Natl. Apprenticeship Service, SENA. See No. C494.

Gold Diadem in Calima Style — A330

Radar Installation A331

Pre-Columbian Art: 3p, Gold statuette, ornamental globe and bird, horiz.

Perf. 13½x14, 14x13½

1967, Oct. 13 Photo.

772 A330 1.60p brt rose lil, gold & brn .80 .25
773 A330 3p dk bl, gold & brn 1.25 .35
Nos. 772-773,C495-C497 (5) 12.25 9.35

Meeting of the UPU Committee of Postal Studies, Bogota, Oct., 1967.

1968, May 14 Litho. *Perf. 13½x14*

1p, Map of communications network.

774 A331 50c brt yel grn, blk & org brn .20 .20
775 A331 1p multi .30 .20
Nos. 774-775,C498-C499 (4) .90 .80

20th anniv. of the National Telecommunications Service (TELECOM).

The Eucharist — A332

St. Augustin, by Gregorio Vasquez — A333

1968, June 6 Litho. *Perf. 13½x14*

776 A332 60c multi .25 .20
Nos. 776,C500-C501 (3) .75

39th Eucharistic Cong., Bogotá, 8/18-25.

1968, Aug. 13 Photo. *Perf. 13*

Designs: 60c, The Gathering of Manna, by Gregorio Vasquez. 1p, The Marriage of the Virgin, by Baltazar de Figueroa. 5p, Jeweled monstrance, c. 1700. 10p, Pope Paul VI, painting by Roman Franciscan nuns.

777 A333 25c multicolored .20 .20
778 A333 60c multicolored .20 .20
779 A333 1p multicolored .20 .20
780 A333 5p multicolored .65 .20
781 A333 10p multicolored 1.25 .45
a. Souvenir sheet of 2 2.75 2.75
Nos. 777-781,C502-C506 (10) 7.95 4.05

39th Eucharistic Congress. Bogotá, Aug. 18-25. No. 781a contains two imperf. stamps similar to Nos. 780-781.

Pope Paul VI — A334

Arms of National University — A335

1968, Aug. 22 Litho. *Perf. 13½x14*

782 A334 25c multi .25 .20
Nos. 782,C507-C509 (4) .95 .80

Visit of Pope Paul VI to Colombia, 8/22-24.

1968, Oct. 29 Litho. *Perf. 13½x14*

783 A335 80c multi .35 .25

Centenary of the founding of the National University. See No. C510.

Stamp of Antioquia, 1868 — A336

Institute Emblem — A337

1968, Nov. 20 Litho. *Perf. 12x12½*

784 A336 30c emer & bl .30 .20

Souvenir Sheet

785 A336 5p lt olive & blue 5.00 5.00

Cent. of the 1st postage stamps of Antioquia and the 7th Natl. Phil. Exhib., Medellin, Nov. 20-29.

1969, Mar. 5 Litho. *Perf. 13½x14*

786 A337 20c multi .35 .25

25th anniv. (in 1967) of the Inter-American Agricultural Sciences Institute. See No. C511.

Battle of Boyaca (Detail), by José Maria Espinosa — A338

Design: 30c, Army of liberation crossing Pisba Pass, by Francisco Antonio Caro.

1969, July 24 Litho. *Perf. 13½x14*

787 A338 20c gold & multi .35 .25
788 A338 30c gold & multi .35 .25
Nos. 787-788,C517 (3) 1.70 .85

Fight for independence, sesquicentennial .

"Poverty" A339

1970, Mar. 1 Litho. *Perf. 14*

789 A339 30c bl & multi .35 .25

Colombian Institute for Family Welfare and 10th anniv. of the Children's Rights Law.

Greek Mask and Pre-Columbian Symbol of Literary Contest — A340

1970, Sept. 12 Litho. *Perf. 14x13½*

790 A340 30c dk brn, red org & ocher .25 .20

3rd Latin American Theatrical Festival of the Universities, Manizales, Sept. 12-20.

Colombian Stamps, Envelope and Emblem A341

1970, Sept. 24 Litho. *Perf. 14x13½*

791 A341 2p brt bl & multi .30 .25

Issued to publicize Philatelic Week.

Arms of Ibague and Discobolus A342

1970, Oct. 13

792 A342 80c buff, emer & sepia .25 .20

9th National Games in Ibague.

St. Theresa, by Baltazar de Figueroa — A343

1970, Oct. 28 Litho. *Perf. 13½x14*

793 A343 2p multi .40 .25

Elevation of St. Theresa (1515-1582), to Doctor of the Church. See No. C568. For overprint see No. C568.

Casa Cural A344

1971, May 20 Litho. *Perf. 14x13½*

794 A344 1.10p multi .30 .20

Fourth centenary (in 1970) of the founding of Guacari, Valle. See No. 809.

Dancers and Music, Currulao — A345

1p, Chicha Maya dancers and music.

1971 Litho. *Perf. 13½x14*

795 A345 1p pink & multi .35 .25
796 A345 1.10p lt bl & multi .35 .25

Souvenir Sheets

Imperf

797	Sheet of 3	3.50	3.50
a.	A345 2.50p Napanga	.35	.35
b.	A345 2.50p Joropo	.35	.35
c.	A345 5p Guabina	.70	.70
798	Sheet of 3	3.50	3.50
a.	A345 4p Bambuco	.55	.55
b.	A345 4p Cumbia	.55	.55
c.	A345 4p Currulao	.55	.55

Issued: #795, 12/20; #796, 8/5; #797-798, 8/10.

Constitutional Assembly, by Delgado A346

1971, Oct. 2 ***Perf. 14***

801 A346 80c multi .25 .20

Sequicentennial of Gran Colombian Constitutional Assembly in Rosario del Cucuta.

See No. C589. For overprint see No. C589.

Arrows Emblem — A347

1972, Feb. 24 ***Perf. 13½x14***

802 A347 60c blk & gray .30 .20

Inter-Governmental Committee on European Migration, 20th anniversary.

Student and World Map A348

1972, Mar. 15 ***Perf. 14x13½***

803 A348 1.10p lt grn & brn .25 .20

20th anniv. of ICETEX, an organization which furnishes financial help for educational purposes and for technical studies abroad.

UN Emblem, Soldier and Frigate A349

1972, Apr. 7

804 A349 1.20p lt bl & multi .25 .20

Colombian Battalion in Korea, 20th anniv.

Mother Francisca Josefa del Castillo — A350

Handicraft A351

1972, Apr. 6 ***Perf. 13½x14***

805 A350 1.20p brn & multi .25 .20

Tercentenary (in 1971) of the birth of Mother Francisca Josefa del Castillo, Poor Clare abbess and writer.

1972, Apr. 11

806 A351 1.10p multi .35 .20

Nos. 806,C569-C571 (4) 1.55 .85

Colombian artisans.

Maxillaria Triloris — A352

Emeralds — A353

1972, Apr. 20

807 A352 20p green & multi 6.50 .75

10th Natl. Phil. Exhib., Medellin.

1972, June 16 Litho. ***Perf. 13½x14***

808 A353 1.10p multi 1.00 .20

Type of 1971

Design: Antonio Nariño House.

1972, June 17 ***Perf. 14x13½***

809 A344 1.10p multi .50 .25

4th centenary, town of Leyva.

San Andres and Providencia Islands — A354

1972, June 24 ***Perf. 13½x14***

810 A354 60c bl & multi .25 .20

Sesquicentennial of annexation by Colombia of San Andres and Providencia Islands.

Postal Service Emblem A355

1972, Nov. 15 Litho. ***Perf. 12½x12***

811 A355 1.10p emerald .25 .20

Family A356

1972, Nov. 23

812 A356 60c orange .25 .20

Social progress.

Radio League Emblem A357

Human Figure, Tamalameque A358

1973, Apr. 6 Litho. ***Perf. 12x12½***

813 A357 60c lt bl, ultra & red .25 .20

40th anniversary of the Colombian Radio Amateurs' League.

1973, June 15 Litho. ***Perf. 13½x14***

Excavated Ceramic Artifacts: 1p, Winged urn, Tairona. 1.10p, Jug, Muisca.

814	A358 60c lt bl & multi	.35	.25
815	A358 1p org & multi	.70	.25
816	A358 1.10p vio bl & multi	.40	.25
	Nos. 814-816,C583-C586 (7)	4.60	2.50

Antonio Nariño, by José M. Espinosa — A359

Child — A360

1973, Dec. 13 Litho. ***Perf. 13½x14***

817 A359 60c multi .25 .20

Sesquicentennial of the death of General Antonio Nariño (1765-1823).

1973, Dec. 17

818 A360 1.10p multi .25 .20

National Campaign for Children's Welfare.

Symbols of Financial Controls A361

1973, Dec. 20 Litho. ***Perf. 14x13½***

819 A361 80c ultra, ocher & blk .25 .20

50th anniv. of Comptroller-general's Office.

Mother Laura Montoya — A362

1974, June 18 Litho. ***Perf. 13½x14***

820 A362 1p multi .25 .20

Mother Laura Montoya (1874-1949), founder and Mother Superior of the Missionaries of Mary Immaculata and St. Catherine of Siena.

Runner and Games' Emblem A363

1974, July 18 Litho. ***Perf. 14x13½***

821 A363 2p ver, yel & brn .35 .20

10th National Games, Pereira.

José Rivera A364

1974, Aug. 3 Litho. ***Perf. 14x13½***

822 A364 10p grn & multi 1.25 .20

50th anniv. of the publication of "La Voragine" (The Whirlpool) by José Eustasio Rivera.

Abstract Pattern — A365

Train Emerging from Tunnel — A366

1974, Oct. 24 Litho. ***Perf. 13½x14***

823 A365 1.10p multi .25 .20

Cent. of Natl. Insurance Co. See No. C610.

1974, Nov. 27 Litho. ***Perf. 13½x14***

824 A366 1.10p multi .25 .20

Centenary of the Antioquia railroad.

Boy, Puppy and Soccer Ball — A367

Christmas: 1p, Girl with racket and kitten.

1974, Dec. 9

825	A367	80c multi	.25	.20
826	A367	1p multi	.25	.20

A368

1975, Apr. 11 Litho. ***Perf. 14x13½***

827	A368	80c Gold Animal	.40	.25
828	A368	1.10p Gold necklace	.40	.25
		Nos. 827-828,C621-C622 (4)	6.20	1.30

Pre-Columbian Sinu culture artifacts.
For surcharge see No. 840.

Guglielmo Marconi — A369

Santa Marta Cathedral — A370

1975, June 2 Litho. ***Perf. 13½x14***

829	A369	3p multi	.30	.20

Birth centenary of Guglielmo Marconi (1874-1937), Italian electrical engineer and inventor.

1975, July 26

830	A370	80c multi	.30	.20

400th anniv. of Santa Marta City. See #C623.

Rafael Nuñez — A371

Arms of Medellin — A372

1975, Sept. 28 Litho. ***Perf. 13½x14***

831	A371	1.10p multi	.20	.20

Rafael Nunez (1825-1894), philosopher, poet, political leader, birth sesquicentenary.
For surcharge see No. 848.

1975-79 ***Perf. 13½x14, 12 (1.20p)***

832	A372	1p	shown	.30	.20
833	A372	1.20p	Ibagué	.20	.20
834	A372	1.20p	Tunja	.20	.20
835	A372	1.50p	Cucuta	.30	.20
836	A372	1.50p	Cartagena	.20	.20
836A	A372	4p	Sogamoso	.50	.20
837	A372	5p	Popayan	.30	.20
838	A372	5p	Barranquilla	.30	.20
839	A372	10p	San Gil	.50	.20
839A	A372	10p	Socorro	.50	.20
			Nos. 832-839A (10)	3.30	2.00

1p for the tercentenary of Medellin; No. 835, the cent. of Cucuta's reconstruction.
Issued: 1p, 11/4; #835, 11/29; #836, 2/10/76; #833, 7/30/76; #834, 12/2076; #837, 8/30/77; #838, 9/20/77; 10p, 8/9/79; 4p, 9/14/79.
See #905-913, C818. For surcharge see #849.

No. 827 Surcharged

1975 ***Perf. 14x13½***

840	A368	1.20p on 80c multi	.20	.20

Purace Indians, Cauca — A373

1976, Nov. 10 Litho. ***Perf. 13½x14***

841	A373	1.50p multi	.20	.20

Callicore A374

5p, Morpho (butterfly). 20p, Anthurium.

1976, Nov. 17 ***Perf. 12***

842	A374	3p multicolored	.85	.20
843	A374	5p multicolored	1.25	.20
844	A374	20p multicolored	3.75	.75
		Nos. 842-844 (3)	5.85	1.15

Rotary Emblem — A375

1976, Dec. 3 Litho. ***Perf. 12***

845	A375	1p multicolored	.20	.20

Rotary Club of Colombia, 50th anniversary.

Declaration of Independence, by John Trumbull — A376

1976, Dec. 21 Litho. ***Perf. 12***

846	A376	Strip of 3	9.00	*10.50*
a.-c.		30p any single	2.75	2.00

American Bicentennial. No. 846 printed in sheets of 4 triptychs.

Policeman with Dog — A377

1976, Dec. 29 ***Perf. 13½x14***

847	A377	1.50p multicolored	.20	.20

Honoring the National Police.
For surcharge see No. 850.

Nos. 831, 834, 847 Surcharged in Light Brown

1977, June Litho. ***Perf. 13½x14, 12***

848	A371	2p on 1.10p multi	.20	.20
849	A372	2p on 1.20p multi	.20	.20
850	A377	2p on 1.50p multi	.25	.20
		Nos. 848-850 (3)	.65	.60

Souvenir Sheet

Postal Museum, Bogota — A378

1977, July 27 Litho. ***Perf. 14***

855	A378	25p multi	2.50	2.50

Postal Museum, Bogotá.

Mother and Child — A379

1977-78 Litho. ***Perf. 12***

856	A379	2p multi	.20	.20
857	A379	2.50p multi ('78)	.90	.20

National good nutrition plan.
Issue dates: 2p, Aug. 30; 2.50p, Jan. 26.

Jacana and Eichhornia A380

Fidel Cano, by Francisco Cano — A381

20p, Mayan cotinga and pyrostegia venusta.

1977, Sept. 6 Litho. ***Perf. 14***

858	A380	10p multicolored	2.00	.25
859	A380	20p multicolored	3.00	.40
		Nos. 858-859,C644-C647 (6)	8.20	1.45

1977, Sept. 16 ***Perf. 14***

860	A381	4p multicolored	.20	.20

90th anniversary of El Espectador, newspaper founded by Fidel Cano.

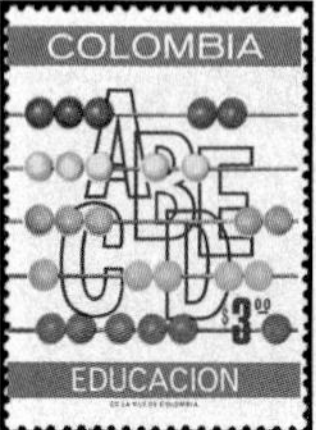

Abacus and Alphabet A382

Cattleya Triannae A383

1977, Sept. 16 ***Perf. 13½x14***

861	A382	3p multicolored	.20	.20

Popular education.

1978-79 Litho. ***Perf. 12***

862	A383	2.50p multi	.20	.20
863	A383	3p multi ('79)	.20	.20

Issue dates: 2.50p, Apr. 18. 3p, May 10.

Sprinting and Games Emblem A384

Sports: a, sprinting. b, basketball. c, baseball. d, boxing. e. bicycling. f, fencing. g, soccer. h, gymnastics. i, judo. j, weight lifting. k, wrestling. l, swimming. m, tennis. n, target shooting. o, volleyball. p, water polo.

1978, June 27 Litho. ***Perf. 14***

868		Sheet of 16	22.50	3.50
a.-p.		A384 10p, any single	.90	.20

13th Central American and Caribbean Games, Medellin.

"Sigma 2" by Alvaro Herrán A385

1978, June 30

869	A385	8p multicolored	.40	.20

Chamber of Commerce, Bogota, centenary.

Gen. Tomás Cipriano de Mosquera (1778-1878), Statesman A386

1978, Oct. 6 Litho. ***Perf. 12***

870	A386	6p multicolored	.40	.20

Anthurium Narinenses — A387

1979, July 23 ***Perf. 12***

871	A387	3p red & multi	.20	.20
872	A387	3p purple & multi	.20	.20
873	A387	3p rose & purple	.20	.20
874	A387	3p white & multi	.20	.20
a.		Block of 4, #871-874	.65	.25

Gen. Rafael Uribe, by Acevedo Bernal — A388

1979, Oct. 31 **Litho.** ***Perf. 12***
875 A388 8p multicolored .40 .20

Gen. Uribe, statesman, 60th death anniv.

Village, by Leonor Alarcon — A389

1979, Nov. 22 ***Perf. 14***
876 A389 15p multicolored 1.00 .35

Community Work Boards, 20th anniversary.

Introduction of Color Television A390

1980, Mar. 4 **Litho.** ***Perf. 14***
877 A390 5p multicolored .35 .20

Bullfight, Arms of Cali A391

1980, Mar. 25
878 A391 5p multicolored .50 .20

Cali Tourist Festival, 12/25/79-1/2/80.

"Learn to Write" — A392

a, shown. b, "a." c, "b." d, "c." e, "ch." f, "d." g, "e." h, "f." i, "g." j, "h." k, "i." l, "j." m, "k." n, "l." o, "ll." p, "m." q, "n." r, "ñ." s, "o." t, "p." u, "q." v, "r." w, "s." x, "t." y, "u." z, "v." aa, "w." ab, "x." ac, "y." ad, "z."

1980, Apr. 25 **Litho.** ***Perf. 12½***
879 Block of 30 22.50 22.50
a.-ad. A392 4p, any single .65 .65

Each stamp shows letter of alphabet and corresponding animal or subject. Issued in sheets of 90 (10x9).

Villavicencio Festival — A393

Design: 9p, Vallenato festival.

1980 **Litho.** ***Perf. 14***
880 A393 5p multicolored .30 .20
881 A393 9p multicolored .30 .20

Issue dates: 5p, July 15; 9p, June 17.

Gustavo Uribe Ramirez and Tree A394

1980, Aug. 5 **Litho.** ***Perf. 12***
882 A394 10p multicolored .30 .20

Gustavo Uribe Ramirez (1893-1968), ecologist.

Narino Palace (Former Presidential Residence) — A395

1980, Sept. 19 **Litho.** ***Perf. 14***
883 A395 5p multicolored .45 .20

Monument to First Pioneers of 1819, Armenia A396

1980, Oct. 14
884 A396 5p multicolored .40 .20

11th National Games, Neiva — A397

Fight against Cancer — A398

1980, Nov. 28 ***Perf. 13½x14***
885 A397 5p multicolored .45 .20

1980, Dec. 9
886 A398 10p multicolored .30 .20

Xavier University Law Faculty, 50th Anniversary A399

1980, Dec. 16 **Litho.** ***Perf. 14½***
887 A399 20p multicolored .55 .20

Death of Bolivar — A400

1980, Dec. 17 ***Perf. 12***
888 A400 25p multicolored 1.00 .60

Simon Bolivar, death sesquicentennial. See No. C696.

José Maria Obando, President of Colombia A401

115th Anniv. of Constitution (Former Presidents): b, Jose Hilario Lopez. c, Manuel Murillo Toro. d, Santiago Perez. e, Rafael Reyes. f, Carlos E. Restrepo. g, Jose Vicente Concha. h, Miguel Abadia Mendez. i, Eduardo Santos. j, Mariano Ospina Perez.

1981, June 9 **Litho.** ***Perf. 12***
889 Strip of 10 *2.00*
a.-j. A401 5p multicolored .25 .20

1981, Sept. 23 **Litho.** ***Perf. 12***

Designs: a, Rafael Nunez (1825-94). b, Marco Fidel Suarez (1855-1927). c, Pedro Nel Ospina (1858-1927). d, Enrique Olaya Herrera (1880-1937). e, Alfonso Lopez Pumarejo (1886-1959). f, Aquileo Parra (1825-1900). g, Santos Gutierrez (1820-72). h, Tomas Cipriano de Mosquera (1789-1878). i, Mariano Ospina Rodriguez. j, Pedro Alcantara Herran (1800-72).

890 Strip of 10 *50.00*
a.-j. A401 7p multicolored 3.00 .50

1981, Aug. 11 **Litho.** ***Perf. 12***

Designs like No. 889.

891 Strip of 10 *50.00*
a.-j. A401 7p multicolored 4.00 1.00

1981, Nov. 11 **Litho.** ***Perf. 12***

Designs: a, Manuel Maria Mallarino. b, Santos Acosta. c, Eustorgio Salgar. d, Julian Trujillo. e, Francisco Javier Zaldua. f, Guillermo Leon Valencia. g, Laureano Gomez. h, Manuel A. Sanclemente. i, Miguel Antonio Caro. j, Jose Eusebio Otalora.

892 Strip of 10 *30.00*
a.-j. A401 7p multicolored 2.00 .40

1981, Dec. 15 **Litho.** ***Perf. 12***

Designs: a, Ruben Piedrahita Arango. b, Jorge Holguin. c, Ramon Gonzalez Valencia. d, Jose Manuel Marroquin. e, Carlos Holguin. f, Bartolome Calvo. g, Sergio Camargo. h, Jose Maria Rojas Garrido. i, J.M. Campo Serrano. j, Eliseo Payan.

893 Strip of 10 22.50
a.-j. A401 7p multicolored 1.75 .30

1982, May 3 ***Perf. 12***

Designs: a, Simon Bolivar. b, Francisco de Paula Santander. c, Joaquin Mosquera. d, Domingo Caicedo. e, Jose Ignacio de Marquez. f, Roberto Urdaneta Arbelaez. g, Carlos Lozano y Lozano. h, Guillermo Quintero Calderon. i, Jose de Obaldia. j, Juan de Dios Aranzazu.

894 Strip of 10 12.50
a.-j. A401 7p multicolored 1.25 .20

See No. 1110.

Jose Maria Villa and West Bridge over Cauca River A404

1981, Nov. 25 **Litho.** ***Perf. 14x13½***
895 A404 60p multicolored 1.00 .25

Agrarian, Mineral and Industrial Credit Bank, 50th Anniv. — A405

Los Nevados Park — A406

1981, Dec. 9 **Litho.** ***Perf. 14***
896 A405 15p multicolored .35 .20

1981, Dec. 10 **Litho.** ***Perf. 13½x14***
897 A406 20p multicolored .60 .20

Girl Sitting on Fence — A407

1982, Feb. 22 **Litho.** ***Perf. 12½x12***
898 Strip of 3 2.00 1.10
a. A407 30p shown .60 .25
b. A407 30p Girl, basket .60 .25
c. A407 30p Boy, wheelbarrow .60 .25

Floral Bouquet — A408

Hipotecario Bank, 50th Anniv. — A409

Various floral arrangements (background): a, Flowers in vase (gray). b, Roses (red). c, Daisies (green). d, Roses (blue). e, Assorted (red). f, Yellow & orange flowers (green). g, Assorted (lilac). h, Roses (gray). i, Pink flowers (green). j, Flowers in basket (gray).

1982, July 28

900	Strip of 10	15.00	15.00
a.-j.	A408 7p, any single	1.50	.30

1982, July 29 ***Perf. 14***

901 A409 9p black & green .20 .20

St. Thomas Aquinas (1225-1274) A410

Paintings by Zurbaran.

1982 Litho. ***Perf. 12***

902	A410 5p multicolored	.20	.20
903	A410 5p St. Teresa of Avila	.20	.20
904	A410 5p St. Francis of Assisi	.20	.20
	Nos. 902-904 (3)	.60	.60

Issued: #902, 8/6; #903, 9/28; #904, 10/4.

Arms Type of 1975

1982-90 Litho. ***Perf. 14, 12 (50p)***

905	A372 10p Buga	.20	.20
905A	A372 10p San Juan de Pasto	.25	.20
906	A372 16p Rionegro	.45	.20
907	A372 20p Santa Fe de Bogota	.40	.20
907A	A372 20p Santiago de Cali	.25	.20
908	A372 23p Honda	.55	.25
911	A372 50p Cartago	.30	.20
913	A372 55p Antioquia ('86)	.60	.25
	Nos. 905-913 (8)	3.00	1.70

Issued: 16p, 23p, #905, 12/7; #907, 3/1/83; #905A, 4/12/83; #907A, 7/25/86; 55p, 8/5/86; 50p, 5/30/90.

See No. C818.

This is an expanding set. Numbers will change if necessary.

Gabriel Marquez, 1982 Nobel Prize, Literature — A412

1982, Dec. 10 ***Perf. 13½x14***

917 A412 7p gray & green .20 .20

See No. C731-C732.

Public Education Bicentenary (Society of Mary for Education) A413

1983, May 6

918 A413 9p gold & blk .35 .20

José Maria Espinosa Prieto, Painter — A414

1983, June 3 ***Perf. 12***

919 A414 9p Self-portrait, 1860 .20 .20

250th Anniv. of City of Cucuta — A415

1983, June 23 Litho. ***Perf. 12***

920 A415 9p multicolored .20 .20

Porfirio Barba-Jacob (1883-1942), Poet — A416

1983, July 29 Litho. ***Perf. 13½x14***

921 A416 9p Portrait .20 .20

Simon Bolivar, 200th Birth Anniv. A417

1983, July 24 ***Perf. 12***

922 A417 9p multicolored .20 .20

See Nos. C736-C737.

Royal Spanish Botanical Expedition, 200th Anniv. — A418

1983, Aug. 18 ***Perf. 14***

923	A418 9p Cinchona lancefolia	.20	.20
924	A418 9p Passiflora laurifolia	.20	.20
925	A418 60p Cinchona cordiflora	1.10	.50
	Nos. 923-925,C738-C740 (6)	3.45	1.70

Dawn in the Andes, by Alejandro Obregon A420

1983, Oct. 5 Litho. ***Perf. 12***

928 A420 20p multicolored .40 .20

See No. C741.

Francisco de Paula Santander (1792-1840), General — A421

1984, Mar. 6 Litho. ***Perf. 14½x14***

929	A421 12p light olive green	.20	.20
930	A421 12p pale carmine	.20	.20
931	A421 12p light ultra	.20	.20
	Nos. 929-931 (3)	.60	.60

Admiral Jose Prudencio Padilla (1784-1831) — A423

1984, May 17 Litho. ***Perf. 12***

933 A423 10p multicolored .20 .20

Luis Antonio Calvo (1882-1945) Composer — A424

1984, July 26

934 A424 18p multicolored .30 .20

Diego Fallon (1834-1905), Educator, Musician, Poet — A425

1984, Aug. 31 ***Perf. 12***

935 A425 20p multicolored .30 .20

Candelario Obeso (1849-1884), Writer — A426

1984, Sept. 4 ***Perf. 14x13½***

936 A426 20p multicolored .30 .20

Site of Marandua, Future City A427

1984, Sept. 28 ***Perf. 12***

937 A427 15p multicolored .25 .20

See No. C744.

Christmas 1984 A428

Nativity and Children Playing, by Jose Uriel Sierra, Age 7.

1984, Dec. 14

938 A428 12p multicolored .20 .20

See No. C746.

Dr. Luis Eduardo Lopez, Education Minister A429

1984, Dec. 21

939 A429 22p multicolored .35 .20

Maria Concepcion Loperena de Fernandez de Castro, Independence War Heroine — A430

1985, Jan. 6

940 A430 12p multicolored .25 .20

Gonzalo Mejia (1885-1956) — A431

1985, Feb. 25

941 A431 12p Portrait, biplane, camera .20 .20

Aviation, motion picture and meat exporting industrialist.

Self-portrait with Wife — A432

1985, Feb. 25

942 A432 37p multicolored .60 .30

Pedro Nel Gomez (1899-1984), painter. See No. C748.

Fauna A433

1985 ***Perf. 14***

943 A433 12p Hydrochaeris hydrochaeris .20 .20

Perf. 13

944	A433 15p Felis pardalis	.20	.20
945	A433 15p Tremarctos ornatus, vert.	.20	.20
946	A433 20p Tapirus pinchaque	.30	.20
	Nos. 943-946,C758 (5)	1.55	1.05

Carlos Gardel (1890-1935), Entertainer A434

Camina Literacy Program — A435

1985, June 23 ***Perf. 14***
947 A434 15p Portrait, Fokker F-31 Trimotor .20 .20

1985, Nov. 25 ***Perf. 13½x14***
948 A435 15p Tree, alphabet .20 .20

Christmas 1985 A436

1985, Dec. 4 Litho. ***Perf. 13***
949 A436 15p multicolored .20 .20

Rafael Pombo Children's Foundation. See No. C755.

Eduardo Carranza (b. 1913), Poet — A437

Colombian Free University, Cent. — A438

1986, Feb. 13
950 A437 18p multicolored .25 .20

1986, Feb. 14
951 A438 18p multicolored .25 .20

Gen. Antonio Ricaurte (b. 1786), Liberator A439

1986, May 7 Litho. ***Perf. 13***
952 A439 18p Leiva birthplace .25 .20

Jose Asuncion Silva (1865-1896), Poet, and Scene from Nocturno — A440

1986, May 30 Litho. ***Perf. 12***
953 A440 18p multicolored .25 .20

Fernando Gomez Martinez (1897-1985), Journalist — A441

1986, June 19
954 A441 24p multicolored .30 .20

Santiago de Cali, 450th Anniv. A442

1986, July 25 Litho. ***Perf. 13***
955 A442 25p La Merced .30 .20

A443

A444

Monsignor Jose Vicente Castro Silva (1885-1968), rector of the Mayor del Rosario School: portrait by Ricardo Gomez.

1986, Aug. 4 Litho. ***Perf. 12***
956 A443 20p multicolored .25 .20

1986, Oct. 14 Litho. ***Perf. 12***
957 A444 40p Natl. University .45 .20

Faculties: Fine Arts, cent., and Architecture, 50th anniv.

Rafael Maya (1897-1980), Poet, and Salamanca University Entrance — A445

1986, Oct. 15
958 A445 25p multicolored .30 .20

See No. C772.

Condor in Flight — A446

Inia goefrenis — A446a

#962, Inia goefrenis. #963, Procyon cancrivorus. #964, Monachus tropicalis. #965, Pteronura brasiliensis. #966, Trichechus manatus. #967, Odocoileus virginianus. #968, Trogon personatos personatos. #962-968 horiz.

1986-89 Litho. ***Perf. 12***
959 A446 20p ultra .25 .20
960 A446 25p ultra ('87) .30 .20

Perf. 14½x14, 14x14½
961 A446a 30p grn ('87) .35 .20
962 A446a 30p dull vio ('87) .35 .20

Engr.
Wmk. 334
963 A446a 35p chest brn ('88) .35 .20
964 A446a 35p dark grn ('88) .35 .20
965 A446a 40p deep org ('88) .40 .20
966 A446a 40p gray ('88) .30 .20
967 A446a 40p tan ('89) .30 .20
968 A446a 45p dark vio ('88) .30 .20
Nos. 959-968 (10) 3.25 2.00

Issued: 20p, 11/6; 25p, 5/25; #961, 6/8; #962, 12/24; #963, 8/6; #964, 9/20; #965, 9/20; #966, 11/29; #967, 4/29; #968, 12/16.
See Nos. 996, 1000, C778-C781.

A447

A448

1987, Jan. 29 Unwmk. ***Perf. 12***
969 A447 25p multicolored .45 .20

Pedro Uribe Mejia (1886-1972), pioneer of Colombian coffee industry.

1987, May 3 ***Perf. 13½x13***
970 A448 500p Santa Barbara Church 4.75 1.60

Mompox, 450th anniv.

Writers A449

Portraits and scenes from works: 70p, Jorge Isaacs (1837-1895), novelist, and scene from *Maria*. 90p, Aurelio Martinez Mutis (1884-1954), poet, and scene from *La Epopeya del Condor*.

1987 ***Perf. 12***
971 A449 70p multicolored .75 .25
972 A449 90p multicolored 1.00 .30

Issue dates: 70p, July 28. 90p, Sept. 2.

A450

A451

Social Security & Communications.

1987 Litho. ***Perf. 13½x13***
973 A450 35p multicolored .40 .20

1988, May 25 Litho. ***Perf. 12***

Natl. Anthem, Cent.: Score, lyricist Rafael Nunez and composer Oreste Sindici. Dated 1987.

974 A451 70p multicolored .65 .25

Human Rights — A452

Perf. 14½x14, 14x14½
1988-89 Engr.
975 A452 30p Life .30 .20
976 A452 35p Suffrage .30 .20
977 A452 40p Association, horiz. .40 .20
978 A452 45p Culture, horiz. .30 .20
Nos. 975-978 (4) 1.30 .80

Issued: 30p, 35p, 5/12; 40p, 7/1; 45p, 10/27/89.
See Nos. C797, C807.

Pasto, 450th Anniv. A453

1988, May 20 Litho. ***Perf. 12***
979 A453 60p Cathedral, Pasto .60 .20

Dated 1987.

Bogota Aqueduct and Sewage System, Cent. — A454

1988, May 20
980 A454 100p Waterfall .95 .30

Maria Currea de Aya (1888-1985), Women's Rights Activist — A455

1988, May 27
981 A455 80p multicolored .75 .25

A456

A457

Sailfish, *Istiaophorus Americanus.*

Perf. 14x13½

1988, July 19 Engr. Wmk. 334

982	A456 (A) dark blue		4.25	2.25
983	A456 (B) Prus blue		1.10	.40

At the time of issue, No. 982 was sold for 400p and No. 983 for 100p. See type A486.

Unwmk.

1988, Aug. 10 Litho. *Perf. 12*

984 A457 120p multicolored 1.10 .35

San Bartolome College, founded in 1604.

Jorge Alvarez Lleras (1885-1952), Engineer and Director of the Natl. Astronomical Observatory — A458

1988, Aug. 17

985 A458 90p multicolored .80 .20

Pres. Eduardo Santos (1888-1974) A459

1988, Aug. 30

986 A459 80p multicolored .70 .20

Andres Bello Seminary A460

Unwmk.

1988, Dec. 27 Litho. *Perf. 12*

987 A460 115p multicolored .80 .30

Adpostal, 25th Anniv. A461

1989, May 3

988 A461 45p multicolored .30 .20

Military Leaders — A462

Bolivar and Santander at the Los Llanos Campaign — A463

1989 Litho. *Perf. 12*

989	A462 40p Santander		.30	.20
990	A462 40p Bolivar		.30	.20
991	A463 45p multicolored		.40	.20
	Nos. 989-991 (3)		1.00	.60

Liberation campaign, 170th anniv.
Issued: #989, 8/25; #990, 7/25; 45p, 8/7.

From Boyaca to Santa Fe — A464

1989, Aug. 7 Litho. *Perf. 12*

992	45p multicolored		.40	.20
993	45p multicolored		.40	.20
a.	A464 Pair, #992-993		.80	.30

Liberation campaign, 170th anniv.

Liberation Campaign Triptych — A466

Designs: a, Gen. Santander, liberation force. b, Simon Bolivar riding mount. c, Insurgent cavalry.

Unwmk.

1989, Aug. 7 Litho. *Perf. 13*

994	A466 Strip of 3		.90	.30
a.-c.	45p any single		.30	.20

Liberation Campaign, 170th anniv.

Tunja, 450th Anniv. A467

1989, Aug. 8 *Perf. 12*

995 A467 45p multicolored .30 .20

Fauna Type of 1988

Designs: No. 996, Harpia harpyja, horiz. No. 997, Urocyon cinereoargenteus. No. 998, Dendrobates histrionicus. No. 1000, Phenacosaurus indenenae. No. 1001, Cebuella pygmaea. No. 1002, Eurypyga helias, horiz.

Perf. 14½x14, 14x14½

1989-90 Engr. Wmk. 334

996	A446a 45p black		.30	.20
997	A446a 50p blue gray		.30	.20
998	A446a 50p deep claret		.30	.20
1000	A446a 55p red brown		.40	.20
1001	A446a 60p brown		.35	.20
1002	A446a 60p org brown		.35	.20
	Nos. 996-1002 (6)		2.00	1.20

Issued: 45p, 9/7; #997, 1001, 3/1/90; #998, 4/25; 55p, 8/18; #1002, 8/6.
This is an expanding set. Numbers will change if necessary.

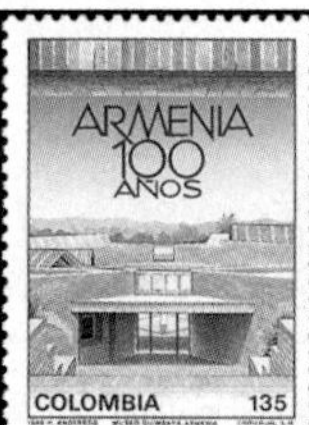

A468

A469

1989, Aug. 30 Unwmk. *Perf. 12*

1011 A468 135p multicolored .90 .30

City of Armenia, cent.

1990, Mar. 28 Litho. *Perf. 12*

1012 A469 60p Espeletia hartwegiana .35 .20

Gen. Francisco De Paula Santander (1792-1840) — A470

1990, May 6 *Perf. 14x13½*

1013	A470 50p multicolored		.30	.20
	Nos. 1013,C823-C827 (6)		3.40	1.65

See Nos. 1046-1047.

General Santander Police Academy, 50th Anniv. — A471

1990, May 16 *Perf. 12*

1014 A471 60p multicolored .35 .20

Department of La Guajira A473

1990, July 1 *Perf. 12*

1016 A473 60p multicolored .35 .20

Ceiba Pentandra A474

1990, July 15 Litho. *Perf. 12*

1017 A474 60p multicolored .35 .20

A475

A476

1990, Aug. 8 Litho. *Perf. 12*

1018 A475 70p Tibouchina lepidota .65 .25

Unwmk.

1990, Aug. 28 Litho. *Perf. 14*

1019 A476 70p Ceroxylon quindiuense .40 .20

A477

A478

1990, Sept. 28 *Perf. 12*

1020 A477 60p St. John Bosco .35 .20

Salesian Order in Colombia, cent.

1991, Mar. 28 Litho. *Perf. 12*

1021 A478 70p multicolored .40 .20

Miraculous Christ, Pilgrimage Church of Buga.

Moths and Butterflies A479

1991, Apr. 18 Litho. *Perf. 14*

1022	A479	70p Callithea philotima	.50	.20
1023	A479	70p Anaea syene, vert.	.50	.20
1024	A479	80p Thecla coronata, vert.	.60	.20
1025	A479	80p Agrias amydon	.65	.20
1026	A479	170p Morpho rhetenor	1.25	.30
1027	A479	190p Heliconius longarenus	1.50	.30
		Nos. 1022-1027 (6)	5.00	1.40

Nos. 1025-1027 are airmail.

New Constitution
A480

1991, July 4 **Litho.** ***Perf. 14***
1028 A480 70p multicolored .35 .20

A481

A482

1991, July 19 ***Perf. 12***
1029 A481 80p multicolored .40 .20

Pres. Dario Echandia Olaya (1897-1989). See No. 1042.

1991, Aug. 7
1030 A482 70p multicolored .35 .20

Col. Antanasio Girardot (1791-1813).

A483

A484

1991, Aug. 15 **Litho.** ***Perf. 14***
1031 A483 80p multicolored .40 .20

Luis Carlos Galan Sarmiento (1943-1989), political reformer.

1991, Aug. 24 ***Perf. 12***

Pre-Columbian Artifacts: 80p, Statue of cat god. No. 1033, Pitcher from tomb of high official. No. 1034, Statue with two heads. 210p, Flying fish, horiz.

1032 A484 80p multicolored .40 .20
1033 A484 90p multicolored .50 .20
1034 A484 90p multicolored .50 .20
1035 A484 210p multicolored 1.10 .30
Nos. 1032-1035 (4) 2.50 .90

Nos. 1034-1035 are airmail.

Colonial Architecture
A485

80p, Cloister of St. Augustine, Tunja. #1037, Community Bridge, Chia. #1038, Roadside Chapel, Pamplona. 190p, Church of Immaculate Conception, Bogota.

1991 **Litho.** ***Perf. 12***
1036 A485 80p multi .40 .20
1037 A485 90p multi .50 .20
1038 A485 90p multi, vert. .45 .20
1039 A485 190p multi, vert. .95 .25
Nos. 1036-1039 (4) 2.30 .85

Issue dates: No. 1037, Sept. 9; others, Sept. 27. Nos. 1038-1039 are airmail.

Istiaphorus Americanus
A486

1991, Sept. 3 ***Perf. 14***
1040 A486 830p multicolored 5.50 1.40

Colombian Police Force, Cent.
A487

1991, Oct. 12 ***Perf. 12***
1041 A487 80p multicolored .40 .20

President Type of 1991

Pres. Alberto Lleras Camargo (1906-1990)

1991, Nov. 5
1042 A481 80p multicolored .40 .20

A489

A490

1991, Dec. 17 **Litho.** ***Perf. 12***
1043 A489 80p Sogamoso City Hall .40 .20

1992 **Litho.** ***Perf. 14***

Designs: No. 1044, Diana Turbay Quintero (1950-91), journalist. No. 1045, Indalecio Lievano Aguirre (1917-82), diplomat.

1044 A490 80p multicolored .40 .20
1045 A490 80p multicolored .40 .20

Issued: #1044, Jan. 24; #1045, Apr. 21.

Santander Type of 1990 and

Battle of Boyaca — A491a

1992, Apr. 2 ***Perf. 14***

Size: 26x37mm

1046 A470 80p Monument .40 .20
1047 A470 190p Portrait .85 .25

Souvenir Sheet

Perf. 13½x14

1047A A491a 950p multicolored 5.00 5.00

Nos. 1047-1047A are airmail. Gen. Francisco de Paula Santander, bicent. of birth.

A492

A493

Ministers of Justice: 100p, Enrique Low Murtra (1939-91). 110p, Rodrigo Lara Bonilla (1946-84).

1992, Apr. 30 **Litho.** ***Perf. 12***
1048 A492 100p multicolored .40 .20
1049 A492 110p multicolored .50 .20

1992, May 18 ***Perf. 14***
1050 A493 110p multicolored .50 .30

15th natl. games, Barranquilla.

Wildlife — A494

1992, Apr. 14 **Litho.** ***Perf. 12***
1051 A494 (B) Oroaetus icidori 1.00 .50
1052 A494 (A) Tremarctos ornatus 5.00 2.25

Nos. 1051-1052 had face values of 200p and 950p respectively on date of issue.

Endangered Species
A495

1992, Aug. 4
1053 A495 100p Crocodylus acatus .45 .30
1054 A495 100p Vultur gryphus, vert. .45 .30

A496

A497

1992, Aug. 24 **Litho.** ***Perf. 14***
1055 A496 100p multicolored .40 .30
1056 A496 110p multicolored .45 .30

Maria Lopez de Escobar, founder of the House of the Mother and Child. No. 1056 is airmail.

1992, Sept. 23 **Litho.** ***Perf. 12***
1057 A497 100p multicolored .40 .30

Conference of First Ladies of the Americas and Caribbean, Cartagena.

Recycling — A498

1992, Oct. 9 **Litho.** ***Perf. 12***
1058 A498 100p multicolored .40 .30

Discovery of America, 500th Anniv. — A499

Paintings: 100p, Zenaida, by Ana Mercedes Hoyos. No. 1060, Estudio Para 1/500, by Beatriz Gonzalez. No. 1061, Blue Eagle, by Alejandro Obregon. 230p, Cantileo, by Luis Luna. 260p, Corn, by Antonio Caro. 400p, Grand Curtain, by Luis Caballero. 440p, Homage to Guatavita, by Alejandro Obregon.

1992, Oct. 5 **Litho.** ***Perf. 13½x14***
1059 A499 100p multicolored .40 .30
1060 A499 110p multicolored .45 .30
1061 A499 110p multicolored .45 .30
1062 A499 230p multicolored .95 .70
1063 A499 260p multicolored 1.10 .80
Nos. 1059-1063 (5) 3.35 2.40

Souvenir Sheets

Perf. 12

1064 A499 400p multicolored 1.60 1.60
1065 A499 440p multicolored 1.75 1.75

Nos. 1061-1063 are airmail.

World Post Day — A500

1992, Oct. 19 Litho. *Perf. 12*

1066 A500 (B) multicolored .95 .65

No. 1066 had face value of 200p on day of issue.

Christmas — A501

Children's paintings of: 100p, Nativity scene. 110p, Adoration of the Magi.

1992, Nov. 20 Litho. *Perf. 12*

1067 A501 100p multicolored .40 .30
1068 A501 110p multicolored .45 .30

No. 1068 is airmail.

Three Musicians, by Fernando Botero A502

1993, Feb. 5 Litho. *Perf. 12*

1069 A502 (B) multicolored .95 .65

No. 1069 had a face value of 250p on day of issue.

Lions Intl. Campaign Against Amblyopia A503

1993, Mar. 26 *Perf. 14*

1070 A503 100p multicolored .40 .30

Holy Week in Popayan A504

1993, Apr. 5 *Perf. 14x13½*

1071 A504 (B) multicolored .95 .65

No. 1071 had a face value of 250p on day of issue.

A505

A506

1993, Apr. 7 *Perf. 12*

1072 A505 (B) multicolored .95 .65

Pan American Health Org., 90th anniv.

No. 1072 had a face value of 250p on day of issue.

1993, Apr. 14

1073 A506 (B) multicolored .95 .65

Franciscans of Mary Immaculate, cent. No. 1073 had a face value of 250p on day of issue.

A507

A508

1993, Apr. 22 Litho. *Perf. 14*

1074 A507 (B) multicolored .90 .60

EXFILBO '93, 18th Natl. Philatelic Exhibition. No. 1074 had a face value of 250p on day issue.

1993, July 2 Litho. *Perf. 12*

1075 A508 250p Guillermo Cano, writer .95 .65

Human Rights A509

Rights: a, 150p, Of prisoners. b, 150p, Of the elderly. c, 200p, Of the infirm. d, 200p, Of children. e, 220p, Of women. f, 220p, Of the poor. g, 460p, To clean environment. h, 520p, Of indigenous people.

Painting: 800p, Peace, Rights, and Freedom, by Alfredo Vivero, vert.

1993, June 10 *Perf. 14*

1076 A509 Block of 8, #a.-h. 8.00 5.50

Souvenir Sheet

1077 A509 800p multicolored 3.00 2.00

Nos. 1076e-1076h are airmail.

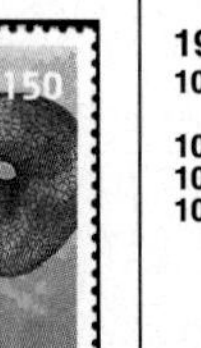

Amazon Region of Colombia — A510

#1078a, Parrot. #1078b, Anaconda. #1079a, Victoria regia. #1079b, Flor ipecacuana. 880p, Map, native, horiz.

1993 Litho. *Perf. 12*

1078 A510 150p Pair, #a.-b. 1.10 .75
1079 A510 220p Pair, #a.-b. 1.60 1.00

Souvenir Sheet

1080 A510 880p multicolored 3.00 2.00

Nos. 1079-1080 are airmail.

Famous People — A511

Designs: a, 150p, Alberto Pumarejo (1893-1970). b, 150p, Lorencita Villegas de Santos (1892-1960). c, 200p, Meliton Rodriguez (1875-1942). d, 200p, Tomas Carrasquilla (1858-1940).

1993 Litho. *Perf. 14x13½*

1081 A511 Block of 4, #a.-d. 2.50 1.60

Christmas A512

1993, Nov. 30 *Perf. 12*

1082 A512 200p Holy Family .70 .50
1083 A512 220p Shepherd 1.50 1.00

No. 1083 is airmail.

Tourism A513

Designs: No. 1084a, San Andres Providence. b, Cocuy Natl. Park. c, Lake Cocha. d, Waterfalls, Serrania de la Macarena. 250p, Lake Otun. No. 1086a, Chicamocha River. b, Sierra Nevada de Santa Marta mountains. 520p, Penol Reservoir.

1993, Dec. 1 Litho. *Perf. 12*

1084 A513 220p Block of 4, #a.-d. 3.00 2.00
1085 A513 250p multicolored .85 .55
1086 A513 460p Pair, #a.-b. 3.00 2.00
1087 A513 520p multicolored 1.75 1.10
Nos. 1084-1087 (4) 8.60 5.65

Nos. 1084, 1086-87 are airmail.

A514

A515

1993, Dec. 21 Litho. *Perf. 14*

1088 A514 150p multicolored .50 .35

Natl. Museum, 170th anniv.

1994, Jan. 25 Litho. *Perf. 14*

1089 A515 300p Marie Poussepin 1.10 .70

A516

A517

Birds: 180p, Ognorhynchus icterotis. 240p, Rallus semiplumbeus. 270p, Semnornis ramphastinus. 560p, Anas cyanoptera.

1994, Mar. 4

1090 A516 180p multi .65 .40
1091 A516 240p multi .85 .55
1092 A516 270p multi, horiz. 1.00 .65
1093 A516 560p multi, horiz. 2.00 1.25
Nos. 1090-1093 (4) 4.50 2.85

Nos. 1092-1093 are airmail.

1994, Apr. 11 Litho. *Perf. 14*

1094 A517 300p multicolored .95 .60

Air Force, 75th anniv.

Latin American Presidential Summit, Cartagena A518

1994, June 14 Litho. *Perf. 14*

1095 A518 300p shown .95 .60
1096 A518 630p Flags 2.00 1.40

No. 1096 is airmail.

1994 World Cup Soccer Championships, US — A519

World Cup Trophy and: 180p, Soccer player, Colombian flag. 270p, Two players with ball. 560p, Soccer ball, Colombian flag, vert.
1110p, Soccer player offering hand to another.

1994, May 26 *Perf. 12*

1097 A519 180p multicolored .60 .40
1098 A519 270p multicolored .90 .55
1099 A519 560p multicolored 1.90 1.25
Nos. 1097-1099 (3) 3.40 2.20

Souvenir Sheet

1100 A519 1110p multicolored 3.75 2.50

Nos. 1098-1099 are airmail.

Ricardo Rendon (1894-1931), Artist — A520

1993 Census — A521

1994, June 30 Litho. *Perf. 12*

1101 A520 240p black .90 .45

1994, Aug. 12 *Perf. 14*

1102 A521 240p multicolored .80 .45

Ministry of Communications Inravision, 30th Anniv. — A522

1994, Aug. 3

1103 A522 180p multicolored .65 .30

Intl. Year of the Family A523

1994, Sept. 1 Litho. *Perf. 14*

1104 A523 300p multicolored 1.00 .65

America Issue — A524

Methods of mail delivery: 270p, Horse, bicycle. 300p, Men holding stamps showing truck, ship, plane.

1994, Oct. 18 Litho. *Perf. 13*

1105 A524 270p multicolored .90 .60
1106 A524 300p multicolored 1.00 .65

No. 1105 is airmail.

Colombian Society of Engineers, Cent. A525

1994, Oct. 20 Litho. *Perf. 12*

1107 A525 180p multicolored .60 .40

Christmas A526

1994, Nov. 22 Litho. *Perf. 13½x13*

1108 A526 270p Magi .90 .60
1109 A526 300p Holy family 1.00 .65

No. 1108 is airmail.

Former President Type of 1981

Miniature Sheet of 20

Designs: a, Jose Miguel Pey. b, Jorge Tadeo Lozano. c, Antonio Narino. d, Camilo Torres. e, Jose Fernandez Madrid. f, Jose Maria del Castillo y Rada. g, Custodio Garcia Rovira. h, Antonio Villavicencio. i, Liborio Mejia. j, Rafael Urdaneta. k, Juan Garcia del Rio. l, Jose Maria Melo. m, Tomas Herrera. n, Froilan Largacha. o, Salvador Camacho Roldan. p, Ezequiel Hurtado. q, Dario Echandia Olaya. r, Alberto Lleras Camargo. s, Gustavo Rojas Pinilla. t, Carlos Lleras Restrepo.

1995, Apr. 4 Litho. *Perf. 12*

1110 A401 270p #a.-t. 18.00 12.00

World Offroad Bicycle Championships, Melgar — A527

1995, Mar. 30 *Perf. 14*

1111 A527 400p multicolored 1.40 .90

A528

A529

1995, Oct. 12 Litho. *Perf. 12*

1112 A528 220p multicolored .45 .30

Gen. Jose Maria Obando (1795-1861), President.

1995, Nov. 28 *Perf. 14*

1113 A529 400p Clean air 1.10 .55
1114 A529 400p Clean water 1.10 .55

Preserve the environment. America issue.

Christmas A530

Stained glass windows: 220p, Flight into Egypt. 330p, Nativity.

1995, Dec. 18 *Perf. 12*

1115 A530 220p multicolored .45 .30
1116 A530 330p multicolored .65 .45

No. 1116 is airmail.

Bogotá to Boyacá World Cycling Championship — A531

1995, Oct. 4 Litho. *Perf. 12*

1117 A531 400p multicolored 1.25 .65

León De Greiff (1895-1976), Poet — A532

1996, May 2 Litho. *Perf. 12*

1118 A532 400p black 1.40 .40

Mosquera Courtyard, Natl. Capitol A533

1996, July 18 Litho. *Perf. 14*

1119 A533 400p multicolored 1.10 .40

Medellin Rapid Transit System A534

1996, July 2 *Perf. 12*

1120 A534 500p multicolored 1.00 .50

A535

A536

1996, June 20

1121 A535 500p multicolored 1.40 .50

Community of St. John of God in Colombia, 400th anniv.

1996, June 25

Arms: a, Santa Maria la Antigua del Darien. b, San Sebastian de Mariquita. c, Villa de la Marinilla. d, Villa of Santa Cruz of Mompox.

1122 A536 400p Block of 4, #a.-d. 4.25 3.00
e. As "d," inscribed AEREO 10.00
f. Block of 4, #1122a-1122c, 1122e 12.00

Issued in sheets of 16 stamps.

1996 Summer Olympic Games, Atlanta — A537

1996, July 16

1123 A537 500p multicolored 1.00 .50

SAYCO (Colombian Authors and Composers Society), 50th Anniv. — A538

1996, Aug. 17 Litho. *Perf. 12*

1124 A538 400p multicolored .80 .40

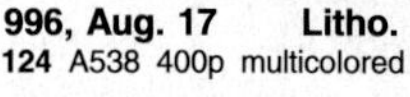

Exfilbo '96, 20th Natl. Philatelic Exhibition A539

Jewelry from Gold Museum, Bogotá.

1996, Oct. 19 **Litho.** ***Perf. 12***
1125 A539 400p multicolored 1.10 .40

Souvenir Sheet

Founders Theater, Manizales, 30th Anniv. — A540

Drop curtain: a, Eagle, people watching man drawing on ground, vert. b, People, animals on hillside.

1996, Oct. 28 ***Perf. 14***
1126 A540 4000p #a.-b. 20.00 20.00

Christmas A541

Designs: No. 1127, Mailman handing woman letter. No. 1128, Woman reading letter, mailman holding bundle of mail.

1996, Nov. 22
1127 A541 400p multicolored 1.10 .40
1128 A541 400p multicolored 1.10 .40

No. 1128 is airmail.

America Issue — A542

1996, Nov. 29 ***Perf. 12***
1129 A542 500p Men's costume 1.40 .50
1130 A542 500p Women's costume 1.40 .50

Historical Landmarks — A543

a, Cemetery, Santa Cruz of Mompox. b, Carved face, San Agustin Archaeological Park. c, Entrance, Palace of the Inquisition, Cartagena de Indias. d, Inside ruins, Tierradentro Archaelogical Park.

1996, Dec. 6 ***Perf. 14***
1131 A543 400p Block of 4, #a.-d. 3.25 1.60

Alvaro Gomez Hurtado (1919-95), Politician, Writer — A544

1997, Mar. 18 **Litho.** ***Perf. 12***
1132 A544 400p multicolored 1.00 .40

Bogotá Journalists Assoc., 50th Anniv. A545

1997, July 10 **Litho.** ***Perf. 12***
1133 A545 400p multicolored 1.00 .40

Natl. Festival of Porro — A546

1997, June 26 ***Perf. 13½x14***
1134 A546 400p multicolored 1.00 .40

Pres. Virgilio Barco (1921-97) — A547

1997, Nov. 27 **Litho.** ***Perf. 14***
1135 A547 500p multicolored 1.25 .40

Colombia in Peace A548

1997, Dec. 30 **Litho.** ***Perf. 12***
1136 A548 500p Children playing 1.10 .40
1137 A548 1100p Children dancing 2.50 .90

No. 1137 is airmail.

America Issue A549

1997, Dec. 30
1138 A549 500p Postman by day 1.10 .40
1139 A549 1100p Postman by night 2.50 .90

No. 1139 is airmail.

Jorge Eliecer Gaitan (1903-48), Politician — A550

1998, Apr. 24 **Litho.** ***Perf. 14***
1140 A550 500p multicolored 1.10 .40

Free University, 75th Anniv. A551

1998, July 1 **Litho.** ***Perf. 14***
1141 A551 500p black & red 1.00 .35

Santander Industrial University, 50th Anniv. — A552

1998, May 14 ***Perf. 12***
1142 A552 500p multicolored 1.10 .35

City of Manizales, 150th Anniv. — A553

1998, July 24 **Litho.** ***Perf. 12***
1143 A553 500p multicolored 1.00 .40

A554

A555

Pre-Columbian art, agency: a, Tairona, Bank of the Republic. b, Malagana, Controller General. c, Quimbaya, Bank Superintendent.

1998, July 24
1144 A554 500p Strip of 3, #a.-c. 3.00 2.00

Natl. financial agencies, 70th anniv.

1998, Aug. 21 ***Perf. 14***
1145 A555 500p multicolored 1.00 .40

Pres. Misael Pastrana Borrero (1923-97).

University of the Andes, 50th Anniv. A556

1998, Sept. 28
1146 A556 500p multicolored .80 .40

Christmas A557

Designs: 500p, Woman kneeling down to get water with bowl, cherubs in sky. No. 1148a, Magi. No. 1148b, Nativity scene.

1998, Nov. 19 **Litho.** ***Perf. 14***
1147 A557 500p multicolored .55 .30
1148 A557 1000p Pair, #a.-b. 2.00 1.00

No. 1148 is airmail.

A558

A559

Emblems of Colombian Academies: a, Language. b, Medicine. c, Law. d, History. e, Science. f, Ecomonics. g, Religion.

1998, Dec. 15 ***Perf. 12***
Sheet of 7 + Label
1149 A558 500p #a.-g. 6.50 5.00

1999, Apr. 16 ***Perf. 14***
1150 A559 1000p multicolored 1.25 .60
Gen. José Hilario López.

Famous Women — A559a

America Issue: 600p, Soledad Román de Nuñez. 1200p, Bertha Herández de Ospina.

1999, Mar. 25 **Litho.** ***Perf. 12***
1151 A559a 600p multicolored 1.10 .35
1152 A559a 1200p multicolored 2.25 .65
No. 1152 is airmail.

Turtles — A560

a, Chelonia mydas. b, Dermochelys coriacea. c, Eretmochelys imbricata.

1999, Apr. 16 ***Perf. 14***
1153 A560 1300p Strip of 3, #a.-c. 7.00 5.00

Dr. Eduardo Zuleta Angel, Diplomat (b. 1899) — A561

1999, Sept. 9 **Litho.** ***Perf. 12***
1154 A561 600p multicolored 1.00 .35

Pamplona, 450th Anniv. A562

1999 **Litho.** ***Perf. 12***
1155 A562 1000p multicolored 1.75 .55

Sovereign Military Order of Malta, 900th Anniv. — A563

1999, June 24 ***Perf. 14***
1156 A563 1200p multicolored 2.10 .65

Japanese Immigration to Colombia — A564

Designs: a, Red at right. b, Red at left.

1999, May 12 ***Perf. 13½x14***
1157 A564 1300p Pair, #a.-b. 4.75 3.00

Pan American Games, Winnipeg, Manitoba A565

Designs: a, Flag, Olympic rings. b, Runner facing right. c, Weight lifter facing left. d, Cyclist facing right. e, Shooter facing left. f, Roller skater facing right. g, Runner facing left. h, Weight lifter facing right. i, Cyclist facing left. j, Shooter facing right. k, Roller skater facing left. l, Like "a," with lilac line under "12."

1999, July 23 **Litho.** ***Perf. 14***
1158 A565 1200p Sheet of 12, #a.-l. 25.00 25.00

Luis A. Robles (b. 1849) — A566

1999, Oct. 27
1159 A566 600p multi .80 .40

Manufacture of Aspirin, Cent. A567

1999, Dec. 1 ***Perf. 12¾***
1160 A567 600p multi .80 .40
Value is for stamp with surrounding selvage.

UPU, 125th Anniv. A568

1999, Oct. 29 ***Perf. 14¼***
1161 A568 1000p "125" 1.25 .65
1162 A568 1300p "1874-1999" 1.75 .85

Inter-American Development Bank, 40th Anniv. — A569

Abstract art: a, "Colombia" in yellow. b, "Colombia" in red.

1999, Nov. 19 ***Perf. 14x14¼***
1163 A569 1000p Pair, #a.-b. 2.60 1.25

America Issue, A New Millennium Without Arms — A570

a, Stylized hands. b, Large flower at LR.

1999, Nov. 9 ***Perf. 14***
1164 A570 1200p Pair, #a.-b. 3.00 1.50

Christmas — A571

a, Holy Family, animals. b, Angel, Magi.

1999, Nov. 29 ***Perf. 13½x14***
1165 A571 600p Pair, #a.-b. 1.60 .80

Millennium — A572

Designs: a, Nude man, flag, dove. b, Globe, rainbow, "2000."

2000, Jan. 3 ***Perf. 14***
1166 A572 1000p Pair, #a.-b. 2.25 1.10

University of Medellin, 50th Anniv. A573

2000 **Litho.** ***Perf. 14***
1167 A573 1000p multi 1.10 .55

Father José Rafael Faría Bermúdez (1896-1970) A574

2000, Mar. 6 **Litho.** ***Perf. 14***
1168 A574 1300p multi 1.50 .75

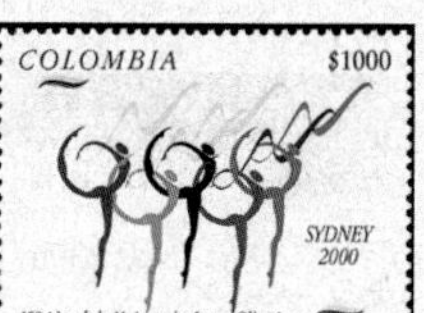
2000 Summer Olympics, Sydney A575

2000, Apr. 21
1169 A575 1000p multi 1.10 .55

Popayán Religious Music Festival A576

2000, July 7
1170 A576 1000p multi 1.10 .55

America Issue, Campaign Against AIDS A577

2000 **Litho.** ***Perf. 14x13½***
1171 A577 1000p multi 1.10 .55

Radio Station HJCK, 50th Anniv. — A578

2000, Sept. 28 **Litho.** ***Perf. 14***
1172 A578 1000p multi 1.10 .55

Birth Registration A579

2000 Litho. *Perf. 14¼*
1173 A579 1000p multi 1.00 .50

Paintings A580

No. 1174: a, Archangel, by Fernando Botero. b, Gypsy Woman With Tamourine, by Jean-Baptiste-Camille Corot. c, Vera Sergine Renoir, by Renoir. d, Man on Horse, by Botero. e, Mother Superior, by Botero. f, A Town, by Botero. g, Flowers, by Botero. h, Cézanne, by Botero. i, Patio, by Botero. j, Absinthe Drinker in Grenelle, by Toulouse-Lautrec. k, A Little Valley, by Corot. l, The Studio, by Botero.

2000 *Perf. 12*
1174 Sheet of 12 7.00 3.50
a.-l. A580 650p Any single .55 .25

Children's Day — A581

2001, Mar. 15 Litho. *Perf. 14*
1175 A581 1100p multi 1.10 .55

Abolition of Slavery, 150th Anniv. — A582

2001, May 21 Litho. *Perf. 14¼x14*
1176 A582 1100p multi 1.10 .55

Discovery of Magdalena River, 500th Anniv. — A583

2001, June 13 Litho. *Perf. 14*
1177 A583 1100p multi 1.10 .55

Copa America Soccer Tournament A584

2001, July 18 Litho. *Perf. 12¾*
1178 A584 1900p multi 2.00 1.00

Values are for copies with surrounding selvage.

America Issue - Los Katios Natl. Park, UNESCO World Heritage Site — A585

2001, Aug. 17 *Perf. 13¾x14*
1179 A585 2100p multi 2.40 1.25

Year of Dialogue Among Civilizations A586

2001, Oct. 9 *Perf. 14*
1180 A586 650p multi .70 .35

Reclining Woman, by Fernando Botero — A587

2001 *Perf. 14¼*
1181 A587 1100p multi 1.25 .60

Christmas A588

2001 *Perf. 14*
1182 A588 1100p multi 1.25 .60

National Beauty Pageant — A589

Flag, Miss Colombia Vanesa A. Mendoza Bustos and: a, Cartagena de Indias. b, St. Francis of Assisi Cathedral, Quibdo.
Illustration reduced.

2002, Jan. 22 *Perf. 14x14¼*
1183 A589 800p Horiz. pair, #a-b 1.60 .80

Natural Riches of Colombia — A590

Parts of map of Colombia, various wildlife and/or natives and: a, Bird and clouds at left. b, Turtle at upper left. c, Fish and whales at left. d, Man on horse at center. e, Volcano at upper left. f, Red and blue parrots at right. g, Flamingos at left. h, Snake at upper left.

2002, Feb. 1 *Perf. 14¼x14*
1184 A590 2300p Sheet of 8, #a-h 18.00 9.00

Children's Day — A591

2002, Feb. 18 *Perf. 12*
1185 A591 1400p multi 1.50 .75

New Emblem of Adpostal — A592

2002, Mar. 7 *Perf. 14*
1186 A592 800p multi .85 .40

7th South American Games A593

2002
1187 A593 2100p multi 2.25 1.10

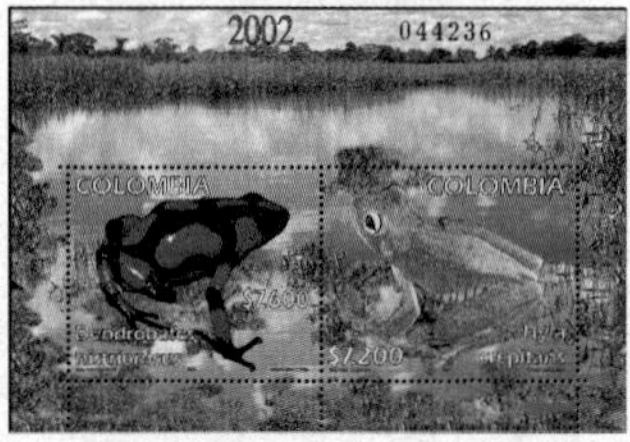

Oxyura Jamaicensis A594

2002, Apr. 30 Litho. *Perf. 12*
1188 A594 3900p multi 4.25 2.10

Souvenir Sheet

Frogs — A595

No. 1189: a, 7200p, Hyla crepitans. b, 7600p, Dendrobates histrionicus.

2002, Apr. 30 *Perf. 13¾x14*
1189 A595 Sheet of 2, #a-b 16.00 8.00

Souvenir Sheet

Butterflies — A596

No. 1190: a, Dryas iulia. b, Dryadula phaetusa, vert.

2002, Apr. 30 *Perf. 12*
1190 A596 13,700p Sheet of 2, #a-b 30.00 15.00

Foundation for Reconstructive Surgery, 25th Anniv. — A597

2002, May 24 *Perf. 14*
1191 A597 1000p multi 1.00 .50

Pre-Columbian Art — A598

No. 1192, 800p: a, Nariño pectoral. b, Nariño disc.
No. 1193, 1400p: a, Calima diadem. b, Calima pectoral.
No. 1194, 2100p: a, Anthropomorphic Tairona pectoral. b, Round Tairona pectoral.
Illustration reduced.

2002, June 7 *Perf. 13½x14*
Horiz. Pairs, #a-b
1192-1194 A598 Set of 3 8.75 4.25

Surgical Society of Bogota San José Hospital, Cent. — A599

No. 1195: a, Early doctors and nurse. b, Hospital.

2002, July 22 *Perf. 14*
1195 A599 800p Horiz. pair, #a-b 1.60 .80

Consuelo Araújo Noguera (1940-2001), Assassinated Former Minister of Culture — A600

2002, Aug. 1

1196 A600 1400p multi 1.50 .70

Union Network International A601

2002, Aug. 12

1197 A601 1000p multi 1.00 .50

America Issue - Youth, Education and Literacy — A602

No. 1198: a, Person reading book. b, Letters amd words.

2002, Oct. 9

1198 A602 2500p Horiz. pair, #a-b 4.50 4.50

Christmas A603

2002, Nov. 6 Litho. *Perf. 14x13¾*

1199 A603 800p multi .75 .40

Colombian History Academy, Cent. — A604

No. 1200: a, Mural scene with Simon Bolivar at UR. b, Mural scene with horsemen at top. c, Mural scene with man with outstretched arms at UL. d, Cafetal, 1956. e, Batalla de Palonegro, 1905. f, Tigre Cazando Sabanera, 1963. g, El Barqueo, 1936. h, Colombia Asesinada, 1902. i, Dos Mujeres, 1951. j, Bearded man at left, Plaza de Santander. k, Carriage, Plaza de Santander. l, Horse, man and woman, Plaza de Santander.

2002, Nov. 19 *Perf. 13¾x14*

1200 A604 800p Sheet of 12, #a-l 9.00 9.00

Peace Treaty Ending War of 1,000 Days, Cent. A605

2002, Nov. 21 *Perf. 14x13¾*

1201 A605 1600p multi 1.50 .75

Carnival A606

No. 1202: a, shown. b, Participants holding masks on sticks. c, Participants on float.

2003, Jan. 4 *Perf. 14*

1202 Horiz. strip of 3 2.75 2.75
a.-b. A606 1000p Either single .85 .85
c. A606 1200p multi 1.00 1.00

Printed in sheets of 3 horizontal strips and 2 horiz. strips of 3 labels.

Articulated Bus, Bogota A607

2003, Mar. 13 *Perf. 12*

1203 A607 1000p multi .75 .40

Departments — A608

No. 1204 — Caldas Department: a, 1200p, Arms. b, 1200p, Government office building, Manizales, horiz. c, 1200p, Campesinos, 1957. d, 2400p, Church, Salamina. e, 2400p, Neira, 1997, horiz. f, 2400p, Enea Chapel, Manizales. g, 2800p, Laguna Verde, Villamaria. h, 2800p, Aguadas, horiz. i, 2800p, Devil's carnival, Riosucio. j, 4100p, Miner, Marmato. k, 4100p, Mariposas del Eje Cafetero, 2001, horiz. l, 4100p, Pacora.

No. 1205, 1000p — Huila Department: a, Arms. b, Government office building, Neiva, horiz. c, La Gaitana. d, Bordones Waterfall, Isnos. e, San Agustín World Heritage Archaeological Park, horiz. f, Lavapatas Spring, San Agustín. g, La Tatacoa Desert, Villavieja. h, Liberty tree, Gigante, horiz. i, Sombrero maker, Suaza. j, Nuestra Señora de los Dolores Church, Aipe. k, Paisaje, horiz. l, Dancers.

2003 *Perf. 12*

Sheets of 12, #a-l, + 8 labels

1204 A608 Caldas 24.00 24.00
1205 A608 Huila 9.50 9.50

Issued: No. 1204, Apr. 11. No. 1205, June 29. Size of horiz. stamps: 46x37mm.

Departments Type of 2003

No. 1206 — 2400p: a, Historic center of Barichara. b, Ophthalmologic Foundation of Santander, Bucaramanga, horiz. c, Girón. d, Santander Industrial University Intl. Piano Festival, 20th anniv. emblem. e, Petroleum Christ Statue, refinery, Barrancabermeja, horiz. f, Church, San Andrés. g, Gustavo Cote Uribe (1918-94), writer. h, Chamber of Commerce, Bucaramanga, horiz. i, Carnival of Eastern Colombia, Bucaramanga. j, Historic center of Albania. k, Chicamocha River Canyon, Cepitá, horiz. l, Entreguerras.

2003 Litho. *Perf. 12*

Sheet of 12, #a-l, + 8 labels

1206 A608 Santander 20.00 20.00

Issued: No. 1206, June 22. Size of horiz. stamps: 46x37mm.

Fish and Coral of the Rosario Islands — A609

2003, Jan. 16 Litho. *Perf. 12*

1207 A609 1000p multi .75 .40

Hapalopsittaca Fuertesi — A610

2003, June 13

1208 A610 1000p multi .75 .40

Souvenir Sheets

Orchids — A611

No. 1209 — 2400p: a, Masdevallia ignea. b, Miltoniopsis vexillaria, horiz.
No. 1210 — 2800p: a, Odontoglossum crispum, horiz. b, Masdevallia macrura.
No. 1211 — 5000p: a, Cimbidium. b, Oncidium obryzatum.
No. 1212 — 7000p: a, Cattleya dowiana. b, Cattleya trianaei (49x49mm).

Perf. 14¼, 13¾x14 (#1212b)

2003, June 13

Sheets of 2, #a-b

1209-1212 A611 Set of 4 25.00 25.00

Tejo, National Sport A612

No. 1213: a, Players, tree in foreground (49x39mm). b, Players, light poles (49x39mm). c, Cacique Turmeque.

2003, July 25 *Perf. 12*

1213 Horiz. strip of 3 5.00 5.00
a.-c. A612 2400p Any single 1.60 .80

America Issue — A613

Flora and fauna: a, Denomination at UR. b, Denomination at LR.

2003, Oct. 9 Litho. *Perf. 12*

1214 A613 1600p Vert. pair, #a-b 2.25 2.25

Printed in sheets of four pairs and four labels.

Souvenir Sheet

Colombia Libraries National Reading Plan — A614

No. 1215: a, 1200p, Building. b, 4100p, Building, diff.

2003, Oct. 30 Litho. *Perf. 12*

1215 A614 Sheet of 2, #a-b 3.75 3.75

General Ramón Arturo Rincón Quiñones (1922-75) — A615

2003, Oct. 31

1216 A615 1000p multi .75 .40

Souvenir Sheet

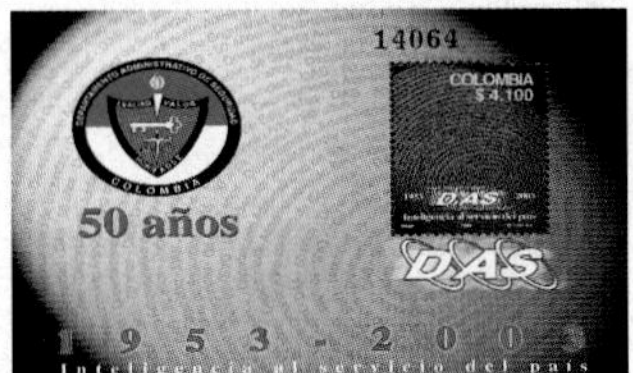

Administrative Security Deparment, 50th Anniv. — A616

2003, Oct. 31

1217 A616 4100p multi 3.00 3.00

Armed Forces A617

No. 1218 — Arms and mottos (#a-d): a, General Command of Military Forces. b, National Army. c, National Navy. d, Air Force. e, Colombian Forces in Korea, 50th anniv.

2003, Nov. 7

1218 Vert. strip of 5 4.25 4.25
a.-e. A617 1200p Any single .85 .45

Christmas — A618

No. 1219: a, Good Shepherd, sheep. b, Tree, comet, airplane, rabbit. c, Rabbits, dog. d, Automobile, angel, reindeer, horse. e, Sheep, woman with basket, swan, house. f, Branch with leaves, horse and rider, duck, Indian with bow and arrow.

2003, Dec. 2 Litho. *Perf. 12*

1219 Block of 6 4.50 4.50
a.-f. A618 1000p Any single .75 .75

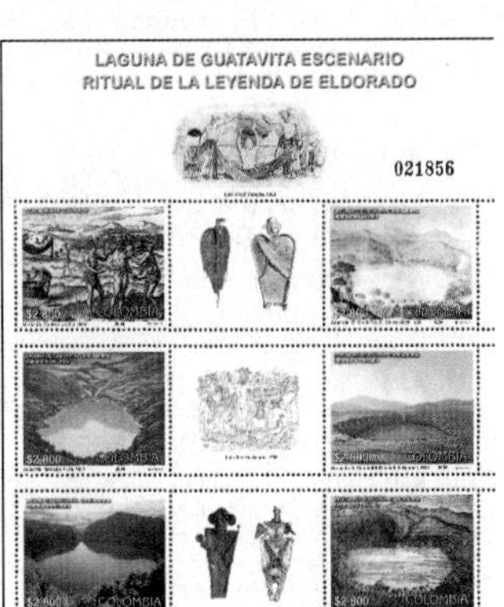

Colombia and the Eldorado Legend — A619

No. 1220: a, Print of Eldorado ceremony, by Teodoro De Bry, 1595. b, Watercolor painting of Lake Guatavita, by M. María Paz, 1855. c, Watercolor painting of Lake Guatavita, by Gonzalo Ariza, 1984. d, Print of Lake Guatavita, by A. Humboldt Thibault and F. Schoell, 1813. e, Photo of Lake Guatavita, by Fernando Urbina Rangel, 1983. f, Print of Lake Guatavita, by Eustacio Barreto, 1883.

No. 1221 — Muisca raft: a, 1700p, Front. b, 2000p, Back, vert.

2004, Mar. 10

1220 A619 2800p Sheet of 6, #a-f, + 3 labels 12.50 12.50

Souvenir Sheet

1221 A619 Sheet of 2, #a-b 2.75 2.75

Locomotives — A620

No. 1222, 1100p: a, 2-8-2. b, 4-8-0.
No. 1223, 1300p: a, 2-6-2. b, 4-6-2.
Illustration reduced.

2004, Mar. 19

Horiz. Pairs, #a-b

1222-1223 A620 Set of 2 3.75 3.75

Nos. 1222-1223 each printed in sheets of four pairs and two pairs of labels.

Departments Type of 2003

No. 1224, 1100p - Nariño Department: a, Galeras Volcano, San Juan de Pasto, horiz. b, Statue of Gen. Antonio Nariño. c, Nariño Government Building, San Juan de Pasto, horiz. d, Farm, Catambuco, horiz. e, Nuestra Señora de las Lajas Sanctuary, Ipiales. f, Sandoná city center, horiz. g, Gallery of Mirrors, horiz. h, Barnizadores de Pasto Chorography Commission. i, Golden palms, horiz. j, El Morro, Tumaco, horiz. k, Virgen de la Playa Sanctuary, San Pablo. l, Festival of Whites and Blacks, horiz.

No. 1225, 2000p — Tolima Department: a, Nevado del Tolima, horiz. b, Tolima arms. c, Ambalema, horiz. d, Bowls, La Chamba, horiz. e, Natural Bridge, Icononzo. f, Hermitage, Mariquita, horiz. g, Matachos, horiz. h, Prison, Ibagué. i, Alberto Castilla Conservatory Room, horiz. j, Fishermen, Magdalena River, horiz. k, Cacique Calarcá. l, Tolima Art Museum, Ibagué.

No. 1226, 3000p — Chocó Department: a, Coat of Arms. b, Quibdó skyline, horiz. c, Indian girls. d, San Pacho Fiesta. e, Carrasquilla College, Quibdó, horiz. f, Houses, Nóvita. g, Canoe on San Juan River. h, Women grinding corn meal, horiz. i, Nuestra Senora del Rosario Church, Condoto. j, Utría Bay. k, Bellavista Church, Bojayá, horiz. l, Goldsmith, Acandi.

Horiz. stamps are 46x37mm.

2004 Litho. *Perf. 13¾x14*

Sheets of 12, #a-l, +8 labels

1224 A608 Nariño 10.50 10.50
1225 A608 Tolima 18.00 18.00
1226 A608 Chocó 30.00 30.00
Nos. 1224-1226 (3) 58.50 58.50

Issued: No. 1224, 8/5; No. 1225, 4/16. No. 1226, 11/17

Maloka Science and Technology Center A621

2004, June 6 Litho. *Perf. 12¾*

1227 A621 1100p multi .80 .80

Values are for stamps with surrounding selvage.

2004 Summer Olympics, Athens — A622

2004, Aug. 5 *Perf. 13¾x14*

1228 A622 4400p multi 3.50 3.50

Natl. Association of Contractors, 60th Anniv. — A623

No. 1229: a, Denomination in white. b, Denomination in black.

2004, Aug. 5 *Perf. 14x13¾*

1229 Pair 4.50 4.50
a.-b. A623 2800p Either single 2.25 2.25

FIFA (Fédération Internationale de Football Association), Cent. — A624

2004, Aug. 25 *Perf. 13¼x14*

1230 A624 3500p multi 2.75 2.75

Women's Citizenship, 50th Anniv. — A625

2004, Sept. 24 *Perf. 14*

1231 A625 15,000p multi 12.00 12.00

Fair and Expositions Corporation, 50th Anniv. — A626

2004, Oct. 14 *Perf. 13½x13*

1232 A626 1300p multi 1.00 1.00

Colombian Radio Announcers Association, 50th Anniv. — A627

2004, Oct. 21 *Perf. 14*

1233 A627 1700p multi 1.40 1.40

SEMI-POSTAL STAMP

Catalogue values for unused stamps in this section are for Never Hinged items.

Girl Giving First Aid — SP1

Perf. 13½x14

1966, Apr. 26 Litho. Unwmk.

B1 SP1 5c + 5c multicolored .20 .20

Issued for the Red Cross.

AIR POST STAMPS

No. 341 Overprinted

1919 Unwmk. *Perf. 14*

C1 A107 2c car rose 2,250. 1,000.
a. Numerals "1" with serifs *4,500. 2,750.*

Used for the first experimental flight from Barranquilla to Puerto Colombia, 6/18/19.

Values are for faulty copies.

Issued by Compania Colombiana de Navegacion Aerea

From 1920 to 1932 the internal airmail service of Colombia was handled by the Compania Colombiana de Navegacion Aerea (1920) and the Sociedad Colombo-Alemana de Transportes Aéreos, known familiarly as "SCADTA" (1920-1932).

These organizations, under government contracts, operated and maintained their own post offices and issued stamps which were the only legal franking for airmail service during this period, both in the internal and international mails. All letters had to bear government stamps as well.

Woman and Boy Watching Plane — AP1

Designs: No. C3, Clouds and small biplane at top. No. C4, Tilted plane viewed close-up from above. No. C5, Flier in plane watching biplane. No. C6, Lighthouse. No. C7, Fuselage and tail of biplane. No. C8, Condor on cliff. No. C9, Plane at rest; pilot foreground. No. C10, Ocean liner.

1920, Feb. Unwmk. Litho. *Imperf.*

Without Gum

C2 AP1 10c multicolored 2,500. 1,500.
C3 AP1 10c multicolored 3,000. 1,500.
C4 AP1 10c multicolored 3,500. 1,500.
C5 AP1 10c multicolored 2,750. 1,500.
C6 AP1 10c multicolored 2,400. 1,500.
C7 AP1 10c multicolored 8,500. 3,000.
C8 AP1 10c multicolored 4,500. 2,400.
a. Without overprint
C9 AP1 10c multicolored 2,750. 1,500.
C10 AP1 10c multicolored 3,500. 2,100.

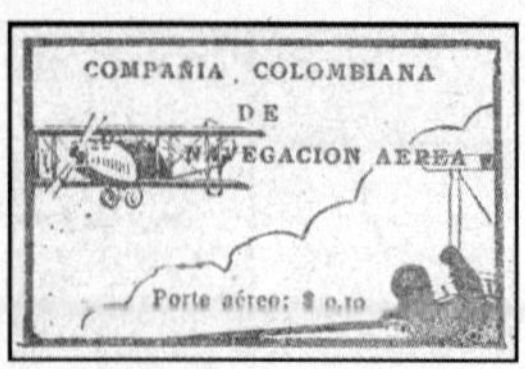

Flier in Plane Watching Biplane — AP2

1920, Mar.

C11	AP2	10c	green	35.00	*70.00*

Four other 10c stamps, similar to No. C11, have two designs showing plane, mountains and water. They are printed in deep green or light brown red. Some authorities state that these four were not used regularly.

Issued by Sociedad Colombo-Alemana de Transportes Aereos (SCADTA)

Seaplane over Magdalena River — AP3

1920-21 Litho. *Perf. 12*

C12	AP3	10c	yellow ('21)	35.00	27.50
C13	AP3	15c	blue ('21)	35.00	30.00
C14	AP3	30c	blk, *rose*	15.00	11.00
C15	AP3	30c	rose ('21)	35.00	27.50
C16	AP3	50c	pale green	35.00	30.00
			Nos. C12-C16 (5)	155.00	126.00

For surcharges see Nos. C17-C24, C36-C37.

No. C16 Handstamp Surcharged in Violet or Black:

(Illustrations of types "a" to "e" are reduced in size.)

VALOR 10 CENTAVOS

a

VALOR 10 CENTAVOS

b

Valor 10 Céntavos

c

VALOR 30 Ctvos
S.C.A.T.A

d

30¢ 30¢

e

$030

f

$030¢

g

1921

C17	AP3 (a)	10c on 50c		450.	450.
C18	AP3 (b)	10c on 50c		450.	450.
C19	AP3 (c)	10c on 50c		*875.*	*700.*
C20	AP3 (b)	30c on 50c		450.	450.
C21	AP3 (d)	30c on 50c		550.	550.
C22	AP3 (e)	30c on 50c		1,000.	1,000.
C23	AP3 (f)	30c on 50c		800.	750.
C24	AP3 (g)	30c on 50c		800.	750.

Plane over Magdalena River — AP4

Plane over Bogota Cathedral AP5

1921 *Perf. 11½*

C25	AP4	5c	orange yellow	2.50	2.50
C26	AP4	10c	slate green	1.10	1.00
C27	AP4	15c	orange brown	1.10	1.10
C28	AP4	20c	red brown	2.50	1.40
a.			Horiz. pair, imperf. vert.	*140.00*	
C29	AP4	30c	green	1.25	.70
C30	AP4	50c	blue	2.10	.75
C31	AP4	60c	vermilion	42.50	22.50
C32	AP5	1p	gray black	12.50	3.75
C33	AP5	2p	rose	22.50	14.00
C34	AP5	3p	violet	70.00	52.50
C35	AP5	5p	olive green	200.00	200.00
			Nos. C25-C35 (11)	358.05	300.20

Exist imperf.

For surcharge see No. C52.

Nos. C16 and C12 Handstamp Surcharged

Illustration of type "h" is reduced in size.

VALOR 20 Ctvs.

h

30 cent.

i

1921-22 *Perf. 12*

C36	AP3 (h)	20c on 50c	1,500.	1,000
C37	AP3 (i)	30c on 10c	425.	300.

Seaplane over Magdalena River — AP6

Plane over Bogota Cathedral AP7

1923-28 Wmk. 116 *Perf. 14x14½*

C38	AP6	5c	orange yellow	1.00	.20
C39	AP6	10c	green	1.00	.20
C40	AP6	15c	carmine	1.00	.20
C41	AP6	20c	gray	1.00	.20
C42	AP6	30c	blue	1.00	.20
C43	AP6	40c	purple ('28)	7.25	5.25
C44	AP6	50c	green	1.25	.20
C45	AP6	60c	brown	2.00	.20
C46	AP6	80c	olive grn ('28)	20.00	19.00
C47	AP7	1p	black	9.00	2.00
C48	AP7	2p	red orange	13.00	4.00
C49	AP7	3p	violet	27.50	17.50
C50	AP7	5p	olive green	45.00	24.00
			Nos. C38-C50 (13)	130.00	73.15

For surcharges and overprints see Nos. C51, C53-C54, CF1.

Nos. C41 and C31 Surcharged in Carmine and Dark Blue:

30 30

No. C51

No. C52

1923

C51	AP6	30c on 20c gray (C)	60.00	35.00
C52	AP4	30c on 60c ver	50.00	27.50

Nos. C41-C42 Overprinted in Black

1928 Wmk. 116 *Perf. 14x14½*

C53	AP6	20c	gray	42.50	40.00
C54	AP6	30c	blue	42.50	40.00

Goodwill flight of Lt. Benjamin Mendez from New York to Bogota.

Magdalena River and Tolíma Volcano AP8

Columbus' Ship and Plane AP9

1929, June 1 Wmk. 127 *Perf. 14*

C55	AP8	5c	yellow org	.65	.20
C56	AP8	10c	red brown	.65	.20
C57	AP8	15c	deep green	.65	.20
C58	AP8	20c	carmine	.65	.20
C59	AP8	30c	gray blue	.65	.20
C60	AP8	40c	dull violet	.65	.25
C61	AP8	50c	dk olive grn	1.25	.25
C62	AP8	60c	orange brown	2.10	.25
C63	AP8	80c	green	5.50	2.25
C64	AP9	1p	blue	6.50	1.75
C65	AP9	2p	brown orange	9.75	4.25
C66	AP9	3p	pale rose vio	21.00	14.00
C67	AP9	5p	olive green	50.00	26.00
			Nos. C55-C67 (13)	100.00	50.00

For surcharges and overprints see Nos. C80-C95, CF2, CF4.

For International Airmail

AP10

AP11

1929, June 1 Wmk. 127 *Perf. 14*

C68	AP10	5c	yellow org	3.50	*4.25*
C69	AP10	10c	red brown	.65	*1.75*
C70	AP10	15c	deep green	.65	*1.75*
C71	AP10	20c	carmine	.65	*2.10*
C72	AP10	25c	violet blue	.65	.35
C73	AP10	30c	gray blue	.65	.55
C74	AP10	50c	dk olive grn	.65	*1.00*
C75	AP10	60c	brown	1.50	*1.75*
C76	AP11	1p	blue	3.00	*4.25*
C77	AP11	2p	red orange	4.50	*5.75*
C78	AP11	3p	violet	55.00	52.50
C79	AP11	5p	olive green	70.00	*75.00*
			Nos. C68-79 (12)	141.40	*151.00*

This issue was sold abroad for use on correspondence to be flown from coastal to interior points of Colombia. Cancellations are those of the country of origin rather than Colombia.

For overprint see No. CF3.

Nos. C63, C66 and C64 Surcharged in Black:

m

1830 1930
SIMON BOLIVAR
30 — 30
cts. — cts.

n

1930, Dec. 15

C80	AP8(m)	10c on 80c	4.25	4.25
C81	AP9(n)	20c on 3p	8.25	*9.00*
C82	AP9(n)	30c on 1p	9.00	9.00
		Nos. C80-C82 (3)	21.50	*22.25*

Simon Bolivar (1783-1830).

Colombian Government Issues

Nos. C55-C67 Overprinted in Black:

o

p

Wmk. 127

1932, Jan. 1 Typo. *Perf. 14*

C83	AP8(o)	5c	yellow org	8.00	8.00
C84	AP8(o)	10c	red brown	1.75	.50
C85	AP8(o)	15c	deep green	3.00	3.00
C86	AP8(o)	20c	carmine	1.50	.30
C87	AP8(o)	30c	gray blue	1.50	.50
C88	AP8(o)	40c	dull violet	2.00	1.00
C89	AP8(o)	50c	dk ol grn	4.00	3.00
C90	AP8(o)	60c	orange brn	3.25	3.00
C91	AP8(o)	80c	green	14.00	14.00
C92	AP9(p)	1p	blue	11.00	9.00
C93	AP9(p)	2p	brown org	30.00	27.50
C94	AP9(p)	3p	pale rose vio	60.00	52.50
C95	AP9(p)	5p	olive green	100.00	*110.00*
			Nos. C83-C95 (13)	240.00	232.30

Coffee AP12

Gold AP16

Designs: 10c, 50c, Cattle. 15c, 60c, Petroleum. 20c, 40c, Bananas. 3p, 5p, Emerald.

1932-39 Wmk. 127 Photo. *Perf. 14*

C96	AP12	5c	org & blk brn	.90	.25
C97	AP12	10c	lake & blk	1.00	.20
C98	AP12	15c	bl grn & vio blk	.45	.20
C99	AP12	15c	ver & vio blk ('39)	2.50	.20
C100	AP12	20c	car & ol blk	.70	.20
C101	AP12	20c	turq grn & ol blk ('39)	3.50	.30
C102	AP12	30c	dk bl & blk brn	1.60	.20
C103	AP12	40c	dk vio & ol bis	.85	.20
C104	AP12	50c	dk grn & brnsh blk	3.50	1.25
C105	AP12	60c	dk brn & blk vio	1.00	.25
C106	AP12	80c	grn & blk brn	5.50	2.00
C107	AP16	1p	dk bl & ol bis	9.00	1.25
C108	AP16	2p	org brn & ol bis	10.00	2.25
C109	AP16	3p	dk vio & emer	17.00	6.25
C110	AP16	5p	gray blk & emer	47.50	20.00
			Nos. C96-C110 (15)	105.00	35.00

For overprint see No. CF5.

Nos. C104, C106-C108 Surcharged:

a

b

1934, Jan. 5

C111 AP12(a) 10c on 50c 3.50 3.50
C112 AP12(a) 15c on 80c 4.75 4.75
C113 AP16(b) 20c on 1p 5.25 5.25
C114 AP16(b) 30c on 2p 5.75 5.75
Nos. C111-C114 (4) 19.25 19.25

400th anniversary of Cartagena.

Nos. C100 and C103 Surcharged in Black or Carmine:

1939, Jan. 15

C115 AP12 5c on 20c (Bk) .35 .35
C116 AP12 5c on 40c (C) .35 .25
C117 AP12 15c on 20c (Bk) 1.50 .50
a. Double surcharge 12.00
b. Pair, one with dbl. surch. 14.00
c. Inverted surcharge 12.00 12.00

No. CF5 Surcharged in Black

C118 AP12 5c on 20c .70 .70
Nos. C115-C118 (4) 2.90 1.80

Nos. C102-C103 Surcharged in Black or Red

1940, Oct. 20

C119 AP12 15c on 30c 1.25 .50
a. Inverted surcharge 12.00
C120 AP12 15c on 40c (R) 2.00 .75
a. Double surcharge 12.00

Pre-Columbian Monument — AP18

Proclamation of Independence — AP22

Designs: 10c, 40c, Symbol of Legend of El Dorado. 15c, 50c, Spanish Fortifications, Cartagena. 20c, 60c, Colonial Bogotá. 2p, 5p, National Library, Bogota.

Unwmk.

1941, Jan. 28 Engr. *Perf. 12*

C121 AP18 5c gray black .20 .20
C122 AP18 10c yellow org .20 .20
C123 AP18 15c carmine rose .20 .20
C124 AP18 20c yellow grn .35 .20
a. Horiz. pair, imperf. vert. 87.50
C125 AP18 30c deep blue .35 .20
C126 AP18 40c rose lake .70 .20
C127 AP18 50c turq green .70 .20
C128 AP18 60c sepia .70 .20
C129 AP18 80c olive blk 1.90 .40
C130 AP22 1p blue & blk 3.25 .50
C131 AP22 2p red org & blk 5.25 2.00
C132 AP22 3p violet & blk 14.00 5.00
C133 AP22 5p lt green & blk 27.50 17.50
Nos. C121-C133 (13) 55.30 27.00

See #C151-C163, C217-C225. For overprints see #C175-C198, C200-C216, C226, C290.

Bay of Santa Maria — AP24

National Capitol, Bogotá AP27

Designs: 5c, 20c, 50c, San Sebastian Fort, Cartagena. 10c, 30c, 60c, Tequendama Waterfall.

Unwmk.

1945, Nov. 3 Litho. *Perf. 11*

C134 AP24 5c blue gray .20 .20
C135 AP24 10c yellow org .20 .20
C136 AP24 15c rose .20 .20
C137 AP24 20c lt yel grn .30 .20
C138 AP24 30c ultra .30 .20
C139 AP24 40c claret .50 .20
C140 AP24 50c bluish grn .55 .20
C141 AP24 60c lt vio brn 2.25 .80
C142 AP24 80c dk slate grn 3.50 .80
C143 AP27 1p dk blue 5.00 .75
C144 AP27 2p red orange 7.00 2.50
Nos. C134-C144 (11) 20.00 6.25

Part-perforate varieties exist for all denominations except 80c.

Imperf., Pairs

C134a AP24 5c 8.50
C135a AP24 10c 8.50
C136a AP24 15c 8.50
C137a AP24 20c 8.50
C138a AP24 30c 8.50
C139a AP24 40c 8.50
C140a AP24 50c 8.50
C141a AP24 60c 8.50
C142a AP24 80c 10.50
C143a AP27 1p 17.50
C144a AP27 2p 60.00

Bello Type of Regular Issue, 1946

Wmk. 255

1946, Sept. 3 Engr. *Perf. 12*

C145 A219 5c deep blue .20 .20

Francisco José de Caldas AP29

Manuel del Socorro Rodriguez AP30

Perf. 12½

1947, May 9 Litho. Unwmk.

C146 AP29 5c dp bl, *grnsh* .35 .20
C147 AP30 10c red org, *grnsh* .50 .45

4th Pan-American Press Congress (1946).

Chancellery Patio — AP31

Capitol, Patio Rafael Nunez AP32

AP33

1948, Apr. 2 Engr. Wmk. 229

C148 AP31 5c dark brown .20 .20
C149 AP32 15c deep blue .90 .90

Miniature Sheet

Imperf

C150 AP33 50c brown 1.40 1.40

9th Pan-American Conference, Bogotá.

Types of 1941

1948, July 21 Unwmk. *Perf. 12*

C151 AP18 5c orange yel .20 .20
C152 AP18 10c scarlet .20 .20
C153 AP18 15c deep blue .20 .20
C154 AP18 20c violet .20 .20
C155 AP18 30c yellow grn .35 .20
C156 AP18 40c gray .40 .20
C157 AP18 50c rose lake .40 .20
C158 AP18 60c olive gray .70 .20
C159 AP18 80c red brn .85 .20
C160 AP22 1p ol grn & vio brn 1.50 .30
C161 AP22 2p dp grn & brt bl 2.50 .65
C162 AP22 3p rose car & blk 5.50 3.75
C163 AP22 5p lt brn & turq grn 14.00 7.00
Nos. C151-C163 (13) 27.00 13.50

"Air Week" 5c Blue

The War and Air Department issued a 5c blue stamp in May, 1949, to publicize Air Week (Semana de Aviacion). This stamp had no franking value and its use was optional during May 16-23.

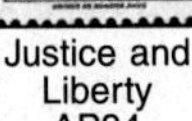

Justice and Liberty AP34

Wing AP35

Design: 10c, Liberty holding tablet of laws.

1949, Oct. 7 Unwmk. *Perf. 13*

C164 AP34 5c blue green .20 .20
C165 AP34 10c orange .20 .20

Issued to honor the new Constitution.

For Domestic Postage

1950, June 22 Litho. *Perf. 12*

C166 AP35 5c orange yellow .25 .25
C167 AP35 10c brown red .35 .30
C168 AP35 15c lt blue .40 .30
C169 AP35 20c lt green .60 *.65*
C170 AP35 30c lilac gray 1.50 *2.00*
C171 AP35 60c chocolate 1.90 *2.50*

With Network as in Parenthesis

C172 AP35 1p gray (buff) 14.00 *16.00*
C173 AP35 2p bl (pale grn) 14.00 *16.00*
C174 AP35 5p red brn (red brn) 40.00 *45.00*
Nos. C166-C174 (9) 73.00 *83.00*

No. C172 was issued both with and without network.

Nos. C151-C157 and C160-C163 Overprinted in Black

1950, July 18

C175 AP18 5c orange yel .20 .20
C176 AP18 10c scarlet .20 .20
C177 AP18 15c deep blue .20 .20
C178 AP18 20c violet .20 .20
C179 AP18 30c yellow green .30 .20
C180 AP18 40c gray .80 .25
C181 AP18 50c rose lake .40 .25
C182 AP22 1p ol grn & vio brn 2.50 2.25
C183 AP22 2p dp grn & brt bl 3.75 3.25
C184 AP22 3p rose car & blk 11.00 11.00
C185 AP22 5p lt brn & turq grn 24.00 24.00
Nos. C175-C185 (11) 43.55 42.00

Nos. C151-C163 Overprinted in Black

1950, July 12

C186 AP18 5c orange yel .20 .20
C187 AP18 10c scarlet .20 .20
C188 AP18 15c deep blue .20 .20
C189 AP18 20c violet .20 .20
C190 AP18 30c yellow green .20 .20
C191 AP18 40c gray .40 .20
C192 AP18 50c rose lake .40 .20
C193 AP18 60c olive gray .70 .20
C194 AP18 80c red brown 1.00 .40
C195 AP22 1p ol grn & vio brn 1.10 .50
C196 AP22 2p dp grn & brt bl 3.00 1.40
C197 AP22 3p rose car & blk 7.25 6.50
C198 AP22 5p lt brn & turq grn 16.00 14.00
Nos. C186-C198 (13) 30.85 24.40

On Nos. C175-C198, "L" stands for LANSA, "A" for AVIANCA.

UPU Type

Miniature Sheet

Unwmk.

1950, Aug. 22 Photo. *Imperf.*

C199 A245 50c gray 1.00 1.00

75th anniv. (in 1949) of the UPU.

Catalogue values for unused stamps in this section, from this point to the end of the section, are for Never Hinged items.

Types of 1941 Overprinted at Lower Right in Black

Unwmk.

1951, Sept. 15 Engr. *Perf. 12*

C200 AP18 40c orange yel 1.50 1.25
C201 AP18 50c ultra 1.50 1.25
C202 AP18 60c gray 1.50 1.25
C203 AP18 80c car rose 1.10 .95
C204 AP22 1p red org & red brn 3.75 3.00
C205 AP22 2p rose car & bl 4.00 3.00
C206 AP22 3p choc & emer 10.00 8.00
C207 AP22 5p org & gray 30.00 30.00
Nos. C200-C207 (8) 53.35 48.70

Types of 1941 Overprinted at Lower Right in Black

1951-54

C208 AP18 40c orange yel 3.25 .55
C209 AP18 50c ultra 4.00 .60
C210 AP18 60c gray 3.00 .45
a. Overprint centered 2.00 .50
C211 AP18 80c car rose .85 .30
C212 AP22 1p red org & red brn 3.25 .50
C213 AP22 1p ol grn & vio brn ('54) 4.00 .75
C214 AP22 2p rose car & bl 3.25 .55
C215 AP22 3p choc & emer 5.00 1.40
C216 AP22 5p org & gray 10.00 1.90
Nos. C208-C216 (9) 36.60 7.00

All values except the 2p and 3p exist without overprint.

Types of 1941

1952, May 10 Engr.

C217 AP18 5c ultra .45 .20
C218 AP18 10c ultra .45 .20
C219 AP18 15c ultra .45 .20
C220 AP18 20c ultra .90 .25
C221 AP18 30c ultra 2.25 .55

Color Change

C222 AP18 5c car rose .45 .20
C223 AP18 10c car rose .45 .20
C224 AP18 20c car rose .85 .20
C225 AP18 30c car rose 1.75 .30
Nos. C217-C225 (9) 8.00 2.30

Type of 1941 Surcharged in Blue

1952, Oct. 30

C226 AP18 70c on 80c car rose 1.50 .70

Latin American Siderurgical Conf., 1952.

Type of Postal Tax Stamps, 1948-50, Nos. 602 and 604 Surcharged or Overprinted in Black

1953 Wmk. 255 *Perf. 12*

C227 PT10 5c on 8c blue .20 .20
C228 PT10 15c on 20c brown .25 .20
C229 PT10 15c on 25c bl grn 1.00 .20
C230 PT10 25c blue green .35 .20
Nos. C227-C230 (4) 1.80 .80

Many varieties of overprint or surcharge exist on Nos. C227-C231.

No. 570 Overprinted "AEREO" in Blue

1953, Aug. Wmk. 229 *Perf. 12½*

C231 A160 10c red .20 .20

"Extra Rapido"

Stamps inscribed "Extra Rapido" are for use on domestic airmail carried by airlines other than AVIANCA.

No. 585 Surcharged and Overprinted "Extra Rapido" in Dark Blue

1953 Unwmk. *Perf. 13*

C232 A244 5c on 11c red .35 .35

Capitol and Arms — AP37

Revenue Stamps Overprinted "Correo Extra-Rapido"

Gray Security Paper

1953 Wmk. 255 Engr. *Perf. 12*

C233 AP37 1c on 2c green .20 .20
C234 AP37 50c red orange .20 .20

AP38

Real Estate Tax Stamps Ovptd. "Correo Extra-Rapido" in Black or Carmine

1953

C235 AP38 5c red orange .20 .20
C236 AP38 20c brown (C) .25 .20

On 20c, overprint is at bottom of stamp and two lines of ornaments cover real estate tax inscription at top.

Castillo y Rada and Map — AP39

Real Estate Tax Stamp Surcharged "Correo Aereo, II Exposicion Filatelica Nacional, Bogota Dicbre 1953, 15 Centavos"

1953, Dec. 12 Engr. & Litho.

C237 AP39 15c on 10p multi .35 .20

2nd Natl. Philatelic Exhib., Bogota, Dec. 1953.

No. RA45 Overprinted in Black

1953

C238 PT10 10c purple .20 .20

Galeras Volcano — AP40

Retreat of San Diego — AP41

Designs: No. C241, Las Lajas Shrine, Narino. No. C242, 50c, Bolivar monument. 20c, 80c, Ruiz mountain, Manizales. 40c, George Isaacs monument, Cali. 60c, Monkey Fountain, Tunja. 1p, Stadium, Medellin. 2p, Pastelillo Fort, Cartagena. 3p, Santo Domingo University gate. 5p, Las Lajas Shrine. 10p, Map of Colombia.

Perf. 13½x13, 13

1954, Jan. 15 Engr. Unwmk.

C239 AP40 5c dp red vio .20 .20
C240 AP41 10c black .20 .20
C241 AP40 15c red orange .20 .20
C242 AP40 15c car rose .20 .20
C243 AP40 20c brown .20 .20
C244 AP40 30c brown org .20 .20
C245 AP40 40c blue .20 .20
C246 AP40 50c dk violet brn .20 .20
C247 AP40 60c dk brown .20 .20
C248 AP40 80c red brown .30 .20

Size: 37x27mm

Center in Black

C249 AP41 1p deep blue 1.90 .20
C250 AP41 2p dark green 2.75 .20
C251 AP41 3p carmine rose 6.00 .90

Size: 38x32mm, 32x38mm

C252 AP41 5p dk grn & red brn 7.25 2.00
C253 AP40 10p gray grn & red org 10.50 4.50
Nos. C239-C253 (15) 30.50 9.80

See Nos. C307-C308. For surcharges and overprints see Nos. 691, C321, C325, C330, C333-C334, C343-C346.

Condor Carrying Shield AP42

Inscribed: "Correo Extra-Rapido"

1954, Apr. 23 Litho. *Perf. 12½*

C254 AP42 5c lilac rose .60 .30

For overprint see No. RA53.

Soldier-Map-Arms Type

1954, June 13 Engr. *Perf. 13*

C255 A259 15c carmine .30 .20

See No. C271a.

Games Type

Design: 20c, Stadium and Athlete holding arms of Colombia.

1954, July 18

C256 A260 15c chocolate .65 .20
C257 A260 20c deep blue green 1.25 .35

Church of St. Peter Claver, Cartagena AP45

1954, Sept. 9

C258 AP45 15c brown .25 .20
a. Souvenir sheet 3.50 3.00

St. Peter Claver, 300th death anniv.

No. C258a contains one stamp similar to No. C258, but printed in red brown.

Mercury Type

1954, Oct. 29

C259 A263 15c deep blue .35 .20

Inscribed "Extra Rapido"

C260 A263 50c scarlet .35 .20

Archbishop Manuel José Mosquera, Death Cent. — AP47

Inscribed: "Correo Extra Rapido"

1954, Nov. 17

C261 AP47 2c yellow green .20 .20

Virgin of Chiquinquira — AP48

Inscribed: "Correo Extra Rapido"

1954, Dec. 4 Engr. & Litho.

C262 AP48 5c org brn & multi .20 .20

See No. C291. For overprint see No. 686.

College Types

Designs: 20c, Brother Cristobal de Torres. 50c, College chapel and arms.

Perf. 12½x11½, 11½x12½

1954, Dec. 6 Engr. Unwmk.

C263 A264 15c orange & blk .25 .20
C264 A264 20c ultra .35 .20
C265 A265 25c dark brown .50 .20
C266 A265 50c black & car 1.25 .60
a. Souvenir sheet 4.75 4.75
Nos. C263-C266 (4) 2.35 1.20

No. C266a contains four stamps similar to Nos. C263-C266, but printed in different colors: 15c red and black, 20c pale purple, 25c brown, 50c black and olive green.

Steel Mill Type

1954, Dec. 12 *Perf. 12½x13*

C267 A266 20c green & blk 1.00 .60

Marti Type

1955, Jan. 28 *Perf. 13½x13*

C268 A267 15c deep green .30 .20

Korean Veterans Type

1955, Mar. 23 *Perf. 12½*

C269 A268 20c dark green .50 .20

Merchant Fleet Types

1955, Apr. 12 *Perf. 12½*

C270 A269 25c black .30 .20
C271 A270 50c dark green .55 .30
a. Souvenir sheet 5.25 5.25

#C271a contains 4 stamps similar to #C255, C269-C271, but printed in different colors; 15c lilac red, 20c olive, 25c bluish black, 50c bluish green.

Marco Fidel Suarez (1855-1927), Pres. 1918-21 — AP56

Inscribed: "Correo Extra Rapido"

1955, April 23 *Perf. 13*

C272 AP56 10c deep blue .20 .20

Hotel-Church Type

1955, May 16 Photo. *Perf. 11½x12*

C273 A271 15c rose brown .25 .20

Rotary Type

Unwmk.

1955, Oct. 17 Engr. *Perf. 13*

C274 A272 15c dk carmine rose .25 .20

Atahualpa, Tisquesuza and Montezuma AP59

Ferdinand the Catholic and Queen Isabella I AP60

Designs: 15c, O'Higgins, Santander and Sucre. 20c, Marti, Hidalgo and Petion. 1p, Artigas, Solano Lopez and Murillo. 2p, Abdon Calderon, Baron de Rio Branco and José de La Mar.

1955, Oct. 12 Engr. & Photo.

Inscribed: "Extra Rapido"

C275	AP59	2c dull brn & blk	.25	.20
C276	AP60	5c dk brn & yel	.25	.20

Regular Air Post

C277	AP59	15c rose car & blk	.30	.20
C278	AP59	20c pale brn & blk	.45	.20
a.		Souvenir sheet of 2	12.50	7.50

Inscribed: "Extra Rapido"

C279	AP60	1p ol gray & brn	10.00	6.00
C280	AP60	2p violet & blk	6.00	4.75
		Nos. C275-C280 (6)	17.25	11.55

7th Cong. of the Postal Union of the Americas and Spain, Bogota, Oct. 12-Nov. 9, 1955.

No. C278a contains one each of Nos. C277-C278 printed in different shades.

Caro Type

1955, Nov. 29 Engr. *Perf. 13½x13*

C281	A275	15c gray green	.25	.20

University of Salamanca AP62

Inscribed: "Extra Rapido"

1955, Nov. 29 Unwmk. *Perf. 13*

C282	AP62	20c dark brown	.20	.20

University of Salamanca, 7th centenary.

Type of Postal Tax Stamp of 1948-50 Surcharged

1956 Wmk. 255 Engr. *Perf. 12*

C283	PT10	2c on 8c blue	.20	.20

No. 617 Overprinted in Black

1956 Unwmk. *Perf. 12½x13*

C284	A256	1p black & emerald	.25	.20

Columbus Type

1956, Oct. 11 Photo. *Perf. 12*

C285	A279	15c intense blue	.50	.20

See No. C306.

St. Elizabeth Type

1956, Nov. 19

C286	A280	15c red brown	.30	.20

St. Ignatius Type

1956, Nov. 26 Engr. *Perf. 12½x13*

C287	A281	5c brown	.20	.20

Javier Pereira — AP63

1956, Dec. 28 Unwmk. *Perf. 12*

C288	AP63	20c rose carmine	.20	.20

Issued to honor 167-year-old Javier Pereira.

No. 649 and Type of 1941 Overprinted in Red "EXTRA RAPIDO"

1957 *Perf. 13½x13*

C289	A276	5c blue & black	6.00	2.50

Perf. 12

C290	AP22	5p orange & gray	5.50	5.00

The overprint measures 14mm.

Virgin Type of 1954

Engraved and Lithographed

1957, May 23 Unwmk. *Perf. 13*

C291	AP48	5c dp plum & multi	.20	.20

Bank Type

#C292, 20c, Emblem & dairy farm. 10c, Emblem & tractor. 15c, Emblem, coffee & corn. #C293, Emblem, cow, horse & herd.

1957 Photo. *Perf. 14x13½*

C292	A283	5c chocolate	.20	.20
C293	A283	5c orange	.20	.20
C294	A283	10c green	.55	.40
C295	A283	15c black	.35	.20
C296	A283	20c dull red	.80	.20
		Nos. C292-C296 (5)	2.10	1.20

No. C292 is inscribed "Extra Rapido."
Issued: #C292, 3/5; others 5/23.

Cyclist AP64

1957, July 6 Unwmk. *Perf. 12*

C297	AP64	2c brown	.20	.20
C298	AP64	5c ultra	.20	.20

Seventh Bicycle Tour of Colombia.

Academy Type

Designs: 15c, Coat of arms and Gen. Rafael Reyes. 20c, Coat of arms and Academy.

1957, July 20 Engr. *Perf. 12½*

C299	A284	15c rose carmine	.20	.20
C300	A284	20c brown	.25	.20

Delgado Type

1957, Sept. 15 Photo. *Perf. 12*

C301	A285	10c slate blue	.20	.20

UPU Type

1957, Oct. 10

C302	A286	15c dark red brown	.20	.20
C303	A286	25c dark blue	.20	.20

St. Vincent de Paul Type

1957, Oct. 18

C304	A287	5c rose brown	.20	.20

Fencing Type

1957, Nov. 23 *Perf. 12*

C305	A288	20c dark red brown	.25	.20

Columbus Type Inscribed "Extra Rapido"

1958, Jan. 8 Unwmk. *Perf. 12*

C306	A279	3c dark green	.20	.20

Scenic Type

Design: 25c, Las Lajas Shrine.

1958, June 20 Engr. *Perf. 13*

C307	AP40	25c dark blue	.30	.20
C308	AP40	25c rose violet	.30	.20

IGY Type

1958, May 12 Photo. *Perf. 12*

C309	A289	25c green	.25	.20

Inscribed "Extra Rapido"

C310	A289	1p purple	.50	.20

No. 659 Overprinted "AEREO" in Carmine

1958, Oct. 16 Engr. *Perf. 13*

C312	A277	50c dk green & blk	.40	.20

Almanza Type

1958, Oct. 23 Photo. *Perf. 14x13*

C313	A290	25c dark gray	.25	.20

Inscribed "Extra Rapido"

C314	A290	10c olive green	.20	.20

Carrasquilla Type

1959, Jan. 22 Photo. *Perf. 14x13*

C315	A291	25c carmine rose	.20	.20
C316	A291	1p dark blue	.60	.20

Miss Universe Type

1959, June 26 Unwmk. *Perf. 11½*

C317	A292	1.20p multicolored	1.40	1.10
C318	A292	5p multicolored	40.00	37.50

Gaitan Type Inscribed "Extra Rapido" and Surcharged in Black or Blue

1959, July 28 Engr. *Perf. 12x13½*

C319	A293	2p on 1p black	1.40	1.25
C320	A293	2p on 1p black (Bl)	1.40	1.25

The 1p black, type A293, exists without surcharge.

No. C247 Surcharged with New Value in Dark Blue; Old Value Obliterated

1959, Aug. 24 Unwmk. *Perf. 13*

C321	AP40	50c on 60c dk brown	1.25	.40

Regular and Air Post Issues of 1948-59 Overprinted in Black or Red

1959-60

C322	A283	5c orange	.35	.25
C323	A287	5c rose brn ('60)	.50	.50
C324	A281	5c brown (R)	.40	.30
C325	AP41	10c black	.25	.20
a.		Double overprint	2.50	2.50
C326	A160	10c red, #C231	.40	.20
a.		Double overprint	1.40	1.40
C328	A284	15c rose car	.25	.20
a.		Inverted overprint	3.00	3.00
C330	AP40	20c brown	.25	.20
a.		Double overprint	1.40	1.40
C331	A284	20c brown	.25	.20
C332	A288	20c dk red brn ('60)	.25	.20
C333	AP40	25c rose vio ('60)	.25	.20
C334	AP40	25c dark blue	.25	.20
C335	A291	25c car rose	.25	.20
C336	A290	25c dark gray	.25	.20
C338	AP40	30c brown org	.25	.20
C340	AP40	50c on 60c dk brn	.40	.20
C341	A291	1p dark blue	.95	.20
a.		Double overprint	2.50	2.50
C342	A292	1.20p brn, ultra, car & ol	1.50	.80
C343	AP41	2p dk grn & blk	2.00	.20
C344	AP41	3p car rose & blk	5.25	.50
a.		Double overprint	8.50	8.50
C345	AP41	5p dk grn & red brn	7.00	1.10
a.		Double overprint	8.50	8.50
b.		Inverted overprint	8.50	8.50
C346	AP40	10p gray grn & red org	8.75	2.25
		Nos. C322-C346 (21)	30.00	8.50

Issued following agreement between the Colombian government and AVIANCA to unify the air postage used on all mail carried by AVIANCA.

Vertical overprint on Nos. C342 and C346.

Airmail Stamp of 1919 and Planes AP66

60c, #C349a, C350a, Planes of 1919 and 1959. #C349b, C350b, Stamp of 1919 and Planes.

Unwmk.

1959, Dec. 5 Photo. *Perf. 12*

C347	AP66	35c lt bl, blk & red	.40	.20
C348	AP66	60c yel grn & gray	.60	.35

Souvenir Sheets

C349		Sheet of 2	7.50	6.75
a.	AP66	1p orange & gray	1.50	1.00
b.	AP66	1p lilac, gray & red	1.50	1.00

Inscribed "Extra Rapido"

1960, May 17

C350		Sheet of 2	7.50	6.75
a.	AP66	1.50p red orange & gray	1.50	1.25
b.	AP66	1.50p olive, gray & rose	1.50	1.25

Nos. C347-C350 for the 40th anniv. of air post service and of the AVIANCA company.

Type of Regular Issue and

1859 Stamp and Seaplane AP67

Tête Bêche 5c Stamps of 1859 — AP68

Designs (various stamps of 1859 and): 10c, Map of Colombia. 25c, Pres. Mariano Ospina. 1.20p, Plane over mountains.

1959, Dec. 1 Photo. *Perf. 12*

C351	A296	25c choc & red	.50	.20
C352	AP67	50c ver & ultra	1.00	.50
C353	AP67	1.20p yel grn & car	2.00	1.10

Inscribed "Extra Rapido"

C354	A296	10c lemon & vio	.20	.20
		Nos. C351-C354 (4)	3.70	2.00

Souvenir Sheet

Wmk. 331

1959, Dec. 23 Litho. *Imperf.*

C355	AP68	5p blue, *pink*	17.50	17.50

Cent. of Colombian postage stamps.

No. C355 exists with inscription "VALOR $5.10" instead of "VALOR $5."

Eldorado Airport, Bogota AP69

1960, Jan. 5 Wmk. 331 *Perf. 12½*

C356	AP69	35c black & ocher	.50	.20
C356A	AP69	60c ver & gray	.65	.35

Inscribed "Extra Rapido"

C356B	AP69	1p Prus bl & gray	.85	.50
		Nos. C356-C356B (3)	2.00	1.05

Ant Bear AP70

1.30p, Armadillo. 1.45p, Parrot fish.

Unwmk.

1960, Feb. 12 Photo. *Perf. 12*

C357	AP70	35c sepia	1.00	.20
C358	AP70	1.30p rose car & dk brn	2.00	1.40
C359	AP70	1.45p lt bl, bl & yel	1.75	1.25
		Nos. C357-C359 (3)	4.75	2.85

Alexander von Humboldt, German naturalist and geographer (1769-1859).

Flower Type

#C360, C362, C366, Passiflora mollissima. #C361, C364, C367, Odontoglossum luteo purpureum. #C363, C369, Anthurium andreanum. #C365, C370, Stanhopea tigrina. #C368, Espeletia grandiflora.

1960, May 10 Photo. *Perf. 12*

Flowers In Natural Colors

C360 A298 5c dark blue .20 .20
C361 A298 35c maroon .40 .20
C362 A298 60c dark blue .75 .55
C363 A298 1.45p dark brown 1.00 .85

Inscribed "Extra Rapido"

C364 A298 5c maroon .20 .20
C365 A298 10c brown .20 .20
C366 A298 1p dark blue 2.00 *2.50*
C367 A298 1p maroon 2.00 *2.50*
C368 A298 1p brown 2.00 *2.50*
C369 A298 1p brown 2.00 *2.50*
C370 A298 1p brown 2.00 *2.50*
Nos. C360-C370 (11) 12.75 *14.70*

See Nos. C420-C425.

Fleeing Family and Uprooted Oak Emblem AP71

Perf. 10, 11

1960, May 24 Litho. Wmk. 331

C371 AP71 60c bl grn & gray .30 .20

World Refugee Year, 7/1/59-6/30/60.

Souvenir Sheet

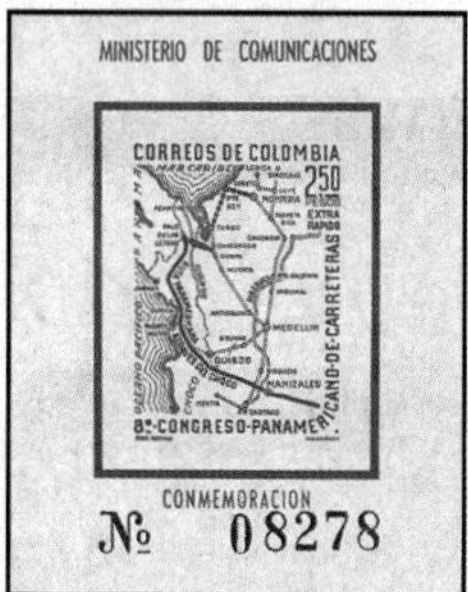

Pan-American Highway Through Colombia — AP72

1960, May 28 Litho. *Imperf.*

C372 AP72 2.50p brn & aqua 5.00 5.00

8th Pan-American Highway Congress, Bogota, May 20-29.

Lincoln Type

1960, June 6 *Perf. 10½*

C375 A299 40c dl red brn & blk .85 .60
C376 A299 60c rose red & blk .25 .20

Type of Regular Issue and

Joaquin Camacho, Jorge Tadeo Lozano and Jose Miguel Pey AP73

Flag, Coins and Arms of Mompox and Cartagena — AP74

No. C378, Arms of Cartagena. 35c, 1.45p, Colombian flag. 60c, Andres Rosillo, Antonio Villavicencio and Joaquin Caicedo. 1p, Manuel de Bernardo Alvarez and Joaquin Gutierrez. 1.20p, Jose Antonio Galan statue. 1.30p, Front page of newspaper La Bagatela, 1811. 1.65p, Antonia Santos, Jose Acevedo y Gomez and Liborio Mejia.

Unwmk.

1960, July 20 Photo. *Perf. 12*

C377 AP73 5c lilac & brn .20 .20
C378 A301 5c dp bl grn & multi .20 .20
C379 AP73 35c multicolored .20 .20
C380 AP73 60c red brn & grn .40 .20
C381 AP73 1p ver & sl grn .85 .60
C382 A301 1.20p ultra & ind .85 .60
C383 AP73 1.30p orange & blk .85 .60
C384 AP73 1.45p multicolored 1.10 .85
C385 AP73 1.65p green & brn .85 .85
Nos. C377-C385 (9) 5.50 4.30

Souvenir Sheet

Stamps Inscribed "Extra Rapido"

C386 AP74 Sheet of 4 4.00 4.00
a. 50c deep claret & multi [illegible] [illegible]
b. 50c green & multi .65 .65
c. 1p brown olive, yel, blue & car .65 .65
d. 1p lilac & gray .65 .65

150th anniv. of Colombia's independence.

St. Isidore Type

Designs: 35c, No. C388a, St. Isidore and farm animals. No. C388b, Nativity.

Unwmk.

1960, Sept. 26 Photo. *Perf. 12*

C387 A302 35c multicolored .20 .20

Souvenir Sheet

Stamps Inscribed "Extra Rapido"

C388 A302 Sheet of 2 6.00 6.00
a. 1.50p multicolored 2.00 2.00
b. 1.50p multicolored 2.00 2.00

See Nos. C439-C440.

Type of Regular Issue, 1959

Wmk. 331

1960, Nov. 23 Litho. *Perf. 12½*

C389 A294 35c Bolivar 3.00 .40

Pan-American Highway Type

1961, Mar. 7 Unwmk. *Perf. 10½x11*

C390 A304 10c rose lil & emer .50 *.50*
C391 A304 20c ver & lt bl .50 *.50*
C392 A304 30c black & emer .50 *.50*

Inscribed "Extra Rapido"

C393 A304 10c dk blue & emer .50 *.50*
Nos. C390-C393 (4) 2.00 *2.00*

8th Pan-American Highway Congress, Bogota, May 20-29, 1960.

Lopez Type

1961, Mar. 22 Photo. *Perf. 12½*

C394 A305 35c blue & brown .50 .20

Inscribed "Extra Rapido"

C395 A305 10c emerald & brn .20 .20

Souvenir Sheet

C396 A305 1p lilac & brn 3.50 3.50

Brother Damian and San Francisco Church, Cali AP75

Designs: 10c, View of Cali, vert. No. 398, Emblem of University del Valle, vert. 1.30p, Fine Arts School, Cali. 1.45p, Agricultural College, Palmira.

Perf. 13x13½, 13½x13

1961, Aug. 17 Photo. Unwmk.

C397 AP75 35c vio brn & ol .30 .20
C398 AP75 35c olive & grn .30 .20
C399 AP75 1.30p sepia & pink .85 .45
C400 AP75 1.45p multicolored .85 .60

Inscribed: "Extra Rapido"

C401 AP75 10c brn & yel grn .20 .20
Nos. C397-C401 (5) 2.50 1.65

50th anniv. (in 1960) of the department of Valle del Cauca.

View of Cucuta AP76

10c, Church of the Rosary, Cucuta, vert.

1961, Aug. 29

C402 AP76 35c brn ol & grn .60 .20

Inscribed: "Extra Rapido"

C403 AP76 10c dk brn & gray grn .20 .20

50th anniv. (in 1960) of the department of North Santander.

Old and New Ships of Barranquilla AP77

Arms and View of San Gil — AP78

Hotel, Popayan AP79

Statue of Christ in Procession AP80

Design: 1.45p, View of Velez.

Perf. 12½x13, 13x12½

1961, Oct. 10 Photo. Unwmk.

C404 AP77 35c gold & bl .45 .20
C405 AP78 35c bl grn, yel & red .45 .20
C406 AP79 35c car & brn .45 .20
C407 AP78 1.45p brown & grn .45 .20

Inscribed: "Extra Rapido"

C408 AP80 10c brown & yel .20 .20
Nos. C404-C408 (5) 2.00 1.00

Types of Regular and Air Post

Souvenir Sheets

Designs, No. C409: 35c, Barranquilla arms. 40c, Popayan arms. c, Arms and view of San Gil. d, Holy Week in Popayan.

No. C410: a, Old and new ships at Barranquilla. b, Hotel, Popayan. c, Bucaramanga arms. d, Holy Week in Popayan.

C409 Sheet of 4 6.00 *6.00*
a. A309 35c gold & multi .55 .55
b. A309 40c gold & multi .55 .55
c. AP78 1p blue, yellow & red 1.10 1.10
d. AP80 1p car rose & yellow 1.10 1.10

Stamps Inscribed: "Extra Rapido"

C410 Sheet of 4 6.00 *6.00*
a. AP77 50c gold & car rose .85 .85
b. AP79 50c gold & blue .85 .85
c. A309 50c pink & multi .85 .85
d. AP80 50c blue & yellow .85 .85

Nos. C404-C408 are in honor of the Atlantico Department. Nos. C409-C410 are in honor of the Departments of Atlantico, Cauca and Santander.

Nos. 713, 716 and 715 Overprinted and Surcharged

1961, Sept. *Perf. 12*

C411 A297 5c grnsh bl & brn .20 .20
C412 A298 5c multicolored .20 .20
C413 A297 10c on 20c cit & gray brn .20 .20
Nos. C411-C413 (3) .60 .60

"Aereo" in script on No. C412.

See Nos. C420-C425.

Sports Type

Designs: No. C414, Women divers. No. C415, Tennis, mixed doubles. 1.45p, No. C419b, Baseball. No. C417, Torch bearer. Nos. C418, C419a, Bolivar statue and flags of six participating nations. No. C419c, Soccer. No. C419d, Basketball.

1961, Dec. 16 Litho. *Perf. 13½x14*

C414 A310 35c ultra, yel & brn .60 .20
C415 A310 35c car, yel & brn .60 .20
C416 A310 1.45p Prus grn, yel & brn .85 .55

Inscribed: "Extra Rapido"

[illegible] [illegible] 10c [illegible], yel & brn .20 .20
C418 A310 10c ol, yel, bl & red .20 .20
Nos. C414-C418 (5) 2.45 1.35

Souvenir Sheet

Stamps Inscribed: "Extra Rapido"

Imperf

C419 Sheet of 4 5.00 5.00
a. A310 50c multi .40 .40
b. A310 50c multi .40 .40
c. A310 1p multi .85 .85
d. A310 1p multi .85 .85

Flower Type of 1960

5c, Passiflora mollissima. 10c, Espeletia grandiflora. 20c, 2p, Odontoglossum luteo purpureum. 25c, Stanhopea tigrina. 60c, Anthurium Andreanum.

Unwmk.

1962, Jan. 30 Photo. *Perf. 12*

Flowers in Natural Colors

C420 A298 5c gray .20 .20
C421 A298 10c gray blue .20 .20
C422 A298 20c rose lilac .20 .20
C423 A298 25c citron .25 .20
C424 A298 60c light brown .25 .20

Inscribed "Extra Rapido"

C425 A298 2p salmon pink 2.50 1.25
Nos. C420-C425 (6) 3.60 2.25

Anti-Malaria Type

Designs: 40c, Colombian anti-malaria emblem. 1p, 1.45p, Malaria eradication emblem and mosquito in swamp.

1962, Apr. 12 Litho. *Perf. 12*

C426 A311 40c yellow & red .25 .20
C427 A311 1.45p gray & ultra .50 .40

Inscribed "Extra Rapido"

C428 A311 1p yel grn & ultra 3.50 3.50
Nos. C426-C428 (3) 4.25 4.10

WHO drive to eradicate malaria.

Type of Regular Issue, 1962 and

Abelardo Ramos and Engineering School, Cauca — AP81

Designs: 10c, Miguel Triana, Andres A. Arroyo and Monserrate shrine with cable cars. 15c, Diodoro Sanchez and first meeting place of Engineers Society. 2p, Engineers Society emblem.

1962, June 12 Photo. *Perf. 11½x12*

C429 AP81 5c blue & dp rose .20 .20
C430 AP81 10c green & sepia .20 .20
C431 AP81 15c lilac & sepia .25 .20

Inscribed: "Extra Rapido"

C432 A312 2p blk, yel, red & bl 1.50 1.50
Nos. C429-C432 (4) 2.15 2.10

75th anniv. of the founding of the Colombian Soc. of Engineers and 6th Natl. Cong. of Engineers.

American States Type

1962, June 28 Photo. *Perf. 13*

Flags in National Colors

C433 A313 35c black & blue .35 .20

Women's Rights Type

Perf. 12x12½

1962, July 20 Litho. Wmk. 229
C434 A314 35c ocher, gray & blk .20 .20

See Nos. C448-C450.

Scout Type

Designs: 15c, No. C438, Scouts at campfire and tents. 40c and No. C437, Girl Scouts.

Perf. 11½x12

1962, July 26 Photo. Unwmk.
C435 A315 15c brown & rose .20 .20
C436 A315 40c dp cl & pink .25 .20
C437 A315 1p blue & buff .80 .35

Inscribed "Extra Rapido"

C438 A315 1p purple & yel 3.75 3.75
Nos. C435-C438 (4) 5.00 4.50

Nos. C435 and C438 for 30th anniv. of the Colombian Boy Scouts. Nos. C436 and C437 for the 25th anniv. of the Girl Scouts.

Nativity by Gregorio Vasquez AP82

Design: 2p, St. Isidore, similar to type A302.

Inscribed "Extra Rapido"

Unwmk.

1962, Aug. 28 Photo. *Perf. 12*
C439 AP82 10c gray & multi .20 .20
C440 AP82 2p gray & multi 3.50 3.50

See Nos. C387-C388.

Type of Regular Issue, 1962 and

Pres. Aquileo Parra and Magdalena River Bridge AP83

Design: 5c, Locomotives of 1854 and 1961. 10c, Railroad map of Colombia.

1962, Sept. 28 Photo. *Perf. 12½*
C441 AP83 5c sep & slate grn .20 .20
C442 A316 10c multicolored .20 .20

Engr.

C443 AP83 1p dull pur & brn 1.40 .20

Inscribed: "Extra Rapido."

C444 AP83 5p bl, brn & dl grn 3.75 3.75
Nos. C441-C444 (4) 5.55 4.35

Progress of Colombian railroads and completion of the Atlantic Line from Santa Maria to Bogota.

UPAE Type

Designs: 50c, Map of Americas and carrier pigeon. 60c, Post horn.

Perf. 13½x14

1962, Oct. 18 Litho. Wmk. 346
C445 A317 50c slate grn & gold .30 .20
C446 A317 60c gold & plum .25 .20

Pope John XXIII AP84

1963, Mar. 11
C447 AP84 60c gold, red brn, buff & red .20 .20

Vatican II, the 21st Ecumenical Council of the Roman Catholic Church.

Women's Rights Type of 1962

1963-64 *Perf. 12x12½*
C448 A314 5c sal, gray & blk ('64) .20 .20
C449 A314 45c pale grn, gray & blk .25 .20
C450 A314 45c brt pink, gray & blk .25 .20
Nos. C448-C450 (3) .70 .60

Games Emblem — AP85

1963, Aug. 12 *Perf. 13x14*
C451 AP85 20c gray & multi .20 .20
C452 AP85 80c buff & multi .20 .20

South American Athletic Championships (22nd for men, 12th for women), Cali, June 30-July 7.

Bolivar Statue by Arenas-Betancourt — AP86

Perf. 14x13½

1963, Aug. 30 Unwmk.
C453 AP86 1.90p olive bis & blue .20 .20

Centenary of the city of Pereira.
For surcharge see No. C574.

Tennis Player — AP87

1963, Oct. 11 *Perf. 13½x14*
C454 AP87 55c multicolored .20 .20

30th South American Tennis Championships, Medellin, Oct. 3-13.

Pres. John F. Kennedy and Alliance for Progress Emblem AP88

1963, Dec. 17 Litho. *Perf. 14x13½*
C455 AP88 10c multicolored .20 .20

President John F. Kennedy (1917-1963).

Church of the True Cross, National Pantheon, Bogota — AP89

2p, Christ of the Martyrs, bell and tomb.

Perf. 13½x14

1964, Mar. 10 Photo. Unwmk.
C459 AP89 1p multicolored .20 .20
C460 AP89 2p multicolored .30 .20

View of Cartagena AP90

1964, Mar. 18 Litho. *Perf. 14x13½*
C461 AP90 3p vio, bl, ocher & brn 1.40 .60

Cartagena's independence in 1811, Simon Bolivar's visit in 1812 and the siege of 1815.

Eleanor Roosevelt AP91

1964, Nov. 10 Photo. *Perf. 12*
C462 AP91 20c ol & dl red brn .20 .20

Eleanor Roosevelt (1884-1962).

Alberto Castilla and Score of "El Bunde" AP92

1964, Nov. 10 Unwmk.
C463 AP92 30c ol bis & Prus grn .20 .20

Department of Tolima and Maestro Alberto Castilla (1878-1937) who in 1906 founded the Tolima Conservatory of Music in Ibague.

Mejia Type

Mejia portrait and: 45c, Women picking coffee. 5p, Mules carrying coffee bags. 10p, Loading coffee on freighter "Manuel Mejia."

1965, Feb. 10 Engr. *Perf. 12½x13*
C464 A320 45c brown & blk .20 .20
C465 A320 5p gray grn & blk 1.75 .25
C466 A320 10p ultra & blk 2.25 .30
Nos. C464-C466 (3) 4.20 .75

ITU Emblem AP93

1965, Oct. 25 Photo. *Perf. 12*
C467 AP93 80c Prus bl, lt bl & red .20 .20

Cent. of the ITU.

Cattleya Truanae — AP94

Cent. of the Telegraph in Colombia — AP95

1965, Oct. 3 Litho. *Perf. 13½x14*
C468 AP94 20c yellow & multi .20 .20

Fifth Philatelic Exhibition.

1965, Nov. 1 *Perf. 13½x14, 14x13½*

#C469, Pres. Manuel Murillo Toro statue, telegraph and orbits. #C470, Telegraph and satellites over South America, horiz.

C469 AP95 60c multicolored .20 .20
C470 AP95 60c multicolored .20 .20

Junkers F-13 Seaplane, 1920 AP96

History of Colombian Aviation: 10c, Dornier Wal, 1924. 20c, Dornier Mercur, 1926. 50c, Trimotor Ford, 1932. 60c, De Havilland biplane, 1930. 1p, Douglas DC-4, 1947. 1.40p, Douglas DC-3, 1944. 2.80p, Superconstellation 1049, 1951. 3p, Boeing 720B jet, 1961.

Perf. 14x13½

1965-66 Photo. Unwmk.
C471 AP96 5c multicolored .20 .20
C472 AP96 10c multicolored .20 .20
C473 AP96 20c multicolored .20 .20
C474 AP96 50c multicolored .20 .20
C475 AP96 60c multicolored .30 .20
C476 AP96 1p multicolored .60 .20
C477 AP96 1.40p multicolored .80 .20
C478 AP96 2.80p multicolored 1.50 .60
C479 AP96 3p multicolored 2.00 .85
Nos. C471-C479 (9) 6.00 2.85
Nos. C471-C479,CE4 (10) 6.35 3.05

Issued: 5c, 60c, 3p, 12/13/65; 10c, 1p, 1.40p, 7/15/66; 20c, 50c, 2.80p, 12/14/66.

Automobile Club Emblem and Car on Road AP97

1966, Feb. 16 Litho. *Perf. 14x13½*
C480 AP97 20c multicolored .20 .20

25th anniv. (in 1965) of the Automobile Club of Colombia.

Fish Type

Fish: 2p, Flying fish. 2.80p, Queen angelfish. 20p, King mackerel.

1966, Aug. 25 Photo. *Perf. 12½x13*
C481 A323 2p multicolored .50 .20
C482 A323 2.80p multicolored 1.10 .90
C483 A323 20p multicolored 14.00 11.00
Nos. C481-C483 (3) 15.60 12.10

Coat of Arms Type

1966, Oct. 11 Litho. *Perf. 14x13½*
C484 A324 1p ultra & multi .25 .20
C485 A324 1.40p red & multi .20 .20

Portrait Type

80c, Father Felix Restrepo Mejia, S.J. (1887-1965), theologian, scholar. 1.70p, José Joaquin Casas (1866-1951), educator, diplomat.

Perf. 13½x14

1967, Jan. 18 Litho. Unwmk.
C486 A325 80c dk bl & bis .20 .20
C487 A325 1.70p blk & bis .25 .20

Declaration of Bogota Type

1967, Feb. 2 Litho. *Perf. 14x13½*
C488 A326 3p multicolored .35 .20

See note after No. 767.

Orchid Type

Orchids: 1p, Cattleya dowiana aurea, vert. 1.20p, Masdevallia coccinea, vert. 5p, Catasetum macrocarpum and bee.

1967, May 23 Litho. *Perf. 14*

C489	A327	1p	multicolored	1.60	.30
C490	A327	1.20p	multicolored	1.10	.25
C491	A327	5p	multicolored	7.50	.90
a.			Souv. sheet of 3, #C489-C491	18.00	18.00
			Nos. C489-C491 (3)	10.20	1.45

Lions Type

1967, July 12 Litho. *Perf. 13½x14*

C492	A328	25c	multicolored	.20	.20

"First Caesarean Section" by Grau AP98

Perf. 14x13½

1967, Sept. 7 Litho. Unwmk.

C493	AP98	80c	multicolored	.20	.20

Issued to publicize the 6th Congress of Colombian Surgeons, Bogota, Sept. 25.

SENA Type

Lithographed and Embossed

1967, Sept. 20 *Perf. 13½x14*

C494	A329	2p	gold, ver & blk	.50	.20

Pre-Columbian Art Type

Designs: 30c, Bird pectoral. 5p Ornamental pectoral. 20p, Pitcher.

1967, Oct. 13 Photo. *Perf. 13½x14*

C495	A330	30c	ver, gold & brn	.20	.20
C496	A330	5p	red, gold & brn	1.75	.30
a.			Souvenir sheet of 2	2.00	1.60
C497	A330	20p	vio, gold & brn	8.25	8.25
			Nos. C495-C497 (3)	10.20	8.75

No. C496a also commemorates the 6th Natl. Phil. Exhib. No. C496a contains 2 imperf. stamps in changed colors similar to Nos. C495-C496 (30c has green background and 5p maroon background).

Telecommunications Type

Designs: 50c, Signal lights. 1p, Early Bird satellite, Southern Cross and radar.

Perf. 13½x14

1968, May 14 Litho. Unwmk.

C498	A331	50c	blk, ver & emer	.20	.20
C499	A331	1p	ultra, yel & gray	.20	.20

Eucharist Type

1968, June 6 Litho. *Perf. 13½x14*

C500	A332	80c	rose lil, red, yel & blk	.20	.20
C501	A332	3p	bl, red, yel & blk	.30	.20

Eucharistic Congress Type

Designs: 80c, The Last Supper, by Gregorio Vasquez, horiz. 1p, St. Francis Xavier Preaching, by Gregorio Vasquez. 2p, The Dream of the Prophet Elias, by Gregorio Vasquez. 3p, Monstrance, c. 1700. 20p, Pope Paul VI, painting by Roman Franciscan nuns.

1968, Aug. 13 Photo. *Perf. 13*

C502	A333	80c	multicolored	.20	.20
C503	A333	1p	multicolored	.25	.20
C504	A333	2p	multicolored	.35	.20
C505	A333	3p	lil & multi	.65	.20
C506	A333	20p	gold & multi	4.00	2.00
			Nos. C502-C506 (5)	5.45	2.80

Shrine of the Eucharist, Bogotá AP99

1.20p, Pope Paul VI giving blessing and Papal arms. 1.80p, Cathedral of Bogotá.

Perf. 14x13½, 13½x14

1968, Aug. 22 Litho.

C507	AP99	80c	multi	.20	.20
C508	AP99	1.20p	multi, vert.	.20	.20
C509	AP99	1.80p	multi, vert.	.30	.20
			Nos. C507-C509 (3)	.70	.60

Visit of Pope Paul VI to Colombia.

Computer Symbols — AP100

1968, Oct. 29 Litho. *Perf. 13½x14*

C510	AP100	30c	buff, car & grn	.30	.20

Cent. of the Natl. University and the 1st Data Processing Cong. in 1967 at the University.

Agriculture Institute Type

1968, Mar. 5 Litho. *Perf. 13½x14*

C511	A337	1p	gray & multi	.20	.20

Microscope and Pen — AP101

1969, Mar. 24 Litho. *Perf. 14*

C512	AP101	5p	blk, yel, ver & pur	2.40	.35

20th anniv. (in 1968) of the University of the Andes.

Alexander von Humboldt and Andes AP102

1969, May 3 Litho. *Perf. 14x13½*

C513	AP102	1p	grn & brn	.65	.35

Alexander von Humboldt (1769-1859), German naturalist and traveler.

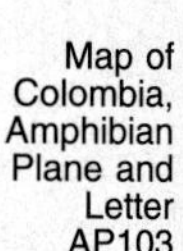

Map of Colombia, Amphibian Plane and Letter AP103

Design: 1.50p, No. C516b, Globe, letter, and jet of Avianca airlines.

1969, June 18 Litho. *Perf. 14x13½*

C514	AP103	1p	multi	.45	.20
C515	AP103	1.50p	multi	.65	.25

Souvenir Sheet

Imperf

C516		Sheet of 2	7.50	7.50
a.	AP103	5p green & multi	1.00	1.00
b.	AP103	5p violet & multi	1.00	1.00

50th anniv. of the 1st air post flight in Colombia. No. C516 also for 8th Natl. Philatelic Exhibition, EXFILBA 69, Barranquilla, June 18-22. No. C516 contains 2 stamps in the designs of the 1p and 1.50p.

Independence Type

2.30p, Simon Bolivar, José Antonio Anzoategui, Francisco de Paula Santander and victorious army entering Bogotá, 9/18/1819; painting by Ignacio Castillo Cervantes.

1969, July 24 Litho. *Perf. 13½x14*

C517	A338	2.30p	gold & multi	1.00	.35

Social Security Emblem — AP104

Neurosurgeons' Congress Emblem — AP105

1969, Oct. 29 Litho. *Perf. 13½x14*

C518	AP104	20c	emer & blk	.25	.20

20th anniv. of the Colombian Institute of Social Security.

1969, Oct. 29

C519	AP105	70c	vio, red & yel	.50	.30

Issued to publicize the 13th Congress of Latin-American Neurosurgeons, Bogotá.

Junkers F-13 AP106

#C521, C522b, Globe with airlines from Bogota & Boeing jet. #C522a, like #C520.

1969, Nov. 28 Litho. *Perf. 14x13½*

C520	AP106	2p	grn & multi	.75	.25
C521	AP106	3.50p	ultra & multi	1.40	.50

Souvenir Sheet

Imperf

C522		Sheet of 2	7.50	7.50
a.	AP106	3.50p lt grn & multi	.75	.75
b.	AP106	5p ultra & multi	1.00	1.00

50th anniv. of AVIANCA; No. C522 also publicizes the 1st Interamerican Phil. Exhib., Bogota, Nov. 28-Dec. 7.

No. C522 contains 2 imperf. stamps.

Child Mailing Letter — AP107

Christmas: 1.50p, Praying child and gifts.

1969, Dec. 16 Litho. *Perf. 13½x14*

C523	AP107	60c	ocher & multi	.80	.20
C524	AP107	1p	multicolored	.85	.25
C525	AP107	1.50p	multicolored	1.10	.25
			Nos. C523-C525 (3)	2.75	.70

Radar Station and Pre-Columbian Head — AP108

1970, Mar. 25 Litho. *Perf. 14x13½*

C526	AP108	1p	dl grn, blk & brick red	.30	.20

Issued to publicize the opening of the communications satellite earth station at Chocontá in Cundinamarca Province.

Emblem of Colombian Youth Sports Institute — AP109

Art Exhibition Emblem — AP110

2.30p, Games' emblem (dove and 3 rings).

1970, Apr. 6 Litho. *Perf. 13½x14*

C527	AP109	1.50p	dk ol grn, yel & blk	.30	.20
C528	AP109	2.30p	red & multi	.40	.20

9th Natl. Youth Games, Ibague, July 10-20.

1970, Apr. 30 Litho. *Perf. 13½x14*

C529	AP110	30c	multicolored	.20	.20

2nd Biennial Art Exhib., Medellin, 6/1-7/14.

Eduardo Santos, Rural and Urban Buildings AP111

1970, June 18 Litho. *Perf. 14x13½*

C530	AP111	1p	grn, yel & blk	.20	.20

Issued to commemorate the founding (in 1939) of the Territorial Credit Institute.

UN Emblem, Scales and Dove — AP112

EXFILCA Emblem — AP113

1970, June 26 *Perf. 13½x14*

C531	AP112	1.50p	dk bl, lt bl & yel	.20	.20

25th anniversary of United Nations.

1970, Nov. Litho. *Perf. 13½x14*

C532	AP113	10p	bl, gold & blk	3.50	.25

EXFILCA 70, 2nd Interamerican Philatelic Exhib., Caracas, Venezuela, Nov. 27-Dec. 6.

Mother Juana Ruperta in Napanga Costume and Music by Efrain Orozco — AP114

Designs: 1p, Dancers from Eastern Plains and music by Alejandro Wills. No. C535, Guabina man, woman and folk song. No. C536, Bambuco man and woman, and music. No. C537, Man and woman dancing the Cumbia, and music.

1970-71 Litho. *Perf. 13½x14*

C533 AP114 60c dp lil rose & multi .50 .20
C534 AP114 1p ultra & multi .30 .20
C535 AP114 1.30p bl & multi .40 .20
C536 AP114 1.30p emer & multi ('71) .40 .20
C537 AP114 1.30p lil & multi ('71) .30 .20
Nos. C533-C537 (5) 1.90 1.00

Athlete and Games Emblem — AP115

Design: 2p, Games emblem.

1971, Mar. 11

C542 AP115 1.50p multicolored .90 .90
C543 AP115 2p blk, org & grn .80 .55

6th Pan-American Games, Cali, 7/30-8/13.

Gilberto Alzate Avendano AP116

1971, Apr. 29 Litho. *Perf. 14x13½*

C544 AP116 1p bl & multi .40 .25

Avendano (1910-60), journalist, popular leader.

Commemorative Medal — AP117

Lithographed and Embossed

1971, June 21 *Perf. 14x13½*

C545 AP117 1p slate grn & gold .50 .30

Centenary (in 1970) of the Bank of Bogota.

Olympic Center — AP118

Soccer — AP119

Designs (Games Emblem and): #C546-C546C, Olympic Center. #547, Soccer. #C548, Wrestling. #C549, Bicycling. #C550, Volleyball. #C551, Diving (women). #C552, Fencing. #C553, Sailing. #C554, Equestrian. #C555, Jumping. #C556, Rowing. #C557, Cali emblem. #C558, Basketball (women). #C559, Stadium. #C560, Baseball. #C561, Hockey. #C562, Weight lifting. #C563, Medals. #C564, Boxing. #C565, Gymnastics (women). #C566, Sharpshooting.

1971, July 16 Litho. *Perf. 13½x14*

Multicolored and Emblem Color:

C546 AP118 1.30p yellow 1.25 .30
C546A AP118 1.30p green 1.25 .30
C546B AP118 1.30p blue 1.25 .30
C546C AP118 1.30p carmine 1.25 .30
C547 AP119 1.30p emerald 1.25 .30
C548 AP119 1.30p lilac 1.25 .30
C549 AP119 1.30p blue 1.25 .30
C550 AP119 1.30p carmine 1.25 .30
C551 AP119 1.30p blue 1.25 .30
C552 AP119 1.30p carmine 1.25 .30
C553 AP119 1.30p blue 1.25 .30
C554 AP119 1.30p gray 1.25 .30
C555 AP119 1.30p green 1.25 .30
C556 AP119 1.30p blue 1.25 .30
C557 AP118 1.30p orange 1.25 .30
C558 AP119 1.30p carmine 1.25 .30
C559 AP118 1.30p light blue 1.25 .30
C560 AP119 1.30p plum 1.25 .30
C561 AP119 1.30p yel grn 1.25 .30
C562 AP119 1.30p pink 1.25 .30
C563 AP118 1.30p deep org 1.25 .30
C564 AP119 1.30p plum 1.25 .30
C565 AP119 1.30p lilac rose 1.25 .30
C566 AP119 1.30p green 1.25 .30
a. Sheet of 25, #C546-C566 32.50 7.00

6th Pan American Athletic Games, Cali. No. C546B appears twice in sheet.

Battle of Carabobo, by Martin Tovar y Tovar — AP120

1971, Nov. 25 Litho. *Perf. 13½x14*

C567 AP120 1.50p multicolored 1.00 .20

Sesquicentennial of the Battle of Carabobo.

St. Theresa Type Overprinted "AEREO"

1972 Litho. *Perf. 13½x14*

C568 A343 2p multicolored .30 .20

See note after No. 793.

Vendor — AP121

Designs: 50c, Woman wearing shawl, and woven shawl. 3p, Fruit vendor (puppet).

1972, Apr. 11 Litho. *Perf. 13½x14*

C569 AP121 50c multicolored .35 .20
C570 AP121 1p multicolored .35 .20
C571 AP121 3p multicolored .50 .25
Nos. C569-C571 (3) 1.20 .65

Colombian artisans.

Mormodes Rolfeanum AP122

1972, Apr. 20 *Perf. 14x13½*

C572 AP122 1.30p multicolored .45 .20

7th World Orchidology Congress, Medellin.

Congo Grande Dancer — AP123

Laureano Gomez, by Ridriguez Cubillos — AP124

1972, June 21 Litho. *Perf. 13½x14*

C573 AP123 1.30p multicolored .50 .20

International Carnival of Barranquilla.

No. C453 Surcharged in Brown

1972, Oct. 5 Litho. *Perf. 14x13½*

C574 AP86 1.30p on 1.90p .55 .20

1972 *Perf. 13½x14*

1.30p (#C576), Guillermo Leòn Valencia Muñoz.

C575 AP124 1.30p multicolored .20 .20
C576 AP124 1.30p multicolored .20 .20

Laureano Gomez (1898-1966), Guillermo Leon Valencia Munoz (1909-71), Presidents of Colombia.

Issued: #C575, 10/17; #C576, 11/28.

Benito Juarez — AP125

Rebecca Fountain AP126

1972, Dec. 12 *Perf. 13½x14*

C577 AP125 1.50p multicolored .20 .20

Benito Juarez (1806-1872), revolutionary leader and president of Mexico.

1972, Dec. 19 Litho.

C578 AP126 80c multicolored .45 .45
C579 AP126 1p multicolored .40 .20

"Bucaramanga" — AP127

1972, Dec. 22 *Perf. 14x13½*

C580 AP127 5p multicolored .85 .20

Founding of Bucaramanga, 350th anniv.

Xavier University AP128

1973, May 8 Litho. *Perf. 14x13½*

C581 AP128 1.30p lt grn & sep .25 .20
C582 AP128 1.50p lt bl & sep .25 .20

350th anniversary of the founding of Xavier University in Bogotá.

Ceramic Type

Excavated Ceramic Artifacts: 1p, Winged urn, Tairona. 1.30p, Woman and child, Sinu. 1.70p, Two-headed figure, Quimbaya. 3.50p, Man, Tumaco.

1973 Litho. *Perf. 13½x14*

C583 A358 1p multicolored 1.00 1.00
C584 A358 1.30p multicolored .50 .20
C585 A358 1.70p multicolored .55 .25
C586 A358 3.50p multicolored 1.10 .30
Nos. C583-C586 (4) 3.15 1.75

Issue dates: 1p, Oct. 11; others, June 15.

Battle of Maracaibo, by Manuel F. Rincon AP129

1973, July 24 Litho. *Perf. 14x13½*

C587 AP129 10p bl & multi 2.00 .20

Battle of Maracaibo, sesquicentennial.

Bank Emblem AP130

1973, Oct. 1 Litho. *Perf. 14x13½*

C588 AP130 2p multicolored .20 .20

50th anniv. of the Bank of the Republic.

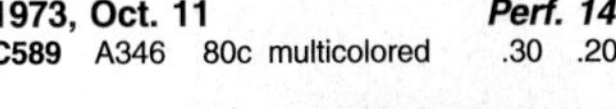

No. 801 Overprinted "AEREO"

1973, Oct. 11 *Perf. 14*

C589 A346 80c multicolored .30 .20

Pres. Pedro Nel Ospina, by Coroleano Leudo — AP131

Arms of Toro — AP132

1973, Nov. 9 *Perf. 13½x14*
C590 AP131 1.50p multicolored .25 .20

50th anniversary of the Ministry of Communications founded under Pres. Ospina.

1973, Dec. 1
C591 AP132 1p multicolored .20 .20

Founding of Toro, Valle del Cauca, 4th cent.

Bolivar, Battle of Bombona AP133

1973, Dec. 7 Litho. *Perf. 14x13½*
C592 AP133 1.30p multicolored .20 .20

Sesquicentennial (in 1972) of the Battle of Bombona.

Nicolaus Copernicus AP134

Andes, Map of South America AP135

1974, Feb. 19 Litho. *Perf. 13½x14*
C593 AP134 2.50p multicolored .50 .20

500th anniversary of the birth of Nicolaus Copernicus (1473-1543), Polish astronomer.

1974, May 11 Litho. *Perf. 14*
C594 AP135 2p multicolored .35 .20

Meeting of Communications Ministers of Members of the Andean Group, Cali, May 7-11, 1974.

Television Set AP136

1974, July 16 Litho. *Perf. 14x13½*
C595 AP136 1.30p org, blk & brn .20 .20

20th anniversary of Colombian television and 10th anniversary of INRAVISION, the National Institute of Radio and Television.

Championship Emblem — AP137

1974, Aug. 5 Litho. *Perf. 14x13½*
C596 AP137 4.50p multicolored .30 .20

2nd World Swimming Championships, Cali.

Condor — AP138

1974, Aug. 28 *Perf. 14*
C597 AP138 1.50p multicolored .25 .20

Bank of Colombia centenary.

UPU Envelope AP139

1974, Sept. 9 Litho. *Perf. 14*
C598 AP139 20p multicolored 2.50 .30

Centenary of Universal Postal Union.

Symbol of Flight — AP140

1974, Sept. *Perf. 12x12½*
C599 AP140 20c olive .20 .20

Gen. José Maria Cordoba — AP141

White-tailed Trogon, Letter — AP142

1974, Oct. 14 Litho. *Perf. 13½x14*
C609 AP141 1.30p multicolored .20 .20

Sesquicentennial of the Battles of Junin and Ayacucho.

Insurance Type

Design: 3p, Abstract pattern.

1974, Oct. 24 Litho. *Perf. 13½x14*
C610 A365 3p multicolored .30 .20

Perf. 13½x14, 14x13½

1974, Nov. 14

Designs (UPU Letter and): 1.30p, Keelbilled Toucan, horiz. 2p, Peruvian cock-of-the-rock, horiz. 2.50p, Scarlet macaw.

C611 AP142 1p multicolored .20 .20
C612 AP142 1.30p multicolored .20 .20
C613 AP142 2p multicolored .30 .20
C614 AP142 2.50p multicolored .30 .20
Nos. C611-C614 (4) 1.00 .80

Centenary of Universal Postal Union.

For surcharge see No. C656.

Forest No. 1, by Roman Roncancio — AP143

Boy with Thorn in Finger, by Gregorio Vazquez AP144

Paintings: 3p, Women Fruit Vendors, by Miguel Diaz Vargas (1886-1956). 5p, Annunciation, Santafereña School, 17th-18th cent.

Perf. 13½x14, 14x13½

1975, Mar. 12 **Litho.**
C615 AP143 2p multicolored .60 .20
C616 AP144 3p multicolored .40 .20
C617 AP144 4p multicolored .50 .20
C618 AP144 5p multicolored 1.00 .25
Nos. C615-C618 (4) 2.50 .85

Modern and Colonial Colombian paintings.

Trees and Lake AP145

Design: 6p, Victoria regia, Amazon River.

1975, Mar. 12 *Perf. 14x13½*
C619 AP145 1p yellow & multi .20 .20
C620 AP145 6p yellow & multi .60 .20

Nature conservation of trees and Amazon Region.

Gold Treasure Type

Designs: 2p, Nose pendant. 10p, Alligator-shaped staff ornament.

1975, Apr. 11 Litho. *Perf. 14x13½*
C621 A368 2p grn, gold & brn .90 .20
C622 A368 10p multicolored 4.50 .60

El Rodadero, Santa Maria AP146

1975, July 26 Litho. *Perf. 14x13½*
C623 AP146 2p multicolored .20 .20

400th anniversary of Santa Maria City.

AP147

AP148

1975, Aug. 31 Litho. *Perf. 13½x14*
C624 AP147 4p multicolored .20 .20

Intl. Women's Year 1975. Maria de Jesus Paramo de Collazos founded 1st normal school for women in Bucaramanga in 1875.

1976, Mar. 12 Litho. *Perf. 13½x14*
C625 AP148 5p "Sugar Cane" .85 .30

4th Congress of Latin-American and Caribbean sugar-exporting countries, Cali, 3/8-12.

View of Bogota — AP149

1976, July 2 Litho. *Perf. 12*
C626 AP149 10p shown 1.25 .90
C627 AP149 10p Barranquilla 1.25 .90
C628 AP149 10p Cali 1.25 .90
C629 AP149 10p Medellin 1.25 .90
a. Block of 4, #C626-C629 5.00 4.00

Habitat, UN Conf. on Human Settlements, Vancouver, Canada, May 31-June 11.

University Emblem and "90" — AP150

1976, Aug. 6 Litho. *Perf. 13½x14*
C630 AP150 5p lt blue & multi .50 .20

Univ. of Colombia day school, 90th anniv.

Miguel Samper — AP151

Telephone, 1895 — AP152

1976, Oct. 29 Litho. *Perf. 13½x14*
C631 AP151 2p multicolored .20 .20

Samper (1825-99), economist and writer.

1976, Nov. 2
C632 AP152 3p multicolored .20 .20

Centenary of first telephone call by Alexander Graham Bell, Mar. 10, 1876.

747 Jumbo Jet AP153

1976, Dec. 3 Litho. *Perf. 12*
C633 AP153 2p multicolored .20 .20

Inauguration of 747 jumbo jet service by Avianca.
For surcharge see No. C636.

Convent, Church and Plaza de San Francisco — AP154

1976, Dec. 29 Litho. *Perf. 14*
C634 AP154 6p multicolored .50 .20

150th anniv. of the Congress of Panama.

Souvenir Sheet

Bank of the Republic Emblem — AP155

1977, June 6 Litho. *Perf. 14*
C635 AP155 25p multicolored 11.00 11.00

Opening of Philatelic Museum of Medellin under auspices of Banco de la Republica.

No. C633 Surcharged in Light Brown

1977, June Litho. *Perf. 12*
C636 AP153 3p on 2p multi .20 .20

Coffee AP156

Coffee Grower, Pack Mule AP157

1977-78 Litho. *Perf. 12½*
C640 AP156 3p multi .20 .20
C641 AP156 3.50p multi ('78) .20 .20

Colombian coffee.

1977, Aug. 9 Litho. *Perf. 13½x14*
C642 AP157 10p multicolored .50 .20

National Federation of Coffee Growers, 50th anniversary.

Beethoven and 9th Symphony AP158

Games' Emblem AP159

1977, Aug. 17
C643 AP158 8p multicolored .50 .20

Sesquicentennial of the death of Ludwig van Beethoven (1770-1827).

Bird Type

Tropical Birds and Plants: No. C644, Woodpecker and Meriania. C645, Purple gallinule and water lilies. No. C646, Xipholaena punicea and Cochlospermum orinocense. No. C647, Crowned flycatcher and Jacaranda copaia.

1977, Sept. 6 Litho. *Perf. 14*
C644 A380 5p multicolored .70 .20
C645 A380 5p multicolored .70 .20
C646 A380 10p multicolored .90 .20
C647 A380 10p multicolored .90 .20
Nos. C644-C647 (4) 3.20 .80

1977, Sept. 9 *Perf. 12x12½*
C648 AP159 6p multicolored .25 .20

13th Central American and Caribbean Games, Medellin, 1978.

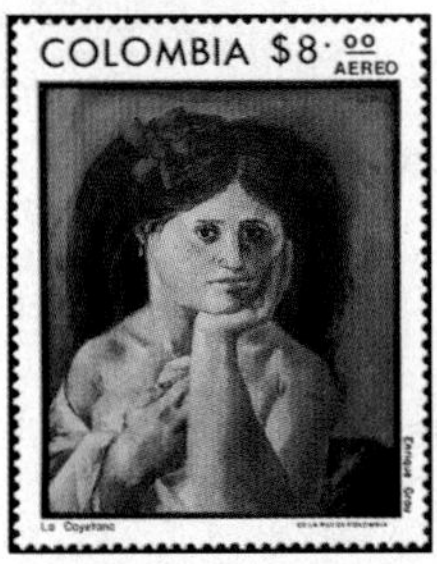
La Cayetana, by Enrique Grau AP160

#C650, Water Nymphs, by Beatriz Gonzalez.

1977, Sept. 13 *Perf. 14x13½*
C649 AP160 8p multicolored .45 .20
C650 AP160 8p multicolored .45 .20

Women's suffrage, 20th anniversary.

Judge Francisco Antonio Moreno, by Joaquin Gutierrez AP161

Design: 25p, Viceroy Manuel de Guirior.

1977, Sept. 13 *Perf. 12*
C651 AP161 20p multicolored 1.25 .75
C652 AP161 25p multicolored 1.75 1.10

Bicentenary of National Library.

Federico Lleras Acosta — AP162

Cauca University Arms — AP163

1977, Sept. 27 Litho. *Perf. 14*
C653 AP162 5p multicolored .25 .20

Dr. Federico Lleras Acosta, veterinarian and bacteriologist; birth centenary.

1977, Oct. 14
C654 AP163 5p multicolored .30 .20

Sesquicentennial of the University of Cauca.

CUDECOM Building, Bogota AP164

1977, Oct. 14
C655 AP164 1.50p multicolored .20 .20

Colombian Society of Engineers, 90th anniv.

No. C612 Surcharged with New Value and Bars in Brown

1977, Dec. 3 Litho. *Perf. 14x13½*
C656 AP142 2p on 1.30p multi .30 .20

Lost City, Tayrona Culture AP165

Creator of Energy, by Arenas Betancourt AP166

1978, Apr. 18 Litho. *Perf. 12½*
C657 AP165 3.50p multicolored .20 .20

1978, Apr. 25 *Perf. 12*
C658 AP166 4p blue & multi .25 .20

Sesquicentennial of Antioquia University Law School.

Column of the Slaves — AP167

Statue of Catalina, Cartagena AP168

1978, May 9
C659 AP167 2.50p multicolored .25 .20

Sesquicentennial of Ocana Convention (meeting of various political groups).

1978, May 30 Litho. *Perf. 12*
C660 AP168 4p blk & lt bl .25 .20

Sesquicentennial of University of Cartagena.

Gold Pendant, Tolima — AP169

1978, July 11 Litho. *Perf. 12x12½*
C661 AP169 3.50p multicolored .20 .20

Apotheosis of Spanish Language, by Luis Alberto Acuña — AP170

1978, Aug. 9 *Perf. 14*
C662 AP170 Strip of 3 4.75 4.75
a.-c. 11p, any single 1.10 1.10

Millennium of Spanish language.

Presidential Guard AP171

Figure, Muisca Culture AP172

1978, Aug. 16 *Perf. 13½x14*

C663 AP171 9p multicolored .45 .45

Presidential Guard Battalion, 50th anniv.

1978, Sept. 12 Litho. *Perf. 12½*

C664 AP172 3.50p multicolored .20 .20

Apse of Carmelite Church — AP173

1978, Oct. 12 *Perf. 13*

C665 AP173 30p multicolored 2.50 .40

Souvenir Sheet

Perf. 13½x14

C666 AP173 50p multicolored 3.25 3.25

ESPAMER '78 Philatelic Exhibition, Bogota, Oct. 12-21.

Owl, Gold Ornament, Calima AP174

Virgin and Child, by Gregorio Vasquez AP175

#C669, Gold frog, Quimbaya culture. #C670, Gold nose pendant, Tairona, horiz.

1978-80 Litho. *Perf. 12½*

C667 AP174 3.50p multi .20 .20
C668 AP174 4p multi ('79) .20 .20
C669 AP174 4p multi ('79) .20 .20
C670 AP174 5p multi ('80) .20 .20
Nos. C667-C670 (4) .80 .80

1978, Nov. 28 *Perf. 13½x14*

C671 AP175 2.50p multicolored .20 .20

Christmas 1978.

Bull Ring, Cathedral, Manizales AP176

1979, Jan. 6 Litho. *Perf. 14*

C672 AP176 7p multicolored .60 .20

Manizales Fair.

Children Playing Hopscotch, and IYC Emblem — AP177

#C674, Child at blackboard and UNESCO emblem. #C675, The Paper Collector, by Omar Gordillo, and UN emblem.

1979, July 19 *Perf. 13½x14, 14x13½*

C673 AP177 8p multi .30 .30
C674 AP177 12p multi, horiz. .45 .45
C675 AP177 12p multi .45 .45
Nos. C673-C675 (3) 1.20 1.20

International Year of the Child.

Rio Prado Hydroelectric Station — AP178

1979, Aug. 24 *Perf. 13½x14*

C676 AP178 5p multicolored .50 .20

Tomb, 6th Century — AP179

1979, Sept. 25 Litho. *Perf. 14*

C677 AP179 8p multicolored .55 .35

San Augustin Archaeological Park.

Gonzalo Jimenez de Quesada, by C. Leudo AP180

1979, Oct. 11 *Perf. 12*

C678 AP180 20p multicolored 1.50 .50

Gonzalo Jimenez de Quesada (1500-1579), Spanish conquistador.

Hill, Penny Black, Colombia No. 1 — AP181

1979, Oct. 23 *Perf. 13½x14*

C679 AP181 15p multicolored .60 .20

Sir Rowland Hill (1795-1879), originator of penny postage.

Amazon Region — AP182

Tourism: 14p, San Fernando Fortress.

1979 Litho. *Perf. 13½x14*

C680 AP182 7p multicolored .35 .20
C681 AP182 14p multicolored .90 .60

Issue dates: 7p, Nov. 16; 14p, Nov. 9. See Nos. C717-C719.

Nativity — AP183

Creche Sculptures: No. C682, Three Kings and soldiers. No. C684, Shepherds.

1979, Nov. 30 *Perf. 12*

C682 AP183 3p multicolored .35 .35
C683 AP183 3p multicolored .35 .35
C684 AP183 3p multicolored .35 .35
a. Strip of 3, #C682-C684 1.15 1.15

Christmas 1979.

AP184

AP185

Magdalena Bridge, Avianca emblem.

1979, Dec. 5 *Perf. 14*

C685 AP184 15p multicolored .60 .20

Barranquilla, 350th anniversary; Avianca National Airline, 60th anniversary.

1980, Feb. 15 *Perf. 13½x14*

Boy Playing Flute, by Judith Leyster.

C686 AP185 6p multicolored .45 .20

2nd Intl. Music Competition, Ibague, Dec. 1979.

Gen. Antonio José de Sucre, 150th Death Anniversary AP186

1980, Feb. 15 Litho. *Perf. 12½x12*

C687 AP186 12p multicolored .45 .20

The Watchman, by Edgar Negret AP187

1980, Feb. 26 *Perf. 12x12½*

C688 AP187 25p multicolored 1.60 .80

Virgin Mary, by Real del Sarte, 1929 AP188

1980, May 23 Litho. *Perf. 14x13½*

C689 AP188 12p multicolored .30 .20

Apparition of the Virgin Mary to Sister Catalina Labouri Gontard, 150th anniv.

San Gil Produce Market, by Luis Roncancio — AP189

1980, May 27 *Perf. 13½x14*

C690 AP189 12p multicolored .50 .25

Pres. Enrique Olaya Herrera, by Miguel Diaz Vargas — AP190

1980, Oct. 28 Litho. *Perf. 12*

C691 AP190 20p multicolored 1.00 .40

Enrique Olaya Herrera (1880-1936), president, 1930-1934.

The Boy Fishing in a Bucket AP191

Christmas (Christmas Stories by Rafael Pombo): #C693, The Frog and the Mouse. #C694, The Seven Lives of the Cat.

1980, Nov. 21 Litho. *Perf. 14½*

C692 AP191 4p multicolored .20 .20
C693 AP191 4p multicolored .20 .20
C694 AP191 4p multicolored .20 .20
Nos. C692-C694 (3) .60 .60

28th World Golf Cup, Cajica — AP192

1980, Dec. 9 Litho. *Perf. 13½x14*
C695 AP192 30p multicolored 1.40 .40

Bolivar Type

Simon Bolivar Death Sesquicentennial: 6p, Portrait, last words to Colombia, vert.

1980, Dec. 17 *Perf. 12*
C696 A400 6p multicolored .60 .45

St. Peter Claver Holding Cross AP193

1981, Jan. 13 *Perf. 14½*
C697 AP193 15p multicolored .50 .20

St. Peter Claver (1580-1654), helped American Indians.

Sculptured Bird, San Augustin AP194

Archaeological Finds: No. C699, Funeral chamber, Tierradentro. No. C700, Chamber hallway, Tierradentro. No. C701, Statue of man, San Augustin.

1981, May 12 Litho. *Perf. 14*
C698 AP194 7p multicolored 1.00 .20
C699 AP194 7p multicolored 1.00 .20
C700 AP194 7p multicolored 1.00 .20
C701 AP194 7p multicolored 1.00 .20
a. Block of 4, #C698-C701 5.00 5.00

See Nos. C707-C710D.

Child with Hobby Horse, by Fernando Botero — AP195

4th Biennial Arts show, Medellin: 20p, Square Abstract, by Omar Rayo. 25p, Flowers, by Alejandro Obregon.

1981, May 15 *Perf. 12*
C702 AP195 20p multicolored .85 .20
C703 AP195 25p multicolored 1.00 .30
C704 AP195 50p multicolored 1.75 .75
Nos. C702-C704 (3) 3.60 1.25

8th South American Swimming Championships, Medellin — AP196

1981, June 5
C705 AP196 15p multicolored .50 .25

Santamaria Bull Ring, 50th Anniv. — AP197

1981, June 9 Litho. *Perf. 12*
C706 AP197 30p multicolored 2.00 1.25

Quimbaya Culture — AP197a

1981, Sept. 23 Litho. *Perf. 14*
Yellow Background
C707 9p Man .45 .20
C708 9p Seated man .45 .20
C709 9p Seal, print .45 .20
C710 9p Jug .45 .20
e. AP197a Block of 4, #C707-C710 1.80 .75

Calima Culture — AP197b

1981, Dec. 17
White Background
C710A 9p Anthropomorphic container .45 .20
C710B 9p Jar .45 .20
C710C 9p Anthropomorphic jar .45 .20
C710D 9p Urn .45 .20
f. AP197b Block of 4, #C710A-C710D 1.80 .75

Fruit AP198

1981, Nov. 3 Litho. *Perf. 14*
C711 Block of 6 22.50 20.00
a.-f. AP198 25p, any single 3.00 .80

Revolt of the Comuneros, 200th Anniv. — AP199

1981, Nov. 21 Litho. *Perf. 12*
C712 AP199 20p multicolored .55 .30

Jose Manuel Restrepo, Historian, 1775?-1860? AP200

Andres Bello, 1780?-1865 AP201

1981, Dec. 1 Litho. *Perf. 12*
C713 AP200 35p multicolored 1.00 .35

1981, Dec. 11 Litho. *Perf. 12*
C714 AP201 18p multicolored .50 .20

Colombia's Admission to UPU, 100th Anniv. AP202

30p, #103. 50p, Hemispheres, #104-108.

1981 Litho. *Perf. 12*
C715 AP202 30p multicolored .70 .35

Size: 100x70mm
Imperf
C716 AP202 50p multicolored 1.40 1.25

Issued: #C715, Dec. 18. #C716, Dec. 28.

Tourism Type of 1979

1982 Litho. *Perf. 12*
C717 AP182 20p Solano Bay .50 .20
C718 AP182 20p Tota Lake, Boyaca .50 .20
C719 AP182 20p Corrales, Boyaca .50 .20
Nos. C717-C719 (3) 1.50 .60

Issued: #C717, 6/2; others, 6/16.

1982 World Cup — AP202a

Players and team emblems: a, "America." b, "A. B." c, "Cali." d, "C." e, "C/D." f, "Junior F.B.C." g, "D/M." h, Stadium. i, "M." j, "Club Atletico Nacional." k, "D/P." l, "Quindio." m, "Santa Fe." n, "T." o, "Santa Marta."

1982, June 21 *Perf. 14*
C720 Sheet of 15 9.00 5.00
a.-o. AP202a 9p, any single .60 .20

Bogota Gun Club Centenary AP202b

1982, July 16 *Perf. 12*
C721 AP202b 20p multicolored .50 .20

Gold Crocodile Figure, Tairona Culture AP202c

Tairona Culture Exhibit, Gold Museum: Various figures. Nos. C723-C727 vert.

1982, July 28
Gold, Black and:
C722 AP202c 25p light brown 1.50 .40
C723 AP202c 25p bright pink 1.50 .40
C724 AP202c 25p green 1.50 .40
C725 AP202c 25p dark blue 1.50 .40
C726 AP202c 25p violet 1.50 .40
C727 AP202c 25p red 1.50 .40
Nos. C722-C727 (6) 9.00 2.40

Government Buildings, Pereira — AP203

1982, Aug. 4 Litho. *Perf. 12*
C728 AP203 35p multicolored 1.00 .40

Biplane in Flight, by Edgar Antonio Bustos AP204

1982, Aug. 5 *Perf. 14*
C729 AP204 18p multicolored .50 .20

American Air Forces Cooperation System.

Magdalena River AP205

1982, Oct. 21 Litho. *Perf. 12*

C730 AP205 30p multicolored 1.25 .35

Marquez Type

1982, Dec. 10 *Perf. 13½x14*

C731 A412 25p gray & blue .60 .20
C732 A412 30p gray & brown .85 .20

San Andres Archipelago — AP206

1983, Apr. 9 Litho. *Perf. 12*

C733 AP206 25p Liberty Fort .50 .20

Opening of Las Gaviotas (The Seagulls) Ecological Center, Bogota — AP207

1983, June 1 Litho.

C734 AP207 12p multicolored .30 .20

50th Anniv. of Radio Amateurs League AP208

1983, June 11 *Perf. 14x13½*

C735 AP208 12p multicolored .30 .20

Bolivar Type

1983, July 24 *Perf. 12*

C736 A417 30p multicolored .60 .20
C737 A417 100p multicolored 2.00 1.50

Botanical Exhibition Type

1983, Aug. 18 *Perf. 14*

C738 A418 12p Begonia guaduensis .35 .20
C739 A418 12p Chinchona ovaliflora .35 .20
C740 A418 40p Begonia urticae 1.25 .40
Nos. C738-C740 (3) 1.95 .80

Cartagena, 450th Anniv. — AP208a

1983, Sept. 9 Litho. *Perf. 12*

C740A AP208a 12p Customs Square .25 .20
C740B AP208a 35p Historic sites, Cartagena .70 .30

Painting Type

1983, Oct. 5 Litho. *Perf. 12*

C741 A420 30p multicolored .50 .20

Scouting Year AP209

Coffee Beans AP210

1983, Oct. 24

C742 AP209 12p multicolored .20 .20

1984, Mar. 28 Litho. *Perf. 14½x14*

C743 AP210 14p multicolored .20 .20

Marandua City Type

1984, Sept. 28 *Perf. 12*

C744 A427 30p multicolored .50 .20

AP211

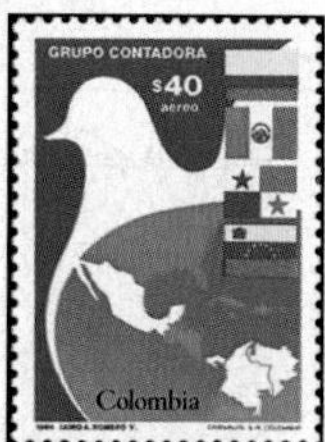

AP212

1984, Nov. 2

C745 AP211 45p multicolored .70 .25

45th Cong. of Americanists, Bogota, 1985.

Christmas Type

1984, Dec. 14

C746 A428 14p multicolored .25 .20

1985, Feb. 15

Design: Dove, map and flags of Colombia, Mexico, Costa Rica and Venezuela.

C747 AP212 40p multicolored .70 .30

Contadora Group of Latin American countries.

Gomez Type

1985, Feb. 25

C748 A432 40p multicolored .70 .30

Birds — AP213

AP214

1985

C749 AP213 14p Dryocopus lineatus nuperus .40 .20
C750 AP213 20p Xiphorhynchus picus .55 .20
C751 AP213 50p Eriocnemis cupreoventris 1.25 .25
C752 AP213 55p Momotus momota 1.50 .25
Nos. C749-C752 (4) 3.70 .90

Issued: 14p, 4/12; 20p, 50p, 8/6; 55p, 8/29.

1985, July 15

C753 AP214 20p multicolored .30 .20

Admiral Padilla Naval School, 50th anniv.

1985 Census AP215

1985, Oct. 15 *Perf. 12*

C754 AP215 20p multicolored .30 .20

Christmas Type

1985, Dec. 4 Litho. *Perf. 13*

C755 A436 20p Girl, Christmas tree .30 .20

Alfonso Lopez Pumarejo (1886-1959), President, 1934-38, 1942-45 — AP216

1986, Jan. 31

C756 AP216 24p multicolored .30 .20

Coffee Berries, Natl. Cycling Team AP217

1986, Feb. 4

C757 AP217 60p multicolored .75 .25

Natl. Coffee Producers Assoc. sponsorship of natl. cycling team, 25th anniv.

Fauna Type of 1985

1986, Feb. 18

C758 A433 50p Pudu mephistophiles .65 .25

World Communications Day — AP218

Intl. Peace Year — AP219

1986, May 17 Litho. *Perf. 13*

C759 AP218 50p multicolored .65 .25

1986, June 13 Litho. *Perf. 13*

C760 AP219 55p multicolored .65 .25

AP220

AP221

1986, July 1 Litho. *Perf. 13*

C761 AP220 24p Portrait, papal arms .30 .20
C762 AP220 55p Portrait, Medellin cathedral, horiz. .65 .25
C763 AP220 60p Blessing crowd, horiz. .70 .25
Nos. C761-C763 (3) 1.65 .70

Souvenir Sheet

C764 AP220 200p Praying, Madonna of Bogota 1.40 1.40

Visit of Pope John Paul II.

Nos. C762-C763 each printed in sheets of 20 with se-tenant labels picturing religious symbols.

1986, July 15 *Perf. 12*

C765 AP221 25p multicolored .30 .20

Enrique Santos Montejo (1886-1971), journalist.

Bach, Handel and Schutz, Composers AP222

1986, July 17 *Perf. 13*

C766 AP222 70p Bach 1.50 .40
C767 AP222 100p Text, music 2.00 .55

Salesian Order Education in Colombia, Cent. AP223

1986, July 23 *Perf. 12*

C768 AP223 25p De La Salle, founder .30 .20

Completion of Coal Mining Complex, El Cerrejon
AP224

1986, July 29 Litho. *Perf. 12*
C769 AP224 55p multi .60 .20

AP225

Natl. Constitution, Cent. — AP226

25p, The Five Signators, by R. Vasquez, detail, & Bogota Cathedral. 200p, Pres. Nunez & Miguel Antonio Caro, Natl. Council of Delegates chairman, & Presidential Palace, constitution.

1986, Aug. 5 Litho. *Perf. 14*
C770 AP225 25p multi .30 .20

Souvenir Sheet
Perf. 12

C771 AP226 200p multi 2.25 .75

Poet Type

Federico Garcia Lorca (1898-1936), poet, and birthplace, Fuentevaqueros, Granada, Spain.

1986, Sept. 26 Litho. *Perf. 12*
C772 A445 60p multi .70 .25

Gratitude for Intl. Aid after the Armero Mudslide Disaster
AP227

1986, Nov. 13
C773 AP227 50p multi .55 .20

Christmas
AP228

Wood sculpture: Virgin Mestiza, Nerina.

1986, Dec. 19 Litho. *Perf. 12*
C774 AP228 25p multi .30 .20

The Apotheosis of Popayan, by Ephrain Martinez Zambrano (1898-1956) — AP229

1987, Jan. 13
C775 100p Popayan riding horse 1.10 .50
C776 100p Onlookers 1.10 .50
a. AP229 Pair, #C775-C776 2.25 2.25

AP230

AP231

1987, Mar. 16 Litho. *Perf. 12*
C777 AP230 30p multi .30 .20

The Conversion of St. Augustine of Hippo, 1600th anniv.

Type of 1987

30p, Phoenicopterus ruber. 35p, Pseudemys scripta, horiz. #C780, Crax alberti. #C781, Symphysodon aequifasciatum, horiz.

Perf. 14½x14, 14x14½

1987-89 Wmk. 334
C778 A446a 30p lake .35 .20
C779 A446a 35p dark red brn .40 .20
C780 A446a 45p dark blue gray .30 .20
C781 A446a 45p blue .30 .20
Nos. C778-C781 (4) 1.35 .80

Issue dates: 30p, June 8. 35p, Dec. 24. No. C780, Dec. 6, 1988. No. C781, June 23, 1989.

Perf. 13½x13

1987, Apr. 10 Unwmk.
C783 AP231 25p multi .30 .20

Natl. University School of Mining, Medellin, cent.

Purebred Horses
AP232

1987, June 17 *Perf. 12*
C784 AP232 60p White horse .70 .25
C785 AP232 70p Black horse .85 .30

El Espectador Newspaper, Cent.
AP233

Design: Frontispieces from 1887, 1915, 1948, 1974 and portraits of founder Don Fidel Cano, editors Don Luis Cano, Luis Gabriel Cano Isaza and Alfonso Cano Isaza.

1987, July 24 *Perf. 12½x12*
C786 AP233 60p multi .70 .25

Intl. Year of Shelter for the Homeless
AP234

1987, Sept. 21 *Perf. 14*
C787 AP234 60p multi .65 .25

Flags
AP235

1987, Nov. 27 Litho. *Perf. 13x13½*
C788 AP235 80p multi .80 .30

Ist Meeting of the eight Latin-American Presidents, Acapulco, Nov.

Christmas
AP236

1987, Dec. 8 Litho. *Perf. 14*
C789 AP236 30p multi .30 .20

Rural Telephone System
AP237

1988, Feb. 4 Litho. *Perf. 14*
C790 AP237 70p multi .80 .30

Founding of Bogota, 450th Anniv. — AP238

1988, Apr. 11 Litho. *Perf. 12*
C791 AP238 70p multi .65 .25

Bogota, 450th Anniv.
AP238a

Unwmk.

1988, July 1 Litho. *Perf. 12*
C792 AP238a 80p Modern district, vert. .75 .25
C793 AP238a 90p Colonial district .85 .30

Gold Artifacts
AP239

Artifacts in the Gold Museum: 70p, Mask. 80p, Two-headed human figure inside a circle, Muisca tribe. 90p, Ritual figure of the Quimbaya.

1988 *Perf. 12*
C794 AP239 70p multi .65 .30
C795 AP239 80p multi .65 .25
C796 AP239 90p multi .70 .35
Nos. C794-C796 (3) 2.00 .90

Issue dates: 70p, May 13; 80p, 90p, Oct. 7.

Human Rights Type
Perf. 14x14½

1988, July 1 Engr. Wmk. 334
C797 A452 40p Communication, horiz. .40 .20

AP240

AP241

1988, Sept. 28 Litho. *Perf. 12*
C798 AP240 80p multi .70 .20

Zipa Tisquesusa (d. 1538), Chibcha Indian leader during revolt against Spanish Conquistadors.

1988, Nov. 23 Litho. *Perf. 12*
C799 AP241 40p multi .35 .20

Christmas.

Agustin Nieto Caballero (1889-1975), Educator — AP242

Unwmk.

1989, Mar. 18 Litho. *Perf. 12*
C800 AP242 100p multi .70 .25

Pres. Laureano Gomez (1889-1965) AP243

1989, Mar. 29
C801 AP243 45p multi .30 .20

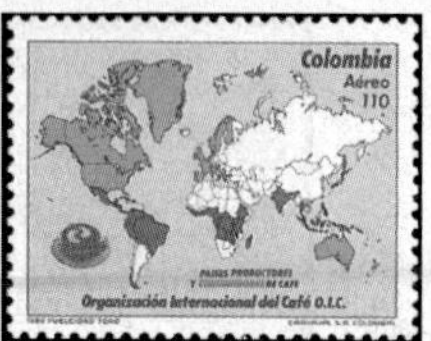

Intl. Coffee Organization — AP244

1989, Apr. 3
C802 AP244 110p multi .80 .30

12th Session of the UN Commission on Human Rights — AP245

1989, Apr. 28
C803 AP245 100p multi .70 .25

French Revolution, Bicent. AP246

1989, June 29 Litho. *Perf. 12*
C804 AP246 100p multi .70 .25

PHILEXFRANCE '89 — AP247

a, Bananas, tropical fruits. b, Fruits, flowers. c, Birds, animals. d, Precious gems, metals and mineral resources. e, View of fields, Colombian carrying produce basket. f, Waterfall. g, Fish, coast. Illustration reduced.

1989 Litho. *Perf. 14*
C805 AP247 Pane of 7 11.00 2.00
a.-g. 110p any single 1.50 .25

No. C805 printed in sheets containing panes of 7, rouletted between.

Souvenir Sheet

Los Lanceros, by R. Arenas Betancur — AP248

1989 Litho. *Perf. 12*
C806 AP248 250p multicolored 1.60 .55

Human Rights Type
Perf. 14½x14

1989, Aug. 18 Engr. Wmk. 334
C807 A452 55p Family .40 .20

Natl. Anti-Drugs Campaign AP249

Unwmk.

1989, Aug. 23 Litho. *Perf. 12*
C808 AP249 115p multicolored .75 .25

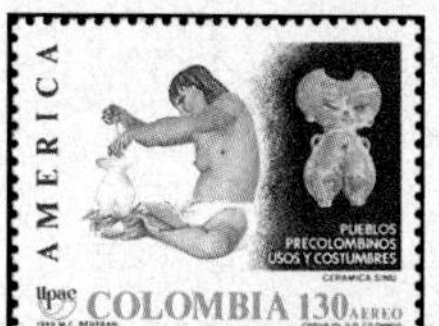

America Issue AP250

UPAE emblem and artifacts or customs of pre-Columbian peoples: 115p, Quimbaya, Calima or Tolima gold smiths. 130p, Potter and Sinu ceramic figurine.

1989 *Perf. 12*
C809 AP250 115p multicolored .75 .25
C810 AP250 130p multicolored .90 .30

Issue dates: 115p, Oct. 12; 130p, Aug. 23.

Joaquin Quijano Mantilla (1878-1944), Journalist — AP251

1989, Sept. 29 *Perf. 12*
C811 AP251 170p multicolored 1.10 .40

Arts and Crafts in Barro-Raquira AP252

1989 Litho. *Perf. 12*
C812 AP252 55p multicolored .40 .20

Christmas.

Boeing 767 AP253

1989, Dec. 5 Litho. *Perf. 12*
C813 AP253 130p multicolored .90 .30

Bolivar Installed at the Congress of Angostura, by Tito Salas — AP254

1989, Dec. 12
C814 AP254 130p multicolored .90 .30

Creation of the Republic, 1819.

Fathers of the Nation Leaving the Constitutional Convention AP255

1989, Dec. 12
C815 AP255 130p shown .90 .30
C816 AP255 130p Arms .90 .30
C817 AP255 130p Temple of the Rosary .90 .30
Nos. C815-C817 (3) 2.70 .90

Constitution of the Republic, 1821.

Arms Type of Regular Issue, 1982

1990, Mar. 1 Litho. *Perf. 12*
C818 A372 60p Velez .30 .20

Presidential Summit, Cartagena AP256

1990, Feb. 15 Litho. *Perf. 12*
C819 AP256 130p Plaza de la Aduana .55 .20

Colombian National Radio, 50th Anniv. — AP257

1990, Feb. 16 Litho. *Perf. 12*
C820 AP257 150p multicolored .65 .20

Teresa Cuervo Borda (1889-1976), Art Historian — AP258

1990, Mar. 28 Litho. *Perf. 12*
C821 AP258 60p multicolored .35 .20

Second Latin American Theater Festival, Bogota — AP259

1990, Apr. 10
C822 AP259 150p buff, tan & gold .80 .25

Santander Type

#C823, Santander holding the Constitution. #C824, Central Cemetery, Bogata and National Pantheon. #C825, Santander, as organizer of public education. #C826, "Postman of New Granada" (Man and burro) by Joseph Brown and Jose Maria del Castillo, horiz. 500p, Santander on death bed.

1990, May 6 *Perf. 14x13½*
C823 A470 60p multicolored .25 .20
C824 A470 60p multicolored .25 .20
C825 A470 70p multicolored .30 .20
C826 A470 70p multicolored .30 .20
Nos. C823-C826 (4) 1.10 .80

Souvenir Sheet
Perf. 12

C827 A470 500p multi 2.00 .65

No. C827 contains one 54x40mm stamp.

First Postage Stamp, 150th Anniv. AP260

1990, May 6 *Perf. 14*
C828 AP260 150p multicolored .65 .25

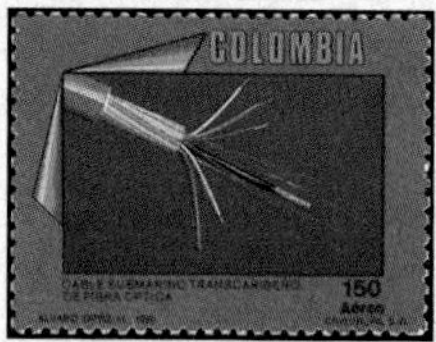

Trans-Caribbean Fiber Optic Cable — AP261

1990, May 19 *Perf. 12*
C829 AP261 150p multicolored .65 .25

Institute of Industrial Development, 25th Anniv. — AP262

1990, May 22
C830 AP262 60p multicolored .35 .20

Souvenir Sheet

World Cup Soccer Championships, Italy — AP263

1990, June 8
C831 AP263 500p multicolored 2.00 .65

AP264

AP265

1990, June 27
C832 AP264 130p multicolored .55 .20

Organization of American States, cent.

1990, July 26
C833 AP265 170p multicolored .70 .25

Museum of Gold, 50th Anniv.

Dolphins, Marine Birds AP266

1990, Oct. 12 Litho. *Perf. 12*
C834 AP266 150p shown 1.00 .20
C835 AP266 170p Jungle fauna, vert. 1.00 .25

AP267

AP268

1990, Nov. 16 Litho. *Perf. 12*
C836 AP267 70p multicolored .40 .20

Monastery of Our Lady of Las Lajas..

1991, Feb. 8 Litho. *Perf. 12*
C837 AP268 170p multicolored .80 .30

Newspaper Publishing, 200th Anniv.

AP269

AP270

1990, Nov. 1 Litho. *Perf. 12*
C838 AP269 70p multicolored .40 .20

Christmas.

1991, May 31 Litho. *Perf. 14*

Whales and Dolphins: 80p, Megaptera novaeangliae, breaching. 170p, Megaptera novaeangliae, diving. 190p, Inia geoffrensis, Sotalia fluviatilis, horiz.

C839 AP270 80p multicolored .35 .20
C840 AP270 170p multicolored .75 .30
C841 AP270 190p multicoloed .90 .30
Nos. C839-C841 (3) 2.00 .80

America Issue AP271

1991, Oct. 11 Litho. *Perf. 14*
C842 AP271 90p shown .45 .20
C843 AP271 190p Ship arriving in New World .85 .25

Adoration of the Magi — AP272

1991, Dec. 20 Litho. *Perf. 14*
C844 AP272 90p multicolored .45 .20

Christmas.

AP273

AP274

1991, Dec. 2
C845 AP273 190p Country flags .85 .25

Fifth summit of Latin American presidents.

1992, Feb. 8 Litho. *Perf. 12*
C846 AP274 210p multicolored .95 .30

8th UNCTAD Conference, Cartagena.

Proclamation of New Constitution, July 4, 1991 — AP275

1991, Nov. 27 Litho. *Perf. 14*
C847 AP275 90p multicolored .40 .20

Export Products AP276

Copyright Protection AP277

1992, Mar. 11 *Perf. 12*
C848 AP276 90p Flowers .40 .20
C849 AP276 210p Fruits, vegetables, horiz. .95 .30

1992, Apr. 13 Litho. *Perf. 12*
C850 AP277 190p multicolored .85 .25

1992 Summer Olympics AP278

1992, June 4 Litho. *Perf. 14*
C851 AP278 110p multicolored .50 .30

Earth Summit '92 AP279

a, Tree, mountain landscape. b, Birds in tree.

1992, June 2 Litho. *Perf. 14*
C852 A279 230p Pair, #a.-b. 2.10 1.40

America Issue AP280

Paintings: 230p, Discovery of America by Christopher Columbus, by Salvador Dali. 260p, Magical America, Myth and Legend, by Alfredo Vivero.

1992, July 22 *Perf. 14x13½*
C853 AP280 230p multicolored 1.00 .70
C854 AP280 260p multicolored 1.10 .75

McDonnell Douglas MD83 AP281

1992, Sept. 22 Litho. *Perf. 12*
C855 AP281 110p multicolored .45 .30

Curtain of Colon Theatre AP282

1992, Oct. 12 Litho. *Perf. 12*
C856 AP282 230p multicolored .95 .65

AP283

AP284

1992, Nov. 27 Litho. *Perf. 12*
C857 AP283 230p Gloria Lara, 1938-82 .95 .65

1993, June 7 Litho. *Perf. 12*
C858 AP284 220p multicolored .85 .60

1993 American Soccer Cup, Ecuador.

Intl. Year of Indigenous People — AP285

1993, July 1 ***Perf. 14***
C859 AP285 460p multicolored 1.75 1.25

South American Eliminations for 1994 World Cup Soccer Championships, US — AP286

1993, July 31 Litho. ***Perf. 12***
C860 AP286 220p multicolored .80 .50

AP287

AP288

America Issue (Endangered species): a, 220p, Saguinus oedipus. b, 220p, Porphyrula martinica. c, 460p, Rupicola peruviana. d, 520p, Trichecus manatus.

1993, Oct. 19 Litho. ***Perf. 12***
C861 AP287 Block of 4, #a.-d. 4.75 3.25

1994, Mar. 21 Litho. ***Perf. 12***
C862 AP288 630p multicolored 2.25 1.40

Intl. Decade for Natural Disaster Reduction.

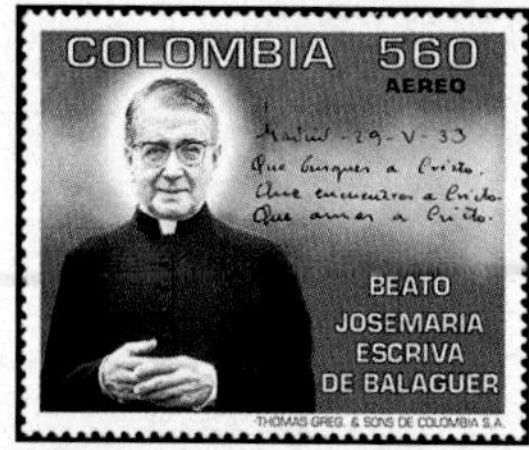

Beatification of Josemaria Escriva de Balaguer — AP289

1994, May 17 Litho. ***Perf. 13½x14***
C863 AP289 560p multicolored 1.90 1.25

First Airmail Delivery, 75th Anniv. AP290

Design: 270p, William Knox Martin, airplane over Port Colombia, 1919.

1994, July 29 Litho. ***Perf. 14***
C864 AP290 270p multicolored .90 .55

Natl. Institute of Medical Law & Forensic Sciences, 80th Anniv. AP291

1994, Oct. 27 Litho. ***Perf. 12***
C865 AP291 560p multicolored 1.90 1.25

Sociedad Colombo-Alemana de Transportes Aereos (SCADTA), 75th Anniv. — AP292

1995, Jan. 2 Litho. ***Perf. 12***
C866 AP292 330p No. C15 1.10 .50

Flora and Fauna — AP293

Iguana iguana: No. C867a, Facing right. b, Facing left.
Rain forest: No. C868a, Nuts on branch, flowers. b, Waterfall, hanging red flower.

1995, Jan. 17
C867 AP293 650p Pair, #a.-b. 4.25 3.00
C868 AP293 750p Pair, #a.-b. 5.00 4.00

Nos. C867-C868 are continuous designs.

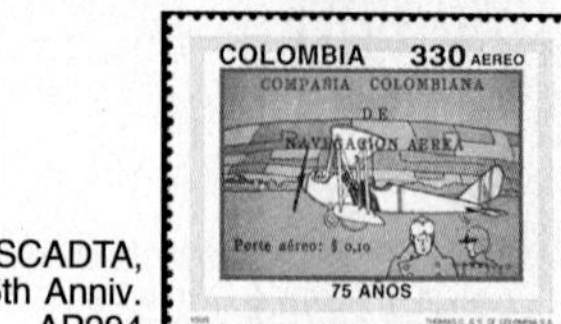

SCADTA, 75th Anniv. AP294

1995, Mar. 30 Litho. ***Perf. 14***
C869 AP294 330p No. C9 1.10 .75

FAO, 50th Anniv. AP295

1995, Apr. 25 Litho. ***Perf. 13x13½***
C870 AP295 750p multicolored 2.25 1.25

Andres Bello Organization, 25th Anniv. — AP296

Colombian Firefighters, Cent. — AP297

1995, Apr. 27 ***Perf. 13½x13***
C871 AP296 650p multicolored 2.00 .85

1995, May 5 ***Perf. 12***
C872 AP297 330p multicolored 1.10 .45

Fenalco, 50th Anniv. — AP298

UN, 50th Anniv. — AP299

1995, May 25 ***Perf. 13½***
C873 AP298 330p multicolored 1.10 .45

1995, June 21 ***Perf. 12***
C874 AP299 750p multicolored 1.50 1.00

First Pacific Ocean Games — AP300

1995, June 23
C875 AP300 750p multicolored 2.25 1.25

11th Summit of Non-Aligned Countries, Cartagena — AP302

1995, Oct. 13 Litho. ***Perf. 12***
C877 AP302 650p multicolored 1.25 .90

Motion Pictures, Cent. AP303

Design: 330p, Charlie Chaplin and Jackie Coogan in "The Kid," Estela López Pomareda in "Maria," first Colombian feature length film.

1995, Oct. 19 ***Perf. 14***
C878 AP303 330p black & sepia .65 .45

AP304

AP305

1995, Nov. 23 ***Perf. 12***
C879 AP304 650p multicolored 1.25 .90

Andes Development Corporation (CAF), 25th Anniv.

1995, Nov. 21 ***Perf. 14***

Fight against illegal drug trafficking: No. C880, Locating illegally grown plants. No. C881, Hands in handcuffs, horiz.

C880 AP305 330p multicolored .65 .45
C881 AP305 330p multicolored .65 .45

Miniature Sheet of 16

Myths and Legends — AP306

Madre-Monte: a.-d.
La Llorna: e.-h.
El Mohán: i.-l.
Hombre Caimán: m.-p.
Background color changes from top to bottom rows. Top row is blue. Row 2 is blue

green. Row 3 is green. Row 4 is lilac. Each design comes in all four colors.

1995, Dec. 6
C882 AP306 750p #a.-p. 24.00 12.00

See No. C886.

José Asunción Silva (1865-96), Poet AP307

1996, Apr. 23 Litho. *Perf. 12*
C883 AP307 400p multicolored .75 .40

Isla de Providencia AP308

Policarpa Salavarrieta (1796-1817), Patriot — AP309

1996, Apr. 25 *Perf. 14*
C884 AP308 800p multicolored 1.50 .75

1996, Apr. 26
C885 AP309 900p multicolored 2.50 .85

Myths and Legends Type

Designs: a, Kogui Creation. b, Yonna Wayu. c, Jaguar Man. d, Master of the Animals.

1996, Aug. 12 Litho. *Perf. 13½x14*
C886 AP306 900p Block of 4, #a.-d. 13.00 10.00

Metropolitan Basilica, Medellin AP310

1996, July 12
C887 AP310 400p multicolored 1.10 .55

National Archives Building AP311

1996, July 30 Litho. *Perf. 14*
C888 AP311 400p multicolored 1.10 .40

CERLALC, 25th Anniv. AP312

1996, Aug. 16 Litho. *Perf. 12*
C889 AP312 800p multicolored 2.10 1.00

UNESCO.

Pioneers in Petroleum Industry — AP313

a, Jorge Isaacs, pumping oil. b, Francisco Burgos Rubio, refinery at night. c, Diego Martínez Camargo, derrick. d, Prisciliano Cabrales Lora, off-shore drilling. e, Manuel María Palacio, oil tanker loading offshore. f, Roberto De Mares, refinery, lake. g, General Virgilio Barco Maldonado, men positioning equipment. h, Roustabout, "ECOPETROL" emblem.

1996, Sept. 5 Litho. *Perf. 13½x14*
C890 AP313 800p Block of 8, #a.-h. 20.00 20.00

Colombian Golf Federation, 50th Anniv. AP314

1996, Sept. 19 Litho. *Perf. 12*
C891 AP314 400p multicolored .80 .40

Covenant for the Children AP315

1997, Feb. 28 Litho. *Perf. 14*
C892 AP315 400p multicolored 1.00 .40

AP316

AP317

1997, Apr. 25 *Perf. 12*
C893 AP316 800p multicolored 2.00 1.00

Motion pictures in Colombia, cent.

1997, May 13 Litho. *Perf. 12*
C894 AP317 400p multicolored 1.10 .40

Social Security Institute, 50th anniv.

Ericsson in Colombia, Cent. — AP318

1997, May 22 *Perf. 13½x14*
C895 AP318 900p multicolored 1.75 .90

Bogatá Colonial Bldg., Home of Natl. Mint and Numismatic Museum — AP319

1997, July 10 *Perf. 12*
C896 AP319 800p multicolored 2.00 1.00

Phytelephas Seemannii — AP320

1997, July 23 *Perf. 13½x14*
C897 AP320 900p multicolored 2.25 .90

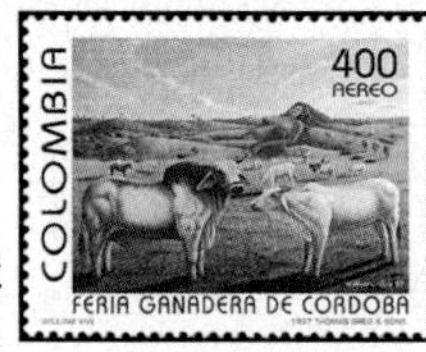

Cordoba Cattle Fair AP321

1997, June 21 *Perf. 14*
C898 AP321 400p multicolored 1.10 .40

Personalities — AP322

No. C899: a, Cacique Gaitana, 16th cent., Indian resistance leader. b, Josefa Acevedo de Gómez (1803-61), writer. c, Domingo Bioho (d. 1621), black leader. d, Soledad Acosta de Samper (1831-1913), historian. e, Maria Cano Márquez (1897-1967), popular leader. f, Manuel Quintín Lame (1880-1967), native leader. g, Ezequiel Uricoechea (1834-80), linguist, naturalist. h, Juan Rodríguez Freyle (1566-1642), colonial reporter. i, Gerardo Reichel-Dolmatoff (1912-94), archaeologist. j, Ramón de Zubiría (1922-95), writer, educator. k, Esteban Jaramillo (1874-1947), economist. l, Pedro Fermín de Vargas (1762-c. 1810), economist.

No. 900: a, Luis Carlos "el turerto" López (1879-1950), poet. b, Aurelio Arturo (1906-74), poet. c, Enrique Pérez Arbeláez (1896-1972), botanist. d, José Maria González Benito (1843-1903), mathematician, astronomer. e, José Manuel Rivas Sacconi (1917-91), diplomat. f, Eduardo Lemaitre Román (1914-94), historian. g, Diójenes Arrieta (1848-93), politician. h, Gabriel Turbay Abunader (1901-47), politician, diplomat. i, Guillermo Echavarría Misas (1888-1985), aviation pioneer. j, Juan Friede Alter (1901-90), historian. k, Fabio Lozano Torrijos (1865-1947), diplomat. l, Lino de Pombo (1797-1862), engineer, diplomat.

1997, Dec. 19 Litho. *Perf. 13½x14*
Sheets of 12
C899 AP322 500p #a.-l. 12.50 12.50
C900 AP322 500p #a.-l. 12.50 12.50

Colombian Society of Orthopedic Surgery and Traumatology, 50th Anniv. — AP323

1997 *Perf. 12*
C901 AP323 1000p multicolored 2.40 .80

AP324

AP325

1998, Apr. 30 Litho. *Perf. 14*
C902 AP324 1000p multicolored 2.75 .75

Organization of American States, 50th anniv.

1998, May 22
C903 AP325 1000p bl & org 2.75 .75

4th Bolivar Philatelic Exhibition, Santa Fe de Bogota.

World Health Organization, 50th Anniv. — AP326

1998, Apr. 7 ***Perf. 12***
C904 AP326 1100p multicolored 2.40 .80

1998 World Cup Soccer Championships, France — AP327

Stylized designs: a, Foot. b. Soccer ball. c, Hand.

1998, June 9 **Litho.** ***Perf. 14***
C905 AP327 1100p Strip of 3, #a.-c. 6.75 6.75

Intl. Year of the Ocean — AP328

1998, May 22 ***Perf. 12***
C906 AP328 1100p ARC Gloria 3.00 .80

Myths and Legends — AP329

Designs: a, Bochica. b, Chimingagua. c, Bachue and Huitica.

Perf. 13¼x12¾
1998, Nov. 27 **Litho.**
C907 AP329 1000p Strip of 3, #a.-c. 11.00 11.00

AIR POST SPECIAL DELIVERY STAMPS

Catalogue values for unused stamps in this section are for Never Hinged items.

Post Horn and Wings APSD1

Unwmk.
1958, May 19 **Litho.** ***Perf. 12***
CE1 APSD1 25c dk bl & red .35 .20

Same Overprinted Vertically in Red

1959
CE2 APSD1 25c dk bl & red .30 .20

Jet Plane and Envelope — AP3D2

1963, Oct. 4 ***Perf. 14***
CE3 APSD2 50c red & blk .20 .20

Aviation Type

80c, Boeing 727 jet, 1966.

Perf. 14x13½
1966, Dec. 14 **Photo.** **Unwmk.**
CE4 AP96 80c crim & multi .35 .20

AIR POST REGISTRATION STAMPS

Issued by Sociedad Colombo-Alemana de Transportes Aereos (SCADTA)

No. C41 Overprinted in Red

R

1923 **Wmk. 116** ***Perf. 14x14½***
CF1 AP6 20c gray 2.50 1.10

No. C58 Overprinted in Black

1929 **Wmk. 127** ***Perf. 14***
CF2 AP8 20c carmine 4.00 1.10

Same Overprint on No. C71

CF3 AP10 20c carmine 6.50 6.00

Colombian Government Issues

Same Overprint on No. C86

1932
CF4 AP8 20c carmine 6.50 6.00

No. C100 Overprinted

CF5 AP12 20c car & ol blk 4.50 1.25

For surcharge see No. C118.

SPECIAL DELIVERY STAMPS

Special Delivery Messenger — SD1

1917 **Unwmk.** **Engr.** ***Perf. 14***
E1 SD1 5c gray green 1.00 1.50

Catalogue values for unused stamps in this section, from this point to the end of the section, are for Never Hinged items.

SD2

1987, July 31 **Litho.** ***Perf. 14***
E2 SD2 25p emerald & ver .30 .30
E3 SD2 30p emerald & ver .35 .35

REGISTRATION STAMPS

R1 R2

1865 **Unwmk.** **Litho.** ***Imperf.***
F1 R1 5c black 80.00 40.00
F2 R2 5c black 75.00 40.00

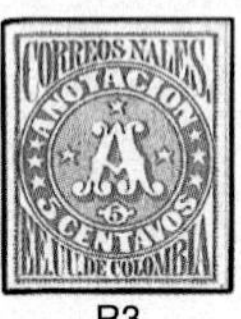

R3 R4

1870

White Paper

Vertical Lines in Background

F3 R3 5c black 2.25 1.90
F4 R4 5c black 2.25 1.90

Horizontal Lines in Background

F5 R3 5c black 7.50 6.50
F6 R4 5c black 2.25 1.90
Nos. F3-F6 (4) 14.25 12.20

Reprints of Nos. F3 to F6 show either crossed lines or traces of lines in background.

R5

R6

1881 ***Imperf.***
F7 R5 10c violet 47.50 40.00
a. Sewing machine perf. 55.00 47.50
b. Perf. 11 60.00 50.00

1883 ***Perf. 12, 13½***
F8 R6 10c red, *orange* 1.50 *1.90*

R7

1889-95 ***Perf. 12, 13½***
F9 R7 10c red, *grysh* 5.25 2.50
F10 R7 10c red, *yelsh* 5.25 2.50
F11 R7 10c dp brn, *rose buff* ('95) 1.50 1.25
F12 R7 10c yel brn, *lt buff* ('92) 1.50 1.25
Nos. F9-F12 (4) 13.50 7.50

Nos. F9-F12 exist imperf. Values same as for perf.

R9

1902 ***Imperf.***
F13 R9 20c red brown, *blue* 1.40 1.40
a. Sewing machine perf. 3.75 3.75
b. Perf. 12 3.75 3.75

Medellin Issue

R10

1902 ***Perf. 12***

Laid Paper

F16 R10 10c blk vio 12.50 12.50
a. Wove paper 17.50 17.50

Regular Issue

1903 ***Imperf.***
F17 R9 20c blue, *blue* 1.40 1.40
a. Sewing machine perf. 4.00 4.00
b. Perf. 12 4.00 4.00

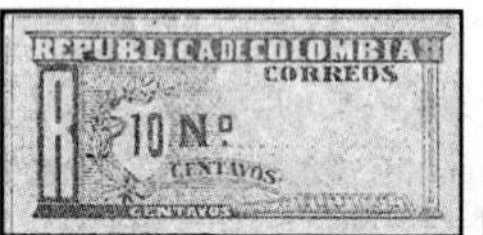

R11

1904 **Pelure Paper** ***Imperf.***
F19 R11 10c purple 3.00 3.00
a. Sewing machine perf. 4.00 3.00
b. Perf. 12 5.00 4.00

R12

Imprint: "J. L. Arango"

1904 ***Perf. 12***

Wove Paper

F20 R12 10c purple 2.00 .50
a. Imperf., pair 6.25 6.25

Imprint: "Lit. Nacional"

1909 ***Perf. 10, 14, 10x14, 14x10***
F21 R12 10c purple 2.25 .70
a. Imperf., pair 5.00 5.00

For overprints see Nos. LF1-LF4.

Execution at Cartagena in 1816 — R13

1910, July 20 Engr. *Perf. 12*

F22 R13 10c red & black 17.50 *75.00*

Centenary of National Independence.

Pier at Puerto Colombia — R14

Tequendama Falls — R15

Perf. 11, 11½, 14, 11½x14

1917, Aug. 25

F23 R14 4c green & ultra .50 *2.50*
a. Center inverted 575.00 575.00
F24 R15 10c deep blue 1.90 .60

R16

1925 Litho. *Perf. 10x13½*

F25 R16 (10c) blue 3.50 1.50
a. Imperf., pair 12.00 10.00
b. Perf. 13½x10 6.00 4.00

ACKNOWLEDGMENT OF RECEIPT STAMPS

AR1

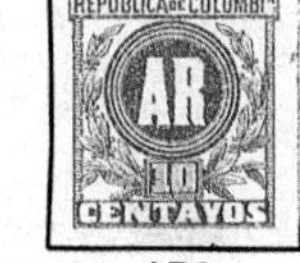

AR2

1893 Unwmk. Litho. *Perf. 13½*

H1 AR1 5c ver, *blue* 4.25 4.25

1894 *Perf. 12*

H2 AR1 5c vermilion 3.50 *4.00*

1902-03 *Imperf.*

H3 AR2 10c blue, *blue* 2.75 2.75
a. 10c, blue, *greenish blue* 2.75 2.75
b. Sewing machine perf. 2.75 2.75
c. Perf. 12 2.75 2.75

The handstamp "AR" in circle is believed to be a postmark.

AR2a

Purple Handstamp

1903 *Imperf.*

H4 AR2a 10c black, *pink* 20.00 20.00

AR3

AR4

1904 Pelure Paper *Imperf.*

H12 AR3 5c pale blue 10.50 10.50
a. Perf. 12 10.50 10.50

No. 307 Overprinted in Black, Green or Violet **A R**

H13 A86 5c carmine 17.50 17.50

1904 *Perf. 12*

H16 AR4 5c blue 3.25 2.75
a. Imperf., pair 8.75 8.75

For overprints see Nos. LH1-LH2.

General José Acevedo y Gómez — AR5

1910, July 20 Engr.

H17 AR5 5c orange & green 5.75 *16.00*

Centenary of National Independence.

Sabana Station AR6

Map of Colombia AR7

1917 *Perf. 14*

H18 AR6 4c bister brown 1.75 *2.00*
H19 AR7 5c orange brown 1.50 *1.75*
a. Imperf., pair 11.00

LATE FEE STAMPS

LF1

LF2

1886 Unwmk. Litho. *Perf. 10½*

I1 LF1 2½c blk, *lilac* 3.25 2.50
a. Imperf., pair 12.00 12.00

1892 *Perf. 12, 13½*

I2 LF2 2½c dk bl, *rose* 2.75 2.00
a. Imperf., pair 12.00
I3 LF2 2½c ultra, *pink* 2.75 2.00

LF3

LF4

1902 *Imperf.*

I4 LF3 5c purple, *rose* .85 .85
a. Perf. 12 1.75 1.75

1914 *Perf. 10, 13½*

I6 LF4 2c vio brown 4.00 4.00
I7 LF4 5c blue green 4.00 3.25

Retardo

Refardo 1921

Overprints illustrated above are unauthorized and of private origin.

POSTAGE DUE STAMPS

These are not, strictly speaking, postage due stamps but were issued to cover an additional fee, "Sobreporte," charged on mail to foreign countries with which Colombia had no postal conventions.

D1

D2

D3

1866 Unwmk. Litho. *Imperf.*

J1 D1 25c black, *blue* 45.00 45.00
J2 D2 50c black, *yellow* 45.00 45.00
J3 D3 1p black, *rose* 125.00 100.00
Nos. J1-J3 (3) 215.00 190.00

DEPARTMENT STAMPS

These stamps are said to be for interior postage, to supersede the separate issues for the various departments.

Regular Issues Handstamped in Black, Violet, Blue or Green — a

On Stamps of 1904

1909 Unwmk. *Perf. 12*

L1 A94 ½c yellow 2.00 2.00
a. Imperf., pair 6.00 6.00
L2 A94 1c yel grn 3.00 2.00
L3 A94 2c red 4.50 3.00
a. Imperf., pair 12.50 12.50
L4 A94 5c blue 5.00 3.25
L5 A94 10c violet 7.00 7.00
L6 A94 20c black 11.00 10.00
L7 A95 1p brown 18.00 17.00

On Stamp of 1902

L8 A83 10p dk brn, *rose* 20.00 20.00
Nos. L1-L8 (8) 70.50 64.25

On Stamps of 1908

Perf. 10, 13, 13½ and Compound

L9 A94 ½c orange 2.00 2.00
a. Imperf., pair 6.00 6.00
L10 A94 1c green 4.00 3.25
a. Without imprint 5.00 5.00
L11 A94 2c red 4.50 3.25
a. Imperf., pair
L12 A94 5c blue 4.50 3.25
a. Imperf., pair 12.50 12.50
L13 A94 10c violet 6.00 6.00

On Tolima Stamp of 1888

Perf. 10½

L14 A23 1p red brn 12.50 12.50
Nos. L9-L14 (6) 33.50 30.25

Regular Issues Handstamped — b

On Stamps of 1904

Perf. 12

L15 A94 ½c yellow 2.00 2.00
L16 A94 1c yellow grn 3.50 3.00
L17 A94 2c red 6.00 5.00
L18 A94 5c blue 6.00 5.00
L19 A94 10c violet 8.00 6.00
L20 A94 20c black 11.00 11.00
L21 A94 1p brown 20.00 20.00
Nos. L15-L21 (7) 56.50 52.00

On Stamps of 1908

Perf. 10, 13, 13½

L22 A94 ½c orange 2.25 2.25
L23 A94 1c yellow grn 6.25 6.25
L24 A94 2c red 5.00 5.00
a. Imperf., pair 12.50 12.50
L25 A94 5c light blue 6.00 5.00
Nos. L22-L25 (4) 19.50 18.50

The handstamps on Nos. L1-L25 are, as usual, found inverted and double.

DEPARTMENT REGISTRATION STAMPS

Registration Stamps Handstamped like Nos. L1-L25

On Registration Stamp of 1904

1909 Unwmk. *Perf. 12*

LF1 R12 (a) 10c purple 25.00 25.00
LF2 R12 (b) 10c purple 25.00 25.00

On Registration Stamp of 1909

Perf. 10, 13

LF3 R12 (a) 10c purple 25.00 25.00
LF4 R12 (b) 10c purple 25.00 25.00
Nos. LF1-LF4 (4) 100.00 100.00

Nos. LF1-LF4 exist imperf. Value per pair, $100.

DEPARTMENT ACKNOWLEDGMENT OF RECEIPT STAMPS

Acknowledgment of Receipt Stamp of 1904 Handstamped like Nos. L1-L25

1909 Unwmk. *Perf. 12*

LH1 AR4 (a) 5c blue 25.00 25.00
a. Imperf., pair 100.00
LH2 AR4 (b) 5c blue 25.00 25.00
a. Imperf., pair 100.00

LOCAL STAMPS FOR THE CITY OF BOGOTA

A1

Pelure Paper

1889 Unwmk. Litho. *Perf. 12*

LX1 A1 ½c black .95 .95
a. Imperf., pair 6.00 6.00

Impressions on bright blue and blue-gray paper were not regularly issued.

A2

A3

White Wove Paper

1896 *Perf. 12, 13½*

LX2 A2 ½c black .95 .95

1903 *Imperf.*

LX3 A3 10c black, *pink* 1.25 1.25
a. Perf. 12 5.00 5.00

OFFICIAL STAMPS

Stamps of 1917-1937 Overprinted in Black or Red:

a

b

1937 Unwmk. *Perf. 11, 12, 13½*

O1	A131 (a)	1c green	.20	.20
O2	A157 (a)	10c dp org	.20	.20
O3	A107 (b)	30c olive bis	1.75	1.00
O4	A129 (b)	40c brn & yel brn	1.50	.80
O5	A114 (b)	50c car	1.00	.50
O6	A107 (b)	1p lt bl	5.00	4.00
O7	A107 (b)	2p org	10.00	6.50
O8	A107 (b)	5p gray	37.50	27.50
O9	A118 (b)	10p dk brn	110.00	100.00

Wmk. 229

Perf. 12½

O10	A132 (a)	2c red	.20	.20
O11	A133 (a)	5c brn	.20	.20
O12	A160 (a)	12c dp bl (R)	1.00	.50
O13	A136 (b)	20c dk bl (R)	1.60	.60
		Nos. O1-O13 (13)	170.15	142.20

Tall, wrong font "I's" in OFICIAL exist on all stamps with "a" overprint.

POSTAL TAX STAMPS

"Greatest Mother" PT1

Perf. 11½

1935, May 27 Unwmk. Litho.

RA1	PT1	5c olive blk & scar	2.10	.75

Required on all mail during Red Cross Week in 1935 (May 27-June 3) and in 1936.

Mother and Child — PT2

Perf. 10½, 10½x11

1937, May 24 Unwmk.

RA2	PT2	5c red	1.50	.60

Required on all mail during Red Cross Week. The tax was for the Red Cross.

PT3

Ministry of Posts and Telegraphs Building — PT4

1939-45 Litho. *Perf. 10½, 12½*

RA3	PT3	¼c dp bl	.20	.20
RA3A	PT3	¼c dk vio brn ('45)	.20	.20
RA4	PT3	½c pink	.20	.20
RA5	PT3	1c violet	.30	.20
RA5A	PT3	1c yel org ('45)	1.50	.60
RA6	PT3	2c pck grn	.40	.20
RA7	PT3	20c lt brn	3.50	1.25
		Nos. RA3-RA7 (7)	6.30	2.85

Obligatory on all mail. The tax was for the construction of the new Communications Building.

The 25c of type PT3 and PT4 were not usable on postal matter.

For overprint see No. 561.

Perf. 12½x13

1940, Jan. 20 Engr. Wmk. 229

RA8	PT4	¼c ultra	.20	.20
RA9	PT4	½c carmine	.20	.20
RA10	PT4	1c violet	.20	.20
RA11	PT4	2c bl grn	.25	.20
RA12	PT4	20c brown	1.00	.20
		Nos. RA8-RA12 (5)	1.85	1.00

See note after No. RA7. See No. RA18.

"Protection" — PT5

1940, Apr. 25 Wmk. 255 *Perf. 12*

RA13	PT5	5c rose carmine	.25	.20

See No. RA17.

Postal Tax Stamps of 1939 Surcharged in Black

1943 Unwmk. *Perf. 10½*

RA14	PT3	½c on 1c violet	.20	.20
a.		Inverted surcharge	1.50	
RA15	PT3	½c on 2c pck grn	.20	.20
RA16	PT3	½c on 20c lt brn	.20	.20
		Nos. RA14-RA16 (3)	.60	.60

Types of 1940

Imprint: "Litografia Colombia Bogota S.A."

1944 Litho. *Perf. 11*

RA17	PT5	5c dark rose	.30	.20

Imprint: "Lito-Colombia Bogota-Colombia"

RA18	PT4	¼c ultra	.20	.20

Ministry of Posts and Telegraphs Building — PT6

1945-48 Wmk. 255 Engr. *Perf. 12*

RA19	PT6	¼c ultra	.20	.20
RA20	PT6	¼c sepia ('46)	.20	.20
RA21	PT6	½c car rose	.20	.20
RA22	PT6	½c dp mag ('46)	.20	.20
RA23	PT6	1c vio ('46)	.20	.20
RA23A	PT6	1c red org ('46)	.20	.20
RA24	PT6	2c grn ('46)	.20	.20
RA25	PT6	20c brn ('46)	.90	.25
a.		20c red brown ('48)	.60	.20
		Nos. RA19-RA25 (8)	2.30	1.65

These stamps were obligatory on all mail. The surtax was for the construction of the new Communications Building. See Nos. 603, RA33. For overprints see Nos. 562-564.

No. 469 Overprinted in Carmine

1946, May 25

RA26	A176	5c dull brown	.35	.20

The surtax was for the Red Cross.

Ministry of Posts and Telegraphs Building — PT7

1946 Unwmk. Litho. *Perf. 11*

RA27	PT7	3c blue	.20	.20

No. 490 Overprinted in Carmine

1947 Wmk. 255 *Perf. 12*

RA28	A196	20c gray black	3.00	1.25

Arms of Colombia and Red Cross — PT8

PT9

Perf. 12½

1947, Sept. Unwmk. Engr.

RA29	PT8	5c car lake	.20	.20

The surtax of Nos. RA29 and RA40 was for the Red Cross. See No. RA40.

No. 466 Overprinted Like No. RA28 in Carmine

RA30	A136	20c dark blue	10.00	7.00

Catalogue values for unused stamps in this section, from this point to the end of the section, are for Never Hinged items.

Type of 1945

1947 Wmk. 255 Engr. *Perf. 12*

RA33	PT6	1c olive bister	.20	.20

Black Surcharge

1948 Unwmk. Litho. *Perf. 11*

RA36	PT9	1c on 5c lt brn	.20	.20
RA37	PT9	1c on 10c lt vio	.20	.20
RA38	PT9	1c on 25c red	.20	.20
RA39	PT9	1c on 50c ultra	.20	.20
		Nos. RA36-RA39 (4)	.80	.80

Type of 1947

1948 *Perf. 10½*

RA40	PT8	5c vermilion	.20	.20

Ministry of Posts and Telegraphs Building — PT10

Mother and Child — PT11

1948-50 Wmk. 255 Engr. *Perf. 12*

RA41	PT10	1c rose car ('49)	.20	.20
RA42	PT10	2c green ('50)	.20	.20
RA43	PT10	3c blue	.20	.20
RA44	PT10	5c gray	.20	.20
RA45	PT10	10c purple	.20	.20
		Nos. RA41-RA45 (5)	1.00	1.00

A 25c stamp of type PT10 was for use on telegrams, later for regular postage. See Nos. 602, 604. For overprints and surcharge see Nos. C227-C230, C238, C283, RA51.

Unwmk.

1950, May 25 Litho. *Perf. 11*

Dark Blue Surcharge

RA46	PT11	5c on 2c gray, red, blk & yel	.75	.30
a.		"195" instead of "1950"	1.40	1.40
b.		Top bar and "19" of "1950" omitted	1.40	1.40

Marginal perforations omitted, creating 26 straight-edged copies in each sheet of 44.

Surtax for Red Cross.

No. 574 Overprinted in Black

1950, May 26 Wmk. 255 *Perf. 12*

RA47	A176	5c blue	.20	.20
a.		Inverted overprint	.90	

Telegraph Stamp Surcharged in Black

RA48	A253a	8c on 50c org yel	.20	.20

Fiscal stamps of type A253a were available for postal use after May 9, 1952. See Nos. 605-608.

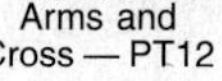

Arms and Cross — PT12

Bartolome de Las Casas Aiding Youth — PT13

Perf. 12½

1951, May Unwmk. Engr.

RA49	PT12	5c red	.25	.20
RA50	PT13	5c carmine	.25	.20

The surtax was for the Red Cross.

No. RA43 Surcharged with New Value in Black

1951 Wmk. 255 *Perf. 12*

RA51	PT10	1c on 3c blue	.20	.20

Type of 1951

Engraved; Cross Lithographed

1953 Unwmk. *Perf. 12½*

RA52	PT13	5c grn & car	.25	.20

Surtax of Nos. RA52-RA60 for the Red Cross.

No. C254 Overprinted with Cross and Bar in Carmine

1954

RA53	AP42	5c lilac rose	.60	.50

St. Peter Claver Offering Gifts to Slaves — PT14

Engraved; Cross Typographed

1955, May 2 Unwmk. *Perf. 13*

RA54	PT14	5c dp plum & red	.25	.20

Death of St. Peter Claver, 300th anniv.

Jean Henri Dunant and Santiago Samper Brush PT15

Photo.; Red Cross & "Cruz Roja" Engr.

1956, June 1 Unwmk. *Perf. 13*

No.	Type	Description	Unused	Used
RA55	PT15	5c brown & red	.25	.20

Nurses and Ambulances PT16

1958, June 2 Photo. *Perf. 12*

No.	Type	Description	Unused	Used
RA56	PT16	5c gray & red	.20	.20

St. Louisa de Marillac and Church PT17

No. RA58, Henri Dunant and battle scene.

1960, Sept. 1 Litho. *Perf. 11*

No.	Type	Description	Unused	Used
RA57	PT17	5c brown & rose	.25	.20
RA58	PT17	5c vio blue & rose	.25	.20

No. RA57 for 3rd cent. of the Sisters of Charity. No. RA58 for cent. (in 1959) of the Red Cross idea.

Manuelita de la Cruz — PT18

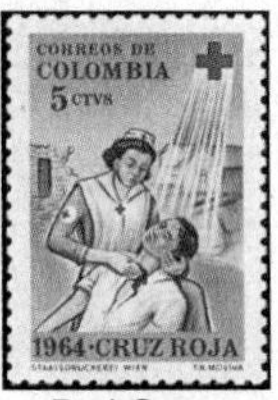

Red Cross Worker, Patient — PT19

1961, Nov. 2 Engr. *Perf. 13*

No.	Type	Description	Unused	Used
RA59	PT18	5c dull pur & red	.20	.20
RA60	PT18	5c brown & red	.20	.20

Issued in memory of Red Cross Nurse Manuelita de la Cruz, who died in the line of duty during the floods of 1955. Obligatory on domestic mail for a month.

1965, Apr. 30 Photo. *Perf. 12*

No.	Type	Description	Unused	Used
RA61	PT19	5c blue gray & red	.20	.20

Obligatory on domestic mail during May.

Nurse's Cap — PT20

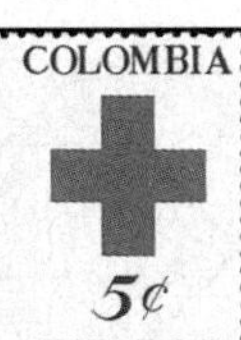

Red Cross — PT21

1967, June 1 Litho. *Perf. 12*

No.	Type	Description	Unused	Used
RA62	PT20	5c brt bl & red	.20	.20

1969, July 1 Litho. *Perf. 12x12½*

No.	Type	Description	Unused	Used
RA63	PT21	5c vio bl & red	.20	.20

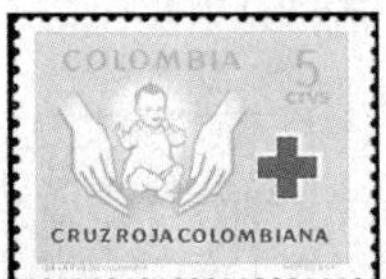

Child Care — PT22

1970, July 1 Litho. *Perf. 12½x12*

No.	Type	Description	Unused	Used
RA64	PT22	5c light bl & red	.20	.20

ANTIOQUIA

ˌant-ē-ˈō-kē-ə

Originally a State, now a Department of the Republic of Colombia. Until the revolution of 1885, the separate states making up the United States of Colombia were sovereign governments in their own right. On August 4, 1886, the National Council of Bogotá, composed of two delegates from each state, adopted a new constitution which abolished the sovereign rights of states, which then became departments with governors appointed by the President of the Republic. The nine original states represented at the Bogotá Convention retained some of their previous rights, as management of their own finances, and all issued postage stamps until as late as 1904. For Panama's issues, see Panama Nos. 1-30.

Coat of Arms
A1 A2

A3

A4

Wove Paper

1868 Unwmk. Litho. *Imperf.*

No.	Type	Description	Unused	Used
1	A1	2½c blue	*1,000.*	*750.*
2	A2	5c green	*750.*	*575.*
3	A3	10c lilac	*3,000.*	*1,000.*
4	A4	1p red	*675.*	*750.*

Reprints of Nos. 1, 3 and 4 are on a bluish white paper and all but No. 3 have scratches across the design.

A5

A6

A7 A8

A9 A10

1869

No.	Type	Description	Unused	Used
5	A5	2½c blue	3.25	2.75
6	A6	5c green	5.00	4.50
7	A7	5c green	5.00	4.50
8	A8	10c lilac	6.25	3.25
9	A9	20c brown	6.25	3.25
10	A10	1p rose red	12.50	11.00
a.		1p vermilion	25.00	22.50
		Nos. 5-10 (6)	38.25	29.25

Reprints of Nos. 7, 8 and 10 are on a bluish white paper; reprints of Nos. 5 and 10a on white paper. The 10c blue is believed to be a reprint.

A11 A12

A13

A14

A15 A16

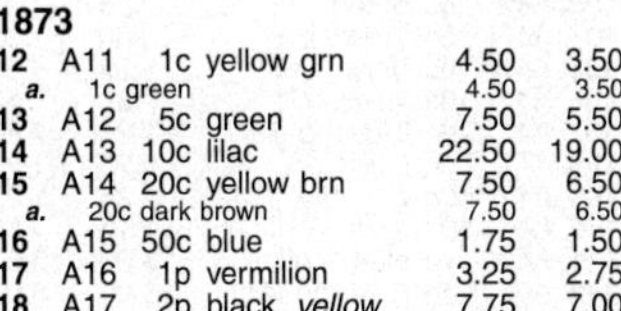

A17 A18

1873

No.	Type	Description	Unused	Used
12	A11	1c yellow grn	4.50	3.50
a.		1c green	4.50	3.50
13	A12	5c green	7.50	5.50
14	A13	10c lilac	22.50	19.00
15	A14	20c yellow brn	7.50	6.50
a.		20c dark brown	7.50	6.50
16	A15	50c blue	1.75	1.50
17	A16	1p vermilion	3.25	2.75
18	A17	2p black, *yellow*	7.75	7.00
19	A18	5p black, *rose*	55.00	47.50

A19

A20

Liberty Head
A21 A22

Pedro Justo Berrio — A23

1875-85

No.	Type	Description	Unused	Used
20	A19	1c blk, *grn,* unglazed ('76)	1.60	1.40
a.		Glazed paper	2.25	1.90
b.		1c blk, *lt grn,* laid paper ('85)	3.75	3.50
21	A19	1c black ('76)	1.10	1.00
a.		Laid paper	140.00	100.00
22	A19	1c bl grn ('85)	2.25	1.90
23	A19	1c red lil, laid paper ('85)	2.25	1.90
24	A20	2½c blue	2.25	1.90
a.		Pelure paper ('78)	*1,700.*	*1,250.*
25	A21	5c green	15.00	12.50
a.		Laid paper	140.00	80.00
26	A22	5c green	15.00	12.50
a.		Laid paper	140.00	80.00
27	A23	10c lilac	22.50	19.00
a.		Laid paper	140.00	110.00
28	A20	10c vio, pelure paper ('78)	*900.00*	675.00

Arms — A24

Liberty — A25

A26

A27

1878-85

No.	Type	Description	Unused	Used
29	A24	2½c blue, pelure paper	2.50	2.25
30	A24	2½c green ('83)	2.25	1.90
a.		Laid paper ('83)	70.00	47.50
31	A24	2½c blk, *buff* ('85)	6.25	5.50
32	A25	5c green ('83)	3.75	3.25
a.		Pelure paper	30.00	25.00
b.		Laid paper ('82)	37.50	11.00
33	A25	5c violet ('83)	8.75	6.50
a.		5c blue violet ('83)	8.75	6.50
34	A26	10c vio, laid paper ('82)	160.00	55.00
35	A26	10c scar ('83)	2.25	1.90
a.		Tete beche pair	50.00	45.00
36	A27	20c brown ('83)	3.75	3.25
a.		Laid paper ('82)	5.00	4.50

A28

A29

Liberty — A30

Coat of Arms — A31

1883-85

No.	Type	Description	Unused	Used
37	A28	5c brown	4.50	3.00
a.		Laid paper	190.00	75.00
38	A28	5c green ('85)	125.00	40.00
a.		Laid paper ('85)	140.00	65.00
39	A28	5c yel, laid paper ('85)	5.00	4.00
40	A29	10c bl grn, laid paper	5.00	4.50
41	A29	10c bl, *bl* ('85)	5.00	4.00
42	A29	10c lil, laid paper ('85)	9.50	6.50
a.		Wove paper ('85)	100.00	40.00
43	A30	20c bl, laid paper ('85)	4.50	4.00

1886

Wove Paper

No.	Type	Description	Unused	Used
55	A31	1c grn, *pink*	.55	.50
56	A31	2½c blk, *orange*	.55	.50
57	A31	5c ultra, *buff*	1.75	1.60
a.		5c blue, *buff*	3.25	2.75
58	A31	10c rose, *buff*	1.60	1.40
a.		Transfer of 50c in stone of 10c	75.00	65.00
59	A31	20c dk vio, *buff*	1.60	1.40
61	A31	50c yel brn, *buff*	2.75	2.50
62	A31	1p yel, *grn*	4.50	4.00
63	A31	2p green, *vio*	4.50	4.00
		Nos. 55-63 (8)	17.80	15.90

1887-88

No.	Type	Description	Unused	Used
64	A31	1c red, *vio*	.45	.40
65	A31	2½c lil, *pale lil*	.45	*.55*
66	A31	5c car, *buff*	.60	.55
67	A31	5c red, *grn*	3.25	1.60
68	A31	10c brn, *grn*	.65	*.80*
		Nos. 64-68 (5)	5.40	3.90

Medellin Issue

A32

A33

A34

A35

1888 **Typeset**

69 A32 2½c blk, *yellow* 14.00 12.50
70 A33 5c blk, *yellow* 7.50 6.75
71 A34 5c red, *yellow* 4.50 4.00
Nos. 69-71 (3) 26.00 23.25

Two varieties of No. 69, six of No. 70 and ten of No. 71.

1889

72 A35 2½c red 7.00 6.00

Ten varieties including "eentavos."

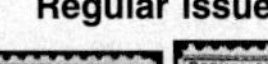

Regular Issue

Coat of Arms
A36 A37

A38

A39

A40

A41

1889 **Litho.** ***Perf. 13½***

73 A36 1c blk, *rose* .25 .25
74 A36 2½c blk, *blue* .25 .25
75 A36 5c blk, *yellow* .30 .30
76 A36 10c blk, *green* .30 .30
Nos. 73-76 (4) 1.10 1.10

1890

78 A37 20c blue 1.25 1.25
79 A38 50c vio brn 2.50 2.50
a. Transfer of 20c in stone of 50c 82.50 82.50
80 A38 50c green 2.00 2.00
81 A39 1p red 1.75 1.75
82 A40 2p blk, *mag* 12.50 12.50
83 A41 5p blk, *org red* 20.00 20.00
Nos. 78-83 (6) 40.00 40.00

Nos. 73-76, 82-83 exist imperf.

The so-called "errors" of Nos. 73 to 76, printed on paper of wrong colors, are essays or, possibly, reprints. They exist perforated and imperforate.

See No. 96.

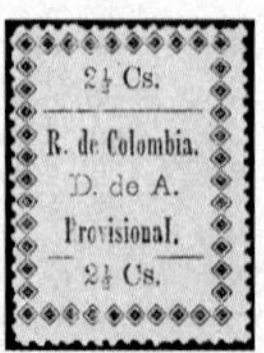
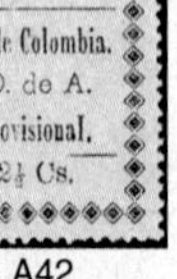

A42

A43

A44

A45

1890 **Typeset** ***Perf. 14***

84 A42 2½c blk, *buff* 2.00 2.00
85 A43 5c blk, *orange* 2.00 2.00
86 A44 10c blk, *buff* 6.00 6.00
87 A44 10c blk, *rose* 7.50 7.50
88 A45 20c blk, *orange* 7.50 7.50
Nos. 84-88 (5) 25.00 25.00

20 varieties of the 5c, 10 each of the other values.

A46

A47

1892 **Litho.** ***Perf. 13½***

89 A46 1c brn, *brnsh* .35 .35
90 A46 2½c pur, *lil* .35 .35
92 A46 5c blk, *gray* 1.00 .50
a. Transfer of 2½c in stone of 5c 150.00
Nos. 89-92 (3) 1.70 1.20

1893

93 A46 1c blue .25 .25
94 A46 2½c green .35 .35
95 A46 5c vermilion .25 .25
96 A36 10c pale brown .25 .25
Nos. 93-96 (4) 1.10 1.10

1896 ***Perf. 14***

97 A47 2c gray .25 .25
98 A47 2c lilac rose .25 .25
99 A47 2½c brown .25 .25
100 A47 2½c steel blue .25 .25
101 A47 3c orange .25 .25
102 A47 3c olive grn .25 .25
103 A47 5c green .25 .25
104 A47 5c yellow buff .30 .30
105 A47 10c brown vio .55 .55
106 A47 10c violet .55 .55
107 A47 20c brown org 1.25 1.25
108 A47 20c blue 1.25 1.25
109 A47 50c gray brn 1.25 1.25
110 A47 50c rose 1.10 1.10
111 A47 1p blue & blk 16.00 16.00
112 A47 1p rose red & blk 16.00 16.00
113 A47 2p orange & blk 47.50 47.50
114 A47 2p dk grn & blk 47.50 47.50
115 A47 5p red vio & blk 82.50 82.50
116 A47 5p purple & blk 82.50 82.50
Nos. 97-116 (20) 300.00 300.00

#115-116 with centers omitted are proofs.

General José María Córdoba — A48

1899 ***Perf. 11***

117 A48 ½c grnsh bl .20 .20
118 A48 1c slate blue .20 .20
119 A48 2c slate brown .20 .20
120 A48 3c red .20 .20
121 A48 4c bister brown .20 .20
122 A48 5c green .20 .20
123 A48 10c scarlet .20 .20
124 A48 20c gray violet .20 .20
125 A48 50c olive bister .20 .20
126 A48 1p greenish blk .20 .20
127 A48 2p olive gray .20 .20
Nos. 117-127 (11) 2.20 2.20

Numerous part-perf. and imperf. varieties of Nos. 117-127 exist.

A49

A50

A50a

1901 **Typeset** ***Perf. 12***

128 A49 1c red .20 .20
129 A50 1c ultra .60 .60
130 A50 1c bister .60 .60
130A A50a 1c dull red .60 .60
130B A50a 1c ultra 4.00 4.00
Nos. 128-130B (5) 6.00 6.00

Eight varieties of No. 128, four varieties of Nos. 129-130B.

A51

A52

Atanasio Girardot
A53

Dr. José Félix Restrepo
A54

1902 **Litho.** **Wove Paper**

131 A51 1c brt rose .20 .20
a. Laid paper .60 .60
b. Imperf., pair 2.50
132 A51 2c blue .20 .20
a. Transfer of 3c in stone of 2c 5.00 5.00
133 A51 3c green .20 .20
a. Imperf., pair 4.00
134 A51 4c dull violet .20 .20
135 A52 5c rose red .20 .20
136 A53 10c rose lilac .20 .20
a. Small head 5.00 5.00
b. 10c rose .20 .20
137 A53 20c gray green .20 .20
138 A53 30c brt rose .20 .20
139 A53 40c blue .20 .20
140 A53 50c brn, *yel* .20 .20

Laid Paper

141 A54 1p purple & blk .70 .70
142 A54 2p rose & blk .70 .70
143 A54 5p sl bl & blk 1.25 1.25
Nos. 131-143 (13) 4.65 4.65

1903

Wove Paper

143A A51 1c blue .20 .20
144 A51 2c violet .20 .20
a. Imperf. 2.50

A55

A56

A57

Designs: 1p, Francisco Antonio Zea. 2p, Custodio Garcia Rovira. 3p, La Pola (Policarpa Salavarrieta). 4p, J. M. Restrepo. 5p, José Fernández Madrid. 10p, Juan del Corral.

1903-04

145 A55 4c yellow brn .20 .20
146 A55 5c blue .20 .20
147 A56 10c yellow .20 .20
148 A56 20c purple .20 .20
149 A56 30c brown .60 .60
150 A56 40c green .60 .60
151 A56 50c rose .20 .20
152 A57 1p olive gray .60 .60
153 A57 2p purple .60 .60
154 A57 3p dark blue .60 .60
155 A57 4p dull red 1.00 1.00
156 A57 5p red brown 3.00 1.50
157 A57 10p scarlet 6.50 3.50
Nos. 145-157 (13) 14.50 10.00

Nos. 145-146, 151, 153-157 exist imperf. Value of pairs, $3 to $4.

Manizales Issue

Stamps of these designs are local private post issues.

OFFICIAL STAMPS Stamps of 1903-04 with overprint "OFICIAL" were never issued.

REGISTRATION STAMPS

R1

1896 **Unwmk.** **Litho.** ***Perf. 14***

F1 R1 2½c rose 1.10 1.10
F2 R1 2½c dull blue 1.10 1.10

Córdoba
R2

R3

R4

1899 ***Perf. 11***

F3 R2 2½c dull blue .25 .25
F4 R3 10c red lilac .25 .25

1902 ***Perf. 12***

F5 R4 10c purple, *blue* .30 .30
a. Imperf.

ACKNOWLEDGMENT OF RECEIPT STAMPS

AR1

1902-03 **Unwmk.** **Litho.** ***Perf. 12***

H1 AR1 5c black, *rose* .90 .90
H2 AR1 5c slate ('03) .30 .30

LATE FEE STAMPS

Córdoba — LF1

1899 Unwmk. Litho. *Perf. 11*

I1	LF1	2½c dark green	.25	.25
a.		Imperf., pair	2.75	

LF2

LF3

1901 Typeset *Perf. 12*

I2	LF2	2½c red violet	.50	.50
a.		2½c purple	.50	.50

1902 Litho.

I3	LF3	2½c violet	.20	.20

City of Medellin

Stamps of the designs shown were not issued by any governmental agency but by the Sociedad de Mejoras Publicas.

BOLIVAR

bə-ˈlē-ˌvär

Originally a State, now a Department of the Republic of Colombia. (See Antioquia.)

A1

1863-66 Unwmk. Litho. *Imperf.*

1	A1	10c green	*1,100.*	*550.00*
a.		Five stars below shield	*2,400.*	*2,200.*
2	A1	10c red ('66)	25.00	*27.50*
a.		Diagonal half used as 5c on cover		55.00
b.		Five stars below shield	75.00	67.50
3	A1	1p red	6.25	*7.25*

Fourteen varieties of each. Counterfeits of Nos. 1 and 1a exist.

Coat of Arms
A2 A3

A4

A5

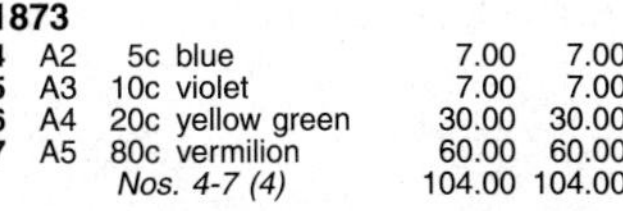

1873

4	A2	5c blue	7.00	7.00
5	A3	10c violet	7.00	7.00
6	A4	20c yellow green	30.00	30.00
7	A5	80c vermilion	60.00	60.00
		Nos. 4-7 (4)	104.00	104.00

A6

A7

A8

Bolívar — A9

1874-78

8	A6	5c blue	25.00	12.50
9	A7	5c blue ('78)	7.75	7.00
10	A8	10c violet ('77)	3.75	3.50
		Nos. 8-10 (3)	36.50	23.00

Dated "1879"

1879 White Wove Paper *Perf. 12½*

11	A9	5c blue	.25	.25
a.		Imperf., pair	.80	
12	A9	10c violet	.20	.20
13	A9	20c red	.25	.25
a.		20c green (error)	10.00	10.00

Bluish Laid Paper

15	A9	5c blue	.30	.30
a.		Imperf., pair	2.00	
16	A9	10c violet	1.60	1.60
a.		Imperf., pair	4.00	
17	A9	20c red	.40	.40
a.		Imperf., pair	1.75	
		Nos. 11-17 (6)	3.00	3.00

Stamps of 80c and 1p on white wove paper and 1p on bluish laid paper were prepared but not placed in use.

Dated "1880"

1880 White Wove Paper *Perf. 12½*

19	A9	5c blue	.25	.25
a.		Imperf., pair	1.60	
20	A9	10c violet	.35	.35
a.		Imperf., pair	1.60	
21	A9	20c red	.35	.35
a.		20c green (error)	13.00	13.00
23	A9	80c green	2.25	2.25
24	A9	1p orange	2.50	2.50
a.		Imperf., pair	5.50	
		Nos. 19-24 (5)	5.70	5.70

Bluish Laid Paper

25	A9	5c blue	.25	.25
a.		Imperf., pair	1.25	
26	A9	10c violet	2.25	2.25
27	A9	20c red	.35	.35
a.		Imperf., pair	2.75	
28	A9	1p orange	400.00	
a.		Imperf.	*450.00*	

A11

A12

A13

A15

A16

Dated "1882"
White Wove Paper

1882 *Perf. 12, 16x12*

29	A11	5c blue	.35	.35
30	A12	10c lilac	.25	.25
31	A13	20c red	.35	.35
33	A15	80c green	.65	.65
34	A16	1p orange	.65	.65
		Nos. 29-34 (5)	2.25	2.25

Nos. 29, 30 and 34 are known imperforate. They are printer's waste and were not issued through post offices.

A17

A18

1882 Engr. *Perf. 12*

35	A17	5p blue & rose red	.60	.60
a.		Imperf., pair	4.75	
b.		Perf. 16	7.50	6.25
c.		Perf. 14	6.25	6.25
36	A17	10p brown & blue	1.60	1.60
a.		Imperf., pair	8.00	
b.		Perf. 16	7.00	5.50
c.		Rouletted	8.00	8.00

Dated "1883"

1883 Litho. *Perf. 12, 16x12*

37	A11	5c blue	.20	.20
a.		Imperf., pair	.80	
b.		Perf. 12	3.00	1.00
38	A12	10c lilac	.25	.25
39	A13	20c red	.25	.25
41	A15	80c green	.30	.30
42	A16	1p orange	.60	.60
a.		Perf. 16x12	2.00	2.00
		Nos. 37-42 (5)	1.60	1.60

Dated "1884"

1884

43	A11	5c blue	.30	.30
a.		Perf. 12	10.00	9.25
44	A12	10c lilac	.20	.20
45	A13	20c red	.20	.20
a.		Perf. 12	4.25	4.25
47	A15	80c green	.25	.25
a.		Perf. 12	2.00	2.00
48	A16	1p orange	.30	.30
		Nos. 43-48 (5)	1.25	1.25

Dated "1885"

1885

49	A11	5c blue	.20	.20
50	A12	10c lilac	.20	.20
51	A13	20c red	.20	.20
53	A15	80c green	.25	.25
54	A16	1p orange	.30	.30
		Nos. 49-54 (5)	1.15	1.15

The note after No. 34 will also apply to imperforate stamps of the 1884-85 issues.

1891 *Perf. 14*

55	A18	1c black	.30	.30
56	A18	5c orange	.30	.30
a.		Imperf., pair	.80	
57	A18	10c carmine	.30	.30
58	A18	20c blue	.60	.60
59	A18	50c green	.90	.90
60	A18	1p purple	.90	.90
		Nos. 55-60 (6)	3.30	3.30

For overprint see Colombia No. 169.

Bolívar
A19

José Fernández Madrid
A20

Manuel Rodriguez Torices
A21

José María García de Toledo
A22

1903 Laid Paper *Imperf.*

62	A19	50c dk bl, *pink*	.60	.60
a.		Bluish paper	.60	.60
63	A19	50c sl grn, *pink*	.60	.60
a.		Rose paper	2.00	2.00
b.		Greenish blue paper	3.00	3.00
c.		Yellow paper	4.00	4.00
d.		Brown paper	4.00	4.00
e.		Salmon paper	7.50	7.50
64	A19	50c pur, *pink*	2.00	2.00
a.		White paper	4.00	4.00
b.		Brown paper	4.00	4.00
c.		Greenish blue paper	4.00	4.00
d.		Lilac paper	4.00	4.00
e.		Rose paper	3.50	3.50
f.		Yellow paper	4.00	4.00
g.		Salmon paper	6.00	6.00
h.		As "a," wove paper	9.00	9.00
65	A20	1p org, *sal*	.60	.60
a.		Yellow paper	4.50	4.50
b.		Greenish blue paper	15.00	15.00
66	A20	1p gray grn, *lil*	1.40	1.40
a.		Yellow paper	6.50	6.50
b.		Salmon paper	7.50	7.50
c.		Green paper	7.50	7.50
d.		White wove paper	10.00	
67	A21	5p car rose, *lil*	.60	.60
a.		Brown paper	1.10	1.10
b.		Yellow paper	1.10	1.10
c.		Greenish blue paper	4.50	4.50
d.		Bluish paper	6.00	6.00
e.		Salmon paper	7.50	7.50
f.		Rose paper	9.00	9.00
68	A22	10p dk bl, *bluish*	1.25	1.25
a.		Greenish blue paper	1.25	1.25
b.		Rose paper	7.50	7.50
c.		Salmon paper	7.50	7.50
d.		Yellow paper	7.50	7.50
e.		Brown paper	8.50	8.50
f.		Lilac paper	10.00	10.00
g.		White paper	9.00	9.00
69	A22	10p pur, *grnsh bl*	3.50	3.50
a.		Bluish paper	7.50	7.50
b.		Rose paper	6.75	6.75
c.		Yellow paper	7.50	7.50
d.		Brown paper	7.50	7.50
		Nos. 62-69 (8)	10.55	10.55

Sewing Machine Perf.
Laid Paper

70	A19	50c dk bl, *pink*	1.00	1.00
a.		Bluish paper	1.00	1.00
71	A19	50c sl grn, *pink*	2.00	2.00
72	A19	50c pur, *grnsh bl*	4.00	4.00
a.		White paper	4.00	4.00
b.		White wove paper	7.50	
73	A20	1p org, *sal*	2.00	2.00
74	A20	1p gray grn, *lil*	9.00	9.00
a.		Yellow paper	9.00	9.00
75	A21	5p car rose, *yel*	1.60	1.60
a.		Lilac paper	4.00	4.00
b.		Brown paper	4.00	4.00
c.		Bluish paper	5.50	5.50
d.		White wove paper	9.00	
76	A22	10p dk bl, *grnsh bl*	4.50	4.50
a.		Bluish paper	7.00	7.00
b.		Yellow paper	9.00	9.00
c.		As "b," wove paper	10.00	
77	A22	10p pur, *grnsh bl*	7.00	7.00
a.		Bluish paper	11.00	11.00
b.		Rose paper	8.00	8.00
c.		Yellow paper	11.00	11.00
		Nos. 70-77 (8)	31.10	31.10

José María del Castillo y Rada — A23

Manuel Anguiano — A24

Pantaleón C. Ribón — A25

1904 *Sewing Machine Perf.*

89	A23	5c black	.25	.25
90	A24	10c brown	.25	.25
91	A25	20c red	.30	.30
92	A25	20c red brown	.60	.60
		Nos. 89-92 (4)	1.40	1.40

Imperf., pairs

89a	A23	5c black	3.50	3.50
90a	A24	10c brown	2.75	2.75
91a	A25	20c red	6.50	6.50
92a	A25	20c red brown	6.50	6.50

A26

A27

A28

1904 ***Imperf.***

93	A26	½c black	.65	.65
a.		Tête bêche pair	3.50	3.50
94	A27	1c blue	1.10	1.10
95	A28	2c purple	1.25	1.25
		Nos. 93-95 (3)	3.00	3.00

REGISTRATION STAMPS

Simón Bolívar
R1 R2

White Wove Paper

Perf. 12½, 16x12

1879 **Unwmk.** **Litho.**

F1	R1	40c brown	.70	.70

Bluish Laid Paper

F2	R1	40c brown	.70	.70
a.		Imperf., pair	3.25	

Dated "1880"

1880

White Wove Paper

F3	R1	40c brown	.30	.30

Bluish Laid Paper

F4	R1	40c brown	.65	.65
a.		Imperf., pair	3.50	

Dated "1882" to "1885"
White Wove Paper

1882-85 ***Perf. 16x12***

F5	R2	40c brown (1882)	.30	.30
F6	R2	40c brown (1883)	.25	.25
F7	R2	40c brown (1884)	.25	.25
F8	R2	40c brown (1885)	.30	.30
		Nos. F5-F8 (4)	1.10	1.10

Perf. 12

F5a	R2	40c	18.00
F6a	R2	40c	9.25
F7a	R2	40c	9.50
F8a	R2	40c	2.50
		Nos. F5a-F8a (4)	39.25

R3

Laid Paper

1903 ***Imperf.***

F9	R3	20c orange, *rose*	.60	.60
a.		Salmon paper	1.10	1.10
b.		Greenish blue paper	6.00	6.00

Sewing Machine Perf.

F10	R3	20c orange, *rose*	2.50	2.50
a.		Salmon paper	2.50	2.50
b.		Greenish blue paper	6.00	6.00

R4

1904

Wove Paper

F11	R4	5c black	3.25	3.25

ACKNOWLEDGMENT OF RECEIPT STAMPS

AR1

AR2

1903 **Unwmk.** **Litho.** ***Imperf.***

Laid Paper

H1	AR1	20c org, *rose*	2.50	2.50
a.		Yellow paper	1.25	1.25
b.		Greenish blue paper	5.00	5.00
H2	AR1	20c dk bl, *yel*	2.00	2.00
a.		Brown paper	3.50	3.50
b.		Rose paper	2.50	2.50
c.		Salmon paper	7.00	7.00
d.		Greenish blue paper	7.00	7.00

Sewing Machine Perf.

H3	AR1	20c org, *grnsh bl*	6.25	6.25
a.		Yellow paper	7.25	7.25
H4	AR1	20c dk bl, *yel*	7.25	7.25
a.		Lilac paper	7.25	7.25
		Nos. H1-H4 (4)	18.00	18.00

1904

Wove Paper

H5	AR2	2c red	1.10	1.10

LATE FEE STAMPS

LF1

1903 **Unwmk.** **Litho.** ***Imperf.***

Laid Paper

I1	LF1	20c car rose, *bluish*	.60	.60
I2	LF1	20c pur, *bluish*	.55	.55
a.		Rose paper	2.00	2.00
b.		Brown paper	2.00	2.00
c.		Lilac paper	2.00	2.00
d.		Yellow paper	6.25	6.25

Sewing Machine Perf.

I3	LF1	20c car rose, *bluish*	3.50	3.50
I4	LF1	20c pur, *bluish*	3.50	3.50
a.		Rose paper	6.00	6.00
b.		Lilac paper	6.00	6.00
c.		Yellow paper	10.00	10.00
		Nos. I1-I4 (4)	8.15	8.15

BOYACA

Originally a State, now a Department of the Republic of Colombia. (See Antioquia.)

Diego Mendoza Pérez — A1

1902 **Unwmk.** **Litho.** ***Perf. 13½***

Wove Paper

1	A1	5c blue green	.70	.70
a.		Bluish paper	90.00	90.00
b.		Imperf., pair	12.50	

Laid Paper

Perf. 12

2	A1	5c green	100.00	100.00

Coat of Arms
A2 A3

Gen. Próspero Pinzón — A4

A5

Monument of Battle of Boyacá — A6

President José Manuel Marroquin — A7

1903 **Litho.** ***Imperf.***

4	A2	10c dark gray	.25	.25
5	A3	20c red brown	.30	.30
6	A5	1p red	3.00	3.00
a.		1p claret	3.50	3.50
8	A6	5p black, *rose*	1.10	1.10
a.		5p black, *buff*	11.00	11.00
9	A7	10p black, *buff*	1.10	1.10
a.		10p black, *rose*	11.00	11.00
b.		Tête bêche pair	15.00	
		Nos. 4-9 (5)	5.75	5.75

Perf. 12

10	A2	10c dark gray	.30	.30
11	A3	20c red brown	.35	.35
12	A4	50c green	.30	.30
13	A4	50c dull blue	2.00	2.00
14	A5	1p red	.30	.30
a.		1p claret	3.00	3.00
16	A6	5p black, *rose*	11.00	11.00
a.		5p black, *buff*	9.50	9.50
17	A7	10p black, *buff*	1.10	1.10
a.		10p black, *rose*	11.00	11.00
b.		Tête bêche pair	12.00	12.00
		Nos. 10-17 (7)	15.35	15.35

Statue of Bolívar — A8

1904

18	A8	10c orange	.25	.25
a.		Imperf., pair	3.50	3.50

CAUCA

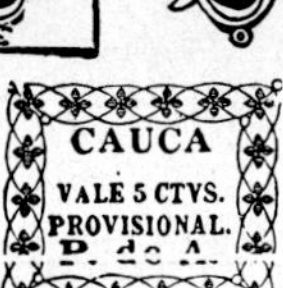

Stamps of these designs were issued by a provincial post between 1879(?) and 1890.

Stamps of this design are believed to be of private origin and without official sanction.

Items inscribed "No hay estampillas" (No stamps available) and others inscribed "Manuel E. Jiménez" are considered by specialists to be receipt labels, not postage stamps.

CUNDINAMARCA

ˌkün-di-nə-ˈmär-kə

Originally a State, now a Department of the Republic of Colombia. (See Antioquia.)

Coat of Arms
A1 A2

1870 **Unwmk.** **Litho.** ***Imperf.***

1	A1	5c blue	4.75	4.75
2	A2	10c red	15.00	15.00

The counterfeits, or reprints, show traces of the cuts made to deface the dies.

A3

A4

A5

A6

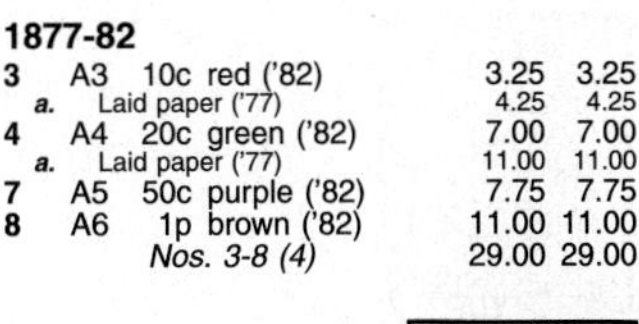

1877-82

3 A3 10c red ('82) 3.25 3.25
a. Laid paper ('77) 4.25 4.25
4 A4 20c green ('82) 7.00 7.00
a. Laid paper ('77) 11.00 11.00
7 A5 50c purple ('82) 7.75 7.75
8 A6 1p brown ('82) 11.00 11.00
Nos. 3-8 (4) 29.00 29.00

A7

1884

10 A7 5c blue .75 .75
11 A7 5c blue (redrawn) .75 .75
a. Tête bêche pair 75.00 75.00

The redrawn stamp has no period after "COLOMBIA."

A8

A9

A10

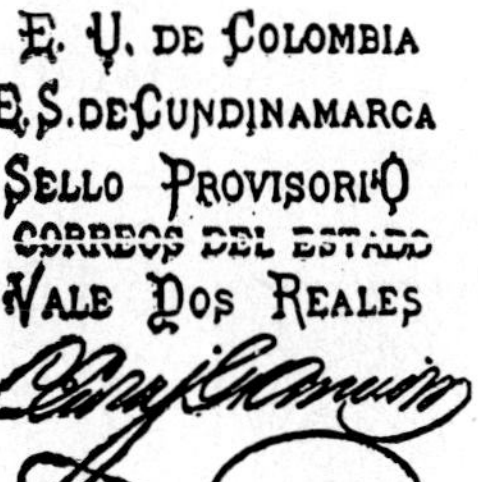

A11

1883 **Typeset**

13 A8 10c black, *yellow* 12.50 12.50
14 A9 50c black, *rose* 12.50 12.50
15 A10 1p black, *brown* 35.00 35.00
16 A11 2r black, *green* *2,000.*

Typeset varieties exist: 4 of the 10c, 2 each of 50c and 1p.

Some experts doubt that No. 16 was issued. The variety without signature and watermarked "flowers" is believed to be a proof. Forgeries exist.

A12

1886 **Litho.**

17 A12 5c blue .75 .75
18 A12 10c red 4.50 4.50
19 A12 10c red, *lilac* 2.50 2.50
20 A12 20c green 3.75 3.75
a. 20c yellow green 4.50 4.50
21 A12 50c purple 5.00 5.00
22 A12 1p orange brown 5.25 5.25
Nos. 17-22 (6) 21.75 21.75

Nos. 17 to 22 have been reprinted. The colors are aniline and differ from those of the original stamps. The impression is coarse and blurred.

A13

A14

A15

A16

A17

A18

A19

A20

A21

1904 ***Perf. 10½, 12***

23 A13 1c orange .25 .25
24 A14 2c gray blue .25 .25
25 A15 3c rose .35 .35
26 A15 5c olive grn .35 .35
27 A16 10c pale brn .35 .35
28 A17 15c pink .35 .35
29 A18 20c blue, *grn* .35 .35
30 A18 20c blue .60 .60
31 A19 40c blue .60 .60
32 A19 40c blue, *buff* 17.50 17.50
33 A20 50c red vio .60 .60
34 A21 1p gray grn .45 .45
Nos. 23-34 (12) 22.00 22.00

Imperf

23a A13 1c orange .75 .75
24a A14 2c blue .75 .75
b. 2c slate 6.00 6.00
25a A15 3c rose .90 .90
26a A15 5c olive green 1.50 1.50
27a A16 10c pale brown 2.00 2.00
28a A17 15c pink .50 .50
29a A18 20c blue, *green* 2.00 2.00
30a A18 20c blue 2.00 2.00
31a A19 40c blue .70 .70
32a A19 40c blue, *buff* 17.50 17.50
33a A20 50c red violet .70 .70
34a A21 1p gray green .70 .70
Nos. 23a-34a (12) 30.00 30.00

REGISTRATION STAMPS

R1

1883 **Unwmk.** ***Imperf.***

F1 R1 black, *orange* 15.00 16.00

R2

1904 ***Perf. 12***

F2 R2 10c bister .80 .80
a. Imperf. 3.50 3.50

Magdalena

Items inscribed "No hay estampillas" (No stamps available) are considered by specialists to be not postage stamps but receipt labels.

Panama

Issues of Panama as a state and later Department of Colombia are listed with the Republic of Panama issues (Nos. 1-30).

SANTANDER

ˌsän-ˌtän-ˈdeˌəˌr

Originally a State, now a Department of the Republic of Colombia.
(See Antioquia.)

Coat of Arms
A1 A2

1884 **Unwmk.** **Litho.** ***Imperf.***

1 A1 1c blue .30 .30
a. 1c gray blue .50 .50
2 A2 5c red .50 .50
3 A2 10c bluish purple 1.75 1.75
a. Tête bêche pair
Nos. 1-3 (3) 2.55 2.55

No. 2 exists unofficially perforated 14.

A3

A4

1886 ***Imperf.***

4 A3 1c blue .90 .90
5 A3 5c red .30 .30
6 A3 10c red violet .50 .50
a. 10c deep violet .50 .50
b. Inscribed "CINCO CENTAVOS" 25.00 25.00
Nos. 4-6 (3) 1.70 1.70

The numerals in the upper corners are omitted on No. 5, while on No. 6 there are no numerals in the side panels. No. 6 exists unofficially perforated 12.

1887

7 A4 1c blue .25 .25
a. 1c ultramarine 1.60 1.60
8 A4 5c red 1.60 1.60
9 A4 10c violet 5.00 5.00
Nos. 7-9 (3) 6.85 6.85

A5

A6

A7

1889 ***Perf. 11½ and 13½***

10 A5 1c blue .30 .30
11 A6 5c red 1.25 1.25
12 A7 10c purple .45 .45
a. Imperf., pair 16.00
Nos. 10-12 (3) 2.00 2.00

A8

A9

1892 ***Perf. 13½***

13 A8 5c red, *rose buff* 1.00 1.00

1895-96

14 A9 5c brown .70 .70
15 A9 5c yel grn ('96) .70 .70

A10

A11

A12

1899 ***Perf. 10***

16 A10 1c black, *green* .35 .35
17 A11 5c black, *pink* .35 .35

Perf. 13½

18 A12 10c blue .70 .70
a. Perf. 12 1.00 1.00
Nos. 16-18 (3) 1.40 1.40

A13

1903 ***Imperf.***

19 A13 50c red .55 .55
a. 50c rose .55 .55
b. "SANTENDER" 2.50 2.50
c. "Corrcos" 2.50 2.50
d. "Corceos" 2.50 2.50
e. Tête bêche pair 4.75 4.75
f. Pair, one without overprint 2.75 2.75

The overprint "Correos de Departmento Bucaramanga" on the 50c red revenue stamp has been proved to be a cancellation.

A14

A15

Arms
A16

Locomotive
A17

A18

A19

A20

1904 *Imperf.*

22	A14	5c dark green	.25	.25
a.		5c yellow green	.40	.40
24	A15	10c rose	.20	.20
25	A16	20c brown violet	.20	.20
26	A17	50c yellow	.20	.20
27	A18	1p black	.20	.20
28	A19	5p dark blue	.35	.35
29	A20	10p carmine	.40	.40
		Nos. 22-29 (7)	1.80	1.80

1905

30	A14	5c pale blue	.40	.40
31	A15	10c red brown	.40	.40
32	A16	20c yellow green	.40	.40
33	A17	50c red violet	.60	.60
34	A18	1p dark blue	.60	.60
35	A19	5p pink	.60	.60
36	A20	10p red	1.60	1.60
		Nos. 30-36 (7)	4.60	4.60

A21

1907 *Imperf.*

37	A21	½c on 50c rose	.55	.55

City of Cucuta

Stamps of these and similar designs on white and yellow paper, with and without surcharges of ½c, 1c or 2c, are believed to have been produced without government authorization.

TOLIMA

tə-lē-mə

Originally a State, now a Department of the Republic of Colombia.
(See Antioquia.)

A1

1870 Unwmk. Typeset *Imperf.*

White Wove Paper

1	A1	5c black	50.00	50.00
2	A1	10c black	75.00	75.00
a.		Vert. se-tenant pair	1,500.	1,500.

Printed from two settings. Setting I, ten types of 5c. Setting II, six types of 5c and four types of 10c.

Blue Laid Batonné Paper

3	A1	5c black	*950.00*	

Buff Laid Batonné Paper

4	A1	5c black	150.00	100.00

Blue Wove Paper

5	A1	5c black	70.00	45.00

Blue Vertically Laid Paper

6	A1	5c black	100.00	75.00
a.		Paper with ruled blue vertical lines		

Blue Horizontally Laid Paper

7	A1	5c black	200.00	150.00

Blue Quadrille Paper

8	A1	5c black	100.00	75.00

Ten varieties each of Nos. 3-5 and 7; 20 varieties each of Nos. 6 and 8.

Official imitations were made in 1886 from new settings of the type. There are only 2 varieties of each value. They are printed on blue and white paper, wove, batonné, laid, etc.

A2

A3

A4

A5

Yellowish White Wove Paper

1871 Litho. *Imperf.*

9	A2	5c deep brown	2.25	2.25
a.		5c red brown	2.25	2.25
b.		Value reads "CINGO"	37.50	37.50
10	A3	10c blue	6.00	6.00
11	A4	50c green	7.75	7.75
12	A5	1p carmine	12.00	12.00
		Nos. 9-12 (4)	28.00	28.00

The 5p stamps, type A2, are bogus varieties made from an altered die of the 5c.

The 10c, 50c and 1 peso stamps have been reprinted on bluish white wove paper. They are from new plates and most copies show traces of fine lines with which the dies had been defaced. Reprints of the 5c have a large cross at the top. The 10c on laid batonné paper is known only as a reprint.

A6

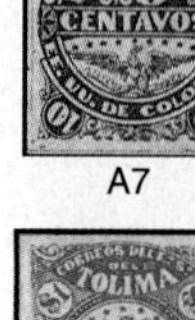
A7

A8

A9

1879

Grayish or White Wove Paper

14	A6	5c yellow brown	.45	.45
a.		5c purple brown	.45	.45
15	A7	10c blue	.50	.50
16	A8	50c green, *bluish*	.50	.50
a.		White paper	1.60	1.60
17	A9	1p vermilion	2.25	2.25
a.		1p carmine rose	9.00	9.00
		Nos. 14-17 (4)	3.70	3.70

A10

Coat of Arms — A12

1883 *Imperf.*

18	A6	5c orange	.45	.45
19	A7	10c vermilion	.90	.90
20	A10	20c violet	1.40	1.40
		Nos. 18-20 (3)	2.75	2.75

1884 *Imperf.*

23	A12	1c gray	.20	.20
24	A12	2c rose lilac	.20	.20
a.		2c slate	.20	.20
25	A12	2½c dull orange	.20	.20
26	A12	5c brown	.20	.20
27	A12	10c blue	.35	.35
a.		10c slate	.25	.25
28	A12	20c lemon	.35	.35
a.		Laid paper	5.00	5.00
29	A12	25c black	.30	.30
30	A12	50c green	.30	.30
31	A12	1p vermilion	.40	.40
32	A12	2p violet	.60	.60
a.		Value omitted	27.50	27.50
33	A12	5p yellow	.40	.40
34	A12	10p lilac rose	1.10	1.10
a.		Laid paper	30.00	30.00
b.		10p gray	*160.00*	
		Nos. 23-34 (12)	4.60	4.60

A13

A14

Condor with Long Wings Touching Flagstaffs
A15 A16

1886 Litho *Perf. 10½, 11*

White Paper

36	A13	5c brown	1.25	1.25
a.		5c yellow brown	1.25	1.25
b.		Imperf., pair	16.00	
37	A14	10c blue	3.50	3.50
a.		Imperf., pair	16.00	
38	A15	50c green	3.00	3.00
a.		Imperf., pair	16.00	
39	A16	1p vermilion	2.50	2.50
a.		Imperf., pair	24.00	
		Nos. 36-39 (4)	10.25	10.25

No. 38 has been reprinted in pale gray green, perforated 10½, and No. 39 in bright vermilion, perforated 11½. The impressions show many signs of wear.

Lilac Tinted Paper

36c	A13	5c orange brown	12.00	12.00
37b	A14	10c blue	12.00	12.00
38b	A15	50c green	9.00	9.00
39b	A16	1p vermilion	8.00	8.00
		Nos. 36c-39b (4)	41.00	41.00

Items similar to A15 and A16 but with condor with long wings and upper flagstaffs omitted are forgeries.

A17

A18

Condor with Short Wings
A19 A20

1886 White Paper *Perf. 12*

44	A19	1c gray	6.25	6.25
45	A17	2c rose lilac	6.50	6.50
46	A18	2½c dull org	19.00	19.00
47	A19	5c brown	8.50	8.00
48	A20	10c blue	8.00	8.00
49	A20	20c lemon	6.50	6.50
a.		Tête bêche pair	225.00	225.00
50	A20	25c black	6.25	6.25
51	A20	50c green	3.50	3.00
52	A20	1p vermilion	5.00	4.25
53	A20	2p violet	7.25	7.25
b.		Tête bêche pair	175.00	175.00
54	A20	5p orange	13.00	13.00
55	A20	10p lilac rose	7.25	7.25
		Nos. 44-55 (12)	97.00	95.25

Imperf., Pairs

44a	A19	1c	16.00
47a	A19	5c	27.50
48a	A20	10c	27.50
52a	A20	1p	20.00
53a	A20	2p	25.00
54a	A20	5p	32.50
55a	A20	10p	16.00

A23

1888 *Perf. 10½*

62	A23	5c red	.20	.20
63	A23	10c green	.30	.30
64	A23	50c blue	.75	.75
65	A23	1p red brown	1.75	1.75
		Nos. 62-65 (4)	3.00	3.00

For overprint see Colombia No. L14.

1895 *Perf. 12, 13½*

66	A23	1c blue, *rose*	.25	.25
67	A23	2c grn, *lt grn*	.25	.25
68	A23	5c red	.20	.20
69	A23	10c green	.50	.50
70	A23	20c blue, *yellow*	.30	.30
71	A23	1p brown	2.00	2.00
		Nos. 66-71 (6)	3.50	3.50

Imperf., Pairs

62a	A23	5c	2.75	
63a	A23	10c	3.25	
64a	A23	50c	4.75	4.75
65a	A23	1p	7.25	
66a	A23	1c	7.25	
67a	A23	2c	7.25	
70a	A23	20c	8.00	

"No Hay Estampillas"

Items inscribed "No hay estampillas" (No stamps available) are considered by specialists to be not postage stamps but receipt labels.

"Honda Issue"

This item seems to be of private origin.

A24

A25

A26 A27

A28

A29

A30

A31

Sewing Machine or Regular Perf. 12

1903-04 **Litho.**

79 A24 4c black, *green* .25 .25
80 A25 10c dull blue .25 .25
81 A26 20c orange .50 .50
82 A27 50c black, *rose* .25 .25
a. 50c black, *buff* .20 .20
84 A28 1p brown .20 .20
85 A29 2p gray .20 .20
86 A30 5p red .20 .20
a. Tête bêche pair 5.00 5.00
87 A31 10p black, *blue* .25 .25
a. 10p black, *light green* .25 .25
b. 10p black, *grn,* glazed 3.50 3.50
Nos. 79-87 (8) 2.10 2.10

Imperf

79a A24 4c black, *green* .25 .25
80a A25 10c dull blue .20 .20
81a A26 20c orange 1.10 1.10
82b A27 50c black, *rose* 1.50 1.50
c. 50c black, *buff* 1.50 1.50
84a A28 1p brown .20 .20
85a A29 2p gray .25 .25
86b A30 5p red .25 .25
c. Tête bêche pair 5.00 5.00
87c A31 10p black, *blue* 2.25 2.25
d. Tête bêche pair
e. 10p black, *light green* 3.50 3.50
f. 10p black, *green,* glazed 18.00 18.00
Nos. 79a-87c (8) 6.00 6.00

COMORO ISLANDS

ˈkä-mə-ˌrō ˈī-ləndz

LOCATION — In Mozambique Channel between Madagascar and Mozambique
GOVT. — Republic
AREA — 838 sq. mi.
POP. — 562,723 (1999 est.)
CAPITAL — Moroni

The Comoro Archipelago consists of the islands of Mayotte, Anjouan, Grand Comoro (Grande Comore) and Moheli, which issued their own stamps as French protectorates or colonies from 1887-1914. The archipelago was attached to Madagascar from 1914 to 1946, when it became a separate French territory. In July 1975, Anjouan, Grand Comoro and Moheli united to declare independence as the State of Comoro. Mayotte remained French.

100 Centimes = 1 Franc

Catalogue values for all unused stamps in this country are for Never Hinged items.

Anjouan Bay — A2

Comoro Woman Grinding Grain — A3

Moroni Mosque on Grand Comoro A4

1950 **Unwmk.** **Engr.** ***Perf. 13***

30 A2 10c blue .25 .25
31 A2 50c green .25 .25
32 A2 1fr dk ol brn .25 .25
33 A3 2fr brt grn .65 .55
34 A3 5fr purple 1.00 .90
35 A3 6fr vio brn 1.25 1.00
36 A4 7fr red 1.25 1.00
37 A4 10fr dk grn 1.25 1.00
38 A4 11fr dp ultra 1.40 1.25
Nos. 30-38 (9) 7.55 6.45

Imperforates

Most Comoro Islands stamps exist imperforate in issued and trial colors, and also in small presentation sheets in issued colors.

Common Design Types pictured following the introduction.

Military Medal Issue
Common Design Type

1952 **Engraved and Typographed**

39 CD101 15fr multi 45.00 25.00

Mosque of Ouani, Anjouan — A5

Coelacanth A6

1952-54 **Engr.**

40 A5 15fr dark brown 2.00 2.00
41 A5 20fr red brown 3.50 3.50
42 A6 40fr aqua & indigo ('54) 21.00 15.00
Nos. 40-42 (3) 26.50 20.50

FIDES Issue
Common Design Type

1956 **Unwmk.** ***Perf. 13x12½***

43 CD103 9fr dp vio 1.60 1.00

Human Rights Issue
Common Design Type

1958 **Engr.** ***Perf. 13***

44 CD105 20fr ol grn & dk bl 8.50 8.50

Flower Issue
Common Design Type

1959 **Photo.** ***Perf. 12½x12***

45 CD104 10fr Colvillea 4.50 3.50

View of Dzaoudzi and Radio Symbol A8

Comoro radio station: 25fr, Radio tower and radio waves over Islands.

1960, Dec. 23 **Engr.** ***Perf. 13***

46 A8 20fr maroon, vio bl & grn 1.25 .90
47 A8 25fr ultra, brn & grn 1.40 1.00

Harpa Conoidalis — A9

Sea Shells: 50c, Cypraecassis rufa. 2fr, Murex ramosus. 5fr, Turbo marmoratus. 20fr, Pterocera scorpio. 25fr, Charonia tritonis.

1962, Jan. 13 **Photo.**

Shells in Natural Colors

48 A9 50c lilac & brn 1.10 1.10
49 A9 1fr yel & red 1.10 1.10
50 A9 2fr pale grn & pink 2.40 2.40
51 A9 5fr yel & grn 3.25 3.25
52 A9 20fr salmon & brn 8.50 8.50
53 A9 25fr bister & pink 10.00 10.00
Nos. 48-53,C5-C6 (8) 54.10 51.10

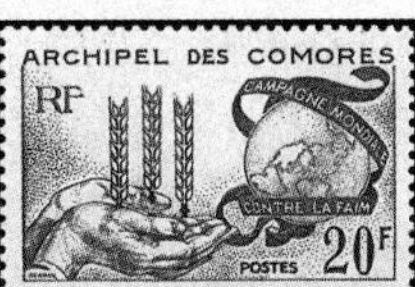

Wheat Emblem and Globe A10

1963, Mar. 21 **Engr.** ***Perf. 13***

54 A10 20fr choc & dk grn 4.00 3.50

FAO "Freedom from Hunger" campaign.

Red Cross Centenary Issue
Common Design Type

1963, Sept. 2 **Unwmk.** ***Perf. 13***

55 CD113 50fr emer, gray & car 6.75 5.75

Human Rights Issue
Common Design Type

1963, Dec. 10 **Engr.**

56 CD117 15fr dk red & yel grn 7.00 5.75

Tobacco Pouch — A13

Grand Comoro Canoe — A14

Designs: 4fr, Censer. 10fr, Carved lamp.

1963, Dec. 27 ***Perf. 13***

Size: 22x36mm

57 A13 3fr multi .70 .70
58 A13 4fr org, dp cl & sl grn .80 .80
59 A13 10fr org brn, dk red brn & grn 1.40 1.40
Nos. 57-59,C8-C9 (5) 13.15 9.65

Philatec Issue
Common Design Type

1964, Mar. 31

60 CD118 50fr dk bl, red & grn 3.50 3.50

1964, Aug. 7 **Photo.** ***Perf. 13x12½***

Design: 30fr, Boutre felucca.

Size: 22x37mm

61 A14 15fr multi 2.00 2.00
62 A14 30fr lt grn & multi 3.50 3.50
Nos. 61-62,C10-C11 (4) 12.25 9.00

Spiny Lobster — A15

Designs: 12fr, Hammerhead shark, horiz. 20fr, Turtle, horiz. 25fr, Merou fish.

1965, Dec. 20 **Engr.** ***Perf. 13***

63 A15 1fr grn, lil & ocher .75 .45
64 A15 12fr org red, slate & gray 1.75 1.25
65 A15 20fr org, red & bl grn 3.25 1.90
66 A15 25fr bl grn, dk brn & red 5.00 2.00
Nos. 63-66 (4) 10.75 5.60

Hotel Itsandra, Moroni A16

Design: 15fr, Lake Salé, Grand Comoro.

1966, Dec. 19 **Photo.** ***Perf. 12½x13***

67 A16 15fr multi 1.00 .60
68 A16 25fr multi 1.25 .80
Nos. 67-68,C18-C19 (4) 11.75 9.40

Comoro Sunbird A17

Birds: 10fr, Malachite kingfisher. 15fr, Rothschild's fody. 30fr, Cuckoo-roller.

1967, June 20 **Photo.** ***Perf. 12½x13***

Size: 36x23mm

69 A17 2fr ocher & multi 1.75 1.75
70 A17 10fr lil & multi 4.25 3.50
71 A17 15fr yel grn & multi 5.25 4.75
72 A17 30fr pink & multi 9.25 9.25
Nos. 69-72,C20-C21 (6) 37.25 30.25

For surcharge see No. 133.

WHO Anniversary Issue
Common Design Type

1968, May 4 **Engr.** ***Perf. 13***

73 CD126 40fr grn, vio & dp car 2.00 1.90

Surgeonfish A19

Design: 25fr, Imperial angelfish.

1968, Aug. 1 **Engr.** ***Perf. 13***

Size: 36x22mm

74 A19 20fr vio bl, yel & red brn 2.75 2.25
75 A19 25fr Prus bl, dk bl & org 3.50 3.50
Nos. 74-75,C23-C24 (4) 17.50 12.25

For surcharge & overprint see #C52, C74.

Human Rights Year Issue
Common Design Type

1968, Aug. 10 **Engr.** ***Perf. 13***

76 CD127 60fr brn, grn & org 2.90 2.90

Msoila Prayer Rug and Praying Man — A20

Each stamp shows a different prayer position.

1969, Feb. 27 **Engr.** ***Perf. 13***

77 A20 20fr bl grn, rose red & pur 1.10 .60
78 A20 30fr pur, rose red & bl grn 1.25 .95
79 A20 45fr rose red, pur & bl grn 2.25 1.40
Nos. 77-79 (3) 4.60 2.95

Vanilla Flower A21

Design: 15fr, Flower of ylang-ylang tree. 25fr, Poinsettia (country name at upper left).

1969-70 **Photo.** ***Perf. 12½x13***

Size: 36x23mm

80 A21 10fr multi 1.60 .60
81 A21 15fr multi 1.75 .70
82 A21 25fr multi ('70) 2.10 1.10
Nos. 80-82,C26-C28 (6) 21.45 12.15

Issue dates: #80-81, Mar. 20. #82, Mar. 5.

ILO Issue
Common Design Type

1969, Nov. 24 Engr. *Perf. 13*
83 CD131 5fr org, emerald & gray 1.25 .80

UPU Headquarters Issue
Common Design Type

1970, May 20 Engr. *Perf. 13*
84 CD133 65fr pur, bl grn & red brn 3.50 2.10

Chiromani Costume, Anjouan — A22

Friday Mosque — A23

25fr, Bouibouí costume, Grand Comoro.

1970, Oct. 30 Photo. *Perf. 12½x13*
85 A22 20fr grn, yel & red 1.10 .85
86 A22 25fr brn, yel & dk bl 1.50 .95

1970, Dec. 18 Engr. *Perf. 13*
87 A23 5fr rose car, grn & grnsh bl .50 .50
88 A23 10fr dp lil, grn & vio .70 .70
89 A23 40fr cop red, grn & dp brn 1.40 1.10
Nos. 87-89 (3) 2.60 2.30

Great White Egret — A24

Pyrostegia Venusta — A25

Birds: 10fr, Comoro pigeon. 15fr, Green-backed heron. 25fr, Comoro blue pigeon. 35fr, Humbolt's flycatcher. 40fr, Allen's gallinule.

1971, Mar. 12 Photo. *Perf. 12½x13*
90 A24 5fr multi .75 .50
91 A24 10fr yel & multi .90 .50
92 A24 15fr bl & multi 1.60 1.25
93 A24 25fr org & multi 2.50 1.40
94 A24 35fr yel grn & multi 3.50 1.60
95 A24 40fr gray & multi 4.25 2.50
Nos. 90-95 (6) 13.50 7.75

For overprint see No. 145.

1971, July 19 Photo. *Perf. 13*

Flowers: 3fr, Dogbane, horiz. 20fr, Frangipani.

Size: 22x36mm, 36x22mm

96 A25 1fr ver & grn .70 .55
97 A25 3fr yel, grn & red 1.00 .80
98 A25 20fr ver & grn 2.90 2.00
Nos. 96-98,C37-C38 (5) 13.10 9.10

For surcharges see Nos. 131-132, C75, C83.

Lithograph Cone A26

Sea Shells: 10fr, Pacific lettered cone. 20fr, Aulicus cone. 35fr, Polita nerita. 60fr, Snake-head cowrie.

1971, Oct. 4
99 A26 5fr lt ultra & multi .90 .80
100 A26 10fr multi 1.25 .95
101 A26 20fr vio & multi 2.50 1.60
102 A26 35fr lt bl & multi 3.75 2.00
103 A26 60fr lt vio & multi 6.75 2.50
Nos. 99-103 (5) 18.15 7.85

For surcharge see No. 150.

De Gaulle Issue
Common Design Type

Designs: 20fr, Gen. de Gaulle, 1940. 35fr, Pres. de Gaulle, 1970.

1971, Nov. 9 Engr. *Perf. 13*
104 CD134 20fr dk car & blk 2.90 2.10
105 CD134 35fr dk car & blk 3.50 2.90

Louis Pasteur, Slides, Microscope A27

1972, Aug. 2
106 A27 65fr indigo, org, & ol brn 4.25 3.50

Sesquicentennial of the birth of Louis Pasteur (1822-1895), chemist.

Type of Air Post Issue 1971

Designs: 10fr, View of Goulaivoini. 20fr, Bay, Mitsamiouli. 35fr, Gate and fountain, Foumbouni. 50fr, View of Moroni.

1973, June 28 Photo. *Perf. 13*
107 AP10 10fr bl & multi .70 .50
108 AP10 20fr grn & multi 1.25 .80
109 AP10 35fr bl & multi 1.75 1.25
110 AP10 50fr bl & multi 2.10 1.75
Nos. 107-110,C53 (5) 14.55 8.55

For overprint see No. 143.

Bank of Madagascar and Comoros — A28

Buildings in Moroni: 15fr, Post and Telecommunications Administration. 20fr, Prefecture.

1973, July 10 Photo. *Perf. 13x12½*
111 A28 5fr multi .50 .35
112 A28 15fr multi .70 .55
113 A28 20fr multi .90 .85
Nos. 111-113 (3) 2.10 1.75

For surcharge see No. 134.

Salimata Hamissi Mosque A29

20fr, Zaouiyat Chaduli Mosque, vert.

Perf. 12½x13, 13x12½
1973, Oct. 20 Photo.
114 A29 20fr multi 1.00 .70
115 A29 35fr multi 1.40 1.00

For surcharges see Nos. 135, 138.

Cheikh Mausoleum A30

Design: 50fr, Mausoleum of President Said Mohamed Cheikh (different view).

1974, Mar. 16 Engr. *Perf. 13*
116 A30 35fr grn, ol brn & blk 1.40 1.00
117 A30 50fr grn, ol brn & blk 2.00 1.40

For surcharge see No. 140.

Koran Stand, Anjouan A31

Designs: 15fr, Carved combs, vert. 20fr, 3-legged table, vert. 75fr, Sugar press.

1974, May 10 Photo. *Perf. 12½x13*
118 A31 15fr emer & multi 1.00 .80
119 A31 20fr grn & multi 1.40 .80
120 A31 35fr multi 1.90 1.25
121 A31 75fr multi 3.50 2.10
Nos. 118-121 (4) 7.80 4.95

For overprints and surcharge see #137, 141, 149.

UPU Emblem, Symbolic Postmark A32

1974, Oct. 9 Engr. *Perf. 13x12½*
122 A32 30fr multi 1.60 1.40

Centenary of Universal Postal Union.
For surcharge see No. 155.

Bracelet A33

1975, Feb. 28 Engr. *Perf. 13*
123 A33 20fr shown .85 .70
124 A33 35fr Diadem 1.40 1.00
125 A33 120fr Saber 3.50 2.75
126 A33 135fr Dagger 5.00 3.25
Nos. 123-126 (4) 10.75 7.70

For surcharges see Nos. 136, 142, 151, 154.

Mohani Village, Moheli — A34

50fr, Djoezi Village, Moheli. 55fr, Chirazi tombs.

1975, May 26 Photo. *Perf. 13*
127 A34 30fr vio bl & multi 1.40 1.00
128 A34 50fr Prus bl & multi 2.10 1.40
129 A34 55fr grn & multi 3.25 2.25
Nos. 127-129 (3) 6.75 4.65

For overprints and surcharge see #139, 146, 148.

Scuba Diver Photographing Coelacanth — A35

1975, June 27 Engr. *Perf. 13*
130 A35 50fr multi 6.50 4.00

1975 coelacanth expedition.

For overprint see No. 147.

STATE OF COMORO

In 1978 the islands' name became the Federal and Islamic Republic of the Comoros.

Issues of 1971-75 Surcharged and Overprinted with Bars and: "ETAT COMORIEN" in Black, Silver or Red.

Tambourine Player — A36

150fr, Woman dancers & tambourine players.

Printing & Perforations as Before, Photogravure (A36)

1975 *Perf. 13 (A36)*
131 A25 5fr on 1fr *.90 .20*
132 A25 5fr on 3fr *.90 .20*
133 A17 10fr on 2fr *.90 .30*
134 A28 15fr on 20fr (R) *.20 .20*
135 A29 15fr on 20fr (S) *.20 .20*
136 A33 15fr on 20fr *.20 .20*
137 A31 20fr *.20 .20*
138 A29 25fr on 35fr *.20 .20*
139 A34 30fr *.35 .25*
140 A30 30fr on 35fr *.75 .25*
141 A31 30fr on 35fr *.75 .25*
142 A33 30fr on 35fr *.35 .25*
143 AP10 35fr *.35 .25*
144 SP2 35fr on 35fr + 10fr *.35 .25*
145 A24 40fr *2.40 .30*
146 A34 50fr *.45 .40*
147 A35 50fr *3.50 .40*
148 A34 50fr on 55fr (S) *.80 .40*
149 A31 75fr *1.90 .60*
150 A26 75fr on 60fr (S) *3.50 .60*
151 A33 100fr on 120fr *1.90 .80*
152 A36 100fr bl & multi *5.25 .80*
153 A36 100fr on 150fr (S) *5.25 .80*
154 A33 200fr on 135fr *4.50 2.00*
155 A32 500fr on 30fr *8.00 5.00*
Nos. 131-155 (25) *44.05 15.30*

Nos. 152-153 exist without overprint or surcharge. No. 155 exists with red surcharge.

Litho. & Embossed "Gold Foil" Stamps
These stamps generally are of a different design format than the rest of the issue. Since there is a commemorative inscription tieing them to the issue a separate illustration is not being shown.

Apollo-Soyuz — A37

Spacecraft and astronauts: 10fr, Soyuz lift-off, Alexei A. Leonov and Valeri N. Kubasov, vert. 30fr, Apollo lift-off, Thomas P. Stafford, Vance D. Brand, Donald K. Slayton, vert. 50fr, Meeting in space. 100fr, Chairman Brezhnev, President Ford talking with astronauts and cosmonauts. 200fr, Spacecraft preparing to dock. 400f, Return to Earth. 500fr, Spacecraft, mission emblems. 1500fr, Apollo-Soyuz crew. No. 164, Preparing to dock, diff.

1975, Dec. 15 Litho. *Perf. 13½*
156 A37 10fr multicolored .20 .20
157 A37 30fr multicolored .45 .25
158 A37 50fr multicolored .75 .55
159 A37 100fr multicolored 1.10 .60
160 A37 200fr multicolored 2.25 1.25
161 A37 400fr multicolored 4.50 2.50
Nos. 156-161 (6) 9.25 5.35

Litho. & Embossed

Size: 45x45mm

162 A37 1500fr gold & multi 15.00 —

Souvenir Sheets
Litho.

163 A37 500fr multicolored 5.00 1.75

Litho. & Embossed

164 A37 1500fr gold & multi 15.00 —

Nos. 159-164 are airmail. No. 163 contains one 64x44mm stamp. No. 164 contains one 45x45mm stamp.
For overprints see Nos. 477-478.

A38

American Revolution, Bicent. — A39

Designs: 15fr, Lewis and Clark, Blackfoot Indian. 25fr, John C. Fremont, Kit Carson, Indian dancer. 35fr, Daniel Boone, Buffalo Bill Cody, wagon train. 40fr, Richard E. Egan, Johnny Frey, Pony Express. 75fr, Henry Wells, William G. Fargo, stagecoach. 400fr, Frontiersman, Indian. 500fr, Leland Stanford, Thomas C. Dunant, transcontinental railroad. 1000fr, George Washington, winter at Valley Forge. 1500fr, John Paul Jones, ship.

1976, Jan. 15 **Litho.**

165 A38 15fr multicolored .20 .20
166 A38 25fr multicolored .35 .25
167 A38 35fr multicolored .65 .35
168 A38 40fr multicolored .75 .45
169 A38 75fr multicolored 1.25 .60
170 A38 500fr multicolored 5.75 2.50
Nos. 165-170 (6) 8.95 4.35

Litho. & Embossed

171 A39 1000fr gold & multi 12.50 —

Souvenir Sheets
Litho.

172 A38 400fr multicolored 5.00 1.75

Litho. & Embossed

173 A39 1500fr gold & multi 15.00 —

Nos. 170-173 are airmail. See Nos. 230, 232 and note after No. 479.

1976 Winter Olympics, Innsbruck — A40

1976, Mar. 30 **Litho.**

174 A40 5fr Women's figure skating .20 .20
175 A40 30fr Slalom skiing .25 .20
176 A40 35fr Speed skating .35 .20
177 A40 50fr Downhill skiing .55 .35
178 A40 200fr Ski jumping 2.00 1.00
179 A40 400fr Cross country skiing 4.00 1.25
Nos. 174-179 (6) 7.35 3.20

Litho. & Embossed
Size: 56x35mm

180 A40 1000fr Downhill skier, hockey *12.00* —

Souvenir Sheets
Litho.

181 A40 500fr Hockey 5.00 1.75

Litho. & Embossed

182 A40 1000fr Olympic Rings *10.00* —

Nos. 178-182 are airmail. Nos. 181-182 contain one 58x35mm stamp. For overprint see No. 471.

1976 Summer Olympics, Montreal — A41

1976, Mar. 30 **Litho.**

183 A41 20fr Runner, Athens, 1896 .20 .20
184 A41 25fr Sprints .25 .20
185 A41 40fr High jump, Paris, 1900 .45 .20
186 A41 75fr High jump .90 .45
187 A41 100fr Women stretching, St. Louis, 1904 1.00 .50
188 A41 500fr Uneven parallel bars 5.50 1.75
Nos. 183-188 (6) 8.30 3.30

Souvenir Sheet

189 A41 400fr Olympic Stadium, Montreal 4.00 1.25

Nos. 187-189 are airmail.
For overprint see No. 476.

Fairy Tales — A42

1976, June 28

190 A42 15fr Hansel & Gretel .20 .20
191 A42 30fr Alice in Wonderland .45 .20
192 A42 35fr Pinocchio .60 .20
193 A42 40fr Good Little Henry .60 .25
194 A42 50fr Peter and the Wolf .80 .25
195 A42 400fr Thousand and One Nights 5.75 2.00
Nos. 190-195 (6) 8.40 3.10

#195 is airmail. #190-191, 193, 195 are vert.

Invention of Telephone, Cent. — A43

Designs: 10fr, A. G. Bell, 1st telephone. 25fr, Charles Bourseul, Paris-London phone service, 1891. 75fr, Philipp Reis, telephone operators. 100fr, Earth to Moon to Earth communications. 200fr, Satellite. 400fr, Ship-to-Satellite communications. No. 201, Satellite in orbit, antenna. No. 203, Global communications.

1976, July 1

196 A43 10fr multicolored .20 .20
197 A43 25fr multicolored .20 .20
198 A43 75fr multicolored .70 .30
199 A43 100fr multicolored 1.00 .50
200 A43 200fr multicolored 2.00 .90
201 A43 500fr multicolored 5.00 1.75
Nos. 196-201 (6) 9.10 3.85

Souvenir Sheets

202 A43 400fr multicolored 4.00 1.25
203 A43 500fr multicolored 5.00 1.75

Nos. 199-203 are airmail. Nos. 202-203 contain a 73x44mm stamp. For overprint see No. 472.

Comoro Flag, Map and Government Buildings — A44

1976, Nov. 18 **Litho.** ***Perf. 13½***

204 A44 30fr multi .70 .30
205 A44 50fr multi 1.10 .30

1st anniversary of independence.
For overprints and surcharges see Nos. 353-356 and footnote after No. 356.

Viking Probe to Mars — A45

Designs: 5fr, Nicolaus Copernicus, rocket launch. 10fr, Albert Einstein, Carl Sagan, Thomas Young, horiz. 25fr, Viking probe orbiting Mars. 35fr, Discovery of America by Vikings, horiz. 100fr, Flag, Viking landing on Mars. 500fr, Viking emblem, surface of Mars, horiz. 400fr, Viking probe. No. 212, Wagon train, frontiersman, rocket launch. No. 214, Viking on Martian surface, robotic shovel.

1976, Nov. 23

206 A45 5fr multicolored .20 .20
207 A45 10fr multicolored .20 .20
208 A45 25fr multicolored .25 .30
209 A45 35fr multicolored 1.00 .30
210 A45 100fr multicolored 1.50 .40
211 A45 500fr multicolored 9.00 1.50
Nos. 206-211 (6) 12.15 2.90

Litho. & Embossed
Size: 57x39mm

212 A45 1500fr gold & multi *12.50* —

Souvenir Sheets
Litho.

213 A45 400fr multicolored *4.50* 1.50

Litho. & Embossed

214 A45 1500fr gold & multi *13.50* —

American Revolution, bicentennial. Nos. 211-214 are airmail. No. 213 contains one 60x42mm stamp.

UN Postal Administration, 25th Anniv. — A46

Designs: 15fr, UN #24, irrigating field. 30fr, UN #43, doctor, nurse. 50fr, UN #162, mother holding child. 75fr, UN #42, communications satellite in orbit. 200fr, UN #32, Concorde, Zeppelin. 400fr, UN #18, cargo plane. 500fr, People passing letters around globe.

1976, Nov. 25 **Litho.**

215 A46 15fr multicolored .20 .20
216 A46 30fr multicolored .25 .20
217 A46 50fr multicolored .55 .30
218 A46 75fr multicolored .75 .30
219 A46 200fr multicolored 2.25 .50
220 A46 400fr multicolored 4.50 1.50
Nos. 215-220 (6) 8.50 3.00

Souvenir Sheet

221 A46 500fr multicolored *4.50* 2.00

Nos. 219-221 are airmail. No. 221 contains one 57x40mm stamp. For overprints see Nos. 282-284, 473.

Comoro Flag, UN Headquarters and Emblem — A47

1976, Nov. 25

222 A47 40fr multi 1.25 .30
223 A47 50fr multi 1.75 .40

1st anniv. of UN membership.

Type of 1976 and

US Bicentennial — A48

Civil War Battles: 10fr, Fort Sumter, Lincoln. 30fr, Bull Run, Gen. P.G.T. Beauregard, vert. 50fr, Antietam, Gen. Joseph E. Johnston. 100fr, Gettysburg, Gen. Meade. 200fr, Chattanooga, Gen. Sherman, vert. 400fr, Appomattox, Gen. Pickett. 500fr, Surrender at Appomattox, Generals Lee and Grant. 1000fr, Lincoln, battlefield. No. 230, Pres. Kennedy, lunar lander.

1976, Dec. 30 **Litho.**

224 A48 10fr multicolored .20 .20
225 A48 30fr multicolored .25 .20
226 A48 50fr multicolored .60 .25
227 A48 100fr multicolored 1.00 .45
228 A48 200fr multicolored 2.25 .80
229 A48 400fr multicolored 4.50 1.50
Nos. 224-229 (6) 8.80 3.40

Litho. & Embossed
Size: 61x51mm

230 A39 1500fr gold & multi *15.00* —

Souvenir Sheets
Litho.

231 A48 500fr multicolored *6.00* 1.75

Litho. & Embossed

232 A39 1000fr gold & multi *8.50* —

American Revolution bicentennial. Nos. 227-232 are airmail. No. 231 contains one 60x42mm stamp.

Endangered Species — A49

1976, Dec. 30 **Litho.**

233 A49 15fr Andean condor, vert. .25 .20
234 A49 20fr Australian tiger cat .35 .20
235 A49 35fr Leopard, vert. .80 .20
236 A49 40fr White rhinoceros 1.00 .45
237 A49 75fr Nyala, vert. 2.25 .55
238 A49 400fr Orangutan 6.25 1.50
Nos. 233-239 (7) 17.15 4.85

Souvenir Sheet

239 A49 500fr Lemur, vert. 6.25 1.75

Nos. 238-239 airmail. No. 239 contains one 40x58mm stamp.
See note after No. 479.

Endangered Species — A50

1977, Apr. 14

240	A50	10fr	Wolf	.20	.20
241	A50	30fr	Aye-aye	.45	.20
242	A50	40fr	Cephalopus zebra	.80	.25
243	A50	50fr	Giant tortoise	.90	.25
244	A50	200fr	Ocelot	2.90	.75
245	A50	400fr	Penguin	5.75	1.50
			Nos. 240-245 (6)	11.00	3.15

Souvenir Sheet

246	A50	500fr	Sumatran tiger	5.25	1.50

Nos. 244-246 airmail. No. 246 contains one 58x40mm stamp.

Giffard Airship, 1851 and Paris-St. Germain Train, 1837, France — A51

Airships & Locomotives: 25fr, Santos-Dumont's airship, 1906, Brazilian Tander 120FIN, Brazil. 50fr, Astra, 1914, Trans-Siberian Express, 1905, Russia. 75fr, R.34, 1919, Southern Belle, 1910, Great Britain. 200fr, Navy airship, Pacific Class locomotive, 1930, US. No. 252, Hindenburg, Rheingold Express, 1933, Germany. No. 253, Graf-Zeppelin, 1928, Nord-Express Type 231, 1925, Germany.

1977, Apr. 14

247	A51	20fr	multicolored	.25	.20
248	A51	25fr	multicolored	.25	.20
249	A51	50fr	multicolored	.70	.25
250	A51	75fr	multicolored	1.00	.25
251	A51	200fr	multicolored	2.40	.60
252	A51	500fr	multicolored	5.75	1.60
			Nos. 247-252 (6)	10.35	3.10

Souvenir Sheet

253	A51	500fr	multi, horiz.	5.25	2.00

Nos. 251-253 are airmail. No. 253 contains one 58x39mm stamp.

Nobel Prize, 75th Anniv. — A52

Nobel Prize winners: 30fr, Medicine. 40fr, Physics. 50fr, Literature. 100fr, Physics. 200fr, Chemistry. 400fr, Peace.

1977, July 7

254	A52	30fr	multicolored	.70	.20
255	A52	40fr	multicolored	.70	.20
256	A52	50fr	multicolored	1.00	.25
257	A52	100fr	multicolored	2.90	.25
258	A52	200fr	multicolored	5.00	.75
259	A52	400fr	multicolored	11.50	1.25
			Nos. 254-259 (6)	21.80	2.90

Souvenir Sheet

260	A52	500fr	Nobel medal	5.00	1.75

Nos. 258-260 are airmail.
See note after No. 479.

Peter Paul Rubens, 400th Birth Anniv. — A53

Portraits: 20fr, Portrait of the Artist's Daughter, Clara. 25fr, Suzanne Fourment. 50fr, Toilet of Venus, (detail). 75fr, Ceres (detail). 200fr, Young Woman with Blonde Braided Hair. No. 266, Helene Fourment in her Wedding Dress. No. 267, Self-portrait.

1977, July 7

261	A53	20fr	multicolored	.20	.20
262	A53	25fr	multicolored	.25	.20
263	A53	50fr	multicolored	.60	.25
264	A53	75fr	multicolored	.90	.30
265	A53	200fr	multicolored	2.25	.60
266	A53	500fr	multicolored	5.75	1.50
			Nos. 261-266 (6)	9.95	3.05

Souvenir Sheet

267	A53	500fr	multicolored	5.00	1.75

Nos. 265-267 are airmail.
See note after No. 479.

Fish A54

1977, Nov. 21

268	A54	30fr	Swordfish	.45	.20
269	A54	40fr	Gaterin	1.00	.20
270	A54	50fr	Sea scorpion	1.50	.20
271	A54	100fr	Chaetodon lunula	3.00	.45
272	A54	200fr	Amphiprion	3.75	.75
273	A54	400fr	Tetrodon	6.75	1.50
			Nos. 268-273 (6)	16.45	3.30

Souvenir Sheet

274	A54	500fr	Coelacanth	7.25	2.00

Nos. 272-274 airmail. No. 274 contains one 52x47mm stamp.

Space Exploration — A55

1977, Nov. 21

275	A55	30fr	Jupiter lander	.25	.20
276	A55	50fr	Voyager probe, Uranus, vert.	.55	.20
277	A55	75fr	Pioneer probe, Venus	.90	.25
278	A55	100fr	Space shuttle, vert.	1.00	.40
279	A55	200fr	Viking III, Mars	2.25	.60
280	A55	400fr	Apollo-Soyuz, vert.	4.50	1.25
			Nos. 275-280 (6)	9.45	2.90

Souvenir Sheet

281	A55	500fr	Allegory of the Sun	4.50	1.75

Nos. 279-281 airmail. No. 281 contains one 52x42mm stamp.

No. 219 Overprinted in One Line in Gold, Silver or Red "Paris-New-York - 22 Nov. 1977"

1977, Nov. 22

282	A46	200fr	multicolored	4.50	2.75
283	A46	200fr	multicolored (S)	27.50	—
284	A46	200fr	multicolored (R)	9.00	—
			Nos. 282-284 (3)	41.00	2.75

Birds — A56

1978, Feb. 6

285	A56	15fr	Porphyrula alleni	.35	.20
286	A56	20fr	M. superciliosus	.55	.20
287	A56	35fr	Alcedo vintsioides johannae	.80	.20
288	A56	40fr	Terpsiphone	1.00	.25
289	A56	75fr	Nectarinia comorensis	1.75	.30
290	A56	400fr	Egretta alba	9.00	1.50
			Nos. 285-290 (6)	13.45	2.65

Souvenir Sheet

291	A56	500fr	Foudia eminentissima, horiz.	6.75	1.75

Nos. 290-291 are airmail. For overprint and surcharges see Nos. 444-448.

World Cup Soccer Championships, Argentina — A57

Designs: 30fr, Greece, 5th. cent. B.C. 50fr, Brittany, 19th cent. 75fr, London, 14th cent. 100fr, Italy, 18th cent. 200fr, England, 19th cent. 400fr, English Cup match, 1891. 500fr, English Cup final, 1962. No. 298, Player, satellite. No. 300, Players.

1978, Feb. 6

292	A57	30fr	multicolored	.25	.20
293	A57	50fr	multicolored	.55	.20
294	A57	75fr	multicolored	.70	.30
295	A57	100fr	multicolored	1.00	.40
296	A57	200fr	multicolored	2.25	.60
297	A57	400fr	multicolored	4.50	1.25
			Nos. 292-297 (6)	9.25	2.95

Litho. & Embossed

Size: 60x42mm

298	A57	1000fr	gold & multi	10.00	—

Souvenir Sheets

Litho.

299	A57	500fr	multicolored	5.50	1.75

Litho. & Embossed

300	A57	1000fr	gold & multi	7.50	4.00

Nos. 296-300 are airmail. No. 300 contains one 60x42mm stamp. For overprints and surcharges see Nos. 402-408, 449-453.

Composers — A58

1978, Apr. 5 **Litho.**

301	A58	30fr	J.S. Bach	.45	.20
302	A58	40fr	W.A. Mozart	.65	.20
303	A58	50fr	Berlioz	.80	.30
304	A58	100fr	Verdi	1.75	.30
305	A58	200fr	Tchaikovsky	2.50	.60
306	A58	400fr	George Gershwin	5.00	1.25
			Nos. 301-306 (6)	11.15	2.85

Souvenir Sheet

307	A58	500fr	Beethoven	5.50	1.75

Nos. 305-307 are airmail. For overprints and surcharges see Nos. 454-458.

Albrecht Durer, 450th Death Anniv. — A59

Portraits: 20fr, Oswolt Krel. 25fr, Elspeth Tucher. 50fr, Hieronymus Holzschuher. 75fr, Young Woman. 200fr, Emperor Maximilian I. No. 313, Young Woman, (detail). No. 314, Self-portrait.

1978, Apr. 5

308	A59	20fr	multicolored	.20	.20
309	A59	25fr	multicolored	.25	.20
310	A59	50fr	multicolored	.60	.30
311	A59	75fr	multicolored	.90	.30
312	A59	200fr	multicolored	2.25	.60
313	A59	500fr	multicolored	5.50	1.60
			Nos. 308-313 (6)	9.70	3.20

Souvenir Sheet

314	A59	500fr	multicolored	5.00	1.75

Nos. 312-314 airmail. No. 314 contains one 42x52mm stamp. See note after No. 479.

Issues Not Valid for Postage

The government changed in May, 1978. A number of sets that had not been issued seem to have been invalid for postage until they were overprinted with the new country name. These are a set of 9 for the 25th anniv. of Elizabeth's coronation, a set of 7 for butterflies, a set of 6 for the 10th Intl. Communications Year, a set of 7 for the history of aviation, a set of 9 for Rubens, and a set of 9 for Durer.

These sets, unoverprinted, exist both mint and cancelled to order. They are no scarcer than the previous listed issues.

See note after No. 479.

Islamic Republic

Nos. 204-205 Surcharged and Overprinted with 3 Lines and: "République / Fédérale / et Islamique / des Comores"

1978, July 24 **Litho.** ***Perf. 13½***

353	A44	30fr	multi	.25	—
354	A44	40fr	on 30fr multi	.25	—
355	A44	50fr	multi	.45	—
356	A44	100fr	on 50fr multi	.80	—
			Nos. 353-356 (3)	1.50	

Nos. 353 and 355 were also overprinted to commemorate Queen Elizabeth II coronation anniversary; Capt. James Cook; World Cup Soccer winner; Albrecht Dürer; First powered flight; Railroad anniversary; Voyager I and II; Intl. Year of the Child; 1980 Olympic Games; World Cup Soccer, Espana '82.

Europe-Africa A66

Various satellites or spacecraft.

1978, Dec. 16

386	A66	10fr	multicolored	.20	.20
387	A66	25fr	multicolored	.20	.20
388	A66	35fr	multicolored	.35	.20
389	A66	50fr	multicolored	.60	.20
390	A66	100fr	multicolored	1.00	.60
391	A66	500fr	multicolored	5.00	1.25
			Nos. 386-391 (6)	7.35	2.65

Souvenir Sheet

392	A66	500fr	multicolored	5.00	1.75

Nos. 390-392 airmail. No. 392 contains one 61x40mm stamp.

Sir Rowland Hill — A67

1978, Dec. 16

393	A67	20fr Saxony #1	.20	.20
394	A67	30fr Netherlands #1	.25	.20
395	A67	40fr Great Britain #2	.55	.20
396	A67	75fr US #2	.70	.30
397	A67	200fr France #33	2.00	.60
398	A67	400fr Basel #3L1	4.25	1.25
		Nos. 393-398 (6)	7.95	2.75

Litho. & Embossed

Size: 39x58mm

399	A67	1500fr British Guiana #13	12.00	—

Souvenir Sheets

Litho.

400	A67	500fr Moheli, Mayotte, Anjouan, Grand Comoro #1	5.00	1.75

Litho. & Embossed

401	A67	1500fr Hill, Mauritius #3	12.00	—

Nos. 397-401 are airmail. No. 400 contains one 57x49mm stamp. No. 401 contains one 58x39mm stamp.

Nos. 292-297 Ovptd. with New Country Name in Black on Silver and
1 ARGENTINE
2 HOLLANDE
3 BRESIL

1978, Dec. 16

402	A57	30fr multicolored	.25	.20
403	A57	50fr multicolored	.55	.20
404	A57	75fr multicolored	.80	.20
405	A57	100fr multicolored	1.00	.45
406	A57	200fr multicolored	2.00	.60
407	A57	400fr multicolored	4.00	1.25
		Nos. 402-407 (6)	8.60	2.90

Souvenir Sheet

408	A57	500fr multicolored	5.00	1.25

Nos. 406-407 are airmail.

Exists with Country name in red on silver. Value approx. triple those of overprints in black.

Galileo and Voyager I — A68

Exploration of Solar System: 30fr, Kepler and Voyager II. 40fr, Copernicus and Voyager I, 100fr, Huygens and Voyager II. 200fr, William Herschel and Voyager II. 400fr, Urbain Leverrier and Voyager II. 500fr, Voyagers I and II, symbolic solar system.

1979, Feb. 19 **Litho.** ***Perf. 13***

409	A68	20fr multi	.20	.20
410	A68	30fr multi	.25	.20
411	A68	40fr multi	.45	.20
412	A68	100fr multi	1.00	.25
413	A68	200fr multi	1.75	.50
414	A68	400fr multi	3.75	1.00
		Nos. 409-414 (6)	7.40	2.35

Souvenir Sheet

415	A68	500fr multi	4.50	1.50

Nos. 413-415 airmail.

Philidor, Anderssen, Steinitz and King — A69

100fr, Chess pieces and board, Venetian chess player. 500fr, Chess Grand Masters Alekhine, Spassky, Fischer, and bishop.

1979, Feb. 19

416	A69	40fr multi	.45	.20
417	A69	100fr multi	1.00	.20
418	A69	500fr multi	4.50	1.50
		Nos. 416-418 (3)	5.95	1.90

Chess Grand Masters. No. 418 airmail.

Nos. 419-425 are reserved for Summer Olympics set of 6 with one souvenir sheet, released Mar. 28, 1979.

Charaxes Defulvata — A71

Birds: 50fr, Leptosomus discolor. 75fr, Bee eater.

1979, Apr. 10 **Litho.** ***Perf. 12½***

426	A71	30fr multi	1.40	.30
427	A71	50fr multi	3.50	.60
428	A71	75fr multi	4.50	1.00
		Nos. 426-428 (3)	9.40	1.90

Otto Lilienthal and Glider — A72

History of Aviation: No. 430, Wright brothers and Flyer A. No. 431, Louis Bleriot and Bleriot XI. 100fr, Claude Dornier and Dornier-Wal hydrofoil. 200fr, Charles Lindbergh and Spirit of St. Louis.

1979, May 2 ***Perf. 13***

Black Overprint and Surcharge

429	A72	30fr multi	.45	.45
430	A72	50fr multi	.75	.75
431	A72	50fr on 75fr multi	.75	.75
432	A72	100fr multi	1.50	1.50
433	A72	200fr multi	2.25	2.25
		Nos. 429-433 (5)	5.70	5.70

No. 433 airmail.

For unoverprinted stamps see note after No. 314.

Papilio Dardanus Cenea A73

Butterflies: 15fr, Papilio dardanus. 30fr, Chrysiridia croesus. 50fr, Precis octavia. 75fr, Bunaea alcinoe.

1979, May 2

Black Overprint and Surcharge

434	A73	5fr on 20fr multi	.20	.20
435	A73	15fr multi	.30	.20
436	A73	30fr multi	.65	.45
437	A73	50fr multi	1.25	.95
438	A73	75fr multi	2.10	1.50
		Nos. 434-438 (5)	4.50	3.30

For unoverprinted stamps see note after No. 314.

Man Reading Proclamation — A74

1979, May 2 **Litho.** ***Perf. 13½***

Black Surcharge and Overprint

439	A74	5fr on 25fr coronation coach	.20	.20
440	A74	10fr Drummer	.25	.25
441	A74	50fr on 40fr with crown, orb, scepter	.65	.65
442	A74	50fr on 200fr shown	1.00	1.00
443	A74	100fr St. Edward's Crown	1.25	1.25
		Nos. 439-443 (5)	3.35	3.35

No. 442 is airmail.

For unoverprinted stamps see note after No. 314.

Nos. 285-289 Overprinted or Surcharged like A72-A74

1979, May 2 **Litho.** ***Perf. 13***

444	A56	15fr multi	.25	.25
445	A56	30fr on 35fr multi	.65	.65
446	A56	50fr on 20fr multi	1.10	1.10
447	A56	50fr on 40fr multi	1.10	1.10
448	A56	200fr on 75fr multi	3.50	3.50
		Nos. 444-448 (5)	6.60	6.60

Nos. 292-296 Overprinted or Surcharged like A72-A74

1979, May 2 **Litho.** ***Perf. 13***

449	A57	1fr on 100fr multi	.20	.20
450	A57	2fr on 75fr multi	.20	.20
451	A57	3fr on 30fr multi	.20	.20
452	A57	50fr multi	.80	.55
453	A57	200fr multi	2.00	2.00
		Nos. 449-453 (5)	3.40	3.15

No. 453 airmail.

Nos. 301-305 Overprinted or Surcharged like A72-A74

1979, May 2 ***Perf. 13½***

454	A58	5fr on 100fr multi	.20	.20
455	A58	30fr multi	.35	.35
456	A58	40fr multi	.45	.45
457	A58	50fr multi	.70	.70
458	A58	50fr on 200fr multi	1.00	1.00
		Nos. 454-458 (5)	2.70	2.70

No. 458 airmail.

Nos. 459-465 are reserved for Intl. Year of the Child set of 6 with one souvenir sheet, released May 30, 1979.

Litchi Nuts — A76

Basketball Players — A77

1979, June 15 **Litho.** ***Perf. 12½***

466	A76	60fr shown	.90	.30
467	A76	70fr Papayas	1.10	.45
468	A76	100fr Avocados	1.25	.55
469	A76	125fr Bananas	1.75	.90
		Nos. 466-469 (4)	5.00	2.20

For surcharges see Nos. 515, 533.

1979, Aug. 28 **Litho.** ***Perf. 13***

470	A77	200fr multi	2.25	1.40

Indian Ocean Olympics.

Nos. 176, 198, 218, 187, 159-160 and Type A78 Overprinted in Black

Nimbus Weather Satellite — A78

No. 475, Apollo-Soyuz. No. 479, Molniya.

Printing & Perfs. as Before, Litho. (A78)

1979, Sept. 15 ***Perf. 13 (A78)***

471	A40	35fr multi	.45	.45
472	A43	75fr multi	.80	.80
473	A46	75fr multi	.80	.80
474	A78	75fr multi	.80	.80
475	A78	100fr multi	1.10	1.10
476	A41	100fr multi	1.10	1.10
477	A37	100fr multi	1.10	1.10
478	A37	200fr multi	2.25	2.25
479	A78	200fr multi	2.25	2.25
		Nos. 471-479 (9)	10.65	10.65

Nos. 476-479 airmail.

For type A78 see note after No. 314.

Nos. 166-167, 169, 235-236, 257, 262, 309, 311, the unissued Rubens set (4 values) and Durer set (5 values) exist with this overprint, supposedly also issued Sept. 15.

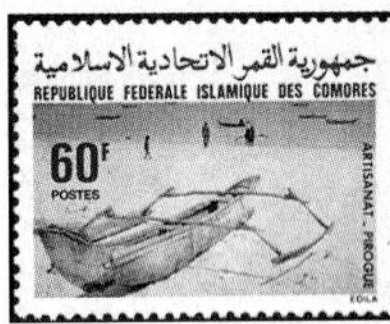

Dugout on Beach A80

Anjouan Puppet — A81

1980, Jan. 4 **Litho.** ***Perf. 13***

498	A80	60fr multi	.90	.25
499	A81	100fr multi	1.25	.45

For surcharge see No. 534.

Sultan Said Ali — A82

1980, Feb. 20 *Perf. 12½x13*

500 A82 40fr shown .55 .20
501 A82 60fr Sultan Ahmed .70 .25

Sherlock Holmes, Doyle — A83

1980, Feb. 25 *Perf. 12½*

502 A83 200fr multi 4.25 1.75

Sir Arthur Conan Doyle (1859-1930), writer.
For surcharge see No. 513.

Grand Mosque, Holy Ka'aba, Mecca — A84

1980, Mar. 12 *Perf. 13x12½*

503 A84 75fr multi .90 .40

Hegira, 1500th anniv.
For surcharge see No. 514.

Year of the Holy City of Jerusalem A85

1980, Mar. 12 *Perf. 13x13½*

504 A85 60fr multi .70 .40

Kepler, Copernicus and Pluto — A86

1980, Apr. 30 **Litho.** *Perf. 12½*

505 A86 400fr multi 4.00 2.25

Discovery of Pluto, 50th anniversary.
For surcharge see No. 531.

Muscle System, Avicenna — A87

1980, Apr. 30 **Engr.** *Perf. 13*

506 A87 60fr multi .70 .40

Avicenna, Arab physician, birth millennium.

Soccer Players — A88

World Cup Soccer 1982; Various soccer scenes. 60fr, 150fr, 500fr, vert.

1981, Feb. 20 **Litho.** *Perf. 12½*

507 A88 60fr multi .60 .20
508 A88 75fr multi .70 .20
509 A88 90fr multi 1.10 .25
510 A88 100fr multi 1.00 .45
511 A88 150fr multi 1.75 .60
Nos. 507-511 (5) 5.15 1.70

Souvenir Sheet

512 A88 500fr multi 4.50 1.50

For overprints & surcharge see #532, 555-560.

Nos. 502-503, 469 Surcharged and

Merops Superciliosus A89

Perf. 12½, 13x12½ (No. 514)

1981, Feb. **Litho.**

Red, Black or Blue Surcharge

513 A83 15fr on 200fr multi .20 .20
514 A84 20fr on 75fr multi .20 .20
515 A76 40fr on 125fr multi (Bk) .35 .35
516 A89 60fr on 75fr multi (Bl) .80 .80
Nos. 513-516 (4) 1.55 1.55

A90

Space Exploration: 50fr, Apollo program, vert. 75fr, 100fr, 500fr, Columbia space shuttle.

1981, July 13 **Litho.** *Perf. 14*

517 A90 50fr multi .55 .20
518 A90 75fr multi .70 .20
519 A90 100fr multi 1.10 .30
520 A90 450fr multi 5.00 1.50
Nos. 517-520 (4) 7.35 2.20

Souvenir Sheet

521 A90 500fr multi 4.50 1.50

For overprints and surcharges see Nos. 599, 804F.

Prince Charles and Lady Diana, Buckingham Palace — A91

1981, Sept. 1 **Litho.** *Perf. 14½*

522 A91 125fr shown 1.00 .30
523 A91 200fr Highwood House 1.60 .60
524 A91 450fr Carnarvon Castle 3.50 1.25
a. Souvenir sheet of 3 6.25 2.00
Nos. 522-524 (3) 6.10 2.15

Royal wedding. No. 524a contains Nos. 522-524 in changed colors.
For overprints see Nos. 551-553.

Official Stamp Flag Type

1981, Oct. **Litho.** *Perf. 13*

526 O1 5fr multi .20 .20
527 O1 15fr multi .20 .20
528 O1 25fr multi .25 .20
529 O1 35fr multi .35 .20
530 O1 75fr multi .70 .35
Nos. 526-530 (5) 1.70 1.15

Nos. 505, 509, 468, 499 Surcharged

1981, Nov. **Litho.** *Perf. 12½*

531 A86 5fr on 400fr multi .20 .20
532 A88 20fr on 90fr multi .20 .20
533 A76 45fr on 100fr multi .45 .20
534 A81 45fr on 100fr multi .45 .20
Nos. 531-534 (4) 1.30 .80

75th Anniv. of Grand Prix — A92

Designs: Winners and their Cars.

1981, Dec. 28 **Litho.** *Perf. 12½*

535 A92 20fr Mercedes, 1914 .25 .20
536 A92 50fr Delage, 1925 .60 .20
537 A92 75fr Rudi Caracciola, 1926 .80 .25
538 A92 90fr Stirling Moss, 1955 1.00 .35
539 A92 150fr Maserati, 1957 1.50 .45
Nos. 535-539 (5) 4.15 1.45

Souvenir Sheet

Perf. 13

540 A92 500fr Changing wheels, vert. 5.50 1.75

For overprint see No. 600.

Scouting Year — A93

1982, Jan. 5 *Perf. 12½*

541 A93 50fr Climbing rocks .55 .20
542 A93 75fr Boating .80 .25
543 A93 250fr Sailing 2.75 .90
544 A93 350fr Sailing, diff. 3.50 1.10
Nos. 541-544 (4) 7.60 2.45

Souvenir Sheet

Perf. 13

545 A93 500fr Baden-Powell 6.00 1.75

For overprint see No. 601.

21st Birthday of Princess of Wales — A94

Various portraits of Princess Diana.

1982, July 1 **Litho.** *Perf. 14*

546 A94 200fr multi 2.25 .60
547 A94 300fr multi 3.00 .90

Souvenir Sheet

548 A94 500fr multi 5.00 1.50

Johannes von Goethe (1749-1832) A95

1982, July

549 A95 75fr multi .70 .25
550 A95 350fr multi 3.50 .90

Nos. 522-524a Overprinted in Blue: "NAISSANCE ROYALE 1982"

1982, July 31 *Perf. 14½*

551 A91 125fr multi 1.40 .60
552 A91 200fr multi 2.25 .90
553 A91 450fr multi 4.00 2.00
a. Souvenir sheet of 3 6.75 6.75
Nos. 551-553 (3) 7.65 3.50

Birth of Prince William of Wales, June 21.

Nos. 507-512 Overprinted with Finalists and Score in Red

1982, Sept. 20 **Litho.** *Perf. 12½*

555 A88 60fr multi .60 .25
556 A88 75fr multi .70 .35
557 A88 90fr multi .90 .45
558 A88 100fr multi 1.00 .45
559 A88 150fr multi 1.25 .60
Nos. 555-559 (5) 4.45 2.10

Souvenir Sheet

560 A88 500fr multi 4.50 1.50

Italy's victory in 1982 World Cup.

Paintings by Norman Rockwell A96

1982, Oct. 11 **Litho.** *Perf. 14*

561 A96 60fr 1931 .65 .25
562 A96 75fr 1925 .70 .25
563 A96 100fr 1922 1.00 .25
564 A96 150fr 1919 1.25 .55
565 A96 200fr 1924 1.75 .60
566 A96 300fr 1918 3.25 1.00
Nos. 561-566 (6) 8.60 2.90

Sultans of Anjouan — A97

1982, Dec. ***Perf. 12½x13, 13x12½***

567 A97 30fr Said Mohamed Sidi, vert. .35 .20
568 A97 60fr Ahmed Abdallah, vert. .70 .25
569 A97 75fr Salim .90 .25
570 A97 300fr Sidi, Abdallah 3.25 1.40
Nos. 567-570 (4) 5.20 2.10

Landscapes — A98

1983, Sept. 30 **Litho.** ***Perf. 13***

571 A98 60fr D'Ziani Lake .70 .30
572 A98 100fr Sunset 1.10 .45
573 A98 175fr Anjouan, vert. 1.75 .75
574 A98 360fr Itsandra 3.50 1.25
575 A98 400fr Anjouan, diff. 4.50 1.60
Nos. 571-575 (5) 11.55 4.35

For surcharge see No. 815S.

Woman from Moheli A99

1983, Oct. 17 **Litho.** ***Perf. 12½x13***

576 A99 30fr shown .35 .20
577 A99 45fr Woman, diff. .50 .20
578 A99 50fr Man from Mayotte .50 .20
Nos. 576-578 (3) 1.35 .60

Horses — A100

1983, Nov. 30 **Litho.** ***Perf. 13***

579 A100 75fr Arabian .70 .25
580 A100 100fr Anglo-Arabian 1.10 .30
581 A100 125fr Lippizaner 1.25 .40
582 A100 150fr Tennessee 1.50 .50
583 A100 200fr Appaloosa 1.75 .70
584 A100 300fr Pure English 3.00 1.00
585 A100 400fr Clydesdale 4.00 1.25
586 A100 500fr Andalusian 5.50 1.50
Nos. 579-586 (8) 18.80 5.90

Double Portrait, by Raphael A101

1983, Dec. 30 **Litho.** ***Perf. 13***

587 A101 100fr shown 1.10 .45
588 A101 200fr Girl, fresco detail 2.25 .80
589 A101 300fr St. George Killing Dragon 3.00 .90
590 A101 400fr Balthazar Castiglione 5.00 1.25
Nos. 587-590 (4) 11.35 3.40

For surcharges see Nos. 703, 800E, 815M.

Ships and Automobiles — A102

1984, Oct. 9 **Litho.** ***Perf. 12½***

591 A102 100fr William Fawcett 1.10 .30
592 A102 100fr De Dion, 1885 1.40 .30
593 A102 150fr Lightning 1.75 .45
594 A102 150fr Benz Victoria, 1893 2.10 .60
595 A102 200fr Rapido 2.25 .75
596 A102 200fr Columbia Electric, 1901 2.75 .75
597 A102 350fr Sindia 4.00 1.00
598 A102 350fr Fiat, 1902 4.50 1.10
Nos. 591-598 (8) 19.85 5.25

For surcharge see No. 812Q.

Souvenir Sheets

Nos. 521, 540, 545, C126, C131 Ovptd. with Exhibition in Black, Blue, Red or Gold

1985, Mar. 11 ***Perf. 14, 13***

599 A90 500fr '85 / HAMBOURG (Bk) 4.50 4.50
600 A92 500fr TSUKUBA EXPO '85 (Bl) 4.50 4.50
601 A93 500fr ARGENTINA '85/BUENOS AIRES (R) 4.50 4.50
602 AP31 500fr Rome, ITALIA '85 emblem (R) 4.50 4.50
603 AP32 500fr OLYMPHILEX/ '85 / LAUSANNE (G) 4.50 4.50
Nos. 599-603 (5) 22.50 22.50

Nos. 602-603 airmail.

Victor Hugo (1802-1885), Author, Pantheon, Paris — A103

Anniversaries and events: 200fr, IYY, Jules Verne (1828-1905), author. 300fr, IYY, Mark Twain (1835-1910), author. 450fr, Queen Mother, 85th birthday, vert. 500fr, Statue of Liberty, cent., vert.

1985, May 27 **Litho.** ***Perf. 13***

604 A103 100fr multi 1.10 .30
605 A103 200fr multi 2.10 .60
606 A103 300fr multi 3.25 .90
607 A103 450fr multi 4.50 1.25
608 A103 500fr multi 5.50 1.50
Nos. 604-608 (5) 16.45 4.55

For surcharges see Nos. 704, 800A.

Sea Shells — A104

1985, Oct. 23 ***Perf. 14***

609 A104 75fr Lambis chiragra .90 .20
610 A104 125fr Strombe lentifinosum 1.25 .35
611 A104 200fr Tonna gala 2.25 .60
612 A104 300fr Cymbium glans 3.50 .90
613 A104 450fr Lambis crocata 5.50 1.40
Nos. 609-613 (5) 13.40 3.45

Comoros Admission to UN, 10th Anniv. — A105

1985, Nov. 12 **Litho.** ***Perf. 13x12½***

614 A105 5fr multi .20 .20
615 A105 30fr multi .25 .20
616 A105 75fr multi .80 .25
617 A105 125fr multi 1.25 .50
618 A105 400fr multi 4.00 1.50
Nos. 614-618 (5) 6.50 2.65

For surcharge see No. 800F.

Moroni Rotary Club, 20th Anniv. — A106

1985, Nov. 30 ***Perf. 13***

619 A106 25fr multi .25 .20
620 A106 75fr multi .80 .40
621 A106 125fr multi 1.25 .45
622 A106 500fr multi 4.50 2.00
Nos. 619-622 (4) 6.80 3.05

Mushrooms — A107

1985, Dec. 24 ***Perf. 13½***

623 A107 75fr Boletus edulis .90 .30
624 A107 125fr Sarcoscypha coccinea 1.40 .45
625 A107 200fr Hypholoma fasciculare 2.25 .60
626 A107 350fr Astraeus hygrometricus 3.50 .90
627 A107 500fr Armillariella mellea 6.50 1.50
Nos. 623-627 (5) 14.55 3.75

For surcharge see No. 815R.

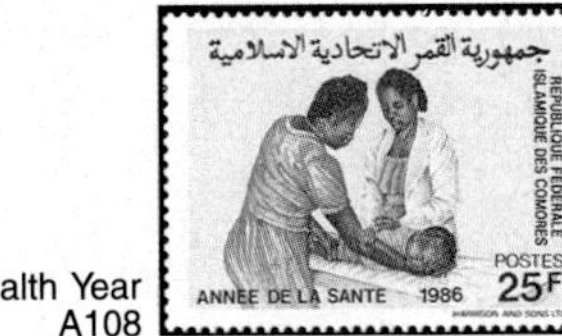

Health Year A108

1986, Oct. 2 **Litho.** ***Perf. 15x14½***

628 A108 25fr Pediatric examination .25 .20
629 A108 100fr Weighing child 1.10 .60
630 A108 200fr Immunization 2.25 1.25
Nos. 628-630 (3) 3.60 2.05

For surcharge see No. 705.

Musical Instruments A109

1986, Dec. 24 **Litho.** ***Perf. 13***

631 A109 75fr Ndzoumara .80 .40
632 A109 125fr Ndzedze 1.10 .60
633 A109 210fr Gaboussi 2.00 .90
634 A109 500fr Ngoma 5.50 1.75
Nos. 631-634 (4) 9.40 3.65

For surcharges see Nos. 796P, 796T, 800L, 815A.

Role of Women in National Development — A110

1987, Mar. 7 **Litho.** ***Perf. 13***

635 A110 75fr Working fields .75 .30
636 A110 125fr Harvesting crops, vert. 1.25 .45
637 A110 1000fr Basketweaving 10.00 3.00
Nos. 635-637 (3) 12.00 3.75

Service Organizations — A111

Emblems and activities: 75fr, Nos. 642, Kiwanis or 643c, Rotary Intl. for child survival. 125fr, Nos. 641, Kiwanis or 643b, Lions Intl. for aid to the handicapped. 210fr, No. 643a, Kiwanis helping poor and homeless children.

1988 **Litho.** ***Perf. 13½***

638 A111 75fr dk bl, lt bl & multi .70 .30
639 A111 125fr dk brn, lt brn & multi 1.25 .45
640 A111 210fr org, yel & multi 2.00 .75
641 A111 425fr red, pink & multi 4.00 1.75
642 A111 500fr bl, yel & multi 5.50 2.00
643 Strip of 3 12.00 6.00
a. A111 210fr grn, lt grn & multi 2.00 .75
b. A111 425fr pur, pink & multi 4.00 1.75
c. A111 500fr red, orange & multi 5.50 2.00
Nos. 638-643 (6) 25.45 11.25

For surcharges see Nos. 654-656, 815B, 815W.

A112

1988 Olympics, Calgary and Seoul — A113

1988 Litho. *Perf. 13½*

644 A112 75fr Women's figure skating .60 .20
645 A112 100fr Running .90 .30
646 A112 125fr Women's speed skating .90 .40
647 A112 150fr Equestrian 1.40 .50
648 A112 350fr Two-man luge 3.00 .90
649 A112 400fr Biathlon 3.75 1.40
650 A112 500fr Pole vault 3.75 1.25
651 A112 600fr Soccer 5.50 1.50
Nos. 644-651 (8) 19.80 6.45

Souvenir Sheets

652 A113 750fr Women's downhill skiing, satellite 7.00 1.50
653 A113 750fr Track, satellite 7.00 1.50

Nos. 649 and 651-653 are airmail.
For surcharges see Nos. 800C, 800M, 815V.

No. 643 and Service Organization Types Surcharged

No. 655, like #643b. No. 656, like #643c.

1988, July 18 Litho. *Perf. 13½*

654 Strip of 3 5.00 5.00
a. A111 75fr on 210fr #643a .60 .45
b. A111 200fr on 425fr #643b 1.60 .90
c. A111 300fr on 500fr #643c 2.50 1.25
655 A111 125fr on 425fr pur, lt pur & multi, blk letters 1.00 .60
656 A111 400fr on 500fr car, pink & multi 3.50 2.00
Nos. 654-656 (3) 9.50 7.60

Nos. 655-656 not issued without surcharge.

Discovery of America, 500th Anniv. (in 1992) — A114

Designs: 75fr, Christopher Columbus, *Santa Maria.* 125fr, Martin Alonzo Pinzon (c. 1441-1493), *Pinta.* 150fr, Vicente Yanez Pinzon (c. 1460-1523), *Nina.* 250fr, Search for Cipango, legendary rich islands off the coast of Asia. 375fr, *Santa Maria* shipwrecked. 450fr, Preparing for 4th voyage. 750fr, Samana Cay landing.

1988, Apr. 18 Litho. *Perf. 13½*

657 A114 75fr multi .60 .20
658 A114 125fr multi 1.00 .30
659 A114 150fr multi 1.40 .45
660 A114 250fr multi 2.00 .75
661 A114 375fr multi 3.50 1.00
662 A114 450fr multi 4.00 1.25
Nos. 657-662 (6) 12.50 3.95

Souvenir Sheet

663 A114 750fr multi, horiz. 7.00 1.50

Nos. 661-663 airmail. No. 663 contains one 42x30mm stamp.
For surcharges see Nos. 702, 815D.

1992 Summer Olympics, Barcelona A115

1988, Apr. 18

664 A115 75fr Discus, vert. .60 .20
665 A115 100fr shown .80 .30
666 A115 125fr Cycling 1.10 .45
667 A115 150fr Wrestling 1.40 .50
668 A115 375fr Basketball, vert. 3.50 1.00
669 A115 600fr Tennis, vert. 5.50 1.25
Nos. 664-669 (6) 12.90 3.70

Souvenir Sheet

670 A115 750fr Marathon, vert. 7.00 1.50

Nos. 668-670 are airmail.

Famous Men — A116

Rotary Intl. — A117

150fr, Yuri Gagarin (1934-68), USSR, cosmonaut. 300fr, Jean-Henri Dunant, Red Cross founder. 400fr, Roger Clemens, baseball player. 500fr, Gary Kasparov, USSR, 1985 world chess champion. 600fr, Paul Harris, US, Rotary founder. 750fr, Neil Armstrong walking on the Moon, John F. Kennedy. #678, The Thinker by Rodin, Rotary Intl. emblem.

1988, Dec. 6 Litho. *Perf. 13½*

671 A116 150fr multi 1.60 .50
672 A116 300fr multi 1.60 .50
673 A116 400fr multi 1.60 .50
674 A116 500fr multi 1.60 .50
675 A116 600fr multi 1.60 .50
a. Souv. sheet of 5, #671-675 + label 9.00 —
Nos. 665-669 (5) 12.30 3.50

Litho. & Embossed

676 A117 1500fr gold & multi 13.50 —

Souvenir Sheets

Litho.

677 A116 750fr multi 7.00 1.50

Litho. & Embossed

678 A117 1500fr gold & multi 13.50 —

Intl. Red Cross, 125th anniv. (300fr), Rotary Intl. (600fr, Nos. 676, 678). Nos. 674-678 are airmail.
#672-673 exist in souv. sheets of 1.

Inventors and Sportsmen A118

Portraits and modes of transportation: Designs: 75fr, Alain Prost, F-1 MacLaren-Honda. 125fr, George Stephenson and locomotive *Borsig of 1935.* 500fr, Ettore Bugatti (1881-1947), 1939 Bugatti Aravis Type 57. 600fr, Rudolf Diesel (1858-1913) and V200 BB diesel-electric locomotive. 750fr, Dennis Conner, captain of the *Stars and Stripes,* winner of the 1987 America's Cup. No. 684, Michael Fay, patron of the *New Zealand,* an entry in the America's Cup. No. 685, Enzo Ferrari and 1989 Ferrari Formula 1, horiz.

1988, Dec. 27 Litho. *Perf. 13½*

679 A118 75fr multi .60 .45
680 A118 125fr multi 1.10 .25
681 A118 500fr multi 4.50 1.25
682 A118 600fr multi 5.50 1.25
683 A118 750fr multi 6.25 1.25
684 A118 1000fr multi 9.00 1.25
Nos. 679-684 (6) 26.95 5.70

Souvenir Sheet

685 A118 1000fr multi 9.00 1.50

Nos. 683-685 are airmail.
#679-684 exist in souv. sheets of 1.

Scouts, Butterflies and Birds — A119

Scouts involved in various activities and species: 50fr, Gathering specimens, *Papilio nireus aristophontes oberthur* female. 75fr, Studying specimen and male. 150fr, Cooking out, *Charaxes fulvescens separanus poulton.* 375fr, Picking mushrooms, *Lonchura cucullatus.* 450fr, Examining specimen, *Charaxes castor comoranus rothschild.* 500fr, Identifying specimen, *Zosterops maderaspatana.* 750fr, Studying specimens, *Foudia omissa* and *Charaxes paradoxa lathy* female. No. 692, Photographing specimen, *Junonia rhadama.* No. 694, Examining specimen, *Agapornis cana cana.*

1989 Litho.

686 A119 50fr multi .50 .20
687 A119 75fr multi .60 .20
688 A119 150fr multi 1.10 .30
689 A119 375fr multi 3.00 .75
690 A119 450fr multi 3.75 1.00
691 A119 500fr multi 4.50 1.25
Nos. 686-691 (6) 13.45 3.70

Litho. & Embossed

692 A119 1500fr gold & multi 12.00 —

Souvenir Sheets

Litho.

693 A119 750fr multi 9.00 1.50

Litho. & Embossed

694 A119 1500fr gold & multi 12.00 —

Nos. 690-694 are airmail. Issue dates: Nos. 692, 694, May 15; others, Mar. 15.
For surcharges see Nos. 800D, 815T.

Gold Medalists of the 1988 Summer Olympics A120

Communication satellites, various equestrians and their mounts: 75fr, Nicole Uphoff, West Germany, individual dressage, and Aussat K3. 150fr, Pierre Durand, France, individual jumping, and Brazilsat. 375fr, Janos Martinek, Hungary, individual modern pentathlon, and ECS 4. 600fr, Mark Todd, New Zealand, individual three-day event, and Olympus. 750fr, Team jumping, West Germany, and satellite. No. 699, Pierre Durand, France, individual show jumping. No. 701, Nicole Uphoff, West Germany, individual dressage.

1989, Apr. 10 Litho. *Perf. 13½*

695 A120 75fr multi .60 .20
696 A120 150fr multi 1.10 .35
697 A120 375fr multi 2.75 .75
698 A120 600fr multi 4.50 1.25
Nos. 695-698 (4) 8.95 2.55

Litho. & Embossed

699 A120 1500fr gold & multi 12.00 —

Souvenir Sheets

Litho.

700 A120 750fr multi 6.25 1.50

Litho. & Embossed

701 A120 1500fr gold & multi 12.00 —

No. 701 contains one 39x38mm stamp. Nos. 698-701 are airmail.
For surcharges see Nos. 796Q, 804I.

Nos. 660, 588, 605 and 630 Surcharged

1989 Litho. *Perfs. as Before*

702 A114 25fr on 250fr #660 .20 .20
703 A101 150fr on 200fr #588 1.00 .50
704 A103 150fr on 200fr #605 1.00 .50
705 A108 150fr on 200fr #630 1.00 .50
Nos. 702-705 (4) 3.20 1.70

1992 Summer Olympics, Barcelona A121

1989, Apr. 26 Litho. *Perf. 13½*

706 A121 75fr Running .60 .20
707 A121 150fr Soccer 1.10 .40
708 A121 300fr Tennis 2.25 .60
709 A121 375fr Baseball 3.00 .80
710 A121 500fr Pommel horse 3.75 1.00
711 A121 600fr Table tennis 4.50 1.25
Nos. 706-711 (6) 15.20 4.25

Souvenir Sheet

712 A121 750fr Equestrian 6.25 1.50

Nos. 710-712 are airmail.
For surcharges see Nos. 796J, 796K, 800J, 812R.

Dr. Joseph-Ignace Guillotin (1738-1814) — A122

French Revolution, Bicent.: 150fr, French artillery, Gen. Francois-Christophe Kellerman (1735-1820). 375fr, Royalist insurgents & leader, Jean Cotterau (1757-94). 600fr, King Louis XVI (1774-92), troops. 1000fr, Storming of the Bastille & Jacques Necker, statesman (1732-1804). #717, Lafayette, Mounier, Sieyes & Declaration of the Rights of Man and Citizen. #719, Robespierre & St. Just before the Convention on 9 Thermidor.

1989, Oct. 25 Litho. *Perf. 13½*

713 A122 75fr multicolored .65 .20
714 A122 150fr multicolored 1.10 .35
715 A122 375fr multicolored 2.75 .60
716 A122 600fr multicolored 4.50 1.25
Nos. 713-716 (4) 9.00 2.40

Litho. & Embossed

717 A122 1500fr gold & multi 12.00 —

Souvenir Sheets

Litho.

718 A122 1000fr multicolored 7.50 1.75

Litho. & Embossed

719 A122 1500fr gold & multi

Philexfrance 1989. No. 716-719 are airmail.
No. 714 incorrectly inscribed "Francois-Etienne."
Nos. 713-717 exist in souvenir sheets of 1.
For surcharges see Nos. 796B, 800W, 804J.

Airport Pavilion A124

Designs: 10fr, 25fr, Airport pavilion. 50fr, 75fr, 150fr, Federal Assembly.

1990, Apr. 1 Litho. *Perf. 13*

722 A124 5fr brn, org & brt red .20 .20
723 A124 10fr brn, org & brt bl .20 .20
724 A124 25fr brn, org & brt grn .20 .20
725 A124 50fr blk & brt red .40 .20
726 A124 75fr blk & brt bl .70 .30
727 A124 150fr blk & grn 1.25 .60
Nos. 722-727 (6) 2.95 1.70

World Cup Soccer Championships, Italy — A125

Players from: 50fr, Brazil. 75fr, England. 100fr, Federal Republic of Germany. 150fr, Belgium. 375fr, Italy. 600fr, Argentina. 750fr, Argentina and Italy.

1990 Litho. Perf. 13½

728	A125	50fr multicolored	.40	.20
729	A125	75fr multicolored	.60	.30
730	A125	100fr multicolored	.75	.35
731	A125	150fr multicolored	1.00	.45
732	A125	375fr multicolored	2.75	1.00
733	A125	600fr multicolored	4.50	1.25
		Nos. 728-733 (6)	10.00	3.55

Litho. & Embossed

734	A125	1500fr gold & multi	12.00	5.00

Souvenir Sheets

Litho.

735	A125	750fr multicolored	6.25	1.50

Litho. & Embossed

736	A125	1500fr gold & multi	12.00	—

Nos. 732-736 are airmail.
For surcharges see Nos. 796L, 796O, 804K.

Telecom '91 A125a

1990, Oct. 29 Litho. Perf. 13½

736A	A125a	75fr Emblem, vert.	1.25	.60
736B	A125a	150fr shown	2.50	1.25

Nos. 736A-736B exist imperf.

A126

Designs: 75fr, Hubble Space Telescope placed in orbit. 150fr, Pope John Paul II, Pres. Gorbachev meet Dec. 3, 1989. 200fr, Kevin Mitchell, San Francisco Giants, Natl. League Most Valuable Player, 1989. 250fr, De Gaulle, France, and Adenauer, West Germany, meet in Sept. 1962. 300fr, Cassini probe to Titan, 2002. 375fr, Bullet train and Concorde, France. 450fr, Gary Kasparov, World Chess Champion. 500fr, Paul Harris (1868-1947), founder of Rotary Intl.

1990, Nov. 26 Litho. Perf. 13½

737	A126	75fr sil & multi	.70	.25
738	A126	150fr sil & multi	1.40	.40
739	A126	200fr sil & multi	1.90	.40
740	A126	250fr sil & multi	2.40	.40
741	A126	300fr sil & multi	2.75	.50
742	A126	375fr sil & multi	3.50	.65
743	A126	450fr sil & multi	4.25	1.00
744	A126	500fr sil & multi	4.75	.75
		Nos. 737-744 (8)	21.65	4.35

Nos. 743-744 are airmail.
#738, 744 exist in souv. sheets of 1.
For surcharges see Nos. 796A, 796R, 800I, 804A, 804L, 815E, 815U.

A127

A128

Winter Olympics participants: 75fr, Edi Reinalter, Switzerland, slalom, 1948. 100fr, Canadian hockey team, 1924. 375fr, Gratia Van der Oye, women's slalom, Holland, 1936. 600fr, Heikki Hasu, Finland, combined cross country and ski jumping, 1948. 750fr, Helene Engelman & Alfred Berger, Austria, pairs figure skating, 1924. No. 751, Speed skater, horiz. No. 751A, Luge, horiz.

1990, Dec. 10

746	A127	75fr multicolored	.55	.20
747	A127	100fr multicolored	.70	.30
748	A127	375fr multicolored	3.25	1.00
749	A127	600fr multicolored	5.50	1.25
		Nos. 746-749 (4)	10.00	2.75

Souvenir Sheet

750	A127	750fr multicolored	7.00	1.50

Litho. & Embossed

751	A127	1500fr gold & multi	15.00	—

Souvenir Sheet

751A	A127	1500fr gold & multi	14.00	—

1992 Winter Olympics, Albertville. Nos. 748-751A are airmail. No. 750 contains one 36x41mm stamp.
For surcharges see Nos. 796M, 800K, 804M, 812S.

1991, May 17 Litho. Perf. 13½

Ground station, Moroni Volo-Volo.

752	A128	75fr multicolored	.90	.20
753	A128	150fr multicolored	1.50	.45
754	A128	225fr multicolored	2.10	.75
755	A128	300fr multicolored	3.00	1.00
756	A128	500fr multicolored	5.00	1.25
		Nos. 752-756 (5)	12.50	3.65

For surcharge see 815N.

Indian Ocean Conference — A129

1991, June 17

757	A129	75fr multicolored	.90	.20
758	A129	150fr multicolored	1.40	.75
759	A129	225fr multicolored	2.00	1.00
		Nos. 757-759 (3)	4.30	1.95

World War II, 50th Anniv. A130

Actors, Films: 150fr, Errol Flynn, Objective Burma. 300fr, Henry Fonda, The Longest Day. 450fr, Humphrey Bogart, Sahara.

1991, Aug. 5

760	A130	150fr sil & multi	1.50	.45
761	A130	300fr sil & multi	3.00	.75
762	A130	450fr sil & multi	4.50	.90
		Nos. 760-762 (3)	9.00	2.10

No. 762 is airmail. Nos. 760-762 exist in souvenir sheets of 1.
For surcharges see Nos. 796D, 800H, 804B, 804G.

A131

Charles de Gaulle A132

De Gaulle and: 125fr, Battle of Koufra. 375fr, Battle of Britain. 500fr, Battle of Monte Cassino. 1000fr, Airplanes. 1500fr, De Gaulle at podium.

1991, Aug. 5 Litho. Perf. 13½

763	A131	125fr multi	1.10	.30
764	A131	375fr multi	2.50	.75
765	A131	500fr multi	4.00	.90
		Nos. 763-765 (3)	7.60	1.95

Souvenir Sheet

766	A131	1000fr multi	11.00	2.00

Litho. & Embossed

767	A132	1500fr gold & multi	15.00	—

Nos. 765-767 are airmail. No. 767 exists in souvenir sheet of 1.
For surcharges see Nos. 796G, 804N, 816I.

Anniversaries and Events — A133

Designs: 100fr, Satellite Columbus in polar orbit. 150fr, Gandhi. 250fr, Jean-Henri Dunant. 300fr, Wolfgang Amadeus Mozart. 375fr, Brandenburg Gate. 400fr, Konrad Adenauer. 450fr, Elvis Presley. 500fr, Ferdinand von Zeppelin.

1991, Nov. 18 Litho. Perf. 13½

768	A133	100fr multicolored	1.10	.30
769	A133	150fr multicolored	1.50	.35
770	A133	250fr multicolored	2.40	.60
771	A133	300fr multicolored	3.00	.60
772	A133	375fr multicolored	4.00	.90
773	A133	400fr multicolored	4.00	.90
774	A133	450fr multicolored	5.00	1.00
a.		Souv. sheet, #771, 774	—	—
775	A133	500fr multicolored	5.00	1.00
a.		Souv. sheet, #772-773, 775	—	—
		Nos. 768-775 (8)	26.00	5.65

Nobel Peace Prize, 90th anniv. (#770). Mozart, bicent. of death (#771). Brandenburg Gate, bicent. (#772). Konrad Adenauer, 25th anniv. of death (#773). Elvis Presley, 15th anniv. of death (in 1992) (#774). Count Zeppelin, 75th anniv. of death (in 1992) (#775).
Nos. 774-775 are airmail. Nos. 768-775 exist in souvenir sheets of 1. Value, set $50.

For surcharges see Nos. 796F, 796H, 800G, 804C, 804O, 815F, 815O, 816J.

Mushrooms — A134

1992, Mar. 23 Litho. Perf. 13½

776	A134	75fr Cepe comestible	.75	.40
777	A134	150fr Geastre en etoile	1.75	.60
778	A134	600fr Pezize ecarlate	7.50	1.50
		Nos. 776-778 (3)	10.00	2.50

No. 778 is airmail. Nos. 776-778 exist imperf. and in souvenir sheets of one.

Shells A135

1992, Mar. 23

779	A135	125fr Conus textile	1.50	.50
780	A135	150fr Cypraecassis rufa	1.90	.65
781	A135	500fr Leporicypraea mappa	6.00	1.90
		Nos. 779-781 (3)	9.40	3.05

Souvenir Sheet

782	A135	750fr Nautilus pompilius	9.50	2.00

Nos. 781-782 are airmail. Nos. 779-781 exist imperf. and in souvenir sheets of one. No. 782 exists imperf.
For surcharges see Nos. 800N, 816K.

Space Programs A136

Designs: 75fr, Mercury rocket, chimpanzee Ham, US. 125fr, Mars Observer, US. No. 785, Veronica rocket, cat Felix, France. No. 786, Mars rover, US, Mars car, USSR. 500fr, Phobos project, USSR. 600fr, Sputnik II, dog Laika, USSR. 1000fr, Viking, US, vert.

1992, Mar. 30 Litho. Perf. 13½

783	A136	75fr multicolored	1.10	.25
784	A136	125fr multicolored	1.60	.30
785	A136	150fr multicolored	2.00	.70
786	A136	150fr multicolored	1.90	.70
787	A136	500fr multicolored	6.00	1.25
a.		Souv. sheet, #784, 786-787	—	—
788	A136	600fr multicolored	7.00	1.40
a.		Souv. sheet, #783, 785, 788	—	—
		Nos. 783-788 (6)	19.60	4.60

Souvenir Sheet

789	A136	1000fr multicolored	12.00	2.25

Nos. 787-789 are airmail. Nos. 783-788 exist imperf. and in souvenir sheets of one. No. 789 contains one 30x42mm stamp.
For surcharges see Nos. 800O, 804Q.

Voyages of Discovery A137

Designs: 75fr, Space shuttle Endeavour, sailing ship Endeavour, Capt. Cook. 100fr, Satellite, sailing ship Golden Hinde, Sir Francis Drake. 150fr, ISO observation satellite, sailing ship Susan Constant, John Smith. 225fr, Probe B, sailing ship Discovery, Robert F. Scott. 375fr, Magellan probe over Venus, sailing ship, Ferdinand Magellan. 500fr, Newton probe, sailing ship Sao Gabriel, Vasco da Gama.

1000fr, Hermes-Columbus space shuttle, Columbus and his fleet.

1992, May 28 Litho. ***Perf. 13½***

790 A137 75fr multicolored 1.10 .25
791 A137 100fr multicolored 1.25 .30
792 A137 150fr multicolored 2.10 .45
793 A137 225fr multicolored 2.50 .75
794 A137 375fr multicolored 4.75 1.00
795 A137 500fr multicolored 5.50 1.25
a. Souvenir sheet of 6, #790-795 14.00 7.00
Nos. 790-795 (6) 17.20 4.00

Souvenir Sheet

796 A137 1000fr multicolored 12.00 2.25

Nos. 794-796 are airmail. Nos. 790-795 exist imperf. in souvenir sheets of one.

For surcharges see Nos. 796E, 800P, 804P.

Various Stamps Surcharged

a — (Obliterator of dots)

Methods and Perfs as Before

1992-95

796A A126 10fr on 300fr #741
796B A122 15fr on 375fr #715
796C AP41 25fr on 210fr #C164
796D A130 25fr on 300fr #761
796E A137 25fr on 375fr #794
796F A133 35fr on 400fr #773
796G A131 50fr on 375fr #764
796H A133 50fr on 375fr #772
796I AP34 50fr on 475fr #C138
796J A121 75fr on 300fr #708
796K A121 75fr on 375fr #709
796L A125 75fr on 375fr #732
796M A127 75fr on 375fr #748
796N AP42 75fr on 600fr #C170
796O A125 100fr on 375fr #732
796P A109 150fr on 210fr #633
796Q A120 150fr on 375fr #697
796R A126 150fr on 375fr #742
796S AP40 150fr on 450fr #C162
796T A109 150fr on 500fr #634
796U AP42 150fr on 500fr #C169

No. 796J exists with quadruple surcharge.

No. 796Q exists with inverted surcharge and with double surcharge, one inverted.

Organization of African Unity, 30th Anniv. — A138

1993, Feb. 15 Litho. ***Perf. 13½x13***

797 A138 25fr blue & multi .20 .20
798 A138 50fr pink & multi .45 .20

Perf. 12

799 A138 75fr green & multi 1.25 .45
800 A138 150fr vermilion & multi 2.00 1.00
Nos. 797-800 (4) 3.90 1.85

Various Stamps Surcharged

b — (Bar obliterator)

Methods and Perfs as Before

1992-95

800A A103 50fr on 450fr #607
x. Zero in surcharge thin at top and bottom
800B AP47 75fr on 800fr #C192
800C A112 100fr on 350fr #648
800D A119 100fr on 375fr #689
y. 150fr on 375fr #689 (error)
800E A101 100fr on 400fr #590
800F A105 100fr on 400fr #618
800G A133 100fr on 400fr #773
800H A130 125fr on 450fr #762
800I A126 150fr on 250fr #740
800J A121 150fr on 375fr #709
z. Zero in surcharge thin at top and bottom —
800K A127 150fr on 375fr #748
a. Zero in surcharge thin at top and bottom —
800L A109 150fr on 500fr #634
800M A112 150fr on 500fr #650
b. Zero in surcharge thin at top and bottom —
800N A135 150fr on 500fr #781
800O A136 150fr on 500fr #787
800P A137 150fr on 500fr #795
c. Zero in surcharge thin at top and bottom —
800Q AP41 150fr on 500fr #C165
d. Zero in surcharge thin at top and bottom —
800R AP44 150fr on 500fr #C177
800S AP45 150fr on 500fr #C181
e. Zero in surcharge thin at top and bottom —
800T AP42 150fr on 500fr #C185
800U AP47 150fr on 500fr #C191
800V AP50 150fr on 500fr #C212
800W A122 150fr on 600fr #716

Surcharge on No. 800W is sideways reading top to bottom. Nos. 800B and 800F exist with inverted surcharge, Nos. 800R and 800W exist with misplaced surcharge.

1994 World Cup Soccer Championships, U.S. — A139

Intl. Telecommunications Day — A140

1993, May 12 Litho. ***Perf. 13x12½***

801 A139 25fr red & multi .20 .20
802 A139 75fr brown & multi .60 .30
803 A139 100fr blue & multi 1.25 .40
804 A139 150fr green & multi 1.50 .60
Nos. 801-804 (4) 3.55 1.50

Various Stamps Surcharged Type "b" in Black or Red

Methods and Perfs as Before

1992-95

804A A126 200fr on 300fr #741
s. Zero in surcharge thin at top and bottom —
804B A130 200fr on 300fr #761
804C A133 200fr on 300fr #771
804D AP45 200fr on 300fr #C180
804E AP47 200fr on 300fr #C190
t. Zero in surcharge thin at top and bottom —
804F A90 200fr on 450fr #520
u. Overprint right side up —
804G A130 200fr on 450fr #762
804H AP40 200fr on 450fr #C162
804I A120 225fr on 375fr #697
804J A122 225fr on 375fr #715
804K A125 225fr on 375fr #732
804L A126 225fr on 375fr #742
804M A127 225fr on 375fr #748
v. "f" in surcharge omitted —
804N A127 225fr on 375fr #764
804O A133 225fr on 375fr #772
804P A137 225fr on 375fr #794
804Q A136 225fr on 500fr #787

Red Surcharge

804R AP40 200fr on 300fr #C161

Surcharge on No. 804F is inverted.

No. 804D exists with "020f" surcharge and with zeroes in surcharge in different sizes. No. 804F exists with zeroes in surcharge in different sizes. No. 804G exists with two obliterators and zeroes in surcharge in different fonts.

1993, May 17

805 A140 50fr red & multi .35 .20
806 A140 75fr blue & multi .60 .30
807 A140 100fr green & multi 1.00 .40
808 A140 150fr black & multi 1.50 .60
Nos. 805-808 (4) 3.45 1.50

Miniature Sheet

Prehistoric Animals A141

Designs: a, 75fr, Edaphosaurus. b, 75fr, Moschops. c, 75fr, Sauroctonus. d, 75fr, Ornitholestes. e, 75fr, Kentrosaurus. f, 75fr, Compsognathus. g, 75fr, Styracosaurus. h, 75fr, Acanthopholis. i, 150fr, Edmontonia. j, 150fr, Struthiomimus. k, 450fr, Dromiceiomimus. l, 450fr, Iguanodon. m, 150fr, Diatryma. n, 150fr, Uintatherium. o, 525fr, Synthetoceras. p, 525fr, Euryapteryx.

1200fr, Tyrannosaurus rex.

1994, Apr. 5 Litho. ***Perf. 13½***

809 A141 Sheet of 16, #a.-p. 20.00 9.00

Souvenir Sheet

810 A141 1200fr multicolored 12.00 3.00

No. 810 is airmail and contains one 42x60mm stamp.

Miniature Sheets

Flora — A142

Orchids: No. 811a, 75fr, Hibiscus syriacus. 150fr, Pyrostegia venusta. 525fr, Allamanda cathartica.

Vegetables: No. 811b, 75fr, Anacardier. 150fr, Manioc. 525fr, Cacao.

Mushrooms: No. 811c, 75fr, Suillus lutens. 150fr, Lycogala epidendron. 525fr, Clathrus ruber.

Butterflies, insects: No. 812a, 75fr, Colotis zoe. b, 150fr, Acherontia atropos. c, 450fr, Danaus chrysippus. d, 75fr, Charaxes comoranus. e, 150fr, Euchloron megaera. f, 450fr, Papilio phorbanta. g, 75fr, Hypurgus ova. h, 150fr, Onthophagus catta. i, 450fr, Echinosoma bolivari.

1994, May 24 Litho. ***Perf. 13½***

811 A142 Sheet of 9 15.00 5.50
a. Strip of 3 4.00 1.50
b. Strip of 3 4.00 1.50
c. Strip of 3 4.00 1.50
d. Souvenir sheet of 3, #811a 15.00 5.00
e. Souvenir sheet of 3, #811b 15.00 5.00
f. Souvenir sheet of 3, #811c 15.00 5.00
812 A142 Sheet of 9, #a.-i. 14.00 5.00
j. Souv. sheet of 3, #812a-812c 15.00 5.00
k. Souv. sheet of 3, #812d-812f 15.00 5.00
l. Souv. sheet of 3, #812g-812i 15.00 5.00

For surcharges see No. 826F.

Independence, 20th Anniv. — A142a

Designs: 100fr, 300fr, Maps of Grand Comoro, Moheli, Mayotte and Anjouan.

1995 (?) Litho. ***Perf. 13x12¾***

812M A142a 100fr multi
812O A142a 300fr multi

An additional stamp was released in this set. The editors would like to examine it.

For surcharge see No. 826M.

Various Stamps Surcharged in Gold

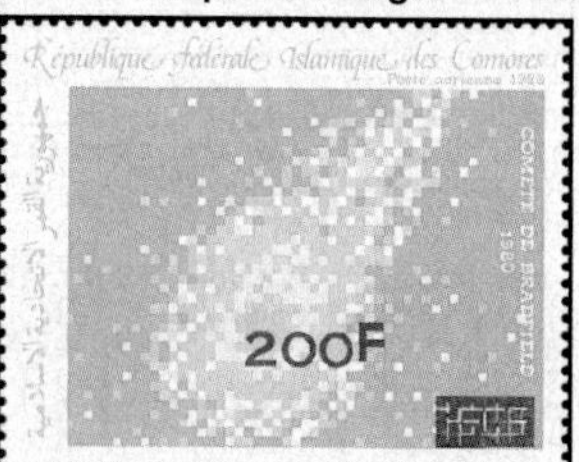

c — (Wide numerals, obliterator of small sqares in grid)

Methods and Perfs as Before

1996, Dec.

812P AP40 200fr on 300fr #C161
812Q A102 200fr on 350fr #598
812R A121 200fr on 375fr #709
v. "2" same size as "0"

812S A127 200fr on 375fr #748
812T AP31 200fr on 400fr #C125
812U AP44 200fr on 500fr #C177

Size of numerals and oblietration grids varies.

A143 A144

Diana, Princess of Wales (1961-97): Various portraits.

1997, Dec. 15 Litho. *Perf. 14*

813 A143 150fr Sheet of 12, #a.-l. 9.00 4.00
814 A143 375fr Sheet of 6, #a.-f. 11.00 5.00

Souvenir Sheet

815 A143 1000fr multicolored 5.00 2.25

Various Stamps Surcharged Type "c" in Black

Methods and Perfs as Before

1996, Dec.

815A A109 200fr on 210fr #633
815B A111 200fr on 210fr #640
815C AP41 200fr on 210fr #C164
815D A114 200fr on 250fr #660
815E A126 200fr on 250fr #740
815F A133 200fr on 250fr #770
815G AP30 200fr on 250fr #C116
815H AP38 200fr on 250fr #C151
815I AP38 200fr on 250fr #C152
x. Pair, #815H-815I + label
815J AP42 200fr on 250fr #C168
815K AP42 200fr on 250fr #C184
815L AP28 200fr on 260fr #C110
815M A101 200fr on 300fr #589
y. With gold obliterator over old value
815N A128 200fr on 300fr #755
815O A133 200fr on 300fr #771
815P AP31 200fr on 300fr #C124
815Q AP37 200fr on 300fr #C150
815R A107 200fr on 350fr #626
815S A98 200fr on 360fr #574
815T A119 200fr on 375fr #689
815U A126 200fr on 375fr #742
815V A112 200fr on 400fr #649
815W A111 200fr on 425fr #641

Size of surcharge numerals and obliteration grid varies. Black surcharge on No. 815My is misplaced. No. 815Q exists with misplaced surcharge that is faintly tripled, a surcharge with thinner zeroes, and a pair containing No. C150 next to No. 815Q with misplaced surcharge that is faintly tripled and has thinner zeroes. No. 815W exists with an inverted surcharge and with a double surcharge, one inverted.

1997, Dec. 15 Litho. *Perf. 14*

816 A144 200fr Mother Teresa (1910-97) .90 .45

No. 816 was issued in sheets of 9.

Aromatic Plants — A144a

Designs: 25fr, 59fr, 1000fr, Piper nigrum. 100fr, 125fr, 200fr, Cinnamomum ceylanicum. 300fr, Syzigium aromaticum. 500fr, Myristica fragrans.

1997, Dec. 15 Litho. *Perf. 14*

816A A144a 25fr multi
816B A144a 50fr multi
816C A144a 100fr multi
816D A144a 125fr multi
816E A144a 200fr multi
816F A144a 300fr multi
816G A144a 500fr multi
816H A144a 1000fr multi

Various Stamps Surcharged Type "c" in Black

Methods and Perfs as Before

1996, Dec.

816I A131 200fr on 500fr #765
816J A133 200fr on 500fr #775
816K A135 200fr on 500fr #781
816L AP42 200fr on 500fr #C169
816M AP42 200fr on 500fr #C185
816N AP42 200fr on 600fr #C170
816O AP42 200fr on 600fr #C186

Size of surcharge and obliteration grid varies.

Vertical Pairs from No. B4 Surcharged with Silver Bar to Obliterate Surtax

Methods and Perfs as before.

1996, Dec.

816P Surcharged pair of #B4a, B4e
t. SP3 200fr on 200fr+10fr Galileo
u. SP3 200fr on 200fr+10fr Planet A & 3 stars
816Q Surcharged pair of #B4b, B4f
v. SP3 200fr on 200fr+10fr Copernicus
w. SP3 200fr on 200fr+10fr ICE
816R Surcharged pair of #B4c, B4g
x. SP3 200fr on 200fr+10fr Kepler
y. SP3 200fr on 200fr+10fr Planet A & 5 stars
816S Surcharged pair of #B4d, B4h
z. SP3 200fr on 200fr+10fr Halley
aa. SP3 200fr on 200fr+10fr Vega

A full sheet of Nos. 816P-816S is not known to exist.

Cats A145

Designs, vert: 75fr, Silver banded. 150fr, Lac de Van. No. 819, 200fr, European short hair. No. 820, 200fr, Somali. No. 821, 375fr, Japanese bobtail. No. 822, 375fr, Egyptian mau.

No. 823: a, Poupée de chiffon. b, Maine coon. c, Norwegian forest cat. d, Persian. e, Droop-eared. f, Marbled American short hair.

No. 824: a, Manx. b, Cashmere. c, British shorthair. d, Cornish rex. e, American curl. f, Ocicat.

No. 825, Silver-chocolate Somali. No. 826, Chocolate Persian, vert.

1998, June 3 Litho. *Perf. 14*

817-822 A145 Set of 6 6.25 6.25

Sheets of 6

823-824 A145 375fr #a.-f., ea 10.00 10.00

Souvenir Sheets

825-826 A145 1500fr each 8.00 3.00

No. C215D Surcharged Type "c" in Red or Black

Methods and Perfs as Before

1997 (?)

826A AP52a 100fr on 225fr
826B AP52a 200fr on 225fr
826C AP52a 200fr on 225fr (Bk)
826D AP52a 500fr on 225fr
826E AP52a 600fr on 225fr

Size of surcharge numerals varies. No. 826B exists with inverted surcharge, No. 826C exists with double surcharge.

No. 811 Surcharged on Six Stamps

d — (Obliterator of Triangles and Wavy Lines)

Methods and Perfs as Before

1998 (?)

826F Sheet of 9
g. A142 200fr on 150fr Pyrostegia venusta
h. A142 200fr on 150fr Manioc
i. A142 200fr on 150fr Lycogala epidendron
j. A142 200fr on 525fr Allamanda cathartica
k. A142 200fr on 525fr Cacao
l. A142 200fr on 525fr Clathrus ruber

The three 75fr stamps on the sheet received no surcharge.

No. 812O Surcharged

e — (Obliterator of Bars, Dots, and Semicircles)

Methods and Perfs as Before

1998 (?)

826M A142a 100fr on 300fr

Size of surcharge numerals varies.

Marine Life A146

No. 827: a, Pomacanthus imperator. b, Cephalopholis miniatus. c, Diver. d, Nautilus pompilius. e, Sphyraena barracuda. f, Manta birostris. g, Lutjanus sebae. h, Chaetodonplus duboulayi. i, Amphiprion bicinctus.

No. 828, vert: a, Istiophorus platypterus. b, Sterna fuscata. c, Larus pipixcan. d, Hippocampus kuda. e, Amphiprion ocellaris (2 fish). f, Octopus vulgaris. g, Chaetodon striatus. h, Actini aquina. i, Acanthurus leucosternon.

No. 829: a, Diomedea exulans. b, Delphinus delphis. c, Sailboat. d, Sphyrna zygaena. e, Loligo forbesi. f, Galeocerdo cuvieri. g, Pomacanthus imperator, diff. h, Amphiprion ocellaris (1 fish). i, Forcipiger flavissimus. j, Electrophorus electricus. k, Dermochelys coriaoea. l, Asterias rubens.

No. 830, Mastigias papua, vert. No. 831, Sepia officinalis. No. 832, Zancius canescens.

1998, Aug. 10 Litho. *Perf. 14*

Sheets of 9 or 12

827-828 A146 150fr #a.-i., each 6.00 6.00
829 A146 200fr #a.-l. 11.00 11.00

Souvenir Sheets

830-832 A146 1500fr each 6.75 6.75

Nos. 830-832 each contain one 51x38mm or 38x51mm stamp.

Betty Boop — A146a

No. 832A: b, Wearing hula skirt, dancing. c, With dog, wearing blue dress, in pink heart. d, Wearing polka dot dress. e, In bathtub. f, Face in red heart. g, Holding top hat. h, With flamingos. i, With dog, Wearing red dress, blue ribbon. j, Wearing hula skirt, on surf board. 1125fr, With fishing pole.

1998 Litho. *Perf. 13¼*

832A A146a 300fr Sheet of 9, #b-j — —

Souvenir Sheet

832K A146a 1125fr multi — —

No. 832A contains nine 35x41mm stamps.

Popeye — A146b

No. 832L: m, Wimpy. n, Popeye, Olive Oyl, ship's wheel. o, Swee'Pea. p, Head of Popeye. q, Popeye. r, Head of Olive Oyl. s, Jeep. t, Olive Oyl. u, Brutus.

No. 832V, 1125fr, Popeye with spinach can. No. 832W, 1125fr, Like #832Ln, horiz.

1998

832L A146b 450fr Sheet of 9, #m-u — —

Souvenir Sheets

832V-832W A146b Set of 2 — —

No. 832L contains nine 35x51mm stamps, No. 832W contains one 60x50mm stamp.

Coelacanth — A147

World Wildlife Fund: a, Swimming right, colored background. b, Swimming right, white background. c, In net. d, Swimming left.

No. 833E: f, Like #833a. g, Like #833d. h, Like #833c. i, Like #833b.

1998

833 A147 200fr Strip of 4, #a-d 3.50 3.50
833E A147 375fr Sheet of 4, #f-i 30.00

No. 833 was issued in sheets of 3 vertical strips.

No. 833E exists imperf.

I Love Lucy — A147a

No. 833F, vert. — Lucy: g, With black ribbon in hair. h, Wearing burlap sack. i, With trapeze in mouth. j, With one arm raised. k, On telephone. l, Wearing red and white apron. m, Wearing bright green dress. n, Wearing blue dress. o, With fishing gear.
1125fr, With Ricky, with fishing gear.

1998 Litho. *Perf. 13¼*

833F A147a 250fr Sheet of 9, #g-o — —

Souvenir Sheet

833P A147a 1125fr multi — —

No. 833F contains nine 35x51mm stamps.

Diana, Princess of Wales (1961-97) A148

Nos. 834-835, 835J, Various portraits.
No. 836, Wearing scarf, green dress. No. 837, Wearing black and white hat and outfit.

1998 Litho. *Perf. 13½*

Sheets of 9

834 A148 250fr #a.-i. 12.00 12.00
835 A148 350fr #a.-i. 17.00 17.00
835J A148 450fr #k.-s. 22.00 22.00

Souvenir Sheets

836-837 A148 1125fr each 6.00 6.00

Nos. 835, 835J contain 42x51mm stamps. Nos. 836-837 each contain one 42x60mm stamp.

Entertainers A149

#838: Various portraits of Grace Kelly (Princess Grace of Monaco) (1929-92).
#839: Various portraits of Frank Sinatra (1915-98).

1998

Sheets of 9

838 A149 300fr #a.-i. 14.50 14.50
839 A149 500fr #a.-i. 24.00 24.00

Classic Automobiles — A150

No. 840: a, 1936 Jaguar SS. b, 1939 Lincoln Continental. c, 1903 Mercedes. d, 1936 MG-TA. e, 1946 Oldsmobile Custom Cruiser 98. f, 1933 Pontiac. g, 1940 Rolls-Royce Silver Ghost 40/50. h, 1950 Studebaker Starlight Coupe. i, 1932 Ford V8.
No. 841: a, 1927 Alfa Romeo RLSS. b, 1933 DuPont Model G. c, Bentley Speed Six. d, 1932 Cadillac 355. e, 1955 Corvette. f, 1934 Chrysler Airflow. g, Buick Coupe deVille. h, Model T Ford. i, 1920 Duesenberg Model A.
No. 842, Rolls-Royce Phantom II Continental. No. 843, 1927 Daimler Double Six.

1998, Oct. 29 Litho. *Perf. 14*

Sheets of 9

840-841 A150 150fr #a.-i., each 6.00 6.00

Souvenir Sheets

842-843 A150 1500fr each 6.75 6.75

Birds — A151

No. 844, 75fr, Macareux moine. No. 845, 75fr, Calliste à tête verte. No. 846, 150fr, Soutmanga de la reine Christine. No. 847, 150fr, Rale d'eau. No. 848, 200fr, Lophophore replendissant. No. 849, 200fr, Francolin noir. No. 850, 375fr, Mesia â oreillonis argentes. No. 851, 375fr, Mérion splendide.
No. 852: a, Canard plongeur austral. b, Garrot a ceil d'or. c, Harle huppé. d, Canard colvert. e, Canard branchu. f, Sarcelle elegante.
No. 853: a, Emérillon. b, Nyctale de tengmalm. c, Aigle royal d, Kétoupa malais. e, Caracara. f, Chouette à lunettes
No. 854, Jacana du mexique. No. 855, Toucan de cuvier.

1999, Jan. 23 Litho. *Perf. 14*

844-851 A151 Set of 8 5.25 5.25

Sheets of 6, #a-f

852-853 A151 375fr Set of 2 20.00 20.00

Souvenir Sheets

854-855 A151 1500fr Set of 2 13.50 13.50

Fauna A152

No. 856, vert: a, Giraffa camaloprdalis. b, Macaca fusata. c, Loxodonta africana. d, Ovis dalli. e, Phoenicopterus ruber. f, Orcinus orca. g, Ursus horribilis. h, Lemur catta.
No. 857, vert: a, Pongo pygmaeus. b, Ceratotherium simum. c, Ailuropoda melanoleuca. d, Tursiops truncartus. e, Felis caracel. g, Eudyptes chrysocome. h, Bison bison. i, Panthera uncia.
No. 858, vert: a, Phascolarctos cinereus. b, Ammotragus levia. c, Hippopatamus amphibius. d, Saimiri boliviensis. e, Acinonyx jubatus. f, Gorilla gorilla. g, Branta sandvicensis. h, Thalarctos maritimus.
No. 859: a, Panthera tigris. b, Phoca groenlandica. c, Acipenser sturio. d, Lepidochelys kempii. e, Ailuropoda melanoleuca. f, Isurus oxyrinchus. g, Chelydra serpentina. h, Eretmochelys imbricata.
No. 860: Pan troglodytes, vert. No. 861, Panthera tigris altaica, vert. No. 862, Oryx gazella, vert. No. 863, Hippotigris zebra. No. 864, Diceros bicornis. No. 865, Panthera leo. No. 866, Amazona viridgenalis. No. 867, Pygoscelis papua, vert.

1999, Jan. 25

Sheets of 8

856-859 A152 150fr #a.-h., ea 5.75 5.75

Souvenir Sheets

860-867 A152 1500fr each 6.75 6.75

Fish A153

No. 868, 75fr, Pomacantus imperator. No. 869, 75fr, Heniochus intermedium. No. 870, 150fr, Mirolaprichthys. No. 871, 150fr, Pomacanthus paru. No. 872, 375fr, Ostzacion tuberculatus. No. 873, 375fr, Colisa calia.
No. 874: a, Coris aygula. b, Chromis caeruleys. c, Euxiphipops navarchus. d, Pseudobalistes fuscus. e, Zebrasoma flavescens. f, Mycteroperca urba. g, Epinephelus flavocaeruleus. h, Equetus lanceolatus. i, Acanthurus leucostemon.
No. 875: a, Chaetodon tinkeri. b, Ostzacidae. c, Seatophagus argus. d, Adioryx coruscus. e, Pygoplites diacanthus. f, Paracanthurus hepatus. g, Chaetodon plebius. h, Lythrypnus dalli. i, Myrichthys oculatus.
No. 876, Amphipzion percula. No. 877, Cymnothorne undulatus.

1998, Oct.-Nov. Litho. *Perf. 14*

868-873 A153 Set of 6 5.50 5.50

Sheets of 9

874-875 A153 150fr #a.-i., each 6.00 6.00

Souvenir Sheets

876-877 A153 1500fr each 6.75 6.75

Marine Life — A154

No. 878, 75fr, Tubastrea aurea. No. 879, 75fr, Condylachtis gigantea. No. 880, 150fr, Paracanthurus hepatus. No. 881, 150fr, Balistoides conspicillum. No. 882, 200fr, Diodon holocanthus. No. 883, 200fr, Sebastes rubrivintus. No. 884, 375fr, Trygonorhina fasciata. No. 885, 375fr, Phocoenoides dalli.
No. 886: a, Epinephelus guttatus. b, Diademichthys lineatus. c, Plotosus lineatus. d, Rhinomuraena quaesita. e, Zanclus cornutus. f, Persephona punctata. g, Murex pecten. h, Tetrosomus gibbosus.
No. 887: a, Lythrpnus dalli. b, Premnas biacilleatus. c, Psendathias tuka. d, Capros aper. e, Balistoides conspicillum. f, Oreaster reticulatus. g, Octopus joubini. h, Fasciolaris tulipa.
No. 888, S. picturatus. No. 889, Megaptera novaeangliae.

1999

878-885 A154 Set of 8 7.25 7.25

Sheets of 8

886-887 A154 150fr #a.-h., ea 6.00 6.00

Souvenir Sheets

888-889 A154 1500fr each 6.75 6.75

Prehistoric Animals — A155

No. 890: a, Meganeura. b, Archaeopteryx. c, Peteinosaurus. d, Eudimorphodon. e, Brachiosaurus. f, Gallimimus. g, Tarbosaurus. h, Parasaurolophus. i, Sauropelta. j, Herrarasaurus. k, Stegosaurus. l, Lambeosaurus.
No. 891: a, Ramphorhinchus. b, Quetzalcoatlus. c, Pterodactylus. d, Pteranodon. e, Dimorphodon. f. Camarasaurus. g, Tenontosaurus. h, Protoceratops. i, Coelurosaurus. j, Mixosaurus. k, Ceresiosaurus. l, Sharovipteryx.

No. 892, Ceratosaurus. No. 893, Mesosaurus. No. 894, Megazostrodon. No. 895, Diatryma.

1999

Sheets of 12

890-891 A155 150fr #a.-l., each 8.00 8.00

Souvenir Sheets

892-895 A155 1500fr each 6.75 6.75

Prehistoric Animals, Lemurs and Butterflies — A156

Prehistoric animals - No. 895A — Prehistoric sea creatures: b, Eurhinodelphis. c, Stenopterygius. d, Ichthyosaurus. e, Pakicetus. f, Xenacanthus. g, Zygorhiza. h, Basilosaurus. i, Mesosaurus. j, Cetotherium.
No. 896: a, Elasmosaurus (b). b, Quetzalcoatl (c). c, Mesadactylus (b). d, Dimorphodon (e). e, Rhamphorhynchus (c, d, f, i). f, Pteranodon (c, i). g, Pterodactylus (h). h, Eudimorphodon (i). i, Ornithodesmus (g, h).
Lemurs - No. 897: a, Haplorhinien primitif. b, Aye aye (c, e, f). c, Lemur vari. d, Indri. e, Makis varis (f, i). f, Potto. g, Lemur catta. h, Lemur macaos. i, Microcebe souris.
Butterflies - No. 898: a, Charaxes nobilis. b, Charaxes eupale. c, Charaxes brutus. d, Lobobunea turlini. e, Papilio nobilis. f, Athletes gigas. g, Papilio antimachus. h, Epiphora albida. i, Papilio zalmoxis.

1998 *Perf. 13¼x13½*

Sheets of 9

895A A156 150fr Sheet of 9, #b-j — —
896 A156 200fr #a.-i. 8.75 8.75
897 A156 250fr #a.-i. 11.00 11.00
898 A156 300fr #a.-i. 13.00 13.00

See Nos. 928-933.

A157

Endangered Species — A157a

Designs: 75fr, Galago crassicaudatus. 150fr, Vulpes vulpes. 200fr, Anomalurus pusillus. 375fr, Loxodonta africana, vert.
Primates, vert: Nos. 903a-903c, Various views of Pan troglodytes. Nos. 903d-903f, Various views of gorilla gorilla. Nos. 903g-903i, Various views of pongo pygmaeus.
No. 904: a, Tragelaphus strepsiceros. b, Capra hircus. c, Egretta alba. d, Tockus flavirostris.
No. 905: a, Ursus maritimus. b, Megaptera novaeangliae. c, Phoca vitulina. d, Aptenodytes forsteri.
No. 906: a, Pelecanus occidentalis. b, Orcinus orca. c, Delphinus delphis. d, Iguana iguana.
No. 907: a, Panthera tigris altaica. b, Camelus bactrianus. c, Canus lupus. d, Cuon alpinus. e, Rangifer tarandus dawsoni. f, Gulo gulo.
No. 908, Loxodonta africana, vert. No. 909, Ursus thibetanus.

Perf. 14, 14½x14 (#904-906)

1999, Jan. 25 Litho.

899-902 A157 Set of 4 3.50 3.50
903 A157 150fr Sheet of 9, #a.-i. 6.00 6.00

Sheets of 4 and 6

904-906 A157a 375fr #a.-d., each 6.75 6.75
907 A157 375fr #a.-f. 10.00 10.00

Souvenir Sheets

908-909 A157 1500fr each 6.75 6.75

Mushrooms
A158 A159

No. 910, 75fr, Russula xerampelina. No. 911, 75fr, Catathelasma imperiale. No. 912, 150fr, Cortinarius violaceus. No. 913, 150fr, Cortinarius camphoratus. No. 914, 200fr, Rozites caperata. No. 915, 200fr, Coprinus picaceus. No. 916, 375fr, Coprinus cromatus. No. 917, 375fr, Russula cavipes.

No. 918: a, Boletus edulis. b, Suillus grevillei. c, Boletinus cavipes. d, Morchella esculenta. e, Morchella conica. f, Clitocybe dealbata. g, Hygrocybe nigrescens. h, Clitocybe geotropa. i, Lepiota cristata.

No. 919: a, Amanita citrina. b, Amanita phalloides. c, Cortinarius praestans. d, Phallus impudicus. e, Cortinarius bicolor. f, Cortinarius renidens. g, Lactarius torminosus. h, Boletus satanas. i, Cystolepiota bucknalii.

No. 920: a, Amanita muscaria. b, Coprinus comatus. c, Clitocybe odora. d, Cantharellus cibarius. e, Mycena epipterygia. f, Marasmius oreades.

No. 921: a, Boletus edulis. b, Laccaria laccata. c, Agaricus campestris. d, Hypholoma fasciculare. e, Lepiota procera. f, Russula aurata.

No. 922, Ramaria aurea, horiz. No. 923, Panellus serotinus. No. 924, Macrolepiota procera. No. 925, Amanita muscaria. No. 926, Hebeloma crustuliniforme. No. 927, Lepiota molybdites.

1999 **Litho.** ***Perf. 14***
910-917 A158 Set of 8 7.25 7.25

Sheets of 9

918-919 A158 150fr #a.-i., ea 6.00 6.00

Sheets of 6

920-921 A159 375fr #a.-f., ea 10.00 10.00

Souvenir Sheets

922-925 A158 1500fr each 6.75 6.75
926-927 A159 1500fr each 6.75 6.75

Raptors — A160

No. 927A — Birds: b, Souimanga royal. c, Martin-pecheur huppe. d, Pie-grieche. e, Barbican a tete roughe. f, Beau-marquet. g, Rollier a poitrine lilas. h, Pintade vulturine. i, Grenadier. j, Outarde korhaon.

No. 928: a, Sparrow hawk. b, Red-tailed buzzard. c, Dark kite. d, African fish eagle. e, Bald eagle. f, Fawn-colored vulture. g, Peregrine falcon. h, Osprey. i, Harpie eagle.

Dinosaurs — No. 929: a, Dilophosaurus. b, Megalosaurus. c, Ceratosaurus. d, Coelophysis. e, Tyrannosaurus. f, Deinonychus. g, Allosaurus. h, Stegosaurus. i, Albertosaurus.

Gems — No. 930: a, Ruby. b, Liroconite. c, Emerald. d, Euclase. e, Diamond. f, Chrysoberyl. g, Plancheite. h, Kasolite. i, Indigolite.

Meteorites — No. 931: a, Martian. b, Antarctic. c, C2 Chondrite. d, Archondrite. e, Octaedrite moyenne. f, Iron. g, Tektite. h, Chondrite olivine. i, Iron, diff.

Mushrooms - No. 932: a, Paxillus atrotomentosus. b, Craterellus cornucopioides. c, Boletus satanas. d, Clavaria truncata. e, Phallus impudicus. f, Scleroderma aurantiacum. g, Amanita citrina. h, Catathe lasma. i, Inocybe fastigiata.

1125fr, Wulfenite.

1998 ***Perf. 13¼x13½***

Sheets of 9

927A A160 175fr Sheet of 9, #b-j — —
928 A160 200fr #a.-i. 8.75 8.75
929 A160 250fr #a.-i. 10.50 10.50
930 A160 375fr #a.-i. 16.00 16.00
931 A160 400fr #a.-i. 17.00 17.00
932 A160 400fr #a.-i. 17.00 17.00

Souvenir Sheet

933 A160 1125fr multicolored 5.25 5.25

No. 933 contains one 36x51mm stamp.
Captions on Nos. 928e and 928h are transposed.
See Nos. 896-898.

"Illegal" Stamps

Comoro Islands postal officials have declared as "illegal" the following items:

Muhammad Ali, sheet of nine 300fr stamps (previously No. 934);

Muhammad Ali, 1125fr souvenir sheet (previously No. 935);

Babe Ruth, sheet of nine 375fr stamps;

Babe Ruth, two 1125fr souvenir sheets;

Ocean Life, sheet of nine stamps with values of 100, 150, 250, 300, 350, 400, 450, and 500fr;

Horses, sheet of nine stamps with values of 100, 150, 250, 300, 350, 400, 450, and 500fr;

Pandas, sheet of nine stamps with values of 100, 150, 250, 300, 350, 400, 450, and 500fr;

Flora and Fauna: 25fr Harpe costata, 25fr Hibiscus, 50fr Volute lapponica, 50fr Tournesol de Comoros, 100fr Ghetonia mydas, 125fr Octopus vulgaris, 150fr Ylang ylang, 300fr Coelacanth, 300fr Tellina variegata.

Famous People: 250fr, Willy Messerschmitt, Messerschmitt BF-109G-6/R6. 300fr, Louis Pasteur, rabies vaccine administered to Joseph Meister. 350fr, Dr. Albert Schweitzer. 400fr, Ferdinand von Zeppelin, flying Zeppelin. 475fr, Henri Dunant, Nobel Prize. 500fr, Albert Einstein, Gravity Probe B. 550fr, Ayrton Senna, race car. 600fr, Pope John Paul II. 750fr, Iranian Pres. Mohammad Khatami, Pope John Paul II. 800fr, Crew of Apollo 11. 1125fr souvenir sheet, Lindbergh, Spirit of St. Louis.

Submarines — A161

No. 934: a, USS Salt Lake City, US. b, Le Terrible, France. c, Amethyste, France.

1999 **Litho.** ***Perf. 13¼***
934 A161 150fr Sheet of 3, #a-c — —

Automobiles — A161a

No. 935: a, Cadillac Eldorado, Cadillac Series 62, US. b, Aston Martin DB2 IV Mark III, Austin Healey. c, Alfa Romeo Superlegera, Alfa Romeo Giuletta.

1125fr, Aston Martin DB5.

1999
935 A161a 200fr Sheet of 3, #a-c — —

Souvenir Sheet

935D A161a 1125fr multi — —

No. 935D contains one 51x30mm stamp.

Motorcycles — A162

No. 935E: f, Honda NR. g, Christian Leliard and motorcycle. h, Joe S. Wright and motorcycle.

1999
935E A162 250fr Sheet of 3, #f-h — —

Helicopters — A162a

No. 936: a, Westland Wessex. b, MIL MI-8. c, Sikorsky 5-76 Spirit.

1999
936 A162a 300fr Sheet of 3, #a-c — —

Dogs and Sleds A163

No. 937: a, Alaskan malamute, US. b, Greenlandic. c, Siberian husky.

1999
937 A163 400fr Sheet of 3, #a-c — —

Airplanes A164

No. 938: a, Tupolev Tu-160. b, Lockheed F-117A. c, Rafale C.01.

No. 939: a, Ilyshin Il-76. b, Boeing E-3. c, Concorde.

1125fr, Concorde, diff.

1999 **Litho.** ***Perf. 13¼***

Sheets of 3

938 A164 375fr #a.-c. 5.50 5.50
939 A164 450fr #a.-c. 6.50 6.50

Souvenir Sheet

940 A164 1125fr mulicolored 5.50 5.50

No. 940 contains one 50x30mm stamp.

Trains A165

No. 941: a, Series E. b, Series 9100. c, Kitson-Still I-C-I.

No. 942: a, HST 125. b, TGV. c, RTG.

1125fr, Sereis DD40AX.

1999 **Litho.** ***Perf. 13¼***

Sheets of 3

941 A165 400fr #a.-c. 5.75 5.75
942 A165 500fr #a.-c. 7.25 7.25

Souvenir Sheet

943 A165 1125fr mulicolored 5.50 5.50

No. 943 contains one 50x30mm stamp.

Space Achievements — A166

#944: a, Shuttles Discovery, Buran. b, Ariane V. c, John Glenn, Saturn V.

#945: a, Valentina Tereshkova, Soyuz 4. b, Dogs Laika, Bielka. c, Yuri Gagarin, Vostok 1.

1999 **Litho.** ***Perf. 13¼***

Sheets of 3

944 A166 500fr #a.-c. 5.50 5.50
945 A166 600fr #a.-c. 6.50 6.50

Space Achievements Type of 1999

Souvenir Sheet

1125fr, Space Shuttle Discovery, John Glenn.

946 A166 1125fr multi — —

No. 946 contains one 51x30mm stamp.

Teams in 1998 World Cup Soccer Tournament — A167

Players in 1998 World Cup Soccer Tournament — A168

No. 947, 150fr: a, Italy. b, Chile, c, Cameroun. d, Austria. e, Netherlands. f, Belgium. g, South Korea. h, Mexico.

No. 948, 250fr: a, Brazil. b, Scotland. c, Morocco. d, Norway. e, Spain. f, Nigeria. g, Paraguay. h, Bulgaria.

No. 949, 300fr: a, France. b, South Africa. c, Saudi Arabia. d, Denmark. e, Germany. f, United States. g, Yugoslavia. h, Iran.

No. 950, 500fr: a, England. b, Colombia. c, Romania. d, Tunisia. e, Argentina. f, Croatia. g, Jamaica. h, Japan.

No. 951, 350fr: a, Desailly, French flag. b, Ronaldo, Brazilian flag. c, Suker, Croatian flag. d, Kluivert, Netherlands flag. e, French players, World Cup trophy. f, Brazilian player (yellow and green shirt). g, Croatian player (checked shirt). h, Netherlands player (orange shirt).

Illustrations reduced.

1998 **Litho.** ***Perf. 13x13½***

Sheets of 8, #a-h

947-950 A167 Set of 4 45.00 45.00
951 A168 multi 13.00 13.00

Trucks — A169

No. 952: a, Truck with ornamentation over cab. b, Blue truck. c, Green truck. d, Yellow truck.

1999 **Litho.** ***Perf. 13¼***
952 A169 350fr Sheet of 4, #a-d — —

Automobile Racing, Chess, Tennis and Table Tennis, Fishing and Diving — A170

No. 953, 250fr — Automobile racing: a, Giuseppe Farina and Alfa 1500. b, Juan Fangio and Mercedes 2.5L. c, Jack Brabham and Cooper Climax 2.5L. d, Jim Clark and Lotus Climax 1.5L.
No. 954, 300fr — Chess players: a, Garry Kasparov. b, Akiba Rubinstein. c, Max Euwe. d, Mikhail Botvinnik.
No. 955, 375fr — Fishing and diving: a, Shark fishing. b, Sport fishing. c, Diver, back half of shark. d, Diver, front half of shark.
No. 956, 500fr — Chess players: a, Bent Larsen. b, José Raúl Capablanca. c, Boris Spassky. d, Bobby Fischer.
No. 957, 600fr — Tennis and table tennis: a, Female tennis player. b, Male table tennis player. c, Female table tennis player. d, Male tennis player.
No. 958, 1125fr — Chess players: a, Samuel Reshevsky. b, Vassili Smyslov.
No. 959, 1125fr — Fishing and diving: a, Sport fishing, diff. b, Divers and marine life.
No. 960, 1125fr — Tennis and table tennis: a, Male table tennis player, diff. b, Women tennis players.

1999 ***Perf. 13¼***

Sheets of 4, #a-d

953-957 A170 Set of 5 — —

Souvenir Sheets of 2, #a-b

958-960 A170 Set of 3 — —

Nos. 816E, 816G Surcharged

Methods and Perfs. As Before

2001, June 16

963 A144a 100fr on 500fr multi — —
964 A144a 125fr on 200fr multi — —

Traditional Costumes A171

Designs: 125fr, Woman. No. 966, 150fr, No. 969, 300fr, Woman, diff. No. 967, 150fr, No. 968, 300fr, Man.

2002, Apr. 8 **Litho.** ***Perf. 13¼x13***

965-969 A171 Set of 5 *7.75 7.75*

Flowers — A172

Designs: 50fr, Cananga odorata. 600fr, Vanilla planifolia.

2003, Oct. 9

970-971 A172 Set of 2 *4.75 4.75*

Marine Mammals A173

Designs: 75fr, Peponocephala electra. 1000fr, Megaptera novaeangliae.

2003, Oct. 9 ***Perf. 13x13¼***

972-973 A173 Set of 2 *8.00 8.00*

Wood Handicrafts A174

Designs: 100fr, Carved door. 300fr, Candleholder.

2003, Oct. 9 ***Perf. 13¼x13***

974-975 A174 Set of 2 *3.00 3.00*

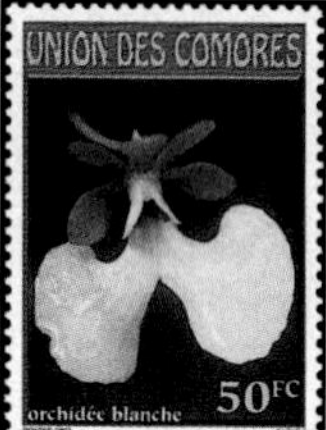

Orchids — A175

Orchid color: 50fr, White. 75fr, Yellow. 100fr, Mauve. 600fr, Red.

2003, Oct. 9

976-979 A175 Set of 4 *6.00 6.00*

SEMI-POSTAL STAMPS

Anti-Malaria Issue
Common Design Type
Perf. 12½x12

1962, Apr. 7 **Engr.** **Unwmk.**

B1 CD108 25fr + 5fr brt pink 2.75 2.75

WHO drive to eradicate malaria.

Nurse Feeding Infant — SP1

Mother and Child — SP2

1967, July 3 **Engr.** ***Perf. 13***

B2 SP1 25fr + 5fr multi 2.25 2.25

For the Red Cross.

1974, Aug. 10 **Engr.** ***Perf. 13***

B3 SP2 35fr + 10fr red & dk brn 2.25 2.25

For the Red Cross.
For surcharge see No. 144.

Miniature Sheet

Space Achievements SP3

World Philatelic Programs emblems (stamp collecting or Halley's Comet) and astronomer or satellite: a, Galileo. b, Copernicus. c, Kepler. d, Halley. e, *Planet A,* Japan, and 3 stars. f, *ICE,* US. g, *Planet A,* 5 stars. h, *Vega,* USSR.

1988 **Litho.** ***Perf. 13½***

B4 Sheet of 8 11.50 11.50
a.-h. SP3 200fr +10fr multi 1.40 1.40

See No. C193.
For surcharges see Nos. 816P-816S.

AIR POST STAMPS

Comoro Village — AP1

Comoro Men and Moroni Mosque — AP2

Design: 200fr, Mosque of Ouani, Anjouan.

1950-54 **Unwmk.** **Engr.** ***Perf. 13***

C1 AP1 50fr grn & red brn 2.25 1.10
C2 AP2 100fr dk brn & red 4.25 1.10
C3 AP1 200fr dk grn, rose brn & pur ('54) 15.00 7.75
Nos. C1-C3 (3) 21.50 9.95

Liberation Issue
Common Design Type

1954, June 6

C4 CD102 15fr sepia & red 25.00 17.50

Madrepora Fructicosa AP3

100fr, Coral, shells and sea anemones.

1962, Jan. 13 **Photo.** ***Perf. 12½x13***

C5 AP3 100fr multi 6.75 6.75
C6 AP3 500fr multi 21.00 18.00

Telstar Issue
Common Design Type

1962, Dec. 5 **Engr.** ***Perf. 13***

C7 CD111 25fr dp vio, dl pur & red lil 4.25 2.75

Type of Regular Issue
Unwmk.

1963, Dec. 27 **Engr.** ***Perf. 13***

Size: 26½x48mm

C8 A13 65fr Baskets 3.50 2.75
C9 A13 200fr Pendant 6.75 4.00

Boat Type of Regular Issue

1964, Aug. 7 **Photo.** ***Perf. 13***

Size: 27x48mm

C10 A14 50fr Mayotte pirogue 2.75 1.25
C11 A14 85fr Schooner 4.00 2.25

Olympic Torch and Boxers — AP4

Order of Star of Grand Comoro — AP5

1964, Oct. 10 **Engr.** ***Perf. 13***

C12 AP4 100fr red brn, dk brn & gray grn 6.00 5.75

18th Olympic Games, Tokyo, Oct. 10-25.

1964, Dec. 10 **Photo.** ***Perf. 13***

C13 AP5 500fr multi 12.00 12.00

ITU Issue
Common Design Type

1965, May 17 **Engr.** ***Perf. 13***

C14 CD120 50fr gray, grnsh bl & ol 16.00 14.00

French Satellite A-1 Issue
Common Design Type

Designs: 25fr, Diamant rocket and launching installations. 30fr, A-1 satellite.

1966, Jan. 17 **Engr.** ***Perf. 13***

C15 CD121 25fr dk pur & ultra 3.50 3.50
C16 CD121 30fr dk pur & ultra 4.00 4.00
a. Strip of 2, #C15-C16 + label 8.50 8.50

French Satellite D-1 Issue
Common Design Type

1966, May 16 **Engr.** ***Perf. 13***

C17 CD122 30fr dk grn, org & brn 3.25 3.25

Old Gun Battery, Dzaoudzi — AP6

200fr, Ksar Castle, Mutsamudu, vert.

1966, Dec. 19 **Photo.** ***Perf. 13***

C18 AP6 50fr multi 3.50 2.25
C19 AP6 200fr multi 6.00 5.75

Bird Type of Regular Issue

Birds: 75fr, Madagascar paradise flycatchers. 100fr, Blue-cheeked bee eaters.

1967, June 20 **Photo.** ***Perf. 13***

Size: 27x48mm

C20 A17 75fr yel grn & multi 7.75 5.00
C21 A17 100fr lt bl & multi 9.00 6.00

Woman Skier — AP7

1968, Apr. 29 **Engr.** ***Perf. 13***
C22 AP7 70fr brt grn, lt bl & choc 4.25 3.50

10th Winter Olympic Games, Grenoble, France, Feb. 6-18, 1968.

Fish Type of Regular Issue

50fr, Moorish idol. 90fr, Diagramma lineatus.

1968, Aug. 1 **Engr.** ***Perf. 13***

Size: 47½x27mm

C23 A19 50fr plum blk & yel 4.50 3.00
C24 A19 90fr brt grn, yel & gray grn 6.75 3.50

For surcharge & overprint see #C52, C74.

Swimmer, Butterfly Stroke — AP8

1969, Jan. 27 **Photo.** ***Perf. 12½***
C25 AP8 65fr ver, grnsh bl & blk 4.00 2.75

19th Olympic Games, Mexico City, 10/12-27.

Flower Type of Regular Issue

50fr, Heliconia sp. 85fr, Tuberose. 200fr, Orchid (angraecum eburneum).

1969, Mar. 20 **Photo.** ***Perf. 13***

Size: 27x48mm

C26 A21 50fr multi, vert. 3.50 2.75
C27 A21 85fr multi, vert. 4.00 2.75
C28 A21 200fr multi, vert. 8.50 4.25
Nos. C26-C28 (3) 16.00 9.75

Concorde Issue

Common Design Type

1969, Apr. 17 **Engr.**
C29 CD129 100fr pur & brn org 16.00 11.00

View of EXPO, Globe and Moon — AP9

90fr, Geisha, map of Japan & EXPO emblem.

1970, Sept. 13 **Photo.** ***Perf. 13***
C30 AP9 60fr slate & multi 2.75 1.60
C31 AP9 90fr multi 3.50 1.90

EXPO '70 International Exposition, Osaka, Japan, Mar. 15-Sept. 13.

Sunset over Mutsamudu — AP10

Map of Archipelago — AP11

Designs: 20fr, Sada Village, Mayotte. 65fr, Old Iconi Palace, Grand Comoro. 85fr, Nioumatchoua Island, Moheli.

1971, May 3 **Photo.** ***Perf. 13***
C32 AP10 15fr dk bl & multi .85 .40
C33 AP10 20fr multi 1.25 .55
C34 AP10 65fr grn & multi 2.75 1.25
C35 AP10 85fr bl & multi 3.50 2.00

Engr.

C36 AP11 100fr brn red, grn & vio bl 5.75 4.00
Nos. C32-C36 (5) 14.10 8.20

See #107-110, C45-C49, C53, C62-C64. For overprints & surcharges see #143, C69, C71, C73, C76-C77, C79-C80, C82, C84.

Flower Type of Regular Issue

Flowers: 60fr, Hibiscus schizopetalus. 85fr, Acalypha sanderii.

1971, July 19 **Photo.** ***Perf. 13***

Size: 27x48mm

C37 A25 60fr grn, ver & yel 3.50 1.75
C38 A25 85fr grn, red & yel 5.00 4.00

For surcharge see No. C75.

Mural, Moroni Airport — AP12

Designs: 85fr, Mural in Arrival Hall, Moroni Airport. 100fr, View of Moroni Airport.

1972, Mar. 30 **Photo.** ***Perf. 13***
C39 AP12 65fr gray & multi 1.40 .55
C40 AP12 85fr gray & multi 1.75 .90

Engr.

C41 AP12 100fr brn, bl & slate grn 2.50 1.75
Nos. C39-C41 (3) 5.65 3.20

New airport in Moroni.

Eiffel Tower and Moroni Telephone Exchange — AP13

75fr, Frenchman and Comoro Islander talking on telephone, radio tower and beacons.

1972, Apr. 24
C42 AP13 35fr dl red & gray .90 .50
C43 AP13 75fr dk car, vio & bl 1.50 .70

First radio-telephone connection between France and Comoro Islands.

Underwater Spear-fishing — AP14

1972, July 5 **Engr.** ***Perf. 13***
C44 AP14 70fr vio bl, brt grn & mar 6.75 4.00

For surcharge see No. C78.

Types of 1971

1972, Nov. 15 **Photo.**

Designs: 20fr, Cape Sima. 35fr, Bambao Palace. 40fr, Domoni Palace. 60fr, Gomajou Peninsula. 100fr, Map of Anjouan Island.

C45 AP10 20fr brn & multi .55 .50
C46 AP10 35fr dk grn & multi .90 .65
C47 AP10 40fr bl & multi 1.40 .80
C48 AP10 60fr grnsh blk & multi 1.75 1.25

Engr.

C49 AP11 100fr mar, bl & sl grn 9.25 4.25
Nos. C45-C49 (5) 13.85 7.45

Pres. Said Mohamed Cheikh (1904-70) AP15

1973, Mar. 16 **Photo.** ***Perf. 13***
C50 AP15 20fr multi .90 .55
C51 AP15 35fr multi 1.40 .75

For overprints see Nos. C70, C72.

No. C24 Surcharged

1973, Apr. 30 **Engr.** ***Perf. 13***
C52 A19 120fr on 90fr multi 8.50 5.00

Intl. Commission for Coelacanth Studies.

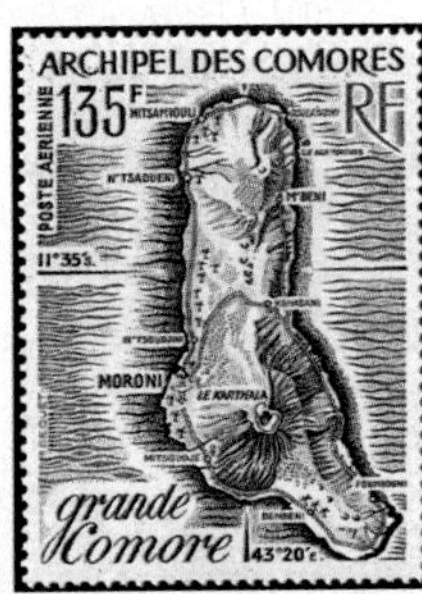

Map of Grand Comoro AP16

1973, June 28 **Engr.** ***Perf. 13***
C53 AP16 135fr vio, bl & dk brn 8.75 4.25

See Nos. C65, C68. For surcharges see Nos. C90-C92.

Karthala Volcano AP17

1973, July 16 **Photo.** ***Perf. 13x12½***
C54 AP17 120fr multi 5.75 3.50

Eruption of Karthala, Sept. 1972.
For surcharge see No. C89.

Armauer G. Hansen — AP18

Design: 150fr, Nicolaus Copernicus (1473-1543), Polish astronomer.

1973, Sept. 5 **Engr.** ***Perf. 13***
C55 AP18 100fr brn, dk bl & sl grn 4.00 2.00
C56 AP18 150fr grnsh bl, vio bl & choc 5.75 3.50

Cent. of the discovery of the Hansen bacillus, the cause of leprosy.
For overprint & surcharge see #C81, C93.

Pablo Picasso (1881-1973) — AP19

1973, Sept. 30 **Photo.**
C57 AP19 200fr blk & multi 8.25 6.00

Souvenir Sheet

C58 AP19 100fr blk & multi 11.50 11.50

For overprint see No. C87.

Order of the Star of Anjouan — AP20

Said Omar ben Soumeth — AP21

1974, Jan. 7 **Photo.** ***Perf. 13***
C59 AP20 500fr brn, bl & gold 10.00 7.00

For overprint see No. C95.

1974, Jan. 31 ***Perf. 13x13½, 13½x13***

135fr, Grand Mufti Said Omar, horiz.

C60 AP21 135fr blk & multi 3.50 2.00
C61 AP21 200fr blk & multi 4.00 2.75

For overprint & surcharge see #C85, C88.

Types of 1971-73

Designs (Views on Mayotte): 20fr, Moya Beach. 35fr, Chiconi. 90fr, Port Mamutzu. 120fr, Map of Mayotte.

1974, Aug. 31 **Photo.** ***Perf. 13***
C62 AP10 20fr bl & multi .85 .65
C63 AP10 35fr grn & multi 3.25 2.00
C64 AP10 90fr multi 5.75 3.50

Engr.

C65 AP16 120fr ultra & grn 6.50 4.25
Nos. C62-C65 (4) 16.35 10.40

Jet Take-off — AP22

1975, Jan. 10 **Engr.** ***Perf. 13***
C66 AP22 135fr multi 5.75 3.50

First direct route Moroni-Hahaya-Paris.
For surcharge see No. C86.

Rotary Emblem, Meeting House, Map — AP23

1975, Feb. 23 **Photo.** ***Perf. 13***
C67 AP23 250fr multi 7.75 5.75

Rotary Intl., 70th anniv., Moroni Rotary Club, 10th anniv.
For surcharge see No. C94.

Map Type of 1973

Design: 230fr, Map of Moheli, horiz.

1975, May 26 **Engr.** ***Perf. 13***
C68 AP16 230fr ocher, ol grn & bl 7.75 5.75

STATE OF COMORO

Issues of 1968-75 Surcharged and Overprinted with Bars and: "ETAT COMORIEN" in Black, Silver, Red or Orange

1975 **Printing & Perfs. as Before**
C69 AP10 10fr on 20fr #C62 *.20 .20*
C70 AP15 20fr (S) *.20 .20*
C71 AP10 30fr on 35fr (R) #C63 *.25 .20*
C72 AP15 35fr (S) *.30 .25*
C73 AP10 40fr (O) *.40 .25*
C74 A19 50fr *.45 .30*
C75 A25 75fr on 60fr *.70 .45*
C76 AP10 75fr on 60fr *.70 .45*
C77 AP10 75fr on 65fr (O) *.70 .45*
C78 AP14 75fr on 70fr *.70 .45*
C79 AP11 100fr #C36 *.90 .60*
C80 AP11 100fr #C49 *.90 .60*
C81 AP18 100fr *.90 .60*
C82 AP10 100fr on 85fr (O) *.90 .60*
C83 A25 100fr on 85fr *.90 .60*
C84 AP10 100fr on 90fr *.90 .60*
C85 AP21 100fr on 135fr (S) *.90 .60*
C86 AP22 100fr on 135fr *.90 .60*
C87 AP19 200fr (S) *1.75 1.25*
C88 AP21 200fr (S) *1.75 1.25*
C89 AP17 200fr on 120fr *1.75 1.25*
C90 AP16 200fr on 120fr *1.75 1.25*
C91 AP16 200fr on 135fr *1.75 1.25*
C92 AP16 200fr on 230fr *1.75 1.25*
C93 AP18 400fr on 150fr *4.00 2.50*
C94 AP23 400fr on 250fr *4.00 2.50*
C95 AP20 500fr *4.50 3.25*
Nos. C69-C95 (27) *34.80 23.75*

See postage section for airmail stamps that are part of joint postage/airmail sets.

Rotary Emblem, Landscape AP26

1979, July 31 **Litho.** ***Perf. 13x12½***
C107 AP26 400fr multi 6.25 3.00

Rotary International.

IYC Emblem, Mother and Child — AP27

1979, July 31 ***Perf. 13x13½***
C108 AP27 250fr multi 3.25 3.25

Intl. Year of the Child. See No. CB1. For surcharges see Nos. C121, C202.

Dimadjou Dispensary, Map of Southern Africa, Emblem AP28

1980, Feb. 23 **Litho.** ***Perf. 12½***
C109 AP28 100fr shown 1.10 .40
C110 AP28 260fr Globe, Concorde, emblem 2.75 1.00

Rotary International, 75th anniv. and Moroni Rotary Club, 15th anniv. (100fr).
For surcharges see Nos. 815L, C119-C120.

First Transatlantic Flight, 50th Anniversary — AP29

1980, May 30 **Litho.** ***Perf. 13***
C111 AP29 200fr multi 2.25 1.25

No. C111 Surcharged in Blue

1981, Feb. **Litho.** ***Perf. 13***
C112 AP29 30fr on 200fr multi .35 .35

The Dove and the Rainbow, by Picasso — AP30

Picasso Birth Centenary: 70fr, Still Life on a Sideboard. 150fr, Studio with Plaster Head. 250fr, Bowl and Pot, vert. 500fr, The Red Tablecloth.

1981, June 30 **Litho.** ***Perf. 12½***
C113 AP30 40fr multi .45 .20
C114 AP30 70fr multi .80 .20
C115 AP30 150fr multi 1.60 .50
C116 AP30 250fr multi 2.75 .70
C117 AP30 500fr multi 5.50 1.50
Nos. C113-C117 (5) 11.10 3.10

For surcharges see Nos. 815G, C118.

#C114, C109-C110, CB1 Surchd.

1981, Nov. **Litho.** ***Perf. 12½, 13***
C118 AP30 10fr on 70fr multi .20 .20
C119 AP28 10fr on 100fr multi .20 .20
C120 AP28 50fr on 260fr multi .45 .20
C121 AP27 50fr on 200fr+30fr multi .45 .20
Nos. C118-C121 (4) 1.30 .80

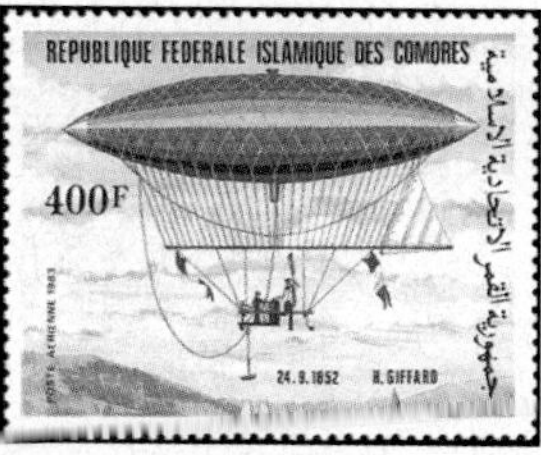

Manned Flight Bicentenary — AP31

Balloons. 100fr, 200fr, 300fr, 500fr vert.

1983, Apr. 20 **Litho.** ***Perf. 13***
C122 AP31 100fr Montgolfiere, 1783 .90 .30
C123 AP31 200fr Lunardi, 1784 1.75 .50
C124 AP31 300fr Blanchard and Jeffries, 1785 2.90 .90
C125 AP31 400fr Giffard, 1852 4.00 1.25
Nos. C122-C125 (4) 9.55 2.95

Souvenir Sheet

C126 AP31 500fr Paris Siege. 1870 5.00 1.50

For overprints and surcharges see Nos. 602, 812T, 815P.

Pre-Olympic Year Sailing — AP32

1983, June 30 **Litho.** ***Perf. 13***
C127 AP32 150fr Type 470 1.25 .40
C128 AP32 200fr Flying Dutchman 1.75 .50
C129 AP32 300fr Type 470, diff. 2.90 .90
C130 AP32 400fr Finn 4.00 1.00
Nos. C127-C130 (4) 9.90 2.80

Souvenir Sheet

C131 AP32 500fr Soling 5.00 1.50

For overprint and surcharge see Nos. 603, C206.

1984 Summer Olympics — AP33

1984, July 10 **Litho.** ***Perf. 13***
C132 AP33 60fr Basketball .45 .20
C133 AP33 100fr Basketball, diff. .80 .40
C134 AP33 165fr Basketball, diff. 1.40 .65
C135 AP33 175fr Baseball, horiz. 1.50 .65
C136 AP33 200fr Baseball, horiz. 1.75 .80
Nos. C132-C136 (5) 5.90 2.70

Souvenir Sheet

C137 AP33 500fr Basketball, diff. 7.00 1.50

Nos. C132-C134 vert.

Development Conference AP34

1984, July 2 **Litho.** ***Perf. 13***
C138 AP34 475fr Tools for development 5.00 2.00

For surcharge see No. 796I.

Audubon Bicentenary — AP35

1985, Jan. 15 **Litho.** ***Perf. 13***
C139 AP35 100fr Hirundo rustica, vert. 1.00 .40
C140 AP35 125fr Icterus galbula, vert. 1.25 .50
C141 AP35 150fr Buteo lineatus 1.60 .60
C142 AP35 500fr Sphyropieus varius 4.00 2.00
Nos. C139-C142 (4) 7.85 3.50

Moroni Port Missile Defense — AP36

No. C146, Ngome Ntsoudjini Scout troop.

1985, May 20 **Litho.** ***Perf. 13x12½***
C145 AP36 200fr multi 2.90 1.25
C146 AP36 200fr multi 2.90 1.25
a. Pair, #C145-C146 + label 6.00 6.00

PHILEXAFRICA '85, Lome.
For surcharges see Nos. C207-C208.

Natl. Flag, Sun, Outline Map of Islands — AP37

1985, July 6
C147 AP37 10fr multi .25 .20
C148 AP37 15fr multi .25 .20
C149 AP37 125fr multi 2.00 .60
C150 AP37 300fr multi 5.00 1.50
Nos. C147-C150 (4) 7.50 2.50

Natl. independence, 10th anniv.
For surcharge see No. 815Q.

Runners — AP38

1985, Nov. 12

C151 AP38 250fr shown 2.50 1.75
C152 AP38 250fr Mining 2.50 1.75
a. Pair, #C151-C152 + label 5.00 5.00

PHILEXAFRICA '85, Lome, Togo, 11/16-24.
For surcharges see Nos. 815H-815I, C204-C205.

Air Transport Union, UTA, 50th Anniv. — AP39

1985, Dec. 30 Litho. *Perf. 13*

C153 AP39 25fr F-AOUL seaplane .20 .20
C154 AP39 75fr Camel driver, DC-8 .70 .30
C155 AP39 100fr Noratlas and Heron DC-4s 1.00 .40
a. Souv. sheet of 3, #C153-C155, perf. 12½ 3.00 2.25
C156 AP39 125fr UTA cargo plane 1.25 .60

Size: 40x52mm

Perf. 12½x13

C157 AP39 1000fr Aircraft, 1935-1985 11.00 6.00
a. Souv. sheet of 2, #C156-C157, perf. 12½ 12.00 8.00
Nos. C153-C157 (5) 14.15 7.50

Halley's Comet — AP40

Comets, astronomers and probes.

1986, Mar. 7 *Perf. 13*

C158 AP40 125fr Edmond Halley, Giotto probe 1.10 .45
C159 AP40 150fr Giacobini-Zinner, 1959 1.40 .50
C160 AP40 225fr Encke, 1961 2.25 .90
C161 AP40 300fr Bradfield, 1980 2.75 1.25
C162 AP40 450fr Planet A probe 4.50 1.75
Nos. C158-C162 (5) 12.00 4.85

For surcharges see Nos. 796S, 804H, 804R, 812P.

1986 World Cup Soccer Championships, Mexico — AP41

Various soccer plays.

1986, June 11 Litho. *Perf. 13*

C163 AP41 125fr multi 1.10 .45
C164 AP41 210fr multi 2.00 .80
C165 AP41 500fr multi 5.00 2.00
C166 AP41 600fr multi 5.50 2.25
Nos. C163-C166 (4) 13.60 5.50

For surcharges see Nos. 796C, 800Q, 815C.

Tennis at the 1988 Summer Olympics — AP42

Various players.

1987, Jan. 28 Litho. *Perf. 13½*

C167 AP42 150fr multi 1.60 .45
C168 AP42 250fr multi 2.75 .75
C169 AP42 500fr multi 5.00 1.50
C170 AP42 600fr multi 6.25 1.75
Nos. C167-C170 (4) 15.60 4.45

For overprints and surcharges see Nos. 796N, 796U, 815J, 816L, 816N, C183-C186, C203.

World Wildlife Fund — AP43

Various pictures of the mongoose lemur.

1987, Feb. 18 *Perf. 13*

C171 AP43 75fr multi, vert. 1.50 .25
C172 AP43 100fr multi 2.25 .35
C173 AP43 125fr multi 3.75 .55
C174 AP43 150fr multi 4.50 .85
Nos. C171-C174 (4) 12.00 2.00

1988 Winter Olympics, Calgary AP44

1987, Apr. 10 Litho. *Perf. 13½*

C175 AP44 150fr Slalom 1.10 .45
C176 AP44 225fr Ski jumping 2.00 .75
C177 AP44 500fr Women's giant slalom 5.00 1.60
C178 AP44 600fr Luge 5.50 2.25
Nos. C175-C178 (4) 13.60 5.05

For surcharges see Nos. 800R, 812U.

AP45

Aviation History AP46

Designs: 200fr, Inventors Didier Daurat and Raymond Vanier with 1935 Air Blue F-ANR1. 300fr, Farman biplane, 1st scheduled airmail delivery, Paris-LeMans-St. Nazaire, Aug. 17, 1918. 500fr, Bleriot aircraft, 1st scheduled airmail delivery, Villacoublay-Vendome-Poitiers-Pauillac, Oct. 15, 1913. 1000fr, Henri Pequet and his aircraft, Feb. 18, 1911.

1987, Dec. 29 Litho. *Perf. 13*

C179 AP45 200fr multi 2.00 .65
C180 AP45 300fr multi 2.90 1.00
C181 AP45 500fr multi 5.00 1.60

Perf. 12½x13

C182 AP46 1000fr multi 10.00 2.25
Nos. C179-C182 (4) 19.90 5.50

Airmail history exposition, Allahabad.
For surcharges see Nos. 800S, 804D.

Nos. C167-C170 Ovptd. in Red for 1988 Olympic Tennis Champions

Overprint includes name of athlete and "Medaille d'or / Seoul" or "Medaille / d'argent / Seoul."

1988, Nov. Litho. *Perf. 13½*

C183 AP42 150fr "Miloslav Mecir / (Tchec.)" 1.10 .75
C184 AP42 250fr "Tim Mayotte / (U.S.A.)" 1.75 1.40
C185 AP42 500fr "Steffi Graf / (R.F.A.)" 4.50 2.75
C186 AP42 600fr "Gabriela Sabatini / (Argentine)" 5.50 3.75
Nos. C183-C186 (4) 12.85 8.65

For surcharges see Nos. 800T, 815K, 816M, 816O.

Early Aviators and Aircraft — AP47

100fr, Alberto Santos-Dumont (1873-1932), & *Bagatelle,* 1st documented power flight in Europe, Oct. 23, 1906. 150fr, Wright Brothers & *Flyer A.* 200fr, Louis Bleriot (1872-1936) & *Bleriot XI,* 1st crossing of the English Channel in a heavier-than-air craft, July 25, 1909. 300fr, Henri Farman (1874-1958) & Voisin biplane, 1st fixed-route 1-kilometer circular flight, Jan. 13, 1908. 500fr, Gabriel (1880-1973) & Charles (1882-1912) Voisin, established 1st biplane factory (1908), & Voisin biplane. 800fr, Roland Garros (1888-1918), 1st trans-Mediterranean flight, Sept. 23, 1913.

1988, Dec. 7 Litho. *Perf. 13*

C187 AP47 100fr pur .90 .45
C188 AP47 150fr brt lil rose 1.40 .60
C189 AP47 200fr blk 1.75 .90
C190 AP47 300fr dark yel org 2.75 .90
C191 AP47 500fr dark blue 4.50 1.50
C192 AP47 800fr lt olive grn 6.75 3.00
Nos. C187-C192 (6) 18.05 7.35

For surcharges see Nos. 800B, 800U, 804E, C209.

Souvenir Sheet

Space Achievements — AP48

Design: World Philatelic Programs stamp collecting emblem, Soviet satellite and Edmond Halley.

1988 Litho. *Perf. 13½*

C193 AP48 750fr multi 7.00 1.50

Nos. C108, C168, C151-C152, C128, C145-C146 and C189 Surcharged

1989 Litho. *Perfs. as Before*

C202 AP27 5fr on 250fr #C108 .20 .20
C203 AP42 25fr on 250fr #C168 .20 .20
C204 AP38 50fr on 250fr #C151 .45 .20
C205 AP38 50fr on 250fr #C152 .45 .20
a. Pair, #C204-C205 + label 1.00 1.00
C206 AP32 150fr on 200fr #C128 1.25 .60
C207 AP36 150fr on 200fr #C145 1.25 .60
C208 AP36 150fr on 200fr #C146 1.25 .60
a. Pair, #C151-C152 + label 2.75 2.75
C209 AP47 150fr on 200fr #C189 1.25 .60
Nos. C202-C209 (8) 6.30 3.20

World Cup Soccer, Championships, Italy — AP50

Various soccer plays and map of Italy.

1990, June Litho. *Perf. 13*

C210 AP50 75fr multicolored .60 .30
C211 AP50 150fr multicolored 1.25 .60
C212 AP50 500fr multicolored 3.75 1.90
C213 AP50 1000fr multicolored 8.00 4.00
Nos. C210-C213 (4) 13.60 6.80

For surcharge see No. 800V.

Souvenir Sheet

Garry Kasparov, Anatoly Karpov, Russian Chess Champions — AP51

Litho. & Embossed

1991, Aug. 5 *Perf. 13½*

C214 AP51 1500fr gold & multi 11.00 —

World Chess Championships.

1992 Summer Olympics, Barcelona AP52

Litho. & Embossed

1992, July 28 *Perf. 13½*
C215 AP52 1500fr gold & multi 24.00 12.00

Sculpted Table — AP52a

1994 (?) Litho. *Perf. 13¼x13½*

Background Color

C215A AP52a 15fr blue
C215B AP52a 75fr green
C215C AP52a 100fr pink
C215D AP52a 225fr orange

For surcharges see Nos. 826A-826E.

Sea Turtles AP53

1995 Litho. *Perf. 13½x13¼*

Frame Color

C216 AP53 10fr blue
C217 AP53 25fr pink
C218 AP53 30fr green
C219 AP53 50fr lilac

No. C215A Surcharged in Blue Violet

Perf. 13¼x13½

2001, June 16 **Litho.**
C220 AP52a 300fr on 15fr — —

AIR POST SEMI-POSTAL STAMP

Type of Air Post 1979

Design: IYC emblem, mother and son.

1979, July 31 Photo. *Perf. 13½x13*
CB1 AP27 200fr + 30fr multi 3.25 3.25

International Year of the Child.
For surcharge see No. C121.

POSTAGE DUE STAMPS

Anjouan Mosque D1

Coelacanth D2

1950 Unwmk. Engr. *Perf. 14x13*
J1 D1 50c deep green .70 .70
J2 D1 1fr black brown .70 .70

1954
J3 D2 5fr dk brown & green .70 .70
J4 D2 10fr gray & red brown 1.00 1.00
J5 D2 20fr indigo & blue 1.60 1.60
Nos. J3-J5 (3) 3.30 3.30

Hibiscus D3

2fr, 15fr, 40fr, 50fr, vertical.

1977, Nov. 19 Litho. *Perf. 13½*
J6 D3 1fr shown .25 .20
J7 D3 2fr Pineapple .25 .20
J8 D3 5fr White butterfly .25 .20
J9 D3 10fr Chameleon .25 .20
J10 D3 15fr Blooming banana .25 .20
J11 D3 20fr Orchids .25 .20
J12 D3 30fr Allamanda cathartica .35 .20
J13 D3 40fr Cashews .70 .20
J14 D3 50fr Custard apple .80 .20
J15 D3 100fr Breadfruit 1.50 .25
J16 D3 200fr Vanilla 3.25 .50
J17 D3 500fr Ylang ylang 8.00 1.25
Nos. J6-J17 (12) 16.10 3.80

OFFICIAL STAMPS

Comoro Flag — O1

Perf. 13x12½

1979-85 Litho. Unwmk.
O1 O1 5fr multi .20 .20
O2 O1 10fr multi .20 .20
O3 O1 20fr multi .20 .20
O4 O1 30fr multi .45 .20
O5 O1 40fr multi .60 .25
O6 O1 60fr multi ('80) .55 .25
O7 O1 75fr multi ('85) .35 .25
O8 O1 100fr multi 1.10 .60
Nos. O1-O8 (8) 3.65 2.15

See Nos. 526-530.

Pres. Said Mohamed Cheikh (1904-1970) — O2

1980-85
O9 O2 100fr multi .60 .40
O10 O2 125fr multi ('85) 3.25 1.50
O11 O2 400fr multi 1.60 .90
Nos. O9-O11 (3) 5.45 2.80

CONGO DEMOCRATIC REPUBLIC

,de-mə-'kra-tik ri-'pə-blik of 'käŋ-(,)gō

LOCATION — Central Africa
GOVT. — Republic
AREA — 895,348 sq. mi. (estimated)
POP. — 22,480,000 (est. 1971)
CAPITAL — Kinshasa (Leopoldville)

Congo was an independent state, founded by Leopold II of Belgium, until 1908 when it was annexed to Belgium as a colony. Congo became an independent republic in 1960. The name was changed to Republic of Zaire, Oct. 28, 1971. In 1998 some issues again used the name Congo Democratic Republic. See Zaire in Vol. 6 for later issues.

100 Centimes = 1 Franc
100 Sengi = 1 Li-Kuta,
100 Ma-Kuta = 1 Zaire (1967)

Catalogue values for all unused stamps in this country are for Never Hinged items.

Belgian Congo Flower Issue of 1952-53 Overprinted or Surcharged

Perf. 11½

1960, June 30 Photo. Unwmk.

Flowers in Natural Colors

Size: 21x25½mm

Granite Paper

323 A86 10c dp plum & ocher .45 .20
324 A86 10c on 15c red & yel grn .45 .20
325 A86 20c grn & gray .45 .20
326 A86 40c grn & sal .45 .20
327 A86 50c on 60c bl grn & pink .45 .20
328 A86 50c on 75c dp plum & gray .45 .20
329 A86 1fr car & yel .45 .20
330 A86 1.50fr vio & ap grn .45 .20
331 A86 2fr ol grn & buff .45 .20
332 A86 3fr ol grn & pink .45 .20
333 A86 4fr choc & lil 1.00 .95
334 A86 5fr dp plum & lt bl grn .45 .20
335 A86 6.50fr dk car & lil .65 .20
336 A86 8fr grn & lt yel .75 .20
337 A86 10fr dp plum & pale ol 1.25 .20
338 A86 20fr vio bl & dl sal 2.25 .80

Nos. 324, 327-328 exist without "CONGO" overprint but with surcharge, also without surcharge but with "CONGO." Inverted and double overprints exist. Values from $10 to $20 each.

Overprinted

Size: 22x32mm

339 A86 50fr dp plum & gray bl 14.50 5.75
340 A86 100fr grn & buff 30.00 9.25
Nos. 323-340 (18) 55.35 19.55

Belgian Congo Animal Issue, Nos. 306-317, Overprinted or Surcharged in Red, Blue, Black or Brown

341 A92 10c bl & brn (R) .20 .20
342 A93 20c red org & sl (Bl) .20 .20
343 A92 40c brn & bl (Bk) .20 .20
344 A93 50c brt ultra, red & sep (R) .20 .20
345 A92 1fr brn, grn & blk (Br) .20 .20
346 A93 1.50fr blk & org yel (R) .20 .20
347 A92 2fr crim, blk & brn (Bl) .40 .20
348 A93 3.50fr on 3fr blk, gray & lil rose (Bk) .60 .20
349 A92 5fr brn, dk brn & brt grn (Br) .80 .20
350 A93 6.50fr bl, brn & org yel (R) 1.00 .20
a. Black overprint 1.75 .60
351 A92 8fr org brn, ol bis & lil (Br) 1.25 .40
352 A93 10fr multi (R) 1.60 .50
Nos. 341-352 (12) 6.85 2.90

See note after No. 340.

Same Overprint on Belgian Congo No. 318

1960

353 A94 50c gldn brn, ocher & red brn .70 .70

Same Overprint and Surcharge of New Value on Belgian Congo Nos. 321-322

Inscription in French

354 A95 3.50fr on 3fr gray & red .70 .45

Inscription in Flemish

355 A95 3.50fr on 3fr gray & red .70 .45
Nos. 353-355 (3) 2.10 1.60

Nos. 353-355 are known with inverted overprints.

Map of Congo A93a

1960 Photo. *Perf. 11½*

356 A93a 20c brown .20 .20
357 A93a 50c rose red .20 .20
358 A93a 1fr green .20 .20
359 A93a 1.50fr red brn .20 .20
360 A93a 2fr rose car .20 .20
361 A93a 3.50fr lilac .20 .20
362 A93a 5fr brt bl .20 .20
363 A93a 6.50fr gray .25 .20
364 A93a 10fr orange .40 .20
365 A93a 20fr ultra .75 .25
Nos. 356-365 (10) 2.80 2.05

Congo's Independence.
For overprints see Nos. 371-380.

Flag, People and Broken Chain — A94

1961, Jan. 4 Unwmk. *Perf. 11½*

Flag in Blue and Yellow

366 A94 2fr rose vio .20 .20
367 A94 3.50fr vermilion .20 .20
368 A94 6.50fr yel brn .20 .20
369 A94 10fr brt grn .25 .20
370 A94 20fr car rose .40 .30
Nos. 366-370 (5) 1.25 1.10

Signing of the Independence Agreement by Belgium, Jan. 4, 1959.

Nos. 356-365 Overprinted in Blue, Black or Red: "Conference Coquilhatville Avril Mai 1961"

1961

371 A93a 20c brn (Bl) 1.40 1.40
372 A93a 50c rose red (Bk) 1.40 1.40
373 A93a 1fr grn (R) 1.40 1.40
374 A93a 1.50fr red brn (Bl) 1.40 1.40
375 A93a 2fr rose car (Bk) 1.40 1.40
376 A93a 3.50fr lil (Bl) 1.40 1.40
377 A93a 5fr brt bl (R) 1.40 1.40
378 A93a 6.50fr gray (R) 1.40 1.40
379 A93a 10fr org (Bk) 1.40 1.40
380 A93a 20fr ultra (R) 1.40 1.40
Nos. 371-380 (10) 14.00 14.00

Coquilhatville Conf., Apr.-May, 1961.
Nos. 371-380 exist with inverted overprints. Value $15 each.

Pres. Joseph Kasavubu — A95

Kasavubu and Map of Congo — A96

10fr-100fr, Kasavubu in uniform and map.

Perf. 11½

1961, June 30 Unwmk. Photo.

Portrait and Inscription in Dark Brown

381 A95 10c yellow .20 .20
382 A95 20c dp rose .20 .20
383 A95 40c bl grn .20 .20
384 A95 50c salmon .20 .20
385 A95 1fr lilac .20 .20
386 A95 1.50fr lt brn .20 .20
387 A95 2fr brt grn .20 .20
388 A96 3.50fr rose pink .20 .20
389 A96 5fr gray *5.75* .20
390 A96 6.50fr ultra .80 .20
391 A96 8fr olive .80 .20
392 A95 10fr lt vio 2.10 .80
393 A95 20fr orange 2.10 .20
394 A95 50fr lt bl 3.50 .35
395 A95 100fr apple green 5.75 .55
Nos. 381-395 (15) 22.40 4.10

First anniversary of independence.

Nos. 381-387, 389 and 392 Overprinted: "REOUVERTURE du PARLEMENT JUILLET 1961"

1961

Portrait and Inscription in Dark Brown

396 A95 10c yellow .20 .20
397 A95 20c dp rose .20 .20
398 A95 40c bl grn .20 .20
399 A95 50c salmon .50 .35
400 A95 1fr lilac .50 .35
401 A95 1.50fr lt brn 1.25 1.00
402 A95 2fr brt grn 1.25 1.00
403 A96 5fr gray 1.25 1.00
404 A95 10fr lt vio 1.25 1.00
Nos. 396-404 (9) 6.60 5.30

Congolese parliament re-opening, 7/1961.
Nos. 396-404 exist with inverted overprints. Value $9 each.

Dag Hammarskjold and Map of Africa with Congo — A97

Malaria Eradication Emblem and Mosquito — A98

1962, Jan. 20 Photo. *Perf. 11½*

Gray Background

405 A97 10c dk brn .20 .20
406 A97 20c Prus bl .20 .20
407 A97 30c brown .20 .20
408 A97 40c dk bl .20 .20
409 A97 50c brn red .20 .20
410 A97 3fr ol grn *4.25* *1.25*
411 A97 6.50fr dk vio 1.25 .35
412 A97 8fr red brn 1.50 .50
Nos. 405-412 (8) 8.00 3.10

Souvenir Sheets

Imperf

413 A97 25fr blk brn 4.00 4.00
a. Overprint in green 4.00 4.00

Dag Hammarskjold, Sec. Gen. of the UN, 1953-61.

No 413a is overprinted "30 Juin 1962" on stamp and "2eme Anniversaire de l'Independance" on sheet margin. Issued June 30, 1962.

For overprints see Nos. 417-424.

1962, June 15

Granite Paper

414 A98 1.50fr yel, blk & dk red .20 .20
415 A98 2fr yel grn, brn & bl grn .25 .20
416 A98 6.50fr ultra, blk & mar .20 .20
Nos. 414-416 (3) .65 .60

WHO drive to eradicate malaria.

Nos. 405-412 Overprinted in Blue, Purple, Black or Carmine

1962, Oct. 15

Gray Background

417 A97 10c dk brn (Bl) .20 .20
418 A97 20c Prus bl (P) .20 .20
419 A97 30c brn (Bk) .20 .20
420 A97 40c dk bl (C) .20 .20
421 A97 50c brn red (Bl) *2.00* *.75*
422 A97 3fr ol grn (P) .20 .20
423 A97 6.50fr dk vio (Bk) .25 .20
424 A97 8fr red brn (C) .35 .20
Nos. 417-424 (8) 3.60 2.15

Reorganization of Adoula administration.

Canceled to Order

Starting in 1963, values in the used column are for "canceled to order" stamps. Postally used copies sell for much more.

A99

1963, Jan. 28 Engr. *Perf. 10½x13*

425 A99 2fr dull purple *.95* *.75*
426 A99 4fr red .20 .20
427 A99 7fr dark blue .20 .20
428 A99 20fr slate green .25 .20
Nos. 425-428 (4) 1.60 *1.35*

Congo's 1st participation at the UPU Cong., New Delhi, Mar. 1963.

For overprints see Nos. 468-471.

Shoebill — A100

Birds: 10c, Pelicans. 20c, Crested guinea fowl, horiz. 30c, Openbill. 40c, White-bellied storks, horiz. 2fr, Marabou. 3fr, Greater flamingos, horiz. 4fr, Congolese peacock. 5fr, Hartlaub ducks, horiz. 6fr, Secretary bird. 7fr, Black-casqued hornbill, horiz. 8fr, Sacred ibis and nest. 10fr, Crowned crane, horiz. 20fr, Saddle-bill stork, horiz.

1963 Unwmk. Photo. *Perf. 11½*

429 A100 10c pink, ultra & ocher .20 .20
430 A100 20c rose red, bl & blk .20 .20
431 A100 30c grn, ocher & blk .20 .20
432 A100 40c gray, org & blk .20 .20
433 A100 1fr brn, emer & gray .20 .20
434 A100 2fr gray, red & ind *2.50* .40
435 A100 3fr ol grn, blk & rose .20 .20

436 A100 4fr car rose, vio bl & grn .20 .20
437 A100 5fr lake, lt bl & blk .30 .20
438 A100 6fr pur, yel & blk *2.50* .40
439 A100 7fr bl grn, blk & ind .40 .20
440 A100 8fr yel, org & blk .50 .20
441 A100 10fr bl, blk & rose .50 .20
442 A100 20fr cit, red & blk .90 .20
Nos. 429-442 (14) 9.00 3.20

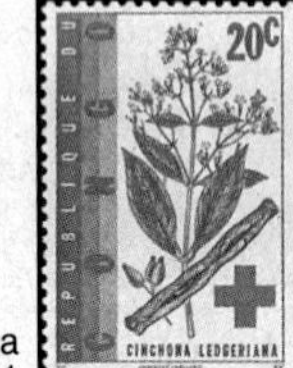

Cinchona Ledgeriana — A101

Red Cross Nurse — A102

10c, 30c, 5fr, Strophanthus sarmentosus.

Perf. 12½x13½, 13½x12½

1963, May 25 Engr. Unwmk.

Cross in Red

443 A101 10c vio & dl grn .20 .20
444 A101 20c magenta & bl .20 .20
445 A101 30c grn & org .20 .20
446 A101 40c bl & vio .20 .20
447 A101 5fr ol & rose claret .20 .20
448 A101 7fr org & blk .20 .20
449 A102 9fr gray olive & red .20 .20
450 A102 20fr purple & red *2.00* .75
Nos. 443-450 (8) 3.40 2.15

International Red Cross centenary.

A souvenir sheet of three contains imperf. 58fr, 7fr, and 20fr stamps similar to Nos. 447, 448 and 450, but in changed colors. Size: 109x75mm. Value $27.50

Men Joining Hands and Map of Congo A103

1963, June 29 Photo. *Perf. 11½*

451 A103 4fr multi .75 .35
452 A103 5fr multi .20 .20
453 A103 9fr multi .20 .20
454 A103 12fr multi .25 .20
Nos. 451-454 (4) 1.40 .95

Issued to celebrate national reconciliation.

Bulldozer and Kabambare Sewer, Leopoldville — A104

Designs: 30c, 5fr, 12fr, Excavator and blueprint. 50c, 9fr, Building Ituri road.

1963, July 1 Engr. Unwmk.

455 A104 20c multi .20 .20
456 A104 30c multi .20 .20
457 A104 50c multi .20 .20
458 A104 3fr multi 1.00 .40
459 A104 5fr multi .20 .20
460 A104 9fr multi .20 .20
461 A104 12fr multi .20 .20
Nos. 455-461 (7) 2.20 1.60

Issued to publicize aid to Congo by the European Economic Community.

Leopoldville Airport N'Djili — A105

5fr, 7fr, 50fr, Tail assembly and airport.

1963, Nov. 30 Photo. *Perf. 11½*

462 A105 2fr gray, yel & red brn .20 .20
463 A105 5fr mag, vio & yel .20 .20
464 A105 6fr bl, yel & dk brn 1.40 .50
465 A105 7fr multi .20 .20
466 A105 30fr lil, yel & ol .40 .25
467 A105 50fr multi .60 .30
Nos. 462-467 (6) 3.00 1.65

Issued to publicize Air Congo.
For surcharge see No. 606.

Nos. 425-428 Overprinted with Silver Frame on Three Sides and Black Inscription: "15e anniversaire / 10 DECEMBRE 1948 / DROITS DE L'HOMME / 10 DECEMBRE 1963"

Engraved and Typographed

1963, Dec. 10 *Perf. 10½x13*

468 A99 2fr dull purple .20 .20
469 A99 4fr red [illegible]
470 A99 7fr dark blue .25 .20
471 A99 20fr slate green .30 .20
Nos. 468-471 (4) .95 .80

Universal Declaration of Human Rights, 15th anniv.

Nos. 468-471 exist with side date panels transposed ("1963" at left, "1948" at right). Value, each $15.

Laboratory Technician and Atomic Emblem A106

1.50fr, 60fr, University. 8fr, 75fr, First African nuclear reactor. 25fr, 100fr, University and crest.

1964, Feb. 1 Photo. *Perf. 14x12½*

472 A106 50c multi .20 .20
473 A106 1.50fr multi .20 .20
474 A106 8fr multi *2.10* *2.00*
475 A106 25fr multi .20 .20
476 A106 30fr multi .30 .20
477 A106 60fr multi .50 .30
478 A106 75fr multi .60 .55
479 A106 100fr multi .80 .70
a. Souv. sheet of 3 5.25 5.25
Nos. 472-479 (8) 4.90 4.35

Lovanium University, Leopoldville, 10th anniv.

No. 479a contains 3 imperf. multicolored stamps: 20fr, design as 50c; 30fr, as 8fr; 100fr.

Belgian Congo Issues of 1952-59 Overprinted "REPUBLIQUE DU CONGO" and Surcharged in Black on Overprinted Metallic Panels

1964 *Perf. 11½*

480 A93 1fr on 20c red org & sl (#307) .20 .20
481 A86 2fr on 1.50fr (#273) *8.75* *3.25*
482 A93 5fr on 6.50fr (#315) .65 .20
483 A86 8fr on 6.50fr (#278) .95 .30

Republic Issues of 1960-61 Surcharged in Black on Overprinted Metallic Rectangles or Ovals

484 A86 1fr on 6.50fr (#335) .20 .20
485 A93 1fr on 20c (#342) .20 .20
486 A86 2fr on 1.50fr (#330) .20 .20
487 A95 3fr on 20c (#382) .35 .20
488 A95 4fr on 40c (#383) .45 .20
489 A93 5fr on 6.50fr ("Congo" red) (#350) .65 .20
a. "Congo" black .65 .20
490 A93a 6fr on 6.50fr (#363) .65 .25
491 A93a 7fr on 20c (#356) .65 .30
Nos. 480-491 (12) 13.90 5.70

Pole Vault A107

7fr, 20fr, Javelin, vert. 8fr, 100fr, Hurdling.

Perf. 11½

1964, July 13 Unwmk. Photo.

Granite Paper

492 A107 5fr gray, dk brn & car .20 .20
493 A107 7fr rose, vio & emer .95 .35
494 A107 8fr org, yel, red brn & vio bl .20 .20
495 A107 10fr bl, vio brn & mag .20 .20
496 A107 20fr gray grn, red brn & ver .25 .20
497 A107 100fr lil, dk brn & grn .95 .25
a. Souv. sheet of 3 8.75 8.75
Nos. 492-497 (6) 2.75 1.40

18th Olympic Games, Tokyo, Oct. 10-25. No. 497a contains 3 imperf. stamps (20fr orange & dark brown, pole vault; 30fr citron and dark brown, hurdling; 100fr dull green and dark brown, javelin). Sheet issued Sept. 10.

National Palace, Leopoldville — A108

1964, Sept. 15

Granite Paper

498 A108 50c lil rose & bl .20 .20
499 A108 1fr bl & lil rose .20 .20
500 A108 2fr brn red & vio .20 .20
501 A108 3fr emer & red .20 .20
502 A108 4fr org & vio bl .20 .20
503 A108 5fr gray vio & emer .20 .20
504 A108 6fr sep & org .20 .20
505 A108 7fr gray ol & red brn .20 .20
506 A108 8fr rose red & vio bl *1.25* .30
507 A108 9fr vio bl & rose red .20 .20
508 A108 10fr brn ol & grn .20 .20
509 A108 20fr bl & brn org .20 .20
510 A108 30fr dk car rose & grn .20 .20
511 A108 40fr ultra & dk car rose .25 .20
512 A108 50fr brn org & grn .30 .20
513 A108 100fr slate & ver .55 .20
Nos. 498-513 (16) 4.75 3.30

For overprints and surcharges see Nos. 574-577, 593-598, 609-615, 670-671, 673-674, 676-677, 680, 684-687.

Pres. John F. Kennedy (1917-63) A109

1964, Dec. 8 Photo. *Perf. 13½*

514 A109 5fr dk bl & blk .20 .20
515 A109 6fr rose claret & blk .20 .20
516 A109 9fr brn & blk .20 .20
517 A109 30fr pur & blk .40 .20
518 A109 40fr dl grn & blk *2.50* .75
519 A109 60fr red brn & blk .90 .25
Nos. 514-519 (6) 4.40 1.80

Souvenir Sheet

520 A109 150fr blk & mar 6.50 6.50

Rocket and Unisphere A110

Basketball A111

Engraved and Typographed

1965, Mar. 1 Unwmk. *Perf. 12*

521 A110 50c lil & blk .20 .20
522 A110 1.50fr bl & lil .20 .20
523 A110 2fr red brn & brt grn .20 .20
524 A110 10fr brt grn & dk red .65 .40
525 A110 18fr vio bl & brn .20 .20
526 A110 27fr rose red & grn .25 .20
527 A110 40fr gray & org .30 .20
Nos. 521-527 (7) 2.00 1.60

New York World's Fair, 1964-65.

1965, Apr. Photo. *Perf. 13½*

6fr, 40fr, Soccer, horiz. 15fr, 60fr, Volleyball.

528 A111 5fr blk, grnsh bl & ocher .20 .20
529 A111 6fr blk, bl gray & crim .20 .20
530 A111 15fr blk, org & yel grn .20 .20
531 A111 24fr blk, rose lil & brt grn .20 .20
532 A111 40fr blk, brt grn & ultra *1.25* .40
533 A111 60fr blk, bl & red lil .35 .20
Nos. 528-533 (6) 2.40 1.40

First African Games, Leopoldville, Mar. 31-Apr. 7, 1965.
For surcharges see Nos. 604-605.

Earth and Satellites A112

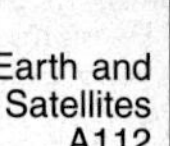

Designs: 9fr, 15fr, 20fr, 40fr, Satellites at left, globe at right.

Perf. 14x14½

1965, June 28 Photo. Unwmk.

534 A112 6fr blk, sal & vio .20 .20
535 A112 9fr blk, lt grn & gray .20 .20
536 A112 12fr org, gray & blk .20 .20
537 A112 15fr grn, ultra & blk .20 .20
538 A112 18fr blk, lt grn & gray 1.10 .30
539 A112 20fr blk, sal & vio .20 .20
540 A112 30fr grn, ultra & blk .25 .20
541 A112 40fr org, gray & blk .30 .20
Nos. 534-541 (8) 2.65 1.70

Cent. of the ITU.

Congolese Paratrooper and Parachutes A113

1965, July 5 *Perf. 13x14*

542 A113 5fr brt bl & brn .20 .20
543 A113 6fr org & brn .20 .20
544 A113 7fr br grn & brn .40 .25
545 A113 9fr brt pink & brn .20 .20
546 A113 18fr lem & brn .20 .20
Nos. 542-546 (5) 1.20 1.05

Fifth anniversary of independence.

Matadi Harbor and ICY Emblem — A114

ICY Emblem and: 8fr, 25fr, Katanga mines. 9fr, 60fr, Tshopo Dam, Stanleyville.

1965, Oct. 25 Photo. *Perf. 13x14*

547 A114 6fr ultra, blk & yel .20 .20
548 A114 8fr org red, blk & bl .20 .20
549 A114 9fr bl grn, blk & brn org .20 .20
550 A114 12fr car rose, blk & gray .75 .30
551 A114 25fr ol, blk & rose red .20 .20
552 A114 60fr gray, blk & org .45 .20
Nos. 547-552 (6) 2.00 1.30

International Cooperation Year, 1965.
For overprints and surcharges see Nos. 559-560, 607-608.

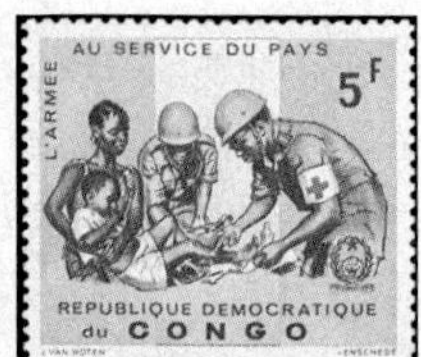

Soldiers Giving First Aid — A115

The Army Serving the Country: 7fr, Bridge building. 9fr, Feeding child. 19fr, Maintenance of telegraph lines. 20fr, House building. 30fr, Soldier and flag. (19fr, 20fr, 30fr, vert.)

Perf. 12½x13, 13x12½

1965, Nov. 17

553 A115 5fr sal, brn & red .20 .20
554 A115 7fr yel & grn .20 .20
555 A115 9fr ol & brn .20 .20
556 A115 19fr brt grn & brn .65 .35

557 A115 20fr lt bl & brn .20 .20
558 A115 30fr multi .25 .20
Nos. 553-558 (6) 1.70 1.35

See Nos. 582-586. For surcharges see Nos. 602, 678-679, 683.

Nos. 551-552 Overprinted with UN Emblem and "6e Journée Météorologique Mondiale / 23.3.66." on Metallic Strip

1966, Mar. 23 Photo. *Perf. 13x14*
559 A114 25fr ol & blk 1.10 .45
560 A114 60fr gray & blk 1.10 .60

6th World Meteorological Day.

Woman's Head and Goat — A116

10fr, Sculptured heads. 12fr, Sitting figure and two heads, vert. 53fr, Figure with earrings and kneeling woman with bowl, vert.

Perf. 11½x13, 13x11½

1966, Apr. 23 Litho. Unwmk.
561 A116 10fr red, blk & gray .20 .20
562 A116 12fr grn, blk & bl .20 .20
563 A116 15fr dp bl, blk & lil .20 .20
564 A116 53fr dp rose, blk & vio bl 1.25 .85
Nos. 561-564 (4) 1.85 1.45

Intl. Negro Arts Festival, Dakar, Senegal, Apr. 1-24.

Pres. Joseph Desiré Mobutu and Fishing Industry
A117

Pres. Mobutu and: 4fr, Pyrethrum harvest. 6fr, Building industry. 8fr, Winnowing rice. 10fr, Cotton harvest. 12fr, Banana harvest. 15fr, Coffee harvest. 24fr, Pineapple harvest. No. 573a, Pres. Mobutu without cap, and men rolling up sleeves.

1966, May 1 Photo. *Perf. 11½*
565 A117 2fr dk brn & dk bl .20 .20
566 A117 4fr dk brn & org .20 .20
567 A117 6fr dk brn & ol .75 .60
568 A117 8fr dk brn & brt grnsh bl .20 .20
569 A117 10fr dk brn & brn red .20 .20
570 A117 12fr dk brn & vio .20 .20
571 A117 15fr dk brn & lt ol grn .20 .20
572 A117 24fr dk brn & lil rose .25 .20
Nos. 565-572 (8) 2.20 2.00

Souvenir Sheet

Perf. 11x11½

573 Sheet of 4 1.75 1.75
a. A117 15fr red, black & ultra .40 .40

Lt. Gen. Joseph Desiré Mobutu, Pres. of Congo, and publicizing the "Back to Work" campaign.
For surcharges see Nos. 601, 603, 616, 619-624, 672, 675, 681-682.

Nos. 510-513 Overprinted

1966, June 13 *Perf. 11½*
574 A108 30fr dk car rose & grn .90 .90
575 A108 40fr ultra & dk car rose 1.00 1.00
576 A108 50fr brn org & grn 1.10 1.10
577 A108 100fr slate & ver 1.10 1.10
Nos. 574-577 (4) 4.10 4.10

Inauguration of WHO Headquarters, Geneva.

Soccer Player — A118

30fr, 2 soccer players. 50fr, 3 soccer players. 60fr, Jules Rimet Cup, soccer ball & globe.

1966, July 25 Photo. *Perf. 14*
578 A118 10fr ocher, vio & brt grn .20 .20
579 A118 30fr brt rose lil, vio & ap grn .35 .20
580 A118 50fr ap grn, Prus bl & tan 1.00 1.00
581 A118 60fr brt grn, dk brn & gold 1.00 .50
Nos. 578-581 (4) 2.55 1.90

World Cup Soccer Championship, Wembley, England, July 11-30.
For overprints see Nos. 587-590.

Army Type of 1965

The Army Serving the Country: 2fr, Soldiers giving first aid. 6fr, Feeding child. 10fr, House building, vert. 18fr, Bridge building. 24fr, Soldier and flag, vert.

1966, Aug. 8 *Perf. 12½x13, 13x12½*
582 A115 2fr ver, ind & red .20 .20
583 A115 6fr ultra red brn .20 .20
584 A115 10fr yel grn & red brn .45 .35
585 A115 18fr car rose & vio .20 .20
586 A115 24fr multi .20 .20
Nos. 582-586 (5) 1.25 1.15

#578-581 Overprinted in Black ("a"), Carmine or Green ("b"): "FINALE / ANGLETERRE-ALLEMAGNE / 4-2"

1966, Nov. 14 Photo. *Perf. 14*
587 A118 10fr pair, B and C .50 .50
588 A118 30fr pair, B and G 1.75 1.75
589 A118 50fr pair, B and C 2.75 2.75
590 A118 60fr pair, B and C 3.00 3.00
Nos. 587-590 (4) 8.00 8.00

England's victory in the World Soccer Cup Championship. The two colors of the overprint alternate in the sheets.

Souvenir Sheets

Pres. John F. Kennedy — A119

1966, Dec. 28 Engr. *Perf. 13*
591 A119 150fr brown 18.00 16.00
592 A119 150fr slate 18.00 16.00

Issued in memory of Pres. John F. Kennedy. No. 591 has slate green, No. 592 deep orange marginal design. Two imperf. sheets exist: 150fr brown with violet blue margin and 150fr slate with lilac margin. Size: 65x76mm. Values, $18 each.

Nos. 498-503 Surcharged in Black, Red or Maroon

1967, Sept. 11 Photo. *Perf. 11½*
593 A108 1k on 2fr .20 .20
a. Inverted overprint 4.00
594 A108 3k on 5fr .20 .20
595 A108 5k on 4fr .25 .20
596 A108 6.60k on 1fr (R) .35 .20
a. Inverted overprint 4.00
597 A108 9.60k on 50c .60 .30
a. Inverted overprint 4.00
598 A108 9.80k on 3fr (M) .70 .50
Nos. 593-598 (6) 2.30 1.60

Souvenir Sheet

Map of Africa, Torch — A120

599 A120 50k grnsh bl, blk & red 2.25 2.25

4th meeting of the Org. for African Unity, Kinshasa (Leopoldville), Sept. 9-11.
No. 599 in other colors was not a postal issue.

Souvenir Sheet

Horn Blower and EXPO Emblem — A121

1967, Sept. 28 Engr. *Perf. 11½*
600 A121 50k dk brn 2.75 2.75

EXPO '67, International Exhibition, Montreal, Apr. 28-Oct. 27, 1967.

Nos. 565-566 and 582 Overprinted: "NOUVELLE CONSTITUTION 1967" and Surcharged with New Value on Metallic Panel in Magenta or Brown

Perf. 11½, 12½x13

1967, Oct. 9 Photo.
601 A117 4k on 2fr (M) .25 .20
602 A115 5k on 2fr (B) .35 .20
603 A117 21k on 4fr (M) 1.25 .70
Nos. 601-603 (3) 1.85 1.10

Promulgation of the Constitution, June 4, 1967.

Nos. 528 and 530 Surcharged with New Value and Overprinted: "1ers Jeux Congolais / 25/6 au 2/7/1967 / Kinshasa"

1967, Oct. 16 Photo. *Perf. 13½*
604 A111 1k on 5fr multi .20 .20
605 A111 9.60k on 15fr multi .65 .55

First Congolese Games, Kinshasa, June 25-July 2, 1967.

No. 465 Surcharged with New Value and Overprinted: "1er VOL BAC / ONE ELEVEN / 14/5/67"

1967, Oct. 16 *Perf. 11½*
606 A105 9.60k on 7fr multi .85 .25

1st flight of the BAC 111 in the service of Air Congo, May 14, 1967.

Nos. 547 and 549 Surcharged in Red or Black: "JOURNEE MONDIALE / DE L'ENFANCE / 8-10-67"

1968, Feb. 10 Photo. *Perf. 13x14*
607 A114 1k on 6fr (R) .20 .20
608 A114 9k on 9fr (B) .80 .60

Intl. Children's Day. The surcharge is on a rectangle printed in metallic ink.

Nos. 498, 504 and 501 Surcharged in Blue or Red: "Année Internationale / du Tourisme 24-10-1967"

1968, Feb. 10 *Perf. 11½*
609 A108 5k on 50c lil rose & bl (Bl) .30 .25
610 A108 10k on 6fr sepia & org (R) .55 .50
611 A108 15k on 3fr emer & red (R) .70 .70
Nos. 609-611 (3) 1.55 1.45

International Tourist Year. The surcharge is on a rectangle printed in metallic ink.

Nos. 500, 498 and 502 Surcharged in Black, Violet Blue or Gold

1968, July Photo. *Perf. 11½*
612 A108 1k on 2fr .25 .20
613 A108 2k on 50c (VBl) .35 .25
614 A108 2k on 50c (G) .35 .25
615 A108 9.60k on 4fr 1.50 1.10
Nos. 612-615 (4) 2.45 1.80

The surcharge on No. 612 consists of a black rectangle and new denomination in upper right corner; the surcharge on No. 613 has a violet blue rectangle with denomination printed in white on it; on No. 614 the rectangle is gold and the denomination black; on No. 615 the rectangle is black and the denomination white.

No. 565 Surcharged in White on Black Rectangle

1968, Oct. Photo. *Perf. 11½*
616 A117 10k on 2fr dk brn & dk bl .70 .20

Leopard
A122

1968, Nov. 5 Litho. *Perf. 10½*
617 A122 2k brt grnsh bl & blk .30 .20
618 A122 9.60k red & blk 1.00 .20

Mobutu Type of 1966 Surcharged

1968, Dec. 20 Photo. *Perf. 11½*
619 A117 15s on 2fr sep & brt bl .20 .20
620 A117 1k on 6fr sep & brn .20 .20
621 A117 3k on 10fr sep & emer .20 .20
622 A117 5k on 12fr sep & org .30 .20
623 A117 20k on 15fr sep & brt grn 1.00 .50
624 A117 50k on 24fr sep & brt lil 2.75 1.40
Nos. 619-624 (6) 4.65 2.70

Human Rights Flame — A123

1968, Dec. 30 ***Perf. 12½x13***

625 A123 2k lt ultra & brt grn .20 .20
626 A123 9.60k grn & dp car .50 .30
627 A123 10k brt lil & brn .60 .30
628 A123 40k org brn & pur 2.00 1.10
Nos. 625-628 (4) 3.30 1.90

International Human Rights Year.

Type of 1968 Overprinted in Gold

1969, Jan. 27 **Photo.** ***Perf. 12½x13***

629 A123 2k ap grn & red brn .20 .20
630 A123 9.60k rose & emer .55 .30
631 A123 10k gray & ultra .55 .30
632 A123 40k grnsh bl & pur 2.10 1.10
Nos. 629-632 (4) 3.40 1.90

4th summit meeting of OCAM (Organisation Communitee Afrique et Malgache), Kinshasa, Jan. 27.

Kinshasa Fair Emblem and Cotton Boll — A124

Fair Emblem and: 6k, Copper. 9.60k, Coffee. 9.80k, Diamond. 11.60k, Oil palm fruits.

1969, May 2 **Photo.** ***Perf. 12½x13***

633 A124 2k brt pur, gold & red lil .20 .20
634 A124 6k grn, gold & bl grn .55 .40
635 A124 9.60k brn, gold & lt brn 1.00 .30
636 A124 9.80k ultra & gold 1.00 .50
637 A124 11.60k hn brn, gold & brn 1.25 .70
Nos. 633-637 (5) 4.00 2.10

Kinshasa Fair, Limete, June 30-July 21.

Fair Entrance, Emblem — A125

Fair Emblem and: 3k, Gecomin Mining Co. Pavilion. 10k, Administration Building. 25k, Pavilion of the Organization for African Unity.

1969, June 30 **Photo.** ***Perf. 11½***
Granite Paper

638 A125 2k brt rose lil & gold .20 .20
639 A125 3k blue & gold .20 .20
640 A125 10k lt ol grn & gold .55 .35
641 A125 25k copper red & gold 1.25 .85
Nos. 638-641 (4) 2.20 1.60

Kinshasa Fair, Limete, June 30-July 21.

Congo Arms — A126

Pres. Mobutu — A127

1969, July-Sept. **Litho.** ***Perf. 14***

642 A126 10s org & blk .20 .20
643 A126 15s ultra & blk .20 .20
644 A126 30s brt grn & blk .20 .20
645 A126 60s brt rose lil & blk .20 .20
646 A126 90s dp bister & blk .20 .20

Perf. 13

647 A127 1k sky bl & multi .20 .20
648 A127 2k org & multi .20 .20
649 A127 3k multi .25 .20
650 A127 5k brt rose & multi .35 .20
651 A127 6k ultra & multi .35 .20
652 A127 9.60k multi .60 .30
653 A127 10k lt lil & multi .75 .35
654 A127 20k yel & multi 1.50 .75
655 A127 50k multi 4.00 2.00
656 A127 100k fawn & multi 7.50 5.00
Nos. 642-656 (15) 16.70 10.40

Well Driller, by Oscar Bonnevalle — A128

Paintings: 4k, Preparation of cocoa, by Jean Van Noten. 8k, Dock workers, by Constantin Meunier. 10k, Poultry shop, by Henri Evenepoel. 15k, Steel industry, by Constantin Meunier.

Perf. 13x14, 14x13 (8k)

1969, Dec. 15 **Litho.**

Size: 41x41mm

657 A128 3k multi .20 .20
658 A128 4k multi .20 .20

Size: 28x41mm

659 A128 8k multi .40 .30

Size: 41x41mm

660 A128 10k multi .60 .35
661 A128 15k multi 1.10 .60
Nos. 657-661 (5) 2.50 1.65

50th anniv. of the ILO.

Souvenir Sheet

Adoration of the Kings, by Rubens — A129

1969, Dec. **Engr.** ***Perf. 13***

662 A129 50k red lilac 4.50 4.50

Issued for Christmas 1969.

Pres. Mobutu, Map and Flag of Congo A130

1970, June 30 **Litho.** ***Perf. 13½x13***

663 A130 10s multi .20 .20
664 A130 90s pur & multi .20 .20
665 A130 1k brn & multi .20 .20
666 A130 2k multi .20 .20
667 A130 7k multi .25 .20
668 A130 10k multi .35 .25
669 A130 20k multi .70 .50
Nos. 663-669 (7) 2.10 1.75

10th anniversary of independence.

Issues of 1964-1966 Surcharged

Perf. 11½, 12½x13, 13x12½

1970, Sept. 24 **Photo.**

670 A108 10s on 1fr (#499) .20 .20
671 A108 20s on 2fr (#500) .20 .20
672 A117 20s on 2fr (#565) .70 .35
673 A108 30s on 3fr (#501) .20 .20
674 A108 40s on 4fr (#502) .20 .20
675 A117 40s on 4fr (#566) .70 .35
676 A108 60s on 7fr (#505) 2.00 1.40
677 A108 90s on 9fr (#507) 2.00 1.40
678 A115 90s on 9fr (#555) .40 .30
679 A115 1k on 7fr (#554) .40 .30
680 A108 1k on 6fr (#504) .30 .20
681 A117 1k on 12fr (#570) 2.00 1.25
682 A117 2k on 24fr (#572) .70 .35
683 A115 2k on 24fr (#586) .70 .35
684 A108 3k on 30fr (#510) 1.25 1.00
685 A108 4k on 40fr (#511) .30 .20
686 A108 5k on 50fr (#512) 5.75 4.00
687 A108 10k on 100fr (#513) 1.40 1.00
Nos. 670-687 (18) 19.40 13.25

Telecommunications Building, Geneva — A131

Designs: 2k, 6.60k, UPU Headquarters, Bern. 9.80k, 10k, 11k, UN Headquarters, NY.

1970, Oct. 24 **Photo.** ***Perf. 11½***

688 A131 1k pink & grn .20 .20
689 A131 2k org & grn .20 .20
690 A131 6.60k grnsh bl & rose car .30 .25
691 A131 9.60k yel & vio bl .40 .30
692 A131 9.80k lt ultra & brn .35 .35
693 A131 10k lt pur & brn .35 .35
694 A131 11k rose & brn .50 .40
Nos. 688-694 (7) 2.30 2.05

ITU; new UPU Headquarters, Bern; 25th anniv. of the UN.

Pres. Mobutu, Congolese Flag and Arch — A132

1970, Nov. 24 **Litho.** ***Perf. 13***

695 A132 2k yel & multi .20 .20
696 A132 10k bl & multi .90 .50
697 A132 20k red & multi 2.10 1.50
Nos. 695-697 (3) 3.20 2.20

Fifth anniversary of new government.

Apollo 11 in Flight A133

Designs: 2k, Astronaut and spacecraft on moon. 7k, Pres. Mobutu decorating astronauts' wives. 10k, Pres. Mobutu with Neil A. Armstrong, Col. Edwin E. Aldrin, Jr. and Lt. Col. Michael Collins. 30k, Armstrong, Aldrin and Collins in space suits.

1970, Dec. 24 ***Perf. 13x13½***

698 A133 1k bl & blk .25 .20
699 A133 2k brt pur & blk .45 .25
700 A133 7k dl org & blk 1.25 .85
701 A133 10k rose red & blk 1.50 1.25
702 A133 30k grn & blk 4.00 3.25
Nos. 698-702 (5) 7.45 5.80

Visit of US Apollo 11 astronauts and their wives to Kinshasa.

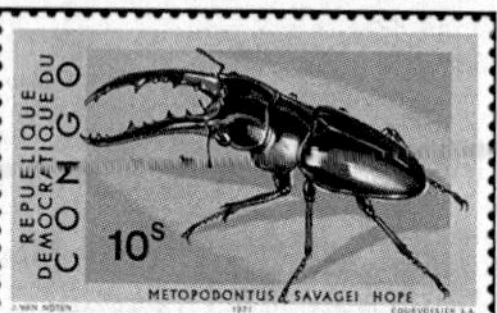

Metopodontus Savagei — A134

Designs: Various insects of Congo.

1971, Jan. 25 **Photo.** ***Perf. 11½***

703 A134 10s dl rose & multi .55 .25
704 A134 50s gray & multi .55 .25
705 A134 90s multi .55 .25
706 A134 1k citron & multi .55 .25
707 A134 2k gray grn & multi .55 .25
708 A134 3k lt vio & multi 1.10 .30
709 A134 5k bl & multi 3.50 1.10
710 A134 10k multi 5.00 1.60
711 A134 30k grn & multi 11.50 4.50
712 A134 40k ocher & multi 17.50 6.50
Nos. 703-712 (10) 41.35 15.25

Colotis Protomedia — A135

Various butterflies and moths of Congo.

1971, Feb. 24

713 A135 10s lt ultra & multi .55 .25
714 A135 20s choc & multi .55 .25
715 A135 70s dp org & multi .55 .25
716 A135 1k vio bl & multi .55 .25
717 A135 3k multi 1.25 .35
718 A135 5k dk grn & multi 3.50 .80
719 A135 10k multi 4.50 1.25
720 A135 15k emer & multi 9.25 2.25
721 A135 25k yel & multi 13.00 3.25
722 A135 40k multi 20.00 6.00
Nos. 713-722 (10) 53.70 14.90

UN Emblem, Racial Unity — A136

1971, Mar. 21 **Photo.** ***Perf. 11½***

723 A136 1k lt grn & multi .20 .20
724 A136 4k gray & multi .20 .20
725 A136 5k lt lil & multi .30 .25
726 A136 10k lt bl & multi .75 .35
Nos. 723-726 (4) 1.45 1.00

Intl. year against racial discrimination.

Hypericum Bequaertii A137

Flowers: 4k, Dissotis brazzae. 20k, Begonia wollastonii. 25k, Cassia alata.

1971, May 24 **Litho.** ***Perf. 14***

727 A137 1k multi 1.00 .25
728 A137 4k multi 1.75 .35
729 A137 20k multi 9.25 1.75
730 A137 25k multi 12.00 2.40
Nos. 727-730 (4) 24.00 4.75

Obelisk at N'sele, Pres. Mobutu A138

1971, May 20 Photo. *Perf. 11½*

731 A138 4k gold & multi .40 .20

4th anniversary of the People's Revolutionary Movement.

Radar Station A139

Designs: 1k, Waves. 6k, Map of Africa with telecommunications network.

1971, June 25 Photo. *Perf. 11½*

732 A139 1k rose & multi .20 .20
733 A139 3k yel & multi .40 .30
734 A139 6k lt bl & multi 1.00 .75
Nos. 732-734 (3) 1.60 1.25

3rd World Telecommunications Day, May 17 (1k); opening of satellite telecommunications ground station, Kinshasa, June 30 (3k); Pan-African telecommunication system (6k).

Grass Monkeys A140

Designs: 20s, Moustached monkeys, vert. 70s, De Brazza's monkeys. 1k, Yellow baboons. 3k, Pygmy chimpanzee, vert. 5k, Mangabeys, vert. 10k, Owlfaced monkeys. 15k, Diana monkeys. 25k, Black-and-white colobus, vert. 40k, L'Hoest's monkeys, vert.

1971, Aug.

735 A140 10s vio & multi .65 .35
736 A140 20s lt bl & multi .65 .35
737 A140 70s ocher & multi .90 .45
738 A140 1k gray & multi .90 .45
739 A140 3k rose & multi 1.50 .75
740 A140 5k brn & multi 3.25 1.60
741 A140 10k multi 6.75 3.25
742 A140 15k multi 11.00 5.50
743 A140 25k brt bl & multi 18.00 9.00
744 A140 40k red & multi 25.00 12.50
Nos. 735-744 (10) 68.60 34.20

Hotel Inter-Continental, Kinshasa — A141

1971, Oct. 2 Photo. *Perf. 13*

745 A141 2k silver & multi .20 .20
746 A141 12k gold & multi .40 .20

Man Reading A142

Designs: 2.50k, Open book and abacus. 7k, Five letters surrounding symbolic head.

1971, Oct. 24

747 A142 50s multi .20 .20
748 A142 2.50k multi .20 .20
749 A142 7k multi 1.25 1.00
Nos. 747-749 (3) 1.65 1.40

Fight against illiteracy.

Succeeding issues are listed in Vol. 6 under Zaire. Beginning in 1998, Zaire reverted back to using the Congo name, at least temporarily. Until the situation is resolved, the current stamps inscribed "Congo" will be listed under Zaire.

SEMI-POSTAL STAMPS

Women Carrying Food, Wheat Emblem, and Tractor SP22

1963, Mar. 21 Photo. *Perf. 14x13*

B48 SP22 5fr + 2fr multi .25 .20
B49 SP22 9fr + 4fr multi .40 .20
B50 SP22 12fr + 6fr multi .45 .25
B51 SP22 20fr + 10fr multi 2.00 1.50
Nos. B48-B51 (4) 3.10 2.15

FAO "Freedom from Hunger" campaign.

CONGO, PEOPLE'S REPUBLIC OF

'pē-pəls ri-'pə-blik of

'käŋ-(,)gō

(ex-French)

LOCATION — West Africa at equator
GOVT. — Republic
AREA — 132,046 sq. mi.
POP. — 2,716,814 (1999 est.)
CAPITAL — Brazzaville

The former French colony of Middle Congo became a member state of the French Community on November 28, 1958, and achieved independence on August 15, 1960. For some years before 1958, the colony was joined with three other French territories to form French Equatorial Africa. Issues of Middle Congo (1907-1933) are listed under that heading.

100 Centimes = 1 Franc

Catalogue values for all unused stamps in this country are for Never Hinged items.

Allegory of New Republic A7

1959 Unwmk. Engr. *Perf. 13*

89 A7 25fr brn, dp claret, org & ol .60 .25

1st anniv. of the proclamation of the Republic.

Imperforates

Most stamps of the Republic of the Congo exist imperforate in issued and trial colors, and also in small presentation sheets in issued colors.

Common Design Types pictured following the introduction.

C.C.T.A. Issue
Common Design Type

1960 Unwmk. *Perf. 13*

90 CD106 50fr dl grn & plum .80 .80

President Fulbert Youlou — A8

Flag, Map and UN Emblem — A9

1960

91 A8 15fr grn, blk & car .35 .35
92 A8 85fr indigo & car 2.00 .45

1961, Mar. 11 *Perf. 13*
Flag in Green, Yellow & Red

93 A9 5fr vio brn & dk bl .25 .20
94 A9 20fr org & dk bl .45 .25
95 A9 100fr grn & dk bl 2.00 .80
Nos. 93-95 (3) 2.70 1.25

Congo's admission to United Nations.

Rainbow Runner A10

Fish: 50c, 3fr, Rainbow runner. 1fr, 2fr, Sloan's viperfish. 5fr, Hatchet fish. 10fr, A deep-sea fish.

1961, Nov. 28 Engr.

96 A10 50c brn, ol grn & sal .25 .20
97 A10 1fr bl grn & sepia .25 .20
98 A10 2fr ultra, sep & dk grn .25 .20
99 A10 3fr dk bl, grn & salmon .35 .20
100 A10 5fr red brn, grn & blk .70 .25
101 A10 10fr blue & red brn 1.40 .30
Nos. 96-101 (6) 3.20 1.35

Brazzaville Market — A11

1962, Mar. 23 Unwmk. *Perf. 13*

102 A11 20fr blk, red & grn .60 .20

Abidjan Games Issue
Common Design Type

20fr, Boxing. 50fr, Running, finish line.

1962, July 21 Photo. *Perf. 12½x12*

103 CD109 20fr car, brt pink, brn & blk .45 .25
104 CD109 50fr car, brt pink, brn & blk .90 .30
Nos. 103-104,C7 (3) 3.85 1.80

African-Malgache Union Issue
Common Design Type

1962, Sept. 8

105 CD110 30fr multicolored 1.00 .40

Waves Around Globe A11a

Design: 100fr, Orbit patterns around globe.

1963, Sept. 19 *Perf. 12½*

106 A11a 25fr org, grn & ultra .50 .30
107 A11a 100fr lt red brn, bl & plum 1.60 .90

Issued to publicize space communications.

King Makoko's Collar — A12

Unwmk.

1963, Oct. 21 Engr. *Perf. 13*

108 A12 10fr showm .45 .25
109 A12 15fr Kebekebe mask .60 .25

UNESCO Emblem, Scales and Tree A12a

1963, Dec. 10 Unwmk. *Perf. 13*

110 A12a 25fr grn, dk bl & brn .70 .30

15th anniv. of the Universal Declaration of Human Rights.

Barograph and WMO Emblem A12b

1964, Mar. 23 Engr.

111 A12b 50fr grn, red brn & ultra 1.00 .60

Fourth World Meteorological Day.

Mechanic with Machine — A13

1964, Apr. 8

112 A13 20fr grnsh bl, mag & dk brn .60 .30

Training of technicians.

Corn and Tools A14

1964, Apr. 24 Unwmk. *Perf. 13*

113 A14 80fr brn, grn & brn car 1.10 .60

Importance of manual labor.

Diaboua Ballet A15

Kébékébé Dance — A16 Carved Figure — A17

1964, May 8 **Engr.**
114 A15 30fr multicolored 1.25 .30
115 A16 60fr multicolored 2.25 .65

1964, May 22
116 A17 50fr brn red & sepia 1.50 .55

Classroom A18

1964, May 26
117 A18 25fr dk brn, red & blue .60 .30

Issued to publicize education.

Type of Air Post Issue, 1963,
Inscribed: "1er ANNIVERSAIRE DE LA REVOLUTION/FETE NATIONALE/15 AOUT 1964"

1964, Aug. 15 **Photo.** ***Perf. 13x12***
118 AP5 20fr lt bl, red, ocher, dk brn & grn .50 .20

1st anniv. of the revolution and Natl. Feast Day, Aug. 15.

Fire Squid A19

15fr, Johnson's deep-sea angler (fish).

1964, Oct. 20 **Engr.** ***Perf. 13***
119 A19 2fr ver, lt grn & brn .50 .20
120 A19 15fr vio, lt ol grn & dp cl 2.25 .80

Cooperation Issue
Common Design Type

1964, Nov. 7 **Unwmk.** ***Perf. 13***
121 CD119 25fr car, brt grn & dk brn .60 .35

Communications Emblems — A20

1965, Jan. 1 **Litho.** ***Perf. 12½x13***
122 A20 25fr ol, red brn & blk .50 .25

Issued to commemorate the establishment of the national postal administration.

Sitatunga — A21 Dancer on Stilts — A22

Design: 20fr, Elephant, horiz.

1965, Mar. 15 **Engr.** ***Perf. 13***
123 A21 15fr redsh brn, dl grn & bl .90 .30
124 A21 20fr blk, dp bl & sl grn .90 .30
125 A22 85fr lil & multi 3.50 1.25
Nos. 123-125 (3) 5.30 1.85

Pres. Alphonse Massamba-Debat A23

1965-66 **Photo.** ***Perf. 12x12½***
126 A23 20fr dk brn, grn & yel .25 .20
127 A23 25fr brn, bl grn, emer & blk ('66) .30 .20
128 A23 30fr brn, bl grn, org & blk ('66) .45 .20
Nos. 126-128 (3) 1.00 .60

Soccer Player A24

Designs: 25fr, Games' emblem (map of Africa and runners). 50fr, Field ball player. 85fr, Runner. 100fr, Bicyclist.

1965, July 17 **Photo.** ***Perf. 12½***
Size: 28x28mm
129 A24 25fr blk, red, yel & grn .50 .30
Size: 34x34mm
130 A24 40fr yel grn & multi .70 .45
131 A24 50fr red & multi .70 .45
132 A24 85fr blk & multi 1.25 .65
133 A24 100fr yel & multi 1.75 .75
a. Min. sheet of 5, #129-133 7.50 7.50
Nos. 129-133 (5) 4.90 2.60

1st African Games, Brazzaville, July 18-25.

Arms of Congo — A25

1965, Nov. 15 **Litho.** ***Perf. 12½x13***
134 A25 20fr multicolored .50 .20

Cooperative Village A26

30fr, Gymnastic drill team with streamers.

1966, Feb. 18 ***Perf. 12½x13***
135 A26 25fr multicolored .50 .25
136 A26 30fr multicolored .50 .30

Sculptured Mask — A27

Designs: 30fr, Weaver, painting. 85fr, String instrument, painting, horiz.

Perf. 13x12½, 12½x13
1966, Apr. 9 **Photo.**
137 A27 30fr multicolored .70 .30
138 A27 85fr multicolored 1.90 .70
139 A27 90fr multicolored 2.25 .90
Nos. 137-139 (3) 4.85 1.90

Intl. Negro Arts Festival, Dakar, Senegal, 4/1-24.

Men and Clocks A28

1966, Apr. 15 ***Perf. 12½x12***
140 A28 70fr pale brn, ocher & dk brn 1.00 .30

Introduction of the shorter work day (less lunch time, earlier quitting time).

WHO Headquarters, Geneva — A29

1966, May 3 **Photo.** ***Perf. 12½x13***
141 A29 50fr org yel, vio & bl .80 .40

Inauguration of the WHO Headquarters, Geneva.

Church of St. Peter Claver A30 Women's Basketball A31

1966, June 15 **Photo.** ***Perf. 13x12½***
142 A30 70fr multicolored 1.00 .40

1966, July 15 **Engr.** ***Perf. 13***

Sport: 1fr, Women's volleyball, horiz. 3fr, Women's field ball, horiz. 5fr, Athletes of various races. 10fr, Torch bearer. 15fr, Soccer and gold medal of First African Games.

143 A31 1fr ultra, choc & ol .20 .20
144 A31 2fr choc, grn & bl .25 .20
145 A31 3fr dk grn, dk car & choc .25 .20
146 A31 5fr slate, emer & choc .25 .20
147 A31 10fr dl bl, dk grn & vio .45 .20
148 A31 15fr vio, car & choc .50 .30
Nos. 143-148 (6) 1.90 1.30

Jules Rimet Cup and Globe A32

1966, July 15 **Photo.** ***Perf. 12½x12***
149 A32 30fr brt red, gold, blk & bl .70 .35

8th World Soccer Cup Championship, Wembley, England, July 11-30.

Savorgnan de Brazza School A33

1966, Sept. 15 **Photo.** ***Perf. 12½x12***
150 A33 30fr dk pur, grn, yel & blk .60 .25

Pointe-Noire Railroad Station — A34

1966, Oct. 15 **Engr.** ***Perf. 13***
151 A34 60fr grn, red & brn 1.25 .60

Student with Microscope A35 Balumbu Mask A36

1966, Nov. 28 **Engr.** ***Perf. 13***
152 A35 90fr brn, grn & ind 1.25 .60

20th anniv. of UNESCO.

1966, Dec. 12 **Engr.** ***Perf. 13***

Masks: 10fr, Kuyu. 15fr, Bakwélé. 20fr, Batéké.

153 A36 5fr car rose & dk brn .45 .20
154 A36 10fr Prus bl & brn .50 .20
155 A36 15fr sep, dl org & dk bl .60 .20
156 A36 20fr dp bl & multi .80 .20
Nos. 153-156 (4) 2.35 .80

Order of the Revolution and Map — A37

Learning the Alphabet A38

Design: 45fr, Harvesting and loading sugar cane, and sugar mill.

Perf. 12x12½, 12½x12
1967, Mar. 15 **Photo.**
157 A37 20fr org & multi .50 .30
158 A38 25fr blk, ocher & dk car .60 .35
159 A38 45fr blk, yel grn & lt bl 1.00 .30
Nos. 157-159 (3) 2.10 .95

Issued to honor the members of the Order of the Revolution (20fr); to publicize the literacy campaign (25fr); to publicize, sugar production (45fr).

Mahatma Gandhi — A39 Fruit Vendor — A40

1967, Apr. 21 **Engr.** ***Perf. 13***
160 A39 90fr bl & blk 1.75 .60

Issued in memory of Mohandas K. Gandhi (1869-1948), Hindu nationalist leader.

1967, June Photo. *Perf. 13x12½*

Dolls: 5fr, "Elegant Lady." 25fr, Woman pounding saka-saka. 30fr, Mother and child.

161 A40 5fr gold & multi .25 .20
162 A40 10fr yel grn & multi .45 .20
163 A40 25fr lt ultra & multi .50 .20
164 A40 30fr multicolored .60 .20
Nos. 161-164 (4) 1.80 .80

ITY Emblem, Village and Waterfall A41

1967, July 5 Engr. *Perf. 13*
165 A41 60fr rose cl, org & ol grn .70 .40

Issued for International Tourist Year, 1967.

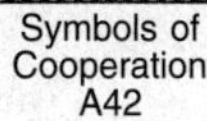

Symbols of Cooperation A42

Arms of Brazzaville A43

Europafrica Issue, 1967

1967, July 20 Photo. *Perf. 12x12½*
166 A42 50fr multicolored .90 .30

1967, Aug. 15 Litho. *Perf. 12½x13*
167 A43 30fr yel & multi .60 .35

Fourth anniversary of the revolution.

UN Emblem, Dove and People — A44

Boy and UNICEF Emblem — A45

1967, Oct. 24 Photo. *Perf. 13x12½*
168 A44 90fr bl, dk brn, red brn & yel 1.60 .60

Issued for United Nations Day, Oct. 24.

1967, Dec. 11 Engr. *Perf. 13*
169 A45 90fr mar, blk & ultra 1.60 .60

21st anniv. of UNICEF.

Albert Luthuli, Dove and Globe A46

1968, Jan. 29 Engr. *Perf. 13*
170 A46 30fr brt grn & ol bis .60 .35

Albert Luthuli (1899-1967) of South Africa, winner of 1960 Nobel Peace Prize.

Arms of Pointe Noire — A47

1968, Feb. 20 Litho. *Perf. 12½x13*
171 A47 10fr brt pink & multi .50 .30

Motherhood A48

Mayombe Viaduct A49

1968, May 25 Engr. *Perf. 13*
172 A48 15fr dk car rose, sky bl & blk .45 .25

Issued for Mother's Day.

1968, June 24
173 A49 45fr maroon, slate grn & bl 1.75 .40

A50

1968, July 29 Photo. *Perf. 13x12½*
174 A50 5fr Daimler, 1889 .45 .20
175 A50 20fr Berliet, 1897 .90 .30
176 A50 60fr Peugeot, 1898 1.75 .40
177 A50 80fr Renault, 1900 2.75 .70
178 A50 85fr Fiat, 1902 3.25 .90
Nos. 174-178,C67-C68 (7) 17.85 6.00

Tanker, Refinery and Map of Area Served — A50a

1968, July 30 *Perf. 12½*
179 A50a 30fr multicolored .70 .25

Issued to commemorate the opening of the Port Gentil (Gabon) Refinery, June 12, 1968.

UN Emblem and Tree of Life — A51

1968, Nov. 28 Engr. *Perf. 13*
180 A51 25fr dk grn, red & dp lil .45 .25

20th anniv. of WHO.

Development Bank Issue
Common Design Type

1969, Sept. 10 Engr. *Perf. 13*
181 CD130 25fr car rose, grn & ocher .35 .20
182 CD130 30fr bl, grn & ocher .35 .20

Bicycle A52

Bicycles & Motorcycles: 75fr, Hirondelle. 80fr, Folding bicycle. 85fr, Peugeot. 100fr, Excelsior Manxman. 150fr, Norton. 200fr, Brough Superior "Old Bill." 300fr, Matchless and N.L.G.-J.A.P.S.

1969, Oct. 6 Engr. *Perf. 13*
183 A52 50fr multicolored 1.25 .30
184 A52 75fr multicolored 1.50 .30
185 A52 80fr multicolored 1.75 .40
186 A52 85fr multicolored 2.00 .45
187 A52 100fr multicolored 2.75 .65
188 A52 150fr multicolored 3.75 .90
189 A52 200fr multicolored 5.00 1.25
190 A52 300fr multicolored 9.00 2.10
Nos. 183-190 (8) 27.00 6.35

Mayombe Train and Tourist Year Emblem A53

40fr, Train and Mbamba Tunnel, vert.

Perf. 13x12½, 12½x13
1969, Oct. 20 Photo.
191 A53 40fr multicolored 1.25 .30
192 A53 60fr multicolored 2.25 .40

Issued for African Tourist Year.

Loutete Cement Works A54

Loutete Cement Works: 15fr, Mixing tower, vert. 25fr, Cable transport, vert. 30fr, General view of plant.

1969, Dec. 10 Engr. *Perf. 13*
193 A54 10fr dk gray, rose cl & dk ol .25 .20
194 A54 15fr Prus bl, red brn & pur .50 .20
195 A54 25fr mar, brn & Prus bl .60 .20
196 A54 30fr vio brn, ultra & blk .70 .20
a. Min. sheet of 4, #193-196 2.50 2.50
Nos. 193-196 (4) 2.05 .80

ASECNA Issue
Common Design Type

1969, Dec. 12
197 CD132 100fr dull brown 1.60 .40

Pineapple Harvest and ILO Emblem A55

30fr, Worker at lathe and ILO emblem.

1969, Dec. 20 Engr. *Perf. 13*
198 A55 25fr bl, olive & brn .35 .25
199 A55 30fr rose red, choc & slate .50 .25

50th anniv. of the ILO.

SOTEXCO Textile Plant, Kinsoundi A56

20fr, Women in spinnery. 25fr, Hand-printing textiles. 30fr, Checking woven cloth.

1970, Jan. 20
200 A56 15fr grn, blk & lil .45 .20
201 A56 20fr plum, car & sl grn .45 .20
202 A56 25fr bl, slate & brn .60 .20
203 A56 30fr gray, car rose & brn .60 .25
Nos. 200-203 (4) 2.10 .85

Hotel Cosmos, Brazzaville A57

1970, Jan. 30
204 A57 90fr slate grn, bl & red brn 1.25 .30

The status of the three sets for Kennedy, etc., Summer Olympics, and Baroque paintings is not certain.

Linzolo Church — A58

Diosso Gorge A59

Design: 90fr, Foulakari waterfall.

1970 Engr. *Perf. 13*
205 A58 25fr multicolored .60 .20
206 A59 70fr multicolored 1.50 .30
207 A59 90fr multicolored 2.25 .40
Nos. 205-207 (3) 4.35 .90

Issue dates: 25fr, Feb. 10; others, Feb. 25.

Volvaria Esculenta — A60

Mushrooms: 10fr, Termitomyces entolomoides. 15fr, Termitomyces microcarpus. 25fr, Termitomyces aurantiacus. 30fr, Termitomyces mammiformis. 50fr, Tremella fuciformis.

1970, Mar. 31 Photo. *Perf. 13*
208 A60 5fr multicolored 6.75 .70
209 A60 10fr multicolored 9.00 1.00
210 A60 15fr multicolored 13.50 1.50
211 A60 25fr multicolored 22.50 3.00
212 A60 30fr multicolored 32.50 4.25
213 A60 50fr multicolored 70.00 7.00
Nos. 208-213 (6) 154.25 17.45

Laying Coaxial Cable A61

Design: 30fr, Full view of rail car; 3 cable layers on railway roadbed.

1970, Apr. 30 Engr. *Perf. 13*
214 A61 25fr dk brn & multi 1.00 .30
215 A61 30fr brn & multi 1.10 .40

Issued to publicize the laying of the coaxial cable linking Brazzaville and Pointe Noire.
For surcharges see Nos. 263-264.

UPU Headquarters Issue
Common Design Type

1970, May 20
216 CD133 30fr dk pur, gray & mag .70 .25

Mother Feeding Child — A62

Dag Hammarskjold, UN Emblem — A63

Design: 90fr, Mother nursing infant.

1970, May 30 **Photo.**
217 A62 85fr vio bl & multi .80 .30
218 A62 90fr lil & multi .95 .40

Issued for Mother's Day.

1970, June 20 **Engr.** ***Perf. 13***

UN Emblem and: No. 220, Trygve Lie, horiz. No. 221, U Thant, horiz.

219 A63 100fr scar, dk red & dk pur 1.25 .60
220 A63 100fr dk red, ultra & ind 1.25 .60
221 A63 100fr grn, emer & dk red 1.25 .60
a. Souv. sheet of 3, #219-221 5.00 5.00
Nos. 219-221 (3) 3.75 1.80

25th anniv. of the UN and to honor its Secretaries General.

Brillantaisia Vogeliana A64

Sternotomis Variabilis — A65

Plants and Beetles: 2fr, Plectranthus decurrens. 3fr, Myrianthemum mirabile. 5fr, Connarus griffonianus. 15fr, Chelorrhina polyphemus. 20fr, Metopodontus savagei.

Perf. 12½x12, 12x12½

1970, June 30 **Photo.**
222 A64 1fr dk grn & multi .45 .20
223 A64 2fr multicolored .45 .20
224 A64 3fr indigo & multi .50 .20
225 A64 5fr lemon & multi 1.00 .20
226 A65 10fr lilac & multi 2.25 .20
227 A65 15fr orange & multi 3.00 .30
228 A65 20fr multicolored 3.25 .50
Nos. 222-228 (7) 10.90 1.80

For surcharge see No. 288.

Stegosaurus — A66

Prehistoric Fauna: 20fr, Dinotherium, vert. 60fr, Brachiosaurus, vert. 80fr, Arsinoitherium.

1970, July 20
229 A66 15fr dl grn, ocher & red brn .80 .30
230 A66 20fr lt bl & multi 2.75 .65
231 A66 60fr lt bl & multi 5.75 .95
232 A66 80fr lt bl & multi 7.50 1.75
Nos. 229-232 (4) 16.80 3.65

Mikado 141, 1932 A67

Locomotives: 60fr, Steam locomotive 130+032, 1947. 75fr, Alsthom BB 1100, 1962. 85fr, Diesel BB BB 302, 1969.

1970, Aug. 20 **Engr.** ***Perf. 13***
233 A67 40fr mag, bl grn & blk 2.75 .80
234 A67 60fr blk, bl & grn 3.00 .90
235 A67 75fr red, bl & blk 4.50 1.25
236 A67 85fr car, sl grn & ocher 7.00 1.75
Nos. 233-236 (4) 17.25 4.70

Cogniauxia Padolaena A68

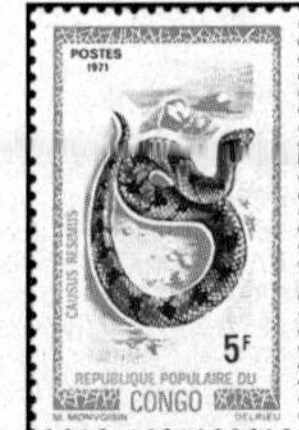
Green Night Adder A69

Tropical Flowers: 2fr, Celosia cristata. 5fr, Plumeria acutifolia. 10fr, Bauhinia variegata. 15fr, Poinsettia. 20fr, Thunbergia grandiflora.

1971, Feb. 10 **Photo.** ***Perf. 12x12½***
237 A68 1fr lil & multi .25 .20
238 A68 2fr yel & multi .25 .20
239 A68 5fr ultra & multi .25 .20
240 A68 10fr yel & multi 1.10 .20
241 A68 15fr multicolored 1.60 .30
242 A68 20fr dk red & multi 2.75 .40
Nos. 237-242 (6) 6.20 1.50

Perf. 12x12½, 12½x12

1971, June 26 **Photo.**

Reptiles: 10fr, African Egg-eating snake, horiz. 15fr, Flap-necked chameleon. 20fr, Nile crocodile, horiz. 25fr, Rock python, horiz. 30fr, Gaboon viper. 40fr, Brown house snake, horiz. 45fr, Jameson's mamba.

243 A69 5fr multicolored .35 .20
244 A69 10fr multicolored .35 .20
245 A69 15fr multicolored 1.25 .20
246 A69 20fr red & multi 2.10 .25
247 A69 25fr grn & multi 2.75 .35
248 A69 30fr multicolored 3.50 .75
249 A69 40fr bis & multi 4.00 .95
250 A69 45fr multicolored 5.25 1.00
Nos. 243-250 (8) 19.55 3.90

Pseudimbrasia Deyrollei — A70

Caterpillars: 15fr, Bunaea alcinoe, vert. 20fr, Epiphora vacuna ploetzi. 25fr, Imbrasia eblis. 30fr, Imbrasia dione, vert. 40fr, Holocera angulata.

1971, July 3 ***Perf. 13***
251 A70 10fr ver, blk & grn 1.00 .20
252 A70 15fr multicolored 1.50 .30
253 A70 20fr yel grn, blk & ocher 2.25 .40
254 A70 25fr multicolored 3.50 .60
255 A70 30fr red, blk & yel 5.00 .90
256 A70 40fr bl, blk & org 6.75 1.25
Nos. 251-256 (6) 20.00 3.65

Boy Scout — A70a

Scouts, Lord Baden-Powell — A70b

Designs: c, Scout facing left. d, Scout facing forward. e, Lord Baden-Powell.

Embossed on Metallic Foil

1971, July 14 ***Die Cut Perf. 10½***
256A A70a 90fr Block of 4, #b.-e, silver *10.00 10.00*
256F A70b 1000fr gold *30.00 30.00*

No. 256F is airmail.

Cymothoe Sangaris A71

Butterflies and Moths: 40fr, Papilio dardanus, vert. 75fr, Iolaus timon. 90fr, Papilio phorcas, vert. 100fr, Euchloron megaera.

1971, Oct. 15 ***Perf. 12½x12, 12x12½***
257 A71 30fr yel & multi 1.50 .40
258 A71 40fr grn & multi 3.00 .65
259 A71 75fr multicolored 5.00 1.25
260 A71 90fr multicolored 6.75 1.90
261 A71 100fr ultra & multi 9.00 2.50
Nos. 257-261 (5) 25.25 6.70

Black and White Men Working Together — A72

1971, Oct. 30 ***Perf. 13x12½***
262 A72 50fr org & multi .60 .30

Intl. Year Against Racial Discrimination.

Nos. 214-215 Surcharged

1971, Nov. 18 **Engr.** ***Perf. 13***
263 A61 30fr on 25fr multicolored .50 .30
264 A61 40fr on 30fr multicolored .60 .35

Inauguration of cable service between Brazzaville and Pointe Noire. Words of surcharge arranged differently on No. 264.

Map of Congo — A73

1971, Dec. 31 **Photo.** ***Perf. 12½x13***
265 A73 30fr bl & multi .35 .20
266 A73 40fr yel grn & multi .45 .20
267 A73 100fr gray & multi 1.10 .40
Nos. 265-267 (3) 1.90 .80

"Labor, Democracy, Peace."

Lion — A74

2fr, African elephants. 3fr, Leopard. 4fr, Hippopotamus. 5fr, Gorilla, vert. 20fr, Potto. 30fr, De Brazza's monkey. 40fr, Pygmy chimpanzee, vert.

1972, Jan. 31 **Engr.** ***Perf. 13***
268 A74 1fr grn & multi .35 .20
269 A74 2fr dk red & multi .50 .20
270 A74 3fr red brn & multi .80 .20
271 A74 4fr vio & multi 1.00 .20
272 A74 5fr brn & multi 1.10 .25
273 A74 20fr org & multi 2.75 .35
274 A74 30fr ocher & multi 3.50 .45
275 A74 40fr Prus bl & multi 5.25 .75
Nos. 268-275 (8) 15.25 2.60

WHO, 25th Anniv. — A75

Perf. 12½x13, 13x12½

1973, June 30 **Typo.**
276 A75 40fr WHO Emblem .60 .20
277 A75 50fr WHO emblem, horiz. .70 .20

Kronenbourg Brewery — A76

Brewery Trademark and: 40fr, Laboratory. 75fr, Vats and controls. 85fr, Automatic control room. 100fr, Pressure room. 250fr, Bottling plant.

1973, July 15 **Engr.** ***Perf. 13***
278 A76 30fr red & multi .50 .20
279 A76 40fr red & multi .60 .20
280 A76 75fr red & multi 1.00 .30
281 A76 85fr red & multi 1.40 .40
282 A76 100fr red & multi 1.50 .55
283 A76 250fr red & multi 3.00 1.00
Nos. 278-283 (6) 8.00 2.65

Kronenbourg Brewery, Brazzaville.

Golwe Locomotive, 1935 — A77

Locomotives: 40fr, Diesel, 1935. 75fr, Diesel Whithcomb, 1946. 85fr, Diesel CC200.

1973, Aug. 1 **Engr.** ***Perf. 13***
284 A77 30fr indigo & multi 1.75 .45
285 A77 40fr vio bl & multi 2.75 .75
286 A77 75fr multicolored 4.00 1.10
287 A77 85fr multicolored 5.00 1.40
Nos. 284-287 (4) 13.50 3.70

No. 225 Surcharged with New Value, 2 Bars, and Overprinted in Ultramarine: "SECHERESSE SOLIDARITE AFRICAINE"

1973, Aug. 16 **Photo.** ***Perf. 12½x12***
288 A64 100fr on 5fr multicolored 1.75 .60

African solidarity in drought emergency.

African Postal Union Issue
Common Design Type

1973, Sept. 12 **Engr.** ***Perf. 13***
289 CD137 100fr bl grn, vio & brn 1.50 .45

Bees, Beehive, Honeycomb A78

1973, Dec. 10 Engr. *Perf. 13*

290 A78 30fr sl grn, dk red & bl 1.10 .20
291 A78 40fr sl bl, sl grn & lt grn 1.50 .20

"Work and economy."

Family, UN and FAO Emblems A79

40fr, Grain, emblems. 100fr, Grain, emblems, vert.

1973, Dec. 10

292 A79 30fr dk car & dk brn .50 .20
293 A79 40fr dk grn, yel & ind .60 .20
294 A79 100fr grn, brn & org 1.40 .40
Nos. 292-294 (3) 2.50 .80

World Food Program, 10th anniversary.

Amilcar Cabral, Cattle and Child — A80

1974, July 15 Engr. *Perf. 13*

295 A80 100fr multicolored 1.00 .50

First death anniversary of Amilcar Cabral (1924-1973), leader of anti-Portuguese guerrilla activity in Portuguese Guinea.

Félix Eboué, Cross of Lorraine A81

1974, Aug. 31 Litho. *Perf. 13*

296 A81 30fr bl & multi .60 .20
297 A81 40fr brt pink & multi .90 .30

Félix A. Eboué (1884-1944), Governor of Chad, first colonial governor to join Free French in WWII, 30th death anniversary.

Pineapples A82

1974, Nov. 12

298 A82 30fr shown .60 .30
299 A82 30fr Bananas .70 .30
300 A82 30fr Safous .70 .30
301 A82 40fr Avocados 1.10 .30
302 A82 40fr Mangos 1.10 .30
303 A82 40fr Papaya 1.10 .30
304 A82 40fr Orange 1.10 .30
Nos. 298-304 (7) 6.40 2.10

Charles de Gaulle and Conference Building — A83

1974, Nov. 25 Engr. *Perf. 13*

305 A83 100fr multicolored 2.75 1.00

Brazzaville Conference, 25th anniversary.

George Stephenson and Various Locomotives — A84

1974, Dec. 15

306 A84 75fr slate green & olive 3.50 .90

George Stephenson (1781-1848), English inventor and railroad founder.

UDEAC Issue

Presidents and Flags of Cameroun, CAR, Congo, Gabon and Meeting Center — A84a

1974, Dec. 8 Photo. *Perf. 13*

307 A84a 40fr gold & multi .60 .20

See note after Cameroun No. 595.
See No. C195.

Irish Setter A85

1974, Dec. 15 Photo. *Perf. 13x13½*

308 A85 30fr shown 1.25 .30
309 A85 40fr Borzoi 1.50 .30
310 A85 75fr Pointer 3.25 .75
311 A85 100fr Great Dane 4.50 .80
Nos. 308-311 (4) 10.50 2.15

1974, Dec. 15

Designs: Cats.

312 A85 30fr Havana chestnut 1.25 .30
313 A85 40fr Red Persian 1.50 .30
314 A85 75fr Blue British 3.25 .75
315 A85 100fr African serval 4.50 .80
Nos. 312-315 (4) 10.50 2.15

Labor Party Flags and People A86

40fr, Hands holding flowers and tools.

1974, Dec. 31 Engr. *Perf. 13x12½*

316 A86 30fr red & multi .50 .20
317 A86 40fr red & multi .60 .25

5th anniversary of Congolese Labor Party and of introduction of red flag.

Symbols of Development — A87

U Thant and UN Headquarters — A88

Paul G. Hoffman and UN Emblem A89

Perf. 13x12½, 12½x13

1975, Feb. 28 Litho.

318 A87 40fr multicolored .60 .25
319 A88 50fr light blue & multi .60 .25
320 A89 50fr yellow & multi .60 .25
Nos. 318-320 (3) 1.80 .75

National economic development.

Map of China and Mao Tse-tung — A90

1975, Mar. 9 Engr. *Perf. 13*

321 A90 75fr multicolored 2.25 .60

25th anniv. of the PRC.

Woman Breaking Bonds, Women's Activities, Map of Congo A91

1975, June 20 Litho. *Perf. 12½*

322 A91 40fr gold & multi .60 .25

Revolutionary Union of Congolese Women, URFC, 10th anniversary.

CARA Soccer Team — A92

Design: 40fr, Team captain and manager receiving trophy, vert.

1975, July 15 Litho. *Perf. 12½*

323 A92 30fr multicolored .50 .25
324 A92 40fr multicolored .60 .25

CARA team, winners of African Soccer Cup 1974.

Citroen, 1935 — A93

Designs: Early autombiles.

1975, July 17 *Perf. 12*

325 A93 30fr shown .90 .30
326 A93 40fr Alfa Romeo, 1911 1.10 .30
327 A93 50fr Rolls Royce, 1926 1.40 .35
328 A93 75fr Duryea, 1893 2.75 .35
Nos. 325-328 (4) 6.15 1.30

Tipoye Transport — A94

1975, Aug. 5

329 A94 30fr shown .90 .40
330 A94 40fr Dugout canoe 1.00 .65

Traditional means of transportation.

Raising Red Flag — A95

1975, Aug. 15

331 A95 30fr shown .50 .20
332 A95 40fr National Conference .60 .25

2nd anniv. of installation of popular power (30fr) and 3rd anniv. of Natl. Conf. (40fr).

Line Fishing — A96

Woman Pounding "Foufou" — A97

Traditional Fishing: 30fr, Trap fishing, horiz. 60fr, Spear fishing. 90fr, Net fishing, horiz.

1975, Aug. 31 Litho. *Perf. 12*

333 A96 30fr multicolored .70 .20
334 A96 40fr multicolored .70 .25
335 A96 60fr multicolored 1.10 .35
336 A96 90fr multicolored 2.25 .65
Nos. 333-336 (4) 4.75 1.45

1975, Sept. 5

Household Tasks: No. 338, Woman chopping wood. 40fr, Woman preparing manioc, horiz.

337 A97 30fr multicolored .60 .20
338 A97 30fr multicolored .60 .20
339 A97 40fr multicolored .90 .25
Nos. 337-339 (3) 2.10 .65

Musical Instruments A98

1975, Sept. 20 *Perf. 12½*

340 A98 30fr Esanga .70 .20
341 A98 40fr Kalakwa 1.00 .25
342 A98 60fr Likembe 1.40 .30
343 A98 75fr Ngongui 1.75 .40
Nos. 340-343 (4) 4.85 1.15

Dzeke (Congolese) Shell Money — A99

Ancient Money: No. 346, like No. 344. Nos. 345, 347, Okengo, Congolese, iron bar. 40fr, Gallic coin, c. 60 B.C. 50fr, Roman denarius, 37 B.C. 60fr, Danubian coin, 2nd cent. B.C. 85fr, Greek stater, 4th cent. B.C.

1975-76 Engr. *Perf. 13*

344 A99 30fr red & multi .60 .20
345 A99 30fr vio & multi .60 .20
346 A99 35fr ol & multi .90 .25
347 A99 35fr dk car rose & multi .90 .25
348 A99 40fr Prus bl & brn .90 .20
349 A99 50fr Prus bl & ol 1.00 .30
350 A99 60fr dk grn & brn 1.25 .35
351 A99 85fr mag & sl grn 2.10 .45
Nos. 344-351 (8) 8.25 2.20

Nos. 346-347 inscribed "1976" and issued Mar. 1976; others issued Oct. 5, 1975.

Moschops — A100

Pre-historic Animals: 70fr, Tyrannosaurus. 95fr, Cryptocleidus. 100fr, Stegosaurus.

1975, Oct. 15 Litho. *Perf. 13*

352 A100 55fr multicolored 2.00 .30
353 A100 75fr multicolored 3.00 .35
354 A100 95fr multicolored 5.25 .75
355 A100 100fr multicolored 7.50 1.25
Nos. 352-355 (4) 17.75 2.65

Albert Schweitzer (1875-1965), Medical Missionary — A101

1975, Oct. 15 Engr.

356 A101 75fr ol, brn & red 1.50 .40

Alexander Fleming A102

Designs: No. 358, André Marie Ampère. No. 359, Clement Ader.

1975, Nov. 15 Engr. *Perf. 13*

357 A102 60fr brn, grn & blk 1.00 .30
358 A102 95fr blk, red & grn 1.40 .40
359 A102 95fr red, blue & indigo 1.60 .40
Nos. 357-359 (3) 4.00 1.10

Fleming (1881-1955), developer of penicillin; Ampère (1775-1836), physicist; Ader (1841-1925), aviation pioneer.

UN Emblem "ONU" and "30" — A103

1975, Dec. 20 Engr. *Perf. 13*

360 A103 95fr car, ultra & grn 1.25 .45

United Nations, 30th anniversary.

Women's Broken Chain — A104

Design: 60fr, Equality between man and woman, globe, IWY emblem.

1975, Dec. 20 Litho. *Perf. 12½*

361 A104 35fr mag, ocher & gray .60 .20
362 A104 60fr ultra, brn & blk .70 .30

International Women's Year, 1975.

Pres. Marien Ngouabi, Flag and Workers — A105

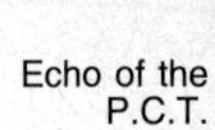

Echo of the P.C.T. A106

1975, Dec. 31 *Perf. 12½x12, 13x12½*

363 A105 30fr multicolored .50 .20
364 A106 35fr multicolored .50 .20

6th anniversary of the Congolese Labor Party (P.C.T.). See No. C215.

A.G. Bell and 1876 Telephone A107

1976, Apr. 25 Litho. *Perf. 12½x13*

365 A107 35fr yel, brn & org brn .50 .20

Cent. of 1st telephone call by Alexander Graham Bell, Mar. 10, 1876. See No. C229.

Women Selling Fruit and Vegetables A108

1976, Sept. 19 Litho. *Perf. 12½x13*

366 A108 35fr shown .50 .20
367 A108 60fr Market scene 1.00 .30

Congolese Coiffure — A109

Designs: Various women's hair styles.

1976, Oct. 10 Litho. *Perf. 13*

368 A109 35fr multicolored .50 .20
369 A109 60fr multicolored .90 .25
370 A109 95fr multicolored 1.40 .35
371 A109 100fr multicolored 1.60 .40
Nos. 368-371 (4) 4.40 1.20

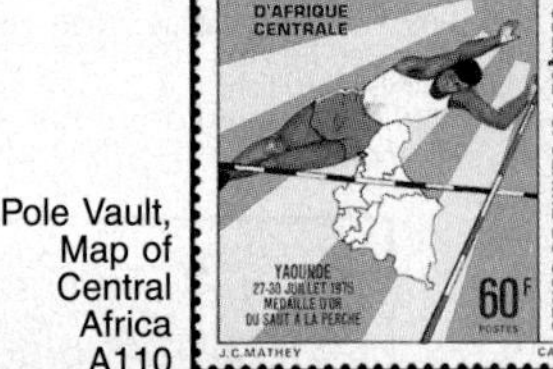

Pole Vault, Map of Central Africa A110

95fr, Long jump and map of Central Africa.

1976, Oct. 25 *Perf. 12½*

372 A110 60fr yel & multi .70 .25
373 A110 95fr yel & multi 1.25 .40
Nos. 372-373,C230-C231 (4) 6.45 2.50

Gold medalists, 1st Central African Games, Yaoundé, July 27-30, 1975.

Antelope A111

1976, Oct. 27 Litho. *Perf. 12½*

Size: 36x36mm

374 A111 5fr shown .25 .20
375 A111 10fr Buffalos .35 .20
376 A111 15fr Hippopotamus .35 .20
377 A111 20fr Wart hog 1.60 .30
378 A111 25fr Elephants 2.00 .35
Nos. 374-378 (5) 4.55 1.25

1976, Dec. 8

Designs: Birds.

Size: 26x36mm

379 A111 5fr Saddle bill storks 1.00 .25

Size: 36x36mm

380 A111 10fr Malachite kingfisher 1.25 .25
381 A111 20fr Crowned cranes 3.00 .60
Nos. 379-381 (3) 5.25 1.10

Bicycling, Map of Participants A112

Heliotrope A113

1976, Dec. 21 Photo. *Perf. 12½x13*

382 A112 35fr shown .35 .20
383 A112 60fr Fieldball .60 .25
384 A112 80fr Running 1.00 .35
385 A112 95fr Soccer 1.25 .40
Nos. 382-385 (4) 3.20 1.20

First Central African Games, Libreville, Gabon, June-July 1976.

1976, Dec. 23 Photo. *Perf. 12½x13*

Flowers: 5fr, Water lilies. 15fr, Bird-of-paradise flower.

386 A113 5fr multicolored .25 .20
387 A113 10fr multicolored .35 .20
388 A113 15fr multicolored .60 .20
Nos. 386-388 (3) 1.20 .60

Torch and Olive Branches A114

1976, Dec. 25 Litho. *Perf. 12½x13*

389 A114 35fr multicolored .45 .20

National Pioneer Movement.

The Spirit of '76 — A115

125fr, Pulling down George III statue. 150fr, Battle of Princeton. 175fr, Generals of Revolutionary War. 200fr, Burgoyne's surrender at Saratoga. 500fr, Battle of Lexington.

1976, Dec. 29 Litho. *Perf. 14*

390 A115 100fr multicolored 1.00 .25
391 A115 125fr multicolored 1.10 .35
392 A115 150fr multicolored 1.60 .40
393 A115 175fr multicolored 2.00 .50
394 A115 200fr multicolored 2.25 .60
Nos. 390-394 (5) 7.95 2.10

Souvenir Sheet

395 A115 500fr multicolored 5.75 1.50

American Bicentennial.

Dugout Canoe Race A116

Design: 60fr, 2-man dugout canoes.

1977, Mar. 27 Litho. *Perf. 13x13½*

396 A116 35fr multicolored .60 .20
397 A116 60fr multicolored 1.00 .35

Dugout canoe races on Congo River.

Lilan Goua A117

Fresh-water Fish: 15fr, Liko ko. 25fr, Liyan ga. 35fr, Mbessi. 60fr, Mongandza.

1977, June 15 Litho. *Perf. 12½*

398 A117 10fr multicolored .60 .20
399 A117 15fr multicolored .70 .20
400 A117 25fr multicolored .90 .20
401 A117 35fr multicolored 1.75 .30
402 A117 60fr multicolored 2.75 .45
Nos. 398-402 (5) 6.70 1.35

Traditional Headdress — A118

1977, June 30 Litho. *Perf. 12½*

403 A118 35fr shown .45 .30
404 A118 60fr Leopard cap .90 .35

See Nos. C234-C235.

Bondjo Wrestling A119

40fr, 50fr, Bondjo wrestling, diff. 40fr, horiz.

1977, July 15

405 A119 25fr multicolored .45 .20
406 A119 40fr multicolored .50 .20
407 A119 50fr multicolored .60 .30
Nos. 405-407 (3) 1.55 .70

"Schwaben" LZ 10, 1911 — A120

Zeppelins: 60fr, "Viktoria Luise." LZ 11, 1913. 100fr, LZ 120. 200fr, LZ 127. 300fr, "Graf Zeppelin II" LZ 130.

1977, Aug. 5 Litho. *Perf. 11*

408 A120 40fr multicolored .45 .20
409 A120 60fr multicolored .70 .25
410 A120 100fr multicolored 1.10 .25
411 A120 200fr multicolored 2.25 .55
412 A120 300fr multicolored 3.50 .80
Nos. 408-412 (5) 8.00 2.05

History of the Zeppelin. Exist imperf. See No. C236.

Coat of Arms and Rising Sun A121

1977, Aug. 15

413 A121 40fr multicolored .45 .20

14th anniversary of the revolution.

Victor Hugo and The Hunchback of Notre Dame — A122

Designs (Hugo and): 60fr, Les Miserables. 100fr, Les Travailleurs de la Mer (octopus).

1977, Aug. 20 Engr. *Perf. 13*

414 A122 35fr multicolored .45 .20
415 A122 60fr multicolored .60 .25
416 A122 100fr multicolored 1.10 .40
Nos. 414-416 (3) 2.15 .85

Victor Hugo (1802-1885), French novelist.

Mao Tse-tung A123

Lithographed; Gold Embossed

1977, Sept. 9 *Perf. 12x12½*

417 A123 400fr red & gold 4.50 1.75

Chairman Mao Tse-tung (1893-1976), Chinese Communist leader, 1st death anniv.

Peter Paul Rubens A124

1977, Sept. 20 Gold Embossed

418 A124 600fr gold & lt bl 10.00 4.50

Peter Paul Rubens (1577-1640), painter.

Child Leading Blind Woman Across Street A125

1977, Oct. 22 Litho. *Perf. 12½x13*

419 A125 35fr multicolored .60 .25

World Health Day: To see is life.

Paul Kamba and Records A126

1977, Oct. 29

420 A126 100fr multicolored 1.00 .45

Paul Kamba (1912-1950), musician.

Trajan Vuia and Flying Machine — A127

Designs: 75fr, Louis Bleriot and plane. 100fr, Roland Garros and plane. 200fr, Charles Lindbergh and Spirit of St. Louis. 300fr, Tupolev Tu-144. 500fr, Lindbergh and Spirit of St. Louis over ship in Atlantic.

1977, Nov. 18 Litho. *Perf. 14*

421 A127 60fr multicolored .60 .20
422 A127 75fr multicolored .90 .25
423 A127 100fr multicolored 1.10 .30
424 A127 200fr multicolored 2.25 .50
425 A127 300fr multicolored 3.25 .70
Nos. 421-425 (5) 8.10 1.95

Souvenir Sheet

426 A127 500fr multicolored 5.75 1.25

History of aviation.

Elizabeth II and Prince Philip A128

Design: 300fr, Elizabeth II wearing Crown.

1977, Dec. 21

427 A128 250fr multicolored 2.25 .65
428 A128 300fr multicolored 2.75 .70

Reign of Queen Elizabeth II, 25th anniv. See #C239. For overprints see #468-469, C244.

King Baudouin A129

Design: No. 430, Charles de Gaulle.

1977, Dec. 21

429 A129 200fr multicolored 2.25 .65
430 A129 200fr multicolored 2.25 .65

King Baudouin of Belgium and Charles de Gaulle, president of France.

Ambete Sculpture A130

Congolese art: 85fr, Babembe sculpture.

1978, Feb. 18 Engr. *Perf. 13*

431 A130 35fr lt brn & multi .60 .25
432 A130 85fr lt grn & multi 1.40 .45

St. Simon, by Rubens A131

Rubens Paintings: 140fr, Duke of Lerma. 200fr, Madonna and Saints. 300fr, Rubens and his Wife Helena Fourment. 500fr, Farm at Laeken.

1978, Mar. 7 Litho. *Perf. 13½x14*

433 A131 60fr gold & multi .60 .20
434 A131 140fr gold & multi 1.50 .30
435 A131 200fr gold & multi 2.25 .45
436 A131 300fr gold & multi 3.25 .65
Nos. 433-436 (4) 7.60 1.60

Souvenir Sheet

437 A131 500fr gold & multi 5.75 1.40

Peter Paul Rubens, 400th birth anniv.

Pres. Ngouabi and Microphones — A132

60fr, Ngouabi at his desk, horiz. 100fr, Portrait.

Perf. 12½x13, 13x12½

1978, Mar. 18 **Litho.**

438 A132 35fr multicolored .45 .20
439 A132 60fr multicolored .50 .25
440 A132 100fr multicolored .90 .40
Nos. 438-440 (3) 1.85 .85

Pres. Marien Ngouabi, 1st death anniv.

Ferenc Puskas and Argentina '78 Emblem — A133

Players and Emblem: 75fr, Giacinto Facchetti. 100fr, Bobby Moore. 200fr, Raymond Kopa. 300fr, Pele. 500fr, Franz Beckenbauer.

1978, Apr. 4 ***Perf. 14x13½***

441 A133 60fr multicolored .60 .20
442 A133 75fr multicolored .70 .25
443 A133 100fr multicolored 1.10 .25
444 A133 200fr multicolored 2.25 .55
445 A133 300fr multicolored 3.25 .75
Nos. 441-445 (5) 7.90 2.00

Souvenir Sheet

446 A133 500fr multicolored 6.25 1.25

11th World Cup Soccer Championship, Argentina, June 1-25.
For overprints see Nos. 481-486.

Pearl S. Buck and Chinese Women — A134

Nobel Prize winners: 75fr, Fridtjof Nansen, refugees and Nansen passport. 100fr, Henri Bergson, book and flame. 200fr, Alexander Fleming and Petri dish. 300fr, Gerhart Hauptmann and book. 500fr, Henri Dunant and Red Cross Station.

1978, Apr. 29

447 A134 60fr multicolored .60 .25
448 A134 75fr multicolored .70 .25
449 A134 100fr multicolored 1.10 .30
450 A134 200fr multicolored 2.00 .50
451 A134 300fr multicolored 2.75 .60
Nos. 447-451 (5) 7.15 1.90

Souvenir Sheet

452 A134 500fr multicolored 5.75 1.40

African Buffalos A135

Endangered animals and Wildlife Fund Emblem: 35fr, Okapi, vert. 85fr, Rhinoceros. 150fr, Chimpanzee, vert. 200fr, Hippopotamus. 300fr, Buffon's kob, vert.

1978 ***Perf. 14½***

453 A135 35fr multicolored .85 .20
454 A135 60fr multicolored 1.40 .30
455 A135 85fr multicolored 3.50 .40
456 A135 150fr multicolored 5.00 .60
457 A135 200fr multicolored 6.75 1.10
458 A135 300fr multicolored 12.50 1.40
Nos. 453-458 (6) 30.00 4.00

Issue dates: 35fr, Aug. 11; others, July 11.

Emblem, Young People, Gun and Fist — A136

1978, July 28 ***Perf. 12½***

459 A136 35fr multicolored .50 .30

11th World Youth Festival, Havana, 7/28-8/5.

Pyramids and Camels — A137

Seven Wonders of the Ancient World: 50fr, Hanging Gardens of Babylon. 60fr, Statue of Zeus, Olympia. 95fr, Colossus of Rhodes. 125fr, Mausoleum of Halicarnassus. 150fr, Temple of Artemis, Ephesus. 200fr, Lighthouse, Alexandria. 300fr, Map of Eastern Mediterranean showing locations. 50fr, 60fr, 95fr, 125fr, 200fr, vertical.

1978, Aug. 12 **Litho.** ***Perf. 14***

460 A137 35fr multicolored .35 .20
461 A137 50fr multicolored .45 .20
462 A137 60fr multicolored .60 .20
463 A137 95fr multicolored .80 .30
464 A137 125fr multicolored 1.00 .40
465 A137 150fr multicolored 1.25 .45
466 A137 200fr multicolored 1.75 .55
467 A137 300fr multicolored 2.25 .80
Nos. 460-467 (8) 8.45 3.10

Nos. 427-428 Overprinted in Silver: "ANNIVERSAIRE DU COURONNEMENT 1953-1978"

1978, Sept. **Litho.** ***Perf. 14***

468 A128 250fr multicolored 2.25 .90
469 A128 300fr multicolored 2.75 1.25

25th anniversary of coronation of Queen Elizabeth II. See No. C244.

Kwame Nkrumah and Map of Africa — A138

1978, Sept. 23 **Litho.** ***Perf. 13x12½***

470 A138 60fr multicolored .60 .25

Nkrumah (1909-72), Pres. of Ghana.

Wild Boar Hunt — A139

Local hunting and fishing: 50fr, Fish smoking. 60fr, Hunter with spears and dog, vert.

1978 **Litho.** ***Perf. 12***

471 A139 35fr multicolored 2.00 .25
472 A139 50fr multicolored .60 .25
473 A139 60fr multicolored 2.00 .25
Nos. 471-473 (3) 4.60 .75

Issue dates: 35fr, 60fr, Oct. 5; 50fr, Oct. 10.

View of Kalchreut, by Dürer — A140

Paintings by Dürer: 150fr, Elspeth Tucher, vert. 250fr, "The Great Piece of Turf," vert. 350fr, Self-portrait, vert.

1978, Nov. 23 **Litho.** ***Perf. 14***

474 A140 65fr multicolored .60 .20
475 A140 150fr multicolored 1.40 .35
476 A140 250fr multicolored 2.25 .65
477 A140 350fr multicolored 3.50 .90
Nos. 474-477 (4) 7.75 2.10

Albrecht Dürer (1471-1528), German painter.

Basketmaker A141

Productive Labor: 90fr, Woodcarver. 140fr, Women hoeing field.

1978, Nov. 18 **Litho.** ***Perf. 12½***

Size: 25x36mm

478 A141 85fr multicolored .70 .40
479 A141 90fr multicolored 1.00 .40

Size: 27x48mm

Perf. 12

480 A141 140fr multicolored 1.50 .65
Nos. 478-480 (3) 3.20 1.45

Nos. 441-446 Overprinted in Silver:
a. "1962 VAINQUEUR: BRESIL"
b. "1966 VAINQUEUR: / GRANDE BRETAGNE"
c. "1970 VAINQUEUR: / BRESIL"
d. "1974 VAINQUEUR: / ALLEMAGNE (RFA)"
e. "1978 VAINQUEUR: / ARGENTINE"
f. "ARGENTINE-PAYS BAS 3-1/25 juin 1978"

1978, Nov. ***Perf. 14x13½***

481 A133 (a) 60fr multicolored .60 .25
482 A133 (b) 75fr multicolored .70 .35
483 A133 (c) 100fr multicolored 1.00 .45
484 A133 (d) 200fr multicolored 2.00 .65
485 A133 (e) 300fr multicolored 2.75 1.00
Nos. 481-485 (5) 7.05 2.70

Souvenir Sheet

486 A133 (f) 500fr multicolored 5.75 2.40

Winners, World Soccer Cup Championships 1962-1978.

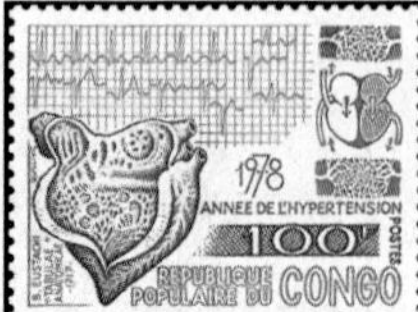

Heart and Charts A142

1978, Dec. 16 **Engr.** ***Perf. 13***

487 A142 100fr multicolored 1.00 .45

Fight against hypertension.

Party Emblem and Road — A143

1978, Dec. 31 **Litho.** ***Perf. 12½x12***

488 A143 60fr multicolored .60 .25

Congolese Labor Party, 9th anniversary.

Capt. Cook, Polynesians and House — A144

Capt. James Cook (1728-1779): 150fr, Island scene. 250fr, Polynesian longboats. 350fr, Capt. Cook's ships off Hawaii.

1979, Jan. 16 ***Perf. 14½***

489 A144 65fr multicolored .60 .20
490 A144 150fr multicolored 1.40 .35
491 A144 250fr multicolored 2.25 .60
492 A144 350fr multicolored 3.50 1.00
Nos. 489-492 (4) 7.75 2.15

Pres. Marien Ngouabi — A145

1979, Mar. 18 **Litho.** ***Perf. 12***

493 A145 35fr multicolored .35 .20
494 A145 60fr multicolored .50 .25

Assassination of President Ngouabi, 2nd anniv.

"1979," IYC Emblem, Child A146

A146a

1979, Apr. 30 Litho. *Perf. 12½x13*

495 A146 45fr multicolored .45 .20
496 A146 75fr multicolored .90 .35

Souvenir Sheet

Perf. 14½

496A A146a 250fr multicolored 2.75 1.00

International Year of the Child.
Issued: 45fr, 75fr, Apr. 30; 250fr, Sept. 5.

Pottery Vases and Solanum — A147

Design: 150fr, Mail runner, Concorde, train, UPU emblem, envelope.

1979, June 8 Litho. *Perf. 13*

497 A147 60fr multicolored 1.25 .60

Engr.

498 A147 150fr multicolored 2.75 1.25

Philexafrique II, Libreville, Gabon, June 8-17. Nos. 497, 498 each printed in sheets of 10 with 5 labels showing exhibition emblem.

Rowland Hill, Diesel Locomotive, Germany No. 78 — A148

Designs (Rowland Hill and): 100fr, Old steam locomotive and France No. B10. 200fr, Diesel locomotive and US No. 245. 300fr, Steam locomotive and England-Australia First Aerialpost vignette, 1919. 500fr, Electric train, Concorde and Middle Congo No. 75.

1979, June 30 *Perf. 14*

499 A148 65fr multicolored .60 .20
500 A148 100fr multicolored 1.00 .25
501 A148 200fr multicolored 2.25 .50
502 A148 300fr multicolored 2.75 .75
Nos. 499-502 (4) 6.60 1.70

Souvenir Sheet

503 A148 500fr multicolored 5.75 1.25

Sir Rowland Hill (1795-1879), originator of penny postage.

Salvador Allende, Flags, Demonstrators — A149

1979, July 21 Litho. *Perf. 12½*

504 A149 100fr multicolored 1.00 .45

Salvador Allende, president of Chile.

Old Man Telling Stories — A150

1979, July 28

505 A150 45fr multicolored .60 .25

Story telling as education.

Handball Players A151

75fr, Players and ball. 250fr, Pres. Ngouabi, cup on map of Africa, player.

1979, July 31 Litho. *Perf. 12½*

Size: 40x30mm, 30x40mm

506 A151 45fr multi .50 .20
507 A151 75fr multi, vert. .90 .25

Size: 22x40mm

Perf. 12x12½

508 A151 250fr multicolored 2.50 1.00

Marien Ngouabi Handball Cup.

Map and Flag of Congo A152

1979, Aug. 15

509 A152 50fr multicolored .45 .25

16th anniversary of revolution.

Souvenir Sheet

Virgin and Child, by Dürer — A153

1979, Aug. 13 *Perf. 13½*

510 A153 500fr red brn & lt grn 6.25 1.50

Albrecht Dürer (1471-1528), German engraver and painter.

Bach and Contemporary Instruments — A155

#512, Albert Einstein, astronauts on moon.

1979, Sept. 10 *Perf. 13½*

511 A155 200fr multicolored 2.25 .75
512 A155 200fr multicolored 2.25 .75

Yoro Fishing Port A156

1979, Sept. 26 Litho. *Perf. 12½*

513 A156 45fr shown .60 .20
514 A156 75fr Port at night .90 .35

Mukukulu Dam — A157

1979, Oct. 5 *Perf. 12½x12*

515 A157 20fr multicolored .25 .20
516 A157 45fr multicolored .70 .25

Emblem, Control Tower, Jets A158

1979, Dec. 12 Litho. *Perf. 12½*

517 A158 100fr multicolored 1.10 .50

ASECNA (Air Safety Board), 20th anniv.

Congolese Labor Party, 10th Anniversary A159

1979, Dec. 31

518 A159 45fr multicolored .45 .20

A160

A161

1980, Mar. 30 Litho. *Perf. 12½*

519 A160 45fr multicolored .45 .20
520 A160 95fr multicolored .90 .30

Post Office, 15th Anniversary.

1980, May 5

521 A161 100fr multicolored 2.00 .30

Visit of Pope John Paul II.

Rotary International, 75th Anniversary — A162

1980, May 10 Litho. *Perf. 12½*

522 A162 150fr multicolored 1.50 .50

Pointe Noire Foundry A163

1980, June 18 Litho. *Perf. 12½*

523 A163 30fr shown .20 .20
524 A163 35fr Different view .50 .20

Claude Chappe, Tower — A164

1980, June 21 Litho. *Perf. 12½*

525 A164 200fr multicolored 2.25 1.00

Claude Chappe (1763-1805), French engineer.

Mossaka Harbor — A165

1980, June 23

532 A165 45fr shown .50 .20
533 A165 90fr Different view 1.00 .25

Papilio Dardanus (Front and Back) — A167

Human Rights Emblem, People — A169

July 31st Hospital — A168

1980, July 12 Litho. *Perf. 12½*

534 A167 5fr shown .70 .20
535 A167 15fr Kalima aethiops .70 .20
536 A167 20fr Papilio demodocus 1.00 .20
537 A167 60fr Euphaedra 3.25 .50
538 A167 90fr Hypolimnas misippus 6.25 .60
Nos. 534-538 (5) 11.90 1.70

Souvenir Sheet

539 A167 300fr Charaxes smaragdalis 17.00 17.00

Nos. 534-536 also exist perf 12½x13. Values the same.

1980, July 31

540 A168 45fr multicolored .60 .25

1980, Aug. 2

541 A169 350fr shown 2.75 1.00
542 A169 500fr Man breaking chain 4.50 1.50

Human Rights Convention, 32nd anniv.

Citizens and Congolese Arms
A170

1980, Aug. 15 *Perf. 12½*

543 A170 75fr shown .70 .30
544 A170 95fr Dove on flag, fists, vert. .90 .30
545 A170 150fr Dove holding Congolese arms 1.40 .60
Nos. 543-545 (3) 3.00 1.20

August 15th Revolution, 17th anniv.

Coffee and Cocoa Trees on Map of Congo — A171

Coffee and Cocoa Day: 95fr, Branches, map of Congo.

1980, Aug. 18 *Perf. 13½x13*

546 A171 45fr multicolored .50 .20
547 A171 95fr multicolored 1.00 .40

Logging
A172

1980, Aug. 28

548 A172 70fr shown .80 .30
549 A172 75fr Wood transport .80 .30

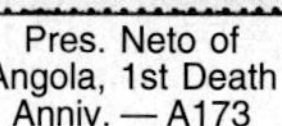

Pres. Neto of Angola, 1st Death Anniv. — A173

Lark — A174

1980, Sept. 11

550 A173 100fr multicolored .90 .30

1980, Sept. 17

Designs: Birds.

551 A174 45fr multi, horiz. .70 .30
552 A174 75fr multi, horiz. 1.00 .30
553 A174 90fr multi, horiz. 1.25 .35
554 A174 150fr multicolored 2.00 .50
555 A174 200fr multicolored 2.75 .90
556 A174 250fr multicolored 3.00 1.00
a Souv. sheet of 6, #551-556 18.00 18.00
Nos. 551-556 (6) 10.70 3.35

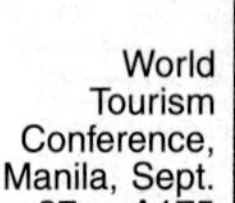

World Tourism Conference, Manila, Sept. 27 A175

1980, Sept. 27 Litho. *Perf. 13½x13*

557 A175 100fr multicolored .90 .35

First Day of School Term — A176

1980, Oct. 2 Photo. *Perf. 13*

558 A176 50fr multicolored .50 .20

First House in Brazzaville — A177

Brazzaville Centenary: 65fr, First native village. 75fr, Old Town Hall, 1912. 150fr, View from bank of Bacongo, 1912. 200fr, Meeting of explorer Savorgnan de Brazza and chief Makoko, 1880.

1980, Oct. 3 Litho. *Perf. 12½*

559 A177 45fr multicolored .50 .20
560 A177 65fr multicolored .70 .30
561 A177 75fr multicolored 1.00 .40
562 A177 150fr multicolored 1.75 .65
563 A177 200fr multicolored 2.25 1.00
Nos. 559-563 (5) 6.20 2.55

Boys on Bank of Congo River — A178

1980, Oct. 30

564 A178 80fr shown .70 .25
565 A178 150fr Djoue Bridge 1.60 .40

Revolutionary Stadium and Athletes — A179

1980, Nov. 20 *Perf. 13x12½*

566 A179 60fr multicolored .70 .25

Rebuilt Railroad Bridge over Congo River
A180

1980, Nov. 29 *Perf. 13x13½*

567 A180 75fr multicolored .90 .30

Mangoes, Loudima Fruit Packing Station
A181

1980, Dec. 2 *Perf. 13*

568 A181 10fr shown .25 .20
569 A181 25fr Oranges .50 .20
570 A181 40fr Citrons .60 .20
571 A181 85fr Mandarins 1.10 .30
Nos. 568-571 (4) 2.45 .90

African Postal Union, 5th Anniversary
A182

1980, Dec. 24 *Perf. 13½*

572 A182 100fr multicolored .90 .30

Moungouni Earth Satellite Station
A183

1980, Dec. 30 *Perf. 12½*

573 A183 75fr multicolored .60 .20

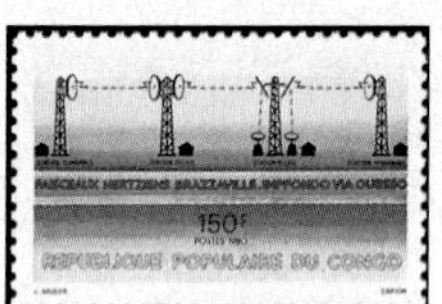

Hertzian Wave Communication, Brazzaville — A184

1980, Dec. 30 *Perf. 12½x12*

574 A184 150fr multicolored 1.25 .40

1980 African Handball Champion Team — A185

Perf. 12½x13, 13x12½

1981, Jan. 26 Litho.

575 A185 100fr Receiving cup, vert. 1.00 .30
576 A185 150fr shown 1.25 .40

Pres. Denis Sassou-Nguesso — A186

1981, Feb. 5 Litho. *Perf. 12½*

577 A186 45fr multicolored .45 .20
578 A186 75fr multicolored .60 .20
579 A186 100fr multicolored .90 .25
Nos. 577-579 (3) 1.95 .65

Columbia Space Shuttle Orbiting Earth — A187

Space Conquest: 100fr, Luna 17, 1970. 200fr, 300fr, 500fr, Columbia space shuttle, 1981.

1981, May 4 Litho. *Perf. 14x13½*

580 A187 100fr multicolored 1.00 .25
581 A187 150fr multicolored 1.40 .40
582 A187 200fr multicolored 2.00 .55
583 A187 300fr multicolored 2.75 .80
Nos. 580-583 (4) 7.15 2.00

Souvenir Sheet

584 A187 500fr multicolored 5.00 1.40

For overprint see No. 725.

Fight Against Apartheid — A188

Twin Palm Tree of Louingui — A189

1981, May 5 Litho. *Perf. 12½*

585 A188 100fr deep blue .90 .25

1981, May 22 *Perf. 12x12½*

586 A189 75fr multicolored 1.00 .25

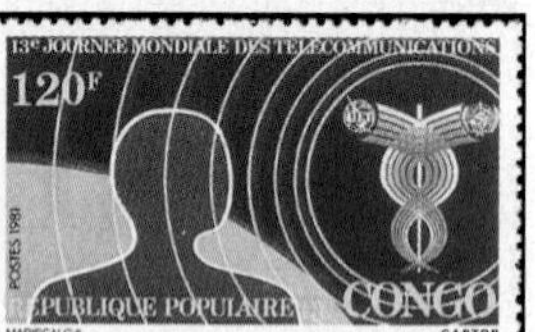

13th World Telecommunications Day — A190

1981, June 6 *Perf. 12½*

587 A190 120fr multicolored 1.25 .30

Rubber Extraction — A191

1981, June 27 *Perf. 13*

588 A191 50fr shown .60 .20
589 A191 70fr Sap draining .90 .30

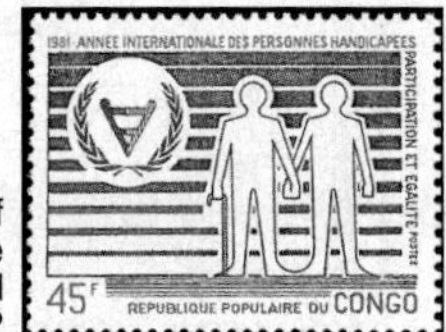

Intl. Year of the Disabled A192

1981, June 29 **Engr.**

590 A192 45fr multicolored .45 .20

See No. B7.

Bird Trap — A194

Designs: Animal traps. 10fr vert.

1981, July

596 A194 5fr multicolored 1.10 .20
597 A194 10fr multicolored 1.10 .20
598 A194 15fr multicolored 1.10 .20
599 A194 20fr multicolored 1.10 .20
600 A194 30fr multicolored 1.60 .25
601 A194 35fr multicolored 2.25 .30
Nos. 596-601 (6) 8.25 1.35

Mausoleum of King Maloango — A195

1981, July 4 **Litho.** *Perf. 12½*

602 A195 75fr shown .70 .20
603 A195 150fr Mausoleum, portrait 1.25 .40

Prince Charles and Lady Diana, Coach A196

Royal wedding: Couple and coaches.

1981, Sept. 1 **Litho.** *Perf. 14½*

604 A196 100fr multicolored 1.00 .25
605 A196 200fr multicolored 2.00 .55
606 A196 300fr multicolored 3.25 .80
Nos. 604-606 (3) 6.25 1.60

Souvenir Sheet

607 A196 400fr multicolored 4.00 1.10

World Food Day — A197

1981, Oct. 16 **Litho.** *Perf. 13½x13*

608 A197 150fr multicolored 1.25 .55

12th World UPU Day A198

1981, Oct. 24 **Engr.** *Perf. 13x12½*

609 A198 90fr multicolored .90 .25

Royal Guard A199

1981, Oct. 31 **Litho.** *Perf. 12½x13*

610 A199 45fr multicolored .60 .20

Eradication of Manioc Beetle — A200

Natl. Red Cross — A201

1981, Nov. 18 **Litho.** *Perf. 12½*

611 A200 75fr multicolored 1.00 .25

1981, Nov. 18 *Perf. 13*

612 A201 10fr Bandaging patient .20 .20
613 A201 35fr Treating child .45 .20
614 A201 60fr Drawing well water .70 .25
Nos. 612-614 (3) 1.35 .65

Giant Baobab ("Tree of Savorgnan de Brazza") A202

1981, Dec. 19 **Litho.** *Perf. 13*

615 A202 45fr multicolored .90 .20
616 A202 75fr multicolored 1.25 .30

Fetish Figure — A203

Designs: Various carved figures.

1981, Dec. 19 *Perf. 13x12½*

617 A203 15fr multicolored .20 .20
618 A203 25fr multicolored .25 .20
619 A203 45fr multicolored .45 .20
620 A203 50fr multicolored .60 .20
621 A203 60fr multicolored .70 .20
Nos. 617-621 (5) 2.20 1.00

Nos. 617, 618 and 620 also exist perf 12½x13. Values the same.

Caves of Bangou A204

1981, Dec. 29 *Perf. 13x13½*

622 A204 20fr multicolored .25 .20
623 A204 25fr multicolored .45 .20

King Makoko and His Queen, Ivory Sculptures by R. Engongodzo — A205

Perf. 13½x13, 13x13½

1982, Feb. 27 **Litho.**

624 A205 25fr Woman, vert. .35 .20
625 A205 35fr Woman, diff., vert. .45 .20
626 A205 100fr shown 1.00 .30
Nos. 624-626 (3) 1.80 .70

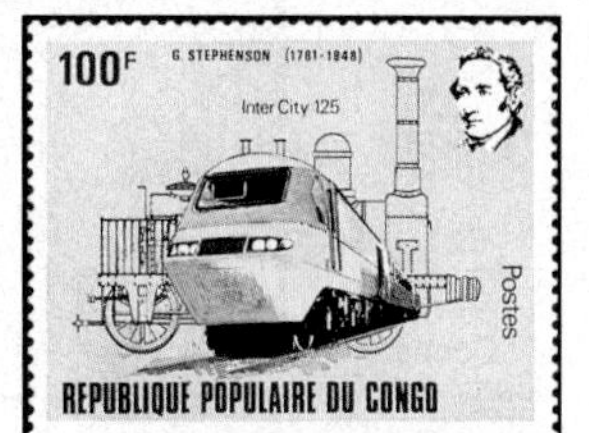

George Stephenson (1781-1848) and Inter City 125, Gt. Britain — A206

Locomotives: 150fr, Sinkansen Bullet Train, Japan. 200fr, Advanced Passenger Train, Gt. Britain. 300fr, TGV-001, France.

1982, Mar. 2 **Litho.** *Perf. 12½*

627 A206 100fr multicolored 1.00 .25
628 A206 150fr multicolored 1.60 .40
629 A206 200fr multicolored 2.25 .55
630 A206 300fr multicolored 3.25 .80
Nos. 627-630 (4) 8.10 2.00

Scouting Year A207

1982, Apr. 13 **Litho.** *Perf. 13*

631 A207 100fr Looking through binoculars 1.00 .25
632 A207 150fr Reading map 1.40 .40
633 A207 200fr Helping woman 2.00 .55
634 A207 300fr Crossing rope bridge 2.75 .80
Nos. 631-634 (4) 7.15 2.00

Souvenir Sheet

635 A207 500fr Hiking, horiz. 5.00 1.75

For overprint see No. 726.

Franklin Roosevelt A208

1982, June 12 **Litho.** *Perf. 13*

636 A208 150fr shown 1.60 .40
637 A208 250fr Washington 2.75 .70
638 A208 350fr Goethe 3.25 .90
Nos. 636-638 (3) 7.60 2.00

21st Birthday of Princess Diana, July 1 — A209

1982, June 12 *Perf. 14*

639 A209 200fr Candles 2.00 .55
640 A209 300fr "21" 2.75 .80

Souvenir Sheet

641 A209 500fr Diana 5.00 1.40

5-Year Plan, 1982-1986 A210

Perf. 13x12½, 12½x13

1982, June 19

642 A210 60fr Road construction .70 .20
643 A210 100fr Communications, vert. 1.10 .30
644 A210 125fr Operating room equipment, vert. 1.40 .35
645 A210 150fr Hydroelectric power, vert. 1.60 .40
Nos. 642-645 (4) 4.80 1.25

ITU Plenipotentiary Conference, Nairobi — A211

1982, June 26 *Perf. 13*

646 A211 300fr multicolored 2.75 .90

Nos. 604-607 Overprinted in Blue: "NAISSANCE ROYALE 1982"

1982, July 30 *Perf. 14½*

647 A196 100fr multicolored	.90	.30
648 A196 200fr multicolored	1.75	.60
649 A196 300fr multicolored	2.75	1.00
Nos. 647-649 (3)	5.40	1.90

Souvenir Sheet

650 A196 400fr multicolored	3.50	2.50

Birth of Prince William of Wales, June 21.

Nutrition Campaign A212

1982, July 24 **Litho.** *Perf. 12½*

651 A212 100fr multicolored 1.00 .25

WHO African Headquarters, Brazzaville — A213

1982, July 24 **Litho.** *Perf. 12½*

652 A213 125fr multicolored 1.00 .35

TB Bacillus Centenary — A214

1982, Aug. 7 *Perf. 12½x12*

653 A214 250fr Koch, bacillus 2.75 .90

Pres. Sassou-Nguesso and 1980 Simba Prize — A215

1982, Oct. 20 **Litho.** *Perf. 13*

654 A215 100fr multicolored .90 .30

Turtles — A216

Various turtles and tortoises.

1982, Dec. 1

655 A216 30fr multicolored	.50	.20
656 A216 45fr multicolored	.90	.25
657 A216 55fr multicolored	1.00	.30
Nos. 655-657 (3)	2.40	.75

Boy Gathering Coconuts — A217

Nest in Tree Trunk — A218

1982, Dec. 11

658 A217 100fr multicolored .90 .30

1982, Dec. 29 *Perf. 12½*

659 A218 40fr shown	1.25	.20
660 A218 75fr Nests in palm tree	1.50	.20
661 A218 100fr Woven nest on thorn branch	1.60	.25
Nos. 659-661 (3)	4.35	.65

Hertzian Wave Communication Network — A219

1982, Dec. 30 *Perf. 13x12½*

662 A219 45fr multicolored	.45	.20
663 A219 60fr multicolored	.50	.20
664 A219 95fr multicolored	.90	.30
Nos. 662-664 (3)	1.85	.70

30th Anniv. of Customs Cooperation Council — A220

1983, Jan. 26 **Litho.** *Perf. 12½x13*

665 A220 100fr Headquarters .90 .30

Mausoleum of Pres. Marien Ngouabi — A221

1983, Feb. 8 *Perf. 13*

666 A221 60fr multicolored	.50	.20
667 A221 80fr multicolored	.80	.20

Ironsmiths — A222

1983 *Perf. 12½*

668 A222 45fr shown	.50	.20
669 A222 150fr Weaver, vert.	1.25	.50

Issue dates: 45fr, Mar. 5; 150fr, Feb. 24.

Carved Chess Pieces, by R. Engongonzo — A223

Various pieces.

1983, Feb. 26 *Perf. 13*

670 A223 40fr multicolored	.25	.20
671 A223 60fr multicolored	.80	.20
672 A223 95fr multicolored	1.50	.50
Nos. 670-672 (3)	2.55	.90

Easter 1983 A224

Raphael drawings. 200fr, 400fr vert.

1983, Apr. 20 **Litho.** *Perf. 13*

673 A224 200fr Transfiguration study	2.00	.50
674 A224 300fr Deposition from Cross	3.00	.65
675 A224 400fr Christ in Glory	4.00	.85
Nos. 673-675 (3)	9.00	2.00

Seashells A225

1983 **Litho.** *Perf. 15x14*

675A A225 25fr multicolored	150.00	65.00
676 A225 35fr multicolored	1.25	.30
677 A225 65fr multicolored	1.60	.35

Dated 1982.

A226 A227

Various traditional combs.

1983, May *Perf. 14*

678 A226 30fr multicolored	.35	.20
679 A226 70fr multicolored	.90	.20
680 A226 85fr multicolored	1.00	.20
Nos. 678-680 (3)	2.25	.60

Litho & Engr.

1983, Aug. 10 *Perf. 12½x13*

681 A227 60fr multicolored	.45	.20
682 A227 100fr multicolored	.90	.30

20th anniv. of revolution.

Centenary of the Arrival of Christian Missionaries — A228

Churches and Clergymen: 150fr, A. Carrie, Church of the Sacred Heart, Loango, vert. 250fr, Msgr. Augouard; St. Louis, Liranga; St. Joseph, Linzolo.

1983, Aug. 23 *Perf. 12½*

683 A228 150fr multicolored	1.60	.40
684 A228 250fr multicolored	2.75	.70

Local Flowers — A229

1984, Jan. 20 **Litho.** *Perf. 12½*

685 A229 5fr Liana thunderaie, vert.	.20	.20
686 A229 15fr Bougainvillea	.35	.20
687 A229 20fr Anthurium, vert.	.50	.20
688 A229 45fr Allamanda	1.00	.20
689 A229 75fr Hibiscus, vert.	1.40	.30
Nos. 685-689 (5)	3.45	1.10

35th Anniv. of World Peace Council A230

1984, Mar. 31 **Litho.** *Perf. 13x12½*

690 A230 50fr multicolored	.45	.20
691 A230 100fr multicolored	.90	.30

Anti-Nuclear Arms Campaign A231

1984, May 31 **Litho.** *Perf. 12x12½*

692 A231 200fr Explosion, victims 1.75 .50

Agriculture Day A232

Perf. 13x13½, 13½x13

1984, June 30 **Litho.**

693 A232 10fr Rice .20 .20
694 A232 15fr Pineapples .20 .20
695 A232 60fr Manioc, vert. .60 .25
696 A232 100fr Palm tree, map, vert. 1.10 .35
Nos. 693-696 (4) 2.10 1.00

Congress Palace — A233

1984, July 27 *Perf. 13*

697 A233 60fr multicolored .50 .20
698 A233 100fr multicolored .90 .30

Chinese-Congolese cooperation.

CFCO-Congo Railways, 50th Anniv. — A234

1984, July 30 *Perf. 13½*

699 A234 10fr Loulombo Station .25 .20
700 A234 25fr Les Bandas Chinese Labor Camp .45 .20
701 A234 125fr "50" 2.00 .70
702 A234 200fr Admin. bldg. 4.50 1.00
Nos. 699-702 (4) 7.20 2.10

Locomotives — A235

Ships on the Congo River — A236

1984, Aug. 24 *Perf. 12½*

703 A235 100fr CC 203 1.10 .35
704 A236 100fr Tugboat 1.10 .35
705 A235 150fr BB 103 1.60 .50
706 A236 150fr Pusher tugboat 1.60 .50
707 A235 300fr BB-BB 301 3.25 1.10
708 A236 300fr Dredger 3.25 1.10
709 A235 500fr BB 420 L'Eclair 5.25 1.75
710 A236 500fr Cargo ship 5.25 1.75
Nos. 703-710 (8) 22.40 7.40

World Fisheries Year A237

1984, Oct. 16 *Perf. 13½*

711 A237 5fr Basket of fish .25 .20
712 A237 20fr Net fishermen in boat .45 .20
713 A237 25fr School of fish .60 .20
714 A237 40fr Net fisherman 1.00 .25
715 A237 55fr Trawler 1.60 .30
Nos. 711-715 (5) 3.90 1.15

Anti-polio Campaign A238

M'Bamou Palace Hotel, Brazzaville A239

1984, Oct. 30

716 A238 250fr Disabled men, hand 2.75 .90
717 A238 300fr Target, disabled women, horiz. 3.25 1.00

1984, Dec. 15 *Perf. 14½*

718 A239 60fr multicolored .45 .20
719 A239 100fr multicolored .90 .30

Fauna A240

1984, Dec. *Perf. 15x14½*

720 A240 30fr Pangolin 3.50 .70
721 A240 70fr Bat 7.50 1.50
722 A240 85fr Civet cat 9.00 1.90
Nos. 720-722 (3) 20.00 4.10

Congo River Logging A241

1984, Dec. *Perf. 13½x13*

723 A241 60fr Log raft, crew hut .60 .25
724 A241 100fr Tugboat pushing logs 1.25 .35

Souvenir Sheets

Nos. 584, 635 Ovptd. with Exhibition in Black or Green

1985, Mar. 8 *Perf. 14x13½, 13*

725 A187 500fr TSUKUBA EXPO '85 5.00 4.50
726 A207 500fr ITALIA '85 emblem, ROME (G) 5.00 4.50

See Nos. C336-C337.

Zonocerus Variegatus — A242

1985, Mar. 15 *Perf. 13*

727 A242 125fr multicolored 1.50 .35

Burial of a Teke Chief — A243

1985, Apr. 30 *Perf. 12½*

728 A243 225fr multicolored 2.25 .75

Edible Fruit A244

Perf. 13½, 13 (#732A), 13½x13¼ (#732B)

1985, June 15

729 A244 5fr Trichoscypha acuminata, vert. .20 .20
730 A244 10fr Aframomum africanum .20 .20
730A A244 90fr like #730
731 A244 125fr Gambeya lacuurtiana 1.40 .40
732 A244 150fr Landolphia jumelei 1.75 .55
732A A244 205fr like #731
732B A244 300fr Like #732 — —

Sizes: #729, 22x36mm, #731, 732A, 36x22mm.

Nos. 730A, 732A, 732B inscribed "Congo" only.

For overprints, see Nos. 1170, 1183-1185.
Compare type A244 with type A352.

Lions Club Intl., 30th Anniv. — A245

1985, June 25 *Perf. 12½*

733 A245 250fr Flag, District 403B 2.25 .70

Russian Soldier, Kremlin, Fall of Berlin A246

1985, July 27 *Perf. 12*

734 A246 60fr multicolored .50 .20

Defeat of Nazi Germany, end of World War II, 40th anniv.

Lady Olave Baden-Powell, Girl Guides Founder — A247

Anniversaries and events: 150fr, Girl Guides, 75th anniv. 250fr, Jacob Grimm, fabulist; Sleeping Beauty. 350fr, Johann Sebastian Bach, composer; European Music Year, St. Thomas Church organ, Leipzig. 450fr, Queen Mother, 85th birthday, vert. 500fr, Statue of Liberty, cent., vert.

1985, Aug. 26 *Perf. 13*

735 A247 150fr multicolored 1.60 .50
736 A247 250fr multicolored 2.25 .90
737 A247 350fr multicolored 2.75 1.25
738 A247 450fr multicolored 3.50 1.50
739 A247 500fr multicolored 5.00 1.90
Nos. 735-739 (5) 15.10 6.05

PHILEXAFRICA '85, Lome, Togo, Nov. 16-24 — A248

1985, Oct. 10 *Perf. 13x12½*

740 A248 250fr shown 2.25 1.00
741 A248 250fr Airport, postal van 2.25 1.00
a. Pair, #740-741 + label 5.25 5.25

Mushrooms — A249

1985, Dec. 14 **Litho.** *Perf. 13*

742 A249 100fr Coprinus, vert. 1.25 .30
743 A249 150fr Cortinarius 2.00 .45
744 A249 200fr Armillariella mellea 2.75 .65
745 A249 300fr Dictyophora 3.50 1.00
746 A249 400fr Crucibulum vulgare 5.25 1.40
Nos. 742-746 (5) 14.75 3.80

Arbor Day — A250

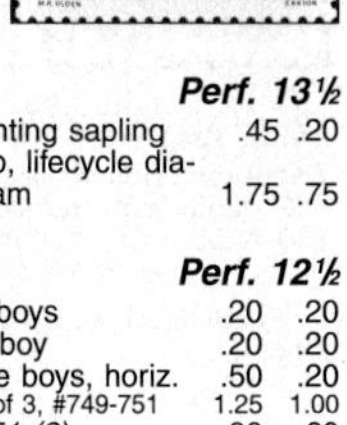

Children's Hoop Races — A251

1986, Mar. 6 *Perf. 13½*

747 A250 60fr Planting sapling .45 .20
748 A250 200fr Map, lifecycle diagram 1.75 .75

1986, Apr. 30 *Perf. 12½*

749 A251 5fr Two boys .20 .20
750 A251 10fr One boy .20 .20
751 A251 60fr Three boys, horiz. .50 .20
a. Souvenir sheet of 3, #749-751 1.25 1.00
Nos. 749-751 (3) .90 .60

A252

A253

1986, June 5 Litho. *Perf. 13½*

752 A252 60fr Garbage disposal .50 .20
753 A252 125fr Dumping garbage 1.00 .40

Intl. Environment Day.

1986, July 15 Litho. *Perf. 13x12½*

Traditional Modes of Transporting Goods: 5fr, Basket on head, child in sling carrier. 10fr, Child in carrier on hip, large basket strapped to forehead. 60fr, Man carrying load on shoulder.

754 A253 5fr multicolored .20 .20
755 A253 10fr multicolored .60 .25
756 A253 60fr multicolored .30 .20
Nos. 754-756 (3) 1.10 .65

Mission of the Sisters of St. Joseph of Cluny, Cent. A254

1986, Aug. 19 Litho. *Perf. 12½x13*

757 A254 230fr multicolored 2.25 .90

A255

A256

1986, Aug. 30 Litho. *Perf. 13½*

758 A255 40fr multicolored .45 .20
759 A255 60fr multicolored .55 .20
760 A255 100fr multicolored 1.00 .35
Nos. 758-760 (3) 2.00 .75

UNESCO intl. communications development program.

1986, Sept. 15 Litho. *Perf. 13½*

761 A256 100fr multicolored .90 .30

Intl. Peace Year.

World Food Day A257

1986, Oct. 16

762 A257 75fr Food staples .80 .25
763 A257 120fr Mother feeding child 1.25 .40

UN Child Survival Campaign A258

Mothers, children and pinwheels in various designs.

1986, Oct. 27

764 A258 15fr multi, vert. .20 .20
765 A258 30fr multi .25 .20
766 A258 70fr multi, vert. .70 .30
Nos. 764-766 (3) 1.15 .70

A258a

A259

1986, Dec. 5 Litho. *Perf. 12x12½*

766A A258a 100fr multicolored 1.50 .35

27th Soviet Communist Party congress.

1987, Feb. 10 Litho. *Perf. 13½*

767 A259 30fr multicolored .25 .20
768 A259 45fr multicolored .45 .20
769 A259 75fr multicolored .70 .25
770 A259 120fr multicolored 1.10 .35
Nos. 767-770 (4) 2.50 1.00

Election of President Sassou-Nguesso, head of the Organization of African States.

Traditional Wedding A260

1987, Feb. 18 Litho. *Perf. 12½x13*

771 A260 5fr multicolored .20 .20
772 A260 15fr multicolored .25 .20
773 A260 20fr multicolored .25 .20
Nos. 771-773 (3) .70 .60

The Blue Lake — A261

1987, July 16 *Perf. 12½*

774 A261 5fr multicolored .20 .20
775 A261 15fr multicolored .20 .20
776 A261 75fr multicolored 1.00 .30
777 A261 120fr multicolored 1.25 .40
Nos. 774-777 (4) 2.65 1.10

Pres. Marien Ngouabi A262

Congress of African Scientists A263

1987, July 18 *Perf. 13*

778 A262 75fr multicolored .70 .25
779 A262 120fr multicolored 1.00 .35

Tenth death anniv.

1987, Sept. 10 *Perf. 13x12½*

780 A263 15fr multicolored .20 .20
781 A263 90fr multicolored .70 .30
782 A263 230fr multicolored 2.00 .80
Nos. 780-782 (3) 2.90 1.30

4th African Games, Nairobi — A264

1987, Oct. 30 *Perf. 12½*

783 A264 75fr multicolored .60 .30
784 A264 120fr multicolored 1.10 .45

Raoul Follereau (1903-1977), Philanthropist — A265

1987, Oct. 20 *Perf. 13½*

785 A265 120fr multicolored 1.10 .45

Cure leprosy.

FAO, 40th Anniv. — A266

1987, Nov. 17 *Perf. 12½*

786 A266 300fr multicolored 2.25 1.10

Anti-Apartheid Campaign A267

Nelson Mandela A268

Perf. 13½x15, 14½x15

1987, Sept. 21 Litho.

787 A267 60fr multicolored .60 .20
788 A268 240fr multicolored 2.25 .75

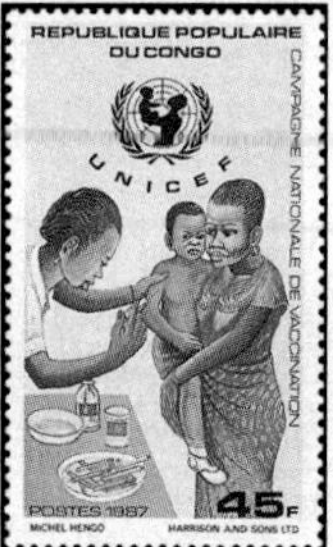
Natl. UNICEF Vaccination Campaign — A269

Africa Fund — A270

Perf. 13½x14½, 14½x13½

1987, Sept. 28

789 A269 30fr Inoculating adults, horiz. .25 .20
790 A269 45fr shown .50 .20
791 A269 500fr Inoculating children, horiz. 5.25 2.00
Nos. 789-791 (3) 6.00 2.40

No. 791 is airmail.

1987, Sept. 28 *Perf. 13½x15*

792 A270 25fr multicolored .20 .20
793 A270 50fr multicolored .35 .20
794 A270 70fr multicolored .70 .25
Nos. 792-794 (3) 1.25 .65

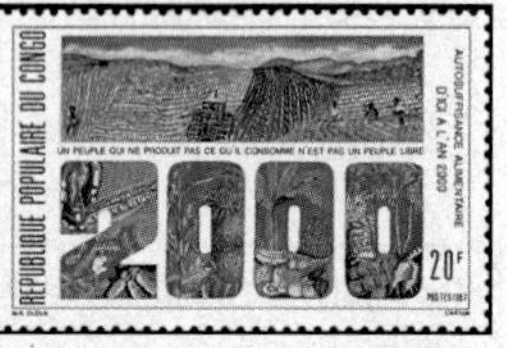
Self-sufficiency in Food Production by the Year 2000 — A271

1987, Nov. 20 Litho. *Perf. 13½*

795 A271 20fr multicolored .25 .20
796 A271 55fr multicolored .60 .20
797 A271 100fr multicolored 1.00 .35
Nos. 795-797 (3) 1.85 .75

Simon Kimbangu (b. 1887), Founder of the Church of Christ on Earth — A272

1987, Nov. 28 *Perf. 12½*

798 A272 75fr Kimbangu, vert. .70 .30
799 A272 120fr Kimbangu, parrot, vert. 1.10 .40
800 A272 240fr Kimbanguist Church, Nkamba 2.75 1.00
a. Souvenir sheet of 3, #798-800 5.75 5.00
Nos. 798-800 (3) 4.55 1.70

October Revolution, Russia, 70th Anniv. — A273

Lenin inspecting revolutionary troops, Red Square, from an unspecified painting.

1988, Feb. 19 Litho. *Perf. 12½x12*

801 A273 75fr multicolored 1.10 .30
802 A273 120fr multicolored 1.60 .40

African Writers Opposing Apartheid — A274

Intl. Fund for Agricultural Development (IFAD), 10th Anniv. — A275

1988, Apr. 6 Litho. *Perf. 13½*

803	A274	15fr multicolored	.20	.20
804	A274	60fr multicolored	.50	.25
805	A274	75fr multicolored	.80	.30
		Nos. 803-805 (3)	1.50	.75

For overprint see #1157.

1988, Apr. 30

806	A275	240fr multicolored	2.00	.85

Invention of the Telegraph by Samuel Morse, 150th Anniv. (in 1987) — A276

1988, Apr. 28

807	A276	90fr Morse, vert.	.90	.30
808	A276	120fr shown	1.10	.40

A277

A278

1988, Sept. 20 Litho. *Perf. 13½*

809	A277	5fr Eucalyptus trees, Brazzaville	.20	.20
810	A277	10fr Stop cutting down trees	.20	.20

Fight against desertification.

1988, Aug. 12 Litho. *Perf. 13½*

Campaigns: No. 812, Return to the Land Campaign (farming). 120fr, Self-sufficiency in food production.

811	A278	75fr shown	.60	.25
812	A278	75fr multicolored	.60	.25
813	A278	120fr multicolored	.90	.40
		Nos. 811-813 (3)	2.10	.90

Congo Revolution, 25th anniv.

Yoro Fishing Village A279

1988, Sept. 1

814	A279	35fr shown	.45	.20
815	A279	40fr Liberty Place	.45	.20

Intl. Day for the Fight Against AIDS A280

1988, Dec. 1 Litho. *Perf. 13½*

816	A280	60fr shown	.45	.20
817	A280	75fr Emblem	.70	.20
818	A280	180fr Modified UN emblem, campaign emblem	1.75	.60
		Nos. 816-818 (3)	2.90	1.00

Natl. Committee for the Fight Against AIDS and Evangelical Anglican Church of Congo anti-AIDS campaign.

February 5 Movement, 10th Anniv. A281

1989, Apr. 21 Litho. *Perf. 13½*

819	A281	75fr Rally	.60	.25
820	A281	120fr Pres. Sassou-Nguesso, natl. achievements	.90	.35

UN Declaration of Human Rights, 40th Anniv. (in 1988) A282

1989, May 19 *Perf. 13*

821	A282	120fr multicolored	.90	.40
822	A282	350fr multicolored	2.25	1.10

Marien Nguabi, Founder of Congo Labor Party A282a

1989, July 31 Litho. *Perf. 12½x13*

822A	A282a	240fr red & yellow	2.00	.75

Red Cross and Red Crescent Societies, 125th Annivs. A283

120fr, Dunant, emblem, Congo Red Cross.

1989, Sept. 19 Litho. *Perf. 13*

823	A283	75fr shown	.60	.35
824	A283	120fr multicolored	1.00	.65

No. 824 is airmail.

Organization of African Unity, 25th Anniv. — A284

1989, Oct. 19 Litho. *Perf. 12½*

825	A284	120fr multicolored	1.10	.40

African Development Bank, 25th Anniv. — A285

1989, Dec. 22 Litho. *Perf. 12½x13*

826	A285	75fr multicolored	.60	.30
827	A285	120fr multicolored	1.00	.40

WHO, 40th Anniv. (in 1988) A286

1989, Dec. 28 Litho. *Perf. 12½*

828	A286	60fr shown	.60	.20
829	A286	75fr Blood donation, vert.	.70	.30

See Nos. 846-847 for overprints.

Congo Labor Party (PCT), 20th Anniv. — A287

1989, Dec. 22 Litho. *Perf. 13x12½*

830	A287	75fr multicolored	.60	.30
831	A287	120fr multicolored	1.10	.40

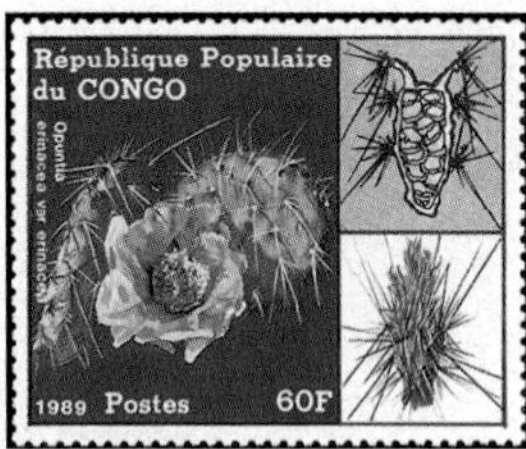

Cacti A288

Perf. 12½x13, 13x12½

1989, Nov. 22

832	A288	35fr *Opuntia phaeacantha discata*	.35	.20
833	A288	40fr *Opuntia ficus indica*	.50	.20
834	A288	60fr *Opuntia erinacea*	.90	.25
835	A288	75fr *Opuntia rufida*	1.25	.30
836	A288	120fr *Opuntia leptocaulis*	1.75	.45
		Nos. 832-836 (5)	4.75	1.40

Souvenir Sheet

Perf. 12½

837	A288	220fr *Opuntia compresa*	5.00	2.10

Nos. 832-833, 835 and 837 vert. No. 837 contains one 32x40mm stamp.

1992 Winter Olympics, Albertville A289

1989, Dec. 22 *Perf. 12½*

838	A289	75fr Ice dancing	.60	.25
839	A289	80fr Nordic skiing	.60	.30
840	A289	100fr Speed skating	.90	.35
841	A289	120fr Luge	1.10	.45
842	A289	200fr Alpine skiing	1.75	.70
843	A289	240fr Ice hockey	2.25	.85
844	A289	400fr Ski jumping	3.25	1.40
		Nos. 838-844 (7)	10.45	4.30

Souvenir Sheet

Perf. 13

845	A289	500fr Bobsled	4.50	2.40

No. 845 contains one 32x40mm stamp.

Nos. 828-829 Ovptd. "NOTRE PLANETE, NOTRE SANTE PENSER GLOBALEMENT AGIR LOCALEMENT" in 3 or 5 Lines

1989, Dec. 28 *Perf. 12½*

846	A286	60fr multicolored	.60	.20
847	A286	75fr multicolored	.70	.30

Health care for everyone.

Intl. Literacy Year — A290

1990, June 26 Litho. *Perf. 13½*

848	A290	75fr bl, blk & yel	.60	.30

Birds A291

Designs: 25fr, Tourterelle des bois. 50fr, Fauvette pitchou, vert. 70fr, Faucon crecerelle, vert. 150fr, Perroquet gris, vert.

1990, July 10

849 A291 25fr multicolored .35 .25
850 A291 50fr multicolored .70 .30
851 A291 70fr multicolored 1.10 .55
852 A291 150fr multicolored 2.10 1.25
Nos. 849-852 (4) 4.25 2.35

Dance Masks — A292

Flowering Plants — A293

1990, July 24 *Perf. 13*

853 A292 120fr Mondo 1.10 .40
854 A292 360fr Bapunu 3.50 1.25
855 A292 400fr Kwele 4.00 1.50
Nos. 853-855 (3) 8.60 3.15

For overprint see #1172.

1990, Sept. 15 Litho. *Perf. 12½*

856 A293 30fr Tournesol (sunflower) .25 .20
857 A293 45fr Cassia alata, horiz. .45 .20
858 A293 75fr Oeillette (opium poppy) .70 .25
859 A293 90fr Acalypha sanderil 1.00 .35
Nos. 856-859 (4) 2.40 1.00

1992 Summer Olympics, Barcelona — A294

1990, June 28 Litho. *Perf. 13½*

860 A294 100fr Street scene, vert. .80 .30
861 A294 150fr shown 1.25 .35
862 A294 200fr Sailing, diff. 1.60 .40
863 A294 240fr Marketplace 2.00 .55
864 A294 350fr Harbor 3.00 .75
865 A294 500fr Monument, vert. 4.25 .90
Nos. 860-865 (6) 12.90 3.25

Souvenir Sheet

866 A294 750fr Cathedral, vert. 5.00 3.50

Nos. 864-865 airmail. Nos. 860-865 exist in miniature sheets of 1.

Royal Necklaces A295

1990, Aug. 18 Litho. *Perf. 13½*

867 A295 75fr shown .60 .25
868 A295 100fr Necklace, diff. .90 .30

Boy Scouts Observing Nature A296

Scout: 35fr, Photographing butterfly, Euphaedra eusimoides. 40fr, Picking mushrooms, Armillaria mellea. 75fr, Drawing butterfly, Palla decius. 80fr, Using magnifying glass, Kallima ansorgei. 500fr, Using microscope, Cortinarius speciosissimus. 600fr, Feeding butterfly, Graphium illyris. 1500fr, Photographing butterfly, Berberia plistonax, horiz. 750fr, Photographing mushrooms, Volvariella bombycina.

1991, June 8 Litho. *Perf. 13½*

869 A296 35fr multicolored .20 .20
870 A296 40fr multicolored .45 .20
871 A296 75fr multicolored .60 .20
872 A296 80fr multicolored .70 .20
873 A296 500fr multicolored 4.00 1.25
874 A296 600fr multicolored 4.00 1.25
a. Min. sheet of 4, #869, 871-872, 874 7.50 3.75
Nos. 869-874 (6) 9.95 3.30

Litho. & Embossed

874B A296 1500fr gold & multi — —

Souvenir Sheet

875 A296 750fr multicolored 5.25 2.25

Nos. 869-874 exist in souvenir sheets of 1. Nos. 873-875 are airmail.

Medicinal Plants — A297

Designs: 15fr, Ocimum viride. 20fr, Kalanchoe pinnata, vert. 30fr, Euphorbia hirta. 60fr, Catharanthus roseus, vert. 75fr, Bidens pilosa, vert. 100fr, Brillantaisia patula, vert. 120fr, Cassia occidentalis, vert.

1991, Jan. 30 Litho. *Perf. 11½*

876 A297 15fr multicolored .20 .20
877 A297 20fr multicolored .20 .20
878 A297 30fr multicolored .25 .20
879 A297 60fr multicolored .50 .20
880 A297 75fr multicolored .60 .25
881 A297 100fr multicolored .80 .30
882 A297 120fr multicolored 1.00 .35
Nos. 876-882 (7) 3.55 1.70

Mushrooms A298

1991, Mar. 25 Litho. *Perf. 13*

883 A298 30fr Amanita rubescens .25 .20
883A A298 45fr Catathelasma imperiale .30 .20
883B A298 75fr Amanita caesarea .60 .25
883C A298 90fr Boletus regius .90 .25
883D A298 120fr Pluteus cervinus 1.00 .40
883E A298 150fr Boletus chrysenteron 1.25 .60
883F A298 200fr Agaricus arvensis 1.75 .75
Nos. 883-883F (7) 6.05 2.65

Souvenir Sheet

Perf. 12½

883G A298 350fr Boletus versipellis, horiz. *3.50 1.90*

No. 883G contains one 40x32mm stamp.

Trains A298a

Designs: 75fr, TGV, France. 120fr, S350, Italy. 200fr, DE24000, Turkey. 250fr, DE1024, Germany.

1991, Apr. 10 Litho. *Perf. 12½x12¼*

883I A298a 75fr multi .60 .25
883J A298a 120fr multi 1.00 .35
883K A298a 200fr multi 1.60 .60
883L A298a 250fr multi 2.10 .80

An additional stamp was issued in this set. The editors would like to examine it.

African Tourism Year — A299

1991, Apr. 15 Litho. *Perf. 13½*

884 A299 75fr shown .60 .30
885 A299 120fr Zebra, map 1.00 .45

Allegory of New Republic — A300

1991, May 13 Litho. *Perf. 13*

888 A300 15fr blue .20 .20
890 A300 30fr brt grn .20 .20
893 A300 60fr org yel .30 .20
894 A300 75fr brt pink .45 .25
898 A300 120fr dk brown .70 .40
Nos. 888-898 (5) 1.85 1.25

This is an expanding set. Numbers will change if necessary.

Trans-Siberian Railroad, Cent. — A301

1991, June 6 Litho. *Perf. 13*

899 A301 120fr Map 1.50 .35
900 A301 240fr Map, train 2.25 .60

Telecom 91 — A302

1991, June 29 Litho. *Perf. 13*

901 A302 75fr multicolored .60 .30
902 A302 120fr multi, vert. 1.00 .45

6th World Forum and Exposition on Telecommunications, Geneva, Switzerland.

Insects — A303

A304

1991, July 2 *Perf. 12½*

903 A303 75fr Peanut beetle .90 .25
904 A303 120fr Centaur, horiz. 1.00 .35
905 A303 200fr Coffee beetle 1.60 .65
906 A303 300fr Goliath beetle 2.75 1.00
Nos. 903-906 (4) 6.25 2.25

1991, July 16 Litho. *Perf. 12½*

907 A304 75fr Water conservation .60 .30

Amnesty Intl., 30th Anniv. A305

Designs: 40fr, Candle, sun, vert. 75fr, "30," broken chains, vert.

1991, Aug. 13 *Perf. 13½*

908 A305 40fr multicolored .35 .20
909 A305 75fr multicolored .60 .25
910 A305 80fr multicolored .70 .35
Nos. 908-910 (3) 1.65 .80

Congo Postage Stamps, Cent. — A306

75fr, Similar to French Congo #1. 120fr, Similar to French Congo #35. 240fr, Similar to Congo Republic #89. 500fr, Similar to French Congo #1, 35 and Congo Republic #89.

Litho. & Engr.

1991, Aug. *Perf. 13x13½*

911 A306 75fr beige & dk grn .80 .30
912 A306 120fr beige, dk grn & brn 1.10 .45
913 A306 240fr multicolored 2.25 1.10
914 A306 500fr multicolored 4.50 2.00
a. Strip of 4, #911-914 10.00 9.00

Ducks A307

1991, Aug. 8 Litho. *Perf. 12½*

915 A307 75fr Anas acuta 1.00 .30
916 A307 120fr Somateria mollissima, vert. 1.25 .45
917 A307 200fr Anas clypeata, vert. 1.75 .75
918 A307 240fr Anas platyrhynchos 3.00 1.00
Nos. 915-918 (4) 7.00 2.50

Automobiles and Space — A308

Designs: 35fr, Ferrari 512S by Pininfarina. 40fr, Vincenzo Lancia, Lancia Stratos by Bertone. 75fr, Maybach Zeppelin type 12, Wilhelm Maybach. 80fr, Mars Observer, 1992. 500fr, Magellan probe surveying Venus. 600fr, Magnification of Sun, Ulysses probe. 750fr, Crew of Apollo 11.

1991, Aug. 23 Litho. *Perf. 13½*

919 A308 35fr multicolored .30 .20
920 A308 40fr multicolored .30 .20
921 A308 75fr multicolored .60 .30
922 A308 80fr multicolored .65 .30
923 A308 500fr multicolored 4.00 2.00
924 A308 600fr multicolored 4.75 2.40
Nos. 919-924 (6) 10.60 5.40

Souvenir Sheet

925 A308 750fr multicolored 6.00 3.00

Nos. 923-925 are airmail. No. 925 contains one 60x42mm stamp.

Butterflies A309

1991, Aug. 31 *Perf. 11½*

926 A309 75fr Petit bleu 1.00 .30
927 A309 120fr Charaxe 1.25 .50
928 A309 240fr Papillon feuille, vert. 1.75 .80
929 A309 300fr Papillon de l'oranger, vert. 3.00 1.00
Nos. 926-929 (4) 7.00 2.60

For overprints see Nos. 1156, 1165.

Celebrities and Organizations — A310

Designs: 100fr, Bo Jackson, baseball and football player. 150fr, Nick Faldo, golfer. 200fr, Rickey Henderson, Barry Bonds, baseball players. 240fr, Garry Kasparov, World Chess Champion. 300fr, Starving child, Lions and Rotary Clubs emblems. 350fr, Wolfgang Amadeus Mozart. 400fr, De Gaulle, Churchill. 500fr, Jean-Henri Dunant, founder of Red Cross. 750fr, De Gaulle, vert.

1991, Sept. 2 *Perf. 13½*

930 A310 100fr multicolored .85 .40
931 A310 150fr multicolored 1.25 .60
932 A310 200fr multicolored 1.60 .80
933 A310 240fr multicolored 1.90 .95
934 A310 300fr multicolored 2.40 1.25
935 A310 350fr multicolored 2.75 1.40
936 A310 400fr multicolored 3.25 1.60
937 A310 500fr multicolored 4.00 2.00
Nos. 930-937 (8) 18.00 9.00

Souvenir Sheet

938 A310 750fr multicolored 6.00 3.00

Nos. 936-938 are airmail. No. 938 contains one 35x50mm stamp.

Gen. Charles de Gaulle in Africa — A311

120fr, De Gaulle, Free French flag, vert. 240fr, De Gaulle, Appeal of Brazzaville, 1940.

1991, Sept. 2 *Perf. 13½x13, 13x13½*

939 A311 75fr multicolored .60 .30
940 A311 120fr multicolored .95 .45
941 A311 240fr multicolored 1.90 .95
Nos. 939-941 (3) 3.45 1.70

A312

Paintings — A313

1991, Oct. 12 *Perf. 11½*

942 A312 75fr multicolored .60 .30
943 A313 120fr multicolored .95 .45

Discovery of America, 500th Anniv. (in 1992) — A314

20fr, Portrait of Christopher Columbus by Sebastian Del Pombo. 35fr, Portrait of Columbus. 40fr, Portrait of Columbus facing right. 55fr, Santa Maria. 75fr, Nina. 150fr, Pinta. 200fr, Arms & signature of Columbus.

1991, May 30 *Perf. 13*

944 A314 20fr multicolored .20 .20
945 A314 35fr multicolored .30 .20
946 A314 40fr multicolored .30 .20
947 A314 55fr multicolored .45 .25
948 A314 75fr multicolored .60 .30
949 A314 150fr multicolored 1.25 .60
950 A314 200fr multicolored 1.60 .80
Nos. 944-950 (7) 4.70 2.55

Primates A315

1991, Dec. 13 Litho. *Perf. 13*

951 A315 30fr Cercopithecus diana .20 .20
952 A315 45fr Pan troglodytes .25 .25
953 A315 60fr Theropithecus gelada .60 .25
954 A315 75fr Papio hamadryas .80 .30
955 A315 90fr Macaca nemestrina 1.00 .40
956 A315 120fr Gorilla gorilla 1.10 .40
957 A315 240fr Mandrillus sphinx 2.25 .50
Nos. 951-957 (7) 6.20 2.30

Nos. 953-957 are vert. A number has been reserved for a souvenir sheet with this set.

Anniversaries and Events A316

Designs: 50fr, Launching of Sputnik II with dog, Laika, 1957. 75fr, Mahatma Gandhi and Martin Luther King, Jr. 1964. 120fr, Launching of Meteosat and ERS-1 over Europe and Africa. 240fr, Maybach Zeppelin automobile and Ferdinand von Zeppelin, 75th death anniversary. 300fr, Konrad Adenauer, 25th death anniversary and opening of the Brandenburg Gate, 1989. 500fr, Pope John Paul II's visit to Africa. 600fr, Elvis Presley, American entertainer.

1992, Feb. 4 Litho. *Perf. 13½*

959 A316 50fr multicolored .40 .20
960 A316 75fr multicolored .60 .30
961 A316 120fr multicolored .95 .50
962 A316 240fr multicolored 1.90 .95
963 A316 300fr multicolored 2.40 1.10
964 A316 500fr multicolored 4.00 2.00
a. Souvenir sheet of 3, #960, 963-964 11.50 5.75
Nos. 959-964 (6) 10.25 5.05

Souvenir Sheet

965 A316 600fr multicolored 4.70 2.35

Nos. 959-964 exist in souvenir sheets of 1. Nos. 962, 964-965 are airmail.

Explorers A317

Birds — A318

Genoa '92: 75fr, Juan de la Cosa, nautical chart. 95fr, Martin Alonso Pinzon, astrolabe. 120fr, Alonso de Ojeda, hour glass. 200fr, Vicente Yanez Pinzon, sun dial. 250fr, Bartholomew Columbus, quadrant.

1992, Oct. 21 Litho. *Perf. 13*

966 A317 75fr multicolored 1.00 .30
967 A317 95fr multicolored 1.10 .30
968 A317 120fr multicolored 1.75 .30
969 A317 200fr multicolored 2.25 .40
970 A317 250fr multicolored 2.75 .50
Nos. 966-970 (5) 8.85 1.80

A number has been reserved for a souvenir sheet with this set.

1992, Oct. 21

Designs: 60fr, Sagittarius serpentarius. 75fr, Ephippiorhynchus senegalensis. 120fr, Bugeranus carunculatus. 200fr, Ardea melanocephala. 250fr, Phoenicopterus ruber roseus.

972 A318 60fr multicolored .70 .20
973 A318 75fr multicolored .80 .20
974 A318 120fr multicolored 1.10 .30
975 A318 200fr multicolored 2.00 .40
976 A318 250fr multicolored 2.75 .50
Nos. 972-976 (5) 7.35 1.60

A number has been reserved for a souvenir sheet with this set.

Wild Cats — A319

1992, Nov. 21 Litho. *Perf. 13*

978 A319 45fr Panthera leo .50 .50
979 A319 60fr Panthera tigris .60 .60
980 A319 75fr Lynx lynx .70 .70
981 A319 95fr Caracal caracal .80 .80
982 A319 250fr Leopardus pardalis 2.25 2.25
Nos. 978-982 (5) 4.85 4.85

Souvenir Sheet

983 A319 400fr Acinonyx jubatus 4.50 1.75

No. 983 contains one 32x40mm stamp.

1992 Winter Olympics, Albertville — A320

1992 Summer Olympics, Barcelona A321

Gold medalists: 150fr, N. Mishkutyonok, A. Dmitriev, pairs figure skating, Unified team. 200fr, I. Appelt, H. Winkler, G. Haldacher, T. Schroll, 4-man bobsled, Austria. 500fr, Gunda Niemann, speed skating, Germany. 600fr, Bjorn Daehlie, cross-country skiing, Norway. 750fr, Alberto Tomba, giant slalom, Italy.

1992, Dec. 21 Litho. *Perf. 13½*

984 A320 150fr multicolored 1.25 1.25
985 A320 200fr multicolored 1.60 1.60
986 A320 500fr multicolored 4.00 4.00
987 A320 600fr multicolored 4.75 4.75
Nos. 984-987 (4) 11.60 11.60

Souvenir Sheet

988 A320 750fr multicolored 6.00 6.00

Nos. 986-988 are airmail. No. 988 contains one 35x50mm stamp. Name on No. 987 spelled incorrectly.

1992, Dec. 21

Barcelona landmarks, Olympic event: 75fr, Steeple of La Sagrada Familia, baseball. 100fr, The Muse, Palace of Music, running. 150fr, Cupola interior, long jump. 200fr, St. Paul Hospital, pole vault. 400fr, Sculpture, by Miro, shot put. 500fr, Galley, Maritime Museum, table tennis. 750fr, La Sagrada Familia, tennis.

989 A321 75fr multicolored .60 .30
990 A321 100fr multicolored .80 .40
991 A321 150fr multicolored 1.25 .60
992 A321 200fr multicolored 1.60 .80
993 A321 400fr multicolored 3.25 3.25
994 A321 500fr multicolored 4.00 4.00
Nos. 989-994 (6) 11.50 9.35

Souvenir Sheet

995 A321 750fr multicolored 6.00 6.00

Nos. 993-995 are airmail.

Christmas A321a

Paintings: 95fr, The Madonna of the Grand Duke, by Raphael. 200fr, The Madonna with a Book, by Botticelli. 250fr, The Madonna Carondelet, by Fra Bartolommeo. 400fr, Madonna and Child, by Raphael.

1992, Dec. 20 Litho. *Perf. 12½*

995A A321 95fr multicolored 1.25 .30
995B A321 200fr multicolored 2.75 .75
995C A321 250fr multicolored 3.25 1.25
Nos. 995A-995C (3) 7.25 2.30

Souvenir Sheet

995D A321 400fr multicolored 4.50 1.90

Nos. 995A-995D were not available until late 1993.

Birds of Prey — A322

A323

1993, Jan. 15 Litho. *Perf. 12½x13*

996 A322 45fr Charognard .50 .20
997 A322 75fr Vulture 1.50 .30
998 A322 120fr Eagle 2.00 .65
Nos. 996-998 (3) 4.00 1.15

1993, Dec. 21 Litho. *Perf. 13½*

Traditional ceramics.

999 A323 45fr Liloko .35 .20
1000 A323 75fr Mbeya .65 .30
1001 A323 120fr Jug with ladles, Mbeya 1.00 .50
Nos. 999-1001 (3) 2.00 1.00

1994 World Cup Soccer Championships, United States — A324

Design: 250fr, Goalie catching ball.

1993, Jan. 15 Litho. *Perf. 12¾*

1006 A324 250fr multi — —

Five additional stamps were issued in this set. The editors would like to examine any examples.

Wild Animals A325

Designs: 60fr, Damaliscus lunatus. 75fr, Gazella granti. 95fr, Equus quagga. 120fr, Panthera pardus. 200fr, Syncerus caffer. 250fr, Hippopotamus ampibius. 350fr, Panthera leo.

1993, Feb. 20 Litho. *Perf. 13*

1008 A325 60fr Damaliscus lunatus .60 .20
1009 A325 75fr Gazella granti .80 .20
1010 A325 95fr Equus quagga 1.10 .25
1011 A325 120fr Panthera pardus 1.25 .25
1012 A325 200fr Syncerus caffer 2.10 .25
1013 A325 250fr Hippopotamus amphibius 2.75 .35
1014 A325 300fr Necrosyrtes monachu 3.00 .35
1015 A325 350fr Panthera leo 3.25 .60
a. Sheet of 8, #1008-1015 20.00 20.00
Nos. 1008-1015 (8) 14.85 2.45

No. 1015a is a continuous design.

Wild Flowers — A326

Designs: 75fr, Hibiscus schizopetalus. 95fr, Pentas lanceolata. 120fr, Ricinus communis. 200fr, Delonix regia. 250fr, Stapelia gigantea.

1993, May 20 Litho. *Perf. 12½*

1016 A326 75fr multicolored *1.25 .30*
1017 A326 95fr multicolored *1.75 .40*
1018 A326 120fr multicolored *3.00 .50*
1019 A326 200fr multicolored *5.25 1.00*
1020 A326 250fr multicolored *6.50 1.60*
Nos. 1016-1020 (5) *17.75 3.80*

Deep Sea Submersibles A327

1993, June 25

1021 A327 75fr Transport PC-1202 *1.60 .75*
1022 A327 95fr J. Sea Link 1 *2.00 1.00*
1023 A327 120fr Nemo *2.50 1.25*
1024 A327 200fr Robot *4.25 2.25*
1025 A327 250fr Alvin *5.50 2.75*
Nos. 1021-1025 (5) *15.85 8.00*

Souvenir Sheet

1026 A327 400fr Star III *9.00 6.75*

No. 1026 contains one 32x40mm stamp.

1996 Summer Olympic Games, Atlanta A329

Designs: 50fr, Equestrian. 75fr, Cycling. 120fr, Sailing. 240fr, shown. 300fr, Hurdles. 500fr, Women's basketball. 750fr, Running.

1993, Apr. 26 Litho. *Perf. 13½*

1030-1035 A329 Set of 6 10.00 4.00
1035a Sheet of 6, #1030-1035 10.00 5.00

Souvenir Sheet

1036 A329 750fr multicolored 6.50 1.50

Nos. 1030-1036 exist imperf. Nos. 1030-1035 exist in souvenir sheets of 1.

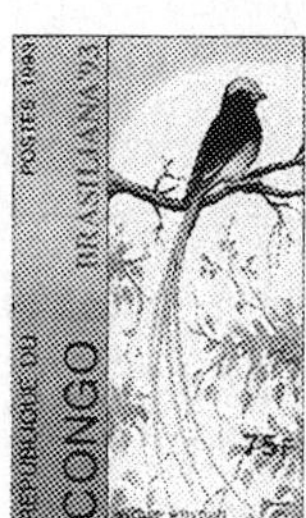

Brasiliana '93 — A330

Birds: 75fr, Vidua whydah. 95fr, Vidua regia. 120fr, Steganura paradisea. 200fr, Vidua macroura. 250fr, Anthreptes platura. 400fr, Coliuspasser macrourus, horiz.

1993, July 15 Litho. *Perf. 12x12½*

1037-1041 A330 Set of 5 13.00 13.00

Souvenir Sheet

1042 A330 400fr multicolored 12.00 12.00

Prehistoric Animals — A331

1993, Aug. 20 Litho. *Perf. 13*

1043 A331 75fr Ichthyostega *1.75 1.25*
1044 A331 95fr Archaeopteryx *2.25 1.60*
1045 A331 120fr Brachiosaurus *3.00 2.10*
1046 A331 200fr Tyrannosaurus *4.75 3.50*
1047 A331 250fr Pteranodon, vert. *6.50 4.25*
Nos. 1043-1047 (5) *18.25 12.70*

Souvenir Sheet

1048 A331 400fr Brontosaurus *13.00 6.50*

No. 1048 contains one 32x40mm stamp.

Powered Flight, 90th Anniv. — A332

Designs: 75fr, Wilbur Wright, Model B airplane, vert. 95fr, Orville Wright and Model B biplane, vert. 120fr, First flight by Orville Wright. 200fr, Flight at Kitty Hawk.

Perf. 12¼x12½, 12½x12¼

1993, Dec. 17 Litho.

1049 A332 75fr multi .90 .90
1050 A332 95fr multi 1.10 1.10
1051 A332 120fr multi 1.25 1.25
1052 A332 200fr multi 2.25 2.25

A number has been reserved for an additional stamp in this set. The editors would like to examine it.

Evolution of the Elephant A333

1994, June 20 Litho. *Perf. 12½*

1054 A333 25fr Palaeomastodon *1.00 .50*
1055 A333 45fr Mammut *1.75 .90*
1056 A333 50fr Amebelodon *2.00 1.00*
1057 A333 75fr Platybelodon *3.00 1.50*
1058 A333 120fr Mammuthus *4.75 2.40*
Nos. 1054-1058 (5) *12.50 6.30*

Protection of Nature — A335

Designs: 50fr, Choeropsis liberiensis. 90fr, Hyemoschus aquaticus. 205fr, Taurotragus euryceros, vert. 300fr, Redunca redunca, vert.

1994, Aug. 27 Litho. *Perf. 12½*

1063 A335 50fr multicolored *.65 .30*
1064 A335 90fr multicolored *1.10 .30*
1065 A335 205fr multicolored *2.50 1.10*
1066 A335 300fr multicolored *3.25 1.60*
Nos. 1063-1066 (4) *7.50 3.30*

For overprint see #1167.

Seaplanes — A336

Designs: 30fr, Cant Z-505, Italy. 45fr, Martin Mariner PBM-3, US. No. 1069, E-59, Russia. No. 1070, Short Sunderland, Great Britain. No. 1071, Martin Mars XPB2M-1, US. 400fr, Boeing 314, US.

1994, Sept. 2 Litho. *Perf. 12½*

1067 A336 30fr multicolored *.40 .40*
1068 A336 45fr multicolored *.65 .65*
1069 A336 90fr multicolored *1.50 1.50*
1070 A336 90fr multicolored *1.50 1.50*
1071 A336 90fr multicolored *1.50 1.50*
Nos. 1067-1071 (5) *5.55 5.55*

Souvenir Sheet

1071A A336 400fr multicolored *5.00 2.50*

No. 1071A contains one 40x32mm stamp.

Intl. Year of the Family — A337

1995, Jan. 28 Litho. *Perf. 12½*

1072 A337 90fr shown *1.10 .40*
1073 A337 205fr African map, child *2.25 1.00*
1074 A337 300fr Family, native huts *3.50 1.50*
Nos. 1072-1074 (3) *6.85 2.90*

For overprint see No. 1168.

Insects — A338

1994, July 24 Litho. *Perf. 12½*

1075 A338 90fr Tarantula *1.90 .40*
1076 A338 205fr Spider *4.50 1.10*
1077 A338 240fr Ladybug *5.00 1.25*
Nos. 1075-1077 (3) *11.40 2.75*

Souvenir Sheet

1078 A338 400fr Bee *4.75 2.00*

Costumes — A338a

1995 Litho. *Perf. 12¾x12½*

1078A A338a 90fr M'Bochi .95 .50
1078B A338a 205fr Téké 1.25 .80
1078C A338a 500fr Loango 3.75 1.40
Nos. 1078A-1078C (3) *5.95 2.70*

Rotary Intl., 90th Anniv. A339

Designs: 90fr, Polio victim. No. 1080, Playing ball with children. No. 1081, Children with food. 300fr, Delivering polio vaccine.
1500fr, Paul Harris, Rotary emblem.

1996, Feb. 6 Litho. *Perf. 14*

1079 A339 90fr multicolored .60 .25
1080 A339 205fr multicolored 1.25 .50
1081 A339 205fr multicolored 1.25 .50
1082 A339 300fr multicolored 1.60 .60
Nos. 1079-1082 (4) 4.70 1.85

Souvenir Sheet

1083 A339 1500fr multicolored 7.50 3.25

18th World Scout Jamboree, The Netherlands - A340

Designs: No. 1084, Handshake. No. 1085, Scout helping another with arm sling. 205fr, Saving life in water. 300fr, Lord Baden-Powell.
1000fr, Scout salute.

1996, Feb. 6 Litho. *Perf. 14*

1084 A340 90fr multicolored .45 .20
1085 A340 90fr multicolored .45 .20
1086 A340 205fr multicolored 1.10 .40
1087 A340 300fr multicolored 1.75 .50
Nos. 1084-1087 (4) 3.75 1.30

Souvenir Sheet

1088 A340 1000fr multicolored 4.25 2.10

1998 World Cup Soccer Tournament A340a

Various players. Denominations: 90fr, 150fr, 205fr, 300fr, 400fr, 500fr.

1996 Litho. *Perf. 12¾*

1088A-1088F A340a Set of 6 7.25 7.25

Souvenir Sheet

Perf. 13¼x13

1088G A340a 1000fr Player's legs 4.50 4.50

No. 1088G contains one 40x31mm stamp.

Antique Automobiles — A341

90fr, 1936 Armstrong Siddeley Twelve. 150fr, 1935 Aston Martin Mark II. 205fr, 1938 Morris 8. 300fr, 1955-62 MG Series MGA. 400fr, 1932 SS1. 500fr, 1938 Alvis 25 SB.

1996, Apr. 30 Litho. *Perf. 12½x12*

1089 A341 90fr multicolored .45 .20
1090 A341 150fr multicolored .75 .40
1091 A341 205fr multicolored 1.00 .50
1092 A341 300fr multicolored 1.50 .75
1093 A341 400fr multicolored 2.00 1.00
1094 A341 500fr multicolored 2.50 1.25
Nos. 1089-1094 (6) 8.20 4.10

Domestic Cats — A342

90fr, Persian. 150fr, Siamese. 205fr, Norwegian forest. 300fr, Exotic shorthair. 400fr, Maine coon. 500fr, Red abyssinian.
1000fr, Turkish Angora.

1996, Mar. 10 *Perf. 13x12½*

1095 A342 90fr multicolored .45 .20
1096 A342 150fr multicolored .75 .40
1097 A342 205fr multicolored 1.00 .50
1098 A342 300fr multicolored 1.50 .75
1099 A342 400fr multicolored 2.00 1.00
1100 A342 500fr multicolored 2.50 1.25
Nos. 1095-1100 (6) 8.20 4.10

Souvenir Sheet

1101 A342 1000fr multicolored 5.00 2.50

No. 1101 contains one 32x40mm stamp.

1996 Summer Olympic Games, Atlanta A343

1996 *Perf. 13x12½, 12½x13*

1102 A343 90fr Fencing, vert. .50 .25
1103 A343 150fr Archery, vert. .80 .40
1104 A343 205fr Basketball, vert. 1.10 .55
1105 A343 300fr Baseball, vert. 1.60 .80
1106 A343 400fr Volleyball 2.25 1.10
1107 A343 500fr 2-man kayak 2.50 1.25
Nos. 1102-1107 (6) 8.75 4.35

Souvenir Sheet

1108 A343 1000fr Judo, vert. 5.25 2.50

No. 1108 contains one 32x40mm stamp.

Flowers — A344

Designs: 90fr, Nerium oleander. 150fr, Eucaliptus globulus. 205fr, Centaurea cyanus. 300fr, Coffea arabica. 400fr, Hibiscus sabdariffa. 500fr, Cassia angustifolia.

1996, May 10 *Perf. 12½*

1109 A344 90fr multicolored .50 .25
1110 A344 150fr multicolored .80 .40
1111 A344 205fr multicolored 1.10 .55
1112 A344 300fr multicolored 1.60 .80
1113 A344 400fr multicolored 2.25 1.10
1114 A344 500fr multicolored 2.50 1.25
Nos. 1109-1114 (6) 8.75 4.35

Mother Carrying Baby — A345

1996 Litho. *Perf. 13*

1115 A345 40fr blue *4.00 2.00*
1116 A345 50fr violet brown *5.00 2.50*
1117 A345 90fr orange *9.00 4.50*
1118 A345 100fr green blue *10.00 5.00*
1119 A345 115fr gray *11.00 5.50*
1120 A345 205fr brown *20.00 10.00*
Nos. 1115-1120 (6) 59.00 29.50

It has been stated that this set was not issued.
See #1145-1150.

A346

Owls — A347

1996, Aug. 31 Litho. *Perf. 13½*

1121 A346 90fr orange & multi .45 .30
1122 A346 205fr green & multi 1.00 .60

Investiture of Pres. Pascal Lissouba, 4th anniv.

1996, Mar. 29 *Perf. 14½*

1123 A347 90fr Tyto alba .70 .25
1124 A347 205fr Bubo poensis 1.40 .50
1125 A347 300fr Scotopelia peli 2.00 .90
1126 A347 500fr Asio capensis 3.25 1.50
Nos. 1123-1126 (4) 7.35 3.15

Military Aircraft — A348

Designs: 90fr, Vought-Sikorsky Vindicator SB2U-1. 150fr, Grumman Wildcat F4F-3. 205fr, North American SNJ-2. 300fr, Brewster Bermuda. 400fr, Blackburn Skua 1. 500fr, Mitsubishi Type 98-1.
1000fr, P-40 Warhawk (Flying Tigers).

1996, June 24 Litho. *Perf. 12½x12*

1127 A348 90fr multicolored .45 .20
1128 A348 150fr multicolored .75 .30
1129 A348 205fr multicolored 1.00 .50
1130 A348 300fr multicolored 1.50 .75
1131 A348 400fr multicolored 2.00 1.00
1132 A348 500fr multicolored 2.50 1.25
Nos. 1127-1132 (6) 8.20 4.00

Souvenir Sheet

Perf. 13

1133 A348 1000fr multicolored 5.00 2.50

No. 1133 contains one 32x40mm stamp.

Aquatic Flowers — A348a

Design: 90fr, Cyrtosperma senegalense.

1996, July 3 Litho. *Perf. 14x14¼*

1133A A348a 90fr multi .50 .50

An additional stamp was issued in this set. The editors would like to examine it.

Crocodilians A348b

1996, July 16 Litho. *Perf. 14*

1133C A348b 205fr Nile crocodile — —
1133D A348b 255fr Gavial — —
1133E A348b 300fr Caiman — —

Arctocebus Calabarensis A349

a, 90fr, With young. b, 205fr, Touching leaf. c, 300fr, Climbing to left. d, 255fr, Walking on branch.

1998, June 3 Litho. *Perf. 14*

1134 A349 Strip of 4, #a.-d. 3.00 3.00

No. 1134 issued in sheets of 12 stamps. World Wildlife Fund.

Endangered Species — A350

#1135, Kabus defassa, vert. #1136, Caphalophus sylvicutor. 205fr, Potamochoerus porcus. 300fr, Tragelaplus spekei.

1996 Litho. *Perf. 14*

1135 A350 90fr multi .55 .25
1136 A350 90fr multi, vert. .55 .25
1137 A350 205fr multi, vert. 1.10 .45
1138 A350 300fr multi 1.60 .65
Nos. 1135-1138 (4) 3.80 1.60

Diana, Princess of Wales (1961-97) A351

#1139-1141: Various portraits with white rose.
Diana, rose, famous people in sheet margin: 750fr, Henry Kissinger, vert. No. 1143, Mother Teresa, vert. No. 1144, Hillary Clinton, vert.

1998, Aug. 31 Litho. *Perf. 14*

Sheets of 6

1139 A351 205fr #a.-f. 4.25 2.00
1140 A351 255fr #a.-f., vert. 5.25 2.75
1141 A351 300fr #a.-f., vert. 6.25 3.00

Souvenir Sheets

1142 A351 750fr multicolored 2.50 1.25
1143-1144 A351 1000fr each 3.50 1.75

Stamps of Type A345 inscribed only "Congo" ovptd.

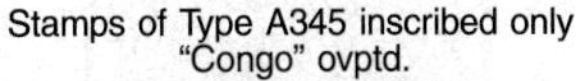

1998 Litho. *Perf. 13*

1145 A345 40fr blue
1146 A345 50fr violet brown
1147 A345 90fr orange
1148 A345 100fr green blue — —
1149 A345 115fr gray
1150 A345 205fr brown

A352

Designs: 90fr, Aframomum africanum. 205fr, Gambeya lacuurtiana (37x24mm). 300fr, Landolphia jumeli.

1998 Litho. *Perf. 13½x13¼*

1151 A352 90fr multi
1152 A352 205fr multi — —
1153 A352 300fr multi

No. 1153 has denomination in yellow.

No. 732A Overprinted

No. 929 Overprinted

1998 Litho. *Perf. 13*

1155 A244 205fr multi — —
1156 A309 300fr multi — —

An additional stamp was issued in this set. The editors would like to examine them.

Nos. 732B, 804, 854, 1066, 1165 Ovptd. Like

A353

Perfs. as before, Perf. 14 (#1164), Perf. 13½x13¼ (#1170)

Methods as before, Litho. (#1164, 1170)

1998

1157 A274 60fr multi
1159 A345 100fr green blue
1164 A353 255fr multi
1165 A309 300fr multi
1167 A335 300fr multi
a. Overprint reading horizontally
1168 A337 300fr multi
1170 A244 300fr multi
a. Overprint reading horizontally — —
1172 A292 360fr multi

Numbers have been reserved for additional overprinted stamps. Overprint reads horizontally on Nos. 1157, 1159 and 1172, vertically reading down on Nos. 1164, 1167, 1168 and 1170, and vertically reading up on No. 1165. No. 1170 has white denomination.

The editors would like to see examples of Nos. 1164 without the overprint.

1998 World Cup Soccer Championships, France — A358

Designs: 90fr, Netherlands, 4th place. 205fr, Croatia, bronze medal. 300fr, Brazil, silver medal. 500fr, France, gold medal.

1998, Nov. 16 Litho. *Perf. 13x13¼*

1175-1178 A358 Set of 4 — —

Masks — A359

Perf. 13¼x13½

1998, Nov. 20 Litho.

1179 A359 90fr Kwele wood mask
1180 A359 150fr Kwele wood mask
1181 A359 205fr Teke/Tsangui wood mask
1182 A359 205fr Kuyu wood mask

No. 732B Overprinted

Type I — Unserifed Upper and Lower Case Letters, 7x3mm

Type II — Serifed Upper and Lower Case Letters, 12x3mm

Type III — Upper Case Letters, 9x2mm

Methods and Perfs as Before

1999 ?

1183 A244 300fr multi (I) — —
1184 A244 300fr multi (II) — —
1185 A244 300fr multi (III) — —

PhilexFrance 99 — A360

Design: 300fr, Woven raffia cloth.

1999, July 2 Litho. *Perf. 13x13¼*

1212 A360 300fr multi — —

An additional stamp was released in this set. The editors would like to examine it.

First French Postage Stamp, 150th Anniv. A361

Litho. With Hologram

1999 *Perf. 13x13¼*

1213 A361 300fr multi — —

Central African Economic and Monetary Community Week — A363

Designs: 90fr, Map and flags. 205fr, Map and circle of flags.

1999 Litho. *Perf. 14½*

1227 A363 90fr multi — —
1228 A363 205fr multi — —

Additional stamps may exist in this set. The editors would like to examine any examples.

Third Pan-African Music Festival — A364

Designs: 120fr, Emblem. 270fr, Map of Africa with drummers.

2001, Aug. 4 Litho. *Perf. 13½x13*

1229-1230 A364 Set of 2 — —

Independence, 40th Anniv. — A365

Designs: 90fr, Dove, vine, map, hands, people. 205fr, Tools, clasped and opened hands, map.

2001, Nov. 15 Litho. *Perf. 13¼x13*

1231-1232 A365 Set of 2 — —

Birds — A366

Designs: 90fr, Egretta garzetta. 120fr, Ardea cenerea. 270fr, Ciconia nigra.

2001 *Perf. 13¼*

1233 A366 90fr multi — —
1234 A366 120fr multi — —
1235 A366 270fr multi — —

Additional stamps may exist in this set. The editors would like to examine any examples.

Type of A345 Inscribed "REPUBLIQUE DU CONGO" Overprinted "LEGAL" Like No. 1145

2001 ? Litho. *Perf. 13*

1236 A345 90fr blue — —

Fruit — A367

Designs: 40fr, Mbila esobe. 50fr, Ikami. 70fr, Tsia, vert. 80fr, Bamou. 120fr, Malombo. 270fr, Ntondolo, vert.

2002, June 25 Litho. *Perf. 13½*

1237-1242 A367 Set of 6 — —

Birds — A368

Designs: 40fr, Calao (hornbill). 80fr, Cigogne blanche (white stork). 120fr, Grue cendrée (gray crane). 270fr, Marabout.

2002, July 23 *Perf. 13½x13*

1243-1246 A368 Set of 4 — —

Elephants A369

Designs; 120fr, Mammoth. 270fr, Elephant on savannah, horiz. 350fr, Elephant, horiz. 500fr, Forest elephant near lake.

Perf. 13¼x13, 13x13¼

2003, June 20

1247-1250 A369 Set of 4 5.75 5.75

Flowers — A370

Designs: 120fr, Muflier (antirrhinum). 270fr, Pivoine (peony). 400fr, Petunia. 600fr, Mauve (mallow), horiz.

2003, July 6

1251-1254 A370 Set of 4 6.50 6.50

SEMI-POSTAL STAMPS

Anti-Malaria Issue

Common Design Type

1962, Apr. 7 Engr. *Perf. 12½x12*

B3 CD108 25fr + 5fr bister .90 .60

Freedom from Hunger Issue

Common Design Type

1963, Mar. 21 Unwmk. *Perf. 13*

B4 CD112 25fr + 5fr vio bl, bl grn & brn .90 .60

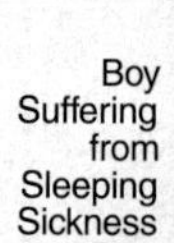
Boy Suffering from Sleeping Sickness SP1

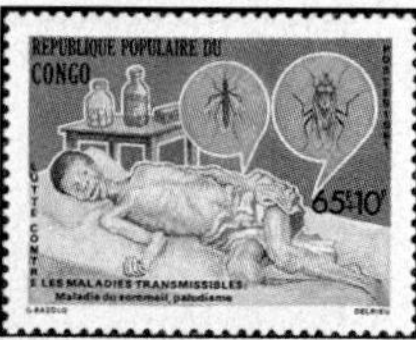

Fight Against Communicable Diseases; 40fr+5fr, Examination, treatment, vert.

1981, June 6 Litho. *Perf. 13*

B5 SP1 40fr + 5fr multi .60 .25
B6 SP1 65fr + 10fr multi 1.00 .30

IYD Type of 1981

1981, June 29 *Perf. 12½*

B7 A192 75fr + 5fr multi .90 .35

AIR POST STAMPS

Olympic Games Issue
French Equatorial Africa No. C37 Surcharged in Red Like Chad No. C1

1960 Unwmk. Engr. *Perf. 13*
C1 AP8 250fr on 500fr grnsh blk, blk & sl 6.75 6.75

17th Olympic Games, Rome, 8/25-9/11.

Helicrysum Mechowiam — AP1

Flowers: 200fr, Cogniauxia podolaena. 500fr, Thesium tencio.

1961, Sept. 28 Engr. *Perf. 13*
C2 AP1 100fr grn, lil & yel 3.25 1.25
C3 AP1 200fr bl grn, yel & brn 5.25 1.75
C4 AP1 500fr brn red, yel & sl grn 16.00 5.00
Nos. C2-C4 (3) 24.50 8.00

Air Afrique Issue
Common Design Type

1961, Nov. 25 Unwmk. *Perf. 13*
C5 CD107 50fr lil rose, sl grn & grn 1.25 .50

Loading Timber, Pointe-Noire Harbor — AP2

1962, June 8 Photo. *Perf. 12½x12*
C6 AP2 50fr multicolored 1.50 .90

Opening of the Intl. Fair and Exhib., Pointe-Noire, June 8-11.

Abidjan Games — AP3

Costus Spectabilis AP4

1962, July 21 *Perf. 12x12½*
C7 AP3 100fr Basketball 2.50 1.25

1963 Unwmk. *Perf. 13*

Design: 250fr, Mountain acanthus.

C8 AP4 100fr multicolored 4.00 1.75
C9 AP4 250fr multicolored 8.00 3.25

Brazzaville City Hall and Pres. Fulbert Youlou — AP4a

1963, Aug. Photo. *Perf. 13x12*
C10 AP4a 100fr multicolored 125.00 125.00

African Postal Union Issue
Common Design Type

1963, Sept. 8 *Perf. 12½*
C13 CD114 85fr pur, ocher & red 1.25 .75

Air Afrique Issue, 1963
Common Design Type
Perf. 13x12

1963, Nov. 19 Unwmk. Photo.
C14 CD115 50fr multicolored .85 .50

Liberty Place, Brazzaville — AP5

1963, Nov. 28
C15 AP5 25fr multicolored .55 .40

See No. 118.

Europafrica Issue
Common Design Type

1963, Nov. 30 *Perf. 12x13*
C16 CD116 50fr gray, yel & dk brn 1.25 .90

Timber Industry — AP6

1964, May 12 Engr. *Perf. 13*
C17 AP6 100fr grn, brn red & blk 2.10 .90

Chiefs of State Issue

Map and Presidents of Chad, Congo, Gabon and CAR AP6a

1964, June 23 Photo. *Perf. 12½*
C18 AP6a 100fr multicolored 1.40 .80

See note after Central African Republic No. C19.

Europafrica Issue, 1964

Sunburst, Wheat, Cogwheel and Globe — AP7

1964, July 20 *Perf. 12x13*
C19 AP7 50fr yel, Prus bl & mar 1.00 .75

See note after Cameroun No. 402.

Hammer Thrower, Olympic Flame and Stadium — AP8

50fr, 100fr, vert.

1964, July 30 Engr. *Perf. 13*
C20 AP8 25fr shown .45 .25
C21 AP8 50fr Weight lifter .80 .45
C22 AP8 100fr Volleyball 1.75 1.00
C23 AP8 200fr High jump 3.25 2.10
a. Min. sheet of 4, #C20-C23 8.00 8.00
Nos. C20-C23 (4) 6.25 3.80

18th Olympic Games, Tokyo, 10/10-25/64.

Communications Symbols — AP8a

1964, Nov. 2 Litho. *Perf. 12½x13*
C24 AP8a 25fr dl rose & dk brn .50 .30

See note after Chad No. C19.

Town Hall, Brazzaville — AP9

1965, Jan. 30 Photo. *Perf. 12½*
C25 AP9 100fr multicolored 1.25 .60

Coupling Hooks — AP10

1965, Feb. 27 Photo. *Perf. 13x12*
C26 AP10 50fr multicolored 1.00 .75

Economic Europe-Africa Association.

Breguet Dial Telegraph, ITU Emblem and Telstar — AP11

1965, May 17 Engr. *Perf. 13*
C27 AP11 100fr dk bl, ocher & brn 2.25 .75

Cent. of the ITU.

Pope John XXIII (1881-1963), St. Peter's Cathedral — AP12

Perf. 12½x13

1965, June 26 Photo. Unwmk.
C28 AP12 100fr gldn brn & multi 1.60 .75

Pres. John F. Kennedy — AP13

Log Rolling — AP14

Portraits: 25fr on 50fr, Patrice Lumumba, premier of Congo Republic (ex-Belgian). 50fr, Sir Winston Churchill. 80fr, Barthélémy Boganda, premier of Central African Republic.

1965, June *Perf. 12½*
C29 AP13 25fr on 50fr dk brn & red .50 .40
a. Surcharge omitted 35.00 35.00
C30 AP13 50fr dk brn & yel grn 1.10 1.00
C31 AP13 80fr dk brn & bl 2.00 1.50
C32 AP13 100fr dk brn & org yel 2.75 2.25
a. Min. sheet of 4, #C29-C32 6.25 6.25
Nos. C29-C32 (4) 6.35 5.15

A second miniature sheet contains one each of Nos. C29a, C30-C32. Value, $50.

Issued: 25fr, 80fr, 6/25; 50fr, 100fr, #C32a, 6/26.

1965, Aug. 14 Engr. *Perf. 13*
C33 AP14 50fr grn, brn & red brn .80 .50

Issued to publicize national unity.

World Map and Symbols of Agriculture and Industry — AP15

1965, Oct. 18 Engr. *Perf. 13*

C34 AP15 50fr dk bl, blk, brn & org 1.10 .75

International Cooperation Year, 1965.

Abraham Lincoln — AP16

1965, Dec. 15 Photo. *Perf. 13*

C35 AP16 90fr pink & multi 1.25 .60

Centenary of death of Abraham Lincoln.

Charles de Gaulle, Torch and Map of Africa — AP17

1966, Feb. 28 Engr. *Perf. 13*

C36 AP17 500fr dk red, dk grn & dk red brn 35.00 26.00

22nd anniv. of the Brazzaville Conf.

D-1 Satellite over Brazzaville Space Tracking Station — AP18

Grain, Atom Symbol and Map of Africa and Europe — AP19

1966, May 15 Engr. *Perf. 13*

C37 AP18 150fr blk, dl red & bl grn 2.25 1.25

1966, July 20 Photo. *Perf. 12x13*

C38 AP19 50fr multicolored .90 .50

See note after Gabon No. C46.

Pres. Massamba-Debat and President's Palace — AP20

3rd anniv. of the Revolution: 30fr, Robespierre and storming of the Bastille. 50fr, Lenin and storming of the Winter Palace.

1966, Aug. 15 Photo. *Perf. 12x12½*

C39 AP20 25fr multicolored .25 .20
C40 AP20 30fr multicolored .35 .25
C41 AP20 50fr multicolored 1.60 .35
a. Souv. sheet of 3, #C39-C41 2.25 2.25
Nos. C39-C41 (3) 2.20 .80

Air Afrique Issue, 1966

Common Design Type

1966, Aug. 31 Photo. *Perf. 13*

C42 CD123 30fr lilac, lemon & blk .60 .25

Dr. Albert Schweitzer — AP21

1966, Sept. 4 Photo. *Perf. 12½*

C43 AP21 100fr red, blk, bl & lilac 1.75 1.10

Issued to honor Dr. Albert Schweitzer (1875-1965), medical missionary.

AP22

AP23

1966, Dec. 26 Photo. *Perf. 13*

C44 AP22 100fr Crab, microscope and pagoda 1.50 1.00

9th Intl. Anticancer Cong., Tokyo. 10/23-29.

1967 Photo. *Perf. 13*

Birds: 50fr, Social Weaver. 75fr, European Bee-eater. 100fr, Lilac-breasted roller. 150fr, Regal sunbird. 200fr, Crowned cranes. 250fr, Secretary bird. 300fr, Knysna touraco.

C45 AP23 50fr multicolored 1.50 .60
C46 AP23 75fr multicolored 3.00 .90
C47 AP23 100fr multicolored 3.00 .90
C48 AP23 150fr multicolored 4.00 2.00
C49 AP23 200fr multicolored 7.00 2.40
C50 AP23 250fr multicolored 9.00 2.75
C51 AP23 300fr multicolored 12.50 4.50
Nos. C45-C51 (7) 40.00 14.05

Issued: #C45-C47, 2/13; others, 6/20.

Shackled Hands AP24

1967, May 24 Photo. *Perf. 12½x13*

C52 AP24 500fr multicolored 8.50 3.00

Issued for African Liberation Day.

Sputnik 1, Explorer 6 and Earth — AP25

Space Craft: 75fr, Ranger 6, Lunik 2 and moon. 100fr, Mars 1, Mariner 4 and Mars. 200fr, Gemini, Vostok and earth.

1967, Aug. 1 Engr. *Perf. 13*

C53 AP25 50fr multicolored .65 .30
C54 AP25 75fr multicolored 1.10 .35
C55 AP25 100fr multicolored 1.60 .60
C56 AP25 200fr multicolored 2.75 1.50
Nos. C53-C56 (4) 6.10 2.75

Space explorations.

African Postal Union Issue, 1967

Common Design Type

1967, Sept. 9 Engr. *Perf. 13*

C57 CD124 100fr ver, ol & emer 1.25 .60

Boy Scouts, Tents and Jamboree Emblem — AP26

Design: 70c, Borah Peak, Idaho; tents, Scout sign and Jamboree emblem.

1967, Sept. 29

C58 AP26 50fr multicolored .90 .30
C59 AP26 70fr multicolored 1.25 .50

12th Boy Scout World Jamboree, Farragut State Park, ID, Aug. 1-9.

Sikorsky S-43 and Map of Africa — AP27

1967, Oct. 2 Photo. *Perf. 13*

C60 AP27 30fr multicolored .60 .30

30th anniv. of the 1st airmail connection by Aeromaritime Lines from Casablanca to Pointe-Noire.

Men of Four Races Dancing on Globe — AP28

1968, Feb 8 Engr. *Perf. 13*

C61 AP28 70fr dk brn, ultra & emer 1.00 .45

Friendship among peoples.

The Oath of the Horatii, by Jacques Louis David — AP29

Paintings: 25fr, On the Barricades, by Delacroix. No. C63, Grandfather and Grandson, by Ghirlandajo, vert. No. C64, The Demolition of the Bastille, by Hubert Robert. 200fr, Negro Woman Arranging Peonies, by Jean F. Bazille.

1968 Photo. *Perf. 12x12½, 12½x12*

C62 AP29 25fr multicolored 1.75 .35
C63 AP29 30fr multicolored .90 .30
C64 AP29 30fr multicolored 1.75 .50
C65 AP29 100fr multicolored 2.25 .90
C66 AP29 200fr multicolored 5.00 1.75
Nos. C62-C66 (5) 11.65 3.80

Issue dates: Nos. C62, C64, Aug. 15. Nos. C63, C65-C66, Mar. 20.

See Nos. C78-C81, C111-C115.

Early Automobile Type

1968, July 29 Photo. *Perf. 13x12½*

C67 A50 150fr Ford, 1915 3.50 1.75
C68 A50 200fr Citroen, 1922 5.25 1.75

Europafrica Issue

Square Knot — AP30

1968, July 20 Photo. *Perf. 13*

C69 AP30 50fr multicolored 1.00 .50

5th anniv. of the economic agreement between the European Economic Community and the African and Malgache Union.

Martin Luther King, Jr. — AP31

Robert F. Kennedy — AP32

1968, Aug. 5 *Perf. 12½*
C70 AP31 50fr lt grn, Prus grn & blk .80 .35

1968, Sept. 30 Photo. *Perf. 13x12½*
C71 AP32 50fr dp car, ap grn & blk .70 .35

Running — AP33

Olympic Rings and: 20fr, Soccer, vert. 60fr, Boxing, vert. 85fr, High jump.

1968, Dec. 27 Engr. *Perf. 13*
C72 AP33 5fr emer, brt bl & choc .20 .20
C73 AP33 20fr dk bl, brn & dk grn .45 .25
C74 AP33 60fr mar, brt grn & choc .90 .50
C75 AP33 85fr blk, car rose & choc 1.50 .75
Nos. C72-C75 (4) 3.05 1.70

19th Olympic Games, Mexico City, 10/12-27.

PHILEXAFRIQUE Issue

G. De Gueidan, by Nicolas de Largillière AP34

1968, Dec. 30 Photo. *Perf. 12½*
C76 AP34 100fr pink & multi 3.00 1.75

Issued to publicize PHILEXAFRIQUE, Philatelic Exhibition, in Abidjan, Feb. 14-23. Printed with alternating pink label.
See Nos. C89-C93.

2nd PHILEXAFRIQUE Issue
Common Design Type

Design: 50fr, Middle Congo No. 72 and Pointe-Noire harbor.

1969, Feb. 14 Engr. *Perf. 13*
C77 CD128 50fr car rose, sl grn & bis brn 1.75 1.75

Painting Type of 1968.

Paintings: 25fr, Battle of Rivoli, by Carle Vernet. 50fr, Battle of Marengo, by Jacques Augustin Pajou. 75fr, Battle of Friedland, by Horace Vernet. 100fr, Battle of Jena, by Charles Thevenin.

1969, May 20 Photo. *Perf. 12x12½*
C78 AP29 25fr vio bl & multi 1.25 .45
C79 AP29 50fr cop red & multi 1.75 .80
C80 AP29 75fr grn & multi 3.00 1.10
C81 AP29 100fr brn & multi 5.00 1.40
Nos. C78-C81 (4) 11.00 3.75

Bicentenary of birth of Napoleon I.

Ernesto Ché Guevara — AP35

1969, June 10 Photo. *Perf. 12½*
C82 AP35 90fr brn, org & blk 1.00 .50

Issued in memory of Ernesto Ché Guevara (1928-1967), Cuban revolutionist.

Doll, Train and Space Toy — AP36

1969, June 20 Engr. *Perf. 13*
C83 AP36 100fr mag, org & gray 1.50 .75

International Toy Fair, Nuremberg, Germany.

Europafrica Issue, 1969

Ribbon Tied Around Bar — AP37

1969, Aug. 5 Photo. *Perf. 13x12*
C84 AP37 50fr bl grn, lil & blk .90 .35

See note after Chad No. C11.

Armstrong, Aldrin and Collins — AP38

Souvenir Sheet

Design: No. C85b, Blast-off from Moon.

Embossed on Gold Foil
1969, Sept. 15 *Imperf.*
C85 AP38 1000fr #a-b 35.00 35.00

See note after Algeria No. 427. No. C85 contains one each of Nos. C85a and C85b with simulated perforations.

Painter, Poto-Poto School — AP39

150fr, Sculpture lesson (man, infant and sculpture). 200fr, Potter working on vase.

1970, Feb. 20 Engr. *Perf. 13*
C86 AP39 100fr multicolored 2.25 .60
C87 AP39 150fr multicolored 3.00 .95
C88 AP39 200fr multicolored 4.50 1.75
Nos. C86-C88 (3) 9.75 3.30

Painting Type (Philexafrique)

Paintings: 150fr, Child with Cherries, by John Russell. 200fr, Erasmus, by Hans Holbein the Younger. 250fr, "Silence" (head), by Bernardino Luini. 300fr, Scene from the Massacre of Scio, by Delacroix. 500fr, The Capture of Constantinople by the Crusaders, by Delacroix.

1970 Photo. *Perf. 12½*
C89 AP34 150fr lil & multi 4.50 1.50
C90 AP34 200fr multicolored 5.75 1.75
C91 AP34 250fr brn & multi 6.25 2.25
C92 AP34 300fr multicolored 8.00 3.25
C93 AP34 500fr brn & multi 13.50 4.50
Nos. C89-C93 (5) 38.00 13.25

Aurichalcite — AP40

1970, Mar. 20
C94 AP40 100fr shown 5.25 1.75
C95 AP40 150fr Dioptase 8.00 2.50

Lenin — AP41

Karl Marx — AP42

1970, June 25 Photo. *Perf. 12½*
C96 AP41 45fr shown 1.00 .35
C97 AP41 75fr Lenin, seated 1.75 .50

Centenary of the birth of Lenin (1870-1924), Russian communist leader.

1970, July 10 Engr. *Perf. 13*

Design: No. C99, Friedrich Engels.

C98 AP42 50fr emer, dk brn & dk red 1.50 .35
C99 AP42 50fr ultra, dk brn & dk red 1.50 .35

Karl Marx (1818-1883) and Friedrich Engels (1820-1895), German socialist writers.

Otto Lilienthal's Glider, 1891 — AP43

Designs: 50fr, "Spirit of St. Louis," Lindbergh's first transatlantic solo flight, 1927. 70fr, Sputnik 1, first satellite in space. 90fr, First man on the moon, Apollo 11, 1969.

1970, Sept. 5 Engr. *Perf. 13*
C100 AP43 45fr dp car, bl & ol bis .90 .30
C101 AP43 50fr emer, sl grn & brn .90 .35
C102 AP43 70fr brt bl, ol bis & dp car 1.25 .50
C103 AP43 90fr brn, bl & ol gray 1.75 .75
Nos. C100-C103 (4) 4.80 1.90

Forerunners of space exploration.

Saint on Horseback AP44

Marilyn Monroe and NYC — AP45

Designs from Stained Glass Windows, Brazzaville Cathedral: 150fr, Saint with staff. 250fr, The Elevation of the Host, from rose window.

1970, Dec. 10 Photo. *Perf. 12½*
C104 AP44 100fr multicolored 1.10 .50
C105 AP44 150fr multicolored 1.75 .75
C106 AP44 250fr multicolored 3.00 1.50
a. Souv. sheet of 3, #C104-C106 6.75 6.75
Nos. C104-C106 (3) 5.85 2.75

Christmas 1970.

1971, Mar. 16 Engr. *Perf. 13*

Portraits: 150fr, Martine Carol and Paris. 200fr, Erich von Stroheim and Vienna. 250fr, Sergei Eisenstein and Moscow.

C107 AP45 100fr brt grn, red brn & ultra 7.00 .50
C108 AP45 150fr brn, brt lil & ultra 7.00 .75
C109 AP45 200fr choc & ultra 7.00 1.10
C110 AP45 250fr brt grn, brn vio & ultra 7.00 1.25
Nos. C107-C110 (4) 28.00 3.60

History of motion pictures.

Painting Type of 1968

Paintings: 100fr, Christ Carrying Cross, by Paolo Veronese. 150fr, Christ on the Cross, Burgundian School, 1500, vert. 200fr, Descent from the Cross, by Rogier van der Weyden. 250fr, Christ Laid in the Tomb, Flemish School, 1500, vert. 500fr, Resurrection, by Hans Memling, vert.

1971, Apr. 26 Photo. *Perf. 13*
C111 AP29 100fr green & multi 1.75 .75
C112 AP29 150fr green & multi 2.75 .90
C113 AP29 200fr green & multi 4.00 1.10
C114 AP29 250fr green & multi 4.50 1.60
C115 AP29 500fr green & multi 10.00 3.00
Nos. C111-C115 (5) 23.00 7.35

Easter 1971.

Map of Africa and Telecommunications System — AP46

1971, June 18 Photo. *Perf. 12½*

C116 AP46 70fr bl, gray & dk brn .60 .30
C117 AP46 85fr bl, lil rose & dk brn 1.00 .35
C118 AP46 90fr grn, yel & dk brn 1.40 .50
Nos. C116-C118 (3) 3.00 1.15

Pan-African telecommunications system.

Globe and Waves — AP47

1971, June 19

C119 AP47 65fr lt bl & multi .70 .30

3rd World Telecommunications Day.

Japanese Mask and Play — AP48

Olympic Torch and Rings — AP49

Design: 150fr, Japanese and African women, symbolic leaves.

1971, June 28 Engr. *Perf. 13*

C120 AP48 75fr lil, blk & mag 1.00 .70
C121 AP48 150fr dk brn, brn red & red lil 1.60 1.10

PHILATOKYO '71 International Stamp Exhibition, Tokyo, Apr. 20-30.

13th World Boy Scout Jamboree, Japan, gold foil 1000fr airmail and silver foil souv. sheet of four 90fr, issued July 14. Nos. 71C01-71C02.

1971, July 20 Engr. *Perf. 13*

350fr, Olympic rings and various sports.

C122 AP49 150fr multi 1.75 .95
C123 AP49 350fr multi, horiz. 4.00 2.25

Pre-Olympic Year, 1971.

Scout Emblem, Japanese Dragon and African Carved Canoe — AP50

Designs (Boy Scout Emblem and): 90fr, Japanese mask and African boy, vert. 100fr, Japanese woman and African drummer, vert. 250fr, Congolese mask.

1971, Aug. 25

C124 AP50 85fr multicolored 1.10 .30
C125 AP50 90fr multicolored 1.25 .35
C126 AP50 100fr multicolored 1.60 .45
C127 AP50 250fr multicolored 3.25 .90
Nos. C124-C127 (4) 7.20 2.00

13th Boy Scout World Jamboree, Asagiri Plain, Japan, Aug. 2-10.

Olympic Rings and Running — AP51

Designs (Olympic Rings and): 85fr, Hurdles. 90fr, Weight lifting, boxing, discus, running, javelin. 100fr, Wrestling. 150fr, Boxing.

1971, Sept. 30

C128 AP51 75fr plum, bl & dk brn .70 .35
C129 AP51 85fr scar, sl & dk brn .80 .35
C130 AP51 90fr vio bl & dk brn .90 .50
C131 AP51 100fr brn & slate 1.10 .50
C132 AP51 150fr grn, red & dk brn 2.00 .90
Nos. C128-C132 (5) 5.50 2.60

75th anniv. of the 1st modern Olympic Games.

Congo No. C36 and de Gaulle — AP52

Pres. Marien Ngouabi's Tribute to de Gaulle — AP53

Design: No. C135, Charles de Gaulle.

1971, Nov. 9

C133 AP52 500fr slate grn & multi 18.00 15.00

Lithographed; Gold Embossed
Perf. 12½

C134 AP53 1000fr gold, grn & red 27.50 20.00
C135 AP53 1000fr gold, grn & red 27.50 20.00
a. Pair, #C134-C135 55.00 55.00

Charles de Gaulle (1890-1970), president of France.

African Postal Union Issue, 1971
Common Design Type

Design: 100fr, Allegory of Congo Republic (woman) and UAMPT Building, Brazzaville.

1971, Nov. 13 Photo. *Perf. 13x13½*

C136 CD135 100fr bl & multi 1.10 .70

Flag of Congo Republic and "Revolution" — AP54

1971, Nov. 30

C137 AP54 100fr red & multi 1.25 .35

8th anniversary of revolution.

Workers and Flag — AP55

40fr, Flag of Congo Republic and sun.

1971, Dec. 31 Photo. *Perf. 13x12½*

C138 AP55 30fr multicolored .45 .20
C139 AP55 40fr red & multi .60 .25

2nd anniv. of founding of Congolese Labor Party (#C138), and adoption of red flag (#C139).

Book Year Emblem — AP56

1972, June 3 Litho. *Perf. 12½*

C140 AP56 50fr red, grn & yel .70 .25

International Book Year 1972.

Congolese Soccer Team — AP57

#C142, Captain of winning team and cup, vert.

1973, Feb. 22 Photo. *Perf. 13*

C141 AP57 100fr ultra, red & blk 1.50 .75
C142 AP57 100fr red, yel & blk 1.50 .75

Girl Holding Bird, Environment Emblem — AP58

1973, Mar. 5 Engr.

C143 AP58 85fr org, slate grn & bl 1.50 .75

UN Conference on Human Environment, Stockholm, Sweden, June 5-16, 1972.

Miles Davis AP59

Designs: 140fr, Ella Fitzgerald. 160fr, Count Basie. 175fr, John Coltrane.

1973, Mar. 5 Photo. *Perf. 13x13½*

C144 AP59 125fr multicolored 4.00 .95
C145 AP59 140fr multicolored 4.00 1.00
C146 AP59 160fr multicolored 5.00 1.50
C147 AP59 175fr multicolored 5.00 1.50
Nos. C144-C147 (4) 18.00 4.95

Black American jazz musicians.

Olympic Rings, Hurdling — AP60

1973, Mar. 15 Engr. *Perf. 13*

C148 AP60 100fr shown 1.10 .60
C149 AP60 150fr Pole vault, vert. 1.75 .90
C150 AP60 250fr Wrestling 2.75 1.50
Nos. C148-C150 (3) 5.60 3.00

20th Olympic Games, Munich, 8/26-9/11/72.

Refinery and Storage Tanks, Djéno — AP61

Designs: 230fr, Off-shore drilling platform, vert. 240fr, Workers assembling drill, vert. 260fr, Off-shore drilling installation.

1973, Mar. 20

C151 AP61 180fr red, bl & indigo 3.25 1.50
C152 AP61 230fr red, bl & blk 4.00 1.50
C153 AP61 240fr red, ind & brn 4.50 1.60
C154 AP61 260fr red, bl & blk 7.25 2.25
Nos. C151-C154 (4) 19.00 6.85

Oil installations, Pointe-Noire.

Astronauts, Landing Module and Lunar Rover on Moon — AP62

1973, Mar. 31

C155 AP62 250fr multicolored 4.50 1.75

Apollo 17 US moon mission, 12/7-19/72.

ITU Emblem, Symbols of Communications AP63

1973, May 24 Engr. *Perf. 13*

C156 AP63 120fr multicolored 2.25 .90

5th International Telecommunications Day.

White Horse, by Delacroix — AP64

Designs: Paintings by Eugene Delacroix.

1973, June 30 Photo. *Perf. 13*
C157 AP64 150fr shown 2.25 1.50
C158 AP64 250fr Lion sleeping 5.00 2.40
C159 AP64 300fr Lion and tiger 5.25 2.50
Nos. C157-C159 (3) 12.50 6.40

See Nos. C169-C171.

Copernicus and Heliocentric System — AP65

1973, June 30 Engr.
C160 AP65 50fr multicolored 1.00 .45

500th anniversary of the birth of Nicolaus Copernicus (1473-1543), Polish astronomer.

Plane, Ship, Rocket, Village, Sun and Clouds — AP66

1973, July
C161 AP66 50fr red & multi 1.00 .50

Cent. of intl. meteorological cooperation.

Pres. Marien Ngouabi — AP67

1973, Aug. 12 Photo. *Perf. 13*
C162 AP67 30fr multicolored .35 .20
C163 AP67 40fr aqua & multi .45 .20
C164 AP67 75fr red & multi 1.00 .35
Nos. C162-C164 (3) 1.80 .75

10th anniversary of independence.

Stamps, Album, African Woman AP68

40fr, #C167, Stamps in shape of map of Congo, album, globe. #C168, Like 30fr.

1973, Aug. 12
C165 AP68 30fr pur & multi 1.90 .30
C166 AP68 40fr multicolored .25 .20
C167 AP68 100fr dk brn & multi 3.75 .80
C168 AP68 100fr ocher & multi .90 .40
Nos. C165-C168 (4) 6.80 1.70

Nos. C165, C168 for the 10th anniv. of the revolution, Nos. C166-C167 the Intl. Philatelic Exhib., Brazzaville.

Painting Type of 1973 Inscribed "EUROPAFRIQUE"

Designs: Details from "Earth and Paradise," by Jan Brueghel, the Elder.

1973, Oct. 10 Photo. *Perf. 13*
C169 AP64 100fr Spotted hyena 3.00 1.50
C170 AP64 100fr Leopard and lion 3.00 1.50
C171 AP64 100fr Elephant and creatures 3.00 1.50
Nos. C169-C171 (3) 9.00 4.50

US and Russian Spacecraft Docking — AP69

Design: 80fr, US and USSR spacecraft docked in space and emblems of 1975 joint space mission.

1973, Oct. 15 Engr. *Perf. 13*
C172 AP69 40fr bl, red & brn .50 .35
C173 AP69 80fr red, grn & bl 1.10 .50

Planned joint US and Soviet space missions.
For overprint see No. C251.

UPU Monument, Satellites, Big Dipper — AP70

1973, Nov. 20 Engr. *Perf. 13*
C174 AP70 80fr vio bl & lt bl 1.00 .35

Universal Postal Union Day.

Astronauts Working in Space — AP71

40fr, Spacecraft & Skylab docking in space.

1973, Nov. 30
C175 AP71 30fr ultra, sl grn & choc .60 .20
C176 AP71 40fr mag, org & sl grn .60 .25

Skylab, first space laboratory.

Goalkeeper, Soccer — AP72

Design: 100fr, Soccer player kicking ball.

1973, Dec. 20
C177 AP72 40fr sl grn, sepia & brn .60 .25
C178 AP72 100fr pur, red & slate grn 1.75 .75

World Soccer Cup, Munich, 1974.

John F. Kennedy (1917-1963) AP73

1973, Dec. 20 Photo. *Perf. 12½*
C179 AP73 150fr ultra, gold & blk 1.75 .90

Runners — AP74

Flag over Map of Congo — AP75

1973, Dec. 20 Engr. *Perf. 13*
C180 AP74 40fr sl grn, red & brn .60 .25
C181 AP74 100fr red, sl grn, & brn 1.75 .75

2nd African Games, Lagos, Nigeria.

1973, Dec. 31 Photo.
C182 AP75 40fr dp grn & multi .50 .25

4th anniversary of Congolese Labor Party and of the Congo Red Flag.

Soccer and Games Emblem — AP76

1974, June 20 Photo. *Perf. 13*
C183 AP76 250fr multicolored 3.75 1.90

World Cup Soccer Championship, Munich, June 13-July 7.

Astronauts Yuri A. Gagarin and Alan B. Shepard — AP77

Designs: 30fr, Space, globe, Russian and American flags with names of astronauts who perished in space. 100fr, Alexei Leonov and Neil A. Armstrong in space and on moon.

1974, June 30 Engr. *Perf. 13*
C184 AP77 30fr red, ultra & brn .45 .20
C185 AP77 40fr red, bl & brn .60 .25
C186 AP77 100fr car, grn & brn 1.40 .90
Nos. C184-C186 (3) 2.45 1.35

For overprint see No. C254.

Soccer Game Superimposed on Ball — AP78

Link-up Emblem, Stages of Link-up — AP79

1974, July 31 Photo. *Perf. 13*
C187 AP78 250fr multicolored 3.50 1.75

Germany's victory in World Cup Soccer Championship.

1974, Aug. 8 Engr. *Perf. 13*

300fr, Spacecraft docking over globe.

C188 AP79 200fr pur, bl & red 2.25 1.10
C189 AP79 300fr multi, horiz. 3.50 1.50

Russo-American space cooperation.
For overprint see No. C255.

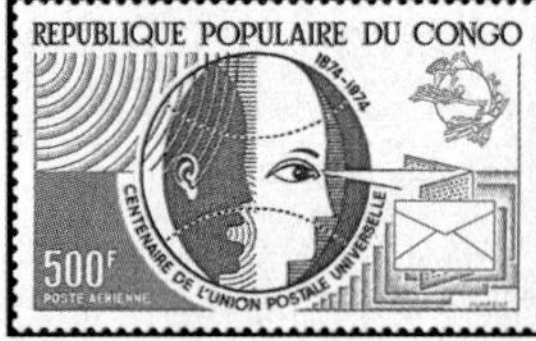

Symbols of Communications, UPU Emblem — AP80

1974, Aug. 10
C190 AP80 500fr blk & red 6.75 3.00

Centenary of Universal Postal Union.
For surcharge see No. C194.

Lenin and Pendulum Trace Pattern — AP81

1974, Sept. 16 Engr. *Perf. 13*
C191 AP81 150fr multicolored 1.60 .75

Lenin (1870-1924).

Churchill and Order of the Garter AP82

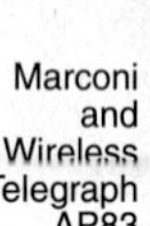

Marconi and Wireless Telegraph AP83

1974, Oct. 1 Litho. *Perf. 13*

C192 AP82 200fr lt grn & multi 2.75 1.25
C193 AP83 200fr lt ultra & multi 2.75 1.25

No. C190 Surcharged in Violet Blue with New Value, 2 Bars and: "9 OCTOBER 1974"

1974, Oct. 9

C194 AP80 300fr on 500fr multi 3.50 1.75

Universal Postal Union Day.

UDEAC Issue

Presidents and Flags of Cameroun, CAR, Gabon and Congo — AP83a

1974, Dec. 8 Photo. *Perf. 13*

C195 AP83a 100fr gold & multi 1.00 .50

See note after Cameroun No. 595.

Regatta at Argenteuil, by Monet — AP84

Impressionist Paintings: 40fr, Seated Dancer, by Degas. 50fr, Girl on Swing, by Renoir. 75fr, Girl with Straw Hat, by Renoir. All vertical.

1974, Dec. 15

C196 AP84 30fr gold & multi 1.50 .35
C197 AP84 40fr gold & multi 1.75 .35
C198 AP84 50fr gold & multi 2.75 .50
C199 AP84 75fr gold & multi 3.00 .80
Nos. C196-C199 (4) 9.00 2.00

National Fair AP85

1974, Dec. 20

C200 AP85 30fr multicolored .90 .35

National Fair, Aug. 24-Sept. 8.

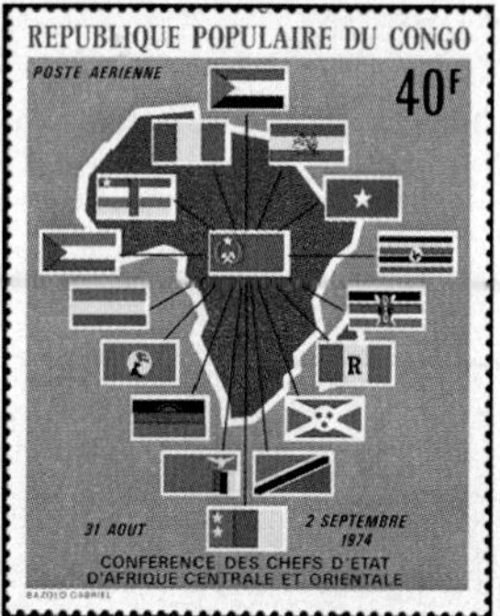

Flags of Participating Nations, Map of Africa — AP86

1974, Dec. 20 *Perf. 13*

C201 AP86 40fr ultra & multi .60 .25

Conference of Chiefs of State of Central and East Africa, Brazzaville, Aug. 31-Sept. 2.

"Five Weeks in a Balloon," by Jules Verne AP87

Design: 50fr, "Around the World in 80 Days," by Jules Verne.

1975, June 30 Litho. *Perf. 12½*

C202 AP87 40fr multicolored .35 .20
C203 AP87 50fr multicolored 1.75 .35

Jules Verne (1828-1905), French science fiction writer, 70th death anniversary.

Paris-Brussels Train, 1890 — AP88

Design: 75fr, Santa Fe, 1880.

1975, June 30

C204 AP88 50fr ocher & multi 2.00 .75
C205 AP88 75fr lt bl & multi 4.25 .90

Soyuz and Apollo-Soyuz Emblem — AP89

Design: 100fr, Apollo and emblem.

1975, July 20 Litho. *Perf. 12½*

C206 AP89 95fr org, blk & mag 1.25 .50
C207 AP89 100fr vio, bl & blk 1.40 .60

Apollo Soyuz space test project (Russo-American space cooperation), launching July 15; link-up, July 17.

For overprints see Nos. C252-C253.

Bicycling and Montreal Olympic Emblem — AP90

Designs (Montreal Olympic Emblem and): 40fr, Boxing, vert. 50fr, Basketball, vert. 95fr, High jump. 100fr, Javelin. 150fr, Running.

Perf. 12½x13, 13x12½

1975, Oct. 30 Photo.

C208 AP90 40fr multicolored .50 .25
C209 AP90 50fr red & multi .60 .25
C210 AP90 85fr bl & multi 1.00 .35
C211 AP90 95fr org & multi 1.10 .45
C212 AP90 100fr multicolored 1.40 .50
C213 AP90 150fr multicolored 1.75 .80
Nos. C208-C213 (6) 6.35 2.60

Pre-Olympic Year 1975.

Map of Africa, Sports and Flags — AP91

Workers and Flag — AP92

1975, Dec. 20 Litho. *Perf. 12½*

C214 AP91 30fr multicolored .60 .35

1st African Games, Brazzaville, 10th anniv.

1975, Dec. 31 Litho. *Perf. 12½*

C215 AP92 60fr multicolored .60 .25

Congolese Labor Party (P.C.T.), 6th anniv.

Alphonse Fondere — AP93

Historic Ships: 5fr, like 30fr. 10fr, 40fr, Hamburg, 1839. 15fr, 50fr, Gomer, 1831. 20fr, 60fr, Great Eastern, 1858. 95fr, J.M. White II, 1878.

1976 Engr. *Perf. 13*

C216 AP93 5fr multicolored .25 .20
C217 AP93 10fr multicolored .25 .20
C218 AP93 15fr multicolored .25 .20
C219 AP93 20fr multicolored .45 .20
C220 AP93 30fr multicolored .60 .25
C221 AP93 40fr multicolored .90 .35
C222 AP93 50fr multicolored .90 .50
C223 AP93 60fr multicolored 1.40 .50
C224 AP93 95fr multicolored 2.00 .80
Nos. C216-C224 (9) 7.00 3.20

Issued: #C216-C219, May; #C220-C224, Mar. 7.

Europafrica Issue 1976

Peasant Family, by Louis Le Nain — AP94

Paintings: 80fr, Boy with Top, by Jean B. Chardin. 95fr, Venus and Aeneas, by Nicolas Poussin. 100fr, The Rape of the Sabine Women, by Jacques Louis David.

1976, Mar. 20 Litho. *Perf. 12½*

C225 AP94 60fr gold & multi .70 .30
C226 AP94 80fr gold & multi 1.00 .45
C227 AP94 95fr gold & multi 1.10 .60
C228 AP94 100fr gold & multi 1.40 .60
Nos. C225-C228 (4) 4.20 1.95

Nos. C225-C228 printed in sheets of 8 stamps and horizontal gutter with commemorative inscription.

Telephone Type of 1976

1976, Apr. 25 Litho. *Perf. 12½x13*

C229 A107 60fr pink, mar & crim .90 .30

Sports Type of 1976

Designs: 150fr, Runner and map of Central Africa. 200fr, Discus and map.

1976, Oct. 25 *Perf. 12½*

C230 A110 150fr multicolored 1.75 .75
C231 A110 200fr multicolored 2.75 1.10

Map of Africa, Flag and OAU Headquarters AP95

1976, Dec. 16 Typo. *Perf. 13x14*

C232 AP95 60fr multicolored .70 .35

13th anniv. of the Organization for African Unity.

Europafrica Issue

Map of Europe and Africa — AP96

1977, June 28 Litho. *Perf. 13*

C233 AP96 75fr multicolored .90 .45

Headdress Type of 1977

1977, June 30 *Perf. 12½*

250fr, Two straw caps. 300fr, Beaded cap.

C234 A118 250fr multicolored 2.75 1.50
C235 A118 300fr multicolored 3.00 1.75

Zeppelin Type of 1977

Souvenir Sheet

Design: 500fr, LZ 127 over US Capitol.

1977, Aug. 5 Litho. *Perf. 11*

C236 A120 500fr multicolored 6.75 2.00

No. C236 exists imperf.

Checkerboard AP97

1977, Aug. 20 Engr. *Perf. 13*
C237 AP97 60fr red & blk .90 .35

Lomé Convention on General Agreement on Tariffs and Trade (GATT).

Newton, Intelsat Satellite and Classical "Planets" — AP98

1977, Aug. 25
C238 AP98 140fr multicolored 2.00 .90

Isaac Newton (1642-1727), natural philosopher and mathematician.

Elizabeth II Type of 1977
Souvenir Sheet

Design: 500fr, Royal family on balcony.

1977, Dec. 21 Litho. *Perf. 14*
C239 A128 500fr multicolored 5.75 1.75

For overprint see No. C244.

Mallard AP99

Birds: 75fr, Purple heron, vert. 150fr, Reed warbler, vert. 240fr, Hoopoe, vert.

1978, May 22 *Perf. 13x12½, 12½x13*
C240 AP99 65fr multicolored 1.00 .50
C241 AP99 75fr multicolored 1.25 .50
C242 AP99 150fr multicolored 3.00 .90
C243 AP99 240fr multicolored 4.50 1.60
Nos. C240-C243 (4) 9.75 3.50

Souvenir Sheet
No. C239 Overprinted in Silver: "ANNIVERSAIRE DU / COURONNEMENT / 1953-1978"

1978, Sept. Litho. *Perf. 14*
C244 A128 500fr multicolored 4.50 3.00

25th anniv. of coronation of Elizabeth II.

Philexafrique II-Essen Issue
Common Design Types

No. C245, Leopard and Congo No. C243. No. C246, Eagle and Wurttemberg No. 1.

1978, Nov. 1 Litho. *Perf. 12½*
C245 CD138 100fr multicolored 2.00 1.10
C246 CD139 100fr multicolored 2.00 1.10
a. Pair, #C245-C246 5.25 5.25

Map of Africa, Satellites AP100

Map of Africa and People — AP101

1978, Nov. 25 Engr. *Perf. 13*
C247 AP100 100fr multicolored 1.25 .50

Pan-African Telecommunications Network, PANAFEL.

1979, Aug. 2 Litho. *Perf. 12½*
C248 AP101 45fr multicolored .45 .20
C249 AP101 75fr multicolored .70 .35

5th Conference of Panafrican Youth Movement, Brazzaville, Aug. 2-7.

Abala Peasant Woman AP102

1979, Aug. 20
C250 AP102 150fr multicolored 1.75 .90

Nos. C173, C206-C207, C186, C189 Overprinted "ALUNISSAGE APOLLO XI / JUILLET 1969" and Emblem

Perf. 13, 12½

1979, Nov. 5 Engr., Litho.
C251 AP69 80fr multicolored .90 .90
C252 AP89 95fr multicolored 1.00 1.00
C253 AP89 100fr multicolored 1.00 1.00
C254 AP77 100fr multicolored 1.00 1.00
C255 AP79 300fr multicolored 2.75 2.75
Nos. C251-C255 (5) 6.65 6.65

Apollo 11 moon landing, 10th anniversary.

Runner, Olympic Rings — AP103

Pre-Olympic Year: 100fr, Boxing. 200fr, Fencing. 300fr, Soccer. 500fr, Moscow '80 emblem.

1979 Litho. *Perf. 13½*
C256 AP103 65fr multi .50 .20
C257 AP103 100fr multi 1.00 .25
C258 AP103 200fr multi, vert. 2.00 .50
C259 AP103 300fr multi 2.50 .75
C260 AP103 500fr multi, vert. 5.00 1.25
Nos. C256-C260 (5) 11.00 2.95

Cross-Country Skiing — AP104

Lake Placid '80 Emblem and: 60fr, Slalom. 200fr, Ski jump, 350fr, Downhill skiing, horiz. 500fr, Woman skier.

1979, Dec *Perf. 14½*
Size: 24x42mm, 42x24mm
C261 AP104 40fr multicolored .45 .20
C262 AP104 60fr multicolored .60 .20
C263 AP104 200fr multicolored 2.00 .45
C264 AP104 350fr multicolored 3.50 .90

Size: 31½x46½mm
Perf. 14
C265 AP104 500fr multicolored 5.00 1.40
Nos. C261-C265 (5) 11.55 3.15

13th Winter Olympic Games, Lake Placid, NY, Feb. 12-24, 1980.

Overprinted with Names of Winners

1980, Apr. 28
C266 AP104 40fr Zimiatov .40 .20
C267 AP104 60fr Moser-Proell .50 .25
C268 AP104 200fr Tomanen 1.90 .75
C269 AP104 350fr Stock 3.50 1.25
C270 AP104 500fr Stenmark-Wenzel 4.75 1.90
Nos. C266-C270 (5) 11.05 4.35

Long Jump, Olympic Rings — AP105

1980, May 2 Litho. *Perf. 14½*
C271 AP105 75fr multi, vert. .90 .20
C272 AP105 150fr multi 1.40 .30
C273 AP105 250fr multi, vert. 2.25 .50
C274 AP105 350fr multi, vert. 3.25 .70
Nos. C271-C274 (4) 7.80 1.70

Souvenir Sheet
C275 AP105 500fr multi 5.00 1.60

22nd Summer Olympic Games, Moscow, July 19-Aug. 3.
For overprints see Nos. C292-C296.

Stadium, Mascot, Madrid Club Emblem — AP106

Stadium, Mascot and Club Emblem: 75fr, Zaragoza. 100fr, Madrid Athletic Club. 150fr, Valencia. 175fr, Spain. 250fr, Barcelona.

1980, June 23 Litho. *Perf. 14x13½*
C276 AP106 60fr multicolored .60 .20
C277 AP106 75fr multicolored .60 .20
C278 AP106 100fr multicolored 1.00 .25
C279 AP106 150fr multicolored 1.40 .35
C280 AP106 175fr multicolored 1.60 .50
Nos. C276-C280 (5) 5.20 1.50

Souvenir Sheet
C281 AP106 250fr multicolored 2.25 .80

World Soccer Cup 1982.
For overprints see Nos. C298-C303.

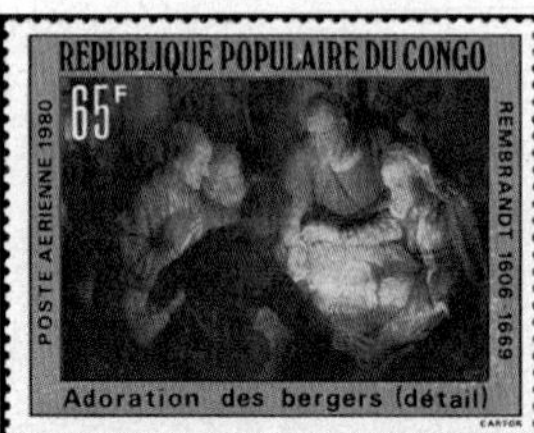

Adoration of the Shepherds — AP107

Rembrandt Paintings: 100fr, The Burial. 200fr, Christ at Emmaus. 300fr, Annunciation, vert. 500fr, Crucifixion, vert.

1980, July 4 *Perf. 12½*
C282 AP107 65fr multicolored .60 .25
C283 AP107 100fr multicolored .90 .35
C284 AP107 200fr multicolored 1.60 .55
C285 AP107 300fr multicolored 2.50 .75
C286 AP107 500fr multicolored 5.25 1.25
Nos. C282-C286 (5) 10.85 3.15

Albert Camus (1913-1960), Writer — AP108

Design: 150fr, Jacques Offenbach (1819-1880), composer, vert.

1980, July 5 Engr. *Perf. 13*
C287 AP108 100fr multicolored 1.25 .50
C288 AP108 150fr multicolored 2.25 1.25

Raffia Dancing Skirts — AP109

Traditional Dancing Costumes: 300fr, Tam-tam dancers, vert. 350fr, Masks.

1980, Aug. 6 Litho. *Perf. 13½*
C289 AP109 250fr multicolored 2.75 .95
C290 AP109 300fr multicolored 3.25 1.50
C291 AP109 350fr multicolored 4.00 1.90
Nos. C289-C291 (3) 10.00 4.35

Nos. C271-C275 Overprinted with Winner and Country

1980, Nov. 14 Litho. *Perf. 14½*
C292 AP105 75fr multicolored .70 .30
C293 AP105 150fr multicolored 1.40 .60
C294 AP105 250fr multicolored 2.25 .90
C295 AP105 350fr multicolored 3.25 1.50
Nos. C292-C295 (4) 7.60 3.30

Souvenir Sheet
C296 AP105 500fr multicolored 5.00 4.00

The Studio by Picasso — AP109a

1981, July 4 *Perf. 12½*
C296A AP109a 100fr shown 1.00 .50
C296B AP109a 150fr Landscape 1.50 .75
C296C AP109a 200fr Cannes Studio 2.00 1.00
C296D AP109a 300fr Still Life 3.00 1.50
C296E AP109a 500fr Still Life, diff. 5.00 2.50
Nos. C296A-C296E (5) 12.50 6.25

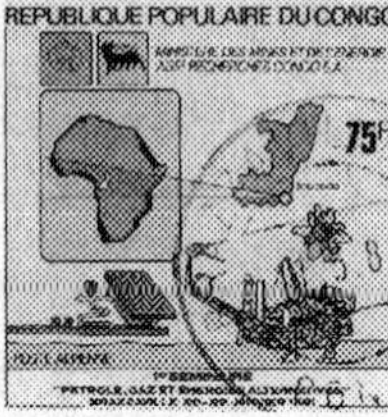

1st Seminar on Petroleum, Gas and Energy Alternatives, Brazzaville AP109b

45fr, Emblem, oil platform, other energy sources. 150fr, Map, other energy sources. 200fr, Maps of Africa, Congo, oil worker.

1981 Litho. *Perf. 12½*

C296F AP109b 45fr multi — —
C296G AP109b 75fr multi 32.50 11.00
C296I AP109b 150fr multi 65.00 32.50
C296J AP109b 200fr multi 90.00 45.00

A number has been reserved for an additional stamp in this set. The editors would like to examine any examples.

1350th Anniv. of Mohamed's Death at Medina — AP110

1982, July 17 Litho. *Perf. 13*

C297 AP110 400fr Medina Mosque minaret 3.75 1.25

Nos. C276-C281 Overprinted with Finalists and/or Scores in Black on Silver

1982, Oct. 7 Litho. *Perf. 14x13½*

C298 AP106 60fr multicolored .50 .25
C299 AP106 75fr multicolored .60 .30
C300 AP106 100fr multicolored .90 .45
C301 AP106 150fr multicolored 1.40 .60
C302 AP106 175fr multicolored 1.50 .60
Nos. C298-C302 (5) 4.90 2.20

Souvenir Sheet

C303 AP106 250fr multicolored 2.25 1.90

30th Anniv. of Amelia Earhart's Transatlantic Flight — AP111

1982, Dec. 4 Engr. *Perf. 13*

C304 AP111 150fr multicolored 1.25 .75

Wind Surfing AP112

Various wind surfing scenes, 1984 Olympic Games, 100fr, 300fr, 400fr vert.

1983, June 4 Litho. *Perf. 13*

C305 AP112 100fr multicolored .90 .25
C306 AP112 200fr multicolored 1.75 .50
C307 AP112 300fr multicolored 2.75 .70
C308 AP112 400fr multicolored 3.50 1.00
Nos. C305-C308 (4) 8.90 2.45

Souvenir Sheet

C309 AP112 500fr multicolored 5.00 2.50

For overprint see No. C336.

Manned Flight Bicentenary AP113

Various balloons.

1983, June 7

C310 AP113 100fr Montgolfiere, 1783 1.10 .20
C311 AP113 200fr Flesselles, 1784 2.10 .40
C312 AP113 300fr Auguste Piccard, 1931 3.00 .60
C313 AP113 400fr Don Piccard 4.50 .90
Nos. C310-C313 (4) 10.70 2.10

Souvenir Sheet

C314 AP113 500fr Mail transport balloon, 1870 5.75 1.60

For overprint see No. C337.

Christmas 1983 AP114

Various Virgin and Child Paintings by Botticelli.

1984, Jan. 21 Litho. *Perf. 13*

C315 AP114 150fr multicolored 1.25 .50
C316 AP114 350fr multicolored 3.00 1.10
C317 AP114 500fr multicolored 4.50 1.50
Nos. C315-C317 (3) 8.75 3.10

Vase of Flowers, by Manet (1832-83) AP115

Paintings: 200fr, Small Holy Family, by Raphael. 300fr, La Belle Jardiniere, by Raphael. 400fr, Virgin of Loretto, by Raphael. 500fr, Portrait of Richard Wagner (1813-83), by Giuseppe Tivoli.

1984, Feb. 24 Litho. *Perf. 13*

C318 AP115 100fr multicolored .90 .30
C319 AP115 200fr multicolored 1.90 .70
C320 AP115 300fr multicolored 2.75 1.00
C321 AP115 400fr multicolored 3.75 1.40
C322 AP115 500fr multicolored 5.00 1.50
Nos. C318-C322 (5) 14.30 4.90

1984 Summer Olympics — AP116

1984, Mar. 31 *Perf. 13*

C323 AP116 45fr Judo, vert. .45 .20
C324 AP116 75fr Judo, diff. .70 .25
C325 AP116 150fr Wrestling 1.40 .50
C326 AP116 175fr Fencing 1.60 .60
C327 AP116 350fr Fencing, diff. 3.25 1.10
Nos. C323-C327 (5) 7.40 2.65

Souvenir Sheet

C328 AP116 500fr Boxing 5.00 2.50

1984 Summer Olympic Gold Medalists — AP117

Sailing/yachting: 100fr, Stephan Van Den Berg, Netherlands, Windglider Class. 150fr, US, Soling Class. 200fr, Spain, 470 Class. 500fr, US, Flying Dutchman Class.

1984, Dec. 18 Litho. *Perf. 13*

C329 AP117 100fr multi, vert. 1.00 .45
C330 AP117 150fr multi 1.40 .65
C331 AP117 200fr multi 2.00 .90
C332 AP117 500fr multi, vert. 4.50 2.25
Nos. C329-C332 (4) 8.90 4.25

Virgin and Child, by Giovanni Bellini (c. 1430-1516) — AP118

Religious paintings: 100fr, Holy Family, by Andrea del Sarto (1486-1530). 400fr, Virgin with Angels, by Cimabue (c. 1240-1302).

1985, Feb. 12 Litho. *Perf. 13*

C333 AP118 100fr multi, vert. 1.00 .45
C334 AP118 200fr multi 2.00 .90
C335 AP118 400fr multi, vert. 3.75 1.75
Nos. C333-C335 (3) 6.75 3.10

Christmas 1984.

Souvenir Sheets
Nos. C309, C314 Ovptd. with Exhibition in Blue or Green

1985, Mar. 8 *Perf. 13*

C336 AP112 500fr OLYMPHILEX '85 / LAUSANNE (B) 5.00 4.00
C337 AP113 500fr MOPHILA '85 / HAMBURG (G) 5.00 4.00

Audubon Birth Bicentenary — AP119

Illustrations of North American bird species by Audubon. Nos. C338-C339 vert.

1985, Apr. 11 *Perf. 13½*

C338 AP119 100fr Passiformes fringillidae 1.00 .45
C339 AP119 150fr Eudocimus ruber 1.50 .65
C340 AP119 200fr Buteo jamaicensis 1.90 .90
C341 AP119 350fr Camptorhynchus labradorius 3.75 1.50
Nos. C338-C341 (4) 8.15 3.50

PHILEXAFRICA '85, Lome — AP120

Youths in public service activities.

1985, May 20 *Perf. 13*

C342 AP120 200fr Community health care 2.25 1.50
C343 AP120 200fr Agriculture 2.25 1.50
a. Pair, #C342-C343 + label 5.75 5.75

Admission to UN, 25th Anniv. — AP121

1985, Aug. 13

C344 AP121 190fr multicolored 1.75 .75

UN, 40th Anniv. — AP122

1985, Oct. 25 *Perf. 12½*

C345 AP122 180fr Rainbow, emblem 1.40 .60

Christmas — AP123

Paintings: 100fr, The Virgin and the Infant Jesus, by David. 200fr, Adoration of the Magi, by Hieronymus Bosch (1450-1516). 400fr, Virgin and Child, by Van Dyck.

1985, Dec. 20 Litho. *Perf. 13*

C346 AP123 100fr multicolored .90 .35
C347 AP123 200fr multicolored 1.90 .75
C348 AP123 400fr multicolored 3.50 1.75
Nos. C346-C348 (3) 6.30 2.85

Nos. C346-C347 vert.

Halley's Comet — AP124

1986, Feb. 17

C349	AP124	125fr Halley, comet	1.00	.50
C350	AP124	150fr West's Comet, 1976	1.25	.60
C351	AP124	225fr Ikeya Seki's Comet, 1965	1.75	.90
C352	AP124	300fr Trajectory diagram	2.25	1.25
C353	AP124	350fr Comet, Vega probe	2.75	1.50
		Nos. C349-C353 (5)	9.00	4.75

Nos. C350-C351 vert.

Cosmos-Frantel Hotel — AP125

1986, May 1 ***Perf. 13½***

C354	AP125	250fr multicolored	2.25	.90

1986 World Cup Soccer Championships, Mexico — AP126

Various soccer plays.

1986, July 22 **Litho.** ***Perf. 13***

C355	AP126	150fr multicolored	1.25	.60
C356	AP126	250fr multicolored	2.00	1.00
C357	AP126	440fr multicolored	3.75	1.75
C358	AP126	600fr multicolored	6.50	2.50
		Nos. C355-C358 (4)	13.50	5.85

Air Africa, 25th Anniv. — AP127

1986, Nov. 29 **Litho.** ***Perf. 13½***

C359	AP127	200fr multicolored	1.75	.75

1988 Winter Pre-Olympics, Calgary — AP128

1986, Dec. 15 ***Perf. 13***

C360	AP128	150fr Downhill skiing	1.25	.60
C361	AP128	250fr Bobsled	2.25	.95
C362	AP128	440fr Women's cross-country skiing	4.00	1.50
C363	AP128	600fr Ski jumping	5.75	2.40
		Nos. C360-C363 (4)	13.25	5.45

Nos. C361-C362 vert.

Christmas AP129

Paintings by Rogier van der Weyden (c.1399-1464): 250fr, Virgin and Child. 440fr, The Nativity. 500fr, Virgin with Carnation.

1986, Dec. 23 ***Perf. 13½***

C364	AP129	250fr multicolored	2.25	1.00
C365	AP129	440fr multicolored	4.50	1.75
C366	AP129	500fr multicolored	5.00	2.10
		Nos. C364-C366 (3)	11.75	4.85

Crocodiles, World Wildlife Fund — AP130

1987, Jan. 22 ***Perf. 13***

C367	AP130	75fr Osteolaemus tetraspis	2.00	.30
C368	AP130	100fr Crocodylus cataphractus	2.25	.35
C369	AP130	125fr Osteolaemus tetraspis, diff.	3.25	.50
C370	AP130	150fr Crocodylus cataphractus, diff.	3.50	.60
		Nos. C367-C370 (4)	11.00	1.75

1988 Summer Olympics, Seoul — AP131

1987, July 11 **Litho.** ***Perf. 13***

C371	AP131	100fr Backstroke	.90	.35
C372	AP131	200fr Freestyle	1.75	.75
C373	AP131	300fr Breaststroke	2.75	1.10
C374	AP131	400fr Butterfly	3.50	1.40
		Nos. C371-C374 (4)	8.90	3.60

Souvenir Sheet

C375	AP131	750fr Start of event	6.75	3.50

Launch of Sputnik, First Artificial Satellite, 30th Anniv. — AP132

1987, June 5 ***Perf. 12½x12***

C376	AP132	60fr multicolored	.50	.25
C377	AP132	240fr multicolored	2.25	1.10

Butterflies — AP133

1987, Sept. 4 ***Perf. 12½***

C378	AP133	75fr Precis epicleli	1.00	.30
C379	AP133	120fr Deilephila nerii	1.75	.45
C380	AP133	450fr Euryphene senegalensis	5.25	1.75
C381	AP133	550fr Precis almanta	7.00	2.40
		Nos. C378-C381 (4)	15.00	4.90

Coubertin, Eternal Flame and Greece No. 125 — AP134

Cameo portrait, athletes and stamps: 120fr, Runners, France No. 198. 350fr, Congo Republic No. C22, hurdler. 600fr, High jump, Congo Republic No. C75.

1987, Nov. 4

C382	AP134	75fr shown	.80	.30
C383	AP134	120fr multicolored	1.10	.45
C384	AP134	350fr multicolored	3.50	1.25
C385	AP134	600fr multicolored	5.25	2.10
		Nos. C382-C385 (4)	10.65	4.10

Pierre de Coubertin (1863-1937), promulgator of the modern Olympics.

Arrival of Schweitzer in Lambarene, 75th Anniv. — AP135

1988, Apr. 17 **Litho.** ***Perf. 12½***

C386	AP135	240fr multicolored	2.25	1.10

Dr. Albert Schweitzer (1875-1965), Nobel Peace Prize winner of 1952, founded Lambarene Hospital, Gabon, in 1913.

1988 Summer Olympics, Seoul — AP136

Pentathlon: 75fr, Swimming. 170fr, Cross-country running, vert. 200fr, Shooting. 600fr, Equestrian. 700fr, Fencing.

1988, June 10 **Litho.** ***Perf. 13***

C387	AP136	75fr multicolored	.50	.25
C388	AP136	170fr multicolored	1.25	.60
C389	AP136	200fr multicolored	1.75	.70
C390	AP136	600fr multicolored	5.00	2.00
		Nos. C387-C390 (4)	8.50	3.55

Souvenir Sheet

C391	AP136	750fr multicolored	6.75	3.75

Elimination Matches, 1990 World Cup Soccer Championships — AP137

Various athletes and cities in Italy.

1989, June 15 **Litho.** ***Perf. 13***

C392	AP137	75fr Bari	.60	.30
C393	AP137	120fr Rome	1.00	.45
C394	AP137	500fr Florence	4.75	1.90
C395	AP137	550fr Naples	5.25	2.00
		Nos. C392-C395 (4)	11.60	4.65

PHILEXFRANCE '89 — AP138

Paintings: 300fr, Storming of the Bastille, July 14, 1789, from a gouache by J.P. Houel. 400fr, Eiffel Tower, by G. Seurat.

1989, June 22

C396	AP138	300fr multicolored	2.75	1.10
C397	AP138	400fr multicolored	3.75	1.50

French revolution, bicent. (300fr); Eiffel Tower, cent. (400fr).

First Moon Landing, 20th Anniv. AP139

Man's first step on the Moon: No. C398, Astronaut on ladder. No. C399, Conducting experiments on the Moon's surface.

1989, June 22

C398	AP139	400fr multicolored	3.75	1.50
C399	AP139	400fr multicolored	3.75	1.50

World Cup Soccer Championships, Italy — AP140

Various soccer plays and architecture.

1990, June 8 **Litho.** ***Perf. 13***

C400	AP140	120fr multicolored	1.00	.50
C401	AP140	240fr multicolored	2.10	.95
C402	AP140	500fr multicolored	4.25	2.00

C403 AP140 600fr multicolored 5.25 2.40
Nos. C400-C403 (4) 12.60 5.85

Pan African Postal Union, 10th Anniv. AP141

1991, Jan. 10 Litho. *Perf. 13½*
C404 AP141 60fr shown .50 .25
C405 AP141 120fr Emblem .95 .50

1992 Winter Olympics, Albertville AP142

1991, June 8 Litho. *Perf. 13½*
C406 AP142 120fr Ice hockey 1.10 .60
C407 AP142 300fr Speed skating 3.00 1.50

Litho. & Embossed
C408 AP142 1500fr Slalom skiing 12.00 12.00

Numbers have been reserved for souvenir sheets in this set.

1992 Summer Olympics, Barcelona AP143

#C411, Equestrian. #C412, Long jump.

1992 Litho. & Embossed *Perf. 13½*
C411 AP143 1500fr gold & multi 12.50 12.50

Souvenir Sheet
C412 AP143 1500fr gold & multi 21.00 21.00

Anniversaries AP144

Designs: 90fr, Victor Schoelcher, missionary, death cent. 205fr, Martin Luther King, civil rights reformer, 25th death anniv. 300fr, Claude Chappe (1763-1805), bicent. of visual telegraph.

1993 Litho. *Perf. 14*
C413 AP144 90fr multicolored *1.00 .50*
C414 AP144 205fr multicolored *2.50 1.25*
C415 AP144 300fr multicolored *3.50 1.75*
Nos. C413-C415 (3) *7.00 3.50*

1994 Winter Olympics, Lillehammer AP145

1993, Apr. 26 Litho. *Perf. 13*
C416 AP145 400fr Ice dancing *3.50 1.10*
C417 AP145 600fr Ice hockey *5.00 1.50*

Souvenir Sheet
C418 AP145 750fr Downhill skiing *6.50 4.00*

Nos. C416-C417 exist in imperf. souvenir sheets of 1. Nos. C416-C418 exist imperf.

AIR POST SEMI-POSTAL STAMPS

Hathor Pillar — SPAP1

Unwmk.
1964, Mar. 9 Engr. *Perf. 13*
CB1 SPAP1 10fr + 5fr vio & chnt .45 .30
CB2 SPAP1 25fr + 5fr org brn & slate grn .70 .60
CB3 SPAP1 50fr + 5fr slate grn & brn red 1.75 1.60
Nos. CB1-CB3 (3) 2.90 2.50

UNESCO world campaign to save historic monuments in Nubia.

POSTAGE DUE STAMPS

Messenger — D6

MH. 1521 Broussard Plane — D7

Early Transportation: 1fr, Litter. 2fr, Canoe. 5fr, Bicyclist. 10fr, Steam locomotive. 25fr, Seaplane.

Unwmk.
1961, Dec. 4 Engr. *Perf. 11*
J34 D6 50c ultra, ol bis & red .20 .20
a. Pair, #J34, J40 .25
J35 D6 1fr red brn, red & grn .20 .20
a. Pair, #J35, J41 .30
J36 D6 2fr grn, ultra & brn .20 .20
a. Pair, #J36, J42 .40
J37 D6 5fr pur & gray brn .25 .25
a. Pair, #J37, J43 .50
J38 D6 10fr bl, grn & chocolate .70 .70
a. Pair, #J38, J44 1.40 1.40
J39 D6 25fr bl, dk grn & dk brn 1.60 1.60
a. Pair, #J39, J45 3.25

Modern transportation: 1fr, Land Rover. 2fr, River boat transporting barge. 5fr, Trailer-truck. 10fr, Diesel locomotive. 25fr, Boeing 707 jet plane.

J40 D7 50c ultra, olive bis & red .20 .20
J41 D7 1fr red & grn .20 .20
J42 D7 2fr ultra, grn & brn .20 .20
J43 D7 5fr pur & gray brn .25 .25
J44 D7 10fr dk grn & chocolate .70 .70
J45 D7 25fr bl, dk grn & sepia 1.60 1.60
Nos. J34-J45 (12) 6.30 6.30

Pairs printed tête bêche, se-tenant at the base.

Flowers — D8

Flowers: 2fr, Phaeomeria magnifica. 5fr, Millettia laurentii. 10fr, Tuberose. 15fr, Pyrostegia venusta. 20fr, Hibiscus.

1971, Mar. 25 Photo. *Perf. 12x12½*
J46 D8 1fr multi .35 .35
J47 D8 2fr multi .45 .45
J48 D8 5fr pink & multi .50 .50
J49 D8 10fr dk grn & multi .60 .60
J50 D8 15fr multi 1.00 1.00
J51 D8 20fr multi 1.25 1.25
Nos. J46-J51 (6) 4.15 4.15

Flowers and Fruit — D9

1986, June 5 Litho. *Perf. 13*
J52 D9 5fr Passiflora quadrangulares .25 .25
J53 D9 10fr Cannaceae, vert. .45 .45
J54 D9 15fr Ananas comosus, vert. .55 .55
Nos. J52-J54 (3) 1.25 1.25

OFFICIAL STAMPS

Coat of Arms — O1

Perf. 14x13
1968-70 Unwmk. Typo.
O1 O1 1fr multi ('70) .20 .20
O2 O1 2fr multi ('70) .20 .20
O3 O1 5fr multi ('70) .20 .20
O4 O1 10fr multi ('70) .25 .20
O5 O1 25fr emer & multi .45 .20
O6 O1 30fr red & multi .60 .20
O7 O1 50fr multi ('70) 1.10 .50
O8 O1 85fr multi ('70) 2.25 .90
O9 O1 100frmulti ('70) 2.75 1.10
O10 O1 200frmulti ('70) 3.75 2.00
Nos. O1-O10 (10) 11.75 5.70

COOK ISLANDS

'kuk 'i-ləndz

(Rarotonga)

LOCATION — South Pacific Ocean, northeast of New Zealand
GOVT. — Internal self-government, linked to New Zealand
AREA — 91 sq. mi.
POP. — 19,103 (1996)
CAPITAL — Avarua

Fifteen islands in Northern and Southern groups extend over 850,000 square miles of ocean.

Separate stamp issues used by Aitutaki (1903-32 and 1972 onward) and Penrhyn Islands (1902-32 and 1973 onward). Niue is included geographically, but administered separately. It continues to issue separate stamps.

12 Pence = 1 Shilling
20 Shillings = 1 Pound
100 Cents = 1 Dollar (1967)

Catalogue values for unused stamps in this country are for Never Hinged items, beginning with Scott 127 in the regular postage section, Scott B1 in the semi-postal section, Scott C1 in the air post section, Scott CB1 in the air post semi-postal section and Scott O16 in the official section.

Watermarks

Wmk. 61 — Single-lined N Z and Star Close Together

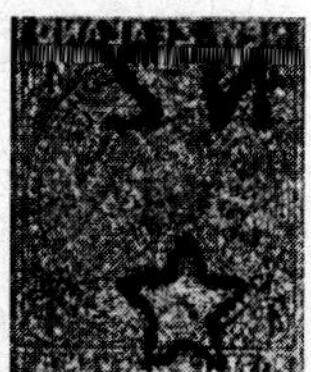

Wmk. 62 — Single-lined N Z and Star Wide Apart

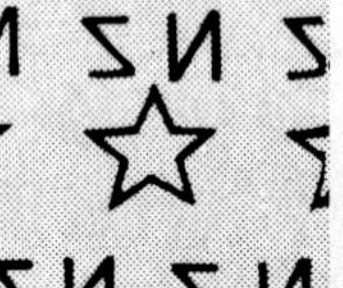

Wmk. 253 — Multiple N Z and Star

A1

1892 Unwmk. Typo. *Perf. 12½*
Toned Paper
1 A1 1p black 32.50 30.00
2 A1 1½p violet 47.50 45.00
a. Imperf, pair *10,500.*
3 A1 2½p blue 47.50 45.00
4 A1 10p carmine 160.00 150.00
Nos. 1-4 (4) 287.50 270.00

White Paper
5 A1 1p black 32.50 30.00
a. Vert. pair, imperf. between *9,750.*
6 A1 1½p violet 47.50 45.00
7 A1 2½p blue 47.50 45.00
8 A1 10p carmine 160.00 150.00
Nos. 5-8 (4) 287.50 270.00

Queen Makea Takau — A2

Wrybill (Torea) — A3

1893-94 Wmk. 62 *Perf. 12x11½*
9 A2 1p brown 47.50 *52.50*
10 A2 1p blue ('94) 10.50 2.50
11 A2 1½p brt violet 9.75 7.50
12 A2 2½p rose 45.00 *27.50*
13 A2 5p olive gray 20.00 15.00
14 A2 10p green 80.00 *55.00*
Nos. 9-14 (6) 212.75 *160.00*

Perf. 12½ examples of Nos. 10, 12 are from a part of the normal perf. 12x11½ sheets. They were caused by a partial deviation of the original perforating.

1898-1900 ***Perf. 11***

15	A3	½p blue ('00)	5.25	*7.00*
a.		"d" omitted at upper right	1,750.	
16	A2	1p brown	19.00	19.00
17	A2	1p blue	5.75	5.25
18	A2	1½p violet	10.50	7.50
19	A3	2p chocolate	9.75	7.50
20	A2	2½p car rose	19.00	10.50
21	A2	5p olive gray	27.50	20.00
22	A3	6p red violet	22.50	*27.50*
23	A2	10p green	21.00	*55.00*
24	A3	1sh car rose	55.00	55.00
		Nos. 15-24 (10)	195.25	214.25

No. 17 Surcharged in Black

1899

25	A2	½p on 1p blue	40.00	*50.00*
a.		Double surcharge	1,000.	*1,050.*
b.		Inverted surcharge	1,850.	*1,900.*

No. 16 Overprinted in Black

1901

26	A2	1p brown	210.00	160.00
a.		Inverted overprint	2,100.	1,650.
c.		Double overprint	1,850.	*1,900.*

Some single stamps were overprinted by favor. Other varieties could exist.

Forgeries exist.

Types of 1893-98

1902 **Unwmk.**

27	A3	½p green	5.00	*5.00*
a.		Vert. pair, imperf. horiz.	1,400.	
28	A2	1p rose	14.00	*12.50*
29	A2	2½p dull blue	15.00	*24.00*
		Nos. 27-29 (3)	34.00	*41.50*

1902 **Wmk. 61** ***Perf. 11***

30	A3	½p green	3.25	*3.75*
31	A2	1p rose	4.75	3.50
32	A2	1½p brt violet	4.75	*10.00*
33	A3	2p chocolate	5.75	*11.50*
a.		Figures of value omitted	*2,750.*	*3,250.*
b.		Perf. 11x14	*1,750.*	
34	A2	2½p dull blue	4.50	*8.00*
35	A2	5p olive gray	40.00	*55.00*
36	A3	6p purple	37.50	32.50
37	A2	10p blue green	55.00	*110.00*
38	A3	1sh car rose	55.00	*80.00*
a.		Perf. 11x14	*1,950.*	
		Nos. 30-38 (9)	210.50	*314.25*

1909-19 ***Perf. 14, 14x14½, 14½x14***

39	A3	½p green, perf 14½x14 ('11)	7.00	*9.25*
a.		½p dp grn, wmk sideways, perf 14 ('15)	5.50	*17.50*
b.		As "a," wmk upright	7.00	*12.50*
40b	A2	1p red	5.50	5.00
41	A2	1½p purple ('15)	10.00	4.75
42	A3	2p dp brown ('19)	5.75	*52.50*
43	A2	10p dp green ('18)	19.00	*100.00*
44	A3	1sh car rose ('19)	32.50	*100.00*
		Nos. 39a,39-44 (7)	85.25	
		Nos. 39-44 (6)		*271.50*

Nos. 39-40 are on both ordinary and chalky paper; Nos. 41-44 on chalky paper.

New Zealand Stamps of 1909-19 Surcharged in Dark Blue or Red

1919 **Typo.** ***Perf. 14x13½, 14x14½***

48	A43	½p yel green (R)	.45	*1.25*
a.		Pair, one without surcharge		
49	A42	1p carmine	1.25	3.50
50	A47	1½p brown org (R)	.60	*.90*
51	A43	2p yellow (R)	1.75	*2.00*
52	A43	3p chocolate	3.25	*15.00*

Engr.

53	A44	2½p dull blue (R)	2.75	*7.50*
54	A45	3p violet brown	2.25	*9.50*
55	A45	4p purple	2.25	*6.50*
56	A44	4½p dark green	2.25	*8.00*
57	A45	6p car rose	3.50	*10.00*
58	A44	7½p red brown	1.75	*6.50*
59	A45	9p ol green (R)	3.75	*17.50*
60	A45	1sh vermilion	13.00	*35.00*
		Nos. 48-60 (13)	38.80	*123.15*

The Polynesian surcharge restates the denomination of the basic stamp.

Landing of Capt. Cook A4

Avarua Waterfront A5

Capt. James Cook — A6

Palm — A7

Houses at Arorangi — A8

Avarua Harbor — A9

1920 **Unwmk.** **Engr.** ***Perf. 14***

61	A4	½p green & black	4.50	*21.00*
62	A5	1p car & black	5.50	*21.00*
a.		Center inverted	*550.00*	
63	A6	1½p blue & black	9.75	9.75
64	A7	3p red brn & blk	2.50	*6.25*
65	A8	6p org & red brn	3.50	*9.75*
66	A9	1sh vio & black	5.75	*20.00*
		Nos. 61-66 (6)	31.50	*87.75*

The stamps overprinted or inscribed "Rarotonga" were used throughout the Cook Islands.

For surcharges see Nos. 78, 79.

New Zealand Postal-Fiscal Stamps of 1906-13 Overprinted in Red or Dark Blue

a

Perf. 14, 14½, 14x14½

1921 **Typo.** **Wmk. 61**

67	PF1	2sh blue (R)	30.00	*62.50*
68	PF1	2sh6p brown	22.50	*60.00*
69	PF1	5sh green (R)	30.00	*75.00*
70	PF1	10sh claret	75.00	*110.00*
71	PF2	£1 rose	100.00	*210.00*
		Nos. 67-71 (5)	257.50	*517.50*

Types of 1920 Issue

1924-26 **Engr.** ***Perf. 14***

72	A4	½p yel grn & black	3.50	5.00
73	A5	1p carmine & black	7.00	2.50

Issued: ½p, 5/13/26; 1p, 11/10/24.

New Zealand Stamps of 1926 Overprinted Type "a" in Red

1926-28 **Typo.** ***Perf. 14, 14½x14***

74	A56	2sh blue ('27)	17.50	*45.00*
a.		2sh dark blue	11.50	*45.00*
75	A56	3sh violet ('28)	18.00	*47.50*

Rarotongan Chief (Te Po) — A10

Avarua Harbor — A11

1927, Oct. 15 **Engr.** ***Perf. 14***

76	A10	2½p dk bl & red brn	5.75	*27.50*
77	A11	4p dull vio & bl grn	9.00	*20.00*

No. 63 Surcharged in Red

1931 **Unwmk.**

78	A6	2p on 1½p blue & blk	10.50	3.00

Same Surcharge on Type of 1920

Wmk. 61

79	A6	2p on 1½p blue & blk	5.25	*12.50*

No. 79 was not issued without surcharge.

New Zealand Postal-Fiscal Stamps of 1931-32 Overprinted Type "a" in Blue or Red

1931, Nov. 12 **Typo.**

80	PF5	2sh6p dp brn (Bl)	11.50	*25.00*
81	PF5	5sh green (R)	21.00	*62.50*
82	PF5	10sh dk car (Bl)	42.50	*110.00*
83	PF5	£1 pink (Bl) ('32)	100.00	*175.00*
		Nos. 80-83 (4)	175.00	372.50

See Nos. 103-108, 124A-126C.

Landing of Capt. Cook — A12

Capt. James Cook — A13

Double Canoe — A14

Islanders Unloading Ship — A15

View of Avarua Harbor — A16

R.M.S. Monowai — A17

King George V — A18

Unwmk.

1932, Mar. 16 **Engr.** ***Perf. 13***

Center in Black

84	A12	½p deep green	4.00	*18.00*
a.		Perf. 14	32.50	*100.00*
85	A13	1p brown lake	7.50	*5.00*
a.		Center inverted	*3,100.*	*3,100.*
b.		Perf. 14	17.50	*24.00*
86	A14	2p brown	3.50	6.25
b.		Perf. 14	10.00	*22.50*
87	A15	2½p dark ultra	12.50	*57.50*
b.		Perf. 14	16.00	*57.50*

Perf. 14

88	A16	4p ultra	11.50	*57.50*
a.		Perf. 13	22.50	*70.00*
b.		Perf. 14x13	35.00	*110.00*
89	A17	6p orange	5.00	*17.50*
a.		Perf. 13	27.50	*55.00*
90	A18	1sh deep violet	9.75	25.00
		Nos. 84-90 (7)	53.75	*186.75*

Nos. 84-90 were available for postage in Aitutaki, Penrhyn and Rarotonga and replaced the special issues for those islands.

Inverted centers of the 2p and 2½p are from printers waste.

1933-36 **Wmk. 61** ***Perf. 14***

91	A12	½p dp grn & blk	1.10	*5.00*
92	A13	1p dk car & black ('35)	1.40	*2.25*
93	A14	2p brn & blk ('36)	1.75	.60
94	A15	2½p dk ultra & blk	1.75	*2.50*
95	A16	4p blue & black	1.75	.60
96	A17	6p org & blk ('36)	2.00	*2.50*
97	A18	1sh dp vio & black ('36)	31.00	*42.50*
		Nos. 91-97 (7)	40.75	*55.95*

See Nos. 116-121.

Silver Jubilee Issue

Types of 1932 Overprinted in Black or Red

1935, May 7

98	A13	1p dk car & brn red	.30	*1.50*
99	A15	2½p dk ultra & bl (R)	.75	*2.50*
100	A17	6p dull org & green	3.00	*6.00*
		Nos. 98-100 (3)	4.05	*10.00*

The vertical spacing of the overprint is wider on No. 100.

New Zealand Stamps of 1926 Overprinted in Black

b

1936, July 15 **Typo.** ***Perf. 14***

101	A56	2sh blue	15.00	*50.00*
102	A56	3sh violet	15.00	*80.00*

New Zealand Postal-Fiscal Stamps of 1931-35 Overprinted Type "b" in Black or Red

1932-36

103	PF5	2sh6p brown ('36)	21.00	*80.00*
104	PF5	5sh grn (R) ('36)	26.00	*100.00*
105	PF5	10sh dk car ('36)	55.00	*200.00*
106	PF5	£1 pink ('36)	85.00	*210.00*
107	PF5	£3 lt grn (R)	300.00	*550.00*
108	PF5	£5 dk blue (R)	210.00	*375.00*
		Nos. 103-108 (6)	697.00	*1,515.*

Issue dates: Mar. 1932, July 15, 1936.

New Zealand Stamps of 1937 Overprinted in Black

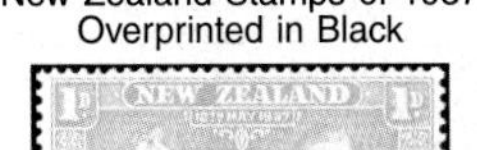

Perf. 14x13½

1937, June 1 **Engr.** **Wmk. 253**

109	A78	1p rose carmine	.20	.20
110	A78	2½p dark blue	.20	.20
111	A78	6p vermilion	.30	.30
		Nos. 109-111 (3)	.70	.70
		Set, never hinged	1.90	

King George VI
A19

Village and Palms
A20

Coastal Scene with Canoe — A21

1938, May 2 **Wmk. 61** ***Perf. 14***

112 A19 1sh dp violet & blk 5.00 *11.00*
113 A20 2sh dk red brn & blk 11.50 14.00
114 A21 3sh yel green & blue 26.00 *35.00*
Nos. 112-114 (3) 42.50 60.00
Set, never hinged 70.00

See Nos. 122-124.

Mt. Ikurangi behind Avarua — A22

Perf. 13½x14

1940, Sept. 2 **Engr.** **Wmk. 253**

115 A22 3p on 1½p violet & blk .70 .70

Issued only with surcharge. Stamps without surcharge are from the printer's archives.

Types of 1932-38

1944-46 **Engr.** ***Perf. 14***

116 A12 ½p dk ol grn & blk ('45) .80 *3.00*
117 A13 1p dk car & blk ('45) 1.10 1.00
118 A14 2p brn & blk ('46) .70 *5.00*
119 A15 2½p dk bl & blk ('45) .40 *1.75*
120 A16 4p blue & black 1.90 *10.00*
121 A17 6p org & black .80 *1.75*
122 A19 1sh dp vio & blk .80 *2.25*
123 A20 2sh dk red brn & blk 17.50 *40.00*
124 A21 3sh yel green & blue ('45) 16.00 *30.00*
Nos. 116-124 (9) 40.00 *94.75*
Set, never hinged 75.00

New Zealand Nos. AR76, AR78, AR85 and Type of 1931 Postal-Fiscal Stamps Overprinted Type "b" in Black or Red

1943-50 **Wmk. 253** **Typo.** ***Perf. 14***

124A PF5 2sh6p brn ('46) 9.00 *17.50*
125 PF5 5sh green (R) 6.00 *17.50*
126 PF5 10sh dp pink ('48) 27.50 *70.00*
126A PF5 £1 pink ('47) 30.00 *75.00*
126B PF5 £3 lt grn (R) ('46) 37.50 *150.00*
126C PF5 £5 dk bl (R) ('50) 140.00 *325.00*
Nos. 124A-126C (6) 250.00 *655.00*
Set, never hinged 425.00

For surcharges see Nos. 192-194.

Catalogue values for unused stamps in this section, from this point to the end of the section, are for Never Hinged items.

Peace Issue

New Zealand Nos. 248, 250, 254 and 255 Overprinted in Black or Blue:

c

d

Perf. 13x13½, 13½x13

1946, June 1 **Engr.**

127 A94 (c) 1p emerald .50 .20
128 A96 (d) 2p rose vio (Bl) .50 .50
129 A100(c) 6p org red & red brn .80 .70
130 A101(c) 8p brn lake & blk (Bl) .80 .70
Nos. 127-130 (4) 2.60 2.10

Ngatangiia Channel, Rarotonga
A23

Capt. James Cook Statue and Map of Cook Islands — A24

Designs: 1p, Cook and map of Hervey Isls. 2p, Rev. John Williams, his ship Messenger of Peace, and map of Rarotonga. 3p, Aitutaki map and palms. 5p, Mail plane landing at Rarotonga airport. 6p, Tongareva (Penrhyn) scene. 8p, Islander's house, Rarotonga. 2sh, Thatched house, mat weaver. 3sh, Steamer Matua offshore.

Perf. 13½x13, 13x13½

1949, Aug.1 **Engr.** **Wmk. 253**

131 A23 ½p brown & violet .20 *1.00*
132 A23 1p green & orange 3.00 2.00
133 A23 2p carmine & brn 1.75 *2.00*
134 A23 3p ultra & green 1.50 *2.00*
135 A23 5p purple & grn 5.00 1.50
136 A23 6p car rose & blk 5.00 2.50
137 A23 8p orange & olive .50 *3.75*
138 A24 1sh chocolate & bl 4.75 3.75
139 A24 2sh rose car & brn 3.50 *12.50*
140 A24 3sh bl grn & lt ultra 9.00 *22.50*
Nos. 131-140 (10) 34.20 *53.50*

For surcharge see No. 147.

Coronation Issue

Type of New Zealand

1953, May 25 **Photo.** ***Perf. 14x14½***

145 A113 3p brown .65 .65
146 A114 6p slate black 1.25 1.25

No. 135 Surcharged with New Value and Two Dots

1960, Apr. 1 **Engr.** ***Perf. 13½x13***

147 A23 1sh6p on 5p purple & grn .50 *.75*

Tiare Maori — A25

Fishing God — A26

Queen Elizabeth II — A27

Island Scene
A28

3sh, Administration building, Mangaia. 5sh, Ship in Rarotonga harbor. 3p, 5p, 6p, 1sh, horiz.

Perf. 13½x13, 13x13½

Litho.; Engr.; (1sh6p)

1963, June 4

148 A25 1p shown .30 *.60*
149 A26 2p shown .20 *.60*
150 A25 3p Frangipani .45 *.60*
151 A26 5p Fairy tern 5.25 1.50
152 A25 6p Hibiscus .65 .65
153 A26 8p Bonito 2.75 1.90
154 A25 1sh Oranges .25 *.65*
155 A27 1sh6p shown 1.75 *2.50*
156 A28 2sh gray & brown .65 *1.00*
157 A28 3sh emer & black .75 *1.25*
158 A28 5sh ultra & brown 7.00 4.75
Nos. 148-158 (11) 20.00 *16.00*

For overprints and surcharges see #167-169, 179-181, 183-184, 186-190.

Solar Eclipse and Palm Tree — A29

1965, May 31 **Litho.** ***Perf. 10x13½***

159 A29 6p black, lt blue & yel .20 .20

Observation of the solar eclipse on Manuae Island, May 30, 1965. Exists imperf.
For surcharge see No. 185.

Flag of New Zealand and Map of Cook Islands
A30

Designs: 10p, London Missionary Society Church and graveyard. 1sh, Reading of Proclamation of Cession, Oct. 8, 1900, and Queen Elizabeth II. 1sh9p, Nikao School and flag of New Zealand.

Perf. 13½x13

1965, Sept. 16 **Litho.** **Wmk. 253**

160 A30 4p blue & red .20 .20
161 A30 10p multicolored .20 .20
162 A30 1sh multicolored .20 .20
163 A30 1sh9p multicolored .50 .50
Nos. 160-163 (4) 1.10 1.10

Establishment of internal self-government.
For surcharges see Nos. 182, 191.

Nos. 160-162 and 156-158 Overprinted in Red: "In Memoriam / Sir Winston Churchill / 1874-1965"

1966, Jan. 24 **Litho.** **Wmk. 253**

164 A30 4p blue & red .75 .30
165 A30 10p multicolored 1.75 .55
a. Inverted overprint 225.00
166 A30 1sh multicolored 1.75 .80
167 A28 2sh gray & brown 1.75 1.50
168 A28 3sh emer & black 1.75 1.50
169 A28 5sh ultra & brown 2.25 2.10
Nos. 164-169 (6) 10.00 6.75

Statesman and WWII leader.

Adoration of the Wise Men, by Fra Angelico — A31

Paintings: 2p, Nativity, by Hans Memling, vert. 4p, Adoration of the Wise Men, by Velazquez. 10p, Adoration of the Wise Men, by Hieronymus Bosch. 1sh6p, Adoration of the Shepherds, by Jose Ribera, vert.

Perf. 13x14½, 14½x13

1966, Nov. 28 **Photo.** **Unwmk.**

170 A31 1p multicolored .20 .20
171 A31 2p multicolored .20 .20
172 A31 4p multicolored .20 .20
173 A31 10p multicolored .30 .30
174 A31 1sh6p multicolored .35 .35
Nos. 170-174 (5) 1.25 1.25

Christmas. Issued in sheets of 6 with ornamental gold border.

Perf. 13x12, 12x13

170a A31 1p .45 *.55*
171a A31 2p 9.50 *10.50*
172a A31 4p .85 *.95*
173a A31 10p 1.60 *4.25*
174a A31 1sh6p 20.00 *6.25*
Nos. 170a-174a (5) 32.40 22.50

Tennis and Queen Elizabeth
A32

Sport: 1p, Women's basketball and Games' emblem. 4p, Boxing and team emblem. 7p, Soccer and Queen Elizabeth II.

1967, Jan. 12 ***Perf. 13½***

175 A32 ½p brt olive & multi .20 .20
176 A32 1p brt blue & multi .20 .20
177 A32 4p purple & multi .20 .20
178 A32 7p red & multi .20 .20
Nos. 175-178,C10-C11 (6) 1.25 1.25

Second South Pacific Games, Noumea, New Caledonia, Dec. 8-18, 1966.

Nos. 148-155, 157-161 Surcharged with New Value or Black or Red

Pair (#181b), with Type I on left (#181) and Type II on right (#181a)

1967

179 A25 1c on 1p .40 1.75
180 A26 2c on 2p .20 .20
181 A25 2½c on 3p (I) .20 .20
a. Type II .20 .20
b. Pair, #181 and #181a .40 .40
182 A30 3c on 4p .20 .20
183 A26 4c on 5p 5.00 .35
184 A25 5c on 6p .20 .20
185 A29 5c on 6p 4.00 .65
186 A26 7c on 8p .25 .20
187 A25 10c on 1sh .20 .20
188 A27 15c on 1sh6p (R) 1.60 1.00
189 A28 30c on 3sh (R) 12.50 5.00
190 A28 50c on 5sh (R) 3.25 2.75
191 A30 $1 on 10p (R) 12.00 10.00
Nos. 179-191 (13) 40.00 22.70

Issued: 2c, 2½c, 3c, 5c, 7c, 10c, 4/3; others 5/4.

No. 191 is surcharged "10/ $1.00" and 3 bars over old value.

Numerous varieties of surcharge include wrong-font "c," thin numerals, etc.

Nos. 126A, 126B and 126C Surcharged in Red

Wmk. 253

1967, June 6 **Typo.** ***Perf. 14***

192 PF5 $2 on £1 pink 60.00 *110.00*
193 PF5 $6 on £3 lt green 110.00 *140.00*
194 PF5 $10 on £5 dk blue 190.00 *225.00*
Nos. 192-194 (3) 360.00 475.00

Frequently found with stained gum.

Stamp of 1892, Village and Queen Victoria
A33

Designs: 3c (4p), PO, Rarotonga, and Elizabeth II. 8c (10p), View of Avarua, Rarotonga, and 10p stamp of 1892. 18c (1sh9p), Map of Cook Islands, DC-3, S.S. Moana Roa and Capt. Cook.

Perf. 13½

1967, July 3 **Photo.** **Unwmk.**

195 A33 1c (1p) multi .20 .20
196 A33 3c (4p) multi .20 .20
197 A33 8c (10p) multi .35 .35
198 A33 18c (1sh9p) multi 1.50 .80
a. Souvenir sheet of 4, #195-198 2.50 2.50
Nos. 195-198 (4) 2.25 1.55

75th anniv. of the first Cook Islands stamps. Issued in sheets of 8 stamps and 1 label with inscription in yellow margin.

Hibiscus — A34

Elizabeth II — A35

Elizabeth II and Flowers — A36

Flowers: 1c, Rose of Sharon. 2c, 15c, Frangipani. 2½c, Butterfly pea. 3c, Suva queen and Queen Elizabeth II. 4c, Water lily. 5c, Bauhania. 6c, Yellow hibiscus. 8c, Alamanda and Queen Elizabeth II. 9c, Stephanotis. 10c, Flaymboyant poinciana. 20c, Thunbergia. 25c, Canna lily and Queen Elizabeth II. 30c, Poinsettia. 50c, Gardenia.

1967-69 Photo. *Perf. 14x13½*

199	A34	½c gold & multi	.30	.20
200	A34	1c gold & multi	.30	.20
201	A34	2c gold & multi	.30	.20
202	A34	2½c gold & multi	.45	.20
203	A34	3c gold & multi	1.00	.20
204	A34	4c *Walter Lily*	1.40	*1.75*
205	A34	4c *Water Lily*	3.75	1.50
206	A34	5c gold & multi	.70	.20
207	A34	6c gold & multi	.75	.20
208	A34	8c gold & multi	.75	.20
209	A34	9c gold & multi	.75	.20
210	A34	10c gold & multi	.75	.20
211	A34	15c gold & multi	.75	.20
212	A34	20c gold & multi	8.50	.50
213	A34	25c gold & multi	1.50	.60
214	A34	30c gold & multi	1.25	.70
215	A34	50c gold & multi	1.90	1.00
216	A35	$1 gold & multi	4.00	2.25
217	A35	$2 gold & multi	9.00	3.50
218	A36	$4 multi ('68)	3.25	*5.50*
219	A36	$6 multi ('68)	3.75	*7.50*
219A	A36	$8 multi ('69)	11.00	*11.00*
220	A36	$10 multi ('68)	7.00	*12.00*
		Nos. 199-220 (23)	63.10	50.00

The $4 exists with "FOUR DOLLARS" in two widths: 32½mm and 33½mm.

Nos. 214-215 were surcharged "Plus 20c United Kingdom Special Mail Service" in 5 lines of capitals for use during the 1971 British mail strike. The strike ended Mar. 8, the day the 50c+20c, was released.

For surcharges see Nos. 290-291, 305-309, B1-B13, B17-B18, B20. For overprints see Nos. 277-283, 302-304, 315, 351-356, O1-O15.

Fluorescence

Since 1968 a number of stamps have been issued with a "fluorescent security underprinting" in a multiple coat of arms pattern. Some issues have this underprint, some do not.

Stamps issued both with and without the underprint are Nos. 199-203, 205-220, 283, 290-291.

From Nos. 292-296 onward, all stamps have this underprint unless otherwise noted.

Ia Orana Maria, by Gauguin A37

Gauguin Paintings: 3c, Riders on the Beach. 5c, Still Life with Flowers. 8c, Whispered Words. 15c, Maternity. 22c, Why Are You Angry?

1967, Oct. 23 Photo. *Perf. 13½*

221	A37	1c gold & multi	.25	.25
222	A37	3c gold & multi	.25	.25
223	A37	5c gold & multi	.25	.25
224	A37	8c gold & multi	.25	.25
225	A37	15c gold & multi	.40	.40
226	A37	22c gold & multi	.60	.60
a.		Souvenir sheet of 6, #221-226	3.00	3.00
		Nos. 221-226 (6)	2.00	2.00

#221-226 are printed in sheets of 6 (3x2).

Holy Family by Rubens — A38

Paintings: 3c, Adoration of the Magi, by Albrecht Durer. 4c, The Lucca Madonna, by Jan Van Eyck. 8c, Adoration of the Shepherds, by Jacopo da Bassano. 15c, Nativity, by El Greco. 25c, Madonna and Child, by Antonio Allegri da Correggio.

1967, Dec. 4 *Perf. 12x13*

227	A38	1c gold & multi	.20	.20
228	A38	3c gold & multi	.20	.20
229	A38	4c gold & multi	.20	.20
230	A38	8c gold & multi	.20	.20
231	A38	15c gold & multi	.30	.30
232	A38	25c gold & multi	.35	.35
		Nos. 227-232 (6)	1.45	1.45

Christmas.

Capt. Cook and Matavai Bay, Tahiti, by Sydney Parkinson A39

1c, Ships off Huahine Island, Tahiti, by John & James Clevely. 2c, town & harbor of Kamchatka, by John Webber, & Queen Elizabeth II. 4c, "The Ice Islands" (Antarctica), by William Hodges.

1968, Sept. 12 Photo. *Perf. 13*

233	A39	½c gold & multi	.20	.20
234	A39	1c gold & multi	.20	.20
235	A39	2c gold & multi	.20	.20
236	A39	4c gold & multi	.20	.20
		Nos. 233-236,C12-C15 (8)	5.55	5.55

Bicent. of Capt. Cook's 1st voyage of discovery. Printed in sheets of 10 stamps and 2 labels (3x4). Labels show portraits of Elizabeth II and Cook.

Gymnast A40

1968, Oct. 21

237	A40	1c Sailing	.20	.20
238	A40	5c shown	.20	.20
239	A40	15c High jump	.20	.20
240	A40	20c Woman diver	.25	.20
241	A40	30c Bicyclist	.50	.20
242	A40	50c Woman hurdler	.40	.25
		Nos. 237-242 (6)	1.75	1.25

19th Olympic Games, Mexico City, Oct. 12-27. Printed in sheets of 10 stamps and 2 labels (3x4).

Virgin and Child, by Titian — A41

Paintings: 4c, Holy Family, by Raphael. 10c, Madonna of the Rosary, by Murillo. 20c, Adoration of the Magi, by Memling. 30c, Adoration of the Magi, by Ghirlandajo.

1968, Dec. 2 Photo. *Perf. 13*

243	A41	1c gold & multi	.20	.20
244	A41	4c gold & multi	.20	.20
245	A41	10c gold & multi	.20	.20
246	A41	20c gold & multi	.30	.30
247	A41	30c gold & multi	.45	.45
a.		Souv. sheet, #243-247 + label	1.75	1.75
		Nos. 243-247 (5)	1.35	1.35

Issued in sheets of 6 (2x3).

Training on Ropeway A42

Designs: ½c, Boy Scouts cooking over campfire. 5c, Training with signal flags, and Queen Elizabeth II. 10c, Planting a tree. 20c, Erecting a hut. 30c, Lord Baden-Powell, lake and mountains (visit to Rarotonga in 1935).

1969, Feb. 6 Photo. *Perf. 13½*

248	A42	½c multicolored	.20	.20
249	A42	1c multicolored	.20	.20
250	A42	5c multicolored	.20	.20
251	A42	10c multicolored	.25	.25
252	A42	20c multicolored	.30	.30
253	A42	30c multicolored	.55	.55
		Nos. 248-253 (6)	1.70	1.70

5th Natl. Boy Scout Jamboree, Christchurch, New Zealand, Jan. 2-12.

Issued in sheets of 10 stamps and 2 labels (4x3).

Soccer — A43

#254b, Pole vault. #255a, Weight lifting. #255b, Basketball, Elizabeth II. #256a, Long jump. #256b, Tennis. #257a, Running. #257b, Javelin, Elizabeth II. #258a, Boxing. #258b, Golf.

Perf. 13½x13

1969, July 7 Photo. Unwmk.

254	A43	½c Pair, #a.-b.	.60	.60
255	A43	1c Pair, #a.-b.	.60	.60
256	A43	4c Pair, #a.-b.	1.25	1.25
257	A43	10c Pair, #a.-b.	1.75	1.75
258	A43	15c Pair, #a.-b.	3.00	3.00
c.		Souv. sheet, #254-258 + 2 labels	8.25	8.25
		Nos. 254-258 (5)	7.20	7.20

3rd South Pacifc Games, Port Moresby, Papua and New Guinea, Aug. 13-23.

Issued in sheets of 10.

Map of Cook Islands and Capt. Cook — A44

Map of Cook Islands and: 5c, Premier Albert Henry of New Zealand. 25c, Coat of arms of New Zealand. 30c, Queen Elizabeth II.

1969, Oct. 8 Photo. *Perf. 13*

264	A44	5c red & multi	.50	.50
265	A44	10c lemon & multi	1.50	1.50
266	A44	25c green & multi	.75	.75
267	A44	30c blue & multi	.75	.75
		Nos. 264-267 (4)	3.50	3.50

South Pacific Conf., Noumea, Oct. 1969.

Madonna and Child, by Filippo Lippi A45

Paintings: 4c, Holy Family, by Baccio della Porta. 10c, Madonna and Child, by Anton Raphael Mengs. 20c, Madonna and Child, by Le Maitre de Flemalle. 30c, Madonna and Child by Correggio.

1969, Nov. 21 Photo. *Perf. 13½*

268	A45	1c buff & multi	.20	.20
269	A45	4c buff & multi	.20	.20
270	A45	10c buff & multi	.20	.20
271	A45	20c buff & multi	.25	.25
272	A45	30c buff & multi	.25	.25
a.		Souv. sheet, #268-272 + label	2.00	2.00
		Nos. 268-272 (5)	1.10	1.10

Issued in sheets of 8 stamps, one label with portrait of Queen Elizabeth II.

Resurrection of Christ, by Raphael — A46

The Resurrection of Christ by: 8c, Dirk Bouts. 20c, Albert Altdorfer. 25c, Murillo.

1970, Mar. 12 Photo. *Perf. 13½*

Size: 25½x56mm

273	A46	4c gold & multi	.20	.20
274	A46	8c gold & multi	.20	.20
275	A46	20c gold & multi	.20	.20
276	A46	25c gold & multi	.25	.25
a.		Souv. sheet, #273-276 + 2 labels	1.50	1.50
		Nos. 273-276 (4)	.85	.85

Easter 1970.

Printed in sheets of 8 stamps and a label (3x3) showing portrait of Queen Elizabeth II and name of painting and painter.

See Nos. 316-318.

Nos. 205, 208, 211-212, 214, 217 Overprinted: "KIA ORANA / APOLLO 13 /ASTRONAUTS / Te Atua to / Tatou Irinakianga"

1970, Apr. Perf. 14x13½

277 A34 4c gold & multi .25 .25
278 A34 8c gold & multi .25 .25
279 A34 15c gold & multi .25 .25
280 A34 20c gold & multi .35 .35
281 A34 30c gold & multi .50 .50
282 A35 $2 gold & multi 1.40 1.40

No. 218 Overprinted: "KIA ORANA / APOLLO 13 /ASTRONAUTS"

283 A36 $4 gold & multi 2.75 2.75
Nos. 277-283 (7) 5.75 5.75

Splashdown of Apollo 13 west of Rarotonga, Apr. 17, 1970.
Issued: #277-282, 4/17; $4, 4/30.
Values for Nos. 283, 290-291 are for stamps with fluorescence. Stamps without fluorescence sell for more.

Queen Elizabeth II, Prince Philip, Princess Anne and Prince Charles — A47

Design: 30c, Wedgwood bust of Capt. Cook and "Endeavour." $1, Royal visit commemorative coin, obverse and reverse.

1970, June 12 Photo. Perf. 13½

284 A47 5c gold & multi .25 .25
285 A47 30c gold & multi 1.50 1.25
286 A47 $1 gold & multi 4.50 4.00
a. Souv. sheet, #284-286 + label 9.00 9.00
Nos. 284-286 (3) 6.25 5.50

Visit of the British royal family.

Nos. 284-286 Overprinted in Silver or Black: "Fifth Anniversary Self-Government August 1970"

1970, Aug. 27 Photo. Perf. 13½

287 A47 5c gold & multi (S) .40 .20
288 A47 30c gold & multi 1.10 .90
289 A47 $1 gold & multi 2.00 1.25
Nos. 287-289 (3) 3.50 2.35

5th anniv. of self-government. The overprint on No. 287 is arranged in one line around 3 sides of the design; the overprint on Nos. 288-289 is in 3 horizontal lines.

Nos. 219A-220 Surcharged

1970, Nov. 11 Photo. Perf. 14x13½

290 A36 $4 on $8 multi *4.25 4.25*
291 A36 $4 on $10 multi *3.00 3.00*

In each sheet of 15, 3 stamps have 2 surcharged bars instead of one. See second note after No. 283.

Nativity A48

Illuminations from 14th Century Robert de Lisle Psalter: 4c, Angel and shepherds. 10c, The Circumcision. 20c, The Adoration of the Kings. 30c, The Presentation at the Temple.

1970, Nov. 30 Photo. Perf. 13½

292 A48 1c gold & multi .20 .20
293 A48 4c gold & multi .20 .20
294 A48 10c gold & multi .30 .30
295 A48 20c gold & multi .35 .35
296 A48 30c gold & multi .45 .45
a. Souv. sheet, #292-296 + label 1.50 1.50
Nos. 292-296 (5) 1.50 1.50

Christmas.
Issued in sheets of 5 stamps and a label (3x2) showing portrait of Queen Elizabeth II and source of design.

Queen Elizabeth II and Prince Philip — A49

Designs: 4c, Royal family at Balmoral. 10c, Prince Philip sailing. 15c, Prince Philip as polo player. 25c, Prince Philip and royal yacht.

1971, Mar. 11 Litho. Perf. 13½

297 A49 1c brt blue & multi .20 .20
298 A49 4c brt blue & multi .25 .25
299 A49 10c brt blue & multi .65 .65
300 A49 15c brt blue & multi 1.00 1.00
301 A49 25c brt blue & multi 1.75 1.75
a. Souv. sheet, #297-301 + 2 labels 4.50 4.50
Nos. 297-301 (5) 3.85 3.85

Visit of Prince Philip, Duke of Edinburgh to Rarotonga, Feb. 27, 1971. Printed in sheets of 10 stamps and 2 labels showing Queen Elizabeth II commemorative coin and a portrait of Prince Philip.

Nos. 210, 213-214 Overprinted

1971, Sept. 8 Photo. Perf. 14x13½

302 A34 10c gold & multi .20 .20
303 A34 25c gold & multi .20 .20
304 A34 30c gold & multi .20 .20
Nos. 302-304 (3) .60 .60

4th South Pacific Games, Papeete, French Polynesia, Sept. 8-19.

Nos. 202, 205, 208-209 and 211 Surcharged with New Value and Three Bars

1971, Oct. 20

305 A34 10c on 2½c multi .20 .20
306 A34 10c on 4c multi .20 .20
307 A34 10c on 8c multi .20 .20
308 A34 10c on 9c multi .20 .20
309 A34 10c on 15c multi .20 .20
Nos. 305-309 (5) 1.00 1.00

Madonna and Child, by Bellini — A50

Christmas: Paintings of the Madonna and Child, by Giovanni Bellini.

1971, Nov. 30 Perf. 13½

310 A50 1c gold & multi .20 .20
311 A50 4c gold & multi .20 .20
312 A50 10c gold & multi .25 .25
313 A50 20c gold & multi .50 .50
314 A50 30c gold & multi .75 .75
a. Souv. sheet, #310-314 + label 2.25 2.25
Nos. 310-314 (5) 1.90 1.90

See No. B14.

No. 216 Overprinted: "SOUTH PACIFIC / COMMISSION / FEB. 1947-1972"

1972, Feb. 17 Photo. Perf. 14x13½

315 A35 $1 gold & multi .90 .90

South Pacific Commission, 25th anniv.

Easter Type of 1970

Illuminations from 14th century Robert de Lisle Psalter: 5c, St. John. 10c, Christ crucified. 30c, Virgin Mary.

1972, Mar. 6 Photo. Perf. 13½

Size: 21x68mm

316 A46 5c gold & multi .20 .20
317 A46 10c gold & multi .20 .20
318 A46 30c gold & multi .50 .50
a. Souvenir sheet of 3, #316-318 1.50 1.50
Nos. 316-318 (3) .90 .90

Printed in sheets of 12.
For surcharges see Nos. B15-B16, B19.

Rocket over Moon — A51

#319a, Shown. #319b, Earth over moon. #320a, Landing module and astronaut. #320b, Astronaut collecting moon rocks. #321a, Earth and rocket over moon. #321b, Lunar rover and astronaut. #322a, Helicopter over raft in Pacific. #322b, Capsule and parachutes.

1972, Apr. 17

319 A51 5c Pair, #a.-b. .20 .20
320 A51 10c Pair, #a.-b. .40 .40
321 A51 25c Pair, #a.-b. 1.00 1.00
322 A51 30c Pair, #a.-b. 1.25 1.25
c. Souvenir sheet of 8 4.25 4.25
Nos. 319-322 (4) 2.85 2.85

Apollo moon explorations.
No. 322c contains Nos. 319-322 arranged in 2 blocks of 4 divided by a map showing splashdown area of Apollo X, XII and XIII.
For surcharges see Nos. B21-B24.

High Jump, Olympic Rings — A52

Rest on Flight to Egypt, by Caravaggio — A53

1972, June 26

327 A52 10c shown .30 .30
328 A52 25c Running .65 .65
329 A52 30c Boxing .65 .65
a. Souv. sheet, #327-329 + label 2.00 2.00
Nos. 327-329 (3) 1.60 1.60

20th Olympic Games, Munich, Aug. 26-Sept. 10. Sheets of 8 stamps and label.
See No. B29.

1972, Oct. 11 Photo. Perf. 13½

Paintings: 5c, Virgin of the Swallows, by Guercino. 10c, Virgin with Green Cushion, by Andrea Solario. 20c, Virgin and Child, by Lorenzo di Credi. 30c, Virgin and Child, by Giovanni Bellini.

330 A53 1c gold & multi .25 .25
331 A53 5c gold & multi .25 .25
332 A53 10c gold & multi .30 .30
333 A53 20c gold & multi .65 .65
334 A53 30c gold & multi 1.10 1.10
a. Souv. sheet, #330-334 + label 3.75 3.75
Nos. 330-334 (5) 2.55 2.55

Christmas. See No. B30.

Princess Elizabeth and Prince Philip — A54

Designs: 5c, Wedding ceremony, Westminster Abbey. 15c, Bridal portrait. 30c, Official wedding picture of royal family.

1972, Nov. 20

Size: 29x40mm

335 A54 5c silver & multi .40 .40
336 A54 10c silver & multi .55 .55

Size: 40x40mm

337 A54 15c silver & multi .70 .70

Size: 66x40mm

338 A54 30c silver & multi .85 .85
Nos. 335-338 (4) 2.50 2.50

25th anniversary of the marriage of Queen Elizabeth II and Prince Philip.
Nos. 335-337 printed in sheets of 8 stamps and one label; No. 338 in sheets of 6.

1c Coin with Queen Elizabeth II and Taro Leaf A55

Queen Elizabeth II Coins: 2c, Pineapples. 5c, Hibiscus. 10c, Oranges. 20c, Fairy terns. 50c, Bonito. $1, Tangaroa, Polynesian god of creation, vert.

1973, Mar. 15 Photo. Perf. 13x13½

Size: 37x24mm

339 A55 1c dp car, blk & gold .20 .20
340 A55 2c blue, blk & gold .20 .20
341 A55 5c green, blk & gold .20 .20

Size: 46x30mm

342 A55 10c vio, blue, blk & sil .25 .25
343 A55 20c dk green, blk & sil .40 .40
344 A55 50c dp car, black & sil .60 .60

Size: 32x54½mm

345 A55 $1 blue, blk & silver .90 .90
Nos. 339-345 (7) 2.75 2.75

Coinage commemorating silver wedding anniversary of Queen Elizabeth II.
Printed in sheets of 20 stamps and label showing Westminster Abbey.

"Noli me Tangere," by Titian — A56

Paintings: 10c, Descent from the Cross, by Rubens. 30c, The Lamentation of Christ, by Dürer.

1973, Apr. 9

346 A56 5c gold & multi .20 .20
347 A56 10c gold & multi .30 .30
348 A56 30c gold & multi .40 .40
a. Souvenir sheet of 3, #346-348 1.40 1.40
Nos. 346-348 (3) .90 .90

Easter. Printed in sheets of 15 stamps and one label.

See Nos. 378-380, B31-B33, B39-B41.

Queen Elizabeth II in Coronation Regalia — A57

1973, June 1 Photo. *Perf. 14x13½*

349 A57 10c gold & multi 1.25 1.25

Souvenir Sheet

Perf. 13½x14½

350 A57 50c gold & multi 3.50 3.50

20th anniv. of the coronation of Queen Elizabeth II. No. 349 printed in sheets of 5 stamps and one label.

Nos. 206, 208, 210, 212-214 Overprinted: "TENTH ANNIVERSARY / CESSATION OF / NUCLEAR TESTING / TREATY"

1973, July 25 Photo. *Perf. 14x13½*

351 A34 5c gold & multi .20 .20
352 A34 8c gold & multi .20 .20
353 A34 10c gold & multi .20 .20
354 A34 20c gold & multi .20 .20
355 A34 25c gold & multi .35 .35
356 A34 30c gold & multi .35 .35
Nos. 351-356 (6) 1.50 1.50

Nuclear Test Ban Treaty, 10th anniv. and as protest against French nuclear testing on Mururoa atoll.

Tipairua — A58

Historic South Pacific sailing vessels.

1973, Sept. 17 Photo. *Perf. 13½x13*

357 A58 ½c shown .25 .25
358 A58 1c Wa'a Kaulua .25 .25
359 A58 1½c Tainui .25 .25
360 A58 5c War canoe .65 .65
361 A58 10c Pahi .80 .80
362 A58 15c Amatasi 1.10 1.10
363 A58 25c Vaka 1.40 1.40
Nos. 357-363 (7) 4.70 4.70

Annunciation A59

Princess Anne — A60

Designs from 15th Century Prayer Book: 5c, The Visitation. 10c, Adoration of the Shepherds. 20c, Adoration of the Kings. 30c, Slaughter of the Innocents.

1973, Oct. 30 Photo. *Perf. 13x13½*

364 A59 1c multicolored .20 .20
365 A59 5c multicolored .20 .20
366 A59 10c multicolored .20 .20
367 A59 20c multicolored .40 .40
368 A59 30c multicolored .65 .65
a. Souv. sheet, #364-368 + label 1.75 1.50
Nos. 364-368 (5) 1.65 1.65

Christmas. See Nos. B34-B38.

1973, Nov. 14 Photo. *Perf. 14*

369 A60 25c shown .40 .40
370 A60 30c Mark Phillips .60 .60
371 A60 50c Princess and Mark Phillips 1.00 1.00
a. Souv. sheet, #369-371 + label 2.50 2.50
Nos. 369-371 (3) 2.00 2.00

Wedding of Princess Anne and Capt. Mark Phillips.

Running and Games Emblem A61

1c, Diving. 3c, Boxing. 10c, Weight lifting. 30c, Bicycling. 50c, Discobolus.

1974, Jan. 24 Photo. *Perf. 14*

372 A61 1c multi, vert. .20 .20
373 A61 3c multi, vert. .20 .20
374 A61 5c multi .20 .20
375 A61 10c multi .25 .25
376 A61 30c multi .75 .75
Nos. 372-376 (5) 1.60 1.60

Souvenir Sheet

377 A61 50c multi, vert. 1.25 1.25

10th British Commonwealth Games, Christchurch, New Zealand, Jan. 24-Feb. 2. No. 377 contains one stamp 35x45mm.

Easter Type of 1973 Dated "1974"

Paintings: 5c, Jesus Carrying Cross, by Raphael. 10c, Jesus in the Arms of God, by El Greco. 30c, Descent from the Cross, by Caravaggio.

1974, Mar. 25 *Perf. 13½x13*

378 A56 5c gold & multi .20 .20
379 A56 10c gold & multi .25 .25
380 A56 30c gold & multi .65 .65
a. Souvenir sheet of 3, #378-380 1.40 1.40
Nos. 378-380 (3) 1.10 1.10

Easter. See Nos. B39-B41.

Phallicium Glaucum A62

Queen Elizabeth II — A63

Queen and Shells — A64

Cook Islands sea shells. The designs of the 2c, 5c, 10c, 30c include portrait of Queen Elizabeth II.

1974-75 Photo. *Perf. 13½*

381 A62 ½c shown .20 .20
382 A62 1c Vasum turbinellus .20 .20
383 A62 1½c Corculum cardissa .20 .20
384 A62 2c Terebellum terebellum .20 .20
385 A62 3c Aulica vespertilio .20 .20
386 A62 4c Strombus gibberulus .20 .20
387 A62 5c Cymatium pileare .20 .20
388 A62 6c Cyprae caputserpentis .20 .20
389 A62 8c Bursa granularis .20 .20
390 A62 10c Tenebra muscaria .20 .20
391 A62 15c Mitra mitra .40 .30
392 A62 20c Natica alapillonis roding .60 .40
393 A62 25c Gloripallium pallium .75 .45
394 A62 30c Conus miles .90 .55
395 A62 50c Conus textile 1.50 1.00
396 A62 60c Oliva sericea roding 1.75 1.10
397 A63 $1 multicolored 2.50 1.90
398 A63 $2 multi ('75) 5.00 3.75

Perf. 14x13½

399 A64 $4 multi ('75) 7.50 5.50
400 A64 $6 multi ('75) 12.00 8.75
401 A64 $8 multi ('75) 15.00 11.00
402 A64 $10 multi ('75) 20.00 15.00
Nos. 381-402 (22) 69.90 51.70

Issued: 50c, 60c, $1, 8/26; $2, 1/27; $4, 3/17; $6, 4/29; $8, 5/30; $10, 6/30; others, 5/17.

For surcharges & overprints see #488-498, 526-528, 991, O16-O26, O30-O31.

Soccer Player and Map of Oceania A65

50c, Munich stadium & map of Oceania. $1, Soccer player, Munich stadium & World Cup.

1974, July 5 Photo. *Perf. 13½*

Size: 31x29mm

403 A65 25c multicolored .45 .45
404 A65 50c multicolored .90 .90

Size: 68x28½mm

405 A65 $1 multicolored 1.75 1.75
a. Souvenir sheet of 3, #403-405 3.75 3.75
Nos. 403-405 (3) 3.10 3.10

World Cup Soccer Championship, Munich, June 13-July 7. Nos. 403-405 printed in sheets of 8 and commemorative label.

$2.50 Capt. Cook Silver Coin — A66

Commemorative Silver Coins: $7.50, $7.50 coin with Queen Elizabeth II on obverse; Capt. Cook, map of Islands and "Resolution" on reverse. $2.50 coin shows "Resolution," "Adventure" and globe on reverse.

1974, July 22 Photo. *Perf. 14*

406 A66 $2.50 sil, vio & blk 11.00 7.25
407 A66 $7.50 grn, sil & blk 29.00 22.50
a. Souvenir sheet of 2, #406-407 47.50 35.00

Bicentenary of Capt. Cook's 2nd voyage of discovery. Nos. 406-407 printed in sheets of 5 and commemorative label.

Cook Islands Nos. 1, 49, 62, 66, 77 — A67

Stamps of Cook Islands: 25c, DC-3 over old Rarotonga landing strip, and No. 19. 30c, Rarotonga Post Office, UPU emblem and No. 65. 50c, UPU emblem and Nos. 1, 19, 49, 62, 65-66 and 77.

1974, Sept. 16 Photo. *Perf. 13½x14*

408 A67 10c gold & multi .20 .20
409 A67 25c gold & multi .55 .55
410 A67 30c gold & multi .65 .65
411 A67 50c gold & multi 1.25 1.25
a. Souv. sheet, #408-411, perf. 13½ 2.75 2.75
Nos. 408-411 (4) 2.65 2.65

Cent. of UPU. Nos. 408-411 printed in sheets of 8 and commemorative label.

Virgin and Child, with St. John, by Raphael — A68

Paintings: 5c, Holy Family, by Andrea del Sarto. 10c, Nativity, by Correggio. 20c, Holy Family, by Rembrandt. 30c, Nativity, by Van der Weyden.

1974, Oct. 15 Photo. *Perf. 13½*

412 A68 1c multicolored .20 .20
413 A68 5c multicolored .20 .20
414 A68 10c multicolored .20 .20
415 A68 20c multicolored .45 .45
416 A68 30c multicolored .65 .65
a. Souv. sheet, #412-416 + label 2.25 2.25
Nos. 412-416 (5) 1.70 1.70

Christmas 1974. Nos. 412-416 printed in sheets of 15 and one label showing Queen Elizabeth II.

See Nos. B42-B46.

Churchill and Blenheim Palace A69

Sir Winston Churchill (1874-1965) and: 10c, Parliament. 25c, Chartwell. 30c, Buckingham Palace. 50c, St. Paul's Cathedral.

1974, Nov. 20 Photo. *Perf. 14*

417 A69 5c violet & multi .20 .20
418 A69 10c maroon & multi .25 .25
419 A69 25c dk blue & multi .65 .65
420 A69 30c brown & multi .85 .85
421 A69 50c multicolored 1.60 1.60
a. Souv. sheet, #417-421 + label 3.75 3.75
Nos. 417-421 (5) 3.55 3.55

Nos. 417-421 printed in sheets of 5 stamps and one label showing $100 commemorative gold coin.

Vasco Nunez de Balboa — A70

5c, Ferdinand Magellan & route around South America. 10c, Juan Sebastian del Cano & ship. 25c, Andres de Urdaneta & ship. 25c, Miguel Lopez de Legaspi & ship.

1975, Feb. 3 *Perf. 13½*

422 A70 1c multicolored .25 .20
423 A70 5c multicolored .25 .20
424 A70 10c multicolored .80 .30
425 A70 25c multicolored 2.10 1.00
426 A70 30c multicolored 2.50 1.10
Nos. 422-426 (5) 5.90 2.80

16th century explorers of the Pacific Ocean.

Apollo and Apollo-Soyuz Emblem — A71

Apollo-Soyuz Emblem &: #427b, Soyuz. #428a, Aleksei A. Leonov & Valery N. Kubasov. #428b, Donald K. Slayton, Vance D. Brand & Thomas P. Stafford. #429a, Cosmonaut inside Soyuz capsule. #429b, American astronauts inside Apollo capsule.

1975, July 15 Photo. *Perf. 13½*

427	A71	25c Pair, #a.-b.	1.00	1.00
428	A71	30c Pair, #a.-b.	1.25	1.25
429	A71	50c Pair, #a.-b.	2.00	2.00
c.		Souvenir sheet of 6, #427-429	4.25	4.25
		Nos. 427-429 (3)	4.25	4.25

Apollo Soyuz space test project (Russo-American space cooperation), launching July 15; link-up, July 17. Printed sheets of 18 stamps and 2 labels showing flags.

$100 Gold Commemorative Coin — A72

1975, Aug. 8 Photo. *Perf. 13½x13*

433	A72	$2 gold & dp violet	6.00	5.75

Bicentenary of the completion of Capt. Cook's second voyage of discovery.

Cook Islands' Flag, Map of Islands and New Zealand A73

Prime Minister Sir Albert Henry — A74

Design: 25c, View of Rarotonga and flag.

1975, Aug. 8 *Perf. 13½x13, 13x13½*

434	A73	5c gold & multi	.50	.20
435	A74	10c gold & multi	.65	.20
436	A73	25c gold & multi	1.60	.50
		Nos. 434-436 (3)	2.75	.90

Tenth anniversary of self-government.

Virgin and Child, 15th Century, Flemish — A75

Paintings: 10c, Madonna in the Field, by Raphael. 15c, Holy Family, by Raphael. 20c, Adoration of the Shepherds, by J. B. Mayno. 35c, Annunciation, by Murillo.

1975, Dec. 1 Photo. *Perf. 13½*

437	A75	6c gold & multi	.20	.20
438	A75	10c gold & multi	.20	.20
439	A75	15c gold & multi	.30	.30
440	A75	20c gold & multi	.40	.40
441	A75	35c gold & multi	.65	.65
a.		Souv. sheet, #437-441 + label	1.75	1.75
		Nos. 437-441 (5)	1.75	1.75

Christmas. See Nos. B47-B51.

Descent from the Cross, by Raphael A76

Paintings: 15c, Pieta, by Veronese. 35c, Pieta, by El Greco.

1976, Mar. 29 Photo. *Perf. 13½*

442	A76	7c gold & multi	.20	.20
443	A76	15c gold & multi	.30	.30
444	A76	35c gold & multi	.70	.70
a.		Souvenir sheet of 3, #442-444	1.90	1.90
		Nos. 442-444 (3)	1.20	1.20

Easter. Nos. 442-444 printed in sheets of 20 with label showing Queen Elizabeth II.
See Nos. B52-B54.

Benjamin Franklin and "Resolution" — A77

Designs: $2, Capt. James Cook and "Resolution." $3, Cook, "Resolution" and Franklin.

1976, May 29 Photo. *Perf. 13½*

445	A77	$1 gold & multi	5.50	3.00
446	A77	$2 gold & multi	11.50	6.25

Souvenir Sheet

Perf. 13

447	A77	$3 gold & multi	14.00	8.00

American Bicentennial. No. 447 contains one stamp 73x31mm. Nos. 445-446 printed in sheets of 5 and corner label with Franklin's request to assist Capt. Cook.
For overprint see No. O29.

Nos. 445-447 Overprinted "Royal Visit July 1976"

1976, July 6 Photo. *Perf. 13½*

448	A77	$1 gold & multi	2.50	2.00
449	A77	$2 gold & multi	6.25	5.75

Souvenir Sheet

Perf. 13

450	A77	$3 gold & multi	13.00	9.00

Visit of Queen Elizabeth II and Prince Philip to the United States.

High Hurdles — A78

15c, Field hockey. 30c, Fencing. 35c, Soccer.

1976, July 22 *Perf. 13½*

451	A78	7c Pair, #a.-b.	.25	.25
452	A78	15c Pair, #a.-b.	.50	.50
453	A78	30c Pair, #a.-b.	1.00	1.00
454	A78	35c Pair, #a.-b.	1.25	1.25
c.		Souvenir sheet of 8, #451-454	3.75	3.75
		Nos. 451-454 (4)	3.00	3.00

21st Olympic Games, Montreal, Canada, 7/17-8/1. Printed in sheets of 10 stamps + 2 labels.

The Visitation — A80

Designs: 10c, Virgin and Child. 15c, Adoration of the Shepherds. 20c, Adoration of the Kings. 35c, Holy Family. After painted Renaissance altar sculptures.

1976, Oct. 12 Photo. *Perf. 14x13½*

459	A80	6c gold & multi	.20	.20
460	A80	10c gold & multi	.20	.20
461	A80	15c gold & multi	.25	.25
462	A80	20c gold & multi	.35	.35
463	A80	35c gold & multi	.60	.60
a.		Souv. sheet, #459-463 + label	1.75	1.75
		Nos. 459-463 (5)	1.60	1.60

Christmas. Nos. 459-463 printed in sheets of 20 with label showing Queen Elizabeth II.
See Nos. B55-B59.

$5 Silver Coin, 1976 — A81

1976, Nov. 15 Photo. *Perf. 13½*

464	A81	$1 multicolored	3.00	2.25

National Wildlife and Conservation Day. Issued in sheets of 5 stamps and commemorative label.
See Nos. 502, 536.

A82

#465a, Crown. #465b, Elizabeth II in Coronation Vestments. #466a, Westminster Abbey. #466b, Coach in procession. #467a, Queen and Prince Philip after coronation. 467b, Investiture of Sir Albert Henry, Premier of Cook Islands, 1974.

1977, Feb. 7 Photo. *Perf. 13½x13*

465	A82	25c Pair, #a.-b.	1.00	.80
466	A82	50c Pair, #a.-b.	2.50	2.00
467	A82	$1 Pair, #a.-b.	5.00	4.00
c.		Souv. sheet, #465-467, perf. 13	8.75	7.50
		Nos. 465-467 (3)	8.50	6.80

Reign of Queen Elizabeth II, 25th anniv. Printed in sheets of 8.
For overprints see No. O27.

Crucifixion, by Rubens — A83

Virgin and Child, by Memling — A84

Paintings by Rubens: 15c, Christ Between the Thieves. 35c, Descent from the Cross.

1977, Mar. 28 Photo. *Perf. 14x13½*

471	A83	7c gold & multi	.35	.35
472	A83	15c gold & multi	.35	.35
473	A83	35c gold & multi	.90	.90
a.		Souv. sheet, #471-473, perf 13	1.65	1.65
		Nos. 471-473 (3)	1.60	1.60

Easter 1977, and 400th birth anniv. of Peter Paul Rubens (1577-1640), Flemish painter. Nos. 471-473 printed in sheets of 24 stamps and corner label with portrait of Queen Elizabeth II and description.
See Nos. B60-B62.

1977, Oct. 3 Photo. *Perf. 13½*

Virgin and Child by: 10c, Hans Memling. 15c, Geertgen Tot Sin Jans. 20c, Carlo Crivelli. 35c, School of Henry Blex.

474	A84	6c gold & multi	.25	.25
475	A84	10c gold & multi	.25	.25
476	A84	15c gold & multi	.25	.25
477	A84	20c gold & multi	.35	.35
478	A84	35c gold & multi	.60	.60
a.		Souv. sheet, #474-478 + label	1.90	1.90
		Nos. 474-478 (5)	1.70	1.70

Christmas. Nos. 474-478 printed in sheets of 24 and label. See Nos. B63-B67.

$5-silver Coin, 1977 — A85

1977, Nov. 15 Photo. *Perf. 13½*

479	A85	$1 silver & multi	3.50	1.60

National Wildlife Conservation Day. No. 479 issued in sheets of 5 and one label.

Capt. Cook, by Nathaniel Dance and "Resolution" — A86

$1, "Capt. Cook Landing at Owyhee" and Capt. Cook. $2, Cook Islands $200 commemorative coin, 1978, and Cook Monument, Hawaii, 1825.

1978, Jan. 20 Litho. *Perf. 13½*

480	A86	50c gold & multi	.75	.75
481	A86	$1 gold & multi	1.50	1.50
482	A86	$2 gold & multi	3.00	3.00
a.		Souvenir sheet of 3, #480-482	6.00	6.00
		Nos. 480-482 (3)	5.25	5.25

Bicentennial of Capt. Cook's arrival in Hawaii.
Nos. 480-482 issued in sheets of 5 with corner label showing ship off Hawaiian coast.
For overprints see Nos. 499-501a.

Pieta, by Rogier van der Weyden A87

Paintings, National Gallery, London: 35c, Burial of Jesus, by Michelangelo. 75c, Jesus at Emmaus, by Caravaggio.

1978, Mar. 20 Photo. *Perf. 13½x13*

483 A87 15c gold & multi .20 .20
484 A87 35c gold & multi .50 .50
485 A87 75c gold & multi 1.10 1.10
a. Souv. sheet, #483-485 + label 1.75 1.75
Nos. 483-485 (3) 1.80 1.80

Easter. Nos. 483-485 printed in sheets of 5 and corner label showing National Gallery.
See Nos. B68-B70.

A88

A89

Souvenir Sheets

1978, June 6 Photo. *Perf. 13*

486 Sheet of 4 + 2 labels 1.00 1.00
a. A88 50c shown .25 .25
b. A88 50c Lion of England .25 .25
c. A88 50c Imperial State Crown .25 .25
d. A88 50c Tangaroa figure .25 .25
487 Sheet of 4 + label 1.00 1.00
a. A88 70c like 486a .25 .25
b. A88 70c Scepter with Cross .25 .25
c. A88 70c St. Edward's Crown .25 .25
d. A88 70c Rarotongan staff god .25 .25
e. Souv. sheet of 8, #486a-487d + label 2.00 2.00

Coronation of Queen Elizabeth II, 25th anniv.

Nos. 381, 383, 388-389, 393-396 Surcharged with New Value and Three Bars in Silver, Black or Gold

1978, Nov. 10 Photo. *Perf. 13½*

488 A62 5c on 1½c multi (S) .25 .25
489 A62 7c on ½c multi .30 .30
490 A62 10c on 6c multi (G) .45 .45
491 A62 10c on 8c multi (G) .45 .45
492 A62 15c on ½c multi .65 .65
493 A62 15c on 25c multi (S) .65 .65
494 A62 15c on 30c multi .65 .65
495 A62 15c on 50c multi (S) .65 .65
496 A62 15c on 60c multi (G) .65 .65
497 A62 17c on ½c multi .80 .80
498 A62 17c on 50c multi (S) .80 .80
Nos. 488-498 (11) 6.30 6.30

See Nos. 526-528.

Nos. 480-482a Overprinted in Black on Silver Panel: "1728--250th ANNIVERSARY OF COOK'S BIRTH--1978"

1978, Nov. 13 Litho. *Perf. 13½*

499 A86 50c gold & multi .75 .75
500 A86 $1 gold & multi 1.50 1.50
501 A86 $2 gold & multi 3.00 3.00
a. Souvenir sheet of 3, #499-501 14.50 14.50
Nos. 499-501 (3) 5.25 5.25

250th anniv. of Capt. Cook's birth. Similar overprint in 4 lines was applied to labels. Label of No. 501a overprinted only with dates 1728, 1978.

Coin Type of 1976

$1, $5 Silver coin, 1978 (Polynesian warbler).

1978, Nov. 15 Photo. *Perf. 13½*

502 A81 $1 multicolored 2.25 2.00

National Wildlife and Conservation Day. Sheets of 24 containing 4 panes of 6.

1978, Dec. 8 Photo. *Perf. 13*

Virgin and Child by: 15c, Rogiervan der Weyden. 17c, Carlo Crivelli. 35c, Murillo.

503 A89 15c multicolored .35 .35
504 A89 17c multicolored .50 .50
505 A89 35c multicolored .80 .80
a. Souvenir sheet of 3, #503-505 1.80 1.80
Nos. 503-505 (3) 1.65 1.65

Christmas. See Nos. B71-B73.

A90

A91

Descent from the Cross, by Gaspar de Crayer (Details): 10c, Pieta. 12c, St. John. 15c, Mary Magdalene. 20c, Cherubs.

1979, Apr. 5 Photo. *Perf. 13*

506 A90 10c multicolored .25 .25
507 A90 12c multicolored .25 .25
508 A90 15c multicolored .30 .30
509 A90 20c multicolored .65 .65
Nos. 506-509 (4) 1.45 1.45

Easter. See No. B74.

1979, July 23 Photo. *Perf. 14x13½*

20c, Capt. Cook, by John Weber. 30c, Resolution, by Henry Roberts. 35c, Endeavour. 50c, Death of Capt. Cook, by George Carter.

510 A91 20c multicolored .40 .40
511 A91 30c multicolored .60 .60
512 A91 35c multicolored .70 .70
513 A91 50c multicolored .95 .95
a. Souvenir sheet of 4 3.00 3.00
Nos. 510-513 (4) 2.65 2.65

Capt. Cook (1728-1779), explorer. No. 513a contains 4 stamps similar to Nos. 510-513 with black frames.

Sir Rowland Hill, Originator of Penny Postage — A92

#514a, Postrider. #514b, Stagecoach. #514c, Automobile. #514d, Streamlined train. #515a, Cap-Horniers, sailing ship. #515b, River steamer. #515c, Liner Deutschland. #515d, Liner United States. #516a, Balloon Neptune. #516b, Junkers F13. #516c, Graf Zeppelin. #516d, Concorde.

1979, Sept. 10 *Perf. 14½*

514 A92 30c Block of 4, #a.-d. 1.25 1.25
515 A92 35c Block of 4, #a.-d. 1.40 1.40
516 A92 50c Block of 4, #a.-d. 2.00 2.00
e. Souv. sheet of 12, #514-516 5.00 5.00
Nos. 514-516 (3) 4.65 4.65

Nos. 381, 383, 396 Surcharged in Gold or Silver

1979, Sept. 12 Photo. *Perf. 13½*

526 A62 6c on ½c multi .20 .20
527 A62 10c on 1½c multi (S) .30 .30
528 A62 15c on 60c multi .40 .40
Nos. 526-528 (3) .90 .90

Nos. 526-528 have 3 thick bars of equal length over old value.

Girl and Baby, IYC Emblem — A93

IYC Emblem and: 50c, Boy playing tree drum. 65c, Children dancing.

1979, Oct. 10 *Perf. 13*

529 A93 30c multicolored .40 .40
530 A93 50c multicolored .70 .70
531 A93 65c multicolored .90 .90
Nos. 529-531 (3) 2.00 2.00

See No. B75.

Apollo 11 Emblem A94

Christmas Tree Ornaments A95

50c, Apollo 11 crew, lunar map. 60c, Astronaut walking on moon. 65c, Splashdown.

1979, Nov. 7 *Perf. 14*

532 A94 30c multicolored .40 .40
533 A94 50c multicolored .60 .60
534 A94 60c multicolored .75 .75
535 A94 65c multicolored .85 .85
a. Souv. sheet, #532-535, perf. 13 3.00 3.00
Nos. 532-535 (4) 2.60 2.60

Apollo 11 moon landing, 10th anniv.

Coin Type of 1976

$1, $5 Silver coin, 1979 (Raratonga fruit dove).

Perf. 13½x14½

1979, Nov. 15 Photo.

536 A81 $1 multicolored 2.00 2.00

National Wildlife and Conservation Day.

1979, Dec. 14 *Perf. 14*

Christmas (Flowers and): 10c, Star. 12c, Bells and candle. 15c, Ancestral statue.

537 A95 6c multicolored .20 .20
538 A95 10c multicolored .20 .20
539 A95 12c multicolored .20 .20
540 A95 15c multicolored .20 .20
Nos. 537-540,B76-B79 (8) 1.80 1.80

A96

Bible illustrations by Gustave Dore, 1833-1883: #541a, Flagellation. #541b, Jesus Wearing Crown of Thorns. #542a, Jesus Mocked. #542b, Jesus Falls. #543a, The Crucifixion. #543b, Descent from the Cross.

1980, Mar. 31 Photo. *Perf. 13*

541 A96 20c Pair, #a.-b. .60 .60
542 A96 30c Pair, #a.-b. .90 .90
543 A96 35c Pair, #a.-b. 1.00 1.00
Nos. 541-543 (3) 2.50 2.50

Easter. See Nos. 553, B80-B83.

Doves with Olive Branch, Rotary Emblem A97

1980, May 27 Photo. *Perf. 14*

547 A97 30c shown .45 .45
548 A97 35c Flowers .50 .50
549 A97 50c Flags, globe .70 .70
Nos. 547-549 (3) 1.65 1.65

Rotary Intl., 75th anniv. See No. B87

Easter Type of 1980 and:

New Zealand No. 1 — A98

#550a, Postrider. #550b, Coach. #550c, Automobile. #550d, Train.
New Zealand #2 and: #551a, Sailing ship. #551b, River steamer. #551c, Transatlantic liner (facing left). #551d, Transatlantic liner (facing right).
New Zealand #3 and: #552a, 1870-71 mail balloon. #552b, 1919 plane. #552c, Graf Zeppelin. #552d, Concorde.

1980, Aug. 22 Photo. *Perf. 14*

550 A98 30c Block of 4, #a.-d. 1.50 1.25
551 A98 35c Block of 4, #a.-d. 2.00 1.75
552 A98 50c Block of 4, #a.-d. 3.00 2.50
e. Souvenir sheet of 12 7.50 6.50
Nos. 550-552 (3) 6.50 5.50

Souvenir Sheet

Perf. 13

553 A96 Sheet of 6, #541-543 5.00 3.50

ZEAPEX '80, New Zealand Intl. Stamp Exhib., Auckland, Aug. 23-31. #552e contains of #550-552 arranged horizontally (4x3). #553 has black on gold overprint: "ZEAPEX / '80 / Auckland / +10c" in margin.

Queen Mother Elizabeth, 80th Birthday — A99

1980, Sept. 22 Photo. *Perf. 13*

554 A99 50c multicolored 1.50 1.00

Souvenir Sheet

555 A99 $2 multicolored 2.75 2.75

No. 554 issued in sheets of 9 (3x3).

Johannes Kepler, Spacecraft — A100

Designs: Nos. 556a, 559a, Kepler, spacecraft (diff.). No. 559b, Kepler, lunar rover, astronaut on moon. Nos. 557a-558b, Jules Verne, various scenes from From Earth to Moon, vert.

1980, Nov. 7 Photo. *Perf. 13*

556 A100 12c Pair, #a-b .60 .60
557 A100 20c Pair, #a-b .60 .60
558 A100 30c Pair, #a-b 1.50 1.50
a. Souvenir sheet, #557-558 2.75 2.75
559 A100 50c Pair, #a-b 2.75 2.75
a. Souv. sheet, #556, 559 3.25 3.25
Nos. 556-559 (4) 5.45 5.45

Death anniversaries of Johannes Kepler, German astronomer and Jules Verne, French science fiction writer.

Burning Bush Coral — A101

Daisy Coral — A102

#564a, 570a, 576a, Siphonogorgia. #564b, 570b, 576b, Pavona practorta. #564c, 570c, 576c, Stylaster echinatus. #564d, 570d, 576d, Stylaster echinatus. #565a, 571a, 577a, Millepora alcicornis. #565b, 571b, 577b, Junceella gemmaea. #565c, 571c, 577c, Fungia fungites. #565d, 571d, 577d, Heliofungia actiniformis. #566a, 572a, 578a, Distichopora violacea. #566b, 572b, 578b, Stylaster. #566c, 572c, 578c, Gonipora. #566d, 572d, 578d, Caulastraea echinulata. #567a, 573a, 579a, Ptilosarcus gurneyi. #567b, 573b, 579b, Stylophora pistillata. #567c, 573c, 579c, Melithaea squamata. #567d, 573d, 579d, Porites andrewsi. #568a, 574a, 580a, Lobophyllia bemprichii. #568b, 574b, 580b, Palauastrea ramosa. #568c, 574c, 580c, Bellonella indica. #568d, 574d, 580d, Pectinia alcicornis. #569a, 575a, 581a, Sarcophyton digitatum. #569b, 575b, 581b, Melithaea albitincta. #569c, 575c, 581c, Plerogyra sinuosa. #569d, 575d, 581d, Dendrophyllia gracilis.

1980-82 *Perf. 13½x13*

Strips of 4

564 A101 1c #a.-d. .25 .25
565 A101 3c #a.-d. .30 .30
566 A101 4c #a.-d. .35 .35
567 A101 5c #a.-d. .45 .45
568 A101 6c #a.-d. .60 .60
569 A101 8c #a.-d. .70 .70
570 A101 10c #a.-d. .90 .90
571 A101 12c #a.-d. 1.10 1.10
572 A101 15c #a.-d. 1.40 1.40
573 A101 20c #a.-d. 1.60 1.60
574 A101 25c #a.-d. 2.25 2.25
575 A101 30c #a.-d. 2.50 2.50
576 A101 35c #a.-d. 3.00 3.00
577 A101 50c #a.-d. 4.00 4.00
578 A101 60c #a.-d. 5.25 5.25
579 A101 70c #a.-d. 5.75 5.75
580 A101 80c #a.-d. 6.25 6.25
581 A101 $1 #a.-d. 7.00 7.00

Perf. 14x13½

582 A102 $2 like #566c 5.50 5.50
583 A102 $3 like #565d 7.75 7.75
584 A102 $4 like #567b 10.00 10.00
585 A102 $6 like #564c 15.00 15.00
586 A102 $10 like #569b 22.50 22.50
Nos. 564-586 (23) 104.40 104.40

Issued: 1-8c, 11/21/80; 10-30c, 12/19/80; 35-60c, 3/16/81; 70c, 80c, 4/13/81; $1, 5/20/81; $2, $3, 11/27/81; $4, $6, 1/11/82; $10, 3/5/82.

For surcharges see Nos. 710-714, 716, 738, 741, 811-815, 953-954, 956-957, 959, 961-962, 964, 978-979, 984-986, B109-B111, O50-O53. For overprints see Nos. 992, 1049.

Annunciation, 13th Century Prayerbook Illustration — A102a

1980, Dec. 1 Photo. *Perf. 14*

652 A102a 15c shown .20 .20
653 A102a 30c Visitation .40 .40
654 A102a 40c Nativity .50 .50
655 A102a 50c Epiphany .70 .70
a. Souvenir sheet of 4, #652-655 2.00 2.00
Nos. 652-655 (4) 1.80 1.80

Christmas. See Nos. B88-B91.

Crucifixion, 12th Cent. Prayerbook Illustration — A103

1981, Apr. 10 *Perf. 14*

656 A103 15c shown .20 .20
657 A103 25c Placing in Tomb .40 .40
658 A103 40c Marys at the Tomb .60 .60
Nos. 656-658 (3) 1.20 1.20

Easter. See Nos. B92-B95.

Prince Charles and Lady Diana — A104

1981, July 29 Photo. *Perf. 14*

659 A104 $1 Charles 1.75 1.75
660 A104 $2 shown 3.50 3.50
a. Souv. sheet of 2, #659-660 5.25 5.25

Royal Wedding. Issued in sheets of 4.

For overprints and surcharges see Nos. 679-680, 715, 835, 980-981, B97-B98.

Soccer Players — A105

Designs: Various soccer players.

1981, Oct 20 Photo. *Perf. 14*

661 A105 20c Pair, #a.-b. .90 .90
662 A105 30c Pair, #a.-b. 1.40 1.40
663 A105 35c Pair, #a.-b. 1.75 1.75
664 A105 50c Pair, #a.-b. 2.25 2.25
Nos. 661-664 (4) 6.30 6.30

ESPANA '82 World Cup Soccer Championships. See No. B96.

Virgin and Child, by Rubens — A107

Christmas: Rubens Paintings.

1981, Dec. 14 Photo. *Perf. 14x13½*

669 A107 8c shown .50 .50
670 A107 15c Coronation of St. Catherine .50 .50
671 A107 40c Adoration of the Shepherds 1.25 1.25
672 A107 50c Adoration of the Kings 1.40 1.40
Nos. 669-672 (4) 3.65 3.65

Souvenir Sheets

1982, Jan. 18

673 A107 75c +5c like #669 1.10 1.10
674 A107 75c +5c like #670 1.10 1.10
675 A107 75c +5c like #671 1.10 1.10
676 A107 75c +5c like #672 1.10 1.10

Surtax was for school children. See No. B99.

21st Birthday of Princess Diana A108

#677a, 21st Birthday. #677b, 1 July 1982. #678a, Wedding portrait. #678b, 1 July 1982. #678d, $1.25, #678e, $2.50, both inscribed "21st Birthday / 1 July 1982."

1982, June 21 Photo. *Perf. 14*

677 A108 $1.25 Pair, #a.-b. 4.00 4.00
678 A108 $2.50 Pair, #a.-b. 8.00 8.00
c. Souv. sheet of 2, #d.-e. 8.00 8.00

Issued in sheets of 4.

See Nos. 681-682. For surcharges and overprints see Nos. 739-740, 833-834, 982.

Nos. 659-660a Overprinted: "ROYAL BIRTH 21 JUNE 1982" (a) or "PRINCE WILLIAM OF WALES" (b)

#680d, $1; #680e, $2, both inscribed "21 JUNE 1982 ROYAL BIRTH."

1982, July 12

679 A104 $1 Pair, #a.-b. 3.00 3.00
680 A104 $2 Pair, #a.-b. 5.50 5.50
c. Souv. sheet of 2, #d.-e. 6.00 6.00

Issued in sheets of 4.

For surcharges see Nos. 987-988.

Design A108 Inscribed: "Royal Birth" (a) or "21 June 1982" (b)

#682d, $1.25; #682e, $2.50, both inscribed "Royal Birth / June 1982."

1982, Aug. 3

681 A108 $1.25 Pair, #a.-b. 3.75 3.75
682 A108 $2.50 Pair, #a.-b. 7.25 7.25
c. Souv. sheet of 2, #d.-e. 6.50 6.50

Issued in sheets of 4.

Serenade, by Norman Rockwell (1894-1978) A109

1982, Sept. 10 Photo. *Perf. 14*

683 A109 5c shown .20 .20
684 A109 10c The Hikers .20 .20
685 A109 20c The Doctor and the Doll .30 .30
686 A109 30c Home From Camp .45 .45
Nos. 683-686 (4) 1.15 1.15

Christmas A110

Princess Diana Holding Prince William. Various Details from Virgin with Garlands, by Rubens.

1982, Nov. 30 Photo. *Perf. 14*

687 A110 35c multicolored 1.10 1.10
688 A110 48c multicolored 1.50 1.50
689 A110 60c multicolored 1.75 1.75
690 A110 $1.70 multicolored 5.25 5.25
Nos. 687-690 (4) 9.60 9.60

Souvenir Sheets

Perf. 13½

691 Sheet of 4 6.00 6.00
a. A110 60c like 35c 1.40 1.40
b. A110 60c like 48c 1.40 1.40
c. A110 60c like #689 1.40 1.40
d. A110 60c like $1.70 1.40 1.40
692 A110 75c + 5c like 35c 2.10 2.10
693 A110 75c + 5c like 48c 2.10 2.10
694 A110 75c + 5c like 60c 2.10 2.10
695 A110 75c + 5c like $1.70 2.10 2.10

No. 691 contains 4 stamps (27x32mm., showing only painting details) plus 2 labels showing Diana and William. Nos. 692-695 show Diana and William (27x39mm), multicolored margins show painting details. Surtax was for child welfare.

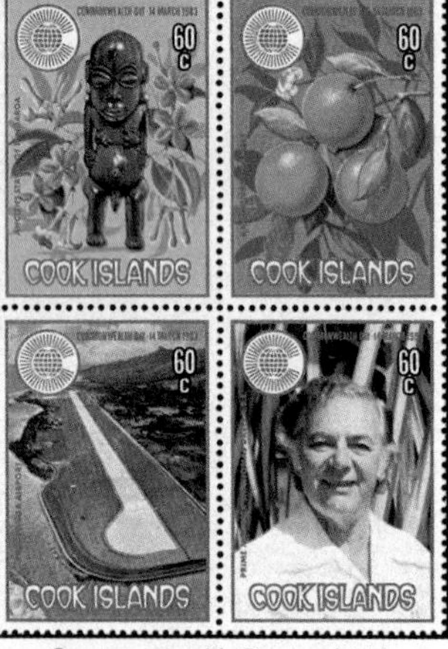

Commonwealth Day — A111

#696a, Tangaroa statue. #696b, Rarotonga oranges. #696c, Rarotonga Airport. #696d, Prime Minister Thomas Davis.

1983, Mar. 14 Photo. *Perf. 14*

696 A111 60c Block of 4, #a.-d. 2.50 2.50

For overprints see No. O46.

Scouting Year — A112

1983, Apr. 5 Photo. *Perf. 13x13½*

700 A112 12c Pair, #a.-b., shown .60 .60
701 A112 36c Pair, #a.-b., Camping 1.90 1.90
702 A112 48c Pair, #a.-b., Rope swing 2.40 2.40
703 A112 60c Pair, #a.-b., Tree planting 3.00 3.00
Nos. 700-703 (4) 7.90 7.90

Souvenir Sheet of 8

704 #a.-d. 6.50 6.50

#704 contains 2 each of #700-703 with 2c surtax.

Nos. 700-704 Overprinted: "XV WORLD JAMBOREE ALBERTA CANADA 1983"

1983, July 4 Photo. *Perf. 13x13½*

705 A112 12c Pair, #a.-b. .50 .50
706 A112 36c Pair, #a.-b. 1.60 1.60
707 A112 48c Pair, #a.-b. 2.00 2.00
708 A112 60c Pair, #a.-b. 2.50 2.50
Nos. 705-708 (4) 6.60 6.60

Souvenir Sheet of 8

709 A112 #a.-d. 6.75 6.75

Nos. 569, 572, 574-575, 579, 587, 660 Surcharged in Black or Gold

Perf. 13½x13, 14x13½, 14

1983, Aug. 12 Photo.

Blocks of 4, #a.-d. (#710-714)

710 A101 18c on 8c #569 1.60 1.60
711 A101 36c on 15c #572 2.50 2.50
712 A101 36c on 30c #575 2.50 2.50
713 A101 48c on 25c #574 4.00 4.00
714 A101 72c on 70c #579 6.00 6.00
715 A104 96c on $2 #660 (G) 2.00 2.00
716 A102 $5.60 on $6 #587 (G) 12.50 12.50
Nos. 710-716 (7) 31.10 31.10

A114

A115

1983, Sept. 9 *Perf. 14*

732 Pair .70 .70
a. A114 6c Gt. Britain .35 .35
b. A115 6c Cook Islds. Group Federal flag .35 .35
733 Pair .90 .90
a. A114 12c Raratonga ensign .45 .45
b. A115 12c New Zealand .45 .45
734 Pair 1.10 1.10
a. A114 15c Cook Islds, 1973-79 .55 .55
b. A115 15c Cook Islds, 1983 .55 .55
c. Souvenir sheet of 6, #732-734 1.40 1.40
735 Pair 1.60 1.60
a. A114 20c like #732a .80 .80
b. A115 20c like #732b .80 .80
736 Pair 2.10 2.10
a. A114 30c like #733a 1.00 1.00
b. A115 30c like #733b 1.00 1.00
737 Pair 2.50 2.50
a. A114 35c like #734a 1.25 1.25
b. A115 35c like #734b 1.25 1.25
c. Souvenir sheet of 6, #735-737 3.25 3.25
Nos. 732-737 (6) 8.90 8.90

Nos. 732-737 have different background landscapes; Nos. 735-737 airmail with silver background. Nos. 734c, 737c perf. 13½.

Nos. 576, 586, 678 Surcharged in Black or Gold

Perf. 13½x13, 14x13½, 14

1983, Aug. 30 Photo.

Block of 4, #a.-d.

738 A101 36c on 35c #576 2.50 2.50

Pair, #a.-b. (#739)

739 A108 96c on $2.50 #678 (G) 4.00 4.00
740 A102 $5.60 on $10 #586 (G) 10.00 10.00
Nos. 738-740 (3) 16.50 16.50

Satellite Earth Station — A116

Designs: Various satellites in orbit.

1983, Oct. 10 Litho. *Perf. 13½*

744 A116 36c multicolored .70 .70
745 A116 48c multicolored .90 .90
746 A116 60c multicolored 1.00 1.00
747 A116 96c multicolored 1.75 1.75
Nos. 744-747 (4) 4.35 4.35

Souvenir Sheet

748 A116 $2 multicolored 4.00 4.00

World Communications Year.

Christmas A117

Manned Flight Bicent. — A118

Raphael Paintings: 12c, La Belle Jardiniere. 18c, Madonna and Child with Five Saints. 36c, Madonna and Child with Saint John. 48c, Madonna of the Fish. 60c, Madonna of the Baldacchino.

1983 Photo. *Perf. 14*

749 A117 12c multicolored .80 .80
750 A117 18c multicolored .80 .80
751 A117 36c multicolored 1.75 1.75
752 A117 48c multicolored 2.10 2.10
753 A117 60c multicolored 3.00 3.00
Nos. 749-753 (5) 8.45 8.45

Souvenir Sheets

Perf. 13½

754 Sheet of 5 3.25 3.25
a. A117 12c + 3c like #749 .25 .25
b. A117 18c + 3c like #750 .30 .30
c. A117 36c + 3c like #751 .60 .60
d. A117 48c + 3c like #752 .75 .75
e. A117 60c + 3c like #753 .95 .95
755 A117 85c + 5c like #749 1.40 1.40
756 A117 85c + 5c like #750 1.40 1.40
757 A117 85c + 5c like #751 1.40 1.40
758 A117 85c + 5c like #752 1.40 1.40
759 A117 85c + 5c like #753 1.40 1.40

Nos. 749-753 issued in sheets of 5 + label. Surtax was for children's charities.

Issued: #749-754, Nov. 14; others, Dec. 9.

1984, Jan. 16 Photo. *Perf. 13*

Various balloons.

760 A118 36c 1st manned flight, 1783 .55 .55
761 A118 48c Ascent of Adorne, Strasbourg, 1784 .75 .75
762 A118 60c 1785 .85 .85
763 A118 72c Man on horse, 1785 1.25 1.25
764 A118 96c Godard's aerial acrobatics, 1850 1.40 1.40
Nos. 760-764 (5) 4.80 4.80

Souvenir Sheets

765 A118 $2.50 Blanchard & Jefferies, 1785 3.75 3.75
766 Sheet of 5 7.75 7.75
a. A118 36c + 5c like 36c .90 .90
b. A118 48c + 5c like 48c 1.10 1.10
c. A118 60c + 5c like 60c 1.50 1.50
d. A118 72c + 5c like 72c 1.75 1.75
e. A118 96c + 5c like 96c 2.25 2.25

#765 contains 1 stamp 30x48mm, perf. 13½.

Save the Whales Campaign A119

1984, Feb. 10 Photo. *Perf. 13*

767 A119 10c Cuvier's beaked whale .35 .35
768 A119 18c Risso's dolphin .50 .50
769 A119 20c True's beaked whale .60 .60
770 A119 24c Long-finned pilot whale .75 .75
771 A119 30c Narwhal .95 .95
772 A119 36c Beluga whale 1.10 1.10
773 A119 42c Common dolphin 1.40 1.40
774 A119 48c Commerson's dolphin 1.50 1.50
775 A119 60c Bottle-nosed dolphin 1.90 1.90
776 A119 72c Sowerby's whale 2.40 2.40
777 A119 96c Common porpoise 2.75 2.75
778 A119 $2 Boutu 6.00 6.00
Nos. 767-778 (12) 20.20 20.20

1984 Summer Olympics A120

Posters of Various Summer Olympics. 72c, 96c, $1.20 airmail.

1984, Mar. 8 Photo. *Perf. 13½*

779 A120 18c Athens, 1896 .25 .25
780 A120 24c Paris, 1900 .30 .30
781 A120 36c St. Louis, 1904 .45 .45
782 A120 48c London, 1948 .60 .60
783 A120 60c Tokyo, 1964 .75 .75
784 A120 72c Berlin, 1936 .90 .90
785 A120 96c Rome, 1960 1.25 1.25
786 A120 $1.20 Los Angeles, 1932 1.50 1.50
Nos. 779-786 (8) 6.00 6.00

For overprints see Nos. 826-828.

Nos. 582-586 Surcharged and:

Coral — A121

1c, Siphonogorgia. 2c, Millepora alcicornis. 3c, Distichopora violacea. 5c, Ptilosarcus gurneyi. 10c, Lobophyllia bemprichii. 12c, Sarcophyton digitatum. 14c, Pavona praetorta. 18c, Junceela gemmacea. 20c, Stylaster. 24c, Stylophora pistillata. 30c, Palauastrea ramosa. 36c, Melithaea albitincta. 40c, Stylaster echinatus. 42c, Fungia fungites. 48c, Gonipora. 50c, Melithaea squamata. 52c, Bellonella indica. 55c, Plerogyra sinuosa. 60c, Tubastraea. 70c, Heliofungia actinformis. 85c, Caulastraea echinulata. 96c, Porites andrewsi. $1.10, Pectinia alcicornis. $1.20, Dendrophyllia gracilis.

1984 *Perf. 13½x13*

787 A121 1c multi .20 .20
788 A121 2c multi .20 .20
789 A121 3c multi .20 .20
790 A121 5c multi .20 .20
791 A121 10c multi .20 .20
792 A121 12c multi .20 .20
793 A121 14c multi .30 .30
794 A121 18c multi .40 .40
795 A121 20c multi .40 .40
796 A121 24c multi .50 .50
797 A121 30c multi .60 .60
798 A121 36c multi .75 .75
799 A121 40c multi .80 .80
800 A121 42c multi .90 .90
801 A121 48c multi .95 .95
802 A121 50c multi 1.00 1.00
803 A121 52c multi 1.00 1.00
804 A121 55c multi 1.10 1.10
805 A121 60c multi 1.25 1.25
806 A121 70c multi 1.40 1.40
807 A121 85c multi 1.60 1.60
808 A121 96c multi 1.75 1.75
809 A121 $1.10 multi 2.25 2.25
810 A121 $1.20 multi 2.50 2.50

Perf. 14x13½

Size: 59½x38½mm

811 A102 $3.60 on $2 #582 6.25 6.25
812 A102 $4.20 on $3 #583 6.75 6.75
813 A102 $5 on $4 #584 8.25 8.25
814 A102 $7.20 on $6 #585 11.50 11.50
815 A102 $9.60 on $10 #586 13.50 13.50
Nos. 787-815 (29) 66.90 66.90

Issued: #787-801, 3/23; #802-810, 5/15; #811-813, 6/28; #814, 7/20; #815, 8/10.

For surcharges & overprints see #948-952, 955, 958, 960, 963, 965-967, B105-B108, O32-O45.

Nos. 784-786 Overprinted With Winners

1984, Aug. 24 Photo. *Perf. 13½*

826 A120 72c Team Dressage, Germany .95 .95
827 A120 96c Daley Thompson, U.K. 1.25 1.25
828 A120 $1.20 Carl Lewis, USA 1.60 1.60
Nos. 826-828 (3) 3.80 3.80

1984 Summer Olympics. Nos. 826-828 airmail.

AUSIPEX '84 — A123

1984, Sept. 20

829 A123 36c Captain Cook's cottage 1.25 1.25
830 A123 48c The Endeavour 1.60 1.60
831 A123 60c Cook's landing 2.00 2.00
832 A123 $2 Portrait, by John Webber 6.50 6.50
a. Souv. sheet, #829-832, 90c ea 10.00 10.00
b. Sheet of 4, STAMPEX '86 emblem 6.50 6.50
Nos. 829-832 (4) 11.35 11.35

No. 832b issued Aug. 4, 1986, for STAMPEX '86, Adelaide, Aug. 4-10; margin ovptd. with exhibition emblem, stamp picturing James Cook ovptd. with gold circle and black "Stampex 86 / Adelaide."

Nos. 677-678 Ovptd.: "Commemorating -/15 Sept. 1984" or "Birth H.R.H./Prince Henry" and Surcharged in Gold.

No. 659 Ovptd. "Royal Birth/Prince Henry/15 Sept. 1984" and Surcharged in Silver.

1984, Oct. 15 Photo. *Perf. 14*

833 A108 $1.25 Pair, #a.-b. 3.00 3.00
834 A108 $2.50 Pair, #a.-b. 6.50 6.50
835 A104 $3 on $1 No. 659 4.00 4.00
Nos. 833-835 (3) 13.50 13.50

Nos. 833-835 printed in sheets of 4 stamps.

A124

A125

Christmas (Paintings): 36c, Virgin on Throne with Child, by Giovanni Bellini (c. 1430-1516). 48c, Virgin and Child, 15th century, artistunknown. 60c, Virgin and Child with Saints, by Alvise Vivarini (c. 1446-1505). 96c, Virgin and Child with Angels, by Hans Memling (c. 1435-1494). $1.20, Adoration of the Magi, by Giovanni Tiepolo (1696-1770).

1984

838 A124 36c multicolored .75 .75
839 A124 48c multicolored .95 .95
840 A124 60c multicolored 1.25 1.25
841 A124 96c multicolored 1.90 1.90
842 A124 $1.20 multicolored 2.25 2.25
Nos. 838-842 (5) 7.10 7.10

Souvenir Sheets

Perf. 13½

843 Sheet of 5 4.25 4.25
a. A124 36c +5c like #838 .50 .50
b. A124 48c +5c like #839 .60 .60
c. A124 60c +5c like #840 .70 .70
d. A124 96c +5c like #841 1.10 1.10
e. A124 $1.20 +5c like #842 1.25 1.25
844 A124 95c + 5c like #838 1.25 1.25
845 A124 95c + 5c like #839 1.25 1.25
846 A124 95c + 5c like #840 1.25 1.25
847 A124 95c + 5c like #841 1.25 1.25
848 A124 95c + 5c like #842 1.25 1.25

Surtax of No. 843 for children's organizations, of Nos. 844-848 for youth education.
Issued: #838-843, 11/21; #844-848, 12/10.

1985, Apr. 23 ***Perf. 13x13½***

Illustrations of North American bird species by artist, naturalist John J. Audubon.

849 A125 30c Downy woodpecker 1.25 1.25
850 A125 55c Black-throated blue warbler 2.25 2.25
851 A125 65c Yellow-throated warbler 2.50 2.50
852 A125 75c Chestnut-sided warbler 3.00 3.00
853 A125 95c Dickcissel 4.00 4.00
854 A125 $1.15 White-crowned sparrow 4.00 4.00
Nos. 849-854 (6) 17.00 17.00

Souvenir Sheets

855 A125 $1.30 Red-cockaded woodpecker 2.10 2.10
856 A125 $2.80 Seaside sparrow 3.75 3.75
857 A125 $5.30 Zenaida dove 7.75 7.75

Audubon birth bicentenary.

Locomotives — A126

1985, May 14 Litho. ***Perf. 14x13½***

858 A126 20c Kingston Flyer, New Zealand .20 .20
859 A126 55c Class 640, Italy .50 .50
860 A126 65c Gotthard, Switzerland .60 .60
861 A126 75c Union Pacific 6900, US .70 .70
862 A126 95c Super Continental, Canada .90 .90
863 A126 $1.15 TGV, France 1.00 1.00
864 A126 $2.20 Flying Scotsman, U.K. 2.00 2.00
865 A126 $3.40 Orient Express, Europe 3.00 3.00
Nos. 858-865 (8) 8.90 8.90

Intl. Youth Year — A127

Paintings: 55c, Helena Fourment, by Rubens. 65c, Vigee-Lebrun and Daughter, by Elizabeth Vigee-Lebrun (1755-1842). 75c, On the Terrace, by Renoir. $1.30, Young Mother Sewing, by Mary Cassatt (1845-1926).

1985, June 6 Photo. ***Perf. 13x13½***

866 A127 55c multicolored 2.40 2.40
867 A127 65c multicolored 2.75 2.75
868 A127 75c multicolored 3.25 3.25
869 A127 $1.30 multicolored 5.25 5.25
Nos. 866-869 (4) 13.65 13.65

Souvenir Sheet

870 Sheet of 4 7.75 7.75
a. A127 55c + 10c like #866 1.25 1.25
b. A127 65c + 10c like #867 1.50 1.50
c. A127 75c + 10c like #868 1.75 1.75
d. A127 $1.30 + 10c like #869 2.75 2.75

Surtax for youth organizations.

Queen Mother, 85th Birthday A128

Portraits: 65c, Lady Elizabeth, 1908, by Mable Hankey. 75c, Duchess of York, 1923, by Savely Sorine. $1.15, Duchess of York, 1925, by Philip De Laslo. $2.80, $5.30, Queen Elizabeth, 1938, by Sir Gerald Kelly.

1985, June 28

871 A128 65c multi .70 .70
872 A128 75c multi .80 .80
873 A128 $1.15 multi 1.25 1.25
874 A128 $2.80 multi 2.75 2.75
874A Sheet of 4 ('86) 5.50 5.50
b.-e. A128 55c, like #871-874 1.25 1.25
Nos. 871-874A (5) 11.00 11.00

Souvenir Sheet

875 A128 $5.30 multi 5.50 5.50

Nos. 871-874 printed in sheets of four.
#874A issued 8/4/86, for 86th birthday.
For surcharges see Nos. B114, B116, B122, B134, B140.

A129

A130

Portraits of prime ministers.

1985, July 29

876 A129 30c Albert Henry, 1965-78 1.10 1.10
877 A129 50c Sir Thomas Davis, 1978-83 2.00 2.00
878 A129 65c Geoffrey Henry, 1983 2.50 2.50
Nos. 876-878 (3) 5.60 5.60

Souvenir Sheet

879 Sheet of 3 11.50 11.50
a. A129 55c like #876 3.50 3.50
b. A129 55c like #877 3.50 3.50
c. A129 55c like #878 3.50 3.50

Self-government, 20th anniv.

1985, July 29 ***Perf. 14***

880 A130 55c Golf 4.25 4.25
881 A130 65c Rugby 4.50 4.50
882 A130 75c Tennis 5.25 5.25
Nos. 880-882 (3) 14.00 14.00

Souvenir Sheet

883 Sheet of 3 9.00 9.00
a. A130 55c + 10c like #880 2.75 2.75
b. A130 65c + 10c like #881 2.75 2.75
c. A130 75c + 10c like #882 2.75 2.75

South Pacific Mini Games, Rarotonga, July 31-Aug. 10. Surtax for the benefit of the Mini Games.

A131

A132

Seahorse & conf. emblems: 55c, South Pacific Bureau for Economic Cooperation. 65c, No. 887b, South Pacific Forum. 75c, No. 887c, Pacific Islands Conf.

1985, July 29 ***Perf. 14***

884 A131 55c blk, scar & gold 1.25 1.25
885 A131 65c blk, vio & gold 1.40 1.40
886 A131 75c blk, brt grn & gold 1.60 1.60
Nos. 884-886 (3) 4.25 4.25

Souvenir Sheet

887 50c Sheet of 3, #a.-c. 3.00 3.00

Pacific islands conf., Rarotonga, 7/30-8/10.

1985

Virgin and Child paintings by Botticelli.

888 A132 55c Madonna of the Magnificent 1.60 1.60
889 A132 65c Madonna with Pomegranate 1.90 1.90
890 A132 75c Madonna with Child & Six Angels 2.10 2.10
891 A132 95c Madonna & Child with St. John 2.75 2.75
Nos. 888-891 (4) 8.35 8.35

Souvenir Sheets

Perf. 13½

892 A132 $2.75 Sheet of 4 4.50 4.50
a. A132 50c like #888 1.00 1.00
b. A132 50c like #888 1.00 1.00
c. A132 50c like #890 1.00 1.00
d. A132 50c like #891 1.00 1.00

Imperf

893 A132 $1.20 like #888 1.90 1.90
894 A132 $1.45 like #889 2.10 2.10
895 A132 $2.20 like #890 3.50 3.50
896 A132 $2.75 like #891 4.00 4.00

Christmas. Issue dates: Nos. 888-892, Nov. 18; Nos. 893-896, Dec. 9.

Halley's Comet — A133

Elizabeth II, 60th Birthday — A134

Paintings: 55c, No. 902a, The Eve of the Deluge, by John Martin (1789-1854). 65c, No. 902b, Lot and His Daughters, by Lucas van Leyden (1494-1533). 75c, No. 902c, Auspicious Comet, 1587, anonymous. $1.25, No. 902d, Events Following Charles I, by Herman Saftleven (1609-1658). $2, No. 902e, Ossian Receiving Napoleonic Officers, by Anne Louis Girodet-Trioson (1764-1824). $4, Halley's Comet over the Thames, 1759, by Samuel Scott (1702-1772).

1986, Mar. 13 Photo. ***Perf. 14***

897 A133 55c multicolored 1.10 1.10
898 A133 65c multicolored 1.40 1.40
899 A133 75c multicolored 1.50 1.50
900 A133 $1.25 multicolored 3.00 3.00
901 A133 $2 multicolored 4.50 4.50
Nos. 897-901 (5) 11.50 11.50

Souvenir Sheets

Perf. 13½

902 Sheet of 5 + label 5.00 5.00
a.-e. A133 70c, each single .95 .95
903 A133 $4 multicolored 6.25 6.25

For surcharges see Nos. B113, B115, B117, B123, B129.

1986, Apr. 21 ***Perf. 13x13½***

Various portraits.

904 A134 95c multi 1.40 1.40
905 A134 $1.25 multi 1.75 1.75
906 A134 $1.50 multi 2.00 2.00
Nos. 904-906 (3) 5.15 5.15

Souvenir Sheets

907 A134 $1.10 like #904 2.25 2.25
908 A134 $1.95 like #905 4.25 4.25
909 A134 $2.45 like #906 6.00 6.00

For surcharges see Nos. 972-974, B118, B124, B127, B136-B137, B139.

AMERIPEX '86 — A135

Designs: $1, US No. 1, The Resolution, Rarotonga. $1.50, Downtown Chicago. $2, No. 398, Benjamin Franklin, The Resolution.

1986, May 21 Photo. ***Perf. 14***

910 A135 $1 multi 3.00 3.00
911 A135 $1.50 multi 4.25 4.25
912 A135 $2 multi 5.50 5.50
Nos. 910-912 (3) 12.75 12.75

For surcharges see Nos. B119, B128, B130.

Statue of Liberty, Cent. — A136

Wedding of Prince Andrew and Sarah Ferguson — A137

1986, July 4

913 A136 $1 Head 1.10 1.10
914 A136 $1.25 Torch 1.40 1.40
915 A136 $2.75 Liberty Is. 3.00 3.00
Nos. 913-915 (3) 5.50 5.50

For surcharges see Nos. B120, B125, B132.

1986, July 23

916 A137 $1 Sarah Ferguson .90 .90
917 A137 $2 Prince Andrew 1.75 1.75

Size: 60x33½mm

Perf. 13½x13

918 A137 $3 Couple 2.75 2.75
Nos. 916-918 (3) 5.40 5.40

Nos. 916-918 each printed in sheets of 4.
For surch. see #975-977, B121, B131, B135.

Christmas A138

Paintings by Rubens: 55c, No. 922a, The Holy Family. $1.30, $6.40, No. 922b, Virgin with Garland. $2.75, No. 922c, Adoration of Magi.

1986, Nov. 17 Litho. *Perf. 13½*

919 A138 55c multi 1.25 1.25
920 A138 $1.30 multi 3.00 3.00
921 A138 $2.75 multi 6.25 6.25
Nos. 919-921 (3) 10.50 10.50

Souvenir Sheets

922 Sheet of 3 13.50 13.50
a.-c. A138 $2.40, any single 4.50 4.50
923 A138 $6.40 multi 13.00 13.00

No. 922 contains 3 stamps 38½x49mm.
For surcharges see Nos. B100-B104, B112, B126, B133, B138, B141.

Stamps of 1980-84 Surcharged in Black

1987, Feb. Litho. *Perfs. as before*
Blocks of 4, #a.-d.
(#953-954, 956-957, 959, 961-962, 964)

948 A121 5c on 1c #787 .20 .20
949 A121 5c on 2c #788 .20 .20
950 A121 5c on 3c #789 .20 .20
951 A121 5c on 12c #792 .20 .20
952 A121 5c on 14c #793 .20 .20
953 A101 10c on 15c #572 .45 .45
954 A101 10c on 25c #574 .45 .45
955 A121 18c on 24c #796 .20 .20
956 A101 18c on 12c #571 .90 .90
957 A101 18c on 20c #573 .90 .90
958 A121 55c on 52c #803 .70 .70
959 A101 55c on 35c #576 2.75 2.75
960 A121 65c on 42c #800 .80 .80
961 A101 65c on 50c #577 3.25 3.25
962 A101 65c on 60c #578 3.25 3.25
963 A121 75c on 48c #801 1.00 1.00
964 A101 75c on 70c #579 3.75 3.75
965 A121 95c on 96c #808 1.25 1.25
966 A121 95c on $1.10 #809 1.25 1.25
967 A121 95c on $1.20 #810 1.25 1.25

Stamps of 1981-86 Surcharged in Black (A102), Black and Gold (#969-970, A137) or Gold (#971, A134, A104, A108)

968 A123 $1.30 on 36c #829 1.60 1.60
969 A123 $1.30 on 48c #830 1.60 1.60
970 A123 $1.30 on 60c #831 1.60 1.60
971 A123 $1.30 on $2 #832 1.60 1.60
972 A134 $2.80 on 95c #904 3.50 3.50
973 A134 $2.80 on $1.25 #905 3.50 3.50
974 A134 $2.80 on $1.50 #906 3.50 3.50
975 A137 $2.80 on $1 #916 3.50 3.50
976 A137 $2.80 on $2 #917 3.50 3.50
977 A137 $2.80 on $3 #918 3.50 3.50
978 A102 $6.40 on $4 #584 7.75 7.75
979 A102 $7.20 on $6 #585 8.75 8.75
980 A104 $9.40 on $1 #659 12.00 12.00
981 A104 $9.40 on $2 #660 12.00 12.00

Pair, #a.-b.

982 A108 $9.40 on $2.50 #678 24.00 24.00
Nos. 948-982 (35) 115.05 115.05

Issued: 5c, #955, 958, 960, 963, 95c, $6.40, $7.20, 2/10; 10c, #956-957, 959, 961-962, 964, 2/11; $12.30, $2.80, $9.40, 2/12.
For surcharge see No. B111.

Stamps of 1980-82 Surcharged in Black (A102) or Gold (A104)

Perfs. as before

1987, June 17 Photo.

984 A102 $2.80 on $2 #582 3.25 3.25
985 A102 $5 on $3 #583 5.50 5.50
986 A102 $9.40 on $10 #586 10.00 10.00

Pairs, #a.-b.

987 A104 $9.40 on $1 #679 20.00 20.00
988 A104 $9.40 on $2 #680 20.00 20.00
Nos. 984-988 (5) 58.75 58.75

Souvenir Sheet

989 A104 $9.20 on #680c 19.00 19.00

Nos. 399 and 584 Ovptd. "ROYAL / WEDDING / FORTIETH / ANNIVERSARY" in Black on Gold Bar

1987, Nov. 20 Photo. *Perf. 14x13½*

991 A64 $4 on #399 5.00 5.00
992 A102 $4 on #584 5.00 5.00

Christmas — A139

The Holy Family, religious paintings by Rembrandt in European museums: $1.25, No. 996a, The Louvre, Paris. $1.50, No. 996b, $6, The Holy Family with Angels, The Hermitage, Leningrad. $1.95, No. 996c, The Alte Pinakothek, Munich.

1987, Dec. 7 Photo. *Perf. 13½*

993 A139 $1.25 multi 2.75 2.75
994 A139 $1.50 multi 3.75 3.75
995 A139 $1.95 multi 4.75 4.75
Nos. 993-995 (3) 11.25 11.25

Souvenir Sheets

996 Sheet of 3 8.50 8.50
a.-c. A139 $1.15 any single 2.75 2.75

Perf. 13x13½

997 A139 $6 multi 10.00 10.00

Size of Nos. 996a-996c: 49½x38½mm. No. 997 contains 1 stamp 39½x31½mm.

1988 Summer Olympics, Seoul A140

Designs: a, Cook Islands commemorative silver coin (obverse and reverse) issued on Aug. 20, 1987, for the '88 Summer Games. b, Seoul Olympic Park, torch and emblem. c, Steffi Graf, women's tennis champion, and '88 gold medal.

1988, Apr. 26 Photo. *Perf. 13½x14*

998 Strip of 3 11.50 11.50
a.-c. A140 $1.50 multicolored 3.75 3.75

Souvenir Sheet

Perf. 13½

999 A140 $10 multi 16.00 16.00

Participation of national athletes in the Olympics for the first time, introduction of tennis as an Olympic gold-medal event.
No. 999 contains one stamp 114x47mm combining the designs of Nos. 998a-998c.

Nos. 998-999 Ovptd. for Olympic Winners

a. "MILOSLAV MECIR CZECHOSLOVAKIA GOLD MEDAL WINNER MEN'S TENNIS"
b. "TIM MAYOTTE UNITED STATES GABRIELA SABATINI ARGENTINA SILVER MEDAL WINNERS"
c. "GOLD MEDAL WINNER STEFFI GRAF WEST GERMANY"
d. "GOLD MEDAL WINNER SEOUL OLYMPIC GAMES STEFFI GRAF - WEST GERMANY"

1988, Oct. 12 Photo. *Perf. 13½x14*

1000 Strip of 3 10.00 10.00
a.-c. A140 $1.50 multicolored 3.25 3.25

Souvenir Sheet

Perf. 13½

1001 A140(d) $10 on No. 999 16.00 16.00

Margin of No. 1001 ovptd.: "STEFFI GRAF, WINNER OF AUSTRALIAN OPEN 24 JULY 1988, FRENCH OPEN / 4 JUNE 1988, WIMBLEDON 2 JULY 1988, U.S. OPEN 10 SEPTEMBER 1988. / FIRST GRAND SLAM WINNER IN 18 YEARS. GOLD MEDAL WINNER SEOUL / OLYMPICS 1 OCTOBER 1988."

Christmas A141

Paintings by Albrecht Durer: 70c, Virgin and Child. 85c, Virgin and Child, diff. 95c, Virgin and Child, diff. $1.25, Virgin and Child, diff. $6.40, The Nativity.

1988, Nov. 11 *Perf. 13½*

1002 A141 70c multi 2.25 2.25
1003 A141 85c multi 2.75 2.75
1004 A141 95c multi 3.00 3.00
1005 A141 $1.25 multi 4.00 4.00
Nos. 1002-1005 (4) 12.00 12.00

Souvenir Sheet

1006 A141 $6.40 multi 8.50 8.50

No. 1006 contains one stamp 45x60mm.

Scene and Left Half of Mission Emblem A142

1st Moon Landing, 20th Anniv. A144

#1007a, Launch vehicle in space. #1007b, *Eagle* landing on Moon. #1008a, Astronaut descending ladder. #1008, Astronaut on Moon. #1009a, Seismic experiment. #1009b, Solar wind experiment. #1010a, Liftoff from Moon. #1010b, Splashdown and recovery.
The "b" stamps have the right half of the emblem.

1989, July 14 Photo. *Perf. 13*

1007 A142 40c Pair, #a.-b. 2.40 2.40
1008 A142 55c Pair, #a.-b. 3.75 3.75
1009 A142 65c Pair, #a.-b. 4.50 4.50
1010 A142 75c Pair, #a.-b. 5.25 5.25
Nos. 1007-1010 (4) 15.90 15.90

Souvenir Sheet

1011 A144 $4.20 Armstrong and Aldrin 7.00 7.00

Printed with continuous designs.

World Wildlife Fund A145

Endangered bird species.

1989, Oct. 4 Photo. *Perf. 13½x13*

1016 A145 15c *Pomarea dimidiata* .95 .95
1017 A145 20c *Pomarea dimidiata* (two) 1.25 1.25
1018 A145 65c *Ptilinopus rarotongensis* (two) 4.25 4.25
1019 A145 70c *Ptilinopus rarotongensis* 4.25 4.25
Nos. 1016-1019 (4) 10.70 10.70

Souvenir Sheets
Without WWF Emblem

Perf. 13½

1020 A145 $1 like 15c 2.00 2.00
1021 A145 $1.25 like 20c 2.25 2.25
1022 A145 $1.50 like 65c 2.75 2.75
1023 A145 $1.75 like 70c 3.25 3.25

World Wildlife Fund. #1020-1023 are airmail and contain one 52x34mm stamp; decorative margins continue the designs.
For overprints see Nos. C24-C27.

Christmas — A146

Details of *Adoration of the Magi*, by Rubens: 70c, Witnesses. 85c, Madonna. 95c, Christ child. $1.50, Attendant. $6.40, Entire painting.

1989, Nov. 24 Photo. *Perf. 13½x13*

1024 A146 70c multicolored 1.90 1.90
1025 A146 85c multicolored 2.25 2.25
1026 A146 95c multicolored 2.50 2.50
1027 A146 $1.50 multicolored 4.00 4.00
Nos. 1024-1027 (4) 10.65 10.65

Souvenir Sheet

Perf. 13½

1028 A146 $6.40 multicolored 11.50 11.50

No. 1028 contains one 45x60mm stamp.

Religious History A147

70c, John Williams, LMS Mission Church. 85c, Bernardine Castanie, Roman Catholic Church. 95c, Osborne J.P. Widstoe, Church of Jesus Christ of Latter Day Saints. $1.60, J.E. Caldwell, Seventh Day Adventist Church.

1990, Feb. 19 Photo. *Perf. 13½x13*

1029 A147 70c multicolored 1.10 1.10
1030 A147 85c multicolored 1.25 1.25
1031 A147 95c multicolored 1.40 1.40
1032 A147 $1.60 multicolored 2.50 2.50
Nos. 1029-1032 (4) 6.25 6.25

Souvenir Sheet

Perf. 13½

1033 Sheet of 4 7.50 7.50
a. A147 90c like 70c 1.75 1.75
b. A147 90c like 85c 1.75 1.75
c. A147 90c like 95c 1.75 1.75
d. A147 90c like $1.60 1.75 1.75

No. 1033 contains 4 36x36mm stamps.

Penny Black, 150th Anniv. — A148

Paintings: 85c, No. 1038a, *Woman Writing a Letter*, by Gerard Terborch (1617-1681). $1.15, No. 1038b, *Portrait of George Gisze*, by

Hans Holbein the Younger. $1.55, No. 1038c, *Portrait of Mrs. John Douglas,* by Thomas Gainsborough. $1.85, No. 1038d, *Portrait of a Gentleman,* by Albrecht Durer.

1990, May 2 Photo. *Perf. 13½*

1034 A148 85c multicolored 1.40 1.40
1035 A148 $1.15 multicolored 2.00 2.00
1036 A148 $1.55 multicolored 2.50 2.50
1037 A148 $1.85 multicolored 3.00 3.00
Nos. 1034-1037 (4) 8.90 8.90

Souvenir Sheet

1038 Sheet of 4 11.00 11.00
a.-d. A148 $1.05 any single 2.50 2.50

The margin of No. 1038 pictures the Stamp World '90 emblem and Great Britain #1-2.

1992 Olympics A149

Designs: a. Summer Games, Barcelona (runners). b. Eternal flame, commemorative coin obverse (Queen Elizabeth II) and reverse (athletes). c. Winter Games, Albertville (skier).

1990, June 15 Photo. *Perf. 14*

1039 Strip of 3 14.50 14.50
a.-c. A149 $1.85 any single 4.50 4.50

Queen Mother, 90th Birthday A150

1990, July 20 Photo. *Perf. 13½*

1040 A150 $1.85 multicolored 4.75 4.75

Souvenir Sheet

1041 A150 $6.40 multicolored 10.50 10.50

Christmas A151

Paintings: 70c, Adoration of the Magi by Memling. 85c, The Holy Family by Lotto. 95c, Madonna and Child with Saints John and Catherine by Titian. $1.50, The Holy Family by Titian. $6.40, Madonna and Child Enthroned, Surrounded by Saints by Vivarini.

1990, Nov. 29 Litho. *Perf. 14*

1042 A151 70c multicolored 1.50 1.50
1043 A151 85c multicolored 1.75 1.75
1044 A151 95c multicolored 1.90 1.90
1045 A151 $1.50 multicolored 3.25 3.25
Nos. 1042-1045 (4) 8.40 8.40

Souvenir Sheet

1046 A151 $6.40 multicolored 11.00 11.00

Souvenir Sheet

1992 Olympic Games — A152

Illustration reduced.

1991, Feb. 12 *Perf. 13½*

1047 A152 $6.40 multicolored 14.50 14.50

Discovery of America 500th Anniv. (in 1992) — A153

1991, Feb. 14 Photo. *Perf. 13½x13*

1048 A153 $1 multicolored 3.00 3.00

No. 586 Ovptd. "65th BIRTHDAY" in Gold

1991, Apr. 22 Litho. *Perf. 14x13½*

1049 A102 $10 multicolored 13.50 13.50

Christmas A154

Paintings: 70c, Adoration of the Child, by Delle Notti (Gerrit van Honthorst). 85c, Birth of the Virgin, by Murillo. $1.15, Adoration of the Shepherds, by Rembrandt. $1.50, Adoration of the Shepherds, by Le Nain. $6.40, Madonna and Child, by Fra Filippo Lippi, vert.

1991, Nov. 12 Litho. *Perf. 14*

1050 A154 70c multicolored 1.60 1.60
1051 A154 85c multicolored 2.00 2.00
1052 A154 $1.15 multicolored 2.75 2.75
1053 A154 $1.50 multicolored 3.50 3.50
Nos. 1050-1053 (4) 9.85 9.85

Souvenir Sheet

1054 A154 $6.40 multicolored 11.50 11.50

Marine Life — A155

A155a

5c, Red-breasted maori wrasse. 10c, Blue sea star. 15c, Black & gold angelfish. 20c, Spotted pebble crab. 25c, Black-tipped cod. 30c, Spanish dancer. 50c, Royal angelfish. 80c, Squirrel fish. 85c, Red pencil sea urchin. 90c, Red-spot rainbow fish. $1, Black-lined maori wrasse. $2, Longnose butterflyfish. $3, Red-spot rainbow fish. $5, Blue sea star. $7, Royal angelfish. $10, Spotted pebble crab. $15, Red pencil sea urchin.

1992-94 Litho. *Perf. 14½x13½*

1058 A155 5c multi .25 .25
1059 A155 10c multi .25 .25
1062 A155 15c multi .25 .25
1064 A155 20c multi .30 .30
1065 A155 25c multi .35 .35
1066 A155 30c multi .40 .40
1071 A155 50c multi .70 .70
1076 A155 80c multi 1.10 1.10
1077 A155 85c multi 1.10 1.10
1078 A155 90c multi 1.10 1.10
1080 A155 $1 multi 1.25 1.25
1081 A155 $2 multi 2.50 2.50
1082 A155a $3 multi 4.00 4.00
1083 A155a $5 multi 6.25 6.25
1085 A155a $7 multi 9.25 9.25
1087 A155a $10 multi 12.50 12.50
1089 A155a $15 multi 20.00 20.00
Nos. 1058-1089 (17) 61.55 61.55

Issued: 85c, 90c, $1, $2, 3/23/92; $3, $5, 10/25/93; $7, 12/6/93; $10, 1/31/94; $15, 9/9/94; others, 1/22/92.

See Nos. 1154-1176 for stamps with buff border. For overprints see Nos. O54-O68.

This is an expanding set. Numbers may change.

Endangered Wildlife — A156

#1095, Tiger. #1096, Asiatic elephant. #1097, Grizzly bear. #1098, Black rhinoceros. #1099, Chimpanzee. #1100, Asian bighorn. #1101, Heavisides dolphin. #1102, Eagle owl. #1103, Bee hummingbird. #1104, Feliscon-color cougar. #1105, European otter. #1106, Red kangaroo.

1992 Litho. *Perf. 14*

1095-1106 $1.15 Set of 12 24.00 24.00

Issued: #1095, 4/6; #1096, 4/7; #1097, 4/8; #1098, 4/9; #1099, 4/10; #1100, 4/11; #1101, 7/13; #1102, 7/14; #1103, 7/15; #1104, 7/16; #1105, 7/17; #1106, 7/18.

See Nos. 1119-1124, 1134-1138.

Discovery of America, 500th Anniv. — A157

1992, May 22 Litho. *Perf. 14x14½*

1107 A157 $6 multicolored 9.25 9.25

Souvenir Sheet

Perf. 15x14

1107A A157 $10 Coming ashore 10.50 10.50

Issued: #1107, May 22. #1107A, Sept. 21.
No. 1107A contains one 40x30mm stamp.

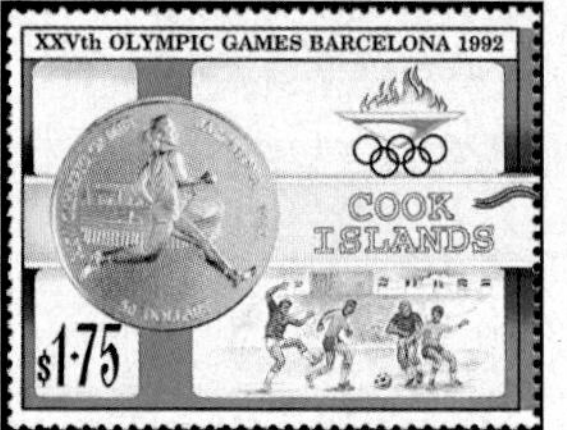

1992 Summer Olympics, Barcelona — A158

Designs: No. 1108a, $50 coin, soccer players. b, Flags of Spain, Cook Islands, Barcelona medal. c, $10 coin, basketball players. No. 1109a, Runners. b, $10, $50 coins. c, Cyclists. $6.40, Javelin.

1992, July 24 Litho. *Perf. 13*

1108 A158 $1.75 Strip of 3, #a.-c. 9.50 9.50
1109 A158 $2.25 Strip of 3, #a.-c. 12.00 12.00

Souvenir Sheet

1110 A158 $6.40 multicolored 12.50 12.50

6th Festival of Pacific Arts, Rarotonga A159

80c, UNESCO poster. 85c, $1, $1.75, Different carvings of Rarotongan fertility god, Tangaroa.

1992, Oct. 16 Litho. *Perf. 15x14*

1111 A159 80c multicolored 1.25 1.25
1112 A159 85c multicolored 1.40 1.40
1113 A159 $1 multicolored 1.60 1.60
1114 A159 $1.75 multicolored 2.75 2.75
Nos. 1111-1114 (4) 7.00 7.00

For overprints see #1231-1234.

Ovptd. "ROYAL VISIT"

1992, Oct. 16

1115 A159 80c on #1111 1.40 1.40
1116 A159 85c on #1112 1.60 1.60
1117 A159 $1 on #1113 1.75 1.75
1118 A159 $1.75 on #1114 3.25 3.25
Nos. 1115-1118 (4) 8.00 8.00

Endangered Wildlife Type of 1992

1992 Litho. *Perf. 14*

1119 A156 $1.15 Jackass penguin 2.00 2.00
1120 A156 $1.15 Asian lion 2.00 2.00
1121 A156 $1.15 Peregrine falcon 2.00 2.00
1122 A156 $1.15 Persian fallow deer 2.00 2.00
1123 A156 $1.15 Key deer 2.00 2.00
1124 A156 $1.15 Alpine ibex 2.00 2.00
Nos. 1119-1124 (6) 12.00 12.00

Issued: #1119, 11/2; #1120, 11/3; #1121, 11/4; #1122, 11/5; #1123, 11/6; #1124, 11/7.

Christmas A160

Paintings by El Parmigianino: 70c, Worship of Shepherds. 85c, $6.40, Virgin with Long Neck. $1.15, Virgin with Rose. $1.90, St. Margaret's Virgin.

1992, Nov. 20 Litho. *Perf. 13½*

1125 A160 70c multicolored 1.25 1.25
1126 A160 85c multicolored 1.50 1.50
1127 A160 $1.15 multicolored 2.00 2.00
1128 A160 $1.90 multicolored 3.50 3.50
Nos. 1125-1128 (4) 8.25 8.25

Souvenir Sheet

1129 A160 $6.40 multicolored 11.00 11.00

No. 1129 contains one 36x47mm stamp.

Queen Elizabeth II's Accession to the Throne, 40th Anniv. — A161

Various portraits of Queen Elizabeth II.

1992, Dec. 10 Litho. *Perf. 14*

1130 A161 80c multicolored 1.25 1.25
1131 A161 $1.15 multicolored 1.75 1.75
1132 A161 $1.50 multicolored 2.50 2.50
1133 A161 $1.95 multicolored 3.25 3.25
Nos. 1130-1133 (4) 8.75 8.75

Endangered Wildlife Type of 1992

1993 Litho. *Perf. 14*

1134 A156 $1.15 English mandrill 2.40 2.40
1135 A156 $1.15 Gorilla 2.40 2.40
1136 A156 $1.15 Vanessa atlanta 2.40 2.40
1137 A156 $1.15 Sichuan takin 2.40 2.40
1138 A156 $1.15 Ring tailed lemur 2.40 2.40
Nos. 1134-1138 (5) 12.00 12.00

Issued: #1134, Feb. 1; #1135, Feb. 2; #1136, Feb. 3; #1137, Feb. 4; #1138, Feb. 5.

Coronation of Queen Elizabeth II, 40th Anniv. — A162

Designs: $1, Coronation ceremony. $2, Coronation portrait. $3, Queen, family on balcony, Buckingham Palace.

1993, June 2 Litho. *Perf. 14*

1139 A162 $1 multicolored 1.50 1.50
1140 A162 $2 multicolored 3.00 3.00
1141 A162 $3 multicolored 4.75 4.75
Nos. 1139-1141 (3) 9.25 9.25

Christmas A163

Paintings: 70c, Virgin with Child, by Filippo Lippi. 85c, Bargellini Madonna, by Lodovico Carracci. $1.15, Virgin of the Curtain, by Raphael. $2.50, Holy Family, by Il Bronzino. $4, Saint Zachary Virgin, by Il Parmigianino.

1993, Nov. 8 Litho. *Perf. 14*

1142 A163 70c multicolored .95 .95
1143 A163 85c multicolored 1.25 1.25
1144 A163 $1.15 multicolored 1.50 1.50
1145 A163 $2.50 multicolored 3.50 3.50

Size: 32x47mm

Perf. 13½

1146 A163 $4.00 multicolored 5.75 5.75
Nos. 1142-1146 (5) 12.95 12.95

1994 Winter Olympics, Lillehammer — A164

Illustration reduced.

1994, Feb. 11 Litho. *Perf. 13½x14*

1147 A164 $5 multicolored 7.25 7.25

1994 World Cup Soccer Championships, US — A165

Illustration reduced.

1994, June 17 Litho. *Perf. 14*

1148 A165 $4.50 multicolored 6.75 6.75

First Manned Moon Landing, 25th Anniv. — A166

Apollo 11 emblem and: No. 1149a, First step onto Moon, US flag. No. 1149b, Astronaut carrying experiment packs on Moon. No. 1150a, Astronaut, US flag. No. 1150b, Flag, reflection shown in astronaut's visor.

1994, July 20

1149 A166 $2.25 Pair, #a.-b. + label 8.00 8.00
1150 A166 $2.25 Pair, #a.-b. + label 8.00 8.00

Living Reef Type of 1992

1994 Litho. *Perf. 14½x13½*

Size: 41x31mm

Buff & Multicolored

1154 A155 5c like #1058 .25 .25
1158 A155 15c like #1062 .25 .25
1160 A155 20c like #1064 .30 .30
1161 A155 25c like #1065 .35 .35
1162 A155 30c like #1066 .45 .45
1167 A155 50c like #1071 .75 .75
1172 A155 80c like #1076 1.10 1.10
1173 A155 85c like #1077 1.25 1.25
1174 A155 90c like #1078 1.40 1.40
1176 A155 $1 like #1080 1.50 1.50
Nos. 1154-1176 (10) 7.60 7.60

Issued: 5c, 15c, 20c, 25c, 30c, 50c, 80c, 85c, 90c, $1, 10/24/94. This is an expanding set. Numbers may change.

Miniature Sheet

The Return of Tommy Tricker — A167

Scenes from film: a, Three people in canoe. b, Traditional dancers. c, Couple walking on beach. d, Aerial view of island. e, Girls performing hand gestures. f, Girls walking along sand bar.

1994, Nov. 23 Litho. *Perf. 14*

1191 A167 85c Sheet of 6, #a.-f. 13.50 13.50

See No. 1213.

Christmas — A168

Paintings: No. 1192a, The Virgin and Child, by Morales. b, Adoration of Kings, by Gerard David. c, Adoration of Kings, by Vinc Foppa. d, The Madonna & Child with St. Joseph & Infant Baptist, by Baroccio.

No. 1193a, Madonna with Iris, in style of Durer. b, Adoration of Shepherds, by Le Nain. c, The Virgin and Child, by follower of Leonardo. d, The Mystic Nativity, by Botticelli.

1994, Nov. 30 Litho. *Perf. 14*

1192 A168 85c Block of 4, #a.-d. 5.25 5.25
1193 A168 $1 Block of 4, #a.-d. 6.25 6.25

Robert Louis Stevenson (1850-94), Writer — A169

Adventure scenes from books: a, "Treasure Island." b, "David Balfour." c, "Dr. Jekyll and Mr. Hyde." d, "Kidnapped."

1994, Dec. 12 *Perf. 14x15*

1194 A169 $1.50 Block of 4, #a.-d. 9.00 9.00

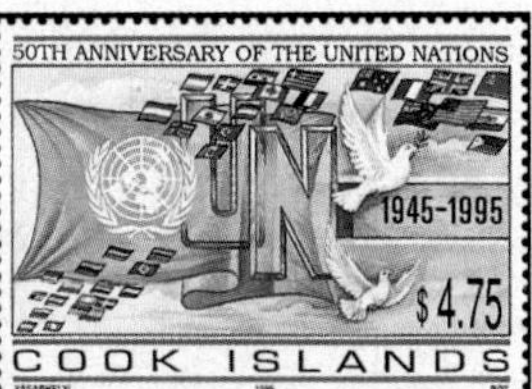

UN, 50th Anniv. — A170

$4.50, FAO, 50th anniv.

1995 Litho. *Perf. 13x13½*

1195 A170 $4.75 multicolored 6.75 6.75

Perf. 13½

1196 A170 $4.50 multicolored 7.25 7.25

Each issued in sheets of 4.
Issued: $4.75, 7/17; $4.50, 10/12.

Queen Mother, 95th Birthday — A172

1995, Aug. 31

1197 A172 $5 multicolored 9.75 9.75

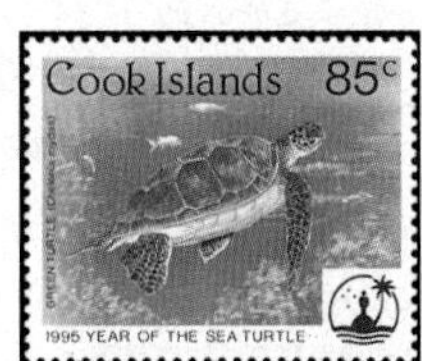

End of World War II, 50th Anniv. — A173

Designs: a, German surrender, Rheims. b, Japanese surrender, Tokyo Bay.

1995, Sept. 4 *Perf. 13*

1198 A173 $3.50 Pair, #a.-b. 17.00 17.00

No. 1198 was issued in sheets of 4 stamps.

Year of the Sea Turtle A174

Designs: 85c, Green turtle in water. $1, Hawksbill turtle in water. $1.75, Green turtle nesting. $2.25, Hawksbill turtle hatchlings leaving nest.

1995, Nov. 20 Litho. *Perf. 14*

1199 A174 85c multicolored 1.60 1.60
1200 A174 $1 multicolored 2.10 2.10
1201 A174 $1.75 multicolored 3.25 3.25
1202 A174 $2.25 multicolored 4.50 4.50
Nos. 1199-1202 (4) 11.45 11.45

1996 Summer Olympics, Atlanta A175

1996, Jan. 12 Litho. *Perf. 14*

1203 A175 85c Discus 1.40 1.40
1204 A175 $1 Torch bearer 1.75 1.75
1205 A175 $1.50 Sprinting 2.50 2.50
1206 A175 $1.85 Gymnastics 3.00 3.00
1207 A175 $2.10 Archery 3.50 3.50
1208 A175 $2.50 Javelin 4.00 4.00
Nos. 1203-1208 (6) 16.15 16.15

Queen Elizabeth II, 70th Birthday — A176

Designs: $1.90, No. 1212a, In blue hat, coat. $2.25, No. 1212b, Wearing tiara. $2.75, No. 1212c, In robes of Order of the Garter.

1996, June 21 Litho. *Perf. 14*

1209 A176 $1.90 multicolored 3.00 3.00
1210 A176 $2.25 multicolored 3.50 3.50
1211 A176 $2.75 multicolored 4.00 4.00
Nos. 1209-1211 (3) 10.50 10.50

Sheet of 3

1212 A176 $2.50 #a.-c. + label 12.00 12.00

Nos. 1209-1211 were issued in sheets of 4.

"The Return of Tommy Tricker" Type of 1994

No. 1213a-1213f, like #1191a-1191f.

1997, Aug. 28 Litho. *Perf. 14*

1213 A167 90c Sheet of 6, #a.-f. 8.00 8.00

Nos. 1213a-1213f Overprinted in Silver

a

b

1997, Sept. 12 Litho. *Perf. 14*

1214 A167 90c Sheet 6, #a.-f. 7.00 7.00

#1214a, 1214d-1214e are overprinted type "a"; #1214b-1214c, 1214f type "b."

Butterflies A177

5c, Lampides boeticus (female). 10c, Vanessa atalanta. 15c, Lampides boeticus (male). 20c, Papilio godeffroyi. 25c, Danaus hamata. 30c, Xois sesara. 50c, Vagrans egista. 70c, Parthenos sylvia. 80c, Hyblaea sanguinea. 85c, Melanitis leda. 90c, Ascalapha odorata. $1, Precis villida. $1.50, Parthenos sylvia. $2, Lampides boeticus. $3, Precis villida. $4, Melanitis leda. $5, Vagrans egista. $7, Hyblaea sanguinea. $10, Vanessa atalanta. $15, Papilio godeffroyi.

1997-98 Litho. *Perf. 13*

1215 A177 5c multi .20 .20
1216 A177 10c multi .20 .20
1217 A177 15c multi .20 .20
1218 A177 20c multi .25 .25
1219 A177 25c multi .30 .30
1220 A177 30c multi .35 .35
1221 A177 50c multi .60 .60
1222 A177 70c multi .85 .85
1223 A177 80c multi 1.00 1.00
1224 A177 85c multi 1.00 1.00
1225 A177 90c multi 1.10 1.10
1226 A177 $1 multi 1.25 1.25

Perf. 13½

Size: 41x25mm

1226A A177 $1.50 multi 1.75 1.75
1226B A177 $2 multi 2.40 2.40
1226C A177 $3 multi 3.50 3.50
1226D A177 $4 multi 5.00 5.00
1226E A177 $5 multi 6.00 6.00

1226F A177 $7 multi 8.50 8.50
1226G A177 $10 multi 12.00 12.00
1226H A177 $15 multi 16.00 16.00
Nos. 1215-1226H (20) 62.45 62.45

Issued: 5c, 10c, 15c, 20c, 25c, 30c, 50c, 70c, 10/22/97; 80c, 85c, 90c, $1, 11/12/97; $1.50, $2, $3, 3/11/98; $4, $5, 6/19/98; $7, $10, 9/18/98; $15, 11/13/98.

For surcharges, see Nos. 1259-1264.

Queen Elizabeth II and Prince Philip, 50th Wedding Anniv.
A178

1997, Nov. 20 *Perf. 14*
1227 A178 $2 multicolored 2.40 2.40

Souvenir Sheet

1228 A178 $5 like #1227, close-up 6.00 6.00

No. 1228 is a continuous design.

Diana, Princess of Wales (1961-97) — A179

1998, Mar. 18 **Litho.** *Perf. 14*
1229 A179 $1.15 shown 1.40 1.40

Souvenir Sheet

1230 A179 $3.50 like #1229 4.25 4.25

No. 1229 was issued in sheets of 5 + label.
See No. B142.

Nos. 1111-1114 Ovptd. "KIA ORANA / THIRD MILLENNIUM"

1231ovpt

Printing Methods and Perfs as before

1999, Dec. 31
1231 A159 80c on #1111 .75 .75
1232 A159 85c on #1112 .80 .80
1233 A159 $1 on #1113 .95 .95
1234 A159 $1.75 on #1114 1.60 1.60
Nos. 1231-1234 (4) 4.10 4.10

Queen Mother, 100th Birthday — A180

No. 1235: a, As child. b, As young woman. c, Wearing green hat. d, Wearing tiara.
Illustration reduced.

2000, Oct. 20 **Litho.** *Perf. 14*
1235 A180 $4.50 Sheet of 4, #a-d 16.00 16.00

Souvenir Sheet

1236 A180 $6 Wearing blue hat 5.50 5.50

2000 Summer Olympics, Sydney — A181

No. 1237: a, Ancient runner. b, Track and field. c, Ancient archery. d, Archery.

2000, Nov. 14
1237 A181 $1.75 Sheet of 4, #a-d 6.25 6.25

Souvenir Sheet

1238 A181 $3.90 Torch bearer 3.50 3.50

Nos. 1095-1106 Surcharged in Gold

2001, Apr. 30 **Litho.** *Perf. 14*
1239 A156 80c on $1.15 #1101 .65 .65
1240 A156 80c on $1.15 #1102 .65 .65
1241 A156 80c on $1.15 #1103 .65 .65
1242 A156 80c on $1.15 #1104 .65 .65
1243 A156 80c on $1.15 #1105 .65 .65
1244 A156 80c on $1.15 #1106 .65 .65
1245 A156 90c on $1.15 #1095 .75 .75
1246 A156 90c on $1.15 #1096 .75 .75
1247 A156 90c on $1.15 #1097 .75 .75
1248 A156 90c on $1.15 #1098 .75 .75
1249 A156 90c on $1.15 #1099 .75 .75
1250 A156 90c on $1.15 #1100 .75 .75
Nos. 1239-1250 (12) 8.40 8.40

Nos. 1042-1045, 1050-1053 Surcharged or Overprinted in Black or Gold

2002, Nov. 11 **Litho.** *Perf. 14*
1251 A151 20c on 70c #1042 .20 .20
1252 A154 20c on 70c #1050 .20 .20
1253 A154 80c on $1.15 #1052 (G) .80 .80
1254 A151 85c #1043 .85 .85
1255 A154 85c #1051 .85 .85
1256 A154 90c on $1.50 #1053 .90 .90
1257 A151 95c #1044 .95 .95
1258 A151 $1 on $1.50 #1045 1.00 1.00
Nos. 1251-1258 (8) 5.75 5.75

Nos. 1226A-1226F Surcharged

Methods and Perfs As Before

2003, June 30
1259 A177 20c on $1.50 #1226A .25 .25
1260 A177 80c on $2 #1226B .95 .95
1261 A177 85c on $3 #1226C 1.00 1.00
1262 A177 85c on $4 #1226D 1.00 1.00
1263 A177 90c on $5 #1226E 1.10 1.10
1264 A177 90c on $7 #1226F 1.10 1.10
Nos. 1259-1264 (6) 5.40 5.40

Obliterator on Nos. 1260-1264 is a Moai head.

United We Stand — A182

2003, Sept. 30 **Litho.** *Perf. 14*
1265 A182 90c multi 1.10 1.10

Printed in sheets of 4.

2004 Summer Olympics, Athens
A183

Designs: 40c, Poster for 1992 Barcelona Olympics. 60c, Pancration, horiz. $1, Cycling, horiz. $2, Gold medal, 1936 Berlin Olympics.

2004, Sept. 29 **Litho.** *Perf. 14¼*
1266-1269 A183 Set of 4 5.50 5.50

SEMI-POSTAL STAMPS

Catalogue values for unused stamps in this section are for Never Hinged items.

Nos. 203-204, 223, 210, 213, 215-216 Surcharged

Perf. 14x13½, 13½

1968, Feb. 12 **Photo.**
B1 A34 3c + 1c multi .20 .20
B2 A34 4c + 1c multi .20 .20
B3 A37 5c + 2c multi .20 .20
B4 A34 10c + 2c multi .25 .25
B5 A34 25c + 5c multi .40 .40
B6 A34 50c + 10c multi .90 .90
B7 A35 $1 + 10c multi 1.75 1.75
Nos. B1-B7 (7) 3.90 3.90

Surtax for the victims of hurricane of Dec. 15-18, 1967. The surcharge on No. B3 is printed on a silver rectangle. The surcharge on No. B7 is in smaller type with serifs, measuring 7½mm in depth.

Nos. 210, 213-214 Surcharged in Ultramarine

1971, Sept. 8 **Photo.** *Perf. 14x13½*
B8 A34 10c + 1c multi .25 .25
B9 A34 10c + 3c multi .25 .25
B10 A34 25c + 1c multi .65 .65
B11 A34 25c + 3c multi .65 .65
B12 A34 30c + 1c multi .75 .75
B13 A34 30c + 3c multi .75 .75
Nos. B8-B13 (6) 3.30 3.30

4th South Pacific Games, Papeete, French Polynesia, Sept. 8-19.

Christmas Type of Regular Issue
Souvenir Sheet

50c+5c, Holy Family in a Garland of Flowers, by Jan Brueghel and Pieter van Avont.

1971, Nov. 30 **Photo.** *Perf. 13½*
B14 A50 50c + 5c gold & multi 1.75 1.75

No. B14 contains one stamp 45x40mm.

Nos. 316-318, 211, 213 and 215 Surcharged in Red or Black

a

b

1972, Mar. 30 **Photo.** *Perf. 13½*
B15 A46(a) 5c + 2c multi (R) .20 .20
B16 A46(a) 10c + 2c multi (R) .20 .20
B17 A34(b) 15c + 5c multi .35 .35
B18 A34(b) 25c + 5c multi .65 .65
B19 A46(a) 30c + 5c multi (R) .75 .75
B20 A34(b) 50c + 10c multi 1.40 1.40
Nos. B15-B20 (6) 3.55 3.55

Surtax for victims of hurricane of Mar. 22-26.

Nos. 319-322c with Surcharge Similar to Type "a"

1972, May 24 Photo. *Perf. 13½*

B21	A51	5c + 2c, pair, #a.-b.	.25	.25
B22	A51	10c + 2c, pair, #a.-b.	.45	.45
B23	A51	25c + 2c, pair, #a.-b.	1.00	1.00
B24	A51	30c + 2c, pair, #a.-b.	1.50	1.50
c.		Souvenir sheet of 8	3.50	3.50
		Nos. B21-B24 (4)	3.20	3.20

Surtax for victims of hurricane of Mar. 22-26. Stamps of No. B24c each surcharged 3c.

Olympic Type of Regular Issue
Souvenir Sheet

50c+5c, Pierre de Coubertin, Olympic rings.

1972, June 26

B29	A52	50c + 5c multi	3.25	3.25

Christmas Type of Regular Issue
Souvenir Sheet

Design: 50c+5c, Nativity, by Correggio.

1972, Oct. 11 Photo. *Perf. 13½*

B30	A53	50c + 5c multi	2.25	2.00

No. B30 contains one stamp 30x40mm.

Easter Type of Regular Issue
Souvenir Sheets

1973, Apr. 30 Photo. *Perf. 13½x14*

B31	A56	50c + 5c like #346	1.10	1.10
B32	A56	50c + 5c like #347	1.10	1.10
B33	A56	50c + 5c like #348	1.10	1.10
		Nos. B31-B33 (3)	3.30	3.30

Surtax was for school children.

Christmas Type of Regular Issue
Souvenir Sheets

1973, Dec. 3 Photo. *Perf. 13x13½*

B34	A59	50c + 5c like #364	.75	.75
B35	A59	50c + 5c like #365	.75	.75
B36	A59	50c + 5c like #366	.75	.75
B37	A59	50c + 5c like #367	.75	.75
B38	A59	50c + 5c like #368	.75	.75
		Nos. B34-B38 (5)	3.75	3.75

Surtax was for school children.

Easter Type of 1973
Dated "1974"
Souvenir Sheets

1974, Apr. 22 *Perf. 13½x14*

B39	A56	50c + 5c like #378	1.00	1.00
B40	A56	50c + 5c like #379	1.00	1.00
B41	A56	50c + 5c like #380	1.00	1.00
		Nos. B39-B41 (3)	3.00	3.00

Christmas Type of 1974
Souvenir Sheets

1974 Photo. *Perf. 13½x13*

B42	A68	50c + 5c like #412	.75	.75
B43	A68	50c + 5c like #413	.75	.75
B44	A68	50c + 5c like #414	.75	.75
B45	A68	50c + 5c like #415	.75	.75
B46	A68	50c + 5c like #416	.75	.75
		Nos. B42-B46 (5)	3.75	3.75

Christmas Type of 1975
Souvenir Sheets

1975, Dec. 1 *Perf. 13½*

B47	A75	75c + 5c like #437	1.10	1.10
B48	A75	75c + 5c like #438	1.10	1.10
B49	A75	75c + 5c like #439	1.10	1.10
B50	A75	75c + 5c like #440	1.10	1.10
B51	A75	75c + 5c like #441	1.10	1.10
		Nos. B47-B51 (5)	5.50	5.50

Size of stamps: 23x40mm.

Easter Type of 1976
Souvenir Sheets

1976, May 3 Photo. *Perf. 13½*

B52	A76	60c + 5c like #442	1.00	1.00
B53	A76	60c + 5c like #443	1.00	1.00
B54	A76	60c + 5c like #444	1.00	1.00
		Nos. B52-B54 (3)	3.00	3.00

Size of stamps: 36x36mm.

Christmas Type of 1976
Souvenir Sheets

1976, Nov. 2 Photo. *Perf. 14x13½*

B55	A80	75c + 5c like #459	1.25	1.25
B56	A80	75c + 5c like #460	1.25	1.25
B57	A80	75c + 5c like #461	1.25	1.25
B58	A80	75c + 5c like #462	1.25	1.25
B59	A80	75c + 5c like #463	1.25	1.25
		Nos. B55-B59 (5)	6.25	6.25

Easter Type of 1977
Souvenir Sheets

1977, Apr. 18 Photo. *Perf. 13½x14*

B60	A83	60c + 5c like #471	1.00	1.00
B61	A83	60c + 5c like #472	1.00	1.00
B62	A83	60c + 5c like #473	1.00	1.00
		Nos. B60-B62 (3)	3.00	3.00

Size of stamps: 30x42mm.

Christmas Type of 1977
Souvenir Sheets

1977, Oct. 31 Photo. *Perf. 14x13½*

B63	A84	75c + 5c like #474	1.10	1.10
B64	A84	75c + 5c like #475	1.10	1.10
B65	A84	75c + 5c like #476	1.10	1.10
B66	A84	75c + 5c like #477	1.10	1.10
B67	A84	75c + 5c like #478	1.10	1.10
		Nos. B63-B67 (5)	5.50	5.50

Easter Type of 1978
Souvenir Sheets

1978, Apr. 10 Photo. *Perf. 14x13½*

B68	A87	60c + 5c like #483	.85	.75
B69	A87	60c + 5c like #484	.85	.75
B70	A87	60c + 5c like #485	.85	.75
		Nos. B68-B70 (3)	2.55	2.25

Christmas Type of 1978
Souvenir Sheets

1979, Jan. 12 Photo. *Perf. 13*

B71	A89	75c + 5c like #503	.90	.90
B72	A89	75c + 5c like #504	.90	.90
B73	A89	75c + 5c like #505	.90	.90
		Nos. B71-B73 (3)	2.70	2.70

Easter Type of 1979
Souvenir Sheet

1979, Apr. 5 Photo. *Perf. 13*

B74		Sheet of 4	1.00	1.00
a.	A90	10c + 2c like #506	.20	.20
b.	A90	12c + 2c like #507	.20	.20
c.	A90	15c + 2c like #508	.25	.25
d.	A90	20c + 2c like #509	.35	.35

IYC Type of 1979
Souvenir Sheet

1979, Oct. 10

B75		Sheet of 3	2.25	2.25
a.	A93	30c + 5c like #529	.45	.45
b.	A93	50c + 5c like #530	.75	.75
c.	A93	65c + 5c like #531	.90	.90

Christmas Type of 1979

1980, Jan. 15 Photo. *Perf. 14*

B76	A95	6c + 2c like #537	.20	.20
B77	A95	10c + 2c like #538	.20	.20
B78	A95	12c + 2c like #539	.25	.25
B79	A95	15c + 2c like #540	.35	.35
		Nos. B76-B79 (4)	1.00	1.00

Easter Type of 1980
Souvenir Sheets

1980, Mar. 31 Photo. *Perf. 13*

B80	A96	Sheet of 6, #a.-f.	2.25	2.25

#B80 contains #541-543, each stamp with 2c surcharge.

1980, Apr. 23

Souvenir Sheets

B81	A96	75c + 5c like #541a	1.00	1.00
B82	A96	75c + 5c like #541b	1.00	1.00
B83	A96	75c + 5c like #542a	1.00	1.00
B84	A96	75c + 5c like #542b	1.00	1.00
B85	A96	75c + 5c like #543a	1.00	1.00
B86	A96	75c + 5c like #543b	1.00	1.00
		Nos. B81-B83 (3)	3.00	3.00

Surtax was for school children.

Rotary Type of 1980
Souvenir Sheet

1980, May 27 Photo. *Perf. 14*

B87		Sheet of 3	1.75	1.75
a.	A97	30c + 3c like #547	.45	.45
b.	A97	35c + 3c like #548	.55	.55
c.	A97	50c + 3c like #549	.75	.75

Christmas Type of 1980
Souvenir Sheets

1981, Jan. 9 Photo. *Imperf.*

B88	A102a	75c + 5c like #652	1.00	1.00
B89	A102a	75c + 5c like #653	1.00	1.00
B90	A102a	75c + 5c like #654	1.00	1.00
B91	A102a	75c + 5c like #655	1.00	1.00
		Nos. B88-B91 (4)	4.00	4.00

Easter Type of 1981
Souvenir Sheets

1981, Apr. 10 Photo. *Perf. 13½*

B92		Sheet of 3	1.50	1.50
a.	A103	15c + 2c like #656	.25	.25
b.	A103	25c + 2c like #657	.50	.50
c.	A103	40c + 2c like #658	.75	.75

1981, Apr. 28 *Imperf.*

B93	A103	75c + 5c like #656	1.50	1.50
B94	A103	75c + 5c like #657	1.50	1.50
B95	A103	75c + 5c like #658	1.50	1.50
		Nos. B93-B95 (3)	4.50	4.50

Surtax was for school children.

Espana '82 Soccer Type
Souvenir Sheet

1981 Photo. *Perf. 13½*

B96	A105	Sheet of 8, #a.-h.	5.75	5.75

#B96 contains #661-664, each stamp with 3c surcharge.

Royal Wedding Type of 1981
Nos. 659-660a Surcharged in Black

1981, Nov. 10 Photo. *Perf. 14*

B97	A104	$1 + 5c multi	2.25	2.25
B98	A104	$2 + 5c multi	4.50	4.50
a.		Souvenir sheet of 2	7.50	7.50

Intl. Year of the Disabled. No. B98a contains Nos. B97-B98 each with 10c surtax, which was for benefit of the disabled; black overprint in margin.

Christmas Type of 1981
Souvenir Sheet

1981, Dec. 14 Photo. *Perf. 13½*

B99		Sheet of 4	3.50	3.50
a.	A107	8c + 3c like #669	.25	.25
b.	A107	15c + 3c like #670	.40	.40
c.	A107	40c + 3c like #671	1.10	1.10
d.	A107	50c + 3c like #672	1.40	1.40

Surtax was for school children.

Nos. 919-923 Surcharged "FIRST PAPAL VISIT TO SOUTH PACIFIC / POPE JOHN PAUL II / *NOV 21-24 1986* " and Value in Silver

1986, Nov. 21 Litho. *Perf. 13½*

B100	A138	55c + 10c multi	1.90	1.90
B101	A138	$1.30 + 10c multi	4.00	4.00
B102	A138	$2.75 + 10c multi	8.00	8.00
		Nos. B100-B102 (3)	13.90	13.90

Souvenir Sheets

B103		Sheet of 3	14.50	14.50
a.-c.		A138 $2.40 + 10c on Nos. 922a-922c, any single	4.75	4.75
B104	A138	$6.40 + 50c multi	14.50	14.50

No. B103 ovptd. in margin "VISIT TO SOUTH PACIFIC / OF POPE JOHN PAUL II" and "FIRST PAPAL VISIT / NOVEMBER 21-24 1986." No. B104 ovptd. around margin only, "*FIRST PAPAL VISIT TO SOUTH PACIFIC NOVEMBER 21-24 1986" and "PRE-CHRISTMAS VISIT OF HIS HOLINESS POPE JOHN PAUL II."

For surcharge see No. B112.

Stamps of 1982 and 1987 Surcharged "HURRICANE RELIEF" in Sans-serif Capitals Plus New Value

Perfs. as before

1987, June 30 Photo.

Surcharged +25c

B105	A121	55c on #958	1.00	1.00
B106	A121	65c on #960	1.10	1.10
B107	A121	75c on #963	1.25	1.25
B108	A121	95c on #965	1.50	1.50

Surcharged +50c

B109	A101	$2.80 on #582	4.00	4.00
B110	A101	$5 on #583	6.75	6.75
B111	A102	$6.40 on #978	8.50	8.50
		Nos. B105-B111 (7)	24.10	24.10

Stamps of 1985-86 Surcharged "HURRICANE RELIEF / +50c" in Silver or Black

1987 *Perfs. as before*

Surcharged +50c

B112	A138	55c on #B100	1.25	1.25
B113	A133	55c on #897 (B)	1.25	1.25
B114	A128	65c on #871	1.40	1.40
B115	A133	65c on #898	1.40	1.40
B116	A128	75c on #872	1.50	1.50
B117	A133	75c on #899	1.50	1.50
B118	A134	95c on #908 (B)	1.75	1.75
B119	A135	$1 on #910	1.90	1.90
B120	A136	$1 on #913	1.90	1.90
B121	A137	$1 on #916	1.90	1.90
B122	A128	$1.15 on #873	2.00	2.00
B123	A133	$1.25 on #900	2.10	2.10
B124	A134	$1.25 on #905	2.10	2.10
B125	A136	$1.25 on #914 (B)	2.10	2.10
B126	A138	$1.30 on #920	2.25	2.25
B127	A134	$1.50 on #906 (B)	2.50	2.50
B128	A135	$1.50 on #911 (B)	2.50	2.50
B129	A133	$2 on #901 (B)	3.00	3.00
B130	A135	$2 on #912 (B)	3.00	3.00
B131	A137	$2 on #917	3.00	3.00
B132	A136	$2.75 on #915	4.00	4.00
B133	A138	$2.75 on #921	4.00	4.00
B134	A128	$2.80 on #874	4.00	4.00
B135	A137	$3 on #918	4.25	4.25
		Nos. B112-B135 (24)	56.55	56.55

Souvenir Sheets

B136	A134	$1.10 on #907 (B)	2.00	2.00
B137	A134	$1.95 on #908	3.00	3.00
B138		on #922, #a.-c.	11.00	11.00
B139	A134	$2.45 on #909 (B)	3.75	3.75
B140	A128	$5.30 on #875	7.25	7.25
B141	A138	$6.40 on #B104	8.50	8.50
		Nos. B136-B141 (6)	35.50	35.50

Issued: #B118, B121, B124, B127, B131, B135-B137, B139-B140, 7/31; others 6/30.

No. 1230 Surcharged "CHILDREN'S / CHARITIES" in Silver
Souvenir Sheet

1998, Nov. 20 Litho. *Perf. 14*

B142	A179	$3.50 +$1 multi	4.75	4.75

AIR POST STAMPS

Catalogue values for unused stamps in this section are for Never Hinged items.

Stamps of 1936-63 Overprinted and Surcharged

Perf. 13x13½, 13½x13

Litho., Engr.

1966, Apr. 22 Wmk. 253

C1	A25	6p on #152	.25	.20
C2	A26	7p on 8p #153	.30	.25
C3	A25	10p on 3p #150	.40	.35
C4	A25	1sh on #154	.50	.45
C5	A27	1sh6p on #155	.75	.65
C6	A28	2sh3p on 3sh #157	1.25	1.00
C7	A28	5sh on #158	2.00	1.75
C8	A28	10sh on 2sh #156	4.00	4.00

Perf. 14

Typo.

C9	PF5	£1 on #106	15.00	14.00
a.		Airplane missing	*30.00*	*42.50*
		Nos. C1-C9 (9)	24.45	22.65

#C9a occurs on all stamps from the right vertical column of the sheet due to a lack of airplane symbols. The size and position of the airplane symbol varies in relation to "Airmail" on the other stamps. The surcharges are printed on silver ovals.

2nd So. Pacific Games' Type

Sport: 10p, Women runners and Games' emblem. 2sh3p, Runner and team emblem.

Perf. 13½

1967, Jan. 12 Unwmk. Photo.

C10	A32	10p org & multi	.20	.20
C11	A32	2sh3p multi	.25	.25

Capt. Cook Type of Regular Issue

6c, The "Resolution" and "Discovery" Beating Through the Ice, by Webber. 10c, The Island of Otaheite, by Hodges, and Queen Elizabeth II. 15c, View of Karakakooa (Kealakekua), Hawaii, by Webber. 25c, The Landing at Middleburg, Tonga, by Hodges, & Captain Cook. (All horiz.)

1968, Sept. 12 Photo. *Perf. 13*

C12	A39	6c gold & multi	.55	.55
C13	A39	10c gold & multi	.85	.85
C14	A39	15c gold & multi	1.10	1.10
C15	A39	25c gold & multi	2.25	2.25
		Nos. C12-C15 (4)	4.75	4.75

See note after No. 236.

Christmas Type of 1979

1979, Dec. 14 Photo. *Perf. 14*

C16	A95	20c like #537	.25	.25
C17	A95	25c like #538	.35	.35
C18	A95	30c like #539	.40	.40
C19	A95	35c like #540	.50	.50
		Nos. C16-C19 (4)	1.50	1.50

Franklin D. Roosevelt — AP1

80c, Benjamin Franklin. $1.40, George Washington, by Gilbert Stuart.

1982, Sept. 30 Photo. *Perf. 14*

C20	AP1	60c multicolored	.90	.90
C21	AP1	80c multicolored	1.10	1.10
C22	AP1	$1.40 multicolored	2.00	2.00
a.		Souvenir sheet of 3	5.25	5.25
		Nos. C20-C22 (3)	4.00	4.00

No. C22a contains Nos. C20-C22, perf. 13½ with portraits in square frames.

No. C22 Overprinted in Gold and Black

1983, Aug. 12 Photo. *Perf. 14*

C23	AP1	96c on $1.40 multi	2.00	2.00

Endangered Bird Species Type

Souvenir Sheets

Nos. 1020-1023 Overprinted

1990, Dec. 5 Litho. *Perf. 13½*

C24	A145	$1 Flycatcher	4.25	4.25
C25	A145	$1.25 Flycatchers	5.00	5.00
C26	A145	$1.50 Fruit dove	6.50	6.50
C27	A145	$1.75 Fruit doves	7.25	7.25
		Nos. C24-C27 (4)	23.00	23.00

Birdpex '90, 20th Intl. Ornithological Cong., New Zealand.

AIR POST SEMI-POSTAL STAMPS

Catalogue values for unused stamps in this section are for Never Hinged items.

Christmas Type of 1979

1980, Jan. 15 Photo. *Perf. 14*

CB1	A95	20c + 4c like #C16	.40	.40
CB2	A95	25c + 4c like #C17	.45	.45
CB3	A95	30c + 4c like #C18	.50	.50
CB4	A95	35c + 4c like #C19	.65	.65
		Nos. CB1-CB4 (4)	2.00	2.00

OFFICIAL STAMPS

Flower Issue of 1967-69 Overprinted or Surcharged in Black on Silver

1975 Photo. Unwmk. *Perf. 14x13½*

O1	A34	1c multi (#200)	.20
O2	A34	2c multi (#201)	.20
O3	A34	3c multi (#203)	.20
O4	A34	4c multi (#205)	.20
O5	A34	5c on 2½c multi (#202)	.20
O6	A34	8c multi (#208)	.25
O7	A34	10c on 6c multi (#207)	.30
O8	A34	18c on 20c multi (#212)	.40
O9	A34	25c on 9c multi (#209)	.60
O10	A34	30c on 15c multi (#211)	.70
O11	A34	50c multi (#215)	1.25
O12	A35	$1 multi (#216)	2.75
O13	A35	$2 multi (#217)	4.75
O14	A36	$4 multi (#218)	8.00
O15	A36	$6 multi (#219)	10.00
		Nos. O1-O15 (15)	30.00

No. O1-O15 were not sold to the public unused. Arrangement of surcharge varies on different denominations.

Silver panel on Nos. O14-O15 measures 26½x6mm and is rounded at both ends.

Issue dates: 1c-$2, Mar. 17, $4-$6, May 19.

Catalogue values for unused stamps in this section, from this point to the end of the section, are for Never Hinged items.

Nos. 381-382, 389, 393-396, 467, 446 Overprinted or Surcharged in Silver or Black

Photo., Litho.

1978, Oct. 19 *Perf. 13½*

O16	A62	1c multi (S)	.85	.20
O17	A62	2c on ½c multi	.85	.20
O18	A62	5c on ½c multi	.95	.20
O19	A62	10c on 8c multi (S)	1.10	.20
O20	A62	15c on 50c multi (S)	1.25	.20
O21	A62	18c on 60c multi (S)	1.25	.20
O22	A62	25c multicolored	1.60	.25
O23	A62	30c multi (S)	1.60	.30
O24	A62	35c on 60c multi (S)	1.60	.35
O25	A62	50c multi (S)	2.10	.50
O26	A62	60c multi (S)	2.40	.60
O27	A82	$1 Pair, #a.-b. (S)	10.00	2.00
O29	A77	$2 multicolored	7.25	2.00
O30	A64	$4 multi ('79)	13.50	4.00
O31	A64	$6 multi ('79)	13.50	6.50
		Nos. O16-O31 (15)	59.80	17.70

Diagonal overprints on No. O27. Overprint on No. O29: 19x4mm.

Nos. 790-791, 795, 797, 799, 805, 807, 809-810 Ovptd. or Surcharged "O.H.M.S." in Silver

1985, July 10 Photo. *Perf. 13½x13*

O32	A121	5c multi	.55	.55
O33	A121	10c multi	.55	.55
O34	A121	20c multi	.65	.65
O35	A121	30c multi	.65	.65
O36	A121	40c multi	.65	.65
O37	A121	55c on 85c multi	.80	.80
O38	A121	60c multi	.80	.80
O39	A121	$1.10 multi	1.25	1.25
O40	A121	$2 on $1.20 multi	2.50	2.50
		Nos. O32-O40 (9)	8.40	8.40

Nos. 792-794, 802, 806, 696 and 583-586 Ovptd. or Surcharged "O.H.M.S." in Silver, Gold (75c) or Black and Silver ($5, $18)

1986-90 Photo. *Perfs. as Before*

O41	A121	12c multi	5.00	5.00
O42	A121	14c multi	5.00	5.00
O43	A121	18c multi	5.00	5.00
O44	A121	50c multi	6.25	6.25
O45	A121	70c multi	6.75	6.75
O46	A111	75c on 60c, #a.-d.	13.50	13.50
O50	A102	$5 on $3 multi	17.00	17.00
O51	A102	$9 on $4 multi	9.00	9.00
O52	A102	$14 on $6 multi	14.00	14.00
O53	A102	$18 on $10 multi	20.00	20.00
		Nos. O41-O53 (10)	101.50	101.50

Issued: $9, 5/30/89; $14, 7/12/89; $18, 6/4/90; others 5/5/86.

Nos. 1058-1059, 1062, 1064-1066, 1071, 1076-1078, 1080-1083, 1085 Ovptd. "O.H.M.S." in Silver

1995-98 Litho. *Perf. 14½x13½*

O54	A155	5c multicolored	.50	.50
O55	A155	10c multicolored	.50	.50
O56	A155	15c multicolored	.65	.65
O57	A155	20c multicolored	.70	.70
O58	A155	25c multicolored	.75	.75
O59	A155	30c multicolored	.80	.80
O60	A155	50c multicolored	1.00	1.00
O61	A155	80c multicolored	1.60	1.60
O62	A155	85c multicolored	1.60	1.60
O63	A155	90c multicolored	1.60	1.60
O64	A155	$1 multicolored	1.90	1.90
O65	A155	$2 multicolored	3.00	3.00
O66	A155a	$3 multicolored	4.75	4.75
O67	A155a	$5 multicolored	5.75	5.75
O68	A155a	$7 multicolored	8.50	8.50
O69	A155a	$10 multi	10.50	10.50
		Nos. O54-O69 (16)	44.10	44.10

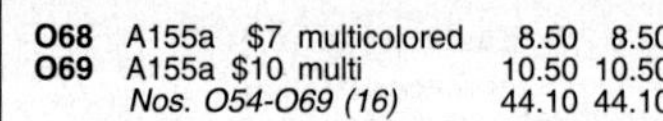

Overprint on Nos. O66-O69 has larger, sans serif letters.

Nos. O66-O69 were not sold unused to local customers.

Issued: 5c-90c, 2/24/95; $1-$2, 5/15/95; $3-$7, 7/17/98, $10, 11/12/98.

CORFU

kor-'fü

LOCATION — An island in the Ionian Sea opposite the Greek-Albanian border
GOVT. — A department of Greece
AREA — 245 sq. mi.
POP. — 114,620 (1938)
CAPITAL — Corfu

In 1922 Italy occupied Corfu (Kerkyra) during a controversy with Greece over the assassination of an Italian official in Epirus. Italy again occupied Corfu in 1941-43.

100 Centesimi = 1 Lira
100 Lepta = 1 Drachma

Watermark

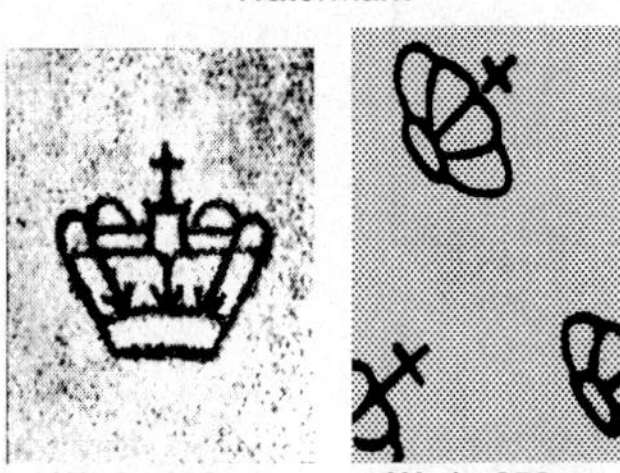

Wmk. 140 — Crown   Wmk. 252 — Crowns

ISSUED UNDER ITALIAN OCCUPATION

Italian Stamps of 1901-23 Overprinted

1923, Sept. 20 Wmk. 140 ***Perf. 14***

No.	Type	Description	Unused	Used
N1	A48	5c green	3.00	2.75
N2	A48	10c claret	3.00	2.75
N3	A48	15c slate	3.00	2.75
N4	A50	20c brown orange	3.00	2.75
N5	A49	30c orange brown	3.00	2.75
N6	A49	50c violet	3.00	2.75
N7	A49	60c blue	3.00	2.75
a.		Vert. pair, one without overprint	*425.00*	
N8	A46	1 l brown & green	3.00	2.75
		Nos. N1-N8 (8)	24.00	22.00
		Set, never hinged	47.50	

Italian Stamps of 1901-23 Surcharged

1923, Sept. 24

No.	Type	Description	Unused	Used
N9	A48	25 l on 10c claret	35.00	13.00
N10	A49	60 l on 25c blue	6.00	
N11	A49	70 l on 30c org brn	6.00	
N12	A49	1.20d on 50c violet	18.00	13.00
N13	A46	2.40d on 1 l brn & grn	18.00	13.00
N14	A46	4.75d on 2 l grn & org	7.00	
		Nos. N9-N14 (6)	90.00	39.00
		Set, never hinged	175.00	

Nos. N10, N11, N14 were not placed in use.

Issue for Corfu and Paxos

Nos. N15-N34, NC1-NC12, NJ1-NJ11 and NRA1-NRA3 have been extensively counterfeited, some with forged cancellations.

Stamps of Greece, 1937-38, Overprinted in Black

Perf. 12x13½, 12½x12, 13½x12

1941, June 5 Wmk. 252

No.	Type	Description	Unused	Used
N15	A69	5 l brn red & blue	2.75	2.50
a.		Inverted overprint	*40.00*	*20.00*
b.		Double overprint	*55.00*	*50.00*
N16	A70	10 l bl & brn red (On 397)	.95	1.25
N17	A70	10 l bl & brn red (On 413)	575.00	300.00
N18	A71	20 l black & grn	1.00	1.40
a.		Inverted overprint	*55.00*	*20.00*
N19	A72	40 l green & blk	1.25	2.10
a.		Inverted overprint	*40.00*	*20.00*
b.		Double overprint	*55.00*	*50.00*
N20	A73	50 l brown & blk	1.00	1.40
a.		Inverted overprint	*40.00*	*20.00*
N21	A74	80 l ind & yel brn	1.10	2.10
N22	A67	1d green	6.00	4.50
N23	A84	1.50d green	4.75	3.75
N24	A75	2d ultra	3.25	2.75
N25	A67	3d red brown	6.00	4.50
N26	A76	5d red	3.25	3.00
N27	A77	6d olive brown	3.25	3.00
N28	A78	7d dark brown	4.25	3.50
N29	A67	8d deep blue	11.00	10.00
N30	A79	10d red brown	375.00	125.00
N31	A80	15d green	14.50	11.50
N32	A81	25d dark blue	11.00	10.50
N33	A84	30d org brn	55.00	45.00
N34	A67	100d carmine lake	175.00	110.00
		Nos. N15-N34 (20)	1,255.	647.75
		Set, never hinged	1,750.	

AIR POST STAMPS

Greece Nos. C37 and C26-C35, Overprinted Like Nos. N15-N34

Perf. 12½x13, 13x12½, 13½x12½

1941, June 5 Unwmk.

No.	Type	Description	Unused	Used
NC1	D3	50 l dk brown	3.00	1.75
NC2	AP16	1d red	275.00	110.00
NC3	AP17	2d gray blue	3.25	1.75
NC4	AP18	5d violet	5.00	2.50
NC5	AP19	7d deep ultra	5.00	2.50
NC6	AP20	10d bister brn (On C26)	450.00	175.00
NC7	AP20	10d brown org (On C35)	27.50	18.00
NC8	AP21	25d rose	40.00	20.00
NC9	AP22	30d dk grn	55.00	27.50
NC10	AP23	50d violet	50.00	27.50
a.		Double overprint		*225.00*
NC11	AP24	100d brown	*475.00*	*250.00*

On No. C36

Serrate Roulette 13½

No.	Type	Description	Unused	Used
NC12	D3	50 l vio brn	24.00	7.50
a.		On No. C36a		
		Nos. NC1-NC12 (12)	*1,412.*	*644.00*
		Set, never hinged	2,400.	

POSTAGE DUE STAMPS

Postage Due Stamps of Greece, 1913-35 Overprinted Like #N15-N34

1941, June 5 Unwmk.

Serrate Roulette 13½

No.	Type	Description	Unused	Used
NJ1	D3	10 l carmine	1.10	1.10
NJ2	D3	25 l ultra	1.40	1.25
NJ3	D3	80 l lilac brown	425.00	225.00

Perf. 12½x13, 13½x12½

No.	Type	Description	Unused	Used
NJ4	D3	1d lt bl (On J80)	*775.00*	*250.00*
NJ5	D3	2d light red	3.00	3.25
NJ6	D3	5d gray	12.00	6.75
NJ7	D3	10d gray green	7.50	5.25
NJ8	D3	15d red brown	7.50	5.25
NJ9	D3	25d light red	9.50	5.25
NJ10	D3	50d orange	9.50	5.25
NJ11	D3	100d slate green	250.00	175.00
		Nos. NJ1-NJ11 (11)	*1,501.*	*683.35*

POSTAL TAX STAMPS

Greece Nos. RA61-RA63, Overprinted Like Nos. N15-N34

Wmk. Unwmk.

1941, June 5 ***Perf. 13½***

No.	Type	Description	Unused	Used
NRA1	PT7	10 l brt rose, *pale rose*	1.00	1.00
NRA2	PT7	50 l gray grn, *pale grn*	1.00	*1.25*
NRA3	PT7	1d dull blue, *lt bl*	12.00	8.25
		Nos. NRA1-NRA3 (3)	14.00	10.50
		Set, never hinged	21.00	

Stamps overprinted "CORFU" were replaced by Italian stamps overprinted "Isole Jonie" (See Ionian Islands).

COSTA RICA

ˌkäs-tə-ˈrē-kə

LOCATION — Central America between Nicaragua and Panama
GOVT. — Republic
AREA — 19,730 sq. mi.
POP. — 3,674,490 (1999 est.)
CAPITAL — San Jose

8 Reales= 100 Centavos= 1 Peso
100 Centimos= 1 Colon (1900)

Catalogue values for unused stamps in this country are for Never Hinged items, beginning with Scott 238 in the regular postage section, Scott C117 in the air post section, Scott CE1 in the air post special delivery section, Scott E1 in the special delivery section, and Scott RA1 in the postal tax section.

Watermarks

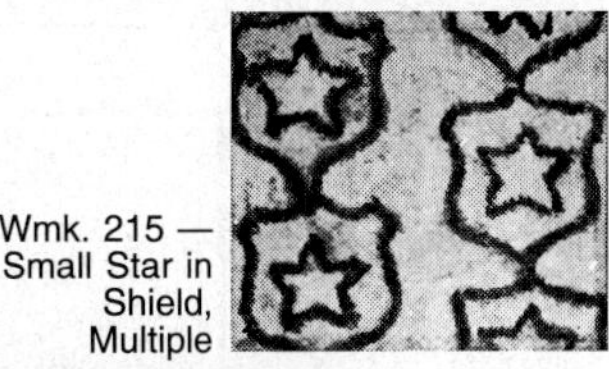

Wmk. 215 — Small Star in Shield, Multiple

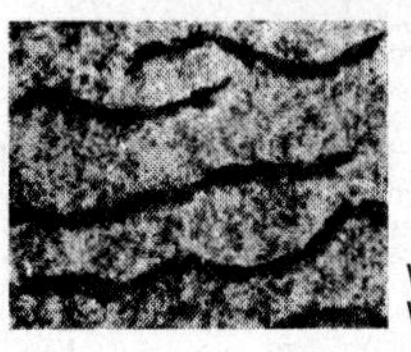

Wmk. 229 — Wavy Lines

Wmk. 334 — Rectangles

Values for unused stamps are for examples with original gum as defined in the catalogue introduction. Very fine examples of Nos. 1-22 will have perforations just clear of the design on one or more sides due to the placement of the stamps on the plates and to imperfect perforating methods.

Coat of Arms — A1

1863 Unwmk. Engr. ***Perf. 12***

No.	Type	Description	Unused	Used
1	A1	½r blue	.30	*1.00*
a.		½r light blue	.30	*1.00*
b.		Pair, imperf. horiz.	*1,500.*	
2	A1	2r scarlet	1.50	*2.00*
3	A1	4r green	15.00	15.00
4	A1	1p orange	40.00	40.00
		Nos. 1-4 (4)	56.80	58.00

The ½r was printed from two plates. The second is in light blue with little or no sky over the mountains.

Imperforate copies of Nos. 1-2 are corner copies from poorly perforated sheets.

Nos. 1-3 Surcharged in Red or Black:

a

b

c

d

e

1881-82

Red or Black Surcharge

No.	Type	Description	Unused	Used
7	A1(a)	1c on ½r ('82)	3.00	
a.		On No. 1a	15.00	
8	A1(b)	1c on ½r ('82)	18.00	
9	A1(c)	2c on ½r, #1a	3.00	
a.		On No. 1	8.00	
12	A1(c)	5c on ½r	8.00	
13	A1(d)	5c on ½r ('82)	55.00	
14	A1(d)	10c on 2r (Bk) ('82)	70.00	
15	A1(e)	20c on 4r ('82)	300.00	

Overprints with different fonts and "OFICIAL" were never placed in use, and are said to have been surcharged to a dealer's order. The ½r surcharged "DOS CTS" is not a postage stamp. It probably is an essay.

Postally used copies of #7-15 are rare. #13-15 exist with a favor cancel having a hyphen between "San" and "Jose." Values same as unused. Fake cancellations exist.

Counterfeits exist of surcharges on #7-15.

Gen. Prospero Fernández
A6

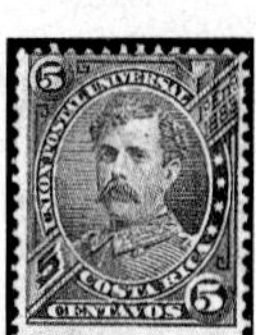

President Bernardo Soto Alfaro
A7

1883, Jan. 1

No.	Type	Description	Unused	Used
16	A6	1c green	3.00	1.50
17	A6	2c carmine	3.00	1.50
18	A6	5c blue violet	30.00	2.00
19	A6	10c orange	140.00	12.00
20	A6	40c blue	2.00	*3.00*
		Nos. 16-20 (5)	178.00	20.00

Unused copies of 40c usually lack gum.

For overprints see Nos. O1-O20, O24, Guanacaste 1-38, 44.

1887

No.	Type	Description	Unused	Used
21	A7	5c blue violet	7.00	.50
22	A7	10c orange	4.00	3.00

Unused copies of 5c usually lack gum.

For overprints see Nos. O22-O23, Guanacaste 42-43, 45.

A8   A9

1889

Black Overprint

No.	Type	Description	Unused	Used
23	A8	1c rose	5.00	3.00
24	A9	5c brown	7.00	3.00

Vertical and inverted overprints are fakes.

For overprints see Guanacaste Nos. 47-54.

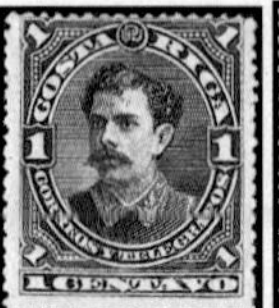

President Soto Alfaro
A10 A11

A12 A13

A14 A15

A16 A17

A18 A19

1889 ***Perf. 14-16 & Compound***

No.	Type	Description	Unused	Used
25	A10	1c brown	.35	*.45*
a.		Horiz. pair, imperf. vert	*100.00*	
b.		Imperf. pair	*75.00*	
c.		Horiz. or vert. pair, imperf. btwn.	*100.00*	
26	A11	2c dark green	.35	*.45*
a.		Imperf., pair	35.00	
b.		Vert. pair, imperf. horiz.	80.00	
c.		Horiz. pair, imperf. btwn.	80.00	
27	A12	5c orange	.45	.35
a.		Imperf., pair		*200.00*
b.		Horiz. pair, imperf. btwn.	*100.00*	
28	A13	10c red brown	.40	.35
a.		Vert. or horiz. pair, imperf. btwn.	*100.00*	
29	A14	20c yellow green	.30	*.35*
a.		Vert. pair, imperf. horiz.	*100.00*	
b.		Horizontal pair, imperf. btwn.	*100.00*	
30	A15	50c rose red	1.00	
		Telegram cancel		.75
31	A16	1p blue	1.25	
		Telegram cancel		.75
32	A17	2p dull violet	6.00	
a.		2p slate	6.00	
		Telegram cancel		4.00
33	A18	5p olive green	25.00	
		Telegram cancel		10.00
34	A19	10p black	100.00	
		Telegram cancel		60.00
		Nos. 25-34 (10)	135.10	

Nos. 30-34 normally were used on telegrams and most copies were removed from the forms and sold by the government.

For overprints see Nos. O25-O30, Guanacaste 55-67.

Arms of Costa Rica
A20 A21

A22 A23

A24 A25

A26 A27

A28 A29

1892 ***Perf. 12-15 & Compound***

No.	Type	Description	Unused	Used
35	A20	1c grnsh blue	.30	*.40*
36	A21	2c yellow	.30	*.40*
37	A22	5c red lilac	.30	.25
a.		5c violet	60.00	.30
38	A23	10c lt green	.75	.35
a.		Horiz. pair, imperf. btwn.	—	*100.00*
39	A24	20c scarlet	12.00	.20
a.		Horiz. pair, imperf. btwn.	—	*100.00*
40	A25	50c gray blue	4.00	*4.25*
41	A26	1p green, *yel*	1.00	1.00
42	A27	2p brown red, *lilac*	3.00	1.00
a.		2p rose red, *pale lil*	12.00	1.00
43	A28	5p dk blue, *blue*	2.00	1.00
44	A29	10p brown, *pale buff*	35.00	5.00
a.		10p brown, *yellow*	8.00	
		Nos. 35-44 (10)	58.65	13.85

Imperfs. of Nos. 35-44 are proofs.

For overprints see Nos. O31-O36.

Statue of Juan Santamaría
A30

Juan Mora Fernández
A31

View of Port Limón — A32

Braulio Carillo ("Branlio" on stamp) — A33

National Theater — A34

José M. Castro — A35

Birris Bridge — A36

Juan Rafael Mora — A37

Jesús Jiménez — A38

Coat of Arms — A39

1901, Jan. ***Perf. 12-15½***

No.	Type	Description	Unused	Used
45	A30	1c green & blk	3.00	.30
a.		Horiz. pair, imperf. btwn.	*150.00*	
46	A31	2c ver & blk	1.00	.30
47	A32	5c gray blue & blk	3.00	.30
a.		Vert. pair, imperf. btwn.	—	*150.00*
48	A33	10c ocher & blk	3.00	.35
49	A34	20c lake & blk	20.00	.25
a.		Vert. pair, imperf. btwn.	*150.00*	
50	A35	50c dull lil & dk bl	5.00	1.00
51	A36	1col ol bis & blk	100.00	3.50
52	A37	2col car rose & dk grn	15.00	3.00
53	A38	5col brown & blk	72.50	3.50
54	A39	10col yel grn & brn red	27.50	3.00
		Nos. 45-54 (10)	250.00	15.50

The 2c exists with center inverted.

Nos. 45-57 in other colors are private reprints made in 1948. They have little value.

For surcharge and overprints see Nos. 58, 78, O37-O44.

Remainders

In 1914 the government sold a large quantity of stamps at very much less than face value. The lot included most regular issues from 1901 to 1911 inclusive, postage due stamps of 1903 and official stamps of 1901-03. These stamps were canceled with groups of five thin parallel bars. The higher valued used stamps, such as Nos. 64, 65-68a, sell for much less than the values quoted which are for stamps with regular postal cancellations. A few sell for much higher prices.

José M. Cañas — A40

Julián Volio — A41

Eusebio Figueroa Oreamuno — A42

1903 ***Perf. 13½, 14, 15***

No.	Type	Description	Unused	Used
55	A40	4c red vio & blk	1.75	.70
56	A41	6c olive grn & blk	7.25	4.00
57	A42	25c gray lil & brn	16.00	.30
		Nos. 55-57 (3)	25.00	5.00

See note on private reprints following #54.

For overprints see Nos. 81, O45-O47.

No. 49 Surcharged in Black:

1905

No.	Type	Description	Unused	Used
58	A34	1c on 20c lake & blk	.50	.50
a.		Inverted surcharge	10.00	10.00
b.		Diagonal surcharge	.50	.50

Specimens surcharged in other colors are proofs.

Statue of Juan Santamaria
A43

Juan Mora Fernández
A44

José M. Cañas
A45

Mauro Fernández
A46

Braulio Carrillo — A47

Julián Volio — A48

Eusebio Figueroa Oreamuno
A49

José M. Castro
A50

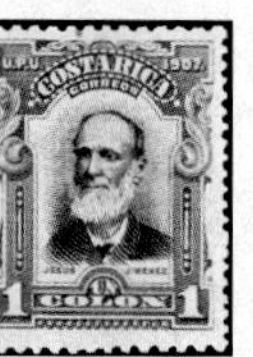

Jesús Jiménez — A51

Juan Rafael Mora — A52

Perf. 11x14, 14 (1c, 5c, 10c, 25c)

1907 **Unwmk.**

No.	Type	Description	Unused	Used
59	A43	1c red brn & ind	3.00	.40
a.		Perf. 11x14	40.00	3.00
b.		Imperf pair	15.00	—
60	A44	2c yel grn & blk	1.50	.30
a.		Perf. 14	1.50	.30
b.		Imperf pair	15.00	—
61	A45	4c car & indigo	12.00	2.50
a.		Perf. 14	450.00	50.00
b.		Imperf pair	15.00	—
62	A46	5c yel & dull bl	3.00	.30
a.		Perf. 11x14	45.00	1.00
b.		Imperf pair	15.00	—
63	A47	10c blue & blk	3.00	.50
a.		Perf. 11x14	20.00	1.00
b.		Imperf pair	30.00	—
64	A48	20c olive grn & blk	25.00	6.00
a.		Perf. 14	25.00	6.00
		Remainder cancel		2.00
b.		Imperf pair	—	
65	A49	25c gray lil & blk	3.00	3.00
		Remainder cancel		1.00
a.		Perf. 11x14	85.00	40.00
b.		Imperf pair	—	
66	A50	50c red lil & blue	50.00	25.00
		Remainder cancel		2.00
a.		Perf. 14	85.00	50.00
b.		Imperf pair	100.00	
67	A51	1col brown & blk	20.00	20.00
a.		Perf. 14	20.00	20.00
		Remainder cancel		2.00
b.		Imperf pair		—

68 A52 2col claret & grn 150.00 100.00
a. Perf. 14 250.00 150.00
Remainder cancel 3.00
b. Imperf pair 200.00
Nos. 59-68 (10) 270.50 158.00
Nos. 59a-68a (16) 1,211. 321.30

The remainder cancel value applies to both perforations.

The imperforate varieties of the above set are valued without gum. Ungummed copies were probably placed on the market in London, while gummed copies appear to have been sent to Costa Rica and accepted for postal use. There is a small premium for gummed copies.

The 1c, 2c, 5c, 20c, 50c, 1 col and 2 col exist with center inverted.

Nos. 59-68 exist with papermaker's watermark.

No. 65b with brown vignette is a proof. Value, pair $40. The actual No. 65b (black vignette) is worth much more.

For overprints see Nos. 77, 79-80, 82-84, O48-O55, O60-O64.

Statue of Juan Santamaria A53

Juan Mora Fernández A54

José M. Cañas A55

Mauro Fernández A56

Braulio Carrillo — A57

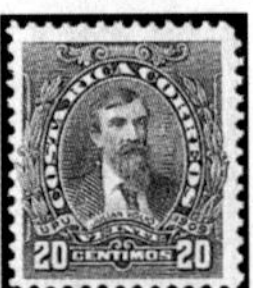

Julián Volio — A58

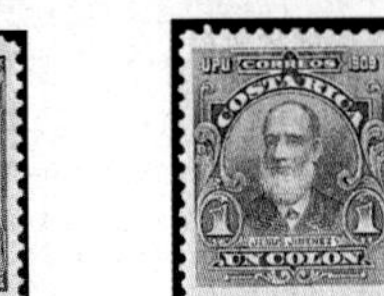

Eusebio Figueroa Oreamuno A59

Jesús Jiménez A60

1910 ***Perf. 12***

69 A53 1c brown .20 .20
70 A54 2c dp green .25 .20
71 A55 4c scarlet .35 .35
72 A56 5c orange 1.00 .20
73 A57 10c deep blue .25 .20
74 A58 20c olive grn .50 .35
75 A59 25c dp violet 17.00 1.50
76 A60 1col dk brown .50 .50
Nos. 69-76 (8) 20.05 3.50

For overprints and surcharge see Nos. 111C-111J, B1, C2, O56-O59.

No. 60a Overprinted in Red

1911 ***Perf. 14***

77 A44 2c yel grn & blk 1.50 1.00
a. Inverted overprint 5.50 5.00
b. Double overprint, both inverted 45.00

Stamps of 1901-07 Overprinted in Red or Black

78 A30 1c grn & blk (R) 2.00 1.00
a. Black overprint 32.50 18.00
b. Inverted overprint
79 A43 1c red brn & ind (Bk) 1.00 .40
a. Inverted overprint 4.50 3.50
b. Double overprint 5.50 5.00
80 A44 2c yel grn & blk (Bk) 1.00 .40
a. Inverted overprint 3.75 3.50
b. Dbl. ovpt., one as on No. 77 40.00 27.50
c. Double overprint, one inverted 15.00 15.00
d. Pair, one stamp No. 77 25.00 18.00
e. Perf. 11x14 30.00 10.00

No. 55 Overprinted in Black

81 A40 4c red vio & blk 1.00 .65

Stamps of 1907 Overprinted in Blue, Black or Rose

Perf. 14, 11x14 (#83, 84)

82 A46 5c yel & bl (Bl) 1.50 .20
a. "Habilitada" 3.25 2.50
b. "2911" 5.50 3.25
c. Roman "I" in "1911" 4.00 2.50
d. Double overprint 5.50 5.00
e. Inverted overprint 6.00 3.75
f. Black overprint — 2.00
g. Triple overprint 6.00
h. Vert. pair, imperf. horiz. 100.00
83 A47 10c blue & blk (Bk) 5.00 1.40
a. As #83, Roman "I" in "1911" 7.00 5.00
c. As #83, double overprint 20.00 11.50
d. Perf. 14 45.00 5.00
84 A47 10c blue & blk (R) 15.00 12.50
a. Roman "I" in "1911" 100.00 100.00
c. Perf. 14 100.00 100.00
Nos. 77-84 (8) 28.00 17.55

Many counterfeits of overprint exist.

A61

A62

A63

Telegraph Stamps Surcharged in Rose, Blue or Black

1911 ***Perf. 12***

86 A61 1c on 10c bl (R) .30 .20
a. "Coereos" 7.75 5.50
b. Inverted surcharge
87 A61 1c on 10c bl (Bk) 200.00 —
88 A61 1c on 25c vio (Bk) .30 .20
a. "Coereos" 8.00 5.50
b. Pair, one without surcharge 20.00
c. Double surcharge 9.00
e. Double surch., one inverted 12.50
89 A61 1c on 50c red brn (Bl) .50 .40
a. Inverted surcharge 5.50 5.00
b. Double surcharge 4.50
90 A61 1c on 1col brn (R) .50 .40
91 A61 1c on 5col red (Bl) .80 .55
92 A61 1c on 10col dk brn (R) 1.00 .70

Perf. 14

93 A62 2c on 5c brn org (Bk) 3.50 1.90
a. Inverted surcharge 9.00 3.75
b. "Correos" inverted 17.50
c. Double surcharge 9.00

Perf. 14x11

94 A62 2c on 10c bl (R) 100.00
a. Perf. 14 300.00
b. "Correos" inverted
c. As "b," perf. 14

95 A62 2c on 50c cl (Bk) .60 .50
a. Inverted surcharge 4.50 3.25
b. Double surcharge 12.50
c. Perf. 14 45.00 20.00
96 A62 2c on 1col brn (Bk) 1.00 .70
a. Inverted surcharge 12.50
b. Double surcharge 16.00
c. Perf. 14 .80 .80
97 A62 2c on 2col car (Bk) .75 .60
a. Inverted surcharge 8.00 5.00
b. "Correos" inverted 10.00 5.50
c. Double surcharge
d. Perf. 14 25.00 15.00
98 A62 2c on 5col grn (Bk) .65 .65
a. Inverted surcharge 10.00 7.00
b. "Correos" inverted 16.00 4.25
c. Perf. 14 6.00 3.00
99 A62 2c on 10col mar (Bk) 1.00 .65
a. "Correos" inverted 7.00
b. Perf. 14 5.00 3.00

Perf. 12

100 A63 5c on 5c org (Bl) .40 .25
a. Double surcharge 25.00 15.00
b. Inverted surcharge 25.00 8.50
c. Pair, one without surcharge 16.00

Counterfeits exist of Nos. 87, 94 and all minor varieties. Genuine "Coereos" errors do not exist on No. 87. Used copies of No. 94 with target cancels are counterfeits.

Nos. 93-99 exist with papermaker's watermark.

Coffee Plantation — A64

1921, June 17 **Litho.** ***Perf. 11½***

103 A64 5c bl & blk 3.00 3.00
a. Tête bêche pair 6.50 6.50
b. Imperf., pair 13.00
c. As "a," imperf. 30.00

Centenary of coffee raising in Costa Rica.

Liberty with Torch of Freedom — A65

1921 **Typo.** ***Perf. 11***

104 A65 5c violet 1.00 .40
a. Imperf, pair 100.00

Cent. of Central American independence.
Beware of trimmed singles that look like No. 104a.
For overprint see No. 111.

Juan Mora and Julio Acosta — A66

1921, Sept. 15 ***Perf. 11½***

105 A66 2c orange & blk 1.40 1.40
106 A66 3c green & blk 1.40 1.40
107 A66 6c scarlet & blk 2.40 2.40
108 A66 15c dk blue & blk 4.25 4.25
109 A66 30c orange brn & blk 5.75 5.75
Nos. 105-109 (5) 15.20 15.20

Centenary of Central American independence. Issue requested by Costa Rican Philatelic Society. Authorized by decree calling for 2,000 of 30c and 5,000 each of other values. Many more were printed illegally including imperforates, color changes and inverted centers.

Each sheet of 20 (4x5) contains 5 tête-bêche pairs.

Simón Bolívar — A67

1921 **Engr.** ***Perf. 12***

110 A67 15c deep violet .75 .20

For overprint No. 110a see set following No. 111. For surcharge see No. 148

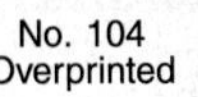

No. 104 Overprinted

1922 ***Perf. 11***

111 A65 5c violet .75 .40
a. Inverted overprint 10.00
b. Double overprint 15.00

Fakes of Nos. 111a and 111b are common.

Stamps of 1910-1921 Overprinted in Blue, Red, Black or Gold

1922 ***Perf. 12***

111C A53 1c brown (Bl) .30 .20
111D A54 2c deep green (R) .40 .20
111E A55 4c scarlet .30 .20
111F A56 5c orange 2.00 .35
111G A57 10c deep blue (R) .75 .35
111H A67 15c deep violet (G) 3.50 2.00
Nos. 111C-111H (6) 7.25 3.30

Inverted overprints occur on all values. Counterfeits are very common for both normal and inverted overprints.

No. 72 Overprinted

1923

111J A56 5c orange 3.00 .75
k. "VD." for "UD." 75.00 75.00

Jesús Jiménez — A68

1923, June 18 **Litho.** ***Perf. 11½***

112 A68 2c brown .30 .30
113 A68 4c green .35 .30
114 A68 5c blue .50 .30
115 A68 20c carmine .75 .40
116 A68 1col violet 1.00 1.00
Nos. 112-116 (5) 2.90 2.30

Pres. Jesús Jiménez (1823-98).

Nos. 112-116, imperf, were not regularly issued. Value, set $5.

For overprints see Nos. O65-O69.

National Monument A70

Harvesting Coffee — A71

Banana Growing — A73

General Post Office A74

Columbus Soliciting Aid of Isabella A75

Christopher Columbus A76

Columbus at Cariari A77

Map of Costa Rica — A78

Manuel M. Gutiérrez — A79

1923-26 Engr. *Perf. 12*

117	A70	1c violet	.25	.20
118	A71	2c yellow	.50	.20
119	A73	4c deep green	.75	.30
120	A74	5c light blue	1.50	.20
121	A74	5c yellow grn ('26)	.50	.20
122	A75	10c red brown	3.00	.20
123	A75	10c car rose ('26)	.50	.20
124	A76	12c carmine rose	10.00	3.00
125	A77	20c deep blue	10.00	.60
126	A78	40c orange	11.00	3.00
127	A79	1col olive green	2.00	.65
		Nos. 117-127 (11)	40.00	8.75

See #151-156. For surcharges & overprints see #136-140, 147, 189, 218, C2.

Rodrigo Arias Maldonado — A80

1924 *Perf. 12½*

128	A80	2c dark green	.20	.20
a.		Perf. 14	.50	.25

See No. 162.

Map of Guanacaste A81

Mission at Nicoya A82

1924 Litho. *Perf. 12*

129	A81	1c carmine rose	.30	.20
130	A81	2c violet	.30	.20
131	A81	5c green	.30	.20
132	A81	10c orange	2.25	.50
133	A82	15c light blue	1.00	.45
134	A82	20c gray black	2.00	1.00
135	A82	25c light brown	3.00	1.50
		Nos. 129-135 (7)	9.15	4.05

Centenary of annexation of Province of Guanacaste to Costa Rica.

Exist imperf. Value, set, $50.

Stamps of 1923 Surcharged:

a

b

1925

136	A74(a)	3c on 5c lt blue	.30	.20
137	A75(a)	6c on 10c red brn	.40	.25
138	A78(a)	30c on 40c orange	1.50	.40
139	A79(b)	45c on 1col ol grn	1.75	.50
a.		Double surcharge	*250.00*	
		Nos. 136-139 (4)	3.95	1.35

No. 124 Surcharged

1926

140	A76	10c on 12c car rose	1.50	.30

College of San Luis, Cartago A83

Chapui Asylum, San José — A84

Normal School, Heredia A85

Ruins of Ujarrás A86

1926 Unwmk. Engr. *Perf. 12½*

143	A83	3c ultra	.50	.20
144	A84	6c dark brown	.50	.20
145	A85	30c deep orange	2.00	.25
146	A86	45c black violet	4.00	1.00
		Nos. 143-146 (4)	7.00	1.65

For surcharges see Nos. 190-190D, 217.

No. 124 Surcharged in Black:

1928, Jan. 7 *Perf. 12*

147	A76	10c on 12c car rose	4.00	4.00

Issued in honor of Col. Charles A. Lindbergh during his Good Will Tour of Central America.

The surcharge has been privately reprinted using an original die. They can be distinguished by distinct dots under the "10s." All errors and inverted surcharges are reprints.

No. 110 Surcharged

1928

148	A67	5(c) on 15c dp violet	.20	.20
a.		Inverted surcharge	27.50	

Type I — A88

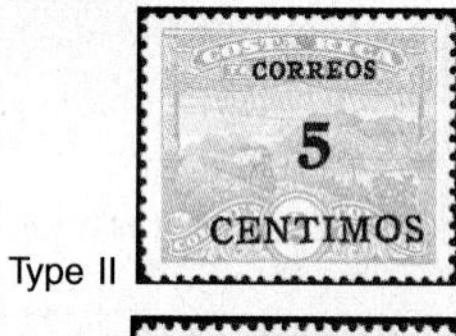

Type II

Type III

Type IV

Type V

Surcharge Typo. (I-V) & Litho. (V)

1929 *Perf. 12½*

149	A88	5c on 2col car (I)	.50	.20
a.-d.		Types II-V (litho.)	.60	.20
e.		Type V (typo.)	3.00	3.00

Telegraph Stamp Surcharged for Postage as in 1929, Surcharge Lithographed

1929

150	A88	13c on 40c deep grn	.30	.20
a.		Inverted surcharge	1.00	1.00

Excellent counterfeits exist of No. 150a.

Types of 1923-26 Issues Dated "1929"
Imprint of Waterlow & Sons

1930 Size: 26x21½mm *Perf. 12½*

151	A70	1c dark violet	.35	.20
155	A74	5c green	.35	.20
156	A75	10c carmine rose	.35	.20
		Nos. 151-156 (3)	1.05	.60

Juan Rafael Mora — A89

1931

157	A89	13c carmine rose	.60	.20

For surcharge see No. 209.

Seal of Costa Rica Philatelic Society ("Octubre 12 de 1932") — A90

1932, Oct. 12 *Perf. 12*

158	A90	3c orange	.25	.20
159	A90	5c dark green	.40	.25
160	A90	10c carmine rose	.50	.25
161	A90	20c dark blue	.85	.30
		Nos. 158-161 (4)	2.00	1.00

Phil. Exhib., Oct. 12, 1932. See #179-183.

Maldonado Type of 1924

1934 *Perf. 12½*

162	A80	3c dark green	.20	.20

Red Cross Nurse — A91

1935, May 31 *Perf. 12*

163	A91	10c rose carmine	7.50	.25

50th anniv. of the founding of the Costa Rican Red Cross Society.

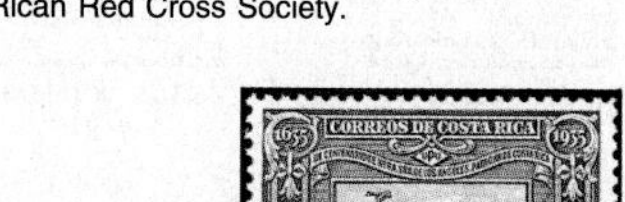

Air View of Cartago A92

Miraculous Statuette and View of Cathedral A93

Vision of 1635 — A94

1935, Aug. *Perf. 12½*

164	A92	5c green	.20	.20
165	A93	10c carmine	.30	.20
166	A92	30c orange	.45	.20
167	A94	45c dark violet	1.10	.55
168	A93	50c blue black	1.75	1.00
		Nos. 164-168 (5)	3.80	2.15

Tercentenary of the Patron Saint, Our Lady of the Angels, of Costa Rica.

Map of Cocos Island A95

1936, Jan. 29 ***Perf. 14, 11½ (25c)***

169	A95	4c ocher	.25	.20
170	A95	8c dark violet	.35	.20
171	A95	25c orange	.50	.20
172	A95	35c brown vio	.75	.20
173	A95	40c brown	1.00	.20
174	A95	50c yellow	1.10	.60
175	A95	2col yellow grn	11.00	10.00
176	A95	5col green	30.00	25.00
		Nos. 169-176 (8)	44.95	36.60

Exist imperf. Value, set, $50.

For surcharges see #196-200, C55-C56.

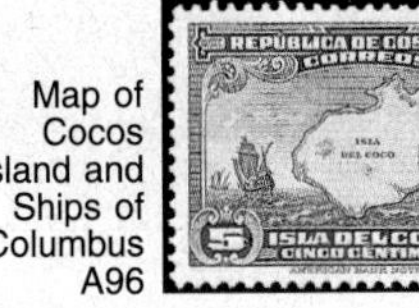

Map of Cocos Island and Ships of Columbus A96

1936, Dec. 5 ***Perf. 12***

177	A96	5c green	.20	.20
178	A96	10c carmine rose	.20	.20

For overprints see Nos. 247, O80-O81.

Seal of Costa Rica Philatelic Society ("Diciembre 1937") — A97

1937

179	A97	2c dark brown	.30	.20
180	A97	3c black	.30	.20
181	A97	5c green	.30	.20
182	A97	10c orange red	.30	.20
		Nos. 179-182 (4)	1.20	.80

Souvenir Sheet

Imperf

183		Sheet of 4	1.50	1.50
a.	A97	2c dark brown	.20	.20
b.	A97	3c black	.20	.20
c.	A97	5c green	.20	.20
d.	A97	10c orange red	.20	.20

Phil. Exhib., Dec. 1937.

Purple Guaria Orchid, National Flower — A98

Tuna — A99

Native with Donkey Carrying Bananas A101

3c, Cacao pod. 10c, Coffee harvesting.

1937-38 **Wmk. 229** ***Perf. 12½***

184	A98	1c green & vio ('38)	.50	.20
185	A98	3c chocolate ('38)	.30	.20

Unwmk. ***Perf. 12***

186	A99	2c olive gray	.35	.20
187	A101	5c dark green	.50	.20
188	A101	10c carmine rose	.75	.20
		Nos. 184-188 (5)	2.40	1.00

National Exposition.

No. 125 Overprinted in Black

1938 **Unwmk.** ***Perf. 12***

189	A77	20c deep blue	1.50	.20

No. 146 Surcharged in Red:

a

b

c

d

e

1940 ***Perf. 12½***

190	A86(a)	15c on 45c blk vio	.50	.20
190A	A86(b)	15c on 45c blk vio	.50	.20
190B	A86(c)	15c on 45c blk vio	.50	.20
190C	A86(d)	15c on 45c blk vio	.50	.20
190D	A86(e)	15c on 45c blk vio	.50	.20
		Nos. 190-190D (5)	2.50	1.00

#190D exists with inverted surcharge. Value, $5.

Allegory A103

Overprinted "Dia Panamericano de la Salud / 2 Diciembre 1940" and Arc

1940, Dec. 2 **Engr.** ***Perf. 12***

191	A103	5c green	.20	.20
192	A103	10c rose carmine	.25	.20
193	A103	20c deep blue	.55	.20
194	A103	40c brown	1.50	1.00
195	A103	55c orange yellow	2.50	2.00
		Nos. 191-195 (5)	5.00	3.60

Pan-American Health Day. See #C46-C54. Exist without overprint.

Stamps of 1936 Surcharged in Black:

1941 ***Perf. 14, 11½***

196	A95	15c on 25c orange	.50	.50
197	A95	15c on 35c brn vio	.50	.50
198	A95	15c on 40c brown	.50	.50
199	A95	15c on 2col yel grn	.50	.50
200	A95	15c on 5col green	1.00	1.00
		Nos. 196-200 (5)	3.00	3.00

Nos. 196-200 exist with surcharge inverted. Value, set of 5, $20.

National Stadium A104

Engr.; Flags Typo. in Natl. Colors

1941, May 8 ***Perf. 12½***

201	A104	5c green	.55	.20
a.		Flags omitted	100.00	
202	A104	10c orange	.40	.20
203	A104	15c car rose	.65	.30
204	A104	25c dk blue	.70	.45
205	A104	40c chestnut	2.75	1.10
206	A104	50c purple	3.50	1.75
207	A104	75c red orange	5.50	5.25
208	A104	1col dk carmine	10.00	10.00
		Nos. 201-208 (8)	24.05	19.25

Caribbean and Central American Soccer Championship. See #C57-C66, C121-C123.

No. 157 Surcharged in Black

1941 ***Perf. 12***

209	A89	5c on 13c car rose	.20	.20

Cleto González Viquez — A105

Design: 5c, José Rodriguez.

1941-45 **Engr.** ***Perf. 12½***

210	A105	3c dp orange	.25	.20
210A	A105	3c dp plum ('43)	.25	.20
210B	A105	3c carmine ('45)	.25	.20
211	A105	5c dp violet	.25	.20
211A	A105	5c brown blk ('43)	.25	.20
		Nos. 210-211A (5)	1.25	1.00

See No. 256.

Old University of Costa Rica A106

New National University A107

1941, Aug. 26 ***Perf. 12***

212	A106	5c green	.35	.20
213	A107	10c yellow org	.40	.20
214	A106	15c lilac rose	.75	.20
215	A107	25c dull blue	1.00	.30
216	A106	50c fawn	7.50	2.10
		Nos. 212-216 (5)	10.00	3.00

National University, founded in 1940. See Nos. C74-C80.

Nos. 144, 189 Surcharged in Black or Red

1942 ***Perf. 12½, 12***

217	A84	5c on 6c dk brn	.35	.20
218	A77	15c on 20c dp bl (R)	.65	.20

Nos. 217-218 exist with inverted surcharge. Value, each $6.

Torch of Freedom, "Victory" and Flags of American Nations A108

Juan Mora Fernández A109

1942, Sept. 25 ***Perf. 12***

219	A108	5c rose	.20	.20
220	A108	5c yellow grn	.20	.20
221	A108	5c purple	.20	.20
222	A108	5c dp blue	.20	.20
223	A108	5c red orange	.20	.20
		Nos. 219-223 (5)	1.00	1.00

For overprints see Nos. 238-241.

1943-47 **Engr.**

Designs: 2c, Bruno Carranza. 3c, Tomas Guardia. 5c, Manuel Aguilar. 15c, Francisco Morazan. 25c, Jose M. Alfaro. 50c, Francisco M. Oreamuno. 1col, Jose M. Castro. 2col, Juan Rafael Mora.

224	A109	1c red lilac	.20	.20
225	A109	2c black	.20	.20
226	A109	3c deep blue	.20	.20
227	A109	5c brt blue grn	.20	.20
a.		5c bright green ('47)	.20	.20
228	A109	15c scarlet	.20	.20
229	A109	25c brt ultra	1.00	.20
230	A109	50c dp violet	3.00	.45
231	A109	1col black brown	4.00	2.00
232	A109	2col deep orange	5.00	3.00
		Nos. 224-232 (9)	14.00	6.65

See Nos. 344-368, C81-C91A, C124-C127, C154-C158, C179-C181, C768-C772, C790-C794, C854-C858. For surcharges see Nos. C154-C158, C182, C184-C185.

View of San Ramón A118

1944, Jan. 19

233	A118	5c dark green	.20	.20
234	A118	10c orange	.20	.20
235	A118	15c rose pink	.25	.20
236	A118	40c gray black	1.00	.75
237	A118	50c deep blue	2.40	1.50
		Nos. 233-237 (5)	4.05	2.85

100th anniv. of the founding of the City of San Ramón. See Nos. C94-C102.

Catalogue values for unused stamps in this section, from this point to the end of the section, are for Never Hinged items.

Nos. 220-223 Overprinted in Red or Black

1944, Sept. 18

238	A108 5c yel green	.20	.20
239	A108 5c purple (R)	.20	.20
240	A108 5c dp blue (R)	.20	.20
241	A108 5c red orange	.20	.20
	Nos. 238-241 (4)	.80	.80

Amicable settlement of a boundary dispute with Panama. This overprint also exists on No. 219.

Mauro Fernández (1844-1905), Statesman — A119

Unwmk.

1945, July 21 Engr. *Perf. 14*

242	A119 20c deep green	.25	.20

For surcharge see No. 246.

Coffee Harvesting — A120

1945, Oct. 9 *Perf. 12*

243	A120 5c dk green & blk	.25	.20
244	A120 10c orange & blk	.25	.20
245	A120 20c car rose & blk	.30	.20
	Nos. 243-245 (3)	.80	.60

No. 242 Surcharged in Red Brown

1946 Unwmk. *Perf. 14*

246	A119 15c on 20c dp green	.25	.20

Exists with inverted surcharge. Value, $6.

No. O80 Overprinted in Red

1947, Mar. 19 *Perf. 12*

247	A96 5c green	.20	.20

Exist with inverted overprint. Value, $6.

Cervantes — A121

A122

Wmk. 215

1947, Nov. 10 Engr. *Perf. 14*

249	A121 30c deep blue	.30	.20
250	A121 55c deep carmine	.40	.25

Miguel de Cervantes Saavedra, novelist, playwright & poet, 400th birth anniv.

1947, Aug. 26 Unwmk. *Perf. 12*

251	A122 5c brt green	.20	.20
252	A122 10c car rose	.20	.20
253	A122 15c ultra	.20	.20
254	A122 25c orange red	.25	.25
255	A122 50c lilac	.40	.30
	Nos. 251-255,C160-C167 (13)	6.65	5.75

Franklin D. Roosevelt. For surcharges see Nos. C224-C226.

Small Portrait Type of 1941

Design: 3c, Bishop Bernardo A. Theil.

1948 *Perf. 12½*

256	A105 3c deep ultra	.20	.20

Old University of Costa Rica A123

1953, June 25 Litho. *Perf. 12*

Black Surcharge

257	A123 5c on 10c green	.25	.20

Revenue Stamp Surcharged in Red or Blue — A124

1955-56 Unwmk. Engr. *Perf. 12*

258	A124 5c on 2c emerald	.20	.20
259	A124 15c on 2c emer (Bl)	.20	.20
260	A124 15c on 2c emer ('56)	.20	.20
	Nos. 258-260,C341-C344 (7)	1.70	1.60

For surcharges see #C341-C344, C431-C433.

Justo A. Facio A125

Anglo-Costa Rican Bank A126

1960, Apr. 20 Photo. *Perf. 13½*

261	A125 10c brown red	.20	.20

Centenary of the birth (in 1859) of Prof. Justo A. Facio. Exists imperf.

Nos. RA12-RA15 Surcharged in Red

1963, Mar.

262	PT3 10c on 5c dk car	.20	.20
263	PT3 10c on 5c sepia	.20	.20
264	PT3 10c on 5c dull grn	.20	.20
265	PT3 10c on 5c blue	.20	.20
	Nos. 262-265 (4)	.80	.80

1963 Unwmk. *Perf. 13½*

266	A126 10c gray	.20	.20

Centenary of the Anglo-Costa Rican Bank.

Arms of San José — A127

Alberto M. Brenes Mora — A128

Coats of Arms: 35c, Cartago. 50c, Heredia. 55c, Alajuela. 65c, Guanacaste. 1col, Puntarenas. 2col, Limon.

1969, Sept. 14 Litho. *Perf. 14x13½*

267	A127 15c multicolored	.20	.20
268	A127 35c multicolored	.20	.20
269	A127 50c gray & multi	.20	.20
270	A127 55c buff & multi	.20	.20
271	A127 65c multicolored	.25	.25
272	A127 1col pink & multi	1.25	.25
273	A127 2col multicolored	1.25	.50
	Nos. 267-273 (7)	3.55	1.80

1976, Mar. 1 Litho. *Perf. 10½*

274	A128 1col violet blue	.25	.20
	Nos. 274,C653-C657 (6)	6.50	3.55

Prof. Alberto Manuel Brenes Mora, botanist, birth centenary.

Map of Costa Rica, Reader with Book — A129

1978, July 17 Litho. *Perf. 13½*

275	A129 50c multicolored	.25	.20

National five-year literacy plan.

A130

A131

1983, May 17 Litho. *Perf. 13x13½*

276	A130 10c multicolored	.20	.20
277	A130 50c multicolored	.20	.20
278	A130 10col multicolored	.70	.25
	Nos. 276-278 (3)	1.10	.65

World Communications Year.

1983, May 30 Litho. *Perf. 10½*

279	A131 20col black	1.40	1.40

1st World Cong. of Human Rights, 1982.

UPU Membership Centenary — A132

1983, June 30 Litho. *Perf. 16*

280	A132 3col #17, monument	.75	.50
281	A132 10col #20, headquarters	1.50	.50

French Alliance Centenary — A133

1983, July 21 Litho. *Perf. 11*

282	A133 12col Scene in San Jose, by Christina Fournier	2.00	.50

Christmas 1983 — A134

Nativity tableau in continuous design. Illustration reduced.

1983, Dec. 5 Litho. *Perf. 13½*

283	1.50col multi	.20	.20
284	1.50col multi	.20	.20
285	1.50col multi	.20	.20
a.	A134 Strip of 3, #283-285	1.00	1.00

Costa Rican Gardens Association.

Fishery Development Administration A135

1983, Dec. 19 Litho. *Perf. 13½*

286	A135 8.50col multi	.65	.25

Local Birds — A136

1984, Jan. 9 Litho. *Perf. 13½*

287	A136 10c Quetzal	.50	.20
288	A136 50c Cyanerpes cyaneus	.50	.20
289	A136 1col Turdus grayi	.50	.20
290	A136 1.50col Momotus momota	.50	.20
291	A136 3col Colibri thalassinus	1.25	.25
292	A136 10col Notiochelindon cyanoleuca	4.25	.30
	Nos. 287-292 (6)	7.50	1.35

Dated 1983. 10c, 1.50col, 3col vert.

José Joaquin Mora, Hero of 1856 Independence Campaign — A137

Paintings, Juan Santamaria Museum, San José: 1.50col, Pancha Carrasco. 3 col, Death of Juan Santamaria, horiz. 8.50col, Juan Rafael Mora Porras.

1984, Apr. 10 Litho. *Perf. 10½*

293 A137 50c multi .20 .20
294 A137 1.50col multi .20 .20
295 A137 3col multi .25 .20
296 A137 8.50col multi .75 .50
Nos. 293-296 (4) 1.40 1.10

For surcharge see No. 440.

Jesus Bonilla Chavarria, Composer A138

Musicians and Composers: 5col, Benjamin Gutierrez (b. 1937). 12col, Pilar Jimenez (1835-1922). 13col, Jose Daniel Zuniga Zeledon (1889-1981).

1984, May 30 Litho. *Perf. 13½*

297 A138 3.50col black & lil .30 .20
298 A138 5col black & pink .40 .25
299 A138 12col black & grn 1.00 .75
300 A138 13col black & yel 1.10 .80
Nos. 297-300 (4) 2.80 2.00

Figurines, Jade Museum — A139

1984 Summer Olympics A140

1984, June 27 Litho. *Perf. 13½*

301 A139 4col Man (pendant) .75 .20
302 A139 7col Seated man 1.50 .35
303 A139 10col Dish, horiz. 1.75 .45
Nos. 301-303 (3) 4.00 1.00

1984, July 27

304 A140 1col Basketball .20 .20
305 A140 8col Swimming .60 .20
306 A140 11col Bicycling .80 .35
307 A140 14col Running 1.10 .60
308 A140 20col Boxing 1.50 1.00
309 A140 30col Soccer 2.40 1.25
Nos. 304-309 (6) 6.60 3.60

Public Street Lighting Centenary A141

1984, Aug. 9 Litho. *Perf. 10½*

310 A141 6col Street scene by Luis Chacon .50 .30

10th Natl. Stamp Exhibition, Sept. 10-16 — A142

1984, Sept. 10 Litho. *Perf. 10½*

311 A142 10col Natl. monument .80 .45
312 A142 10col Juan Mora Fernandez monument .80 .45
a. Min. sheet, 2 each #311-312 15.00

Natl. Arms — A143

1984, Oct. 29 Engr. *Perf. 14x13½*

313 A143 100col dk green 6.50 3.00
314 A143 100col yel org 6.50 3.00

Detail from Sistine Virgin by Raphael — A144

1984, Dec. 7 Litho. *Perf. 10½*

315 3col multicolored .25 .20
316 3col multicolored .25 .20
a. A144 Pair, #315-316 2.00 2.00

20th Intl. Bicycle Race, Costa Rica — A146

1984, Dec. 19 Litho. *Perf. 13½*

317 A146 6col multi .50 .30

Intl. Youth Year A147

1985, Jan. 31 *Perf. 10½*

322 A147 11col IYY emblem, #C476 1.40 .45

Scouting Movement, 75th anniv.

Labor Monument, San Jose — A148

Natl. values: 11col, Freedom of speech-wooden hand printing press. 13col, Neutrality-dove, natl. flag, outline map.

1985, Feb. 28

323 A148 6col shown .75 .30
324 A148 11col bl, blk & yel 1.10 .45
325 A148 13col multi 1.25 .50

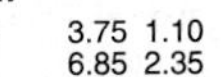

Size: 68x38mm

326 A148 30col Nos. 323-325 3.75 1.10
Nos. 323-326 (4) 6.85 2.35

Natl. Red Cross Cent., UN 40th Anniv. A149

1985, May 3 *Perf. 10½*

327 A149 3col No. 163, horiz. 2.00 .20
328 A149 5col No. C120 3.00 .25

Club Emblem A150

1st Club Pres., Ricardo Saprissa Ayma A151

Design: No. 330, Hands holding soccer ball.

1985, July 16 *Perf. 10½*

329 A150 3col multi .25 .20
330 A150 3col multi .25 .20
a. Pair, #329-330 .50 .50
331 A151 6col multi .50 .30
Nos. 329-331 (3) 1.00 .70

Saprissa Soccer Club, 50th Anniv.

Orchids — A152

1985, Dec. 3

332 A152 6col Brassia arcuigera 1.25 .50
333 A152 6col Encyclia peraltensis 1.25 .50
334 A152 6col Maxillaria especie 1.25 .50
a. Strip of 3, #332-334 6.50 2.75
335 A152 13col Oncidium turialbae 1.25 .90
336 A152 13col Trichopilia marginata 1.25 .90
337 A152 13col Stanhopea ecornuta 1.25 .90
a. Strip of 3, #335-337 6.50 2.75
Nos. 332-337 (6) 7.50 4.20

11th Natl. Philatelic Exposition A153

1985, Dec. 3 Litho. *Perf. 13½*

338 A153 20col No. C41 1.00 .45

Christmas 1985 — A153a

1985, Dec. 12 Litho. *Perf. 10½*

338A A153a 3col multi .20 .20

Compulsory Education, Cent. A154

Designs: 3col, Primary school, horiz. 30col, Mauro Fernandez Acuna, founder.

1986, Feb. 28 *Perf. 13½*

339 A154 3col pale yel & brn .20 .20
340 A154 30col pale pink & brn 1.25 .60

Agriculture Students — A155

1986, Mar. 21 *Perf. 10½*

341 10col shown .40 .20
342 10col IDB emblem .40 .20
343 10col Capo Bianco fisherman .40 .20
a. A155 Strip of 3, #341-343 2.50 2.50
Nos. 341-343 (3) 1.20 .60

Inter-American Development Bank Annual Governors' Assembly, San Jose.

Presidents Type of 1943

Designs: Nos. 344, 349, 354, 359, 364, Francisco J. Orlich Bolmarcich, 1962-66.

Nos. 345, 350, 355, 360, 365, Jose Joaquin Trejos Fernandez, 1966-70.

Nos. 346, 351, 356, 361, 366, Daniel Oduber Quiros, 1974-78.

Nos. 347, 352, 357, 362, 367, Rodrigo Carazo Oido, 1978-82.

Nos. 348, 353, 358, 363, 368, Luis Alberto Monge Alvarez, 1982-86.

1986, May 12 Litho. *Perf. 10½*

344 A109 3col turq blue .35 .20
345 A109 3col turq blue .35 .20
346 A109 3col turq blue .35 .20
347 A109 3col turq blue .35 .20
348 A109 3col turq blue .35 .20
a. Strip of 5, #344-348 2.00 1.75
349 A109 6col yel brn .50 .25
350 A109 6col yel brn .50 .25
351 A109 6col yel brn .50 .25
352 A109 6col yel brn .50 .25
353 A109 6col yel brn .50 .25
a. Strip of 5, #349-353 4.00 3.50
354 A109 10col brn org .60 .30
355 A109 10col brn org .60 .30
356 A109 10col brn org .60 .30
357 A109 10col brn org .60 .30
358 A109 10col brn org .60 .30
a. Strip of 5, #354-358 5.25 5.00
359 A109 11col slate gray .75 .40
360 A109 11col slate gray .75 .40
361 A109 11col slate gray .75 .40
362 A109 11col slate gray .75 .40
363 A109 11col slate gray .75 .40
a. Strip of 5, #359-363 6.25 5.50
364 A109 13col olive 1.00 .45
365 A109 13col olive 1.00 .45
366 A109 13col olive 1.00 .45
367 A109 13col olive 1.00 .45
368 A109 13col olive 1.00 .45
a. Strip of 5, #364-368 8.50 6.50
Nos. 344-368 (25) 16.00 8.00
Nos. 348a-368a (5) 25.00

1986 World Cup Soccer Championships, Mexico — A156

1986, May 30 Litho. *Perf. 13½*

369 A156 1col Players .20 .20
370 A156 1col Character trademark, vert. .30 .20
371 A156 4col as No. 370 1.00 .20
372 A156 6col as No. 369 1.50 .20
373 A156 11col Players, diff. 3.00 .20
Nos. 369-373 (5) 6.00 1.00

A second printing of No. 370 differs in paper and shade from the first printing, but the most obvious difference is in the absence of the initials "LIL" by the left foot of the soccer player. Unused copies are rare. Value for used, $3.

Intl. Peace Year — A157

Gold Museum, Central Bank of Costa Rica — A158

Peace in many languages: a, "Hoa binh," etc. b, "Vrede," etc. c, "Paz," etc.

1986, July 31 Litho. *Perf. 10½*

374	Strip of 3	*4.00*	.20
a.-c.	A157 5col, any single	.50	.20

1986, Sept. 19 *Perf. 10½*

Designs: Various undescribed works of Pre-Columbian art.

375	Strip of 5	1.75	.30
a.-e.	A158 6col any single	.25	.20
376	Strip of 5	3.25	.60
a.-e.	A158 13col any single	.50	.20

Exist perf 13½, value $8 for the two strips of 5 unused

A159

Fauna and Flora — A160

1986, Dec. 16 Litho. *Perf. 13x13½*

377	A159	2col	Centurio senex	.20	.20
378	A159	3col	Glossophaga soricina	.25	.20
379	A159	4col	Ectophylla alba	.30	.20
380	A159	5col	Ectophylla alba, diff.	.40	.20
381	A159	6col	Agalychnis callidryas	.50	.20
382	A159	10col	Dendrobates pumilio	.85	.20
383	A159	11col	Hyla ebraccata	.90	.20
384	A159	20col	Phyllobates lugubris	1.60	.20
			Nos. 377-384 (8)	5.00	1.60

Souvenir Sheet

Perf. 12½x12

385	A160	50col	Agalychnis callidryas, diff.	*35.00*	*25.00*

Natl. Science and Technology Day — A161

Mural (detail), by Francisco Amighetti, Clorito Picado Social Security Clinic.

1987, July 31 Litho. *Perf. 10½*

386	A161	8col	multi	*3.75*	.25

Natl. Museum, Cent. A162

Artifacts: No. 387a, Dowel-shaped figure of a man. No. 387b, Ape-like carved stone figurine. No. 387c, Polished stone ritual figure. No. 387d, Carved granite capital. No. 387e, Two-legged pot. No. 388a, Bowl. No. 388b, Sculpture. No. 388c, Water jar.

1987, Aug. 7

387	Strip of 5	2.25	.40
a.-e.	A162 8col any single, vert.	.30	.20
388	Strip of 3	2.75	.45
a.-c.	A162 15col any single	.60	.20
	Nos. 387-388 (2)	5.00	.85

Horse-drawn Wagon — A163

1987, Oct. 26

389	A163	20col	shown	.75	.20
390	A163	20col	Street in old San Jose	.75	.20
391	A163	20col	Provincial coat of arms	.75	.20
			Nos. 389-391 (3)	2.25	.60

City of San Jose, 250th anniv. Rotary Club, 60th anniv.

Columbus Day A164

1987, Oct. 26 *Perf. 10½*

392	A164	30col	Map, 16th cent.	2.00	.30

Day of the Race; 495th anniv. of Columbus's departure from Palos, Spain, on first journey to the New World.

Discovery of America, 500th Anniv. (in 1992) — A165

Pres. Oscar Arias, 1987 Nobel Peace Prize Winner — A166

Maps of Honduras, Nicaragua, Costa Rica and Panama, believed to be Asia by Columbus: No. 393, Costa Rica, 16th cent. No. 394, Map of "Asia" by Bartholomeu Columbus (1461-1514).

1987, Nov. 20 Litho. *Perf. 13½*

393	A165	4col	yel & dk red brn	.20	.20
394	A165	4col	yel & dk red brn	.20	.20
a.			Pair, #393-394	1.50	.20

1987, Dec. 2 *Perf. 10½*

395	A166	10col	multi	*1.50*	.20

Two Houses, a Watercolor by Fausto Pacheco (1899-1966) A167

1987, Dec. 22 Litho. *Perf. 10½*

396	A167	1col	multi	.20	.20

Intl. Year of Shelter for the Homeless.

17th General Conference for the Preservation of Natural Resources A168

1988, Feb. 1 Litho. *Perf. 13½*

397	A168	5col	Green turtle	.60	.20
398	A168	5col	Emblem, golden toad	.60	.20
399	A168	5col	Blue butterfly	.60	.20
a.			A168 Strip of 3, #397-399	2.00	2.00

Intl. Red Cross and Red Crescent Organizations, 125th Annivs. — A169

1988, Apr. 18 Litho. *Perf. 10½*

400	A169	30col	lt blue & dark red	1.00	.25

North and South Campaign A170

1988, June 6 Photo. *Perf. 11½*

Granite Paper

401	A170	18col	Adult education	.60	.20
402	A170	20col	Cultural radio programs	.70	.20

Cultural cooperation with Liechtenstein. See Liechtenstein #886-887. For overprint see #C921.

A171

A172

1988, June 27 Litho. *Perf. 10½*

403	A171	3col	dk blue, dark red & yel	.20	.20

Anglo-Costa Rican Bank, 125th anniv.

1988, Sept. 16 Litho. *Perf. 13½*

404	A172	25col	Character trademark	.70	.20
405	A172	25col	Games emblem	.70	.20
a.			Pair, #404-405	1.40	.40

1988 Summer Olympics, Seoul.

Girls' High School, Cent. A173

1988, Oct. 17 Litho. *Perf. 10½*

406	A173	10col	Student, courtyard	.35	.20

A174

A175

1988, Nov. 18

407	A174	10col	gray, greenish bl & red brn	.35	.20

Educator Omar Dengo (1888-1928) and the Teachers' College, Heredia.

1988, Nov. 28 *Perf. 13½*

Indian glass-bead and lion-tooth necklace.

408	A175	4col	multi	.20	.20

Discovery of America, 500th anniv. (in 1992).

A176

A177

1988, Dec. 26 Litho. *Perf. 10½*

409	A176	2col	Observation tower	.20	.20

Natl. Meteorological Institute, cent. For surcharge see No. 439.

1989, Feb. 28

Designs: Indigenous flora.

410	A177	5col	*Eschweilera costarricensis*	.20	.20
411	A177	10col	*Heliconia wagneriana*	.25	.20
412	A177	15col	*Heliconia lophocarpa*	.40	.20
413	A177	20col	*Aechmea magdalenae*	.50	.20
414	A177	25col	*Psammisia ramiflora*	.60	.20
415	A177	30col	*Passiflora vitifolia*	.75	.20
			Nos. 410-415 (6)	2.70	1.20

A178

A179

1989, July 1 Litho. *Perf. 10½*

416	A178	30col	Nation at Arms	.75	.20

French Revolution, bicent.

1989, Aug. 28 Litho. *Perf. 13½*

417	A179	10col	Sugar mill	.25	.20

Grecia County, 151st anniv. For overprints see Nos. RA106-RA109.

America Issue — A180

UPAE emblem and pre-Columbian stone carvings: 50col, Three-footed bench for grinding corn. 100col, Sphere.

Litho. & Engr.
Perf. 12½x12

1989, Oct. 12 **Wmk. 334**
418 A180 50col multi 2.50 1.10
419 A180 100col multi 5.00 1.75

For overprint see No. C916.

A181 A182

Perf. 10½

1989, Oct. 23 **Litho.** **Unwmk.**
420 A181 10col Orchid *1.75* .20

"100 Years of Democracy" summit of Presidents.

Perf. 13½

1989, Nov. 27 **Litho.** **Unwmk.**
421 A182 18col Map, H.F. Pittier, emblem .45 .20

Natl. Geographic Institute, cent.
For surcharge see No. 452.

America Issue — A183

Pre-Columbian gold frog figurine and facing portraits of Ferdinand V and Isabella I on gold coin struck by Spain from 1476 to 1516.

1989, Dec. 4 ***Perf. 10½***
422 A183 4col multicolored .20 .20

Discovery of America, 500th anniv. (in 1992).

Natl. Theater, Cent. A184

Perf. 10½

1990, Feb. 27 **Litho.** **Unwmk.**
423 A184 5col *Coffee Allegory* .20 .20

World Cup Soccer Championships, Italy — A185

1990, June 1 **Litho.** ***Perf. 10½***
424 A185 5col multicolored .25 .20

Univ. of Costa Rica, 50th Anniv. A187

1990, Aug. 24 **Litho.** ***Perf. 10½***
426 A187 18col multicolored .40 .20

Education, Democracy, Peace — A188

Litho. & Engr.

1990, Oct. 31 ***Perf. 12½***
427 A188 100col shown 2.25 1.10
428 A188 200col Flag as map 4.50 1.75
429 A188 500col National arms 11.50 6.00
Nos. 427-429 (3) 18.25 8.85

"Invisible" security printing is sometimes visible.
For overprints see Nos. 448, C920.

Hospitals A190 America Issue A191

#431, St. Vincent de Paul Hospital, Heredia. #432, Natl. Psychiatric hospital.

1990, Dec. 18 **Engr.** ***Perf. 13x12½***
431 A190 50col multicolored 1.10 .30
432 A190 100col multicolored 2.25 .55

1990, Dec. 21 **Litho.** ***Perf. 10½***
433 A191 18col Ara macao .50 .20
434 A191 18col Ara ambigua .50 .20
a. Pair, #433-434 3.00 3.00
435 A191 24col Cassia grandis 1.00 .20
436 A191 24col Tabebuia ochracea 1.00 .20
a. Pair, #435-436 3.00 3.00
Nos. 433-436 (4) 3.00 .80

Costa Rica-Panama Border Treaty, 50th Anniv. — A192

Designs: a, Flags, national arms. b, Presidents. c, Map.

1991, May 24 **Litho.** ***Perf. 10½***
437 A192 10col Strip of 3, #a.-c. .70 .20

Discovery of America, 500th Anniv. (in 1992) — A193

1991, Oct. 11 **Litho.** ***Perf. 13½***
438 A193 4col multicolored 1.00 .20

Nos. 409, 296 Surcharged

1991, Oct. 21 **Litho.** ***Perf. 10½***
439 A176 1col on 2col #409 .20 .20
440 A137 3col on 8.50col #296 .20 .20

Former Presidents, Supreme Court of Justice — A194

Designs: a, Benito Serrano Jimenez. b, Luis Davila Solera. c, Fernando Baudrit Solera. d, Alejandro Alvarado Garcia.

Perf. 14½x13½

1992, Feb. 28 **Litho.**
441 A194 5col Strip of 4, #a.-d. 1.40 .35

DINADECO, Natl. Directorate of Community Development, 25th Anniv. A195

1992, Apr. 28 **Litho.** ***Perf. 10½***
442 A195 15col multicolored 1.10 .30

Compare with No. C505.

A196 A197

1992, May 26 **Litho.** ***Perf. 13½***
443 A196 15col lake & black 1.10 .30

Dr. Solon Nunez Frutos, public health pioneer.

1992, July 17 **Litho.** ***Perf. 13***

Solar Eclipse: a, Total eclipse. b, Post Office Bldg. during eclipse. c, Partial eclipse.

444 A197 45col Strip of 3, #a.-c. 6.00 1.00

A198 A199

1992, Aug. 14 **Litho.** ***Perf. 13½***
445 A198 35col multicolored 1.00 .25

Interamerican Institute for Agricultural Cooperation, 50th anniv.

1992, Nov. 5 **Litho.** ***Perf. 10½***
446 A199 2col Waterfall .25 .20
447 A199 15col Coastline .25 .20

Cocos Island, 450th anniv. of discovery.

No. 427 Ovptd. "CENTENARIO / DE LIMON"

Litho. & Engr.

1992, Nov. 27 ***Perf. 12½***
448 A188 100col black & blue 2.10 1.00

America Issue A200

1992, Dec. 15 **Litho.** ***Perf. 10½***
449 A200 15col Anolis townsendi *1.00* .20
450 A200 35col Pinaroloxias inornata *3.00* .25

Natl. Theater A201

Detail from painting "Allegory of Fine Arts," by Roberto Fontana.

1993, Jan. 29 **Litho.** ***Perf. 10½***
451 A201 20col multicolored .50 .20

No. 421 Surcharged

1993, Mar. 26 **Litho.** ***Perf. 13½***
452 A182 5col on 18col multi .50 .20

50,000 stamps originally were overprinted with a tiny block and four thin bars over the value, but this was considered unacceptable. So these stamps plus 1,550,000 unoverprinted stamps were overprinted with the large black square and surcharge, as shown.

Protection of the Dolphin A202

1993, May 17 **Litho.** ***Perf. 10½***
453 A202 10col Delphinus delphis .60 .20
454 A202 20col Stenella coeruleoalbus 1.40 .25

Costa Rican Civil Service, 40th Anniv. — A203

1993, May 28 **Litho.** ***Perf. 13½***
455 A203 5col multicolored .20 .20

Costa Rican Chamber of Industries, 50th Anniv. A204

1993, July 15 ***Perf. 10½***
456 A204 45col multicolored 1.00 .60

School of Communication Sciences, University of Costa Rica, 25th Anniv. — A205

1993, Aug. 19 **Litho.** ***Perf. 13½***
457 A205 20col black, blue & red .35 .20

Protection of the Tropical Rain Forest — A206

1993, Aug. 27 ***Perf. 10½***
458 A206 2col Passiflora vitifolia .30 .20
459 A206 35col Gurania megistantha .70 .25

Social Guarantees and Labor Code, 50th Anniv. A207

1993, Sept. 14 **Litho.** ***Perf. 10½***
460 A207 20col multicolored .40 .20

A208

A209

1993, Oct. 25 **Litho.** ***Perf. 13½***
461 A208 45col multicolored .90 .45

Intl. Assoc. of Professional Custom-House Agents, 15th Congress.

1993, Nov. 26 ***Perf. 10½***
462 A209 20col multicolored .40 .20

Miguel Angel Castro Carazo (1893-1960), educator and humanitarian.

For surcharge see No. 481.

A211

A212

1993, Dec. 23 **Litho.** ***Perf. 10½***
464 A211 20col multicolored .40 .20

Law School of Costa Rica, 150th anniv.

1994, Mar. 8 **Litho.** ***Perf. 13***
465 A212 20col Natl. Theater .40 .20

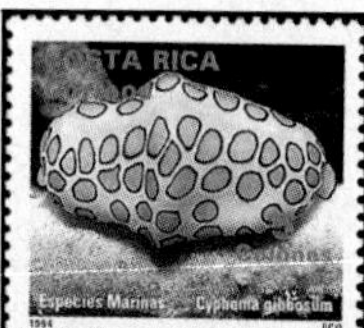

Marine Life — A213

5col, Cyphoma gibbosum. 10col, Ophioderma rubicundum. 15col, Myripristis jacobus. 20col, Holocanthus passer. 35col, Paranthias furcifer. 45col, Tubastraea coccinea. 50col, Acanthaster planci. 55col, Ocypode. 70col, Arothron meleagris. 100col, Thalassoma lucasanum.

Litho. & Embossed

1994, Apr. 29 ***Perf. 12½x12***

466	A213	5col	multicolored	.20	.20
467	A213	10col	multicolored	.25	.20
468	A213	15col	multicolored	.60	.20
469	A213	20col	multicolored	.80	.25
470	A213	35col	multicolored	1.25	.40
471	A213	45col	multicolored	1.75	.55
472	A213	50col	multicolored	1.90	.65
473	A213	55col	multicolored	2.25	.70
474	A213	70col	multicolored	3.00	.90
	Nos. 466-474 (9)			12.00	4.05

Souvenir Sheet

Perf. 13

475 A213 100col multicolored 3.00 3.00

America Issue A214

Illustrations from 19th century Book of Figueroa: a, Man on horseback. b, Back of ox carrying bundles.

1994, Dec. 19 **Litho.** ***Perf. 10½***
476 A214 20col Pair, #a.-b. + label 1.00 .45

No. 476 is a continuous design.

Rotary Intl., 90th Anniv. — A215

1995, Mar. **Litho.** ***Perf. 13½***
477 A215 20col multicolored .75 .25

Antonio Jose de Sucre (1795-1830) A216

Guanacaste Institute, 50th Anniv. A217

Design: 30col, Jose Marti (1853-95).

1995, June **Litho.** ***Perf. 10½***
478 A216 10col multicolored [illegible] [illegible]
479 A216 30col multicolored .50 .25

1995, July 24 ***Perf. 13½***
480 A217 50col grn, blk & bis .80 .40

No. 462 Surcharged in Blue or Black

1995, Sept. 11 **Litho.** ***Perf. 10½***
481 A209 5col on 20col multi .20 .20

UN, 50th Anniv. — A218

13th Natl. Philatelic Expo — A219

1995, Oct. 24 **Litho.** ***Perf. 10½***
482 A218 5col multicolored .20 .20

1995, Dec. 1

Paintings by Lola Fernández: No. 483, Noviembre. No. 484, Enero.

483	A219	50col	multicolored	.80	.40
484	A219	50col	multicolored	.80	.40
a.			Pair, Nos. 483-484	1.60	.80

America Issue A220

30col, Jabiru mycteria. #486, View of coast. #487, River, trees. 50col, Atta cephalotes.

1995, Dec. 25 **Litho.** ***Rouletted 13½***

485	A220	30col	multicolored	.50	.25
486	A220	40col	multicolored	.65	.30
487	A220	40col	multicolored	.65	.30
a.			Pair, #486-487	1.30	.65
488	A220	50col	multicolored	.80	.80
a.			Souvenir sheet, #485-488	2.50	1.25
	Nos. 485-488 (4)			2.60	1.65

Seaport City of Limón A221

Designs: a, Early picture of steam train. b, Photo of ship in port, 1922. c, Aerial view of seaport, 1995. d, Painting of fruit seller, by Diego Villalobos. e, Drawing of Calipso singers, by Jorge Esquivel.

1996, Jan. 31 **Litho.** ***Perf. 10½***
489 A221 30col Strip of 5, #a.-e. 2.50 1.25

Jerusalem, 3000th Anniv. — A222

1996, May 17 **Litho.** ***Perf. 13½***
490 A222 30col multicolored .45 .25

1996 Summer Olympic Games, Atlanta A223

Olympic swimmers, coaches from Costa Rica: a, F. Rivas, M.M. Paris. b, S. Poll, R. Yglesias. c, C. Poll, A. Cruz.

1996, July 18 **Litho.** ***Perf. 10½***
491 A223 5col Strip of 3, #a.-c. .50 .20

No. 491 is a continuous design.

A224

A225

First lady, presidents: a, Juana del Castillo. b, Juan Mora Fernández. c, J.M. Castro Madriz. d, Pacífica Fernández.

1996, Sept. 13 **Litho.** ***Perf. 10½***
492 A224 30col Block of 4, #a.-d. 2.25 1.00

Independence, 175th anniv. No. 492 was issued in sheets of 16 stamps.

1996, Oct. 4 **Litho.** ***Perf. 13½***
493 A225 15col multicolored .25 .20

Aqueducts and sewage systems, 35th anniv. Exists imperf.

A226

America issue (Paintings): No. 494, Black from Lemon, by Manuel da la Cruz González. No. 495, Peasant Women, by Gonzalo Morales Alvarado, vert.

1996, Dec. 16 ***Perf. 10½***
494 A226 45col multicolored .70 .35
495 A226 45col multicolored .70 .35

A227

Entrance of the Saints at San Ramón, parade of people: a, Building with palm trees on top. b, Church on hill. c, Tree, holy family.

1997, Aug. 14 Litho. *Perf. 13½*
496 A227 30col Strip of 3, #a.-c. 1.25 1.25

Costa Rican traditions.

School of Fine Arts, Cent. A228

1997, Sept. 24 *Perf. 10½*
497 A228 50col multicolored .40 .20

Radio Netherlands, 50th Anniv. — A229

1997, Sept. 26 *Perf. 13½*
498 A229 45col multicolored .60 .40

Exists imperf.

14th Natl. Philatelic Exhibition A230

1997, Oct. 9 *Perf. 10½*
499 A230 30col Postmen .35 .25

America Issue.

Church of the Immaculate Conception, Heredia, Bicent. — A231

1997, Nov. 10 Litho. *Perf. 10½*
502 A231 50col multicolored .90 .70

Second Republic, 50th Anniv. — A232

Former Pres. José Figueres demolishing wall of Fort Bellavista: 10col, 45col, Complete photo. 30col, Detail of Figueres' head. 50col, Hammer head hitting wall.

Litho. & Engr.

1998, Mar. 30 *Perf. 12½*
503 A232 10col multicolored .20 .20
504 A232 30col multicolored .30 .20
505 A232 45col multicolored .45 .20
506 A232 50col multicolored .50 .25
a. Souvenir sheet of 2, #504, 506 1.00 1.00

Natl. University, 25th Anniv. — A233

1998, July 27 Litho. *Perf. 10½*
507 A233 50col multicolored .90 .75

Butterflies A234

10col, Caligo memnon. 15col, Morpho peleides. 20col, Papilio thoas. 30col, Siproeta stelenes. 35col, Ascia monuste. 40col, Parides iphidamas. 45col, Smyrna blonfildia. 50col, Callicore pitheas. 55col, Historis odius. 60col, Danaus plexippus.

1998, July
508 A234 10col multicolored .25 .20
509 A234 15col multicolored .30 .25
510 A234 20col multicolored .45 .35
511 A234 30col multicolored .65 .50
512 A234 35col multicolored .80 .55
513 A234 40col multicolored .90 .60
514 A234 45col multicolored 1.00 .65
515 A234 50col multicolored 1.10 .75
516 A234 55col multicolored 1.25 .85
517 A234 60col multicolored 1.40 1.00
Nos. 508-517 (10) 8.10 5.70

1998 World Cup Soccer Championships, France — A235

1998, Feb. 27 Litho. *Perf. 10½*
518 A235 50col multicolored 1.00 .80

A236

A237

1998, Nov. 30 Litho. *Perf. 13½*
519 A236 50col brn, yel brn & lt yel .45 .35

Carmen Lyra (1888-1949), author.

1998, Dec. 11 Litho. *Perf. 13½*
520 A237 50col multicolored .75 .50

Gandhi (1869-1948).

Intl. Union for the Conservation of Nature, 50th Anniv. A238

Turtles: a, 70col, Rhinociemmys pulcherrima. b, 60col, Trachemys scripta. c, 70col, Chelydra serpentina.

1998, Dec. 1
521 A238 Strip of 3, #a.-c. 4.50 4.50

Mushrooms A239

a, Morchella esculenta. b, Boletus edulis.

1999, July 2 Litho. *Perf. 10½*
522 A239 50col Pair, #a.-b. 1.50 1.50

SOS Children's Villages, 50th Anniv. — A240

1999, June Litho. *Perf. 10½*
523 A240 50col multicolored .60 .40

Costa Rican Institute of Electricity, 50th Anniv. A241

1999, Sept. 21 Litho. *Perf. 13¼*
524 A241 75col multi .50 .35

A242

A243

1999, Oct. 7 Engr. *Perf. 13¾x14*
525 A242 300col violet 2.25 2.00

Archbishop Víctor M. Sanabria (1899-1952). See No. 538.

1999, Oct. 29 Litho. *Perf. 13¼*
526 A243 50col multi .45 .25

Intl. Year of Older Persons.

Supreme Election Tribunal, 50th Anniv. A244

1999, Nov. 5 *Perf. 10½*
527 A244 70col multi .75 .25

UPU, 125th Anniv. A245

Carmen Granados (1915-99), Humorist A246

1999, Dec. 1 *Perf. 13¼*
528 A245 75col multi .50 .25

1999, Dec. 1
529 A246 50col multi .35 .20

America Issue, A New Millennium Without Arms — A247

1999, Dec. 1
530 A247 50col shown .35 .20
531 A247 70col Face, hands, diff. .50 .25

PhilexFrance '99 — A248

1999, Dec. 1
532 A248 300col shown 3.00 1.00
533 A248 300col Flower, Eiffel Tower 3.00 1.00

Natl. Bank, 50th Anniv. — A249

No. 534 — Pre-Columbian artifacts: a, Jaguar. b, Scorpion. c, Bat. d, Crab. e, Beast with horns.

No. 535 — Obverse and reverse of coins: a, Gold, from 1825. b, Gold, from 1850. c, Silver one-eighth peso. d, Gold 20-peso. e, 1935 1-colon.

2000, Jan. 28 Litho. *Perf. 13¼*
534 Vert. strip of 5 7.50 6.00
a.-e. A249 60col Any single 1.00 .50
535 Vert. strip of 5 15.00 10.00
a.-e. A249 90col Any single 2.00 1.00

2000 Summer Olympics, Sydney — A250

No. 536, 60col: a, Taekwando. b, Cycling. c, Swimming. d, Soccer.

No. 537, 70col: a, Running. b, Boxing. c, Men's rings. d, Tennis.

Illustration reduced.

2000, Aug. 31

Blocks of 4, #a-d

536-537 A250 Set of 2 7.00 7.00

There were two printings of Nos. 536-537. In the first printing, colors are paler, and the green Olympic ring is misregistered on Nos. 536a-536d. In the second, colors are more intense, and the green ring is properly registered. Values the same.

Famous Person Type of 1999

Pres. Rafael A. Calderón Guardia (1900-70).

2000 Engr. *Perf. 12½*

538 A242 100col deep blue 1.00 .20
a. Perf 13¾x14 3.00 .50

Paintings by Max Jiménez — A251

No. 539: a, Fishermen in Cojimar. b, Adamant.
Illustration reduced.

2000, Nov. Litho. *Perf. 10½*

539 Horiz. pair 2.00 2.00
a.-b. A251 50col Any single .75 .40

America Issue, Fight Against AIDS — A252

Designs: 60col, Stylized people. 90col, Stylized person.

2000, Dec. *Perf. 13¼*

540-541 A252 Set of 2 1.40 1.25

Christmas — A253

2000, Dec.

542 A253 100col multi 1.00 .70

America Issue — UNESCO World Heritage A254

Birds form Cocos Island Natl. Park: 95col, Coccyzus ferrugineus. 115col, Pinaroloxias inornata.

2001, Apr. 5 Litho. *Perf. 10½*

543-544 A254 Set of 2 3.50 2.50

Costa Rica — Netherlands Diplomatic Relations, 150th Anniv. — A255

2001, July

545 A255 65col multi .60 .40

No. 429 Surcharged

2001 Method and Perf. As Before

546 A188 65col on 500col multi .50 .50
547 A188 80col on 500col multi .70 .70
548 A188 95col on 500col multi .80 .80
Nos. 546-548 (3) 2.00 2.00

Issued: No. 846, 8/24. Nos. 547-548, 9/7.

Third Hispanic-Costa Rican Exposition — A256

Orchids: a, Guaria turrialba. b, Tricopilia.
Illustration reduced.

2001, Oct. 5 Litho. *Perf. 13¼*

549 A256 65col Horiz. pair, #a-b 2.00 2.00

Campaign Against Child Labor — A257

2001, Nov. 15 *Perf. 13¼*

550 A257 100col multi 1.00 .65

Pres. Tomás Guardia (1832-82) and Locomotive — A258

2001, Nov. 21

551 A258 65col multi 1.00 .60

A second printing of No. 551 was issued in 2002. It features a lighter beige and has yellow gum. This printing of 500 sheets of 15 stamps was made to complete the contract. Value, unused $25.

Costa Rican Team for 2002 World Cup Soccer Championships, Japan and Korea — A259

Illustration reduced.

2002, Mar. *Perf. 10½*

552 A259 65col multi .60 .40

No. 428 Surcharged in Red

Litho. & Engr.

2002, Jan. 24 *Perf. 12½*

553 A188 65col on 200col multi .60 .40

America Issue — Youth, Education and Literacy — A260

Designs: 65col, Children and globe. 100col, Blind person reading Braille.

Litho. & Embossed

2002, Mar. *Perf. 10½*

554-555 A260 Set of 2 1.75 1.25

Taiwan Friendship Bridge A261

2002, Apr. 3 Litho.

556 A261 95col multi 1.00 .75

16th Rio Group Congress A262

2002, Apr. 10

557 A262 65col blue & green .65 .40

Pan-American Health Organization, Cent. — A263

No. 558: a, People (red denomination at UR). b, Emblem. c, Mother and child (black denomination at LR). d, Child and man (red denomination at LR).
50col, Emblem.

2002, July 5

558 A263 10col Block of 4, #a-d .50 .50
559 A263 50col multi .50 .40

In Remembrance of Sept. 11, 2001 Terrorist Attacks — A264

Litho. & Embossed

2002, Sept. 11

560 A264 110col multi 1.10 1.10

Marine Life of Uvita Island A265

Designs: No. 561, 75col, Gorgona flabellum. No. 562, 75col, Ulva lactuca. No. 563, 75col, Cittarium pica. No. 564, 75col, Liriope tetraphyla.

Litho & Embossed

2002, Sept. 25

561-564 A265 Set of 4 4.50 4.50

Space Exploration — A266

No. 565: a, Dr. Franklin Chang-Diaz, astronaut, and space shuttle. b, Phanaeus changdiazi and satellite.
Illustration reduced.

Litho. & Embossed

2003, June 15 *Perf. 10½*

565 A266 115col Horiz. pair, #a-b 1.10 1.10

Coco Island National Park — A267

No. 566: a, Denomination at UR. b, Denomination at UL.
Illustration reduced.

2003, Aug. 1

566 A267 75col Horiz. pair, #a-b .75 .75

America Issue - Fish — A268

No. 567: a, Archocentrus sajica. b, Astatheros diquis.
Illustration reduced.

2003

567 A268 110col Horiz. pair, #a-b 5.00 1.50

Scenes from Cocorí, by Joaquín Gutiérrez — A269

No. 568: a, Boy, turtle, monkey and bird. b, Boy looking at reflection in water. c, Toucan in tree, boy and monkey on ground. d, Sailor, girl and boy. e, Boy, bird on branch. f, Jaguar, turtle armadillo, monkey, boy and father. g, Boy and monkey pushing turtle. h, Monkey with open arms, turtle, boy. i, Mother and boy. j, Mother, boy, rose bush. k, Boy, father playing musical instrument (80x150mm).

Litho. & Embossed

2003, Sept. 3 *Perf. 10½*

568 A269 Sheet of 11 2.40 2.40
a.-j. 25col Any single .20 .20
k. 225col multi 1.10 1.10

National Anthem, Cent. — A270

No. 569: a, Lyricist José Maria Zeledón (24x35mm). b, Flag, text of anthem (49x35mm).

2003, Sept. 10 Litho.

569 A270 75col Horiz. pair, #a-b .75 .75

Election of Pope John Paul II, 25th Anniv. — A271

2003, Oct. 16 Litho. ***Perf. 13¼x13½***
570 A271 130col multi .65 .65

Charles Lindbergh's Flight to Costa Rica, 75th Anniv. — A272

Litho. & Embossed

2003, Dec. 16 ***Perf. 13½x13¼***
571 A272 110col multi .55 .55

Guayabo de Turrialba Archaeological Monument — A273

2003, Dec. 18
572 A273 110col multi .55 .55

America Issue A274

Flora: No. 573, 75col, Ceiba pentandra. No. 574, 75col, Tetranema floribundum. 90col, Ceiba pentandra, diff. 110col, Tetranema gamboanum.

2004, Mar. 23 Litho. ***Perf. 10½***
573-576 A274 Set of 4 1.75 1.75

Volcanoes A275

Designs: 85col, Arenal. 120col, Irazú. 140col, Poás.

2004, June 24
577-579 A275 Set of 3 1.60 1.60

2004 Summer Olympics, Athens A276

No. 580 — Various athletes in: a, Blue. b, Yellow orange. c, Green. d, Red.

2004, July 15
580 Horiz. strip of 4 2.25 2.25
a.-d. A276 120col Any single .55 .55

Dr. Miguel Angel Rodríguez, Organization of American States President A277

2004, Sept. 15
581 A277 120col multi .55 .55

POSTAL-FISCAL STAMPS

From April 1884 through September 1889 revenue stamps were permitted for postal use, when post offices exhausted supplies of regular postage stamps.

Used values are for stamps with postal cancels.

PF1

PF2

1884 Engr. ***Perf. 12***
AR1 PF1 1c rose .50 *5.00*
AR2 PF1 2c light blue *20.00* 5.00

1888
AR3 PF2 5c brown .50 *3.00*
AR4 PF2 10c blue .25 *3.00*

SEMI-POSTAL STAMPS

No. 72 Surcharged in Red

1922 Unwmk. ***Perf. 12***
B1 A56 5c + 5c orange 1.00 .40

Issued for the benefit of the Costa Rican Red Cross Society. In 1928, owing to a temporary shortage of the ordinary 5c stamp, No. B1 was placed on sale as a regular 5c stamp, the surtax being disregarded.

Discus Thrower — SP1

Trophy — SP2

Parthenon SP3

1924 Litho. ***Imperf.***
B2 SP1 5c dark green 1.50 *2.00*
B3 SP2 10c carmine 1.50 *2.00*
B4 SP3 20c dark blue 3.50 *3.00*
a. Tête bêche pair 14.00 *16.00*

Perf. 12
B5 SP1 5c dark green 1.50 *2.00*
B6 SP2 10c carmine 1.50 *2.00*
B7 SP3 20c dark blue 3.00 *3.50*
a. Tête bêche pair 14.00 *16.00*
Nos. B2-B7 (6) 12.50 *14.50*

These stamps were sold at a premium of 10c each, to help defray the expenses of athletic games held at San José in Dec. 1924.

AIR POST STAMPS

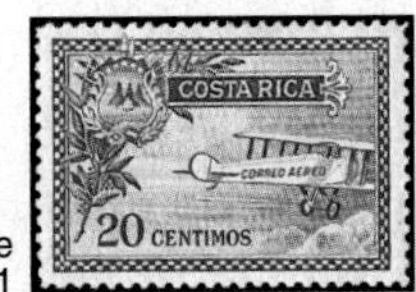

Airplane AP1

Perf. 12½

1926, June 4 Unwmk. Engr.
C1 AP1 20c ultramarine 3.00 .50

No. 123 Overprinted

1930, Mar. 14 ***Perf. 12***
C2 A75 10c carmine rose 2.00 .25

Inverted or double overprints are fakes.

AP3

1930-32 ***Perf. 12½***
C3 AP3 5c on 10c dk brn ('32) .40 .25
C4 AP3 20c on 50c ultra .50 .25
C5 AP3 40c on 50c ultra .60 .25
Nos. C3-C5 (3) 1.50 .75

The existence of genuine inverted or double surcharges of Nos. C3-C5 is in doubt.

Telegraph Stamp Overprinted

1930, Mar. 19
C6 AP3 1col orange 2.00 .50

No. O79 Surcharged in Red

1930, Mar. 11
C7 O7 8c on 1col lilac & blk .60 .50
C8 O7 20c on 1col lilac & blk .90 .50
C9 O7 40c on 1col lilac & blk 1.75 1.50
C10 O7 1col on 1col lilac & blk 2.75 1.50
Nos. C7-C10 (4) 6.00 4.00

AP6

AP7

Red Surcharge on Revenue Stamps

1931-32 ***Perf. 12***
C11 AP6 2col on 2col gray grn 35.00 35.00
C12 AP6 3col on 5col lil brn 35.00 35.00
C13 AP6 5col on 10col gray blk 35.00 35.00
Nos. C11-C13 (3) 105.00 105.00

There were two printings of this issue which were practically identical in the colors of the stamps and the surcharges.

Nos. C11 and C13 have the date "1929" on the stamp, No. C12 has "1930."

Black Overprint on Telegraph Stamp

1932, Mar. 8 ***Perf. 12½***
C14 AP7 40c green 3.00 .30
a. Inverted overprint 30.00

Unofficial "proofs," inverts and double overprints were made from a defaced plate.

Mail Plane about to Land AP8

Allegory of Flight AP9

1934, Mar. 14 ***Perf. 12***
C15 AP8 5c green .20 .20
C16 AP8 10c carmine rose .20 .20
C17 AP8 15c chocolate .35 .20
C18 AP8 20c deep blue .40 .20
C19 AP8 25c deep orange .50 .20
C20 AP8 40c olive blk 1.75 .20
C21 AP8 50c gray blk .85 .20
C22 AP8 60c orange yel 1.50 .20
C23 AP8 75c dull violet 2.75 .45
C24 AP9 1col deep rose 1.50 .20
C25 AP9 2col lt blue 6.00 .90
C26 AP9 5col black 5.00 4.75
C27 AP9 10col red brown 9.00 8.00
Nos. C15-C27 (13) 30.00 15.90

Stamps Nos. C15 to C27 with holes punched through were for use of government officials.

See Nos. C216-C219. For overprints see Nos. C67-C73, C92-C93, C103-C116, CO1-CO13.

Airplane over Poás Volcano — AP10

1937, Feb. 10
C28 AP10 1c black .35 .35
C29 AP10 2c brown .35 .35
C30 AP10 3c dk violet .35 .35
Nos. C28-C30 (3) 1.05 1.05

First Fair of Costa Rica.

Puntarenas — AP11

National Bank AP12

Perf. 12, 12½

1937, Dec. 15 Unwmk.

C31 AP11 2c black gray .20 .20
C32 AP11 5c green .20 .20
C33 AP11 20c deep blue .30 .20
C34 AP11 1.40col olive brn 2.50 2.50
Nos. C31-C34 (4) 3.20 3.10

1938, Jan. 11 Wmk. 229 *Perf. 12½*

C35 AP12 1c purple .20 .20
C36 AP12 3c red orange .20 .20
C37 AP12 10c carmine rose .30 .20
C38 AP12 75c brown 2.50 2.00
Nos. C35-C38 (4) 3.20 2.60

Nos. C31-C38 for the Natl. Products Exposition held at San José, Dec. 1937.

Airport Administration Building, La Sabana — AP13

1940, May 2 Engr. Unwmk.

C39 AP13 5c green .20 .20
C40 AP13 10c rose pink .20 .20
C41 AP13 25c lt blue .20 .20
C42 AP13 35c red brown .20 .20
C43 AP13 60c red org .30 .30
C44 AP13 85c violet 1.40 .90
C45 AP13 2.35col turq grn 6.00 5.50
Nos. C39-C45 (7) 8.50 7.50

Opening of the Intl. Airport at La Sabana.

Duran Sanatorium AP14

Overprinted "Dia Panamericano de la Salud / 2 Diciembre 1940" and Bar in Black

1940, Dec. 2 *Perf. 12*

C46 AP14 10c scarlet .20 .20
C47 AP14 15c purple .20 .20
C48 AP14 25c lt blue .35 .35
C49 AP14 35c bister brn .50 .50
C50 AP14 60c pck green .75 .75
C51 AP14 75c olive 2.00 2.00
C52 AP14 1.35col red org 6.00 6.00
C53 AP14 5col sepia 40.00 40.00
C54 AP14 10col red lilac 125.00 100.00
Nos. C46-C54 (9) 175.00 150.00

Pan-American Health Day. Exist without overprint. Few copies of C53-C54 were sold for postal purposes, nearly all having been obtained by philatelic speculators.

No. 174 Surcharged in Black or Blue

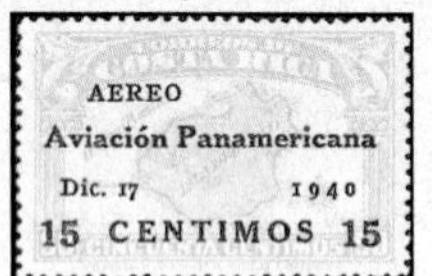

1940, Dec. 17 *Perf. 14*

C55 A95 15c on 50c yel (Bk) .75 .75
C56 A95 30c on 50c yel (Bl) .75 .75

Pan-American Aviation Day, proclaimed by President F. D. Roosevelt.

The 15c surcharge exists normal and inverted on #171, value, normal, $30.

International Soccer Game at National Stadium — AP15

1941, May 8 *Perf. 12*

C57 AP15 15c red .75 .20
C58 AP15 30c dp ultra .85 .25
C59 AP15 40c red brn .85 .35
C60 AP15 50c purple 1.25 .75
C61 AP15 60c brt green 1.50 .85
C62 AP15 75c yel org 2.50 1.40
C63 AP15 1col dull vio 4.25 4.25
C64 AP15 1.40col rose 8.75 8.75
C65 AP15 2col blue grn 20.00 17.50
C66 AP15 5col black 50.00 37.50
Nos. C57-C66 (10) 90.70 71.80

Caribbean and Central American Soccer Championship. See Nos. C121-C123. For surcharges see Nos. C145-C147.

Air Post Stamps of 1934 Overprinted or Surcharged in Black with New Values and Bars

1941, June 2

C67 AP8 5c on 20c dp bl .20 .20
C68 AP8 15c on 20c dp bl .20 .20
C69 AP8 40c on 75c dl vio .35 .20
C70 AP9 65c on 1col dp rose .50 .50
C71 AP9 1.40col on 2col lt bl 3.25 3.00
C72 AP9 5col black 11.00 11.00
C73 AP9 10col red brn 14.50 12.50
Nos. C67-C73 (7) 30.00 27.60

Issued in commemoration of the settlement of the Costa Rica-Panama border dispute.

Nos. C67-C73 are found with hyphen omitted in overprint. Nos. C67-C69 with inverted overprint.

University Types of 1941

1941, Aug. 26 *Perf. 12*

C74 A107 15c salmon .20 .20
C75 A106 30c lt blue .30 .20
C76 A107 40c orange .40 .30
C77 A106 60c turq green .45 .40
C78 A107 1col violet 1.90 1.90
C79 A106 2col black 4.75 4.75
C80 A107 5col sepia 16.00 16.00
Nos. C74-C80 (7) 24.00 23.75

Portrait Type of 1943-47

Designs: 40c, Manuel Aguilar. No. C83, Francisco Morazan. No. C83A, Jose R. De Gallegos. 50c, Jose M. Alfaro. 60c, Francisco M. Oreamuno. 65c, Jose M. Castro. 85c, Juan Rafael Mora. 1col, Jose M. Montealegre. 1.05col, Braulio Carrillo. 1.15col, Jesus Jimenez. 1.40col, Bruno Carranza. 2col, Tomas Guardia.

1943-45 Engr.

C81 A109 10c rose pink .20 .20
C82 A109 40c blue .20 .20
C82A A109 40c car rose .20 .20
C83 A109 45c magenta .30 .20
C83A A109 45c black .20 .20
C84 A109 50c turq grn 1.50 .20
C84A A109 50c red org .30 .20
C85 A109 60c brt ultra .40 .20
C85A A109 60c brt green .20 .20
C86 A109 65c scarlet .75 .20
C86A A109 65c brt ultra .20 .20
C87 A109 85c dp org .90 .30
C87A A109 85c dull pur 1.10 .40
C88 A109 1col black 1.10 .40
C88A A109 1col scarlet .45 .20
C88B A109 1.05col bis brn .60 .40
C89 A109 1.15col red brn 1.50 1.40
C89A A109 1.15col green 2.00 1.10
C90 A109 1.40col dp vio 2.25 1.90
C90A A109 1.40col org yel 1.40 1.25
C91 A109 2col black 3.50 1.10
C91A A109 2col olive grn 1.10 .35
Nos. C81-C91A (22) 20.35 11.00

Issued: #C82A, C83A, C84A, C85A, C86A, C87A, C88A, C88B, C89A, C90A, C91A, 1945.

See #C124-C127, C179-C181. For surcharges see #C154-C158, C182, C184-C185.

Nos. C26-C27 Overprinted in Red or Blue

1943, Sept. 16

C92 AP9 5col black (R) 4.25 3.00
C93 AP9 10col red brown (Bl) 5.00 3.25

Mercury and Plane AP31

1944, Jan. 19

C94 AP31 10c red orange .20 .20
C95 AP31 15c dk carmine .20 .20
C96 AP31 40c brt ultra .30 .20
C97 AP31 45c dp red lil .35 .30
C98 AP31 60c turq green .45 .40
C99 AP31 1col dk red brn 1.00 .80
C100 AP31 1.40col gray blk 7.50 5.00
C101 AP31 5col violet 20.00 15.00
C102 AP31 10col black 70.00 62.50
Nos. C94-C102 (9) 100.00 84.60

City of San Ramón founding, 100th anniv.

Very few copies of the 5col or 10col stamps were sold for postal purposes, nearly all having been obtained by philatelic speculators.

No. CO10 With Additional Overprint in Black

1944, Nov. 22

C103 AP9 1col deep rose 2.00 .35
a. Blue overprint 75.00 75.00

Nos. CO1-CO13 Overprinted in Carmine or Black

1945, Jan. 12 Unwmk. *Perf. 12*

C104 AP8 5c green .60 .50
C105 AP8 10c car rose (Bk) .60 .55
C106 AP8 15c chocolate .60 .55
C107 AP8 20c deep blue .50 .40
C108 AP8 25c dp org (Bk) .60 .60
C109 AP8 40c olive blk .35 .35
C110 AP8 50c gray blk .60 .60
C111 AP8 60c org yel (Bk) .90 .35
C112 AP8 75c dull violet .75 .50
C113 AP9 1col dp rose (Bk) .75 .35
C114 AP9 2col light blue 8.00 4.50
C115 AP9 5col black 8.00 5.50
C116 AP9 10col red brn (Bk) 11.00 8.25
Nos. C104-C116 (13) 33.25 23.00

#C104 exists inverted & overprinted in black. This is probably a trial color. Value, $50.

Catalogue values for unused stamps in this section, from this point to the end of the section, are for Never Hinged items.

AP32

Telegraph Stamps Overprinted in Black or Carmine

1945, Feb. 20 Unwmk. *Perf. 12½*

C117 AP32 40c green (C) .25 .20
C118 AP32 50c ultra (C) .30 .20
C119 AP32 1col orange (Bk) 1.00 .40
Nos. C117-C119 (3) 1.55 .80

#C117 exists with inverted overprint. Value, $10.

Florence Nightingale and Edith Cavell AP33

1945 Engr.

C120 AP33 1col black & car 1.00 .50

Costa Rican Red Cross Soc., 60th anniv

For surcharge see No. C183.

Soccer Type of 1941
Inscribed: "Febrero 1946"

1946, May 13 *Perf. 12*

C121 AP15 25c green 1.00 .60
C122 AP15 30c dull yellow 1.00 .60
C123 AP15 55c deep blue 1.40 .60
Nos. C121-C123 (3) 3.40 1.80

Portrait Type of 1943-47

Designs: 25c, Aniceto Esquivel. 30c, Vicente Herrera. 55c, Prospero Fernandez. 75c, Bernardo Soto.

1946, May 12

C124 A109 25c blue .20 .20
C125 A109 30c red brown .25 .20
C126 A109 55c plum .40 .30
C127 A109 75c blue green .60 .40
Nos. C124-C127 (4) 1.45 1.10

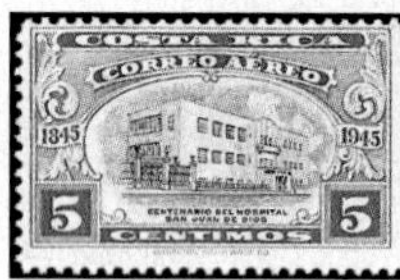

Hospital of St. John of God AP38

1946, June 24 Unwmk. *Perf. 12½*

Center in Black

C128 AP38 5c yellow grn .20 .20
C129 AP38 10c dk brown .20 .20
C130 AP38 15c carmine .20 .20
C131 AP38 25c dk blue .20 .20
C132 AP38 30c dp orange .45 .25
C133 AP38 40c olive grn .20 .20
C134 AP38 50c violet .30 .25
C135 AP38 60c dk sl grn .60 .55
C136 AP38 75c brown .50 .40
a. Horiz. pair, imperf. btwn. 100.00
C137 AP38 1col blue .60 .35
C138 AP38 2col brn org 1.00 .70
C139 AP38 3col dk vio brn 2.00 1.75
C140 AP38 5col yellow 2.50 2.25
Nos. C128-C140 (13) 8.95 7.50

Nos. C128, C129, C132 and C135 exist imperf.

Rafael Iglesias — AP39

3col, Ascensión Esquivel. 5col, Cleto González Viquez. 10col, Ricardo Jiménez Oreamuno.

1947, Jan. 15 Wmk. 215 *Perf. 14*

Center in Black

C141 AP39 2col blue 1.50 1.00
C142 AP39 3col dp car 2.25 1.40
C143 AP39 5col dk green 3.75 1.90
C144 AP39 10col orange 6.50 4.50
Nos. C141-C144 (4) 14.00 8.80

#C141-C144 also exist in a souvenir sheet of 4. Value, $500. The sheet in sepia is a proof and worth less.

Nos. C121-C123 Surcharged in Black

1947, May 5 Unwmk. *Perf. 12*

C145	AP15	15c on 25c green	.90	.75
C146	AP15	15c on 30c dull yel	.90	.75
C147	AP15	15c on 55c dp blue	.90	.75
		Nos. C145-C147 (3)	2.70	2.25

Exist with inverted surcharge.

Columbus in Cariari AP43

1947, May 19 Engr. *Perf. 12½*

Center in Black

C148	AP43	25c green	.25	.20
C149	AP43	30c dp ultra	.25	.20
C150	AP43	40c red orange	.35	.20
C151	AP43	45c violet	.45	.25
C152	AP43	50c brt carmine	.50	.20
C153	AP43	65c brown org	1.40	.70
		Nos. C148-C153 (6)	3.20	1.75

For surcharges see Nos. C178, C220-C223.

Nos. C84A, C85A, C127, C88A, and C88B Surcharged with New Value in Black or Red

1947, June 3 *Perf. 12*

C154	A109	15c on 50c red org	.25	.20
C155	A109	15c on 60c brt grn (R)	.25	.20
C156	A109	15c on 75c bl grn (R)	.25	.20
C157	A109	15c on 1col scar	.30	.20
C158	A109	15c on 1.05col bis brn	.25	.20
		Nos. C154-C158 (5)	1.30	1.00

#C155 is known with black surcharge. Value, $10. #C156 with inverted surcharge. Value, $10.

Early Steam Locomotive — AP44

1947, Nov. 10 *Perf. 12½*

C159	AP44	35c bl grn & blk	2.25	.50

Electric railroad to the Pacific coast, 50th anniv.

Roosevelt Type of Regular Issue

1947, Aug. 26 *Perf. 12*

C160	A122	15c green	.20	.20
C161	A122	30c car rose	.20	.20
C162	A122	45c red brown	.20	.20
C163	A122	65c orange yel	.25	.20
C164	A122	75c blue	.30	.20
C165	A122	1col olive grn	.50	.35
C166	A122	2col black	1.25	1.00
C167	A122	5col scarlet	2.50	2.25
		Nos. C160-C167 (8)	5.40	4.60

For surcharges see Nos. C224-C226.

National Theater AP46

Rafael Iglesias AP47

1948, Jan. 26 *Perf. 12½*

Center in Black

C168	AP46	15c brt ultra	.20	.20
C169	AP46	20c red	.20	.20
C170	AP47	35c dk green	.30	.20
C171	AP46	45c purple	.40	.25
C172	AP46	50c carmine	.40	.25
C173	AP46	75c red violet	.90	.70
C174	AP46	1col olive	1.90	1.10
C175	AP46	2col red brn	3.00	1.50
C176	AP47	5col org yel	4.75	3.00
C177	AP47	10col brt blue	11.00	6.00
		Nos. C168-C177 (10)	23.05	13.40

50th anniversary of National Theater.

No. C150 Surcharged in Carmine

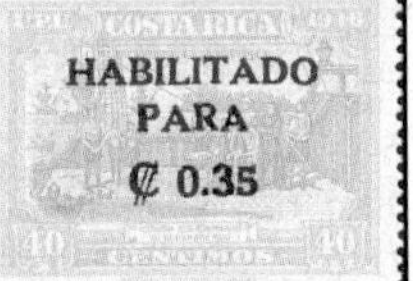

1948, Apr. 21

C178	AP43	35c on 40c	1.10	.45

Exists with surcharge inverted.

Portrait Type of 1943-47

5c, Salvador Lara. 15c, Carlos Duran.

1948 Engr. *Perf. 12*

C179	A109	5c sepia	.20	.20
C180	A109	10c olive brown	.20	.20
C181	A109	15c violet	.20	.20
		Nos. C179-C181 (3)	.60	.60

Nos. C88B, C120, C89A and C90A Surcharged in Carmine or Black

Perf. 12½, 12

1949, Aug. 28 Unwmk.

C182	A109	35c on 1.05col bis brn	.35	.20
C183	AP33	50c on 1col blk & car	.60	.45
a.		2nd & 3rd lines both read "125 Aniversario"	.85	.70
C184	A109	55c on 1.15col grn	.85	.70
C185	A109	55c on 1.40col org yel (Bk)	.90	.60
		Nos. C182-C185 (4)	2.70	1.95

125th anniv. of the annexation of the province of Guanacaste.

Overprint differs on No. C183, with "Guanacaste" in capitals, and lower case "a" in "Anexión."

The variety "I" for "i" in "Anexion" is found on Nos. C182, C184 and C185.

Symbols of UPU AP48

1950, Jan. 11 Photo. *Perf. 11½*

C186	AP48	15c lilac rose	.20	.20
C187	AP48	25c chalky blue	.20	.20
C188	AP48	1col gray green	.30	.20
		Nos. C186-C188 (3)	.70	.60

75th anniv. of the UPU.

Battle of El Tejar, Cartago AP49

Occupation of Limón — AP50

Bull (Cattle Raising) — AP51

25c, Lucha ranch. 35c, Trenches of San Isidro Battalion. 55c, 75c, Observation post. 80c, 1col, Dr. Carlos Luis Valverde.

Inscribed: "Guerra de Liberacion Nacional 1948"

Engraved; Center Photogravure

1950, July 20 *Perf. 12½*

Center in Black

C189	AP49	15c brt car	.20	.20
C190	AP50	20c dull green	.20	.20
C191	AP49	25c dull blue	.30	.20
C192	AP49	35c chestnut	.40	.20
C193	AP49	55c lilac	.70	.20
C194	AP49	75c red org	1.10	.30
C195	AP50	80c gray	1.10	.50
C196	AP50	1col org yel	1.50	.55
		Nos. C189-C196 (8)	5.50	2.35

2nd anniv. of the War for Natl. Liberation.

Inscribed: "Feria Nacional Agricola Ganadera e Industrial Cartago 1950"

1950, July 27

1c, 10c, 2col, Bull. 2c, 30c, 3col, Tuna fishing. 3c, 65c, Pineapple. 5c, 50c, 5col, Bananas. 45c, 80c, 10col, Coffee picker.

Center in Black

C197	AP51	1c brt green	.20	.20
C198	AP51	2c brt blue	.20	.20
C199	AP51	3c chocolate	.20	.20
C200	AP51	5c dp ultra	.20	.20
C201	AP51	10c green	.20	.20
C202	AP51	30c purple	.20	.20
C203	AP51	45c vermilion	.20	.20
C204	AP51	50c blue gray	.35	.20
C205	AP51	65c dk blue	.40	.20
C206	AP51	80c dp rose	.85	.60
C207	AP51	2col org yel	2.25	1.60
C208	AP51	3col blue	6.25	4.00
C209	AP51	5col carmine	7.25	6.00
C210	AP51	10col dp claret	7.25	6.00
		Nos. C197-C210 (14)	26.00	20.00

National Agricultural, Livestock and Industrial Fair, Cartago, 1950.

For surcharge see No. RA1.

Queen Isabella I and Caravels of Columbus AP52

Unwmk.

1952, Mar. 4 Engr. *Perf. 13*

C211	AP52	15c carmine	.25	.20
C212	AP52	20c orange	.45	.20
C213	AP52	25c ultra	.70	.20
C214	AP52	55c dp green	2.25	.25
C215	AP52	2col violet	4.75	.45
		Nos. C211-C215 (5)	8.40	1.30

Birth of Queen Isabella I of Spain, 500th anniv.

Mail Plane Type of 1934

1952-53 *Perf. 12*

C216	AP8	5c blue	.30	.20
C217	AP8	10c green	.30	.20
C218	AP8	15c car rose ('53)	.40	.20
C219	AP8	35c purple	1.00	.20
		Nos. C216-C219 (4)	2.00	.80

#C216-C217 were reprinted in 1953 in different shades. Values the same.

Nos. C149-C151, C153 Surcharged in Red: "HABILITADO PARA CINCO CENTIMOS 1953"

1953, Apr. 24 *Perf. 12½*

Center in Black

C220	AP43	5c on 30c dp ultra	1.00	.85
C221	AP43	5c on 40c red org	.20	.20
C222	AP43	5c on 45c vio	.20	.20
C223	AP43	5c on 65c brn org	.20	.20
		Nos. C220-C223 (4)	1.60	1.45

Nos. C161-C163 Surcharged in Black

1953, Apr. 11 *Perf. 12*

C224	A122	15c on 30c car rose	.25	.20
C225	A122	15c on 45c red brn	.25	.20
C226	A122	15c on 65c org yel	.25	.20
		Nos. C224-C226 (3)	.75	.60

Refinery of Vegetable Oils and Fats — AP53

Industries: 10c, Pottery. 15c, Sugar. 20c, Soap. 25c, Lumber. 30c, Matches. 35c, Textiles. 40c, Leather. 45c, Tobacco. 50c, Preserving. 55c, Canning. 60c, General. 65c, Metals. 75c, Pharmaceuticals. 80c, Pharmaceuticals. 1col, Paper. 2col, Rubber. 3col, Airplane maintenance. 5col, Marble. 10col, Beer.

Engraved; Center Photogravure

1954-59 Unwmk. *Perf. 13x12½*

Center in Black

C227	AP53	5c red	.20	.20
C228	AP53	10c dk blue	.20	.20
C229	AP53	15c green	.20	.20
C230	AP53	20c violet	.20	.20
C231	AP53	25c magenta	.20	.20
C232	AP53	30c purple	.50	.30
C233	AP53	35c red vio	.20	.20
C234	AP53	40c black	.50	.30
C235	AP53	45c dk green	.90	.30
C236	AP53	50c vio brown	.60	.20
C237	AP53	55c yellow	.45	.20
C238	AP53	60c brown	1.10	.55
C239	AP53	65c carmine	1.40	.80
C240	AP53	75c violet	2.10	.65
C240A	AP53	80c pur & gray	1.10	.65
C241	AP53	1col blue	.60	.30
a.		Imperf., pair	90.00	
C242	AP53	2col rose pink	1.90	1.00
C243	AP53	3col ol grn	2.75	1.50
C244	AP53	5col black	4.00	1.25
C245	AP53	10col yellow	12.00	8.00
		Nos. C227-C245 (20)	31.10	17.20

Issued: 30c, 35c, 60c, 65c, 75c, 2col, 3col, Oct. 20; 80c, Oct. 2, 1959; others, Sept. 1.

See #C252-C255. For surcharges and overprint see #C314-C315, C334-C336, RA2, RA11.

Globe, Rotary Emblem AP54

Map of Costa Rica AP55

25c, Hand protecting boy. 40c, 2col, Hospital. 45c, Globe & palm leaves. 60c, Lighthouse.

1956, Feb. 7 Engr. *Perf. 12*

C246	AP54	10c green	.20	.20
C247	AP54	25c dk blue	.20	.20
C248	AP54	40c dk brown	.35	.25
C249	AP54	45c brt red	.25	.20
C250	AP54	60c dk red vio	.30	.25
C251	AP54	2col yel org	1.25	.50
		Nos. C246-C251 (6)	2.55	1.60

50th anniv. of Rotary Intl. (in 1955).

Industries Type of 1954

Designs as in 1954.

Engraved; Center Photogravure

1956, Feb. 17 ***Perf. 12***

Center in Black

C252 AP53 5c ultra .25 .20
C253 AP53 10c violet blue .25 .20
C254 AP53 15c orange yel .25 .20
C255 AP53 75c red orange .45 .30
Nos. C252-C255 (4) 1.20 .90

1957, June 21 Engr. ***Perf. 13½x13***

10c, Map of Guanacaste. 15c, Inn. 20c, House of Santa Rosa. 25c, Gen. Jose Manuel Quiros. 30c, Old Presidential Palace. 35c, Joaquin Bernardo Calvo. 40c, Luis Molina. 45c, Gen. Jose Joaquin Mora. 50c, Gen. Jose Maria Canas. 55c, Juan Santamaria monument. 60c, National monument. 65c, Antonio Vallerriestra. 70c, Ramon Castilla y Marquesado. 75c, San Carlos fortress. 80c, Francisco Maria Oreamuno. 1col, Pres. Juan Rafael Mora.

C256 AP55 5c lt blue .20 .20
C257 AP55 10c green .20 .20
C258 AP55 15c dp orange .20 .20
C259 AP55 20c lt brown .25 .20
C260 AP55 25c vio blue .25 .20
C261 AP55 30c violet .35 .20
C262 AP55 35c car rose .35 .20
C263 AP55 40c slate .35 .20
C264 AP55 45c rose red .40 .20
C265 AP55 50c ultra .45 .20
C266 AP55 55c ocher .85 .20
C267 AP55 60c brt car .65 .25
C268 AP55 65c carmine .75 .25
C269 AP55 70c orange yel .95 .30
C270 AP55 75c emerald .85 .30
C271 AP55 80c dk brown 1.10 .35
C272 AP55 1col black 1.25 .35
Nos. C256-C272 (17) 9.40 4.00

Centenary of War of 1856-57.

Cleto Gonzalez Viquez — AP56

Highway and Gonzalez Viquez AP57

Designs: 10c, Ricardo Jimenez Oreamuno. 20c, Puntarenas wharf and Jimenez. 35c, Post and Telegraph Bldg. and Jimenez. 55c, Pipeline and Gonzalez Viquez. 80c, National Library and Gonzalez Viquez. 1col, Electric train and Jimenez. 2col, Gonzales and Jimenez.

1959, Nov. 23 Engr. ***Perf. 13½***

C274 AP56 5c car & ultra .20 .20
C275 AP56 10c red & gray .20 .20

Perf. 13½x13

C276 AP57 15c dk bl grn & blk .20 .20
C277 AP57 20c car & brn .40 .20
C278 AP57 35c rose lil & bl .20 .20
C279 AP57 55c olive & vio .40 .20
C280 AP57 80c ultra .50 .30
C281 AP57 1col orange & mar .75 .45
C282 AP57 2col gray & mar 1.75 1.40
Nos. C274-C282 (9) 4.60 3.35

For surcharge and overprint see #C337, C339.

Soccer AP58

Designs: Various soccer scenes.

Perf. 13½

1960, Mar. 7 Unwmk. Photo.

C283 AP58 10c black .20 .20
C284 AP58 25c ultra .20 .20
C285 AP58 35c red orange .25 .25
C286 AP58 50c red brown .30 .25
C287 AP58 85c Prus green .75 .60
C288 AP58 5col dp claret 1.60 1.60
Nos. C283-C288 (6) 3.30 3.10

Souvenir Sheet

Imperf

C289 AP58 2col blue 4.60 4.50

3rd Pan-American Soccer Games, San José, Mar. 1960.
Nos. C283-C288 exist imperf.

WRY Uprooted Oak Emblem — AP59

1960, Apr. 7 Unwmk. ***Perf. 11½***

Granite Paper

C290 AP59 35c vio bl, blk & yel .30 .25
C291 AP59 85c black & brt pink .60 .50

Refugee Year, July 1, 1959-June 30, 1960.

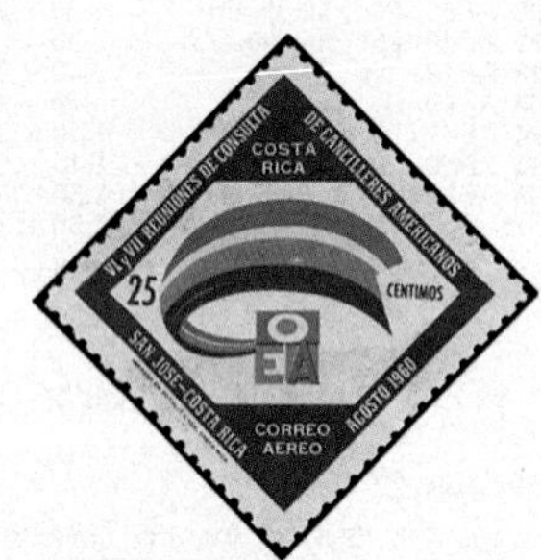

Banner and "OEA" — AP60

35c, "OEA" in oval. 55c, Clasped hands. 2col, "OEA" & map of Americas. 5col, Flags forming bird. 10col, Map of Costa Rica, flags & "OEA."

1960, Aug. 15 Litho. ***Perf. 10***

C292 AP60 25c black & multi .20 .20
a. Multi, impression sideways 45.00
C293 AP60 35c multicolored .30 .30
a. Pair, imperf. between 45.00
C294 AP60 55c multicolored .50 .40
C295 AP60 5col multicolored 3.00 2.75
C296 AP60 10col black & multi 5.00 4.00
Nos. C292-C296 (5) 9.00 7.65

Souvenir Sheet

Imperf

C297 AP60 2col multicolored 2.75 2.75

Pan-American Conf., San Jose, Aug. 15.

St. Louisa de Marillac and Orphanage — AP61

St. Vincent de Paul — AP62

25c, St. Vincent & old seminary. 50c, St. Louisa & sickroom. 1col, St. Vincent & new seminary.

1960, Oct. 26 Engr. ***Perf. 14x13½***

C298 AP61 10c green .20 .20
C299 AP61 25c carmine .20 .20
C300 AP61 50c dk blue .20 .20
C301 AP61 1col brown org .40 .30
C302 AP62 5col brown 2.00 1.60
Nos. C298-C302 (5) 3.00 2.50

St. Vincent (1581?-1660) and St. Louisa (1591-1660). Exist imperf.

Runner AP63

Sports: 2c, Woman swimmer. 3c, Bicyclist. 4c, Weight lifter. 5c, Woman tennis player. 10c, Boxers. 25c, Soccer player. 85c, Basketball player. 1col, Baseball batter. 5col, Romulus and Remus statue. 10col, Pistol marksman.

Perf. 13½x14

1960, Dec. 14 Photo. Unwmk.

Designs in Black

C303 AP63 1c brt yellow .20 .20
C304 AP63 2c lt ultra .20 .20
C305 AP63 3c dp rose .20 .20
C306 AP63 4c yellow .20 .20
C307 AP63 5c brt yel grn .20 .20
C308 AP63 10c pink .20 .20
C309 AP63 25c lt bl grn .20 .20
C310 AP63 85c lilac 1.10 .75
C311 AP63 1col gray 1.25 .95
C312 AP63 10col lt violet 10.00 7.25
Nos. C303-C312 (10) 13.75 10.35

Souvenir Sheets

Perf. 14x13½

C313 AP63 5col multi 5.50 5.50

17th Olympic Games, Rome, 8/25-9/11.
Nos. C303-C313 exist imperf.

No. C255 Surcharged and Overprinted in Blue or Ultramarine: "XV Campeonato Mundial de Beisbol de Aficionados"

Engraved and Photogravure

1961, Apr. 21 ***Perf. 12***

Center in Black

C314 AP53 25c on 75c red org (Bl) .25 .20
C315 AP53 75c red orange (U) .55 .20

15th Amateur Baseball Championships.

Alberto Brenes C. AP64

Miguel Obregon AP65

#C317, Manuel Aguilar. #C318, Agustin Gutierrez L. #C319, Vicente Herrera.

1961, June 12 Photo. ***Perf. 12***

C316 AP64 10c deep claret .25 .20
C317 AP64 10c blue .25 .20
C318 AP64 25c bright violet .25 .20
C319 AP64 25c gray .25 .20
Nos. C316-C319 (4) 1.00 .80

First Continental Congress of Lawyers, San José, June 11-15. Exist imperf.
See Nos. C330-C333.

1961, July 19 Litho. ***Perf. 13½***

C320 AP65 10c Prussian green .20 .20

Birth centenary of Prof. Miguel Obregon L. Exists imperf. Value $90.

UN Food and Agriculture Organization AP66

UN day (UN Organizations): 20c, WHO. 25c, ILO. 30, ITU. 35c, World Meteorological Organization. 45c, UNESCO. 85c, ICAO. 5col, "United Nations" holding the world. 10col, Int. Bank for Reconstruction and Development.

Perf. 11½

1961, Oct. 24 Unwmk. Engr.

C321 AP66 10c lt green .20 .20
C322 AP66 20c orange .20 .20
C323 AP66 25c Prus grn .20 .20
C324 AP66 30c dk blue .20 .20
C325 AP66 35c carmine rose .85 .20
C326 AP66 45c violet .30 .20
C327 AP66 85c blue .65 .50
C328 AP66 10col dk sl grn 4.75 4.00
Nos. C321-C328 (8) 7.35 5.70

Souvenir Sheet

Imperf

C329 AP66 5col ultra 3.00 3.00

For overprint see No. C338.

Portrait Type of 1961

#C330, Dr. José Maria Soto Alfaro. #C331, Dr. Elias Rojas Roman. #C332, Dr. Andres Saenz Llorente. #C333, Dr. Juan José Ulloa Giralt.

1961 Photo. ***Perf. 13½***

C330 AP64 10c blue green .25 .20
C331 AP64 10c violet .25 .20
C332 AP64 25c dark gray .25 .20
C333 AP64 25c deep claret .25 .20
Nos. C330-C333 (4) 1.00 .80

9th Congress of Physicians of Central America and Panama.

Nos. C229, C236 and C280 Surcharged in Black, Orange or Red

Engraved; Center Photogravure

1962 ***Perf. 13x12½, 13½x13***

C334 AP53 10c ("10") on 15c .20 .20
C334A AP53 10c ("c0.10") on 15c (R) .20 .20
C335 AP53 25c on 15c .20 .20
C336 AP53 35c on 50c (O) .25 .20

Engr.

C337 AP57 85c on 80c (R) .70 .55
Nos. C334-C337 (5) 1.55 1.35

No. C336 exists with double surcharge. Value, $25.

Nos. C324 and C282 Overprinted in Red: "II CONVENCION FILATELICA CENTROAMERICANA SETIEMBRE 1962"

1962, Sept. 12 ***Perf. 11½, 13½x13***

C338 AP66 30c dark blue .50 .40
C339 AP57 2col gray & mar 1.50 1.10

2nd Central American Phil. Convention.

Revenue Stamp Surcharged with New Values and "CORREO AEREO" in Red

1962 Engr. ***Perf. 12***

C341 A124 25c on 2c emer .20 .20
C342 A124 35c on 2c emer .20 .20
C343 A124 45c on 2c emer .25 .20
C344 A124 85c on 2c emer .45 .40
Nos. C341-C344 (4) 1.10 1.00

Arms and Malaria Eradication Emblem AP67

1963, Feb. 14 Photo. ***Perf. 11½***

C345 AP67 25c brt rose .20 .20
C346 AP67 35c brown org .25 .20
C347 AP67 45c ultra .30 .25
C348 AP67 85c blue grn .60 .40
C349 AP67 1col dk blue 1.00 .50
Nos. C345-C349 (5) 2.35 1.55

WHO drive to eradicate malaria.

Central American Tapir — AP68

Designs: 5c, Paca. 25c, Jaguar. 30c, Ocelot. 35c, Whitetail deer. 40c, Manatee. 85c, White-throated capuchin monkey. 5col, White-lipped peccary.

Perf. 13½

1963, May Unwmk. Photo.

C354	AP68	5c yel ol & brn	.25	.20
C355	AP68	10c orange & sl	.25	.20
C356	AP68	25c blue & yel	.40	.20
C357	AP68	30c lt yel grn & brn	.60	.35
C358	AP68	35c bis & red brn	.90	.35
C359	AP68	40c emer & sl bl	1.10	.50
C360	AP68	85c green & blk	3.50	.50
C361	AP68	5col gray grn & choc	10.50	3.50
		Nos. C354-C361 (8)	17.50	5.80

Stamp of 1863 and Packet "Monarch" — AP69

Issue of 1863 and: 2col, Recaredo Bonilla Carrillo, Postmaster, 1862-63. 3col, Burros, overland mail transport, 1839. 10col, Burro railway car.

1963, June 26 Litho.

C362	AP69	25c dl rose & chlky bl	.25	.20
C363	AP69	2col gray bl & org	1.60	1.10
C364	AP69	3col bister & emer	2.75	1.75
C365	AP69	10col dl grn & ocher	9.75	5.00
		Nos. C362-C365 (4)	14.35	8.05

Centenary of Costa Rica's stamps.

No. C362 is inscribed "William Le Lacheur," the builder and captain of the "Monarch."

Souvenir Sheets

Stamps of 1863 and San José Postmark — AP70

Perf. 13½, Imperf.

1963, June 26 Unwmk.

C366	AP70	5col bl, red, grn & org	4.25	4.25

Cent. of Costa Rica's stamps.

In 1968 copies of No. C366 were overprinted "2-4 Agosto 1968" and "III Exposicion Filatelica Nacional / 'Costa Rica 68'." Value, each $10.

Animal Type of 1963 Surcharged in Red

#C367, Little anteater. #C368, Gray fox. #C369, Armadillo. #C370, Great anteater.

1963, Sept. 14 Photo. *Perf. 13½*

C367	AP68	10c on 1c brt grn & org brn	1.00	.25
C368	AP68	25c on 2c org yel & ol grn	1.00	.25
C369	AP68	35c on 3c bluish grn & brn	1.25	.25
C370	AP68	85c on 4c dp rose & dk brn	2.50	.50
		Nos. C367-C370 (4)	5.75	1.25

Copies of #C370 exist without surcharge.

Pres. Kennedy AP71

Ancestral Figure AP72

Portraits- Presidents: 25c, Francisco J. Orlich, Costa Rica. 30c, Julio A. Rivera, El Salvador. 35c, Miguel Ydigoras F., Guatemala. 85c, Dr. Ramon Villeda M., Honduras. 1col, Luis A. Somoza, Nicaragua. 3col, Roberto F. Chiari, Panama.

1963, Dec. 7 Unwmk. *Perf. 14*
Portraits in Black Brown

C371	AP71	25c violet brn	.20	.20
C372	AP71	30c brt lil rose	.20	.20
C373	AP71	35c ocher	.20	.20
C374	AP71	85c gray blue	.30	.20
C375	AP71	1col orange brn	.35	.25
C376	AP71	3col lt ol grn	1.50	1.50
C377	AP71	5col gray	2.25	2.25
		Nos. C371-C377 (7)	5.00	4.80

Meeting of Central American Presidents with Pres. John F. Kennedy, San José, Mar. 18-20, 1963.

1963-64 Photo. *Perf. 12*

Ancient Art: 5c, Dog, horiz. 10c, Ornamental stool, horiz. 25c, Male figure. 30c, Ceremonial dancer. 35c, Ceramic vase. 50c, Frog. 55c, Bell. 75c, Six-limbed figure. 85c, Seated man. 90c, Bird-shaped jug. 1col, Twin human beaker, horiz. 2col, Alligator, horiz. 3col, Twin-tailed lizard. 5col, Figure under arch. 10col, Polished stone figure.

C378	AP72	5c lt yel grn & Prus grn	.20	.20
C379	AP72	10c buff & dk grn	.20	.20
C380	AP72	25c rose & dk brn	.20	.20
C381	AP72	30c ocher & Prus grn ('64)	.25	.20
C382	AP72	35c sal & sl grn	.25	.20
C383	AP72	45c lt bl & dk brn	.25	.20
C384	AP72	50c dl bl & dk brn	.35	.20
C385	AP72	55c yel grn & dk brn	.50	.20
C386	AP72	75c ocher & dk red brn	.50	.20
C387	AP72	85c yel & red brn	1.25	1.25
C388	AP72	90c cit & red brn	1.60	1.60
C389	AP72	1col lt bl & dk brn	.95	.30
C390	AP72	2col buff & dk grn	1.50	.60
C391	AP72	3col yel grn & dk brn	5.00	.90
C392	AP72	5col cit & sep	5.00	5.00
C393	AP72	10col rose lil & sl grn	8.00	8.00
		Nos. C378-C393 (16)	26.00	19.45

For surcharges and overprint see Nos. C395, C397-C398, C400, C426-C428.

Flags of Central American States — AP73

Alfredo Gonzalez F. — AP74

1964 *Perf. 14*

C394	AP73	30c bl, gray, red & blk	.75	.25

Central American Independence issue. For surcharge see No. C396.

Nos. C381, C394 and C387 Surcharged

1964, Oct. *Perf. 12, 14*

C395	AP72	5c on 30c	.50	.25
C396	AP73	15c on 30c	.50	.25
C397	AP72	15c on 85c	.50	.25
		Nos. C395-C397 (3)	1.50	.75

No. C388 Surcharged: "C 0.15 / CONFERENCIA POSTAL / DE PARIS - 1864"

1964 *Perf. 12*

C398	AP72	15c on 90c cit & red brn	.25	.20

Paris Postal Conference.

1965, June Photo. *Perf. 12*

C399	AP74	35c dk blue green	*3.00*	.25

50th anniv. of the National Bank and honoring Alfredo Gonzalez F., 1st governor of the bank.

No. C390 Overprinted: "75 ANIVERSARIO / ASILO CHAPUI / 1890-1965"

1965, Aug. 14 Unwmk. *Perf. 12*

C400	AP72	2col buff & dk grn	1.25	.60

75th anniv. of Chapui Asylum, San José.

Girl, FAO Emblem and Hands Holding Grain — AP75

Church of Nicoya — AP76

FAO Emblem and: 15c, Map of Costa Rica and silos, horiz. 50c, World population chart and children. 1col, Plane over map of Costa Rica, horiz.

1965 Litho. *Perf. 14*

C401	AP75	15c lt brn & blk	.25	.20
C402	AP75	35c black & yel	.25	.20
C403	AP75	50c ultra & dk grn	.25	.20
C404	AP75	1col grn, blk & sil	.40	.25
		Nos. C401-C404 (4)	1.15	.85

FAO "Freedom from Hunger" campaign.

1965, Dec. 20 *Perf. 13½x14*

5c, Leonidas Briceno B. 15c, Scroll dated "25 de Julio de 1964." 35c, Map of Guanacaste and Nicoya peninsula. 50c, Dancing couple. 1col, Map showing local products.

C405	AP76	5c red brn & blk	.35	.20
C406	AP76	10c blue & gray	.35	.20
C407	AP76	15c bis & slate	.35	.20
C408	AP76	35c blue & slate	.35	.20
C409	AP76	50c gray & vio bl	.50	.20
C410	AP76	1col buff & slate	1.10	.35
		Nos. C405-C410 (6)	3.00	1.35

Acquisition of the Nicoya territory.

Runner and Olympic Rings AP77

Pres. Kennedy Speaking in San José Cathedral AP78

Olympic Rings and Emblem: 10c, Bicyclists. 40c, Judo. 65c, Basketball. 80c, Soccer. 1col, Hands holding torches, and Mt. Fuji.

1965, Dec. 23 *Perf. 13x13½*

C411	AP77	5c bister & multi	.20	.20
C412	AP77	10c lt lil & multi	.20	.20
C413	AP77	40c multicolored	.20	.20
C414	AP77	65c lemon & multi	.25	.20
C415	AP77	80c tan & multi	.35	.20
C416	AP77	1col multicolored	.45	.30
	a.	Souvenir sheet of 2	3.00	3.00
		Nos. C411-C416 (6)	1.65	1.30

18th Olympic Games, Tokyo, Oct. 10-25, 1964. No. C416a contains two 1col stamps, one like No. C416, the other with gray background replacing yellow orange.

#C416a was issued both perf and imperf. Same values.

#C411-C416 exist imperf.

Perf. 13½x13, 13x13½

1965, Dec. 23 Litho. Unwmk.

Designs: 45c, Friendship 7 capsule circling globe, and Kennedy, horiz. 85c, Kennedy and John, Jr. 1col, Curtis-Lee Mansion and flame from Kennedy grave, Arlington, Va.

C417	AP78	45c brt bl & lil	.25	.20
C418	AP78	55c org & brt bl	.30	.20
C419	AP78	85c gray, dk brn & red brn	.50	.30
C420	AP78	1col multicolored	.60	.40
	a.	Souvenir sheet of 2	1.10	1.10
		Nos. C417-C420 (4)	1.65	1.10

President John F. Kennedy (1917-63). No. C420a contains two 1col stamps, one like No. C420, the other with green background replacing dark blue. Exists with light blue background instead of green; value $150.

#C420a was issued both perf and imperf. Same values.

#C417-C420 exist imperf.

For surcharges see Nos. C429-C430.

Firemen with Hoses — AP79

Designs: 5c, Fire engine "Knox," horiz. 10c, 1866 fire pump. 35c, Fireman's badge. 50c, Emblem and flags of Confederation of Central American Fire Brigades.

1966, Mar. 12 Litho. *Perf. 11*

C421	AP79	5c black & red	.30	.20
C422	AP79	10c bister & red	.35	.20
C423	AP79	15c blk, red brn & red	.55	.20
C424	AP79	35c black & yel	.90	.25
C425	AP79	50c dk blue & red	1.90	.35
		Nos. C421-C425 (5)	4.00	1.20

Centenary of San José Fire Brigade.

Nos. C381, C383, C386 and C418-C419 Surcharged

a

b

1966 Photo. *Perf. 12*

C426	AP72(a)	15c on 30c	.20	.20
C427	AP72(a)	15c on 45c	.20	.20
C428	AP72(a)	35c on 75c	.20	.20

Litho. *Perf. 13x13½*

C429	AP78(a)	35c on 55c	.20	.20
C430	AP78(b)	50c on 85c	.35	.20
		Nos. C426-C430 (5)	1.15	1.00

Revenue Stamps (Basic Type of A124) Surcharged

1966, Dec. Engr. *Perf. 12*

C431 A124 15c on 5c blue .20 .20
C432 A124 35c on 10c claret .25 .20
C433 A124 50c on 20c rose red .35 .25
Nos. C431-C433 (3) .80 .65

Central Bank of Costa Rica — AP80

1967, Mar. Litho. *Perf. 11*

C434 AP80 5c brt green .25 .20
C435 AP80 15c brown .25 .20
C436 AP80 35c scarlet .25 .20
Nos. C434-C436 (3) .75 .60

Power Lines — AP81

Telecommunications Building, San Pedro — AP82

Electrification Program: 15c, Telephone Central. 25c, La Garita Dam. 35c, Rio Mache Reservoir. 50c, Cachi Dam.

1967, Apr. 24 Litho. *Perf. 11*

C437 AP81 5c dark gray .25 .20
C438 AP82 10c brt rose .25 .20
C439 AP81 15c brown org .25 .20
C440 AP82 25c brt ultra .25 .20
C441 AP81 35c brt green .25 .20
C442 AP82 50c red brown .30 .25
Nos. C437-C442 (6) 1.55 1.25

Chondrorhyncha Aromatica AP83

Institute Emblem AP84

Orchids: 10c, Miltonia endresii. 15c, Stanhopea cirrhata. 25c, Trichopilia suavis. 35c, Odontoglossum schlieperianum. 50c, Cattleya skinneri. 1col, Cattleya dowiana. 2col, Odontoglossum chiriquense.

1967, June 15 Engr. *Perf. 13x13½*
Orchids in Natural Colors

C443 AP83 5c multicolored .20 .20
C444 AP83 10c olive & multi .35 .20
C445 AP83 15c multicolored .35 .20
C446 AP83 25c multicolored .80 .20
C447 AP83 35c dull vio & multi .80 .20
C448 AP83 50c brown & multi 1.00 .20
C449 AP83 1col vio & multi 2.75 .75
C450 AP83 2col dk ol bis & multi 4.25 1.50
Nos. C443-C450 (8) 10.50 3.45

Issued for the University Library.

1967, Oct. 6 Litho. *Perf. 13x13½*

C451 AP84 50c vio bl, lt bl & bl .25 .20

Inter-American Agriculture Institute, 25th anniv.

Church of Solitude — AP85

LACSA Emblem — AP86

Costa Rican Churches: 10c, Basilica of Santo Domingo, Heredia. 15c, Cathedral of Tilaran. 25c, Cathedral of Alajuela. 30c, Mercy Church. 35c, Basilica of Our Lady of Angels. 40c, Church of St. Raphael, Heredia. 45c, Ujarras ruins. 50c, Ruins of parish church, Cartago. 55c, Cathedral of San José. 65c, Parish church, Puntarenas. 75c, Church of Orosi. 80c, Cathedral of St. Isidro, the General. 85c, St. Ramon Church. 90c, Church of the Abandoned. 1col, Coronado Church. 2col, Church of St. Teresita. 3col, Parish Church, Heredia. 5col, Carmelite Church. 10col, Limon Cathedral.

1967, Dec. 15 Engr. *Perf. 12½*

C452 AP85 5c green .20 .20
C453 AP85 10c blue .20 .20
C454 AP85 15c lilac .20 .20
C455 AP85 25c dull yel .20 .20
C456 AP85 30c orange brn .20 .20
C457 AP85 35c lt blue .25 .20
C458 AP85 40c dp orange .25 .20
C459 AP85 45c dl bl grn .25 .20
C460 AP85 50c olive .30 .20
C461 AP85 55c brown .30 .20
C462 AP85 65c car rose .55 .25
C463 AP85 75c sepia .60 .30
C464 AP85 80c yellow 1.10 .40
C465 AP85 85c violet blk 1.25 .40
C466 AP85 90c emerald 1.25 .60
C467 AP85 1col slate 1.00 .30
C468 AP85 2col brt green 4.75 1.65
C469 AP85 3col orange 6.75 2.75
C470 AP85 5col vio blue 6.75 2.75
C471 AP85 10col carmine 8.75 4.00
Nos. C452-C471 (20) 35.10 15.40

Nos. C452 and C454 exist imperf; Nos. C455 and C470 exist imperf horiz.

See Nos. C561-C576.

Perf. 13x13½, 13½x13
1967, Dec. 12 Litho. & Engr.

45c, LACSA emblem, jet, horiz. 50c, Decorated wheel, anniversary emblem.

C472 AP86 40c ultra, grnsh bl & gold .25 .20
C473 AP86 45c blk, pale grn, ultra & gold .25 .20
C474 AP86 50c blue & multi .25 .20
Nos. C472-C474 (3) .75 .60

20th anniv. (in 1966) of Lineas Aereas Costaricenses, LACSA, Costa Rican Airlines.

Scout Directing Traffic AP87

Runner AP88

Designs: 25c, Campfire under palm tree. 35c, Flag of Costa Rica, Scout flag and emblem. 50c, Encampment, horiz. 65c, Photograph of first Scout troop, horiz.

1968, Mar. 15 *Perf. 13*

C475 AP87 15c lt bl, blk & lt brn .20 .20
C476 AP87 25c lt ultra, vio bl & org .25 .20
C477 AP87 35c blue & multi .35 .20
C478 AP87 50c multicolored .60 .30
C479 AP87 65c sal, dk bl & brn .75 .35
Nos. C475-C479 (5) 2.15 1.25

Costa Rican Boy Scouts, 50th anniversary.

1968, Jan. 17 Litho. *Perf. 10x11*

Sports: 40c, Women's running. 55c, Boxing. 65c, Bicycling. 75c, Weight lifting. 1col, High diving. 3col, Rifle shooting.

C481 AP88 30c multi .20 .20
C482 AP88 40c multi .20 .20
C483 AP88 55c multi .25 .20
C484 AP88 65c lil & multi .30 .20
C485 AP88 75c multi .30 .20
C486 AP88 1col multi .35 .25
C487 AP88 3col multi 1.50 .90
Nos. C481-C487 (7) 3.10 2.15

19th Olympic Games, Mexico City, 10/12-27.

Philatelic Exhibition Emblem — AP89

1969, June 5 Litho. *Perf. 11x10*

C488 AP89 35c multicolored .20 .20
C489 AP89 40c pink & multi .20 .20
C490 AP89 50c lt blue & multi .25 .20
C491 AP89 2col multicolored .90 .50
Nos. C488-C491 (4) 1.55 1.10

4th Natl. Philatelic Exhib., San José, 6/5-8.

ILO Emblem AP90

1969, Oct. 29 Litho. *Perf. 10*

C492 AP90 35c bl grn & blk .25 .20
C493 AP90 50c scarlet & blk .25 .20

50th anniv. of the ILO.

Soccer — AP91

Stylized Crab — AP92

Designs: 65c, Soccer ball, map of North and Central America. 85c, Soccer player. 1col, Two players in action.

1969, Nov. 23 Litho. *Perf. 11x10*

C494 AP91 65c gray & multi .30 .20
C495 AP91 75c multicolored .30 .20
C496 AP91 85c multicolored .35 .30
C497 AP91 1col pink & multi .50 .35
Nos. C494-C497 (4) 1.45 1.05

Issued to publicize the 4th Soccer Championships (CONCACAF), Nov. 23-Dec. 7.

1970, May 14 Litho. *Perf. 12½*

C498 AP92 10c blk & lil rose .25 .20
C499 AP92 15c blk & yel .25 .20
C500 AP92 50c blk & brn org .25 .20
C501 AP92 1.10col blk & emer .50 .20
Nos. C498-C501 (4) 1.25 .80

10th Inter-American Cancer Cong., 5/22-29.

Costa Rica No. 124, Magnifying Glass and Stamps — AP93

2col, Father, son with stamps, album.

1970, Sept. 14 Litho. *Perf. 11*

C502 AP93 1col ultra, brn & car rose .95 .20
C503 AP93 2col blk, pink & ultra 1.10 .50

The 5th National Philatelic Exhibition.

EXPO Emblem and Costa Rican Cart — AP94

EXPO Emblem and: 10c, Japanese floral arrangement, vert. 35c, Pavilion and Tower of the Sun. 40c, Japanese tea ceremony. 45c, Woman picking coffee, vert. 55c, Earth seen from moon, vert.

1970, Oct. 22 Litho. *Perf. 13x13½*

C504 AP94 10c multicolored .20 .20
C505 AP94 15c green & multi .20 .20
C506 AP94 35c blue & multi .35 .20
C507 AP94 40c gray & multi .50 .20
C508 AP94 45c multicolored .50 .20
C509 AP94 55c black & multi .50 .20
Nos. C504-C509 (6) 2.25 1.20

EXPO '70 International Exhibition, Osaka, Japan, Mar. 15-Sept. 13.

Escazu Valley, by Margarita Bertheau — AP95

Paintings: 25c, "Irazu," by Rafael A. Garcia, vert. 80c, Shore landscape, by Teodorico Quiros. 1col, "The Other Face," by Cesar Valverde. 2.50col, Mother and Child, by Luis Daell, vert.

1970, Nov. 4 Litho. *Perf. 12½*

C510 AP95 25c multi .75 .30
C511 AP95 45c multi .75 .30
C512 AP95 80c multi 1.10 .55
C513 AP95 1col multi 1.10 .60
C514 AP95 2.50col multi 2.40 2.00
Nos. C510-C514 (5) 6.10 3.75

Arms of Costa Rica, 1964 — AP96

COSTA RICA
2
COLONES
CORREO AEREO

National Theater AP97

Various Coats of Arms, dated: 10c, Nov. 27, 1906. 15c, Sept. 29, 1848. 25c, Apr. 21, 1840. 35c, Nov. 22, 1824. 50c, Nov. 2, 1824. 1col, Mar. 6, 1824. 2col, May 10, 1823.

1971, Feb. 10 Litho. *Perf. 14x13½*

C515 AP96 5c buff & multi .35 .20
C516 AP96 10c multi .35 .20
C517 AP96 15c yel & multi .45 .20
C518 AP96 25c pink & multi .45 .20
C519 AP96 35c multi .60 .20
C520 AP96 50c rose & multi .70 .20
C521 AP96 1col beige & multi .75 .40
C522 AP96 2col multi 1.50 .80
Nos. C515-C522 (8) 5.15 2.40

1971, Apr. 14 Litho. *Perf. 11*

C523 AP97 2col plum .40 .30

Organization of American States meeting.

José Matias Delgado, Manuel José Arce AP98

Flag of Costa Rica — AP99

Independence Leaders: 10c, Miguel Larreinaga and Manuel Antonio de la Cerda, Nicaragua. 15c, José Cecilio del Valle, Dionisio de Herrera, Honduras. 35c, Pablo Alvarado and Florencio del Castillo, Costa Rica. 50c, Antonio Larrazabal and Pedro Molina, Guatemala. 2col, Costa Rica coat of arms.

1971, Sept. 14 ***Perf. 13***

C524 AP98 5c multi .20 .20
C525 AP98 10c multi .20 .20
C526 AP98 15c gray, brn & blk .20 .20
C527 AP98 35c multi .20 .20
C528 AP98 50c multi .20 .20
C529 AP99 1col multi .20 .20
C530 AP99 2col multi .40 .40
Nos. C524-C530 (7) 1.60 1.60

Central American independence, sesqui.

Soccer Federation Emblem — AP100

Children of the World — AP101

1971, Dec. 6

C531 AP100 50c multi .30 .20
C532 AP100 60c multi .30 .20

50th anniv. of Soccer Federation of Costa Rica.

1972, Jan. 11 ***Perf. 12½***

C533 AP101 50c multi .25 .20
C534 AP101 1.10col red & multi .40 .25

25th anniv. (in 1971) of UNICEF.

Tree of Guanacaste AP102

Designs: 40c, Hermitage, Liberia. 55c, Petroglyphs, Rincón Brujo. 60c, Painted head, sculpture from Curubandé, vert.

1972, Feb. 28 ***Perf. 11***

C535 AP102 20c brn, ol & brt grn .35 .20
C536 AP102 40c brn & ol .35 .20
C537 AP102 55c blk & brn .35 .20
C538 AP102 60c blk, buff & ver .35 .20
Nos. C535-C538 (4) 1.40 .80

Bicentenary of the founding of the city of Liberia, Guanacaste.

Farm and Family — AP103

Inter-American Exhibitions AP104

Designs: 45c, Cattle, dairy products and meat, horiz. 50c, Kneeling figure with plant. 10col, Farmer and map of Americas.

1972, June 30 **Litho.** ***Perf. 12½***

C539 AP103 20c multi .30 .20
C540 AP103 45c multi .30 .20
C541 AP103 50c dp yel, grn & blk .30 .20
C542 AP103 10col brn, org & blk 2.40 1.75
Nos. C539-C542 (4) 3.30 2.35

30th anniversary of the Inter-American Institute of Agricultural Sciences.

1972, Aug. 26 **Litho.** ***Perf. 13***

C543 AP104 50c orange & brn .20 .20
C544 AP104 2col blue & vio .40 .30

4th Interamerican Philatelic Exhibition, EXFILBRA, Rio de Janeiro, Aug. 26-Sept. 2.

First Book Printed in Costa Rica — AP105

Intl. Book Year: 50c, 5col, Natl. Library, horiz.

1972, Dec. 7 **Litho.** ***Perf. 12½***

C545 AP105 20c brt blue .35 .20
C546 AP105 50c gold & multi .35 .20
C547 AP105 75c multicolored .35 .20
C548 AP105 5col multicolored 1.75 .95
Nos. C545-C548 (4) 2.80 1.55

Road to Irazú Volcano AP106

1972-73 ***Perf. 11x11½, 11½x11***

C549 AP106 5c like 20c .30 .20
C550 AP106 15c Coco-Culebra Bay .30 .20
C551 AP106 20c shown .30 .20
C552 AP106 25c like 15c .30 .20
C553 AP106 40c Manuel Antonio Beach .30 .20
C554 AP106 45c Tourist Office emblem .30 .20
C555 AP106 50c Lindora Lake .30 .20
C556 AP106 60c San Jose P.O., vert. .30 .20
C557 AP106 80c like 40c .35 .20
C558 AP106 90c like 45c .35 .20
C559 AP106 1col like 50c .35 .20
C560 AP106 2col like 60c .65 .45
Nos. C549-C560 (12) 4.10 2.65

Tourism year of the Americas.
Issued: 20c, 25c, 80c, 90c, 1col, 2col, 12/26; others, 3/21/73.
No. C555 exists with inverted center, used only.

Church Type of 1967

Designs as before.

1973, July 16 **Engr.** ***Perf. 12½***

C561 AP85 5c slate grn .20 .20
C562 AP85 10c olive .20 .20
C563 AP85 15c orange .20 .20
C564 AP85 25c brown .20 .20
C565 AP85 30c rose claret .20 .20
C566 AP85 35c violet .20 .20
C567 AP85 40c brt green .20 .20
C568 AP85 45c dull yellow .20 .20
C569 AP85 50c rose magenta .20 .20
C570 AP85 55c blue .25 .20
C571 AP85 65c black .30 .20
C572 AP85 75c rose red .30 .20
C573 AP85 80c yellow grn .30 .20
C574 AP85 85c lilac .35 .25
C575 AP85 90c brt pink .35 .25
C576 AP85 1col dark blue .35 .25
Nos. C561-C576 (16) 4.00 3.35

Human Rights Flame — AP107

OAS Emblem — AP108

1973, Dec. 10 **Photo.** ***Perf. 10½***

C577 AP107 50c black & red .25 .20

25th anniversary of the Universal Declaration of Human Rights.

1973, Dec. 17 **Litho.** ***Perf. 10½***

C578 AP108 20c dk bl & dp car .25 .20

25th anniv. of the OAS.

Joaquin Vargas Calvo — AP109

AP110

1974, Jan. 14

C579 AP109 20c shown .35 .20
C580 AP109 20c Alejandro Monestel .35 .20
C581 AP109 20c Julio Mata .35 .20
C582 AP109 60c Julio Fonseca .35 .20
C583 AP109 2col Rafael A. Chaves .80 .30
C584 AP109 5col Manuel M. Gutierrez 1.90 1.10
Nos. C579-C584 (6) 4.10 2.20

Costa Rican composers honored by the National Symphony Orchestra.

Revenue Stamps Overprinted "Habilitado para Correo Aereo"

1974, Apr. 5 **Engr.** ***Perf. 12***

C585 AP110 50c brown .20 .20
C586 AP110 1col violet .30 .20
C587 AP110 2col orange .70 .35
C588 AP110 5col olive 1.60 1.60
Nos. C585-C588 (4) 2.80 2.35

Telephone Building, San Pedro — AP111

EXFILMEX 74 Emblem AP112

Designs: 65c, Rio Macho Control, horiz. 85c, Turbines, Rio Macho Center. 1.25col, Cachi Dam and reservoir, horiz. 2col, I.C.E. Headquarters.

1974, July 30 **Litho.** ***Perf. 10½***

C589 AP111 50c gold & multi .20 .20
C590 AP111 65c gold & multi .25 .20
C591 AP111 85c gold & multi .30 .20
C592 AP111 1.25col gold & multi .35 .20
C593 AP111 2col gold & multi .75 .30
Nos. C589-C593 (5) 1.85 1.10

25th anniversary of Costa Rican Electrical Institute (I.C.E.).

1974, Aug. 22 ***Perf. 13***

C594 AP112 65c green .20 .20
C595 AP112 3col lilac rose .60 .40

5th Inter-American Philatelic Exhibition, EXFILMEX-74 UPU, Mexico City, Oct. 26-Nov. 3.

Map of Costa Rica, 4-S Emblem AP113

50c, Young harvesters and 4-S emblem.

1974, Oct. 7 **Litho.** ***Perf. 12x11***

C596 AP113 20c brt green .35 .20
C597 AP113 50c multicolored .35 .20

25th anniversary of 4-S Clubs of Costa Rica (similar to US 4-H Clubs).

Roberto Brenes Mesen — AP114

"Life Insurance" AP115

Designs: 85c, "Love and Death," manuscript. 5col, Hands of writer, horiz.

1974, Oct. 14 **Litho.** ***Perf. 10½***

C598 AP114 20c black & brn .20 .20
C599 AP114 85c black & red .25 .20
C600 AP114 5col black & red brn 1.50 .85
Nos. C598-C600 (3) 1.95 1.25

Mesen, educator & writer, birth centenary.

1974, Oct. 30 ***Perf. 14***

Designs: 20c, Ricardo Jiménez Oreamuno and Tomás Soley Güell, horiz. 50c, Harvest Insurance (hand holding shovel), horiz. 85c, Maritime insurance (hand holding paper boat). 1.25col, INS emblem. 2col, Workers rehabilitation (arm with crutch). 2.50col, Workers' Compensation (hand holding wrench). 20col, Fire insurance (hands protecting house).

C601 AP115 20c multi .20 .20
C602 AP115 50c multi .20 .20
C603 AP115 65c multi .20 .20
C604 AP115 85c multi .20 .20
C605 AP115 1.25col multi .30 .20
C606 AP115 2col multi .55 .25
C607 AP115 2.50col multi .60 .40
C608 AP115 20col multi 3.75 3.75
Nos. C601-C608 (8) 6.00 5.40

Costa Rican Insurance Institute (Instituto Nacional de Seguros, INS), 50th anniversary.
For surcharges see Nos. C721-C722.

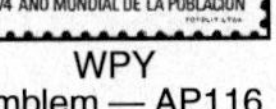

WPY Emblem — AP116

Oscar J. Pinto F. — AP117

1974, Nov. 13 Litho. *Perf. 11x11½*

C609 AP116 2col vio bl & red .45 .25

World Population Year.

1974, Dec. 2 *Perf. 13*

Designs: 50c, Alberto Montes de Oca D., champion sharpshooter. 1col, Eduardo Garnier, sports promoter. O. J. Pinto, introducer of soccer.

C610 AP117 20c gray & dk bl .20 .20
C611 AP117 50c gray & dk bl .20 .20
C612 AP117 1col gray & dk bl .45 .20
Nos. C610-C612 (3) .85 .60

First Central American Olympic Games, held in Guatemala, 1973.

Mormodes Buccinator AP118

Masdevallia Ephippium AP119

Designs: Orchids.

1975, Mar. 7 Litho. *Perf. 10½, 13½*

C613 AP118 25c *shown* .60 .20
C614 AP118 25c *Gongora clavi-odora* .60 .20
C615 AP119 25c *shown* .60 .20
C616 AP119 25c *Encyclia spondiadum* .60 .20
a. Block of 4, #C613-C616 2.40 1.00
b. As "a," perf. 10½ 1.60
C617 AP118 65c *Lycaste skinneri alba* 1.50 .20
C618 AP118 65c *Peristeria elata* 1.50 .20
C619 AP119 65c *Miltonia roezelii* 1.50 .20
C620 AP119 65c *Brassavola digbyana* 1.50 .20
a. Block of 4, #C617-C620, perf. 13½ 6.00 2.00
b. As "a," perf. 10½ 16.00
C621 AP118 80c *Epidendrum mirabile* 2.00 .30
C622 AP118 80c *Barkeria lindleyana* 2.00 .30
C623 AP119 80c *Cattleya skinneri* 2.00 .30
C624 AP119 80c *Sobralia macrantha* 2.00 .30
a. Block of 4, #C621-C624 8.00 2.50
b. As "a," perf. 10½ 10.00
C625 AP118 1.40col *Lycaste cruenta* 2.50 .35
C626 AP118 1.40col *Oncidium obryzatum* 2.50 .35
C627 AP119 1.40col *Gongora armeniaca* 2.50 .35
C628 AP119 1.40col *Sievekingia suavis* 2.50 .35
a. Block of 4, #C625-C628 8.00 4.00
b. As "a," perf. 10½ 8.00

Perf. 13½

C629 AP118 1.75col *Hexisea imbricata* 1.50 .35
C630 AP118 2.15col *Warcewiczella discolor* 1.50 .50
C631 AP119 2.50col *Oncidium kramerianum* 2.50 1.00
C632 AP119 3.25col *Cattleya dowiana* 3.00 1.25
Nos. C613-C632 (20) 34.90 7.30

5th National Orchid Exhibition.

Nos. C613-C628 were printed in both perforations on two different papers: dull finish and shiny. Nos. C629-C632 were printed on shiny paper.

Most copies of Nos. C617-C620, perf 10½, were surcharged.

For overprints and surcharges see Nos. C715-C720, C723-C728.

Radio Club Emblem AP120

Members' Flags and Emblem — AP121

Design: 2col, Federation emblem.

1975, Apr. 16 Litho. *Perf. 13½*

C633 AP120 1col blk & red lil .45 .20
C634 AP121 1.10col multi .55 .20
C635 AP120 2col black & bl .90 .25
Nos. C633-C635 (3) 1.90 .65

16th Central American Radio Amateurs' Convention, San José, May 2-4.

Nicoya Beach AP122

Designs: 75c, Driving cattle. 1col, Colonial Church, Nicoya. 3col, Savannah riders, vert.

1975, Aug. 1 Litho. *Perf. 13½*

C636 AP122 25c gray & multi .20 .20
C637 AP122 75c gray & multi .25 .20
C638 AP122 1col gray & multi .30 .20
C639 AP122 3col gray & multi .90 .75
Nos. C636-C639 (4) 1.65 1.35

Sesqui. of annexation of Nicoya District.

Costa Rica #158 AP123

Designs (Type A90 of 1932): No. C641, #159. No. C642, #160. No. C643, #161.

1975, Aug. 14 Litho. *Perf. 12*

C640 AP123 2.20col blk & org .40 .35
C641 AP123 2.20col blk & dk grn .40 .35
C642 AP123 2.20col blk & car rose .40 .35
C643 AP123 2.20col blk & dk bl .40 .35
a. Block of 4, #C640-C643 3.00 3.00

6th Natl. Phil. Exhib., San José, Aug. 14-17.

For surcharges see Nos. C885-C892.

IWY Emblem AP124

1975, Oct. 9 Litho. *Perf. 10½*

C644 AP124 40c vio bl & red .20 .20
C645 AP124 1.25col blk & ultra .35 .20

International Women's Year 1975.

UN Emblem AP125

UN, 30th Anniv.: 60c, UN General Assembly, horiz. 1.20col, UN Headquarters, NY.

1975, Oct. 24 *Perf. 12*

C646 AP125 10c bl & blk .20 .20
C647 AP125 60c multi .20 .20
C648 AP125 1.20col multi .20 .20
Nos. C646-C648 (3) .60 .60

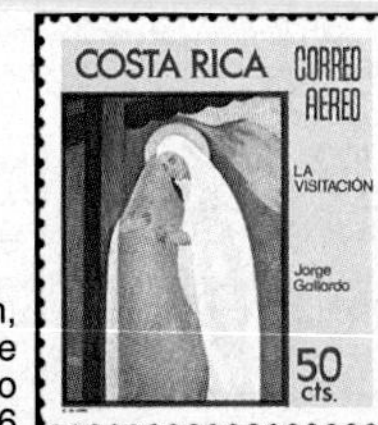

The Visitation, by Jorge Gallardo AP126

"20-30" Club Emblem — AP127

Paintings by Jorge Gallardo: 1col, Nativity and Star. 5col, St. Joseph in his Workshop, Virgin and Child.

1975, Nov. 3 *Perf. 10½*

C649 AP126 50c multi .30 .20
C650 AP126 1col multi .45 .20
C651 AP126 5col multi 1.60 .70
Nos. C649-C651 (3) 2.35 1.10

Christmas 1975.

1976, Jan. 16 Litho. *Perf. 12*

C652 AP127 1col multi .25 .20

"20-30" Club of Costa Rica, 20th anniv.

Quercus Brenessi Trel — AP128

"Literary Development" AP129

Plants: 30c, Maxillaria albertii schecht. 55c, Calathea brenesii standl. 2col, Brenesia costaricensis schlecht. 10col, Philodendron brenesii standl.

1976, Mar. 1 *Perf. 10½*

C653 AP128 5c multi .45 .20
C654 AP128 30c multi .45 .20
C655 AP128 55c multi .45 .20
C656 AP128 2col tan & multi .90 .35
C657 AP128 10col multi 4.00 2.40
Nos. C653-C657 (5) 6.25 3.35

Prof. Alberto Manuel Brenes Mora, botanist, birth centenary.

1976, Apr. 9 Litho. *Perf. 16*

Designs: 1.10col, Man holding book, stylized. 5col, Costa Rican flag emanating from book, horiz.

C658 AP129 15c multi .20 .20
C659 AP129 1.10col multi .20 .20
C660 AP129 5col multi .90 .70
Nos. C658-C660 (3) 1.30 1.10

Publishing in Costa Rica.

Postrider, 1839 — AP130

Costa Rica No. 13, Post Office AP131

Designs: 65c, Costa Rica No. 14 and Post Office. 85c, Costa Rica No. 15 and Post Office. 2col, UPU Monument, Bern, vert.

1976, May 24 *Perf. 10½*

C661 AP130 20c apple grn & blk .30 .20
C662 AP131 50c bister & multi .30 .20
C663 AP131 65c multi .30 .20
C664 AP131 85c multi .30 .20
C665 AP130 2col blk & lt bl .75 .40
Nos. C661-C665 (5) 1.95 1.20

Cent. of UPU (in 1974).

Nos. C662-C664 exist without the surcharges on reproductions of Nos. 13-15.

Telephones, 1876 and 1976 — AP132

Designs: 2col, Wall telephone. 5col, Alexander Graham Bell.

1976, June 28

C666 AP132 1.60col lt bl & blk .35 .20
C667 AP132 2col multicolored .45 .20
C668 AP132 5col yellow & blk 1.10 .90
Nos. C666-C668 (3) 1.90 1.30

Centenary of first telephone call by Alexander Graham Bell, Mar. 10, 1876.

Inverted Center Stamp of 1901 and Association Emblems — AP133

Design: 5col, 1901 stamp between Costa Rican Philatelic Society and Interamerican Philatelic Federation emblems.

1976, Nov. 11 Litho. *Perf. 10½*

C669 AP133 50c multi .20 .20
C670 AP133 1col multi .20 .20
C671 AP133 2col multi .35 .20
Nos. C669-C671 (3) .75 .60

Souvenir Sheet

Perf. 12

C672 AP133 5col multi 2.40 2.40

7th Natl. Phil. Exhib. and 9th Plenary Assembly of the Interamerican Phil. Fed. (FIAF), San José, Nov. 1976.

No. C672 was issued both perf and imperf. Same values.

No. C670 exists in colors of No. C671.

"Seeing Eye" and Map of Costa Rica
AP134

Amadeo Quiros Blanco — AP135

1976, Nov. 22 ***Perf. 16***

C673 AP134 35c black & blue	.20	.20
C674 AP135 2col multicolored	.50	.35

General Audit Office, 25th anniversary.

Nurse Attending Child — AP136

LACSA Circling Globe — AP137

1.10col, National Children's Hospital, horiz.

1976, Nov. 29

C675 AP136 90c multi	.25	.20
C676 AP136 1.10col multi	.35	.25

5th Panamerican Congress of Pediatric Surgery and 12th Congress of Pediatrics.

1976, Dec. 1 ***Perf. 10½***

Designs: 1.20col, Route map. 3col, LACSA emblem and Costa Rican flag.

C677 AP137 1col multi	.25	.20
C678 AP137 1.20col multi	.35	.20
C679 AP137 3col multi	1.00	.60
Nos. C677-C679 (3)	1.60	1.00

Costa Rican Air Lines (LACSA), 30th anniversary.

Boston Tea Party
AP138

US Bicent.: 5col, Declaration of Independence. 10col, Ringing Liberty Bell to announce Independence, vert.

1976, Dec. 24

C680 AP138 2.20col multi	.35	.30
C681 AP138 5col multi	.90	.70
C682 AP138 10col multi	1.75	1.40
Nos. C680-C682 (3)	3.00	2.40

Tree of Guanacaste
AP139

Felipe J. Alvarado
AP140

Designs (Rotary Emblem and): 60c, Dr. Paul Blanco Cervantes Hospital, horiz. 3col, Map of Costa Rica, horiz. 10col, Paul Harris.

1977, Mar. 31 **Litho.** ***Perf. 16***

C683 AP139 40c multi	.20	.20
C684 AP140 50c multi	.20	.20
C685 AP139 60c multi	.20	.20
C686 AP139 3col multi	.90	.50
C687 AP140 10col multi	3.00	2.10
Nos. C683-C687 (5)	4.50	3.20

Rotary Club of San José, 50th anniversary.

Boruca Cloth
AP141

Design: 1.50col, Painted wood ornament.

1977, Feb. 22

C688 AP141 75c multi	.20	.20
C689 AP141 1.50col multi	.30	.20

Natl. Artisan & Small Industry Program.

Juana Pereira
AP142

Alonso de Anguciana de Gamboa
AP143

Designs: 1col, First Church of Our Lady of the Angels, horiz. 1.10col, Our Lady of the Angels (gold sculpture). 1.25col, Crown of Our Lady of the Angels.

1977, June 6 **Litho.** ***Perf. 10½***

C690 AP142 50c multi	.20	.20
C691 AP142 1col multi	.20	.20
C692 AP142 1.10col multi	.20	.20
C693 AP142 1.25col multi	.25	.20
Nos. C690-C693 (4)	.85	.80

50th anniv. of the coronation of Our Lady of the Angels, patron saint of Costa Rica.

1977, July 4 **Litho.** ***Perf. 10½***

Designs: 75c, Church of Esparza. 1col, Statue of Our Lady of Candlemas. 2col, Statue of Diego de Artieda y Chirino.

C694 AP143 35c multi	.20	.20
C695 AP143 75c multi	.20	.20
C696 AP143 1col multi	.30	.20
C697 AP143 2col multi	.55	.30
Nos. C694-C697 (4)	1.25	.90

400th anniv. of the founding of Esparza.
For surcharge see No. C883.

CARE Emblem and Child — AP144

1col, CARE emblem and soybeans, horiz.

1977, Sept. 14 **Litho.** ***Perf. 16***

C698 AP144 80c multi	.25	.20
C699 AP144 1col multi	.35	.20

20th anniversary of CARE (relief organization) in Costa Rica.

Institute's Emblem — AP145

First Map of Americas, 1540 — AP146

1977, Oct. 21 **Litho.** ***Perf. 16***

C700 AP145 50c blk & multi	.45	.20
C701 AP146 1.40col blk & multi	.90	.35

Hispanic Cultural Institute of Costa Rica, 25th anniversary.

Mercy Church, by Ricardo Ulloa B.
AP147

Health Ministry Emblem
AP148

Paintings: 1col, Christ, by Floria Pinto de Herrero. 5col, St. Francis and the Birds, by Louisa Gonzalez Y Saenz.

1977, Nov. 9 **Litho.** ***Perf. 10½***

C702 AP147 50c multi	.35	.20
C703 AP147 1col multi	.35	.20
C704 AP147 5col multi	1.60	.70
Nos. C702-C704 (3)	2.30	1.10

1977, Nov. 16 ***Perf. 16***

C705 AP148 1.40col multi	.35	.20

Creation of Ministry of Health.

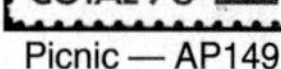

Picnic — AP149

San Martin — AP150

Designs: 50c, Weaver. 2col, Beach scene. 5col, Fruit and vegetable market. 10col, Swans on lake.

1978, Mar. 21 **Litho.** ***Perf. 10½***

C706 AP149 50c blk & multi	.20	.20
C707 AP149 1col blk & multi	.20	.20
C708 AP149 2col blk & multi	1.00	.20
C709 AP149 5col blk & multi	1.90	.75
C710 AP149 10col blk & multi	1.90	1.90
Nos. C706-C710 (5)	5.20	3.25

Conf. of Latin American Tourist Organizations.

1978, Aug. 7 **Litho.** ***Perf. 10½***

C711 AP150 5col multi	1.25	.65

Gen. José de San Martin (1778-1850), soldier and statesman, fought for South American independence.

Geographical Institute Emblem — AP151

University Federation Emblem — AP152

1978, Aug. 28 **Litho.** ***Perf. 12½***

C712 AP151 5col multi	1.10	.60

Pan-American Geography and History Institute, 50th anniversary. Exists imperf.

1978, Sept. 18 ***Perf. 11***

C713 AP152 80c ultra	.25	.20

Central American University Federation, 30th anniversary.

Emblems — AP153

1978, Oct. 24 ***Perf. 16***

C714 AP153 2col aqua, blk & gold	.50	.35

6th Interamerican Philatelic Exhibition, Argentina 78, Buenos Aires, Oct. 1978.

Nos. C629-C631 Overprinted: "50 Aniversario del / primer vuelo de PAN AM / en Costa Rica / 1928-1978"

1978, Nov. 1 **Litho.** ***Perf. 13½***

C715 AP118 1.75col multi	.45	.30
C716 AP118 2.15col multi	.60	.30
C717 AP119 2.50col multi	.80	.40
Nos. C715-C717 (3)	1.85	1.00

1st Pan Am flight in Costa Rica, 50th anniv.

Nos. C629-C631 Overprinted: "50 Aniversario de la / visita de Lindbergh a / Costa Rica 1928-1978"

1978, Nov. 1

C718 AP118 1.75col multi	1.25	.30
C719 AP118 2.15col multi	1.40	.35
C720 AP119 2.50col multi	1.75	.45
Nos. C718-C720 (3)	4.40	1.10

50th anniversary of Lindbergh's visit.

Nos. C603 and C607 Surcharged with New Value, 4 Bars and: "Centenario del / Asilo Carlos / Maria Ulloa / 1878-1978"

1978, Nov. 8 ***Perf. 14***

C721 AP115 50c on 65c multi	.20	.20
C722 AP115 2col on 2.50col multi	.50	.25

Asilo Carlos Maria Ulloa, birth centenary.

No. C617-C620, C630-C631 Surcharged with New Value and 4 Bars

Perf. 10½, 13½

1978, Nov. 13 **Litho.**

C723 AP118 50c on 65c	.50	.50
C724 AP118 50c on 65c	.50	.50
C725 AP119 50c on 65c	.50	.50
C726 AP119 50c on 65c	.50	.50
a. Block of 4, #C723-C726	2.00	2.00
C727 AP118 1.20col on 2.15col	1.25	.50
C728 AP119 2col on 2.50col	1.25	.50
Nos. C723-C728 (6)	4.50	3.00

#C723-C726, perf. 13½, value *$20*, unused, *$10*, used, each. #C726a, unused, *$350*.

Star over Map of Costa Rica — AP154

"Flying Men," Chorotega AP155

1978, Nov. 13 *Perf. 10½*

C729	AP154	50c blue & blk	.20	.20
C730	AP154	1col rose lil & blk	.20	.20
C731	AP154	5col orange & blk	1.25	.60
a.		Strip of 3, #C729-C731	1.75	1.75

Christmas 1978. #C729-C731 printed in sheets of 100 and se-tenant in sheet of 15 (3x5).

1978, Nov. 20 *Perf. 11½*

Designs: 1.20col, Oviedo giving his History of Indies to Duke of Calabria, horiz. 10col, Lord of Oviedo's coat of arms.

C732	AP155	85c multi	.20	.20
C733	AP155	1.20col blk & lt bl	.20	.20
C734	AP155	10col multi	1.90	1.90
		Nos. C732-C734 (3)	2.30	2.30

500th birth anniv. of Gonzalo Fernandez de Oviedo, 1st chronicler of Spanish Indies.

Msgr. Domingo Rivas AP156

San José Cathedral AP157

1978, Dec. 6 *Perf. 16, 13½ (20col)*

C735	AP156	1col black & indigo	.20	.20
C736	AP157	20col multicolored	3.50	3.25

Centenary of the Cathedral of San José.

View of Coco Island AP158

Designs: 2.10, 3, 5 col, various views of Coco Island. 10col, Installation of memorial plaque, people and flag. 5, 10col vert.

1979, Apr. 30 **Litho.** *Perf. 10½*

C737	AP158	90c multi	.20	.20
C738	AP158	2.10col multi	.90	.35
C739	AP158	3col multi	1.25	.45
C740	AP158	5col multi	1.90	1.75
C741	AP158	10col multi	3.75	3.75
a.		Souv. sheet, #C737-C741	15.00	15.00
		Nos. C737-C741 (5)	8.00	6.50

Visit of Pres. Rodrigo Carazo Odio to Coco Island, June 24, 1978, in the interest of national defense.

No. C741a exists imperf.

Shrimp AP159

Designs: 85c, Mahogany snapper. 1.80col, Corvina. 3col, Crayfish. 10col, Tuna.

1979, May 14 **Litho.** *Perf. 13½*

C742	AP159	60c multi	.20	.20
C743	AP159	85c multi	.20	.20
C744	AP159	1.80col multi	.45	.20
C745	AP159	3col multi	.65	.40
C746	AP159	10col multi	2.50	2.50
		Nos. C742-C746 (5)	4.00	3.50

Marine life protection.

Hungry Nestlings, IYC Emblem AP160

Microwave Transmitters, Mt. Irazu AP161

1979, May 24 *Perf. 11*

C747	AP160	1col multi	.50	.20
C748	AP160	2col multi	1.50	1.00
C749	AP160	20col multi	10.00	5.00
		Nos. C747-C749 (3)	12.00	6.20

International Year of the Child.

1979, June 28 **Litho.** *Perf. 14*

Design: 1col, Arenal Dam, horiz.

C750	AP161	1col multi	.20	.20
C751	AP161	5col multi	1.00	.60

Costa Rican Electricity Institute, 30th anniversary.

Costa Rica No. 1 and Rowland Hill AP162

Design: 10col, Penny Black and Hill.

1979, July 16 *Perf. 13*

C752	AP162	5col lil rose & bl gray	1.10	.50
C753	AP162	10col dl bl & blk	2.25	1.00

Sir Rowland Hill (1795-1879), originator of penny postage.

Poverty, by Juan Ramon Bonilla AP163

National Sculpture Contest: 60c, Hope, by Hernan Gonzalez. 2.10col, Cattle, by Victor M. Bermudez, horiz. 5col, Bust of Clorito Picado, by Juan Rafael Chacon. 20col, Mother and Child, by Francisco Zuniga.

1979, July 16 **Litho.** *Perf. 12*

C754	AP163	60c multi	.20	.20
C755	AP163	1col multi	.20	.20
C756	AP163	2.10col multi	.50	.25
C757	AP163	5col multi	1.40	1.10
C758	AP163	20col multi	4.50	2.25
		Nos. C754-C758 (5)	6.80	4.00

Danaus Plexippus — AP164

Butterflies: 1col, Phoebis philea. 1.80col, Rothschildia. 2.10col, Prepona omphale. 2.60col, Marpesia marcella. 4.05col, Morpho cypris.

1979, Aug. 31 **Litho.** *Perf. 13½*

C759	AP164	60c multi	*2.00*	.30
C760	AP164	1col multi	*4.00*	.30
C761	AP164	1.80col multi	*6.00*	.50
C762	AP164	2.10col multi	*8.00*	1.00
C763	AP164	2.60col multi	*8.00*	2.00
C764	AP164	4.05col multi	*12.00*	3.00
		Nos. C759-C764 (6)	*40.00*	7.10

SOS Emblem, Houses AP165

Children's Drawings: 5col, 5.50col, Landscapes, diff.

1979, Sept. 18

C765	AP165	2.50col multi	.50	.35
C766	AP165	5col multi	1.10	.70
C767	AP165	5.50col multi	1.50	1.10
		Nos. C765-C767 (3)	3.10	2.15

SOS Children's Villages, 30th anniversary.

President Type of 1943

Presidents of Costa Rica: 60c, Rafael Iglesias C. 85c, Ascension Esquivel Ibarra. 1col, Cleto Gonzalez Viquez. 2col, Ricardo Jimenez Oreamuno.

1979, Oct. 8 **Litho.** *Perf. 13½*

C768	A109	10c dk blue	.20	.20
C769	A109	60c dull purple	.20	.20
C770	A109	85c red orange	.25	.20
C771	A109	1col red orange	.30	.20
C772	A109	2col brown	.60	.30
a.		Strip of 5, #C768-C772	1.40	1.10
		Nos. C768-C772 (5)	1.55	1.10

Printed in sheets of 100 and se-tenant in sheets of 25 (5x5).

See Nos. C790-C794.

Holy Family, Creche AP167

Reforestation AP168

1979, Nov. 16 **Litho.** *Perf. 12½*

C773	AP167	1col multi	.25	.20
C774	AP167	1.60col multi	.65	.25

Christmas 1979.

1980, Jan. 14 **Litho.** *Perf. 11*

C775	AP168	1col multi	.20	.20
C776	AP168	3.40col multi	.55	.40

Anatomy Lesson, by Rembrandt AP169

1980, Feb. 7 **Litho.** *Perf. 10½*

C777	AP169	10col multi	3.75	1.50

Legal medicine teaching in Costa Rica, 50th anniversary.

Rotary Intl., 75th Anniv. — AP170

Gulf of Nicoya, Satellite Photo — AP171

1980, Feb. 26 *Perf. 16*

C778	AP170	2.10col multi	.35	.25
C779	AP170	5col multi	1.00	.60

1980, Mar. 10 **Litho.** *Perf. 12½*

C780	AP171	2.10col Puerto Limon	.35	.25
C781	AP171	5col shown	1.00	.60

14th Intl. Symposium on Remote Sensing of the Environment, San José, Apr. 23-30. Exist imperf.

Soccer, Moscow '80 Emblem — AP172

Poas Volcano AP173

1980, Apr. 16 **Litho.** *Perf. 10½*

C782	AP172	1col shown	*.50*	.20
C783	AP172	3col Bicycling	*6.50*	.50
C784	AP172	4.05col Baseball	*6.50*	.75
C785	AP172	20col Swimming	*6.50*	5.00
		Nos. C782-C785 (4)	*20.00*	6.45

22nd Summer Olympic Games, Moscow, July 19-Aug. 3.

1980, May 14 **Litho.** *Perf. 10½*

C786	AP173	1col shown	.20	.20
C787	AP173	2.50col Cahuita Beach	.40	.30

National Parks Service, 10th anniversary.

José Maria Zeledon Brenes, Score — AP174

Design: 10col, Manuel Maria Gutierrez.

1980, June 25 **Litho.** *Perf. 12½*

C788	AP174	1col multi	.20	.20
C789	AP174	10col multi	1.50	1.25

National anthem composed by Brenes (words) and Gutierrez (music). Exist imperf.

President Type of 1943

1col, Alfredo Gonzalez F. 1.60col, Federico Tinoco G. 1.80col, Francisco Aguilar B. 2.10col, Julio Acosta G. 3col, Leon Cortes C.

1980, Aug. 14 **Litho.** *Perf. 11*

C790	A109	1col dk red	.20	.20
C791	A109	1.60col slate bl	.25	.20
C792	A109	1.80col brown	.30	.20
C793	A109	2.10col dull green	.35	.25
C794	A109	3col dark purple	.45	.35
		Nos. C790-C794 (5)	1.55	1.20

8th Natl. Phil. Exhib. — AP175

Fruits — AP176

1980, Sept. 11 *Perf. 13½*

C795	AP175	5col multi	.80	.60
C796	AP175	20col multi	3.25	2.75

1980, Sept. 24 *Perf. 10½*

C797 AP176 10c shown .20 .20
C798 AP176 60c Cacao .20 .20
C799 AP176 1col Coffee .20 .20
C800 AP176 2.10col Bananas .30 .25
C801 AP176 3.40col Flowers .55 .40
C802 AP176 5col Sugar cane .80 .20
Nos. C797-C802 (6) 2.25 1.45

Giant Tree, by Jorge Carvajal
AP177

Virgin and Child, by Raphael
AP178

Paintings: 2.10col, Secret Look, by Rolando Cubero. 2.45col, Consuelo, by Fernando Carballo. 3col, Volcano, by Lola Fernandez. 4.05col, attending Mass, by Francisco Amighetti.

1980, Oct. 22 Litho. *Perf. 10½*

C803 AP177 1col multi .20 .20
C804 AP177 2.10col multi .30 .25

Size: 28x30mm

C805 AP177 2.45col multi .40 .30

Size: 22x36mm

C806 AP177 3col multi .55 .35
C807 AP177 4.05col multi .80 .45
Nos. C803-C807 (5) 2.25 1.55

1980, Nov. 11 *Perf. 13½*

Christmas 1980: 10col, Virgin and Child and St. John, by Raphael.

C808 AP178 1col multi .20 .20
C809 AP178 10col multi 1.50 1.50

Juan Santamaria International Airport
AP179

1980, Dec. 11 Litho. *Perf. 10½*

Sizes: 30x30mm, 31x25mm (1.30col), 25x32mm (2.60col)

C810 AP179 1col Caldera Harbor .25 .20
C811 AP179 1.30col shown .30 .20
C812 AP179 2.10col Rio Frio Railroad Bridge .45 .25
C813 AP179 2.60col Highway to Colon .55 .35
C814 AP179 5col Huetar post office 1.25 .60
Nos. C810-C814 (5) 2.80 1.60

Paying your taxes means progress.
For surcharge see No. C884.

Repertorio Americano Cover, J. Garcia Monge and Signature — AP180

1981, Jan. 2 Litho. *Perf. 10½*

C815 AP180 1.60col multi .25 .20
C816 AP180 3col multi .50 .30

Birth centenary of J. Garcia Monge, founder of Repertorio Americano journal.

Arms of Aserri (Site of Cornea Bank)
AP181

Harpia Harpyja
AP182

1981, Jan. 28 Litho. *Perf. 13½*

C817 AP181 1col shown .20 .20
C818 AP181 1.80col Eye .30 .20
C819 AP181 5col Rojas .90 .60
Nos. C817-C819 (3) 1.40 1.00

Establishment of human cornea bank, founded by Abelardo Rojas.

1980, Dec. 23 *Perf. 11*

C820 AP182 2.10col shown 1.00 .25
C821 AP182 2.50col Ara macao 1.25 .40
C822 AP182 3col Felis concolor 1.75 .50
C823 AP182 5.50col Ateles geoffrovi 3.50 .85
Nos. C820-C823 (4) 7.50 2.00

Medical and Surgical Clinic
AP183

10c, Physiology class. 50c, Medical school, A. Chavarria (1st dean). 1.30col, Music school. 3.40col, Carlos Monge Alfaro Library. 4.05col, R.F. Brenes, rector (1952-61).

1981, Apr. 8 Litho. *Perf. 10½*

C824 AP183 5c multi .20 .20
C825 AP183 10c multi .20 .20
C826 AP183 50c multi .20 .20
C827 AP183 1.30col multi .25 .20
C828 AP183 3.40col multi .30 .20
C829 AP183 4.05col multi, vert. .35 .20
Nos. C824-C829 (6) 1.50 1.20

University of Costa Rica, 40th anniversary.

Mail Transport by Horse — AP184

1981, May 6 Litho. *Perf. 10½*

C830 AP184 1col shown .20 .20
C831 AP184 2.10col Train, 1857 .30 .25
C832 AP184 10col Mail carriers, 1858 1.50 1.25
Nos. C830-C832 (3) 2.00 1.70

Heinrich von Stephan (1831-97), UPU founder.

13th World Telecommunications Day — AP185

1981, May 18 *Perf. 11*

C833 AP185 5col multi .80 .60
C834 AP185 25col multi 4.00 4.00

Bishop Bernardo Thiel
AP186

Juan Santamaria
AP187

1981, June 8 Litho. *Perf. 10½*

C835 Strip of 5, stained glass windows .50 .40
a. AP186 1col Sts. Peter & Paul .20 .20
b. AP186 1col St. Vincent de Paul .20 .20
c. AP186 1col Death of St. Joseph .20 .20
d. AP186 1col Archangel Michael .20 .20
e. AP186 1col Holy Family .20 .20
C836 AP186 2col shown .20 .20

Consecration of Bernardo Augusto Thiel as Bishop of San Jose.

1981, June 26 *Perf. 13½*

C837 AP187 1col shown .20 .20
C838 AP187 2.45col Alajuela Cathedral, horiz. .25 .20

Alajuela province.

Potters — AP188

1981, July 10 Litho. *Perf. 10½*

C839 AP188 15c shown .20 .20
C840 AP188 1.60col Bricklayers .20 .20
C841 AP188 1.80col Farmers .20 .20
C842 AP188 2.50col Fishermen .25 .20
C843 AP188 3col Nurse, patient .35 .20
C844 AP188 5col Children, traffic policeman .65 .25
Nos. C839-C844 (6) 1.85 1.25

Model of New Natl. Archives
AP189

Natl. Archives Centenary: 1.40col, Leon Fernandez Bonilla, founder, vert. 2col, Arms, vert. 3col, St. Thomas University, former headquarters.

1981, Aug. 24 Litho. *Perf. 13½*

C845 AP189 1.40col multi .20 .20
C846 AP189 2col multi .20 .20
C847 AP189 3col multi .20 .20
C848 AP189 3.50col multi .25 .20
Nos. C845-C848 (4) .85 .80

Men Reaching for Sun, Map
AP190

1981, Sept. 9 Litho. *Perf. 11*

C849 AP190 1col Man in wheelchair, stairs, vert. .30 .20
C850 AP190 2.60col Man reaching for scale, vert. .70 .20
C851 AP190 10col shown 3.00 1.00
Nos. C849-C851 (3) 4.00 1.40

Intl. Year of the Disabled.

World Food Day — AP191

1981, Oct. 16 Litho. *Perf. 10½*

C852 AP191 5col multi .40 .25
C853 AP191 10col multi .70 .50

President Type of 1943

1col, Rafael A. Calderon Guardia, 1940. 2col, Teodoro Picado Michalski, 1944. 3col, José Figueres Ferrer, 1953. 5col, Otilio Ulate Blanco, 1949. 10col, Mario Echandi Jimenez, 1958.

1981, Dec. 7 Litho. *Perf. 13½*

C854 A109 1col pink .20 .20
C855 A109 2col orange .20 .20
C856 A109 3col green .20 .20
C857 A109 5col dk bl .35 .25
C858 A109 10col blue .70 .55
Nos. C854-C858 (5) 1.65 1.40

Bar Assoc. of Costa Rica Centenary (1981)
AP192

1982, Mar. 22 Litho. *Perf. 13½*

C859 AP192 1col Emblem, horiz. .20 .20
C860 AP192 2col E. Figueroa, 1st pres. .20 .20
C861 AP192 20col Bar building, horiz. 1.25 1.10
Nos. C859-C861 (3) 1.65 1.50

National Progress
AP193

1982 *Perf. 10½*

C862 AP193 95c Housing .20 .20
C863 AP193 1.15col Agricultural fair .20 .20
C864 AP193 1.45col Education .20 .20
C865 AP193 1.65col Drinkable water .20 .20
C866 AP193 1.80col Rural medical care .20 .20
C867 AP193 2.10col Recreational areas .20 .20
C868 AP193 2.35col Natl. Theater Square .20 .20
C869 AP193 2.60col Communications .20 .20
C870 AP193 3col Electric railroad .20 .20
C871 AP193 4.05col Irrigation .20 .20
Nos. C862-C871 (10) 2.00 2.00

Issue dates: 1.80col, 2.10col, 2.60col, 3col, 4.05col, May 5; others, June 16.

City of Alajuela Bicentenary
AP194

Perez Zeledon County, 50th Anniv. (1981)
AP195

Designs: 5col, Central Park Fountain. 10col, Juan Santamaria Historical and Cultural Museum, horiz. 15col, Church of Christ of Esquipulas. 20col, Monsignor Esteban Lorenzo de Tristan, 25col, Father Juan Manuel Lopez del Corral.

1982, Aug. 9

C872 AP194 5col multi .30 .20
C873 AP194 10col multi .55 .25
C874 AP194 15col multi .80 .60
C875 AP194 20col multi 1.10 1.10
C876 AP194 25col multi 1.40 1.40
Nos. C872-C876 (5) 4.15 3.55

1982, Aug. 30

Designs: 10c, Saint's Stone. 50c, Monument to Mothers. 1col, Pedro Perz Zeledon. 1.25col, St. Isidore Labrador Church. 3.50col, Municipal Building, horiz. 4.25col, Arms.

C877 AP195 10c multi .20 .20
C878 AP195 50c multi .20 .20
C879 AP195 1col multi .20 .20
C880 AP195 1.25col multi .20 .20
C881 AP195 3.50col multi .20 .20
C882 AP195 4.25col multi .25 .20
Nos. C877-C882 (6) 1.25 1.20

Nos. C695 and C813 Surcharged

1982, Oct. 28 Litho. *Perf. 10½*

C883 AP143 3col on 75c multi .20 .20
C884 AP179 5col on 2.60col multi .30 .20

Nos. C640-C643 Surcharged and Overprinted: "IX EXPOSICION FILATELICA - 1982"

1982, Oct. 28 *Perf. 12*

C885 AP123 8.40col on #C640 .50 .40
C886 AP123 8.40col on #C641 .50 .40
C887 AP123 8.40col on #C642 .50 .40
C888 AP123 8.40col on #C643 .50 .40
C889 AP123 9.70col on #C640 .60 .50
C890 AP123 9.70col on #C641 .60 .50
C891 AP123 9.70col on #C642 .60 .50
C892 AP123 9.70col on #C643 .60 .50
Nos. C885-C892 (8) 4.40 3.60

9th Natl. Stamp Exhibition.

TB Bacillus Centenary AP196

Pan-American Blood Donors' Society, 7th Cong. — AP197

1982, Nov. 19 *Perf. 13½*

C893 AP196 1.50col Koch .20 .20
C894 AP196 3col Koch, slide .20 .20
C895 AP196 3.30col Health Ministry .20 .20
Nos. C893-C895 (3) .60 .60

1982, Nov. 25 *Perf. 11*

C896 AP197 30col Natl. Blood Assoc. emblem 1.50 1.50
C897 AP197 50col Cong. emblem 2.50 2.50

AP198 AP199

1982, Dec. 13 Litho. *Perf. 10½*

C898 AP198 8.40col Emblem, horiz. .40 .20
C899 AP198 9.70col Emblem, diff. .50 .25
C900 AP198 11.70col Handshake, horiz. .60 .25
C901 AP198 13.05col Emblem, diff., horiz. .65 .30
Nos. C898-C901 (4) 2.15 1.00

Inter-Governmental Migration Committee, 30th anniv.

1983, Jan. 3 *Perf. 16*

4.80col, St. Francis of Assisi, by El Greco. 7.40col, Portrait, diff.

C902 AP199 4.80col multi .25 .20
C903 AP199 7.40col multi .35 .20

For surcharges see Nos. C908-C911.

Visit of Pope John Paul II AP200

Bolivar, by Francisco Zuniga Chavarria AP201

1983, Mar. 1 Litho. *Perf. 10½*

C904 AP200 5col multi *1.75* .20
C905 AP200 10col multi *1.75* .40
C906 AP200 15col multi *4.25* .60
Nos. C904-C906 (3) *7.75* 1.20

1983, July 22 Litho. *Perf. 16*

C907 AP201 10col multi .55 .20

Nos. C902-C903 Surcharged

1983, Sept. 23 Litho. *Perf. 16*

C908 AP199 10c on 4.80col .20 .20
C909 AP199 50c on 4.80col .20 .20
C910 AP199 1.50col on 7.40col .20 .20
C911 AP199 3col on 7.40col .20 .20
Nos. C908-C911 (4) .80 .80

LACSA Costa Rica Airlines, 40th Anniv. — AP202

Various childrens' drawings.

1986, Dec. 12 Litho. *Perf. 13½*

C912 AP202 1col Adriana E. Hidalgo *.50* .20
C913 AP202 7col Osvaldo A.G. Vega *2.50* .30
C914 AP202 16col David V. Rodriguez *7.00* .75
Nos. C912-C914 (3) *10.00* 1.25

Nos. C912-C913 exist perf 11. Unused copies are rare. Value used, $5 each.

Roman Macaya Lahmann, Aviation Pioneer AP203

1988, Sept. 26 Litho. *Perf. 10½*

C915 AP203 10col multi .30 .20

No. 418 Ovptd.

1990, Nov. 5

C916 A180 50col multicolored 1.10 .30

Bagging Coffee Beans — AP204

Perf. 10½

1990, Nov. 16 Litho. Unwmk.

C917 AP204 50col multicolored 1.10 .30

AP205

AP206

1990, Dec. 6

C918 AP205 50col blue & black 1.10 .30

First postage stamps, 150th anniv.

1991, Mar. 25 Litho. *Perf. 10½*

Banana Picker, 1897, by Alleardo Villa.

C919 AP206 30col multicolored .65 .20

National Theater.

No. 428 Overprinted

Litho. & Engr.

1991, Sept. 13 *Perf. 12½*

C920 A188 200col 4.50 1.10

12th Natl. Philatelic Exposition.

No. 402 Overprinted

1991, Oct. 11 Litho. *Perf. 11½*

Granite Paper

C921 A170 20col multicolored 4.75 1.00

Basketball, cent.

Social Security Administration, 50th Anniv. AP207

1991, Nov. 1 Litho. *Perf. 13½*

C922 AP207 15col multicolored 1.00 .30

La Poesia by Vespaciano Bignami — AP208

1992, Jan. 24 Litho. *Perf. 10½*

C923 AP208 35col multicolored 2.50 .65

National Theater.

Discovery of America, 500th Anniv. AP209

Columbus' ships: a, Nina. b, Santa Maria. c, Pinta.

1992, Oct. 8 Litho. *Perf. 13½*

C924 AP209 45col Strip of 3, #a.-c. 2.00 .50

Intl. Arts Festival — AP210

1993, Mar. 15 Litho. *Perf. 13½*

C925 AP210 45col multicolored 1.00 .35

Telecommunications Institute, 30th Anniv. — AP211

1993, Nov. 25 Litho. *Perf. 13½*

C926 AP211 45col multicolored .90 .45

Ministry of the Interior, 150th Anniv. AP212

1994, Mar. 8 Litho. *Perf. 10½*

C927 AP212 45col multicolored .90 .45

Intl. Year of the Family — AP213

1994, May 5 Litho. *Perf. 10½*

C928 AP213 45col multicolored 1.00 1.00

LACSA, 50th Anniv. AP214

1996, Mar. 29 Litho. *Perf. 10½*

C929	AP214	5col Douglas DC-3	.20	.20
C930	AP214	10col Curtiss C-46	.20	.20
C931	AP214	20col Beechcraft	.30	.20
C932	AP214	30col DC-6B	.45	.20
C933	AP214	35col BAC 1-11	.55	.25
C934	AP214	40col Convair CV 440	.65	.30
C935	AP214	45col Electra L-188	.70	.35
C936	AP214	50col Boeing 727-200	.80	.40
C937	AP214	55col Douglas DC-8	.90	.45
C938	AP214	60col Airbus A320	.95	.45
		Nos. C929-C938 (10)	5.70	3.00

No. C932 Surcharged

2001, Oct. 5 Litho. *Perf. 10½*

C939	AP214	5col on 30col multi	.20	.20

AIR POST SPECIAL DELIVERY STAMPS

Catalogue values for unused stamps in this section are for Never Hinged items.

UPU Headquarters and Monument, Bern — APSD1

Perf. 10x11

1970, May 20 Litho. Unwmk.

CE1	APSD1	35c multi	.75	.25
CE2	APSD1	60c multi	.75	.25

Opening of the UPU Headquarters in Bern. The red and black label attached to the 60c is inscribed "EXPRES." Values are for stamps with label attached.

Stamps with labels removed were used for regular airmail.

AIR POST OFFICIAL STAMPS

Air Post Stamps of 1934 Overprinted in Red

1934 Unwmk. *Perf. 12*

CO1	AP8	5c green	.20	.20
CO2	AP8	10c car rose	.20	.20
CO3	AP8	15c chocolate	.35	.35
CO4	AP8	20c deep blue	.55	.55
CO5	AP8	25c deep org	.55	.55
CO6	AP8	40c olive blk	1.00	.60
CO7	AP8	50c gray blk	1.00	.60
CO8	AP8	60c org yel	1.25	.75
CO9	AP8	75c dull vio	1.25	.75
CO10	AP9	1col deep rose	5.00	1.10
CO11	AP9	2col light blue	8.00	3.50
CO12	AP9	5col black	9.00	6.50
CO13	AP9	10col red brown	8.00	8.00
		Nos. CO1-CO13 (13)	36.35	23.65

For overprints see Nos. C103-C116.

SPECIAL DELIVERY STAMPS

Catalogue values for unused stamps in this section are for Never Hinged items.

Winged Letter SD1

Unwmk.

1972, Mar. 20 Litho. *Perf. 11*

E1	SD1	75c brown & red	.30	.30
E2	SD1	1.50col blue & red	.50	.40

1973 *Perf. 11x12*

E3	SD1	75c green & red	.30	.30

1973, Nov. 5 Litho. *Perf. 12*

E4	SD1	75c lilac & orange	1.50	.75

Exists perf 11x11½.

Concorde SD2

1976, May 17 Litho. *Perf. 16*

E5	SD2	1col vermilion & multi	.30	.30

SD3

SD4

1979, June 15 Litho. *Perf. 12½*

E6	SD3	2col multi	.60	.40

1980, Dec. 18 Litho. *Perf. 12½*

E7	SD4	2col multi	.60	.40

1982, Dec. 20 Litho. *Perf. 11*

E8	SD4	4col multi	.60	.40

POSTAGE DUE STAMPS

D1

D2

1903 Unwmk. Engr. *Perf. 14*

Numerals in Black

J1	D1	5c slate blue	6.00	.90
J2	D1	10c brown orange	6.00	.65
J3	D1	15c yellow green	3.00	1.75
J4	D1	20c carmine	4.00	1.60
J5	D1	25c slate gray	4.00	1.75
J6	D1	30c brown	5.00	2.50
J7	D1	40c olive bister	6.00	2.50
J8	D1	50c red violet	6.00	2.00
		Nos. J1-J8 (8)	40.00	13.65

1915 Litho. *Perf. 12*

J9	D2	2c orange	1.00	.50
J10	D2	4c dark blue	1.00	.50
J11	D2	8c gray green	1.00	.50
J12	D2	10c violet	1.00	.50
J13	D2	20c brown	1.00	.50
		Nos. J9-J13 (5)	5.00	2.50

OFFICIAL STAMPS

Values for unused stamps are for examples with original gum as defined in the catalogue introduction. Very fine examples of Nos. O1-O24 will have perforations just clear of the design on one or more sides.

Official stamps, to about 1915, normally were not canceled when affixed to official mail. Occasionally they were canceled in a foreign country of destination. Used values are for favor-canceled specimens or for stamps without gum.

Regular Issues Overprinted

Overprinted in Red, Black, Blue or Green

1883-85 Unwmk. *Perf. 12*

O1	A6	1c green (R)	2.00	1.00
O2	A6	1c green (Bk)	4.00	1.00
O3	A6	2c carmine (Bk)	4.00	1.25
O4	A6	2c carmine (Bl)	2.00	1.40
O5	A6	5c blue vio (R)	7.00	2.75
O6	A6	10c orange (G)	10.00	3.50
O7	A6	40c blue (R)	10.00	3.50
		Nos. O1-O7 (7)	39.00	14.40

Overprinted

1886

O8	A6	1c green (Bk)	3.00	1.00
O9	A6	2c carmine (Bk)	3.00	1.50
O10	A6	5c blue vio (R)	20.00	10.00
O11	A6	10c orange (Bk)	20.00	10.00
		Nos. O8-O11 (4)	46.00	22.50

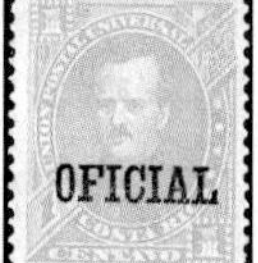

Overprinted

O12	A6	1c green (Bk)	3.00	.90
O13	A6	2c carmine (Bk)	3.00	1.25
O14	A6	5c blue vio (R)	20.00	10.00
O15	A6	10c orange (Bk)	20.00	10.00
		Nos. O12-O15 (4)	46.00	22.15

Nos. O8-O11 and O12-O15 exist se-tenant in vertical pairs.

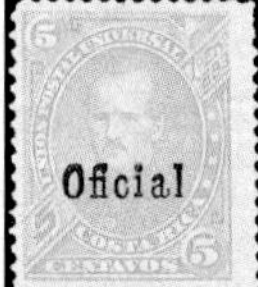

Overprinted in Black

O16	A6	5c blue vio	50.00	30.00
O17	A6	10c orange	—	250.00

Overprinted

1887

O18	A6	1c green	1.00	.50
O19	A6	2c carmine	1.00	.45
O21	A6	10c orange	32.50	20.00
c.		Double overprint	37.50	
O22	A7	5c blue vio	10.00	3.00
O23	A7	10c orange	.75	.45
c.		Double overprint	25.00	
O24	A6	40c blue	1.00	.45
		Nos. O18-O24 (6)	46.25	24.85

Overprinted "OFICAL"

O18a	A6	1c green		
O19a	A6	2c carmine	12.00	12.00
O22a	A7	5c blue violet	12.00	
O23a	A7	10c orange	12.00	2.75
O24a	A6	40c blue	15.00	15.00
		Nos. O18a-O24a (4)	51.00	

Dangerous counterfeits exist of Nos. O18a-O24a.

Without Period

O18b	A6	1c green	2.00	1.50
O19b	A6	2c carmine	2.00	1.50
O22b	A7	5c blue violet	12.00	8.00
O23b	A7	10c orange	2.00	1.50
		Nos. O18b-O23b (4)	18.00	12.50

Nos. O18b-O23b are from a separate plate without periods. No. O23 exists without period (position 32). These must be collected in pairs.

Issues of 1889-1901 Overprinted

1889 *Perf. 14, 15*

O25	A10	1c brown	.20	.20
O26	A11	2c dk green	.20	.20
O27	A12	5c orange	.20	.20
O28	A13	10c red brown	.20	.20
O29	A14	20c yellow grn	.20	.20
O30	A15	50c rose red	1.00	1.00
		Nos. O25-O30 (6)	2.00	2.00

1892

O31	A20	1c grnsh blue	.25	.25
O32	A21	2c yellow	.25	.25
O33	A22	5c violet	.25	.25
O34	A23	10c lt green	1.00	1.00
O35	A24	20c scarlet	.20	.20
O36	A25	50c gray blue	.50	.50
		Nos. O31-O36 (6)	2.45	2.45

1901-02

O37	A30	1c green & blk	.35	.35
O38	A31	2c ver & blk	.35	.35
O39	A32	5c gray bl & blk	.35	.35
O40	A33	10c ocher & blk	.60	.60
O41	A34	20c lake & blk	.85	.85
O42	A35	50c lilac & dk bl	2.75	2.75
O43	A36	1col ol bis & blk	10.00	10.00
		Nos. O37-O43 (7)	15.25	15.25

No. 46 Overprinted in Green

1903

O44	A31	2c ver & blk	2.25	2.25
b.		"PROVISIORO"	8.00	8.00
d.		Inverted overprint	8.00	8.00
f.		As "b," inverted	10.00	8.00

Counterfeit overprints exist.

Regular Issue of 1903 Overprinted Like Nos. O25-O43

1903 *Perf. 14, 12½x14*

O45	A40	4c red vio & blk	1.10	1.10
O46	A41	6c ol grn & blk	1.25	1.25
O47	A42	25c gray lil & brn	8.00	4.50
		Nos. O45-O47 (3)	10.35	6.85

Counterfeit overprints exist.

Regular Issue of 1907 Overprinted

1908 *Perf. 14*

O48 A43 1c red brn & ind .20 .20
O49 A44 2c yel grn & blk .20 .20
O50 A45 4c car & ind .20 .20
O51 A46 5c yel & dull bl .20 .20
O52 A47 10c blue & blk .90 .90
O53 A49 25c gray lil & blk .20 .20
O54 A50 50c red lil & bl .30 .30
O55 A51 1col brown & blk .70 .70
Nos. O48-O55 (8) 2.90 2.90

Various varieties of the overprint exist.
Imperfs exist of Nos. O48, O49 and O53. The Nos. O49 and O53 imperfs were found in 1970 (one sheet of each) and are much scarcer than No. O48 imperf.

Regular Issue of 1910 Overprinted in Black

1917

O56 A56 5c orange .25 .25
a. Inverted overprint 5.00 3.00
O57 A57 10c deep blue .20 .20
a. Inverted overprint 3.00 3.00

No. 74 Surcharged

1920 **Red Surcharge** *Perf. 12*

O58 A58 15c on 20c olive grn .50 .50

Nos. 72, 61, 59, 65-67 Surcharged or Overprinted

A56

O60

A43

1921 **Black Surcharge** *Perf. 12*

O59 A56 10c on 5c orange .30 .25
a. "10 CTS." inverted 16.00

Perf. 14

O60 A45 4c car & indigo .30 .30
a. "1291" for "1921" 11.00
O61 A43 6c on 1c red brn & ind .40 .40
O62 A49 20c on 25c gray lil & blk .40 .40

Overprinted like No. O60

O63 A50 50c red lil & bl 1.50 1.50
O64 A51 1col brown & blk 2.75 2.75
Nos. O59-O64 (6) 5.65 5.60

Nos. O60 to O64 exist with date and new values inverted. These may be printer's waste but probably were deliberately made.

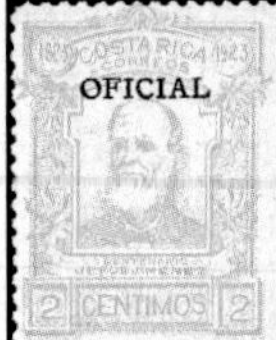

Regular Issue of 1923 Overprinted

1923 *Perf. 11½*

O65 A68 2c brown .20 .20
O66 A68 4c green .20 .20
O67 A68 5c blue .20 .20
O68 A68 20c carmine .20 .20
O69 A68 1col violet .30 .30
Nos. O65-O69 (5) 1.10 1.10

Nos. O65 to O69 exist imperforate but were not regularly issued in that condition.

O7

1926 **Unwmk.** **Engr.** *Perf. 12½*

O70 O7 2c ultra & blk .20 .20
O71 O7 3c mag & blk .20 .20
O72 O7 4c lt bl & blk .20 .20
O73 O7 5c grn & blk .20 .20
O74 O7 6c ocher & blk .20 .20
O75 O7 10c rose red & blk .20 .20
O76 O7 20c ol grn & blk .20 .20
O77 O7 30c red org & blk .20 .20
O78 O7 45c brown & blk .20 .20
O79 O7 1col lilac & blk .20 .20
Nos. O70-O79 (10) 2.00 2.00

See #O82-O94. For surcharges see #C7-C10.

Regular Issue of 1936 Overprinted in Black

1936 **Unwmk.** *Perf. 12*

O80 A96 5c green .20 .20
O81 A96 10c carmine rose .20 .20

Type of 1926

1937 *Perf. 12½*

O82 O7 2c vio & blk .20 .20
O83 O7 3c bis brn & blk .20 .20
O84 O7 4c rose car & blk .20 .20
O85 O7 5c ol grn & blk .20
O86 O7 8c blk brn & blk .20
O87 O7 10c rose lake & blk .20
O88 O7 20c ind & blk .20 .20
O89 O7 40c red org & blk .20 .20
O90 O7 55c dk vio & blk .30
O91 O7 1col brn vio & blk .25 .25
O92 O7 2col gray bl & blk .50 .50
O93 O7 5col dl yel & blk 2.50 2.50
O94 O7 10col blue & blk 20.00 20.00
Nos. O82-O94 (13) 25.15

Nine stamps of this series exist with perforated star (2c, 3c, 4c, 20c, 40c, 1col, 2col, 5col, 10col). These were issued to officials for postal purposes. Unpunched copies were sold to collectors but had no franking power. Values for unused are for unpunched.

POSTAL TAX STAMPS

Catalogue values for unused stamps in this section are for Never Hinged items.

Most postal tax issues were to benefit the Children's Village and were obligatory on all mail during Dec.

No. C198 Surcharged in Red: "Sello de Navidad Pro-Ciudad de Los Niños 5 5"

Engraved; Center Photogravure

1958 **Unwmk.** *Perf. 12½*

RA1 AP51 5c on 2c brt bl & blk .20 .20

Similar Surcharge in Green on Type of 1954

Design: Like No. C228, pottery.

RA2 AP53 5c on 10c dk bl & blk .35 .20
a. Inverted surcharge 7.50

Father Edward J. Flanagan PT1

Father Peralta PT2

Paintings: No. RA4, Boy by El Greco. No. RA5, Boy by Jose Ribera. No. RA6, Girl by Amadeo Modigliani.

Perf. 13½

1959, Nov. 25 **Unwmk.** **Photo.**

RA3 PT1 5c green .25 .20
RA4 PT1 5c dl gray vio .25 .20
RA5 PT1 5c olive .25 .20
RA6 PT1 5c lilac rose .25 .20
Nos. RA3-RA6 (4) 1.00 .80

Exist imperf.

1960 **Litho.** *Perf. 14*

Designs: No. RA8, Girl by Renoir. No. RA9, Boys with cups by Velazquez. No. RA10, Singing children, sculpture by F. Zuñiga.

RA7 PT2 5c chocolate .25 .20
RA8 PT2 5c dp org .25 .20
RA9 PT2 5c plum .25 .20
RA10 PT2 5c grysh bl .25 .20
Nos. RA7-RA10 (4) 1.00 .80

Exist imperf.

#C229 Surcharged Like #RA1-RA2

Engraved; Center Photogravure

1961 *Perf. 13x12½*

RA11 AP53 5c on 15c grn & blk .25 .20

Nicolas, Son of Rubens — PT3

Boys in Workshop — PT4

Designs: No. RA13, Madonna by Bellini. RA14, Angel playing stringed instrument by Melozzo. RA15, Msgr. Rubén Odio H.

1962 **Photo.** *Perf. 13½*

RA12 PT3 5c dark carmine .25 .20
RA13 PT3 5c sepia .25 .20
RA14 PT3 5c dull green .25 .20
RA15 PT3 5c blue .25 .20
Nos. RA12-RA15 (4) 1.00 .80

For surcharges see Nos. 262-265.

Type of 1962, Inscribed "1963"
Designs as before

1963 **Photo.** *Perf. 13½*

RA16 PT3 5c sepia (RA12) .25 .20
RA17 PT3 5c ultra (RA13) .25 .20
RA18 PT3 5c dk car (RA14) .25 .20
RA19 PT3 5c black (RA15) .25 .20
Nos. RA16-RA19 (4) 1.00 .80

1964 **Litho.** *Perf. 12½*

Designs: No. RA21, Two playing boys. No. RA22, Teacher and children. No. RA23, Priest with boys.

RA20 PT4 5c bright green .25 .20
RA21 PT4 5c rose lilac .25 .20
RA22 PT4 5c blue .25 .20
RA23 PT4 5c brown .25 .20
Nos. RA20-RA23 (4) 1.00 .80

Brother Casiano de Madrid PT5

Christmas Ornaments PT6

Designs: No. RA25, National Children's Hospital. No. RA26, Poinsettia. No. RA27, Santa Claus with children (diamond).

1965, Dec. 10 **Litho.** *Perf. 10*

RA24 PT5 5c red brown .20 .20
RA25 PT5 5c green .20 .20
RA26 PT5 5c red .20 .20
RA27 PT5 5c ultra .20 .20
Nos. RA24-RA27 (4) .80 .80

1966 **Litho.** *Perf. 11*

RA28 PT6 5c shown .20 .20
RA29 PT6 5c Angel .20 .20
RA30 PT6 5c Church .20 .20
RA31 PT6 5c Reindeer .20 .20
Nos. RA28-RA31 (4) .80 .80

General Post Office, San José — PT7

1967, Mar. **Litho.** *Perf. 11*

RA32 PT7 10c blue .20 .20

No. RA32 was issued as a postal tax stamp to be used by organizations normally allowed free postage. On Dec. 15, 1972, it was authorized for use as an ordinary postage stamp.

Madonna and Child — PT8

Star of Bethlehem, Mother and Child — PT9

1967 **Litho.** *Perf. 11*

RA33 PT8 5c olive green .20 .20
RA34 PT8 5c dp lil rose .20 .20
RA35 PT8 5c brt blue .20 .20
RA36 PT8 5c grnsh blue .20 .20
Nos. RA33-RA36 (4) .80 .80

1968, Dec. **Litho.** *Perf. 12½*

RA37 PT9 5c gray .20 .20
RA38 PT9 5c rose red .20 .20
RA39 PT9 5c dk rose brn .20 .20
RA40 PT9 5c bister brn .20 .20
Nos. RA37-RA40 (4) .80 .80

Madonna and Child — PT10

Christ Child, Star — PT11

1969, Dec. **Litho.** *Perf. 12½*

RA41 PT10 5c dk blue .20 .20
RA42 PT10 5c orange .20 .20
RA43 PT10 5c brown red .20 .20
RA44 PT10 5c blue green .20 .20
Nos. RA41-RA44 (4) .80 .80

1970, Dec. **Litho.** *Perf. 12½*

RA45 PT11 5c brt purple .20 .20
RA46 PT11 5c lilac rose .20 .20
RA47 PT11 5c olive .20 .20
RA48 PT11 5c ocher .20 .20
Nos. RA45-RA48 (4) .80 .80

Christ Child and "PAX" — PT12

Madonna and Child — PT13

1971, Nov. 29

RA49 PT12 10c dk blue	.20	.20
RA50 PT12 10c orange	.20	.20
RA51 PT12 10c brown	.20	.20
RA52 PT12 10c green	.20	.20
Nos. RA49-RA52 (4)	.80	.80

1972, Nov. 30 ***Perf. 11x11½***

RA53 PT13 10c dk blue	.20	.20
RA54 PT13 10c brt red	.20	.20
RA55 PT13 10c lilac	.20	.20
RA56 PT13 10c green	.20	.20
Nos. RA53-RA56 (4)	.80	.80

Madonna and Child — PT14

Boys Eating Cake, by Murillo — PT15

1973, Nov. 30 **Litho.** ***Perf. 12½***

RA57 PT14 10c purple	.20	.20
RA58 PT14 10c car rose	.20	.20
RA59 PT14 10c gray	.20	.20
RA60 PT14 10c orange brn	.20	.20
Nos. RA57-RA60 (4)	.80	.80

1974, Nov. 25 ***Perf. 13***

Paintings: No. RA62, Virgin and Child, with St. John, by Raphael. No. RA63, Maternity, by Juan R. Bonilla. No. RA64, Praying Child, by Reynolds.

RA61 PT15 10c brt pink	.20	.20
RA62 PT15 10c rose lilac	.20	.20
RA63 PT15 10c dk gray	.20	.20
RA64 PT15 10c violet bl	.20	.20
Nos. RA61-RA64 (4)	.80	.80

See No. RA110.

"Happy Dreams," by Sonia Romero PT16

Virgin and Child, by Hans Memling PT17

Paintings: No. RA66, Virgin with Carnation, by Leonardo da Vinci. No. RA67, Children with Tortoise, by Francisco Amighetti. No. RA68, Boy with Pigeon, by Picasso.

1975, Nov. 25 **Litho.** ***Perf. 10½***

RA65 PT16 10c gray	.20	.20
RA66 PT16 10c red lilac	.20	.20
RA67 PT16 10c orange brown	.20	.20
RA68 PT16 10c brt blue	.20	.20
Nos. RA65-RA68 (4)	.80	.80

1976, Nov. 24 **Litho.** ***Perf. 10½***

Paintings: No. RA70, Girl with Sombrero, by Auguste Renoir. No. RA71, Meditation (boy), by Floria Pinto de Herrero. No. RA72, Gaston de Mezerville (boy), by Lolita Zeller de Peralta.

RA69 PT17 10c rose lilac	.20	.20
RA70 PT17 10c rose carmine	.20	.20
RA71 PT17 10c gray	.20	.20
RA72 PT17 10c violet blue	.20	.20
Nos. RA69-RA72 (4)	.80	.80

Boy's Head, by Amparo Cruz — PT18

Boy with Kite — PT19

Paintings: No. RA74, Girl's head, by Rubens. No. RA75, Girl and infant, by Cristina Fournier. No. RA76, Mariano Goya, by Goya.

1977, Nov. **Litho.** ***Perf. 10½***

RA73 PT18 10c gray olive	.20	.20
RA74 PT18 10c rose red	.20	.20
RA75 PT18 10c brt ultra	.20	.20
RA76 PT18 10c brt rose lil	.20	.20
Nos. RA73-RA76 (4)	.80	.80

1978, Nov. 20 **Litho.** ***Perf. 12½***

Designs: Nos. RA78-RA79, Girl flying kite.

RA77 PT19 10c magenta	.20	.20
RA78 PT19 10c slate	.20	.20
RA79 PT19 10c lilac	.20	.20
RA80 PT19 10c violet blue	.20	.20
Nos. RA77-RA80 (4)	.80	.80

Boy Leaning on Tree — PT20

Boy on Swing — PT21

1979, Nov. 19 **Litho.** ***Perf. 12½***

RA81 PT20 10c blue	.20	.20
RA82 PT20 10c orange	.20	.20
RA83 PT20 10c magenta	.20	.20
RA84 PT20 10c green	.20	.20
Nos. RA81-RA84 (4)	.80	.80

1980, Nov. 18 **Litho.** ***Perf. 12½***

RA85 PT21 10c brt blue	.20	.20
RA86 PT21 10c brt yellow	.20	.20
RA87 PT21 10c crimson rose	.20	.20
RA88 PT21 10c brt green	.20	.20
Nos. RA85-RA88 (4)	.80	.80

Boy Riding Toy Car PT22

Youth Running Machine PT23

1981, Nov. 19 **Litho.** ***Perf. 11***

RA89 PT22 10c blue	.20	.20
RA90 PT22 10c green	.20	.20
RA91 PT22 10c red	.20	.20
RA92 PT22 10c orange	.20	.20
Nos. RA89-RA92 (4)	.80	.80

1982, Nov. 19 **Litho.** ***Perf. 10½***

RA93 PT23 10c red	.20	.20
RA94 PT23 10c gray	.20	.20
RA95 PT23 10c purple	.20	.20
RA96 PT23 10c grnsh blue	.20	.20
Nos. RA93-RA96 (4)	.80	.80

Youths Working on Wheelchair PT24

Girl on Bicycle PT25

1983, Nov. 24 **Litho.** ***Perf. 16***

RA97 PT24 10c red	.20	.20
RA98 PT24 10c orange	.20	.20
RA99 PT24 10c ultra	.20	.20
RA100 PT24 10c green	.20	.20
Nos. RA97-RA100 (4)	.80	.80

Christmas 1983.

1984, Nov. 20 **Litho.** ***Perf. 10½***

RA101 PT25 10c violet	.20	.20

Christmas 1984.

Taking a Child in Out of the Cold PT26

Depressed Child PT27

1985, Dec. 1 **Litho.** ***Perf. 13***

RA102 PT26 10c dull brown	.20	.20

Christmas 1985.

1986, Dec. 1 **Litho.** ***Perf. 10½***

RA103 PT27 10c lemon	.20	.20

Christmas stamps, 25th anniv.; Christmas 1986.

Christmas PT28

Teaching Children PT29

1987, Dec. 1 **Litho.** ***Perf. 10½***

RA104 PT28 10c dk ol bis & brt bl	.20	.20

No postal tax stamp was issued for 1988.

1989, Dec. 1 **Litho.** ***Perf. 13½***

RA105 PT29 1col blue, blk & brt apple grn	.20	.20

Christmas 1989.

No. 417 Ovptd. in Red, Blue, Green, or Orange

LEY 7157 PRO-CIUDAD DE LOS NIÑOS 1990

1990, Nov. 16 **Litho.** ***Perf. 13½***

RA106 A179 10col multi (R)	.25	.20
RA107 A179 10col multi (Bl)	.25	.20
RA108 A179 10col multi (G)	.25	.20
RA109 A179 10col multi (O)	.25	.20
Nos. RA106-RA109 (4)	1.00	.80

No. RA109 exists with a silver overprint.

Art Type of 1974

Design: 10col, Praying Child, by Reynolds.

1991, Nov. 18 **Litho.** ***Perf. 10½***

RA110 PT15 10col dark ultra	.70	.20

PT30

PT31

Boy in workshop.

1992, Dec. 1 **Litho.** ***Perf. 10½***

RA111 PT30 10col red	.20	.20

Christmas.

1993, Nov. 17

RA112 PT31 10col multicolored	.20	.20

Christmas.

PT32

PT33

1994, Nov. 23 **Litho.** ***Perf. 10½***

RA113 PT32 11col lilac & slate	.20	.20

Christmas.

1995, Dec. 1 ***Perf. 13½***

Painting of mother and child, by Claudio Carazo.

RA114 PT33 12col multicolored	.20	.20
a. Miniature sheet, #RA114 + 5 labels	1.75	.90

No. RA114a contains 4 progressive proofs of No. RA114 + one label of text and sold for 112col.

Christmas.

PT34

PT35

1996, Dec. 1 **Litho.** ***Perf. 10½***

RA115 PT34 14col Sculpture	.25	.20

1997, Dec. 1

Bust of Antonio Obando Chan, by Olger Villegas Cruz.

RA116 PT35 15col multicolored	.20	.20

Christmas.

PT36

Designs: a, Flower. b, Flower up close, one in background. c, Berries on branch.

1998 **Litho.** ***Perf. 13½***

RA117 PT36 16col Strip of 3, #a.-c.	.45	.20

Christmas.

Children's Village PT37

1999, Dec. 1 Litho. *Perf. 13¼*
RA118 PT37 17col multi .20 .20

Child — PT38

Color: a, Green. b, Red. c, Blue. d, Brown.

2000, Dec. 1 Litho. *Perf. 10½*
RA119 Horiz. strip of 4 .55 .55
a.-d. PT38 20col Any single .20 .20

Child Examining Stamp — PT39

Panel color: a, Purple. b, Green. c, Red. d, Orange.

2001, Dec. 1 Litho. *Perf. 10½*
RA120 Horiz. strip of 4 .55 .55
a.-d. PT39 21col Any single .20 .20

Child — PT40

Panel color: a, Purple. b, Blue. c, Orange. d, Green.

2002 Litho. *Perf. 10½*
RA121 Horiz strip of 4 .50 .50
a.-d. PT40 22col Any single .20 .20

Child Pointing at Star — PT41

No. RA122 — Background color: a, Purple. b, Green. c, Red. d, Yellow orange.

2003, Dec. 1 Litho. *Perf. 13½x13¼*
RA122 Horiz. strip of 4 .45 .45
a.-d. PT41 23col Any single .20 .20

GUANACASTE

ˌgwä-nə-ˈkästā

(A province of Costa Rica)

LOCATION — Northwestern coast of Central America
AREA — 4,000 sq. mi. (approx.)
POP. — 69,531 (estimated)
CAPITAL — Liberia

Residents of Guanacaste were allowed to buy Costa Rican stamps, overprinted "Guanacaste," at a discount from face value because of the province's isolation and climate, which makes it difficult to keep mint stamps. Use was restricted to the province.

Counterfeits of most Guanacaste overprints are plentiful.

For 1c and 2c stamps between Nos. 19-36, unused values are for examples with or without gum. For 5c stamps between Nos. 5-43, unused examples without gum sell for slightly more than the used value.

Very fine examples of Nos. 1-54 will have perforations just clear of the design on one or more sides.

Dangerous counterfeits exist of Nos. 1-54.

On Issue of 1883
Overprinted Horizontally in Black

16mm

1885 Unwmk. *Perf. 12*
1 A6 1c green 4.00 3.00
2 A6 2c carmine 4.00 3.00
a. "Gnanacaste" *150.00*
3 A6 10c orange 30.00 18.00
a. "Gnanacaste" *500.00*

Same Overprint in Red
4 A6 1c green 4.00 3.00
a. "Gnanacaste" *150.00*
b. Overprinted in black & red *250.00*
5 A6 5c blue violet 20.00 3.50
a. "Gnanacaste" *350.00*
6 A6 40c blue 20.00 18.00

Overprinted Horizontally in Black

17½mm

7 A6 1c green 7.00 7.00
8 A6 2c carmine 7.00 7.00
9 A6 5c blue violet 40.00 15.00
10 A6 10c orange 50.00 30.00
11 A6 40c blue 55.00 55.00

Same Overprint in Red
12 A6 5c blue violet 350.00 75.00
13 A6 40c blue *2,000.*

Overprinted Horizontally in Black

18½mm — c

14 A6 2c carmine 10.00 7.00
15 A6 10c orange 70.00 60.00

Same Overprint in Red
16 A6 1c green 7.00 7.00
a. Double ovpt., one in blk 125.00
17 A6 5c blue violet 40.00 15.00
18 A6 40c blue 60.00 60.00

Same Overprint, Vertically in Black
19 A6 1c green *4,500.*
20 A6 2c carmine *4,250.*
21 A6 5c blue violet 500.00 175.00
22 A6 10c orange 100.00 100.00

Guanacaste GUANACASTE GUANACASTE GUANACASTE GUANACASTE
e f g h i

Overprinted Type e, Vertically
23 A6 1c green 1,500. 1,500.
24 A6 2c carmine 500.00 300.00
25 A6 5c blue violet 250.00 75.00
26 A6 10c orange 60.00 60.00

Overprinted Type f, Vertically
27 A6 1c green 1,500. 1,500.
28 A6 2c carmine 500.00 400.00
29 A6 5c blue violet 400.00 125.00
30 A6 10c orange 80.00 80.00

Overprinted Type g, Vertically
31 A6 1c green 1,500. 1,500.
32 A6 2c carmine 700.00 700.00
33 A6 5c blue violet 550.00 200.00
34 A6 10c orange 150.00 150.00

Overprinted Type h, Vertically
35 A6 1c green 850.00 800.00
36 A6 2c carmine 300.00 275.00
37 A6 5c blue violet 250.00 75.00
38 A6 10c orange 60.00 60.00

Overprinted Type i, Vertically
39 A6 1c green —
39A A6 2c carmine 275.00
40 A6 5c blue violet 20.00
41 A6 10c orange 175.00

On Issues of 1883-87

Overprinted Horizontally in Black

1888-89
42 A7 5c blue violet 15.00 3.00

Overprinted Horizontally in Black

43 A7 5c blue violet 15.00 3.00

Overprinted Horizontally in Black

44 A6 2c carmine 3.00
45 A7 10c orange 3.00

Inverted overprints are fakes.

On Issue of 1889
Overprinted Like Nos. 7-13, Horizontally

1889
47 A8 2c blue 20.00

Vertically
48 A8 2c blue (c) 200.00
49 A8 2c blue (e) 60.00
51 A8 2c blue (f) 75.00
52 A8 2c blue (g) 200.00
54 A8 2c blue (h) 75.00

Nos. 47-54 are overprinted "Correos." Copies without "Correos" are known postally used. Unused examples are valued the same as Nos. 47-54, unused. The 1c without "Correos" is known postally used. The 1c with "Correos" is counterfeit.

On Nos. 25-33

Overprinted Horizontally in Black

1889 *Perf. 14 and 15*
55 A10 1c brown 5.00 3.00
56 A11 2c dark green 3.00 1.50
57 A12 5c orange 4.00 1.50
58 A13 10c red brown 4.00 1.50
59 A14 20c yellow green 1.00 1.50
60 A15 50c rose red 1.50 1.50
61 A16 1p blue 2.50 2.50
62 A17 2p violet 5.00 5.00
63 A18 5p olive green 35.00 30.00
Nos. 55-63 (9) 61.00 48.00

#61-63 with remainder cancels sell for about half the used values shown.

Overprinted "GUAGACASTE"
60a A15 50c rose red *300.00 300.00*
61a A16 1p blue *300.00 300.00*
62a A17 2p violet *350.00 350.00*
63a A18 5p olive green *500.00 500.00*

Values for #60a-63a used are for examples with remainder cancels.

Overprinted Horizontally in Black

64 A10 1c brown 2.00 1.50
a. Vert. pair, imperf. between
65 A11 2c dark green 2.00 1.50
66 A12 5c orange 2.00 1.50
67 A13 10c red brown 2.00 1.50
Nos. 64-67 (4) 8.00 6.00

CRETE

ˈkrēt

LOCATION — An island in the Mediterranean Sea south of Greece
GOVT. — A department of Greece
AREA — 3,235 sq. mi.
POP. — 336,150 (1913)
CAPITAL — Canea

Formerly Crete was a province of Turkey. After an extended period of civil wars, France, Great Britain, Italy and Russia intervened and declaring Crete an autonomy, placed it under the administration of Prince George of Greece as High Commissioner. In October, 1908, the Cretan Assembly voted for union with Greece and in 1913 the union was formally effected.

40 Paras = 1 Piaster
4 Metallik = 1 Grosion (1899)
100 Lepta = 1 Drachma (1900)

Issued Under Joint Administration of France, Great Britain, Italy and Russia
British Sphere of Administration
District of Heraklion (Candia)

A1

A2

Handstamped
1898 Unwmk. *Imperf.*
1 A1 20pa violet 425.00 240.00

1898 Litho. *Perf. 11½*
2 A2 10pa blue 8.50 3.00
Never hinged 17.00
a. Horiz. pair, imperf. btwn.
b. Imperf., pair 260.00
3 A2 20pa green 13.50 3.00
Never hinged 20.00
a. Imperf., pair 260.00

1899
4 A2 10pa brown 8.75 3.00
Never hinged 17.50
a. Horiz. pair, imperf. btwn.
b. Imperf., pair 260.00
5 A2 20pa rose 19.00 3.00
Never hinged 24.00
a. Imperf., pair 260.00

Used values for Nos. 2-5 are for stamps canceled by the straight-line "Heraklion" town postmark. Stamps canceled with any other postmark used for postal duty are scarce and worth much more.

Counterfeits exist of Nos. 1-5.

Russian Sphere of Administration District of Rethymnon

Coat of Arms
A3 A4

1899 Handstamped *Imperf.*

10	A3	1m green	6.50	4.50
11	A3	2m black	6.50	4.50
12	A3	2m rose	250.00	200.00
13	A4	1m blue	80.00	18.00

Nos. 10-13 exist on both wove and laid papers. Counterfeits exist.

Poseidon's Trident—A5a
A5

1899 Litho. *Perf. 11½*

With Control Mark Overprinted in Violet

Without Stars at Sides

14	A5	1m orange	80.	60.
15	A5	2m orange	80.	60.
16	A5	1gr orange	80.	60.
17	A5	1m green	80.	60.
18	A5	2m green	80.	60.
19	A5	1gr green	80.	60.
20	A5	1m yellow	80.	60.
21	A5	2m yellow	80.	60.
22	A5	1gr yellow	80.	60.
23	A5	1m rose	80.	60.
24	A5	2m rose	80.	60.
25	A5	1gr rose	80.	60.
26	A5	1m violet	80.	60.
27	A5	2m violet	80.	60.
28	A5	1gr violet	80.	60.
29	A5	1m blue	80.	60.
30	A5	2m blue	80.	60.
31	A5	1gr blue	80.	60.
32	A5	1m black	1,000.	900.
33	A5	2m black	1,000.	900.
34	A5	1gr black	1,000.	900.

With Stars at Sides

35	A5a	1m blue	25.00	15.00
36	A5a	2m blue	7.00	5.25
37	A5a	1gr blue	4.50	3.25
38	A5a	1m rose	50.00	40.00
39	A5a	2m rose	7.00	5.25
40	A5a	1gr rose	4.50	3.25
41	A5a	1m green	24.00	15.00
42	A5a	2m green	7.00	5.25
43	A5a	1gr green	7.00	5.25
44	A5a	1m violet	24.00	15.00
45	A5a	2m violet	7.00	5.25
46	A5a	1gr violet	4.50	4.25
		Nos. 35-46 (12)	171.50	122.00

Nearly all of Nos. 14 to 46 may be found without control mark, with double control marks and in various colors.

Counterfeits exist of Nos. 14-46.

Issued by the Cretan Government

Hermes — A6 Hera — A7

Prince George of Greece — A8

Talos — A9

Minos — A10

St. George and the Dragon — A11

1900, Mar. 1 Engr. *Perf. 14*

50	A6	1 l violet brown	.20	.20
51	A7	5 l green	.95	.20
52	A8	10 l red	1.10	.20
53	A7	20 l carmine rose	4.75	.90
		Nos. 50-53 (4)	7.00	1.50

See #64-71. For overprints and surcharges see #54-63, 72-73, 85, 88, 93, 97-99, 108, 111.

Overprinted

Red Overprint

54	A8	25 l blue	2.00	.85
55	A6	50 l lilac	2.00	1.25
56	A9	1d gray violet	13.00	11.00
57	A10	2d brown	25.00	25.00
58	A11	5d green & blk	85.00	85.00
		Nos. 54-58 (5)	127.00	123.10

Black Overprint

59	A8	25 l blue	2.00	.85
60	A6	50 l lilac	2.00	1.25
61	A9	1d gray violet	12.50	4.50
a.		Inverted overprint	*450.00*	*450.00*
62	A10	2d brown	22.50	22.50
63	A11	5d green & blk	47.50	47.50
		Nos. 59-63 (5)	86.50	76.60

1901

Without Overprint

64	A6	1 l bister		.90
65	A7	20 l orange	4.75	.90
66	A8	25 l blue	8.50	.45
67	A6	50 l lilac	30.00	22.50
68	A6	50 l ultra	13.50	13.00
69	A9	1d gray violet	27.50	25.00
70	A10	2d brown	9.00	7.75
71	A11	5d green & blk	9.25	8.00
		Nos. 64-71 (8)		78.50
		Nos. 65-71 (7)	102.50	

No. 64 is a revenue stamp that was used for postage for a short time. Unused, it can only be considered as a revenue.

Types A6 to A8 in olive yellow, and types A9 to A11 in olive yellow and black are revenue stamps.

See note following No. 53.

Surcharges with the year "1922" on designs A6, A8, A9, A11, A13, A15-A23 and D1 are listed under Greece.

No. 66 Overprinted in Black

1901

72	A8	25 l blue	32.50	.80
a.		First letter of ovpt. invtd.	300.00	200.00

No. 65 Surcharged in Black

1904, Dec.

73	A7	5 l on 20 l orange	4.50	.85
a.		Without "5" at right	100.00	50.00

Mycenaean Seal — A12

Britomartis (Cortyna Coin) — A13

Prince George — A14

Kydon and Dog (Cydonia Coin) — A15

Triton (Itanos Coin) — A16

Ariadne (Knossos Coin) — A17

Zeus as Bull Abducting Europa (Cortyna Coin) A18

Palace of Minos Ruins, Knossos A19

Arkadi Monastery and Mt. Ida — A20

1905, Feb. 15

74	A12	2 l dull violet	1.90	.45
75	A13	5 l yellow grn	4.75	.45
76	A14	10 l red	5.00	.45
77	A15	20 l blue grn	5.25	1.00
78	A16	25 l ultra	4.75	1.00
79	A17	50 l yellow brn	7.00	4.75
80	A18	1d rose car & dp brn	50.00	50.00
81	A19	3d orange & blk	50.00	40.00
82	A20	5d ol grn & blk	25.00	20.00
		Nos. 74-82 (9)	153.65	118.10

For overprints see Nos.86-87, 89, 91-92, 94-95, 104, 106, 109-110, 112-113, 115-120.

The so-called revolutionary stamps of 1905 were issued for sale to collectors and, so far as can be ascertained, were of no postal value whatever.

A. T. A. Zaimis A21

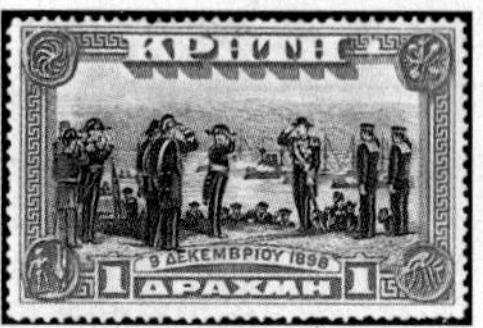

Prince George Landing at Suda A22

1907, Aug. 28

83	A21	25 l blue & blk	37.50	.65
84	A22	1d green & blk	10.00	9.00

Administration under a High Commissioner.

For overprints see Nos. 90, 105, 107.

Stamps of 1900-1907 Overprinted in Black

1908, Sept. 21

85	A6	1 l violet brn	.60	.50
86	A12	2 l dull violet	.65	.50
87	A13	5 l yellow grn	.65	.50
88	A8	10 l red	1.10	.65
89	A15	20 l blue grn	4.50	.70
90	A21	25 l blue & blk	11.00	2.50
91	A17	50 l yellow brn	11.00	4.00
92	A18	1d rose car & dp brn	55.00	55.00
93	A10	2d brown	10.50	10.50
94	A19	3d orange & blk	30.00	30.00
95	A20	5d ol grn & blk	30.00	30.00
		Nos. 85-95 (11)	155.00	134.85

This overprint exists inverted and double, as well as with incorrect, reversed, misplaced and omitted letters. Similar errors are found on the Postage Due and Official stamps with this overprint.

Hermes by Praxiteles — A23

1908

96	A23	10 l brown red	2.50	.85
a.		Pair, one without overprint	25.00	
b.		Inverted overprint	25.00	
c.		Double overprint	35.00	

Nos. 96 and 114 were not regularly issued without overprint.

For overprints see Nos. 103, 114.

No. 53 Surcharged

1909

97	A7	5 l on 20 l car rose	100.00	*125.00*

Forgeries exist of No. 97.

On No. 65

98	A7	5 l on 20 l orange	1.75	1.00
a.		Inverted surcharge		

Overprinted on Nos. 64, J1

99	A6	1 l bister	1.75	1.75
100	D1	1 l red	1.75	1.75

No. J4 Surcharged

101	D1	2 l on 20 l red	1.75	1.75
b.		Inverted surcharge	75.00	
c.		Second letter of surcharge "D" instead of "P"	50.00	50.00

No. J4 Surcharged

102	D1	2 l on 20 l red	1.60	1.40

Overprinted in Black:

a

ΕΛΛΑΣ

b

c

103	A23(a)	10 l brown red	4.75	1.25
a.		Inverted overprint	85.00	
104	A15(a)	20 l blue grn	6.25	1.25
105	A21(c)	25 l blue & blk	12.50	4.00
106	A17(a)	50 l yellow brn	10.00	5.25
107	A22(b)	1d green & blk	11.00	11.00
108	A10(a)	2d brown	11.00	11.00
109	A19(b)	3d org & blk	80.00	75.00
110	A20(b)	5d ol grn & blk	22.50	22.50
		Nos. 103-110 (8)	158.00	131.25

Stamps of 1900-08 Overprinted in Red or Black

1909-10

111	A6	1 l violet brown	.45	.25
112	A12	2 l dull violet	.45	.25
113	A13	5 l yellow green	.45	.25
114	A23	10 l brown red (Bk)	.85	.25
115	A15	20 l blue green	3.00	.70
116	A16	25 l ultra	3.50	.75
117	A17	50 l yellow brn	9.00	6.75
118	A18	1d rose car & dp brn (Bk)	60.00	60.00
119	A19	3d orange & blk	50.00	50.00
120	A20	5d ol grn & blk	45.00	40.00
		Nos. 111-120 (10)	172.70	159.20

POSTAGE DUE STAMPS

D1

1901 Unwmk. Litho. *Perf. 14*

J1	D1	1 l red	.25	.25
J2	D1	5 l red	.65	.40
J3	D1	10 l red	1.10	.40
J4	D1	20 l red	1.40	1.10
J5	D1	40 l red	14.00	14.00
J6	D1	50 l red	14.00	14.00
J7	D1	1d red	14.00	14.00
J8	D1	2d red	14.00	14.00
		Nos. J1-J8 (8)	59.40	58.15

For overprints and surcharges see Nos. 100-102, J9-J26.

Surcharged in Black

1901

J9	D1	1d on 1d red	10.00	10.00

Overprinted

1908

J10	D1	1 l red	.45	.45
J11	D1	5 l red	.85	.85
J12	D1	10 l red	.90	.85
J13	D1	20 l red	2.40	2.25
J14	D1	40 l red	9.25	9.25
J15	D1	50 l red	9.25	9.25
J16	D1	1d red	95.00	100.00
J17	D1	1d on 1d red	9.25	9.25
J18	D1	2d red	13.50	13.50
		Nos. J10-J18 (9)	140.85	145.65

Nos. J10-J18 exist with inverted overprint. See note after No. 95.

Counterfeits of No. J16 exist.

Overprinted

1910

J19	D1	1 l red	.50	.20
J20	D1	5 l red	1.40	.25
J21	D1	10 l red	.85	.45
J22	D1	20 l red	3.75	1.50
J23	D1	40 l red	10.00	9.00
J24	D1	50 l red	12.50	11.00
J25	D1	1d red	22.50	22.50
J26	D1	2d red	22.50	22.50
		Nos. J19-J26 (8)	74.00	67.40

OFFICIAL STAMPS

O1

O2

Unwmk.

1908, Jan. 14 Litho. *Perf. 14*

O1	O1	10 l dull claret	16.00	2.00
O2	O2	30 l blue	35.00	2.00

Nos. O1-O2 exist imperf.

Overprinted

O3	O1	10 l dull claret	16.00	2.00
O4	O2	30 l blue	35.00	2.00

See note after No. 95.

Overprinted

1910

O5	O1	10 l dull claret	2.25	2.00
O6	O2	30 l blue	2.25	2.00

Nos. O5-O6 remained in use until 1922, nine years after union with Greece.

CROATIA

krō-ˈā-sh,ē,-ə

LOCATION — Southeastern Europe
GOVT. — Independent state
AREA — 44,453 sq. mi.
POP. — 7,000,000 (approx.)
CAPITAL — Zagreb

The Independent Croatian State of 1941-45 became part of the Yugoslav Federation in 1945.

Croatia declared its independence in 1991.

100 Paras = 1 Dinar
100 Banica = 1 Kuna

Catalogue values for unused stamps in this country are for Never Hinged items, beginning with Scott 1 in the regular postage section, Scott B1 in the semi-postal section, Scott C1 in the airmail section and Scott RA1 in the postal tax section.

Watermark

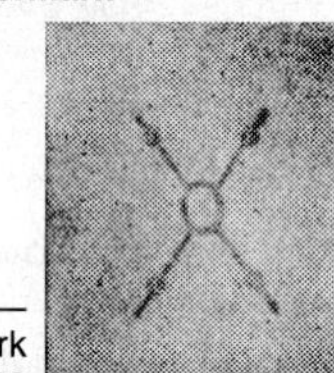

Wmk. 278 — Network Connecting Circles

Yugoslavia Nos. 143 to 148B Overprinted in Black

Perf. 12½

1941, Apr. 12 Unwmk. Typo.

1	A16	50p orange	1.90	*2.50*
2	A16	1d yellow grn	1.90	*2.50*
3	A16	1.50d red	1.90	1.40
4	A16	2d deep magenta	1.90	*2.25*
5	A16	3d dull red brn	3.50	*5.00*
6	A16	4d ultra	3.50	*5.75*
7	A16	5d dark blue	4.75	*6.00*
8	A16	5.50d dk violet brn	4.75	*7.00*
		Nos. 1-8 (8)	24.10	*32.40*

The overprint exists inverted on Nos. 1-6; double on Nos. 2, 3 and 5.

Counterfeit overprints exist of Nos. 1-8, especially the inverted overprint varieties.

Yugoslavia Nos. 142 to 154 Overprinted in Black

1941, Apr. 21

9	A16	25p black	.20	*.40*
10	A16	50p orange	.20	*.40*
11	A16	1d yellow grn	.20	*.40*
12	A16	1.50d red	.20	*.40*
13	A16	2d deep magenta	.20	*.40*
14	A16	3d dull red brn	.20	*.75*
15	A16	4d ultra	.65	*1.10*
16	A16	5d dark blue	.95	*1.10*
17	A16	5.50d dk violet brn	.95	*1.10*
18	A16	6d slate blue	1.10	*1.90*
19	A16	8d sepia	1.60	*1.90*
20	A16	12d brt violet	2.25	*2.50*
21	A16	16d dull violet	2.25	*3.75*
22	A16	20d blue	3.00	*4.50*
23	A16	30d bright pink	4.75	*8.25*
		Nos. 9-23 (15)	18.70	*28.85*

The overprint exists inverted on Nos. 9-11, 17 and 20; double on Nos. 9, 11, 12, 16 and 17; and double, one inverted, on Nos. 16 and 18.

Yugoslavia Nos. 147, 148 Surcharged in Black

1941, May 16

24	A16	1d on 3d dull red brn	.30	.30
25	A16	2d on 4d ultra	.30	.30

The overprint exists inverted and double on Nos. 24-25.

Postage Due Stamps of Yugoslavia, Nos. J28, J30 to J32, Overprinted in Black

1941, May 17

26	D4	50p violet	.40	.40
27	D4	2d deep blue	.75	*.95*
28	D4	5d orange	.75	*.95*
29	D4	10d chocolate	1.10	*1.25*
		Nos. 26-29 (4)	3.00	*3.55*

Counterfeit cancellations exist for Nos. 1-29 on cover.

Imperforates

Nearly all Croatian stamps, from No. 30 through 80, B3 through B76, J6 through J25, O1 through O24 and RA1 through RA7 exist imperforate, or imperforate vertically or horizontally. These are primarily from the special Ministerial Albums issued by the State Printing Office.

Ozalj Castle — A1

Designs: 50b, City of Jajce. 75b, Old Warasdin. 1k, Velebit Mountains. 1.50k, Zelanjak. 2k, Zagreb Cathedral. 3k, Osjek Cathedral. 4k, Drina River. No. 38, Konjica. No. 39, Zemun. 6k, Dubrovnik. 7k, Save River. 8k, Sarajevo. 10k, Plitvice. 12k, Klis Fortress, Split. 20k, Hvar. 30k, Syrmia. 50k, Senj. 100k, Banjaluka (without "F.I.").

Perf. 11¼.

1941-43 Unwmk. Photo.

Ordinary Paper

30	A1	25b henna	.20	.20
31	A1	50b slate blue	.20	.20
32	A1	75b dk olive grn	.20	.20
33	A1	1k Prussian green	.20	.20
34	A1	1.50k deep green	.20	.20
35	A1	2k carmine lake	.20	.20
36	A1	3k brown red	.20	.20
37	A1	4k deep ultra	.20	.20
38	A1	5k black	1.60	.95
39	A1	5k blue	.20	.20
40	A1	6k lt olive brn	.20	.20
41	A1	7k orange red	.20	.20
42	A1	8k chestnut	.40	.20
43	A1	10k dark plum	.75	.40
44	A1	12k olive brown	.75	.30
45	A1	20k golden brown	.75	.30
46	A1	30k black brown	1.00	.45

47	A1	50k dk slate green	1.90	1.25
48	A1	100k violet	3.25	2.75
		Nos. 30-48 (19)	12.60	*8.80*

Nos. 30-48 exist with a variety of perforations, including 11¾x10¾ and 12.

Nos. 31, 35 and 43 exist on thin to pelure paper, as does No. 32, though the latter was not issued to the public. Shades of all values exist.

For overprints and surcharge see #49-51, 53.

Tête bêche Pairs

30a	A1	25b	1.00	.80
31a	A1	50b	1.00	.90
33a	A1	1k	1.00	.95
34a	A1	1.50k	1.00	*1.25*
35a	A1	2k	1.00	*1.40*
37a	A1	4k	1.25	*1.50*
38a	A1	5k	7.00	4.00
40a	A1	6k	2.00	1.60
41a	A1	7k	2.00	1.75
42a	A1	8k	2.00	1.90
43a	A1	10k	2.50	2.50
45a	A1	20k	4.00	2.50
46a	A1	30k	6.75	4.50
47a	A1	50k	12.50	10.00
		Nos. 30a-47a (14)	45.00	*35.55*

Types of 1941 Overprinted in Brown or Green

1942, Apr. 9

49	A1	2k dark brown	.30	.30
50	A1	5k dark carmine	.45	*.65*
51	A1	10k dark blue green (G)	.85	*.95*
		Nos. 49-51 (3)	1.60	*1.90*

First anniversary of Croatian independence.

Tête bêche pairs of Nos. 49-51 are from Ministerial Albums.

Banjaluka ("F.I." at upper right) — A20

1942, June 13

52	A20	100k violet	3.25	*3.50*

Banjaluka Philatelic Exhibition.

Exists in se-tenant pair with No. 48. Value unused, $160.

No. 35 Surcharged in Red Brown with New Value and Bar

1942, June 23

53	A1	25b on 2k carmine lake	.45	.45
a.		Tête bêche pair	2.50	2.50

No. 53 exists with double surcharge. It is not scarce.

Trakoscan Castle — A21

Catherine Zrinski — A23

Design: 12.50k, Citadel of Veliki Tabor.

1943, Mar. 28

Pelure Paper

54	A21	3.50k brown carmine	.55	.40
55	A21	12.50k violet black	.75	.65

Nos. 54 was reissued in 1944 on ordinary paper, perf 12. Value the same for both varieties. No. 55 also exists on ordinary paper. It is scarce.

1943, June 7 Engr. *Perf. 12½*

2k, Fran Krsto Frankopan. 3.50k, Peter Zrinski.

Various Frames

56	A23	1k dark blue	.30	.30
57	A23	2k dark olive green	.30	.30
58	A23	3.50k dark red	.40	.45
		Nos. 56-58 (3)	1.00	*1.05*

Rugjer Boscovich — A26

Ante Pavelich — A27

1943, Dec. 13 *Perf. 11*

59	A26	3.50k copper red	.30	.30
60	A26	12.50k dk violet brn	.45	.45

Rugjer Boscovich (1711-1787). Mathematician and physicist.

1943-44 Litho. *Perf. 12½, 14*

61	A27	25b orange ver	.20	.20
62	A27	50b Prus blue	.20	.20
63	A27	75b olive green	.20	.20
64	A27	1k lt green	.20	.20
65	A27	1.50k dull gray vio	.20	.20
66	A27	2k rose lake	.20	.20
67	A27	3k rose brown	.20	.20
68	A27	3.50k bright blue	.20	.20
a.		3.50k dark blue, perf. 11½	2.25	*2.50*
69	A27	4k brt red violet	.20	.20
70	A27	5k ultra	.20	.20
71	A27	8k orange brn	.20	.20
72	A27	9k rose pink	.20	.20
73	A27	10k violet brn	.20	.20
74	A27	12k dk olive bis	.20	.20
75	A27	12.50k gray black	.20	.20
76	A27	18k dull brown	.20	.20
77	A27	32k dark brown	.20	.20
78	A27	50k grnsh blue	.20	.20
79	A27	70k orange	.50	.50
80	A27	100k violet	1.25	1.25
		Nos. 61-80 (20)	5.35	*5.35*

Nos. 61 and 63 measure 20½x26mm. Nos. 62 and 64-80 measure 22x27½mm.

Nos. 61, 63, 67, 70, 71 and 72 are perf 12½. Nos. 62, 64-66, 68, 69, 73 and 75-80 are perf 14. No. 74 exists either perf 12½ or 14.

Issue dates: 2k, 1943; No. 68a, June 13, 1943, Pavelich's birthday; others, 1944.

"Labor Day 1945" — A28

1945 Photo. *Perf. 11½*

81	A28	3.50k red brown	.50	*1.10*

From 1951 to 1972 44 labels were circulated by a Croatian Government in Exile. These had no postal value.

GOVT. — Independent state
AREA — 21,823 sq. mi.
POP. — 4,676,865 (1999 est.)
CAPITAL — Zagreb

Croatia declared its independence from Yugoslavia in 1991.

100 Paras = 1 Dinar (1991)
100 Lipa = 1 Kuna (1994)

Nos. RA20, RA20a Surcharged in Black and Gold

1991, Nov. 21 Litho. *Perf. 14*

100	PT10	4d on 1.20d #RA20	*.35*	*.35*
a.		Perf. 11x10½	*.35*	*.35*

A35

A36

1991, Dec. 10 *Perf. 12*

101	A35	30d multicolored	*1.60*	*.35*

Declaration of independence, 10/8/91.

1991, Dec. 11 *Perf. 12*

Christmas: Creche figures of the Holy Family from Kosljun Monastery.

102	A36	4d multicolored	*.60*	*.60*

No. RA21 Surcharged in Black and Gold

1992, Jan. 3 *Perf. 10½x11*

103	PT11	20d on 1.70d #RA21	*4.00*	*3.00*

Croatian Arms — A37

1992, Jan. 15 *Perf. 11x10½*

104	A37	10d multicolored	*.25*	*.25*
a.		Perf. 14	*.20*	*.20*

See No. RA22.

1992 Winter Olympics, Albertville A38

1992, Feb. 4 *Perf. 11x10½*

105	A38	30d multicolored	*1.60*	*1.60*

Croatian Cities and Landmarks A39

A39a

Designs: 6d, Knin. 7d, Eltz Castle, Vukovar. 20d, Church, Ilok. 30d, Starcevic Street, Gospic. 45d, Rector's Palace, Dubrovnik. 50d, St. Jakov's Cathedral, Sibenik. 100d, Vinkovci. 200d, Pazin, vert. No. 115, Beli Monastery. 500d, Slavonski Brod. 1000d, Varazdin. 2000d, Karlovac. 5000d, Zadar, vert. 10,000d, Vis.

1992-94 *Perf. 14*

107	A39	6d multicolored	*.20*	*.20*
108	A39	7d multicolored	*.20*	*.20*
109	A39	20d multicolored	*.25*	
a.		Perf. 11x10½	*1.00*	
110	A39	30d multicolored	*.60*	*.60*
111	A39	45d multicolored	*1.10*	*1.10*
112	A39	50d multicolored	*1.10*	*1.10*
113	A39a	100d multicolored	*.45*	
114	A39a	200d multicolored	*.35*	
115	A39	300d multicolored	*4.00*	
117	A39a	500d multicolored	*1.25*	
118	A39a	1000d multicolored	*1.90*	
119	A39a	2000d multicolored	*2.25*	
120	A39a	5000d multicolored	*2.50*	
121	A39a	10,000d multicolored	*4.50*	
		Nos. 107-121 (14)	*20.65*	

Issued: 6d, 4/18; 7d, 4/8; #109, 2/28; #109a, 9/9; 30d, 5/21; 45d, 4/14; 50d, 4/28; 115, 6/26; 100d, 12/14; 500d, 2/9/93; 1000d, 3/16/93; 200d, 4/22/93; 2000d, 5/20/93; 5000d, 9/24/93; 10,000d, 2/22/94.

See Nos. 355-356, 437A, 456.

Statue of King Tomislav — A40

1992, May 5 Engr. *Perf. 12½ Horiz.*

Coil Stamp

124	A40	10d dark green	*.25*

Railroad Station, Zagreb, Cent. — A41

1992, June 30 Litho. *Perf. 14*

125	A41	30d multicolored	*.75*

Matica, Society of Knowledge and Literacy, 150th Anniv. — A42

1992, July 8

126	A42	20d red, gold & black	*.35*

Bishop Josip Juraj Strossmayer, Founder — A43

1992, July 9

127	A43	30d multicolored	*.45*

Croatian Academy of Arts and Sciences, 125th anniv., in 1991.

1992 Summer Olympics, Barcelona A44

Design: 105d, Abstract design.

1992, July 25

128 A44 40d shown .50
129 A44 105d multicolored *1.25*

Flowers A45

Designs: 30d, Edraianthus pumilio. 85d, Degenia velebitica, vert.

1992, July 28

130 A45 30d multicolored .40
131 A45 85d multicolored 1.00

Wildlife — A46

40d, Monticola solitarius. 75d, Elaphe situla.

1992, July 31

132 A46 40d multicolored .50
133 A46 75d multicolored .90

Discovery of America, 500th Anniv. — A47

Europa: 30d, 60d, Sailing ship. 75d, 130d, Indian in Chicago, by Ivan Mestrovic (1883-1962).

1992, Sep. 4 Litho. *Perf. 14*

134 A47 30d multicolored .35
135 A47 60d multicolored .75
136 A47 75d red & black .90
137 A47 130d red, blk & gold 1.60
Nos. 134-137 (4) 3.60

Issued: 30d, 75d, July 31; others, Sept. 4.

A48

A49

1992, Oct. 2

138 A48 40d multicolored .35
139 A48 130d multi, diff. *1.00*

Declaration of Croatian Literary Language, 25th Anniv. (#133). Spelling reform by Dr. Ivan Broz, cent. (#104).

1992, Oct. 16

140 A49 90d multicolored .60

City of Samobor, 750th Anniv.

Gift of the St. Juraj Church by Archbishop Mucimir, 1100th Anniv. — A50

1992, Oct. 30

141 A50 60d multicolored .40

Reign of King Bela IV, 750th Anniv. — A51

1992, Nov. 16 Litho. *Perf. 14*

142 A51 180d multicolored .95

Christmas A52

1992, Dec. 7

143 A52 80d multicolored .40

Blaz Lorkovic (1839-1892), Scientist — A53

Kolo Literature Review, 150th Anniv. — A54

1992, Dec. 21

144 A53 250d multicolored .85

1992, Dec. 22

145 A54 300d multicolored 1.10

Ivan Bunic-Vucic (1592-1658) A55

1992, Dec. 29

146 A55 350d multicolored *1.25*

— A55a

800th Anniversary of Krapina

1993, Jan. 15

146A A55a 300d multicolored .80 .80

Nikola Tesla (1856-1943), Physicist A56

1993, Jan. 30

147 A56 250d multicolored 70

Self-Portrait, by Ferdo Quiquerez (1845-1893) A57

1993, Feb. 10

148 A57 100d multicolored .25

Wildlife — A58

1993, Feb. 23 Litho. *Perf. 14*

149 A58 500d Cervus elaphus 1.10
150 A58 550d Haliaeetus albicilla 1.25

Self-Portrait, by Zlatko Sulentic (1893-1971) A59

1993, Mar. 17

151 A59 350d multicolored .65

Lipik Health and Convalescent Home, Cent. — A60

1993, Apr. 22 Litho. *Perf. 14*

152 A60 400d multicolored .75

Ivan Goran Kovacic (1913-1943), Author — A61

1993, Apr. 24

153 A61 200d multicolored .35

59th PEN Congress, Dubrovnik A62

1993, Apr. 24

154 A62 800d multicolored *1.25*

Ivan Kukuljevic (1816-89), Politician, Historian, Writer — A63

1993, May 2 Litho. *Perf. 14*

155 A63 500d multicolored .75

Croatian Natl. Theatre, Split, Cent. — A64

Pag, 500th Anniv. — A65

1993, May 6 Litho. *Perf. 14*

156 A64 600d multicolored .85

1993, May 18

157 A65 800d multicolored .95

Croatian Membership in United Nations, 1st Anniv. — A66

1993, May 22

158 A66 500d multicolored .60

Europa
A67

Contemporary paintings by: 700d, Ivo Dulcic (1916-75). 1000d, Miljenko Stancic (1926-77). 1100d, Ljubo Ivancic (b. 1925).

1993, June 5

159 A67 700d multicolored .65 .65
160 A67 1000d multicolored .90 .90
161 A67 1100d multicolored 1.00 1.00
a. Min. sheet, 2 each #159-161 5.25 5.25
Nos. 159-161 (3) 2.55 2.55

Intl. Art Biennial, Venice — A68

Works of art by: 250d, Milivoj Bijelic. 600d, Ivo Dekovic. 1000d, Zeljko Kipke.

1993, June 10 Litho. *Perf. 14*

162 A68 250d multicolored .25
a. Souvenir sheet of 4 1.00
163 A68 600d multicolored .75
a. Souvenir sheet of 4 3.00
164 A68 1000d multicolored 1.00
a. Souvenir sheet of 4 4.00
Nos. 162-164 (3) 2.00

1993 Mediterranean Games — A69

1993, June 15 Litho. *Perf. 14*

165 A69 700d multicolored .75

Adolf Waldinger (1843-1904), Painter — A70

1993, June 16

166 A70 300d multicolored .30

Famous Croatian Battles
A71

1993, July 6 Litho. *Perf. 14*

167 A71 800d Krbavskom, 1493 .65
168 A71 1300d Sisak, 1593 1.00

Miroslav Krleza (1893-1981), Writer — A72

1993, July 7

169 A72 400d multicolored .35

Croatian Membership in UPU, 1st Anniv. — A73

1993, July 20 Litho. *Perf. 14*

170 A73 1800d multicolored 1.40

Vlaho Paljetak (1893-1944), Composer
A74

1993, Aug. 7

171 A74 500d multicolored .35

Stamp Day — A75

1993, Sept. 9 Litho. *Perf. 14*

172 A75 600d multicolored .35

Map of Istria, 1620 — A76

1993, Sept. 20

173 A76 2200d multicolored 1.10

Incorporation of Istria, Rijeka and Zadar into Croatia, 50th anniv.

Tadija Smiciklas (1843-1914), Historian — A77

1993, Oct. 1

174 A77 800d black, gold & red .40

Archaelogical Museum, Split, Cent. — A78

1993, Oct. 27

175 A78 1000d multicolored .45

A79

A80

1993, Nov. 17 Litho. *Perf. 14*

176 A79 3000d multicolored 1.40

Uprising of 13th Pioneer Battalion, Villefranche-de-Rouergue, France, 50th anniv.

1993, Nov. 18

900d, Josip Eugen Tomic (1843-1906), writer.

177 A80 900d multicolored .40

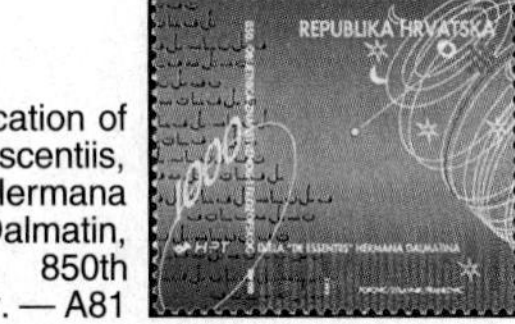

Publication of De Esscentiis, by Hermana Dalmatin, 850th Anniv. — A81

1993, Nov. 30

178 A81 1000d multicolored .45

Christmas
A82

Paintings: 1000d, Christmas at the Front, by Miroslav Sutej. 4000d, Birth of Christ, 15th cent. fresco, Marienkirch of Dvigrad.

1993, Dec. 3

179 A82 1000d multicolored .40
180 A82 4000d multicolored 1.75

Organized Skiing in Croatia, Cent. — A83

1993, Dec. 15

181 A83 1000d multicolored .40

Croatian Natl. Guard, 125th Anniv.
A84

1993, Dec. 22

182 A84 1100d multicolored .45

Printers of Senj, 500th Anniv. — A85

1994, Jan. 29

183 A85 2200d multicolored .95

1994 Winter Olympics, Lillehammer
A86

1994, Feb. 12

184 A86 4000d multicolored 1.75

Dinosaurs from Western Istria — A87

a, 2400d, Iguanodons. b, 4000d, Map, skeleton.

1994, Mar. 7

185 A87 Pair, #a.-b. 2.75

Nos. 185a-185b are a continuous design.

Zora Dalmatinska Magazine, 150th Anniv. — A88

1994, Mar. 15

186 A88 800d multicolored .40

Croatian University, Zagreb, 325th Anniv. — A89

Design: 2200d, University building, Emperor Leopold I's seal, vice-chancellor's chain.

1994, Apr. 19 Litho. *Perf. 14*

187 A89 2200d multicolored 1.00

Protect the Environment
A90

ILO, 75th Anniv. — A91

1994, Apr. 22 Litho. *Perf. 14*
188 A90 3800d Canis lupus 1.75

1994, May 2
189 A91 1000d multicolored .50

A92

Europa — A93

European inventions, discoveries: 3800d, Faust Vrancic (1551-1617), parachute. 4000d, Slavoljub Penkala (1871-1922), fountain pen.

1994, May 16
190 A92 3800d multicolored 1.75
191 A93 4000d multicolored 1.90

A94

A95

1994, June 3
192 A94 2.40k Iris croatica 1.10
193 A94 4k Colchicum visianii 1.90

1994, June 7

Drazen Petrovic (1964-93), basketball player.

194 A95 1k multicolored .50

Tourism in Croatia, 150th Anniv. — A96

Designs: 80 l, Plitvice Lakes Natl. Park. 1k, Waterfalls, Krka River. 1.10k, Kornati Islands Natl. Park. 2.20k, Kopacki Trscak nature reserve. 2.40k Sailboats, Opatijska Riviera resort. 3.80k, Brijuni islands. 4k, Trakoscan castle, Zagorje.

1994, June 15 Litho. *Perf. 14*
196 A96 80 l multicolored .40
197 A96 1k multicolored .45
198 A96 1.10k multicolored .50
200 A96 2.20k multicolored 1.00
201 A96 2.40k multicolored 1.10
206 A96 3.80k multicolored 1.75
207 A96 4k multicolored 1.90
a. Min. sheet of 7, #196-198, 200-201, 206-207 + 2 labels 7.25
Nos. 196-207 (7) 7.10

Issued: 80 l, 1k, 1.10k, 2.20k, 2.40k, 3.80k, 4k, 6/15/94. This is an expanding set. Numbers may change.

Croatian Musicians A97

Designs: 1k, Kresimir Baranovic (1894-1975), composer, vert. 2.20k, Vatroslav Lisinski (1819-54), composer, vert. 2.40k, Pauline Liederbuch (b.1644), harpist.

1994, June 20
211 A97 1k multicolored .45
212 A97 2.20k multicolored 1.00
213 A97 2.40k multicolored 1.10
Nos. 211-213 (3) 2.55

Croatian Fraternal Union, Cent. — A98

1994, Aug. 15 Litho. *Perf. 14*
214 A98 2.20k multicolored 1.10

A99

A100

1994, Aug. 31
215 A99 80 l multicolored .40

Intl. Year of the Family.

1994, Sept. 10
216 A100 1k multicolored .50

Intl. Olympic Committee, cent.

Visit of Pope John Paul II — A101

1994, Sept. 10
217 A101 1k multicolored .50

No. 217 printed with se-tenant label.

Antoine de Saint-Exupery (1900-44), Aviator, Author A102

1994, Sept. 20
218 A102 3.80k multicolored 1.90

13th Intl. Congress on Early Christian Archeology A103

1994, Sept. 23
219 A103 4k multicolored 2.00

No. 219 printed with se-tenant label.

Modern Croatian Paintings A104

Designs: 2.40k, Still Life with Fruits and Basket, by Marino Tartaglia, 1926. 3.80k, In the Park, by Milan Steiner, c. 1918. 4k, Self-portrait, by Vilko Gecan, 1929.

1994, Oct. 12
220 A104 2.40k multicolored 1.25
221 A104 3.80k multicolored 1.90
222 A104 4k multicolored 2.00
Nos. 220-222 (3) 5.15

Ivan Belostenec (1594-1675), Writer & Lexicographer A105

1994, Nov. 9
223 A105 2.20k multicolored 1.10

City of Zagreb, Zagreb Bishopric, 900th Anniv. — A106

Designs: No. 224a, 1k, Zagreb exchange building, designed by V. Kovacic, S. Penkala's airplane, Cibona office tower, designed by Hrzic, Pitesa and Serbetic. b, 1k, Maxi Cat, by Zlatko Grgic, Zagreb School of Animated Film. c, 1k, St. Mark's Church, Gradec; photo of gas lantern, by Toso Dabac. d, 4k, Late Gothic bishop's staff, Valvasor's view of Zagreb.
13.50k, Zagreb street scene, Penkala's airplane, vert.

1994, Nov. 16
224 A106 Strip of 4, #a.-d. 3.50

Souvenir Sheet

225 A106 13.50k multicolored 6.75

No. 224 is a continuous design. No. 225 contains one 24x48mm stamp.

Christmas A107

Design: 1k, Epiphany, by unknown sculptor.

1994, Dec. 1 Litho. *Perf. 14*
226 A107 1k multicolored .50

Virgin Mary's Sanctuary, Loreto, 700th Anniv. — A108

Design: 4k, The Moving of the Holy House, by Giovanni Battista Tiepolo.

1994, Dec. 10
227 A108 4k multicolored 1.90

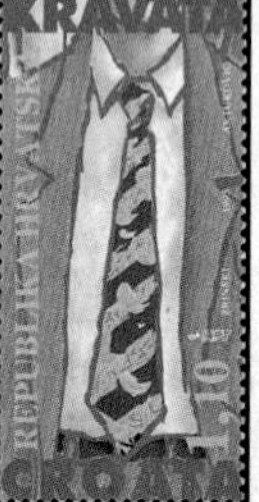
Necktie in Croatia — A109

Tie designs: 1.10k, Businessman's, 1995. 3.80k, English Dandy, 1810. 4k, Croatian soldier, 1630.

1995, Jan. 19 Litho. *Perf. 14*
228 A109 1.10k multicolored .40
229 A109 3.80k multicolored 1.40
230 A109 4k multicolored 1.50
a. Souvenir sheet of 3, #228-230 3.25
Nos. 228-230 (3) 3.30

Croatian Monasteries — A110

1k, Jesuit Monastery, Zagreb, 350th anniv. 2.40k, Franciscan Monastery, Visovac, 550th anniv.

1995, Feb. 16
231 A110 1k multicolored .35
232 A110 2.40k multicolored .90

Hunting Dogs — A111

Designs: 2.20k, Istrian short-haired. 2.40k, Posavinian. 3.80k, Istrian wire-haired.

1995, Mar. 9 Litho. *Perf. 14*
233 A111 2.20k multicolored .90
234 A111 2.40k multicolored .95
235 A111 3.80k multicolored 1.50
Nos. 233-235 (3) 3.35

Town of Split, 1700th Anniv. — A112

#236: a, 1k, Drawing of reconstruction of Diocletian's Palace. b, 2.20k, "Split Harbour," by Emanuel Vidovic, 1937. c, 4k, Modern view of town, bust of Marko Marulic by Ivan Mestrovic.
13.40k, Buildings, vert.

1995, Apr. 20 Litho. *Perf. 14*
236 A112 Strip of 3, #a.-c. 3.00

Souvenir Sheet

237 A112 13.40k multicolored 5.50

No. 237 contains one 24x48mm stamp.

World Team Handball Championships, Iceland — A113

1995, May 4
238 A113 4k multicolored 1.60

Peace & Freedom A114

Europa: 2.40k, Clearing storm clouds. 4k, Hands of angel, by Francisco Robba.

1995, May 9
239 A114 2.40k multicolored 1.00
240 A114 4k multicolored 1.60

Anti-Austria Demonstrations, 150th Anniv. — A115

1995, May 15
241 A115 1.10k multicolored .45
242 A115 3.80k multicolored 1.50

Croatian surrender to British forces at Bleiburg, 50th anniv. (#242).

Independence Day — A116

1995, May 30 Litho. *Perf. 14*
243 A116 1.10k multicolored .45

Croatian Sculptures at Venice Biennial, 1995 — A117

2.20k, Installation (a part), by Martina Kramer. 2.40k, Paracelsus Paraduchamps, by Mirko Zrinscak, vert. 4k, Shadows, by Goran Petercol.

1995, June 8 Litho. *Perf. 14*
244 A117 2.20k multicolored .90
245 A117 2.40k multicolored 1.00
246 A117 4k multicolored 1.60
Nos. 244-246 (3) 3.50

St. Anthony of Padua (1195-1231) — A118

1995, June 13
247 A118 1k multicolored .40

Marine Life — A119

1995, June 29 Litho. *Perf. 14*
248 A119 2.40k Caretta caretta .95
249 A119 4k Tursiops truncatus 1.60

Liberation of the City of Knin — A120

1995, Aug. 5 Litho. *Perf. 14*
250 A120 1.30k multicolored .50

Krka River Hydroelectric Power Plant, Cent. — A121

1995, Aug. 28
251 A121 3.60k multicolored 1.40

Stamp Day — A122

1995, Sept. 9 Litho. *Perf. 14*
252 A122 1.30k multicolored .50

Franz von Suppe (1819-95), Composer A123

1995, Sept. 15
253 A123 6.50k multicolored 2.50

See Austria Nos. 1686-1687.

Liberation of Petrinja from Turkish Rule, 400th Anniv. — A124

1995, Sept. 21
254 A124 2.20k multicolored .85

Croatian Music — A125

Composers, conductors: 1.20k, Ivo Tijardovic (1895-1976). 1.40k, Lovro Von Matacic (1899-1985). 6.50k, Jakov Gotovac (1895-1982).

1995, Sept. 23
255 A125 1.20k multicolored .45
256 A125 1.40k multicolored .55
257 A125 6.50k multicolored 2.50
Nos. 255-257 (3) 3.50

Herman Bollé (1845-1926), Architect — A126

2.40k, Izidor Krsnjavi (1845-1927), painter. 3.60k, Croatian National Theatre, cent.

1995, Oct. 14 Litho. *Perf. 14*
258 A126 1.80k multicolored .70
259 A126 2.40k multicolored .90
260 A126 3.60k multicolored 1.40
Nos. 258-260 (3) 3.00

Croatian Towns — A127

1995, Oct. 20
261 A127 1k Bjelovar .40
262 A127 1.30k Osijek, vert. .50
263 A127 1.40k Cakovec, vert. .55
264 A127 2.20k Rovinj .85
265 A127 2.40k Korcula .90
266 A127 3.60k Zupanja 1.40
Nos. 261-266 (6) 4.60

See No. 448.

UN, FAO, 50th Anniv. — A128

No. 268, "5, 0" in form of cracker, FAO.

1995, Oct. 24
267 A128 3.60k multicolored 1.40
268 A128 3.60k multicolored 1.40
a. Pair, #267-268 2.80

Croatian Scientists — A129

1k, Spiro Brusina (1845-1908). 2.20k, Bogoslav Sulek (1816-95). 6.50k, Front of European language dictionary, published by Faust Vrancic (1551-1617).

1995, Oct. 30
269 A129 1k multicolored .40
270 A129 2.20k multicolored .85
271 A129 6.50k multicolored 2.50
Nos. 269-271 (3) 3.75

Institute for Blind Children, Cent. — A130

1995, Nov. 23 Litho. *Perf. 14*
272 A130 1.20k multicolored .45

Christmas A131

1995, Dec. 1
273 A131 1.30k multicolored .50

Maroc Polo's Return from China, 700th Anniv. A132

1995, Dec. 7
274 A132 3.60k multicolored 1.25

Liberated Towns A133

1995, Dec. 16
275 A133 20 l Hrvatska Kostajnica .20
276 A133 30 l Slunj .20
277 A133 50 l Gracac .20
278 A133 1.20k Drnis, vert. .45
279 A133 6.50k Glina 2.50
280 A133 10k Obrovac, vert. 3.75
Nos. 275-280 (6) 7.30

Incunabula A134

Designs: 1.40k, Lectionary of Bernardin of Split. 3.60k, Spovid Opcena (General Confession).

1995, Dec. 28
281 A134 1.40k multicolored .55
282 A134 3.60k multicolored 1.25

Spirituality of the Croats
A135

Political Anniversaries
A136

Designs: No. 283, Mosaic of St. Marko Krizevcanin (1589-1619), Catholic martyr. No. 284, Veneration of Miraculous Crucifix, St. Guido's Church, Rijeka, 700th anniv. No. 285, Ivan Merz (1896-1928), Catholic educator.

1996, Jan. 18 Litho. *Perf. 14*

283 A135 1.30k multicolored *.50*
284 A135 1.30k multicolored *.50*
285 A135 1.30k multicolored *.50*
a. Strip of 3, Nos. 283-285 *1.50*

1996, Feb. 28

1.20k, Rakovica Uprising by Eugen Kvaternik, 125th anniv., horiz. 1.40k, Ante Starcevic (1823-96). 2.20k, Constitution of Neutral Peasant Republic of Croatia, 75th anniv., Stjepan Radic (1871-1928). 3.60k, Labin Republic, 75th anniv.

286 A136 1.20k multicolored *.45*
287 A136 1.40k multicolored *.55*
288 A136 2.20k multicolored *.75*
289 A136 3.60k multicolored *1.25*
Nos. 286-289 (4) *3.00*

Institute for Pharmacognosy, University of Zagreb, Cent. — A137

1996, Mar. 23 Litho. *Perf. 14*

290 A137 6.50k multicolored *2.25*

Croatian Music — A138

a, Vinko Jelíc (1596-1636), composer. b, First performance of opera "Love and Music." c, Josip Stolcer Slavenski (1896-1955), composer. d, "Lijepa Nasa," Croatian national anthem, 150th anniv.

1996, Mar. 28

291 A138 2.20k Strip of 4, #a.-d. 3.25

A139

A140

Famous Women Writers (Europa): 2.20k, Cvijeta Zuzoric (b. 1551 or 1552). 3.60k, Ivana Brlic Mazuranic (1874-1938).

1996, Apr. 11 Litho. *Perf. 14*

292 A139 2.20k multicolored *.80*
293 A139 3.60k multicolored *1.25*

1996, Apr. 30

The Zrinskis and The Frankopans: 1.30k, Nikola Subic Zrinski of Sziget (1508-56). 1.40k, Nikola Zrinski (1620-64). 2.20k, Petar Zrinski (1621-71). 2.40k, Katarina Zrinski (1625-73). 3.60k, Fran Krsto Frankopan (1643-71).

294 A140 1.30k multicolored *.45*
295 A140 1.40k multicolored *.50*
296 A140 2.20k multicolored *.80*
297 A140 2.40k multicolored *.90*
298 A140 3.60k multicolored *1.25*
a. Sheet of 5, #294-298 4.50
Nos. 294-298 (5) *3.90*

Natl. Guard, 5th Anniv.
A141

Flowers
A142

1996, May 28 Litho. *Perf. 14*

299 A141 1.30k multicolored *.55*

1996, June 5

Designs: 2.40k, Campanula istriaca. 3.60k, Centaurea ragusina.

300 A142 2.40k multicolored *1.00*
301 A142 3.60k multicolored *1.50*

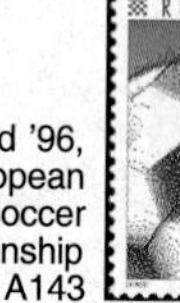

England '96, European Soccer Championship
A143

1996, June 8

302 A143 2.20k red & black *.90*

Father Ferdinand Konscak's Expedition to Lower California, 250th Anniv. — A144

1996, June 10

303 A144 2.40k multicolored *1.00*

1996 Summer Olympics, Atlanta
A145

1996, July 4

304 A145 3.60k multicolored *1.50*

A146

A147

1996, July 4

305 A146 1.40k multicolored *.60*

Josip Fon, founder of Croatian Sokol Gymnastics Society, 150th birth anniv.

1996, Sept. 9 Litho. *Perf. 14*

306 A147 1.30k multicolored *.55*

Croatian postage stamps, 5th anniv.

1st Written Reference, Zumberak Region, 700th Anniv. — A148

1996, Sept. 14

307 A148 2.20k multicolored *.90*

A149

A150

1996, Sept. 19

308 A149 1.30k multicolored *.55*

First written record of fishing in Croatia, 1000th anniv.

1996, Sept. 19

Events of the early Middle Ages: 1.20k, Vekenega's Book of Gospels, 900th anniv. 1.40k, Visit by Saxon Benedictine abbot Gottschalk (805-870), to Duke Trpimir's court, 1150th anniv.

309 A150 1.20k multicolored *.50*
310 A150 1.40k multicolored *.60*

Scientists
A151

Designs: a, Gjuro Pilar (1846-93), geologist. b, Frane Bulic (1846-1934), archeologist. c, Ante Sercer (1896-1968), otolaryngologist.

1996, Oct. 4 Litho. *Perf. 14*

311 A151 2.40k Strip of 3, #a.-c. *2.75*

Beginning of Higher Education in Croatia, 600th Anniv. — A152

Oldest preserved Croatian text written in Latin script, "Order and Law" of Dominican nuns, Zadar.

1996, Oct. 16 *Perf. 13½*

312 A152 1.40k multicolored .50

Paintings — A153

Designs: 1.30k, Rain, by Menci Clement Crncic (1865-1930). 1.40k, The Peljesac-Korcula Channel, by Mato Celestin Medovic (1857-1919). 3.60k, Pink Dream, by Vlaho Bukovac (1855-1922).

1996, Nov. 7 Litho. *Perf. 14*

313 A153 1.30k multicolored *.45*
314 A153 1.40k multicolored *.50*
315 A153 3.60k multicolored *1.25*
Nos. 313-315 (3) *2.20*

UNICEF, 50th Anniv. — A154

1996, Nov. 15

316 A154 3.60k multicolored *1.25*

City of Osijek, 800th Anniv.
A155

Christmas
A156

Views of city: No. 317, River bank, church, coat of arms. No. 318, Boats in water, view looking down covered walkway through building.

1996, Dec. 2 Litho. *Perf. 14*

317 A155 2.20k multicolored *.80*
318 A155 2.20k multicolored *.80*
a. Pair, #317-318 *1.60*

1996, Dec. 3

319 A156 1.30k multicolored *.45*

First Croatian Savings Bank, Zagreb, 150th Anniv. — A157

Design: 3.60k, Publishing of "The Bases of Corn Trade," by Josip Sipus, bicent.

1996, Dec. 14

320 A157 2.40k multicolored *.85*
321 A157 3.60k multicolored *1.25*

Motion Pictures, Cent. — A158

Designs: a, Shooting of film, "Vatroslav Lisinski," Oktavijan Miletic, cameraman, director. b, Characters from animated series, "Professor Baltazar." c, Mirjana Bohanec, Relja Basic in "Who Sings Means No Harm."

1997, Jan. 16 Litho. *Perf. 14*

322 A158 1.40k Strip of 3, #a.-c. 1.40

Great Europeans
A159

Designs: 2.20k, Miguel de Cervantes (1547-1676), author. 3.60k, Johannes Gutenberg (1397-1468), printer, horiz.

1997, Feb. 7

323 A159 2.20k multicolored .75
324 A159 3.60k multicolored 1.25

Legends A160

Europa: 1.30k, Home Genies, from story, "Stribor's Forest." 3.60k, "Vili Joze," by Vladimir Nazor, vert.

1997, Mar. 6 **Litho.** ***Perf. 14***
325 A160 1.30k multicolored .45
326 A160 3.60k multicolored 1.25

Fauna of Croatia — A161

1997, Apr. 22 **Litho.** ***Perf. 14***
327 A161 1.40k Pinna nobilis .45
328 A161 2.40k Radziella styx .80
329 A161 3.60k Tonna galea 1.25
Nos. 327-329 (3) 2.50

Admission of Croatia to UN, 5th Anniv. A162

1997, May 22 **Litho.** ***Perf. 14***
330 A162 6.50k Pres. Franjo Tudjman 2.10

First Croatian Esperantist Conference, 90th Anniv. A163

Ludwig Lazarus Zamenhof, conf. logo.

1997, May 31
331 A163 1.20k multicolored .40

Congress of Intl. Amateur Rugby Federation, Dubrovnik A164

1997, June 6
332 A164 2.20k multicolored .70

Siege of Vukovar, Serbo-Croatian War, 1991 — A165

Painting by Zlatko Kauzlaric Atac. Illustration reduced.

1997, June 8 **Litho.** ***Perf. 14***
333 A165 6.50k multicolored 2.10

Croatian Kings — A166

1.30k, King Peter Svacic, 900th death anniv. 2.40k, King Stephen Drzislav, 1000th death anniv.

1997, July 3
334 A166 1.30k multicolored .45
335 A166 2.40k multicolored .80

16th Century Courier from Dubrovnik A167

1997, Sept. 9 **Litho.** ***Perf. 14***
336 A167 2.30k multicolored .75

Stamp Day.

Croatian Olympic Medals — A168

Designs: 1k, Tennis, bronze, Barcelona, 1992. 1.20k, Basketball, silver, Barcelona 1992. 1.40k, Water polo, silver, Atlanta, 1996. 2.20k, Handball, gold, Atlanta, 1996.

1997, Sept. 10
337 A168 1k multicolored .35
338 A168 1.20k multicolored .40

Size: 27x31mm

339 A168 1.40k multicolored .45
340 A168 2.20k multicolored .70
Nos. 337-340 (4) 1.90

Defense of Sibenik — A169

Designs: No. 341, Fort, airplanes. No. 342, Turkish cavalry, fort.

1997, Sept. 18
341 A169 1.30k multicolored .45
342 A169 1.30k multicolored .45
a. Pair, #341-342 .90

Serbo-Croatian War, 1991 (#341). War with the Turks, 350th anniv. (#342).

Anniversaries A170

No. 343: a, Frane Petríc (1529-97), philosopher. b, Vicko Lovrin, 16th century painter. c, Frano Krsiníc (1897-1982), sculptor. d, Dubravko Dujsin (1894-1947), actor.

1997, Oct. 17 **Litho.** ***Perf. 14***
343 A170 1.40k Strip of 4, #a.-d. 1.75 1.75

A171

A172

1997, Oct. 23
344 A171 2.20k multicolored .70 .35
345 A172 3.60k multicolored 1.25 .65

Use of Croatian language in parliament, 150th anniv. (#344).
Croatian Grammar School, Zadar, cent. (#345).

Palaeontological Finds in Croatia — A173

Designs: 1.40k, Gomphotherium angustidens. 2.40k, Viviparus novskaensis.

1997, Nov. 6
346 A173 1.40k multicolored .45 .25
347 A173 2.40k multicolored .80 .40

Modern Art A174

Paintings: 1.30k, Painter in the Pond, by Nikola Masic (1852-1902). 2.20k, Angelus, by Emanuel Vidovic (1870-1953). 3.60k, Tree in the Snow, by Slava Raskaj (1877-1906).

1997, Nov. 14
348 A174 1.30k multicolored .45 .25
349 A174 2.20k multicolored .70 .35
350 A174 3.60k multicolored 1.25 .60
Nos. 348-350 (3) 2.40 1.20

Contemporary Christmas Painting, by Ivan Antolcic — A175

"Birth of Jesus," by Isidor Krsnjavi A176

1997, Nov. 28 **Litho.** ***Perf. 13½***
351 A175 1.30k multicolored .40 .20

Perf. 14

352 A176 3.60k multicolored 1.10 .55

Croatian Literature — A177

1997, Dec. 18 ***Perf. 14***
353 A177 1k shown .30 .20
354 A177 1.20k Book, words .40 .20

Printing of the translation of "Electra," by Dominko Zlataric, 400th anniv. (No. 353). Publication of "The Best of Folk Speech and the Illyric or Croatian Language," by Filip Grabovac, 250th anniv. (No. 354).

Cities and Landmarks Type of 1992

1997 **Litho.** ***Perf. 14***
355 A39 5 l Ilok .20
356 A39 10 l Dubrovnik .20

Events and Festivals — A178

Europa: 1.45k, Varazdin Baroque Evenings, musical notes. 4k, Dubrovnik Summer Festival.

1998, Jan. 23 ***Perf. 13½***
357 A178 1.45k multicolored .45
358 A178 4k multicolored 1.25

1998 Winter Olympic Games, Nagano — A179

1998, Feb. 7 ***Perf. 14***
359 A179 2.45k multicolored .75

Croatian Events of 1848 — A180

a, 1.60k, Flag, battle near Moor. b, 4k, Portrait of Ban Josip Jelacic. c, 1.60k, Croatian Assembly.

1998, Mar. 25 Litho. *Perf. 14*
360 A180 Strip of 3, #a.-c. *2.25*

No. 360b is 21x32mm.

Ante Topic Mimara (1898-1987), Art Collector, Painter A181

1998, Apr. 7 Litho. *Perf. 14*
361 A181 2.65k multicolored .85

A182

A183

Mushrooms: a, 1.30k, Amanita caesarea. b, 7.20k, Morchella conica. c, 1.30k, Lactarius deliciosus.

1998, Apr. 22
362 A182 Strip of 3, #a.-c. 3.00

1998, May 8
363 A183 1.50k multicolored .50

Cardinal of Zagreb, Alojzije Stepinac (1898-1960).

27th European Regional Conference of Interpol, Dubrovnik A184

1998, May 13
364 A184 2.45k multicolored .75

Souvenir Sheet

Expo '98, Lisbon — A185

Illustration reduced.

1998, June 3 Litho. *Perf. 14*
365 A185 14.85k Fishing boat, Falkusa 4.50

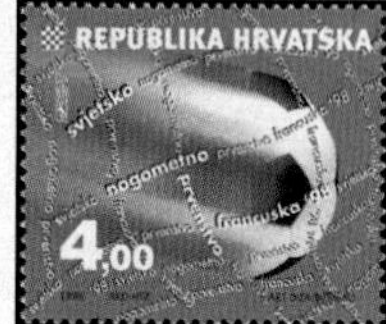

1998 World Cup Soccer Championships, France — A186

1998, June 10
366 A186 4k multicolored 1.25

Writers A187

1.20k, Juraj Barakovic (1548-1628). 1.50k, Milan Begovic (1876-1948). 1.60k, Mate Balota (Mijo Mirkovic, 1898-1963). 2.45k, Antun Gustav Matos (1873-1914). 2.65k, Matija Antun Relkovic (1732-98). 4.00k, Antun Branko Simic (1898-1925).

1998, June 13 Litho. *Perf. 14*
367 A187 1.20k multicolored .40
368 A187 1.50k multicolored .50
369 A187 1.60k multicolored .50
370 A187 2.45k multicolored .75
371 A187 2.65k multicolored .80
372 A187 4k multicolored 1.25
Nos. 367-372 (6) 4.20

19th Conference of the Countries of the Danube Region, Osijek — A188

1998, June 15
373 A188 1.80k multicolored .55

Stjepan Betlheim (1898-1970), Psychiatrist A189

1998, July 22
374 A189 1.50k multicolored .50

Souvenir Sheet

Croatian Soccer Team, Bronze Medalists at 1998 World Cup Soccer Championships, France — A190

Portions of team picture, denomination: a, red, LL. b, yellow, CR (player in yellow & blue shirt). c, yellow, CL. d, yellow, LR.

1998, July 24
375 A190 4k Sheet of 4, #a.-d. 5.00

Croatian Ships — A191

1.20k, Serilia Liburnica. 1.50k, Condura Croatica. 1.60k, Dubrovnik carrack. 1.80k, Bracera. 2.45k, Ship from the Neretva. 2.65k, Bark. 4k, Training ship, "Villa Velebita." 7.20k, Passenger ship, "Amorella." 20k, Missile gun boat, "Kralj Petar Kresimir IV."

1998, Aug. 27 Litho. *Perf. 14*
376 A191 1.20k multi .40 .40
376A A191 1.50k multi .50 .50
376B A191 1.60k multi .55 .55
376C A191 1.80k multi .60 .60
376D A191 2.45k multi .80 .80
376E A191 2.65k multi .90 .90
376F A191 4k multi 1.25 1.25
376G A191 7.20k multi 2.25 2.25
376H A191 20k multi 6.50 6.50
i. Sheet of 9, #376-376H + 3 labels 14.00
Nos. 376-376H (9) 13.75 13.75

Stamp Day — A192

1998, Sept. 9
377 A192 1.50k multicolored .50

Bishopric of Sibenik, 700th Anniv. — A193

1998, Sept. 29 Litho. *Perf. 14*
378 A193 4k multicolored 1.25 1.25

Pope John Paul II, Second Visit to Croatia A194

1998, Oct. 2
379 A194 1.50k multicolored .50 .50

History of Public Transportation A195

Designs: a, 1.50k, Horse tram. b, 1.50k, First automobile in Zagreb, 1901. c, 7.20k, Zagreb funicular. d, 1.50k, Karlovac-Rijeka Railway Line, 1873. e, 1.50k, New Highway, Zagreb-Rijeka.

1998, Oct. 23 Litho. *Perf. 14*
380 A195 Strip of 5, #a.-e. 4.25 4.25

No. 380c is 20x24mm.

Christmas — A196

Adoration of the Shepherds, by Juraj Julije Klovic (1498-1578).

1998, Nov. 21 *Perf. 14x13*
381 A196 1.50k multicolored .50 .50

See Vatican City No. 1088.

Father Luka Ibrisimovic (1620-98) A197

1998, Nov. 30 Litho. *Perf. 14*
382 A197 1.90k multicolored .60 .60

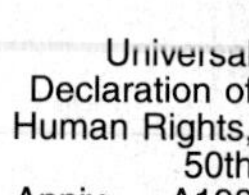

Universal Declaration of Human Rights, 50th Anniv. — A198

1998, Dec. 10
383 A198 5k multicolored 1.60 1.60

Modern Art A199

Paintings: 1.90k, Paromlin Road, by Josip Vanista. 2.20k, Cypresses, by Frano Simunovic, vert. 5k, Koma, by Dalibor Martinis, vert.

1998, Dec. 15
384 A199 1.90k multicolored .60 .60
385 A199 2.20k multicolored .70 .70
386 A199 5k multicolored 1.60 1.60
Nos. 384-386 (3) 2.90 2.90

Zagreb Intl. Trade Fair — A200

1999, Jan. 21 Litho. *Perf. 14*
387 A200 1.80k multicolored .55 .55

Cardinal Juraj Haulik (1788-1869), Archbishop of Zagreb — A201

Photo. & Engr.

1999, Jan. 28 *Perf. 11½*
388 A201 5k multicolored 1.50 1.50

See Slovakia 321.

National Parks — A202

Europa: 1.80k, Mljet Island. 5k, Lonja River Field.

1999, Mar. 12 Litho. *Perf. 14*
389 A202 1.80k multicolored .50 .50
390 A202 5k multicolored 1.40 1.40

Vipera Ursinii — A203

World Wildlife Fund: a, One coiled in grass and rock. b, Two. c, Head. d, One coiled on rock.

1999, Apr. 27 Litho. *Perf. 14*
391 A203 2.20k Strip of 4, #a.-d. 2.10 2.10

Council of Europe, 50th Anniv. — A204

1999, May 5
392 A204 2.80k multicolored .80 .80

19th Convention of the Foundation of European Carnival Cities, Dubrovnik — A205

1999, May 8
393 A205 2.30k multicolored .65 .65

Croatian Coins — A206

Designs: a, 2.30k, Obv., rev. of 1849 kreutzer. b, 5k, One kuna.

1999, May 30 Litho. *Perf. 14*
394 A206 Pair, #a.-b. 2.00 2.00

Minting of Jelacic kreutzer, 150th anniv. (#394a). Croatian kuna, 5th anniv. (#394b).

Famous Croats — A207

1.80k, Vladimir Nazor (1876-1949), poet. 2.30k, Ferdo Livadic (1799-1879), composer. 2.50k, Ivan Rendic (1849-1932), sculptor. 2.80k, Milan Lenuci (1849-1924), architect. 3.50k, Vjekoslav Klaic (1849-1929), historian, muscician. 4k, Emilij Laszowski (1868-1949), historian. 5k, Antun Kanizlic (1699-1777), poet, missionary.

1999, June 18
395 A207 1.80k multicolored .45 .45
396 A207 2.30k multicolored .65 .65
397 A207 2.50k multicolored .70 .70
398 A207 2.80k multicolored .75 .75
399 A207 3.50k multicolored .95 .95
400 A207 4k multicolored 1.10 1.10
401 A207 5k multicolored 1.40 1.40
Nos. 395-401 (7) 6.00 6.00

Euphrasian Basilica, Porec — A208

1999, June 25
402 A208 4k multicolored 1.10 1.10

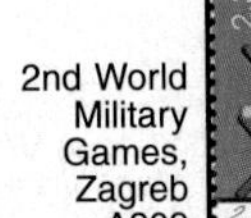

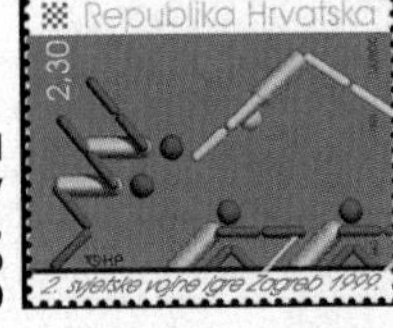

2nd World Military Games, Zagreb A209

1999, Aug. 7 Litho. *Perf. 14*
403 A209 2.30k multicolored .65 .65

Discovery of Early Krapina Man, Cent. — A210

Designs: a, 1.80k, Bones, rendition of Krapina man. b, 4k, Ancient bones, paleontologist Dragutin Gorjanovic-Kramberger.

1999, Aug. 23
404 A210 Pair, #a.-b. 1.60 1.60

Stamp Day and UPU, 125th Anniv. — A211

1999, Sept. 9 Litho. *Perf. 14*
405 A211 2.30k multicolored .65 .65

Paulist Order in Lepoglava, 600th Anniv. — A212

a, Lace, Jesus Expelling the Money Changers from Temple, by Ivan Ranger, altar angel from St. Mary's Church, Lepoglava. b, St. Mary's Church facade, altar angel. c, St. Elizabeth, lace.

1999, Sept. 11 Litho.
406 A212 5k Strip of 3, #a.-c. 4.25 4.25

150th Anniv. of "Jelacic March" by Johann Strauss the Elder — A213

1999, Sept. 16 Litho.
407 A213 3.50k multicolored 1.00 1.00

World Ozone Layer Protection Day A214

1999, Sept. 16 Litho.
408 A214 5k multicolored 1.40 1.40

Grammar School Anniversaries A215

1999, Oct. 15 Litho. *Perf. 14*
409 A215 2.30k Pazin, cent. .65 .65
410 A215 3.50k Pozega, 300th anniv. .95 .95

Andrija Hebrang (1899-1949), Politician — A216

1999, Oct. 21
411 A216 1.80k multicolored .50 .50

Our Lady of the Rose Garden, by Blaz Jurjev Trogiranin A217

1999, Oct. 28
412 A217 5k multicolored 1.40 1.40

Christmas, opening of exhibition of Croatian religious art and artifacts, Vatican City.

Christmas A218

1999, Nov. 24 Litho. *Perf. 14*
413 A218 2.30k multicolored .60 .60

Modern Art A219

Designs: 2.30k, Winter Landscape, by Gabrijel Jurkic (1886-1974). 3.50k, Klek, by Oton Postruznik (1900-78). 5k, Stone Table, by Ignjat Job (1895-1936), vert.

1999, Dec. 15
414 A219 2.30k multicolored .60 .60
415 A219 3.50k multicolored .90 .90
416 A219 5k multicolored 1.40 1.40
Nos. 414-416 (3) 2.90 2.90

Pres. Franjo Tudjman (1922-99) — A220

1999, Dec. 16 Vignette Color
417 A220 2.30k black .60 .60
418 A220 5k blue 1.40 1.40

Millennium A221

2000, Jan. 1 Litho. *Perf. 14*
419 A221 2.30k multi .55 .55

Valentine's Day — A222

2000, Feb. 1
420 A222 2.30k multi .55 .55

Split Grammar School, 300th Anniv. — A223

2000, Mar. 25 Litho. *Perf. 14*
421 A223 2.80k multi .65 .65

Croatian Writers' Assoc., 100th Anniv. — A224

2000, Apr. 22 Litho. *Perf. 14*
422 A224 2.30k black & red .55 .55

A225 A226

A227 A228

A229

2000, Apr. 22
423 A225 1.80k multi .40 .40
424 A226 2.30k multi .55 .55
425 A227 2.80k multi .65 .65
426 A228 3.50k multi .80 .80
427 A229 5k multi 1.25 1.25
Nos. 423-427 (5) 3.65 3.65

Lo Schiavone (Andrija Medulic, c. 1500-63), painter (1.80k); Matija Petar Katancic (1750-

1825), writer (2.30k); Marija Ruzicka-Strozzi (1850-1937), actress (2.80k); Marko Marulic (1450-1524), writer (3.50k); Blaz Jurjev Trogiranin (c. 1390-1450), painter (5k).

Europa, 2000

Common Design Type and

A230

2000, May 9

428 A230	2.30k multi	.55	.55
429 CD17	5k multi	1.25	1.25

Independence Day — A231

2000, May 30 Litho. *Perf. 14*

430 A231	2.30k multi	.55	.55

Souvenir Sheet

Expo 2000, Hanover — A232

Illustration reduced.

2000, June 1

431 A232	14.40k multi	3.50	3.50

Flora — A233

No. 432: a, 3.50k, Micromeria croatica. b, 5k, Geranium dalmaticum.
Illustration reduced.

2000, June 5

432 A233	Pair, #a-b	2.10	2.10
c.	Booklet pane of 10 #432a	8.50	
	Booklet, #432c	8.50	
d.	Booklet pane of 10 #432b	12.50	
	Booklet, #432d	12.50	

Kastav Statute, 600th Anniv. — A234

2000, June 6

433 A234	1.80k multi	.45	.45

World Mathematics Year — A235

2000, June 15

434 A235	3.50k multi	.85	.85

Ivan Ranger (1700-53), Artist — A236

2000, June 19

435 A236	1.80k multi	.45	.45

Souvenir Sheet

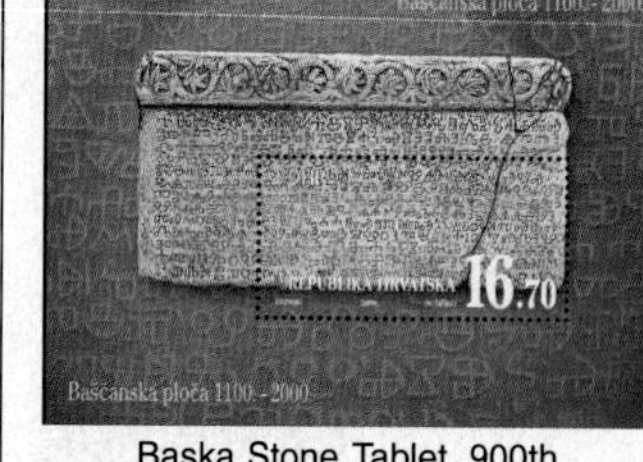

Baska Stone Tablet, 900th Anniv. — A237

Illustration reduced.

2000, June 24

436 A237	16.70k multi	4.00	4.00

Archdeacon Toma of Split (1200-68) A238

2000, July 10

437 A238	3.50k multi	.85	.85

Type of 1992-94 Redrawn

2000, Aug. 1 Litho. *Perf. 14*

437A A39a	3.50k Vis	.85	.85

No. 437A has "HP" and post horn in LR corner.

Stamp Day — A239

No. 438: a, 2.30k, Austria #5. b, 2.30k, Automatic mail sorting equipment.

2000, Sept. 9 Litho. *Perf. 14*

438 A239	Pair, #a-b	1.10	1.10

First stamps used in Croatia, 150th anniv. (#438a).

2000 Summer Olympics, Sydney A240

2000, Sept. 15

439 A240	5k multicolored	1.25	1.25

Altarpiece, Church of the Blessed Virgin Mary, Ostarije A241

2000, Nov. 23

440 A241	2.30k multi	.55	.55
a.	Booklet pane of 10	5.50	
	Booklet, #440a	5.50	

Modern Art A242

Designs: 1.80k, Korcula, by Vladimir Varlaj. 2.30k, Brusnik, by Duro Tiljak. 5k, Boats, by Ante Kastelacic.

2000, Dec. 1

441-443 A242	Set of 3	2.25	1.10

Start of New Millennium A243

2001, Jan. 1 Litho. *Perf. 14*

444 A243	2.30k multi	.55	.55

Souvenir Sheet

Equestrian Statue of Charlemagne — A244

2001, Jan. 19

445 A244	14.40k multi	3.50	3.50

Crowning of Charlemagne as Emperor of the Romans, 1200th anniv. (in 2000).

Dzore Drzic (1461-1501), Writer — A245

2001, Mar. 15 Litho. *Perf. 14*

446 A245	2.80k multi	.70	.70

Comic Strip "Black Rider," by Andrija Maurovic (1901-81) A246

2001, Mar. 29

447 A246	5k multi	1.25	1.25

Makarska A247

2001, Mar. 30

448 A247	2.30k multi	.55	.55

Janica Kostelic, Skier — A248

2001, Apr. 19 Litho. *Perf. 14*

449 A248	2.80k multi	.70	.70

Kastel Stafilic Olive Trees, 1500th Anniv. — A249

2001, Apr. 20

450 A249	1.80k multi	.45	.45

Europa — A250

No. 451: a, 3.50k, Denomination at R. b, 5k, Denomination at L.

2001, May 9

451 A250	Horiz. pair, #a-b	2.00	2.00

World No Smoking Day — A251

2001, May 31

452 A251	2.50k multi	.60	.60

Butterflies A252

Designs: 2.50k, Parnassius apollo. 2.80k, Maculinea teleius. 5k, Coenonympha oedippus.

2001, June 5

453-455 A252	Set of 3	2.50	2.50

Type of 1992 Redrawn

2001, June 21 Litho. *Perf. 14*

456 A39	2.80k Eltz Castle, Vukovar	.70	.70

No. 456 has "1991-2001" inscription, and "HP" and post horn at LL.

Souvenir Sheet

Trsteno Arboretum — A253

2001, July 12 Litho. *Perf. 14*
457 A253 14.40k multi 3.50 3.50

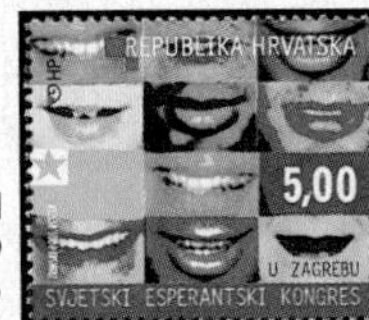

World Esperanto Congress, Zagreb — A254

2001, July 21
458 A254 5k multi 1.25 1.25

Refugee Organizations, 50th Annivs. A255

Designs: 1.80k, UN High Commissioner for Refugees. 5k, Intl. Organization for Migration.

2001, July 28
459-460 A255 Set of 2 1.75 1.75

Victory of Goran Ivanisevic at Wimbledon A256

2001, Aug. 31
461 A256 2.50k multi .60 .60

Printed in sheets of 9 + label.

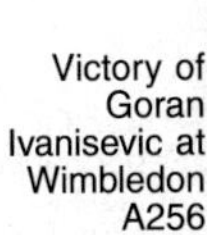

Stamp Day — A257

2001, Sept. 9
462 A257 2.50k multi .60 .60

Printed in sheets of 16 + 4 labels.

Native Dog Breeds A258

Designs: 1.80k, Croatian sheepdog. 5k, Dalmatian.

2001, Oct. 4
463-464 A258 Set of 2 1.75 1.75

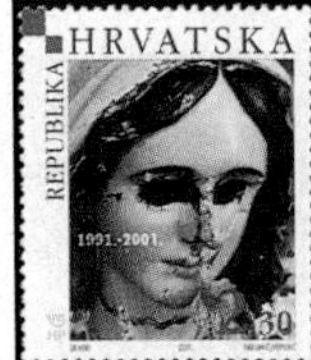

Independence, 10th Anniv. — A259

2001, Oct. 8
465 A259 2.30k multi .55 .55

Printed in sheets of 25 + 5 labels.

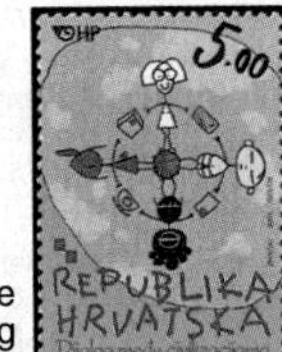

Year of Dialogue Among Civilizations — A260

2001, Oct. 9
466 A260 5k multi 1.25 1.25

Fortresses — A261

Designs: 1.80k, Klis, 16th cent. 2.50k, Ston, 14th-15th cents. 3.50k, Sisak, 16th cent.

2001, Oct. 26 Litho. *Perf. 14*
467-469 A261 Set of 3 1.90 1.90

Adoration of the Magi Altarpeice, Church of the Visitation of Mary, Cucerje — A262

2001, Nov. 22 Litho. *Perf. 14*
470 A262 2.30k multi .55 .55

Modern Art Type of 2000

Designs: No. 471, 2.50k, Maternité du Port-Royal, by Leo Junek. No. 472, 2.50k, Amphitheater Ruins, by Vjekoslav Parac. 5k, Nude with a Baroque Figure, by Slavko Sohaj, vert.

2001, Dec. 1
471-473 A242 Set of 3 2.40 2.40

Croatian Nobel Laureates — A263

Laureates: 2.80k, Lavoslav (Leopold) Ruzicka, Chemistry, 1939. 3.50k, Vladimir Prelog, Chemistry, 1975. 5k, Ivo Andric, Literature, 1961.

2001, Dec. 5
474-476 A263 Set of 3 2.75 2.75

Famous Croats and Events — A264

Designs: 1.80k, Ivan Gucetic (1451-1502), writer. 2.30k, Dobrisa Cesaric (1902-80), writer. 2.50k, Publishing of Juraj Rattkay's *History of Croatian Rulers,* 350th anniv. 2.80k, Franjo Vranjanin Laurana (c. 1420-1502), sculptor. 3.50k, Beatification of Bishop Augustin Kazotic (c. 1260-1323), 300th anniv. 5k, Matko Laginja (1852-1930), politician and writer.

2002, Jan. 24 Litho. *Perf. 14*
477-482 A264 Set of 6 4.25 4.25

2002 Winter Olympics, Salt Lake City — A265

2002, Feb. 8
483 A265 5k multi 1.25 1.25

Croatian Chamber of Economy, 150th Anniv. — A266

2002, Feb. 16
484 A266 2.50k multi .60 .60

Souvenir Sheet

Trpimir's Deed of Gift, 1150th Anniv. — A267

2002, Mar. 4
485 A267 14.40k multi 3.50 3.50

Franjo Cardinal Kuharic (1919-2002) A268

2002, Mar. 25
486 A268 2.30k multi .55 .55

Divan, by Vlaho Bukovac — A269

Litho. & Engr.

2002, Apr. 23 *Perf. 11¾*
487 A269 5k multi 1.25 1.25

See Czech Republic No. 3169.

Royal Borough of Krizevci, 750th Anniv. — A270

2002, Apr. 24 Litho. *Perf. 14*
488 A270 1.80k multi .45 .45

Varazdin Post Office, Cent. — A271

2002, Apr. 26
489 A271 2.30k multi .55 .55

Europa — A272

Clown color: a, 3.50k, Orange. b, 5k, Blue. Illustration reduced.

2002, May 9 Litho. *Perf. 14*
490 A272 Horiz. pair, #a-b 2.10 2.10

2002 World Cup Soccer Championships, Japan and Korea — A273

Stylized players facing: a, 3.50k, Left. b, 5k, Right.

2002, May 15
491 A273 Horiz. pair, #a-b 2.10 2.10

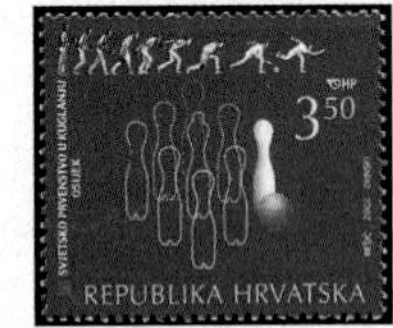

World Bowling Championships, Osijek — A274

2002, May 18
492 A274 3.50k multi .90 .90

Oak Trees — A275

Designs: 1.80k, Quercus rober. 2.50k, Quercus petraea. 2.80k, Quercus ilex.

2002, June 5

493-495 A275	Set of 3	1.90	1.90
493a	Booklet pane of 10	4.75	—
	Complete booklet, #493a	4.75	
494a	Booklet pane of 10	6.50	—
	Complete booklet, #494a	6.50	
495a	Booklet pane of 10	7.50	—
	Complete booklet, #495a	7.50	

15th World Animated Films Festival, Zagreb — A276

2002, June 18
496 A276 5k multi 1.25 1.25

Lace — A277

Lace from: 3.50k, Pag Island, Croatia. 5k, Liedekerke, Belgium.

2002, July 13 Photo. *Perf. 11½*
497-498 A277 Set of 2 2.25 2.25

See Belgium Nos. 1927-1928.

Fortresses Type of 2001

Designs: No. 499, 2.50k, Nehaj, 16th cent. No. 500, 2.50k, Skocibuha, 16th cent. 5k, Veliki Tabor, 16th cent.

2002, Sept. 20 Litho. *Perf. 14*
499-501 A261 Set of 3 2.75 2.75

Old Slavonic Academy, Krk, Cent. — A278

2002, Oct. 3 Litho. & Embossed
502 A278 4k red & black 1.10 1.10

Children's Help Line 48 26 051, 5th Anniv. — A279

2002, Oct. 15 Litho.
503 A279 2.30k multi .60 .60

Christmas A280

2002, Nov. 21
504 A280 2.30k multi .60 .60
a. Booklet pane of 10 6.00 —
Complete booklet, #504a 6.00

Modern Art Type of 2002

Designs: No. 505, 2.50k, Flowers on the Window, by Antun Motika (1902-92), vert. No. 506, 2.50k, The Girl in the Boat, by Milivoj Uzelac (1897-1977), vert. 5k, On the Drava River, by Krsto Hegedusic (1901-75).

2002, Dec. 2 Litho. *Perf. 14*
505-507 A242 Set of 3 2.75 2.75

Zagreb Bishopric, 150th Anniv. — A281

2002, Dec. 11
508 A281 2.80k multi .80 .80

Printed in sheets of 19 + label.

Pavao Ritter Vitezovic (1652-1713), Writer — A282

2002, Dec. 13
509 A282 2.30k multi .65 .65

Pacta Conventa, 900th Anniv. — A283

2002, Dec. 14
510 A283 3.50k multi 1.00 1.00

Fairies From Stories by Ivana Brlic Mazuranic — A284

No. 511: a, 2.30k, Kosjenka, fairy character from *Regoc*. b, 2.80k, Tintilinic, fairy character from *Suma Striborova*.
Illustration reduced.

2003, Jan. 15
511 A284 Horiz. pair, #a-b 1.50 1.50

St. Valentine's Day — A285

Litho. With Foil Application
2003, Feb. 1
512 A285 2.30k multi .65 .65

Astronomy and Meteorology A286

No. 513: a, 1.80k, Zagreb Astronomical Observatory, cent. b, 3.50k, Meteorological measurements in Zagreb, 150th anniv.; Meteorological station on Zavizan, 50th anniv.

2003, Feb. 17 Litho.
513 A286 Pair, #a-b 1.50 1.50

Souvenir Sheet

Croatia, 2003 World Handball Champions — A287

No. 514: a, Five team members, one wearing red shirt. b, Eight team members, one with arm extended. c, Six team members. d, Four team members, one wearing blue shirt.

2003, Feb. 20
514 A287 4k Sheet of 4, #a-d 4.50 4.50

Paulist High School, Lepoglava, 500th Anniv. — A288

2003, Mar. 1
515 A288 5k multi 1.40 1.40

Missal of Hrvoje Vukcic Hrvatinic, 600th Anniv. — A289

2003, Mar. 25
516 A289 5k multi 1.40 1.40

Land Mine Danger A290

2003, Apr. 8
517 A290 2.30k multi .65 .65

Alpine Skiing World Cup Victories of Janica and Ivica Kostelic A291

No. 518: a, Janica. b, Ivica.

2003, Apr. 16
518 A291 3.50k Pair, #a-b 2.00 2.00

Printed in sheets containing 4 vertical pairs and 2 labels.

Christian Institutions in Rome Founded by Croatian Roman Brotherhood of St. Jerome, 550th Anniv. — A292

2003, Apr. 22
519 A292 2.80k multi .85 .85

Famous Croatians A293

Designs: 1.80k, Antun Soljan (1932-93), writer. 2.30k, Hanibal Lucic (1485-1553), writer. 5k, Federiko Benkovic (1667-1753), painter.

2003, Apr. 22
520-522 A293 Set of 3 2.75 2.75

Poster for Performance of Marya Delvard, by Tomislav Krizman, 1907. — A294

Poster for Performance of "The Firebird," by Boris Bucan, 1983 — A295

2003, May 9 Litho. *Perf. 14*
523 A294 3.50k multi 1.10 1.10
524 A295 5k multi 1.50 1.50

Europa.

Fortresses Type of 2001

Designs; 1.80k, Kostajnica, 15th-18th cent. 2.80k, Slavonski Brod, 18th cent. 5k, Minceta Tower, 15th cent., vert.

2003, May 13
525-527 A261 Set of 3 3.00 3.00

Visit of Pope John Paul II — A296

2003, June 2
528 A296 2.30k multi .75 .75

Rodents A297

Designs: 2.30k, Sciuris vulgaris. 2.80k, Glis glis. 3.50k, Castor fiber.

2003, June 5
529-531 A297 Set of 3 2.75 2.75
531a Booklet pane, 6 #529, 2 each #530-531 8.25 —
Complete booklet, #531a 8.25

Souvenir Sheet

Robe of King Ladislaus, 11th Cent. — A298

2003, June 13
532 A298 10k multi 3.25 3.25

Stamp Day — A299

2003, Sept. 9 **Litho.** ***Perf. 14***
533 A299 2.30k multi .70 .70

Souvenir Sheet

Primosten Vineyards — A300

Litho. with Foil Application
2003, Sept. 19
534 A300 10k multi 3.00 3.00

Ursuline Sisters in Croatia, 300th Anniv. — A301

2003, Oct. 20 **Litho.**
535 A301 2.50k multi .75 .75

Christmas A302

2003, Nov. 20 **Litho.** ***Perf. 14***
536 A302 2.30k multi .75 .75

Self-Adhesive
Serpentine Die Cut 5¼
537 A302 2.30k multi .75 .75

Modern Art A304

Designs: 1.80k, Flower Girl II, by Slavko Kopac, vert. No. 539, 3.50k, Dry Stone Wall 5-71, by Oton Gliha. No. 540, 3.50k, Pont des Arts, by Josip Racic.

2003, Nov. 21 ***Perf. 14***
538-540 A304 Set of 3 2.75 2.75

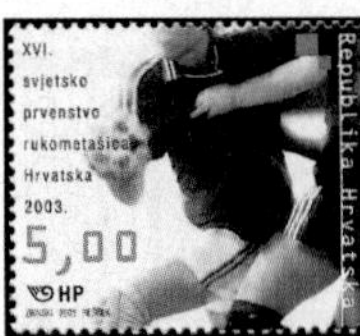

18th World Women's Handball Championships — A305

2003, Dec. 1
541 A305 5k multi 1.60 1.60

Musicians — A306

No. 542: a, Josip Hatze (1879-1959), composer. b, Zagreb Soloists, 50th anniv.

2004, Jan. 5 **Litho.** ***Perf. 14***
542 A306 5k Horiz. pair, #a-b 3.50 3.50

Hval's Manuscript, 600th Anniv. — A307

2004, Jan. 22
543 A307 2.30k multi .75 .75

European Boxing Championships, Pula — A308

2004, Feb. 19 **Litho.** ***Perf. 14***
544 A308 2.80k multi .95 .95

Worldwide Fund for Nature (WWF) — A309

Ardea purpurea: a, In grass. b, Standing with head extended. c, With young. d, In flight.

2004, Mar. 22
545 Strip or block of 4 6.50 6.50
a.-d. A309 5k Any single 1.60 1.60

Famous Croats — A310

Designs: 2.30k, Ivan Lucic (1604-79), historian. No. 547, 3.50k, Antun Vrancic (1504-75), archbishop, writer. No. 548, 3.50k, St. Jerome, sculpture by Andrija Alesi (c. 1425-1504). 10k, Printing of Croatian grammar book, by Bartol Kasic (1575-1650), 400th anniv.

2004, Apr. 22
546-549 A310 Set of 4 6.25 6.25

Souvenir Sheet

Risnjak National Park — A311

2004, Apr. 22
550 A311 10k multi 3.25 3.25

Martyrdom of St. Domnio, 1700th Anniv. — A312

2004, May 7
551 A312 3.50k multi 1.10 1.10

Europa A313

Designs: No. 552, 3.50k, Summer vacation items. No. 553, 3.50k, Winter vacation items.

2004, May 9
552-553 A313 Set of 2 2.25 2.25

FIFA (Fédération Internationale de Football Association), Cent. A314

2004, May 21 **Litho.** ***Perf. 14***
554 A314 2.50k multi .85 .85

Medicinal Herbs — A315

Designs: 2.30k, Rosa canina. 2.80k, Viola odorata. 3.50k, Mentha piperita.

2004, June 5
555-557 A315 Set of 3 2.75 2.75
555a Booklet pane of 10 7.50 —
Complete booklet, #555a 7.50
556a Booklet pane of 10 9.00 —
Complete booklet, #556a 9.00
557a Booklet pane of 10 11.00 —
Complete booklet, #557a 11.00

Nos. 555-557 are impregnated with a floral scent.

Intl. Marionette Union Congress, Intl. Puppetry Art Festival, Rijeka A316

2004, June 6
558 A316 3.50k multi 1.10 1.10

European Soccer Championships, Portugal — A317

2004, June 12
559 A317 3.50k multi 1.25 1.25

Values are for stamps with surrounding selvage.

Restoration of Old Bridge, Mostar, Bosnia & Herzegovina A318

2004, July 23 **Litho.** ***Perf. 14***
560 A318 3.50k multi 1.10 1.10

2004 Summer Olympics, Athens — A319

2004, Aug. 13
561 A319 3.50k multi 1.25 1.25

Virovitica A320

2004, Aug. 16
562 A320 5k multi 1.75 1.75

Zagreb Post Office, Cent. A321

2004, Sept. 9
563 A321 2.30k multi .80 .80

Printed in sheets of 16 + 4 labels.

Father Andrija Kacic Miosic (1704-60), Poet — A322

2004, Sept. 15

564 A322 2.80k multi .95 .95

Fortresses Type of 2001

Designs: No. 565, 3.50k, Dubovac, 15th-19th cent. No. 566, 3.50k, Gripe, 17th cent. No. 567, 3.50k, Valpovo, 15th-18th cent.

2004, Sept. 29

565-567 A261 Set of 3 3.50 3.50

Modern Art Type of 2003

Designs: No. 568, 2.30k, Self-portrait, by Miroslav Kraljevic, vert. No. 569, 2.30k, Noon in Supetar, by Jerolim Mise, vert. No. 570, 2.30k, Stari Grad, by Juraj Plancic, vert.

2004, Nov. 15 Litho. *Perf. 14*

568-570 A304 Set of 3 2.50 2.50

Christmas A323

2004, Nov. 25

571 A323 2.30k multi .85 .85

SEMI-POSTAL STAMPS

Catalogue values for unused stamps in this section are for Never Hinged items.

Types of Yugoslavia, 1941, Overprinted in Gold "NEZAVISNA / DRZAVA / HRVATSKA"

Perf. 11½

1941, May 10 Unwmk. Engr.

B1 SP80 1.50d + 1.50d bl blk 13.00 13.00
B2 SP81 4d + 3d choc 13.00 13.00

Sheets of 16 stamps and 9 labels.
This overprint exists on Yugoslavia No. B124. Value $2,500.

Five thousand sets of Yugoslavia Nos. 142-154 were overprinted "NEZAVISNA DRZAVA HRVATSKA 10. IV. 1941" and small shield in red or blue, in 1941. Sold for double face value. Value, set, $225.

Costume of Sinj, Dalmatia — SP1

Soldiers with Arms of the Axis States — SP4

Designs (Costumes): 2k+2k, Travnik, Bosnia. 4k+4k, Turopolje, Croatia.

1941, Oct. 12 Photo. *Perf. 10½x10*

B3 SP1 1.50k + 1.50k Prus bl & red .80 .35
B4 SP1 2k + 2k ol brn & red 1.10 .45
B5 SP1 4k + 4k brn lake & red 1.10 1.10
Nos. B3-B5 (3) 3.00 *1.90*

The surtax aided the Croatian Red Cross.

Sheets of 20 stamps and 5 labels.

1941, Dec. 3 *Perf. 11*

B6 SP4 4k + 2k blue 1.75 *2.00*

The surtax was used for Croatian Volunteers in the East.

Model Plane — SP5

Model Plane — SP6

Designs: 3k+3k, Boy with model plane. 4k+4k, Model seaplane in flight.

1942, Mar. 25

B7 SP5 2k + 2k sepia 1.25 1.25
B8 SP6 2.50k + 2.50k dl grn 1.25 1.25
B9 SP5 3k + 3k brn car 1.25 1.25
B10 SP6 4k + 4k dp bl 1.25 1.25
Nos. B7-B10 (4) 5.00 *5.00*

Nos. B7-B10 were issued in sheets of 25 and in sheets of 24 plus label.

Values for used souvenir sheets are for those with special philatelic cancels. Sheets with normal postal cancels are very scarce and sell for much more.

Souvenir Sheets

Perf. 11

B11 Sheet of 2 32.50 30.00
 a. SP5 2k+8k brown carmine 9.00 *10.00*
 b. SP5 3k+12k deep blue 9.00 *10.00*

Imperf

B12 Sheet of 2 40.00 37.50
 a. SP5 2k+8k deep blue 12.00 12.00
 b. SP5 3k+12k brown carmine 12.00 12.00

The sheets measure 125x110mm.
Aviation Exposition of Zagreb. The surtax aided society of Croatian Wings (Hrvatska Krila).
Nos. B11-B12 exist with colors of stamps and inscriptions transposed, with missing colors and with one stamp missing.

Boy Trumpeters SP10

Triumphal Arch — SP11

Mother and Child — SP12

1942, July 5 *Perf. 11½*

B13 SP10 3k + 1k lake 1.25 1.25
B14 SP11 4k + 2k dk brn 1.25 1.25
B15 SP12 5k + 5k dp bl grn 1.25 1.25
Nos. B13-B15 (3) 3.75 *3.75*

The surtax was for national welfare.

Matthew Gubec SP13

Ante Starcevich SP14

SP15

1942, Nov. 22 *Perf. 14½*

B16 SP13 3k + 6k dark red .65 .65
B17 SP14 4k + 7k sepia .65 .65

Souvenir Sheets

Perf. 12, Imperf.

B18 SP15 5k + 20k dull blue 9.00 *9.00*

Heroes of Senj, May 9, 1937. Nos. B16-B17 were printed in sheets of 16 + 9 labels, each bearing a hero's name. The surtax aided the Natl. Youth Soc.

Sestine Peasant SP16

Croatian Labor Corpsman SP20

Designs: 3k+1k, Slavonian peasant. 4k+2k, Bosnian peasant. 10k+5k, Dalmatian peasant. 13k+6k, Sestine peasant.

1942, Oct. 4 *Perf. 11½*

B20 SP16 1.50k + 50b org brn & red 1.10 1.10
B21 SP16 3k + 1k dl pur & red 1.10 1.10
B22 SP16 4k + 2k dp bl & red 1.40 1.40
B23 SP16 10k + 5k dk ol bis & red 2.25 2.25
B24 SP16 13k + 6k rose lake & red 4.25 4.25
Nos. B20-B24 (5) 10.10 *10.10*

The surtax aided the Croatian Red Cross.
Issued in sheets of 24 stamps plus label.

1943, Jan. 17 Wmk. 278 *Perf. 11*

Designs: 3k+3k, Corpsman with wheelbarrow. 7k+4k, Corpsman plowing.

B25 SP20 2k + 1k ol gray & sepia 3.00 *3.25*
B26 SP20 3k + 3k brn & sepia 3.00 *3.25*
B27 SP20 7k + 4k gray bl & sepia 3.00 *3.25*
Nos. B25-B27 (3) 9.00 *9.75*

The surtax aided the State Labor Service (Drzavna Radna Sluzba). Issued in sheets of 9.

Arms of Zagreb and "Golden Bull" — SP23

1943, Mar. 23 Unwmk.

B28 SP23 3.50k (+ 6.50k) ultra 2.75 *3.00*

700th anniversary of Zagreb's "Golden Bull," a Magna Carta of civic rights and privileges granted to the city in 1242 by King Bela because the Croats annihilated Tartar hordes at Grobnik.
Issued in sheets of 8 with marginal inscriptions.

Ante Pavelich — SP24

Sailor at Sea of Azov — SP26

1943, Apr. 10 *Perf. 14*

B29 SP24 5k + 3k copper red .50 .50
B30 SP24 7k + 5k dark green .50 .50

Surtax aided the National Youth Society.
Issued in sheets of 100, and in miniature sheets of 16 stamps + 9 labels.

Souvenir Sheets

1943, May 17 *Perf. 12, Imperf.*

B31 SP24 12k + 8k dp ultra 10.00 10.00

1943, July 1 *Perf. 11*

Designs: 2k+1k, Flier at Sevastopol and Rzhev. 3.50k+1.50k, Infantrymen at Stalingrad. 9k+4.50k, Panzer Division at Don River.

B33 SP26 1k + 50b grn .35 .25
B34 SP26 2k + 1k dk red .35 .25
B35 SP26 3.50k + 1.50k dk bl .35 .25
B36 SP26 9k + 4.50k chestnut .35 .25
Nos. B33-B36 (4) 1.40 *1.00*

Souvenir Sheets

Perf. 11, Imperf.

B37 Sheet of 4 4.50 4.50
 a. SP26 1k+50b dark blue .80 *.80*
 b. SP26 2k+1k green .80 *.80*
 c. SP26 3.50k+1.50k dk red brown .80 *.80*
 d. SP26 9k+4.50k bluish black .80 *.80*

Issued to honor the Croatian Legion which fought with the Germans in Russia.
The surtax aided the Croatian Legion.

St. Mary's Church and Cistercian Cloister, Zagreb, in 1650 SP31

1943, Sept. 12 Engr. *Perf. 14½*

B39 SP31 18k + 9k dl gray vio 3.00 *3.50*

Souvenir Sheet

Perf. 12½

B40 SP31 18k + 9k blk brn 6.50 6.50

Croatian Phil. Soc. Exhibition at Zagreb.

No. B39 Overprinted in Red

HRVATSKO MORE 8. IX. 1943.

1943, Sept. 12

B41 SP31 18k + 9k dl gray vio	7.00	7.00

Return to Croatia of the Dalmatian and Croatian coasts.

Mother and Children — SP33

Nurse and Patient — SP34

1943, Oct. 3 Litho. *Perf. 11*

Cross in Red

B42 SP33 1k + 50b bl grn	.45	.45
B43 SP33 2k + 1k bril car	.45	.45
B44 SP33 3.50k + 1.50k brt bl	.45	.45
B45 SP34 8k + 3k red brn	.60	.60
B46 SP34 9k + 4k yel grn	.65	.65
B47 SP33 10k + 5k dp vio	.65	.65
B48 SP34 12k + 6k brt ultra	.65	.65
B49 SP33 12.50k + 6k dk brn	1.10	1.10
B50 SP34 18k + 8k brn org	1.10	1.10
B51 SP34 32k + 12k dk gray	1.10	1.10
Nos. B42-B51 (10)	7.20	*7.20*

The surtax aided the Croatian Red Cross.

Post Horn and Arms — SP35

Carrier Pigeon and Plane — SP36

Mercury — SP37

Winged Wheel — SP38

1944, Feb. 3

B52 SP35 7k + 3.50k ol bis & red	.60	.60
B53 SP36 16k + 8k bl & dk bl	.60	.60
B54 SP37 24k + 12k red & rose red	.60	.60
B55 SP38 32k + 16k gray & red	.60	.60
Nos. B52-B55 (4)	2.40	*2.40*

The surtax benefited communications and railway employees. Sheets of 9.

St. Sebastian — SP39

War Invalids SP40

Statue of Ancient Croatian King — SP41

Death of King Peter Svacic, 1097 — SP42

1944, Feb. 15

B56 SP39 7k + 3.50k org red & rose car	.60	.60
B57 SP40 16k + 8k yel grn & dk grn	.60	.60
B58 SP41 24k + 12k yel brn & red	.60	.60
B59 SP42 32k + 16k bl & dk bl	.60	.60
Nos. B56-B59 (4)	2.40	*2.40*

The surtax aided wounded war victims.

Issued in sheets of eight stamps, with marginal inscriptions and a central label picturing St. Sebastian.

Black Legion in Combat — SP43

Guarding the Drina — SP44

Jure Francetich SP45

1944, May 22 Photo. *Imperf.*

B60 SP43 3.50k + 1.50k brn red	.20	.20
B61 SP44 12.50k + 6.50k slate bl	.20	.20
B62 SP45 18k + 9k olive brn	.20	.20
Nos. B60-B62 (3)	.60	.60

Third anniversary of Croatian independence.

The surtax aided the National Youth Society. Sheets of 20.

Perf. 14½

B63 SP45 12.50k + 287.50k int blk	10.00	10.00

Issued to commemorate Jure Francetich.

Labor Corpsmen Marching SP46

Corpsman Digging SP47

Designs: 18k+9k, Officer instructing corpsman. 32k+16k, Pavelich reviewing Labor Corps. Sheets of 8 plus label.

Perf. 11½, 12½, 14½

1944, Aug. 20 Engr.

B65 SP46 3.50k + 1k dk red	.50	.50
B66 SP47 12.50k + 6k sepia	.50	.50
B67 SP47 18k + 9k dk bl	.50	.50
B68 SP47 32k + 16k gray grn	.50	.50
Nos. B65-B68 (4)	2.00	2.00

Nos. B68 exists only perf 12½, while B65-B67 exist perf 11½, 12½ or 14½. Values are for copies perf 11½ or 12½. Values Nos. B65-B67 perf 14½, $5 each unused or used.

Souvenir Sheet

Perf. 12½

B69 SP47 32k + 16k dk brn, *cr*	4.00	*4.50*

The surtax aided the State Labor Service (Drzavna Radna Sluzba).

Palm Leaf — SP51

1944, Nov. 12 Litho. *Perf. 11*

B70 SP51 2k + 1k dl grn & red	.35	.35
B71 SP51 3.50k + 1.50k car lake & red	.35	.35
B72 SP51 12.50k + 6k ind & red	.35	.35
Nos. B70-B72 (3)	1.05	1.05

The surtax aided the Croatian Red Cross. Sheets of 16.

Men of Storm Division — SP52

70k+70k, Soldiers of Storm Division in action. 100k+100k, Storm Division emblem.

1944 Unwmk. Litho. *Perf. 11*

B73 SP52 50k + 50k brick red	100.00	*110.00*
B74 SP52 70k + 70k sepia	100.00	*110.00*
B75 SP52 100k + 100k chlky, pale & dp bl	100.00	*110.00*
Nos. B73-B75 (3)	300.00	*330.00*

Souvenir Sheet

B76 Sheet of 3	1,450.	1,450.
a. SP52 50k + 50k brick red	400.00	400.00
b. SP52 70k + 70k sepia	400.00	400.00
c. SP52 100k + 100k chalky, pale & deep blue	400.00	400.00

Nos. B76a to B76c are inscribed "O. A." in brick red at right below design. The sheet measures 216x132mm. The surtax aided the First Croatian Storm Division. Counterfeits are plentiful.

Postman SP55

Telephone Line Repairman SP56

24k+12k, Switchboard operator. 50k+25k, 100k+50k, Postman delivering parcel.

1945 Photo.

B77 SP55 3.50k + 1.50k sl gray	.30	*.30*
B78 SP56 12.50k + 6k brn car	.30	*.30*
B79 SP56 24k + 12k dk grn	.30	*.30*
B80 SP56 50k + 25k brn vio	.30	.30
Nos. B77-B80 (4)	1.20	*1.20*

Souvenir Sheet

B81 SP56 100k + 50k dp brn	8.00	8.00

The surtax on #B77-B81 aided employees of the P.T.T. Sheets of 8.

Famous Croatians SP60

#B100, Ban Josip Jelacic (1801-59). #B101, Dr. Ante Starcevic (1823-96). 7d + 3d, Stjepan Radic (1871-1928).

1992 Litho. *Perf. 11x10½*

B100 SP60 4d +2d multi	*.35*	*.35*
B101 SP60 4d +2d multi	*.40*	*.35*

Perf. 14

B102 SP60 7d +3d multi	*.25*	*.25*
Nos. B100-B102 (3)	*1.00*	*.95*

Issued: #B100, 2/1; #B101, 3/4; #B102, 4/2.

The surcharge on Nos. B100-B102 was initially an obligatory tax on all internal and overseas mail. From May 15, 1992, these stamps were valid for postage at their 6d or 10d face values.

AIR POST STAMPS

Catalogue values for unused stamps in this section are for Never Hinged items.

Airplane, Zagreb Cathedral and Port of Dubrovnik AP1

Airplane Over Ruins of Diocletian's Palace, Split — AP2

Coat of Arms, Aiplane, Zagreb Cathedral and Pula Amphitheatre AP3

Paper Airplane Made From Picture of Osijek Cathedral AP4

1991-92 Litho. *Perf. 11x10½*

C1 AP1 1d multicolored	*.20*
a. Perf. 14	*.20*
C2 AP2 2d multicolored	*.30*
a. Perf. 14	*.20*
C3 AP3 3d multicolored	*.30*
C4 AP4 4d multicolored	*.30*
Nos. C1-C4 (4)	*1.10*

Issued: #C1, 9/9/91; #C1a, 6/24/92; #C2, 10/9/91; #C2a, 1992; #C3, 11/20/91; #C4, 2/14/92.

POSTAGE DUE STAMPS

Yugoslavia Nos. J28-J32 Overprinted in Black

1941, Apr. 26 Unwmk. *Perf. 12½*

J1 D4 50p violet .20 *.30*
a. 50p rose violet 4.00 *9.50*
J2 D4 1d deep magenta .20 *.30*
J3 D4 2d deep blue 5.00 *20.00*
J4 D4 5d orange .50 *1.10*
J5 D4 10d chocolate 3.00 *8.00*
Nos. J1-J5 (5) 8.90 *29.70*
Set, never hinged 17.50

The overprint on the 50p and 1d exist inverted. Counterfeit overprints exist, particularly of Nos. J3 and J5.

D1

D2

1941, Sept. 12 Litho. *Perf. 11*

J6 D1 50b carmine lake .20 *.40*
J7 D1 1k carmine lake .20 *.40*
J8 D1 2k carmine lake .20 *.55*
J9 D1 5k carmine lake .30 *.80*
J10 D1 10k carmine lake .45 *1.10*
Nos. J6-J10 (5) 1.35 *3.25*
Set, never hinged 2.00

1943 *Perf. 11½, 12x12½, 12½*
Size: 24x24mm

J11 D2 50b lt blue & gray .20 .20
J12 D2 1k lt blue & gray .20 .20
J13 D2 2k lt blue & gray .20 *.20*
J14 D2 4k lt blue & gray .20 *.20*
J15 D2 5k lt blue & gray .20 *.30*
J16 D2 6k lt blue & gray .20 *.40*
J17 D2 10k blue & indigo .20 *.30*
J18 D2 15k blue & indigo .20 *.45*
J19 D2 20k blue & indigo .65 *1.25*
Nos. J11-J19 (9) 2.25 *3.50*
Set, never hinged 2.50

1942, July 30 *Perf. 10½, 11½*
Size: 25x24¼mm

J20 D2 50b lt blue & gray .20 *.20*
J21 D2 1k lt blue & gray .20 *.20*
J22 D2 2k lt blue & gray .20 *.35*
J23 D2 5k lt blue & gray .20 *.35*
J24 D2 10k lt blue & blue .55 *.95*
J25 D2 20k lt blue & blue .85 *1.40*
Nos. J20-J25 (6) 2.20 *3.45*
Set, never hinged 2.75

Nos. J21-J25 exist both perf 10½ and 11½. No. J20 exists only perf 11½.

OFFICIAL STAMPS

Croatian Coat of Arms
O1 O2

Perf. 10½, 11½
1942-43 Unwmk. Litho.
Ordinary Paper

O1 O1 25b rose lake .20 .20
O2 O1 50b slate blk .20 .20
O3 O1 75b gray grn .20 .20
O4 O1 1k orange brn .20 .20
O5 O1 2k turq blue .20 *.20*
O6 O1 3k vermilion .20 .20
O7 O1 4k brown vio .20 .20
O8 O1 5k ultra .20 *.20*
a. Thin paper 4.50 *2.00*
O9 O1 6k brt violet .20 .20
O10 O1 10k lt green .20 .20
O11 O1 12k brown rose .20 *.20*
O12 O1 20k dark blue .20 *.20*
O13 O2 30k brn vio & gray .20 *.20*
O14 O2 40k vio blk & gray .20 *.20*
O15 O2 50k brn lake & gray .30 *.30*
O16 O2 100k black & pink .30 *.30*
Nos. O1-O16 (16) 3.40 *3.40*
Set, never hinged 4.00

Nos. O1-O16 exist perf 10½ and 11½. No. O8a exists only perf 11½.

1943-44 Thin Paper *Perf. 11½*

O17 O1 25b claret .20 .20
O18 O1 50b gray .20 .20
O19 O1 75b dull green .20 .20
O20 O1 1k orange brn .20 .20
O21 O1 2k slate blue .20 .20
O22 O1 3.50k car rose .20 .20
a. Ordinary paper 3.00 *3.00*
O23 O1 6k brt red vio .20 .20
O24 O1 12.50k deep orange .20 .20
a. Ordinary paper 2.00 *2.00*
Set, never hinged .75

POSTAL TAX STAMPS

Catalogue values for unused stamps in this section are for Never Hinged items.

Nurse and Soldier — PT1 Wounded Soldier — PT2

Unwmk.
1942, Oct. 4 Litho. *Perf. 11*

RA1 PT1 1k olive grn & red .50 .40

The tax aided the Croatian Red Cross. Issued in sheets of 24 plus label.

1943, Oct. 3

RA2 PT2 2k blue & red .45 *.45*

The tax aided the Croatian Red Cross.

Ruins — PT3

Wounded Soldier — PT4

1944, Jan. 1 Photo. *Perf. 12*

RA3 PT3 1k dk slate green .20 *.20*
RA4 PT4 2k carmine lake .25 *.20*
RA5 PT4 5k black .25 *.20*
RA6 PT4 10k deep blue .45 .25
RA7 PT4 20k brown .60 .45
Nos. RA3-RA7 (5) 1.75 *1.30*

Interior of Zagreb Cathedral PT10

1991, Apr. 1 Litho. *Perf. 14*

RA20 PT10 1.20d black & gold *.40*
a. Perf. 11x10½ .40
b. Perf. 11 13.50
c. Imperf .40

Worker's Fund. Required on mail during April 1991.
For surcharges see Nos. 100, 100a.

Shrine of the Virgin, 700th Anniv. PT11

1991, May 16 *Perf. 10½x11*

RA21 PT11 1.70d multicolored .55
a. Imperf .55

Workers' Fund. Required on mail May 16-31.

Croatian Arms Type of 1992

1991, July 1 *Perf. 11x10½*

RA22 A37 2.20d multicolored *.65*
a. Imperf .90

Required on mail during July.

Members of Parliament PT12

1991, Aug. 1 *Perf. 11x10½*

RA23 PT12 2.20d multicolored *.65*
a. Imperf .90

Worker's Fund. Required on mail during Aug.

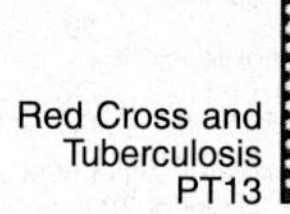

Red Cross and Tuberculosis PT13

1991, Sept 14 *Perf. 11*

RA24 PT13 2.20d blue & red *.70*

Required on mail Sept. 14-21.

Re-erection of Ban Josip Jelacic Equestrian Statue, Zagreb PT14

1991, Nov. 1 *Perf. 11x10½*

RA25 PT14 2.20d multicolored *.40*
a. Imperf. *.70*

Worker's Fund. Required on mail during Nov.

"VUKOVAR" with Barbed Wire — PT16

1992, Jan. 1 Litho. *Perf. 11x10½*

RA32 PT16 2.20d black & brown *.30*
a. Imperf. *.55*

Vukovar Refugee's Fund. Required on mail during Jan.

Red Cross PT17 Red Cross and Solidarity PT18

1992 *Perf. 11*

RA33 PT17 3d red & black *.20*
RA34 PT18 3d red & black *.20*

Issued: No. RA33, May 8. No. RA34, June 1.
No. RA33 was required on mail May 8-15; No. RA34, June 1-7.

Madonna of Bistrica — PT19

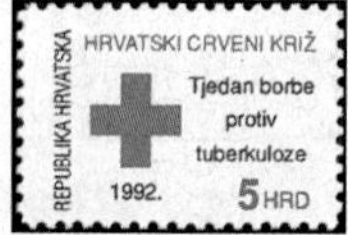

Red Cross — PT20

1992, Aug. 1 Litho. *Perf. 14*

RA35 PT19 5d blue & gold *.20*

Required on mail, Aug. 1-8.

1992, Sept. 21 Litho. *Perf. 11*

RA36 PT20 5d black & red *.25*

Required on mail Sept. 14-21.

St. George Slaying Dragon PT21

1992, Nov. 4 *Perf. 14*

RA37 PT21 15d multicolored *.20*

Cancer Research League. Required on mail Nov. 4-11.
See No. RA43.

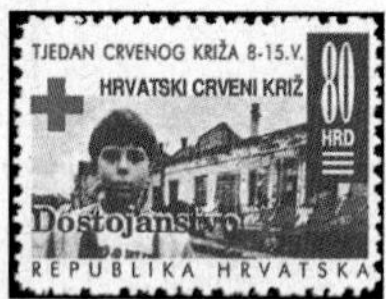

Red Cross — PT22

1993, May 8 Litho. *Rough Perf. 11*

RA38 PT22 80d black & red *.20*

Required on mail May 8-15.

Red Cross and Solidarity PT23

1993, June 1
RA39 PT23 100d black & red *1.10*

Required on mail June 1-7.

Cardinal Stepinac (1898-1960) PT24

1993, July 15 Litho. *Perf. 14*
RA40 PT24 150d multicolored *.20*

Required on mail July 15-22.

Zrinski-Frankopan Foundation — PT25

Design: 200d, Gen. Peter Zrinski (1621-1671), Politician and Fran Krsto Frankopan, Count of Tersat (1643-1671), Poet.

1993, Aug. 12 Litho. *Perf. 14*
RA41 PT25 200d gray & blue *.20*

Required on mail Aug. 12-19.

Red Cross Campaign Against Tuberculosis PT26

1993, Sept. 14 Litho. *Perf. 11*
RA42 PT26 300d gray, red & black *.20*

Required on mail Sept. 14-21.

St. George Slaying Dragon Type of 1992

1993, Oct. 11 Litho. *Perf. 14*
RA43 PT21 400d multicolored *.25*

Cancer Research League. Required on mail Oct. 11-31.

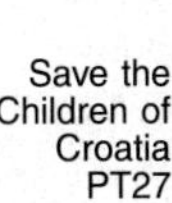

Save the Children of Croatia PT27

1993, Nov. 1 *Perf. 13½x14*
RA44 PT27 400d multicolored *.25*

Required on mail Nov. 1-30.

Croatian Red Cross — PT28

1994, May 5 Litho. *Perf. 11*
RA45 PT28 500d multicolored *.25*

Required on mail May 8-15.

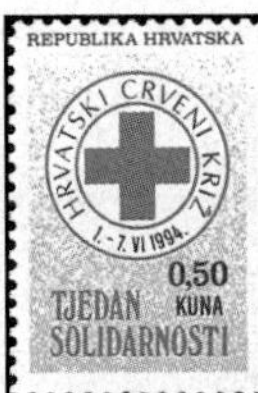

Red Cross Solidarity PT29

Ludberg Church PT30

1994, May 5 Litho. *Perf. 11*
RA46 PT29 50 l multicolored *.25*

Required on mail June 1-7.

1994, July 15 *Perf. 14*
RA47 PT30 50 l multicolored *.25*

Required on mail July 15-22.

Save the Children of Croatia — PT31

St. George Slaying Dragon — PT32

1994, Aug. 16 Litho. *Perf. 14*
RA48 PT31 50 l multicolored *.25*

Required on mail Aug. 16-29.

1994, Sept. 1
RA49 PT32 50 l multicolored *.25*

Cancer Research League. Required on mail Sept. 1-8.

PT33 PT34

1994, Sept. 14 *Perf. 11*
RA50 PT33 50 l blk, grn & red *.40*

Red Cross Campaign against Tuberculosis. Required on mail Sept. 14-21.

1994, Oct. 15 Litho. *Perf. 14*
RA51 PT34 50 l multicolored *.30*

Town of Slavonski Brod, 750th anniv.

Homage to Olympia, by Ivan Lackovic PT35

Intl. Olympic Committee, Cent. — PT36

Designs: a, Tennis. b, Soccer. c, Basketball. d, Team handball. e, Canoeing, kayaking. f, Water polo. g, Track and field. h, Gymnastics.

1994, Nov. 2 Litho. *Perf. 14*
RA52 PT35 50 l Pair, #a.-b. *1.40*

Miniature Sheets of 8

RA53 PT36 50 l #a.-h. *5.75*
RA54 PT36 50 l #a.-h. *5.75*

Nos. RA52b, RA53a, RA53d-RA53e, RA53h, RA54b-RA54c, RA54f-RA54g have IOC centennial emblem. Others have emblem of Croatian Olympic Committee.
Required on mail Nov. 2-15.

Natl. Olympic Committee PT37

Designs: a, Rowing. b, Pétanque. c, Monument to Drazen Petrovic, Olympic Park, Lausanne. d, Tennis. e, Basketball.

1995, Apr. 17 Litho. *Perf. 14*
RA55 PT37 50 l Strip of 5, #a.-e. *1.00*

Required on mail Apr. 17-30.

Red Cross Stamps
PT38 PT39

1995, May 8 *Perf. 11*
RA56 PT38 50 l multicolored *.20*

Required on mail May 8-15.

1995, June 1
RA57 PT39 50 l multicolored *.20*

Required on mail June 1-7.

Sts. Peter and Paul Cathedral, Osijek — PT40

1995, July 17 *Perf. 14*
RA58 PT40 65 l multicolored *.25*

Required on mail July 17-30.

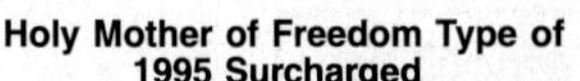

Holy Mother of Freedom Type of 1995 Surcharged

Design: No. RA59, Like No. RA60, but with black surcharge on white panel.

1995, Aug. 14 Litho. *Perf. 14*
RA59 PT41 65 l on 50 l multi *1.25 1.25*

No. RA59 not issued without surcharge. Examples without surcharge are printer's waste. Required on mail Aug. 14-27.

Holy Mother of Freedom PT41

#RA60, Croatian Pieta, by Ivan Lackovic.
#RA61, Gedenkstatte Church Project.

1995, Aug. 14
RA60 PT41 65 l multicolored *.25*
RA61 PT41 65 l multicolored *.25*

Required on mail Aug. 14-27.

A number has been reserved for an additional value in this set.

Red Cross and Tuberculosis PT42

Save the Croatian Children PT43

1995, Sept. 14 Litho. *Perf. 11*
RA62 PT62 65 l multicolored *.25*

Required on mail Sept. 14-21.

1995, Oct. 16 *Perf. 14*
RA63 PT43 65 l multicolored *.25*

Required on mail Oct. 16-29.

PT44

PT45

Performance scene: a, Woman seated at top of steps. b, Gathering of people. c, People, large statue in background.

1995, Oct. 16
RA64 PT44 65 l Strip of 3, #a.-c. *.80*

Croatian Natl. Theater, Zagreb, cent. No. RA64 has continuous design. Required on mail 10/16-29.

1995, Nov. 6 Litho. *Perf. 14*
RA65 PT45 65 l multicolored *.25*

Fight against drugs. Required on mail Nov. 20-30.

PT46

1995, Nov. 20 Litho. *Perf. 14x13¾*
RA66 PT46 65 l multicolored .25

Croatian Anti-Cancer League. Required on mail Nov. 20-30.

PT47

PT48

1996, Feb. 15 Litho. *Perf. 14x13½*
RA67 PT47 65 l multicolored .25

Croatian Anti-Cancer League. Required on mail Feb. 15-28.

1996, Mar. 18 Litho. *Perf. 14*
RA68 PT48 65 l multicolored .25

Sanctuary of the Virgin Mary of Bistrica. Required on mail Mar. 18-31.

Croatian Olympic Committee
PT49

1996, Apr. 17 Litho. *Perf. 14*
RA69 PT49 65 l multi .20 .20

No. RA69 exists imperf. and in booklets, which were not placed on sale. Required on mail Apr. 17-30.

PT50

PT51

1996, May 8 Litho. *Perf. 11*
RA70 PT50 65 l multicolored .25

Red Cross. Required on mail May 8-15.

1996, June 6 Litho. *Perf. 11*
RA71 PT51 65 l multicolored .25

Red Cross Solidarity Week. Required on mail June 1-7.

PT52

1996, June 14 Litho. *Perf. 14x13½*
RA72 PT52 65 l multicolored .25

For Croatian children. Required on mail 6/14-27.

PT53

1996, July 3 Litho. *Perf. 14*
RA73 PT53 65 l multicolored .25

Osijek, 800th anniv. Required on mail July 3-16.

PT54

PT55

1996, July 17 Litho. *Perf. 14*
RA74 PT54 65 l multicolored .25

Renovation of Dakovaska Cathedral. Required on mail July 17-30.

1996, Aug. 1 Litho. *Perf. 14*
RA75 PT55 65 l multicolored .25

Split, 1700th anniv. Required on mail Aug. 1-14.

PT56

PT57

1996, Aug. 16 Litho. *Perf. 14x13½*
RA76 PT56 65 l multicolored .25

Aid to Vukovar. Required on mail 8/16-29.

1996, Sept. 1 Litho. *Perf. 14*
RA77 PT57 65 l multicolored .25

Fight against drugs. Required on mail Sept. 1-12.

PT58

1996, Sept. 14 Litho. *Perf. 11*
RA78 PT58 65 l multicolored .25

Red Cross Tuberculosis Week. Required on mail Sept. 14-21.

PT59

1996, Oct. 10 Litho. *Perf. 14*
RA79 PT59 65 l multicolored .25

Isolation of insulin, 75th anniv. Required on mail Oct. 10-17.

PT60

PT61

1996, Nov. 11 Litho. *Perf. 14*
RA80 PT60 65 l multicolored .25

Remete pilgrimage. Required on mail Nov. 11-24.

1997, Jan. 6 Litho. *Perf. 14*
RA81 PT61 65 l multicolored .25

Antun Mihanovic (1796-1861), natl. anthem lyricist. Required on mail Jan. 6-26.

House of Dr. Ante Starcevic
PT62

1997, Jan. 27 Litho. *Perf. 14*
RA82 PT62 65 l multicolored .25

Required on mail Jan. 27-Feb. 14.

PT63

PT64

1997, Feb. 15 Litho. *Perf. 14*
RA83 PT63 65 l multicolored .25

Croatian Anti-Cancer League. Required on mail Feb. 15-28.

1997, May 8 Litho. *Perf. 10½x11*
RA84 PT64 65 l multicolored .25
a. Perf 10½ .25
b. Perf 11 35.00

Red Cross. Required on mail May 8-15.

CUBA

'kyü-bə

LOCATION — The largest island of the West Indies; south of Florida
GOVT. — Former Spanish possession
AREA — 44,206 sq. mi.
POP. — 11,096,395 (1999 est.)
CAPITAL — Havana

Formerly a Spanish possession, Cuba made several unsuccessful attempts to gain her freedom, which finally led to the intervention of the US in 1898. In that year under the Treaty of Paris, Spain relinquished the island to the US in trust for its inhabitants.

In 1902 a republic was established and the Cuban Congress took over the government from the military authorities.

8 Reales Plata = 1 Peso
100 Centesimos = 1 Escudo or Peseta (1867)
1000 Milesimas = 100 Centavos = 1 Peso

Catalogue values for unused stamps in this country are for Never Hinged items, beginning with Scott 402 in the regular postage section, Scott B3 in the semi-postal section, Scott C38 in the airpost section, Scott CB1 in the airpost semi-postal section, Scott E13 in the special delivery section, and Scott RA1 in the postal tax section.

Pen cancellations are common on the earlier stamps of Cuba. Stamps so canceled sell for very much less than those with postmark cancellations.

Watermarks

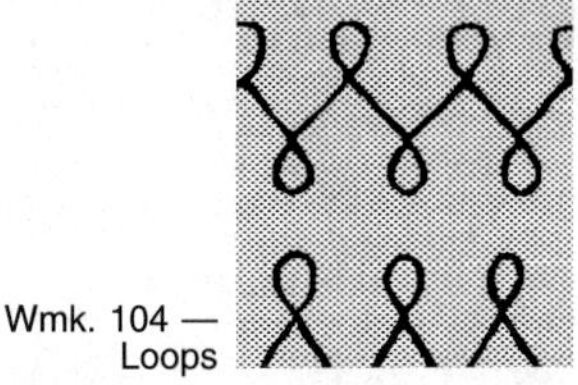

Wmk. 104 — Loops

Loops from different rows may or may not be directly opposite each other.

Wmk. 105 — Crossed Lines

Wmk. 106 — Star

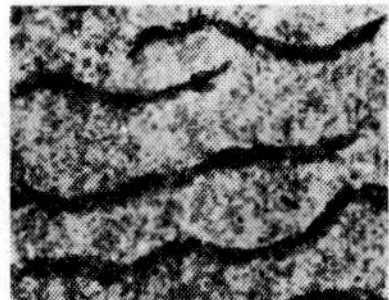

Wmk. 229 — Wavy Lines

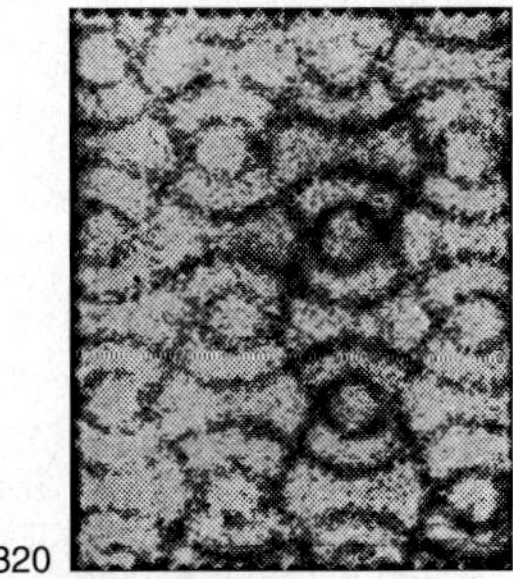

Wmk. 320

Wmk. 321 — "R de C"

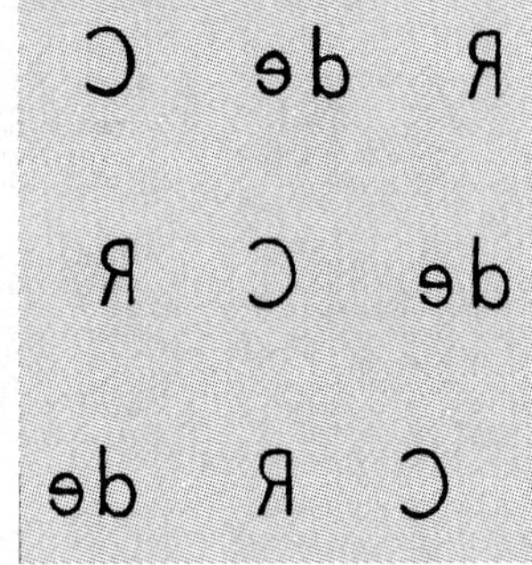

Wmk. 376 — "R de C"

Issued under Spanish Dominion

Used also in Puerto Rico: Nos. 1-3, 9-14, 17-21, 32-34, 35A-37, 39-41, 43-45, 47-49, 51-53, 55-57.

Used also in the Philippines: Nos. 2-3.

Identifiable cancellations of those countries will increase the value of the stamps.

Queen Isabella II — A1

Blue Paper

1855 Typo. Wmk. 104 *Imperf.*

1 A1 ½r p blue green 60.00 5.00
a. ½r p blackish green 65.00 8.25
2 A1 1r p gray green 50.00 3.50
3 A1 2r p carmine 275.00 10.00
4 A1 2r p orange red 700.00 15.00
Nos. 1-4 (4) 1,085. 33.50

See #9-14. For surcharges see #5-8, 15.

Counterfeit surcharges are plentiful.

Nos. 3-4 Surcharged Y ¼

1855-56

5 A1 ¼r p on 2r p car 625.00 175.00
a. Without fraction bar *1,250.* 500.00
6 A1 ¼r p on 2r p org red 525.00

Surcharged Y ¼

7 A1 ¼r p on 2r p car 550.00 175.00
a. Without fraction bar 675.00
8 A1 ¼r p on 2r p org red 825.00 375.00
a. Without fraction bar 1,050.

The "Y ¼" surcharge met the "Ynterior" rate for delivery within the city of Havana.

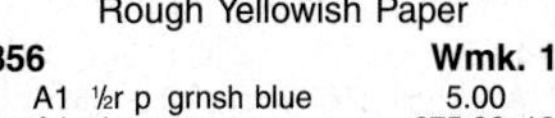

Rough Yellowish Paper

1856 Wmk. 105

9 A1 ½r p grnsh blue 5.00 .75
10 A1 1r p green 675.00 13.50
a. 1r p emerald *1,000.* 18.00
11 A1 2r p orange red 325.00 14.00

White Smooth Paper

1857 Unwmk.

12 A1 ½r p blue 3.25 .65
13 A1 1r p gray green 3.00 .65
a. 1r p pale yellow green 2.75 .65
14 A1 2r p dull rose 17.50 3.00
Nos. 12-14 (3) 23.75 4.30

Surcharged

1860

15 A1 ¼r p on 2r p dl rose 210.00 72.50
a. 1 of ¼ inverted 325.00 140.00
b. "1 ⅘" instead of 1 ¼ —

22 overprint varieties exist.

Queen Isabella II
A2 A3

1862-64 *Imperf.*

16 A2 ¼r p black 21.00 17.00
17 A3 ¼r p blk, *buff* ('64) 21.00 16.00
18 A3 ½r p green ('64) 4.75 .70
19 A3 ½r p grn, *pale rose* ('64) 11.00 2.00
20 A3 1r p bl, *sal* ('64) 4.75 1.00
a. Diagonal half used as ½r p on cover 125.00
21 A3 2r p ver, *buff* ('64) 25.00 6.00
a. 2r p red, *buff* 30.00 6.75
Nos. 16-21 (6) 87.50 42.70

No. 17 Overprinted in Black

1866

22 A3 ¼r p black, *buff* 65.00 70.00

Exists with handstamped "1866."

A5

A6

1866

23 A5 5c dull violet 40.00 26.00
24 A5 10c blue 2.50 1.00
25 A5 20c green 1.50 1.00
a. Diag. half used as 10c on cover 150.00
26 A5 40c rose 9.50 8.00
Nos. 23-26 (4) 53.50 36.00

For the Type A5 20c in dull lilac, see Spain No. 87.

Stamps Dated "1867"

1867 *Perf. 14*

27 A5 5c dull violet 37.50 19.00
28 A5 10c blue 17.50 1.25
a. Imperf., pair 100.00 6.00
b. Diagonal half used as 5c on cover 125.00
29 A5 20c green 11.00 1.75
a. Imperf., pair 100.00 65.00
b. Diag. half used as 10c on cover 140.00
30 A5 40c rose 14.00 9.00
Nos. 27-30 (4) 80.00 31.00

Stamps Dated "1868"

1868

31 A6 5c dull violet 20.00 8.25
32 A6 10c blue 3.75 1.75
a. Diagonal half used as 5c on cover 140.00
33 A6 20c green 5.50 3.00
a. Diag. half used as 10c on cover 140.00
34 A6 40c rose 14.00 8.00
a. Diag. half used as 20c on cover 175.00
Nos. 31-34 (4) 43.25 21.00

Nos. 31-34 Overprinted in Black

1868

35 A6 5c dull violet 57.50 26.00
35A A6 10c blue 57.50 26.00
b. Diag. half used as 5c on cover *250.00*
36 A6 20c green 57.50 26.00
37 A6 40c rose 57.50 26.00
Nos. 35-37 (4) 230.00 104.00

1869 Stamps Dated "1869"

38 A6 5c rose 37.50 12.00
39 A6 10c red brown 3.75 1.75
a. Diag. half used as 5c on cover 125.00
40 A6 20c orange 6.50 2.25
41 A6 40c dull violet 30.00 9.50
Nos. 38-41 (4) 77.75 25.50

Nos. 38-41 Ovptd. Like Nos. 35-37

42 A6 5c rose 125.00 37.50
43 A6 10c red brown 42.50 30.00
a. Diag. half used as 5c on cover —
44 A6 20c orange 35.00 30.00
a. Diag. half used as 10c on cover —
45 A6 40c dull violet 60.00 30.00
Nos. 42-45 (4) 262.50 127.50

"Espana"
A8 A9

1870 *Perf. 14*

46 A8 5c blue 140.00 50.00
47 A8 10c green 2.50 .80
a. Diagonal half used as 5c on cover 140.00
48 A8 20c red brown 2.50 .80
a. Diag. half used as 10c on cover 200.00
49 A8 40c rose 175.00 27.50

1871

50 A9 12c red lilac 18.00 10.00
a. Imperf., pair 85.00 —
51 A9 25c ultra 2.25 .85
a. Imperf., pair 40.00 —
b. Diagonal half used as 12c on cover 140.00
52 A9 50c gray green 2.25 .85
a. Imperf., pair 15.00 —
b. Diagonal half used as 25c on cover 140.00
53 A9 1p pale brown 27.50 9.00
a. Imperf., pair 125.00 —
Nos. 50-53 (4) 50.00 20.70

King Amadeo — A10

1873 *Perf. 14*

54 A10 12½c dark green 22.50 12.50
55 A10 25c gray 2.00 .80
a. Diagonal half used as 12½c on cover 75.00
b. 25c lilac 5.50 1.00
c. As "b," half used as 12½c on cover 100.00
56 A10 50c brown 1.40 .75
a. Imperf., pair 50.00 —
b. Half used as 25c on cover 82.50
57 A10 1p red brown 300.00 40.00
a. Diagonal half used as 50c on cover 240.00

"España"
A11

Coat of Arms
A12

1874

58 A11 12½c brown 17.00 7.50
a. Half used as 5c on cover 125.00
59 A11 25c ultra .85 .50
a. Diagonal half used as 12½c on cover 90.00
60 A11 50c dp violet 1.50 .75
a. Diagonal half used as 25c on cover 100.00
61 A11 50c gray 1.50 .75
a. Diagonal half used as 25c on cover 100.00
62 A11 1p carmine 190.00 55.00
a. Imperf., pair 550.00 190.00
Nos. 58-62 (5) 210.85 64.50

1875

63 A12 12½c lt violet .90 .90
a. Imperf., pair 75.00
64 A12 25c ultra .40 .30
a. Imperf., pair 75.00
b. Diagonal half used as 12½c on cover 70.00
65 A12 50c blue green .50 .40
a. Imperf., pair 75.00
b. Diag. half used as 25c on cover 65.00
66 A12 1p brown 8.00 5.00
b. Diag. half used as 50c on cover 125.00
Nos. 63-66 (4) 9.80 6.60

King Alfonso XII
A13 A14

1876

67 A13 12½c green 1.75 1.50
a. 12½c emerald green 2.00 2.00
68 A13 25c gray .75 .35
a. Diagonal half used as 12½c on cover 80.00
b. 25c pale violet 1.50 .25
d. 25c bluish gray 2.25 .35
69 A13 50c ultra .75 .40
a. Imperf., pair 14.00
b. Diag. half used as 25c on cover 65.00
70 A13 1p black 8.50 3.75
a. Imperf., pair 35.00
b. Diag. half used as 50c on cover 100.00
Nos. 67-70 (4) 11.75 6.00

1877

71 A14 10c lt green 22.50
72 A14 12½c gray 6.00 2.75
a. Imperf., pair 35.00
b. Diagonal half used on cover 65.00
73 A14 25c dk green .55 .45
a. Imperf., pair 35.00
b. Diagonal half used as 12½c on cover 65.00
74 A14 50c black .55 .45
a. Imperf., pair 35.00
b. Half used as 25c on cover 75.00
75 A14 1p brown 25.00 12.50
Nos. 71-75 (5) 54.60

No. 71 was not placed in use.

Stamps Dated "1878"

1878

76 A14 5c blue .55 .45
77 A14 10c black 62.50
78 A14 12½c brown bis 3.25 1.75
a. 12½c gray bister 4.00 1.50
c. Diagonal half used on cover 65.00
79 A14 25c yel green .20 .20
b. No. 79 or 79c, diagonal half used as 12½c on cover 60.00
c. 25c deep green .20 .20
80 A14 50c dk blue grn .35 .20
b. Diagonal half used as 25c on cover 60.00
81 A14 1p carmine 10.00 4.50
b. 1p rose 6.75 3.50
Nos. 76-81 (6) 76.85 7.10

No. 77 was not placed in use.

Imperf., Pairs

76a	A14	5c blue	21.00
77a	A14	10c black	125.00
78b	A14	12½c brown bister	21.00
79a	A14	25c deep green	21.00
80a	A14	50c dk blue green	100.00
81a	A14	1p carmine	72.50

Stamps Dated "1879"

1879

82 A14 5c slate black .55 .25
83 A14 10c orange 125.00 65.00
84 A14 12½c rose .55 .25
85 A14 25c ultra .45 .25
a. Diagonal half used as 12½c on cover 65.00
b. Imperf., pair 40.00 —
86 A14 50c gray .45 .25
a. Diag. half used as 25c on cover 65.00
87 A14 1p olive bister 16.00 8.50
Nos. 82-87 (6) 143.00 74.50

A15

A16

A17

1880

88 A15 5c green .35 .20
89 A15 10c lake 72.50
90 A15 12½c gray .35 .20
91 A15 25c gray blue .35 .20
a. Diagonal half used as 12½c on cover 75.00
92 A15 50c brown .40 .20
a. Diagonal half used as 25c on cover 65.00
93 A15 1p yellow brn 5.50 2.50
a. Diagonal half used as 50c on cover 90.00
Nos. 88-93 (6) 79.45 3.30

No. 89 was not placed in use.

1881

94 A16 1c green .25 .20
95 A16 2c lake 35.00
96 A16 2½c olive bister .45 .30
97 A16 5c gray blue .25 .20
a. Diag. half used as 2½c on cover 55.00
98 A16 10c yellow brown .35 .20
a. Diag. half used as 5c on cover 55.00
99 A16 20c dark brown 5.00 4.00
Nos. 94-99 (6) 41.30 4.90

No. 95 was not placed in use.

1882

100 A17 1c green .40 .35
a. Diag. half used as ½c on cover 50.00
101 A17 2c lake 2.40 .35
a. Diag. half used as 1c on cover 50.00
102 A17 2½c dk brown 5.25 1.75
103 A17 5c gray blue 2.40 .50
a. Diag. half used as 2½c on cover 65.00
104 A17 10c olive brown .60 .20
a. Diag. half used as 5c on cover 50.00
105 A17 20c red brown 80.00 27.50
a. Diag. half used as 10c on cover 110.00
Nos. 100-105 (6) 91.05 30.65

See #121-131. For surcharges see #106-120.

Issue of 1882 Surcharged or Overprinted in Black, Blue or Red:

a

b

c

d

e

1883

Type "a"

106 A17 5 on 5c (R) 1.75 .90
a. Triple surcharge
b. Double surcharge 17.50 17.50
c. Inverted surcharge 22.50 22.50
d. Without "5" in surcharge 12.50 12.50
e. Dbl. surch., types "a" & "d"
107 A17 10 on 10c (Bl) 1.75 1.00
a. Inverted surcharge
b. Double surcharge 20.00 20.00
108 A17 20 on 20c 22.50 19.00
a. "10" instead of "20" 60.00 60.00
b. Double surcharge

Type "b"

109 A17 5 on 5c (R) 1.75 .90
a. Inverted surcharge 20.00 20.00
b. Double surcharge 17.50 17.50
110 A17 10 on 10c (Bl) 5.00 2.00
a. Inverted surcharge 25.00 25.00
b. Double surcharge
111 A17 20 on 20c 50.00 25.00
a. Double surcharge
b. Dbl. surch., types "b" & "c"

Type "c"

112 A17 5 on 5c (R) 1.50 .90
a. Inverted surcharge 25.00 25.00
b. Dbl. surch., types "c" & "d" —
113 A17 10 on 10c (Bl) 5.00 2.25
a. Inverted surcharge 30.00 30.00
b. Double surcharge 30.00 30.00
114 A17 20 on 20c 35.00 18.00
a. "10" instead of "20" 75.00 60.00
b. Double surcharge 75.00 75.00
c. Dbl. surch., types "a" & "c"

Type "d"

115 A17 5 on 5c (R) 1.40 .85
a. Inverted surcharge 25.00 25.00
b. Double surcharge 20.00 20.00
116 A17 10 on 10c (Bl) 2.00 1.50
a. Inverted surcharge 25.00 25.00
b. Double surcharge 22.50 22.50
117 A17 20 on 20c 50.00 20.00
a. Dbl. surch., types "a" & "d"

Type "e"

118 A17 5c gray blue (R) 1.75 1.25
a. Double overprint 27.50 27.50
119 A17 10c olive bis (Bl) 4.25 4.25
a. Double overprint 30.00 30.00
120 A17 20c red brown 125.00 32.50
a. Double overprint 100.00 100.00
Nos. 106-120 (15) 308.65 130.30

Handstamped overprints and surcharges are counterfeits.

Numerous other varieties exist.

Type of 1882

Original

1st retouch

2d retouch

The differences between the stamps of 1882 and the various retouches are as follows:

Original state: The medallion is surrounded by a heavy line of color of nearly even thickness, touching the horizontal line below the word "Cuba" (or "Filipinas," "Puerto Rico," as the case may be); the opening in the hair above the temple is narrow and pointed.

1st retouch: The line around the medallion is thin, except at the upper right, and does not touch the horizontal line above it; the opening in the hair is slightly wider and a trifle rounded; the lock of hair above the forehead is shaped like a broad "V" and ends in a point; there is a faint white line below it, which is not found on the stamps in the original state. Owing to wear of the plate the shape of the lock of hair and the width of the white line below it vary.

2nd retouch: The opening in the hair forms a semi-circle; the lock above the forehead is nearly straight, having only a slight wave, and the white line is much broader than before.

1883-86

121 A17 1c grn, 2nd retouch *95.00 37.50*
122 A17 2½c olive bister .40 .20
124 A17 2½c violet .40 .25
a. 2½c red lilac ('85) .85 .50
b. 2½c ultramarine 95.00 —
125 A17 5c gray bl, 1st retouch 2.25 .30
a. Diag. half used as 2½c on cover 45.00
126 A17 5c gray bl, 2nd retouch 17.50 2.50
a. Diag. half used as 2½c on cover 50.00
127 A17 10c brn, 1st retouch 1.75 .50
a. Diagonal half used as 5c on cover 40.00
128 A17 20c olive bister 13.00 2.75
Nos. 121-128 (7) 130.30 44.00

1888

129 A17 2½c red brown 1.60 .90
130 A17 10c blue 1.25 .80
a. Diagonal half used as 5c on cover 175.00
131 A17 20c brnsh gray 12.00 4.00
Nos. 129-131 (3) 14.85 5.70

King Alfonso XIII
A18 A19

1890-97

132 A18 1c gray brown 12.00 6.00
133 A18 1c ol gray ('91) 7.25 3.25
134 A18 1c ultra ('94) 3.00 .35
135 A18 1c dk vio ('96) .85 .25
136 A18 2c slate blue 6.75 2.00
137 A18 2c lilac brn ('91) 1.40 .45
138 A18 2c rose ('94) 29.00 5.00
139 A18 2c claret ('96) 7.50 .75
140 A18 2½c emerald 9.25 4.00
141 A18 2½c salmon ('91) 42.50 9.00
142 A18 2½c lilac ('94) 2.75 .25
143 A18 2½c rose ('96) .60 .20
144 A18 5c olive gray .70 .60
145 A18 5c emerald ('91) .85 .40
146 A18 5c sl blue ('96) .45 .20
147 A18 10c brown violet 2.50 .75
148 A18 10c claret ('91) 1.60 .40
149 A18 10c emerald ('96) 2.10 .20
150 A18 20c dk violet .70 .55
151 A18 20c ultra ('91) 8.50 7.25
152 A18 20c red brn ('94) 22.50 9.50
153 A18 20c violet ('96) 13.50 4.75
154 A18 40c orange brn ('97) 27.50 11.00
155 A18 80c lilac brn ('97) 50.00 17.00
Nos. 132-155 (24) 253.75 84.10

Imperf., Pairs

134a	A18	1c ultramarine	80.00
138a	A18	2c rose	85.00
142a	A18	2½c lilac	80.00
145a	A18	5c emerald	85.00
148a	A18	10c claret	75.00
152a	A18	20c red brown	125.00

1898

156 A19 1m orange brn .20 .20
157 A19 2m orange brn .20 .20
158 A19 3m orange brn .20 .20
159 A19 4m orange brn 3.75 1.40
160 A19 5m orange brn .20 .20
161 A19 1c black vio .20 .20
162 A19 2c dk blue grn .20 .20
163 A19 3c dk brown .20 .20
164 A19 4c orange 11.00 3.50
165 A19 5c car rose .75 .20
a. Imperf., pair 100.00
166 A19 6c dk blue .20 .20
a. Imperf., pair 100.00
167 A19 8c gray brown .80 .35
168 A19 10c vermilion .80 .35
169 A19 15c slate green 3.75 .35
170 A19 20c maroon .45 .20
171 A19 40c dark lilac 1.75 .35
172 A19 60c black 1.75 .35
173 A19 80c red brown 11.50 6.75
174 A19 1p yel green 11.50 6.75
175 A19 2p slate blue 22.50 6.75
Nos. 156-175 (20) 71.90 28.90

Nos. 156-160 were issued for use on newspapers.

For surcharges see #176-189C, 196-200.

Issued under Administration of the United States

Puerto Principe Issue

Issues of Cuba of 1898 and 1896 Surcharged:

HABILITADO 1 cent. (a)	HABILITADO 1 cents. (b)
HABILITADO 2 cents. (c)	HABILITADO 2 cents. (d)
HABILITADO 3 cents. (e)	HABILITADO 3 cents. (f)
HABILITADO 5 cents. (g)	HABILITADO 5 cents. (h)
HABILITADO 5 cents. (i)	HABILITADO 5 cents. (j)
HABILITADO 3 cents. (k)	HABILITADO 3 cents. (l)
(m)	HABILITADO 10 cents.

Types a, c, d, e, f, g and h are 17½mm high, the others are 19½mm high.

Black Surcharge On Nos. 156, 157, 158 and 160

1898-99

#176-189 are Orange Brown

No.	Type	Description	Unused	Used
176	A19 (a)	1c on 1m	50.00	30.00
177	A19 (b)	1c on 1m	45.00	35.00
a.		Broken figure "l"	75.00	65.00
b.		Inverted surcharge		200.00
d.		As "a," inverted		*250.00*
178	A19 (c)	2c on 2m	22.50	18.00
a.		Inverted surcharge	250.00	50.00
179	A19 (d)	2c on 2m	40.00	35.00
a.		Inverted surcharge	350.00	100.00
179B	A19 (k)	3c on 1m	300.00	175.00
c.		Double surcharge	1,500.	750.00
179D	A19 (l)	3c on 1m	*1,500.*	*750.00*
e.		Double surcharge	—	—
179F	A19 (e)	3c on 2m		*1,500.*

Value is for copy with minor faults.

No.	Type	Description	Unused	Used
179G	A19 (f)	3c on 2m	—	*2,000.*

Value is for copy with minor faults.

No.	Type	Description	Unused	Used
180	A19 (e)	3c on 3m	27.50	*30.00*
a.		Inverted surcharge		*110.00*
181	A19 (f)	3c on 3m	75.00	75.00
a.		Inverted surcharge		*200.00*
182	A19 (g)	5c on 1m	700.00	200.00
a.		Inverted surcharge		*500.00*
183	A19 (h)	5c on 1m	*1,300.*	*500.00*
a.		Inverted surcharge		*700.00*
184	A19 (g)	5c on 2m	750.00	250.00
185	A19 (h)	5c on 2m	1,500.	500.00
186	A19 (g)	5c on 3m	650.00	175.00
a.		Inverted surcharge	1,200.	700.00
187	A19 (h)	5c on 3m		400.00
a.		Inverted surcharge		1,000.
188	A19 (g)	5c on 5m	80.00	60.00
a.		Inverted surcharge	400.00	200.00
b.		Double surcharge	—	—
189	A19 (h)	5c on 5m	350.00	250.00
a.		Inverted surcharge		400.00
b.		Double surcharge	—	—

The 2nd printing of Nos. 188-189 has shiny ink. Values are for the 1st printing.

No.	Type	Description	Unused	Used
189C	A19 (i)	5c on 5m		*7,500.*

Black Surcharge on No. P25

No.	Type	Description	Unused	Used
190	N2 (g)	5c on ½m bl grn	250.00	75.00
a.		Inverted surcharge	500.00	150.00
b.		Pair, right stamp without surcharge		500.00

Value for No. 190b is for pair with unsurcharged copy at right. Exists with unsurcharged stamp at left.

No.	Type	Description	Unused	Used
191	N2 (h)	5c on ½m bl grn	300.00	90.00
a.		Inverted surcharge		200.00
192	N2 (i)	5c on ½m bl grn	550.00	200.00
a.		Dbl. surch., one diagonal		*11,500.*
193	N2 (j)	5c on ½m bl grn	800.00	300.00

Red Surcharge on No. 161

No.	Type	Description	Unused	Used
196	A19 (k)	3c on 1c blk vio	65.00	35.00
a.		Inverted surcharge		300.00
197	A19 (l)	3c on 1c blk vio	125.00	55.00
a.		Inverted surcharge		300.00
198	A19 (i)	5c on 1c blk vio	25.00	*30.00*
a.		Inverted surcharge		125.00
b.		Surcharge vert. up		*3,500.*
c.		Double surcharge	*400.00*	*600.00*
d.		Dbl. invtd. surch.		—

No. 198b exists reading down.

No.	Type	Description	Unused	Used
199	A19 (j)	5c on 1c blk vio	55.00	55.00
a.		Inverted surcharge		250.00
b.		Vertical surcharge		*2,000.*
c.		Double surcharge	1,000.	600.00
200	A19 (m)	10c on 1c blk vio	20.00	*50.00*
a.		Broken figure "l"	40.00	*100.00*

Black Surcharge on Nos. P26-P30

No.	Type	Description	Unused	Used
201	N2 (k)	3c on 1m bl grn	350.	350.
a.		Inverted surcharge		450.
b.		"EENTS"	550.	450.
c.		As "b," inverted		850.
202	N2 (l)	3c on 1m bl grn	550.	400.
a.		Inverted surcharge		850.
203	N2 (k)	3c on 2m bl grn	850.	350.
a.		"EENTS"	1,250.	500.
b.		Inverted surcharge		850.
c.		As "a," inverted		950.
204	N2 (l)	3c on 2m bl grn	1,250.	600.
a.		Inverted surcharge		750.
205	N2 (k)	3c on 3m bl grn	900.	350.
a.		Inverted surcharge		500.
b.		"EENTS"	1,250.	450.
c.		As "b," inverted		700.
206	N2 (l)	3c on 3m bl grn	1,200.	550.
a.		Inverted surcharge		700.
211	N2 (i)	5c on 1m bl grn		1,800.
a.		"EENTS"	—	2,500.
212	N2 (j)	5c on 1m bl grn		2,250.
213	N2 (i)	5c on 2m bl grn		1,800.
a.		"EENTS"	—	1,900.
214	N2 (j)	5c on 2m bl grn		1,750.
215'	N2 (i)	5c on 3m bl grn		550.
a.		"EENTS"		1,000.
216	N2 (j)	5c on 3m bl grn	—	1,000.
217	N2 (i)	5c on 4m bl grn	*2,500.*	900.
a.		"EENTS"	*3,000.*	1,500.
b.		Inverted surcharge		*2,000.*
c.		As "a," inverted		2,000.
218	N2 (j)	5c on 4m bl grn		*1,250.*
a.		Inverted surcharge		*2,000.*
219	N2 (i)	5c on 8m bl grn	*2,500.*	1,250.
a.		Inverted surcharge		1,500.
b.		"EENTS"	—	1,800.
c.		As "b," inverted		2,500.
220	N2 (j)	5c on 8m bl grn		2,000.
a.		Inverted surcharge		2,500.

Beware of forgeries of the Puerto Principe issue. Obtaining expert opinions is recommended.

United States Nos. 279, 267, 267b, 279Bf, 279Bh, 268, 281, 282C and 283 Surcharged in Black

1899 Wmk. 191 *Perf. 12*

No.	Type	Description	Unused	Used
221	A87	1c on 1c yel grn	5.25	.35
222	A88	2c on 2c red-dish car, type III	10.00	.75
b.		2c on 2c vermilion, type III	10.00	.75
222A	A88	2c on 2c red-dish car, type IV	5.75	.40
c.		2c on 2c vermilion, type IV	5.75	.40
d.		As #222A, inverted surcharge	*3,500.*	*3,500.*
223	A88	2½c on 2c red-dish car, type III	5.00	.80
b.		2½c on 2c vermilion, type III	5.00	.80
223A	A88	2½c on 2c red-dish car, type IV	3.50	.50
c.		2½c on 2c vermilion	3.50	.50
224	A89	3c on 3c purple	12.50	1.75
a.		"CUB.A"	37.50	35.00
225	A91	5c on 5c blue	12.50	2.00
226	A94	10c on 10c brn, type I	22.50	6.50
b.		"CUBA" omitted	*4,000.*	*4,000.*
226A	A94	10c on 10c brn, type II	*6,000.*	
		Nos. 221-226 (8)	77.00	13.05

The 2½c was sold and used as a 2c stamp.

Excellent counterfeits of this and the preceding issue exist, especially inverted and double surcharges.

Issues of the Republic under U.S. Military Rule

Statue of Columbus A20

Royal Palms A21

"Cuba" — A22

Ocean Liner — A23

Cane Field — A24

Wmk. US-C (191C)

1899 Engr. *Perf. 12*

No.	Type	Description	Unused	Used
227	A20	1c yel grn	3.50	.20
228	A21	2c carmine	3.50	.20
a.		2c scarlet	3.50	.20
b.		Booklet pane of 6 ('02)	*2,000.*	
229	A22	3c purple	3.50	.20
230	A23	5c blue	4.50	.20
231	A24	10c brown	11.00	.50
		Nos. 227-231 (5)	26.00	1.30

No. 228b was issued by the Republic. See #233-237. For surcharge see #232.

Issues of the Republic

No. 229 Surcharged in Carmine

1902, Sept. 30

No.	Type	Description	Unused	Used
232	A22	1c on 3c purple	1.00	.50
a.		Inverted surcharge	150.00	150.00
b.		Surcharge sideways (numeral horizontal)		
c.		Double surcharge	200.00	200.00

Counterfeits of the errors are plentiful.

Re-engraved

The re-engraved stamps of 1905-07 may be distinguished from the issue of 1899 as follows:

ORIGINAL

RE-ENGRAVED

1c — The ends of the label inscribed "Centavo" are rounded instead of square.

2c — The foliate ornaments, inside the oval disks bearing the numerals of value, have been removed.

5c — Two lines forming a right angle have been added in the upper corners of the label bearing the word "Cuba."

10c — A small ball has been added to each of the square ends of the label bearing the word "Cuba."

1905 Unwmk. *Perf. 12*

No.	Type	Description	Unused	Used
233	A20	1c green	1.60	.20
234	A21	2c rose	1.10	.20
a.		Booklet pane of 6	140.00	
236	A23	5c blue	35.00	1.00
237	A24	10c brown	3.00	.45
		Nos. 233-237 (4)	40.70	1.85

Maj. Gen. Antonio Maceo — A26

1907

No.	Type	Description	Unused	Used
238	A26	50c gray bl & blk	1.10	.75

Bartolomé Masó A27

Máximo Gómez A28

Julio Sanguily A29

Ignacio Agramonte A30

Calixto García A31

José M. Rodriquez y Rodriquez (Mayia) A32

Carlos Roloff — A33

1910, Feb. 1

239 A27 1c grn & vio .80 .20
a. Center inverted 250.00 *250.00*
240 A28 2c car & grn 1.60 .20
a. Center inverted 550.00 *550.00*
241 A29 3c vio & bl 1.10 .20
242 A30 5c bl & grn 15.00 .80
243 A31 8c ol & vio 1.10 .30
244 A32 10c brn & bl 6.50 .65
a. Center inverted 800.00
245 A26 50c vio & blk 1.60 .50
246 A33 1p slate & blk 7.25 4.00
Nos. 239-246 (8) 34.95 6.85
Set, never hinged 45.00

1911-13

247 A27 1c green .50 .20
248 A28 2c car rose .65 .20
a. Booklet pane of 6 ('13) 75.00
250 A30 5c ultra 1.60 .20
251 A31 8c ol grn & blk 1.00 .60
252 A33 1p black 4.50 2.00
Nos. 247-252 (5) 8.25 3.20
Set, never hinged 15.00

Map of Cuba — A34

1914-15

253 A34 1c green .40 .20
a. Booklet pane of 6 80.00
254 A34 2c car rose .60 .20
a. Booklet pane of 6 80.00
255 A34 2c red ('15) 1.25 .20
a. Booklet pane of 6 80.00
256 A34 3c violet 4.00 .30
257 A34 5c blue 5.75 .20
258 A34 8c ol grn 4.50 .60
259 A34 10c brown 8.50 .30
260 A34 10c ol grn ('15) 10.00 .45
261 A34 50c orange 65.00 8.75
262 A34 1p gray 90.00 20.00
Nos. 253-262 (10) 190.00 31.20
Set, never hinged 250.00

Complete set of eight 1914 stamps, imperf. pairs, value $1,150.

Nos. 253, 254, 256 and E5 exist with "1917 GOB./CONSTITUCIONAL/CAMAGUEY" overprint. These were not authorized.

Gertrudis Gómez de Avellaneda, Cuban Poetess (1814-73) A34a

1914

263 A34a 5c blue 14.00 5.00
Never hinged 19.00

José Martí A35

Máximo Gómez A36

José de la Luz Caballero A37

Calixto García A38

Ignacio Agramonte A39

Tomás Estrada Palma A40

José A. Saco — A41

Antonio Maceo — A42

Carlos Manuel de Céspedes — A43

1917-18 Unwmk. *Perf. 12*

264 A35 1c bl grn .75 .20
a. Booklet pane of 6 40.00
b. Booklet pane of 30 250.00
265 A36 2c rose .75 .20
a. Booklet pane of 6 50.00
b. Booklet pane of 30 210.00
266 A36 2c lt red ('18) .60 .20
a. Booklet pane of 6 50.00
267 A37 3c violet .75 .20
a. Imperf. pair 275.00
b. Booklet pane of 6 50.00
268 A38 5c dp bl .75 .20
269 A39 8c red brn 3.50 .20
270 A40 10c yel brn 2.25 .20
271 A41 20c gray grn 14.00 1.60
272 A42 50c dl rose 14.00 .70
273 A43 1p black 14.50 .70
Nos. 264-273 (10) 51.85 4.40
Set, never hinged 75.00

1925-28 Wmk. 106 *Perf. 12*

274 A35 1c blue green 1.00 .20
a. Booklet pane of 6 325.00
275 A36 2c brt rose 1.10 .20
a. Booklet pane of 6 70.00
b. Booklet pane of 30 325.00
276 A38 5c dp bl 2.25 .20
277 A39 8c red brn ('28) 5.25 .60
278 A40 10c yel brn ('27) 6.50 .70
279 A41 20c olive grn 10.00 1.10
Nos. 274-279 (6) 26.10 3.00

1926 *Imperf.*

280 A35 1c blue green 1.40 1.00
281 A36 2c brt rose 1.40 1.00
282 A38 5c deep blue 1.75 1.40
Nos. 280-282 (3) 4.55 3.40
Set, never hinged 5.00

See Nos. 304-310. For overprint and surcharge see Nos. 317-318, 644.

Arms of Republic A44

1927, May 20 Unwmk. *Perf. 12*

283 A44 25c violet 14.00 3.50
Never hinged 19.00

25th anniversary of the Republic.
For surcharges see Nos. 355, C3.

Tomás Estrada Palma A45

Designs: 2c, Gen. Gerardo Machado. 5c, Morro Castle. 8c, Havana Railway Station. 10c, Presidential Palace. 13c, Tobacco Plantation. 20c, Treasury Building. 30c, Sugar Mill. 50c, Havana Cathedral. 1p, Galician Clubhouse, Havana.

1928, Jan. 2 Wmk. 106

284 A45 1c deep green .45 .20
285 A45 2c brt rose .50 .20
286 A45 5c deep blue .75 .30
287 A45 8c lt red brn 3.00 .90
288 A45 10c bister brn .75 .55
289 A45 13c orange 1.50 .55
290 A45 20c olive grn 1.75 .65
291 A45 30c dk violet 4.00 .55
292 A45 50c carmine rose 6.50 2.10
293 A45 1p gray black 13.00 5.00
Nos. 284-293 (10) 32.45 11.00
Set, never hinged 50.00

Sixth Pan-American Conference.

Capitol, Havana A55

1929, May 18

294 A55 1c green .25 .25
295 A55 2c carmine rose .30 .30
296 A55 5c blue .45 .30
297 A55 10c bister brn .75 .50
298 A55 20c violet 3.25 2.75
Nos. 294-298 (5) 5.00 4.10
Set, never hinged 9.00

Opening of the Capitol, Havana.

Hurdler — A56

1930, Mar. 15 Engr.

299 A56 1c green .40 .35
300 A56 2c carmine .40 .40
301 A56 5c deep blue .55 .40
302 A56 10c bister brn .90 .85
303 A56 20c violet 7.00 3.00
Nos. 299-303 (5) 9.25 5.00
Set, never hinged 14.00

2nd Central American Athletic Games.

Types of 1917 Portrait Issue
Flat Plate Printing

1930-45 Wmk. 106 Engr. *Perf. 10*

304 A35 1c blue green .75 .25
a. Booklet pane of 6 50.00
b. Booklet pane of 30 —
305 A36 2c brt rose 75.00 —
a. Booklet pane of 6 1,200.
305B A37 3c dk rose vio ('42) 2.25 .30
c. Booklet pane of 6 42.50
306 A38 5c dk blue 2.75 .20
306A A39 8c red brn ('45) 2.75 .25
307 A40 10c brown 2.75 .25
a. 10c yellow brown ('35) 3.50 .75
307B A41 20c olive grn ('41) 4.75 .75
Nos. 304-307B (7) 91.00 2.00

Nos. 305 and 305B were printed for booklet panes and all copies have straight edges.
For surcharge see No. 644.

Rotary Press Printing

308 A35 1c blue grn 1.10 .20
309 A36 2c brt rose 1.10 .20
a. Booklet pane of 50
310 A37 3c violet 1.50 .20
a. 3c dull violet ('38) 1.10 .20
b. 3c rose violet ('41) 1.10 .20
c. Booklet pane of 50
Nos. 308-310 (3) 3.70 .60

Flat plate stamps measure 18½x21½mm; rotary press, 19x22mm.

The Mangos of Baragua — A57

War Memorial — A61

Battle of Mal Tiempo A58

Battle of Coliseo A59

Maceo, Gómez and Zayas A60

Wmk. 229

1933, Apr. 23 Photo. *Perf. 12½*

312 A57 3c dk brown 1.40 .30
313 A58 5c dk blue 1.25 .35
314 A59 10c emerald 2.25 .35
315 A60 13c red 2.75 .90
316 A61 20c black 5.50 2.10
Nos. 312-316 (5) 13.15 4.00

War of Independence and dedication of the "Soldado Invasor" (the American Army that came to the aid of the revolution against Spain)monument.

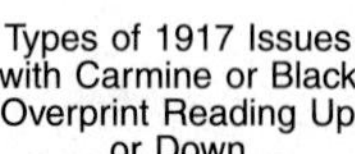

Types of 1917 Issues with Carmine or Black Overprint Reading Up or Down

Rotary Press Printing
Wmk. 106

1933, Dec. 23 Engr. *Perf. 10*

317 A35 1c blue green (C) .50 .20

With Additional Surcharge of New Value and Bars

318 A37 2c on 3c vio (Bk) .50 .20

Establishment of a revolutionary junta.
Catalogue values for Nos. 317-318 unused are for examples with overprint reading up. Values for overprint reading down, $5.

Dr. Carlos J. Finlay — A62

1934, Dec. 3 Engr. *Perf. 10*

319 A62 2c dark carmine .75 .20
320 A62 5c dark blue 2.50 .50
Set, never hinged 4.00

Cent. of the birth of Dr. Carlos J. Finlay (1833-1915), physician-biologist who found that a mosquito transmitted yellow fever.

Pres. José Miguel Gómez — A63

Gómez Monument A64

1936, May ***Perf. 10***

322 A63 1c green 1.50 .20
323 A64 2c carmine 2.25 .25
Set, never hinged 7.00

Unveiling of a monument to Gen. José Miguel Gómez, ex-president.

Matanzas Issue

Map of Cuba A65

2c, Map of Free Zone. 4c, S. S. "Rex" in Matanzas Bay. 5c, Ships in Matanzas Bay. 8c, Caves of Bellamar. 10c, Valley of Yumuri. 20c, Yumuri River. 50c, Ships Leaving Port.

Wmk. 229

1936, May 5 Photo. ***Perf. 12½***

324	A65 1c blue green	.40	.20
325	A65 2c red	.60	.20
326	A65 4c claret	1.00	.20
327	A65 5c ultra	1.50	.20
328	A65 8c orange brn	2.50	.55
329	A65 10c emerald	2.75	.55
330	A65 20c brown	5.25	2.10
331	A65 50c slate	9.75	3.00
	Nos. 324-331,C18-C21 (12)	36.65	12.40
	Set, never hinged	60.00	

Issued both perf and imperf. Same values.

"Peace and Work" A73

Máximo Gómez Monument — A74

Torch — A75

"Independence" — A76

"Messenger of Peace" — A77

1936, Nov. 18 ***Perf. 12½***

332	A73 1c emerald	.50	.20
333	A74 2c crimson	.60	.20
334	A75 4c maroon	.70	.20
335	A76 5c ultra	2.75	.35
336	A77 8c dk green	4.00	.75
	Nos. 332-336,C22-C23,E9 (8)	17.80	3.40
	Set, never hinged	35.00	

Maj. Gen. Máximo Gómez, birth centenary.

Issued both perf and imperf. Values for imperfs are approx. 50% higher.

Sugar Cane — A78

Primitive Sugar Mill — A79

Modern Sugar Mill — A80

Wmk. 106

1937, Oct. 2 Engr. ***Perf. 10***

337	A78 1c yellow green	.45	.30
338	A79 2c red	.25	.20
339	A80 5c bright blue	.55	.30
	Nos. 337-339 (3)	1.25	.80
	Set, never hinged	2.25	

Cuban sugar cane industry, 400th anniv.

Argentine Emblem — A81

Mountain Scene (Bolivia) — A82

Arms of Brazil — A83

Canadian Scene — A84

Camilo Henriquez (Chile) A85

Gen, Francisco de Paula Santander (Colombia) A86

Natl. Monument (Costa Rica) — A87

Autograph of José Marti (Cuba) — A88

Columbus Lighthouse (Dominican Rep.) — A89

Juan Montalvo (Ecuador) — A90

Abraham Lincoln (US) A91

Quetzal and Scroll (Guatemala) A92

Arms of Haiti A93

Francisco Morazán (Honduras) A94

Fleet of Columbus — A95

Wmk. 106

1937, Oct. 13 Engr. ***Perf. 10***

340	A81 1c deep green	.55	.55
341	A82 1c green	.55	.55
342	A83 2c carmine	.55	.55
343	A84 2c carmine	.55	.55
344	A85 3c violet	1.50	1.50
345	A86 3c violet	1.50	1.50
346	A87 4c bister brown	1.75	1.75
347	A88 4c bister brown	3.25	3.25
348	A89 5c blue	1.60	1.60
349	A90 5c blue	1.60	1.60
350	A91 8c citron	11.50	11.50
351	A92 8c citron	2.75	2.75
352	A93 10c maroon	2.75	2.75
353	A94 10c maroon	2.75	2.75
354	A95 25c rose lilac	27.50	27.50
	Nos. 340-354,C24-C29,E10-E11 (23)	114.65	114.65
	Set, never hinged	160.00	

Nos. 340-354 were sold by the Cuban PO for 3 days, Oct. 13-15, during which no other stamps were sold. They were postally valid for the full face value. Proceeds from their three-day sale above 30,000 pesos were paid by the Cuban POD to the Assoc. of American Writers and Artists. Remainders were overprinted "SVP" (Without Postal Value).

No. 283 Surcharged in Green

1937, Nov. 19 Unwmk. ***Perf. 12***

355 A44 10c on 25c violet 12.50 2.00
Never hinged 17.50

Centenary of Cuban railroads.

Ciboney Indian and Cigar — A96

Cigar and Globe — A97

Tobacco Plant and Cigars — A98

1939, Aug. 28 Wmk. 106 ***Perf. 10***

356	A96 1c yellow green	.35	.20
357	A97 2c red	.50	.20
358	A98 5c brt ultra	.90	.25
	Nos. 356-358 (3)	1.75	.65
	Set, never hinged	3.00	

General Calixto García A99 A100

1939, Nov. 6 ***Perf. 10, Imperf.***

359 A99 2c dark red .35 .20
360 A100 5c deep blue .65 .30
Set, never hinged 2.00

Birth centenary of General Garcia.

Gonzalo de Quesada — A101

1940, Apr. 30 Engr. ***Perf. 10***

361 A101 2c rose red .60 .25
Never hinged 1.50

Pan American Union, 50th anniversary.

Rotary Club Emblem, Cuban Flag and Tobacco Plant — A102

Lions Emblem, Cuban Flag and Royal Palms — A103

1940, May 18 Wmk. 106 *Perf. 10*

362 A102 2c rose red 1.00 .50
Never hinged 1.60

Rotary Intl. Convention held at Havana.

1940, July 23

363 A103 2c orange vermilion 1.00 .50
Never hinged 1.60

Lions International Convention, Havana.

Dr. Nicolás J. Gutiérrez A104

1940, Oct. 28

364 A104 2c orange ver .50 .25
365 A104 5c blue .75 .25
a. Sheet of four, imperf., unwmkd. 3.00 2.50
Never hinged 4.75
b. As "a," black overprint ('51) 3.50 3.00
Never hinged 5.50
Set, never hinged 2.00

100th anniv. of the publication of the 1st Cuban Medical Review, "El Repertorio Medico Habanero."

No. 365a contains 2 each of Nos. 364-365 imperf. and sold for 25c.

For overprint see No. C43A.

In 1951 No. 365a was overprinted in black: "50 Aniversario Descubrimiento Agente Transmisor de la Flebre Amarilla por el Dr. Carlos J. Finlay Honor a los Martires de la Ciencia 1901 1951." The overprint is illustrated over No. C43A, but does not include the plane and "Correo Aereo."

Major General Guillermo Moncada — A105

Moncada Riding into Battle A106

1941, June 25

366 A105 3c dk brown, *buff* .70 .30
367 A106 5c bright blue .70 .30
Set, never hinged 2.25

Maj. Gen. Guillermo Moncada (1841-96).

Globe Showing Western Hemisphere A107

"Labor: Wealth of America" — A109

Maceo, Bolívar, Juárez, Lincoln and Arms of Cuba A108

Tree of Fraternity, Havana A110

Statue of Liberty — A111

Perf. 10, Imperf.

1942, Feb. 23 Wmk. 106

368 A107 1c emerald .20 .20
369 A108 3c orange brown .25 .20
370 A109 5c blue .35 .20
371 A110 10c red violet 1.00 .40
372 A111 13c red 1.00 .65
Nos. 368-372 (5) 2.80 1.65
Set, never hinged 4.25

Spirit of Democracy in the Americas.

The imperforate varieties are without gum. Value, set $6.00.

Ignacio Agramonte Loynaz — A112

Rescue of Sanguily by Agramonte A113

1942, Apr. 10 *Perf. 10*

373 A112 3c bister brn .50 .25
374 A113 5c brt blue, *bluish* 1.00 .30
Set, never hinged 2.40

100th anniv. of the birth of Ignacio Agramonte Loynaz, patriot.

"Unmask the Fifth Columnists" — A114

"Be Careful, The Fifth Column is Spying on You" — A115

"Destroy it. The Fifth Column is like a Serpent" — A116

"Fulfill your Patriotic Duty by Destroying the Fifth Column" — A117

"Don't be Afraid of the Fifth Column. Attack it" — A118

1943, July 5

375 A114 1c dk blue grn .35 .20
376 A115 3c red .55 .20
377 A116 5c brt blue .60 .20
378 A117 10c dull brown 2.00 .60
379 A118 13c dull rose vio 3.00 1.25
Nos. 375-379 (5) 6.50 2.45
Set, never hinged 10.00

General Eloy Alfaro and Flags of Cuba and Ecuador A119

1943, Sept. 20

380 A119 3c green .80 .25
Never hinged 1.50

General Eloy Alfaro of Ecuador, 100th birth anniv.

Retirement Security A120

1943, Nov. 8 Wmk. 106 *Perf. 10*

381 A120 1c yellow green .35 .20
382 A120 3c vermilion .35 .20
383 A120 5c bright blue .50 .25

1944, Mar. 18

384 A120 1c bright yel grn .80 .30
385 A120 3c salmon .80 .30
386 A120 5c light blue 1.60 .75
Nos. 381-386 (6) 4.40 2.00
Set, never hinged 7.00

Half the proceeds from the sale of Nos. 381-386 were used for the Communications Ministry Employees' Retirement Fund.

Portrait of Columbus — A121

Bartolomé de Las Casas — A122

First Statue of Columbus at Cárdenas — A123

Discovery of Tobacco A124

Columbus Sights Land A125

1944, May 19

387 A121 1c dk yellow grn .20 .20
a. Pair, imperf horiz. 75.00
388 A122 3c brown .30 .20
389 A123 5c brt blue .55 .20
390 A124 10c dark violet 1.75 .60
391 A125 13c dark red 2.10 1.40
Nos. 387-391,C36-C37 (7) 6.75 3.40
Set, never hinged 7.50

450th anniv. of the discovery of America.

Major General Carlos Roloff — A126

Americas Map and 1st Brazilian Postage Stamps — A127

1944, Aug. 21

392 A126 3c violet .35 .20
Never hinged .65

Maj. Gen. Carlos Roloff, 100th birth anniv.

1944, Dec. 20 **Engr.**

393 A127 3c brown orange .85 .30
Never hinged 1.25

Cent. of the 1st postage stamps of the Americas, issued by Brazil in 1843.

Seal of the Society — A128

Luis de las Casas and Luis Maria Penalyer A129

1945, Oct. 5 **Wmk. 106** ***Perf. 10***

394 A128 1c yellow green .20 .20
395 A129 2c scarlet .25 .20
Set, never hinged .75

Sesquicentenary of the founding of the Economic Society of Friends of the Country.

Aged Couple A130

1945, Dec. 27

396 A130 1c dk yellow grn .20 .20
397 A130 2c scarlet .40 .20
398 A130 5c cobalt blue .90 .20

1946, Mar. 26

399 A130 1c brt yellow grn .75 .20
400 A130 2c salmon pink .45 .20
401 A130 5c light blue .75 .25
Nos. 396-401 (6) 3.45 1.25
Set, never hinged 5.00

See note after No. 386.

Catalogue values for unused stamps in this section, from this point to the end of the section, are for Never Hinged items.

Gabriel de la Concepcion Valdés Plácido A131

1946, Feb. 5

402 A131 2c scarlet 1.00 .30

Cent. of the death of the poet Gabriel de la Concepcion Valdés.

Manuel Marquez Sterling — A132

Globe and Cross — A133

1946, Apr. 30

403 A132 2c scarlet 1.00 .30

Founding of the Manuel Marquez Sterling Professional School of Journalism, 3th anniv.

1946, July 4 **Engr.**

404 A133 2c scarlet, *pink* 1.00 .20

80th anniv. of the Intl. Red Cross.

Cow and Milkmaid — A134

Franklin D. Roosevelt — A135

1947, Feb. 20 **Wmk. 106** ***Perf. 10***

405 A134 2c scarlet .75 .20

1947 National Livestock Exposition.

1947, Apr. 12

406 A135 2c vermilion .35 .20

2nd anniv. of the death of Franklin D. Roosevelt.

Antonio Oms Sarret and Aged Couple A136

1947, Oct. 20

407 A136 1c dp yellow grn .20 .20
408 A136 2c scarlet .20 .20
409 A136 5c lt blue .45 .40
Nos. 407-409 (3) .85 .80

See note after No. 386.

Marta Abreu Arenabio de Estevez — A137

"Charity" — A138

Marta Abreu Monument, Santa Clara A139

"Patriotism" A140

1947, Nov. 29

410 A137 1c dp yellow grn .20 .20
411 A138 2c scarlet .30 .20
412 A139 5c brt blue .50 .25
413 A140 10c dk violet 1.00 .50
Nos. 410-413 (4) 2.00 1.15

Birth cent. of Marta Abreu Arenabio de Estevez, philanthropist and humanitarian.

Armauer Hansen A141

1948, Apr. 9

414 A141 2c rose carmine .75 .20

International Leprosy Congress, Havana.

Mother and Child A142

1948, Oct. 15 **Engr.**

415 A142 1c yellow grn .30 .20
416 A142 2c scarlet .40 .20
417 A142 5c brt blue .90 .20
Nos. 415-417 (3) 1.60 .60

See note after No. 386.

Death of José Martí — A143

Martí Rowing to Shore — A144

1948, Nov. 10 **Wmk. 106** ***Perf. 10***

418 A143 2c scarlet .35 .20
419 A144 5c brt blue .80 .20

50th anniversary of the death of José Martí, patriot (in 1945).

Tobacco Picking — A145

Liberty Carrying Flag and Cigars — A146

Cigar and Arms of Cuba — A147

1948, Dec. 6

Size: 22½x26mm

420 A145 1c green .20 .20
421 A146 2c rose car .30 .20
422 A147 5c brt blue .40 .20
Nos. 420-422 (3) .90 .60

Cuba's tobacco industry. See Nos. 445-447. For overprints and surcharge see Nos. 448-451, 512.

Equestrian Statue of Gen. Antonio Maceo — A148

Sword Salute to Maceo A149

Designs: 2c, Portrait of Maceo. 5c, Mausoleum, El Cacahual. 10c, East to West invasion. 20c, Battle of Peralejo. 50c, Declaration of Baragua. 1p, Death of Maceo at San Pedro.

1948, Dec. 15 **Wmk. 229** ***Perf. 12½***

423 A148 1c blue green .20 .20
424 A148 2c red .20 .20
425 A148 5c blue .30 .20
426 A149 8c black & brown .45 .30
427 A149 10c brown & bl grn .45 .20
428 A149 20c blue & car 1.75 .90
429 A149 50c car & ultra 2.75 2.00
430 A149 1p black & violet 6.00 2.75
Nos. 423-430 (8) 12.10 6.75

Birth cent. (in 1945) of Maceo.

Symbol of Pharmacy A150

Morro Lighthouse A151

1948, Dec. 28 ***Perf. 10***
431 A150 2c rose carmine .75 .20

1st Pan-American Congress of Pharmacy, Havana, Dec. 1948.

1949, Jan. 17 Wmk. 229 ***Perf. 12½***
432 A151 2c carmine .85 .20

Centenary (in 1944) of the erection of the Morro Lighthouse.

Jagua Castle, Cienfuegos A152

1949, Jan. 27 Wmk. 106 ***Perf. 10***
433 A152 1c yellow green .40 .20
434 A152 2c rose red .80 .20

200th anniv. of the construction of Jagua Castle and the cent. of the publication of the 1st newspaper in Cienfuegos.

Manuel Sanguily y Garritt — A153

Map of Isle of Pines — A154

1949, Mar. 31
435 A153 2c rose red .35 .20
436 A153 5c blue .75 .20

Manuel Sanguily y Garritt (1848-1925), cabinet member, editor, author.

1949, Apr. 26
437 A154 5c blue .90 .70

20th anniv. of the recognition of Cuban ownership of the Isle of Pines.

Ismael Cespedes — A155

1949, Sept. 28
438 A155 1c yellow green .40 .20
439 A155 2c scarlet .40 .20
440 A155 5c brt blue .90 .20
Nos. 438-440 (3) 1.70 .60

See note after No. 386.

Gen. Enrique Collazo — A156

Enrique José Varona — A157

1950, Feb. 28 Engr. ***Perf. 10***
441 A156 2c scarlet .50 .20
442 A156 5c brt blue 1.00 .20

Centenary (in 1948) of the birth of General Enrique Collazo.

1950, Feb. 28
443 A157 2c scarlet .40 .20
444 A157 5c brt blue .80 .20

Centenary of the birth of Enrique José Varona, writer and patriot.

Tobacco Types of 1948

1950, June 20 Re-engraved
Size: 21x25mm
445 A145 1c green .55 .20
446 A146 2c rose red .55 .20
447 A147 5c blue .90 .20
Nos. 445-447 (3) 2.00 .60

The re-engraved stamps show slight differences in many minor details.
For overprints and surcharge see #448-451, 512.

No. 446 Overprinted in Black

1950, Apr. 27
448 A146 2c rose red .75 .20

Natl. Bank of Cuba opening, Apr. 27, 1950.

Re-engraved Tobacco Types of 1950 Overprinted in Carmine

1950, May 18
449 A145 1c yellow green .20 .20
450 A146 2c lilac rose .25 .20
451 A147 5c light blue .55 .20
Nos. 449-451 (3) 1.00 .60

75th anniv. (in 1949) of the UPU.
No. 451 exists with surcharge inverted.

Manuel Balanzategui, Antonio L. Pausa and Train Wreck A158

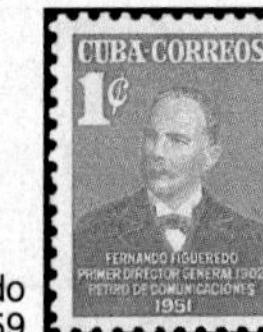
Fernando Figueredo — A159

1950, Sept. 21 Engr.
452 A158 1c yellow grn .35 .20
453 A158 2c scarlet .35 .20
454 A158 5c brt blue .75 .20
Nos. 452-454 (3) 1.45 .60

1951, Mar. 17 Wmk. 106 ***Perf. 10***
455 A159 1c green .40 .20
456 A159 2c scarlet .40 .20
457 A159 5c brt blue .75 .20
Nos. 455-457 (3) 1.55 .60

Three-fourths of the proceeds from the sale of these stamps were used for the Communication Ministry Employees' Retirement Fund.
See Nos. 474, C51-C56, E15. For surcharges see Nos. 474, C51-C56, E15.

Miguel Teurbe Tolón and Flag — A160

Narciso Lopez — A161

Emilia Teurbe Tolón Sewing Flag — A162

Cuban Flag — A163

Engraved and Lithographed
1951, July 3 Wmk. 229 ***Perf. 13***
458 A160 1c Prus grn, ultra & red .50 .30
459 A161 2c red & gray blk .70 .30
460 A162 5c ultra & red 1.50 .45
461 A163 10c rose vio, bl & red 2.25 .60
Nos. 458-461,C41-C43,E13 (8) 19.55 5.40

Centenary of adoption of Cuba's flag.

Clara Louise Maass and Hospitals A164

Hospitals: Lutheran Memorial, Newark, N.J. and Las Animas, Havana.

Wmk. 106
1951, Aug. 24 Engr. ***Perf. 10***
462 A164 2c scarlet .90 .20

75th anniv. of the birth of Clara Louise Maass, (1876-1901), American nurse and martyr in yellow fever fight.

Airmail Type and

José Raul Capablanca — A165

Capablanca Club, Havana A166

Wmk. 229
1951, Nov. 1 Photo. ***Perf. 13***
463 A165 1c blue grn & org 2.40 .60
464 AP27 2c rose car & dk brn 3.00 1.10
465 A166 5c black & dp ultra 6.00 1.75
Nos. 463-465,C44-C46,E14 (7) 44.90 12.30

Jose Raul Capablanca, World Chess titlist (1921). Value imperf., set of 7 pairs, $1,500.

Antonio Guiteras Holmes — A167

Guiteras Preparing Social Legislation A168

Fort of the Morrillo A169

Wmk. 106
1951, Oct. 22 Engr. ***Perf. 10***
466 A167 1c yellow green .20 .20
467 A168 2c rose carmine .35 .20
468 A169 5c deep blue .60 .20
Nos. 466-468,C47-C49 (6) 9.25 3.35

16th anniv. of the Action of the Morrillo and to honor Antonio Guiteras Holmes, who was killed there.
Souvenir sheets containing stamps similar to Nos. 466-468, but in different colors, are listed as Nos. C49a-C49b.

Poinsettia A170

Maj. Gen. José Maceo A171

1951, Dec. 1 Engr. and Typo.
469 A170 1c green & car 1.75 .25
470 A170 2c rose car & grn 2.00 .40

See Nos. 498-499.

1952, Feb. 6 Engr.
471 A171 2c yellow brown .40 .20
472 A171 5c indigo .90 .20

Birth centenary of Maceo.
See note after No. C49.

Isabella I — A172

Receipt of Autonomy A173

1952, Feb. 22
473 A172 2c bright red .60 .20

500th anniv. of the birth of Queen Isabella I of Spain.

Souvenir sheets containing 2c stamps of type A172 are listed as Nos. C50a-C50b.

Type of 1951 Surcharged in Green

1952, Mar. 18
474 A159 10c on 2c yel brn 1.25 .25

Wmk. 106
1952, May 27 Engr. *Perf. 12½*

Designs: 2c, Tomas Estrada Palma and Luis Estevez Romero. 5c, Barnet, Finlay, Guiteras and Nuñez. 8c, Capitol. 20c, Map, Central Highway. 50c, Sugar Mill.

Centers in Black
475 A173 1c dk green .20 .20
476 A173 2c dk carmine .25 .20
477 A173 5c dk blue .35 .20
478 A173 8c dk brown car .55 .20
479 A173 20c dk olive grn 1.40 .40
480 A173 50c dp orange 2.75 .80
Nos. 475-480,C57-C60,E16 (11) 11.90 4.35

50th anniv. of the Republic of Cuba.

Hands Holding Coffee Beans A174

Designs: 2c, Map and man picking coffee beans. 5c, Farmer with pan of beans.

1952, Aug. 22 Wmk. 229 *Perf. 13½*
481 A174 1c green .40 .20
482 A174 2c rose red .70 .20
483 A174 5c dk vio bl & aqua .90 .20
Nos. 481-483 (3) 2.00 .60

Bicentenary of coffee cultivation.

Col. Charles Hernandes y Sandrino A175

Alonso Alvarez de la Campa A176

1952, Oct. 7 Wmk. 106 *Perf. 10*
484 A175 1c yellow grn .30 .20
485 A175 2c scarlet .50 .20
486 A175 5c blue .55 .20
487 A175 8c black 1.50 .30
488 A175 10c brown red 1.50 .30
489 A175 20c brown 5.50 2.50
Nos. 484-489,C63-C72,E17 (17) 42.65 16.30

See note after No. 457.

Frame Engraved; Center in Black
1952, Nov. 27

Portraits: 2c, Carlos A. Latorre. 3c, Anacleto Bermudez. 5c, Eladio G. Toledo. 8c, Angel Laborde. 10c, Jose M. Medina. 13c, Pascual Rodriguez. 20c, Carlos Verdugo.

490 A176 1c green .30 .20
491 A176 2c carmine .55 .20
492 A176 3c purple .65 .20
493 A176 5c blue .65 .20
494 A176 8c bister brn 1.40 .35
495 A176 10c orange brn 1.10 .25
496 A176 13c lilac rose 2.10 .40
497 A176 20c olive grn 3.25 .70
Nos. 490-497,C73-C74 (10) 14.75 4.10

Execution of 8 medical students, 81st anniv.

Christmas Type of 1951
Dated "1952-1953"
Frame Engr.; Center Typo.
1952, Dec. 1

Centers: Tree.

498 A170 1c yel grn & car 4.00 1.00
499 A170 3c vio & dk grn 4.00 1.00

Birthplace of José Martí — A177

Marti at St. Lazarus Quarry — A178

#501, Court martial. #502, Martiano house, Havana. #504, El Abra ranch, Isle of Pines. #505, Symbols, "Marti the Poet." #506, Marti and Bolivar statue, Caracas. #507, At desk in New York. #508, House where revolutionary party was formed. #509, 1st issue of "Patria."

1953 Engr. *Perf. 10*
500 A177 1c dk grn & red brn .25 .20
501 A177 1c dk grn & red brn .25 .20
502 A177 3c purple & brn .30 .20
503 A178 3c purple & brn .30 .20
504 A177 5c dp bl & dk brn .50 .20
505 A178 5c ultra & brn .50 .20
506 A178 10c red brn & blk 1.10 .35
507 A178 10c dk brn & blk 1.10 .35
508 A178 13c dk ol grn & dk brn 1.75 .80
509 A177 13c dk ol grn & brn 1.75 1.00
Nos. 500-509,C79-C89 (21) 28.10 12.30

Centenary of birth of José Marti.

Rafael Montoro Valdez — A179

Francisco Carrera Justiz — A180

1953, Mar. 5
510 A179 3c dark violet .35 .20

Rafael Montoro Valdez, statesman, birth cent.

1953, Mar. 9
511 A180 3c rose red .25 .20

Francisco Carrera Justiz, educator, statesman.

No. 446 Surcharged with New Value
1953, June 16
512 A146 3c on 2c rose red .60 .20

Board of Accounts Bldg., Havana — A181

1953, Nov. 3 Engr.
513 A181 3c blue .40 .20
Nos. 513,C90-C91 (3) 5.65 1.60

1st Intl. Cong. of Boards of Accounts, Havana, Nov. 2-9.

Miguel Coyula Llaguno — A182

Communications Assoc. Flag — A183

Designs: 3c, 8c, Enrique Calleja Hensell. 10c, Antonio Ginard Rojas.

1954 Dated 1953
514 A182 1c green .30 .20
515 A182 3c rose red .30 .20
516 A183 5c blue 1.40 .20
517 A182 8c brn car 2.25 .30
518 A182 10c brown 3.50 .50
Nos. 514-518,C92-C95,E19 (10) 25.05 12.65

Nos. 515 and 517 show the same portrait, but inscriptions are arranged differently.
See note after No. 457.

Carlos J. Finlay A184

Serafin Sanchez A184a

Portraits: 1c, José Marti. 2c, Maximo Gomez. 3c, José de la Luz Caballero. 4c, Miguel Aldama. 5c, Calixto Garcia. 8c, Ignacio Agramont. 10c, Tomas Estrada Palma. 20c, José Antonio Saco. 50c, Antonio Maceo. 1p, Carlos Manuel de Cespedes.

1954-56 Wmk. 106 *Perf. 10*
519 A184 1c green .30 .20
520 A184a 2c rose car .30 .20
521 A184 3c violet .30 .20
521A A184 4c red lil ('56) .35 .20
522 A184a 5c slate bl .40 .20
523 A184a 8c car lake .60 .20
524 A184 10c sepia .60 .20
525 A184 13c org red .90 .20
525A A184a 14c gray ('56) 1.25 .20
526 A184 20c olive 1.75 .20
527 A184a 50c org yel 3.00 .25
528 A184a 1p orange 6.00 .40
Nos. 519-528 (12) 15.75 2.65

See Nos. 674-680. For surcharges see Nos. 636, 641-643.

Maj. Gen. José M. Rodriguez — A185

Design: 5c, Gen. Rodriguez on horseback.

1954, June 8 Engr. *Perf. 12½*
Center in Dark Brown
529 A185 2c dark carmine .80 .20
530 A185 5c deep blue 1.90 .20

Cent. of the birth of Maj. Gen. José Maria Rodriguez (in 1851).

Gen. Batísta Sanatorium — A186

1954, Sept. 21 Wmk. 106 *Perf. 10*
531 A186 3c deep blue .75 .20

See No. C107.

Santa Claus — A187

Maria Luisa Dolz — A188

1954, Dec. 15
532 A187 2c dk grn & car 4.00 .35
533 A187 4c car & dk grn 3.50 .35

Christmas 1954.

1954, Dec. 23
534 A188 4c deep blue .75 .20

Cent. of the birth of Maria Luisa Dolz, educator and defender of women's rights. See No. C108.

Cuban Flag and Scouts Saluting A189

1954, Dec. 27 *Perf. 12½*
535 A189 4c dark green .85 .20

Issued to publicize the national patrol encampment of the Boy Scouts of Cuba.

Rotary Emblem and Paul P. Harris — A190

1955, Feb. 23 Engr. Wmk. 106
536 A190 4c blue 1.00 .20

Rotary International, 50th anniversary.
See No. C109.

Maj. Gen. Francisco Carrillo — A191

Portrait: 5c, Gen. Carrillo standing.

1955, Mar. 8 *Perf. 10*
537 A191 2c brt red & dk bl .40 .20
538 A191 5c dk bl & dk brn .75 .20

Cent. of the birth of Maj. Gen. Francisco Carrillo (1851-1926).

Stamp of 1885 and Convent of San Francisco — A192

Designs (including 1855 stamp): 4c, Volanta carriage. 10c, Havana, 19th century. 14c, Captain general's residence.

1955, Apr. *Perf. 12½*
539 A192 2c lil rose & dk grnsh bl .95 .20
540 A192 4c ocher & dk grn 1.25 .20
541 A192 10c ultra & dk red 3.00 .85
542 A192 14c grn & dp org 7.00 1.00
Nos. 539-542,C110-C113 (8) 20.55 5.35

Cent. of Cuba's 1st postage stamps.

Maj. Gen. Mario G. Menocal A193

Gen. Emilio Nuñez A194

Portraits: 10c, J. G. O. Gomez. 14c, A. Sanchez de Bustamente.

1955, June 22

543 A193	2c dark green	.65	.20
544 A194	4c lilac rose	.75	.20
545 A193	10c deep blue	1.25	.25
546 A194	14c gray violet	2.50	.35
Nos. 543-546,C114-C116,E20 (8)		17.85	5.05

See note after No. 457.

Turkey — A195

Gen. Emilio Nuñez — A196

1955, Dec. 15 **Engr.**

547 A195 2c slate grn & dk car 3.75 .40
548 A195 4c rose lake & brt grn 3.75 .30

Christmas 1955.

1955, Dec. 27

549 A196 4c claret .80 .20
Nos. 549,C127-C128 (3) 4.70 1.10

Cent. of the birth of Gen. Emilio Nunez, Cuban revolutionary hero.

Francisco Cagigal de la Vega (1695-1777) A197

Julian del Casal A198

1956, Mar. 27 ***Perf. 12½***

552 A197 4c rose brn & slate bl 1.10 .20

Cuban post bicent. See No. C129.

1956, May 2

Portraits: 4c, Luisa Perez de Zambrana. 10c, Juan Clemente Zenea. 14c, José Joaquin Palma.

Portraits in Black

553 A198	2c green	.30	.20
554 A198	4c rose lilac	.30	.20
555 A198	10c blue	.70	.20
556 A198	14c violet	.90	.20
Nos. 553-556,C131-C133,E21 (8)		11.10	3.50

See note after No. 457.

Victor Muñoz — A199

Masonic Temple, Havana — A200

1956, May 13

557 A199 4c brown & green .50 .20

Victor Munoz (1873-1922), founder of Mother's Day in Cuba. See No. C134.

1956, June 5

558 A200 4c blue 1.00 .20

See No. C135.

Virgin of Charity, El Cobre — A201

"The Cry of Yara" — A202

1956, Sept. 8 ***Perf. 12½***

559 A201 4c brt blue & yel .40 .20

Issued in honor of Our Lady of Charity of Cobre, patroness of Cuba. See No. C149.

1956, Oct. 10

560 A202 4c dk grn & brn .25 .20

Cuba's independence from Spain.

Raimundo G. Menocal A203

The Three Wise Men — A204

1956, Dec. 3 **Wmk. 106** ***Perf. 12½***

561 A203 4c dark brown .25 .20

Cent. of the birth of Prof. Raimundo G. Menocal, physician.

1956, Dec. 1

562 A204 2c red & slate grn 2.00 .60
563 A204 4c slate grn & red 2.00 .40

Christmas 1956.

Martin Morua Delgado — A205

Boy Scouts at Campfire — A206

1957, Jan. 30

564 A205 4c dark green .25 .20

Delgado, patriot, birth cent.

1957, Feb. 22 **Wmk. 106** ***Perf. 12½***

565 A206 4c slate grn & red 1.00 .20

Cent. of the birth of Lord Baden-Powell, founder of the Boy Scouts. See No. C152.

"The Blind," by M. Vega A207

Paintings: 4c, "The Art Critics" by M. Melero. 10c, "Volanta in Storm" by A. Menocal. 14c, "The Convalescent" by L. Romañach.

1957, Mar. **Engr.** ***Perf. 12½***

Side and Lower Inscriptions in Dark Brown

566 A207	2c olive green	.30	.20
567 A207	4c orange red	.40	.20
568 A207	10c olive green	.65	.25
569 A207	14c ultra	.90	.25
Nos. 566-569,C153-C155,E22 (8)		13.00	3.00

See note after No. 457.

Emblem of Philatelic Club of Cuba A208

Juan F. Steegers A209

1957, Apr. 24

570 A208 4c ocher, blue & red .75 .25

Issued for Stamp Day, Apr. 24, and the National Philatelic Exhibition. See No. C156.

1957, Apr. 30

571 A209 4c blue .60 .25

Juan Francisco Steegers y Perera (1856-1921), dactyloscopy pioneer. See No. C157.

Victoria Bru Sanchez A210

Joaquin de Aguero in Battle of Jucaral A211

1957, June 3 **Wmk. 106** ***Perf. 12½***

572 A210 4c indigo .25 .20

1957, July 4

573 A211 4c dark green .25 .20

Issued to honor Joaquin de Aguero, Cuban freedom fighter and patriot. See No. C162.

Boy, Dogs and Cat — A212

Col. Rafael Manduley del Rio — A213

1957, July 17

574 A212 4c Prus green 2.00 .40

Mrs. Jeanette Ryder, founder of the Humane Society of Cuba. See Nos. C163-C163a.

1957, July 31

575 A213 4c Prus green 1.00 .50

Issued to honor Col. Manduley del Rio, patriot, on the cent. of his birth (in 1856).

Palace of Justice A214

1957, Sept. 2 **Engr.** ***Perf. 12½***

576 A214 4c blue gray .75 .25

Opening of the new Palace of Justice in Havana. See No. C165.

Generals of the Liberation — A215

1957, Sept. 26

577 A215	4c dl grn & red brn	.50	.20
578 A215	4c dl bl & red brn	.50	.20
579 A215	4c rose & brown	.50	.20
580 A215	4c org yel & brn	.50	.20
581 A215	4c lt violet & brn	.50	.20
Nos. 577-581 (5)		2.50	1.00

Generals of the army of liberation.

1st Publication Printed in Cuba — A216

Patio — A217

1957, Oct. 18 **Wmk. 106** ***Perf. 12½***

582 A216 4c slate blue .75 .25
Nos. 582,C167-C168 (3) 3.25 .85

José Marti National Library.

1957, Nov. 19

583 A217 4c red brn & grn .60 .25
Nos. 583,C173-C174 (3) 4.50 1.15

Cent. of the 1st Cuban Normal School.

Trinidad, Founded 1514 — A218

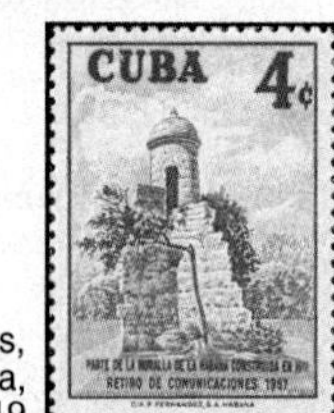

Fortifications, Havana, 1611 — A219

Views: 10c, Padre Pico street, Santiago de Cuba. 14c, Church of Our Lady, Camaguey.

1957, Dec. 17 **Engr.** ***Perf. 12½***

584 A218	2c brown & indigo	.30	.20
585 A219	4c slate grn & brn	.70	.20
586 A219	10c sepia & red	1.10	.20
587 A219	14c green & dk red	1.75	.20
Nos. 584-587,C175-C177,E23 (8)		11.50	3.15

See note after No. 457.

Nativity — A220

1957, Dec. 20
588 A220 2c multicolored 1.75 .50
589 A220 4c multicolored 1.75 .40

Christmas 1957.

Dayton Hedges and Ariguanabo Textile Factory A221

1958, Jan. 30 Wmk. 106 *Perf. 12½*
590 A221 4c blue .50 .25

Issued to honor Dayton Hedges, founder of Cuba's textile industry. See No. C178.

Dr. Francisco Dominguez Roldan — A222

José Ignacio Rivero y Alonso — A223

1958, Feb. 21
591 A222 4c green .75 .25

Roldan (1864-1942), who introduced radiotherapy and physiotherapy to Cuba.

1958, Apr. 1
592 A223 4c lt olive green .50 .50

José Ignacio Rivero y Alonso, editor of Diario de la Marina, 1919-44. See No. C179.

Map of Cuba and Mail Route, 1756 A224

1958, Apr. 24 *Perf. 12½*
593 A224 4c dk grn, aqua & buff .50 .25

Issued for Stamp Day, Apr. 24 and the National Philatelic Exhibition. See No. C180.

Maj. Gen. José Miguel Gomez A225

Nicolas Ruiz Espadero A226

1958, June 6 Wmk. 106 *Perf. 12½*
594 A225 4c slate .50 .25

Maj. Gen. José Miguel Gomez, President of Cuba, 1909-13. See No. C181.

1958, June 27 *Perf. 12½*

Indigo Emblem

Musicians: 4c, Ignacio Cervantes. 10c, José White. 14c, Brindis de Salas.

595 A226 2c brown .50 .20
596 A226 4c dark gray .50 .20
597 A226 10c olive green .80 .20
598 A226 14c red 1.10 .25

Green Emblem

Physicians: 2c, Tomas Romay Chacon. 4c, Angel Arturo Aballi. 10c, Fernando Gonzalez del Valle. 14c, Vicente Antonio de Castro.

599 A226 2c brown .70 .20
600 A226 4c gray 1.10 .20
601 A226 10c dark carmine .80 .20
602 A226 14c dark blue 1.10 .20

Red Emblem

Lawyers: 2c, Jose Maria Garcia Montes. 4c, Jose A. Gonzalez Lanuza. 10c, Juan B. Hernandez Barreiro. 14c, Pedro Gonzalez Llorente.

603 A226 2c sepia .50 .20
604 A226 4c gray .80 .20
605 A226 10c olive grn 1.00 .20
606 A226 14c slate blue 1.10 .20
Nos. 595-606 (12) 10.00 2.45

For surcharges see Nos. 629-631.

Carlos de la Torre — A227

1958, Aug. 29 Engr. Wmk. 321
607 A227 4c violet blue .60 .25
Nos. 607,C182-C184 (4) 14.60 4.65

Dr. Carlos de la Torre y Huerta (1858-1950), naturalist. For surcharge see No. 632.

Poey's "Memorias" Title Page — A228

Felipe Poey — A229

1958, Sept. 26 Wmk. 106
608 A228 2c black & lt violet .60 .25
609 A229 4c brown black .70 .25
Nos. 608-609,C185-C191,E26-E27 (11) 60.05 19.75

Felipe Poey (1799-1891), naturalist.

Theodore Roosevelt — A230

Cattleyopsis Lindenii Orchid — A231

1958, Oct. 27 *Perf. 12½*
610 A230 4c gray green .50 .25

Theodore Roosevelt, birth cent. See #C192.

Engraved and Photogravure

1958, Dec. 16 Wmk. 321 *Perf. 12½*

4c, Oncidium Guibertianum Orchid.

611 A231 2c multicolored 3.00 .75
612 A231 4c multicolored 3.00 .75

Christmas. For surcharge see #633.

Flag and Revolutionary A232

Gen. Adolfo Flor Crombet (1848-95) A233

Engr. & Typo.

1959, Jan. 28 Wmk. 321
613 A232 2c car rose & gray .50 .25

Day of Liberation, Jan. 1, 1959.

1959, Mar. 18 Engr. Wmk. 106
614 A233 4c slate green .60 .25

For surcharge see No. 634.

Maria Teresa Garcia Montes A234

Carlos Manuel de Cespedes A235

1959, Nov. 11 *Perf. 12½*
615 A234 4c brown .30 .25

Maria Teresa Garcia Montes (1880-1930), founder of the Musical Arts Society. See No. C198. For surcharge see No. 635.

1959, Oct. 10 Wmk. 106 *Perf. 12½*

Presidents: No. 617, Salvador Cisneros Betancourt. No. 618, Manuel de Jesus Calvar. No. 619, Bartolomé Maso. No. 620, Juan B. Spotorno. No. 621, Tomas Estrada Palma. No. 622, Francisco Javier de Céspedes. No. 623, Vicente Garcia.

616 A235 2c slate blue .30 .20
617 A235 2c green .30 .20
618 A235 2c deep violet .30 .20
619 A235 2c orange brown .30 .20
620 A235 4c dark carmine .40 .20
621 A235 4c deep brown .40 .20
622 A235 4c dark gray .40 .20
623 A235 4c dark violet .40 .20
Nos. 616-623 (8) 2.80 1.60

Issued to honor former Cuban presidents.

No. B3 Surcharged in Red: "HABILITADO PARA / 2¢"

1960
624 SP2 2c on 2c + 1c car & ultra .55 .20

See No. C199.

Rebel Attack on Moncada Barracks A236

Designs: 2c, Rebels disembarking from "Granma." 10c, Battle of the Uvero. 12c, Map of Cuba and rebel ("The Invasion").

1960, Jan. 28 Wmk. 320
625 A236 1c gray ol, bl & ver .20 .20
626 A236 2c bl, gray ol & brn .20 .20
627 A236 10c bl, gray ol & red .35 .20
628 A236 12c brt bl, brn & grn .50 .20
Nos. 625-628,C200-C202 (7) 5.10 2.80

First anniversary of revolution.

Stamps of 1956-59 Surcharged with New Value in Carmine or Silver

1960, Feb. 3
629 A226 1c on 4c dk gray & ind .35 .20
630 A226 1c on 4c gray & grn .55 .25
631 A226 1c on 4c gray & red .35 .20
632 A227 1c on 4c violet bl .35 .20
633 A231 1c on 4c multi (S) .90 .50
634 A233 1c on 4c slate grn .30 .20
635 A234 1c on 4c brown .35 .20
636 A184a 2c on 14c gray .45 .20
Nos. 629-636,C203-C204 (10) 5.10 2.55

Tomas Estrada Palma Statue, Havana — A237

17th Olympic Games, Rome, Aug. 25-Sept. 11 — A238

Statues: 2c, Mambi Victorioso (Battle of San Juan Hill), Santiago de Cuba. 10c, Marta Abreo de Estevez. 12c, Ignacio Agramonte, Camaguey.

Wmk. 321

1960, Mar. 28 Engr. *Perf. 12½*
637 A237 1c brn & dk bl .20 .20
638 A237 2c green & red .30 .20
639 A237 10c choc & red .75 .20
640 A237 12c gray ol & vio .90 .20
Nos. 637-640,C206-C208 (7) 5.65 2.30

See note after No. 386.

Nos. 521A, 522 and 525 Surcharged "HABILITADO / PARA / 2¢" in Violet Blue, Red or Black

1960 Wmk. 106 *Perf. 10*
641 A184 2c on 4c red lil (VB) .50 .20
642 A184a 2c on 5c sl bl (R) .60 .20
643 A184 2c on 13c org red .75 .20

No. 307B Surcharged "HABILITADO / 10¢"

644 A41 10c on 20c ol grn .50 .20
Nos. 641-644 (4) 2.35 .80

Wmk. 321

1960, Sept. 22 Engr. *Perf. 12½*
645 A238 1c Sailboats .20 .20
646 A238 2c Marksman .25 .20
Nos. 645-646,C212-C213 (4) 1.30 1.00

For souvenir sheet see No. C213a.

Camilo Cienfuegos and View of Escolar A239

1960, Oct. 27 Litho. Unwmk.
647 A239 2c brn, bl, grn & red .20 .20

1st anniv. of the death of Camilo Cienfuegos, revolutionary hero.

Morning Glory A240

Tobacco and Christmas Hymn A241

1960 Litho. *Perf. 12½*
648 A240 1c red .55 .50
649 A241 1c Tobacco .75 .75
650 A241 1c Mariposa .75 .75
651 A241 1c Guaiacum .75 .75

652 A241 1c Coffee .75 .75
a. Block of 4, #649-652 4.50
653 A240 2c ultra .75 .75
654 A241 2c Tobacco 2.00 2.00
655 A241 2c Mariposa 2.00 2.00
656 A241 2c Guaiacum 2.00 2.00
657 A241 2c Coffee 2.00 2.00
a. Block of 4, #654-657 12.00
658 A240 10c ocher 2.25 2.00
659 A241 10c Tobacco 5.50 5.00
660 A241 10c Mariposa 5.50 5.00
661 A241 10c Guaiacum 5.50 5.00
662 A241 10c Coffee 5.50 5.00
a. Block of 4, #659-662 35.00
Nos. 648-662 (15) 36.55 34.25

Issued for Christmas 1960.

Nos. 648-662 were printed in three sheets of 25. Nine stamps of type A240 form a center cross, stamps of type A241 form a block of four in each corner with the musical bars joined in an oval around the floral designs.

"Public Capital for Economic Benefit" — A242

Designs: 2c, Chart and symbols of agriculture and industry. 6c, Cogwheels.

Perf. 11½

1961, Jan. 10 Unwmk. Photo.
663 A242 1c yel, blk & org .20 .20
664 A242 2c bl, blk & red .20 .20
665 A242 6c yel, red org & blk .50 .25
Nos. 663-665,C215-C218 (7) 4.40 2.55

Issued to publicize the conference of underdeveloped countries, Havana.

Jesus Menéndez and Sugar Cane — A243

1961, Jan. 22 Litho. *Perf. 12½*
666 A243 2c dk grn & brn .20 .20

Jesus Menéndez, leader in sugar industry.

Same Overprinted in Red: "PRIMERO DE MAYO 1961 ESTAMOS VENCIENDO"

1961, May 2
667 A243 2c dk grn & brn .30 .25

Issued for May Day, 1961.

Dove and UN Emblem — A244

1961, Apr. 12 Litho. *Perf. 12½*
668 A244 2c red brn & yel grn .30 .20
669 A244 10c emer & rose lil .50 .20
a. Souv. sheet, #668-669, imperf. 1.00
Nos. 668-669,C222-C223 (4) 1.70 .90

15th anniv. (in 1960) of the UN.

Maceo Stamp of 1907 and 1902 Simulated Cancel
A245

Stamp Day: 1c, Revolutionary 10c stamp of 1874, 1868 "cancel." 10c, #613, "cancel."

1961, Apr. 24 Unwmk.
670 A245 1c dull rose & dk grn .20 .20
671 A245 2c salmon & dk grn .20 .20
672 A245 10c pale grn, car rose & blk .40 .25
Nos. 670-672 (3) .80 .65

For overprint see No. 681.

Hand Releasing Dove — A246

1961, July 26 *Perf. 12½*
673 A246 2c blk, red, yel & gray .30 .20

26th of July (1953) movement, Castro's revolt against Fulgencio Batista.

Burelage on back consisting of wavy lines and diagonal rows of "CUBA CORREOS" in pale salmon.

Portrait Type of 1954

Designs: Same as before. On the 2c, "1833" is replaced by "?."

Wmk. 321 (Nos. 674, 676); Unwmkd.
Perf. 12½ (Nos. 674, 676); Rouletted
1961-69 Engr.
674 A184 1c brown red
675 A184 1c lt blue ('69)
676 A184a 2c slate green
677 A184a 2c yel grn ('69)
678 A184 3c org ('64)
679 A184 13c brn ('64)
680 A184 20c lilac ('69)

Issued: #674, 676, 8/1; #678-679, 12/764; others, 9/69.

For Nos. 675, 677-680, see embargo note following No. 702.

No. 672 Ovptd. in Red

Perf. 12½

1961, Oct. 7 Litho. Unwmk.
681 A245 10c pale grn, car rose & blk

1st Official Phil. Exhib., Havana, Oct. 7-17.

Education Year — A247

Designs: One letter (per stamp) of "CUBA," book and various quotations by Jose Marti about the virtues of literacy.

1961, Nov. 22
682 A247 1c pale grn, red & blk
683 A247 2c blue, red & blk
684 A247 10c vio, red & blk
685 A247 12c org, red & blk

A248

Christmas A249

1c, Snails. 2c, Birds, vert. 10c, Butterflies.

1961, Dec. 1
686 A248 1c Polymita flammulata
687 A249 1c Polymita fulminata
688 A249 1c Polymita nigrofasciata
689 A249 1c Polymita fuscolimbata
690 A249 1c Polymita roseolimbata
a. Block of 5 + label, Nos. 686-690
691 A248 2c Cuban grassquit
692 A249 2c Cuban macaw
693 A249 2c Cuban trogon
694 A249 2c Bee hummingbird
695 A249 2c Ivory-billed woodpecker
a. Block of 5 + label, Nos. 691-695
696 A248 10c Othreis toddi
697 A249 10c Uranidia boisduvalii
698 A249 10c Phoebis avellaneda
699 A249 10c Phaloe cubana
700 A249 10c Papilio gundlachianus
a. Block of 5 + label, Nos. 696-700

Stamps of the same denomination printed se-tenant in sheets of 20 stamps plus 5 labels picturing bells and star. Stamps of Type A249 are arranged in blocks of 4; Type A248 stamps and labels form a cross in sheet.

See #760-774, 912-926, 1025-1039, 1179-1193, 1303-1317, 1464-1478, 1572-1586.

3rd Anniv. of the Revolution A250

1962, Jan. 3
701 A250 1c multi
702 A250 2c multi

See Nos. C226-C228.

Importation Prohibited

Cuban stamps issued after No. 673 have not been valued because the embargo on trade with Cuba, proclaimed Feb. 7, 1962, by President Kennedy, prohibits the importation from any country of stamps of Cuban origin, used or unused.

Natl. Militia A251

Silhouettes of militiamen and women and their peace-time occupations: 1c, Farmer. 2c, Welder. 3c, Seamstress.

1962, Feb. 26
703 A251 1c blue grn & blk
704 A251 2c deep blue & blk
705 A251 10c brt org & blk

Bay of Pigs Invasion, 1st Anniv. — A252

1962, Apr. 17
706 A252 2c multi
707 A252 3c multi
708 A252 10c multi

1st West Indies Packet A253

1962, Apr. 24
709 A253 10c red & gray

Stamp Day. See No. E32.

Intl. Labor Day — A254

1962, May 1
710 A254 2c ocher & blk
711 A254 3c ver & blk
712 A254 10c greenish blue & blk

Natl. Sports Institute (INDER) Emblem and Athletes — A255

1962, July 25 Wmk. 321
713 A255 1c Judo
714 A255 1c Discus
715 A255 1c Gymnastics
716 A255 1c Wrestling
717 A255 1c Weight lifting
718 A255 2c Roller skating
719 A255 2c Equestrian
720 A255 2c Archery
721 A255 2c Bicycling
722 A255 2c Bowling
723 A255 3c Power boating
724 A255 3c One-man kayak
725 A255 3c Swimming
726 A255 3c Sculling
727 A255 3c Yachting
728 A255 9c Soccer
729 A255 9c Volleyball
730 A255 9c Baseball
731 A255 9c Basketball
732 A255 9c Tennis
733 A255 10c Boxing
734 A255 10c Underwater fishing
735 A255 10c Model-plane flying
736 A255 10c Pistol shooting
737 A255 10c Water polo
738 A255 13c Paddleball
739 A255 13c Fencing
740 A255 13c Sports Palace
741 A255 13c Chess
742 A255 13c Jai alai

Stamps of the same denomination printed se-tenant in sheets of 25. Various combinations possible.

9th Anniv. of the Revolution A256

Attack on Moncada Barracks: Abel Santamaria and: 2c, Barracks under siege. 3c, Children at Moncada School.

1962, July 26
743 A256 2c brn car & dark ultra
744 A256 3c dark ultra & brn car

8th World Youth Festival for Peace and Friendship, Helsinki, July 28-Aug. 6 — A257

1962, July 28
745 A257 2c Dove, emblem
746 A257 3c Hand grip, emblem
a. Min. sheet of 2, Nos. 745-746, imperf.

9th Central American and Caribbean Games, Kingston, Jamaica, Aug. 11 - 25 — A258

1962, Aug. 27
747 A258 1c Boxing
748 A258 2c Tennis
749 A258 3c Baseball
750 A258 13c Fencing

A259

First Natl. Congress of the Federation of Cuban Women — A260

1962, Oct. 1
751 A259 9c rose, blk & grn
752 A260 13c blk, grn & lt blue

Latin American University Games — A261

1962, Oct. 13 **Wmk. 106**
753 A261 1c Running
754 A261 2c Baseball
755 A261 3c Basketball
756 A261 13c World map

World Health Organization Campaign to Eradicate Malaria — A262

Designs: 1c, Magnified specimen of the parasitic protozoa, microscope. 2c, Swamp and mosquito. 3c, Chemist's structural formulas for quinine, cinchona plant.

1962, Dec. 14
757 A262 1c multi
758 A262 2c multi
759 A262 3c multi

Christmas Type of 1961

2c, Reptiles. 3c, Insects, vert. 10c, Rodents.

1962, Dec. 21 **Unwmk.**
760 A248 2c Epicrates angulifer
761 A249 2c Cricosaurus typica
762 A249 2c Anolis equestris
763 A249 2c Tropidophis wrighti
764 A249 2c Cyclura macleayi
a. Block of 5 + label, Nos. 760-764
765 A248 3c Cubispa turquino
766 A249 3c Chrysis superba
767 A249 3c Essostruta roberto
768 A249 3c Hortensia conciliata
769 A249 3c Lachnopus argus
a. Block of 5 + label, Nos. 765-769
770 A248 10c Monophyllus cubanus
771 A249 10c Capromys pilorides
772 A249 10c Capromys pre-hensilis
773 A249 10c Solenodon cubensis
774 A249 10c Capromys pilorides (Blanca)
a. Block of 5 + label, Nos. 770-774

Christmas 1962. See note after No. 700.

Around 1962 a 1ctv. label picturing Fidel Castro was used as a voluntary contribution stamp. It is not inscribed "Correos" and was not valid for postage.

Soviet Space Flights — A263

Spacecraft and cosmonauts: 1c, Vostok 1, Yuri A. Gagarin, Apr. 12, 1961. 2c, Vostok 2, Gherman S. Titov, Aug. 6-7, 1961. 3c, Vostok 3, Andrian G. Nikolaev, Aug. 11-15, 1962, and Vostok 4, Pavel R. Popovich, Aug. 12-15, 1962. 9c, Vostok 5, Valery F. Bykovsky, June 14-19, 1963. 13c, Vostok 6, Valentina V. Tereshkova, June 16-19, 1963.

1963-64 **Wmk. 321**
775 A263 1c ultra, red & yel
776 A263 2c grn, yel & rose lake
777 A263 3c yel, vio & ver
778 A263 9c red, dark vio & yel
779 A263 13c dark blue green, dull red brown & yel

Issued: 1c, 2c, 3c, 2/26/63; others, 8/15/64.

Attack of the Presidential Palace, 6th Anniv. — A264

9c, Guerillas attacking palace. 13c, Four student leaders. 30c, Jose A. Echeverria, Menelad Mora.

1963, Mar. 13
780 A264 9c dark red & blk
781 A264 13c chalky blue & sep
782 A264 30c org & grn

4th Pan American Games, Sao Paulo, Brazil, Apr. 20-May 5 — A265

1963, Apr. 20
783 A265 1c Baseball
784 A265 13c Boxing

Stamp Day A266

3c, Mask mailbox, 19th cent. 10c, Mask mailbox at the Plaza de la Catedral, Havana.

1963, Apr. 25
785 A266 3c black & dark org
786 A266 10c black & pur

See Nos. 828-829, 956-957 and 1102-1103.

Labor Day — A267

1963, May 1
787 A267 3c shown
788 A267 13c Four workers

Intl. Children's Week, June 1-7 — A268

1963, June 1
789 A268 3c blue blk & bister brn
790 A268 30c blue blk & red

Ritual Effigy — A269

Broken Chains at Moncada A270

Taino Civilization artifacts: 3c, Wood-carved throne, horiz. 9c, Stone-carved figurine.

1963, June 29
791 A269 2c org & red brn
792 A269 3c ultra & red brn
793 A269 9c rose & gray

Montane Anthropology Museum, 60th anniv.

1963, July 26

2c, Attack on the Presidential Palace. 3c, The insurrection. 7c, Strike of April 9. 9c, Triumph of the revolution. 10c, Agricultural reform and nationalization of industry. 13c, Bay of Pigs victory.

794 A270 1c pink & blk
795 A270 2c lt blue & vio brn
796 A270 3c lt vio & brn
797 A270 7c apple green & rose
798 A270 9c olive bister & rose vio
799 A270 10c beige & sage grn
800 A270 13c pale org & slate blue

Indigenous Fruit — A271

1963, Aug. 19
801 A271 1c Star apple
802 A271 2c Cherimoya
803 A271 3c Cashew nut
804 A271 10c Custard apple
805 A271 13c Mangoes

Geometric Shapes A272

View of a Town — A273

Designs: No. 806, Circle, triangle, square, vert. No. 807, Roof, window, vert. No. 808, View of a town. No. 809, View of a town in blue. No. 810, View of a town in olive bister and red. No. 811, Circle, triangle, vert. No. 812, House, roof and doorway, vert. No. 813, House, girders.

1963, Sept. 29 **Unwmk.**
806 A272 3c multi
807 A272 3c multi
808 A273 3c multi
809 A273 3c multi
810 A273 13c multi
811 A272 13c multi
812 A272 13c multi
813 A272 13c multi

7th Intl. Congress of the Intl. Union of Architects.

Ernest Hemingway (1899-1961), American Author — A274

Hemingway and: 3c, The Old Man and the Sea. 9c, For Whom the Bell Tolls. 13c, Hemingway Museum (former residence), San Francisco de Paula, near Havana.

1963, Dec. 5 **Wmk. 321**
814 A274 3c brn & lt blue
815 A274 9c sage grn & pink
816 A274 13c blk & yel grn

Natl. Museum, 50th Anniv. — A275

Works of art: 2c, El Zapateo (Dance), by Victor P. Landaluze. 3c, Abduction of the Mulatto Women, by Carlos Enriquez, vert. 9c, Greek Panathean amphora, vert. 13c, My Beloved (bust of a young woman), by Jean Antoine Houdon, vert.

1964, Mar. 19 **Unwmk.**
817 A275 2c multi
818 A275 3c multi
819 A275 9c multi
820 A275 13c multi

General Strike on Apr. 9, 6th Anniv. — A276

Rebel leaders: 2c, Bernardo Juan Borrell. 3c, Marcelo Salado. 10c, Oscar Lucero. 13c, Sergio Gonzalez.

1964, Apr. 9

821 A276 2c blk, yel grn & dull org
822 A276 3c blk, red & dull org
823 A276 10c blk, pur & beige
824 A276 13c blk, brt blue & beige

Bay of Pigs Invasion, 3rd Anniv. A277

Designs: 3c, Fish in net. 10c, Victory Monument. 13c, Fallen eagle, vert.

1964, Apr. 17

825 A277 3c multi
826 A277 10c multi
827 A277 13c multi

Stamp Day Type of 1963

3c, Vicente Mora Pera, 1st postal director. 13c, Unissued provisional stamp, 1871.

1964, Apr. 24

828 A266 3c ocher & dull lil
829 A266 13c dull vio & lt olive grn

Labor Day — A278

Diplomatic Relations with China — A279

1964, May 1

830 A278 3c Industry
831 A278 13c Agriculture

1964, May 15

Designs: 1c, China Monument, Havana. 2c, Cuban and Chinese farmers. 3c, Natl. flags.

832 A279 1c multi
833 A279 2c org brn, blk & apple grn
834 A279 3c multi

15th UPU Congress, Vienna, May-June A280

1964, May 29

835 A280 13c Hemispheres on world map
836 A280 30c Heinrich von Stephan
837 A280 50c UPU Monument, Bern

Development of Natl. Industry A281

1964, June 16

838 A281 1c Fish
839 A281 2c Cow
840 A281 13c Chickens

Merchant Fleet — A282

1964, June 30

841 A282 1c Rio Jibacoa
842 A282 2c Camilo Cienfuegos
843 A282 3c Sierra Maestra
844 A282 9c Bahia de Siguanea
845 A282 10c Oriente

Unification of Viet Nam — A283

Designs: 2c, Vietnamese guerrilla, American soldier. 3c, Northerner and southerner shaking hands over map of united Viet Nam. 10c, Ox-drawn plow, machinised harvester. 13c, Natl. flags and profiles of Cuban and Vietnamese farmers.

1964, July 20

846 A283 2c multi
847 A283 3c multi
848 A283 10c multi
849 A283 13c multi

11th Anniv. of the Revolution A284

1964 Summer Olympics, Tokyo, Oct. 10-25 A285

Designs: 3c, Raul Gomez Garcia and poem. 13c, Cover of La Historia Me Absolvera, by Fidel Castro.

1964, July 25

850 A284 3c red, tan & blk
851 A284 13c multi

1964, Oct. 10 Wmk. 376 ***Perf. 10***

852 A285 1c Gymnastics
853 A285 2c Rowing
854 A285 3c Boxing
855 A285 7c Running, horiz.
856 A285 10c Fencing, horiz.
857 A285 13c Foil, cleats, oar, boxing glove, sun, horiz.

Satellite and Globe A286

Satellite and Partial Globe A287

No. C31 and Partial Globe A288

Various satellites and rockets.

1964, Oct. 15

858 A286 1c shown
859 A287 1c shown
860 A287 1c Globe LL
861 A287 1c Globe UR
862 A287 1c Globe UL
a. Block of 5 + label, Nos. 858-862
863 A286 2c Spacecraft and globe
864 A287 2c Globe LR
865 A287 2c Globe LL
866 A287 2c Globe UR
867 A287 2c Globe UL
a. Block of 5 + label, Nos. 863-867
868 A286 3c Satellite and globe
869 A287 3c Globe LR
870 A287 3c Globe LL
871 A287 3c Globe UR
872 A287 3c Globe UL
a. Block of 5 + label, Nos. 868-872
873 A286 9c Satellite and globe, diff
874 A287 9c Globe LR
875 A287 9c Globe LL
876 A287 9c Globe UR
877 A287 9c Globe UL
a. Block of 5 + label, Nos. 873-877
878 A286 13c Satellite and globe, diff.
879 A287 13c Globe LR
880 A287 13c Globe LL
881 A287 13c Globe UR
882 A287 13c Globe UL
a. Block of 5 + label, Nos. 878-882
883 A288 50c blk & lt grn
a. Souvenir sheet of one, Wmk. 321

Experimental Cuban postal rocket flight, 25th anniv. Stamps of the same denomination printed se-tenant in sheets of 20 stamps and 5 inscribed labels. Stamps of Type A287 arranged in blocks of 4 with a complete globe in center of block; Type A286 stamps and labels form a cross in center of sheet. Inscribed "1939-Cohete Postal Cubano-1964." No. 883a contains one 46x28mm stamp.

Type of A288 Ovptd. in Silver

1964, Oct. 17 **Unwmk.**

884 A288 50c dark red brown & lt grn

No. 884 not issued without overprint.

40th Death Anniv. of Lenin — A289

Havana Zoo — A290

Designs: 13c, Lenin Mausoleum, horiz. 30c, Lenin, star, hammer and sickle.

1964, Nov. 7 **Wmk. 376**

885 A289 3c org & blk
886 A289 13c pur, pink & blk
887 A289 30c blue & blk

1964, Nov. 25

888 A290 1c Leopard, horiz.
889 A290 2c Elephant
890 A290 3c Fallow deer
891 A290 4c Kangaroo, horiz.
892 A290 5c Lions, horiz.
893 A290 6c Eland, horiz.
894 A290 7c Zebra, horiz.
895 A290 8c Hyena, horiz.
896 A290 9c Tiger, horiz.
897 A290 10c Guanaco, horiz.
898 A290 13c Chimpanzees, horiz.
899 A290 20c Peccary, horiz.
900 A290 30c Raccoon
901 A290 40c Hippopotamus, horiz.
902 A290 50c Tapir, horiz.
903 A290 60c Dromedary
904 A290 70c Bison, horiz.
905 A290 80c Black bear
906 A290 90c Water buffalo, horiz.

Size: 47x32mm

907 A290 1p Deer in nature park, horiz.

Heroes of the 1895 War of Independence — A291

1964, Dec. 7

908 A291 1c Jose Marti
909 A291 2c Antonio Maceo
910 A291 3c Maximo Gomez
911 A291 13c Calixto Garcia

Christmas Type of 1961

2c, Coral. 3c, Jellyfish. 10c, Starfish, sea-urchins.

1964, Dec. 18

912 A248 2c Dwarf cup coral
913 A249 2c Eusmilia fastigiata
914 A249 2c Acropora palmata
915 A249 2c Acropora profilera
916 A249 2c Diploria labyrinthiformis
a. Block of 5 + label, Nos. 912-916
917 A248 3c Condylactis gigantea
918 A249 3c Physalia physalis
919 A249 3c Aurelia aurita
920 A249 3c Linuche unguiculata
921 A249 3c Cassiopea frondosa
a. Block of 5 + label, Nos. 917-921
922 A248 10c Neocrinus blakei
923 A249 10c Eucidaris tribuloidas
924 A249 10c Tripneutes
925 A249 10c Ophiocoma echinata
926 A249 10c Oreaster celiculatus
a. Block of 5 + label, Nos. 922-926

Christmas 1964. See note after No. 700.

Dr. Tomas Romay (1764-1849), Physician and Scientist — A292

Romay Monument — A293

Designs: 2c, First vaccination against smallpox. 3c, Portrait and treatise on vaccination.

1964, Dec. 21

927 A292 1c blk & olive brn
928 A292 2c blk & tan
929 A293 3c olive & dark red brown
930 A293 10c bister & blk

Second Declaration of Havana A294

Map of Latin America and ripples or map of Cuba and peasant breaking shackles under text from the Declaration of Havana: No. 931a, 932a "Visperas de su muerte..." No. 931b, 932b, "Un continente, que juntos suponen representos..." No. 931c, 932c, "Y no se ocultaran ni el gobierna..." No. 931d, 932d, "Millones de mulatos latinamericanos que saben..." No. 931e, "A labran la tierra en condiciones..."

1964, Dec. 23

931 Strip of 5
a.-e. A294 3c any single
932 Strip of 5
a.-e. A294 13c any single

Nos. 931-932 printed in sheets of 25 (5x5).

Dioramas in New Cuban Postal Museum — A295

1965, Jan. 4

Yellow & Black Border

933 A295 13c Maritime Post
934 A295 30c Insurrection Post

Souvenir Sheet

Imperf

935 Sheet of 2
a. A295 13c like #933, blue & blk border
b. A295 30c like #934, blue & blk border

Stamps in #935 have simulated perforations; buff margin is inscribed "PRECIO 50c" LR.

Fishing Fleet — A296

1965, May 1

936 A296 1c Schooner
937 A296 2c Omicron
938 A296 3c Victoria
939 A296 9c Cardenas
940 A296 10c Sigma
941 A296 13c Lambda

Intl. Women's Day — A297

1965, Mar. 8

942 A297 3c Lidia Doce
943 A297 13c Clara Zetkin

Technical Revolution — A298

Designs: 3c, Jose Antonio Echeverria University School. 13c, Stylized symbols of science and research, molecular structure and satellite dish.

1965, Mar. 31

944 A298 3c tan, blk & dark red brn
945 A298 13c multi

Cosmonauts, Rocket — A299

30c, Cosmonauts Pavel I. Balyayev, Aleksei A. Leonov taking first space walk.

1965, Apr. 2

946 A299 30c dark blue, blk & brn
947 A299 50c brt pink & blue blk

Flight of Voskhod 2, the first man to walk in space, Mar. 17.

Abstract Wood Carving by Eugenio Rodriguez — A300

Abraham Lincoln — A301

Paintings in the Natl. Museum, Havana: 3c, Garden with Sunflowers, by Victor Manuel. 10c, Abstract, by Wilfredo Lam, horiz. 13c, Children, by Enrique Ponce, horiz.

1965, Apr. 12

948 A300 2c multi

Size: 35x46mm

949 A300 3c multi

Size: 46x35mm

950 A300 10c multi

Size: 43x37mm

951 A300 13c multi

1965, Apr. 15

Designs: 1c, Log cabin, birth site, horiz. 2c, Memorial, Washington, DC, horiz. 3c, Monument, Washington, DC. 13c, Portrait, quote.

952 A301 1c yel bister, red brn & gray
953 A301 2c lt blue & dark blue
954 A301 3c red org, blk & blue blk
955 A301 13c org, blk & blue blk

Stamp Day Type of 1963

Stamp Day 1965: 3c, 18th Cent. postmarks and packet. 13c, No. C16 and airplanes over capital.

1965, Apr. 24

956 A266 3c sep & dark org
957 A266 13c brt blue, sal rose & blk

Intl. Quiet Sun Year — A302

Intl. Telecommunications Union, Cent. — A303

1965, May 10

958 A302 1c Sun, Earth's magnetic pole, horiz.
959 A302 2c Sun Year emblem
960 A302 3c Earth's magnetic field, horiz.
961 A302 6c Atmospheric currents, horiz.
962 A302 30c Solar rays on planet surface
963 A302 50c Effect on satellite orbits, horiz.
a. Souv. sheet of one, imperf.
b. As "a," changed colors

Stamps in Nos. 963a-963b have simulated perforations.

Stamp in No. 963b is blue blk, Prus blue, org yel & red. Issued Oct. 10 for the Philatelic Space Exhibition, Havana, Oct. 10-17.

1965, May 17

964 A303 1c Station, horiz.
965 A303 2c Satellite
966 A303 3c Telstar, horiz.
967 A303 10c Telstar, receiving station
968 A303 30c ITU emblem, horiz.

9th Communist World Youth and Students Congress — A304

1965, June 10

969 A304 13c Flags of Cuba and Algeria, emblem
970 A304 30c Flags, guerrillas

Matias Perez, Cuban Aeronautics Pioneer — A305

1965, June 23

971 A305 3c pink & blk
972 A305 13c dull vio & blk, diff.

Flowers and Maps of Their Locations A306

1965, July 20

973 A306 1c Rosa canina, Europe
974 A306 2c Chrysanthemum hortorum, Asia
975 A306 3c Strelitzia reginae, Africa
976 A306 4c Dahlia pinnata, No. America
977 A306 5c Cattleya labiata, So. America
978 A306 13c Grevillea banksii, Oceania
979 A306 30c Brunfelsia nitida, Cuba

1st Natl. Games — A307

1965, July 25

980 A307 1c Swimming
981 A307 2c Basketball
982 A307 3c Gymnastics
983 A307 30c Hurdling

Revolution Museum Opening A308

1965, July 26

984 A308 1c Anti-tank guns
985 A308 2c Tanks
986 A308 3c Bazookas
987 A308 10c Uniform, guerillas
988 A308 13c Compass, yacht Granma

A309

1965, Aug. 20

989 A309 1c Finlay's signature
990 A309 2c Anopheles mosquito
991 A309 3c Portrait
992 A309 7c Microscope
993 A309 9c Dr. Claudio Delgado
994 A309 10c Monument
995 A309 13c Discussing theory with doctors

Carlos J. Finlay (1833-1915), discovered transmission of yellow fever via aedes aegypti (not anopheles) mosquito. Nos. 990-995 vert.

Butterflies A310

1965, Sept. 22 **Unwmk.**

996 A310 2c Dismorphia cubana
997 A310 2c Anetia numidia briarea
998 A310 2c Carathis gortynoides
999 A310 2c Hymenitis cubana
1000 A310 2c Eubaphe heros
a. Strip of 5, Nos. 996-1000
1001 A310 3c Lycorea ceres demeter
1002 A310 3c Eubaphe disparitis
1003 A310 3c Siderone nemesis
1004 A310 3c Syntomidopsis variegata
1005 A310 3c Ctenuchidia virgo
a. Strip of 5, Nos. 1001-1005
1006 A310 13c Prepona antimache crossina
1007 A310 13c Sylepta reginalis
1008 A310 13c Chlosyne perezi perezi
1009 A310 13c Anaea clytemnestra iphigenia
1010 A310 13c Anetia cubana
a. Strip of 5, Nos. 1006-1010

Cuban Mint, 50th Anniv. A311

Coins (obverse and reverse).

1965, Oct. 13

1011 A311 1c 20 centavos, 1962
1012 A311 2c 1 peso, 1934
1013 A311 3c 40 centavos, 1962
1014 A311 8c 1 peso, 1915
1015 A311 10c Marti peso, 1953
1016 A311 13c 20 pesos, 1915

Tropical Fruit — A312

1965, Nov. 15 ***Perf. 12½***

1017 A312 1c Oranges
1018 A312 2c Custard apples
1019 A312 3c Papayas
1020 A312 4c Bananas
1021 A312 10c Avocado
1022 A312 13c Pineapple
1023 A312 20c Guavas
1024 A312 50c Marmalade plums

Christmas Type of 1961

Birds.

1965, Dec. 1

1025 A248 3c Icterus galbula
1026 A249 3c Passerina ciris
1027 A249 3c Setophaga ruticillar
1028 A249 3c Dendroica tusca
1029 A249 3c Pheucticus ludovicianus
a. Block of 5 + label, Nos. 1025-1029
1030 A248 5c Pyranga olivacea
1031 A249 5c Dendroica dominica
1032 A249 5c Vermivora pinus
1033 A249 5c Protonotaria citrea
1034 A249 5c Wilsonia citrina
a. Block of 5 + label, Nos. 1030-1034
1035 A248 13c Passerina cyanea
1036 A249 13c Anas discors
1037 A249 13c Aix sponsa
1038 A249 13c Spatula clypeata
1039 A249 13c Nycticorax hoactli
a. Block of 5 + label, Nos. 1035-1039

Christmas 1965. See note after No. 700.

Intl. Athletic Competition, Havana, 7th Anniv. — A313

1965, Dec. 11 **Wmk. 376** ***Perf. 10***

1040 A313 1c Hurdling
1041 A313 2c Discus
1042 A313 3c Shot put
1043 A313 7c Javelin
1044 A313 9c High jump
1045 A313 10c Hammer throw
1046 A313 13c Running

Fish in the Natl. Aquarium — A314

1965, Dec. 5 **Unwmk.** ***Perf. 12½***

1047 A314 1c Echeneis naucrates
1048 A314 2c Katsuwonus pelamis
1049 A314 3c Abudefduf saxatilis
1050 A314 4c Istiophorus
1051 A314 5c Epinephelus striatus
1052 A314 10c Lutianus analis
1053 A314 13c Ocyurus chrysurus
1054 A314 30c Holocentrus ascensionis

Andre Voisin (d. 1964), French Naturalist — A315

1965, Dec. 21 **Wmk. 376**

1055 A315 3c shown
1056 A315 13c Portrait, flags, microscope, plant

Transportation — A316

1965, Dec. 30

1057 A316 1c Skoda bus, Czechoslovakia
1058 A316 2c Ikarus bus, Hungary
1059 A316 3c Leyland bus, G.B.
1060 A316 4c TEM-4 locomotive, USSR
1061 A316 7c BB-69.000 locomotive, France
1062 A316 10c Remolcador tugboat, DDR
1063 A316 13c 15 de Marzo freighter, Spain
1064 A316 20c Ilyushin 18 jet, USSR

A317

7th Anniv. of the Revolution A318

1966, Jan. 2

1065 A317 1c Guerrillas
1066 A317 2c Commander and tank
1067 A317 3c Sailor, patrol boat
1068 A318 10c Jet aircraft
1069 A318 13c Rocket

Conference of Asian, African and South American Countries, Havana — A319

1966, Jan. 3

1070 A319 2c Emblem at R
1071 A319 3c Emblem at L
1072 A319 13c Emblem at center

Guardalabarca Beach — A320

1966, Feb. 10

1073 A320 1c shown
1074 A320 2c Gran Piedra mountain
1075 A320 3c Guama Village
1076 A320 13c Soroa waterfall, vert.

11th Medical and 7th Natl. Dental Congresses — A321

1966, Feb. 28 **Wmk. 376**

1077 A321 3c multi
1078 A321 13c multi, diff.

Folk Art A322

1966, Feb. 28 **Unwmk.**

1079 A322 1c Afro-cuban ritual puppet
1080 A322 2c Sombreros
1081 A322 3c Ceramic vase
1082 A322 7c Lanterns, lamp
1083 A322 9c Table lamp
1084 A322 10c Shark, wood sculpture
1085 A322 13c Snail-shell necklace, earrings

Nos. 1079-1083 vert.

Chelsea College, by Canaletto — A323

Ceramics and paintings in the National Museum: 1c, Ming vase. 3c, Portrait of a Lady, by Goya. 13c, Portrait of Fayum, encaustic painting. Nos. 1086, 1088-1089 vert.

1966, Mar. 31 **Wmk. 376**

1086 A323 1c multi
1087 A323 2c multi
1088 A323 3c multi
1089 A323 13c multi

First Man in Space, 5th Anniv. A324

Designs: 1c, Konstantin Eduardovich Tsiolkovsky (1857-1935), Soviet rocket and space sciences pioneer. 2c, Cosmonauts in training, vert. 3c, Yuri Gagarin, rocket, Earth. 7c, Cosmonauts Nikolaev and Popovich, vert. 9c, Tereshkova and Bykovsky. 10c, Komarov, Feoktistov and Yegarov. 13c, Leonov taking first space walk.

1966, Apr. 12

1090 A324 1c multi
1091 A324 2c multi
1092 A324 3c multi
1093 A324 7c multi
1094 A324 9c multi
1095 A324 10c multi
1096 A324 13c multi

Bay of Pigs Invasion, 5th Anniv. A325

1966, Apr. 17

1097 A325 2c Tank
1098 A325 3c Burning ship, plane crash
1099 A325 9c Tank in ditch
1100 A325 10c Soldier, gunners
1101 A325 13c Operations map

Stamp Day Type of 1963

Designs: 3c, Cuban Postal Museum interior. 13c, No. 613 and stamp collector.

1966, Apr. 24

1102 A266 3c sage grn & sal rose
1103 A266 13c brn, sal rose & blk

Stamp Day 1966. 1st Anniv. of the Cuban Postal Museum (No. 1102); 1st anniv. of the Cuban Philatelic Federation (No. 1103).

Flowers and Symbols of Industry — A326

1966, May 1

1104 A326 2c Anvil
1105 A326 3c Machete
1106 A326 10c Hammer
1107 A326 13c Hemisphere, gearwheel

Labor Day.

Opening of the World Health Organization Headquarters, Geneva — A327

Views of WHO headquarters and emblem or emblem on flag.

1966, May 3

1108 A327 2c blk & yel org
1109 A327 3c blk, lt blue & yel org
1110 A327 13c blk, lt blue & yel org

10th Central American and Caribbean Games, Puerto Rico, June 11-25
A328

1966, June 11

1111 A328 1c Running, vert.
1112 A328 2c Rifle shooting
1113 A328 3c Baseball, vert.
1114 A328 7c Volleyball, vert.
1115 A328 9c Soccer, vert.
1116 A328 10c Boxing, vert.
1117 A328 13c Basketball, vert.

Progress in Education
A329

Designs: 1c, Makarenko School, Playa de Tarara. 2c, Natl. Literacy Campaign Museum. 3c, Lantern, literacy campaign emblem for 1961. 10c, Frank Pais education team in the mountains. 13c, Farmer, factory worker.

1966, June 15

1118 A329 1c grn & blk
1119 A329 2c yel, olive bister & blk
1120 A329 3c brt blue, lt blue & blk
1121 A329 10c golden brn, brn & blk
1122 A329 13c multi

1st Graduating class of Makarenko School (1c), 5th anniv. of the Natl. Literacy Campaign (3c), 4th anniv. of agricultural and industrial trade education (13c).

12th Congress of the Cuban Labor Organization — A330

1966, Aug. 12

1123 A330 3c multi

Sea Shells — A331

1966, Aug. 25 **Unwmk.**

1124 A331 1c Liguus flammellus
1125 A331 2c Cypraea zebra
1126 A331 3c Strombus pugilis
1127 A331 7c Aequipecten muscosu
1128 A331 9c Liguus fasciatus crenatus
1129 A331 10c Charonia variegata
1130 A331 13c Liguus fasciatus archeri

Breeding Messenger Pigeons — A332

1966, Sept. 18 **Wmk. 376**

1131 A332 1c shown
1132 A332 2c Timer
1133 A332 3c Coops
1134 A332 7c Breeder tending coops
1135 A332 9c Pigeons in yard
1136 A332 10c Two men, message

Size: 47x32mm

1137 A332 13c Baracoa to Havana championship flight, July 26, 1959

Provincial and Natl. Coats of Arms, Map of Cuba — A333

17th World Chess Olympiad, Havana — A334

1966, Oct. 10

1138 A333 1c Pinar del Rio
1139 A333 2c Havana
1140 A333 3c Matanzas
1141 A333 4c Las Villas
1142 A333 5c Camaguey
1143 A333 9c Oriente

Size: 30x48mm

1144 A333 13c National arms

1966, Oct. 18

1145 A334 1c Pawn
1146 A334 2c Rook
1147 A334 3c Knight
1148 A334 9c Bishop
1149 A334 10c Queen, games, horiz.
1150 A334 13c King and emblem, horiz.

Souvenir Sheet

Imperf

1151 A334 30c Capablanca Vs. Lasker, 1914, horiz.

No. 1151 contains one 49½x31mm stamp.

Cuban-Soviet Diplomatic Relations — A335

1966, Nov. 7

1152 A335 2c Lenin Hospital
1153 A335 3c Oil tanker, world map
1154 A335 10c Workers, gearwheels
1155 A335 13c Agriculture

2nd Song Festival
A336

Cuban composers and their compositions.

1966, Nov. 18

1156 A336 1c Amadeo Roldan
1157 A336 2c Eduardo Sanchez de Fuentes
1158 A336 3c Moises Simons
1159 A336 7c Jorge Anckermann
1160 A336 9c Alejandro G. Caturla
1161 A336 10c Eliseo Grenet
1162 A336 13c Ernesto Lecuona

Viet Nam War — A337

Flag of Viet Nam and: 2c, US aircraft discharging bombs, dead cattle. 3c, Gas mask and victims. 13c, US bombs, women and children.

1966, Nov. 23

1163 A337 2c multi
1164 A337 3c multi
1165 A337 13c multi

10th Anniv. of Successful Revolution Campaigns — A338

Revolution leaders, scenes of the insurrection.

1966, Nov. 30

1166 A338 1c Antonio Fernandez
1167 A338 2c Candido Gonzalez
1168 A338 3c Jose Tey
1169 A338 7c Tony Aloma
1170 A338 9c Otto Paralleda
1171 A338 10c Juan Manuel Marquez
1172 A338 13c Frank Pais

Intl. Leisure Time and Recreation Seminar — A339

1966, Dec. 2

1173 A339 3c shown
1174 A339 9c World map, stopwatch, eye
1175 A339 13c Earth, clock, emblem

1st Natl. Telecommunications Forum — A340

1966, Dec. 12

1176 A340 3c shown
1177 A340 10c Satellite in orbit
1178 A340 13c Shell, satellite
a. Souv. sheet of 3, #1176-1178, imperf,

No. 1178a sold for 30c.

Christmas Type of 1961

1966, Dec. 20 **Unwmk.**

1179 A248 1c Cypripedium eurylochus
1180 A249 1c Cattleya speciosissima
1181 A249 1c Cattleya mendelii majestica
1182 A249 1c Cattleya trianae amesiana
1183 A249 1c Cattleya labiata macfarlanei
a. Block of 5 + label, #1179-1183
1184 A248 3c Cypripedium morganiae burfordense
1185 A249 3c Cattleya Countess of Derby
1186 A249 3c Cypripedium hookerae volunteanum
1187 A249 3c Cattleya warscewiczii reginae burfordense
1188 A249 3c Cypripedium stonei cannartae
a. Block of 5 + label, #1184-1188
1189 A248 13c Cattleya mendelii Duchess of Montrose
1190 A249 13c Oncidium macranthum
1191 A249 13c Cypripedium stonei platytoenium
1192 A249 13c Cattleya dowiana aurea
1193 A249 13c Laelia anceps
a. Block of 5 + label, #1189-1193

Christmas 1966. See note after No. 700.

8th Anniv. of the Revolution — A341

1967, Jan. 2

1194 A341 3c Liberation, 1959
1195 A341 3c Agrarian Reform, 1960
1196 A341 3c Education, 1961
1197 A341 3c Agriculture, 1965
a. Strip of 4, Nos. 1194-1197
1198 A341 13c Rodin's Thinker, Planning, 1962
1199 A341 13c Organization, 1963
1200 A341 13c Economy, 1964
1201 A341 13c Solidarity, 1966
a. Strip of 4, Nos. 1198-1201

Nos. 1198-1201 vert.

Spring, by Jorge Arche — A342

Paintings in the Natl. Museum: 1c, Coffee Machine, by Angel Acosta Leon, vert. 2c, Country People, by Eduardo Abela, vert. 13c, Still-life, by Amelia Pelaez, vert. 30c, Landscape, by Gonzalo Escalante.

1967, Feb. 27

1202 A342 1c multi
1203 A342 2c multi
1204 A342 3c multi
1205 A342 13c multi
1206 A342 30c multi

Natl. Events, Mar. 13, 1957
A343

1967, Mar. 13 **Wmk. 376**

1207 A343 3c Attack on Presidential Palace

Size: 41x28mm

1208 A343 13c Landing of Corynthia
1209 A343 30c Cienfuegos revolt

Evolution of Man — A344

Prehistoric men: 2c, Australopithecus. 3c, Pithecanthropus erectus. 4c, Sinanthropus pekinensis. 5c, Neanderthal man. 13c, Cro-magnon man carving tusk. 20c, Cro-magnon man painting petroglyph.

1967, Mar. 31 **Unwmk.**

1210 A344 1c multi
1211 A344 2c multi
1212 A344 3c multi
1213 A344 4c multi
1214 A344 5c multi
1215 A344 13c multi
1216 A344 20c multi

Stamp Day A345

Carriages.

1967, Apr. 24

1217 A345 3c Victoria
1218 A345 9c Volante
1219 A345 13c Quitrin

EXPO '67, Montreal, Apr. 28-Oct. 27 — A346

1967, Apr. 28

1220 A346 1c Cuban pavilion
1221 A346 2c Space exploration
1222 A346 3c Petroglyph, hieroglyph
1223 A346 13c Agriculture, computer technology
1224 A346 20c Athletes

Botanical Gardens, Sequicentennial A347

Flowering plants.

1967, May 30

1225 A347 1c Eugenia malaccencis
1226 A347 2c Jacaranda filicifolia
1227 A347 3c Coroupita guianensis
1228 A347 4c Spathodea campanulata
1229 A347 5c Cassia fistula
1230 A347 13c Plumieria alba
1231 A347 20c Erythrina poeppigiana

Natl. Ballet — A348

1967, June 15

1232 A348 1c Giselle
1233 A348 2c Swan Lake
1234 A348 3c Don Quixote
1235 A348 4c Calaucan
1236 A348 13c Swan Lake
1237 A348 20c Nutcracker

Intl. Ballet Festival, Havana.

5th Pan American Games, Winnipeg, Canada, July 22-Aug. 7 — A349

1st Conference of Latin American Solidarity Organization (OLAS) — A350

1967, July 22

1238 A349 1c Baseball, horiz.
1239 A349 2c Swimming, horiz.
1240 A349 3c Basketball
1241 A349 4c Gymnastic rings
1242 A349 5c Water polo
1243 A349 13c Weight lifting, horiz.
1244 A349 20c Javelin

1967, July 28 **Wmk. 376**

Portrait of representative, map of South American homeland: No. 1245, Camilo Torres, Colombia. No. 1246, Luis de la Puente Uceda, Peru. No. 1247, Luis A. Turcios Lima, Guatemala. No. 1248, Fabricio Ojeda, Venezuela.

1245 A350 13c pale grn, blk & red
1246 A350 13c lil, blk & red
1247 A350 13c dark chalky blue, blk & red
1248 A350 13c golden brn, blk & red

Portrait of Sonny Rollins, by Alan Davie — A351

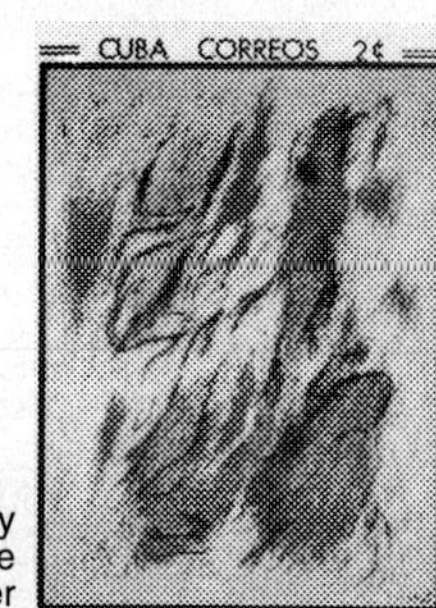

Bathers, by Gustave Singier A352

Modern Art: No. 1250, Twelve Selenities, by Felix Labisse. No. 1251, Night of the Drinker, by Friedensreich Hundertwasser. No. 1252, Figure, by Mariano. No. 1253, All-Souls, by Wilfredo Lam. No. 1254, Darkness and Cracks, by Antonio Tapies. No. 1256, Torso of a Muse, by Jean Arp. No. 1257, Figure, by M.W. Svanberg. No. 1258, Oppenheimer's Information, by Erro. No. 1259, Where Cardinals Are Born, by Max Ernst. No. 1260, Havana Landscape, by Portocarrero. No. 1261, EG 12, by Victor Vasarely. No. 1262, Frisco, by Alexander Calder. No. 1263, The Man with the Pipe, by Picasso. No. 1264, Abstract Composition, by Sergei Poliakoff. No. 1265, Painting, by Bram van Velde. No. 1266, Sower of Fires, by R. Matta. No. 1267, The Art of Living, by Rene Magritte. No. 1268, Poem, by Joan Miro. No. 1269, Young Tigers, by Jean Messagier. No. 1270, Painting, by M. Vieira da Silva. No. 1271, Live Cobra, by Pierre Alechinsky. No. 1272, Stalingrad, by Asger Jorn. 30c, Warriors, by Edouard Pignon. 50c, Cloister, a mural at the exhibition representing the Salon de Mayo pictures.

1967, July 29 **Unwmk.**

1249 A351 1c shown
1250 A351 1c multi
1251 A351 1c multi
1252 A351 1c multi
1253 A351 1c multi
a. Strip of 5, Nos. 1249-1253

Sizes: 36½x54mm, 36½x53mm, 36½x45mm, 36½x41mm

1254 A352 2c multi
1255 A352 2c shown
1256 A352 2c multi
1257 A352 2c multi
1258 A352 2c multi
a. Strip of 5, Nos. 1254-1258

Sizes: 36½x54mm, 36½x40mm, 36½x42mm, 36½x49mm

1259 A352 3c multi
1260 A352 3c multi
1261 A352 3c multi
1262 A352 3c multi
1263 A352 3c multi
a. Strip of 5, Nos. 1259-1263

Sizes: 35x15mm, 35x67mm, 35x46½mm, 35x55mm

1264 A352 4c multi
1265 A352 4c multi
1266 A352 4c multi
1267 A352 4c multi
1268 A352 4c multi
a. Strip of 5, Nos. 1264-1268

Sizes: 49x32mm, 49x35mm, 49x46mm

1269 A351 13c multi
1270 A351 13c multi
1271 A351 13c multi
1272 A351 13c multi
a. Strip of 4, Nos. 1269-1272

Size: 54x32mm

1273 A351 30c multi

Souvenir Sheet

Imperf

1274 A351 50c multi

Salon de Mayo Art Exhibition, Havana. No. 1274 contains one 88x45mm stamp with simulated perforations. Issued Oct. 7.

World Underwater Fishing Championships — A353

1967, Sept. 5

1275 A353 1c Green moray
1276 A353 2c Octopus
1277 A353 3c Great barracuda
1278 A353 4c Blue shark
1279 A353 5c Spotted jewfish
1280 A353 13c Sting ray
1281 A353 20c Green turtle

Soviet Space Program A354

1967, Oct. 4 **Wmk. 376**

1282 A354 1c Sputnik 1
1283 A354 2c Lunik 3
1284 A354 3c Venusik
1285 A354 4c Cosmos
1286 A354 5c Mars 1
1287 A354 9c Electron 1 & 2
1288 A354 10c Luna 9
1289 A354 13c Luna 10
a. Souv. sheet of 8, #1282-1289, imperf.

Stamps in #1289a have simulated perfs.

50th Anniv. of the October Revolution, Russia A355

Paintings: 1c, Storming the Winter Palace, by Sokolov, Skalia and Miasnikov. 2c, Lenin Addressing Congress, by W.A. Serov. 3c, Lenin, by H.D. Nalbandian. 4c, Lenin Explaining Electrification Map, by L.A. Schmatko. 5c, Dawn of the Five-Year Plan, by J.D. Romas. 13c, Kusnetzkroi Steel Furnace No. 1, by P. Kotov. 30c, Victory, by A. Krivonogov.

1967, Nov. 7 **Unwmk.**

1290 A355 1c 64x36mm
1291 A355 2c 48x36mm
1292 A355 3c
1293 A355 4c 48x36mm
1294 A355 5c 50x36mm
1295 A355 13c 36x50mm
1296 A355 30c 50x36mm

Castle of the Royal Forces, Havana — A356

Historic architecture: 2c, Iznaga Tower, Trinidad, vert. 3c, Castle of Our Lady of the Angels, Cienfuegos. 4c, St. Francis de Paula Church, Havana. 13c, St. Francis Convent, Havana. 30c, Castle del Morro, Santiago de Cuba.

1967, Nov. 7 **Wmk. 376**

Sizes: 26x47mm (1c), 41x29mm (3c, 4c), 38½x31mm (13c)

1297 A356 1c multi
1298 A356 2c multi
1299 A356 3c multi
1300 A356 4c multi
1301 A356 13c multi
1302 A356 30c multi

Christmas Type of 1961

Birds.

1967, Dec. 20

1303 A248 1c Struthia camelus australis
1304 A249 1c Chysolophus pictus
1305 A249 1c Ciconia ciconia ciconia
1306 A249 1c Balearica pavonina

1307 A249 1c Dromiceius novaehollandiae
a. Block of 5 + label, Nos. 1303-1307
1308 A248 3c Anodorhynchus hyacinthus
1309 A249 3c Psittacus erithacus
1310 A249 3c Domicella garrula
1311 A249 3c Ramphastos sulfuratus
1312 A249 3c Kakatoe galerita galerita
a. Block of 5 + label, Nos. 1308-1312
1313 A248 13c Phoenicopterus ruber
1314 A249 13c Pelecanus erythrorhynchos
1315 A249 13c Alopochen aegyptiacus
1316 A249 13c Dendronessa galericulata
1317 A249 13c Chenopsis atrata
a. Block of 5 + label, Nos. 1313-1317

Christmas 1967. See note after No. 700.

Ernesto "Che" Guevara (1928-1967), Revolution Leader — A356a

1968, Jan. 3
1318 A356a 13c blk, dark red & buff

Cultural Congress, Havana — A357

Abstract designs: No. 1319, Independence fostering culture. No. 1320, Integral formation of man. No. 1321, Responsibility of intellectuals. No. 1322, Relationship between culture and the mass media. No. 1323, The arts versus science and technology.

1968, Jan. 4
1319 A357 3c multi, vert.
1320 A357 3c multi, vert.
1321 A357 13c multi, vert.
1322 A357 13c multi, vert.
1323 A357 30c multi

Canaries and Breeding Cycles A358

1968, Apr. 13
1324 A358 1c F.C.C. 4016
1325 A358 2c A.C.C. 774
1326 A358 3c A.C.C. 122
1327 A358 4c F.C.C. 4477
1328 A358 5c A.C.C 117
1329 A358 13c A.N.R. 1175
1330 A358 20c A.C.C. 777

Stamp Day A359

Paintings: 13c, The Village Postman, by J. Harris. 30c, The Philatelist, by G. Sciltian.

1968, Apr. 24 **Unwmk.**
1331 A359 13c multi
1332 A359 30c multi

World Health Organization, 20th Anniv. — A360

1968, May 10 **Wmk. 376**
1333 A360 13c Nurse, mother, child
1334 A360 30c Surgeons

Intl. Children's Day — A361

1968, June 1
1335 A361 3c multi

Seville Camaguey Flight, 35th Anniv. — A362

1968, June 20
1336 A362 13c Plane Four Winds
1337 A362 30c Capt. Barberan, Lt. Collar, pilots

Natl. Food Production — A363

1968, June 29
1338 A363 1c Yellow tuna, can
1339 A363 2c Cow, dairy products
1340 A363 3c Rooster, eggs
1341 A363 13c Rum, sugar cane
1342 A363 20c Crayfish, box

Attack of Moncada Barracks, 15th Anniv. A364

1968, July 26
Size: 43x29mm (13c)
1343 A364 3c Siboney farmhouse
1344 A364 13c Assault route, Santiago de Cuba
1345 A364 30c Students, school

Committee for the Defense of the Revolution, 8th Anniv. — A365

1968, Sept. 28
1346 A365 3c multi

Guerilla Day A366

Che Guevara and: 1c, Rifleman and "En Cualquier Lugar..." 3c, Machine gunners and "Crear tres muchos Viet Nam." 9c, Silhouette of battalion and "Este Tipo De Lucha..." 10c, Guerillas cheering and "Hoy aquilatamos..." 13c, Map of Caribbean, So. America and "Hasta La Victoria Siempre."

1968, Oct. 8
1347 A366 1c gold, brt blue grn & blk
1348 A366 3c gold, org brn blk
1349 A366 9c multi
1350 A366 10c gold, lt olive grn & blk
1351 A366 13c gold, red org & blk

Cuban War of Independence, Cent. — A367

Independence fighters and scenes.

1968, Oct. 10 **Unwmk.**
1352 A367 1c C.M. de Cespedes, broken wheel
1353 A367 1c E. Betances, horsemen, flag
1354 A367 1c I. Agramonte, Clavellinas Monument
1355 A367 1c A. Maceo, Baragua Protest
1356 A367 1c J. Marti, horsemen
a. Strip of 5, Nos. 1352-1356
1357 A367 3c M. Gomez, The Invasion
1358 A367 3c J.A. Mella, declaration
1359 A367 3c A. Guiteras, El Morrillo monument
1360 A367 3c A. Santamaria, attack on Moncada Barracks
1361 A367 3c F. Paiz memorial
a. Strip of 5, Nos. 1357-1361
1362 A367 9c J. Echeverria, student protest
1363 A367 13c C. Cienfuegos, insurrection
1364 A367 30c Che Guevara, 1st Declaration of Havana

Souvenir Sheet

The Burning of Bayamo, by J.E. Hernandez Giro — A368

1968, Oct. 18 ***Imperf.***
1365 A368 50c multi

Natl. Philatelic Exhibition, independence cent. Stamp in No. 1365 has simulated perforations.

19th Summer Olympics, Mexico City, Oct. 12-27 — A369

1968, Oct. 21 ***Perf. 12½***
1366 A369 1c Parade of athletes
1367 A369 2c Women's basketball, vert.
1368 A369 3c Hammer throw, vert.
1369 A369 4c Boxing
1370 A369 5c Water polo
1371 A369 13c Pistol shooting

Size: 32x50mm
1372 A369 30c Mexican flag, calendar stone

Souvenir Sheet
Imperf
1373 A369 50c Running

Stamp in #173 has simulated perforations.

Civilian Activities of the Armed Forces A370

1968, Dec. 2 **Wmk. 376** ***Perf. 12½***
1374 A370 3c Crop dusting
1375 A370 9c Che Guevara's Brigade
1376 A370 10c Road building
1377 A370 13c Plowing, harvesting

San Alejandro School of Painting, Sesquicentennial — A371

Paintings: 1c, Manrique de Lara's Family, by Jean Baptiste Vermay, vert. 2c, Seascape, by Leopoldo Romanach. 3c, Wild Cane, by Antonio Rodriguez, vert. 4c, Self-portrait, by Miguel Melero, vert. 5c, The Lottery List, by Jose Joaquin Tejada. 13c, Portrait of Nina, by Armando B. Menocal, vert. 30c, Landscape, by Esteban B. Chartrand. 50c, Siesta, by Guillermo Collazo.

1968, Dec. 30 **Unwmk.**
Sizes: 38x48mm (1c, 3c), 39x50mm (4c, 13c), 53x36mm (30c)
1378 A371 1c multi
1379 A371 2c multi
1380 A371 3c multi
1381 A371 4c multi
1382 A371 5c multi
1383 A371 13c multi
1384 A371 30c multi

Souvenir Sheet

Imperf

1385 A371 50c multi

No. 1385 contains one 52x41½mm stamp that has simulated perforations.

10th Anniv. of the Revolution A372

1969, Jan. 3 Wmk. 376 *Perf. 12½*

1386 A372 13c multi

Villaclarenos Rebellion, Cent. — A373

1969, Feb. 6

1387 A373 3c Gutierrez and Sanchez

Women's Day — A374

Design: Mariana Grajales, rose and statue.

1969, Mar. 8

1388 A374 3c multi

Cuban Pioneers and Young Communists Unions — A375

1969, Apr. 4

1389 A375 3c Pioneers
1390 A375 13c Young Communists

Guaimaro Assembly, Cent. — A376

1969, Apr. 10

1391 A376 3c dark brn

The Postman, by Jean C. Cazin A377

Paintings: 30c, Portrait of a Young Man, by George Romney.

1969, Apr. 24 Unwmk.

1392 A377 13c multi

Size: 35½x43½mm

1393 A377 30c multi

Stamp Day.

Agrarian Reform, 10th Anniv. A378

1969, May 17 Wmk. 376

1394 A378 13c multi

Marine Life A379

1969, May 20 Unwmk.

1395 A379 1c Petrochirus bahamensis
1396 A379 2c Stenopus hispidus
1397 A379 3c Panulirus argus
1398 A379 4c Callinectes sapidus
1399 A379 5c Gecarcinus ruricola
1400 A379 13c Macrobrachium carcinus
1401 A379 30c Carpilius coralinus

Intl. Labor Organization, 50th Anniv. — A380

1969, June 6 Wmk. 376

1402 A380 3c shown
1403 A380 13c Blacksmith breaking chains

Paintings in the Natl. Museum — A381

Designs: 1c, Flowers, by Raul Milian, vert. 2c, Annunciation, by Antonia Eiriz. 3c, Factory, by Marcelo Pogolotti, vert. 4c, Territorial Waters, by Luis Martinez Pedro, vert. 5c, Miss Sarah Gale, by John Hoppner, vert. 13c, Two Women Wearing Mantilla, by Ignacio Zuloaga. 30c, Virgin and Child, by Francisco de Zurburan.

1969, June 15 Unwmk.

1404 A381 1c 39x59mm
1405 A381 2c
1406 A381 3c 39½x49mm
1407 A381 4c 39½x43mm
1408 A381 5c 39½x45½mm
1409 A381 13c 38x41½mm
1410 A381 30c 39x45mm

Broadcasting Institute — A382

1969, July 5 Wmk. 376

1411 A382 3c shown
1412 A382 13c Hemispheres, tower
1413 A382 1p Waves on graph

Fish A383

1969, July 20 Unwmk.

1414 A383 1c Apogon maculatus
1415 A383 2c Bodianus rufus
1416 A383 3c Microspathodon chrysurus
1417 A383 4c Gramma loreto
1418 A383 5c Chromis marginatus
1419 A383 13c Myripristis jacobus
1420 A383 30c Nomeus gronovii, vert.

Natl. Film Industry, 10th Anniv. — A384

1969, Aug. 5 Wmk. 376

1421 A384 1c Poster
1422 A384 3c Documentaries
1423 A384 13c Cartoons
1424 A384 30c Entertainers

Napoleon in Milan, by Andrea Appiani — A385

Paintings in the Napoleon Museum, Havana: 2c, Hortensia de Beauharnais, by Francois Gerard. 3c, Napoleon as First Consul, by J.B. Regnault. 4c, Elisa Bonaparte, by Robert Lefevre. 5c, Napoleon Planning Coronation Ceremony, by J.G. Vibert, horiz. 13c, Napoleon as Cuirassier Corporal, by Jean Meissonier. 30c, Napoleon Bonaparte, by LeFevre.

1969, Aug. 20 Unwmk.

1425 A385 1c
1426 A385 2c 41½x55mm
1427 A385 3c 45½x56mm
1428 A385 4c 43x62½mm
1429 A385 5c 63x47½mm
1430 A385 13c 43x62½mm
1431 A385 30c 45x59½mm

See Nos. 2448-2453.

Cuba's Victory at the 17th World Amateur Baseball Championships, Santo Domingo — A386

1969, Sept. 11

1432 A386 13c multi

No. 1432 printed se-tenant with inscribed label listing finalists.

Alexander von Humboldt (1769-1859), German Naturalist — A387

1969, Sept. 14

1433 A387 3c Surinam eel
1434 A387 13c Night ape
1435 A387 30c Condors

World Fencing Championships, Havana — A388

Designs: 1c, Ancient Egyptians in combat. 2c, Roman gladiators. 2c, Viking and Norman. 4c, Medieval tournament. 5c, French musketeers. 13c, Japanese samurai. 30c, Mounted Cubans, War of Independence. 50c, Modern fencers.

1969, Oct. 2

1436 A388 1c multi
1437 A388 2c multi
1438 A388 3c multi
1439 A388 4c multi
1440 A388 5c multi
1441 A388 13c multi
1442 A388 30c multi

Souvenir Sheet

Imperf

1443 A388 50c multi

Stamp in No. 1443 has simulated perforations.

Natl. Revolutionary Militia, 10th Anniv. — A389

1969, Oct. 26 Wmk. 376

1444 A389 3c multi

Disappearance of Maj. Camilo Cienfuegos, 10th Anniv. — A390

1969, Oct. 28
1445 A390 13c multi

Agriculture — A391

1969, Nov. 2 **Unwmk.**
1446 A391 1c Strawberries, grapes
1447 A391 1c Onions, asparagus
1448 A391 1c Rice
1449 A391 1c Banana
a. Strip of 4, #1446-1449
1450 A391 3c Pineapple, vert.
1451 A391 3c Tobacco, vert.
1452 A391 3c Citrus fruits, vert.
1453 A391 3c Coffee, vert.
1454 A391 3c Rabbits, vert.
a. Strip of 5, #1450-1454
1455 A391 10c Pigs, vert.
1456 A391 13c Sugar cane
1457 A391 30c Bull

Sporting Events — A392

1969, Nov. 15
1458 A392 1c 2nd Natl. Games
1459 A392 2c 11th Anniv. Games
1460 A392 3c Barrientos Commemorative, vert.
1461 A392 10c 2nd Olympic Trials, vert.
1462 A392 13c 6th Socialist Bicycle Race, vert.
1463 A392 30c 6th Capablanca Memorial Chess Championships, vert.

Christmas Type of 1961

Flowering plants.

1969, Dec. 1
1464 A248 1c Plumbago capensis
1465 A249 1c Petrea volubilis
1466 A249 1c Clitoria ternatea
1467 A249 1c Duranta repens
1468 A249 1c Ruellia tuberosa
a. Block of 5 + label, Nos. 1464-1468
1469 A248 3c Turnera ulmifolia
1470 A249 3c Thevetia peruviana
1471 A249 3c Hibiscus elatus
1472 A249 3c Allamanda cathartica
1473 A249 3c Cosmos sulphureus
a. Block of 5 + label, Nos. 1469-1473
1474 A248 13c Delonix regia
1475 A249 13c Neriun oleander
1476 A249 13c Cordia sebestena
1477 A249 13c Lochnera rosea
1478 A249 13c Jatropha integerrima
a. Block of 5 + label, Nos. 1474-1478

Christmas 1969. See note after No. 700.

Zapata Swamp Fauna — A393

1969, Dec. 15
1479 A393 1c Trelanorhynus variabilis
1480 A393 2c Hyla insulsa
1481 A393 3c Atractosteus tristoechus
1482 A393 4c Capromys nana
1483 A393 5c Crocodylus rhombifer
1484 A393 13c Amazona leucocephala
1485 A393 30c Agelaius phoeniceus assimilis

Nos. 1482, 1484-1485 vert.

Tourism A394

1970, Jan. 25 **Wmk. 376**
1486 A394 1c Jibacoa Beach
1487 A394 3c Trinidad City
1488 A394 13c Santiago de Cuba
1489 A394 30c Vinales Valley

Medicinal Plants — A395

1970, Feb. 10 **Unwmk.**
1490 A395 1c Guarea guara
1491 A395 3c Ocimum sanctum
1492 A395 10c Canella winterana
1493 A395 13c Bidens pilosa
1494 A395 30c Turnera ulmifolia
1495 A395 50c Picramnia pentandra

11th Central American and Caribbean Games, Panama, Feb. 28-Mar. 14 — A396

1970, Feb. 28 **Wmk. 376**
1496 A396 1c Weight lifting
1497 A396 3c Boxing
1498 A396 10c Gymnastics
1499 A396 13c Running
1500 A396 30c Fencing

Souvenir Sheet

Imperf

1501 A396 50c Baseball

No. 1501 contains one 50x37mm stamp that has simulated perforations.

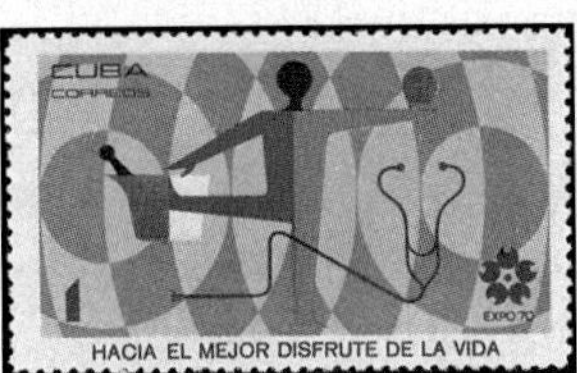

EXPO '70, Osaka, Japan, Mar. 15-Sept. 13 — A397

1970, Mar. 15
1502 A397 1c Enjoying life
1503 A397 2c Improving on nature, vert.
1504 A397 3c Better living standard
1505 A397 13c Intl. cooperation, vert.
1506 A397 30c Cuban pavilion

Speleological Soc., 30th Anniv. — A398

Petroglyphs in Cuban caves: 1c, Ambrosio Cave, Varadero Matanzas. 2c, Cave No. 1, Punta del Este, Isle of Pines. 3c, Pichardo Cave, Cubitas Camaguey Mountains. 4c, Ambrosio Cave, diff. 5c, Cave No. 1, diff. 13c, Garcia Ribiou Cave, Havana. 30c, Cave No. 2, Punta del Este.

1970, Mar. 28 **Unwmk.**

Sizes: 29x45mm (1c, 3c, 4c, 13c)

1507 A398 1c multi
1508 A398 2c shown
1509 A398 3c multi
1510 A398 4c multi
1511 A398 5c multi
1512 A398 13c multi
1513 A398 30c multi

Aviation Pioneers — A399

1970, Apr. 10
1514 A399 3c Jose D. Blino
1515 A399 13c Adolfo Teodore

Lenin Birth Centenary — A400

Paintings and quotes: 1c, Lenin in Kazan, by O. Vishniakov. 2c, Young Lenin, by V. Prager. 3c, Second Socialist Party Congress, by Y. Vinagradov. 4c, First Manifesto, by F. Golubkov. 5c, First Day of Soviet Power, by N. Babasiuk. 13c, Lenin in Smolny, by M. Sokolov. 30c, Autumn in Gorky, by A. Varlamov. 50c, Lenin at Gorky, by N. Bashkakov.

1970, Apr. 22

Sizes: 67½x46mm (1c, 4c, 5c)

1516 A400 1c multi
1517 A400 2c shown
1518 A400 3c multi
1519 A400 4c multi
1520 A400 5c multi
1521 A400 13c multi
1522 A400 30c multi

Souvenir Sheet

Imperf

1523 A400 50c multi

No. 1523 contains one 48x46mm stamp that has simulated perforations.

Stamp Day — A401

1970, Apr. 24
1524 A401 13c The Letter, by J. Arche

Size: 30x44mm

1525 A401 30c Portrait of A Cadet, Anonymous

Da Vinci's Anatomical Drawing, Earth, Moon — A402

1970, May 17 **Wmk. 376**
1526 A402 30c multi

World Telecommunications Day.

Ho Chi Minh (1890-1969), President of North Viet Nam — A403

1970, May 19 **Unwmk.**
1527 A403 1c Vietnamese fisherman

Size: 32x44mm

1528 A403 3c Two women
1529 A403 3c Plowing field

Size: 33x45mm

1530 A403 3c Teacher, students in air-raid shelter
1531 A403 3c Nine women in paddy

Size: 34x41½mm

1532 A403 3c Camouflaged machine shop

Size: 34x39mm

1533 A403 13c shown

Cuban Cigar Industry A404

1970, July 5
1534 A404 3c Plantation, Eden cigar band
1535 A404 13c Factory, El Mambi band
1536 A404 30c Packing cigars, Lopez Hermanos band

Projected Sugar Production: Over 10 Million Tons — A405

1970, July 26

1537 A405 1c Cane-crushing
1538 A405 2c Sowing and crop dusting
1539 A405 3c Cutting sugar cane
1540 A405 10c Transporting cane
1541 A405 13c Modern cutting machine
1542 A405 30c Intl. Brigade, cane cutters, vert.
1543 A405 1p Sugar warehouse

Pedro Figueredo (d. 1870), Composer — A406

Versions of the Natl. Anthem.

1970, Aug. 17

1544 A406 3c 1868 Version
1545 A406 20c 1898 Version

Women's Federation, 10th Anniv. — A407

1970, Aug. 23

1546 A407 3c multi

Militia, by Servando C. Moreno — A408

Paintings in the Natl. Museum: 2c, Washerwomen, by Aristides Fernandez. 3c, Puerta del Sol, Madrid, by L. Paret Y Alcazar. 4c, Fishermen's Wives, by Joaquin Sorolla. 5c, Portrait of a Woman, by Thomas de Keyser. 13c, Mrs. Edward Foster, by Sir Thomas Lawrence. 30c, Tropical Gypsy, by Victor M. Garcia.

1970, Aug. 31

1547 A408 1c shown

Size: 45x41mm

1548 A408 2c multi
1549 A408 3c multi

Size: 40x41mm

1550 A408 4c multi

Size: 38x45½mm

1551 A408 5c multi
1552 A408 13c multi
1553 A408 30c multi

See #1640-1646, 1669-1675, 1773-1779.

Havana Declaration, 10th Anniv. — A409

1970, Sept. 2

1554 A409 3c Jose Marti Square

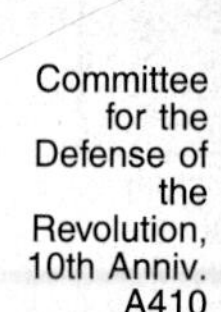

Committee for the Defense of the Revolution, 10th Anniv. A410

1970, Sept. 28

1555 A410 3c multi

39th Sugar Technician's Assoc. (ATAC) Conference — A411

1970, Oct. 11

1556 A411 30c multi

Wildlife — A412

1970, Oct. 20

1557 A412 1c Numida meleagris galeata
1558 A412 2c Dendrocygna arborea
1559 A412 3c Phasianus colchicus torquatus
1560 A412 4c Zenaida macroura macroura
1561 A412 5c Colinus virginianus cubanensis
1562 A412 13c Sus scrofa
1563 A412 30c Odocoileus virginianus

Black-magic Feast, by M. Puente — A413

Afro-Cuban folk paintings: 3c, Hat Dance, by V.P. Landaluze. 10c, Los Hoyos Conga Dance, by Domingo Ravenet. 13c, Climax of the Rumba, by Eduardo Abela.

1970, Nov. 5

Sizes: 36x48½mm (3c, 13c), 44½x44mm (10c)

1564 A413 1c shown
1565 A413 3c multi
1566 A413 10c multi
1567 A413 13c multi

Road Safety Week A414

1970, Nov. 15

1568 A414 3c Zebra, road signs
1569 A414 9c Prudence the Bear

Intl. Education Year — A415

1970, Nov. 20

1570 A415 13c Abacus, "a"
1571 A415 30c Cow, microscope

Christmas Type of 1961

Birds.

1970, Dec. 1

1572 A248 1c Dives atroviolaceus
1573 A249 1c Glaucidium siju siju
1574 A249 1c Todus multicolor
1575 A249 1c Xiphidiopicus percussus percussus
1576 A249 1c Ferminia cerverai
a. Block of 5 + label, Nos. 1572-1576
1577 A248 3c Teretistris fornsi
1578 A249 3c Myadestes elisabeth elisabeth
1579 A249 3c Polioptila lembeyei
1580 A249 3c Vireo gundlachii gundlachii
1581 A249 3c Teretistris fernandinae
a. Block of 5 + label, Nos. 1577-1581
1582 A248 13c Torreornis inexpectata inexpectata
1583 A249 13c Chondrohierax wilsonii
1584 A249 13c Accipiter gundlachi
1585 A249 13c Starnoenas cyanocephala
1586 A249 13c Aratinga euops
a. Block of 5 + label, Nos. 1582-1586

Christmas 1970. See note after No. 700.

Camilo Cienfuegos Military Academy — A416

1970, Dec. 2

1587 A416 3c multi

7th Congress of the Intl. Organization of Journalists — A417

1971, Jan. 4

1588 A417 13c multi

World Meteorology Day — A418

1971, Feb. 16

Size: 39½x35½mm (3c)

1589 A418 1c Class, weather chart, computer, vert.
1590 A418 3c Weather map
1591 A418 8c Equipment, vert.
1592 A418 30c shown

6th Pan American Games, Cali, Colombia — A419

1971, Feb. 20

1593 A419 1c Emblem, vert.
1594 A419 2c Women's running, vert.
1595 A419 3c Rifle shooting
1596 A419 4c Gymnastics, vert.
1597 A419 5c Boxing, vert.
1598 A419 13c Water polo
1599 A419 30c Baseball

Porcelain and Mosaics in the Metropolitan Museum, Havana — A420

Designs: 1c, Parisian vase, 19th cent. 3c, Mexican bowl, 17th cent. 10c, Parisian vase, diff. 13c, Colosseum, Italian mosaic, 19th cent. 20c, Mexican bowl, 17th cent. 30c, St. Peter's Square, Italian mosaic, 19th cent.

1971, Mar. 11

Sizes: 34½x53mm (1c, 10c), 46x53mm (3c), 42x48mm (20c)

1600 A420 1c multi
1601 A420 3c multi
1602 A420 10c multi
1603 A420 13c shown
1604 A420 20c multi
1605 A420 30c multi

See Nos. 1699-1705.

Natl. Child Centers, 10th Anniv. — A421

1971, Apr. 10

1606 A421 3c multi

Manned Space Flight 10th Anniv. — A422

Cosmonauts in training.

1971, Apr. 12

1607 A422 1c multi
1608 A422 2c multi, diff.
1609 A422 3c multi, diff.
1610 A422 4c multi, diff.
1611 A422 5c multi, diff.

1612 A422 13c multi, diff.
1613 A422 30c multi, diff.

Souvenir Sheet

Imperf

1614 A422 50c multi

Stamp in #1614 has simulated perf.

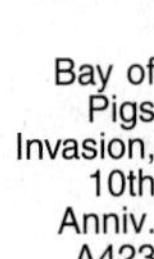

Bay of Pigs Invasion, 10th Anniv. A423

1971, Apr. 17
1615 A423 13c multi

Stamp Day — A424

Packets: 13c, Jeune Richard attacking the Windsor Castle, 1807. 30c, Orinoco.

1971, Apr. 24
1616 A424 13c multi
1617 A424 30c multi

Cuban Intl. Broadcast Service, 10th Anniv. — A425

1971, May 1 **Wmk. 376**
1618 A425 3c multi
1619 A425 50c multi

Orchids A426

1971, May 15
1620 A426 1c Cattleya skinnerii
1621 A426 2c Vanda hibrida
1622 A426 3c Cypripedium collossum
1623 A426 4c Cypripedium gloucophyllum
1624 A426 5c Vanda tricolor
1625 A426 13c Cypripedium mowgh
1626 A426 30c Cypripedium solum

See Nos. 1677-1683 and 1780-1786.

Enrique Loynaz del Castillo (b. 1861), Composer — A427

1971, June 5 **Wmk. 376**
1627 A427 3c Portrait, Invasion Hymn

Bee Keeping — A428

1971, June 20 **Unwmk.**
1628 A428 1c Egg, larvae, pupa
1629 A428 3c Worker
1630 A428 9c Drone
1631 A428 13c Defense of hive
1632 A428 30c Queen

Children's Drawings — A429

1971, Aug. 30

Size: 45x39mm

1633 A429 1c Sailboat
1634 A429 3c The Little Train

Sizes: 45½x35½mm (9c, 13c), 47x37½mm (10c)

1635 A429 9c Sugar Cane Cutter
1636 A429 10c Return of the Fishermen
1637 A429 13c The Zoo

Size: 47x42mm

1638 A429 20c House and Garden

Size: 31½x50mm

1639 A429 30c Landscape

Art Type of 1970

Paintings in the Natl. Museum: 1c, St. Catherine of Alexandria, by F. Zurburan. 2c, The Cart, by Federico Americo. 3c, St. Christopher and Child, by J. Bassano. 4c, Little Devil, by Rene Portocarrero. 5c, Portrait of a Woman, by Nicolas Maes. 13c, Phoenix, by Raul Martinez. 30c, Sir William Pitt, by Thomas Gainsborough.

1971, Sept. 20
1640 A408 1c 31x55mm
1641 A408 2c 48x37mm
1642 A408 3c 31x55mm
1643 A408 4c 37x48mm
1644 A408 5c 37x48mm
1645 A408 13c 39x48½mm
1646 A408 30c 39x48½mm

Sport Fishing — A431

1971, Oct. 30
1647 A431 1c Albula vulpes
1648 A431 2c Seriola species
1649 A431 3c Micropterus salmoides
1650 A431 4c Coryphaena hippurus
1651 A431 5c Megalops atlantica
1652 A431 13c Acanthocybium solandri
1653 A431 30c Makaira ampla

19th World Amateur Baseball Championships — A432

1971, Nov. 22 **Wmk. 376**
1654 A432 3c shown
1655 A432 1p Globe as baseball

Execution of Medical Students, Cent. A433

Paintings: 3c, Dr. Fermin Valdez Dominguez, anonymous. 13c, Execution of the Medical Students, by M. Mesa. 30c, Capt. Federico Capdevila, anonymous.

1971, Nov. 27 **Unwmk.**

Size: 61½x46mm (13c)

1656 A433 3c multi
1657 A433 13c multi
1658 A433 30c multi

Spindalis Zena Pretrei — A434

Birds: 1c, Falco sparverius sparverioides vigors. 2c, Glaucidium siju siju. 3c, Priotelus temnurus temnurus. 4c, Saurothera merlini merlini. 5c, Nesoceleus fernandinae. 30c, Mimocichla plumbea rubripes. 50c, Chlorostilbon ricordii ricordii and Archilochus colubris. Nos. 1659-1663 vert.

1971, Dec. 10
1659 A434 1c multi
1660 A434 2c multi
1661 A434 3c multi
1662 A434 4c multi
1663 A434 5c multi
1664 A434 13c shown
1665 A434 30c multi

Size: 55½x29mm

1666 A434 50c multi

Death centenary of Ramon de la Sagra, naturalist.

Cuba's Victory at the World Amateur Baseball Championships — A435

1971, Dec. 8 **Wmk. 376**
1667 A435 13c multi

UNICEF, 25th Anniv. A436

1971, Dec. 11
1668 A436 13c multi

Art Type of 1970

Paintings in the Natl. Museum: 1c, Arrival of an Ambassador, by Vittore Carpaccio. 2c, Senora Malpica, by G. Collazo. 3c, La Chorrera Tower, by Esteban Chartrand. 4c, Creole Landscape, by Carlos Enriquez. 5c, Sir William Lemon, by George Romney. 13c, Landscape, by Henry Cleenewerk. 30c, Valencia Beach, by Joaquin Sorolla y Bastida.

1972, Jan. 25 **Unwmk.**
1669 A408 1c 50x33mm
1670 A408 2c 27½x52mm
1671 A408 3c 50x33mm
1672 A408 4c 35x43mm
1673 A408 5c 35x43mm
1674 A408 13c 43x33mm
1675 A408 30c 43x33mm

Academy of Sciences, 10th Anniv. — A437

1972, Feb. 20 **Wmk. 376**
1676 A437 13c Capitol Type of 1929

Orchid Type of 1971

1972, Feb. 25 **Unwmk.**
1677 A426 1c Brasso cattleya sindorossiana
1678 A426 2c Cypripedium doraeus
1679 A426 3c Cypripedium exul
1680 A426 4c Cypripedium rosy dawn
1681 A426 5c Cypripedium champolliom
1682 A426 13c Cypripedium bucolique
1683 A426 30c Cypripedium sullanum

Eduardo Agramonte (1849-1872), Physicist A438

1972, Mar. 8
1684 A438 3c Portrait by F. Martinez

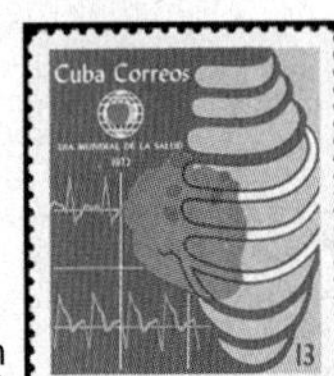

World Health Day — A439

1972, Apr. 7 **Wmk. 376**
1685 A439 13c multi

Soviet Space Program — A440

1972, Apr. 12 **Unwmk.**

1686 A440 1c Sputnik 1
1687 A440 2c Vostok 1
1688 A440 3c Valentina Tereshkova
1689 A440 4c Alexei Leonov
1690 A440 5c Lunokhod 1, moon vehicle
1691 A440 13c Linking Soyuz capsules
1692 A440 30c Victims of Soyuz 11 accident

Stamp Day — A441

Designs: 13c, Postmaster-Gen. Vicente Mora Pera, by Ramon Loy. 30c, Soldier's Letter, Cuba to Venezuela, 1897.

1972, Apr. 24

1693 A441 13c shown

Size: 48x39mm

1694 A441 30c multi

Labor Day — A442

Jose Marti, Ho Chi Minh — A443

3rd Conference Against War in Indo-China, May 19 — A444

1972, May 1 **Wmk. 376**

1695 A442 3c multi

1972, May 19

1696 A443 3c shown
1697 A444 13c shown
1698 A443 30c Roses, conference emblem

Metropolitan Museum Type of 1971

Portraits: 1c, Salvador del Muro, by J. Del Rio. 2c, Luis de las Casas, by Del Rio. 3c, Cristopher Columbus, anonymous. 4c, Tomas Gamba, by V. Escobar. 5c, Maria Galarraga, by Escobar. 13c, Isabel II, by Federico Madrazo. 30c, Carlos III, by Miguel Melero.

1972, May 25 **Unwmk.**

Size: 34x43½mm

1699 A420 1c multi
1700 A420 2c multi
1701 A420 3c multi
1702 A420 4c multi
1703 A420 5c multi

Size: 34x51½mm

1704 A420 13c multi
1705 A420 30c multi

Children's Songs Competition, Natl. Library A445

1972, June 5 **Wmk. 376**

1706 A445 3c multi

Thoroughbred Horses — A446

1972, June 30 **Unwmk.**

1707 A446 1c Tarpan
1708 A446 2c Kertag
1709 A446 3c Creole
1710 A446 4c Andalusian
1711 A446 5c Arabian
1712 A446 13c Quarter horse
1713 A446 30c Pursang

Frank Pais (d. 1957), Educator, Revolutionary — A447

1972, July 26 **Wmk. 376**

1714 A447 13c blk & red

1972 Summer Olympics, Munich, Aug. 26-Sept. 10 — A448

1972, Aug. 26 **Unwmk.**

1715 A448 1c Athlete, emblems, vert.
1716 A448 2c "M," boxing
1717 A448 3c "U," weight lifting
1718 A448 4c "N," fencing
1719 A448 5c "I," rifle shooting
1720 A448 13c "C," running
1721 A448 30c "H," basketball

Souvenir Sheet

Imperf

1722 A448 50c Gymnastics

Stamp in No. 1722 has simulated perforations.

Intl. Hydrological Decade — A449

Landscapes: 1c, Tree Trunks, by Domingo Ramos. 3c, Cyclone, by Tiburcio Lorenzo. 8c, Vinales, by Ramos. 30c, Forest and Brook, by Antonio R. Morey, vert.

1972, Sept. 20

1723 A449 1c multi
1724 A449 3c multi
1725 A449 8c multi
1726 A449 30c multi

Butterflies from the Gundlach Collection — A450

1972, Sept. 25

1727 A450 1c Papilio thoas oviedo
1728 A450 2c Papilio devilliers
1729 A450 3c Papilio polixenes polixenes
1730 A450 4c Papilio androgeus epidaurus
1731 A450 5c Papilio cayguanabus
1732 A450 13c Papilio andraemon hernandezi
1733 A450 30c Papilio celadon

A451

Miguel de Cervantes Saavedra (1547-1616), Spanish Author — A452

Paintings by A. Fernandez: 3c, In La Mancha, vert. 13c, Battle with Wine Skins. 30c, Don Quixote de La Mancha, vert. 50c, Scene from Don Quixote, by Jose Moreno Carbonero.

1972, Sept. 29

Size: 34½x46mm (3c, 30c)

1734 A451 3c multi
1735 A451 13c shown
1736 A451 30c multi

Souvenir Sheet

Perf. 12½ on 3 Sides

1737 A452 50c shown

Guerrilla Day, 5th Anniv. — A453

1972, Oct. 8

1738 A453 3c Ernesto "Che" Guevara
1739 A453 13c Tamara "Tania" Bunke
1740 A453 30c Guido "Inti" Peredo

Traditional Musical Instruments A454

1972, Oct. 25

1741 A454 3c Abwe (rattles)
1742 A454 13c Bonko enchemiya (drum)
1743 A454 30c Iya (drum)

MATEX '72, 3rd Natl. Philatelic Exhibition, Matanzas — A455

1972, Nov. 18 **Wmk. 376**

1744 A455 13c No. 467
1745 A455 30c No. C49

Nos. 1744-1745 printed se-tenant with insribed labels picturing Type A232, emblem of the Cuban Philatelic Federation.

Historic Ships A456

1972, Nov. 30 **Unwmk.**

1746 A456 1c Viking long boat, 6th-9th cent.
1747 A456 2c Caravel, 15th cent., vert.
1748 A456 3c Galleass, 16th cent.
1749 A456 4c Galleon, 17th cent., vert.
1750 A456 5c Clipper, 19th cent.
1751 A456 13c Steam packet, 19th cent.

Size: 52½x29mm.

1752 A456 30c Atomic icebreaker Lenin

UNESCO Save Venice Campaign — A457

1972, Dec. 8

1753 A457 3c Lion of St. Mark
1754 A457 13c Bridge of Sighs, vert.
1755 A457 30c St. Mark's Cathedral

Cuba, World Amateur Baseball Champion in 1972 — A458

Sport Events, 1972 — A459

1972, Dec. 15
1756 A458 3c Umpire

1972, Dec. 22
1757 A459 1c shown
1758 A458 2c Pole vault
1759 A458 3c like No. 1756
1760 A458 4c Wrestling
1761 A458 5c Fencing
1762 A458 13c Boxing
1763 A458 30c Marlin

Barrientos Memorial Athletics Championships, 11th Amateur Baseball Championships, Cerro Pelado Intl. Tournament, Central American and Caribbean Fencing Tournament, Giraldo Cordova Tournament, Ernest Hemingway Natl. Fishing Contest.
No. 1759 inscribed "XI serie nacional de beisbol aficionado."

Medals Won by Cubans at the 1972 Summer Olympics, Munich A460

1c, Bronze, Women's 100-meter. 2c, Bronze, women's relay. 3c, Gold, 54kg boxing. 4c, Silver, 81kg boxing. 5c, Bronze, 51kg boxing. 13c, Gold, 87kg boxing. 30c, Gold, silver cup, heavyweight boxing. 50c, Bronze, basketball.

1973, Jan. 28
1764 A460 1c multi
1765 A460 2c multi
1766 A460 3c multi
1767 A460 4c multi
1768 A460 5c multi
1769 A460 13c multi
1770 A460 30c multi

Souvenir Sheet
Imperf

1771 A460 50c multi

Stamp in No. 1771 has simulated perforations.

A461

A462

Portrait by A.M. Esquivel.

1973, Feb. 10
1772 A461 13c multi

Gertrudis Gomez de Avellaneda (1814-1873), poet.

Art Type of 1970

Paintings in the Natl. Museum: 1c, Bathers in the Lagoon, by C. Enriquez. 2c, Still-life, by W.C. Heda. 3c, Gallantry, by P. Landaluze. 4c, Return in the Late Afternoon, by C. Troyon. 5c, Elizabetta Mascagni, by F.X. Fabre. 13c, The Picador, by De Lucas Padilla, horiz. 30c, In the Garden, by Arburu Morell.

1973, Feb. 28
Sizes: 36x46mm, 46x36mm
1773 A408 1c multi
1774 A408 2c multi
1775 A408 3c multi
1776 A408 4c multi
1777 A408 5c multi
1778 A408 13c multi
1779 A408 30c multi

Orchid Type of 1971

1973, Mar. 26
1780 A426 1c Dendrobium hybrid
1781 A426 2c Cypripedium exul
1782 A426 3c Vanda miss. joaquin rose marie
1783 A426 4c Phalaenopsis schilleriana
1784 A426 5c Vanda gilbert tribulet
1785 A426 13c Dendrobium hybrid, diff.
1786 A426 30c Arachnis catherine

1973, Apr. 7 **Wmk. 376**
1787 A462 10c multi, *buff*

World Health Day. World Health Organization, 25th anniv.

Anti-Polio Campaign — A463

1973, Apr. 9 **Unwmk.**
1788 A463 3c multi

Soviet Space Program — A464

1973, Apr. 12
1789 A464 1c Soyuz rocket launch, vert.
1790 A464 2c Luna 1, Moon
1791 A464 3c Luna 16 taking-off from Moon, vert.
1792 A464 4c Venus 7
1793 A464 5c Molnia 1, vert.
1794 A464 13c Mars 3
1795 A464 30c Radar observation ship, Yuri Gagarin

Stamp Day A465

Postmarks: 13c, Santiago de Cuba, 1760. 30c, Havana, 1760.

1973, Apr. 24
1796 A465 13c multi
1797 A465 30c multi

See Nos. 1888-1891.

Portrait by A. Espinosa A466

1973, May 11
1798 A466 13c multi

Maj.-Gen. Ignacio Agramonte (1841-1873).

Birthplace, Torun, and Inventions — A467

Copernicus Monument, Warsaw — A468

1973, May 25
1799 A467 3c shown
1800 A467 13c Copernicus, spacecraft
1801 A467 30c Manuscript, Frombork Tower

Souvenir Sheet
Perf. 12½ on 3 Sides

1802 A468 50c shown

500th anniversary of the birth of Nicolaus Copernicus (1473-1543), Polish astronomer.

Improvement of School Education — A469

1973, June 12 **Wmk. 376**
1803 A469 13c multi

Cattle — A470

1973, June 28 **Unwmk.**
1804 A470 1c Jersey
1805 A470 2c Charolaise
1806 A470 3c Creole
1807 A470 4c Swiss
1808 A470 5c Holstein
1809 A470 13c Santa Gertrudis
1810 A470 30c Brahman

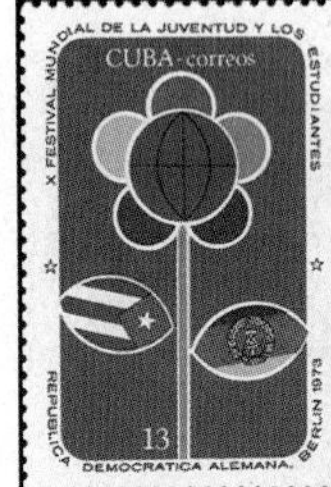

A471

A472

1973, July 10 **Wmk. 376**
1811 A471 13c multi

10th Communist Festival of Youths and Students, East Berlin.

1973, July 26 **Unwmk.**
1812 A472 3c Siboney Farm, Santiago de Cuba
1813 A472 13c Moncada Barracks
1814 A472 30c Revolution Plaza, Havana

20th anniv. of the Revolution.

10th Anniv. of the Revolutionary Navy — A473

1973, Aug. 3 **Wmk. 376**
1815 A473 3c Midshipman, missile frigate

Interior, by Manuel Vicens A474

Paintings in the Natl. Museum: 1c, Amalia of Saxony, by J.K. Rossler. 3c, Margarita of Austria, by J. Pantoja de la Cruz. 4c, City Hall Official, anonymous. 5c, View of Santiago de Cuba, by Hernandez Giro. 13c, The Catalan, by J.J. Tejada. 30c, Alley in Guayo, by Tejada.

1973, Aug. 30 **Unwmk.**

Sizes: 26½x41mm (1c, 3c), 28½x39mm (4c, 13c, 30c)

1816 A474 1c multi
1817 A474 2c multi
1818 A474 3c multi
1819 A474 4c multi
1820 A474 5c multi
1821 A474 13c multi
1822 A474 30c multi

WMO Emblem, Paintings by J. Madrazo A475

1973, Sept. 4

1823 A475 8c Spring
1824 A475 8c Summer
1825 A475 8c Fall
1826 A475 8c Winter

World Meterorogical Organization, cent. Nos. 1823-1826 printed se-tenant in strips of 4; frame reversed on 2nd and 4th stamp in strip.

A476

A477

27th World and 1st Pan American Weight Lifting Championships: Various weightlifting positions.

1973, Sept. 12

1827 A476 1c multi, diff.
1828 A476 2c shown
1829 A476 3c multi, diff.
1830 A476 4c multi, diff.
1831 A476 5c multi, diff.
1832 A476 13c multi, diff.
1833 A476 30c multi, diff.

1973, Sept. 28

Flowering plants.

1834 A477 1c Erythrina standleyana
1835 A477 2c Lantana camara
1836 A477 3c Canavalia maritima
1837 A477 4c Dichromena colorata
1838 A477 5c Borrichia arborescens
1839 A477 13c Anguria pedata
1840 A477 30c Cordia sebestena

8th World Trade Union Congress, Varna, Bulgaria — A478

1973, Oct. 5 **Wmk. 376**

1841 A478 13c multi

Cuban Natl. Ballet, 25th Anniv. — A479

Sea Shells — A480

1973, Oct. 28 **Unwmk.**

1842 A479 13c gold & brt ultra

1973, Oct. 29

1843 A480 1c Liguus fasciatus fasciatus
1844 A480 2c Liguus fasciatus guitarti
1845 A480 3c Liguus fasciatus whartoni
1846 A480 4c Liguus fasciatus angelae
1847 A480 5c Liguus fasciatus trinidadense
1848 A480 13c Liguus blainianus
1849 A480 30c Liguus vittatus

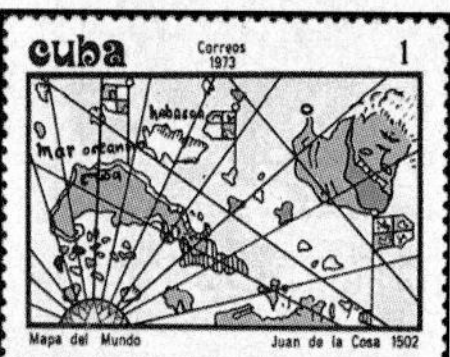

Maps of Cuba A481

1973, Oct. 29

1850 A481 1c Juan de la Cosa, 1502
1851 A481 3c Ortelius, 1572
1852 A481 13c Bellini, 1762
1853 A481 40c 1973

15th Anniversary of the Revolution — A482

1974, Jan. 2

1854 A482 1c No. 625
1855 A482 3c No. 626
1856 A482 13c No. C200
1857 A482 40c No. C201

Woman, by F. Ponce de Leon — A483

Amilcar Cabral — A484

Portraits in the Camaguey Museum: 3c, Mexican Girls, by J. Arche. 8c, Young Woman, by A. Menocal. 10c, Mulatto Woman Drinking from Coconut, by L. Romanach. 13c, Head of an Old Man, by J. Arburu.

1974, Jan. 10

1858 A483 1c multi
1859 A483 3c multi
1860 A483 8c multi
1861 A483 10c multi
1862 A483 13c multi

1974, Jan. 20

1863 A484 13c multi

Amilcar Cabral, Guinea-Bissau freedom fighter, 1st death anniv.

Lenin, by I.V. Kosmin — A485

12th Central American and Caribbean Games, Santo Domingo — A486

1974, Jan. 21

1864 A485 30c multi

50th death anniv. of Lenin.

1974, Feb. 8

1865 A486 1c Emblem
1866 A486 2c Javelin
1867 A486 3c Boxing
1868 A486 4c Baseball, horiz.
1869 A486 13c Basketball, horiz.
1870 A486 30c Volleyball, horiz.

Portrait by F. Martinez — A487

Portrait of a Man, by J.B. Vermay — A488

1974, Feb. 27

1871 A487 13c multi

Carlos M. de Cespedes (d. 1874), patriot.

1974, Mar. 7

Paintings in the Natl. Museum: 2c, The Wet Nurse, by C.A. Van Loo. 3c, Cattle in River, by R. Morey. 4c, Village, by Morey. 13c, Faun and Bacchus, by Rubens. 30c, Young Woman Playing Cards, by R. Madrazo.

1872 A488 1c shown
1873 A488 2c multi
1874 A488 3c multi
1875 A488 4c multi
1876 A488 13c multi
1877 A488 30c multi

Council for Mutual Economic Assistance (COMECON), 25th Anniv. — A489

1974, Mar. 15

1878 A489 30c Comecon building, Moscow

Visit of Leonid I. Brezhnev to Cuba, Jan. 28-Feb. 3 — A490

1974, Mar. 28

1879 A490 13c Jose Marti, Lenin, flags
1880 A490 30c Brezhnev, Fidel Castro

Science Fiction A491

Paintings by A. Sokolov.

1974, Apr. 12

1881 A491 1c Martian Crater
1882 A491 2c Fiery Labyrinth
1883 A491 3c Amber Wave
1884 A491 4c Flight Through Space
1885 A491 13c Planet in Nebula
1886 A491 30c World of Two Suns

Cosmonauts Day.

UPU, Cent. A492

1974, Apr. 15

1887 A492 30c Letter, 1874

Stamp Day Type of 1973

Postmarks.

1974, Apr. 24

1888 A465 1c Havana
1889 A465 3c Matanzas
1890 A465 13c Trinidad
1891 A465 20c Guana Vacoa

18th Sports Congress of Friendly Armies — A493

1974, May 5 **Wmk. 376**

1892 A493 3c multi

Felipe Poey (1799-1891), Naturalist — A494

Designs: 1c, 4c, Butterflies. 2c, 13c, Sea shells. 3c, 30c, 50c, Fish.

1974, May 26 ***Perf. 12½x12***

1893 A494 1c Eumaeus atala atala
1894 A494 2c Pineria terebra
1895 A494 3c Chaetodon sedentarius
1896 A494 4c Eurema dina dina
1897 A494 13c Hemitrochus fusco-labiata
1898 A494 30c Eupomacentrus partitus

Souvenir Sheet

Imperf

1899 A494 50c Apogon binotatus

Stamp in #1899 has simulated perforations.

Havana Philharmonic Orchestra, 50th Anniv. — A495

1c, Antonio Mompo, cello. 3c, Cesar Perez Sentenat, piano. 5c, Pedro Mercado, trumpet. 10c, Pedro Sanjuan, Havana Philharmonic emblem. 13c, Roberto Ondina, flute.

1974, June 8 ***Perf. 12½***

1900 A495 1c multi
1901 A495 3c multi
1902 A495 5c multi
1903 A495 10c multi
1904 A495 13c multi

Garden Flowers — A496

1974, June 12

1905 A496 1c Heliconia humilis
1906 A496 2c Anthurium andraeanum
1907 A496 3c Canna generalis
1908 A496 4c Alpinia purpurata
1909 A496 13c Gladiolus grandiflorus
1910 A496 30c Amomum capitatum

A497

A498

World Amateur Boxing Championships: Emblem and various boxers.

Perf. 12x12½

1974, Aug. 24 **Litho.** **Unwmk.**

1911 A497 1c multi
1912 A497 3c multi
1913 A497 13c multi

1974, Aug. 28 ***Perf. 13***

Extinct birds.

1914 A498 1c Dodo
1915 A498 3c Ara de Cuba (parrot)
1916 A498 8c Passenger pigeon
1917 A498 10c Moa
1918 A498 13c Great auk

Pres. Salvador Allende of Chile (d. 1973) A499

1974, Sept. 11

1919 A499 13c multi

Wildflowers A500

Model Aircraft — A501

1974, Sept. 14 ***Perf. 13x12½***

1920 A500 1c Suriana maritima
1921 A500 3c Cassia ligustrina
1922 A500 8c Flaveria linearis
1923 A500 10c Stachytarpheta jamaicensis
1924 A500 13c Bacopa monnieri

1974, Sept. 22 ***Perf. 12½***

1925 A501 1c shown
1926 A501 3c Sky diving
1927 A501 8c Glider
1928 A501 10c Crop dusting
1929 A501 13c Commercial aviation

Civil Aeronautic Institute, 10th anniv. Nos. 1927-1929 horiz.

History of Cuban Baseball — A502

1974, Oct. 3 ***Perf. 13***

1930 A502 1c Indians playing ball
1931 A502 3c 1st Official game, 1874
1932 A502 8c Emilio Sabourin
1933 A502 10c Umpire, players, 1974
1934 A502 13c Latin-American Stadium, Havana

Nos. 1930-1932 vert.

Mambi 10c Stamp (Revolutionary Junta Issue), Cent. — A503

1974, Oct. 10

1935 A503 13c multi

16th Conference of Customs Organizations of Socialist Countries — A504

1974, Oct. 15

1936 A504 30c Comecon Building, Moscow

Disappearance of Major Camilo Cienfuegos, 15th Anniv. — A505

Wmk. 376

1974, Oct. 28 **Litho.** ***Perf. 13***

1937 A505 3c multi

8th World Mining Conference — A506

1974, Nov. 3

1938 A506 13c multi

Petroleum Institute, 15th Anniv. — A507

1974, Nov. 20

1939 A507 3c multi

Intersputnik Earth Station Opening — A508

1974, Nov. 30 **Unwmk.**

1940 A508 3c shown
1941 A508 13c Satellite, satellite dish
1942 A508 1p Satellite, flags

Philatelic Federation, 10th Anniv. — A509

1974, Nov. 30 ***Perf. 12½x13***

1943 A509 30c multi

Souvenir Sheet

Mercury — A510

1974, Dec. 6 ***Imperf.***

1944 A510 50c multi

4th Natl. Phil. Exhib., Havana.

1st World Peace Congress, 25th Anniv. — A511

1974, Dec. 16 **Wmk. 376** ***Perf. 13***

1945 A511 30c *F. Joliot-Curie*, by Picasso

Ruben Martinez Villena (b. 1899), Revolutionary — A512

1974, Dec. 20 **Unwmk.**
1946 A512 3c red org & yel

Souvenir Sheet

Cuban Victories, 1st Amateur Boxing Championships — A513

1975, Jan. 6 **Litho.** ***Imperf.***
1947 A513 50c Trophy

The World, by Marcelo Pogolotti A514

Paintings in the Natl. Museum: 2c, *The Silk-Cotton Tree,* by Henry Cleenewerk. 3c, *Landscape,* by Guillermo Collazo. 5c, *Still-life,* by Francisco Peralta. 13c, *Maria Wilson,* by Federico Martinez, vert. 30c, *The Couple,* by Mariano Fortuny.

1975, Jan. 20 ***Perf. 13***
1948 A514 1c multi
1949 A514 2c multi
1950 A514 3c multi
1951 A514 5c multi
1952 A514 13c multi
1953 A514 30c multi

Intl. Women's Year A515

1975, Feb. 6
1954 A515 13c multi

Fishing Industry A516

Various fish and fishing vessels.

1975, Feb. 22
1955 A516 1c Long-finned tuna
1956 A516 2c Tuna
1957 A516 3c Mediterranean grouper
1958 A516 8c Hake
1959 A516 13c Prawn
1960 A516 30c Lobster

Minerals — A517

1975, Mar. 15 **Litho.** ***Perf. 13x12½***
1961 A517 3c Nickel
1962 A517 13c Copper
1963 A517 30c Chromium

Cosmonaut's Day — A518

1975, Apr. 12 ***Perf. 13x12½, 12½x13***
1964 A518 1c Cosmodrome
1965 A518 2c Probe, vert.
1966 A518 3c Eclipse
1967 A518 5c Threshold to Space
1968 A518 13c Midday on Mars
1969 A518 30c Cosmonaut's view of Earth

The future of space.

Stamp Day A519

Various covers.

1975, Apr. 24 ***Perf. 13***
1970 A519 3c multi
1971 A519 13c multi
1972 A519 30c multi

Victory Over Fascism, 30th Anniv. — A520

Design: Raising red flag over Reichstag, Berlin.

1975, May 9 ***Perf. 13x12½***
1973 A520 30c multi

A521

Works in the Decorative Art Museum — A522

1c, Sevres porcelain vase, vert. 2c, Meissen porcelain statue *Shepherdess and Dancers,* vert. 3c, Chinese porcelain dish *Lady with Parasol.* 5c, Chinese screen detail *The Phoenix,* vert. 13c, *Allegory of Music,* by Francois Boucher (1703-70), vert. 30c, *Portrait of a Lady,* by L. Tocque, vert. 50c, *The Swing,* by Hubert Robert (1733-1808).

1975, May 10 ***Perf. 12½x13, 13x12½***
1974 A521 1c multi
1975 A521 2c multi
1976 A521 3c shown
1977 A521 5c multi
1978 A521 13c multi
1979 A521 30c multi

Souvenir Sheet

Perf. 13x12½ on 3 Sides

1980 A522 50c shown

No. 1980 contains one 25x39mm stamp.

Intl. Children's Day — A523

Wmk. 376

1975, May 31 **Litho.** ***Perf. 13***
1981 A523 3c multi

Indigenous Birds — A524

1975, June 18 **Unwmk.**
1982 A524 1c *Vireo gundlachi*
1983 A524 2c *Gymnoglaux lawrenci*
1984 A524 3c *Aratingo eoups*
1985 A524 5c *Staroenas cyanocephala*
1986 A524 13c *Chondrohierax wilsoni*
1987 A524 30c *Cyanolimnas cerverai*

See #2121-2125, 2180-2182, C276-C276.

Scientific Investigation Center, 10th Anniv. — A525

1975, July 1 ***Perf. 12½***
1988 A525 13c multi

Irrigation and Drainage Commission, 25th Anniv. — A526

1975, Aug. 2 ***Perf. 13***
1989 A526 13c multi

Afforestation A527

1975, Aug. 20
1990 A527 1c *Cedrela mexicana*
1991 A527 3c *Swietenia mahagoni*
1992 A527 5c *Calophyllum brasiliense*
1993 A527 13c *Hibiscus tiliaceus*
1994 A527 30c *Pinus caribaea*

Cuban Women's Federation, 15th Anniv. — A528

1975, Aug. 23
1995 A528 3c multi

Intl. Conference on the Independence of Puerto Rico — A529

1975, Sept. 5 **Litho.**
1996 A529 13c multi

A530

A531

7th Pan American Games, Mexico: Aztec calendar stone and various athletes.

1975, Sept. 20 ***Perf. 12½x13***

1997 A530 1c Baseball
1998 A530 3c Boxing
1999 A530 5c Basketball
2000 A530 13c High jump
2001 A530 30c Weight lifting

Souvenir Sheet

Imperf

2002 A530 50c Stone, emblem

1975, Sept. 28 ***Perf. 12½x13***

2003 A531 3c multi

Revolutionary Defense Committees (CDR), 15th anniv.

Friendship Among the Peoples Institute, 15th Anniv. A532

1975, Oct. 8 ***Perf. 12½x13***

2004 A532 3c multi

Natl. Bank, 25th Anniv. A533

Designs: 1-peso coins and banknotes identified by serial numbers.

1975, Oct. 13 ***Perf. 13x12½***

2005 A533 13c Coin, 1915
2006 A533 13c C882736A, 1934
2007 A533 13c A000387A, 1946
2008 A533 13c 933906, 1964
2009 A533 13c K000000, 1976
a. Strip of 5, Nos. 2005-2009

Locomotives — A534

1975, Oct. 28 **Unwmk.** ***Perf. 12½***

2010 A534 1c *La Junta,* 1837
2011 A534 3c Steam engine 2-8-0 *No. 12*
2012 A534 5c Diesel TEM 4 *No. 51010*
2013 A534 13c Diesel DVM 9 *I-7 55*
2014 A534 30c Diesel M 62K *No. 61601*

Railway history.

Development of the Textile Industry — A535

1975, Nov. 10 ***Perf. 13x12½***

2015 A535 13c Bobbins, flag, loom operator

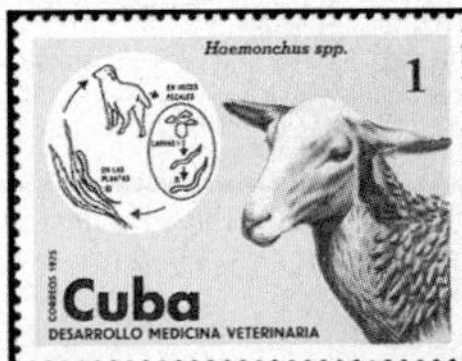
Veterinary Medicine — A536

Parasites and host species.

1975, Nov. 25 **Litho.** ***Perf. 13***

2016 A536 1c *Haemonchus,* lamb
2017 A536 2c *Ancylostoma caninum,* dog
2018 A536 3c *Dispharynx nasuta,* rooster
2019 A536 5c *Gasterophilus intestinalis,* horse
2020 A536 13c *Ascaris lumbricoides,* pig
2021 A536 30c *Boophilus microplus,* bull

Manuel Ascunce Domenech Educational Detachment A537

1975, Nov. 27 **Litho.**

2022 A537 3c multi

Development of Agriculture and Animal Husbandry — A538

1975, Dec. 15 **Litho.** ***Perf. 13x12½***

2023 A538 13c Irrigation

1st Communist Party Congress — A539

1975, Dec. 17 ***Perf. 12½x13, 13x12½***

2024 A539 3c "1," revolutionaries, vert.
2025 A539 13c shown
2026 A539 30c Party leaders

8th Latin-American Obstetrics and Gynecology Congress — A540

1976, Jan. 24 ***Perf. 13***

2027 A540 3c multi

Paintings in Natl. Museums — A541

Designs: 1c, *Seated Woman,* by Victor Manuel, vert. 2c, *Garden,* by Santiago Rusinol. 3c, *Guadalquivir River,* by Manuel Barron y Carrillo. 5c, *Self-portrait,* by Jan Havicksz Steen, vert. 13c, *Portrait of a Woman,* by Louis Michel Van Loo, vert. 30c, *La Chula,* by Jose Arburu Morell, vert.

Perf. 13, 12½ (3c, 30c)

1976, Jan. 30

Sizes: 29x40mm (1c, 5c, 13c), 40x29mm (2c), 44x27mm (3c), 27x44mm (30c)

2028 A541 1c multi
2029 A541 2c multi
2030 A541 3c multi
2031 A541 5c multi
2032 A541 13c multi
2033 A541 30c multi

10th Cong. of Ministers from Socialist Communications Organizations, Feb. 12, Havana — A542

1976, Feb. 12 **Litho.** ***Perf. 13***

2034 A542 13c multi

Hunting Dogs A543

1976, Feb. 20

2035 A543 1c American foxhound
2036 A543 2c Labrador retriever
2037 A543 3c Borzoi
2038 A543 5c Irish setter
2039 A543 13c Pointer
2040 A543 30c Cocker spaniel

Socialist Constitution — A544

1976, Feb. 24 ***Perf. 12½***

2041 A544 13c Natl. flag, arms, anthem

Chess Champions — A545

Designs: 1c, Ruy Lopez Segura and chessboard. 2c, Francois Philidor and frontispiece of his book, *Analysis of the Game of Chess.* 3c, Wilhelm Steinitz and knight. 13c, Emanuel Lasker and king. 30c, Jose Raul Capablanca learning to play chess as a small boy.

1976, Mar. 15 ***Perf. 13x12½***

2042 A545 1c multi
2043 A545 2c multi
2044 A545 3c multi
2045 A545 13c multi
2046 A545 30c multi

Havana Radio Intl. Broadcasts, 15th Anniv. — A546

1976, Mar. 26

2047 A546 50c multi

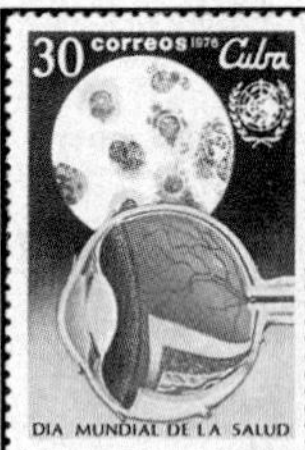
World Health Day — A547

Child Care Centers, 15th Anniv. — A548

1976, Apr. 7

2048 A547 30c multi

1976, Apr. 10 ***Perf. 12½x13***

2049 A548 3c multi

1st Manned Space Flight, 15th Anniv. A549

1976, Apr. 12 ***Perf. 13***

2050 A549 1c Gagarin, lift-off
2051 A549 2c V. Tesreshkova, rockets
2052 A549 3c A. Leonov's space walk, vert.
2053 A549 5c Spacecraft, vert.
2054 A549 13c Spacecraft, diff., vert.
2055 A549 30c Space link-up

Bay of Pigs Invasion, 15th Anniv. — A550

1976, Apr. 17 ***Perf. 13x12½, 12½x13***

2056 A550 3c shown
2057 A550 13c Bomber, pilot
2058 A550 30c Soldiers exulting, vert.

Natl. Militia, 17th anniv. (3c); Air Force, 15th anniv. (13c); proclamation of the socialist revolution, 15th anniv. (30c).

Nat. Assoc. of Small Farmers (ANAP), 15th Anniv. — A551

1976, May 17 ***Perf. 13x12½***
2059 A551 3c multi

1976 Summer Olympics, Montreal — A552

1976, May 25 ***Perf. 12½x13***
2060 A552 1c Volleyball
2061 A552 2c Basketball
2062 A552 3c Long jump
2063 A552 4c Boxing
2064 A552 5c Weight lifting
2065 A552 13c Judo
2066 A552 30c Swimming

Souvenir Sheet

Imperf

2067 A552 50c Character trademark (beaver)

See Nos. 2106, 2112.

Modern Secondary Schools — A553

1976, June 12 **Litho.** ***Perf. 13***
2068 A553 3c red, pale grn & blk

Indigenous Birds — A554

1976, June 15 ***Perf. 13x12½***
2069 A554 1c *Teretistris fornsi*
2070 A554 2c *Glaucidium siju*
2071 A554 3c *Nesoceleus fernandinae*
2072 A554 5c *Todus mutlicolor*
2073 A554 13c *Accipiter gundlachi*
2074 A554 30c *Priotelus temnurus*

EXPO '76, USSR A555

1976, July 5 ***Perf. 12½x13, 13x12½***
2075 A555 1c Anatomical scanning device
2076 A555 3c Child, doe
2077 A555 10c Cosmonauts
2078 A555 30c Tupolev supersonic jet

Public health and industrial safety (1c), environmental protection (3c), space exploration (10c) and modern transportation (30c). Nos. 2075-2077 vert.

Death Cent. of "El Inglesito" A556

1976, Aug. 4 ***Perf. 13***
2079 A556 13c Henry M. Reeve

Portrait of G. Collazo, by Jean Dabour — A557

Paintings by Collazo: 2c, *The Art Lovers,* horiz. 3c, *The Patio.* 5c, *Coconut Tree.* 13c, *New York Studio,* horiz. 30c, *R. Emelina Collazo.*

Perf. 13, 12½x13 (5c, 30c), 13x12½ (13c)

1976, Sept. 2

Sizes: 33x44mm, 44x33mm (2c), 31x46mm (5c, 30c), 46x31mm (13c)

2080 A557 1c multi
2081 A557 2c multi
2082 A557 3c multi
2083 A557 5c multi
2084 A557 13c multi
2085 A557 30c multi

Camilo Cienfuegos Military Schools, 10th Anniv. — A558

1976, Sept. 23 ***Perf. 13***
2086 A558 3c multi

Development of the Merchant Marine — A559

Various cargo and passenger ships.

1976, Oct. 2 ***Perf. 12½***
2087 A559 1c multi
2088 A559 2c multi
2089 A559 3c multi
2090 A559 5c multi
2091 A559 13c multi
2092 A559 30c multi

8th Intl. Health Film Festival of Socialist Countries, Havana — A560

1976, Oct. 4 ***Perf. 13x12½***
2093 A560 3c multi

5th Intl. Ballet Festival, Havana A561

Scenes from ballets. 2c, 5c, 13c, 30c vert.

1976, Nov. 6 ***Perf. 13***
2094 A561 1c *Apollo*
2095 A561 2c *The River and the Forest*
2096 A561 3c *Giselle*
2097 A561 5c *Oedipus Rex*
2098 A561 13c *Carmen*
2099 A561 30c *Vital Song*

3rd Military Games A562

1976, Nov. 25 ***Perf. 13***
2100 A562 3c multi

Granma Landings, 20th Anniv. — A563

1976, Dec. 2 ***Perf. 13x12½***
2101 A563 1c Landing craft
2102 A563 3c Landing force
2103 A563 13c Castro, soldiers
2104 A563 30c Globe, rifles

Souvenir Sheet

Cuban Landscape, by F. Cadava — A564

1976, Dec. 8 ***Perf. 13x13½***
2105 A564 50c multi

CIENFUEGOS '76, 5th natl. phil. exhib.

Summer Olympics Type of 1976 and

Victory of Cuban Athletes at the Montreal Games — A565

1976, Dec. 10 ***Perf. 12½x13***
2106 A565 1c Volleyball
2107 A565 2c Hurdles
2108 A565 3c Running (starting blocks)
2109 A565 8c Boxing
2110 A565 13c Running (finish line)
2111 A565 30c Judo

Souvenir Sheet

Imperf

2112 A552 50c like No. 2063

Paintings in the Natl. Museum A566

1c, *Golden Cross Inn,* by S. Scott. 3c, *Portrait of a Man,* by J.C. Verspronck, vert. 5c, *Venetian Landscape,* by Francesco Guardi. 10c, *Valley Corner,* by H. Cleenewerck, vert. 13c, *F. Xaviera Paula,* anonymous, vert. 30c, *F. de Medici,* by C. Allori, vert.

Perf. 13, 12½x13 (3c, 10c, 30c), 12½ (13c)

1977, Jan. 18

Sizes: 40x29mm, 27x42mm (3c, 10c, 30c), 27x43½mm (13c)

2113 A566 1c multi
2114 A566 3c multi
2115 A566 5c multi
2116 A566 10c multi
2117 A566 13c multi
2118 A566 30c multi

Rural Transport A567

1977, Feb. 15 ***Perf. 13***
2119 A567 3c multi

Constitution of Popular Government — A568

1976, Dec. 1 ***Perf. 13x12½***
2120 A568 13c multi

Bird Type of 1975

1977, Feb. 25 ***Perf. 13***
2121 A524 1c *Xiphidiopicus percussus*
2122 A524 4c *Tiaris canora*
2123 A524 10c *Dives atroviolaceus*
2124 A524 13c *Ferminia cerverai*
2125 A524 30c *Mellisuga helenae*

Lenin Park Aquarium, Havana — A569

1977, Mar. 15

2126 A569 1c *Chichlasoma meeki*
2127 A569 3c *Barbus tetrazona tetrazona*
2128 A569 5c *Cyprinus carpio*
2129 A569 10c *Betta splendens*
2130 A569 13c *Pterophyllum scalare*, vert.
2131 A569 30c *Hemigrammus caudovittatus*

Sputnik (1st Artificial Satellite), 20th Anniv. — A570

1c, DDR No. 370, *Sputnik.* 3c, Hungary No. 1216, *Luna 16.* 5c, North Korean Intl. Geophysical Year 10-won stamp of 1958, *Cosmos.* 10c, Poland No. 822, *Sputnik 3.* 13c, Yugoslavia No. 870, Earth, Moon. 30c, Cuba No. 866, Earth, Moon. 50c, Russia No. 2021, *Sputnik.*

1977, Apr. 12 ***Perf. 13x12½***

2132 A570 1c multi
2133 A570 3c multi
2134 A570 5c multi
2135 A570 10c multi
2136 A570 13c multi
2137 A570 30c multi

Souvenir Sheet

Imperf

2138 A570 50c multi

No. 2138 has simulated perfs.

Antonio Maria Romeu (1876-1955), Composer — A571

1977, May 10 **Litho.** ***Perf. 13***

2139 A571 3c multi

See No. C251.

Flowering Plants — A572

1977, May 31

2140 A572 1c *Hibiscus rosa sinensis*
2141 A572 2c *Nerium oleander*
2142 A572 5c *Allamanda cathartica*
2143 A572 10c *Pelargonium zonale*

Dr. Juan Tomas Roig (b. 1877), botanist. See Nos. C252-C254.

Fire Prevention Week — A573

1977, June 20

2144 A573 1c shown
2145 A573 2c Horse-drawn fire pump, diff.
2146 A573 6c Early motorized vehicle
2147 A573 10c Modern truck
2148 A573 13c Turntable-ladder truck
2149 A573 30c Crane vehicle

Natl. Decorations (Ribbons and Medals of Honor) — A574

1977, July 26 ***Perf. 12x12½***

2150 A574 1c shown
2151 A574 3c multi, diff.

See Nos. C255-C256.

Paintings by Jorge Arche — A575

Perf. 13x12½, 12½x13 (10c), 13 (5c)

1977, Aug. 25

Sizes: 26x38mm, 29x40mm (5c), 38x26mm (10c)

2152 A575 1c *Portrait of Mary*
2153 A575 3c *Jose Marti*
2154 A575 5c *Portrait of Aristides*
2155 A575 10c *Bathers*

Nos. 2152-2154 vert. See Nos. C257-C259.

4th Military Spartakiad (Summer Sports) — A576

1977, Sept. 10 ***Perf. 13***

2156 A576 1c Boxing
2157 A576 3c Volleyball
2158 A576 5c Parachuting
2159 A576 10c Running

See Nos. C260-C261.

Intl. Airmail Service, 50th Anniv. A577

Designs: 1c, Biplane and No. C62. 2c, Three-engine plane and Cuba-Key West 1st flight cancel, Oct. 28, 1927. 5c, Flying boat and intl. airmail service 1st flight cachet. 10c, Jet aircraft and Havana-Madrid cachet, Apr. 26, 1948.

1977, Oct. 27 **Litho.** ***Perf. 12x12½***

2160 A577 1c multi
2161 A577 2c multi
2162 A577 5c multi
2163 A577 10c multi

See Nos. C263-C264.

October Revolution, Russia, 60th Anniv. — A578

1977, Nov. 7 ***Perf. 13x12½***

2164 A578 3c Cruiser *Aurora*
2165 A578 13c Lenin, Flags
2166 A578 30c Hammer, sickle, symbols of agriculture, technology

Felines, Havana Zoo — A579

1977, Nov. 24 **Litho.** ***Perf. 13***

2167 A579 1c Cat
2168 A579 2c Black panther
2169 A579 8c Puma
2170 A579 10c Leopard

See Nos. C266-C267.

Martyrs of the Revolution, 20th Death Annivs. — A580

1977, Dec. 2 ***Perf. 12½x12***

2171 A580 3c Cienfuegos Uprising
2172 A580 20c Siege on the Presidential Palace

See No. C268.

Intl. Measurement System — A581

1977, Dec. 9

2173 A581 3c multi

Havana University, 250th Anniv. — A582

1978, Jan. 5 ***Perf. 13x12½***

2174 A582 3c multi

See Nos. C270-C271.

Landscape with Figures, by J. Pilliment — A583

Paintings in the Natl. Museum of Art: 1c, *Seated Woman,* by R. Mandrazo, vert. 4c, *Girl,* by J. Sorolla, vert. 10c, *The Cow,* by E. Abela.

Perf. 12x12½, 13 (4c, 6c, 10c)

1978, Feb. 20

Sizes: 27x42mm, 29x40mm (4c), 40x29mm (6c, 10c)

2175 A583 1c multi
2176 A583 4c multi
2177 A583 6c shown
2178 A583 10c multi

See Nos. C273-C274.

Frontier Troops, 15th Anniv. — A584

1978, Mar. 5 ***Perf. 13***

2179 A584 13c multi

Bird Type of 1975

Perf. 13, 12½x12 (4c)

1978, Mar. 10 **Size: 42x27mm**

2180 A524 1c *Myadestes elisabeth*
2181 A524 4c *Palioptila lembeyei*
2182 A524 10c *Teretistris fernandinae*

Name of bird inscribed below vignette. See Nos. C275-C276.

Cosmonaut's Day — A585

1978, Apr. 12 ***Perf. 13***

2183 A585 1c Intercosmos, vert.
2184 A585 2c Luna 24
2185 A585 5c Venus 9, vert.
2186 A585 10c Cosmos

See Nos. C278-C279.

9th World Trade Unions Congress, Prague — A586

1978, Apr. 16

2187 A586 30c ver, deep brn & blk

Cactus Flowers — A587

1978, May 15 ***Perf. 12½x13 (1c), 13***

2188 A587 1c *Melocactus guitarti*
2189 A587 4c *Leptocereus wrightii*
2190 A587 6c *Opuntia militaris*
2191 A587 10c *Cylindropuntia hystrix*

Natl. Botanical Gardens. See #C281-C282.

Lenin Park Aquarium, Havana — A588

1978, June 15 ***Perf. 13***

2192 A588 1c *Barbus arulios*
2193 A588 4c *Hiphessobrycon flammeus*
2194 A588 6c *Poecilia reticulata*
2195 A588 10c *Colis lalia*

See Nos. C286-C287.

MEDELLIN '78, 13th Central American and Caribbean Games — A589

1978, July 1

2196 A589 1c Basketball, vert.
2197 A589 3c Boxing, vert.
2198 A589 5c Weight lifting, vert.
2199 A589 10c Fencing

See Nos. C288-C289.

Attack on Moncada Barracks, 25th Anniv. — A590

1978, July 26

2200 A590 3c multi

See Nos. C290-C291.

World Youth and Students Festival, Havana A591

Natl. flags and views of host cities.

1978, July 28

2201 A591 3c Prague, 1947
2202 A591 3c Budapest, 1949
2203 A591 3c Berlin, 1951
2204 A591 3c Bucharest, 1953
2205 A591 3c Warsaw, 1955
a. Strip of 5, Nos. 2201-2205

See Nos. C292-C297.

Young Workers' Army, 5th Anniv. — A592

1978, Aug. 3

2206 A592 3c multi

Tuna Industry A593

1978, Aug. 30 ***Perf. 12½x12***

2207 A593 1c Tuna boat
2208 A593 2c Processing ship
2209 A593 5c Shrimp boat
2210 A593 10c Inshore stern trawler

See Nos. C298-C299.

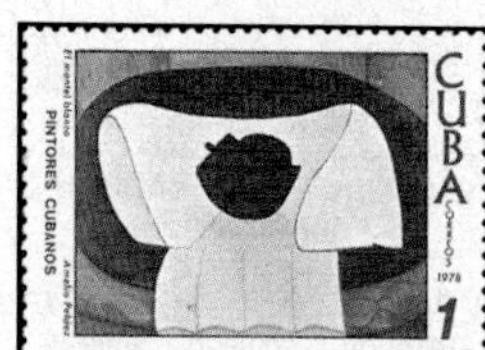

Paintings by Amelia Pelaez del Casal (1896-1968) — A594

Perf. 13x12½, 13 (3c, 6c), 12½x13
1978, Sept. 15

2211 A594 1c *The White Mantle*
2212 A594 3c *Still-life with Flowers*, vert.
2213 A594 6c *Women*, vert.
2214 A594 10c *Fish*, vert.

See Nos. C301-C303.

African Fauna, Havana Zoo A595

1978, Oct. 20 ***Perf. 13***

2215 A595 1c Rhinoceros
2216 A595 4c Okapi, vert.
2217 A595 6c Mandrill
2218 A595 10c Giraffe, vert.

See Nos. C307-C308.

Natl. Ballet, 30th Anniv. — A596

1978, Oct. 28 ***Perf. 13x12½***

2219 A596 3c *Grande Pas de Quatre*

See Nos. C309-C310.

A597

A598

Flowers of the Pacific: Various species.

1978, Nov. 30 **Litho.** ***Perf. 13***

2220 A597 1c multi
2221 A597 4c multi
2222 A597 6c multi
2223 A597 10c multi

See Nos. C311-C312.

1979, Jan. 1 ***Perf. 12½x13 (3c), 13***

2224 A598 3c Castro, soldier
2225 A598 13c Industry
2226 A598 1p Flag, globe, flame

Triumph of the Revolution, 20th anniv.

Doves and Pigeons A599

1979, Jan. 30 ***Perf. 13***

2227 A599 1c *Starnoenas cyanocephala*
2228 A599 3c *Geotrygon chysia*
2229 A599 7c *Geotrygon caniceps*
2230 A599 8c *Geotrygon montana*
2231 A599 13c *Columba leucocephala*
2232 A599 30c *Columba inornata*

Paintings in the Natl. Museum of Art A600

Designs: 1c, *Genre Scene,* by David Teniers. 3c, *Arrival of Spanish Troops,* by J. Louis Meissonier. 6c, *A Joyful Gathering,* by Sir David Wilkie. 10c, *A Robbery,* by E. De Lucas Padilla. 13c, *Tea Time,* by R. Madrazo, vert. 30c, *Peasants in Front of a Tavern,* by Adriaen van Ostade.

1979, Feb. 20

2233 A600 1c multi
2234 A600 3c multi
2235 A600 6c multi
2236 A600 10c multi
2237 A600 13c multi
2238 A600 30c multi

See Nos. 2262-2267, C317.

Marine Flora — A601

1979, Mar. 20

2239 A601 3c *Nymphaea capensis*
2240 A601 10c *Nymphaea ampla*
2241 A601 13c *Nymphaea coerulea*
2242 A601 30c *Nymphaea rubra*

All are incorrectly inscribed "Nymphaca."

A602

A603

1979, Mar. 24

2243 A602 3c multi

Cuban film industry, 20th anniv.

1979, Apr. 12

2244 A603 1c Rocket launch
2245 A603 4c Soyuz
2246 A603 6c Salyut
2247 A603 10c Link-up
2248 A603 13c Soyuz, Salyut
2249 A603 30c Parachute landing

Cosmonaut's Day. See No. C315.

6th Summit Meeting of Non-Aligned Countries — A604

1979, Apr. 17

2250 A604 3c Understanding, cooperation
2251 A604 13c Fight colonialism
2252 A604 30c New world economic order

House of the Americas Museum, 20th Anniv. — A605

1979, Apr. 28 ***Perf. 13x12½***

2253 A605 13c Cuna Indian tapestry

Agrarian Reform, 20th Anniv. — A606

1979, May 17 ***Perf. 12½x12***

2254 A606 3c multi

Souvenir Sheet

The Party, by Jules Pascin — A607

1979, May 18 ***Perf. 13***

2255 A607 50c multi

PHILASERDICA '79 phil. exhib., Sofia.

Nocturnal Butterflies — A608

1979, May 25

2256 A608 1c *Eulepidotis rectimargo*
2257 A608 4c *Othreis materna*
2258 A608 6c *Noropsis hieroglyphica*
2259 A608 10c *Heterochroma*
2260 A608 13c *Melanchroia regnatrix*
2261 A608 30c *Attera gemmata*

Art Type of 1979

Paintings by Victor Emmanuel Garcia (d. 1969): 1c, *Main Avenue, Paris.* 3c, *Portrait of Enmita.* 6c, *San Juan River, Matanzas.* 10c, *Woman Carrying Hay.* 13c, *Still-life with Vase.* 30c, *Street at Night.* Nos. 2262-2267 vert.

1979, June 15

2262 A600 1c multi
2263 A600 3c multi
2264 A600 6c multi
2265 A600 10c multi
2266 A600 13c multi
2267 A600 30c multi

See No. C317.

World Peace Council, 30th Anniv. A609

1979, June 29 ***Perf. 12½x13***

2268 A609 30c multi

1980 Summer Olympics, Moscow — A610

1979, July 30 ***Perf. 13x12½***

2269 A610 1c Wrestling
2270 A610 4c Boxing
2271 A610 6c Women's volleyball
2272 A610 10c Shooting
2273 A610 13c Weight lifting
2274 A610 30c High jump

Roses — A611

A612

1979, Aug. 20 ***Perf. 13***

2275 A611 1c *Rosa eglanteria*
2276 A611 2c *Rosa centifolia anemonoides*
2277 A611 3c *Rosa indica vulgaris*
2278 A611 5c *Rosa eglanteria punicea*
2279 A611 10c *Rosa sulfurea*
2280 A611 13c *Rosa muscosa alba*
2281 A611 20c *Rosa gallica purpurea velutina*

1979, Aug. 30

2282 A612 13c multi

Council for Mutual Economic Assistance, 30th anniv.

Cubana Airlines, 50th Anniv. A613

Various aircraft.

1979, Oct. 8

2283 A613 1c Ford trimotor
2284 A613 2c Sikorsky S-38
2285 A613 3c Douglas DC-3
2286 A613 4c Douglas DC-6
2287 A613 13c Ilyushin IL-14
2288 A613 40c Tupolev TU-104

Disappearance of Camilo Cienfuegos, 20th Anniv. — A614

1979, Oct. 28

2289 A614 3c multi

Reinoso, Sugar Cane and Blossom A615

1979, Nov. 12

2290 A615 13c multi

Sugar Cane Research Institute, 15th anniv., and sesquicentennial of the birth of Alvaro Reinoso.

Zoo Animals A616

1979, Nov. 15

2291 A616 1c Chimpanzees
2292 A616 2c Leopards
2293 A616 3c Deer
2294 A616 4c Lion cubs
2295 A616 5c Bear cubs
2296 A616 13c Squirrels
2297 A616 30c Pandas
2298 A616 50c Tiger cubs

Insects A617

1980, Jan. 25

2299 A617 1c *Rhina oblita*
2300 A617 5c *Odontocera josemartii,* vert.
2301 A617 6c *Pinthocoelium columbinum*
2302 A617 10c *Calasoma splendida,* vert.
2303 A617 13c *Homophileurus cubanus,* vert.
2304 A617 30c *Heterops dimidiata,* vert.

1980 Summer Olympics, Moscow — A618

1980, Feb. 20 ***Perf. 12½***

2305 A618 1c Weight lifting
2306 A618 2c Shooting
2307 A618 5c Javelin
2308 A618 6c Wrestling
2309 A618 8c Judo
2310 A618 10c Running
2311 A618 13c Boxing
2312 A618 30c Women's volleyball

Souvenir Sheet

Imperf

2313 A618 50c Mischa character

No. 2313 contains one 32x40mm stamp.

Paintings in the Natl. Museum A619

Designs: 1c, *The Oak Trees,* by Henry Joseph Harpignies, vert. 4c, *Family Reunion,* by Willem van Mieris. 6c, *Domestic Fowl,* by Melchior De Hondecoeter, vert. 9c, *Innocence,* by William A. Bougereau, vert. 13c, *Venetial Scene II,* by Michele Marieschi. 30c, *Spanish Peasant Woman,* by Joaquin Dominguez Bequer, vert.

Perf. 12½, 13 (9c, 30c), 12½x13 (13c)

1980, Mar. 11

Sizes: 29x40mm, 40x29mm (4c), 28x42mm (9c, 30c), 38x26mm (13c)

2314 A619 1c multi
2315 A619 4c multi
2316 A619 6c multi
2317 A619 9c multi
2318 A619 13c multi
2319 A619 30c multi

Souvenir Sheet

LONDON '80 — A620

1980, Apr. 1 ***Perf. 13***

2320 A620 50c *Malvern Hall,* by John Constable

Intercosmos Program — A621

1980, Apr. 12

2321 A621 1c Emblem, flags
2322 A621 4c Astrophysics
2323 A621 6c Satellite communications
2324 A621 10c Meteorology
2325 A621 13c Biology and medicine
2326 A621 30c Surveying satellite

Cuban Postage Stamps, 125th Anniv. — A622

1980, Apr. 24 ***Perf. 12½***

2327 A622 30c Nos. 1, 7 and 613

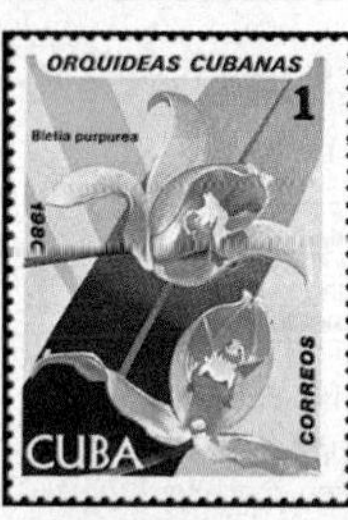

Orchids — A623

1980, May 20 *Perf. 13*

2328 A623 1c *Bletia purpurea*
2329 A623 4c *Oncidium leiboldii*
2330 A623 6c *Epidendrum cochieatum*
2331 A623 10c *Cattleyopsis lindenii*
2332 A623 13c *Encyclia fucata*
2333 A623 30c *Encyclia phoenicea*

Marine Mammals — A624

1980, June 20

2334 A624 1c *Tursiops truncatus*
2335 A624 3c *Megaptera novaeangliae,* vert.
2336 A624 13c *Ziphius cavirostris*
2337 A624 30c *Monachus tropicalis*

Urban Reform Campaign, 20th Anniv. — A625

Nationalization of Foreign Industry, 20th Anniv. — A626

1980, July 26 *Perf. 13x12½, 12½x13*

2338 A625 3c multi
2339 A626 13c multi

Moncada Program.

Colonial Copperware A627

Perf. 12½, 12½x13 (13c)

1980, July 29

Sizes: 27x43½mm, 38x26mm (13c)

2340 A627 3c Wine pitcher, 19th cent.
2341 A627 13c Oil jar, 18th cent.
2342 A627 30c Lidded pitcher, 19th cent.

Cuban Women's Federation, 20th Anniv. — A628

1980, Aug. 23 *Perf. 13*

2343 A628 3c multi

Souvenir Sheet

ESPAMER '80, Madrid — A629

Design: *Clotilde Passing Through the Country Garden,* by Joaquin Sorolla y Bastida.

1980, Aug. 29

2344 A629 50c multi

Postage stamps of Spain, 130th anniv.

1st Havana Declaration, 20th Anniv. — A630

1980, Sept. 2

2345 A630 13c multi

Construction of Naval Vessels in Cuba, 360th Anniv. — A631

Ships under construction: 1c, *Our Lady of Atocha,* galleon, 1620. 3c, *El Rayo,* warship, 1749. 7c, *Santisima Trinidad,* 1769. 10c, *Santisima Trinidad,* diff., 1805, vert. 13c, Steamships *Congreso* and *Colon,* 1851. 30c, Cardenas and Chullima shipyards.

1980, Sept. 15

2346 A631 1c multi
2347 A631 3c multi
2348 A631 7c multi
2349 A631 10c multi
2350 A631 13c multi
2351 A631 30c multi

A633

A634

1980, Sept. 26 *Perf. 13*

2354 A633 13c multi

Fidel Castro's 1st speech before the UN General Assembly, 20th anniv.

1980, Sept. 28 *Perf. 13x12½*

2355 A634 3c multi

Revolutionary defense committees, 20th anniv.

Souvenir Sheet

ESSEN '80, 49th Intl. Philatelic Federation Congress — A635

Painting: *Portrait of a Lady,* by Ludger Tom Ring The Younger.

1980, Oct. 2 **Litho.** *Perf. 13*

2356 A635 50c multi

Early Locomotives — A636

1980, Oct. 15

2357 A636 1c Josefa
2358 A636 2c Chaparra Sugar Co. No. 22
2359 A636 7c Steam storage locomotive
2360 A636 10c 2-4-2 locomotive
2361 A636 13c 2-4-0 locomotive
2362 A636 30c Oil combustion engine, 1909

Lighthouses A637

1980, Oct. 30

2363 A637 3c Roncali, San Antonio
2364 A637 13c Jagua, Cienfuegos
2365 A637 30c Maisi Point, Guantanamo

See Nos. 2440-2442, 2553-2555, 2614-2616.

Victory of Cuban Athletes at the 1980 Summer Olympics, Moscow — A638

1980, Nov. 10 **Litho.** *Perf. 12½x12*

2366 A638 13c Bronze medals
2367 A638 30c Silver medals
2368 A638 50c Gold medals

Nos. 2366-2368 each printed se-tenant with label containing statistical data.

Wildflowers A639

1980, Nov. 20 *Perf. 13*

2369 A639 1c *Pancratium arenicolum*
2370 A639 4c *Urechites lutea*
2371 A639 6c *Solanum elaegnifolium*
2372 A639 10c *Hamelia patens*
2373 A639 13c *Morinda royoc*
2374 A639 30c *Centrosema virginianum*

Souvenir Sheet

7th Natl. Stamp Exhibition — A640

1980, Nov. 22

2375 A640 50c Mail train

2nd Communist Party Congress A641

1980, Dec. 17

2376 A641 3c shown
2377 A641 13c Industry, communication
2378 A641 30c Athletics, elderly, education

Paintings in the Natl. Museum of Art A642

Designs: 1c, *Lady Mayo,* by Anton Van Dyck, vert. 6c, *The Spinner,* by Giovanni Battista Piazzeta, vert. 10c, *Daniel Collyer,* by Francis Cotes, vert. 13c, *Gardens, Palma de Mallorca,* by Santiago Rusinol Prats. 20c, *Landscape with Roadway and Houses,* by Frederick Waters Watts. 50c, *Landscape with Sheep,* by Jean-Francois Millet.

1981, Jan. 20

2379 A642 1c multi
2380 A642 6c multi
2381 A642 10c multi
2382 A642 13c multi
2383 A642 20c multi
2384 A642 50c multi

See Nos. 2510-2515.

Pelagic Fish A643

1981, Feb. 25

2385 A643 1c *Isurus oxyrhynchus*
2386 A643 3c *Lampris regius*
2387 A643 10c *Istiophorus platypterus*
2388 A643 13c *Mola mola,* vert.
2389 A643 30c *Coruphaena hippurus*
2390 A643 50c *Tetrapturus albidus*

1982 World Cup Soccer Championships, Spain — A644

Globe and various soccer players.

1981, Mar. 20 ***Perf. 12½***

2391 A644 1c multi
2392 A644 2c multi
2393 A644 3c multi
2394 A644 10c multi, vert.
2395 A644 13c multi, vert.
2396 A644 50c multi

Souvenir Sheet

Perf. 13

2397 A644 1p Soccer ball, flag

No. 2397 contains one 40x32mm stamp.

Opening of the 1st Kindergarten, 20th Anniv. — A645

1981, Apr. 10 ***Perf. 13***

2398 A645 3c multi

1st Man in Space, 20th Anniv. A646

Designs: 1c, Jules Verne, Russian scientist Konstantin E. Tsiolkovski, and Sergei P. Korolev, designer of the 1st Soviet spacecraft, vert. 2c, Yuri Gagarin, 1st man in space. 3c, Valentina Tereshkova, 1st woman in space, and *Vostok 6.* 5c, Aleksei A. Leonov, 1st man to walk in space. 13c, Konstantin Feoktistov, Boris Yegorov and Vladimir Komarov, *Voskhod 1* crew, 1st 3-man orbital flight. 30c, Valeri Ryumen and Leonid Popov, set a space endurance record. 50c, Arnaldo Tamayo, 1st Cuban cosmonaut, and Soviet cosmonaut Yuri Romanenko on joint space flight, vert.

1981, Apr. 12 ***Perf. 12½***

2399 A646 1c multi
2400 A646 2c multi
2401 A646 3c multi
2402 A646 5c multi
2403 A646 13c multi
2404 A646 30c multi
2405 A646 50c multi

A647

Designs: 3c, Rocket, aircraft. 13c, Hand raising gun.

1981, Apr. 19 **Litho.** ***Perf. 13***

2406 A647 3c multi, vert.
2407 A647 13c multi, vert.
2408 A647 30c multi

Creation of armed forces (DAAFAR) (3c), Bay of Pigs Invasion, 20th Anniv. (13c), Proclamation of the socialist revolution (30c).

Attack on Goicuria Barracks, 25th Anniv. — A648

1981, Apr. 29

2409 A648 3c multi

Natl. Assoc. of Small Farmers (ANAP), 20th Anniv. A649

1981, May 17

2410 A649 3c multi

Souvenir Sheet

WIPA '81 — A650

1981, May 22 **Litho.**

2411 A650 50c Austria No. 643

Fighting Cocks A651

1981, May 25 ***Perf. 12½x13, 13x12½***

2412 A651 1c Canelo, vert.
2413 A651 3c Cenizo
2414 A651 7c Blanco, vert.
2415 A651 13c Pinto, vert.
2416 A651 30c Giro
2417 A651 50c Jabao, vert.

Ministry of the Interior, 20th Anniv. — A652

1981, June 6 ***Perf. 13***

2418 A652 13c multi

Souvenir Sheet

Mother and Child, by Zlatka Dabova — A653

1981, June 14

2419 A653 50c gold, sil & blk

Bulgaria, 1300th anniv. BULGARIA '81 phil. exhib.

Horse-drawn Carriages — A654

1981, June 25

2420 A654 1c Streetcar
2421 A654 4c Bus
2422 A654 9c Breake
2423 A654 13c Landau
2424 A654 30c Phaeton
2425 A654 50c Funeral coach

House in the Country, by Mario Caridad — A655

1981, July 15 ***Perf. 12½***

2426 A655 30c multi

Intl. Year of the Disabled.

Sandinistas, 25th Anniv. — A656

1981, July 23 ***Perf. 13***

2427 A656 13c multi

State Institutions, 20th Annivs. — A657

1981, July 26 ***Perf. 12½***

2428 A657 3c multi
2429 A657 13c multi, diff.
2430 A657 30c multi, diff.

Institute for Sports, Physical Education and Recreation (3c); Radio Havana (13c); and Ministry of Foreign Trade (MINCEX) (30c).

Carlos J. Finlay and Cent. of His Theory of Biological Vectors — A658

1981, Aug. 14 ***Perf. 13***

2431 A658 13c multi

Nonaligned Countries Movement, 20th Anniv. — A659

1981, Sept. 1

2432 A659 50c multi

Horses — A660

Illustration reduced. Nos. 2433-2437 vert.

1981, Sept. 15 ***Perf. 13***

Size: 29x40mm

2433 A660 1c multi
2434 A660 3c multi, diff.
2435 A660 8c multi, diff.
2436 A660 13c multi, diff.
2437 A660 30c multi, diff.

Size: 68x27mm

Perf. 12½

2438 A660 50c Herd

Souvenir Sheet

Idyll in a Tea House, by Kitagawa Utamaro — A661

1981, Oct. 9 ***Perf. 13***
2439 A661 50c multi

PHILATOKYO '81.

Lighthouse Type of 1980

1981, Oct. 15 **Litho.**
2440 A637 3c North Rock
2441 A637 13c Lucrecia Point
2442 A637 40c East Guano

Jose Marti Natl. Library, 80th Anniv. — A662

Sugar mills, lithographs from *Los Ingenios,* by Eduardo Laplante (b. 1818): 3c, Flor de Cuba, 1838. 13c, El Progreso, 1845. 30c, Santa Teresa, 1847.

1981, Oct. 18 ***Perf. 12½x12***
2443 A662 3c multi
2444 A662 13c multi
2445 A662 30c multi

Pablo Picasso (b. 1881) and No. 1263 A663

1981, Oct. 25 ***Perf. 12½x13***
2446 A663 30c multi

Souvenir Sheet

ESPAMER '81, Buenos Aires — A664

1981, Nov. 13 ***Perf. 13***
2447 A664 1p Packet

Art Type of 1969

Paintings in the Napoleon Museum: 1c, *Napoleon in Coronation Costume,* anonymous. 3c, *Napoleon with Landscape in the Background,* by Jean Horace Vernet. 10c, *Bonaparte in Egypt,* by Edouard Detaille. 13c, *Napoleon on Horseback,* by Hippolyte Bellange. 30c, *Napoleon in Normandy,* by Bellange. 50c, *Death of Napoleon,* anonymous.

1981, Dec. 1 ***Perf. 12½***
Sizes: 42x58mm, 58x42mm (3c, 13c, 30c, 50c)
2448 A385 1c multi
2449 A385 3c multi, horiz.
2450 A385 10c multi
2451 A385 13c multi, horiz.
2452 A385 30c multi, horiz.
2453 A385 50c multi, horiz.

Napoleon Museum, 20th anniv.

25th Annivs. A665

1981, Dec. 2 ***Perf. 13***
2454 A665 3c Revolutionaries, vert.
2455 A665 20c Marksman
2456 A665 1p Yacht *Granma*

November 30th insurrection (3c); creation of the revolutionary armed forces (20c); and disembarking of revolutionary forces (1p).

Fauna — A666

1981, Dec. 14 **Litho.** ***Perf. 12½x12***
2457 A666 1c Hummingbird
2458 A666 2c Parakeet
2459 A666 5c Hutia
2460 A666 20c Almiqui
2461 A666 35c Manatee
2462 A666 40c Crocodile

Fernando Ortiz, Folklorist, Birth Cent. A667

1981, Dec. 20 ***Perf. 12½x13***
2463 A667 3c Portrait by Jorge Arche y Silva
2464 A667 10c Hanging idol
2465 A667 30c Arara drum
2466 A667 50c Chango statue

Literacy Campaign, 20th Anniv. — A668

1981, Dec. 25 ***Perf. 12½x12***
2467 5c Conrado Benitez
2468 5c Manuel Asunce
a. A668 Pair, #2467-2468

A669

1982 World Cup Soccer Championships, Spain — A670

Various athletes.

1982, Jan. 15 ***Perf. 13***
2469 A669 1c multi, vert.
2470 A669 2c multi, vert.
2471 A669 5c multi, vert.
2472 A669 10c multi, vert.
2473 A669 20c shown
2474 A669 40c multi
2475 A669 50c multi, vert.

Souvenir Sheet

2476 A670 1p shown

No. 2476 contains one 32x40mm stamp.

10th World Trade Unions Congress, Havana — A671

1982, Feb. 10 **Litho.**
2477 A671 30c Lazaro Pena, delegate

Butterflies — A672

1982, Feb. 25 ***Perf. 12½***
2478 A672 1c *Euptoieta hegesia*
2479 A672 4c *Metamorpha stelenes insularis*
2480 A672 5c *Heliconius charithonius ramsdeni*
2481 A672 20c *Phoebis avellaneda*
2482 A672 30c *Hamadryas ferox diasia*
2483 A672 50c *Marpesia eleuchea*

Exports — A673

3c, Sugar (processing plant). 4c, Lobster (fishing boat). 6c, Canned fruits. 7c, Agricultural machinery. 8c, Nickel (passenger jet, industrial complex, car). 9c, Rum. 10c, Coffee. 30c, Fresh fruit. 50c, Tobacco. 1p, Cement. Nos. 2489-2493 vert.

1982, Feb. 26 ***Perf. 12x12½, 12½x12***
2484 A673 3c lt grn
2485 A673 4c car rose
2486 A673 6c dull blue
2487 A673 7c brt org
2488 A673 8c brt vio
2489 A673 9c slate
2490 A673 10c dull red brn
2491 A673 30c bister
2492 A673 50c orange
2493 A673 1p olive bister

Tulips A674

1982, Mar. 30 ***Perf. 12½x13***
2494 A674 1c Greenland
2495 A674 3c Mariette
2496 A674 8c Ringo
2497 A674 20c La Tulipe Noire
2498 A674 30c Jewel of Spring
2499 A674 50c Orange Parrot

Communist Youth Organization, 20th Anniv. — A675

1982, Apr. 4 ***Perf. 13***
2500 A675 5c multi

2nd UN Congress on the Peaceful Use of Outer Space — A676

1982, Apr. 12
2501 A676 1c *Mars*
2502 A676 3c *Venera*
2503 A676 6c *Salyut-Soyuz* link-up
2504 A676 20c *Lunokhod* moon vehicle
2505 A676 30c *Venera* with heat shield
2506 A676 50c *Cosmos*

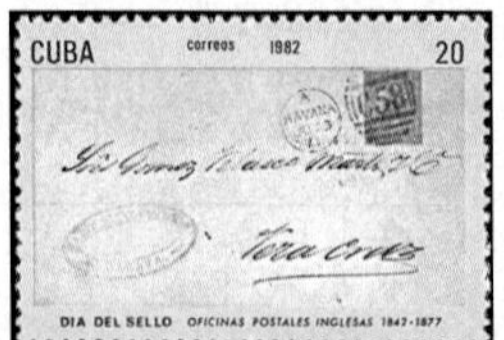

Cover A677

1982, Apr. 24 ***Perf. 12½x12***
2507 A677 20c Havana-Veracruz
2508 A677 30c Havana-Tampico

Stamp Day. English post office, 1842-1877 (20c); and French post office, 1862-1877 (30c).

Broadcasting and Television Institute (ICRT), 20th Anniv. — A678

1982, May 24 ***Perf. 12x12½***
2509 A678 30c multi

Art Type of 1981
With Larger Type

Paintings in the Natl. Museum of Art: 1c, *Portrait of a Youth* (girl), by Jean B. Greuze, vert. 3c, *Procession in Brittany*, by Jules Breton. 9c, *Landscape*, by Jean Piliment. 20c, *Late Afternoon*, by William A. Bourgueran, vert. 30c, *Tiger*, by Ferdinand V.E. Delacroix. 40c, *The Chair*, by Wilfredo Lam, vert.

Perf. 13, 13x12½ (3c), 12x12½ (20c, 40c), 12½x12 (30c)

1982, May 31 **Litho.**
2510 A642 1c 29x40mm
2511 A642 3c 46x36mm
2512 A642 9c 40x29mm
2513 A642 20c 27x42mm
2514 A642 30c 42x27mm
2515 A642 40c 27x42mm

Souvenir Sheet

PHILEXFRANCE '82 — A679

1982, June 7 ***Perf. 13***
2516 A679 1p Steamship *Louisiana* at St. Nazaire

DEPORFILEX '82 — A680

1982, June 10 ***Perf. 13x12½***
2517 A680 20c Hurdler, No. 300

Reptiles A681

1982, June 15 ***Perf. 13***
2518 A681 1c *Pseudemys decussata*
2519 A681 2c *Tropidophis pardalis*
2520 A681 3c *Crocodylus rhombifer*
2521 A681 20c *Cyclura nubila*
2522 A681 30c *Anolis allisonis*
2523 A681 50c *Alsophis canthergerus*

George Dimitrov (1882-1949), Bulgarian Prime Minister — A682

1982, June 18
2524 A682 30c multi

Koch, Bacillus A683

1982, July 18
2525 A683 20c multi

Discovery of the tubercle bacillus by Dr. Robert Koch, cent.

14th Central American and Caribbean Games — A684

1982, Aug. 1
2526 A684 1c Baseball
2527 A684 2c Boxing
2528 A684 10c Water polo
2529 A684 20c Javelin
2530 A684 35c Weight lifting
2531 A684 50c Volleyball

Hydraulic Development Plan, 20th Anniv. — A685

5c, Fruit, *Eichornia crassipes*, ship. 20c, Arid soil, *Nymphaea alba*, irrigation & reservoir systems.

1982, Aug. 9
2532 A685 5c multi
2533 A685 20c multi

Souvenir Sheet

DEPORFILEX '82, Intl. Stamp and Coin Exhibition — A686

1982, Aug. 10 **Litho.**
2534 A686 1p Cuco, character trademark

14th Central American and Caribbean Games.

Namibia Day — A687

1982, Aug. 26
2535 A687 50c multi

1982 World Cup Soccer Championships, Spain — A688

Various athletes.

1982, Aug. 30
2536 A688 5c multi
2537 A688 20c multi
2538 A688 30c multi
2539 A688 50c multi

Also exist in miniature sheets of 16 + 9 labels containing 4 each Nos. 2536-2539 in blocks of 4.

Natl. Folklore Ensemble, 20th Anniv. — A689

Paintings by V.P. Landaluze.

1982, Sept. 10
2540 A689 20c *Little Devil*, vert.
2541 A689 30c *Day of Kings*

Prehistoric Fauna — A690

1982, Sept. 15 **Litho.**
2542 A690 1c *Ornimegalonyx oteroi*, vert.
2543 A690 5c *Crocodylus rhombifer*
2544 A690 7c *Aquila borrasi*, vert.
2545 A690 20c *Geocapromys colombianus*
2546 A690 35c *Megalocnus rodens*, vert.
2547 A690 50c *Nesophontes micrus*

15th Death Anniv. of Che Guevara — A691

1982, Oct. 8 ***Perf. 13x12½***
2548 A691 20c multi

Discovery of America, 490th Anniv. — A692

1982, Oct. 12 ***Perf. 13***
2549 A692 5c shown
2550 A692 20c *Santa Maria*, vert.
2551 A692 35c *Pinta*, vert.
2552 A692 50c *Nina*, vert.

Lighthouse Type of 1980

1982, Oct. 25
2553 A637 5c Jutias Caye
2554 A637 20c Paredon Grande Caye
2555 A637 30c Morro Santiago de Cuba

George Washington, 250th Birth Anniv. — A693

Designs: Quotations and anonymous oil paintings, 18th-19th cent.

1982, Oct. 29 ***Perf. 12x12½***
2556 A693 5c multi
2557 A693 20c multi, diff.

Souvenir Sheet

8th Natl. Philatelic Exposition, Ciego de Avila — A694

1982, Nov. 13
2558 A694 1p Paddle steamer *Almendares*

8th Congress of the Cuban Philatelic Federation, Nov. 13-22.

Lenin Natl. Park, 10th Anniv. A695

1982, Dec. 28
2559 A695 5c multi

Chess Champion Jose Raul Capablanca and King — A696

1982, Dec. 29
2560 A696 5c shown
2561 A696 20c Rook
2562 A696 30c Knight

2563 A696 50c Queen
a. Bklt. pane of 4, Nos. 2560-2563

Exist in sheets of 4+2 labels picturing chessmen.

USSR, 60th Anniv. — A697

1982, Dec. 30 *Perf. 13x12½*
2564 A697 30c multi

World Communications Year — A698

1983, Jan. 24 Litho. *Perf. 13*
2565 A698 20c multi

No. 507 and Birthplace — A699

1983, Jan. 28 *Perf. 13x12½*
2566 A699 5c multi

Jose Marti (b. 1853), writer, revolution leader.

1984 Summer Olympics, Los Angeles A700

1983, Jan. 31 *Perf. 13*
2567 A700 1c Javelin
2568 A700 5c Volleyball
2569 A700 6c Basketball
2570 A700 20c Weight lifting
2571 A700 30c Wrestling
2572 A700 50c Boxing

Souvenir Sheet

Perf. 13½x13

2573 A700 1p Judo

No. 2573 contains one 32x40mm stamp.

Radio Rebelde, 25th Anniv. — A701

1983, Feb. 24 *Perf. 13*
2574 A701 20c multi

Karl Marx, Death Cent. A702

1983, Mar. 14
2575 A702 30c multi

1st Manned Balloon Flight, Bicent. — A703

Various balloons.

1983, Mar. 30
2576 A703 1c multi
2577 A703 3c multi
2578 A703 5c multi
2579 A703 7c multi
2580 A703 30c multi
2581 A703 50c multi

Souvenir Sheet

2582 A703 1p Jose D. Blino

No. 2582 contains one 32x40mm stamp.

Cosmonauts' Day — A704

1983, Apr. 12 Litho.
2583 A704 1c *Vostok 1*
2584 A704 4c Satellite *Frances D1*
2585 A704 5c *Mars 2*
2586 A704 20c *Soyuz*
2587 A704 30c Meteorological satellite
2588 A704 50c Intercosmos satellite

Stamp Day A705

1983, Apr. 24
2589 A705 20c Havana-Key West cover
2590 A705 30c Spain-Havana cover

1st Intl. airmail services.

Souvenir Sheet

TEMBAL '83, Basel — A706

1983, May 21 *Perf. 13½x13*
2591 A706 1p Weasel

Simon Bolivar, Liberator of South America A707

1983, July 24 *Perf. 12½x13*
2592 A707 5c Jose Rafael de las Heras
2593 A707 20c Bolivar

Attack of Moncada Barracks, 30th Anniv. — A708

Designs: 5c, Jose Marti, Moncada barracks. 20c, Abel Santamaria, Jose Luis Tasende and Boris Luis Santa Coloma, martyrs, vert. 30c, *History Will Absolve Me,* declaration of Fidel Castro, vert.

1983, July 26 *Perf. 13*
2594 A708 5c multi
2595 A708 20c multi
2596 A708 30c multi

Souvenir Sheet

Alberto Santos-Dumont (1873-1932) — A709

1983, July 29 *Perf. 13x13½*
2597 A709 1p Dumont's aircraft

BRASILIANA '83, Rio; 140th anniv. of 1st stamp issued in the Americas.

9th Pan American Games, Caracas — A710

1983, Aug. 14 *Perf. 13x12½*
2598 A710 1c Weight lifting
2599 A710 2c Volleyball
2600 A710 3c Baseball
2601 A710 20c High jump
2602 A710 30c Basketball
2603 A710 50c Boxing

Port, by Claude Joseph Vernet — A711

1983, Sept. 5
2604 A711 30c multi

French alliance, cent.

Pres. Salvador Allende of Chile (d. 1973) — A712

1983, Sept. 12
2605 A712 20c multi

1st Congress of Farmers at Arms, 25th Anniv. — A713

1983, Sept. 21 *Perf. 12½x12*
2606 A713 5c multi

Raphael, 500th Birth Anniv. — A714

1983, Sept. 30 Litho. *Perf. 13*
2607 A714 1c *Girl with Veil*
2608 A714 2c *The Cardinal*
2609 A714 5c *Francesco M. Della Rovere*
2610 A714 20c *Portrait of a Youth*
2611 A714 30c *Magdalena Doni*
2612 A714 50c *La Fornarina*

State Quality Seal A715

1983, Oct. 14
2613 A715 5c multi

Lighthouse Type of 1980

1983, Oct. 20

2614 A637 5c Carapachibey
2615 A637 20c Cadiz Bay
2616 A637 30c Gobernadora Point

Turtles A716

1983, Nov. 15

2617 A716 1c *Eretmochelys imbricata*
2618 A716 2c *Lepidochelys kempi*
2619 A716 5c *Chrysemys decussata*
2620 A716 20c *Caretta caretta*
2621 A716 30c *Chelonia mydas*
2622 A716 50c *Dermochelys coriacea*

World Communications Year — A717

1983, Nov. 23

2623 A717 1c Bell's Gallow Frame, telephone
2624 A717 5c Telegram, airmail
2625 A717 10c Satellite, satellite dish
2626 A717 20c Television, radio
2627 A717 30c 24th Communications conf.

Nos. 319 and 990 A718

1983, Dec. 3 ***Perf. 13x12½***

2628 A718 20c multi

See note after No. 320.

Flowers, Birds A719

Flowers A720

1983, Dec. 20 ***Perf. 13***

2629 A719 5c *Opuntia dillenii*
2630 A719 5c *Euphorbia podocarpifolia*
2631 A719 5c *Dinema cubincola*
2632 A719 5c *Guaiacum officinale*
2633 A719 5c *Magnolia cubensis*
a. Strip of 5, Nos. 2629-2633
2634 A719 5c *Jatropha angustifolia*
2635 A719 5c *Cochlospermum vitifolium*
2636 A719 5c *Tabebuia lepidota*
2637 A719 5c *Kalmiella ericoides*
2638 A719 5c *Jatropha integerrima*
2639 A719 5c *Melocactus actinacanthus*
2640 A719 5c *Cordia sebestana*
2641 A719 5c *Tabernae - montana apoda*
2642 A719 5c *Lantana camara*
2643 A719 5c *Cordia gerascanthus*
a. Block of 10, Nos. 2634-2643
2644 A719 5c *Tiaris canora*
2645 A719 5c *Phaethon lepturus*
2646 A719 5c *Myadestes elisabeth*
2647 A719 5c *Saurothera merlini*
2648 A719 5c *Polioptila lembeyei*
a. Strip of 5, Nos. 2644-2648
2649 A719 5c *Mellisuga helenae*
2650 A719 5c *Mimus polyglottos*
2651 A719 5c *Todus multicolor*
2652 A719 5c *Amazona leucocephala*
2653 A719 5c *Ferminia cerverai*
2654 A719 5c *Pelecanus occidentalis*
2655 A719 5c *Melanerpes superciliaris*
2656 A719 5c *Mimocichla plumbea*
2657 A719 5c *Aratinga euops*
2658 A719 5c *Sturnella magna*
a. Block of 10, Nos. 2649-2658

Souvenir Sheets

2658B A719 100c *Hedychium coronarium*
2658C A719 100c *Priotelus temnurus*

1983, Dec. 30 ***Perf. 12½***

2659 A720 60c Tobacco
2660 A720 70c Lily
2661 A720 80c Mariposa
2662 A720 90c Orchid

25th Anniv. of the Revolution — A721

1983, Dec. 31 **Litho.** ***Perf. 13***

2663 A721 5c shown
2664 A721 20c Flags, Santa Clara Rlwy. tracks

25th Anniv. of the Revolution — A722

1984, Jan. 8

2665 20c Guevara, Castro
2666 20c Star
2667 20c PCC emblem, workers
a. A722 Strip of 3, #2665-2667

Lenin, 60th Death Anniv. A723

1984, Jan. 21 ***Perf. 12½x12***

2668 A723 30p Spasski Tower, Russia Nos. 295, 265

Cuban Labor Union, 45th Anniv. A724

1984, Jan. 28 ***Perf. 13***

2669 A724 5c multi

Butterflies — A725

1984, Jan. 31 ***Perf. 13x12½***

2670 A725 1c *Ixias balice*
2671 A725 2c *Phoebis avellaneda*
2672 A725 3c *Anthocaris sara*
2673 A725 5c *Victorina*
2674 A725 20c *Heliconius cydno cydnides*
2675 A725 30c *Parides gundlachianus calzadillae*
2676 A725 50c *Catagramma sorana*

Marine Mammals — A726

1984, Feb. 15 ***Perf. 12x12½, 12½x12***

2677 A726 1c *Grampus griseus*, vert.
2678 A726 2c *Delphinus delphis*, vert.
2679 A726 5c *Physeter catodon*
2680 A726 6c *Stenella plagiodon*, vert.
2681 A726 10c *Pseudorca crassidens*
2682 A726 30c *Tursiops truncatus*, vert.
2683 A726 50c *Megaptera novaeangliae*

Augusto C. Sandino (1893-1934), Nicaraguan Revolutionary — A727

1984, Feb. 21 ***Perf. 13***

2684 A727 20c multi

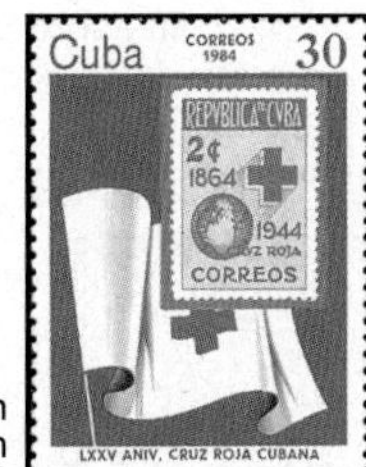

Red Cross in Cuba, 75th Anniv. — A728

1984, Mar. 10

2685 A728 30c Flag, No. 404

Cuban Film Industry, 25th Anniv. A729

1984, Mar. 24

2686 A729 20c multi

Caribbean Flowers — A730

1984, Mar. 29

2687 A730 1c *Brownea grandiceps*
2688 A730 2c *Couroupita guianensis*
2689 A730 5c *Triplaris surinamensis*
2690 A730 20c *Amherstia nobilis*
2691 A730 30c *Plumieria alba*
2692 A730 50c *Delonix regia*

Cosmonauts' Day — A731

1984, Apr. 12

2693 A731 2c *Electron 1*, 1964
2694 A731 3c *Electron 2*, 1964
2695 A731 5c *Intercosmos 1*, 1969
2696 A731 10c *Mars 5*, 1974
2697 A731 30c *Soyuz*, 1969
2698 A731 50c USSR-Bulgaria space flight, 1979

Souvenir Sheet

Perf. 12½

2699 A731 1p *Luna 1*, 1959

No. 2699 contains one 32x40mm stamp.

Mothers' Day — A732

1984, Apr. 19 ***Perf. 13***

2700 A732 20c Red roses
2701 A732 20c Pink roses

Stamp Day — A733

Designs: Mural, by R. Rodriguez Radillo (details).

1984, Apr. 24 *Perf. 13x12½*
2702 A733 20c Mexican runner
2703 A733 30c Egyptian boatman

See Nos. 2787-2788, 2860-2861, 3025-3026, 3122-3123, 3213-3214.

Souvenir Sheet

ESPANA '84, Madrid — A734

1984, Apr. 27 *Perf. 13x13½*
2704 A734 1p Clipper ship

Women's Basketball, 1984 Summer Olympics A735

1984, May 5 *Perf. 13*
2705 A735 20c multi

Agrarian Reform Act, 25th Anniv. — A736

1984, May 17 *Perf. 13½x13*
2706 A736 5c multi

Banco Popular de Ahorro, 1st Anniv. — A737

1984, May 18 *Perf. 13*
2707 A737 5c multi

Early Locomotives — A738

1984, June 11 *Perf. 12½x12*
2708 A738 1c multi
2709 A738 4c multi, diff.
2710 A738 5c multi, diff.
2711 A738 10c multi, diff.
2712 A738 30c multi, diff.
2713 A738 50c multi, diff.

Souvenir Sheet

19th UPU Congress, HAMBURG '84 — A739

1984, June 19 *Perf. 13x13½*
2714 A739 1p Nos. 73, 232

Intl. Olympic Committee, 90th Anniv. — A740

1984, June 23 *Perf. 13*
2715 A740 30c Coubertin, torchbearer

Children's Day A741

1984, July 15 *Perf. 12½x13*
2716 A741 5c multi

1984 Summer Olympics, Los Angeles A742

1984, July 28 *Perf. 13*
2717 A742 1c Wrestling
2718 A742 3c Discus
2719 A742 5c Volleyball
2720 A742 20c Boxing
2721 A742 30c Basketball
2722 A742 50c Weight lifting

Souvenir Sheet

Perf. 12½

2723 A742 1p Baseball

No. 2723 contains one 32x40mm stamp.

Emilio Roig de Leuchsenring (1889-1964), Historian A743

1984, Aug. 8 *Perf. 13*
2724 A743 5c multi

Friendship Games, Aug. 18-26, Havana — A744

1984, Aug. 18
2725 A744 3c Volleyball
2726 A744 5c Women's volleyball
2727 A744 8c Water polo
2728 A744 30c Boxing

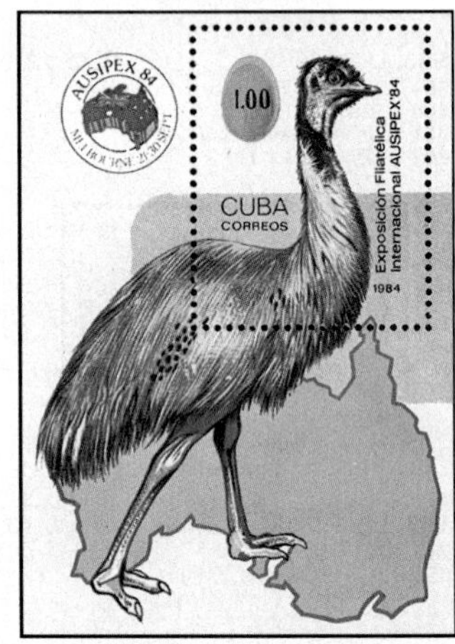

Cattle Breeding A745

1984, Sept. 20
2729 A745 2c Artificial pastures
2730 A745 3c Cuban carib
2731 A745 5c Charolaise, vert.
2732 A745 30c Cuban cebu, vert.
2733 A745 50c White-udder

Souvenir Sheet

AUSIPEX '84, Sept. 21-30, Melbourne — A746

1984, Sept. 21 *Perf. 12½*
2734 A746 1p Emu

Fauna — A747

1984, Oct. 10 *Perf. 13*
2735 A747 1c *Polymita*
2736 A747 2c *Solenodon cubanus*
2737 A747 3c *Alsophis cantherigerus*
2738 A747 4c *Osteopilus septentrionalis*
2739 A747 5c *Mellisuga helenae*
2740 A747 10c *Capromys melanurus*
2741 A747 30c *Todus multicolor*
2742 A747 50c Parrots (cotorra)

Souvenir Sheet

ESPAMER '85, Havana A748

1984, Oct. 12
2743 Sheet of 4+2 labels
a. A748 5c Ferdinand, Isabella
b. A748 20c Departure from Palos
c. A748 30c *Nina, Pinta, Santa Maria*
d. A748 50c Landing in America

Columbus Day.

Souvenir Sheet

9th Natl. Phil. Exhibition, Oct. 20-28, Santiago de Cuba — A749

1984, Oct. 20 *Perf. 12½*
2744 A749 1p multicolored

Natl. Revolutionary Militia, 25th Anniv. — A750

1984, Oct. 26 *Perf. 12½x13*
2745 A750 5c multi

Disappearance of Camilo Cienfuegos, 25th Anniv. — A751

1984, Oct. 28 *Perf. 13x12½*
2746 A751 5c multi

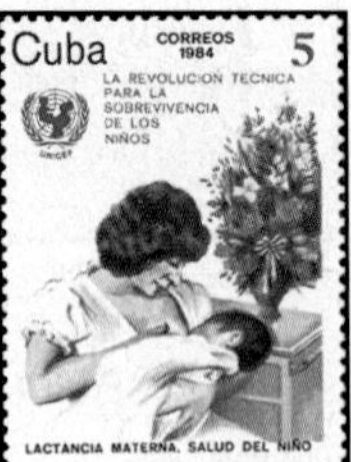

UN Child Survival Campaign A752

1984, Nov. 11 *Perf. 13*
2747 A752 5c Breast-feeding

Classic Automobiles — A753

1984, Nov. 25

2748 A753 1c 1909 Morgan
2749 A753 2c 1922 Austin
2750 A753 5c 1903 De Dion-Bouton
2751 A753 20c 1908 Ford Model T
2752 A753 30c 1885 Benz
2753 A753 50c 1910 Benz

Postal Museum, 20th Anniv. — A754

1985, Jan. 2 ***Perf. 13x12½***

2754 A754 20c multi

Portrait of Celia Sanchez, by E. Escobedo A755

1985, Jan. 11 ***Perf. 13***

2755 A755 5c multi

Celia Sanchez (1920-1980), party leader.

PORTO '85, Intl. Pigeon Exhibition — A756

1985, Jan. 23

2756 A756 20c multi

1986 World Cup Soccer Championships, Mexico — A757

Athletes and Flags of previous host nations.

1985, Jan. 25

2757 A757 1c Chile, 1962
2758 A757 2c Great Britain, 1966
2759 A757 3c Mexico, 1970
2760 A757 4c Federal Republic of Germany, 1974
2761 A757 5c Argentina, 1978
2762 A757 30c Spain, 1982
2763 A757 50c Sweden, 1958

Souvenir Sheet

Perf. 12½

2764 A757 1p Mexico, 1986

No. 2764 contains one 40x32mm stamp.

Bacanao Natl. Park — A758

Dinosaurs.

1985, Feb. 14 ***Perf. 13x12½***

2765 A758 1c Pteranodon
2766 A758 2c Brontosaurus
2767 A758 4c Iguanodontus
2768 A758 5c Estegosaurus
2769 A758 8c Monoclonius
2770 A758 30c Corythosaurus
2771 A758 50c Tyrannosaurus

13th Congress of the Postal Unions of the Americas, Havana — A759

Design: Uruguay #196, congress emblem and Brazil #287. Illustration reduced.

1985, Mar. 11 ***Perf. 12½x12***

2772 A759 20c multi

ESPAMER '85 — A760

Indian activities: 1c, Playing ball. 2c, Medicine man preparing calumet and other ritual items. 5c, Net and spear fishing. 20c, Potter. 30c, Hunting. 50c, Hollowing-out canoe, decorating paddle. 1p, Cooking.

1985, Mar. 19 ***Perf. 12½x13***

2773 A760 1c multi
2774 A760 2c multi
2775 A760 5c multi
2776 A760 20c multi
2777 A760 30c multi
2778 A760 50c multi

Souvenir Sheet

Perf. 12½

2779 A760 1p multi

No. 2779 contains one 32x40mm stamp.
An imperf. souvenir sheet exists containing Nos. 2773-2779.

Cosmonauts' Day — A761

Designs: 2c, Spacecraft orbiting Moon. 3c, Two spacecraft. 10c, Space walkers linked. 13c, Space walkers welding. 20c, *Vostok 2.* 50c, *Lunokhod 1* moon vehicle.

1985, Apr. 12 ***Perf. 13x12½***

2780 A761 2c multi
2781 A761 3c multi
2782 A761 10c multi
2783 A761 13c multi
2784 A761 20c multi
2785 A761 50c multi

12th Youth and Students Festival, Moscow A762

1985, Apr. 19 ***Perf. 13***

2786 A762 30c Lenin Mausoleum

Stamp Day Type of 1984

Mural, by R. Rodriguez Radillo (1967), details: 20c, Roman charioteer (courier of *Cursus Publicus*). 35c, Medieval nobleman, monks (monastic messenger mail).

1985, Apr. 24 ***Perf. 13x12½***

2787 A733 20c multi
2788 A733 35c multi

Mothers' Day — A763

1985, May 2 ***Perf. 13***

2789 A763 1c Peonies
2790 A763 4c Carnations
2791 A763 5c Dahlias
2792 A763 13c Roses
2793 A763 20c Roses, diff.
2794 A763 50c Tulips

50th Death Anniv. of Antonio Guiteras and Carlos Aponte, Revolutionaries — A764

1985, May 9 ***Perf. 12½x12***

2795 A764 5c multi

End of WWII, 40th Anniv. A765

1985, May 10

2796 A765 5c shown
2797 A765 20c Soviet memorial, Berlin-Treptow
2798 A765 30c Dove

Souvenir Sheet

ARGENTINA '85, Buenos Aires — A766

1985, June 5 ***Perf. 13½x13***

2799 A766 1p *Vulture gryphus*

Motorcycle, Cent. — A767

1985, June 28 ***Perf. 13***

2800 A767 2c 1885 Daimler
2801 A767 5c 1910 Kaiser Tricycle
2802 A767 10c 1925 Fanomobile
2803 A767 30c 1926 Mars A20
2804 A767 50c 1936 Simson BSW

Development of Health Care Since the Revolution — A768

1985, July 18 ***Perf. 12½x12***

2805 A768 5c Hospitals

Federation of Cuban Women (FMC), 25th Anniv. — A769

1985, Aug. 23

2806 A769 5c multi

No. 2806 printed se-tenant with label picturing federation emblem.

Universiade Games, Japan — A770

1985, Aug. 27 ***Perf. 13***

2807 A770 50c multi

1st Havana Declaration, 25th Anniv. — A771

1985, Sept. 2
2808 A771 5c Jose Marti statue, revolutionaries

Souvenir Sheet

ITALIA '85 — A772

1985, Sept. 25 ***Perf. 12½***
2809 A772 1p Roman galley

Revolutionary Defense Committees (CDR), 25th Anniv. — A773

1985, Sept. 28 ***Perf. 13***
2810 A773 5c multi

Aquarium Fish — A774

1985, Sept. 30 **Litho.**
2811 A774 1c *Centropyge argi*
2812 A774 3c *Holacanthus tricolor*
2813 A774 5c *Chaetodon capistratus*
2814 A774 10c *Chaetodon sedentarius*
2815 A774 20c *Chaetodon ocellatus*
2816 A774 50c *Holacanthus ciliaris*

Communist Party Central Committee, 20th Anniv. — A775

1985, Oct. 1
2817 A775 5c multi

Souvenir Sheet

EXFILNA '85 — A776

1985, Oct. 18
2818 A776 1p Spain No. C45, Cuba No. 387

UN, 40th Anniv. — A777

1985, Oct. 24
2819 A777 20c multi

Sites on the UNESCO World Heritage List — A778

Designs: 2c, Plaza Vieja, 16th cent. 5c, Royal Army Castle, c. 1558. 20c, Havana Cathedral, c. 1748. 30c, Captains-General Palace (Havana City Museum), 1776. 50c, The Temple, 1827.

1985, Nov. 25
2820 A778 2c multi
2821 A778 5c multi
2822 A778 20c multi
2823 A778 30c multi
2824 A778 50c multi

1986 World Cup Soccer Championships, Mexico — A779

Various athletes.

1986, Jan. 20
2825 A779 1c multi
2826 A779 4c multi
2827 A779 5c multi
2828 A779 10c multi
2829 A779 30c multi
2830 A779 50c multi

Souvenir Sheet
Perf. 13½x13

2831 A779 1p multi

No. 2831 contains one 32x40mm stamp.

3rd Communist Party Congress, Havana — A780

1986, Feb. 4 ***Perf. 13***
2832 A780 5c shown
2833 A780 20c Party and natl. flags, emblem

Natl. Sports Institute (INDER), 25th Anniv. A781

1986, Feb. 23
2834 A781 5c multi

A782 A783

1986, Feb. 23
2835 A782 5c multi

Ministry of Domestic Trade, 25th anniv.

1986, Feb. 25 ***Perf. 12½x12***

Exotic flowers in the Botanical Gardens.

2836 A783 1c *Tecomaria capensis*
2837 A783 3c *Michelia champaca*
2838 A783 5c *Thunbergia grandiflora*
2839 A783 8c *Dendrobium phalaenopsis*
2840 A783 30c *Allamanda violacea*
2841 A783 50c *Rhodactus bleo*

Gundlach and Birds — A784

1986, Mar. 14 **Litho.** ***Perf. 13½x13***
2842 A784 1c *Agelaius assimilis*
2843 A784 3c *Dendroica pityophila*
2844 A784 7c *Myiarchus sagrae*
2845 A784 9c *Dendroica petechia gundlachi*
2846 A784 30c *Geotrygon caniceps*
2847 A784 50c *Colaptes auratus chrysocaulosus*

Juan Cristobal Gundlach (d. 1896), ornithologist.

Pioneers Youth Organization, 25th Anniv. — A785

1986, Apr. 3 ***Perf. 13***
2848 A785 5c Induction

150th Birth Anniv. of Maximo Gomez — A786

1986, Apr. 4
2849 A786 20c multi

A787

A788

1986, Apr. 10 ***Perf. 12½***
2850 A787 5c multi

Kindergartens, 25th anniv.

1986, Apr. 12 ***Perf. 13x13½***

1st Man in Space, 25th Anniv.: 1c, *Vostok* and rocket designer Sergei Korolev. 2c, Yuri Gagarin, *Vostok 1*. 5c, Valentina Tereshkova, *Vostok 6*. 20c, *Salyut-Soyuz* space link. 30c, Capsule landing. 50c, *Soyuz* rocket launch. 1p, Konstantin Tsiolkovski (1857-1935), rocket scientist.

2851 A788 1c multi
2852 A788 2c multi
2853 A788 5c multi
2854 A788 20c multi
2855 A788 30c multi
2856 A788 50c multi

Souvenir Sheet
Perf. 12½

2857 A788 1p multi

No. 2857 contains one 32x40mm stamp.

Natl. Flag and No. 2407 A789

1986, Apr. 19 ***Perf. 13***
2858 A789 5c shown
2859 A789 20c Banners, natl. crest

Bay of Pigs invasion, 25th anniv. (5c); Proclamation of Socialist Revolution, 25th anniv. (20c).

Stamp Day Type of 1984

Mural, by R. Rodriguez Radillo (1967), details.

1986, Apr. 24 ***Perf. 13x12½***
2860 A733 20c Mail coach, 18th-19th cent.
2861 A733 30c Pony Express

Radio Havana, 25th Anniv. — A790

1986, May 1

2862 A790 5c multi

EXPO '86, Vancouver — A791

Locomotives: 1c, *Stourbridge Lion,* 1829, US. 4c, Stephenson's *Rocket,* 1829, GB. 5c, 1st Russian locomotive, 1845. 8c, Seguin's locomotive, 1830, France. 30c, 1st Canadian locomotive, 1836. 50c, Urban locomotive, Belgian Grand Central Rlwy., 1872. 1p, US locomotive pulling Cuban sugar train, 1837.

1986, May 2 Litho. ***Perf. 12½x12***

2863 A791 1c multi
2864 A791 4c multi
2865 A791 5c multi
2866 A791 8c multi
2867 A791 30c multi
2868 A791 50c multi

Souvenir Sheet

Perf. 13x13½

2869 A791 1p multi

No. 2869 contains one 40x32mm stamp.

Assoc. of Small Farmers, (ANAP), 25th Anniv. — A792

1986, May 17 ***Perf. 13***

2870 A792 5c multi

Intl. Peace Year A793

1986, June 2

2871 A793 30c multi

Ministry of the Interior (MININT), 25th Anniv. — A794

1986, June 6

2872 A794 5c multi

Martin Luther King, Jr. A795

1986, June 27 ***Perf. 13½x13***

2873 A795 20c multi

Bonifacio Byrne (d. 1936), Poet A796

1986, July 5 ***Perf. 13***

2874 A796 5c multi

Cuban Union of Writers and Artists (UNEAC), 25th Anniv. — A797

Sandinista Movement in Nicaragua (FSLN), 25th Anniv. — A798

1986, July 10 ***Perf. 13x12½***

2875 A797 5c multi

1986, July 23 ***Perf. 13x12***

Augusto Cesar Sandino and Carlos Fonseca.

2876 A798 20c multi

Ministry of Transportation, 25th Anniv. — A799

1986, Aug. 1 ***Perf. 13***

2877 A799 5c multi

7th University Games of Central America and the Caribbean A800

1986, Aug. 9

2878 A800 20c multi

Souvenir Sheet

STOCKHOLMIA '86 — A801

Designs: a, 2c Mambi Revolutionary stamp of 1897. b, Sweden Type A7, cancellation.

1986, Aug. 28 ***Perf. 12½***

2879 A801 Sheet of 2
a.-b. 50c multi

Nonaligned Countries Movement, 25th Anniv. — A802

1986, Sept. 1 ***Perf. 13½x13***

2880 A802 50c multi

Orchids — A803

1986, Sept. 15 ***Perf. 12½***

2881 A803 1c *Cattleya hardyana*
2882 A803 4c *Brassolaelio cattleya*
2883 A803 5c *Phalaenopsis marget moses*
2884 A803 10c *Laelio cattleya prism palette*
2885 A803 30c *Phalaenopsis violacea*
2886 A803 50c *Disa uniflora*

Latin American History — A804

Pre-Columbian artifacts: No. 2887, Mayan dwelling and votive jade sculpture. No. 2888, Inca vase and Tiahuanacu sun gate (Bolivia). No. 2889, Spain No. C47, discovery of America 500th anniv. emblem, scroll. No. 2890, Diaguitan duck-shaped pitcher and Pucara de Quitor ruins (Chile). No. 2891, San Agustin Archaeological Park megaliths and Quimbayan sculpture (Colombia). No. 2892, Moler grinding stone and Chorotega ceramic figurine. No. 2893, Tabaco idol and Indian dwelling (Cuba). No. 2894, Spain No. C38. No. 2895, Taino dwelling and chair (Dominica). No. 2896, Tolita statue and Ingapirca Castle ruins. No. 2897, Maya vase and Tikal Temple (Guatemala). No. 2898, Copan ruins and Maya idol. No. 2899, Spain No. C37. No. 2900, Chichen Itza Temple and Zapotecan urn (Mexico). No. 2901, Punta de Zapote megaliths and Ometepe ceramic figurine. No. 2902, Tonosi lidded ceramic bowl and Barriles monoliths. No. 2903, Ruins at Machu-Picchu and Inca statue (Peru). No. 2904, Spain No. C49. No. 2905, Teepees and triangular sculpture (Puerto Rico). No. 2906, Fertility statue from Santa Ana and Santo Domingo Cave.

1986, Oct. 12 ***Perf. 13***

2887 A804 1c multi
2888 A804 1c multi
2889 A804 1c multi
2890 A804 1c multi
2891 A804 1c multi
a. Strip of 5, Nos. 2887-2891
2892 A804 5c multi
2893 A804 5c multi
2894 A804 5c multi
2895 A804 5c multi
2896 A804 5c multi
a. Strip of 5, Nos. 2892-2896
2897 A804 10c multi
2898 A804 10c multi
2899 A804 10c multi
2900 A804 10c multi
2901 A804 10c multi
a. Strip of 5, Nos. 2897-2901
2902 A804 20c multi
2903 A804 20c multi
2904 A804 20c multi
2905 A804 20c multi
2906 A804 20c multi
a. Strip of 5, Nos. 2902-2906

Discovery of America, 500th anniv. (in 1992). See Nos. 2966-2985, 3065-3084, 3253-3272, 3463-3466.

Intl. Brigades, Spain, 50th Anniv. — A805

1986, Oct. 14 ***Perf. 12½x12***

2907 A805 30c multi

Paintings in the Natl. Museum A806

Designs: 2c, *Two Children,* by Gutierrez de la Vega, vert. 4c, *Sed,* by Jean-Georges Vibert. 6c, *Virgin and Child,* by Niccolo Abbate, vert. 10c, *Bullfight,* by Eugenio de Lucas Velazquez. 30c, *The Five Senses,* anonymous. 50c, *Arrival at Thomops Castle,* by Jean Louis Ernest.

1986, Nov. 5 ***Perf. 13***

2908 A806 2c multi
2909 A806 4c multi
2910 A806 6c multi
2911 A806 10c multi
2912 A806 30c multi
2913 A806 50c multi

Anniversaries — A807

1986, Dec. 2 Litho. ***Perf. 12½***

2914 A807 5c *Granma*

Size: 26x38mm

2915 A807 20c Soldier, rifle, flag

Granma Landings, 30th anniv. (5c); Revolutionary Armed Forces, 30th anniv. (20c).

Scholarship Program, 25th Anniv. — A808

1986, Dec. 22 ***Perf. 13***

2916 A808 5c Guevara, students

Natl. Literacy Campaign, 25th Anniv. — A809

1986, Dec. 25 ***Perf. 13x12½***

2917 A809 5c Marti, man learning to write

Siege of La Plata, 30th Anniv. A810

1987, Jan. 17 ***Perf. 12½x12***

2918 A810 5c Map, revolutionaries

Paintings in the Natl. Museum A811

3c, *Gypsy,* by Joaquin Sorolla. 5c, *Sir Walter Scott,* by Sir John W. Gordon. 10c, *Farm Meadows,* by Alfred de Breanski. 20c, *Still-life,* by Isaac van Duynen. 30c, *Landscape with Figures,* by Francesco Zuccarelli. 40c, *The Failure* (defeated bullfighter), by Ignacio Zuloaga.

1987, Feb. 5 ***Perf. 13***

2919 A811 3c multi, vert.
2920 A811 5c multi, vert.
2921 A811 10c multi
2922 A811 20c multi
2923 A811 30c multi
2924 A811 40c multi, vert.

Siege of the Presidential Palace, 30th Anniv. — A812

1987, Mar. 13 ***Perf. 12½x12***

2925 A812 5c Palace, van, Echeverra

Lazarus Ludwig Zamenhof and Russia Type A77 — A813

1987, Mar. 16 ***Perf. 13½x13***

2926 A813 30c multi

Esperanto, cent.

Souvenir Sheet

EXFILNA '87, 10th Natl. Stamp Exposition, Holguin — A814

1987, Mar. 28 ***Perf. 13x13½***

2927 A814 1p Nos. 552, C129

25th Anniv. and 5th Cong. of the Youth Communist League (U.J.C.) — A815

1987, Apr. 4 ***Perf. 13***

2928 A815 5c multi

Intercosmos, 20th Anniv. — A816

1987, Apr. 12 Litho. ***Perf. 12½x12***

2929 A816 3c *Intercosmos 1*
2930 A816 5c *Intercosmos 2*
2931 A816 10c *TD*
2932 A816 20c *Cosmos 93*
2933 A816 30c *Molniya*
2934 A816 50c *Vostok 3*

Souvenir Sheet

Perf. 13½x13

2935 A816 1p Rocket, *Vostok 3*

No. 2935 contains one 32x40mm stamp.

Stamp Day A817

Stamped covers and canceled stamps.

1987, Apr. 24 ***Perf. 13***

2936 A817 30c Havana, 1890
2937 A817 50c Santiago de Cuba, 1869

Mothers' Day — A818

Various dahlias and roses.

1987, May 2

2938 A818 3c multi
2939 A818 5c multi
2940 A818 10c multi
2941 A818 13c multi
2942 A818 30c multi
2943 A818 50c multi

Bone-lengthening Procedure (Femur in Frame) — A819

1987, May 4

2944 A819 5c multi

ORTOPEDIA '87, medical congress for orthopedists from Spanish and Portuguese-speaking countries, Havana.

Cuban Broadcasting and Television Institute, 25th Anniv. — A820

1987, May 24 ***Perf. 13***

2945 A820 5c multi

Battle of Uvero, 30th Anniv. A821

1987, May 28 ***Perf. 13½x13***

2946 A821 5c Views of monument, Sierra Maestra Mts.

CAPEX '87 — A822

Natl. flags, stamps and 19th cent. mail carriers pictured on cigarette cards: 3c, Messenger, llamas and Bolivia Type A9. 5c, Early p.o., automobile and France Type A17. 10c, Messengers riding elephants and Thailand Type A2. 20c, Messenger riding camel and stamp of Egypt, 1879. 30c, Mail troika and stamp of Russia. 50c, Post rider and stamp of Indo-China. 1p, Post rider and Mambi Revolutionary stamp.

1987, June 15 ***Perf. 12½x13***

2947 A822 3c multi
2948 A822 5c multi
2949 A822 10c multi
2950 A822 20c multi
2951 A822 30c multi
2952 A822 50c multi

Souvenir Sheet

Perf. 13½x13

2953 A822 1p multi

No. 2953 contains one 32x40mm stamp.

Dinosaur Exhibits, Bacanao Natl. Park A823

1987, June 25 ***Perf. 13***

2954 A823 3c multi
2955 A823 5c multi
2956 A823 10c multi
2957 A823 20c multi
2958 A823 35c multi
2959 A823 40c multi

Frank Pais (d. 1957), Teacher and Student Leader — A824

1987, July 30 ***Perf. 12½x12***

2960 A824 5c Pais, Rafael Maria Mendive University

10th Pan American Games, Indianapolis — A825

1987, Aug. 8

2961 A825 50c multi

Printed se-tenant with inscribed label picturing the 1991 Havana Games character trademark.

Siege of Cienfuegos, 30th Anniv. — A826

1987, Sept. 5 ***Perf. 13***

2962 A826 5c Memorial

Souvenir Sheet

HAFNIA '87, Denmark — A827

1987, Sept. 16 ***Perf. 13½x13***

2963 A827 1p Danish mailman, 1887, Type A6

Souvenir Sheet

ESPAMER '87, La Coruna, Oct. 2-12 — A828

1987, Oct. 2
2964 A828 1p La Coruna Port, 1525

20th Heroic Guerrillas Day — A829

1987, Oct. 8 ***Perf. 12½x12***
2965 A829 50c Coins, #1364

Latin American History Type of 1986

Indians and birds: #2966, Tehuelche Indian of Argentina, *Habia rubica.* #2967, *Ramphastos cuvieri,* Tibirica Indian of Brazil. #2968, Spain #C31 & discovery of America 500th anniv. emblem. #2969, *Vulture gryphus,* Lautaro Indian of Chile. #2970, Calarca Indian of Colombia, *Opisthocomus hoazin.* #2971, *Priotelus temnurus,* Hatuey Indian of Cuba. #2972, *Columbigallina passerina,* Enriquillo Indian of the Dominican Republic. #2973, Spain #427. #2974, *Semnornis ramphastinus,* Ruminahui Indian of Ecuador. #2975, *Pharomachrus mocinno,* Tecum Uman Indian of Guatemala. #2976, Anacaona Indian of Haiti, *Aramas guarauna.* #2977, Lempira Indian of Honduras, *Diglossa baritula.* #2978, Spain #C42. #2979, *Onychorhinchus mexicanus,* Cuauhtemoc Indian of Mexico. #2980, *Setofaga picta,* Nicarao Indian of Nicaragua. #2981, *Rupicola peruviana,* Atahualpa Indian of Peru. #2982, Atlacatl Indian of El Salvador, *Bluteo jamaicensis.* #2983, Spain #432. #2984, Abayuba Indian of Uruguay, *Phytotoma rutila.* #2985, Guaycaypuro Indian of Venezuela, *Ara arauna.*

1987, Oct. 12 ***Perf. 13***
2966 A804 1c multi
2967 A804 1c multi
2968 A804 1c multi
2969 A804 1c multi
2970 A804 1c multi
a. Strip of 5, Nos. 2966-2970
2971 A804 5c multi
2972 A804 5c multi
2973 A804 5c multi
2974 A804 5c multi
2975 A804 5c multi
a. Strip of 5, Nos. 2971-2975
2976 A804 10c multi
2977 A804 10c multi
2978 A804 10c multi
2979 A804 10c multi
2980 A804 10c multi
a. Strip of 5, Nos. 2976-2980
2981 A804 20c multi
2982 A804 20c multi
2983 A804 20c multi
2984 A804 20c multi
2985 A804 20c multi
a. Strip of 5, Nos. 2981-2985

Discovery of America, 500th anniv. (in 1992). *Vultur* is spelled incorrectly on No. 2969.

October Revolution, Russia, 70th Anniv. — A830

1987, Nov. 7 ***Perf. 12½x12***
2986 A830 30c Soviet spacecraft, Russia No. 379

Cuban Railway, 150th Anniv. — A831

Stamps on stamps.

1987, Nov. 19 ***Perf. 13x12½***
2987 A831 3c No. 453
2988 A831 5c No. 1061
2989 A831 10c No. 2010
2990 A831 20c No. 2011
2991 A831 35c No. 2360
2992 A831 40c No. 2361

Souvenir Sheet

Perf. 13x13½

2993 A831 1p No. 355

No. 2993 contains 40x32mm one stamp.

An imperf. sheet containing Nos. 2987-2992 exists, inscribed to promote the 17th Pan American Railway Congress.

San Alejandro Art School, 170th Anniv. — A832

Paintings: 1c, *Landscape,* by Domingo Ramos. 2c, *Portrait of Rodriguez Morey,* by Eugenio Gonzalez Olivera. 3c, *Landscape with Malangas and Palm Trees,* by Valentin Sanz Carta. 5c, *Wagons,* by Eduardo Morales. 10c, *Portrait of Elena Herrera,* by Armando Menocal, vert. 30c, *Rape of Dejanira,* by Miguel Melero, vert. 50c, *The Card Player,* by Leopoldo Romanach.

1988, Jan. 12 ***Perf. 13x12½, 12½x13***
2994 A832 1c multi
2995 A832 2c multi
2995A A832 3c multi
2996 A832 5c multi
2997 A832 10c multi
2998 A832 30c multi
2999 A832 50c multi

Poisonous Mushrooms A833

1988, Feb. 15 ***Perf. 13***
3000 A833 1c *Boletus satanas*
3001 A833 2c *Amanita citrina*
3002 A833 3c *Tylopilus felleus*
3003 A833 5c *Paxillus involutus*
3004 A833 10c *Inocybe patouillardii*
3005 A833 30c *Amanita muscaria*
3006 A833 50c *Hypholoma fasciculare*

Radio Rebelde, 30th Anniv. — A834

1988, Feb. 24 ***Perf. 12½x12***
3007 A834 5c multi

Monuments A835

1988 **Litho.** ***Perf. 13***
3008 A835 5c Mario Munoz, Santiago de Cuba
3009 A835 5c Frank Pais Memorial, eternal flame

Battle fronts, 30th annivs. Issue dates: No. 3008, Mar. 5. No. 3009, Mar. 11.

Mothers' Day — A836

1988, Mar. 30
3010 A836 1c Red roses
3011 A836 2c Pale pink roses
3012 A836 3c Daisies
3013 A836 5c Dahlias
3014 A836 13c White roses
3015 A836 35c Carnations
3016 A836 40c Pink roses

Cosmonauts' Day — A837

1988, Apr. 12
3017 A837 2c *Gorizont*
3018 A837 3c *Mir-Kvant* space link
3019 A837 4c *Signo 3*
3020 A837 5c Mars, space probe
3021 A837 10c *Phobos*
3022 A837 30c *Vega*
3023 A837 50c Spacecraft

Souvenir Sheet

Perf. 13½x13

3024 A837 1p Spacecraft, diff.

No. 3024 contains one 32x40mm stamp.

Stamp Day Type of 1984

Mural, by R. Rodriguez Radillo (1967) details: 30c, Mail coach, telegraph operator. 50c, Passenger pigeon.

1988, Apr. 24 ***Perf. 13x12½***
3025 A733 30c multi
3026 A733 50c multi

Institute for Research on Sugar Cane and Byproducts (ICIDCA), 25th Anniv. — A838

1988, May 23 ***Perf. 12½x12***
3027 A838 5c multi

Cubana Airlines Transatlantic Flights — A839

1988, May 25
3028 A839 2c Madrid, 1948
3029 A839 4c Prague, 1961
3030 A839 5c Berlin, 1972
3031 A839 10c Luanda, 1975
3032 A839 30c Paris, 1983
3033 A839 50c Moscow, 1987

Souvenir Sheet

FINLANDIA '88 — A840

1988, June 1 ***Perf. 12½***
3034 A840 1p Steam packet *Furst Menschikoff*

Postal Union of the Americas and Spain (UPAE) Conference on Stamps of the Americas, Havana — A841

Illustration reduced.

1988, June 20 ***Perf. 12½x12***
3035 A841 20c multi

Beetles A842

1988, June 30 ***Perf. 13***
3036 A842 1c *Megasoma elephas fabricus*
3037 A842 3c *Platycoelia flavoscutellata ohaus,* vert.
3038 A842 4c *Plusiotis argenteola bates*
3039 A842 5c *Heterosternus oberthuri ohaus*
3040 A842 10c *Odontotaenius zodiacus truqui*
3041 A842 35c *Chrysophora chrysochlora latreille,* vert.
3042 A842 40c *Phanaeus leander waterhouse*

Jose Raul Capablanca (1888-1942), Chess Champion — A843

1988, July 15 ***Perf. 12½x13, 13x12½***
3043 A843 30c Chessmen, vert.
3044 A843 40c J. Corza, Capablanca

3045 A843 50c Lasker, Capablanca
3046 A843 1p Winning configuration, 1921, vert.
3047 A843 3p Portrait by E. Valderrama, vert.
3048 A843 5p Chessmen, Capablanca

Souvenir Sheets

3049 Sheet of 2
a. A843 30c No. 464, vert.
b. like No. 3043, size: 32x40mm
3050 Sheet of 2
a. A843 40c No. 465
b. like No. 3044, size: 40x32mm
3051 Sheet of 2
a. A843 50c No. C44
b. like No. 3045, size: 40x32mm
3052 Sheet of 2
a. A843 1p No. 464, vert.
b. like No. 3046, size: 32x40mm
3053 Sheet of 2
a. A843 3p No. C46, vert.
b. like No. 3047, size: 32x40mm
3054 Sheet of 2
a. A843 5p No. C45, vert.
b. like No. 3048, size: 32x40mm

Attack on Moncada Barracks, 35th Anniv. A844

1988, July 26 *Perf. 13*
3055 A844 5c blk, yel ocher & red

Souvenir Sheet

PRAGA '88 — A845

1988, Aug. 26 *Perf. 12½*
3056 A845 1p Czechoslovakia #45

Czechoslovakian postage stamps, 70th anniv.

Revolutionary Invasion Force, 30th Anniv. — A846

1988, Aug. 31 *Perf. 12½x12*
3057 A846 5c multi

World Marxist Review, 30th Anniv. A847

1988, Sept. 1 *Perf. 13*
3058 A847 30c multi

Locomotives — A848

1988, Sept. 19 *Perf. 12½x13*
3059 A848 20c Stephenson's *Rocket*, 1837
3060 A848 30c Miller, US, 1839
3061 A848 50c *La Junta*
3062 A848 1p J.G. Brill trolley, US, 1922
3063 A848 2p TEM 4K, USSR, c. 1960
3064 A848 5p CAP 9 electric, c. 1988

Latin American History Type of 1986

Natl. arms & patriots: #3065, San Martin, Argentina. #3066, M.A. Padilla, Bolivia. #3067, #390 & discovery of America 500th anniv. emblem. #3068, Tiradentes, Brazil. #3069, O'Higgins, Chile. #3070, A. Narino, Colombia. #3071, Marti, Cuba. #3072, #391 & emblem. #3073, Duarte, Dominican Republic. #3074, Sucre, Ecuador. #3075, M.J. Arce, El Salvador. #3076, Dessalines, Haiti. #3077, #C36 & emblem. #3078, Hidalgo, Mexico. #3079, J.D. Estrada, Nicaragua. #3080, Diaz, Paraguay. #3081, F. Bolognesi, Peru. #3082, #C37 & emblem. #3083, Artigas, Uruguay. #3084, Bolivar, Venezuela.

1988, Oct. 12 *Perf. 13*
3065 A804 1c multi
3066 A804 1c multi
3067 A804 1c multi
3068 A804 1c multi
3069 A804 1c multi
a. Strip of 5, Nos. 3065-3069
3070 A804 5c multi
3071 A804 5c multi
3072 A804 5c multi
3073 A804 5c multi
3074 A804 5c multi
a. Strip of 5, Nos. 3070-3074
3075 A804 10c multi
3076 A804 10c multi
3077 A804 10c multi
3078 A804 10c multi
3079 A804 10c multi
a. Strip of 5, Nos. 3075-3079
3080 A804 20c multi
3081 A804 20c multi
3082 A804 20c multi
3083 A804 20c multi
3084 A804 20c multi
a. Strip of 5, Nos. 3080-3084

Discovery of America, 500th anniv. (in 1992).

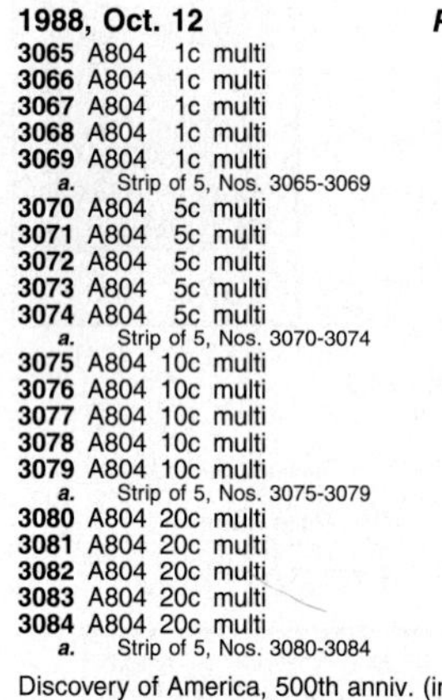

Havana Museum, 20th Anniv. — A849

Design: Captain-General's Palace and Maces of Municipal Havana.

1988, Oct. 16 Litho. *Perf. 12½x12*
3085 A849 5c multi + label

Anniversaries — A850

1988, Oct. 28 *Perf. 13*
3086 A850 5c *Swan Lake*
3087 A850 5c Theater in 1838 and 1988
a. Pair, Nos. 3086-3087

Natl. Ballet, 40th anniv. (No. 3086); Grand Theater of Havana, 150th anniv. (No. 3087).

Intl. Literacy Year A851

1988, Dec. 5
3088 A851 5c multi

UN Declaration of Human Rights, 40th Anniv. — A851a

1988, Dec. 10
3088A A851a 30c multi

Battle of Santa Clara, 30th Anniv. — A852

1988, Dec. 28 *Perf. 13x12½*
3089 A852 30c Monument, Che Guevara Plaza

30th Anniv. of the Revolution — A853

1989, Jan. 1 *Perf. 13*
3090 A853 5c multi
3091 A853 20c multi
3092 A853 30c multi
3093 A853 50c multi

Edible Mushrooms — A854

1989, Jan. 10
3094 A854 2c *Pleurotus levis*
3095 A854 3c *Pleurotus floridanus*
3096 A854 5c *Amanita caesarea*
3097 A854 10c *Lentinus cubensis*
3098 A854 40c *Pleurotus ostreatus* (brown)
3099 A854 50c *Pleurotus ostreatus* (yellow)

2c, 3c, 5c, 40c, 50c, vert.

Souvenir Sheet

INDIA '89 — A855

1989, Jan. 20
3100 A855 1p Indian River Post, 1858

Central Organization of Cuban Trade Unions (CTC), 50th Anniv. — A856

1989, Jan. 28 *Perf. 12½*
3101 A856 5c No. 2477, CTC emblem

Butterflies A857

1989, Feb. 15
3102 A857 1c *Metamorpho dido*
3103 A857 3c *Callithea saphhira*
3104 A857 5c *Papilio zagreus*
3105 A857 10c *Mynes sestia*
3106 A857 30c *Papilio dardanus*
3107 A857 50c *Catagranma sorana*

1990 World Cup Soccer Championships, Italy — A858

Various athletes.

1989, Mar. 15 *Perf. 13*
3108 A858 1c multi
3109 A858 3c multi, diff.
3110 A858 5c multi, diff.
3111 A858 10c multi, diff.
3112 A858 30c multi, diff.
3113 A858 50c multi, diff.

Souvenir Sheet

Perf. 12½

3114 A858 1p multi, diff., horiz.

No. 3114 contains one 40x32mm stamp.

Natl. Revolutionary Police (PNR), 30th Anniv. — A859

1989, Mar. 23 *Perf. 13*
3115 A859 5c multi

Cosmonauts' Day — A860

Spacecraft and rocket mail covers: 1c, *Zodiac* and cover, Australia 1934. 3c, Lighthouse and cover, India, 1934. 5c, Cover, England, 1934. 10c, *Icarus* and cover, The Netherlands, 1935. 40c, *La Douce France* and cover, France, 1935. 50c, Rocket mail cover, Cuba, 1939.

1989, Apr. 12

3116 A860 1c multi
3117 A860 3c multi
3118 A860 5c multi
3119 A860 10c multi
3120 A860 40c multi
3121 A860 50c multi

Stamp Day Type of 1984

Details of mural by R. Rodriguez Radillo (1967): 30c, Mail coach, Satellite dish. 50c, Galleon, longboats, train, passenger pigeon, horses.

1989, Apr. 24 Litho. ***Perf. 13x12½***

3122 A733 30c multi
3123 A733 50c multi

Casa de Las Americas, 30th Anniv. A861

1989, Apr. 28 ***Perf. 12½x13***

3124 A861 5c multi

BULGARIA '89 — A862

1989, May 1 ***Perf. 12½***

3125 A862 1p Bulgaria No. 346

58th FIP Congress and 101st anniv. of Bulgarian Railways.

Cuban Postal Code A863

1989, May 5 ***Perf. 13***

3126 A863 5c multi

Mothers' Day — A864

Perfume bottles and flowers.

1989, May 10

3127 A864 1c Habano, tobacco
3128 A864 3c Violeta, violets
3129 A864 5c Mariposa, mariposa
3130 A864 13c Coral Negro, roses
3131 A864 30c Ala Alonso, jasmine
3132 A864 50c D'Man, lemon blossoms

Agrarian Reform Law, 30th Anniv. — A865

1989, May 17 ***Perf. 12x12½***

3133 A865 5c multi

Council for Mutual Economic Assistance (CAME), 40th Anniv. A866

1989, June 1 Litho. ***Perf. 12½x13***

3134 A866 30c multi

13th World Communist Youth and Student Festival, Pyongyang — A867

1989, July 1 Litho. ***Perf. 12½***

3135 A867 30c multi

Souvenir Sheet

Rouget de Lisle Singing La Marseillaise, by Pils — A868

1989, July 7 ***Perf. 13***

3136 A868 1p multi

PHILEXFRANCE '89, French revolution bicent. and Cuban revolution 30th anniv.

BRASILIANA '89 — A869

Exotic birds. Illustration reduced.

1989, July 28 Litho. ***Perf. 12½***

3137 A869 1c *Ramphastos toco*
3138 A869 3c *Agamia agami*
3139 A869 5c *Eudocimus ruber*
3140 A869 10c *Psophia leucoptera*
3141 A869 35c *Harpia harpyja*
3142 A869 50c *Cephatopterus ornatus*

Warships A870

1989, Sept. 29 Litho. ***Perf. 12½***

3143 A870 1c *El Fenix*
3144 A870 3c *Triunfo*
3145 A870 5c *El Rayo*
3146 A870 10c *San Carlos*
3147 A870 30c *San Jose*
3148 A870 50c *San Genaro*

America Issue — A871

UPAE emblem and pre-Columbian art: 5p, Stone carving, Indians in dugout canoe. 20p, Petroglyph, Indian drawing on stone wall.

1989, Oct. 12 ***Perf. 12½x12***

3149 A871 5c multi
3150 A871 20c multi

Latin American History — A872

Writers and orchids: No. 3151, Domingo Sarmiento (1811-1888), Argentine educator, and *Govenia utriculata.* No. 3152, Joaquim Maria Machado de Assis (1839-1908), Brazilian novelist, and *Laelia grandis.* No. 3153, Salvador No. 69 and discovery of America anniv. emblem. No. 3154, Jorge Isaacs (1837-1895), Colombian novelist, and *Cattleya trianae.* No. 3155, Alejo Carpentier, Cuban writer, and *Cochleanthes discolor.* No. 3156, Pablo Neruda (1904-1973), Chilean poet, and *Oxalis adenophylla.* No. 3157, Pedro Urena, Dominican writer, and *Epidendrum fragrans.* No. 3158, Salvador No. 86 and anniv. emblem. No. 3159, Juan Montalvo (1832-1889), Ecuadorian satirist, and *Miltonia vexillaria.* No. 3160, Miguel Asturias (1899-1974), Guatemalan writer awarded the 1966 Lenin Peace Prize and 1967 Nobel Prize for literature, and *Odontoglossum rossii.* No. 3161, Jose C. del Valle, Honduran writer, and *Laelia anceps.* No. 3162, Alfonso Reyes (1889-1959), Mexican poet, and *Laelia anceps alba.* No. 3163, Salvador No. 87 and anniv. emblem. No. 3164, Ruben Dario (1867-1917), Nicaraguan poet, and *Brassavola acaulis.* No. 3165, Belisario Porras (1856-1942), president of Panama, and *Pescatorea celina.* No. 3166, Ricardo Palma (1833-1919), Peruvian writer, and *Coryanthes leucocorys.* No. 3167, Eugenio Maria de Hostos (1839-1903), Puerto Rican writer, and *Guzmania berteroniana.* No. 3168, Salvador No. 88 and anniv. emblem. No. 3169, Jose E. Rodo (1872-1917), Uruguayan philosopher, essayist, and *Cypella hebertii.* No. 3170, Romulo Gallegos, Venezuelan writer, and *Cattleya mossiae.*

1989, Oct. 27 Litho. ***Perf. 13***

3151 A872 1c multicolored
3152 A872 1c multicolored
3153 A872 1c multicolored
3154 A872 1c multicolored
3155 A872 1c multicolored
a. Strip of 5, Nos. 3151-3155
3156 A872 5c multicolored
3157 A872 5c multicolored
3158 A872 5c multicolored
3159 A872 5c multicolored
3160 A872 5c multicolored
a. Strip of 5, Nos. 3156-3160
3161 A872 10c multicolored
3162 A872 10c multicolored
3163 A872 10c multicolored
3164 A872 10c multicolored
3165 A872 10c multicolored
a. Strip of 5, Nos. 3161-3165
3166 A872 20c multicolored
3167 A872 20c multicolored
3168 A872 20c multicolored
3169 A872 20c multicolored
3170 A872 20c multicolored
a. Strip of 5, Nos. 3166-3170

Discovery of America 500th anniv. (in 1992).

Disappearance of Camilo Cienfuegos, 30th Anniv. — A873

1989, Oct. 28

3171 A873 5c multicolored

Founding of the City of Trinidad, 475th Anniv. A874

1989, Nov. 6 ***Perf. 12½x13***

3172 A874 5c multicolored

Paintings in the Natl. Museum — A875

Designs: 1p, *Familiar Scene,* by Antoine Faivre. 2p, *Flowers,* by Emile Jean Horace Vernet (1789-1863). 5p, *The Judgement of Paris,* by Charles Le Brun (1619-1690). 20p, *Outskirts of Nice,* by Eugene Louis Boudin (1824-1898). 30p, *Portrait of Sarah Bernhardt,* by G.J.V. Clairin. 50p, *Fishermen in Port,* by C.J. Vernet.

Perf. 12½, 12½x13 (30p)

1989, Nov. 20 Litho.

Size of 30p: 36x46mm

3173 A875 1c multicolored
3174 A875 2c multicolored
3175 A875 5c multicolored
3176 A875 20c multicolored
3177 A875 30c multicolored
3178 A875 50c multicolored

11th Pan-American Games, Havana, 1991 — A876

1989, Dec. 15 Litho. ***Perf. 12½***

3179 A876 5c Cycling
3180 A876 5c Fencing
3181 A876 5c Water polo
3182 A876 5c Shooting
3183 A876 5c Archery
3184 A876 20c Tennis, vert.
3185 A876 30c Swimming, vert.
3186 A876 35c Diving, vert.
3187 A876 40c Field hockey
3188 A876 50c Basketball, vert.

Jose Marti's *Golden Age*, Cent. — A877

1989, Dec. 20 ***Perf. 13***
3189 A877 5c scar, light blue & blk

Cuban Postal Museum, 25th Anniv. — A878

1990, Jan. 2 ***Perf. 13x12½***
3190 A878 5c *Almendares*
3191 A878 30c Mail train

Speleological Soc., 50th Anniv. — A879

Illustration reduced.

1990, Jan. 15 ***Perf. 12½***
3192 A879 30c multicolored

1990 World Cup Soccer Championships, Italy — A880

Various Italian architecture and athletes: No. 3193a, Dribbling (in red and blue). No. 3193b, Heading (in red and green). No. 3193c, Kicking (in green). 10c, Goalie catching ball. 30c, Dribbling, diff. 50c, Kicking, diff. 1p, Goalie catching ball, diff.

1990, Jan. 30 Litho. ***Perf. 12½***
3193 Strip of 3
a.-c. A880 5c any single
3194 A880 10c multicolored
3195 A880 30c multicolored
3196 A880 50c multicolored

Souvenir Sheet

3197 A880 1p multicolored

No. 3193 has a continuous design picturing The Colosseum.

1992 Summer Olympics, Barcelona — A881

1990, Feb. 20 Litho. ***Perf. 12½***
3198 A881 1c Baseball
3199 A881 4c Running
3200 A881 5c Basketball
3201 A881 10c Women's volleyball
3202 A881 30c Wrestling
3203 A881 50c Boxing

Souvenir Sheet

3204 A881 1p High jump

Nos. 3198-3201 and 3203 are vert. No. 3204 contains one 40x32mm stamp.

75th Universal Esperanto Congress — A882

1990, Mar. 7
3205 A882 30c Tower of Babel

No. 3205 printed se-tenant with inscribed label publicizing the congress.

Souvenir Sheet

1992 Winter Olympics, Albertville — A883

1990, Mar. 30 Litho. ***Perf. 13***
3206 A883 1p multicolored

Cosmonauts' Day — A884

Spacecraft and rocket mail covers: 1c, Austria, 1932. 2c, Germany, 1933. 3c, Netherlands, 1934. 10c, Belgium, 1935. 30c, Yugoslavia, 1935. 50c, United States, 1936.

1990, Apr. 12 ***Perf. 12½***
3207 A884 1c multicolored
3208 A884 2c multicolored
3209 A884 3c multicolored
3210 A884 10c multicolored
3211 A884 30c multicolored
3212 A884 50c multicolored

Stamp Day Type of 1984

Details of mural by R. Rodriguez Radillo (1967): 30c, Train station. 50c, Jet aircraft in flight.

1990, Apr. 24 ***Perf. 13x12½***
3213 A733 30c multicolored
3214 A733 50c multicolored

Labor Day, Cent. A885

1990, Apr. 30 ***Perf. 13***
3215 A885 5c multicolored

Souvenir Sheet

Great Britain No. 1 on Cover — A886

1990, May 3
3216 A886 1p multicolored

Stamp World London '90, Penny Black 150th anniv.

Penny Black, 150th Anniv. A887

Portraits of Sir Rowland Hill and stamps of Great Britain.

1990, May 6 Litho. ***Perf. 12½x12***
3217 A887 2c No. 1
3218 A887 3c No. 2
3219 A887 5c Type A5
3220 A887 10c No. 5
3221 A887 30c First day postmark
3222 A887 50c 5 #1 on Mulready envelope

Celia Sanchez Manduley (1920-1980) — A888

1990, May 9 ***Perf. 12½x13***
3223 A888 5c multicolored

Ho Chi Minh (1890-1969), Vietnamese Communist Party Leader — A889

1990, May 19 ***Perf. 12½***
3224 A889 50c multicolored

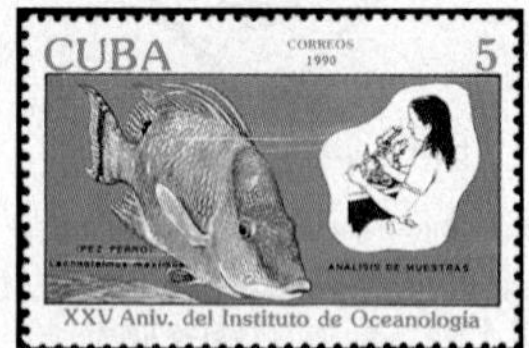

Oceanography Institute, 25th Anniv. — A890

Designs: 5c, Specimen analysis and *Lachnolaimus maximus.* 30c, Research ship, fish, coral reef. 50c, Specimen collection and *Panullrus argus.*

1990, June 18 Litho. ***Perf. 12½***
3225 A890 5c multicolored
3226 A890 30c multicolored
3227 A890 50c multicolored

5th Latin American Botanical Conference A891

1990, June 25 Litho. ***Perf. 12½***
3228 A891 3c Banara minutiflora
3229 A891 5c Oplonia nanophylla
3230 A891 10c Jacquinia brunnescens
3231 A891 30c Rondeletia brachycarpa
3232 A891 50c Rondeletia odorata

Tourism A892

1990, June 30
3233 A892 5c Wind surfing
3234 A892 10c Spear fishing
3235 A892 30c Deep sea fishing
3236 A892 40c Hunting

Nos. 3233, 3236 vert.

Art Treasures A893

5c, "La Flauta Del Dios Pan." 20c, "Un Pastor." 50c, "Ganimedes." 1p, "Venus Anadiomena."

1990, July 20
3237 A893 5c multicolored
3238 A893 20c multicolored
3239 A893 50c multicolored
3240 A893 1p multicolored

Birds A894

1990, Aug. 24 Litho. ***Perf. 13***
3241 A894 2c Podiceps cristatus
3242 A894 3c Gallirallus australis
3243 A894 5c Nestor notabilis
3244 A894 10c Xenicus longipes
3245 A894 30c Cracticus torquatus
3246 A894 50c "Prosthemadera" novaeseelandiae

Souvenir Sheet

3247 A894 1p Kiwi

New Zealand '90. No. 3247 contains one 39x31mm stamp.

8th UN Congress on Crime Prevention A895

1990, Aug. 27 Litho. *Perf. 12½*
3248 A895 50c blue, silver & red

Discovery of America, 500th Anniv. (in 1992) — A896

1990, Oct. 12 Litho. *Perf. 12½*
3249 A896 5c Ship, shore
3250 A896 20c Columbus, village

Cuban Television, 40th Anniv. — A897

1990, Oct. 12 Litho. *Perf. 13*
3251 A897 5c multicolored

Nationalization of Railroads, 30th Anniv. — A898

1990, Oct. 13 *Perf. 13x12½*
3252 A898 50c multicolored

Latin American History Type of 1986

Latin American stamps or flags and costumes: No. 3253, Argentina. No. 3254, Bolivia. No. 3255, Argentina No. 91. No. 3256, Colombia. No. 3257, Costa Rica. No. 3258, Cuba. No. 3259, Chile. No. 3260, Dominican Republic No. 110. No. 3261, Ecuador. No. 3262, El Salvador. No. 3263, Guatemala. No. 3264, Mexico. No. 3265, Puerto Rico No. 133. No. 3266, Nicaragua. No. 3267, Panama. No. 3268, Paraguay. No. 3269, Peru. No. 3270, El Salvador No. 103. No. 3271, Puerto Rico. No. 3272, Venezuela.

1990, Oct. 27 *Perf. 12½*
3253 A804 1c multicolored
3254 A804 1c multicolored
3255 A804 1c multicolored
3256 A804 1c multicolored
3257 A804 1c multicolored
a. Strip of 5, Nos. 3253-3257
3258 A804 5c multicolored
3259 A804 5c multicolored
3260 A804 5c multicolored
3261 A804 5c multicolored
3262 A804 5c multicolored
a. Strip of 5, Nos. 3258-3262
3263 A804 10c multicolored
3264 A804 10c multicolored
3265 A804 10c multicolored
3266 A804 10c multicolored
3267 A804 10c multicolored
a. Strip of 5, Nos. 3263-3267
3268 A804 20c multicolored
3269 A804 20c multicolored
3270 A804 20c multicolored
3271 A804 20c multicolored
3272 A804 20c multicolored
a. Strip of 5, Nos. 3268-3272

Discovery of America, 500th anniv. (in 1992).

11th Jai Alai World Championships A899

1990, Nov. 14 Litho. *Perf. 12½*
3273 A899 30c multicolored

No. 3273 printed with se-tenant label.

11th Pan American Games, Havana — A900

1990, Nov. 15 Litho. *Perf. 12½*
3274 A900 5c Judo
3275 A900 5c Sailing
3276 A900 5c Kayak
3277 A900 5c Rowing
3278 A900 5c Equestrian
3279 A900 10c Table tennis
3280 A900 20c Men's gymnastics, vert.
3281 A900 30c Baseball, vert.
3282 A900 35c Team handball, vert.
3283 A900 50c Soccer, vert.

See Nos. 3311-3320.

A901

Butterflies A902

1990, Nov. 20 Litho. *Perf. 13*
3284 A901 5c Boxing
3285 A901 30c Baseball
3286 A901 50c Volleyball

16th Central American and Caribbean Games, Mexico.

1991, Jan. 25 Litho. *Perf. 12½*
3287 A902 2c Chioides marmorosa
3288 A902 3c Composia fidelissima
3289 A902 5c Danaus plexippus
3290 A902 10c Hypolimnas misippus
3291 A902 30c Hypna iphigenia
3292 A902 50c Hemiargus ammon

Jose Luis Guerra Aguiar (1914-1990), Director of Postal Museum — A903

1991, Feb. 17 Litho. *Perf. 12½*
3293 A903 5c multicolored

A904

A905

1991, Feb. 20
3294 A904 1c Long jump
3295 A904 2c Javelin
3296 A904 3c Field hockey
3297 A904 5c Weight lifting
3298 A904 40c Cycling
3299 A904 50c Gymnastics

Souvenir Sheet

3300 A904 1p Torchbearer

1992 Summer Olympics, Barcelona.

1991, Apr. 12 Litho. *Perf. 13*

1st Man in Space, 30th anniv.: 5c, Yuri Gagarin. No. 3302, Cosmonaut Y. Romanenko. No. 3303, Cosmonaut A. Tamayo. No. 3304, Mir space station. No. 3305, Mir space station, docked Soyuz, earth. 50c, Soviet space shuttle Buran.

3301 A905 5c multicolored
3302 A905 10c multicolored
3303 A905 10c multicolored
a. Pair, #3302-3303
3304 A905 30c multicolored
3305 A905 30c multicolored
a. Pair, #3304-3305
3306 A905 50c multicolored

Proclamation of the Socialist Revolution, 30th Anniv. — A906

Design: 50c, Ship, jet on fire.

1991, Apr. 19 *Perf. 12½*
3307 A906 5c multicolored
3308 A906 50c multicolored

Bay of Pigs invasion, 30th anniv., No. 3308.

Stamp Day A907

Details from mural by R. Rodriguez Radillo: 30c, Rocket lift-off. 50c, Dish antenna, horiz.

1991, Apr. 24 *Perf. 12½x13, 13x12½*
3309 A907 30c multicolored
3310 A907 50c multicolored

11th Pan American Games Type of 1990

1991, May 15 Litho. *Perf. 12½*
3311 A900 5c Volleyball
3312 A900 5c Rhythmic gymnastics
3313 A900 5c Synchronized swimming
3314 A900 5c Weight lifting
3315 A900 5c Baseball
3316 A900 10c Bowling
3317 A900 20c Boxing
3318 A900 30c Running
3319 A900 35c Wrestling
3320 A900 50c Karate

Nos. 3311-3315 & 3317 are vert.

Airships A908

Designs: 5c, First ellipsoidal, 1784, J.B.M. Meusnier. 10c, First with steam engine, 1852, H. Giffard. 20c, First with gas engine, 1872, P. Haenlein. 30c, First with gasoline engine, 1896, H. Wolfert. 50c, First rigid aluminum, 1897, D. Schwarz. 1p, LZ-129 Hindenburg, 1936, F. von Zeppelin.

1991, July 1 Litho. *Perf. 13*
3321 A908 5c multicolored
3322 A908 10c multicolored
3323 A908 20c multicolored
3324 A908 30c multicolored
3325 A908 50c multicolored
3326 A908 1p multicolored

Espamer '91, Buenos Aires, Argentina.

Simon Bolivar A909

1991, June 22 Litho. *Perf. 12½x13*
3327 A909 50c multicolored

Amphictyonic Cong. of Panama, 165th anniv.

Birds A910

Designs: 45c, Melanerpes superciliaris. 50c, Myadestes elisabeth. 2p, Priotelus temnurus. 4p, Tiaris canora. 5p, Campephilus principalis. 10p, Amazona leucocephala, horiz. 16.45p, Mellisuga helenae, horiz.

1991, July 15 ***Perf. 12½x13, 13x12½***

3328 A910 45c multicolored
3329 A910 50c multicolored
3330 A910 2p multicolored
3331 A910 4p multicolored
3332 A910 5p multicolored
3333 A910 10p multicolored
3334 A910 16.45p multicolored

Tourism — A911

Designs: No. 3335, Varadero Beach, vert. No. 3336, Cayo Largo, vert. No. 3337, Artillerymen at fortress San Carlos de la Cabana. No. 3338, Tres Reyes del Morro Castle.

1991, July 30

3335 A911 20c multicolored
3336 A911 20c multicolored
3337 A911 30c multicolored
3338 A911 30c multicolored

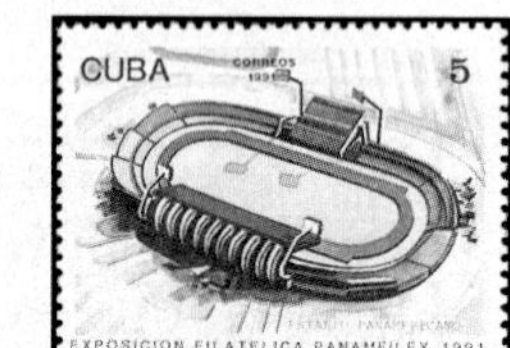

Panamfilex '91 — A912

11th Pan American Games venues: 5c, Pan American Stadium. 20c, Swimming venue. 30c, Multisports center. 50c, Velodrome. 1p, Havana City Coliseum and Sports Center.

1991, Aug. 4 **Litho.** ***Perf. 12½***

3339 A912 5c multicolored
3340 A912 20c multicolored
3341 A912 30c multicolored
3342 A912 50c multicolored

Souvenir Sheet

3343 A912 1p multicolored

No. 3343 contains one 40x32mm stamp.

Paintings A913

5c, Kataoka Dengoemon Takafusa, by Utagawa Kuniyoshi. 10c, Evening Walk, by Hosoda Eishi. 20c, Courtesans, by Torii Kiyonaga. 30c, Conversation, by Utamaro. 50c, Bridge at Inari-bashi, by Hiroshige. 1p, On the Terrace, by Kiyonaga.

1991, Sept. 9 **Litho.** ***Perf. 12½x13***

3344 A913 5c multicolored
3345 A913 10c multicolored
3346 A913 20c multicolored
3347 A913 30c multicolored
3348 A913 50c multicolored
3349 A913 1p multicolored

Phila Nippon '91, Tokyo.

Souvenir Sheet

1992 Winter Olympics, Albertville — A914

1991, Sept. 25 **Litho.** ***Perf. 12½***

3350 A914 1p multicolored

Cuban Communist Party, 4th Congress A915

1991, Oct. 10

3351 A915 5c shown
3352 A915 50c Congress symbol

Discovery of America, 500th Anniv. (in 1992) — A916

Designs: 5c, Columbus, Vicente and Martin Pinzon. 20c, Santa Maria, Nina and Pinta.

1991, Oct. 12

3353 A916 5c multicolored
3354 A916 20c multicolored

Jose Marti A917

1991, Oct. 15 ***Perf. 13x12½***

3355 A917 50c multicolored

Publication of "Simple Verses," cent.

Latin American History A918

Stamps or musicians and instruments: No. 3356, Julian Aguirre, Argentina, charango. No. 3357, Eduardo Caba, Bolivia, antara. No. 3358, Chile #2. No. 3359, Heitor Villalobos, Brazil, resonator trumpet. No. 3360, Guillermo Uribe-Holguin, Colombia, drum. No. 3361, Miguel Failde, Cuba, claves. No. 3362, Enrique Soro, Chile, drum. No. 3363, Chile #57. No. 3364, Segundo L. Moreno, Ecuador, xylophone. No. 3365, Ricardo Castillo, Guatemala, marimba. No. 3366, Carlos Chavez, Mexico, guitar. No. 3367, Luis A. Delgadillo, Nicaragua, maracas. No. 0000, Chile #60. No. 3369, Alfredo De Saint-Malo, Panama, mejorana. No. 3370, Jose Asuncion Flores, Paraguay, harp. No. 3371, Daniel Alomia, Peru, flute. No. 3372, Juan Morell y Campos, Puerto Rico, cuatro. No. 3373, Chile #72. No. 3374, Eduardo Farini, Uruguay, drums. No. 3375, Juan V. Lecuna, Venezuela, cuatro, diff.

1991, Oct. 27 ***Perf. 13***

3356 A918 1c multicolored
3357 A918 1c multicolored
3358 A918 1c multicolored
3359 A918 1c multicolored
3360 A918 1c multicolored
a. Strip of 5, #3356-3360
3361 A918 5c multicolored
3362 A918 5c multicolored
3363 A918 5c multicolored
3364 A918 5c multicolored
3365 A918 5c multicolored
a. Strip of 5, #3361-3365
3366 A918 10c multicolored
3367 A918 10c multicolored
3368 A918 10c multicolored
3369 A918 10c multicolored
3370 A918 10c multicolored
a. Strip of 5, #3366-3370
3371 A918 20c multicolored
3372 A918 20c multicolored
3373 A918 20c multicolored
3374 A918 20c multicolored
3375 A918 20c multicolored
a. Strip of 5, #3371-3375

Discovery of America, 500th anniv. in 1992 (Nos. 3358, 3363, 3368, 3373).

Jose Marti Pioneers Organization, 1st Congress A919

1991, Oct. 29

3376 A919 5c multicolored

Toussaint L'Ouverture (1743-1803) — A920

1991, Nov. 20 ***Perf. 12½x13***

3377 A920 50c multicolored

Haitian Revolution, Bicent.

Cuban Revolutionary Armed Forces, 35th Anniv. — A921

Design: 50c, Landing of the Granma expedition, 35th anniv., vert.

Perf. 12½x12, 12x12½

1991, Dec. 2 **Litho.**

3378 A921 5c multicolored
3379 A921 50c multicolored

Gen. Ignacio Agramonte (1841-1873), Revolutionary Hero — A922

1991, Dec. 23 **Litho.** ***Perf. 12½x13***

3380 A922 5c multicolored

Souvenir Sheet

1992 Winter Olympics, Albertville — A923

1992, Jan. 15 ***Perf. 13***

3381 A923 1p multicolored

1992 Summer Olympics, Barcelona — A924

1992, Jan. 20 **Litho.** ***Perf. 13x12½***

3382 A924 3c Table tennis
3383 A924 5c Handball
3384 A924 10c Shooting
3385 A924 20c Long jump, vert.
3386 A924 35c Judo
3387 A924 50c Fencing

Souvenir Sheet

Perf. 12½

3388 A924 100c Rhythmic gymnastics, vert.

No. 3388 contains one 32x40mm stamp.

Environmental Protection A925

1992, Feb. 10 ***Perf. 13***

3389 A925 5c Terraced hillsides
3390 A925 20c Save the whales
3391 A925 35c Ozone hole over Antarctica
3392 A925 40c Nuclear disarmament

Dogs
A926

1992, Mar. 10 Litho. *Perf. 13x12½*

3393 A926 5c Boxer
3394 A926 10c Great dane
3395 A926 20c German shepherd
3396 A926 30c Various breeds
3397 A926 35c Doberman pinscher
3398 A926 40c Fox terrier
3399 A926 50c Poodle

Souvenir Sheet

Perf. 12½

3400 A926 1p Bichon frise, vert.

No. 3400 contains one 32x40mm stamp.
Nos. 3401-3404 will not be assigned.

Union of Young Communists, 30th Anniv. — A928

1992, Apr. 4 Litho. *Perf. 13*

3405 A928 5c multicolored

Cuban Revolutionary Party, Cent. — A929

1992, Apr. 10 *Perf. 13x12½*

3406 A929 5c multicolored
3407 A929 50c multicolored

Discovery of America, 500th Anniv. — A930

1992, Apr. 14 *Perf. 12½*

3408 A930 5c Landing at Bariay
3409 A930 20c Landing at San Salvador

Granada '92 Philatelic Exhibition — A931

Views of the Alhambra, Granada: 5c, With Sierra Nevada mountains beyond. 10c, Arches at sunset. 20c, Interior architecture. 30c, Patio, fountain of lions. 35c, Bedroom. 50c, View of Albaicin.

1992, Apr. 17 *Perf. 13*

3410 A931 5c multicolored
3411 A931 10c multicolored
3412 A931 20c multicolored
3413 A931 30c multicolored
3414 A931 35c multicolored
3415 A931 50c multicolored

La Bodeguita Del Medio Restaurant, 50th Anniv. — A932

1992, Apr. 26

3416 A932 50c multicolored

Fish
A933

1992, May 15 Litho. *Perf. 12½*

3417 A933 5c Holacanthus isabelita
3418 A933 10c Equetus lanceolatus
3419 A933 20c Acanthurus coeruleus
3420 A933 30c Abudefduf saxatilis
3421 A933 50c Microspathodon chrysurus

Orchids — A934

1992, June 20 Litho. *Perf. 12½*

3422 A934 3c Cattleya hibrida
3423 A934 5c Phalaenopsis
3424 A934 10c Cattleyopsis lindenii
3425 A934 30c Bletia purpurea
3426 A934 35c Oncidium luridum
3427 A934 40c Vanda hibrida

Soroa Orchid Garden, 40th anniv.

Mellisuga Helenae — A935

1992, July 7 *Perf. 13*

3428 A935 5c Sitting on nest
3429 A935 10c Wings extended
3430 A935 20c Sitting on branch
3431 A935 30c In flight

World Wildlife Fund.

Tourism
A936

1992, July 15 Litho. *Perf. 12½*

3432 A936 10c Guardalavaca Beach
3433 A936 20c Bucanero Hotel
3434 A936 30c Sailing ship, Havana
3435 A936 50c Varadero Beach

Souvenir Sheet

Expo '92, Seville — A937

1992, July 27 Litho. *Perf. 13*

3436 A937 1.50p multicolored

1992 Summer Olympics, Barcelona
A938

Athlete, sport: 5c, Eligio (Kid Chocolate) Sardinas, boxing. 35c, Ramon Fonst, fencing. 40c, Sergio Martinez, cycling. 50c, Martin Dihigo, baseball.

1992, July 20 Litho. *Perf. 12½x13*

3437 A938 5c multicolored
3438 A938 35c multicolored
3439 A938 40c multicolored
3440 A938 50c multicolored

Olymphilex '92.

Discovery of America, 500th Anniv. — A939

5c, Alvarez Cabral. 10c, Alonso Pinzon. 20c, Alonso de Ojeda. 30c, Amerigo Vespucci. 35c, Prince Henry the Navigator. 40c, Bartolomeu Dias. 1p, Columbus' fleet.

1992, Sept. 18 Litho. *Perf. 12½*

3441 A939 5c multicolored
3442 A939 10c multicolored
3443 A939 20c multicolored
3444 A939 30c multicolored
3445 A939 35c multicolored
3446 A939 40c multicolored

Souvenir Sheet

Perf. 13

3447 A939 1p multi, vert.

Genoa '92. No. 3447 contains one 32x40mm stamp.

1992 Summer Olympics Medal Winners, Barcelona — A940

Medals and participants in events: No. 3448, Bronze, 4x100-meter relay, women's high jump, and women's 800-meter. No. 3449, Gold, high jump, women's discus. No. 3450, Silver, 4x400-meter relay, bronze, discus. No. 3451, Gold and silver, boxing. No. 3452, Gold, baseball. No. 3453, Gold, women's volleyball. No. 3454, Gold, silver, and bronze, judo. No. 3455, Gold and bronze, Greco-Roman and freestyle wrestling. No. 3456, Silver and bronze, fencing, silver, weight lifting.

1992, Sept. 24 Litho. *Perf. 13*

3448 A940 5c multicolored
3449 A940 5c multicolored
3450 A940 5c multicolored
3451 A940 20c multicolored
3452 A940 20c multicolored
3453 A940 20c multicolored
3454 A940 50c multicolored
3455 A940 50c multicolored
3456 A940 50c multicolored

6th World Track and Field Cup, Havana
A941

1992, Sept. 24 Litho. *Perf. 13*

3457 A941 5c High jump
3458 A941 20c Javelin
3459 A941 30c Hammer throw
3460 A941 40c Long jump, vert.
3461 A941 50c Hurdles, vert.

Souvenir Sheet

3462 A941 1p Women's relay

No. 3462 contains one 40x32mm stamp.

Latin American History Type of 1986

Discovery of America: No. 3463a, Columbus, Queen Isabella. b, Columbus at Rabida Monastery. c, Columbus, pointing up, outlining his plan. d, Columbus, with scroll, before Salamanca Council. e, Departure of Columbus' fleet from Palos.

No. 3464a, Three ships stopping at Canary Islands. b, Columbus speaking to crew. c, Land sighted, Oct. 12, 1492. d, Columbus landing in New World. e, Meeting natives.

No. 3465a, Grounding of Santa Maria at Hispanola. b, Arrival of Nina at Palos. c, Columbus welcomed in Barcelona. d, Columbus describes his voyage to Ferdinand and Isabella. e, Departure of fleet from Cadiz on second voyage.

No. 3466a, King and Queen welcome Columbus. b, Fleet on Columbus' third voyage. c, Columbus deported from Hispanola to Spain as prisoner. d, Columbus on ship, fourth voyage. e, Death of Columbus, May 20, 1506 in Valladolid.

1992, Oct. 3 *Perf. 13*

3463 A804 1c Strip of 5, #a.-e.
3464 A804 5c Strip of 5, #a.-e.
3465 A804 10c Strip of 5, #a.-e.
3466 A804 20c Strip of 5, #a.-e.

Jose Maria Chacon y Calvo (1892-1969), Historian
A942

1992, Oct. 29 *Perf. 13*

3467 A942 30c multicolored

Churches
A943

Designs: 5c, Basilica of Nuestra Senora de la Caridad del Cobre. 20c, Santa Maria del Rosario Church. 30c, Espiritu Santo Church. 50c, Santo Angel Custodio Church.

1992, Nov. 10 Litho. *Perf. 12½*

3468 A943 5c multicolored
3469 A943 20c multicolored
3470 A943 30c multicolored
3471 A943 50c multicolored

Development of the Diesel Engine — A944

1993, Jan. 20 Litho. *Perf. 12½*

3472 A944 5c Truck
3473 A944 10c Automobile
3474 A944 30c Tugboat
3475 A944 40c Locomotive
3476 A944 50c Tractor

Souvenir Sheet

3477 A944 1p Rudolf Diesel

No. 3477 contains one 40x32mm stamp. Rudolf Diesel, 80th anniv. of death (#3477).

Davis Cup Tennis Competition — A945

Various tennis players in action.

Perf. 12x12½, 12½x12

1993, Feb. 10 Litho.

3478 A945 5c multi, vert.
3479 A945 20c multi, vert.
3480 A945 30c multi, vert.
3481 A945 35c multicolored
3482 A945 40c multicolored

Souvenir Sheet

Perf. 12½

3483 A945 1p multicolored

No. 3483 contains one 40x32mm stamp.

Scientists A946

Designs: 3c, Pierre-Paul-Emile Roux (1853-1933), bacteriologist. 5c, Carlos J. Finlay (1833-1915), suggested mosquito as carrier of yellow fever. 10c, Ivan Petrovich Pavlov (1849-1936), physiologist, investigated conditioned reflexes. 20c, Louis Pasteur, chemist, developer of pasteurization. 30c, Santiago Ramon y Cajal (1852-1934), histologist, isolated the neuron. 35c, Sigmund Freud, psychoanalyst. 40c, Wilhelm Conrad Roentgen, physicist, discoverer of x-ray. 50c, Joseph Lister, surgeon, introduced principle of antisepsis. 1p, Robert Koch, bacteriologist, developer of tuberculin, vert.

1993, Mar. 3 Litho. *Perf. 12½*

3484 A946 3c multicolored
3485 A946 5c multicolored
3486 A946 10c multicolored
3487 A946 20c multicolored
3488 A946 30c multicolored
3489 A946 35c multicolored
3490 A946 40c multicolored
3491 A946 50c multicolored

Souvenir Sheet

3492 A946 1p multicolored

Bicycles — A947

Bicycles designed by: 3c, Leonardo da Vinci, 15th cent. 5c, Karl Von Drais de Sauerbrun, 1813. 10c, Ernest Michaux, 1856. 20c, James Starley, 1869. 30c, Harry Lawson, 1879. 35c, Guaso (Cuba), 1992.

1993, Apr. 14 *Perf. 13*

3493 A947 3c multicolored
3494 A947 5c multicolored
3495 A947 10c multicolored
3496 A947 20c multicolored
3497 A947 30c multicolored
3498 A947 35c multicolored

Cuban Natl. Museum, 80th Anniv. A948

Paintings by Joaquin Sorolla y Bastida (1863-1923): 3c, Child Eating Watermelon, 1920, vert. 5c, Valencian Fisherwomen, 1909. 10c, Regattas. 20c, Contadina, 1889. 40c, Summer, 1904. 50c, Boats on the Ocean, 1908.

1993, May 29 Litho. *Perf. 13x12½*

3499 A948 3c multicolored

Perf. 12½x13

3500 A948 5c multicolored
3501 A948 10c multicolored
3502 A948 20c multicolored
3503 A948 40c multicolored
3504 A948 50c multicolored

Water Birds A949

Perf. 12½, 13x12½ (5, 30c)

1993, June 15

3505 A949 3c Jacana spinosa
3506 A949 5c Ardea herodias, vert.
3507 A949 10c Himantopus mexicanus
3508 A949 20c Nycticorax nycticorax
3509 A949 30c Grus canadensis, vert.
3510 A949 50c Aramus guarauna

Brasiliana '93. Nos. 3506, 3510 are 27x44mm.

Anniversaries — A950

#3511, Jose Marti, Moncada Barracks. #3512, "History Will Absolve Me," declaration of Fidel Castro, Marti. #3513, Jose Marti, Rafael M. Mendive, vert. #3514, Carlos Manuel de Cespedes, gear wheels.

1993, July 26 Litho. *Perf. 13*

3511 A950 5c multicolored
3512 A950 5c multicolored
3513 A950 5c multicolored
3514 A950 5c multicolored

Attack on Moncada Barracks, 40th anniv. (#3511). Declaration of Fidel Castro, 40th anniv. (#3512). Birth of Jose Marti, 140th anniv. (#3513). Declaration of the Ten Years' War, 125th anniv. (#3514).

Flowers from Cienfuegos Botanical Gardens A951

1993, Aug. 20

3515 A951 3c Sedum allantoides
3516 A951 5c Heliconia caribaea
3517 A951 10c Anthurium andraeanum
3518 A951 20c Pseudobombax ellipticum
3519 A951 35c Ixora coccinea
3520 A951 50c Callistemon specious

Bangkok '93, Intl. Philatelic Exhibition A952

Butterflies: 3c, Battus devillievs. 5c, Anteos maerula. 20c, Ascia monuste evonima. 30c, Junonia coenia. 35c, Anartia jatrophae guantanamo. 50c, Hypolimnas misippus.

1993, Sept. 10 Litho. *Perf. 13*

3521 A952 3c multicolored
3522 A952 5c multicolored
3523 A952 20c multicolored
3524 A952 30c multicolored
3525 A952 35c multicolored
3526 A952 50c multicolored

Endangered Species A953

1993, Oct. 12 Litho. *Perf. 13*

3527 A953 5c Phoenicopterus ruber
3528 A953 50c Ajaia ajaja

Latin American Revolutionaries A954

Flags, map and: No. 3529, Simon Bolivar. No. 3530, Jose Marti. No. 3531, Benito Juarez, Mexican President. No. 3532, Ernesto "Che" Guevara.

1993, Oct. 27 Litho. *Perf. 13*

3529 A954 50c multicolored
3530 A954 50c multicolored
3531 A954 50c multicolored
3532 A954 50c multicolored
a. Block of 4, #3529-3532

17th Central American and Caribbean Games, Ponce, Puerto Rico — A955

1993, Nov. 10 Litho. *Perf. 12½*

3533 A955 5c Swimming
3534 A955 10c Pole vault
3535 A955 20c Boxing
3536 A955 35c Gymnastics, vert.
3537 A955 50c Baseball, vert.

Souvenir Sheet

3538 A955 1p Basketball

No. 3538 contains one 40x32mm stamp.

Mariana Grajales (1808-93), Patriot — A956

Peter I. Tchaikovsky (1840-93), Composer A957

1993, Nov. 27 *Perf. 13*

3539 A956 5p multicolored

1993, Nov. 30

3540 A957 5c Portrait
3541 A957 20c Swan Lake Ballet
3542 A957 30c Statue
3543 A957 50c Museum, horiz.

A958

A959

1994, Jan. 1 Litho. *Perf. 13*

3544 A958 5c multicolored

35th anniv. of the Revolution.

1994, Jan. 1

Various soccer players.

3545 A959 5c multicolored
3546 A959 20c multicolored
3547 A959 30c multicolored
3548 A959 35c multicolored
3549 A959 40c multicolored

3550 A959 50c multicolored

Souvenir Sheet

3551 A959 1p multicolored

1994 World Cup Soccer Championships, US. No. 3551 contains one 40x31mm stamp.

Cats A960

1994, Feb. 15 Litho. *Perf. 12½*
3552 A960 5c Blue Persian
3553 A960 10c Havana
3554 A960 20c Maine coon
3555 A960 30c Blue British shorthair
3556 A960 35c Bicolor Persian
3557 A960 50c Gold chinchilla

Souvenir Sheet

Perf. 13

3558 A960 1p Abyssinian, vert.

No. 3558 contains one 30x38mm stamp.

Medicinal Plants — A961

Designs: 5c, Salvia officinalis. 10c, Aloe barbadensis. 20c, Helianthus annuus. 30c, Matricaria chamomilla. 40c, Calendula officinalis. 50c, Tilia platyphyllos.

1994, Mar. 30 Litho. *Perf. 12½*
3559 A961 5c multicolored
3560 A961 10c multicolored
3561 A961 20c multicolored
3562 A961 30c multicolored
3563 A961 40c multicolored
3564 A961 50c multicolored

Carriages — A962

Designs: 5c, Public coach, 1860. 10c, Coach of Ferdinand VII, Maria Louisa. 30c, Louis XV-style coach. 35c, Elizabeth II gala day's coach. 40c, Catalina II's summer coach. 50c, Volanta habanera.

1994, Apr. 20 *Perf. 12½x12*
3565 A962 5c multicolored
3566 A962 10c multicolored
3567 A962 30c multicolored
3568 A962 35c multicolored
3569 A962 40c multicolored
3570 A962 50c multicolored

No. 3570 is 68x37mm.

Aquaculture — A963

Designs: 5c, Crassostrea rhizophorae. 20c, Cardisoma guanhumi. 30c, Tilapia melanopleura. 35c, Hippospongia lachne. 40c, Panulirus argus. 50c, Cyprinus carpio.

1994, May 10 Litho. *Perf. 12½*
3571 A963 5c multicolored
3572 A963 20c multicolored
3573 A963 30c multicolored
3574 A963 35c multicolored
3575 A963 40c multicolored
3576 A963 50c multicolored

Intl. Olympic Committee, Cent. — A964

1994, June 23 Litho. *Perf. 12½*
3577 A964 5c Flag, runners
3578 A964 30c Flag, world map
3579 A964 50c Flag, Olympic flame

Scientists A965

Designs: 5c, Michael Faraday (1791-1867), physicist. 10c, Marie Curie (1867-1934), physical chemist. 20c, Pierre Curie (1859-1906), chemist. 30c, Albert Einstein (1879-1955), physicist, mathematician. 40c, Max Planck (1858-1947), theoretical physicist. 50c, Otto Hahn (1879-1968), physical chemist.

1994, July 20 Litho. *Perf. 12½*
3580 A965 5c multicolored
3581 A965 10c multicolored
3582 A965 20c multicolored
3583 A965 30c multicolored
3584 A965 40c multicolored
3585 A965 50c multicolored

Cactus Flowers A966

Designs: 5c, Opuntia dillenii. 10c, Opuntia millspaughii, vert. 30c, Leptocereus santamarinae. 35c, Pereskia marcanoi. 40c, Dendrocereus nudiflorus, vert. 50c, Pilocereus robinii.

1994, Aug. 15 Litho. *Perf. 12½*
3586 A966 5c multicolored
3587 A966 10c multicolored
3588 A966 30c multicolored
3589 A966 35c multicolored
3590 A966 40c multicolored
3591 A966 50c multicolored

Souvenir Sheet

2nd Spanish-Cuban Philatelic Exhibition, Havana — A967

Design: 1p, Cuban postal rocket, #C31.

1994, Sept. 18
3592 A967 1p multicolored

Experimental postal rocket flight, 55th anniv.

Dogs A968

1994, Sept. 20
3593 A968 5c Rough collie
3594 A968 20c American cocker spaniel
3595 A968 30c Dalmatian
3596 A968 40c Afghan hound
3597 A968 50c English cocker spaniel

Cayo Largo Island A969

Fauna: 15c, Carpilius corallinus. 65c, Cyclura nubila, vert. 75c, Pelecanus occidentalis. 4p, Chelonia mydas.

1994, Sept. 30 Litho. *Perf. 12½*
3598 A969 15c multicolored
3599 A969 65c multicolored
3600 A969 75c multicolored
3601 A969 1p multicolored

A970

A971

1994, Oct. 28
3602 A970 15c multicolored

Camilo Cienfuegos Gorriaran, revolutionary, 35th anniv. of disappearance.

1994, Oct. 30

Fauna of the Caribbean: 10c, Epinephelus flavolimbatus, horiz. No. 3604, Phoenicopterus ruber. No. 3605, Aetobatus narinari. No. 3606, Istiophorus platypterus, horiz. No. 3607, Tursiops truncatus, horiz. No. 3608, Pelecanus occidentalis.

3603 A971 10c multicolored
3604 A971 15c multicolored
3605 A971 15c multicolored
3606 A971 15c multicolored
3607 A971 65c multicolored
3608 A971 65c multicolored

ICAO, 50th Anniv. A972

1994, Nov. 9
3609 A972 65c multicolored

Zoological Garden, Havana, 55th Anniv. — A973

1994, Nov. 14 Litho. *Perf. 13*
3610 A973 15c Bronze monument
3611 A973 65c Ara chloroptera
3612 A973 75c Carduelis carduelis

Cuban Philatelic Federation, 30th Anniv. — A974

1994, Nov. 20
3613 A974 15c multicolored

America Issue — A975

Postal transportation: 15c, 18th Cent. Spanish galleon, maritime postal service, vert. 65c, 19th Cent. postal rider, insurgent postal service.

1994, Dec. 12
3614 A975 15c multicolored
3615 A975 65c multicolored

Postal Museum, 30th Anniv. — A976

1995, Jan. 2
3616 A976 15c multicolored

Lizards — A977

Designs: 15c, Anolis baracoae. 65c, Sphaerodactylus ramsdeni. 75c, Leiocephalus raviceps. 85c, Sphaerodactylus ruibali. 90c, Anolis ophiolepis. 1p, Sphaerodactylus armasi.

1994, Nov. 30 Litho. *Perf. 12½*
3617 A977 15c multicolored
3618 A977 65c multicolored
3619 A977 75c multicolored
3620 A977 85c multicolored
3621 A977 90c multicolored
3622 A977 1p multicolored

Cuban War of Independence, Cent. — A978

1995, Feb. 24 Litho. *Perf. 12½*
3623 A978 15c Jose Marti, flag

Pan American Games, Mar del Plata, Argentina — A979

1995, Mar. 11 Litho. *Perf. 13*
3624 A979 10c Boxing, vert.
3625 A979 15c Weight lifting, vert.
3626 A979 65c Volleyball, vert.
3627 A979 75c Wrestling
3628 A979 85c Baseball
3629 A979 90c High jump

National Aquarium, 35th Anniv. — A980

Fish: 10c, Holacanthus cillaris. 15c, Hypoplectrus guttavarius. 65c, Anisotremus virginicus. 75c, Amblycirrhitus pinos. 85c, Pomaacanthus paru. 90c, Acanthurus coeruleus.

1995, Apr. 28 Litho. *Perf. 13*
3630 A980 10c multicolored
3631 A980 15c multicolored
3632 A980 65c multicolored
3633 A980 75c multicolored
3634 A980 85c multicolored
3635 A980 90c multicolored

FAO, 50th Anniv. A981

1995, Apr. 7 Litho. *Perf. 13*
3636 A981 75c multicolored

First Cuban Postage Stamp, 140th Anniv. — A982

65c, Ornamental letter drop, envelope.

1995. Apr. 24 Litho. *Perf. 12½*
3637 A982 15c black & blue green
3638 A982 65c multicolored

Jose Marti, Death Cent. A983

Designs: 15c, Marti killed in combat, signature, portrait. 65c, Landing of Marti, Cuban patriots on Playitas beach. 75c, Montecristi Manifesto signed in Domincan Republic, Marti. 85c, Meeting of Marti, Maceo, Gomez at La Mejorana Farm. 90c, Marti's mausoleum, Santiago, Cuba, vert.

1995, May 19 *Perf. 12½x13, 13x12½*
3639 A983 15c multicolored
3640 A983 65c multicolored
3641 A983 75c multicolored
3642 A983 85c multicolored
3643 A983 90c multicolored

Antonio Maceo (1845-96), Revolutionary — A984

1995, June 14 Litho. *Perf. 12½*
3644 A984 15c multicolored

Butterflies — A985

Designs: 10c, Dione vanillae. 15c, Eunica tatila. 65c, Melete salacia. 75c, Greta cubana. 85c, Eurema daira. 90c, Phoebis sennae.

1995, June 20 *Perf. 12½x13*
3645 A985 10c multicolored
3646 A985 15c multicolored
3647 A985 65c multicolored
3648 A985 75c multicolored
3649 A985 85c multicolored
3650 A985 90c multicolored

World War II Combat Planes — A986

Designs: 10c, Supermarine "Spitfire," Great Britain. 15c, IL-2, Russia. 65c, Curtiss P-40, US. 75c, Messerschmitt Bf-109, Germany. 85c, Morane-Sauinier 406, France.

1995, July 30 Litho. *Perf. 12½*
3651 A986 10c multicolored
3652 A986 15c multicolored
3653 A986 65c multicolored
3654 A986 75c multicolored
3655 A986 85c multicolored

A987

A988

1995, Aug. 6 Litho. *Perf. 12½*
3656 A987 15c multicolored

Ernesto Lecuona, composer, pianist, birth cent.

1995, Aug. 10
Color of Horse or Horses
3657 A988 10c golden brown, white
3658 A988 15c white, horiz.
3659 A988 65c dark brown, white
3660 A988 75c red brown
3661 A988 85c tan
3662 A988 90c white

Singapore '95.

Souvenir Sheet

Beijing Intl. Stamp & Coin Expo '95 — A989

Illustration reduced.

1995, Aug. 28 *Perf. 13*
3663 A989 50c multicolored

1996 Summer Olympics, Atlanta — A990

1995, Sept. 25 Litho. *Perf. 13*
3664 A990 10c Wrestling
3665 A990 15c Weight lifting
3666 A990 65c Women's volleyball
3667 A990 75c Women's athletics
3668 A990 85c Baseball
3669 A990 90c Women's judo

Souvenir Sheet
3670 A990 1p Boxing

No. 3670 contains one 30x36mm stamp.

Cuban Sugar Industry, 400th Anniv. A991

Paintings from "Los Ingenios," by Edouard Laplante, 1852: 15c, Steam train, sugar factory. 65c, Sugar factory, tower, bridge.

1995, Oct. 3
3671 A991 15c multicolored
3672 A991 65c multicolored

UN, 50th Anniv. A992

1995, Oct. 24 Litho. *Perf. 13*
3673 A992 65c multicolored

Zoological Gardens, Havana — A993

Designs: 10c, Panthera leo, vert. 15c, Equus grevyi. 65c, Pongo pygmaeus, vert. 75c, Elephas maximus. 85c, Sciurus vulgaris. 90c, Procyon lotor.

1995, Oct. 30 Litho. *Perf. 13*
3674 A993 10c multicolored
3675 A993 15c multicolored
3676 A993 65c multicolored
3677 A993 75c multicolored
3678 A993 85c multicolored
3679 A993 90c multicolored

UNESCO, 50th Anniv. — A994

UNESCO World Culture and National Heritage sites: 65c, Santa Clara de Asis Convent. 75c, San Francisco de Asis Minor Basilica.

1995, Nov. 4
3680 A994 65c multicolored
3681 A994 75c multicolored

Orchids — A995

Designs: 5c, Epidendrum porpax. 10c, Cyrtopodium punctatum. 15c, Polyrrhiza lindeni. 40c, Bletia patula. 45c, Galeandra beyrichii. 50c, Vanilla dilloniana. 65c, Macradenia lutescens. 75c, Oncidium luridum. 85c, Ionopsis utricularioides.

1995, Nov. 10 *Perf. 12½*
3681A A995 5c multicolored
3681B A995 10c multicolored
3681C A995 15c multicolored
3682 A995 40c multicolored
3683 A995 45c multicolored
3684 A995 50c multicolored

3685 A995 65c multicolored
3686 A995 75c multicolored
3687 A995 85c multicolored

Issued: 40c-85c, 11/10/95; 5c-15c, 6/28/96.

Motion Pictures, Cent. — A996

1995, Dec. 7 *Perf. 13*

3688 A996 15c Lumiere Brothers
3689 A996 15c Marilyn Monroe
3690 A996 15c Marlene Dietrich
3691 A996 15c Vittorio DeSica
3692 A996 15c Charlie Chaplin
3693 A996 15c Greta Garbo
3694 A996 65c Humphrey Bogart
3695 A996 75c Montaner
3696 A996 85c Cantinflas

Souvenir Sheet

4th Cuban-Spanish Philatelic Exhibition, Havana — A997

Illustration reduced.

1995, Dec. 11 **Litho.** *Perf. 13*

3697 A997 1p multicolored

America Issue — A998

1995, Dec. 12

3698 A998 15c Centurus superciliaris
3699 A998 65c Todus multicolor

Generals Who Died in 1895 War — A999

Designs: No. 3700, Alfonso Goulet Goulet, Francisco Adolfo Crombet Ballon. No. 3701, Jesus Calvar O, Jose Guillermo Moncada, Tomas Jordan. No. 3702, Francisco Borrero Lavadi, Francisco Inchaustegui Cabrera.

1995, Dec. 20 *Perf. 12½*

3700 A999 15c multicolored
3701 A999 15c multicolored
3702 A999 15c multicolored
a. Strip of 3, #3700-3702

See Nos. 3758-3760.

Island of Coco Cay, Jardines del Rey A1000

Bird, scenic view: 10c, Sterna antillarum, aerial view of island. 15c, Eudocimus albus, people on beach. 45c, Spindalis zena, couple on steps of resort complex. 50c, Turdus plumbeus, resort. 65c, Mimus polyglottos, resort. 75c, Phoenicopterus ruber, couple in pool at resort.

1995, Dec. 23

3703 A1000 10c multicolored
3704 A1000 15c multicolored
3705 A1000 45c multicolored
3706 A1000 50c multicolored
3707 A1000 65c multicolored
3708 A1000 75c multicolored

Patriots — A1001

Designs: 15c, Carlos M. de Céspedes (1819-74). 65c, José Marti (1853-95). 75c, Antonio Maceo (1845-96). 1.05p, Ignacio Agramonte (1841-73). 2.05p, Máximo Gómez (1836-1905). 3p, Calixto Garcia (1839-98).

1996, Jan. 10

3709 A1001 15c green
3710 A1001 65c blue
3711 A1001 75c carmine
3712 A1001 1.05p lilac
3713 A1001 2.05p brown
3714 A1001 3p light brown

See Nos. 3755-3757.

Organization of Solidarity of the Peoples of Africa, Asia and Latin America (OSPAAAL), 30th Anniv. — A1002

1996, Jan. 14

3715 A1002 65c multicolored

Scientists — A1003

10c, Leonardo da Vinci (1452-1519). 15c, Mikhail V. Lomonosov (1711-65), atmospheric scientist. 65c, James Watt (1736-1819), engineer, inventor. 75c, Guglielmo Marconi (1874-1937), physicist. 85c, Charles R. Darwin (1809-82), naturalist.

1996, Jan. 30 **Litho.** *Perf. 12½*

3716 A1003 10c multicolored
3717 A1003 15c multicolored
3718 A1003 65c multicolored
3719 A1003 75c multicolored
3720 A1003 85c multicolored

1996 Summer Olympics, Atlanta — A1004

1996, Feb. 15 **Litho.** *Perf. 12½*

3721 A1004 10c Athletics, vert.
3722 A1004 15c Weight lifting, vert.
3723 A1004 65c Judo, vert.
3724 A1004 75c Wrestling
3725 A1004 85c Boxing

Souvenir Sheet

3726 A1004 1p Baseball, vert.

No. 3726 contains one 40x32mm stamp.

Espamer '96, Aviation and Space, Philatelic Exhibition, Seville — A1005

1996, Mar. 4

3727 A1005 15c C-4 Autogiro
3728 A1005 65c CASA C-352
3729 A1005 75c Alcotan C-201
3730 A1005 85c CASA C-212

Juan C. Gundlach (1810-1896), Ornithologist — A1006

Birds: 10c, Ceryle alcyon. 15c, Setophaga ruticilla. 65c, Geothlypis trichas. 75c, Passerina ciris. 85c, Bombycilla cedrorum.
1p, Vireo gundlachi.

1996, Mar. 15 *Perf. 12½*

3731 A1006 10c multicolored
3732 A1006 15c multicolored
3733 A1006 65c multicolored
3734 A1006 75c multicolored
3735 A1006 85c multicolored

Souvenir Sheet

3736 A1006 1p multicolored

No. 3736 contains one 40x32mm stamp.

Souvenir Sheet

ESPAMER '96, Stamp Exhibition of America and Europe, Seville — A1007

Illustration reduced.

1996, Mar. 14 **Litho.** *Perf. 12½*

3737 A1007 1p multicolored

First Man in Space, 35th Anniv. — A1008

Designs: 15c, Yuri A. Gagarin (1934-68). 65c, Spaceship, map showing orbital route.

1996, Apr. 12 **Litho.** *Perf. 12½*

3738 A1008 15c multi
3739 A1008 65c multi, horiz.

Socialist Revolution, 35th Anniv. — A1009

1996, Apr. 19

3740 A1009 15c shown
3741 A1009 65c Natl. flags

Cuban Sailing Ships A1010

Designs: 10c, Bahama. 15c, Santísima Trinidad. 65c, Principe de Asturias. 75c, San Pedro de Alcántara. 85c, Santa Ana.
1p, San Genaro.

1996, May 8 **Litho.** *Perf. 12½*

3742 A1010 10c multicolored
3743 A1010 15c multicolored
3744 A1010 65c multicolored
3745 A1010 75c multicolored
3746 A1010 85c multicolored

Souvenir Sheet

3747 A1010 1p multicolored

CAPEX '96. No. 3747 contains one 40x32mm stamp.

Fauna of the Caribbean A1011

Designs: 10c, Todus multicolor. No. 3749, Eulampis jugularis. No. 3750, Aix sponsa. No. 3751, Chaetodon ocellatus. No. 3752, Papilio cresphontes. No. 3753, Hypoplectrus indigo.

1996, June 18 **Litho.** *Perf. 12½*

3748 A1011 10c multicolored
3749 A1011 15c multicolored
3750 A1011 15c multicolored
3751 A1011 15c multicolored
3752 A1011 65c multicolored
3753 A1011 65c multicolored

Jose M. Maceo Grajales (1849-96), Revolutionary War Leader — A1012

1996, July 5
3754 A1012 15c multicolored

Patriot Type of 1996

Designs: 10c. Serafin Sánchez. 85c, Juan Gualberto Gomez. 90c, Quintin Bandera.

1996, July 10
3755 A1001 10c orange
3756 A1001 85c olive
3757 A1001 90c olive brown

Generals Who Died in 1895 War Type of 1995

#3758, Esteban Tamayo (1843-96), Angel Guerra (1842-96). #3759, Juan Fernández Ruz (1821-96), José Maria Aguirre (1843-96), Serafin Sánchez (1846-96). #3760, Juan Bruno Zayas (1867-96), Pedro Vargas Sotomayor (1868-96).

1996, July 30
3758 A999 15c multicolored
3759 A999 15c multicolored
3760 A999 15c multicolored
a. Strip of 3, #3758-3760

Santiago de Cuba — A1013

Flower, scenic view: 15c, Jacaranda arborea, beach. 65c, Begonia bissei, Fort San Pedro de la Roca. 75c, Byrsonima crassifolia, palm trees, mountains, vert. 85c, Pereskia zinniiflora, church, vert.

Perf. 13x12½, 12½x13
1996, Sept. 27 **Litho.**
3761 A1013 15c multicolored
3762 A1013 65c multicolored
3763 A1013 75c multicolored
3764 A1013 85c multicolored

Steam Locomotives — A1014

Designs: 10c, Baldwin 0-4-2, 1878. 15c, American 2-6-0, 1904. 65c, Baldwin 4-6-0, 1906. 75c, Rogers 2-4-4, 1914. 90c, Baldwin 2-8-0, 1920.

1996, Sept. 30 ***Perf. 12½***
3765 A1014 10c multicolored
3766 A1014 15c multicolored
3767 A1014 65c multicolored
3768 A1014 75c multicolored
3769 A1014 90c multicolored

Traditional Costumes A1015

America Issue: 15c, Free black couple, 19th cent. 65c, Guayabera couple, 20th cent.

1996, Oct. 12 **Litho.** ***Perf. 12½***
3770 A1015 15c multicolored
3771 A1015 65c multicolored

UNICEF, 50th Anniv. — A1016

1996, Nov. 8 **Litho.** ***Perf. 12½***
3772 A1016 15c multicolored

World Chess Championship Won by José Raúl Capablanca, 75th Anniv. — A1017

Designs: 15c, Portrait, chess board. 65c, Portrait, seated at chess board. 75c, Rook with top shaped as world, portrait. 85c, Playing chess as a child. 90c, In championship match, 1921.

1996, Nov. 30 **Litho.** ***Perf. 12½***
3773 A1017 15c multicolored
3774 A1017 65c multicolored
3775 A1017 75c multicolored
3776 A1017 85c multicolored
3777 A1017 90c multicolored

Revolutionary Armed Forces and Return of Castro from Mexico, 40th Anniv. — A1018

1996, Dec. 2
3778 A1018 15c Yacht Granma
3779 A1018 65c Armed forces

Maj. Gen. Antonio Maceo (1845-96) — A1019

Designs: 10c, Monument, Santiago, vert. No. 3781, Portrait, vert. No. 3782, Monument, Duaba. 65c, Detail of painting showing Maceo dying from combat wounds. 75c, Maceo, young man and monument, San Pedro.

1996, Dec. 7
3780 A1019 10c multicolored
3781 A1019 15c multicolored
3782 A1019 15c multicolored
3783 A1019 65c multicolored
3784 A1019 75c multicolored

Medals Won at 1996 Summer Olympic Games, Atlanta — A1020

Medal, sport: No. 3785a, Gold, judo. b, Bronze, wrestling.
No. 3786: a, Gold, weight lifting. b, Gold, wrestling. c, Silver, fencing. d, Silver, swimming.
No. 3787: a, Gold, women's volleyball. b, Gold, boxing. c, Silver, women's running. d, Gold, baseball.

1996, Dec. 10
3785 A1020 10c Pair, #a-b + 4 labels
3786 A1020 15c Block, #a-d + 2 labels
3787 A1020 65c Block, #a-d + 2 labels

New Year 1996 (Year of the Rat) — A1021

1996, Dec. 28 **Litho.** ***Perf. 12½***
3788 A1021 15c multicolored

Espamer '98 — A1022

Locomotives: 15c, Minho Douro 0-6-0, Portugal. No. 3790, Vulcan Iron Works 0-4-0, Brazil. No. 3791, Baldwin 2-6-0, Dominican Republic. No. 3792, American Locomotive Co. 2-6-4, Panama. No. 3793, Baldwin 0-4-0, Puerto Rico. No. 3794, Slaughter, Gruning Co. 0-4-0, Spain. No. 3795, Yorkshire Engine Co. 4-4-0, Argentina. No. 3796, 2-6-0 Paraguay. No. 3797, H.K. Porter Co. 2-8-2, Chile. No. 3798, 2-6-0, Mexico.
1p, Baldwin 0-4-2 (1884), Cuba.

1996, Dec. 30
3789 A1022 15c multicolored
3790 A1022 65c multicolored
3791 A1022 65c multicolored
3792 A1022 65c multicolored
3793 A1022 65c multicolored
3794 A1022 65c multicolored
3795 A1022 75c multicolored
3796 A1022 75c multicolored
3797 A1022 75c multicolored
3798 A1022 75c multicolored

Souvenir Sheet

3799 A1022 1p multicolored

No. 3799 contains one 36x28mm.

Hong Kong '97, Intl. Philatelic Exhibition — A1023

Cats: 10c, Brown-point Siamese, vert. No. 3801, Japanese bobtail. No. 3802, Burmese, vert. No. 3803, Singapore. No. 3804, Korat.
1p, Blue-point Siamese.

1997, Jan. 15 **Litho.** ***Perf. 12½***
3800 A1023 10c multicolored
3801 A1023 15c multicolored
3802 A1023 15c multicolored
3803 A1023 65c multicolored
3804 A1023 75c multicolored

Souvenir Sheet

3805 A1023 1p multicolored

No. 3805 contains one 40x31mm stamp.

Motion Pictures, Cent. A1024

Film scenes from: 15c, "El Romance del Palmar," directed by Ramón Peón. 65c, "Memorias del Subdesarrollo," directed by Tomás Gutiérrez Alea, vert.

1997, Jan. 24 **Litho.** ***Perf. 13***
3806 A1024 15c multicolored
3807 A1024 65c multicolored

Zoo Animals A1025

Designs: 10c, Camelus dromedarius. No. 3809, Ailuropada melanoleuca. No. 3810, Cerothoterium simun. 75c, Pongo pygmaeus. 90c, Bison bonasus.

1997, Feb. 20 **Litho.** ***Perf. 12½***
3808 A1025 10c multicolored
3809 A1025 15c multicolored
3810 A1025 15c multicolored
3811 A1025 75c multicolored
3812 A1025 90c multicolored

New Year 1997 (Year of the Ox) — A1026

1997, Feb. 22
3813 A1026 15c multicolored

Attack on the Presidential Palace, 40th Anniv. — A1027

1997, Mar. 13 **Litho.** ***Perf. 12½***
3814 A1027 15c Menelao Mora Morales

F

1998 World Cup Soccer Championships, France — A1028

Action scenes: 10c, Three players. No. 3816, Player in green, player in blue & yellow. No. 3817, Player in yellow & black, player in green. 65c, Player in yellow & blue, player in

blue and red. 75c, Player in red & blue, player in yellow & black.
1p, Player down.

1997, Mar. 25

3815 A1028 10c multicolored
3816 A1028 15c multicolored
3817 A1028 15c multicolored
3818 A1028 65c multicolored
3819 A1028 75c multicolored

Souvenir Sheet

3820 A1028 1p multicolored

No. 3820 contains one 40x31mm stamp.

Young Communist League (UJC), 35th Anniv. — A1029

1997, Apr. 4

3821 A1029 15c multicolored

Paddle Steamer Caledonia — A1030

Stamp Day: 15c, Maritime Postal Service, 170th anniv. 65c, Air Postal Service, 70th anniv.

1997, Apr. 24 **Litho.** ***Perf. 12½***

3822 A1030 15c multicolored
3823 A1030 65c multicolored

Death of Generals in War of 1895, 102nd Anniv. — A1031

#3824, Adolfo de Castillo, Enrique del Junco Cruz-Muñoz. #3825, Alberto Rodríguez Acosta, Mariano Sánchez Vaillant.

1997, May 18 **Litho.** ***Perf. 12½***

3824 A1031 15c multicolored
3825 A1031 15c multicolored
a. Pair, #3824-3825

Gen. Gregorio Luperon, Death Cent. — A1032

1997, May 20

3826 A1032 65c multicolored

Butterflies — A1033

Designs: 10c, Eurema nicippe. No. 3828, Eurema dina. No. 3829, Colobura dirce clementi. 65c, Vanesa atalanta. 85c, Kricogonia castalia.

1997, May 20

3827 A1033 10c multicolored
3828 A1033 15c multicolored
3829 A1033 15c multicolored
3830 A1033 65c multicolored
3831 A1033 85c multicolored

Cuban Assoc. of the UN, 50th Anniv. A1034

1997, May 31

3832 A1034 65c multicolored

Chinese In Cuba, 150th Anniv. — A1035

1997, May 29 ***Perf. 13***

3833 A1035 15c multicolored

14th World Festival of Youth and Students A1036

Designs: 10c, Dove holding olive twig, rainbow. No. 3835, Children playing on playground equipment, vert. No. 3836, Monument with arms extended. 65c, Maj. Ernesto "Che" Guevara, revolutionary hero. 75c, Monument, diff.

1997, July 28 **Litho.** ***Perf. 12½***

3834 A1036 10c multicolored
3835 A1036 15c multicolored
3836 A1036 15c multicolored
3837 A1036 65c multicolored
3838 A1036 75c multicolored

Frank País (1934-57), Revolutionary Hero — A1037

1997, July 30

3839 A1037 15c multicolored

Seven Wonders of the Ancient World A1038

Designs: 10c, Lighthouse of Alexandria. No. 3841, Pyramids of Egypt. No. 3842, Gardens of Semiramis at Babylon. No. 3843, Colossus at Rhodes. No. 3844, Mausoleum of Halicarnassus. No. 3845, Statue of Zeus at Olympia. 75c, Temple of Artemis at Ephesus.

1997, July 30

3840 A1038 10c multicolored
3841 A1038 15c multicolored
3842 A1038 15c multicolored
3843 A1038 15c multicolored
3844 A1038 65c multicolored
3845 A1038 65c multicolored
3846 A1038 75c multicolored

Independence of India, 50th Anniv. — A1039

1997, Aug. 15

3847 A1039 15c Mahatma Gandhi

Caribbean Birds — A1040

#3848, Sicalis flaveola. #3849, Eubucco bourcierii. #3850, Trogon curucui. #3851, Amazona leucocephala. #3852, Amazona ochrocephala. #3853, Hylocharis eliciae. #3854, Carduelis carduelis.

1997, Aug. 15

3848 A1040 15c multicolored
3849 A1040 15c multicolored
3850 A1040 15c multicolored
3851 A1040 15c multicolored
3852 A1040 65c multicolored
3853 A1040 65c multicolored
3854 A1040 75c multicolored

Famous Composers — A1041

10c, Liszt. #3856, Chopin. #3857, Bach. #3858, Beethoven. 65c, Ignacio Cervantes (1847-1905). 75c, Mozart.

1997, Sept. 15 **Litho.** ***Perf. 12½***

3855 A1041 10c multicolored
3856 A1041 15c multicolored
3857 A1041 15c multicolored
3858 A1041 15c multicolored
3859 A1041 65c multicolored
3860 A1041 75c multicolored

Tourism in Pinar del Rio — A1042

Bird, scene: 10c, Myadestes elisabeth, Viñales Valley. 15c, Corvus nasicus, Jutia Key. 65c, Dendroica pityophila, Soroa Falls. 75c, Tyrannus cubensis, San Juan River.

1997, Sept. 27 **Litho.**

3861 A1042 10c multi
3862 A1042 15c multi
3863 A1042 65c multi, vert.
3864 A1042 75c multi, vert.

Caribbean Flowers — A1043

Designs: No. 3865, Hibiscus elatus (majagua). No. 3866, Cordia sebestena (vomitel). No. 3867, Bidens pilosa (romerillo). No. 3868, Catharanthus roseus (vicaria). 65c, Reullia tuberosa (salta perico). 75c, Turnera ulmifolia (marilope).

1997, Sept. 30

3865 A1043 15c multicolored
3866 A1043 15c multicolored
3867 A1043 15c multicolored
3868 A1043 15c multicolored
3869 A1043 65c multicolored
3870 A1043 75c multicolored

Eastern University, 50th Anniv. — A1044

1997, Oct. 1 ***Perf. 13***

3871 A1044 15c multicolored

Che Guevara (1928-67), 5th Cuban Communist Party Congress A1045

1997, Oct. 8

3872 A1045 15c Flags
3873 A1045 15c Text, Guevara
3874 A1045 75c Portrait of Guevara

America Issue — A1046

1997, Oct. 12 **Litho.** ***Perf. 13***

3875 A1046 15c 19th cent. postman
3876 A1046 65c 20th cent. postman

Hominids — A1047

Designs: 10c, Australopithecus. No. 3878, Pithecanthropus (Java man). No. 3879, Sinanthropus (Peking man). No. 3880, Neanderthal. 65c, Cro-magnon man. 75c, Oberkassel man.

1997, Oct. 30 *Perf. 12½*

3877 A1047 10c multicolored
3878 A1047 15c multicolored
3879 A1047 15c multicolored
3880 A1047 15c multicolored
3881 A1047 65c multicolored
3882 A1047 75c multicolored

October Revolution, 80th Anniv. — A1048

1997, Nov. 7 *Perf. 12½*

3884 A1048 75c multicolored

Cuban Railroad, 160th Anniv. — A1049

10c, John Bull, 1830, UK. No. 3886, Old Ironsides, Baldwin, 1832, US. No. 3887, Baldwin Pacific Type 4-6-2, 1910-13, US. 65c, TE.M4:1 diesel electric, 1970, USSR. 75c, TE.114-K, diesel electric, 1975, USSR.

1997, Nov. 19 **Litho.** *Perf. 12½*

3885 A1049 10c multicolored
3886 A1049 15c multicolored
3887 A1049 15c multicolored
3888 A1049 65c multicolored
3889 A1049 75c multicolored

UN Conference on Commerce and Employment, Havana, 50th Anniv. — A1050

1997, Nov. 21

3890 A1050 65c multicolored

Victor Manuel Garcia, Painter, Birth Cent. A1051

1997, Dec. 29 **Litho.** *Perf. 12½*

3891 A1051 15c #1553, Garcia

Visit of Pope John Paul II A1052

Pope John Paul II, different coats of arms, and: 65c, Havana Cathedral. 75c, Basilica of Our Lady of Charity, Cobre, vert.

No. 3894, vert: a, Pope John Paul II greeting Fidel Castro. b, Pope waving.

1998, Jan. 18 **Litho.** *Perf. 12½*

3892 A1052 65c multicolored
3893 A1052 75c multicolored

Souvenir Sheet of 2

3894 A1052 50c #a.-b.

Nos. 3894a-3894b are 32x40mm.

Assassination of Jesus Menendez, 50th Anniv. — A1053

1998, Jan. 22

3895 A1053 15c multicolored

1998 World Cup Soccer Championships, France — A1054

Various soccer plays: 10c, 2 players. #3897, Player in black & yellow. #3898, Player on ground, 1 in striped shirt. #3899, 3 players, 2 in striped shirts. #3900, 3 players, 2 in blue shirts.

1p, Player with #11 on sleeve.

1998, Feb. 10 **Litho.** *Perf. 12½*

3896 A1054 10c multi, vert.
3897 A1054 15c multi, vert.
3898 A1054 15c multi, vert.
3899 A1054 65c multi
3900 A1054 65c multi

Souvenir Sheet

Perf. 13

3901 A1054 1p multicolored

No. 3901 contains one 40x32mm stamp.

Capt. Isabel Rubio Diaz, Medical Aide During Revolution, Death Cent. — A1055

1998, Feb. 15 *Perf. 13*

3902 A1055 15c multicolored

Brig. Gen. Vidal Ducasse Reeve (1852-98) A1056

1998, Feb. 19 *Perf. 12½*

3903 A1056 15c multicolored

No. 3903 inscribed "Revee."

"Radio Rebelde," 40th Anniv. — A1057

1998, Feb. 23

3904 A1057 15c multicolored

Fire Engines A1058

Designs: 10c, 1901 Shand Mason & Co., London. No. 3905, 1905 Horse-drawn municipal fire wagon, Havana, 1905. No. 3906, 1921 American-La France Fire Engine Co. 65c, 1952 Chevrolet 6400, US. 75c, 1956 American-La France Foamite Co., US.

1998, Mar. 10

3905 A1058 10c multicolored
3906 A1058 15c multicolored
3907 A1058 15c multicolored
3908 A1058 65c multicolored
3909 A1058 75c multicolored

Protest of Baragua, 120th Anniv. — A1059

1998, Mar. 15

3910 A1059 15c multicolored

Victory at Cuito Cuanavale, Angola, 10th Anniv. — A1060

1998, Mar. 23 **Litho.** *Perf. 12½*

3911 A1060 15c multicolored

New Year 1998 (Year of the Tiger) — A1061

1998, Mar. 30

3912 A1061 15c multicolored

Dogs — A1062

1998, Apr. 15 **Litho.** *Perf. 12½*

3913 A1062 10c Chihuahua
3914 A1062 15c Beagle
3915 A1062 15c Xoloitzcuintle
3916 A1062 65c German pointer
3917 A1062 75c Chow chow

Evolution of the Chimpanzee A1063

Pan troglodytes and: 10c, Proconsul. No. 3919, Cranium. No. 3920, Right hand and foot. 65c, New-born chimpanzee. 75c, Map of Africa showing chimpanzee's range.

1998, May 15 **Litho.** *Perf. 12½*

3918 A1063 10c multicolored
3919 A1063 15c multicolored
3920 A1063 15c multicolored
3921 A1063 65c multicolored
3922 A1063 75c multicolored

Lisbon '98, World Stamp Exhibition — A1064

Deep sea fish: No. 3923, Raja batis. No. 3924, Eurypharynx pelecanoides. 65c, Caulophryne. 75c, Chauliodus sloani.

1998, May 22 **Litho.** *Perf. 12½*

3923 A1064 15c multicolored
3924 A1064 15c multicolored
3925 A1064 65c multicolored
3926 A1064 75c multicolored

Souvenir Sheet

Juvalux '98, World Stamp Exhibition for Youth Philately and Postal History, Luxembourg — A1065

Illustration reduced.

1998, May 20 **Litho.** *Perf. 12½*

3927 A1065 1p Postman on bicycle

Federico Garcia Lorca (1898-1936), Poet — A1066

1998, June 2
3928 A1066 75c multicolored

Intl. Year of the Oceans A1067

#3929, Canarreos flower coral, coral crab, small fish. #3030, French angel fish, brain coral, gorgonia.

1998, June 5
3929 A1067 65c multicolored
3930 A1067 65c multicolored
a. Pair, #3929-3930

Diana, Princess of Wales (1961-97) A1068

Various portraits, color of clothes: No. 3931, Pale yellow and pink. No. 3932, Black and white. No. 3933, Multicolored print. No. 3934, Red. No. 3935, Pink and black plaid. 65c, White. 75c, Blue.

1998, June 30 Litho. *Perf. 13*
3931 A1068 10c multicolored
3932 A1068 10c multicolored
3933 A1068 10c multicolored
3934 A1068 15c multicolored
3935 A1068 15c multicolored
3936 A1068 65c multicolored
3937 A1068 75c multicolored

Expo 2000, Hanover A1069

#3938, Mascot, "Twipsy." #3939, Mascot in London, 1851. #3940, Mascot in Brussels, 1958. #3941, German flag, map of Germany. 65c, Mascot in Paris, 1889. 75c, Mascot on top of world, fireworks.

1998, July 31 *Perf. 12½*
3938 A1069 15c multi, vert.
3939 A1069 15c multi
3940 A1069 15c multi
3941 A1069 15c multi
3942 A1069 65c multi, vert.
3943 A1069 75c multi

Maracaibo '98, 18th Central America and Caribbean Games — A1070

1998, Aug. 8
3944 A1070 15c multicolored

Attack on Moncada Barracks, 45th Anniv. — A1071

Designs: 15c, Siboney farmhouse, Abel Santamaría. 65c, Barracks, José Martí.

1998, July 26 Litho. *Perf. 13*
3945 A1071 15c multicolored
3946 A1071 65c multicolored

Democratic Republic of Korea, 50th Anniv. — A1072

1998, Sept. 8 Litho. *Perf. 13*
3947 A1072 75c Kim Il Sung (1912-94)

Japanese Immigration to Cuba, Cent. — A1073

1998, Sept. 9 Litho. *Perf. 13*
3948 A1073 75c multicolored

Orchids A1074

10c, Coelogyne flaccida. #3950, Dendrobium fimbriatum. #3951, Arunding graminifolia. #3952, Bletia patula. #3953, Phaius tankervilliaea.

1998, Sept. 10
3949 A1074 10c multicolored
3950 A1074 15c multicolored
3951 A1074 15c multicolored
3952 A1074 65c multicolored
3953 A1074 65c multicolored

5th Congress of the Revolution Defense Committees A1075

1998, Sept. 25 Litho. *Perf. 13*
3954 A1075 15c multicolored

World Tourism Day — A1076

Holguin Province, reptiles: 10c, Looking through gateway, city of Gibara, anolis equestris, vert. 15c, Mayabe Valley, anolis vermiculatus, vert. 65c, Guardalavaca Beach, anolis allisoni. 75c, Mayari pine forest, anolis mestrei.

1998, Sept. 27
3955 A1076 10c multicolored
3956 A1076 15c multicolored
3957 A1076 65c multicolored
3958 A1076 75c multicolored

Women Who Aided Cuban Revolutionary Movements A1077

America Issue: 65c, Bernarda Toro Pelegrin (1852-1911). 75c, Maria Magdalena Cabrales Issac (1842-1905).

1998, Oct. 12
3959 A1077 65c multicolored
3960 A1077 75c multicolored

World Wildlife Fund Protected Fauna — A1078

Cuban Natl. Ballet, 50th Anniv. — A1079

Arantinga Euops: 10c, Two on tree branch. 15c, One looking out of nest. 65c, One on tree branch. 75c, One up close.

1998, Oct. 21
3961 A1078 10c multicolored
3962 A1078 15c multicolored
3963 A1078 65c multicolored
3964 A1078 75c multicolored

1998, Oct. 28
3965 A1079 15c Swan Lake
3966 A1079 65c Giselle

Massacre of O'Farrill and Goicuria, 40th Anniv. — A1080

Rogelio Perea, Angel Ameijeiras, Pedro Gutiérrez.

1998, Nov. 8
3967 A1080 15c multicolored

Battle of Guisa, 40th Anniv. A1081

Design: Capt. Braulio Coroneaux, tank.

1998, Nov. 30 Litho. *Perf. 12½*
3968 A1081 15c multicolored

A1082

A1083

1998, Dec. 10 Litho. *Perf. 12½*
3969 A1082 65c multicolored

Universal Declaration of Human Rights, 50th anniv.

1998, Dec. 11 *Perf. 13*

Calixto Garcia Iñiguez (1839-98), revolutionary Major General.

3970 A1083 65c multicolored

Padre Félix Varela (1788-1853) — A1084

1998, Dec. 16
3971 A1084 75c multicolored

War for Independence, Cent. — A1085

War heroes, historical scene: No. 3972, Carlos Manuel de Céspedes. No. 3973, Ignacio Agramonte. No. 3974, Máximo Gómez. No. 3975, José Maceo. No. 3976, Salvador Cisneros. No. 3978, Calixto Garcia. No. 3979, Adolfo Flor. No. 3980, Serafin Sánchez. 65c, José Marti. 75c, Antonio Maceo.

1998, Dec. 25 Litho. ***Perf. 12½***
3972 A1085 15c multicolored
3973 A1085 15c multicolored
3974 A1085 15c multicolored
3975 A1085 15c multicolored
3976 A1085 15c multicolored
3977 A1085 15c multicolored
3978 A1085 15c multicolored
3979 A1085 15c multicolored
3980 A1085 65c multicolored
3981 A1085 75c multicolored

Battle for Palma Soriano, 40th Anniv. A1086

1998, Dec. 27 Litho. ***Perf. 13***
3982 A1086 15c multicolored

Cuban Revolution, 40th Anniv. — A1087

a, Boat, soldiers in water. b, Fidel Castro with soldier. c, Castro giving speech, pigeons.

1999, Jan. 1
3983 A1087 65c Strip of 3, #a.-c.

Natl. Revolutionary Police, 40th Anniv. — A1088

1999, Jan. 5
3984 A1088 15c multicolored

Cuban Workers' Trade Union Organization, 60th Anniv. — A1089

1999, Jan. 28 Litho. ***Perf. 12½***
3985 A1089 15c multicolored

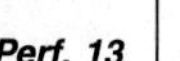

New Year 1999 (Year of the Rabbit) — A1090

1999, Feb. 5 ***Perf. 13***
3986 A1090 75c multicolored

Lenin (1870-1924) — A1091

1999, Feb. 21 Litho. ***Perf. 12½***
3987 A1091 75c multicolored

Dinosaurs — A1092

1999, Mar. 10
3988 A1092 10c Ornithosuchus
3989 A1092 15c Saltopus
3990 A1092 15c Bactrosaurus
3991 A1092 65c Protosuchus
3992 A1092 75c Mussaurus

Cuban Musicians — A1093

1999, Mar. 22 ***Perf. 13***
3993 A1093 5c Dámaso Pérez Prado
3994 A1093 15c Benny Moré
3995 A1093 15c Chano Pozo
3996 A1093 35c Miguelito Valdés
3997 A1093 65c Bola de Nieve
3998 A1093 75c Rita Montaner

Simón Bolivar's Visit to Cuba, Bicent. A1094

1999, Mar. 25
3999 65c Portrait
4000 65c Monument
a. A1094 Pair, #3999-4000

State Security Organization, 40th Anniv. — A1095

1999, Mar. 26 Litho. ***Perf. 12½***
4001 A1095 65c multicolored

Souvenir Sheet

China '99 World Philatelic Exhibition — A1096

Illustration reduced.

1999, Apr. 10 Litho. ***Perf. 12½***
4002 A1096 1p Giant panda

Stamp Day A1097

1999, Apr. 24
4003 A1097 15c Postal rocket
4004 A1097 65c Post rider

Test of Cuban Postal Rocket, 60th anniv. Insurgent Postal Service, 130th anniv.

Casa de las Américas, 40th Anniv. — A1098

1999, Apr. 24
4005 A1098 65c multicolored

Souvenir Sheet

IBRA '99, World Philatelic Exhibition, Nuremberg — A1099

Illustration reduced.

1999, Apr. 27
4006 A1099 1p Train

Agrarian Reform Law, 40th Anniv. A1100

1999, May 17
4007 A1100 65c multicolored

Felipe Poey, Scientist, Birth Bicent. A1101

Fish: 5c, Gramma loreto Poey. 15c, Liopropoma rubre Poey. #4010, Hypoplectrus gummigutta. #74011, Stegastes dorsopunicans. 1p, Portrait of Poey, hypoplectrus guttavarius.

1999, May 26 Litho. ***Perf. 12½***
4008 A1101 5c multicolored
4009 A1101 15c multicolored
4010 A1101 65c multicolored
4011 A1101 65c multicolored

Souvenir Sheet

Perf. 13¼x13

4012 A1101 1p multicolored

No. 4012 contains one 32x40mm stamp.

Souvenir Sheet

Philexfrance '99, World Philatelic Exhibition — A1102

Sculpture in sheet margin: "1814," by Jean Louis Meissonier (1815-1891). Illustration reduced.

1999, June 2 ***Perf. 13***
4013 A1102 1p multicolored

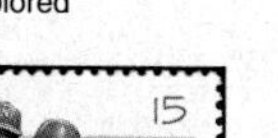

1999 Pan-American Games, Winnipeg — A1103

1999, June 25 Litho. ***Perf. 13***
4014 A1103 15c Baseball
4015 A1103 65c Volleyball, vert
4016 A1103 75c Boxing

People's Republic of China, 50th Anniv. A1104

5c, Victory at Wioming, by Gao Hong. 15c, Nanchang Insurrection, by Cai Lang. 40c, Red Army Crossing a Swamp, by Gao Quan. 65c, Occupation of the Presidential Palace, by Cheng Yifei and Wei Jingshan. 75c, Proclamation of the People's Republic of China, by Dong Xiwen.

1999, Aug. 21 Litho. ***Perf. 12¾***

4017 A1104 5c multicolored
4018 A1104 15c multicolored
4019 A1104 40c multicolored
4020 A1104 65c multicolored
4021 A1104 75c multicolored

China 1999 World Philatelic Exhibition, Beijing — A1105

No. 4022, Morning Glories, by Qi Baishi. No. 4023, Three Galloping Horses, by Xu Beihong. No. 4024, Hunan Woman, by Fu Baoshi. No. 4025, Birthplace of Luxun, by Wu Guanzhong. No. 4026, Horse Riders, by Huangzhou. 40c, Pine Tree, by He Xiangning. 65c, Sleep, by Jin Shangyi. 75c, Poetic Scene in Xun Yang, by Chen Yifei.

1999, Aug. 22 Litho. ***Perf. 13***

4022 A1105 5c multicolored
4023 A1105 5c multicolored
4024 A1105 15c multicolored
4025 A1105 15c multicolored
4026 A1105 15c multicolored
4027 A1105 40c multicolored
4028 A1105 65c multicolored
4029 A1105 75c multicolored

UPU, 125th Anniv. A1106

1999, Sept. 16 Litho. ***Perf. 12¾***

4030 A1106 75c multicolored

World Tourism Day A1107

Butterflies and Havana tourist sites: 10c, Antia numidia, Morro Castle. 15c, Papilio polyxenes, Havana Cathedral. 65c, Dryas julia, Convent of San Francisco. 75c, Eueides cleobaea, Capitol.

1999, Sept. 27 ***Perf. 12½x12¾***

4031 A1107 10c multicolored
4032 A1107 15c multicolored
4033 A1107 65c multicolored
4034 A1107 75c multicolored

Expo 2000, Hanover, Germany A1108

5c, World map, Expo 2000 emblem. #4036, "Twipsy" mascot, vert. #4037, "Twipsy" and 1876 Philadelphia Exposition. #4038, "Twipsy" and 1970 Osaka Exposition. 65c, "Twipsy" and 2000 Exposition. 75c, "Twipsy" and 1967 Montreal Exposition.

1999, Oct. 1 ***Perf. 12¾***

4035 A1108 5c multicolored
4036 A1108 15c multicolored
4037 A1108 15c multicolored
4038 A1108 15c multicolored
4039 A1108 65c multicolored
4040 A1108 75c multicolored

Cubana Airlines, 70th Anniv. — A1109

1999, Oct. 8 ***Perf. 12½x12¼***

4041 A1109 15c Fokker
4042 A1109 15c DC-10
4043 A1109 65c A-320
4044 A1109 75c DC-3

America Issue, A New Millennium Without Arms — A1110

1999, Oct. 12 ***Perf. 12¾***

4045 A1110 15c Pigeon, mushroom cloud
4046 A1110 65c Dove, globe

National Instiutions, 40th Anniv. — A1111

1999, Oct. 16 ***Perf. 12¾***

4047 A1111 15c MINFAR
4048 A1111 65c Natl. Revolutionary Militia

Disappearance of Camilo Cienfuegos, 40th Anniv. — A1112

1999, Oct. 28 Litho. ***Perf. 12¾***

4049 A1112 15c multicolored

Souvenir Sheet

12th Congress of Cuban Philatelic Federation — A1113

Illustration reduced.

1999, Dec. 11 ***Perf. 13***

4050 A1113 1p multicolored

Ernest Hemingway (1899-1961), Writer — A1114

1999, Dec. 15 ***Perf. 12½x12¼***

4051 A1114 65c multicolored

9th Summit of Ibero-American Heads of State and Government, Havana — A1115

Designs: 65c, Plaza Vieja. 75c, Plaza of St. Francis of Assisi.
1p, Plaza de Armas.

1999, Nov. 5 Litho. ***Perf. 12¾x12½***

4052 A1115 65c multi
4053 A1115 75c multi

Souvenir Sheet

Perf. 13

4054 A1115 1p multi

No. 4054 contains one 40x31mm stamp.

Rubén Martínez Villena (1899-1934), Revolutionary — A1116

1999, Dec. 20 ***Perf. 12½x12¾***

4055 A1116 15c multi

Dr. Tomás Romay Chacón (1764-1849) A1117

1999, Dec. 21 ***Perf. 13***

4056 A1117 65c multi

New Year 2000 (Year of the Dragon) — A1118

2000, Jan. 10 ***Perf. 12½***

4057 A1118 15c multi

Folklore A1119

Paintings depicting Cuban folklore by Concepción Ferrant (1882-1968): 10c, Rumba Caliente. 15c, Cachumba. 65c, En Casa de un Babalao. 75c, Tata Cuñengue.

2000, Jan. 26 ***Perf. 12½x12¾***

4058 A1119 10c multi
4059 A1119 15c multi
4060 A1119 65c multi
4061 A1119 75c multi

Butterflies — A1120

10c, Helcyra superba. No. 4063, Pantaporia punctata. No. 4064, Neptis themis. 65c, Curetis acuta. 75c, Chrysozephyrus ataxus.

2000, Feb. 25 ***Perf. 12¾***

4062 A1120 10c multi
4063 A1120 15c multi
4064 A1120 15c multi
4065 A1120 65c multi
4066 A1120 75c multi

Bangkok 2000 Stamp Exhibition.

Group of 77 South Summit, Havana — A1121

2000, Apr. 7 Litho. ***Perf. 13x12½***
4067 A1121 75c multi

Lenin, 130th Anniv. of Birth — A1122

2000, Apr. 22 ***Perf. 12¾***
4068 A1122 75c multi

Che Guevara in Congo, 35th Anniv. A1123

2000, Apr. 24
4069 A1123 65c multi

Stamp Day — A1124

Designs: 65c, Cuba #2, building. 90c, Airplane, cover, Jaime Gonzáles, pilot of first experimental airmail flight in Cuba.

2000, Apr. 24
4070 A1124 65c multi
4071 A1124 90c multi

Capt. San Luis (Elisio Reyes), Military Hero (1940-67) A1125

2000, Apr. 27
4072 A1125 65c multi

The Stamp Show 2000, London A1126

Locomotives: 5c, 1882 Baldwin 0-6-0. 10c, 1895 Baldwin 2-8-0. 15c, 1912 Baldwin 2-8-0. 65c, 1919 Alco 2-8-0. 75c, 1925 Alco 2-8-2.

1p, 1920 Henschel 2-6-0.

2000, May 5 ***Perf. 12¾***
4073 A1126 5c multi
4074 A1126 10c multi
4075 A1126 15c multi
4076 A1126 65c multi
4077 A1126 75c multi

Souvenir Sheet

Perf. 13

4078 A1126 1p multi

No. 4078 contains one 40x32mm stamp.

WIPA 2000 Philatelic Exhibition, Vienna — A1127

Airships of: 10c, Henri Giffart, 1852. 15c, Albert and Gaston Tissandier, 1883, vert. 50c, Charles Renard and Arthur Krebs, 1884. 65c, Pierre and Paul Lebaudy, 1903. 75c, August von Perseval, 1906.

1p, Ferdinand von Zeppelin.

Perf. 12½x12¼, 12¼x12½
2000, May 18
4079 A1127 10c multi
4080 A1127 15c multi
4081 A1127 50c multi
4082 A1127 65c multi
4083 A1127 75c multi

Souvenir Sheet

Perf. 12½

4084 A1127 1p multi

No. 4084 contains one 40x32mm stamp.

Second World Meeting of Friendship and Solidarity With Cuba — A1128

2000, June 23 Litho. ***Perf. 12¾***
4085 A1128 65c multi

José de la Luz y Caballero (1800-62), Educator — A1129

2000, July 11 ***Perf. 12½x12¼***
4086 A1129 65c multi

Amadeo Roldan (1900-39), Violinist — A1130

2000, July 12 ***Perf. 12¾***
4087 A1130 65c multi

La Edad de Oro, by José Marti — A1131

5c, Bebé y El Señor Don Pomposo. 10c, La Muñeca Negra. 15c, Nene Traviesa. 50c, Los Dos Ruiseñores. 65c, Frontispiece of La Edad de Oro. 75c, El Camarón Encantado.

2000, July 20
4088-4093 A1131 Set of 6

Latin American Association for Integration — A1132

2000, Aug. 12
4094 A1132 65c multi

Souvenir Sheet

Olymphilex 2000, Sydney — A1133

Illustration reduced.

2000, Aug. 17 ***Perf. 13***
4095 A1133 1p multi

2000 Summer Olympics, Sydney A1134

Designs: 5c, Runners. 15c, Soccer. 65c, Baseball. 75c, Cycling.

2000, Aug. 20 ***Perf. 12¾***
4096-4099 A1134 Set of 4

Dr. Pedro Kouri Esmeja (1900-64) A1135

2000, Aug. 21 **Litho.**
4100 A1135 65c multi

Federation of Cuban Women, 40th Anniv. — A1136

2000, Aug. 23
4101 A1136 15c multi

España 2000 Intl. Philatelic Exhibition — A1137

Designs: 10c, 1851 Havana-Bilbao stampless cover, ship. No. 4103, 15c, Spain #1, Cibeles Fountain, Madrid. No. 4104, 15c, 1850 Zaragoza-Cadiz cover, Palacio de Cristal, Madrid. 65c, Spain #1-5, Palacio de Comunicaciones, Madrid. 75c, Cuba #1, Centro Gallego, Havana.

2000, Sept. 7 ***Perf. 12¾x12½***
4102-4106 A1137 Set of 5

Souvenir Sheet

Perf. 12½

4107 A1137 100c Queen Isabella II, vert.

No. 4107 contains one 32x40mm stamp.

Beaches — A1138

#4108, Coconuts Bay, PRC. #4109, Varadero Beach, Cuba.

2000, Sept. 26 ***Perf. 12½x12¼***
4108-4109 A1138 15c Set of 2
4109a Pair, #4108-4109

See People's Republic of China No. 3052.

World Tourism Day — A1139

Marine life: 10c, Eretmochelys imbricata, vert. 15c, Epinephelus striatus, vert. 65c, Pomacanthus paru. 75c, Anisotremus surinamensis.

Perf. 12½x12¾, 12¾x12½
2000, Sept. 27
4110-4113 A1139 Set of 4

Committees of Defense of the Revolution, 40th Anniv. — A1140

2000, Sept. 28 ***Perf. 12¾***
4114 A1140 15c multi

America Issue - AIDS Prevention A1141

Ribbon, heart-shaped map and: 15c, Family. 65c, Couple.

2000, Oct. 12
4115-4116 A1141 Set of 2

Cuban Military in Angola, 25th Anniv. — A1142

2000, Nov. 7
4117 A1142 75c multi

Visit by Alexander von Humboldt, Bicent. — A1143

Humboldt and: 15c, House in Trinidad. 65c, House in Havana, Political Essay on the Island of Cuba.

2000, Dec. 19 **Litho.** ***Perf. 12¾***
4118-4119 A1143 Set of 2

20th Pan-American Railway Congress A1144

2000, Sept. 18 **Litho.** ***Perf. 12¾***
4120 A1144 65c multi

Millennium — A1145

Snails: a, Polymita versicolor. b, Polymita picta iolimbata. c, Polymita picta roseolimbata. d, Polymita picta picta. e, Polymita picta nigrolimbata.
Illustration reduced.

2000, Dec. 20
4121 A1145 65c Block of 5, #a-e, + label

New Year 2001 (Year of the Snake) — A1146

Illustration reduced.

2001, Jan. 10
4122 A1146 15c multi

Hong Kong 2001 Stamp Exhibition — A1147

Birds: 5c, Aix galericulata. 10c, Chrysolophus pictus. 15c, Ardea cinerea. 65c, Gallus gallus. 75c, Streptotelia decaocto.

2001, Jan. 25 ***Perf. 12¾***
4123-4127 A1147 Set of 5

Souvenir Sheet

Perf. 12½

4128 A1147 1p Grus grus

No. 4128 contains one 32x40mm stamp.

National Institute for Sport Physical Education and Recreation, 40th Anniv. — A1148

2001, Feb. 23 ***Perf. 12½x12¼***
4129 A1148 65c multi

UN High Commissioner for Refugees, 50th Anniv. — A1149

2001, Mar. 15 ***Perf. 12¾x12½***
4130 A1149 65c multi

Antique Locomotives — A1150

Locomotives from, 10c, 1863. 15c, 1876. 40c, 1885. 65c, 1914. 75c, 1932.

2001, Mar. 20 ***Perf. 12½x12¼***
4131-4135 A1150 Set of 5

105th Interparliamentary Union Congress, Havana — A1151

2001, Mar. 30 ***Perf. 12¾***
4136 A1151 65c multi

Bay of Pigs Invasion, 40th Anniv. — A1152

2001, Apr. 19 ***Perf. 12¾x12½***
4137 A1152 65c multi

Cats and Dogs A1153

Designs: 10c, Cats, emblem of Cat Aficionados Association. No. 4139, 15c, Dogs, Cats, emblem of Aniplant. No. 4140, 15c, Dogs, emblem of Cynological Federation of Cuba. 65c, Dogs, emblem of Sporting Dog Federation of Cuba. 75c, Dogs, cats.

2001, Apr. 25 ***Perf. 12½x12¾***
4138-4142 A1153 Set of 5

Radio Havana, 40th Anniv. — A1154

2001, May 1 ***Perf. 12½x12¼***
4143 A1154 65c multi

Tourism Convention — A1155

2001, May 7 ***Perf. 12¾x12½***
4144 A1155 65c multi

Belgica 2001 Intl. Stamp Exhibition, Brussels A1156

Designs: 5c, St. Michel Cathedral. 10c, Sablon Church, horiz. 15c, Royal Residence, horiz. 65c, Sacred Heart Basilica, horiz. 75c, Atomium.
1p, Royal Palace.

2001, May 10 ***Perf. 12¾***
4145-4149 A1156 Set of 5

Souvenir Sheet

Perf. 12½

4150 A1156 100c multi

No. 4150 contains one 32x40mm stamp.

Interior Ministry, 40th Anniv. A1157

2001, June 6 ***Perf. 12¾***
4151 A1157 65c multi

Phila Nippon '01, Japan A1158

Japanese trains: 5c., JR 500. 10c, JR 700. 15c, MAX 1. 65c, MAX 2. 75c, 300.

2001, June 20 **Litho.** ***Perf. 12¾***
4152-4156 A1158 Set of 5

Souvenir Sheet

Perf. 12½

4157 A1158 100c Zero

No. 4157 contains one 40x32mm stamp.

Republic of San Marino, 1700th Anniv. — A1159

2001, July 20 Litho. ***Perf. 12½x12¼***
4158 A1159 75c multi

Aquaculture — A1160

Designs: 5c, Tinca tinca. 10c, Rana temporaria. 15c, Cardisoma guanhumi. 65c, Mytius edulis. 75c, Tilapia mariae.
1p, Potamobius pallipes.

2001, Sept. 17 ***Perf. 12¾***
4159-4163 A1160 Set of 5

Souvenir Sheet

Perf. 12½

4164 A1160 1p multi

No. 4164 contains one 40x32mm stamp.

Recovery of Raw Materials, 40th Anniv. — A1161

2001, Sept. 21 ***Perf. 12¾x12½***
4165 A1161 65c multi

Tourism — A1162

Designs: 10c, Valle de Viñales. 15c, Trinidad. 65c, Sirena Beach, Cayo Largo del Sur. 75c, Morro Castle, Havana.

2001, Sept. 27
4166-4169 A1162 Set of 4

Year of Dialogue Among Civilizations A1163

2001, Oct. 9 ***Perf. 12¾***
4170 A1163 65c multi

America Issue - UNESCO World Heritage A1164

Flora and fauna from Desembarco del Granma Natl. Park: 15c, Tetramicra malpighiarum. 65c, Liggus vittatus.

2001, Oct. 12 ***Perf. 13¼x13¾***
4171-4172 A1164 Set of 2

José Marti National Library, Cent. A1165

2001, Oct. 18 ***Perf. 12¾***
4173 A1165 15c multi

Cuban Airliner Explosion Near Barbados, 25th Anniv. — A1166

Various details of painting.

2001, Oct. 22
4174 Horiz. strip of 5
a. A1166 5c shown
b. A1166 10c multi
c. A1166 15c multi
d. A1166 50c multi
e. A1166 65c multi

Eduardo R. Chibas, Communist Leader, Cent. of Birth — A1167

2001, Nov. 27 Litho. ***Perf. 13***
4175 A1167 65c multi

Napoleonic Museum, 40th Anniv. — A1168

Equestrian statues of Napoleon and map of battle of: No. 4176, 10c, Eylau. No. 4177, 10c, Marengo. 65c, Waterloo. 75c, Aboukir.

2001, Dec. 1 ***Perf. 12¾x12½***
4176-4179 A1168 Set of 4

Pablo de la Torriente Brau (1901-36), Poet — A1169

2001, Dec. 12 ***Perf. 12¾***
4180 A1169 75c multi

Cuban Federation of Pigeon Fanciers, 4th Congress A1170

Pigeons: No. 4181, 65c, Empedrado oscura 2021-61-ME. No. 4182, 65c, Empedrado claro 2241-55-ME. No. 4183, 65c, Mosaico 1561-66-HM. No. 4184, 65c, Mosaico, 3013-67-HM. No. 4185, 65c Bronceado, 338-59-HE.

2001, Dec. 14 ***Perf. 12½***
4181-4185 A1170 Set of 5

CUBA correos 2001 5

Film Stars Who Never Won Academy Awards A1171

Designs: 5c, Tyrone Power. No. 4187, 10c, Ava Gardner. No. 4188, 10c, Steve McQueen. No. 4189, 15c, Rita Hayworth. No. 4190, 15c, Marilyn Monroe. No. 4191, 15c, James Dean. No. 4192, 65c, Rock Hudson. No. 4193, 65c, Natalie Wood. 75c, Richard Burton.

2001, Dec. 20
4186-4194 A1171 Set of 9
a. Sheet of 9, #4186-4194

New Year 2002 (Year of the Horse) — A1172

2002, Jan. 21 Litho. ***Perf. 12½x12¾***
4195 A1172 15c multi

Cigar Production — A1173

Cigars and: 5c, Hat, Cuba No. 358, tobacco leaf. 10c, Clock, cigar cylinder. 15c, Map of Cuba, Simon Bolivar. 65c, Cuba Nos. 356, 357, map, cigar smoker. 75c, Flag, tobacco field, man.
1p, Fidel Castro, map, star.

2002, Feb. 15 ***Perf. 12¾***
4196-4200 A1173 Set of 5

Souvenir Sheet

Perf. 13131/4

4201 A1173 1p multi

Fourth Havana Festival, Cohiba brand, 36th anniv. No. 4201 contains one 40x32mm stamp.

Second UPAEP Information Workshop — A1174

Illustration reduced.

2002, Feb. 21 ***Perf. 12½x12¼***
4202 A1174 65c multi

Explorers A1175

Explorers: 5c, Reading map. 15c, Tying knots. 50c, Starting campfire for cooking. 65c, Starting fire. 75c, Using orientation techniques.

2002, Mar. 20 ***Perf. 12½***
4203-4207 A1175 Set of 5
a. Sheet of 5, #4203-4207, + label

Union of Young Communists, 40th Anniv. — A1176

2002, Apr. 4 ***Perf. 12½x12¼***
4208 A1176 15c multi

ExpoVid 2002 Wine Event — A1177

Designs: 15c, Cigar smokers, wine bottles and glasses, map of wine producing areas. 65c, Wine glass and barrels. 75c, Wine glass and vineyard.

2002, June 5 ***Perf. 12¾x12½***
4209-4211 A1177 Set of 3

2002 World Cup Soccer Championships, Japan and Korea — A1178

Player and flag from: No. 4212, 15c, South Korea. No. 4213, 15c, France. No. 4214, 15c, Germany. No. 4215, 15c, Brazil. No. 4216, 15c, Spain. 65c, Argentina. 75c, Italy. 85c, Japan.

2002, Apr. 21 **Litho.** ***Perf. 12½***
4212-4219 A1178 Set of 8
4219a Sheet, #4212-4219

Souvenir Sheet

Hispano-Cubano Philatelic Exposition — A1179

2002, Apr. 27 ***Perf. 13***
4220 A1179 1p multi

Juan Tomas Roig, Botanist, 125th Anniv. of Birth A1180

Designs: 5c, Bust of Roig, experimental agronomic station, Santiago de las Vegas. 10c, Bust and house of Roig. 15c, Roig, laboratory glassware and Nicotiana tabacum. 50c, Building, Allophyllum roiggi, and sculpture of Roig. 65c, Roig, laboratory glassware and botanical dictionary.

2002, May 10 ***Perf. 12½x12¾***
4221-4225 A1180 Set of 5
4225a Sheet, #4221-4225, + label

Medi Cuba Suiza — A1181

2002, June 18 ***Perf. 12¾x12½***
4226 A1181 75c multi

Mushrooms A1182

Designs: 5c, Amanita junquillea. 15c, Lepiota puellaris. 45c, Cortinarius cumatilis. 65c, Pholliota adiposa. 75c, Coprinus comatus.

2002, June 20 ***Perf. 12¾***
4227-4231 A1182 Set of 5
4231a Sheet, #4227-4231, + label

Nicolás Guillén (1902-89), Poet — A1183

2002, July 10 ***Perf. 12¾x12½***
4232 A1183 65c multi

Dockers, By Marcelo Pogolotti (1902-88) A1184

2002, July 12 ***Perf. 12¾***
4233 A1184 15c multi

Agostinho Neto (1922-79), Pres. of Angola — A1185

2002, Sept. 17 ***Perf. 12¾x12½***
4234 A1185 65c multi

España 2002 Youth Philatelic Exposition, Salamanca — A1186

Birds: 5c, Calidris minutilla. 10c, Tringa melanoleucas. 15c, Charadius semipalmatus. 65c, Plurialis squatarola. 75c, Arenaria interpres.
1p, Porzana carolina.

2002, Sept. 20 ***Perf. 12½x12¼***
4235-4239 A1186 Set of 5
4239a Sheet, #4235-4239, + label

Souvenir Sheet
Perf. 13

4240 A1186 1p multi

No. 4240 contains one 40x31mm stamp.

Third Intl. Meeting of War Correspondents — A1187

2002, Oct. 7 ***Perf. 12¾***
4241 A1187 65c multi

Ernesto "Che" Guevara (1928-67), Revolutionary Leader — A1188

Various depictions of Guevara: 5c, 10c, 15c, 50c, 65c, 75c.

2002, Oct. 8 **Litho.**
4242-4247 A1188 Set of 6
4247a Sheet, #4242-4247

America Issue - Youth, Education and Literacy — A1189

Designs: 15c, Emblem of Literacy Army, man with book, teacher with student. 65c, Building, flag, children at computer.

2002, Oct. 12 ***Perf. 12½x12¼***
4248-4249 A1189 Set of 2

Old Automobiles — A1190

Designs: No. 4250, 5c, 1956 Pontiac Catalina. No. 4251, 5c, 1957 Mercury Monterrey. 15c, 1959 Cadillac Fleetwood. 65c, Hudson Hornet. 75c, 1957 Chevrolet Bel Air. 85c, 1957 Mercedes-Benz 190SL.

2002, Oct. 19 ***Perf. 12¾***
4250-4255 A1190 Set of 6
a. Sheet, #4250-4255, + 6 labels

15th Intercontinental Baseball Cup — A1191

Baseball players: 5c, G. Mesa. 15c, A. Pacheco. 50c, O. Linares. 65c, O. Kindelan. 75c, L. Ulacia.

2002, Nov. 1
4256-4260 A1191 Set of 5

20th Havana Intl. Fair — A1192

2002, Nov. 3
4261 A1192 65c multi

Railroads, 165th Anniv. — A1193

Designs: 5c, Rocket. 15c, Miller. 50c, Vulcan. 65c, Consolidation. 75c, Mikado.

2002, Nov. 12 ***Perf. 12½x12¼***
4262-4266 A1193 Set of 5
a. Sheet, #4262-4266, + label

Camagüey Ballet, 35th Anniv. — A1194

Designs: 65c, Twelve dancers. 75c, Two dancers.

2002, Dec. 1 ***Perf. 12¾***
4267-4268 A1194 Set of 2

Pan-American Health Organization, Cent. — A1195

2002, Dec. 2
4269 A1195 65c multi

Paintings of Wilfredo Lam (1902-82) A1196

Designs: 15c, Emi Cosinca, 1950. 45c, Yo Soy, 1949. 65c, Retrado de H.H., 1941-42. 75c, Mujer Sentada, 1951.

2002, Dec. 8 ***Perf. 12¾***
4270-4273 A1196 Set of 4
a. Sheet, #4270-4273, + 4 labels

Dulce M. Loynaz (1902-97), Writer A1197

Perf. 12½x12¾

2002, Dec. 19 **Litho.**
4274 A1197 65c multi

Souvenir Sheet

Tursiops Truncatus — A1198

2002, Dec. 20 ***Perf. 12½***
4275 A1198 1p multi

Fifth National Philatelic Competition.

Prehistoric and Modern-Day Animals — A1199

Designs: 5c, Megaloceros, Cervus elaphus. 10c, Theropithecus, Papio anubis. 15c, Coelodonta, Diceros bicornis. 45c, Canis dirus, Canis lupus. 65c, Ursus spelaeus, Ursus arctos. 75c, Smilodon, Panthera leo.
1p, Mammuthus primigenius.
Illustration reduced.

2002, Dec. 27 ***Perf. 12½x12¼***
4276-4281 A1199 Set of 6

Souvenir Sheet
Perf. 13

4282 A1199 1p multi

No. 4282 contains one 40x32mm stamp.

New Year 2003 (Year of the Ram) A1200

Ram with background in: No. 4283, 15c, Green. No. 4284, 15c, Red.

2003, Jan. 6 ***Perf. 12½***
4283-4284 A1200 Set of 2

San Alejandro Academy for Arts, 185th Anniv. — A1201

Paintings by: 5c, Amelia Pelaez. 15c, René Portocarrero. 65c, Mario Carreña, horiz. 75c, Servando Cabrera.

2003, Jan. 12 ***Perf. 12¾***
4285-4288 A1201 Set of 4

José Martí (1853-95), Patriot — A1202

Designs: 15c, Birthplace. No. 4290, 65c, Martí and text. No. 4291, 65c, Martí, sky and text, horiz. 75c, Portrait.
1p, Martí, horiz.

2003, Jan. 28 ***Perf. 12¾***
4289-4292 A1202 Set of 4

Souvenir Sheet
Perf. 12½

4293 A1202 1p multi

No. 4293 contains one 40x32mm stamp.

Arrival of Europeans at Havana, 510th Anniv. — A1203

Various Cuban stamps and: No. 4294, 15c, Woman with Cigar boxes, map of Cuba (diamond-shaped). No. 4295, 15c, Men at table holding cigars and drinks (diamond-shaped). 50c, Tobacco farmer, field, hands rolling cigar. 65c, Building, Trinidad. 75c, Cigar, building, palm tree, people in room.
1p, Indian lighting cigar, vert.

2003, Feb. 6 ***Perf. 12½***
4294-4298 A1203 Set of 5

Souvenir Sheet

4299 A1203 1p multi

No. 4299 contains one 32x40mm stamp.

Radio Rebelde, 45th Anniv. A1204

2003, Feb. 13 ***Perf. 12¾***
4300 A1204 65c multi

Félix Varela (1788-1853), Priest — A1205

2003, Feb. 25 ***Perf. 12½***
4301 A1205 65c multi

Military Units, 45th Anniv. — A1206

Designs: No. 4302, 15c, 2nd Frank Pais Front. No. 4303, 15c, 3rd Mario Muñoz Front.

2003 ***Perf. 12¾***
4302-4303 A1206 Set of 2

Issued: No. 4302, 3/5; No. 4303, 3/11.

16th World Sexology Congress A1207

2003, Mar. 11
4304 A1207 65c multi

Transportation and Shipping — A1208

Designs: 5c, Container ship. 10c, Truck. 15c, Train. 65c, Airplane and delivery van. 75c, Airplane and delivery van, diff.

2003, Apr. 10 ***Perf. 12½***
4305-4309 A1208 Set of 5

Flora & Fauna — A1209

Designs: 5c, Nymphaea ampla, Lepisosteus tristoechus. 10c, Magnolia grandiflora, Spindalis zena pretrei. 15c, Lillium candidum, Polymita picta. 65c, Strelitzia regiae, Solenodon cubanus. 75c, Hibiscus rosasinensis, Mellysuga helenae.

2003, May 15
4310-4314 A1209 Set of 5

Pan American Games, Santo Domingo, Dominican Republic A1210

Designs: 5c, Kayaking. 15c, Judo. 50c, Track. 65c, Volleyball.

2003, June 27 ***Perf. 12½x12¾***
4315-4318 A1210 Set of 4

Attack on Moncada Barracks, 50th Anniv. — A1211

Designs; 15c, Men and barracks. 65c, Fidel Castro, text.

2003, July 26 ***Perf. 12¾***
4319-4320 A1211 Set of 2

Railroads A1212

Designs: 5c, Three-wheeled handcar, 1930-35. 10c, Crane, 1920. 15c, B-B 120/120 E locomotive, 1925. 65c, DVM-9 Ganz Mavag locomotive, 1969. 75c, 2-6-0 locomotive, 1905.

2003, Aug. 7
4321-4325 A1212 Set of 5

UN Conference to Combat Desertification — A1213

Illustration reduced.

2003, Aug. 25 ***Perf. 12½x12¼***
4326 A1213 65c multi

Expo Bangkok A1214

Wildlife: 5c, Nyctea scandiaca. 10c, Fratercula arctica. 15c, Sula bassana. 65c, Ursus maritimus. 75c, Alopex lagopus.
1p, Pagolphilus groenlandicus.

2003, Aug. 28 ***Perf. 12¾***
4327-4331 A1214 Set of 5

Souvenir Sheet
Perf. 12½

4332 A1214 1p multi

No. 4332 contains one 32x40mm stamp.

Butterflies and Flowers — A1215

Designs: 5c, Dione juno, Gardenia jasminoides. 15c, Apatura ilia, Chrysanthemus sinence. 65c, Inachis io, Hibiscus rosasinensis. 75c, Marpesia iole, Althaea rosea.
1p, Danaus plexippus, Zantedeschia aethiopica, vert.

2003, Sept. 11 **Litho.** ***Perf. 12½***
4333-4336 A1215 Set of 4

Souvenir Sheet

4337 A1215 1p multi

No. 4337 contains one 32x40mm stamp.

Ecotourism — A1216

Bird and location: 10c, Aratinga eops, Baracoa. 15c, Xiphiopicus percussus, Valle de los Ingenios. 65c, Tiaris canora, Sierra Maestra. 75c, Priotelus temnurus, Granma.

2003, Sept. 27 ***Perf. 12¾x12½***
4338-4341 A1216 Set of 4

Worldwide Fund for Nature (WWF) — A1217

Crocodylus rhombifer: No. 4342, 15c, Eggs and hatchling. No. 4343, 15c, Adult at water's edge. 65c, Capturing prey. 75c, With open mouth.

2003, Sept. 30 **Litho.** ***Perf. 12¾***
4342-4345 A1217 Set of 4

America Issue - Flora and Fauna — A1218

Designs: 15c, Xiphidiopicus percussus. 65c, Encyclia phoenicea.

2003, Oct. 12
4346-4347 A1218 Set of 2

35th Baseball World Cup — A1219

Cuban players: 5c, Antonio Muñoz. 10c, Lourdes Gourriel. No. 4350, 15c, Jorge L. Valdes. No. 4351, 15c, Lazaro Vargas. 65c, Lazaro Valle. 75c, Javier Mendez.
1p, Players celebrating, vert.

2003, Oct. 17 ***Perf. 12½x12¼***
4348-4353 A1219 Set of 6

Souvenir Sheet

Perf. 12½

4354 A1219 1p multi

No. 4354 contains one 32x40mm stamp.

Ballet — A1220

Designs: No. 4355, 65c, National Ballet of Cuba, 55th anniv. No. 4356, 65c, Alicia Alonso as Giselle, 60th anniv., vert.

Perf. 12¾x12½, 12½x12¾

2003, Oct. 28
4355-4356 A1220 Set of 2

Powered Flight, Cent. — A1221

Emblem and: 5c, Wright Brothers. 15c, Pitcairn PA-5. 65c, Stearman C-3MB. 75c, Douglas M-2.

2003, Dec. 17 ***Perf. 12½x12¼***
4357-4360 A1221 Set of 4

Cuban Revolution, 45th Anniv. A1222

2004, Jan. 1 ***Perf. 12¾***
4361 A1222 65c multi

Expocuba, 15th Anniv. — A1223

Illustration reduced.

2004, Jan. 4 ***Perf. 12½x12¼***
4362 A1223 65c multi

2004 Summer Olympics, Athens — A1224

Sports: 10c, Baseball. 65c, Boxing. 75c, Equestrian.
Illustration reduced.

2004, Jan. 6 **Litho.**
4363-4365 A1224 Set of 3

New Year 2004 (Year of the Monkey) A1225

Monkey with denomination in: No. 4366, 15c, Blue. No. 4367, 15c, Orange.

2004, Jan. 9 ***Perf. 12¾***
4366-4367 A1225 Set of 2

Julio A. Mella (1903-29), Communist Leader A1226

2004, Jan. 10
4368 A1226 65c multi

José Martí (1853-95) — A1227

Designs: No. 4369, 5c, Martí in 1862, Colegio San Pablo, Prado No. 88. No. 4370, 5c, Martí's father, Mariano, Tapineria No. 16, Valencia. No. 4371, 5c, Martí's mother, Leonor Pérez, birthplace, Paula No. 41. No. 4372, 10c, Martí's high school, 1862, Martí, Fermín Valdés Domínguez, 1869. No. 4373, 10c, Martí in 1869, Havana Royal Jail. No. 4374, 15c, Martí in 1870, El Abra farm, Isle of Pines. No. 4375, 15c, Martí in 1870, Martí Forge. No. 4376, 15c, Martí and son, José Francisco, 1879, Guanabacoa Lyceum. 65c, Martí and son, 1879, Mercaderes Law Offices. 75c, Martí in 1895, La Jatía farm, Oriente.

2004, Jan. 28 ***Perf. 12½x12¼***
4369-4378 A1227 Set of 10

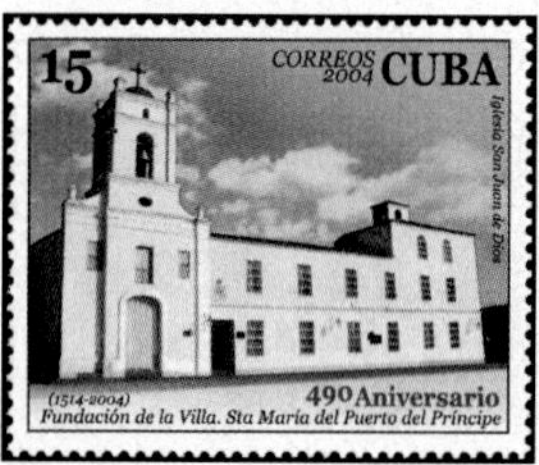

Town of Santa María de Puerto del Principe, 490th Anniv. — A1228

2004, Feb. 2 ***Perf. 12¾x12½***
4379 A1228 15c multi

Trolleys A1229

Designs: 5c, Santiago. 10c, Havana. 15c, Camagüey. 65c, Matanzas. 75c, Camagüey, diff.
1p, Havana, diff.

2004, Feb. 20 ***Perf. 12¾***
4380-4384 A1229 Set of 5

Souvenir Sheet

Perf. 12½

4385 A1229 1p multi

No. 4385 contains one 40x32mm stamp.

Souvenir Sheet

Cuba — Mexico Binational Philatelic Exhibition — A1230

2004, Feb. 25 ***Perf. 12½***
4386 A1230 1p multi

EGREM Recording Co., 40th Anniv. — A1231

Recording artists: 10c, Cascarita, Julio Cuevas. 15c, Carlos Puebla. 65c, Benny Maré. 75c, Compay Segundo.

2004, Mar. 24 ***Perf. 12¾***
4387-4390 A1231 Set of 4

España 2004 Intl. Philatelic Exhibition — A1232

Dogs: 5c, Spanish pointer. 10c, Spanish hound. 15c, Mallorquin bulldog. 65c, Catalan sheepdog. 75c, Pyrenean mastiff.
1p, Spanish mastiff.

2004, Mar. 24 ***Perf. 12½x12¼***
4391-4395 A1232 Set of 5

Souvenir Sheet

Perf. 12½

4396 A1232 1p multi

No. 4396 contains one 40x32mm stamp.

National Police, 45th Anniv. — A1233

Illustration reduced.

2004, Mar. 26 ***Perf. 12½x12¼***
4397 A1233 15c multi + label

Souvenir Sheet

Second Cuban Sports Olympiad — A1234

2004, Apr. 18 *Perf. 12½*
4398 A1234 1p multi

Nature and Man Foundation, 10th Anniv. — A1235

2004, May 16 Litho. *Perf. 12¼x12½*
4399 A1235 65c multi

FIFA (Fédération Internationale de Football Association), Cent. — A1236

FIFA emblem and various players: 10c, 15c, 65c, 75c.

2004, May 21 *Perf. 12¾*
4400-4403 A1236 Set of 4

Pets A1237

Designs: 5c, Parakeets. 10c, Fish. 15c, Dogs. 65c, Cats. 75c, Finches. 1p, Horse, horiz.

2004, June 25 *Perf. 12½x12¾*
4404-4408 A1237 Set of 5

Souvenir Sheet
Perf. 12½
4409 A1237 1p multi

No. 4409 contains one 40x32mm stamp.

Intl. Chess Federation, 80th Anniv. — A1238

Chess players: 15c, Maria Teresa Mora. 65c, José Raúl Capablanca, horiz. 75c, Ernesto "Che" Guevara.

2004, July 20 *Perf. 12¾*
4410-4412 A1238 Set of 3

Minerals — A1239

Designs: 5c, Corundum. 10c, Thenardite. 15c, Uraninite. 65c, Realgar. 75c, Fluorite. 1p, Copper.

2004, July 30 *Perf. 13*
4413-4417 A1239 Set of 5

Souvenir Sheet
Perf. 12½
4418 A1239 1p multi

No. 4418 contains one 40x32mm stamp.

Convention Hall, 25th Anniv. — A1240

2004, Sept. 3 *Perf. 12¾*
4419 A1240 65c multi

Cuban Aviation, 75th Anniv. — A1241

Designs: 15c, Lockheed Constellation. 65c, IL-62M. 75c, Airbus 330.

2004, Oct. 8 *Perf. 12½x12¼*
4420-4422 A1241 Set of 3

America Issue — A1242

Map of Cuba and: 15c, Bird over islands. 65c, Fish and marine life.

2004, Oct. 12
4423-4424 A1242 Set of 2

Marine Mammals — A1243

Designs: 5c, Delphinus delphis. 10c, Lagenorhynchus obliquidens. 15c, Stenella attenuata. 65c, Grampus griseus. 75c, Tursiops truncatus.
1p, Orcinus orca.

2004, Oct. 20 *Perf. 12½x12¼*
4425-4429 A1243 Set of 5

Souvenir Sheet
Perf. 13
4430 A1243 1p multi

No. 4430 contains one 40x32mm stamp.

Disappearance of Camilo Cienfuegos, 45th Anniv. A1244

2004, Oct. 28 *Perf. 12¾*
4431 A1244 65c multi

Railroad Stations, Cent. — A1245

Designs: 15c, Agramonte Station, 1906 ALCO No. 48 4-6-0. 65c, Aguacate Station, 1907 BLW No. 57 4-6-0. 75c, Guira de Melina Station, 1903 ALCO No. 7 4-4-0.

2004, Nov. 10 *Perf. 13*
4432-4434 A1245 Set of 3

SEMI-POSTAL STAMPS

Common Design Types pictured following the introduction.

Curie Issue
Common Design Type
Wmk. 106

1938, Nov. 23 Engr. *Perf. 10*

B1	CD80	2c + 1c salmon	3.25	1.00
B2	CD80	5c + 1c deep ultra	3.25	1.25

40th anniv. of the discovery of radium by Pierre and Marie Curie. Surtax for the benefit of the Intl. Union for the Control of Cancer.

Catalogue values for unused stamps in this section, from this point to the end of the section, are for Never Hinged items.

"Agriculture" Supporting "Industry" SP2

Engr., Center Typo.
1959, May 7 Wmk. 321 *Perf. 12½*
B3 SP2 2c + 1c car & ultra .50 .20

Agricultural reforms. See No. CB1. For surcharges see Nos. 624, C199.

Nurse — SP3

Wmk. 229
1959, Sept. 22 Photo. *Perf. 12½*
B4 SP3 2c + 1c crimson rose .35 .25

Exists imperf, value about double.

AIR POST STAMPS

Seaplane over Havana Harbor AP1

Wmk. 106
1927, Nov. 1 Engr. *Perf. 12*
C1 AP1 5c dark blue 3.00 .25

For overprint see No. C30.

Type of 1927 Issue Overprinted

1928, Feb. 8
C2 AP1 5c carmine rose 1.60 1.60

No. 283 Surcharged in Red

1930, Oct. 27 **Unwmk.**
C3 A44 10c on 25c violet 1.60 1.60

Airplane and Coast of Cuba — AP3

For Foreign Postage

1931, Feb. 26 Wmk. 106 *Perf. 10*

C4	AP3	5c green	.45	.20
C5	AP3	10c dk blue	.45	.20
C6	AP3	15c rose	.90	.30
C7	AP3	20c brown	.90	.20
C8	AP3	30c dk violet	1.25	.20
C9	AP3	40c dp orange	2.75	.35
C10	AP3	50c olive grn	3.25	.35
C11	AP3	1p black	5.25	.90
		Nos. C4-C11 (8)	15.20	2.70

See No. C40. For surcharges see Nos. C16-C17, C203, C225.

Airplane AP4

For Domestic Postage

1931-46

C12	AP4	5c rose vio ('32)	.35	.20
a.		5c brown violet ('36)	.35	.20
C13	AP4	10c gray blk	.35	.20
C14	AP4	20c car rose	2.50	.85
C14A	AP4	20c rose pink ('46)	1.10	.20
C15	AP4	50c dark blue	4.25	.90
		Nos. C12-C15 (5)	8.55	2.35

See #C130. For overprints see #C31, E29-E30.

Type of 1931 Surcharged in Black

1935, Apr. 24 ***Perf. 10***

C16 AP3 10c + 10c red	11.00	7.50
a. Double surcharge	110.00	

Imperf

C17 AP3 10c + 10c red	25.00	*25.00*

Matanzas Issue

Air View of Matanzas
AP5

10c, Airship "Macon." 20c, Airplane "The Four Winds." 50c, Air View of Fort San Severino.

Wmk. 229

1936, May 5 **Photo.** ***Perf. 12½***

C18 AP5 5c violet	.75	.25
C19 AP5 10c yellow orange	.90	.40
C20 AP5 20c green	3.25	1.75
C21 AP5 50c greenish slate	8.00	3.00
Nos. C18-C21 (4)	12.90	5.40
Set, never hinged	20.00	

Exist imperf. Value 20% more.

"Lightning"
AP9

Allegory of Flight
AP10

1936, Nov. 18

C22 AP9 5c violet	1.25	.25
C23 AP10 10c orange brown	2.00	.35
Set, never hinged	4.25	

Major Gen. Maximo Gomez, birth cent.

Flat Arch (Panama) — AP11

Carlos Antonio López (Paraguay) — AP12

Inca Gate, Cuzco (Peru) — AP13

Atlacatl (Salvador)
AP14

José Enrique Rodó (Uruguay)
AP15

Simón Bolívar (Venezuela)
AP16

Wmk. 106

1937, Oct. 13 **Engr.** ***Perf. 10***

C24 AP11 5c red	6.25	6.25
C25 AP12 5c red	6.25	6.25
C26 AP13 10c blue	6.25	6.25
C27 AP14 10c blue	6.25	6.25
C28 AP15 20c green	8.75	8.75
C29 AP16 20c green	8.75	8.75
Nos. C24-C29 (6)	42.50	42.50
Set, never hinged	45.00	

See note after No. 354.

Type of 1927 Overprinted in Black

1938, May **Wmk. 106**

C30 AP1 5c dark orange	2.75	1.50
Never hinged	3.50	

1st airplane flight from Key West to Havana, made by Domingo Rosillo, 1913.

Type of 1931-32 Overprinted

1939, Oct. 15

C31 AP4 10c emerald	21.00	6.00
Never hinged	27.50	

Issued in connection with an experimental postal rocket flight held at Havana.

Sir Rowland Hill, Map of Cuba and First Stamps of Britain, Spanish Cuba and Republic of Cuba — AP17

1940, Nov. 28 **Engr.** **Wmk. 106**

C32 AP17 10c brown	3.00	2.00
Never hinged	4.00	

Souvenir Sheet

Unwmk. ***Imperf.***

C33 Sheet of 4	11.00	11.00
Never hinged	16.00	
a. AP17 10c light brown	2.75	1.25
Never hinged	3.50	

Cent. of the 1st postage stamp.

Sheet sold for 60c.

No. C33 exists with each of the four stamps overprinted in black: "Exposicion de la ACNU/24 de Octubre de 1951/Dia de las Naciones" and "Historia de la Aviacion" in lower margin. Value, $60.

For overprints see Nos. C39, C211.

Poet José Heredia and Palms
AP18

Heredia and Niagara Falls — AP19

1940, Dec. 30 **Wmk. 106**

C34 AP18 5c emerald	1.40	1.00
C35 AP19 10c greenish slate	2.40	1.50

Death cent. of José Maria Heredia y Campuzano (1803-39), poet and patriot.

First Cuban Land Sighted by Columbus
AP20

Columbus Lighthouse
AP21

1944, May 19

C36 AP20 5c olive green	.60	.30
C37 AP21 10c slate black	1.25	.50

450th anniv. of the discovery of America.

Catalogue values for unused stamps in this section, from this point to the end of the section, are for Never Hinged items.

Conference of La Mejorana (Meceo, Gomez and Marti)
AP22

1948, May 21 **Wmk. 229** ***Perf. 12½***

C38 AP22 8c org yel & blk	2.00	.75

50th anniv. of the start of the War of 1895.

Souvenir Sheet

No. C33 Overprinted in Ultramarine

1948, May 21 **Unwmk.** ***Imperf.***

C39 AP17 Sheet of 4	15.00	10.00

The overprint is applied in the center of the four 10c stamps, so that a portion falls on each.

American Air Mail Soc. Convention, Havana, May 21 to 23, 1948. The sheets sold for 60c each.

Type of 1931

1948, June 15 **Wmk. 106** ***Perf. 10***

C40 AP3 8c orange brown	1.40	.30

Narciso Lopez Landing at Cárdenas
AP23

Flag on Cuban Fort — AP24

Flag on Morro Castle, Havana — AP25

Engraved and Lithographed

1951, July 3 **Wmk. 229** ***Perf. 13***

C41 AP23 5c ol grn, ultra & red	1.60	.30
C42 AP24 8c red brn, bl & red	2.50	.30
C43 AP25 25c gray blk, bl & red	3.50	1.90
Nos. C41-C43 (3)	7.60	2.50

Centenary of adoption of Cuba's flag.

Souvenir Sheet

No. 365a Overprinted in Green

Illustration reduced.

1951, Aug. 24 **Unwmk.** ***Imperf.***

C43A Sheet of 4	10.00	8.50

50th anniv. of the discovery of the cause of yellow fever by Dr. Carlos J. Finlay, and to honor the martyrs of science.

Postage Type and

Resignation Play of Dr. Lasker
AP26

Capablanca Making "The Exact Play" — AP27

Wmk. 229

1951, Nov. 1 **Photo.** ***Perf. 13***

C44 AP26 5c shown	3.25	.75
C45 AP27 8c shown	5.75	1.10
C46 A165 25c Capablanca	10.50	3.00
Nos. C44-C46 (3)	19.50	4.85

30th anniv. of the winning of the World Chess title by José Raul Capablanca.

Morrillo Types of Regular Issue

Wmk. 106

1951, Nov. 22 **Engr.** ***Perf. 10***

C47 A167 5c violet	1.60	.50
C48 A168 8c deep green	2.25	.75
C49 A169 25c dark brown	4.25	1.50
a. Souv. sheet of 6, black brown, perf. 13	50.00	50.00
b. Souv. sheet of 6, green, imperf.	200.00	200.00
Nos. C47-C49 (3)	8.10	2.75

Nos. C49a and C49b contain one each of the 1c, 2c and 5c of types A167-A169 and of the 5c, 8c and 25c airmail stamps of types A167-A169. Sheets are unwatermarked and measure 124x133mm.

Isabella Type of Regular Issue, 1952

1952, Feb. 22

C50	A172	25c purple	2.50	1.00
a.		Souv. sheet of 2, perf. 11	17.50	17.50
b.		Souv. sheet of 2, imperf.	20.00	20.00

Nos. C50a and C50b contain one each of a 2c of type A172 and a 25c air-mail stamp of type A172. In No. C50a, the 2c and marginal inscriptions are brown carmine; the 25c, dark blue. In No. C50b, the 2c and marginal inscriptions are dark blue; the 25c, brown carmine. Sheets measure 108x18mm.

Type of Regular Issue of 1951 Surcharged in Various Colors

1952, Mar. 18

Color: Yellow Brown

C51	A159	5c on 2c	.85	.25
C52	A159	8c on 2c (C)	1.75	.25
C53	A159	10c on 2c (Bl)	1.75	.25
C54	A159	25c on 2c (V)	2.75	1.25
C55	A159	50c on 2c (C)	8.50	2.50
C56	A159	1p on 2c (Bl)	19.00	10.00
		Nos. C51-C56 (6)	34.60	14.50

Country School AP32

Entrance, University of Havana — AP33

10c, Presidential Mansion. 25c, Banknote.

Wmk. 106

1952, May 27 Engr. *Perf. 12½*

Centers Various Shades of Green

C57	AP32	5c dark purple	.35	.20
C58	AP33	8c dark red	.55	.20
C59	AP32	10c deep blue	1.10	.20
C60	AP32	25c dark violet brn	1.90	1.00
		Nos. C57-C60 (4)	3.90	1.60

Foundation of the Republic of Cuba, 50th anniv.

Plane and Map — AP34

Agustín Parlá — AP35

1952, July 22 Engr. *Perf. 10*

C61	AP34	8c black	1.50	.55
a.		Souv. sheet, 8c deep blue	15.00	15.00
b.		Souv. sheet, 8c deep green	15.00	15.00
C62	AP35	25c ultra	4.00	1.60
a.		Souv. sheet, 25c deep blue	15.00	15.00
b.		Souv. sheet, 25c deep green	15.00	15.00

30th anniv. of the Key West-Mariel flight of Agustin Parla.

The four souvenir sheets are perf. 11.

Col. Charles Hernandes y Sandrino — AP36

1952, Oct. 7

C63	AP36	5c orange	.70	.20
C64	AP36	8c brt yel grn	.70	.20
C65	AP36	10c dk brown	.90	.20
C66	AP36	15c dk Prus grn	1.75	.50
C67	AP36	20c aqua	2.25	.65
C68	AP36	25c crimson	1.75	.65
C69	AP36	30c dk vio bl	4.50	1.60
C70	AP36	45c rose lilac	4.50	2.25
C71	AP36	50c indigo	2.75	1.60
C72	AP36	1p bister	9.00	3.25
		Nos. C63-C72 (10)	28.80	11.10

Three-fourths of the proceeds from the sale were used for the Communications Ministry Employees' Retirement Fund.

Entrance, University of Havana — AP37

F. V. Dominguez, M. Estebanez and F. Capdevila — AP38

Engr.; Center Typo.

1952, Nov. 27

C73	AP37	5c indigo & dk blue	1.25	.35
C74	AP38	25c org & dk grn	3.50	1.25

Execution of 8 medical students, 81st anniv.

AP39

Lockheed Constellation Airliners — AP40

1953, May 22 Engr.

C75	AP39	8c orange brn	1.00	.20
C76	AP39	15c scarlet	2.10	.70

Typographed and Engraved

C77	AP40	2p dp green & dk brn	25.00	10.00
C78	AP40	5p blue & dk brn	47.50	17.50
		Nos. C75-C78 (4)	75.60	28.40

See #C120-C121. For surcharge see #C224.

Page of Manifesto of Montecristi — AP42

House of Maximo Gomez AP43

#C79, Marti in Kingston, Jamaica, #C80, With Workers in Tampa, Florida. #C83, Marti addressing liberating army. #C84, Portrait. #C85, Dos Rios obelisk. #C86, Marti's first tomb. #C87, Present tomb. #C88, Monument in Havana. #C89, Martian forge.

1953 Engr. *Perf. 10*

C79	AP42	5c dk car & blk	.35	.20
C80	AP42	5c dk car & blk	.35	.20
C81	AP43	8c dk green & blk	.80	.20
C82	AP42	8c dk green & blk	.80	.20
C83	AP43	10c dk blue & dk car	1.75	.50
C84	AP42	10c dk blue & dk car	1.75	.50
C85	AP42	15c violet & gray	1.25	.90
C86	AP42	15c violet & gray	1.25	.90
C87	AP42	25c brown & car	3.25	1.25
C88	AP42	25c brown & car	3.25	1.25
C89	AP43	50c yellow & bl	5.50	2.50
		Nos. C79-C89 (11)	20.30	8.60

Cent. of the birth of José Marti.

Board of Accounts Building — AP44

25c, Plane above Board of Accounts Bldg.

1953, Nov. 3

C90	AP44	8c rose carmine	1.75	.50
C91	AP44	25c dk gray grn	3.50	.90

1st Intl. Cong. of Boards of Account, Havana, Nov. 2-9, 1953.

Miguel Coyula Llaguno AP45

Antonio Ginard Rojas AP46

Designs: 10c, Gregorio Hernandez Saez. 1p, Communications Association Flag.

1954

C92	AP45	5c dark blue	.50	.25
C93	AP46	8c red violet	.65	.25
C94	AP46	10c orange	1.40	.35
C95	AP45	1p black	9.50	9.50
		Nos. C92-C95 (4)	12.05	10.35

See note after No. C72.

Alvaro Reinoso — AP47

Plane and Harvesters Cutting Cane AP48

Designs in Lower Triangle: 5c, Four-engine Plane and Cane Field. 10c, Tractor pulling loaded wagons. 15c, Train of sugar cane. 20c, Modern mill. 25c, Evaporators. 30, Sacks of sugar. 40c, Loading sugar on ship. 45c, Ox cart. 50c, Primitive sugar mill.

1954, Apr. 27 Engr.

C96	AP47	5c yellow green	.40	.20
C97	AP48	8c brown	1.10	.30
C98	AP48	10c dark green	1.10	.30
C99	AP48	15c henna brn	2.50	.40
C100	AP48	20c blue	1.10	.20
C101	AP48	25c scarlet	.80	.20
C102	AP48	30c lilac rose	2.25	.95
C103	AP48	40c deep blue	4.25	1.25
C104	AP48	45c violet	3.50	2.50
C105	AP48	50c brt blue	3.50	1.60
C106	AP47	1p dk gray blue	9.50	3.25
		Nos. C96-C106 (11)	30.00	11.15

For surcharges see Nos. C204.

Sanatorium Type of Regular Issue

1954, Sept. 21 Wmk. 106 *Perf. 10*

C107	A186	9c deep green	2.00	.50

Dolz Type of Regular Issue, 1954

1954, Dec. 23

C108	A188	12c carmine	2.00	.60

Rotary Type of Regular Issue, 1955

1955, Feb. 23

C109	A190	12c carmine	2.00	.50

Stamps of 1855 and 1905, Palace of Fine Arts AP52

Designs (including 2 stamps): 12c, Plaza de la Fraternidad. 24c, View of Havana. 30c, Plaza de la Republica.

1955, Apr. 24 *Perf. 12½*

C110	AP52	8c dk grnsh bl & grn	1.00	.35
C111	AP52	12c dk ol grn & red	1.10	.35
C112	AP52	24c dk red & ultra	2.00	.90
C113	AP52	30c dp org & brn	4.25	1.50
		Nos. C110-C113 (4)	8.35	3.10

Cent. of Cuba's 1st postage stamps.

Mariel Bay — AP53

Views: 12c, Varadero beach. 1p, Vinales valley.

1955, June 22 Wmk. 106

C114	AP53	8c dk car & dk grn	.95	.25
C115	AP53	12c dk ocher & brt bl	1.25	.35
C116	AP53	1p dk grn & ocher	7.50	2.50
		Nos. C114-C116 (3)	9.70	3.10

See note after No. C72.

Map of Crocier's 1914 Flight — AP54

Design: 30c, Crocier in plane.

1955, July 4 *Perf. 10*

C117	AP54	12c red & dk grn	1.00	.25
C118	AP54	30c dk grn & mag	3.00	.60

35th anniv. of the death of Jaime Gonzalez Crocier, aviation pioneer.

Cuban Museum, Tampa, Fla. — AP55

1955, July 1 Engr. *Perf. 12½*

C119	AP55	12c red & dk brn	2.00	.50

Cent. of Tampa's incorporation as a town.

Lockheed Type of 1953

Typographed and Engraved

1955, Sept. 21 Wmk. 106

C120	AP40	2p bl & ol grn	20.00	6.00
C121	AP40	5p dp rose & ol grn	42.50	15.00

Wright Brothers' Plane and Stamps AP56

Designs: 12c, Spirit of St. Louis. 24c, Graf Zeppelin. 30c, Constellation passenger plane. 50c, Convair jet fighter.

Engraved and Photogravure
1955, Nov. 12 Wmk. 106 *Perf. 12½*
Inscription and Plane in Black

C122	AP56	8c car & bl	1.00	.35
C123	AP56	12c yel grn & car	2.25	.70
C124	AP56	24c vio & car	6.75	2.50
C125	AP56	30c bl & red org	5.75	3.25
C126	AP56	50c ol grn & red org	7.75	4.00
a.		Souvenir sheet of 5	27.50	27.50
		Nos. C122-C126 (5)	23.50	10.80

International Centenary Philatelic Exhibition in Havana, Nov. 12-19, 1955.

No. C126a is printed on thick paper and measures 140x178mm. It contains one each of Nos. C122-C126 with the background of each stamp printed in a different color from the perforated stamps.

"Three Friends" and Gen. Emilio Nuñez AP57

Design: 12c, Landing on the Cuban Coast.

1955, Dec. 27 Engr. Unwmk.

C127	AP57	8c ultra & dk car	1.50	.40
C128	AP57	12c grn & dk red brn	2.40	.50

Gen. Emilio Nuñez, Cuban revolutionary hero, birth cent.

Post Type of Regular Issue, 1956

Bishop P. A. Morell de Santa Cruz (1694-1768).

1956, Mar. 27 Wmk. 106

C129	A197	12c dk brn & grn	1.75	.40

Plane Type of 1931-46

1956 Engr. *Perf. 10*

C130	AP4	50c greenish blue	3.00	1.00

Portrait Type of Regular Issue, 1956

1956, May 2 *Perf. 12½*

Portraits: 8c, Gen. Julio Sanguily. 12c, Gen. José Maria Aguirre. 30c, Col. Ernesto Ponts Sterling.

Portraits in Black

C131	A198	8c brown	.90	.20
C132	A198	12c dull yellow	1.50	.25
C133	A198	30c indigo	2.75	1.50
		Nos. C131-C133 (3)	5.15	1.95

See note after No. C72.

Mother and Child — AP60

Masonic Temple Havana — AP61

1956, May 13 Wmk. 106 *Perf. 12½*

C134	AP60	12c ultra & red	2.00	.25

Issued in honor of Mother's Day 1956.

1956, June 5

C135	AP61	12c olive green	2.00	.40

Pigeon AP62

Gundlach Hawk — AP63

Birds: 8c, Wood duck. 19c, Herring gulls. 24c, White pelicans. 29c, Common merganser. 30c, Quail. 50c, Herons (great white, great blue and Wurdemann's). 1p, Northern caracara. 2p, Middle American jacana. 5p, Ivory-billed woodpecker.

1956

C136	AP62	8c blue	.50	.20
C137	AP62	12c gray blue	7.50	.20
C138	AP63	14c green	1.75	.25
C139	AP63	19c redsh brn	1.10	.55
C140	AP63	24c lilac rose	1.25	.55
C141	AP62	29c green	1.90	.55
C142	AP62	30c dk olive bis	2.25	.80
C143	AP63	50c slate blk	4.25	1.10
C144	AP63	1p dk car rose	6.50	2.25
C145	AP62	2p rose violet	13.00	4.25
C146	AP63	5p brt red	35.00	8.75
		Nos. C136-C146 (11)	75.00	19.45

See Nos. C205, C235-C237. For surcharges and overprints see #C147, C151, C197, C209-C210

Type of 1956 Surcharged

Design: 24c, White pelicans.

1956, July 13

C147	AP63	8c on 24c deep org	1.00	.40

Opening of the new building of the Cuba Philatelic Club, Havana, July 14, 1956.

Hubert de Blanck — AP64

Church of Our Lady of Charity — AP65

1956, July 6

C148	AP64	12c ultra	1.25	.30

Hubert de Blanck (1856-1932), composer.

1956, Sept. 8

C149	AP65	12c green & carmine	2.00	.40
a.		Souvenir sheet of 2, imperf.	8.00	7.00

Issued in honor of Our Lady of Charity of Cobre, patroness of Cuba.

No. C149a contains one each of Nos. 559 and C149. No. C149a exists with yellow of No. 559 omitted.

Benjamin Franklin AP66

1956, Oct. 5 Engr. *Perf. 12½*

C150	AP66	12c red brown	2.00	.40

Type of 1956 Surcharged in Blue

Design: 2p, Middle American jacana.

1956, Oct. 26 Wmk. 106

C151	AP62	12c on 2p dark gray	2.00	.75

Issued in honor of the 12th Inter-American Press Association Conference, Havana.

Lord Baden-Powell AP67

1957, Feb. 22

C152	AP67	12c slate	2.40	.50

Centenary of the birth of Lord Baden-Powell, founder of the Boy Scouts.

Hanabanilla Waterfall AP68

12c, Sierra de Cubitas. 30c, Puerto Boniato.

1957, Mar. 29

C153	AP68	8c blue & red	.75	.20
C154	AP68	12c green & red	3.00	.30
C155	AP68	30c ol grn & dk pur	3.25	.50
		Nos. C153-C155 (3)	7.00	1.00

See note after No. 457.

Philatelic Club, Havana AP69

Fingerprint AP70

1957, Apr. 24 Wmk. 106 *Perf. 12½*

C156	AP69	12c yel, grn & brn	1.75	.30

Stamp Day, and the Natl. Phil. Exhib.

1957, Apr. 30

C157	AP70	12c claret brown	1.75	.30

Birth cent. (in 1856) of Juan Francisco Steegers y Perera, dactyloscopy pioneer.

Baseball Player — AP71

1957, May 17 Wmk. 106 *Perf. 12½*

C158	AP71	8c shown	1.00	.35
C159	AP71	12c Ballerina	1.75	.40
C160	AP71	24c Girl diver	2.50	1.00
C161	AP71	30c Boxers	3.50	1.50
		Nos. C158-C161 (4)	8.75	3.25

Issued to honor young Cuban athletes.

Joaquin de Aguero AP72

Jeanette Ryder AP73

1957, July 4

C162	AP72	12c indigo	.90	.25

Issued to honor Joaquin de Aguero, Cuban freedom fighter and patriot.

1957, July 17

C163	AP73	12c dk red brn	4.00	.40
a.		Pair, #574, C163	7.00	7.00

Mrs. Jeanette Ryder, founder of the Humane Society of Cuba.

José M. de Heredia y Girard — AP74

John Robert Gregg — AP75

1957, Aug. 16 Engr. Wmk. 106

C164	AP74	8c dk blue vio	1.00	.25

José Maria de Heredia y Girard (1842-1905), Cuban born French poet.

Justice Type of Regular Issue, 1957

1957, Sept. 2 *Perf. 12½*

C165	A214	12c green	2.00	.50

1957, Oct. 1

C166	AP75	12c dark green	2.00	.50

90th anniv. of the birth of John Robert Gregg, inventor of the Gregg shorthand system.

D. Figarola Caneda — AP76

José Marti National Library AP77

1957, Oct. 18 Wmk. 106 *Perf. 12½*

C167	AP76	8c ultra	.60	.25
C168	AP77	12c chocolate	1.90	.35

José Marti National Library.

Map of Cuba and UN Emblem AP78

1957, Oct. 24

C169	AP78	8c dk green & brn	1.00	.25
C170	AP78	12c car rose & grn	1.50	.40
C171	AP78	30c ind & brt pink	3.50	1.00
		Nos. C169-C171 (3)	6.00	1.65

Issued for United Nations Day, 1957.

Map of Cuba and Florida AP79

1957, Oct. 28
C172 AP79 12c dk red brn & bl 1.75 .50

30th anniv. of airmail service from Key West to Havana.

Type of Regular Issue, 1957 and

Stairway and Bell Tower AP80

Design: 12c, Facade of Normal School.

1957, Nov. 19 Engr. ***Perf. 12½***
C173 A217 12c indigo & ocher 1.40 .30
C174 AP80 30c dk car & gray 2.50 .60

View Types of Regular Issue, 1957

Views: 8c, El Viso Fort, El Caney. 12c, Sancti Spiritus Church. 30c, Concordia Bridge, Matanzas.

1957, Dec. 17 ***Perf. 12½***
C175 A218 8c dk gray & red .75 .30
C176 A219 12c brown & gray 1.40 .30
C177 A218 30c red brn & bl gray 2.75 .75
Nos. C175-C177 (3) 4.90 1.35

See note after No. C72.

Hedges Types of Regular Issue, 1958

8c, Dayton Hedges & Matanzas rayon factory.

1958, Jan. 30 Wmk. 106 ***Perf. 12½***
C178 A221 8c green 2.00 .50

Diario de la Marina Building — AP81

1958, Apr. 1
C179 AP81 29c black 3.50 2.00

Jose Ignacio Rivero y Alonso, editor of the newspaper, Diario de la Marina.

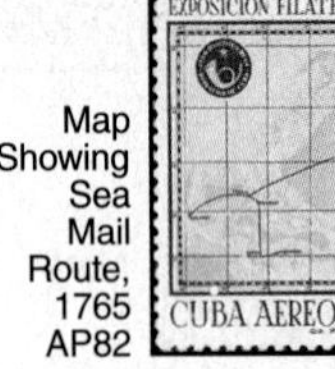

Map Showing Sea Mail Route, 1765 AP82

1958, Apr. 24 Wmk. 106 ***Perf. 12½***
C180 AP82 29c dk bl aqua & buff 3.50 1.25

Issued for Stamp Day, Apr. 24, and the National Philatelic Exhibition.

Gen. Gomez in Battle — AP83

Snail (Polymita Picta) — AP84

1958, June 6 **Engr.**
C181 AP83 12c slate green 1.40 .35

Issued in honor of Maj. Gen. José Miguel Gomez, President of Cuba, 1909-13.

1958, Aug. 29 Wmk. 321 ***Perf. 12½***

12c, Megalocnus Rodens. 30c, Ammonite.

C182 AP84 8c gray, red & yel 3.00 .90
C183 AP84 12c brn, *yel grn* 4.75 1.50
C184 AP84 30c grn, *pink* 6.25 2.00
Nos. C182-C184 (3) 14.00 4.40

Centenary of the birth of Dr. Carlos de la Torre, naturalist.

Papilio Caiguanabus AP85

Cuban Sea Bass — AP86

12c, Teria gundlachia. 14c, Teria ebriola. 19c, Nathalis felicia. 29c, Butter Hamlet. 30c, Tattler.

1958, Sept. 26 Wmk. 106 ***Perf. 12½***
C185 AP85 8c multicolored 2.25 .50
C186 AP85 12c emer, blk & org 2.75 .50
C187 AP85 14c multicolored 4.00 .75
C188 AP85 19c bl, blk & yel 5.00 1.00
C189 AP86 24c multicolored 5.75 1.00
C190 AP86 29c blk, brn & ultra 8.25 1.25
C191 AP86 30c blk, yel grn & sep 12.00 1.75
Nos. C185-C191 (7) 40.00 6.75

Felipe Poey (1799-1891), naturalist.

Battle of San Juan Hill, 1898 — AP87

Wmk. 106
1958, Oct. 27 Engr. ***Perf. 12½***
C192 AP87 12c black brown 1.50 .30

Birth centenary of Theodore Roosevelt.

UNESCO Building, Paris — AP88

Design: 30c, "UNESCO" and map of Cuba.

1958, Nov. 7
C193 AP88 12c dk slate grn 1.50 .40
C194 AP88 30c dp ultra 3.00 1.25

UNESCO Headquarters in Paris opening, Nov. 3.

Postal Notice of 1765 — AP89

Musical Arts Building — AP90

Design: 30c, Administrative postal book of St. Cristobal, Havana, 1765.

1959, Apr. 24 Wmk. 321 ***Perf. 12½***
C195 AP89 12c Prus blue & sep 1.50 .25
C196 AP89 30c sepia & Prus bl 2.50 1.00

Issued for Stamp Day, Apr. 24, and the National Philatelic Exhibition.

Type of 1956 Surcharged with New Value, Bar and "ASTA" Emblem in Dark Blue

1959, Oct. 17 Wmk. 321 ***Perf. 12½***
C197 AP63 12c on 1p emerald 2.00 1.00

Issued to publicize the meeting of the American Soc. of Travel Agents, Oct. 17-23.

Wmk. 106
1959, Nov. 11 Engr. ***Perf. 12½***
C198 AP90 12c yellow green 1.50 .45

40th anniversary of the Musical Arts Society.

No. CB1 Surcharged in Red: "HABILITADO PARA / 12c"

Engr. & Typo.
1960 Wmk. 321 ***Perf. 12½***
C199 SPAP1 12c on 12 + 3c car & grn 1.50 .75

Type of Regular Issue, 1960

8c, Battle of Santa Clara. 12c, Rebel forces entering Havana. 29c, Bank-note changing hands ("Clandestine activities in the cities").

Wmk. 320
1960, Jan. 28 Engr. ***Perf. 12½***
C200 A236 8c bl, gray ol & sal .75 .25
C201 A236 12c gray ol & ocher 1.10 .25
C202 A236 29c gray & car 2.00 1.50
Nos. C200-C202 (3) 3.85 2.00

Nos. C9 and C104 Surcharged "12c" in Red

1960, Feb. 3 **Wmk. 106**
C203 AP3 12c on 40c dp org .75 .30
C204 AP48 12c on 45c vio .75 .30

Pigeon Type of 1956

1960, Feb. 12 **Wmk. 321**
C205 AP62 12c brt blue grn .50 .20

Statue Type of Regular Issue, 1960.

Statues: 8c, José Marti, Matanzas. 12c, Heroes of the Cacarajicara, Pinar del Rio. 30c, Cosme de la Torriente, Isle of Pines, horiz.

1960, Mar. 28 ***Perf. 12½***
C206 A237 8c gray & car .60 .25
C207 A237 12c blue & car .90 .25
C208 A237 30c violet & brn 2.00 1.00
Nos. C206-C208 (3) 3.50 1.50

See note after No. 386.

Type of 1956 and No. C33 Overprinted in Dark Blue

1960, Apr. 24 Wmk. 321 ***Perf. 12½***
C209 AP62 8c orange yel .30 .20
C210 AP62 12c cerise .50 .20

Souvenir Sheet

C211 AP17 Sheet of 4 20.00 20.00

Stamp Day, 4/24/60, and Natl. Phil. Exhib.
No. C211 has added marginal inscription in dark blue for cent. of the ¼r on 2r (No. 15).

Type of Olympic Games Issue, 1960

Wmk. 321
1960, Sept. 22 Engr. ***Perf. 12½***
C212 A238 8c Boxer .35 .20
C213 A238 12c Runner .50 .40
a. Souvenir sheet of 4 3.00

17th Olympic Games, Rome, Aug. 25-Sept. 11. No. C213a contains one each imperf. of types of Nos. 645-646 and Nos. C212-C213 in dark blue.

No. C3 and Flight Symbols of 1930, 1960 — AP91

1960, Oct. 30 Litho. **Unwmk.**
C214 AP91 8c multicolored 2.00 1.50

30th anniv. of national air mail service.

Sword of Sheaf of Wheat — AP92

12c, Two workers, horiz. 30c, Three maps, horiz. 50c, Hand inscribed "Peace" in 5 languages.

1961, Jan. 10 Photo. ***Perf. 11½***
Granite Paper
C215 AP92 8c multicolored .30 .20
C216 AP92 12c multicolored .45 .20
C217 AP92 30c black & red 1.25 .50
C218 AP92 50c blk, bl & red 1.50 1.00
Nos. C215-C218 (4) 3.50 1.90

Conf. of Underdeveloped Countries, Havana.

José Marti and "Declaration of Havana" — AP93

Background in Spanish, English or French.

1961, Jan. 28 Litho. ***Perf. 12½***
C219 AP93 8c pale grn, blk & red 1.00 .60
C220 AP93 12c org yel, blk & pale vio 1.50 1.00
C221 AP93 30c pale bl, blk & pale brn 2.50 1.50
a. Souvenir sheet of 3 11.00 11.00
Nos. C219-C221 (3) 5.00 3.10

Declaration of Havana, Sept. 1, 1960.
Sheets of 25 are imprinted in margin "E" for Spanish, "I" for English or "F" for French.
No. C221a contains one each of Nos. C219-C221, imperf. The 8c has background in Spanish, the 12c in English and the 30e in French.

UN Type of 1961

1961, Apr. 12 Unwmk. ***Perf. 12½***
C222 A244 8c dp car & yel .30 .20
C223 A244 12c brt ultra & org .60 .30
a. Souv. sheet of 2, #C222-C223, imperf. 2.00

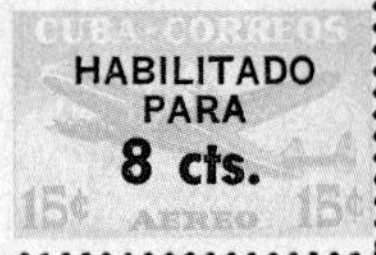

Nos. C76 and C7 Surcharged

Wmk. 106
1961, Oct. 1 Engr. ***Perf. 10***
C224 AP39 8c on 15c No. C76
C225 AP3 8c on 20c No. C7

Revolution Anniv. Type of 1962

Perf. 12½
1962, Jan. 3 Litho. **Unwmk.**
C226 A250 8c multi
C227 A250 12c multi
C228 A250 30c multi

1st Sugarcane Harvest in Socialist Cuba, 1st Anniv. — AP94

1962, Jan. 16
C229 AP94 8c salmon pink & dark brn
C230 AP94 12c bluish lil & blk

Importation Prohibited
Cuban stamps issued after No. C230 have not been valued because the embargo on trade with Cuba, proclaimed Feb. 7, 1962, by President Kennedy, prohibits the importation from any country of stamps of Cuban origin, used or unused.

Intl. Radio Service AP95

1962, Mar. 26 **Wmk. 321**
C231 AP95 8c multi
C232 AP95 12c multi
C233 AP95 30c multi
C234 AP95 1p multi

Bird Type of 1956

1962, July 20 **Engr.** **Wmk. 321**
C235 AP63 1p like #C144, royal blue
C236 AP62 2p like #C145, dark red
C237 AP63 5p like #C146, rose lake

PRAGA '62 — AP96

1962, Aug. 18 **Litho.**
C238 AP96 31c Czechoslovakia No. 1080

Souvenir Sheet
Imperf

C239 AP96 31c like No. C238

No. C239 contains one 60x35½mm stamp.

Achievements of the Revolution — AP97

1966, July 26 **Wmk. 376** ***Perf. 12½***
C240 AP97 1c Agrarian reform
C241 AP97 2c Industrialization
C242 AP97 3c Urban reform
C243 AP97 7c Eradication of unemployment
C244 AP97 9c Education
C245 AP97 10c Public health
C246 AP97 13c Excerpt from *La Historia Me Absolvera,* by Castro

Camaguey-Seville Flight, 35th Anniv. — AP98

1971, Jan. 12 **Unwmk.**
C247 AP98 13c Aircraft
C248 AP98 30c Map, Lieut. Menendez Palaez

Havana-Santiago de Chile Direct Air Service, 1st Anniv. — AP99

1972, June 26 **Wmk. 376**
C249 AP99 25c multi

6th Congress of Latin American and Caribbean Exporters of Sugar, Havana — AP100

Perf. 12½x12

1977, Feb. 28 **Unwmk.**
C250 AP100 13c multi

Composer Type of 1977

1977, May 10 ***Perf. 13***
C251 A571 13c Jorge Ankerman and score

Flower Type of 1977

1977, May 31
C252 A572 13c *Caesalpinia pulcherrima*
C253 A572 30c *Catharanthus roseus*

Souvenir Sheet
Perf. 13½x13

C254 A572 50c Juan Tomas Roig

No. C254 contains one 32x40mm stamp.

Natl. Decorations Type of 1977

1977, July 26 ***Perf. 12x12½***
C255 A574 13c multi, diff.
C256 A574 30c multi, diff.

Art Type of 1977

Paintings by Jorge Arche: 13c, *My Wife and I,* vert. 30c, *Domino Players.* 50c, *Self-portrait,* vert.

1977, Aug. 25 ***Perf. 13x12½***
Size: 26x38mm
C257 A575 13c multi
Size: 40x29mm
Perf. 13
C258 A575 30c multi

Souvenir Sheet
Perf. 13½x13

C259 A575 50c multi

No. C259 contains one 32x40mm stamp.

Spartakiad Type of 1977

1977, Sept. 10 ***Perf. 13***
C260 A576 13c Grenade-throwing
C261 A576 30c Rifle-shooting, horiz.

10th Heroic Guerrilla's Day AP101

1977, Oct. 8 ***Perf. 12½x13***
C262 AP101 13c Guerrilla fighters

Airmail Service Type of 1977

1977, Oct. 27 ***Perf. 12x12½***
C263 A577 13c Havana-Mexico cachet
C264 A577 30c Havana-Prague cachet

Souvenir Sheet

Adoration of the Magi, by Rubens — AP102

1977, Nov. 18 ***Perf. 13***
C265 AP102 50c multi

Ruben's 400th birth anniv.

Havana Zoo Type of 1977

1977, Nov. 24
C266 A579 13c Tiger
C267 A579 30c Lion

Revolution Martyrs Type of 1977

1977, Dec. 2 ***Perf. 12½x12***
C268 A580 13c *Corynthia* landing

Pan American Health Organization (OPS), 75th Anniv. — AP103

1977, Dec. 2
C269 AP103 13c multi

Havana University Type of 1978

1978, Jan. 5 ***Perf. 13x12½***
C270 A582 13c Crossed sabres, university
C271 A582 30c University, statue, crowd

Portrait of Jose Marti (b. 1853), by A. Menocal AP104

1978, Jan. 28
C272 AP104 13c multi

Art Type of 1978

Paintings in the Nat. Museum of Art: 13c, *El Guadalquivir,* by M. Barron. 30c, *Portrait of H.E. Ridley,* by J.J. Masqueries, vert.

1978, Feb. 20 ***Perf. 12½x12, 13***
Sizes: 42x27mm, 29x40mm
C273 A583 13c multi
C274 A583 30c multi

Bird Type of 1975

1978, Mar. 10 ***Perf. 12½x12, 13***
Size: 42x27mm, 27x42mm
C275 A524 13c *Torreornis inexpectata,* horiz.
C276 A524 30c *Ara tricolor*

Baragua Protest, Cent. — AP105

1978, Mar. 15 ***Perf. 13x13½***
C277 AP105 13c *Antonio Maceo,* by A. Melero

Cosmonaut's Day Type of 1978

1978, Apr. 12 ***Perf. 13***
C278 A585 13c *Venus 10*
Size: 36x46mm
Perf. 12½x13
C279 A585 30c *Lunokhod 2,* vert.

SOCFILEX '78, Budapest — AP106

1978, May 7 ***Perf. 13x12½***
C280 AP106 30c Parliament, Hungary No. 217

Cactus Type of 1978

1978, May 15 ***Perf. 13***
C281 A587 13c *Rhodocactus cubensis*
C282 A587 30c *Harrisia taetra*

World Telecommunications Day — AP107

1978, May 17
C283 AP107 30c multi

Organization of African Unity, 15th Anniv. — AP108

1978, May 25 ***Perf. 13x12½***
C284 AP108 30c multi

Souvenir Sheet

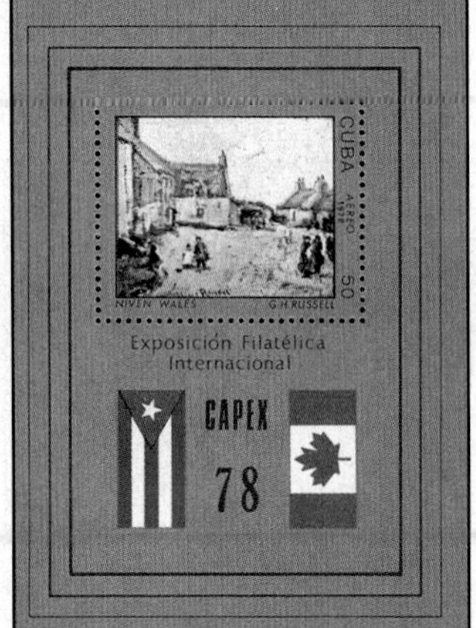

CAPEX '78, Toronto — AP109

1978, June 9 ***Perf. 13x13½***
C285 AP109 50c *Niven, Wales,* by G.H. Russell

Aquarium Type of 1978

1978, June 15 ***Perf. 13***
C286 A588 13c *Carassius auratus,* vert.
C287 A588 30c *Symphysodon aequifasciata axelrodi*

MEDELLIN Games Type of 1978

1978, July 1
C288 A589 13c Volleyball
C289 A589 30c Running

Attack on Moncada Type of 1978

1978, July 26
C290 A590 13c Soldiers bearing rifles
C291 A590 30c Stylized dove, banners

Youth Festival Type of 1978

Natl. flags and views of host cities.

1978, July 28
C292 A591 13c Moscow, 1957
C293 A591 13c Vienna, 1959
C294 A591 13c Helsinki, 1962
C295 A591 13c Sofia, 1968
C296 A591 13c Berlin, 1973
a. Strip of 5, Nos. C292-C296

Size: 46x36mm

Perf. 13x12½

C297 A591 30c Havana, 1978

Tuna Industry Type of 1978

1978, Aug. 30 ***Perf. 12½x12***
C298 A593 13c Stern trawler
C299 A593 30c Refrigerator ship

Souvenir Sheet

PRAGA '78 — AP110

1978, Sept. 8 ***Perf. 13***
C300 AP110 50c *Marina,* by A. Brandeis

Art Type of 1978

Paintings by Amelia Pelaez del Casal (1896-1968).

1978, Sept. 15 ***Perf. 12x12½, 13***
C301 A594 13c *Yellow Flowers,* vert.
C302 A594 30c *Still-life in Blue,* vert.

Souvenir Sheet

Perf. 13½x13

C303 A594 50c *Portrait of Amelia,* by L. Romanach, vert.

No. C303 contains one 32x40mm stamp.

Socialist Communication Organizations Congress (OSS), 20th Anniv. — AP111

1978, Sept. 25 ***Perf. 13***
C304 AP111 30c multi

Souvenir Sheet

EXFILNA '78, 6th Natl. Philatelic Exposition — AP112

1978, Oct. 10 ***Imperf.***
C305 AP112 50c 1st Postal Card, issued in 1878

No. C305 has simulated perfs.

Intl. Anti-Apartheid Year — AP113

1978, Oct. 16 ***Perf. 12½***
C306 AP113 13c multi

Zoo Type of 1978

1978, Oct. 20 ***Perf. 13***
C307 A595 13c *Acinonyx jubatos*
C308 A595 30c *Loxodonta africana,* vert.

Natl. Ballet Type of 1978

1978, Oct. 28 ***Perf. 12½x13***
C309 A596 13c *Giselle,* vert.
C310 A596 30c *Genesis,* vert.

Pacific Flora Type of 1978

1978, Nov. 30 ***Perf. 13***
C311 A597 13c multi, diff.
C312 A597 30c multi, diff.

25th Death Anniv. of Julius and Ethel Rosenberg, American Communists Executed for Espionage — AP114

1978, Dec. 20
C313 AP114 13c multi

Julio A. Mella (d. 1929) AP115

1979, Jan. 10
C314 AP115 13c multi

Cosmonaut's Day Type of 1979
Souvenir Sheet

1979, Apr. 12 ***Perf. 13½x13***
C315 A603 50c Orbital complex

No. C315 contains one 32x40mm stamp.

Intl. Year of the Child — AP116

1979, June 1 ***Perf. 13x12½***
C316 AP116 13c multi

Art Type of 1979

1979, June 15 ***Perf. 13½x13***
C317 A600 50c *Portrait of Victor Emmanuel Garcia,* by J. Arche, vert.

No. C317 contains one 32x40mm stamp.

CARIFESTA '79, Festival of Caribbean Peoples, Havana AP117

1979, July 16 ***Perf. 12½x13***
C318 AP117 13c multi

10th World Universiade Games, Mexico City — AP118

1979, Sept. 1 ***Perf. 13x12½***
C319 AP118 13c grn, pale grn & gold

6th Conference of Nonaligned Countries — AP119

1979, Sept. 3
C320 AP119 50c Convention Palace

Sir Rowland Hill (d. 1879), Originator of Penny Postage — AP120

1979, Sept. 4 ***Perf. 13½x13***
C321 AP120 30c Hill, casket

SOCFILEX '79, Bucharest — AP121

Illustration reduced.

1979, Oct. 25 ***Perf. 12½***
C322 AP121 30c Romania No. 683, flags

Intl. Radio Consultative Committee (CCIR), 50th Anniv. — AP122

1979, Nov. 30 ***Perf. 12½x12***
C323 AP122 30c Ground receiving station

1st Soviet-Cuban Joint Space Flight — AP123

1980, Sept. 23 ***Perf. 12½***
C324 AP123 13c multi
C325 AP123 30c multi

Capt. Mariano Barberan, Lt. Joaquin Collar, and Their Airplane Cuatro Vientos. — AP124

1993, June 11 Litho. *Perf. 13*
C326 AP124 30c multicolored

1st Flight Seville-Camaguey, 60th anniv.

AIR POST SEMI-POSTAL STAMP

Catalogue values for unused stamps in this section are for Never Hinged items.

Farm Couple and Factory SPAP1

Engr. & Typo.
1959, May 7 Wmk. 321 *Perf. 12½*
CB1 SPAP1 12c + 3c car & grn 1.25 .50

Agricultural reforms. See No. C199.

AIR POST SPECIAL DELIVERY STAMP

Matanzas Issue

Matanzas Harbor APSD1

Wmk. 229
1936, May 5 Photo. *Perf. 12½*
CE1 ASPD1 15c light blue 3.25 2.25
Never hinged 4.50

Exists imperf. Value $5 unused, $2.50 used.

SPECIAL DELIVERY STAMPS

Issued under US Administration

US No. E5 Surcharged in Red

1899 Wmk. 191 *Perf. 12*
E1 SD3 10c on 10c blue 130.00 100.00
a. No period after "CUBA" 450.00 400.00

Issues of the Republic under US Military Rule

Special Delivery Messenger SD2

Inscribed: "Immediata"

1899 Wmk. U S-C (191C) Engr.
E2 SD2 10c orange 55.00 15.00

Issues of the Republic

Inscribed: "Inmediata"

1902 *Perf. 12*
E3 SD2 10c orange 1.00 .75

J. B. Zayas SD3

1910 Unwmk.
E4 SD3 10c orange & blue 14.00 3.25
a. Center inverted 1,250.

Airplane and Morro Castle SD4

1914, Feb. 24 *Perf. 12*
E5 SD4 10c dark blue 15.00 1.25

Exists imperf. Value, pair $500.

1927 Wmk. Star (106)
E6 SD4 10c deep blue 12.00 .50

1935 *Perf. 10*
E7 SD4 10c blue 12.00 .40

Matanzas Issue

Mercury SD5

Wmk. Wavy Lines (229)
1936, May 5 Photo. *Perf. 12½*
E8 SD5 10c deep claret 3.25 1.40
Never hinged 4.50

Exists imperf. Value $6 unused, $2.50 used.

"Triumph of the Revolution" — SD6

1936, Nov. 18
E9 SD6 10c red orange 6.00 1.10
Never hinged 8.00

Maj. Gen. Máximo Gómez (1836-1905).

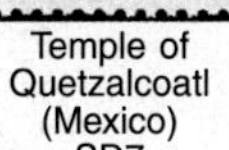

Temple of Quetzalcoatl (Mexico) SD7

Ruben Dario (Nicaragua) SD8

Wmk. 106
1937, Oct. 13 Engr. *Perf. 10*
E10 SD7 10c deep orange 5.75 5.75
E11 SD8 10c deep orange 5.75 5.75
Set, never hinged 11.00

See note after No. 354.

Letter and Symbols of Transportation — SD9

1945, Oct. 30
E12 SD9 10c olive brown 1.40 .25
Never hinged 2.00

Catalogue values for unused stamps in this section, from this point to the end of the section, are for Never Hinged items.

Governor's Building, Cárdenas SD10

Engraved and Lithographed

1951, July 3 Wmk. 229 *Perf. 13*
E13 SD10 10c henna brn, ultra & red 7.00 1.25

Cent. of the adoption of Cuba's flag.

Chess Type of Regular Issue, 1951

1951, Nov. 1 Photo.
E14 A166 10c dk grn & rose brn 14.00 4.00

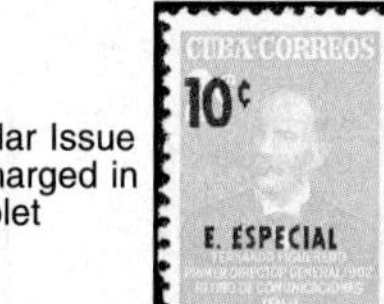

Type of Regular Issue of 1951 Surcharged in Red Violet

Wmk. 106
1952, Mar. 18 Engr. *Perf. 10*
E15 A159 10c on 2c yel brn 6.00 1.25

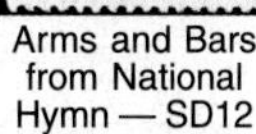

Arms and Bars from National Hymn — SD12

Roseate Tern — SD13

1952, May 27 *Perf. 12½*
E16 SD12 10c dp org & bl 2.50 .75

Republic of Cuba founding, 50th anniv.

Type of Air Post Stamps of 1952 Inscribed: "Entrega Especial"

1952, Oct. 7 *Perf. 10*
E17 AP36 10c pale olive grn 4.00 1.50

Three-fourths of the proceeds from the sale of No. E17 were used for the Communications Ministry Employees' Retirement Fund.

1953, July 28
E18 SD13 10c blue 2.75 .75

Gregorio Hernandez Saez SD14

Felix Varela SD15

1954, Feb. 23
E19 SD14 10c olive green 5.25 .90

1955, June 22 *Perf. 12½*
E20 SD15 10c brown car 3.00 .95

See note after No. E17.

Portrait Type of Regular Issue, 1956 Inscribed: "Entrega Especial"

Portrait: 10c, Jose Jacinto Milanes.

1956, May 2 Wmk. 106
E21 A198 10c dk car rose & blk 3.75 .75

See note after No. E17.

Painting Type of Regular Issue, 1957, Inscribed: "Entrega Especial"

10c, "Yesterday" by E. Garcia Cabrera.

1957, Mar. 15 Engr. *Perf. 12½*
E22 A207 10c dk brn & turq bl 3.75 1.10

See note after No. E17.

View Type of Regular Issue, 1957, Inscribed: "Entrega Especial."

10c, Independence square, Pino del Rio.

1957, Dec. 17
E23 A218 10c dk pur & brn 2.75 1.00

See note after No. E17.

View in Havana and Messenger SD16

1958, Jan. 10 Engr.
E24 SD16 10c blue 2.00 .75
E25 SD16 20c green 2.50 .75

See Nos. E28, E31.

Fish Type of Air Post Issue, 1958, Inscribed "Entrega Especial."

Fish: 10c, Blackfish snapper. 20c, Mosquitofish.

1958, Sept. 26 Wmk. 106 *Perf. 12½*
E26 AP86 10c blk, bl, pink & yel 4.75 2.50
E27 AP86 20c blk, ultra & pink 14.00 10.00

See note after No. C191.

Messenger Type of 1958

1960 Wmk. 321 *Perf. 12½*
E28 SD16 10c brt vio 1.75 .50

Plane Type of Air Post Issue, of 1931-46, Surcharged in Black or Red: "HABILITADO ENTREGA ESPECIAL 10¢"

1960 Wmk. 106 *Perf. 10*
E29 AP4 10c on 20c car rose 1.40 .50
E30 AP4 10c on 50c grnsh bl (R) 1.10 .50

Messenger Type of 1958

1961, June 28 Wmk. 321 *Perf. 12½*
E31 SD16 10c orange 1.75 .65

West Indies Packet Type of 1962

Perf. 12½
1962, Apr. 24 Litho. Unwmk.
E32 A253 10c buff, dull ultra & brn

POSTAGE DUE STAMPS

Issued under Administration of the United States

Postage Due Stamps of the US Nos. J38, J39, J41 and J42 Surcharged in Black like Nos. 221-226A

1899 Wmk. 191 *Perf. 12*

J1	D2	1c on 1c dp claret	45.00	5.25
J2	D2	2c on 2c dp claret	45.00	5.25
a.		Inverted surcharge		*2,750.*
J3	D2	5c on 5c dp claret	45.00	5.25
J4	D2	10c on 10c dp claret	27.50	2.50
		Nos. J1-J4 (4)	162.50	18.25

Issues of the Republic

D1

1914 Unwmk. Engr. *Perf. 12*

J5	D1	1c carmine rose	6.50	1.00
J6	D1	2c carmine rose	8.00	1.00
J7	D1	5c carmine rose	12.00	2.00
		Nos. J5-J7 (3)	26.50	4.00

1927-28

J8	D1	1c rose red	3.50	.70
J9	D1	2c rose red	5.50	.70
J10	D1	5c rose red	6.50	1.00
		Nos. J8-J10 (3)	15.50	2.40

NEWSPAPER STAMPS

Issued under Spanish Dominion

N1

N2

1888 Unwmk. Typo. *Perf. 14*

P1	N1	½m black	.20	*.25*
P2	N1	1m black	.20	*.30*
P3	N1	2m black	.20	*.30*
P4	N1	3m black	1.50	1.00
P5	N1	4m black	1.90	*2.00*
P6	N1	8m black	7.25	*8.50*
		Nos. P1-P6 (6)	11.25	*12.35*

1890

P7	N2	½m red brown	.45	*.60*
P8	N2	1m red brown	.45	*.60*
P9	N2	2m red brown	.75	*.90*
P10	N2	3m red brown	.95	*1.00*
P11	N2	4m red brown	7.25	5.25
P12	N2	8m red brown	7.25	5.25
		Nos. P7-P12 (6)	17.10	13.60

1892

P13	N2	½m violet	.20	*.30*
P14	N2	1m violet	.20	*.30*
P15	N2	2m violet	.20	*.30*
P16	N2	3m violet	.95	.30
P17	N2	4m violet	3.50	1.75
P18	N2	8m violet	7.50	2.75
		Nos. P13-P18 (6)	12.55	5.70

1894

P19	N2	½m rose	.20	*.30*
a.		Imperf. pair	22.50	
P20	N2	1m rose	.40	.30
P21	N2	2m rose	.45	.30
P22	N2	3m rose	1.75	1.25
P23	N2	4m rose	3.00	1.50
P24	N2	8m rose	5.25	3.75
		Nos. P19-P24 (6)	11.05	7.40

1896

P25	N2	½m blue green	.20	*.30*
P26	N2	1m blue green	.20	*.30*
P27	N2	2m blue green	.20	*.30*
P28	N2	3m blue green	2.50	1.50
P29	N2	4m blue green	5.25	*7.00*
P30	N2	8m blue green	9.50	*10.00*
		Nos. P25-P30 (6)	17.85	*19.40*

For surcharges see Nos. 190-193, 201-220.

POSTAL TAX STAMPS

Catalogue values for unused stamps in this section are for Never Hinged items.

Mother and Child — PT1

Nurse with Child — PT2

Wmk. Star. (106)

1938, Dec. 1 Engr. *Perf. 10*

RA1	PT1	1c bright green	1.25	.20

The tax benefited the National Council of Tuberculosis fund for children's hospitals. Obligatory on all mail during December and January. This note applies also to Nos. RA2-RA4, RA7-RA10, RA12-RA15, RA17-RA21.

1939, Dec. 1

RA2	PT2	1c orange vermilion	.75	.20

"Health" Protecting Children — PT3

1940, Dec. 1

RA3	PT3	1c deep blue	.75	.20

Mother and Child — PT4

Victory — PT5

1941, Dec. 1

RA4	PT4	1c olive bister	.75	.20

1942-44

RA5	PT5	½c orange	.30	.20
RA6	PT5	½c gray ('44)	.45	.20

Issued: #RA5, 7/1/42; #RA6, 10/3/44.

Type of 1941 Overprinted "1942" in Black

1942, Dec. 1

RA7	PT4	1c salmon	.80	.25
a.		Inverted overprint	60.00	50.00

As PT3 — PT6

As PT4 — PT7

1943, Dec. 1

RA8	PT6	1c brown	.75	.20

1949, Dec. 9

RA9	PT7	1c blue	.50	.20

Type of 1949 Inscribed: "1950"

1950, Dec. 1 Engr.

RA10	PT7	1c rose red	.50	.20

Proposed Communications Building

PT8 PT10

Woman Holding Child Aloft — PT9

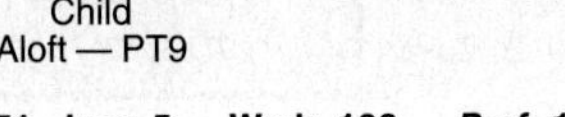
Child — PT11

1951, June 5 Wmk. 106 *Perf. 10*

RA11	PT8	1c violet	.75	.20

The tax was to help build a new Communications Building. This note applies also to Nos. RA16, RA34, RA43.

1951, Dec. 1

RA12	PT9	1c violet blue	.45	.20
RA13	PT9	1c brown carmine	.45	.20
RA14	PT9	1c olive bister	.45	.20
RA15	PT9	1c deep green	.45	.20
		Nos. RA12-RA15 (4)	1.80	.80

1952, Feb. 8

RA16	PT10	1c slate blue	.30	.20

See Nos. RA34, RA43.

1952, Dec. 1

RA17	PT11	1c rose carmine	.75	.20
RA18	PT11	1c yellow green	.75	.20
RA19	PT11	1c blue	.75	.20
RA20	PT11	1c orange	.75	.20
		Nos. RA17-RA20 (4)	3.00	.80

Hands Reaching for Lorraine Cross PT12

Child's Head, Lorraine Cross PT13

1953, Dec. 1 *Perf. 9½*

RA21	PT12	1c rose carmine	.50	.20

1954, Nov. 1 *Perf. 9½x10*

RA22	PT13	1c rose red	.75	.20
RA23	PT13	1c violet	.75	.20
RA24	PT13	1c bright blue	.75	.20
RA25	PT13	1c emerald	.75	.20
		Nos. RA22-RA25 (4)	3.00	.80

The tax benefited the Natl. Council of Tuberculosis fund for children's hospitals. Obligatory on all mail during Nov., Dec., Jan. & Feb. This note applies also to #RA26-RA33, RA35-RA42.

Rose and Watering Can PT14

Child and Protective Hands PT15

1955, Nov. 1

RA26	PT14	1c red orange	.75	.20
RA27	PT14	1c red lilac	.75	.20
RA28	PT14	1c bright blue	.75	.20
RA29	PT14	1c orange yellow	.75	.20
		Nos. RA26-RA29 (4)	3.00	.80

1956, Nov. 1

RA30	PT15	1c rose red	.75	.20
RA31	PT15	1c yellow brown	.75	.20
RA32	PT15	1c bright blue	.75	.20
RA33	PT15	1c emerald	.75	.20
		Nos. RA30-RA33 (4)	3.00	.80

Building Type of 1952

1957, Jan. 18 *Perf. 10*

RA34	PT10	1c rose red	.30	.20

Mother and Child by Silvia Arrojo Fernandez PT16

National Council of Tuberculosis PT17

Wmk. 321

1957, Nov. 1 Engr. *Perf. 10*

RA35	PT16	1c dull rose	.70	.20
RA36	PT16	1c bright blue	.70	.20
RA37	PT16	1c gray	.70	.20
RA38	PT16	1c emerald	.70	.20
		Nos. RA35-RA38 (4)	2.80	.80

1958

RA39	PT17	1c rose red	.40	.20
RA40	PT17	1c red brown	.40	.20
RA41	PT17	1c gray	.40	.20
RA42	PT17	1c emerald	.40	.20
		Nos. RA39-RA42 (4)	1.60	.80

Building Type of 1952

1958 Wmk. 321

RA43	PT10	1c rose red	.30	.20

CYPRUS

'sī-prəs

LOCATION — An island in the Mediterranean Sea off the coast of Turkey
GOVT. — Republic
AREA — 3,572 sq. mi.
POP. — 754,064 (1999 est.)
CAPITAL — Nicosia

The British Crown Colony of Cyprus became a republic in 1960.

Turkey invaded Cyprus in 1974 resulting in the northern 40% of the island becoming the Turkish Republic of Northern Cyprus. No other country recognizes this division of the island.

See Turkey in Volume 6.

12 Pence = 1 Shilling
40 Paras = 1 Piaster
9 Piasters = 1 Shilling
20 Shillings = 1 Pound
1000 Milliemes = 1 Pound (1955)
100 Cents = 1 Cyprus Pound (1983)

Catalogue values for unused stamps in this country are for Never Hinged items, beginning with Scott 156 in the regular postage section and Scott RA1 in the postal tax section.

Values for unused stamps are for examples with original gum as defined in the catalogue introduction. Very fine examples of Nos. 1, 2 and 7-10 will have perforations touching the design on at least one or more sides due to the narrow spacing of the stamps on the plates and to imperfect perforation methods. Stamps with perfs clear on all four sides are scarce and will command higher prices.

Watermark

Wmk. 344 — Map of Cyprus and KC/K Delta

Queen Victoria — A1

A2

A3

A4

A5

A6

A7

Various Watermarks as in Great Britain (#20, 23, 25, 27 & 29)

1880 **Typo.** *Perf. 14*

1 A1 ½p rose (P 15) 125.00 110.00
Plate 12 210.00 *300.00*
Plate 19 5,750. 950.00
b. Double overprint (P 15) *15,500.*
2 A2 1p red (P 216) 19.00 *45.00*
Plate 217 13.00 *45.00*
Plate 174 1,400. 1,400.
Plate 181 400.00 200.00
Plate 184 14,500. 2,750.
Plate 193 800.00
Plate 196 700.00
Plate 201 14.00 *57.50*
Plate 205 65.00 57.50
Plate 208 110.00 65.00
Plate 215 13.00 *57.50*
Plate 218 21.00 *65.00*
Plate 220 550.00 475.00
b. Double overprint (P 218) 5,400.
Double overprint (P 208) *17,500.*
c. Pair, one without ovpt. (P 208) *22,000.*
3 A3 2½p claret (P 14) 2.75 *9.25*
Plate 15 4.00 *27.50*
4 A4 4p lt ol grn (P 16) 140.00 *240.00*
5 A5 6p ol gray (P 16) 575.00 *750.00*
6 A6 1sh green (P 13) 750.00 525.00

Black Surcharge

7 A7 30 paras on 1p red (P 216) 110.00 *95.00*
Plate 201 140.00 100.00
Plate 217 200.00 200.00
Plate 220 175.00 *190.00*
b. Dbl. surch., one invtd. (P 220) 1,500. *1,350.*
Dbl. surch., one invtd. (P 216) 4,250.

No. 2 Surcharged

18mm Long

1881

8 A2 ½p on 1p (205, 216) 80.00 *100.00*
Plate 174 175.00 *350.00*
Plate 181 175.00 *200.00*
Plate 201 110.00 *140.00*
Plate 205 80.00 *100.00*
Plate 208 190.00 *325.00*
Plate 215 750.00 *800.00*
Plate 217 925.00 825.00
Plate 218 525.00 *640.00*
Plate 220 300.00 *375.00*

16mm Long

9 A2 ½p on 1p (P 201) 140.00 *190.00*
Plate 216 400.00 *450.00*
Plate 218 *11,500.*
a. Double surcharge (P 201, 216) 3,200. 2,900.

13mm Long

10 A2 ½p on 1p red (P 215) 52.50 *75.00*
Plate 205 290.00
Plate 217 150.00 92.50
Plate 218 80.00 *110.00*
c. Double surcharge (P 215) 550.00 700.00
Double surcharge (P 205) 800.00
e. Triple surcharge (P 215) 800.00
Triple surcharge (P 205) *4,000.*
Triple surcharge (P 217) —
Triple surcharge (P 218) *4,000.*
h. Quadruple surch. (P 205, 215) *5,000.*
j. "CYPRUS" double (P 218) *5,500.*

A8

1881, July **Typo.** **Wmk. 1**

11 A8 ½pi emerald green 210.00 52.50
12 A8 1pi rose 425.00 37.50
13 A8 2pi ultramarine 525.00 37.50
14 A8 4pi olive green 1,050. 325.00
15 A8 6pi olive gray 1,750. 500.00

Postage and revenue stamps of Cyprus with "J.A.B." (the initials of Postmaster J.A. Bulmer) in manuscript, or with "POSTAL SURCHARGE" (with or without "J. A. B."), were not Postage Due stamps but were employed for accounting purposes between the chief PO at Larnaca and the sub-offices.

See Nos. 19-25, 28-37. For surcharges see Nos. 16-18, 26-27.

A9

A10

Black Surcharge

1882 **Wmk. 1**

16 A9 ½pi on ½pi grn 700.00 85.00
17 A10 30pa on 1pi rose 1,750. 125.00

1884 **Wmk. 2**

18 A9 ½pi on ½pi green 160.00 10.00
a. Double surcharge 3,200.

See Nos. 26, 27.

1882-94 **Die B**

For explanation of Dies A and B, see back of this section of the Catalogue.

19 A8 ½pi green 5.75 .80
20 A8 30pa violet 5.75 5.75
21 A8 1pi rose 13.00 2.25
22 A8 2pi blue 16.00 2.00
23 A8 4pi pale ol grn 25.00 *27.50*
24a A8 6pi 190.00 *650.00*
25a A8 12pi 150.00 *375.00*
Nos. 19-25a (7) 405.50 *1,063.*

Die A

19a A8 ½pi 18.00 1.75
b. ½pi emerald *5,750.* 475.00
20a A8 30pa lilac 70.00 22.50
21a A8 1pi 100.00 2.25
22a A8 2pi 140.00 2.25
23a A8 4pi 400.00 27.50
24 A8 6pi olive gray 55.00 19.00
25 A8 12pi brown org 200.00 40.00
Nos. 19a-25 (7) 983.00 115.25

A11

Type I — Figures "½" 8mm apart.
Type II — Figures "½" 6mm apart.
The space between the fraction bars varies from 5½ to 8½mm but is usually 6 or 8mm.

Black Surcharge Type I

1886 **Wmk. 2**

26 A11 ½pi on ½pi grn 400.00 15.00
a. Type II 250.00 80.00
b. Double surcharge, type II

Wmk. 1

27 A11 ½pi on ½pi grn *8,750.* 500.00
a. Type II *19,500.*

No. 27a probably is a proof.

1894-96 **Wmk. 2**

28 A8 ½pi grn & car rose 4.75 1.50
29 A8 30pa violet & green 2.75 1.50
30 A8 1pi rose & ultra 6.50 1.50
31 A8 2pi ultra & mar 7.50 1.50
32 A8 4pi ol green & vio 16.00 5.25
33 A8 6pi ol gray & grn 13.00 *16.00*
34 A8 9pi brown & rose 18.00 20.00
35 A8 12pi brn org & blk 20.00 *57.50*
36 A8 18pi slate & brown 52.50 52.50
37 A8 45pi dk vio & ultra 110.00 *150.00*
Nos. 28-37 (10) 251.00 *307.25*

King Edward VII A12

King George V A13

1903 **Typo.**

38 A12 ½pi grn & car rose 4.50 1.40
39 A12 30pa violet & green 9.50 3.00
40 A12 1pi carmine rose & ultra 19.00 3.50
41 A12 2pi ultra & mar 62.50 11.50
42 A12 4pi ol green & vio 32.50 22.50
43 A12 6pi ol brown & grn 45.00 *140.00*
44 A12 9pi brn & car rose 110.00 *225.00*
45 A12 12pi org brn & blk 15.00 *62.50*
46 A12 18pi black & brown 92.50 *175.00*
47 A12 45pi dk vio & ultra 225.00 *575.00*
Nos. 38-47 (10) 615.50 *1,219.*

1904-07 **Wmk. 3**

48 A12 5pa bis & blk ('07) 1.10 .80
49 A12 10pa org & grn ('07) 3.50 .55
50 A12 ½pi grn & car rose 5.25 .20
51 A12 30pa violet & green 16.00 1.75
52 A12 1pi car rose & ultra 5.75 1.10
53 A12 2pi ultra & maroon 7.00 2.00
54 A12 4pi ol grn & red vio 12.50 9.25
55 A12 6pi ol brn & green 16.00 *17.00*
56 A12 9pi brn & car rose 35.00 9.75
57 A12 12pi org brn & blk 29.00 *45.00*
58 A12 18pi black & brown 35.00 12.50
59 A12 45pi dk vio & ultra 85.00 *160.00*
Nos. 48-59 (12) 251.10 *259.90*

1912

61a A13 10pa org yellow & green 2.50 1.40
62 A13 ½pi grn & car rose 2.00 .20
63 A13 30pa violet & green 2.90 .70
64 A13 1pi car & ultra 4.50 2.00
65 A13 2pi ultra & maroon 7.50 2.25
66 A13 4pi ol grn & red vio 4.75 *5.50*
67 A13 6pi ol brn & green 4.00 *9.75*
68 A13 9pi brn & car rose 27.50 *30.00*
69 A13 12pi org brn & blk 17.50 *40.00*
70 A13 18pi black & brown 30.00 *35.00*
71 A13 45pi dl vio & ultra 92.50 *140.00*
Nos. 61a-71 (11) 195.65 *266.80*

1921-23 **Wmk. 4**

72 A13 10pa orange & grn 7.00 *8.50*
73 A13 10pa gray & yellow 14.00 7.50
74 A13 30pa violet & grn 2.90 .45
75 A13 30pa green 8.00 .45
76 A13 1pi rose & ultra 20.00 *30.00*
77 A13 1pi violet & car 3.50 *4.50*
78 A13 1½pi orange & blk 5.75 *5.50*
79 A13 2pi ultra & red vio 22.50 15.00
80 A13 2pi rose & ultra 11.00 *25.00*
81 A13 2¾pi ultra & red vio 8.00 *10.50*
82 A13 4pi ol grn & red vio 14.00 *20.00*
83 A13 6pi ol brn & green 18.00 *75.00*
84 A13 9pi brn & carmine 30.00 *80.00*
85 A13 18pi black & brn 70.00 *150.00*
86 A13 45pi dl vio & ultra 200.00 *290.00*
Nos. 72-86 (15) 434.65 *722.40*

Wmk. 3

87 A13 10sh grn & red, *yel* 425.00 *875.00*
88 A13 £1 vio & black, *red* 1,150. *2,100.*

Years of issue: Nos. 73, 75, 77-78, 80-81, 87-88, 1923; others, 1921.

A14

1924-28 **Chalky Paper** **Wmk. 4**

89 A14 ¼pi gray & brn org 1.10 .20
90 A14 ½pi gray blk & blk 3.00 *10.00*
91 A14 ½pi grn & dp grn ('25) 2.50 1.10
92 A14 ¾pi grn & dp grn 2.50 1.10
93 A14 ¾pi gray blk & blk ('25) 2.25 .20
94 A14 1pi brn vio & org brown 2.25 .80
95 A14 1½pi org & black 2.25 *8.50*
96 A14 1½pi carmine ('25) 2.90 .35
97 A14 2pi car & green 2.50 *15.00*
98 A14 2pi org & black ('25) 7.00 3.75
99 A14 2½pi ultra ('25) 3.50 .35
100 A14 2¾pi ultra & dull vio 3.75 3.50
101 A14 4pi ap grn & vio 3.75 3.00
102 A14 4½pi black & yel, *emer* 4.00 4.00
103 A14 6pi grn ol & grn 4.25 *6.25*
104 A14 9pi brn & dk vio 7.00 5.00
105 A14 12pi org brn & blk 10.50 *62.50*
106 A14 18pi blk & org 22.50 5.75
Revenue cancel 1.00
107 A14 45pi gray vio & ultra 42.50 *42.50*
Revenue cancel 1.50
108 A14 90pi grn & red, *yel* 100.00 *200.00*
Revenue cancel 3.00
109 A14 £5 blk, *yel* ('28) 3,200. *7,000.*
Revenue cancel 175.00

Wmk. 3

110 A14 £1 vio & black, *red* 350.00 *800.00*
Revenue cancel 10.00
Nos. 89-108 (20) 230.00 *373.85*

Nos. 96 and 99 are on ordinary paper.

Silver Coin of Amathus — A15

Philosopher Zeno — A16

Map of Cyprus — A17

Discovery of Body of St. Barnabas — A18

Cloisters of Bella Paise Monastery — A19

Badge of the Colony — A20

Hospice of Umm Haram at Larnaca — A21

Statue of Richard Coeur de Lion, London — A22

St. Nicholas Cathedral, Famagusta — A23

King George V — A24

Perf. 12

1928, Feb. 1 Engr. Wmk. 4

114 A15 ¾pi dark violet 3.00 1.10
115 A16 1pi Prus bl & blk 3.50 1.75
116 A17 1½pi red 5.00 2.25
117 A18 2½pi ultramarine 4.00 *2.50*
118 A19 4pi dp red brown 6.25 *7.00*
119 A20 6pi dark blue 8.50 *24.00*
120 A21 9pi violet brown 8.50 *12.50*
121 A22 18pi dk brn & blk 21.00 *21.00*
122 A23 45pi dp blue & vio 45.00 *55.00*
123 A24 £1 ol brn & deep blue 225.00 *350.00*
Nos. 114-123 (10) 329.75 *477.10*

50th year of Cyprus as a British colony.

Ruins of Vouni Palace — A25

Columns at Salamis — A26

Peristerona Church — A27

Soli Theater — A28

Kyrenia Castle and Harbor — A29

Kolossi Castle — A30

St. Sophia Cathedral — A31

Bairakdar Mosque — A32

Queen's Window, St. Hilarion Castle — A33

Buyuk Khan, Nicosia — A34

Forest Scene — A35

1934, Dec. 1 Engr. Perf. 12½

125 A25 ¼pi yel brn & ultra 1.10 .55
Never hinged 1.50
a. Vert. pair, imperf. between *26,500.* *18,500.*
126 A26 ½pi green 1.40 1.10
Never hinged 1.75
a. Vert. pair, imperf. between *12,750.* *14,000.*
127 A27 ¾pi violet & blk 1.75 .20
Never hinged 3.00
a. Vert. pair, imperf. between *29,000.*
128 A28 1pi brown & blk 1.10 .90
Never hinged 2.50
a. Vert. pair, imperf. between *15,000.* *15,000.*
b. Horiz. pair, imperf. btwn. *11,750.*
129 A29 1½pi rose red 2.25 .60
Never hinged 4.25
130 A30 2½pi dark ultra 2.25 2.00
Never hinged 4.50
131 A31 4½pi dk car & blk 3.50 *4.25*
Never hinged 10.00
132 A32 6pi blue & black 10.00 *14.00*
Never hinged 21.00
133 A33 9pi dl vio & blk brown 8.00 *5.50*
Never hinged 19.00
134 A34 18pi ol grn & black 45.00 32.50
Never hinged 95.00
135 A35 45pi blk & emer 75.00 *57.50*
Never hinged 150.00
Nos. 125-135 (11) 151.35 *119.10*
Set, optd. "SPECIMEN" 325.00

Common Design Types pictured following the introduction.

Silver Jubilee Issue

Common Design Type

1935, May 6 Perf. 11x12

136 CD301 ¾pi gray blk & ultra 1.90 .40
137 CD301 1½pi car & dk bl 3.75 2.75
138 CD301 2½pi ultra & brn 4.00 *1.60*
139 CD301 9pi brn vio & ind 14.00 *14.00*
Nos. 136-139 (4) 23.65 *18.75*
Set, never hinged 37.50

Coronation Issue

Common Design Type

1937, May 12 Perf. 11x11½

140 CD302 ¾pi dark gray .35 .20
141 CD302 1½pi dark carmine .50 .85
142 CD302 2½pi deep ultra 1.00 *1.40*
Nos. 140-142 (3) 1.85 2.45
Set, never hinged 3.75

Ruins of Vouni Palace — A36

Columns at Salamis — A37

Peristerona Church — A38

Soli Theater — A39

Kyrenia Castle and Harbor — A40

Kolossi Castle — A41

Map of Cyprus — A42

Bairakdar Mosque — A43

Citadel, Famagusta — A44

Buyuk Khan — A45

Forest Scene A46

King George VI A47

1938-44 Wmk. 4 Perf. 12½

143 A36 ¼pi yel brn & ultra .20 .20
144 A37 ½pi green .30 .20
145 A38 ¾pi violet & blk 7.00 .55
146 A39 1pi orange .40 .20
a. Perf. 13½x12½ ('44) 350.00 30.00
Never hinged 460.00
147 A40 1½pi rose car 2.50 1.60
147A A40 1½pi lt vio ('43) .25 .30
147B A38 2pi carmine & blk ('42) .35 .20
c. Perf. 12½x13½ ('44) 2.00 *7.50*
Never hinged 2.50
148 A41 2½pi ultramarine 10.00 3.50
148A A41 3pi dp ultra ('42) .80 .20
149 A42 4½pi gray .35 .20
150 A43 6pi blue & black .60 *1.10*
151 A44 9pi dk vio & blk 1.00 .20
152 A45 18pi ol grn & blk 2.00 .90
153 A46 45pi blk & emer 9.00 2.75
154 A47 90pi blk & brt vio 16.00 5.50
155 A47 £1 ind & dl red 35.00 26.00
Nos. 143-155 (16) 85.75 43.60
Set, never hinged 175.00

See Nos. 164-166.

Catalogue values for unused stamps in this section, from this point to the end of the section, are for Never Hinged items.

Peace Issue

Common Design Type

1946, Oct. 21 Engr. Perf. 13½x14

156 CD303 1½pi purple .20 .20
157 CD303 3pi deep blue .20 .20

Silver Wedding Issue

Common Design Types

1948, Dec. 20 Photo. Perf. 14x14½

158 CD304 1½pi purple .55 .20

Engr.; Name Typo.

Perf. 11½x11

159 CD305 £1 dark blue 45.00 *55.00*

UPU Issue

Common Design Types

Perf. 13½, 11x11½

1949, Oct. 10 Engr. Wmk. 4

160 CD306 1½pi violet .45 *.75*
161 CD307 2pi deep carmine 1.75 1.75
162 CD308 3pi indigo .80 *1.10*
163 CD309 9pi rose violet 1.75 1.75
Nos. 160-163 (4) 4.75 5.35

Types of 1938-43

1951, July 2 Engr. Perf. 12½

164 A37 ½pi purple 2.40 .20
165 A40 1½pi deep green 3.00 .55
166 A41 4pi deep ultra 3.25 .25
Nos. 164-166 (3) 8.65 1.00

Coronation Issue

Common Design Type

1953, June 2 Perf. 13½x13

167 CD312 1½pi brt grn & black .90 .25

Carobs A48

Copper Pyrites Mine A49

St. Hilarion Castle A50

Queen Elizabeth II and Cyprian Coin Devices — A51

Designs: 3m, Grapes. 5m, Oranges. 15m, Troodos forest. 20m, Aphrodite beach. 25m, Coin of Paphos. 30m, Kyrenia. 35m, Harvest in Mesaoria. 40m, Famagusta harbor. 100m, Hala Sultan Tekke. 250m, Kanakaria church. £1, Queen Elizabeth II and devices of Byzantium, Lusignan, Ottoman Empire and Venice.

Perf. 11½

1955, Aug. 1 Engr. Wmk. 4

168	A48	2m chocolate	.20	.30
169	A48	3m violet blue	.20	.20
170	A48	5m orange	.65	.20
171	A49	10m gray grn & chocolate	.95	.20
172	A49	15m indigo & olive	2.40	.35
173	A49	20m ultra & brown	.95	.25
174	A49	25m aquamarine	1.90	.45
175	A49	30m carmine & blk	1.40	.20
176	A49	35m aqua & orange	.60	.30
177	A49	40m choc & dk grn	.95	.45

Perf. 13½

178	A50	50m red brn & aqua	.80	.25
179	A50	100m bl green & mag	11.50	.45
180	A50	250m vio brn & dk blue gray	8.50	6.75

Perf. 11x11½

181	A51	500m lilac rose & grnsh gray	26.00	8.75
182	A51	£1 grnsh gray & brn red	22.50	*30.00*
		Revenue cancel		1.00
		Nos. 168-182 (15)	79.50	49.10

Republic

Nos. 168-182 Overprinted in Dark Blue

1960, Aug. 16 Ovpt. 10x6½mm

183	A48	2m chocolate	.20	.20
184	A48	3m violet blue	.20	.20
185	A48	5m orange	.20	.20

Overprint 12½x11mm

186	A49	10m gray grn & choc	.25	.20
187	A49	15m indigo & ol	.45	.20
188	A49	20m ultra & brn	.50	.20
a.		Double overprint		*8,500.*
189	A49	25m aquamarine	.60	.35
190	A49	30m car & black	.75	.30
a.		Double overprint		*13,500.*
191	A49	35m aqua & org	1.00	.45
192	A49	40m choc & dk grn	1.10	.65

2-line overprint 2½mm apart

193	A50	50m red brown & aqua	1.25	.75
194	A50	100m bl grn & mag	3.00	2.00
195	A50	250m vio brn & dk blue gray	10.50	6.00

2-line overprint 22mm apart

196	A51	500m lil rose & grnsh gray	45.00	18.00
197	A51	£1 grnsh gray & brn red	85.00	45.00
		Nos. 183-197 (15)	150.00	74.70

The overprint, in Greek and Turkish, reads "Republic of Cyprus."

Map of Cyprus — A52

Wmk. 314

1960, Aug. 16 Engr. *Perf. 11½*

198	A52	10m brown & green	.25	.20
199	A52	30m blue & brown	1.00	.70
200	A52	100m purple & black	2.50	2.10
		Nos. 198-200 (3)	3.75	3.00

Independence of Republic of Cyprus.

Europa Issue, 1961

Nineteen Doves Flying as One CD4

Perf. 14x13½

1962, Mar. 19 Litho. Unwmk.

201	CD4	10m lilac	.20	.20
202	CD4	40m deep ultra	.40	.20
203	CD4	100m emerald	.40	.25
		Nos. 201-203 (3)	1.00	.65

Admission of Cyprus to Council of Europe.

Malaria Eradication Emblem A54

1962, May 14 *Perf. 14x13½*

204	A54	10m gray green & blue	.25	.20
205	A54	30m red brown & black	.50	.50

WHO drive to eradicate malaria.

Iron Age Jug — A55

St. Barnabas Church, Salamis A56

Designs: 5m, Grapes. 10m, Head of Apollo. 15m, St. Sophia Church, Nicosia. 30m, Temple of Apollo. 35m, Head of Aphrodite. 40m, Skiing on Mt. Troodos. 50m, Ruins of Gymnasium, Salamis. 100m, Hala Sultan Tekke (sheep, Salt Lake Larnaca and tomb). 250m, Bella Paise Monastery. 500m, Cyprus mouflon. £1, St. Hilarion Castle.

Perf. 13½x14, 14x13½

1962, Sept. 17 Wmk. 344

206	A55	3m dk brn & sal	.20	.30
207	A55	5m dull green & red lilac	.20	.20
208	A55	10m dk slate grn & yel green	.20	.20
209	A55	15m dk brn & rose vio	.45	.20
210	A56	25m salmon & brn	.45	.20
211	A56	30m lt bl & dk bl	.25	.20
212	A55	35m dk bl & pale grn	.45	.20
213	A56	40m vio bl & dk bl	1.50	1.75
214	A56	50m olive bis & dk grn	.60	.20
215	A55	100m brn & yel brn	4.25	.30
216	A56	250m tan & black	10.50	2.25
217	A55	500m brown & olive	19.00	8.50
218	A56	£1 gray & green	20.00	*27.50*
		Nos. 206-218 (13)	58.05	42.00

Wmk. 344 is found in two positions: normal or inverted on vertical stamps, and reading up or down on horizontal stamps.

For overprints see Nos. 232-236, 265-268. For surcharge see No. 273.

Europa Issue, 1962

Common Design Type

Perf. 14x13½

1963, Jan. 28 Wmk. 344

Size: 36x20mm

219	CD5	10m ultra & black	*6.25*	.30
220	CD5	40m red & black	*27.50*	2.25
221	CD5	150m green & black	*92.50*	6.00
		Nos. 219-221 (3)	*126.25*	8.55

Cypriot Farm Girl — A57

Cub Scout and Tents — A58

75m, Statue of Demeter, goddess of agriculture.

1963, Mar. 21 *Perf. 13½x14*

222	A57	25m blk, ultra & ocher	.55	.40
223	A57	75m dk car, gray & blk	3.00	1.50

FAO "Freedom from Hunger" campaign.

1963, Aug. 21 Wmk. 344

20m, Sea Scout. 150m, Boy Scout & mouflon.

224	A58	3m multicolored	.20	.20
225	A58	20m multicolored	.40	.25
226	A58	150m multicolored	2.00	2.50
a.		Souvenir sheet of 3	140.00	140.00
		Nos. 224-226 (3)	2.60	2.95

Boy Scout movement in Cyprus, 50th anniv. #226a contains 3 imperf. stamps similar to #224-226 with simulated perforations. Sold for 250m.

Red Cross Nurse — A59

Children's Home, Kyrenia A60

Perf. 13½x14, 14x13½

1963, Sept. 9 Litho. Wmk. 344

227	A59	10m multicolored	1.00	.20
228	A60	100m multicolored	4.00	4.00

Intl. Red Cross, cent.

Europa Issue, 1963

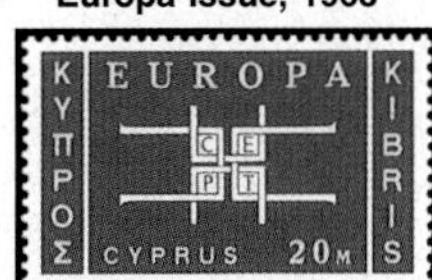

Stylized Links, Symbolizing Unity — CD6

1963, Nov. 4 *Perf. 14x13½*

229	CD6	20m multicolored	*9.50*	.60
230	CD6	30m multicolored	*10.50*	.60
231	CD6	150m multicolored	*90.00*	9.00
		Nos. 229-231 (3)	*110.00*	10.20

Nos. 208, 211, 213-215 Overprinted in Ultramarine

1964, May 5 *Perf. 13½x14, 14x13½*

232	A55	10m dk sl grn & yel grn	.20	.20
233	A55	30m lt blue & dk blue	.25	.20
234	A55	40m vio bl & dull bl	.35	.30
235	A55	50m ol bis & dk grn	.45	.35
236	A55	100m brn & yel brown	.75	.75
		Nos. 232-236 (5)	2.00	1.80

Decision by the UN and its Security Council to help restore the country to normality and to seek a solution of its problems.

Clay Mask and Soli Theater A62

Designs: 35m, Curium theater. 50m, Salamis theater. 100m, Performance of "Othello" in front of Othello Tower.

1964, June 15 *Perf. 13½x14*

237	A62	15m multicolored	.40	.20
238	A62	35m multicolored	.40	.25
239	A62	50m multicolored	.40	.25
240	A62	100m multicolored	1.50	1.75
		Nos. 237-240 (4)	2.70	2.45

400th anniversary of Shakespeare's birth.

Boxers A63

14th century B.C. art: 10m, Runners, vert. 75m, Chariot.

1964, July 6 *Perf. 13½x14, 14x13½*

241	A63	10m brn, bis & blk	.20	.20
242	A63	25m gray bl, bl & brn	.30	.25
243	A63	75m brick red, blk & brn	.75	.80
a.		Souvenir sheet of 3	9.00	*12.50*
		Nos. 241-243 (3)	1.25	1.25

18th Olympic Games, Tokyo, Oct. 10-25, 1964. No. 243a contains three imperf. stamps similar to Nos. 241-243 with gray marginal inscription. Sheet sold for 250m; the difference between face value and selling price went for the promotion of classical athletics in Cyprus.

Symbolic Daisy CD7

Satyr Drinking Wine, 5th Century B.C. Statuette A65

Modern Winery A66

Europa Issue, 1964

Perf. 13½x14

1964, Sept. 14 Litho. Wmk. 344

244 CD7 20m bis brn & red brn 5.50 .35
245 CD7 30m lt blue & dk blue 7.00 .35
246 CD7 150m grn & ol grn 72.50 5.50
Nos. 244-246 (3) 85.00 6.20

CEPT, 5th anniv. The 22 petals of the flower symbolize the 22 members of the organization.

Perf. 14x13½, 13½x14

1964, Oct. 26 Wmk. 344

Cypriot Wine Industry: 10m, Dionysus and Acme drinking wine, 3rd century mosaic. 50m, Commandaria wine, Knight Templar and Kolossi Castle.

247 A66 10m multicolored .40 .20
248 A65 40m multicolored .85 1.25
249 A65 50m multicolored .85 .30
250 A66 100m multicolored 2.40 2.00
Nos. 247-250 (4) 4.50 3.75

Pres. John F. Kennedy (1917-1963) — A67

Perf. 14x13½

1965, Feb. 15 Litho. Wmk. 344

251 A67 10m violet blue .20 .20
252 A67 40m green .40 .40
253 A67 100m rose claret .45 .40
a. Souvenir sheet of 3 4.25 6.00
Nos. 251-253 (3) 1.05 1.00

No. 253a contains 3 imperf. stamps similar to Nos. 251-253 with simulated perforations. Sold for 250m, 100m going to charitable organizations in Cyprus.

Old Couple — A68

Mother and Children by A. Diamantis — A69

45m, Man with broken leg (accident insurance).

1965, Apr. 12 *Perf. 13½x14*

254 A68 30m dull green & tan .30 .20
255 A68 45m dk vio bl, bl & gray .50 .30

Perf. 13½x12½

256 A69 75m buff & red brown 1.50 2.00
Nos. 254-256 (3) 2.30 2.50

Introduction of Social Insurance Law.

ITU Emblem, Old and New Communication Equipment — A70

1965, May 17 Litho. *Perf. 14x13½*

257 A70 15m brn, yel & black .75 .25
258 A70 60m grn, lt grn & black 8.00 3.00
259 A70 75m dk & lt bl & black 9.25 4.25
Nos. 257-259 (3) 18.00 7.50

ITU, cent.

ICY Emblem A71

1965, May 17 Wmk. 344

260 A71 50m multicolored 1.00 .20
261 A71 100m multicolored 1.75 .75

International Cooperation Year.

Europa Issue, 1965

Leaves and Fruit CD8

Perf. 14x13½

1965, Sept. 27 Litho. Wmk. 344

262 CD8 5m org, org brn & black 1.00 .20
263 CD8 45m lt grn, org brn & black 7.00 1.25
264 CD8 150m gray, org brn & black 22.50 4.00
Nos. 262-264 (3) 30.50 5.45

Nos. 206, 208, 211 and 216 Overprinted in Dark Blue

1966, Jan. 31 *Perf. 13½x14, 14x13½*

265 A55 3m dk brn & salmon .25 .30
266 A55 10m dk sl grn & yel green .25 .20
267 A56 30m lt bl & dk blue .25 .20
268 A56 250m tan & black .75 2.00
Nos. 265-268 (4) 1.50 2.70

UN General Assembly's resolution to mediate the dispute between Greeks and Turks on Cyprus, Dec. 18, 1965.

St. Barnabas, Ancient Icon — A73

Chapel over Tomb of St. Barnabas A74

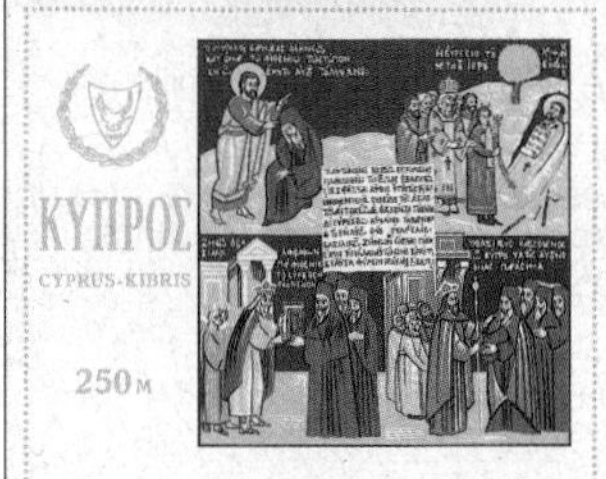

Bishop Anthemios of Constantine Dreaming of St. Barnabas, Discovering Tomb, etc. — A75

Design: 15m, Discovery of body of St. Barnabas (scene as in type A18).

Perf. 13x14, 14x13

1966, Apr. 25 Litho. Wmk. 344

269 A73 15m multicolored .20 .20
270 A74 25m multicolored .20 .20
271 A73 100m multicolored .75 1.50

Size: 110x91mm

Imperf

272 A75 250m multicolored 6.00 11.00
Nos. 269-272 (4) 7.15 12.90

1900th anniv. of the death of St. Barnabas.

No. 206 Surcharged with New Value and Three Bars

Perf. 13½x14

1966, May 30 Litho. Wmk. 344

273 A55 5m on 3m dk brn & sal .20 .20

Gen. K. S. Thimayya A76

1966, June 6 *Perf. 14x13½*

274 A76 50m tan & black .35 .25

In memory of Gen. Kodendera Subayya Thimayya (1906-1965), commander of the UN Peace-keeping Force on Cyprus.

Europa Issue, 1966

Symbolic Sailboat — CD9

Perf. 13½x14

1966, Sept. 26 Litho. Wmk. 344

275 CD9 20m multicolored .75 .20
276 CD9 30m multicolored .75 .30
277 CD9 150m multicolored 5.00 2.75
Nos. 275-277 (3) 6.50 3.25

Stavrovouni Monastery A78

St. Nicholas Cathedral, Famagusta A79

Ingot Bearer, Bronze Age — A80

Designs: 5m, St. James' Church, Tricomo, vert. 10m, Zeno of Citium, marble bust, vert. 15m, Ship from 7th cent. BC vase, horiz. 20m, Silver coin, 4th cent. BC (head of Hercules with lion skin). 25m, Sleeping Eros (1st cent. marble statue; horiz.). 35m, Hawks on 11th cent. gold and enamel scepter from Curium. 40m, Marriage of David (7th cent. silver disc). 50m, Silver coin of Alexander the Great showing Hercules and Zeus, horiz. 100m, Bird catching fish on 7th cent. BC jug. 500m, The Rape of Ganymede (3rd cent. mosaic). £1, Aphrodite (1st cent. marble statue).

Perf. 12x12½, 12½x12

1966, Nov. 21 Litho. Wmk. 344

278 A78 3m bl, dl yel, grn & black .60 .20
279 A78 5m dk bl, ol & blk .20 .20
280 A78 10m olive & black .25 .20

Perf. 14x13½, 13½x14

281 A79 15m org brn, blk & red brn .25 .20
282 A79 20m red brn & blk 1.75 1.40
283 A79 25m red brn, gray & black .55 .20
284 A79 30m aqua, tan & blk .75 .30
285 A79 35m dk car, yel & blk .75 .45
286 A79 40m brt bl, gray & blk 1.00 .45
287 A79 50m org brn, gray & blk 1.50 .20
288 A79 100m gray, buff, blk & red 5.00 .20

Perf. 13x14

289 A80 250m dull yel, grn & blk 1.50 .50
290 A80 500m multicolored 3.50 1.00
291 A80 £1 gray, lt gray & black 3.00 7.00
Nos. 278-291 (14) 20.60 12.50

Electric Power Station, Limassol — A81

Arghaka-Maghounda Dam — A82

Designs: 35m, Troodos Highway. 50m, Cyprus Hilton Hotel. 100m, Ships in Famagusta Harbor.

Perf. 14x13½, 13½x14

1967, Apr. 10 Litho. Wmk. 344

292 A81 10m lt brn, dark brn & yellow .20 .20
293 A82 15m lt bl, bl & grn .25 .25
294 A82 35m dark gray, indigo & dark grn .35 .35
295 A82 50m gray, olive & blue .35 .35
296 A82 100m gray, ind & bl .35 .35
Nos. 292-296 (5) 1.50 1.50

1st development program, 1962-66, completion.

Europa Issue, 1967

Common Design Type

1967, May 2 *Perf. 13x14*

Size: 21x37mm

297 CD10 20m yel grn & olive 1.25 .20
298 CD10 30m rose vio & pur 1.25 .25
299 CD10 150m pale brn & brn 5.00 2.00
Nos. 297-299 (3) 7.50 2.45

Javelin Thrower, Map of Eastern Mediterranean and "Victory" — A83

Map of Eastern Mediterranean, Victory Statue and: 35m, Runner. 100m, High jumper. 250m, Amphora, map of Eastern Mediterranean and Victory statue.

Perf. 13½x13

1967, Sept. 4 Litho. Wmk. 344

300 A83 15m multicolored .20 .20
301 A83 35m multicolored .30 .25
302 A83 100m multicolored .60 .60

Size: 97x77mm

Imperf

303	A83	250m multicolored	3.00	*5.50*
		Nos. 300-303 (4)	4.10	6.55

Cyprus-Crete-Salonika Athletic Games.

Marble Forum at Salamis, Church of St. Barnabas and Bellapais Abbey A84

ITY Emblem and: 40m, Famagusta Beach. 50m, Plane and Nicosia International Airport. 100m, Youth Hostel and skiing on Mt. Troodos.

Perf. 13½x13

1967, Oct. 16 Litho. Wmk. 344

304	A84	10m multicolored	.20	.20
305	A84	40m multicolored	.20	*1.00*
306	A84	50m multicolored	.30	.20
307	A84	100m multicolored	.50	*1.00*
		Nos. 304-307 (4)	1.20	2.40

Intl. Tourist Year, 1967.

St. Andrew, 6th Century Mosaic — A85

Crucifixion, 15th Century — A86

The Three Kings, 15th Century Fresco — A87

1967, Nov. 8 ***Perf. 13x13½***

308	A85	25m multicolored	.20	.20
309	A86	50m multicolored	.20	.20
310	A87	75m multicolored	.20	.20
		Nos. 308-310 (3)	.60	.60

St. Andrew's Monastery, cent. (25m); Exhibition of Art of Cyprus, Paris, Nov. 7, 1967-Jan. 3, 1968 (50m); 20th anniv. of UNESCO (75m).

Human Rights Flame and Stars — A88

Designs: 90m, Human Rights flame and UN emblem. 250m, Scroll showing Article One of the Declaration of Human Rights.

Perf. 13½x14

1968, Mar. 18 Litho. Wmk. 344

311	A88	50m multicolored	.20	.20
312	A88	90m multicolored	.40	.60

Size: 110x90mm

Imperf

313	A88	250m multicolored	1.25	*4.00*
		Nos. 311-313 (3)	1.85	4.80

Intl. Human Rights Year.

Europa Issue, 1968

Common Design Type

1968, Apr. 29 ***Perf. 14x13½***

314	CD11	20m multicolored	*1.75*	.35
315	CD11	30m dk car rose, gray brn & blk	*.75*	.35
316	CD11	150m multicolored	*1.75*	2.00
		Nos. 314-316 (3)	4.25	2.70

Boy Holding Milk, UNICEF Emblem A89

Aesculapius and WHO Emblem — A90

Perf. 14x13½, 13½x14

1968, Sept. 2 Wmk. 344

317	A89	35m dk red, lt brn & blk	.20	.20
318	A90	50m gray ol, blk & grn	.20	.20

21st anniv. of UNICEF (No. 317), 20th anniv. of the WHO (No. 318).

Discus Thrower — A91

ILO Emblem — A92

25m, Runners. 100m, Stadium, Mexico City.

Perf. 13½x14, 14x13½

1968, Oct. 24 Litho.

319	A91	10m multicolored	.20	.20
320	A91	25m vio blue & multi	.20	.20
321	A91	100m blue & multi, horiz.	.30	*1.00*
		Nos. 319-321 (3)	.70	1.40

19th Olympic Games, Mexico City, 10/12-27.

Perf. 12x13½

1969, Mar. 3 Wmk. 344

322	A92	50m bl, vio bl & org brn	.20	.20
323	A92	90m gray, blk & org brn	.25	.25

ILO, 50th anniv.

Ancient Map of Cyprus A93

Design: 50m, Medieval map of Cyprus.

Perf. 13½x13

1969, Apr. 7 Wmk. 344

324	A93	35m multicolored	.20	.20
325	A93	50m olive & multi	.20	.20

1st Intl. Congress of Cypriot Studies.

Europa Issue, 1969

"EUROPA" and "CEPT" CD12

1969, Apr. 28 Litho. ***Perf. 14x13½***

326	CD12	20m bl, blk & gray	*.75*	.20
327	CD12	30m cop red, blk & ocher	*.75*	.20
328	CD12	150m grn, blk & yel	*3.25*	1.50
		Nos. 326-328 (3)	4.75	1.90

CEPT, 10th anniv.

European Roller — A95

Birds: 15m, Audouin's gull. 20m, Cyprus warbler. 30m, Eurasian jay, vert. 40m, Hoopoe, vert. 90m, Eleonora's falcon, vert.

Perf. 13½x12, 12x13½

1969, July 7 Wmk. 344

329	A95	5m multicolored	.50	.20
330	A95	15m multicolored	.70	.20
331	A95	20m multicolored	.70	.20
332	A95	30m multicolored	.70	.25
333	A95	40m multicolored	.80	.25
334	A95	90m multicolored	1.75	4.00
		Nos. 329-334 (6)	5.15	5.10

Nativity, Mural, 1192 A96

Christmas: 45m, Nativity, mural in Church of Ayios Nicolaos tis Steghis, 14th century. 250m, Virgin and Child between Archangels Michael and Gabriel, mosaic in Church of Panayia Angeloktistos, 6th-7th centuries. Design of 20m is a mural in Church of Panayia tou Arakos, Lagoudhera.

1969, Nov. 24 Litho. ***Perf. 13½x13***

335	A96	20m multicolored	.20	.20
336	A96	45m multicolored	.30	.25

Size: 109x89mm

Imperf

337	A96	250m dk blue & multi	5.00	*10.00*
		Nos. 335-337 (3)	5.50	10.45

Mahatma Gandhi A97

1970, Jan. 26 ***Perf. 14x13½***

338	A97	25m multicolored	.20	.20
339	A97	75m multicolored	.40	.50

Birth cent. of Mohandas K. Gandhi (1869-1948), leader in India's struggle for independence.

Europa Issue, 1970

Interwoven Threads CD13

1970, May 4 Litho. Wmk. 344

340	CD13	20m brn, yel & org	*.30*	.30
341	CD13	30m brt bl, yel & org	*.30*	.30
342	CD13	150m brt rose lil, yel & orange	*3.75*	3.75
		Nos. 340-342 (3)	4.35	4.35

Landscape with Flowers — A99

Designs: Various landscapes with flowers.

Perf. 13x14

1970, Aug. 3 Litho. Wmk. 344

343	A99	10m multicolored	.20	.20
344	A99	50m multicolored	.20	.20
345	A99	90m multicolored	.70	*1.00*
		Nos. 343-345 (3)	1.10	1.40

European Nature Conservation Year.

Education Year Emblem — A100

Grapes and Partridge (Mosaic) A101

UN Emblem, Dove, Globe and Wheat A102

Perf. 13x14, 14x13

1970, Sept. 7 Litho. Wmk. 344

346	A100	5m tan, blk & brn	.20	.20
347	A101	15m multicolored	.20	.20
348	A102	75m multicolored	.20	.20
		Nos. 346-348 (3)	.60	.60

Intl. Education Year (No. 346); 50th General Assembly of the Intl. Vine and Wine Office (No. 347); 25th anniv. of the UN (No. 348).

Virgin and Child, Mural from Podhithou Church, 16th Century — A103

Perf. 14x14½

1970, Nov. 23 Photo. Unwmk.

349	A103	Strip of three	.40	.40
a.		25m Left angel	.20	.20
b.		25m Virgin and Child	.20	.20
c.		25m Right angel	.20	.20
350	A103	75m multicolored	.30	.30

Christmas.

Design of No. 349 is same as No. 350, but divided by perforation into 3 stamps with 25m denomination each. Size of No. 349: 71x46mm; size of No. 350: 42x31mm.

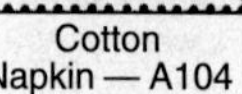

Cotton Napkin — A104

Festive Costume — A105

Drinking Cup, 7th Cent. B.C. A106

Mouflon from Mosaic Pavement, 3rd Century — A107

Cypriot Art: 5m, St. George, bas-relief on pine board, 19th cent. 20m, kneeling donors, painting, Church of St. Mamas, 1465. 25m, Mosaic head, 5th cent. A.D. 30m, Athena mounting horse-drawn chariot, terracotta figurine, 5th cent. B.C. 40m, Shepherd playing pipe, 14th cent. fresco. 50m, Woman's head, limestone, 3rd cent. B.C. 75m, Angel, mosaic, 6th cent. 90m, Mycenaean silver bowl, 14th cent. B.C. 500m, Woman and tree, decoration from amphora, 7th-6th cent. B.C. £1, God statue (horned helmet), from Enkomi, 12th cent. B.C., vert.

Perf. 12½x13½ (A104), 13x14 (A105), 14x13 (A106), 13½x13, 13x13½ (A107)

1971, Feb. 22 Litho. Wmk. 344

351 A104 3m blk, red & brn .40 .50
352 A104 5m citron, red brn & black .20 .20
353 A105 10m multicolored .20 .30
354 A106 15m bister brn, blk & slate .25 .20
355 A105 20m slate, red brn & black .45 .50
356 A105 25m multicolored .35 .20
357 A106 30m multicolored .35 .20
358 A105 40m gray & multi 1.25 1.10
359 A105 50m bl, bis & blk 1.00 .20
360 A105 75m cit & multi 2.25 1.25
361 A106 90m multicolored 2.50 2.50
362 A107 250m lt red brn, brn & black 1.90 .40
363 A107 500m tan & multi 1.00 .50
364 A107 £1 multicolored 1.90 .75
Nos. 351-364 (14) 14.00 8.80

For surcharges & overprints see #403, 424-427, 444, RA1.

Europa Issue, 1971

"Fraternity, Co-operation, Common Effort" — CD14

1971, May 3 Litho. *Perf. 14x13½*
Size: 36½x23½mm

365 CD14 20m lt bl, vio bl & blk *.35* .20
366 CD14 30m brt yel grn, grn & blk *.35* .20
367 CD14 150m yel, grn & blk *3.00* 2.50
Nos. 365-367 (3) *3.70* 2.90

Archbishop Kyprianos, 1821 — A109

Paintings: 30m, Young Greek Taking Oath, horiz. 100m, Bishop Germanòs of Patras Declaring Greek Independence.

Perf. 13x13½, 13½x13

1971, July 9 Wmk. 344

368 A109 15m multicolored .20 .20
369 A109 30m multicolored .20 .20
370 A109 100m multicolored .30 .30
Nos. 368-370 (3) .70 .70

150th anniversary of Greek independence.

Arch and Castle A110

Tourist Publicity: 25m, Decorated gourd and sun over shore, vert. 60m, Mountain road, vert. 100m, Village church.

Perf. 13½x13, 13x13½

1971, Sept. 20

371 A110 15m vio bl & multi .20 .20
372 A110 25m ocher & multi .20 .20
373 A110 60m green & multi .25 .25
374 A110 100m blue & multi .25 .25
Nos. 371-374 (4) .90 .90

Virgin and Child — A111

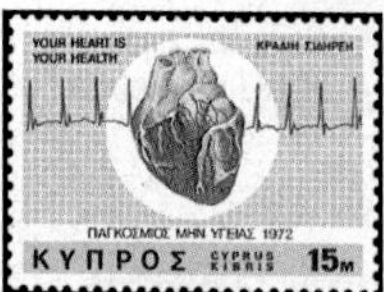

Heart and Electrocardiogram — A112

1971, Nov. 22 *Perf. 13½x14*

375 A111 10m shown .20 .20
376 A111 50m The Three Kings .20 .20
377 A111 100m Shepherds .30 .30
a. Strip of 3, Nos. 375-377 .75 .75

Christmas.

1972, Apr. 11 *Perf. 13½x12½*

378 A112 15m bister & multi .20 .20
379 A112 50m brown & multi .30 .30

"Your heart is your health," World Health Day.

Europa Issue 1972

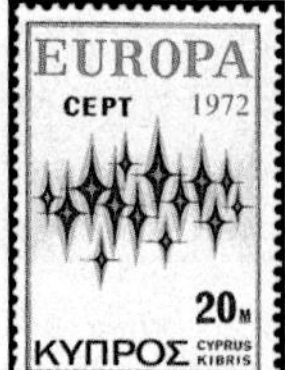

Sparkles, Symbolic of Communications CD15

1972, May 22 *Perf. 12½x13½*

380 CD15 20m brn, org & fawn .50 .20
381 CD15 30m pur, org & lilac .50 .45
382 CD15 150m dk ol, org & brt green 3.00 2.50
Nos. 380-382 (3) 4.00 3.15

Archery, Olympic and Motion Emblems A114

1972, July 24 *Perf. 14x13½*

383 A114 10m shown .20 .20
384 A114 40m Wrestling .25 .25
385 A114 100m Soccer .55 .55
Nos. 383-385 (3) 1.00 1.00

20th Olympic Games, Munich, 8/26-9/11.

Apollo, Silver Stater, Marion, 5th Century B.C. A115

Silver Staters of Cyprus: 30m, Eagle's head, Paphos, c. 460 B.C. 40m, Pallas Athena, Lapithos, 388-387 B.C. 100m, Sphinx (obverse) and lotus flower (reverse), Idalion, c. 460 B.C.

1972, Sept. 25 Litho. Wmk. 344
Coins in Silver

386 A115 20m lt grnsh bl & blk .20 .20
387 A115 30m pale bl & silver .20 .20
388 A115 40m ol bister & black .35 .30
389 A115 100m pale brn & blk 1.25 1.10
Nos. 386-389 (4) 2.00 1.80

Bathing the Christ Child — A116

Christmas: 20m, The Three Kings. 100m, Nativity. 250m, The Nativity, 1466, mural in Church of the Holy Cross, Platanistasa. The designs of the 10m, 20m, 100m, show details from mural shown entirely on 250m.

1972, Nov. 20 Litho. *Perf. 13½x14*

390 A116 10m multicolored .30 .30
391 A116 20m multicolored .30 .30
392 A116 100m multicolored .40 .40

Size: 110x90mm
Imperf

393 A116 250m multicolored 3.00 3.00
Nos. 390-393 (4) 4.00 4.00

Landscape, Troodos Mountains A117

100m, FIS Congress emblem and map of Cyprus.

Perf. 14x13½

1973, Mar. 13 Wmk. 344

394 A117 20m blue & multi .20 .20
395 A117 100m blue & multi .40 .40

29th Meeting of the Intl. Ski Fed. (FIS), Nicosia, June 1973.

Europa Issue 1973

Post Horn of Arrows CD16

1973, May 7 Size: 37x21mm

396 CD16 20m lt bl & multi .20 .20
397 CD16 30m multicolored .40 .30
398 CD16 150m multicolored 2.25 2.00
Nos. 396-398 (3) 2.85 2.50

Archbishop's Palace, Nicosia — A119

Traditional Architecture: 30m, Konak, Nicosia, 18th century, vert. 50m, House, Gourri, 1850, vert. 100m, House, Rizokarpaso, 1772.

1973, July 23 *Perf. 14x13, 13x14*

399 A119 20m multicolored .20 .20
400 A119 30m multicolored .20 .20
401 A119 50m multicolored .20 .20
402 A119 100m multicolored .50 .50
Nos. 399-402 (4) 1.10 1.10

No. 354 Surcharged

1973, Sept. 24 *Perf. 14x13*

403 A106 20m on 15m multi .25 .25

Cyprus Scout Emblem — A120

EEC Emblem A122

Cyprus Airways Emblem — A121

35m, FAO emblem. 100m, INTERPOL emblem.

1973, Sept. 24 *Perf. 13x14, 14x13*

404 A120 10m brn ol, ol & buff .25 .25
405 A121 25m pur, bl & plum .25 .25
406 A121 35m grn, gray grn & citron .25 .25
407 A122 50m black & blue .25 .25
408 A120 100m brown & fawn .50 .50
Nos. 404-408 (5) 1.50 1.50

60th anniv. of Cyprus Boy Scout Organ.; association of Cyprus with EEC; 10th anniv. of FAO; 25th anniv. of Cyprus Airways; 50th anniv. of Intl. Criminal Police Organization.

Archangel Gabriel — A123

Virgin and Child — A124

Christmas: 100m, Panaya tou Araka Church, horiz. Designs of 10m, 20m are from wall paintings in Arakas Church.

1973, Nov. 26 **Wmk. 344**

409	A123	10m multicolored	.20	.20
410	A124	20m multicolored	.20	.20
411	A124	100m multicolored	.60	.60
		Nos. 409-411 (3)	1.00	1.00

Grapes — A125

Rape of Europa — A126

1974, Mar. 18 **Litho.** ***Perf. 13x14***

412	A125	25m shown	.20	.20
413	A125	50m Grapefruit	.20	.20
414	A125	50m Oranges	.20	.20
415	A125	50m Lemons	.30	.30
a.		Strip of 3, #413-415	.90	.90
		Nos. 412-415 (4)	.90	.90

Europa Issue 1974

1974, Apr. 29

Design shows a silver stater of Marion, second half of 5th century B.C.

416	A126	10m org brn & multi	.30	.30
417	A126	40m multicolored	.60	.60
418	A126	150m dk car & multi	2.10	2.10
		Nos. 416-418 (3)	3.00	3.00

Solon, 3rd Century Mosaic A127

Designs: 10m, Front page of "History of Cyprus," by Archimandrite Kyprianos, 1788, vert. 100m, St. Neophytos, mural, vert. 250m, Maps of Cyprus and Greek Islands, by Abraham Ortelius, 1584.

Perf. 13x14, 14x13

1974, July 22 **Litho.** **Wmk. 344**

419	A127	10m multicolored	.20	.20
420	A127	25m multicolored	.20	.20
421	A127	100m multicolored	.85	.85

Size: 110x90mm

Imperf

422	A127	250m multicolored	2.75	*3.00*
		Nos. 419-422 (4)	4.00	4.25

2nd Intl. Congress of Cypriot Studies, Nicosia, Sept. 15-21. No. 422 has simulated perforations.

Nos. 353, 358-359, 362 Overprinted

Perf. 13x14, 13½x13

1974, Oct. 14 **Litho.**

424	A105	10m multicolored	.25	.25
425	A105	40m multicolored	.35	.35
426	A105	50m multicolored	.35	.35
427	A107	250m multicolored	.80	.80
		Nos. 424-427 (4)	1.75	1.75

UN Security Council Resolution No. 353 to end hostilities on Cyprus. Overprint is in 3 lines on No. 427.

Virgin and Child, 1466 A129

Adoration of the Kings, c. 1500 — A130

Christmas: 100m, Flight into Egypt, mural, Monastery Church of Ayios Meophytos, c. 1500. (50m is from same church). Mural on 10m is in Church of Stavros tou Ahiasmati.

Perf. 14x13, 13x14

1974, Dec. 2 **Wmk. 344**

429	A129	10m multicolored	.20	.20
430	A130	50m multicolored	.20	.20
431	A129	100m multicolored	.40	.40
		Nos. 429-431 (3)	.80	.80

Disabled Persons, Emblem — A131

Council of Europe Flag — A132

1975, Feb. 17 **Unwmk.** ***Perf. 14½***

432	A131	30m ocher & ultra	.20	.20
433	A132	100m multicolored	.70	.60

8th European Meeting of the Intl. Society for the Rehabilitation of Disabled Persons (30m; design shows society's emblem); 25th anniv. of Council of Europe (100m).

First Mail Coach in Cyprus A133

1975, Feb. 17

434	A133	20m multicolored	.20	.20
435	A133	50m ultra & multi	1.10	.40

Centenary (in 1974) of UPU.

The Distaff, by Michael Kashalos — A134

Europa (Paintings): 30m, Still Life, by Christoforos Savva. 150m, Virgin and Child of Liopetri, by Georghios P. Georghiou.

Perf. 13½x14½

1975, Apr. 28 **Photo.**

436	A134	20m multicolored	.20	.20
437	A134	30m multicolored	.20	.20
438	A134	150m multicolored	1.00	.85
a.		Strip of 3, #436-438	1.40	1.40

Red Cross Flag over Cyprus — A135

Nurse and Nurses Emblem A136

Steatite Female Figure, c. 3000 B.C. — A137

Perf. 12½x13½, 13½x12½

1975, Aug. 4 **Litho.** **Wmk. 344**

439	A135	25m blue green & red	.20	.20
440	A136	30m dp blue & lt grn	.25	.25
441	A137	75m multicolored	.40	.40
		Nos. 439-441 (3)	.85	.85

Cyprus Red Cross, 25th anniv.; Intl. Nurses' Day 1975; IWY.

Submarine Cable — A138

International Telephone A139

Perf. 12½x13½, 13½x12½

1975, Oct. 13 **Litho.**

442	A138	50m multicolored	.25	.20
443	A139	100m purple & org	.50	.45

Telecommunications achievements.

No. 351 Surcharged

1976, Jan. 5 ***Perf. 12½x13½***

444	A104	10m on 3m multi	.20	.20

Vessel in Shape of Woman, 19th Century — A140

Composite Vessel, 2100-2000 B.C. — A141

Europa: 100m, Byzantine goblet, 15th cent.

Perf. 13x14

1976, May 3 **Litho.** **Wmk. 344**

445	A140	20m violet & multi	.25	.20
446	A141	60m gray & multi	.70	.70
447	A140	100m brown & multi	1.25	1.25
		Nos. 445-447 (3)	2.20	2.15

Self-help Housing A142

Cyprus Airways Jet — A143

Designs: 25m, Women sewing in front of tents. 30m, Aforestation.

1976, May 3 ***Perf. 14x13***

448	A142	10m multicolored	.20	.20
449	A142	25m multicolored	.20	.20
450	A142	30m multicolored	.20	.20
451	A143	60m multicolored	.30	.30
		Nos. 448-451 (4)	.90	.90

Re-activation of the economy.

Terracotta Statue, 7th-6th Centuries B.C. — A144

Bronze Plate with Inscription, Idalion, 5th Century B.C. A145

Designs: 10m, Limestone head of bearded man, 5th cent. B.C. 20m, Gold necklace, Lamboussa, 6th cent. A.D. 25m, Terracotta warrior on horseback, 7th cent. B.C. 30m, Limestone figure, priest of Aphrodite, 5th cent. B.C. 50m, Mycenaean crater, 13th cent. B.C. 60m, Limestone sarcophagus, Amathus, 550-500 B.C. 100m, Gold bracelet, Lamboussa, 6th cent. A.D. 250m, Silver dish, Lamboussa, 6th cent. A.D. 500m, Bronze stand, 12th cent. B.C. £1, Marble statue of Artemis, Larnaca, 4th cent. B.C.

Perf. 12x13½

1976, June 7 **Wmk. 344**

Size: 22x33mm

452	A144	5m brn & multi	.20	.20
453	A144	10m gray & multi	.20	.20

Size: 24x37mm, 37x24mm

Perf. 13x14, 14x13

454	A144	20m red & multi	.20	.20
455	A144	25m lt brn & blk	.20	.20
456	A144	30m green & multi	.20	.20
457	A145	40m bis gray & blk	.20	.20
458	A145	50m brn & multi	.20	.20
459	A145	60m dk brn & multi	.25	.20
460	A145	100m crim & multi	.40	.35

Size: 28x40mm

Perf. 13x12½

461	A144	250m	dk bl & multi	.90	.80
462	A144	500m	yel & multi	1.75	1.75
463	A144	£1	slate & multi	3.75	3.50
			Nos. 452-463 (12)	8.45	8.00

George Washington A146

1976, July 5 ***Perf. 13x13½***

464	A146	100m	multicolored	.70	.60

American Bicentennial.

Montreal Olympic Games Emblem — A147

Various Sports A148

100m, like 60m, with different sports.

1976, July 5 **Unwmk.** ***Perf. 14***

465	A147	20m	yel, blk & dk car	.20	.20
466	A148	60m	ultra & multi	.30	.30
467	A148	100m	lilac & multi	.50	.50
			Nos. 465-467 (3)	1.00	1.00

21st Olympic Games, Montreal, Canada, July 17-Aug. 1.

Children in Library — A149

Low-cost Housing Development A150

Hands Shielding Eye — A151

Perf. 13½x14, 13x13½

1976, Sept. 27 **Litho.** **Wmk. 344**

468	A149	40m	black & multi	.30	.30
469	A150	50m	multicolored	.25	.20
470	A151	80m	ultra & multi	.45	.35
			Nos. 468-470 (3)	1.00	.85

Books for Children (40m); Habitat, UN Conference on Human Settlements, Vancouver, Canada, May 31-June 11 (50m); World Health Day: Foresight prevents blindness (80m).

Archangel Michael — A152

Christmas: 15m, Archangel Gabriel. 150m, Nativity. Icons in Ayios Neophytis Monastery, 16th century.

1976, Nov. 15 **Unwmk.** ***Perf. 12½***

471	A152	10m	multicolored	.20	.20
472	A152	15m	multicolored	.20	.20
473	A152	150m	multicolored	.85	.75
			Nos. 471-473 (3)	1.25	1.15

Landscape, by A. Diamantis — A154

Europa (Paintings): 60m, Trees and Meadow, by T. Kanthos. 120m, Harbor, by V. Ioannides.

Perf. 13½x13

1977, May 2 **Litho.** **Unwmk.**

475	A154	20m	multicolored	.20	.20
476	A154	60m	multicolored	.45	.45
477	A154	120m	multicolored	.90	.80
			Nos. 475-477 (3)	1.55	1.45

Cyprus No. 196 — A155

Perf. 13x13½

1977, June 13 **Litho.** **Wmk. 344**

478	A155	120m	multicolored	.55	.40

25th anniv. of reign of Queen Elizabeth II.

Silver Tetradrachm of Demetrios Poliorcetes — A156

Ancient Coins of Cyprus: 10m, Bronze coin of Emperor Trajan. 60m, Silver Tetradrachm of Ptolemy VIII. 100m, Gold octadrachm of Arsinoe II.

1977, June 13 **Unwmk.** ***Perf. 14***

479	A156	10m	multicolored	.20	.20
480	A156	40m	multicolored	.25	.20
481	A156	60m	multicolored	.35	.30
482	A156	100m	multicolored	.50	.50
			Nos. 479-482 (4)	1.30	1.20

Archbishop Makarios (1913-1977), Pres. of Cyprus — A157

20m, Archbishop in full vestments. 250m, Head.

Perf. 13x14

1977, Sept. 10 **Litho.** **Unwmk.**

483	A157	20m	multicolored	.20	.20
484	A157	60m	multicolored	.25	.20
485	A157	250m	multicolored	.95	.85
			Nos. 483-485 (3)	1.40	1.25

Handicrafts A158

Sputnik over Earth — A159

Designs: 40m, Map of Cyprus. 60m, Gold medals and sports emblems.

Perf. 13½x12

1977, Oct. 17 **Wmk. 344**

486	A158	20m	multicolored	.20	.20
487	A158	40m	multicolored	.20	.20
488	A158	60m	multicolored	.25	.25
489	A159	80m	multicolored	.35	.30
			Nos. 486-489 (4)	1.00	.95

Revitalization of handicrafts (20m); Man and the biosphere (40m); Gold medals won by secondary school students in France for long jump and 200 meter race (60m); 60th anniv. of Bolshevik Revolution (80m).

Nativity A160

Christmas (Children's Drawings): 10m, Three Kings following the star. 150m, Flight into Egypt.

Perf. 14x13½

1977, Nov. 21 **Litho.** **Unwmk.**

490	A160	10m	multicolored	.20	.20
491	A160	40m	multicolored	.20	.20
492	A160	150m	multicolored	.75	.70
			Nos. 490-492 (3)	1.15	1.10

Demetrios Libertis (1866-1937) — A161

150m, Vasilis Michaelides (1849-1917).

1978, Mar. 6 **Wmk. 344** ***Perf. 14x13***

493	A161	40m	bister & olive	.20	.20
494	A161	150m	gray, ver & blk	.60	.55

Cypriot poets.

Chrysorrhogiatissa Monastery — A162

Europa: 75m, Kolossi Castle. 125m, Municipal Library, Paphos.

Perf. 14½x13

1978, Apr. 24 **Litho.** **Unwmk.**

495	A162	25m	multicolored	.20	.20
496	A162	75m	multicolored	.40	.40
497	A162	125m	multicolored	.90	.90
			Nos. 495-497 (3)	1.50	1.50

Makarios as Archbishop 1950-1977 A163

"The Great Leader" — A164

Archbishop Makarios: 25m, Exiled, Seychelles, 1956-1957. 50m, President of Cyprus, 1960-1977. 75m, Soldier of Christ. 100m, Freedom fighter.

Perf. 14x14½

1978, Aug. 3 **Litho.** **Unwmk.**

498	A163	15m	multicolored	.20	.20
499	A163	25m	multicolored	.20	.20
500	A163	50m	multicolored	.25	.25
501	A163	75m	multicolored	.35	.35
502	A163	100m	multicolored	.50	.50
a.			Strip of 5, #498-502	1.50	1.50

Size: 110x80mm

Imperf

503	A164	300m	multicolored	5.00	4.00
			Nos. 498-503 (6)	6.50	5.50

Archbishop Makarios, President of Cyprus.

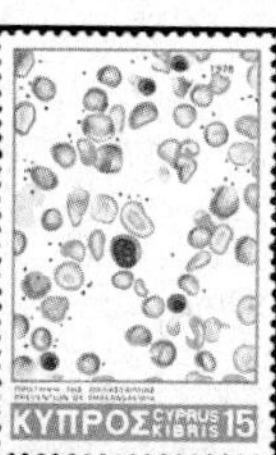

Blood Cells with Low Hemoglobin A165

Bust of Aristotle A166

Heads and Human Rights Emblem A167

Wilbur and Orville Wright, Flyer I A168

Perf. 13x14, 14x13

1978, Oct. 23 Unwmk. Litho.

504 A165 15m multicolored .20 .20
505 A166 35m multicolored .20 .20
506 A167 75m black .35 .35
507 A168 125m multicolored .50 .50
Nos. 504-507 (4) 1.25 1.25

Anemia prevention (15m); 2300th birth anniv. of Aristotle (35m); 30th anniv. of Universal Declaration of Human Rights (75m); 75th anniv. of first powered flight (125m).

Kiti Icon Stand — A169

Christmas: 35m, Athienou icon stand. 150m, Omodhos icon stand.

1978, Dec. 4 *Perf. 14x14½*

508 A169 15m multicolored .20 .20
509 A169 35m multicolored .20 .20
510 A169 150m multicolored .75 .75
Nos. 508-510 (3) 1.15 1.15

Venus Statue from Soli A170

125m, Birth of Venus, by Botticelli (detail).

1979, Mar. 12 Litho. *Perf. 14x13½*

511 A170 75m multicolored .35 .35
512 A170 125m multicolored .55 .55

Mail Coach, Envelope and Truck A171

Europa: 75m, Old telephone, dish antenna and satellite. 125m, Steamship, jet and envelopes.

1979, Apr. 30 Litho. *Perf. 14x13½*

513 A171 25m multicolored .35 .35
514 A171 75m multicolored .65 .65
515 A171 125m multicolored 1.50 1.50
Nos. 513-515 (3) 2.50 2.50

Peacock Wrasse A172

Designs: 50m, Black partridge, vert. 75m, Cyprus cedar, vert. 125m, Mule.

Perf. 13½x12½, 12½x13½

1979, June 25 Litho.

516 A172 25m multicolored .20 .20
517 A172 50m multicolored .25 .20
518 A172 75m multicolored .35 .30
519 A172 125m multicolored .55 .50
Nos. 516-519 (4) 1.35 1.20

Children Holding Globe, UNESCO Emblem — A173

Dove, Magnifying Glass, Album A174

Lord Kitchener, Map of Cyprus A175

Smiling Child, IYC Emblem A176

Soccer A177

Rotary Emblem — A178

1979, Oct. 1 Litho. *Perf. 12½*

520 A173 15m multicolored .20 .20
521 A174 25m multicolored .20 .20
522 A175 50m multicolored .25 .25
523 A176 75m multicolored .30 .25
524 A177 100m multicolored .50 .45
525 A178 125m multicolored .55 .50
Nos. 520-525 (6) 2.00 1.85

Intl. Bureau of Education, Geneva, 50th anniv.; Cyprus Philatelic Society, 20th anniv.; Horatio Herbert Kitchener's survey of Cyprus, cent.; IYC; European Soccer Assoc., 25th anniv.; Rotary Club of Cyprus, 75th anniv.

Jesus, Icon, 12th Century — A179

Christmas (Icons): 35m, Nativity, 16th cent. 150m, Virgin and Child, 12th cent.

Perf. 13½x14, 13x14

1979, Nov. 5 Litho.

Sizes: 24x37mm; 27x40mm (35m)

526 A179 15m multicolored .20 .20
527 A179 35m multicolored .20 .20
528 A179 150m multicolored .50 .40
Nos. 526-528 (3) .90 .80

Cyprus No. 1, Nicosia Cancel A180

Cyprus Stamp Centenary: 125m, #3, Kyrenia cancel. 175m, #6, Larnaca cancel. 500m, #1-6.

1980, Mar. 17 Litho. *Perf. 14x13*

529 A180 40m multicolored .20 .20
530 A180 125m multicolored .50 .50
531 A180 175m multicolored .75 .75

Size: 105x85mm

Imperf

532 A180 500m multicolored 2.25 2.25
Nos. 529-532 (4) 3.70 3.70

Holy Cross, St. Barnabas Church, Ayiasmati — A181

Europa: 125m, Zenon of Citium, Ny Carsberg Glyptothek, Copenhagen.

1980, Apr. 28 *Perf. 12½*

533 A181 40m multicolored .20 .20
534 A181 125m multicolored .40 .40

Sailing, Moscow '80 Emblem A182

1980, June 23 Litho. *Perf. 14x13*

535 A182 40m shown .20 .20
536 A182 125m Swimming .40 .40
537 A182 200m Gymnast .70 .70
Nos. 535-537 (3) 1.30 1.30

22nd Summer Olympic Games, Moscow, July 19-Aug. 3.

Gold Necklace — A183

Clay Amphora — A184

Archaeological finds on Cyprus, 12th cent. B.C. to 3rd cent. A.D. 15m, 40m, 150m, 500m, horiz.

Perf. 13½x14, 14x13½

1980, Sept. 15 Litho. Wmk. 344

538 A183 10m shown .30 .30
539 A184 15m Bronze cow .30 .30
540 A184 25m shown .30 .30
541 A184 40m Lion, gold ring .40 .40
542 A184 50m Bronze caul-dron .40 .40
543 A184 75m Stele 1.25 1.25
544 A184 100m Clay jug .90 .90
545 A184 125m Warrior, terra-cotta bust .90 .90
546 A184 150m Lions attack-ing bull 1.50 1.50
547 A184 175m Faience and enamel vase 1.00 1.00
548 A184 200m Warrior god, bronze 1.00 1.00
549 A184 500m Stone bowl 1.00 1.00
550 A183 £1 Ivory plaque 1.25 1.25
551 A183 £2 Leda and the swan, mosaic 2.50 2.50
Nos. 538-551 (14) 13.00 13.00

For surcharges see Nos. 584, 600-611.

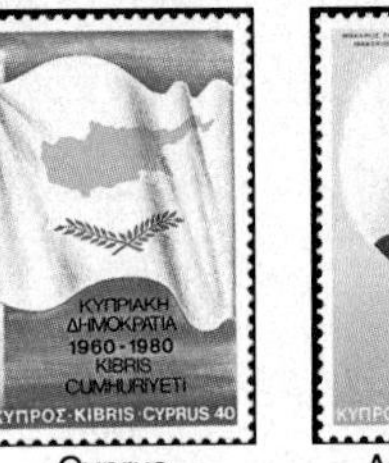

Cyprus Flag — A185

Archbishop Makarios — A187

Treaty Signing Establishing Republic, 20th Anniversary — A186

1980, Oct. 1 *Perf. 13½x14, 14x13*

552 A185 40m multicolored .20 .20
553 A186 125m multicolored .45 .45
554 A187 175m multicolored .65 .65
Nos. 552-554 (3) 1.30 1.30

Dove and Woman A188

Perf. 14x13

1980, Nov. 29 Litho. Wmk. 344

555 A188 40m shown .20 .20
556 A188 125m Dove and man .60 .60
a. Pair, #555-556 .80 .80

Intl. Palestinian Solidarity Day.

Pulpit, Tripiotis Church, Nicosia — A189

Christmas: 100m, Iconostatis (Holy Door), Panayia Church, Paralimni. 125m, Pulpit, Ayios Lazaros Church, Larnaca.

1980, Nov. 29 *Perf. 13½x14*

557 A189 25m multicolored .20 .20

Size: 24x37mm

558 A189 100m multicolored .40 .40

Size: 21x37mm

559 A189 125m multicolored .50 .50
Nos. 557-559 (3) 1.10 1.10

Europa Issue 1981

Folk Dance — A190

1981, May 4 Photo. *Perf. 14*

560 A190 40m shown .20 .20
561 A190 175m Dance, diff. .90 .90

Self-portrait, by Leonardo Da Vinci — A191

The Last Supper, by Da Vinci — A192

Perf. 13½x14, 12½x13½

1981, June 15 Wmk. 344 Litho.

562 A191 50m shown .25 .25
563 A192 125m shown .65 .65
564 A191 175m Lace pattern, Milan Cathedral .90 .90
Nos. 562-564 (3) 1.80 1.80

Da Vinci's visit to Cyprus, 500th anniv.

Ophrys Kotschyi — A193

Designs: Orchids.

1981, July 6 *Perf. 13½x14*

565 A193 25m shown .25 .20
566 A193 50m Orchis puntulata .45 .40
567 A193 75m Ophrys argolica elegantis .65 .60
568 A193 150m Epipactis veratrifolia 1.40 1.25
a. Block of 4, #565-568 3.25 3.25

Prince Charles and Lady Diana, St. Paul's Cathedral A194

Perf. 14x13

1981, Sept. 28 Wmk. 344

569 A194 200m multicolored 1.00 1.00

Royal wedding.

Heinrich von Stephan (1831-1897), UPU Founder — A195

World Food Day (Oct. 16) A196

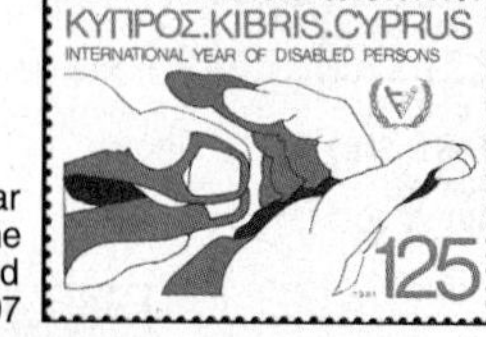

Intl. Year of the Disabled A197

European Campaign for Urban Renaissance — A198

1981, Sept. 28

570 A195 25m multicolored .20 .20
571 A196 40m multicolored .20 .20
572 A197 125m multicolored .55 .55
573 A198 150m multicolored .60 .60
Nos. 570-573 (4) 1.55 1.55

Our Lady of the Angels, Transfiguration Church, Palekhori A199

Christmas (Frescoes): 100m, Christ, Madonna of Arakas Church, Lagoudera, vert. 125m, Baptism of Christ, Our Lady of Assinou Church, Nikitari.

1981, Nov. 16 *Perf. 12½*

574 A199 25m multicolored .25 .20
575 A199 100m multicolored .60 .30
576 A199 125m multicolored .75 .40
Nos. 574-576 (3) 1.60 .90

Bathing Aphrodite, Sculpture, Soloi, 250 B.C. — A200

Design: 175m, Aphrodite Emerging from the Water, by Titian, 16th cent.

Perf. 13½x14

1982, Apr. 12 Litho. Wmk. 344

577 A200 125m multicolored .80 .65
578 A200 175m multicolored 1.00 .90

Europa Issue 1982

Liberation by Emperor Nicephorus II Phocas, 965 A.D. A201

Perf. 12½

1982, May 3 Photo. Unwmk.

579 A201 40m shown .70 .20
580 A201 175m Conversion of Sergius Paulus, 45 A.D. 1.10 1.10

Mosaic Chrismon A202

Cultural Heritage: 125m, King of Palaepaphos (High Priest of Aphrodite), sculpture, vert. 225m, Theseus Struggling with the Minotaur, mosaic.

1982, July 5 Litho. Wmk. 344

581 A202 50m multicolored .20 .20
582 A202 125m multicolored .50 .50
583 A202 225m multicolored .95 .95
Nos. 581-583 (3) 1.65 1.65

No. 543 Surcharged

1982, Sept. 6 Litho. *Perf. 13½x14*

584 A184 100m on 75m multi .40 .40

Scouting Year A203

Christmas A204

Perf. 13½x12½, 12½x13½

1982, Nov. 8 Wmk. 344

585 A203 100m Emblem, horiz. .40 .40
586 A203 125m Baden-Powell .50 .50
587 A203 175m Camp site, horiz. .70 .70
Nos. 585-587 (3) 1.60 1.60

Perf. 12½, 13½x14 (100m)

1982, Dec. 6

Designs: 25m, 250m, Christ Giving Holy Communion (bread, 25m; wine, 250m) to the Apostles, St. Neophytos Monastery Church, Paphos, horiz. 100m, Chalice, Church of St. Savvas, Nicosia.

588 A204 25m multicolored .20 .20
589 A204 100m multicolored .40 .40
590 A204 250m multicolored 1.00 1.00
Nos. 588-590 (3) 1.60 1.60

A204a

1983, Mar. 14 *Perf. 14x13½*

591 A204a 50m Cyprus Forest Industries, Ltd. .20 .20
592 A204a 125m Mosaic, 3rd cent. .35 .35
593 A204a 150m Dancers .45 .45
594 A204a 175m Royal Exhibition Building, Melbourne .50 .50
Nos. 591-594 (4) 1.50 1.50

Commonwealth Day.

Europa A205

50m, Cyprosyllabic script funerary stele, 6th cent. B.C. 200m, Copper ore, Enkomi ingot, 1400-1250 BC, bronze jug, 2nd cent.

1983, May 3 Photo. *Perf. 14½x14*

595 A205 50m multicolored .20 .20
596 A205 200m multicolored .80 .80

Local Butterflies A206

Wmk. 344

1983, June 28 Litho. *Perf. 12½*

597 A206 60m Pararge aegeria .40 .40
598 A206 130m Aricia medon .80 .80
599 A206 250m Glaucopsyche paphos 1.60 1.60
Nos. 597-599 (3) 2.80 2.80

Nos. 538-549 Surcharged

Perf. 13½x14, 14x13½

1983, Oct. 3 Litho. Wmk. 344

600 A183 1c on 10m multi .20 .20
601 A184 2c on 15m multi .20 .20
602 A184 3c on 25m multi .20 .20
603 A184 4c on 40m multi .20 .20
604 A184 5c on 50m multi .25 .25
605 A184 6c on 75m multi .25 .25
606 A184 10c on 100m multi .45 .45
607 A184 13c on 125m multi .60 .60
608 A184 15c on 150m multi .70 .70
609 A184 20c on 200m multi .90 .90
610 A184 25c on 175m multi 1.25 1.25
611 A184 50c on 500m multi 2.25 2.25
Nos. 600-611 (12) 7.45 7.45

Electricity Authority of Cyprus, 30th Anniv. — A207

World Communications Year — A208

Intl. Maritime Org., 25th Anniv. — A209

Universal Declaration of Human Rights, 35th Anniv. — A210

Nicos Kazantzakis, 100th Birth Anniv. — A211

Archbishop Makarios III, 70th Birth Anniv. — A212

1983, Oct. 31 Litho. *Perf. 13½x14*

612 A207 3c multicolored .20 .20
613 A208 6c multicolored .20 .20
614 A209 13c multicolored .40 .40
615 A210 15c multicolored .45 .45
616 A211 20c multicolored .65 .65
617 A212 25c multicolored .80 .80
Nos. 612-617 (6) 2.70 2.70

Christmas — A213

Designs: 4c, Belfry, St. Lazaros Church, Larnaca. 13c, Belfry, St. Varvara Church, Kaimakli, Nicosia. 20c, Belfry, St. Ioannis Church, Larnaca.

1983, Dec. 12 *Perf. 12½x14*

618 A213 4c multicolored .20 .20
619 A213 13c multicolored .55 .55
620 A213 20c multicolored .80 .80
Nos. 618-620 (3) 1.55 1.55

Waterside Cafe at the Marina, Larnaca — A214

19th Century engravings. Size of 6c: 41x27mm; 75c, 110x85mm.

Perf. 14½x14 (6c), 14, Imperf. (75c)

1984, Mar. 6

621 A214 6c shown .20 .20
622 A214 20c Bazaar, Larnaca .60 .60
623 A214 30c East Gate, Nicosia .85 .85
624 A214 75c St. Lazarus Church Interior, Larnaca 2.25 2.25
Nos. 621-624 (4) 3.90 3.90

Europa (1959-1984) — A215

1984, Apr. 30 Wmk. 344 *Perf. 12½*
625 A215 6c multicolored .50 .25
626 A215 15c multicolored 1.25 1.25

1984 Summer Olympics A216

1984, June 18 Litho. *Perf. 14*
627 A216 3c Running .20 .20
628 A216 4c Olympic column .20 .20
629 A216 13c Swimming .60 .60
630 A216 20c Gymnastics .90 .90
Nos. 627-630 (4) 1.90 1.90

Turkish Invasion, 10th Anniv. A217

1984, July 20 Litho. *Perf. 14x13½*
631 A217 15c Prisoners, barbed wire .45 .45
632 A217 20c Map .60 .60

Cyprus Philatelic Society, 25th Anniv. — A218

Cyprus Soccer Assoc., 50th Anniv. A219

George Papanicolaou (1883-1962), Cancer Researcher — A220

Medieval Map A221

1984, Oct. 15 Wmk. 344 *Perf. 12½*
633 A218 6c multicolored .25 .25
634 A219 10c multicolored .45 .45
635 A220 15c multicolored .75 .75
636 A221 25c multicolored 1.40 1.40
Nos. 633-636 (4) 2.85 2.85

Intl. Symposium of Cyprus Cartography and First Intl. Symposium on Medieval Paleography (25c).

Christmas — A222

1984, Nov. 26 Litho. *Perf. 12½*
637 A222 4c St. Mark .30 .30
638 A222 13c Gospel page (St. Mark) 1.00 1.00
639 A222 20c St. Luke 1.50 1.50
Nos. 637-639 (3) 2.80 2.80

Landscapes — A223

Perf. 15x14, 14x15
1985, Mar. 18 Litho.
640 A223 1c Autumn at Platania .20 .20
641 A223 2c Ayia Napa Monastery .20 .20
642 A223 3c Phine Village .20 .20
643 A223 4c Kykko Monastery .20 .20
644 A223 5c Beach at Makronissos .20 .20
645 A223 6c Village Street, Omodhos, vert. .20 .20
646 A223 10c Sea view .30 .30
647 A223 13c Water sports .40 .40
648 A223 15c Beach at Protaras .50 .50
649 A223 20c Forestry, vert. .60 .60
650 A223 25c Sunrise at Protaras, vert. .90 .75
651 A223 30c Village houses, Pera Orinis 1.25 .90
652 A223 50c Apollo Hylates Sanctuary 2.50 1.50
653 A223 £1 Troodos Mountain, vert. 5.00 5.00
654 A223 £5 Personification of Autumn, Dionyssos House, vert. 17.00 15.00
Nos. 640-654 (15) 29.65 26.15

For surcharges see Nos. 684-685, 712.

Europa A224

6c, Ceramic figures playing the double flute, lyre and tambourine, 7th-6th cent. B.C. 15c, Cypriot violin, lute, flute, the Fourth Women's Dance from the Cyprus Suite.

1985, May 6 Litho. *Perf. 12½*
655 A224 6c multicolored .90 .60
656 A224 15c multicolored 1.60 1.60

Republic of Cyprus, 25th Anniv. — A225

UN 40th Anniv. — A229

Natl. Liberation Movement, 30th Anniv. — A226

Intl. Youth Year A227

Solon Michaelides (1905-1979), Conductor, European Music Year — A228

Perf. 14½ (#657), 14½x14, 15 (#661)
1985, Sept. 23 Litho.
657 A225 4c multicolored .30 .30
658 A226 6c multicolored .45 .45
659 A227 13c multicolored .95 .95
660 A228 15c multicolored 1.10 1.10
661 A229 20c multicolored 1.40 1.40
Nos. 657-661 (5) 4.20 4.20

Christmas — A230

Murals of the St. Ioannis Lampadistis Monastery, Kalopanyiotis: 4c, Virgin Mary's Visit to Elizabeth. 13c, The Nativity. 20c, The Candlemas, Church of Our Lady of Assinous, Nikitari.

1985, Nov. 18 Litho. *Perf. 12½*
662 A230 4c multicolored .35 .35
663 A230 13c multicolored 1.00 1.00
664 A230 20c multicolored 1.65 1.65
Nos. 662-664 (3) 3.00 3.00

Hellenistic Platinum Spoon A231

Designs: 20c, Ionian helmet, foot of a sculpture. 25c, Union of Eros and Intellect personified, abstract. 30c, Statue profile.

1986, Feb. 17 *Perf. 15x14*
665 A231 15c multicolored .75 .75
666 A231 20c multicolored 1.10 1.10
667 A231 25c multicolored 1.40 1.40
668 A231 30c multicolored 1.75 1.75
a. Souv. sheet of 4, #665-668 16.00 16.00
Nos. 665-668 (4) 5.00 5.00

Construction of the New Archaeological Museum, Nicosia. Department of Antiquities, 50th anniv. No. 668a sold for £1.

Europa Issue

Mouflon, Cedar Trees A232

1986, Apr. 28 Litho. *Perf. 14x13*
669 A232 7c shown .50 .50
670 A232 17c Flamingos, Larnaca Salt Lake 2.10 2.10

Seashells A233

1986, July 1 *Perf. 14x13½*
671 A233 5c Chlamys pesfelis .45 .45
672 A233 7c Charonia variegata .55 .55
673 A233 18c Murex brandaris 1.25 1.25
674 A233 25c Cypraea spurca 1.75 1.75
Nos. 671-674 (4) 4.00 4.00

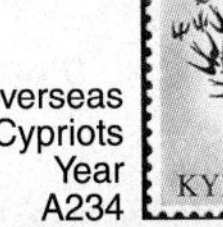

Overseas Cypriots Year A234

Halley's Comet A235

Anniversaries and events.

Perf. 13½x13
1986, Oct. 13 Litho. Wmk. 344
675 A234 15c multicolored 1.25 1.25
676 A235 18c shown 1.75 1.75
677 A235 18c Comet tail, Edmond Halley 1.75 1.75
a. Pair, #676-677 3.50 3.50
Nos. 675-677 (3) 4.75 4.75

No. 677a has continuous design.

Road Safety A236

1986, Nov. 10 *Perf. 14x13*
678 A236 5c Pedestrian crossing .75 .75
679 A236 7c Helmet, motorcycle controls 1.25 1.25
680 A236 18c Seatbelt, rearview mirror 3.00 3.00
Nos. 678-680 (3) 5.00 5.00

Intl. Peace Year, Christmas A237

Nativity frescoes (details): 5c, Church of Panayia tou Araka. 15c, Church of Panayia tou Moutoulla. 17c, Church of St. Nicholaos tis Steyis.

1986, Nov. 24 *Perf. 13½x14*
681 A237 5c multicolored .50 .50
682 A237 15c multicolored 1.50 1.50
683 A237 17c multicolored 1.75 1.75
Nos. 681-683 (3) 3.75 3.75

Nos. 645 and 647 Surcharged

Perf. 14x15, 15x14
1986, Oct. 13 Litho. Wmk. 344
684 A223 7c on 6c multi .75 .75
685 A223 18c on 13c multi 1.75 1.75

Miniature Sheet

Troodos Churches on UNESCO World Heritage List — A238

Churches and frescoes: a, Assinou, Nikitari. b, Moutoulla, Moutoullas. c, Podithou, Galata. d, Ayios Ioannis Lampadistis, Kalopanayiotis. e, Timios Stavros, Pelentri. f, Stavros Ayiasmati, Platanistasa. g, Archangelos Pedoula, Pedoulas. h, Ayios Nicolaos tis Steyis, Kakopetria. i, Araka, Lagoudera.

Perf. 12½

1987, Apr. 22 Photo. Unwmk.

686 Sheet of 9 10.00 10.00
a.-i. A238 15c any single 1.00 1.00

Europa Issue

Modern Architecture A239

Perf. 14x13½

1987, May 11 Litho. Wmk. 344

687 A239 7c Central Bank of Cyprus .70 .70
688 A239 18c Cyprus Communications Authority 1.50 1.50

Ships Named Kyrenia A240

1987, Oct. 3

689 A240 2c The Kyrenia, Kyrenia Castle .30 .20
690 A240 3c Kyrenia II, Perama Shipyard .40 .75
691 A240 5c Kyrenia II, Paphos .60 .25
692 A240 17c Kyrenia II, NY Harbor 1.50 1.00
Nos. 689-692 (4) 2.80 2.20

Blood Donation Coordinating Committee, 10th Anniv. — A241

European Campaign for Countryside — A242

TROODOS '87 — A243

Perf. 14x13½

1987, Nov. 2 Litho. Wmk. 344

693 A241 7c multicolored .55 .55
694 A242 15c multicolored 1.25 1.25
695 A243 20c multicolored 1.60 1.60
Nos. 693-695 (3) 3.40 3.40

Christmas A244

1987, Nov. 30 *Perf. 14*

696 A244 5c Babe in a manger .35 .35
697 A244 15c Ornament 1.25 1.25
698 A244 17c Fruit bowl 1.40 1.40
Nos. 696-698 (3) 3.00 3.00

Cyprus Customs Union in Cooperation with the EEC — A245

Perf. 13x13½

1988, Jan. 11 Wmk. 344

699 A245 15c Natl. and EEC flags 1.25 1.25
700 A245 18c Maps 1.60 1.60

A246

Europa (Communication and transportation): No. 701, Electronic mail (Intelpost). No. 702, Cellular telephone system. No. 703, Cyprus Airways, technology vs. ecology (jet, 3 flamingos). No. 704, Cyprus Airways (jet, 4 flamingos).

1988, May 9 *Perf. 14x14½*

701 A246 7c multicolored .75 .75
702 A246 7c multicolored .75 .75
a. Pair, #701-702 1.50 1.50
703 A246 18c multicolored 2.75 2.75
704 A246 18c multicolored 2.75 2.75
a. Pair, #703-704 5.50 5.50
Nos. 701-704 (4) 7.00 7.00

1988 Summer Olympics, Seoul — A247

Unwmk.

1988, June 27 Photo. *Perf. 12*

Granite Paper

705 A247 5c Sailing .40 .25
706 A247 7c Track .45 .45
707 A247 10c Marksmanship .50 .50
708 A247 20c Judo 1.10 1.10
Nos. 705-708 (4) 2.45 2.30

Non-Aligned Foreign Minister's Conference — A248

Designs: 10c, Natl. coat of arms. 50c, Jawaharlal Nehru, Tito, Gamal Abdel Nasser and Makarios III (1913-77).

Perf. 14x13½

1988, Sept. 5 Litho. Wmk. 344

709 A248 1c shown .20 .20
710 A248 10c multicolored .50 .50
711 A248 50c multicolored 2.75 2.75
Nos. 709-711 (3) 3.45 3.45

No. 643 Surcharged **15c**

1988, Oct. 3 Litho. *Perf. 15x14*

712 A223 15c on 4c multi 1.60 1.25

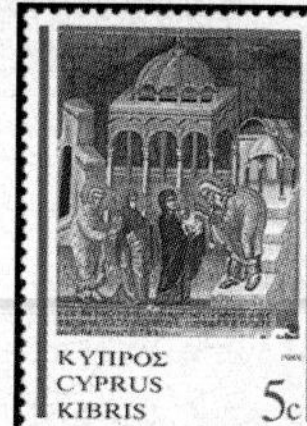

A249

A250

Christmas.

Perf. 13½x14

1988, Nov. 28 Litho. Wmk. 344

713 A249 5c Candlemas .45 .25
714 A249 15c Madonna and child .95 .30
715 A249 17c Adoration of the Magi 1.40 1.40
Nos. 713-715 (3) 2.80 1.95

1988, Dec. 10

716 A250 25c lt ultra & int blue 1.10 1.10

UN Declaration of Human Rights, 40th anniv.

3rd Games of Small European States, Nicosia A251

Perf. 13½

1989, Apr. 10 Litho. Unwmk.

717 A251 1c Discus .20 .20
718 A251 5c Javelin .20 .20
719 A251 15c Wrestling .65 .65
720 A251 18c Running .80 .80

Size: 110x80mm

Imperf

721 A251 £1 Mythological woman, laurel, bird 6.00 6.00
Nos. 717-721 (5) 7.85 7.85

Various Children's Games A252

Perf. 13x13½

1989, May 8 Litho. Unwmk.

722 A252 7c multi (5 boys) 1.00 1.00
723 A252 7c multi (6 boys) 1.00 1.00
a. Pair, #722-723 2.00 2.00
724 A252 18c multi (6 boys) 1.10 1.10
725 A252 18c multi (5 boys) 1.10 1.10
a. Pair, #724-725 2.25 2.25
Nos. 722-725 (4) 4.20 4.20

Europa.

French Revolution, Bicent. — A253

Perf. 11½

1989, July 7 Litho. Unwmk.

Granite Paper

726 A253 18c multicolored .80 .80

A254

A255

1989, Sept. 4 *Perf. 13½*

727 A254 15c multicolored .60 .60
728 A255 30c multicolored 1.25 1.25

15c for Interparliamentary Union, cent. 30c for 9th Non-Aligned Summit Conf., Belgrade.

Apiculture A256

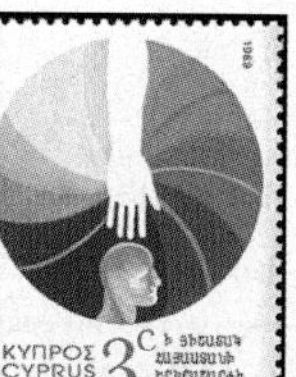

Annivs. & Events — A257

1989, Oct. 15 *Perf. 13½x14*

729 A256 3c Honeycomb .25 .20
730 A256 10c Gathering nectar .55 .45
731 A256 15c Gathering nectar, diff. .75 .45
732 A256 18c Queen, worker bees .85 .85
Nos. 729-732 (4) 2.40 1.95

1989, Nov. 13

Designs: 3c, Armenian earthquake. 5c, Cyprus Philatelic Society. 7c, European Cancer Year. 17c, World Food Day.

733 A257 3c multicolored .25 .25
734 A257 5c multicolored .35 .20
735 A257 7c multicolored .60 .60
736 A257 17c multicolored .90 .90
Nos. 733-736 (4) 2.10 1.95

A258

A259

Mosaics, 3rd-5th Cent. A260

Details: 1c, Winter, from *The Four Seasons,* House of Dionysos. 2c, Personification of Crete, from *Theseus Slaying the Minotaur,* Villa of Theseus. 3c, Centaur and Maenad, from *The Dionysiac Procession,* House of Aion, vert. 4c, *Poseidon and Amymone,* House of Dionysos. 5c, Leda, from *Leda and the Swan,* House of Aion. 7c, Apollon, from *Apollo and Marsyas,* House of Aion. 10c, Hermes and Dionysos, from *Hermes Presenting Dionysos to Tropheus,* House of Aion, vert. 15c, Cassiopeia, from *Cassiopeia and the Nereids,* House of Aion. 18c, *Orpheus Playing the Lyre,* House of Orpheus. 20c, Nymphs preparing bath, from *Hermes Presenting Dionysos to Tropheus,* vert. 25c, Amazon holding double ax and reins, House of Orpheus, vert. 40c, Doris, one of 3 Nereids in *Cassiopeia and the Nereids.* 50c, Hercules and the lion, from *The First Labor of Hercules,* House of Orpheus. £1, *Apollon and Daphne,* House of Dionysos. £3, Cupid hunting, Villa of Theseus.

Perf. 13, 13x13½ (2c, 4c, 18c, 40c), 13½x13 (3c, 10c, 20c, 25c)

1989, Dec. 29

737	A258	1c multicolored	.30	1.10
738	A259	2c multicolored	.35	1.10
739	A259	3c multicolored	.45	1.25
740	A259	4c multicolored	.60	1.25
741	A258	5c multicolored	.60	.25
742	A258	7c multicolored	.70	.30
743	A259	10c multicolored	.90	.35
744	A258	15c multicolored	1.50	.55
745	A259	18c multicolored	1.50	.60
746	A259	20c multicolored	1.75	.90
747	A259	25c multicolored	1.75	.95
748	A259	40c multicolored	2.50	1.75

Perf. 13½x14

749	A260	50c multicolored	2.00	1.75
750	A260	£1 multicolored	4.00	3.50
751	A260	£3 multicolored	9.00	9.00
		Nos. 737-751 (15)	27.90	24.60

UNESCO World Literacy Year — A261

83rd Interparliamentary Conference, Nicosia — A262

Lions Europa Forum A263

Anniversaries & events.

1990, Apr. 3 ***Perf. 14x13½***

752	A261	15c multicolored	.80	.80
753	A262	17c multicolored	.95	.95
754	A263	18c multicolored	1.10	1.10
		Nos. 752-754 (3)	2.85	2.85

Europa A264

Post Offices.

1990, May 10 Litho. ***Perf. 13x13½***

755	A264	7c Paphos	*1.10*	.35
756	A264	18c Limassol City Center	*1.50*	1.50

European Year of Tourism — A265

Designs: 5c, Hotel and Catering Institute, 25th anniv. 7c, Holy Church of St. Lazarus, 1100th anniv. 15c, Female silhouette, butterflies. 18c, Male silhouette, birds.

1990, July 9 ***Perf. 14***

757	A265	5c multicolored	.60	.60
758	A265	7c multicolored	.80	.80
759	A265	15c multicolored	1.75	1.75
760	A265	18c multicolored	2.10	2.10
		Nos. 757-760 (4)	5.25	5.25

Republic of Cyprus, 30th Anniv. A266

1990, Sept. 29 Photo. ***Perf. 11½***

761	A266	15c Sun	.60	.60
762	A266	17c shown	.65	.65
763	A266	18c Fish	.75	.75
764	A266	40c Birds, flowers	1.75	1.75

Size: 90x90mm

Imperf

765	A266	£1 Stylized bird	5.00	5.00
		Nos. 761-765 (5)	8.75	8.75

Flowers — A267 Christmas — A268

1990, Nov. 5 Litho. ***Perf. 13½x13***

766	A267	2c Chionodoxa lochiae	.20	.20
767	A267	3c Pancrayium maritimum	.45	.45
768	A267	5c Paeonia mascula	.55	.55
769	A267	7c Cyclamen cyprium	.80	.80
770	A267	15c Tulipa cypria	1.75	1.75
771	A267	18c Crocus cyprius	2.00	2.00
		Nos. 766-771 (6)	5.75	5.75

1990, Dec. 3 ***Perf. 13½x14***

772	A268	5c Nativity	.40	.20
773	A268	15c Virgin and Child	1.10	.30
774	A268	17c Nativity, diff.	1.25	1.25
		Nos. 772-774 (3)	2.75	1.75

Mosaics From Kanakaria Church — A269

1991, Mar. 28 Photo. ***Perf. 12***

Granite Paper

775	A269	5c Archangel	.20	.20
776	A269	15c Christ Child	.75	.75
777	A269	17c St. James	1.50	1.50
778	A269	18c St. Matthew	1.75	1.75
		Nos. 775-778 (4)	4.20	4.20

Europa A270

1991, May 6 Litho. ***Perf. 13x13½***

779	A270	7c Spacecraft Ulysses	.75	.35
780	A270	18c Spacecraft Giotto	1.25	1.25

Oenanthe Cypriaca (Cyprus Wheatear) A271

1991, July 4 Litho. ***Perf. 13½***

781	A271	5c Juvenile bird	.75	.35
782	A271	7c Autumn plumage	.80	.35
783	A271	15c Male bird	1.10	.50
784	A271	30c Female bird	1.75	1.75
		Nos. 781-784 (4)	4.40	2.95

UN High Commissioner for Refugees, 40th Anniv. — A272

1991, Oct. 7 Litho. ***Perf. 14x13½***

785	A272	5c shown	.40	.25
786	A272	15c Legs	1.40	.70
787	A272	18c Faces	1.75	1.75
		Nos. 785-787 (3)	3.55	2.70

Christmas A273

A274

1991, Nov. 25 Litho. ***Perf. 13½***

788	A273	5c Nativity scene	.20	.20
789	A273	15c St. Basil	.65	.65
790	A273	17c Baptism of Jesus	.75	.75
a.		Strip of 3, #788-790	1.75	1.75

Strips of 3 are from sheets of 9.

1992, Apr. 3 Litho. ***Perf. 12***

Granite Paper

791	A274	10c Swimming	.70	.40
792	A274	20c Long jump	1.10	.85
793	A274	30c Running	1.60	1.60
794	A274	35c Discus	1.90	1.90
		Nos. 791-794 (4)	5.30	4.75

1992 Summer Olympics, Barcelona.

Expo '92, Seville A275

10th Youth Under 16 European Soccer Tournament — A276

Opening of University of Cyprus A277

1992, Apr. 20 Litho. ***Perf. 14***

795	A275	20c multicolored	1.75	.85
796	A276	25c multicolored	1.90	1.10
797	A277	30c multicolored	1.90	1.90
		Nos. 795-797 (3)	5.55	3.85

Discovery of America, 500th Anniv. A278

1992, May 29 Litho. ***Perf. 13x13½***

798	A278	10c Map	1.40	1.40
799	A278	10c Embarkation at Palos	1.40	1.40
a.		Pair, #798-799	3.00	3.00
800	A278	30c Three ships	1.90	1.90
801	A278	30c Columbus	1.90	1.90
a.		Pair, #800-801	4.00	4.00
		Nos. 798-801 (4)	6.60	6.60

Europa.

Reptiles A279

Designs: 7c, Chamaeleo chamaeleon. 10c, Lacerta laevis troodica. 15c, Mauremys caspica. 20c, Coluber cypriensis.

1992, Sept. 14 Litho. ***Perf. 14x13½***

802	A279	7c multicolored	.70	.35
803	A279	10c multicolored	.90	.55
804	A279	15c multicolored	1.25	.75
805	A279	20c multicolored	1.40	1.40
		Nos. 802-805 (4)	4.25	3.05

Intl. Maritime and Shipping Conference — A280

Unwmk.

1992, Nov. 9 Litho. ***Perf. 14***

806	A280	50c multicolored	3.50	3.50

Christmas A281

Church wall paintings: 7c, , "Virgin Mary Greeting Elizabeth," Church of Timios Stavros, Pelendri. 15c, "The Virgin and Child," Church of Panayia tou Araka. 20c, "Holy Mother Odigitria," Church of Ayios Nicolaos tis Steyis.

1992, Nov. 9 *Perf. 13½x14*

807 A281 7c multicolored .50 .35
808 A281 15c multicolored .85 .70
809 A281 20c multicolored 1.25 1.25
Nos. 807-809 (3) 2.60 2.30

A282

A283

1993, Feb. 15 **Litho.** *Perf. 14*

810 A282 10c multicolored .95 .75

Pancyprian Gymnasium, cent.

1993, Apr. 3 *Perf. 13½x14, 14x13½*

Europa: 10c, Bronze sculpture, Motherhood, by N. Dymiotis (1930-1990). 30c, Applique, Motherhood, by Savva (1924-1968), horiz.

811 A283 10c multicolored 1.10 .60
812 A283 30c multicolored 2.10 2.10

13th European Cup for Women Athletes A284

Scouting in Cyprus, 80th Anniv. — A285

Water Skiing Moufflon Encouragement Cup — A286

Archbishop Makarios III, 80th Anniv. of Birth — A287

Perf. 13½x14, 14x13½

1993, May 24 **Litho.**

813 A284 7c multicolored .55 .35
814 A285 10c multicolored .75 .50
815 A286 20c multicolored 1.25 1.25
a. Inscribed "MUFFLON" 25.00
816 A287 25c multicolored 1.90 1.90
Nos. 813-816 (4) 4.45 4.00

Fish — A288

1993, Sept. 6 **Litho.** *Perf. 14x13½*

817 A288 7c Holocentrus ruber .60 .30
818 A288 15c Scorpaena scrofa .95 .60
819 A288 20c Serranus scriba 1.10 1.10
820 A288 30c Balistes capriscus 2.10 2.10
Nos. 817-820 (4) 4.75 4.10

Maritime Cyprus A289

1993, Oct. 4 *Perf. 14*

821 A289 25c multicolored 2.25 2.25

12th Commonwealth Summit Conference — A290

1993, Oct. 4 *Perf. 14x13½*

822 A290 35c red brown & tan 2.40 2.40
823 A290 40c olive brown & tan 2.75 2.75

Christmas A291

7c, Carved wooden cross, Stavrovouni Monastery. 20c, Crucifixion, cross from Lefkara Church. 25c, Nativity, cross from Pedoulas Church.

1993, Nov. 22 **Litho.** *Perf. 13½x14*

824 A291 7c multicolored .40 .30
825 A291 20c multicolored .95 .95

Perf. 14x13½

826 A291 25c multi, horiz. 1.25 1.25
Nos. 824-826 (3) 2.60 2.50

Copper Industry A292

Europa: 10c, Early smelting of copper. 30c, Map, boat, copper ingot.

1994, Mar. 1 **Litho.** *Perf. 13x13½*

827 A292 10c multicolored .75 .45
828 A292 30c multicolored 1.75 1.75

Persons with Special Needs — A293

Intl. Olympic Committee, Cent. — A294

World Gymnasiade, Nicosia — A295

Intl. Year of the Family — A296

1994, May 9 **Litho.** *Perf. 13*

829 A293 7c multicolored .60 .30
830 A294 15c multicolored 1.00 .60
831 A295 20c multicolored 1.25 1.25
832 A296 25c multicolored 1.60 1.60
Nos. 829-832 (4) 4.45 3.75

Turkish Invasion and Occupation of Cyprus, 20th Anniv. — A297

1994, June 27 **Litho.** *Perf. 14*

833 A297 10c Human rights .90 .40
834 A297 50c Cultural heritage 3.50 3.50

Trees — A298

7c, Pinus nigra. 15c, Cedrus libani. 20c, Quercus alnifolia. 30c, Arbutus andrachne.

1994, Oct. 10 **Litho.** *Perf. 13½*

835 A298 7c multicolored .55 .30
836 A298 15c multicolored .85 .60
837 A298 20c multicolored 1.00 1.00
838 A298 30c multicolored 1.60 1.60
Nos. 835-838 (4) 4.00 3.50

ICAO, 50th Anniv. A299

1994, Nov. 21 **Litho.** *Perf. 14*

839 A299 30c multicolored 2.50 2.50

Christmas A300

Designs: 7c, Virgin Mary (Vlahernitissa). 20c, Nativity. 25c, Archangel Michael.

1994, Nov. 21 *Perf. 13½*

840 A300 7c multicolored .55 .30
841 A300 20c multicolored 1.25 .80
842 A300 25c multicolored 1.50 1.50
Nos. 840-842 (3) 3.30 2.60

Traditional Costumes — A301

Costumess: 1c, Female, Phapos. 2c, Bridal, Karpess. 3c, Female, Phapos, diff. 5c, Female, Messaoria. 7c, Bridegroom's. 10c, Shepherd's, Messaoria. 15c, Festive female, Nicosia. 20c, Festive female, Karpass. 25c, Female, Mountain-Pitsillia. 30c, Festive female, Karpass, diff. 35c, Rural male. 40c, Plain festive male, Messaoria. 50c, Urban male. £1, Urban festive female, Sarka.

1994, Dec. 27 **Litho.** *Perf. 13½x13*

843 A301 1c multicolored .25 .25
844 A301 2c multicolored .35 .35
845 A301 3c multicolored .40 .40
846 A301 5c multicolored .50 .50
847 A301 7c multicolored .55 .55
848 A301 10c multicolored .70 .70
849 A301 15c multicolored 1.25 1.25
850 A301 20c multicolored 1.25 1.25
851 A301 25c multicolored 1.40 1.40
852 A301 30c multicolored 1.40 1.40
853 A301 35c multicolored 1.40 1.40
854 A301 40c multicolored 1.60 1.60
855 A301 50c multicolored 2.40 2.40
856 A301 £1 multicolored 4.75 4.75
Nos. 843-856 (14) 18.20 18.20

No. 856 exists imscribed "1998."

Third Intl. Congress of Cypriot Studies — A302

Excavations: 20c, Hearth room, Ashlar building, Paliotaverna. 30c, Hall, Agios Demetrios area, Kalavasos. £1, Old Nicosia Archbishorpic building, 18th cent.

1995, Feb. 27 **Litho.** *Perf. 14*

859 A302 20c multicolored 1.40 1.40
860 A302 30c multicolored 1.75 1.75

Size: 107x71mm

Imperf

861 A302 £1 multicolored 6.00 6.00
Nos. 859-861 (3) 9.15 9.15

A303

A304

Liberation Monument, Nicosia: a, People walking left. b, Statue of Liberty, prisoners leaving prison. c, People walking right.

1995, Mar. 31 Litho. *Perf. 13x14*

862 Strip of 3	4.00	4.00
a.-c. A303 20c any single	1.25	1.25

No. 862 is a continuous design.
Formation of EOKA (Natl. Organization of Cypriot Struggle), 40th anniv.

1995, May 8 Litho. *Perf. 13½*

Europa: 10c, Concentration camp prisoners, dove, rainbow, map of Europe. 30c, Prisoner, dove.

863 A304 10c multicolored	1.10	.55
864 A304 30c multicolored	2.50	2.50

Liberation of the concentration camps, 50th anniv.

Health A305

7c, Proper nutrition, exercise. 10c, Fight against AIDS. 15c, Fight against illegal drugs. 20c, Stop smoking campaign.

1995, June 26 Litho. *Perf. 13½*

865 A305 7c multi, vert.	.35	.30
866 A305 10c multi	.75	.75
867 A305 15c multi	.80	.80
868 A305 20c multi, vert.	1.10	1.10
Nos. 865-868 (4)	3.00	2.95

European Cultural Month A306

1995, Sept. 18 Litho. *Perf. 13x13½*

869 A306 20c shown	.95	.95
870 A306 25c Map of Europe, building	1.25	1.25

Souvenir Sheet

Eurofilex '95 A307

Designs: a, Dove carrying letter, stars. b, Stars, exhibition emblem. Illustration reduced.

1995, Sept. 18 Litho. *Perf. 14*

871 Sheet of 2	6.00	6.00
a.-b. A307 50c any single	3.00	3.00

A limited number were surcharged £5 on each stamp and sold at "Europhilex '95" on Oct. 27 and 28, 1995.

UN, 50th Anniv. A308

Volleyball, Cent. — A309

European Conservation Year — A310

World Clay Target Shooting Championships — A311

Perf. 13x13½, 13½x13

1995, Oct. 24 Litho.

872 A308 10c multicolored	.50	.45
873 A309 15c multicolored	.70	.65
874 A310 20c multicolored	1.00	.90
875 A311 25c multicolored	1.25	1.25
Nos. 872-875 (4)	3.45	3.25

Christmas A312

Various reliquaries, Kykko Monastery.

1995, Nov. 27 Litho. *Perf. 13½x13*

876 A312 7c multicolored	.30	.30
877 A312 20c multicolored	.90	.90
878 A312 25c multicolored	1.10	1.10
Nos. 876-878 (3)	2.30	2.30

A313

A314

A315

Anniversaries and Events — A316

1996, Jan. 4 Litho. *Perf. 13½x13*

879 A313 10c multicolored	.65	.40
880 A314 20c multicolored	1.25	.80
881 A315 35c multicolored	1.90	1.90
882 A316 40c multicolored	2.00	2.00
Nos. 879-882 (4)	5.80	5.10

Pancyprian Organization of Large Families, 25th anniv. (#879). Motion pictures, cent. (#880). UNICEF, 50th anniv. (#881). 13th Conf. of Commonwealth Speakers and Presiding Officers (#882).

Portraits of Women
A317 A318

1996, Apr. 8 Litho. *Perf. 14*

883 A317 10c multicolored	.65	.35
884 A318 30c multicolored	1.75	1.75

Europa.

1996 Summer Olympics, Atlanta A319

1996, June 10 Litho. *Perf. 13*

885 A319 10c High jump	.90	.35
886 A319 20c Javelin	1.25	.70
887 A319 25c Wrestling	1.75	1.00
888 A319 30c Swimming	1.90	1.90
Nos. 885-888 (4)	5.80	3.95

Mills of Cyprus — A320

1996, Sept. 23 Litho. *Perf. 13*

889 A320 10c Watermill	.55	.50
890 A320 15c Olivemill	.85	.75
891 A320 20c Windmill	1.10	1.00
892 A320 25c Handmill	1.40	1.40
Nos. 889-892 (4)	3.90	3.65

Icons, Religious Landmarks A321

Designs: No. 893, Icon of Our Lady of Iberia, Moscow. No. 894, Holy Monastery of Stavrovouni, Cyprus. No. 895, Icon of St. Nicholas, Cyprus. No. 896, Iveron Mother of God Resurrection Gate, Moscow.

1996, Nov. 13 Litho. *Perf. 11½*

893 A321 30c multicolored	1.75	1.75
894 A321 30c multicolored	1.75	1.75
895 A321 30c multicolored	1.75	1.75
896 A321 30c multicolored	1.75	1.75
a. Block of 4, #893-896	7.50	7.50

See Russia No. 6356.

Christmas A322

Paintings from Church of the Virgin of Asinou: 7c, Detail from Nativity. 20c, Virgin Mary between Archangels Gabriel and Michael. 25c, Christ bestowing blessings, vert.

1996, Dec. 2 *Perf. 13x13½, 13½x13*

897 A322 7c multicolored	.60	.30
898 A322 20c multicolored	1.50	.90
899 A322 25c multicolored	1.90	1.90
Nos. 897-899 (3)	4.00	3.10

Easter A323

1997, Mar. 24 Litho. *Perf. 13x13½*

900 A323 15c The Last Supper	1.10	.60
901 A323 25c The Crucifixion	1.40	1.40

A324

A325

1997, Mar. 24 *Perf. 13½x13*

902 A324 30c multicolored	2.10	2.00

European Men's Clubs Basketball Cup finals.

1997, May 5 Litho. *Perf. 13½x13*

Europa (Stories and Legends): 30c, Man in red cape fighting Death, eagle above.

903 A325 15c shown	.90	.50
904 A325 30c multicolored	1.60	1.60

Insects
A326

10c, Oedipoda miniata. 15c, Acherontia atropos. 25c, Daphnis nerii. 35c, Ascalaphus macaronius.

1997, June 30 Litho. *Perf. 13x13½*

905 A326 10c multicolored .50 .40
906 A326 15c multicolored .75 .50
907 A326 25c multicolored 1.25 1.00
908 A326 35c multicolored 1.40 1.40
Nos. 905-908 (4) 3.90 3.30

Archbishop Makarios III (1913-77), 1st Pres. of Cyprus Republic
A327

1997, Aug. 1 Litho. *Perf. 13x13½*

909 A327 15c multicolored .95 .65

Christmas
A328

Frescoes from Church of Ayios Ioannis Lambadestis: 10c, Nativity. 25c, Magi on way to Bethlehem. 30c, Flight into Egypt.

1997, Nov. 17 Litho. *Perf. 13½x13*

910 A328 10c multicolored .55 .40
911 A328 25c multicolored 1.60 1.00
912 A328 30c multicolored 1.75 1.75
Nos. 910-912 (3) 3.90 3.15

Minerals
A329

1998, Mar. 9 Litho. *Perf. 13x13½*

913 A329 10c Green jasper .60 .40
914 A329 15c Iron pyrite .90 .65
915 A329 25c Gypsum 1.25 1.25
916 A329 30c Chalcedony 1.50 1.50
Nos. 913-916 (4) 4.25 3.80

1998 World Cup Soccer Championships, France — A330

1998, May 4 Litho. *Perf. 14*

917 A330 35c multicolored 2.50 1.50

Europa
A331

Festivals, holidays: 15c, "Katakklysmos" Larnaca. 30c, People watching proclamation of independence, 1960.

1998, May 4

918 A331 15c multicolored 1.00 .60
919 A331 30c multicolored 1.60 1.60

Ovis Gmelini Ophion
A332

World Wildlife Fund: No. 920, Male, female, calf. No. 921, Group running. No. 922, Male up close. No. 923, Male with front legs up on rock, one grazing.

1998, June 22 Litho. *Perf. 13x13½*

920 A332 25c multicolored 1.25 1.25
921 A332 25c multicolored 1.25 1.25
922 A332 25c multicolored 1.25 1.25
923 A332 25c multicolored 1.25 1.25
a. Block of 4, #920-923 5.50 5.50

Issued in sheets of 16.

World Stamp Day
A333

1998, Oct. 9 Litho. *Perf. 14*

924 A333 30c multicolored 1.25 1.25
a. Booklet pane of 8 10.00
Complete booklet, #924a 10.00

A334

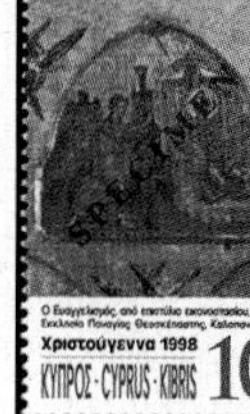

A335

1998, Oct. 9

925 A334 50c multicolored 2.00 2.00

Universal Declaration of Human Rights, 50th anniv.

1998, Nov. 16 Litho. *Perf. 14*

Christmas (Scenes from paintings in the Church of the Virgin of Théoskèpasti, Kalopanayiotis): 10c, The Annunciation. 25c, The Nativity. 30c, Baptism of Christ.

926 A335 10c multicolored .40 .40
927 A335 25c multicolored 1.10 1.10
928 A335 30c multicolored 3.25 3.25
a. Souvenir sheet, #926-928 2.75 2.75
Nos. 926-928 (3) 4.75 4.75

Mushrooms — A336

10c, Pleurotus eryngii. 15c, Lactarius deliciosus. 25c, Sparassis crispa. 30c, Morchella elata.

1999, Mar. 4 Litho. *Perf. 13½x13*

929 A336 10c multicolored .45 .45
930 A336 15c multicolored .95 .60
931 A336 25c multicolored 1.40 1.40
932 A336 30c multicolored 1.50 1.50
Nos. 929-932 (4) 4.30 3.95

Natl. Parks and Nature Preserves
A337

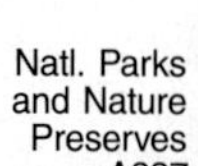

1999, May 6 Litho. *Perf. 14*

933 A337 15c Tripylos Reserve .75 .50
934 A337 30c Lara Reserve 1.25 1.25
a. Booklet pane, 4 each #933-934 9.00
Complete booklet, #934a 9.00

Europa.

Council of Europe, 50th Anniv.
A338

1999, May 6

935 A338 30c multicolored 1.25 1.25

4000 Years of Hellenism — A339

a, Sanctuary of Apollo Hylates, Kourion. b, Mycenaean "Krater of the Warriors," Athens. c, Mycenaean amphoral krater, Cyprus Museum. d, Sanctuary of Apollo Epikourios, Delphi.

1999, June 28 Litho. *Perf. 13½x13*

936 A339 25c Block of 4, #a.-d. 4.00 4.00

See Greece No. 1938.

UPU, 125th Anniv.
A340

1999, Sept. 30 Litho. *Perf. 14*

937 A340 15c shown .60 .60
938 A340 35c "125" 1.40 1.40

Souvenir Sheet

Maritime Cyprus Shipping Conference
A341

Cyprus flag and: a, Container ship. b, Binoculars, chart, cap. c, Ship with yellow stripe on tower. d, Tanker.

1999, Sept. 30

939 A341 25c Sheet of 4, #a.-d. 4.00 4.00

Souvenir Sheet

Turkish Invasion of Cyprus, 25th Anniv. — A342

Illustration reduced.

1999, Nov. 11 Litho. *Imperf.*

940 A342 30c multicolored 1.60 1.60

A343

A344

1999, Nov. 11 *Perf. 14*

941 A343 10c Angel .40 .40
942 A343 25c Magi .95 .95
943 A343 30c Madonna and child 1.10 1.10
Nos. 941-943 (3) 2.45 2.45

Christmas.

Souvenir Sheet

2000, Mar. 30 Litho. *Perf. 13¼x13*

Miss Universe 2000: a, 15c, Woman, stars. b, 35c, Armless nude statue of woman.

944 A344 Sheet of 2, #a.-b. 1.90 1.90

Jewelry — A345

Various pieces of jewelry. #945-952 vert.

2000, Mar. 30 Litho. *Perf. 14*

945 A345 10c multi .40 .40
946 A345 15c multi .55 .55
947 A345 20c multi .75 .75
948 A345 25c multi .95 .95
949 A345 30c multi 1.10 1.10
950 A345 35c multi 1.25 1.25
951 A345 40c multi 1.50 1.50
952 A345 50c multi 2.00 2.00
953 A345 75c multi 2.75 2.75
954 A345 £1 multi 3.75 3.75
955 A345 £2 multi 7.50 7.50
956 A345 £3 multi 11.50 11.50
Nos. 945-956 (12) 34.00 34.00

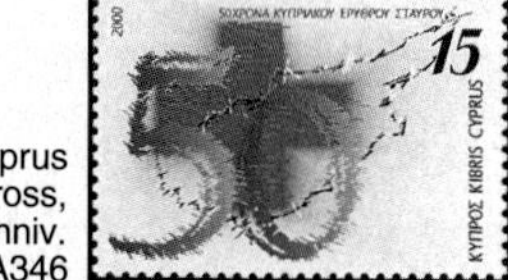

Cyprus Red Cross, 50th Anniv.
A346

2000, May 9 Litho. *Perf. 13x13¼*

957 A346 15c multi .95 .55

Memorial to Heroes of 1955-59 Independence Struggle — A347

2000, May 9 *Perf. 13¼x13*

958 A347 15c multi .55 .55

Europa, 2000

Common Design Type

2000, May 9 *Perf. 14*

959 CD17 30c multi 1.25 1.25

World Meteorological Org., 50th Anniv. — A348

2000, May 9

960 A348 30c multi 1.25 1.25

European Convention of Human Rights, 50th Anniv. A349

2000, June 29 Litho. ***Perf. 13x13¼***

961 A349 30c multi 1.25 1.25

Churches Damaged Under Turkish Occupation A350

Designs: 10c, Monastery of Antifonitis, Kalograia, vert. 15c, Church of St. Themonianos, Lysi, vert. 25c, Church of Panagia Kanakaria, Lytrhagkomi. 30c, Avgasida Monastery Church, Milia.

Perf. 13¼x13, 13x13¼

2000, June 29

962 A350 10c multi	.55	.35
963 A350 15c multi	.75	.50
964 A350 25c multi	1.00	.80
965 A350 30c multi	1.10	1.10
Nos. 962-965 (4)	3.40	2.75

2000 Summer Olympics, Sydney A351

Designs: 10c, Archery. 15c, Pommel horse. 25c, Diving. 35c, Trampoline.

2000, Sept. 14 Litho. ***Perf. 13x13½***

966-969 A351 Set of 4 3.50 3.50

Christmas — A352

Gospel covers: 10c, Annunciation. 25c, Nativity. 30c, Baptism of Jesus.

2000, Nov. 2 ***Perf. 13½x13***

970-972 A352 Set of 3 2.75 2.75

Pavlos Liasides (1901-85), Poet — A353

2001, Mar. 12 Litho. ***Perf. 13¼x13***

973 A353 13c multi .55 .40

Commonwealth Day, 25th Anniv. — A354

2001, Mar. 12 ***Perf. 13x13¼***

974 A354 30c multi 1.25 1.25

UN High Commissioner for Refugees, 50th Anniv. — A355

2001, Mar. 12

975 A355 30c multi 1.25 1.25

Europa A356

Designs: 20c, Bridge over Diarizos River. 30c, Akaki River.

2001, May 3

976-977 A356 Set of 2	1.75	1.75
977a Booklet pane, 4 each #976-977	7.00	
Booklet, #977a	7.00	

Crabs A357

Designs: 13c, Parthenope massena. 20c, Calappa granulata. 25c, Ocypode cursor. 30c, Pagurus bernhardus.

2001, June 7

978-981 A357 Set of 4 2.75 2.75

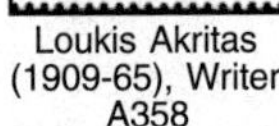

Loukis Akritas (1909-65), Writer A358

Christmas A359

2001, Oct. 25 Litho. ***Perf. 13½x13***

982 A358 20c multi .85 .65

2001, Oct. 25

Holy Monastery of Macheras, 800th anniv.: 13c, Icon of Madonna. 25c, Monastery building. 30c, Crucifix.

983-985 A359 Set of 3 2.50 2.50

Cats — A360

No. 986, 20c: a, Red brown panel. b, Green panel.

No. 987, 25c: a, Dark brown panel. b, Orange brown panel.

Illustration reduced.

2002, Mar. 21 Litho. ***Perf. 13x13½***

Horiz. Pairs, #a-b

986-987 A360 Set of 2 4.25 4.25

Europa — A361

Designs: 20c, Equestrian act. 30c, Tightrope walker.

2002, May 9 ***Perf. 13½x13***

988-989 A361 Set of 2	2.10	2.10
a. Booklet pane, 4 each #988-989	8.50	—
Booklet, #989a	8.50	

Medicinal Plants A362

Designs: 13c, Myrtus communis. 20c, Lavandula stoechas. 25c, Capparis spinosa. 30c, Ocimum basilicum.

2002, June 13 ***Perf. 13x13½***

990-993 A362 Set of 4 4.25 4.25

Mother Teresa (1910-97) — A363

2002, Sept. 12 Litho. ***Perf. 13½x13***

994 A363 40c multi 2.10 2.10

Intl. Teachers' Day — A364

No. 995: a, 13c, Blackboard and teachers. b, 30c, Computer and teachers.

Illustration reduced.

2002, Sept. 12 ***Perf. 13x13½***

995 A364 Horiz. pair, #a-b 2.25 2.25

Cyprus-Europhilex 02 Philatelic Exhibition — A365

No. 996: a, Seal, 490-470 B.C. (red brown background). b, Silver coin of Timoharis, 5th-4th cent B.C. (blue background) c, Silver coin of Stasioikos, 449 B.C. (yellow background).

No. 997: a, Clay oil lamp, 2nd cent. A.D. (olive green background). b, Clay statue of Europa on a bull, 7th-6th cent. B.C. (yellow background). c, Clay oil lamp, 1st cent. B.C. (lilac background)

No. 998: a, 15th cent. map of eastern Crete and western Cyprus, and statue of Aphrodite, 1st cent. B.C. b, Map of eastern Cyprus, and Abduction of Europe, by Francesco di Giorgio.

2002, Sept. 22

996 Horiz. strip of 3	3.00	3.00
a.-c. A365 20c Any single	1.00	1.00
997 Horiz. strip of 3	4.50	4.50
a.-c. A365 30c Any single	1.50	1.50

Souvenir Sheet

998 Sheet of 2, #a-b	5.25	5.25
a.-b. A365 50c Any single	2.50	2.50

Christmas A366

Wall painting in Church of Metamorphosis Sotiros, Palechori: 13c, Nativity, detail. 25c, Angels, detail. 30c, Entire painting (37x37mm).

Perf. 13x13½, 13¾ (30c)

2002, Nov. 21

999-1001 A366 Set of 3 2.40 2.40

Antique Automobiles A367

No. 1002: a, 20c, 1946 Triumph Roadster 1800. b, 25c, 1917 Ford Model T. c, 30c, 1932 Baby Ford.

2003, Mar. 20 Litho. ***Perf. 13x13½***

1002 A367 Vert. strip of 3, #a-c 2.75 2.75

Europa — A368

2003, May 8 ***Perf. 13½x13***

Color of Triangles

1003 A368 20c yellow	.75	.75
a. Perf. 13½x13¾ on 3 sides	.75	.75
1004 A368 30c red	1.25	1.25
a. Perf. 13½x13¾ on 3 sides	1.25	1.25
b. Booklet pane, 4 each #1003a-1004a	8.00	—
Complete booklet, #1004b	8.00	

European Ministers of Education, 7th Conference — A369

2003, June 12 Litho. ***Perf. 13½x13***

1005 A369 30c multi 1.25 1.25

Worldwide Fund for Nature (WWF) — A370

Mediterranean horseshoe bat: a, In flight. b, Close-up. c, Hanging from rock. d, With open mouth.
Illustration reduced.

2003, June 12 *Perf. 13x13½*
1006 A370 25c Block of 4, #a-b 4.00 4.00

Birds of Prey — A371

No. 1007, 20c: a, Eleonora's falcon. b, Eleonora's falcons in flight.
No. 1008, 25c: a, Head of Imperial eagle. b, Imperial eagles in flight.
No. 1009, 30c: a, Owl on branch. b, Owl in flight, eggs.

2003, Sept. 25 Litho. *Perf. 14*
Horiz. pairs, #a-b
1007-1009 A371 Set of 3 6.00 6.00

Famous Men A372

Designs: No. 1010, 5c, Constantinos Spyridakis (1903-76), Education minister. No. 1011, 5c, Tefkros Anthias (1903-68), poet (23x31mm).

Perf. 13x13¼, 13¼x13
2003, Nov. 13
1010-1011 A372 Set of 2 .45 .45

Christmas A373

Details of Nativity icon from church in Kourdali: 13c, Angels. 30c, Three Magi on horses. 40c, Entire icon (37x60mm).

Perf. 13¾x13¼, 13¾x14 (40c)
2003, Nov. 13
1012-1014 A373 Set of 3 3.50 3.50

FIFA (Fédération Internationale de Football Association), Cent. — A374

Perf. 13¼x13¾
2004, Mar. 11 **Litho.**
1015 A374 30c multi 1.25 1.25

UEFA (European Soccer Union), 50th Anniv. — A375

2004, Mar. 11 *Perf. 13¼x13*
1016 A375 30c multi 1.25 1.25

Yiannos Kranidiotis (1947-99), Politician A376

2004, May 1 *Perf. 13¼x13½*
1017 A376 20c multi .85 .85

Admission to European Union — A377

2004, May 1 *Perf. 14¼x14*
1018 A377 30c multi 1.25 1.25

Europa A378

Cliff and: 20c, Amphitheater, ship. 30c, Family at seashore, sculpture

2004, May 1 *Perf. 13¾x13¼*
1019 A378 20c multi .85 .85
a. Perf. 13¾ on 3 sides .85 .85
1020 A378 30c multi 1.25 1.25
a. Perf. 13¾ on 3 sides 1.25 1.25
b. Booklet pane, 4 each #1019a, 1020a 8.50 —
Complete booklet, #1020b 8.50

2004 Summer Olympics, Athens — A379

Designs: 13c, Equestrian. 20c, Runners. 30c, Swimmers. 40c, Athletes, man in robe.
Illustration reduced.

2004, June 10 Litho. *Perf. 13¼x13*
1021-1024 A379 Set of 4 4.25 4.25

Mammals — A380

No. 1025, 20c — Tursiops truncatus: a, Blue background. b, White background.
No. 1026, 30c — Vulpes vulpes indutus: a, Green background. b, White background.
No. 1027, 40c, Lepus europaeus cyprium: a, Orange brown background. b, White background.
Illustration reduced.

2004, Sept. 9 Litho. *Perf. 13¾x13½*
Horiz. Pairs, #a-b
1025-1027 A380 Set of 3 7.75 7.75

Georgios Philippou Pierides (1904-99), Writer — A381

Emilios Chourmouzios (1904-73), Writer — A382

2004, Nov. 11 *Perf. 13¼x13*
1028 A381 5c multi .25 .25
1029 A382 5c multi .25 .25

Christmas A383

Details from icon depicting the birth of Christ, Monastery of Chrysoroyiatissa: 13c, Angels. 30c, Magi on horseback. 40c, Annunciation, vert. (37x60mm).
£1, Adoration of the Shepherds.

Perf. 13¾x13¼, 13¾x14 (40c)
2004, Nov. 11
1030-1032 A383 Set of 3 3.75 3.75

Souvenir Sheet
Perf. 13¾ on 3 Sides
1033 A383 £1 multi 4.50 4.50

No. 1033 contains one 37x38mm stamp.

POSTAL TAX STAMPS

Catalogue values for unused stamps in this section are for Never Hinged items.

Unless otherwise stated, Cyprus postal tax stamps are for the Refugee Fund.

No. 352 Surcharged

Perf. 12x12½
1974, Dec. 2 **Wmk. 344**
RA1 A104 10m on 5m multi .20 .20

Old Woman and Child — PT1

Child and Barbed Wire — PT2

1974, Oct. 1 *Perf. 12½x13½*
RA2 PT1 10m gray & black .20 .20

Perf. 13x12½
1977, Jan. 10 Litho. Wmk. 344
RA3 PT2 10m black .20 .20

Inscribed 1984
1984, June 18 *Perf. 13x12½*
RA4 PT2 1c black .20 .20

There are two types of No. RA4.

Inscribed 1988 — PT3

1988-99 *Perf. 13x12½*
Design Size 22x28mm
RA5 PT3 1c black & pale gray .20 .20

Perf. 11½x12
RA6 PT3 1c Inscribed 1989 .20 .20
RA7 PT3 1c Inscribed 1990 .20 .20

Unwmk.
Perf. 13
RA8 PT3 1c Inscribed 1991 .20 .20
RA9 PT3 1c Inscribed 1992 .20 .20
RA10 PT3 1c Inscribed 1993 .20 .20
RA11 PT3 1c Inscribed 1994 .20 .20

Perf. 14½x13¾
Design Size 21x24.5mm
RA12 PT3 1c Inscribed 1995 .20 .20
RA13 PT3 1c Inscribed 1996 .20 .20
RA14 PT3 1c Inscribed 1997 .20 .20
RA15 PT3 1c Inscribed 1998 .20 .20
RA16 PT3 1c Inscribed 1999 .20 .20
RA17 PT3 1c Inscribed 2000 .20 .20
RA18 PT3 1c Inscribed 2001 .20 .20

Size: 22x27mm
Perf. 12¾
RA19 PT3 1c Inscribed 2002 .20 .20
RA20 PT3 1c Inscribed 2003 .20 .20

Perf. 12¾x13
RA21 PT3 1c Inscribed 2004 .20 .20
Nos. RA5-RA21 (17) 3.40 3.40

Issued: #RA5, 9/12/88; #RA6, 9/4/89; #RA7, 9/29/90; #RA8, 10/7/91; #RA9, 11/9/92; #RA10, 1993; #RA11, 11/21/94; #RA12, 10/24/95; #RA13, 6/10/96; #RA14, 6/30/97; #RA15, 1998; #RA16, 1999; #RA17, 2000; #RA18, 2001. #RA19, 2002. #RA19, 2003. #RA20, 2003. #RA21, 11/11/04.

CYRENAICA

ˌsir-ə-ˈnā-ə-kə

LOCATION — In northern Africa bordering on the Mediterranean Sea
GOVT. — Italian colony
AREA — 75,340 sq. mi.
POP. — 225,000 (approx. 1934)
CAPITAL — Bengasi (Benghazi)

Cyrenaica was an Italian Colony. In 1949 Great Britain granted the Amir of Cyrenaica autonomy in internal affairs. Cyrenaica was incorporated into the kingdom of Libya in 1951.

100 Centesimi = 1 Lira
1000 Milliemes = 1 Pound (1950)

Catalogue values for unused stamps in this country are for Never Hinged items, beginning with Scott 65 in the regular postage section, Scott J1 in the postage due section.

Used values in italics are for postally used stamps. CTO's sell for about the same as unused, hinged stamps.

Watermark

Wmk. 140 — Crown

Propagation of the Faith Issue

Italy Nos. 143-146 Overprinted

1923, Oct. 24 Wmk. 140 *Perf. 14*

No.	Type	Description	Unused	Used
1	A68	20c ol grn & brn org	4.50	*24.00*
2	A68	30c claret & brn org	4.50	*24.00*
3	A68	50c vio & brn org	3.00	*27.50*
4	A68	1 l bl & brn org	3.00	*37.50*
		Nos. 1-4 (4)	15.00	*113.00*
		Set, never hinged	37.50	

Fascisti Issue

Italy Nos. 159-164 Overprinted in Red or Black

1923, Oct. 29 Unwmk. *Perf. 14*

No.	Type	Description	Unused	Used
5	A69	10c dk grn (R)	5.25	*10.00*
6	A69	30c dk vio (R)	5.25	*10.00*
7	A69	50c brn car	5.25	*11.75*

Wmk. 140

No.	Type	Description	Unused	Used
8	A70	1 l blue	5.25	*27.50*
9	A70	2 l brown	5.25	*32.50*
10	A71	5 l blk & bl (R)	5.25	*47.50*
		Nos. 5-10 (6)	31.50	*139.25*
		Set, never hinged	75.00	

Manzoni Issue

Italy Nos. 165-170 Overprinted in Red

1924, Apr. 1 *Perf. 14*

No.	Type	Description	Unused	Used
11	A72	10c brn red & blk	7.25	*27.50*
12	A72	15c bl grn & blk	7.25	*27.50*
13	A72	30c blk & slate	7.25	*27.50*
14	A72	50c org brn & blk	7.25	*27.50*
15	A72	1 l bl & blk	57.50	*180.00*
a.		Double overprint	1,000.	
		Never Hinged	2,000.	
16	A72	5 l vio & blk	475.00	*1,750.*
		Nos. 11-16 (6)	561.50	*2,040.*
		Set, never hinged	1,425.	

Vertical overprints on Nos. 11-14 are essays. On Nos. 15-16 the overprint is vertical at the left.

All examples of #15a are poorly centered.

Victor Emmanuel Issue

Italy Nos. 175-177 Overprinted

1925-26 Unwmk. *Perf. 11*

No.	Type	Description	Unused	Used
17	A78	60c brn car	.35	*6.50*
18	A78	1 l dark blue	.55	*6.50*
19	A78	1.25 l dk bl ('26)	2.75	*12.75*
a.		Perf. 13½	150.00	*300.00*
		Never hinged	300.00	
		Nos. 17-19 (3)	3.65	*25.75*
		Set, never hinged	9.00	

Issue dates: Nov. 1925, July 1926.

Saint Francis of Assisi Issue

Italian Stamps of 1926 Overprinted

1926, Apr. 12 Wmk. 140 *Perf. 14*

No.	Type	Description	Unused	Used
20	A79	20c gray green	1.60	*8.75*
21	A80	40c dark violet	1.60	*8.75*
22	A81	60c red brown	1.60	*16.00*

Overprinted in Red

Unwmk.

No.	Type	Description	Unused	Used
23	A82	1.25 l dk bl, perf. 11	1.60	*23.50*
24	A83	5 l + 2.50 l ol grn	4.50	*47.50*
		Nos. 20-24 (5)	10.90	*104.50*
		Set, never hinged	16.00	

Volta Issue

Type of Italy 1927, Overprinted

1927, Oct. 10 Wmk. 140 *Perf. 14*

No.	Type	Description	Unused	Used
25	A84	20c purple	5.50	*22.00*
26	A84	50c dp org	7.25	*14.50*
27	A84	1.25 l brt bl	11.00	*37.50*
		Nos. 25-27 (3)	23.75	*74.00*
		Set, never hinged	60.00	

#25 exists with overprint omitted. See Italy.

Monte Cassino Issue

Types of 1929 Issue of Italy, Overprinted in Red or Blue

1929, Oct. 14

No.	Type	Description	Unused	Used
28	A96	20c dk grn (R)	4.00	*11.50*
29	A96	25c red org (Bl)	4.00	*11.50*
30	A98	50c + 10c crim (Bl)	4.00	*13.00*
31	A98	75c + 15c ol brn (R)	4.00	*13.00*
32	A96	1.25 l + 25c dk vio (R)	8.00	*22.00*
33	A98	5 l + 1 l saph (R)	8.00	*25.00*

Overprinted in Red

Unwmk.

No.	Type	Description	Unused	Used
34	A100	10 l + 2 l gray brn	8.00	*35.00*
		Nos. 28-34 (7)	40.00	*131.00*
		Set, never hinged	100.00	

Royal Wedding Issue

Type of Italian Stamps of 1930 Overprinted

1930, Mar. 17 Wmk. 140

No.	Type	Description	Unused	Used
35	A101	20c yel grn	1.10	*3.50*
36	A101	50c + 10c dp org	.90	*5.75*
37	A101	1.25 l + 25c rose red	.90	*13.00*
		Nos. 35-37 (3)	2.90	*22.25*
		Set, never hinged	7.25	

#35 exists with overprint omitted. See Italy.

Ferrucci Issue

Types of Italian Stamps of 1930, Overprinted in Red or Blue

1930, July 26

No.	Type	Description	Unused	Used
38	A102	20c violet (R)	1.80	*2.20*
39	A103	25c dk grn (R)	1.80	*2.20*
40	A103	50c black (R)	1.80	*5.00*
41	A103	1.25 l dp bl (R)	1.80	*10.00*
42	A104	5 l + 2 l dp car	5.50	*18.00*
		Nos. 38-42 (5)	12.70	*37.40*
		Set, never hinged	35.00	

Virgil Issue

Types of Italian Stamps of 1930 Overprinted in Red or Blue

1930, Dec. 4

No.	Type	Description	Unused	Used
43	A106	15c vio blk	.90	*5.00*
44	A106	20c org brn (Bl)	.90	*2.20*
45	A106	25c dk grn	.90	*1.90*
46	A106	30c lt brn (Bl)	.90	*2.25*
47	A106	50c dl vio	.90	*1.90*
48	A106	75c rose red (Bl)	.90	*3.50*
49	A106	1.25 l gray bl	.90	*5.00*

Unwmk.

No.	Type	Description	Unused	Used
50	A106	5 l + 1.50 l dk vio	6.25	*30.00*
51	A106	10 l + 2.50 l ol brn (Bl)	6.25	*42.50*
		Nos. 43-51 (9)	18.80	*94.25*
		Set, never hinged	40.00	

Saint Anthony of Padua Issue

Types of Italian Stamps of 1931 Overprinted in Blue or Red

1931, May 7 Wmk. 140

No.	Type	Description	Unused	Used
52	A116	20c brown (Bl)	1.50	*11.00*
53	A116	25c green (R)	1.50	*3.50*
54	A118	30c gray brn (Bl)	1.50	*3.50*
55	A118	50c dl vio (Bl)	1.50	*3.50*
56	A120	1.25 l slate bl (R)	1.50	*22.00*

Overprinted like Nos. 23-24 in Red or Black

Unwmk.

No.	Type	Description	Unused	Used
57	A121	75c black (R)	1.50	*11.00*
58	A122	5 l + 2.50 l dk brn	2.75	*50.00*
		Nos. 52-58 (7)	11.75	*104.50*
		Set, never hinged	26.00	

Carabineer
A1

1934, Oct. 16 Photo. Wmk. 140

No.	Type	Description	Unused	Used
59	A1	5c dk ol grn & brn	3.00	*13.00*
60	A1	10c brn & blk	3.00	*13.00*
61	A1	20c scar & indigo	3.00	*10.00*
62	A1	50c pur & brn	3.00	*10.00*
63	A1	60c org brn & ind	3.00	*16.00*
64	A1	1.25 l dk bl & grn	3.00	*25.00*
		Nos. 59-64 (6)	18.00	*87.00*
		Set, never hinged	47.50	

2nd Colonial Art Exhibition held at Naples. See Nos. C24-C29.

Catalogue values for unused stamps in this section, from this point to the end of the section, are for Never Hinged items.

Autonomous State

Senussi Warrior
A2 A3

Perf. 12½

1950, Jan. 16 Unwmk. Engr.

No.	Type	Description	Unused	Used
65	A2	1m dark brown	.60	*2.25*
66	A2	2m rose car	.70	*1.90*
67	A2	3m orange	.70	*2.00*
68	A2	4m dark green	1.40	*3.25*
69	A2	5m gray	1.00	*.90*
70	A2	8m red orange	.90	*.85*
71	A2	10m purple	.90	*.85*
72	A2	12m red	.90	*.85*
73	A2	20m deep blue	.90	*.80*
74	A3	50m choc & ultra	2.00	*4.00*
75	A3	100m bl blk & car rose	5.00	*12.00*
76	A3	200m vio & pur	10.00	*32.50*
77	A3	500m dk grn & org	35.00	*85.00*
		Nos. 65-77 (13)	60.00	*147.15*

SEMI-POSTAL STAMPS

Many issues of Italy and Italian Colonies include one or more semipostal denominations. To avoid splitting sets, these issues are generally listed as regular postage unless all values carry a surtax.

Holy Year Issue

Italian Semi-Postal Stamps of 1924 Overprinted in Black or Red

1925, June 1 Wmk. 140 ***Perf. 12***

B1 SP4 20c + 10c dk grn & brn 2.75 *14.50*
B2 SP4 30c + 15c dk brn & brn 2.75 *16.00*
B3 SP4 50c + 25c vio & brn 2.75 *14.50*
B4 SP4 60c + 30c dp rose & brn 2.75 *20.00*
B5 SP8 1 l + 30c dp bl & vio (R) 2.75 *25.00*
B6 SP8 5 l + 2.50 l org brn & vio (R) 2.75 *40.00*
Nos. B1-B6 (6) 16.50 *130.00*
Set, never hinged 40.00

Colonial Institute Issue

"Peace" Substituting Spade for Sword — SP1

1926, June 1 Typo. ***Perf. 14***

B7 SP1 5c + 5c brown .65 *4.75*
B8 SP1 10c + 5c olive grn .65 *4.75*
B9 SP1 20c + 5c blue grn .65 *4.75*
B10 SP1 40c + 5c brown red .65 *4.75*
B11 SP1 60c + 5c orange .65 *4.75*
B12 SP1 1 l + 5c blue .65 *9.25*
Nos. B7-B12 (6) 3.90 *33.00*
Set, never hinged 13.50

Surtax for Italian Colonial Institute.

Types of Italian Semi-Postal Stamps of 1926 Overprinted like Nos. 17-19

1927, Apr. 21 Unwmk. ***Perf. 11***

B13 SP10 40c + 20c dk brn & blk 2.00 *20.00*
B14 SP10 60c + 30c brn red & ol brn 2.00 *20.00*
B15 SP10 1.25 l + 60c dp bl & blk 2.00 *37.50*
B16 SP10 5 l + 2.50 l dk grn & blk 3.25 *50.00*
Nos. B13-B16 (4) 9.25 *127.50*
Set, never hinged 22.50

The surtax on these stamps was for the charitable work of the Voluntary Militia for Italian National Defense.

Allegory of Fascism and Victory — SP2

1928, Oct. 15 Wmk. 140 ***Perf. 14***

B17 SP2 20c + 5c bl grn 1.90 *7.25*
B18 SP2 30c + 5c red 1.90 *7.25*
B19 SP2 50c + 10c purple 1.90 *13.50*
B20 SP2 1.25 l + 20c dk bl 2.00 *14.50*
Nos. B17-B20 (4) 7.70 *42.50*
Set, never hinged 19.00

46th anniv. of the Societa Africana d'Italia. The surtax aided that society.

Types of Italian Semi-Postal Stamps of 1926 Overprinted in Red or Black like Nos. 52-56

1929, Mar. 4 Unwmk. ***Perf. 11***

B21 SP10 30c + 10c red & blk 3.25 *13.00*
B22 SP10 50c + 20c vio & blk 3.25 *14.50*
B23 SP10 1.25 l + 50c brn & bl 4.00 *25.00*
B24 SP10 5 l + 2 l ol grn & blk (Bk) 4.00 *47.50*
Nos. B21-B24 (4) 14.50 *100.00*
Set, never hinged 37.50

Surtax for the charitable work of the Voluntary Militia for Italian Natl. Defense.

Types of Italian Semi-Postal Stamps of 1926 Overprinted in Black or Red like Nos. 52-56

1930, Oct. 20 ***Perf. 14***

B25 SP10 30c + 10c dk grn & bl grn (Bk) 14.50 *20.00*
B26 SP10 50c + 10c dk grn & vio 14.50 *27.50*
B27 SP10 1.25 l + 30c ol brn & red brn 14.50 *40.00*
B28 SP10 5 l + 1.50 l ind & grn 47.50 *87.50*
Nos. B25-B28 (4) 91.00 *175.00*
Set, never hinged 225.00

Surtax for the charitable work of the Voluntary Militia for Italian Natl. Defense.

Sower — SP3

1930, Nov. 27 Photo. Wmk. 140

B29 SP3 50c + 20c ol brn 2.50 *13.50*
B30 SP3 1.25 l + 20c dp bl 2.50 *13.50*
B31 SP3 1.75 l + 20c green 2.50 *14.50*
B32 SP3 2.55 l + 50c purple 6.50 *27.50*
B33 SP3 5 l + 1 l dp car 6.50 *37.50*
Nos. B29-B33 (5) 20.50 *106.50*
Set, never hinged 29.00

25th anniv. of the Italian Colonial Agricultural Institute. The surtax was for the aid of that institution.

AIR POST STAMPS

Air Post Stamps of Tripolitania, 1931, Overprinted in Blue like Nos. 38-42

1932, Jan. 7 Wmk. 140 ***Perf. 14***

C1 AP1 50c rose car .70 .35
C2 AP1 60c dp org 4.50 *8.75*
C3 AP1 80c dl vio 4.50 *17.00*
Nos. C1-C3 (3) 9.70 *26.10*
Set, never hinged 24.00

Air Post Stamps of Tripolitania, 1931, Overprinted in Blue

1932, May 12

C4 AP1 50c rose car 1.10 1.75
C5 AP1 80c dull violet 4.50 *17.00*
Set, never hinged 14.00

This overprint was also applied to the 60c, Tripolitania No. C9. The overprinted stamp was never used in Cyrenaica, but was sold at Rome in 1943 by the Postmaster General for the Italian Colonies. Value $5.

Arab on Camel — AP2

Airplane in Flight AP3

1932, Aug. 8 Photo.

C6 AP2 50c purple 3.75 .20
C7 AP2 75c brn rose 5.50 *7.25*
C8 AP2 80c deep blue 5.50 *13.50*
C9 AP3 1 l black 1.75 .20
C10 AP3 2 l green 2.25 *7.50*
C11 AP3 5 l deep car 4.00 *13.50*
Nos. C6-C11 (6) 22.75 *42.15*
Set, never hinged 57.50

For surcharges and overprint see #C20-C33.

Graf Zeppelin Issue

Zeppelin and Clouds forming Pegasus AP4

Zeppelin and Ancient Galley AP5

Zeppelin and Giant Bowman AP6

1933, Apr. 15

C12 AP4 3 l dk brn 6.50 *80.00*
C13 AP5 5 l purple 6.50 *80.00*
C14 AP6 10 l dp grn 6.50 *140.00*
C15 AP5 12 l deep blue 6.50 *160.00*
C16 AP4 15 l carmine 6.50 *160.00*
C17 AP6 20 l black 6.50 *175.00*
Nos. C12-C17 (6) 39.00 *795.00*
Set, never hinged 95.00

North Atlantic Crossing Issue

Airplane Squadron and Constellations — AP7

1933, June 1

C18 AP7 19.75 l grn & dp bl 12.50 *400.00*
C19 AP7 44.75 l red & indigo 12.50 *400.00*
Set, never hinged 65.00

Type of 1932 Overprinted and Surcharged

1934, Jan. 20

C20 AP3 2 l on 5 l org brn 2.25 *42.50*
C21 AP3 3 l on 5 l yel grn 2.25 *42.50*
C22 AP3 5 l ocher 2.25 *50.00*
C23 AP3 10 l on 5 l rose 2.50 *50.00*
Nos. C20-C23 (4) 9.25 *185.00*
Set, never hinged 22.50

For use on mail to be carried on a special flight from Rome to Buenos Aires.

Transport Plane AP8

Venus of Cyrene AP9

1934, Oct. 9

C24 AP8 25c sl bl & org red 3.00 *20.00*
C25 AP8 50c dk grn & ind 3.00 *16.00*
C26 AP8 75c dk brn & org red 3.00 *8.75*
a. Imperf. 1,475.
Never hinged 1,825.
C27 AP9 80c org brn & ol grn 3.00 *20.00*
C28 AP9 1 l scar & ol grn 3.00 *22.50*
C29 AP9 2 l dk bl & brn 3.00 *37.50*
Nos. C24-C29 (6) 18.00 *124.75*
Set, never hinged 47.50

2nd Colonial Arts Exhib. held at Naples.

AIR POST SEMI-POSTAL STAMPS

King Victor Emmanuel III SPAP1

Wmk. 104

1934, Nov. 5 Photo. ***Perf. 14***

CB1 SPAP1 25c + 10c gray grn 3.75 *8.75*
CB2 SPAP1 50c + 10c brn 3.75 *8.75*
CB3 SPAP1 75c + 15c rose red 3.75 *8.75*
CB4 SPAP1 80c + 15c brn blk 3.75 *8.75*
CB5 SPAP1 1 l + 20c red brn 3.75 *8.75*
CB6 SPAP1 2 l + 20c brt bl 3.75 *8.75*
CB7 SPAP1 3 l + 25c pur 17.00 *50.00*
CB8 SPAP1 5 l + 25c org 17.00 *50.00*
CB9 SPAP1 10 l + 30c dp vio 17.00 *50.00*
CB10 SPAP1 25 l + 2 l dp grn 17.00 *50.00*
Nos. CB1-CB10 (10) 90.50 *252.50*
Set, never hinged 225.00

65th birthday of King Victor Emmanuel III and the non-stop flight, Rome-Mogadiscio.

AIR POST SEMI-POSTAL OFFICIAL STAMP

Type of Air Post Semi-Postal Stamps, 1934, Overprinted Crown and "SERVIZIO DI STATO" in Black

1934, Nov. 5 Wmk. 140 ***Perf. 14***

CBO1 SPAP1 25 l + 2 l cop red *2,000.*
Never hinged *2,550.*

POSTAGE DUE STAMPS

Catalogue values for unused stamps in this section are for Never Hinged items.

D1

Perf. 12½

1950, July 1		Unwmk.		Engr.
J1	D1	2m dark brown	50.00	*110.00*
J2	D1	4m deep green	50.00	*110.00*
J3	D1	8m scarlet	50.00	*110.00*
J4	D1	10m vermilion	50.00	*110.00*
J5	D1	20m orange yel	50.00	*110.00*
J6	D1	40m deep blue	50.00	*110.00*
J7	D1	100m dark gray	50.00	*110.00*
		Nos. J1-J7 (7)	350.00	*770.00*

CZECHOSLOVAKIA

ˌche-kə-slō-ˈvä-kē-ə

LOCATION — Central Europe
GOVT. — Republic
AREA — 49,355 sq. mi.
POP. — 15,395,970 (1983 est.)
CAPITAL — Prague

The Czechoslovakian Republic consists of Bohemia, Moravia and Silesia, Slovakia and Ruthenia (Carpatho-Ukraine). In March 1939, a German protectorate was established over Bohemia and Moravia, as well as over Slovakia which had meanwhile declared its independence. Ruthenia was incorporated in the territory of Hungary. These territories were returned to the Czechoslovak Republic in 1945, except for Ruthenia, which was ceded to Russia. Czechoslovakia became a federal state on Jan. 2, 1969. On Jan. 1, 1993 Czechoslovakia separated into Slovakia and the Czech Republic. See Volume 5 for the stamps of Slovakia.

100 Haleru = 1 Koruna

Catalogue values for unused stamps in this country are for Never Hinged items, beginning with Scott 142 in the regular postage section, B144 in the semi-postal section, Scott C19 in the air post section, Scott EX1 in the personal delivery section, and Scott J58 in the postage due section, Scott O1 int he officials section, and Scott P14 in the newspaper section.

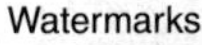
Watermarks

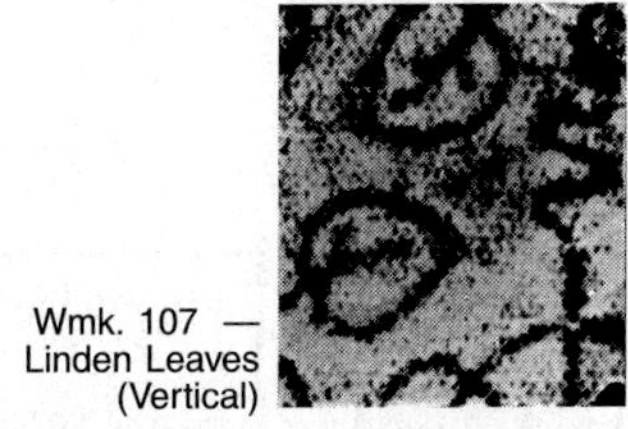
Wmk. 107 — Linden Leaves (Vertical)

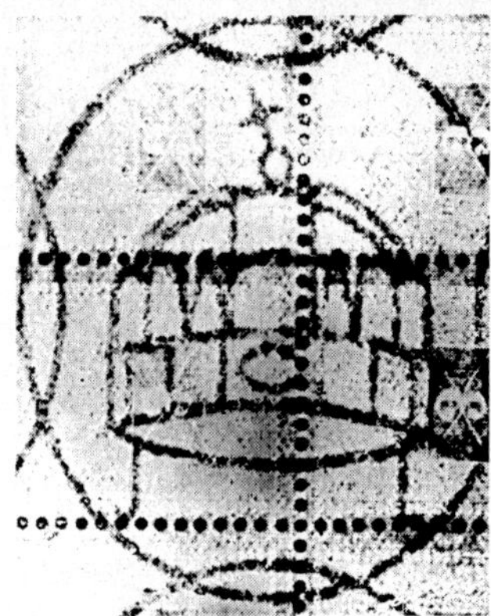
Wmk. 135 — Crown in Oval or Circle, Sideways

Wmk. 136

Wmk. 136a

Wmk. 341 — Striped Ovals

Stamps of Austria overprinted "Ceskoslovenska Republika," lion and "Cesko Slovensky Stat," "Provisorni Ceskoslovenska Vlada" and Arms, and "Ceskoslovenska Statni Posta" and Arms were made privately. A few of them were passed through the post but all have been pronounced unofficial and unauthorized by the Postmaster General.

During the occupation of part of Northern Hungary by the Czechoslovak forces, stamps of Hungary were overprinted "Cesko Slovenska Posta," "Ceskoslovenska Statni Posta" and Arms, and "Slovenska Posta" and Arms. These stamps were never officially issued though copies have passed the post.

Hradcany at Prague — A1

1918-19		Unwmk. Typo.		*Imperf.*
1	A1	3h red violet	.20	.20
2	A1	5h yellow green	.20	.20
3	A1	10h rose	.20	.20
4	A1	20h bluish green	.20	.20
5	A1	25h deep blue	.20	.20
6	A1	30h bister	.30	.20
7	A1	40h red orange	.30	.20
8	A1	100h brown	.95	.20
9	A1	200h ultra	1.60	.20
10	A1	400h purple	2.50	.20

On the 3h-40h "Posta Ceskoslovenska" is in white on a colored background; on the higher values the words are in color on a white background.

The 25h in ultramarine was not valid for postage.

Nos. 1-6 exist as tete-beche gutter pairs.

See #368, 1554, 1600. For surcharges see #B130, C1, C4, J15, J19-J20, J22-J23, J30.

Perf. 11½, 13½

13	A1	5h yellow green	.65	.20
a.		Perf. 11½x10¾	1.90	.45
14	A1	10h rose	.30	.20
15	A1	20h bluish green	.30	.20
a.		Perf. 11½	.30	.20
16	A1	25h deep blue	.45	.20
a.		Perf. 11½	1.25	.65
20	A1	200h ultra	3.25	.20
		Nos. 1-10,13-16,20 (15)	11.60	3.00

All values of this issue exist with various private perforations and copies have been used on letters.

The 3, 30, 40, 100 and 400h formerly listed are now known to have been privately perforated.

For overprints see Eastern Silesia Nos. 2, 5, 7-8, 14, 16, 18, 30.

A2

Type II — Sun behind cathedral. Colorless foliage in foreground.

Type III — Without sun. Shaded foliage in foreground.

Type IV — No foliage in foreground. Positions of buildings changed. Letters redrawn.

1919				*Imperf.*
23	A2	1h dark brown (II)	.20	.20
25	A2	5h blue green (IV)	.30	.20
27	A2	15h red (IV)	.65	.20
29	A2	25h dull violet (IV)	.55	.20
30	A2	50h dull violet (II)	.30	.20
31	A2	50h dark blue (IV)	.30	.20
32	A2	60h orange (III)	.95	.20
33	A2	75h slate (IV)	.65	.20
34	A2	80h olive grn (III)	.95	.20
36	A2	120h gray black (IV)	1.90	.30
38	A2	300h dark green (III)	4.75	.65
39	A2	500h red brown (IV)	5.25	.50
40	A2	1000h violet (III)	14.00	.75
a.		1000h bluish violet	32.50	1.60
		Nos. 23-40 (13)	30.75	4.00

For overprints see Eastern Silesia Nos. 1, 3-4, 6, 9-13, 15, 17, 20-21.

1919-20		***Perf. 11½, 13¾, 13¾x11½***		
41	A2	1h dk brown (II)	.20	.20
42	A2	5h blue grn (IV), perf. 13½	.30	.20
a.		Perf. 11½	16.00	3.25
43	A2	10h yellow grn (IV)	.30	.20
a.		Imperf.	19.00	19.00
b.		Perf. 11¾	9.50	1.25
44	A2	15h red (IV)	.30	.20
a.		Perf. 11½x10¾	12.50	3.75
b.		Perf. 11½x13¾	65.00	19.00
c.		Perf. 13¾x10¾	110.00	26.00
45	A2	20h rose (IV)	.30	.20
a.		Imperf.	82.50	77.50
46	A2	25h dull vio (IV), perf. 11½	.65	.25
a.		Perf. 11½x10¾	3.75	.95
b.		Perf. 13¾x10¾	175.00	32.50
47	A2	30h red violet (IV)	.25	.20
a.		Imperf.	190.00	190.00
b.		Perf. 13¾x13½	425.00	160.00
c.		30h deep violet	.30	.20
d.		As "c," perf. 13¾x13½	475.00	190.00
e.		As "c," imperf.	190.00	140.00
50	A2	60h orange (III)	.30	.20
a.		Perf. 13¾x13½	12.50	6.25
53	A2	120h gray black (IV)	3.75	.95
		Nos. 41-53 (9)	6.35	2.60

Nos. 43a, 45a, 47a and 47e were imperforate by accident and not issued in quantities as were Nos. 23 to 40.

Rouletted stamps of the preceding issues are said to have been made by a postmaster in a branch post office at Prague, or by private firms, but without authority from the Post Office Department.

The 50, 75, 80, 300, 500 and 1000h have been privately perforated.

Unlisted color varieties of types A1 and A2 were not officially released, and some are printer's waste.

For surcharges and overprints see Nos. B131, C2-C3, C5-C6, J16-J18, J21, J24-J29, J31, J42-J43, Eastern Silesia 22-29.

Pres. Thomas Garrigue Masaryk — A4

1920				***Perf. 13½***
61	A4	125h gray blue	.65	.20
a.		125h ultramarine	19.00	19.00
62	A4	500h slate, *grysh*	2.50	1.50
63	A4	1000h blk brn, *brnsh*	4.50	2.40
		Nos. 61-63 (3)	7.65	4.10

#61-63 imperf were not regularly issued. Values, unused singles, #61, $15; #61a, $55; #62, $20; #63, $40.

For surcharge and overprints see Nos. B131, Eastern Silesia 31-32.

Carrier Pigeon with Letter — A5

Czechoslovakia Breaking Chains to Freedom — A6

Hussite Priest — A7

Agriculture and Science — A8

Two types of 40h:
Type I: 9 leaves by woman's hip.
Type II: 10 leaves by woman's hip.

1920				***Perf. 14***
65	A5	5h dark blue	.20	.20
a.		Perf. 13¾	*325.00*	*150.00*
66	A5	10h blue green	.20	.20
a.		Perf. 13¾	*225.00*	110.00
67	A5	15h red brown	.20	.20
68	A6	20h rose	.20	.20
69	A6	25h lilac brown	.20	.20
70	A6	30h red violet	.20	.20
71	A6	40h red brown	.30	.20
a.		Tête bêche pair	3.00	2.00
b.		Perf. 13½	.75	.20
c.		Type II	.20	.20
72	A6	50h carmine	.20	.20
73	A6	60h dark blue	.20	.20
a.		Tête bêche pair	4.00	3.00
b.		Perf. 13½	1.25	.25
		Photo.		
74	A7	80h purple	.20	.20
75	A7	90h black brown	.30	.20
		Typo.		
76	A8	100h dark green	.50	.20
77	A8	200h violet	.70	.20
78	A8	300h vermilion	1.40	.20
a.		Perf. 13¾x13½	4.00	.35
79	A8	400h brown	3.50	.45
80	A8	500h deep green	4.25	.45
a.		Perf. 13¾x13½	100.00	5.50
81	A8	600h deep violet	5.75	.45
a.		Perf. 13¾x13½	200.00	7.00
		Nos. 65-81 (17)	18.50	4.15

No. 69 has background of horizontal lines.

Imperfs. were not regularly issued.

Nos. 71 and 73 exist as tete-beche gutter pairs.

For surcharges and overprint see Nos. C7-C9, J44-J56.

1920-25 *Perf. 14*

Two types of 20h:
Type I: Base of 2 is long, interior of 0 is angular.
Type II: Base of 2 is short, interior of 0 is an oval.
Two types of 25h:
Type I: Top of 2 curves up.
Type II: Top of 2 curves down.

82 A5 5h violet .20 .20
a. Tête bêche pair 1.25 1.00
b. Perf. 13½ .60 .35
83 A5 10h olive bister .20 .20
a. Tête bêche pair 2.25 1.50
b. Perf. 13½ .30 .20
84 A5 20h deep orange .20 .20
a. Tête bêche pair 17.50 14.00
b. Perf. 13½ 3.50 .60
c. Type II .20 .20
85 A5 25h blue green .20 .20
a. Type II .20 .20
86 A5 30h deep violet ('25) 1.75 .20
87 A6 50h yellow green .35 .20
a. Tête bêche pair 30.00 27.50
b. Perf. 13½ 9.00 2.00
88 A6 100h dark brown .45 .20
a. Perf. 13½ 15.00 .25
89 A6 150h rose 2.50 .50
a. Perf. 13½ 37.50 1.10
90 A6 185h orange 1.25 .20
91 A6 250h dark green 3.50 .25
Nos. 82-91 (10) 10.60 2.35

Imperfs. were not regularly issued.
#82-84, 87 exist as tete-beche gutter pairs.

Type of 1920 Issue Redrawn

Type I — Rib of leaf below "O" of POSTA is straight and extends to tip. White triangle above book is entirely at left of twig. "P" has a stubby, abnormal appendage.
Type II — Rib is extremely bent; does not reach tip. Triangle extends at right of twig. "P" like Type I.
Type III — Rib of top left leaf is broken in two. Triangle like Type II. "P" has no appendage.

1923 *Perf. 13¾, 13¾x13½*
92 A8 100h red, *yellow,* III, perf. 14x13½ 1.00 .20
a. Type I, perf. 13¾ 1.25 .20
b. Type I, perf. 13¾x13½ 1.25 .20
c. Type II, perf. 13¾ 1.50 .20
d. Type II, perf. 13¾x13½ 1.50 .20
e. Type III, perf. 13¾ 7.00 .20
93 A8 200h blue, *yellow,* II, perf. 14 5.00 .20
a. Type II, perf. 13¾x13½ 8.50 .25
b. Type III, perf. 13¾ 8.50 .25
c. Type III, perf. 13¾x13½ 52.50 .50
94 A8 300h violet, *yellow,* I, perf. 13¾ 3.75 .20
a. Type II, perf. 13¾ 35.00 .25
b. Type II, perf. 13¾x13½ 50.00 .50
c. Type III, perf. 13¾x13½ 7.00 .20
d. Type III, perf. 13¾ 24.00 .35
Nos. 92-94 (3) 9.75 .60

President Masaryk
A9 A10

Perf. 13¾x13½, 13¾
1925 **Photo.** **Wmk. 107**
Size: 19½x23mm

95 A9 40h brown orange .75 .20
96 A9 50h olive green 1.50 .20
97 A9 60h red violet 1.75 .20
Nos. 95-97 (3) 4.00 .60

Distinctive Marks of the Engravings.
I, II, III — Background of horizontal lines in top and bottom tablets. Inscriptions in Roman letters with serifs.
IV — Crossed horizontal and vertical lines in the tablets. Inscriptions in Antique letters without serifs.
I, II, IV — Shading of crossed diagonal lines on the shoulder at the right.
III — Shading of single lines only.
I — "T" of "Posta" over middle of "V" of "Ceskoslovenska." Three short horizontal lines in lower part of "A" of "Ceskoslovenska."
II — "T" over right arm of "V." One short line in "A."
III — "T" as in II. Blank space in lower part of "A."
IV — "T" over left arm of "V."

Engr.
I. First Engraving
Wmk. Horizontally (107)
Size: 19¾x22½mm

98 A10 1k carmine .85 .20
99 A10 2k deep blue 2.00 .25
100 A10 3k brown 4.00 .65
101 A10 5k blue green 1.40 .45
Nos. 98-101 (4) 8.25 1.55

Wmk. Vertically (107)
Size: 19¼x23mm

101A A10 1k carmine 100.00 4.00
101B A10 2k deep blue 100.00 12.50
101C A10 3k brown 250.00 12.50
101D A10 5k blue green 5.00 2.00
Nos. 101A-101D (4) 455.00 31.00

II. Second Engraving
Wmk. Horizontally (107)
Size: 19x21½mm

102 A10 1k carmine 42.50 .50
103 A10 2k deep blue 3.50 .25
104 A10 3k brown 3.50 .50
Nos. 102-104 (3) 49.50 1.25

III. Third Engraving
Size: 19-19½x21½-22mm
Perf. 10

105 A10 1k carmine rose 1.00 .20
a. Perf. 14 12.50 .20

IV. Fourth Engraving
Size: 19x22mm

1926 *Perf. 10*
106 A10 1k carmine rose 1.00 .20
Perf. 14
108 A10 3k brown 4.50 .20

There is a 2nd type of No. 106: with long mustache. Same values. See No. 130, design SP3.

Karlstein Castle — A11

1926, June 1 **Engr.** *Perf. 10*
109 A11 1.20k red violet .50 .30
110 A11 1.50k car rose .30 .20
111 A11 2.50k dark blue 3.00 .30
Nos. 109-111 (3) 3.80 .80

See Nos. 133, 135.

Karlstein Castle — A12

Pernstein Castle — A13

Orava Castle
A14

Masaryk
A15

Strahov Monastery — A16

Hradcany at Prague
A17

Great Tatra — A18

1926-27 **Engr.** **Wmk. 107**
114 A13 30h gray green 1.25 .20
115 A14 40h red brown .50 .20
116 A15 50h deep green .50 .20
117 A15 60h red vio, *lil* .85 .20
118 A16 1.20k red violet 4.00 1.50

Perf. 13½
119 A17 2k blue .75 .20
a. 2k ultramarine 5.50 .75
120 A17 3k deep red 1.50 .20
121 A18 4k brn vio ('27) 3.50 .40
122 A18 5k dk grn ('27) 12.50 2.25
Nos. 114-122 (9) 25.35 5.35

No. 116 exists in two types. The one with short, straight mustache at left sells for several times as much as that with longer wavy mustache.
See Nos. 137-140.

Coil Stamps
Perf. 10 Vertically

123 A12 20h brick red .50 .40
a. Vert. pair, imperf. horiz. 100.00
124 A13 30h gray green .35 .20
a. Vert. pair, imperf. horiz. 100.00
125 A15 50h deep green .25 .20
Nos. 123-125 (3) 1.10 .80

See No. 141.

1927-31 **Unwmk.** *Perf. 10*
126 A13 30h gray green .25 .20
127 A14 40h deep brown .70 .20
128 A15 50h deep green .20 .20
129 A15 60h red violet .70 .20
130 A10 1k carmine rose 1.10 .20
131 A15 1k deep red .75 .20
132 A16 1.20k red violet .40 .20
133 A11 1.50k carmine ('29) .55 .20
134 A13 2k dp grn ('29) .50 .20
135 A11 2.50k dark blue 5.50 .30
136 A14 3k red brown ('31) .60 .20
Nos. 126-136 (11) 11.25 2.30

No. 130 exists in two types. The one with longer mustache at left sells for several times as much as that with the short mustache.

1927-28 *Perf. 13½*
137 A17 2k ultra .85 .20
138 A17 3k deep red ('28) 1.90 .65
139 A18 4k brown violet ('28) 6.00 1.00
140 A18 5k dark green ('28) 6.25 .50
Nos. 137-140 (4) 15.00 2.35

Coil Stamp
1927 *Perf. 10 Vertically*
141 A12 20h brick red .50 .20

Catalogue values for unused stamps in this section, from this point to the end of the section, are for Never Hinged items.

Hradec Castle
A19

Brno Cathedral
A25

Masaryk — A27

10th anniv. of Czech. independence: 40h, Town Hall, Levoca. 50h, Telephone exchange, Prague. 60h, Town of Jasina. 1k, Hluboka Castle. 1.20k, Pilgrims' House, Velehrad. 2.50k, Great Tatra. 5k, Old City Square, Prague.

1928, Oct. 22 *Perf. 13½*
142 A19 30h black .20 .20
143 A19 40h red brown .20 .20
144 A19 50h dark green .20 .20
145 A19 60h orange red .20 .20

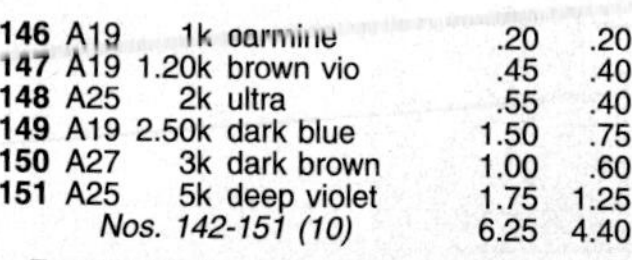

146 A19 1k carmine .20 .20
147 A19 1.20k brown vio .45 .40
148 A25 2k ultra .55 .40
149 A19 2.50k dark blue 1.50 .75
150 A27 3k dark brown 1.00 .60
151 A25 5k deep violet 1.75 1.25
Nos. 142-151 (10) 6.25 4.40

From one to three sheets each of Nos. 142-148, perf 12½, appeared on the market in the early 1950's.

Coat of Arms — A29

1929-37 *Perf. 10*
152 A29 5h dark ultra ('31) .20 .20
153 A29 10h bister brn ('31) .20 .20
154 A29 20h red .20 .20
155 A29 25h green .20 .20
156 A29 30h red violet .20 .20
157 A29 40h dk brown ('37) .40 .20
a. 40h red brown ('29) 1.00 .20
Nos. 152-157 (6) 1.40 1.20

Coil Stamp
Perf. 10 Vertically
158 A29 20h red .20 .20

For overprints see Bohemia and Moravia Nos. 1-5, Slovakia 2-6.

St. Wenceslas
A30

Founding St. Vitus' Cathedral
A31

Design: 3k, 5k, St. Wenceslas martyred.

1929, May 14 *Perf. 13½*
159 A30 50h gray green .40 .20
160 A30 60h slate violet .60 .20
161 A31 2k dull blue 1.25 .40
162 A30 3k brown 1.50 .20
163 A30 5k brown violet 5.50 1.50
Nos. 159-163 (5) 9.25 2.50

Millenary of the death of St. Wenceslas.

Statue of St. Wenceslas and National Museum, Prague — A33

1929 *Perf. 10*
164 A33 2.50k deep blue .65 .20

Brno Cathedral
A34

Tatra Mountain Scene
A35

Design: 5k, Old City Square, Prague.

1929, Oct. 15 *Perf. 13½*
165 A34 3k red brown 1.75 .20
166 A35 4k indigo 4.50 .50
167 A35 5k gray green 5.00 .30
Nos. 165-167 (3) 11.25 1.00

See No. 183.

A37

Type I 

Type II 

Two types of 50h:
I — A white space exists across the bottom of the vignette between the coat, shirt and tie and the "HALERU" frame panel.
II — An extra frame line has been added just above the "HALERU" panel which finishes off the coat and tie shading evenly.

1930, Jan. 2 *Perf. 10*
168 A37 50h myrtle green (II) .20 .20
a. Type I .75 .20
169 A37 60h brown violet .50 .20
170 A37 1k brown red .20 .20
Nos. 168-170 (3) .90 .60

See No. 234.

Coil Stamp

1931 *Perf. 10 Vertically*
171 A37 1k brown red .75 .40

President Masaryk — A38

St. Nicholas' Church, Prague — A39

1930, Mar. 1 *Perf. 13½*
175 A38 2k gray green 1.00 .25
176 A38 3k red brown 1.50 .25
177 A38 5k slate blue 5.25 1.50
178 A38 10k gray black 13.00 3.00
Nos. 175-178 (4) 20.75 5.00

Eightieth birthday of President Masaryk.

1931, May 15
183 A39 10k black violet 10.00 2.50

Krivoklat Castle — A40

Krumlov Castle — A42

Design: 4k, Orlik Castle.

1932, Jan. 2 *Perf. 10*
184 A40 3.50k violet 2.00 .80
185 A40 4k deep blue 2.25 .35
186 A42 5k gray green 2.50 .35
Nos. 184-186 (3) 6.75 1.50

A43

A44

Miroslav Tyrs — A45

1932, Mar. 16
187 A43 50h yellow green .35 .20
188 A43 1k brown carmine .90 .20
189 A44 2k dark blue 6.25 .35
190 A44 3k red brown 12.50 .35
Nos. 187-190 (4) 20.00 1.10

1933, Feb. 1
191 A45 60h dull violet .25 .20

Miroslav Tyrs (1832-84), founder of the Sokol movement; and the 9th Sokol Congress (#187-190).

First Christian Church at Nitra
A46 A47

1933, June 20
192 A46 50h yellow green .35 .20
193 A47 1k carmine rose 3.50 .20

Prince Pribina who introduced Christianity into Slovakia and founded there the 1st Christian church in A.D. 833.
All gutter pairs are vertical.

Bedrich Smetana, Czech Composer and Pianist, 50th Death Anniv. — A48

1934, Mar. 26 **Engr.** *Perf. 10*
194 A48 50h yellow green .30 .20

Consecration of Legion Colors at Kiev, Sept. 21, 1914 — A49

Ensign Heyduk with Colors A51

Legionnaires A52

1k, Legion receiving battle flag at Bayonne.

1934, Aug. 15 *Perf. 10*
195 A49 50h green .30 .20
196 A49 1k rose lake .45 .20
197 A51 2k deep blue 1.75 .20
198 A52 3k red brown 2.50 .20
Nos. 195-198 (4) 5.00 .80

20th anniv. of the Czechoslovakian Legion which fought in WWI.

Antonin Dvorák, (1841-1904), Composer — A53

1934, Nov. 22
199 A53 50h green .30 .20

Pastoral Scene — A54

1934, Dec. 17 *Perf. 10*
200 A54 1k claret .40 .20
a. Souv. sheet of 15, perf. 13½ 150.00 *200.00*
b. As "a," single stamp 7.00 6.00
201 A54 2k blue 1.10 .35
a. Souv. sheet of 15, perf. 13½ 500.00 *750.00*
b. As "a," single stamp 30.00 17.50

Centenary of the National Anthem.
Nos. 200a & 201a have thick paper, darker shades, no gum. Forgeries exist.

A55

President Masaryk — A56

1935, Mar. 1
202 A55 50h green, *buff* .35 .20
203 A55 1k claret, *buff* .40 .20
204 A56 2k gray blue, *buff* 2.00 .25
205 A56 3k brown, *buff* 3.25 .25
Nos. 202-205 (4) 6.00 .90

85th birthday of President Masaryk. See No. 235.

Monument to Czech Heroes at Arras, France — A57

1935, May 4
206 A57 1k rose .75 .20
207 A57 2k dull blue 1.50 .35

20th anniversary of the Battle of Arras.

Gen. Milan Stefánik A58

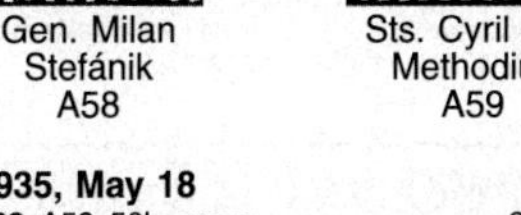
Sts. Cyril and Methodius A59

1935, May 18
208 A58 50h green .20 .20

1935, June 22
209 A59 50h green .25 .20
210 A59 1k claret .35 .20
211 A59 2k deep blue 1.40 .25
Nos. 209-211 (3) 2.00 .65

Millenary of the arrival in Moravia of the Apostles Cyril and Methodius.

Masaryk — A60

Statue of Macha, Prague — A61

1935, Oct. 20 *Perf. 12½*
212 A60 1k rose lake .20 .20

No. 212 exists imperforate. See No. 256. For overprints see Bohemia and Moravia Nos. 9-10, Slovakia 12.

1936, Apr. 30
213 A61 50h deep green .20 .20
214 A61 1k rose lake .30 .20

Karel Hynek Macha (1810-1836), Bohemian poet.

Jan Amos Komensky (Comenius) — A61a

Pres. Eduard Benes A62

Gen. Milan Stefánik A63

1936
215 A61a 40h dark blue .20 .20
216 A62 50h dull green .20 .20
217 A63 60h dull violet .20 .20
Nos. 215-217 (3) .60 .60

See #252, 255. For overprints see Bohemia and Moravia #6, 8, Slovakia 7, 9-11.

Castle Palanok near Mukacevo A64

Town of Banska Bystrica A65

Castle at Zvikov — A66

Ruins of Castle at Strecno — A67

Castle at Cesky Raj A68

Palace at Slavkov (Austerlitz) A69

Statue of King George of Podebrad A70

Town Square at Olomouc — A71

Castle Ruins at Bratislava A72

1936, Aug. 1

218 A64 1.20k rose lilac .20 .20
219 A65 1.50k carmine .20 .20
220 A66 2k dark blue green .20 .20
221 A67 2.50k dark blue .30 .20
222 A68 3k brown .30 .20
223 A69 3.50k dark violet 1.00 .30
224 A70 4k dark violet .50 .20
225 A71 5k green .45 .20
226 A72 10k blue 1.10 .30
Nos. 218-226 (9) 4.25 2.00

For overprints and surcharge see Nos. 237-238, 254A, Bohemia and Moravia 11-12, 14-19, Slovakia 13-14, 16-23.

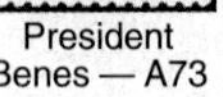

President Benes — A73

Soldiers of the Czech Legion — A74

1937, Apr. 26 Unwmk. *Perf. 12½*

227 A73 50h deep green .20 .20

For overprints see Nos. 236, Slovakia 8.

1937, June 15

228 A74 50h deep green .20 .20
229 A74 1k rose lake .25 .20

20th anniv. of the Battle of Zborov.

Cathedral at Prague — A75

Jan Evangelista Purkyne — A76

1937, July 1

230 A75 2k green .75 .20
231 A75 2.50k blue 1.00 .50

Founding of the "Little Entente," 16th anniv

1937, Sept. 2

232 A76 50h slate green .20 .20
233 A76 1k dull rose .20 .20

150th anniv. of the birth of Purkyne, Czech physiologist.

Masaryk Types of 1930-35

1937, Sept. *Perf. 12½*

234 A37 50h black .20 .20

With date "14.IX. 1937" in design

235 A56 2k black .30 .20

Death of former President Thomas G. Masaryk on Sept. 14, 1937.

International Labor Bureau Issue

Stamps of 1936-37 Overprinted in Violet or Black

1937, Oct. 6 *Perf. 12½*

236 A73 50h dp green (Bk) .25 .20
237 A65 1.50k carmine (V) .35 .20
238 A66 2k dp green (V) .50 .35
Nos. 236-238 (3) 1.10 .75

Bratislava Philatelic Exhibition Issue

Souvenir Sheet

A77

1937, Oct. 24 *Perf. 12½*

239 A77 Sheet of 2 1.75 *2.00*
a. 50h dark blue .50 .50
b. 1k brown carmine .50 .50

The stamps show a view of Poprad Lake (50h) and the tomb of General Milan Stefanik (1k).

No. 239 overprinted with the Czechoslovak arms and "Czecho-Slovak Participation New York World's Fair 1939, Czecho-Slovak Pavilion" were privately produced to finance Czechoslovak participation in the exhibition. The overprint exists in black, green, red, blue, gold and silver.

No. 239 overprinted "Liberation de la Tchechoslovaquie, 28-X-1945" etc., was sold at a philatelic exhibition in Brussels, Belgium.

St. Barbara's Church, Kutna Hora — A79

Peregrine Falcon, Sokol Emblem — A80

1937, Dec. 4

240 A79 1.60k olive green .20 .20

For overprints see Bohemia and Moravia Nos. 13, Slovakia 15.

1938, Jan. 21

241 A80 50h deep green .20 .20
242 A80 1k rose lake .25 .20

10th Intl. Sokol Games. Imperf. copies of No. 242 are essays. Nos. 241-242 se-tenant with labels sell slightly higher.

Legionnaires
A81 A82

Legionnaire — A83

1938

243 A81 50h deep green .20 .20
244 A82 50h deep green .20 .20
245 A83 50h deep green .20 .20
Nos. 243-245 (3) .60 .60

20th anniv. of the Battle of Bachmac, Vouziers and Doss Alto. #243-245 se-tenant with label sell slightly higher.

Jindrich Fügner, Co-Founder of Sokol Movement — A84

1938, June 18 *Perf. 12½*

246 A84 50h deep green .20 .20
247 A84 1k rose lake .20 .20
248 A84 2k slate blue .40 .20
Nos. 246-248 (3) .80 .60

10th Sokol Summer Games. Nos. 246-248 se-tenant with labels sell slightly higher.

View of Pilsen — A85

Cathedral of Kosice — A86

1938, June 24

249 A85 50h deep green .20 .20

Provincial Economic Council meeting, Pilsen.
For overprint see Bohemia & Moravia #7.

1938, July 15 *Perf. 12½*

250 A86 50h deep green .20 .20

Kosice Cultural Exhibition.

Prague Philatelic Exhibition Issue

Souvenir Sheet

Vysehrad Castle - Hradcany — A87

1938, June 26 *Perf. 12½*

251 A87 Sheet of 2 4.00 3.00
a. 50h dark blue 1.25 1.25
b. 1k deep carmine 1.25 1.25

See No. 3036.

Stefánik Type of 1936

1938, Nov. 21

252 A63 50h deep green .20 .20

Allegory of the Republic — A89

1938, Dec. 19 Unwmk.

253 A89 2k lt ultra .30 .20
254 A89 3k pale brown .30 .20

20th anniv. of Independence. See No. B153.

"Wir sind frei!"

Stamps of Czechoslovakia, 1918-37, overprinted with a swastika in black or red and "Wir sind frei!" were issued locally and unofficially in 1938 as Czech authorities were evacuating and German authorities arriving. They appeared in the towns of Asch, Karlsbad, Reichenberg-Maffersdorf, Rumburg, etc.

The overprint, sometimes including a surcharge or the town name (as in Karlsbad), exists on many values of postage, air post, semi-postal, postage due and newspaper stamps.

No. 226 Surcharged in Orange Red

1939, Jan. 18 Unwmk. *Perf. 12½*

254A A72 300h on 10k blue 1.00 *1.50*

Opening of the Slovakian Parliament.

View of Jasina — A89a

Perf. 12½

1939, Mar. 15 Engr. Unwmk.

254B A89a 3k ultra 11.00 *25.00*

Inauguration of the Carpatho-Ukraine Diet, Mar. 2, 1939.

Printed for use in the province of Carpatho-Ukraine but issued in Prague at the same time.

Used value is for red commemorative cancel.

Stefánik Type of 1936

1939 Engr. *Perf. 12½*

255 A63 60h dark blue 40.00 20.00

Used exclusively in Slovakia.

Masaryk Type of 1935 with hyphen in Cesko-Slovensko

1939, Apr. 23

256 A60 1k rose lake .20 .20

Linden Leaves and Buds — A90

1945 Photo. *Perf. 14*

256A A90 10h black .20 .20
257 A90 30h yellow brown .20 .20
258 A90 50h dark green .20 .20
258A A90 60h dark blue .20 .20

Engr.

(Buds Open)

Perf. 12½

259 A90 60h blue .20 .20
259A A90 80h orange ver .20 .20
260 A90 1.20k rose .20 .20
261 A90 3k violet brown .20 .20
262 A90 5k green .20 .20
Nos. 256A-262 (9) 1.80 1.80

Thomas G. Masaryk — A91

Coat of Arms — A92

1945-46 Photo. *Perf. 12*

262A A91 5h dull violet ('46) .20 .20
262B A91 10h orange yel ('46) .20 .20
262C A91 20h dk brown ('46) .20 .20
263 A91 50h brt green .20 .20
264 A91 1k orange red .20 .20
265 A91 2k chalky blue .25 .25
Nos. 262A-265 (6) 1.25 1.25

1945 *Imperf.*

266 A92 50h olive gray .20 .20
267 A92 1k brt red vio .20 .20
268 A92 1.50k dk carmine .20 .20
269 A92 2k deep blue .20 .20
269A A92 2.40k henna brn .30 .20
270 A92 3k brown .20 .20

No.	Type	Denom.	Color	Unused	Used
270A	A92	4k	dk slate grn	.20	.20
271	A92	6k	violet blue	.25	.20
271A	A92	10k	sepia	.40	.20
			Nos. 266-271A (9)	2.15	1.80

Nos. 266-271A exist in 2 printings. Stamps of the 1st printing are on thin, hard paper in sheets of 100; those of the 2nd printing on thick, soft wove paper in sheets of 200.

Staff Capt. Ridky (British Army) — A93

Dr. Miroslav Novak (French Army) — A94

Capt. Otakar Jaros (Russian Army) — A95

Staff Capt. Stanislav Zimprich (Foreign Legion) — A96

2nd Lt. Jiri Kral (French Air Force) A97

Josef Gabcik (Parachutist) A98

Staff Capt. Alois Vasatko (Royal Air Force) A99

Private Frantisek Adamek (British Colonial Service) A100

1945, Aug. 18 Engr. *Perf. 11½x12½*

No.	Type	Denom.	Color	Unused	Used
272	A93	5h	intense blue	.20	.20
273	A94	10h	dark brown	.20	.20
274	A95	20h	brick red	.20	.20
275	A96	25h	rose red	.20	.20
276	A97	30h	purple	.20	.20
277	A98	40h	sepia	.20	.20
278	A99	50h	dark olive	.20	.20
279	A100	60h	violet	.20	.20
280	A93	1k	carmine	.20	.20
281	A94	1.50k	lake	.20	.20
282	A95	2k	ultra	.20	.20
283	A96	2.50k	deep violet	.20	.20
284	A97	3k	sepia	.20	.20
285	A98	4k	rose lilac	.20	.20
286	A99	5k	myrtle green	.20	.20
287	A100	10k	brt ultra	.65	.20
			Nos. 272-287 (16)	3.65	3.20

Flags of Russia, Great Britain, US and Czechoslovakia — A101

View of Banská Bystrica A102

Patriot Welcoming Russian Soldier, Turciansky A103

Ruins of Castle at Sklabina A104

Czech Patriot, Strecno A105

1945, Aug. 29 Photo. *Perf. 10*

No.	Type	Denom.	Color	Unused	Used
288	A101	1.50k	brt carmine	.20	.20
289	A102	2k	brt blue	.20	.20
290	A103	4k	dark brown	.20	.20
291	A104	4.50k	purple	.25	.25
292	A105	5k	deep green	.50	.50
			Nos. 288-292 (5)	1.35	1.35

National uprising against the Germans.

A card contains one each of Nos. 288-292 on thin cardboard, ungummed. Size: 148x210mm. Sold for 50k. Value, $18 unused, $100 used.

A106

A107

Stefánik — Benes — Masaryk — A108

1945-47 Engr. *Perf. 12, 12½*

No.	Type	Denom.	Color	Unused	Used
293	A106	30h	rose violet	.20	.20
294	A107	60h	blue	.20	.20
294A	A106	1k	red org ('47)	.20	.20
295	A108	1.20k	car rose	.20	.20
295A	A108	1.20(k)	rose lil ('46)	.20	.20
296	A106	2.40(k)	rose	.20	.20
297	A107	3k	red violet	.20	.20
297A	A108	4k	dark blue ('46)	.20	.20
298	A108	5k	Prus green	.20	.20
299	A107	7k	gray	.20	.20
300	A106	10k	gray blue	.35	.20
300A	A106	20k	sepia ('46)	.75	.20
			Nos. 293-300A (12)	3.10	2.40

1945 Photo. *Perf. 14*

No.	Type	Denom.	Color	Unused	Used
301	A108	50h	brown	.20	.20
302	A106	80h	dark green	.20	.20
303	A107	1.60(k)	olive green	.20	.20
304	A108	15k	red violet	.55	.20
			Nos. 301-304 (4)	1.15	.80

Statue of Kozina and Chod Castle, Domazlice A109

Red Army Soldier A110

1945, Nov. 28 Engr. *Perf. 12½*

No.	Type	Denom.	Color	Unused	Used
305	A109	2.40k	rose carmine	.20	.20
306	A109	4k	blue	.20	.20

250th anniv. of the death of Jan Sladky Kozina, peasant leader.

1945, Mar. 26 Litho. *Imperf.*

No.	Type	Denom.	Color	Unused	Used
307	A110	2k	crimson rose	.35	.30
308	A110	5k	slate black	1.50	1.40
309	A110	6k	ultramarine	.40	.30
			Nos. 307-309 (3)	2.25	2.00

Souvenir Sheet

1945, July 16

Gray Burelage

No.	Type	Denom.	Color	Unused	Used
310			Sheet of 3	2.00	2.50
a.	A110	2k	crimson rose	.40	.30
b.	A110	5k	slate black	.40	.30
c.	A110	6k	ultramarine	.40	.30

Return of Pres. Benes, Apr., 1945.

Clasped Hands — A112

Karel Havlícek Borovsky — A113

1945 *Rouletted 12½*

No.	Type	Denom.	Color	Unused	Used
311	A112	1.50k	brown red	2.25	2.25
312	A112	9k	red orange	.50	.50
313	A112	13k	orange brown	.65	.65
314	A112	20k	blue	1.75	1.75
			Nos. 311-314 (4)	5.15	5.15

1946, July 5 Engr. *Perf. 12½*

No.	Type	Denom.	Color	Unused	Used
315	A113	1.20k	gray black	.20	.20

Borovsky (1821-56), editor and writer.

Old Town Hall, Brno — A114

Hodonin Square — A115

Perf. 12½x12, 12x12½

1946, Aug. 3 Engr. Unwmk.

No.	Type	Denom.	Color	Unused	Used
316	A114	2.40k	deep rose	.20	.20
317	A115	7.40k	dull violet	.30	.20

See No. B159.

President Eduard Benes — A116

1946, Oct. 28

No.	Type	Denom.	Color	Unused	Used
318	A116	60h	indigo	.20	.20
319	A116	1.60k	dull green	.20	.20
320	A116	3k	red lilac	.20	.20
321	A116	8k	sepia	.25	.20
			Nos. 318-321 (4)	.85	.80

Flag, Symbols — A117

Saint Adalbert — A118

1947, Jan. 1 *Perf. 12½*

No.	Type	Denom.	Color	Unused	Used
322	A117	1.20k	Prus green	.20	.20
323	A117	2.40k	deep rose	.20	.20
324	A117	4k	deep blue	.30	.20
			Nos. 322-324 (3)	.70	.60

Czechoslovakia's two-year reconstruction and rehabilitation program.

1947, Apr. 23

No.	Type	Denom.	Color	Unused	Used
326	A118	1.60k	gray	.50	.30
327	A118	2.40k	rose carmine	.80	.65
328	A118	5k	blue green	1.00	.40
			Nos. 326-328 (3)	2.30	1.35

950th anniv. of the death of Saint Adalbert, Bishop of Prague.

Grief — A119

Allegorical Figure — A120

1947, June 10 Engr.

No.	Type	Denom.	Color	Unused	Used
329	A119	1.20k	black	.30	.25
330	A119	1.60k	slate black	.40	.40
331	A120	2.40k	brown violet	.50	.50
			Nos. 329-331 (3)	1.20	1.15

Destruction of Lidice, 5th anniversary.

World Federation of Youth Symbol — A121

Thomas G. Masaryk — A122

1947, July 20

No.	Type	Denom.	Color	Unused	Used
332	A121	1.20k	violet brown	.30	.20
333	A121	4k	slate	.35	.20

World Youth Festival held in Prague, July 20-Aug. 17.

1947, Sept. 14

No.	Type	Denom.	Color	Unused	Used
334	A122	1.20k	gray blk, *buff*	.20	.20
335	A122	4k	blue blk, *cream*	.40	.20

Death of Masaryk, 10th anniv.

Msgr. Stefan Moyses A123

1947, Oct. 19

No.	Type	Denom.	Color	Unused	Used
336	A123	1.20k	rose violet	.20	.20
337	A123	4k	deep blue	.35	.20

150th anniversary of the birth of Stefan Moyses, first Slovakian chairman of the Slavic movement.

"Freedom from Social Oppression" A124

1947, Oct. 26 Photo. *Perf. 14*

No.	Type	Denom.	Color	Unused	Used
338	A124	2.40k	brt carmine	.20	.20
339	A124	4k	brt ultra	.35	.20

Russian revolution of Oct., 1917, 30th anniv.

Benes
A125

"Czechoslovakia" Greeting Sokol Marchers
A126

1948, Feb. 15 Photo.

Size: 17½x21½mm

340 A125 1.50k brown .20 .20

Size: 19x23mm

341 A125 2k deep plum .20 .20
342 A125 5k brt ultra .20 .20
Nos. 340-342 (3) .60 .60

1948, Mar. 7 Engr. *Perf. 12½*

343 A126 1.50k brown .20 .20
344 A126 3k rose carmine .20 .20
345 A126 5k blue .30 .20
Nos. 343-345 (3) .70 .60

The 11th Sokol Congress.

King Charles IV — A127

St. Wenceslas, King Charles IV — A128

1948, Apr. 7

346 A127 1.50k black brown .20 .20
347 A128 2k dark brown .20 .20
348 A128 3k brown red .20 .20
349 A127 5k dark blue .40 .20
Nos. 346-349 (4) 1.00 .80

600th anniv. of the foundation of Charles University, Prague.

Czech Peasants in Revolt
A129

Jindrich Vanicek
A130

Unwmk.

1948, May 14 Photo. *Perf. 14*

350 A129 1.50k dk olive brown .20 .20

Centenary of abolition of serfdom.

1948, June 10 Engr. *Perf. 12½*

Designs: 1.50k, 2k, Josef Scheiner.

351 A130 1k dark green .20 .20
352 A130 1.50k sepia .20 .20
353 A130 2k gray blue .20 .20
354 A130 3k claret .25 .20
Nos. 351-354 (4) .85 .80

11th Sokol Congress, Prague, 1948.

Frantisek Palacky & F. L. Rieger — A131

Miloslav Josef Hurban — A132

1948, June 20 Unwmk.

355 A131 1.50k gray .20 .20
356 A131 3k brown carmine .20 .20

Constituent Assembly at Kromeriz, cent.

1948, Aug. 27 *Perf. 12½*

3k, Ludovit Stur. 5k, Michael M. Hodza.

357 A132 1.50k dark brown .20 .20
358 A132 3k carmine lake .20 .20
359 A132 5k indigo .25 .20
Nos. 357-359 (3) .65 .60

Cent. of 1848 insurrection against Hungary.

Eduard Benes
A133

Czechoslovak Family
A134

1948, Sept. 28

360 A133 8k black .20 .20

President Eduard Benes, 1884-1948.

1948, Oct. 28 *Perf. 12½x12*

361 A134 1.50k deep blue .20 .20
362 A134 3k rose carmine .20 .20

Czechoslovakia's Independence, 30th anniv.

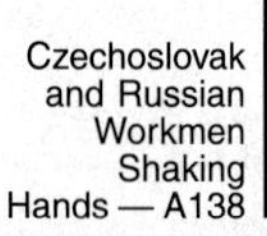
Pres. Klement Gottwald — A135

1948-49 *Perf. 12½*

Size: 18½x23½mm

363 A135 1.50k dk brown .20 .20
364 A135 3k car rose .25 .20
a. 3k rose brown .40 .20
365 A135 5k gray blue .25 .20

Size: 23½x29mm

366 A135 20k purple 1.10 .20
Nos. 363-366 (4) 1.80 .80

See Nos. 373, 564, 600-604.

Souvenir Sheet

1948, Nov. 23 Unwmk. *Imperf.*

367 A135 30k rose brown 3.50 2.75

52nd birthday of Pres. Klement Gottwald (1896-1953).

Hradcany Castle Type of 1918
Souvenir Sheet

1948, Dec. 18

368 A1 10k dk blue violet 1.75 .90

1st Czech postage stamp, 30th anniv.

Czechoslovak and Russian Workmen Shaking Hands — A138

Lenin — A139

1948, Dec. 12 *Perf. 12½*

369 A138 3k rose carmine .20 .20

5th anniv. of the treaty of alliance between Czechoslovakia and Russia.

1949, Jan. 21 Engr. *Perf. 12½*

370 A139 1.50k violet brown .25 .20
371 A139 5k deep blue .25 .20

25th anniversary of the death of Lenin.

Gottwald Type of 1948 Inscribed: "UNOR 1948" and

Gottwald Addressing Meeting
A140

1949, Feb. 25 Photo. *Perf. 14*

372 A140 3k red brown .20 .20

Perf. 12½

Engr.

Size: 23½x29mm

373 A135 10k deep green .60 .25

1st anniv. of Gottwald's speech announcing the appointment of a new government. No. 372 exists in a souvenir sheet of 1. It was not sold to the public.

A141

A142

Writers: 50h, P. O. Hviezdoslav. 80h, V. Vancura. 1k, J. Sverma. 2k, Julius Fucik. 4k, Jiri Wolker. 8k, Alois Jirasek.

1949 Photo. *Perf. 14*

374 A141 50h violet brown .20 .20
375 A141 80h scarlet .20 .20
376 A141 1k dk olive green .20 .20
377 A141 2k brt blue .40 .20

Perf. 12½

Engr.

378 A141 4k violet brown .40 .20
379 A141 8k brown black .50 .20
Nos. 374-379 (6) 1.90 1.20

1949, May 20

3k, Stagecoach and Train. 5k, Postrider and post bus. 13k, Sailing ship and plane.

380 A142 3k brown carmine 1.10 1.10
381 A142 5k deep blue .60 .35
382 A142 13k deep green 1.10 .65
Nos. 380-382 (3) 2.80 2.10

75th anniv. of the UPU.

Reaping
A143

Communist Emblem and Workers
A144

Workman, Symbol of Industry — A145

Perf. 12½x12, 12x12½

1949, May 24 Unwmk.

383 A143 1.50k deep green .50 .45
384 A144 3k brown carmine .25 .20
385 A145 5k deep blue .50 .45
Nos. 383-385 (3) 1.25 1.10

No. 384 for the 9th meeting of the Communist Party of Czechoslovakia, 5/25/49.

Bedrich Smetana and Natl. Theater, Prague — A146

Aleksander Pushkin — A147

1949, June 4 *Perf. 12½x12*

386 A146 1.50k dull green .20 .20
387 A146 5k deep blue .55 .20

Birth of Bedrich Smetana, composer, 125th anniv.

1949, June 6 *Perf. 12x12½*

388 A147 2k olive gray .30 .25

Birth of Aleksander S. Pushkin, 150th anniv.

Frederic Chopin and Conservatory, Warsaw
A148

1949, June 24 *Perf. 12½x12*

389 A148 3k dark red .30 .20
390 A148 8k violet brown .75 .40

Cent. of the death of Frederic F. Chopin.

Globe and Ribbon — A149

Zvolen Castle — A150

1949, Aug. 20 *Perf. 12½x12*

391 A149 1.50k violet brown .25 .20
392 A149 5k ultra .60 .40

50th Prague Sample Fair, Sept. 11-18, 1949.

Starting in 1949, commemorative stamps which are valued in italics were issued in smaller quantities than those in the balance of the set and sold at prices higher than face value.

1949, Aug. 28 *Perf. 12½*

393 A150 10k rose lake .65 .20

Early Miners — A151

Miner of Today — A152

Design: 5k, Mining Machine.

1949, Sept. 11 **Perf. 12½**

394 A151 1.50k sepia .65 .45
395 A152 3k carmine rose 5.00 1.50
396 A151 5k deep blue 4.00 1.25
Nos. 394-396 (3) 9.65 3.20

700th anniv. of the Czechoslovak mining industry; 150th anniv. of the miner's laws.

Construction Workers — A153

Joseph V. Stalin — A154

1949, Dec. 11 **Perf. 12½**

397 A153 1k shown 2.50 .75
398 A153 2k Machinist 1.50 .40

2nd Trade Union Congress, Prague, 1949.

1949, Dec. 21 **Unwmk.**

Design: 3k, Stalin facing left.

Cream Paper

399 A154 1.50k greenish gray 1.25 .60
400 A154 3k claret 3.50 1.40

70th birthday of Joseph V. Stalin.

Skier — A155

Efficiency Badge — A156

Engr., Photo. (3k)

1950, Feb. 15 **Perf. 12½, 13½**

401 A155 1.50k gray blue 1.75 .50
402 A156 3k vio brn, cr 1.75 1.00
403 A155 5k ultramarine 2.25 1.25
Nos. 401-403 (3) 5.75 2.75

51st Ski Championship for the Tatra cup, Feb. 15-26, 1950.

Vladimir V. Mayakovsky, Poet, 20th Death Anniv. — A157

1950, Apr. 14 **Engr.** **Perf. 12½**

404 A157 1.50k dark brown 1.90 .75
405 A157 3k brown red 1.90 .65

See Nos. 414-417, 422-423, 432-433, 464-465, 477-478.

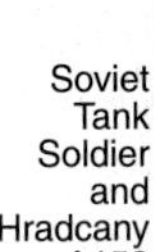

Soviet Tank Soldier and Hradcany A158

2k, Hero of Labor medal. 3k, Two workers (militiamen) and Town Hall, Prague. 5k, Text of government program and heraldic lion.

1950, May 5

406 A158 1.50k gray green .35 .20
407 A158 2k dark brown .80 .50
408 A158 3k brown red .25 .20
409 A158 5k dark blue .45 .20
Nos. 406-409 (4) 1.85 1.10

5th anniv. of the Czechoslovak People's Democratic Republic.

Factory and Young Couple with Tools A159

Designs: 2k, Steam shovel. 3k, Farmer and farm scene. 5k, Three workers leaving factory.

1950, May 9 **Engr.**

410 A159 1.50k dark green .90 .75
411 A159 2k dark brown 1.00 .75
412 A159 3k rose red .45 .35
413 A159 5k deep blue .45 .35
Nos. 410-413 (4) 2.80 2.20

Canceled to Order

The government philatelic department started about 1950 to sell canceled sets of new issues. Values in the second ("used") column are for these canceled-to-order stamps. Postally used copies are worth more.

Portrait Type of 1950

Design: S. K. Neumann.

1950, June 5 **Unwmk.** **Perf. 12½**

414 A157 1.50k deep blue .20 .20
415 A157 3k violet brown .95 .75

Stanislav Kostka Neumann (1875-1947), journalist and poet.

1950, June 21

Design: Bozena Nemcova.

416 A157 1.50k deep blue 1.25 .75
417 A157 7k dark brown .30 .20

Bozena Nemcova (1820-1862), writer.

Liberation of Colonies A160

Designs: 2k, Allegory, Fight for Peace. 3k, Group of Students. 5k, Marching Students with flags.

1950, Aug. 14

418 A160 1.50k dark green .20 .20
419 A160 2k sepia .85 .55
420 A160 3k rose carmine .20 .20
421 A160 5k ultra .40 .35
Nos. 418-421 (4) 1.65 1.30

2nd International Students World Congress, Prague, Aug. 12-24, 1950.

Portrait Type of 1950

Design: Zdenek Fibich.

1950, Oct. 15

422 A157 3k rose brown .90 .55
423 A157 8k gray green .35 .20

Zdenek Fibich, musician, birth centenary.

Miner, Soldier and Farmer A161

Czech and Soviet Soldiers A162

1950, Oct. 6

424 A161 1.50k slate .60 .60
425 A162 3k carmine rose .30 .30

Issued to publicize Czech Army Day.

Prague Castle, 16th Century A163

Prague, 1493 A164

3k, Prague, 1606. 5k, Prague, 1794.

1950, Oct. 21 **Perf. 14**

426 A163 1.50k black 3.25 3.00
427 A164 2k chocolate 3.25 3.00
428 A164 3k brown car 3.25 3.00
429 A164 5k gray 3.25 3.00
a. Block of 4, #426-429 17.50 16.00

See Nos. 434-435.

Communications Symbols — A165

1950, Oct. 25 **Perf. 12½**

430 A165 1.50k chocolate .20 .20
431 A165 3k brown carmine .85 .30

1st anniv. of the foundation of the Intl. League of P.T.T. Employees.

Portrait Type of 1950

Design: J. Gregor Tajovsky.

1950, Oct. 26

432 A157 1.50k brown 1.00 .60
433 A157 5k deep blue .65 .30

10th anniversary of the death of J. Gregor Tajovsky (1874-1940), Slovakian writer.

Scenic Type of 1950

Design: Prague, 1950.

1950, Oct. 28

434 A164 1.50k indigo .35 .20
a. Souvenir sheet of 4, imperf. 17.50 10.00
435 A164 3k brown car .65 .50

Czech and Soviet Steel Workers A166

1950, Nov. 4 **Unwmk.**

436 A166 1.50k chocolate .30 .20
437 A166 5k deep blue .65 .50

Issued to publicize the 2nd meeting of the Union of Czechoslovak-Soviet Friendship.

Dove by Picasso A167

1951, Jan. 20 **Photo.** **Perf. 14**

438 A167 2k deep blue 3.50 2.25
439 A167 3k rose brown 2.25 1.50

1st Czechoslovak Congress of Fighters for Peace, held in Prague.

Julius Fucik — A168

1951, Feb. 17 **Engr.** **Perf. 12½**

440 A168 1.50k gray .40 .30
441 A168 5k gray blue 1.10 .75

Drop Hammer — A169

Installing Gear — A170

1951, Feb. 24

442 A169 1.50k gray blk .20 .20
443 A170 3k violet brn .20 .20
444 A169 4k gray blue .60 .50
Nos. 442-444 (3) 1.00 .90

Women Machinists A171

Apprentice Miners A172

Designs: 3k, Woman tractor operator. 5k, Women of different races.

1951, Mar. 8 **Photo.** **Perf. 14**

445 A171 1.50k olive brown .25 .20
446 A171 3k brown car .90 .50
447 A171 5k blue .40 .20
Nos. 445-447 (3) 1.55 .90

International Women's Day, Mar. 8.

1951, Apr. 12 **Engr.** **Perf. 12½**

448 A172 1.50k gray .45 .25
449 A172 3k red brown .20 .20

Plowing A173

Collective Cattle Breeding A174

1951, Apr. 28 **Photo.** **Perf. 14**

450 A173 1.50k brown .50 .50
451 A174 2k dk green .75 .65

Tatra Mountain Recreation Center — A175

Mountain Recreation Centers: 2k, Beskydy (Beskids). 3k, Krkonose (Carpathians).

1951, May 5 Engr. *Perf. 12½*

452 A175 1.50k deep green .20 .20
453 A175 2k dark brown *.75 .50*
454 A175 3k rose brown .30 .20
Nos. 452-454 (3) *1.25 .90*

Issued to publicize the summer opening of trade union recreation centers.

Klement Gottwald and Joseph Stalin A176

Factory Militiaman A177

Red Army Soldier and Partisan A178

Marx, Engels, Lenin and Stalin A179

1951 Unwmk. *Perf. 12½*

455 A176 1.50k olive gray .65 .25
456 A177 2k red brown .25 .20
457 A178 3k rose brown .25 .20
458 A176 5k deep blue *2.00 1.40*
459 A179 8k gray .60 .25
Nos. 455-459 (5) *3.75 2.30*

30th anniv. of the founding of the Czechoslovak Communist Party.

A180 A181

Design: 1k, 2k, Antonin Dvorák. 1.50k, 3k, Bedrich Smetana.

1951, May 30

460 A180 1k redsh brown .25 .20
461 A180 1.50k olive gray *.70 .30*
462 A180 2k dk redsh brn *.85 .70*
463 A180 3k rose brown .25 .20
Nos. 460-463 (4) *2.05 1.40*

International Music Festival, Prague.

Portrait Type of 1950

1951, June 21

Portrait: Bohumir Smeral (facing right).

464 A157 1.50k dark gray *.45 .35*
465 A157 3k rose brown .40 .20

10th anniv. of the death of Bohumir Smeral, political leader.

1951, June 21

466 A181 1k shown .65 .30
467 A181 1.50k Discus .45 .30
468 A181 3k Soccer 1.10 .30
469 A181 5k Skier *2.25 1.25*
Nos. 466-469 (4) *4.45 2.15*

Issued to honor the 9th Congress of the Czechoslovak Sokol Federation.

Scene from "Fall of Berlin" A182

Scene from "The Great Citizen" A183

1951, July 14

470 A182 80h rose brown .30 .20
471 A183 1.50k dark gray .30 .20
472 A182 4k gray blue *1.25 .75*
Nos. 470-472 (3) *1.85 1.15*

Intl. Film Festival, Karlovy Vary, July 14-29.

Alois Jirásek — A184

"Fables and Fate" A185

Design: 4k, Scene from "Reign of Tabor."

1951, Aug. 23 Engr. *Perf. 12½*

473 A184 1.50k gray .35 .20
474 A184 5k dark blue *1.60 1.25*

Photo.

Perf. 14

475 A185 3k dark red .35 .20
476 A185 4k dark brown .35 .20
Nos. 473-476 (4) *2.65 1.85*

Cent. of the birth of Alois Jirásek, author.

Portrait Type of 1950

Design: Josef Hybes (1850-1921), co-founder of Czech Communist Party.

1951, July 21 Engr.

477 A157 1.50k chocolate .20 .20
478 A157 2k rose brown *.55 .35*

"Ostrava Region" — A186

Mining Iron Ore — A187

1951, Sept. 9

479 A186 1.50k dk brown .20 .20
480 A187 3k rose brown .20 .20
481 A186 5k deep blue *1.10 .90*
Nos. 479-481 (3) *1.50 1.30*

Miner's Day, Sept. 9, 1951.

Soldiers on Parade — A188

1k, Gunner and field gun. 1.50k, Klement Gottwald. 3k, Tankman and tank. 5k, Aviators.

Photo. (80h, 5k), Engr.

1951, Oct. 6 *Perf. 14 (80h, 5k), 12½*

Inscribed: "Den CS Armady 1951"

482 A188 80h olive brown .25 .25
483 A188 1k dk olive grn .25 .25
484 A188 1.50k sepia .40 .25
485 A188 3k claret .50 .25
486 A188 5k blue *1.10 .75*
Nos. 482-486 (5) *2.50 1.75*

Issued to publicize Army Day, Oct. 6, 1951.

Stalin and Gottwald — A189

Lenin, Stalin and Soldiers — A190

1951, Nov. 3 Engr. *Perf. 12½*

487 A189 1.50k sepia .20 .20
488 A190 3k red brown .20 .20
489 A189 4k deep blue *1.10 .40*
Nos. 487-489 (3) *1.50 .80*

Issued to publicize the month of Czechoslovak-Soviet friendship, 1951.

Peter Jilemnicky A191

Ladislav Zapotocky A192

1951, Dec. 5 Unwmk.

491 A191 1.50k redsh brown .25 .20
492 A191 2k dull blue *.50 .35*

Peter Jilemnicky (1901-1949), writer.

1952, Jan. 12 *Perf. 11½*

493 A192 1.50k brown red .20 .20
494 A192 4k gray *.45 .45*

Centenary of the birth of Ladislav Zapotocky, Bohemian socialist pioneer.

Jan Kollar — A193

Lenin and Lenin Hall — A194

1952, Jan. 30 Unwmk. *Perf. 11½*

495 A193 3k dark carmine .20 .20
496 A193 5k violet blue *.65 .50*

Jan Kollar (1793-1852), poet.

1952, Jan. 30 *Perf. 12½*

497 A194 1.50k rose carmine .20 .20
498 A194 5k deep blue *.65 .35*

6th All-Russian Party Conf., 40th anniv.

Emil Holub and African — A195

Gottwald Metallurgical Plant — A196

1952, Feb. 21 *Perf. 11½*

499 A195 3k red brown .50 .30
500 A195 5k gray *1.75 1.10*

Death of Emil Holub, explorer, 50th anniv.

1952, Feb. 25 Photo. *Perf. 14*

Designs: 2k, Foundry. 3k, Chemical plant.

501 A196 1.50k sepia .25 .20
502 A196 2k red brown *1.00 .60*
503 A196 3k scarlet .20 .20
Nos. 501-503 (3) *1.45 1.00*

Student, Soldier and Worker — A197

Youths of Three Races — A198

1952, Mar. 21 Unwmk. *Perf. 14*

504 A197 1.50k blue .20 .20
505 A198 2k olive black .25 .20
506 A197 3k lake *.85 .50*
Nos. 504-506 (3) *1.30 .90*

International Youth Day, Mar. 25, 1952.

Similar to Type of 1951

Portrait: Otakar Sevcik.

1952, Mar. 22 Engr. *Perf. 12½*

507 A184 2k choc, *cr* *.50 .40*
508 A184 3k rose brn, *cr* .20 .20

Otakar Sevcik, violinist, birth cent.

Jan A. Komensky A199

Industrial and Farm Women A200

1952, Mar. 28

509 A199 1.50k dk brown, *cr* *1.25 .60*
510 A199 11k dk blue, *cr* .25 .20

360th anniv. of the birth of Jan Amos Komensky (Comenius), teacher and philosopher.

1952, Mar. 8

511 A200 1.50k dp blue, *cr* *1.00 .50*

International Women's Day Mar. 8, 1952.

Woman and Children A201

Antifascist A202

1952, Apr. 12

512 A201 2k chocolate, *cr* *.75* .40
513 A201 3k dp claret, *cr* .20 .20

Intl. Conf. for the Protection of Children, Vienna, Apr. 12-16, 1952.

1952, Apr. 11 Photo. *Perf. 14*

514 A202 1.50k red brown .20 .20
515 A202 2k ultra *.60* *.45*

Day of International Solidarity of Fighters against Fascism, Apr. 11, 1952.

Harvester A203

Design: 3k, Tractor and Seeders.

1952, Apr. 30

516 A203 1.50k deep blue *.90* *.60*
517 A203 2k brown .20 .20
518 A203 3k brown red .20 .20
Nos. 516-518 (3) *1.30* *1.00*

Youths Carrying Flags — A204

1952, May 1

519 A204 3k brown red .55 .40
520 A204 4k dk red brown *.70* *.60*

Issued to publicize Labor Day, May 1, 1952.

Crowd Cheering Soviet Soldiers — A205

1952, May 9

521 A205 1.50k dark red .60 .50
522 A205 5k deep blue *1.25* *1.00*

Liberation of Czechoslovakia from German occupation, 7th anniversary.

Children A206

J. V. Myslbek — A207

Design: 3k, "Pioneer" teaching children.

1952, May 31 Engr. *Perf. 12½*

523 A206 1.50k dk brn, *cr* .20 .20
524 A206 2k Prus grn, *cr* *.90* *.45*
525 A206 3k rose brn, *cr* .20 .20
Nos. 523-525 (3) *1.30* *.85*

International Children's Day May 31, 1952.

1952, June 2

Design: 8k, Allegory, "Music."

526 A207 1.50k red brown .20 .20
527 A207 2k dark brown *.95* *.95*
528 A207 8k gray green .20 .20
Nos. 526-528 (3) *1.35* *1.35*

Joseph V. Myslbek (1848-1922), sculptor.

Beethoven — A208

House of Artists — A209

1952, June 7 Unwmk. *Perf. 11½*

529 A208 1.50k sepia .35 .25
530 A209 3k red brown .40 .25
531 A208 5k indigo *1.25* *.75*
Nos. 529-531 (3) *2.00* *1.25*

International Music Festival, Prague, 1952.

Lidice, Symbol of a New Life — A210

1952, June 10 *Perf. 12½*

532 A210 1.50k dk violet brn .25 .20
533 A210 5k dark blue *.75* *.50*

Destruction of Lidice, 10th anniversary.

Jan Hus — A211

Bethlehem Chapel — A212

1952, July 5

534 A211 1.50k brown .20 .20
535 A212 3k red brown .20 .20
536 A211 5k black *.85* *.60*
Nos. 534-536 (3) *1.25* *1.00*

550th anniv. of the installation of Jan Hus as pastor of Bethlehem Chapel, Prague.

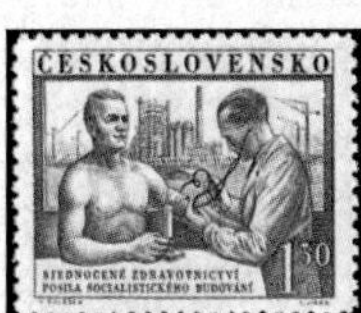

Doctor Examining Patient — A213

2k, Doctor, Nurse, Mother and child.

1952, July 31

537 A213 1.50k dark brown *.70* *.50*
538 A213 2k blue violet .20 .20
539 A213 3k rose brown .20 .20
Nos. 537-539 (3) *1.10* *.90*

Czechoslovakia's Unified Health Service.

Relay Race — A214

1952, Aug. 2 *Perf. 11½*

540 A214 1.50k shown .65 .35
541 A214 2k Canoeing *1.75* *.75*
542 A214 3k Cycling .35 .35
543 A214 4k Hockey *2.25* *2.00*
Nos. 540-543 (4) *5.00* *3.45*

Issued to publicize Czechoslovakia's Unified Physical Education program.

F. L. Celakovski A215

Mikulas Ales A216

1952, Aug. 5 *Perf. 12½*

544 A215 1.50k dark brown .20 .20
545 A215 2k dark green *.75* *.50*

Centenary of the death of Frantisek L. Celakovski, poet and writer.

Perf. 11x11½

1952, Aug. 30 Engr. Unwmk.

546 A216 1.50k dk gray grn .35 .25
547 A216 6k red brown *2.00* *1.50*

Birth centenary of Mikulas Ales, painter.

17th Century Mining Towers — A217

Jan Zizka — A218

Designs: 1.50k, Coal Excavator. 2k, Peter Bezruc mine. 3k, Automatic coaling crane.

1952, Sept. 14 *Perf. 12½*

548 A217 1k sepia *.85* *.50*
549 A217 1.50k dark blue .20 .20
550 A217 2k olive gray .20 .20
551 A217 3k violet brown .20 .20
Nos. 548-551 (4) *1.45* *1.10*

Miners' Day, Sept. 14, 1952. No. 550 also for the 85th anniv. of the birth of Peter Bezruc (Vladimir Vasek), poet.

1952, Oct. 5 Engr. *Perf. 11½*
Inscribed: ". . . . Armady 1952,"

Designs: 2k, Fraternization with Russians. 3k, Marching with flag.

552 A218 1.50k rose lake .20 .20
553 A218 2k olive bister .20 .20
554 A218 3k dk car rose .20 .20
555 A218 4k gray *1.10* *.85*
Nos. 552-555 (4) *1.70* *1.45*

Issued to publicize Army Day, Oct. 5, 1952.

Souvenir Sheet

Statues to Bulgarian Partisans and to Soviet Army — A219

1952, Oct. 18 Unwmk. *Perf. 12½*

556 A219 Sheet of 2 110.00 17.50
a. 2k deep carmine 24.00 6.50
b. 3k ultramarine 24.00 6.50

National Philatelic Exhibition, Bratislava, Oct. 18-Nov. 2, 1952.

Danube River, Bratislava A220

1952, Oct. 18

557 A220 1.50k dark brown .20 .20

National Philatelic Exhibition, Bratislava.

Conference with Lenin and Stalin — A221

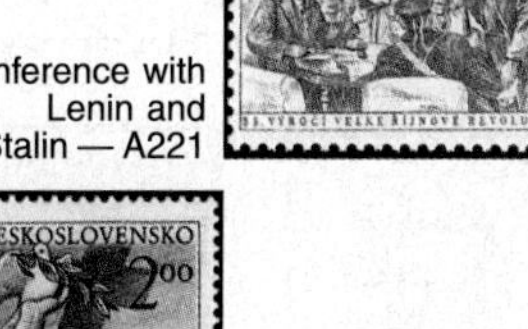

Worker and Nurse Holding Dove and Olive Branch — A222

1952, Nov. 7

558 A221 2k brown black *1.00* *.75*
559 A221 3k carmine .20 .20

35th anniv. of the Russian Revolution and to publicize Czechoslovak-Soviet friendship.

1952, Nov. 15 Photo. *Perf. 14*

560 A222 2k brown *.85* *.50*
561 A222 3k red .20 .20

Issued to publicize the first State Congress of the Czechoslovak Red Cross.

Matej Louda, Hussite Leader, Painted by Mikulas Ales A223

3k, Dragon-killer Trutnov, painted by Ales.

1952, Nov. 18 Engr. *Perf. 11½*

562 A223 2k red brown .20 .20
563 A223 3k grnsh gray *.30* *.20*

Mikulas Ales, painter, birth cent.

Gottwald Type of 1948-49

1952, June 2 Unwmk. *Perf. 12½*
Size: 19x24mm

564 A135 1k dark green .20 .20

"Peace" Flags — A224

Dove by Picasso — A225

1952, Dec. 12 Photo. *Perf. 14*

565 A224 3k red brown .25 .20
566 A224 4k deep blue *.80 .50*

Issued to publicize the Congress of Nations for Peace, Vienna, Dec. 12-19, 1952.

1953, Jan. 17

Design: 4k, Czech Family.

567 A225 1.50k dark brown .20 .20
568 A225 4k slate blue *.60 .30*

2nd Czechoslovak Peace Congress.

Smetana Museum — A226

Design: 4k, Jirásek Museum.

1953, Feb. 10 Engr. *Perf. 11½*

569 A226 1.50k dk violet brn .20 .20
570 A226 4k dark gray *1.00 .65*

Prof. Zdenek Nejedly, 75th birth anniv.

Martin Kukucin — A227

Jaroslav Vrchlicky — A228

Designs: 2k, Karel Jaromir Erben. 3k, Vaclav Matej Kramerius. 5k, Josef Dobrovsky.

1953, Feb. 28

571 A227 1k gray .20 .20
572 A228 1.50k olive .20 .20
573 A228 2k rose lake .20 .20
574 A228 3k lt brown .20 .20
575 A228 5k slate blue *1.10 1.10*
Nos. 571-575 (5) 1.90 1.90

Issued to honor Czech writers and poets: 1k, 25th anniv. of death of Kukucin. 1.50k, birth cent. of Vrchlicky. 2k, cent. of completion of "Kytice" by Erben. 3k, birth bicent. of Kramerius. 5k, birth bicent. of Dobrovsky.

Militia — A229

Gottwald — A230

Design: 8k, Portraits of Stalin and Gottwald and Peoples Assembly.

Perf. 13½x14

1953, Feb. 25 Photo. Unwmk.

576 A229 1.50k deep blue .20 .20
577 A230 3k red .20 .20
578 A229 8k dark brown *1.10 .75*
Nos. 576-578 (3) 1.50 1.15

5th anniv. of the defeat of the attempt to reinstate capitalism.

Book and Torch — A231

Design: 3k, Bedrich Vaclavek.

1953, Mar. 5 Engr. *Perf. 11½*

579 A231 1k sepia *.70 .50*
580 A231 3k orange brown .20 .20

Bedrich Vaclavek (1897-1943), socialist writer.

Stalin Type of 1949
Inscribed "21 XII 1879-5 III 1953"

1953, Mar. 12

581 A154 1.50k black .25 .20

Death of Joseph Stalin, Mar. 5, 1953.

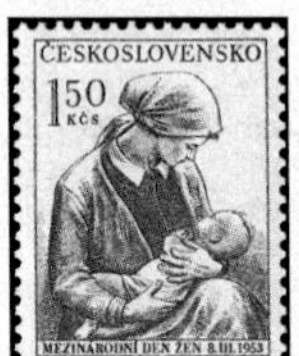

Mother and Child — A232

Girl Revolutionist A233

1953, Mar. 8

582 A232 1.50k ultra .20 .20
583 A233 2k brown red *.75 .35*

International Women's Day.

Klement Gottwald — A234

1953, Mar. 19

584 A234 1.50k black .20 .20
585 A234 3k black .20 .20

Souvenir Sheet

Imperf

586 A234 5k black 2.25 1.75

Death of Pres. Klement Gottwald, 3/14/53.

Josef Pecka, Ladislav Zapotocky and Josef Hybes — A236

1953, Apr. 7 Unwmk. *Perf. 11½*

587 A236 2k lt violet brn .20 .20

75th anniversary of the first congress of the Czech Social Democratic Party.

Cyclists — A237

1953, Apr. 29

588 A237 3k deep blue .45 .25

6th International Peace Bicycle Race, Prague-Berlin-Warsaw.

Medal of "May 1, 1890" A238

Designs: 1.50k, Lenin and Stalin. 3k, May Day Parade. 8k, Marx and Engels.

Engraved and Photogravure

1953, Apr. 30 *Perf. 11½x11, 14*

589 A238 1k chocolate *1.00 .70*
590 A238 1.50k dark gray .20 .20
591 A238 3k carmine lake .20 .20
592 A238 8k dk gray green .25 .20
Nos. 589-592 (4) 1.65 1.30

Issued to publicize Labor Day, May 1, 1953.

Sowing Grain — A239

1953, May 8 Photo. *Perf. 14*

593 A239 1.50k shown .30 .20
594 A239 7k Reaper *.95 .75*

Socialization of the village.

Dam — A240

Welder — A241

Design: 3k, Iron works.

1953, May 8 *Perf. 11½*

595 A240 1.50k gray *.50 .45*
596 A241 2k blue gray .20 .20
597 A240 3k red brown .20 .20
Nos. 595-597 (3) .90 .85

Josef Slavik — A242

Leos Janacek — A243

1953, June 19 Photo.

598 A242 75h dp gray blue *.40 .20*
599 A243 1.60k dark brown .85 .20

Issued on the occasion of the International Music Festival, Prague, 1953.

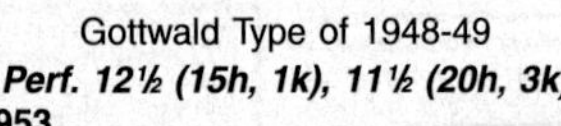

Gottwald Type of 1948-49

Perf. 12½ (15h, 1k), 11½ (20h, 3k)

1953

600 A135 15h yellow green .20 .20
601 A135 20h dk violet brn .20 .20
602 A135 1k purple .60 .20
603 A135 3k brown car .20 .20
604 A135 3k gray .65 .20
Nos. 600-604 (5) 1.85 1.00

Nos. 600-604 vary slightly in size.

Pres. Antonin Zapotocky — A244

1953, June 19 *Perf. 14*

605 A244 30h violet blue .45 .20
606 A244 60h cerise .25 .20

Julius Fucik A245

Book and Carnation A246

1953, Sept. 8 Engr. *Perf. 12½*

607 A245 40h dk violet brn .25 .20
608 A246 60h pink *.40 .25*

10th anniv. of the death of Julius Fucik, Communist leader executed by the Nazis.

Miner and Flag — A247

Design: 60h, Oil field and workers.

1953, Sept. 10 *Perf. 11½*

609 A247 30h gray .20 .20
610 A247 60h brown vio *.75 .50*

Miner's Day, Sept. 10, 1953.

Volleyball Game — A248

Motorcyclist A249

Design: 60h, Woman throwing javelin.

1953, Sept. 15

611 A248 30h brown red *1.25 1.25*
612 A249 40h dk violet brn 2.50 .75
613 A248 60h rose violet 2.50 .75
Nos. 611-613 (3) 6.25 *2.75*

Hussite Warrior A250

Pres. Antonin Zapotocky A251

Designs: 60h, Soldier presenting arms. 1k, Red army soldiers.

1953, Oct. 8

614 A250 30h brown .30 .20
615 A250 60h rose lake .65 .20
616 A250 1k brown red *1.25 .70*
Nos. 614-616 (3) 2.20 1.10

Issued to publicize Army Day, Oct. 3, 1953.

1953 Unwmk. *Perf. 11½, 12½*

617 A251 30h violet blue .25 .20
618 A251 60h carmine rose .50 .20

#617 is perf. 11½ & measures 19x23mm, #618 perf. 12½ & 18½x23½mm.
See No. 780.

Charles Bridge and Prague Castle — A252

Korean and Czech Girls — A253

1953, Aug. 15 Engr. *Perf. 11½*

619 A252 5k gray 2.25 .20

1953, Oct. 11 *Perf. 11x11½*

620 A253 30h dark brown 2.25 1.00

Czechoslovakia's friendship with Korea.

Flags, Hradcany Castle and Kremlin — A254

Designs: 60h, Lomonosov University, Moscow. 1.20k, Lenin Ship Canal.

1953, Nov. 7

621 A254 30h dark gray *.90 .65*
622 A254 60h dark brown 1.00 .75
623 A254 1.20k ultra 2.00 1.25
Nos. 621-623 (3) 3.90 2.65

Czechoslovak-Soviet friendship month.

Emmy Destinn, Opera Singer — A255

National Theater, Prague — A256

Portrait: 2k, Eduard Vojan, actor.

1953, Nov. 18 *Perf. 14*

624 A255 30h blue black .85 .40
625 A256 60h brown .25 .20
626 A255 2k sepia *2.25 .65*
Nos. 624-626 (3) 3.35 1.25

Natl. Theater founding, 70th anniv.

Josef Manes — A257

Vaclav Hollar — A258

1953, Nov. 28 *Perf. 11x11½*

627 A257 60h brown carmine .35 .20
628 A257 1.20k deep blue *1.10 .50*

Issued to honor Josef Manes, painter.

1953, Dec. 5

Portrait: 1.20k, Head framed, facing right.

629 A258 30h brown black .20 .20
630 A258 1.20k dark brown *.80 .45*

Vaclav Hollar, artist and etcher.

Leo N. Tolstoi — A259

1953, Dec. 29 Unwmk.

631 A259 60h dark green .20 .20
632 A259 1k chocolate *1.10 .65*

Leo N. Tolstoi, 125th birth anniv.

Locomotive — A260

Design: 1k, Plane loading mail.

Engraved, Center Photogravure

1953, Dec. 29 *Perf. 11½x11*

633 A260 60h brn org & gray vio 1.00 .30
634 A260 1k org brn & brt bl *2.50 .75*

Lenin — A261

Lenin Museum, Prague — A262

1954, Jan. 21 Engr. *Perf. 11½*

635 A261 30h dark brown .45 .20
636 A262 1.40k chocolate *1.00 .90*

30th anniversary of the death of Lenin.

Klement Gottwald — A263

Design: 2.40k, Revolutionist with flag.

1954, Feb. 18 *Perf. 11x11½, 14x13½*

637 A263 60h dark brown .30 .20
638 A263 2.40k rose lake *4.25 1.50*

25th anniversary of the fifth congress of the Communist Party in Czechoslovakia.

Gottwald Mausoleum, Prague — A264

Gottwald and Stalin A265

1.20k, Lenin & Stalin mausoleum, Moscow.

1954, Mar. 5 *Perf. 11½, 14x13½*

639 A264 30h olive brown .20 .20
640 A265 60h dee, ultra .25 .20
641 A264 1.20k rose brown *1.25 .85*
Nos. 639-641 (3) 1.70 1.25

1st anniv. of the deaths of Stalin and Gottwald.

Two Runners — A266

Group of Hikers — A267

Design: 1k, Woman swimmer.

1954, Apr. 24 *Perf. 11½*

642 A266 30h dark brown 1.40 .60
643 A267 80h dark green *5.00 2.75*
644 A266 1k dk violet blue 1.00 .65
Nos. 642-644 (3) 7.40 4.00

Nurse — A268

Designs: 15h, Construction worker. 40h, Postwoman. 45h, Ironworker. 50h, Soldier. 75h, Lathe operator. 80h, Textile worker. 1k, Farm woman. 1.20k, Scientist and microscope. 1.60k, Miner. 2k, Physician and baby. 2.40k, Engineer. 3k, Chemist.

1954 *Perf. 12½x12, 11½x11*

645 A268 15h dark green .30 .20
646 A268 20h lt violet .35 .20
647 A268 40h dark brown .45 .20
648 A268 45h dk gray blue .20 .20
649 A268 50h dk gray green .35 .20
650 A268 75h deep blue .35 .20
651 A268 80h violet brown .35 .20
652 A268 1k green .60 .20
653 A268 1.20k dk violet blue .35 .20
654 A268 1.60k brown blk .90 .20
655 A268 2k orange brown 1.10 .20
656 A268 2.40k violet blue 1.00 .20
657 A268 3k carmine 1.40 .20
Nos. 645-657 (13) 7.70 2.60

Antonin Dvorák — A269

Prokop Divis — A270

40h, Leos Janacek. 60h, Bedrich Smetana.

1954, May 22 *Perf. 11x11½*

658 A269 30h violet brown .85 .20
659 A269 40h brick red *1.40 .20*
660 A269 60h dark blue .90 .20
Nos. 658-660 (3) 3.15 .60

"Year of Czech Music," 1954.

1954, June 15

661 A270 30h gray .20 .20
662 A270 75h violet brown *.65 .50*

200th anniv. of the invention of a lightning conductor by Prokop Divis.

Slovak Insurrectionist A271

Anton P. Chekhov A272

Design: 1.20k, Partisan woman.

1954, Aug. 28 *Perf. 11½*

663 A271 30h brown orange .20 .20
664 A271 1.20k dark blue *.80 .75*

Slovak national uprising, 10th anniv.

1954, Sept. 24

665 A272 30h dull gray grn .20 .20
666 A272 45h dull gray brn *.90 .65*

50th anniv. of the death of Chekhov, writer.

Soviet Representative Giving Agricultural Instruction — A273

Designs: 60h, Soviet industrial instruction. 2k, Dancers (cultural collaboration).

1954, Nov. 6 *Perf. 11½x11*

667 A273 30h yellow brown .20 .20
668 A273 60h dark blue .20 .20
669 A273 2k vermilion *1.25 1.25*
Nos. 667-669 (3) 1.65 1.65

Czechoslovak-Soviet friendship month.

Jan Neruda — A274

60h, Janko Jesensky. 1.60k, Jiri Wolker.

1954, Nov. 25 *Perf. 11x11½*

670 A274 30h dark blue .85 .20
671 A274 60h dull red *1.40 .50*
672 A274 1.60k sepia .35 .20
Nos. 670-672 (3) 2.60 .90

Issued to honor Czechoslovak poets.

View of Telc A275

Views: 60h, Levoca. 3k, Ceske Budejovice.

1954, Dec. 10 **Engr. & Photo.**

673 A275 30h black & bis .35 .20
674 A275 60h brown & bis .35 .20
675 A275 3k black & bis *2.00 1.50*
Nos. 673-675 (3) 2.70 1.90

Pres. Antonin Zapotocky A276

Attacking Soldiers A278

1954, Dec. 18 **Engr.** ***Perf. 11½***

676 A276 30h black brown .45 .20
677 A276 60h dark blue .25 .20

Souvenir Sheet

Imperf

678 A276 2k deep claret 5.00 3.00

70th birthday of Pres. Antonin Zapotocky. See Nos. 829-831.

1954, Oct. 3 ***Perf. 11½***

Design: 2k, Soldier holding child.

679 A278 60h dark green .30 .20
680 A278 2k dark brown *1.00 .95*

Army Day, Oct. 6, 1954.

Woman Holding Torch — A279

Comenius University Building A280

Design: 45h, Ski jumper.

1955, Jan. 20 **Engr.**

681 A279 30h red 1.90 .25

Engraved and Photogravure

682 A279 45h black & blue 2.50 .20

First National Spartacist Games, 1955.

1955, Jan. 28 **Engr.** ***Perf. 11½***

Design: 75h, Jan A. Komensky medal.

683 A280 60h deep green .20 .20
684 A280 75h chocolate *.90 .45*

35th anniversary of the founding of Comenius University, Bratislava.

Czechoslovak Automobile A281

60h, Textile worker. 75h, Lathe operator.

1955, Mar. 15 **Unwmk.**

685 A281 45h dull green *.65 .45*
686 A281 60h dk violet blue .20 .20
687 A281 75h sepia .35 .20
Nos. 685-687 (3) 1.20 .85

Woman Decorating Soviet Soldier — A282

Stalin Memorial, Prague — A283

Designs: 35h, Tankman with flowers. 60h, Children greeting soldier.

1955, May 5 **Engr.** ***Perf. 11½***

688 A282 30h blue .25 .20
689 A282 35h dark brown *.75 .50*
690 A282 60h cerise .25 .20

Photo.

691 A283 60h sepia .40 .20
Nos. 688-691 (4) 1.65 1.10

10th anniv. of Czechoslovakia's liberation.

Music and Spring — A284

Foundry Worker — A285

Design: 1k, Woman with lyre.

1955, May 12 **Engr. & Photo.**

692 A284 30h black & pale blue .35 .25
693 A284 1k black & pale rose *1.10 1.00*

International Music Festival, Prague, 1955.

1955, May 12 **Engr.**

Design: 45h, Farm workers.

694 A285 30h violet .20 .20
695 A285 45h green *.60 .45*

Issued to publicize the third congress of the Trade Union Revolutionary Movement.

Woman Athlete — A286

Jakub Arbes — A287

60h, Dancing couple. 1.60k, Athlete.

1955, June 21

696 A286 20h violet blue *.65 .35*
697 A286 60h green .25 .20
698 A286 1.60k red .65 .25
Nos. 696-698 (3) 1.55 .80

Issued to publicize the first National Spartacist Games, Prague, June-July, 1955.

1955

Portraits: 30h, Jan Stursa. 40h, Elena Marothy-Soltesova. 60h, Josef Vaclav Sladek. 75h, Alexander Stepanovic Popov. 1.40k, Jan Holly. 1.60k, Pavel Josef Safarik.

699 A287 20h brown .25 .20
700 A287 30h black .25 .20
701 A287 40h gray green .75 .20
702 A287 60h black .50 .20
703 A287 75h claret *1.10 .70*
704 A287 1.40k black, *cr* .50 .20
705 A287 1.60k dark blue .50 .20
Nos. 699-705 (7) 3.85 1.90

Various anniversaries of prominent Slavs.

Girl and Boy of Two Races — A288

Costume of Ocova, Slovakia — A289

1955, July 20

706 A288 60h violet blue .30 .20

5th World Festival of Youth in Warsaw, July 31-Aug. 14.

1955, July 25

Regional Costumes: 75h, Detva man, Slovakia. 1.60k, Chodsko man, Bohemia. 2k, Hana woman, Moravia.

Frame and Outlines in Brown

707 A289 60h orange & rose *8.25 5.75*
708 A289 75h orange & lilac *4.75 3.00*
709 A289 1.60k blue & orange *8.00 4.75*
710 A289 2k yellow & rose *9.00 6.50*
Nos. 707-710 (4) 30.00 20.00

Carp A290

Designs: 30h, Beetle. 35h, Gray Partridge. 1.40k, Butterfly. 1.50k, Hare.

1955, Aug. 8 **Engr. & Photo.**

711 A290 20h sepia & lt bl 1.50 .20
712 A290 30h sepia & pink 1.00 .20
713 A290 35h sepia & buff 1.00 .20
714 A290 1.40k sepia & cream *5.00 2.00*
715 A290 1.50k sepia & lt grn 1.50 .25
Nos. 711-715 (5) 10.00 2.85

Tabor A291

45h, Prachatice. 60h, Jindrichuv Hradec.

1955, Aug. 26 **Engr.**

716 A291 30h violet brown .20 .20
717 A291 45h rose carmine *.75 .60*
718 A291 60h sage green .20 .20
Nos. 716-718 (3) 1.15 1.00

Issued to publicize the architectural beauty of the towns of Southern Bohemia.

Souvenir Sheet

Various Views of Prague — A292

1955, Sept. 10 **Engr.** ***Perf. 14x13½***

719 A292 Sheet of 5 18.00 16.00
a. 30h gray black 3.00 3.00
b. 45h gray black 3.00 3.00
c. 60h rose lake 3.00 3.00
d. 75h rose lake 3.00 3.00
e. 1.60k gray black 3.00 3.00

International Philatelic Exhibition, Prague, Sept. 10-25, 1955. Size: 145x110mm. Exists imperf., value $40.

Motorcyclists A293

Workers, Soldier and Pioneer A294

1955, Aug. 28

720 A293 60h violet brown 2.25 .50

30th International Motorcycle Races at Gottwaldov, Sept. 13-18, 1955.

1955, Oct. 6 **Unwmk.** ***Perf. 11½***

Army Day: 60h, Tanks and planes.

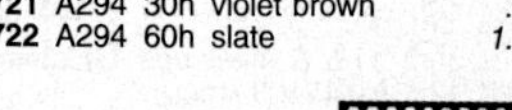

721 A294 30h violet brown .25 .20
722 A294 60h slate *1.25 1.25*

Hans Christian Andersen — A295

Portraits: 40h, Friedrich von Schiller. 60h, Adam Mickiewicz. 75h, Walt Whitman.

1955, Oct. 27

723 A295 30h brown red .20 .20
724 A295 40h dark blue *.95 .65*
725 A295 60h deep claret .20 .20
726 A295 75h greenish black .30 .20
Nos. 723-726 (4) 1.65 1.25

Issued in honor of these four poets and to mark the 100th anniversary of the publication of Walt Whitman's "Leaves of Grass."

Railroad Bridge A296

30h, Train crossing bridge. 60h, Train approaching tunnel. 1.60k, Miners' housing project.

Inscribed: "Stavba Socialismu"

1955, Dec. 15

727 A296 20h dull green .25 .20
728 A296 30h violet brown .25 .20
729 A296 60h slate .25 .20
730 A296 1.60k carmine rose .50 .20
Nos. 727-730 (4) 1.25 .80

Issued to publicize socialist public works.

Hydroelectric Plant — A297

Jewelry — A298

2nd Five Year Plan: 10h, Miner with drill. 25h, Building construction. 30h, Harvester. 60h, Metallurgical plant.

Inscribed: "Druhy Petilety Plan 1956-1960."

1956, Feb. 20 ***Perf. 11½x11***

731 A297 5h violet brown .20 .20
732 A297 10h gray black .20 .20
733 A297 25h dk car rose .20 .20
734 A297 30h green .20 .20
735 A297 60h violet blue .20 .20
Nos. 731-735 (5) 1.00 1.00

1956, Mar. 17 ***Perf. 11x11½***

736 A298 30h shown .25 .20
737 A298 45h Glassware *3.75 2.00*
738 A298 60h Ceramics .65 .20
739 A298 75h Textiles .25 .20
Nos. 736-739 (4) *4.90 2.60*

Products of Czechoslovakian industries.

Karlovy Vary (Karlsbad) A299

"We Serve our People" A300

Various Spas: 45h, Marianske Lazne (Marienbad). 75h, Piestany. 1.20k, Tatry Vysne Ruzbachy (Tatra Mountains).

1956, Mar. 17

740 A299 30h olive green 1.10 .25
741 A299 45h brown .85 .20
742 A299 75h claret *6.00 4.00*
743 A299 1.20k ultra .40 .20
Nos. 740-743 (4) *8.35 4.65*

Issued to publicize Czechoslovakian spas.

1956, Apr. 9 **Photo.** ***Perf. 11x11½***

Designs: 60h, Russian War Memorial, Berlin. 1k, Tank crewman with standard.

744 A300 30h olive brown .30 .20
745 A300 60h carmine rose .30 .20
746 A300 1k ultra *4.75 3.00*
Nos. 744-746 (3) *5.35 3.40*

Exhibition: "The Construction and Defense of our Country," Prague, Apr., 1956.

Cyclists — A301

Girl Basketball Players — A302

Athletes and Olympic Rings — A303

Engraved and Photogravure

1956, Apr. 25 **Unwmk.** ***Perf. 11½***

747 A301 30h green & lt blue *2.50 .20*
748 A302 45h dk blue & car 1.00 .20
749 A303 75h brown & lemon 1.00 .20
Nos. 747-749 (3) *4.50 .60*

9th Intl. Peace Cycling Race, Warsaw-Berlin-Prague, May 1-15, 1956 (No. 747). 5th European Womens' Basketball Championship (No. 748). Summer Olympics, Melbourne, Nov. 22-Dec. 8, 1956 (No. 749).

Mozart — A304

Home Guard — A305

45h, Josef Myslivecek. 60h, Jiri Benda. 1k, Bertramka House, Prague. 1.40k, Xaver Dusek (1731-99) and wife Josepha. 1.60k, Nostic Theater, Prague.

1956, May 12 **Engr.**

Design in Gray Black

750 A304 30h bister 1.25 .50
751 A304 45h gray green *12.00 8.50*
752 A304 60h pale rose lilac 1.25 .20
753 A304 1k salmon 1.50 .30
754 A304 1.40k lt blue 3.50 .50
755 A304 1.60k lemon 2.50 .25
Nos. 750-755 (6) *22.00 10.25*

200th anniv. of the birth of Wolfgang Amadeus Mozart and to publicize the International Music Festival in Prague.

1956, May 25

756 A305 60h violet blue .60 .20

Issued to commemorate the first meeting of the Home Guard, Prague, May 25-27, 1956.

Josef Kajetan Tyl — A306

River Patrol — A307

Portraits: 20h, Ludovit Stur. 30h, Frana Sramek. 1.40k, Karel Havlicek Borovsky.

1956, June 23

757 A306 20h dull purple .55 .20
758 A306 30h blue .30 .20
759 A306 60h black .30 .20
760 A306 1.40k claret *2.75 1.40*
Nos. 757-760 (4) *3.90 2.00*

Issued to honor various Czechoslovakian writers. See Nos. 781-784, 873-876.

1956, July 8 ***Perf. 11x11½***

Design: 60h, Guard and dog.

761 A307 30h ultra *.85 .25*
762 A307 60h green .20 .20

Issued to honor men of Frontier Guard.

Type of 1956 and

Steeplechase — A308

1956, Sept. 8 **Unwmk.** ***Perf. 11½***

763 A308 60h indigo & bister *1.75 .40*
764 A308 80h brown vio & vio 1.00 .20
765 A303 1.20k slate & orange .75 .20
Nos. 763-765 (3) *3.50 .80*

Steeplechase, Pardubice, 1956 (No. 763). Marathon race, Kosice, 1956 (No. 764). Olympic Games, Melbourne, Nov. 22-Dec. 8 (No. 765).

Woman Gathering Grapes — A309

Fishermen — A310

35h, Women gathering hops. 95h, Logging.

1956, Sept. 20 **Engr.**

766 A309 30h brown lake .25 .20
767 A309 35h gray green .25 .20
768 A310 80h dark blue .45 .20
769 A310 95h chocolate *1.50 1.40*
Nos. 766-769 (4) *2.45 2.00*

Issued to publicize natural resources.

European Timetable Conf., Prague, Nov. 9-13 — A311

A312

Locomotives: 10h, 1846. 30h, 1855. 40h, 1945. 45h, 1952. 60h, 1955. 1k, 1954.

1956, Nov. 9 **Unwmk.** ***Perf. 11½***

770 A311 10h brown 1.25 .20
771 A312 30h gray 2.50 .20
772 A312 40h green 3.50 .30
773 A312 45h brown car *11.00 5.50*
774 A312 60h indigo 2.50 .20
775 A312 1k ultra 4.25 .30
Nos. 770-775 (6) *25.00 6.70*

Costume of Moravia — A313

Regional Costumes (women): 1.20k, Blata, Bohemia. 1.40k, Cicmany, Slovakia. 1.60k, Novohradsko, Slovakia.

1956, Dec. 15 ***Perf. 13½***

776 A313 30h brn, ultra & car 2.00 .60
777 A313 1.20k brn, car & ultra 2.50 .25
778 A313 1.40k brn, ocher & ver *6.50 1.75*
779 A313 1.60k brn, car & grn 2.00 .40
Nos. 776-779 (4) *13.00 3.00*

See Nos. 832-835.

Zapotocky Type of 1953

1956, Oct. 7 **Unwmk.** ***Perf. 12½***

780 A251 30h blue .30 .20

Portrait Type of 1956

15h, Ivan Olbracht. 20h, Karel Toman. 30h, F. X. Salda. 1.60k, Terezia Vansova.

1957, Jan. 18 **Engr.** ***Perf. 11½***

781 A306 15h dk red brn, *cr* .20 .20
782 A306 20h dk green, *cr* .20 .20
783 A306 30h dk brown, *cr* .20 .20
784 A306 1.60k dk blue, *cr* .40 .20
Nos. 781-784 (4) 1.00 .80

Issued in honor of Czechoslovakian writers.

Kolin Cathedral — A315

Views: No. 786, Banska Stiavnica. No. 787, Uherske Hradiste. No. 788, Karlstein. No. 789, Charles Bridge, Prague. 1.25k, Moravska Trebova.

1957, Feb. 23

785 A315 30h dk blue gray .20 .20
786 A315 30h rose violet .20 .20
787 A315 60h deep rose .35 .20
788 A315 60h gray green .35 .20
789 A315 60h brown .25 .20
790 A315 1.25k gray *1.25 1.25*
Nos. 785-790 (6) *2.60 2.25*

Anniversaries of various towns and landmarks.

Komensky Mausoleum, Naarden A316

Jan A. Komensky A317

Farm Woman — A318

Old Prints: 40h, Komensky teaching. 1k, Sun, moon, stars and earth.

Perf. 11½x11, 14 (A317)

1957, Mar. 28 **Engr.** **Unwmk.**

791 A316 30h pale brown .25 .20
792 A316 40h dark green .25 .20
793 A317 60h chocolate *1.25 .75*
794 A316 1k carmine rose .45 .20
Nos. 791-794 (4) *2.20 1.35*

300th anniv. of the publication of "Didactica Opera Omnia" by J. A. Komensky (Comenius). No. 793 issued in sheets of four.

1957, Mar. 22 ***Perf. 11½***

795 A318 30h lt blue green .35 .20

3rd Cong. of Agricultural Cooperatives.

Cyclists A319

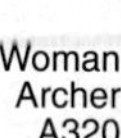

Woman Archer A320

Boxers — A321

Rescue Team A322

1957, Apr. 30 ***Perf. 11½x11, 11x11½***

796 A319 30h sepia & ultra .25 .20
797 A319 60h dull grn & bis *1.50 1.25*
798 A320 60h gray & emer .25 .20
799 A321 60h sepia & org .25 .20
800 A322 60h violet & choc .25 .20
Nos. 796-800 (5) *2.50 2.05*

10th Intl. Peace Cycling Race, Prague-Berlin-Warsaw (#796-797). Intl. Archery Championships (#798). European Boxing Championships, Prague (#799). Mountain Climbing Rescue Service (#800).

Jan V. Stamic — A323

Musicians: No. 802, Ferdinand Laub. No. 803, Frantisek Ondricek. No. 804, Josef B. Foerster. No. 805, Vitezslav Novak. No. 806, Josef Suk.

1957, May 12 ***Perf. 11½***

801 A323 60h purple .25 .20
802 A323 60h black .25 .20
803 A323 60h slate blue .25 .20
804 A323 60h brown .25 .20
805 A323 60h dull red brn .60 .20
806 A323 60h blue green .25 .20
Nos. 801-806 (6) 1.85 1.20

Spring Music Festival, Prague.

Josef Bozek — A324

School of Engineering A325

60h, F. J. Gerstner. 1k, R. Skuhersky.

1957, May 25

807 A324 30h bluish black .20 .20
808 A324 60h gray brown .25 .20
809 A324 1k rose lake .25 .20
810 A325 1.40k blue violet .55 .20
Nos. 807-810 (4) 1.25 .80

School of Engineering in Prague, 250th anniv.

Pioneer and Philatelic Symbols A326

Design: 60h, Girl and carrier pigeon.

Engraved and Photogravure

1957, June 8 ***Perf. 11½***

811 A326 30h olive grn & org .50 .20

Engr. ***Perf. 13½***

812 A326 60h brn & vio bl *1.25 1.00*

Youth Philatelic Exhibition, Pardubice.

"Grief" A327

Motorcyclists A328

Design: 60h, Rose, symbol of new life.

1957, June 10

813 A327 30h black .25 .20
814 A327 60h blk & rose red *.55 .25*

Destruction of Lidice, 15th anniversary.

1957, July 5 ***Perf. 11½***

815 A328 60h dk gray & blue .60 .20

32nd International Motorcycle Race.

Karel Klic — A329

Josef Ressel — A330

1957, July 5

816 A329 30h gray black .20 .20
817 A330 60h violet blue .25 .20

Klic, inventor of photogravure, and Ressel, inventor of the ship screw.

Chamois — A331

Gentian A332

Designs: 30h, Brown bear. 60h, Edelweiss. 1.25k, Tatra Mountains.

1957, Aug. 28 **Engr.** ***Perf. 11½***

818 A331 20h emer & brnsh gray .60 .35
819 A331 30h lt blue & brn .50 .20
820 A332 40h gldn brn & vio bl .75 .20
821 A332 60h yellow & grn .35 .20

Size: 48x28½mm

822 A332 1.25k ol grn & bis *1.50 1.25*
Nos. 818-822 (5) *3.70 2.20*

Tatra Mountains National Park.

"Marycka Magdonova" A333

Man Holding Banner of Trade Union Cong. A334

Engraved and Photogravure

1957, Sept. 15 **Unwmk.** ***Perf. 11½***

823 A333 60h black & dull red .30 .20

90th birthday of Petr Bezruc, poet and author of "Marycka Magdonova."

1957, Sept. 28 **Engr.**

824 A334 75h rose red .40 .20

4th Intl. Trade Union Cong., Leipzig, 10/4-15.

Television Transmitter and Antennas — A335

Design: 60h, Family watching television.

1957, Oct. 19 **Engr.** ***Perf. 11½***

825 A335 40h dk blue & car .20 .20
826 A335 60h redsh brown & emer .25 .20

Issued to publicize the television industry.

Worker, Globe and Lenin A336

60h, Worker, factory, hammer and sickle.

1957, Nov. 7 ***Perf. 12x11½***

827 A336 30h claret .20 .20
828 A336 60h gray blue .25 .20

Russian Revolution, 40th anniversary.

Zapotocky Type of 1954 dated: 19 XII 1884-13 XI 1957

1957, Nov. 18 **Unwmk.** ***Perf. 11½***

829 A276 30h black .20 .20
830 A276 60h black .25 .20

Souvenir Sheet

Imperf

831 A276 2k black 1.00 .75

Death of Pres. Antonin Zapotocky.

Costume Type of 1956

Regional Costumes: 45h, Pilsen woman, Bohemia. 75h, Slovacko man, Moravia. 1.25k, Hana woman, Moravia. 1.95k, Teshinsko woman, Silesia.

1957, Dec. 18 **Engr.** ***Perf. 13½***

832 A313 45h brn, bl & dk red 2.50 1.00
833 A313 75h dk brn, red & grn 1.75 .80
834 A313 1.25k dk brn, scar & ocher 2.50 .75
835 A313 1.95k sepia, bl & ver *3.00 2.00*
Nos. 832-835 (4) *9.75 4.55*

A337

A338

Designs: 30h, Radio telescope and observatory. 45h, Meteorological station in High Tatra. 75h, Sputnik 2 over Earth.

1957, Dec. 20 ***Perf. 11½***

836 A337 30h violet brn & yel 1.75 .65
837 A338 45h sepia & lt bl .45 .35
838 A337 75h claret & blue 2.50 1.00
Nos. 836-838 (3) 4.70 2.00

IGY, 1957-58. No. 838 also for the launching of Sputnik 2, Nov. 3, 1957.

Girl Skater — A339

Litomysl Castle — A340

Designs: 40h, Canoeing. 60h, Volleyball. 80h, Parachutist. 1.60k, Soccer.

1958, Jan. 25 **Engr.** ***Perf. 11½x12***

839 A339 30h rose violet 1.25 .25
840 A339 40h blue .25 .20
841 A339 60h redsh brown .25 .20
842 A339 80h violet blue *1.50 .50*
843 A339 1.60k brt green .45 .20
Nos. 839-843 (5) *3.70 1.35*

Issued to publicize various sports championship events in 1958.

1958, Feb. 10 ***Perf. 11½***

Design: 60h, Bethlehem Chapel.

844 A340 30h green .20 .20
845 A340 60h redsh brown .20 .20

80th anniversary of the birth of Zdenek Nejedly, restorer of Bethlehem Chapel.

Giant Excavator A341

Jewelry — A342

Peace Dove and: 60h, Soldiers, flame and banner, horiz. 1.60k, Harvester and rainbow, horiz.

1958, Feb. 25

846 A341 30h gray violet & yel .20 .20
847 A341 60h gray brown & car .30 .20
848 A341 1.60k green & dull yel .50 .20
Nos. 846-848 (3) 1.00 .60

10th anniv. of the "Victorious February."

Engraved and Photogravure

1958 Unwmk. *Perf. 11½*

Designs: 45h, Dolls. 60h, Textiles. 75h, Kaplan turbine. 1.20k, Glass.

849 A342 30h rose car & blue .20 .20
850 A342 45h rose red & pale lil .20 .20
851 A342 60h violet & aqua .20 .20
852 A342 75h ultra & salmon *1.10* *.75*
853 A342 1.20k blue grn & pink .30 .20
Nos. 849-853 (5) *2.00* *1.55*

Issued for the Universal and International Exposition at Brussels.

King George of Podebrad — A343

Design: 60h, View of Prague, 1628.

1958, May 19 Engr.

854 A343 30h carmine rose .35 .20
855 A343 60h violet blue .30 .20

Issued to publicize the National Archives Exhibition, Prague, May 15-Aug. 15.

"Towards the Stars" — A344

Women of Three Races — A345

Boy, Girl and Globes A346

1958, May 26

856 A344 30h carmine rose *.75* *.35*
857 A345 45h rose violet .20 .20
858 A346 60h blue .20 .20
Nos. 856-858 (3) *1.15* *.75*

The Soc. for Dissemination of Political and Cultural Knowledge (#856). 4th Cong. of the Intl. Democratic Women's Fed. (#857). 1st World Trade Union Conf. of Working Youths, Prague, July 14-20 (#858).

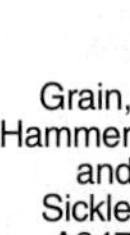

Grain, Hammer and Sickle A347

Atomic Reactor A348

45h, Map of Czechoslovakia, hammer & sickle.

1958, May 26

859 A347 30h dull red .20 .20
860 A347 45h green .20 .20
861 A348 60h dark blue .20 .20
Nos. 859-861 (3) .60 .60

11th Congress of the Czech Communist Party and the 15th anniv. of the Russo-Czechoslovakian Treaty.

Karlovy Vary A349

Various Spas: 40h, Podebrady. 60h, Marianske Lazne. 80h, Luhacovice. 1.20k, Strbske Pleso. 1.60k, Trencianske Teplice.

1958, June 25

862 A349 30h rose claret .20 .20
863 A349 40h redsh brown .20 .20
864 A349 60h gray green .20 .20
865 A349 80h sepia .20 .20
866 A349 1.20k violet blue .30 .20
867 A349 1.60k lt violet *1.10* *.80*
Nos. 862-867 (6) *2.20* *1.80*

Telephone Operator A350

Pres. Novotny A351

Design: 45h, Radio transmitter.

1958, June 20

868 A350 30h black & brn org .25 .20
869 A350 45h black & lt grn .35 .20

Conference of Postal Ministers of Communist Countries, Prague, June 30-July 9.

1958-59 *Perf. 12½*

870 A351 30h brt violet blue .20 .20
b. Perf. 11½ .20 .20
870A A351 30h lt violet ('59) *1.50* *.50*
871 A351 60h carmine rose .25 .20

Perf. 11½

Redrawn

871A A351 60h rose red .20 .20
Nos. 870-871A (4) *2.15* *1.10*

On No. 871 the top of the "6" turns down; on No. 871A it is open.

Czechoslovak Pavilion, Brussels — A352

1958, July 15 Engr. & Photo.

872 A352 1.95k lt blue & bis brn .90 .20

Czechoslovakia Week at the Universal and International Exhibition at Brussels.

Portrait Type of 1956

30h, Julius Fucik. 45h, G. K. Zechenter 60h, Karel Capek. 1.40k, Svatopluk Cech.

1958, Aug. 20 Engr. *Perf. 11½*

873 A306 30h rose red .25 .20
874 A306 45h violet *1.25* *.50*
875 A306 60h dk blue gray .20 .20
876 A306 1.40k gray .50 .20
Nos. 873-876 (4) *2.20* *1.10*

Death anniversaries of four famous Czechs.

The Artist and the Muse — A353

1958, Aug. 20 *Perf. 14*

877 A353 1.60k black 2.75 1.25

85th birthday of Max Svabinsky, artist and engraver.

Children's Hospital, Brno — A354

Designs: 60h, New Town Hall, Brno. 1k, St. Thomas Church. 1.60k, View of Brno.

1958, Sept. 6 Unwmk. *Perf. 11½*

Size: 40x23mm

878 A354 30h violet .20 .20
879 A354 60h rose red .20 .20
880 A354 1k brown .45 .20

Perf. 14

Size: 50x28mm

881 A354 1.60k dk slate grn *1.90* *1.75*
Nos. 878-881 (4) *2.75* *2.35*

Natl. Phil. Exhib., Brno, Sept. 9.
No. 881 sold for 3.10k, including entrance ticket to exhibition. Issued in sheets of four.

Lepiota Procera — A355

Children on Beach — A356

Mushrooms: 40h, Boletus edulis. 60h, Krombholzia rufescens. 1.40k, Amanita muscaria L. 1.60k, Armillariella mellea.

1958, Oct. 6 *Perf. 14*

882 A355 30h dk brn, grn & buff 1.00 .20
883 A355 40h vio brn & brn org 1.00 .20
884 A355 60h black, red & buff 1.00 .20
885 A355 1.40k brown, scar & grn 2.00 .30
886 A355 1.60k blk, red brn & ol *10.00* *1.10*
Nos. 882-886 (5) *15.00* *2.00*

1958, Oct. 24 Unwmk. *Perf. 14*

45h, Mother, child and bird. 60h, Skier.

887 A356 30h blue, yel & red .20 .20
888 A356 45h ultra & carmine .25 .20
889 A356 60h brown, blue & yel .35 .20
Nos. 887-889 (3) .80 .60

UNESCO Headquarters in Paris opening, Nov. 3.

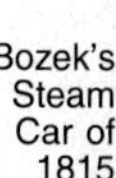

Bozek's Steam Car of 1815 A357

Designs: 45h, "Präsident" car of 1897. 60h, "Skoda" sports car. 80h, "Tatra" sedan. 1k, "Autocar Skoda" bus. 1.25k, Trucks.

Engraved and Photogravure

1958, Dec. 1 *Perf. 11½x11*

890 A357 30h vio blk & buff .50 .20
891 A357 45h ol & lt ol grn .40 .20
892 A357 60h ol gray & sal .55 .20
893 A357 80h claret & bl grn .40 .20
894 A357 1k brn & lt yel grn .40 .20
895 A357 1.25k green & buff *2.00* *.60*
Nos. 890-895 (6) *4.25* *1.60*

Issued to honor the automobile industry.

Stamp of 1918 and Allegory — A358

1958, Dec. 18 Engr. *Perf. 11x11½*

896 A358 60h dark blue gray .30 .20

1st Czechoslovakian postage stamp, 40th anniv.

Ice Hockey A359

30h, Girl throwing javelin. 60h, Ice hockey. 1k, Hurdling. 1.60k, Rowing. 2k, High jump.

1959, Feb. 14 *Perf. 11½x11*

897 A359 20h dk brown & gray .25 .20
898 A359 30h red brn & org brn .25 .20
899 A359 60h dk bl & pale grn .20 .20
900 A359 1k maroon & citron .40 .20
901 A359 1.60k dull vio & lt bl .55 .20
902 A359 2k red brn & lt bl *1.75* *1.00*
Nos. 897-902 (6) *3.40* *2.00*

Congress Emblem — A360

"Equality of All Races" — A361

60h, Industrial & agricultural workers, emblem.

1959, Feb. 27 *Perf. 11½*

903 A360 30h maroon & lt blue .20 .20
904 A360 60h dk blue & yellow .20 .20

4th Agricultural Cooperative Cong. in Prague.

1959, Mar. 23

Designs: 1k, "Peace." 2k, Mother and Child: "Freedom for Colonial People."

905 A361 60h gray green .20 .20
906 A361 1k gray .25 .20
907 A361 2k dk gray blue *1.25* *.50*
Nos. 905-907 (3) *1.70* *.90*

10th anniversary of the signing of the Universal Declaration of Human Rights.

Girl Holding Doll — A362

Frederic Joliot Curie — A363

40h, Pioneer studying map. 60h, Pioneer with radio. 80h, Girl pioneer planting tree.

1959, Mar. 28 **Engr. & Photo.**

908 A362 30h violet bl & yel .20 .20
909 A362 40h indigo & ultra .20 .20
910 A362 60h black & lilac .20 .20
911 A362 80h brown & lt green .30 .20
Nos. 908-911 (4) .90 .80

10th anniv. of the Pioneer organization.

1959, Apr. 17 **Engr.**

912 A363 60h sepia .75 .25

Frederic Joliot Curie and the 10th anniversary of the World Peace Movement.

"Reaching for the Moon" — A364

Town Hall Pilsen — A365

1959, Apr. 17

913 A364 30h violet blue .95 .25

2nd Cong. of the Czechoslovak Assoc. for the Propagation of Political and Cultural knowledge.

1959, May 2

Designs: 60h, Part of steam condenser turbine. 1k, St. Bartholomew's Church, Pilsen. 1.60k, Part of lathe.

914 A365 30h lt brown .20 .20
915 A365 60h violet & lt grn .25 .20
916 A365 1k violet blue .30 .20
917 A365 1.60k black & yellow *1.25* *.85*
Nos. 914-917 (4) *2.00* *1.45*

2nd Pilsen Stamp Exhib. in connection with the centenary of the Skoda (Lenin) armament works.

Factory and Emblem A366

Inscribed: "IV Vseodborovy sjezd, 1959"

1959, May 13

918 A366 30h shown .20 .20
919 A366 60h Dam .20 .20

4th Trade Union Congress.

Zvolen Castle A367

1959, June 13

920 A367 60h gray olive & yel .30 .20

Regional Stamp Exhibition, Zvolen, 1959.

Frantisek Benda — A368

Aurel Stodola — A369

30h, Vaclav Kliment Klicpera. 60h, Karel V. Rais. 80h, Antonin Slavicek. 1k, Peter Bezruc.

1959, June 22 ***Perf. 11½x11***

921 A368 15h violet blue .20 .20
922 A368 30h orange brown .20 .20
923 A369 40h dull green .20 .20
924 A369 60h dull red brn .25 .20
925 A369 80h dull violet .25 .20
926 A368 1k dark brown .25 .20
Nos. 921-926 (6) 1.35 1.20

View of the Fair Grounds A370

Designs: 60h, Fair emblem and world map. 1.60k, Pavilion "Z."

Inscribed: "Mezinarodni Veletrh Brne 6.-20.IX. 1959"

Engraved and Photogravure

1959, July 20 **Unwmk.** ***Perf. 11½***

927 A370 30h lilac & yellow .20 .20
928 A370 60h dull blue .25 .20
929 A370 1.60k dk blue & bister .40 .20
Nos. 927-929 (3) .85 .60

International Fair at Brno, Sept. 6-20.

Revolutionist and Flag — A371

Slovakian Fighter — A372

1.60k, Linden leaves, sun and factory.

Perf. 11½

1959, Aug. 29 **Unwmk.** **Engr.**

930 A371 30h black & rose .20 .20
931 A372 60h carmine rose .25 .20
932 A371 1.60k dk blue & yel .45 .20
Nos. 930-932 (3) .90 .60

Natl. Slovakian revolution, 15th anniv. and Slovakian Soviet Republic, 40th anniv.

Alpine Marmots A373

1959, Sept. 25 **Engr. & Photo.**

933 A373 30h shown 1.00 .20
934 A373 40h Bison 1.00 .20
935 A373 60h Lynx, vert. 2.00 .20
936 A373 1k Wolf *1.75* *.80*
937 A373 1.60k Red deer 1.25 .20
Nos. 933-937 (5) *7.00* *1.60*

Tatra National Park, 10th anniv.

Lunik 2 Hitting Moon and Russian Flag A374

1959, Sept. 23 ***Perf. 11½***

938 A374 60h dk red & lt ultra .85 .25

Issued to commemorate the landing of the Soviet rocket on the moon, Sept. 13, 1959.

Stamp Printing Works, Peking A375

1959, Oct. 1

939 A375 30h pale green & red .20 .20

10 years of Czechoslovakian-Chinese friendship.

Haydn — A376

Great Spotted Woodpecker A377

Design: 3k, Charles Darwin.

1959, Oct. 16 **Engr.** ***Perf. 11½***

940 A376 60h violet black .45 .20
941 A376 3k dark red brown *1.10* *.50*

150th death anniv. of Franz Joseph Haydn, Austrian composer, and 150th birth anniv. of Charles Darwin, English naturalist.

1959, Nov. 16 ***Perf. 14***

Birds: 30h, Blue tits. 40h, Nuthatch. 60th, Golden oriole. 80h, Goldfinch. 1k, Bullfinch. 1.20k, European kingfisher.

942 A377 20h multicolored .85 .20
943 A377 30h multicolored .85 .20
944 A377 40h multicolored *5.00* *1.00*
945 A377 60h multicolored .85 .20
946 A377 80h multicolored 1.60 .20
947 A377 1k multicolored .85 .20
948 A377 1.20k multicolored *5.00* *.50*
Nos. 942-948 (7) *15.00* *2.50*

Nikola Tesla A378

Designs: 30h, Alexander S. Popov. 35h, Edouard Branly. 60h, Guglielmo Marconi. 1k, Heinrich Hertz. 2k, Edwin Howard Armstrong and research tower, Alpine, N. J.

Engraved and Photogravure

1959, Dec. 7 ***Perf. 11½***

949 A378 25h black & pink *.50* *.20*
950 A378 30h black & orange .20 .20
951 A378 35h black & lt vio .20 .20
952 A378 60h black & blue .20 .20
953 A378 1k black & lt grn .25 .20
954 A378 2k black & bister *1.50* *.40*
Nos. 949-954 (6) *2.85* *1.40*

Issued to honor inventors in the fields of telegraphy and radio.

Gymnast — A379

2nd Winter Spartacist Games: 60h, Skier. 1.60k, Basketball players.

1960, Jan. 20 ***Perf. 11½***

955 A379 30h salmon pink & brn .50 .20
956 A379 60h lt blue & blk .20 .20
957 A379 1.60k bister & brn .30 .25
Nos. 955-957 (3) 1.00 .65

1960, June 15 **Unwmk.**

Designs: 30h, Two girls in "Red Ball" drill. 60h, Gymnast with stick. 1k, Three girls with hoops.

958 A379 30h lt grn & rose claret .20 .20
959 A379 60h pink & black .25 .20
960 A379 1k ocher & vio bl .45 .20
Nos. 958-960 (3) .90 .60

2nd Summer Spartacist Games, Prague, June 23-July 3.

River Dredge Boat A380

Ships: 60h, River tug. 1k, Tourist steamer. 1.20k, Cargo ship "Lidice."

1960, Feb. 22 ***Perf. 11½***

961 A380 30h slate grn & sal 1.00 .20
962 A380 60h maroon & pale bl .50 .20
963 A380 1k dk violet & yel 1.00 .20
964 A380 1.20k lilac & pale grn *2.00* *.90*
Nos. 961-964 (4) *4.50* *1.50*

Ice Hockey Players — A381

Design: 1.80k, Figure skaters.

1960, Feb. 27

965 A381 60h sepia & lt blue .30 .25
966 A381 1.80k black & lt green *3.25* *2.50*

8th Olympic Winter Games, Squaw Valley, Calif., Feb. 18-29, 1960.

1960, June 15 **Unwmk.**

Designs: 1k, Running. 1.80k, Women's gymnastics. 2k, Rowing.

967 A381 1k black & orange .40 .20
968 A381 1.80k black & sal pink 1.00 .25
969 A381 2k black & blue *1.60* *.95*
Nos. 967-969 (3) *3.00* *1.40*

17th Olympic Games, Rome, 8/25-9/11.

Trencin Castle — A382

Castles: 10h, Bezdez. 20h, Kost. 30h, Pernstein. 40h, Kremnica. 50h, Krivoklát castle. 60h, Karlstein. 1k, Smolenice. 1.60k, Kokorin.

1960-63 **Engr.** ***Perf. 11½***

970 A382 5h gray violet .20 .20
971 A382 10h black .20 .20
972 A382 20h brown org .30 .20
973 A382 30h green .20 .20
974 A382 40h brown .20 .20
974A A382 50h black ('63) .20 .20

1115 A424 1.40k carmine rose .50 .20
1116 A424 1.60k lt brown *1.75 .90*
Nos. 1111-1116 (6) 3.50 1.90

Child and Grieving Mother — A425 Klary's Fountain, Teplice — A426

60h, Flowers growing from ruins of Lezáky.

1962, June 9 Engr. & Photo.
1118 A425 30h black & red .30 .20
1119 A425 60h black & dull bl .35 .20

20th anniversary of the destruction of Lidice and Lezáky by the Nazis.

1962, June 9
1120 A426 60h dull grn & yel .35 .20

1,200th anniversary of the discovery of the medicinal springs of Teplice.

Malaria Eradication Emblem, Cross and Dove A427 Soccer Goalkeeper A428

3k, Dove and malaria eradication emblem.

1962, June 18
1121 A427 60h black & crimson .20 .20
1122 A427 3k dk blue & yel *1.25 .60*

WHO drive to eradicate malaria.

1962, June 20 Unwmk. *Perf. 11½*
1123 A428 1.60k green & yellow 1.10 .20

Czechoslovakia's participation in the World Cup Soccer Championship, Chile, May 30-June 17. See No. 1095.

Soldier in Swimming Relay Race A429 "Agriculture" A430

Designs: 40h, Soldier hurdling. 60h, Soccer player. 1k, Soldier with rifle in relay race.

1962, July 20
1124 A429 30h green & lt ultra .20 .20
1125 A429 40h dk purple & yel .20 .20
1126 A429 60h brown & green .20 .20
1127 A429 1k dk blue & sal pink .35 .20
Nos. 1124-1127 (4) .95 .80

2nd Summer Spartacist Games of Friendly Armies, Prague, Sept., 1962.

1962 Engr. *Perf. 13½*

Designs: 60h, Astronaut in capsule. 80h, Boy with flute, horiz. 1k, Workers of three races, horiz. 1.40k, Children dancing around tree. 1.60k, Flying bird, horiz. 5k, View of Prague, horiz.

1128 A430 30h multicolored 1.50 .90
1129 A430 60h multicolored .65 .55
a. Miniature sheet of 8 *15.00 12.50*
1130 A430 80h multicolored 2.00 1.25
1131 A430 1k multicolored 2.00 2.25
1132 A430 1.40k multicolored 2.00 2.25
1133 A430 1.60k multicolored *2.00 3.50*
Nos. 1128-1133 (6) 10.15 10.70

Souvenir Sheet

1134 A430 5k multicolored *12.00 10.00*
a. Imperf. *42.50 30.00*

"PRAGA 1962 World Exhib. of Postage Stamps," 8/18-9/2/62. No. 1133 also for FIP Day, Sept. 1. Printed in sheets of 10.

No. 1129a contains 4 each of Nos. 1128-1129 and 2 labels arranged in 2 rows of 2 se-tenant pairs of Nos. 1128-1129 with label between. Sold for 5k, only with ticket.

No. 1134 contains one 51x30mm stamp. Sold only with ticket.

Children in Day Nursery and Factory A431

Sailboat and Trade Union Rest Home, Zinkovy — A432

Engraved and Photogravure
1962, Oct. 29 Unwmk. *Perf. 11½*
1135 A431 30h black & lt blue .20 .20
1136 A432 60h brown & yellow .20 .20

Cruiser "Aurora" A433

1962, Nov. 7
1137 A433 30h black & gray bl .20 .20
1138 A433 60h black & pink .20 .20

Russian October revolution, 45th anniv.

Cosmonaut and Worker — A434

Lenin — A435

1962, Nov. 7
1139 A434 30h dark red & blue .20 .20
1140 A435 60h black & dp rose .20 .20

40th anniversary of the USSR.

Symbolic Crane — A436

40h, Agricultural products, vert. 60h, Factories.

1962, Dec. 4
1141 A436 30h dk red & yel .20 .20
1142 A436 40h gray blue & yel .20 .20
1143 A436 60h black & dp rose .30 .20
Nos. 1141-1143 (3) .70 .60

Communist Party of Czechoslovakia, 12th cong.

Ground Beetle — A437

Table Tennis — A438

Beetles: 30h, Cardinal beetle. 60h, Stag beetle, vert. 1k, Great water beetle. 1.60k, Alpine longicorn, vert. 2k, Ground beetle, vert.

1962, Dec. 15 Engr. *Perf. 14*
1144 A437 20h multicolored .80 .20
1145 A437 30h multicolored .80 .20
1146 A437 60h multicolored 1.00 .20
1147 A437 1k multicolored 1.40 .20
1148 A437 1.60k multicolored 3.00 .30
1149 A437 2k multicolored *4.00 1.25*
Nos. 1144-1149 (6) 11.00 2.35

Engraved and Photogravure
1963, Jan. *Perf. 11½*

Sports: 60h, Bicyclist. 80h, Skier. 1k, Motorcyclist. 1.20k, Weight lifter. 1.60k, Hurdler.

1150 A438 30h black & dp grn .20 .20
1151 A438 60h black & orange .20 .20
1152 A438 80h black & ultra .20 .20
1153 A438 1k black & violet .25 .20
1154 A438 1.20k blk & pale brn .30 .20
1155 A438 1.60k blk & car .40 .20
Nos. 1150-1155 (6) 1.55 1.20

Various 1963 sports events.

Industrial Plant, Laurel and Star — A439 Symbol of Child Welfare Home — A440

Industrial Plant and Symbol of Growth — A441

1963, Feb. 25 Unwmk. *Perf. 11½*
1156 A439 30h carmine & lt bl .20 .20
1157 A440 60h black & car .20 .20
1158 A441 60h black & red .20 .20
Nos. 1156-1158 (3) .60 .60

15th anniv. of the "Victorious February" and 5th Trade Union Cong.

Artists' Guild Emblem — A442 Juraj Jánosik — A443

Eduard Urx — A444

National Theater, Prague — A445

#1163, Woman reading to children. #1164, Juraj Pálkovic. 1.60k, Max Svabinsky.

Engr. & Photo.; Engr. (A444)
1963, Mar. 25 Unwmk. *Perf. 11½*
1159 A442 20h black & Prus bl .20 .20
1160 A443 30h car & lt bl .20 .20
1161 A444 30h carmine .20 .20
1162 A445 60h dl red brn & lt bl .20 .20
1163 A444 60h green .20 .20
1164 A444 60h black .25 .20
1165 A444 1.60k brown .50 .20
Nos. 1159-1165 (7) 1.75 1.40

Various cultural personalities and events.

Boy and Girl with Flag A446 Television Transmitter A447

Engraved and Photogravure
1963, Apr. 18 *Perf. 11½*
1166 A446 30h slate & rose red .20 .20

The 4th Congress of Czechoslovak Youth.

1963, Apr. 25

40h, Television camera, mast and set, horiz.

1167 A447 40h buff & slate .20 .20
1168 A447 60h dk red & lt blue .25 .20

Czechoslovak television, 10th anniversary.

Rocket to the Sun A448

50h, Rockets & Sputniks leaving Earth. 60h, Spacecraft to & from Moon. 1k, 3k, Interplanetary station & Mars 1. 1.60k, Atomic rocket & Jupiter. 2k, Rocket returning from Saturn.

1963, Apr. 25
1169 A448 30h red brn & buff .20 .20
1170 A448 50h slate & bluish grn .20 .20
1171 A448 60h dk green & yel .25 .20
1172 A448 1k dk gray & sal .45 .20
1173 A448 1.60k gray brn & lt grn .75 .20
1174 A448 2k dk purple & yel *2.50 .75*
Nos. 1169-1174 (6) 4.35 1.75

Souvenir Sheet

Imperf

1175 A448 3k Prus grn & org red *3.00 2.50*

No. 1175 issued for 1st Space Research Exhib., Prague, Apr. 1963.

Studio and Radio A449

1k, Globe inscribed "Peace" & aerial mast, vert.

1963, May 18 Unwmk. *Perf. 11½*

1176 A449 30h choc & pale grn .20 .20
1177 A449 1k bluish grn & lilac .30 .20

40th anniversary of Czechoslovak radio.

Tupolev Tu-104B Turbojet A450

Design: 1.80k, Ilyushin Il-18 Moskva.

1963, May 25

1178 A450 80h violet & lt bl .35 .20
1179 A450 1.80k dk blue & lt grn .75 .20

40th anniversary of Czechoslovak airlines.

9th Cent. Ring, Map of Moravian Settlements A451

Woman Singing A452

1.60k, Falconer, 9th cent. silver disk.

1963, May 25

1180 A451 30h lt green & blk .20 .20
1181 A451 1.60k dull yel & blk .45 .20

1100th anniversary of Moravian empire.

1963, May 25 Engr.

1182 A452 30h bright red .40 .20

60th anniversary of the founding of the Moravian Teachers' Singing Club.

Kromeriz Castle and Barley — A453

Centenary Emblem, Nurse and Playing Child — A454

Engraved and Photogravure

1963, June 20 Unwmk. *Perf. 11½*

1183 A453 30h slate grn & yel .30 .20

Natl. Agricultural Exhib. and 700th anniv. of Kromeriz.

1963, June 20

1184 A454 30h dk gray & car .40 .20

Centenary of the International Red Cross.

Bee, Honeycomb and Emblem A455

Liberec Fair Emblem — A456

1963, June 20

1185 A455 1k brown & yellow .40 .20

19th Intl. Beekeepers Cong., Apimondia, 1963.

1963, July 13

1186 A456 30h black & dp rose .35 .20

Liberec Consumer Goods Fair.

Town Hall, Brno — A457

Cave, Moravian Karst — A458

Design: 60h, Town Hall tower, Brno.

1963, July 29

1187 A457 30h lt blue & maroon .20 .20
1188 A457 60h pink & dk blue .25 .20

International Trade Fair, Brno.

1963, July 29

#1190, Trout, Hornad Valley. 60h, Great Hawk Gorge. 80h, Macocha mountains.

1189 A458 30h brown & lt bl .20 .20
1190 A458 30h dk bl & dull grn .20 .20
1191 A458 60h green & blue .20 .20
1192 A458 80h sepia & pink .25 .20
Nos. 1189-1192 (4) .85 .80

Blast Furnace A459

1963, Aug. 15 Unwmk. *Perf. 11½*

1193 A459 60h blk & bluish grn .25 .20

30th Intl. Cong. of Iron Founders, Prague.

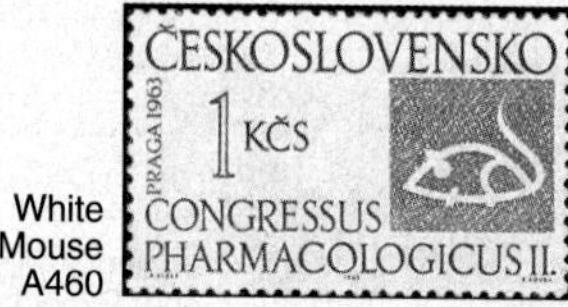
White Mouse A460

1963, Aug. 15

1194 A460 1k black & carmine .40 .20

2nd Intl. Pharmacological Cong., Prague.

Farm Machinery for Underfed Nations — A461

Wooden Toys — A462

1963, Aug. 15 Engr.

1195 A461 1.60k black .40 .20

FAO "Freedom from Hunger" campaign.

1963, Sept. 2 Engr. *Perf. 13½*

Folk Art (Inscribed "UNESCO"): 80h, Cock and flowers. 1k, Flowers in vase. 1.20k, Janosik, Slovak hero. 1.60k, Stag. 2k, Postilion.

1196 A462 60h red & vio bl .25 .20
1197 A462 80h multi .35 .20
1198 A462 1k multi .45 .25
1199 A462 1.20k multi .45 .20
1200 A462 1.60k multi .45 .20
1201 A462 2k multi 2.50 .95
Nos. 1196-1201 (6) 4.45 2.00

Sheets of 10.

Canoeing A463

Tree and Star — A464

Sports: 40h, Volleyball. 60h, Wrestling. 80h, Basketball. 1k, Boxing. 1.60k, Gymnastics.

Engraved and Photogravure

1963, Oct. 26 *Perf. 11½*

1202 A463 30h indigo & grn .25 .20
1203 A463 40h red brn & lt bl .25 .20
1204 A463 60h brn red & yel .25 .20
1205 A463 80h dk pur & dp org .25 .20
1206 A463 1k ultra & dp rose .25 .20
1207 A463 1.60k vio bl & ultra 2.00 1.00
Nos. 1202-1207 (6) 3.25 2.00

1964 Olympic Games, Tokyo.

1963, Dec. 11 Unwmk. *Perf. 11½*

Design: 60h, Star, hammer and sickle.

1208 A464 30h bis brn & lt bl .20 .20
1209 A464 60h carmine & gray .20 .20

Russo-Czechoslovakian Treaty, 20th anniv.

Atom Diagrams Surrounding Head — A465

Chamois — A466

1963, Dec. 12 Engr.

1210 A465 60h dark purple .40 .20

3rd Congress of the Association for the Propagation of Scientific Knowledge.

1963, Dec. 14 *Perf. 14*

40h, Alpine ibex. 60h, Mouflon. 1.20k, Roe deer. 1.60k, Fallow deer. 2k, Red deer.

1211 A466 30h multi .50 .25
1212 A466 40h multi .55 .35
1213 A466 60h brn, yel & grn .70 .30
1214 A466 1.20k multi .75 .25
1215 A466 1.60k multi 1.25 .35
1216 A466 2k multi 6.00 2.00
Nos. 1211-1216 (6) 9.75 3.50

Figure Skating — A467

Ice Hockey — A468

80h, Skiing, horiz. 1k, Field ball player.

Engraved and Photogravure

1964, Jan. 20 Unwmk. *Perf. 11½*

1217 A467 30h violet bl & yel .20 .20
1218 A467 80h dk blue & org .20 .20
1219 A467 1k brown & lilac .35 .20
Nos. 1217-1219 (3) .75 .60

Intl. University Games (30h, 80h) and the World Field Ball Championships (1k).

1964, Jan. 20

1220 A468 1k shown .85 .35
1221 A468 1.80k Toboggan 1.00 .60
1222 A468 2k Ski jump 2.50 2.25
Nos. 1220-1222 (3) 4.35 3.20

9th Winter Olympic Games, Innsbruck, Jan. 29-Feb. 9, 1964.

Magura Rest Home, High Tatra — A469

Design: 80h, Slovak National Insurrection Rest Home, Low Tatra.

1964, Feb. 19 Unwmk. *Perf. 11½*

1223 A469 60h green & yellow .20 .20
1224 A469 80h violet bl & pink .20 .20

Skiers and Ski Lift
A470

60h, Automobile camp, Telc. 1k, Fishing, Spis Castle. 1.80k, Lake & boats, Cesky Krumlov.

1964, Feb. 19 Engr. & Photo.
1225 A470 30h dk vio brn & bl .20 .20
1226 A470 60h slate & car .25 .20
1227 A470 1k brown & olive .40 .20
1228 A470 1.80k slate grn & org .65 .25
Nos. 1225-1228 (4) 1.50 .85

Moses, Day and Night by Michelangelo — A471

Designs: 60h, "A Midsummer Night's Dream," by Shakespeare. 1k, Man, telescope and heaven, vert. 1.60k, King George of Podebrad (1420-71).

1964, Mar. 20
1229 A471 40h black & yel grn .20 .20
1230 A471 60h slate & car .20 .20
1231 A471 1k black & lt blue .35 .20
1232 A471 1.60k black & yellow .45 .20
a. Souvenir sheet of 4 ('88) 2.00 2.00
Nos. 1229-1232 (4) 1.20 .80

400th anniv. of the death of Michelangelo (40h); 400th anniv. of the birth of Shakespeare (60h); 400th anniv. of the birth of Galileo (1k); 500th anniv. of the pacifist efforts of King George of Podebrad (1.60k).
No. 1232a for PRAGA '88.

Yuri A. Gagarin — A472

Astronauts: 60h, Gherman Titov. 80h, John H. Glenn, Jr. 1k, Scott M. Carpenter, vert. 1.20k, Pavel R. Popovich and Andrian G. Nikolayev. 1.40k, Walter M. Schirra, vert. 1.60k, Gordon L. Cooper, vert. 2k, Valentina Tereshkova and Valeri Bykovski, vert.

1964, Apr. 27 Unwmk. *Perf. 11½*
Yellow Paper
1233 A472 30h black & vio bl .50 .25
1234 A472 60h dk grn & dk car .25 .20
1235 A472 80h dk car & vio .50 .20
1236 A472 1k ultra & rose vio .25 .25
1237 A472 1.20k ver & ol gray .50 .35
1238 A472 1.40k black & dl grn 1.25 .50
1239 A472 1.60k pale pur & Prus grn *3.00 1.50*
1240 A472 2k dk blue & red 1.00 .40
Nos. 1233-1240 (8) *7.25 3.65*

World's first 10 astronauts.

Creeping Bellflower
A473

Film "Flower" and Karlovy Vary Colonnade
A474

Flowers: 80h, Musk thistle. 1k, Chicory. 1.20k, Yellow iris. 1.60k, Gentian. 2k, Corn poppy.

1964, June 15 Engr. *Perf. 14*
1241 A473 60h dk grn, lil & org 1.25 .25
1242 A473 80h blk, grn & red lil 1.25 .25
1243 A473 1k vio bl, grn & pink 1.25 .45
1244 A473 1.20k black, yel & grn 1.25 .30
1245 A473 1.60k violet & grn 3.00 .40
1246 A473 2k vio, red & grn *7.00 2.00*
Nos. 1241-1246 (6) *15.00 3.65*

Engraved and Photogravure
1964, June 20 Unwmk. *Perf. 13½*
1247 A474 60h black, blue & car 1.25 .20

14th Intl. Film Festival at Karlovy Vary, July 4-19.

Silesian Coat of Arms — A475

Young Miner of 1764 — A476

1964, June 20 *Perf. 11½*
1248 A475 30h black & yel .25 .20

150th anniv. of the Silesian Museum, Opava.

1964, June 20
1249 A476 60h sepia & lt grn .25 .20

Mining School at Banska Stiavnica, bicent.

Skoda Fire Engine
A477

1964, June 20
1250 A477 60h car rose & lt bl .35 .20

Voluntary fire brigades in Bohemia, cent.

Gulls, Hradcany Castle, Red Cross — A478

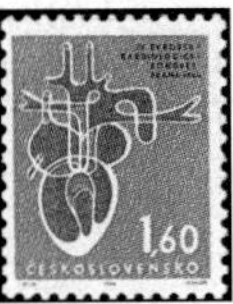

Human Heart — A479

1964, July 10
1251 A478 60h car & bluish gray .35 .20

4th Czechoslovak Red Cross Congress at Prague.

1964, July 10
1252 A479 1.60k ultra & car .60 .20

4th European Cardiological Cong. at Prague.

Partisans, Girl and Factories
A480

Battle Scene, 1944 — A481

Design: 60h, Partisans and flame.

Engraved and Photogravure
1964, Aug. 17 Unwmk. *Perf. 11½*
1253 A480 30h brown & red .20 .20
1254 A480 60h dk blue & red .20 .20
1255 A481 60h black & red .20 .20
Nos. 1253-1255 (3) .60 .60

20th anniv. of the Slovak Natl. Uprising; No. 1255, 20th anniv. of the Battles of Dukla Pass.

Hradcany at Prague — A482

Discus Thrower and Pole Vaulter — A483

Design: 5k, Charles Bridge and Hradcany.

1964, Aug. 30 *Perf. 11½x12*
1256 A482 60h black & red .50 .20

Souvenir Sheet
Engr. *Imperf.*
1257 A482 5k deep claret 1.90 1.50

Millenium of the Hradcany, Prague.
No. 1257 stamp size: 30x50mm.

Engraved and Photogravure
1964, Sept. 2 *Perf. 13½*

Designs: 60h, Bicycling, horiz. 1k, Soccer. 1.20k, Rowing. 1.60k, Swimming, horiz. 2.80k, Weight lifting, horiz.

1258 A483 60h multi .35 .25
1259 A483 80h multi .50 .25
1260 A483 1k multi .50 .25
1261 A483 1.20k multi .60 .30
1262 A483 1.60k multi .75 .35
1263 A483 2.80k multi *4.00 2.00*
Nos. 1258-1263 (6) *6.70 3.40*

Issued to commemorate the 18th Olympic Games, Tokyo, Oct. 10-25. Sheets of 10.

Miniature Sheet

Space Ship Voskhod I, Astronauts and Globe — A484

1964, Nov. 12 Unwmk. *Perf. 11½*
1264 A484 3k dk bl & dl lil, *buff* 4.50 3.50

Russian 3-man space flight of Vladimir M. Komarov, Boris B. Yegorov and Konstantin Feoktistov, Oct. 12-13.

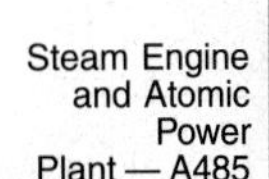

Steam Engine and Atomic Power Plant — A485

Diesel Engine "CKD Praha" — A486

1964, Nov. 16 Engr.
1265 A485 30h dull red brown .20 .20

Engraved and Photogravure
1266 A486 60h green & salmon .20 .20

Traditions and development of engineering; No. 1265 for 150th anniv. of the First Brno Engineering Works, No. 1266 for the engineering concern CKD Praha.

European Redstart — A487

Birds: 60h, Green woodpecker. 80h, Hawfinch. 1k, Black woodpecker. 1.20k, European robin. 1.60k, European roller.

1964, Nov. 16 Litho. *Perf. 10½*
1267 A487 30h multicolored .50 .20
1268 A487 60h black & multi .50 .20
1269 A487 80h multicolored 1.00 .20
1270 A487 1k multicolored 1.00 .25
1271 A487 1.20k lt vio bl & blk 1.00 .25
1272 A487 1.60k yellow & blk 2.00 .60
Nos. 1267-1272 (6) 6.00 1.70

Dancer
A488

"In the Sun" Pre-school Children
A489

Designs: 60h, "Over the Obstacles," teenagers. 1k, "Movement and Beauty," woman flag twirler. 1.60k, Runners at start.

Engraved and Photogravure
1965 Unwmk. *Perf. 11½*
1273 A488 30h red & lt blue .20 .20

Perf. 11½x12
1274 A489 30h vio bl & car .20 .20
1275 A489 60h brown & ultra .20 .20
1276 A489 1k black & yellow .25 .20
1277 A489 1.60k maroon & gray .60 .20
Nos. 1273-1277 (5) 1.45 1.00

3rd Natl. Spartacist Games. Issue dates: No. 1273, Jan. 3; Nos. 1274-1277, May 24.

Mountain Rescue Service — A490

Arms and View, Beroun — A491

Designs: No. 1279, Woman gymnast. No. 1280, Bicyclists. No. 1281, Women hurdlers.

1965, Jan. 15 Unwmk. *Perf. 11½*
1278 A490 60h violet & blue .25 .20
1279 A490 60h maroon & ocher .25 .20
1280 A490 60h black & carmine .25 .20
1281 A490 60h green & yellow .25 .20
Nos. 1278-1281 (4) 1.00 .80

Mountain Rescue Service (#1278); 1st World Championship in Artistic Gymnastics,

Prague, Dec. 1965 (#1279); World Championship in Indoor Bicycling, Prague, Oct. 1965 (#1280); "Universiada 1965," Brno (#1281).

1965, Feb. 15

Designs: No. 1283, Town Square, Domazlice. No. 1284, Old and new buildings, Frydek-Mystek. No. 1285, Arms and view, Lipnik. No. 1286, Fortified wall, City Hall and Arms, Policka. No. 1287, View and hops, Zatek. No. 1288, Small fortress and rose, Terezin.

1282	A491	30h vio bl & lt bl	.20	.20
1283	A491	30h dull pur & yel	.20	.20
1284	A491	30h slate & gray	.20	.20
1285	A491	30h green & bis	.20	.20
1286	A491	30h brown & tan	.20	.20
1287	A491	30h dk blue & cit	.20	.20
1288	A491	30h black & rose	.20	.20
		Nos. 1282-1288 (7)	1.40	1.40

Nos. 1282-1287 for 700th anniv. of the founding of various Bohemian towns; No. 1288 the 20th anniv. of the liberation of the Theresienstadt (Terezin) concentration camp.

Sun's Corona A492

Space Research: 30h, Sun. 60h, Exploration of the Moon. 1k, Twin space craft, vert. 1.40k, Space station. 1.60k, Exploration of Mars, vert. 2k, USSR and US Meteorological collaboration.

1965, Mar. 15 ***Perf. 12x11½, 11½x12***

1289	A492	20h rose & red lilac	.25	.20
1290	A492	30h rose red & yel	.25	.20
1291	A492	60h bluish blk & yel	.25	.20
1292	A492	1k pur & pale bl	.50	.20
1293	A492	1.40k black & salmon	.50	.20
1294	A492	1.60k black & pink	.50	.20
1295	A492	2k bluish blk & lt bl	*1.50*	*1.00*
		Nos. 1289-1295 (7)	*3.75*	*2.20*

Space research; Nos. 1289-1290 also for the Intl. Quiet Sun Year, 1964-65.

Frantisek Ventura, Equestrian; Amsterdam, 1928 — A493

Czechoslovakian Olympic Victories: 30h, Discus, Paris, 1900. 60h, Running, Helsinki, 1952. 1k, Weight lifting, Los Angeles, 1932. 1.40k, Gymnastics, Berlin, 1936. 1.60k, Double sculling, Rome, 1960. 2k, Women's gymnastics, Tokyo, 1964.

1965, Apr. 16 ***Perf. 11½x12***

1296	A493	20h choc & gold	.25	.20
1297	A493	30h indigo & emer	.25	.20
1298	A493	60h ultra & gold	.25	.20
1299	A493	1k red brn & gold	.35	.25
1300	A493	1.40k dk sl grn & gold	.75	.60
1301	A493	1.60k black & gold	.80	.60
1302	A493	2k maroon & gold	1.10	.45
		Nos. 1296-1302 (7)	3.75	2.50

Astronauts Virgil Grissom and John Young — A494

Designs: No. 1304, Alexei Leonov floating in space. No. 1305, Launching pad at Cape Kennedy. No. 1306, Leonov leaving space ship.

1965, Apr. 17 ***Perf. 11x11½***

1303	A494	60h slate bl & lil rose	.25	.20
1304	A494	60h vio blk & blue	.25	.20
1305	A494	3k slate bl & lil rose	1.50	1.00
a.		Pair, #1303, 1305	1.75	1.20
1306	A494	3k vio blk & blue	1.50	1.00
a.		Pair, #1304, 1306	1.75	1.20
		Nos. 1303-1306 (4)	3.50	2.40

Issued to honor American and Soviet astronauts. Printed in sheets of 25; one sheet contains 20 No. 1303 and 5 No. 1305, the other sheet contains 20 No. 1304 and 5 No. 1306.

Russian Soldier, View of Prague and Guerrilla Fighters A495

Designs: No. 1308, Blast furnace, workers and tank. 60h, Worker and factory. 1k, Worker and new constructions. 1.60k, Woman farmer, new farm buildings and machinery.

1965, May 5 **Engr.** ***Perf. 13½***

1307	A495	30h dk red, blk & ol	.20	.20
1308	A495	30h multicolored	.20	.20
1309	A495	60h vio bl, red & blk	.25	.20
1310	A495	1k dp org, blk & brn	.40	.20
1311	A495	1.60k yel, red & blk	.70	.20
		Nos. 1307-1311 (5)	1.75	1.00

20th anniv. of liberation from the Nazis.

Slovakian Kopov Dog A496

Dogs: 40h, German shepherd. 60h, Czech hunting dog with pheasant. 1k, Poodle. 1.60k, Czech terrier. 2k, Afghan hound.

1965, June 10 ***Perf. 12x11½***

1312	A496	30h black & red org	.40	.20
1313	A496	40h black & yellow	.40	.20
1314	A496	60h black & ver	.65	.20
1315	A496	1k black & dk car rose	.90	.20
1316	A496	1.60k yel & orange	1.25	.25
1317	A496	2k black & orange	2.50	1.00
		Nos. 1312-1317 (6)	6.10	2.05

World Dog Show at Brno and the International Dog Breeders Congress, Prague.

UN Headquarters Building, NY — A497

Emblems: 60h, UN & inscription. 1.60k, ICY.

1965, June 24 ***Perf. 12x11½***

1318	A497	60h dk red brn & yel	.20	.20
1319	A497	1k ultra & lt blue	.30	.20
1320	A497	1.60k gold & dk red	.50	.35
		Nos. 1318-1320 (3)	1.00	.75

20th anniv. of the UN and the ICY, 1965.

Trade Union Emblem A498

1965, June 24 **Engr.**

1321	A498	60h dk red & ultra	.25	.20

Intl. Trade Union Federation, 20th anniv.

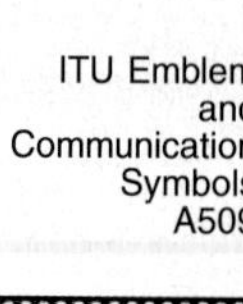

Women and Globe — A499

1965, June 24 ***Perf. 11½x12***

1322	A499	60h violet blue	.25	.20

20th anniv. of the Intl. Women's Federation.

Children's House (Burgraves' Palace), Hradcany A500

Matthias Tower — A501

1965, June 25 ***Perf. 11½***

1323	A500	30h slate green	.20	.20
1324	A501	60h dark brown	.25	.20

Issued to publicize the Hradcany, Prague.

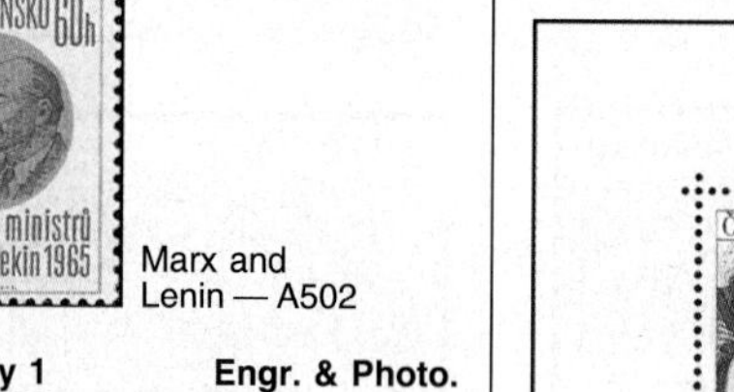

Marx and Lenin — A502

1965, July 1 **Engr. & Photo.**

1325	A502	60h car rose & gold	.20	.20

6th conf. of Postal Ministers of Communist Countries, Peking, June 21-July 15.

Joseph Navratil — A503

Jan Hus — A504

Gregor Johann Mendel A505

Costume Jewelry A506

Bohuslav Martinu A507

Seated Woman and University of Bratislava A508

ITU Emblem and Communication Symbols A509

Macromolecular Symposium Emblem A510

Design: No. 1327, Ludovit Stur (diff. frame).

1965 **Unwmk.** ***Perf. 11½***

1326	A503	30h black & fawn	.20	.20
1327	A503	30h black & dull grn	.20	.20
1328	A504	60h black & crimson	.20	.20
1329	A505	60h vio bl & red	.20	.20
1330	A506	60h purple & gold	.20	.20
1331	A507	60h black & orange	.20	.20
1332	A508	60h brn, *yel*	.20	.20
1333	A509	1k orange & blue	.35	.20
1334	A510	1k black & dp org	.35	.20
		Nos. 1326-1334 (9)	2.10	1.80

No. 1326, Navratil (1798-1865), painter; No. 1327, Stur (1815-56), Slovak author and historian; No. 1328, the 550th anniv. of the death of Hus, religious reformer;

No. 1329, cent. of publication of Mendel's laws of inheritance; No. 1330 publicizes the "Jablonec 1965" costume jewelry exhib.; No. 1331, Martinu (1890-1959), composer; No. 1332, 500th anniv. of the founding of the University of Bratislava as Academia Istropolitana; No. 1333, cent. of the ITU; No. 1334, Intl. Symposium on Macromolecular Chemistry, Prague, Sept. 1-8.

Issued: No. 1333, 7/10.

"Young Woman at her Toilette," by Titian — A512

Miniature Sheet

1965, Aug. 12

1336	A512	5k multicolored	3.75	2.00

Hradcany Art Gallery. #1336 contains one stamp.

Help for Flood Victims — A513

Rescue of Flood Victims A514

1965, Sept. 6 **Engr.**

No.	Type	Denomination / Color	Unused	Used
1337	A513	30h violet blue	.20	.20

Engraved and Photogravure

No.	Type	Denomination / Color	Unused	Used
1338	A514	2k dk ol grn & ol	.65	.45

Help for Danube flood victims in Slovakia.

Dotterel A515

Mountain Birds: 60h, Wall creeper, vert. 1.20k, Lesser redpoll. 1.40k, Golden eagle, vert. 1.60k, Ring ouzel. 2k, Eurasian nutcracker, vert.

1965, Sept. 20 **Litho.** ***Perf. 11***

No.	Type	Denomination / Color	Unused	Used
1339	A515	30h multi	.75	.20
1340	A515	60h multi	.75	.20
1341	A515	1.20k multi	.75	.20
1342	A515	1.40k multi	1.50	.25
1343	A515	1.60k multi	1.00	.30
1344	A515	2k multi	3.25	1.25
		Nos. 1339-1344 (6)	8.00	2.40

Levoca — A516   Medicinal Plants — A517

Views of Towns: 10h, Jindrichuv Hradec. 20h, Nitra. 30h, Kosice. 40h, Hradec Králové. 50h, Telc. 60h, Ostrava. 1k, Olomouc. 1.20k, Ceske Budejovice. 1.60k, Cheb. 2k, Brno. 3k, Bratislava. 5k, Prague.

Engraved and Photogravure

1965-66 ***Perf. 11½x12***

Size: 23x19mm

No.	Type	Denomination / Color	Unused	Used
1345	A516	5h black & yel	.20	.20
1346	A516	10h ultra & ol bis	.20	.20
1347	A516	20h black & lt bl	.20	.20
1348	A516	30h vio bl & lt grn	.20	.20
1348A	A516	40h dk brn & lt bl ('66)	.20	.20
1348B	A516	50h black & ocher ('66)	.20	.20
1348C	A516	60h red & gray ('66)	.25	.20
1348D	A516	1k pur & pale grn ('66)	.30	.20

Perf. 11½x11

Size: 30x23mm

No.	Type	Denomination / Color	Unused	Used
1349	A516	1.20k slate & lt bl	.35	.20
1350	A516	1.60k indigo & yel	.45	.20
1351	A516	2k sl grn & pale yel	.55	.20
1352	A516	3k brn & yel	.75	.20
1353	A516	5k black & pink	1.25	.20
		Nos. 1345-1353 (13)	5.10	2.60

1965, Dec. 3 **Engr.** ***Perf. 14***

No.	Type	Denomination / Color	Unused	Used
1354	A517	30h Coltsfoot	.50	.20
1355	A517	60h Meadow saffron	.50	.20
1356	A517	80h Corn poppy	.50	.20
1357	A517	1k Foxglove	1.00	.20
1358	A517	1.20k Arnica	3.00	.30
1359	A517	1.60k Cornflower	1.50	.40
1360	A517	2k Dog rose	*6.00*	*1.50*
		Nos. 1354-1360 (7)	*13.00*	*3.00*

Strip of "Stamps" — A518

Engraved and Photogravure

1965, Dec. 18 ***Perf. 11½***

No.	Type	Denomination / Color	Unused	Used
1361	A518	1k dark red & gold	2.75	2.25

Issued for Stamp Day, 1965.

Romain Rolland (1866-1944), French Writer A519

Symbolic Musical Instruments & Names of Composers A520

Portraits: No. 1362, Stanislav Sucharda (1866-1916), sculptor. No. 1363, Ignac Josef Pesina (1766-1808), veterinarian. No. 1365, Donatello (1386-1466), Italian sculptor.

1966, Feb. 14 **Engr.** ***Perf. 11½***

No.	Type	Denomination / Color	Unused	Used
1362	A519	30h deep green	.20	.20
1363	A519	30h violet blue	.20	.20
1364	A519	60h rose lake	.20	.20
1365	A519	60h brown	.20	.20
		Nos. 1362-1365 (4)	.80	.80

1966, Jan. 15 **Engr. & Photo.**

No.	Type	Denomination / Color	Unused	Used
1366	A520	30h black & gold	.30	.20

Czech Philharmonic Orchestra, 70th anniv.

Figure Skating Pair A521

#1368, Man skater. #1369, Volleyball player, spiking, vert. 1k, Volleyball player, saving, vert. 1.60k, Woman skater. 2k, Figure skating pair.

1966, Feb. 17

No.	Type	Denomination / Color	Unused	Used
1367	A521	30h dk car rose	.20	.20
1368	A521	60h green	.20	.20
1369	A521	60h carmine & buff	.20	.20
1370	A521	1k vio & lt bl	.30	.20
1371	A521	1.60k brown & yellow	.40	.20
1372	A521	2k blue & grnsh bl	*2.00*	*.40*
		Nos. 1367-1372 (6)	*3.30*	*1.40*

#1367-1368, 1371-1372 for the European Figure Skating Championships, Bratislava; #1369-1370 for the World Volleyball Championships.

Souvenir Sheet

Girl Dancing — A522

1966, Mar. 21 **Engr.** ***Imperf.***

No.	Type	Denomination / Color	Unused	Used
1373	A522	3k slate bl, red & bl	2.50	1.50

Cent. of the opera "The Bartered Bride" by Bedrich Smetana.

"Ajax" 1841 A523

Locomotives: 30h, "Karlstejn" 1865. 60h, Steam engine, 1946. 1k, Steam engine with tender, 1946. 1.60k, Electric locomotive, 1964. 2k, Diesel locomotive, 1964.

1966, Mar. 21 ***Perf. 11½x11***

Buff Paper

No.	Type	Denomination / Color	Unused	Used
1374	A523	20h sepia	1.00	.20
1375	A523	30h dull violet	1.25	.20
1376	A523	60h dull purple	.90	.20
1377	A523	1k dark blue	1.00	.40
1378	A523	1.60k dk blue grn	1.75	.30
1379	A523	2k dark red	*3.50*	*1.50*
		Nos. 1374-1379 (6)	*9.40*	*2.80*

European Perch A524

30h, Brown trout, vert. 1k, Carp. 1.20k, Northern pike. 1.40k, Grayling. 1.60k, Eel.

Perf. 13x13½, 13½x13

1966, Apr. 22 **Litho.** **Unwmk.**

No.	Type	Denomination / Color	Unused	Used
1380	A524	30h multi	.25	.20
1381	A524	60h multi	.35	.20
1382	A524	1k multi	.50	.20
1383	A524	1.20k multi	.50	.20
1384	A524	1.40k multi	.85	.25
1385	A524	1.60k multi	*2.75*	*1.10*
		Nos. 1380-1385 (6)	*5.20*	*2.15*

Intl. Fishing Championships, Svit, Sept. 3-5.

WHO Headquarters, Geneva — A525

Engraved and Photogravure

1966, Apr. 25 ***Perf. 12x11½***

No.	Type	Denomination / Color	Unused	Used
1386	A525	1k dk blue & lt blue	.40	.20

Opening of the WHO Headquarters, Geneva.

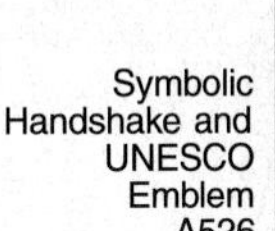

Symbolic Handshake and UNESCO Emblem A526

1966, Apr. 25 ***Perf. 11½***

No.	Type	Denomination / Color	Unused	Used
1387	A526	60h bister & olive gray	.20	.20

20th anniv. of UNESCO.

Prague Castle Issue

Belvedere Palace and St. Vitus' Cathedral A527

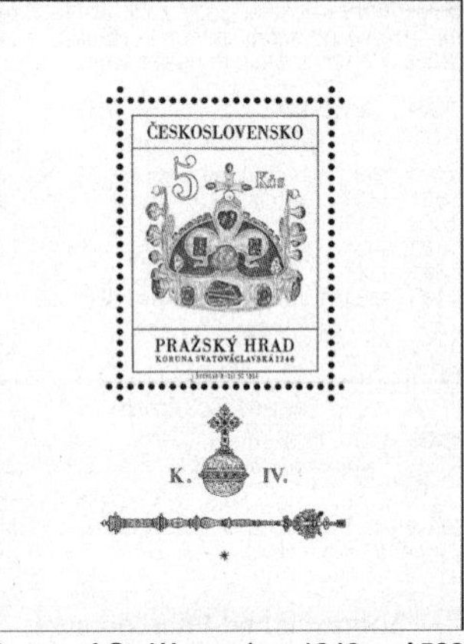

Crown of St. Wenceslas, 1346 — A528

Design: 60h, Madonna, altarpiece from St. George's Church.

1966, May 9 **Engr.** ***Perf. 11½***

No.	Type	Denomination / Color	Unused	Used
1388	A527	30h dark blue	.20	.20

Engraved and Photogravure

No.	Type	Denomination / Color	Unused	Used
1389	A527	60h blk & yel bis	.50	.20

Souvenir Sheet

Engr.

No.	Type	Denomination / Color	Unused	Used
1390	A528	5k multi	2.75	2.50

See Nos. 1537-1539.

Tiger Swallowtail A529

Butterflies and Moths: 60h, Clouded sulphur. 80h, European purple emperor. 1k, Apollo. 1.20k, Burnet moth. 2k, Tiger moth.

1966, May 23 **Engr.** ***Perf. 14***

No.	Type	Denomination / Color	Unused	Used
1391	A529	30h multi	.60	.25
1392	A529	60h multi	.60	.25
1393	A529	80h multi	1.25	.40
1394	A529	1k multi	1.90	.60
1395	A529	1.20k multi	1.90	.50
1396	A529	2k multi	*3.50*	*1.50*
		Nos. 1391-1396 (6)	*9.75*	*3.50*

Sheets of ten.

Flags of Russia and Czechoslovakia — A530

Designs: 60h, Rays surrounding hammer and sickle "sun." 1.60k, Girl's head and stars.

Engraved and Photogravure

1966, May 31 ***Perf. 11½***

No.	Type	Denomination / Color	Unused	Used
1397	A530	30h dk bl & crim	.20	.20
1398	A530	60h dk bl & red	.20	.20
1399	A530	1.60k red & dk bl	.50	.20
		Nos. 1397-1399 (3)	.90	.60

13th Congress of the Communist Party of Czechoslovakia.

Dakota Chief — A531

Model of Molecule — A532

Designs: 20h, Indians, canoe and tepee, horiz. 30h, Tomahawk. 40h, Haida totem poles. 60h, Kachina, good spirit of the Hopis. 1k, Indian on horseback hunting buffalo, horiz. 1.20k, Calumet, Dakota peace pipe.

1966, June 20

Size: 23x40mm

No.	Type	Description	Unused	Used
1400	A531	20h vio bl & dp org	.20	.20
1401	A531	30h blk & dl org	.20	.20
1402	A531	40h blk & lt bl	.20	.20
1403	A531	60h grn & yel	.25	.20
1404	A531	1k pur & emer	.25	.20
1405	A531	1.20k vio bl & rose lil	.30	.30

Perf. 14

Engr.

Size: 23x37mm

No.	Type	Description	Unused	Used
1406	A531	1.40k multi	*1.60*	*.90*
		Nos. 1400-1406 (7)	*3.00*	*2.20*

Cent. of the Náprstek Ethnographic Museum, Prague, and "The Indians of North America" exhibition.

Engraved and Photogravure

1966, July 4 Unwmk. *Perf. 11½*

No.	Type	Description	Unused	Used
1407	A532	60h blk & lt bl	.20	.20

Czechoslovak Chemical Society, cent.

"Guernica" by Pablo Picasso — A533

1966, July 5

Size: 75x30mm

No.	Type	Description	Unused	Used
1408	A533	60h blk & pale bl	1.75	1.25

30th anniversary of International Brigade in Spanish Civil War.

Sheets of 15 stamps and 5 labels inscribed "Picasso-Guernica 1937."

Pantheon, Bratislava A534

Atom Symbol and Sun A535

Designs: No. 1410, Devin Castle and Ludovit Stur. No. 1411, View of Nachod. No. 1412, State Science Library, Olomouc.

1966, July 25 Engr.

No.	Type	Description	Unused	Used
1409	A534	30h dl pur	.20	.20
1410	A534	60h dk bl	.25	.20
1411	A534	60h green	.25	.20
1412	A534	60h sepia	.30	.20
		Nos. 1409-1412 (4)	1.00	.80

No. 1409, Russian War Memorial, Bratislava; No. 1410, the 9th cent. Devin Castle as symbol of Slovak nationalism; No. 1411, 700th anniv. of the founding of Nachod; No. 1412, the 400th anniv. of the State Science Library, Olomouc.

Engraved and Photogravure

1966, Aug. 29 *Perf. 11½*

No.	Type	Description	Unused	Used
1413	A535	60h blk & red	.20	.20

Issued to publicize Jachymov (Joachimsthal), where pitchblende was first discovered, "cradle of the atomic age."

Brno Fair Emblem — A536

Olympia Coin and Olympic Rings — A537

1966, Aug. 29

No.	Type	Description	Unused	Used
1414	A536	60h blk & red	.20	.20

8th International Trade Fair, Brno.

1966, Aug. 29

Design: 1k, Olympic flame, Czechoslovak flag and Olympic rings.

No.	Type	Description	Unused	Used
1415	A537	60h blk & gold	.20	.20
1416	A537	1k dk bl & red	.50	.30

70th anniv. of the Olympic Committee.

Missile Carrier, Tank and Jet Plane A538

1966, Aug. 31

No.	Type	Description	Unused	Used
1417	A538	60h blk & apple grn	.30	.20

Issued to commemorate the maneuvers of the armies of the Warsaw Pact countries.

Mercury A539

30h, Moravian silver thaler, 1620, reverse & obverse, vert. 1.60k, Old & new buildings of Brno State Theater. 5k, Intl. Trade Fair Administration Tower & postmark, vert.

1966, Sept. 10

No.	Type	Description	Unused	Used
1418	A539	30h dk red & blk	.25	.20
1419	A539	60h org & blk	.25	.20
1420	A539	1.60k blk & brt grn	.75	.25
		Nos. 1418-1420 (3)	1.25	.65

Souvenir Sheet

No.	Type	Description	Unused	Used
1421	A539	5k multi	2.50	2.50

Brno Philatelic Exhibition, Sept. 11-25. No. 1421 contains one 30x40mm stamp.

First Meeting in Orbit — A540

30h, Photograph of far side of Moon & Russian satellite. 60h, Photograph of Mars & Mariner 4. 80th, Soft landing on Moon. 1k, Satellite, laser beam & binary code. 1.20k, Telstar over Earth & receiving station.

1966, Sept. 26 *Perf. 11½*

No.	Type	Description	Unused	Used
1422	A540	20h vio & lt grn	.20	.20
1423	A540	30h blk & sal pink	.20	.20
1424	A540	60h slate & lilac	.25	.20
1425	A540	80h dk pur & lt bl	.25	.20
1426	A540	1k blk & vio	.30	.20
1427	A540	1.20k red & bl	*1.60*	*.45*
		Nos. 1422-1427 (6)	*2.80*	*1.45*

Issued to publicize American and Russian achievements in space research.

Badger A541

Game Animals: 40h, Red deer, vert. 60h, Lynx. 80h, Hare. 1k, Red fox. 1.20k, Brown bear, vert. 2k, Wild boar.

1966, Nov. 28 Litho. *Perf. 13½*

No.	Type	Description	Unused	Used
1428	A541	30h multi	.40	.20
1429	A541	40h multi	.40	.20
1430	A541	60h multi	.30	.20
1431	A541	80h multi *(europaens)*	.75	.25
a.		80h multi *(europaeus)*	4.75	3.50
1432	A541	1k multi	.60	.30
1433	A541	1.20k multi	.75	.50
1434	A541	2k multi	*2.00*	*1.00*
		Nos. 1428-1434 (7)	*5.20*	*2.65*

The sheet of 50 of the 80h contains 40 with misspelling "europaens" and 10 with "europaeus."

"Spring" by Vaclav Hollar, 1607-77 A542

Paintings: No. 1436, Portrait of Mrs. F. Wussin, by Jan Kupecky (1667-1740). No. 1437, Snow Owl by Karel Purkyne (1834-1868). No. 1438, Tulips by Vaclav Spála (1885-1964). No. 1439, Recruit by Ludovít Fulla (1902-1980).

1966, Dec. 8 Engr. *Perf. 14*

No.	Type	Description	Unused	Used
1435	A542	1k black	3.75	3.50
1436	A542	1k multicolored	5.25	1.90
1437	A542	1k multicolored	2.40	1.90
1438	A542	1k multicolored	2.40	1.90
1439	A542	1k multicolored	*19.00*	*16.00*
		Nos. 1435-1439 (5)	*32.80*	*25.20*

Printed in sheets of 4 stamps and 2 labels. The labels in sheet of No. 1435 are inscribed "Vaclav Hollar 1607-1677" in fancy frame. Other labels are blank.

See No. 1484.

Symbolic Bird — A543

Engraved and Photogravure

1966, Dec. 17 *Perf. 11½*

No.	Type	Description	Unused	Used
1440	A543	1k dp blue & yel	.65	.65

Issued for Stamp Day.

Youth — A544

1967, Jan. 16 *Perf. 11½*

No.	Type	Description	Unused	Used
1441	A544	30h ver & lt bl	.20	.20

5th Cong. of the Czechoslovak Youth Org.

Symbolic Flower and Machinery A545

1967, Jan. 16

No.	Type	Description	Unused	Used
1442	A545	30h carmine & yel	.20	.20

6th Trade Union Congress, Prague.

Parents with Dead Child — A545a

1967, Jan. 16 *Perf. 11½*

No.	Type	Description	Unused	Used
1442A	A545a	60h black & salmon	.25	.20

"Peace and Freedom in Viet Nam."

View of Jihlava and Tourist Year Emblem A546

Views and Tourist Year Emblem: 40h, Spielberg Castle and churches, Brno. 1.20k, Danube, castle and churches, Bratislava. 1.60k, Vlatava River bridges, Hradcany and churches, Prague.

1967, Feb. 13 Engr. *Perf. 11½*

Size: 40x23mm

No.	Type	Description	Unused	Used
1443	A546	30h brown violet	.20	.20
1444	A546	40h maroon	.20	.20

Size: 75x30mm

No.	Type	Description	Unused	Used
1445	A546	1.20k violet blue	.40	.20
1446	A546	1.60k black	*1.10*	*.50*
		Nos. 1443-1446 (4)	*1.90*	*1.10*

International Tourist Year, 1967.

Black-tailed Godwit — A547

Birds: 40h, Shoveler, horiz. 60h, Purple heron. 80h, Penduline tit. 1k, Avocet. 1.40k, Black stork. 1.60k, Tufted duck, horiz.

1967, Feb. 20 Litho. *Perf. 13½*

No.	Type	Description	Unused	Used
1447	A547	30h multi	.50	.20
1448	A547	40h multi	.50	.20
1449	A547	60h multi	.50	.20
1450	A547	80h multi	.50	.20
1451	A547	1k multi	.75	.20
1452	A547	1.40k multi	1.00	.20
1453	A547	1.60k multi	*4.00*	*1.00*
		Nos. 1447-1453 (7)	*7.75*	*2.20*

Solar Research and Satellite — A548

Space Research: 40h, Space craft, rocket and construction of station. 60h, Man on moon and orientation system. 1k, Exploration of solar system and rocket. 1.20k, Lunar satellites and moon photograph. 1.60k, Planned lunar architecture and moon landing.

Engraved and Photogravure

1967, Mar. 24 *Perf. 11½*

1454 A548 30h yel & dk red .20 .20
1455 A548 40h vio bl & blk .20 .20
1456 A548 60h lilac & grn .20 .20
1457 A548 1k brt pink & sl .20 .20
1458 A548 1.20k lt violet & blk .30 .20
1459 A548 1.60k brn lake & blk *1.10 .60*
Nos. 1454-1459 (6) 2.20 1.60

Gothic Painting, by Master Theodoric A549

Designs: 40h, "Burning of Master Hus," from Litomerice Hymnal. 60h, Modern glass sculpture. 80h, "The Shepherdess and the Chimney Sweep," Andersen fairy tale, painting by J. Trnka. 1k, Section of pressure vessel from atomic power station. 1.20k, Three ceramic figurines, by P. Rada. 3k, Montreal skyline and EXPO '67 emblem.

1967, Apr. 10 **Engr.** *Perf. 14*

Size: 37x23mm

1460 A549 30h multi .20 .20
1461 A549 40h multi .20 .20
1462 A549 60h multi .20 .20
1463 A549 80h multi .25 .20
1464 A549 1k multi .25 .25
1465 A549 1.20k multi *1.10 .60*
Nos. 1460-1465 (6) 2.20 1.65

Souvenir Sheet

Perf. 11½

Size: 40x30mm

1466 A549 3k multi 2.00 1.50

EXPO '67, International Exhibition, Montreal, Apr. 28-Oct. 27, 1967.

Canoe Race A550

Women Playing Basketball — A551

#1468, Wheels, dove & emblems of Warsaw, Berlin, Prague. 1.60k, Canoe slalom.

Perf. 12x11½, 11½x12

1967, Apr. 17 **Engr. & Photo.**

1467 A550 60h black & brt bl .20 .20
1468 A550 60h black & salmon .20 .20
1469 A551 60h blk & grnsh bl .20 .20
1470 A551 1.60k black & brt vio *1.25 .50*
Nos. 1467-1470 (4) 1.85 1.10

No. 1467, 5th Intl. Wild-Water Canoeing Championships; No. 1468, 20th Warsaw-Berlin-Prague Bicycle Race: No. 1469, Women's Basketball Championships; No. 1470, 10th Intl. Water Slalom Championships.

"Golden Street" — A552

Designs: 60h, Interior of Hall of King Wenceslas. 5k, St. Matthew, from illuminated manuscript, 11th century.

1967, May 9 *Perf. 11½x11*

1471 A552 30h rose claret .20 .20
1472 A552 60h bluish black .45 .20

Souvenir Sheet

Perf. 11½

1473 A552 5k multicolored 2.75 2.50

Issued to publicize the Castle of Prague.

Stylized Lyre with Flowers — A553

Old-New Synagogue, Prague — A554

1967, May 10 *Perf. 11½*

1474 A553 60h dull pur & brt grn .30 .20

Prague Music Festival.

1967, May 22 *Perf. 11½*

30h, Detail from Torah curtain, 1593. 60h, Prague Printer's emblem, 1530. 1k, Mikulov jug, 1804. 1.40k, Memorial for Concentration Camp Victims 1939-45, Pincas Synagogue (menorah & tablet). 1.60k, Tombstone of David Gans, 1613.

1475 A554 30h dull red & lt bl .20 .20
1476 A554 60h blk & lt grn .20 .20
1477 A554 1k dk bl & rose lil .20 .20
1478 A554 1.20k dk brn & mar .30 .20
1479 A554 1.40k black & yellow .30 .20
1480 A554 1.60k green & yel *3.50 2.75*
Nos. 1475-1480 (6) 4.70 3.75

Issued to show Jewish relics. The items shown on the 30h, 60h and 1k are from the State Jewish Museum, Prague.

"Lidice" A555

Prague Architecture A556

1967, June 9 **Unwmk.** *Perf. 11½*

1481 A555 30h black & brt rose .20 .20

Destruction of Lidice by the Nazis, 25th anniv.

1967, June 10 **Engr. & Photo.**

1482 A556 1k black & gold .45 .20

Issued to publicize the 9th Congress of the International Union of Architects, Prague.

Peter Bezruc A557

1967, June 21

1483 A557 60h dull rose & blk .25 .20

Peter Bezruc, poet & writer, birth cent.

Painting Type of 1966

2k, Henri Rousseau (1844-1910), self-portrait.

1967, June 22 **Engr.** *Perf. 11½*

1484 A542 2k multicolored 1.75 1.25

Praga 68, World Stamp Exhibition, Prague, June 22-July 7, 1968. Printed in sheets of 4 stamps (2x2), separated by horizontal gutter with inscription and picture of Natl. Gallery, site of Praga 68.

View of Skalitz — A558

#1486, Mining tower & church steeple, Pribram. #1487, Hands holding book & view of Presov.

1967, Aug. 21 **Engr.** *Perf. 11½*

1485 A558 30h violet blue .20 .20
1486 A558 30h slate green .20 .20
1487 A558 30h claret .20 .20
Nos. 1485-1487 (3) .60 .60

Towns of Skalitz, Pribram, Presov, annivs.

Colonnade and Spring, Karlovy Vary and Communications Emblem — A559

1967, Aug. 21 **Engr. & Photo.**

1488 A559 30h violet bl & gold .30 .20

5th Sports & Cultural Festival of the Employees of the Ministry of Communications, Karlovy Vary.

Ondrejov Observatory and Galaxy — A560

1967, Aug. 22 **Engr.**

1489 A560 60h vio bl, rose lil & sil 1.50 .25

13th Cong. of the Intl. Astronomical Union.

Orchid — A561

Flowers from the Botanical Gardens: 30h, Cobaea scandens. 40h, Lycaste deppei. 60h, Glottiphyllum davisii. 1k, Anthurium. 1.20k, Rhodocactus. 1.40k, Moth orchid.

1967, Aug. 30 **Litho.** *Perf. 12½*

1490 A561 20h multicolored .20 .20
1491 A561 30h pink & multi .20 .20
1492 A561 40h multicolored .25 .20
1493 A561 60h lt blue & multi .30 .20
1494 A561 1k multicolored .50 .20
1495 A561 1.20k lt yellow & multi .60 .30
1496 A561 1.40k multicolored *1.75 .45*
Nos. 1490-1496 (7) 3.80 1.75

Red Squirrel A562

Animals from the Tatra National Park: 60h, Wild cat. 1k, Ermine. 1.20k, Dormouse. 1.40k, Hedgehog. 1.60k, Pine marten.

Engraved and Photogravure

1967, Sept. 25 *Perf. 11½*

1497 A562 30h black, yel & org .25 .20
1498 A562 60h black & buff .25 .20
1499 A562 1k black & lt blue .30 .20
1500 A562 1.20k brn, pale grn & yel .50 .20
1501 A562 1.40k blk, pink & yel .60 .20
1502 A562 1.60k black, org & yel *2.50 1.00*
Nos. 1497-1502 (6) 4.40 2.00

Rockets and Weapons — A563

1967, Oct. 6 **Engr.** *Perf. 11½*

1503 A563 30h slate green .30 .20

Day of the Czechoslovak People's Army.

Cruiser "Aurora" Firing at Winter Palace A564

Designs: 60h, Hammer and sickle emblems and Red Star, vert. 1k, Hands reaching for hammer and sickle, vert.

1967, Nov. 7 **Engr. & Photo.**

1504 A564 30h black & dk car .20 .20
1505 A564 60h black & dk car .20 .20
1506 A564 1k black & dk car .20 .20
Nos. 1504-1506 (3) .60 .60

Russian October Revolution, 50th anniv.

The Conjurer, by Frantisek Tichy A565

Paintings: 80h, Don Quixote, by Cyprian Majernik. 1k, Promenade in the Park, by Norbert Grund. 1.20k, Self-portrait, by Peter J. Brandl. 1.60k, Saints from Jan of Jeren Epitaph, by Czech Master of 1395.

1967, Nov. 13 **Engr.** *Perf. 11½*

1507 A565 60h multi .30 .20
1508 A565 80h multi .40 .25
1509 A565 1k multi .65 .40
1510 A565 1.20k multi .65 .40
1511 A565 1.60k multi *2.75 2.25*
Nos. 1507-1511 (5) 4.75 3.50

Sheets of 4. See Nos. 1589-1593, 1658-1662, 1711-1715, 1779-1783, 1847-1851, 1908-1913, 2043-2047, 2090-2093, 2147-2151, 2265-2269, 2335-2339, 2386-2390, 2437-2441, 2534-2538, 2586-2590, 2634-2638, 2810-2813, 2843-2847, 2872-2874, 2908-2910, 2936-2938, 2973-2975, 2995, 3001-3002, 3028-3030, 3054-3055, 3075-3076, 3105-3107.

Pres. Antonin Novotny — A566

1967, Dec. 9 **Engr.** *Perf. 11½*

1512 A566 2k blue gray .90 .20
1513 A566 3k brown 1.40 .20

Czechoslovakia Nos. 65, 71 and 81 of 1920 A567

1967, Dec. 18
1514 A567 1k maroon & silver .95 .75

Issued for Stamp Day.

Symbolic Flag and Dates — A568

1968, Jan. 15 Engr. *Perf. 11½*
1515 A568 30h red, dk bl & ultra .25 .20

50th anniversary of Czechoslovakia.

Figure Skating and Olympic Rings — A569

Olympic Rings and: 1k, Ski course. 1.60k, Toboggan chute. 2k, Ice hockey.

1968, Jan. 29 Engr. & Photo.
1516 A569 60h blk, yel & ocher .20 .20
1517 A569 1k ol grn, lt bl & lem .25 .20
1518 A569 1.60k blk, lil & bl grn .40 .20
1519 A569 2k blk, ap grn & lt bl *1.25 .55*
Nos. 1516-1519 (4) *2.10 1.15*

10th Winter Olympic Games, Grenoble, France, Feb. 6-18.

Factories and Rising Sun — A570

Design: 60h, Workers and banner.

1968, Feb. 25 *Perf. 11½x12*
1520 A570 30h car & dk bl .20 .20
1521 A570 60h car & dk bl .20 .20

20th anniversary of February Revolution.

Map of Battle of Sokolow A571

Human Rights Flame — A572

1968, Mar. 8 *Perf. 11½*
1522 A571 30h blk, brt bl & car .25 .20

Engr.
1523 A572 1k rose carmine .65 .30

25th anniv. of the Battle of Sokolow, Mar. 8, 1943, against the German Army, No. 1522; Intl. Human Rights Year, No. 1523.

Janko Kral and Liptovsky Mikulas — A573

Karl Marx — A574

Girl's Head — A575

Arms and Allegory — A576

Head — A577

1968, Mar. 25 Engr.
1524 A573 30h green .20 .20
1525 A574 30h claret .20 .20

Engraved and Photogravure
1526 A575 30h dk red & gold .20 .20
1527 A576 30h dk blue & dp org .20 .20
1528 A577 1k multicolored .50 .20
Nos. 1524-1528 (5) 1.30 1.00

The writer Janko Kral and the Slovak town Liptovsky Mikulas (No. 1524); 150th anniv. of the birth of Karl Marx (No. 1525); cent. of the cornerstone laying of the Prague Natl. Theater (No. 1526); 150th anniv. of the Prague Natl. Museum (No. 1527); 20th anniv. of WHO (1k).

Symbolic Radio Waves A578

No. 1530, Symbolic television screens.

1968, Apr. 29 *Perf. 11½*
1529 A578 30h blk, car & vio bl .20 .20
1530 A578 30h blk, car & vio bl .20 .20

45th anniv. of Czechoslovak broadcasting (#1529), 15th anniv. of television (#1530).

Olympic Rings, Mexican Sculpture and Diver — A579

Olympic Rings and: 40h, Runner and "The Sanctification of Quetzalcoatl." 60h, Volleyball and Mexican ornaments. 1k, Czechoslovak and Mexican Olympic emblems and carved altar. 1.60k, Soccer and ornaments. 2k, View of Hradcany, weather vane and key.

1968, Apr. 30
1531 A579 30h black, bl & car .20 .20
1532 A579 40h multi .20 .20
1533 A579 60h multi .25 .20
1534 A579 1k multi .35 .20
1535 A579 1.60k multi .50 .20
1536 A579 2k black & multi *2.00 .55*
Nos. 1531-1536 (6) *3.50 1.55*

19th Olympic Games, Mexico City, 10/12-27.

Prague Castle Types of 1966

Designs: 30h, Tombstone of Bretislav I. 60h, Romanesque door knocker, St. Wenceslas Chapel. 5k, Head of St. Peter, mosaic from Golden Gate of St. Vitus Cathedral.

1968, May 9 *Perf. 11½*
1537 A527 30h multicolored .20 .20
1538 A527 60h black, red & cit .20 .20

Souvenir Sheet
Engr.
1539 A528 5k multicolored 2.50 2.50

Pres. Ludvik Svoboda — A580

1968-70 Engr. *Perf. 11½*
1540 A580 30h ultramarine .20 .20
1540A A580 50h green ('70) .20 .20
1541 A580 60h maroon .20 .20
1541A A580 1k rose car ('70) .30 .20
Nos. 1540-1541A (4) .90 .80

Shades exist of No. 1541A.

"Business," Sculpture by Otto Gutfreund A581

Cabaret Performer, by Frantisek Kupka — A582

Designs (The New Prague): 40h, Broadcasting Corporation Building. 60h, New Parliament. 1.40k, Tapestry by Jan Bauch "Prague 1787." 3k, Presidential standard.

Engr. & Photo.; Engr. (2k)
1968, June 5
1542 A581 30h black & multi .20 .20
1543 A581 40h black & multi .30 .20
1544 A581 60h dk brn & multi .30 .20
1545 A581 1.40k dk brn & multi .45 .20
1546 A582 2k indigo & multi *1.00 1.75*
1547 A581 3k black & multi 1.00 .45
Nos. 1542-1547 (6) *3.25 3.00*

1968, June 21 *Perf. 11½*

Designs (The Old Prague): 30h, St. George's Basilica. 60h, Renaissance fountain. 1k, Villa America-Dvorak Museum, 18th cent. building. 1.60k, Emblem from the House of Three Violins, 18th cent. 2k, Josefina, by Josef Manes. 3k, Emblem of Prague, 1475.

1548 A581 30h green, gray & yel .20 .20
1549 A581 60h dk vio, ap grn & gold .20 .20
1550 A581 1k black, lt bl & pink .30 .20
1551 A581 1.60k slate grn & multi .55 .20
1552 A582 2k brown & multi *1.25 .60*
1553 A581 3k blk, yel, bl & pink 1.25 .60
Nos. 1548-1553 (6) *3.75 2.00*

Nos. 1542-1553 publicized the Praga 68 Philatelic Exhibition. Nos. 1542-1545, 1547-1551, 1553 issued in sheets of 15 + 15 labels with Praga 68 emblem and inscription. Nos. 1546, 1552 issued in sheets of 4 (2x2) with one horizontal label between top and bottom rows showing Praga 68 emblem.

Souvenir Sheet

View of Prague and Emblems — A583

Engraved and Photogravure
1968, June 22 *Imperf.*
1554 A583 10k multicolored 3.75 3.50

Praga 68 and 50th anniv. of Czechoslovak postage stamps. Sold only together with a 5k admission ticket to the Praga 68 philatelic Exhibition.

Madonna with the Rose Garlands, by Dürer — A584

1968, July 6 *Perf. 11½*
1555 A584 5k multicolored 3.75 2.25

FIP Day, July 6. Issued in sheets of 4 (2x2) with one horizontal label between, showing Praga 68 emblem.

Stagecoach on Rails — A585

Design: 1k, Steam and electric locomotives.

1968, Aug. 6
1556 A585 60h multicolored .30 .20
1557 A585 1k multicolored .45 .20

No. 1556: 140th anniv. of the horse-drawn railroad Ceské Budejovice to Linz; No. 1557: cent. of the Ceské Budejovice to Plzen railroad.

6th Intl. Slavonic Cong. in Prague — A586

1968, Aug. 7 *Perf. 11½*
1558 A586 30h vio blue & car .50 .20

Ardspach Rocks and Ammonite — A587

60h, Basalt formation & frog skeleton fossil. 80h, Rocks, basalt veins & polished agate. 1k, Pelecypoda (fossil shell) & Belanske Tatra mountains. 1.60k, Trilobite & Barrande rock formation.

1968, Aug. 8
1559 A587 30h black & citron .20 .20
1560 A587 60h black & rose cl .20 .20
1561 A587 80h black, lt vio & pink .20 .20
1562 A587 1k black & lt blue .25 .20
1563 A587 1.60k black & bister *1.40 .65*
Nos. 1559-1563 (5) *2.25 1.45*

Issued to publicize the 23rd International Geological Congress, Prague, Aug. 8-Sept. 3.

Raising Slovak Flag A588

60h, Slovak partisans, and mountain.

1968, Sept. 9 **Engr.** *Perf. 11½*
1564 A588 30h ultra .20 .20
1565 A588 60h red .20 .20

No. 1564 for the Slovak Natl. Council, No. 1565 the 120th anniv. of the Slovak national uprising.

Flowerpot, by Jiri Schlessinger (age 10) — A589

Drawings by Children in Terezin Concentration Camp: 30h, Jew and Guard, by Jiri Beutler (age 10). 60h, Butterflies, by Kitty Brunnerova (age 11).

Engraved and Photogravure
1968, Sept. 30 *Perf. 11½*
Size: 30x23mm
1566 A589 30h blk, buff & rose lil .20 .20
1567 A589 60h black & multi .20 .20

Perf. 12x11½
Size: 41x23mm
1568 A589 1k black & multi .30 .20
Nos. 1566-1568 (3) .70 .60

30th anniversary of Munich Pact.

Arms of Regional Capitals A590

Arms of Prague — A591

1968, Oct. 21 *Perf. 11½*
1569 A590 60h Banská Bystrica .20 .20
1570 A590 60h Bratislava .20 .20
1571 A590 60h Brno .20 .20
1572 A590 60h Ceské Budejovice .20 .20
1573 A590 60h Hradec Králové .20 .20
1574 A590 60h Kosice .20 .20
1575 A590 60h Ostrava (horse) .20 .20
1576 A590 60h Plzen .20 .20
1577 A590 60h Ustí nad Labem .20 .20

Perf. 11½x16
1578 A591 1k shown .75 .20
Nos. 1569-1578 (10) 2.55 2.00

#1578 issued in sheets of 10. See #1652-1657, 1742-1747, 1886-1888, 2000-2001.

Flag and Linden Leaves A592

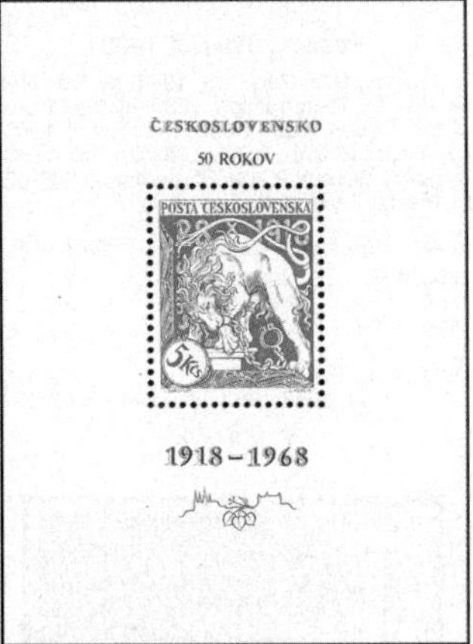

Bohemian Lion Breaking Chains (Type SP1 of 1919) — A593

Design: 60h, Map of Czechoslovakia, linden leaves, Hradcany in Prague and Castle in Bratislava.

1968, Oct. 28 *Perf. 12x11½*
1579 A592 30h dp blue & mag .20 .20
1580 A592 60h blk, gold, red & ultra .20 .20

Souvenir Sheet
Engr.
Perf. 11½x12
1581 A593 5k red 2.50 2.25

Founding of Czechoslovakia, 50th anniv.

Ernest Hemingway A594

Cinderlad A595

Caricatures: 30h, Karel Capek (1890-1938), writer. 40h, George Bernard Shaw. 60h, Maxim Gorki. 1k, Pablo Picasso. 1.20k, Taikan Yokoyama (1868-1958), painter. 1.40k, Charlie Chaplin.

Engraved and Photogravure
1968, Nov. 18 *Perf. 11½x12*
1582 A594 20h black, org & red .20 .20
1583 A594 30h black & multi .20 .20
1584 A594 40h blk, lic & car .20 .20
1585 A594 60h black, sky bl & grn .20 .20
1586 A594 1k black, brn & yel .30 .20
1587 A594 1.20k black, dp car & vio .30 .20
1588 A594 1.40k black, brn & dp org *1.50 .50*
Nos. 1582-1588 (7) *2.90 1.70*

Cultural personalities of the 20th cent. and UNESCO. See Nos. 1628-1633.

Painting Type of 1967

Czechoslovakian Art: 60h, Cleopatra II, by Jan Zrzavy (1890-1977). 80h, Black Lake (man and horse), by Jan Preisler (1872-1918). 1.20k, Giovanni Francisci as a Volunteer, by Peter Michal Bohun (1822-1879). 1.60k, Princess Hyacinth, by Alfons Mucha (1860-1939). 3k, Madonna and Child, woodcarving, 1518, by Master Paul of Levoca.

1968, Nov. 29 **Engr.** *Perf. 11½*
1589 A565 60h multi .40 .40
1590 A565 80h multi .40 .40
1591 A565 1.20k multi 1.10 .45
1592 A565 1.60k multi .75 .50
1593 A565 3k multi *4.50 3.00*
Nos. 1589-1593 (5) *7.15 4.75*

Sheets of 4.

1968, Dec. 18 **Engr. & Photo.**

Slovak Fairy Tales: 60h, The Proud Lady. 80h, The Ruling Knight. 1k, Good Day, Little Bench. 1.20k, The Spellbound Castle. 1.80k, The Miraculous Hunter. The designs are from illustrations by Ludovit Fulla for "Slovak Stories."

1594 A595 30h multi .20 .20
1595 A595 60h multi .20 .20
1596 A595 80h multi .25 .20
1597 A595 1k multi .30 .20
1598 A595 1.20k multi .30 .20
1599 A595 1.80k multi *1.50 .65*
Nos. 1594-1599 (6) *2.75 1.65*

Czechoslovakia Nos. 2 and 3 — A596

1968, Dec. 18
1600 A596 1k violet bl & gold .75 .65

50th anniv. of Czechoslovakian postage stamps.

Crescent, Cross and Lion and Sun Emblems A597

ILO Emblem A598

60h, 12 crosses in circles forming large cross.

1969, Jan. 31 *Perf. 11½*
1601 A597 60h black, red & gold .20 .20
1602 A597 1k black, ultra & red .35 .20

No. 1601: 50th anniv. of the Czechoslovak Red Cross. No. 1602: 50th anniv. of the League of Red Cross Societies.

1969, Jan. 31
1603 A598 1k black & gray .30 .20

50th anniv. of the ILO.

Cheb Pistol A599

Historical Firearms: 40h, Italian pistol with Dutch decorations, c. 1600. 60h, Wheellock rifle from Matej Kubik workshop c. 1720. 1k, Flintlock pistol, Devieuxe workshop, Liege, c. 1760. 1.40k, Duelling pistols, from Lebeda workshop, Prague, c. 1835. 1.60k, Derringer pistols, US, c. 1865.

1969, Feb. 18
1604 A599 30h black & multi .20 .20
1605 A599 40h black & multi .20 .20
1606 A599 60h black & multi .20 .20
1607 A599 1k black & multi .25 .20
1608 A599 1.40k black & multi .35 .20
1609 A599 1.60k black & multi *1.00 .50*
Nos. 1604-1609 (6) *2.20 1.50*

Bratislava Castle, Muse and Book — A600

#1611, Science symbols & emblem (Brno University). #1612, Harp, laurel & musicians' names. #1613, Theatrical scene. #1614, Arms of Slovakia, banner & blossoms. #1615, School, outstretched hands & woman with linden leaves.

1969, Mar. 24 **Engr.** *Perf. 11½*
1610 A600 60h violet blue .20 .20

Engraved and Photogravure
1611 A600 60h blk, gold & slate .20 .20
1612 A600 60h gold, blue, blk & red .20 .20
1613 A600 60h black & rose red .20 .20
1614 A600 60h rose red, sil & bl .20 .20
1615 A600 60h black & gold .20 .20
Nos. 1610-1615 (6) 1.20 1.20

50th anniv. of: Komensky University in Bratislava (#1610); Brno University (#1611); Brno Conservatory of Music (#1612); Slovak Natl. Theater (#1613); Slovak Soviet Republic (#1614); cent. of the Zniev Gymnasium (academic high school) (#1615).

Baldachin-top Car and Four-seat Coupé of 1900-1905 — A601

Designs: 1.60k, Laurin & Klement Voiturette, 1907, and L & K touring car with American top, 1907. 1.80k, First Prague bus, 1907, and sectionalized Skoda bus, 1967.

1969, Mar. 25 **Engr. & Photo.**
1616 A601 30h blk, lil & lt grn .20 .20
1617 A601 1.60k blk, org brn & lt bl .40 .20
1618 A601 1.80k multi *1.25 .75*
Nos. 1616-1618 (3) *1.85 1.15*

Peace, by Ladislav Guderna — A602

1969, Apr. 21 *Perf. 11*
1619 A602 1.60k multi .50 .35

20th anniv. of the Peace Movement. Issued in sheets of 15 stamps and 5 tabs.

Horse and Rider, by Vaclav Hollar — A603

Old Engravings of Horses: 30h, Prancing Stallion, by Hendrik Goltzius, horiz. 80h, Groom Leading Horse, by Matthäus Merian, horiz. 1.80k, Horse and Soldier, by Albrecht Dürer. 2.40k, Groom and Horse, by Johann E. Ridinger.

1969, Apr. 24 ***Perf. 11x11½, 11½x11***

Yellowish Paper

1620 A603 30h dark brown .20 .20
1621 A603 80h violet brown .20 .20
1622 A603 1.60k slate .40 .20
1623 A603 1.80k sepia .45 .20
1624 A603 2.40k multi 2.25 .60
Nos. 1620-1624 (5) 3.50 1.40

M. R. Stefánik as Astronomy Professor and French General — A604

1969, May 4 **Engr.** ***Perf. 11½***

1625 A604 60h rose claret .20 .20

Gen. Milan R. Stefánik, 50th death anniv.

St. Wenceslas Pressing Wine, Mural by the Master of Litomerice — A605

Design: No. 1627, Coronation banner of the Estates, 1723, with St. Wenceslas and coats of arms of Bohemia and Czech Crown lands.

1969, May 9 **Engr.** ***Perf. 11½***

1626 A605 3k multicolored 1.50 1.40
1627 A605 3k multicolored 1.50 1.40

Issued to publicize the art treasures of the Castle of Prague. See Nos. 1689-1690.

Caricature Type of 1968

Caricatures: 30h, Pavol Orszagh Hviezdoslav (1849-1921), Slovak writer. 40h, Gilbert K. Chesterton (1874-1936), English writer. 60h, Vladimir Mayakovski (1893-1930), Russian poet. 1k, Henri Matisse (1869-1954), French painter. 1.80k, Ales Hrdlicka (1869-1943), Czech-born American anthropologist. 2k, Franz Kafka (1883-1924), Austrian writer.

Engraved and Photogravure

1969, June 17 ***Perf. 11½x12***

1628 A594 30h blk, red & bl .20 .20
1629 A594 40h blk, bl & lt vio .20 .20
1630 A594 60h blk, rose & yel .20 .20
1631 A594 1k black & multi .30 .20
1632 A594 1.80k blk, ultra & ocher .35 .20
1633 A594 2k blk, yel & brt grn 1.50 .50
Nos. 1628-1633 (6) 2.75 1.50

Issued to honor cultural personalities of the 20th century and UNESCO.

"Music," by Alfons Mucha — A606

Paintings by Mucha: 60h, "Painting." 1k, "Dance." 2.40k, "Ruby" and "Amethyst."

1969, July 14 ***Perf. 11½x11***

Size: 30x49mm

1634 A606 30h black & multi .20 .20
1635 A606 60h black & multi .20 .20
1636 A606 1k black & multi .20 .20

Size: 39x51mm

1637 A606 2.40k black & multi 1.40 1.10
Nos. 1634-1637 (4) 2.00 1.70

Alfons Mucha (1860-1930), painter and stamp designer (Type A1).

Pres. Svoboda and Partisans A607

No. 1639, Slovak fighters and mourners.

1969, Aug. 29 ***Perf. 11***

1638 A607 30h ol grn & red, *yel* .20 .20
1639 A607 30h vio bl & red, *yel* .20 .20

25th anniversary of the Slovak uprising and of the Battle of Dukla.

Tatra Mountain Stream and Gentians — A608

Designs: 60h, Various views in Tatra Mountains. No. 1644, Mountain pass and gentians. No. 1645, Houses, Krivan Mountain and autumn crocuses.

1969, Sept. 8 **Engr.** ***Perf. 11***

Size: 71x33mm

1640 A608 60h gray .25 .20
1641 A608 60h dark blue .25 .20
1642 A608 60h dull gray vio .25 .20

Perf. 11½

Size: 40x23mm

1643 A608 1.60k multi .35 .20
1644 A608 1.60k multi 1.50 .50
1645 A608 1.60k multi .40 .20
Nos. 1640-1645 (6) 3.00 1.50

20th anniv. of the creation of the Tatra Mountains Natl. Park. Nos. 1640-1642 are printed in sheets of 15 (3x5) with 5 labels showing mountain plants. Nos. 1643-1645 issued in sheets of 10.

Bronze Belt Ornaments A609

Archaeological Treasures from Bohemia and Moravia: 30h, Gilt ornament with 6 masks. 1k, Jeweled earrings. 1.80k, Front and back of lead cross with Greek inscription. 2k, Gilt strap ornament with human figure.

Engraved and Photogravure

1969, Sept. 30 ***Perf. 11½x11***

1646 A609 20h gold & multi .20 .20
1647 A609 30h gold & multi .20 .20
1648 A609 1k red & multi .20 .20
1649 A609 1.80k dull org & multi .40 .20
1650 A609 2k gold & multi 1.25 .40
Nos. 1646-1650 (5) 2.25 1.20

"Mail Circling the World" A610

1969, Oct. 1 **Engr.** ***Perf. 12***

1651 A610 3.20k multi 1.40 .90

16th UPU Cong., Tokyo, Oct. 1-Nov. 14. Issued in sheets of 4.

Coat of Arms Type of 1968

Engraved and Photogravure

1969, Oct. 25 ***Perf. 11½***

1652 A590 50h Bardejov .20 .20
1653 A590 50h Hranice .20 .20
1654 A590 50h Kezmarok .20 .20
1655 A590 50h Krnov .20 .20
1656 A590 50h Litomerice .20 .20
1657 A590 50h Manetin .20 .20
Nos. 1652-1657 (6) 1.20 1.20

Painting Type of 1968

Designs: 60h, Requiem, 1944, by Frantisek Muzika. 1k, Resurrection, 1380, by the Master of the Trebon Altar. 1.60k, Crucifixion, 1950, by Vincent Hloznik. 1.80k, Girl with Doll, 1863, by Julius Bencur. 2.20k, St. Jerome, 1357-67, by Master Theodorik.

1969, Nov. 25 ***Perf. 11½***

1658 A565 60h multi .25 .20
1659 A565 1k multi .25 .20
1660 A565 1.60k multi .35 .20
1661 A565 1.80k multi .65 .30
1662 A565 2.20k multi 2.50 1.10
Nos. 1658-1662 (5) 4.00 2.00

Sheets of 4.

Symbolic Sheet of Stamps — A611

1969, Dec. 18 ***Perf. 11½x12***

1663 A611 1k dk brn, ultra & gold .40 .40

Issued for Stamp Day 1969.

Ski Jump — A612

Designs: 60h, Long distance skier. 1k, Ski jump and slope. 1.60k, Woman skier.

1970, Jan. 6 ***Perf. 11½***

1664 A612 50h multi .20 .20
1665 A612 60h multi .20 .20
1666 A612 1k multi .20 .20
1667 A612 1.60k multi 1.00 .30
Nos. 1664-1667 (4) 1.60 .90

Intl. Ski Championships "Tatra 1970."

Ludwig van Beethoven — A613

Portraits: No. 1669, Friedrich Engels (1820-95), German socialist. No. 1670, Maximilian Hell (1720-92), Slovakian Jesuit and astronomer. No. 1671, Lenin, Russian Communist leader. No. 1672, Josef Manes (1820-71), Czech painter. No. 1673, Comenius (1592-1670), theologian and educator.

1970, Feb. 17 **Engr.** ***Perf. 11x11½***

1668 A613 40h black .20 .20
1669 A613 40h dull red .20 .20
1670 A613 40h yellow brn .20 .20
1671 A613 40h dull red .20 .20
1672 A613 40h brown .20 .20
1673 A613 40h black .20 .20
Nos. 1668-1673 (6) 1.20 1.20

Anniversaries of birth of Beethoven, Engels, Hell, Lenin and Manes, 300th anniv. of the death of Comenius, and to honor UNESCO.

Bells A614

80h, Machine tools & lathe. 1k, Folklore masks. 1.60k, Angel & Three Wise Men, 17th cent. icon from Koniec. 2k, View of Orlik Castle, 1787, by F. K. Wolf. 3k, "Passing through Koshu down to Mishima" from Hokusai's 36 Views of Fuji.

Engraved and Photogravure

1970, Mar. 13 ***Perf. 11½x11***

Size: 40x23mm

1674 A614 50h multi .20 .20
1675 A614 80h multi .20 .20
1676 A614 1k multi .25 .20

Size: 50x40mm

Perf. 11½

1677 A614 1.60k multi .45 .30
1678 A614 2k multi .60 .35
1679 A614 3k multi 1.60 1.00
Nos. 1674-1679 (6) 3.30 2.25

EXPO '70 Intl. Exhib., Osaka, Japan, Mar. 15-Sept. 13, 1970. Nos. 1674-1676 issued in sheets of 50, Nos. 1677-1679 in sheets of 4.

Kosice Townhall, Laurel and Czechoslovak Arms — A615

1970, Apr. 5 ***Perf. 11***

1680 A615 60h slate, ver & gold .25 .20

Government's Kosice Program, 25th anniv.

"The Remarkable Horse" by Josef Lada — A616

Lenin — A617

Paintings by Josef Lada: 60h, Autumn, 1955, horiz. 1.80k, "The Water Sprite." 2.40k, Children in Winter, 1943, horiz.

1970, Apr. 21 *Perf. 11½*

1681 A616 60h black & multi .20 .20
1682 A616 1k black & multi .30 .20
1683 A616 1.80k black & multi .50 .20
1684 A616 2.40k black & multi *1.00 .50*
Nos. 1681-1684 (4) *2.00 1.10*

1970, Apr. 22

Design: 60h, Lenin without cap, facing left.

1685 A617 30h dk red & gold .20 .20
1686 A617 60h black & gold .20 .20

Lenin (1870-1924), Russian communist leader.

Fighters on the Barricades — A618

No. 1688, Lilac, Russian tank and castle.

1970, May 5 *Perf. 11x11½*

1687 A618 30h dull pur, gold & bl .20 .20
1688 A618 30h dull grn, gold & red .20 .20

No. 1687: 25th anniv. of the Prague uprising. No. 1688: 25th anniv. of the liberation of Czechoslovakia from the Germans.

Prague Castle Art Type of 1969

#1689, Bust of St. Vitus, 1486. #1690, Hermes and Athena, by Bartholomy Springer (1546-1611), mural from White Tower.

1970, May 7 **Engr.** *Perf. 11½*

1689 A605 3k maroon & multi 1.75 1.50
1690 A605 3k lt blue & multi 1.75 1.50

Compass Rose, UN Headquarters and Famous Buildings of the World — A619

Engraved and Photogravure

1970, June 26 *Perf. 11*

1691 A619 1k black & multi .25 .20

25th anniv. of the UN. Issued in sheets of 15 (3x5) and 5 labels showing UN emblem.

Cannon from 30 Years' War and Baron Munchhausen — A620

Historical Cannons: 60h, Cannon from Hussite war and St. Barbara. 1.20k, Cannon from Prussian-Austrian war, and legendary cannoneer Javurek. 1.80k, Early 20th century cannon and spaceship "La Colombiad" (Jules Verne). 2.40k, World War I cannon and "Good Soldier Schweik."

1970, Aug. 31 *Perf. 11½*

1692 A620 30h black & multi .20 .20
1693 A620 60h black & multi .20 .20
1694 A620 1.20k black & multi .35 .20
1695 A620 1.80k black & multi .35 .20
1696 A620 2.40k black & multi *1.60 .65*
Nos. 1692-1696 (5) *2.70 1.45*

"Rude Pravo" (Red Truth) A621

1970, Sept. 21 *Perf. 11½x11*

1697 A621 60h car, gold & blk .20 .20

50th anniv. of the Rude Pravo newspaper.

"Great Sun" House Sign and Old Town Tower Bridge, Prague — A622

60h, "Blue Lion" & Town Hall Tower, Brno. 1k, Gothic corner stone & Town Hall Tower, Bratislava. 1.40k, Coat of Arms & Gothic Tower, Bratislava, & medallion. 1.60k, Moravian Eagle & Gothic Town Hall Tower, Brno. 1.80k, "Black Sun" & "Green Frog" house signs & New Town Hall, Prague.

1970, Sept. 23 *Perf. 11x11½*

1698 A622 40h black & multi .20 .20
1699 A622 60h black & multi .20 .20
1700 A622 1k black & multi .20 .20
1701 A622 1.40k black & multi *1.10 .50*
1702 A622 1.60k black & multi .25 .20
1703 A622 1.80k black & multi .80 .20
Nos. 1698-1703 (6) *2.75 1.50*

Germany-Uruguay Semifinal Soccer Match — A623

Designs: 20h, Sundisk Games' emblem and flags of participating nations. 60h, England-Czechoslovakia match and coats of arms. 1k, Romania-Czechoslovakia match and coats of arms. 1.20k, Brazil-Italy, final match and emblems. 1.80k, Brazil-Czechoslovakia match and emblems.

1970, Oct. 29 *Perf. 11½*

1704 A623 20h blk & multi .20 .20
1705 A623 40h blk & multi .20 .20
1706 A623 60h blk & multi .20 .20
1707 A623 1k blk & multi .30 .20
1708 A623 1.20k blk & multi .35 .20
1709 A623 1.80k blk & multi *1.75 .45*
Nos. 1704-1709 (6) *3.00 1.45*

9th World Soccer Championships for the Jules Rimet Cup, Mexico City, 5/30-6/21.

Congress Emblem — A624

1970, Nov. 9 **Engr. & Photo.**

1710 A624 30h blk, gold, ultra & red .20 .20

Congress of the Czechoslovak Socialist Youth Federation.

Painting Type of 1967

Paintings: 1k, Seated Mother, by Mikulas Galanda. 1.20k, Bridesmaid, by Karel Svolinsky. 1.40k, Walk by Night, 1944, by Frantisek Hudecek. 1.80k, Banska Bystrica Market, by Dominik Skutecky. 2.40k, Adoration of the Kings, from the Vysehrad Codex, 1085.

1970, Nov. 27 **Engr.** *Perf. 11½*

1711 A565 1k multi .25 .25
1712 A565 1.20k multi .35 .35
1713 A565 1.40k multi .40 .30
1714 A565 1.80k multi .50 .35
1715 A565 2.40k multi *2.25 1.75*
Nos. 1711-1715 (5) *3.75 3.00*

Sheets of 4.

Radar A625

Designs: 40h, Interkosmos 3, geophysical satellite. 60h, Molniya meteorological satellite. 1k, Astronaut and Vostok satellite. No. 1720, Interkosmos 4, solar research satellite. No. 1720A, Space satellite (Sputnik) over city. 1.60k, Two-stage rocket on launching pad.

1970-71 **Engr. & Photo.** *Perf. 11*

1716 A625 20h black & multi .20 .20
1717 A625 40h black & multi .20 .20
1718 A625 60h black & multi .20 .20
1719 A625 1k black & multi .25 .20
1720 A625 1.20k black & multi .35 .20
1720A A625 1.20k black & multi ('71) .40 .20
1721 A625 1.60k black & multi *1.40 .35*
Nos. 1716-1721 (7) *3.00 1.55*

"Interkosmos," the collaboration of communist countries in various phases of space research.

Issued: #1720A, 11/15/71; others, 11/30/70.

Face of Christ on Veronica's Veil — A626

Slovak Ikons, 16th-18th Centuries: 60h, Adam and Eve in the Garden, vert. 2k, St. George and the Dragon. 2.80k, St. Michael, vert.

1970, Dec. 17 **Engr.** *Perf. 11½*

Cream Paper

1722 A626 60h multi .20 .20
1723 A626 1k multi .30 .25
1724 A626 2k multi .50 .50
1725 A626 2.80k multi *1.60 1.60*
Nos. 1722-1725 (4) *2.60 2.55*

Sheets of 4.

Carrier Pigeon Type of 1920 — A627

Engraved and Photogravure

1970, Dec. 18 *Perf. 11x11½*

1726 A627 1k red, blk & yel grn .50 .50

Stamp Day.

Song of the Barricades, 1938, by Karel Stika — A628

Czech and Slovak Graphic Art: 50h, Fruit Grower's Barge, 1941, by Cyril Bouda. 60h, Moon (woman) Searching for Lilies of the Valley, 1913, by Jan Zrzavy. 1k, At the Edge of Town (working man and woman), 1931, by Koloman Sokol. 1.60k, Summer, 1641, by Vaclav Hollar. 2k, Gamekeeper and Shepherd of Orava Castle, 1847, by Peter M. Bohun.

Engr. & Photo.; Engr. (40h, 60h, 1k)

1971, Jan. 28 *Perf. 11½*

1727 A628 40h brown .20 .20
1728 A628 50h black & multi .20 .20
1729 A628 60h slate .20 .20
1730 A628 1k black .30 .20
1731 A628 1.60k black & buff .50 .20
1732 A628 2k black & multi *1.25 .30*
Nos. 1727-1732 (6) *2.65 1.30*

Saris Church A629 — Bell Tower, Hronsek A630

Designs: 1k, Roofs and folk art, Horácko. 2.40k, House, Jicin. 3k, House and folk art, Melnik. 3.60k, Church of St. Bartholomew, Chrudim. 5k, Watch Tower, Nachod. 5.40k, Baroque house, Posumavi. 6k, Cottage, Orava. 9k, Cottage, Turnov. 10k, Old houses, Liptov. 14k, House and wayside bell stand. 20k, Houses, Cicmany.

Engraved and Photogravure

1971-72 *Perf. 11½x11, 11x11½*

1733 A630 1k multi .20 .20
1734 A629 1.60k multi .85 .20
1735 A630 2k multi 1.25 .20
1736 A629 2.40k multi .80 .50
1736A A630 3k multi ('72) 1.25 .20
1737 A629 3.60k multi 1.00 .20
1737A A630 5k multi ('72) 1.25 .20
1738 A629 5.40k multi .65 .20
1739 A630 6k multi 2.25 .20
1740 A630 9k multi .85 .20
1740A A629 10k multi ('72) 2.00 .20
1741 A629 14k multi 2.25 .25
1741A A629 20k multi ('72) 2.40 .50
Nos. 1733-1741A (13) 17.00 3.25

Nos. 1736A, 1738, 1740 are horizontal.

See No. 2870.

Coat of Arms Type of 1968

1971, Mar. 26 *Perf. 11½*

1742 A590 60h Zilina .20 .20
1743 A590 60h Levoca .20 .20
1744 A590 60h Ceska Trebova .20 .20
1745 A590 60h Uhersky Brod .20 .20
1746 A590 60h Trutnov .20 .20
1747 A590 60h Karlovy Vary .20 .20
Nos. 1742-1747 (6) 1.20 1.20

"Fight of the Communards and Rise of the International" — A631

Design: No. 1749, World fight against racial discrimination, and "UNESCO."

1971, Mar. 18 *Perf. 11*

1748 A631 1k multicolored .30 .20
1749 A631 1k multicolored .30 .20

No. 1748 for cent. of the Paris Commune. No. 1749 for the Year against Racial Discrimination. Issued in sheets of 15 stamps and 5 labels.

A632

A633

Edelweiss, mountaineering map & equipment.

1971, Apr. 27 *Perf. 11½x11*

1750 A632 30h multicolored .20 .20

50th anniversary of Slovak Alpine Club.

1971, Apr. 27 *Perf. 11½*

1751 A633 30h Singer .20 .20

50th anniversary of Slovak Teachers' Choir.

Abbess' Crosier, 16th Century A634

#1753, Allegory of Music, 16th cent. mural.

1971, May 9

1752 A634 3k gold & multi 1.50 1.25
1753 A634 3k blk, dk brn & buff 1.50 1.25

See Nos. 1817-1818, 1884-1885, 1937-1938, 2040-2041, 2081-2082, 2114-2115, 2176-2177, 2238-2239, 2329-2330, 2384-2385, 2420-2421.

Lenin A635

40h, Hammer & sickle allegory. 60h, Raised fists. 1k, Star, hammer & sickle.

1971, May 14 *Perf. 11*

1754 A635 30h blk, red & gold .20 .20
1755 A635 40h blk, ultra, red & gold .20 .20
1756 A635 60h blk, ultra, red & gold .20 .20
1757 A635 1k blk, ultra, red & gold .30 .20
Nos. 1754-1757 (4) .90 .80

Czechoslovak Communist Party, 50th anniv.

Star, Hammer-Sickle Emblems — A636

60h, Hammer-sickle emblem, fist & people, vert.

Perf. 11½x11, 11x11½

1971, May 24 **Engr. & Photo.**

1758 A636 30h blk, red, gold & yel .20 .20
1759 A636 60h blk, red, gold & bl .20 .20

14th Congress of Communist Party of Czechoslovakia.

Ring-necked Pheasant — A637

Designs: 60h, Rainbow trout. 80h, Mouflon. 1k, Chamois. 2k, Stag. 2.60k, Wild boar.

1971, Aug. 17 *Perf. 11½x11*

1760 A637 20h orange & multi .20 .20
1761 A637 60h lt blue & multi .20 .20
1762 A637 80h yellow & multi .20 .20
1763 A637 1k lt green & multi .20 .20
1764 A637 2k lilac & multi .45 .20
1765 A637 2.60k bister & multi *1.90 .65*
Nos. 1760-1765 (6) *3.15 1.65*

World Hunting Exhib., Budapest, Aug. 27-30.

Diesel Locomotive A638

Gymnasts and Banners A639

1971, Sept. 2 *Perf. 11x11½*

1766 A638 30h lt bl, blk & red .20 .20

Cent. of CKD, Prague Machine Foundry.

1971, Sept. 2 *Perf. 11½x11*

1767 A639 30h red brn, gold & ultra .20 .20

50th anniversary of Workers' Physical Exercise Federation.

Road Intersections and Bridge — A640

1971, Sept. 2 **Engr. & Photo.**

1768 A640 1k blk, gold, red & bl .30 .20

14th World Highways and Bridges Congress. Sheets of 25 stamps and 25 labels printed se-tenant with continuous design.

Chinese Fairytale, by Eva Bednarova A641

Designs: 1k, Tiger and other animals, by Mirko Hanak. 1.60k, The Miraculous Bamboo Shoot, by Yasuo Segawa, horiz.

Perf. 11½x11, 11x11½

1971, Sept. 10

1769 A641 60h multi .20 .20
1770 A641 1k multi .35 .20
1771 A641 1.60k multi .85 .25
Nos. 1769-1771 (3) 1.40 .65

Bratislava BIB 71 biennial exhibition of illustrations for children's books.

Apothecary Jars and Coltsfoot — A642

Intl. Pharmaceutical Cong.: 60h, Jars and dog rose. 1k, Scales and adonis vernalis. 1.20k, Mortars and valerian. 1.80k, Retorts and chicory. 2.40k, Mill, mortar and henbane.

1971, Sept. 20 *Perf. 11½x11*

Yellow Paper

1772 A642 30h multi .20 .20
1773 A642 60h multi .20 .20
1774 A642 1k multi .30 .20
1775 A642 1.20k multi .40 .20
1776 A642 1.80k multi .70 .25
1777 A642 2.40k multi *1.50 .45*
Nos. 1772-1777 (6) *3.30 1.50*

Painting Type of 1967

Paintings: 1k, "Waiting" (woman's head), 1967, by Imro Weiner-Král. 1.20k, Resurrection, by Master of Vyssi Brod, 14th century. 1.40k, Woman with Pitcher, by Milos Bazovsky. 1.80k, Veruna Cudova (in folk costume), by Josef Mánes. 2.40k, Detail from "Feast of the Rose Garlands," by Albrecht Dürer.

1971, Nov. 27 *Perf. 11½*

1779 A565 1k multi .30 .25
1780 A565 1.20k multi .45 .35
1781 A565 1.40k multi .55 .25
1782 A565 1.80k multi .70 .45
1783 A565 2.40k multi *2.25 .70*
Nos. 1779-1783 (5) *4.25 2.00*

Sheets of 4.

Workers Revolt in Krompachy, by Julius Nemcik — A643

1971, Nov. 28 *Perf. 11x11½*

1784 A643 60h multi .20 .20

History of the Czechoslovak Communist Party.

Wooden Dolls and Birds — A644

Folk Art and UNICEF Emblem: 80h, Jug handles, carved. 1k, Horseback rider. 1.60k, Shepherd carrying lamb. 2k, Easter eggs and rattle. 3k, "Zbojnik," folk hero.

1971, Dec. 11 *Perf. 11½*

1785 A644 60h multi .20 .20
1786 A644 80h multi .30 .20
1787 A644 1k multi .40 .20
1788 A644 1.60k multi .60 .20
1789 A644 2k multi 1.25 .40
1790 A644 3k multi 2.25 .55
Nos. 1785-1790 (6) 5.00 1.75

25th anniv. of UNICEF.

Runners, Parthenon, Czechoslovak Olympic Emblem — A645

Designs: 40h, Women's high jump, Olympic emblem and plan for Prague Stadium. 1.60k, Cross-country skiers, Sapporo '72 emblem and ski jump in High Tatras. 2.60k, Discus thrower, Discobolus and St. Vitus Cathedral.

1971, Dec. 16 **Engr. & Photo.**

1791 A645 30h multi .20 .20
1792 A645 40h multi .20 .20
1793 A645 1.60k multi .45 .20
1794 A645 2.60k multi 1.75 .65
Nos. 1791-1794 (4) 2.60 1.25

75th anniversary of Czechoslovak Olympic Committee (30h, 2.00k); 20th Summer Olympic Games, Munich, Aug. 26-Sept. 10, 1972 (40h); 11th Winter Olympic Games, Sapporo, Japan, Feb. 3-13, 1972 (1.60k).

Post Horns and Lion — A646

1971, Dec. 17 *Perf. 11x11½*

1795 A646 1k blk, gold, car & bl .30 .20

Stamp Day.

Figure Skating — A647

"Ležáky" — A648

Olympic Emblems and: 50h, Ski jump. 1k, Ice hockey. 1.60k, Sledding, women's.

1972, Jan. 13 *Perf. 11½*

1796 A647 40h pur, org & red .20 .20
1797 A647 50h dk bl, org & red .20 .20
1798 A647 1k mag, org & red .35 .20
1799 A647 1.60k bl grn, org & red *1.25 .30*
Nos. 1796-1799 (4) *2.00 .90*

11th Winter Olympic Games, Sapporo, Japan, Feb. 3-13.

1972, Feb. 16

No. 1801, Boy's head behind barbed wire, horiz. No. 1802, Hand rising from ruins. No. 1803, Soldier and banner, horiz.

1800 A648 30h blk, dl org & red .20 .20
1801 A648 30h blk & brn org .20 .20
1802 A648 60h blk, yel & red .20 .20
1803 A648 60h sl grn & multi .20 .20
Nos. 1800-1803 (4) .80 .80

30th anniv. of: destruction of Ležáky (No. 1800) and Lidice (No. 1802); Terezin concentration camp (No. 1801); Czechoslovak Army unit in Russia (No. 1803).

Book Year Emblem A649

Steam and Diesel Locomotives A650

1972, Mar. 17 ***Perf. 11½x11***
1804 A649 1k blk & org brn .30 .20

International Book Year 1972.

1972, Mar. 17 ***Perf. 11½x11***
1805 A650 30h multi .20 .20

Centenary of the Kosice-Bohumin railroad.

"Pasture," by Vojtech Sedlacek A651

Designs: 50h, Dressage, by Frantisek Tichy. 60th, Otakara Kubina, by Vaclav Fiala. 1k, The Three Kings, by Ernest Zmetak. 1.60k, Woman Dressing, by Ludovit Fulla.

1972, Mar. 27 ***Perf. 11½x11***
1806 A651 40h multi .20 .20
1807 A651 50h multi .20 .20
1808 A651 60h multi .20 .20
1809 A651 1k multi .30 .20
1810 A651 1.60k multi *.85 .85*
Nos. 1806-1810 (5) *1.75 1.65*

Czech and Slovak graphic art. 1.60k issued in sheets of 4. See #1859-1862, 1921-1924.

Ice Hockey A652

Design: 1k, Two players.

1972, Apr. 7 ***Perf. 11***
1811 A652 60h blk & multi .20 .20
1812 A652 1k blk & multi .35 .20

World and European Ice Hockey Championships, Prague.
For overprint see Nos. 1845-1846.

Bicycling, Olympic Rings and Emblem A653

1972, Apr. 7
1813 A653 50h shown .20 .20
1814 A653 1.60k Diving .60 .20
1815 A653 1.80k Canoeing .70 .20
1816 A653 2k Gymnast *1.40 .50*
Nos. 1813-1816 (4) *2.90 1.10*

20th Olympic Games, Munich, 8/26-9/11.

Prague Castle Art Type of 1971

Designs: No. 1817, Adam and Eve, column capital, St. Vitus Cathedral. No. 1818, Czech coat of arms (lion), c. 1500.

1972, May 9 ***Perf. 11½***
1817 A634 3k blk & multi *2.25 1.75*
1818 A634 3k blk, red, sil & gold 1.25 .75

Sheets of 4.

Andrej Sladkovic (1820-1872), Poet — A654

#1820, Janko Kral (1822-1876), poet. #1821, Ludmilla Podjavorinska (1872-1951), writer. #1822, Antonin Hudecek (1872-1941), painter. #1823, Frantisek Bilek (1872-1941), sculptor. #1824, Jan Preisler (1872-1918), painter.

1972, June 14 ***Perf. 11***
1819 A654 40h pur, ol & bl .20 .20
1820 A654 40h dk grn, bl & yel .20 .20
1821 A654 40h blk & multi .20 .20
1822 A654 40h brn, grn & bl .20 .20
1823 A654 40h choc, grn & org .20 .20
1824 A654 40h grn, sl & dp org .20 .20
Nos. 1819-1824 (6) 1.20 1.20

Men with Banners — A655

1972, June 14 ***Perf. 11x11½***
1825 A655 30h dk vio bl, red & yel .20 .20

8th Trade Union Congress, Prague.

Art Forms of Wire A656

Ornamental Wirework: 60h, Plane and rosette. 80h, Four-headed dragon and ornament. 1k, Locomotive and loops. 2.60k, Tray and owl.

1972, Aug. 28 ***Perf. 11½x11***
1826 A656 20h sal & multi .20 .20
1827 A656 60h multi .20 .20
1828 A656 80h pink & multi .30 .20
1829 A656 1k multi .40 .20
1830 A656 2.60k rose & multi *1.40 .45*
Nos. 1826-1830 (5) *2.50 1.25*

"Jiskra" A657

Engr. & Photo.

1972, Sept. 27 ***Perf. 11½x11***

Size: 40x22mm

Multicolored Design on Blue Paper

1831 A657 50h shown .20 .20
1832 A657 60h "Mir" .20 .20
1833 A657 80h "Republika" .25 .20

Size: 48x29mm

Perf. 11x11½

1834 A657 1k "Kosice" .30 .20
1835 A657 1.60k "Dukla" .45 .20
1836 A657 2k "Kladno" *1.75 .55*
Nos. 1831-1836 (6) *3.15 1.55*

Czechoslovak sea-going vessels.

Hussar, 18th Century Tile — A658

1972, Oct. 24 ***Perf. 11½x11***
1837 A658 30h shown .20 .20
1838 A658 60h Janissary .20 .20
1839 A658 80h St. Martin .20 .20
1840 A658 1.60k St. George .45 .20
1841 A658 1.80k Nobleman's guard .50 .20
1842 A658 2.20k Slovakian horseman *1.75 .60*
Nos. 1837-1842 (6) *3.30 1.60*

Horsemen from 18th-19th century tiles or enamel paintings on glass.

Worker, Flag Hoisted on Bayonet A659

Star, Hammer and Sickle A660

1972, Nov. 7 ***Perf. 11x11½***
1843 A659 30h gold & multi .20 .20
1844 A660 60h rose car & gold .20 .20

55th anniv. of the Russian October Revolution (30h); 50th anniv. of the Soviet Union (60h).

Nos. 1811-1812 Overprinted in Violet Blue or Black

1972 ***Perf. 11***
1845 A652 60h multi (VBl) 5.25 4.50
1846 A652 1k multi (Bk) 5.25 4.50

Czechoslovakia's victorious ice hockey team. The overprint on the 60h (shown) is in Czech and reads CSSR/MISTREM/SVETA; the overprint on the 1k is in Slovak.

Painting Type of 1967

Designs: 1k, "Nosegay" (nudes and flowers), by Max Svabinsky. 1.20k, Struggle of St. Ladislas with Kuman nomad, anonymous, 14th century. 1.40k, Lady with Fur Hat, by Vaclav Hollar. 1.80k, Midsummer Night's Dream, 1962, by Josef Liesler. 2.40k, Pablo Picasso, self-portrait.

1972, Nov. 27 **Engr. & Photo.**
1847 A565 1k multi .55 .35
1848 A565 1.20k multi .70 .50
1849 A565 1.40k blk & cream .85 .65
1850 A565 1.80k multi 1.10 1.00
1851 A565 2.40k multi *2.50 2.50*
Nos. 1847-1851 (5) *5.70 5.00*

Sheets of 4.

Goldfinch A661

Songbirds: 60h, Warbler feeding young cuckoo. 80h, Cuckoo. 1k, Black-billed magpie. 1.60k, Bullfinch. 3k, Song thrush.

1972, Dec. 15

Size: 30x48½mm

1852 A661 60h yel & multi .20 .20
1853 A661 80h multi .25 .20
1854 A661 1k lt bl & multi .25 .20

Engr.

Size: 30x23mm

1855 A661 1.60k multi .35 .20
1856 A661 2k multi .45 .20
1857 A661 3k multi *2.50 .75*
Nos. 1852-1857 (6) *4.00 1.75*

Post Horn and Allegory — A662

1972, Dec. 18 **Engr. & Photo.**
1858 A662 1k blk, red lil & gold .30 .30

Stamp Day.

Art Type of 1972

Designs: 30h, Flowers in Window, by Jaroslav Grus. 60h, Quest for Happiness, by Josef Balaz. 1.60k, Balloon, by Kamil Lhotak. 1.80k, Woman with Viola, by Richard Wiesner.

1973, Jan. 25 ***Perf. 11½x11***
1859 A651 30h multi .20 .20
1860 A651 60h multi .20 .20
1861 A651 1.60k multi .45 .20
1862 A651 1.80k multi *1.25 .60*
Nos. 1859-1862 (4) *2.10 1.20*

Czech and Slovak graphic art.

Tennis Player — A663

Figure Skater — A664

Torch and Star — A665

1973, Feb. 22 ***Perf. 11***
1863 A663 30h vio & multi .20 .20
1864 A664 60h blk & multi .20 .20
1865 A665 1k multi .30 .20
Nos. 1863-1865 (3) .70 .60

80th anniversary of the tennis organization in Czechoslovakia (30h); World figure skating championships, Bratislava (60h); 3rd summer army Spartakiad of socialist countries (1k).

Star and Factories A666

Workers' Militia, Emblem and Flag — A667

1973, Feb. 23

1866	A666 30h multi	.20	.20
1867	A667 60h multi	.20	.20

25th anniversary of the Communist revolution in Czechoslovakia and of the Militia.

Capt. Jan Nalepka, Major Antonin Socnor and Laurel
A668

Torch &: 40h, Evzen Rosicky, Mirko Nespor & ivy leaves. 60h, Vlado Clementis, Karol Smidke & linden leaves. 80h, Jan Osoha, Josef Molak & oak leaves. 1k, Marie Kuderikova, Jozka Jaburkova & rose. 1.60k, Vaclav Sinkule, Eduard Urx & palm leaf.

1973, Mar. 20 ***Perf. 11½x11***

Yellow Paper

1868	A668	30h blk, ver & gold	.20	.20
1869	A668	40h blk, ver & grn	.20	.20
1870	A668	60h blk, ver & gold	.20	.20
1871	A668	80h blk, ver & gold	.20	.20
1872	A668	1k blk, ver & grn	.30	.20
1873	A668	1.60k blk, ver & sil	*.60*	*.20*
		Nos. 1868-1873 (6)	*1.70*	*1.20*

Fighters against and victims of Fascism and Nazism during German Occupation.

Virgil I. Grissom, Edward H. White, Roger B. Chaffee — A669

Designs: 20h, Soviet planetary station "Venera." 30h, "Intercosmos" station. 40h, Lunokhod on moon. 3.60k, Vladimir M. Komarov, Georgi T. Dobrovolsky, Vladislav N. Volkov, Victor I. Patsayev. 5k, Yuri A. Gagarin.

1973, Apr. 12 ***Perf. 11½x11***

Size: 40x22mm

1874	A669	20h multi	.20	.20
1875	A669	30h multi	.20	.20
1876	A669	40h multi	.20	.20

Engr.

Perf. 11½

Size: 49x30mm

1877	A669	3k multi	1.25	.55
1878	A669	3.60k multi	1.60	1.10
1879	A669	5k multi	*3.75*	*3.50*
		Nos. 1874-1879 (6)	*7.20*	*5.75*

In memory of American and Russian astronauts.

Radio — A670

Telephone and Map of Czechoslovakia
A671

Television
A672

1973, May 1 ***Perf. 11½x11***

1880	A670 30h blk & multi	.20	.20
1881	A671 30h lt bl, pink & blk	.20	.20
1882	A672 30h dp bl & multi	.20	.20
	Nos. 1880-1882 (3)	.60	.60

Czechoslovak anniversaries: 50 years of broadcasting (No. 1880); 20 years of telephone service to all communities (No. 1881); 20 years of television (No. 1882).

Coat of Arms and Linden Branch — A673

1973, May 9 ***Perf. 11x11½***

1883	A673 60h red & multi	.20	.20

25th anniv. of the Constitution of May 9.

Prague Castle Art Type of 1971

No. 1884, Royal Legate, 14th century. No. 1885, Seal of King Charles IV, 1351.

1973, May 9 ***Perf. 11½***

1884	A634 3k blue & multi	.85	1.00
1885	A634 3k gold, grn & dk brn	1.25	1.75

Sheets of 4.

Coat of Arms Type of 1968

1973, June 20

1886	A590 60h Mikulov	.20	.20
1887	A590 60h Zlutice	.20	.20
1888	A590 60h Smolenice	.20	.20
	Nos. 1886-1888 (3)	.60	.60

Coats of arms of Czechoslovakian cities.

Heraldic Colors of Olomouc and Moravia — A674

Anthurium — A675

1973, Aug. 23 **Engr. & Photo.**

1889	A674 30h multi	.20	.20

University of Olomouc, 400th anniv.

1973, Aug. 23 ***Perf. 11½***

Sizes: 60h, 1k, 2k, 30x50mm; 1.60k, 1.80k, 3.60k, 23x39mm.

1890	A675	60h Tulips	.75	.75
1891	A675	1k Rose	.35	.25
1892	A675	1.60k shown	.35	.20
1893	A675	1.80k Iris	.35	.20
1894	A675	2k Chrysanthemum	*2.25*	*2.25*
1895	A675	3.60k Cymbidium	.75	.35
		Nos. 1890-1895 (6)	*4.80*	*4.00*

Flower Show, Olomouc, Aug. 18-Sept. 2. 60h, 1k, 2k issued in sheets of 4, others in sheets of 10.

Hunting Dogs
A676

1973, Sept. 5

1896	A676	20h Irish setter	.30	.20
1897	A676	30h Czech terrier	.30	.20
1898	A676	40h Bavarian hunting dog	.40	.20
1899	A676	60h German pointer	.40	.20
1900	A676	1k Cocker spaniel	.60	.20
1901	A676	1.60k Dachshund	*1.50*	*.50*
		Nos. 1896-1901 (6)	*3.50*	*1.50*

Czechoslovak United Hunting Org., 50th anniv.

St. John, the Baptist, by Svabinsky
A677

Works by Max Svabinsky: 60h, "August Noon" (woman). 80h, "Marriage of True Minds" (artist and muse). 1k, "Paradise Sonata I" (Adam dreaming of Eve). 2.60k, Last Judgment, stained glass window, St. Vitus Cathedral.

1973, Sept. 17 **Litho. & Engr.**

1902	A677	20h blk & pale grn	.20	.20
1903	A677	60h black & buff	.20	.20

Engr.

1904	A677	80h black	.25	.20
1905	A677	1k slate green	.30	.25
1906	A677	2.60k multi	*1.50*	*1.25*
		Nos. 1902-1906 (5)	*2.45*	*2.10*

Centenary of the birth of Max Svabinsky (1873-1962), artist and stamp designer. 20h and 60h issued in sheets of 25; 80h and 1k se-tenant in sheets of 4 checkerwise; 2.60k in sheets of 4.

Trade Union Emblem
A678

1973, Oct. 15 **Engr. & Photo.**

1907	A678 1k red, bl & yel	.25	.20

8th Congress of the World Federation of Trade Unions, Varna, Bulgaria.

Painting Type of 1967

1k, Boy from Martinique, by Antonin Pelc. 1.20k, "Fortitude" (mountaineer), by Martin Benka. 1.80k, Rembrandt, self-portrait. 2k, Pierrot, by Bohumil Kubista. 2.40k, Ilona Kubinyiova, by Peter M. Bohun. 3.60k, Virgin and Child (Veveri Madonna), c. 1350.

1973, Nov. 27 ***Perf. 11½***

1908	A565	1k multi, vio bl inscriptions	*1.75*	*1.10*
a.		1k multi, black inscriptions	*15.00*	*14.00*
1909	A565	1.20k multi	*1.75*	*1.10*
1910	A565	1.80k multi	.50	.30
1911	A565	2k multi	.75	.45
1912	A565	2.40k multi	.75	.45
1913	A565	3.60k multi	1.00	.60
		Nos. 1908-1913 (6)	*6.50*	*4.00*

Sheets of 4. Nos. 1910-1913 printed se-tenant with gold and black inscription on gutter.

Central background bluish gray on No. 1908, light bluish green on No. 1908a.

Postilion — A679

1973, Dec. 18

1914	A679 1k gold & multi	.25	.20

Stamp Day 1974 and 55th anniversary of Czechoslovak postage stamps. Printed with 2 labels showing telephone and telegraph.

Bedrich Smetana — A681

Pablo Neruda, Chilean Flag — A682

"CSSR" — A680

Comecon Building, Moscow — A683

1974, Jan. 1

1915	A680 30h red, gold & ultra	.20	.20

5th anniversary of Federal Government in the Czechoslovak Socialist Republic.

1974, Jan. 4 ***Perf. 11x11½***

1916	A681 60h shown	.20	.20
1917	A681 60h Josef Suk	.20	.20
1918	A682 60h shown	.20	.20
	Nos. 1916-1918 (3)	.60	.60

Smetana (1824-84), composer; Suk (1874-1935), composer, and Pablo Neruda (Neftali Ricardo Reyes, 1904-73), Chilean poet.

1974, Jan. 23

1919	A683 1k gold, red & vio bl	.25	.20

25th anniversary of the Council of Mutual Economic Assistance (COMECON).

Symbols of Postal Service — A684

1974, Feb. 20 ***Perf. 11½***

1920	A684 3.60k multi	.95	.45

BRNO '74 National Stamp Exhibition, Brno, June 8-23.

Art Type of 1972

Designs: 60h, Tulips 1973, by Josef Broz. 1k, Structures 1961 (poppy and building), by Orest Dubay. 1.60k, Bird and flowers (Golden Sun-Glowing Day), by Adolf Zabransky. 1.80k, Artificial flowers, by Frantisek Gross.

1974, Feb. 21 ***Perf. 11½x11***

1921	A651	60h multi	.20	.20
1922	A651	1k multi	.30	.20
1923	A651	1.60k multi	.45	.20
1924	A651	1.80k multi	.90	.30
		Nos. 1921-1924 (4)	1.85	.90

Czech and Slovak graphic art.

Oskar Benes and Vaclav Prochazka — A685

40h, Milos Uher, Anton Sedlacek. 60h, Jan Hajecek, Marie Sedlackova. 80h, Jan Sverma, Albin Grznar. 1k, Jaroslav Neliba, Alois Hovorka. 1.60k, Ladislav Exnar, Ludovit Kukorelli.

1974, Mar. 21 *Perf. 11½x11*

1925	A685	30h indigo & multi	.20	.20
1926	A685	40h indigo & multi	.20	.20
1927	A685	60h indigo & multi	.20	.20
1928	A685	80h indigo & multi	.20	.20
1929	A685	1k indigo & multi	.25	.20
1930	A685	1.60k indigo & multi	.75	.25
		Nos. 1925-1930 (6)	1.80	1.25

Partisan commanders and fighters.

"Water, the Source of Energy" A686

Symbolic Designs: 1k, Importance of water for agriculture. 1.20k, Study of the oceans. 1.60k, "Hydrological Decade." 2k, Struggle for unpolluted water.

1974, Apr. 25 **Engr.** *Perf. 11½*

1931	A686	60h multi	.20	.20
1932	A686	1k multi	.25	.20
1933	A686	1.20k multi	.35	.30
1934	A686	1.60k multi	.45	.40
1935	A686	2k multi	1.50	1.50
		Nos. 1931-1935 (5)	2.75	2.60

Hydrological Decade (UNESCO), 1965-1974. Sheets of 4.

Allegory Holding "Molniya," and Ground Station — A687

Sousaphone A688

1974, Apr. 30 **Engr. & Photo.**

1936	A687	30h vio bl & multi	.20	.20

"Intersputnik," first satellite communications ground station in Czechoslovakia.

Prague Castle Art Type of 1971

#1937, Golden Cock, 17th century locket. #1938, Glass monstrance, 1840.

1974, May 9 **Engr.** *Perf. 11½*

1937	A634	3k gold & multi	1.40	1.25
1938	A634	3k blk & multi	1.40	1.25

Sheets of 4.

Engraved and Photogravure

1974, May 12 *Perf. 11x11½*

1939	A688	20h shown	.20	.20
1940	A688	30h Bagpipe	.20	.20
1941	A688	40h Violin, by Martin Benka	.20	.20
1942	A688	1k Pyramid piano	.30	.20
1943	A688	1.60k Tenor quinton, 1754	.80	.20
		Nos. 1939-1943 (5)	1.70	1.00

Prague and Bratislava Music Festivals. The 1.60k also commemorates 25th anniversary of Slovak Philharmonic Orchestra.

Child — A689

1974, June 1 *Perf. 11½*

1944	A689	60h multi	.20	.20

Children's Day. Design is from illustration for children's book by Adolf Zabransky.

Globe, People and Exhibition Emblems — A690

Design: 6k, Rays and emblems symbolizing "Oneness and Mutuality."

1974, June 1

1945	A690	30h multi	.20	.20
1946	A690	6k multi	1.50	1.00

BRNO 74 Natl. Stamp Exhib., Brno, June 8-23. Sheets of 16 stamps and 14 labels.

Resistance Fighter — A691

Actress Holding Tragedy and Comedy Masks — A692

1974, Aug. 29 *Perf. 11½*

1947	A691	30h multi	.20	.20

Slovak National Uprising, 30th anniversary.

1974, Aug. 29

1948	A692	30h red, sil & blk	.20	.20

Bratislava Academy of Music and Drama, 25th anniversary.

Slovak Girl with Flower — A693

1974, Aug. 29

1949	A693	30h multi	.20	.20

SLUK, Slovak folksong and dance ensemble, 25th anniversary.

Hero and Leander A694

Design: 2.40k, Hero watching Leander swim the Hellespont. No. 1952, Leander reaching shore. No. 1953, Hero mourning over Leander's body. No. 1954, Hermione, Leander's sister. No. 1955, Mourning Cupid. Designs are from 17th century English tapestries in Bratislava Council Palace.

1974-76

1950	A694	2k multi	1.25	1.10
1951	A694	2.40k multi	1.50	1.25
1952	A694	3k multi	.90	.45
1953	A694	3k multi	1.75	1.75
1954	A694	3.60k multi	2.25	1.10
1955	A694	3.60k multi	.85	.60
		Nos. 1950-1955 (6)	8.50	6.25

Issued: #1950-1951, 9/25/74; #1952, 1954, 8/29/75; #1953, 1955, 5/9/76.

Soldier Standing Guard, Target, 1840 — A695

Painted Folk-art Targets: 60h, Landscape with Pierrot and flags, 1828. 1k, Diana crowning champion marksman, 1832. 1.60k, Still life with guitar, 1839. 2.40k, Salvo and stag in flight, 1834. 3k, Turk and giraffe, 1831.

1974, Sept. 26 *Perf. 11½*

Size: 30x50mm

1956	A695	30h black & multi	.20	.20
1957	A695	60h black & multi	.20	.20
1958	A695	1k black & multi	.25	.20

Engr.

Perf. 12

Size: 40x50mm

1959	A695	1.60k green & multi	.40	.35
1960	A695	2.40k sepia & multi	.70	.60
1961	A695	3k multi	*2.25*	*2.25*
		Nos. 1956-1961 (6)	*4.00*	*3.80*

UPU Emblem and Postilion — A696

UPU Cent. (UPU Emblem and): 40h, Mail coach. 60h, Railroad mail coach, 1851. 80h, Early mail truck. 1k, Czechoslovak Airlines mail plane. 1.60k, Radar.

Engraved and Photogravure

1974, Oct. 9 *Perf. 11½*

1962	A696	30h multi	.20	.20
1963	A696	40h multi	.20	.20
1964	A696	60h multi	.20	.20
1965	A696	80h multi	.20	.20
1966	A696	1k multi	.30	.20
1967	A696	1.60k multi	1.00	.25
		Nos. 1962-1967 (6)	2.10	1.25

Sealed Letter — A697

Post Rider — A699

Stylized Bird — A698

Postal Code Symbol — A698a

20h, Post Horn, Old Town Bridge Tower. #1971, Carrier pigeon. #1979, Map of Czechoslovakia with postal code numbers.

1974, Oct. 31 *Perf. 11½x11*

1968	A699	20h multi	.20	.20
1969	A697	30h brn, bl & red	.20	.20
1970	A699	40h multi	.20	.20
1971	A697	60h bl, yel & red	.20	.20
		Nos. 1968-1971 (4)	.80	.80

See No. 2675.

Coil Stamps

1975 **Photo.** *Perf. 14*

1976	A698	30h brt bl	.20	.20
1977	A698	60h carmine	.20	.20

1976 *Perf. 11½*

1978	A698a	30h emer	.20	.20
1979	A698a	60h scar	.20	.20

Nos. 1976-1979 have black control number on back of every fifth stamp.

Ludvik Kuba, Self-portrait, 1941 — A700

Paintings: 1.20k, Violinist Frantisek Ondricek, by Vaclav Brozik. 1.60k, Vase with Flowers, by Otakar Kubin. 1.80k, Woman with Pitcher, by Janko Alexy. 2.40k, Bacchanalia, c. 1635, by Karel Skreta.

1974, Nov. 27 **Engr.** *Perf. 11½*

1980	A700	1k multi	.30	.25
1981	A700	1.20k multi	.50	.30
1982	A700	1.60k multi	.55	.40
1983	A700	1.80k multi	.55	.50
1984	A700	2.40k multi	2.25	2.00
		Nos. 1980-1984 (5)	4.15	3.45

Czech and Slovak art. Sheets of 4.

See Nos. 2209-2211, 2678-2682, 2721-2723, 2743, 2766-2768.

Post Horn — A701

Engraved and Photogravure

1974, Dec. 18 *Perf. 11x11½*

1985	A701	1k multicolored	.30	.20

Stamp Day.

Still-life with Hare, by Hollar — A702

Designs: 1k, The Lion and the Mouse, by Vaclav Hollar. 1.60k, Deer Hunt, by Philip Galle. 1.80k, Grand Hunt, by Jacques Callot.

1975, Feb. 26 ***Perf. 11½x11***

1988	A702	60h blk & buff	.20	.20
1989	A702	1k blk & buff	.25	.20
1990	A702	1.60k blk & yel	.45	.20
1991	A702	1.00k blk & buff	1.00	.50
		Nos. 1988-1991 (4)	1.90	1.10

Hunting scenes from old engravings.

Guns Pointing at Family A703

Young Woman and Globe — A704

Designs: 1k, Women and building on fire. 1.20k, People and roses. All designs include names of destroyed villages.

1975, Feb. 26 ***Perf. 11***

1992	A703	60h multi	.20	.20
1993	A703	1k multi	.30	.20
1994	A703	1.20k multi	.30	.20
		Nos. 1992-1994 (3)	.80	.60

Destruction of 14 villages by the Nazis, 30th anniversary.

1975, Mar. 7 ***Perf. 11½x11***

1995	A704	30h red & multi	.20	.20

International Women's Year 1975.

Little Queens, Moravian Folk Custom A705

Folk Customs: 1k, Straw masks (animal heads and blackened faces), Slovak. 1.40k, The Tale of Maid Dorothea (executioner, girl, king and devil). 2k, Drowning of Morena, symbol of death and winter.

1975, Mar. 26 **Engr.** ***Perf. 11½***

1996	A705	60h blk & multi	.20	.20
1997	A705	1k blk & multi	.35	.35
1998	A705	1.40k blk & multi	.50	.50
1999	A705	2k blk & multi	1.25	1.25
		Nos. 1996-1999 (4)	2.30	2.30

Sheets of four.

Coat of Arms Type of 1968

Engraved and Photogravure

1975, Apr. 17 ***Perf. 11½***

2000	A590	60h Nymburk	.20	.20
2001	A590	60h Znojmo	.20	.20

Coats of arms of Czechoslovakian cities.

Czech May Uprising — A706

Liberation by Soviet Army — A707

Czechoslovak-Russian Friendship — A708

Engr. & Photo.; Engr. (A707)

1975, May 9

2002	A706	1k multi	.25	.20
2003	A707	1k multi	.25	.20
2004	A708	1k multi	.25	.20
		Nos. 2002-2004 (3)	.75	.60

30th anniv. of the May uprising of the Czech people and of liberation by the Soviet Army; 5th anniv. of the Czechoslovak-Soviet Treaty of Friendship, Cooperation and Mutual Aid.

Adolescents' Exercises — A709

Designs: 60th, Children's exercises. 1k, Men's and women's exercises.

Engraved and Photogravure

1975, June 15 ***Perf. 12x11½***

2005	A709	30h lil & multi	.20	.20
2006	A709	60h multi	.20	.20
2007	A709	1k vio & multi	.25	.20
		Nos. 2005-2007 (3)	.65	.60

Spartakiad 1975, Prague, June 26-29. Nos. 2005-2007 each issued in sheets of 30 stamps and 40 labels, showing different Spartakiad emblems.

Datrioides Microlepis and Sea Horse — A710

Tropical Fish (Aquarium): 1k, Beta splendens regan and pterophyllum scalare. 1.20k, Carassius auratus. 1.60k, Amphiprion percula and chaetodon sp. 2k, Pomacanthodes semicirculatus, pomocanthus maculosus and paracanthorus hepatus.

1975, June 27 ***Perf. 11½***

2008	A710	60h multi	.20	.20
2009	A710	1k multi	.35	.20
2010	A710	1.20k multi	.40	.20
2011	A710	1.60k multi	.55	.20
2012	A710	2k multi	*1.75*	*.50*
		Nos. 2008-2012 (5)	3.25	1.30

Pelicans, by Nikita Charushin — A711

Book Illustrations: 30h, The Dreamer, by Lieselotte Schwarz. 40h, Hero on horseback, by Val Muntenau. 60h, Peacock, by Klaus Ensikat. 80h, Man on horseback, by Robert Dubravec.

1975, Sept. 5

2013	A711	20h multi	.20	.20
2014	A711	30h multi	.20	.20
2015	A711	40h multi	.20	.20
2016	A711	60h multi	.20	.20
2017	A711	80h multi	*.40*	*.20*
		Nos. 2013-2017 (5)	1.20	1.00

Bratislava BIB 75 biennial exhibition of illustrations for children's books.

Nos. 2013-2017 issued in sheets of 25 stamps and 15 labels with designs and inscriptions in various languages.

Strakonice, 1951 — A712

Designs: Motorcycles.

1975, Sept. 29 ***Perf. 11½***

2018	A712	20h shown	.20	.20
2019	A712	40h Jawa 250, 1945	.20	.20
2020	A712	60h Jawa 175, 1935	.20	.20
2021	A712	1k ITAR, 1921	.20	.20
2022	A712	1.20k ORION, 1903	.25	.20
2023	A712	1.80k Laurin & Klement, 1898	1.40	.40
		Nos. 2018-2023 (6)	2.45	1.40

Study of Shortwave Solar Radiation — A713

Soyuz-Apollo Link-up in Space — A714

60h, Study of aurora borealis & Oréol satellite. 1k, Study ofionosphere & cosmic radiation. 2k, Copernicus, radio map of the sun & satellite.

1975, Sept. 30

2024	A713	30h multi	.20	.20
2025	A713	60h yel, rose red & vio	.20	.20
2026	A713	1k bl, yel & vio	.30	.20
2027	A713	2k red, vio & yel	.45	.20

Engr.

2028	A714	5k vio & multi	*2.50*	*2.50*
		Nos. 2024-2028 (5)	*3.65*	*3.30*

International cooperation in space research. No. 2028 issued in sheets of 4.

The design of No. 2026 appears to be inverted.

Slovnaft, Petrochemical Plant — A715

Designs: 60h, Atomic power station. 1k, Construction of Prague subway. 1.20k, Construction of Friendship pipeline. 1.40k, Combine harvesters. 1.60k, Apartment house construction.

Engraved and Photogravure

1975, Oct. 28

2029	A715	30h multi	.20	.20
2030	A715	60h multi	.20	.20
2031	A715	1k multi	.30	.20
2032	A715	1.20k multi	.35	.20
2033	A715	1.40k multi	.40	.20
2034	A715	1.60k multi	*.75*	*.40*
		Nos. 2029-2034 (6)	2.20	1.40

Socialist construction, 30th anniversary. Nos. 2029-2034 printed se-tenant with labels.

Pres. Gustav Husak — A716

1975, Oct. 28 **Engr.**

2035	A716	30h ultra	.20	.20
2036	A716	60h rose red	.20	.20

Prague Castle Art Type of 1971

3k, Gold earring, 9th cent. 3.60k, Arms of Premysl Dynasty & Bohemia from lid of leather case containing Bohemian crown, 14th cent.

1975, Oct. 29

2040	A634	3k blk, grn, pur & gold	.75	.60
2041	A634	3.60k red & multi	*2.00*	*1.50*

Sheets of 4.

Miniature Sheet

Ludvik Svoboda, Road Map, Buzuluk to Prague, Carnations — A717

1975, Nov. 25

2042	A717	10k multi	10.00	10.00

Pres. Ludvik Svoboda, 80th birthday.

Exists imperf. Value, $45 unused, $30 used.

Art Type of 1967

Paintings: 1k, "May 1975" (Woman and doves for 30th anniv. of peace), by Zdenek Sklenar. 1.40k, Woman in national costume, by Eugen Nevan. 1.80k, "Liberation of Prague," by Alena Cermakova, horiz. 2.40k, "Fire 1938" (woman raising fist), by Josef Capek. 3.40k, Old Prague, 1828, by Vincenc Morstadt.

1975, Nov. 27 **Engr.** ***Perf. 11½***

2043	A565	1k blk, buff & brn	.30	.25
2044	A565	1.40k multi	.60	.30
2045	A565	1.80k multi	.60	.30
2046	A565	2.40k multi	1.50	.95
2047	A565	3.40k multi	1.50	1.50
		Nos. 2043-2047 (5)	4.50	3.30

Sheets of 4.

Carrier Pigeon — A718

Engraved and Photogravure

1975, Dec. 18 ***Perf. 11½***
2048 A718 1k red & multi .30 .20

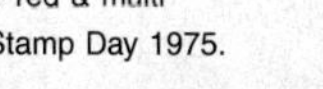
Stamp Day 1975.

Frantisek Halas — A719

Wilhelm Pieck — A720

Frantisek Lexa — A721

Jindrich Jindrich — A722

Ivan Krasko — A723

1976, Feb. 25 ***Perf. 11½***
2049 A719 60h multi .20 .20
2050 A720 60h multi .20 .20
2051 A721 60h multi .20 .20
2052 A722 60h multi .20 .20
2053 A723 60h multi .20 .20
Nos. 2049-2053 (5) 1.00 1.00

Halas (1901-49), poet; Pieck (1876-1960), pres. of German Democratic Republic; Lexa (1876-1960), professor of Egyptology; Jindrich (1876-1967), composer and writer; Krasko (1876-1958), Slovak poet. No. 2051 printed in sheets of 10, others in sheets of 50.

Ski Jump, Olympic Emblem A724

Winter Olympic Games Emblem and: 1.40k, Figure skating, women's. 1.60k, Ice hockey.

1976, Mar. 22 ***Perf. 12x11½***
2054 A724 1k gold & multi .25 .20
2055 A724 1.40k gold & multi .35 .20
2056 A724 1.60k gold & multi *.40* *.25*
Nos. 2054-2056 (3) *1.00* *.65*

12th Winter Olympic Games, Innsbruck, Austria, Feb. 4-15.

Javelin and Olympic Rings — A725

1976, Mar. 22 ***Perf. 11½***
2057 A725 2k shown .65 .20
2058 A725 3k Relay race .95 .30
2059 A725 3.60k Shot put *1.40* *.65*
Nos. 2057-2059 (3) *3.00* *1.15*

21st Olympic Games, Montreal, Canada, July 17-Aug. 1.

Table Tennis — A726

1976, Mar. 22 ***Perf. 11x12***
2060 A726 1k multi .30 .20

European Table Tennis Championship, Prague, Mar. 26-Apr. 4.

Symbolic of Communist Party — A727

Worker, Derrick, Emblem — A728

1976, Apr. 12 ***Perf. 11x12***
2061 A727 30h gold & multi .20 .20
2062 A728 60h gold & multi .20 .20

15th Congress of the Communist Party of Czechoslovakia.

Radio Prague Orchestra A729

Dancer, Violin, Tragic Mask — A730

Actors — A731

Folk Dancers A732

Film Festival — A733

1976, Apr. 26 ***Perf. 11½***
2063 A729 20h gold & multi .20 .20
2064 A730 20h pink & multi .20 .20
2065 A731 20h lt bl & multi .20 .20
2066 A732 30h blk & multi .20 .20
2067 A733 30h vio bl, rose & grn .20 .20
Nos. 2063-2067 (5) 1.00 1.00

Czechoslovak Radio Symphony Orchestra, Prague, 50th anniv. (No. 2063); Academy of Music and Dramatic Art, Prague, 50th anniv. (No. 2064); Nova Scena Theater Co., Bratislava, 30th anniv. (No. 2065); Intl. Folk Song and Dance Festival, Straznice, 30th anniv. (No. 2066); 20th Intl. Film Festival, Karlovy Vary (No. 2067).

Hammer and Sickle
A734 A735

Design: 6k, Hammer and sickle, horiz.

1976, May 14
2068 A734 30h gold, red & dk bl .20 .20
2069 A735 60h gold, red & dp car .25 .20

Souvenir Sheet

2070 A735 6k red & multi 1.50 1.50

Czechoslovak Communist Party, 55th anniv. #2070 contains a 50x30mm stamp.

Ships in Storm, by Frans Huys (1522-1562) A736

Old Engravings of Ships: 60h, by Václav Hollar (1607-77). 1k, by Regnier Nooms Zeeman (1623-68). 2k, by Francois Chereau (1680-1729).

Engraved and Photogravure

1976, July 21 ***Perf. 11x11½***
2071 A736 40h buff & blk .20 .20
2072 A736 60h gray, buff & blk .20 .20
2073 A736 1k lt grn, buff & blk .20 .20
2074 A736 2k lt bl, buff & blk *1.10* *.40*
Nos. 2071-2074 (4) *1.70* *1.00*

"UNESCO" A737

1976, July 30 ***Perf. 11½***
2075 A737 2k gray & multi .50 .45

30th anniversary of UNESCO. Sheets of 10.

Souvenir Sheet

Hands Holding Infant, Globe and Dove A738

1976, July 30
2076 Sheet of 2 5.50 4.50
a. A738 6k multi 2.50 2.00

European Security and Cooperation Conference, Helsinki, Finland, 2nd anniv.

Merino Ram — A739

Couple Smoking, WHO Emblem and Skull — A740

Designs: 40h, Bern-Hana milk cow. 1.60k, Kladruby stallion Generalissimus XXVII.

1976, Aug. 28 ***Perf. 11½x12***
2077 A739 30h multi .20 .20
2078 A739 40h multi .20 .20
2079 A739 1.60k multi .35 .20
Nos. 2077-2079 (3) .75 .60

Bountiful Earth Exhibition, Ceske Budejovice, Aug. 28-Sept. 12.

1976, Sept. 7 ***Perf. 12x11½***
2080 A740 2k multi .75 .40

Fight against smoking, WHO drive against drug addiction. Printed in sheets of 10 (2x5) with WHO emblems and inscription in margin.

Prague Castle Art Type of 1971

Designs: 3k, View of Prague Castle, by F. Hoogenberghe, 1572. 3.60k, Faun and Satyr, sculptured panel, 16th century.

1976, Oct. 22 **Engr.** ***Perf. 11½***
2081 A634 3k multi 2.00 1.75
2082 A634 3.60k multi .75 .50

Sheets of 4.

Guernica 1937, by Imro Weiner-Kral A741

1976, Oct. 22
2083 A741 5k multi 1.25 .60

40th anniv. of the Intl. Brigade in Spain.

Zebras A742

20h, Elephants. 30h, Cheetah. 40h, Giraffes. 60h, Rhinoceros. 3k, Bongos.

Engraved and Photogravure

1976, Nov. 3 ***Perf. 11½x11, 11x11½***

2084 A742 10h multi .20 .20
2085 A742 20h multi, vert. .20 .20
2086 A742 30h multi .20 .20
2087 A742 40h multi, vert. .20 .20
2088 A742 60h multi .20 .20
2089 A742 3k multi, vert. 1.25 .50
Nos. 2084-2089 (6) 2.25 1.50

African animals in Dvur Kralove Zoo.

Art Type of 1967

Paintings of Flowers: 1k, by Peter Matejka. 1.40k, by Cyril Bouda. 2k, by Jan Breughel. 3.60k, J. Rudolf Bys.

1976, Nov. 27 **Engr.** ***Perf. 11½***

2090 A565 1k multi .80 .60
2091 A565 1.40k multi 1.00 .80
2092 A565 2k multi 1.60 1.25
2093 A565 3.60k multi .90 .75
Nos. 2090-2093 (4) 4.30 3.40

Sheets of 4. Emblem and name of Praga 1978 on horizontal gutter.

Postrider, 17th Century, and Satellites — A743

1976, Dec. 18 **Engr. & Photo.**

2094 A743 1k multi .25 .20

Stamp Day 1976.

Ice Hockey — A744

Arms of Vranov — A745

1977, Feb. 11 ***Perf. 11½***

2095 A744 60h shown .20 .20
2096 A744 1k Biathlon .30 .20
2097 A744 1.60k Ski jump *1.25* *.25*
2098 A744 2k Downhill skiing .55 .30
Nos. 2095-2098 (4) *2.30* *.95*

6th Winter Spartakiad of Socialist Countries' Armies.

1977, Feb. 20

Coats of Arms of Czechoslovak towns.

2099 A745 60h shown .20 .20
2100 A745 60h Kralupy & Vltavou .20 .20
2101 A745 60h Jicin .20 .20
2102 A745 60h Valasske Mezirici .20 .20
Nos. 2099-2102 (4) .80 .80

See Nos. 2297-2300.

Window, Michna Palace — A746

Prague Renaissance Windows: 30h, Michna Palace. 40h, Thun Palace. 60h, Archbishop's Palace, Hradcany. 5k, St. Nicholas Church.

1977, Mar. 10

2103 A746 20h multi .20 .20
2104 A746 30h multi .20 .20
2105 A746 40h multi .20 .20
2106 A746 60h multi .20 .20
2107 A746 5k multi *1.75* *.75*
Nos. 2103-2107 (5) *2.55* *1.55*

PRAGA 1978 International Philatelic Exhibition, Prague, Sept. 8-17, 1978.

Children, Auxiliary Police A747

1977, Apr. 21 ***Perf. 11½***

2108 A747 60h multi .20 .20

Auxiliary Police, 25th anniversary.

Warsaw, Polish Flag, Bicyclists A748

Congress Emblem — A749

Designs: 60h, Berlin, DDR flag, bicyclists. 1k, Prague, Czechoslovakian flag, victorious bicyclist. 1.40k, Bicyclists on highways, modern views of Berlin, Prague and Warsaw.

1977, May 7

2109 A748 30h multi .20 .20
2110 A748 60h multi .20 .20
2111 A748 1k multi *.50* *.25*
2112 A748 1.40k multi .35 .20
Nos. 2109-2112 (4) *1.25* *.85*

30th International Bicycle Peace Race Warsaw-Prague-Berlin.

1977, May 25 ***Perf. 11½***

2113 A749 30h car, red & gold .20 .20

9th Trade Union Congress, Prague 1977.

Prague Castle Art Type of 1971

Designs: 3k, Onyx footed bowl, 1350. 3.60k, Bronze horse, 1619.

1977, June 7 **Engr.**

2114 A634 3k multi 1.10 1.00
2115 A634 3.60k multi 1.60 1.50

Sheets of 4.

French Postrider, 19th Century, PRAGA '78 Emblem — A750

Postal Uniforms: 1k, Austrian, 1838. 2k, Austrian, late 18th century. 3.60k, Germany, early 18th century.

1977, June 8 **Engr. & Photo.**

2116 A750 60h multi .20 .20
2117 A750 1k multi .25 .20
2118 A750 2k multi .45 .20
2119 A750 3.60k multi *1.90* *.75*
Nos. 2116-2119 (4) *2.80* *1.35*

PRAGA 1978 International Philatelic Exhibition, Prague, Sept. 8-17, 1978.

Nos. 2116-2119 issued in sheets of 50 and sheets of 4 with 4 labels and horizontal gutter.

Coffeepots, Porcelain Mark — A751

Mlada Boleslav Costume — A752

Czechoslovak Porcelain and Porcelain Marks: 30h, Urn. 40h, Vase. 60h, Cup and saucer, jugs. 1k, Candlestick and plate. 3k, Cup and saucer, coffeepot.

1977, June 15

2120 A751 20h multi .20 .20
2121 A751 30h multi .20 .20
2122 A751 40h multi .20 .20
2123 A751 60h multi .20 .20
2124 A751 1k multi .25 .20
2125 A751 3k multi *1.10* *.65*
Nos. 2120-2125 (6) *2.15* *1.65*

1977, Aug. 31 **Engr.** ***Perf. 11½***

PRAGA Emblem and Folk Costumes from: 1.60k, Vazek. 3.60k, Zavadka. 5k, Belkovice.

2126 A752 1k multi .25 .25
2127 A752 1.60k multi *2.00* *2.00*
2128 A752 3.60k multi .75 .70
2129 A752 5k multi .85 .85
Nos. 2126-2129 (4) *3.85* *3.80*

Issued in sheets of 10 and in sheets of 8 plus 2 labels showing PRAGA '78 emblem.

Old Woman, Devil and Spinner, by Viera Bombova A753

Book Illustrations: 60h, Bear and tiger, by Genadij Pavlisin. 1k, Coach drawn by 4 horses (Hans Christian Andersen), by Ulf Lovgren. 2k, Bear and flamingos (Lewis Carroll), by Nicole Claveloux. 3k, King with keys, and toys, by Jiri Trnka.

1977, Sept. 9 **Engr. & Photo.**

2130 A753 40h multi .20 .20
2131 A753 60h multi .20 .20
2132 A753 1k multi .25 .20
2133 A753 2k multi .50 .20
2134 A753 3k multi *1.75* *.50*
Nos. 2130-2134 (5) *2.90* *1.30*

Prize-winning designs, 6th biennial exhibition of illustrations for children's books, Bratislava.

Globe, Violin, Doves, View of Prague — A754

1977, Sept. 28 ***Perf. 11½***

2135 A754 60h multi .20 .20

Congress of International Music Council of UNESCO, Prague and Bratislava.

Souvenir Sheets

"For a Europe of Peace" A755

1.60k, "For a Europe of Cooperation." 2.40k, "For a Europe of Social Progress."

1977, Oct. 3

2136 Sheet of 2 .65 .50
a. A755 60h multi .25 .25
2137 Sheet of 2 1.25 1.00
a. A755 1.60k multi .40 .35
2138 Sheet of 2 2.00 1.75
a. A755 2.40k multi .70 .60

2nd European Security and Cooperation Conference, Belgrade. Nos. 2136-2138 each contain 2 stamps and 2 blue on buff inscriptions and ornaments.

S. P. Korolev, Sputnik I Emblem — A756

Sailors, Cruiser Aurora — A757

30h, Yuri A. Gagarin & Vostok I. 40h, Alexei Leonov. 1k, Neil A. Armstrong & footprint on moon. 1.60k, Construction of orbital space station.

1977, Oct. 4

2139 A756 20h multi .20 .20
2140 A756 30h multi .20 .20
2141 A756 40h multi .20 .20
2142 A756 1k multi .30 .20
2143 A756 1.60k multi .80 .20
Nos. 2139-2143 (5) 1.70 1.00

Space research, 20th anniv. of 1st earth satellite.

1977, Nov. 7

2144 A757 30h multi .20 .20

60th anniv. of Russian October Revolution.

"Russia," Arms of USSR, Kremlin A758

"Science" A759

1977, Nov. 7

2145 A758 30h multi .20 .20

55th anniversary of the USSR.

1977, Nov. 17

2146 A759 3k multi .75 .35

Czechoslovak Academy of Science, 25th anniversary.

Art Type of 1967

Paintings: 2k, "Fear" (woman), by Jan Murdoch. 2.40k, Jan Francisci, portrait by Peter M. Bohun. 2.60k, Vaclav Hollar, self-portrait, 1647. 3k, Young Woman, 1528, by Lucas Cranach. 5k, Cleopatra, by Rubens.

1977, Nov. 27 **Engr.** ***Perf. 11½***

2147 A565 2k multi .75 .40
2148 A565 2.40k multi *1.10* *1.00*
2149 A565 2.60k multi 1.10 1.00
2150 A565 3k multi .75 .60
2151 A565 5k multi 1.50 1.50
Nos. 2147-2151 (5) *5.20* *4.50*

Sheets of 4.

View of Bratislava, by Georg Hoefnagel — A760

Design: 3.60k, Arms of Bratislava, 1436.

1977, Dec. 6

2152 A760 3k multi 1.90 1.50
2153 A760 3.60k multi .90 .65

Sheets of 4. See Nos. 2174-2175, 2270-2271, 2331-2332, 2364-2365, 2422-2423, 2478-2479, 2514-2515, 2570-2571, 2618-2619.

Stamp Pattern and Post Horn — A761

1977, Dec. 18 **Engr. & Photo.**

2154 A761 1k multi .25 .20

Stamp Day.

Zdenek Nejedly — A762

Karl Marx — A763

1978, Feb. 10 ***Perf. 11½***

2155 A762 30h multi .20 .20
2156 A763 40h multi .20 .20

Zdenek Nejedly (1878-1962), musicologist and historian; Karl Marx (1818-1883), political philosopher.

Civilians Greeting Guardsmen — A764

Intellectual, Farm Woman and Steel Worker, Flag — A765

1978, Feb. 25

2157 A764 1k gold & multi .25 .20
2158 A765 1k gold & multi .25 .20

30th anniv. of "Victorious February" (No. 2157), and Natl. Front (No. 2158). See note after 2190.

Yuri A. Gagarin, Vostok I — A766

10k Coin, 1964, and 25k Coin, 1965 — A767

Design: 30h, 3.60k, like No. 2140.

Engraved; Overprint Photogravure (Blue and carmine on 30h, green and lilac rose on 3.60k)

1978, Mar. 2 ***Perf. 11½x12***

2159 A766 30h dk red .25 .25
2160 A766 3.60k vio bl *4.50 4.00*

Capt. V. Remek, 1st Czechoslovakian cosmonaut on Russian spaceship Soyuz 28, Mar. 2-9.

1978, Mar. 14 **Engr. & Photo.**

40h, Medal for Culture, 1972. 1.40k, Charles University medal, 1948. 3k, Ferdinand I medal, 1568. 5k, Gold florin, 1335.

2161 A767 20h sil & multi .20 .20
2162 A767 40h sil & multi .20 .20
2163 A767 1.40k gold & multi *2.00 .30*
2164 A767 3k gold & multi .60 .40
2165 A767 5k gold & multi 1.00 .50
Nos. 2161-2165 (5) *4.00 1.60*

650th anniversary of Kremnica Mint.

Tire Tracks and Ball — A768

Congress Emblem — A769

1978, Mar. 15

2166 A768 60h multi .20 .20

Road safety.

1978, Apr. 16 ***Perf. 11½***

2167 A769 1k multi .25 .20

9th World Trade Union Cong., Prague 1978.

Shot Put and Praha '78 Emblem A770

1k, Pole vault. 3.60k, Women runners.

1978, Apr. 26

2168 A770 40h multi .20 .20
2169 A770 1k multi .30 .20
2170 A770 3.60k multi 1.25 .75
Nos. 2168-2170 (3) 1.75 1.15

5th European Athletic Championships, Prague 1978.

Ice Hockey — A771

Designs: 30h, Hockey. 2k, Ice hockey play.

1978, Apr. 26

2171 A771 30h multi .20 .20
2172 A771 60h multi .20 .20
2173 A771 2k multi .40 .20
Nos. 2171-2173 (3) .80 .60

5th European Ice Hockey Championships and 70th anniversary of Bandy hockey.

Bratislava Type of 1977

Designs: 3k, Bratislava, 1955, by Orest Dubay. 3.60k, Fishpound Square, Bratislava, 1955, by Imro Weiner-Kral.

1978, May 9 **Engr.** ***Perf. 11½***

2174 A760 3k multi 1.10 1.00
2175 A760 3.60k multi 1.60 1.50

Sheets of 4.

Prague Castle Art Type of 1971

3k, King Ottokar II, detail from tomb. 3.60k, Charles IV, detail from votive panel by Jan Ocka.

1978, May 9

2176 A634 3k multi .75 .50
2177 A634 3.60k multi 2.00 2.00

Sheets of 4.

Ministry of Post, Prague A772

Engraved and Photogravure

1978, May 29 ***Perf. 12x11½***

2178 A772 60h multi .20 .20

14th session of permanent COMECOM Commission (Ministers of Post and Telecommunications of Socialist Countries).

Palacky Bridge A773

Prague Bridges and PRAGA '78 Emblem: 40h, Railroad bridge. 1k, Bridge of May 1. 2k, Manes Bridge. 3k, Svatopluk Cech Bridge. 5.40k, Charles Bridge.

1978, May 30

2179 A773 20h blk & multi .20 .20
2180 A773 40h blk & multi .20 .20
2181 A773 1k blk & multi .25 .20
2182 A773 2k blk & multi .50 .25
2183 A773 3k blk & multi .70 .35
2184 A773 5.40k blk & multi 3.00 1.00
Nos. 2179-2184 (6) 4.85 2.20

PRAGA 1978 International Philatelic Exhibition, Prague, Sept. 8-17.

St. Peter and Apostles, Clock Tower, and Emblem A774

Town Hall Clock, Prague, by Josef Manes, and PRAGA '78 Emblem: 1k, Astronomical clock. 2k, Prague's coat of arms. 3k, Grape harvest (September). 3.60k, Libra. 10k, Arms surrounded by zodiac signs and scenes symbolic of 12 months, horiz. 2k, 3k, 3.60k show details from design of 10k.

1978, June 20 ***Perf. 11½x11***

2185 A774 40h multi .20 .20
2186 A774 1k multi .30 .20
2187 A774 2k multi .50 .20
2188 A774 3k multi *2.00 .75*
2189 A774 3.60k multi .75 .25
Nos. 2185-2189 (5) *3.75 1.60*

Souvenir Sheet

Perf. 12x12

2190 A774 10k multi 8.00 6.00

PRAGA'78 Intl. Philatelic Exhibition, Prague, Sept. 8-17. No. 2190 contains one 50x40mm stamp. Sheet exists imperf. Value $25.

A non-valid souvenir sheet contains 4 imperf. copies of No. 2157. Sold only with PRAGA ticket.

Folk Dancers — A775

1978, July 7 ***Perf. 11½x12***

2191 A775 30h multi .20 .20

25th Folklore Festival, Vychodna.

Overpass and PRAGA Emblem — A776

1k, 2k, Modern office buildings, diff. 6k, Old & new Prague. 20k, Charles Bridge & Old Town, by Vincent Morstadt, 1828.

1978 ***Perf. 12x11½***

2192 A776 60h blk & multi .20 .20
2193 A776 1k blk & multi .25 .20
2194 A776 2k blk & multi .50 .25
2195 A776 6k blk & multi 2.75 1.10
Nos. 2192-2195 (4) 3.70 1.75

Souvenir Sheet

Engr.

2196 A776 20k multi 6.50 6.50

PRAGA 1978 Intl. Phil. Exhib., Prague, Sept. 8-17. No. 2196 also for 60th anniv. of Czechoslovak postage stamps. No. 2196 contains one 61x45mm stamp.

Issued: #2192-2195, 9/8; #2196, 9/10.

Souvenir Sheet

Apollo's Companion, by Titian — A777

#2197b, King Midas. Stamps show details from "Apollo Flaying Marsya" by Titian.

1978, Sept. 12 ***Perf. 11½***

2197 Sheet of 2 7.50 7.50
a. A777 10k multi 3.00 3.00
b. A777 10k multi 3.00 3.00

Titian (1488-1576), Venetian painter. No. 2197 with dark blue marginal inscription "FIP" was sold only with entrance ticket to PRAGA Philatelic Exhibition. Value $25.

Exhibition Hall — A778

Engraved and Photogravure

1978, Sept. 13 *Perf. 11½x11*
2198 A778 30h multi .20 .20

22nd International Engineering Fair, Brno.

Postal Newspaper Service — A779

TV Screen, Headquarters and Logo — A780

Newspaper, Microphone A781

1978, Sept. 21 *Perf. 11½*
2199 A779 30h multi .20 .20
2200 A780 30h multi .20 .20
2201 A781 30h multi .20 .20
Nos. 2199-2201 (3) .60 .60

Postal News Service, 25th anniv.; Czechoslovakian television, 25th anniv.; Press, Broadcasting and Television Day.

Sulky Race A782

Pardubice Steeplechase: 10h, Falling horses and jockeys at fence. 30h, Race. 40h, Horses passing post. 1.60k, Hurdling. 4.40k, Winner.

1978, Oct. 6 *Perf. 12x11½*
2202 A782 10h multi .20 .20
2203 A782 20h multi .20 .20
2204 A782 30h multi .20 .20
2205 A782 40h multi .20 .20
2206 A782 1.60k multi .40 .25
2207 A782 4.40k multi 1.75 .80
Nos. 2202-2207 (6) 2.95 1.85

Woman Holding Arms of Czechoslovakia A783

1978, Oct. 28 *Perf. 11½*
2208 A783 60h multi .20 .20

60th anniversary of independence.

Art Type of 1974

2.40k, Flowers, by Jakub Bohdan (1660-1724). 3k, The Dream of Salas, by Ludovit Fulla, horiz. 3.60k, Apostle with Censer, Master of the Spissko Capitals (c. 1480-90).

1978, Nov. 27 **Engr.**
2209 A700 2.40k multi .60 .45
2210 A700 3k multi .70 .65
2211 A700 3.60k multi 2.50 2.00
Nos. 2209-2211 (3) 3.80 3.10

Slovak National Gallery, 30th anniversary.

Musicians, by Jan Könyves — A784

Slovak Ceramics: 30h, Janosik on Horseback, by Jozef Franko. 40h, Woman in Folk Costume by Michal Polasko. 1k, Three Girls Singing, by Ignac Bizmayer. 1.60k, Janosik Dancing, by Ferdis Kostka.

Engraved and Photogravure

1978, Dec. 5 *Perf. 11½x12*
2212 A784 20h multi .20 .20
2213 A784 30h multi .20 .20
2214 A784 40k multi .20 .20
2215 A784 1k multi .20 .20
2216 A784 1.60k multi 1.00 .30
Nos. 2212-2216 (5) 1.80 1.10

Alfons Mucha and his Design for 1918 Issue — A785

1978, Dec. 18 *Perf. 11½*
2217 A785 1k multi .25 .20

60th Stamp Day.

COMECON Building, Moscow — A786

1979, Jan. 1 *Perf. 11½*
2218 A786 1k multi .25 .20

Council for Mutual Economic Aid (COMECON), 30th anniversary.

Woman's Head and Grain — A787

Woman, Workers, Child, Doves — A788

1979, Jan. 1
2219 A787 30h multi .20 .20
2220 A788 60h multi .20 .20

United Agricultural Production Assoc., 30th anniv. (30h); Czechoslovakian Federation, 10th anniv. (60h).

Soyuz 28, Rockets and Capsule — A789

60h, Astronauts Aleksei Gubarev and Vladimir Remek on launching pad, vert. 1.60k, Soviet astronauts J. Romanenko and G. Grecko, Salyut 6 and recovery ship. 2k, Salyut-Soyuz orbital complex, post office in space and Czechoslovakia No. 2153. 4k, Soyuz 28, crew after landing and trajectory map, vert. 10k, Gubarev and Remek, Intercosmos emblem, arms of Czechoslovakia and USSR.

1979, Mar. 2
2221 A789 30h multi .20 .20
2222 A789 60h multi .20 .20
2223 A789 1.60k multi .35 .20
2224 A789 2k multi 1.50 .40
2225 A789 4k multi .60 .30
Nos. 2221-2225 (5) 2.85 1.30

Souvenir Sheet

2226 A789 10k multi 3.50 3.50

1st anniv. of joint Czechoslovak-Soviet space flight. Size of No. 2226: 76x93mm (stamp 39x55mm). No. 2226 has Cyrillic inscription, No. 2455a does not. No. 2226 exists imperf. Value, $15.

Alpine Bellflowers A790

Stylized Satellite, Dial, Tape A791

Mountain Flowers: 20h, Crocus. 30h, Pinks. 40h, Alpine hawkweed. 3k, Larkspur.

1979, Mar. 23 *Perf. 11½*
2227 A790 10h multi .20 .20
2228 A790 20h multi .20 .20
2229 A790 30h multi .20 .20
2230 A790 40h multi .20 .20

Perf. 14

2231 A790 3k multi 1.40 .75
Nos. 2227-2231 (5) 2.20 1.55

Mountain Rescue Service, 25th anniversary. The 3k exists perf. 11½. Value, $40 unused, $20 used.

1979, Apr. 2
2232 A791 10h multi .20 .20

Telecommunications research, 30th anniv.

Artist and Model, Dove, Bratislava Castle — A792

Cog Wheels, Transformer and Student — A793

Musical Instruments, Bratislava Castle — A794

Pioneer Scarf, IYC Emblem — A795

Red Star, Man, Child and Doves — A796

1979, Apr. 2
2233 A792 20h multi .20 .20
2234 A793 20h multi .20 .20
2235 A794 30h multi .20 .20
2236 A795 30h multi .20 .20
2237 A796 60h multi .20 .20
Nos. 2233-2237 (5) 1.00 1.00

Fine Arts Academy, Bratislava, 30th anniv.; Slovak Technical University, 40th anniv.; Radio Symphony Orchestra, Bratislava, 30th anniv.; Young Pioneers, 30th anniv. and IYC; Peace Movement, 30th anniversary.

Prague Castle Art Type of 1971

3k, Burial crown of King Ottokar II. 3.60k, Portrait of Mrs. Reitmayer, by Karel Purkyne.

1979, May 9 *Perf. 11½*
2238 A634 3k multi 1.75 1.40
2239 A634 3.60k multi .85 .50

Sheets of 4.

Arms of Vlachovo Brezi, 1538 — A797

Animals in Heraldry: 60h, Jesenik, 1509 (bear and eagle). 1.20k, Vysoke Myto, 1471 (St. George slaying dragon). 1.80k,Martin, 1854 (St. Martin giving coat to beggar). 2k, Zebrak, 1674 (mythological beast).

1979, May 25 *Perf. 11½x12*
2240 A797 30h multi .20 .20
2241 A797 60h multi .20 .20
2242 A797 1.20k multi .30 .20
2243 A797 1.80k multi *1.00 .30*
2244 A797 2k multi .40 .20
Nos. 2240-2244 (5) *2.10 1.10*

Forest, Thriving and Destroyed A798

Designs: 1.80k, Water. 3.60k, City. 4k, Cattle. All designs show good and bad environment, separated by exclamation point; Man and Biosphere emblem.

1979, June 22 **Engr.** *Perf. 11½*
2245 A798 60h multi .20 .20
2246 A798 1.80k multi .30 .25
2247 A798 3.60k multi *1.75 .75*
2248 A798 4k multi .75 .40
Nos. 2245-2248 (4) *3.00 1.60*

Man and Biosphere Program of UNESCO.

Blast Furnace — A799

Engraved and Photogravure

1979, Aug. 29 *Perf. 11x11½*

2249 A799 30h multi .20 .20

Slovak National Uprising, 35th anniversary.

Frog and Goat A800

Book Illustrations (IYC Emblem and): 40h, Knight on horseback. 60h, Maidens. 1k, Boy with sled following rooster. 3k, King riding flying beast.

1979, Apr. 2 *Perf. 11½x11*

2250 A800 20h multi .20 .20
2251 A800 40h multi .20 .20
2252 A800 60h multi .20 .20
2253 A800 1k multi .30 .20
2254 A800 3k multi *1.75* *.50*
Nos. 2250-2254 (5) 2.65 1.30

Prize-winning designs, 7th biennial exhibition of illustrations for children's books, Bratislava; International Year of the Child. Printed with labels showing story characters.

"Bone Shaker" Bicycles, 1870 A801

Bicycles from: 20h, 1978. 40h, 1910. 60h, 1886. 3.60k, 1820.

1979, Sept. 14 *Perf. 12x11½*

2255 A801 20h multi .20 .20
2256 A801 40h multi .20 .20
2257 A801 60h multi .20 .20
2258 A801 2k multi .50 .20
2259 A801 3.60k multi 1.60 .50
Nos. 2255-2259 (5) 2.70 1.30

Bracket Clock, 18th Century A802

Designs: 18th century clocks.

1979, Oct. 1 *Perf. 11½*

2260 A802 40h multi .20 .20
2261 A802 60h multi .20 .20
2262 A802 80h multi .85 .20
2263 A802 1k multi .25 .20
2264 A802 2k multi .50 .20
Nos. 2260-2264 (5) 2.00 1.00

Art Type of 1967

Paintings: 1.60k, Sunday by the River, by Alois Moravec. 2k, Self-portrait, by Gustav Mally. 3k, Self-portrait, by Ilia Yefimovic Repin. 3.60k, Horseback Rider, by Jan Bauch. 5k, Dancing Peasants, by Albrecht Dürer.

1979, Nov. 27 **Engr.** *Perf. 12*

2265 A565 1.60k multi .35 .30
2266 A565 2k multi .45 .45
2267 A565 3k multi .60 .45
2268 A565 3.60k multi 3.25 1.50
2269 A565 5k multi 1.10 1.10
Nos. 2265-2269 (5) 5.75 3.80

Bratislava Type of 1977

Designs: 3k, Bratislava Castle on the Danube, by L. Janscha, 1787. 3.60k, Bratislava Castle, stone engraving by Wolf, 1815.

1979, Dec. 5

2270 A760 3k multi .70 .65
2271 A760 3.60k multi 1.90 1.90

Stamp Day — A803

Engraved and Photogravure

1979, Dec. 18 *Perf. 11½x12*

2272 A803 1k multi .25 .20

Electronic Circuits — A804

Designs: 50h, Satellite dish. 2k, Airplane. 3k, Computer punch tape.

1979-80 **Photo.** *Perf. 11½x12*

Coil Stamps

2273 A804 50h red .20 .20
2274 A804 1k brown .25 .20
2275 A804 2k green ('80) .50 .20
2276 A804 3k lake ('80) .70 .25
Nos. 2273-2276 (4) 1.65 .85

The 1k comes in two shades.

Runners and Dove A805

Engraved and Photogravure

1980, Jan. 29 *Perf. 12x11½*

2289 A805 50h multi .20 .20

50th Intl. Peace Marathon, Kosice, Oct. 4.

Downhill Skiing — A806

1980, Jan. 29 *Perf. 11½x12*

2290 A806 1k shown .25 .20
2291 A806 2k Speed skating .80 .30
2292 A806 3k Four-man bobsled .65 .30
Nos. 2290-2292 (3) 1.70 .80

13th Winter Olympic Games, Lake Placid, NY, Feb. 12-24.

Basketball — A807

1980, Jan. 29 *Perf. 11½*

2293 A807 40h shown .20 .20
2294 A807 1k Swimming .30 .20
2295 A807 2k Hurdles 1.75 .40
2296 A807 3.60k Fencing .75 .35
Nos. 2293-2296 (4) 3.00 1.15

22nd Olympic Games, Moscow, 7/19-8/3.

Arms Type of 1977

1980, Feb. 20 *Perf. 11½*

2297 A745 50h Bystrice Nad Pernstejnem .20 .20
2298 A745 50h Kunstat .20 .20
2299 A745 50h Rozmital Pod Tremsinem .20 .20
2300 A745 50h Zlata Idka .20 .20
Nos. 2297-2300 (4) .80 .80

Theatrical Mask — A808

Slovak National Theater, Actors — A809

1980, Mar. 1

2301 A808 50h multi .20 .20
2302 A809 1k multi .25 .20

50th Jiraskuv Hronov Theatrical Ensemble Review; Slovak National Theater, Bratislava, 60th anniversary.

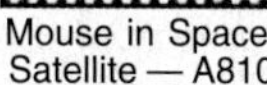

Mouse in Space, Satellite — A810

Police Corps Banner, Emblem — A811

Intercosmos: 1k, Weather map, satellite. 1.60k, Intersputnik television transmission. 4k, Camera, satellite. 5k, Czech satellite station, 1978, horiz. 10k, Intercosmos emblem, horiz.

1980, Apr. 12 *Perf. 11½x12, 12x11½*

2303 A810 50h multi .20 .20
2304 A810 1k multi .30 .20
2305 A810 1.60k multi 1.75 .20
2306 A810 4k multi .75 .40
2307 A810 5k multi 1.00 .50
Nos. 2303-2307 (5) 4.00 1.50

Souvenir Sheet

2308 A810 10k multi 3.25 2.50

Intercosmos cooperative space program.
No. 2308 exists imperf. Value, $30.

1980, Apr. 17 *Perf. 11½*

2309 A811 50h multi .20 .20

National Police Corps, 35th anniversary.

Lenin's 110th Birth Anniversary — A812

Design: #2311, Engels's 160th birth anniv.

1980, Apr. 22

2310 A812 1k tan & brn .25 .20
2311 A812 1k lt grn & brn .25 .20

Old and Modern Prague, Czech Flag, Bouquet A813

Boy Writing "Peace" A814

Pact Members' Flags, Dove — A815

Czech and Soviet Arms, Prague and Moscow Views A816

1980, May 6 *Perf. 12x11½*

2312 A813 50h multi .20 .20
2313 A814 1k multi .25 .20
2314 A815 1k multi .25 .20
2315 A816 1k multi .30 .20
Nos. 2312-2315 (4) 1.00 .80

Liberation by Soviet army, 35th anniv.; Soviet victory in WWII, 35th anniv.; Signing of Warsaw Pact (Bulgaria, Czechoslovakia, German Democratic Rep., Hungary, Poland, Romania, USSR), 25th anniv.; Czechoslovak-Soviet Treaty of Friendship, Cooperation and Mutual Aid, 10th anniv.

Souvenir Sheet

UN, 35th Anniv. A817

1980, June 3 **Engr.** *Perf. 12*

2316 Sheet of 2 2.75 2.75
a. A817 4k multicolored 1.25 1.25

Athletes Parading Banners in Strahov Stadium, Prague, Spartakiad Emblem — A818

Engraved and Photogravure

1980, June 3 *Perf. 12x11½*

2317 A818 50h shown .20 .20
2318 A818 1k Gymnast, vert. .25 .20

Spartakiad 1980, Prague, June 26-29.

Aechmea Fasciata — A819

A820

1980, Aug. 13 *Perf. 12*

2319 A819 50h *Gerbera Jamesonii* .20 .20
2320 A819 1k *Aechmea fasciata* 1.60 .25
2321 A819 2k *Strelitzia reginae* .70 .25
2322 A819 4k *Paphiopedilum* 1.40 .50
Nos. 2319-2322 (4) *3.90* *1.20*

Olomouc and Bratislava Flower Shows.

1980, Sept. 24 *Perf. 11½x12*

Designs: Folktale character embroideries.

2323 A820 50h Chad girl .20 .20
2324 A820 1k Punch and dog .25 .20
2325 A820 2k Dandy and Posy .50 .20
2326 A820 4k Lion and moon *2.50 .75*
2327 A820 5k Wallachian dance 1.00 .40
Nos. 2323-2327 (5) *4.45 1.75*

National Census A821

1980, Sept. 24 *Perf. 12x11½*
2328 A821 1k multi .25 .20

Prague Castle Type of 1971

Designs: 3k, Old Palace gateway. 4k, Armorial lion, 16th century.

1980, Oct. 28 *Perf. 12*
2329 A634 3k multi 2.00 1.90
2330 A634 4k multi .75 .65

Sheets of 4.

Bratislava Type of 1977

3k, View across the Danube, by J. Eder, 1810. 4k, The Old Royal Bridge, by J.A. Lantz, 1820.

1980, Oct. 28
2331 A760 3k multi 2.00 1.90
2332 A760 4k multi .75 .65

10th Anniversary of Socialist Youth Federation — A822

1980, Nov. 9 *Perf. 12x11½*
2333 A822 50h multi .20 .20

No. 2137 Overprinted in Red: 3. / MEZINARODNI VELETRH ZNAMEK / ESSEN '80

1980, Nov. 18
2334 A755 1.60k multi *14.00 14.00*

Czechoslovak Day/ ESSEN '80, 3rd International Stamp Exhibition, No. 2334 has overprinted red marginal inscription.

Art Type of 1967

Designs: 1k, Pavel Jozef Safarik, by Jozef B. Klemens. 2k, Peasant Revolt mosaic, Anna Podzemna. 3k, St. Lucia, 14th century statue. 4k, Waste Heaps, by Jan Zrzavy, horiz. 5k, Labor, sculpture by Jan Stursa.

1980, Nov. 27 **Engr.** *Perf. 12*
2335 A565 1k multi 1.10 1.10
2336 A565 2k multi 2.25 2.25
2337 A565 3k multi .50 .50
2338 A565 4k multi .85 .85
2339 A565 5k multi 1.00 1.00
Nos. 2335-2339 (5) 5.70 5.70

Stamp Day — A823

Engraved and Photogravure

1980, Dec. 18 *Perf. 11½x12*
2340 A823 1k multi .25 .20

7th Five-year Plan, 1981-1985 A824

1981, Jan. 1 *Perf. 11½*
2341 A824 50h multi .20 .20

International Year of the Disabled A825

1981, Feb. 24
2342 A825 1k multi .25 .20

Landau, 1800 A826

1981, Feb. 25 *Perf. 12x11½*
2343 A826 50h shown .20 .20
2344 A826 1k Mail coach, 1830 .30 .25
2345 A826 3.60k Mail sled, 1840 *4.00 1.75*
2346 A826 5k 4-horse mail coach, 1860 1.00 1.00
2347 A826 7k Open carriage, 1840 1.50 1.50
a. Sheet of 4 *12.50 10.00*
Nos. 2343-2347 (5) *7.00 4.70*

WIPA '81 Intl. Philatelic Exhibition, Vienna, Austria, May 22-31. #2347a issued May 10.

Wolfgang Amadeus Mozart — A827

Famous Men: #2348, Joesph Hlavka (1831-1908). #2349, Juraj Hronec (1881-1959). #2350, Jan Sverma (1901-44). #2351, Mikulas Schneider-Trnavsky (1881-1958). #2352, B. Bolzano (1781-1848). #2353, Dimitri Shostakovich, composer. #2354, George Bernard Shaw, playwright.

1981, Mar. 10 *Perf. 11½*
2348 A827 50h multi .20 .20
2349 A827 50h multi .20 .20
2350 A827 50h multi .20 .20
2351 A827 50h multi .20 .20
2352 A827 1k multi .80 .25
2353 A827 1k multi .35 .20
2354 A827 1k multi .35 .20
2355 A827 1k multi .35 .20
Nos. 2348-2355 (8) 2.65 1.65

Souvenir Sheet

Yuri Gagarin A828

1981, Apr. 5 *Perf. 12*
2356 Sheet of 2 4.25 3.00
a. A828 6k multicolored 1.75 1.10

20th anniv. of 1st manned space flight.

Workers and Banner A829

1981, Apr. 6 *Perf. 12x11½*
2357 A829 50h shown .20 .20
2358 A829 1k Hands holding banner .25 .20
2359 A829 4k Worker holding banner, vert. 1.00 .35
Nos. 2357-2359 (3) 1.45 .75

Czechoslovakian Communist Party, 60th anniv.

Congress Emblem, View of Prague — A830

1981, Apr. 6
2360 A830 50h shown .20 .20
2361 A830 1k Bratislava .25 .20

16th Communist Party Congress.

Agriculture Museum, 90th Anniv. A831

Natl. Assembly Elections A832

1981, May 14 *Perf. 11½x12*
2362 A831 1k multi .25 .20

1981, June 1
2363 A832 50h multi .20 .20

Bratislava Type of 1977

Designs: 3k, Bratislava Castle, by G.B. Probst, 1760. 4k, Grassalkovic Palace, by C. Bschor, 1815.

1981, June 10 *Perf. 12*
2364 A760 3k multi 2.00 2.00
2365 A760 4k multi .75 .50

Uran and Red October Hotels A833

Successes of Socialist Achievements Exhibition: 1k, Brno-Bratislava Highway, Jihlava. 2k, Nuclear power station, Jaslovske Bohunice.

1981, June 10 *Perf. 12x11½*
2366 A833 80h multi .20 .20
2367 A833 1k multi .30 .20
2368 A833 2k multi .50 .20
Nos. 2366-2368 (3) 1.00 .60

Border Defense Units, 30th Anniv. A834

Civil Defense, 30th Anniv. A835

Army Cooperation, 30th Anniv. — A836

Rysy Youth Mountain Climbing Contest A837

Engraved and Photogravure

1981, July 11 *Perf. 11½*
2369 A834 40h multi .20 .20
2370 A835 50h multi .20 .20
2371 A836 1k multi .25 .20
2372 A837 3.60k multi .90 .30
Nos. 2369-2372 (4) 1.55 .90

30th Natl. Festival of Amateur Puppet Ensembles — A838

1981, July 2 *Perf. 11½*
2373 A838 2k Punch and Devil .50 .20

Souvenir Sheet

Guernica, by Pablo Picasso — A839

1981, July 2 **Engr.** *Perf. 11½x12*
2374 A839 10k multi 3.50 2.50

Picasso's birth centenary; 45th anniv. of Intl. Brigades in Spain.

Cat Holding Flower, by Etienne Delessert A840

8th Biennial Exhibition of Children's Book Illustrations (Designs by): 50h, Albin Brunovsky, vert. 1k, Adolf Born. 2k, Vive Tolli. 10k, Suekichi Akaba.

Engraved and Photogravure

1981, Sept. 5 *Perf. 11½*
2375 A840 50h multi .20 .20
2376 A840 1k multi .25 .20
2377 A840 2k multi .40 .20
2378 A840 4k multi .95 .40
2379 A840 10k multi 4.00 2.00
Nos. 2375-2379 (5) 5.80 3.00

Prague Zoo, 50th Anniv. — A841

1981, Sept. 28 *Perf. 11½x12*
2380 A841 50h Gorillas .20 .20
2381 A841 1k Lions .20 .20
2382 A841 7k Przewalski's horses 1.60 .80
Nos. 2380-2382 (3) 2.00 1.20

Anti-smoking Campaign A842

1981, Oct. 27 ***Perf. 12***
2383 A842 4k multi 1.00 .60

No. 2383 se-tenant with label.

Prague Castle Art Type of 1971

Designs: 3k, Carved dragon, Palais Lobkovitz, 16th cent. 4k, St. Vitus Cathedral, by J. Sember and G. Dobler, 19th cent.

1981, Oct. 28
2384 A634 3k multi .65 .65
2385 A634 4k multi 2.00 2.00

Sheets of 4.

Art Type of 1967

Designs: 1k, View of Prague, by Vaclav Hollar (1607-1677). 2k, Czechoslovak Academy medallion, engraved by Otakar Spaniel (1881-1955). 3k, Jihoceska Vysivka, by Zdenek Sklenar (b. 1910). 4k, Still Life, by A.M. Gerasimov (1881-1963). 5k, Standing Woman, by Pablo Picasso (1881-1973).

1981, Nov. 27 **Engr.** ***Perf. 12***
2386 A565 1k multi 2.25 1.40
2387 A565 2k multi .50 .20
2388 A565 3k multi .75 .40
2389 A565 4k multi 1.00 .40
2390 A565 5k multi 1.25 1.10
Nos. 2386-2390 (5) 5.75 3.50

Sheets of 4. Sheets of No. 2390 exist with center gutter inscribed with Philexfrance 82 and FIP emblems. Value, $15.

Stamp Day — A843

Engraved and Photogravure

1981, Dec. 18 ***Perf. 11½x12***
2391 A843 1k Engraver Edward Karel .25 .20

Russian Workers' Party, Prague Congress, 70th Anniv. — A844

1982, Jan. 18 ***Perf. 12***
2392 A844 2k Lenin .50 .35
a. Sheet of 4 *4.00 4.00*

No. 2392 issued in sheet of 8.

1982 World Cup Soccer A845

Designs: Various soccer players.

1982, Jan. 29 ***Perf. 12x11½***
2393 A845 1k multi .25 .20
2394 A845 3.60k multi .70 .30
2395 A845 4k multi 1.40 .50
Nos. 2393-2395 (3) 2.35 1.00

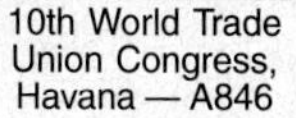

10th World Trade Union Congress, Havana — A846

Arms of Hrob — A847

1982, Feb. 10 ***Perf. 11½***
2396 A846 1k multi .25 .20

1982, Feb. 10 ***Perf. 12x11½***

Arms of various cities.

2397 A847 50h shown .20 .20
2398 A847 50h Nove Mesto Nad Metuji .20 .20
2399 A847 50h Trencin .20 .20
2400 A847 50h Mlada Boleslav .20 .20
Nos. 2397-2400 (4) .80 .80

See Nos. 2499-2502, 2542-2544, 2595-2597, 2783-2786.

50th Anniv. of the Great Strike at Most — A848

1982, Mar. 23 ***Perf. 11½***
2401 A848 1k multi .25 .20

60th Intl. Railway Union Congress — A849

1982, Mar. 23 ***Perf. 12x11½***
2402 A849 6k Steam locomotive, 1922, electric, 1982 1.50 .75

10th Workers' Congress, Prague A850

George Dimitrov A851

1982, Apr. 15
2403 A850 1k multi .25 .20

1982, May 1
2404 A851 50h multi .20 .20

A852

10th Lidice Intl. Children's Drawing Contest — A853

Engravings: 40h, The Muse Euterpe Playing a Flute, by Crispin de Passe (1565-1637). 50h, The Lute Player, by Jacob de Gheyn (1565-1629). 1k, Woman Flautist, by Adriaen Collaert (1560-1618). 2k, Musicians in a Hostel, by Rembrandt (1606-1669). 3k, Hurdy-gurdy Player, by Jacques Callot (1594-1635).

1982, May 18 ***Perf. 11½x12***
2405 A852 40h multi .20 .20
2406 A852 50h multi .20 .20
2407 A852 1k multi .20 .20
2408 A852 2k multi .30 .20
2409 A852 3k multi 1.10 .60
Nos. 2405-2409 (5) 2.00 1.40

1982, May 18
2410 A853 2k multi 1.00 1.00

Issued in sheets of 6.

40th Anniv. of Destruction of Lidice and Lezaky — A854

1982, June 4 ***Perf. 11½***
2411 A854 1k Girl, rose .25 .20
2412 A854 1k Hands, barbed wire .25 .20

Souvenir Sheet

UN Disarmament Conference — A855

1982, June 4 ***Perf. 12***
2413 Sheet of 2 7.50 6.00
a. A855 6k Woman holding doves 3.50 2.75

Souvenir Sheet

2nd UN Conference on Peaceful Uses of Outer Space, Vienna, Aug. 9-21 — A856

1982, Aug. 9 **Engr. & Photo.**
2414 Sheet of 2 7.50 7.00
a. A856 5k multi 3.50 3.00

Krivoklat Castle A857

1982, Aug. 31 ***Perf. 12x11½***
2415 A857 50h shown .20 .20
2416 A857 1k Statues (Krivoklat) .25 .20
2417 A857 2k Nitra Castle .50 .25
2418 A857 3k Pottery, lock (Nitra) .75 .35
a. Souv. sheet of 4, #2415-2418 2.00 1.50
Nos. 2415-2418 (4) 1.70 1.00

50th Anniv. of Zizkov Hill Natl. Monument — A858

1982, Sept. 16
2419 A858 1k multi .25 .20

Prague Castle Art Type of 1971

Designs: 3k, St. George and the Dragon, 1373. 4k, Tomb of King Vratislav I, 10th cent.

1982, Sept. 28 ***Perf. 12***
2420 A634 3k multi 2.00 .65
2421 A634 4k multi .75 .75

Sheets of 4.

Bratislava Type of 1977

Designs: 3k, Paddle steamer, Parnik, 1818. 4k, View from Bridge, 19th cent.

1982, Sept. 29
2422 A760 3k multi 2.00 .65
2423 A760 4k multi .75 .75

European Danube Commission — A859

1982, Sept. 29 ***Perf. 11½x12***
2424 A859 3k Steamer, Bratislava Bridge .75 .35
a. Souvenir sheet of 4 5.00 4.00
2425 A859 3.60k Ferry, Budapest .95 .50
a. Souvenir sheet of 4 7.00 6.00

16th Communist Party Congress — A860

1982, Oct. 28 ***Perf. 12x11½***
2426 A860 20h Agriculture .20 .20
2427 A860 1k Industry .25 .20
2428 A860 3k Engineering .75 .35
Nos. 2426-2428 (3) 1.20 .75

30th Anniv. of Academy of Sciences — A861

1982, Oct. 29 ***Perf. 11½***
2429 A861 6k Emblem 1.50 .75

65th Anniv. of October Revolution — A862

Design: 1k, 60th anniv. of USSR.

1982, Nov. 7 ***Perf. 12x11½***
2430 A862 50h multi .20 .20
2431 A862 1k multi .25 .20

Jaroslav Hasek, Writer, Sculpture by Josef Malejovsky — A863

Sculptures: 2k, Jan Zrzavy, freedom fighter, by Jan Simota. 4.40k, Leos Janacek, composer, by Milos Axman. 6k, Martin Kukucin, freedom fighter, by Jan Kulich. 7k, Peaceful Work, by Rudolf Pribis.

Engraved and Photogravure

1982, Nov. 26 ***Perf. 11½x12***
2432 A863 1k multi .25 .20
2433 A863 2k multi .50 .20
2434 A863 4.40k multi 1.00 .50
2435 A863 6k multi 1.25 .70
2436 A863 7k multi 3.00 1.50
Nos. 2432-2436 (5) 6.00 3.10

Art Type of 1967

1k, Revolution in Spain, by Josef Sima (1891-1971). 2k, Woman Dressing, by Rudolf Kremlicka (1886-1932). 3k, The Girl Bride, by Dezider Milly (1906-1971). 4k, Performers, by

Jan Zelibsky (b. 1907). 5k, The Complaint of the Birds, by Emil Filla (1882-1953).

1982, Nov. 27 *Perf. 12*

2437 A565 1k multi 1.00 .25
2438 A565 2k multi 2.00 .60
2439 A565 3k multi .75 .75
2440 A565 4k multi 1.00 1.00
2441 A565 5k multi 1.25 1.00
Nos. 2437-2441 (5) 6.00 3.50

Stamp Day — A864

1982, Dec. 8 *Perf. 11½*

2442 A864 1k Engraver Jaroslav Goldschmied (1890-1977) .25 .20

A865

A866

1983, Jan. 10 Engr. *Perf. 12x11½*

2443 A865 50h dark blue .20 .20

Pres. Gustav Husak, 70th birthday. See No. 2686.

1983, Feb. 24 Engr. & Photo.

Designs: 50h, Jaroslav Hasek (1882-1923), writer. 1k, Julius Fucik (1903-1943), antifascist martyr. 2k, Martin Luther (1483-1546). 5k, Johannes Brahms (1833-1897), composer.

2444 A866 50h multi .20 .20
2445 A866 1k multi .25 .20
2446 A866 2k multi .45 .20
a. Souvenir sheet of 4 *12.00 9.00*
2447 A866 5k multi 1.10 .40
Nos. 2444-2447 (4) 2.00 1.00

Nordposta '83 Intl. Stamp Exhibition, Hamburg.
No. 2446a issued Nov. 1.

Workers Marching A867

Family — A868

1983, Feb. 25 *Perf. 11½*

2448 A867 50h multi .20 .20
2449 A868 1k multi .25 .20

35th anniv. of "Victorious February" (50h), and Natl. Front (1k).

World Communications Year — A869

Perf. 11½, 12x11½ (2k)

1983, Mar. 16

2450 A869 40h multi .20 .20
2451 A869 1k multi .25 .20
2452 A869 2k multi .45 .20
2453 A869 3.60k multi .90 .40
Nos. 2450-2453 (4) 1.80 1.00

Various wave patterns. 2k, 40x23mm; 3.60k, 49x19mm.

7th World Ski-jumping Championships A870

1983, Mar. 16 *Perf. 11½*

2454 A870 1k multi .25 .20

Souvenir Sheet

5th Anniv. of Czechoslovak-USSR Intercosmos Cooperative Space Program — A871

1983, Apr. 12 *Perf. 12*

2455 Sheet of 2 11.00 6.00
a. A871 10k multi 4.75 2.50

See No. 2226.

Protected Species — A872

1983, Apr. 28 *Perf. 12x11½*

2456 A872 50h Butterfly, violets .30 .20
2457 A872 1k Water lilies, frog .65 .20
2458 A872 2k Pine cones, crossbill .65 .30
2459 A872 3.60k Herons .80 .35
2460 A872 5k Gentians, lynx 1.10 .45
2461 A872 7k Stag 2.50 1.00
Nos. 2456-2461 (6) 6.00 2.50

A873

A874

Soviet Marshals.

1983, May 5 *Perf. 11½*

2462 A873 50h Ivan S. Konev .20 .20
2463 A873 1k Andrei I. Sheremenko .30 .20
2464 A873 2k Rodion J. Malinovsky .50 .20
Nos. 2462-2464 (3) 1.00 .60

30th anniv. of Czechoslovak-Soviet defense treaty.

1983, July 13 *Perf. 12*

2465 A874 2k multi .50 .20
a. Souvenir sheet of 4 5.00 4.00

World Peace and Life Congress, Prague.
No. 2465 issued in sheets of 8.

Emperor Rudolf II by Adrian De Vries (1560-1626) A875

Art treasures of the Prague Castle: 5k, Kinetic relief, Timepiece, Rudolf Svoboda.

1983, Aug. 25 *Perf. 11½*

2466 A875 4k multi 1.00 .40
2467 A875 5k multi 1.25 .50

See Nos. 2518-2519, 2610-2611, 2654-2655, 2717-2718, 2744-2745, 2792-2793.

9th Biennial of Illustrations for Children and Youth — A876

Illustrators: 50h, Oleg K. Zotov, USSR. 1k, Zbigniew Rychlicki, Poland. 4k, Lisbeth Zwerger, Austria. 7k, Antonio Dominques, Angola.

1983, Sept. 9 Engr. & Photo.

2468 A876 50h multi .20 .20
2469 A876 1k multi .20 .20
2470 A876 4k multi .30 .20
2471 A876 7k multi .65 .30
a. Souv. sheet of 4, #2468-2471 5.00 3.00
Nos. 2468-2471 (4) 1.35 .90

World Communications Year — A877

Emblems and aircraft.

1983, Sept. 30 *Perf. 11½*

2472 A877 50h red & black .20 .20
2473 A877 1k red & black, vert. .25 .20
2474 A877 4k red & black 1.00 .75
Nos. 2472-2474 (3) 1.45 1.15

60th anniv. of the Czechoslovak Airlines.

16th Party Congress Achievements — A878

1983, Oct. 20 *Perf. 12x11½*

2475 A878 50h Civil engineering construction .20 .20
2476 A878 1k Chemical industry .25 .20
2477 A878 3k Health services .75 .40
Nos. 2475-2477 (3) 1.20 .80

Bratislava Type of 1977

Designs: 3k, Two sculptures, Viktor Tilgner (1844-96). 4k, Mirbachov Palace, 1939, by Julius Schubert (1888-1947).

1983, Oct. 28 *Perf. 12*

2478 A760 3k multi 2.00 .65
2479 A760 4k multi 1.00 1.00

Natl. Theater, Prague, Centenary — A879

1983, Nov. 8 Engr. *Perf. 11½*

2480 A879 50h Natl. Theater building .20 .20
2481 A879 2k State Theater, Natl. Theater .50 .20

Messenger of Mourning, by Mikolas Ales — A880

Designs: 2k, Genius, theater curtain by Vojtech Hynais (1854-1925). 3k, Music, Lyric drawings by Frantisek Zenisek (1849-1916). 4k, Symbolic figure of Prague, by Vaclay Brozik (1851-1901). 5k, Hradcany Castle, by Julius Marak (1832-1899).

1983, Nov. 18 Engr.

2482 A880 1k multi 1.40 .30
2483 A880 2k multi 2.75 .60
2484 A880 3k multi .75 .65
2485 A880 4k multi 1.00 .85
2486 A880 5k multi 1.25 1.00
Nos. 2482-2486 (5) 7.15 3.40

Warrior with Sword and Shield, Engraving, 17th Cent. — A881

Engravings of Costumes: 50h, Bodyguard of Rudolf II, by Jacob de Gheyn (1565-1629). 1k, Lady with Lace Collar, by Jacques Callot (1592-1635). 4k, Lady, by Vaclav Hollar (1607-77). 5k, Man, by Antoine Watteau (1684-1721).

Engraved and Photogravure

1983, Dec. 2 *Perf. 11½x12*

2487 A881 40h multi .20 .20
2488 A881 50h multi .20 .20
2489 A881 1k multi .25 .20
2490 A881 4k multi .75 .40
2491 A881 5k multi 2.25 .75
Nos. 2487-2491 (5) 3.65 1.75

Stamp Day — A882

1983, Dec. 18

2492 A882 1k Karl Seizinger (1889-1978), #114 .25 .20

Czechoslovak Federation, 15th Anniv. — A883

1984, Jan. 1 *Perf. 11½*
2493 A883 50h Bratislava, Prague Castles .20 .20

35th Anniv. of COMECON A884

1984, Jan. 23
2494 A884 1k Headquarters, Moscow .25 .20

1984 Winter Olympics A885

1984, Feb. 7 *Perf. 12x11½*
2495 A885 2k Cross-country skiing .50 .25
2496 A885 3k Hockey .75 .30
a. Souvenir sheet of 4 3.75 3.00
2497 A885 5k Biathlon 1.25 .45
Nos. 2495-2497 (3) 2.50 1.00

Intl. Olympic Committee, 90th Anniv. — A886

1984, Feb. 7 *Perf. 11½x12*
2498 A886 7k Rings, runners, torch 1.75 .70

City Arms Type of 1982

1984, Mar. 1 *Perf. 12x11½*
2499 A847 50h Kutna Hora .20 .20
2500 A847 50h Turnov .20 .20
2501 A847 1k Martin .25 .20
2502 A847 1k Milevsko .25 .20
Nos. 2499-2502 (4) .90 .80

Intercosmos Space Program — A887

Various satellites. Nos. 2503-2507 se-tenant with labels showing flags.

1984, Apr. 12 *Perf. 11½x12*
2503 A887 50h multi .20 .20
2504 A887 1k multi .20 .20
2505 A887 2k multi .35 .20
2506 A887 4k multi .75 .40
2507 A887 5k multi 1.40 .50
Nos. 2503-2507 (5) 2.90 1.50

Resistance Heroes — A888

Designs: 50h, Vendelin Opatrny (1908-44). 1k, Ladislav Novomesky (1904-44). 2k, Rudolf Jasiok (1919-44). 4k, Jan Nalepka (1912-43).

1984, May 9 *Perf. 11x11½*
2508 A888 50h multi .20 .20
2509 A888 1k multi .30 .20
2510 A888 2k multi .50 .25
2511 A888 4k multi 1.00 .35
Nos. 2508-2511 (4) 2.00 1.00

Music Year — A889

1984, May 11 *Perf. 11½*
2512 A889 50h Instruments .20 .20
2513 A889 1k Organ pipes, vert. .25 .20

Bratislava Type of 1977

Designs: 3k, Vintners' Guild arms, 19th cent. 4k, View of Bratislava (painting commemorating shooting competition, 1827).

1984, June 1 *Perf. 12*
2514 A760 3k multi .75 .75
2515 A760 4k multi 1.00 1.00

Issued in sheet of 4.

Central Telecommunications Building, Bratislava — A890

1984, June 1 *Perf. 11½*
2516 A890 2k multi .45 .20

A891 A893

1984, June 12 *Perf. 12*
2517 A891 5k UPU emblem, dove, globe 1.75 1.25

1984 UPU Congress. Issued in sheet of 4 with and without Philatelic Salon text. Values, $10 with text, $25 without text.

Prague Castle Type of 1983

Designs: 3k, Crowing rooster, St. Vitus Cathedral, 19th cent. 4k, King David from the Roundnice, Book of Psalms illuminated manuscript, Bohemia, 15th cent.

1984, Aug. 9 **Engr. & Photo.**
2518 A875 3k multi .65 .40
2519 A875 4k multi .90 .65

1984, Aug. 28 *Perf. 11½x12*

Playing cards.

2520 A893 50h Jack of Spades, 16th cent. .20 .20
2521 A893 1k Queen of spades, 17th cent. .20 .20
2522 A893 2k 9 of hearts, 18th cent. .25 .20
2523 A893 3k Jack of clubs, 18th cent. .35 .20
2524 A893 5k King of hearts, 19th cent. 1.25 .60
Nos. 2520-2524 (5) 2.25 1.40

Slovak Natl. Uprising, 40th Anniv. A894

1984, Aug. 29 *Perf. 12x11½*
2525 A894 50h Family, factories, flowers .20 .20

Battle of Dukla Pass (Carpathians), 40th Anniv. — A895

1984, Sept. 8 *Perf. 11½x12*
2526 A895 2k Soldiers, flag .40 .20

1984 Summer Olympics A896

1984, Sept. 9 *Perf. 12x11½*
2527 A896 1k Pole vault .20 .20
2528 A896 2k Bicycling .40 .20
2529 A896 3k Rowing .60 .35
2530 A896 5k Weight lifting 1.00 .45
a. Souv. sheet of 4, #2527-2530 3.00 2.00
Nos. 2527-2530 (4) 2.20 1.20

16th Party Congress Goals and Projects — A897

1984, Oct. 28 *Perf. 12x11½*
2531 A897 1k Communications .20 .20
2532 A897 2k Transportation .30 .20
2533 A897 3k Transgas pipeline .50 .30
a. Souvenir sheet of 3 2.00 1.50
Nos. 2531-2533 (3) 1.00 .70

Art Type of 1967

1k, The Milevsky River, by Karel Stehlik (b. 1912). 2k, Under the Trees, by Viktor Barvitius (1834-1902). 3k, Landscape with Flowers, by Zolo Palugyay (1898-1935). 4k, King in Palace, Visehrad Codex miniature, 1085. 5k, View of Kokorin Castles, by Antonin Manes. #2534-2537 horiz.; issued in sheets of 4.

1984, Nov. 16 *Perf. 11½*
2534 A565 1k multi 1.10 .50
2535 A565 2k multi 1.10 .50
2536 A565 3k multi .85 .30
2537 A565 4k multi 1.10 .35
2538 A565 5k multi 1.10 .35
Nos. 2534-2538 (5) 5.25 2.00

Students' Intl., 45th Anniv. A898 — Birth Cent., Antonin Zapotocky A899

1984, Nov. 17
2539 A898 1k Head, dove .20 .20

Engr. & Photo.

1984, Dec. 18 *Perf. 11½*
2540 A899 50h multi .20 .20

Stamp Day — A900

1984, Dec. 18 *Perf. 11½x12*
2541 A900 1k Engraver Bohumil Heinz (1894-1940) .20 .20

City Arms Type of 1982

1985, Feb. 5 *Perf. 12x11½*
2542 A847 50h Kamyk nad Vltavou .20 .20
2543 A847 50h Havirov .20 .20
2544 A847 50h Trnava .20 .20
Nos. 2542-2544 (3) .60 .60

University of Applied Arts, Prague, Centenary — A901

1985, Feb. 6 *Perf. 11½x12*
2545 A901 3k Art and Pleasure, sculpture .60 .30

Trnava University, 350th Anniv. — A902

1985, Feb. 6 *Perf. 11½x12*
2546 A902 2k Town of Trnava .40 .20

Military Museum Exposition — A903

1985, Feb. 7 *Perf. 11½x12, 12x11½*
2547 A903 50h Armor, crossbow, vert. .20 .20
2548 A903 1k Medals, vert. .20 .20
2549 A903 2k Biplane, spacecraft .40 .20
Nos. 2547-2549 (3) .80 .60

Vladimir I. Lenin (1870-1924), 1st Chairman of Russia — A904

1985, Mar. 15 **Engr.** *Perf. 12*
2550 A904 2k multi .50 .30

No. 2550 printed in sheets of 6.

UN 40th Anniv., Peace Year 1986 A905

1985, Mar. 15
2551 A905 6k UN, Peace Year emblems *1.75 1.50*

Issued in sheets of 4.

A906 A907

Engraved and Photogravure

1985, Apr. 5 *Perf. 11½*

2552 A906 4k Natl. arms, twig, crowd .80 .40

Kosice govt. plan, Apr. 5, 1945.

1985, Apr. 5

2553 A907 50h Natl. arms, flag, soldiers .20 .20

Natl. Security Forces, 40th anniv.

Halley's Comet, INTERCOSMOS Project Vega — A908

Design: Emblem, space platform, interstellar map, intercept data.

1985, Apr. 12 *Perf. 12x11½*

2554 Sheet of 2 *7.50 6.75*
a. A908 5k multicolored *1.75 1.50*

Project Vega, a joint effort of the USSR, France, German Democratic Republic, Austria, Poland, Bulgaria and CSSR, was for the geophysical study of Halley's Comet, Dec. 1984-Mar. 1986.

European Ice Hockey Championships, Prague, Apr. 17-May 3 — A909

1985, Apr. 13

2555 A909 1k Hockey players, emblem .20 .20

No. 2555 Ovptd. "CSSR MISTREM SVETA" in Violet Blue

1985, May 31 *Perf. 12x11½*

2556 A909 1k multi *2.50 2.50*

Natl. Chess Org., 80th Anniv. — A910

1985, Apr. 13 *Perf. 11½*

2557 A910 6k Emblem, game board, chessmen .90 .50

Anniversaries — A911

1985, May 5 *Perf. 11½x12*

2558 A911 1k May Uprising, 1945 .20 .20
2559 A911 1k Soviet Army in CSSR, 1945 .20 .20
2560 A911 1k Warsaw Treaty, 1950 .20 .20
2561 A911 1k Czech-Soviet Treaty, 1970 .20 .20
Nos. 2558-2561 (4) .80 .80

Spartakiad '85, Strahov Stadium, Prague, June 27 — A912

Designs: 50h, Gymnasts warming up with rackets and balls. 1k, Rhythmic gymnastics floor exercise, Prague Castle.

1985, June 3 *Perf. 11½, 11½x12*

2562 A912 50h multi .20 .20

Size: 53x22mm

2563 A912 1k multi .20 .20

WWII Anti-Fascist Political Art — A913

Drawings and caricatures: 50h, Fire, and From the Concentration Camp, by Joseph Capek (1887-1945). 2k, The Conference on Disarmament in Geneva, 1927 and The Prophecy of Three Parrots, 1933, by Frantisek Bidlo (1895-1945). 4k, The Unknown Warrior to Order, 1936, and The Almost Peaceful Dove, 1937, by Antonin Pelc (1895-1967).

1985, June 4 *Perf. 12x11½*

2564 A913 50h multi .20 .20
2565 A913 2k multi .30 .20
2566 A913 4k multi .60 .40
Nos. 2564-2566 (3) 1.10 .80

Helsinki Conference on European Security and Cooperation, 10th Anniv. — A914

1985, July 1 **Engr. & Photo.**

2567 A914 7k multi 1.50 1.00
a. Souvenir sheet of 4 8.00 8.00

An Imperf. souv. sheet similar to No. 2567a was issued June 1, 1988 for FINLANDIA '88 and PRAGA '88. Value $35.

12th World Youth Festival, Moscow A915

1985, July 2

2568 A915 1k Kremlin, youths .20 .20

A916

A918

1985, Sept. 3 *Perf. 11½*

2569 A916 50h multi .20 .20

Federation of World Trade Unions, 40th anniv.

Bratislava Type of 1977

Designs: 3k, Castle and river, lace embroidery by Elena Holeczyova (1906-1983). 4k, Pottery cups and mugs, 1600-1500 B.C.

1985, Sept. 4 **Engr.** *Perf. 12*

2570 A760 3k multi .55 .45
2571 A760 4k multi .75 .60

Issued in sheets of 4.

Engraved and Photogravure

1985, Sept. 5 *Perf. 11½*

Children's book illustrations: 1k, Rocking Horse, by Kveta Pacovska, USSR. 2k, Fairies, by Gennadij Spirin, USSR. 3k, Butterfly and Girl, by Kaarina Kaila, Finland. 4k, Boy and Animals, by Erick Ingraham, US.

2572 A918 1k multi .20 .20
2573 A918 2k multi .30 .20
2574 A918 3k multi .45 .25
2575 A918 4k multi .60 .35
a. Souv. sheet of 4, #2572-2575 3.50 2.75
Nos. 2572-2575 (4) 1.55 1.00

10th biennial of illustrations.

5-Year Development Plan — A919

1985, Oct. 28 *Perf. 12x11½*

2576 A919 50h Construction machinery .20 .20
2577 A919 1k Prague subway, map .20 .20
2578 A919 2k Modern textile spinning .30 .25
Nos. 2576-2578 (3) .70 .65

16th Communist Party Congress goals.

Prague Castle — A920 A921

Engr., Engr. & Photo. (3k)

1985, Oct. 28 *Perf. 12*

2579 A920 2k Presidential Palace Gate, 1768 .30 .25
2580 A920 3k St. Vitus' Cathedral .45 .40

Sheets of 6.

Engraved and Photogravure

1985, Nov. 23 *Perf. 11½x12*

Glassware: 50h, Pitcher, Near East, 4th cent. 1k, Venetian pitcher, 16th cent. 2k, Bohemian goblet, c. 1720. 4k, Harrachov Bohemian vase, 18th cent. 6k, Jablonec Bohemian vase, c. 1900.

2581 A921 50h multi .20 .20
2582 A921 1k multi .20 .20
2583 A921 2k multi .30 .25
2584 A921 4k multi .60 .40
2585 A921 6k multi .90 .70
Nos. 2581-2585 (5) 2.20 1.75

Arts and Crafts Museum, Prague, cent.

Art Type of 1967

Designs: 1k, Young Woman in a Blue Gown, by Jozef Ginovsky (1800-1857). 2k, Lenin on the Charles Bridge, Prague, 1952, by Martin Sladky (b. 1920). 3k, Avenue of Poplars, 1935, by Vaclav Rabas (1885-1954). 4k, The Martyrom of St. Dorothea, 1516, by Hans Baldung Grien (c. 1484-1545). 5k, Portrait of Jasper Schade van Westrum, 1645, by Frans Hals (c. 1581-1666).

1985, Nov. 27 **Engr.** *Perf. 12*

2586 A565 1k multi *1.60 .80*
2587 A565 2k multi 1.10 .35
2588 A565 3k multi 1.50 .35
2589 A565 4k multi .90 .50
2590 A565 5k multi .90 .50
Nos. 2586-2590 (5) *6.00 2.50*

Sheets of 4.

Bohdan Roule (1921-1960), Engraver — A922

Engraved and Photogravure

1985, Dec. 18 *Perf. 11½x12*

2591 A922 1k multicolored .20 .20

Stamp Day 1985.

Intl. Peace Year — A923

1986, Jan. 2

2592 A923 1k multi .20 .20

Philharmonic Orchestra, 90th Anniv. — A924

EXPO '86, Vancouver A925

1986, Jan. 2 *Perf. 11½*

2593 A924 1k Victory Statue, Prague .20 .20

1986, Jan. 23 *Perf. 11½*

Design: Z 50 LS monoplane, Cenyerth Prague-Kladno locomotive, Sahara Desert rock drawing, 5th-6th cent. B.C.

2594 A925 4k multicolored .60 .40

City Arms Type of 1982

1986, Feb. 10 *Perf. 12x11½*

Size: 42x54mm

2595 A847 50h Myjava .20 .20
2596 A847 50h Vodnany .20 .20
2597 A847 50h Zamberk .20 .20
Nos. 2595-2597 (3) .60 .60

17th Natl. Communist Party Congress, Prague, Mar. 24 — A926

1986, Mar. 20 *Perf. 11½*

2598 A926 50h shown .20 .20
2599 A926 1k Industry .20 .20

Natl. Communist Party, 65th Anniv. — A927

1986, Mar. 20 *Perf. 12x11½*

2600 A927 50h Star, man, woman .20 .20
2601 A927 1k Hammer, sickle, laborers .20 .20

Natl. Front Election Program A928

1986, Mar. 28

2602 A928 50h multi .20 .20

Karlovy Vary Intl. Film Festival, 25th Anniv. — A929

1986, Apr. 3 ***Perf. 11½***
2603 A929 1k multi .20 .20

A930

A931

1986, Apr. 8 **Engr. & Photo.**
2604 A930 1k multi .20 .20

Spring of Prague Music Festival.

1986, Apr. 25
2605 A931 50h multi .20 .20

Prague-Moscow air service, 50th anniv.

Intl. Olympic Committee, 90th Anniv. — A932

1986, May 12 ***Perf. 11½x12***
2606 A932 2k multi .30 .20

1986 World Cup Soccer Championships, Mexico — A933

1986, May 15 ***Perf. 12x11½***
2607 A933 4k multi .60 .40

Women's World Volleyball Championships, Prague — A934

1986, May 19
2608 A934 1k multi .20 .20

Souvenir Sheet

Intl. Philatelic Federation, FIP, 60th Anniv. — A935

1986, June 3 **Engr.** ***Perf. 12***
2609 A935 20k multi 5.00 5.00

Exists imperf and with perforations between stamps omitted. Values, $12 and $25, respectively.

Prague Castle Type of 1983

Designs: 2k, Jewelled funerary pendant, 9th cent. 3k, Allegory of Blossoms, sculpture by Jaroslav Horejc (1886-1983), St. Vitus' Cathedral.

1986, June 6 **Engr.** ***Perf. 12***
2610 A875 2k multi .30 .30
2611 A875 3k multi .70 .45

UN Child Survival Campaign — A937

Toys.

Engraved and Photogravure
1986, Sept. 1 ***Perf. 11½***
2612 A937 10h Rooster .20 .20
2613 A937 20h Horse and rider .20 .20
2614 A937 1k Doll .25 .20
2615 A937 2k Doll, diff. .50 .30
2616 A937 3k Tin omnibus, c. 1910 .75 .50
Nos. 2612-2616 (5) 1.90 1.40

UNICEF, 40th anniv.

Registration, Cent. — A938

1986, Sept. 2 ***Perf. 11½x12***
2617 A938 4k Label, mail coach .60 .45

Bratislava Type of 1977

1986, Sept. 11 **Engr.** ***Perf. 12***
2618 A760 3k Sigismund Gate .55 .40
2619 A760 4k St. Margaret, bas-relief .70 .50

Sheets of four.

Owls — A939

Engraved and Photogravure
1986, Sept. 18 ***Perf. 11½***
2620 A939 50h Bubo bubo .20 .20
2621 A939 2k Asio otus .30 .25
2622 A939 3k Strix aluco .50 .25
2623 A939 4k Tyto alba .65 .35
2624 A939 5k Asio flammeus .80 .50
Nos. 2620-2624 (5) 2.45 1.55

Souvenir Sheet

Intl. Brigades in Spain — A940

Theater curtain: Woman Savaged by Horses, 1936, by Vladimir Sychra (1903-1963), Natl Gallery, Prague.

1986, Oct. 1 **Engr.** ***Perf. 12***
2625 Sheet of 2 3.00 2.75
a. A940 5k multi 1.25 1.00

Locomotives and Streetcars — A941

Engraved and Photogravure
1986, Oct. 6 ***Perf. 12x11½***
2626 A941 50h KT-8 .20 .20
2627 A941 1k E458.1 .20 .20
2628 A941 3k T466.2 .50 .30
2629 A941 5k M152.0 .80 .50
Nos. 2626-2629 (4) 1.70 1.20

Paintings in the Prague and Bratislava Natl. Galleries — A942

Designs: 1k, The Circus Rider, 1980, by Jan Bauch (b. 1898). 2k, The Ventriloquist, 1954, by Frantisek Tichy (1896-1961). 3k, In the Circus, 1946, by Vincent Hloznik (b. 1919). 6k, Clown, 1985, by Karel Svolinsky (1896-1986).

1986, Oct. 13 **Engr.** ***Perf. 12***
2630 A942 1k multi .20 .20
2631 A942 2k multi .40 .30
2632 A942 3k multi .50 .40
2633 A942 6k multi 1.10 .90
Nos. 2630-2633 (4) 2.20 1.80

Art Type of 1967

1k, The Czech Lion, May 1918, by Vratislav H. Brunner (1886-1928). 2k, Boy with Mandolin, 1945, by Jozef Sturdik (b. 1920). 3k, Metra Building, 1984, by Frantisek Gross (1909-1985). 4k, Portrait of Maria Maximiliana at Sternberk, 1665, by Karel Skreta (1610-1674). 5k, Adam & Eve, 1538, by Lucas Cranach (1472-1553).

1986, Nov. 3 **Engr.** ***Perf. 12***
2634 A565 1k multi *.40 .20*
2635 A565 2k multi *.75 .55*
2636 A565 3k multi *1.25 .75*
2637 A565 4k multi *1.60 1.00*
2638 A565 5k multi *2.00 1.25*
Nos. 2634-2638 (5) *6.00 3.75*

Sheets of 4.

Stamp Day — A943

Design: V.H. Brunner (1886-1928), stamp designer, and No. 88.

Photo. & Engr.
1986, Dec. 18 ***Perf. 11½x12***
2639 A943 1k multicolored .20 .20

World Cyclocross Championships, Jan. 24-25, Central Bohemia — A944

1987, Jan. 22 ***Perf. 11½***
2640 A944 6k multi 1.00 .60

Czechoslovakian Bowling Union, 50th Anniv. — A945

1987, Jan. 22 ***Perf. 11½***
2641 A945 2k multi .35 .20

State Decorations — A946

Designs: 50h, Gold Stars of Socialist Labor and Czechoslovakia. 2k, Order of Klement Gottwald. 3k, Order of the Republic. 4k, Order of Victorious February. 5k, Order of Labor.

1987, Feb. 4 ***Perf. 12x11½***
2642 A946 50h multi .20 .20
2643 A946 2k multi .35 .25
2644 A946 3k multi .50 .45
2645 A946 4k multi .70 .40
2646 A946 5k multi .85 .50
Nos. 2642-2646 (5) 2.60 1.80

Butterflies — A947

1987, Mar. 4
2647 A947 1k Limenitis populi .20 .20
2648 A947 2k Smerinthus ocellatus .30 .25
2649 A947 3k Pericallia matronula .45 .30
2650 A947 4k Saturnia pyri .60 .40
Nos. 2647-2650 (4) 1.55 1.15

Natl. Nuclear Power Industry A948

1987, Apr. 6
2651 A948 5k multi .75 .50

11th Revolutionary Trade Union Movement Congress, Apr. 14-17, Prague — A949

1987, Apr. 7 ***Perf. 11½***
2652 A949 1k multi .20 .20

Souvenir Sheet

INTERCOSMOS, 20th Anniv. — A950

Cosmonauts Alexei Gubarev of the USSR & Vladimir Remek of Czechoslovakia, rocket & emblem.

1987, Apr. 12 Engr. *Perf. 12*

2653 Sheet of 2 3.50 3.50
a. A950 10k multi 1.75 1.75
b. Souv. sheet of 4, litho. & engr., imperf. 7.00 7.00

No. 2653b issued Nov. 15, 1987.

Prague Castle Art Treasures Type of 1983

Designs: 2k, Three Saints, stained-glass window detail, c. 1870, St. Vitus Cathedral, by Frantisek Sequens (1830-1896). 3k, Coat of Arms, New Land Rolls Hall, 1605.

1987, May 9 *Perf. 11½*

2654 A875 2k multi .30 .20
2655 A875 3k dk red, slate gray & yel org .45 .30

Nos. 2654-2655 each printed in sheets of 6.

PRAGA '88 A951

Photo. & Engr.

1987, May 12 *Perf. 12x11½*

2656 A951 3k Telephone, 1894 .50 .30
2657 A951 3k Postal van, 1924 .50 .35
2658 A951 4k Locomotive tender, 1907 .75 .40
2659 A951 4k Tram, 1900 .75 .45
2660 A951 5k Steam roller, 1936 .85 .50
Nos. 2656-2660 (5) 3.35 2.00

Printed in sheets of 8 + 2 labels picturing telephone or vehicles. Value $25.

Nos. 2657-2658 were also printed in sheets of 4 + label picturing vehicles. Value, $12 for both sheets.

Destruction of Lidice and Lezaky, 45th Anniv. — A952

Drawings: No. 2661, When the Fighting Ended, 1945, by Pavel Simon. No. 2662, The End of the game, 1945, by Ludmila Jirincova.

1987, June *Perf. 11½*

2661 A952 1k blk, cerise & vio .20 .20
2662 A952 1k blk, gold, pale lil & cerise .20 .20

Union of Czechoslovakian Mathematicians and Physicists, 125th Anniv. — A953

Designs: No. 2663, Prague Town Hall mathematical clock, Theory of Functions diagram. No. 2664, J.M. Petzval (1807-1891), J. Strouhal (1850-1922) and V. Jarnik (1897-1970). No. 2665, Geographical measurement from A.M. Malletta's book, 1672, earth fold and Brownian motion diagrams.

1987, July 6 *Perf. 11½x12*

2663 A953 50h multi .20 .20
2664 A953 50h multi .20 .20
2665 A953 50h multi .20 .20
Nos. 2663-2665 (3) .60 .60

A954

A955

Award-winning illustrations.

1987, Sept. 3 *Perf. 11½*

2666 A954 50h Asun Balzola, Spain .20 .20
2667 A954 1k Frederic Clement, France .20 .20
2668 A954 2k Elzbieta Gaudasinska, Poland .40 .25
a. Souv. sheet of 2 + label .80 .60
2669 A954 4k Marija Lucija Stupica, Yugoslavia .80 .50
Nos. 2666-2669 (4) 1.60 1.15

11th Biennial of Children's Book Illustration, Sept. 11-Oct. 30, Bratislava.

1987, Sept. 23

2670 A955 50h Eternal flame, flower .20 .20

Theresienstadt Memorial for the victims from 23 European countries who died in the Small Fortress, Terezin, a Nazi concentration camp.

Socialist Communications Organization, 30th Anniv. — A956

1987, Sept. 23

2671 A956 4k Emblem, satellite, dish receiver .65 .40

Jan Evangelista Purkyne (1787-1869), Physiologist A957

1987, Sept. 30

2672 A957 7k multicolored 1.10 .75

Views of Bratislava — A958

Designs: 3k, Male and female figures supporting an oriel, Arkier Palace, c. 1552. 4k, View of Bratislava from Ware Conterfactur de Stadt Presburg, from an engraving by Hans Mayer, 1563.

1987, Oct. 1 Engr. *Perf. 12*

2673 A958 3k multicolored .50 .35
2674 A958 4k multicolored .70 .45

Printed in sheets of 4 with Bratislava Castle (from Mayer's engraving) between.

See #2719-2720, 2763-2764, 2800-2801.

Type of 1974

Photo. & Engr.

1987, Nov. 1 *Perf. 12x11½*

2675 A699 1k Post rider .20 .20

PRAGA '88, Aug. 26-Sept. 4, 1988. No. 2675 printed se-tenant with label picturing exhibition emblem.

October Revolution, Russia, 70th Anniv. — A959

Establishment of the Union of Soviet Socialist Republics, 65th Anniv. — A960

1987, Nov. 6 *Perf. 12x11½*

2676 A959 50h multicolored .20 .20
2677 A960 50h multicolored .20 .20

Art Type of 1974

Paintings in national galleries: 1k, Enclosure of Dreams, by Kamil Lhotak (b. 1912). 2k, Tulips, by Ester Simerova-Martincekova (b. 1909). 3k, Triptych with Bohemian Landscape, by Josef Lada (1887-1957). 4k, Accordion Player, by Josef Capek (1887-1945). 5k, Self-portrait, by Jiri Trnka (1912-1969).

1987, Nov. 18 Engr. *Perf. 12*

2678 A700 1k multi .20 .20
2679 A700 2k multi .40 .25
2680 A700 3k multi .55 .30
2681 A700 4k multi .75 .45
2682 A700 5k multi .95 .60
Nos. 2678-2682 (5) 2.85 1.80

Czech and Slovak art. Issued in sheets of 4.

69th Stamp Day — A961

Portrait of Jacob Obrovsky (1882-1949), stamp designer, Bohemian Lion (Type SP1), sketch of a lion and PRAGA '88 emblem.

Photo. & Engr.

1987, Dec. 18 *Perf. 11½x12*

2683 A961 1k multicolored .20 .20

No. 2683 printed in sheet of four with eight labels se-tenant with stamps, inscribed "100 Years of the National Philatelic Movement in Czechoslovakia" in Czech. The four labels between the "blocks of six" are blank.

Czechoslovak Republic, 70th Anniv. — A962

1988, Jan. 1 *Perf. 12x11½*

2684 A962 1k Woman, natl. arms, linden branch .20 .20

Natl. Front, 40th Anniv. — A963

1988, Feb. 25 *Perf. 11½*

2685 A963 50h multicolored .20 .20

Husak Type of 1983

Photo. & Engr.

1988, Jan. 10 *Perf. 12x11½*

2686 A865 1k brt rose & dk carmine .20 .20

Olympics — A965

1988, Feb. 1 *Perf. 11½x12*

2687 A965 50h Ski jumping, ice hockey .20 .20
2688 A965 1k Basketball, soccer .20 .20
2689 A965 6k Discus, weight lifting 1.00 .85
Nos. 2687-2689 (3) 1.40 1.25

Exist in souv. sheets of 2, imperf. between and in souv. sheets of 2, imperf.

Victorious February, 40th Anniv. — A966

Statue of Klement Gottwald by Rudolf Svoboda.

1988, Feb. 25 *Perf. 11½*

2690 A966 50h multicolored .20 .20

No. 2690 exists in a souvenir sheet of two No. 2690 and two postally invalid copies of No. 637, imperf. Sheet exists imperf.

Classic Automobiles — A967

1988, Mar. 1 *Perf. 12x11½*

2691 A967 50h 1914 Laurin & Klement .20 .20
2692 A967 1k 1902 Tatra NW Type B .20 .20
2693 A967 2k 1905 Tatra NW Type E .30 .20
2694 A967 3k 1929 Tatra 12 Normandie .60 .25
2695 A967 4k 1899 Meteor .80 .40
a. Bklt. pane, 2 3k, 3 4k + label 4.00 4.00
Nos. 2691-2695 (5) 2.10 1.25

Postal Museum, 70th Anniv. A968

Praga '88 emblem and: 50h, Postman, Malostranske Namesti Square p.o., Prague, c. 1742, and Velka Javorina television transmitter, 1979. 1k, Telecommunications Center, Mlada Boleslav, 1986, and Carmelite Street p.o., Prague, c. 1792. 2k, Prague 1 (1873) and Bratislava 56 (1984) post offices. 4k, Communications Center, Prachatice (1982), postman and Maltetske Nameski Square p.o., Prague, c. 1622.

1988, Mar. 10

2696 A968 50h multi .20 .20
2697 A968 1k multi .25 .20
2698 A968 2k multi .40 .30
2699 A968 4k multi .90 .60
a. Souv. sheet, 2 ea #2698-2699 2.75 1.50
Nos. 2696-2699 (4) 1.75 1.30

In No. 2699a the top pair of Nos. 2698-2699 is imperf. at top and sides.

A969

A970

1988, Mar. 29 *Perf. 11½*
2700 A969 50h multicolored .20 .20

Matice Slovenska Cultural Assoc., 125th anniv.

1988, May 12 **Photo. & Engr.**

PRAGA '88. (Exhibition emblem and aspects of the Museum of Natl. Literature, Prague): 1k, Gate and distant view of museum. 2k, Celestial globe, illuminated manuscript, bookshelves and ornately decorated ceiling. 5k, Illuminated "B" and decorated binder of a medieval Bible. 7k, Celestial globe, illuminated manuscript, Zodiacal signs (Aries and Leo), view of museum.

2701 A970 1k multicolored .25 .20
a. Souvenir sheet of 4 1.00 .75
2702 A970 2k multicolored .50 .30
a. Souvenir sheet of 4 2.10 1.50
2703 A970 5k multicolored 1.25 .75
a. Souvenir sheet of 4 5.50 3.75
2704 A970 7k multicolored 1.50 .75
a. Souvenir sheet of 4 6.00 4.00
b. Souv. sheet of 4, imperf., #2701-2704 3.50 2.50
Nos. 2701-2704 (4) 3.50 2.00

PRAGA '88 — A971

Exhibition emblem and fountains, Prague.

1988, June 1 *Perf. 11½x12*
2705 A971 1k Waldstein Palace .25 .20
2706 A971 2k Old town square .50 .25
2707 A971 3k Charles University .80 .40
2708 A971 4k Prague Castle 1.10 .50
a. Souv. sheet of 4, #2705-2708 2.75 1.75
Nos. 2705-2708 (4) 2.65 1.35

Souvenir Sheet

Soviet-US Summit Conference on Arms Reduction, Moscow — A972

Design: The capital, Washington, and the Kremlin, Moscow.

1988, June 1 *Perf. 12x11½*
2709 A972 4k blue blk, dark red & gold 2.25 1.25

Exists imperf. Value $6.

PRAGA '88 A973

Exhibition emblem and modern architecture, Prague: 50h, Trade Unions Central Recreation Center. 1k, Koospol foreign trade company. 2k, Motol Teaching Hospital. 4k, Culture Palace.

1988, July 1 *Perf. 12x11½*
2710 A973 50h multicolored .20 .20
2711 A973 1k blk, lt blue & bister .25 .20
2712 A973 2k multicolored .45 .25
a. Souv. sheet, 2 1k, 2 2k + 4 labels, imperf. 1.25 .60
2713 A973 4k multicolored .95 .50
a. Souv. sheet, 2 50h, 2 4k + 4 labels, imperf. 1.75 .90
Nos. 2710-2713 (4) 1.85 1.15

Souvenir Sheet

PRAGA '88 — A974

Design: Exhibition emblem and Alfons Mucha (1860-1939), designer of first Czech postage stamp.

1988, Aug. 18 **Engr.** *Perf. 12*
2714 A974 Sheet of 2 3.00 1.75
a. 5k multicolored 1.50 .85

Czech postage stamps, 70th anniv.

Souvenir Sheets

PRAGA '88 A975

5k, *Turin, Monte Superga,* by Josef Navratil (1798-1865), Postal Museum, Prague.

Details of *Bacchus and Ariadne,* by Sebastiano Ricci (1659-1734), Natl. Gallery, Prague: No. 2716a, Ariadne. No. 2716b, Bacchus and creatures.

1988
2715 Sheet of 2 2.75 1.50
a. A975 5k multi 1.50 .85
2716 Sheet of 2 5.50 3.25
a.-b. A975 10k any single 2.75 1.50

#2716 exists with emblem and inscription "DEN F.I.P. JOURNEE DE LA FEDERATION INTERNATIONALE DE PHILATELIE."

Issue dates: 5k, Aug. 19; 10k, Aug. 26.

Prague Castle Type of 1983

2k, Pottery jug, 17th cent. 3k, *St. Catherine with Angel,* 1580, by Paolo Veronese.

1988, Sept. 28 **Engr.** *Perf. 12*
2717 A875 2k shown .95 .50
2718 A875 3k multi 1.25 .70

Issued in sheets of 6.

Bratislava Views Type of 1987

3k, *Hlavne Square, circa 1840* an etching by R. Alt-Sandman, 1840. 4k, *Ferdinand House, circa 1850,* a pen-and-ink drawing by V. Reim.

1988, Oct. 19
2719 A958 3k multicolored .95 .50
2720 A958 4k multicolored 1.25 .70

Issued in sheets of 4.

Art Type of 1974

Paintings in natl. galleries: 2k, *With Bundles,* 1931, by Martin Benka (1888-1971). 6k, *Blue Bird,* 1903, by Vojtech Preissig (1873-1944). 7k, *A Jaguar Attacking a Rider,* c. 1850, by Eugene Delacroix (1798-1863).

1988, Nov. 17 **Engr.** *Perf. 12*
2721 A700 2k multicolored .30 .20
2722 A700 6k multicolored .90 .35
2723 A700 7k multicolored 1.00 .45
Nos. 2721-2723 (3) 2.20 1.00

Czech and Slovak art. Issued in sheets of 4.

Stamp Day — A978

Design: 1k, Jaroslav Benda (1882-1970), illustrator and stamp designer.

Photo. & Engr.

1988, Dec. 18 *Perf. 11½x12*
2724 A978 1k multicolored .20 .20

Paris-Dakar Rally — A979

Trucks: 50h, Earth, Motokov Liaz. 1k, Liaz, globe. 2k, Earth, Motokov Tatra. No. 607. 4k, Map of racecourse, turban, Tatra.

1989, Jan. 2 *Perf. 12x11½*
2725 A979 50h multicolored .20 .20
2726 A979 1k multicolored .20 .20
2727 A979 2k multicolored .25 .20
2728 A979 4k multicolored .50 .25
Nos. 2725-2728 (4) 1.15 .85

Czechoslovakian Federation, 20th Anniv. — A980

1989, Jan. 1
2729 A980 50h multicolored .20 .20

Jan Botto (1829-1881) A981

Taras Grigorievich Shevchenko (1814-1861) A982

Jean Cocteau (1889-1963) A983

Charlie Chaplin (1889-1977) A984

Jawaharlal Nehru (1889-1964) and "UNESCO" — A985

Famous men: No. 2732, Modest Petrovich Musorgsky (1839-1881).

Photo. & Engr.

1989, Mar. 9 *Perf. 12x11½*
2730 A981 50h brn blk & lt blue green .20 .20
2731 A982 50h shown .20 .20
2732 A982 50h multicolored .20 .20
2733 A983 50h red brn, grnh blk & org brn .20 .20
2734 A984 50h blk, int blue & dark red .20 .20
2735 A985 50h brn blk & lt yel green .20 .20
Nos. 2730-2735 (6) 1.20 1.20

Shipping Industry A986

1989, Mar. 27
2736 A986 50h *Republika* .20 .20
2737 A986 1k *Pionyr,* flags .20 .20
2738 A986 2k *Brno,* flags .25 .20
2739 A986 3k *Trinec* .35 .20
2740 A986 4k Flags, mast, *Orlik* .45 .25
2741 A986 5k *Vltava,* communication hardware .55 .30
Nos. 2736-2741 (6) 2.00 1.35

Pioneer Organization, 40th Anniv. — A987

Photo. & Engr.

1989, Apr. 20 *Perf. 11½*
2742 A987 50h multi .20 .20

Art Type of 1974

Details of *Feast of Rose Garlands,* 1506, by Albrecht Durer, Natl. Gallery, Prague: a, Virgin and Child. b, Angel playing mandolin.

1989, Apr. 21 **Engr.** *Perf. 12*

Miniature Sheet

2743 Sheet of 2 5.00 4.50
a.-b. A700 10k any single 2.50 2.00

Prague Castle Art Type of 1983

2k, Bas-relief picturing Kaiser Karl IV, from Kralovske tomb by Alexander Colin (c. 1527-1612). 3k, Self-portrait, by V.V. Reiner (1689-1743).

1989, May 9 **Photo. & Engr.**
2744 A875 2k dark red, sepia & buff .30 .20
2745 A875 3k multi .45 .25

Printed in sheets of 6.

Souvenir Sheet

PHILEXFRANCE '89, French Revolution Bicent. — A988

1989, July 14 **Engr.** *Perf. 12*
2746 A988 5k brt blue, blk & dk red 1.50 1.10

Haliaeetus albicilla — A989

Photo. & Engr.

1989, July 17 *Perf. 12x11½*
2747 A989 1k multicolored .20 .20

World Wildlife Fund — A990

Toads and newts.

1989, July 18 *Perf. 11½x12*
2748 A990 2k *Bombina bombina* 1.00 .20
2749 A990 3k *Bombina variegata* 1.25 .25
2750 A990 4k *Triturus alpestris* 1.40 .35
2751 A990 5k *Triturus montandoni* 1.60 .45
Nos. 2748-2751 (4) 5.25 1.25

Slovak Folk Art Collective, 40th Anniv. — A991

1989, Aug. 29 *Perf. 12x11½*
2752 A991 50h multicolored .20 .20

Slovak Uprising, 45th Anniv. — A992

Photo. & Engr.

1989, Aug. 29 *Perf. 11½x12*
2753 A992 1k multicolored .20 .20

A993 A994

Award-winning illustrations.

1989, Sept. 4 *Perf. 11½*
2754 A993 50h Hannu Taina, Finland .20 .20
2755 A993 1k Aleksander Aleksov, Bulgaria .20 .20
2756 A993 2k Jurgen Spohn, West Berlin .25 .20
2757 A993 4k Robert Brun, Czechoslovakia .50 .25
a. Souvenir sheet of 2 1.25 .60
Nos. 2754-2757 (4) 1.15 .85

12th Biennial of Children's Book Illustration, Bratislava.

1989, Sept. 5 Engr. *Perf. 11½x12*

Poisonous mushrooms.

2758 A994 50h *Nolanea verna* .25 .20
2759 A994 1k *Amanita phalloides* .30 .30
2760 A994 2k *Amanita virosa* .45 .40
2761 A994 3k *Cortinarius orellanus* .70 .55
2762 A994 5k *Galerina marginata* .80 .55
Nos. 2758-2762 (5) 2.50 2.00

Bratislava Views Type of 1987

Views of Devin, a Slavic castle above the Danube, Bratislava.

1989, Oct. 16 Engr. *Perf. 12*
2763 A958 3k Castle, flower 1.60 .75
2764 A958 4k Castle, urn 2.25 1.25

Printed in sheets of 4.

Jan Opletal (1915-39) — A996

Photo. & Engr.

1989, Nov. 17 *Perf. 12x11½*
2765 A996 1k multicolored .20 .20

Intl. Student's Day. Funeral of Opletal, a Nazi victim, on Nov. 15, 1939, sparked student demonstrations that resulted in the closing of all universities in occupied Bohemia and Moravia.

Art Type of 1974

Paintings in Natl. Galleries: 2k, *Nirvana*, c. 1920, by Anton Jasusch (1882-1965). 4k, *Winter Evening in Town*, c. 1907, by Jakub Schikaneder (1855-1924), horiz. 5k, *The Bakers*, 1926, by Pravoslav Kotik (1889-1970), horiz.

1989, Nov. 27 Engr. *Perf. 12*
2766 A700 2k multicolored .90 .55
2767 A700 4k multicolored 1.60 1.10
2768 A700 5k multicolored 1.50 1.10
Nos. 2766-2768 (3) 4.00 2.75

Printed in sheets of 4.

Stamp Day — A997

Design: Portrait of Cyril Bouda, stamp designer, art tools and falcon.

Photo. & Engr.

1989, Dec. 18 *Perf. 11½x12*
2769 A997 1k multicolored .20 .20

A998

A999

Photo. & Engr.

1990, Jan. 8 *Perf. 11½x12*
2770 A998 1k multicolored .20 .20

UNESCO World Literacy Year. Printed se-tenant with inscribed label picturing UN and UNESCO emblems.

1990, Jan. 9 *Perf. 11½*

Famous men: No. 2771, Karel Capek, writer. No. 2772, Thomas G. Masaryk. 1k, Lenin. 2k, Emile Zola, French writer. 3k, Jaroslav Heyrovsky (1890-1987), chemical physicist. 10k, Bohuslav Martinu (1890-1959), composer.

2771 A999 50h multicolored .20 .20
2772 A999 50h multicolored .20 .20
2773 A999 1k multicolored .20 .20
2774 A999 2k multicolored .30 .20
2775 A999 3k multicolored .50 .30
2776 A999 10k multicolored 1.60 .90
Nos. 2771-2776 (6) 3.00 2.00

#2771, 2775-2776 inscribed "UNESCO."

Pres. Vaclav Havel A1000 Handball Players A1001

1990, Jan. 9 *Perf. 12x11½*
2777 A1000 50h red, brt vio & bl .20 .20

See Nos. 2879, 2948.

1990, Feb. 1 *Perf. 11½*
2778 A1001 50h multicolored .20 .20

1990 Men's World Handball Championships, Czechoslovakia.

Flora — A1002 A1003

Photo. & Engr.

1990, Mar. 1 *Perf. 11½*
2779 A1002 50h *Antirrhinum majus* .25 .20
2780 A1002 1k *Zinnia elegans* .40 .40
2781 A1002 3k *Tigridia pavonia* .85 .50

Perf. 12x12½

2782 A1002 5k *Lilium candidum* 1.50 .90
Nos. 2779-2782 (4) 3.00 2.00

City Arms Type of 1982

Photo. & Engr.

1990, Mar. 28 *Perf. 12x11½*
2783 A847 50h Prostejov .20 .20
2784 A847 50h Bytca .20 .20
2785 A847 50h Sobeslav .20 .20
2786 A847 50h Podebrady .20 .20
Nos. 2783-2786 (4) .80 .80

1990, Apr. 16 *Perf. 11½x12*
2787 A1003 1k brn vio, rose & buff .20 .20

Visit of Pope John Paul II.

World War II Liberation A1004

Photo. & Engr.

1990, May 5 *Perf. 11½*
2788 A1004 1k multicolored .20 .20

Souvenir Sheet

150th Anniv. of the Postage Stamp — A1005

1990, May 6 Engr. *Perf. 12*
2789 A1005 7k multicolored 2.50 1.50

Stamp World London 90.

A1006

A1007

Photo. & Engr.

1990, May 8 *Perf. 11½*
2790 A1006 1k multicolored .20 .20

World Cup Soccer Championships, Italy.

1990, June 1
2791 A1007 1k multicolored .20 .20

Free elections.

Prague Castle Type of 1983

1990, June 6, 1990 Engr.
2792 A875 2k Gold and jeweled hand .35 .20
2793 A875 3k Medallion .50 .25

Art treasures of Prague Castle. Printed in sheets of 6.

Helsinki Conference, 15th Anniv. — A1008

Photo & Engr.

1990, June 21 *Perf. 12x11½*
2794 A1008 7k multicolored 1.10 .60

Dr. Milada Horakova A1009

1990, June 25 *Perf. 12x11½*
2795 A1009 1k multicolored .20 .20

Intercanis Dog Show, Brno — A1010

Designs: 50h, Poodles, 1k, Afghan hound, Irish wolfhound, greyhound. 4k, Czech terrier, bloodhound, Hannoverian hound. 7k, Cavalier King Charles Spaniel, cocker spaniel, American cocker spaniel.

1990, July 2
2796 A1010 50h multicolored .25 .20
2797 A1010 1k multicolored .35 .25
2798 A1010 4k multicolored 1.00 .40
2799 A1010 7k multicolored 1.90 .65
Nos. 2796-2799 (4) 3.50 1.50

Bratislava Art Type of 1987

1990 Engr. *Perf. 12*
2800 A958 3k Ancient Celtic coin .50 .30
2801 A958 4k Gen. Milan Stefanik .70 .30

Issue dates: 3k, Sept. 29. 4k, July 21. Printed in sheets of 4.

Grand Pardubice Steeplechase, Cent. — A1011

Photo. & Engr.

1990, Sept. 7 *Perf. 12x11½*

2802 A1011 50h multicolored .20 .20
2803 A1011 4k multi, diff. .70 .35

Protected Animals — A1012

Litho. & Engr.

1990, Oct. 1 *Perf. 12x11*

2804 A1012 50h Marmota marmota .75 .20
2805 A1012 1k Felis silvestris 1.25 .20
2806 A1012 4k Castor fiber 1.40 .35
2807 A1012 5k Plecotus auritus 1.75 .50
Nos. 2804-2807 (4) 5.15 1.25

Conf. of Civic Associations, Helsinki — A1013

Litho. & Engr.

1990, Oct. 15 *Perf. 12x11½*

2808 A1013 3k blue, gold & yel .50 .30

Christmas — A1014

Photo. & Engr.

1990, Nov. 15 *Perf. 11½x12*

2809 A1014 50h multicolored .20 .20

Art Type of 1967

Works of art: 2k, Krucemburk by Jan Zrzavy (1890-1977), horiz. 3k, St. Agnes of Bohemia from the St. Wenceslas Monument, Prague by Josef V. Myslbek (1848-1922). 4k, The Slavs in their Homeland by Alfons Mucha (1860-1939). 5k, St. John the Baptist by Auguste Rodin (1840-1917).

1990, Nov. 27 **Engr.** *Perf. 11½*

2810 A565 2k multicolored .65 .50
2811 A565 3k multicolored 1.10 .75
2812 A565 4k multicolored 1.25 .75
2813 A565 5k multicolored 1.75 1.50
Nos. 2810-2813 (4) 4.75 3.50

Karel Svolinsky (1896-1986), Vignette from No. 1182 — A1016

1990, Dec. 18 **Photo. & Engr.**

2814 A1016 1k multicolored .20 .20

Stamp Day.

A1017 A1018

1991, Jan. 10 *Perf. 11½*

2815 A1017 1k multicolored .20 .20

European Judo Championships, Prague.

1991, Jan. 10

Design: A. B. Svojsik (1876-1938), Czech Scouting Founder.

2816 A1018 3k multicolored 1.00 .20

Scouting in Czechoslovakia, 80th Anniv.

Bethlehem Chapel, Prague, 600th Anniv. — A1019

1991, Feb. 4 *Perf. 12x11½*

2817 A1019 50h multicolored .20 .20

Wolfgang Amadeus Mozart (1756-1791), Old Theatre — A1020

1991, Feb. 4

2818 A1020 1k multicolored .20 .20

Steamship Bohemia, 150th Anniv. — A1021

1991, Feb. 4 *Perf. 11½x12*

2819 A1021 5k multicolored .50 .25

Famous Men A1022

Designs: No. 2820, Antonin Dvorak (1841-1904), composer. No. 2821, Andrej Kmet (1841-1908), botanist. No. 2822, Jaroslav Seifert (1901-1986), poet, Nobel laureate for Literature. No. 2823, Jan Masaryk (1886-1948), diplomat. No. 2824, Alois Senefelder (1771-1834), lithographer.

1991, Feb. 18 *Perf. 12x11½*

2820 A1022 1k multicolored .20 .20
2821 A1022 1k multicolored .30 .20
2822 A1022 1k multicolored .40 .20
2823 A1022 1k multicolored .50 .20
2824 A1022 1k multicolored .60 .20
Nos. 2820-2824 (5) 2.00 1.00

#2820-2824 printed with se-tenant labels. See No. 2831.

Europa — A1023 A1024

Photo. & Engr.

1991, May 6 *Perf. 11½x12*

2825 A1023 6k blk, bl & red 2.00 .50

Photo. & Engr.

1991, May 10 *Perf. 11½x12*

2826 A1024 1k multicolored .20 .20

General Exhibition in Prague, cent.

Antarctic Treaty, 30th Anniv. A1025

1991, May 20 *Perf. 12x11½*

2827 A1025 8k multicolored .80 .40

Castles — A1026 Scenic Views — A1027

1991, June 3 *Perf. 11½*

2828 A1026 50h Blatna .40 .20
2829 A1026 1k Bouzov .50 .20
2830 A1026 3k Kezmarok .60 .20
Nos. 2828-2830 (3) 1.50 .60

Famous Men Type

Design: Jan Palach (1948-1969), Student.

Photo. & Engr.

1991, Aug. 9 *Perf. 12x11½*

2831 A1022 4k black 1.00 .20

Printed se-tenant with label.

Photo. & Engr.

1991, Aug. 28 *Perf. 11½*

2832 A1027 4k Krivan mountains 1.00 .60
2833 A1027 4k Rip mountain 1.00 .60

A1028 A1029

Illustrations by: 1k, Binette Schroeder, Germany. 2k, Stasys Eidrigevicius, Poland.

Photo. & Engr.

1991, Sept. 2 *Perf. 11½*

2834 A1028 1k multicolored .50 .25
2835 A1028 2k multicolored .50 .25

13th Biennial Exhibition of Children's Book Illustrators, Bratislava.

1991, Sept. 27 **Engr.** *Perf. 11½*

Design: Father Andrej Hlinka (1864-1938), Slovak nationalist.

2836 A1029 10k blue black 3.00 .55

Art of Prague and Bratislava A1030

Designs: No. 2837, Holy Infant of Prague. No. 2838, Blue Church of Bratislava.

1991, Sept. 30

2837 A1030 3k multicolored 1.00 .75
2838 A1030 3k multicolored 1.00 .75

Flowers A1031 Christmas A1033

Photo. & Engr.

1991, Nov. 3 *Perf. 12x11½*

2839 A1031 1k Gagea bohemica .30 .20
2840 A1031 2k Aster alpinus .60 .20
2841 A1031 5k Fritillaria meleagris 1.60 .25
2842 A1031 11k Daphne cneorum 2.50 .35
Nos. 2839-2842 (4) 5.00 1.00

Art Type of 1967

Paintings: 2k, Everyday Homelife by Max Ernst. 3k, Lovers by Auguste Renoir. 4k, Head of Christ by El Greco. 5k, Coincidence by Ladislav Guderna. 7k, Two Maidens by Utamaro.

1991, Nov. 3 **Engr.** *Perf. 11½*

2843 A565 2k multicolored .65 .35
2844 A565 3k multicolored .85 .80
2845 A565 4k multicolored 1.10 1.00
2846 A565 5k multicolored 1.40 1.25
2847 A565 7k multicolored 2.00 1.60
Nos. 2843-2847 (5) 6.00 5.00

1991, Nov. 19

2848 A1033 50h multicolored .20 .20

Stamp Day — A1034

Martin Benka (1888-1971), stamp engraver.

Photo. & Engr.

1991, Dec. 18 *Perf. 11½x12*

2849 A1034 2k multicolored .20 .20

1992 Winter Olympics, Albertville — A1035

1992, Jan. 6 *Perf. 11½*

2850 A1035 1k Biathlon .20 .20

Photo. & Engr.

1992, May 21 *Perf. 11½*

2851 A1035 2k Tennis .25 .20

1992 Summer Olympics, Barcelona.

Souvenir Sheet

Jan Amos Komensky (Comenius), Educator — A1036

1992, Mar. 5 **Engr.**
2852 A1036 10k multicolored 3.00 3.00

World Ice Hockey Championships, Prague and Bratislava — A1037

1992, Mar. 31 **Photo. & Engr.**
2853 A1037 3k multicolored .35 .20

Traffic Safety A1038

1992, Apr. 2
2854 A1038 2k multicolored .25 .20

Expo '92, Seville — A1039

1992, Apr. 2
2855 A1039 4k multicolored .45 .25

Discovery of America, 500th Anniv. — A1040

1992, May 5 **Engr.**
2856 A1040 22k multicolored 5.00 4.00

Europa. Printed in sheets of 8. Value $50.

Czechoslovak Military Actions in WWII — A1041

Designs: 1k, J. Kubis and J. Gabcik, assassins of Reinhard Heydrich, 1942. 2k, Pilots flying for France and Great Britain. 3k, Defense of Tobruk. 6k, Capture of Dunkirk, 1944-45.

1992, May 21 **Engr.** ***Perf. 12x11½***

2857	A1041	1k multicolored	.50	.20
2858	A1041	2k multicolored	.60	.20
2859	A1041	3k multicolored	.75	.25
2860	A1041	6k multicolored	1.60	.35
		Nos. 2857-2860 (4)	3.45	1.00

A1042

A1043

Photo. & Engr.

1992, June 10 ***Perf. 11½***
2861 A1042 2k multicolored .25 .20

Czechoslovakian Red Cross.

1992, June 30
2862 A1043 1k multicolored .20 .20

Junior European Table Tennis Championships, Topolcany.

Beetles A1044

1992, July 15

2863	A1044	1k Polyphylla fullo	.35	.20
2864	A1044	2k Ergates faber	.70	.20
2865	A1044	3k Meloe violaceus	1.10	.25
2866	A1044	4k Dytiscus latissimus	1.40	.35
		Nos. 2863-2866 (4)	3.55	1.00

The 1k exists with denomination omitted.

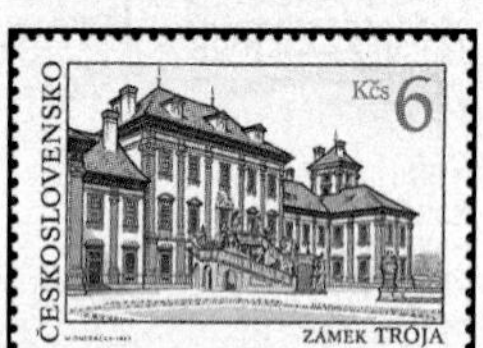

Troja Castle A1045

1992, Aug. 28 **Engr.** ***Perf. 11½***

2867	A1045	6k shown	1.40	.75
2868	A1045	7k Statue of St. Martin, vert.	1.60	1.00
2869	A1045	8k Lednice Castle	2.00	1.25
		Nos. 2867-2869 (3)	5.00	3.00

Chrudim Church Type of 1971

Photo. & Engr.

1992, Aug. 28 ***Perf. 11½x11***
2870 A629 50h multicolored .20 .20

Postal Bank — A1045a

Photo. & Engr.

1992, Aug. 28 ***Perf. 11½x12***
2870A A1045a 20k multicolored 5.00 1.10

Antonius Bernolak, Georgius Fandly — A1046

Photo. & Engr.

1992, Oct. 6 ***Perf. 12x11½***
2871 A1046 5k multicolored 1.50 .50

Slovakian Educational Society, bicent.

Cesky Krumlov — A1046a

Photo. & Engr.

1992, Oct. 19 ***Perf. 11½x12***
2871A A1046a 3k brick red & brn .35 .20

See No. 2890.

Painting Type of 1967

6k, Old Man on a Raft, by Koloman Sokol. 7k, Still Life of Grapes and Raisins, by Georges Braque, horiz. 8k, Abandoned Corset, by Toyen.

Perf. 11½x12, 12x11½

1992, Nov. 2 **Engr.**

2872	A565	6k multicolored	1.00	.30
2873	A565	7k multicolored	2.00	.40
2874	A565	8k multicolored	2.00	.45
		Nos. 2872-2874 (3)	5.00	1.15

Christmas — A1047

Photo. & Engr.

1992, Nov. 9 ***Perf. 12x11½***
2875 A1047 2k multicolored .40 .20

Jindra Schmidt (1897-1984), Graphic Artist and Engraver — A1048

Photo. & Engr.

1992, Dec. 18 ***Perf. 11½x12***
2876 A1048 2k multicolored .40 .20

Stamp Day.

On January 1, 1993, Czechoslovakia split into Czech Republic and Slovakia. Czech Republic listings continue here. Slovakia can be found in Volume 5.

CZECH REPUBLIC

AREA — 30,449 sq. mi.
POP. — 10,280,513 (1999 est.)

Natl. Arms A1049

Photo. & Engr.

1993, Jan. 20 ***Perf. 11***
2877 A1049 3k multicolored .30 .20

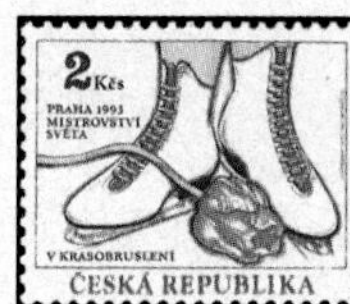

1993 World Figure Skating Championships, Prague A1050

1993, Feb. 25 ***Perf. 11½x11***
2878 A1050 2k multicolored .20 .20

Havel Type of 1990 Inscribed "Ceska Republika"

Photo. & Engr.

1993, Mar. 2 ***Perf. 12x11½***
2879 A1000 2k vio, vio brn & blue .20 .20

St. John Nepomuk, Patron Saint of Czechs, 600th Death Anniv. — A1051

1993, Mar. 11
2880 A1051 8k multicolored .75 .35

See Germany No. 1776; Slovakia No. 158.

Holy Hunger, by Mikulas Medek — A1052

1993, Mar. 11 ***Perf. 11½***
2881 A1052 14k multicolored 5.00 3.00

Europa.

Sacred Heart Church, Prague A1053

1993, Mar. 30 **Engr.** ***Perf. 11½***
2882 A1053 5k multicolored .50 .35

Brevnov Monastery, 1000th Anniv. — A1054

Litho. & Engr.

1993, Apr. 12 ***Perf. 12x11½***
2883 A1054 4k multicolored .35 .20

1993 Intl. Junior Weight Lifting Championships, Cheb — A1055

Photo. & Engr.

1993, May 12 ***Perf. 11½***
2884 A1055 6k multicolored .50 .30

Clock Tower and Church, Brno — A1056

1993, June 16 Engr. ***Perf. 12x11½***
2885 A1056 8k multicolored .75 .40

Brno, 750th anniv.

Arrival of St. Cyril and St. Methodius, 1130th Anniv. — A1057

1993, June 22 Photo. & Engr.
2886 A1057 8k multicolored .65 .40

See Slovakia No. 167.

Souvenir Sheet

State Arms — A1058

1993, June 22 ***Perf. 11½***
2887 A1058 8k Sheet of 2 1.40 1.00

Architecture Type of 1992 Inscribed "Ceska Republika" and

A1059

Cities: 1k, Ceske Budejovice. 2k, Usti Nad Labem. #2890, like #2871A. #2890A, Brno. 5k, Plzen. 6k, Slany. 7k, Ostrava. 8k, Olomouc. 10k, Hradec Kralove. 20k, Prague. 50k, Opava.

Perf. 12x11½, 11½x12

1993-94 Photo. & Engr.

2888	A1059	1k dp cl & org	.20	.20
2889	A1059	2k red vio & bl	.20	.20
2890	A1046a	3k gray bl & red	.30	.20
		Complete booklet, 5 #2890	1.40	
2890A	A1059	3k dk bl & red	.25	.20
		Complete booklet, 5 #2890A	1.25	
2891	A1059	5k bluish green & brn	.40	.25
2891A	A1059	6k grn & org yel	.55	.30
2891B	A1059	7k blk brn & grn	.60	.30
2892	A1059	8k dp vio & yel	.60	.30
2893	A1059	10k olive gray & red	.75	.40
2894	A1059	20k red & blue	1.50	.75
2895	A1059	50k brn & grn	3.25	1.75
		Nos. 2888-2895 (11)	8.60	4.85

Issued: No. 2890A, 3/30/94; 6k, 10/1/94; 7k, 11/23/94; others, 7/1/93. This is an expanding set. Numbers may change.

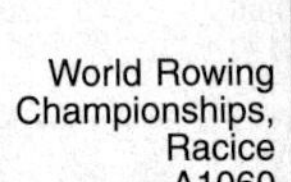

World Rowing Championships, Racice A1060

Photo. & Engr.

1993, Aug. 18 ***Perf. 11½***
2901 A1060 3k multicolored .30 .20

A1061

Trees — A1062

Famous men: 2k, August Sedlacek (1843-1926), historian. 3k, Eduard Cech (1893-1960), mathematician.

1993, Aug. 26 ***Perf. 12x11½***
2902 A1061 2k multicolored .25 .20
2903 A1061 3k multicolored .30 .20

1993, Oct. 26 ***Perf. 11½***
2904 A1062 5k Quercus robur .55 .30
2905 A1062 7k Carpinus betulus .75 .40
2906 A1062 9k Pinus silvestris 1.00 .50
Nos. 2904-2906 (3) 2.30 1.20

Christmas — A1063

A1064

Photo. & Engr.

1993, Nov. 8 ***Perf. 11½***
2907 A1063 2k multicolored .20 .20

Art Type of 1967 Inscribed "CESKA REPUBLIKA"

Paintings: 9k, Strahovska Madonna, by "Bohemian Master" in the year 1350. 11k, Composition, by Miro, horiz. 14k, Field of Green, by Van Gogh, horiz.

1993 Engr. ***Perf. 11½x12***
2908 A565 9k multicolored .55 .30

Perf. 12x11½
2909 A565 11k multicolored 1.00 .50
2910 A565 14k multicolored 1.25 .65
Nos. 2908-2910 (3) 2.80 1.45

Issued: 11k, 14k, Nov. 8; 9k, Dec. 15.

Photo. & Engr.

1994, Jan. 19 ***Perf. 11½***
2911 A1064 2k multicolored .20 .20

Intl. Year of the Family.

Jan Kubelik (1880-1940), Composer A1065

Photo. & Engr.

1994, Jan. 19 ***Perf. 11½***
2912 A1065 3k multicolored .25 .20

UNESCO — A1065a

Designs: 2k, Voltaire (1694-1778), philosopher. 6k, Georgius Agricola (1494-1555), mineralogist, humanist.

1994, Feb. 2 ***Perf. 12x11½***
2913 A1065a 2k multicolored .20 .20
2914 A1065a 6k multicolored .50 .25

A1066

A1067

Photo. & Engr.

1994, Feb. 2 ***Perf. 11½***
2915 A1066 5k multicolored .40 .20

1994 Winter Olympics, Lillehammer.

Photo. & Engr.

1994, May 4 ***Perf. 11½***

Europa (Marco Polo &): #2916, Stylized animals, Chinese woman. #2917, Stylized animals.

2916 A1067 14k multicolored 1.50 1.25
2917 A1067 14k multicolored 1.50 1.25
a. Pair, #2916-2917 3.00 2.50

A1068

A1070

Architectural Sights — A1069

1994, May 18
2918 A1068 5k Eduard Benes .40 .20

1994, May 18

UNESCO: 8k, Houses at the square, Telc. 9k, Cubist house designed by Chochol, Prague.

2919 A1069 8k multicolored .65 .30
2920 A1069 9k multicolored .75 .35

Photo. & Engr.

1994, June 1 ***Perf. 11½***
2921 A1070 2k Children's Day .20 .20

Dinosaurs — A1071

Perf. 11½x11, 11x11½

1994, June 1 Litho.
2922 A1071 2k Stegosaurus .75 .20
2923 A1071 3k Apatosaurus 1.00 .20
2924 A1071 5k Tarbosaurus, vert. 1.25 .25
Nos. 2922-2924 (3) 3.00 .65

A1072

A1073

Photo. & Engr.

1994, June 1 ***Perf. 11½x11***
2925 A1072 8k multicolored .75 .40

1994 World Cup Soccer Championships, US.

1994, June 15 ***Perf. 11x11½***
2926 A1073 2k multicolored .20 .20

12th Pan-Sokol Rally, Prague.

Intl. Olympic Committee, Cent. — A1074

1994, June 15
2927 A1074 7k multicolored .65 .30

UPU, 120th Anniv. A1075

1994, Aug. 3 Engr. ***Perf. 11½***
2928 A1075 11k multicolored 1.25 .65

Songbirds — A1076

Designs: 3k, Saxicola torquata. 5k, Carpodacus erythrinus. 14k, Luscinia svecica.

Photo. & Engr.

1994, Aug. 24 ***Perf. 11x11½***
2929 A1076 3k multicolored .30 .20
2930 A1076 5k multicolored .55 .30
2931 A1076 14k multicolored 1.60 .80
Nos. 2929-2931 (3) 2.45 1.30

Historic Race Cars — A1077

Photo. & Engr.

1994, Oct. 5 *Perf. 11½*

2932 A1077 2k 1900 NW .25 .20
2933 A1077 3k 1908 L&K .35 .20
Complete booklet, 5 #2933 1.60
2934 A1077 9k 1912 Praga 1.00 .50
Nos. 2932-2934 (3) 1.60 .90

Christmas — A1078

Photo. & Engr.

1994, Nov. 9 *Perf. 11½*

2935 A1078 2k multicolored .25 .20

Art Type of 1967 Inscribed "CESKA REPUBLIKA"

Engraving or paintings: 7k, Stary Posetilec A Zena, by Lucas Van Leyden. 10k, Moulin Rouge, by Henri de Toulouse-Lautrec. 14k, St. Vitus Madonna, St. Vitus Cathedral, Prague.

1994, Nov. 9 Engr. *Perf. 12*

2936 A565 7k multicolored .75 .40
2937 A565 10k multicolored 1.00 .50
2938 A565 14k multicolored 1.40 .70
Nos. 2936-2938 (3) 3.15 1.60

Nos. 2936-2938 printed in sheets of 4.

World Tourism Organization, 20th Anniv. A1079

Czech Stamp Production A1080

Photo. & Engr.

1995, Jan. 2 *Perf. 11x12*

2939 A1079 8k green blue & red .75 .40

1995, Jan. 20

2940 A1080 3k Design N1 .30 .20

Czech Republic & European Union Association Agreement A1081

1995, Jan. 20 Litho. *Perf. 13½x12½*

2941 A1081 8k multicolored .75 .40

Famous Men A1082

Designs: 2k, Johannes Marcus Marci (1595-1667). 5k, Ferdinand Peroutka (1895-1978). 7k, Premysl Pitter (1895-1976).

Photo. & Engr.

1995, Feb. 1 *Perf. 12x11*

2942 A1082 2k multicolored .20 .20
2943 A1082 5k multicolored .45 .25
2944 A1082 7k multicolored .65 .30
Nos. 2942-2944 (3) 1.30 .75

Theater Personalities — A1083

Designs: No. 2945, Jiri Voskovec (1905-81). No. 2946, Jan Werich (1905-80). No. 2947, Jaroslav Jezek (1906-42). 22k, Caricatures of Voskovec, Werich, and Jezek with piano.

1995 Photo. & Engr. *Perf. 12x11*

2945 A1083 3k multicolored .30 .20
Complete booklet, 3 #2945 .90
2946 A1083 3k multicolored .30 .20
Complete booklet, 3 #2946 .90
2947 A1083 3k multicolored .30 .20
Complete booklet, 3 #2947 .90
a. Strip of 3, #2945-2947 .90 .45
Complete booklet, 2 #2947a 1.80
Nos. 2945-2947 (3) .90 .60

Souvenir Sheet

Photo.

Perf. 12

2947B A1083 22k yellow & black 2.00 1.00

Issued: 3k, 3/15; 22k, 9/20.

Havel Type of 1990 Inscribed "Ceska Republika"

Photo. & Engr.

1995, Mar. 22 *Perf. 12x11½*

2948 A1000 3.60k bl, vio & mag .30 .20
Complete booklet, 5 #2948 1.50

Rural Architecture A1084

1995, Mar. 22 *Perf. 11½*

2949 A1084 40h shown .20 .20
2950 A1084 60h Homes, diff. .20 .20

European Nature Conservation Year — A1085

1995, Apr. 12

2951 A1085 3k Bombus terrestris .20 .20
Complete booklet, 5 #2951 1.00
2952 A1085 5k Mantis religiosa .40 .20
Complete booklet, 5 #2952 2.00
2953 A1085 6k Calopteryx splendens .40 .25
Complete booklet, 5 #2953 2.25
Nos. 2951-2953 (3) 1.00 .65

Peace & Freedom A1086

Photo. & Engr.

1995, May 3 *Perf. 11½*

2954 A1086 9k Rose, profiles .70 .30
2955 A1086 14k Butterfly, profiles 1.10 .40

Europa.

Natural Beauties in Czech Republic A1087

Designs: 8k, "Stone Organ" scenic mountain. 9k, Largest sandstone bridge in Europe.

Photo. & Engr.

1995, May 3 *Perf. 11½*

2956 A1087 8k multicolored .65 .30
2957 A1087 9k multicolored .70 .35

Children's Day — A1088

Photo. & Engr.

1995, June 1 *Perf. 11½*

2958 A1088 3.60k multicolored .35 .20

First Train from Vienna to Prague, 150th Anniv. A1089

3k, Chocen Tunnel. 9.60k, Entering Prague.

1995, June 21

2959 A1089 3k multicolored .25 .20
Complete booklet, 5 #2959 1.25
2960 A1089 9.60k multicolored .85 .40

World Wrestling Championships, Prague A1090

Photo. & Engr.

1995, Sept. 6 *Perf. 11½*

2961 A1090 3k multicolored .30 .20

Cartoon Characters A1091

Designs: 3k, Man playing violin, woman washing, by Vladimir Rencin. 3.60k, Angel, naked man, by Vladimir Jiranek. 5k, Circus trainer holding ring for champagne cork to pop through, by Jiri Sliva.

1995, Sept. 6

2962 A1091 3k multicolored .30 .20
Complete booklet, 5 #2962 1.50
2963 A1091 3.60k multicolored .35 .20
Complete booklet, 5 #2963 1.75
2964 A1091 5k multicolored .45 .25
Complete booklet, 5 #2964 2.25
Nos. 2962-2964 (3) 1.10 .65

A1092 A1093

1995, Sept. 20 Litho. *Perf. 13½x13*

2965 A1092 3k multicolored .35 .20

SOS Children's Villages, 25th anniv.

Photo. & Engr.

1995-97 *Perf. 12x11½*

Designs: 2.40k, Gothic. 3k, Secession. 3.60k, Romance. 4k, Classic portal; 4.60k, Rococo. 9.60k, Renaissance Portal. 12.60k, Cubist. 14k, Baroque.

2966 A1093 2.40k red & green .20 .20
2967 A1093 3k grn & bl .25 .20
2967A A1093 3.60k pur & grn .35 .20
2968 A1093 4k blue & red .35 .20
Complete booklet, 5 #2967A 2.25
2968A A1093 4.60k multicolored .35 .20
2969 A1093 9.60k blue & red .70 .45
2969A A1093 12.60k red brn & bl .70 .45
2970 A1093 14k grn & pur 1.10 .60
Nos. 2966-2970 (8) 4.00 2.50

Issued: 9.60k, 9/27; 2.40k, 14k, 10/11; 3k, 3.60k, 10/25; 4k, 6/12/96; 4.60k, 3/26/97; 12.60k, 6/25/97.

UN, 50th Anniv. A1094

1995, Oct. 11 Litho. *Perf. 12x11½*

2971 A1094 14k multicolored 1.60 .80

Wilhelm Röntgen (1845-1923), Discovery of the X-Ray, Cent. — A1095

1995, Oct. 11 Photo. & Engr.

2972 A1095 6k blk, buff & bl vio .75 .35

Art Type of 1967 Inscribed "CESKA REPUBLIKA"

Designs: 6k, Parisiene, by Ludek Marold. 9k, Vase of Flowers, by J.K. Hirschely. 14k, Portrait of J. Malinsky, by Antoinín Machek.

1995, Nov. 8 *Perf. 12*

2973 A565 6k multicolored .75 .35
2974 A565 9k multicolored 1.00 .50
2975 A565 14k multicolored 1.60 .80
Nos. 2973-2975 (3) 3.35 1.65

Nos. 2973-2975 printed in sheets of 4.

Christmas — A1096

1995, Nov. 8 *Perf. 11½*

2976 A1096 3k multicolored .35 .20
Complete booklet, 3 #2976 1.05

Czech Philharmonic Orchestra, Cent. — A1097

Photo. & Engr.

1996, Jan. 2 *Perf. 12x11½*

2977 A1097 3.60k multicolored .40 .20

Tradition of Czech Stamp Production — A1098

Photo. & Engr.

1996, Jan. 20 *Perf. 11½x12*

2978 A1098 3.60k Design A5 of 1920 .40 .20

Vera Mencikova (1906-44), Chess Player — A1099

Photo. & Engr.

1996, Feb. 14 *Perf. 12x11½*
2979 A1099 6k multicolored .65 .30

Easter — A1100

1996, Mar. 13 *Perf. 11½x12*
2980 A1100 3k multicolored .35 .20
Complete booklet, 5 #2980 1.75

Josef Sudek (1896-1976), Photographer A1101

Photo. & Engr.

1996, Mar. 13 *Perf. 11*
2981 A1101 9.60k multicolored 1.10 .55

Rulers from House of Luxembourg — A1102

Designs: a, John of Luxembourg (1296-1346). b, Charles IV (1316-78). c, Wenceslas IV. (1361-1419). d, Sigismund (1368-1437).

1996, Mar. 27 **Engr.** *Perf. 11½*
2982 A1102 14k Sheet of 4, #a.-d. + label 6.00 3.00

Jiri Guth-Jurkovsky, Participant in First Modern Olympic Games, Athens A1103

Photo. & Engr.

1996, Mar. 27 *Perf. 11½*
2983 A1103 9.60k multicolored 1.10 .55

Modern Olympic Games, cent.

World Wildlife Fund — A1104

Ema Destinnova (1878-1930), Singer — A1105

Designs: a, 3.60k, Eliomys quercinus. b, 5k, Dryomys nitedula. c, 6k, Spermophilus citellus. d, 8k, Sicista betulina.

Photo. & Engr.

1996, Apr. 24 *Perf. 11½x12*
2984 A1104 Block of 4, #a.-d. 2.50 2.00

Issued in sheets of 8 stamps.

1996, May 2 *Perf. 11½*
2985 A1105 8k multicolored .75 .50

Europa.

A1106

A1107

Photo. & Engr.

1996, May 15 *Perf. 11x11½*
2986 A1106 12k multicolored 1.40 .65

Jean Gaspart Deburau (1796-1846), mime.

1996, May 29
2987 A1107 3k multicolored .35 .20

1996 Summmer Olympic Games, Atlanta.

Intl. Children's Day — A1108

Photo. & Engr.

1996, May 29 *Perf. 11½*
2988 A1108 3k multicolored .35 .20

Architectural Sites — A1109

UNESCO: 8k, St. Nepomuk Church, Zelena Hora. 9k, Loretta Tower, Prague.

1996, June 26 **Engr.** *Perf. 11½*
2989 A1109 8k multicolored .90 .45
2990 A1109 9k multicolored 1.00 .50

See Nos. 3056-3057.

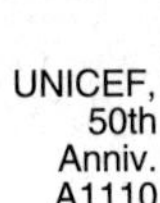

UNICEF, 50th Anniv. A1110

Photo. & Engr.

1996, Sept. 11 *Perf. 12x11*
2991 A1110 3k multicolored .35 .20

Horses

A1111 A1112

Photo. & Engr.

1996, Sept. 25 *Perf. 11x11½*
2992 A1111 3k multicolored .35 .20
2993 A1112 3k multicolored .35 .20
a. Pair, #2992-2993 .70 .40
Complete booklet, 3 #2992, 2 #2993 1.75
Complete booklet, 2 #2992, 3 #2993 1.75

Souvenir Sheet

Vaclav Havel, 60th Birthday — A1113

Illustration reduced.

1996, Oct. 5
2994 A1113 Sheet of 2 1.35 .65
a. 6k red & blue .65 .30

Art Type of 1967 Inscribed "CESKA REPUBLICA"

The Baroque Chair, by Endre Nemes (1909-85).

1996, Oct. 5 **Engr.** *Perf. 11½*
2995 A565 20k multicolored 2.25 1.10

See Slovakia No. 255; Sweden No. 2199.

Tycho Brahe (1546-1601), Astronomer — A1114

Photo. & Engr.

1996, Oct. 9 *Perf. 11½x11*
2996 A1114 5k multicolored .55 .30

Biplanes A1115

1996, Oct. 9
2997 A1115 7k Letov S1 (1920) .80 .40
2998 A1115 8k Aero A11 (1925) .90 .45
2999 A1115 10k Avia BH21 (1925) 1.10 .55
Nos. 2997-2999 (3) 2.80 1.40

Christmas A1116

Photo. & Engr.

1996, Nov. 13 *Perf. 11½*
3000 A1116 3k multicolored .35 .20
Complete booklet, 5 #3000 2.50

Art Type of 1967 Inscribed "CESKA REPUBLICA"

Designs: 9k, Garden of Eden, by Josef Váchal (1884-1969), horiz. 11k, Breakfast, by Georg Flegel (1566-1638).

1996, Nov. 13 **Engr.** *Perf. 11½*
3001 A565 9k multicolored .95 .45
3002 A565 11k multicolored 1.10 .60

Czech Stamp Production — A1117

Photo. & Engr.

1997, Jan. 20 *Perf. 11½x12*
3003 A1117 3.60k #68, bl & red .40 .25

Easter — A1118

Flowers — A1119

Photo. & Engr.

1997, Mar. 12 *Perf. 11½*
3004 A1118 3k multicolored .35 .20
Complete booklet, 5 #3004 1.75

1997, Mar. 12 *Perf. 11x11½*

3.60k, Erythronium dens-canis. 4k, Calla palustris. 5k, Cypripedium calceolus. 8k, Iris pumila.

3005 A1119 3.60k multicolored .40 .20
Complete booklet, 5 #3005 2.00
3006 A1119 4k multicolored .45 .25
Complete booklet, 5 #3006 2.25
3007 A1119 5k multicolored .55 .30
Complete booklet, 5 #3007 2.75
3008 A1119 8k multicolored .90 .45
Complete booklet, 5 #3008 4.50
Nos. 3005-3008 (4) 2.30 1.20

A1120

A1121

Jewish Monuments in Prague: 8k, Altneuschul Synagogue. 10k, Tombstone of Rabbi Judah Loew MaHaRal.

1997, Apr. 30 *Perf. 11½*
3009 A1120 8k multicolored .90 .45
3010 A1120 10k multicolored 1.10 .55
a. Sheet, 4 each #3009-3010 8.00 4.00

See Israel Nos. 1302-1303.

1997, Mar. 26 **Litho.** *Perf. 13x13½*

Greetings stamp.

3011 A1121 4k Girl with cats .45 .25

A1122

A1123

1997, Apr. 23 Engr. *Perf. 11½*
3012 A1122 7k deep violet .75 .40

St. Adalbert (956-97). See Germany No. 1964, Hungary No. 3569, Poland No. 3337, Vatican City No. 1040.

Photo. & Engr.
1997, Apr. 30 *Perf. 11½x12*

Europa (Stories and Legends): No. 3013, Queen, knight with sword, lion, snakes. No. 3014, Man riding in chariot drawn by chickens, King looking through window.

3013 A1123 8k multicolored .75 .35
3014 A1123 8k multicolored .75 .35

Souvenir Sheet

Collections of Rudolf II (1522-1612), Prague Exhibition A1124

Designs: a, 6k, Musical instruments, flowers, face of bearded man. b, 8k, Rudolf II wearing laurel wreath, holding rose, Muses. c, 10k, Rudolf II, skull, moth's wings, tree, flowers, leaves, fruit.

1997, May 14 Engr. *Perf. 12*
3015 A1124 Sheet of 3, #a.-c. 2.25 1.10

Intl. Children's Day — A1125

Photo. & Engr.
1997, May 28 *Perf. 11½*
3016 A1125 4.60k multicolored .45 .25

Frantisek Krizik (1847-1941), Electrical Engineer, Inventor of Arc Lamp — A1126

Photo. & Engr.
1997, June 25 *Perf. 12x11½*
3017 A1126 6k multicolored .35 .20

European Swimming & Diving Championships, Prague — A1127

Photo. & Engr.
1997, Aug. 27 *Perf. 11½*
3018 A1127 11k multicolored 1.75 .85

"The Good Soldier Schweik," by Jaroslav Hasek, 110th Anniv. — A1128

4k, Mrs. Müller, Schweik in wheelchair. 4.60k, Lt. Lukás, Col. Kraus von Zillergut, dog. 6k, Schweik smoking pipe, winter scene.

Photo. & Engr.
1997, Sept. 10 *Perf. 12x11½*
3019 A1128 4k multicolored .35 .20
a. Booklet pane of 8 + 4 labels 2.75
Complete booklet, #3019a 2.75
3020 A1128 4.60k multicolored .45 .20
a. Booklet pane of 8 + 4 labels 3.75
Complete booklet, #3020a 3.75
3021 A1128 6k multicolored .55 .30
a. Booklet pane of 8 + 4 labels 4.50
Complete booklet, #3021a 4.50
Nos. 3019-3021 (3) 1.35 .70

Praga 1998, Intl. Stamp Exhibition — A1129

#3022, Lesser Town, Prague Castle. #3023, Old Town, bridges over Vltava River.

Photo. & Engr.
1997, Sept. 24 *Perf. 11½*
3022 A1129 15k multicolored 1.40 .70
3023 A1129 15k multicolored 1.40 .70
a. Souvenir sheet, #3022-3023 + 2 labels 2.80 1.40

Historic Service Vehicles A1130

Designs: 4k, Postal bus, Prague. 4.60k, Sentinel truck, Skoda. 8k, Fire truck, Tatra.

1997, Oct. 8 *Perf. 12x11½*
3024 A1130 4k multicolored .40 .20
3025 A1130 4.60k multicolored .45 .25
3026 A1130 8k multicolored .80 .40
Complete booklet, 5 #3026 4.00
Nos. 3024-3026 (3) 1.65 .85

A1131

A1132

Photo. & Engr.
1997, Nov. 12 *Perf. 11½*
3027 A1131 4k multicolored .40 .20
Complete booklet, 5 #3027 2.00

Christmas.

Art Type of 1967 Inscribed "CESKA REPUBLIKA"

7k, Landscape with Chateau in Chantilly, by Antonín Chittussi (1847-91). 12k, The Prophets Came Out of the Desert, by Frantisek Bílek (1872-1941). 1 6k, Parisian Antiquarians, by T. F. Simon (1877-1942).

1997, Nov. 12 Engr. *Perf. 12*
3028 A565 7k multi, horiz. .65 .35
3029 A565 12k multi 1.10 .55
3030 A565 16k multi 1.50 .75
Nos. 3028-3030 (3) 3.25 1.65

1998, Jan. 20 Litho. *Perf. 11½x12*
3031 A1132 7k multicolored .60 .30

1998 Winter Olympic Games, Nagano.

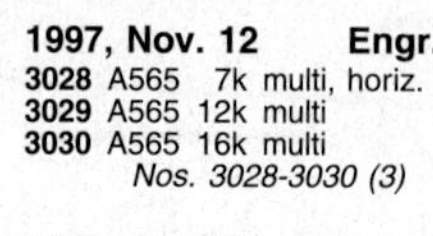
Tradition of Czech Stamp Production — A1133

Photo. & Engr.
1998, Jan. 20 *Perf. 12x11½*
3032 A1133 12.60k Type A8 1.10 .55
a. Booklet pane of 8 + 4 labels 8.75
Complete booklet, #3032a 8.75

Pres. Václav Havel A1134

Love A1135

1998, Jan. 22
3033 A1134 4.60k dark grn & red .40 .20

See No. 3114.

1998, Feb. 4 *Perf. 11½*
3034 A1135 4k multicolored .35 .20
Complete booklet, #3034 1.75

Skibob World Championship, Spindleruv Mlyn — A1136

1998, Feb. 25
3035 A1136 8k multicolored .70 .35

Prague Philatelic Exhibition Type of 1938
Souvenir Sheet

1998, Feb. 25 Engr. *Perf. 12x11½*
3036 A87 Sheet of 2 5.25 2.60
a. 30k like #251a 2.60 1.25

Prague '98, Intl. Philatelic Exhibition.

Easter — A1137

Photo. & Engr.
1998, Mar. 25 *Perf. 11x11½*
3037 A1137 4k multicolored .40 .20

Ondrejov Observatory, Cent. — A1138

1998, Mar. 25 *Perf. 12x11½*
3038 A1138 4.60k multicolored .45 .20

Czech Ice Hockey Team, Gold Medalists at Nagano Winter Olympic Games — A1139

1998, Apr. 1 Litho. *Perf. 11½x12*
3039 A1139 23k Dominik Hasek 2.20 1.10

No. 3039 was issued in a sheet with two labels.

Charles University and New Town, Prague, 650th Anniv. — A1140

Designs: a, 15k, Hands forming arch, University seal. b, 22k, Charles IV (1316-78), Holy Roman Emperor, King of Bohemia. c, 23k, Groin vault, St. Vitus Cathedral, Prague.

1998, Apr. 1 Engr. *Perf. 12*
3040 A1140 Sheet of 3, #a.-c. 5.25 2.75

World Book and Copyright Day — A1141

1998, Apr. 23 Litho. *Perf. 12x11½*
3041 A1141 10k multicolored .90 .45

Nature Conservation A1142

1998, Apr. 23 *Perf. 13x13½*
3042 A1142 4.60k Perdix perdix .40 .20
3043 A1142 4.60k Lyrurus tetrix .40 .20
a. Pair, #3042-3043 .80 .40
3044 A1142 8k Cervus elaphus .70 .35
3045 A1142 8k Alces alces .70 .35
a. Pair, #3044-3045 1.40 .70
Nos. 3042-3045 (4) 2.20 1.10

Natl. Festivals and Holidays A1143

Europa: 11k, King's Ride. 15k, Wearing masks for Carnival.

Litho. & Engr.
1998, May 5 *Perf. 11½*
3046 A1143 11k multicolored .90 .75
3047 A1143 15k multicolored 1.10 1.00

Intl. Children's Day — A1144

Designs: 4k, Two satyr musicians. 4.60k, Character riding on fish.

Photo. & Engr.

1998, May 27 *Perf. 11½*

3048 A1144 4k multicolored .35 .20
a. Booklet of 6 +4 labels 2.10
Complete booklet, #3048a 2.10
3049 A1144 4.60k multicolored .40 .20
a. Booklet of 6 + 4 labels 2.50
Complete booklet, #3049a 2.50

Famous Men — A1145

Designs: 4k, Frantisek Kmoch (1848-1912), bandleader, composer. 4.60k, Frantisek Palacky (1798-1876), historian, politician. 6k, Rafael Kubelík (1914-96), composer, conductor.

1998, May 27 *Perf. 11½x12*

3050 A1145 4k multicolored .35 .20
3051 A1145 4.60k multicolored .40 .20
3052 A1145 6k multicolored .55 .25
Nos. 3050-3052 (3) 1.30 .65

Revolt of 1848, 150th Anniv. A1146

1998, May 27 *Perf. 12x11½*

3053 A1146 15k multicolored 1.25 .65

Art Type of 1967 Inscribed "CESKA REPUBLIKA"

Praga 1998 Intl. Stamp Exhibition, works of art: 22k, Amorfa Dvoubarevna Fuga, by Frantisek Kupka (1871-1957), horiz. 23k, Escape, by Paul Gauguin (1848-1903), horiz.

1998, June 17 **Engr.** *Perf. 12*

3054 A565 22k multicolored 2.00 1.00
3055 A565 23k multicolored 2.00 1.00

Nos. 3054-3055 printed in sheets of 4.

UNESCO World Heritage Sites Type of 1996

8k, St. Barbara Cathedral, Kutná Hora, horiz. 11k, The Chateau of Valtice, horiz.

1998, Oct. 7 **Engr.** *Perf. 11½x12*

3056 A1109 8k multicolored .80 .40
3057 A1109 11k multicolored 1.10 .55

Czechoslovak Republic, 80th Anniv. — A1147

Designs based on World War I recruitment posters by Vojtech Preissig (1873-1944): 4.60k, Soldiers holding flags, guns. 5k, Three soldiers marching. 12.60k, Flags waving from city buildings.

Perf. 11½x11¾

1998, Oct. 28 **Litho. & Engr.**

3058 A1147 4.60k multicolored .40 .20
3059 A1147 5k multicolored .45 .25
3060 A1147 12.60k multicolored 1.10 .55
Nos. 3058-3060 (3) 1.95 1.00

No. 3060 was issued in sheets of 6+2 labels.

Christmas A1148

Designs: 4k, People following star. 6k, Angel blowing trumpet over town, vert.

Photo. & Engr.

1998, Nov. 18 *Perf. 11½*

3061 A1148 4k multicolored .40 .20
Complete booklet, 5 #3061 2.00
3062 A1148 6k multicolored .55 .25
Complete booklet, 5 #3062 2.75

Signs of the Zodiac — A1149

1998-2000 *Perf. 12x11½*

3063 A1149 1k Capricorn .20 .20
3064 A1149 10k Aquarius .95 .45
3065 A1149 9k Libra .75 .40
3066 A1149 8k Cancer .65 .30
3067 A1149 20k Sagittarius 1.60 .80

Photo. & Engr.

Perf. 11¾x11¼

3068 A1149 5k Taurus .40 .20
Booklet, 5 #3068 2.00
3069 A1149 5.40k Scorpio .40 .20
Booklet, 5 #3069 2.00
3070 A1149 2k Virgo .20 .20
3071 A1149 40h Pisces .20 .20
3072 A1149 12k Leo .85 .40
3073 A1149 17k Gemini 1.25 .65
3074 A1149 26k Aries 1.90 .95
Nos. 3063-3074 (12) 9.35 4.95

Issued: 1k, 10k, 11/18; 9k, 5/5/99; 8k, 20k, 9/8/99; 5k, 5.40k, 12/8/99; 2k, 5/9/00. 40h, 1/20/01. 12k, 2/21/01. 17k, 9/1/02. 26k, 2/12/03.

Art Type of 1967 Inscribed "CESKA REPUBLIKA"

15k, Painting from the Greater Cycle, 1902, by Jan Preisler (1872-1918), horiz. 16k, Spinner, by Josef Navrátil (1798-1865).

1998, Dec. 9 *Perf. 12*

3075 A565 15k multicolored 1.40 .70
3076 A565 16k multicolored 1.50 .75

A1150

A1151

Photo. & Engr.

1999, Jan. 20 *Perf. 11½x11¾*

3077 A1150 4.60k #164 .40 .20
a. Booklet pane of 8 + 4 labels 3.25
Complete booklet, #3077a 3.25

Tradition of Czech stamp production.

Photo. & Engr.

1999, Feb. 17 *Perf. 11½*

Domestic cats.

3078 A1151 4.60k shown .40 .20
Complete booklet, 5 #3078 2.00
3079 A1151 5k Adult, kitten .45 .25
Complete booklet, 5 #3079 2.25
3080 A1151 7k Two cats .60 .30
Complete booklet, 5 #3080 3.00
Nos. 3078-3080 (3) 1.45 .75

Easter — A1152

A1153

Photo. & Engr.

1999, Mar. 10 *Perf. 11¼x11½*

3081 A1152 3k multicolored .25 .20

Perf. 12¾x13¼

1999, Mar. 10 **Litho.**

Protected birds: No. 3082, Merops apiaster. No. 3083, Upupa epops.
Protected butterflies: No. 3084, Catocala electa. No. 3085, Euphydryas maturna.

3082 A1153 4.60k multicolored .40 .20
3083 A1153 4.60k multicolored .40 .20
a. Pair, #3082-3083 .80 .40
Complete booklet, 3 #3082, 2 #3083 2.00
3084 A1153 5k multicolored .45 .20
3085 A1153 5k multicolored .45 .20
a. Pair, #3084-3085 .90 .40
Complete booklet, 3 #3084, 2 #3085 2.25

Nature conservation.

Czech Republic's Entry Into NATO — A1154

Photo. & Engr.

1999, Mar. 12 *Perf. 12x11½*

3086 A1154 4.60k multicolored .40 .20

Council of Europe, 50th Anniv. A1155

Photo. & Engr.

1999, Apr. 14 *Perf. 11¾x11¼*

3087 A1155 7k multicolored .55 .25

Natl. Olympic Committee, Cent. — A1156

Design: Josef Rössler-Orovsky (1869-1933), founder of Czech Olympic Committee.

1999, Apr. 14 *Perf. 11¼x11¾*

3088 A1156 9k multicolored .75 .35

Europa A1157

Natl. Parks: 11k, Sumava. 17k, Podyji.

1999, May 5 *Perf. 11¾x11¼*

3089 A1157 11k multicolored .75 .45
3090 A1157 17k multicolored 1.25 .70

Ferda the Ant, Pytlik the Beetle and Ladybird A1158

Photo. & Engr.

1999, May 26 *Perf. 11½x11¼*

3091 A1158 4.60k multicolored .40 .20

Bridges A1159

1999, May 26 **Engr.** *Perf. 11¾*

3092 A1159 8k Stádlec, vert. .70 .35
3093 A1159 11k Cernvír .90 .45

Souvenir Sheet

Paleontologist Joachim Barrande (1799-1883) and Trilobite Fossils — A1160

a, 13k, Barrande, fossils. b, 31k, Delphon forbesi, Ophioceras simplex, Carolicrinus barrandei.

1999, June 23 **Engr.** *Perf. 11¾*

3094 A1160 Sheet of 2, #a.-b. + 2 labels 3.75 1.90

Jihlava Mining Rights, 750th Anniv. A1161

Photo. & Engr.

1999, June 23 *Perf. 11¾x11¼*

3095 A1161 8k multicolored .70 .35
a. Bklt. pane of 8 + 4 labels 5.75
Complete booklet, #3095a 5.75

UPU, 125th Anniv. — A1162

Litho. & Engr.

1999, June 23 *Perf. 11¾*

3096 A1162 9k multicolored .75 .35

Issued se-tenant with two labels.

Vincenc Preissnitz (1799-1851), Hydrotherapy Advocate A1163

Photo. & Engr.

1999, Sept. 8 ***Perf. 11¼***
3097 A1163 4.60k multicolored .40 .20

UNESCO.

Carved Beehives A1164

Cartoons by Miroslav Bartak A1165

Designs: 4.60k, Woman. 5k, St. Joseph and Infant Jesus. 7k, Chimney sweep.

Photo. & Engr.

1999, Sept. 29 ***Perf. 11¼x11½***
3098 A1164 4.60k multi .35 .20
Complete booklet, 5 #3098 1.75
3099 A1164 5k multi .40 .20
Complete booklet, 5 #3099 2.00
3100 A1164 7k multi .55 .25
Complete booklet, 5 #3100 2.75
Nos. 3098-3100 (3) 1.30 .65

1999, Oct. 20

Designs: 4.60k, Doctor in clown mask, infant. 5k, Dog with pipe. 7k, Night seeping through window sill.

3101 A1165 4.60k multi .35 .20
3102 A1165 5k multi .40 .20
3103 A1165 7k multi .55 .25
Nos. 3101-3103 (3) 1.30 .65

Souvenir Sheet

Beuron Art School — A1166

Designs: a, 11k, Mater Dei, 1898. b, 13k, Pantocrator, 1911.

Litho. & Engr.

1999, Oct. 20 ***Perf. 11¾***
3104 A1166 Sheet of 2, #a.-b. 1.90 .95

Art Type of 1967 Inscribed "CESKA REPUBLIKA"

Designs: 13k, Red Orchid, by Jindrich Styrsky (1899-1942). 17k, Landscape with Marsh, by Julius Marák (1832-99). 26k, Monument, by Frantisek Hudecek (1909-90).

1999, Nov. 10 **Engr.** ***Perf. 11¾***
3105 A565 13k multi 1.00 .50
3106 A565 17k multi 1.25 .65
3107 A565 26k multi 2.00 1.00
Nos. 3105-3107 (3) 4.25 2.15

A1167 A1168

Photo. & Engr.

1999, Nov. 10 ***Perf. 11¼x11½***
3108 A1167 3k multi .25 .20

Christmas.

Photo. & Engr.

2000, Jan. 20 ***Perf. 11¼x11¾***
3109 A1168 5.40k #B151 .40 .20
a. Bklt. pane of 8 + 4 labels 3.25
Booklet, #3109a 3.25

Tradition of Czech stamp production.

Brno 2000 Philatelic Exhibition — A1169

Designs: 5k, 1593 view of Brno. 50k, St. James's Church, vert.

2000, Jan. 20 ***Perf. 11¾x11¼***
3110 A1169 5k multi .40 .20

Souvenir Sheet

Perf. 11¼x11¾
3111 A1169 50k multi 3.50 1.75

No. 3110 printed in sheets of 35 stamps and 30 labels.

Kutna Hora Royal Mining Law, 700th Anniv. — A1170

2000, Mar. 1 ***Perf. 11¼x11¾***
3112 A1170 5k multi .40 .20
a. Booklet pane of 8 + 4 labels 3.25
Booklet, #3112a 3.25

Souvenir Sheet

Pres. Thomas Garrigue Masaryk (1850-1937) — A1171

Illustration reduced.

2000, Mar. 1 **Engr.** ***Perf. 11¾***
3113 A1171 17k multi 1.25 .65

Pres. Havel Type of 1998

Photo & Engr.

2000, Mar. 1 ***Perf. 11¾x11¼***
3114 A1134 5.40k Prus bl & org brn .40 .20

Easter — A1172

Photo. & Engr.

2000, Apr. 5 ***Perf. 11¼x11½***
3115 A1172 5k multi .40 .20

Souvenir Sheet

Prague, 2000 European City of Culture — A1173

No. 3116: a, 9k, Statue of man. b, 11k, Statue of harpist. c, 17k, Statue of King Charles IV.
Illustration reduced.

Litho. & Engr.

2000, Apr. 5 ***Perf. 11¾***
3116 A1173 #a-c + 3 labels 2.75 1.40

Souvenir Sheet

Trains — A1174

No. 3117: a, 8k, Train from 1900. b, 15k, Train from 2000.
Illustration reduced.

Litho. & Engr.

2000, May 5 ***Perf. 11¾***
3117 A1174 Sheet of 2, #a-b, +3 labels 1.50 .75

Czech Personalities A1175

5k, Vítezslav Nezval (1900-58), writer. 8k, Gustav Mahler (1860-1911), composer.

Photo. & Engr.

2000, May 5 ***Perf. 11¼x11¾***
3118-3119 A1175 Set of 2 .95 .45

Europa, 2000

Common Design Type

2000, May 5 **Litho.** ***Perf. 12¾x13¼***
3120 CD17 9k multi .60 .25

Intl. Children's Year — A1176

Photo. & Engr.

2000, May 31 ***Perf. 11½x11¼***
3121 A1176 5.40k multi .40 .20
a. Booklet pane of 8 + 2 labels 3.25
Booklet, #3121a 3.25

1995 Proof of Fermat's Last Theorem by Andrew Wiles A1177

2000, May 31 ***Perf. 11¾x11¼***
3122 A1177 7k multi .50 .25

Intl. Mathematics Year.

Prague Landmarks — A1178

Designs: 9k, Charles Bridge tower. 11k, St. Nicholas's Church. 13k, Town Hall.

2000, June 28 **Engr.** ***Perf. 11¾***
3123-3125 A1178 Set of 3 2.25 1.10

Mushrooms — A1179

No. 3126, 5k: a, Geastrum pouzarii. b, Boletus satanoides.
No. 3127, 5.40k: a, Morchella pragensis. b, Verpa bohemica.

Photo. & Engr.

2000, June 28 ***Perf. 11¼x11½***

Pairs, #a-b

3126-3127 A1179 Set of 2 1.40 .70
Booklet, 3 #3126a, 2 #3126b 3.25
Booklet, 3 #3127b, 2 #3127a 3.75

Meeting of Intl. Monetary Fund and World Bank Group, Prague — A1180

2000, Aug. 30 ***Perf. 11¾x11¼***
3128 A1180 7k multi .50 .25

Ancient Olympics
A1181

2000, Aug. 30
3129 A1181 9k multi .60 .30

2000 Summer Olympics, Sydney — A1182

2000, Aug. 30
3130 A1182 13k multi .90 .45

Hunting — A1183

No. 3131: a, 5k, Falconry. b, 5k, Deer at feed trough.
No. 3132: a, 5.40k, Ducks and blind. b, 5.40k, Deer and blind.

Photo. & Engr.

2000, Oct. 4 ***Perf. 11¼x11¾***

Horiz. Pairs, #a-b

3131-3132	A1183	Set of 2	1.10	.55
		Booklet, 3 #3131a, 2 #3131b		
		Booklet, 3 #3132a, 2 #3132b		

Art Type of 1967 Inscribed "CESKA REPUBLIKA"

Designs: 13k, St. Luke the Evangelist, by Master Theodoricus. 17k, Simeon With Infant Jesus, by Petr Jan Brandl. 26k, Brunette, by Alfons Mucha.

2000, Nov. 15 **Engr.** ***Perf. 11¾***
3133-3135 A565 Set of 3 4.25 2.10

Christmas — A1184

Photo. & Engr.

2000, Nov. 15 ***Perf. 11¼x11½***
3136 A1184 5k multi .40 .20

End of Millennium
A1185

Advent of New Millennium
A1186

2000, Nov. 22
3137 A1185 9k multi .65 .30

2001, Jan. 2
3138 A1186 9k multi .65 .30

Tradition of Czech Stamp Production
A1187

2001, Jan. 20 ***Perf. 11¼x11¾***

3139	A1187 5.40k #474		.40	.20
a.	Booklet pane of 8 + 4 labels		3.25	
	Booklet, #3139a		3.25	

Jan Amos Komensky (Comenius, 1592-1670), Theologian — A1188

Photo. & Engr.

2001, Mar. 14 ***Perf. 11¼x11½***
3140 A1188 9k red & black .55 .25

Souvenir Sheet

Architecture — A1189

No. 3141: a, 13k, Church and decorations, Jakub. b, 17k, Arcade decorations, Bucovice Castle. c, 31k, Dance Hall, Prague.

2001, Mar. 28 **Engr.** ***Perf. 11¾x11½***
3141 A1189 Sheet of 3, #a-c 3.50 1.75

Easter — A1190

Photo. & Engr.

2001, Mar. 28 ***Perf. 11¼x11½***
3142 A1190 5.40k multi .35 .20

Souvenir Sheet

Allegory of Art, by Vaclav Vavrinec Reiner — A1191

Litho. & Engr.

2001, Apr. 18 ***Perf. 11¾***
3143 A1191 50k multi 3.00 1.50

Europa
A1192

Photo. & Engr.

2001, May 9 ***Perf. 11¾x11¼***
3144 A1192 9k pur & lilac .55 .35

European Men's Volleyball Championships, Ostrova — A1193

Photo. & Engr.

2001, May 9 ***Perf. 11¼x11½***
3145 A1193 12k multi .85 .40

Intl. Children's Day — A1194

Famous Men — A1195

Photo. & Engr.

2001, May 30 ***Perf. 11¼x11½***

3146	A1194 5.40k multi		.40	.20
a.	Booklet pane of 8 + 2 labels		3.25	—
	Booklet, #3146a		3.25	

2001, May 30

Designs: 5.40k, Frantisek Skroup (1801-62), composer. 16k, Frantisek Halas (1901-49), writer.

3147-3148 A1195 Set of 2 1.60 .80

Congratulations
A1196

2001, June 20

3149	A1196 5.40k multi		.35	.20
	Booklet, 5 #3149		1.75	

Dogs — A1197

No. 3150: a, West Highland terrier. b, Beagle.
No. 3151: a, German shepherd. b, Golden retriever.

Photo. & Engr.

2001, June 20 ***Perf. 11½x11¼***

3150	Pair		.70	.35
a.-b.	A1197 5.40k Any single		.35	.20
	Booklet, 3 #3150a, 2 #3150b		1.75	
	Booklet, 3 #3150b, 2 #3150a		1.75	
3151	Pair		.70	.35
a.-b.	A1197 5.40k Any single		.35	.20
	Booklet, 3 #3151a, 2 #3151b		1.75	

Zoo Animals
A1198

No. 3152: a, Pongo pygmaeus. b, Panthera tigris altaica.

No. 3153: a, Ailurus fulgens. b, Fennecus zerda.

Photo. & Engr.

2001, Sept. 5 ***Perf. 11¾x11¼***

3152	Pair		.80	.40
a.-b.	A1198 5.40k Any single		.40	.20
	Booklet, 3 #3152b, 2 #3152a		2.00	
3153	Pair		.80	.40
a.-b.	A1198 5.40k Any single		.40	.20
	Booklet, 3 #3153b, 2 #3153a		2.00	

UNESCO World Heritage Sites
A1199

Designs: 12k, Kormeríz Castle and Gardens. 14k, Holasovice Historical Village Restoration.

2001, Oct. 9 **Engr.** ***Perf. 11½x11¾***
3154-3155 A1199 Set of 2 1.90 .95

Year of Dialogue Among Civilizations
A1200

Photo. & Engr.

2001, Oct. 9 ***Perf. 11¼x11½***
3156 A1200 9k multi .60 .30

Mills
A1201

Christmas
A1202

Designs: 9k, Windmill. 14.40k, Water mill.

2001, Oct. 9
3157-3158 A1201 Set of 2 1.60 .80

Photo. & Engr.

2001, Nov. 14 ***Perf. 11¼x11½***
3159 A1202 5.40k multi .40 .20

Art Type of 1967 Inscribed "CESKA REPUBLIKA"

Designs: 12k, The Annunciation of the Virgin Mary, by Michael J. Rentz. 17k, The Sans Souci Bar in Nimes, by Cyril Bouda. 26k, The Goose Keeper, by Vaclav Brozík.

2001, Nov. 14 **Engr.** ***Perf. 11¾***
3160-3162 A565 Set of 3 4.00 2.00

Tradition of Czech Stamp Production — A1203

Photo. & Engr.

2002, Jan. 20 ***Perf. 11¼x11¾***

3163	A1203 5.40k Type A89		.40	.20
a.	Booklet pane of 8 + 4 labels		3.25	—
	Booklet, #3163a		3.25	

2002 Winter Olympics, Salt Lake City — A1204

2002, Jan. 30 ***Perf. 11¼***
3164 A1204 12k multi .90 .45

For overprint, see No. 3168.

2002 Winter Paralympics, Salt Lake City — A1205

2002, Jan. 30 ***Perf. 11¼x11½***
3165 A1205 5.40k multi .40 .20

Composers Jaromír Vejvoda (1902-88), Josef Poncar (1902-86) and Karel Vacek (1902-82) — A1206

2002, Mar. 6 ***Perf. 11¾x11¼***
3166 A1206 9k multi .75 .35

Easter — A1207

2002, Mar. 6 ***Perf. 11¼x11½***
3167 A1207 5.40k multi .40 .20

No. 3164 Overprinted in Blue

Photo. & Engr.

2002, Mar. 8 ***Perf. 11¼***
3168 A1204 12k multi .90 .45

Divan, by Vlaho Bukovac (1855-1922) — A1208

Litho. & Engr.

2002, Apr. 23 ***Perf. 11¾***
3169 A1208 17k multi 1.25 .65

Printed in sheets of 4 + 2 labels.
See Croatia No. 487.

Europa A1209

Photo. & Engr.

2002, May 7 ***Perf. 11¾x11¼***
3170 A1209 9k multi .70 .35

Souvenir Sheet

Czech Culture and France — A1210

No. 3171: a, 23k, Klávesy Piana-Jezero, by Frantisek Kupka. b, 31k, Man with Broken Nose, sculpture by Auguste Rodin.

Perf. 11¾x11½

2002, May 7 **Litho. & Engr.**
3171 A1210 Sheet of 2, #a-b 4.25 2.10

Intl. Children's Day — A1211

Photo. & Engr.

2002, May 29 ***Perf. 11¼x11½***
3172 A1211 5.40k multi .40 .20
a. Booklet pane of 8 + 2 labels 3.25 —
Complete booklet, #3172a 3.25

Margaritifera Margaritifera A1212

2002, June 6
3173 A1212 9k multi .70 .35

Jan Hus (1372-1415), Religious Leader — A1213

2002, June 19
3174 A1213 9k multi + label .70 .35

Souvenir Sheet

Worldwide Fund for Nature (WWF) — A1214

Butterflies: a, 5.40k, Maculinea nausithous. b, 5.40k, Maculinea alcon. c, 9k, Maculinea teleius. d, 9k, Maculinea arion.

Litho. & Engr.

2002, June 19 ***Perf. 11¾***
3175 A1214 Sheet of 4, #a-d + 4 labels 2.25 1.10

Pansy — A1215

Photo. & Engr.

2002, Sept. 1 ***Perf. 11¾x11¼***
3176 A1215 6.40k multi .50 .25

World Heritage Sites Type of 2001

Designs: 12k, Litomysl Castle. 14k, Holy Trinity Column, Olomouc, vert.

Perf. 11½x11¾, 11¾x11½

2002, Sept. 11 **Engr.**
3177-3178 A1199 Set of 2 2.10 1.10

Emil Zátopek (1922-2000), Olympic Long Distance Runner — A1216

Photo. & Engr.

2002, Sept. 11 ***Perf. 11¼x11¾***
3179 A1216 9k multi .70 .35

Pres. Havel Type of 1998

Photo. & Engr.

2002, Nov. 6 ***Perf. 11¾x11¼***
3180 A1134 6.40k pur & blue .45 .20

St. Nicholas' Day A1217

Christmas A1218

2002, Nov. 6 ***Perf. 11¼x11½***
3181 A1217 6.40k multi .45 .20
a. Booklet pane of 8 + 2 labels 3.75 —
Complete booklet, #3181a 3.75

2002, Nov. 13
3182 A1218 6.40k multi .45 .20

NATO Summit, Prague — A1219

2002, Nov. 14 ***Perf. 11¼x11¾***
3183 A1219 9k multi .60 .30

Furniture — A1220

Designs: 6.40k, Armchair, 17th cent. 9k, Sewing table with hemispheric cover, 1820. 12k, Dressing table with mirror, 1860. 17k, Art deco amchair, 1923.

2003, Dec. 11
3184-3187 A1220 Set of 4 3.00 1.50

Art Type of 1967 Inscribed "CESKA REPUBLIKA"

Designs: 12k, The Abandoned, by Jaroslav Panuska, horiz. 20k, St. Wenceslas, by Mikolás Ales. 26k, Portrait of a Young Man with a Lute, by Jan Petr Molitor.

2002, Dec. 11 **Engr.** ***Perf. 11¾***
3188-3190 A565 Set of 3 4.00 2.00

Souvenir Sheet

Czech Republic, 10th Anniv. — A1221

Litho. & Engr.

2003, Jan. 1 ***Perf. 11¾***
3191 A1221 25k multi 1.75 .85

Tradition of Czech Stamp Production — A1222

Photo. & Engr.

2003, Jan. 20 *Perf. 11¼x11¾*
3192 A1222 6.40k Type A75 .45 .20
a. Booklet pane of 8 + 2 labels 3.75 —
Complete booklet, #3192a 3.75

Famous Men — A1223

Designs: 6.40k, Jaroslav Vrchlicky (1853-1912), poet. 8k, Josef Thomayer (1853-1927), physician and writer.

2003, Feb. 12 *Perf. 11½x11¼*
3193-3194 A1223 Set of 2 1.00 .50

Easter — A1224

2003, Mar. 26 *Perf. 11¼x11½*
3195 A1224 6.40k multi .45 .20

Roses Above Prague — A1225

Perf. 12¾x13¼
2003, Mar. 26 **Litho.**
3196 A1225 6.40k multi + label .45 .20

Labels could be personalized.

Lace A1226

Designs: 6.40k, Netted lace. 9k, Bobbin lace.

Photo. & Engr.

2003, Mar. 26 *Perf. 11¼*
3197 A1226 6.40k bl, dk bl & red .45 .20
a. Booklet pane of 6 + 4 labels 2.75 —
Complete booklet, #3197a 2.75
3198 A1226 9k dk bl, bl & red .60 .30
a. Booklet pane of 6 + 4 labels 3.75 —
Complete booklet, #3197a 3.75

Europa — A1227

Litho. & Engr.

2003, May 7 *Perf. 11¾*
3199 A1227 9k multi .65 .35

Geologic Attractions — A1228

Designs: 12k, Sandstone towers, Hrubá Skála Region. 14k, Punkva Caves, Moravian karst area.

2003, May 7 **Engr.** *Perf. 11½x11¾*
3200-3201 A1228 Set of 2 1.90 .95

Mach and Sebestova, Children's Television Show Characters — A1229

Photo. & Engr.

2003, May 28 *Perf. 11¼x11½*
3202 A1229 6.40k multi .50 .25

First Electric Railway, Tábor — Bechyne, Cent. A1230

2003, May 28 *Perf. 11¾x11¼*
3203 A1230 10k multi .75 .40

A1231

A1233

A1232

Observation towers: No. 3204, 6.40k, Klet. No. 3205, 6.40k, Slovanka.

2003, May 28 *Perf. 11¼x11½*
3204-3205 A1231 Set of 2 .95 .50

2003, June 25 *Perf. 11¾x11¼*
3206 A1232 9k multi .65 .35

European Shooting Championships, Plzen and Brno.

2003, June 25 *Perf. 11¼x11½*
3207 A1233 9k multi .65 .35

Josef Dobrovsky (1753-1829), linguist.

Pres. Vaclav Klaus — A1234

Photo. & Engr.

2003 *Perf. 11¾x11¼*
3208 A1234 6.40k buff, red & vio bl .45 .25
3209 A1234 6.50k Prus bl & pur .50 .25

Issued: 6.40k, 7/30; 6.50k, 11/5.

Souvenir Sheet

Tropical Fish — A1235

No. 3210: a, 12k, Betta splendens (27x44mm). b, 14k, Pterophyllum scalare (27x44mm). c, 16k, Carassius auratus (54x44mm). d, 20k, Symphysodon aequifasciatus (54x44mm).

Litho. & Engr.

2003, Sept. 10 *Perf. 11¾*
3210 A1235 Sheet of 4, #a-d 4.50 2.25

Oriental Carpets A1236

Designs: 9k, Turkish prayer carpet, 19th cent. 12k, Turkish carpet, 18th cent.

2003, Oct. 1 **Engr.** *Perf. 11¾*
3211-3212 A1236 Set of 2 1.60 .80

Tympanum, Porta Coeli Monastery, Predklásterí — A1237

Photo. & Engr.

2003, Oct. 15 *Perf. 11¾x11¼*
3213 A1237 6.50k multi .50 .25
a. Booklet pane of 8 + 4 labels 4.00 —
Complete booklet, #3213a 4.00

Birds of Prey — A1238

Designs: 6.50k, Milvus milvus. 8k, Falco peregrinus. 9k, Hieraaetus pennatus.

2003, Oct. 15 *Perf. 11¼x11½*
3214 A1238 6.50k multi .50 .25
Booklet, 5 #3214 2.50
3215 A1238 8k multi .60 .30
Booklet, 5 #3215 3.00
3216 A1238 9k multi .65 .30
Booklet, 5 #3216 3.25
Nos. 3214-3216 (3) 1.75 .85

Czech Fire Fighters, 140th Anniv. A1239

Fire engines: 6.50k, Wooden fire engine, 1822. 9k, Motorized fire engine, 1933. 12k, CAS 8/Avia Daewoo fire truck, 2002.

2003, Oct. 15 *Perf. 11¾x11¼*
3217-3219 A1239 Set of 3 2.00 1.00

Flower Type of 2002

Designs: 50h, Cornflower (chrpa). 6.50k, Dahlia (jirina).

2003, Oct. 22
3220 A1215 50h multi .20 .20
3221 A1215 6.50k multi .50 .25

Roses Over Prague Type of 2003 and

Prague Castle Lantern — A1240

2003, Oct. 22 **Litho.** *Perf. 12¾x13¼*
3222 A1225 6.50k multi + label .50 .25
3223 A1240 9k multi + label .65 .30

Labels could be personalized.

Art Type of 1967 Inscribed "CESKA REPUBLIKA"

Designs: 17k, Poor Countryside, by Max Svabinsky, horiz. 20k, Autumn in Veltrusy, by Antonín Slavícek. 26k, Eleanora de Toledo, by Agnolo Bronzino.

2003, Nov. 5 **Engr.** *Perf. 11¾*
3224-3226 A565 Set of 3 4.50 2.25

Christmas A1241

Photo. & Engr.

2003, Nov. 5 *Perf. 11¼x11½*
3227 A1241 6.50k multi .50 .25

Tradition of Czech Stamp Production A1242

Photo. & Engr.

2004, Jan. 20 *Perf. 11¼x11¾*
3228 A1242 6.50k Vignette of #1703 .50 .25
a. Booklet pane of 8 + 4 labels 4.00 —
Complete booklet, #3228a 4.00

Church of the Assumption of the Virgin Mary, Brno — A1243

2004, Feb. 18 **Engr.** *Perf. 11¾*
3229 A1243 17k multi 1.25 .65

Brno 2005 Philatelic Exhibition.

Industrial Building Historical Preservation A1244

Designs: 6.50k, Busek's Water Forging Hammer, Lniste. 17k, Iron Furnace, Stará Hut u Adamova.

Photo. & Engr.

2004, Feb. 18 ***Perf. 11½x11¼***

3230-3231	A1244	Set of 2	1.75	.90

Easter A1245

2004, Mar. 17

3232	A1245	6.50k multi	.50	.25

Art Type of 1967 Inscribed "CESKA REPUBLIKA"

Design: Prometheus, by Antonín Procházka.

2004, Mar. 17 **Engr.** ***Perf. 11¾***

3233	A565	26k multi	1.90	.95

World Ice Hockey Championships, Prague and Ostrava — A1246

Photo. & Engr.

2004, Apr. 14 ***Perf. 11¼x11¾***

3234	A1246	12k multi	.90	.45

Admission to European Union A1247

Photo. & Engr.

2004, May 1 ***Perf. 11¼***

3235	A1247	9k multi	.70	.35

Admission to the European Union — A1248

2004, May 1 **Litho.** ***Perf. 11¾x11¼***

3236	A1248	9k multi	.70	.35

Europa A1249

2004, May 5 ***Perf. 11¼***

3237	A1249	9k multi	.70	.35

Composers of Czech Operas — A1250

Designs: 6.50k, Dalibor, by Bedrich Smetana (1824-84). 8k, Jakobín, by Antonín Dvorák (1841-1904). 10k, Její Pastorkyna, by Leos Janácek (1854-1928).

Photo. & Engr.

2004, May 5 ***Perf. 11¼x11¾***

3238-3240	A1250	Set of 3	1.90	.95

For Children A1251

Photo. & Engr.

2004, May 26 ***Perf. 11½x11¼***

3241	A1251	6.50k multi	.55	.25
a.		Booklet pane of 8 + 2 labels	4.50	—
		Complete booklet, #3241a	4.50	

Statue of Radegast, by Albín Polásek — A1252

2004, May 26 ***Perf. 11¼x11½***

3242	A1252	6.50k multi	.55	.25

Brno 2005 Philatelic Exhibition.

Tourist Attractions — A1253

Designs: 12k, Holy Mountain, Príbram. 14k, Holy Shrine, Bystrice pod Hostynem.

2004, May 26 **Engr.** ***Perf. 11½x11¾***

3243-3244	A1253	Set of 2	2.00	1.00

A1254

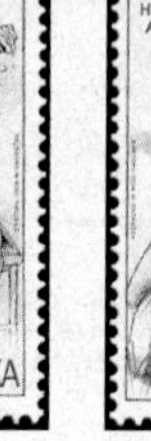

A1255

Photo. & Engr.

2004, June 23 ***Perf. 11¼x11¾***

3245	A1254	6.50k multi	.55	.25

2004 Paralympics, Athens.

2004, June 23

3246	A1255	9k multi	.70	.35

2004 Summer Olympics, Athens.

Petrarch (1304-74), Poet — A1256

2004, June 23 ***Perf. 11¾x11¼***

3247	A1256	14k multi	1.10	.55

SEMI-POSTAL STAMPS

Nos. B1-B123 were sold at 1½ times face value at the Philatelists' Window of the Prague P.O. for charity benefit. They were available for ordinary postage.

Almost all stamps between Nos. B1-B123 are known with misplaced or inverted overprints and/or in pairs with one stamp missing the overprint.

The overprints of Nos. B1-B123 have been well forged.

Austrian Stamps of 1916-18 Overprinted in Black or Blue

a

1919 ***Perf. 12½***

B1	A37	3h brt violet	.20	*.25*
B2	A37	5h lt green	.20	*.25*
B3	A37	6h dp org (Bl)	.60	.50
B4	A37	6h dp org (Bk)	*2,000.*	*2,000.*
B5	A37	10h magenta	.60	*.75*
B6	A37	12h lt blue	.60	*.65*
B7	A42	15h dull red	.20	*.25*
B8	A42	20h dark green	.20	*.25*
a.		20h green	100.00	100.00
B9	A42	25h blue	.30	*.40*
B10	A42	30h dull violet	.30	*.40*
B11	A39	40h olive grn	.30	*.40*
B12	A39	50h dk green	.30	*.40*
B13	A39	60h dp blue	.30	*.40*
B14	A39	80h orange brn	.30	*.40*
B15	A39	90h red violet	.70	*.75*
B16	A39	1k car, *yel* (Bl)	.50	*.60*
B17	A39	1k car, *yel* (Bk)	125.00	100.00
B18	A40	2k light blue	1.90	1.90
a.		2k dark blue	2,750.	1,750.
B19	A40	3k carmine rose	50.00	27.50
a.		3k claret	2,500.	900.00
B20	A40	4k yellow grn	20.00	15.00
a.		4k deep green	45.00	35.00
B21	A40	10k violet	300.00	160.00
a.		10k deep violet	375.00	275.00
b.		10k black violet	450.00	300.00

The used value of No. B18a is for copies which have only a Czechoslovakian cancellation. Some of the copies of Austria No. 160 which were officially overprinted with type "a" and sold by the post office, had previously been used and lightly canceled with Austrian cancellations. These canceled-before-overprinting copies, which were postally valid, sell for about one-fourth as much.

Granite Paper

B22	A40	2k light blue	2.00	2.00
B23	A40	3k carmine rose	7.25	6.00

The 4k and 10k on granite paper with this overprint were not regularly issued.

Excellent counterfeits of Nos. B1-B23 exist.

Austrian Newspaper Stamps Overprinted

b

Imperf

On Stamp of 1908

B26	N8	10h carmine	2,250.	2,000.

On Stamps of 1916

B27	N9	2h brown	.20	.20
B28	N9	4h green	.25	.25
B29	N9	6h deep blue	.20	.20
B30	N9	10h orange	2.75	2.75
B31	N9	30h claret	1.10	1.10
		Nos. B27-B31 (5)	4.50	4.50

Austrian Special Handling Stamps Overprinted in Blue or Black

Stamps of 1916 Overprinted

c

Perf. 12½

B32	SH1	2h claret, *yel* (Bl)	40.00	35.00
B33	SH1	5h dp grn, *yel* (Bk)	*1,200.*	*900.00*

Stamps of 1917 Overprinted

d

B34	SH2	2h cl, *yel* (Bl)	.25	*.35*
a.		Vert. pair, imperf. btwn.	*250.00*	
B35	SH2	2h cl, *yel* (Bk)	60.00	35.00
B36	SH2	5h grn, *yel* (Bk)	.25	.25

Austrian Air Post Stamps, #C1-C3, Overprinted Type "c" Diagonally

B37	A40	1.50k on 2k lil	200.00	200.00
B38	A40	2.50k on 3k ocher	200.00	200.00
B39	A40	4k gray	1,000.	900.

1919

Austrian Postage Due Stamps of 1908-13 Overprinted Type "b"

B40	D3	2h carmine	*4,500.*	*2,750.*
B41	D3	4h carmine	25.00	15.00
B42	D3	6h carmine	12.50	8.00
B43	D3	14h carmine	90.00	35.00
B44	D3	25h carmine	45.00	20.00
B45	D3	30h carmine	375.00	300.00
B46	D3	50h carmine	875.00	825.00

Austria Nos. J49-J56 Overprinted Type "b"

B47	D4	5h rose red	.20	*.30*
B48	D4	10h rose red	.20	*.30*
B49	D4	15h rose red	.20	*.30*
B50	D4	20h rose red	2.00	1.50
B51	D4	25h rose red	1.25	1.00
B52	D4	30h rose red	.50	.50
B53	D4	40h rose red	2.00	1.75
B54	D4	50h rose red	400.00	250.00

Austria Nos. J57-J59 Overprinted Type "a"

B55	D5	1k ultra	12.50	10.00
B56	D5	5k ultra	55.00	35.00
B57	D5	10k ultra	375.00	200.00

Austria Nos. J47-J48, J60-J63 Overprinted Type "c" Diagonally

B58	A22	1h gray	32.50	30.00
B59	A23	15h on 2h vio	125.00	110.00
B60	A38	10h on 24h blue	90.00	85.00
B61	A38	15h on 36h vio	1.00	1.00
B62	A38	20h on 54h org	90.00	85.00
B63	A38	50h on 42h choc	1.00	1.00

Hungarian Stamps Ovptd. Type "b"

1919 **Wmk. 137** ***Perf. 15***

On Stamps of 1913-16

B64	A4	1f slate	2,400.	1,600.
B65	A4	2f yellow	3.50	2.50
B66	A4	3f orange	45.00	25.00
B67	A4	6f olive green	4.50	4.50
B68	A4	50f lake, *bl*	1.25	1.00
B69	A4	60f grn, *sal*	50.00	20.00
B70	A4	70f red brn, *grn*	2,400.	1,600.

On Stamps of 1916

B71 A8 10f rose 300.00 175.00
B72 A8 15f violet 160.00 100.00

On Stamps of 1916-18

B73 A9 2f brown org .20 .20
B74 A9 3f red lilac .20 .20
B75 A9 5f green .20 .20
B76 A9 6f grnsh blue .60 .60
B77 A9 10f rose red 1.40 *2.25*
B78 A9 15f violet .25 .25
B79 A9 20f gray brown 5.50 5.00
B80 A9 25f dull blue .80 .75
B81 A9 35f brown 6.75 6.75
B82 A9 40f olive green 1.75 1.50

Overprinted Type "d"

B83 A10 50f red vio & lil .80 .80
B84 A10 75f brt bl & pale bl .75 .75
B85 A10 80f yel grn & pale grn 1.10 1.10
B86 A10 1k red brn & cl 1.40 1.40
B87 A10 2k ol brn & bis 5.50 5.50
B88 A10 3k dk vio & ind 37.50 37.50
B89 A10 5k dk brn & lt brn 140.00 90.00
B90 A10 10k vio brn & vio 1,250. 800.00

Overprinted Type "b"

On Stamps of 1918

B91 A11 10f scarlet .25 .25
B92 A11 20f dark brown .30 .30
B93 A11 25f deep blue 1.40 1.25
B94 A12 40f olive grn 1.50 1.25
B95 A12 50f lilac 67.50 25.00

On Stamps of 1919

B96 A13 10f red 7.00 6.00
B97 A13 20f dk brn *6,750.* —

Same Overprint On Hungarian Newspaper Stamp of 1914

Imperf

B98 N5 (2f) orange .20 *.30*

Same Overprint On Hungarian Special Delivery Stamp

Perf. 15

B99 SD1 2f gray grn & red .25 *.35*

Same Ovpt. On Hungarian Semi-Postal Stamps

B100 SP3 10f + 2f rose red .55 *.60*
B101 SP4 15f + 2f violet .90 .90
B102 SP5 40f + 2f brn car 7.00 3.50
Nos. B98-B102 (5) 8.90 5.65

Hungarian Postage Due Stamps of 1903-18 Overprinted Type "b"

1919 Wmk. 135 ***Perf. 11½, 12***

B103 D1 50f green & black *525.00 525.00*

Wmk. Crown (136, 136a)

Perf. 11½x12, 15

B104 D1 1f green & black *1,200. 1,000.*
B105 D1 2f green & black *1,000. 750.*
B106 D1 12f green & black *4,250. 3,000.*
B107 D1 50f green & black 275. 150.

Wmk. Double Cross (137)

Perf. 15

On Stamps of 1914

B110 D1 1f green & black 1,250. 600.
B111 D1 2f green & black 700. 550.
B112 D1 5f green & black 1,325. 900.
B113 D1 12f green & black *5,250. 4,000.*
B114 D1 50f green & black 275. 150.

On Stamps of 1915-18

B115 D1 1f green & red 175.00 140.00
B116 D1 2f green & red 1.00 .80
B117 D1 5f green & red 12.50 10.00
B118 D1 6f green & red 1.50 1.50
B119 D1 10f green & red .60 .60
a. Pair, one without overprint
B120 D1 12f green & red 2.00 2.00
B121 D1 15f green & red 7.50 5.00
B122 D1 20f green & red 1.00 1.00
B123 D1 30f green & red 80.00 70.00
Nos. B115-B123 (9) 281.10 230.90

Excellent counterfeits of Nos. B1-B123 exist.

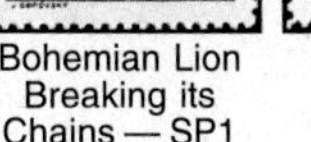

Bohemian Lion Breaking its Chains — SP1

Mother and Child — SP2

Perf. 11½, 13¾ and Compound

1919 Typo. Unwmk.

Pinkish Paper

B124 SP1 15h gray green .20 .20
B125 SP1 25h dark brown .20 .20
a. 25h light brown *5.00* 2.50
B126 SP1 50h dark blue .20 .20

Photo.

Yellowish Paper

B127 SP2 75h slate .20 .20
B128 SP2 100h brn vio .20 .20
B129 SP2 120h vio, *yel* .20 .20
Nos. B124-B129 (6) 1.20 1.20

Nos. B124-B126 commemorate the 1st anniv. of Czechoslovak independence. Nos. B127-B129 were sold for the benefit of Legionnaires' orphans. Imperforates exist.
See No. 1581.

Regular Issues of Czechoslovakia Surcharged in Red:

a

b

1920 ***Perf. 13¾***

B130 A1(a) 40h + 20h bister .50 .50
B131 A2(a) 60h + 20h green .50 .50
B132 A4(b) 125h + 25h gray bl 1.00 1.00
Nos. B130-B132 (3) 2.00 *2.00*

President Masaryk — SP3

Wmk. Linden Leaves (107)

1923 Engr. ***Perf. 13¾x14¾***

B133 SP3 50h gray green .75 .50
B134 SP3 100h carmine 1.00 .60
B135 SP3 200h blue 3.00 1.25
B136 SP3 300h dark brown 3.25 2.25
Nos. B133-B136 (4) 8.00 4.60

5th anniv. of the Republic.
The gum was applied through a screen and shows the monogram "CSP" (Ceskoslovenska Posta). These stamps were sold at double their face values, the excess being given to the Red Cross and other charitable organizations.

International Olympic Congress Issue

Semi-Postal Stamps of 1923 Overprinted in Blue or Red

1925

B137 SP3 50h gray green 5.00 4.50
B138 SP3 100h carmine 8.50 7.75
B139 SP3 200h blue (R) 55.00 50.00
Nos. B137-B139 (3) 68.50 62.25
Set, never hinged 100.00

These stamps were sold at double their face values, the excess being divided between a fund for post office clerks and the Olympic Games Committee.

Sokol Issue

Semi-Postal Stamps of 1923 Overprinted in Blue or Red

1926

B140 SP3 50h gray green 1.60 1.00
B141 SP3 100h carmine 3.25 1.50
B142 SP3 200h blue (R) 15.00 19.50
a. Double overprint
B143 SP3 300h dk brn (R) 20.00 16.00
Nos. B140-B143 (4) 39.85 38.00

These stamps were sold at double their face values, the excess being given to the Congress of Sokols, June, 1926.

Catalogue values for unused stamps in this section, from this point to the end of the section, are for Never Hinged items.

Midwife Presenting Newborn Child to its Father; after a Painting by Josef Manes
SP4 SP5

1936 Unwmk. Engr. ***Perf. 12½***

B144 SP4 50h + 50h green .45 .20
B145 SP5 1k + 50h claret .45 .35
B146 SP4 2k + 50h blue 1.90 .95
Nos. B144-B146 (3) 2.80 1.50

SP6

"Lullaby" by Stanislav Sucharda SP7

1937 ***Perf. 12½***

B147 SP6 50h + 50h dull green .50 .20
B148 SP6 1k + 50h rose lake .75 .50
B149 SP7 2k + 1k dull blue 1.75 1.00
Nos. B147-B149 (3) 3.00 1.70

President Masaryk and Little Girl in Native Costume — SP8

1938 ***Perf. 12½***

B150 SP8 50h + 50h deep green .25 *.20*
B151 SP8 1k + 50h rose lake .35 *.25*

Souvenir Sheet

Imperf

B152 SP8 2k + 3k black 3.50 *2.40*

88th anniv. of the birth of Masaryk (1850-1937).

Allegory of the Republic Type Souvenir Sheet

1938 ***Perf. 12½***

B153 A89 2k (+ 8k) dark blue 2.50 2.50

The surtax was devoted to national relief for refugees.

"Republic" and Congress Emblem SP10

St. George Slaying the Dragon SP11

1945 Engr.

B154 SP10 1.50k + 1.50k car rose .20 .20
B155 SP10 2.50k + 2.50k blue .25 .20

Students' World Cong., Prague, 11/17/45.

1946

B156 SP11 2.40k + 2.60k car rose .20 .20
B157 SP11 4k + 6k blue .45 .20

Souvenir Sheet

Imperf

B158 SP11 4k + 6k blue 1.00 1.00

1st anniv. of Czechoslovakia's liberation. The surtax aided WW II orphans.

Old Town Hall Type of 1946 Souvenir Sheet

1946, Aug. 3 ***Imperf.***

B159 A114 2.40k rose brown .80 .50

Brno Natl. Stamp Exhib., Aug., 1946. The sheet was sold for 10k.

"You Went Away" — SP14

"You Remained Ours" — SP15

"You Came Back" — SP16

1946, Oct. 28 Photo. ***Perf. 14***

B160 SP14 1.60k + 1.40k red brn .45 .45
B161 SP15 2.40k + 2.60k scarlet .20 .20
B162 SP16 4k + 4k deep blue .35 .35
Nos. B160-B162 (3) 1.00 *1.00*

The surtax was for repatriated Slovaks.

Barefoot Boy — SP17

Woman and Child — SP18

2k+1k, Mother and child. 3k+1k, Little girl.

Perf. 12½

1948, Dec. 18 Unwmk. Engr.

B163 SP17 1.50k + 1k rose lilac .20 .20
B164 SP17 2k + 1k dp blue .20 .20
B165 SP17 3k + 1k rose car .20 .20
Nos. B163-B165 (3) .60 .60

The surtax was for child welfare.
Labels alternate with stamps in sheets of Nos. B163-B165.

1949, Dec. 18 *Perf. 12½*

Design: 3k+1k, Man lifting child.

B166 SP18	1.50k + 50h gray	*2.25*	*.75*
B167 SP18	3k + 1k claret	*4.25*	*1.25*

The surtax was for child welfare.

SP19

Dove Carrying Olive Branch — SP20

1949, Dec. 18

B168 SP19	1.50k + 50h claret	*3.25*	*1.25*
B169 SP20	3k + 1k rose red	*3.25*	*1.25*

The surtax was for the Red Cross.

AIR POST STAMPS

Nos. 9, 39-40, 20, and Types of 1919 Surcharged in Red, Blue or Green:

1920 **Unwmk.** ***Imperf.***

C1	A1 14k on 200h (R)	15.00	15.00
a.	Inverted surcharge	125.00	
C2	A2 24k on 500h (Bl)	40.00	30.00
a.	Inverted surcharge	225.00	
C3	A2 28k on 1000h (G)	30.00	30.00
a.	Inverted surcharge	150.00	
b.	Double surcharge	200.00	
	Nos. C1-C3 (3)	85.00	*75.00*

Perf. 13¾, 13¾x 13 ½ (#C6)

C4	A1 14k on 200h (R)	22.50	14.00
a.	Perf. 13¾x13½	90.00	52.50
C5	A2 24k on 500h (Bl)	45.00	32.50
a.	Perf. 13¾x13½	100.00	77.50
C6	A2 28k on 1000h (G)	20.00	25.00
a.	Inverted surcharge	400.00	—
b.	Perf. 13¾	475.00	350.00
c.	As "b," invtd. surcharge	350.00	—
	Nos. C4-C6 (3)	87.50	71.50
	Nos. C1-C6 (6)	172.50	*146.50*

Excellent counterfeits of the overprint are known.

Stamps of 1920 Surcharged in Black or Violet:

1922, June 15 ***Perf. 13¾***

C7	A8 50h on 100h dl grn	1.50	1.50
a.	Inverted surcharge	150.00	
b.	Double surcharge	160.00	
C8	A8 100h on 200h vio	2.00	*3.25*
a.	Inverted surcharge	150.00	
C9	A8 250h on 400h brn (V)	5.00	*7.50*
a.	Inverted surcharge	275.00	
	Nos. C7-C9 (3)	8.50	*12.25*

Fokker Monoplane AP3

Smolik S 19 AP4

Smolik S 19 — AP5

Fokker over Prague AP6

1930, Dec. 16 **Engr.** ***Perf. 13½***

C10	AP3	50h deep green	.20	.20
C11	AP3	1k deep red	.25	.25
C12	AP4	2k dark green	.60	.55
C13	AP4	3k red violet	1.25	1.00
C14	AP5	4k indigo	1.00	.80
C15	AP5	5k red brown	1.50	1.50
C16	AP6	10k vio blue	3.50	3.50
a.		10k ultra	6.25	*6.50*
C17	AP6	20k gray violet	4.50	3.00
		Nos. C10-C17 (8)	12.80	10.80

Two types exist of the 50h, 1k and 2k, and three types of the 3k, differing chiefly in the size of the printed area. A "no hill at left" variety of the 3k exists.

Imperf. copies of Nos. C10-C17 are proofs.

Perf. 12

C10a	AP3	50h deep green	1.90	1.90
C11a	AP3	1k deep red	18.00	18.00
C12a	AP4	2k dark green	14.00	14.00
C14a	AP5	4k indigo	6.00	*6.25*
C17a	AP6	20k gray violet	4.00	3.00

Perf. 12x13½, 13½x12

C11b	AP3	1k deep red	2.75	2.75
C12b	AP4	2k dark green	9.25	9.25

Perf. 13¾x12¼

C17b	AP6	20k gray violet	*1,100.*	

Perf. 12½

C15a	AP5	5k red brown	*2,000.*	

Type of 1930 with hyphen in Cesko-Slovensko

1939, Apr. 22 ***Perf. 13½***

C18	AP3 30h rose lilac	.20	.20

Catalogue values for unused stamps in this section, from this point to the end of the section, are for Never Hinged items.

Capt. Frantisek Novak — AP7

Plane over Bratislava Castle — AP8

Plane over Charles Bridge, Prague — AP9

1946-47 ***Perf. 12½***

C19	AP7	1.50k rose red	.20	.20
C20	AP7	5.50k dk gray bl	.30	.20
C21	AP7	9k sepia ('47)	.60	.20
C22	AP8	10k dl grn	.60	.25
C23	AP7	16k violet	1.00	.40
C24	AP8	20k light blue	1.10	.70
C25	AP9	24k dk bl, *cr*	.70	.45
C26	AP9	24k rose lake	1.10	.75
C27	AP9	50k dk gray bl	2.40	1.10
		Nos. C19-C27 (9)	8.00	4.25

No. C25 was issued June 12, 1946, for use on the first Prague-New York flight.

Nos. C19-C24, C26-C27 Surcharged with New Value and Bars in Various Colors

1949, Sept. 1 ***Perf. 12½***

C28	AP7	1k on 1.50k (Bl)	.20	.20
C29	AP7	3k on 5.50k (C)	.25	.20
C30	AP7	6k on 9k (Br)	.35	.20
C31	AP7	7.50k on 16k (C)	.50	.20
C32	AP8	8k on 10k (G)	.50	.30
C33	AP8	12.50k on 20k (Bl)	.70	.30
C34	AP9	15k on 24k rose lake (Bl)	1.75	.50
C35	AP9	30k on 50k (Bl)	1.25	.60
		Nos. C28-C35 (8)	5.50	2.50

Karlovy Vary (Karlsbad) — AP10

1951, Apr. 2 **Engr.** ***Perf. 13½***

C36	AP10	6k shown	2.00	.50
C37	AP10	10k Piestany	2.00	.50
C38	AP10	15k Marienbad	4.00	.50
C39	AP10	20k Silac	*5.25*	*3.00*
		Nos. C36-C39 (4)	*13.25*	*4.50*

View of Cesky Krumlov — AP11

Views: 1.55k, Olomouc. 2.35k, Banska Bystrica. 2.75k, Bratislava. 10k, Prague.

1955 ***Perf. 11½***

Cream Paper

C40	AP11	80h olive green	.80	.20
C41	AP11	1.55k violet brn	1.00	.25
C42	AP11	2.35k violet blue	1.40	.20
C43	AP11	2.75k rose brown	2.00	.25
C44	AP11	10k indigo	3.00	1.10
		Nos. C40-C44 (5)	8.20	2.00

Issue dates: 10k, Feb. 20. Others, Mar. 28.

Airline: Moscow-Prague-Paris — AP12

2.35k, Airline: Prague-Cairo-Beirut-Damascus.

Engraved and Photogravure

1957, Oct. 15 **Unwmk.** ***Perf. 11½***

C45	AP12	75h ultra & rose	.40	.20
C46	AP12	2.35k ultra & org yel	.85	.20

Planes at First Czech Aviation School, Pardubice — AP13

Design: 1.80k, Jan Kaspar and flight of first Czech plane, 1909.

1959, Oct. 15

C47	AP13	1k gray & yel	.20	.20
C48	AP13	1.80k blk & pale bl	.70	.20

50th anniv. of Jan Kaspar's 1st flight Aug. 25, 1909, at Pardubice.

Mail Coach, Plane and Arms of Bratislava — AP14

Design: 2.80k, Helicopter over Bratislava.

1960, Sept. 24 **Unwmk.** ***Perf. 11½***

C49	AP14	1.60k dk bl & gray	*1.50*	*.90*
C50	AP14	2.80k grn & buff	*2.00*	*1.10*

Issued to publicize the National Stamp Exhibition, Bratislava, Sept. 24-Oct. 9.

AP15

AP16

Designs: 60h, Prague hails Gagarin. 1.80k, Gagarin, rocket and dove.

1961, June 22

C51	AP15	60h gray & car	.20	.20
C52	AP15	1.80k gray & blue	.40	.20

No. C51 commemorates Maj. Gagarin's visit to Prague, Apr. 28-29; No. C52 commemorates the first man in space, Yuri A. Gagarin, Apr. 12, 1961.

1962, May 14 **Engr.** ***Perf. 14***

"PRAGA" emblem and: 80h, Dove & Nest of Eggs. 1.40k, Dove. 2.80k, Symbolic flower with five petals. 4.20k, Five leaves.

C53	AP16	80h multicolored	.60	.35
C54	AP16	1.40k blk, dk red & bl	1.25	1.10
C55	AP16	2.80k multicolored	1.25	1.10
C56	AP16	4.20k multicolored	1.90	1.10
		Nos. C53-C56 (4)	5.00	3.65

PRAGA 1962 World Exhibition of Postage Stamps, Aug. 18-Sept. 2, 1962.

Vostok 5 and Lt. Col. Valeri Bykovski AP17

2.80k, Vostok VI & Lt. Valentina Tereshkova.

1963, June 26

C57	AP17	80h slate bl & pink	.35	.20
C58	AP17	2.80k dl red brn & lt bl	1.40	.25

Space flights of Valeri Bykovski, June 14-19, and Valentina Tereshkova, first woman astronaut, June 16-19, 1963.

PRAGA 1962 Emblem, View of Prague and Plane — AP18

Designs: 60h, Istanbul '63 (Hagia Sophia). 1k, Philatec Paris 1964 (Ile de la Cité). 1.40k, WIPA 1965 (Belvedere Palace, Vienna). 1.60k, SIPEX 1966 (Capitol, Washington). 2k, Amphilex '67 (harbor and old town, Amsterdam). 5k, PRAGA 1968 (View of Prague).

Engraved and Photogravure

1967, Oct. 30 ***Perf. 11½***

Size: 30x50mm

C59	AP18	30h choc, yel & rose	.20	.20
C60	AP18	60h dk grn, yel & lil	.20	.20
C61	AP18	1k blk, brick red & lt bl	.35	.20
C62	AP18	1.40k vio, yel & dp org	.40	.20
C63	AP18	1.60k ind, tan & lil	.35	.20
C64	AP18	2k dk grn, org & red	.40	.25

Size: 40x50mm

C65	AP18	5k multi	2.00	1.25
		Nos. C59-C65 (7)	*3.90*	*2.50*

PRAGA 1968 World Stamp Exhibition, Prague, June 22-July 7, 1968. No. C59-C64 issued in sheets of 15 stamps and 15 bilingual labels. No. C65 issued in sheets of 4 stamps and one center label.

Glider L-13 — AP19

Airplanes: 60h, Sports plane L-40. 80h, Aero taxi L-200. 1k, Crop-spraying plane Z-37. 1.60k, Aerobatics trainer Z-526. 2k, Jet trainer L-29.

1967, Dec. 11

C66	AP19	30h multi	.20	.20
C67	AP19	60h multi	.20	.20
C68	AP19	80h multi	.20	.20
C69	AP19	1k multi	.25	.20
C70	AP19	1.60k multi	.40	.20
C71	AP19	2k multi	1.25	.55
		Nos. C66-C71 (6)	*2.50*	*1.55*

Charles Bridge, Prague, and Balloon — AP20

Designs: 1k, Belvedere, fountain and early plane. 2k, Hradcany, Prague, and airship.

1968, Feb. 5 **Unwmk.** ***Perf. 11½***

C72	AP20	60h multicolored	.25	.20
C73	AP20	1k multicolored	.35	.25
C74	AP20	2k multicolored	.65	.25
		Nos. C72-C74 (3)	1.25	.70

PRAGA 1968 World Stamp Exhibition, Prague, June 22-July 7, 1968.

Astronaut, Moon and Manhattan AP21

Design: 3k, Lunar landing module and J. F. Kennedy Airport, New York.

1969, July 21

C75	AP21	60h blk, vio, yel & sil	.20	.20
C76	AP21	3k blk, bl, ocher & sil	1.00	.50

Man's 1st landing on the moon, July 20, 1969, US astronauts Neil A. Armstrong and Col. Edwin E. Aldrin, Jr., with Lieut. Col. Michael Collins piloting Apollo 11.

Nos. C75-C76 printed with label inscribed with names of astronauts and European date of moon landing.

TU-104A over Bitov Castle AP22

Designs: 60h, IL-62 over Bezdez Castle. 1.40k, TU-13A over Orava Castle. 1.90k, IL-18 over Veveri Castle. 2.40k, IL-14 over Pernstejn Castle. 3.60k, TU-154 over Trencin Castle.

1973, Oct. 24 **Engr.** ***Perf. 11½***

C77	AP22	30h multi	.20	.20
C78	AP22	60h multi	.20	.20
C79	AP22	1.40k multi	.25	.20
C80	AP22	1.90k multi	.40	.20
C81	AP22	2.40k multi	1.50	.75
C82	AP22	3.60k multi	.70	.20
		Nos. C77-C82 (6)	*3.25*	*1.75*

50 years of Czechoslovakian aviation.

Old Water Tower and Manes Hall — AP23

Designs (Praga 1978 Emblem, Plane Silhouette and): 1.60k, Congress Hall. 2k, Powder Tower, vert. 2.40k, Charles Bridge and Old Bridge Tower. 4k, Old Town Hall on Old Town Square, vert. 6k, Prague Castle and St. Vitus' Cathedral, vert.

Engraved and Photogravure

1976, June 23 ***Perf. 11½***

C83	AP23	60h ind & multi	.20	.20
C84	AP23	1.60k ind & multi	.25	.20
C85	AP23	2k ind & multi	.35	.20
C86	AP23	2.40k ind & multi	.40	.20
C87	AP23	4k ind & multi	.80	.30
C88	AP23	6k ind & multi	2.00	.80
		Nos. C83-C88 (6)	4.00	1.90

PRAGA 1978 International Philatelic Exhibition, Prague, Sept. 8-17, 1978.

Zeppelin, 1909 and 1928 — AP24

PRAGA '78 Emblem and: 1k, Ader, 1890, L'Eole & Dunn, 1914. 1.60k, Jeffries-Blanchard balloon, 1785. 2k, Otto Lilienthal's glider, 1896. 4.40k, Jan Kaspar's plane, Pardubice, 1911.

1977, Sept. 15 ***Perf. 11½***

C89	AP24	60h multi	.20	.20
C90	AP24	1k multi	.20	.20
C91	AP24	1.60k multi	.25	.20
C92	AP24	2k multi	.30	.20
C93	AP24	4.40k multi	*1.40*	*.50*
		Nos. C89-C93 (5)	*2.35*	*1.30*

History of aviation.

SPECIAL DELIVERY STAMPS

Doves — SD1

1919-20 **Unwmk.** **Typo.** ***Imperf.***

E1	SD1	2h red vio, *yel*	.20	.20
E2	SD1	5h yel grn, *yel*	.20	.20
E3	SD1	10h red brn, *yel* ('20)	.40	.40
		Nos. E1-E3 (3)	.80	.80

For overprints and surcharge see Nos. P11-P13, Eastern Silesia E1-E2.

1921 **White Paper**

E1a	SD1	2h red violet	8.00
E2a	SD1	5h yellow green	5.25
E3a	SD1	10h red brown	100.00
		Nos. E1a-E3a (3)	113.25

It is doubted that Nos. E1a-E3a were regularly issued.

PERSONAL DELIVERY STAMPS

Catalogue values for unused stamps in this section are for Never Hinged items.

PD1

Design: No. EX2, "D" in each corner.

1937 **Unwmk.** **Photo.** ***Perf. 13½***

EX1	PD1	50h blue	.20	*.25*
EX2	PD1	50h carmine	.20	*.25*

PD3

1946 ***Perf. 13½***

EX3	PD3	2k deep blue	.50	.50

POSTAGE DUE STAMPS

D1

1918-20 **Unwmk.** **Typo.** ***Imperf.***

J1	D1	5h deep bister	.20	.20
J2	D1	10h deep bister	.20	.20
J3	D1	15h deep bister	.20	.20
J4	D1	20h deep bister	.20	.20
J5	D1	25h deep bister	.20	.20
J6	D1	30h deep bister	.30	.20
J7	D1	40h deep bister	.30	.25
J8	D1	50h deep bister	.30	.20
J9	D1	100h blk brn	1.25	.20
J10	D1	250h orange	4.75	1.40
J11	D1	400h scarlet	6.50	1.40
J12	D1	500h gray grn	2.50	.20
J13	D1	1000h purple	3.50	.25
J14	D1	2000h dark blue	15.00	.60
		Nos. J1-J14 (14)	35.40	5.70

For surcharges and overprints see Nos. J32-J41, J57, Eastern Silesia J1-J11.

Nos. 1, 33-34, 10 Surcharged in Blue

1922

J15	A1	20h on 3h red vio	.20	.20
J16	A2	50h on 75h slate	.60	.20
J17	A2	60h on 80h olive grn	.45	.20
J18	A2	100h on 80h olive grn	1.50	.20
J19	A1	200h on 400h purple	2.25	.20
		Nos. J15-J19 (5)	5.00	1.00

Same Surcharge on Nos. 1, 10, 30-31, 33-34, 36, 40 in Violet

1923-26

J20	A1	10h on 3h red vio	.20	.20
J21	A1	20h on 3h red vio	.50	.20
J22	A1	30h on 3h red vio	.20	.20
J23	A1	40h on 3h red vio	.20	.20
J24	A2	50h on 75h slate	1.60	.20
J25	A2	60h on 50h dk vio ('26)	4.50	1.25
J26	A2	60h on 50h dk bl ('26)	4.50	1.50
J27	A2	60h on 75h slate	.50	.20
J28	A2	100h on 80h ol grn	27.50	.20
J29	A2	100h on 120h gray blk	1.10	.20
J30	A1	100h on 400h pur ('26)	1.10	.20
J31	A2	100h on 1000h dp vio ('26)	1.60	.20
		Nos. J20-J31 (12)	43.50	4.75

Postage Due Stamp of 1918-20 Surcharged in Violet

1924

J32	D1	50h on 400h scar	.75	.20
J33	D1	60h on 400h scar	2.75	.50
J34	D1	100h on 400h scar	1.75	.20
		Nos. J32-J34 (3)	5.25	.90

Postage Due Stamps of 1918-20 Surcharged with New Values in Violet as in 1924

1925

J35	D1	10h on 5h bister	.20	.20
J36	D1	20h on 5h bister	.20	.20
J37	D1	30h on 15h bister	.20	.20
J38	D1	40h on 15h bister	.20	.20
J39	D1	50h on 250h org	.95	.20
J40	D1	60h on 250h org	1.25	.50
J41	D1	100h on 250h org	1.90	.20
		Nos. J35-J41 (7)	4.90	1.70

Stamps of 1918-19 Surcharged with New Values in Violet as in 1922

1926 ***Perf. 14, 11½***

J42	A2	30h on 15h red	.50	.30
J43	A2	40h on 15h red	.50	.30

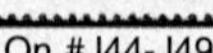
On #J44-J49

On #J50-J56

1926 Violet Surcharge *Perf. 14*
J44 A8 30h on 100h dk grn .20 .20
J45 A8 40h on 200h violet .25 .20
J46 A8 40h on 300h ver .95 .25
a. Perf. 14x13½ 60.00
J47 A8 50h on 500h dp grn .50 .20
a. Perf. 14x13½ 2.75
J48 A8 60h on 400h brown 1.00 .20
J49 A8 100h on 600h dp vio 2.50 .35
a. Perf. 14x13½ 30.00 1.25
Nos. J44-J49 (6) 5.40 1.40

1927 Violet Overprint
J50 A6 100h dark brown .55 .20
a. Perf. 13½ *200.00* 10.00

Surcharged with New Value in Violet
J51 A6 40h on 185h org .20 .20
J52 A6 50h on 20h car .20 .20
a. 50h on 50h carmine (error) *35,000.*
J53 A6 50h on 150h rose .20 .20
a. Perf. 13½ 12.50 2.00
J54 A6 60h on 25h brown .25 .20
J55 A6 60h on 185h orange .55 .20
J56 A6 100h on 25h brown .55 .20
Nos. J50-J56 (7) 2.50 1.40

No. J52a is known only used.

No. J12 Surcharged in Violet

1927 *Imperf.*
J57 D1 200h on 500h gray grn 6.00 2.50

Catalogue values for unused stamps in this section, from this point to the end of the section, are for Never Hinged items.

D5

1928 *Perf. 14x13½*
J58 D5 5h dark red .20 .20
J59 D5 10h dark red .20 .20
J60 D5 20h dark red .20 .20
J61 D5 30h dark red .20 .20
J62 D5 40h dark red .20 .20
J63 D5 50h dark red .20 .20
J64 D5 60h dark red .20 .20
J65 D5 1k ultra .20 .20
J66 D5 2k ultra .50 .20
J67 D5 5k ultra .75 .20
J68 D5 10k ultra 1.90 .20
J69 D5 20k ultra 3.75 .30
Nos. J58-J69 (12) 8.50 2.50

D6

1946-48 Photo. *Perf. 14*
J70 D6 10h dark blue .20 .20
J71 D6 20h dark blue .20 .20
J72 D6 50h dark blue .35 .20
J73 D6 1k carmine rose .35 .20
J74 D6 1.20k carmine rose .35 .20
J75 D6 1.50k carmine rose ('48) .35 .20
J76 D6 1.60k carmine rose .35 .20
J77 D6 2k carmine rose ('48) .35 .20
J78 D6 2.40k carmine rose .35 .20
J79 D6 3k carmine rose .70 .20
J80 D6 5k carmine rose .70 .20
J81 D6 6k carmine rose ('48) 1.00 .20
Nos. J70-J81 (12) 5.25 2.40

D7

D8

1954-55 Engr. *Perf. 12½, 11½*
J82 D7 5h gray green ('55) .20 .20
J83 D7 10h gray green ('55) .20 .20
J84 D7 30h gray green .20 .20
J85 D7 50h gray green ('55) .20 .20
J86 D7 60h gray green ('55) .20 .20
J87 D7 95h gray green .35 .20
J88 D8 1k violet .35 .20
J89 D8 1.20k violet ('55) .35 .20
J90 D8 1.50k violet .70 .20
J91 D8 1.60k violet ('55) .45 .20
J92 D8 2k violet .85 .20
J93 D8 3k violet 1.10 .20
J94 D8 5k violet ('55) 1.40 .25
Nos. J82-J94 (13) 6.55 2.65

Perf. 11½ stamps are from a 1963 printing which lacks the 95h, 1.60k, and 2k.

Stylized Flower — D9

Designs: Various stylized flowers.

Engraved and Photogravure
1971-72 *Perf. 11½*
J95 D9 10h vio bl & pink .20 .20
J96 D9 20h vio & lt bl .20 .20
J97 D9 30h emer & lil rose .20 .20
J98 D9 60h pur & emer .20 .20
J99 D9 80h org & vio bl .20 .20
J100 D9 1k dk red & emer .25 .20
J101 D9 1.20k grn & org .20 .20
J102 D9 2k blue & red .40 .20
J103 D9 3k blk & yel .50 .20
J104 D9 4k brn & ultra .85 .20
J105 D9 5.40k red & lilac 1.00 .20
J106 D9 6k brick red & org 1.40 .20
Nos. J95-J106 (12) 5.60 2.40

All except 5.40k issued in 1972.

OFFICIAL STAMPS

Catalogue values for unused stamps in this section are for Never Hinged items.

Coat of Arms — O1

1945 Unwmk. Litho. *Perf. 10½x10*
O1 O1 50h dp slate grn .20 .20
O2 O1 1k dp bl vio .20 .20
O3 O1 1.20k plum .20 .20
O4 O1 1.50k crimson rose .20 .20
O5 O1 2.50k bright ultra .20 .20
O6 O1 5k dk vio brn .30 .20
O7 O1 8k rose pink .30 .30
Nos. O1-O7 (7) 1.60 1.50

Redrawn
1947 Photo. *Perf. 14*
O8 O1 60h red .20 .20
O9 O1 80h dk olive grn .20 .20
O10 O1 1k dk lilac gray .20 .20
O11 O1 1.20k dp plum .20 .20
O12 O1 2.40k dk car rose .20 .20
O13 O1 4k brt ultra .20 .20
O14 O1 5k dk vio brn .20 .20
O15 O1 7.40k purple .20 .20
Nos. O8-O15 (8) 1.60 1.60

There are many minor changes in design, size of numerals, etc., of the redrawn stamps.

NEWSPAPER STAMPS

Windhover — N1

1918-20 Unwmk. Typo. *Imperf.*
P1 N1 2h gray green .20 .20
P2 N1 5h green ('20) .20 .20
a. 5h dark green .40 .20
P3 N1 6h red .30 .25
P4 N1 10h dull violet .20 .20
P5 N1 20h blue .20 .20
P6 N1 30h gray brown .20 .20
P7 N1 50h orange ('20) .30 .20
P8 N1 100h red brown ('20) .40 .20
Nos. P1-P8 (8) 2.00 1.65

Nos. P1-P8 exist privately perforated.
For surcharges and overprints see Nos. P9-P10, P14-P16, Eastern Silesia P1-P5.

Stamps of 1918-20 Surcharged in Violet

1925-26
P9 N1 5h on 2h gray green .50 .40
P10 N1 5h on 6h red ('26) .25 *.40*

Special Delivery Stamps of 1918-20 Overprinted in Violet

1926
P11 SD1 5h apple grn, *yel* .20 .20
a. 5h dull green, *yellow* .50 .40
P12 SD1 10h red brn, *yel* .20 .20

With Additional Surcharge of New Value
P13 SD1 5h on 2h red vio, *yel* .35 .35
Nos. P11-P13 (3) .75 .75

Catalogue values for unused stamps in this section, from this point to the end of the section, are for Never Hinged items.

Newspaper Stamps of 1918-20 Overprinted in Violet

1934
P14 N1 10h dull violet .20 .20
P15 N1 20h blue .20 .20
P16 N1 30h gray brown .20 .20
Nos. P14-P16 (3) .60 .60

Overprinted for use by commercial firms only.

Carrier Pigeon — N2

1937 *Imperf.*
P17 N2 2h bister brown .20 .20
P18 N2 5h dull blue .20 .20
P19 N2 7h red orange .20 .20
P20 N2 9h emerald .20 .20
P21 N2 10h henna brown .20 .20
P22 N2 12h ultra .20 .20
P23 N2 20h dark green .20 .20
P24 N2 50h dark brown .20 .20
P25 N2 1k olive gray .20 .20
Nos. P17-P25 (9) 1.80 1.80

For overprint see Slovakia Nos. P1-P9.

Bratislava Philatelic Exhibition Issue
Souvenir Sheet
1937 *Imperf.*
P26 N2 10h henna brn, sheet of 25 4.00 4.00

Newspaper Delivery Boy — N4

1945 Unwmk. Typo. *Imperf.*
P27 N4 5h dull blue .20 .20
P28 N4 10h red .20 .20
P29 N4 15h emerald .20 .20
P30 N4 20h dark slate green .20 .20
P31 N4 25h bright red vio .20 .20
P32 N4 30h ocher .20 .20
P33 N4 40h red orange .20 .20
P34 N4 50h brown red .20 .20
P35 N4 1k slate gray .20 .20
P36 N4 5k deep vio blue .20 .20
Nos. P27-P36 (10) 2.00 2.00

CZECHOSLOVAK LEGION POST

The Czechoslovak Legion in Siberia issued these stamps for use on its mail and that of local residents. Forgeries exist.

Urn and Cathedral at Irkutsk — A1

Armored Railroad Car — A2

Sentinel — A3

Lion of Bohemia — A4

1919 Litho. *Perf. 11½*
1 A1 25k carmine 10.50
a. Imperf. 10.50
2 A2 50k yellow green 10.50
a. Imperf. 10.50
3 A3 1r red brown 14.00
a. Imperf. 14.00
Nos. 1-3 (3) 35.00
Nos. 1a-3a (3) 35.00

Originals of Nos. 1-3 and 1a-3a have yellowish gum. Ungummed remainders, which were given a white gum, exist imperforate and perforated 11½ and 14. Value per set, $3.

Embossed
Perce en Arc in Blue
4 A4 (25k) blue & rose 4.00

Two types: I- 6 points on star-like mace head at right of goblet; large saber handle; measures 19½x24¾mm. II- 5 points on mace head; small saber handle; measures 20x25mm.

No. 4 Overprinted

1920

No.	Type	Description	Unused
5	A4	(25k) bl & rose	7.00

Both types of No. 4 received overprint.

No. 5 Surcharged with New Values in Green

No.	Type	Description	Unused
6	A4	2k bl & rose	30.00
7	A4	3k bl & rose	30.00
8	A4	5k bl & rose	30.00
9	A4	10k bl & rose	30.00
10	A4	15k bl & rose	30.00
11	A4	25k bl & rose	30.00
12	A4	35k bl & rose	30.00
13	A4	50k bl & rose	30.00
14	A4	1r bl & rose	30.00
		Nos. 6-14 (9)	270.00

BOHEMIA AND MORAVIA

Catalogue values for unused stamps in this country are for never hinged items, beginning with Scott 20 in the regular postage section, Scott B1 in the semi-postal section, Scott J1 in the postage due section, Scott O1 in the official section, and Scott P1 in the newspaper section.

German Protectorate

Stamps of Czechoslovakia, 1928-39, Overprinted in Black

Perf. 10, 12½, 12x12½

1939, July 15 **Unwmk.**

No.	Type	Description	Unused	Used
1	A29	5h dk ultra	.20	.20
2	A29	10h brown	.20	.20
3	A29	20h red	.20	.20
4	A29	25h green	.20	.20
5	A29	30h red vio	.20	.20
6	A61a	40h dk bl	2.50	4.75
7	A85	50h dp grn	.20	.20
8	A63	60h dl vio	2.50	4.75
9	A60	1k rose lake (212)	.75	1.75
10	A60	1k rose lake (256)	.30	.85
11	A64	1.20k rose lilac	3.00	6.25
12	A65	1.50k carmine	2.50	4.75
13	A79	1.60k olive grn	2.50	4.75
a.		"Mähnen"	16.00	27.50
14	A66	2k dk bl grn	1.10	1.75
15	A67	2.50k dk bl	3.00	4.50
16	A68	3k brown	3.00	4.75
17	A70	4k dk vio	3.50	5.00
18	A71	5k green	3.50	5.75
19	A72	10k blue	4.75	9.50
		Nos. 1-19 (19)	34.10	60.30

Overprint size varies; #1-10 measure 17½x15½mm, #11-16 19x18mm, #17, 19 28x17½mm, #18 23½x23mm.

Catalogue values for unused stamps in this section, from this point to the end of the section, are for never hinged items.

Linden Leaves and Closed Buds — A1

1939-41 **Photo.** ***Perf. 14***

No.	Type	Description	Unused	Used
20	A1	5h dark blue	.20	.20
21	A1	10h blk brn	.20	.20
22	A1	20h crimson	.20	.20
23	A1	25h dk bl grn	.20	.20
24	A1	30h dp plum	.20	.20
24A	A1	30h golden brn ('41)	.20	.20
25	A1	40h orange ('40)	.20	.20
26	A1	50h slate grn ('40)	.20	.20
		Nos. 20-26 (8)	1.60	1.60

See Nos. 49-51.

Castle at Zvikov — A2

Karlstein Castle — A3

St. Barbara's Church, Kutna Hora — A4

Cathedral at Prague — A5

Brno Cathedral — A6

Town Square, Olomouc — A7

1939 **Engr.** ***Perf. 12½***

No.	Type	Description	Unused	Used
27	A2	40h dark blue	.20	.20
28	A3	50h dk bl grn	.20	.20
29	A4	60h dl vio	.20	.20
30	A5	1k dp rose	.20	.20
31	A6	1.20k rose lilac	.40	.60
32	A6	1.50k rose car	.20	.20
33	A7	2k dk bl grn	.20	.20
34	A7	2.50k dark blue	.20	.20
		Nos. 27-34 (8)	1.80	2.00

No. 31 measures 23½x29½mm, No. 42 measures 18½x23mm.

See #52-53, 53B. For overprints see #60-61.

Zlin — A8

Iron Works at Moravská Ostrava — A9

Prague — A10

1939-40

No.	Type	Description	Unused	Used
35	A8	3k dl rose vio	.20	.20
36	A9	4k slate ('40)	.20	.20
37	A10	5k green	.40	.40
38	A10	10k lt ultra	.30	.65
39	A10	20k yel brn	.90	1.25
		Nos. 35-39 (5)	2.00	2.70

Types of 1939 and

Neuhaus A11

Lainsitz Bridge near Bechyne A14

Pernstein Castle — A12

Samson Fountain, Budweis — A15

Pardubice Castle — A13

Kromeriz A16

Wallenstein Palace, Prague — A17

1940 **Engr.** ***Perf. 12½***

No.	Type	Description	Unused	Used
40	A11	50h dk bl grn	.20	.20
41	A12	80h dp bl	.25	.40
42	A6	1.20k vio brn	.40	.25
43	A13	2k gray grn	.20	.20
44	A14	5k dk bl grn	.20	.20
45	A15	6k brn vio	.20	.25
46	A16	8k slate grn	.20	.30
47	A17	10k blue	.45	.30
48	A10	20k sepia	1.10	1.50
		Nos. 40-48 (9)	3.20	3.60

No. 42 measures 18½x23mm; No. 31, 23½x29½mm.

Types of 1939-40

1941

No.	Type	Description	Unused	Used
49	A1	60h violet	.20	.20
50	A1	80h red org	.20	.20
51	A1	1k brown	.20	.20
52	A5	1.20k rose red	.20	.20
53	A4	1.50k lil rose	.20	.20
53A	A13	2k light blue	.20	.20
53B	A6	2.50k ultra	.20	.20
53C	A12	3k olive	.20	.20
		Nos. 49-53C (8)	1.60	1.60

Nos. 49-51 show buds open. Nos. 52 and 53B measure 18¾x23½mm and have no inscriptions below design.

For overprints see Nos. 60-61.

Antonin Dvorák — A18

1941, Aug. 25 **Engr.** ***Perf. 12½***

No.	Type	Description	Unused	Used
54	A18	60h dull lilac	.20	.20
55	A18	1.20k sepia	.25	.25

Antonin Dvorák (1841-1904), composer.

Labels alternate with stamps in sheets of #54-55.

Farming Scene — A19

Factories — A20

1941, Sept. 7 **Photo.** ***Perf. 13½***

No.	Type	Description	Unused	Used
56	A19	30h dk red brn	.20	.20
57	A19	60h dark green	.20	.20
58	A20	1.20k dk plum	.20	.25
59	A20	2.50k sapphire	.25	.35
		Nos. 56-59 (4)	.85	1.00

Issued to publicize the Prague Fair.

Nos. 52 and 53B Overprinted in Blue or Red

1942, Mar. 15 ***Perf. 12½***

No.	Type	Description	Unused	Used
60	A5	1.20k rose red (Bl)	.30	.50
61	A6	2.50k ultra (R)	.45	.50

3rd anniv. of the Protectorate of Bohemia and Moravia.

Adolf Hitler A21

17th Century Messenger A22

1942 **Photo.** ***Perf. 14***

Size: 17½x21½mm

No.	Type	Description	Unused	Used
62	A21	10(h) gray blk	.20	.20
63	A21	30(h) bister brn	.20	.20
64	A21	40(h) slate blue	.20	.20
65	A21	50(h) slate grn	.20	.20
66	A21	60(h) purple	.20	.20
67	A21	80(h) org ver	.20	.20

Perf. 12½

Engr.

Size: 18x21mm

No.	Type	Description	Unused	Used
68	A21	1k dl brn	.20	.20
69	A21	1.20(k) carmine	.20	.20
70	A21	1.50(k) claret	.20	.20
71	A21	1.60(k) Prus grn	.20	.50
72	A21	2k light blue	.20	.25
73	A21	2.40(k) fawn	.20	.25

Size: 18½x24mm

No.	Type	Description	Unused	Used
74	A21	2.50(k) ultra	.20	.25
75	A21	3k olive grn	.20	.25
76	A21	4k brt red vio	.20	.25
77	A21	5k myrtle grn	.20	.25
78	A21	6k claret brn	.20	.25
79	A21	8k indigo	.20	.25

Size: 23½x29¾mm

No.	Type	Description	Unused	Used
80	A21	10k dk gray grn	.20	1.00
81	A21	20k gray vio	.30	1.00
82	A21	30k red	.75	1.50
83	A21	50k deep blue	1.50	3.00
		Nos. 62-83 (22)	6.35	10.80

1943, Jan. 10 **Photo.** ***Perf. 13½***

No.	Type	Description	Unused	Used
84	A22	60h dark rose violet	.20	.20

Stamp Day.

Scene from "Die Meistersinger" A23

Richard Wagner A24

Scene from "Siegfried" — A25

1943, May 22

85 A23 60h violet .20 .20
86 A24 1.20k carmine rose .20 .20
87 A25 2.50k deep ultra .20 .20
Nos. 85-87 (3) .60 .60

Richard Wagner (1813-83).

St. Vitus' Cathedral, Prague — A26

Adolf Hitler — A27

1944, Nov. 21 Engr. *Perf. 12½*

88 A26 1.50k dull rose brn .20 .20
89 A26 2.50k dull lilac blue .20 *.25*

1944

90 A27 4.20k green .20 *.50*

SEMI-POSTAL STAMPS

Catalogue values for unused stamps in this section are for never hinged items.

Nurse and Wounded Soldier — SP1

Perf. 13½

1940, June 29 Photo. Unwmk.

B1 SP1 60h + 40h indigo .55 *.60*
B2 SP1 1.20k + 80h deep plum .70 .65

Surtax for German Red Cross.

Labels alternate with stamps in sheets of #B1-B2.

Red Cross Nurse and Patient — SP2

1941, Apr. 20

B3 SP2 60h + 40h indigo .40 *.60*
B4 SP2 1.20k + 80h dp plum .40 *.65*

Surtax for German Red Cross.

Labels alternate with stamps in sheets of #B3-B4.

Old Theater, Prague — SP3

Mozart — SP4

1941, Oct. 26

B5 SP3 30h + 30h brown .20 .20
B6 SP3 60h + 60h Prus grn .20 .20
B7 SP4 1.20k + 1.20k scar .25 *.45*
B8 SP4 2.50k + 2.50k dk bl .45 *.55*
Nos. B5-B8 (4) 1.10 *1.40*

150th anniversary of Mozart's death.

Labels alternate with stamps in sheets of Nos. B5-B8. The labels with Nos. B5-B6 show two bars of Mozart's opera "Don Giovanni." Those with Nos. B7-B8 show Mozart's piano.

Adolf Hitler — SP5

Nurse and Soldier — SP6

1942, Apr. 20 Engr. *Perf. 12½*

B9 SP5 30h + 20h dl brn vio .20 .20
B10 SP5 60h + 40h dl grn .20 .20
B11 SP5 1.20k + 80h dp claret .20 .25
B12 SP5 2.50k + 1.50k dl bl .20 *.35*
Nos. B9-B12 (4) .80 *1.00*

Hitler's 53rd birthday.

1942, Sept. 4 *Perf. 13½*

B13 SP6 60h + 40h deep blue .20 .20
B14 SP6 1.20(k) + 80(h) dp plum .20 .20

The surtax aided the German Red Cross.

Emperor Charles IV SP7

Peter Parler SP8

John the Blind, King of Bohemia — SP9

Adolf Hitler — SP10

1943, Jan. 29

B15 SP7 60h + 40h violet .20 .20
B16 SP8 1.20k + 80h carmine .20 .20
B17 SP9 2.50k + 1.50k vio bl .20 .20
Nos. B15-B17 (3) .60 *.60*

The surtax was for the benefit of the German wartime winter relief.

1943, Apr. 20 Engr. *Perf. 12½*

B18 SP10 60h + 1.40k dl vio .20 *.20*
B19 SP10 1.20k + 3.80k carmine .20 *.25*

Hitler's 54th birthday.

Deathmask of Reinhard Heydrich — SP11

Eagle and Red Cross — SP12

1943, May 28 Photo. *Perf. 13½*

B20 SP11 60h + 4.40k black .30 *.40*

No. B20 exists in a miniature sheet containing a single copy. It was given to officials attending Heydrich's funeral.

1943, Sept. 16 *Perf. 13*

B21 SP12 1.20k + 8.80k blk & car .20 .20

The surtax aided the German Red Cross.

Native Costumes SP13

Nazi Emblem, Arms of Bohemia, Moravia SP14

1944, Mar. 15 *Perf. 13½*

B22 SP13 1.20(k) + 3.80(k) rose lake .20 .20
B23 SP14 4.20(k) + 10.80(k) golden brn .20 .20
B24 SP13 10k + 20k saph .20 *.30*
Nos. B22-B24 (3) .60 *.70*

Fifth anniversary of protectorate.

Adolf Hitler — SP15

Bedrich Smetana — SP16

1944, Apr. 20

B25 SP15 60h + 1.40k olive blk .20 .20
B26 SP15 1.20k + 3.80k slate grn .20 .20

1944, May 12 Engr. *Perf. 12½*

B27 SP16 60h + 1.40k dk gray grn .20 .20
B28 SP16 1.20k + 3.80k brn car .20 .20

Bedrich Smetana (1824-84), Czech composer and pianist.

PERSONAL DELIVERY STAMPS

PD1

1939-40 Unwmk. Photo. *Perf. 13½*

EX1 PD1 50h indigo & blue ('40) .45 *.80*
EX2 PD1 50h carmine & rose .55 *1.10*

POSTAGE DUE STAMPS

Catalogue values for unused stamps in this section are for never hinged items.

D1

1939-40 Unwmk. Typo. *Perf. 14*

J1 D1 5h dark carmine .20 .20
J2 D1 10h dark carmine .20 .20
J3 D1 20h dark carmine .20 .20
J4 D1 30h dark carmine .20 .20
J5 D1 40h dark carmine .20 .20
J6 D1 50h dark carmine .20 .20
J7 D1 60h dark carmine .20 .20
J8 D1 80h dark carmine .20 .20
J9 D1 1k bright ultra .20 *.30*
J10 D1 1.20k brt ultra ('40) .25 *.35*
J11 D1 2k bright ultra .70 *.80*
J12 D1 5k bright ultra .85 .85
J13 D1 10k bright ultra 1.25 1.25
J14 D1 20k bright ultra 2.40 2.40
Nos. J1-J14 (14) 7.25 *7.55*

OFFICIAL STAMPS

Catalogue values for unused stamps in this section are for never hinged items.

Numeral O1

Eagle O2

Unwmk.

1941, Jan. 1 Typo. *Perf. 14*

O1 O1 30h ocher .20 .20
O2 O1 40h indigo .20 .20
O3 O1 50h emerald .20 .20
O4 O1 60h slate grn .20 .20
O5 O1 80h org red .55 .20
O6 O1 1k red brn .25 .20
O7 O1 1.20k carmine .25 .20
O8 O1 1.50k dp plum .40 .20
O9 O1 2k brt bl .40 .20
O10 O1 3k olive .40 .20
O11 O1 4k red vio .55 .45
O12 O1 5k org yel 1.40 .90
Nos. O1-O12 (12) 5.00 3.35

1943, Feb. 15

O13 O2 30(h) bister .20 .20
O14 O2 40(h) indigo .20 .20
O15 O2 50(h) yel grn .20 .20
O16 O2 60(h) dp vio .20 .20
O17 O2 80(h) org red .20 .20
O18 O2 1k chocolate .20 .20
O19 O2 1.20(k) carmine .20 .20
O20 O2 1.50(k) brn red .20 .20
O21 O2 2k lt bl .20 .20
O22 O2 3k olive .20 .20
O23 O2 4k red vio .20 .20
O24 O2 5k dk grn .20 *.30*
Nos. O13-O24 (12) 2.40 2.50

NEWSPAPER STAMPS

Catalogue values for unused stamps in this section are for never hinged items.

Carrier Pigeon — N1

1939 Unwmk. Typo. *Imperf.*

P1 N1 2h ocher .20 .20
P2 N1 5h ultra .20 .20
P3 N1 7h red orange .20 .20
P4 N1 9h emerald .20 .20
P5 N1 10h henna brown .20 .20
P6 N1 12h dark ultra .20 .20
P7 N1 20h dark green .20 *.25*
P8 N1 50h red brown .20 *.35*
P9 N1 1k greenish gray .20 *.35*
Nos. P1-P9 (9) 1.80 *2.15*

No. P5 Overprinted in Black

1940

P10 N1 10h henna brown .20 *.30*

Overprinted for use by commercial firms.

N2

1943, Feb. 15

P11	N2	2(h)	ocher	.20	.20
P12	N2	5(h)	light blue	.20	.20
P13	N2	7(h)	red orange	.20	.20
P14	N2	9(h)	emerald	.20	.20
P15	N2	10(h)	henna brown	.20	.20
P16	N2	12(h)	dark ultra	.20	.20
P17	N2	20(h)	dark green	.20	.20
P18	N2	50(h)	red brown	.20	.20
P19	N2	1k	slate green	.20	.20
			Nos. P11-P19 (9)	1.80	1.80

DAHOMEY

də-'hō-mē

LOCATION — West coast of Africa
AREA — 43,483 sq. mi.
POP. — 3,030,000 (est. 1974)
CAPITAL — Porto-Novo

Formerly a native kingdom including Benin, Dahomey was annexed by France in 1894. It became part of the colonial administrative unit of French West Africa in 1895. Stamps of French West Africa superseded those of Dahomey in 1945. The Republic of Dahomey was proclaimed Dec. 4, 1958.

The republic changed its name to the People's Republic of Benin on Nov. 30, 1975. See Benin for stamps issued after that date.

100 Centimes = 1 Franc

Catalog values for unused stamps in this country are for Never Hinged items, beginning with Scott 137 in the regular postage section, Scott B15 in the semi-postal section, Scott C14 in the airpost section, Scott CQ1 in the airpost parcel post section, Scott J29 in the postage due section, and Scott Q1 int he parcel post section.

See French West Africa No. 71 for stamp inscribed "Dahomey" and "Afrique Occidentale Francaise."

Navigation and Commerce — A1

Perf. 14x13½

1899-1905 Typo. Unwmk.

Name of Colony in Blue or Carmine

No.	Type	Description	Unused	Used
1	A1	1c black, *lil bl* ('01)	.95	.95
2	A1	2c brown, *buff* ('04)	1.60	1.00
3	A1	4c claret, *lav* ('04)	1.75	1.40
4	A1	5c yellow grn ('04)	4.25	2.40
5	A1	10c red ('01)	3.50	2.40
6	A1	15c gray ('01)	3.50	1.25
7	A1	20c red, *grn* ('04)	13.00	9.50
8	A1	25c black, *rose* ('99)	11.50	5.00
9	A1	25c blue ('01)	12.50	11.00
10	A1	30c brown, *bis* ('04)	17.00	8.75
11	A1	40c red, *straw* ('04)	18.00	11.00
12	A1	50c brn, *az* (name in red) ('01)	16.00	14.50
12A	A1	50c brn, *az* (name in bl) ('05)	25.00	16.00
13	A1	75c dp vio, *org* ('04)	65.00	42.50
14	A1	1fr brnz grn, *straw* ('04)	32.50	22.50
15	A1	2fr violet, *rose* ('04)	80.00	55.00
16	A1	5fr red lilac, *lav* ('04)	100.00	77.50
		Nos. 1-16 (17)	406.05	282.65

Perf. 13½x14 stamps are counterfeits.
For surcharges see Nos. 32-41.

Gen. Louis Faidherbe A2

Oil Palm — A3

Dr. Noel Eugène Ballay A4

1906-07 *Perf. 13½x14*

Name of Colony in Red or Blue

No.	Type	Description	Unused	Used
17	A2	1c slate	.95	.80
18	A2	2c chocolate	1.25	.85
19	A2	4c choc, *gray bl*	2.25	1.75
20	A2	5c green	6.50	1.75
21	A2	10c carmine (B)	16.00	2.75
22	A3	20c black, *azure*	10.00	8.95
23	A3	25c blue, *pnksh*	10.00	9.00
24	A3	30c choc, *pnksh*	11.50	9.00
25	A3	35c black, *yellow*	65.00	9.00
26	A3	45c choc, *grnsh* ('07)	14.50	10.00
27	A3	50c deep violet	14.50	11.00
28	A3	75c blue, *orange*	17.50	13.50
29	A4	1fr black, *azure*	21.00	16.00
30	A4	2fr blue, *pink*	85.00	85.00
31	A4	5fr car, *straw* (B)	75.00	75.00
		Nos. 17-31 (15)	350.95	254.35

#2-3, 6-7, 9-13 Surcharged in Black or Carmine

1912 *Perf. 14x13½*

No.	Description	Unused	Used
32	5c on 2c brn, *buff*	1.25	1.25
33	5c on 4c claret, *lav* (C)	1.10	1.10
a.	Double surcharge	200.00	
34	5c on 15c gray (C)	1.25	1.25
35	5c on 20c red, *grn*	1.10	1.10
36	5c on 25c blue (C)	1.25	1.25
a.	Inverted surcharge	160.00	
37	5c on 30c brown, *bis* (C)	1.25	1.25
38	10c on 40c red, *straw*	1.25	1.25
a.	Inverted surcharge	250.00	
39	10c on 50c brn, *az*, name in bl (C)	1.60	1.60
40	10c on 50c brn, *az*, name in red (C)	850.00	900.00
41	10c on 75c violet, *org*	4.25	4.25
a.	Double surcharge	*4,500.*	
	Nos. 32-39,41 (9)	14.30	14.30

Two spacings between the surcharged numerals are found on Nos. 32 to 41.

Man Climbing Oil Palm — A5

1913-39 *Perf. 13½x14*

No.	Type	Description	Unused	Used
42	A5	1c violet & blk	.20	.20
43	A5	2c choc & rose	.20	.20
44	A5	4c black & brn	.20	.20
45	A5	5c yel grn & bl grn	.80	.35
46	A5	5c vio brn & vio ('22)	.35	.35
47	A5	10c org red & rose	.80	.45
48	A5	10c yel grn & bl grn ('22)	.50	.50
49	A5	10c red & ol ('25)	.20	.20
50	A5	15c brn org & dk vio ('17)	.45	.35
51	A5	20c gray & choc	.35	.35
52	A5	20c bluish grn & grn ('26)	.20	.20
53	A5	20c mag & blk ('27)	.20	.20
54	A5	25c ultra & dp blue	1.40	.95
55	A5	25c vio brn & org ('22)	.70	.70
56	A5	30c choc & vio	2.00	1.60
57	A5	30c red org & rose ('22)	2.10	2.10
58	A5	30c yellow & vio ('25)	.20	.20
59	A5	30c dl grn & grn ('27)	.20	.20
60	A5	35c brown & blk	.60	.45
61	A5	35c bl grn & grn ('38)	.20	.20
62	A5	40c black & red org	.45	.45
63	A5	45c gray & ultra	.45	.45
64	A5	50c chocolate & brn	4.25	4.00
65	A5	50c ultra & bl ('22)	1.00	1.00
66	A5	50c brn red & bl ('26)	.85	.85
67	A5	55c gray grn & choc ('38)	.50	.35
68	A5	60c vio, *pnksh* ('25)	.20	.20
69	A5	65c yel brn & ol grn ('26)	.80	.80
70	A5	75c blue & violet	.80	.80
71	A5	80c henna brn & ultra ('38)	.20	.20
72	A5	85c dk bl & ver ('26)	1.00	1.00
73	A5	90c rose & brn red ('30)	.60	.50
74	A5	90c yel bis & red org ('39)	.75	.35
75	A5	1fr blue grn & blk	.80	.55
76	A5	1fr dk bl & ultra ('26)	1.00	1.00
77	A5	1fr yel brn & lt red ('28)	1.10	.80
78	A5	1fr dk red & red org ('38)	.75	.65
79	A5	1.10fr vio & bis ('28)	3.50	3.00
80	A5	1.25fr dp bl & dk brn ('33)	13.00	5.00
81	A5	1.50fr dk bl & lt bl ('30)	.95	.55
82	A5	1.75fr dk brn & dp buff ('33)	3.00	1.50
83	A5	1.75fr ind & ultra ('38)	1.00	.55
84	A5	2fr yel org & choc	.80	.80
85	A5	3fr red violet ('30)	2.00	.55
86	A5	5fr violet & dp bl	1.60	1.50
		Nos. 42-86 (45)	53.20	37.35

The 1c gray and yellow green and 5c dull red and black are Togo Nos. 193a, 196a.
For surcharges see #87-96, B1, B8-B11.

Type of 1913 Surcharged

1922-25

No.	Type	Description	Unused	Used
87	A5	60c on 75c vio, *pnksh*	.80	.80
a.		Double surcharge	140.00	
88	A5	65c on 15c brn org & dk vio ('25)	1.25	1.25
89	A5	85c on 15c brn org & dk vio ('25)	1.10	1.10
		Nos. 87-89 (3)	3.15	3.15

Stamps and Type of 1913-39 Surcharged with New Value and Bars

1924-27

No.	Type	Description	Unused	Used
90	A5	25c on 2fr org & choc	.80	.80
91	A5	90c on 75c cer & brn red ('27)	1.10	1.10
92	A5	1.25fr on 1fr dk bl & ultra (R) ('26)	.95	.95
93	A5	1.50fr on 1fr dk bl & grnsh bl ('27)	1.50	1.50
94	A5	3fr on 5fr olvn & dp org ('27)	7.25	7.25
95	A5	10fr on 5fr bl vio & red brn ('27)	5.75	5.75
96	A5	20fr on 5fr ver & dl grn ('27)	5.75	5.75
		Nos. 90-96 (7)	23.10	23.10

Common Design Types pictured following the introduction.

Colonial Exposition Issue

Common Design Types

1931 Engr. *Perf. 12½*

Name of Country in Black

No.	Type	Description	Unused	Used
97	CD70	40c deep green	4.25	4.25
98	CD71	50c violet	4.25	4.25
99	CD72	90c red orange	4.25	4.25
100	CD73	1.50fr dull blue	4.25	4.25
		Nos. 97-100 (4)	17.00	17.00

Paris International Exposition Issue

Common Design Types

1937 Engr. *Perf. 13*

No.	Type	Description	Unused	Used
101	CD74	20c deep violet	1.10	1.10
102	CD75	30c dark green	1.10	1.10
103	CD76	40c carmine rose	1.25	1.25
104	CD77	50c dark brown	1.25	1.25
105	CD78	90c red	1.25	1.25
106	CD79	1.50fr ultra	1.25	1.25
		Nos. 101-106 (6)	7.20	7.20

Souvenir Sheet

Imperf

No.	Type	Description	Unused	Used
107	CD77	3fr dp blue & blk	5.75	*7.25*

Caillié Issue

Common Design Type

1939, Apr. 5 Engr. *Perf. 12½x12*

No.	Type	Description	Unused	Used
108	CD81	90c org brn & org	.90	.90
109	CD81	2fr brt violet	.90	.90
110	CD81	2.25fr ultra & dk blue	1.10	1.10
		Nos. 108-110 (3)	2.90	2.90

New York World's Fair Issue

Common Design Type

1939 Engr.

No.	Type	Description	Unused	Used
111	CD82	1.25fr carmine lake	.80	.80
112	CD82	2.25fr ultra	.80	.80

Man Poling a Canoe — A7

Pile House A8

Sailboat on Lake Nokoué — A9

Dahomey Warrior — A10

1941 *Perf. 13*

No.	Type	Description	Unused	Used
113	A7	2c scarlet	.20	.20
114	A7	3c deep blue	.20	.20
115	A7	5c brown violet	.45	.45
116	A7	10c green	.20	.20
117	A7	15c black	.20	.20
118	A8	20c violet brown	.20	.20
119	A8	30c dk violet	.20	.20
120	A8	40c scarlet	.50	.50
121	A8	50c slate green	.80	.80
122	A8	60c black	.20	.20
123	A8	70c brt red violet	.80	.80
124	A9	80c brown black	.80	.80
125	A9	1fr violet	.80	.80
126	A9	1.30fr brown violet	.95	.95
127	A9	1.40fr green	.80	.80
128	A9	1.50fr brt rose	.80	.80
129	A9	2fr brown orange	1.00	1.00
130	A10	2.50fr dark blue	1.00	1.00
131	A10	3fr scarlet	.80	.80
132	A10	5fr slate green	.80	.80
133	A10	10fr violet brown	1.50	1.50
134	A10	20fr black	1.75	1.75
		Nos. 113-134 (22)	14.95	14.95

Nos. 121, 122 without "RF," see Nos. 136A-136B.

Pile House and Marshal Pétain A11

1941 *Perf. 12½x12*

No.	Type	Description	Unused	Used
135	A11	1fr green	.55	—
136	A11	2.50fr blue	.55	—

For surcharges see Nos. B14A-B14B.

Type of 1941 without "RF"

1944 ***Perf. 13***

136A A8 50c slate green .75
136B A8 60c black .75

Nos. 136A-136B were issued by the Vichy government in France, but were not placed on sale in Dahomey.

Catalogue values for unused stamps in this section, from this point to the end of the section, are for Never Hinged items.

Republic

Village Ganvié — A12

Unwmk.

1960, Mar. 1 **Engr.** ***Perf. 12***

137 A12 25fr dk blue, brn & red .55 .20

For overprint see No. 152.

Imperforates
Most Dahomey stamps from 1960 onward exist imperforate in issued and trial colors, and also in small presentation sheets in issued colors.

C.C.T.A. Issue
Common Design Type

1960, May 16

138 CD106 5fr rose lilac & ultra .45 .20

Emblem of the Entente — A13

Prime Minister Hubert Maga — A14

Council of the Entente Issue

1960, May 29 **Photo.** ***Perf. 13x13½***

139 A13 25fr multicolored .55 .30

1st anniv. of the Council of the Entente (Dahomey, Ivory Coast, Niger and Upper Volta).

1960, Aug. **Engr.** ***Perf. 13***

140 A14 85fr deep claret & blk 1.10 .60

Issued on the occasion of Dahomey's proclamation of independence, Aug. 1, 1960.
For surcharge see No. 149.

Weaver — A15

Doves, UN Building and Emblem — A16

2fr, 10fr, Wood sculptor. 3fr, 15fr, Fisherman and net, horiz. 4fr, 20fr, Potter, horiz.

1961, Feb. 17 **Engr.** ***Perf. 13***

141 A15 1fr rose, org & red lilac .20 .20
142 A15 2fr bister brn & choc .20 .20
143 A15 3fr green & orange .20 .20
144 A15 4fr olive bis & claret .20 .20
145 A15 6fr rose, lt vio & ver .30 .20
146 A15 10fr blue & green .45 .30
147 A15 15fr red lilac & violet .60 .30
148 A15 20fr bluish vio & Prus bl .75 .45
Nos. 141-148 (8) 2.90 2.05

For surcharges see Nos. Q1-Q7.

No. 140 Surcharged with New Value, Bars and: "Président de la République"

1961, Aug. 1

149 A14 100fr on 85fr dp cl & blk 2.10 2.10

First anniversary of Independence.

1961, Sept. 20 **Unwmk.** ***Perf. 13***

150 A16 5fr multicolored .25 .20
151 A16 60fr multicolored .90 .65

1st anniv. of Dahomey's admission to the UN. See #C16 and souvenir sheet #C16a.

No. 137 Overprinted: "JEUX SPORTIFS D'ABIDJAN 24 AU 31 DECEMBRE 1961"

1961, Dec. 24

152 A12 25fr dk blue, brn & red .55 .30

Abidjan Games, Dec 24-31.

Interior of Burned-out Fort Ouidah and Wrecked Car — A17

1962, July 31 **Photo.** ***Perf. 12½***

153 A17 30fr multicolored .40 .30
154 A17 60fr multicolored .90 .40

Evacuation of Fort Ouidah by the Portuguese, and its occupation by Dahomey. 1st anniv.

African and Malgache Union Issue
Common Design Type

1962, Sept. 8 ***Perf. 12½x12***

155 CD110 30fr red lil, bluish grn, red & gold .75 .45

Red Cross Nurses and Map — A18

1962, Oct. 5 **Engr.** ***Perf. 13***

156 A18 5fr blue, choc & red .25 .20
157 A18 20fr blue, dk grn & red .45 .35
158 A18 25fr blue, brown & red .50 .35
159 A18 30fr blue, black & red .65 .55
Nos. 156-159 (4) 1.85 1.45

Ganvié Woman in Canoe — A19

Peuhl Herdsman and Cattle — A20

Designs: 3fr, 65fr, Bariba chief of Nikki. 15fr, 50fr, Ouidah witch doctor, rock python. 20fr, 30fr, Nessoukoué women carrying vases on heads, Abomey. 25fr, 40fr, Dahomey girl. 60fr, Peuhl herdsman and cattle. 85fr, Ganvié woman in canoe.

1963, Feb. 18 **Unwmk.** ***Perf. 13***

160 A19 2fr grnsh blue & vio .20 .20
161 A19 3fr blue & black .20 .20
162 A20 5fr brown, blk & grn .45 .20
163 A19 15fr brn, bl grn & red brn .45 .20
164 A19 20fr green, blk & car .35 .20
165 A20 25fr dk brn, bl & bl grn .45 .20
166 A19 30fr brn org, choc & mag .50 .35
167 A20 40fr choc, grn & brt bl .80 .35
168 A19 50fr blk, grn, brn & red brn 1.25 .45
169 A20 60fr choc, org red & ol 2.25 .85
170 A19 65fr orange brn & choc 1.50 .55
171 A19 85fr brt blue & choc 2.25 .85
Nos. 160-171 (12) 10.65 4.60

For surcharges see Nos. 211, 232, Benin 655A, 690F, 700, 722.

Boxers — A21

Designs: 1fr, 20fr, Soccer goalkeeper, horiz. 2fr, 5fr, Runners.

1963, Apr. 11 **Engr.**

172 A21 50c green & blue .20 .20
173 A21 1fr olive, blk & brn .20 .20
174 A21 2fr olive, blue & brn .20 .20
175 A21 5fr brown, crim & blk .20 .20
176 A21 15fr dk violet & brn .35 .20
177 A21 20fr multicolored .55 .45
Nos. 172-177 (6) 1.70 1.45

Friendship Games, Dakar, Apr. 11-21.
For surcharge & overprint see Benin #697, 704.

President's Palace, Cotonou — A22

1963, Aug. 1 **Photo.** ***Perf. 12½x12***

178 A22 25fr multicolored .45 .20

Third anniversary of independence.

Gen. Toussaint L'Ouverture — A23

UN Emblem, Flame, "15" — A24

1963, Nov. 18 **Unwmk.** ***Perf. 12x13***

179 A23 25fr multicolored .35 .20
180 A23 30fr multicolored .55 .20
181 A23 100fr ultra, brn & red 1.10 .65
Nos. 179-181 (3) 2.00 1.05

Pierre Dominique Toussaint L'Ouverture (1743-1803), Haitian gen., statesman and descendant of the kings of Allada (Dahomey).

1963, Dec. 10 ***Perf. 12***

182 A24 4fr multicolored .20 .20
183 A24 6fr multicolored .20 .20
184 A24 25fr multicolored .45 .20
Nos. 182-184 (3) .85 .60

15th anniversary of the Universal Declaration of Human Rights.

Somba Dance — A25

Regional Dances: 3fr, Nago dance, Pobe-Ketou, horiz. 10fr, Dance of the baton. 15fr, Nago dance, Ouidah, horiz. 25fr, Dance of the Sakpatassi. 30fr, Dance of the Nessouhouessi, horiz.

1964, Aug. 8 **Engr.** ***Perf. 13***

185 A25 2fr red, emerald & blk .20 .20
186 A25 3fr dull red, blue & grn .20 .20
187 A25 10fr purple, blk & red .35 .20
188 A25 15fr magenta, blk & grn .35 .20
189 A25 25fr Prus blue, brn & org .65 .25
190 A25 30fr dk red, choc & org .85 .35
Nos. 185-190 (6) 2.60 1.40

Runner — A26

1964, Oct. 20 **Photo.** ***Perf. 11***

191 A26 60fr shown 1.25 .70
192 A26 85fr Bicyclist 2.00 .90

18th Olympic Games, Tokyo, Oct. 10-25.

Cooperation Issue
Common Design Type

1964, Nov. 7 **Engr.** ***Perf. 13***

193 CD119 25fr org, vio & dk brn .65 .20

UNICEF Emblem, Mother and Child — A27

IQSY Emblem and Apollo — A28

25fr, Mother holding child in her arms.

1964, Dec. 11 **Unwmk.** ***Perf. 13***

194 A27 20fr yel grn, dk red & blk .30 .20
195 A27 25fr blue, dk red & blk .45 .35

18th anniv. of UNICEF.

1964, Dec. 22 **Photo.** ***Perf. 13x12½***

100fr, IQSY emblem, Nimbus weather satellite.

196 A28 25fr green & lt yellow .35 .20
197 A28 100fr deep plum & yellow 1.00 .60

International Quiet Sun Year, 1964-65.

Abomey Tapestry — A29

Designs (Abomey tapestries): 25fr, Warrior and fight scenes. 50fr, Birds and warriors, horiz. 85fr, Animals, ship and plants, horiz.

1965, Apr. 12 Photo. *Perf. 12½*

198 A29 20fr multicolored .65 .20
199 A29 25fr multicolored .70 .35
200 A29 50fr multicolored 1.10 .70
201 A29 85fr multicolored 2.25 .90
a. Min. sheet of 4, #198-201 6.50 6.50
Nos. 198-201 (4) 4.70 2.15

Issued to publicize the local rug weaving industry.

Baudot Telegraph Distributor and Ader Telephone A30

1965, May 17 Engr. *Perf. 13*

202 A30 100fr lilac, org & blk 1.50 1.10

Cent. of the ITU.

Cotonou Harbor — A31

100fr, Cotonou Harbor, denomination at left.

1965, Aug. 1 Photo. *Perf. 12½*

203 A31 25fr multicolored .75 .20
204 A31 100fr multicolored 1.75 .90
a. Pair, #203-204 3.25 1.60

The opening of Cotonou Harbor. No. 204a has a continuous design.

For surcharges see Nos. 219-220.

Cybium Tritor A32

Fish: 25fr, Dentex filosus. 30fr, Atlantic sailfish. 50fr, Blackish tripletail.

1965, Sept. 20 Engr. *Perf. 13*

205 A32 10fr black & brt blue .45 .20
206 A32 25fr brt blue, org & blk .65 .45
207 A32 30fr violet bl & grnsh bl 1.25 .65
208 A32 50fr black, gray bl & org 2.00 .90
Nos. 205-208 (4) 4.35 2.20

For surcharge see Benin No. 911.

Independence Monument — A33

1965, Oct. 28 Photo. *Perf. 12x12½*

209 A33 25fr gray, black & red .30 .20
210 A33 30fr lt ultra, black & red .45 .20

October 28 Revolution, 2nd anniv.

No. 165 Surcharged

1965, Nov. Engr. *Perf. 13*

211 A20 1fr on 25fr .30 .20

Porto Novo Cathedral A34

Designs: 50fr, Ouidah Pro-Cathedral, vert. 70fr, Cotonou Cathedral.

1966, Mar. 21 Engr. *Perf. 13*

212 A34 30fr Prus bl, vio brn & grn .45 .20
213 A34 50fr vio brn, Prus bl & brn .50 .35
214 A34 70fr grn, Prus bl & vio brn .90 .55
Nos. 212-214 (3) 1.85 1.10

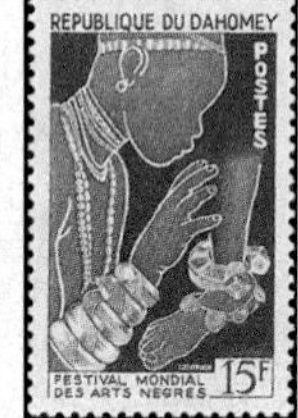

Jewelry — A35

Designs: 30fr, Architecture. 50fr, Musician. 70fr, Crucifixion, sculpture.

1966, Apr. 4 Engr. *Perf. 13*

215 A35 15fr dull red brn & blk .35 .20
216 A35 30fr dk brn, ultra & brn red .55 .35
217 A35 50fr brt blue & dk brn .90 .45
218 A35 70fr red brown & blk 1.75 .65
Nos. 215-218 (4) 3.55 1.65

International Negro Arts Festival, Dakar, Senegal, Apr. 1-24.

Nos. 203-204 Surcharged

1966, Apr. 24 Photo. *Perf. 12½*

219 A31 15fr on 25fr multi .55 .35
220 A31 15fr on 100fr multi .55 .35
a. Pair, #219-220 1.50 1.10

Fifth anniversary of the Cooperation Agreement between France and Dahomey.

WHO Headquarters from the East — A36

1966, May 3 *Perf. 12½x13*

Size: 35x22½mm

221 A36 30fr multicolored .55 .20

Inauguration of the WHO Headquarters, Geneva. See No. C32.

Boy Scout Signaling A37

Designs: 10fr, Patrol standard with pennant, vert. 30fr, Campfire and map of Dahomey, vert. 50fr, Scouts building foot bridge.

1966, Oct. 17 Engr. *Perf. 13*

222 A37 5fr dk brn, ocher & red .20 .20
223 A37 10fr black, grn & rose cl .20 .20
224 A37 30fr org, red brn & pur .55 .35
225 A37 50fr vio bl, grn & dk brn .95 .45
a. Min. sheet of 4, #222-225 2.25 2.25
Nos. 222-225 (4) 1.90 1.20

Clappertonia Ficifolia — A38

Lions Emblem, Dancing Children, Bird — A39

Flowers: 3fr, Hewittia sublobata. 5fr, Butterfly pea. 10fr, Water lily. 15fr, Commelina forskalaei. 30fr, Eremomastax speciosa.

1967, Feb. 20 Photo. *Perf. 12x12½*

226 A38 1fr multicolored .20 .20
227 A38 3fr multicolored .30 .20
228 A38 5fr multicolored .45 .20
229 A38 10fr multicolored .75 .30
230 A38 15fr multicolored 1.00 .45
231 A38 30fr multicolored 1.75 .75
Nos. 226-231 (6) 4.45 2.10

For surcharges see Benin Nos. 707, 715.

Nos. 170-171 Surcharged with New Value and Heavy Bar

1967, Mar. 1 Engr. *Perf. 13*

232 A19 30fr on 65fr .65 .45
a. Double surcharge 29.00
233 A19 30fr on 85fr .65 .45
a. Double surcharge 42.50
b. Inverted surcharge 42.50

1967, Mar. 20

234 A39 100fr dl vio, dp bl & grn 1.60 .70

50th anniversary of Lions International.

EXPO '67 "Man in the City" Pavilion A40

Design: 70fr, "The New Africa" exhibit.

1967, June 12 Engr. *Perf. 13*

235 A40 30fr green & choc .55 .20
236 A40 70fr green & brn red 1.10 .50

EXPO '67, International Exhibition, Montreal, Apr. 28-Oct. 27, 1967. See No. C57 and miniature sheet No. C57a.

For surcharges see Benin No. 897.

Europafrica Issue, 1967

Trade (Blood) Circulation, Map of Europe and Africa — A41

1967, July 20 Photo. *Perf. 12x12½*

237 A41 30fr multicolored .45 .20
238 A41 45fr multicolored .65 .35

Scouts Climbing Mountain, Jamboree Emblem A42

70fr, Jamboree emblem, Scouts launching canoe.

1967, Aug. 7 Engr. *Perf. 13*

239 A42 30fr brt bl, red brn & sl .50 .20
240 A42 70fr brt bl, sl grn & dk brn 1.25 .65

12th Boy Scout World Jamboree, Farragut State Park, Idaho, Aug. 1-9. For souvenir sheet see No. C59a.

For surcharges see Benin Nos. 902, 912.

Rhone River and Olympic Emblems A43

Designs (Olympic Emblems and): 45fr, View of Grenoble, vert. 100fr, Rhone Bridge, Grenoble, and Pierre de Coubertin.

1967, Sept. 2 Engr. *Perf. 13*

241 A43 30fr bis, dp bl & grn .55 .35
242 A43 45fr ultra, grn & brn .75 .45
243 A43 100fr choc, grn & brt bl 1.60 .85
a. Min. sheet of 3, #241-243 3.25 3.25
Nos. 241-243 (3) 2.90 1.65

10th Winter Olympic Games, Grenoble, Feb. 6-18, 1968.

For surcharge see Benin No. 903.

Monetary Union Issue

Common Design Type

1967, Nov. 4 Engr. *Perf. 13*

244 CD125 30fr grn, dk car & dk brn .55 .35

Cape Buffalo A45

Animals from the Pendjari Reservation: 30fr, Lion. 45fr, Buffon's kob. 70fr, African slender-snouted crocodile. 100fr, Hippopotamus.

1968, Mar. 18 Photo. *Perf. 12½x13*

245 A45 15fr multicolored .35 .20
246 A45 30fr purple & multi .55 .35
247 A45 45fr blue & multi 1.10 .45
248 A45 70fr multicolored 2.00 .55
249 A45 100fr multicolored 3.50 1.50
Nos. 245-249 (5) 7.50 3.05

For surcharges see #310, Benin 655E, 725.

WHO Emblem A46

1968, Apr. 22 Engr. *Perf. 13*

250 A46 30fr multicolored .45 .20
251 A46 70fr multicolored 1.00 .50

20th anniv. of WHO.

Leopard A47

Animals: 5fr, Warthog. 60fr, Spotted hyena. 75fr, Anubius baboon. 90fr, Hartebeest.

1969, Feb. 10 Photo. *Perf. 12½x12*

252 A47 5fr dark brown & multi .20 .20
253 A47 30fr deep ultra & multi .55 .35
254 A47 60fr dark green & multi 1.10 .50

255 A47 75fr dark blue & multi 2.25 .65
256 A47 90fr dark green & multi 3.00 1.50
Nos. 252-256 (5) 7.10 3.20

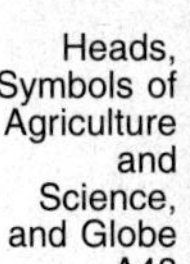

Heads, Symbols of Agriculture and Science, and Globe A48

1969, Mar. 10 Engr. *Perf. 13*

257 A48 30fr orange & multi .35 .20
258 A48 70fr maroon & multi 1.10 .50

50th anniv. of the ILO.
For surcharges see Benin Nos. 904, 913.

Arms of Dahomey — A49

1969, June 30 Litho. *Perf. 13½x13*

259 A49 5fr yellow & multi .35 .30
260 A49 30fr orange red & multi 1.25 .45

See No. C101.

Development Bank Issue

Cornucopia and Bank Emblem — A50

1969, Sept. 10 Photo. *Perf. 13*

261 A50 30fr black, grn & ocher .55 .35

African Development Bank, 5th anniv.
For surcharge see Benin No. 905.

Europafrica Issue

Ambary (Kenaf) Industry, Cotonou A51

Design: 45fr, Cotton industry, Parakou.

1969, Sept. 22 Litho. *Perf. 14*

262 A51 30fr multicolored .75 .35
263 A51 45fr multicolored .90 .55

See Nos. C105-C105a.

Sakpata Dance and Tourist Year Emblem — A52

Dances and Tourist Year Emblem: 30fr, Guelede dance. 45fr, Sato dance.

1969, Dec. 15 Litho. *Perf. 14*

264 A52 10fr multicolored .45 .30
265 A52 30fr multicolored .90 .45
266 A52 45fr multicolored 1.25 .55
Nos. 264-266 (3) 2.60 1.30

See No. C108. For surcharge see Benin No. 690J.

UN Emblem, Garden and Wall — A53

1970, Apr. 6 Engr. *Perf. 13*

267 A53 30fr ultra, red org & slate .50 .20
268 A53 40fr ultra, brn & sl grn .65 .35

25th anniversary of the United Nations.
For surcharges see Nos. 294, Benin 647B.

ASECNA Issue
Common Design Type

1970, June 1 Engr. *Perf. 13*

269 CD132 40fr red & purple .65 .25

For surcharge see Benin No. 906.

Mt. Fuji, EXPO '70 Emblem, Monorail Train — A54

1970, June 15 Litho. *Perf. 13½x14*

270 A54 5fr green, red & vio bl .25 .20

EXPO '70 International Exhibition, Osaka, Japan, 3/15-9/13/70. See Nos. C124-C125.

Alkemy, King of Ardres — A55

40fr, Sailing ships "La Justice" & "La Concorde," Ardres, 1670. 50fr, Matheo Lopes, ambassador of the King of Ardres & his coat of arms. 200fr, Louis XIV & fleur-de-lis.

1970, July 6 Engr. *Perf. 13*

271 A55 40fr brt grn, ultra & brn .55 .20
272 A55 50fr dk car, choc & emer .75 .35
273 A55 70fr gray, lemon & choc 1.10 .55
274 A55 200fr Prus bl, dk car & choc 3.00 1.10
Nos. 271-274 (4) 5.40 2.20

300th anniv. of the mission from the King of Ardres to the King of France, and of the audience with Louis XIV on Dec. 19, 1670.
For surcharge see Benin No. 914.

Star of the Order of Independence A56

Bariba Warrior A57

1970, Aug. 1 Photo. *Perf. 12*

275 A56 30fr multicolored .40 .20
276 A56 40fr multicolored .60 .20

10th anniversary of independence.
For surcharge see Benin No. 720.

1970, Aug. 24 *Perf. 12½x13*

Designs: 2fr, 50fr, Two horsemen. 10fr, 70fr, Horseman facing left.

277 A57 1fr yellow & multi .20 .20
278 A57 2fr gray grn & multi .30 .20
279 A57 10fr blue & multi .35 .20
280 A57 40fr yellow grn & multi 1.40 .35
281 A57 50fr gold & multi 1.75 .50
282 A57 70fr lilac rose & multi 2.10 .80
Nos. 277-282 (6) 6.10 2.25

For surcharges see Benin Nos. 350-351, 613, 703.

Globe and Heart A58

Design: 40fr, Hands holding heart, vert.

1971, June 7 Engr. *Perf. 13*

283 A58 40fr red, green & dk brn .90 .35
284 A58 100fr green, red & blue 1.75 .90

For surcharges see Benin Nos. 617, 647A, 712, 907.

Intl. year against racial discrimination.

Ancestral Figures and Lottery Ticket — A59

King Behanzin's Emblem (1889-1894) A60

1971, June 24 Litho. *Perf. 14*

285 A59 35fr multicolored .65 .20
286 A59 40fr multicolored .80 .35

4th anniv. of the National Lottery.
For overprint see Benin #710.

Photo.; Litho. (25fr, 135fr)
1971-72 *Perf. 12½*

Emblems of the Kings of Abomey: 25fr, Agoliagbo (1894-1900). 35fr, Ganyehoussou (1620-45), bird and cup, horiz. 100fr, Guezo (1818-58), bull, tree and birds. 135fr, Ouegbadja (1645-85), horiz. 140fr, Glèle (1858-89), lion and sword, horiz.

287 A60 25fr multicolored .35 .20
288 A60 35fr green & multi .55 .20
289 A60 40fr green & multi .75 .35
290 A60 100fr red & multi 1.40 .55
291 A60 135fr multicolored 2.00 .90
292 A60 140fr brown & multi 2.25 1.10
Nos. 287-292 (6) 7.30 3.30

Issued: 25fr, 135fr, 7/17/72; others, 8/3/71.
For surcharges, see Benin #614, 634B, 726, 791.

Kabuki Actor, Long-distance Skiing — A61

Brahms and "Soir d'été" — A62

1972, Feb. Engr. *Perf. 13*

293 A61 35fr dk car, brn & bl grn 1.60 .75

11th Winter Olympic Games, Sapporo, Japan, Feb. 3-13. See No. C153.

No. 268 Surcharged

1972

294 A53 35fr on 40fr multi .65 .35

1972, June 29 Engr. *Perf. 13*

65fr, Brahms, woman at piano & music, horiz.

295 A62 30fr red brn, blk & lilac 1.75 .55
296 A62 65fr red brn, blk & lilac 3.00 1.25

75th anniversary of the death of Johannes Brahms (1833-1897), German composer.
For surcharge see Benin Nos. 654B, 718.

The Hare and The Tortoise, by La Fontaine — A63

Fables: 35fr, The Fox and The Stork, vert. 40fr, The Cat, The Weasel and Rabbit.

1972, Aug. 28 Engr. *Perf. 13*

297 A63 10fr multicolored 1.75 .75
298 A63 35fr dark red & multi 3.25 1.25
299 A63 40fr ultra & multi 4.25 1.75
Nos. 297-299 (3) 9.25 3.75

Jean de La Fontaine (1621-1695), French fabulist.

West African Monetary Union Issue
Common Design Type

1972, Nov. 2 Engr. *Perf. 13*

300 CD136 40fr choc, ocher & gray .65 .20

Dr. Hansen, Microscope, Bacilli — A65

Design: 85fr, Portrait of Dr. Hansen.

1973, May 14 Engr. *Perf. 13*

301 A65 35fr ultra, vio brn & brn .50 .35
302 A65 85fr yel grn, bis & ver 1.10 .75

Centenary of the discovery by Dr. Armauer G. Hansen of the Hansen bacillus, the cause of leprosy.
For surcharges see Benin Nos. 655G, 1084.

Arms of Dahomey — A66

1973, June 25 Photo. *Perf. 13*

303 A66 5fr ultra & multi .20 .20
304 A66 35fr ocher & multi .40 .20
305 A66 40fr red orange & multi .60 .20
Nos. 303-305 (3) 1.20 .60

For surcharge see Benin No. 690A.

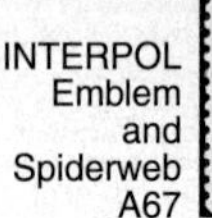

INTERPOL Emblem and Spiderweb A67

Design: 50fr, INTERPOL emblem and communications symbols, vert.

1973, July Engr.

306 A67 35fr ver, grn & brn .60 .30
307 A67 50fr green, brn & red 1.00 .45

50th anniversary of International Criminal Police Organization (INTERPOL).
For surcharges see Benin Nos. 634A, 810.

Education in Hygiene and Nutrition A68

WHO, 25th Anniv.: 100fr, Prenatal examination and care, WHO emblem.

1973, Aug. 2 Photo. *Perf. 12½x13*

308 A68 35fr multicolored .50 .30
309 A68 100fr multicolored 1.50 .65

No. 248 Surcharged with New Value, 2 Bars, and Overprinted in Red: "SECHERESSE SOLIDARITE AFRICAINE"

1973, Aug. 16

310 A45 100fr on 70fr multi 2.10 1.00

African solidarity in drought emergency.

African Postal Union Issue

Common Design Type

1973, Sept. 12 Engr. *Perf. 13*

311 CD137 100fr red, purple & blk 1.25 .55

For surcharge see Benin No. 690I.

Epinephelus Aeneus — A69

Fish: 15fr, Drepane africana. 35fr, Pragus ehrenbergi.

1973, Sept. 18

312 A69 5fr slate blue & indigo 1.00 .30
313 A69 15fr black & brt blue 1.50 .35
314 A69 35fr emerald, ocher & sep 3.50 .60
Nos. 312-314 (3) 6.00 1.25

Chameleon A70

40fr, Emblem over map of Dahomey, vert.

1973, Nov. 30 Photo. *Perf. 13*

315 A70 35fr olive & multi .55 .30
316 A70 40fr multicolored 1.25 .35

1st anniv. of the Oct. 26 revolution.

The Chameleon in the Tree — A71

Designs: 5fr, The elephant, the hen and the dog, vert. 10fr, The sparrowhawk and the dog, vert. 25fr, The chameleon in the tree. 40fr, The eagle, the viper and the hen.

1974, Feb. 14 Photo. *Perf. 13*

317 A71 5fr emerald & multi .40 .20
318 A71 10fr slate blue & multi .50 .20
319 A71 25fr slate blue & multi .90 .30
320 A71 40fr light blue & multi 1.40 .45
Nos. 317-320 (4) 3.20 1.15

Folktales of Dahomey.
For surcharges see Benin Nos. 709, 908.

German Shepherd — A72

1974, Apr. 25 Photo. *Perf. 13*

321 A72 40fr shown 1.50 .35
322 A72 50fr Boxer 1.75 .35
323 A72 100fr Saluki 3.50 .80
Nos. 321-323 (3) 6.75 1.50

Council Issue

Map and Flags of Members A73

1974, May 29 Photo. *Perf. 13x12½*

324 A73 40fr blue & multi .80 .20

15th anniversary of the Council of Accord.

Locomotive 232, 1911 — A74

Designs: Locomotives.

1974, Sept. 2 Photo. *Perf. 13x12½*

325 A74 35fr shown .75 .30
326 A74 40fr Freight, 1877 1.50 .30
327 A74 100fr Crampton, 1849 2.25 1.00
328 A74 200fr Stephenson, 1846 4.50 1.60
Nos. 325-328 (4) 9.00 3.20

For surcharges see Benin Nos. 654E, 690K, 727, 909.

Globe, Money, People in Bank A75

1974, Oct. 31 Engr. *Perf. 13*

329 A75 35fr multicolored .50 .35

World Savings Day.

Dompago Dance, Hissi Tribe — A76

Flags of Dahomey and Nigeria over Africa — A77

Folk Dances: 25fr, Fetish Dance, Vaudou-Tchinan. 40fr, Bamboo Dance, Agbehoun. 100fr, Somba Dance, Sandoua, horiz.

1975, Aug. 4 Litho. *Perf. 12*

330 A76 10fr yellow & multi .50 .20
331 A76 25fr dk green & multi 1.00 .20
332 A76 40fr red & multi 1.25 .50
333 A76 100fr multicolored 2.25 .60
Nos. 330-333 (4) 5.00 1.50

For surcharge and overprint see Benin Nos. 655D, 713.

1975, Aug. 11 Photo. *Perf. 12½x13*

Design: 100fr, Arrows connecting maps of Dahomey and Nigeria, horiz.

334 A77 65fr multicolored .75 .25
335 A77 100fr green & multi 1.00 .45

Year of intensified cooperation between Dahomey and Nigeria.
For surcharges & overprint see Benin Nos. 690H, 701, 899, 901.

Map, Pylons, Emblem — A78

Benin Electric Community Emblem and Pylon — A79

1975, Aug. 18

336 A78 40fr multicolored .75 .35
337 A79 150fr multicolored 2.00 1.00

Benin Electric Community and Ghana-Togo-Dahomey cooperation.
For surcharges see Benin #601, 900, 910.

Map of Dahomey, Rising Sun — A80

Albert Schweitzer, Nurse, Patient — A81

1975, Aug. 25 Photo. *Perf. 12½x13*

338 A80 35fr multicolored .50 .20

Cooperation Year for the creation of a new Dahoman society.
For overprint see Benin No. 690E.

1975, Sept. 22 Engr. *Perf. 13*

339 A81 200fr olive, grn & red brn 5.00 1.50

Birth centenary of Albert Schweitzer (1875-1965), medical missionary and musician.
For surcharge see Benin No. 655F.

Woman Speaking on Telephone, IWY Emblem — A82

150fr, IWY emblem and linked rings.

1975, Oct. 20 Engr. *Perf. 12½x13*

340 A82 50fr Prus blue & lilac .75 .35
341 A82 150fr emerald, brn & org 2.00 .80

International Women's Year 1975.
For surcharge see Benin No. 655C.

SEMI-POSTAL STAMPS

Regular Issue of 1913 Surcharged in Red

1915 Unwmk. *Perf. 14x13½*

B1 A5 10c + 5c orange red & rose .90 .90

Curie Issue

Common Design Type

1938 *Perf. 13*

B2 CD80 1.75fr + 50c brt ultra 7.25 7.25

French Revolution Issue

Common Design Type

1939 Photo.

Name and Value Typo. in Black

B3 CD83 45c + 25c green 6.50 6.50
B4 CD83 70c + 30c brown 6.50 6.50
B5 CD83 90c + 35c red org 6.50 6.50
B6 CD83 1.25fr + 1fr rose pink 6.50 6.50
B7 CD83 2.25fr + 2fr blue 6.50 6.50
Nos. B3-B7 (5) 32.50 32.50

Postage Stamps of 1913-38 Surcharged in Black

1941 ***Perf. 13½x14***

B8 A5 50c + 1fr brn red & bl 1.50 1.50
B9 A5 80c + 2fr hn brn & ultra 5.00 5.00
B10 A5 1.50fr + 2fr dk bl & lt bl 5.00 5.00
B11 A5 2fr + 3fr yel org & choc 5.00 5.00
Nos. B8-B11 (4) 16.50 16.50

Common Design Type and

Radio Operator — SP1

Senegalese Artillerymen SP2

1941 **Photo.** ***Perf. 13½***

B12 SP1 1fr + 1fr red .95
B13 CD86 1.50fr + 3fr claret .95
B14 SP2 2.50fr + 1fr blue 1.00
Nos. B12-B14 (3) 2.90

Surtax for the defense of the colonies.
Nos. B12-B14 were issued by the Vichy government in France, but were not placed on sale in Dahomey.

Nos. 135-136
Surcharged in Black or Red

1944 **Engr.** ***Perf. 12½x12***

B14A 50c + 1.50fr on 2.50fr deep blue (R) .55
B14B + 2.50fr on 1fr green .55

Colonial Development Fund.
Nos. B14A-B14B were issued by the Vichy government in France, but were not placed on sale in Dahomey.

Catalogue values for unused stamps in this section, from this point to the end of the section, are for Never Hinged items.

Republic

Anti-Malaria Issue

Common Design Type

1962, Apr. 7 **Engr.** ***Perf. 12½x12***

B15 CD108 25fr + 5fr orange brn .55 .55

Freedom from Hunger Issue

Common Design Type

1963, Mar. 21 **Unwmk.** ***Perf. 13***

B16 CD112 25fr + 5fr ol, brn red & brn .65 .65

AIR POST STAMPS

Common Design Type

1940 **Unwmk.** **Engr.** ***Perf. 12½***

C1 CD85 1.90fr ultra .20 .25
C2 CD85 2.90fr dk red .35 .35
C3 CD85 4.50fr dk gray grn .55 .55
C4 CD85 4.90fr yel bister .70 .70
C5 CD85 6.90fr deep org 1.00 1.00
Nos. C1-C5 (5) 2.80 2.85

Common Design Types

1942

C6 CD88 50c car & bl .20
C7 CD88 1fr brn & blk .20
C8 CD88 2fr dk grn & red brn .35
C9 CD88 3fr dk bl & scar .80
C10 CD88 5fr vio & brn red .80

Frame Engr., Center Typo.

C11 CD89 10fr ultra, ind & org .80
C12 CD89 20fr rose car, mag & gray blk .80
C13 CD89 50fr yel grn, dl grn & dp bl 1.50 *3.25*
a. 50fr yellow green, dull green & pale blue 2.00 *3.75*
Nos. C6-C13 (8) 5.45

Nos. C6-C12 were issued by the Vichy government in France, but were not placed on sale in Dahomey.

Catalogue values for unused stamps in this section, from this point to the end of the section, are for Never Hinged items.

Republic

Somba House — AP4

Design: 500fr, Royal Court of Abomey.

Unwmk.

1960, Apr. 1 **Engr.** ***Perf. 13***

C14 AP4 100fr multi 3.25 .80
C15 AP4 500fr multi 13.50 4.00

For overprint see Benin No. C419.

Type of Regular Issue, 1961

1961, Sept. 20

C16 A16 200fr multi 3.00 2.25
a. Souv. sheet of 3, #150-151, C16 6.00 6.00

Air Afrique Issue

Common Design Type

1962, Feb. 17 ***Perf. 13***

C17 CD107 25fr ultra, blk & org brn .70 .30

Palace of the African and Malgache Union, Cotonou — AP5

1963, July 27 **Photo.** ***Perf. 13x12***

C18 AP5 250fr multi 4.00 2.00

Assembly of chiefs of state of the African and Malgache Union held at Cotonou in July.

African Postal Union Issue

Common Design Type

1963, Sept. 8 **Unwmk.** ***Perf. 12½***

C19 CD114 25fr brt bl, ocher & red .60 .25

See note after Cameroun No. C47.

Boeing 707 — AP6

Boeing 707: 200fr, On the ground. 300fr, Over Cotonou airport. 500fr, In the air.

1963, Oct. 25 **Engr.** ***Perf. 13***

C20 AP6 100fr multi 2.00 .60
C21 AP6 200fr multi 3.00 2.00
C22 AP6 300fr multi 5.00 2.00
C23 AP6 500fr multi 10.00 2.50
Nos. C20-C23 (4) 20.00 7.10

For surcharges see Nos. CQ1-CQ5.

Priests Carrying Funerary Boat, Isis Temple, Philae — AP7

1964, Mar. 9 **Unwmk.** ***Perf. 13***

C24 AP7 25fr vio bl & brn 1.50 .75

UNESCO world campaign to save historic monuments in Nubia.

Weather Map and Symbols — AP8

1965, Mar. 23 **Photo.** ***Perf. 12½***

C25 AP8 50fr multi .80 .55

Fifth World Meteorological Day.

ICY Emblem and Men of Various Races — AP9

1965, June 26 **Engr.** ***Perf. 13***

C26 AP9 25fr dl pur, mar & grn .40 .20
C27 AP9 85fr dp bl, mar & sl grn .90 .65

International Cooperation Year, 1965

Winston Churchill — AP10

1965, June 15 **Photo.** ***Perf. 12½***

C28 AP10 100fr multi 1.65 1.10

Abraham Lincoln — AP11

1965, July 15 ***Perf. 13***

C29 AP11 100fr multi 1.65 1.00

Centenary of death of Lincoln
For surcharge see No. C55.

John F. Kennedy and Arms of Dahomey — AP12

1965, Nov. 22 **Photo.** ***Perf. 12½***

C30 AP12 100fr dp grn & blk 2.25 1.10

President John F. Kennedy (1917-63).
For surcharge see No. C56.

Dr. Albert Schweitzer and Patients — AP13

1966, Jan. 17 **Photo.** ***Perf. 12½***

C31 AP13 100fr multi 2.50 1.25

Dr. Albert Schweitzer (1875-1965), medical missionary, theologian and musician.
For surcharge see Benin No. C435.

WHO Type of Regular Issue

Design: WHO Headquarters from the West.

1966, May 3 **Unwmk.** ***Perf. 13***
Size: 47x28mm

C32 A36 100fr ultra, yel & blk 1.15 .90

Pygmy Goose — AP14

Broad-billed Rollers — AP15

Birds: 100fr, Fiery-breasted bush-shrike. 250fr, Emerald cuckoos. 500fr, Emerald starling.

1966-67 ***Perf. 12½***

C33 AP14 50fr multi 2.00 .55
C34 AP14 100fr multi 3.00 .85
C35 AP15 200fr multi 10.00 2.25

C36 AP15 250fr multi 10.00 3.00
C37 AP14 500fr multi 15.00 6.00
Nos. C33-C37 (5) 40.00 12.65

Issued: 50fr, 100fr, 500fr, 6/13/66; others, 1/20/67.
For surcharges see Nos. C107, Benin C353-C355, C357, C368, C436, C448.

Industrial Symbols — AP16

1966, July 21 Photo. *Perf. 12x13*
C38 AP16 100fr multi 1.60 .80

Agreement between European Economic Community & the African & Malagache Union, 3rd anniv.

Pope Paul VI and St. Peter's, Rome — AP17

Pope Paul VI and UN General Assembly AP18

70fr, Pope Paul VI and view of NYC.

1966, Aug. 22 Engr. *Perf. 13*
C39 AP17 50fr multi .75 .45
C40 AP17 70fr multi .95 .55
C41 AP18 100fr multi 1.75 1.00
a. Min. sheet of 3, #C39-C41 4.50 4.50
Nos. C39-C41 (3) 3.45 2.00

Pope Paul's appeal for peace before the UN General Assembly, Oct. 4, 1965.

Air Afrique Issue, 1966
Common Design Type

1966, Aug. 31 Photo. *Perf. 12½*
C42 CD123 30fr dk vio, blk & gray 1.50 .50

"Science" — AP20

Designs: 45fr, "Art" (carved female statue), vert. 100fr, "Education" (book and letters).

1966, Nov. 4 Engr. *Perf. 13*
C43 AP20 30fr mag, ultra & vio brn .45 .20
C44 AP20 45fr mar & grn .80 .55
C45 AP20 100fr blk, mar & brt bl 1.90 1.00
a. Min. sheet of 3, #C43-C45 3.25 3.25
Nos. C43-C45 (3) 3.15 1.75

20th anniversary of UNESCO.

Madonna by Alessio Baldovinetti AP21

Christmas: 50fr, Nativity after 15th century Beaune tapestry. 100fr, Adoration of the Shepherds, by José Ribera.

1966, Dec. 25 Photo. *Perf. 12½x12*
C46 AP21 50fr multi 3.25 2.25
C47 AP21 100fr multi 4.50 3.25
C48 AP21 200fr multi 9.00 5.00
Nos. C46-C48 (3) 16.75 10.50

See Nos. C95-C96, C109-C115. For surcharge see No. C60.

1967, Apr. 10 *Perf. 12½x12*

Paintings by Ingres: No. C49, Self-portrait, 1804. No. C50, Oedipus and the Sphinx.

C49 AP21 100fr multi 3.00 1.50
C50 AP21 100fr multi 3.00 1.50

Jean Auguste Dominique Ingres (1780-1867), French painter.

Three-master Suzanne — AP22

Windjammers: 45fr, Three-master Esmeralda, vert. 80fr, Schooner Marie Alice, vert. 100fr, Four-master Antonin.

1967, May 8 *Perf. 13*
C51 AP22 30fr multi 1.00 .50
C52 AP22 45fr multi 1.25 .75
C53 AP22 80fr multi 2.25 1.25
C54 AP22 100fr multi 3.00 1.50
Nos. C51-C54 (4) 7.50 4.00

For overprint & surcharge see Benin Nos. C369, C420.

Nos. C29-C30 Surcharged

1967, May 29 Photo. *Perf. 13, 12½*
C55 AP11 125fr on 100fr 2.00 1.25
C56 AP12 125fr on 100fr 2.00 1.25

50th anniv. of the birth of Pres. John F. Kennedy.

EXPO '67 "Man In Space" Pavilion — AP23

1967, June 12 Engr. *Perf. 13*
C57 AP23 100fr dl red & Prus bl 2.25 .75
a. Min. sheet of 3, #235-236, C57 4.00 4.00

EXPO '67, International Exhibition, Montreal, Apr. 28-Oct. 27, 1967.

Europafrica Issue, 1967

Konrad Adenauer, by Oscar Kokoschká AP24

1967, July 19 Photo. *Perf. 12½x12*
C58 AP24 70fr multi 1.50 .75
a. Souv. sheet of 4 7.00 7.00

Konrad Adenauer (1876-1967), chancellor of West Germany (1949-1963).

Jamboree Emblem, Ropes and World Map — AP25

1967, Aug. 7 Engr. *Perf. 13*
C59 AP25 100fr lil, sl grn & dp bl 1.90 .75
a. Souv. sheet of 3, #239-240, C59 4.00 4.00

12th Boy Scout World Jamboree, Farragut State Park, Idaho, Aug. 1-9.

No. C48 Surcharged in Red

1967, Aug. 12 Photo. *Perf. 12½x12*
C60 AP21 150fr on 200fr 3.00 2.25
a. "150F" omitted 300.00 300.00

Riccione, Italy Stamp Exhibition.

African Postal Union Issue, 1967
Common Design Type

1967, Sept. 9 Engr. *Perf. 13*
C61 CD124 100fr red, brt lil & emer 1.25 .75

For surcharge see Benin No. C471.

Charles de Gaulle AP26

1967, Nov. 21 Photo. *Perf. 12½x13*
C62 AP26 100fr multi 3.25 2.00
a. Souv. sheet of 4 15.00 15.00

Pres. Charles de Gaulle of France on the occasion of Pres. Christophe Soglo's state visit to Paris, Nov. 1967.

Madonna, by Matthias Grunewald AP27

Paintings: 50fr, Holy Family by the Master of St. Sebastian, horiz. 100fr, Adoration of the Magi by Ulrich Apt the Elder. 200fr, Annunciation, by Matthias Grunewald.

1967, Dec. 11 Photo. *Perf. 12½*
C63 AP27 30fr multi .55 .45
C64 AP27 50fr multi 1.10 .60
C65 AP27 100fr multi 2.00 1.25
C66 AP27 200fr multi 5.00 2.00
Nos. C63-C66 (4) 8.65 4.30

Christmas 1967.

Venus de Milo and Mariner 5 — AP28

Gutenberg Monument, Strasbourg Cathedral AP29

#C68, Venus de Milo and Venus 4 Rocket.

1968, Feb. 17 Photo. *Perf. 13*
C67 AP28 70fr grnsh bl & multi 1.50 .75
C68 AP28 70fr dp bl & multi 1.50 .75
a. Souv. sheet of 2, #C67-C68 3.50 3.50

Explorations of the planet Venus, Oct. 18-19, 1967.
For surcharges see Nos. C103-C104.

1968, May 20 Litho. *Perf. 14x13½*

Design: 100fr, Gutenberg Monument, Mainz, and Gutenberg press.

C69 AP29 45fr grn & org 1.00 .40
C70 AP29 100fr dk & lt bl 2.00 1.00
a. Souv. sheet of 2, #C69-C70 3.75 3.75

500th anniv. of the death of Johann Gutenberg, inventor of printing from movable type.
For surcharge see Benin #C516.

Martin Luther King, Jr. — AP30

Designs: 30fr, "We must meet hate with creative love" in French, English and German. 100fr, Full-face portrait.

Perf. 12½, 13½x13

1968, June 17 — Photo.

Size: 26x46mm

No.	Type	Description	Unused	Used
C71	AP30	30fr red brn, yel & blk	.55	.35

Size: 26x37mm

No.	Type	Description	Unused	Used
C72	AP30	55fr multi	.85	.45
C73	AP30	100fr multi	1.25	.90
a.		Min. sheet of 3, #C71-C73	3.75	3.75
		Nos. C71-C73 (3)	2.65	1.70

Martin Luther King, Jr. (1929-68), American civil rights leader.

Robert Schuman — AP31

45fr, Alcide de Gasperi. 70fr, Konrad Adenauer.

1968, July 20 — Photo. — *Perf. 13*

No.	Type	Description	Unused	Used
C74	AP31	30fr dp yel, blk & grn	.40	.40
C75	AP31	45fr org, dk brn & ol	.85	.50
C76	AP31	70fr multi	1.40	.50
		Nos. C74-C76 (3)	2.65	1.40

5th anniversary of the economic agreement between the European Economic Community and the African and Malgache Union.

For surcharge see Benin No. C462.

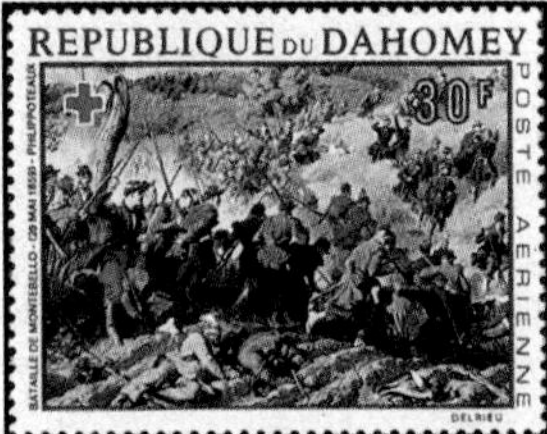

Battle of Montebello, by Henri Philippoteaux — AP32

Paintings: 45fr, 2nd Zouave Regiment at Magenta, by Riballier. 70fr, Battle of Magenta, by Louis Eugène Charpentier. 100fr, Battle of Solferino, by Charpentier.

1968, Aug. 12 — *Perf. 12½x12*

No.	Type	Description	Unused	Used
C77	AP32	30fr multi	.90	.50
C78	AP32	45fr multi	1.25	.65
C79	AP32	70fr multi	2.50	1.25
C80	AP32	100fr multi	3.25	1.00
		Nos. C77-C80 (4)	7.90	3.40

Issued for the Red Cross.

Mail Truck in Village — AP33

Designs: 45fr, Mail truck stopping at rural post office. 55fr, Mail truck at river bank. 70fr, Mail truck and train.

1968, Oct. 7 — Photo. — *Perf. 13x12½*

No.	Type	Description	Unused	Used
C81	AP33	30fr multi	.80	.50
C82	AP33	45fr multi	1.00	.55
C83	AP33	55fr multi	1.50	.55
C84	AP33	70fr multi	3.75	1.00
		Nos. C81-C84 (4)	7.05	2.60

For surcharges see Benin Nos. C352, C357A.

Aztec Stadium, Mexico City — AP34

45fr, Ball player, Mayan sculpture, vert. 70fr, Wrestler, sculpture from Uxpanapan, vert. 150fr, Olympic Stadium, Mexico City.

1968, Nov. 20 — Engr. — *Perf. 13*

No.	Type	Description	Unused	Used
C85	AP34	30fr dp cl & sl grn	.60	.30
C86	AP34	45fr ultra & dk rose brn	1.10	.60
C87	AP34	70fr sl grn & dk brn	1.60	.65
C88	AP34	150fr dk car & dk brn	2.25	1.25
a.		Min. sheet of 4, #C85-C88	5.50	5.50
		Nos. C85-C88 (4)	5.55	2.80

19th Olympic Games, Mexico City, Oct. 12-27. No. C88a is folded down the vertical gutter separating Nos. C85-C86 se-tenant at left and Nos. C87-C88 se-tenant at right.

For overprint and surcharges see Benin Nos. C457, C461, C513.

The Annunciation, by Foujita — AP35

Paintings by Foujita: 30fr, Nativity, horiz. 100fr, The Virgin and Child. 200fr, The Baptism of Christ.

Perf. 12x12½, 12½x12

1968, Nov. 25 — Photo.

No.	Type	Description	Unused	Used
C89	AP35	30fr multi	.80	.55
C90	AP35	70fr multi	1.60	.80
C91	AP35	100fr multi	1.75	1.25
C92	AP35	200fr multi	4.00	2.75
		Nos. C89-C92 (4)	8.15	5.35

Christmas 1968.

PHILEXAFRIQUE Issue

Painting: Diderot, by Louis Michel Vanloo.

1968, Dec. 16 — *Perf. 12½x12*

No.	Type	Description	Unused	Used
C93	AP35	100fr multi	3.50	3.50

PHILEXAFRIQUE, Philatelic Exhibition in Abidjan, Feb. 14-23. Printed with alternating label.

2nd PHILEXAFRIQUE Issue

Common Design Type

50fr, Dahomey #119 and aerial view of Cotonou.

1969, Feb. 14 — Engr. — *Perf. 13*

No.	Type	Description	Unused	Used
C94	CD128	50fr bl, brn & pur	2.10	2.10

For surcharge see Benin No. C467.

Christmas Painting Type

Paintings: No. C95, Virgin of the Rocks, by Leonardo da Vinci. No. C96, Virgin with the Scales, by Cesare da Sesto.

1969, Mar. 17 — Photo. — *Perf. 12½x12*

No.	Type	Description	Unused	Used
C95	AP21	100fr vio & multi	1.75	1.00
C96	AP21	100fr grn & multi	1.75	1.00

Leonardo da Vinci (1452-1519).

General Bonaparte, by Jacques Louis David AP36

Paintings: 60fr, Napoleon I in 1809, by Robert J. Lefevre. 75fr, Napoleon on the Battlefield of Eylau, by Antoine Jean Gros, horiz. 200fr, Gen. Bonaparte at Arcole, by Gros.

1969, Apr. 14 — Photo. — *Perf. 12½x12*

No.	Type	Description	Unused	Used
C97	AP36	30fr multi	1.50	1.25
C98	AP36	60fr multi	2.75	1.75
C99	AP36	75fr multi	3.00	2.50
C100	AP36	200fr multi	7.25	5.50
		Nos. C97-C100 (4)	14.50	11.00

Bicentenary of the birth of Napoleon I.

Arms Type of Regular Issue, 1969

1969, June 30 — Litho. — *Perf. 13½x13*

No.	Type	Description	Unused	Used
C101	A49	50fr multi	.55	.30

For overprint see Benin No. C417.

Apollo 8 Trip Around the Moon — AP37

Embossed on Gold Foil

1969, July — *Die-cut Perf. 10½*

No.	Type	Description	Unused	Used
C102	AP37	1000fr gold	20.00	20.00

US Apollo 8 mission, which put the 1st men into orbit around the moon, Dec. 21-27, 1968.

Nos. C67-C68 Surcharged

1969, Aug. 1 — Photo. — *Perf. 13*

No.	Type	Description	Unused	Used
C103	AP28	125fr on 70fr, #C67	2.00	1.75
C104	AP28	125fr on 70fr, #C68	2.00	1.75

Man's 1st landing on the moon, July 20, 1969; US astronauts Neil A. Armstrong, Col. Edwin E. Aldrin, Jr., with Lieut. Col. Michael Collins piloting Apollo 11.

Europafrica Issue

Type of Regular Issue, 1969

Design: 100fr, Oil palm industry, Cotonou.

1969, Sept. 22 — Litho. — *Perf. 14*

No.	Type	Description	Unused	Used
C105	A51	100fr multi	3.00	1.10
a.		Souv. sheet of 3, #262-263, C105	4.25	4.25

For surcharge see No. C523.

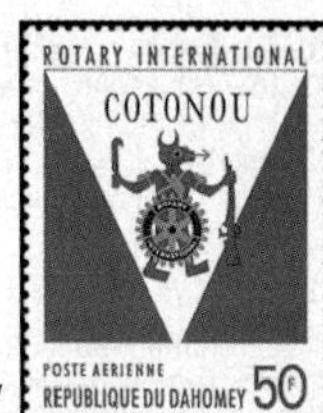

Dahomey Rotary Emblem — AP38

1969, Sept. 25 — *Perf. 14x13½*

No.	Type	Description	Unused	Used
C106	AP38	50fr multi	1.00	.75

For surcharge see Benin No. C468.

No. C33 Surcharged

1969, Nov. 15 — Photo. — *Perf. 12½*

No.	Type	Description	Unused	Used
C107	AP14	10fr on 50fr multi	.45	.20

Dance Type of Regular Issue

Design: Teke dance and Tourist Year emblem.

1969, Dec. 15 — Litho. — *Perf. 14*

No.	Type	Description	Unused	Used
C108	A52	70fr multi	1.75	.80

For surcharge see Benin No. C398.

Painting Type of 1966

Christmas: 30fr, Annunciation, by Vrancke van der Stockt. 45fr, Nativity, Swabian School, horiz. 110fr, Madonna and Child, by the Master of the Gold Brocade. 200fr, Adoration of the Kings, Antwerp School.

1969, Dec. 20 — *Perf. 12½x12, 12x12½*

No.	Type	Description	Unused	Used
C109	AP21	30fr multi	.45	.40
C110	AP21	45fr red & multi	.80	.65
C111	AP21	110fr multi	2.00	1.25
C112	AP21	200fr multi	3.50	2.25
		Nos. C109-C112 (4)	6.75	4.55

For surcharges see Benin #C425, C463, C475.

1969, Dec. 27 — *Perf. 12½x12*

Paintings: No. C113, The Artist's Studio (detail), by Gustave Courbet. No. C114, Self-portrait with Gold Chain, by Rembrandt. 150fr, Hendrickje Stoffels, by Rembrandt.

No.	Type	Description	Unused	Used
C113	AP21	100fr red & multi	2.25	1.25
C114	AP21	100fr grn & multi	2.25	1.25
C115	AP21	150fr multi	3.50	1.75
		Nos. C113-C115 (3)	8.00	4.25

For overprint and surcharge see Benin Nos. C458, C472.

Franklin D. Roosevelt AP39

Astronauts, Rocket, US Flag — AP40

1970, Feb. Photo. *Perf. 12½*
C116 AP39 100fr ultra, yel grn & blk 1.60 .60

25th anniversary of the death of Pres. Franklin Delano Roosevelt (1882-1945)

1970, Mar. 9 Photo. *Perf. 12½*

Astronauts: 50fr, Riding rocket through space. 70fr, In landing module approaching moon. 110fr, Planting US flag on moon.

C117 AP40 30fr multi .65 .25

Souvenir Sheet

C118 Sheet of 4 8.00 8.00
a. AP40 50fr violet blue & multi .75 .75
b. AP40 70fr violet blue & multi 1.00 1.00
c. AP40 110fr violet blue & multi 1.25 1.25

See note after No. C104. No. C118 contains Nos. C117, C118a, C118b and C118c.
For surcharge see No. C120.

Walt Whitman and Dahoman Huts — AP41

1970, Apr. 30 Engr. *Perf. 13*
C119 AP41 100fr Prus bl, brn & emer 1.25 .60

Walt Whitman (1818-92), American poet.

No. C117 Surcharged in Silver with New Value, Heavy Bar and: "APOLLO XIII / SOLIDARITE / SPATIALE / INTERNATIONALE"

1970, May 15 Photo. *Perf. 12½*
C120 AP40 40fr on 30fr multi 1.20 .75

The flight of Apollo 13.
For surcharge see Benin No. C464.

Soccer Players and Globe — AP42

Designs: 50fr, Goalkeeper catching ball. 200fr, Players kicking ball.

1970, May 19
C121 AP42 40fr multi .75 .40
C122 AP42 50fr multi .95 .50
C123 AP42 200fr multi 3.50 1.25
Nos. C121-C123 (3) 5.20 2.15

9th World Soccer Championships for the Jules Rimet Cup, Mexico City, May 30-June 21, 1970.
For surcharge see No. C126.

EXPO '70 Type of Regular Issue

EXPO '70 Emblems and: 70fr, Dahomey pavilion. 120fr, Mt. Fuji, temple and torii.

1970, June 15 Litho. *Perf. 13½x14*
C124 A54 70fr yel, red & dk vio 1.25 .60
C125 A54 120fr yel, red & grn 2.25 1.00

For surcharges see Benin Nos. C470, C477.

No. C123 Surcharged with New Value and Overprinted: "Bresil-Italie / 4-1"

1970, July 13 Photo. *Perf. 12½*
C126 AP42 100fr on 200fr multi 2.10 1.00

Brazil's victory in the 9th World Soccer Championships, Mexico City.
For surcharge see Benin No. C515.

Mercury, Map of Africa and Europe — AP43

Ludwig van Beethoven AP44

Europafrica Issue, 1970

1970, July 20 Photo. *Perf. 12x13*
C127 AP43 40fr multi .80 .40
C128 AP43 70fr multi 1.25 .60

For surcharges see Benin #C429, C488.

1970, Sept. 21 Litho. *Perf. 14x13½*
C129 AP44 90fr brt bl & vio blk 1.40 .45
C130 AP44 110fr yel grn & dk brn 1.75 .65

Bicentenary of the birth of Ludwig van Beethoven (1770-1827), composer.
For surcharge see Benin No. C476.

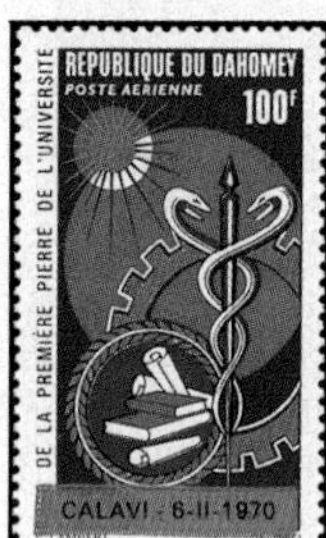

Symbols of Learning — AP45

1970, Nov. 6 Photo. *Perf. 12½*
C131 AP45 100fr multi 1.75 .75

Laying of the foundation stone for the University at Calavi.
For overprint see Benin No. C356.

Annunciation, Rhenish School, c.1340 — AP46

Paintings of Rhenish School, circa 1340: 70fr, Nativity. 110fr, Adoration of the Kings. 200fr, Presentation at the Temple.

1970, Nov. 9 *Perf. 12½x12*
C132 AP46 40fr gold & multi .55 .40
C133 AP46 70fr gold & multi 1.00 .55
C134 AP46 110fr gold & multi 2.40 1.25
C135 AP46 200fr gold & multi 4.00 2.00
Nos. C132-C135 (4) 7.95 4.20

Christmas 1970.
For surcharge see Benin No. C479.

Charles de Gaulle, Arc de Triomphe and Flag — AP47

Design: 500fr, de Gaulle as old man and Notre Dame Cathedral, Paris.

1971, Mar. 15 Photo. *Perf. 12½*
C136 AP47 40fr multi .80 .45
C137 AP47 500fr multi 6.50 3.25

Gen. Charles de Gaulle (1890-1970), President of France.
For surcharge see Benin No. C465.

L'Indifférent, by Watteau — AP48

Painting: No. C139, Woman playing stringed instrument, by Watteau.

1971, May 3 Photo. *Perf. 13*
C138 AP48 100fr red brn & multi 3.25 1.75
C139 AP48 100fr red brn & multi 3.25 1.75

For overprints see Nos. C151-C152, Benin C357D, C456.

1971, May 29 Photo. *Perf. 13*

Dürer Paintings: 100fr, Self-portrait, 1498. 200fr, Self-portrait, 1500.

C140 AP48 100fr bl grn & multi 2.25 1.25
C141 AP48 200fr dk grn & multi 4.50 2.25

Albrecht Dürer (1471-1528), German painter and engraver. See #C151-C152, C174-C175. For surcharge and overprint see Benin #C357B, C381.

Johannes Kepler and Diagram — AP49

200fr, Kepler, trajectories, satellite and rocket.

1971, July 12 Engr. *Perf. 13*
C142 AP49 40fr brt rose lil, blk & vio bl .90 .55
C143 AP49 200fr red, blk & dk bl 3.25 1.75

Kepler (1571-1630), German astronomer.
For overprint and surcharges see Benin Nos. C342, C348, C466, C480.

Europafrica Issue

Jet Plane, Maps of Europe and Africa — AP50

100fr, Ocean liner, maps of Europe and Africa.

1971, July 19 Photo. *Perf. 12½x12*
C144 AP50 50fr blk, lt bl & org 1.00 .60
C145 AP50 100fr multi 1.60 1.00

For surcharges see Benin #C374, C404, C421.

African Postal Union Issue, 1971

Common Design Type

Design: 100fr, Dahomey coat of arms and UAMPT building, Brazzaville, Congo.

1971, Nov. 13 *Perf. 13x13½*
C146 CD135 100fr bl & multi 1.40 .60

For overprint see Benin No. C357E.

Flight into Egypt, by Van Dyck — AP51

Paintings: 40fr, Adoration of the Shepherds, by the Master of the Hausbuch, c. 1500, vert. 70fr, Adoration of the Kings, by Holbein the Elder, vert. 200fr, The Birth of Christ, by Dürer.

1971, Nov. 22 *Perf. 13*
C147 AP51 40fr gold & multi .80 .45
C148 AP51 70fr gold & multi 1.25 .55
C149 AP51 100fr gold & multi 2.00 .80
C150 AP51 200fr gold & multi 4.75 1.75
Nos. C147-C150 (4) 8.80 3.55

Christmas 1971
For overprint and surcharges see Benin Nos. C394, C397, C403, C405, C481, C503.

Painting Type of 1971 Inscribed: "25e ANNIVERSAIRE DE L'UNICEF"

Paintings: 40fr, Prince Balthazar, by Velasquez. 100fr, Infanta Margarita Maria, by Velázquez.

1971, Dec. 11
C151 AP48 40fr gold & multi 1.00 .55
C152 AP48 100fr gold & multi 2.00 .85

25th anniv. of UNICEF.
For surcharges see Benin #C366, C418.

Olympic Games Type

Design: 150fr, Sapporo '72 emblem, ski jump and stork flying.

1972, Feb. Engr. *Perf. 13*
C153 A61 150fr brn, dp rose lil & bl 3.00 1.25

11th Winter Olympic Games, Sapporo, Japan, Feb. 3-13.
For overprint and surcharge see Benin Nos. C347, C433.

Boy Scout and Scout Flag — AP52

Designs: 40fr, Scout playing marimba. 100fr, Scouts doing farm work.

1972, Mar. 19 Photo. *Perf. 13*

Size: 26x35mm

C154 AP52 35fr multi .50 .25
C155 AP52 40fr multi .85 .40

Size: 26x46mm

C156 AP52 100fr yel & multi 1.75 .85
a. Souvenir sheet of 3, #C154-C156, perf. 12½ 4.25 4.25
Nos. C154-C156 (3) 3.10 1.50

World Boy Scout Seminar, Cotonou, Mar. 1972.
For overprint and surcharge see Benin Nos. C373, C414.

Workers Training Institute and Friedrich Naumann — AP53

Design: 250fr, Workers Training Institute and Pres. Theodor Heuss of Germany.

1972, Mar. 29 Photo. *Perf. 13x12*

C157 AP53 100fr brt rose, blk & vio 1.25 .65
C158 AP53 250fr bl, blk & vio 2.75 1.25

Laying of foundation stone for National Workers Training Institute.
For surcharges see Benin Nos. C380, C473.

Mosaic Floor, St. Mark's, Venice — AP54

12th Century Mosaics from St. Mark's Basilica: 40fr, Roosters carrying fox on a pole. 65fr, Noah sending out dove.

1972, Apr. 10 *Perf. 13*

C159 AP54 35fr gold & multi 1.10 .75
C160 AP54 40fr gold & multi 1.25 .90
C161 AP54 65fr gold & multi 2.10 1.50
Nos. C159-C161 (3) 4.45 3.15

UNESCO campaign to save Venice.
For surcharge see Benin No. 690G.

Neapolitan and Dahoman Dancers — AP55

1972, May 3 *Perf. 13½x13*

C162 AP55 100fr multi 1.50 .65

12th Philatelic Exhibition, Naples.
For surcharge see Benin No. C395.

Running, German Eagle, Olympic Rings — AP56

85fr, High jump and Glyptothek, Munich. 150fr, Shot put and Propylaeum, Munich.

1972, June 12 Engr. *Perf. 13*

C163 AP56 20fr ultra, grn & brn .40 .25
C164 AP56 85fr brn, grn & ultra .95 .60
C165 AP56 150fr grn, brn & ultra 2.00 1.00
a. Min. sheet of 3, #C163-C165 4.00 4.00
Nos. C163-C165 (3) 3.35 1.85

20th Olympic Games, Munich, 8/26-9/10.
For overprints and surcharges see Nos. C170-C172, Benin C343, C346, C370.

Louis Blériot and his Plane — AP57

1972, June 26

C166 AP57 100fr vio, cl & brt bl 3.00 1.75

Birth centenary of Louis Blériot (1872-1936), French aviation pioneer.
For surcharge see Benin No. C386.

Adam, by Lucas Cranach — AP58

Design: 200fr, Eve, by Lucas Cranach.

1972, Oct. 24 Photo.

C167 AP58 150fr multi 1.90 .65
C168 AP58 200fr multi 3.25 1.25

Cranach (1472-1553), German painter.
For surcharge see Benin No. C402.

Pauline Borghese, by Canova — AP59

1972, Nov. 8

C169 AP59 250fr multi 4.00 1.75

Antonio Canova (1757-1822), Italian sculptor.

Nos. C163-C165 Overprinted:
a. 5.000m-10.000m. / VIREN / 2 MEDAILLES D'OR
b. HAUTEUR DAMES / MEYFARTH / MEDAILLE D'OR
c. POIDS / KOMAR / MEDAILLE D'OR

1972, Nov. 13 Engr. *Perf. 13*

C170 AP56(a) 20fr multi .45 .25
C171 AP56(b) 85fr multi 1.25 .60
C172 AP56(c) 150fr multi 2.25 1.25
a. Miniature sheet of 3 5.25 5.25
Nos. C170-C172 (3) 3.95 2.10

Gold medal winners in 20th Olympic Games: Lasse Viren, Finland, 5,000m. and 10,000m. races (20fr); Ulrike Meyfarth, Germany, women's high jump (85fr); Wladyslaw Komar, Poland, shot put (150fr).

Louis Pasteur — AP60

1972, Nov. 30

C173 AP60 100fr brt grn, lil & brn 2.25 1.00

Pasteur (1822-95), chemist and bacteriologist.
For surcharge see Benin No. C344.

Painting Type of 1971

Paintings by Georges de La Tour (1593-1652), French painter: 35fr, Vielle player. 150fr, The Newborn, horiz.

1972, Dec. 11 Photo.

C174 AP48 35fr multi .80 .40
C175 AP48 150fr multi 2.25 1.25

For surcharges see Benin #C364, C490.

Annunciation, School of Agnolo Gaddi — AP61

Paintings: 125fr, Nativity, by Simone dei Crocifissi. 140fr, Adoration of the Shepherds, by Giovanni di Pietro. 250fr, Adoration of the Kings, by Giotto.

1972, Dec. 15

C176 AP61 35fr gold & multi .55 .25
C177 AP61 125fr gold & multi 1.50 .65
C178 AP61 140fr gold & multi 2.00 1.00
C179 AP61 250fr gold & multi 3.25 1.50
Nos. C176-C179 (4) 7.30 3.40

Christmas 1972. See Nos. C195-C198, C234, C251, C253-C254. For overprint and surcharge see Benin Nos. C384, C401.

Statue of St. Teresa, Basilica of Lisieux — AP62

100fr, St. Teresa, roses, and globe, vert.

1973, May 14 Photo. *Perf. 13*

C180 AP62 40fr blk, gold & lt ultra .75 .45
C181 AP62 100fr gold & multi 2.00 1.00

St. Teresa of Lisieux (Therese Martin, 1873-97), Carmelite nun.
For surcharge see Benin No. C390.

Scouts, African Scout Emblem — AP63

Designs (African Scout Emblem and): 20fr, Lord Baden-Powell, vert. 40fr, Scouts building bridge.

1973, July 2 Engr. *Perf. 13*

C182 AP63 15fr bl, grn & choc .45 .20
C183 AP63 20fr ol & Prus bl .75 .25
C184 AP63 40fr grn, Prus bl & brn .90 .35
a. Souvenir sheet of 3 3.00 3.00
Nos. C182-C184 (3) 2.10 .80

24th Boy Scout World Conference, Nairobi, Kenya, July 16-21. No. C184a contains 3 stamps similar to Nos. C182-C184 in changed colors (15fr in ultramarine, slate green and chocolate; 20fr in chocolate, ultramarine and indigo; 40fr in slate green, indigo and chocolate).
For surcharges see Nos. C217-C218, Benin C365, C409.

Copernicus, Venera and Mariner Satellites — AP64

125fr, Copernicus, sun, earth & moon, vert.

1973, Aug. 20 Engr. *Perf. 13*

C185 AP64 65fr blk, dk brn & org 1.25 .55
C186 AP64 125fr bl, slate grn & pur 2.00 1.00

For surcharges see Benin Nos. C345, C375.

Head and City Hall, Brussels AP64a

1973, Sept. 17 Engr. *Perf. 13*

C187 AP64a 100fr blk, Prus bl & dk grn 1.10 .60

African Weeks, Brussels, Sept. 15-30, 1973.
For surcharge see Benin No. C400.

WMO Emblem, World Weather Map — AP65

1973, Sept. 25

C188 AP65 100fr ol grn & lt brn 1.25 .75

Cent. of intl. meteorological cooperation.
For surcharge and overprint see Nos. C199, Benin C382.

Europafrica Issue

AP66

Design: 40fr, similar to 35fr.

1973, Oct. 1 Engr. *Perf. 13*

C189 AP66 35fr multi .55 .35
C190 AP66 40fr bl, sepia & ultra .70 .40

For overprint see Benin No. C411.

John F. Kennedy — AP67

1973, Oct. 18

C191 AP67 200fr bl grn, vio & sl grn 2.75 2.75
a. Souvenir sheet 5.00 5.00

Pres. John F. Kennedy (1917-63). No. C191a contains one stamp in changed colors (bright blue, magenta & brown).

For surcharge see Benin No. C377.

Soccer — AP68

40fr, 2 soccer players. 100fr, 3 soccer players.

1973, Nov. 19 Engr. *Perf. 13*

C192 AP68 35fr multi .55 .25
C193 AP68 40fr multi .65 .25
C194 AP68 100fr multi 1.25 .65
Nos. C192-C194 (3) 2.45 1.15

World Soccer Cup, Munich 1974.

For surcharges and overprint see Nos. C219-C220, Benin C396.

Painting Type of 1972

Christmas: 35fr, Annunciation, by Dirk Bouts. 100fr, Nativity, by Giotto. 150fr, Adoration of the Kings, by Botticelli. 200fr, Adoration of the Shepherds, by Jacopo Bassano, horiz.

1973, Dec. 20 Photo. *Perf. 13*

C195 AP61 35fr gold & multi .65 .40
C196 AP61 100fr gold & multi 1.25 .65
C197 AP61 150fr gold & multi 2.40 1.10
C198 AP61 200fr gold & multi 2.75 1.75
Nos. C195-C198 (4) 7.05 3.90

For surcharges see Benin Nos. C378, C388, C410, C434.

No C188 Surcharged in Violet with New Value and: "OPERATION SKYLAB / 1973-1974"

1974, Feb. 4 Engr. *Perf. 13*

C199 AP65 200fr on 100fr multi 2.10 1.25

Skylab US space missions, 1973-74.

Skiers, Snowflake, Olympic Rings — AP69

1974, Feb. 25 Engr. *Perf. 13*

C200 AP69 100fr vio bl, brn & brt bl 1.75 1.10

50th anniversary of first Winter Olympic Games, Chamonix, France.

Marie Curie AP70

1974, June 7 Engr. *Perf. 13*

C201 AP70 50fr Lenin 1.40 .65
C202 AP70 125fr shown 1.75 .90
C203 AP70 150fr Churchill 2.00 1.40
Nos. C201-C203 (3) 5.15 2.95

50th anniv. of the death of Lenin; 40th anniv. of the death of Marie Sklodowska Curie; cent. of the birth of Winston Churchill.

For surcharge see Benin No. C489.

Bishop, Persian, 18th Century — AP71

Frederic Chopin — AP72

200fr, Queen, Siamese chess piece, 19th cent.

1974, June 14 Photo. *Perf. 12½x13*

C204 AP71 50fr org & multi 2.00 .75
C205 AP71 200fr brt grn & multi 4.50 2.00

21st Chess Olympiad, Nice, 6/6-30/74.

For surcharges and overprint see Benin Nos. C469, C482, Q11.

1974, June 24 Engr. *Perf. 13*

Design: No. C207, Ludwig van Beethoven.

C206 AP72 150fr blk & copper red 2.50 1.10
C207 AP72 150fr blk & copper red 2.50 1.10

Famous musicians: Frederic Chopin and Ludwig van Beethoven.

For surcharges see Benin #C376, C452, C459.

Astronaut on Moon, and Earth AP73

1974, July 10 Engr. *Perf. 13*

C208 AP73 150fr multi 2.75 1.50

5th anniversary of the first moon walk.

For surcharge and overprint see Benin Nos. C391, C460.

Litho. & Embossed 'Gold Foil' Stamps

These stamps generally are of a different design format than the rest of the issue. Since there is a commemorative inscription tying them to the issue a separate illustration is not being shown.

There is some question as to the status of 4 sets, Nos. C209-C216, C225-C232, C238-C249.

World Cup Soccer Championships, Munich — AP74

World Cup trophy and players and flags of: 35fr, West Germany, Chile, Australia, DDR. 40fr, Zaire, Scotland, Brazil, Yugoslavia. 100fr, Sweden, Bulgaria, Uruguay, Netherlands. 200fr, Italy, Haiti, Poland, Argentina. 300fr, Stadium. 500fr, Trophy and flags.

Perf. 14x13, 13x14

1974, July 16 Litho.

C209 AP74 35fr multicolored
C210 AP74 40fr multicolored
C211 AP74 100fr multicolored
C212 AP74 200fr multicolored
C213 AP74 300fr multi, horiz.

Souvenir Sheet

C215 AP74 500fr multi, horiz.

It is uncertain if this issue was valid for postage or recognized by the Dahomey government.

Nos. C182-C183 Surcharged and Overprinted in Black or Red: "XIe JAMBOREE PANARABE DE BATROUN-LIBAN"

1974, July 19

C217 AP63 100fr on 15fr multi 1.25 .60
C218 AP63 140fr on 20fr multi (R) 1.75 .90

11th Pan-Arab Jamboree, Batrun, Lebanon, Aug. 1974. Overprint includes 2 bars over old denomination; 2-line overprint on No. C217, 3 lines on No. C218.

Nos. C193-C194 Overprinted and Surcharged with New Value and Two Bars: "R F A 2 / HOLLANDE 1"

1974, July 26 Engr. *Perf. 13*

C219 AP68 100fr on 40fr 1.10 .65
C220 AP68 150fr on 100fr 1.60 1.00

World Cup Soccer Championship, 1974, victory of German Federal Republic.

Earth and UPU Emblem — AP75

Designs (UPU Emblem and): 65fr, Concorde in flight. 125fr, French railroad car, c. 1860. 200fr, African drummer and Renault mail truck, pre-1939.

1974, Aug. 5 Engr. *Perf. 13*

C221 AP75 35fr rose cl & vio .55 .40
C222 AP75 65fr Prus grn & cl 1.10 .95
C223 AP75 125fr multi 2.50 1.50
C224 AP75 200fr multi 2.50 2.00
Nos. C221-C224 (4) 6.65 4.85

Centenary of Universal Postal Union.

For surcharge see Benin No. C422.

UPU, Cent. — AP76

Communications and transportation: 50fr, Rocket, Indian shooting arrow. 100fr, Airplane, dog sled, vert. 125fr, Rocket launch, balloon. 150fr, Rocket re-entry into Earth's atmosphere, drum. 200fr, Locomotive, Pony Express rider. 500fr, UPU headquarters. No. C230, Train, 1829. No. C232, Astronaut canceling envelope on moon.

1974 Litho. *Perf. 13x14, 14x13*

C225 AP76 50fr multicolored
C226 AP76 100fr multicolored
C227 AP76 125fr multicolored
C228 AP76 150fr multicolored
C229 AP76 200fr multicolored

Litho. & Embossed
Perf. 13½
Size: 48x60mm

C230 AP76 1000fr gold & multi

Souvenir Sheets
Litho.
Perf. 13x14

C231 AP76 500fr multicolored

Litho. & Embossed
Perf. 13½

C232 AP76 1000fr gold & multi

Issued: #C230, C232, Oct. 9; others, Aug. 5.

It is uncertain if this issue was valid for postage or recognized by the Dahomey government.

Painting Type of 1972 and

Lion of Belfort by Frederic A. Bartholdi — AP77

Painting: 250fr, Girl with Falcon, by Philippe de Champaigne.

1974, Aug. 20 Engr. *Perf. 13*

C233 AP77 100fr rose brn 2.50 1.00
C234 AP61 250fr multi 4.00 2.40

For surcharges see Benin Nos. C363, C445.

Prehistoric Animals — AP78

1974, Sept. 23 Photo.

C235 AP78 35fr Rhamphorhynchus 1.50 .80
C236 AP78 150fr Stegosaurus 5.00 2.25
C237 AP78 200fr Tyrannosaurus 7.00 2.75
Nos. C235-C237 (3) 13.50 5.80

For surcharges see Benin #C349, C350.

Conquest of Space — AP79

Various spacecraft and: 50fr, Mercury. 100fr, Venus. 150fr, Mars. 200fr, Jupiter. 400fr, Sun.

1974, Oct. 31 Litho. *Perf. 13x14*

C238 AP79 50fr multicolored
C239 AP79 100fr multicolored
C240 AP79 150fr multicolored
C241 AP79 200fr multicolored

Souvenir Sheet

C242 AP79 400fr multicolored

It is uncertain if this issue was valid for postage or recognized by the Dahomey government.

West Germany, World Cup Soccer Champions — AP80

Designs: 100fr, Team. 125fr, Paul Breitner. 150fr, Gerd Muller. 300fr, Presentation of trophy. 500fr, German team positioned on field.

1974, Nov. Litho. *Perf. 13x14*

C243 AP80 100fr multicolored
C244 AP80 125fr multicolored
C245 AP80 150fr multicolored
C246 AP80 300fr multicolored

Souvenir Sheet

C248 AP80 500fr multicolored

It is uncertain if this issue was valid for postage or recognized by the Dahomey government.

Europafrica Issue

Globe, Cogwheel, Emblem — AP81

1974, Dec. 20 Typo. *Perf. 13*

C250 AP81 250fr red & multi 3.25 2.75

Printed tête bêche in sheets of 10.
For surcharges see Benin Nos. C430, C509.

Christmas Type of 1972 and

Nativity, by Martin Schongauer — AP82

Paintings: 35fr, Annunciation, by Schongauer. 100fr, Virgin in Rose Arbor, by Schongauer. 250fr, Virgin and Child, with St. John the Baptist, by Botticelli.

1974, Dec. 23 Photo. *Perf. 13*

C251	AP61	35fr gold & multi	.45	.30
C252	AP82	40fr gold & multi	.45	.40
C253	AP61	100fr gold & multi	1.25	.55
C254	AP61	250fr gold & multi	3.25	1.75
		Nos. C251-C254 (4)	5.40	3.00

For surcharges, see Benin Nos. C439, C446.

Apollo and Soyuz Spacecraft AP83

200fr, American and Russian flags, rocket take-off. 500fr, Apollo-Soyuz link-up.

1975, July 16 Litho. *Perf. 12½*

C255	AP83	35fr multi	.50	.30
C256	AP83	200fr vio bl, red & bl	2.40	1.25
C257	AP83	500fr vio bl, ind & red	5.00	3.00
		Nos. C255-C257 (3)	7.90	4.55

Apollo Soyuz space test project (Russo-American cooperation); launching July 15; link-up, July 17.
For surcharges see Benin #C406, C415-C416, C451.

Nos. C255-C256 Surcharged in Silver or Black: "RENCONTRE / APOLLO-SOYOUZ / 17 Juil. 1975"

1975, July 17 Litho. *Perf. 12½*

C258	AP83	100fr on 35fr (S)	1.25	.60
C259	AP83	300fr on 200fr	3.25	1.40

Apollo-Soyuz link-up in space, July 17, 1975.

ARPHILA Emblem, "Stamps" and Head of Ceres — AP84

1975, Aug. 22 Engr. *Perf. 13*

C260 AP84 100fr blk, bl & lilac 1.25 .75

ARPHILA 75, International Philatelic Exhibition, Paris, June 6-16.
For surcharge see Benin No. C474.

Holy Family, by Michelangelo AP85

Infantry and Stars — AP86

Europafrica Issue

1975, Sept. 29 Litho. *Perf. 12*

C261 AP85 300fr gold & multi 3.50 1.50

For surcharge see Benin No. C447.

1975, Nov. 18 Engr. *Perf. 13*

American bicentennial (Stars and): 135fr, Drummers and fifer. 300fr, Artillery with cannon. 500fr, Cavalry.

C262	AP86	75fr grn car & pur	.85	.45
C263	AP86	135fr bl, mag & sep	1.50	.90
C264	AP86	300fr vio bl, ver & choc	2.75	1.75
C265	AP86	500fr ver, dk grn & brn	5.00	2.50
		Nos. C262-C265 (4)	10.10	5.60

For overprint and surcharges see Benin Nos. C247-C249, C385, C408, C412, C453, C478.

Diving and Olympic Rings AP87

Design: 250fr, Soccer and Olympic rings.

1975, Nov. 24

C266	AP87	40fr vio, grnsh bl & ol brn	.55	.25
C267	AP87	250fr red, emer & brn	2.25	1.25

Pre-Olympic Year 1975.
For surcharge see Benin No. C341.

AIR POST SEMI-POSTAL STAMPS

Maternity Hospital, Dakar — SPAP1

Dispensary, Mopti — SPAP2

Nurse Weighing Baby — SPAP3

Perf. 13½x12½, 13 (#CB3)
Photo, Engr. (#CB3)

1942, June 22

CB1	SPAP1	1.50fr + 3.50fr green	.55	*3.50*
CB2	SPAP2	2fr + 6fr brown	.55	*3.50*
CB3	SPAP3	3fr + 9fr car red	.55	*3.50*
		Nos. CB1-CB3 (3)	1.65	*10.50*

Native children's welfare fund.

Colonial Education Fund
Common Design Type
Perf. 12½x13½

1942, June 22 Engr.

CB4 CD86a 1.20fr + 1.80fr blue & red .55 *3.50*

AIR POST PARCEL POST STAMPS

Catalogue values for unused stamps in this section are for Never Hinged items.

Nos. C20-C23, C14 Surcharged in Black or Red

1967-69 Engr. *Perf. 13*

CQ1	AP6	200fr on 200fr	4.75	3.50
CQ2	AP6	300fr on 100fr	5.25	4.25
CQ3	AP6	500fr on 300fr	10.00	8.00
CQ4	AP6	1000fr on 500fr	21.00	16.00
CQ5	AP4	5000fr on 100fr (R) ('69)	80.00	80.00
		Nos. CQ1-CQ5 (5)	121.00	111.75

On No. CQ5, "Colis Postaux" is at top, bar at right.

POSTAGE DUE STAMPS

Dahomey Natives — D1

D2

1906 Unwmk. Typo. *Perf. 14x13½*

J1	D1	5c grn, *grnsh*	1.75	1.75
J2	D1	10c red brn	3.00	3.00
J3	D1	15c dark blue	5.75	5.75
J4	D1	20c blk, *yellow*	4.25	4.25
J5	D1	30c red, *straw*	6.00	6.00
J6	D1	50c violet	17.50	17.50
J7	D1	60c blk, *buff*	10.00	10.00
J8	D1	1fr blk, *pinkish*	27.50	27.50
		Nos. J1-J8 (8)	75.75	75.75

1914

J9	D2	5c green	.20	.20
J10	D2	10c rose	.35	.35
J11	D2	15c gray	.35	.35
J12	D2	20c brown	.80	.80
J13	D2	30c blue	.95	.95
J14	D2	50c black	1.10	1.10
J15	D2	60c orange	1.40	1.40
J16	D2	1fr violet	1.40	1.40
		Nos. J9-J16 (8)	6.55	6.55

Type of 1914 Issue Surcharged

1927

J17	D2	2fr on 1fr lilac rose	4.00	4.00
J18	D2	3fr on 1fr org brn	4.00	4.00

Carved Mask — D3

1941 Engr. *Perf. 14x13*

J19	D3	5c black	.20	.20
J20	D3	10c lilac rose	.20	.20
J21	D3	15c dark blue	.20	.20
J22	D3	20c bright yel green	.20	.20
J23	D3	30c orange	.35	.35
J24	D3	50c violet brown	.55	.55
J25	D3	60c slate green	.95	.95
J26	D3	1fr rose red	1.10	1.10
J27	D3	2fr yellow	1.25	1.25
J28	D3	3fr dark purple	1.60	1.60
		Nos. J19-J28 (10)	6.60	6.60

Type D3 without "RF"

1944

J28A D3 10c lilac rose .20
J28B D3 15c dark blue .20
J28C D3 20c bright yel green .20
Nos. J28A-J28C (3) .60

Nos. J28A-J28C were issued by the Vichy government in France, but were not placed on sale in Dahomey.

Catalogue values for unused stamps in this section, from this point to the end of the section, are for Never Hinged items.

Republic

Panther and Man — D4

Perf. 14x13½

1963, July 22 Typo. Unwmk.

J29 D4 1fr green & rose .20 .20
J30 D4 2fr brn & emerald .20 .20
J31 D4 5fr org & vio bl .20 .20
J32 D4 10fr magenta & blk .50 .50
J33 D4 20fr vio bl & org .75 .75
Nos. J29-J33 (5) 1.85 1.85

Mail Boat — D5

No. J35, Heliograph. No. J36, Morse receiver. No. J37, Mailman on bicycle. No. J38, Early telephone. No. J39, Autorail. No. J40, Mail truck. No. J41, Radio tower. No. J42, DC-8F jet plane. No. J43, Early Bird communications satellite.

1967, Oct. 24 Engr. *Perf. 11*

J34 D5 1fr brn, dl pur & bl .20 .20
J35 D5 1fr dl pur, brn & bl .20 .20
a. Pair, #J34-J35 .25
J36 D5 3fr dk brn, dk grn & org .20 .20
J37 D5 3fr dk grn, dk brn & org .20 .20
a. Pair, #J36-J37 .25
J38 D5 5fr ol bis, lil & bl .35 .35
J39 D5 5fr lil, ol bis & bl .35 .35
a. Pair, #J38-J39 .75
J40 D5 10fr brn org, vio & grn .50 .50
J41 D5 10fr vio, brn org & grn .50 .50
a. Pair, #J40-J41 1.10
J42 D5 30fr Prus bl, mar & vio 1.00 1.00
J43 D5 30fr vio, Prus bl & mar 1.00 1.00
a. Pair, #J42-J43 2.25
Nos. J34-J43 (10) 4.50 4.50

Pairs printed tete beche, se-tenant at the base.

PARCEL POST STAMPS

Catalogue values for unused stamps in this section are for Never Hinged items.

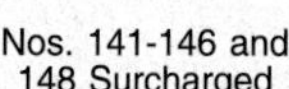

Nos. 141-146 and 148 Surcharged

1967, Jan. Unwmk. Engr. *Perf. 13*

Q1 A15 5fr on 1fr multi .25 .25
Q2 A15 10fr on 2fr multi .35 .35
Q3 A15 20fr on 6fr multi .60 .60
Q4 A15 25fr on 3fr multi .70 .70
Q5 A15 30fr on 4fr multi .80 .80
Q6 A15 50fr on 10fr multi 1.25 1.25
a. "20" instead of "50" 100.00
Q7 A15 100fr on 20fr multi 2.50 2.50
Nos. Q1-Q7 (7) 6.45 6.45

The surcharge is arranged to fit the shape of the stamp.

No. Q6a occurred once on the sheet.

DALMATIA

dal-'mā-sh,ē-ə

LOCATION — A promontory in the northwestern part of the Balkan Peninsula, together with several small islands in the Adriatic Sea.
GOVT. — Part of the former Austro-Hungarian crownland of the same name.
AREA — 113 sq. mi.
POP. — 18,719 (1921)
CAPITAL — Zara.

Stamps were issued during Italian occupation. This territory was subsequently annexed by Italy.

100 Centesimi = 1 Corona = 1 Lira

Used values are for postally used copies.

Issued under Italian Occupation

Italy No. 87 Surcharged

1919, May 1 Wmk. 140 *Perf. 14*

1 A46 1cor on 1 l brn & grn 1.90 *5.75*

Italian Stamps of 1906-08 Surcharged — a

1921-22

2 A48 5c on 5c green 1.50 *1.00*
3 A48 10c on 10c claret 1.50 *1.00*
4 A49 25c on 25c blue ('22) 3.75 2.75
5 A49 50c on 50c vio ('22) 4.50 3.75

Italian Stamps of 1901-10 Surcharged — b

6 A46 1cor on 1 l brn & grn ('22) 7.50 6.50
7 A46 5cor on 5 l bl & rose ('22) 55.00 47.50
8 A51 10cor on 10 l gray grn & red ('22) 55.00 47.50
Nos. 2-8 (7) 128.75 110.00

Surcharges similar to these but differing in style or arrangement of type were used in Austria under Italian occupation.

SPECIAL DELIVERY STAMPS

Italian Special Delivery Stamp No. E1 Surcharged type "a"

1921 Wmk. 140 *Perf. 14*

E1 SD1 25c on 25c rose red 3.00 *3.75*
a. Double surcharge 110.00 150.00

Italian Special Delivery Stamp Surcharged **LIRE 1,20 DI CORONA**

1922

E2 SD2 1.20 l on 1.20 l 75.00 150.00

No. E2 was not placed in use.

POSTAGE DUE STAMPS

Italian Postage Due Stamps and Type Surcharged types "a" or "b"

1922 Wmk. 140 *Perf. 14*

J1 D3 (a) 50c on 50c buff & mag 1.90 *1.90*
J2 D3 (b) 1cor on 1 l bl & red 5.50 *5.50*
J3 D3 (b) 2cor on 2 l bl & red 37.50 *37.50*
J4 D3 (b) 5cor on 5 l bl & red 37.50 *37.50*
Nos. J1-J4 (4) 82.40 *82.40*

DANISH WEST INDIES

'dā-nish 'west 'in-dēs

LOCATION — A group of islands in the West Indies, lying east of Puerto Rico
GOVT. — A former Danish colony
AREA — 132 sq. mi.
POP. — 27,086 (1911)
CAPITAL — Charlotte Amalie

The US bought these islands in 1917 and they became the US Virgin Islands, using US stamps and currency.

100 Cents = 1 Dollar
100 Bit = 1 Franc (1905)

Watermarks

Wmk. 111 — Small Crown

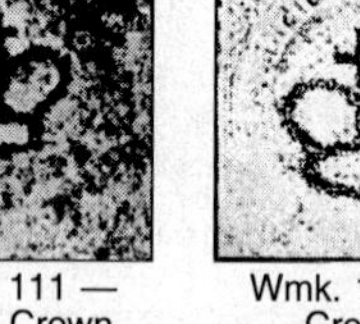

Wmk. 112 — Crown

Wmk. 113 — Crown

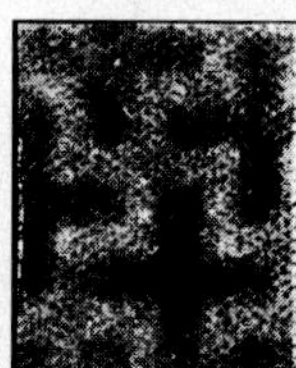

Wmk. 114 — Multiple Crosses

Coat of Arms — A1

Yellowish Paper
Yellow Wavy-line Burelage, UL to LR

1856 Wmk. 111 Typo. *Imperf.*

1 A1 3c dk car, brn gum 190. 210.
a. 3c dark car, yellow gum 200. 210.
b. 3c carmine, white gum 4,000. —

Reprint: 1981, carmine, back-printed across two stamps ("Reprint by Dansk Post og Telegrafmuseum 1978"), value, pair, $10.

White Paper
Yellow Wavy-line Burelage, UR to LL

1866

2 A1 3c rose 40.00 *67.50*

No. 2 reprints unwatermarked: 1930 carmine, value $100. 1942 rose carmine, back-printed across each row ("Nytryk 1942 G. A. Hagemann Danmark og Dansk Vestindiens Friemaerker Bind 2"), value $50.

1872 *Perf. 12½*

3 A1 3c rose 75.00 *200.00*

1873

Without Burelage

4 A1 4c dull blue 200.00 *400.00*
a. Imperf., pair 750.00
b. Horiz. pair, imperf. vert. 550.00

#4 reprints, unwatermarked, imperf.: 1930, ultramarine, value $85. 1942, blue back-printed like 1942 reprint of #2, value $50.

A2

Normal Frame

Inverted Frame

The arabesques in the corners have a main stem and a branch. When the frame is in normal position, in the upper left corner the branch leaves the main stem half way between two little leaflets. In the lower right corner the branch starts at the foot of the second leaflet. When the frame is inverted the corner designs are, of course, transposed.

White Wove Paper
Varying from Thin to Thick

1874-79 Wmk. 112 *Perf. 14x13½*

5 A2 1c green & brn red 15.00 *22.50*
a. 1c grn & rose lilac, thin paper 75.00 *125.00*
b. 1c grn & red vio, medium paper 40.00 65.00
c. 1c green & violet, thick paper 15.00 *22.50*
e. Inverted frame 15.00 *22.50*
f. As "a,"Inverted frame *425.00*
6 A2 3c blue & carmine 20.00 16.00
a. 3c lt bl & rose car, thin paper 65.00 50.00
b. 3c dp bl & dk car, medium paper 35.00 16.00
c. 3c greenish blue & lake, thick paper 20.00 16.00
d. Imperf., pair 325.00 —
e. Inverted frame 19.00 14.00
f. As "a,"Inverted frame *350.00*
7 A2 4c brn & dull blue 14.00 *16.00*
b. 4c brown & ultramarine 150.00 200.00
c. Diagonal half used as 2c on cover 125.00
d. As "b," inverted frame *750.00* *1,250.*
8 A2 5c grn & gray ('76) 17.50 17.50
a. 5c yel grn & dk gray, thin paper 45.00 30.00
b. Inverted frame 17.50 17.50
9 A2 7c lilac & orange 22.50 *85.00*
a. 7c lilac & yellow 77.50 77.50
b. Inverted frame 52.50 *125.00*
10 A2 10c blue & brn ('76) 21.00 *22.50*
a. 10c dk bl & blk brn, thin paper 70.00 45.00
b. "cent.s" 30.00 30.00
c. Inverted frame 21.00 *25.00*
11 A2 12c red lilac & yel green ('77) 37.50 *125.00*
a. 12c lilac & deep green 125.00 *140.00*
12 A2 14c lilac & green 500.00 *850.00*
a. Inverted frame *2,000.* *2,750.*
13 A2 50c violet, thin paper ('79) 160.00 *260.00*
a. 50c gray vio, thick porous paper ('85) 210.00 *350.00*
Nos. 5-13 (9) 807.50 *1,414.*

The central element in the fan-shaped scrollwork at the outside of the lower left corner of Nos. 5a and 7b looks like an elongated diamond.

See Nos. 16-20. For surcharges see Nos. 14-15, 23-28, 40.

Nos. 9 & 13 Surcharged in Black

1887-95

14 A2 1c on 7c lilac & org 72.50 *175.00*
a. 1c on 7c lilac & yellow 72.50 *175.00*
b. Double surcharge 175.00 *350.00*
c. Inverted frame 90.00 *300.00*
15 A2 10c on 50c violet, thin paper ('95) 37.50 *60.00*

Type of 1874-79

1896-1901 *Perf. 13*

16 A2 1c grn & red vio ('98) 12.00 *18.00*
a. Normal frame 225.00 *325.00*
17 A2 3c blue & lake ('98) 10.00 *13.00*
a. Normal frame 200.00 *325.00*
18 A2 4c bis & dl bl ('01) 12.50 12.50
a. Diagonal half used as 2c on cover 90.00
b. Inverted frame 45.00 *75.00*
c. As "b," diagonal half used as 2c on cover 300.00
19 A2 5c green & gray 30.00 30.00
a. Normal frame 600.00 *850.00*
20 A2 10c blue & brn ('01) 65.00 *110.00*
a. Inverted frame 750.00 1,300.
b. "cent.s" 160.00 150.00
Nos. 16-20 (5) 129.50 *183.50*

Arms — A5

1900

21 A5 1c light green 2.75 2.75
22 A5 5c light blue 15.00 *20.00*

See #29-30. For surcharges see #41-42.

Nos. 6, 17, 20 Surcharged

c

d

Surcharge "c" in Black

1902 *Perf. 14x13½*

23 A2 2c on 3c blue & car 350.00 *400.00*
a. "2" in date with straight tail 375.00 *425.00*
b. Normal frame *3,500.*

Perf. 13

24 A2 2c on 3c blue & lake 9.00 *20.00*
a. "2" in date with straight tail 11.50 *22.50*
b. Dated "1901" 400.00 *450.00*
c. Normal frame 150.00 *225.00*
d. Dark green surcharge 1,750.
e. As "d" & "a" — —
f. As "d" & "c" —
25 A2 8c on 10c blue & brn 20.00 *32.50*
a. "2" with straight tail 22.50 *35.00*
b. On No. 20b 20.00 *37.50*
c. Inverted frame 200.00 *325.00*

Only one copy of No. 24f can exist.

Surcharge "d" in Black

27 A2 2c on 3c blue & lake 11.00 *30.00*
a. Normal frame 225.00 *375.00*
28 A2 8c on 10c blue & brn 11.00 11.00
a. On No. 20b 17.50 *20.00*
b. Inverted frame 175.00 *350.00*
Nos. 23-28 (5) 401.00 493.50

1903 Wmk. 113

29 A5 2c carmine 6.00 *17.50*
30 A5 8c brown 22.50 *42.50*

King Christian IX — A8

St. Thomas Harbor — A9

1905 Typo. *Perf. 13*

31 A8 5b green 3.50 3.00
32 A8 10b red 3.50 3.00
33 A8 20b green & blue 8.00 7.50
34 A8 25b ultramarine 8.00 9.50
35 A8 40b red & gray 8.00 7.50
36 A8 50b yellow & gray 9.00 *11.00*

Frame Typo., Center Engr.
Wmk. Two Crowns (113)

Perf. 12

37 A9 1fr green & blue 17.50 *40.00*
38 A9 2fr org red & brown 30.00 *55.00*
39 A9 5fr yellow & brown 70.00 *225.00*
Nos. 31-39 (9) 157.50 *361.50*

Favor cancels exist on #37-39. Value 25% less.

Nos. 18, 22, 30 Surcharged in Black

1905 Wmk. 112 *Perf. 13*

40 A2 5b on 4c bis & dl bl 13.50 *40.00*
a. Inverted frame 40.00 *75.00*
41 A5 5b on 5c light blue 12.50 *32.50*

Wmk. 113

42 A5 5b on 8c brown 12.50 *32.50*
Nos. 40-42 (3) 38.50 *105.00*

Favor cancels exist on #40-42. Value 25% less.

Frederik VIII A10

Christian X A11

Frame Typo., Center Engr.

1907-08 Wmk. 113 *Perf. 13*

43 A10 5b green 1.75 1.75
44 A10 10b red 1.75 1.75
45 A10 15b violet & brown 3.50 3.50
46 A10 20b green & blue 30.00 25.00
47 A10 25b blue & dk blue 1.75 2.10
48 A10 30b claret & slate 45.00 45.00
49 A10 40b ver & gray 5.25 *8.50*
50 A10 50b yellow & brown 5.25 *12.00*
Nos. 43-50 (8) 94.25 99.60

1915 Wmk. 114 *Perf. 14x14½*

51 A11 5b yellow green 3.50 3.00
52 A11 10b red 3.50 *35.00*
53 A11 15b lilac & red brown 3.50 *40.00*
54 A11 20b green & blue 3.50 *40.00*
55 A11 25b blue & dark blue 3.50 *10.00*
56 A11 30b claret & black 3.50 *70.00*
57 A11 40b orange & black 3.50 *70.00*
58 A11 50b yellow & brown 3.50 *70.00*
Nos. 51-58 (8) 28.00 *338.00*

Forged and favor cancellations exist.

POSTAGE DUE STAMPS

Royal Cipher, "Christian 9 Rex" D1

1902 Unwmk. Litho. *Perf. 11½*

J1 D1 1c dark blue 4.00 *13.00*
J2 D1 4c dark blue 9.00 *20.00*
J3 D1 6c dark blue 17.50 *55.00*
J4 D1 10c dark blue 15.00 *55.00*
Nos. J1-J4 (4) 45.50 *143.00*

There are five types of each value. On the 4c they may be distinguished by differences in the figures "4"; on the other values the differences are minute.

Used values of Nos. J1-J4 are for canceled copies. Uncanceled examples without gum have probably been used. Value 60% of unused.

Counterfeits of Nos. J1-J4 exist.

D2

1905-13 *Perf. 13*

J5 D2 5b red & gray 4.00 *6.25*
J6 D2 20b red & gray 7.00 *12.50*
J7 D2 30b red & gray 6.00 *12.50*
J8 D2 50b red & gray 5.50 *32.50*
a. Perf. 14x14½ ('13) 35.00 *125.00*
b. Perf. 11½ 300.00
Nos. J5-J8 (4) 22.50 *63.75*

All values of this issue are known imperforate, but were not regularly issued.

Used values of Nos. J5-J8 are for canceled copies. Uncanceled examples without gum have probably been used. Value 60% of unused.

Counterfeits of Nos. J5-J8 exist.

Danish West Indies stamps were replaced by those of the US in 1917, after the US bought the islands.

DANZIG

'dan,ţ-sig

LOCATION — In northern Europe bordering on the Baltic Sea
AREA — 754 sq. mi.
POP. — 407,000 (approx. 1939)
CAPITAL — Danzig

Established as a "Free City and State" under the protection of the League of Nations in 1920, Danzig was seized by Germany in 1939. It became a Polish province in 1945.

100 Pfennig = 1 Gulden (1923)
100 Pfennig = 1 Mark

Watermarks

Wmk. 108 — Honeycomb

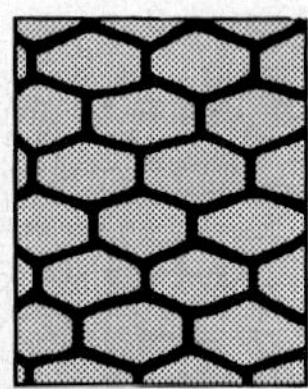

Wmk. 109 — Webbing

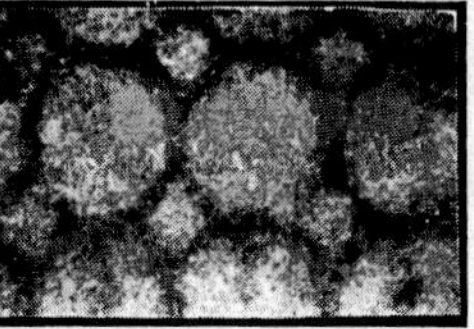

Wmk. 110 — Octagons

Wmk. 125 — Lozenges

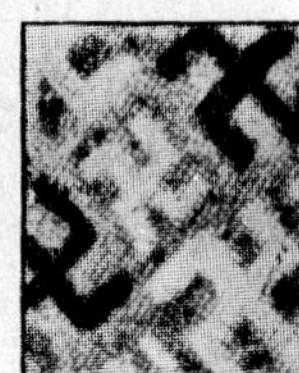

Wmk. 237 — Swastikas

Used Values of 1920-23 are for favor-canceled stamps unless otherwise noted. Postally used copies bring much higher prices.

For additional varieties, see the *Scott Classic Catalogue.*

German Stamps of 1906-20 Overprinted in Black

Perf. 14, 14½, 15x14½

1920 Wmk. 125

1 A16 5pf green .25 .25
2 A16 10pf car rose .25 .25
3 A22 15pf violet brown .25 .25
4 A16 20pf blue violet .25 *1.00*
5 A16 30pf org & blk, *buff* .25 .25
6 A16 40pf car rose .25 .25
7 A16 50pf pur & blk, *buff* .50 .25
8 A17 1m red .50 .55
9 A17 1.25m green .50 .55
10 A17 1.50m yellow brn .90 .85
11 A21 2m blue 2.75 *4.25*
a. Double overprint *350.00*
Never hinged *750.00*
12 A21 2.50m lilac rose 1.50 *3.25*
13 A19 3m black violet 7.00 *9.00*
14 A16 4m black & rose 4.75 5.25
15 A20 5m slate & car 1.75 1.75
a. Center & "Danzig" invtd. *10,500.*
Never hinged —
b. Inverted overprint *17,500.*
Nos. 1-15 (15) 21.65 27.95
Set, never hinged 100.00

The 5pf brown, 10pf orange and 40pf lake and black with this overprint were not regularly issued. Value for trio, $450.

Frame is inverted on No. 15a.

For surcharges see Nos. 19-23, C1-C3.

Issued: 40pf, 9/13; 1.50m, 3m 7/20; 4m, 12/21; others 6/14.

Nos. 5, 4 Surcharged in Various Sizes

1920

19 A16 5pf on 30pf (V) .20 .20
20 A16 10pf on 20pf (R) .20 .20
  a. Double surcharge 87.50 —
  Never hinged 200.00
21 A16 25pf on 30pf (G) .20 .20
  a. Inverted surcharge 75.00 —
  Never hinged 190.00
22 A16 60pf on 30pf (Br) .70 .80
  a. Double surcharge 75.00 240.00
  Never hinged 190.00
23 A16 80pf on 30pf (V) .70 *.80*

German Stamps Surcharged in Various Styles

Gray Burelage with Points Up

25 A16 1m on 30pf org & blk, *buff* (Bk) .70 *1.10*
  a. Pair, one without surcharge
26 A16 1¼m on 3pf brn (R) .70 *1.10*
27 A22 2m on 35pf red brn (Bl) .85 *1.10*
  d. Surcharge omitted 70.00 —
  Never hinged 225.00
28 A22 3m on 7½pf org (G) .85 *1.10*
29 A22 5m on 2pf gray (R) .85 *1.10*
30 A22 10m on 7½pf org (Bk) 3.00 *7.00*
  Nos. 19-30 (11) 8.95 *14.70*
  Set, never hinged 43.00

Issued: #21, 8/10; #20, 8/17; #19, 22-23, 11/1.

Gray Burelage with Points Down

26a A16 1¼m on 3pf brown 24.00 *37.50*
27a A22 2m on 35pf red brn 240.00 *300.00*
28a A22 3m on 7½pf org 11.00 *13.00*
29a A22 5m on 2pf gray 10.50 *26.00*
30a A22 10m on 7½pf org 4.50 *11.00*
  Nos. 26a-30a (5) 290.00 *387.50*
  Set, never hinged 1,150.

Violet Burelage with Points Up

25b A16 1m on 30pf org & blk, *buff* 45.00 37.50
26b A16 1¼m on 3pf brown 4.25 *6.25*
27b A22 2m on 35pf red brown 10.50 *37.50*
28b A22 3m on 7½pf org 1.75 *2.25*
29b A22 5m on 2pf gray 1.00 *2.00*
30b A22 10m on 7½pf org 1.00 *1.90*
  Nos. 25b-30b (6) 63.50 *87.40*
  Set, never hinged 250.00

Violet Burelage with Points Down

25c A16 1m on 30pf org & blk, *buff* 1.10 2.25
26c A16 1¼m on 3pf brown 5.50 *10.50*
27c A22 2m on 35pf red brown 18.00 *42.50*
28c A22 3m on 7½pf org 35.00 *80.00*
29c A22 5m on 2pf gray 3.50 *8.00*
30c A22 10m on 7½pf org 11.00 *18.00*
  Nos. 25c-30c (6) 74.10 *161.25*
  Set, never hinged 325.00

Excellent counterfeits of the surcharges are known.

German Stamps of 1906-20 Overprinted in Blue

1920

31 A22 2pf gray 100.00 *175.00*
32 A22 2½pf gray 125.00 *250.00*
33 A16 3pf brown 10.00 *40.00*
  a. Double overprint 55.00 —
  Never hinged 140.00
34 A16 5pf green .35 .35
  a. Double overprint 72.50
  Never hinged 190.00
35 A22 7½pf orange 40.00 *57.50*
36 A16 10pf carmine 3.75 *7.00*
37 A22 15pf dk violet .50 *.75*
  b. Double overprint 70.00
  Never hinged 175.00
38 A16 20pf blue violet .50 *.75*

Overprinted in Carmine or Blue

39 A16 25pf org & blk, *yel* .50 *.75*
40 A16 30pf org & blk, *buff* 45.00 *82.50*
42 A16 40pf lake & blk 1.60 *2.25*
  a. Inverted overprint —
  b. Double overprint —
43 A16 50pf pur & blk, *buff* 140.00 *250.00*
44 A16 60pf mag (Bl) 1,250. *1,800.*
45 A16 75pf green & blk .50 *.75*
46 A16 80pf lake & blk, *rose* 3.00 4.25
47 A17 1m carmine 1,000. *1,750.*
  a. Double overprint *3,750.*

Overprinted in Carmine

48 A21 2m gray blue 1,000. *1,750.*

Counterfeit overprints of Nos. 31-48 exist.
Nos. 44, 47 and 48 were issued in small quantities and usually affixed directly to the mail by the postal clerk.
For surcharge see No. 62.

Hanseatic Trading Ship
A8 A9

Serrate Roulette 13½

1921, Jan. 31 Typo. Wmk. 108

49 A8 5pf brown & violet .25 .20
50 A8 10pf orange & dk vio .25 .20
51 A8 25pf green & car rose .45 .65
52 A8 40pf carmine rose 3.25 3.25
53 A8 80pf ultra .50 .50
54 A9 1m car rose & blk 1.40 1.40
55 A9 2m dk blue & dk grn 6.00 4.75
56 A9 3m blk & grnsh bl 1.40 *1.60*
57 A9 5m indigo & rose red 1.40 *1.60*
58 A9 10m dk grn & brn org 2.25 *4.25*
  Nos. 49-58 (10) 17.15 *18.40*
  Set, never hinged 77.50

Issued in honor of the Constitution.
Nos. 49 and 50 with center in red instead of violet and Nos. 49-51, 54-58 with center inverted are probably proofs. All values of this issue exist imperforate but are not known to have been regularly issued in that condition.

1921, Mar. 11 *Perf. 14*

59 A8 25pf green & car rose .70 *1.10*
60 A8 40pf carmine rose 1.10 1.10
61 A8 80pf ultra 5.25 *10.50*
  Nos. 59-61 (3) 7.05 *12.70*
  Set, never hinged 27.50

No. 45 Surcharged in Black

1921, May 6 Wmk. 125

62 A16 60pf on 75pf .50 *.90*
  Never hinged 3.00
  a. Double surcharge 82.50 *92.50*
  Never hinged 175.00

Arms — A11 Coat of Arms — A12

Wmk. 108 (Vert. or Horiz.)

1921-22 *Perf. 14*

63 A11 5(pf) orange .20 .20
64 A11 10(pf) dark brown .20 .20
65 A11 15(pf) green .20 .20
66 A11 20(pf) slate .20 .20
67 A11 25(pf) dark green .20 .20
68 A11 30(pf) blue & car .25 .20
  a. Center inverted 27.50
  Never hinged 70.00
69 A11 40pf green & car .20 .20
  a. Center inverted 42.50
  Never hinged 70.00
70 A11 50pf dk green & car .20 .20
71 A11 60pf carmine .45 .35
72 A11 80pf black & car .35 *.45*

Paper With Faint Gray Network

73 A11 1m orange & car .20 *.35*
  a. Center inverted 42.50
  Never hinged 70.00
74 A11 1.20m blue violet 1.25 1.00
75 A11 2m gray & car 3.25 *3.50*
76 A11 3m violet & car 9.00 8.75

Serrate Roulette 13½

77 A12 5m grn, red & blk 1.25 *2.50*
78 A12 9m rose, red & org ('22) 2.50 *7.75*
79 A12 10m ultra, red & blk 1.25 *2.50*
80 A12 20m red & black 1.25 *2.50*
  Nos. 63-80 (18) 22.40 *31.25*
  Set, never hinged 70.00

In this and succeeding issues the mark values usually have the face of the paper covered with a gray network. This network is often very faint and occasionally is omitted.
Nos. 64-76 exist imperf. Value, each $10-$37.50 unused, $30-$100 never hinged.
See Nos. 81-93, 99-105. For surcharges and overprints see Nos. 96-98, O1-O33.

Type of 1921 and

A13

Coat of Arms — A13a

1922 Wmk. 108 *Perf. 14*

81 A11 75(pf) deep violet .20 .20
82 A11 80(pf) green .20 .20
83 A11 1.25m violet & car .20 .20
84 A11 1.50m slate gray .20 .20
85 A11 2m car rose .20 .20
86 A11 2.40m dk brn & car .70 *1.40*
87 A11 3m car lake .20 *.35*
88 A11 4m dark blue .70 *1.40*
89 A11 5m deep green .20 *.35*
90 A11 6m car lake .20 *.35*
  a. 6m car rose, wmk. 109 horiz. *1,800.*
  Never hinged *3,900.*
91 A11 8m light blue .20 *.70*
92 A11 10m orange .20 *.35*
93 A11 20m orange brn .20 *.35*
94 A13 50m gold & car 1.40 *3.50*
  a. 50m gold & red 52.50 *85.00*
  Never hinged 190.00
95 A13a 100m metallic grn & red 3.25 *10.00*
  Nos. 81-95 (15) 8.25 *19.75*
  Set, never hinged 32.50

No. 95 has buff instead of gray network.
Nos. 81-83, 85-86, 88 exist imperf. Value, each $12.50.
Nos. 94-95 exist imperf. Value, each $50

Nos. 87, 88 and 91 Surcharged in Black or Carmine

1922

96 A11 6m on 3m car lake .20 *.45*
  a. Double surcharge
97 A11 8m on 4m dk blue .20 *.70*
  a. Double surcharge 50.00 62.50
  Never hinged 100.00
98 A11 20m on 8m lt bl (C) .20 *.45*
  Nos. 96-98 (3) .60 *1.60*
  Set, never hinged 1.75

1922-23 Wmk. 109 (Horiz.) *Perf. 14*

99 A11 4m dark blue .20 *.35*
100 A11 5m dark green .20 *.35*
102 A11 10m orange .20 *.35*
103 A11 20m orange brn .20 *.35*

Paper Without Network

104 A11 40m pale blue .20 .50
105 A11 80m red .20 .50
  Nos. 99-105 (6) 1.20 *2.40*
  Set, never hinged 3.60

Nos. 100, 102 and 103 also exist with watermark vertical. Values slightly higher.
Nos. 104-105 exist imperf. Value, each $17.50.

A15

A15a

Coat of Arms A16

1923 *Perf. 14*

Paper With Gray Network

106 A15 50m pale bl & red .20 *.35*
107 A15a 100m dk grn & red .20 *.35*
108 A15a 150m violet & red .20 *.35*
109 A16 250m violet & red .20 *.35*
110 A16 500m gray blk & red .20 *.35*
111 A16 1000m brown & red .20 *.35*
112 A16 5000m silver & red 1.00 *4.25*

Paper Without Network

113 A15 50m pale blue .20 *.50*
114 A15a 100m deep green .20 *.50*
115 A15 200m orange .20 *.50*
  Nos. 106-115 (10) 2.80 *7.85*
  Set, never hinged 13.00

#108-112 exist imperf. Value, each $35 unused, $85 never hinged.
Nos. 113-115 exist imperf. Value, each $35 unused, $92.50 never hinged.
See Nos. 123-125. For surcharges and overprints see Nos. 126, 137-140, 143, 156-167, O35-O38.

A17

1923 *Perf. 14*

Paper With Gray Network

117 A17 250m violet & red .20 *.35*
118 A17 300m blue grn & red .20 *.35*
119 A17 500m gray & red .20 *.35*
120 A17 1000m brown & red .20 *.35*
121 A17 3000m violet & red .20 *.35*
123 A16 10,000m orange & red .35 *.50*
124 A16 20,000m pale bl & red .35 *.90*
125 A16 50,000m green & red .35 *.90*
  Nos. 117-125 (8) 2.05 *4.05*
  Set, never hinged 10.00

#117, 119-121 exist imperf. Value, each $10.50 unused, $27.50 never hinged; #123-125 also exist imperf. Values each, $11.50 unused, $27.50 never hinged.
See #127-135. For surcharges & overprints see #141-142, 144-155, O39-O41.

No. 124 Surcharged in Red

1923, Aug. 14
126 A16 100,000m on 20,000m 1.10 *7.00*
Never hinged 3.50

No. 126 exists imperf. Value $14.50 unused, $42.50 never hinged.

1923 ***Perf. 14***
Paper Without Network
127 A17 1000m brown .20 *.35*
129 A17 5000m rose .20 *.35*
131 A17 20,000m pale blue .20 *.35*
132 A17 50,000m green .20 *.35*
Paper With Gray Network
133 A17 100,000m deep blue .20 *.35*
134 A17 250,000m violet .20 *.35*
135 A17 500,000m slate .20 *.35*
Nos. 127-135 (7) 1.40 2.45
Set, never hinged 3.15

Nos. 127, 129, 131-135 exist imperf. Value each, $14.50 unused, $35 never hinged.

Abbreviations: th=(tausend) thousand mil=million

Nos. 115, 114, 132, and Type of 1923 Surcharged

1923 ***Perf. 14***
Paper Without Network
137 A15 40th m on 200m .70 *1.75*
a. Double surcharge 70.00
Never hinged 140.00
138 A15 100th m on 200m .70 *1.75*
139 A15 250th m on 200m 6.00 *10.50*
140 A15a 400th m on 100m .35 .35
141 A17 500th m on 50,000m .25 .25
142 A17 1mil m on 10,000m org 2.75 *6.00*

The surcharges on Nos. 140-142 differ in details from those on Nos. 137-139.

Type of 1923 Surcharged

Paper With Gray Network
143 A16 10mil m on 1,000,000m org 1.40 1.40
Nos. 137-143 (7) 12.15 *22.00*
Set, never hinged 73.50

#142-143 exist imperf. Value: #142 unused $21, never hinged $50; #143 unused $19, never hinged $42.50.

Type of 1923 Surcharged

Paper Without Network
10,000m rose
144 A17 1mil m on 10,000m .20 *.35*
145 A17 2mil m on 10,000m .20 *.35*
146 A17 3mil m on 10,000m .20 *.35*
147 A17 5mil m on 10,000m .20 *.35*
b. Double surcharge 70.00
Never hinged 140.00
10,000m gray lilac
148 A17 10mil m on 10,000m .35 *.65*
149 A17 20mil m on 10,000m .35 *.65*
150 A17 25mil m on 10,000m .20 *.65*
151 A17 40mil m on 10,000m .20 *.65*
a. Double surcharge 52.50
Never hinged 140.00
152 A17 50mil m on 10,000m .20 *.65*

Type of 1923 Surcharged in Red

10,000m gray lilac
153 A17 100mil m on 10,000m .20 *.65*
154 A17 300mil m on 10,000m .20 *.65*
155 A17 500mil m on 10,000m .20 *.65*
Nos. 144-155 (12) 2.70 *6.60*
Set, never hinged 12.00

#144-147 exist imperf. Value, each $12.50 unused, $29 never hinged.. #148-155 exist imperf. Value, each $10.50 unused, $26 never hinged.

Types of 1923 Surcharged

1923 **Wmk. 110** ***Perf. 14***
156 A15 5pf on 50m rose .60 .35
157 A15 10pf on 50m rose .60 .35
158 A15a 20pf on 100m rose .60 .35
159 A15 25pf on 50m rose 5.75 *9.00*
160 A15 30pf on 50m rose 4.00 1.75
161 A15a 40pf on 100m rose 3.50 1.75
162 A15a 50pf on 100m rose 3.50 *2.50*
163 A15a 75pf on 100m rose 9.25 *14.50*

Type of 1923 Surcharged

164 A16 1g on 1mil m rose 6.25 5.25
165 A16 2g on 1mil m rose 14.50 *17.50*
166 A16 3g on 1mil m rose 32.50 *60.00*
167 A16 5g on 1mil m rose 30.00 *62.50*
Nos. 156-167 (12) 111.05 *175.80*
Set, never hinged 375.00

Coat of Arms — A19

1924-37 **Wmk. 109** ***Perf. 14***
168 A19 3pf brn, *yelsh* ('36) 1.25 1.25
a. 3pf dp brn, *white* ('27) 2.00 1.75
Never hinged 5.75
170 A19 5pf org, *yelsh* ('36) 3.25 .45
a. White paper 4.25 .50
Never hinged 12.50
c. Tête bêche pair 275.00
Never hinged 650.00
d. Syncopated perf., #170 ('37) 10.50 9.00
Never hinged 29.00
e. Syncopated perf., #170a ('32) 20.00 10.50
Never hinged 60.00
171 A19 7pf yel grn ('33) 1.75 *2.40*
172 A19 8pf yel grn ('37) 3.25 *4.25*
173 A19 10pf grn, *yelsh* ('36) 7.75 .45
a. White paper 7.75 .45
Never hinged 20.00
c. 10pf blue grn, *yellowish* ('37) 4.50 .85
Never hinged 12.50
d. Tête bêche pair 275.00
Never hinged 650.00
e. Syncopated perf., #173 ('37) 18.00 10.50
Never hinged 50.00
f. Syncopated perf., #173a (132) 24.00 13.00
Never hinged 70.00
g. Syncopated perf., #173c ('37) 10.50 *14.50*
Never hinged 26.00
175 A19 15pf gray 8.75 .45
176 A19 15pf red, *yelsh* ('36) 2.75 1.00
a. White paper ('25) 2.75 .70
Never hinged 12.50
177 A19 20pf carmine & red 12.50 .65
178 A19 20pf gray ('35) 2.00 1.75
179 A19 25pf slate & red 20.00 3.00
180 A19 25pf carmine ('35) 20.00 1.40
181 A19 30pf green & red 10.50 .75
182 A19 30pf dk violet ('35) 2.00 *4.25*
183 A19 35pf ultra ('25) 2.25 1.10
184 A19 40pf dk blue & blue 9.25 1.00
185 A19 40pf yel brn & red ('35) 7.00 *13.00*
186 A19 40pf dk blue ('35) 1.40 *3.50*
a. Imperf. 35.00
Never hinged 100.00
187 A19 50pf blue & red 12.50 7.00
a. Yellowish paper ('36) 12.50 7.00
Never hinged 37.50
188 A19 55pf plum & scar ('37) 7.25 *14.00*
189 A19 60pf dk grn & red ('35) 8.25 *16.00*
190 A19 70pf yel grn & red ('35) 3.25 *5.25*
191 A19 75pf violet & red, *yellowish* ('36) 5.75 *7.00*
a. White paper 12.50 *7.00*
Never hinged 40.00
192 A19 80pf dk org brn & red ('35) 3.50 *7.00*
Nos. 168-192 (23) 156.15 *96.90*
Set, never hinged 450.00

The 5pf and 10pf with syncopated perforations (Netherlands type C) are coils.

See Nos. 225-232. For overprints and surcharges see Nos. 200-209, 211-215, 241-252, B9-B11, O42-O52.

Oliva Castle and Cathedral A20

St. Mary's Church A23

Council Chamber on the Langenmarkt A24

2g, Mottlau River & Krantor. 3g, View of Zoppot.

1924-32 **Engr.** **Wmk. 125**
193 A20 1g yel grn & blk 18.00 *37.50*
Parcel post cancel 18.00
194 A20 1g org & gray blk ('25) 14.00 3.25
a. 1g red orange & blk ('32) 14.00 7.00
Never hinged 50.00
Parcel post cancel 1.00
195 A20 2g red vio & blk 37.50 *95.00*
Parcel post cancel 40.00
196 A20 2g rose & blk ('25) 3.50 *6.25*
Parcel post cancel 1.75
197 A20 3g dk blue & blk 3.50 *5.00*
Parcel post cancel 2.25
198 A23 5g brn red & blk 3.50 *6.25*
Parcel post cancel 1.90
199 A24 10g dk brn & blk 18.00 *75.00*
Parcel post cancel 18.00
Nos. 193-199 (7) 98.00 *228.25*
Set, never hinged 385.00

See No. 233. For overprints and surcharges see Nos. 210, 253-254, C31-C35.

Stamps of 1924-25 Overprinted in Black, Violet or Red

1930, Nov. 15 **Typo.** **Wmk. 109**
200 A19 5pf orange 2.50 *3.50*
201 A19 10pf yellow grn (V) 4.50 4.25
202 A19 15pf red 6.00 *10.50*
203 A19 20pf carmine & red 3.00 *5.25*
204 A19 25pf slate & red 4.75 *10.50*
205 A19 30pf green & red 10.50 *24.00*
206 A19 35pf ultra (R) 40.00 *75.00*
207 A19 40pf dk bl & bl (R) 11.50 *35.00*
208 A19 50pf dp blue & red 40.00 *75.00*
209 A19 75pf violet & red 40.00 *75.00*

Wmk. Lozenges. (125)
Engr.
210 A20 1g orange & blk (R) 40.00 *75.00*
Nos. 200-210 (11) 202.75 *393.00*
Set, never hinged 540.00

10th anniv. of the Free State. Counterfeits exist.

Nos. 171 and 183 Surcharged in Red Blue or Green:

Nos. 211-214

No. 215

1934-36
211 A19 6pf on 7pf (R) .80 *1.40*
212 A19 8pf on 7pf (Bl) ('35) 2.00 *2.00*
213 A19 8pf on 7pf (R) ('36) 1.10 1.70
214 A19 8pf on 7pf (G) ('36) .80 *1.70*
215 A19 30pf on 35pf (Bl) 12.00 *20.00*
Nos. 211-215 (5) 16.70 *26.80*
Set, never hinged 42.50

Bathing Beach, Brösen A25

View of Brösen Beach A26

War Memorial at Brösen — A27

Skyline of Danzig — A28

1936, June 23 **Typo.** **Wmk. 109**
216 A25 10pf deep green .70 *.70*
217 A26 25pf rose red 1.00 *2.40*
218 A27 40pf bright blue 1.75 *4.50*
Nos. 216-218 (3) 3.45 *7.60*
Set, never hinged 11.50

Village of Brösen, 125th anniversary.
Exist imperf. Value each, $35 unused, $85 never hinged.

1937, Mar. 27
219 A28 10pf dark blue .45 *1.40*
220 A28 15pf violet brown 1.40 *2.00*
Set, never hinged 5.50

Air Defense League.

Danzig Philatelic Exhibition Issue
Souvenir Sheet

St. Mary's Church — A29

1937, June 6 **Wmk. 109** ***Perf. 14***
221 A29 50pf dark opal green 3.25 *16.00*
Never hinged 9.50

Danzig Philatelic Exhib., June 6-8, 1937.

Arthur Schopenhauer
A30 A31

Design: 40pf, Full-face portrait, white hair.

Unwmk.

1938, Feb. 22 Photo. *Perf. 14*

222 A30 15pf dull blue 1.60 *3.00*
223 A31 25pf sepia 3.25 *7.25*
224 A31 40pf orange ver 1.70 *4.25*
Nos. 222-224 (3) 6.55 *14.50*
Set, never hinged 17.50

150th anniv. of the birth of Schopenhauer.

Type of 1924-35

1938-39 Typo. Wmk. 237 *Perf. 14*

225 A19 3pf brown .90 *4.00*
226 A19 5pf orange .90 *1.40*
b. Syncopated perf. 1.40 *7.00*
Never hinged 5.25
227 A19 8pf yellow grn 4.00 *16.00*
228 A19 10pf blue green .90 *1.25*
b. Syncopated perf. 3.00 *8.75*
Never hinged 10.50
229 A19 15pf scarlet 2.50 *6.25*
230 A19 25pf carmine 2.50 *6.25*
231 A19 40pf dark blue 3.00 *7.00*
232 A19 50pf brt bl & red ('39) 3.00 *10.50*

Engr.

233 A20 1g red org & blk 5.75 *11.50*
Nos. 225-233 (9) 23.45 *64.15*
Set, never hinged 60.00

Sizes: #233, 32½x21¼mm; #194, 31x21mm.

Nos. 226b and 228b are coils with Netherlands type C perforation.

Knights in Tournament, 1500 — A33

French Leaving Danzig, 1814 — A35

Stamp Day: 10pf, Signing of Danzig-Sweden neutrality treaty, 1630. 25pf, Battle of Weichselmünde, 1577.

Unwmk.

1939, Jan. 7 Photo. *Perf. 14*

234 A33 5pf dark green .80 *2.25*
235 A33 10pf copper brown 1.00 *2.50*
236 A35 15pf slate black 1.25 *3.25*
237 A35 25pf brown violet 1.40 *3.50*
Nos. 234-237 (4) 4.45 *11.50*
Set, never hinged 12.50

Gregor Mendel — A37

15pf, Dr. Robert Koch. 25pf, Wilhelm Roentgen.

1939, Apr. 29 Photo. *Perf. 13x14*

238 A37 10pf copper brown .40 *1.10*
239 A37 15pf indigo .65 *2.00*
240 A37 25pf dark olive green 1.00 *2.50*
Nos. 238-240 (3) 2.05 *5.60*
Set, never hinged 5.50

Issued in honor of the achievements of Mendel, Koch and Roentgen.

Issued under German Administration

Stamps of Danzig, 1925-39, Surcharged in Black:

a

b

c

1939 Wmk. 109 *Perf. 14*

241 A19(b) 4rpf on 35pf ultra .75 *2.00*
242 A19(b) 12rpf on 7pf yel grn 1.00 *2.00*
243 A19(a) 20rpf gray 2.50 *7.00*

Wmk. 237

244 A19(a) 3rpf brown 1.00 *2.00*
245 A19(a) 5rpf orange 1.00 *2.00*
246 A19(a) 8rpf yellow grn 1.75 *3.50*
247 A19(a) 10rpf blue grn 2.25 *3.50*
248 A19(a) 15rpf scarlet 5.25 *8.75*
249 A19(a) 25rpf carmine 5.75 *10.50*
250 A19(a) 30rpf dk violet 2.25 *3.75*
251 A19(a) 40rpf dk blue 3.00 *5.25*
252 A19(a) 50rpf brt bl & red 4.50 *7.00*
253 A20(c) 1rm on 1g red org & blk 12.50 *40.00*

Wmk. 125

254 A20(c) 2rm on 2g rose & blk 15.00 *37.50*
Nos. 241-254 (14) 58.50 *134.75*
Set, never hinged 175.00

#241-254 were valid throughout Germany.

SEMI-POSTAL STAMPS

St. George and Dragon — SP1

Wmk. 108

1921, Oct. 16 Typo. *Perf. 14*

Size: 19x22mm

B1 SP1 30pf + 30pf grn & org .45 .70
B2 SP1 60pf + 60pf rose & org 1.25 1.25

Size: 25x30mm

Serrate Roulette 13½

B3 SP1 1.20m + 1.20m dk bl & org 2.25 1.90
Nos. B1-B3 (3) 3.95 3.85
Set, never hinged 11.50

Nos. B1-B3 exist imperf. Value each, $17.50 unused, $42.50 never hinged.

Aged Pensioner SP2

1923, Mar. Wmk. 109 *Perf. 14*

Paper With Gray Network

B4 SP2 50m + 20m lake .20 *.50*
B5 SP2 100m + 30m red violet .20 *.50*
Set, never hinged 1.25

Philatelic Exhibition Issue

Neptune Fountain — SP3

Various Frames.

1929, July 7 Engr. Unwmk.

B6 SP3 10pf yel grn & gray 2.00 *2.25*
B7 SP3 15pf car & gray 2.00 *2.25*
B8 SP3 25pf ultra & gray 7.50 7.00
a. 25pf violet blue & black 29.00 *55.00*
Never hinged 87.50
Nos. B6-B8 (3) 11.50 11.50
Set, never hinged 32.50

These stamps were sold exclusively at the Danzig Philatelic Exhibition, June 7-14, 1929, at double their face values, the excess being for the aid of the exhibition.

Regular Issue of 1924-25 Surcharged in Black

1934, Jan. 15 Wmk. 109

B9 A19 5pf + 5pf orange 11.50 *20.00*
B10 A19 10pf + 5pf yel grn 35.00 *45.00*
B11 A19 15pf + 5pf carmine 22.50 *37.50*
Nos. B9-B11 (3) 69.00 *102.50*
Set, never hinged 145.00

Surtax for winter welfare. Counterfeits exist.

Stock Tower — SP4

George Hall — SP6

City Gate, 16th Century SP5

1935, Dec. 16 Typo. *Perf. 14*

B12 SP4 5pf + 5pf orange .65 *1.25*
B13 SP5 10pf + 5pf green 1.00 *2.00*
B14 SP6 15pf + 10pf scarlet 2.00 *3.25*
Nos. B12-B14 (3) 3.65 *6.50*
Set, never hinged 10.00

Surtax for winter welfare.

Milk Can Tower SP7

Frauentor SP8

Krantor — SP9

Langgarter Gate — SP10

High Gate SP11

1936, Nov. 25

B15 SP7 10pf + 5pf dk bl 1.60 *3.00*
a. Imperf. 52.50
Never hinged 140.00
B16 SP8 15pf + 5pf dull green 1.60 *4.25*
B17 SP9 25pf + 10pf red brown 2.75 *5.75*
B18 SP10 40pf + 20pf brn & red brn 3.75 *9.50*
B19 SP11 50pf + 20pf bl & dk bl 6.25 *14.50*
Nos. B15-B19 (5) 15.95 *37.00*
Set, never hinged 45.00

Surtax for winter welfare.

SP12

SP13

1937, Oct. 30

B20 SP12 25pf + 25pf dk car 2.50 *5.25*
B21 SP13 40pf + 40pf blue & red 2.50 *5.25*
a. Souv. sheet of 2, #B20-B21 35.00 *70.00*
Never hinged 100.00
Set, never hinged 18.00

Founding of Danzig community at Magdeburg.

Madonna SP14

Mercury SP15

Weather Vane, Town Hall SP16

Neptune Fountain SP17

St. George and Dragon — SP18

1937, Dec. 13

B23 SP14 5pf + 5pf brt violet 3.50 *5.25*
B24 SP15 10pf + 10pf dk brn 3.50 *5.25*
B25 SP16 15pf + 5pf bl & yel brn 4.00 *5.25*
B26 SP17 25pf + 10pf bl grn & grn 4.00 *7.00*
B27 SP18 40pf + 25pf brt car & bl 7.50 *16.00*
Nos. B23-B27 (5) 22.50 *38.75*
Set, never hinged 52.50

Surtax for winter welfare. Designs are from frieze of the Artushof.

"Peter von Danzig" Yacht Race — SP19

Ships: 10pf+5pf, Dredger Fu Shing. 15pf+10pf, S. S. Columbus. 25pf+10pf, S. S. City of Danzig. 40pf+15pf, Peter von Danzig, 1472.

1938, Nov. 28 **Photo.** **Unwmk.**

B28	SP19	5pf + 5pf dk blue grn	1.25	*1.90*
B29	SP19	10pf + 5pf gldn brown	1.40	*3.00*
B30	SP19	15pf + 10pf ol grn	1.90	*3.00*
B31	SP19	25pf + 10pf indigo	2.50	*4.00*
B32	SP19	40pf + 15pf vio brn	3.25	*7.00*
		Nos. B28-B32 (5)	10.30	*18.90*
		Set, never hinged	29.00	

Surtax for winter welfare.

AIR POST STAMPS

No. 6 Surcharged in Blue or Carmine

1920, Sept. 29 **Wmk. 125** ***Perf. 14***

C1	A16	40pf on 40pf	1.00	*2.50*
	a.	Double surcharge	110.00	*200.00*
		Never hinged	300.00	
C2	A16	60pf on 40pf (C)	1.00	*2.50*
	a.	Double surcharge	110.00	*200.00*
		Never hinged	300.00	
C3	A16	1m on 40pf	1.00	*2.50*
		Nos. C1-C3 (3)	3.00	*7.50*
		Set, never hinged	9.75	

Plane faces left on No. C2.

AP3

Plane over Danzig AP4

Wmk. Honeycomb (108)

1921-22 **Typo.** ***Perf. 14***

C4	AP3	40(pf) blue green	.25	*.45*
C5	AP3	60(pf) dk violet	.25	*.45*
C6	AP3	1m carmine	.25	*.45*
C7	AP3	2m orange brown	.25	*.45*

Serrate Roulette 13½

Size: 34½x23mm

C8	AP4	5m violet blue	1.00	*1.75*
C9	AP4	10m dp grn ('22)	2.00	*3.75*
		Nos. C4-C9 (6)	4.00	*7.30*
		Set, never hinged	14.00	

Nos. C4-C9 exist imperf. Value, each $26.00 unused, $70 never hinged.

1923 **Wmk. Webbing (109)** ***Perf. 14***

C10	AP3	40(pf) blue green	.35	*1.75*
C11	AP3	60(pf) dk violet	.35	*1.75*
	a.	Double impression		—
C12	AP3	1m carmine	.35	*1.75*
C13	AP3	2m org brown	.35	*1.75*
C14	AP3	25m pale blue	.25	*.45*

Serrate Roulette 13½

Size: 34½x23mm

C15	AP4	5m violet blue	.35	*.80*
C16	AP4	10m deep green	.35	*.80*

Paper With Gray Network

C17	AP4	20m orange brown	.35	*.80*

Size: 40x23mm

C18	AP4	50m orange	.25	*.50*
C19	AP4	100m red	.25	*.50*
C20	AP4	250m dark brown	.25	*.50*
C21	AP4	500m carmine rose	.25	*.50*
		Nos. C10-C21 (12)	3.70	*11.85*
		Set, never hinged	11.50	

#C11, C12, C14-C21 exist imperf. Value, #C11, C12, C15-C17, each $5.75 unused, $17.50 never hinged. Value, #C14, C18-C21, each $21 unused, $50 never hinged.

Issued: #C10, C13, C15-C16, 1/3/23. #C14, C18, C20-C21, 4/27/23. #C17, 1/10/23. #C19, 2/5/23.

Nos. C18, C19 and C21 exist with wmk. sideways, both perf and imperf. Value each, $40 unused, $140 never hinged.

Post Horn and Airplanes — AP5

1923, Oct. 18 ***Perf. 14***

Paper Without Network

C22	AP5	250,000m scarlet	.25	*1.00*
C23	AP5	500,000m scarlet	.25	*1.00*
		Set, never hinged	1.80	

Exist imperf. Value, each $42.50.

Surcharged

C24	AP5	2mil m on 100,000m	.25	*1.00*
C25	AP5	5mil m on 50,000m	.25	*1.00*
	b.	Cliché of 10,000m in sheet of 50,000m	30.00	*70.00*
		Never hinged	90.00	
		Set, never hinged	1.80	

Value, each $100 unused, $260 never hinged.

Nos. C24 and C25 were not regularly issued without surcharge, although copies have been passed through the post. Values: C24 unused $7, never hinged $21; C25 unused $12, never hinged $21.

AP6

Plane over Danzig — AP7

1924

C26	AP6	10(pf) vermilion	22.50	4.75
C27	AP6	20(pf) carmine rose	2.00	1.10
C28	AP6	40(pf) olive brown	4.50	1.75
C29	AP6	1g deep green	4.50	1.75
C30	AP7	2½g violet brown	22.50	*32.50*
		Nos. C26-C30 (5)	56.00	*41.85*
		Set, never hinged	125.00	

Exist imperf. Value #C26, C30, $70 unused, $175 never hinged; others, each $35 unused, $85 never hinged.

Nos. 193, 195, 197-199 Surcharged in Various Colors

1932 **Wmk. 125**

C31	A20	10pf on 1g (G)	10.50	*20.00*
C32	A20	15pf on 2g (V)	10.50	*20.00*
C33	A20	20pf on 3g (Bl)	10.50	*20.00*
C34	A23	25pf on 5g (R)	10.50	*20.00*
C35	A24	30pf on 10g (Br)	10.50	*20.00*
		Nos. C31-C35 (5)	52.50	*100.00*
		Set, never hinged	175.00	

Intl. Air Post Exhib. of 1932. The surcharges were variously arranged to suit the shapes and designs of the stamps. The stamps were sold at double their surcharged values, the excess being donated to the exhibition funds.

No. C31 exists with inverted surcharge and with double surcharge. Value each, $70 unused, $175.00 never hinged.

Airplane
AP8 AP9

1935 **Wmk. 109**

C36	AP8	10pf scarlet	2.00	.70
C37	AP8	15pf yellow	2.00	1.00
C38	AP8	25pf dark green	2.00	1.75
C39	AP8	50pf gray blue	8.00	*9.25*
C40	AP9	1g magenta	4.00	*9.25*
		Nos. C36-C40 (5)	18.00	*21.95*
		Set, never hinged	50.00	

Nos. C36 and C40 exist imperf. Values: C36 unused $17.50, never hinged $50; C40 unused $26, never hinged $70.

See Nos. C42-C45.

Souvenir Sheet

St. Mary's Church — AP10

1937, June 6 ***Perf. 14***

C41	AP10	50pf dark grayish blue	2.75	*13.50*
		Never hinged	8.00	

Danzig Phil. Exhib., June 6-8, 1937.

Type of 1935

1938-39 **Wmk. 237**

C42	AP8	10pf scarlet	2.25	*5.75*
C43	AP8	15pf yellow ('39)	2.25	*5.75*
C44	AP8	25pf dark green	2.25	*7.00*
C45	AP8	50pf gray blue ('39)	3.50	*17.50*
		Nos. C42-C45 (4)	10.25	*36.00*
		Set, never hinged	32.50	

POSTAGE DUE STAMPS

Danzig Coat of Arms
D1 D2

Wmk. Honeycomb (108)

1921-22 **Typo.** ***Perf. 14***

Paper Without Network

J1	D1	10(pf) deep violet	.25	*.35*
J2	D1	20(pf) deep violet	.25	*.35*
J3	D1	40(pf) deep violet	.25	*.35*
J4	D1	60(pf) deep violet	.25	*.35*
J5	D1	75(pf) dp violet ('22)	.25	*.35*
J6	D1	80(pf) deep violet	.25	*.35*
J7	D1	120(pf) deep violet	.25	*.35*
J8	D1	200(pf) dp violet ('22)	1.00	*1.25*
J9	D1	240(pf) deep violet	.25	*.35*
J10	D1	300(pf) dp violet ('22)	1.00	*1.25*
J11	D1	400(pf) deep violet	1.00	*1.25*
J12	D1	500(pf) deep violet	1.00	*1.25*
J13	D1	800(pf) dp violet ('22)	1.00	*1.25*
J14	D1	20m dp violet ('22)	1.00	*1.25*
		Nos. J1-J14 (14)	8.00	*10.30*
		Set, never hinged	20.00	

Nos. J1-J14 exist imperf. Value, each $15 unused, $42.50 never hinged.

1923 **Wmk. 109**

J15	D1	100(pf) deep violet	.60	*.70*
J16	D1	200(pf) deep violet	2.10	*3.50*
J17	D1	300(pf) deep violet	.60	*.70*
J18	D1	400(pf) deep violet	.60	*.70*
J19	D1	500(pf) deep violet	.60	*.70*
J20	D1	800(pf) deep violet	1.40	*3.50*
J21	D1	10m deep violet	.60	*.80*
J22	D1	20m deep violet	.60	*.80*
J23	D1	50m deep violet	.60	*.90*

Paper With Gray Network

J24	D1	100m deep violet	.60	*.85*
J25	D1	500m deep violet	.60	*.85*
		Nos. J15-J25 (11)	8.90	14.00
		Set, never hinged	24.00	

#J15, J17, J22-J25 exist imperf. Value each, $8.50 unused, $26 never hinged.

Nos. J22-J23 and Type of 1923 Surcharged

1923, Oct. 1

Paper without Network

J26	D1	5000m on 50m	.35	*.70*
J27	D1	10,000m on 20m	.35	*.70*
J28	D1	50,000m on 500m	.35	*.70*
J29	D1	100,000m on 20m	.75	*1.25*
		Nos. J26-J29 (4)	1.80	*3.35*
		Set, never hinged	5.50	

On No. J26 the numerals of the surcharge are all of the larger size.

A 1000(m) on 100m deep violet was prepared but not issued. Value, $145, never hinged $350.

Nos. J26-J28 exist imperf. Value each, $14.50 unused, $35 never hinged.

1923-28 **Wmk. 110**

J30	D2	5(pf) blue & blk	.90	.80
J31	D2	10(pf) blue & blk	.60	*.75*
J32	D2	15(pf) blue & blk	1.40	1.10
J33	D2	20(pf) blue & blk	1.75	*2.25*
J34	D2	30(pf) blue & blk	7.25	2.25
J35	D2	40(pf) blue & blk	2.00	*3.00*
J36	D2	50(pf) blue & blk	2.00	*2.25*
J37	D2	60(pf) blue & blk	13.00	*17.50*
J38	D2	100(pf) blue & blk	14.00	7.00
J39	D2	3g blue & car	7.25	*45.00*
	a.	"Guldeu" instead of "Gulden"	300.00	*900.00*
		Never hinged	900.00	
		Nos. J30-J39 (10)	50.15	*81.90*
		Set, never hinged	145.00	

Used values of Nos. J30-J39 are for postally used copies.

See Nos. J43-J47.

Postage Due Stamps of 1923 Issue Surcharged in Red

1932, Dec. 20

J40	D2	5pf on 40(pf)	2.00	*10.50*
J41	D2	10pf on 60(pf)	40.00	10.50
J42	D2	20pf on 100(pf)	2.00	*8.00*
		Nos. J40-J42 (3)	44.00	*29.00*
		Set, never hinged	105.00	

Type of 1923

1938-39 **Wmk. 237** ***Perf. 14***

J43	D2	10(pf) bl & blk ('39)	1.10	*14.00*
J44	D2	30(pf) blue & black	1.90	*14.50*
J45	D2	40(pf) bl & blk ('39)	5.50	*32.50*
J46	D2	60(pf) bl & blk ('39)	6.75	*32.50*
J47	D2	100(pf) blue & black	10.50	*50.00*
		Nos. J43-J47 (5)	25.75	*143.50*
		Set, never hinged	87.50	

OFFICIAL STAMPS

Regular Issues of 1921-22 Overprinted

a

1921-22 Wmk. 108 *Perf. 14x14½*

No.	Type	Description	Unused	Used
O1	A11	5(pf) orange	.25	.20
O2	A11	10(pf) dark brown	.20	*.20*
a.		Inverted overprint	35.00	
		Never hinged	100.00	—
O3	A11	15(pf) green	.20	*.20*
O4	A11	20(pf) slate	.20	*.20*
O5	A11	25(pf) dark green	.20	*.20*
O6	A11	30(pf) blue & car	.50	*.70*
O7	A11	40(pf) green & car	.25	*.25*
O8	A11	50(pf) dk grn & car	.25	*.25*
O9	A11	60(pf) carmine	.25	*.25*
O10	A11	75(pf) dp vio ('22)	.20	*.35*
O11	A11	80(pf) black & car	1.00	*1.10*
O12	A11	80(pf) green ('22)	.20	*1.75*

Paper With Faint Gray Network

No.	Type	Description	Unused	Used
O14	A11	1m orange & car	.20	*.25*
O15	A11	1.20m blue violet	1.60	1.10
O16	A11	1.25m vio & car ('22)	.20	*.35*
O17	A11	1.50m sl gray ('22)	.20	*.35*
O18	A11	2m gray & car	18.00	13.50
a.		Inverted overprint		
		Never hinged	130.00	
O19	A11	2m car rose ('22)	.20	*.35*
O20	A11	2.40m dk brn & car ('22)	1.25	*2.50*
O21	A11	3m violet & car	12.50	*13.00*
O22	A11	3m car lake ('22)	.20	*.35*
O23	A11	4m dk blue ('22)	1.00	.75
O24	A11	5m dp grn ('22)	.20	*.35*
O25	A11	6m car lake ('22)	.20	*.35*
O26	A11	10m orange ('22)	.20	*.35*
O27	A11	20m org brn ('22)	.20	*.35*
		Nos. O1-O27 (25)	39.65	*39.35*
		Set, never hinged	130.00	

Double overprints exist on Nos. O1-O2, O5-O7, O10 and O12.

Same Overprint on No. 96

No.	Type	Description	Unused	Used
O28	A11	6m on 3m	.20	*.65*
		Never hinged	.50	
a.		Inverted overprint	26.00	
		Never hinged	70.00	

No. 77 Overprinted

1922 *Serrate Roulette 13½*

No.	Type	Description	Unused	Used
O29	A12	5m grn, red & blk	3.25	*5.50*
		Never hinged	12.00	

Nos. 99-103, 106-107 Overprinted Type "a"

1923 Wmk. 109 *Perf. 14*

No.	Type	Description	Unused	Used
O30	A11	4m dark blue	.20	*.50*
O31	A11	5m dark green	.20	*.85*
O32	A11	10m orange	.20	*.50*
O33	A11	20m orange brn	.20	*.50*
O34	A15	50m pale bl & red	.20	*.50*
O35	A15a	100m dk grn & red	.20	*.50*

Nos. 113-115, 118-120 Overprinted Type "a"

No.	Type	Description	Unused	Used
O36	A15	50m pale blue	.20	*.45*
a.		Inverted overprint	21.00	
		Never hinged	52.50	
O37	A15a	100m dark green	.20	*.45*
O38	A15	200m orange	.20	*.45*
a.		Inverted overprint	21.00	
		Never hinged	52.50	

Paper With Gray Network

No.	Type	Description	Unused	Used
O39	A17	300m bl grn & red	.20	*.50*
O40	A17	500m gray & red	.20	*.45*
O41	A17	1000m brown & red	.20	*.45*
		Nos. O30-O41 (12)	2.40	*6.10*
		Set, never hinged	8.75	

Regular Issue of 1924-25 Overprinted

1924-25 *Perf. 14x14½*

No.	Type	Description	Unused	Used
O42	A19	5pf orange	2.50	*3.00*
O43	A19	10pf yellow grn	2.50	2.25
O44	A19	15pf gray	2.25	1.90
O45	A19	15pf red ('25)	22.50	8.75
O46	A19	20pf car & red	2.50	1.40
O47	A19	25pf slate & red	26.00	26.00
O48	A19	30pf green & red	3.75	2.50
O49	A19	35pf ultra ('25)	52.50	50.00
O50	A19	40pf dk bl & dull bl	7.25	7.00
O51	A19	50pf dp blue & red	21.00	*32.50*
O52	A19	75pf violet & red	42.50	*100.00*
		Nos. O42-O52 (11)	185.25	*235.30*
		Set, never hinged	500.00	

Double overprints exist on Nos. O42-O44, O47, O50-O52.

DENMARK

'den-,märk

LOCATION — Northern part of a peninsula which separates the North and Baltic Seas, and includes the surrounding islands
GOVT. — Kingdom
AREA — 16,631 sq. mi.
POP. — 5,294,860 (1/1/1999)
CAPITAL — Copenhagen

96 Skilling = 1 Rigsbank Daler
100 Ore = 1 Krone (1875)

Catalogue values for unused stamps in this country are for Never Hinged items, beginning with Scott 297 in the regular postage section, Scott B15 in the semi-postal section, and Scott Q28 in the parcel post section.

Values for unused stamps are for examples with original gum as defined in the catalogue introduction. Very fine examples of Nos. 9-37 and O1-O9 will have perforations clear of the framelines but with the design noticeably off center. Well centered stamps are quite scarce and will command substantial premiums.

Watermarks

Wmk. 111 — Small Crown

Wmk. 112 — Crown

Wmk. 113 — Crown

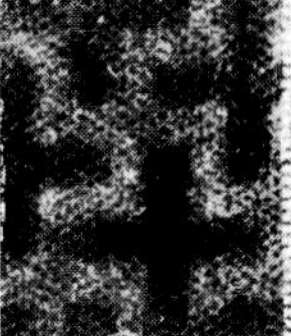
Wmk. 114 — Multiple Crosses

A1

Royal Emblems — A2

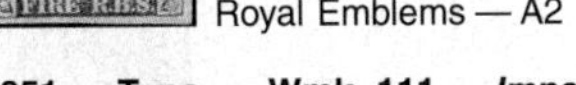

1851 Typo. Wmk. 111 *Imperf.*
With Yellow Brown Burelage

1	A1 2rs blue	*2,250.*	975.00
a.	First printing	*6,750.*	*1,850.*
2	A2 4rs brown	475.00	32.50
a.	First printing	575.00	57.50
b.	4rs yellow brown	825.00	47.50

The first printing of Nos. 1 and 2 had the burelage printed from a copper plate, giving a clear impression with the lines in slight relief. The subsequent impressions had the burelage typographed, with the lines fainter and not rising above the surface of the paper.

Nos. 1-2 were reprinted in 1885 and 1901 on heavy yellowish paper, unwatermarked and imperforate, with a brown burelage. No. 1 was also reprinted without burelage, on both yellowish and white paper. Value for least costly reprint of No. 1, $50.

No. 2 was reprinted in 1951 in 10 shades with "Colour Specimen 1951" printed on the back. It was also reprinted in 1961 in 2 shades without burelage and with "Farve Nytryk 1961" printed on the back. Value for least costly reprint of No. 2, $8.50.

Dotting in Spandrels
A3

Wavy Lines in Spandrels
A4

1854-57

3	A3 2s blue ('55)	55.00	50.00
4	A3 4s brown	250.00	11.00
a.	4s yellow brown	275.00	11.00
5	A3 8s green ('57)	250.00	55.00
a.	8s yellow green	250.00	60.00
6	A3 16s gray lilac ('57)	475.00	150.00
	Nos. 3-6 (4)	1,030.	266.00

See No. 10. For denominations in cents see Danish West Indies Nos. 1-4.

1858-62

7	A4 4s yellow brown	57.50	8.00
a.	4s brown	60.00	8.50
b.	Wmk. 112 ('62)	55.00	9.00
8	A4 8s green	625.00	82.50

Nos. 2 to 8 inclusive are known with unofficial perforation 12 or 13, and Nos. 4, 5, 7 and 8 with unofficial roulette 9½.

Nos. 3, 6-8 were reprinted in 1885 on heavy yellowish paper, unwatermarked, imperforate and without burelage. Nos. 4-5 were reprinted in 1924 on white paper, unwatermarked, imperforate, gummed and without burelage. Value for No. 3, $11; Nos. 4-5, each $100; No. 6, $15; Nos. 7-8, each $10.

1863 Wmk. 112 *Rouletted 11*

9	A4 4s brown	77.50	13.00
a.	4s deep brown	77.50	13.00
10	A3 16s violet	1,300.	450.00

Royal Emblems — A5

1864-68 *Perf. 13*

11	A5 2s blue ('65)	55.00	27.50
12	A5 3s red vio ('65)	72.50	67.50
13	A5 4s red	35.00	7.00
14	A5 8s bister ('68)	250.00	90.00
15	A5 16s olive green	425.00	160.00
	Nos. 11-15 (5)	837.50	352.00

Nos. 11-15 were reprinted in 1886 on heavy yellowish paper, unwatermarked, imperforate and without gum. The reprints of all values except the 4s were printed in two vertical rows of six, inverted with respect to each other, so that horizontal pairs are always tête bêche. Value $10 each.

Nos. 13 and 15 were reprinted in 1942 with printing on the back across each horizontal row: "Nytryk 1942. G. A. Hagemann: Danmarks og Vestindiens Frimaerker, Bind 2." Value, $65 each.

Imperf

11a	A5	2s blue	90.00	90.00
12a	A5	3s red violet	125.00	
13a	A5	4s red	72.50	85.00
14a	A5	8s bister	350.00	
15a	A5	16s olive green	425.00	

1870 *Perf. 12½*

11b	A5	2s blue	240.00	310.00
12b	A5	3s red violet	400.00	575.00
14b	A5	8s bister	400.00	400.00
15b	A5	16s olive green	625.00	*1,250.*
		Nos. 11b-15b (4)	1,665.	2,535.

A6

NORMAL FRAME

INVERTED FRAME

The arabesques in the corners have a main stem and a branch. When the frame is in normal position, in the upper left corner the branch leaves the main stem half way between two little leaflets. In the lower right corner the branch starts at the foot of the second leaflet. When the frame is inverted the corner designs are, of course, transposed.

1870-71 Wmk. 112 *Perf. 14x13½*
Paper Varying from Thin to Thick

16	A6 2s gray & ultra ('71)	45.00	22.50
a.	2s gray & blue	45.00	22.50
17	A6 3s gray & brt lil ('71)	72.50	85.00
18	A6 4s gray & car	35.00	7.00
19	A6 8s gray & brn ('71)	160.00	65.00
20	A6 16s gray & grn ('71)	225.00	150.00

Perf. 12½

21	A6 2s gray & bl ('71)	1,750.	*2,900.*
22	A6 4s gray & car	125.00	100.00
24	A6 48s brn & lilac	400.00	250.00

Nos. 16-20, 24 were reprinted in 1886 on thin white paper, unwatermarked, imperforate and without gum. These were printed in sheets of 10 in which 1 stamp has the normal frame (value $32.50 each) and 9 the inverted (value $11 each).

Imperf

16b	A6	2s	*210.00*	
17a	A6	3s	*190.00*	
18a	A6	4s	*175.00*	
19a	A6	8s	*200.00*	
20a	A6	16s	*350.00*	
24a	A6	48s	*350.00*	—

Inverted Frame

16c	A6	2s	825.00	625.00
17b	A6	3s	1,900.	1,500.
18b	A6	4s	625.00	77.50
19b	A6	8s	1,250.	725.00
20b	A6	16s	1,700.	1,250.
24b	A6	48s	2,100.	1,450.

1875-79 *Perf. 14x13½*

25	A6 3o gray blue & gray	13.00	9.00
a.	1st "A" of "DANMARK" missing	45.00	*125.00*
b.	Imperf.	*750.00*	
c.	Inverted frame	13.00	10.50
26	A6 4o slate & blue	20.00	.40
a.	4o gray & blue	20.00	.90
b.	4o slate & ultra	70.00	12.00
c.	4o gray & ultra	60.00	9.50
d.	Imperf	60.00	—
e.	Inverted frame	20.00	.40
27	A6 5o rose & blue ('79)	25.00	62.50
a.	Ball of lower curve of large "5" missing	87.50	225.00
b.	Inverted frame	825.00	*1,850.*
28	A6 8o slate & car	17.50	.40
a.	8o gray & carmine	35.00	4.00
b.	Imperf	70.00	—
c.	Inverted frame	17.50	.40
29	A6 12o sl & dull lake	8.50	3.50
a.	12o gray & bright lilac	35.00	6.75
b.	12o gray & dull magenta	42.50	8.75
c.	Inverted frame	8.00	3.00
30	A6 16o slate & brn	32.50	3.00
a.	16o light gray & brown	40.00	4.00
b.	Inverted frame	26.00	3.25
31	A6 20o rose & gray	70.00	26.00
a.	20o carmine & gray	70.00	26.00
b.	Inverted frame	70.00	26.00
32	A6 25o gray & green	42.50	26.00
a.	Inverted frame	70.00	57.50
33	A6 50o brown & vio	47.50	22.50
a.	50o brown & blue violet	325.00	110.00
b.	Inverted frame	47.50	25.00
34	A6 100o gray & org ('77)	80.00	45.00
a.	Imperf	225.00	
b.	Inverted frame	87.50	45.00
	Nos. 25-34 (10)	356.50	198.30
	Set, never hinged	800.00	

The stamps of this issue on thin semi-transparent paper are far scarcer than those on thicker paper.

See Nos. 41-42, 44, 46-47, 50-52. For surcharges see Nos. 55, 79-80, 136.

Arms — A7

Two types of numerals in corners:

1882

Small Corner Numerals

35 A7 5o green 210.00 82.50
Never hinged 400.00
37 A7 20o blue 160.00 35.00
Never hinged 450.00

1884-88

Larger Corner Numerals

38 A7 5o green 11.00 1.40
a. Imperf. —
39 A7 10o carmine ('85) 11.00 1.40
a. Small numerals in corners ('88) 400.00 *525.00*
b. Imperf., single 140.00
c. Pair, Nos. 39, 39a 475.00 *775.00*
40 A7 20o blue 17.50 1.75
a. Pair, Nos. 37, 40 300.00 *675.00*
b. Imperf. —
Nos. 38-40 (3) 39.50 4.55
Set, never hinged 110.00

Stamps with large corner numerals have white line around crown and lower oval touches frame.

The plate for No. 39, was damaged and 3 clichés in the bottom row were replaced by clichés for post cards, which had small numerals in the corners.

Two clichés with small numerals were inserted in the plate of No. 40.

See Nos. 43, 45, 48-49, 53-54. For surcharge see No. 56.

1895-1901 Wmk. 112 *Perf. 13*

41 A6 3o blue & gray 3.75 2.25
42 A6 4o slate & bl ('96) 3.00 .30
43 A7 5o green 5.00 .55
44 A6 8o slate & car 3.00 .35
45 A7 10o rose car 17.50 .55
46 A6 12o sl & dull lake 3.50 3.00
47 A6 16o slate & brown 12.50 3.00
48 A7 20o blue 17.50 1.75
49 A7 24o brown ('01) 5.00 2.75
50 A6 25o gray & grn ('98) 52.50 9.00
51 A6 50o brown & vio ('97) 35.00 12.50
52 A6 100o slate & org 45.00 22.50
Nos. 41-52 (12) 203.25 58.50
Set, never hinged 425.00

Inverted Frame

41b A6 3o 7.25 4.25
42a A6 4o 3.00 .35
44a A6 8o 3.00 .40
46a A6 12o 8.00 3.00
47a A6 16o 15.00 3.00
50a A6 25o 30.00 13.50
51a A6 50o 55.00 14.50
52a A6 100o 45.00 22.50
Nos. 41b-52a (8) 166.25 61.50
Set, never hinged 300.00

1902-04 Wmk. 113

41c A6 3o blue & gray 2.50 2.25
42b A6 4o slate & blue 11.00 13.50
43a A7 5o green 1.60 .20
44d A6 8o slate & carmine 275.00 210.00
45a A7 10o rose carmine 2.40 .20
48a A7 20o blue 13.00 2.50
50b A6 25o gray & green 5.75 3.00
51b A6 50o brown & violet 20.00 11.50
52b A6 100o slate & orange 18.00 9.00
Nos. 41c-52b (9) 349.25 252.15
Set, never hinged 625.00

Inverted Frame

41d A6 3o 45.00 32.50
42c A6 4o 95.00 62.50
50c A6 25o 125.00 40.00
51c A6 50o 160.00 97.50
52c A6 100o 125.00 100.00
Nos. 41d-52c (5) 550.00 332.50
Set, never hinged 1,200.

1902 Wmk. 113

53 A7 1o orange .60 .45
a. Imperf. — —
54 A7 15o lilac 9.00 .55
a. Imperf, single *3,750.*

Nos. 44d, 44, 49 Surcharged:

a

b

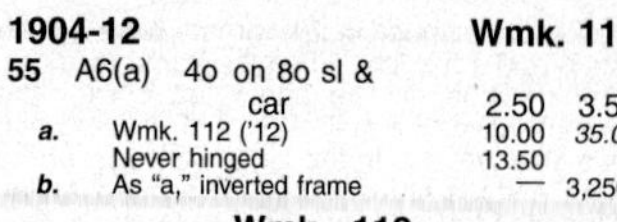

1904-12 Wmk. 113

55 A6(a) 4o on 8o sl & car 2.50 3.50
a. Wmk. 112 ('12) 10.00 *35.00*
Never hinged 13.50
b. As "a," inverted frame — 3,250.

Wmk. 112

56 A7(b) 15o on 24o brown 3.00 5.00
a. Short "15" at right 15.00 *50.00*
Never hinged 32.50
Set, never hinged 9.00

A10

King Christian IX
A11

King Frederik VIII
A12

1905-17 Wmk. 113 *Perf. 13*

57 A10 1o orange ('06) 1.25 .40
58 A10 2o carmine 2.50 .25
a. Perf. 14x14½ ('17) 2.25 *11.00*
59 A10 3o gray 5.25 .45
60 A10 4o dull blue 4.50 .45
a. Perf. 14x14½ ('17) 6.50 *20.00*
61 A10 5o dp green ('12) 2.50 .20
62 A10 10o dp rose ('12) 3.50 .20
63 A10 15o lilac 13.00 1.25
64 A10 20o dk blue ('12) 22.50 .50
Nos. 57-64 (8) 55.00 3.70
Set, never hinged 160.00

The three wavy lines in design A10 are symbolical of the three waters which separate the principal Danish islands. Compare with design A32.

See Nos. 85-96. For surcharges and overprints see Nos. 163, 181, J1, J38, Q1-Q2.

1904-05 Engr.

65 A11 10o scarlet 1.60 .20
66 A11 20o blue 13.00 1.75
67 A11 25o brown ('05) 17.50 2.50
68 A11 50o dull vio ('05) 45.00 *52.50*
69 A11 100o ocher ('05) 8.75 *35.00*
Nos. 65-69 (5) 85.85 *91.95*
Set, never hinged 225.00

1905-06 Re-engraved

70 A11 5o green 2.75 .20
71 A11 10o scarlet ('06) 9.00 .20
Set, never hinged 28.00

The re-engraved stamps are much clearer than the originals, and the decoration on the king's left breast has been removed.

1907-12

72 A12 5o green 1.00 .20
a. Imperf.
73 A12 10o red 1.75 .20
a. Imperf.
74 A12 20o indigo 6.00 .20
a. 20o bright blue ('11) 8.00 .70
75 A12 25o olive brn 10.00 .40
76 A12 35o dp org ('12) 2.50 2.50
77 A12 50o claret 15.00 3.25
78 A12 100o bister brn 50.00 1.90
Nos. 72-78 (7) 86.25 8.65
Set, never hinged 305.00

Nos. 47, 31 and O9 Surcharged:

c

d

Dark Blue Surcharge

1912 Wmk. 112 *Perf. 13*

79 A6(c) 35o on 16o 8.00 *35.00*
a. Inverted frame 150.00 *375.00*

Perf. 14x13½

80 A6(c) 35o on 20o 16.00 *55.00*
a. Inverted frame 55.00 *125.00*

Black Surcharge

81 O1(d) 35o on 32o 15.00 *60.00*
Nos. 79-81 (3) 39.00 *150.00*
Set, never hinged 71.00

General Post Office, Copenhagen — A15

1912 Engr. Wmk. 113 *Perf. 13*

82 A15 5k dark red 300.00 100.00
Never hinged 525.00

See Nos. 135, 843.

Perf. 14x14½

1913-30 Typo. Wmk. 114

85 A10 1o dp org ('14) .20 .20
a. Bklt. pane, 2 ea #85, 91 + 2 labels 18.00
86 A10 2o car ('13) 1.25 .20
a. Imperf. 100.00 *200.00*
b. Booklet pane, 4 + 2 labels 24.00
87 A10 3o gray ('13) 2.25 .20
88 A10 4o blue ('13) 3.25 .20
a. Half used as 2o on cover 1,000.
89 A10 5o dk brown ('21) .55 .20
a. Imperf. 150.00
b. Booklet pane, 4 + 2 labels 12.50
90 A10 5o lt green ('30) .90 .20
a. Booklet pane, 4 + 2 labels 12.50
b. Booklet pane of 50
91 A10 7o apple grn ('26) 2.25 .90
a. Booklet pane, 4 + 2 labels 15.00
92 A10 7o dk violet ('30) 7.50 2.25
93 A10 8o gray ('21) 3.00 1.25
94 A10 10o green ('21) .75 .20
a. Imperf. 150.00
b. Booklet pane, 4 + 2 labels 32.50
95 A10 10o bister brn ('30) 1.25 .20
a. Booklet pane, 4 + 2 labels 14.00
b. Booklet pane of 50
96 A10 12o violet ('26) 12.50 4.00
Nos. 85-96 (12) 35.65 10.00
Set, never hinged 97.00

No. 88a was used with No. 97 in Faroe Islands, Jan. 3-23, 1919.

See surcharge and overprint note following #64.

King Christian X
A16 A17

1913-28 Typo. *Perf. 14x14½*

97 A16 5o green .90 .20
a. Booklet pane of 4 10.00
98 A16 7o orange ('18) 1.75 .95
99 A16 8o dk gray ('20) 4.50 3.50
100 A16 10o red 1.25 .20
a. Imperf. 175.00
b. Booklet pane of 4 10.00
101 A16 12o gray grn ('18) 5.00 6.00
102 A16 15o violet 1.25 .20
103 A16 20o dp blue 6.25 .20
104 A16 20o brown ('21) .60 .20
105 A16 20o red ('26) .90 .20
106 A16 25o dk brown 7.50 .35
107 A16 25o brn & blk ('20) 40.00 3.00
108 A16 25o red ('22) 2.25 .60
109 A16 25o yel grn ('25) 2.50 .35
110 A16 27o ver & blk ('18) 18.00 *32.50*
111 A16 30o grn & blk ('18) 14.00 1.40
112 A16 30o orange ('21) 1.75 1.40
113 A16 30o dk blue ('25) 1.25 .35
114 A16 35o orange 11.00 1.75
115 A16 35o yel & blk ('19) 4.00 3.50
116 A16 40o vio & blk ('18) 8.00 2.25
117 A16 40o gray bl & blk ('20) 25.00 4.25
118 A16 40o dk blue ('22) 3.50 .75
119 A16 40o orange ('25) 1.25 .60
120 A16 50o claret 27.50 2.00
121 A16 50o claret & blk ('19) 40.00 .95
122 A16 50o lt gray ('22) 5.50 .20
a. 50o dark gray ('21) 35.00 3.00
Never hinged 100.00
123 A16 60o brn & bl ('19) 25.00 3.00
a. 60o brown & ultra ('19) 125.00 9.00
Never hinged 350.00
124 A16 60o grn bl ('21) 6.00 .60
125 A16 70o brn & grn ('20) 15.00 1.40
126 A16 80o bl grn ('15) 27.50 9.00
127 A16 90o brn & red ('20) 8.00 2.25
128 A16 1k brn & bl ('22) 30.00 1.40
129 A16 2k gray & cl ('25) 35.00 11.00
130 A16 5k vio & brn ('27) 4.50 4.25
131 A16 10k ver & yel grn ('28) 165.00 30.00
Nos. 97-131 (35) 551.40 130.75
Set, never hinged 1,475.

#97 surcharged "2 ORE" is Faroe Islands #1.

Nos. 87 and 98, 89 and 94, 89 and 104, 90 and 95, 97 and 103, 100 and 102 exist se-tenant in coils for use in vending machines.

For surcharges and overprints see Nos. 161-162, 176-177, 182-184, J2-J8, M1-M2, Q3-Q10.

1913-20 Engr.

132 A17 1k yellow brown 57.50 .60
133 A17 2k gray 65.00 3.00
134 A17 5k purple ('20) 8.00 7.00
Nos. 132-134 (3) 130.50 10.60
Set, never hinged 420.00

For overprint see No. Q11.

G.P.O. Type of 1912

Perf. 14x14½

1915 Wmk. 114 Engr.

135 A15 5k dark red ('15) 250.00 90.00
Never hinged 550.00

Nos. 46 and O10 Surcharged in Black type "c" and:

e

1915 Wmk. 112 Typo. *Perf. 13*

136 A6 (c) 80o on 12o 18.00 *67.50*
a. Inverted frame 275.00 *500.00*
Never hinged 400.00
137 O1 (e) 80o on 8o 30.00 *80.00*
a. "POSTERIM" 40.00 *160.00*
Never hinged 52.50
Set, never hinged 71.50

Newspaper Stamps Surcharged

On Issue of 1907

1918 Wmk. 113 *Perf. 13*

138 N1 27o on 1o olive 60.00 *200.00*
139 N1 27o on 5o blue 60.00 *200.00*
140 N1 27o on 7o car 60.00 *200.00*
141 N1 27o on 10o dp lil 60.00 *200.00*
142 N1 27o on 68o yel brn 4.00 *22.50*
143 N1 27o on 5k rose & yel grn 3.50 *12.50*
144 N1 27o on 10k bis & bl 4.00 *20.00*
Nos. 138-144 (7) 251.50 *855.00*
Set, never hinged 462.50

On Issue of 1914-15

Wmk. Multiple Crosses (114)

Perf. 14x14½

145 N1 27o on 1o ol gray 2.50 *9.50*
146 N1 27o on 5o blue 4.75 *20.00*
147 N1 27o on 7o rose 2.50 *6.50*
148 N1 27o on 8o green 3.50 *9.50*
149 N1 27o on 10o dp lil 2.50 *7.75*
150 N1 27o on 20o green 3.50 *9.00*
151 N1 27o on 29o org yel 2.50 *6.50*
152 N1 27o on 38o orange 18.00 *65.00*
153 N1 27o on 41o yel brn 6.00 *32.50*
154 N1 27o on 1k bl grn & mar 2.50 *6.50*
Nos. 145-154 (10) 48.25 *172.75*
Set, never hinged 76.50

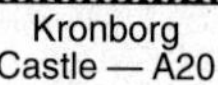

Kronborg Castle — A20

Sonderborg Castle — A21

Roskilde Cathedral — A22

Perf. 14½x14, 14x14½

1920, Oct. 5 Typo.

156 A20 10o red 2.25 .25
157 A21 20o slate 1.75 .25
158 A22 40o dark brown 7.00 3.00
Nos. 156-158 (3) 11.00 3.50
Set, never hinged 23.75

Reunion of Northern Schleswig with Denmark.

See #159-160. For surcharges see #B1-B2.

1921

159 A20 10o green 3.25 .35
160 A22 40o dark blue 25.00 4.25
Set, never hinged 70.00

Stamps of 1918 Surcharged in Blue

1921-22

161 A16 8o on 7o org ('22) 1.40 *2.50*
162 A16 8o on 12o gray grn 1.40 *6.00*
Set, never hinged 9.00

No. 87 Surcharged

1921

163 A10 8o on 3o gray 1.75 *2.25*
Never hinged 3.25

Christian X A23

Christian IV A24

A25

A26

1924, Dec. 1 ***Perf. 14x14½***

164 A23 10o green 4.00 3.50
165 A24 10o green 4.00 3.50
166 A25 10o green 4.00 3.50
167 A26 10o green 4.00 3.50
a. Block of 4, #164-167 20.00 *35.00*
168 A23 15o violet 4.00 3.50
169 A24 15o violet 4.00 3.50
170 A25 15o violet 4.00 3.50
171 A26 15o violet 4.00 3.50
a. Block of 4, #168-171 20.00 *35.00*
172 A23 20o dark brown 4.00 3.50
173 A24 20o dark brown 4.00 3.50
174 A25 20o dark brown 4.00 3.50
175 A26 20o dark brown 4.00 3.50
a. Block of 4, #172-175 20.00 *35.00*
Nos. 164-175 (12) 48.00 42.00
Set, never hinged 87.00
#167a, 171a, 175a, never hinged 120.00

300th anniv. of the Danish postal service.

Stamps of 1921-22 Surcharged:

k

l

1926

176 A16 (k) 20o on 30o org 3.50 *8.00*
177 A16 (l) 20o on 40o dk bl 4.00 *11.00*
Set, never hinged 12.50

A27

A28

1926, Mar. 11 ***Perf. 14x14½***

178 A27 10o dull green .60 .20
179 A28 20o dark red 1.00 .20
180 A28 30o dark blue 3.75 .45
Nos. 178-180 (3) 5.35 .85
Set, never hinged 8.75

75th anniv. of the introduction of postage stamps in Denmark.

Stamps of 1913-26 Surcharged in Blue or Black

No. 181

Nos. 182-184

1926-27 ***Perf. 14x14½***

181 A10 7o on 8o gray (Bl) .60 *2.00*
182 A16 7o on 27o ver & blk 3.00 *7.50*
183 A16 7o on 20o red ('27) .55 .40
184 A16 12o on 15o violet 2.00 *3.25*

Surcharged on Official Stamps of 1914-23

185 O1 (e) 7o on 1o org 3.00 *6.50*
186 O1 (e) 7o on 3o gray 4.50 *16.00*
187 O1 (e) 7o on 4o blue 2.50 *6.50*
188 O1 (e) 7o on 5o grn 35.00 *77.50*
189 O1 (e) 7o on 10o grn 2.50 *6.50*
190 O1 (e) 7o on 15o vio 2.25 *6.50*
191 O1 (e) 7o on 20o ind 10.00 *32.50*
a. Double surcharge *525.00* *675.00*
Nos. 181-191 (11) 65.90 *165.15*
Set, never hinged 105.00

Caravel A30

Christian X A31

1927 **Typo.** ***Perf. 14x14½***

192 A30 15o red 2.50 .20
193 A30 20o gray 6.00 .65
194 A30 25o light blue .60 .20
195 A30 30o ocher .50 .20
196 A30 35o red brown 11.50 .65
197 A30 40o yel green 10.00 .20
Nos. 192-197 (6) 31.10 2.10
Set, never hinged 90.50

See #232-238J. For surcharges & overprints see #244-245, 269-272, Q12-Q14, Q19-Q25.

1930, Sept. 26

210 A31 5o apple grn 1.60 .20
a. Booklet pane, 4 + 2 labels 17.50
211 A31 7o violet 6.00 2.25
212 A31 8o dk gray 15.00 15.00
213 A31 10o yel brn 2.75 .20
a. Booklet pane, 4 + 2 labels 25.00
214 A31 15o red 5.50 .20
215 A31 20o lt gray 16.00 3.00
216 A31 25o lt blue 6.00 .60
217 A31 30o yel buff 6.00 1.50
218 A31 35o red brown 8.00 2.50
219 A31 40o dp green 7.50 .80
Nos. 210-219 (10) 74.35 26.25
Set, never hinged 165.50

60th birthday of King Christian X.

Wavy Lines and Numeral of Value — A32

Type A10 Redrawn

1933-40 **Unwmk.** **Engr.** ***Perf. 13***

220 A32 1o gray blk .20 .20
221 A32 2o scarlet .20 .20
222 A32 4o blue .25 .20
223 A32 5o yel grn .65 .20
a. 5o gray green 16.00 *20.00*
b. Tête bêche gutter pair 5.50 *10.00*
c. Booklet pane of 4 8.00
d. Bklt. pane, 1 #223a, 3 #B6 25.00
e. As "b," without gutter, never hinged 12.00
224 A32 5o rose lake ('38) .20 .20
a. Booklet pane of 4 .30
b. Booklet pane of 10 .65
224C A32 6o orange ('40) .20 .20
225 A32 7o violet .80 .20
226 A32 7o yel grn ('38) .70 .20
226A A32 7o lt brown ('40) .20 .20
227 A32 8o gray .50 .20
227A A32 8o yellow grn ('40) .20 .20
228 A32 10o yellow org 7.00 .20
a. Tête bêche gutter pair 20.00 20.00
b. Booklet pane of 4 57.50
c. As "a," without gutter, never hinged 45.00
229 A32 10o lt brown ('37) 4.50 .20
a. Booklet pane of 4 50.00
b. Booklet pane of 4, 1 #229, 3 #B7 22.50
230 A32 10o violet ('38) .50 .20
a. Booklet pane of 4 2.50
b. Bklt. pane, 2 #230, 2 #B10 4.00
Nos. 220-230 (14) 16.10 2.80
Set, never hinged 28.00

Design A10 was typographed. They had a solid background with groups of small hearts below the heraldic lions in the upper corners and below "DA" and "RK" of "DANMARK." The numerals of value were enclosed in single-lined ovals.

Design A32 is line-engraved and has a background of crossed lines. The hearts have been removed and the numerals of value are now in double-lined ovals. Two types exist of some values.

The 1ö, No. 220, was issued on fluorescent paper in 1969.

No. 230 with wide margins is from booklet pane No. 230b.

Surcharges of 20, 50 & 60öre on #220, 224 & 224C are listed as Faroe Islands #2-3, 5-6.

See Nos. 318, 333, 382, 416, 437-437A, 493-498, 629, 631, 688-695, 793-795, 883-886, 1111, 1114. For overprints and surcharges see Nos. 257, 263, 267-268, 355-356, Q15-Q17, Q31, Q43.

Certain Tête Bêche pairs of 1938-55 issues which reached the market in 1971, and were not regularly issued, are not listed. This group comprises 24 different major-number vertical pairs of types A32, A47, A61 and SP3 (13 with gutters, 11 without), and pairs of some minor numbers and shades. They were removed from booklet pane sheets.

Type of 1927 Issue

Type I

Type I — Two columns of squares between sail and left frame line.

1933-34 **Engr.** ***Perf. 13***

232 A30 20o gray 8.50 .20
233 A30 25o blue 45.00 15.00
234 A30 25o brown ('34) 17.50 .20
235 A30 30o orange yel .60 .80
236 A30 30o blue ('34) .75 .20
237 A30 35o violet .30 .20
238 A30 40o yellow grn 3.00 .20
Nos. 232-238 (7) 75.65 16.80
Set, never hinged 167.50

Type II

Type II — One column of squares between sail and left frame line.

1933-40

238A A30 15o deep red 2.00 .20
k. Booklet pane of 4 22.50
l. Bklt. pane, 1 #238A, 3 #B8 35.00
238B A30 15o yel grn ('40) 5.00 .20
238C A30 20o gray blk ('39) 3.00 .20
238D A30 20o red ('40) .40 .20
238E A30 25o dp brown ('39) .40 .20
238F A30 30o blue ('39) 1.50 .25
238G A30 30o orange ('40) .40 .20
238H A30 35o violet ('40) .50 .30
238I A30 40o yel grn ('39) 8.00 .20
238J A30 40o blue ('40) .80 .20
Nos. 238A-238J (10) 22.00 2.15
Set, never hinged 41.00

Nos. 232-238J, engraved, have crosshatched background. Nos. 192-197, typographed, have solid background.

No. 238A surcharged 20 ore is listed as Faroe Islands No. 4.

See note on surcharges and overprints following No. 197.

King Christian X — A33

1934-41 ***Perf. 13***

239 A33 50o gray .75 .20
240 A33 60o blue grn 1.50 .20
240A A33 75o dk blue ('41) .30 .20
241 A33 1k lt brown 2.50 .20
242 A33 2k dull red 3.75 .65
243 A33 5k violet 5.00 2.25
Nos. 239-243 (6) 13.80 3.70
Set, never hinged 39.50

For overprints see Nos. Q26-Q27.

Nos. 233, 235 Surcharged in Black

1934, June 9

244 A30 4o on 25o blue .40 .40
245 A30 10o on 30o org yel 1.50 *1.75*
Set, never hinged 3.25

"The Ugly Duckling" A34

Andersen A35

"The Little Mermaid" — A36

1935, Oct. 4 ***Perf. 13***

246 A34 5o lt green 1.75 .20
a. Tête bêche gutter pair 8.50 *9.00*
b. Booklet pane of 4 17.50
c. As "a," without gutter, never hinged 19.00
247 A35 7o dull vio 1.50 *2.00*
248 A36 10o orange 3.00 .20
a. Tête bêche gutter pair 11.50 *15.00*
b. Booklet pane of 4 30.00
c. As "a," without gutter, never hinged 29.00
249 A35 15o red 7.50 .20
a. Tête bêche gutter pair 30.00 *24.00*
b. Booklet pane of 4 75.00
c. As "a," without gutter, never hinged 62.50
250 A35 20o gray 8.50 1.10
251 A35 30o dl bl 1.75 .30
Nos. 246-251 (6) 24.00 *4.00*
Set, never hinged 66.00

Centenary of the publication of the earliest installment of Hans Christian Andersen's "Fairy Tales."

Nikolai Church A37

Hans Tausen A38

Ribe Cathedral — A39

1936 ***Perf. 13***

252 A37 5o green .90 .20
a. Booklet pane of 4 17.50
253 A37 7o violet 1.00 *1.75*
254 A38 10o lt brown 1.25 .20
a. Booklet pane of 4 18.00
255 A38 15o dull rose 2.00 .20
256 A39 30o blue 8.00 1.00
Nos. 252-256 (5) 13.15 3.35
Set, never hinged 33.75

Church Reformation in Denmark, 400th anniv.

No. 229 Overprinted in Blue

1937, Sept. 17

257 A32 10o lt brown .85 *1.50*
Never hinged 1.40

Jubilee Exhib. held by the Copenhagen Phil. Club on their 50th anniv. The stamps were on sale at the Exhib. only, each holder of a ticket of admission (1k) being entitled to purchase 20 stamps at face value; of a season ticket (5k), 100 stamps.

Yacht and Summer Palace, Marselisborg
A40

Christian X in Streets of Copenhagen
A41

Equestrian Statue of Frederik V and Amalienborg Palace — A42

1937, May 15 ***Perf. 13***
258 A40 5o green .65 .20
a. Booklet pane of 4 10.50
259 A41 10o brown .65 .20
a. Booklet pane of 4 10.50
260 A42 15o scarlet .65 .20
a. Booklet pane of 4 12.00
261 A41 30o blue 11.50 1.75
Nos. 258-261 (4) 13.45 2.35
Set, never hinged 27.75

25th anniv. of the accession to the throne of King Christian X.

Emancipation Column, Copenhagen — A43

1938, June 20 ***Perf. 13***
262 A43 15o scarlet .40 .20
Never hinged .80

Abolition of serfdom in Denmark, 150th anniv.

No. 223 Overprinted in Red on Alternate Stamps

1938, Sept. 2
263 A32 5o yellow grn, pair 2.75 *5.25*
Never hinged 3.75

10th Danish Philatelic Exhibition.

Bertel Thorvaldsen
A44

Statue of Jason
A45

1938, Nov. 17 **Engr.** ***Perf. 13***
264 A44 5o rose lake .20 .20
265 A45 10o purple .45 .20
266 A44 30o dark blue 1.10 .30
Nos. 264-266 (3) 1.75 .70
Set, never hinged 3.50

The return to Denmark in 1838 of Bertel Thorvaldsen, Danish sculptor.

Stamps of 1933-39 Surcharged with New Values in Black:

a

b

c

1940
267 A32 (a) 6o on 7o yel grn .20 .20
268 A32 (a) 6o on 8o gray .20 .20
269 A30 (b) 15o on 40o #238 .60 *3.00*
270 A30 (b) 15o on 40o #238I .60 .65
271 A30 (c) 20o on 15o dp red .80 .20
272 A30 (b) 40o on 30o #238F .60 .20
Nos. 267-272 (6) 3.00 *4.45*
Set, never hinged 4.45

Bering's Ship — A46

1941, Nov. 27 **Engr.** ***Perf. 13***
277 A46 10o dk violet .30 .20
278 A46 20o red brown .60 .25
279 A46 40o dk blue .35 .30
Nos. 277-279 (3) 1.25 .75
Set, never hinged 1.85

Death of Vitus Bering, explorer, 200th anniv.

King Christian X — A47

1942-46 **Unwmk.** ***Perf. 13***
280 A47 10o violet .20 .20
281 A47 15o yel grn .30 .20
282 A47 20o red .30 .20
283 A47 25o brown ('43) .55 .30
284 A47 30o orange ('43) .40 .20
285 A47 35o brt red vio ('44) .35 .20
286 A47 40o blue ('43) .40 .20
286A A47 45o ol brn ('46) .30 .20
286B A47 50o gray ('45) .40 .20
287 A47 60o bluish grn ('44) .40 .20
287A A47 75o dk blue ('46) .35 .20
Nos. 280-287A (11) 3.95 2.30
Set, never hinged 7.00

For overprints see Nos. Q28-Q30.

Round Tower — A48

Condor Plane — A49

1942, Nov. 27
288 A48 10o violet .20 .20
Never hinged .20

300th anniv. of the Round Tower, Copenhagen.
For surcharge see No. B14.

1943, Oct. 29
289 A49 20o red .20 .20
Never hinged .25

25th anniv. of the Danish Aviation Company (Det Danske Luftfartsselskab).

Ejby Church — A50

15ö, Oesterlars Church. 20ö, Hvidbjerg Church.

1944 **Engr.** ***Perf. 13***
290 A50 10o violet .20 .20
291 A50 15o yellow grn .25 .35
292 A50 20o red .20 .20
Nos. 290-292 (3) .65 .75
Set, never hinged .65

Ole Roemer
A53

Christian X
A54

1944, Sept. 25
293 A53 20o henna brown .20 .20
Never hinged .25

Birth of Ole Roemer, astronomer, 300th anniv.

1945, Sept. 26
294 A54 10o lilac .20 .20
295 A54 20o red .20 .20
296 A54 40o deep blue .40 .25
Nos. 294-296 (3) .80 .65
Set, never hinged 1.00

75th birthday of King Christian X.

Catalogue values for unused stamps in this section, from this point to the end of the section, are for Never Hinged items.

Small State Seal — A55

Tycho Brahe — A56

1946-47 **Unwmk.** ***Perf. 13***
297 A55 1k brown .85 .20
298 A55 2k red ('47) .70 .20
299 A55 5k dull blue 1.25 .20
Nos. 297-299 (3) 2.80 .60

Nos. 297-299 issued on ordinary and fluorescent paper. Values for ordinary paper are much higher.

See Nos. 395-400, 441A-444D, 499-506, 643-650, 716-720A, 804-815, 909. For overprints see Nos. Q35, Q40, Q46-Q48.

1946, Dec. 14 **Engr.**
300 A56 20o dark red .25 .20

Birth of Tycho Brahe, astronomer, 400th anniv.

First Danish Locomotive
A57

Modern Steam Locomotive
A58

Diesel Locomotive
A59

1947, June 27
301 A57 15o steel blue .30 .25
302 A58 20o red .50 .20
303 A59 40o deep blue 2.00 .55
Nos. 301-303 (3) 2.80 1.00

Inauguration of the Danish State Railways, cent.

Jacobsen
A60

Frederik IX
A61

1947, Nov. 10 ***Perf. 13***
304 A60 20o dark red .30 .20

60th anniv. of the death of Jacob Christian Jacobsen, founder of the Glyptothek Art Museum, Copenhagen.

1948-50 **Unwmk.** ***Perf. 13***

Three types among 15ö, 20ö, 30ö:
I — Background of horizontal lines. No outline at left for cheek and ear. King's uniform textured in strong lines.
II — Background of vertical and horizontal lines. Contour of cheek and ear at left. Uniform same.
III — Background and facial contour lines as in II. Uniform lines double and thinner.

306 A61 15(o) green (II) 2.00 .20
a. Type III ('49) 1.00 .20
307 A61 20(o) dk red (I) .75 .20
a. Type II ('49) .85 .20
308 A61 25(o) lt brown 1.10 .20
309 A61 30(o) org (II) 11.00 .20
a. Type III ('50) 12.50 .20
310 A61 40(o) dl blue ('49) 4.25 .50
311 A61 45(o) olive ('50) 1.60 .20
312 A61 50(o) gray ('49) 1.60 .20
313 A61 60(o) grnsh bl ('50) 2.25 .20
314 A61 75(o) lil rose ('50) 1.25 .20
Nos. 306-314 (9) 25.80 2.10

See Nos. 319-326, 334-341, 354. For surcharges see Nos. 357-358, 370, B20, B24-B25, Q32-Q34, Q36-Q39.

Legislative Assembly, 1849 — A62

Symbol of UPU — A63

1949, June 5
315 A62 20o red brown .30 .20

Adoption of the Danish constitution, cent.

1949, Oct. 9
316 A63 40o dull blue .65 .50

75th anniv. of the UPU.

Kalundborg Radio Station and Masts — A64

1950, Apr. 1 **Engr.** ***Perf. 13***
317 A64 20o brown red .40 .20

Radio broadcasting in Denmark, 25th anniv.

Types of 1933-50

1950-51 **Unwmk.** ***Perf. 13***
318 A32 10o green .20 .20
319 A61 15(o) lilac .75 .20
b. 15(o) gray lilac 3.25 .25
320 A61 20(o) lt brown .45 .20
321 A61 25(o) dark red 3.75 .20
322 A61 35(o) gray grn ('51) .60 .20
323 A61 40(o) gray .85 .20
324 A61 50(o) dark blue 2.75 .20
325 A61 55(o) brown ('51) 21.00 1.60
326 A61 70(o) deep green 2.25 .20
Nos. 318-326 (9) 32.60 3.20

Warship of 1701 — A65

Oersted — A66

1951, Feb. 26 Engr. *Perf. 13*

327 A65 25o dark red .50 .25
328 A65 50o deep blue 2.75 .75

250th anniv. of the foundation of the Naval Officers' College.

1951, Mar. 9 Unwmk.

329 A66 50o blue 1.40 .45

Cent. of the death of Hans Christian Oersted, physicist.

Post Chaise ("Ball Post") — A67

Marine Rescue — A68

1951, Apr. 1 *Perf. 13*

330 A67 15o purple .60 .25
331 A67 25o henna brown .60 .25

Cent. of Denmark's 1st postage stamp.

1952, Mar. 26

332 A68 25o red brown .45 .30

Cent. of the foundation of the Danish Lifesaving Service.

Types of 1933-50

1952-53 *Perf. 13*

333 A32 12o lt yel grn .30 .20
334 A61 25(o) lt blue 1.00 .20
335 A61 30(o) brown red .55 .20
336 A61 50(o) aqua ('53) .55 .20
337 A61 60(o) dp blue ('53) .75 .20
338 A61 65(o) gray ('53) .55 .20
339 A61 80(o) orange ('53) .85 .20
340 A61 90(o) olive ('53) 3.00 .20
341 A61 95(o) red org ('53) .75 .25
Nos. 333-341 (9) 8.30 1.85

Jelling Runic Stone — A69

Designs: 15o, Vikings' camp, Trelleborg. 20o, Church of Kalundborg. 30o, Nyborg castle. 60o, Goose tower, Vordinborg.

1953-56 *Perf. 13*

342 A69 10o dp green .20 .20
343 A69 15o lt rose vio .20 .20
344 A69 20o brown .20 .20
345 A69 30o red ('54) .25 .20
346 A69 60o dp blue ('54) .40 .20

Designs: 10o, Manor house, Spottrup. 15o, Hammershus castle ruins. 20o, Copenhagen stock exchange. 30o, Statue of Frederik V, Amalienborg. 60o, Soldier statue at Fredericia.

347 A69 10o green ('54) .20 .20
348 A69 15o lilac ('55) .20 .20
349 A69 20o brown ('55) .20 .20
350 A69 30o red ('55) .25 .20
351 A69 60o deep blue ('56) .50 .20
Nos. 342-351 (10) 2.60 2.00

1000th anniv. of the Kingdom of Denmark. Each stamp represents a different century.

Telegraph Equipment of 1854 A70

Frederik V A71

1954, Feb. 2 *Perf. 13*

352 A70 30o red brown .40 .25

Cent. of the telegraph in Denmark.

1954, Mar. 31

353 A71 30o dark red .55 .25

200th anniv. of the founding of the Royal Academy of Fine Arts.

Type of 1948-50

1955, Apr. 27

354 A61 25o lilac .20 .20

Nos. 224C and 226A Surcharged with New Value in Black. Nos. 307 and 321 Surcharged with New Value and 4 Bars

1955-56

355 A32 5o on 6o org .20 .20
356 A32 5o on 7o lt brn .20 .20
357 A61 30(o) on 20(o) dk red (I) .25 .20
a. Type III .35 .20
b. Double surcharge *1,050.* *1,050.*
c. Inverted surcharge *650.00*
358 A61 30(o) on 25(o) dk red ('56) .50 .20
a. Double surcharge *1,050.*
Nos. 355-358 (4) 1.15 .80

A72

A73

1955, Nov. 11 Unwmk.

359 A72 30o dark red .30 .20

100th anniv. of the death of Sören Kierkegaard, philosopher and theologian.

1956, Sept. 12 Engr.

360 A73 30o Ellehammer's plane .50 .20

50th anniv. of the 1st flight made by Jacob Christian Hansen Ellehammer in a heavier-than-air craft.

Northern Countries Issue

Whooper Swans — A74

1956, Oct. 30 *Perf. 13*

361 A74 30o rose red 1.50 .20
362 A74 60o ultramarine 1.25 .55

Issued to emphasize the close bonds among the northern countries: Denmark, Finland, Iceland, Norway and Sweden.

Prince's Palace A75

Harvester A76

Design: 60ö, Sun God's Chariot.

1957, May 15 Unwmk.

363 A75 30o dull red .75 .20
364 A75 60o dark blue .75 .35

150th anniv. of the National Museum.

1958, Sept. 4 Engr. *Perf. 13*

365 A76 30o fawn .25 .20

Centenary of the Royal Veterinary and Agricultural College.

Frederik IX A77

Ballet Dancer A78

1959, Mar. 11

366 A77 30o rose red .40 .20
367 A77 35o rose lilac .40 .35
368 A77 60o ultra .40 .20
Nos. 366-368 (3) 1.20 .75

King Frederik's 60th birthday.

1959, May 16

369 A78 35o rose lilac .25 .20

Danish Ballet and Music Festival, May 17-31. See Nos. 401, 422.

No. 319 Surcharged

1960, Apr. 7

370 A61 30o on 15o purple .25 .20

World Refugee Year, 7/1/59-6/30/60.

Seeder and Farm A79

30ö, Harvester combine. 60ö, Plow.

1960, Apr. 28 Engr. *Perf. 13*

371 A79 12o green .20 .20
372 A79 30o dull red .30 .20
373 A79 60o dk blue .50 .20
Nos. 371-373 (3) 1.00 .60

King Frederik IX and Queen Ingrid — A80

1960, May 24 Unwmk.

374 A80 30o dull red .45 .20
375 A80 60o blue .45 .20

25th anniversary of the marriage of King Frederik IX and Queen Ingrid.

Bascule Light — A81

Finsen — A82

1960, June 8 Engr.

376 A81 30o dull red .25 .20

400th anniv. of the Lighthouse Service.

1960, Aug. 1 *Perf. 13*

377 A82 30o dark red .25 .20

Centenary of the birth of Dr. Niels R. Finsen, physician and scientist.

Nursing Mother — A83

DC-8 Airliner — A84

1960, Aug. 16 Unwmk.

378 A83 60o ultra .55 .20

10th meeting of the regional committee for Europe of WHO, Copenhagen, Aug. 16-20.

Europa Issue, 1960

Common Design Type

1960, Sept. 19 *Perf. 13*

Size: 28x21mm

379 CD3 60o ultra .55 .45

1961, Feb. 24

380 A84 60o ultra .65 .50

10th anniv. of the Scandinavian Airlines System, SAS.

Landscape A85

Frederik IX A86

1961, Apr. 21 *Perf. 13*

381 A85 30o copper brown .25 .20

Denmark's Soc. of Nature Lovers, 50th anniv.

Fluorescent Paper

as well as ordinary paper, was used in printing many definitive and commemorative stamps, starting in 1962. These include No. 220, 224; the 15, 20, 25, 30, 35 (Nos. 386 and 387), 50 and 60ö, 1.20k, 1.50k and 25k definitives of following set, and Nos. 297-299, 318, 333, 380, 401-427, 429-435, 438-439, 493, 543, 548, B30.

Only fluorescent paper was used for Nos. 436-437, 437A and 440 onward; in semipostals from B31 onward.

1961-63 Engr. *Perf. 13*

382 A32 15o green ('63) .20 .20
383 A86 20o brown .50 .20
384 A86 25o brown ('63) .25 .20
385 A86 30o rose red .65 .20
386 A86 35o olive grn .65 .50
387 A86 35o rose red ('63) .25 .20
388 A86 40o gray 1.00 .20
389 A86 50o aqua .65 .20
390 A86 60o ultra .85 .20
391 A86 70o green 1.60 .20
392 A86 80o red orange 1.60 .20
393 A86 90o olive bister 4.00 .20
394 A86 95o claret ('63) 1.00 .70
Nos. 382-394 (13) 13.20 3.40

See Nos. 417-419, 438-441. For overprints see Nos. Q41-Q42, Q44-Q45.

State Seal Type of 1946-47

1962-65

395 A55 1.10k lilac ('65) 3.75 1.25
396 A55 1.20k gray 3.25 .20
397 A55 1.25k orange 3.25 .20
398 A55 1.30k green ('65) 3.75 1.25
399 A55 1.50k red lilac 1.10 .20
400 A55 25k yellow grn 7.00 .25
Nos. 395-400 (6) 22.10 3.35

Dancer Type of 1959 Inscribed "15-31 MAJ"

1962, Apr. 26

401 A78 60o ultra .30 .20

Issued to publicize the Danish Ballet and Music Festival, May 15-31.

Old Mill — A87

M.S. Selandia — A88

1962, May 10 Unwmk. *Perf. 13*

402 A87 10o red brown .20 .20

Cent. of the abolition of mill monopolies.

1962, June 14 Engr.

403 A88 60o dark blue 1.50 1.25

M.S. Selandia, the 1st Diesel ship, 50th anniv.

Violin Scroll, Leaves, Lights and Balloon A89

1962, Aug. 31

404 A89 35o rose violet .30 .20

150th anniv. of the birth of Georg Carstensen, founder of Tivoli amusement park, Copenhagen.

Cliffs on Moen Island — A90

Germinating Wheat — A91

1962, Nov. 22

405 A90 20o pale brown .20 .20

Issued to publicize preservation of natural treasures and landmarks.

1963, Mar. 21 Engr.

406 A91 35o fawn .25 .20

FAO "Freedom from Hunger" campaign.

Railroad Wheel, Tire Tracks, Waves and Swallow — A92

Sailing Vessel, Coach, Postillions and Globe — A93

1963, May 14 Unwmk. *Perf. 13*

407 A92 15o green .20 .20

Inauguration of the "Bird Flight Line" railroad link between Denmark and Germany.

1963, May 27

408 A93 60o dark blue .45 .20

Cent. of the 1st Intl. Postal Conf., Paris, 1863.

Niels Bohr and Atom Diagram — A94

Early Public School Drawn on Slate — A95

1963, Nov. 21 Engr.

409 A94 35o red brown .30 .20
410 A94 60o dark blue .55 .20

50th anniv. of Prof. Niels Bohr's (1885-1962) atom theory.

1964, June 19 Unwmk. *Perf. 13*

411 A95 35o red brown .20 .20

150th anniversary of the royal decrees for the public school system.

Fish and Chart — A96

Danish Watermarks and Perforations A97

1964, Sept. 7 Engr.

412 A96 60o violet blue .35 .20

Conference of the International Council for the Exploration of the Sea, Copenhagen.

1964, Oct. 10 *Perf. 13*

413 A97 35o pink .25 .20

25th anniv. of Stamp Day and to publicize the Odense Stamp Exhibition, Oct. 10-11.

Landscape A98

Calculator, Ledger and Inkwell — A99

1964, Nov. 12 Engr.

414 A98 25o brown .20 .20

Issued to publicize preservation of natural treasures and landmarks.

1965, Mar. 8 Unwmk.

415 A99 15o light olive green .20 .20

First Business School in Denmark, cent.

Types of 1933 and 1961

1965, May 15 Engr. *Perf. 13*

416 A32 25o apple green .25 .20
417 A86 40o brown .25 .20
418 A86 50o rose red .30 .20
419 A86 80o ultra .85 .20
Nos. 416-419 (4) 1.65 .80

For overprints see Nos. Q41-Q42.

ITU Emblem, Telegraph Key, Teletype Paper A100

Carl Nielsen (1865-1931), Composer A101

1965, May 17

420 A100 80o dark blue .35 .20

Cent. of the ITU.

1965, June 9 Engr.

421 A101 50o brown red .25 .20

Dancer Type of 1959 Inscribed "15-31 MAJ"

1965, Sept. 23

422 A78 50o rose red .25 .20

Issued to publicize the Danish Ballet and Music Festival, May 15-31.

Bogo Windmill A102

Mylius Dalgas Surveying Wasteland A103

1965, Nov. 10 Engr. *Perf. 13*

423 A102 40o brown .25 .20

Issued to publicize the preservation of natural treasures and landmarks.

1966, Feb. 24

424 A103 25o olive green .20 .20

Cent. of the Danish Heath Soc. (reclamation of wastelands), founded by Enrico Mylius Dalgas.

Christen Kold (1816-70), Educator — A104

1966, Mar. 29 *Perf. 13*

425 A104 50o dull red .25 .20

Poorhouse, Copenhagen A105

Holte Allée, Bregentved A106

Dolmen (Grave) in Jutland — A107

1966 Unwmk.

426 A105 50o dull red .25 .20
427 A106 80o dk blue .55 .20
428 A107 1.50k dk slate grn .80 .20
Nos. 426-428 (3) 1.60 .60

Publicizing preservation of national treasures and ancient monuments. Issued: 50o, May 12; 80o, June 16; 1.50k, Nov. 24.

George Jensen by Ejnar Nielsen A108

Music Bar and Instruments A109

1966, Aug. 31 Engr. *Perf. 13*

429 A108 80o dark blue .60 .20

George Jensen, silversmith, birth cent.

1967, Jan. 9

430 A109 50o dark red .25 .20

Royal Danish Academy of Music, cent.

Cogwheels, Broken Customs Duty Ribbon — A110

1967, Mar. 2

431 A110 80o dark blue .70 .20

European Free Trade Association. Industrial tariffs were abolished Dec. 31, 1966, among EFTA members: Austria, Denmark, Finland, Great Britain, Norway, Portugal, Sweden and Switzerland.

Windmill and Medieval Fortress — A111

Designs: 40ö, Ship's rigging and baroque house front. 50ö, Old Town Hall. 80ö, New building construction.

1967 Engr. *Perf. 13*

432 A111 25o green .30 .20
433 A111 40o sepia .25 .20
434 A111 50o red brown .25 .20
435 A111 80o dk blue .75 .25
Nos. 432-435 (4) 1.55 .85

The 800th anniversary of Copenhagen. Issued: #432-433, 4/6; #434-435, 5/11.

Princess Margrethe and Prince Henri — A112

1967, June 10

436 A112 50o red .30 .20

Marriage of Crown Princess Margrethe and Prince Henri de Monpezat.

Types of 1933-1961

1967-71 Engr. *Perf. 13*

437 A32 30o dk green .20 .20
437A A32 40o orange ('71) .20 .20
438 A86 50o brown .35 .20
439 A86 60o rose red .35 .20
440 A86 80o green .35 .20
441 A86 90o ultra .35 .20
441A A55 1.20k Prus grn ('71) 1.00 .25
442 A55 2.20k orange 1.50 .20
443 A55 2.80k gray 1.50 .20
444 A55 2.90k rose vio 2.50 .20
444A A55 3k dk sl grn ('69) .55 .20
444B A55 3.10k plum ('70) 4.50 .20

444C A55 4k gray ('69) .80 .20
444D A55 4.10k olive ('70) 4.50 .20
Nos. 437-444D (14) 18.65 2.85

Issued: #437-441, 6/30/67; #442-443, 7/8/67; #444, 4/29/68; #444A, 444C, 8/28/69; #444B, 444D, 8/27/70; #437A, 441A, 6/24/71.
For overprints see Nos. Q44-Q45.

Sonne — A113

Cross-anchor and Porpoise — A114

1967, Sept. 21
445 A113 60o red .25 .20

150th anniv. of the birth of Hans Christian Sonne, pioneer of the cooperative movement in Denmark.

1967, Nov. 9 Engr. *Perf. 13*
446 A114 90o dk blue .35 .25

Centenary of the Danish Seamen's Church in Foreign Ports.

Esbjerg Harbor — A115

Koldinghus A116

1968, Apr. 24
447 A115 30o dk yellow grn .20 .20

Centenary of Esbjerg Harbor.

1968, June 13
448 A116 60o copper red .25 .20

700th anniversary of Koldinghus Castle.

Shipbuilding Industry A117

Sower A118

Designs: 50o, Chemical industry. 60o, Electric power. 90o, Engineering.

1968, Oct. 24 Engr. *Perf. 13*
449 A117 30o green .25 .20
450 A117 50o brown .25 .20
451 A117 60o red brown .25 .20
452 A117 90o dark blue .40 .25
Nos. 449-452 (4) 1.15 .85

Issued to publicize Danish industries.

1969, Jan. 29
453 A118 30o gray green .20 .20

Royal Agricultural Soc. of Denmark, 200th anniv.

Five Ancient Ships A119

Frederik IX A120

Nordic Cooperation Issue

1969, Feb. 28 Engr. *Perf. 13*
454 A119 60o brown red .80 .20
455 A119 90o blue 1.25 .70

50th anniv. of the Nordic Soc. and cent. of postal cooperation among the northern countries: Denmark, Finland, Iceland, Norway and Sweden. The design is taken from a coin found at the site of Birka, an ancient Swedish town.

1969, Mar. 11
456 A120 50o sepia .20 .20
457 A120 60o dull red .20 .20

70th birthday of King Frederik IX.

Common Design Types pictured following the introduction.

Europa Issue, 1969
Common Design Type

1969, Apr. 28
Size: 28x20mm
458 CD12 90o chalky blue .70 .55

Kronborg Castle — A121

Danish Flag — A122

1969, May 22 Engr. *Perf. 13*
459 A121 50o brown .25 .20

Association of Danes living abroad, 50th anniv.

1969, June 12
460 A122 60o bluish blk, red & gray .30 .20

750th anniversary of the fall of the Dannebrog (Danish flag) from heaven.

Nexo A123

Stensen A124

1969, Aug. 28
461 A123 80o deep green .30 .20

Centenary of the birth of Martin Andersen Nexo (1869-1954), novelist.

1969, Sept. 25
462 A124 1k deep brown .35 .20

300th anniv. of the publication of Niels Stensen's geological work "On Solid Bodies."

Abstract Design — A125

Symbolic Design — A126

1969, Nov. 10 Engr. *Perf. 13*
463 A125 60o rose, red & ultra .25 .20

1969, Nov. 20
464 A126 30o olive green .25 .20

Valdemar Poulsen (1869-1942), electrical engineer and inventor.

Post Office Bank — A127

School Safety Patrol — A128

1970, Jan. 15 Engr. *Perf. 13*
465 A127 60o dk red & org .25 .20

50th anniv. of post office banking service.

1970, Feb. 19
466 A128 50o brown .25 .20

Issued to publicize road safety.

Candle in Window A129

Deer A130

1970, May 4 Engr. *Perf. 13*
467 A129 50o slate, dull bl & yel .25 .20

25th anniv. of liberation from the Germans.

1970, May 28
468 A130 60o yel grn, red & brn .25 .20

Tercentenary of Jaegersborg Deer Park.

Elephant Figurehead, 1741 A131

"The Homecoming" by Povl Christensen A132

1970, June 15 *Perf. 11½*
469 A131 30o multicolored .25 .20

Royal Naval Museum, tercentenary.

1970, June 15 *Perf. 13*
470 A132 60o org, dl vio & ol grn .25 .20

Union of North Schleswig and Denmark, 50th anniv.

Electromagnet A133

1970, Aug. 13 Engr.
471 A133 80o gray green .30 .20

150th anniversary of Hans Christian Oersted's discovery of electromagnetism.

Bronze Age Ship A134

Ships: 50o, Viking shipbuilding, from Bayeux tapestry. 60o, Thuroe schooner with topgallant. 90o, Tanker.

1970, Sept. 24
472 A134 30o ocher & brown .25 .20
473 A134 50o brn red & rose brn .25 .20
474 A134 60o gray ol & red brn .45 .20
475 A134 90o blue grn & ultra .75 .60
Nos. 472-475 (4) 1.70 1.20

UN Emblem A135

1970, Oct. 22 Engr. *Perf. 13*
476 A135 90o blue, grn & red .65 .50

25th anniversary of the United Nations.

Bertel Thorvaldsen A136

Mathide Fibiger A137

1970, Nov. 19
477 A136 2k slate blue .60 .20

Bicentenary of the birth of Bertel Thorvaldsen (1768-1844), sculptor.

1971, Feb. 25
478 A137 80o olive green .30 .20

Danish Women's Association centenary.

Refugees A138

Hans Egede A139

1971, Mar. 26 Engr. *Perf. 13*
479 A138 50o brown .25 .20
480 A138 60o brown red .35 .20

Joint northern campaign for the benefit of refugees.

1971, May 27
481 A139 1k brown .40 .20

250th anniversary of arrival of Hans Egede in Greenland and beginning of its colonization.

A140

A141

1971, Oct. 14
482 A140 30o Swimming .20 .20
483 A140 50o Gymnastics .30 .20
484 A140 60o Soccer .40 .20
485 A140 90o Sailing .60 .40
Nos. 482-485 (4) 1.50 1.00

1971, Nov. 11 Engr. *Perf. 13*
486 A141 90o dark blue .35 .20

Centenary of first lectures given by Georg Brandes (1842-1927), writer and literary critic.

A142

A143

1972, Jan. 27
487 A142 80o slate green .35 .20

Centenary of Danish sugar production.

1972, Mar. 11 Engr. *Perf. 13*
488 A143 60o red brown .30 .20

Frederik IX (1899-1972).

Abstract Design A144

1972, Mar. 11
489 A144 1.20k brt rose lil, bl gray & brn .60 .50

Danish Meteorological Institute, cent.

Nikolai F. S. Grundtvig A145

Locomotive, 1847, Ferry, Travelers A146

1972, May 4 Engr. *Perf. 13*
490 A145 1k sepia .40 .20

Nikolai Frederik Severin Grundtvig (1783-1872), theologian and poet.

1972, June 26
491 A146 70o rose red .30 .20

125th anniversary of Danish State Railways.

Rebild Hills A147

"Tinker Turned Politician" A148

1972, June 26
492 A147 1k bl, sl grn & mar .35 .20

Types of 1933-46

1972-78 Engr. *Perf. 13*
493 A32 20o slate bl ('74) .20 .20
494 A32 50o sepia ('74) .20 .20
a. Bklt. pane of 12 (4 #318, 4 #493, 4 #494) ('85) 2.00
495 A32 60o apple grn ('76) 1.00 .30
496 A32 60o gray ('78) .40 .35
497 A32 70o red .50 .20
498 A32 70o apple grn ('77) .20 .20
499 A55 2.50k orange 1.00 .20
500 A55 2.80k olive ('75) .70 .45
501 A55 3.50k lilac 1.10 .20
502 A55 4.5k olive 2.75 .20
503 A55 6k vio blk ('76) 1.00 .20
504 A55 7k red lilac ('78) 1.25 .20
505 A55 9k brown ol ('77) 1.75 .20
506 A55 10k lemon ('76) 1.60 .20
Nos. 493-506 (14) 13.65 3.30

1972, Sept. 14
507 A148 70o dark red .30 .20

250th anniv. of the comedies of Ludvig Holberg (1684-1754) on the Danish stage.

WHO Building, Copenhagen — A149

1972, Sept. 14
508 A149 2k bl, blk & lt red brn .60 .30

Opening of WHO Building, Copenhagen.

Bridge Across Little Belt A150

Aeroskobing House c. 1740 A151

Highway engineering (Diagrams): 60o, Hanstholm Harbor. 70o, Lim Fjord Tunnel. 90o, Knudshoved Harbor.

1972, Oct. 19 Engr. *Perf. 13*
509 A150 40o dk green .20 .20
510 A150 60o dk brown .30 .20
511 A150 70o dk red .30 .20
512 A150 90o dk blue grn .40 .20
Nos. 509-512 (4) 1.20 .80

1972, Nov. 23

Danish Architecture: 60o, East Bornholm farmhouse, 17th century, horiz. 70o, House, Christianshavn, c. 1710. 1.20k, Hvide Sande Farmhouse, c. 1810, horiz.

Size: 20x28mm, 27x20mm
513 A151 40o red, brn & blk .35 .25
514 A151 60o blk, vio bl & grn .35 .25

Size: 18x37mm, 36x20mm
515 A151 70o red, dk red & blk .45 .20
516 A151 1.20k dk brn, red & grn .60 .55
Nos. 513-516 (4) 1.75 1.25

Jensen A152

Guard Rails, Cogwheels A153

1973, Feb. 22 Engr. *Perf. 13*
517 A152 90o green .35 .20

Centenary of the birth of Johannes Vilhelm Jensen (1873-1950), lyric poet and novelist.

1973, Mar. 22
518 A153 50o sepia .25 .20

Centenary of first Danish Factory Act for labor protection.

Abildgaard A154

Rhododendron A155

1973, Mar. 22
519 A154 1k dull blue .35 .35

Bicentenary of Royal Veterinary College, Christianshaven, founded by Prof. P. C. Abildgaard.

1973, Apr. 26

Design: 70o, Dronningen of Denmark rose.

520 A155 60o brn, grn & vio .40 .20
521 A155 70o dk red, rose & grn .40 .20

Centenary of the founding of the Horticultural Society of Denmark.

Nordic Cooperation Issue 1973

Nordic House, Reykjavik A156

1973, June 26 Engr. *Perf. 13*
522 A156 70o multicolored .40 .20
523 A156 1k multicolored 1.40 .30

A century of postal cooperation among Denmark, Finland, Iceland, Norway and Sweden, and in connection with the Nordic Postal Conference, Reykjavik.

Sextant, Stella Nova, Cassiopeia A157

St. Mark, from 11th Cent. Book of Dalby A158

1973, Oct. 18 Engr. *Perf. 13*
524 A157 2k dark blue .60 .20

400th anniversary of the publication of "De Nova Stella," by Tycho Brahe.

1973, Oct. 18 Photo. *Perf. 14x14½*
525 A158 120o buff & multi .60 .55

300th anniversary of Royal Library.

Devil and Gossips, Fanefjord Church, 1480 — A159

Frescoes: No. 527, Queen Esther and King Ahasuerus, Tirsted Church, c.1400. No. 528, Miraculous Harvest, Jetsmark Church, c.1474. No. 529, Jesus carrying cross, and wearing crown of thorns, Biersted Church, c.1400. No. 530, Creation of Eve, Fanefjord Church, c.1480.

1973, Nov. 28 Engr. *Perf. 13*
Cream Paper
526 A159 70o dk red, yel & grn 1.25 .30
527 A159 70o dk red, yel & grn 1.25 .30
528 A159 70o dk red, yel & grn 1.25 .30
529 A159 70o dk red, yel & grn 1.25 .30
530 A159 70o dk red, yel & grn 1.25 .30
a. Bklt. pane, 2 each #526-530 35.00
b. Strip of 5, #526-530 6.25

Blood Donors A160

Queen Margrethe A161

1974, Jan. 24
531 A160 90o purple & red .35 .20

"Blood Saves Lives."

1974-81 Engr. *Perf. 13*
532 A161 60o brown .35 .30
533 A161 60o orange .30 .20
534 A161 70o red .30 .20
535 A161 70o dk brown .30 .20
536 A161 80o green .35 .20
537 A161 80o dp brn ('76) .30 .20
538 A161 90o red lilac .35 .20
539 A161 90o dull red .30 .20
540 A161 90o slate grn ('76) .35 .20
541 A161 100o dp ultra .35 .20
542 A161 100o gray ('75) .35 .20
543 A161 100o red ('76) .35 .20
544 A161 100o brown ('77) .35 .20
a. Bklt. pane of 5 (#544, #494, 2 #493, #318) 1.50
545 A161 110o orange ('78) .40 .20
546 A161 120o slate .50 .35
547 A161 120o red ('77) .35 .20
548 A161 130o ultra ('75) 1.10 .85
549 A161 150o vio bl ('78) .50 .55
550 A161 180o slate grn ('77) .35 .25
551 A161 200o blue ('81) .70 .75
Nos. 532-551 (20) 8.20 5.85

See #630, 632-642. For overprint see #Q49.

Pantomime Theater — A162

Hverringe A163

1974, May 16
552 A162 100o indigo .45 .20

Cent. of the Pantomime Theater, Tivoli.

1974, June 20 Engr. *Perf. 13*

Views: 60o, Norre Lyndelse, Carl Nielsen's childhood home. 70o, Odense, Hans Chr. Andersen's childhood home. 90o, Hesselagergaard, vert. 120o, Hindsholm.

553 A163 50o brown & multi .40 .20
554 A163 60o sl grn & multi .35 .25
555 A163 70o red brn & multi .35 .25
556 A163 90o dk green & mar .50 .20
557 A163 120o red org & dk grn .65 .40
Nos. 553-557 (5) 2.25 1.30

Emblem, Runner with Map — A164

Iris — A165

1974, Aug. 22 Engr. *Perf. 13*
558 A164 70o shown .35 .25
559 A164 80o Compass .35 .25

World Orienteering Championships 1974.

1974, Sept. 19
560 A165 90o shown .35 .20
561 A165 120o Purple orchid .55 .25

Copenhagen Botanical Garden centenary.

Mailman, 1624, and Postilion, 1780 — A166

Carrier Pigeon — A167

Design: 90o, Balloon and sailing ships.

1974, Oct. 9 Engr. *Perf. 13*

562 A166 70o lemon & dk brn .30 .35
563 A166 90o dull grn & sepia .40 .20
564 A167 120o dark blue .55 .30
Nos. 562-564 (3) 1.25 .85

350th anniv. of Danish PO (70o, 90o) and cent. of UPU (120o).

Souvenir Sheet

Ferslew's Essays, 1849 and 1852 — A168

Engraved and Photogravure

1975, Feb. 27 *Perf. 13*

565 A168 Sheet of 4 5.25 *6.00*
a. 70o Coat of arms 1.25 *1.40*
b. 80o King Frederik VII 1.25 *1.40*
c. 90o King Frederik VII 1.25 *1.40*
d. 100o Mercury 1.25 *1.40*

HAFNIA 76 Intl. Stamp Exhib., Copenhagen, Aug. 20-29, 1976. Sold for 5k.
See No. 585.

Early Radio Equipment A169

Flora Danica Plate A170

1975, Mar. 20 Engr. *Perf. 13*

566 A169 90o dull red .35 .20

Danish broadcasting, 50th anniversary.

1975, May 22

Danish China: 90o, Flora Danica tureen. 130o, Vase and tea caddy, blue fluted china.

567 A170 50o slate grn .30 .20
568 A170 90o brown red .60 .20
569 A170 130o violet bl .90 .90
Nos. 567-569 (3) 1.80 1.30

Church of Moravian Brethren, Christiansfeld A171

120o, Kongsgaard farmhouse, Lejre. 150o, Anna Queenstraede, Helsingor, vert.

1975, June 19

570 A171 70o sepia .30 .25
571 A171 120o olive green 1.10 .30
572 A171 150o violet black .50 .20
Nos. 570-572 (3) 1.90 .75

European Architectural Heritage Year 1975.

Andersen A172

Watchman's Square, Abenra A173

Designs: 70o, Numbskull Jack, drawing by Vilh. Pedersen. 130o, The Marshking's Daughter, drawing by L. Frohlich.

1975, Aug. 28 Engr. *Perf. 13*

573 A172 70o brown & blk .55 .50
574 A172 90o brn red & dk brn 1.00 .25
575 A172 130o blue blk & sepia 1.25 1.25
Nos. 573-575 (3) 2.80 2.00

Hans Christian Andersen (1805-75), writer.

1975, Sept. 25

Designs: 90o, Haderslev Cathedral, vert. 100o, Mögeltönder Polder. 120o, Mouth of Vidaaen at Höjer Floodgates.

576 A173 70o multicolored .30 .25
577 A173 90o multicolored .40 .20
578 A173 100o multicolored .40 .25
579 A173 120o multicolored .55 .30
Nos. 576-579 (4) 1.65 1.00

European Kingfisher A174

1975, Oct. 23 Engr. *Perf. 13*

580 A174 50o shown .45 .25
581 A174 70o Hedgehog .45 .25
582 A174 90o Cats .45 .20
583 A174 130o Avocets .85 .75
584 A174 200o Otter .70 .20
Nos. 580-584 (5) 2.90 1.65

Protected animals, and for the centenary of the Danish Society for the Prevention of Cruelty to Animals (90o).

HAFNIA Type of 1974
Souvenir Sheet

1975, Nov. 20 Engr. & Photo.

585 A168 Sheet of 4 2.75 *3.50*
a. 50o buff & brown, No. 2 .65 *.85*
b. 70o buff, brown & blue, No. 1 .65 *.85*
c. 90o buff, blue & brown, No. 11 .65 *.85*
d. 130o olive, brown & buff, No. 19 .65 *.85*

HAFNIA 76 Intl. Stamp Exhib., Copenhagen, Aug. 20-29, 1976. Sold for 5k.

Copenhagen, Center — A175

View from Round Tower — A176

Copenhagen, Views: 100o, Central Station, interior. 130o, Harbor.

1976, Mar. 25 Engr. *Perf. 12½*

586 A175 60o multicolored .50 .20
587 A176 80o multicolored .50 .20
588 A176 100o multicolored .30 .20
589 A175 130o multicolored 1.50 1.50
Nos. 586-589 (4) 2.80 2.10

Postilion, by Otto Bache A177

Emil Chr. Hansen, Physiologist, in Laboratory A178

1976, June 17 Engr. *Perf. 12½*

590 A177 130o multicolored 1.25 1.25

Souvenir Sheet

591 A177 130o multicolored 7.00 *8.25*

HAFNIA 76 Intl. Stamp Exhib., Copenhagen, Aug. 20-29. No. 591 contains one stamp similar to No. 590 with design continuous into sheet margin. Sheet shows painting "A String of Horses Outside an Inn" of which No. 590 shows a detail. Sheet sold for 15k including exhibition ticket.

1976, Sept. 23 Engr. *Perf. 13*

592 A178 100o orange red .40 .20

Carlsberg Foundation (art and science), centenary.

Glass Blower Molding Glass — A179

Five Water Lilies — A180

Danish Glass Production: 80o, Finished glass removed from pipe. 130o, Glass cut off from foot. 150o, Glass blown up in mold.

1976, Nov. 18 Engr. *Perf. 13*

593 A179 60o slate .20 .20
594 A179 80o dk brown .25 .20
595 A179 130o dk blue .70 .65
596 A179 150o red brown .50 .20
Nos. 593-596 (4) 1.65 1.25

Photogravure and Engraved

1977, Feb. 2 *Perf. 12½*

597 A180 100o brt green & multi .45 .25
598 A180 130o ultra & multi 1.40 1.25

Nordic countries cooperation for protection of the environment and 25th Session of Nordic Council, Helsinki, Feb. 19.

Road Accident — A181

Europa — A182

1977, Mar. 24 Engr. *Perf. 12½*

599 A181 100o brown red .35 .20

Road Safety Traffic Act, May 1, 1977.

1977, May 2 Engr. *Perf. 12½*

600 A182 1k Allinge .50 .25
601 A182 1.30k View, Ringsted 2.50 *3.00*

Kongeaen A183

Hammers and Horseshoes A184

Landscapes, Southern Jutland: 90o, Skallingen. 150o, Torskind. 200o, Jelling.

1977, June 30 Engr. *Perf. 12½*

602 A183 60o multicolored .85 .75
603 A183 90o multicolored .40 .25
604 A183 150o multicolored .50 .30
605 A183 200o multicolored .60 .20
Nos. 602-605 (4) 2.35 1.50

See Nos. 616-619, 655-658, 666-669.

1977, Sept. 22 Engr. *Perf. 12½*

Designs: 1k, Chisel, square and plane. 1.30k, Trowel, ceiling brush and folding ruler.

606 A184 80o dk brown .30 .25
607 A184 1k red .40 .20
608 A184 1.30k violet bl .70 .30
Nos. 606-608 (3) 1.40 .75

Danish crafts.

Globe Flower — A185

Handball — A186

Endangered Flora: 1.50k, Cnidium dubium.

1977, Nov. 17 Engr. *Perf. 12½*

609 A185 1k multicolored .40 .20
610 A185 1.50k multicolored .90 .55

1978, Jan. 19 *Perf. 12½*

611 A186 1.20k red .30 .20

Men's World Handball Championships.

Christian IV, Frederiksborg Castle A187

Frederiksborg Museum A188

1978, Mar. 16

612 A187 1.20k brown red .40 .20
613 A188 1.80k black .70 .30

Frederiksborg Museum, centenary.

Europa Issue

Jens Bang's House, Aalborg A189

Frederiksborg Castle, Ground Plan and Elevation A190

1978, May 11 Engr. *Perf. 12½*

614 A189 1.20k red *.60* .20
615 A190 1.50k dk bl & vio bl *1.40* *.75*

Landscape Type of 1977

Landscapes, Central Jutland: 70o, Kongenshus Memorial Park. 120o, Post Office, Old Town in Aarhus. 150o, Lignite fields, Soby. 180o, Church wall, Stadil Church.

1978, June 15 Engr. *Perf. 12½*
616 A183 70o multicolored .25 .20
617 A183 120o multicolored .45 .20
618 A183 150o multicolored .55 .40
619 A183 180o multicolored .60 .35
Nos. 616-619 (4) 1.85 1.15

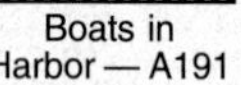

Boats in Harbor — A191

Edible Morel — A192

Danish fishing industry: 1k, Eel traps. 1.80k, Boats in berth. 2.50k, Drying nets.

1978, Sept. 7 Engr. *Perf. 12½*
620 A191 70o olive gray .40 .20
621 A191 1k redsh brown .40 .20
622 A191 1.80k slate .40 .20
623 A191 2.50k sepia .90 .30
Nos. 620-623 (4) 2.10 .90

1978, Nov. 16 Engr. *Perf. 12½*

Design: 1.20k, Satan's mushroom.

624 A192 1k sepia .35 .30
625 A192 1.20k dull red .50 .30

Telephones — A193

1979, Jan. 25 Engr. *Perf. 12½*
626 A193 1.20k dull red .40 .20

Centenary of Danish telephone.

University Seal A194

Pentagram: University Faculties A195

1979, Apr. 5 Engr. *Perf. 12½*
627 A194 1.30k vermilion .45 .20
628 A195 1.60k dk vio blue .60 .55

University of Copenhagen, 500th anniv.

Types of 1933-1974

1979-82 Engr. *Perf. 13*
629 A32 80o green .25 .20
630 A161 90o slate 1.25 1.10
631 A32 100o dp green ('81) .30 .20
632 A161 110o brown .40 .20
a. Bklt. pane, #493-494, 632, 2 #318 ('79) 1.00
633 A161 130o red .35 .20
a. Bklt. pane, 2 ea #494, 629, 632, 4 #633 ('79) 4.00
634 A161 130o brown ('81) .40 .25
635 A161 140o red org ('80) .90 .85
636 A161 150o red org ('81) .45 .40
637 A161 160o ultra .60 .55
638 A161 160o red ('81) .40 .20
a. Bklt. pane, 2 ea #318, 634, 638, 8 #494) 8.00
639 A161 180o ultra ('80) .75 .70
640 A161 210o gray ('80) .90 .85
641 A161 230o ol grn ('81) .75 .25
642 A161 250o blue grn ('81) .80 .45
643 A55 2.80k dull grn .60 .20
644 A55 3.30k brn red ('81) .75 .35
645 A55 3.50k grnsh bl ('82) 1.25 1.25
646 A55 4.30k brn red ('80) 1.25 1.25
647 A55 4.70k rose lil ('81) 1.60 1.60
648 A55 8k orange 1.50 .20
649 A55 12k red brn ('81) 2.50 .35
650 A55 14k dk red brn ('82) 2.75 .45
Nos. 629-650 (22) 20.70 12.05

A196

A197

Europa: 1.30k, Mail cart, 1785. 1.60k, Morse key and amplifier.

1979, May 10 *Perf. 12½*
651 A196 1.30k red .90 .20
652 A196 1.60k dark blue 1.40 .75

1979, June 14 Engr. *Perf. 13*

Viking Art: 1.10k, Gripping beast pendant. 2k, Key with gripping beast design.

653 A197 1.10k sepia .40 .20
654 A197 2k grnsh gray .60 .20

Landscape Type of 1977

Landscapes, Northern Jutland: 80o, Mols Bjerge. 90o, Orslev Kloster. 200o, Trans. 280o, Bovbjerg.

1979, Sept. 6 Engr. *Perf. 12½*
655 A183 80o multicolored .25 .25
656 A183 90o multicolored .60 .50
657 A183 200o multicolored .50 .20
658 A183 280o multicolored .65 .45
Nos. 655-658 (4) 2.00 1.40

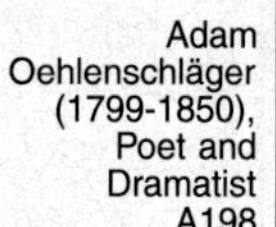

Adam Oehlenschläger (1799-1850), Poet and Dramatist A198

1979, Oct, 4 Engr. *Perf. 13*
659 A198 1.30k dk carmine .40 .20

Score, Violin, Dancing Couple — A199

Ballerina — A200

1979, Nov. 8 Engr. *Perf. 13x12½*
660 A199 1.10k brown .35 .20
661 A200 1.60k ultra .65 .30

Jacob Gade (1879-63), composer; August Bournonville (1805-79), ballet master.

Royal Mail Guards' Office, Copenhagen, 1779 — A201

1980, Feb. 14 Engr. *Perf. 13*
662 A201 1.30k brown red .30 .20

National Postal Service, 200th anniversary.

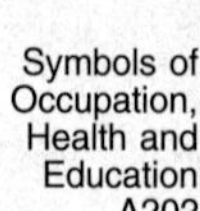

Symbols of Occupation, Health and Education A202

1980, May 5 Engr. *Perf. 13*
663 A202 1.60k dark blue .40 .40

World Conference of the UN Decade for Women, Copenhagen, July 14-30.

Karen Blixen (1885-1962), Writer (Pen Name Isak Dinesen) — A203

Europa: 1.60k, August Krogh (1874-1949), physiologist.

1980, May 5
664 A203 1.30k red *.60* .20
665 A203 1.60k blue *1.25* .60

Landscape Type of 1977

Northern Jutland: 80o, Viking ship burial grounds, Lindholm Hoje. 110o, Lighthouse, Skagen, vert. 200o, Boreglum Monastery. 280o, Fishing boats, Vorupor Beach.

1980, June 19 Engr. *Perf. 13*
666 A183 80o multicolored .25 .25
667 A183 110o multicolored .30 .30
668 A183 200o multicolored .45 .20
669 A183 280o multicolored 1.00 1.00
Nos. 666-669 (4) 2.00 1.75

Nordic Cooperation Issue

Silver Tankard, by Borchardt Rollufse, 1641 — A204

1980, Sept. 9 Engr. *Perf. 13*
670 A204 1.30k shown .30 .20
671 A204 1.80k Bishop's bowl, Copenhagen faience, 18th cent. .65 *.65*

Frisian Sceat Facsimile, Obverse and Reverse, 9th Century A205

Coins: 1.40k Silver coin of Valdemar the Great and Absalom, 1157-1182, 1.80k, Gold 12-mark coin of Christian VII, 1781.

1980, Oct. 9 Engr. *Perf. 13*
672 A205 1.30k red & redsh brn .30 .25
673 A205 1.40k ol gray & sl grn .70 *.70*
674 A205 1.80k dk bl & sl bl .60 *.60*
Nos. 672-674 (3) 1.60 *1.55*

Tonder Lace Pattern, North Schleswig — A206

Designs: Tonder lace patterns.

1980, Nov. 13 Engr. *Perf. 13*
675 A206 1.10k brown .30 .35
676 A206 1.30k brown red .35 .20
677 A206 2k olive gray .50 .20
Nos. 675-677 (3) 1.15 .75

Nyboder Development, Copenhagen, 350th Anniversary A207

Design: 1.30k, View of Nyboder, diff.

1981, Mar. 19
678 A207 1.30k dp org & ocher .50 .50
679 A207 1.60k dp org & ocher .35 .20

Tilting at a Barrel on Shrovetide A208

Design: 2k, Midsummer's Eve bonfire.

1981, May 4 Engr. *Perf. 13*
680 A208 1.60k brown red *.50* .20
681 A208 2k dk blue *.90* .50

Soro Lake and Academy, Zealand — A209

Designs: Views of Zealand.

1981, June 18 Engr. *Perf. 13*
682 A209 100o shown .25 .25
683 A209 150o Poet N.F.S. Grundtvig's home, Udby .40 .40
684 A209 160o Kaj Munk's home, Opager .40 .20
685 A209 200o Gronsund .55 .55
686 A209 230o Bornholm Isld. .60 .55
Nos. 682-686 (5) 2.20 1.95

European Urban Renaissance Year — A210

1981, Sept. 10 Engr. *Perf. 12½x13*
687 A210 1.60k dull red .40 .20

Type of 1933

1981-85 Engr. *Perf. 13*
688 A32 30o orange .20 .20
a. Bklt. pane 10 (2 #318, 2 #688, 6 #494)('84) 1.75
689 A32 40o purple .20 .20
a. Bklt. pane of 10 (4 #318, 2 #689, 4 #494) ('89) 1.25
690 A32 80o ol bis ('85) .30 .30
691 A32 100o blue ('83) .40 .20
b. Bklt. pane of 8 (2 #494, 4 #691, 2 #706) ('83) 6.00
692 A32 150o dk green ('82) .30 .20
693 A32 200o green ('83) .40 .40
694 A32 230o brt yel grn ('84) .50 .20
695 A32 250o brt yel grn ('85) .65 .40
Nos. 688-695 (8) 2.95 2.10

Ellehammer's 18-horsepower Biplane, 1906 — A211

1981, Oct. 8 Engr. *Perf. 13*
696 A211 1k shown .30 .30
697 A211 1.30k R-1 Fokker CV reconnaissance plane, 1926 .65 .65
698 A211 1.60k Bellanca J-300, 1931 .35 .20
699 A211 2.30k DC-7C, 1957 .55 .45
Nos. 696-699 (4) 1.85 1.60

Queen Margrethe II, 10th Anniv. of Accession — A212

1982-85 Engr. *Perf. 13*
700 A212 1.60k dull red .45 .20
701 A212 1.60k dk ol grn 1.60 1.60
702 A212 1.80k sepia .50 .35
703 A212 2k dull red .65 .20
b. Bklt. pane, 4 #494, 2 ea #493, 702, 703 10.00
704 A212 2.20k ol grn ('83) .60 .25
705 A212 2.30k violet .50 .20
706 A212 2.50k org red ('83) 2.10 2.10
707 A212 2.70k dk blue .60 .50
708 A212 2.70k cop red ('84) .90 .20
c. Booklet pane, 3 #688, 2 #494, 3 #708 ('84) 5.00
709 A212 2.80k cop red ('85) .75 .20
b. Booklet pane, 3 #493, 2 #494, 3 #709 ('85) 4.00
710 A212 3k violet ('83) .75 .20
711 A212 3.30k bluish blk ('84) 1.10 .45
712 A212 3.50k blue ('83) 1.60 1.60
713 A212 3.50k dk vio ('85) 1.25 .70
714 A212 3.70k dp blue ('84) .95 .25
715 A212 3.80k dk blue ('85) 1.10 .20

See Nos. 796-803, 887, 889, 896, 899.

Arms Type of 1946

Engr. *Perf. 13*

716	A55 4.30k dk ol grn ('84)	3.00	3.00
717	A55 5.50k dk bl grn ('84)	1.75	1.75
718	A55 16k cop red ('83)	3.50	.50
719	A55 17k cop red ('84)	5.00	1.00
720	A55 18k brn vio ('85)	5.00	.75
720A	A55 50k dk red ('85)	10.00	1.50
	Nos. 700-720A (22)	43.65	17.70

World Figure Skating Championships A213

1982, Feb. 25

721 A213 2k dark blue .60 .25

A214

A215

1982, Feb. 25 Engr. *Perf. 12½*

722 A214 1.60k Revenue schooner Argus .45 .20

Customs Service centenary

1982, May 3 Engr. *Perf. 12½*

723 A215 2k Abolition of ad-scription, 1788 *1.10* .20

724 A215 2.70k Women's voting right, 1915 *1.40* .65

Europa.

Butter Churn, Barn, Hjedding — A216

Records Office, 400th Anniv. — A217

1982, June 10 Engr. *Perf. 13*

725 A216 1.80k brown .45 .45

Cooperative dairy farming centenary.

1982, June 10

726 A217 2.70k green .70 .30

Steen Steensen Blicher (1782-1848), Poet, by J.V. Gertner — A218

1982, Aug. 26 Engr. *Perf. 13*

727 A218 2k brown red .50 .20

Robert Storm Petersen (1882-1949), Cartoonist A219

Printing in Denmark, 500th Anniv. A220

Characters: 1.50k, Three little men and the number man. 2k, Peter and Ping the penguin, horiz.

1982, Sept. 23 Engr. *Perf. 12½*

728 A219 1.50k dk bl & red .45 .30

729 A219 2k red & ol grn .60 .25

1982, Sept. 23

730 A220 1.80k Press, text, ink balls .50 .50

A221

A222

1982, Nov. 4

731 A221 2.70k Library seal .65 .35

500th anniv. of University Library.

1983, Jan. 27 Engr. *Perf. 13*

732 A222 2k multicolored .50 .20

World Communications Year.

Amusement Park, 400th Anniv. A223

Badminton Championship A224

1983, Feb. 24

733 A223 2k multicolored .50 .20

1983, Feb. 24

734 A224 2.70k multicolored .65 .25

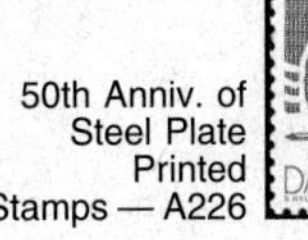

Nordic Cooperation Issue — A225

1983, Mar. 24

735 A225 2.50k Egeskov Castle .60 .25

736 A225 3.50k Troll Church, North Jutland .80 .45

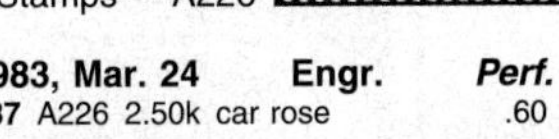

50th Anniv. of Steel Plate Printed Stamps — A226

1983, Mar. 24 Engr. *Perf. 13*

737 A226 2.50k car rose .60 .25

Europa 1983 — A227

Weights and Measures Ordinance, 300th Anniv. — A228

2.50k, Kildekovshallen Recreation Center, Copenhagen. 3.50k, Salling Sound Bridge.

1983, May 5 Engr. *Perf. 13*

738 A227 2.50k multicolored *1.10* .20

739 A227 3.50k multicolored *1.40* .50

1983, June 16

740 A228 2.50k red .55 .20

A229

A230

1983, Sept. 8 Engr.

741 A229 5k Codex titlepage 1.10 .40

Christian V Danish law, 300th anniv.

1983, Oct. 6 Engr. *Perf. 13*

742 A230 1k Car crash, police .25 .20

743 A230 2.50k Fire, ambulance service .55 .25

744 A230 3.50k Sea rescue .80 .50

Nos. 742-744 (3) 1.60 .95

Life saving and salvage services.

Elderly in Society — A231

1983, Oct. 6

745 A231 2k Stages of life .50 .40

746 A231 2.50k Train passengers .60 .20

N.F.S. Grundtvig (1783-1872), Poet — A232

Street Scene, by C.W. Eckersberg (1783-1853) — A233

1983, Nov. 3 Engr.

747 A232 2.50k brown red .55 .20

748 A233 2.50k brown red .55 .20

A234

A235

1984, Jan. 26 Litho. & Engr.

749 A234 2.70k Shovel, sapling .60 .20

Plant a tree campaign.

1984, Jan. 26 Engr.

750 A235 3.70k Game .80 .35

1984 Billiards World Championships, Copenhagen, May 10-13.

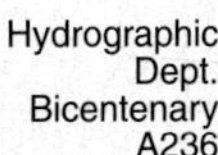

Hydrographic Dept. Bicentenary A236

Pilotage Service, 300th Anniv. — A237

1984, Mar. 22 Engr. *Perf. 13*

751 A236 2.30k Compass .60 .60

752 A237 2.70k Boat .65 .20

2nd European Parliament Elections A238

Scouts Around Campfire, Emblems A239

Litho. & Engr.

1984, Apr. 12 *Perf. 13*

753 A238 2.70k org & dk bl .65 .20

754 A239 2.70k multi .65 .20

Europa (1959-84) A240

1984, May 3 Engr. *Perf. 12½*

755 A240 2.70k red *1.25* .20

756 A240 3.70k blue *1.90* .90

Prince Henrik, 50th Birthday A241

D Day, 40th Anniv. A242

1984, June 6 Engr.

757 A241 2.70k brown red .65 .25

758 A242 2.70k War Memorial, Copenhagen .65 .20

See Greenland No. 160.

17th Cent. Inn — A243

1984, June 6

759 A243 3k multicolored .75 .60

Fishing and Shipping A244

1984, Sept. 6 Engr.

760 A244 2.30k Research (Herring) .80 .80

761 A244 2.70k Sea transport .65 .35

762 A244 3.30k Deep-sea fishing .85 .85

763 A244 3.70k Deep-sea, diff. .90 .80

Nos. 760-763 (4) 3.20 2.80

A245

A246

1984, Oct. 5 Litho. & Engr.

764 A245 1k Post bird .25 .20

1984, Oct. 5

Holberg Meets with an Officer, by Wilhelm Marstrand (1810-73).

765 A246 2.70k multicolored .65 .20

Ludvig Holberg (1684-1754), writer.

Jewish Community in Copenhagen, 300th Anniv. — A247

1984, Oct. 5

766 A247 3.70k Woman blessing Sabbath candles .85 .60

Carnival in Rome, by Christoffer W. Eckersberg (1783-1853) — A248

Paintings: 10k, Ymer and Odhumble (Nordic mythology figures), by Nicolai A. Abildgaard (1743-1809), vert.

Perf. 12½x13, 13x12½

1984, Nov. 22 Litho. & Engr.

767 A248 5k multicolored 1.50 1.50
768 A248 10k multicolored 3.00 3.00

German and French Reform Church, 300th Anniv. — A249

1985, Jan. 24 Engr. *Perf. 13*

769 A249 2.80k magenta .65 .20

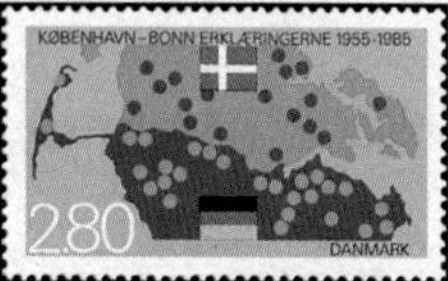

Bonn-Copenhagen Declaration, 30th Anniv. — A250

1985, Feb. 21 Litho. *Perf. 14*

770 A250 2.80k Map, flags .80 .35

A251

A252

1985, Mar. 14 *Perf. 13*

771 A251 3.80k multicolored .85 .60

Intl. Youth Year.

Souvenir Sheet

Early postal ordinances.

1985, Mar. 14 Litho. & Engr.

772 Sheet of 4 3.50 *3.50*
- ***a.*** A252 1k Christian IV's Ordinance on Postmen, 1624 .80 *.90*
- ***b.*** A252 2.50k Plague Mandate, 1711 .80 *.90*
- ***c.*** A252 2.80k Ordinance on Prohibition of Mail by Means other than the Post, 1775 .80 *.90*
- ***d.*** A252 3.80k Act on Postal Articles, 1831 .80 *.90*

HAFNIA '87 phil. exhib. Sold for 15k.

Europa 1985 — A253

1985, May 2

773 A253 2.80k Musical staff *1.40* .40
774 A253 3.80k Musical staff, diff. *1.60* 1.00

Arrival of Queen Ingrid in Denmark, 50th Anniv. — A254

1985, May 21

775 A254 2.80k Queen Mother, chrysanthemums .65 .20

See Greenland No. 163.

Opening of the Faro Bridges — A255

1985, May 21 Litho. *Perf. 13*

776 A255 2.80k Faro-Falster Bridge .65 .20

St. Cnut's Land Grant to Lund Cathedral, 900th Anniv. — A256

Seal of King Cnut and: 2.80k, Lund Cathedral. 3k, City of Helsingdorg, Sweden.

1985, May 21 Engr.

777 A256 2.80k multi .65 .25
778 A256 3k multi .80 .80

See Sweden Nos. 1538-1539.

UN Decade for Women A257

Sports A258

1985, June 27 Litho. & Engr.

779 A257 3.80k Cyclist .90 .90

1985, June 27

780 A258 2.80k Women's floor exercise .70 .20
781 A258 3.80k Canoe & kayak .90 .50
782 A258 6k Cycling 1.40 1.00
Nos. 780-782 (3) 3.00 1.70

Kronborg Castle, Elsinore, 400th Anniv. — A259

UN 40th Anniv. — A260

1985, Sept. 5

783 A259 2.80k multi .65 .20

1985, Sept. 5

784 A260 3.80k Dove, emblem .90 .50

Niels Bohr (1885-1962), Physicist — A261

1985, Oct. 3 *Perf. 13x12½*

785 A261 2.80k With wife Margrethe .80 .90

Winner of 1922 Nobel Prize in Physics for theory of atomic structure.

Hand Signing "D" — A262

Boat, by Helge Refn — A263

1985, Nov. 7 Engr. *Perf. 13*

786 A262 2.80k multicolored .70 .20

Danish Assoc. for the Deaf, 50th anniv.

1985, Nov. 7 Litho.

787 A263 2.80k multicolored .65 .20

Abstract Iron Sculpture by Robert Jacobsen A264

Lithographed and Engraved

1985, Nov. 7 *Perf. 13x12½*

788 A264 3.80k multicolored 1.75 2.00

Painting by Bjorn Wiinblad A265

1986, Jan. 23 Litho. *Perf. 13x12½*

789 A265 2.80k multicolored .80 .80

Amnesty Intl., 25th Anniv. A266

Lithographed and Engraved

1986, Jan. 23 *Perf. 13*

790 A266 2.80k multicolored .65 .20

Miniature Sheet

HAFNIA '87 — A267

1986, Feb. 20

791 Sheet of 4 5.00 5.50
- ***a.*** A267 100o Holstein carriage, c. 1840 1.10 1.25
- ***b.*** A267 250o Iceboat, c. 1880 1.10 1.25
- ***c.*** A267 280o 1st mail van, 1908 1.10 1.25
- ***d.*** A267 380o Airmail service 1919 1.10 1.25

Sold for 15k.

Changing of the Guard — A268

1986, Mar. 20 *Perf. 13*

792 A268 2.80k multicolored .65 .20

Royal Danish Life Guards barracks and Rosenborg Drilling Ground, bicent.

Types of 1933-82

1986-90 Engr. *Perf. 13*

793	A32	5o	brn org ('89)	.20	.20
794	A32	270o	brt yel grn	.65	.50
b.			Bklt. pane, 6 #318, 2 #691, 2 #794	3.00	
795	A32	300o	brt yel grn	.70	.25
796	A212	3k	cop red	.70	.20
797	A212	3.20k	deep vio	.80	.50
798	A212	3.20k	carmine	.80	.20
c.			Bklt. pane, 2 #693, 4 #798	5.00	
799	A212	3.40k	dk grn	1.50	1.50
800	A212	3.80k	dark vio	1.00	1.00
801	A212	4.10k	dark blue	1.00	.30
802	A212	4.20k	dk pur	1.50	1.25
803	A212	4.40k	dp bl	1.00	.25
804	A55	4.60k	gray	2.00	2.00
805	A55	6.50k	dp grn	1.60	.50
806	A55	6.60k	green	1.60	1.75
807	A55	7.10k	brn vio	2.00	1.40
808	A55	7.30k	green	2.25	2.25
809	A55	7.70k	dk brn vio	1.90	.90
810	A55	11k	brown	2.25	1.75
811	A55	20k	dp ultra	4.50	.45
812	A55	22k	henna brn	4.50	1.00
813	A55	23k	dark olive grn	5.00	.75
814	A55	24k	dark olive grn	5.00	.50
815	A55	26k	dark olive grn	5.50	1.25
			Nos. 793-815 (23)	47.95	20.65

Issued: 6.50k, 20k, 1/9/86; 22k, 1/3/87; 270o, 3k, #797, 3.80k, 4.10k, 4.60k, 6.60k, 7.10k, 24k, 1/7/88; #794b, 1/28/88; 300o, #798, 3.40k, 4.20k, 4.40k, 7.30k, 7.70k, 11k, 26k, 1/26/89; 5o, 1989; 23k, 1/11/90.

No. 793 issued for use in lieu of currency of the same face value.

Soro Academy, 400th Anniv. — A269

1986, Apr. 28 Litho. & Engr.

816 A269 2.80k multi .70 .20

A270

A271

1986, Apr. 28

817 A270 3.80k multi .90 .65

Intl. Peace Year.

1986, May 26 Litho.

818 A271 2.80k multi .80 .30

Crown Prince Frederik, 18th birthday.

Nordic Cooperation Issue
1986 — A272

Sister towns.

1986, May 27 **Engr.**
819 A272 2.80k Aalborg Harbor .65 .30
820 A272 3.80k Thisted Church and Town Hall .90 .50

Hoje Tastrup Train Station Opening, May 31 — A273

1986, May 27 **Litho.**
821 A273 2.80k multi .65 .20

Mailbox, Telegraph Lines, Telephone
A274

Natl. Bird Candidates
A275

1986, June 19 **Litho.** ***Perf. 13***
822 A274 2.80k multi .65 .20

19th European Intl. PTT Congress, Copenhagen, Aug. 12-16.

1986, June 19 **Litho. & Engr.**

Finalists: a, Corvus corax. b, Sturnus vulgaris. c, Cygnus olor (winner). d, Vanellus vanellus. e, Alauda arvensis.

823 Strip of 5 5.00 5.50
a.-e. A275 2.80k any single .90 .75

A276

HAFNIA '87 — A277

1986, June 19
824 A276 2.80k multi .65 .20

Danish Rifle, Gymnastics and Sports Club, 125th anniv.

Souvenir Sheet

1986, Sept. 4
825 Sheet of 4 5.25 5.25
a. A277 100o Mailcoach, c. 1841 1.10 1.10
b. A277 250o Postmaster, c. 1840 1.10 1.10
c. A277 280o Postman, c. 1851 1.10 1.10
d. A277 380o Rural postman, c. 1893 1.25 1.25

Sold for 15k.

Europa
1986 — A278

Cupid — A279

1986, Sept. 4 **Engr.**
826 A278 2.80k Street sweeper *1.50* .20
827 A278 3.80k Garbage truck *1.75* .75

1986, Oct. 9 **Litho.**
828 A279 3.80k multi .85 .45

Premiere of The Whims of Cupid and the Ballet Master, by Vincenzo Galeotti, bicent.

Refugee — A280

A281

1986, Oct. 9 **Litho. & Engr.**
829 A280 2.80k multi .65 .20

Danish Refugee Council Relief Campaign.

1986, Oct. 9 **Litho.** ***Perf. 13***

Protestant Reformation in Denmark, 450th Anniv.: Sermon, altarpiece detail, 1561, Thorslunde Church, Copenhagen.

830 A281 6.50k multi 1.60 .75

A282

Abstract by Lin Utzon — A283

1986, Nov. 6 **Litho. & Engr.**
831 A282 3.80k multi 1.25 1.25

Organization for Economic Cooperation and Development, 25th anniv.

1987, Jan. 22 **Litho.** ***Perf. 13***
832 A283 2.80k multi .65 .20

Art appreciation.

A284

A285

1987, Feb. 26 **Engr.** ***Perf. 13***
833 A284 2.80k lake & black .65 .20

Danish Consumer Council, 40th anniv.

1987, Apr. 9 **Litho.** ***Perf. 13***

Religious art (details) from Ribe Cathedral.

834 A285 3k Fresco .70 .50
835 A285 3.80k Stained-glass window 1.00 .80
836 A285 6.50k Mosaic 1.60 1.60
Nos. 834-836 (3) 3.30 2.90

Ribe Cathedral redecoration, 1982-1987, by Carl-Henning Pedersen.

A286

A287

Europa (Modern architecture): 2.80k, Central Library, Gentofte, 1985. 3.80k, Hoje Tastrup High School, 1985, horiz.

1987, May 4 **Engr.** ***Perf. 13***
837 A286 2.80k rose claret *1.50* .40
838 A286 3.80k bright ultra *2.00* 1.00

1987, May 4
839 A287 2.50k dk red & bl blk .70 .80

Danish Academy of Technical Sciences (ATV), 50th anniv.

8th Gymnaestrada, Herning, July 7-11 — A288

1987, June 18 **Litho. & Engr.**
840 A288 2.80k multi .70 .20

A289

A290

1987, June 18
841 A289 3.80k multi .90 .60

Danish Cooperative Bacon Factories, cent.

1987, Aug. 27 **Litho.**
842 A290 3.80k Single-sculler .90 .50

World Rowing Championships, Aug. 23-30.

HAFNIA '87, Bella Center, Copenhagen, Oct. 16-25 — A291

Litho. & Engr.

1987, Aug. 27 ***Perf. 13x12½***
843 A291 280o Type A15, mail train c. 1912 .70 .75

Souvenir Sheet

843A A291 280o like No. 843, green lawn and locomotive 14.00 14.00

Purchase of No. 843A included admission to the exhibition. Sold for 45k.

Abstact by Ejler Bille — A292

1987, Sept. 24 **Litho.** ***Perf. 13***
844 A292 2.80k multi .65 .20

Rasmus Rask (1787-1832), Linguist — A293

1987, Oct. 15 **Engr.** ***Perf. 13x12½***
845 A293 2.80k dark henna brown .65 .20

A294

A295

Emblem: Miraculous Catch (Luke 5:4-7), New Testament.

1987, Oct. 15 ***Perf. 13***
846 A294 3k carmine lake .70 .25

Clerical Assoc. for the Home Mission in Denmark, 125th anniv.

Photo. & Engr., Litho. (4.10k)

1988, Feb. 18 ***Perf. 13***

Designs: 3k, Two lions from the gate of Rosenburg Castle around the monogram of Christian IV. 4.10k, Portrait of the monarch painted by P. Isaacsz, vert.

847 A295 3k blue gray & gold .70 .25
848 A295 4.10k multi 1.00 .50

Accession of Christian IV (1577-1648), King of Denmark and Norway (1588-1648), 400th anniv.

Ole Worm (1588-1654), Archaeologist, and Runic Artifacts — A296

1988, Feb. 18 **Engr.**
849 A296 7.10k chocolate 1.60 1.60

Odense, 1000th Anniv. — A297

A298

Design: St. Cnut's Church and statue of Hans Christian Andersen, Odense.

1988, Mar. 10 **Engr.**
850 A297 3k multi .70 .20

1988, Apr. 7 **Litho.**
851 A298 2.70k multi .65 .50

Danish Civil Defense and Emergency Planning Agency, 50th Anniv.

WHO, 40th Anniv. — A299

Abolition of *Stavnsbaand*, 200th Anniv. — A300

1988, Apr. 7 **Litho. & Engr.**
852 A299 4.10k multi .90 .60

1988, May 5 **Litho.**

Painting: King Christian VII riding past the Liberty Memorial, Copenhagen, by C.W. Eckersberg (1783-1853).

853 A300 3.20k multi .80 .60

Stavnsbaand (adscription) provided that all Danish farmers' sons from age 4 to 40 would be bound as villeins to the estates on which they were born, thus providing landowners with free labor.

A301

A302

Europa: Transport and communication.

1988, May 5

854 A301 3k Postwoman on bicycle *1.10* .20
855 A301 4.10k Mobile telephone *1.90* .75

1988, June 16 **Litho.**

856 A302 4.10k multi .90 .50

1988 Individual Speedway World Motorcycle Championships, Denmark, Sept. 3.

Federation of Danish Industries, 150th Anniv. — A303

Painting (detail): *The Industrialists,* by P.S. Kroyer.

1988, June 16 ***Perf. 13½x13***

857 A303 3k multi .70 .40

Danish Metalworkers' Union, Cent. — A304

1988, Aug. 18 **Litho.** ***Perf. 13***

858 A304 3k Glass mosaic by Niels Winkel .70 .25

Tonder Teachers' Training College, 200th Anniv. — A305

1988, Aug. 18 **Engr.** ***Perf. 13x12½***

859 A305 3k lake .70 .20

Homage to Leon Degand, Sculpture by Robert Jacobsen A306

1988, Sept. 22 ***Perf. 11½x13***

860 A306 4.10k blk, lake & gray 1.50 *1.90*

Danish-French cultural exchange program, 10th anniv. See France No. 2130.

Preservation of Historic Sites — A307

1988, Oct. 13 **Engr.** ***Perf. 13x12½***

861 A307 3k Lumby Windmill, 1818 .80 .20
862 A307 7.10k Vejstrup Water Mill, 1837 1.60 1.00

Paintings in the State Museum of Art, Copenhagen — A308

4.10k, *Bathing Boys,* 1902, by Peter Hansen (1868-1928). 10k, *The Hill at Overkaerby,* 1917, by Fritz Syberg (1862-1939).

Litho. & Engr.

1988, Nov. 3 ***Perf. 13***

863 A308 4.10k multi 1.60 *1.75*
864 A308 10k multi 3.25 *3.75*

See #881-882, 951-952, 972-973, 1018-1019.

The Little Mermaid, Sculpture by Edvard Eriksen — A309

1989, Feb. 16 **Engr.**

865 A309 3.20k dark green .80 .20

Tourism industry, cent.

Danish Soccer Assoc., Cent. — A310

NATO Membership, 40th Anniv. — A311

1989, Mar. 16 **Litho.**

866 A310 3.20k multi .80 .20

1989, Mar. 16

867 A311 4.40k dk blue, gold & lt blue 1.00 .80

Nordic Cooperation Issue — A312

Folk costumes.

1989, Apr. 20 **Litho. & Engr.**

868 A312 3.20k Woman from Valby .80 .25
869 A312 4.40k Pork butcher 1.00 .80

European Parliament 3rd Elections A313

1989, May 11 **Litho.**

870 A313 3k blue & yellow .75 .75

Europa 1989 — A314

Children's toys.

1989, May 11 **Litho. & Engr.**

871 A314 3.20k Lego blocks *1.40* .20
872 A314 4.40k Wooden soldiers, by Kay Bojesen *1.90* .60

Agricultural Museum, Cent. A315

1989, June 15 **Engr.** ***Perf. 13***

873 A315 3.20k Tractor, 1889 .80 .20

Interparliamentary Union, Cent. — A316

1989, June 15 **Litho. & Engr.**

874 A316 3.40k Folketing Chamber layout 1.50 1.60

Danish Fishery and Marine Research Institute, Cent. A317

1989, Aug. 24 **Litho. & Engr.**

875 A317 3.20k multi .80 .25

Bernhard Severin Ingemann (1789-1862), Poet and Novelist — A318

1989, Aug. 24 **Engr.**

876 A318 7.70k dark green 1.75 1.00

A319

A320

Danish Film Office, 50th Anniv.: 3k, Scene from the short feature film *They Reached the Ferry,* 1948. 3.20k, Bodil Ipsen (d. 1964), actress. 4.40k, Carl Th. Dreyer (1889-1968), screenwriter and director.

1989, Sept. 28 **Litho.**

877 A319 3k multi .80 .80
878 A319 3.20k multi .80 .35
879 A319 4.40k multi 1.00 .60
Nos. 877-879 (3) 2.60 1.75

1989, Nov. 10 **Litho. & Engr.**

880 A320 3.20k multi .80 .30

Stamp Day, 50th anniv.

Art Type of 1988

Paintings: 4.40k, *Part of the Northern Gate of the Citadel Bridge,* c. 1837, by Christen Kobke (1810-1848). 10k, *A Little Girl, Elise Kobke, With a Cup in Front of Her,* c. 1850, by Constantin Hansen (1804-1880).

1989, Nov. 10 ***Perf. 12½x13***

881 A308 4.40k multi 1.25 *1.40*
882 A308 10k multi 3.00 *3.25*

Types of 1933-82 and:

A321

A321a Queen Margrethe II

Perf. 12½, 13 (A321a)

1990-98 **Engr.**

883 A32 25o bluish black .20 .20
a. Bklt. pane, 4 #691, 2 #883 1.75
884 A32 125o carmine lake .40 .20
885 A32 325o lt yel grn 1.00 1.00
886 A32 350o yellow green .80 .60
887 A212 3.50k dark red .80 .20
a. Bklt. pane, 2 each #691, 885, 887 5.00
888 A321 3.50k henna brown .80 .20
b. Bklt. pane, 4 each #883, #884, #888 ('91) 7.25
889 A212 3.75k dark green 1.00 1.00
890 A321 3.75k green 1.60 1.50
891 A321 3.75k red .80 .20
a. Bklt. pane, 4 each #884, #891 7.25
b. Booklet pane, 2 each #691, 883, 891 3.75
Complete booklet, #891b 3.75
892 A321a 3.75k red .80 .20
a. Booklet pane, 2 each #691, 883, 892 3.50
Complete booklet, #892a 3.50
b. Booklet pane, 2 #883, 4 #494, 2 #892 3.50
Complete booklet, #892b 3.50
893 A321 4k brown .90 .50
894 A321a 4k deep bl grn .90 .20
895 A321a 4.25k olive brown .90 .60
896 A212 4.50k brown violet 1.10 1.10
897 A321 4.50k violet 1.10 1.00
898 A321a 4.50k deep bl blk 1.00 .60
899 A212 4.75k dark blue 1.10 .25
900 A321 4.75k blue 1.10 .25
901 A321 4.75k violet 1.10 1.00
902 A321a 4.75k brown 1.00 .80
903 A321a 5k violet 1.10 .20
904 A321 5k blue 1.10 .30
905 A321 5.25k black 1.10 .80
906 A321a 5.25k deep blue 1.10 .20
907 A321 5.50k green 1.10 1.10
908 A321a 5.50k henna brown 1.10 1.00
909 A55 7.50k dark bl grn 1.60 1.40
Nos. 883-909 (27) 26.60 16.60

Queen Margrethe II's 50th birthday (No. 888).

Issued: #888, 4/5; #890, 897, 900, 1990; #888a, 2/14/91; #886, 891, 891a, 901, 904, 6/10/92; 5.50k, 1/13/94; 4k, 5.25k, 6/27/96; #892, 892a, 1/14/97; #894, 902, 903, 906, 8/28/97; #895, 898, 908, 909, 3/26/98; others, 1/11/90.

See Nos. 1120, 1127, 1135.

A322

A323

Design: Silver coffee pot designed by Axel Johannes Kroyer, Copenhagen, 1726.

1990, Feb. 15 **Engr.** ***Perf. 13***

911 A322 3.50k dark blue & blk .75 .20

Museum of Decorative Art, cent.

1990, Feb. 15

Steam engine, 200th anniv.: Steam engine built by Andrew Mitchell, 1790.

912 A323 8.25k dull red brown 1.75 1.00

Nyholm, 300th Anniv. A324

1990, Apr. 5 **Engr.**

913 A324 4.75k black 1.10 .70

Europa 1990 — A325

1990, Apr. 5 **Litho.**

914 A325 3.50k Royal Monogram, Haderslev P.O. 2.00 .20
915 A325 4.75k Odense P.O. 3.00 .75

A326

A327

Pieces from the Flora Danica Banquet Service produced for King Christian VII.

1990, May 3 **Litho.**

916 A326 3.50k Bell-shaped lid, dish 1.00 1.10
917 A326 3.50k Gravy boat, dish 1.00 1.10
918 A326 3.50k Ice pot, casserole, lid 1.00 1.10
919 A326 3.50k Serving dish 1.00 1.10
a. Strip of 4, #916-919 4.50

Flora Danica porcelain, 200th anniv.

1990, June 14

Endangered plant species.

920 A327 3.25k Marshmallow .80 .80
921 A327 3.50k Red helleborine 1.40 .25
922 A327 3.75k Purple orchis 1.00 1.00
923 A327 4.75k Lady's slipper 1.10 .60
Nos. 920-923 (4) 4.30 2.65

Village Churches, Jutland — A328

Perf. 13x12½, 12½x13

1990, Aug. 30 **Engr.**

924 A328 3.50k Gjellerup .80 .25
925 A328 4.75k Veng 1.10 .60
926 A328 8.25k Bredsten, vert. 2.00 1.50
Nos. 924-926 (3) 3.90 2.35

Fredericia, "The Town for Everybody" A329

Engr. & Embossed

1990, Oct. 5 ***Perf. 13***

927 A329 3.50k black & red .80 .40

Tordenskiold (Peter Wessel, 1690-1720), Admiral — A330

1990, Oct. 5 **Litho.** ***Perf. 13½x13***

928 A330 3.50k multicolored .80 .35

Prevent Bicycle Thefts — A331

Design: 3.50k, Stop drunk driving.

1990, Nov. 8 **Litho.** ***Perf. 13x12½***

930 A331 3.25k shown .80 .80
931 A331 3.50k Automobile, wine glass .80 .25

Locomotives — A332

1991, Mar. 14 **Engr.** ***Perf. 13***

932 A332 3.25k IC3 1990 1.00 1.00
933 A332 3.50k Class A 1882 .80 .50
934 A332 3.75k Class MY 1954 .95 .80
935 A332 4.75k Class P 1907 1.25 .75
Nos. 932-935 (4) 4.00 3.05

Europa — A333

Jutland Law, 750th Anniv. — A334

Satellite photographs showing temperatures of Danish: 3.50k, Waters. 4.75k, Land.

1991, May 2 **Litho.** ***Perf. 13***

936 A333 3.50k multicolored 1.25 .25
937 A333 4.75k multicolored 1.75 .75

1991, May 2

938 A334 8.25k multicolored 2.00 2.00

Danish Islands — A335

1991, June 6

939 A335 3.50k Fano 1.00 .20
940 A335 4.75k Christianso 1.10 .50

Decorative Art — A336

Keep Denmark Clean — A337

Designs: 3.25k, Earthenware bowl and jars by Christian Poulsen. 3.50k, Chair by Hans Wegner, vert. 4.75k, Silver cutlery by Kay Bojesen, vert. 8k, Lamp by Poul Henningsen.

1991, Aug. 22 **Litho.** ***Perf. 13***

941 A336 3.25k multicolored .80 .80
942 A336 3.50k multicolored .80 .25
943 A336 4.75k multicolored 1.10 .75
944 A336 8.25k multicolored 2.00 2.00
Nos. 941-944 (4) 4.70 3.80

1991, Sept. 19 **Engr.** ***Perf. 13***

Designs: 3.50k, Cleaning up after dog. 4.75k, Picking up litter.

945 A337 3.50k red .80 .20
946 A337 4.75k blue 1.10 .80

Posters from Danish Museum of Decorative Arts — A338

Posters for: 3.50k, Nordic Advertising Congress, by Arne Ungermann (1902-1981). 4.50k, Poster Exhibition at Copenhagen Zoo (baboon), by Valdemar Andersen (1875-1928). 4.75k, Danish Air Lines, by Ib Andersen (1907-1969). 12k, The Sinner, by Sven Brasch (1886-1970).

1991, Sept. 19 **Litho.**

947 A338 3.50k multicolored .80 .25
948 A338 4.50k multicolored 1.40 1.40
949 A338 4.75k multicolored 1.10 1.10
950 A338 12k multicolored 2.75 1.60
Nos. 947-950 (4) 6.05 4.35

Art Type of 1988

Designs: 4.75k, Lady at her Toilet by Harald Giersing (1881-1927), vert. 14k, Road through a Wood by Edvard Weie (1879-1943), vert.

Litho. & Engr.

1991, Nov. 7 ***Perf. 13x12½***

951 A308 4.75k multicolored 1.40 1.40
952 A308 14k multicolored 3.50 3.50

A339

A340

Treasures of Natl. Museum: 3.50k, Earthenware bowl, Skarpsalling. 4.50k, Bronze dancer, Grevensvaenge. 4.75k, Bottom plate of silver cauldron, Gundestrup. 8.25k, Flint knife, Hindsgavl.

1992, Feb. 13 **Engr.** ***Perf. 13***

953 A339 3.50k dk vio & brown .80 .25
954 A339 4.50k dk bl & dk ol green 1.50 1.50
955 A339 4.75k brown & black 1.10 1.00
956 A339 8.25k dk ol grn & vio brown 2.00 2.00
Nos. 953-956 (4) 5.40 4.75

1992, Mar. 12 ***Perf. 13½x13***

957 A340 3.50k rose carmine .80 .35

Danish Society of Chemical, Civil, Electrical, and Mechanical Engineers, cent.

Souvenir Sheet

Queen Margaret I (1353-1412) — A341

Litho. & Engr.

1992, Mar. 12 ***Perf. 12½***

958 A341 Sheet of 2 4.00 4.50
a. 3.50k Fresco 1.50 1.50
b. 4.75k Alabaster bust 2.00 2.00

Nordia '94, Scandinavian Philatelic Exhibition. No. 958 sold for 12k to benefit the exhibition.

Discovery of America, 500th Anniv. — A342

1992, May 7 **Engr.** ***Perf. 12½***

959 A342 3.50k Potato plant *1.60* .40
960 A342 4.75k Ear of corn *2.75* 1.25

Europa.

Protect the Environment — A343

Litho. & Engr.

1992, June 10 ***Perf. 13***

961 A343 3.75k Hare beside road .90 .20
962 A343 5k Fish, water pollution 1.10 .50
963 A343 8.75k Cut trees, vert. 2.00 1.60
Nos. 961-963 (3) 4.00 2.30

Queen Margrethe II and Prince Henrik, 25th Wedding Anniv. — A344

1992, June 10 **Litho.** ***Perf. 12½x13***

964 A344 3.75k multicolored 1.00 .80

A345

A346

1992, July 16 ***Perf. 13***

965 A345 3.75k multicolored 1.00 .25

Denmark, European soccer champions.

1992, Aug. 27 **Engr.** ***Perf. 13***

966 A346 3.75k blue .80 .35

Danish Pavilion, Expo '92, Seville.

A347

A348

1992, Oct. 8 **Litho. & Engr.** ***Perf. 13***

967 A347 3.75k blue & org .80 .60

Single European market.

Litho. & Engr.

1992, Oct. 8 ***Perf. 12½***

Cartoon characters: 3.50k, A Hug, by Ivar Gjorup. 3.75k, Love Letter, by Phillip Stein Jonsson. 4.75k, Domestic Triangle, by Nikoline Werdelin. 5k, Poet and His Little Wife, by Jorgen Mogensen.

968 A348 3.50k multicolored 1.00 .80

Engr.

969 A348 3.75k red & purple .80 .20
970 A348 4.75k blk & red brn 1.25 1.25
971 A348 5k blue & red brn 1.25 .50
Nos. 968-971 (4) 4.30 2.75

Art Type of 1988

5k, Landscape from Vejby, 1843, by John Thomas Lundbye. 10k, Motif from Halleby Brook, 1847, by Peter Christian Skovgaard.

Litho. & Engr.

1992, Nov. 12 ***Perf. 12½x13***

972 A308 5k multicolored 1.40 1.40
973 A308 10k multicolored 2.40 2.40

A349

A350

1992, Nov. 12 ***Perf. 13***

974 A349 3.75k Jacob's fight with angel .80 .20

Publication of new Danish bible.

Litho. & Engr.

1993, Feb. 4 ***Perf. 13***

Archaeological Treasures. Anthropomorphic gold foil figures found in: 3.75k, Lundeborg, horiz. 5k, Bornholm.

975 A350 3.75k multicolored .80 .20
976 A350 5k multicolored 1.25 .50

A351

A352

Butterflies.

1993, Mar. 11 **Litho.**

977 A351 3.75k Small tortoise-shell .80 .20
978 A351 5k Large blue 1.25 .50
979 A351 8.75k Marsh fritillary 2.40 1.60
980 A351 12k Red admiral 2.75 2.00
Nos. 977-980 (4) 7.20 4.30

1993, May 6 **Litho.** ***Perf. 12½***

Posters: 3.75k, Pierrot, by Thor Bogelund, 1947, horiz. 5k, Balloons, by Wilhelm Freddie, 1987.

981 A352 3.75k multicolored .80 .20
982 A352 5k multicolored 1.25 .60

Tivoli Gardens, 150th anniv.

A353

A354

Europa (Contemporary paintings by): 3.75k, Troels Worsel, horiz. 5k, Stig Brogger.

1993, May 6 ***Perf. 13***

983 A353 3.75k multicolored .80 .50
984 A353 5k multicolored 1.25 .60

1993, June 17 **Engr.** ***Perf. 13***

985 A354 5k dark blue green 1.25 .50

Danish-Russian relations, 500th anniv. See Russia No. 6154.

Training Ships
A355 A356

Perf. 13, 13½x13 (#987)

1993, June 17 **Litho. & Engr.**

986 A355 3.75k Danmark .80 .20
987 A356 4.75k Jens Krogh 1.25 1.25
988 A355 5k Georg Stage, horiz. 1.25 .80

Size: 39x28mm

Perf. 13x13½

989 A356 9.50k Marilyn Anne, horiz. 2.40 2.75
Nos. 986-989 (4) 5.70 5.00

Child's Drawing of Viking Ships — A357

Letter Writing Campaign — A358

1993, Aug. 19 **Litho.** ***Perf. 13***

990 A357 3.75k multicolored .80 .20
991 A358 5k lt & dk bl & blk 1.25 .60

Ethnic Jewelry — A359

1993, Sept. 16 **Litho.** ***Perf. 13***

992 A359 3.50k Falster .80 .60
993 A359 3.75k Amager .80 .20
994 A359 5k Laeso 1.25 .50
995 A359 8.75k Romo 2.00 1.60
Nos. 992-995 (4) 4.85 2.90

Cubist Paintings A360

5k, Assemblage, by Vilhelm Lundstrom, 1929. 15k, Composition, by Franciska Clausen, 1929.

Litho. & Engr.

1993, Nov. 11 ***Perf. 12½***

996 A360 5k multicolored 1.25 1.25
997 A360 15k multicolored 3.25 3.25

See Nos. 1080-1081.

Conservation — A361

1994, Jan. 27 **Litho.** ***Perf. 13***

998 A361 3.75k Save water .80 .20
999 A361 5k CO2 1.10 .35

Castles A362

Castles: 3.50k, Marselisborg, Aarhus. 3.75k, Amalienborg, Copenhagen. 5k, Fredensborg, North Zealand. 8.75k, Graasten, South Jutland.

Litho. & Engr.

1994, Mar. 17 ***Perf. 13x12½***

1000 A362 3.50k multicolored .80 .60
1001 A362 3.75k multicolored .80 .20
1002 A362 5k multicolored 1.25 .40
1003 A362 8.75k multicolored 2.00 2.00
a. Bklt. pane, #1000-1003 6.50 6.50

No. 1003a printed with 2 different labels. One shows a marching band, the other shows a ship.

Danmark Expedition, 1906-08 — A363

Europa: 3.75k, Expedition ship, Danmark, Alfred Wegener's weather balloon. 5k, Theodolite, Johan Peter Koch, cartographer.

1994, May 5 **Engr.** ***Perf. 13***

1004 A363 3.75k deep brn vio .90 .20
1005 A363 5k dp slate grn 1.25 .50

Trams — A364

Designs: 3.75k, Copenhagen tram (Engelhardt). 4.75k, Aarhus car. 5k, Odense tram, vert. 12k, Horse-drawn tram.

Litho. & Engr.

1994, June 9 ***Perf. 13***

1006 A364 3.75k multicolored .90 .20
1007 A364 4.75k multicolored 1.25 1.25
1008 A364 5k multicolored 1.25 .60

Size: 38x21mm

1009 A364 12k multicolored 2.75 2.40
Nos. 1006-1009 (4) 6.15 4.45

Children's Stamp Competition A365

ILO, 75th Anniv. A366

1994, Aug. 25 **Litho.** ***Perf. 12½***

1010 A365 3.75k multicolored .80 .20

1994, Aug. 25 ***Perf. 13***

1011 A366 5k multicolored 1.10 .30

A367

A368

Wild animals.

Litho. & Engr.

1994, Oct. 20 ***Perf. 12½***

1012 A367 3.75k House sparrows .80 .20
1013 A367 4.75k Badger 1.00 1.00
1014 A367 5k Squirrel, vert. 1.25 .50
1015 A367 9.50k Black grouse 2.50 2.00

Size: 36x26mm

Perf. 13

1016 A367 12k Grass snake 3.00 2.75
Nos. 1012-1016 (5) 8.55 6.45

1994, Nov. 10 **Litho.** ***Perf. 13***

1017 A368 3.75k multicolored 1.00 .20

Folk High Schools, 150th anniv.

Painting Type of 1988

Designs: 5k, Study of Italian Woman and Sleeping Child, by Wilhelm Marstrand. 15k, Interior from Amaliegade with the Artist's Brothers, by Wilhelm Bendz.

Litho. & Engr.

1994, Nov. 10 ***Perf. 12½x13***

1018 A308 5k multicolored 1.25 1.25
1019 A308 15k multicolored 3.50 3.25

Aarhus Cathedral School, 800th Anniv. — A369

Litho. & Engr.

1995, Jan. 26 ***Perf. 13***

1020 A369 3.75k multicolored .90 .20

UN, 50th Anniv. — A370

Litho. & Engr.

1995, Jan. 26 ***Perf. 13***

1021 A370 5k multicolored 1.25 .35
Complete booklet, 10 #1021 20.00

Danish Islands A371

1995, Mar. 16 **Engr.** ***Perf. 13***

1022 A371 3.75k Avernako 1.10 .20
Complete booklet, 10 #1022 11.00
1023 A371 4.75k Fejo 1.25 1.00
1024 A371 5k Fur 1.40 .60
1025 A371 9.50k Endelave 2.25 1.75
a. Booklet pane, #1022-1025 + 2 labels 7.00
Complete booklet, 2 #1025a 15.00
Nos. 1022-1025 (4) 6.00 3.55

No. 1025a printed with four different large labels. Labels with one pane are MF Faaborg II and MF Endelave. The other pane has MF Bukken-bruse and MF Fursund.

Liberation of Denmark, 50th Anniv. A372

Designs: 3.75k, Gen. Montgomery, Town Hall Square, vert. 5k, White busses returning from concentration camps. 8.75k, Airplane dropping supplies to resistance. 12k, Jews escape across the Sound to Sweden.

1995, May 4 **Litho.** ***Perf. 13***

1026 A372 3.75k multicolored .90 .20
Complete booklet, 10 #1026 11.00

1027 A372 5k multicolored 1.25 .60
1028 A372 8.75k multicolored 2.10 1.50
1029 A372 12k multicolored 3.00 2.75
Nos. 1026-1029 (4) 7.25 5.05

Europa (Nos. 1026-1027).

A373

A374

1995, June 8 Litho. *Perf. 13*
1030 A373 3.50k multicolored .90 .50

Danish Rhymed Chronicle, 500th anniv.

1995, June 8

3.75k, Roskilde Festival. 5k, Tonder Festival.

1031 A374 3.75k multi, horiz. .90 .20
Complete booklet, 10 #1031 14.00
1032 A374 5k multi 1.25 .40

No. 1031 is 28x21mm.

Paintings A375

Designs: 10k, "Sct. Hans Aften, 1955," by Jens Sondergaard. 15k, "Landskab-Gudhjem, 1939," by Niels Lergaard.

Litho. & Engr.

1995, Aug. 24 *Perf. 13x12½*
1033 A375 10k multicolored 2.50 2.50
1034 A375 15k multicolored 3.50 3.50

Tycho Brahe (1546-1601), Astronomer A376

3.75k, Uranienborg Observatory. 5.50k, Sextant.

Litho. & Engr.

1995, Oct. 27 *Perf. 13*
1035 A376 3.75k multicolored .90 .20
1036 A376 5.50k multicolored 1.40 1.10

See Sweden Nos. 2149-2150.

Toys A377

Designs: 3.75k, Tekno cars. 5k, Dolls, teddy bear. 8.75k, Model trains. 12k, Glud & Marstrand tin horse-drawn carriage & fire pumper.

1995, Nov. 9 *Perf. 13x12½*
1037 A377 3.75k multicolored .90 .20
Complete booklet, 10 #1037 10.00
1038 A377 5k multicolored 1.25 .65
1039 A377 8.75k multicolored 2.10 1.50
1040 A377 12k multicolored 3.00 3.00
Nos. 1037-1040 (4) 7.25 5.35

A378

A379

Cartoonlike views of Copenhagen: 3.75k, Round Tower as music box. 5k, Christiansborg Castle. 8.75k, Marble Church as top of balloon. 12k, The Little Mermaid statue on stage.

1996, Jan. 25 Litho. *Perf. 13*
1041 A378 3.75k multicolored .90 .20
Complete booklet, 10 #1041 11.00
1042 A378 5k multicolored 1.25 .60
1043 A378 8.75k multicolored 2.25 1.50
1044 A378 12k multicolored 3.00 2.50
Nos. 1041-1044 (4) 7.40 4.80

Copenhagen, 1996 cultural capital of Europe.

1996, Mar. 21 Litho. *Perf. 13*
1045 A379 3.75k Sports for disabled .90 .20
Complete booklet, 10 #1045 11.00
1046 A379 4.75k Swimming 1.10 .90
1047 A379 5k Sailing 1.25 .40
1048 A379 9.50k Cycling 2.25 2.25
a. Bklt. pane of 4, #1045-1048 + 2 labels 6.50
Complete booklet, 2 #1048a 13.00

No. 1048a printed with two different large labels. One shows hands and soccer ball, second shows tennis racket and tennis balls.

Danish Federation for Sports for the Disabled (No. 1045). Modern Olympic Games, cent., Sports Confederation of Denmark, cent., 1996 Summer Olympics, Atlanta (Nos. 1046-1048).

A380

A381

1996, May 9 Litho. *Perf. 13*
1049 A380 3.75k multicolored .90 .20

Danish Employers' Confederation, cent.

1996, May 9

Famous Danish Women (Europa): 3.75k, Karen Blixen (1885-1962), writer. 5k, Asta Nielsen (1881-1972), silent screen actress.

1050 A381 3.75k lt brn & dk brn .90 .20
1051 A381 5k gray & dk blue 1.25 .40
Complete booklet, 10 #1051 16.00

A382

A383

Wooden Dinghies: 3.50k, Roskilde Fjord sail boat. 3.75k, Limfjorden skiff. 12.25k, Two-masted smack, South Funen Archipelago.

Perf. 13, 12½ (#1053)

1996, June 13 Engr.
1052 A382 3.50k multicolored .90 .75
1053 A382 3.75k multicolored .90 .20
Complete booklet, 10 #1053 11.00
1054 A382 12.25k multicolored 3.00 2.75
Nos. 1052-1054 (3) 4.80 3.70

No. 1053 is 20x39mm.

Litho. & Engr.

1996, Sept. 12 *Perf. 13x12½*

Lighthouses.

1055 A383 3.75k Fornaes .90 .20
Complete booklet, 10 #1055 11.00
1056 A383 5k Blavandshuk 1.25 .30
a. Bklt. pane, 8 #1055, 2 #1056 12.50
Complete booklet, #1056a 15.00
1057 A383 5.25k Bovbjerg 1.40 .90
1058 A383 8.75k Mon 2.25 1.25
Nos. 1055-1058 (4) 5.80 2.65

Art Works of Thorvald Bindesboll (1846-1908) — A384

Litho. & Engr.

1996, Oct. 10 *Perf. 13*
1059 A384 3.75k Pitcher .90 .20
Complete booklet, 10 #1059 11.00

Litho.

1060 A384 4k Portfolio cover 1.00 .70

Paintings A385

Designs: 10k, "At Lunch," by P.S. Kroyer, 1893. 15k, "The Girl with Sunflowers," by Michael Ancher, 1889.

Litho. & Engr.

1996, Nov. 7 *Perf. 13x12½*
1061 A385 10k multicolored 3.50 1.75
1062 A385 15k multicolored 5.25 2.60

A386

A387

Queen Margrethe II: 3.50k, With Prince Henrik. 3.75k, With Crown Prince Frederik. 4k, Delivering New Year speech. 5.25k, Waving to crowd.

1997, Jan. 14 Litho. *Perf. 13*
1063 A386 3.50k multicolored .70 .40
1064 A386 3.75k multicolored .75 .20
Complete booklet, 10 #1064 11.00
1065 A386 4k multicolored .85 .40
1066 A386 5.25k multicolored 1.75 .85
a. Sheet of 4, #1063-1066 + 2 labels 4.50 4.50
Nos. 1063-1066 (4) 4.05 1.85

Queen Margrethe II, 25th anniv. of coronation.

1997, Mar. 13 Engr. *Perf. 13*

Open Air Museum, Copenhagen, Cent.: 3.50k, Kalstrup post mill. 3.75k, Ellested water mill. 5k, Fjellerup manor barn. 8.75k, Romo farm.

1067 A387 3.50k multicolored .85 .20
1068 A387 3.75k multicolored .85 .20
Complete booklet, 10 #1068 9.00
1069 A387 5k multicolored 1.25 .75
Complete booklet, 10 #1069 12.50
1070 A387 8.75k multicolored 2.10 1.75
a. Booklet pane, #1067-1070 + label 5.00
Complete booklet, 2 #1070a 10.00
Nos. 1067-1070 (4) 5.05 2.90

No. 1070a printed with two different large labels. One shows a view of Ellested water mill, the other shows a farm in Ejersted.

Great Belt Railway Link — A388

A389

1997, May 15 Litho. *Perf. 13*
1071 A388 3.75k East Tunnel 1.10 .20
Complete booklet, 10 #1071 11.50
1072 A388 4.75k West Bridge 1.50 .75

1997, June 12 Litho. *Perf. 13*

Kalmar Union, 600th Anniv.: No. 1073, Margrete I and Eric of Pomerania. No. 1074, The Three Graces symbolizing Denmark, Norway and Sweden.

1073 A389 4k multicolored 1.40 .50
1074 A389 4k multicolored 1.40 .50
a. Pair, #1073-1074 3.00 1.20

No. 1074a is a continuous design.

Copenhagen-Roskilde Railway, 150th Anniv. — A390

Designs: 3.75k, Two modern trains under Carlsberg Bridge. 8.75k, Early steam train going under Carlsberg Bridge.

Litho. & Engr.

1997, June 12 *Perf. 13*
1075 A390 3.75k multicolored 1.25 .20
Complete booklet, 10 #1075 12.50
1076 A390 8.75k multicolored 3.00 1.25

End of Railway Mail Service A391

1997, June 12 Litho.
1077 A391 5k multicolored 1.75 .60

Stories and Legends A392

Europa: 3.75k, Large cat on top of treasure chest, from "The Tinder Box." 5.25k, Butterfly, pond, frog, from "Thumbelina."

1997, Aug. 28 Engr. *Perf. 13*
1078 A392 3.75k multicolored 1.25 .20
1079 A392 5.25k multicolored 1.75 1.00

Painting Type of 1993

Designs: 9.75k, "Dust Dancing in the Sun," by Vilhelm Hammershoi (1864-1916). 13k, "Woman Mountaineer," by J.F. Willumsen (1863-1958).

Litho. & Engr.

1997, Sept. 18 *Perf. 13x12½*
1080 A360 9.75k multicolored 3.25 1.40
1081 A360 13k multicolored 4.50 1.75

A393

Danish Design: 3.75k, Faaborg chair, vert. 4k, Margrethe bowl, vert. 5k, The Ant (chair). 12.25k, Georg Jensen silver bowl, vert.

1997, Nov. 6 Litho. *Perf. 13*

1082 A393 3.75k multicolored 1.25 .20
Complete booklet, 10 #1082 12.50
1083 A393 4k multicolored 1.40 .60
1084 A393 5k multicolored 1.75 .35
1085 A393 12.25k multicolored 4.25 2.10
Nos. 1082-1085 (4) 8.65 3.25

A394

A395

Danish Confederation of Trade Unions, Cent.: 3.50k, General Workers Union in Denmark (SiD). 3.75k, Danish Confederation of Trade Unions (LO). 4.75k, Danish Nurse's Organization. 5k, Union of Commercial and Clerical Employees in Denmark (HK).

1998, Jan. 22 Litho. *Perf. 13*

1086 A394 3.50k multicolored 1.25 .65
1087 A394 3.75k multicolored 1.25 .20
Complete booklet, 10 #1087 12.50
1088 A394 4.75k multicolored 1.60 .90
1089 A394 5k multicolored 1.75 .35
Complete booklet, 10 #1089 17.50
Nos. 1086-1089 (4) 5.85 2.10

Litho. & Engr.

1998, Mar. 26 *Perf. 13*

1090 A395 3.75k multicolored 1.25 .55
Complete booklet, 10 #1090 12.50

City of Roskilde, 1000th anniv.

A396

A397

1998, Mar. 26 Litho. *Perf. 13*

1091 A396 5k Ladybug 1.75 .20

Reduce poison.

1998, May 28 Litho. *Perf. 13*

New Post & Tele Museum, Copenhagen: 3.75k, Postman, 1922. 4.50k, Morse code operator, c. 1910. 5.50k, Telephone operator, 1910. 8.75k, Modern postman.

1092 A397 3.75k multicolored 1.25 .20
Complete booklet, 10 #1092 12.50
a. Booklet pane, 2 each #1087, 1089, 3 ea. 1090, 1092 13.50
Complete booklet, #1092a 13.50
1093 A397 4.50k multicolored 1.50 .75
1094 A397 5.50k multicolored 1.90 .90
1095 A397 8.75k multicolored 3.00 1.25
a. Booklet pane, #1092-1095 7.50
Complete booklet, 2 #1095a 15.00
Nos. 1092-1095 (4) 7.65 3.10

No. 1095a is printed with two backgrounds. One shows part of King Christian IV's "Order Concerning Postmen," 1624. The other shows part of Copenhagen c. 1923. Complete booklets contain panes with each background.

Bridges over Great Belt A398

1998, May 28 Engr. *Perf. 13*

1096 A398 5k West Bridge (shown) 1.75 .75
1097 A398 5k East Bridge (suspension) 1.75 .75
a. Pair, #1096-1097 + label 3.50 1.50

Nordic Stamps — A399

Shipping: No. 1098, Signal flags, harbor master with binoculars. No. 1099, Radar image of entrance to Copenhagen harbor, sextant.

1998, May 28 Litho. *Perf. 13*

1098 A399 6.50k multicolored 2.25 .95
1099 A399 6.50k multicolored 2.25 .95
a. Pair, #1098-1099 4.50 1.90
b. Souvenir sheet, #1099a 4.50 1.90

National Festivals — A400

Europa: 3.75k, Horse at Danish agricultural show. 4.50k, Theater, tents at Arhus Festival Week, Arhus.

Litho. & Engr.

1998, Sept. 3 *Perf. 13*

1100 A400 3.75k multicolored 1.25 .60
Complete booklet, 10 #1100 12.50
1101 A400 4.50k multicolored 1.50 .70

Contemporary Art — A401

Paintings: 3.75k, Danish Autumn, by Per Kirkeby. 5k, Alpha, by Mogens Andersen, vert. 8.75k, Imagery, by Ejler Bille, vert. 19k, Celestial Horse, by Carl-Henning Pedersen.

Perf. 12½x13, 13x12½

1998, Oct. 15 Litho. & Engr.

1102 A401 3.75k multicolored 1.25 .20

Litho.

1103 A401 5k multicolored 1.75 .60
1104 A401 8.75k multicolored 3.00 .60
1105 A401 19k multicolored 6.50 1.50
Nos. 1102-1105 (4) 12.50 2.90

See Nos. 1160-1161, 1190-1191.

A402

Fossil, name of Danish geologist: 3.75k, Ammonite, Ole Worm (1588-1654). 4.50k, Shark's teeth, Niels Stensen (1638-86). 5.50k, Sea Urchin, Soren Abildgaard (1718-91). 15k, Slit-shell snail, Erich Pontoppidan (1698-1764).

1998, Nov. 5 Engr. *Perf. 13*

1106 A402 3.75k multicolored 1.25 .20
Complete booklet, 10 #1106 12.50
1107 A402 4.50k multicolored 1.50 .60
1108 A402 5.50k multicolored 1.90 .60
1109 A402 15k multicolored 5.25 1.50
a. Souvenir sheet, #1106-1109 10.00 4.75

Wavy Lines and Queen Types of 1933, 1997 and:

Queen Margrethe II — A402a

1999-2000 Engr. *Perf. 12¾*

1111 A32 150o purple .50 .20
1114 A32 375o green 1.25 .60
1115 A32 400o green 1.10 .55
1116 A321a 4k red 1.40 .20
a. Booklet pane, 4 #883, 2 #494, 2 #1120 3.75
Complete booklet, #1120a 3.75
1117 A402a 4k red 1.40 .20
a. Booklet pane, 2 each #494, 1121, 4 #883 2.25
b. Booklet pane, 4 #883, 2 #494, 2 #1121 2.25
Booklet, #1121b 2.25
c. Sheet of 8 + label 11.50
1118 A32 425o green 1.40 .25
1119 A402a 4.25k blue 1.50 .20
1120 A402a 4.25k red 1.25 .60
b. Booklet pane, 6 #883, 2 #1122A 3.00
c. Sheet of 8 + central label 10.00 —
1121 A402a 4.50k orange 1.50 .20
a. Vert. strip of 10 + 10 etiquettes 11.50
1122 A402a 4.50k red 1.50 .25
a. Booklet pane, 2 #494, 2 #1122 3.50 —
Complete booklet, #1122a 3.50
1123 A402a 4.75k sepia 1.60 .55
1124 A402a 5k dk green 1.75 .20
a. Sheet of 8 + 8 etiquettes 10.00 —
1125 A402a 5.25k ultra 1.75 .30
1126 A402a 5.50k violet 1.90 .30
a. Sheet of 8 + label 12.00
b. Sheet of 8 + 8 etiquettes 13.00 13.00
1127 A321a 5.75k blue 2.00 .50
1128 A402a 5.75k emerald 2.00 .40
1129 A402a 6k bister 2.00 .40
1129A A402a 6.25k green 1.75 .90
1130 A402a 6.50k slate grn 2.25 .75
a. Sheet of 8 + 8 etiquettes 15.00 15.00
b. Sheet of 8 + central label 14.00 —
1135 A321a 6.75k slate green 2.25 .50
1136 A402a 6.75k henna brn 2.25 .85
1137 A402a 7k rose lilac 2.40 .40
1139 A402a 8.50k bright blue 2.40 1.25
1140 A55 10.50k dk bl gray 3.50 1.25
1141 A55 11.50k dk bl gray 3.25 1.60
1141A A55 12.50k gray 4.25 1.50
1141B A55 13k orange 4.50 1.60
1142 A55 15k blue 5.00 1.90
Nos. 1111-1142 (28) 59.60 18.40

Issued: 375o, #1120, 1135, 1/13/99; #1127, 1/3/00; #1121, 1121a, 4.25k, 4.50k, 5k, 5.25k, 5.50k, #1128, 1136, 4/12/00; No. 1121b, 6k, 7k, 5/9/01; Nos. 1121c, 1123a, 1126a, 4/17/01; 150o, 4.75k, 6.50k, 10.50k, 1/2/02. 400o, No. 1122A, 6.25k, 8.50k, 11.50k, 1/2/03. No. 1122Ab, 3/12. Nos. 1126b, 1130a, 3/12/03. Nos. 1122Ab, 1129Ab, 1/2/03; No. 1124a, 4/2/02; 425o, No. 1122, 12.50k, 13k, 15k, 1/2/04.

This is an expanding set. Numbers may change.

A403

1999, Jan. 13 Litho. *Perf. 13*

1143 A403 4k Oersted Satellite 1.40 .50

Deciduous Trees A404

4k, Fagus sylvatica. 5k, Fraxinus excelsior, vert. 5.25k, Tilia cordata, vert. 9.25k, Quercus robur.

1999, Jan. 13 Litho. & Engr.

1144 A404 4k multicolored 1.40 .20
Complete booklet, 10 #1144 14.00
1145 A404 5k multicolored 1.75 .50
1146 A404 5.25k multicolored 1.75 .50
1147 A404 9.25k multicolored 3.25 1.10
Nos. 1144-1147 (4) 8.15 2.30

50th Anniversaries — A405

Litho. & Engr.

1999, Feb. 24 *Perf. 13*

1148 A405 3.75k Home Guard 1.25 .20
1149 A405 4.25k NATO 1.50 .50

A406

A407

Harbingers of spring.

1999, Feb. 24 Litho.

1150 A406 4k Lapwing in flight 1.40 .20
Complete booklet, 10 #1150 14.00
1151 A406 5.25k Geese 1.75 .80
a. Souvenir sheet, #1150-1151 4.50 1.50

Litho. & Engr.

1999, Apr. 28 *Perf. 13*

Nature Reserves.

1152 A407 4.50k Vejlerne 1.50 .40
1153 A407 5.50k Langli 1.90 .60

Europa.

Council of Europe, 50th Anniv. A408

1999, Apr. 28 Engr.

1154 A408 9.75k blue 3.25 1.10

Danish Constitution, 150th Anniv. — A409

1999, June 2 Litho. *Perf. 13*

1155 A409 4k red & black 1.40 .20

Danish Revue, 150th Anniv. A410

Performers: 4k, Kjeld Petersen and Dirch Passer, comedians. 4.50k, Osvald Helmuth, singer. 5.25k, Preben Kaas and Jorgen Ryg, comedians, singers. 6.75k, Liva Weel, singer.

1999, June 2 Engr. *Perf. 13*

1156 A410 4k deep red 1.40 .20
Complete booklet, 10 #1156 14.00
1157 A410 4.50k slate 1.50 .40
1158 A410 5.25k deep blue 1.75 .75
Complete booklet, 10 #1158 17.50
1159 A410 6.75k deep claret 2.25 .95
a. Bklt. pane, #1156-1159 + 2 labels 7.00
Complete booklet, 2 #1159a 14.00
Nos. 1156-1159 (4) 6.90 2.30

No. 1159a printed with two different pairs of labels. One version has showgirl label at left, the second version has showgirl label at right. Complete booklets contain one of each pane.

Contemporary Paintings Type

9.25k, Fire Farver, by Thomas Kluge. 16k, Dreng, by Lise Malinovsky.

1999, Aug. 25 Litho. *Perf. 12¾*
1160 A401 9.25k multi, vert. 3.25 1.40
1161 A401 16k multi, vert. 5.50 2.25

Opening of New Extension of the Royal Library, "The Black Diamond" A411

1999, Aug. 25 Engr. *Perf. 13¾*
1162 A411 8.75k black 3.00 1.25

Migratory Birds — A412

Litho. & Engr.

1999, Sept. 29 *Perf. 12¾*
1163 A412 4k Swallows 1.40 .20
Complete booklet, 10 #1163 14.00
1164 A412 5.25k Gray-lag geese 1.75 .70
a. Souvenir sheet, #1163-1164 3.25 1.25
1165 A412 5.50k Common eider 1.90 .75
1166 A412 12.25k Arctic tern 4.00 1.75
a. Souvenir sheet, #1165-1166 6.00 2.50
Nos. 1163-1166 (4) 9.05 3.40

Stamps from Nos. 1164a and 1166a lack white border found on Nos. 1163-1166.

New Year 2000 — A413

1999, Nov. 10 Litho. *Perf. 13¼*
1167 A413 4k Hearts 1.40 .20
1168 A413 4k Wavy lines 1.40 .20
a. Bklt. pane, 5 ea #1167-1168 14.00
Complete booklet, #1168a 14.00

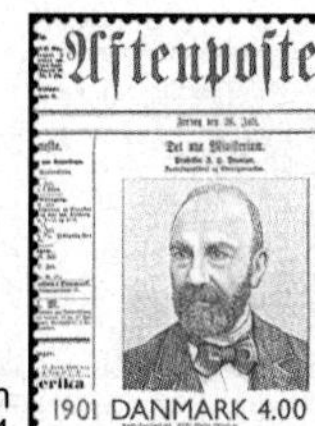

The 20th Century — A414

4k, Prof. J.H. Deuntzer on front page of newspaper, 1901. 4.50k, Newspaper illustration, 1903. 5.25k, Asta Nielsen and Poul Reumert in the film "The Abyss," 1910. 5.75k, Advertising sticker showing woman on telephone, 1914.

See sheet of 16, #1184a.

2000, Jan. 12 Litho. & Engr.
1169 A414 4k buff & blk 1.40 .20
Complete booklet, 10 #1169 14.00
1170 A414 4.50k multicolored 1.50 .40
1171 A414 5.25k multicolored 1.75 .75
Complete booklet, 10 #1171 17.50
1172 A414 5.75k multicolored 2.00 .80
Nos. 1169-1172 (4) 6.65 2.15

2000, May 9

4k, Allegory of women suffrage on front page of newspaper, 1915. 5k, Newspaper caricature of the Kanslergade Agreement, 1933. 5.50k, Film "Long and Short," 1927. 6.75k, Front page of Radio Weekly Review, 1925.

1173 A414 4k multi 1.40 .45
Booklet, 10 #1173 14.00
1174 A414 5k multi 1.75 .55
1175 A414 5.50k multi 1.90 .65
1176 A414 6.75k multi 2.25 .75
Nos. 1173-1176 (4) 7.30 2.40

2000, Aug. 23

4k, Liberation of Denmark on front page of newspaper, 1945. 5.75k, Newspaper caricature of new constitution, 1953. 6.75k, Poster for film "Café Paradise," 1950. 12.25k, Advertisement for Arena television, 1957.

1177 A414 4k multi 1.40 .45
Booklet, 10 #1177 14.00
1178 A414 5.75k multi 2.00 .70
1179 A414 6.75k multi 2.25 .75
1180 A414 12.25k multi 4.25 1.40
Nos. 1177-1180 (4) 9.90 3.30

2000, Nov. 8

4k, Entry of Denmark into European Community on front page of newspaper, 1972. 4.50k, Newspaper caricature of youth revolt, 1969. 5.25k, Poster for film "The Olsen Gang," 1968. 5.50k, Denmark Post website on Internet, 1999.

1181 A414 4k multi 1.40 .45
Booklet, 10 #1181 14.00
1182 A414 4.50k multi 1.50 .50
1183 A414 5.25k multi 1.75 .60
Booklet, 10 #1183 17.50
a. Booklet pane, #1171, 1175, 1179, 1183 + label 7.50
Booklet, 2 #1183a 15.00
1184 A414 5.50k multi 1.90 .65
a. Sheet of 16, #1169-1184 30.00 11.50
Nos. 1181-1184 (4) 6.55 2.20

No. 1183a comes with two different labels. Booklet contains one of each.

60th Birthday of Queen Margrethe II — A415

2000, Apr. 12 Litho. *Perf. 12¾*
1185 A415 4k blk & car 1.40 .50
Complete booklet, 10 #1185 14.00
1186 A415 5.25k blk & blue 1.75 .70
a. Souvenir sheet, #1185-1186 3.25 1.25

Oresund Bridge, Sweden-Denmark — A416

Illustration reduced.

Litho. & Engr.

2000, May 9 *Perf. 12¾*
1187 A416 4.50k shown 1.50 .50

Litho.

1188 A416 4.50k Map 1.50 .50
a. Pair, #1187-1188 3.00 1.00

See Sweden Nos. 2391-2393.

Europa, 2000
Common Design Type

2000, May 9 Litho. *Perf. 13*
1189 CD17 9.75k multi 3.25 1.10

Contemporary Art Type of 1998

Designs: 4k, Pegasus, by Kurt Trampedach. 5.25k, Landscape, by Nina Sten-Knudsen.

2000, Sept. 27 *Perf. 12¾*
1190 A401 4k multi 1.40 .45
1191 A401 5.25k multi 1.75 .65

Royal Danish Air Force, 50th Anniv. A417

2000, Sept. 27 Engr.
1192 A417 9.75k black & red 3.25 1.10
a. Souvenir sheet of 1 3.25 1.10

Botanical Gardens, Copenhagen — A418

Litho. & Engr.

2001, Jan. 24 *Perf. 12¾*
1193 A418 4k Palm House 1.40 .50
Booklet, 10 #1193 14.00

Size: 28x21mm

1194 A418 6k Lake 2.00 .75
1195 A418 12.25k Water lilies 4.25 1.60
Nos. 1193-1195 (3) 7.65 2.85

"Use the Language" A419

2001, Mar. 28 Litho. *Perf. 13*
1196 A419 4k "A," text 1.40 .45
Booklet, 10 #1196 14.00
1197 A419 7k "Z," text 2.40 .80

Danish Postage Stamps, 150th Anniv. — A420

Portion of #2 and: 4k, Engraver Martinus William Ferslew. 5.50k, Printer Andreas Thiele. 6k, Head Copenhagen postmaster Frantz Christopher von Jessen. 10.25k, Postmaster General Magrius Otto Spohus Count Danneskjold-Samsoe.

Litho. & Engr.

2001, Apr. 1 *Perf. 13¼x13*
1198 A420 4k multi 1.40 .45
1199 A420 5.50k multi 1.90 .65
Booklet, 10 #1199 19.00
1200 A420 6k multi 2.00 .70
1201 A420 10.25k multi 3.50 1.25
a. Booklet pane, #1198-1201 + label 8.75
Booklet, 2 #1201a 17.50
Nos. 1198-1201 (4) 8.80 3.05

No. 1201a printed with two different labels. One version has proof of stamp design, sketch of proposed design and Ferslew's letter to Danneskjold-Samsoe, and other shows two essays and letter from M. T. C. Bartholdy.

Europa — A421

Designs: 4.50k, Hands in water. 9.75k, Woman's head, water.

2001, May 9 Litho. *Perf. 13¼x13*
1202 A421 4.50k multi 1.50 .50
a. Booklet pane of 5 + 5 etiquettes 7.50
Booklet, 2 #1202a 15.00
1203 A421 9.75k multi 3.25 1.10

Contemporary Paintings Type of 1998

Designs: 18k, Missus, by Jorn Larsen, horiz. 22k, Postbillede, by Henning Damgaard-Sorensen.

Perf. 13x12½, 12½x13
2001, Aug. 22 Litho.
1204 A401 18k multi 6.25 2.25
1205 A401 22k multi 7.50 2.75

Youth Culture A422

Designs: 4k, Skateboarding. 5.50k, Kissing. 6k, Creating music. 10.25k, Tongue piercing.

2001, Aug. 22 *Perf. 13*
1206 A422 4k multi 1.40 .50
Booklet, 10 #1206 14.00
1207 A422 5.50k multi 1.90 .70
Booklet, 10 #1207 19.00
1208 A422 6k multi 2.00 .75
1209 A422 10.25k multi 3.50 1.25
a. Souvenir sheet, #1206-1209 9.00 3.25
Nos. 1206-1209 (4) 8.80 3.20

Hafnia 01 Philatelic Exhibition, Copenhagen A423

Monarch and stamps: 4k, Queen Margrethe II, #757, 1000. 4.50k, King Frederik IX, #775, 1003. 5.50k, King Christian X, #1001, B10. 7k, King Christian IX, #1002, 66.

Litho. & Engr.

2001, Oct. 16 *Perf. 13x13¼*
1210 A423 4k multi 1.40 .50
1211 A423 4.50k multi 1.50 .55
1212 A423 5.50k multi 1.90 .70
1213 A423 7k multi 2.40 .85
a. Souvenir sheet, #1210-1213 7.25 2.60
b. Strip, #1210-1213 + central label 7.25 2.60
Nos. 1210-1213 (4) 7.20 2.60

Island Ferries A424

Designs: 3.75k, Bukken-Bruse. 4k, Ouro. 4.25k, Hjarno. 6k, Barsofaergen.

2001, Nov. 7 *Perf. 12¾*
1214 A424 3.75k multi 1.25 .45
1215 A424 4k multi 1.40 .50
Booklet, 10 #1215 14.00
1216 A424 4.25k multi 1.50 .50
1217 A424 6k multi 2.00 .75
Nos. 1214-1217 (4) 6.15 2.20

Comics and Cartoons — A425

Designs: 4k, Rasmus Klump, by Vilhelm Hansen. 5.50k, Valhalla, by Peter Madsen. 6.50k, Jungledyret Hugo, by Flemming Quist Moller. 10.50k, Cirkeline, by Hanne Hastrup.

2002, Jan. 16 Litho. *Perf. 13¼x13*
1218 A425 4k multi 1.40 .45
Booklet, 10 #1218 14.00
a. Sheet of 8 + label 11.50 3.75
1219 A425 5.50k multi 1.90 .65
Booklet, 10 #1219 19.00
a. Sheet of 8 + label 16.00 5.25
1220 A425 6.50k multi 2.25 .75
1221 A425 10.50k multi 3.50 1.25
a. Souvenir sheet, #1218-1221 9.00 3.25
Nos. 1218-1221 (4) 9.05 3.10

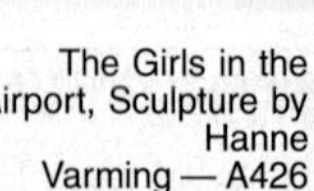

The Girls in the Airport, Sculpture by Hanne Varming — A426

Designs: 4k, Rear view. 5k, Front view.

Photo. & Engr.

2002, Mar. 13 ***Perf. 12¾***

1222 A426 4k multi, *greenish* 1.40 .45
Booklet, 10 #1222 14.00
1223 A426 5k multi, *greenish* 1.75 .60

Europa — A427

Winning drawings in children's stamp design contest: 4k, Clown, by Luna Ostergard. 5k, Clown, by Camille Wagner Larsen.

2002, May 15 **Litho.** ***Perf. 13***

1224 A427 4k multi 1.40 .50
Booklet, 10 #1224 14.00
1225 A427 5k multi 1.75 .60
a. Booklet pane of 5 + 5 etiquettes 8.75 —
Booklet, 2 #1225a 17.50

Landscapes A428

2002, May 15 **Engr.**

1226 A428 4k Bornholm 1.40 .50
1227 A428 6k West Jutland 2.00 .75
1228 A428 6.50k Langeland 2.25 .80
1229 A428 12.50k Thy 4.25 1.50
Nos. 1226-1229 (4) 9.90 3.55

Historic Postal Vehicles A429

Designs: 4k, 1953 Nimbus motorcycle. 5.50k, 1962 Bedford van. 10k, 1984 Renault 4 van. 19k, 1998 Volvo FH12 tractor trailer.

Litho. & Engr.

2002, Aug. 21 ***Perf. 13x13¼***

1230 A429 4k multi 1.40 .50
Booklet, 10 #1230 14.00
a. Sheet of 8 + central label 8.00 —
1231 A429 5.50k multi 1.90 .70
Booklet, 10 #1231 19.00
1232 A429 10k multi 3.50 1.25
1233 A429 19k multi 6.25 2.50
a. Booklet pane of 4, #1230-1233 13.00
Booklet, 2 #1233a 26.00
Nos. 1230-1233 (4) 13.05 4.95

No. 1233a is printed with two different labels. One shows a 1908 Berliet van and the other a 2002 Peugeot Partner. Both are included in the booklet.

Opening of Copenhagen Metro — A430

2002, Sept. 25 **Engr.** ***Perf. 12¾***

1234 A430 5.50k multi, *tan* 1.90 .75

Contemporary Paintngs Type of 1998

Designs: 5k, Children's Corner, by Jens Birkemose, vert. 6.50k, Maleren og Modellen, by Frans Kannik, vert.

2002, Sept. 25 ***Perf. 13x12½***

1235 A401 5k red & blue 1.75 .70
1236 A401 6.50k multi 2.25 .85

Intl. Council for the Exploration of the Sea, Cent. — A431

Atlantic cod and: 4k, Exploration ship Dana. 10.50k, Hirtshals lighthouse.

Litho. & Engr.

2002, Sept. 25 ***Perf. 13¼x13***

1237 A431 4k multi 1.40 .55
1238 A431 10.50k multi 3.50 1.40
a. Souvenir sheet, #1237-1238 5.00 2.00

See Faroe Islands No. 426, Greenland Nos. 401-402.

Danish House Architecture A432

Designs: 4k, Dianas Have, Horsholm, by Vandkusten Design Studio, 1992. 4.25k, Blangstedgard, Odense, by Poul Ingemann, 1988. 5.50k, Dansk Folkeferie, Karrebaeksminde, by Stephan Kappel, 1979. 6.50k, Fredensborg Terraces, Fredensborg, by Jorn Utzon, 1963. 9k, Soholm, Klampenborg, by Arne Jacobsen, 1950.

Litho. & Engr.

2002, Nov. 8 ***Perf. 12¾***

1239 A432 4k multi 1.40 .55
Booklet, 10 #1239 14.00
1240 A432 4.25k multi 1.50 .60
1241 A432 5.50k multi 1.90 .75
1242 A432 6.50k multi 2.25 .90
1243 A432 9k multi 3.00 1.25
Nos. 1239-1243 (5) 10.05 4.05

Youth Sports — A433

2003, Jan. 15 **Litho.** ***Perf. 12¾***

1244 A433 4.25k Soccer 1.25 .60
Booklet, 10 #1244 12.50
a. Sheet of 8 + central label 10.00 —
1245 A433 5.50k Swimming 1.60 .80
Booklet, 10 #1245 16.00
1246 A433 8.50k Gymnastics 2.50 1.25
1247 A433 11.50k Handball 3.50 1.75
Nos. 1244-1247 (4) 8.85 4.40

Danish Literary Greenland Expedition, Cent. — A434

Designs: 4.25k, Expedition members Harald Moltke, Knud Rasmussen, Jorgen Bronlund, Ludvig Mylius-Erichsen and Gabriel Olsen. 7k, Campsite.

2003, Mar. 12 **Engr.** ***Perf. 12¾***

1248 A434 4.25k blue gray 1.25 .60

Size: 61x22mm

1249 A434 7k multi 2.00 1.00
a. Souvenir sheet, #1248-1249 + label 3.25 1.60

See Greenland Nos. 407-408.

Europa A435

Insects A436

Poster art: 4.25k, Poster for Copenhagen International Theater Festival, by Ole Fick, 1985. 5.50k, Poster for Bertel Thorvaldsen Museum, by Ole Woldbye, 1970.

2003, May 14 **Litho.** ***Perf. 12¾***

1250 A435 4.25k multi 1.40 .70
Booklet, 10 #1250 14.00

Engr.

1251 A435 5.50k black 1.75 .85
Booklet, 10 #1251 17.50
a. Sheet of 8 + central label 14.00 —

2003, May 14 **Litho. & Engr.**

Designs: 4.25k, Ephemera danica. 6.50k, Dytiscus latissimus. 12k, Cordulegaster boltoni, vert.

1252 A436 4.25k multi 1.40 .70
a. Sheet of 8 + central label 11.50 —
1253 A436 6.50k multi 2.00 1.00
a. Sheet of 8 + central label 16.00 —

Size: 21x39mm

1254 A436 12k multi 3.75 1.90
a. Souvenir sheet, #1252-1254 7.25 7.25
Nos. 1252-1254 (3) 7.15 3.60

Contemporary Art Type of 1998

Designs: 5.50k, Baering, by Sys Hindsbo. 19k, Det Forjaettede Land, by Poul Anker Bech.

Litho. & Engr.

2003, Aug. 27 ***Perf. 12½x13***

1255 A401 5.50k multi 1.75 .85

Litho.

1256 A401 19k multi 5.75 3.00

Danish House Architecture Type of 2002

Designs: 4k, Bellahoj Apartment Complex, Copenhagen, by Tage Nielsen and Mogens Irming, 1944-58. 4.25k, Anchersvej, Klampenborg, by Mogens Lassen, 1935. 5.25k, Gerthasminde, Odense, by Anton Rosen, 1912-35. 9k, Solvang, Vallekilde College, by Andreas Bentsen and Martin Nyrop, 1889. 15k, Stenbrogard, Brorup, by Peter Holdensen, 1868.

Litho. & Engr.

2003, Aug. 27 ***Perf. 12¾***

1257 A432 4k multi 1.25 .60
1258 A432 4.25k multi 1.40 .70
Complete booklet, 10 #1258 14.00
1259 A432 5.25k multi 1.60 .80
1260 A432 9k multi 2.75 1.40
1261 A432 15k multi 4.50 2.25
Nos. 1257-1261 (5) 11.50 5.75

A437

A438

2003, Nov. 7 **Engr.** ***Perf. 12¾***

1262 A437 6.50k gray blue 2.00 1.00

Awarding of first Nobel Prize to a Dane (Niels Finsen for Physiology and Medicine), cent.

2003, Nov. 7 **Litho. & Engr.**

Artifacts from Royal Jelling World Heritage Site: 4.25k, Queen Thyra's stone. 5.50k, King Gorm's cup. 8.50k, King Harald's stone. 11.50k, Wall paintings, Jelling Church.

1263 A438 4.25k multi 1.40 .70
Booklet, 10 #1263 14.00
1264 A438 5.50k multi 1.75 .85
Booklet, 10 #1264 17.50
1265 A438 8.50k multi 2.60 1.40
1266 A438 11.50k multi 3.75 1.90
Nos. 1263-1266 (4) 9.50 4.85

A spiral-bound booklet, enclosed in a slipcase, with four booklet panes containing single stamps of Nos. 1263-1266, and a booklet pane containing a strip of Nos. 1263-1266, sold for 99k.

Danish House Architecture Type of 2002

Designs: 4.50k, Spurveskjul, Virum, by Nicolai Abildgaard, 1805. 6k, Liselund, Mon, by Andreas Kirkerup, 1792. 7k, Kampmann's Yard, Varde, by Hans Wolff Ollgaard, Hack Kampmann and Mikkel Stobberup, 1781. 12.50k, Harsdorff's House, Copenhagen, by Caspar Frederik Harsdorff, 1780. 15k, Nyso Manor, Praesto, by Jens Lauridsen.

Litho. & Engr.

2004, Jan. 14 ***Perf. 12¾***

1267 A432 4.50k multi 1.50 .75
Booklet, 10 #1267 15.00
1268 A432 6k multi 2.00 1.00
1269 A432 7k multi 2.40 1.25
1270 A432 12.50k multi 4.25 2.10
1271 A432 15k multi 5.00 2.50
Nos. 1267-1271 (5) 15.15 7.60

Academy of Fine Arts, Copenhagen, 250th Anniv. — A439

Litho. & Engr.

2004, Mar. 26 ***Perf. 13¼x13***

1272 A439 5.50k multi 1.90 .95
Booklet, 10 #1272 19.00

Norse Gods — A440

Designs: 4.50k, Heimdal guarding Bifrost bridge. 6k, Gefion plowing Sjaelland out of Sweden.

2004, Mar. 26

1273 A440 4.50k multi 1.50 .75
a. Sheet of 8 + central label 12.00 12.00
1274 A440 6k multi 2.00 1.00
a. Souvenir sheet, #1273-1274 3.50 1.75
b. Sheet of 8 + central label 16.00 16.00

Wedding of Crown Prince Frederik and Mary Donaldson — A441

No. 1275: a, Couple facing right. b, Couple facing left.

Litho. & Photo.

2004, May 14 ***Perf. 13x13¼***

1275 A441 Horiz. pair 3.00 1.50
Booklet, 5 #1275 15.00
a.-b. 4.50k Either single, denomination 8½ mm wide 1.50 .75
c.-d. 4.50k Either single, denomination 7½ mm wide 1.50 .75
e. Souvenir sheet, #1275c-1275d + central label 3.00 1.50

Frederiksberg Palace, 300th Anniv. — A442

Designs: 4.25k, Doorway overlooking Sondermarken Park. 4.50k, Gatehouse archway, castle yard. 6.50k, Aerial view.

Litho. & Engr.

2004, May 14 *Perf. 13*

1276 A442 4.25k multi 1.40 .70
1277 A442 4.50k multi 1.50 .75

Size: 55x32mm

1278 A442 6.50k multi 2.10 1.00
a. Souvenir sheet, #1276-1278 5.00 2.50
Nos. 1276-1278 (3) 5.00 2.45

Prince Henrik, 70th Birthday — A443

2004, June 9 **Litho.** *Perf. 12¾*

1279 A443 4.50k multi 1.50 .75

Europa A444

2004, June 9 *Perf. 13*

1280 A444 6k Cyclists 2.00 1.00
1281 A444 9k Sailboats 3.00 1.50

Contemporary Paintings Type of 1998

Designs: 13k, Senses the Body Landscape, by Lars Ravn, vert. 21k, The Dog Bites, by Lars Norgard, vert.

Litho. & Engr.

2004, Aug. 25 *Perf. 13x12½*

1282 A401 13k multi 4.25 2.25

Litho.

1283 A401 21k multi 7.00 3.50

Viking Ship Museum, Roskilde A445

Designs: 4.50k, Skuldelev 1 on Roskilde Fjord. 5.50k, Reconstruction of Skuldelev 2. 6.50k, Cross-section of ship. 12.50k, Excavation of archaeological site where ships were found.

Litho. & Engr.

2004, Aug. 25 *Perf. 13x13¼*

1284 A445 4.50k multi 1.50 .75
Complete booklet, 10 #1284 15.00
1285 A445 5.50k multi 1.90 .95
Complete booklet, 10 #1285 19.00
1286 A445 6.50k multi 2.10 1.10
1287 A445 12.50k multi 4.25 2.10
Nos. 1284-1287 (4) 9.75 4.90

A spiral-bound booklet, enclosed in a slipcase, with four booklet panes containing single stamps of Nos. 1284-1287 and a booklet pane containing a strip of Nos. 1284-1287, sold for 99k.

Birds of Prey A446

Designs: 4.50k, Falco tinnunculus. 5.50k, Accipiter nisus. 6k, Buteo buteo. 7k, Circus aeruginosus.

Litho. & Engr.

2004, Nov. 5 *Perf. 13*

1288 A446 4.50k multi 1.60 .80
Complete booklet, 10 #1288 16.00
1289 A446 5.50k multi 1.90 .95
1290 A446 6k multi 2.10 1.10
1291 A446 7k multi 2.50 1.25
Nos. 1288-1291 (4) 8.10 4.10

SEMI-POSTAL STAMPS

Nos. 159, 157 Surcharged in Red

Wmk. Multiple Crosses (114)

1921, June 17 *Perf. 14½x14*

B1 A20 10o + 5o green 9.00 *32.50*
B2 A21 20o + 10o slate 11.00 *40.00*
Set, never hinged 52.50

Crown and Staff of Aesculapius SP1

Dybbol Mill SP2

1929, Aug. 1 **Engr.**

B3 SP1 10o yellow green 2.50 *3.50*
a. Booklet pane of 2 21.00
B4 SP1 15o brick red 4.00 *6.00*
a. Booklet pane of 2 25.00
B5 SP1 25o deep blue 17.50 *21.00*
a. Booklet pane of 2 100.00
Nos. B3-B5 (3) 24.00 *30.50*
Set, never hinged 43.00

These stamps were sold at a premium of 5 öre each for benefit of the Danish Cancer Committee.

1937, Jan. 20 **Unwmk.** *Perf. 13*

B6 SP2 5o + 5o green .40 *.75*
B7 SP2 10o + 5o lt brown 1.75 *3.00*
B8 SP2 15o + 5o carmine 1.75 *3.00*
Nos. B6-B8 (3) 3.90 *6.75*
Set, never hinged 8.75

The surtax was for a fund in memory of H. P. Hanssen, statesman.

Nos. 223a and B6, Nos. 229 and B7, Nos. 238A and B8 are found se-tenant in booklets. For booklet panes, see Nos. 223d, 229b and 238e.

Queen Alexandrine SP3

Princesses Ingrid and Margrethe SP4

1939-40 *Perf. 13*

B9 SP3 5o + 3o rose lake & red ('40) .20 .20
a. Booklet pane of 4 2.00 2.00
B10 SP3 10o + 5o dk violet & red .20 .20
B11 SP3 15o + 5o scarlet & red .30 *.50*
Nos. B9-B11 (3) .70 .90
Set, never hinged 1.25

The surtax was for the Danish Red Cross.

Nos. 230 and B10 have been issued se-tenant in booklets. See No. 230b. In this pane No. 230 measures 23½x31mm from perf. to perf.

1941-43

B12 SP4 10o + 5o dk violet .20 .25
a. Booklet pane of 10 19.00
B13 SP4 20o + 5o red ('43) .20 .25
Set, never hinged .45

Surtax for the Children's Charity Fund.

No. 288 Surcharged in Red

1944, May 11

B14 A48 10o + 5o violet .20 .20
a. Booklet pane of 10 27.50
Never hinged .20

The surtax was for the Danish Red Cross.

Catalogue values for unused stamps in this section, from this point to the end of the section, are for Never Hinged items.

Symbols of Freedom SP5

Explosions at Rail Junction SP6

Danish Flag SP7

Princess Anne-Marie SP8

1947, May 4 **Engr.** *Perf. 13*

B15 SP5 15o + 5o green .35 .30
B16 SP6 20o + 5o dark red .35 .30
B17 SP7 40o + 5o deep blue .90 .75
Nos. B15-B17 (3) 1.60 1.35

Issued in memory of the Danish struggle for liberty and the liberation of Denmark. The surtax was for the Liberty Fund.

For surcharges see Nos. B22-B23.

1950, Oct. 19 **Unwmk.**

B18 SP8 25o + 5o rose brown .55 .50

The surtax was for the National Children's Welfare Association.

S. S. Jutlandia — SP9

1951, Sept. 13 *Perf. 13*

B19 SP9 25o + 5o red .65 .60

The surtax was for the Red Cross.

No. 335 Surcharged in Black

1953, Feb. 13

B20 A61 30o + 10o brown red 1.50 1.25

The surtax was for flood relief in the Netherlands.

Stone Memorial — SP10

1953, Mar. 26 *Perf. 13*

B21 SP10 30o + 5o dark red 1.40 1.25

The surtax was for cultural work of the Danish Border Union.

Nos. B15 and B16 Surcharged with New Value and Ornamental Screen in Black

1955, Feb. 17

B22 SP5 20o + 5o on No. B15 1.00 .85
B23 SP6 30o + 5o on No. B16 1.00 .85

The surtax was for the Liberty Fund.

No. 341 Surcharged

1957, Mar. 25

B24 A61 30o + 5o on 95o red org .65 .65

The surtax went to the Danish Red Cross for aid to Hungary.

#335 Surcharged: "Gronlandsfonden + 10"

1959, Feb. 23

B25 A61 30o + 10o brown red .85 .85

The surtax was for the Greenland Fund.

Globe Encircled by Red Cross Flags — SP11

Queen Ingrid — SP12

1959, June 24 **Engr.** *Perf. 13*

B26 SP11 30o + 5o rose red .45 .40
B27 SP11 60o + 5o lt ultra & car .80 .75

Centenary of the Intl. Red Cross idea. The surtax was for the Red Cross. Crosses photogravure on No. B27.

1960, Oct. 25 **Unwmk.**

B28 SP12 30o + 10o dark red .75 *.85*

Queen Ingrid's 25th anniv. as a Girl Scout. The surtax was for the Scouts' fund for needy and sick children.

African Mother, Child — SP13

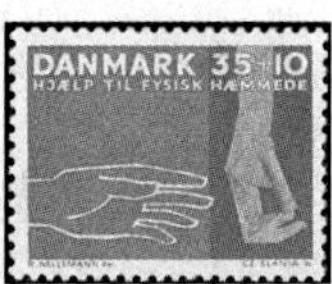
Healthy and Crippled Hands — SP14

1962, May 24

B29 SP13 30o + 10o dark red .75 *1.00*

Issued to aid underdeveloped countries.

1963, June 24 *Perf. 13*

B30 SP14 35o + 10o dark red 1.10 1.10

The surtax was for the benefit of the Cripples' Foundation.

Old Bridge at Danish-German Border — SP15

1964, May 28 **Engr.**

B31 SP15 35o + 10o henna brn .85 *.90*

Surtax for the Danish Border Union.

Princesses Margrethe, Benedikte, Anne-Marie — SP16

Happy Child — SP17

1964, Aug. 24

B32 SP16 35o + 10o dull red .75 .75
B33 SP16 60o + 10o dk bl & red .95 .95

The surtax was for the Red Cross.

1965, Oct. 21 **Engr.** ***Perf. 13***

B34 SP17 50o + 10o brick red .50 .50

The surtax was for the National Children's Welfare Association.

"Red Cross" in 32 Languages and Red Cross, Red Lion and Sun, and Red Crescent Emblems SP18

1966, Jan. 20 **Engr.** ***Perf. 13***

B35 SP18 50o + 10o red .40 .40

Engraved and Photogravure

B36 SP18 80o + 10o dk bl & red .80 .80

The surtax was for the Red Cross.

"Refugees 66" — SP19

Symbolic Rose — SP20

1966, Oct. 24 **Engr.** ***Perf. 13***

B37 SP19 40o + 10o sepia .80 .80
B38 SP19 50o + 10o rose red .80 .80
B39 SP19 80o + 10o blue 1.10 1.10
Nos. B37-B39 (3) 2.70 2.70

The surtax was for aid to refugees.

1967, Oct. 12

B40 SP20 60o + 10o brown red .45 .45

The surcharge was for the Salvation Army.

Two Greenland Boys in Round Tower — SP21

1968, Sept. 12 **Engr.** ***Perf. 13***

B41 SP21 60o + 10o dark red .55 .55

The surtax was for child welfare work in Greenland.

Princess Margrethe and Prince Henrik with Prince Frederik — SP22

1969, Dec. 11

B42 SP22 50o + 10o brn & red .65 .65
B43 SP22 60o + 10o brn red & red .65 .65

The surtax was for the Danish Red Cross.

Child Seeking Help — SP23

1970, Mar. 13

B44 SP23 60o + 10o brown red .55 .55

Surtax for "Save the Children Fund."

Child — SP24

Marsh Marigold — SP25

1971, Apr. 29 **Engr.** ***Perf. 13***

B45 SP24 60o + 10o copper red .55 .55

Surtax was for the National Children's Welfare Association.

1972, Aug. 17

B46 SP25 70o + 10o green & yel .45 .45

Soc. and Home for the Disabled, cent.

Heimaey Town and Volcano — SP26

1973, Oct. 17 **Engr.** ***Perf. 13***

B47 SP26 70o + 20o vio blue & red .55 .55

The surtax was for the victims of the eruption of Heimaey Volcano, Jan. 23, 1973.

Queen Margrethe, IWY Emblem — SP27

1975, Mar. 20 **Engr.** ***Perf. 13***

B48 SP27 90o + 20o red & buff .65 .65

International Women's Year 1975. Surtax was for a foundation to benefit women primarily in Greenland and Faroe Islands.

Skuldelev I SP28

Ships: 90o+20o, Thingvalla, emigrant steamer. 100o+20o, Liner Frederick VIII, c. 1930. 130o+20o, Three-master Danmark.

1976, Jan. 22 **Engr.** ***Perf. 13***

B49 SP28 70 + 20o olive brown .75 *.85*
B50 SP28 90 + 20o brick red .75 *.85*
B51 SP28 100 + 20o olive green .85 *1.10*
B52 SP28 130 + 20o violet blue .85 *1.10*
Nos. B49-B52 (4) 3.20 *3.90*

American Declaration of Independence, 200th anniv.

People and Red Cross SP29

Invalid in Wheelchair SP30

1976, Feb. 26 **Engr.** ***Perf. 13***

B53 SP29 100o + 20o red & black .65 .65
B54 SP29 130o + 20o bl, red & blk .80 .80

Centenary of Danish Red Cross.

1976, May 6 **Engr.** ***Perf. 13***

B55 SP30 100o + 20o ver & blk .55 .55

The surtax was for the Foundation to Aid the Disabled.

Mother and Child — SP31

Anti-Cancer Campaign — SP32

1977, Mar. 24 **Engr.** ***Perf. 12½***

B56 SP31 1k + 20o multicolored .55 .55

Danish Society for the Mentally Handicapped, 25th anniv. Surtax was for the Society.

1978, Oct. 12 **Engr.** ***Perf. 13***

B57 SP32 120o + 20o red .55 .55

Danish Anti-Cancer Campaign, 50th anniversary. Surtax was for campaign.

Child and IYC Emblem — SP33

1979, Jan. 25 **Engr.** ***Perf. 12½***

B58 SP33 1.20k + 20o red & brown .55 .55

International Year of the Child.

Foundation for the Disabled, 25th Anniversary SP34

1980, Apr. 10 **Engr.** ***Perf. 13***

B59 SP34 130o + 20o brown red .50 .50

Children Playing Ball SP35

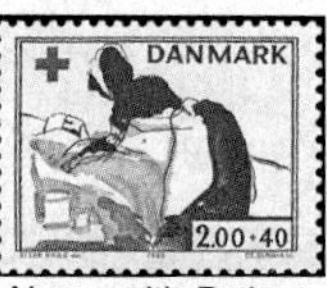

Intl. Year of the Disabled SP36

1981, Feb. 5 **Engr.** ***Perf. 12½x13***

B60 SP35 1.60k + 20o brown red .65 .65

Surtax was for child welfare.

1981, Sept. 10 **Engr.** ***Perf. 12½x13***

B61 SP36 2k + 20o dark blue .65 .65

Stem and Broken Line — SP37

1982, May 3 **Engr.** ***Perf. 13***

B62 SP37 2k + 40o dull red .65 .65

Surtax was for Danish Multiple Sclerosis Society.

Nurse with Patient SP38

1984 Olympic Games SP39

1983, Jan. 27 **Engr.**

B63 SP38 2k + 40o multicolored .75 .75

1984, Feb. 23 **Litho. & Engr.**

B64 SP39 2.70k + 40o multi 1.00 1.00

Electrocardiogram Reading, Heart — SP40

1984, Sept. 6 **Engr.** ***Perf. 12½***

B65 SP40 2.70k + 40o red 1.00 1.00

Surtax was for Heart Foundation.

SP41

SP42

1985, May 2 **Litho.** ***Perf. 13***

B66 SP41 2.80k + 50o multi 1.00 1.00

Liberation from German Occupation, 40th Anniv. Surtax for benefit of World War II veterans.

1985, Oct. 3 **Litho. & Engr.**

Design: Tapestry detail, by Caroline Ebbeson (1852-1936), former patient, St. Hans Hospital, Roskilade.

B67 SP42 2.80k + 40o multi .85 .85

Natl. Soc. for the Welfare of the Mentally Ill, 25th Anniv. Surtax benefited the mentally ill.

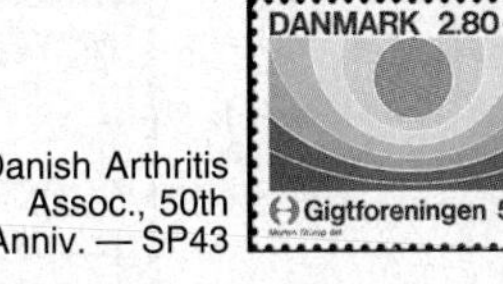

Danish Arthritis Assoc., 50th Anniv. — SP43

1986, Mar. 20 **Litho.** ***Perf. 13***
B68 SP43 2.80k + 50o multicolored .70 .70

Surtax for the Arthritis Assoc.

Poul Reichhart (1913-1985), as Papageno in The Magic Flute — SP44

1986, Feb. 6 **Litho.** ***Perf. 13***
B69 SP44 2.80k + 50o multicolored .70 .70

Surtax for the physically handicapped.

Danish Society for the Blind, 75th Anniv. — SP45

Litho. & Engr.

1986, Feb. 20 ***Perf. 13***
B70 SP45 2.80k +50o blk, vio brn & dk red .70 .70

Danish Assoc. of Epileptics, 25th Anniv. SP46

1987, Sept. 24 **Engr.** ***Perf. 13***
B71 SP46 2.80k +50o dk red, brt ultra & dk grn .95 .95

Folkekirkens Nodhjaelp Relief Organization — SP47

1988, Mar. 10 **Engr.**
B72 SP47 3k +50o multicolored 1.10 1.10

Surtax for the relief organization.

Natl. Council for Unwed Mothers, 5th Anniv. — SP48

1988, Sept. 22 **Photo.**
B73 SP48 3k +50o dk rose brn 1.10 1.10

SP49

SP50

1989, Feb. 16 **Litho.**
B74 SP49 3.20k +50o multi 1.25 1.25

Salvation Army.

1990, Aug. 30 **Litho.** ***Perf. 13***
B75 SP50 3.50k +50o Insulin crystal 1.40 1.40

Danish Diabetes Assoc., 50th anniv.

Children's Telephone SP51

1991, June 6 **Engr.** ***Perf. 13***
B76 SP51 3.50k +50o dark blue 1.10 1.10

Surtax benefits Borns Vilkar, children's welfare organization.

Danish Dyslexia Assoc., 50th Anniv. SP52

Litho. & Engr.

1992, Aug. 27 ***Perf. 13***
B77 SP52 3.75k +50o multi 1.40 1.40

SP53

SP54

1993, Aug. 19 **Litho.** ***Perf. 13***
B78 SP53 3.75k +50o multi 1.10 1.10

YMCA Social Work, 75th anniv.

Litho. & Engr.

1994, June 9 ***Perf. 13***
B79 SP54 3.75k +50o multi 1.25 1.25

Prince Henrik, 60th birthday. Surtax for Danish Red Cross.

Natl. Society of Polio and Accident Victims, 50th Anniv. SP55

1995, June 8 **Litho.** ***Perf. 13***
B80 SP55 3.75k +50o red 1.25 1.25

SP56

SP57

1996, Oct. 10 **Litho.** ***Perf. 13***
B81 SP56 3.75k +50o red & black 1.25 1.25

The AIDS Foundation.

1997, May 15 **Litho.** ***Perf. 13***
B82 SP57 3.75k +50o multi 1.25 1.25

Asthma-Allergy Assoc.

Danish Cancer Society SP58

1998, Sept. 3 **Litho.** ***Perf. 13***
B83 SP58 3.75k +50o multi 1.25 1.25

SP59

SP60

1999, Aug. 25 **Litho.** ***Perf. 13***
B84 SP59 4k +50o blue & red 1.25 1.25

For the Alzheimer's Association.

2000, Sept. 27 **Engr.** ***Perf. 13***
B85 SP60 4k +50o red & blue 1.00 1.00

For the Cerebral Palsy Association.

Amnesty International — SP61

2001, Jan. 24 **Engr.** ***Perf. 12¾***
B86 SP61 4k +50o blk & red 1.10 1.10

LEV National Association SP62

2002, Mar. 13 **Engr.** ***Perf. 12¾***
B87 SP62 4k + 50o multi, *greenish* 1.10 1.10

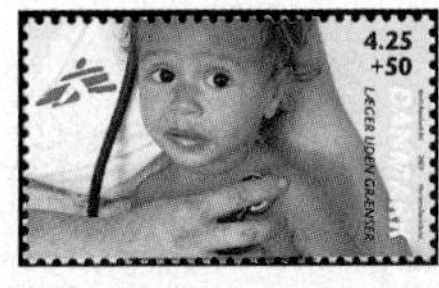

Doctors Without Borders SP63

2003, Mar. 12 **Litho.** ***Perf. 12¾***
B88 SP63 4.25k +50o multi 1.40 1.40
Booklet, 10 #B88 14.00

Children's Aid Day — SP64

2004, Jan. 14 **Litho.** ***Perf. 12¾***
B89 SP64 4.50k +50o multi 1.75 1.75
Booklet, 10 #B89 17.50

AIR POST STAMPS

Airplane and Plowman AP1

Towers of Copenhagen AP2

Wmk. Multiple Crosses (114)

1925-29 **Typo.** ***Perf. 12x12½***

C1	AP1	10o yellow green	16.00	*25.00*
C2	AP1	15o violet ('26)	32.50	*42.50*
C3	AP1	25o scarlet	27.50	*37.50*
C4	AP1	50o lt gray ('29)	65.00	*125.00*
C5	AP1	1k choc ('29)	55.00	*125.00*
		Nos. C1-C5 (5)	196.00	*355.00*
		Set, never hinged	450.00	

Unwmk.

1934, June 9 **Engr.** ***Perf. 13***

C6	AP2	10o orange	.50	*1.00*
C7	AP2	15o red	1.75	*3.50*
C8	AP2	20o Prus blue	2.00	*4.00*
C9	AP2	50o olive black	2.00	*4.00*
C10	AP2	1k brown	8.00	*15.00*
		Nos. C6-C10 (5)	14.25	*27.50*
		Set, never hinged	26.00	

LATE FEE STAMPS

LF1

Coat of Arms — LF2

Perf. 14x14½

1923 **Typo.** **Wmk. 114**
I1 LF1 10o green 8.00 1.00
Never hinged 24.00
a. Double overprint

No. I1 was, at first, not a postage stamp but represented a tax for the services of the post office clerks in filling out postal forms and writing addresses. In 1923 it was put into use as a Late Fee stamp.

1926-31

I2	LF2	10o green	3.75	.95
I3	LF2	10o brown ('31)	3.50	.35
		Set, never hinged	29.50	

1934 **Unwmk.** **Engr.** ***Perf. 13***

I4	LF2	5o green	.20	.20
I5	LF2	10o orange	.20	.20
		Set, never hinged	.50	

POSTAGE DUE STAMPS

Regular Issues of 1913-20 Overprinted

Perf. 14x14½

1921, May 1 **Wmk. 114**

J1	A10	1o deep orange	1.00	*1.50*
J2	A16	5o green	3.00	2.25
J3	A16	7o orange	2.50	1.75
J4	A16	10o red	13.50	7.50
J5	A16	20o deep blue	8.00	4.50
J6	A16	25o brown & blk	20.00	2.50
J7	A16	50o claret & blk	6.50	3.00
		Nos. J1-J7 (7)	54.50	23.00
		Set, never hinged	125.00	

Same Overprint in Dark Blue On Military Stamp of 1917

1921, Nov. 23
J8 A16 10o red 8.50 6.00
Never hinged 16.50
a. "S" inverted 100.00 *150.00*
Never hinged 190.00

Numeral of Value — D1

Typographed (Solid Panel)

1921-30 ***Perf. 14x14½***
J9 D1 1o orange ('22) .50 .40
J10 D1 4o blue ('25) 2.00 1.10
J11 D1 5o brown ('22) 2.00 .65
J12 D1 5o lt green ('30) .75 .60
J13 D1 7o apple grn ('27) 10.50 10.50
J14 D1 7o dk violet ('30) 22.50 22.50
J15 D1 10o yellow grn ('22) 2.00 .40
J16 D1 10o lt brown ('30) 1.00 .35
J17 D1 20o grnsh blue ('21) 1.25 .50
a. Double impression 2,100.
J18 D1 20o gray ('30) 1.25 .85
J19 D1 25o scarlet ('23) 2.00 .70
J20 D1 25o violet ('26) 1.75 .90
J21 D1 25o lt blue ('30) 3.75 2.25
J22 D1 1k dk blue ('21) 45.00 4.50
J23 D1 1k brn & dk bl ('25) 7.00 3.50
J24 D1 5k purple ('25) 15.00 7.00
Nos. J9-J24 (16) 118.25 56.70
Set, never hinged 265.00

Engraved (Lined Panel)

1934-55 **Unwmk.** ***Perf. 13***
J25 D1 1o slate .20 .20
J26 D1 2o carmine .20 .20
J27 D1 5o yellow green .20 .20
J28 D1 6o dk olive ('41) .40 .20
J29 D1 8o magenta ('50) 1.25 *1.50*
J30 D1 10o orange .20 .20
J31 D1 12o dp ultra ('55) .30 .25
J32 D1 15o violet ('37) .40 .20
J33 D1 20o gray .35 .20
J34 D1 25o blue .40 .20
J35 D1 30o green ('53) .40 .20
J36 D1 40o claret ('49) .50 .20
J37 D1 1k brown .65 .25
Nos. J25-J37 (13) 5.45 *4.00*
Set, never hinged 7.00

No. 96 Surcharged in Black

1934 **Wmk. 114** ***Perf. 14x14½***
J38 A10 15o on 12o violet 1.50 .70
Never hinged 6.25

MILITARY STAMPS

Nos. 97 and 100 Overprinted in Blue

1917 **Wmk. 114** ***Perf. 14x14½***
M1 A16 5o green 7.50 *16.00*
a. "S" inverted 190.00 *275.00*
M2 A16 10o red 8.00 *13.00*
a. "S" inverted 150.00 *200.00*
Set, never hinged 34.00
#M1a, M2a, never hinged *575.00*

The letters "S F" are the initials of "Soldater Frimaerke" (Soldier's Stamp).
For overprint see No. J8.

OFFICIAL STAMPS

Small State Seal — O1

Wmk. Crown (112)

1871 **Typo.** ***Perf. 14x13½***
O1 O1 2s blue 75.00 62.50
a. 2s ultra 75.00 52.50
b. Imperf *250.00*
O2 O1 4s carmine 45.00 9.00
a. Imperf *200.00*
O3 O1 16s green 310.00 210.00
a. Imperf *300.00*

Perf. 12½
O4 O1 4s carmine 4,100. 360.00
O5 O1 16s green 310.00 360.00
#O1-O3, O5, never hinged 1,850.

Nos. O4-O5 values are for copies with defective perfs.
Nos. O1-O3 were reprinted in 1886 upon white wove paper, unwatermarked and imperforate. Value $10 each.

1875 ***Perf. 14x13½***
O6 O1 3o violet 6.00 10.00
O7 O1 4o grnsh blue 6.00 2.50
O8 O1 8o carmine 6.00 1.25
a. Imperf —
O9 O1 32o green 20.00 20.00
Nos. O6-O9 (4) 38.00 33.75
Set, never hinged 95.00

For surcharge see No. 81.

1899-02 ***Perf. 13***
O9A O1 3o red lilac ('02) 2.75 *3.75*
c. Imperf *210.00*
O9B O1 4o blue 1.75 1.60
O10 O1 8o carmine 11.00 11.00
Nos. O9A-O10 (3) 15.50 16.35
Set, never hinged 45.00

For surcharge see No. 137.

1902-06 **Wmk. 113**
O11 O1 1o orange 1.10 *1.60*
O12 O1 3o red lilac ('06) .70 .65
O13 O1 4o blue ('03) 1.50 1.25
O14 O1 5o green 1.25 .55
O15 O1 10o carmine 1.25 1.10
Nos. O11-O15 (5) 5.80 5.15
Set, never hinged 13.50

1914-23 **Wmk. 114** ***Perf. 14x14½***
O16 O1 1o orange 1.10 *1.25*
O17 O1 3o gray ('18) 3.00 3.00
O18 O1 4o blue ('16) 30.00 *50.00*
O19 O1 5o green ('15) .75 .35
O20 O1 5o choc ('23) 3.50 *5.00*
O21 O1 10o red ('17) 5.50 .75
O22 O1 10o green ('21) 1.00 *1.50*
O23 O1 15o violet ('19) 10.00 *27.50*
O24 O1 20o indigo ('20) 12.50 6.25
Nos. O16-O24 (9) 67.35 *95.60*
Set, never hinged 113.40

Used value for No. O20 is for a CTO.
For surcharges see Nos. 185-191.
Official stamps were discontinued 4/1/24.

NEWSPAPER STAMPS

Numeral of Value — N1

1907 **Typo.** **Wmk. 113** ***Perf. 13***
P1 N1 1o olive 10.00 2.75
P2 N1 5o blue 21.00 14.00
P3 N1 7o carmine 9.00 1.25
P4 N1 10o deep lilac 20.00 3.00
P5 N1 20o green 19.00 1.40
P6 N1 38o orange 25.00 1.50
P7 N1 68o yellow brown 60.00 25.00
P8 N1 1k bl grn & claret 19.00 3.00
P9 N1 5k rose & yel grn 160.00 37.50
P10 N1 10k bister & blue 160.00 37.50
Nos. P1-P10 (10) 503.00 126.90
Set, never hinged 2,620.

For surcharges see Nos. 138-144.

1914-15 **Wmk. 114** ***Perf. 14x14½***
P11 N1 1o olive gray 7.00 1.40
P12 N1 5o blue 21.00 7.00
P13 N1 7o rose 21.00 1.40
P14 N1 8o green ('15) 20.00 1.40
P15 N1 10o deep lilac 25.00 1.50
P16 N1 20o green 225.00 2.75
a. Imperf., pair *825.00*
P17 N1 29o orange yel ('15) 35.00 2.75
P18 N1 38o orange 1,550. 125.00
Never hinged 2,250.
P19 N1 41o yellow brn ('15) 40.00 2.00
P20 N1 1k blue grn & mar 77.50 2.50
Nos. P11-P17,P19-P20 (9) 471.50 22.70
Set, never hinged 2,400.

For surcharges see Nos. 145-154.

PARCEL POST STAMPS

These stamps were for use on postal packets sent by the Esbjerg-Fano Ferry Service.

Regular Issues of 1913-30 Overprinted

1919-41 **Wmk. 114** ***Perf. 14x14½***
Q1 A10 10o green ('22) 8.00 *13.00*
Q2 A10 10o bister brn ('30) 9.00 6.50
Q3 A16 10o red 27.50 *55.00*
a. "POSFFAERGE" 150.00 *350.00*
Q4 A16 15o violet 11.50 *27.50*
a. "POSFFAERGE" 150.00 *350.00*
Q5 A16 30o orange ('22) 10.00 *21.00*
Q6 A16 30o dk blue ('26) 3.00 3.00
Q7 A16 50o cl & blk ('20) 165.00 165.00
Q8 A16 50o lt gray ('22) 18.00 11.00
a. 50o dark gray ('22) 125.00 *250.00*
Q9 A16 1k brn & bl ('24) 40.00 17.00
Q9A A16 5k vio & brn ('41) 1.50 1.50
Q10 A16 10k ver & grn ('30) 55.00 *85.00*

Engr.
Q11 A17 1k yellow brn 75.00 *140.00*
a. "POSFFAERGE" 1,400. *2,250.*
Nos. Q1-Q11 (12) 423.50 *545.50*
Set, never hinged 865.00

1927-30
Q12 A30 15o red ('27) 13.00 10.50
Q13 A30 30o ocher ('27) 11.00 11.00
Q14 A30 40o yel grn ('30) 12.50 10.50
Nos. Q12-Q14 (3) 36.50 *32.00*
Set, never hinged 75.00

Overprinted on Regular Issues of 1933-40

1936-42 **Unwmk.** ***Perf. 13***
Q15 A32 5o rose lake ('42) .20 .20
Q16 A32 10o yellow org 15.00 *25.00*
Q17 A32 10o lt brown ('38) 1.00 *1.40*
Q18 A32 10o purple ('39) .20 .20
Q19 A30 15o deep red .40 *1.00*
Q20 A30 30o blue, I 3.25 *4.25*
Q21 A30 30o blue, II ('40) 6.00 *12.00*
Q22 A30 30o org, II ('42) .35 *.60*
Q23 A30 40o yel grn, I 3.25 *4.25*
Q24 A30 40o yel grn, II ('40) 6.00 *11.00*
Q25 A30 40o blue, II ('42) .40 *1.00*
Q26 A33 50o gray 1.00 *1.50*
Q27 A33 1k lt brown .80 *1.25*
Nos. Q15-Q27 (13) 37.85 *63.65*
Set, never hinged 75.00

Catalogue values for unused stamps in this section, from this point to the end of the section, are for Never Hinged items.

Overprinted on Nos. 284, 286, 286B

1945
Q28 A47 30o orange 2.00 1.40
Q29 A47 40o blue 1.40 1.00
Q30 A47 50o gray 1.50 1.25
Nos. Q28-Q30 (3) 4.90 3.65

Ovptd. on #318, 309, 310, 312, 297

1949-53
Q31 A32 10o green ('53) .25 .25
Q32 A61 30o orange 2.00 1.50
Q33 A61 40o dull blue 2.25 1.50
Q34 A61 50o gray ('50) 14.00 3.25
Q35 A55 1k brown ('50) 1.50 1.40
Nos. Q31-Q35 (5) 20.00 7.90

Ovptd. on #335, 323, 336, 326, 397

1955-65
Q36 A61 30o brown red .90 *1.00*
Q37 A61 40o gray .90 *1.00*
Q38 A61 50o aqua .90 *1.00*
Q39 A61 70o deep green .90 *1.00*
Q40 A55 1.25k orange ('65) 6.00 *9.00*
Nos. Q36-Q40 (5) 9.60 *13.00*

Overprinted on Nos. 417 and 419

1967 **Engr.** ***Perf. 13***
Q41 A86 40o brown .55 .55
Q42 A86 80o ultra .55 .55

Nos. 224, 438, 441, 297-299 Overprinted

1967-74 **Engr.** ***Perf. 13***
Q43 A32 5o rose lake .35 .35
Q44 A86 50o brown ('74) .50 .50
Q45 A86 90o ultra ('70) 1.10 1.10
Q46 A55 1k brown 2.50 2.50
Q47 A55 2k red ('72) 2.25 2.25
Q48 A55 5k dull bl ('72) 6.00 6.00
Nos. Q43-Q48 (6) 12.70 12.70

Nos. Q44-Q45, Q47-Q48 are on fluorescent paper.

Overprinted on No. 541

1975, Feb. 27
Q49 A161 100o deep ultra 1.25 1.25

DIEGO-SUAREZ

dē-ˌā-gō ˈswär-əs

LOCATION — A town at the northern end of Madagascar
GOVT. — French colony
POP. — 12,237

From 1885 to 1896 Diego-Suarez, (Antsirane), a French naval base, was a separate colony and issued its own stamps. These were succeeded by stamps of Madagascar.

100 Centimes = 1 Franc

Values for unused stamps are for examples with original gum as defined in the catalogue introduction except for Nos. 6-10 and J1-J2 which are valued without gum.

Stamps of French Colonies Handstamp Surcharged in Violet

1890 **Unwmk.** ***Perf. 14x13½***
1 A9 15c on 1c blk, *bl* 210.00 67.50
2 A9 15c on 5c grn, *grnsh* 550.00 67.50
3 A9 15c on 10c blk, *lav* 210.00 67.50
4 A9 15c on 20c red, *grn* 550.00 67.50
5 A9 15c on 25c blk, *rose* 90.00 35.00

This surcharge is found inverted, double, etc. See the *Scott Classic Catalogue.* Counterfeits exist.

Ship Flying French Flag — A2

France — A5

Symbolical of Union of France and Madagascar
A3 A4

1890 **Litho.** ***Imperf.***
6 A2 1c black 775.00 175.00
7 A3 5c black 775.00 150.00
8 A4 15c black 175.00 67.50
9 A5 25c black 200.00 77.50

Counterfeits exist of Nos. 6-9.

A6

1891

10 A6 5c black 250.00 70.00

Excellent counterfeits exist of No. 10.

Stamps of French Colonies Surcharged in Red or Black:

No. 11

No. 12

1892 *Perf. 14x13½*

11 A9 5c on 10c blk, *lav* (R) 150.00 80.00
a. Inverted surcharge 350.00 325.00
12 A9 5c on 20c red, *grn* 140.00 55.00
a. Inverted surcharge 350.00 325.00

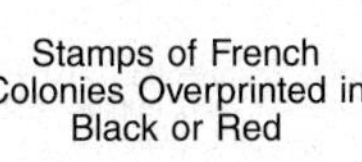
Stamps of French Colonies Overprinted in Black or Red

1892

13 A9 1c blue (R) 21.00 12.50
14 A9 2c brown, *buff* 21.00 12.50
15 A9 4c claret, *lav* 35.00 27.50
16 A9 5c green, *grnsh* 77.50 60.00
17 A9 10c black, *lavender* 27.50 21.00
b. Double overprint 140.00 110.00
18 A9 15c blue, *pale blue* 21.00 13.00
19 A9 20c red, *grn* 25.00 21.00
20 A9 25c black, *rose* 21.00 12.00
21 A9 30c brown, *bis* (R) 925.00 675.00
22 A9 35c black, *yellow* 925.00 675.00
23 A9 75c carmine, *rose* 50.00 32.50
a. Double overprint 325.00
24 A9 1fr brnz grn, *straw* (R) 57.50 40.00
a. Double overprint 160.00 150.00

Inverted Overprint

13a A9 1c 160.00 125.
14a A9 2c 160.00 125.
15a A9 4c 250.
16a A9 5c 160.00 125.
17a A9 10c 160.00 125.
20a A9 25c 160.00 125.
21a A9 30c 1,250.
22a A9 35c 1,250.

Navigation and Commerce
A10 A11

1892 **Typo.** *Perf. 14x13½*

Name of Colony in Blue or Carmine

25 A10 1c black, *blue* 1.75 1.75
26 A10 2c brown, *buff* 1.90 1.90
27 A10 4c claret, *lav* 2.10 2.10
28 A10 5c green, *grnsh* 4.50 4.50
29 A10 10c black, *lavender* 6.00 4.25
30 A10 15c bl, quadrille paper 10.50 6.50
31 A10 20c red, *green* 16.00 10.50
32 A10 25c black, *rose* 11.50 10.00
33 A10 30c brown, *bister* 16.00 11.00
34 A10 40c red, *straw* 19.00 14.00
35 A10 50c carmine, *rose* 35.00 21.00
36 A10 75c violet, *org* 35.00 27.50
37 A10 1fr brnz grn, *straw* 52.50 35.00
Nos. 25-37 (13) 211.75 150.00

Perf. 13½x14 stamps are counterfeits.

1894 *Perf. 14x13½*

38 A11 1c black, *blue* 1.25 1.25
39 A11 2c brown, *buff* 2.00 1.60
40 A11 4c claret, *lav* 2.10 1.75
41 A11 5c green, *grnsh* 4.00 3.50
42 A11 10c black, *lavender* 5.75 4.50
43 A11 15c blue, quadrille paper 8.50 4.25
44 A11 20c red, *grn* 14.00 9.25
45 A11 25c black, *rose* 7.25 5.75
46 A11 30c brown, *bister* 8.50 4.25
47 A11 40c red, *straw* 8.50 4.25
48 A11 50c carmine, *rose* 13.50 9.25
49 A11 75c violet, *org* 8.50 5.75
50 A11 1fr brnz grn, *straw* 20.00 16.00
Nos. 38-50 (13) 103.85 71.35

Bisected stamps of type A11 are mentioned in note after Madagascar No. 62.

For surcharges see Madagascar #56-57, 61-62.

Perf. 13½x14 stamps are counterfeits.

POSTAGE DUE STAMPS

D1

D2

1891 **Unwmk.** **Litho.** ***Imperf.***

J1 D1 5c violet 160.00 57.50
J2 D2 50c black 175.00 67.50

Excellent counterfeits exist of Nos. J1-J2.

Postage Due Stamps of French Colonies Overprinted Like Nos. 13-24

1892

J3 D1 1c black 95.00 52.50
J4 D1 2c black 95.00 45.00
a. Inverted overprint 275.00 325.00
J5 D1 3c black 95.00 47.50
J6 D1 4c black 95.00 47.50
J7 D1 5c black 95.00 47.50
J8 D1 10c black 25.00 21.00
a. Inverted overprint 325.00 210.00
J9 D1 15c black 25.00 21.00
a. Double overprint 475.00 400.00
J10 D1 20c black 160.00 92.50
a. Double overprint 475.00 400.00
J11 D1 30c black 85.00 47.50
a. Inverted overprint 325.00 210.00
J12 D1 60c black 875.00 650.00
J13 D1 1fr brown 2,200. 1,150.

DJIBOUTI

jə-'bü-tē

LOCATION — East Africa
GOVT. — Republic
AREA — 8,958 sq. mi.
POP. — 447,439 (1999 est.)
CAPITAL — Djibouti

The French territory of Afars and Issas became the Republic of Djibouti June 27, 1977. For 1894-1902 issues with "Djibouti" or "DJ," see Somali Coast.

Catalogue values for all unused stamps in this country are for Never Hinged items.

Afars and Issas Issues of 1972-1977 Overprinted and Surcharged with Bars and "REPUBLIQUE DE DJIBOUTI" in Black, Dark Green, Blue or Brown

Printing and Perforations as Before

1977

439 A63 1fr on 4fr (#358;B) 2.00 .25
440 A81 2fr on 5fr (#433;B) 2.00 .25
441 A75 5fr on 20fr (#421;B) .25 .20
442 A70 8fr (#380;B) .35 .25
443 A71 20fr (#387;DG) 3.50 .65
444 A81 30fr (#434;B) 3.75 .80
445 A71 40fr (#388;DG) 4.50 1.10
446 A71 45fr (#389;Bl) 5.00 1.25
447 A78 45fr (#428;B) 7.50 1.25
448 A72 50fr (#394;B) 8.00 1.60
449 A71 60fr (#391;Br) 7.00 1.60
450 A79 70fr (#430;B) 8.00 1.90
451 A81 70fr (#435;B) 5.50 2.25
452 A74 100fr(#418;B) 11.00 3.00
453 A72 150fr(#399;B) 11.50 3.50
454 A76 200fr(#422;B) 5.00 3.50
455 A80 200fr(#432;B) 5.75 4.00
456 A74 300fr(#419;B) 9.25 6.50
Nos. 439-456,C106-C108 (21) 122.10 52.10

Map and Flag of Djibouti — A83

Water Pipe — A84

Design: 65fr, Map and flag of Djibouti, map of Africa, horiz.

1977, June 27 **Litho.** ***Perf. 12½***

457 A83 45fr multicolored 1.10 .40
458 A83 65fr multicolored 1.40 .60

Independence, June 27.

1977, July 4

459 A84 10fr Headrest, horiz. .25 .20
460 A84 20fr shown .50 .20
461 A84 25fr Pitcher .70 .30
Nos. 459-461 (3) 1.45 .70

Ostrich — A85

1977, Aug. 11 **Litho.** ***Perf. 12½***

462 A85 90fr shown 2.75 .80
463 A85 100fr Weaver 4.00 1.10

Snail A86

Designs: 15fr, Fiddler crab. 50fr, Klipspringers. 70fr, Green turtle. 80fr, Priacanthus hamrur (fish). 150fr, Dolphinfish.

1977 **Litho.** ***Perf. 12½***

464 A86 15fr multicolored .50 .20
465 A86 45fr multicolored 1.25 .30
466 A86 50fr multicolored 1.60 .40
467 A86 70fr multicolored 1.75 .40
468 A86 80fr multicolored 2.25 .45
469 A86 150fr multicolored 4.00 1.25
Nos. 464-469 (6) 11.35 3.00

Issued: 45fr, 70fr, 80fr, 9/14; others, 12/5.

Pres. Hassan Gouled Aptidon and Djibouti Flag — A87

1978, Feb. 12 **Litho.** ***Perf. 13***

470 A87 65fr multicolored 1.00 .35

Charaxes Hansali — A88

Necklace — A89

Butterflies: 20fr, Colias electo. 25fr, Acraea chilo. 150fr, Junonia hierta.

1978, Mar. 13 **Litho.** ***Perf. 12½x13***

471 A88 5fr multicolored .25 .20
472 A88 20fr multicolored 1.00 .25
473 A88 25fr multicolored 1.50 .50
474 A88 150fr multicolored 5.75 1.75
Nos. 471-474 (4) 8.50 2.70

1978, May 29 **Litho.** ***Perf. 12½x13***

Design: 55fr, Necklace, diff.

475 A89 45fr pink & multi 1.00 .35
476 A89 55fr blue & multi 1.25 .40

Bougainvillea A90

Flowers: 35fr, Hibiscus schizopetalus. 250fr, Caesalpinia pulcherrima.

1978, July 10 **Photo.** ***Perf. 12½x13***

477 A90 15fr multicolored .45 .20
478 A90 35fr multicolored .90 .25
479 A90 250fr multicolored 5.25 .90
Nos. 477-479 (3) 6.60 1.35

Charonia Nodifera — A91

Sea Shell: 80fr, Charonia variegata.

1978, Oct. 9 **Litho.** ***Perf. 13***

480 A91 10fr multicolored 1.10 .35
481 A91 80fr multicolored 3.75 .90

Chaetodon A92

30fr, Yellow surgeonfish. 40fr, Harlequinfish.

1978, Nov. 20 **Litho.** ***Perf. 13x12½***

482 A92 8fr multicolored .60 .20
483 A92 30fr multicolored 1.25 .25
484 A92 40fr multicolored 2.50 .45
Nos. 482-484 (3) 4.35 .90

Alsthom BB 1201 at Dock — A93

55fr, Steam locomotive 231. 60fr, Steam locomotive 130 and map of route. 75fr, Diesel.

1979, Jan. 29 Litho. *Perf. 13*

485	A93 40fr multicolored		1.00	.20
486	A93 55fr multicolored		1.10	.25
487	A93 60fr multicolored		1.60	.25
488	A93 75fr multicolored		2.00	.30
	Nos. 485-488 (4)		5.70	1.00

Djibouti-Addis Ababa railroad.

Children and IYC Emblem — A94

Design: 200fr, Mother, child, IYC emblem.

1979, Feb. 26 Litho. *Perf. 13*

489	A94 20fr multicolored	.45	.20
490	A94 200fr multicolored	3.50	1.10

International Year of the Child.

Plane over Ardoukoba Volcano — A95

30fr, Helicopter over Ardoukoba Volcano.

1979, Mar. 19

491	A95 30fr multi, vert.	.90	.35
492	A95 90fr multi	2.50	.60

Rowland Hill, Postal Clerks, No. C109 — A96

100fr, Somali Coast #22, Djibouti #457, letters, Rowland Hill. 150fr, Letters hoisted onto ship, smoke signals, Rowland Hill.

1979, Apr. 17 Litho. *Perf. 13x12½*

493	A96 25fr multicolored	.35	.20
494	A96 100fr multicolored	1.75	.45
495	A96 150fr multicolored	2.75	.70
	Nos. 493-495 (3)	4.85	1.35

Sir Rowland Hill (1795-1879), originator of penny postage.

View of Djibouti, Bird and Local Woman — A97

Design: 80fr, Map and flag of Djibouti, UPU emblem, Concorde, train and mail runner.

1979, June 8 Litho. *Perf. 13x12½*

496	A97 55fr multicolored	2.10	.70
497	A97 80fr multicolored	2.75	.95

Philexafrique II, Libreville, Gabon, June 8-17. Nos. 496, 497 each printed in sheets of 10 with 5 labels showing exhibition emblem.

Solanacea A98

Flowers: 2fr, Opuntia, vert. 15fr, Trichodesma. 45fr, Acacia etbaica. 50fr, Thunbergia alata, vert.

Perf. 13x13½, 13½x13

1979, June 18

498	A98 2fr multicolored	.20	.20
499	A98 8fr multicolored	.25	.20
500	A98 15fr multicolored	.50	.20
501	A98 45fr multicolored	1.00	.30
502	A98 50fr multicolored	1.25	.25
	Nos. 498-502 (5)	3.20	1.05

Running — A99

Olympic Emblem and: 70fr, Basketball, vert. 200fr, Soccer.

Perf. 12½x13, 13x12½

1979, Oct. 22 Litho.

503	A99 70fr multicolored	1.40	.25
504	A99 120fr multicolored	2.10	.50
505	A99 200fr multicolored	3.50	.75
	Nos. 503-505 (3)	7.00	1.50

Pre-Olympic Year.

Cypraecassis Rufa — A100

Shells: 40fr, Lambis chiragra arthritica. 300fr, Harpa connaidalis.

1979, Dec. 22 Litho. *Perf. 13*

506	A100 10fr multicolored	.20	.20
507	A100 40fr multicolored	.90	.20
508	A100 300fr multicolored	5.75	1.50
	Nos. 506-508 (3)	6.85	1.90

Rotary International, 75th Anniversary — A101

1980, Feb. 19 Litho. *Perf. 13x12½*

509	A101 90fr multicolored	1.75	.50

Lions Club of Djibouti — A102

1980, Feb. 19

510	A102 100fr multicolored	2.25	.75

Colotis Danae — A103

1980, Mar. 17 *Perf. 13x13½*

511	A103 5fr *shown*	.70	.45
512	A103 55fr *Danaus chrysippus*	3.25	1.40

Chess Players, Knight — A104

Chess Federation Creation: 75fr, Chess Game, Florence, 1493.

1980, June 9 Litho. *Perf. 13*

513	A104 20fr multicolored	.80	.20
514	A104 75fr multicolored	2.25	.30

Cribraria A105

1980, Aug. 12 Litho. *Perf. 13*

515	A105 15fr *shown*	.50	.20
516	A105 85fr *Nautilius pompilius*	2.00	.40

Alexander Fleming, Discoverer of Penicillin — A106

Design: 130fr, Jules Verne, French science fiction writer; earth, moon and spacecraft.

1980, Sept. 1

517	A106 20fr multicolored	.80	.25
518	A106 130fr multicolored	2.25	.50

Capt. Cook and Endeavor — A107

Capt. James Cook Death Bicentenary: 90fr, Ships and Maps of voyages.

1980, Nov. 20 Litho. *Perf. 13*

519	A107 55fr multicolored	1.00	.25
520	A107 90fr multicolored	1.75	.40

Souvenir sheets of 1 exist, perf. 12½x12.

Angel Fish A108

1981, Apr. 13 Litho. *Perf. 12½*

521	A108 25fr shown	.90	.20
522	A108 55fr Moorish idol	2.10	.35
523	A108 70fr Scad	2.25	.90
	Nos. 521-523 (3)	5.25	1.45

13th World Telecommunications Day — A109

1981, May 17 Litho. *Perf. 13*

524	A109 140fr multicolored	2.25	.60

Type 231 Steam Locomotive, Germany, 1958 and Amtrak, US, 1980 — A110

Locomotives: 55fr, Stephenson and his Rocket, Djibouti Railways 230 engine. 65fr, Type TGV, France, Type 962, Japan.

1981, June 9 Litho. *Perf. 13*

525	A110 40fr multicolored	1.25	.30
526	A110 55fr multicolored	1.75	.35
527	A110 65fr multicolored	2.25	.40
	Nos. 525-527 (3)	5.25	1.05

Radio Amateurs Club — A111

1981, June 25

528	A111 250fr multicolored	4.50	1.00

Prince Charles and Lady Diana — A112

1981, June 29

529	A112 180fr shown	3.50	.90
530	A112 200fr Couple, diff.	4.00	1.00

Royal Wedding.

Lord Nelson and Victory — A113

1981, July 6 Litho. *Perf. 13x12½*

531	A113 100fr multicolored	1.75	.45
532	A113 175fr multicolored	3.00	.90

Lord Horatio Nelson (1758-1805).

Scout Tending Campfire — A114

1981, July 16 Litho. *Perf. 13*

533 A114 60fr shown 2.75 .60

534 A114 105fr Scout giving sign 3.50 .70

28th World Scouting Conference, Dakar, Aug. (60fr); 4th Pan-African Scouting Conference, Abidjan, Aug. (105fr).

Pawn and Queen, Swedish Bone Chess Pieces, 13th Cent. — A115

1981, Oct. 15 Litho. *Perf. 13*

535 A115 50fr shown 1.40 .30

536 A115 130fr Pawn, knight, Chinese, 19th cent., vert. 2.25 .70

For overprints see Nos. 542-543.

Sheraton Hotel Opening — A116

1981, Nov. 15 Litho. *Perf. 13x12½*

537 A116 75fr multicolored 1.25 .35

For surcharge see No. 623.

Acacia Mellifera A117

1981, Dec. 21 *Perf. 13*

538 A117 10fr Clitoria ternatea, vert. .35 .20

539 A117 30fr shown .70 .20

540 A117 35fr Punica granatum 1.00 .20

541 A117 45fr Malvaceous plant, vert. 1.25 .30

Nos. 538-541 (4) 3.30 .90

See Nos. 558-560.

Nos. 535-536 Overprinted with Winners' Names

1981, Dec. Litho. *Perf. 13*

542 A115 50fr multicolored 1.00 .35

543 A115 130fr multicolored 2.75 .75

World Chess Championship.

TB Bacillus Centenary A117a

1982 Litho. *Perf. 13*

544 A117a 305fr Koch, slide, microscope 5.75 1.50

A117b

A118

1982, Apr. 8 Litho. *Perf. 13*

545 A117b 125fr Ivory bishop 2.75 .65

546 A117b 175fr Queen, pawn, 19th cent. 3.75 1.00

1982 World Chess Championship.

1982, May 17

547 A118 150fr multicolored 2.25 .65

14th World Telecommunications Day.

For surcharge see No. 647.

Bus and Jeep — A119

1982, July 27 Litho. *Perf. 13*

548 A119 20fr shown .45 .20

549 A119 25fr Dhow, ferry .60 .20

550 A119 55fr Train, jet 1.25 .35

Nos. 548-550 (3) 2.30 .75

Shells from the Red Sea A120

1982, Nov. 20 Litho. *Perf. 12½*

551 A120 10fr Cypraea erythraeensis .25 .20

552 A120 15fr Conus sumatrensis .35 .20

553 A120 25fr Cypraea pulchra .60 .20

554 A120 30fr Conus inscriptus .80 .20

555 A120 70fr Casmaria ponderosa 1.75 .40

556 A120 150fr Cypraea exusta 3.50 .60

Nos. 551-556 (6) 7.25 1.80

See Nos. 563-567.

Intl. Palestinian Solidarity Day — A121

1982, Nov. 29 Litho. *Perf. 13*

557 A121 40fr multicolored .60 .20

Local Flowers type of 1981

Various flowers. 5fr, 55fr, vert.

1983, Apr. 14 Litho. *Perf. 13*

558 A117 5fr multicolored .20 .20

559 A117 50fr multicolored 1.10 .40

560 A117 55fr multicolored 1.25 .40

Nos. 558-560 (3) 2.55 1.00

World Communications Year — A123

1983, June 20 Litho. *Perf. 13*

561 A123 500fr multicolored 7.50 2.00

Conference of Donors, Nov. 21-23 — A124

1983, Nov. 21 Litho. *Perf. 13x12½*

562 A124 75fr multicolored 1.25 .40

Shell Type of 1982

1983, Dec. 20 Litho. *Perf. 12½*

563 A120 15fr Marginella obtusa .45 .20

564 A120 30fr Conus jickelli .90 .20

565 A120 55fr Cypraea macandrewi 1.40 .40

566 A120 80fr Conus cuvieri 2.00 .50

567 A120 100fr Turbo petholatus 2.10 .65

Nos. 563-567 (5) 6.85 1.95

Local Butterflies A125

1984, Jan. 24 Litho. *Perf. 13½x13*

568 A125 5fr Colotis chrysonome .25 .20

569 A125 20fr Colias erate .70 .25

570 A125 30fr Junonia orithyia 1.25 .35

571 A125 75fr Acraea doubledayi 3.75 1.00

572 A125 110fr Byblia ilithya 5.00 1.50

Nos. 568-572 (5) 10.95 3.30

Landscapes and Animals — A126

1984, Apr. 29 Litho. *Perf. 13*

573 A126 2fr Randa Klipspringer .20 .20

574 A126 8fr Ali Sabieh, gazelles .20 .20

575 A126 10fr Lake Assal, oryx .20 .20

576 A126 15fr Tadjoura, gazelle .25 .20

577 A126 40fr Alaila Dada, jackal, vert. .60 .20

578 A126 45fr Lake Abbe, warthog .60 .25

579 A126 55fr Obock, seagull 1.60 .60

580 A126 125fr Presidential Palace, bird 3.25 1.10

Nos. 573-580 (8) 6.90 2.95

For surcharges see #646, 657-658, 660.

Fire Prevention — A127

1984, Sept. 9 Litho. *Perf. 13*

581 A127 25fr Fire truck .80 .20

582 A127 95fr Hook & ladder 2.50 .45

583 A127 100fr Fire plane 2.75 .95

Nos. 581-583 (3) 6.05 1.60

International Olympic Committee Membership A128

1984, July 22 Litho. *Perf. 13*

584 A128 45fr Runners .90 .35

Motor Carriage, 1886 A128a

1984, Nov. 11 Litho. *Perf. 12½*

585 A128a 35fr shown .70 .30

586 A128a 65fr Cabriolet, 1896 1.40 .65

587 A128a 90fr Phoenix, 1900 2.00 .95

Nos. 585-587 (3) 4.10 1.90

Gottlieb Daimler (1834-1900), pioneer automobile manufacturer.

Marie and Pierre Curie — A129

1984, Dec. 3 Litho. *Perf. 12½*

588 A129 150fr Pierre Curie 2.75 1.10

589 A129 150fr Marie Curie 2.75 1.10

A130

Audubon Bicentenary — A130a

Illustration A130a reduced.

1985, Jan. 27 Litho. *Perf. 13*

590 A130 5fr Merops al-bicollis .70 .30
591 A130 15fr Pterocles exustus 3.00 .80
592 A130 20fr Trachyphonus mar-garitatus somalicus 3.50 .95
593 A130 25fr Coracias garrulus 4.25 1.00
Nos. 590-593 (4) 11.45 3.05

Souvenir Sheet
Self-Adhesive
Perf. 12½

593A A130a 200fr Pandion haliaetus, vert. 26.00 26.00

No. 593A is airmail and printed on wood.

Intl. Youth Year — A131

1985, Mar. 26 Litho. *Perf. 13*

594 A131 10fr multicolored .20 .20
595 A131 30fr multicolored .50 .30
596 A131 40fr multicolored .70 .40
Nos. 594-596 (3) 1.40 .90

German Railways, 150th Anniv. — A132

Designs: 55fr, Engine No. 29, Addis Ababa-Djibouti Railways. 75fr, Adler, museum facsimile of the first German locomotive.

1985, Apr. 22 Litho. *Perf. 13*

597 A132 55fr multicolored 2.00 .65
598 A132 75fr multicolored 3.00 .90

A133

A134

1985, May 23

599 A133 35fr Planting saplings .80 .35
600 A133 65fr Hygiene, family health care 1.50 .65

Scouting.

1985, June 24 Litho.

80fr, Victor Hugo (1802-1885), Novelist. 100fr, Arthur Rimbaud (1854-1891), poet.

601 A134 80fr brt blue & slate 1.40 .80
602 A134 100fr multicolored 1.60 1.00

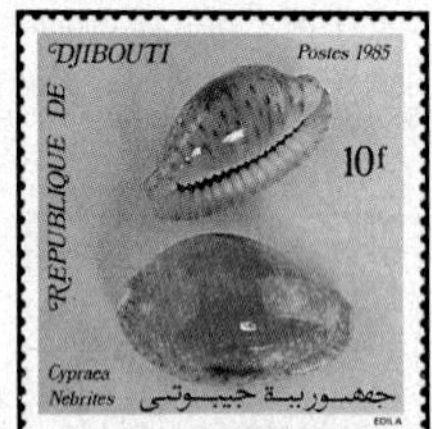

Sea Shells A135

1985, July 15 Litho. *Perf. 12½*

603 A135 10fr Cypraea nebrites .25 .20
604 A135 15fr Cypraea turdus .45 .20
605 A135 30fr Conus acuminatus 1.10 .25
606 A135 40fr Cypraea camelo-pardalis 1.25 .45
607 A135 55fr Conus terebra 2.10 .60
Nos. 603-607 (5) 5.15 1.70

1st World Cup Marathon '85, Hiroshima A136

1985, Sept. 2 *Perf. 12½x13*

608 A136 75fr Winners 1.25 .75
609 A136 100fr Approaching finish 2.00 1.00

Halley's Comet — A137

Designs: 85fr, Bayeux Tapestry, Comet and Halley. 90fr, Vega I, Giotto space probes, map of planets, comet trajectory.

1986, Jan. 27 Litho. *Perf. 13*

610 A137 85fr multicolored 1.25 .45
611 A137 90fr multicolored 1.60 .80

ISERST Solar Energy Installation — A138

Designs: 50fr, Runners on beach. 150fr, Windmill, headquarters, power control station.

1986, Mar. 20

612 A138 50fr multicolored .80 .40
613 A138 150fr multicolored 2.25 1.25

Ships from Columbus's Fleet, 1492 — A139

1986, Apr. 14

614 A139 60fr Santa Maria 1.40 .45
615 A139 90fr Nina, Pinta 2.25 .75

Fish, Red Sea — A140

1986, June 16 Litho. *Perf. 13½x13*

616 A140 20fr Elagatis bipinnulatus .45 .20
617 A140 25fr Valamugil seheli .50 .20
618 A140 55fr Lutjanus rivulatus 1.40 .40
Nos. 616-618 (3) 2.35 .80

Public Buildings — A141

105fr, People's Palace. 115fr, Ministry of the Interior, Posts & Telecommunications.

1986, July 21 Litho. *Perf. 13*

619 A141 105fr multicolored 1.50 .90
620 A141 115fr multicolored 1.75 1.00

Sea-Me-We Building, Keyboard — A142

1986, Sept. 8 Litho. *Perf. 13*

621 A142 100fr multicolored 2.00 .70

Souvenir Sheet
Perf. 12½

622 A142 250fr multicolored 13.50 13.50

Southeast Asia, Middle East, Western Europe Submarine Cable System inauguration.

No. 537 Surcharged "5e ANNIVERSAIRE."

1986, Nov. 15 *Perf. 13x12½*

623 A116 55fr on 75fr multi 1.00 .40

Pasteur Institute, Cent. — A143

1987, Feb. 19 Litho. *Perf. 13*

624 A143 220fr multicolored 4.00 1.50

Natl. Vaccination Campaign.

Edible Mushrooms A144

1987, Apr. 16 Litho. *Perf. 13x12½*

625 A144 35fr Macrolepiota imbricata 1.00 .40
626 A144 50fr Lentinus squarrosulus 1.75 .50
627 A144 95fr Terfezia boudieri 2.50 1.00
Nos. 625-627 (3) 5.25 1.90

Wildlife A145

1987, May 14 *Perf. 12½x13*

628 A145 5fr Hare .25 .20
629 A145 30fr Dromedary 1.00 .30
630 A145 140fr Cheetah 4.50 1.00
Nos. 628-630 (3) 5.75 1.50

1988 Olympics, Seoul and Calgary — A146

85fr, Pierre de Coubertin (1863-1937), founder of the modern Olympics, & lighting of the flame. 135fr, Ski jumping. 140fr, Running.

1987, July 16 *Perf. 13*

631 A146 85fr multicolored 1.50 .55
632 A146 135fr multicolored 2.50 .95
633 A146 140fr multicolored 2.75 1.00
Nos. 631-633 (3) 6.75 2.50

Traditional Art — A147

UN Universal Immunization by 1990 Campaign A148

1988, Jan. 31 Litho. *Perf. 13*

634 A147 30fr Nomad's comb .60 .30
635 A147 70fr Wash jug 1.25 .60

1988, Mar. 12 *Perf. 12½*

636 A148 125fr multicolored 2.25 1.00

16th Africa Cup Soccer Championships, Morocco — A149

1988, Mar. 12 *Perf. 13*

637 A149 55fr Athletes, view of Rabat 1.10 .50

1988 Winter Olympics, Calgary — A150

1988, Mar. 27 Litho. *Perf. 13*

638 A150 45fr Ski jump .90 .40

Campaign Against Thirst A151

1988, Sept. 10 Litho. *Perf. 12½x13*

639 A151 50fr multicolored 1.00 .40

Intl. Fund for Agricultural Development, 10th Anniv. — A152

1988, Nov. 14 *Perf. 13*

640 A152 135fr multicolored 2.25 1.00

Michel Lafoux Air Club, 40th Anniv. — A153

1988, Dec. 6

641 A153 145fr 1948 Tiger Moth, 1988 Tobago-10 2.75 1.00

Marine Life A154

1989, Jan. 29 Litho. *Perf. 12½*

642 A154 90fr *Lobophyllia costata* 1.75 .25
643 A154 160fr *Lambis truncata* 3.25 1.10

Colotis protomedia A155

1989, Feb. 2

644 A155 70fr multicolored 2.50 1.25

Nos. 573 and 547 Surcharged

1989, Mar. 5 *Perf. 13*

646 A126 70fr on 2fr No. 573 2.25 .50
647 A118 70fr on 150fr No. 547 2.25 .50

Folk Dances — A157

Francolin of Djibouti — A159

1989, Jan. 29

648 A157 30fr shown .50 .25
649 A157 70fr multicolored, diff. 1.40 .50

1989, Apr. 25 Litho. *Perf. 12½*

651 A159 35fr multicolored 1.40 .35

Rare Flora A160

1989, June 12

652 A160 25fr *Calotropis procera* .45 .20

A161

A162

1989, Aug. 9 Litho. *Perf. 13*

653 A161 70fr multicolored 1.25 .50

Interparliamentary Union, cent.

1989, Oct. 1

654 A162 145fr multicolored 2.75 1.10

Intl. Literacy Year.

Petroglyph — A163

1989, Nov. 18 Litho. *Perf. 13*

655 A163 5fr multicolored .35 .20

Girl — A164

1989, Dec. 6

656 A164 55fr multicolored 1.00 .40

Nos. 574, 576-577 Surcharged

1990 Litho. *Perf. 13*

657 A126 30fr on 8fr multi .50 .30
658 A126 50fr on 40fr multi 2.00 .55
660 A126 120fr on 15fr multi 2.00 .80
Nos. 657-660 (3) 4.50 1.65

Issue dates: 50fr, July 3; 120fr, Mar. 17.

Water Conservation — A165

1990, Mar. 17 Litho. *Perf. 11½*

665 A165 120fr multicolored 1.75 .70

Traditional Jewelry A166

1990, Mar. 21

666 A166 70fr multicolored 1.25 .45

Commiphora — A167

1990, Apr. 16 *Perf. 12*

667 A167 30fr multicolored .60 .35

Baskets — A168

1990, May 5

668 A168 30fr multicolored .50 .20

A169

A170

1990, June 12 *Perf. 11½*

669 A169 100fr multicolored 1.50 .60

World Cup Soccer Championships, Italy.

1990, July 3 *Perf. 11½*

670 A170 55fr shown 1.00 .40

20 kilometer race of Djibouti.

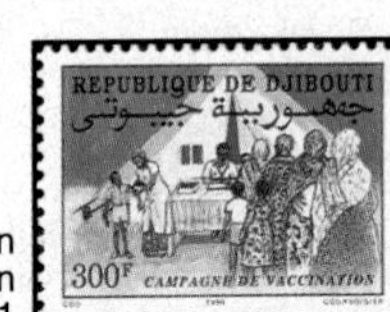

Vaccination Campaign A171

1990, Aug. 22 Litho. *Perf. 11½*
Granite Paper

671 A171 300fr multicolored 4.50 1.75

Charles de Gaulle — A172

African Tourism Year — A173

1990, Sept. 16

Granite Paper

672 A172 200fr multicolored 3.50 1.25

1991, Jan. 23 Litho. ***Perf. 13***

673 A173 115fr multicolored 2.00 .80

Corals — A174

Aquatic Birds — A175

1991, Jan. 28 ***Perf. 12½***

674 A174 40fr Acropora .80 .40
675 A174 45fr Seriatopora hytrise 1.00 .40

1991, Feb. 12

676 A175 10fr Pelecanus rufescens .60 .20
677 A175 15fr Egretta gularis 1.40 .25
678 A175 20fr Ardea goliath, horiz. 1.60 .30
679 A175 25fr Platalea leucorodia, horiz. 1.75 .35
Nos. 676-679 (4) 5.35 1.10

UNO Development Conference A176

Fossils A177

1990, Oct. 9 Litho. ***Perf. 11½x12***

Granite Paper

680 A176 45fr multicolored .90 .40

1990, Nov. 12

Granite Paper

681 A177 90fr pur, org & blk 5.25 1.75

Papio Hamadryas — A178

1990, Dec. 6

Granite Paper

682 A178 50fr multicolored .90 .30

Pandion Haliaetus A179

1991, Mar. 27 Litho. ***Perf. 12x11½***

683 A179 200fr multicolored 3.25 1.10

Traditional Game A180

1991, Apr. 4

684 A180 250fr multicolored 3.50 2.25

See No. 696.

Djibouti-Ethiopia Railroad — A181

1991, May 25 Litho. ***Perf. 11½***

685 A181 85fr multicolored 1.25 .70

World Environment Day — A182

1991, June 10

686 A182 110fr multicolored 2.00 .50

Philexafrique — A183

1991 Litho. ***Perf. 11½***

687 A183 120fr Islands 1.75 1.00

A184

A185

1991

688 A184 175fr Handball 2.25 1.60

Pre-Olympic year.

1991 Litho. ***Perf. 11½x12***

689 A185 105fr multicolored 2.10 1.10

World Food Day.

Underwater Cable Network — A186

1991, Nov. 23 ***Perf. 12x11½***

690 A186 130fr multicolored 2.10 .80

Discovery of America, 500th Anniv. A187

1991, Dec. 19 Litho. ***Perf. 11½***

691 A187 145fr multicolored 2.25 1.40

Arthur Rimbaud (1854-1891) Poet and Merchant — A188

1991-92 ***Perf. 11½***

692 A188 90fr Young man, ship 2.00 .75
693 A188 150fr Old man, camels 2.25 .75

Issued: 90fr, 2/5/92; 150fr, 12/23/91.

Djibouti-Ethiopia Railroad — A189

Design: 250fr, Locomotive, map.

1992 Litho. ***Perf. 12x11½***

694 A189 70fr multicolored 1.50 .60

Souvenir Sheet

Perf. 13x12½

695 A189 250fr multicolored 4.50 4.50

Issue dates: 70fr, Feb. 2; 250fr, Jan. 30.

Traditional Game Type of 1991

1992, Feb. 10 ***Perf. 11½***

696 A180 100fr Boys playing Go 1.50 .60

A190

A191

1992, Apr. 24 Litho. ***Perf. 14***

697 A190 80fr multicolored 1.10 .70

1992 Summer Olympics, Barcelona.

1992, June 9 Litho. ***Perf. 14x13½***

Traditional food preparation.

698 A191 30fr Pounding grain .50 .30
698A A191 45fr Preparing mofo
699 A191 70fr Winnowing grain 1.10 .60

An additional stamp was released in this set. The editors would like to examine it. Date of issue of No. 698A is not known.

Discovery of America, 500th Anniv. A192

1992, May 16 Litho. ***Perf. 11½***

700 A192 125fr multicolored 2.10 .75

African Soccer Championships A193

Intl. Space Year — A194

1992, July 22 ***Perf. 14***

701 A193 15fr multicolored .25 .20

Perf. 14x13½, 13½x14

1992, Sept. 28

702 A194 120fr Rocket, satellite 1.75 .60
703 A194 135fr Astronaut, satellite, horiz. 2.00 .70

Wildlife — 704

1992, Nov. 11 *Perf. 14*

704 A195 5fr Dik-dik .70 .20
705 A195 200fr Caretta caretta 3.25 1.25

Taeniura Lymma — A195a

1993 (?) Litho. *Perf. 11½x11¾*

Panel Color

705A A195a 70fr yellow
705B A195a 100fr green
705C A195a 120fr lilac — —

Nomad Girls in Traditional Costumes A196

1993, Feb. 10 Litho. *Perf. 13*

706 A196 70fr Girl beside hut 1.25 .35
707 A196 120fr shown 2.10 .60

White-eyed Seagull A197

1993, Mar. 10 Litho. *Perf. 12½*

708 A197 300fr multicolored 4.25 1.60

Amin Salman Mosque — A198

1993, Feb. 17 Litho. *Perf. 13¾x14*

709 A198 500fr multicolored *52.50 4.25*

Handcrafts — A199

Handicrafts Type of 1993

1993, Apr. 23 Litho. *Perf. 13¾x14*

710 A199 100fr Neck rest 1.10 1.10

1993, Apr. 23 Litho. *Perf. 13¾x14*

711 A199 125fr Sword 1.50 1.50

A number has been reserved for a 100fr stamp in this set. The editors would like to examine it.

Water Carriers — A202

1993, July 6 Litho. *Perf. 14x13¾*

714 A202 30fr Woman .35 .35
715 A202 50fr Man .60 .60

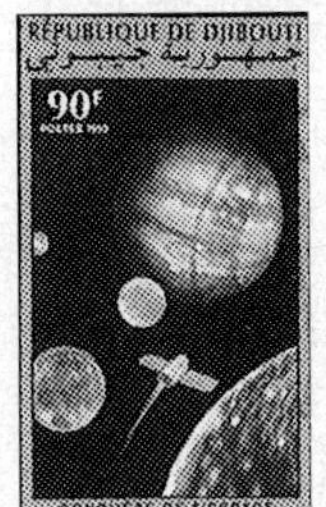

Conquest of Space — A203

1993, Sept. 30 Litho. *Perf. 14x13¾*

716 A203 90fr multicolored 1.10 1.10

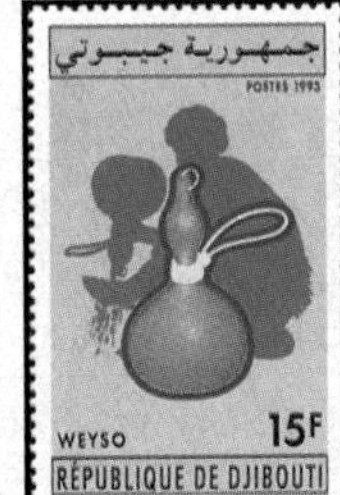

A204

A205

Traditional utensils.

1993, Sept. 30 Litho. *Perf. 13½*

717 A204 15fr Weyso .25 .20
718 A204 20fr Hangol .45 .20
719 A204 25fr Saqaf .50 .20
720 A204 30fr Subrar .70 .25
Nos. 717-720 (4) 1.90 .85

1993, Nov. 10 Litho. *Perf. 14*

Traditional musical instruments.

721 A205 5fr Flute .20 .20
722 A205 10fr Drum .20 .20

Souvenir Sheet

Wedding of Japan's Crown Prince Naruhito and Masako Owada — A206

1994, Jan. 10 Litho. *Perf. 13x12½*

Self-Adhesive

723 A206 500fr multicolored 13.50 13.50

No. 723 printed on wood.

20 Kilometer Race of Djibouti A207

Promotion of Breastfeeding A208

1994 Litho. *Perf. 11½*

724 A207 50fr multicolored 1.00 .40

1994

725 A208 40fr shown 1.25 .40
726 A208 45fr Mother, infant 1.40 .40

Hassan Gouled Aptidon Stadium A209

1994

727 A209 70fr multicolored 1.25 .55

Stenella Longirostris — A210

1994, May 1 Litho. *Perf. 11¾x11½*

728 A210 120fr multicolored 1.25 1.25

Eupodotis Senegalensis — A212

Perf. 11¾x11½

1994, June 16 Litho.

730 A212 10fr multicolored

1994 World Cup Soccer Tournament — A213

1994, Sept. 7

731 A213 200fr multicolored *160.00 1.60*

Traditional Nomad Costume — A214

Design: 150fr, Dress of a village leader.

Perf. 11½x11¾

1994, Sept. 18 Litho.

732 A214 100fr multicolored 1.00 1.00

Perf. 11¾

733 A214 150fr multicolored 1.60 1.60

Canis Aureus A215

Perf. 11¾x11½

1994, Sept. 28 Litho.

734 A215 400fr multi *100.00 3.25*

World Walking Day A216

1994, Oct. 19 Litho. *Perf. 11¾x11½*

735 A216 75fr multicolored

A217

1994, Nov. 26 Litho. *Perf. 11¾*

736 A217 55fr Book stand

A218

1994, Dec. 6 Litho. *Perf. 11½x11¾*

737 A218 35fr Traditional dance

A219

A220

1995, Feb. 25 Litho. *Perf. 11¾*

738 A219 70fr multicolored

Volleyball, cent.

1995, Feb. 25

739 A220 120fr multicolored

United Nations, 50th anniv.

Fight Against Thirst A221

Perf. 11¾x11½

1995, Mar. 29 Litho.

740 A221 100fr multicolored

Threskiornis Aethiopica — A222

1995, Apr. 5 Litho. *Perf. 11¾*

742 A222 50fr multicolored

A number has been reserved for a 30fr stamp in this set. The editors would like to examine it.

World Telecommunications Day — A223

Perf. 11¾x11½

1995, June 10 Litho.

743 A223 125fr multicolored *50.00* .90

People Meeting Under Tree A225

1995, July 3 Litho. *Perf. 11¾x11½*

745 A225 150fr multi *50.00* 1.10

A226 A227

1995, Aug. 9 *Perf. 11¾*

746 A226 45fr Nomads around fire *50.00* .30

1995, Sept. 27 *Perf. 11½x11¾*

747 A227 250fr multi *50.00* 2.00

FAO, 50th anniv.

Traditional Costume — A228

1995, Dec. 6 Litho. *Perf. 11¾*

748 A228 90fr multicolored

African Development Bank, 30th Anniv. — A229

Perf. 11¾x11½

1995. Dec. 18 Litho.

749 A229 300fr multi *50.00* 2.50

African Soccer Cup — A230

1996, Feb. 28 Litho *Perf. 11¾*

750 A230 70fr multicolored *160.00* .50

Leopard A232

1996, May 6 Litho. *Perf. 11¾*

752 A232 70fr multi

1996 Summer Olympic Games, Atlanta — A234

Perf. 11½x11¾

1996, Sept. 21 Litho.

754 A234 105fr multicolored *100.00* 1.00

Commicarpus Grandiflorus A236

1996, Oct. 6 Litho. *Perf. 11½x11¾*

756 A236 350fr multi *50.00* 2.75

Legend of the Lion and Three Bulls A238

1996, Nov. 28 Litho. *Perf. 11¾*

758 A238 95fr multi *100.00* .80

Children's Day A239

1996, Dec. 17 *Perf. 11¾x11½*

759 A239 130fr multi *50.00* 1.00

A240 A241

Legend of the Tortoise and the Fox: No. 760, Tortoise and fox at starting line. No. 761, Fox leaves tortoise behind. No. 762, Tortoise passes sleeping fox.

1997, Jan. 17 *Perf. 11¾*

760 A240 60fr multi

761 A240 60fr multi

762 A240 60fr multi

a. Horiz. strip, #760-762 *100.00*

1997, Feb. 9 Litho. *Perf. 11¾*

763 A241 80fr Mother, child *52.50*

764 A241 90fr Hands around globe *52.50*

UNICEF, 50th anniv.

Dancers — A242

1997, May 14 Litho. *Perf. 11¾*

765 A242 70fr multi *50.00*

Fortune Teller A243

Design: 300fr, Fortune teller, camel.

1997, May 29 Litho. *Perf. 11¾*

767 A243 300fr multi — —

An additional stamp was issued in this set. The editors would like to examine it.

Woman's Day — A244

1997, May 30 Litho. *Perf. 11¾*

768 A244 250fr multi *160.00*

Traditional Objects Type of 1997

Design: 30fr, Writing board, horiz.

1997, June 5 Litho. *Perf. 11¾*

769 A245 30fr multi — —

Traditional Objects — A245

Design: 400fr, Bowl and spoon.

1997, June 5 Litho. *Perf. 11¾*

770 A245 400fr multi — —

An additional stamp was issued in this set. The editors would like to examine it.

Telecommunications — A246

Designs: 30fr, Arta post office. 100fr, Map, building with antenna and satellite dishes.

1997, June 27 Litho. *Perf. 11¾*

771 A246 30fr multi — —

772 A246 100fr multi

An additional stamp was issued in this set. The editors would like to examine it.

A248

A249

Portrait of Diana: a, 125fr. b, 130fr. c, 150fr.

1998, Mar. 25 Litho. *Perf. 13½*

775 A248 Strip of 3, #a.-c. 5.75 5.75

Diana, Princess of Wales (1961-97). No. 775 was isssued in sheets of 6 stamps.

1998 Litho. *Perf. 13½*

776 A249 130fr multicolored 1.50 1.10

Mother Teresa (1910-97). No. 776 was issued in sheets of 4.

Intl. Year of the Ocean A250

a, Tangara chilensis. b, Agalychnis callidryas. c, Delphinus delphis, megaptera novaeangliae. d, Cercopithecus aethiops (h). e, Laticaudia colubrina (i), sphyrna mokarran. f, Lactoria cornuta, delphinus delphis (g). g, Delphinus delphis (k). h, Aspidontus taeniatus, lo vulpinus. i, Sepioteuthis lessoniana. j, Prionace glauca (i), chaetodon ornatissimus. k, Eupagurus bernherdus. l, Octopus vulgaris (k).

1998, Apr. 20 Litho. *Perf. 13½*

777 A250 75fr Sheet of 12, #a.-l. 14.00 14.00

Mahatma Gandhi (1869-1948) A251

1998, Apr. 20 **Litho.** ***Perf. 11¾***
778 A251 250fr multi 50.00

Traditional Art — A252

1998, Apr. 25 **Litho.** ***Perf. 11½x11¾***
779 A252 30fr multicolored

Women's Rights and International Peace — A253

1998, May 3 ***Perf. 11¾x11½***
780 A253 70fr multicolored 50.00 —

World Water Day A254

1998, May 10 **Litho.** ***Perf. 11¾***
781 A254 45fr multi 50.00 —

Marine Life — A256

Cats and Bush — A257

Perf. 11½x11¾, 11¾x11½
1998, July 2 **Litho.**
783 A256 20fr Octopus 100.00 —
784 A256 25fr Shark, horiz. 100.00 —

1998, Aug. 30 ***Perf. 11½x11¾***
785 A257 120fr multi 100.00 —

National Bank — A259

1998, Sept. 30 **Litho.** ***Perf. 11¾***
787 A259 100fr multi

Flags and IGAD Emblem — A260

Perf. 11½x11¾
1998, Sept. 30 **Litho.**
788 A260 85fr multi 50.00 —

Traditional Game Goos A261

1998, Oct. 1 ***Perf. 11¾x11½***
789 A261 110fr multi 50.00 —

Fishing Port A262

1998
790 A262 100fr multi 50.00 —

Maskali Island A263

1998
791 A263 500fr multi 100.00 —

Fish A264

1999 **Litho.** ***Perf. 13¼x13½***
792 A264 70fr multi 100.00 —

Djibouti Franc, 50th Anniv. A265

1999
793 A265 100fr multi 50.00

World Telecommunications Day — A266

1999
794 A266 125fr multi 50.00 —

Worldwide Fund for Nature (WWF) — A267

Phacochoerus africanus aeliani: a, Adult and young. b, Adult standing. c, Head. d, Adult walking.
Illustration reduced.

2000, Apr. 13 **Litho.** ***Perf. 14***
795 A267 100fr Block of 4, #a-d 5.00 5.00

Wild Animals — A268

No. 796: a, Flamingo. b, Ostrich. c, Sifaka. d, Yellow-billed stork. e, Scarlet macaw. f, Dwarf puff adder. g, Toucan. h, Whooping crane.

2000, Apr. 13
796 A268 100fr Sheet of 8, #a-h 9.00 9.00

Butterflies — A269

No. 797: a, Doxocopa cherubina. b, Heliconius charitonius. c, Cantonephele numili. d, Danaus gilippus. e, Morpho peleides. f, Heliconius doris.
No. 798, 250fr, Agraulis vanillae. No. 799, 250fr, Strymon melinus.

2000, Apr. 13
797 A269 100fr Sheet of 6, #a-f 9.00 9.00

Souvenir Sheets

798-799 A269 Set of 2 9.00 9.00

No. 797 contains six 28x42mm stamps.

Water Resources — A270

2000, Apr. 13
800 A270 500fr multi 7.25 7.25

Trains and Landmarks — A271

No. 801: a, 5fr, Class OJ 2-10-2, China. b, 25fr, Eurostar, France-England. c, 15fr, Glacier Express, Switzerland. d, 40fr, Unidentified train. e, 35fr, Class WP 4-6-2, India.
No. 802, 110fr: a, Nord Chapelon Pacific, France. b, Class 23 2-6-2, Germany. c, Class GS-4 4-8-4, US. d, Class A4 4-6-2, Great Britain. e, Pacific 4-6-2, South Africa. f, Class HP, India.
No. 803, 120fr: a, VT601, Germany. b, ICIII Bo-Bo EMU, Netherlands. c, TGV, France. d, ETR 450, Italy. e, AVE, Spain. f, Bullet Train, Japan.
No. 804, 250fr, GM War Bonnet, US. No. 805, 250fr, Class 8 Pacific, Great Britain.

2000, Apr. 28
801 A271 Horiz. strip of 5, #a-e 1.75 1.75

Sheets of 6, #a-f

802-803 A271 Set of 2 16.00 16.00

Souvenir Sheets

804-805 A271 Set of 2 7.00 7.00

Dancers A272

2000, Apr. 28
806 A272 75fr multi 1.10 1.10

Blacksmith — A273

2000, May 14
807 A273 100fr multi 1.50 1.50

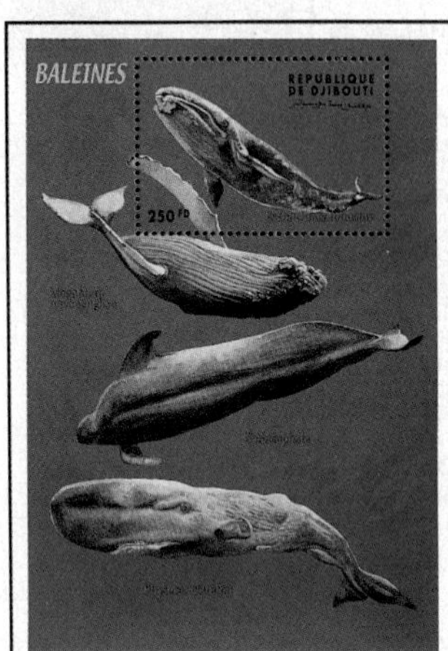

Marine Life — A274

No. 808, vert.: a, Dendrochirus biocellatus. b, Hippocampus. c, Amphiprion ocellaris, Amphiprion percula. d, Periclimenes imperator. e, Pomacnetridae. f, Octopus vulgaris.
No. 809, 50fr: a, Cephalopholis miniata. b, Ptereleotris hanae. c, Sphyraena genie. d, Tripterygion segmentatum. e, Odontaspididae. f, Cirrhitidae. g, Amphiprion. h, Capros aper. i, Balistidae. j, Trygonorhina fasciata. k, Cephalopholis. l, Corythoichthys ocellatus.
No. 810, 60fr: a, Lutjanus kasmira. b, Chaetodon fasciatus. c, Epinephelinae. d,

Hypoplectrus gutavarius. e, Loligo opalescens. f, Diodontinae. g, Coelenterata. h, Sargocentron xantherythrum. i, Thalassoma lunare. j, Hemichromis bimaculatus. k, Dasyatis. l, Fromia monilis.

No. 811, 250fr, Eschrichtis robustus. No. 812, 250fr, Cheloniidae.

2000, May 14

808 A274 55fr Sheet of 6, #a-f 5.50 5.50

Sheets of 12, #a-l

809-810 A274 Set of 2 20.00 20.00

Souvenir Sheets

811-812 A274 Set of 2 8.00 8.00

Camels and Tender A275

2000, June 26

813 A275 35fr multi .65 .65

Ships A276

Designs: 10fr, Thomas W. Lawson, 1902. 15fr, BT Global Challenge, 2000. 20fr, Reliance and Shamrock III, 1903. 25fr, Archibald Russell, 1905. 50fr, Greek merchantman, 8th cent. B.C.

No. 819, 130fr: a, Norman warship, 1066. b, Hanseatic cog, c. 1300. c, Santa Maria, 1492. d, Mary Rose, 1510. e, Golden Hind, 1577. f, Sovereign of the Seas, 1637.

No. 820:, 135fr: a, HMS Endeavour, 1768. b, USS Constitution, 1797. c, Chasse-Maree, 1800. d, Baltimore clipper, 1812. e, Lightning, 1853. f, Bluenose, 1921.

No. 821, 250fr, HM Yacht Britannia, 1893. No. 822, 250fr, Herzogin Cecilie, 1902.

2000, June 26

814-818 A276 Set of 5 2.00 2.00

Sheets of 6, #a-f

819-820 A276 Set of 2 25.00 25.00

Souvenir Sheets

821-822 A276 Set of 2 8.00 8.00

Millennium A277

2000, July 18

823 A277 125fr multi 2.00 2.00

Birds A278

2000, Aug. 23

824	Horiz. strip of 5	2.00	2.00
a.	A278 5fr Lanius excubitor	.20	.20
b.	A278 10fr Phoenicopterus minor	.20	.20
c.	A278 15fr Eupodatis senegalensis	.20	.20
d.	A278 40fr Noephron perchopterus	.45	.45
e.	A278 50fr Pterocles lichtensteinii	.55	.55

Space Exploration A279

No. 825, 100fr, vert.: a, John Glenn and Mercury capsule, 1962. b, Soyuz capsule, Apollo-Soyuz mission, 1975. c, Hubble Telescope, 1990. d, Apollo capsule, Apollo-Soyuz mission. e, Glenn at speaker's stand, 1974. f, Space Shuttle Columbia, 1981.

No. 826, 100fr, vert.: a, Apollo 11 service module, 1969. b, Telstar, 1962. c, Ariane 4, 1988. d, Apollo 11 lunar module. e, Neil Armstrong, 1969. f, Splashdown of Apollo 11, 1969.

No. 827, 200fr, Astronaut on moon saluting. No. 828, 250fr, Astronauts conducting experiments on moon. No. 829, 250fr, Space Shuttle Challenger.

2000, Aug. 23 **Sheets of 6, #a-f**

825-826 A279 Set of 2 20.00 20.00

Souvenir Sheets

827-829 A279 Set of 3 12.00 12.00

2000 Summer Olympics, Sydney A280

Olympic flame, flag and: 80fr, Runner. 90fr, Tennis player.

2000 ***Perf. 14***

830-831 A280 Set of 2 2.75 2.75

AIR POST STAMPS

Afars and Issas Nos. C104-C105, C103 Overprinted with Bars and "REPUBLIQUE DE DJIBOUTI" in Brown or Black

1977 **Engr.** ***Perf. 13***

C106 AP37 55fr multi (Br) 1.75 1.75

C107 AP37 75fr multi 7.00 3.00

Litho. ***Perf. 12***

C108 AP36 500fr multi 13.50 13.50

Nos. C106-C108 (3) 22.25 18.25

Map of Djibouti, Dove, UN Emblem — AP38

1977, Oct. 19 **Photo.** ***Perf. 13***

C109 AP38 300fr multi 5.25 2.75

Djibouti's admission to the United Nations.

Marcel Brochet MB 101, 1955 — AP39

Djibouti Aero Club: 85fr, Tiger Moth, 1960. 200fr, Rallye-Commodore, 1973.

1978, Feb. 27 **Litho.** ***Perf. 13***

C110 AP39 60fr multi 1.10 .35

C111 AP39 85fr multi 1.60 .60

C112 AP39 200fr multi 3.50 1.00

Nos. C110-C112 (3) 6.20 1.95

Old Man, by Rubens AP40

500fr, Hippopotamus Hunt, by Rubens.

1978, Apr. 24 **Photo.** ***Perf. 13***

C113 AP40 50fr multi 1.00 .35

C114 AP40 500fr multi, horiz. 10.00 3.25

Peter Paul Rubens (1577-1640).

Player Holding Soccer Cup — AP41

Design: 300fr, Soccer player, map of South America with Argentina, Cup and emblem.

1978, June 20 **Litho.** ***Perf. 13***

C115 AP41 100fr multi 1.75 .35

C116 AP41 300fr multi 5.25 1.00

11th World Cup Soccer Championship, Argentina, June 1-25.

For overprints see Nos. C117-C118.

Nos. C115-C116 Overprinted:
a. ARGENTINE/CHAMPION 1978
b. ARGENTINE/HOLLANDE/3-1

1978, Aug. 20 **Litho.** ***Perf. 13***

C117 AP41 (a) 100fr multi 1.75 .40

C118 AP41 (b) 300fr multi 5.25 1.25

Argentina's victory in 1978 Soccer Championship.

Tahitian Women, by Gauguin — AP42

Young Hare, by Dürer AP43

Perf. 13x12½, 12½x13

1978, Sept. 25 **Litho.**

C119 AP42 100fr multi 2.25 .40

C120 AP43 250fr multi 5.25 1.50

Paul Gauguin (1848-1903) and Albrecht Dürer (1471-1528), painters.

Common Design Types pictured following the introduction.

Philexafrique II-Essen Issue

Common Design Types

Designs: No. C121, Lynx and Djibouti No. 456. No. C122, Jay and Brunswick No. 3.

1978, Dec. 13 **Litho.** ***Perf. 13x12½***

C121 CD138 90fr multi 3.00 1.25

C122 CD139 90fr multi 3.00 1.25

a. Pair, Nos. C121-C122 + label 6.25 6.25

UPU Emblem, Map of Djibouti, Dove — AP44

1978, Dec. 18 **Engr.** ***Perf. 13***

C123 AP44 200fr multi 3.00 1.10

Centenary of Congress of Paris.

Junkers JU-52 and Dewoitine D-338 — AP45

Powered Flight, 75th Anniversary: 250fr, Potez P63-11, 1941 and Supermarine Spitfire HF-VII, 1942. 500fr, Concorde, 1969 and Sikorsky S-40 "American Clipper," 1931.

1979, May 21 **Litho.** ***Perf. 13x12½***

C124 AP45 140fr multi 2.75 .60

C125 AP45 250fr multi 4.00 1.00

C126 AP45 500fr multi 8.50 1.75

Nos. C124-C126 (3) 15.25 3.35

The Laundress, by Honore Daumier AP46

1979, July 10 **Litho.** ***Perf. 12½x13***

C127 AP46 500fr multi 10.50 2.75

Olympic Emblem, Skis, Sleds — AP47

1980, Jan. 21 Litho. *Perf. 13*
C128 AP47 150fr multi 2.75 .60

13th Winter Olympic Games, Lake Placid, N.Y., Feb. 12-24.
For surcharges see Nos. C133-C134.

Cathedral of the Archangel, Basketball, Moscow '80 Emblem — AP48

120fr, Lomonossov Univ., Moscow, soccer. 250fr, Cathedral of the Annunciation, running.

1980, Apr. 10 Litho. *Perf. 13*
C129 AP48 60fr multi 1.00 .25
C130 AP48 120fr multi 2.00 .40
C131 AP48 250fr multi 4.00 1.00
Nos. C129-C131 (3) 7.00 1.65

22nd Summer Olympic Games, Moscow, July 18-Aug. 3.

Air Djibouti, 1st Anniversary — AP49

1980, Mar. 29 Litho. *Perf. 13x12½*
C132 AP49 400fr multi 7.50 2.00

No. C128 Surcharged in Black and Blue or Purple:
80fr. A.M. MOSER-PROEL / AUTRICHE / DESCENTE DAMES / MEDAILLE D'OR
200fr. HEIDEN / USA / 5 MEDAILLES D'OR / PATINAGE DE VITESSE

1980, Apr. 5 Litho. *Perf. 13*
C133 AP47 80fr on 150fr 1.40 .40
C134 AP47 200fr on 150fr (P) 3.50 1.25

Apollo 11 Moon Landing, 10th Anniversary — AP50

Space Conquests: 300fr, Apollo-Soyuz space project, 5th anniversary.

1980, May 8
C135 AP50 200fr multi 3.50 .60
C136 AP50 300fr multi 5.25 1.00

Satellite Earth Station Inauguration — AP51

1980, July 3 Litho. *Perf. 13*
C137 AP51 500fr multi 9.00 1.75

Graf Zeppelin — AP52

1980, Oct. 2 Litho. *Perf. 13*
C138 AP52 100fr shown 2.25 .40
C139 AP52 150fr Ferdinand von Zeppelin, blimp 2.75 .60

Zeppelin flight, 80th anniversary.

Voyager Passing Saturn — AP53

1980, Dec. 21 Litho. *Perf. 13*
C140 AP53 250fr multi 5.00 1.00

AP54

AP55

World Cup Soccer Preliminary Games: 200fr, Players, diff.

1981, Jan. 14
C141 AP54 80fr multi 1.40 .30
C142 AP54 200fr multi 3.50 .65

1981, Feb. 10 Litho. *Perf. 13*
C143 AP55 100fr multi 2.50 .50

European-African Economic Convention.

5th Anniversary of Viking I Take-off to Mars — AP56

20th Anniversary of Various Space Flights: 75fr, Vostok I, Yuri Gagarin, vert. 150fr, Freedom 7, Alan B. Shepard, vert.

1981, Mar. 9 Litho. *Perf. 13*
C144 AP56 75fr multi 1.40 .30
C145 AP56 120fr multi 2.00 .40
C146 AP56 150fr multi 2.75 .60
Nos. C144-C146 (3) 6.15 1.30

Football Players, by Picasso (1881-1973) — AP57

Design: 400fr Man Wearing a Turban, by Rembrandt (1606-1669), vert.

Perf. 13x12½, 12½x13
1981, Aug. 3 Litho.
C147 AP57 300fr multi 6.25 1.40
C148 AP57 400fr multi 7.00 1.75

Columbia Space Shuttle — AP58

1981, Sept. 24 Litho. *Perf. 13*
C149 AP58 90fr Shuttle, diff., vert. 1.75 .40
C150 AP58 120fr shown 2.25 .60

Nos. C149-C150 Overprinted in Brown with Astronauts' Names and Dates

1981, Nov. 12 Litho. *Perf. 13*
C151 AP58 90fr multi 1.75 .50
C152 AP58 120fr multi 2.25 .75

1982 World Cup Soccer — AP59

Designs: Various soccer players.

1982, Jan. 20
C153 AP59 110fr multi 2.10 .60
C154 AP59 220fr multi 4.00 1.25

For overprints see Nos. C166-C167.

Space Anniversaries — AP60

Designs: 40fr, Luna 9 moon landing, 15th, vert. 60fr, John Glenn's flight, 20th, vert. 180fr, Viking I Mars landing, 5th.

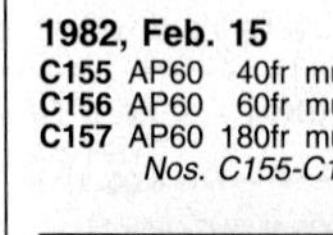
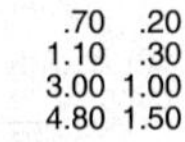

1982, Feb. 15
C155 AP60 40fr multi .70 .20
C156 AP60 60fr multi 1.10 .30
C157 AP60 180fr multi 3.00 1.00
Nos. C155-C157 (3) 4.80 1.50

21st Birthday of Princess Diana of Wales AP61

1982, Apr. 29 Litho. *Perf. 12½x13*
C158 AP61 120fr Portrait 2.00 .75
C159 AP61 180fr Portrait, diff. 3.00 1.00

For overprints see Nos. C168-C169.

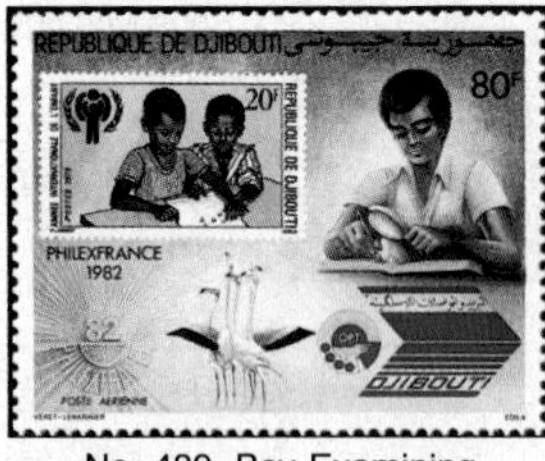
No. 489, Boy Examining Collection — AP62

1982, May 10 *Perf. 13x12½*
C160 AP62 80fr shown 1.40 .50
C161 AP62 140fr No. 495 2.75 .90
a. Pair, Nos. C160-C161 + label 4.50 4.50

PHILEXFRANCE '82 Stamp Exhibition, Paris, June 11-21.

1350th Anniv. of Mohammed's Death at Medina — AP63

1982, June 8 Litho. *Perf. 13*
C162 AP63 500fr Medina Mosque 7.50 2.00

Scouting Year — AP64

1982, June 28
C163 AP64 95fr Baden-Powell 1.50 .50
C164 AP64 200fr Camp, scouts 3.50 1.25

2nd UN Conference on Peaceful Uses of Outer Space, Vienna, Aug. 9-21 — AP65

1982, Aug. 19
C165 AP65 350fr multi 3.00 1.40

Nos. C153-C154 Overprinted with Winner's Name and Scores

1982, July 21 Litho. *Perf. 13*

C166 AP59 110fr multi 2.00 .60
C167 AP59 220fr multi 4.00 1.10

Italy's victory in 1982 World Cup.

Nos. C158-C159 Overprinted in Blue or Red with Date, Name and Title

1982, Aug. 9 *Perf. 12½x13*

C168 AP61 120fr multi 2.25 .75
C169 AP61 180fr multi (R) 3.25 1.00

Birth of Prince William of Wales, June 21.

Franklin D. Roosevelt (1882-1945)
AP66

1982, Oct. 7 Litho. *Perf. 13*

C170 AP66 115fr shown 1.75 .50
C171 AP66 250fr George Washington 4.50 1.00

Manned Flight Bicentenary
AP67

Pre-olympic Year — AP68

1983, Jan. 20 Litho.

C172 AP67 35fr Montgolfiere, 1783 .65 .25
C173 AP67 45fr Giffard, Paris Exposition, 1878 1.10 .30
C174 AP67 120fr Double Eagle II, 1978 2.75 .80
Nos. C172-C174 (3) 4.50 1.35

1983, Feb. 15

C175 AP68 75fr Volleyball 1.40 .50
C176 AP68 125fr Wind surfing 2.40 .80

50th Anniv. of Air France — AP69

1983, Mar. 20 Litho. *Perf. 13*

C177 AP69 25fr Bloch 220 .40 .20
C178 AP69 100fr DC-4 1.75 .70
C179 AP69 175fr Boeing 747 3.25 1.10
Nos. C177-C179 (3) 5.40 2.00

AP70

AP71

180fr, Martin Luther King, Jr. (1929-68), civil rights leader. 250fr, Alfred Nobel (1833-96)

1983, May 18 Litho. *Perf. 13*

C180 AP70 180fr multi 2.75 1.25
C181 AP70 250fr multi 3.75 2.00

1983, July 18 Litho. *Perf. 13*

Service Clubs: 90fr, Rotary Club Intl., Sailing Show, Toronto, June 5-9. 150fr, Lions Club Intl., Honolulu Meeting, June 22-24, Djibouti lighthouse.

C182 AP71 90fr multi 1.40 .60
C183 AP71 150fr multi 2.25 1.00
a. Pair, Nos. C182-C183 + label 5.00 1.75

Vintage Motor Cars — AP72

1983, July 18 Litho. *Perf. 13x12½*

C184 AP72 60fr Renault, 1904 1.50 .40
C185 AP72 80fr Mercedes, 1910, vert. 2.00 .55
C186 AP72 110fr Lorraine-Dietrich, 1912 2.50 .75
Nos. C184-C186 (3) 6.00 1.70

Souvenir Sheet

Air France, 50th Anniv. — AP73

Illustration reduced.

1983, Oct. 7 Litho. *Perf. 12½*
Self-Adhesive

C187 AP73 250fr multicolored 25.00 2.10

Printed on wood.

Vostok VI
AP74

1983, Oct. 20 Litho. *Perf. 12*

C188 AP74 120fr shown 2.00 .80
C189 AP74 200fr Explorer I 3.50 1.10

1984 Winter Olympics — AP75

1984, Feb. 14 Litho. *Perf. 13*

C190 AP75 70fr Speed skating 1.40 .50
C191 AP75 130fr Figure skating 2.25 1.00

For overprints see Nos. C196-C197.

Souvenir Sheet

Ship — AP76

1984, Feb. 14 Litho. *Perf. 12½*

C192 AP76 250fr multi 11.00 1.75

Sea-Me-We (South-east Asia-Middle East-Western Europe) submarine cable construction agreement.

Motorized Hang Gliders — AP77

Various hang gliders.

1984, Mar. 12 *Perf. 13x12½*

C193 AP77 65fr multi 1.25 .50
C194 AP77 85fr multi 1.60 .60
C195 AP77 100fr multi 2.10 .75
Nos. C193-C195 (3) 4.95 1.85

Nos. C190-C191 Overprinted with Winners' Names and Country

1984, Mar. 28 *Perf. 13*

C196 AP75 70fr multi 1.25 .50
C197 AP75 130fr multi 2.40 1.00

Portrait of Marguerite Matisse, 1910, by Henri Matisse
AP78

Design: 200fr, Portrait of Mario Varvogli, by Amedeo Modigliani.

1984, Apr. 15 Litho. *Perf. 12½x13*

C198 AP78 150fr multi 3.25 1.00
C199 AP78 200fr multi 4.00 1.40

1984 Summer Olympics — AP79

1984, May 24 *Perf. 13*

C200 AP79 50fr Running 1.00 .40
C201 AP79 60fr High jump 1.25 .40
C202 AP79 80fr Swimming 1.50 .60
Nos. C200-C202 (3) 3.75 1.40

Battle Scene — AP80

1984, June 16 Litho. *Perf. 13x12½*

C203 AP80 300fr multi 5.50 2.25

125th anniv. of Battle of Solferino and 120th anniv. of Red Cross.

Bleriot's Flight over English Channel, 75th Anniv. — AP81

1984, July 8

C204 AP81 40fr 14-Bis plans .80 .30
C205 AP81 75fr Britten-Norman Islander 1.40 .55
C206 AP81 90fr Air Djibouti jet 1.50 .65
Nos. C204-C206 (3) 3.70 1.50

375th Anniv., Galileo's Telescope
AP82

1984, Oct. 7 Litho. *Perf. 13*

C207 AP82 120fr Telescopes, spacecraft 2.25 .80
C208 AP82 180fr Galileo, telescopes 3.25 1.10

1984 Soccer Events — AP83

1984, Oct. 20 Litho. *Perf. 13*

C209 AP83 80fr Euro Cup 1.75 .60
C210 AP83 80fr Los Angeles Olympics 1.75 .60
a. Pair, Nos. C209-C210 + label 4.25 1.25

Service Clubs — AP84

1985, Feb. 23 Litho. *Perf. 13*
C211 AP84 50fr Lions, World Leprosy Day 1.10 .40
C212 AP84 60fr Rotary, chess board, pieces 1.25 .45

#C211-C212 exist in souvenir sheets of 1.

Telecommunications Technology — AP85

No. C213, Technician, researchist, operator. No. C214, Offshore oil rig, transmission tower, government building.

1985, July 2 *Perf. 13x12½*
C213 AP85 80fr multi 2.00 .55
C214 AP85 80fr multi 2.00 .55
a. Pair, Nos. C213-C214 + label 4.50 1.10

PHILEXAFRICA '85, Lome.

Telecommunications Development — AP86

1985, Oct. 2 *Perf. 13*
C215 AP86 50fr Intl. transmission center .90 .35
C216 AP86 90fr Ariane rocket, vert. 1.60 .65
C217 AP86 120fr ARABSAT satellite 2.00 .90
Nos. C215-C217 (3) 4.50 1.90

Youths Windsurfing, Playing Tennis — AP87

No. C219, Tadjoura Highway construction.

1985, Nov. 13 *Perf. 13x12½*
C218 AP87 100fr multi 2.00 .70
C219 AP87 100fr multi 2.00 .70
a. Pair, Nos. C218-C219 + label 4.50 1.50

PHILEXAFRICA '85, Lome, Togo, 11/16-24.

1986 World Cup Soccer Championships, Mexico — AP88

1986, Feb. 24 Litho. *Perf. 13*
C220 AP88 75fr shown 1.50 .50
C221 AP88 100fr Players, stadium 2.00 .70

For overprints see Nos. C223-C224.

Statue of Liberty, Cent. — AP89

1986, May 21
C222 AP89 250fr multi 4.00 1.75

Nos. C220-C221 Ovptd. with Winners

1986, Sept. 15 Litho. *Perf. 13*
C223 75fr "FRANCE - BELGIQUE / 4-2" 1.10 .55
C224 100fr "3-2 ARGENTINE-RFA" 1.50 .70

1986 World Chess Championships, May 1-19 — AP89a

Malayan animal chess pieces.

1986, Oct. 13 Litho. *Perf. 13*
C225 AP89a 80fr Knight, bishops 1.75 .60
C226 AP89a 120fr Rook, king, pawn 2.75 .90

Yuri Gagarin, Sputnik Spacecraft — AP90

1986, Nov. 27 Litho. *Perf. 13*
C227 AP90 150fr shown 3.00 1.10
C228 AP90 200fr Space rendezvous, 1966 3.25 1.25

First man in space, 25th anniv.; Gemini 8-Agena link-up, 20th anniv.

Historic Flights — AP91

1987, Jan. 22 Litho. *Perf. 13*
C229 AP91 55fr Amiot 370 1.25 .40
C230 AP91 80fr Spirit of St. Louis 1.75 .55
C231 AP91 120fr Voyager 2.50 .90
Nos. C229-C231 (3) 5.50 1.85

First flight from Istria to Djibouti, 1942; Lindbergh's Transatlantic flight, 1927; nonstop world circumnavigation without refueling.
For surcharge see No. C240.

Souvenir Sheet

Fight Against Leprosy — AP91a

Design: Raoul Follereau (b. 1903), care giver to lepers, Gerhard Hansen (1841-1912), discoverer of bacillus of leprosy.
Illustration reduced.

1987, Mar. 23 Litho. *Perf. 13x12½*
Self-Adhesive
C231A AP91a 500fr multi 17.00 4.25

No. C231A printed on wood.

Pres. Aptidon, Natl. Crest and Flag AP92

1987, June 27 Litho. *Perf. 12½x13*
C232 AP92 250fr multi 4.00 1.50

Natl. independence, 10th anniv.

Telstar, 25th Anniv. — AP93

1987, Oct. 1 *Perf. 13*
C233 AP93 190fr shown 3.00 1.25
C234 AP93 250fr Samuel Morse, telegraph key 3.75 1.50

Invention of the telegraph, 150th anniv. (250fr).

City of Djibouti, Cent. — AP94

100fr, Djibouti Creek & quay, 1887. 150fr, Aerial view of city, 1987. 250fr, Somali Coast #6, 20, postmarks of 1898 & 1903.

1987, Nov. 15 Litho. *Perf. 13x12½*
C235 AP94 100fr blk & buff 2.00 1.10
C236 AP94 150fr multi 3.00 1.60
a. Pair, Nos. C235-C236 + label 6.00 2.75

Souvenir Sheet

237 AP94 250fr multi 5.50 2.75

No. C237 has decorative margin like design of 100fr.

Intl. Red Cross and Red Crescent Organizations, 125th Anniv. — AP95

1988, Feb. 17 Litho. *Perf. 13*
C238 AP95 300fr multi 6.00 3.25

1988 Summer Olympics, Seoul — AP96

1988, June 15 Litho. *Perf. 13*
C239 AP96 105fr multi 2.50 1.00

For overprint see No. C242.

No. C229 Surcharged in Black

1988, June 28
C240 AP91 70fr on 55fr multi 1.75 .70

Air race in memory of the Paris-Djibouti-St. Denis flight of French aviator Roland Garros (1888-1913).

World Post Day — AP97

1988, Oct. 9 Litho. *Perf. 13*
C241 AP97 1000fr multi 15.00 10.00

No. C239 Ovptd. "AHMED SALAH / 1re MEDAILLE OLYMPIQUE"

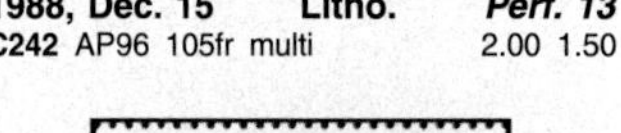

1988, Dec. 15 Litho. *Perf. 13*
C242 AP96 105fr multi 2.00 1.50

World Telecommunications Day — AP98

1989, May 17 Litho. *Perf. 12½*
C243 AP98 150fr multi 2.75 1.50

PHILEXFRANCE '89, Declaration of Human Rights and Citizenship Bicent. — AP99

1989, July 7 Litho. *Perf. 12½x13*
C244 AP99 120fr multi 2.25 1.25

Salt, Lake Assal — AP100

1989, Sept. 15 Litho. *Perf. 13*
C245 AP100 300fr multicolored 4.50 3.00

POSTAGE DUE STAMP

Urn for Milking Camel — D1

1988, Jan. 31 Litho. *Perf. 13*
J1 D1 60fr multi .90 .65

DOMINICA

ˌdä-mə-ˈnē-kə

LOCATION — The largest island of the Windward group in the West Indies. Southeast of Puerto Rico.
GOVT. — Republic in British Commonwealth
AREA — 290 sq. mi.
POP. — 64,881 (1999 est.)
CAPITAL — Roseau

Formerly a Presidency of the Leeward Islands, Dominica became a separate colony under the governor of the Windward Islands on January 1, 1940. Dominica joined the West Indies federation April 22, 1958. In 1968, Dominica became an associate state of Britain; in 1978, an independent nation.

12 Pence = 1 Shilling
20 Shillings = 1 Pound
100 Cents = 1 Dollar (1949)

Catalogue values for unused stamps in this country are for Never Hinged items, beginning with Scott 112.

Watermark

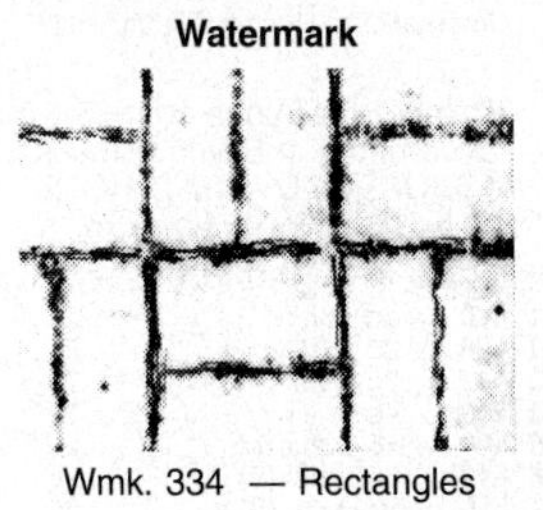

Wmk. 334 — Rectangles

Queen Victoria — A1

Perf. 12½

1874, May 4 Typo. Wmk. 1

No.	Type	Description	Unused	Used
1	A1	1p violet	170.00	55.00
2	A1	6p green	625.00	115.00
3	A1	1sh deep lilac rose	375.00	80.00
		Nos. 1-3 (3)	1,170.	250.00

During 1875-87 some issues were manuscript dated with village names. These are considered postally used. Stamps with entire village names sell for much more, starting at $100.

1877-79 *Perf. 14*

No.	Type	Description	Unused	Used
4	A1	½p bister ('79)	14.50	*57.50*
5	A1	1p violet	7.00	2.30
a.		Diagonal or vertical half used as ½p on cover		2,100.
6	A1	2½p red brown ('79)	260.00	32.50
7	A1	4p blue ('79)	125.00	4.00
8	A1	6p green	170.00	22.50
9	A1	1sh dp lilac rose	140.00	57.50
		Nos. 4-9 (6)	716.50	176.30

For surcharges see Nos. 10-15.

No. 5 Bisected and Surcharged in Black or Red:

a b c

1882

No.	Type	Description	Unused	Used
10	A1(a)	½p on half of 1p	210.00	47.50
a.		Inverted surcharge	1,150.	900.00
b.		Surcharge tete beche pair	*1,900.*	*1,750.*
11	A1(b)	½p on half of 1p	72.50	27.50
a.		Surch. reading downward	72.50	27.50
b.		Double surcharge	900.00	
12	A1(c)	½p on half of 1p (R)	35.00	19.00
a.		Inverted surcharge	1,150.	550.00
b.		Double surcharge	1,850.	750.00
		Nos. 10-12 (3)	317.50	94.00

The existence of genuine copies of No. 10b has been questioned.

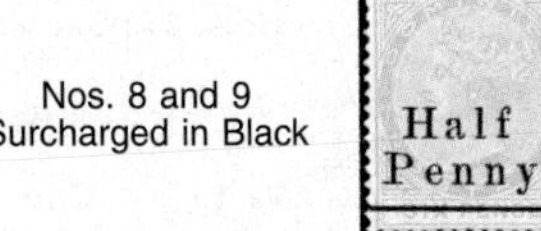

Nos. 8 and 9 Surcharged in Black

1886

No.	Type	Description	Unused	Used
13	A1	½p on 6p green	6.50	6.00
14	A1	1p on 6p green	*24,000.*	*12,500.*
15	A1	1p on 1sh	16.00	*19.00*
a.		Double surcharge	6,250.	3,500.

All copies of No. 14 may have small pin marks which may have been part of the surcharging process.

1883-88 Wmk. 2

No.	Type	Description	Unused	Used
16	A1	½p bister ('83)	3.75	*11.50*
17	A1	½p green ('86)	1.70	*6.25*
18	A1	1p violet ('86)	32.50	14.00
a.		Half used as ½p on cover		2,200.
19	A1	1p car rose ('87)	3.25	*7.50*
a.		1p rose	18.00	*20.00*
b.		Vert. half used as ½p on cover		2,100.
20	A1	2½p red brn ('84)	160.00	3.00
21	A1	2½p ultra ('88)	4.25	*5.75*
22	A1	4p gray ('86)	3.75	*5.75*
23	A1	6p orange ('88)	11.00	*55.00*
24	A1	1sh dp lil rose ('88)	180.00	*325.00*
		Nos. 16-24 (9)	400.20	*433.75*

Roseau, Capital of Dominica — A6

King Edward VII — A7

1903 Wmk. 1 *Perf. 14*

No.	Type	Description	Unused	Used
25	A6	½p gray green	4.75	2.90
26	A6	1p car & black	9.50	.90
27	A6	2p brn & gray grn	3.00	*5.25*
28	A6	2½p ultra & blk	6.00	4.75
29	A6	3p black & vio	9.50	4.00
30	A6	6p org brn & blk	5.25	21.00
31	A6	1sh gray grn & red vio	32.50	*47.50*
32	A6	2sh red vio & blk	30.00	*32.50*
33	A6	2sh6p ocher & gray grn	21.00	*85.00*
34	A7	5sh brown & blk	105.00	*160.00*
		Nos. 25-34 (10)	226.50	*363.80*

Nos. 25 to 29 and 31 are on both ordinary and chalky paper. For detailed listings, see the *Scott Classic Specialized Catalogue of Stamps & Covers.*

1907-20 Wmk. 3

Chalky Paper

No.	Type	Description	Unused	Used
35	A6	½p gray green	4.00	3.75
36	A6	1p car & black	2.40	.50
37	A6	2p brn & gray grn	6.25	*19.00*
38	A6	2½p ultra & black	5.25	25.00
39	A6	3p black & vio	4.75	*16.00*
40	A6	3p vio, *yel* ('09)	3.50	*5.00*
41	A6	6p org brn & blk ('08)	60.00	*95.00*
42	A6	6p vio & dl vio ('09)	11.50	*17.50*
43	A6	1sh gray grn & red vio	4.50	*62.50*
44	A6	1sh blk, *green* ('10)	3.50	3.25
45	A6	2sh red vio & blk ('08)	27.50	*37.50*
46	A6	2sh ultra & vio, *bl* ('19)	30.00	*97.50*
47	A6	2sh6p ocher & gray grn ('08)	25.00	*70.00*
48	A6	2sh6p red & blk, *bl* ('20)	30.00	*100.00*
49	A7	5sh brn & blk ('08)	70.00	70.00
		Nos. 35-49 (15)	288.15	*622.50*

Nos. 40, 42 and 44 are on both ordinary and chalky paper. For detailed listings, see the *Scott Classic Specialized Catalogue of Stamps & Covers.*
For type surcharged see No. 55.

1908-09 Ordinary Paper

No.	Type	Description	Unused	Used
50	A6	½p green	3.25	2.75
51	A6	1p scarlet	1.75	.55
a.		1p carmine	3.50	.35
52	A6	2p gray ('09)	4.00	*14.00*
53	A6	2½p ultramarine	9.50	*7.00*
a.		2½p bright blue ('18)	5.75	*10.50*
		Nos. 50-53 (4)	18.50	*24.30*

King George V — A8

1914 Chalky Paper *Perf. 14*

No.	Type	Description	Unused	Used
54	A8	5sh grn & scar, *yel*	70.00	*92.50*

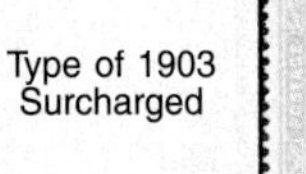

Type of 1903 Surcharged

1920

No.	Type	Description	Unused	Used
55	A6	1½p on 2½p orange	3.00	*5.25*

1921 Wmk. 4

Ordinary Paper

No.	Type	Description	Unused	Used
56	A6	½p green	3.00	*17.50*
57	A6	1p rose red	2.25	*4.50*
58	A6	1½p orange	4.00	*12.50*
59	A6	2p gray	3.50	*4.00*
60	A6	2½p ultra	2.25	*10.00*
61	A6	6p vio & dl vio	3.00	*42.50*
62	A6	2sh ultra & vio, *bl*	37.50	*105.00*
63	A6	2sh6p red & blk, *bl*	37.50	*110.00*
		Nos. 56-63 (8)	93.00	*306.00*

No. 61 is on chalky paper.

Seal of Colony and George V — A9

1923-33 Chalky Paper Wmk. 4

No.	Type	Description	Unused	Used
65	A9	½p green & blk	2.00	.70
66	A9	1p violet & blk	2.30	1.90
67	A9	1p scar & black	10.50	1.15
68	A9	1½p car & black	3.25	.75
69	A9	1½p dp brn & blk	10.50	.80
70	A9	2p gray & black	2.00	.55
71	A9	2½p org & black	1.70	*10.50*
72	A9	2½p ultra & black	4.75	2.30
73	A9	3p ultra & black	1.75	*14.00*
74	A9	3p red & blk, *yel*	1.75	1.15
75	A9	4p brown & blk	2.75	*6.25*
76	A9	6p red vio & blk	4.00	*8.00*
77	A9	1sh blk, *emerald*	2.60	*3.25*
78	A9	2sh ultra & blk, *bl*	11.50	*22.50*
79	A9	2sh6p red & blk, *bl*	21.00	*22.50*
80	A9	3sh vio & blk, *yel*	3.75	*14.00*
81	A9	4sh red & blk, *emer*	12.50	*25.00*
82	A9	5sh grn & blk, *yel*	25.00	*55.00*
		Nos. 65-82 (18)	123.60	*190.30*

Issue years: Nos. 80, 82, 1927; Nos. 72, 74, 1928; Nos. 67, 69, 1933; others, 1923.

1923 Wmk. 3

No.	Type	Description	Unused	Used
83	A9	3sh vio & blk, *yel*	5.00	*72.50*
84	A9	5sh grn & blk, *yel*	11.00	*57.50*
85	A9	£1 vio & blk, *red*	275.00	*400.00*
		Nos. 83-85 (3)	291.00	*530.00*

Common Design Types pictured following the introduction.

Silver Jubilee Issue

Common Design Type

Perf. 13½x14

1935, May 6 Wmk. 4 Engr.

No.	Type	Description	Unused	Used
90	CD301	1p car & blue	.25	.25
91	CD301	1½p gray blk & ultra	.85	1.25
92	CD301	2½p blue & brn	3.00	*3.25*
93	CD301	1sh brt vio & ind	3.00	*4.50*
		Nos. 90-93 (4)	7.10	9.25
		Set, never hinged	13.50	

Coronation Issue

Common Design Type

1937, May 12 *Perf. 11x11½*

No.	Type	Description	Unused	Used
94	CD302	1p dark carmine	.20	.20
95	CD302	1½p brown	.20	.20
96	CD302	2½p deep ultra	.35	*.60*
		Nos. 94-96 (3)	.75	1.00
		Set, never hinged	1.25	

Fresh-Water Lake — A10

Layou River — A11

Picking Limes — A12

Boiling Lake — A13

1938-47 Wmk. 4 *Perf. 12½*

No.	Type	Description	Unused	Used
97	A10	½p grn & red brn	.20	.20
98	A11	1p car & gray	.20	.20
99	A12	1½p rose vio & grn	.20	*.75*
100	A13	2p brn blk & dp rose	.40	*1.00*
101	A12	2½p ultra & rose vio	3.25	1.90
102	A11	3p red brn & ol	.20	*.40*
103	A12	3½p red vio & brt ultra	1.00	*1.60*
104	A10	6p vio & yel grn	.50	*1.25*
105	A10	7p org brn & grn	.85	*1.40*
106	A13	1sh olive & vio	1.75	1.25
107	A11	2sh red vio & blk	4.00	*8.25*
108	A10	2sh6p scar ver & blk	8.75	5.00
109	A11	5sh dk brn & bl	4.75	*8.25*
110	A13	10sh dl org & blk	9.75	*14.50*
		Nos. 97-110 (14)	35.80	*45.95*
		Set, never hinged	50.00	

Issued: 3½p, 7p, 2sh, 10sh, 10/15/47; others, 8/15/38.

King George VI — A14

1940, Apr. 15 Photo. *Perf. 14½x14*

No.	Type	Description	Unused	Used
111	A14	¼p brown violet	.20	.20

Catalogue values for unused stamps in this section, from this point to the end of the section, are for Never Hinged items.

Peace Issue

Common Design Type

1946, Oct. 14 Engr. *Perf. 13½x14*

No.	Type	Description	Unused	Used
112	CD303	1p carmine	.20	.20
113	CD303	3½p deep blue	.20	.20

Silver Wedding Issue
Common Design Types

1948, Dec. 1 Photo. *Perf. 14x14½*
114 CD304 1p scarlet .20 .20

Engraved; Name Typographed
Perf. 11½x11
115 CD305 10sh orange brn 11.00 *22.50*

UPU Issue
Common Design Types
Engr.: Name Typo. on 6c and 12c
1949, Oct. 10 *Perf. 13½, 11x11½*
116 CD306 5c blue .20 .20
117 CD307 6c chocolate 1.00 1.00
118 CD308 12c rose violet .45 .45
119 CD309 24c olive .25 .25
Nos. 116-119 (4) 1.90 1.90

University Issue
Common Design Types
1951, Feb. 16 Engr. *Perf. 14x14½*
120 CD310 3c purple & green .60 .40
121 CD311 12c dp car & dk bl grn .80 .60

George VI A15

Drying Cocoa A16

Picking Oranges — A17

Designs: 2c and 60c, Carib Baskets. 3c and 48c, Lime Plantation. 4c, Picking Oranges. 5c, Bananas. 6c, Botanical Gardens. 8c, Drying Vanilla Beans. 12c and $1.20, Fresh Water Lake. 14c, Layou River. 24c, Boiling Lake.

Perf. 14½x14
1951, July 1 Photo. Wmk. 4
122 A15 ½c brown .20 .20

Perf. 13x13½
Engr.
123 A16 1c red org & blk .20 .25
124 A16 2c dp grn & red brn .20 .20
125 A16 3c red vio & bl grn .20 .60
126 A16 4c dk brn & brn org .40 .70
127 A16 5c rose red & blk .95 .25
128 A16 6c org brn & ol grn 1.00 .25
129 A16 8c dp bl & dp grn .65 .60
130 A16 12c emer & gray .50 1.60
131 A16 14c pur & blue 1.10 1.60
132 A16 24c rose car & red vio .90 .25
133 A16 48c red org & bl grn 3.00 *7.25*
134 A16 60c gray & car 3.00 *6.00*
135 A16 $1.20 gray & emer 4.75 *6.00*

Perf. 13½x13
136 A17 $2.40 gray & org 26.00 *35.00*
Nos. 122-136 (15) 43.05 *60.75*

Nos. 125, 127, 129 and 131 Overprinted in Black or Carmine

1951, Oct. 15 *Perf. 13x13½*
137 A16 3c red vio & bl green .20 .20
138 A16 5c rose red & black .35 .35
139 A16 8c dp blue & dp grn (C) .45 .45
140 A16 14c purple & blue (C) .70 .70
Nos. 137-140 (4) 1.70 1.70

Adoption of a new constitution for the Windward Islands, 1951.

Coronation Issue
Common Design Type
1953, June 2 Engr. *Perf. 13½x13*
141 CD312 2c dk green & black .20 .20

Types of 1951 with Portrait of Queen Elizabeth II

1954, Oct. 1 Photo. *Perf. 14½x14*
142 A15 ½c brown .20 .20

Perf. 13x13½
Engr.
143 A16 1c red org & blk .20 .20
144 A16 2c dp grn & red brn .70 .20
145 A16 3c red vio & bl grn 1.50 .40
146 A16 4c dk brn & brn org .20 .20
147 A16 5c rose red & blk 1.50 .55
148 A16 6c org brn & ol grn .45 .20
149 A16 8c dp bl & dp grn 1.00 .20
150 A16 12c emer & gray .60 .20
151 A16 14c pur & bl .25 .25
152 A16 24c rose car & red vio .45 *.40*
153 A16 48c red org & bl grn 1.90 *8.50*
154 A16 60c gray & car 1.25 *1.50*
155 A16 $1.20 gray & emer 19.00 3.50

Perf. 13½x13
156 A17 $2.40 gray & org 19.00 8.00
Nos. 142-156 (15) 48.20 24.50

Mat Making — A18

5c, Canoe making. 10c, Bananas.

1957, Oct. 15 Wmk. 4 *Perf. 13x13½*
157 A18 3c car rose & black 2.40 *1.75*
158 A18 5c brown & blue 7.50 .80
159 A18 10c redsh brn & brt grn 4.00 1.60
160 A18 48c violet & brown 1.00 *.85*
Nos. 157-160 (4) 14.90 5.00

West Indies Federation
Common Design Type
Perf. 11½x11
1958, Apr. 22 Wmk. 314
161 CD313 3c green .20 .20
162 CD313 6c blue .20 .20
163 CD313 12c car rose .40 .40
Nos. 161-163 (3) .80 .80

Sailing Canoe — A19

Traditional Costume — A20

Designs: 1c, Seashore, Rosalie. 2c, 5c, Queen Elizabeth II by Annigoni. 4c, Sulphur Springs. 6c, Road making. 8c, Dugout canoe. 10c, Frog (mountain chicken). 12c, Boats and Scotts Head. 15c, Bananas. 24c, Imperial parrot. 48c, View of Goodwill. 60c, Cacao tree. $1.20, Coat of Arms. $2.40, Trafalgar Falls. $4.80, Coconut palm.

Two types of 14c:
I — Mountain light violet. Girl's eyes look straight out.
II — Mountain blue. Eyes look sideways.

Perf. 14½x14, 14x14½
1963, May 16 Photo. Wmk. 314
164 A19 1c bl, brn & grn .20 *1.00*
165 A20 2c ultramarine .20 .20
166 A19 3c lt ultra & blk 1.00 1.25
167 A19 4c sl, grn & brn .20 .20
168 A20 5c magenta .20 .20
169 A19 6c lt grn, vio & buff .20 .20
170 A19 8c tan, blk & lt grn .20 .20
171 A19 10c pink & brn .20 .20
172 A19 12c bl, blk, grn & brn .65 .20
173 A20 14c multi (II) .65 .20
a. Type I .50 .70
174 A19 15c grn, yel & brn 1.00 .20
175 A20 24c multicolored 7.50 .20
176 A19 48c bl, blk & grn .70 .50
177 A19 60c blk, grn, org & brn 1.00 .85
178 A19 $1.20 multicolored 6.25 1.25
179 A20 $2.40 grn, bl, brn & blk 3.00 3.00
180 A20 $4.80 bl, brn & grn 8.50 *22.50*
Nos. 164-180 (17) 31.65 32.35

For overprints see Nos. 211-232.

1966-67 Wmk. 314 Sideways
167a A19 4c ('67) .20 .20
169a A19 6c .25 .25
170a A19 8c .60 .60
171a A19 10c ('67) .65 .65
174a A19 15c ('67) 1.00 1.00
Nos. 167a-174a (5) 2.70 2.70

Freedom from Hunger Issue
Common Design Type
1963, June 4 *Perf. 14x14½*
181 CD314 15c lilac .25 .25

Red Cross Centenary Issue
Common Design Type
Wmk. 314
1963, Sept. 2 Litho. *Perf. 13*
182 CD315 5c black & red .20 .20
183 CD315 15c ultra & red .70 *.90*

Shakespeare Issue
Common Design Type
1964, Apr. 23 Photo. *Perf. 14x14½*
184 CD316 15c lilac rose .30 .30

ITU Issue
Common Design Type
1965, May 17 Litho. *Perf. 11x11½*
185 CD317 2c emerald & blue .20 .20
186 CD317 48c grnsh blue & slate .60 .60

Intl. Cooperation Year Issue
Common Design Type
1965, Oct. 25 *Perf. 14½*
187 CD318 1c blue grn & claret .20 .20
188 CD318 15c lt violet & grn .30 .30

Churchill Memorial Issue
Common Design Type
1966, Jan. 24 Photo. *Perf. 14*
Design in Black, Gold and Carmine Rose
189 CD319 1c bright blue .20 .20
a. Gold omitted *750.00*
190 CD319 5c green .20 .20
191 CD319 15c brown .30 .30
192 CD319 24c violet .40 .40
Nos. 189-192 (4) 1.10 1.10

Royal Visit Issue
Common Design Type
1966, Feb. 4 Litho. *Perf. 11x12*
193 CD320 5c violet blue .75 .20
194 CD320 15c dk car rose 2.25 .40

World Cup Soccer Issue
Common Design Type
1966, July 1 Litho. *Perf. 14*
195 CD321 5c multicolored .25 .20
196 CD321 24c multicolored .75 .45

WHO Headquarters Issue
Common Design Type
1966, Sept. 20 Litho. *Perf. 14*
197 CD322 5c multicolored .20 .20
198 CD322 24c multicolored .45 .45

UNESCO Anniversary Issue
Common Design Type
1966, Dec. 1 Litho. *Perf. 14*
199 CD323 5c "Education" .20 .20
200 CD323 15c "Science" .30 .20
201 CD323 24c "Culture" .50 .20
Nos. 199-201 (3) 1.00 .60

Carib, Negro and Caucasian Children — A21

10c, Columbus' ship Santa Maria & banderol. 15c, Hands with banderol. 24c, Belaire dancers.

Perf. 14½x14
1967, Nov. 3 Photo. Wmk. 314
202 A21 5c multicolored .20 .20
203 A21 10c multicolored .30 .20
204 A21 15c multicolored .20 .20
205 A21 24c multicolored .20 .20
Nos. 202-205 (4) .90 .80

Issued for National Day, Nov. 3.

John F. Kennedy and Human Rights Flame — A22

Human Rights Flame and: 10c, Cecil E. A. Rawle (1891-1938), Dominican crusader for human rights. 12c, Pope John XXIII. 48c, Florence Nightingale. 60c, Dr. Albert Schweitzer.

Wmk. 314 Sideways
1968, Apr. 20 Litho. *Perf. 14*
206 A22 1c multicolored .20 .20
207 A22 10c multicolored .20 .20
208 A22 12c multicolored .45 .20
209 A22 48c multicolored .30 .25
210 A22 60c multicolored .30 .25
Nos. 206-210 (5) 1.45 1.10

International Human Rights Year.

Stamps and Types of 1963-67 Overprinted in Silver or Black: "ASSOCIATED / STATEHOOD"

Perf. 14½x14, 14x14½
1968, July 8 Photo. Wmk. 314
211 A19 1c multi .20 .20
212 A20 2c ultra .20 .20
213 A19 3c lt ultra & blk .20 .20
214 A19 4c multi .20 .20
215 A20 5c magenta .20 .20
216 A19 6c multi (B) .20 .20
217 A19 8c multi (B) .20 .20
218 A19 10c pink & brn .55 1.10
219 A19 12c multi .20 .20
a. Watermark upright .20 .20
220 A20 14c multi (II) .20 .20
221 A19 15c multi .20 .20
222 A20 24c multi 3.25 .20
223 A19 48c multi .55 1.00
a. Watermark upright .50 *1.00*
224 A19 60c multi (B) .90 1.75
225 A19 $1.20 multi (B) 1.00 2.00
226 A20 $2.40 multi 1.00 2.00
227 A20 $4.80 multi 1.25 2.50
Nos. 211-227 (17) 10.50 12.55

In this set, overprint was applied to 2c, 3c, 12c, 14c, 24c, 48c, 60c, $1.20, $2.40 and $4.80 with watermark upright. A reprinting of the 1c, 4c, 6c, 8c, 10c, 12c, No. 219, 15c and 48c, No. 223 on paper with watermark sideways was made. Same value.

Nos. 164-166, 173 and 178 Overprinted: "NATIONAL DAY / 3 NOVEMBER 1968"

Perf. 14½x14, 14x14½
1968, Nov. 3 Photo. Wmk. 314
228 A19 1c blue, brn & grn .20 .20
229 A20 2c ultra .20 .20
230 A19 3c lt ultra & blk .20 .20
231 A20 14c multi (I) .20 .20
232 A19 $1.20 multicolored .70 .70
Nos. 228-232 (5) 1.50 1.50

A23

#233a, 3 soccer players. #233b, Soccer player, goalie. #234a, Swimmers at start. #234b, Divers. #235a, Javelin thrower, hurdlers. #235b, Hurdlers. #236a, Basketball. #236b, 3 basketball players.

Perf. 11½
1968, Nov. 23 Unwmk. Litho.
233 A23 1c Pair, #a-b .20 .20
234 A23 5c Pair, #a-b .20 .20
235 A23 48c Pair, #a-b .45 .45
236 A23 60c Pair, #a-b 1.50 1.50
Nos. 233-236 (4) 2.35 2.35

19th Olympic Games, Mexico City, 10/12-27.

The Small Cowper Madonna, by Raphael
A24

Perf. 12½x12

1968, Dec. 23 Photo. Unwmk.

241 A24 5c multicolored .20 .20

Christmas. No. 241 printed in sheets of 20. Sheets of 6 (3x2) exist containing two each of 12c, 24c, and $1.20 stamps, each picturing a different madonna painting. Value $2.50.

Venus and Adonis, by Rubens — A25

Citrus Fruit Picker — A26

Paintings: 15c, The Death of Socrates, by Louis Jacques David. 24c, Christ at Emmaus, by Velazquez. 50c, Pilate Washing his Hands, by Rembrandt.

Perf. 14½x15

1969, Jan. 30 Litho. Wmk. 314

242 A25 5c lilac & multi .20 .20
243 A25 15c emerald & multi .25 .25
244 A25 24c lt blue & multi .25 .25
245 A25 50c crimson & multi .40 .40
Nos. 242-245 (4) 1.10 1.10

20th anniv. (in 1968) of the WHO.

1969, Mar. 10 ***Perf. 14½***

#247, Woman and child. #248, Hotel. #249, Red-necked parrots. #250, Calypso band. #251, Women dancers. #252, Tropical fish and coelenterates. #253, Diver and turtle.

246 A26 10c multicolored .20 .20
247 A26 10c multicolored .20 .20
a. Pair, #246-247 .25
248 A26 12c multicolored .20 .20
249 A26 12c multicolored .20 .20
a. Pair, #248-249 .25
250 A26 24c multicolored .25 .25
251 A26 24c multicolored .25 .25
a. Pair, #250-251 .50
252 A26 48c multicolored .70 .70
253 A26 48c multicolored .70 .70
a. Pair, #252-253 1.40
Nos. 246-253 (8) 2.70 2.70

Tourist publicity.

Spinning, by Millet, Flags and ILO Emblem — A27

50th anniv. of the ILO (Etchings by Jean F. Millet, Flags and ILO Emblem): 30c, Threshing. 30c, Flax pulling.

1969, July Unwmk. ***Perf. 13½***

254 A27 15c multicolored .20 .20
255 A27 30c multicolored .25 .25
256 A27 38c multicolored .25 .25
Nos. 254-256 (3) .70 .70

"Strength in Unity," Bananas and Cacao
A28

"Strength in Unity" Emblem and: 8c, Map of Dominica and Hawker Siddeley 748. 12c, Map of Caribbean. 24c, Ships in harbor.

1969, July Litho.

257 A28 5c orange & multi .20 .20
258 A28 8c gray & multi .20 .20
259 A28 12c lilac & multi .20 .20
260 A28 24c lt blue & multi .40 .40
Nos. 257-260 (4) 1.00 1.00

Caribbean Free Trade Area (CARIFTA).

Gandhi at Spinning Wheel and Big Ben, London
A29

38c, Gandhi, Nehru and Fatehpur Sikri Mausoleum. $1.20, Gandhi & Taj Mahal.

1969, Oct. Litho. ***Perf. 14½***

261 A29 6c multicolored .45 .20
262 A29 38c multicolored .75 .25
263 A29 $1.20 multicolored .80 .80
Nos. 261-263 (3) 2.00 1.25

Mohandas K. Gandhi (1869-1948), leader in India's fight for independence. "Gandhi" is misspelled "Ghandi" on Nos. 261-263.

St. Joseph — A30

Stained Glass Windows, from 17th Century French Churches: 8c, St. John. 12c, St. Peter. 60c, St. Paul.

1969, Nov. 10 Litho. ***Perf. 14***

264 A30 6c black & multi .20 .20
265 A30 8c black & multi .20 .20
266 A30 12c black & multi .20 .20
267 A30 60c black & multi .40 .40
Nos. 264-267 (4) 1.00 1.00

National Day, Nov. 3. Issued in sheets of 16 (4x4) with control numbers and 4 tabs with a patriotic poem by W. O. M. Pond.

Queen Elizabeth II — A31

Purplethroated Carib (Hummingbird) — A32

2c, Poinsettia. 3c, Red-necked pigeon. 4c, Imperial parrot. 5c, Swallowtail butterfly. 6c, Brown Julia butterfly. 8c, Banana shipment. 10c, Portsmouth Harbor. 12c, Copra processing plant. 15c, Women with straw work. 25c, Timber plant. 30c, Mining pumice. 38c, Cricket, Grammar School. 50c, Roman Catholic Cathedral. 60c, Government headquarters. $1.20, Melville Hall Airport. $2.40, Coat of Arms. $4.80, Queen Elizabeth II.

Perf. 13½

1969, Nov. 26 Unwmk. Photo.

268 A31 ½c silver & multi .20 .20
269 A32 1c yellow & multi .20 .20
270 A32 2c yellow & multi .20 .20
271 A32 3c yellow & multi .20 .20
272 A32 4c yellow & multi .20 .20
273 A32 5c yellow & multi .20 .20
274 A32 6c brown & multi .20 .20
275 A32 8c brown & multi .20 .20
276 A32 10c yellow & multi .20 .20
277 A32 12c citron & multi .20 .20
278 A32 15c blue & multi .25 .25
279 A32 25c pink & multi .55 .55
280 A32 30c olive & multi .70 .65
281 A32 38c multicolored .90 .95
282 A32 50c brown & multi 1.00 1.10

Wmk. Rectangles (334)

Perf. 14

Size: 38x26mm, 26x38mm

283 A32 60c yel & multi 1.40 1.25
284 A32 $1.20 yel & multi 2.75 2.75
285 A32 $2.40 gold & multi 6.25 6.00
286 A31 $4.80 gold & multi 12.00 12.50
Nos. 268-286 (19) 27.80 28.00

Madonna and Child, by Filippino Lippi — A33

Paintings: 10c, Holy Family with Lamb, by Raphael. 15c, Virgin and Child, by Perugino. $1.20, Madonna of the Rose Hedge, by Botticelli.

Perf. 14½

1969, Dec. Unwmk. Litho.

287 A33 6c lt blue & multi .20 .20
288 A33 10c multicolored .20 .20
289 A33 15c lilac & multi .20 .20
290 A33 $1.20 lt grn & multi .60 .60
a. Souvenir sheet of 2 1.50 1.50
Nos. 287-290 (4) 1.20 1.20

Christmas. No. 290a contains 2 imperf. stamps with simulated perforations similar to Nos. 289-290.

Neil A. Armstrong, First Man on the Moon — A34

Designs: 5c, American flag and astronauts on moon. 8c, Astronauts collecting moon rocks. 30c, Landing module, moon and earth. 50c, Memorial tablet left on moon. 60c, Astronauts Armstrong, Aldrin and Collins.

1970, Feb. 2 Litho. ***Perf. 12½***

291 A34 ½c lilac & multi .20 .20
292 A34 5c lt blue & multi .20 .20
293 A34 8c orange & multi .20 .20
294 A34 30c blue & multi .25 .25
295 A34 50c red brn & multi .50 .50
296 A34 60c rose & multi .65 .65
a. Souvenir sheet of 4 2.50 2.50
Nos. 291-296 (6) 2.00 2.00

See note after US No. C76. No. 296a contains 4 stamps similar to Nos. 293-296, but imperf. with simulated perforations.

Giant Green Turtle — A35

Designs: 24c, Flying fish. 38c, Anthurium lily. 60c, Imperial and red-necked parrots.

1970, Sept. 6 Litho. ***Perf. 13½x13***

297 A35 6c lt green & multi .55 .55
298 A35 24c multicolored .70 .70
299 A35 38c green & multi .85 .85
300 A35 60c yellow & multi 3.50 3.50
a. Souvenir sheet of 4, #297-300 9.00 9.00
Nos. 297-300 (4) 5.60 5.60

Women in 18th Century Dress
A36

Natl. Day: 8c, Carib mace & wife leader, 18th cent. $1, Map & flag of Dominica.

1970, Nov. 3 Litho. ***Perf. 14***

301 A36 5c yellow & multi .20 .20
302 A36 8c green & multi .20 .20
303 A36 $1 lt blue & multi .60 .60
a. Souv. sheet of 3, #301-303 + 3 labels 1.75 2.00
Nos. 301-303 (3) 1.00 1.00

Marley's Ghost — A37

Designs (from A Christmas Carol, by Dickens): 15c, Fezziwig's Ball. 24c, Scrooge and his Nephew's Christmas Party. $1.20, The Ghost of Christmas Present.

1970, Nov. 23 Litho. ***Perf. 14x14½***

304 A37 2c blue & multi .20 .20
305 A37 15c multicolored .30 .30
306 A37 24c red & multi .30 .30
307 A37 $1.20 multicolored 1.00 1.00
a. Souvenir sheet of 4, #304-307 3.00 3.00
Nos. 304-307 (4) 1.80 1.80

Christmas; Charles Dickens (1812-1870).

Hands and Red Cross
A38

Designs: 8c, The Doctor, by Sir Luke Fildes. 15c, Dominica flag and Red Cross. 50c, The Sick Child, by Edvard Munch.

1970, Dec. 28 ***Perf. 14½x14***

308 A38 8c multicolored .20 .20
309 A38 10c multicolored .20 .20
310 A38 15c multicolored .20 .20
311 A38 50c multicolored .50 .50
a. Souvenir sheet of 4, #308-311 2.00 2.25
Nos. 308-311 (4) 1.10 1.10

Centenary of the British Red Cross Society.

Marigot Primary School — A39

Education Year Emblem and: 8c, Goodwill Junior High School. 14c, University of the West Indies. $1, Trinity College, Cambridge, England.

1971, Mar. 1 Litho. *Perf. 13½*

312 A39 5c multicolored .20 .20
313 A39 8c multicolored .20 .20
314 A39 14c multicolored .20 .20
315 A39 $1 multicolored .65 .65
a. Souvenir sheet of 2, #314-315 1.00 1.00
Nos. 312-315 (4) 1.25 1.25

International Education Year.

Waterfall and Bird-of-Paradise Flower — A40

Tourist Publicity: 10c, Boat building. 30c, Sailboat along North Coast. 50c, Speed boat and steamer.

1971, Mar. 22 *Perf. 13½x14*

316 A40 5c multicolored .20 .20
317 A40 10c multicolored .20 .20
318 A40 30c multicolored .25 .25
319 A40 50c multicolored .60 .60
a. Souvenir sheet of 4, #316-319 1.00 1.00
Nos. 316-319 (4) 1.25 1.25

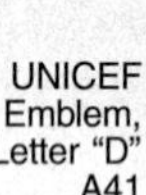

UNICEF Emblem, Letter "D" A41

1971, June 14 Litho. *Perf. 14*

320 A41 5c multicolored .20 .20
321 A41 10c multicolored .20 .20
322 A41 38c multicolored .20 .20
323 A41 $1.20 multicolored .50 .50
a. Souvenir sheet of 2, #321, 323 1.00 1.00
Nos. 320-323 (4) 1.10 1.10

25th anniv. of UNICEF.

Boy Scout, Jamboree Emblem, Torii, Camp and Mt. Fuji — A42

24c, British Scout, flag. 30c, Japanese Scout, flag. $1, Dominican Scout, flag.

1971, Oct. 18 Unwmk. *Perf. 11*

324 A42 20c bister & multi .25 .25
325 A42 24c green & multi .30 .30
326 A42 30c red lilac & multi .45 .45
327 A42 $1 blue & multi 1.75 1.75
a. Souvenir sheet of 2, #326-327 2.25 2.25
Nos. 324-327 (4) 2.75 2.75

13th Boy Scout World Jamboree, Asagiri Plain, Japan, Aug. 2-10.

Boats at Portsmouth — A43

15c, Carnival street scene. 20c, $1.20, Anthea Mondesire, Carifta Queen. 50c, Rock of Atkinson.

Perf. 13½x14, 14x13½

1971, Nov. 15 Litho.

328 A43 8c multi .20 .20
329 A43 15c multi .20 .20
330 A43 20c multi, vert. .20 .20
331 A43 50c multi, vert. .30 .30
Nos. 328-331 (4) .90 .90

Souvenir Sheet

Perf. 15

332 A43 $1.20 multi, vert. 1.00 1.00

National Day.

First Dominica Coin, 8 Reals, 1761 — A44

Early Dominica Coins: 30c, Eleven and 3-bit pieces, 1798. 35c, Two-real coin, 1770, vert. 50c, Three "mocos" and piece of 8, 1798.

1972, Feb. 7 Litho. *Perf. 14*

333 A44 10c violet, silver & blk .20 .20
334 A44 30c green, silver & blk .20 .20
335 A44 35c ultra, silver & blk .25 .25
336 A44 50c red, silver & blk .35 .35
a. Souvenir sheet of 2, #335-336 1.25 1.25
Nos. 333-336 (4) 1.00 1.00

Margin of #336a inscribed "Christmas 1971."

Common Opossum, Environment Emblem — A45

Environment Emblem and: 35c, Agouti. 60c, Oncidium papillo (orchid). $1.20, Hibiscus.

1972, June 5

337 A45 ½c yel grn & multi .20 .20
338 A45 35c org brn & multi .35 .35
339 A45 60c lt blue & multi 2.75 2.75
340 A45 $1.20 yellow & multi 2.40 2.40
a. Souvenir sheet of 4, #337-340 7.75 7.75
Nos. 337-340 (4) 5.70 5.70

UN Conf. on Human Environment, Stockholm, June 5-16.

100-meter Sprint, Olympic Rings — A46

Olympic Rings and: 35m, 400-meter hurdles. 58c, Hammer throw, vert. 72c, Broad jump, vert.

1972, Oct. 9 Litho. *Perf. 14*

341 A46 30c dp org & multi .20 .20
342 A46 35c blue & multi .30 .30
343 A46 58c lilac rose & multi .40 .40
344 A46 72c yel green & multi .85 .85
a. Souv. sheet, #343-344, perf. 15 1.50 1.50
Nos. 341-344 (4) 1.75 1.75

20th Olympic Games, Munich, Aug. 26-Sept. 11.

General Post Office — A47

1972, Nov. 1 *Perf. 13½*

345 A47 10c shown .20 .20
346 A47 20c Morne Diablotin Mountain .20 .20
347 A47 30c Rodney's Rock .20 .20
a. Souv. sheet, #346-347, perf. 15 .75 .75
Nos. 345-347 (3) .60 .60

National Day.

Adoration of the Shepherds, by Caravaggio A48

Paintings: 14c, Madonna and Child, by Rubens. 30c, Madonna and Child, with St. Anne by Orazio Gentileschi. $1, Adoration of the Kings, by Jan Mostaert. (On 8c, painting is mistakenly attributed to Boccaccino, according to Fine Arts Philatelist.)

1972, Dec. 4.

348 A48 8c gold & multi .20 .20
349 A48 14c gold & multi .20 .20
350 A48 30c gold & multi .20 .20
351 A48 $1 gold & multi .65 .65
a. Souvenir sheet of 2 1.50 1.50
Nos. 348-351 (4) 1.25 1.25

Christmas. No. 351a contains one each of Nos. 350-351 with simulated perforations.

Silver Wedding Issue, 1972

Common Design Type

Design: Queen Elizabeth II, Prince Philip, bananas, sisseron parrot.

Perf. 14x14½

1972, Nov. 13 Photo. Wmk. 314

352 CD324 5c olive & multi .20 .20
353 CD324 $1 multicolored .60 .60

See note after Antigua No. 296.

Launching of Tiros Weather Satellite — A49

1c, Nimbus satellite. 2c, Radiosonde balloon & equipment. 30c, Radarscope. 35c, General circulation of atmosphere. 50c, Picture of hurricane transmitted by satellite. $1, Computer weather map. 30c, 35c, 50c, $1, horiz.

Perf. 14½

1973, July 16 Unwmk. Litho.

354 A49 ½c black & multi .20 .20
355 A49 1c black & multi .20 .20
356 A49 2c black & multi .20 .20
357 A49 30c black & multi .20 .20
358 A49 35c black & multi .20 .20
359 A49 50c black & multi .35 .35
360 A49 $1 black & multi .65 .65
a. Souvenir sheet of 2, #359-360 1.50 1.50
Nos. 354-360 (7) 2.00 2.00

Intl. meteorological cooperation, cent.

Going to the Hospital A50

WHO Emblem and: 1c, Maternity and infant care. 2c, Inoculation against smallpox. 30c, Emergency service. 35c, Waiting patients. 50c, Examination. $1, Traveling physician.

1973, Aug. 20 Unwmk. *Perf. 14½*

361 A50 ½c lt blue & multi .20 .20
362 A50 1c gray grn & multi .20 .20
363 A50 2c yellow & multi .20 .20
364 A50 30c lt vio & multi .25 .25
365 A50 35c yel grn & multi .30 .30
366 A50 50c multicolored .40 .40
367 A50 $1 bister & multi .70 .70
a. Souvenir sheet of 2, #366-367, perf. 14x14½ 1.75 1.75
Nos. 361-367 (7) 2.25 2.25

WHO, 25th anniv. #367a exists perf. 14½.

Cyrique Crab — A51

1973, Oct.

368 A51 ½c shown .20 .20
369 A51 22c Blue land crab .35 .35
370 A51 25c Breadfruit .45 .45
371 A51 $1.20 Sunflower 2.00 2.00
a. Souvenir sheet of 4, #368-371 4.00 4.00
Nos. 368-371 (4) 3.00 3.00

Princess Anne and Mark Phillips — A52

1973, Nov. 14 *Perf. 13½*

372 A52 25c salmon & multi .20 .20
373 A52 $2 blue & multi .80 .80
a. Souv. sheet of 2 (75c, $1.20) 1.00 1.00

Wedding of Princess Anne and Capt. Mark Phillips.

#372-373 were issued in sheets of 5 + label.

No. 373a contains 2 stamps of type A52: 75c in colors of the 25c, and $1.20 in colors of the $2.

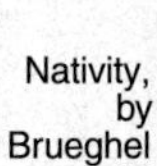

Nativity, by Brueghel A53

Paintings of the Nativity by: 1c, Botticelli. 2c, Dürer. 12c, Botticelli. 22c, Rubens. 35c, Dürer. $1, Giorgione (inscribed "Giorgeone").

1973 Unwmk. *Perf. 14½x15*

374 A53 ½c gray & multi .20 .20
375 A53 1c gray & multi .20 .20
376 A53 2c gray & multi .20 .20
377 A53 12c gray & multi .20 .20
378 A53 22c gray & multi .20 .20
379 A53 35c gray & multi .25 .25
380 A53 $1 gray & multi .75 .75
a. Souvenir sheet of 2 1.75 1.75
Nos. 374-380 (7) 2.00 2.00

Christmas. No. 380a contains one each of Nos. 379-380 in changed colors.

Carib Basket Weaving — A54

Designs: 10c, Staircase of the Snake. 50c, Miss Caribbean Queen, Kathleen Telemacque, vert. 60c, Miss Carifta Queen, Esther Fadelle, vert. $1, La Jeune Etoille Dancers.

1973, Dec. 17 ***Perf. 13½x14, 14x13½***

381 A54 5c buff & multi .20 .20
382 A54 10c multicolored .20 .20
383 A54 50c multicolored .25 .25
384 A54 60c multicolored .25 .25
385 A54 $1 multicolored .35 .35
a. Souv. sheet of 3, #381-382, 385 1.10 1.10
Nos. 381-385 (5) 1.25 1.25

National Day.

U.W.I. Center, Dominica — A55

30c, Graduation. $1, University coat of arms.

1974, Jan. 21 Litho. ***Perf. 13½x14***

386 A55 12c dp orange & multi .20 .20
387 A55 30c violet & multi .20 .20
388 A55 $1 multicolored .50 .50
a. Souvenir sheet of 3, #386-388 .85 *1.25*
Nos. 386-388 (3) .90 .90

University of the West Indies, 25th anniv.

Dominica No. 1 and Map of Island A56

Designs: 1c, 50c, No. 8 and post horn. 2c, $1.20, No. 9 and coat of arms. 10c, Like ½c.

1974, May 4 Litho. ***Perf. 14½***

389 A56 ½c brt pur & multi .20 .20
390 A56 1c salmon & multi .20 .20
391 A56 2c ultra & multi .20 .20
392 A56 10c violet & multi .20 .20
393 A56 50c yel grn & multi .50 .50
394 A56 $1.20 rose & multi 1.10 1.10
a. Souv. sheet, #392-394, perf. 15 2.00 2.00
Nos. 389-394 (6) 2.40 2.40

Centenary of Dominican postage stamps.

Soccer Player and Cup, Brazilian Flag — A57

Soccer cup, various players and flags.

1974, July Litho. ***Perf. 14½***

395 A57 ½c shown .20 .20
396 A57 1c Germany, Fed. Rep. .20 .20
397 A57 2c Italy .20 .20
398 A57 30c Scotland .55 .55
399 A57 40c Sweden .55 .55
400 A57 50c Netherlands .75 .75
401 A57 $1 Yugoslavia 1.10 1.10
a. Souvenir sheet of 2, #400-401, perf. 13½ 1.90 1.90
Nos. 395-401 (7) 3.55 3.55

World Cup Soccer Championship, Munich, June 13-July 7.

Indian Hole A58

40c, Teachers' Training College. $1, Petite Savane Co-operative Bay Oil Distillery.

1974, Nov. 1 Litho. ***Perf. 13½x14***

402 A58 10c multicolored .20 .20
403 A58 40c multicolored .35 .35
404 A58 $1 multicolored .75 .75
a. Souvenir sheet of 3, #402-404 1.00 1.00
Nos. 402-404 (3) 1.30 1.30

Churchill at Race Track A59

Sir Winston Churchill (1874-1965): 1c, with Gen. Eisenhower. 2c, with Franklin D. Roosevelt. 20c, as First Lord of the Admiralty. 45c, painting outdoors. $2, giving "V" sign.

1974, Nov. 25 Litho. ***Perf. 14½***

405 A59 ½c multicolored .20 .20
406 A59 1c multicolored .20 .20
407 A59 2c multicolored .20 .20
408 A59 20c multicolored .20 .20
409 A59 45c multicolored .30 .30
410 A59 $2 multicolored .75 .75
a. Souvenir sheet of 2, #409-410, perf. 13½ 1.75 1.75
Nos. 405-410 (6) 1.85 1.85

Virgin and Child, by Oronzo Tiso — A60

Paintings (Virgin and Child): 1c, by Lorenzo Costa. 2c, by unknown Master. 10c, by G. F. Romanelli. 25c, Holy Family, by G. S. da Sermoneta. 45c, Adoration of the Shepherds, by Guido Reni. $1, Adoration of the Kings, by Cristoforo Caselli.

1974, Dec. 16 Litho. ***Perf. 14***

411 A60 ½c multicolored .20 .20
412 A60 1c multicolored .20 .20
413 A60 2c multicolored .20 .20
414 A60 10c multicolored .35 .20
415 A60 25c multicolored .50 .40
416 A60 45c multicolored .65 .20
417 A60 $1 multicolored .90 .50
a. Souvenir sheet of 2, #416-417 2.25 2.25
Nos. 411-417 (7) 3.00 1.90

Christmas.

Seamail, "Orinoco," 1851, and "Geesthaven," 1966 — A61

Cent. of UPU: $2, $2.40, Airmail, De Havilland 4, 1918, and Boeing 747, 1974.

1974, Dec. 4 Litho. ***Perf. 13½***

418 A61 10c multicolored .20 .20
419 A61 $2 multicolored 1.75 1.75

Souvenir Sheet

419A Sheet of 2 2.25 2.25
b. A61 $1.20 multicolored .75 .75
c. A61 $2.40 multicolored 1.50 1.50

Oldwife A62

1975, June 2 Litho. ***Perf. 14½***

421 A62 ½c shown .20 .20
422 A62 1c Ocyurus chrysurus .20 .20
423 A62 2c Blue marlin .20 .20
424 A62 3c Swordfish .20 .20
425 A62 20c Great barracuda 1.50 1.00
426 A62 $2 Grouper 5.25 2.75
a. Souvenir sheet, perf. 13½ 5.25 *5.00*
Nos. 421-426 (6) 7.55 4.55

Myscelia Antholia A63

Designs: Butterflies.

1975, July 28 Litho. ***Perf. 14½***

427 A63 ½c shown .20 .20
428 A63 1c Lycorea ceres .20 .20
429 A63 2c Siderone nemesis .25 .25
430 A63 6c Battus polydamas 1.00 .85
431 A63 30c Anartia lytrea 3.00 1.00
432 A63 40c Morpho peleides 3.00 1.00
433 A63 $2 Dryas julia 4.00 *6.50*
a. Souvenir sheet, perf. 13½ 6.25 6.25
Nos. 427-433 (7) 11.65 10.00

Royal Mail Ship Yare A64

Ships Tied in with Dominican History: 1c, Royal mail ship Thames. 2c, Canadian National S.S. Lady Nelson. 20c, C.N. S.S. Lady Rodney. 45c, Harrison Line M.V. Statesman. 50c, Geest Line M.V. Geestcape. $2, Geest Line M.V. Geeststar.

1975, Sept. 1 ***Perf. 14***

434 A64 ½c black & multi .45 .35
435 A64 1c black & multi .45 .35
436 A64 2c black & multi .50 .40
437 A64 20c black & multi 1.75 .75
438 A64 45c black & multi 2.25 1.00
439 A64 50c black & multi 2.25 1.25
440 A64 $2 black & multi 4.00 *4.50*
a. Souvenir sheet of 2, #439-440 6.50 4.00
Nos. 434-440 (7) 11.65 8.60

IWY Emblem, Farm Women A65

$2, IWY emblem, dressmaker & saleswoman.

1975, Oct. 30 Litho. ***Perf. 14***

441 A65 10c pink & multi .20 .20
442 A65 $2 yellow & multi 1.10 1.10

International Women's Year.

Public Library — A66

5c, Miss Caribbean Queen 1975. 30c, Citrus factory. $1, National Day Cup.

1975, Nov. 6

443 A66 5c multi, vert. .30 .30
444 A66 10c multi .30 .30
445 A66 30c multi .30 .30
446 A66 $1 multi, vert. .85 .85
a. Souvenir sheet of 3 1.00 1.50
Nos. 443-446 (4) 1.75 1.75

National Day. No. 446a contains 3 stamps similar to Nos. 444-446 with simulated perforations.

Virgin and Child, by Mantegna — A67

Christmas: Paintings of the Virgin and Child.

1975, Nov. 24

447 A67 ½c shown .20 .20
448 A67 1c Fra Filippo Lippi .20 .20
449 A67 2c Bellini .20 .20
450 A67 10c Botticelli .20 .20
451 A67 25c Bellini .25 .25
452 A67 45c Correggio .30 .30
453 A67 $1 Durer .65 .65
a. Souvenir sheet of 2, #452-453 1.75 1.75
Nos. 447-453 (7) 2.00 2.00

Hibiscus A68

Queen Elizabeth II — A69

Designs: 1c, African tulip. 2c, Castor oil tree. 3c, White cedar flower. 4c, Eggplant. 5c, Garfish. 6c, Okra. 8c, Zenaida doves. 10c, Screw pine. 20c, Mangoes. 25c, Crayfish. 30c, Manicou. 40c, Bay leaf groves. 50c, Tomatoes. $1, Lime factory. $2, Rum distillery. $5, Bay oil distillery.

1975, Dec. 8 Litho. ***Perf. 14½***

454 A68 ½c ultra & multi .20 *.40*
455 A68 1c lilac & multi .25 *.40*
456 A68 2c orange & multi .25 *.40*
457 A68 3c multicolored .25 *.40*
458 A68 4c pink & multi .25 *.40*
459 A68 5c multicolored .30 *.40*
460 A68 6c gray & multi .30 *.50*
461 A68 8c multicolored 4.00 .50
462 A68 10c violet & multi .25 .20
463 A68 20c yellow & multi .50 .20
464 A68 25c lemon & multi .55 .20
465 A68 30c salmon & multi 1.50 .75
466 A68 40c multicolored 1.50 .75
467 A68 50c red & multi .65 .45
468 A68 $1 citron & multi .90 .55
469 A68 $2 multicolored 1.60 *3.00*
470 A68 $5 multicolored 2.00 *4.50*

Perf. 14

471 A69 $10 blue & multi 2.75 *13.00*
Nos. 454-471 (18) 18.00 *27.00*

For overprints see Nos. 584-601, 640-643.

American Infantry — A70

Rowing — A71

Designs: 1c, English three-decker, 1782. 2c, George Washington. 45c, English sailors. 75c, English ensign with regimental flag. $2, Admiral Hood. All designs have old maps in background.

1976, Apr. 12 Litho. *Perf. 14½*

472 A70 ½c green & multi .20 .20
473 A70 1c purple & multi .20 .20
474 A70 2c orange & multi .20 .20
475 A70 45c brown & multi .90 .20
476 A70 75c ultra & multi 1.50 1.00
477 A70 $2 red & multi 1.75 *3.00*
a. Souvenir sheet of 2 4.50 *6.00*
Nos. 472-477 (6) 4.75 4.80

American Bicentennial. No. 477a contains 2 stamps similar to Nos. 476-477, perf. 13.

1976, May 24 Litho. *Perf. 14½*

1c, Shot put. 2c, Swimming. 40c, Relay race. 45c, Gymnastics. 60c, Sailing. $2, Archery.

478 A71 ½c ocher & multi .20 .20
479 A71 1c ocher & multi .20 .20
480 A71 2c ocher & multi .20 .20
481 A71 40c ocher & multi .20 .20
482 A71 45c ocher & multi .20 .20
483 A71 60c ocher & multi .30 .30
484 A71 $2 ocher & multi .80 .80
a. Souv. sheet, #483-484, perf 13 2.00 2.00
Nos. 478-484 (7) 2.10 2.10

21st Olympic Games, Montreal, Canada, July 17-Aug. 1.

Ringed Kingfisher A72

Birds: 1c, Mourning dove. 2c, Green heron. 15c, Broad-winged hawk. 30c, Blue-headed hummingbird. 45c, Banana-quit. $2, Imperial parrot. 15c, 30c, 45c, $2, vert.

1976, June 28

485 A72 ½c multicolored .25 .25
486 A72 1c multicolored .25 .25
487 A72 2c multicolored .25 .25
488 A72 15c multicolored 1.50 1.50
489 A72 30c multicolored 2.25 2.25
490 A72 45c multicolored 2.75 2.75
491 A72 $2 multicolored 5.75 5.75
a. Souv. sheet of 3, #489-491, perf. 13 9.50 9.50
Nos. 485-491 (7) 13.00 13.00

Map of West Indies, Bats, Wicket and Ball A72a

Prudential Cup — A72b

1976, July 26 Litho. *Perf. 14*

492 A72a 15c lt blue & multi .50 .50
493 A72b 25c lilac rose & black 1.00 1.00

World Cricket Cup, won by West Indies Team, 1975.

Viking Spacecraft — A73 Virgin and Child, by Giorgione — A74

1c, Titan launch center, horiz. 2c, Titan 3-D & Centaur D-IT. 3c, Orbiter & landing capsule. 45c, Capsule with closed parachute. 75c, Capsule with open parachute. $1, Landing capsule descending on Mars, horiz. $2, Viking on Mars, horiz.

1976, Sept. 20 Litho. *Perf. 15*

494 A73 ½c multicolored .20 .20
495 A73 1c multicolored .20 .20
496 A73 2c multicolored .20 .20
497 A73 3c multicolored .20 .20
498 A73 45c multicolored .35 .35
499 A73 75c multicolored .45 .45
500 A73 $1 multicolored .55 .55
501 A73 $2 multicolored .85 .85
a. Souvenir sheet of 2, #500, 501, perf. 13½ 2.00 2.00
Nos. 494-501 (8) 3.00 3.00

Viking mission to Mars.

1976, Nov. 1 Litho. *Perf. 14*

Virgin and Child by: 1c, Bellini. 2c, Mantegna. 6c, Mantegna. 25c, Memling. 45c, 50c, Correggio. $1, $3, Raphael.

502 A74 ½c multicolored .20 .20
503 A74 1c multicolored .20 .20
504 A74 2c multicolored .20 .20
505 A74 6c multicolored .20 .20
506 A74 25c multicolored .20 .20
507 A74 45c multicolored .25 .25
508 A74 $3 multicolored 1.25 1.25
Nos. 502-508 (7) 2.50 2.50

Souvenir Sheet

509 Sheet of 2 1.60 1.60
a. A74 50c multicolored .40
b. A74 $1 multicolored .80

Christmas.

Island Craft Co-operative — A75

National Day: 50c, Banana harvest, Castle Bruce Co-operative. $1, Banana shipping plant, Bourne Farmers' Co-operative.

1976, Nov. 22 Litho. *Perf. 13½x14*

510 A75 10c multicolored .20 .20
511 A75 50c multicolored .25 .25
512 A75 $1 multicolored .55 .55
a. Souvenir sheet of 3, #510-512 1.25 1.25
Nos. 510-512 (3) 1.00 1.00

Common Sundial — A76

Sea Shells: 1c, Flame helmet. 2c, Mouse cone. 20c, Caribbean vase. 40c, West Indian fighting conch. 50c, Short coral shell. $2, Long-spined star shell. $3, Apple murex.

1976, Dec. 20 Litho. *Perf. 14*

513 A76 ½c black & multi .20 .20
514 A76 1c black & multi .20 .20
515 A76 2c black & multi .20 .20
516 A76 20c black & multi .35 .20
517 A76 40c black & multi .70 .50
518 A76 50c black & multi .75 .60
519 A76 $3 black & multi 5.00 3.25
Nos. 513-519 (7) 7.40 5.15

Souvenir Sheet

520 A76 $2 black & multi 3.00 3.00

Queen Enthroned — A77

Designs: 1c, Imperial crown. 45c, Elizabeth II and Princess Anne. $2, Coronation ring. $2.50, Ampulla and spoon. $5, Royal visit to Dominica.

1977, Feb. 7 *Perf. 14*

521 A77 ½c multicolored .20 .20
522 A77 1c multicolored .20 .20
523 A77 45c multicolored .25 .25
524 A77 $2 multicolored 1.10 1.10
525 A77 $2.50 multicolored 1.40 1.40
Nos. 521-525 (5) 3.15 3.15

Souvenir Sheet

526 A77 $5 multicolored 2.50 2.50

25th anniv. of the reign of Elizabeth II.

Nos. 521-525 were printed in sheets of 40 (4x10), perf. 14, and sheets of 5 plus label, perf. 12, in changed colors.

For overprints see Nos. 549-554.

Joseph Haydn — A78

Designs: 1c, Fidelio, act I, scene IV. 2c, Dancer Maria Casentini. 15c, Beethoven working on Pastoral Symphony. 30c, "Wellington's Victory." 40c, Soprano Henriette Sontag. $2, Young Beethoven.

1977, Apr. 25 Litho. *Perf. 14*

527 A78 ½c multicolored .20 .20
528 A78 1c multicolored .20 .20
529 A78 2c multicolored .20 .20
530 A78 15c multicolored .40 .40
531 A78 30c multicolored .40 .40
532 A78 40c multicolored .40 .40
533 A78 $2 multicolored 2.50 2.50
a. Souvenir sheet of 3, #531-533 3.50 3.50
Nos. 527-533 (7) 4.30 4.30

Ludwig van Beethoven (1770-1827), composer.

Boy Scouts on Hike A79

Saluting Boy Scout and: 1c, First aid. 2c, Scouts setting up camp. 45c, Rock climbing. 50c, Kayaking. 75c, Map reading. $2, Campfire. $3, Sailing.

1977, Aug. 8 Litho. *Perf. 14*

534 A79 ½c multicolored .20 .20
535 A79 1c multicolored .20 .20
536 A79 2c multicolored .20 .20
537 A79 45c multicolored .40 .40
538 A79 50c multicolored .50 .50
539 A79 $3 multicolored 2.25 2.25
Nos. 534-539 (6) 3.75 3.75

Souvenir Sheet

540 Sheet of 2 2.50 2.50
a. A79 75c multicolored .75
b. A79 $2 multicolored 1.75

6th Caribbean Jamboree, Kingston, Jamaica, Aug. 5-14.

Nativity A80

Christmas: 1c, Annunciation to the Shepherds. 2c, 45c, Presentation at the Temple (different). 6c, $2, $3, Flight into Egypt (different). 15c, Adoration of the Kings. 50c, Virgin and Child with Angels. ½c to 45c are illustrations from De Lisle Psalter, 14th century. 50c, $2, $3 are from other Psalters.

1977, Nov. 14 Litho. *Perf. 14*

541 A80 ½c multicolored .20 .20
542 A80 1c multicolored .20 .20
543 A80 2c multicolored .20 .20
544 A80 6c multicolored .20 .20
545 A80 15c multicolored .20 .20
546 A80 45c multicolored .40 .40
547 A80 $3 multicolored 1.10 1.10
Nos. 541-547 (7) 2.50 2.50

Souvenir Sheet

548 Sheet of 2 1.75 1.75
a. A80 50c multicolored .25
b. A80 $2 multicolored 1.50

Nos. 521-526 Overprinted "ROYAL VISIT / W.I. 1977"

1977, Nov. 24 Litho. *Perf. 12, 14*

549 A77 ½c multicolored .20 .20
550 A77 1c multicolored .20 .20
551 A77 45c multicolored .20 .20
552 A77 $2 multicolored .60 .60
553 A77 $2.50 multicolored .65 .65
Nos. 549-553 (5) 1.85 1.85

Souvenir Sheet

Perf. 14

554 A77 $5 multicolored 1.50 1.50

Caribbean visit of Queen Elizabeth II. #549-550 are perf. 12, others perf. 12 and 14.

Two types of No. 554: I. Overprinted only on stamp. II. Overprinted "W.I. 1977" on stamp and "Royal Visit W.I. 1977" on margin.

Masqueraders — A81

Designs: 1c, Sensay costume. 2c, Street musicians. 45c, Douiette band. 50c, Pappy Show wedding. $2, $2.50, Masquerade band.

1978, Jan. 9 *Perf. 14*

555 A81 ½c multicolored .20 .20
556 A81 1c multicolored .20 .20
557 A81 2c multicolored .20 .20
558 A81 45c multicolored .30 .30
559 A81 50c multicolored .35 .35
560 A81 $2 multicolored 1.40 1.40
Nos. 555-560 (6) 2.65 2.65

Souvenir Sheet

561 A81 $2.50 multicolored 1.75 1.75

History of Carnival.

Lindbergh and Spirit of St. Louis A82

Designs: 10c, Spirit of St. Louis take-off, Long Island, May 20, 1927. 15c, Lindbergh and map of route New York to Paris. 20c, Lindbergh and plane in Paris. 40c, 1st Zeppelin, trial over Lake Constance. 50c, Spirit of St. Louis. 60c, Count Zeppelin and Zeppelin LZ-2, 1906. $2, Graf Zeppelin, 1928. $3, LZ-127, 1928.

1978, Mar. 13 Litho. *Perf. 14½*

562 A82	6c	multicolored	.20	.20
563 A82	10c	multicolored	.20	.20
564 A82	15c	multicolored	.20	.20
565 A82	20c	multicolored	.20	.20
566 A82	40c	multicolored	.45	.45
567 A82	60c	multicolored	.70	.70
568 A82	$3	multicolored	3.50	3.50
		Nos. 562-568 (7)	5.45	5.45

Souvenir Sheet

569	Sheet of 2	2.75	2.75
a.	A82 50c multicolored	.50	
b.	A82 $2 multicolored	2.00	

Charles A. Lindbergh's solo transatlantic flight from New York to Paris, 50th anniv., and flights of Graf Zeppelin.

Royal Family on Balcony — A83

Designs: 45c, Coronation. $2.50, Elizabeth II and Prince Philip. $5, Elizabeth II.

1978, June 2 Litho. *Perf. 14*

570 A83	45c	multicolored	.20	.20
571 A83	$2	multicolored	.95	.95
572 A83	$2.50	multicolored	1.10	1.10
		Nos. 570-572 (3)	2.25	2.25

Souvenir Sheet

573 A83	$5	multicolored	2.00	2.00

Coronation of Queen Elizabeth II, 25th anniv. Nos. 570-572 were issued in sheets of 50, and in sheets of 3 stamps and label, in changed colors, perf. 12.

Wright Plane Coming out of Hangar A84

Designs: 40c, 1908 plane. 60c, Flyer I gliding. $2, Flyer I taking off. $3, Wilbur and Orville Wright and Flyer I.

1978, July 10 Litho. *Perf. 14½*

574 A84	30c	multicolored	.20	.20
575 A84	40c	multicolored	.30	.30
576 A84	60c	multicolored	.40	.40
577 A84	$2	multicolored	1.50	1.50
		Nos. 574-577 (4)	2.40	2.40

Souvenir Sheet

578 A84	$3	multicolored	2.50	2.50

75th anniv. of first powered flight.

Two Apostles, by Rubens — A85

Rubens Paintings: 45c, Descent from the Cross. 50c, St. Ildefonso Receiving Chasuble. $2, Holy Family. $3, Assumption of the Virgin.

1978, Oct. 16 Litho. *Perf. 14*

579 A85	20c	multicolored	.20	.20
580 A85	45c	multicolored	.30	.30
581 A85	50c	multicolored	.35	.35
582 A85	$3	multicolored	2.00	2.00
		Nos. 579-582 (4)	2.85	2.85

Souvenir Sheet

583 A85	$2	multicolored	1.50	1.50

Christmas.

Nos. 454-471 Overprinted: "INDEPENDENCE/ 3rd NOVEMBER 1978"

1978 Nov. 1 Litho. *Perf. 14½*

584 A68	½c	ultra & multi	.20	.20
585 A68	1c	lilac & multi	.20	.20
586 A68	2c	orange & multi	.20	.20
587 A68	3c	multicolored	.20	.20
588 A68	4c	pink & multi	.20	.20
589 A68	5c	multicolored	.20	.20
590 A68	6c	gray & multi	.20	.20
591 A68	8c	multicolored	.20	.20
592 A68	10c	violet & multi	.20	.20
a.		Perf. 13½ ('79)	.20	.20
593 A68	20c	yellow & multi	.20	.20
594 A68	25c	lemon & multi	.20	.20
595 A68	30c	salmon & multi	.25	.25
596 A68	40c	multicolored	.35	.50
597 A68	50c	red & multi	.50	.70
598 A68	$1	citron & multi	.90	1.25
599 A68	$2	multicolored	1.90	2.50
600 A68	$5	multicolored	4.00	5.00

Perf. 14

601 A69	$10	blue & multi	8.00	11.50
		Nos. 584-601 (18)	18.10	23.90

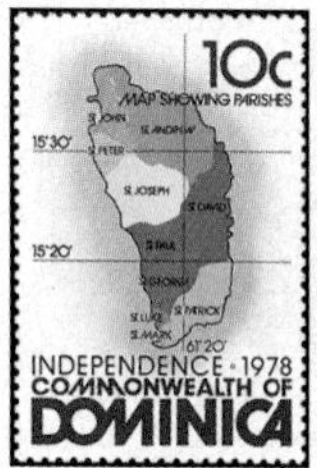

Map of Dominica with Parishes — A86

Rowland Hill — A87

25c, Sabinea carinalis, natl. flower, & map. 45c, New flag & map. 50c, Coat of arms & map. $2, Prime Minister Patrick John.

1978, Nov. 1 *Perf. 14*

602 A86	10c	multicolored	.20	.20
603 A86	25c	multicolored	.20	.20
604 A86	45c	multicolored	.65	.65
605 A86	50c	multicolored	.75	.75
606 A86	$2	multicolored	3.00	3.00
		Nos. 602-606 (5)	4.80	4.80

Souvenir Sheet

607 A86	$2.50	multicolored	*3.00*	*3.25*

Dominican independence.

1979, Mar. 19

45c, Great Britain #2. 50c, Dominica #1. $2, Maltese Cross handstamps. $5, Penny Black.

608 A87	25c	multicolored	.20	.20
609 A87	45c	multicolored	.20	.20
610 A87	50c	multicolored	.25	.25
611 A87	$2	multicolored	.95	.95
		Nos. 608-611 (4)	1.60	1.60

Souvenir Sheet

612 A87	$5	multicolored	2.50	2.50

Sir Rowland Hill (1795-1879), originator of penny postage.

Nos. 608-611 printed in sheets of 5 plus label, perf. 12x12½, in changed colors.

For overprints see Nos. 663A-663D.

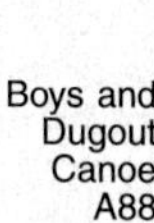

Boys and Dugout Canoe A88

IYC Emblem and: 40c, Children carrying bananas. 50c, Boys playing cricket. $3, Child feeding rabbits. $5, Boy showing catch of fish.

1979, Apr. 23 Litho. *Perf. 14*

613 A88	30c	multicolored	.25	.25
614 A88	40c	multicolored	.35	.35
615 A88	50c	multicolored	.40	.40
616 A88	$3	multicolored	2.50	2.50
		Nos. 613-616 (4)	3.50	3.50

Souvenir Sheet

617 A88	$5	multicolored	4.50	4.50

Grouper A89

30c, Striped dolphin. 50c, White-tailed tropic birds. 60c, Brown pelicans. $1, Pilot whale. $2, Brown booby. $3, Elkhorn coral.

1979, May 21 Litho. *Perf. 14*

618 A89	10c	multicolored	.20	.20
619 A89	30c	multicolored	.95	.95
620 A89	50c	multicolored	1.60	1.60
621 A89	60c	multicolored	1.90	1.90
622 A89	$1	multicolored	3.25	3.25
623 A89	$2	multicolored	6.50	6.50
		Nos. 618-623 (6)	14.40	14.40

Souvenir Sheet

624 A89	$3	multicolored	3.25	3.25

Wildlife protection.

Capt. Cook, Bark Endeavour — A90

Capt. Cook and: 50c, Resolution, map of 2nd voyage. 60c, Discovery, map of 3rd voyage. $2, Cook's map of New Zealand, 1770. $5, Portrait.

1979, July 16 Litho. *Perf. 14*

625 A90	10c	multicolored	.20	.20
626 A90	50c	multicolored	.90	.90
627 A90	60c	multicolored	1.10	1.10
628 A90	$2	multicolored	3.50	3.50
		Nos. 625-628 (4)	5.70	5.70

Souvenir Sheet

629 A90	$5	multicolored	3.00	3.00

200th death anniv. of Capt. James Cook (1728-1779).

Girl Guides Cooking A91

Girl Guides: 20c, Setting up emergency rain tent. 50c, Raising flag of independent Dominica. $2.50, Playing accordion and singing. $3, Leader and Guides of different ages.

1979, July 30

630 A91	10c	multicolored	.20	.20
631 A91	20c	multicolored	.20	.20
632 A91	50c	multicolored	.40	.40
633 A91	$2.50	multicolored	2.00	2.00
		Nos. 630-633 (4)	2.80	2.80

Souvenir Sheet

634 A91	$3	multicolored	3.00	3.00

50th anniv. of Dominican Girl Guides.

Colvillea — A92

Flowering Trees: 40c, Lignum vitae. 60c, Dwarf poinciana. $2, Fern tree. $3, Perfume tree.

1979, Sept. 3 Litho. *Perf. 14*

635 A92	20c	multicolored	.20	.20
636 A92	40c	multicolored	.25	.25
637 A92	60c	multicolored	.40	.40
638 A92	$2	multicolored	1.40	1.40
		Nos. 635-638 (4)	2.25	2.25

Souvenir Sheet

639 A92	$3	multicolored	2.40	2.40

Nos. 459, 466, 470-471 Overprinted: "HURRICANE / RELIEF"

Perf. 14½, 13½, 13½x14, 14

1979, Oct. 29 Litho.

640 A68	5c	multicolored	.20	.20
641 A68	40c	multicolored	.40	.40
642 A68	$5	multicolored	5.00	5.00
643 A68	$10	multicolored	10.00	10.00
		Nos. 640-643 (4)	15.60	15.60

Hurricane devastation, Aug. 29. Vertical overprint on No. 643, others horizontal.

Music Scenes A92a

1979, Nov. 2 Litho. *Perf. 11*

644 A92a	½c	Mickey Mouse	.20	.20
645 A92a	1c	Goofy playing guitar	.20	.20
646 A92a	2c	Mickey Mouse and Goofy	.20	.20
647 A92a	3c	Donald Duck	.20	.20
648 A92a	4c	Minnie Mouse	.20	.20
649 A92a	5c	Goofy playing accordion	.20	.20
650 A92a	10c	Horace Horsecollar and Dale	.20	.20
651 A92a	$2	Huey, Dewey, Louie	2.50	2.50
652 A92a	$2.50	Donald and Huey	3.00	3.00
		Nos. 644-652 (9)	6.90	6.90

Souvenir Sheet

Perf. 13

653 A92a	$3	Mickey Mouse playing piano	4.25	4.25

Cathedral of the Assumption — A93

Cathedrals: 40c, St. Patrick's, New York. 45c, St. Paul's, London, vert. 60c, St. Peter's, Rome. $2, Cologne Cathedral. $3, Notre Dame, Paris, vert.

1979, Nov. 26 Litho. *Perf. 14*

654 A93	6c	multicolored	.20	.20
655 A93	45c	multicolored	.30	.30
656 A93	60c	multicolored	.40	.40
657 A93	$3	multicolored	2.00	2.00
		Nos. 654-657 (4)	2.90	2.90

Souvenir Sheet

658	Sheet of 2	1.00	1.00
a.	A93 40c multicolored	.25	.25
b.	A93 $2 multicolored	.75	.75

Christmas.

Nurse and Patients, Rotary Emblem A94

1980, Mar. 31 Litho. *Perf. 14*

659 A94 10c shown .20 .20
660 A94 20c Electrocardiogram machine .20 .20
661 A94 40c Mental hospital .30 .30
662 A94 $2.50 Paul Harris, founder 1.75 1.75
Nos. 659-662 (4) 2.45 2.45

Souvenir Sheet

663 A94 $3 Map of Africa and Europe 2.25 2.25

Rotary International, 75th anniv. Nos. 659-662 each contain quadrant of Rotary emblem.

Nos. 608-611 Overprinted "LONDON 1980"

1980, May 6 Litho. *Perf. 12*

663A A87 25c multicolored .50 .50
663B A87 45c multicolored .90 .90
663C A87 50c multicolored 1.00 1.00
663D A87 $2 multicolored 4.00 4.00
Nos. 663A-663D (4) 6.40 6.40

London 80 Intl. Stamp Exhib., May 6-14.

Shot Put, Moscow '80 Emblem A95

1980, May 27 Litho. *Perf. 14*

664 A95 30c shown .20 .20
665 A95 40c Basketball .30 .30
666 A95 60c Swimming .40 .40
667 A95 $2 Gymnast 1.40 1.40
Nos. 664-667 (4) 2.30 2.30

Souvenir Sheet

668 A95 $3 Running 2.00 2.00

22nd Summer Olympic Games, Moscow, July 19-Aug. 3.

Embarkation for Cythera, by Watteau — A96

Paintings: 20c, Supper at Emmaus, by Caravaggio. 25c, Charles I Hunting, by Van Dyck, vert. 30c, The Maids of Honor, by Velazquez, vert. 45c, Rape of the Sabine Women, by Poussin. $1, Embarkation for Cythera, by Watteau. $3, Holy Family, by Rembrandt. $5, Girl before a Mirror, by Picasso, vert.

Perf. 14x13½, 13½x14

1980, July 22 Litho.

669 A96 20c multicolored .20 .20
670 A96 25c multicolored .20 .20
671 A96 30c multicolored .20 .20
672 A96 45c multicolored .25 .25
673 A96 $1 multicolored .55 .55
674 A96 $5 multicolored 2.00 2.00
Nos. 669-674 (6) 3.40 3.40

Souvenir Sheet

675 A96 $3 multicolored 1.50 1.50

Queen Mother Elizabeth, 80th Birthday A97

1980, Aug. 4 *Perf. 12, 14*

676 A97 40c multicolored .25 .25
677 A97 $2.50 multicolored 1.00 1.00

Souvenir Sheet

678 A97 $3 multicolored 1.25 1.75

Tinkerbell — A98

Designs: Scenes from Disney's Peter Pan.

1980, Oct. 1 Litho. *Perf. 11*

679 A98 ½c multicolored .20 .20
680 A98 1c multicolored .20 .20
681 A98 2c multicolored .20 .20
682 A98 3c multicolored .20 .20
683 A98 4c multicolored .20 .20
684 A98 5c multicolored .20 .20
685 A98 10c multicolored .20 .20
686 A98 $2 multicolored 3.00 1.50
687 A98 $2.50 multicolored 3.00 1.75
Nos. 679-687 (9) 7.40 4.65

Souvenir Sheet

688 A98 $4 multicolored 6.00 6.00

Christmas.

Douglas Bay A99

1981, Feb. 12 Litho. *Perf. 14*

689 A99 20c shown .20 .20
690 A99 30c Valley of Desolation .20 .20
691 A99 40c Emerald Pool, vert. .20 .20
692 A99 $3 Indian River, vert. 1.50 1.50
Nos. 689-692 (4) 2.10 2.10

Souvenir Sheet

693 A99 $4 Trafalgar Falls 2.00 2.00

Pluto and Fifi — A100

$4, Pluto in Blue Note (1947 cartoon).

1981, Apr. 30 Litho. *Perf. 13½x14*

694 A100 $2 multicolored 2.00 2.00

Souvenir Sheet

695 A100 $4 multicolored 4.00 4.00

50th anniversary of Walt Disney's Pluto.

Forest Thrush A101

1981, Apr. 30 *Perf. 14*

696 A101 20c shown .20 .20
697 A101 30c Stolid flycatcher .35 .35
698 A101 40c Blue-hooded euphonia .50 .50
699 A101 $5 Lesser antillean peewee 6.25 6.25
Nos. 696-699 (4) 7.30 7.30

Souvenir Sheet

700 A101 $3 Sisserou parrot 4.25 4.25

Royal Wedding Issue
Common Design Type

1981, June 16 Litho. *Perf. 14*

701 CD331 45c Couple .25 .25
702 CD331 60c Windsor Castle .30 .30
703 CD331 $4 Charles 2.00 2.00
Nos. 701-703 (3) 2.55 2.55

Souvenir Sheet

704 CD331 $5 Helicopter 2.00 2.00

Booklet

705 CD331 8.25
a. Pane of 6 (3x25c, Lady Diana, 3x$2, Charles) 4.75
b. Pane of 1, $5, Couple 3.50

No. 705 contains imperf., self-adhesive stamps.

Nos. 701-703 also printed in sheets of 5 plus label, perf. 12, in changed colors.

Elves Repairing Santa's Sleigh — A102

Christmas: Scenes from Walt Disney's Santa's Workshop.

1981, Nov. 2 Litho. *Perf. 14*

706 A102 ½c multicolored .20 .20
707 A102 1c multicolored .20 .20
708 A102 2c multicolored .20 .20
709 A102 3c multicolored .20 .20
710 A102 4c multicolored .20 .20
711 A102 5c multicolored .20 .20
712 A102 10c multicolored .20 .20
713 A102 45c multicolored .60 .60
714 A102 $5 multicolored 6.50 6.50
Nos. 706-714 (9) 8.50 8.50

Souvenir Sheet

715 A102 $4 multicolored 6.25 6.25

Ixora A103

1981, Dec. 1 Litho. *Perf. 14*

716 A103 1c shown .20 .20
717 A103 2c Flamboyant .20 .20
718 A103 4c Poinsettia .20 .20
719 A103 5c Sabinea carinalis .20 .20
720 A103 8c Annatto roucou .20 .20
721 A103 10c Passion fruit .20 .20
722 A103 15c Breadfruit .20 .20
723 A103 20c Allamanda buttercup .20 .20
724 A103 25c Cashew .20 .20
725 A103 35c Soursop .25 .25
726 A103 40c Bougainvillea .30 .60
727 A103 45c Anthurium .35 .65
728 A103 60c Cacao .45 .85
729 A103 90c Pawpaw tree .65 1.25
730 A103 $1 Coconut palm .70 1.40
731 A103 $2 Coffee tree 1.40 2.50
732 A103 $5 Lobster claw 3.50 6.50
a. Perf. 12½x12 ('85) 2.25 2.25
733 A103 $10 Banana fig 7.00 13.50
Nos. 716-733 (18) 16.40 29.30

Nos. 721-722, 728, 732 exist dated "1985." For overprints see Nos. 852-853.

1984 *Perf. 12*

721a A103 10c .80 .80
730a A103 $1 1.00 1.00
732a A103 $5 3.50 3.50
733a A103 $10 7.50 7.50

Dated "1984."

Intl. Year of the Disabled — A104

Bathers, by Picasso — A105

1981, Dec. 22 Litho. *Perf. 14*

734 A104 45c Ramp curb .30 .30
735 A104 60c Bus steps .40 .40
736 A104 75c Hand-operated car .55 .55
737 A104 $4 Bus lift 2.75 2.75
Nos. 734-737 (4) 4.00 4.00

Souvenir Sheet

738 A104 $5 Elevator buttons 5.75 5.75

1981, Dec. 30 *Perf. 14½*

739 A105 45c Olga in Armchair .35 .35
740 A105 60c shown .45 .45
741 A105 75c Woman in Spanish Costume .55 .55
742 A105 $4 Dog and Cock 3.00 3.00
Nos. 739-742 (4) 4.35 4.35

Souvenir Sheet

743 A105 $5 Sleeping Peasants 5.75 5.75

1982 World Cup Soccer — A106

Various Disney characters playing soccer.

1982, Jan. 29 *Perf. 14*

744 A106 ½c multicolored .20 .20
745 A106 1c multicolored .20 .20
746 A106 2c multicolored .20 .20
747 A106 3c multicolored .20 .20
748 A106 4c multicolored .20 .20
749 A106 5c multicolored .20 .20
750 A106 10c multicolored .20 .20
751 A106 60c multicolored .85 .85
752 A106 $5 multicolored 7.25 7.25
Nos. 744-752 (9) 9.50 9.50

Souvenir Sheet

753 A106 $4 multicolored 6.25 6.25

Golden Days, by Norman Rockwell A107

1982, Mar. 10 Litho. *Perf. 14x13½*

754 A107 10c shown .20 .20
755 A107 25c The Morning News .20 .20
756 A107 45c The Marbles Champ .35 .35
757 A107 $1 Speeding Along .75 .75
Nos. 754-757 (4) 1.50 1.50

Intl. Decade for Women (1975-85) A108

Famous Women: 10c, Elma Napier (1890-1973), first woman elected to Legislative Council in British West Indies, 1940. 45c, Margaret Mead (1901-1978), anthropologist. $1, Mabel Caudiron (1909-1968), musician and folk historian. $3, Florence Nightingale, founder of modern nursing. $4, Eleanor Roosevelt.

1982, Apr. 15 Litho. *Perf. 14*

758 A108 10c multicolored .20 .20
759 A108 45c multicolored .35 .35
760 A108 $1 multicolored .75 .75
761 A108 $4 multicolored 3.00 3.00
Nos. 758-761 (4) 4.30 4.30

Souvenir Sheet

762 A108 $3 multicolored 3.25 3.25

George Washington and Independence Hall, Philadelphia — A109

Washington or Roosevelt and: 60c, Capitol Building. 90c, The Surrender of Cornwallis, by John Trumbull. $2, Dam construction during New Deal (mural by William Gropper). $5, Washington, Roosevelt.

1982, May 1 *Perf. 14½*

763 A109 45c multicolored .35 .35
764 A109 60c multicolored .45 .45
765 A109 90c multicolored .70 .70
766 A109 $2 multicolored 1.50 1.50
Nos. 763-766 (4) 3.00 3.00

Souvenir Sheet

767 A109 $5 multicolored 3.25 3.25

George Washington's 250th birth anniv. and Franklin D. Roosevelt's birth cent.

Godman's Leaf Butterfly — A110

1982, June 1 **Litho.** *Perf. 14*

768 A110 15c shown .50 .50
769 A110 45c Zebra 2.10 2.10
770 A110 60c Mimic 2.40 2.40
771 A110 $3 Red rim 9.50 9.50
Nos. 768-771 (4) 14.50 14.50

Souvenir Sheet

772 A110 $5 Southern dagger tail 7.25 7.25

Princess Diana Issue
Common Design Type

1982, July 1 **Litho.** *Perf. 14½x14*

773 CD332 45c Buckingham Palace .35 .35
774 CD332 $2 Engagement portrait 1.50 1.50
775 CD332 $4 Wedding 3.00 3.00
Nos. 773-775 (3) 4.85 4.85

Souvenir Sheet

776 CD332 $5 Diana, diff. 4.25 4.25

Also issued in sheet of 5 plus label.
For overprints see Nos. 782-785.

Scouting Year A111

1982, July 1 **Litho.** *Perf. 14*

777 A111 45c Cooking .95 .95
778 A111 60c Meteorological study 1.25 1.25
779 A111 75c Sisserou parrot, cub scouts 1.50 1.50
780 A111 $3 Canoeing, Indian River 6.00 6.00
Nos. 777-780 (4) 9.70 9.70

Souvenir Sheet

781 A111 $5 Flagbearer 4.25 4.25

Nos. 773-776 Overprinted: "ROYAL BABY / 21.6.82"

1982, Sept. 1 **Litho.** *Perf. 14½x14*

782 CD332 45c multicolored .35 .35
783 CD332 $2 multicolored 1.50 1.50
784 CD332 $4 multicolored 3.00 3.00
Nos. 782-784 (3) 4.85 4.85

Souvenir Sheet

785 CD332 $5 multicolored 3.75 3.75

Birth of Prince William of Wales, June 21.
Also issued in sheet of 5 plus label.

Christmas — A112

Holy Family Paintings by Raphael.

1982, Oct. 18 **Litho.** *Perf. 14*

786 A112 25c multicolored .20 .20
787 A112 30c multicolored .20 .20
788 A112 90c multicolored .60 .60
789 A112 $4 multicolored 2.75 2.75
Nos. 786-789 (4) 3.75 3.75

Souvenir Sheet

790 A112 $5 multicolored 3.75 3.75

Goosebeak Whale Eating Squid — A113

1983, Feb. 15 **Litho.** *Perf. 14*

791 A113 45c shown 1.25 1.25
792 A113 60c Humpback whale 1.75 1.75
793 A113 75c Great right whale 2.25 2.25
794 A113 $3 Melonhead whale 9.25 9.25
Nos. 791-794 (4) 14.50 14.50

Souvenir Sheet

795 A113 $5 Pygmy sperm whale 6.75 6.75

A113a

1983, Mar. 14

796 A113a 25c Banana industry .20 .20
797 A113a 30c Road construction .20 .20
798 A113a 90c Community nursing .55 .55
799 A113a $3 Basket weavers 1.75 1.75
Nos. 796-799 (4) 2.70 2.70

Commonwealth Day.

World Communications Year — A114

1983, Apr. 18 **Litho.** *Perf. 14*

800 A114 45c Hurricane pattern, map .35 .35
801 A114 60c Air-to-ship communication .45 .45
802 A114 90c Columbia shuttle, dish antenna .70 .70
803 A114 $2 Walkie-talkie 1.50 1.50
Nos. 800-803 (4) 3.00 3.00

Souvenir Sheet

804 A114 $5 Satellite 3.25 3.25

Manned Flight Bicentenary — A115

1983, July 19 **Litho.** *Perf. 15*

805 A115 45c Mayo Composite .50 .50
806 A115 60c Macchi M-39 .65 .65
807 A115 90c Fairey Swordfish 1.00 1.00
808 A115 $4 Zeppelin LZ-3 4.25 4.25
Nos. 805-808 (4) 6.40 6.40

Souvenir Sheet

809 A115 $5 Double Eagle II, vert. 3.75 3.75

Duesenberg SJ, 1935 — A116

1983, Sept. 1 **Litho.** *Perf. 14*

810 A116 10c shown .20 .20
811 A116 45c Studebaker Avanti, 1962 .35 .35
812 A116 60c Cord 812, 1936 .45 .45
813 A116 75c MG-TC, 1945 .55 .55
814 A116 90c Camaro 350-SS, 1967 .70 .70
815 A116 $3 Porsche 356, 1948 2.25 2.25
Nos. 810-815 (6) 4.50 4.50

Souvenir Sheet

816 A116 $5 Ferrari 312-T, 1975 3.50 3.50

Christmas — A117

Raphael Paintings.

1983, Oct. 4 **Litho.** *Perf. 13½*

817 A117 45c multicolored .35 .35
818 A117 60c multicolored .50 .50
819 A117 90c multicolored .75 .75
820 A117 $4 multicolored 3.25 3.25
Nos. 817-820 (4) 4.85 4.85

Souvenir Sheet

821 A117 $5 multicolored 3.75 3.75

23rd Olympic Games, Los Angeles, July 28-Aug. 12 — A118

1984, Mar. **Litho.** *Perf. 14*

822 A118 30c Gymnastics .25 .25
823 A118 45c Javelin .35 .35
824 A118 60c Diving .50 .50
825 A118 $4 Fencing 3.25 3.25
Nos. 822-825 (4) 4.35 4.35

Souvenir Sheet

826 A118 $5 Equestrian 3.50 3.50

Local Birds A119

1984, May **Litho.**

827 A119 5c Plumbeous warbler 2.75 2.75
828 A119 45c Imperial parrot 7.50 7.50
829 A119 60c Blue-headed hummingbird 11.00 11.00
830 A119 90c Red-necked parrot 16.00 16.00
Nos. 827-830 (4) 37.25 37.25

Souvenir Sheet

831 A119 $5 Roseate flamingoes 4.50 4.50

Easter A120

Various Disney characters and Easter bunnies.

1984, Apr. 15 **Litho.** *Perf. 11*

832 A120 ½c multicolored .20 .20
833 A120 1c multicolored .20 .20
834 A120 2c multicolored .20 .20
835 A120 3c multicolored .20 .20
836 A120 4c multicolored .20 .20
837 A120 5c multicolored .20 .20
838 A120 10c multicolored .20 .20
839 A120 $2 multicolored 3.50 3.50
840 A120 $4 multicolored 6.75 6.75
Nos. 832-840 (9) 11.65 11.65

Souvenir Sheet
Perf. 14

841 A120 $5 multicolored 6.50 6.50

Ships A121

1984, June 14 **Litho.** *Perf. 14*

842 A121 45c Atlantic Star 1.10 1.10
843 A121 60c Atlantic 1.40 1.40
844 A121 90c Carib fishing pirogue 2.25 2.25
845 A121 $4 Norway 9.75 9.75
Nos. 842-845 (4) 14.50 14.50

Souvenir Sheet

846 A121 $5 Santa Maria 5.50 5.50

Local Plants — A122

Correggio & Degas — A122a

1984, Aug. 13

847 A122 45c Guzmania lingulata .40 .40
848 A122 60c Pitcairnia angustifolia .50 .50
849 A122 75c Tillandsia fasciculata .60 .60
850 A122 $3 Aechmea smithiorum 2.75 2.75
Nos. 847-850 (4) 4.25 4.25

Souvenir Sheet

851 A122 $5 Tillandsia utriculata 3.50 3.50

Ausipex Intl. Stamp Exhibition.

Nos. 721, 732 Overprinted: "19th UPU / CONGRESS HAMBURG"

1984 **Litho.** *Perf. 14*

852 A103 10c multicolored .20 .20
853 A103 $5 multicolored 5.00 5.00

1984, Nov. **Litho.** *Perf. 15*

Correggio: 25c, Virgin and Child with Young St. John. 60c, Christ Bids Farewell to the Virgin Mary. 90c, Do Not Touch Me. $4, The Mystical Marriage of St. Catherine. No. 862, Adoration of the Magi,

Degas, horiz.: 30c, Before the Start. 45c, On the Racecourse. $1, Jockeys at the Flagpole. $3, Racehorses at Longchamp. No. 863, Self-portrait.

854 A122a 25c multicolored .20 .20
855 A122a 30c multicolored .20 .20
856 A122a 45c multicolored .35 .35
857 A122a 60c multicolored .45 .45
858 A122a 90c multicolored .65 .65
859 A122a $1 multicolored .75 .75
860 A122a $3 multicolored 2.25 2.25
861 A122a $4 multicolored 3.00 3.00
Nos. 854-861 (8) 7.85 7.85

Souvenir Sheets

862 A122a $5 multicolored 3.75 3.75
863 A122a $5 multicolored 3.75 3.75

A123

A124

1984, Dec. *Perf. 14*

864 A123 30c Avro 748 .20 .20
865 A123 60c Twin Otter 1.40 1.40
866 A123 $1 Islander 2.25 2.25
867 A123 $3 Casa 6.75 6.75
Nos. 864-867 (4) 10.60 10.60

Souvenir Sheet

868 A123 $5 Boeing 747 7.25 7.25

Intl. Civil Aviation Org., 40th anniv.

1984, Nov. **Litho.**

Scenes from various Donald Duck movies.

869 A124 45c multicolored .85 .85
870 A124 60c multicolored 1.10 1.10
871 A124 90c multicolored 1.75 1.75
872 A124 $2 multicolored, perf. 12x12½ 3.75 3.75
873 A124 $4 multicolored 7.25 7.25
Nos. 869-873 (5) 14.70 14.70

Souvenir Sheet

Perf. 13½x14

874 A124 $5 multicolored 6.50 6.50

Christmas and 50th anniv. of Donald Duck.

Cats A125

1984, Nov. 12 **Litho.** *Perf. 15*

875 A125 10c Tabby .20 .20
876 A125 15c Calico shorthair .20 .20
877 A125 20c Siamese .20 .20
878 A125 25c Manx .20 .20
879 A125 45c Abyssinian .45 .45
880 A125 60c Tortoise shell longhair .55 .55
881 A125 $1 Rex .90 .90
882 A125 $2 Persian 2.00 2.00
883 A125 $3 Himalayan 3.00 3.00
884 A125 $5 Burmese 4.50 4.50
Nos. 875-884 (10) 12.20 12.20

Souvenir Sheet

885 A125 $5 Gray Burmese, Persian, American shorthair 6.00 6.00

Girl Guides, 75th Anniv. A126

1985, Feb. 18 *Perf. 14*

886 A126 35c Lady Baden-Powell .45 .45
887 A126 45c Inspecting Dominican troop .65 .65
888 A126 60c With Dominican troop leaders .85 .85
889 A126 $3 Lord and Lady Baden-Powell, vert. 4.25 4.25
Nos. 886-889 (4) 6.20 6.20

Souvenir Sheet

890 A126 $5 Flag ceremony 6.00 6.00

John James Audubon A127

1985, Apr. 4

891 A127 45c King rails .85 .85
892 A127 $1 Black & white warbler, vert. 1.75 1.75
893 A127 $2 Broad-winged hawks, vert. 3.50 3.50
894 A127 $3 Ring-necked ducks 5.25 5.25
Nos. 891-894 (4) 11.35 11.35

Souvenir Sheet

895 A127 $5 Reddish egrets, vert. 5.50 5.50

Nos. 891-894 exist vertically se-tenant with labels showing additional bird species.

See Nos. 965-969.

Duke of Edinburgh Awards, 1984 — A128

1985, Apr. 30

896 A128 45c Woman at computer terminal .55 .55
897 A128 60c Medical staff, patient .70 .70
898 A128 90c Runners 1.10 1.10
899 A128 $4 Family jogging 4.75 4.75
Nos. 896-899 (4) 7.10 7.10

Souvenir Sheet

900 A128 $5 Duke of Edinburgh 4.25 4.25

Intl. Youth Year A129

1985, July 8 **Litho.** *Perf. 14*

901 A129 45c Cricket match 1.60 1.60
902 A129 60c Environmental study, parrot 2.10 2.10
903 A129 $1 Stamp collecting 3.00 3.00
904 A129 $3 Boating, leisure 10.50 10.50
Nos. 901-904 (4) 17.20 17.20

Souvenir Sheet

905 A129 $5 Youths join hands 4.25 4.25

Queen Mother, 85th Birthday — A130

Johann Sebastian Bach — A131

1985, July 15

906 A130 60c Visiting Sadlers Wells .45 .45
907 A130 $1 Fishing .90 .90
908 A130 $3 At Clarence House, 1984 2.75 2.75
Nos. 906-908 (3) 4.10 4.10

Souvenir Sheet

909 A130 $5 Attending Windsor Castle Garter Ceremony 4.00 4.00

1985, Sept. 2

Portrait, signature, music from Explication and: 45c, Cornett 60c, Coiled trumpet. $1, Piccolo. $3, Violoncello piccolo.

910 A131 45c multicolored .75 .75
911 A131 60c multicolored 1.00 1.00
912 A131 $1 multicolored 1.60 1.60
913 A131 $3 multicolored 6.25 6.25
Nos. 910-913 (4) 9.60 9.60

Souvenir Sheet

914 A131 $5 Portrait 4.50 4.50

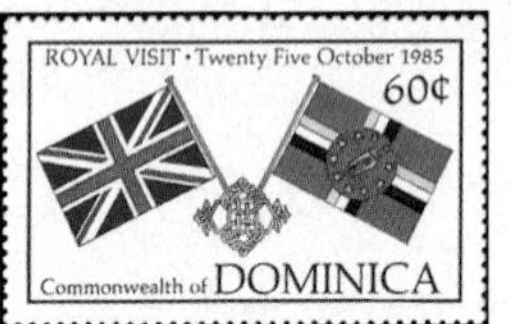

State Visit of Elizabeth II, Oct. 25 — A132

1985, Oct. 25 *Perf. 14½*

915 A132 60c Flags of UK, Dominica .55 .55
916 A132 $1 Elizabeth II, vert. .95 .95
917 A132 $4 HMS Britannia 4.00 4.00
Nos. 915-917 (3) 5.50 5.50

Souvenir Sheet

918 A132 $5 Map 4.00 4.00

Mark Twain — A133

Disney characters in Tom Sawyer.

1985, Nov. 11 **Litho.** *Perf. 14*

919 A133 20c multicolored .45 .45
920 A133 60c multicolored 1.00 1.00
921 A133 $1 multicolored 1.75 1.75
922 A133 $1.50 multicolored 3.25 3.25
923 A133 $2 multicolored 4.50 4.50
Nos. 919-923 (5) 10.95 10.95

Souvenir Sheet

924 A133 $5 multicolored 7.00 7.00

Christmas.

The Brothers Grimm — A134

Disney characters in Little Red Cap (Little Red Riding Hood).

1985, Nov. 11

925 A134 10c multicolored .40 .40
926 A134 45c multicolored .85 .85
927 A134 90c multicolored 1.60 1.60
928 A134 $1 multicolored 1.90 1.90
929 A134 $3 multicolored 5.75 5.75
Nos. 925-929 (5) 10.50 10.50

Souvenir Sheet

930 A134 $5 multicolored 8.25 8.25

Christmas.

UN, 40th Anniv. A135

Stamps of UN, famous men and events: 45c, No. 442 and Lord Baden-Powell. $2, No. 157 and Maimonides (1135-1204) Judaic scholar. $3, No. 278 and Sir Rowland Hill. $5, Apollo-Soyuz Mission, 10th anniv.

1985, Nov. 22 *Perf. 14½*

931 A135 45c multicolored .45 .45
932 A135 $2 multicolored 2.75 2.75
933 A135 $3 multicolored 4.00 4.00
Nos. 931-933 (3) 7.20 7.20

Souvenir Sheet

934 A135 $5 multicolored 4.25 4.25

1986 World Cup Soccer Championships, Mexico — A136

Various soccer plays.

1986, Mar. 26 *Perf. 14*

935 A136 45c multicolored .90 .90
936 A136 60c multicolored 1.25 1.25
937 A136 $1 multicolored 2.25 2.25
938 A136 $3 multicolored 6.75 6.75
Nos. 935-938 (4) 11.15 11.15

Souvenir Sheet

939 A136 $5 multicolored 9.00 9.00

For overprints see Nos. 974-978.

Statue of Liberty, Cent. A137

Statue and: 15c, New York police pursuing river pirates, c. 1890. 25c, Police patrol boat. 45c, Hoboken Ferry Terminal, c. 1890. $4, Holland Tunnel.

1986, Mar. 26

940 A137 15c multicolored .50 .50
941 A137 25c multicolored .50 .50
942 A137 45c multicolored .75 .75
943 A137 $4 multicolored 7.50 7.50
Nos. 940-943 (4) 9.25 9.25

Souvenir Sheet

944 A137 $5 Statue, vert. 5.75 5.75

Halley's Comet A138

5c, Jantal Mantar Observatory, Delhi, India, Nasir al Din al Tusi (1201-1274), astronomer. 10c, US Bell X-1 rocket plane breaking sound barrier. 45c, Astronomicum Caesareum, 1540, manuscript diagram of comet's trajectory,

1531. $4, Mark Twain, comet appeared at birth and death. $5, Comet.

1986, Apr. 17
945 A138 5c multicolored .20 .20
946 A138 10c multicolored .20 .20
947 A138 45c multicolored .45 .45
948 A138 $4 multicolored 4.50 4.50
Nos. 945-948 (4) 5.35 5.35

Souvenir Sheet

949 A138 $5 multicolored 4.00 4.00

For overprints see Nos. 984-988.

Queen Elizabeth II, 60th Birthday
Common Design Type

1986, Apr. 21 Litho. *Perf. 14*
950 CD339 2c Wedding, 1947 .25 .25
951 CD339 $1 With Pope John Paul II, 1982 .75 .75
952 CD339 $4 Royal visit, 1971 2.50 2.50
Nos. 950-952 (3) 3.50 3.50

Souvenir Sheet

953 CD339 $5 Age 10 3.75 3.75

AMERIPEX '86 — A139

Walt Disney characters involved in stamp collecting.

1986, May 22 *Perf. 11*
954 A139 25c Mickey Mouse and Pluto .20 .20
955 A139 45c Donald Duck .70 .70
956 A139 60c Chip-n-Dale .85 .85
957 A139 $4 Donald, nephews 5.75 5.75
Nos. 954-957 (4) 7.50 7.50

Souvenir Sheet
Perf. 14

958 A139 $5 Uncle Scrooge 6.50 6.50

British Monarchs — A140

1986, June 9 *Perf. 14*
959 A140 10c William I .20 .20
960 A140 40c Richard II .35 .35
961 A140 50c Henry VIII .45 .45
962 A140 $1 Charles II .95 .95
963 A140 $2 Queen Anne 1.90 1.90
964 A140 $4 Queen Victoria 4.00 4.00
Nos. 959-964 (6) 7.85 7.85

Audubon Type of 1985
Perf. 12½x12, 12x12½

1986, June 18
965 A127 25c Black-throated diver .40 .40
966 A127 60c Great blue heron 1.00 1.00
967 A127 90c Yellow-crowned night heron 1.50 1.50
968 A127 $4 Shoveler duck 7.25 7.25
Nos. 965-968 (4) 10.15 10.15

Souvenir Sheet
Perf. 14

969 A127 $5 Goose 10.50 10.50

Nos. 966-967 vert.

Royal Wedding Issue, 1986
Common Design Type

1986, July 23 *Perf. 14*
970 CD340 45c Couple .30 .30
971 CD340 60c Prince Andrew .45 .45
972 CD340 $4 Prince, aircraft 2.75 2.75
Nos. 970-972 (3) 3.50 3.50

Souvenir Sheet

973 CD340 $5 Couple, diff. 4.00 4.00

Nos. 935-939 Ovptd. "WINNERS / Argentina 3 / W. Germany 2" in Gold

1986, Sept. 15 Litho. *Perf. 14*
974 A136 45c multicolored .75 .75
975 A136 60c multicolored 1.10 1.10
976 A136 $1 multicolored 1.90 1.90
977 A136 $3 multicolored 6.00 6.00
Nos. 974-977 (4) 9.75 9.75

Souvenir Sheet

978 A136 $5 multicolored 9.25 9.25

Paintings by Albrecht Durer — A141

A142

1986, Dec. 2 Litho. *Perf. 14*
979 A141 45c Virgin in Prayer .90 .90
980 A141 60c Madonna and Child 1.10 1.10
981 A141 $1 Madonna and Child, diff. 2.00 2.00
982 A141 $3 Madonna and Child with St. Anne 6.00 6.00
Nos. 979-982 (4) 10.00 10.00

Souvenir Sheet

983 A142 $5 Nativity 9.25 9.25

Nos. 945-949 Printed with Halley's Comet Logo in Black or Silver

1986, Dec. 16
984 A138 5c multicolored .20 .20
985 A138 10c multicolored .20 .20
986 A138 45c multicolored .45 .45
987 A138 $4 multicolored 4.25 4.25
Nos. 984-987 (4) 5.10 5.10

Souvenir Sheet

988 A138 $5 multi (S) 5.25 5.25

Birds — A143

1987, Jan. 20 Litho. *Perf. 15*
989 A143 1c Broad-winged hawk .20 .20
990 A143 2c Ruddy quail dove .20 .20
991 A143 5c Red-necked pigeon .20 .20
992 A143 10c Green heron .20 .20
993 A143 15c Common gallinule .20 .20
994 A143 20c Ringed kingfisher .20 .20
995 A143 25c Brown pelican .20 .20
996 A143 35c White-tailed tropicbird .30 .30
997 A143 45c Red-legged thrush .35 .35
998 A143 60c Purple throated carib .50 .50
999 A143 90c Magnificent frigatebird .70 .70
1000 A143 $1 Trembler .80 .80
1001 A143 $2 Black-capped petrel 1.60 1.60
1002 A143 $5 Barn owl 4.00 4.00
1003 A143 $10 Imperial parrot 8.00 8.00
Nos. 989-1003 (15) 17.65 17.65

Inscribed "1989" and "Questa"

1989, Aug. 31 Litho. *Perf. 14*
990a A143 2c .20 .20
991a A143 5c .20 .20
992a A143 10c .20 .20
993a A143 15c .20 .20
994a A143 20c .20 .20
995a A143 25c .30 .30
996a A143 35c .45 .45
997a A143 45c .55 .55
998a A143 60c .75 .75
1000a A143 $1 1.25 1.25
1001a A143 $2 2.50 2.50
1002a A143 $5 6.25 6.25
1003a A143 $10 12.50 12.50
Nos. 990a-1003a (13) 25.55 25.55

Inscribed "1989" and "Questa"

1990 Litho. *Perf. 12*
990b A143 2c .20 .20
991b A143 5c .20 .20
992b A143 10c .20 .20
993b A143 15c .20 .20
994b A143 20c .20 .20
995b A143 25c .30 .30
996b A143 35c .45 .45
997b A143 45c .55 .55
998b A143 60c .75 .75
1000b A143 $1 1.25 1.25
1001b A143 $2 2.50 2.50
1002b A143 $5 6.25 6.25
1003b A143 $10 12.50 12.50
Nos. 990b-1003b (13) 25.55 25.55

Inscribed "1989" and "Questa"

1991 Litho. *Perf. 13x11½*
990c A143 2c .20 .20
991c A143 5c .20 .20
992c A143 10c .20 .20
993c A143 15c .20 .20
994c A143 20c .20 .20
995c A143 25c .35 .35
996c A143 35c .50 .50
997c A143 45c .60 .60
998c A143 60c .85 .85
1000c A143 $1 1.40 1.40
1001c A143 $2 2.75 2.75
1002c A143 $5 6.75 6.75
1003c A143 $10 13.50 13.50
Nos. 990c-1003c (13) 27.70 27.70

Paintings by Marc Chagall (1887-1985) A144

Designs: 25c, Artist and His Model. 35c, Midsummer Night's Dream. 45c, Joseph the Shepherd. 60c, the Cellist. 90c, Woman with Pigs. $1, the Blue Circus. $3, For Vava. $4, the Rider. No. 1012, Purim. No. 1013, Firebird design for the curtain of the Stravinsky Ballet production.

1987, Mar. 2 *Perf. 14*
1004 A144 25c multicolored .20 .20
1005 A144 35c multicolored .30 .30
1006 A144 45c multicolored .35 .35
1007 A144 60c multicolored .50 .50
1008 A144 90c multicolored .70 .70
1009 A144 $1 multicolored .80 .80
1010 A144 $3 multicolored 2.40 2.40
1011 A144 $4 multicolored 3.25 3.25

Size: 110x95mm
Imperf

1012 A144 $5 multicolored 4.00 4.00
1013 A144 $5 multicolored 4.00 4.00
Nos. 1004-1013 (10) 16.50 16.50

A145

Conch Shells — A147

America's Cup — A146

1987, Feb. 5 *Perf. 15*
1014 A145 45c Reliance, 1903 .45 .45
1015 A145 60c Freedom, 1980 .55 .55
1016 A145 $1 Mischief, 1881 1.00 1.00
1017 A145 $3 Australia, 1977 3.00 2.00
Nos. 1014-1017 (4) 5.00 4.00

Souvenir Sheet

1018 A146 $5 Courageous, Australia, 1977 4.00 4.00

1987, Apr. 13 Litho.

Designs: 35c, Morch Poulsen's triton. 45c, Swainson globe purple sea snail. 60c, Banded tulip. No. 1022, Lamarck deltoid rock shell. No. 1023, Junoia volute.

1019 A147 35c multicolored .30 .30
1020 A147 45c multicolored .40 .40
1021 A147 60c multicolored .55 .55
1022 A147 $5 multicolored 4.00 4.00
Nos. 1019-1022 (4) 5.25 5.25

Souvenir Sheet

1023 A147 $5 multicolored 4.75 4.75

CAPEX '87 A148

Mushrooms.

1987, June 15 Litho. *Perf. 14*
1024 A148 45c Cantharellus cinnabarinus .80 .80
1025 A148 60c Boletellus cubenis 1.10 1.10
1026 A148 $2 Eccilia cystiophorus 4.25 4.25
1027 A148 $3 Xerocomus guadelupae 6.25 6.25
Nos. 1024-1027 (4) 12.40 12.40

Souvenir Sheet

1028 A148 $5 Gymnopilus chrysopellus 11.50 11.50

A149

Discovery of America, 500th Anniv. (in 1992) — A150

Explorations of Christopher Columbus: 10c, Discovery of Dominica. 15c, Ships greeted by Carib Indians. 45c, Claiming New World for Spain. 60c, Wrecking of the Santa Maria. 90c, Fleet setting sail. $1, Sighting land. $3, Trading with the Indians. No. 1036, First settlement. No. 1037, Arrival of Second Fleet at Dominica, Nov. 3, 1493. No. 1038, Map of exploration of the Leeward Islands.

1987, July 27 *Perf. 15*

1029 A149 10c multicolored .25 .25
1030 A149 15c multicolored .25 .25
1031 A149 45c multicolored .45 .45
1032 A149 60c multicolored .60 .60
1033 A149 90c multicolored .90 .90
1034 A149 $1 multicolored 1.00 1.00
1035 A149 $3 multicolored 3.00 3.00
1036 A149 $5 multicolored 5.00 5.00
Nos. 1029-1036 (8) 11.45 11.45

Souvenir Sheets

1037 A150 $5 multicolored 4.00 4.00
1038 A150 $5 multicolored 4.00 4.00

For overprints see Nos. 1083-1084.

Transportation — A151

10c, Warrior, 1st iron-clad warship. 15c, Maglev-MLU 001, fastest passenger train. 25c, Clipper Flying Cloud, fastest NYC-San Francisco voyage, 1852. 35c, 1st elevated railway, NYC. 45c, Tom Thumb, 1st US passenger train locomotive. 60c, Joshua Slocum, 1st solo circumnavigation of the world in a sloop. 90c, Se-Land Commerce, fastest Pacific crossing. $1, 1st cable car, San Francisco. $3, Orient Express. $4, The North River Steamboat of Clermont, invented by Robert Fulton, 1st successful commercial steamboat.

1987 **Litho.** *Perf. 14*

1039 A151 10c multicolored .20 .20
1040 A151 15c multicolored .20 .20
1041 A151 25c multi, vert. .40 .40
1042 A151 35c multi, vert. .50 .50
1043 A151 45c multicolored .60 .60
1044 A151 60c multi, vert. .90 .90
1045 A151 90c multi, vert. 1.25 1.25
1046 A151 $1 multicolored 1.50 1.50
1047 A151 $3 multicolored 4.50 4.50
1048 A151 $4 multicolored 5.50 5.50
Nos. 1039-1048 (10) 15.55 15.55

Issued: 10c, 15c, 45c, 60c, $4, 9/28; others 8/1.

For overprints see Nos. 1081-1082.

Christmas — A152

Paintings (details): 20c, Virgin and Child with St. Anne, by Durer. 25c, The Virgin and Child, by Murillo. $2, Madonna and Child, by Vincenzo Foppa (c. 1427-1516). $4, Madonna and Child, by Paolo Veronese (1528-1588). $5, Angel of the Annunciation, anonymous.

1987, Nov. 16

1049 A152 20c multicolored .30 .30
1050 A152 25c multicolored .30 .30
1051 A152 $2 multicolored 2.10 2.10
1052 A152 $4 multicolored 4.25 4.25
Nos. 1049-1052 (4) 6.95 6.95

Souvenir Sheet

1053 A152 $5 multicolored 4.00 4.00

Mickey Mouse, 60th Anniv. A153

Disney theme parks and trains: 20c, People Mover, Disney World. 25c, Horse-drawn Trolley, Disneyland. 45c, Roger E. Broggie, Disney World. 60c, Big Thunder Mountain, Disneyland. 90c, Walter E. Disney, Disneyland. $1, Monorail, Disney World. $3, Casey Jr. from Dumbo. $4, Lilly Belle, Disney World. No. 1062, Rainbow Caverns Mine Train, Disneyland, horiz. No. 1063, Toy train from movie Out of Scale, horiz.

1987, Dec. 7 **Litho.** *Perf. 14*

1054 A153 20c multicolored .40 .40
1055 A153 25c multicolored .40 .40
1056 A153 45c multicolored .70 .70
1057 A153 60c multicolored 1.00 1.00
1058 A153 90c multicolored 1.25 1.25
1059 A153 $1 multicolored 1.50 1.50
1060 A153 $3 multicolored 4.50 4.50
1061 A153 $4 multicolored 6.00 6.00
Nos. 1054-1061 (8) 15.75 15.75

Souvenir Sheets

1062 A153 $5 multicolored 4.25 4.25
1063 A153 $5 multicolored 4.25 4.25

40th Wedding Anniv. of Queen Elizabeth II and Prince Philip — A154

1988 Summer Olympics, Seoul — A155

1988, Feb. 15 **Litho.** *Perf. 14*

1064 A154 45c Couple, wedding party, 1947 .45 .45
1065 A154 60c Elizabeth, Charles, c. 1952 .60 .60
1066 A154 $1 Royal Family, c. 1952 1.10 1.10
1067 A154 $3 Queen with tiara, c. 1960 3.00 3.00
Nos. 1064-1067 (4) 5.15 5.15

Souvenir Sheet

1068 A154 $5 Elizabeth, 1947 3.50 3.50

1988, Mar. 15

1069 A155 45c Kayaking .65 .65
1070 A155 60c Tae kwon-do .85 .85
1071 A155 $1 Diving 1.50 1.50
1072 A155 $3 Parallel bars 4.00 4.00
Nos. 1069-1072 (4) 7.00 7.00

Souvenir Sheet

1073 A155 $5 Soccer 3.50 3.50

For overprints see Nos. 1151-1155.

Reunion '88 Tourism Campaign A156

1988, Apr. 13 **Litho.** *Perf. 15*

1074 A156 10c Carib Indian, vert. .20 .20
1075 A156 25c Mountainous interior .20 .20
1076 A156 35c Indian River, vert. .25 .25
1077 A156 60c Belaire dancer, vert. .40 .40
1078 A156 90c The Boiling Lake, vert. .60 .60
1079 A156 $3 Coral reef 2.00 2.00
Nos. 1074-1079 (6) 3.65 3.65

Souvenir Sheet

1080 A156 $5 Belaire dancer, diff., vert. 3.25 3.25

Independence, 10th anniv.

Nos. 1046-1047, 1037-1038 Ovptd. for Philatelic Exhibitions in Black

a

b

c

d

1988, June 1 **Litho.** *Perf. 14*

1081 A151(a) $1 multi 1.25 1.25
1082 A151(b) $3 multi 4.00 4.00

Souvenir Sheets

Perf. 15

1083 A150(c) $5 multi 3.75 3.75
1084 A150(d) $5 multi 3.75 3.75

Miniature Sheet

Rain Forest Flora and Fauna — A157

Designs: a, White-tailed tropicbirds. b, Blue-throated euphonia. c, Smooth-billed ani. d, Scaly-breasted thrasher. e, Purple-throated carib. f, Southern daggertail and Clench's hairstreak. g, Trembler. h, Imperial parrot. i, Mangrove cuckoo. j, Hercules beetle. k, Orion. l, Red-necked parrot. m, Tillandsia. n, Polystacha luteola and bananaquit. o, False chameleon. p, Iguana. q, Hypolimnas. r, Green-throated carib. s, Heliconia. t, Agouti.

1988, July 25 *Perf. 14½*

1085 Sheet of 20 14.00 14.00
a.-t. A157 45c any single .70 .70

Intl. Fund for Agricultural Development (IFAD), 10th Anniv. — A158

1988, Sept. 5 **Litho.** *Perf. 14*

1086 A158 45c Hen house .60 .60
1087 A158 60c Pig farm .75 .75
1088 A158 90c Cattle 1.10 1.10
1089 A158 $3 Black-belly sheep 3.75 3.75
Nos. 1086-1089 (4) 6.20 6.20

Souvenir Sheet

1090 A158 $5 Mixed crops, vert. 4.00 4.00

Entertainers A159

1988, Sept. 8

1091 A159 10c Gary Cooper .20 .20
1092 A159 35c Josephine Baker .35 .35
1093 A159 45c Maurice Chevalier .40 .40
1094 A159 60c James Cagney .50 .50
1095 A159 $1 Clark Gable .85 .85
1096 A159 $2 Louis Armstrong 1.75 1.75
1097 A159 $3 Liberace 2.50 2.50
1098 A159 $4 Spencer Tracy 3.25 3.25
Nos. 1091-1098 (8) 9.80 9.80

Souvenir Sheets

1099 A159 $5 Elvis Presley 4.50 4.50
1100 A159 $5 Humphrey Bogart 4.50 4.50

Flowering Trees and Shrubs A160

1988, Sept. 29 **Litho.** *Perf. 14*

1101 A160 15c Sapodilla .20 .20
1102 A160 20c Tangerine .20 .20
1103 A160 25c Avocado pear .20 .20
1104 A160 45c Amherstia .30 .30
1105 A160 90c Lipstick tree .60 .60
1106 A160 $1 Cannonball tree .60 .60
1107 A160 $3 Saman 1.90 1.90
1108 A160 $4 Pineapple 2.50 2.50
Nos. 1101-1108 (8) 6.50 6.50

Souvenir Sheets

1109 A160 $5 Lignum vitae 3.75 3.75
1110 A160 $5 Sea grape 3.75 3.75

Paintings by Titian A161

Designs: 25c, Jacopo Strada, c. 1567. 35c, Titian's Daughter Lavinia, c. 1565. 45c, Andrea Navagero, c. 1515. 60c, Judith with Head of Holoferenes, c. 1570. $1, Emilia di Spilimbergo, c. 1560. $2, Martyrdom of St. Lawrence, c. 1548. $3, Salome With the Head of St. John the Baptist, 1560. $4, St. John the Baptist, c. 1540. No. 1119, Self-portrait, c. 1555. No. 1120, Sisyphus, 1549.

1988, Oct. 10 Litho. *Perf. 13½x14*

1111 A161 25c multicolored .20 .20
1112 A161 35c multicolored .30 .30
1113 A161 45c multicolored .35 .35
1114 A161 60c multicolored .45 .45
1115 A161 $1 multicolored .75 .75
1116 A161 $2 multicolored 1.50 1.50
1117 A161 $3 multicolored 2.25 2.25
1118 A161 $4 multicolored 3.00 3.00
Nos. 1111-1118 (8) 8.80 8.80

Souvenir Sheets

1119 A161 $5 multicolored 3.75 3.75
1120 A161 $5 multicolored 3.75 3.75

A162

A163

1988, Oct. 31 Litho. *Perf. 14*

1121 A162 20c Imperial parrot .35 .35
1122 A162 45c No. 1, landscape .55 .55
1123 A162 $2 No. 602, waterfall 2.40 2.40
1124 A162 $3 Carib wood 3.75 3.75
Nos. 1121-1124 (4) 7.05 7.05

Souvenir Sheet

1125 A162 $5 Natl. band performing 4.00 4.00

Independence, 10th Anniv. Nos. 1122-1123 horiz.

1988, Nov. 22

1126 A163 20c With Jackie .20 .20
1127 A163 25c Sailing Vicuna .20 .20
1128 A163 $2 Walking in Hyannis Port 1.10 1.10
1129 A163 $4 Berlin Wall speech 2.25 2.25
Nos. 1126-1129 (4) 3.75 3.75

Souvenir Sheet

1130 A163 $5 Portrait 3.75 3.75

John F. Kennedy. #1126-1128 horiz.

Miniature Sheet

Christmas, Mickey Mouse 60th Anniv. — A164

#1131: a, Huey, Dewey, Louie. b, Daisy Duck. c, Winnie-the-Pooh. d, Goofy. e, Donald Duck. f, Mickey Mouse. g, Minnie Mouse. h, Chip-n-Dale.

#1132, Mickey, Morty and Ferdy. #1133, Characters visiting shopping mall Santa.

1988, Dec. 1 *Perf. 13½x14*

1131 A164 Sheet of 8 7.00 7.00
a.-h. 60c any single .85 .85

Souvenir Sheets

1132 A164 $6 multi 5.25 5.25
1133 A164 $6 multi, horiz. 5.25 5.25

UN Declaration of Human Rights, 40th Anniv. — A165

Designs: $3, Flag of Sweden and Raoul Wallenberg, who helped save 100,000 Jews in Budapest from deportation to Nazi concentration camps. $5, Human Rights Flame.

1988, Dec. 12 *Perf. 14*

1134 A165 $3 multicolored 3.00 3.00

Souvenir Sheet

1135 A165 $5 multi, vert. 4.25 4.25

Coastal Game Fish A166

1988, Dec. 22 Litho. *Perf. 14*

1136 A166 10c Greater amberjack .30 .30
1137 A166 15c Blue marlin .30 .30
1138 A166 35c Cobia .45 .45
1139 A166 45c Dolphin .50 .50
1140 A166 60c Cero .65 .65
1141 A166 90c Mahogany snapper 1.00 1.00
1142 A166 $3 Yellowfin tuna 3.25 3.25
1143 A166 $4 Rainbow parrotfish 4.50 4.50
Nos. 1136-1143 (8) 10.95 10.95

Souvenir Sheets

1144 A166 $5 Manta ray 5.50 5.50
1145 A166 $5 Tarpon 5.50 5.50

Caribbean Insects and Reptiles A167

1988, Dec. 29

1146 A167 10c Leatherback turtle .30 .30
1147 A167 25c Monarch butterfly .70 .70
1148 A167 60c Green anole 1.60 1.60
1149 A167 $3 Praying mantis 8.00 8.00
Nos. 1146-1149 (4) 10.60 10.60

Souvenir Sheet

1150 A167 $5 Hercules beetle 5.25 5.25

Nos. 1069-1072 Ovptd. for Olympic Winners

a. "Men's c-1,500m O. Heukrodt DDR"

b. "Women's Flyweight N.Y. Choo S. Korea"

c. "Women's Platform Y. Xu China"

d. "V. Artemov USSR"

e. "USSR defeated Brazil 3-2 on penalty kicks after a 1-1 tie"

1989, Mar. 20 Litho. *Perf. 14*

1151 A155(a) 45c multi .35 .35
1152 A155(b) 60c multi .45 .45
1153 A155(c) $1 multi .80 .80
1154 A155(d) $3 multi 2.00 2.00
Nos. 1151-1154 (4) 3.60 3.60

Souvenir Sheet

1155 A155(e) $5 multi 3.75 3.75

Pre-Columbian Societies and Their Customs — A168

UPAE and discovery of America anniv. emblems and: 20c, Carib Indians canoeing. 35c, Bow hunting. $1, Canoe making. $3, Shield wrestling. $6, Dancing.

1989, May 8 Litho. *Perf. 14*

1156 A168 20c multicolored .25 .25
1157 A168 35c multicolored .35 .35
1158 A168 $1 multicolored .90 .90
1159 A168 $3 multicolored 2.75 2.75
Nos. 1156-1159 (4) 4.25 4.25

Souvenir Sheet

1160 A168 $6 multicolored 4.50 4.50

Discovery of America 500th anniv. (in 1992).

Paintings by Yokoyama Taikan (1868-1958) A169

Designs: 10c, Lao-tzu. 20c, Red Maple Leaves (panels 1-2). 45c, King Wen Learns a Lesson from His Cook. 60c, Red Maple Leaves (panels 3-4). $1, Wild Flowers. $2, Red Maple Leaves (panels 5-6). $3, Red Maple Leaves (panels 7-8). $4, The Indian Ceremony of Floating Lamps on the River. No. 1169, Innocence. No. 1170, Red Maple Leaves (4 panels).

1989, Aug. 8 Litho. *Perf. 13½x14*

1161 A169 10c multicolored .20 .20
1162 A169 20c multicolored .20 .20
1163 A169 45c multicolored .30 .30
1164 A169 60c multicolored .40 .40
1165 A169 $1 multicolored .65 .65
1166 A169 $2 multicolored 1.25 1.25
1167 A169 $3 multicolored 1.90 1.90
1168 A169 $4 multicolored 2.50 2.50
Nos. 1161-1168 (8) 7.40 7.40

Souvenir Sheets

1169 A169 $5 multicolored 4.00 4.00
1170 A169 $5 multicolored 4.00 4.00

Hirohito (1901-89) and enthronement of Akihito as emperor of Japan.

PHILEXFRANCE '89, July 7-17, Paris — A170

Designs: 10c, Map of Dominica with French place names, 1766. 35c, French coin, 1688. $1, French ship, 1720. $4, Introduction of coffee to Dominica by the French, 1772. $5, Text.

1989, July 17 Litho. *Perf. 14*

1171 A170 10c multi, vert. .20 .20
1172 A170 35c shown .40 .40
1173 A170 $1 multicolored 1.10 1.10
1174 A170 $4 multicolored 4.25 4.25
Nos. 1171-1174 (4) 5.95 5.95

Souvenir Sheet

1175 A170 $5 multicolored 5.50 5.50

Butterflies A171

Designs: 10c, Homerus swallowtail. 15c, *Morpho peleides*. 25c, Julia. 35c, Gundlach's swallowtail. 60c, Monarch. $1, Gulf fritillary. $3, Red-splashed sulphur. $5, *Papilio andraemon*. No. 1184, *Heliconius doris, Adelpha cytherea, Calliona argenissa, Eurema proterpia*. No. 1185, *Adelpha iphicla, Dismorphia spio, Lucinia sida*.

1989, Sept. 11 Litho. *Perf. 14*

1176 A171 10c multicolored .20 .20
1177 A171 15c multicolored .20 .20
1178 A171 25c multicolored .40 .40
1179 A171 35c multicolored .60 .60
1180 A171 60c multicolored 1.00 1.00
1181 A171 $1 multicolored 1.50 1.50
1182 A171 $3 multicolored 4.00 4.00
1183 A171 $5 multicolored 7.25 7.25
Nos. 1176-1183 (8) 15.15 15.15

Souvenir Sheets

1184 A171 $6 multicolored 6.25 6.25
1185 A171 $6 multicolored 6.25 6.25

Misspellings: No. 1181, "Frittillary"; No. 1182, "Sulper."

Orchids — A172

1989, Sept. 28

1186 A172 10c *Oncidium pusillum* .20 .20
1187 A172 35c *Epidendrum cochleata* .55 .55
1188 A172 45c *Epidendrum ciliare* .60 .60
1189 A172 60c *Cyrtopodium andersonii* .90 .90
1190 A172 $1 *Habenaria pauciflora* 1.50 1.50
1191 A172 $2 *Maxillaria alba* 3.00 3.00
1192 A172 $3 *Selenipedium palmifolium* 4.50 4.50
1193 A172 $4 *Brassavola cucullata* 6.00 6.00
Nos. 1186-1193 (8) 17.25 17.25

Souvenir Sheets

1194 A172 $5 *Oncidium lanceanum* 6.25 6.25
1195 A172 $5 *Comparettia falcata* 6.25 6.25

1st Moon Landing, 20th Anniv. A173

1989, Oct. 31 Litho. *Perf. 14*

1196 A173 10c *Columbia* in lunar orbit .20 .20
1197 A173 60c Aldrin descending ladder .75 .75
1198 A173 $2 Aldrin, Sea of Tranquillity 2.40 2.40
1199 A173 $3 Flag raising 3.75 3.75
Nos. 1196-1199 (4) 7.10 7.10

Souvenir Sheet

1200 A173 $6 Liftoff 7.25 7.25

Souvenir Sheets

A174

1990 World Cup Soccer Championships, Italy — A175

Past championship match scenes, flags and soccer ball: a, Brazil vs. Italy, Mexico, 1970. b, England vs. West Germany, England, 1966. c, West Germany vs. Netherlands, West Germany, 1974. d, Italy vs. West Germany, Spain, 1982.

1989, Nov. 7 *Perf. 14*

1201 A174 Sheet of 4 8.50 8.50
a.-d. $1 any single 2.00 2.00

Perf. 14

1202 A175 $6 shown 6.25 6.25

Souvenir Sheet

The Capitol, Washington, DC — A176

1989, Nov. 17 Litho. *Perf. 14*

1203 A176 $4 multicolored 4.00 4.00

World Stamp Expo '89.

Miniature Sheets

American Presidency, 200th Anniv. — A177

US presidents, historic events and monuments.

No. 1204: a, Washington, 1st inauguration. b, John Adams, presidential mansion, 1800. c, Jefferson, Graff House in Philadelphia, excerpt from the 1st draft of the Declaration of Independence. d, Madison, USS *Constitution* at the defeat of HMS *Guerriere,* 1812. e, Monroe, freed slaves settle Liberia, 1822. f, John Quincy Adams, opening of the Erie Canal, 1825.

No. 1205: a, Fillmore, Commodore Perry laying groundwork for US trade agreement with Japan. b, Pierce, Jefferson Davis and San Xavier del Bac mission, Tucson, AZ, Gadsden Purchase, 1853. c, Buchanan, Pony Express stamp, Buffalo Bill Cody as express rider. d, Lincoln, UPU emblem, Intl. Postal Congress, Paris, 1863. e, Andrew Johnson, polar bear, purchase of Alaska from Russia, 1867. f, Grant, 1st transcontinental railway link, Promontory Point, Utah, 1869.

No. 1206: a, Theodore Roosevelt, construction of the Panama Canal, 1904. b, Taft, Adm. Peary becomes 1st man to reach the North Pole, 1909. c, Wilson, US #C3, cancel commemorating 1st scheduled airmail service, 1918. d, Harding, airship USS *Shenandoah* at Lakehurst, NJ. e, Coolidge, Lindbergh's solo transatlantic flight, 1927. f, Mt. Rushmore, by Gutzon Borglum, 1927.

No. 1207: a, Lyndon B. Johnson, space exploration. b, Nixon visiting PRChina, 1971. c, Ford, tall ship in NY Harbor for Operation Sail, 1976, US bicentennial celebrations. d, Carter, Sadat of Egypt and Begin of Israel during the Camp David Accords, 1979. e, Reagan, European Space Agency emblem, flags and *Columbia* space shuttle. f, Bush, Grumman Avenger bomber he piloted during WWII.

1989, Nov. 17 *Perf. 14*

1204 Sheet of 6 5.25 5.25
a.-f. A177 60c any single .85 .85
1205 Sheet of 6 5.25 5.25
a.-f. A177 60c any single .85 .85
1206 Sheet of 6 5.25 5.25
a.-f. A177 60c any single .85 .85
1207 Sheet of 6 5.25 5.25
a.-f. A177 60c any single .85 .85

Mickey Mouse as a Hollywood Star — A178

Walt Disney characters: 20c, Reading script. 35c, Television interview. 45c, Named a star in tabloid headline. 60c, Signing autographs. $1, In dressing room, holding fans at bay. $2, Riding in limousine. $3, With Minnie in the limelight. $4, Accepting award. No. 1216, Giving interview during celebrity tennis tournament. No. 1217, Footprint impression in cement outside theater.

1989, Nov. 30 Litho. *Perf. 14x13½*

1208 A178 20c multicolored .30 .30
1209 A178 35c multicolored .45 .45
1210 A178 45c multicolored .55 .55
1211 A178 60c multicolored .70 .70
1212 A178 $1 multicolored 1.25 1.25
1213 A178 $2 multicolored 2.40 2.40
1214 A178 $3 multicolored 3.50 3.50
1215 A178 $4 multicolored 4.75 4.75
Nos. 1200 1215 (8) 13.90 13.90

Souvenir Sheets

1216 A178 $5 multicolored 6.00 6.00
1217 A178 $5 multicolored 6.00 6.00

Christmas — A179

Religious paintings by Botticelli: 20c, *Madonna in Glory with Seraphim.* 25c, *The Annunciation.* 35c, *Madonna of the Pomegranate.* 45c, *Madonna of the Rose Garden.* 60c, *Madonna of the Book.* $1, *Madonna and Child Under a Baldachin with Three Angels.* $4, *Madonna and Child with Angels.* No. 1225, *Bardi Madonna.* No. 1226, *The Mystic Nativity.* No. 1227, *The Adoration of the Magi.*

1989, Dec. 4 *Perf. 14*

1218 A179 20c multicolored .30 .30
1219 A179 25c multicolored .30 .30
1220 A179 35c multicolored .45 .45
1221 A179 45c multicolored .55 .55
1222 A179 60c multicolored .70 .70
1223 A179 $1 multicolored 1.10 1.10
1224 A179 $4 multicolored 4.50 4.50
1225 A179 $5 multicolored 5.50 5.50
Nos. 1218-1225 (8) 13.40 13.40

Souvenir Sheets

1226 A179 $5 multicolored 5.25 5.25
1227 A179 $5 multicolored 5.25 5.25

Nehru — A180

Girl Guides — A181

1989, Dec. 27 Litho. *Perf. 14*

1228 A180 60c shown 2.10 2.10

Souvenir Sheet

1229 A180 $5 Parliament House, New Delhi, horiz. 5.75 5.75

Jawaharlal Nehru (1889-1964), 1st prime minister of independent India.

1989, Dec. 29

Guide movement in Dominica, 60th anniv.: 60c, Lady Baden-Powell and Agatha Robinson, former Guide leader on Dominica. $5, Dorris Stockmann, chairman of the world committee of the World Assoc. of Girl Guides and Girl Scouts, and Judith Pestaina, chief commissioner of the Dominica Girl Guides Assoc., horiz.

1230 A181 60c multicolored 1.50 1.50

Souvenir Sheet

1231 A181 $5 multi, horiz. 5.75 5.75

Miniature Sheet

Marine Life A182

Designs: a, Cocoa damselfish. b, Stinging jellyfish. c, Dolphin. d, Queen angelfish. e, French angelfish. f, Blue striped grunt. g, Pork fish. h, Hammerhead shark. i, Spadefish. j, Great barracuda. k, Stingray. l, Black grunt. m, Two-spotted butterflyfish. n, Dog snapper. o, Southern puffer. p, Four-eyed butterflyfish. q, Lane snapper. r, Green moray.

1990 Litho. *Perf. 14*

1232 Sheet of 18 9.50 9.50
a.-r. A182 45c any single .50 .50

Penny Black, 150th Anniv. A183

Stamp World London '90: 50c, Post Office accelerator, 1830. 60c, $4, No. 1239, London skyline, St. Paul's Cathedral. 90c, Railway post car, 1838. $3, Center cycle, 1883. No. 1240, Mail truck, 1899.

1990, May 3 Litho. *Perf. 13½*

1233 A183 45c green & black .45 .45
1234 A183 50c blk & slate blue .55 .55
1235 A183 60c dk blue & blk .60 .60
1236 A183 90c black & green .90 .90
1237 A183 $3 blk & dk bl vio 3.00 3.00
1238 A183 $4 dk bl vio & blk 4.00 4.00
Nos. 1233-1238 (6) 9.50 9.50

Souvenir Sheet

1239 A183 $5 beige & black 4.50 4.50
1240 A183 $5 gray & red brn 4.50 4.50

A184

A185

Birds: 10c, Blue-headed hummingbird. 20c, Black-capped petrel. 45c, Red-necked parrot. 60c, Black swift. $1, Troupial. $2, Brown noddy. $4, Lesser Antillean pewee. $5. Little blue heron. No. 1249, House wren. No. 1250, Imperial parrot.

1990, July 16 Litho. *Perf. 14*

1241 A184 10c multicolored .40 .40
1242 A184 20c multicolored .55 .55
1243 A184 45c multicolored .80 .80
1244 A184 60c multicolored 1.00 1.00
1245 A184 $1 multicolored 1.60 1.60
1246 A184 $2 multicolored 2.50 2.50
1247 A184 $4 multicolored 4.00 4.00
1248 A184 $5 multicolored 4.50 4.50
Nos. 1241-1248 (8) 15.35 15.35

Souvenir Sheets

1249 A184 $6 multicolored 7.75 7.75
1250 A184 $6 multicolored 7.75 7.75

1990, July 19

Shells: 10c, Reticulated cowrie-helmet. 20c, West Indian chank. 35c, West Indian fighting conch. 60c, True tulip. $1, Sunrise tellin. $2, Crown cone. $3, Common dove shell. $4, Atlantic fig shell. No. 1259, Giant tun. No. 1260, King helmet.

1251 A185 10c multicolored .40 .40
1252 A185 20c multicolored .55 .55
1253 A185 35c multicolored .70 .70
1254 A185 60c multicolored 1.00 1.00
1255 A185 $1 multicolored 1.40 1.40
1256 A185 $2 multicolored 2.50 2.50
1257 A185 $3 multicolored 3.25 3.25
1258 A185 $4 multicolored 3.75 3.75
Nos. 1251-1258 (8) 13.55 13.55

Souvenir Sheets

1259 A185 $5 multicolored 5.00 5.00
1260 A185 $5 multicolored 5.00 5.00

A186

A187

Queen Mother, 90th Birthday: various photos.

1990, Sept. 10

1261 A186 20c multicolored .25 .25
1262 A186 45c multicolored .40 .40
1263 A186 60c multicolored .55 .55
1264 A186 $3 multicolored 2.75 2.75
Nos. 1261-1264 (4) 3.95 3.95

Souvenir Sheet

1265 A186 $5 multicolored 3.50 3.50

1990, Nov. 5 Litho. *Perf. 14*

1266 A187 45c Men's singles, tennis .85 .85
1267 A187 60c Men's foil fencing 1.25 1.25
1268 A187 $2 100m freestyle swimming 2.50 2.50
1269 A187 $3 Star class yachting 3.75 3.75
Nos. 1266-1269 (4) 8.35 8.35

Souvenir Sheet

1270 A187 $5 Coxless pairs, rowing 7.00 7.00

1992 Summer Olympics, Barcelona.

Christmas A188

Walt Disney characters on carousel animals: 10c, Mickey, frog. 15c, Huey, Dewey & Louie, white elephant. 25c, Donald, polar bear. 45c, Goofy, goat. $1, Donald, giraffe. $2, Daisy, stork. $4, Goofy, lion. $5, Daisy, horse. No. 1279, Mickey, swan chariot, horiz. No. 1280, Mickey, Minnie & Goofy, griffin chariot.

1990, Dec. 13 *Perf. 13½x14*

1271 A188 10c multicolored .20 .20
1272 A188 15c multicolored .20 .20
1273 A188 25c multicolored .30 .30
1274 A188 45c multicolored .55 .55
1275 A188 $1 multicolored 1.10 1.10
1276 A188 $2 multicolored 2.10 2.10
1277 A188 $4 multicolored 4.25 4.25
1278 A188 $5 multicolored 5.25 5.25
Nos. 1271-1278 (8) 13.95 13.95

Souvenir Sheets

Perf. 14x13½

1279 A188 $6 multicolored 7.00 7.00
1280 A188 $6 multicolored 7.00 7.00

World Cup Soccer Championships, Italy — A189

Players and coaches from participating countries.

1990, Dec. 28 Litho. *Perf. 14*

1281 A189 15c England .35 .35
1282 A189 45c Brazil .55 .55
1283 A189 60c West Germany .90 .90
1284 A189 $4 Austria 5.25 5.25
Nos. 1281-1284 (4) 7.05 7.05

Souvenir Sheets

1285 A189 $6 Ireland, vert. 5.25 5.25
1286 A189 $6 USSR, vert. 5.25 5.25

Cog Trains of Switzerland — A190

Designs: 10c, Glion-Roches de Naye, 1890. 35c, Electric cog rail car ascending Mt. Pilatus. 45c, Cog railway to Schynige Platte, view of Eiger, Monch and Jungfrau Mountains. 60c, Furka-Oberalp train on Bugnli Viaduct, vert. $1, 1910 Jungfraubahn Cog Railway, Jungfrau Mountain, 1910. $2, Testing Swiss rail cars built for Pike's Peak on Arth-Rigibahn, 1963. $4, Brienz-Rothorn Bahn, 1991. $5, Private 1870 Rigi-Scheideck Hotel post stamp, 1890 Arth-Rigi Railway Engine. No. 1295, Sherlock Holmes watching Brunigline train descending from Brunig Pass. No. 1296, Switzerland #738 and first passenger train to ascend Mt. Rigi, 1871.

1991, Mar. 26 Litho. *Perf. 14*

1287 A190 10c multicolored .25 .25
1288 A190 35c multicolored .35 .35
1289 A190 45c multicolored .40 .40
1290 A190 60c multicolored .55 .55
1291 A190 $1 multicolored .90 .90
1292 A190 $2 multicolored 1.75 1.75
1293 A190 $4 multicolored 3.50 3.50
1294 A190 $5 multicolored 4.50 4.50
Nos. 1287-1294 (8) 12.20 12.20

Souvenir Sheets

Perf. 13½

1295 A190 $6 multicolored 5.75 5.75
1296 A190 $6 multicolored 5.75 5.75

Nos. 1295-1296 each contain one 50x37mm stamp.

Voyages of Discovery A191

Explorer's ships: 10c, Gil Eannes, 1433-1434. 25c, Alfonso Gonclaves Baldaya, 1436. 45c, Bartolomeu Dias, 1487. 60c, Vasco da Gama, 1497-1499. $1, Vallarte the Dane. $2, Aloisio Cadamosto, 1456-1458. $4, Diogo Gomes, 1457. $5, Diogo Cao, 1482-1485.

1991, Apr. 8 Litho. *Perf. 14*

1297 A191 10c multicolored .25 .25
1298 A191 25c multicolored .40 .40
1299 A191 45c multicolored .55 .55
1300 A191 60c multicolored .70 .70
1301 A191 $1 multicolored .95 .95
1302 A191 $2 multicolored 1.75 1.75
1303 A191 $4 multicolored 3.50 3.50
1304 A191 $5 multicolored 4.00 4.00
Nos. 1297-1304 (8) 12.10 12.10

Souvenir Sheets

1305 A191 $6 Blue and yellow macaw 5.50 5.50
1306 A191 $6 Red and yellow macaw 5.50 5.50

Discovery of America, 500th anniv. (in 1992).

Japanese Costumes — A192

Walt Disney characters wearing Japanese costumes: 10c, Donald as soldier. 15c, Mickey as Kabuki actor. 25c, Mickey, Minnie in traditional wedding clothes. 45c, Daisy as Geisha girl, vert. $1, Mickey in sokutai dress of high government official, vert. $2, Goofy as mino farmer, vert. $4, Pete as shogun, vert. $5, Donald as warlord. No. 1315, Mickey, as Noh player, vert. No. 1316, Goofy as Kabubei-Jishi street performer, vert.

1991, May 22 Litho. *Perf. 14*

1307 A192 10c multicolored .20 .20
1308 A192 15c multicolored .20 .20
1309 A192 25c multicolored .30 .30
1310 A192 45c multicolored .60 .60
1311 A192 $1 multicolored 1.10 1.10
1312 A192 $2 multicolored 2.25 2.25
1313 A192 $4 multicolored 4.25 4.25
1314 A192 $5 multicolored 5.50 5.50
Nos. 1307-1314 (8) 14.40 14.40

Souvenir Sheets

1315 A192 $6 multicolored 7.50 7.50
1316 A192 $6 multicolored 7.50 7.50

Phila Nippon '91.

Mushrooms A193

1991, June 3 Litho. *Perf. 14*

1318 A193 10c Horn of plenty .20 .20
1319 A193 15c Shaggy mane .25 .25
1320 A193 45c Yellow morel .35 .35
1321 A193 60c Chanterelle .55 .55
1322 A193 $1 Blewit .90 .90
1323 A193 $2 Slippery jack 1.90 1.90
1324 A193 $4 Emetic russula 3.75 3.75
1325 A193 $5 Honey mushroom 4.50 4.50
Nos. 1318-1325 (8) 12.40 12.40

Souvenir Sheets

1326 A193 $6 Beefsteak polypore 5.25 5.25
1327 A193 $6 Voluminous-latex milky 5.25 5.25

Royal Family Birthday, Anniversary

Common Design Type

1991, June 17 Litho. *Perf. 14*

1328 CD347 10c multicolored .50 .50
1329 CD347 15c multicolored .40 .40
1330 CD347 40c multicolored .55 .55
1331 CD347 60c multicolored 1.10 1.10
1332 CD347 $1 multicolored 1.40 1.40
1333 CD347 $2 multicolored 3.75 3.75
1334 CD347 $4 multicolored 5.75 5.75
1335 CD347 $5 multicolored 9.75 9.75
Nos. 1328-1335 (8) 23.20 23.20

Souvenir Sheets

1336 CD347 $5 Elizabeth, Philip 4.50 4.50
1337 CD347 $5 Charles, Diana, sons 6.00 6.00

10c, 60c, $2, $4, No. 1336, Queen Elizabeth II, 65th birthday. Others, Charles and Diana, 10th wedding anniversary.

Vincent Van Gogh (1853-1890), Painter — A194

Paintings: 10c, Thatched Cottages. 25c, The House of Pere Eloi. 45c, The Midday Siesta. 60c, Portrait of a Young Peasant, vert. $1, Still Life: Vase with Irises Against a Yellow Background, vert. $2, Still Life Vase with Irises. $4, Blossoming Almond Tree. $5, Irises. No. 1346, A Meadow in the Mountains: Le Mas De Saint-Paul. No. 1347, Doctor Gachet's Garden in Auvers, vert.

1991, July 8 Litho. *Perf. 13½*

1338 A194 10c multicolored .25 .25
1339 A194 25c multicolored .25 .25
1340 A194 45c multicolored .35 .35
1341 A194 60c multicolored .55 .55
1342 A194 $1 multicolored .90 .90
1343 A194 $2 multicolored 1.90 1.90
1344 A194 $4 multicolored 3.75 3.75
1345 A194 $5 multicolored 4.50 4.50
Nos. 1338-1345 (8) 12.45 12.45

Size: 101x75mm

Imperf

1346 A194 $6 multicolored 6.00 6.00
1347 A194 $6 multicolored 6.00 6.00

Intl. Literacy Year — A195

Scenes from Walt Disney's "The Little Mermaid": 10c, Ariel with Flounder and Sebastian. 25c, King Triton. 45c, Sebastian drums in "Kiss De Girl" concert. 60c, Flotsam and Jetsam taunt Ariel. $1, Scuttle, Flounder and Ariel. $2, Ariel and Flounder discover a book. $4, Prince Eric, dog Max, manservant Grimsby, and crew. $5, Ursula the sea witch. No. 1356, Ariel transformed into human being. No. 1357, Ariel and Prince Eric dancing in town, vert.

1991, Aug. 6 *Perf. 14*

1348 A195 10c multicolored .20 .20
1349 A195 25c multicolored .30 .30
1350 A195 45c multicolored .50 .50
1351 A195 60c multicolored .70 .70
1352 A195 $1 multicolored 1.25 1.25
1353 A195 $2 multicolored 2.40 2.40
1354 A195 $4 multicolored 4.75 4.75
1355 A195 $5 multicolored 6.00 6.00
Nos. 1348-1355 (8) 16.10 16.10

Souvenir Sheets

1356 A195 $6 multicolored 6.25 6.25
1357 A195 $6 multicolored 6.25 6.25

World Landmarks — A196

Designs: 10c, Empire State Building, US, vert. 25c, Kremlin, USSR. 45c, Buckingham Palace, United Kingdom. 60c, Eiffel Tower, France, vert. $1, Taj Mahal, India. $2, Sydney Opera House, Australia. $4, Colosseum, Italy. $5, Pyramids, Egypt. No. 1366, Galileo demonstrating laws of physics from Tower of Pisa, Italy. No. 1367, Great Wall of China and Emperor Shi Huang Ti.

1991, Aug. 12 Litho. *Perf. 14*

1358 A196 10c multicolored .20 .20
1359 A196 25c multicolored .30 .30
1360 A196 45c multicolored .50 .50
1361 A196 60c multicolored .70 .70
1362 A196 $1 multicolored 1.25 1.25
1363 A196 $2 multicolored 2.40 2.40
1364 A196 $4 multicolored 4.75 4.75
1365 A196 $5 multicolored 6.00 6.00
Nos. 1358-1365 (8) 16.10 16.10

Souvenir Sheets

1366 A196 $6 multicolored 7.75 7.75
1367 A196 $6 multicolored 7.75 7.75

Japanese Attack on Pearl Harbor, 50th Anniv. A197

Designs: 10c, 6:00am, First wave of Japanese planes leave carrier Akagi. 15c, 6:40am, Destroyer Ward and PBY attack midget submarine. 45c, 7:00am, Second wave of Japanese planes leave carriers. 60c, 7:48am, Japanese Zeros attack on Kaneohe Air Station. $1, 8:30am, Destroyers Breeze, Medusa and Curtiss sink midget submarine. $2, 8:45am, Damaged battleship Nevada sorties. $4, 8:10am, Battleship Arizona explodes, killing 1,177 men. $5, 9:45am, Japanese attack ends. No. 1376, 8:00am, Japanese fighters and bombers attack Hickam Air Base. No. 1377, 7:55am, Pearl Harbor attack begins.

1991, Sept. 2

1368 A197 10c multicolored .20 .20
1369 A197 15c multicolored .25 .25
1370 A197 45c multicolored .35 .35
1371 A197 60c multicolored .55 .55
1372 A197 $1 multicolored .90 .90
1373 A197 $2 multicolored 1.90 1.90
1374 A197 $4 multicolored 3.75 3.75
1375 A197 $5 multicolored 4.50 4.50
Nos. 1368-1375 (8) 12.40 12.40

Souvenir Sheets

1376 A197 $6 multicolored 5.25 5.25
1377 A197 $6 multicolored 5.25 5.25

Butterflies — A198 A199

Perf. 13½x13, 13½x14 (2c, 10c, 15c, 25c, 45c, 90c, $1, $20)

1991-93

1378 A198 1c Little yellow .20 .20
1379 A198 2c Gulf fritillary .20 .20
1380 A198 5c Monarch .20 .20
1381 A198 10c Red rim .20 .20
1382 A198 15c Flambeau .20 .20
1383 A198 20c Large orange sulphur .20 .20
1384 A198 25c Caribbean buckeye .20 .20
1385 A198 35c Polydamas swallowtail .25 .25
1386 A198 45c Cassius blue .30 .30
1386A A198 55c Great southern white .40 .40
1387 A198 60c Godman's leaf .45 .45
1387A A198 65c Hanno blue .50 .50
1388 A198 90c Mimic .70 .70
1389 A198 $1 Long-tailed skipper .75 .75
1389A A198 $1.20 Orion .90 .90
1390 A198 $2 Cloudless sulphur 1.50 1.50
1391 A198 $5 Painted lady 3.75 3.75
1391A A198 $10 Southern daggertail 8.50 8.50
1391B A198 $20 White peacock 16.00 16.00
Nos. 1379-1391B (18) 35.20 35.20

Issued: 55c, 65c, $1.20, 1/11/93; others, 10/14/91.

1991, Nov. 1

1392 A199 45c shown 1.75 1.75

Souvenir Sheet

1393 A199 $5 blk & bl, horiz. 5.75 5.75

Charles de Gaulle, birth cent.

Creole Week — A200 Credit Union, 40th Anniv. — A201

45c, Man in 18th cent. costume. 60c, Accordion player. $1, Dancers. $5, Stick fight c. 1785.

1991, Nov. 1 *Perf. 14*

1394 A200 45c multicolored .60 .60
1395 A200 60c multicolored .90 .90
1396 A200 $1 multicolored 1.50 1.50
Nos. 1394-1396 (3) 3.00 3.00

Souvenir Sheet

1397 A200 $5 multicolored 7.00 7.00

1991, Nov. 1

1398 A201 10c black .45 .45
1399 A201 60c Emblem, founder, horiz. 1.00 1.00

Year of the Environment and Shelter — A202

15c, Keep the beaches clean. 60c, No. 1402, Amazona imperalis. No. 1403, Lagoon outlet.

1991, Nov. 18

1400 A202 15c multicolored .95 .95
1401 A202 60c multicolored 2.10 2.10

Souvenir Sheets

1402 A202 $5 multicolored 7.00 7.00
1403 A202 $5 multicolored 7.00 7.00

Christmas A203

Paintings by Jan van Eyck: 10c, The Virgin Enthroned with Child (detail). 20c, The Madonna at the Fountain. 35c, The Virgin in a Church. 45c, The Madonna with Canon van der Paele. 60c, The Madonna with Canon van der Paele (detail). $1, The Madonna in an Interior. $3, The Annunciation. $5, The Annunciation, diff. No. 1412, The Madonna with Chancellor Rolin. No. 1413, Virgin and Child with Saints and Donor.

1991, Dec. 2 ***Perf. 12***

1404 A203 10c multicolored .20 .20
1405 A203 20c multicolored .35 .35
1406 A203 35c multicolored .40 .40
1407 A203 45c multicolored .50 .50
1408 A203 60c multicolored .75 .75
1409 A203 $1 multicolored 1.25 1.25
1410 A203 $3 multicolored 3.75 3.75
1411 A203 $5 multicolored 6.00 6.00
Nos. 1404-1411 (8) 13.20 13.20

Souvenir Sheets

Perf. 14x14½

1412 A203 $6 multicolored 6.25 6.25
1413 A203 $6 multicolored 6.25 6.25

Queen Elizabeth II's Accession to the Throne, 40th Anniv.

Common Design Type

1992, Feb. 6 Litho. ***Perf. 14***

1414 CD348 10c multicolored .20 .20
1415 CD348 15c multicolored .20 .20
1416 CD348 $1 multicolored .65 .65
1417 CD348 $5 multicolored 3.25 3.25
Nos. 1414-1417 (4) 4.30 4.30

Souvenir Sheets

1418 CD348 $6 River scene 3.75 3.75
1419 CD348 $6 Seaside village 3.75 3.75

Botanical Gardens, Cent. — A204

Designs: 10c, Cricket match. 15c, Scenic entrance. 45c, Traveller's tree. 60c, Bamboo house. $1, Old pavilion. $2, Ficus benjamina. $4, Cricket ground. $5, Thirty-five steps. No. 1428, Fountain. No. 1429, Cricket masters.

1992, Mar. 30 Litho. ***Perf. 14***

1420 A204 10c multicolored .20 .20
1421 A204 15c multicolored .20 .20
1422 A204 45c multicolored .35 .35
1423 A204 60c multicolored .50 .50
1424 A204 $1 multicolored .85 .85
1425 A204 $2 multicolored 1.75 1.75
1426 A204 $4 multicolored 3.50 3.50
1427 A204 $5 multicolored 4.25 4.25
Nos. 1420-1427 (8) 11.60 11.60

Souvenir Sheets

1428 A204 $6 multicolored 4.50 4.50
1429 A204 $6 multicolored 4.50 4.50

Spanish Art — A205

Paintings or details from paintings by Velazquez: 10c, Pope Innocent X. 15c, 45c The Forge of Vulcan (different details). 60c, Queen Mariana of Austria. $1, Pablo de Valladolid. $2, Sebastian de Morra. $3, Felipe IV (detail). $4, Felipe IV. No. 1438, Surrender of Breda. No. 1439, The Drunkards.

1992, May 4 ***Perf. 13***

1430 A205 10c multicolored .20 .20
1431 A205 15c multicolored .20 .20
1432 A205 45c multicolored .40 .40
1433 A205 60c multicolored .45 .45
1434 A205 $1 multicolored .75 .75
1435 A205 $2 multicolored 1.50 1.50
1436 A205 $3 multicolored 2.25 2.25
1437 A205 $4 multicolored 3.25 3.25

Size: 120x95mm

Imperf

1438 A205 $6 multicolored 5.00 5.00
1439 A205 $6 multicolored 5.00 5.00
Nos. 1430-1439 (10) 19.00 19.00

Granada '92.

Easter — A206

Paintings: 10c, The Supper at Emmaus, studio of Gerrit Van Honthorst. 15c, Christ before Caiaphas, by Van Honthorst, vert. 45c, The Taking of Christ, by Valentin de Boulogne. 60c, Pilate Washing his Hands, by Mattia Preti, vert. $1, The Last Supper (detail), by Master of the Reredos of The Chapel of the Church of S. Francisco D'Evora. $2, The Three Marys at the Tomb (detail), by Adolphe William Bouguereau, vert. $3, Denial of St. Peter, by Hendrik Terbrugghen. $5, Doubting Thomas, by Bernardo Strozzi, vert. No. 1448, The Crucifixion (detail), by Mathias Grunewald, vert. No. 1449, The Resurrection (detail), by Caravaggio, vert.

1992 ***Perf. 14***

1440 A206 10c multicolored .20 .20
1441 A206 15c multicolored .20 .20
1442 A206 45c multicolored .35 .35
1443 A206 60c multicolored .50 .50
1444 A206 $1 multicolored .85 .85
1445 A206 $2 multicolored 1.75 1.75
1446 A206 $3 multicolored 2.50 2.50
1447 A206 $5 multicolored 4.25 4.25
Nos. 1440-1447 (8) 10.60 10.60

Souvenir Sheets

1448 A206 $6 multicolored 5.25 5.25
1449 A206 $6 multicolored 5.25 5.25

Columbus and New World Flora and Fauna — A207

1992, May 18

1450 A207 10c Hercules beetle .20 .20
1451 A207 25c Crapaud frog .25 .25
1452 A207 75c Parrot .70 .70
1453 A207 $2 Anole 1.90 1.90
1454 A207 $4 Royal gramma 3.75 3.75
1455 A207 $5 Hibiscus 4.75 4.75
Nos. 1450-1455 (6) 11.55 11.55

Souvenir Sheets

1456 A207 $6 Giant katydid 5.00 5.00
1457 A207 $6 Columbus' fleet 5.00 5.00

Nos. 1456-1457 are horiz.

Hummingbirds — A208

10c, Purple throated carib. 15c, Rufous breasted hermit. 45c, Puerto Rican emerald. 60c, Antillean mango. $1, Green throated carib. $2, Blue headed. $4, Eastern streamertail. $5, Antillean crested. #1466, Green mango. #1467, Vervain hummingbird.

1992, May 28

1458 A208 10c multicolored .20 .20
1459 A208 15c multicolored .20 .20
1460 A208 45c multicolored .35 .35
1461 A208 60c multicolored .55 .55
1462 A208 $1 multicolored .90 .90
1463 A208 $2 multicolored 1.90 1.90
1464 A208 $4 multicolored 3.75 3.75
1465 A208 $5 multicolored 4.75 4.75
Nos. 1458-1465 (8) 12.60 12.60

Souvenir Sheets

1466 A208 $6 multicolored 7.00 7.00
1467 A208 $6 multicolored 7.00 7.00

Genoa '92.

Dinosaurs A209

1992, June 23 Litho. ***Perf. 14***

1468 A209 10c Camptosaurus .20 .20
1469 A209 15c Edmontosaurus .20 .20
1470 A209 25c Corythosaurus .25 .25
1471 A209 60c Stegosaurus .50 .50
1472 A209 $1 Torosaurus .85 .85
1473 A209 $3 Euoplocephalus 2.50 2.50
1474 A209 $4 Tyrannosaurus 3.25 3.25
1475 A209 $5 Parasaurolophus 4.25 4.25
Nos. 1468-1475 (8) 12.00 12.00

Souvenir Sheets

1476 A209 $6 like #1472 5.50 5.50
1477 A209 $6 like #1470 5.50 5.50

Marine Life A210

No. 1478: a, Copper sweeper (b). b, Sea wasp (c). c, Nassau grouper. d, Glasseye snapper, margate. e, Green moray (f). f, Reef squid. g, Octopus. h, Porkfish (g, i). i, Reef squirrelfish (h). j, Coral crab, flower coral. k, Red coral shrimp, sea star, pillar coral (l, n). l, Cubbyu, brain coral (o). m, Basket starfish, thick finger coral. n, Belted cardinal fish, boulder coral (k, m). o, Fire worm, crenelated fire coral.

No. 1479: a, Trumpetfish, blue chromis. b, Queen triggerfish. c, Hawksbill turtle. d, Sergeant major, rock beauty. e, Sharksucker. f, Lemon shark. g, Spotted trunkfish, bluehead. h, Blue tang, yellowtail damselfish. i, Queen angelfish, banded butterflyfish. j, Spotted seahorse, flower coral. k, Stoplight parrotfish, pillar coral. l, Smallmouth grunt, brain coral. m, Flamingo tongue, thick finger coral. n, Arrow crab, boulder coral. o, Sharknose goby, crenelated fire coral.

No. 1480, Harlequin bass. No. 1481, Flamefish.

1992, July 20 Litho. ***Perf. 14***

1478 A210 65c Sheet of 15, #a.-o. 9.00 9.00
1479 A210 65c Sheet of 15, #a.-o. 9.00 9.00

Souvenir Sheets

1480 A210 $6 multicolored 7.25 7.25
1481 A210 $6 multicolored 7.25 7.25

A211

A212

1992, Aug. 10 Litho. ***Perf. 14***

1482 A211 10c Archery .20 .20
1483 A211 15c Two-man canoeing .20 .20
1484 A211 25c 110-meter hurdles .25 .25
1485 A211 60c Men's high jump .50 .50
1486 A211 $1 Greco-Roman wrestling .80 .80
1487 A211 $2 Men's rings 1.60 1.60
1488 A211 $4 Men's parallel bars 3.50 3.50
1489 A211 $5 Equestrian 4.25 4.25
Nos. 1482-1489 (8) 11.30 11.30

Souvenir Sheets

1490 A211 $6 Field hockey 5.75 5.75
1491 A211 $6 Women's platform diving 5.75 5.75

1992 Summer Olympics, Barcelona.

1992 Litho. ***Perf. 14½***

1492 A212 $1 Coming ashore 1.00 1.00
1493 A212 $2 Natives, ships 2.00 2.00

Discovery of America, 500th anniv. Organization of East Caribbean States.

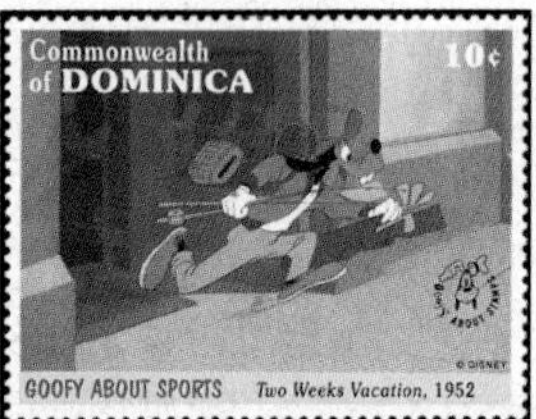

Walt Disney's Goofy, 60th Anniv. — A213

Scenes from Disney cartoon films: 10c, Two Weeks Vacation, 1952. 15c, Aquamania, 1961. 25c, Goofy Gymnastics, 1949. 45c, How to Ride a Horse, 1941. $1, Foul Hunting, 1947. $2, For Whom the Bulls Toil, 1953. $4, Tennis Racquet, 1949. $5, Double Dribble, 1946. No. 1502, Aquamania, 1961, vert. No. 1503, The Goofy Sports Story, 1956, vert.

1992, Nov. 11 Litho. ***Perf. 14x13½***

1494 A213 10c multicolored .20 .20
1495 A213 15c multicolored .20 .20
1496 A213 25c multicolored .35 .35
1497 A213 45c multicolored .65 .65
1498 A213 $1 multicolored 1.25 1.25
1499 A213 $2 multicolored 2.50 2.50
1500 A213 $4 multicolored 5.00 5.00
1501 A213 $5 multicolored 6.00 6.00
Nos. 1494-1501 (8) 16.15 16.15

Souvenir Sheets

Perf. 13½x14

1502 A213 $6 multicolored 8.00 8.00
1503 A213 $6 multicolored 8.00 8.00

Model Trains A214

15c, Brass Reno 4-4-0, HO scale, c. 1963. 25c, Union Pacific Golden Classic, G gauge, 1992. 55c, LMS 3rd class brake coach, OO scale, 1970s. 65c, Brass Wabash 2-6-0, HO scale, c. 1958. 75c, Pennsylvania RR T-1 duplex, O gauge, 1991. $1, Streamline engine 2-6-0, O gauge, post World War II. $3, Japanese Natl. Railways class C62, HO scale, c. 1960. $5, Tinplate friction-drive floor trains, 1960s. No. 1512, 1st "toy" train in Japan, 1854. No. 1513, Stephenson's Rocket, 1:26 scale, c. 1972, vert.

1992, Nov. 11 *Perf. 14*

1504 A214 15c multicolored .20 .20
1505 A214 25c multicolored .25 .25
1506 A214 55c multicolored .45 .45
1507 A214 65c multicolored .60 .60
1508 A214 75c multicolored .70 .70
1509 A214 $1 multicolored .90 .90
1510 A214 $3 multicolored 2.75 2.75
1511 A214 $5 multicolored 4.50 4.50
Nos. 1504-1511 (8) 10.35 10.35

Souvenir Sheets

Perf. 13

1512 A214 $6 multicolored 5.00 5.00
1513 A214 $6 multicolored 5.00 5.00

No. 1512 contains one 52x40mm stamp, No. 1513 one 39x51mm stamp.

Hummel Figurines — A215

Angel: 20c, Playing violin. 25c, Playing horn. 55c, Playing mandolin. 65c, Seated, playing trumpet. 90c, On cloud with lantern. $1, Holding candle. $1.20, Flying. $6, On cloud with candle.

1992, Nov. 2 *Perf. 14*

1514 A215 20c multicolored .20 .20
1515 A215 25c multicolored .25 .25
1516 A215 55c multicolored .45 .45
1517 A215 65c multicolored .55 .55
a. Sheet of 4, #1514-1517 2.25 2.25
1518 A215 90c multicolored .70 .70
1519 A215 $1 multicolored .85 .85
1520 A215 $1.20 multicolored 1.00 1.00
1521 A215 $6 multicolored 5.00 5.00
a. Sheet of 4, #1518-1521 8.00 8.00
Nos. 1514-1521 (8) 9.00 9.00

Anniversaries and Events
A216 A217

Designs: 25c, Graf Zeppelin, 1929. No. 1523, Elderly man, plant. No. 1524, Elderly man on bicycle. No. 1525, Elderly man helping boy bait hook. No. 1526, Konrad Adenauer. No. 1527, Space shuttle. No. 1528, Wolfgang Amadeus Mozart. No. 1529, Snowy egret. No. 1530, Sir Thomas Lipton, Shamrock V, 1930. $2, Men pulling fishing net toward beach. $3, Helen Keller. No. 1533, Earth Resources Satellite. No. 1534, Map of Germany, 1949. No. 1535, Eland. $5, Count Ferdinand von Zeppelin. No. 1537, Cologne Cathedral, Germany. No. 1538, Scene from the Magic Flute. No. 1539, MIR Space Station. No. 1540, Engine of Graf Zeppelin. No. 1541, Rhinoceros hornbill.

1992 **Litho.** *Perf. 14*

1522 A216 25c multicolored .20 .20
1523 A216 45c multicolored .35 .35
1524 A216 45c multicolored .35 .35
1525 A216 45c multicolored .35 .35
1526 A216 90c multicolored .65 .65
1527 A216 90c multicolored .65 .65
1528 A217 $1.20 multicolored .90 .90
1529 A216 $1.20 multicolored .90 .90
1530 A216 $1.20 multicolored .90 .90
1531 A216 $2 multicolored 1.50 1.50
1532 A216 $3 multicolored 2.25 2.25
1533 A216 $4 multicolored 3.00 3.00
1534 A216 $4 multicolored 3.00 3.00
1535 A216 $4 multicolored 3.00 3.00
1536 A216 $5 multicolored 3.75 3.75
Nos. 1522-1536 (15) 21.75 21.75

Souvenir Sheets

1537 A216 $6 multicolored 4.50 4.50
1538 A217 $6 multicolored 4.50 4.50
1539 A216 $6 multicolored 4.50 4.50
1540 A216 $6 multicolored 4.50 4.50
1541 A216 $6 multicolored 4.50 4.50

Konrad Adenauer, 25th anniv. of death (#1526, 1534, 1537). Intl. Space Year (#1527, 1533, 1539). Mozart, 200th anniv. of death (in 1991) (#1528, 1538). Count Zeppelin, 75th anniv. of death (#1522, 1536, 1540). Intl. Day of the Elderly (#1523-1525). UN Earth Summit, Rio (#1529, 1535, 1541). America's Cup yacht race (#1530). WHO Intl. Conference on Nutrition, Rome (#1531). Lions Intl., 75th anniv. (#1532).

Issued: #1528, 1539, Oct.; #1523-1527, 1533-1534, 1537-1538, Nov.; #1522, 1529, 1535-1536, 1540-1541, Dec.

Miniature Sheet

Louvre Museum, Bicent. — A218

Details or entire paintings by Titian: a-b, Madonna and Child with St. Catherine and a Rabbit (diff. details). c, A Woman at Her Toilet. d-e, The Supper at Emmaus (diff. details). f, The Pastoral Concert. g-h, An Allegory, Perhaps of Marriage (diff. details).

Painting by Hieronymus Bosch: $6, The Ship of Fools.

1993, Mar. 24 **Litho.** *Perf. 12*

1542 A218 $1 Sheet of 8, #a.-h. + label 8.00 8.00

Souvenir Sheet

Perf. 14½

1543 A218 $6 multicolored 6.00 6.00

No. 1543 contains one 55x88mm stamp.

Elvis Presley, 15th Anniv. of Death (in 1992) A219

a, Portrait. b, With guitar. c, Holding microphone.

1993, Feb. *Perf. 14*

1544 A219 $1 Strip of 3, #a.-c. 3.25 3.25

Miniature Sheet

Birds of Dominica — A220

a, Plumbeous warbler. b, Black swift. c, Blue-hooded euphonia. d, Rufous-throated solitaire. e, Ringed kingfisher. f, Blue-headed hummingbird. g, Bananaquit. h, Trembler. i, Forest thrush. j, Purple-throated carib. k, Ruddy quail dove. l, Least bittern.

No. 1546, Imperial parrot. No. 1547, Red-necked parrot (Amazona arausiaca).

1993, Apr. 30

1545 A220 90c Sheet of 12, #a.-l. 14.00 14.00

Souvenir Sheet

1546 A220 $6 multicolored 5.75 5.75
1547 A220 $6 multicolored 5.75 5.75

Turtles A221

25c, Leatherback laying eggs. 55c, Hawksbill. 65c, Atlantic Ridley. 90c, Green turtle laying eggs. $1, Green turtle at sea. $2, Hawksbill, diff. $4, Loggerhead. $5, Leatherback at sea. #1556, Green turtle hatchling. #1557, Head of hawksbill.

1993, May 26 **Litho.** *Perf. 14*

1548 A221 25c multicolored .25 .25
1549 A221 55c multicolored .50 .50
1550 A221 65c multicolored .65 .65
1551 A221 90c multicolored .85 .85
1552 A221 $1 multicolored .95 .95
1553 A221 $2 multicolored 1.90 1.90
1554 A221 $4 multicolored 3.75 3.75
1555 A221 $5 multicolored 4.75 4.75
Nos. 1548-1555 (8) 13.60 13.60

Souvenir Sheets

1556 A221 $6 multicolored 6.25 6.25
1557 A221 $6 multicolored 6.25 6.25

For overprints see Nos. 2103-2107.

Automobiles — A222

Designs: 90c, 1928 Model A Ford. $1.20, Mercedes-Benz winning Swiss Grand Prix, 1936. $4, Mercedes-Benz winning German Grand Prix, 1935. $5, 1915 Model T Ford.

#1562: a, 1993 Mercedes-Benz coupe/roadster. b, 1893 Benz Viktoria.

No. 1563, Ford GT-40.

1993, May **Litho.** *Perf. 14*

1558 A222 90c multicolored .80 .80
1559 A222 $1.20 multicolored 1.00 1.00
1560 A222 $4 multicolored 3.50 3.50
1561 A222 $5 multicolored 4.25 4.25
Nos. 1558-1561 (4) 9.55 9.55

Souvenir Sheets

1562 A222 $3 Sheet of 2, #a.-b. 5.00 5.00
1563 A222 $6 multicolored 5.00 5.00

No. 1563 contains one 57x42mm stamp.

First Ford gasoline engine, cent. (#1558, 1561, 1563). Benz's first four-wheeled vehicle, cent. (#1559-1560, 1562).

Dominica Grammar School, Cent. A223

Designs: 25c, School crest. 30c, V. A. A. Archer, first West Indian headmaster. 65c, Hubert A. Charles, first Dominican headmaster. 90c, Present school building.

1993, May

1564 A223 25c multicolored .25 .25
1565 A223 30c multicolored .30 .30
1566 A223 65c multicolored .65 .65
1567 A223 90c multicolored .85 .85
Nos. 1564-1567 (4) 2.05 2.05

Aviation Anniversaries — A224

Designs: 25c, New York ticker tape parade, 1928. 55c, BAC Lightning F2. 65c, Graf Zeppelin over Sphinx, pyramids, 1929. $1, Boeing 314 flying boat. $2, Astronaut stepping onto moon. $4, Viktoria Louise over Kiel harbor, 1912. $5, Supermarine Spitfire, vert. No. 1575, Royal Air Force Crest, vert. No. 1576, Hugo Eckener in airship cockpit, vert. No. 1577, Jean-Pierre Blanchard's hot air balloon, 1793, vert.

1993, May 28 **Litho.** *Perf. 14*

1568 A224 25c multicolored .40 .40
1569 A224 55c multicolored .45 .45
1570 A224 65c multicolored .95 .95
1571 A224 $1 multicolored .70 .70
1572 A224 $2 multicolored 1.60 1.60
1573 A224 $4 multicolored 5.75 5.75
1574 A224 $5 multicolored 4.25 4.25
Nos. 1568-1574 (7) 14.10 14.10

Souvenir Sheets

1575 A224 $6 multicolored 7.00 7.00
1576 A224 $6 multicolored 4.75 4.75
1577 A224 $6 multicolored 4.75 4.75

Zeppelin Capt. Hugo Eckener, 125th anniv. of birth (#1568, 1570, 1573, 1576). Royal Air Force, 75th anniv. (#1569, 1574-1575).

Nos. 1575-1576 each contain one 42x57mm stamp.

Miniature Sheet

Coronation of Queen Elizabeth II, 40th Anniv. A225

Designs: No. 1578a, 20c, Official coronation photograph. b, 25c, Ceremony. c, 65c, Gold State Coach. d, $5, Queen Elizabeth II, Queen Mother.

$6, Portrait, by Norman Hutchinson, 1969.

1993, June 2 **Litho.** *Perf. 13½x14*

1578 A225 Sheet, 2 each #a.-d. 14.00 14.00

Souvenir Sheet

Perf. 14

1579 A225 $6 multicolored 7.00 7.00

No. 1579 contains one 28x42mm stamp.

For overprints see Nos. 1688-1689.

Wedding of Japan's Crown Prince Naruhito and Masako Owada
A226

Cameo photos of couple and: 90c, Crown Prince holding flowers. $5, Princess wearing full-length coat.
$6, Princess riding in limousine.

1993, June 14 Litho. *Perf. 14*

1580 A226 90c multicolored .95 .95
1581 A226 $5 multicolored 5.00 5.00

Souvenir Sheet

1582 A226 $6 multicolored 6.25 6.25

Inauguration of Pres. William J. Clinton — A227

$5, Bill, Hillary Clinton. $6, Bill Clinton, vert.

1993, July 30 Litho. *Perf. 14*

1583 A227 $5 multicolored 4.50 4.50

Souvenir Sheet

1584 A227 $6 multicolored 6.25 6.25

Willy Brandt (1913-92), German Chancellor — A228

Brandt and: 65c, Pres. Eisenhower, 1959. $5, N.K. Winston, 1964. $6, Portrait.

1993, July 30

1585 A228 65c black & brown .70 .70
1586 A228 $5 black & brown 5.25 5.25

Souvenir Sheet

1587 A228 $6 black & brown 6.25 6.25

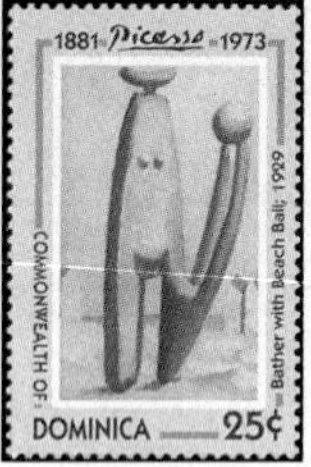

Picasso (1881-1973)
A229

Polska '93
A230

Paintings: 25c, Bather with Beach Ball, 1929. 90c, Portrait of Leo Stein, 1906. $5, Portrait of Wilhelm Unde, 1910. $6, Man with a Pipe, 1915.

1993, July 30

1588 A229 25c multicolored .25 .25
1589 A229 90c multicolored .95 .95
1590 A229 $5 multicolored 5.00 5.00
Nos. 1588-1590 (3) 6.20 6.20

Souvenir Sheet

1591 A229 $6 multicolored 6.25 6.25

1993, July 30

Paintings: 90c, Self-portrait, by Marian Szczyrbula, 1921. $3, Portrait of Bruno Jasienski, by Tytus Czyzewski, 1921. $6, Miser, by Tadeusz Makowski, 1973.

1592 A230 90c multicolored 1.10 1.10
1593 A230 $3 multicolored 3.50 3.50

Souvenir Sheet

1594 A230 $6 multicolored 6.25 6.25

A231

A232

90c, Monika Holzner, speedskating, 1984. $4, US hockey players, Ray Leblanc, Tim Sweeney, 1992. $6, Men's ski jump.

1993, July 30

1595 A231 90c multicolored 1.10 1.10
1596 A231 $4 multicolored 4.75 4.75

Souvenir Sheet

1597 A231 $6 multicolored 6.00 6.00

1994 Winter Olympics, Lillehammer, Norway.

1993, July 30

Designs: $1.20, Astronomer using quadrant. $3, Observatory. $5, Copernicus.

1598 A232 $1.20 multicolored 1.75 1.75
1599 A232 $3 multicolored 4.25 4.25

Souvenir Sheet

1600 A232 $5 multicolored 6.50 6.50

Copernicus (1473-1543).

Opening of New General Post Office
A233

New General Post Office and: 25c, Prince Philip. 90c, Queen Elizabeth II.

1993, July 30

1601 A233 25c multicolored .25 .25
1602 A233 90c multicolored 1.00 1.00

1994 World Cup Soccer Championships, US — A234

1993, Sept. 8 Litho. *Perf. 14*

1603 A234 25c Maradona, Buchwald .30 .30
1604 A234 55c Gullit .55 .55
1605 A234 65c Chavarria, Bliss .70 .70
1606 A234 90c Maradona .95 .95
1607 A234 90c Alvares .95 .95
1608 A234 $1 Altobelli, Yong-hwang 1.00 1.00
1609 A234 $2 Referee, Stopyra 2.10 2.10
1610 A234 $5 Renquin, Yaremtchuk 5.25 5.25
Nos. 1603-1610 (8) 11.80 11.80

Souvenir Sheets

1611 A234 $6 Brehme 5.25 5.25
1612 A234 $6 Fabbri 5.25 5.25

Taipei '93 — A235

Chinese kites: No. 1617a, Chang E Rising up to the Moon. b, Red Phoenix and Rising Sun. c, Heavenly Judge. d, Monkey King. e, Goddess of the Luo River. f, Heavenly Maiden Scatters Flowers.

1993, Oct. 4 Litho. *Perf. 13½x14*

1613 A235 25c Tiger Balm Gardens .25 .25
1614 A235 65c Building, Kenting Park .60 .60
1615 A235 90c Tzu-en Tower .85 .85
1616 A235 $5 Villa, Lan Tao Island 4.50 4.50
Nos. 1613-1616 (4) 6.20 6.20

Miniature Sheet

1617 A235 $1.65 Sheet of 6, #a.-f. 10.50 10.50

Souvenir Sheet

1618 A235 $6 Jade Girl, Liao Dynasty 5.25 5.25

With Bangkok '93 Emblem

Puppets: No. 1623a, Thai, Rama and Sita. b, Burmese, Tha Khi Lek. c, Burmese, diff. d, Thai, Demons, Wat Phra Kaew. e, Thai, Hun Lek performing Khun Chang, Khun Phaen. f, Thai, Hun Lek performing Ramakien.

1993

1619 A235 25c Tugu Monument, Java .25 .25
1620 A235 55c Candi Cangkuang, West Java .60 .60
1621 A235 90c Pura Taman Ayun, Mengwi .85 .85
1622 A235 $5 Stone mosaics, Ceto 4.50 4.50
Nos. 1619-1622 (4) 6.20 6.20

Miniature Sheet

1623 A235 $1.65 Sheet of 6, #a.-f. 10.50 10.50

Souvenir Sheet

1624 A235 $6 Stone carving, Thailand 5.25 5.25

With Indopex '93 Emblem

Designs: 25c, Ornate Chedi, Wat Phra Boromathat Chaiya. 55c, Preserved temple ruins, Sukhothai Historical Park. 90c, Prasat Hin Phimai, Thailand. $5, Main sanctuary, Prasat Phanom Rung, Thailand.
Indonesian puppets — #1629: a, Arjuna & Prabu Gilling Wesi. b, Loro Blonyo. c, Yogyanese puppets, Menak cycle. d, Wayang gedog, Ng Setro. e, Wayang golek, Kencana Wungu. f, Wayang gedog, Raden Damar Wulan.
$6, Sculpture of Majapahit noble, Pura Sada, Kapel.

1993, Oct. 4 Litho. *Perf. 13½x14*

1625 A235 25c multicolored .25 .25
1626 A235 55c multicolored .60 .60
1627 A235 90c multicolored .85 .85
1628 A235 $5 multicolored 4.50 4.50
Nos. 1625-1628 (4) 6.20 6.20

Miniature Sheet

1629 A235 $1.65 Sheet of 6, #a.-f. 10.50 10.50

Souvenir Sheet

1630 A235 $6 multicolored 5.25 5.25

Miniature Sheet

Willie the Operatic Whale — A236

Nos. 1631-1633, Characters and scenes from Disney's animated film Willie the Operatic Whale.

1993, Nov. 1 Litho. *Perf. 14x13½*

1631 A236 $1 Sheet of 9, #a.-i. 12.50 12.50

Souvenir Sheets

1632 A236 $6 multicolored 5.00 5.00

Perf. 13½x14

1633 A236 $6 multi, vert. 5.00 5.00

Christmas
A237

25c, 55c, 65c, 90c (#1637), Details or entire woodcut, The Adoration of the Magi, by Durer.
90c (#1638), $1, $3, $5, Details or entire painting, The Foligni Madonna, by Raphael.
Souvenir Sheets: #1642, $6, The Adoration of the Magi, by Durer. #1643, $6, The Foligni Madonna, by Raphael.

1993, Nov. 8 Litho. *Perf. 13*

1634-1643 A237 Set of 10 21.00 21.00

A238

Hong Kong '94 — A239

Stamps, scene from Peak Tram: No. 1644, Hong Kong #527, city buildings, trees. No. 1645, Trees, tram, #1292.
Chinese jade: No. 1646a, Horse. b, Cup with handle. c, Vase with birthday peaches. d, Vase. e, Fu dog and puppy. f, Drinking vessel.

1994, Feb. 18 Litho. *Perf. 14*

1644 A238 65c multicolored .60 .60
1645 A238 65c multicolored .60 .60
a. Pair, #1644-1645 1.25 1.25

Miniature Sheet

1646 A239 65c Sheet of 6, #a.-f. 3.50 3.50

Nos. 1644-1645 issued in sheets of 5 pairs. No. 1645a is a continuous design.
New Year 1994 (Year of the Dog) (#1646e).

Insects, Butterflies, & Birds — A240

Various Hercules beetles: 20c, 25c, 65c, Male. 90c, Female.
$1, Imperial parrot. $2, Southern dagger tail. $3, The mimic. $5, Purple-throated carib.
No. 1655, Snout butterfly. No. 1656, Blue-headed hummingbird.

1994, Mar. 15 **Litho.** ***Perf. 14***
1647-1654 A240 Set of 8 11.00 11.00
1650a Min. sheet, 3 each #1647-1650 5.50 5.50

Souvenir Sheets

1655-1656 A240 $6 each 5.50 5.50

World Wildlife Fund (#1647-1650).

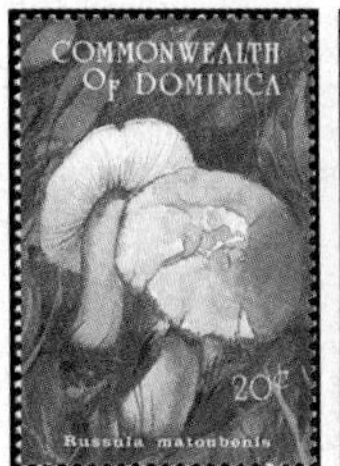

Mushrooms A241

Orchids A242

Designs: 20c, Russula matoubenis. 25c, Leptonia caeruleocapita. 65c, Inocybe littoralis. 90c, Russula hygrophytica. $1, Pyrrhoglossum lilaceipes. $2, Hygrocybe konradii. $3, Inopilus magnificus. $5, Boletellus cubensis.
No. 1665, Gerronema citrinum. No. 1666, Lentinus strigosus.

1994, Apr. 18

1657	A241	20c multicolored	.20	.20
1658	A241	25c multicolored	.20	.20
1659	A241	65c multicolored	.50	.50
1660	A241	90c multicolored	.75	.75
1661	A241	$1 multicolored	.85	.85
1662	A241	$2 multicolored	1.75	1.75
1663	A241	$3 multicolored	2.50	2.50
1664	A241	$5 multicolored	4.00	4.00
		Nos. 1657-1664 (8)	10.75	10.75

Souvenir Sheets

1665	A241	$6 multicolored	5.25	5.25
1666	A241	$6 multicolored	5.25	5.25

1994, May 3

Designs: 20c, Laeliocattleya. 25c, Sophrolaeliocattleya. 65c, Odontocidium. 90c, Laeliocattleya, diff. $1, Cattleya. $2, Odontocidium, diff. $3, Epiphronitis. $4, Oncidium.
#1675, Schombocattleya. #1676, Cattleya, diff.

1667-1674 A242 Set of 8 10.50 10.50

Souvenir Sheets

1675-1676 A242 $6 each 5.50 5.50

New Year 1994 (Year of the Dog) — A243

Designs: 20c, Dachshund. 25c, Beagle. 55c, Greyhound. 90c, Jack Russell terrier. $1, Pekingese. $2, White fox terrier. $4, English toy spaniel. $5, Irish setter.
#1686, Welsh corgi. #1687, Labrador retriever.

1994, May 17

1678	A243	20c multicolored	.20	.20
1679	A243	25c multicolored	.20	.20
1680	A243	55c multicolored	.40	.40
1681	A243	90c multicolored	.65	.65
1682	A243	$1 multicolored	.75	.75
1683	A243	$2 multicolored	1.50	1.50
1684	A243	$4 multicolored	3.00	3.00
1685	A243	$5 multicolored	3.75	3.75
		Nos. 1678-1685 (8)	10.45	10.45

Souvenir Sheets

1686	A243	$6 multicolored	5.25	5.25
1687	A243	$6 multicolored	5.25	5.25

Nos. 1578-1579 Ovptd. "ROYAL VISIT / FEBRUARY 19, 1994" in Black or Silver

1994, June 27 **Litho.** ***Perf. 13½x14***
1688 A225 Sheet, 2 ea #a-d 15.00 15.00

Souvenir Sheet

1689 A225 $6 multicolored (S) 7.50 7.50

Overprint on No. 1689 appears in sheet margin.

Miniature Sheet

1994 World Cup Soccer Championships, US — A244

No. 1690: a, Dos Armstrong, US. b, Dennis Bergkamp, Netherlands. c, Roberto Baggio, Italy. d, Rai, Brazil. e, Cafu, Brazil. f, Marco Van Baston, Netherlands.
No. 1691, Roberto Mancini, Italy. No. 1692, Stanford Stadium, Palo Alto.

1994, July 5 ***Perf. 14***
1690 A244 $1 Sheet of 6, #a.-f. 6.00 6.00

Souvenir Sheets

1691-1692 A244 $6 each 5.50 5.50

Butterflies A245

1994, May 3 **Litho.** ***Perf. 14***

1693	A245	20c Florida white	.20	.20
1694	A245	25c Red rim	.20	.20
1695	A245	55c Barred sulphur	.45	.45
1696	A245	65c Mimic	.55	.55
1697	A245	$1 Large orange sulphur	.85	.85
1698	A245	$2 Southern dagger tail	1.75	1.75
1698A	A245	$3 Dominican snout butterfly	2.50	2.50
1699	A245	$5 Caribbean buckeye	4.25	4.25
		Nos. 1693-1699 (8)	10.75	10.75

Souvenir Sheets

1700	A245	$6 Clench's hairstreak	5.25	5.25
1701	A245	$6 Painted lady	5.25	5.25

10th Caribbean Scout Jamboree A246

Designs: 20c, Backpacking. 25c, Cooking over campfire. 55c, Making camp. 65c, Camping. $1, Scout drum unit. $2, Planting trees. $4, Sailing. $5, Scout salute.
No. 1710, Early Scout troop. No. 1711, Pres. C.A. Sorhaindo, vert.

1994, July 18 **Litho.** ***Perf. 14***
1702-1709 A246 Set of 8 13.00 13.00

Souvenir Sheets

1710-1711 A246 $6 each 6.50 6.50

For overprints see Nos. 1762-1766.

D-Day, 50th Anniv. A247

Designs: 65c, US Waco glider brings reinforcements. $2, British Horsa gliders land more troops. $3, Glider troops take Pegasus Bridge.
$6, Hadrian glider.

1994, July 26
1712-1714 A247 Set of 3 5.75 5.75

Souvenir Sheet

1715 A247 $6 multicolored 5.25 5.25

A248

Intl. Olympic Committee, Cent. — A249

Designs: 55c, Ulrike Meyfarth, Germany, high jump, 1984. $1.45, Dieter Baumann, Germany, 5000-meter run, 1992.
$6, Ji Hoon Chae, South Korea, 500-meter short track speed skating, 1994.

1994, July 26

1716	A248	55c multicolored	.60	.60
1717	A248	$1.45 multicolored	1.60	1.60

Souvenir Sheet

1718 A249 $6 multicolored 5.50 5.50

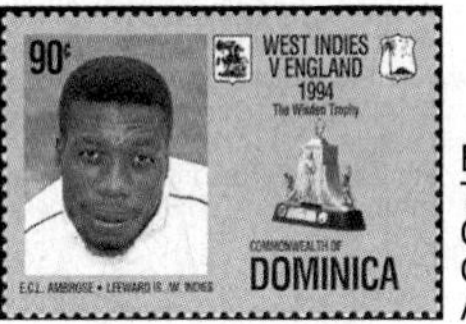

English Touring Cricket, Cent. A250

Designs: 55c, D.I. Goweer Leics, England, vert. 90c, E.C.L. Ambrose, Leeward Islands. $1, G.A. Gooch, England, vert.
$3, First English team, 1895.

1994, July 26
1719-1721 A250 Set of 3 2.50 2.50

Souvenir Sheet

1722 A250 $3 multicolored 5.00 5.00

Miniature Sheet of 6

First Manned Moon Landing, 25th Anniv. A251

#1723: a, Apollo 14 crew. b, Apollo 14 patch. c, Apollo 14 lunar module Antares at Fra Mauro Crater. d, Apollo 15 crew. e, Apollo 15 patch. f, Apollo 15 mission, Mount Hadley from rover.
$6, 25th anniv. emblem, lunar surface.

1994, July 26
1723 A251 $1 #a.-f. 5.50 5.50

Souvenir Sheet

1724 A251 $6 multicolored 6.25 6.25

A252

PHILAKOREA '94 — A253

Designs: 65c, P'alsang-jon Hall, Korea. 90c, Popchu-sa Temple. $2, Uhwajong Pavillion, Korea.
Screen, Late Choson Dynasty showing flowers and: No. 1728a, c, e, Birds. b, g, Butterfly. d, Roosters. f, Duck. h, Pheasant. i, Cranes. j, Deer.
$4, Stylized "spirit post" guardian.

1994, July 26 ***Perf. 14, 13 (#1728)***
1725-1727 A252 Set of 3 2.75 2.75

Miniature Sheet of 10

1728 A253 55c #a.-j. 4.25 4.25

Souvenir Sheet

1729 A252 $4 multicolored 3.00 3.00

Mickey Mouse, 65th Birthday A254

Disney characters: 20c, Dippy dawg. 25c, Clarabelle Cow. 55c, Horace Horsecollar. 65c, Mortimer Mouse. $1, Joe Piper. $3, Mr. Casey. $4, Chief O'Hara. $5, Mickey and the Blot.
No. 1738, Minnie, Tanglefoot. No. 1739, Pluto, Minnie, horiz.

Perf. 13½x14, 14x13½ (#1739)

1994, Oct. 3
1730-1737 A254 Set of 8 15.00 15.00

Souvenir Sheets

1738-1739 A254 $6 each 7.50 7.50

A255

A256

Local Entertainers: 20c, Sonia Llyod, folk singer. 25c, Ophelia Marie, singer. 55c, Edney Francis, accordionist. 65c, Norman Letang, saxophonist. 90c, Edie Andre, steel drummer

1994, Dec. 1 **Litho.** ***Perf. 14***
1740-1744 A255 Set of 5 1.90 1.90

Miniature Sheet of 9

1994, Dec. 1

Marilyn Monroe (1926-62), Actress: #1745a-1745i, Various portraits. #1746, Hands above head. #1747, Holding hat.

1745 A256 90c #a.-i. 12.0012.00

Souvenir Sheets

1746-1747 A256 $6 each 5.75 5.75

Christmas A257

Details or entire Spanish paintings: 20c, Madonna and child, by Luis de Morales. 25c, Madonna and Child with Yarn Winder, by Morales. 55c, Our Lady of the Rosary, by Zurbaran. 65c, Dream of the Patrician, by Bartolome Murillo. 90c, Madonna of Charity, by El Greco. $1, The Annunciation, by Zurbaran. $2, Mystical Marriage of St. Catherine, by Jusepe de Ribera. $3, The Holy Family with St. Bruno and Other Saints, by Ribera.
No. 1756, Vision of the Virgin to St. Bernard, by Murillo. No. 1757, Adoration of the Shepherds, by Murillo.

1994, Dec. 2 *Perf. 13½x14*
1748-1755 A257 Set of 8 8.50 8.50

Souvenir Sheets

1756-1757 A257 $6 each 4.50 4.50

Order of the Caribbean Community — A258

First award recipients: 25c, Sir Shridath Ramphal, statesman, Guyana. 65c, William Gilbert Demas, economist, Trinidad & Tobago. 90c, Derek Walcott, writer, St. Lucia.

1994, Dec. 16 *Perf. 14*
1758-1760 A258 Set of 3 2.00 2.00

Jeffrey Edmund, 1994 World Cup Soccer Player, Dominica A259

1994, Dec. 28
1761 A259 25c multicolored .20 .20

Nos. 1705, 1708-1711 Ovptd.

18th World Scout Jamboree Mondial, Holland, May 6, 1995

1995, Mar. 21 Litho. *Perf. 14*
1762-1764 A246 Set of 3 8.25 8.25

Souvenir Sheets

1765-1766 A246 $6 each 6.00 6.00

Location of overprint varies.

New Year 1995 (Year of the Boar) — A260

Stylized boars: a, 25c, Facing right. b, 65c, Facing forward. c, $1, Facing left.
$2, Two facing each other, horiz.

1995, Apr. 15 Litho. *Perf. 14½*
1767 A260 Strip of 3, #a.-c. 1.75 1.75
d. Souv. sheet of 3, #1767a-1767c 1.75 1.75

Souvenir Sheet

1768 A260 $2 multicolored 1.50 1.50

No. 1767 was issued in sheets of 4 strips.

Birds A261

Designs: 25c, Wood duck. 55c, Mallard. 65c, Blue-winged teal. $5, Blood eared parakeet.
No. 1773, vert.: a, Cattle egret. b, Snow goose (a, c). c, Peregrine falcon. d, Barn owl. e, Black-crowned night heron. f, Common grackle. g, Brown pelican. h, Great egret. i, Ruby-throated hummingbird. j, Laughing gull. k, Greater flamingo. l, Common moorhen.
No. 1774, Trumpeter swan, vert. No. 1775, White-eyed vireo.

1995, Apr. 15 Litho. *Perf. 14*
1769-1772 A261 Set of 4 5.00 5.00

Miniature Sheet of 12

1773 A261 65c #a.-l. 15.0015.00

Souvenir Sheets

1774 A261 $5 multicolored 4.75 4.75
1775 A261 $6 multicolored 5.75 5.75

Miniature Sheets of 6 or 8

End of World War II, 50th Anniv. A262

No. 1776: a, Mitsubishi A6M2 Zero. b, Aichi D3A1 Type 99 "Val." c, Nakajima 97-B5N "Kate." d, Zuikaku. e, Akagi. f, Ryuho.
No. 1777: a, German Panther tank, Ardennes. b, Allied fighter bomber. c, Patton's army crosses the Rhine. d, Rocket-powered ME 163. e, V-2 rocket on launcher. f, German U-boat surrenders in North Atlantic. g, Round the clock bombardment of Berlin. h, Soviet soldiers reach center of Berlin.
No. 1778, Statue atop Dresden's town hall after Allied bombing. No. 1779, Japanese attack plane.

1995 Litho. *Perf. 14*
1776 A262 $2 #a.-f. + label 10.50 10.50
1777 A262 $2 #a.-h. + label 14.50 14.50

Souvenir Sheets

1778-1779 A262 $6 each 6.50 6.50

Issued: #1777-1778, 5/18; others, 7/21.

1996 Summer Olympics, Atlanta A263

Designs: 15c, Mark Breland, boxing. 20c, Lou Banach, Joseph Atiyeh, freestyle wrestling. 25c, Judo. 55c, Fencing. 65c, Matt Biondi, swimming. $1, Gushiken on rings, vert. $2, Cycling, vert. $5, Volleyball.
No. 1788, Joe Cargis on Touch of Class, equestrian. No. 1789, Soccer, vert.

1995, July 21
1780-1787 A263 Set of 8 8.75 8.75

Souvenir Sheets

1788-1789 A263 $6 each 5.75 5.75

UN, 50th Anniv. — A264

No. 1790: a, 65c, Signatures on UN charter, attendee. b, $1, Attendee. $2, Attendees.
$6, Winston Churchill.

1995, Aug. 16 Litho. *Perf. 14*
1790 A264 Strip of 3, #a.-c. 2.75 2.75

Souvenir Sheet

1791 A264 $6 multicolored 5.00 5.00

No. 1790 is a continuous design.

Souvenir Sheets

FAO, 50th Anniv. — A265

Street market scene: a, 90c, Woman in red dress. b, $1, Woman seated. c, $2, Vendors, women.
$6, Woman in field, woman holding water cans, vert.

1995, Aug. 16
1792 A265 Sheet of 3, #a.-c. 2.75 2.75
1793 A265 $6 multicolored 4.50 4.50

No. 1792 is a continuous design.

Queen Mother, 95th Birthday A266

No. 1794: a, Drawing. b, Wearing crown, green dress. c, Formal portrait. d, Blue dress.
$6, Portrait as younger woman.

1995, Aug. 16 *Perf. 13½x14*
1794 A266 $1.65 Strip of block of 4, #a.-d. 9.25 9.25

Souvenir Sheet

1795 A266 $6 multicolored 4.50 4.50

No. 1794 was issued in sheets of 8 stamps.
Sheet margins of Nos. 1794-1795 exist with black frame and text "In Memoriam - 1900-2002" overprinted in sheet margins.

Rotary, 90th Anniv. A267

1995 *Perf. 14*
1796 A267 $1 Paul Harris, emblem .75 .75

Souvenir Sheet

1797 A267 $6 Rotary emblems 4.50 4.50

Dinosaurs A268

20c, Monoclonius. 25c, Euoplocephalus. 55c, Coelophysis. 65c, Compsognathus.
No. 1802: a, Dimorphodon. b, Ramphorynchus. c, Giant alligator. d, Pentaceratops.
No. 1803, vert: a, Ceratosaurus. b, Comptosaurus (a). c, Stegosaur. d, Camarasaurs. e, Baronyx. f, Dilophosaurus. g, Dromaeosaurids (f). h, Deinonychus. i, Dinicthys. j, Carcharodon (k). k, Nautiloid. l, Trilobite.
$5, Sauropelta. $6, Triceratops, vert.

1995, Sept. 8
1798-1801 A268 Set of 4 1.25 1.25
1802 A268 90c Strip of 4, #a.-b. 2.75 2.75

Miniature Sheet of 12

1803 A268 $1 #a.-l. 9.00 9.00

Souvenir Sheets

1804 A268 $5 multicolored 3.75 3.75
1805 A268 $6 multicolored 4.50 4.50

Singapore '95 (#1798-1801, #1803-1805).

Miniature Sheets of 6

Nobel Prize Fund Established, Cent. — A269

Recipients: No. 1806a, Oscar A. Sanchez, peace, 1987. b, Ernst B. Chain, medicine, 1945. c, Aage Bohr, physics, 1975. d, Jaroslav Seifert, literature, 1984. e, Joseph E. Murray, medicine, 1990. f, Jaroslav Heyrovsky, chemistry, 1959.
No. 1807: a, Adolf von Baeyer, chemistry, 1905. b, Edward Buchner, chemistry, 1907. c, Carl Bosch, chemistry, 1931. d, Otto Hahn, chemistry, 1944. e, Otto Paul Herman Diels, chemistry, 1950. f, Kurt Alder, chemistry, 1950.
No. 1808, Emil A. von Behring, medicine, 1901.

1995, Oct. 24 Litho. *Perf. 14*
1806-1807 A269 $2 #a.-f., each 9.00 9.00

Souvenir Sheet

1808 A269 $2 multicolored 1.50 1.50

Christmas A270

Details or entire paintings: 20c, Madonna and Child, by Pontormo. 25c, The Immaculate Conception, by Murillo. 55c, The Adoration of the Magi, by Filippino Lippi. 65c, Rest on the Flight into Egypt, by Van Dyck. 90c, Sacred Family, by Van Dyck. $5, The Annunciation, by Van Eyck.
No. 1815, The Virgin and the Infant, by Van Eyck. No. 1816, The Holy Family, by Ribera.

1995, Nov. 30 Litho. *Perf. 13½x14*
1809-1814 A270 Set of 6 5.75 5.75

Souvenir Sheets

1815 A270 $5 multicolored 3.75 3.75
1816 A270 $6 multicolored 4.50 4.50

Miniature Sheets of 9

Sierra Club, Cent. A271

Designs: No. 1817: a, Florida panther with mouth open. b, Florida panther looking right. c, Manatee. d, Two manatees. e, Three sockeye salmon. f, Group of sockeye salmon. g, Two southern sea otters. h, Southern sea otter. i, Southern sea otter showing both front paws.

No. 1818, vert: a, Florida panther. b, Manatee. c, Sockeye salmon. d, Key deer facing left. e, Key deer. f, Key deer with antlers, up close. g, Wallaby with young in pouch. h, Wallaby. i, Wallaby with young.

1995, Dec. 10 *Perf. 14*

1817-1818 A271 $1 #a.-i., each 6.75 6.75

Chinese Paintings, A City of Cathay A272

No. 1819, brown lettering: a, Boats docked, people on shore. b, River, bridge. c, Two boats on river. d, River, pavilion along shore. e, Open sea, people in courtyard.

No. 1820, black lettering: a, City scene. b, City scene, wall. c, Outside wall, river. d, Large boat on river. e, People crossing over bridge.

No. 1821: a, Boat on river, city above. b, People walking across bridge.

No. 1822: a, Lifting ramp to another boat, vert. b, Holding lines in water, tree, vert.

1995, Dec. 27 Litho. *Perf. 14½*

Strips of 5

1819-1820 A272 90c #a.-e., each 3.50 3.50

Souvenir Sheets of 2

1821-1822 A272 $2 #a-b, ea 3.00 3.00

Nos. 1819-1822 are each continuous designs.

Classic Western Art — A273

Paintings by Raphael: No. 1823, Agony in the Garden. No. 1824, Pope Leo with Nephews. No. 1825, Bindo Altoviti.

$6, Triumphant entry of Constantine into Rome, by Rubens.

1995, Dec. 27 *Perf. 14*

1823-1825 A273 $2 Set of 3 4.50 4.50

Souvenir Sheet

1826 A273 $6 multicolored 4.50 4.50

New Year 1996 (Year of the Rat) — A274

Stylized rats, Chinese inscriptions: No. 1827a, 25c, purple & brown. b, 65c, orange & green. c. $1, red lilac & blue.

$2, Two rats, horiz.

1996, Jan. 16 *Perf. 14½*

1827 A274 Strip of 3, #a.-c. 1.40 1.40

Miniature Sheet

1828 A274 Sheet of 1 #1827 1.40 1.40

Souvenir Sheet

1829 A274 $2 multicolored 1.50 1.50

No. 1827 was issued in sheets of 12 stamps.

Miniature Sheet

Disney Lunar New Year — A275

Disney characters representing year of the: No. 1830a, Rat. b, Ox. c, Tiger. d, Hare. e, Dragon. f, Snake. g, Horse. h, Sheep. i, Monkey. j, Rooster. k, Dog. l, Pig.

$3, Rat character. $6, Pig, rat, ox characters on lunar calendar wheel.

1996, Jan. 16 *Perf. 14x13½*

1830 A275 55c Sheet of 12, #a.-l. 8.00 8.00

Souvenir Sheets

1831 A275 $3 multicolored 3.50 3.50
1832 A275 $6 multicolored 7.25 7.25

Methods of Transportation — A276

Designs: 65c, Donkey cart, 1965. 90c, 1910 Car. $2, 1950 Taxi. $3, 1955 Bus.

1996, Jan. 29 Litho. *Perf. 14*

1833-1836 A276 Set of 4 5.00 5.00

Miniature Sheets

Locomotives — A277

No. 1837: a, "Dragon," Hawaii. b, "Regina," Italy. c, Calazo to Padua, Italy. d, "Mogul," Philippines. e, Nuremberg, Germany. f, "Stanislas," French Natl. Railway. g, "Black Five," Scotland. h, SNCF diesel electric, France. i, "Sir Nigel Gresley," England.

No. 1838: a, Hohi Line 9600 class, Japan. b, Peloponnese Express, Greece. c, Porter 2-4-0S, Hawaii. d, Norway-Swedish Jodemans Railway. e, 220 Diesel, Federal German Railway. f, 2-8-4T Indian Railways. g, East African Railways. h, Electrical trains, USSR. i, 0-8-0, Austria.

$5, "Duchess of Hamilton," England. $6, Diesel engine, China.

1996, Jan. 29

1837-1838 A277 $2 #a-i, ea 14.00 14.00

Souvenir Sheets

1839 A277 $5 multicolored 3.75 3.75
1840 A277 $6 multicolored 4.50 4.50

No. 1837h has a face value of $1.

Giant Panda A278

Designs: a, With right leg up on rock. b, Front legs up on rock. c, Seated. d, Holding head down.

1996, May 15 Litho. *Perf. 13½x14*

1841 A278 55c Block of 4, #a.-d. 3.75 3.75

Souvenir Sheet

Perf. 14x13½

1842 A278 $3 Panda, horiz. 2.25 2.25

CHINA '96, 9th Asian Intl. Philatelic Exhibition. No. 1841 was issued in sheets of 8 stamps.

See No. 1911.

Queen Elizabeth II, 70th Birthday A279

No. 1843: a, Portrait. b, Wearing regalia of Order of the Garter. c, Wearing bright blue dress, pearls.

$6, In uniform.

1996, May 16 Litho. *Perf. 13½x14*

1843 A279 $2 Strip of 3, #a.-c. 4.50 4.50

Souvenir Sheet

1844 A279 $6 multicolored 4.50 4.50

No. 1843 was issued in sheets of 9 stamps.

Legendary Film Detectives A280

Designs: a, Humphrey Bogart as Sam Spade. b, Sean Connery as James Bond. c, Warren Beatty as Dick Tracy. d, Basil Rathbone as Sherlock Holmes. e, William Powell as the Thin Man. f, Sidney Toler as Charlie Chan, g, Peter Sellers as Inspector Clouseau. h, Robert Mitchum as Philip Marlowe. i, Peter Ustinov as Inspector Poirot.

$6, Margaret Rutherford as Miss Marple.

1996, July

1845 A280 $1 Sheet of 9, #a.-i. 9.50 9.50

Souvenir Sheet

1846 A280 $6 multicolored 6.50 6.50

1996 Summer Olympics, Atlanta A281

Designs: 20c, Olympic Stadium, Moscow, 1980. 25c, Hermine Joseph, vert. 55c, Women's field hockey, Zimbabwe, 1980. 90c, Jerome Romain, vert. $1, Polo, discontinued sport, vert. $2, Greg Louganis, diving.

1996 *Perf. 14*

1847-1852 A281 Set of 6 3.75 3.75

Local Entertainers A282

Designs: 25c, Irene Peltier, national dress of Dominica. 55c, Rupert Bartley, street band player. 65c, Rosemary Cools-Lartigue, pianist. 90c, Celestine "Orion" Theophile, belle queen, Grand Bay. $1, Cecil Bellot, former government band master.

1996, July 31 Litho. *Perf. 14*

1853-1857 A282 Set of 5 2.50 2.50

Jerusalem, 3000th Anniv. — A283

Designs: a, 90c, Shrine of the Book, Israel Museum. b, $1, Church of All Nations. c, $2, The Great Synagogue.

$5, Hebrew University, Mount Scopus.

1996, July 31

1858 A283 Sheet of 3, #a.-c. 3.00 3.00

Souvenir Sheet

1859 A283 $5 multicolored 3.75 3.75

Radio, Cent. A284

Entertainers: 90c, Artie Shaw. $1, Benny Goodman. $2, Duke Ellington. $4, Harry James.

$6, Tommy Dorsey, Jimmy Dorsey, horiz.

1996, July 31

1860-1863 A284 Set of 4 6.00 6.00

Souvenir Sheet

1864 A284 $6 multicolored 4.50 4.50

UNICEF, 50th Anniv. A285

20c, Girl looking at globe. 55c, Boy with stethoscope, syringe. $5, Doctor examining child.

No. 1868, Girl, vert.

1996, July 31

1865-1867 A285 Set of 3 4.25 4.25

Souvenir Sheet

1868 A285 $5 multicolored 3.75 3.75

World Post Day — A286

Scenes of 18th cent. life in Dominica: 10c, Captain of ship taking letters by hand. 25c, Anthony Trollope vists Dominica to organize postal service. 55c, Steam vessel "Yare" carries mail around island. 65c, Post offices and agencies. 90c, Country postman carrying mail around mountain tracks. $1, West Indies Federation stamp, first airmail sent on German "goose" seaplane. $2, #602, General Post Office, old and new.
$5, Captain of ship.

1996, Oct. 1 Litho. *Perf. 14*
1869-1875 A286 Set of 7 4.25 4.25

Souvenir Sheet

1876 A286 $5 multicolored 3.75 3.75

Fish — A287

Designs: 1c, Scrawled filefish. 2c, Lion fish. 5c, Porcupine fish. 10c, Powder blue surgeonfish. 15c, Red hind. 20c, Golden butterfly fish. 25c, Long-nosed butterfly fish. 35c, Pennant butterfly fish. 45c, Spotted drum. 55c, Blue-girdled angelfish. 60c, Scorpion fish. 65c, Harlequin sweetlips. 90c, Flame angelfish. $1, Queen trigger. $1.20, Stoplight parrot. $1.45, Black durgon. $2, Glasseye snapper. $5, Balloon fish. $10, Creole wrasse. $20, Seabass.

1996, Oct. 1 Litho. *Perf. 14*

No.	Type	Value	Color	Unused	Used
1877	A287	1c	multicolored	.20	.20
1878	A287	2c	multicolored	.20	.20
1879	A287	5c	multicolored	.20	.20
1880	A287	10c	multicolored	.20	.20
1881	A287	15c	multicolored	.20	.20
1882	A287	20c	multicolored	.20	.20
1883	A287	25c	multicolored	.20	.20
1884	A287	35c	multicolored	.25	.25
1885	A287	45c	multicolored	.35	.35
1886	A287	55c	multicolored	.40	.40
1887	A287	60c	multicolored	.45	.45
1888	A287	65c	multicolored	.50	.50
1889	A287	90c	multicolored	.70	.70
1890	A287	$1	multicolored	.75	.75
1891	A287	$1.20	multicolored	.90	.90
1892	A287	$1.45	multicolored	1.10	1.10
1893	A287	$2	multicolored	1.50	1.50
1894	A287	$5	multicolored	3.75	3.75
1895	A287	$10	multicolored	7.50	7.50
1896	A287	$20	multicolored	15.00	15.00
	Nos. 1877-1896 (20)			34.55	34.55

See Nos. 2024-2039B for size 20x18mm stamps.

1996 Summer Olympic Games Type

Past Olympic medalists, vert: No. 1897a, Ulrike Meyfarth, high jump. b, Pat McCormick, diving. c, Takeichi Nishi, equestrian. d, Peter Farkas, Greco-Roman wrestling. e, Carl Lewis, track & field. f, Agnes Keleti, gymnastics. g, Yasuhiro Yamashita, judo. h, John Kelly, single sculls. i, Naim Suleymanoglu, weight lifting.
No. 1898, vert.: a, Sammy Lee, diving. b, Bruce Jenner, decathlon. c, Olga Korbut, gymnastics. d, Steffi Graf, tennis. e, Florence Griffith-Joyner, track and field. f, Mark Spitz, swimming. g, Li Ning, gymnastics. h, Erika Salumae, cycling. i, Abebe Bikila, marathon.
#1899, Joan Benoit, 1st women's marathon, vert.
#1900, Milt Campbell, discus.

1996, June 7 Litho. *Perf. 14*
1897-1898 A281 90c Sheets of 9, #a.-i., each 6.25 6.25

Souvenir Sheets

1899-1900 A281 $5 each 3.75 3.75

A288 A289

Christmas (Details or entire paintings): 25c, Enthroned Madonna and Child, by Stefano Veneziano. 55c, Noli Me Tangere, by Beato Angelico. 65c, Madonna and Child, by Angelico. 90c, Madonna of Corneta Tarquinia, by Filippo Lippi. $2, Annunciation, by Angelico. $5, Madonna with Child, by Angelico, diff.
No. 1907, Coronation of the Virgin, by Beato Angelico. No. 1908, Holy Family with St. Barbara, by Veronese, horiz.

1996, Nov. 25
1901-1906 A288 Set of 6 7.00 7.00

Souvenir Sheet

1907-1908 A288 $6 each 4.50 4.50

1997 Litho. *Perf. 14*

Paintings of "Herdboy and Buffalo," by Li Keran (1907-89): No. 1909: a, f, Herdboy Plays the Flute. b, g, Playing Cricket in the Autumn. c, h, Listen to the Summer Cicada. d, i, Grazing in the Spring.
$2, Return in Wind and Rain.

1909 A289 90c Strip of 4, #a.-d. 2.75 2.75

Souvenir Sheets

1909E A289 55c Sheet of 4, #f.-i. 1.60 1.60

Perf. 15x14½

1910 A289 $2 multicolored 1.50 1.50

New Year 1997 (Year of the Ox).
No. 1909 was printed in sheets of 8 stamps.
No. 1910 contains one 34x52mm stamp.

Souvenir Sheet

Huangshan Mountain, China — A290

Illustration reduced.

1996, May 15 Litho. *Perf. 12*
1911 A290 $2 multicolored 1.50 1.50

China '96. No. 1911 was not available until March 1997.

A291

Lee Lai-Shan, 1996 Olympic Gold Medalist in Wind Surfing — A291a

Illustration A291a reduced.

1997 Litho. *Perf. 15x14*
1912 A291 $2 multicolored 1.50 1.50

Souvenir Sheet

Perf. 14

1913 A291 $5 multicolored 3.75 3.75

No. 1912 was issued in sheets of 3.
No. 1913 contains one 38x51mm stamp.

Litho. & Embossed

Perf. 9

Without Gum

1913A A291a $35 gold & multi, like #1913

Butterflies A292

No. 1914: a, Meticalla metis. b, Coeliades forestan. c, Papilio dardanus. d, Mylothris chloris. e, Poecilmitis thyshe. f, Myrina silenus. g, Bematistes aganice. h, Euphaedra neophron. i, Precis hierta.
No. 1915, vert: a, Striped policeman. b, Mountain sandman. c, Brown-veined white. d, Bowker's widow. e, Foxy charaxes. f, Pirate. g, African clouded yellow. h, Garden inspector.
No. 1916, Acraea natalica. No. 1917, Eurytela dryope.

1997, Apr. 1 Litho. *Perf. 14*
1914 A292 55c Sheet of 9, #a.-i. 3.75 3.75
1915 A292 90c Sheet of 8, #a.-h. 5.50 5.50

Souvenir Sheets

1916-1917 A292 $6 each 4.50 4.50

UNESCO, 50th Anniv. A293

55c, View from temple, China. 65c, Palace of Diocletian, Croatia. 90c, St. Mary's Cathedral, Hildesheim, Germany. $1, Monastery of Rossanou, Mount Athos, Greece. $2, Scandola Nature Reserve, France. $4, Church of San Antao, Portugal.
No. 1924: a, Ruins of Copan, Honduras. b, Cuzco Cathedral, Peru. c, Olinda, Brazil, d, Canaima Natl. Park, Venezuela. e, Galapagos Islands Natl. Park, Ecuador. f, Ruins of Church, Jesuit missions of Santisima, Paraguay. g, Fortress, San Lorenzo, Panama. h, Natl. Park, Fortress, Haiti.
No. 1925, Chengde Lakes, China. No. 1926, Kyoto, Japan.

1997, Apr. 7 *Perf. 13½x14*
1918-1923 A293 Set of 6 6.75 6.75
1924 A293 $1 Sheet of 8, #a.-h. + label 6.00 6.00

Souvenir Sheets

1925-1926 A293 $6 each 4.50 4.50

Disney Scenes "Sealed with a Kiss" A294

Cartoon film, year released: 25c, Mickey's Horse, Tanglefoot, 1933. 35c, Shanghaied, 1935. 55c, Pluto's Judgment Day, 1935. 65c, Race for Riches, 1935. 90c, Elmer Elephant, 1936. $1, Brave Little Tailor, 1938. $2, Donald's Crime, 1945. $4, In Dutch, 1946.
No. 1935, Nifty Nineties, 1941. No. 1936, Mickey's Surprise Party, 1939.

1997, Apr. 15 *Perf. 13½x14*
1927-1934 A294 Set of 8 7.25 7.25

Souvenir Sheets

1935-1936 A294 $6 each 4.50 4.50

Cats — A295 Dogs — A296

25c, Cream Burmese. $1, Snowshoe. $2, Sorrell Abyssinian. $5, Torbie Persian.
No. 1941: a, British bicolor shorthair (d, e). b, Maine coon kitten, Somali kitten (c). c, Maine coon kitten, diff. d, Lynx point Siamese (e). e, Blue Burmese kitten, white Persian (odd-eyed) (f). f, Persian kitten.
No. 1942, Silver tabby.

1997, Apr. 24 *Perf. 14*
1937-1940 A295 Set of 4 6.25 6.25
1941 A295 $2 Sheet of 6, #a.-f. 9.00 9.00

Souvenir Sheet

1942 A295 $6 multicolored 4.50 4.50

1997, Apr. 24

Designs: 20c, Afghan hound. 55c, Cocker spaniel. 65c, Smooth fox terrier. 90c, West Highland white terrier.
No. 1947a, St. Bernard. b, Boy with grand basset. c, Rough collie. d, Golden retriever. e, Golden retriever, Tibetan spaniel, smooth fox terrier. f, Smooth fox terrier, diff.
$6, Shetland sheepdog.

1943-1946 A296 Set of 4 1.75 1.75
1947 A296 90c Sheet of 6, #a.-f. 4.50 4.50

Souvenir Sheet

1948 A296 $6 multicolored 4.50 4.50

Queen Elizabeth II and Prince Philip, 50th Wedding Anniv. A297

No. 1949: a, Queen Elizabeth II. b, Royal Arms. c, Prince, Queen walking among crowd. d, Queen, Prince in military attire. e, Buckingham Palace. f, Prince Philip.
$6, Portrait of Queen and Prince on balcony.

1997, May 29 Litho. *Perf. 14*
1949 A297 $1 Sheet of 6, #a.-f. 4.50 4.50

Souvenir Sheet

1950 A297 $6 multicolored 4.50 4.50

Paintings by Hiroshige (1797-1858) A298

#1951: a, Ichigaya Hachiman Shrine. b, Blossoms on the Tama River Embankment. c, Kumano Junisha Shrine, Tsunohazu ("Juniso"). d, Benkei Moat from Soto-Sakurada to Kojimachi. e, Kinokuni Hill & View of Akasak Tameike. f, Naito Shinjuku, Yotsuya.

No. 1952, Kasumigaseki. No. 1952A, Sanno Festival Procession at Kojimachi I-chome.

1997, May 29

1951 A298 $1.55 Sheet of 6, #a.-f. 7.00 7.00

Souvenir Sheets

1952-1952A A298 $6 each 4.50 4.50

Orchids A299

Designs, vert: 20c, Oncidium altissimum. 25c, Oncidium papilio. 55c, Epidendrum fragrans. 65c, Oncidium lanceanum. 90c, Campylocentrum micranthum. $4, Pogonia rosea.

No. 1959: a, Brassavola cucculata. b, Epidendrum ibaguense. c, Ionopsis utriculari-odes. d, Rodriguezia lanceolata. e, Oncidium cebolleta. f, Epidendrum ciliare.

No. 1960, Stanhopea grandiflora. No. 1961, Oncidium ampliatum.

1997, May 10 Litho. *Perf. 14*

1953-1958 A299 Set of 6 4.90 4.90
1959 A299 $1 Sheet of 6, #a.-f. 4.50 4.50

Souvenir Sheets

1960-1961 A299 $5 each 3.75 3.75

Paul P. Harris (1868-1947), Founder of Rotary, Intl. — A300

Portrait of Harris and: $2, Rotary Village Corps, irrigation project, Honduras. $6, Emblems, world community service.

1997, May 29

1962 A300 $2 multicolored 1.50 1.50

Souvenir Sheet

1963 A300 $6 multicolored 4.50 4.50

Heinrich von Stephan (1831-97) A301

Portraits of Von Stephan and: No. 1964 a, Kaiser Wilhelm II. b, UPU emblem. c, Postal messenger, ancient Japan.

$6, Von Stephan, Russian dog team carrying post, 1859.

1997, May 29

1964 A301 $2 Sheet of 3, #a.-c. 4.50 4.50

Souvenir Sheet

1965 A301 $6 multicolored 4.50 4.50

PACIFIC 97.

Chernobyl Disaster, 10th Anniv. A302

Designs: No. 1966, Chabad's Children of Chernobyl. No. 1967, UNESCO.

1997, May 29 *Perf. 13½x14*

1966 A302 $2 multicolored 1.50 1.50
1967 A302 $2 multicolored 1.50 1.50

Grimm's Fairy Tales A303

Mother Goose Rhymes — A304

The Goose Girl: No. 1968: a, Girl with horse. b, Geese, pond, castle. c, Girl. No. 1969, Girl, horiz.

No. 1970: Mary, Mary, Quite Contrary.

1997, May 29 *Perf. 13½x14*

1968 A303 $2 Sheet of 3, #a.-c. 4.50 4.50

Souvenir Sheets

Perf. 14x13½

1969 A303 $6 multicolored 4.50 4.50

Perf. 14

1970 A304 $6 multicolored 4.50 4.50

Return of Hong Kong to China — A305

Designs: $1, View of Hong Kong at night. $1.45, View of Hong Kong in daytime. $2, View of Hong Kong at night, diff.

Hong Kong skyline at dusk: No. 1974: a, 65c. b, 90c. c, $1. d, $3.

1997, July 1 *Perf. 14*

1971-1973 A305 Set of 3 3.40 3.40
1974 A305 Sheet of 4, #a.-d. 4.25 4.25

#1971-1973 were issued in sheets of 4.

1998 Winter Olympics, Nagano — A306

Medal winners: 20c, Yukio Kasaya, 1972 ski jump. 25c, Jens Weissflog, 1994 ski jump. No. 1977, 55c, Anton Maier, 1968 men's speed skating. No. 1978, 55c, Ljubov Egorova, 1994 women's cross-country skiing. 65c, 1994 Ice hockey, Sweden. 90c, Bernhard Glass, 1980 men's luge. $4, Frank-Peter Roetsch, 1988 men's biathlon.

No. 1982: a, like #1975. b, like #1976. c, like #1977. d, Christa Rothenburger, 1988 women's speed skating.

No. 1983, Jacob Tullin Thams, 1924 ski jumping. No. 1984, Charles Jewtraw, 1924 men's speed skating.

1997, July 15

1975-1981 A306 Set of 7 5.25 5.25
1982 A306 $1 Strip or block of 4, #a.-d. 3.00 3.00

Souvenir Sheets

1983-1984 A306 $5 each 3.75 3.75

No. 1982 issued in sheets of 8 stamps.

1998 World Cup Soccer Championships, France — A307

Players, vert: 20c, Klinsmann, Germany. 55c, Bergkamp, Holland. 65c, Ravanelli, Italy. 90c, Kinkladze, Georgia. $2, Shearer, England. $4, Dani, Portugal.

Stadiums: No. 1991: a, Wembley, England. b, Bernabeu, Spain. c, Maracana, Brazil. d, Torino, Italy. e, Centenary, Uruguay. f, Olympic, Germany. g, Rose Bowl, US. h, Azteca, Mexico.

Team Captains: No. 1992: a, Meazza, Italy, 1934. b, Matthaus, Germany, 1990. c, Walter, W. Germany, 1954. d, Maradona, Argentina, 1986. e, Beckenbauer, Germany, 1974. f, Moore, England, 1966. g, Dunga, Brazil, 1994. h, Zoff, Italy, 1982.

$5, Mario Kempes, Argentina, vert. $6, Ally McCoist, Scotland, vert.

1997, July 21 Litho. *Perf. 14*

1985-1990 A307 Set of 6 7.00 7.00

Sheets of 8 + Label

1991-1992 A307 65c #a.-h., each 4.00 4.00

Souvenir Sheets

1993 A307 $5 multicolored 3.75 3.75
1994 A307 $6 multicolored 4.50 4.50

Dominica Credit Union — A308

25c, Joffre Robinson, former Credit Union president. 55c, Sister Alicia, founder credit union movement in Dominica. 65c, Lorrel Bruce, 1st Cooperative Credit Union president. 90c, Roseau Credit Union Building.

$5, Bruce, Robinson, Sister Alicia.

1997, Aug. 15 Litho. *Perf. 14x13½*

1995-1998 A308 Set of 4 1.75 1.75

Souvenir Sheet

Perf. 14

1999 A308 $5 multicolored 3.75 3.75

No. 1999 contains one 28x60mm stamp.

A309 A310

Medical Pioneers: 20c, Louis Pasteur, father of bacteriology. 25c, Christiaan Barnard, performed first heart transplant. 55c, Sir Alexander Fleming, developer of penicillin. 65c, Camillo Golgi, neurologist. 90c, Jonas Salk, developer of polio vaccine. $1, Har Ghobind Khorana, geneticist. $2, Elizabeth Blackwell, first woman physician. $3, Sir Frank Macfarlane Burnet, immunologist.

$5, Fleming, diff. $6, Pasteur, diff.

1997, Sept. 1 Litho. *Perf. 14*

2000-2007 A309 Set of 8 6.50 6.50

Souvenir Sheets

2008 A309 $5 multicolored 3.75 3.75
2009 A309 $6 multicolored 4.50 4.50

1997, Oct. 20 Litho. *Perf. 14*

Diana, Princess of Wales (1961-97): Various portraits.

2010 A310 $2 Sheet of 4, #a.-d. 6.00 6.00

Souvenir Sheet

2011 A310 $5 multicolored 3.75 3.75

Christmas — A311

Entire paintings or details: 20c, Echo and Narcissus, by Poussin. 55c, Angel Departing from the Family of Tobias, by Rembrandt. 65c, Seated Nymphs with Flute, by Francois Boucher. 90c, Angel, by Rembrandt. $2, Dispute of the Holy Sacrament, by Raphael. $4, Garden of Love, by Rubens.

No. 2018, Annunciation, by Botticelli. No. 2019, Christ on the Mount of Olives, by El Greco.

1997, Nov. 10 Litho. *Perf. 14*

2012-2017 A311 Set of 6 6.25 6.25

Souvenir Sheets

2018-2019 A311 $6 each 4.50 4.50

The $4 is incorrectly inscribed Holy Trinity, by Raphael. No. 2018 is incorrectly inscribed Study of a Muse, by Raphael.

A312

A313

Paintings of tigers, by Ling-Nan School: No. 2020: a, 55c, Gao Qifeng. b, 65c, Zhao Shao'ang. c, 90c, Gao Jianfu. d, $1.20, Gao Jianfu, diff.

$3, Tiger running down mountain, by Gao Jianfu.

1998, Jan. 5 Litho. *Perf. 14½*

2020 A312 Sheet of 4, #a.-d. 2.50 2.50

Souvenir Sheet

Perf. 14x14½

2021 A312 $3 multicolored 2.25 2.25

New Year 1998 (Year of the Tiger). No. 2021 contains one 44x36mm stamp.

Fish Type of 1996

1998 *Perf. 13x13½*

Size: 20x18mm

2024	A287	5c Porcupine fish	.20	.20
2025	A287	10c Powder-blue surgeonfish	.20	.20
2026	A287	15c Red hind	.20	.20
2027	A287	20c Golden butterflyfish	.20	.20
2028	A287	25c Long-nosed butterflyfish	.20	.20
2029	A287	35c Pennant butterflyfish	.25	.25
2030	A287	45c Spotted drum	.35	.35
2031	A287	55c Blue-girdled angelfish	.40	.40
2032	A287	60c Scorpion fish	.45	.45
2033	A287	65c Harlequin sweetlips	.50	.50
2034	A287	90c Flame angelfish	.65	.65
2035	A287	$1 Queen trigger	.75	.75
2036	A287	$1.20 Stoplight parrot	.90	.90
2037	A287	$1.45 Black durgon	1.00	1.00
2038	A287	$2 Glasseye snapper	1.50	1.50
2039	A287	$5 Balloon fish	3.75	3.75
2039A	A287	$10 Creole wrasse	7.50	7.50
2039B	A287	$20 Seabass	15.00	15.00
		Nos. 2024-2039B (18)	34.00	34.00

Numbers have been reserved for additional values in this set.

1998, Feb. 9 Litho. *Perf. 14*

Famous 20th cent. athletes - #2040: a, Jesse Owens. b, Owens jumping in 1936 Summer Olympic Games, Berlin. c, Isaac Berger lifting weights. d, Berger. e, Boris Becker. f, Becker playing tennis. g, Arthur Ashe playing tennis, holding Wimbledon trophy. h, Ashe.

No. 2041, Franz Beckenbauer, soccer player, horiz.

Sheet of 8

2040 A313 $1 #a.-h. 6.00 6.00

Souvenir Sheet

2041 A313 $6 multi 4.50 4.50

Nos. 2040b-2040c, 2040f-2040g are each 53x38mm.

A314

A315

Japanese Cinema Stars - No. 2042: a, Akira Kurosawa. b, Kurosawa's 1950 film, "Rashomon." c, Toshiro Mifune in 1954 film, "Seven Samurai." d, Mifune. e, Yasujiro Ozu. f, Ozu's 1949 film, "Late Spring." g, Sessue Hayakawa in 1957 film, "Bridge on the River Kwai." h, Hayakawa.

No. 2043, Akira Kurosawa, director.

1998, Feb. 9 Litho. *Perf. 14*

Sheet of 8

2042 A314 $1 #a.-h. 6.00 6.00

Souvenir Sheet

2043 A314 $6 multi 4.50 4.50

Nos. 2042b-2042c, 2042f-2042g are each 53x38mm.

1998, Mar. 2 Litho. *Perf. 14*

Mushrooms: 10c, Omphalotus illudens. 15c, Inocybe fastigiata. 20c, Marasmius plicatulus. 50c, Mycena lilacifolia. 55c, Armillaria straminea. 90c, Tricholomopsis rutilans.

No. 2050: a, Lepiota naucina. b, Cortinarius violaceus. c, Boletus aereus. d, Tricholoma aurantium. e, Lepiota procera. f, Clitocybe geotropa. g, Lepiota acutesquamosa. h, Tricholoma saponaceum. i, Lycoperdon gemmatum.

No. 2051: a, Boletus ornatipes. b, Russula xerampelina. c, Cortinarius collinitus. d, Agaricus meleagris. e, Coprinus comatus. f, Amanita caesarea. g, Amanita brunnescens. h, Amanita muscaria. i, Morchella esculenta.

$6, Cortinarius violaceus.

2044-2049 A315 Set of 6 1.75 1.75

Sheets of 9

2050-2051 A315 $1 #a.-i., each 6.75 6.75

Souvenir Sheet

2052 A315 $6 multicolored 4.50 4.50

Sailing Ships A316

Designs: 65c, Greek bireme. 90c, Egyptian felucca. $1, Viking longboat. $2, Chinese junk.

No. 2057: a, Two-masted topsail schooner. b, The Golden Hinde. c, Roman merchant ship. d, Gazela Primeriro. e, Moshulu. f, Bluenose.

No. 2058, Pinta. No. 2059, Chesapeake Bay skipjack.

1998, Mar. 16 Litho. *Perf. 14*

2053-2056 A316 Set of 4 3.50 3.50

2057 A316 55c Block of 6, #a.-f. 2.50 2.50

Souvenir Sheets

2058-2059 A316 $5 each 3.75 3.75

No. 2053 incorrectly inscribed "Egyptian felucca."

No. 2057 was issued in sheets of 12 stamps.

Mickey & Minnie Mouse's 70th Anniv. — A317

25c, Steamboat Willie, 1928. 55c, The Brave Little Tailor, 1938. 65c, Nifty Nineties, 1941. 90c, Mickey Mouse Club, 1955. $1, Mickey, Minnie at the opening of Walt Disney World, 1971. $1.45, Mousercise Mickey & Minnie, 1980.

No. 2061, Walt Disney, Mickey, Minnie. No. 2062, Surprise Party for Mickey & Minnie.

1998, June 16 Litho. *Perf. 14x13½*

2060A	A317	25c black	.20	.20
2060B	A317	55c multicolored	.40	.40
2060C	A317	65c multicolored	.50	.50
2060D	A317	90c multicolored	.70	.70
2060E	A317	$1 multicolored	.75	.75
2060F	A317	$1.45 multicolored	1.10	1.10
		Nos. 2060A-2060F (6)	3.65	3.65

Souvenir Sheet of 7

2060G #2060A-2060F, 2060h 7.50 7.50
h. $5 Runaway brain, perf 13½ at left 3.75 3.75

Size: 130x104mm

Imperf

2061-2062 A317 $5 each 3.75 3.75

Souvenir Sheet

Disney's The Lion King — A318

1998, June 16 Litho. *Perf. 13½x14*

2063 A318 $5 multicolored 3.75 3.75

Sea Birds A319

25c, Erect crested penguin. 65c, Humboldt penguin. 90c, Red knot. $1, Audubon's shearwater.

No. 2068: a, Crested tern. b, Franklin's gull. c, Australian pelican. d, Fairy prion. e, Andean gull. f, Imperial shag. g, Red phalarope. h, Hooded grebe. i, Least auklet. j, Little grebe. k, Cape petrel. l, Horned grebe.

No. 2069, Sula nebouxii. No. 2070, Fulmarus glacialis.

1998, Aug. 4 *Perf. 14*

2064-2067 A319 Set of 4 2.00 2.00

2068 A319 90c Sheet of 12, #a.-l. 8.25 8.25

Souvenir Sheets

2069-2070 A319 $5 each 3.75 3.75

Airplanes A320

20c, Jetstar II. 25c, AN 225. 55c, Dash-8. 65c, Beech-99. 90c, American Eagle. $2, HFB 320 Itansa Jet.

No. 2077: a, SR 71 "Blackbird." b, Stealth bomber. c, Northrop YF23. d, F-14 A "Tomcat." e, F-15 "Eagle S." f, MiG 29 "Fulcrum." g, Europa X5. h, Camion.

No. 2078: a, E400. b, CL-215 C-GKDN Amphibian. c, Piper jet. d, Beech Hawker. e, Lockheed YF22. f, Piper Seneca V. g, CL-215 Amphibian. h, Vantase.

No. 2079, F-1 Fighter. No. 2080, Sea Hopper.

1998, Aug. 17

2071-2076 A320 Set of 6 3.50 3.50

Sheets of 8

2077-2078 A320 $1 #a.-h., each 6.00 6.00

Souvenir Sheets

2079-2080 A320 $6 each 4.50 4.50

Intl. Year of the Ocean A321

Marine life: 25c, Fridman fish. 55c, Hydrocoral. 65c, Feather star. 90c, Royal angelfish.

No. 2085: a, Monk seal. b, Galapagos penguin. c, Manta ray. d, Hawksbill turtle. e, Moorish idol. f, Nautilus. g, Giant clam. h, Tubeworms. i, Nudibranch.

No. 2086: a, Spotted dolphin. b, Atlantic sailfish. c, Sailfin flying fish. d, Fairy basslet. e, Atlantic spadefish. f, Leatherback turtle. g, Blue tang. h, Coral banded shrimp. i, Rock beauty.

No. 2087, Humpback whale. No. 2088, Leafy sea dragon.

1998, Sept. 7 Litho. *Perf. 14*

2081-2084 A321 Set of 4 1.75 1.75

Sheets of 9

2085-2086 A321 $1 #a.-i., each 6.75 6.75

Souvenir Sheets

2087 A321 $5 multicolored 3.75 3.75

2088 A321 $6 multicolored 4.50 4.50

Organization of American States, 50th Anniv. A322

1998, Sept. 1 Litho. *Perf. 14*

2089 A322 $1 multicolored .75 .75

Ferrari Sports Cars A323

55c, 365 GT 2+2. 90c, Boano/Ellena 250 GT. $1, 375 MM coupe. $5, 212.

1998, Sept. 1

2090-2092 A323 Set of 3 1.90 1.90

Souvenir Sheet

2093 A323 $5 multicolored 3.75 3.75

No. 2093 contains one 91x35mm stamp.

Gandhi — A324

1998, Sept. 1

2094 A324 90c shown .70 .70

Souvenir Sheet

2095 A324 $6 Seated 4.50 4.50

No. 2094 was issued in sheets of 4.

Pablo Picasso A325

Paintings: 90c, The Painter and His Model, 1926. $1, The Crucifixion, 1930. $2, Nude with Raised Arms, 1908, vert.

$6, Cafe at Royan, 1940.

1998, Sept. 1 *Perf. 14½*

2096-2098 A325 Set of 3 3.00 3.00

Souvenir Sheet

2099 A325 $6 multicolored 4.50 4.50

Royal Air Force, 80th Anniv. A326

No. 2100: a, Nimrod MR2P. b, C-130 Hercules Mk3. c, Panavia Tornado GR1. d, C-130 Hercules landing.
$5, Biplane, hawk. $6, Hawker Hart, jet.

1998, Sept. 1 *Perf. 14*
2100 A326 $2 Sheet of 4, #a.-d. 6.00 6.00

Souvenir Sheets

2101 A326 $5 multicolored 3.75 3.75
2102 A326 $6 multicolored 4.50 4.50

No. 2100d incorrectly inscribed Panavia Tornado GR1.

Nos. 1548-1549, 1551-1552, 1554 Ovptd. "Save the Turtles"

1998, Sept. 14
2103-2107 A221 Set of 5 5.00 5.00

A327

A328

1998 World Scouting Jamboree, Chile: 65c, Scout sign. $1, Scout handshake. $2, World Scout flag.
$5, Lord Baden-Powell.

1998
2108-2110 A327 Set of 3 2.75 2.75

Souvenir Sheet

2111 A327 $5 multicolored 3.75 3.75

1998, Dec. 1 **Litho.** *Perf. 14*

Birds: 25c, Northern cardinal. 55c, Eastern bluebird. 65c, Carolina wren. 90c, Blue jay. $1, Evening grosbeak. $2, Bohemian waxwing.
$5, Northern parula. $6, Painted bunting.

2112-2117 A328 Set of 6 4.00 4.00

Souvenir Sheets

2118 A328 $5 multicolored 3.75 3.75
2119 A328 $6 multicolored 4.50 4.50

Christmas.

New Year 1999 (Year of the Rabbit) A329

Painting by Tsui Po (1050-1080).

1999, Jan. 4 **Litho.** *Perf. 14*
2120 A329 $1.50 multicolored 1.10 1.10

No. 2120 was issued in sheets of 4.

Orchids — A330

55c, Broughtonia sanguinea. 65c, Cattleyonia Keith Roth "Roma." 90c, Comparettia falcata. $2, Cochleanthes discolor.
No. 2125: a, Dracula erythiochaete. b, Lycasle aromatica. c, Masdevallia marguerile. d, Encyclia marfae. e, Laelia gouldiana. f, Huntleya meleagris. g, Galeandria baueri. h, Lycale deppei.
No. 2126: a, Anguloa clowesii. b, Lemboglossum cervantesii. c, Oncidium cebolleta. d, Millonia. e, Pescatorea lehmannll. f, Sophronitis coccinea. g, Pescatorea cerina. h, Encyclia vitellina.
No. 2127, Lepanthes ovalis. No. 2128, Encyclia cochleata.

1999, Apr. 26 **Litho.** *Perf. 14*
2121-2124 A330 Set of 4 3.00 3.00

Sheets of 8

2125-2126 A330 $1 #a.-h., each 6.00 6.00

Souvenir Sheets

2127-2128 A330 $5 each 3.75 3.75

Trains A331

No. 2129: a, Class 103.1 Co-Co, Germany. b, Class .24, "Trans Pennine," UK. c, GG1 2-Co-Co-2, US. d, LRC Bo-Bo, Canada. e, Class EW, New Zealand. f, Class SS1 "Shao-Shani," China. g, Gulf, Mobile Ohio, US. h, Class 9100 2-Do-2, France.
No. 2130: a, County Donegal Petrol Rail Car No. 10, Ireland. b, RDC Single Rail Car, US. c, WDM Class Co-Co, India. d, Bi-Polar No. E-2, US. e, Class X Co-Co, Australia. f, Beijing Bo-Bo, China. g, Class E428 2-Bo-Bo-2, Italy. h, Class 581 Twelve-Car Train, Japan.
$5, X-2000 Tilting Express Train, Sweden, vert. $6, Class 87 Bo-Bo, Great Britain, vert.

1999, May 10 **Litho.** *Perf. 14*

Sheets of 8

2129-2130 A331 $1 #a.-h., each 6.00 6.00

Souvenir Sheets

2131 A331 $5 multicolored 3.75 3.75
2132 A331 $6 multicolored 4.50 4.50

Australia '99, World Stamp Expo.

Prehistoric Animals — A332

25c, Tyrannosaurus, vert. 65c, Hypacrosaurus. 90c, Sauropelta. $2, Zalambdalestes.
No. 2137: a, Barosaurus. b, Rhamphorhynchus. c, Apatosaurus. d, Archaeopteryx. e, Diplodocus. f, Ceratosaurus. g, Stegosaurus. h, Elaphrosaurus. i, Vulcanodon.
No. 2138: a, Psittacosaurus. b, Pteranodon. c, Ichthyornis. d, Spinosaurus. e, Parasaurolophus. f, Ornithomimus. g, Anatosaurus. h, Triceratops. i, Baronyx.
$5, Yangchuanosaurus. $6, Brachiosaurus.

1999, June 1 **Litho.** *Perf. 14*
2133-2136 A332 Set of 4 2.75 2.75

Sheets of 9

2137-2138 A332 $1 #a.-i., each 6.75 6.75

Souvenir Sheets

2139 A332 $5 multicolored 3.75 3.75
2140 A332 $6 multicolored 4.50 4.50

Wedding of Prince Edward and Sophie Rhys-Jones A333

No. 2141: a, Sophie. b, Sophie, Edward. c, Edward.
$6, like No. 2141b.

1999, June 19 **Litho.** *Perf. 13½*
2141 A333 $3 Sheet of 3, #a.-c. 6.75 6.75

Souvenir Sheet

2142 A333 $6 multicolored 4.50 4.50

IBRA '99, World Philatelic Exhibition, Nuremberg — A334

Exhibition emblem, sailing ship Eendraght and: 65c, Cameroun #58, #56. 90c, Cameroun #11, #9.
Emblem, early German train and: $1, Cameroun #19. $2, Cameroun #6.
$6, Cover with Cameroun #19.
Illustration reduced.

1999, June 22 *Perf. 14*
2143-2146 A334 Set of 4 3.50 3.50

Souvenir Sheet

2147 A334 $6 multicolored 4.50 4.50

Souvenir Sheets

PhilexFrance '99 — A335

Trains: $5, L'Aigle, 1855. $6, Mainline diesel locomotive, 1963.
Illustration reduced.

1999, June 22 *Perf. 13¾*
2148 A335 $5 multicolored 3.75 3.75
2149 A335 $6 multicolored 4.50 4.50

Apollo 11 Moon Landing, 30th Anniv. A336

No. 2150: a, Command Module separation b, Service Module separation. c, 3rd Stage Booster separation. d, Landing, Command Modules go to the moon. e, Apollo Ground Tracker. f, Goldstone Radio Telescope.
$6, Apollo 11 after splashdown.

1999, June 22 *Perf. 14*
2150 A336 $1.45 Sheet of 6, #a.-f. 6.50 6.50

Souvenir Sheet

2151 A336 $6 multicolored 4.50 4.50

Paintings by Hokusai (1760-1849) A337

Details or entire paintings — No. 2152: a, Pilgrims at Kirifuri Waterfall. b, Kakura-Sato (rats looking at book, pulling on rope). c, Travelers on the Bridge by Ono Waterfall. d, Fast Cargo Boat Battling the Waves. e, Kakura-Sato (rats working with bales). f, Buufinfinh and Weeping cherry.
No. 2153: a, Cuckoo and Azalea. b, Soldiers (spear in left hand). c, Lover in the snow. d, Ghost of Koheiji. e, Soldiers (spear in right hand). f, Chinese Poet in Snow.
$5, Empress Jitó. $6, One Hundred Poems by One Hundred Poets.

Perf. 13½x13¾
1999, June 22 **Litho.**

Sheets of 6

2152-2153 A337 $2 #a.-f., each 9.25 9.25

Souvenir Sheets

2154 A337 $5 multicolored 3.75 3.75
2155 A337 $6 multicolored 4.50 4.50

Johann Wolfgang von Goethe (1749-1832), Poet — A338

No. 2156: a, Faust perceives an astrological sign. b, Portrait of Goethe and Friedrich von Schiller (1759-1805). c, Faust tempted by Mephistopheles.
$6, Profile portrait of Goethe.

1999, June 22 *Perf. 14*
2156 A338 $2 Sheet of 3, #a.-c. 4.50 4.50

Souvenir Sheet

2157 A338 $6 multicolored 4.50 4.50

Rights of the Child — A339

No. 2158: a, Woman, child. b, Child in blue sweater. c, Two children.
$6, Dove, horiz.

1999, June 22 **Litho.** *Perf. 14*
2158 A339 $3 Sheet of 3, #a.-c. 6.75 6.75

Souvenir Sheet

2159 A339 $6 multicolored 4.50 4.50

Queen Mother (b. 1900) — A340

A340a

Gold Frames

No. 2160: a, In 1939. b, In Australia, 1958. c, At Badminton, 1982. d, Hatless, in 1982.

$6, In 1953.

1999, Aug. 4 *Perf. 14*

2160 A340 $2 Sheet of 4, #a.-d. + label 6.00 6.00

Souvenir Sheet

Perf. 13¾

2161 A340 $6 multicolored 4.50 4.50

No. 2161 contains one 38x51mm stamp. Compare with Nos. 2345-2346. Backdrop of photo is more pink on No. 2161 than on No. 2346. No. 2161 has embossed arms in margin, while No. 2346 does not.

Litho. & Embossed

Die Cut Perf. 8¾

Without Gum

2161A A340a $20 gold & multi

Flora & Fauna A341

Designs: 25c, Heliconia lobster claw. 65c, Broad winged hawk. $1, Anthurium. $1.55, Blue-headed hummingbird. $2, Bananaquit. $4 Agouti.

No. 2168: a, White-throated sparrow. b, Blue-winged teal. c, Raccoon. d, Alfalf butterfly. e, Bridge. f, Whitetail deer. g, Gray squirrel. h, Banded purple butterfly. i, Snowdrop. j, Bullfrog. k, Mushrooms. l, Large-blotched ensatina.

$5, Eastern chipmunk. $6, Black-footed ferret.

1999

2162-2167 A341 Set of 6 7.00 7.00

Sheet of 12

2168 A341 90c #a.-l. 8.00 8.00

Souvenir Sheets

2169 A341 $5 multicolored 3.75 3.75
2170 A341 $6 multicolored 4.50 4.50

A342 A343

Dominica Festival Commission: 25c, Domfesta. 55c, $5, Dominica's 21st anniv. as a republic. 65c, Carnival development committee. 90c, World Creole Music Festival.

1999 *Perf. 12½*

2171-2174 A342 Set of 4 1.60 1.60

Souvenir Sheet

Perf. 13¼

2175 A342 $5 multicolored 3.75 3.75

No. 2175 contains one 38x51mm stamp.

1999, Aug. 4 *Perf. 14*

Intl. Year of the Elderly: 25c, Family. 65c, Four people. 90c, Four people, one in chair.

2176 A343 Sheet of 3, #a.-c. 1.40 1.40

A345

A346

Christmas: 25c, Yellow-crowned parrot. 55c, Red bishop. 65c, Troupial. 90c, Puerto Rican woodpecker. $2, Mangrove cuckoo. $3, American robin.

$6, Mary with Child Beside the Wall, by Albrecht Dürer.

1999, Dec. 7 **Litho.** *Perf. 14*

2178-2183 A345 Set of 6 5.50 5.50

Souvenir Sheet

2184 A345 $6 multi 4.50 4.50

Inscription on No. 2181 is misspelled.

Perf. 12¾x12½

1999, Dec. 31 **Litho.**

Millennium (Highlights of the early 13th Cent.) — #2185: a, Leonardo Fibonacci publishes "Liber Abaci," 1202. b, St. Francis of Assisi. c, Mongols conquer China. d, Children's Crusade begins, 1212. e, Magna Carta signed, 1215. f, Founding of Salamanca University, 1218. g, Snorri Sturluson writes "Prose Edda". h, Chinese painter Ma Yuan dies, 1225. i, Genghis Khan dies, 1227. j, Zen Buddhism in Japan. k, Sixth Crusade. l, Lubeck-Hamburg League. m, Inquisitions begin, 1231. n, Cordoba conquered by Castilians, 1236. o, Democracy in San Marino. p, Maimonides (60x40mm). q, Notre Dame Cathedral, Paris.

Highlights of the 1940s — No. 2186: a, Japan bombs Pearl Harbor. b, Churchill becomes Prime Minister of Great Britain. c, Regular television broadcasting begins in the US. d, Anne Frank hid in Amsterdam. e, D-Day Invasion. f, Yalta Conference. g, Establishment of the UN. h, Germany surrenders, concentration camps exposed. i, Russians hoist flag over gutted Reichstag building. j, Eniac computer. k, Independence for India. l, Bell Laboratories produce 1st transistor. m, Gandhi assassinated. n, Israel achieves statehood. o, Blockade of West Berlin, Berlin Airlift. p, Atomic bomb tested in New Mexico (60x40mm). q, Establishment of People's Republic of China.

Sheets of 17

2185 A346 55c #a.-q. + label 7.00 7.00
2186 A346 55c #a.-q. + label 7.00 7.00

See Nos. 2249-2252.

New Year 2000 (Year of the Dragon) A347

2000, Feb. 5 *Perf. 13¾*

2187 A347 $1.50 shown 1.10 1.10

Souvenir Sheet

2188 A347 $4 Dragon, horiz. 3.00 3.00

No. 2187 printed in sheets of 4.

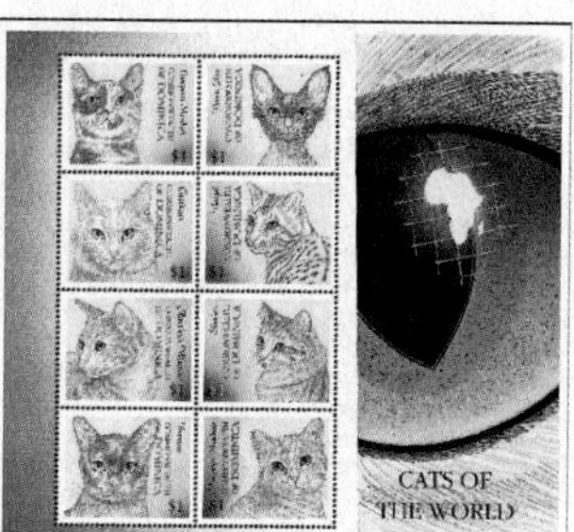

Cats — A348

No. 2189: a, European Shorthair. b, Devon Rex. c, Chartreux. d, Bengal. e, American Wirehair. f, Siberian. g, Burmese. h, American Shorthair.

No. 2190: a, Asian Longhair. b, Burmilla. c, Snowshoe. d, Pekeface Persian. e, Himalayan Persian. f, Japanese Bobtail. g, Seychelles Longhair. h, Exotic Shorthair.

No. 2191, Awake cat. No. 2192, Sleeping cat.

2000, Feb. 21 *Perf. 14¼*

Sheets of 8, #a.-h.

2189-2190 A348 $1 each 6.00 6.00

Souvenir Sheets

2191-2192 A348 $6 each 4.50 4.50

Puppies — A349

No. 2193: a, Jack Russell Terrier. b, Shar Peis. c, Basset Hound. d, Boxers. e, Wirehaired Terrier. f, Golden Retrievers.

No. 2194, Beagle.

2000, Feb. 21 *Perf. 14½x14¼*

2193 A349 $1 Sheet of 6, #a.-f. 4.50 4.50

Souvenir Sheet

2194 A349 $6 multi 4.50 4.50

Flowers A350

Various flowers making up a photomosaic of Princess Diana.

2000, Apr. 3 *Perf. 13¾*

2195 A350 $1 Sheet of 8, #a.-h. 6.00 6.00

See No. 2225.

Butterflies A351

No. 2196: a, Giant swallowtail. b, Tiger pierid. c, Orange theope. d, White peacock. e, Blue tharops. f, Mosaic.

No. 2197: a, Banded king shoemaker. b, Figure-of-eight. c, Grecian shoemaker. d, Blue night. e, Monarch. f, Common morpho.

No. 2198: a, Orange-barred sulphur. b, Clorinde. c, Small flambeau. d, Small lacewing. e, Polydamas swallowtail. f, Atala.

No. 2199, Polydamas swallowtail, vert. No. 2200, Sloane's urania, vert. No. 2201, Blue-green reflector, vert.

2000, Apr. 10 *Perf. 14*

Sheets of 6, #a.-f.

2196-2198 A351 $1.50 each 6.75 6.75

Souvenir Sheets

2199-2201 A351 $6 each 4.50 4.50

Flowers — A352

Designs: 65c, Passion flower. 90c, Spray orchid. $1, Peach angel's trumpet. $4, Allamanda.

No. 2206: a, Bird of paradise. b, Lobster claw heliconia. c, Candle bush. d, Flor de San Miguel. e, Hibiscus. f, Oleander.

No. 2207: a, Anthurium. b, Fire ginger. c, Shrimp plant. d, Sky vine thunbergia. e, Ceriman. f, Morning glory.

No. 2208, Bird of paradise, diff. No. 2109, Hibiscus, diff.

2000, Apr. 25 **Litho.** *Perf. 14*

2202-2205 A352 Set of 4 5.00 5.00

Sheets of 6, #a-f

Perf. 13¾

2206-2207 A352 $1.65 each 7.50 7.50

Souvenir Sheets

Perf. 13½x 13¾

2208-2209 A352 $6 each 4.50 4.50

Size of stamps: Nos. 2106-2107, 32x48mm; Nos. 2108-2109, 38x51mm.

Paintings of Anthony Van Dyck — A353

No. 2210: a, Lady Jane Goodwin. b, Philip Herbert, 4th Earl of Pembroke. c, Philip, Lord Wharton. d, Sir Thomas Hammer. e, Olivia Porter, Wife of Enymion Porter. f, Sir Thomas Chaloner.

No. 2211, horiz.: a, Ladies in Waiting. b, Thomas Wentworth, Earl of Strafford, with Sir Philip Mainwaring. c, Dorothy Rivers Savage, Viscountess Andover and Her Sister Lady Elizabeth Thimbleby. d, Mountjoy Blount, Earl of Newport, and Lord George Goring with a Page. e, Thomas Killigrew and an Unidentified Man. f, Elizabeth Villiers, Lady Dalkeith, and Cecilia Killigrew.

No. 2212, horiz.: a, The Ages of Man. b, Portrait of a Girl as Erminia Accompanied by Cupid. c, Cupid and Psyche. d, Vertumnus and Pomona. e, The Continence of Scipio. f, Diana and Endymion Surprised by a Satyr.

No. 2213, Achilles and the Daughters of Lycomedes. No. 2214, Amaryllis and Mirtillo. No. 2215, Thomas Howard, 2nd Earl of Arundel, with Alathea, Countess of Arundel.

Illustration reduced.

2000, May 29 *Perf. 13¾*

Sheets of 6, #a-f

2210-2212 A353 $1.65 each 7.50 7.50

Souvenir Sheets

2213-2214 A353 $5 each 3.75 3.75
2215 A353 $6 multi 4.50 4.50

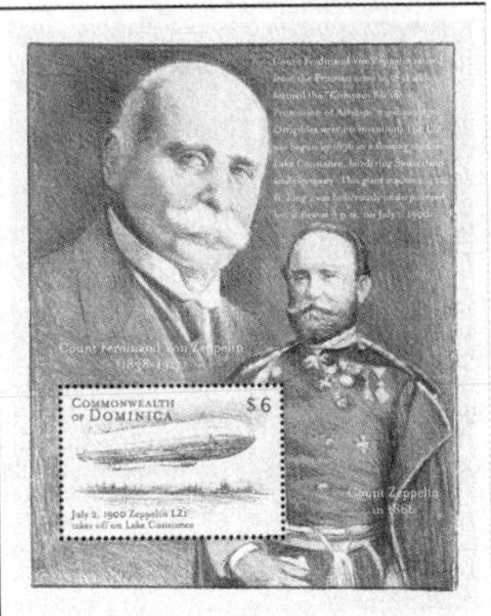

First Zeppelin Flight, Cent. — A354

No. 2216: a, Count Ferdinand von Zeppelin (1838-1917). b, First takeoff of LZ-1. c, LZ-10 over field. d, LZ-6 and Deutschland in hangar. e, Arrival of Z-4 at Luneville. f, Victoria Luise.
No. 2217, LZ-1, diff.
Illustration reduced.

2000, June 21 Litho. *Perf. 14*
2216 A354 $1.65 Sheet of 6, #a-f 7.50 7.50

Souvenir Sheet

2217 A354 $6 multi 4.50 4.50

Berlin Film Festival, 50th Anniv. — A355

No. 2218: a, Director Satyajit Ray. b, Mahangar. c, Fanfan La Tulipe. d, Le Salaire de la Peur. e, Les Cousins. f, Hon Dansade en Sommar.
No. 2219, Buffalo Bill and the Indians.
Illustration reduced.

2000, June 21
2218 A355 $1.65 Sheet of 6, #a-f 7.50 7.50

Souvenir Sheet

2219 A355 $6 multi 4.50 4.50

100th Test Match at Lord's Ground — A356

2000, June 21
2220 A356 $4 Norbert Philip 3.00 3.00

Souvenir Sheet

2221 A356 $6 Lord's Ground 4.50 4.50

Souvenir Sheets

2000 Summer Olympics, Sydney — A357

a, Jesse Owens. b, Pole vault. c, Lenin Stadium Moscow, Soviet Union flag. d, Ancient Greek discus thrower.
Illustration reduced.

2000, June 21
2222 A357 $2 Sheet of 4, #a-d 6.00 6.00

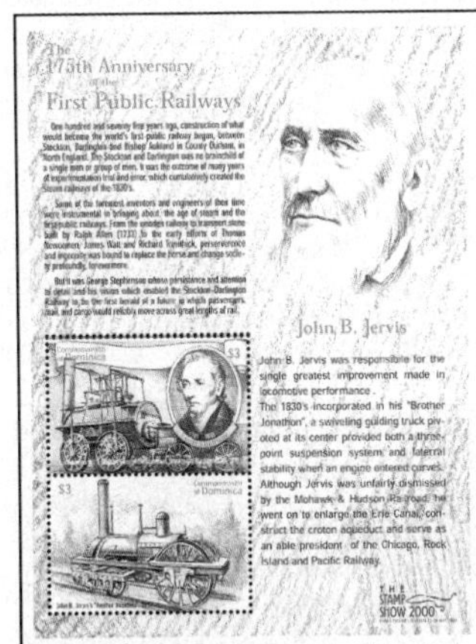

Public Railways, 175th Anniv. — A358

No. 2223: a, Locomotion No. 1, George Stephenson. b, Brother Jonathon.
Illustration reduced.

2000, June 21
2223 A358 $3 Sheet of 2, #a-b 4.50 4.50

The Stamp Show 2000, London.

Johann Sebastian Bach — A359

Illustration reduced.

2000, June 21
2224 A359 $6 multi 4.50 4.50

Flower Type of 2000

Various pictures of religious sites making up a photomosaic of Pope John Paul II.

2000, June 21 Litho. *Perf. 13¾*
2225 A350 $1 Sheet of 8, #a-h 6.00 6.00

Apollo-Soyuz Mission, 25th Anniv. — A360

No. 2226, vert.: a, Saturn IB launch vehicle. b, Apollo 18. c, Donald K. Slayton.
$6, Apollo and Soyuz docking.
Illustration reduced.

2000, June 21 *Perf. 14*
2226 A360 $3 Sheet of 3, #a-c 6.75 6.75

Souvenir Sheet

2227 A360 $6 multi 4.50 4.50

Souvenir Sheet

Albert Einstein (1879-1955) — A361

2000, June 21 *Perf. 14¼*
2228 A361 $6 multi 4.50 4.50

Prince William, 18th Birthday — A362

No. 2229: a, In ski gear. b, In jacket and red sweater. c, In suit and tie. d, In plaid shirt.
$6, With Prince Harry.
Illustration reduced.

2000, June 22 *Perf. 14*
2229 A362 $1.65 Sheet of 4, #a-d 5.00 5.00

Souvenir Sheet
Perf. 13¾

2230 A362 $6 multi 4.50 4.50

No. 2229 contains four 28x42mm stamps.

Bob Hope — A363

No. 2231: a, Microphone at right. b, Entertaining troops. c, Wearing bowler. d, Standing in cake. e, Microphone at left. f, With moon.
Illustration reduced.

2000, Aug. 7 *Perf. 14*
2231 A363 $1.65 Sheet of 6, #a-f 7.25 7.25

Monty Python and the Holy Grail, 25th Anniv. — A364

No. 2232: a, Close-up of Eric Idle. b, Terry Jones, Graham Chapman and John Cleese as three-headed giant, horiz. c, Knights facing castle wall. d, Chapman as King Arthur, with helmeted knight. e, Beheaded knight. f, Armless and legless Black Knight and King Arthur.

2000, Aug. 7 *Perf. 13¾*
2232 A364 90c Sheet of 6, #a-f 4.00 4.00

Popes — A365

No. 2233: a, Clement X, 1670-76. b, Innocent X, 1644-55. c, Nicholas V, 1447-55. d, Martin V, 1417-31. e, Julius III, 1550-55. f, Innocent XII, 1691-1700.
$6, Clement XIV, 1796-74.
Illustration reduced.

2000, Sept. 5
2233 A365 $1.65 Sheet of 6, #a-f 7.25 7.25

Souvenir Sheet

2234 A365 $6 multi 4.50 4.50

Monarchs — A366

No. 2235: a, Edward IV of England, 1461-83. b, Peter the Great of Russia, 1682-1725. c, Henry VI of England, 1422-61. d, Henry III of England, 1216-72. e, Richard III of England, 1483-85. f, Edward I of England, 1272-1307.
$6, Henry VIII of England, 1509-47.
Illustration reduced.

2000, Sept. 5
2235 A366 $1.65 Sheet of 6, #a-f 7.25 7.25

Souvenir Sheet

2236 A366 $6 multi 4.50 4.50

World Stamp Expo 2000, Anaheim — A367

Spacecraft - No. 2237, $1.65: a, Explorer 14. b, Luna 16. c, Copernicus. d, Explorer 16. e, Luna 10. f, Arybhattan.

No. 2238, $1.65: a, Essa 8. b, Echo 1. c, Topex Poseidon. d, Diademe. e, Early Bird. f, Molnya.

#2239, $6, Hipparcos. #2240, $6, Eole.

Illustration reduced.

2000, June 21 Litho. *Perf. 14¼x14*

Sheets of 6, #a-f

2237-2238 A367 Set of 2 15.00 15.00

Souvenir Sheets

2239-2240 A367 Set of 2 9.00 9.00

David Copperfield, Magician — A368

2000, Aug. 8 *Perf. 14*

2241 A368 $2 multi 1.50 1.50

Printed in sheets of 4.

Souvenir Sheet

Female Recording Groups of the 1960s — A369

No. 2242 — The Crystals, yellow spotlight covering: a, UR, LL and LR corners. b, UL and LL corners. c, UR and LR corners. d, UL, LL and LR corners.

Illustration reduced.

2000, Aug. 8

2242 A369 90c Sheet of 4, #a-d 2.75 2.75

Christmas — A370

Angel: 25c, No. 2247a, Looking right, purple and yellow green background. 65c, No. 2247b, At left, looking left, purple background. 90c, No. 2247c, At right, purple and orange background. $5, No. 2247d, At center, blue and purple background.

2000, Dec. 4

2243-2246 A370 Set of 4 5.00 5.00

Sheet of 4

2247 A370 $1.90 #a-d 5.75 5.75

Souvenir Sheet

2248 A370 $6 Angel 4.50 4.50

Millennium Type of 1999

Chinese Art — No. 2249, 55c: a, Eight Prize Steeds, by Giuseppe Castiglione. b, Oleanders, by Wu Hsi Tsai. c, Mynah and Autumn Flowers, by Chang Hsiung. d, Hen and Chicks Beneath Chrysanthemums, by Chu Ch'ao. e, Long Living Pine and Crane, by Xugu. f, Flowers and Fruits, by Chu Lien. g, Lotus and Willow, by Pu Hua. h, Kuan-Yin, by Ch'ien Hui-An. i, Human Figures, by Jen hsun. j, Han-Shan and Shih-Te, by Ren Yi. k, Landscape and Human Figure, by Jen Yu. l, Poetic Thoughts While Walking With a Staff, by Wangchen. m, Peony, by Chen Heng-Ko. n, Plum and Orchids, by Wu Chang-Shih. o, Monkey, by Kao Chi-Feng. p, Grapes and Locust, by Ch'i Pai-Shih and Galloping Horse, by Xu Beihong (60x40mm). q, The Beauty, by Lin Fengmian.

History of Change — No. 2250, 55c: a, Star charts. b, Precision tools. c, Science of the stars. d, Investigation into healing a human being. e, Sharing of medical information. f, Church. g, Water alarm clock. h, Weighted clock. i, Spring-loaded miniature clock. j, New technology of glass blowing. k, First screws. l, Wood lathe. m, New systems for assembly blocks for ships. n, Interchangeable parts for rifles. o, Study of movement. p, Efficiency and the Industrial Revolution (60x40mm). q, Concept of effieciency.

Highlights of the 1960s — No. 2251, 55c: a, First birth control pill developed. b, Yuri Gagarin becomes first man in space. c, The first hit for the Beatles in Britain. d, Assassination of John F. Kennedy. e, Dr. Martin Luther King's "I Have a Dream" speech. f, Betty Friedan writes "The Feminine Mystique." g, Kenya gains independence. h, U.S. Surgeon General warns about smoking-related health hazards. i, U.S. Congress passes Civil Rights Act. j, U.S. increases military presence in South Viet Nam. k, Ernesto "Che" Guevara. l, First heart transplant. m, Israel wins Six-day War. n, Ho Chi Minh dies. o, First man on the Moon. p, Communists build wall to divide East and West Berlin (60x40mm). q, Woodstock rock concert.

Highlights of the late 14th Century — No. 2252: a, Minnesingers. b, Acampitzin, King of the Aztecs. c, Black Death eases. d, Giotto's campanile built. e, First French franc. f, Ming Dynasty in China. g, Tamerlane begins conquest of Asia. h, Triumph of Death painted by Francesco Traini. i, Robin Hood. j, Geoffrey Chaucer writes "The Canterbury Tales." k, Succession dispute in Japan. l, Jewish exodus from France. m, Temple of the Golden Pavilion built . n, Strasbourg Cathedral built. o, Alhambra Palace (60x40mm). p, Ife bronzes in Nigeria.

2000, Dec. 31 *Perf. 12¾x12½*

Sheets of 17, #a-q

2249-2251 A346 Set of 3 21.00 21.00
2252 A347 65c Sheet of 17, #a-h, j-p, 2 #i 8.25 8.25

Hummingbirds — A371

No. 2253, $1.25: a, Green-throated carib. b, Bee, on branch. c, Bee, in flight. d, Bahama woodstar. e, Antillean mango. f, Blue-headed.

No. 2254, $1.65: a, Eastern streamertail. b, Purple-throated carib. c, Vervain. d, Bahama woodstar. e, Puerto Rican emerald. f, Antillean crested.

No. 2255, $5, Feeders. No. 2256, $6, Hispaniolan.

Illustration reduced.

2000, Dec. 18 Litho. *Perf. 14*

Sheets of 6, #a-f

2253-2254 A371 Set of 2 13.00 13.00

Souvenir Sheets

2255-2256 A371 Set of 2 8.25 8.25

Misspellings abound on Nos. 2253-2254.

New Year 2001 (Year of the Snake) A372

2001, Jan. 2 *Perf. 12x12¼*

2257 A372 $1.20 multi .90 .90

Printed in sheets of 4.

Fauna A373

Designs: 15c, Puerto Rican crested toad. 20c, Axolotl. $1.90, Panamanian golden frog. $2.20, Manatee.

No. 2262, $1.45: a, St. Vincent parrot. b, Indigo macaw. c, Cock of the rock. d, Cuban solenodon. e, Cuban hutia. f, Chinchilla.

No. 2263, $1.45: a, South American flamingo. b, Golden conure. c, Ocelot. d, Giant armadillo. e, Margay. f, Maned wolf.

No. 2264, $6, Anteater. No. 2265, $6, Hawksbill turtle.

2000, Dec. 18 Litho. *Perf. 14*

2258-2261 A373 Set of 4 3.50 3.50

Sheets of 6, #a-f

2262-2263 A373 Set of 2 13.00 13.00

Souvenir Sheets

2264-2265 A373 Set of 2 9.00 9.00

Pokémon — A374

No. 2266, horiz.: a, Butterfree. b, Bulbasaur. c, Caterpie. d, Charmander. e, Squirtle. f, Pidgeotto.

2001, Feb. *Perf. 13¾*

2266 A374 $1.65 Sheet of 6, #a-f 7.50 7.50

Souvenir Sheet

2267 A374 $6 Nidoking 4.50 4.50

A375

Marine Life A376

Designs: No. 2268, 15c, Banded sea snake. 25c, Soldier fish. 55c, Banner fish. No. 2271, 90c, Crown of thorns starfish.

No. 2272, 15c, Fish. 65c, Ray. No. 2274, 90c, Octopus. $3, Fish, diff.

No. 2276, $1.65: a, White-tip reef shark, lionfish, sergeant major. b, Blue-striped snappers. c, Great hammerhead shark, stovepipe sponge, pink vase sponge. d, Hawaiian monk seal, blue tube coral. e, Seahorse, common clownfish, red feather star coral. f, Bat starfish, brown octopus.

No. 2277, $1.65: a, Red sponge, shoal of Anthias. b, Orange-striped triggerfish. c, Coral grouper, soft tree coral. d, Peacock fan worms, gorgonian sea fan. e, Sweetlips, sea fan. f, Giant clam, golden cup coral.

No. 2278: a, Shark. b, Starfish. c, Seahorse. d, Fish. e, Crab. f, Eel.

No. 2279, $5, Royal angelfish. No. 2280, $5, Pink anemone fish. No. 2281, Turtle.

2001, Feb. 27 *Perf. 14*

2268-2271 A375 Set of 4 1.40 1.40
2272-2275 A376 Set of 4 3.50 3.50

Sheets of 6, #a-f

2276-2277 A375 Set of 2 15.00 15.00
2278 A376 $2 Sheet of 6, #a-f 9.00 9.00

Souvenir Sheets

2279-2280 A375 Set of 2 7.50 7.50
2281 A376 $5 multi 3.75 3.75

DOMINICA 25¢

Phila Nippon '01, Japan — A377

Art: 25c, Gathering of Chinese Women, by Tsuji Kako. 55c, Village by Bamboo Grove, by Takeuchi Seiho. 65c, Mountain Village in Spring, by Suzuki Hyakunen. 90c, Gentleman Amusing Himself, by Domoto Insho. $1, Calmness of Spring Light, by Seiho. $2, Su's Embankment on a Spring Morning, by Tomioka Tessai.

No. 2288, $1.65: a, Thatched Cottages in the Willows, by Kako. b, Joy in the Garden, by Kako. c, Azalea and butterfly, by Kikuchi Hobun. d, Pine Grove, by Kako. e, Woodcutters Talking in Autumn Valley, by Kubota Beisen.

No. 2289, $1.65: a, Waterfowl in Snow, by Kako. b, Heron and Willow, by Kako. c, Crow and Cherry Blossoms, by Hobun. d, Chrysanthemum Immortal, by Yamamoto Shunkyo. e, Cranes of Immortality, by Kako.

No. 2290, $6, Kamo Riverbank in the Misty Rain, by Kako. No. 2291, $6, Diamond Gate, by Kako. No. 2292, $6, Woman, by Suzuki Harunobu.

2001, May 15 Litho. *Perf. 14*

2282-2287 A377 Set of 6 4.00 4.00

Sheets of 5, #a-e

2288-2289 A377 Set of 2 12.50 12.50

Souvenir Sheets

Perf. 13¾

2290-2292 A377 Set of 3 13.50 13.50

Nos. 2290-2292 each contain one 38x51mm stamp.

Queen Victoria (1819-1901) — A378

No. 2293: a, Prince Albert in uniform. b, Victoria with silver crown. c, Victoria with gold crown. d, Albert in suit.
$6, Victoria as old woman.

2001, May 15 ***Perf. 14***

2293 A378 $2 Sheet of 4, #a-d 6.00 6.00

Souvenir Sheet

Perf. 13¾

2294 A378 $6 multi 4.50 4.50

No. 2294 contains one 38x51mm stamp.

Queen Elizabeth II, 75th Birthday — A379

No. 2295: a, With crown. b, With white dress. c, Formal portrait by Pietro Annigoni. d, With orange coat. e, With child. f, With green dress.
$6, In uniform.

2001, May 15 ***Perf. 14***

2295 A379 $1.20 Sheet of 6, #a-f 5.50 5.50

Souvenir Sheet

2296 A379 $6 multi 4.50 4.50

Toulouse-Lautrec Paintings — A380

No. 2297: a, Two Women Waltzing. b, The Medical Inspection. c, The Two Girlfriends. d, Woman Pulling Up Her Stocking.

2001, May 15 **Litho.** ***Perf. 13¾***

2297 A380 $2 Sheet of 4, #a-d 6.00 6.00

Souvenir Sheet

2298 A380 $6 Self-portrait 4.50 4.50

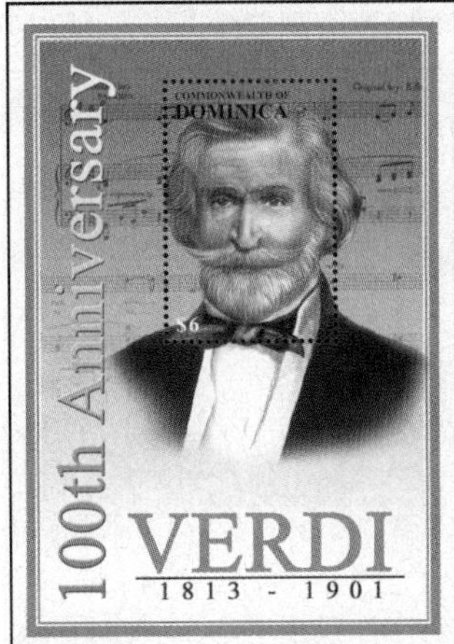

Giuseppe Verdi (1813-1901), Opera Composer — A381

No. 2299: a, Verdi. b, Lady Macbeth. c, Orchestra. d, Score.

2001, May 15 ***Perf. 14***

2299 A381 $2 Sheet of 4, #a-d 6.00 6.00

Souvenir Sheet

2300 A381 $6 Verdi, score 4.50 4.50

Mushrooms A382

Designs: 15c, Cantharellus cibarius. 25c, Hygrocybe pratensis. 55c, Leccinum aurantiacum. $3, Mycena haematopus.
No. 2305, 90c, horiz.: a, Caesar's amanita. b, Agaricus augustus. c, Clitocybe nuda. d, Hygrocybe plavescens. e, Stropharia kaufmanii. f, Hygrophorus speciosus.
No. 2306, $2: a, Marasmiellus candidus. b, Calostoma cinnabarina. c, Cantharellus infundibuliformis. d, Hygrocybe punicea. e, Basket stinkhorn. f, Agrocybe praecox.
No. 2307, $5, Fly agaric, horiz. No. 2308, $5, Gymnopilus spectabilis, horiz.

2001, June 18

2301-2304 A382 Set of 4 3.00 3.00

Sheets of 6, #a-f

2305-2306 A382 Set of 2 13.00 13.00

Souvenir Sheets

2307-2308 A382 Set of 2 7.50 7.50

Mao Zedong (1893-1976) — A383

No. 2309 - Picture from: a, 1945. b, 1926. c, 1949.
$3, 1930.

2001, May 15 **Litho.** ***Perf. 14***

2309 A383 $2 Sheet of 3, #a-c 4.50 4.50

Souvenir Sheet

2310 A383 $3 multi 2.25 2.25

Monet Paintings — A384

No. 2311, horiz.: a, The Basin of Argenteuil. b, The Bridge at Argenteuil. c, The Railway Bridge, Argenteuil. d, The Seine Bridge at Argenteuil.
$6, Woman with a Parasol - Madame Monet and Her Son.

2001, May 15 ***Perf. 13¾***

2311 A384 $2 Sheet of 4, #a-d 6.00 6.00

Souvenir Sheet

2312 A384 $6 multi 4.50 4.50

Fauna — A385

No. 2313: a, St. Vincent parrot. b, Painted bunting. c, Jamaican giant anole. d, White-fronted capuchin. e, Strand racerunner. f, Agouti.
No. 2314: a, Cook's tree boa. b, Tamandua. c, Common iguana. d, Solenodon.
No. 2315, $5, Purple gallinule. No. 2316, $5, Rufous-tailed jacamar. No. 2317, $5, Ruby-throated hummingbird, horiz. No. 2318, $5, Bottlenose dolphins, horiz.

2001, Sept. 3 ***Perf. 14***

2313 A385 $1.45 Sheet of 6, #a-f 6.50 6.50

2314 A385 $2 Sheet of 4, #a-d 6.00 6.00

Souvenir Sheets

2315-2318 A385 Set of 4 15.00 15.00

Birds — A386

Designs: 5c, Yellow warbler. 10c, Palmchat. 15c, Snowy cotinga. 20c, Blue-gray gnatcatcher. 25c, Belted kingfisher. 55c, Red-legged thrush. 65c, Bananaquit. 90c, Yellow-bellied sapsucker. $1, White-tailed tropicbird. $1.45, Ruby-throated hummingbird. $1.90, Painted bunting. $2, Great frigatebird. $5, Brown trembler. $10, Red-footed booby. $20, Sooty tern.

2001, Sept. 3 **Litho.** ***Perf. 14¾x14***

2319	A386	5c	multi	.20	.20
2320	A386	10c	multi	.20	.20
2321	A386	15c	multi	.20	.20
2322	A386	20c	multi	.20	.20
2323	A386	25c	multi	.20	.20
2324	A386	55c	multi	.40	.40
2325	A386	65c	multi	.45	.45
2326	A386	90c	multi	.65	.65
2327	A386	$1	multi	.75	.75
2328	A386	$1.45	multi	1.10	1.10
2329	A386	$1.90	multi	1.40	1.40
2330	A386	$2	multi	1.50	1.50
2331	A386	$5	multi	3.75	3.75
2332	A386	$10	multi	7.50	7.50
2333	A386	$20	multi	15.00	15.00
	Nos. 2319-2333 (15)			33.50	33.50

Photomosaic of Queen Elizabeth II — A387

2001, Nov. 15 ***Perf. 14***

2334 A387 $1 multi .75 .75

Issued in sheets of 8.

Christmas — A388

Paintings by Giovanni Bellini: 25c, Madonna and Child. 65c, Madonna and Child, diff. 90c, Baptism of Christ. $1.20, Madonna and Child, diff. $4, Madonna and Child, diff.
$6, Madonna and Child with Sts. Catherine and Mary Magdalene.

2001, Dec. 3

2335-2339 A388 Set of 5 5.25 5.25

Souvenir Sheet

2340 A388 $6 multi 4.50 4.50

2002 World Cup Soccer Championships, Japan and Korea — A389

No. 2341, $2: a, US team, 1950. b, Poster, 1954. c, Poster, 1958. d, Zozimo, 1962. e, Gordon Banks, 1966. f, Pelé, 1970.
No. 2342, $2: a, Daniel Passarella, 1978. b, Paolo Rossi, 1982. c, Diego Maradona, 1986. d, Poster, 1990. e, Seo Jungulon, 1994. f, Jürgen Klinsmann, 1998.
No. 2343, $5, Face on World Cup, 1930. No. 2344, $5, Face and globe on Jules Rimet Trophy, 2002.

2001, Dec. 13 ***Perf. 13¾x14¼***

Sheets of 6, #a-f

2341-2342 A389 Set of 2 18.00 18.00

Souvenir Sheets

Perf. 14¼

2343-2344 A389 Set of 2 7.50 7.50

Queen Mother Type of 1999 Redrawn

No. 2345: a, In 1939. b, In Australia, 1958. c, At Badminton, 1982. d, Hatless, in 1982.
$6, In 1953.

2001, Dec. ***Perf. 14***

Yellow Orange Frames

2345 A340 $2 Sheet of 4, #a-d, + label 6.00 6.00

Souvenir Sheet

Perf. 13¾

2346 A340 $6 multi 4.50 4.50

Queen Mother's 101st birthday. No. 2346 contains one 38x51mm stamp with a bluer backdrop than that found on No. 2161. Sheet margins of Nos. 2345-2346 lack embossing and gold arms and frames found on Nos. 2160-2161.

Souvenir Sheets

Betty Boop — A390

Betty Boop: No. 2347, $5, In chair, pink rose background. No. 2348, $5, Wearing blue blouse, in jungle. No. 2349, $5, With heart and stars, cat with film reel. No. 2350, $5, Wearing nurse's cap.

2001, Oct. 1 Litho. *Perf. 13¾*

2347-2350 A390 Set of 4 15.00 15.00

The Three Stooges — A391

No. 2351: a, Man, Larry, Moe with sledgehammer, Joe Besser. b, Larry, woman, Joe Besser, Moe. c, Joe Besser, Larry and Moe on hands and knees. d, Larry grabbing throat of woman holding Joe Besser and Moe. e, Joe Besser drinking from baby bottle, pony, Moe and Larry. f, Military policeman, Joe Besser, Larry, woman. g, Larry. h, Joe Besser. i, Moe.

No. 2352, $5, Moe and Larry, "On the air" sign. No. 2353, $5, Larry and pony.

2001, Oct. 1 Litho. *Perf. 13¾*

2351 A391 $1 Sheet of 9, #a-i 6.75 6.75

Souvenir Sheets

2352-2353 A391 Set of 2 7.50 7.50

Souvenir Sheet

New Year 2002 (Year of the Horse) — A392

No. 2354: a, Man with pole, horse. b, Horses grazing. c, Man currying horse. d, Horses with heads up.

2001, Dec. 17 *Perf. 14*

2354 A392 $1.65 Sheet of 4, #a-d 5.00 5.00

Reign of Queen Elizabeth II, 50th Anniv. — A393

No. 2355: a, Wearing blue coat. b, With Prince Philip. c, Wearing tiara. d, Wearing flowered hat.

$6, With Prince Philip, diff.

2002, Feb. 6 *Perf. 14¼*

2355 A393 $2 Sheet of 4, #a-d 6.00 6.00

Souvenir Sheet

2356 A393 $6 multi 4.50 4.50

United We Stand — A394

2002, Feb. *Perf. 13½x13¼*

2357 A394 $2 multi 1.50 1.50

Printed in sheets of 4.

Shirley Temple in "Just Around the Corner" — A395

No. 2358, horiz.: a, Temple, woman with dogs. b, Temple, man and woman. c, Temple and man. d, Boy eating turkey leg, Temple carving turkey. e, Temple with old man. f, Temple with group of boys.

No. 2359: a, Boy, Temple with purse. b, Man and Temple using fingers as guns. c, Temple and man. d, Temple cutting boy's hair.

$6, Temple with black man on toadstool.

2002, Apr. 8 *Perf. 12¼*

2358 A395 $1.90 Sheet of 6, #a-f 8.50 8.50

2359 A395 $2 Sheet of 4, #a-d 6.00 6.00

Souvenir Sheet

2360 A395 $6 multi 4.50 4.50

Japanese Art — A396

No. 2361, $1.20: a, The Courtesan Tsukioka of the Teahouse Hyogo-Ya, by Eisui Ichirakutei. b, Woman and Servant in the Snow, by Choki Eishosai. c, The Courtesan Shiratsuyu of the Teahouse Wakana-Ya, by Eisho Chokosai. d, Ohisa of the Takashima-Ya, by Toyokuni Utagawa. e, Woman and a Cat, by Kunimasa Utagawa. f, One of "Genre Scenes of Beauties," by Eisen Keisai.

No. 2362, $1.65: a, Women Inside and Outside a Mosquito Net, by Harushige Suzuki. b, Komachi at Shimizu, by Harushige Suzuki. c, Women Viewing Plum Blossoms, by Harunobu Suzuki. d, Women Cooling Themselves at Shijogawara in Kyoto, by Toyohiro Utagawa. e, Woman Reading a Letter, by Utamaro Kitagawa. f, Women Dressed for the Kashima Dance at the Niwaka Festival, by Utamaro Kitagawa.

No. 2363, $1.90: a, Actor Kiyotaro Iwai, by Kunimasa Utagawa. b, Actors Hiriji Otani III and Ryuzo Arashi, by Sharaku Toshusai. c, Actor Komazo Ichikawa II, by Shunko Katsukawa. d, Actors Yaozo Ichikawa and Hangoro Sakata III, by Sharaku Toshusai. e, Actor Torazo Tanimura, by Sharaku Toshusai. f, Actor Kiyotaro Iwai as Oishi, by Toyokuni Utagawa.

No. 2464, $5, Actor Riko Nakamura, by Shunsho Katsukawa. No. 2365, $5, Actors Hanshiro Iwai IV and Sojuro Sawamura III, by Kiyonaga Torii, horiz. No. 2366, $6, Ofuji, Daughter of the Motoyanagi-Ya, by Harunobu Suzuki.

2002, June 17 *Perf. 14¼*

Sheets of 6, #a-f

2361-2363 A396 Set of 3 21.00 21.00

Souvenir Sheets

2364-2366 A396 Set of 3 12.00 12.00

Souvenir Sheet

Intl. Year of Mountains — A397

No. 2367: a, Mt. Everest. b, Mt. Kilimanjaro. c, Mt. McKinley.

2002, July 15 *Perf. 14*

2367 A397 $2 Sheet of 3, #a-c 4.50 4.50

2002 Winter Olympics, Salt Lake City A398

Designs: No. 2368, $2, Skiing. No. 2369, $2, Bobsled.

2002, July 15 *Perf. 13½*

2368-2369 A398 Set of 2 3.00 3.00

a. Souvenir sheet, #2368-2369 3.00 3.00

First Solo Trans-Atlantic Flight, 75th Anniv. — A399

No. 2370: a, Charles Lindbergh and Spirit of St. Louis. b, Charles and Anne Morrow Lindbergh.

$6, Charles Lindbergh and Spirit of St. Louis, diff.

2002, July 15 *Perf. 14*

2370 A399 $3 Sheet of 2, #a-b 4.50 4.50

Souvenir Sheet

2371 A399 $6 multi 4.50 4.50

Popeye in New York — A400

No. 2372, $1: a, Olive Oyl. b, Brutus. c, Sweet Pea. d, Wimpy. e, Jeep. f, Popeye.

No. 2373, $1.90: a, Popeye and Olive Oyl, giraffe at Bronx Zoo. b, Popeye and Olive Oyl, Statue of Liberty. c, Popeye, Olive Oyl, Empire State Building. d, Popeye skating at Rockefeller Center. e, Popeye at Yankee Stadium. f, Popeye helping firefighters.

No. 2374, $6, Popeye, Atlas Statue, Rockefeller Center. No. 2375, $6, Popeye, Olive Oyl and Radio City Music Hall Rockettes, horiz.

2002, July 22

Sheets of 6, #a-f

2372-2373 A400 Set of 2 13.00 13.00

Souvenir Sheets

2374-2375 A400 Set of 2 9.00 9.00

20th World Scout Jamboree, Thailand — A401

No. 2376: a, Lord Robert Baden-Powell (facing forward). b, Lady Olave Baden-Powell. c, Maceo Johnson.
$6, Lord Baden-Powell (profile).

2002, July 15 Litho. *Perf. 14¼x14*

2376 A401 $3 Sheet of 3, #a-c 6.75 6.75

Souvenir Sheet

2377 A401 $6 multi 4.50 4.50

Birds, Insects, Moths and Whales — A402

No. 2378, $1.50, vert. — Birds: a, Brown trembler. b, Snowy ctinga. c, Bananaquit. d, Painted bunting. e, Belted kingfisher. f, Ruby-throated hummingbird.
No. 2379, $1.50, vert. — Insects: a, Field cricket. b, Migratory grasshopper. c, Honey bee. d, Hercules beetle. e, Black ant. f, Cicada.
No. 2380, $1.50, vert. — Moths: a, Carolina sphinx. b, White-lined sphinx. c, Orizaba silkmoth. d, Hieroglyphic moth. e, Hickory tussock moth. f, Diva moth.
No. 2381, $1.50, vert. — Whales: a, Sei. b, Killer. c, Blue. d, White. e, Pygmy. f, Sperm.
No. 2382, $6, Yellow-bellied sapsucker. No. 2383, $6, Bumble bee. No. 2384, $6, Ornate moth. No. 2385, $6, Gray whale.

2002, July 29 *Perf. 14*

Sheets of 6, #a-f

2378-2381 A402 Set of 4 27.50 27.50

Souvenir Sheets

2382-2385 A402 Set of 4 18.00 18.00

A403

A404

Amphilex 2002 Intl. Stamp Exhibition, Amsterdam — A405

No. 2386 — Dutch Nobel Prize winners: a, Willem Einthoven, Medicine, 1924. b, Nobel Economics medal. c, Peter J. W. Debye, Chemistry, 1936. d, Frits Zernike, Physics, 1953. e, Jan Tinbergen, Economics, 1969. f, Simon van der Meer, Physics, 1984.
No. 2387 — Dutch lighthouses: a, Marken. b, Harlingen. c, Den Oever. d, De Ven. e, Urk. f, Oosterleek.
No. 2388 — Traditional women's costumes: a, South Holland woman with small white head covering (facing forward). b, Zeeland woman with large white head covering (facing backwards). c, Limburg woman with black scarf.

2002, Aug. 30 *Perf. 13½x13¼*

2386 A403 $1.50 Sheet of 6, #a-f 6.75 6.75

2387 A404 $1.50 Sheet of 6, #a-f 6.75 6.75

Perf. 13½

2388 A405 $3 Sheet of 3, #a-c 6.75 6.75

Intl. Year of Ecotourism A406

Island scenes and cartoon characters: 45c, Detective H2O. 50c, Factman. 55c, B.B. 60c, Stanley the Starfish. 90c, Toxi. $1.20, Adopt. $6, Litterbit.

2002, Oct. 16 *Perf. 14¼*

2389-2394 A406 Set of 6 3.25 3.25

Souvenir Sheet

2395 A406 $6 multi 4.50 4.50

Elvis Presley (1935-77) A407

2002, Oct. 28 *Perf. 13¾*

2396 A407 $1.50 multi 1.10 1.10

Printed in sheets of 6 stamps with slightly differing frames.

Amerigo Vespucci (1454-1512), Explorer — A408

No. 2397: a, Compass rose. b, Vespucci with map. c, Map scroll.
$5, Two men.

2002, Nov. 28 *Perf. 13¾*

2397 A409 $3 Sheet of 3, #a-c 6.75 6.75

Souvenir Sheet

Perf. 14

2398 A409 $5 multi 3.75 3.75

No. 2397 contains three 50x38mm stamps.

Pres. John F. Kennedy (1917-63) — A409

No. 2399, $1.90: a, Wearing military uniform. b, With red denomination at UL. c, With blue denomination at UR. d, Wearing tan suit.
No. 2400, $1.90 (denominations at UL in blue): a, Wearing red tie. b, Wearing blue tie (profile). c, Wearing black tie. d, With hand on chin.

2002, Dec. 16 *Perf. 14*

Sheets of 4, #a-d

2399-2400 A409 Set of 2 11.50 11.50

Pres. Ronald Reagan — A410

No. 2401, $1.90: a, Wearing cowboy hat. b, Wearing blue green sweater. c, Wearing red sweater. d, Wearing blue sweater.
No. 2402, $1.90, horiz.: a, Wearing blue shirt, and with wife, Nancy. b, Nancy and US flag. c, Ronald. d, Wearing pink shirt, and with wife.

2002, Dec. 16 Litho. *Perf. 14*

Sheets of 4, #a-d

2401-2402 A410 Set of 2 11.50 11.50

Princess Diana (1961-97) — A411

2002, Dec. 16

2403 A411 $1.90 Sheet of 4, #a-d 5.75 5.75

Souvenir Sheet

2404 A411 $5 multi 3.75 3.75

Elizabeth "Ma Pampo" Israel, 128th Birthday — A412

2003, Jan. 27 *Perf. 13½x13¼*

2405 A412 90c multi .70 .70

New Year 2003 (Year of the Ram) — A413

2003, Feb. 10 *Perf. 13¾*

2406 A413 $1.65 multi 1.25 1.25

Printed in sheets of 4.

Souvenir Sheets

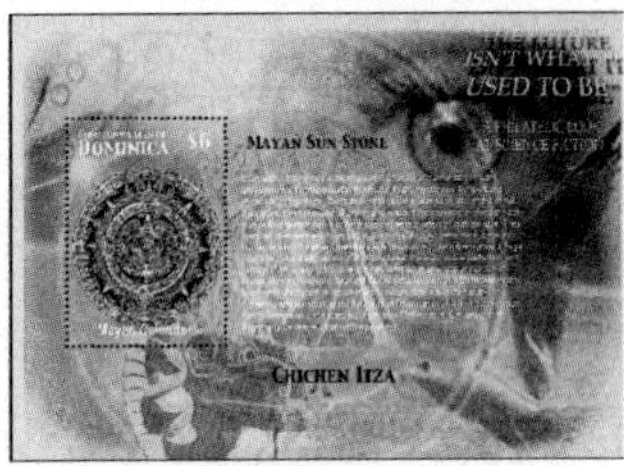

Science Fiction — A414

Designs: No. 2407, $6, Mayan calendar. No. 2408, $6, Atlas. No. 2409, $6, Confucius. No. 2410, $6, Nazca Lines. No. 2411, $6, Pres. Franklin D. Roosevelt and Pres. John F. Kennedy. No. 2412, $6, Zoroaster.

2003, Feb. 10 *Perf. 13¼*

2407-2412 A414 Set of 6 27.50 27.50

A415

Coronation of Queen Elizabeth II, 50th Anniv. — A416

No. 2413: a, Wearing white dress, no crown. b, Wearing black robe. c, Wearing crown.
$6, Wearing crown, diff. $20, Wearing red robe.

2003 Litho. *Perf. 14*
2413 A415 $3 Sheet of 3, #a-c 6.75 6.75

Souvenir Sheet

2414 A415 $6 multi 4.50 4.50

Miniature Sheet

Litho. & Embossed

Perf. 13¼x13

2415 A416 $20 gold & multi 15.00 15.00

Issued: Nos. 2413-2414, 5/13; No. 2415, 2/24.

Prince William, 21st Birthday — A417

No. 2416: a, Wearing dark blue shirt. b, Wearing blue suit, holding flowers. c, In polo uniform.
$6, Wearing black suit.

2003, June 21 Litho. *Perf. 14*
2416 A417 $3 Sheet of 3, #a-c 6.75 6.75

Souvenir Sheet

2417 A417 $6 multi 4.50 4.50

Intl. Year of Fresh Water — A418

No. 2418: a, Trafalgar Falls. b, YS Falls. c, Dunn's River.
$6, Annandale Falls.

2003, June 21 *Perf. 13½*
2418 A418 $3 Sheet of 3, #a-c 6.75 6.75

Souvenir Sheet

2419 A418 $6 multi 4.50 4.50

Teddy Bears, Cent. — A419

No. 2420 — Bear with: a, Purple shirt. b, Pink shirt and party favor. c, Green shirt and party favor. d, Black hat. e, Purple hat. f, Pink shirt and birthday cake.
No. 2421 — Bear with: a, Reindeer sweater, text at top. b, Santa Claus costume, text at top. c, Santa Claus costume, text at bottom. d, Reindeer sweater, text at bottom.

2003, June 21 *Perf. 13½*
2420 A419 $1.65 Sheet of 6, #a-f 7.50 7.50
2421 A419 $2 Sheet of 4, #a-d 6.00 6.00

No. 2421 contains four 37x51mm stamps.

General Motors Automobiles — A420

No. 2422, $2 — Cadillacs: a, 1903 Model A Runabout. b, 1912 Model 30. c, 1918 Type 57 Victoria Coupe. d, 1927 Lasalle Convertible Coupe.
No. 2423, $2 — Corvettes: a, 1953. b, 1956. c, 1957. d, 1962.
No. 2424, $5, 1933 Cadillac 355-C V8 sedan. No. 2425, $5, 1959 Corvette.

2003, June 21 *Perf. 13¼*

Sheets of 4, #a-d

2422-2423 A420 Set of 2 12.00 12.00

Souvenir Sheets

2424-2425 A420 Set of 2 7.50 7.50

Tour de France Bicycle Race, Cent. — A421

No. 2426 — Champions: a, Firmin Lambot, 1919. b, Phillippe Thys, 1920. c, Léon Scieur, 1921. d, Lambot, 1922.
$5, François Faber.

2003, June 21
2426 A421 $2 Sheet of 4, #a-d 6.00 6.00

Souvenir Sheet

2427 A421 $5 multi 3.75 3.75

History of Aviation — A422

No. 2428: a, Sputnik, first orbiting satellite, 1957. b, Yuri Gagarin, first man in space, 1961. c, Neil Armstrong, first man on the Moon, 1969. d, Skylab 1, 1973.
$6, Flight over Mt. Everest, 1933.

2003, June 21 *Perf. 14*
2428 A422 $2 Sheet of 4, #a-d 6.00 6.00

Souvenir Sheet

2429 A422 $6 multi 4.50 4.50

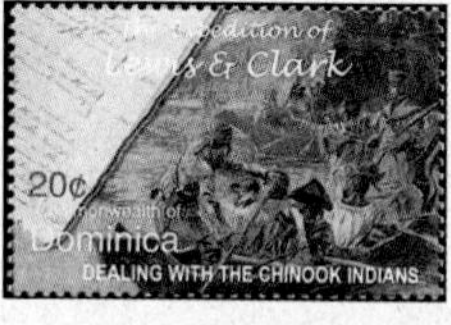

Lewis & Clark Expedition A423

Designs: 20c, Dealing with the Chinook Indians. 50c, Compass used in expedition. 55c, Rocky Mountains. 65c, Medals presented to the Indians, vert. 90c, First encounter with grizzly bear. $1, Befriending Shoshone Indians. $2, Lewis after the expedition, vert. $4, Lewis & Clark, vert.
No. 2438, $5, Meriwether Lewis, vert. No. 2439, $5, William Clark, vert.

2003, June 21
2430-2437 A423 Set of 8 7.50 7.50

Souvenir Sheets

2438-2439 A423 Set of 2 7.50 7.50

2002 World Cup Soccer Championships, Japan and Korea — A424

No. 2440, $1.45: a, Danny Mills. b, Paul Scholes. c, Darius Vassell. d, Michael Owen. e, Emile Heskey. f, Rio Ferdinand.
No. 2441, $1.45: a, Bobby Moore. b, Roger Hunt. c, Gordon Banks. d, Bobby Charlton. e, Alan Ball. f, Geoff Hurst.
No. 2442, $3: a, Ashley Cole. b, David Seaman.
No. 2443, $3: a, Sven-Goran Eriksson. b, Nikki Butt.
No. 2444, $3: a, Robbie Fowler. b, Sol Campbell.
No. 2445, $3: a, Charlton, Ball and Hunt. b, Nobby Stiles.
No. 2446, $3: a, Franz Beckenbauer. b, Oliver Kahn.

2003, June 21 *Perf. 13¼*

Sheets of 6, #a-f

2440-2441 A424 Set of 2 13.00 13.00

Souvenir Sheets of 2, #a-b

2442-2446 A424 Set of 5 22.50 22.50

CARICOM, 30th Anniv. — A425

2003, July 25 *Perf. 13½*
2447 A425 $1 multi .75 .75

Christmas A426

Painting details: 50c, Madonna and Child with the Young St. John, by Correggio. 90c, Madonna in Glory with the Christ Child and Sts. Frances and Alvise with the Donor, by Titian. $1.45, Madonna and Child with Angels Playing Musical Instruments, by Correggio. $3, Madonna of the Cherries, by Titian.
$6, Holy Family with John the Baptist, by Andrea del Sarto.

2003, Nov. 17 Litho. *Perf. 14¼*
2448-2451 A426 Set of 4 4.50 4.50

Souvenir Sheet

2452 A426 $6 multi 4.50 4.50

New Year 2004 (Year of the Monkey) — A427

No. 2453: a, Orange monkey, hindquarters of brown monkey. b, Monkey with brown face. c, Brown monkey drinking water. d, Monkey with blue face.

2004, Jan. 5 Litho. *Perf. 14*
2453 A427 $1.50 Sheet of 4, #a.-d. 4.50 4.50

Paintings of Pablo Picasso — A428

No. 2454, vert.: a, Portrait of Manuel Pallarés. b, Woman with Vase of Flowers. c, Woman with a Fan (Fernande). d, Portrait of Clovis Sagot.
$5, Brick Factory at Torosa (The Factory).

2004, Mar. 8 *Perf. 14¼*
2454 A428 $1 Sheet of 4, #a.-d. 3.00 3.00

Imperf

2455 A428 $5 multi 3.75 3.75

No. 2454 contains four 38x50mm stamps.

Paintings of Paul Gauguin — A429

No. 2456: a, Village Tahitien avec la Femme en Marche. b, La Barriere. c, Bonjour, Monsieur Gauguin. d, Vegetation Tropicale.
$5, Petites Bretonnes Devant la Mer. Illustration reduced.

2004, Mar. 8 *Perf. 14¼*
2456 A429 $2 Sheet of 4, #a.-d. 6.00 6.00

Imperf

2457 A429 $5 multi 3.75 3.75

No. 2456 contains four 38x50mm stamps.

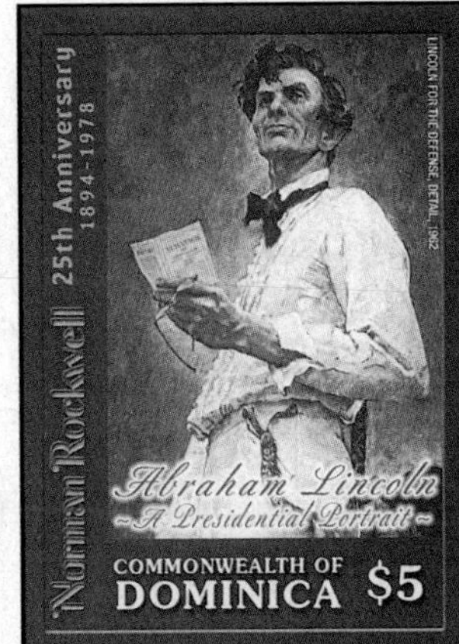

Paintings of Presidents by Norman Rockwell — A430

No. 2458: a, Dwight D. Eisenhower. b, John F. Kennedy. c, Lyndon B. Johnson. d, Richard M. Nixon.
$5, Abraham Lincoln.

2004, Mar. 8 *Perf. 14¼*
2458 A430 $2 Sheet of 4, #a.-d. 6.00 6.00

Imperf

2459 A430 $5 multi 3.75 3.75

No. 2458 contains four 38x50mm stamps.

Paintings of James McNeill Whistler — A431

Designs: 50c, Symphony in White No. 3. $1, The Artist's Studio, vert. $1.65, The Thames in Ice, vert. No. 2463, $2, Arrangement in Black: Portrait of F. R. Leyland, vert.
No. 2464, $2, vert.: a, Arrangement in Brown & Black: Portrait of Miss Rosa Corder. b, Harmony in Red: Lamplight. c, Symphony in Flesh Color & Pink: Portrait of Mrs. Frances Leyland. d, Arrangement in Yellow & Gray: Effie Deans.
$5, Harmony in Gray and Green: Miss Cicely Alexander, vert.

2004, Mar. 8 *Perf. 14¼*
2460-2463 A431 Set of 4 4.00 4.00

Perf. 13½

2464 A431 $2 Sheet of 4, #a-d 6.00 6.00

Imperf

Size: 71x103mm

2465 A431 $5 multi 3.75 3.75

No. 2464 contains four 35x70mm stamps.

Fish A432

Designs: 20c, Banded butterflyfish. 25c, Queen angelfish. 55c, Porkfish. No. 2469, $5, Redband parrotfish.
No. 2470: a, Beaugregory. b, Porkfish, diff. c, Bicolor cherubfish. d, Rock beauty. e, Blackfin snapper. f, Blue tang.
No. 2471, $5, Indigo hamlet.

2004, Mar. 8 *Perf. 14¼x14¾*
2466-2469 A432 Set of 4 4.50 4.50

Perf. 14

2470 A432 $2 Sheet of 6, #a-f 9.00 9.00

Souvenir Sheet

2471 A432 $5 multi 3.75 3.75

Nos. 2470-2471 each contain 42x28mm stamps.

Shells A433

Designs: 20c, Siratus perelegans. 90c, Polystira albida. $1.45, Cypraea cervus. $2, Strombus gallus.
No. 2476: a, Strombus pugilis. b, Cittarium pica. c, Distorsio clathrata. d, Melongena morio. e, Prunum labiata. f, Chione paphia.
$5, Strombus alatus, vert.

2004, Mar. 8 *Perf. 14¼x14¾*
2472-2475 A433 Set of 4 3.50 3.50

Perf. 14

2476 A433 $1.90 Sheet of 6, #a-f 8.50 8.50

Souvenir Sheet

2477 A433 $5 multi 3.75 3.75

No. 2476 contain six 42x28mm stamps; No. 2477 contains one 28x42mm stamp.

Orchids — A434

Designs: 25c, Epidendrum pseudepidendrum. 55c, Aspasia epidendroides. $1.50, Cochleanthes discolor. $4, Brassavola nodosa.
No. 2482: a, Laelia anceps. b, Caularthron bicornutum. c, Cattleya velutina. d, Cattleya warneri. e, Oncidium splendidum. f, Psychlis atropurpurea.
$5, Maxillaria cuculata, vert.

2004, Mar. 8 *Perf. 14¼x14¾*
2478-2481 A434 Set of 4 4.75 4.75

Perf. 14

2482 A434 $1.90 Sheet of 6, #a-f 8.50 8.50

Souvenir Sheet

2483 A434 $5 multi 3.75 3.75

No. 2482 contains six 42x28mm stamps; No. 2483 contains one 28x42mm stamp.

Butterflies — A435

Designs: 50c, Small flambeau. 90c, Tiger pierid. $1, White peacock. No. 2469, $2, Cramer's mesene.
No. 2488, $2: a, Figure-of-eight. b, Orange theope. c, Clorinde. d, Grecian shoemaker. e, Orange-barred sulphur. f, Common morpho.
$5, Giant swallowtail, vert.

2004, Mar. 8 *Perf. 14¼x14¾*
2484-2487 A435 Set of 4 3.25 3.25

Perf. 14

2488 A435 $2 Sheet of 6, #a-f 9.00 9.00

Souvenir Sheets

2489 A435 $5 multi 3.75 3.75

No. 2488 contains six 42x28mm stamps; No. 2489 contains one 28x42mm stamp.

Olympic Gold Medalists A436

Designs: 20c, Elizabeth Robinson, Amsterdam, 1928. 25c, Károly Takács, London, 1948. 55c, Bob Beamon, Mexico City, 1968. 65c, Mildred Didrikson, Los Angeles, 1932. $1, Ville Ritola, Paris, 1924. $1.65, Alfred Hajós (Guttman), Athens, 1896. $2, Paavo Nurmi, Antwerp, 1920. $4, Nedo Nadi, Antwerp, 1920.

2004, Apr. 12 *Perf. 13¼*
2490-2497 A436 Set of 8 7.75 7.75

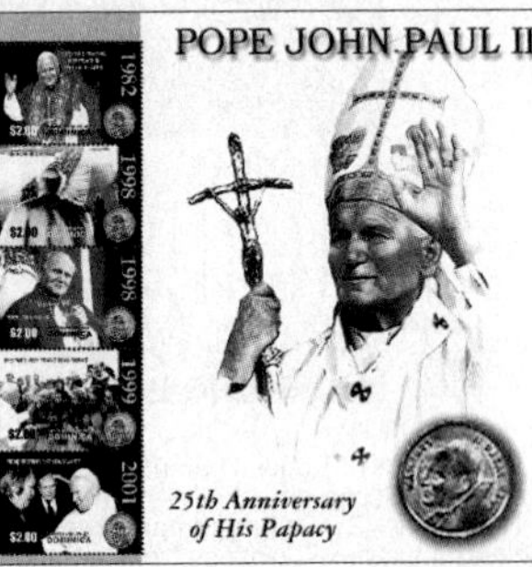

Election of Pope John Paul II, 25th Anniv. (in 2003) — A437

No. 2498: a, Praying for peace in Falkland Islands, 1982. b, In Croatia, 1998. c, Seated, 1998. d, With Franciscan monks, 1999. e, Remembering the Holocaust, 2001.

2004, June 21 Litho. *Perf. 14*
2498 A437 $2 Sheet of 5, #a-e 7.50 7.50

European Soccer Championships, Portugal — A438

No. 2499, vert.: a, Jose Luis Villalonga. b, Lev Yashin. c, Marcelino Martinez. d, Santiago Bernabeu Stadium.
$6, 1964 Spain team.

2004, June 21 *Perf. 14*
2499 A438 $2 Sheet of 4, #a-d 6.00 6.00

Souvenir Sheet

Perf. 14¼

2500 A438 $6 multi 4.50 4.50

No. 2499 contains four 28x42mm stamps.

Trains — A439

No. 2501, $1: a, Engine #22, V7 T4-4-0, V7T4-6-0. b, Don J12. c, Baldwin 2-D-D. d, Southern Engine #20. e, 143-890 2DB class electric locomotive. f, Engine #1.

No. 2502, $1: a, Canadian Pacific freight train. b, Queensland Rail IM U railroad. c, Green and white Shinkansen locomotive. d, Amtrak locomotive. e, Shinkansen locomotive in station. f, YPDMU rail cars.

No. 2503, $1: a, Santa Fe Railroad locomotive. b, Via Rail train, Canada. c, Two Conrail road switchers. d, Strasburg Railroad #90. e, Deltic diesel-electric engine. f, Brighton Belle.

No. 2504, $6, Golsdorf two cylinder compound locomotive 4-4-0. No. 2505, $6, Southern Pacific 4449 4-8-4. No. 2506, $6, White, yellow and blue Shinkansen.

2004, July 12 ***Perf. 13¼x13½***

Sheets of 6, #a-f

2501-2503 A439 Set of 3 13.50 13.50

Souvenir Sheets

2504-2506 A439 Set of 3 13.50 13.50

D-Day, 60th Anniv. A440

Designs: $1, Eddie Hannath. $4, Pres. Franklin D. Roosevelt.

No. 2509: a, Rangers make their way towards the cliffs of Pointe du Hoc. b, Rangers begin scaling the cliffs of Pointe du Hoc. c, British troops advance on Sword Beach. d, An AVRE Petard heads inland off Sword Beach.

$6, British troops landing on Sword Beach.

2004, July 22 ***Perf. 14***

Stamp + Label (#2507-2508)

2507-2508 A440 Set of 2 3.75 3.75
2509 A440 $2 Sheet of 4, #a-d 6.00 6.00

Souvenir Sheet

2510 A440 $6 multi 4.50 4.50

George Herman "Babe" Ruth (1895-1948), Baseball Player — A441

No. 2511: a, Swinging bat. b, Swinging bat, looking up. c, Holding three bats. d, Hand on knee.

2004, Aug. 18 ***Perf. 13½x13¼***

2511 A441 $2 Sheet of 4, #a-d 6.00 6.00

Marilyn Monroe (1926-62), Actress — A442

No. 2512: a, Wearing earrings and necklace. b, Wearing earrings. c, Wearing no earrings or necklace. d, Wearing necklace.

2004, Aug. 18

2512 A442 $2 Sheet of 4, #a-d 6.00 6.00

Bird Type of 2001

2004, Sept. 3 ***Perf. 14¾x14***

2513 A386 50c Baltimore oriole .40 .40

Queen Juliana of the Netherlands (1909-2004) A443

2004, Sept. 21 ***Perf. 13¼***

2514 A443 $2 multi 1.50 1.50

Printed in sheets of 6.

Intl. Year of Peace — A444

No. 2515: a, Mother Teresa, UN emblem. b, Mother Teresa feeding poor. c, Dove.

2004, Sept. 21 ***Perf. 14***

2515 A444 $2 Sheet of 3, #a-c 4.50 4.50

Souvenir Sheet

Deng Xiaoping (1904-97) and Mao Zedong (1893-1976), Chinese Leaders — A445

2004, Sept. 21 ***Perf. 14***

2516 A445 $6 multi 4.50 4.50

WAR TAX STAMPS

No. 50 Surcharged in Red

1916 **Wmk. 3** ***Perf. 14***

MR1 A6 ½p on ½p green .80 *.80*

No. 50 Overprinted in Black

1918

MR2 A6 ½p green 3.25 *6.75*

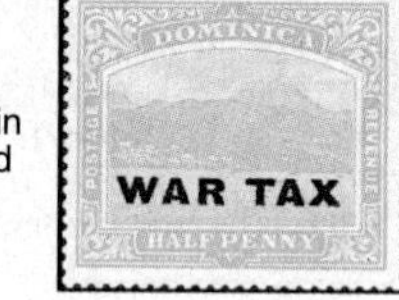

Nos. 50, 40 in Black or Red

1918

MR3 A6 ½p green .20 *.55*
MR4 A6 3p violet, *yel* (R) 1.60 *4.50*

Type of 1908-09 Surcharged in Red

1919

MR5 A6 1½p on 2½p orange .20 *.60*

DOMINICAN REPUBLIC

də-'mi-ni-kən ri-'pə-blik

LOCATION — Comprises about two-thirds of the island of Hispaniola in the West Indies
GOVT. — Republic
AREA — 18,700 sq. mi.
POP. — 8,129,734 (1999 est.)
CAPITAL — Santo Domingo

8 Reales = 1 Peso
100 Centavos = 1 Peso (1880)
100 Centimos = 1 Franco (1883)
100 Centavos = 1 Peso (1885)

Catalogue values for unused stamps in this country are for Never Hinged items, beginning with Scott 437 in the regular postage section, Scott B1 in the semi-postal section, Scott C75 in the airpost section, Scott CB1 in the airpost semi-postal section, Scott E7 in the special delivery section, Scott G13 in the insured letter section, Scott J14 in the postage due section, Scott O26 in the officials section, and Scott RA20 in the postal tax section.

Watermarks

Wmk. 115 — Diamonds

Wmk. 116 — Crosses and Circles

Coat of Arms
A1 A2

1865 **Unwmk.** **Typo.** ***Imperf.***

Wove Paper

1 A1 ½r black, *rose* 600. 600.
2 A1 1r black, *dp green* 950. 950.

Twelve varieties of each.

Laid Paper

3 A2 ½r black, *pale green* 525. 475.
4 A2 1r black, *straw* 1,700. 1,100.

Twelve varieties of the ½r, ten of the 1r.

A3

A4

1866 **Laid Paper** **Unwmk.**

5 A3 ½r black, *straw* 175. 150.
6 A3 1r black, *pale green* 775. 775.
7 A4 1r black, *pale green* 150. 125.

Nos. 5-8 have 21 varieties (sheets of 21).

Wmk. 115

8 A3 1r black, *pale green* 7,000. 7,000.

1866-67 **Wove Paper** **Unwmk.**

9 A3 ½r black, *rose* ('67) 47.50 47.50
10 A3 1r blk, *pale green* 85.00 75.00
a. Inscription dbl., top & bottom *400.00* *400.00*
11 A3 1r black, *blue* ('67) 40.00 30.00
a. 1r black, *light blue* ('67) 40.00 30.00
b. No space btwn. "Un" and "real" 225.00 200.00
c. Without inscription at top & bottom 400.00 200.00
d. Inscription invtd., top & bottom
Nos. 9-11 (3) 172.50 152.50

1867-71

Pelure Paper

13 A3 ½r black, *rose* 100.00 75.00
15 A3 ½r black, *lav* ('68) 210.00 210.00
a. Without inscription at top and bottom 525.00
b. Dbl. inscriptions, one invtd. *425.00*
16 A3 ½r black, *grnsh gray* ('68) 225.00 225.00
18 A3 ½r black, *ol* ('69) 2,500. 2,500.
23 A3 1r black, *lavender* 225.00 200.00
24 A4 1r black, *rose* ('68) 225.00 225.00
25 A4 1r black, *mag* ('69) 1,300. 1,300.
26 A4 1r black, *sal* ('71) 225.00 225.00

1870-73

Ordinary Paper

27 A3 ½r black, *magenta* 1,000. 1,000.
28 A3 ½r blue, *rose* (blk inscription) ('71) 50.00 42.50
a. Blue inscription 500.00 500.00
b. Without inscription at top and bottom
29 A3 ½r black, *yel* ('73) 30.00 21.00
a. Without inscription at top and bottom 375.00 375.00
30 A4 1r black, *vio* ('73) 30.00 21.00
a. Without inscription at top and bottom 700.00 700.00
31 A4 1r black, *dk grn* 60.00 50.00

Nos. 9-31 have 21 varieties (sheets of 21). Nos. 29 and 30 are known pin-perforated, unofficially.

Bisects are known of several of the early 1r stamps.

A5

A6

1879 *Perf. 12½x13*

32 A5 ½r violet 2.50 1.50
a. Imperf., pair 9.00 9.00
b. Horiz. pair, imperf. vert. 17.00
33 A5 ½r violet, *bluish* 2.50 1.50
a. Imperf., pair 9.00 7.50
34 A5 1r carmine 3.50 1.50
a. Imperf., pair 11.50 9.00
b. Perf. 13 11.50 7.50
c. Perf. 13x12½ 11.50 7.50
35 A5 1r carmine, *sal* 2.50 1.50
a. Imperf., pair 8.25 8.25
Nos. 32-35 (4) 11.00 6.00

In 1891 15 stamps of 1879-83 were surcharged "U P U," new values and crossed diagonal lines.

1880 Typo. ***Rouletted in Color***

36 A6 1c green 1.25 .90
b. Laid paper 50.00 50.00
37 A6 2c red 1.00 .75
a. Pelure paper 40.00 40.00
b. Laid paper 40.00 40.00
38 A6 5c blue 1.25 .60
39 A6 10c rose 3.25 .90
40 A6 20c brown 2.00 .75
41 A6 25c violet 2.25 1.10
42 A6 50c orange 2.50 1.50
43 A6 75c ultra 5.00 2.50
a. Laid paper 40.00 40.00
44 A6 1p gold 6.50 4.00
a. Laid paper 50.00 50.00
b. Double impression 42.50 42.50
Nos. 36-44 (9) 25.00 13.00

1881

Network Covering Stamp

45 A6 1c green .90 .45
46 A6 2c red .90 .45
47 A6 5c blue 1.25 .45
48 A6 10c rose 1.50 .60
49 A6 20c brown 1.50 .80
50 A6 25c violet 1.75 .90
51 A6 50c orange 2.00 1.25
52 A6 75c ultra 6.00 4.00
53 A6 1p gold 8.00 6.50
Nos. 45-53 (9) 23.80 15.40

Preceding Issues (Type A6) Surch. with Value in New Currency:

5 céntimos.
a

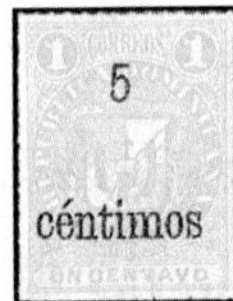
5 céntimos
b

5 céntimos.
c

1 franco.
d

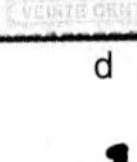

1 Franco.
e

1 franco
f

1 franco, 25 céntimos.
g

5 francos
h

5 francos.
i

1883

Without Network

54 (a) 5c on 1c green 1.40 1.50
b. Inverted surcharge 21.00 21.00
c. Surcharged "25 céntimos" 50.00 50.00
d. Surcharged "10 céntimos" 27.50 27.50
55 (b) 5c on 1c green 25.00 9.00
b. Double surcharge 100.00
c. Inverted surcharge 65.00 65.00
56 (c) 5c on 1c green 17.00 9.50
b. Surcharged "10 céntimos" 35.00 35.00
c. Surcharged "25 céntimos" 37.50 37.50
57 (a) 10c on 2c red 5.00 3.00
a. Inverted surcharge 27.50 27.50
d. Surcharged "5 céntimos" 52.50 52.50
e. Surcharged "25 céntimos" 75.00 75.00
58 (c) 10c on 2c red 4.50 3.50
a. "Céntimso"
b. Inverted surcharge 37.50 37.50
c. Surcharged "25 céntimos" 60.00 60.00
d. "10" omitted 60.00
59 (a) 25c on 5c blue 6.50 4.00
a. Surcharged "5 céntimos" 52.50
b. Surcharged "10 céntimos" 52.50 52.50
c. Surcharged "50 céntimos" 75.00 75.00
d. Inverted surcharge 50.00 50.00
60 (c) 25c on 5c blue 7.50 3.50
a. Inverted surcharge 45.00 37.50
b. Surcharged "10 céntimos" 45.00 37.50
e. "25" omitted 75.00
f. Surcharged on back 75.00
61 (a) 50c on 10c rose 25.00 11.50
a. Inverted surcharge 50.00 45.00
62 (c) 50c on 10c rose 35.00 17.50
a. Inverted surcharge 52.50 52.50
63 (d) 1fr on 20c brown 15.00 9.75
64 (e) 1fr on 20c brown 17.50 9.75
a. Comma after "Franco," 27.50 27.50
65 (f) 1fr on 20c brown 25.00 17.50
a. Inverted surcharge 75.00
66 (g) 1fr25c on 25c violet 21.00 15.00
a. Inverted surcharge 65.00 65.00
67 (g) 2fr50c on 50c orange 15.00 10.50
a. Inverted surcharge 35.00 27.50
68 (g) 3fr75c on 75c ultra 27.50 25.00
b. Inverted surcharge 60.00 60.00
c. Laid paper 75.00 75.00
70 (i) 5fr on 1p gold 550.00 500.00
a. "s" of "francos" inverted 700.00 700.00

With Network

71 (a) 5c on 1c green 3.00 2.50
b. Inverted surcharge 22.50 22.50
c. Double surcharge 22.50 22.50
d. Surcharged "25 céntimos" 42.50 42.50
e. "5" omitted 75.00 75.00
72 (b) 5c on 1c green 21.00 9.00
b. Inverted surcharge 60.00 60.00
73 (c) 5c on 1c green 27.50 11.50
b. Surcharged "10 céntimos" 50.00 42.50
c. Surcharged "25 céntimos" 60.00
74 (a) 10c on 2c red 3.75 2.25
a. Surcharged "5 céntimos" 52.50 45.00
b. Surcharged "25 céntimos" 67.50 67.50
c. "10" omitted 57.50
75 (c) 10c on 2c red 3.00 2.00
a. Inverted surcharge 30.00 17.00
76 (a) 25c on 5c blue 7.50 3.50
a. Surcharged "10 céntimos" 75.00
b. Surcharged "5 céntimos" 60.00
c. Surcharged "50 céntimos" 67.50
77 (c) 25c on 5c blue 60.00 30.00
a. Inverted surcharge
b. Surcharged on back
78 (a) 50c on 10c rose 25.00 7.50
a. Inverted surcharge 50.00 30.00
b. Surcharged "25 céntimos" 60.00
79 (c) 50c on 10c rose 30.00 9.50
a. Inverted surcharge 60.00
80 (d) 1fr on 20c brown 12.00 9.75
81 (e) 1fr on 20c brown 14.50 12.50
a. Comma after "Franco" 35.00 35.00
b. Inverted surcharge 75.00
82 (f) 1fr on 20c brown 25.00 20.00
83 (g) 1fr25c on 25c violet 45.00 30.00
a. Inverted surcharge 75.00
84 (g) 2fr50c on 50c orange 19.00 12.50
a. Inverted surcharge 35.00 27.50
85 (g) 3fr75c on 75c ultra 45.00 42.50
86 (h) 5fr on 1p gold 140.00 140.00
a. Inverted surcharge
87 (i) 5fr on 1p gold 190.00 190.00

Many minor varieties exist in Nos. 54-87: accent on "i" of "centimos"; "5" with straight top; "1" with straight serif.

A7

A7a

1885-91 Engr. ***Perf. 12***

88 A7 1c green .90 .45
89 A7 2c vermilion .90 .45
90 A7 5c blue 1.25 .45
91 A7a 10c orange 2.00 .60
92 A7a 20c dark brown 2.00 .75
93 A7a 50c violet ('91) 7.00 6.00
94 A7 1p carmine ('91) 18.00 12.00
95 A7 2p red brown ('91) 22.50 14.00
Nos. 88-95 (8) 54.55 34.70

Nos. 93, 94, 95 were issued without gum.
Imperf. varieties are proofs.
For surcharges see Nos. 166-168.

Coat of Arms — A8

1895 ***Perf. 12½x14***

96 A8 1c green 1.10 .45
97 A8 2c orange red 1.10 .45
98 A8 5c blue 1.10 .45
99 A8 10c orange 2.25 1.40
Nos. 96-99 (4) 5.55 2.75

Exist imperforate but were not issued.

1897 ***Perf. 14***

96a A8 1c green 1.40 .50
97a A8 2c orange red 8.00 .75
98a A8 5c blue 1.40 .75
99a A8 10c orange 2.75 1.50
Nos. 96a-99a (4) 13.55 3.50

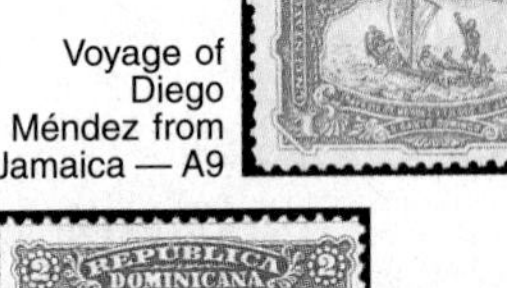
Voyage of Diego Méndez from Jamaica — A9

Enriquillo's Revolt — A10

Sarcophagus of Columbus A11

"Española" Guarding Remains of Columbus A12

Toscanelli Replying to Columbus A13

Bartolomé de las Casas Defending Indians — A14

Columbus at Salamanca A15

Columbus' Mausoleum A16

1899, Feb. 27 Litho. ***Perf. 11½***

100 A9 1c brown violet 5.00 4.00
102 A10 2c rose red 1.75 .70
103 A11 5c blue 2.00 .70
104 A12 10c orange 4.25 1.25
a. Tête bêche pair 42.50 42.50
105 A13 20c brown 6.50 5.00
106 A14 50c yellow green 8.00 6.00
a. Tête bêche pair 57.50 57.50
107 A15 1p black, *gray bl* 20.00 15.00
108 A16 2p bister brown 37.50 37.50

1900, Jan.

109 A11 ¼c black .70 *1.25*
110 A15 ½c black .70 *1.25*
110A A9 1c gray green .70 .50
Nos. 100-110A (11) 87.10 73.15

Nos. 100-110A were issued to raise funds for a Columbus mausoleum.

Imperf., Pairs

100a A9 1c brown violet 15.00
102a A10 2c rose red 5.00
103a A11 5c blue 5.75
104b A12 10c orange 8.75
105a A13 20c brown 15.00
106b A14 50c yellow green 17.50
c. As "b," tête bêche pair 125.00
107a A15 1p black, *gray blue* 42.50
108a A16 2p bister brown 70.00
109a A11 ¼c black 2.10 *2.50*
110b A15 ½c black 2.10 *2.50*
110c A9 1c gray green 3.50

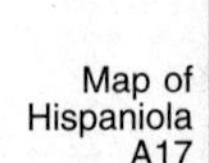

Map of Hispaniola A17

A18

1900, Oct. 21 Unwmk. ***Perf. 14***

111 A17 ¼c dark blue .65 .40
112 A17 ½c rose .65 .40
113 A17 1c olive green .65 .40
114 A17 2c deep green .65 .40
115 A17 5c red brown .65 .40
a. Vertical pair, imperf. between 17.50

Perf. 12

116 A17 10c orange .65 .40
117 A17 20c lilac 2.75 2.10
a. 20c rose (error) 5.75 5.75
118 A17 50c black 2.50 2.25
119 A17 1p brown 2.75 2.25
Nos. 111-119 (9) 11.90 9.00

Several varieties in design are known in this issue. They were deliberately made. Counterfeits of Nos. 111-119 abound.

1901-06 Typo. ***Perf. 14***

120 A18 ½c carmine & vio .65 .35
121 A18 ½c blk & org ('05) 1.50 .85
122 A18 ½c grn & blk ('06) .80 .30
123 A18 1c ol grn & vio .65 .20
124 A18 1c blk & ultra ('05) 1.50 .70
125 A18 1c car & blk ('06) 1.00 .45
126 A18 2c dp grn & vio .70 .20
127 A18 2c blk & vio ('05) 2.00 .60
128 A18 2c org brn & blk ('06) 1.00 .20
129 A18 5c org brn & vio .75 .25
130 A18 5c black & cl ('05) 2.25 1.00
131 A18 5c blue & blk ('06) 1.25 .30
132 A18 10c orange & vio 1.25 .35
133 A18 10c blk & grn ('05) 3.75 2.00
134 A18 10c red vio & blk ('06) 1.25 .35
135 A18 20c brn vio & vio 2.25 .70
136 A18 20c blk & ol ('05) 11.50 7.50
137 A18 20c ol grn & blk ('06) 6.50 2.50
138 A18 50c gray blk & vio 7.00 5.00
139 A18 50c blk & red brn ('05) 40.00 30.00
140 A18 50c brn & blk ('06) 7.50 7.00
141 A18 1p brn & vio 16.00 9.50
142 A18 1p blk & gray ('05) 175.00 *200.00*
143 A18 1p violet & blk ('06) 17.50 12.00
Nos. 120-143 (24) 303.55 282.30

Issued: 11/15/01; 5/11/05; 8/17/06.
See #172-176. For surcharges see #151-156.

Francisco Sánchez — A19

Juan Pablo Duarte — A20

Ramón Mella — A21

Ft. Santo Domingo — A22

1902, Feb. 25 Engr. *Perf. 12*

144 A19 1c dk green & blk .25 .25
145 A20 2c scarlet & blk .25 .25
146 A20 5c blue & blk .25 .25
147 A19 10c orange & blk .25 .25
148 A21 12c purple & blk .25 .25
149 A21 20c rose & blk .35 .35
150 A22 50c brown & blk .50 .50
Nos. 144-150 (7) 2.10 2.10

Center Inverted

144a A19 1c 5.00 3.50
145a A20 2c 5.00 3.50
146a A20 5c 5.00 3.50
148a A21 12c 5.00 3.50
149a A21 20c 5.00 3.50
150a A22 50c 5.00 3.50
Nos. 144a-150a (6) 30.00 21.00

400th anniversary of Santo Domingo.
Imperforate varieties of Nos. 144 to 150 were never sold to the public.

Nos. 138, 141 Surcharged in Black

1904, Aug.

151 A18 2c on 50c 7.00 6.00
152 A18 2c on 1p 10.50 7.00
b. "2" omitted 50.00 50.00
153 A18 5c on 50c 3.75 2.10
154 A18 5c on 1p 4.00 3.50
155 A18 10c on 50c 7.00 6.50
156 A18 10c on 1p 7.00 6.50
Nos. 151-156 (6) 39.25 31.60

Inverted Surcharge

151a A18 2c on 50c 14.00 14.00
152a A18 2c on 1p 14.00 14.00
c. As "a," "2" omitted 80.00 80.00
153a A18 5c on 50c 5.00 3.50
154a A18 5c on 1p 7.00 6.50
155a A18 10c on 50c 14.00 14.00
156a A18 10c on 1p 10.00 10.00
Nos. 151a-156a (6) 64.00 62.00

Official Stamps of 1902 Overprinted

Red Overprint

1904, Aug. 16

157 O1 5c dk blue & blk 5.00 2.75
a. Inverted overprint 6.50 5.50

Black Overprint

158 O1 2c scarlet & blk 12.50 4.00
a. Inverted overprint 15.00 5.00
159 O1 5c dk blue & blk 3,500. 3,500.
160 O1 10c yellow grn & blk 9.25 9.00
a. Inverted overprint 12.50 12.50

Surcharged

161 O1 1c on 20c yellow & blk 4.00 2.75
a. Inverted surcharge 6.50 5.00

Nos. J1-J2 Surcharged or Overprinted

Surcharged "CENTAVOS"

1904-05

Black Surcharge

162 D1 1c on 2c olive gray 100.00 100.00
a. "entavos"
b. "Dominican" 200.00 200.00
c. "Centavo" 200.00 200.00

Carmine Surcharge or Overprint

163 D1 1c on 2c olive gray 2.25 1.00
a. Inverted surcharge 3.50 2.50
b. "Domihicana" 15.00 15.00
c. As "b," inverted 40.00 40.00
d. "Dominican" 10.50 10.50
e. "Centavos" omitted 30.00 30.00
g. "entavos" 30.00
163F D1 1c on 4c olive gray 35.00 7.00
164 D1 2c olive gray .80 .50
a. "Domihicana" 11.00 11.00
b. Inverted overprint 1.90 1.90
c. As "a," inverted 25.00 25.00
d. "Dominican" 5.75 5.75
e. "Centavo" omitted 12.50 10.00
f. "entavos" 12.50 12.50
g. As "f," inverted 40.00 40.00
h. As "d," inverted 40.00 40.00

Surcharged "CENTAVO"

165 D1 1c on 4c olive gray .80 .65
a. "Domihicana" 10.00 10.00
c. Inverted surcharge 1.75 1.75
d. "1" omitted 3.50 3.50
e. As "a," inverted 32.50 32.50
f. As "d," inverted 40.00 40.00
g. Double surcharge 30.00 30.00

No. 92 Surcharged in Red

1905, Apr. 4

166 A7a 2c on 20c dk brown 7.00 5.00
a. Inverted surcharge 15.00 15.00
167 A7a 5c on 20c dk brown 4.00 1.75
a. Inverted surcharge 16.00 16.00
b. Double surcharge 25.00 25.00
168 A7a 10c on 20c dk brown 7.00 5.00
Nos. 166-168 (3) 18.00 11.75

Nos. 166-168 exist with inverted "A" for "V" in "CENTAVOS" in surcharge.

Nos. J2, J4, J3 Surcharged:

REPUBLICA DOMINICANA. UN centavo.

REPUBLICA DOMINICANA. DOS centavos.

1906, Jan. 16 *Perf. 14*

Red Surcharge

169 D1 1c on 4c olive gray .85 .50
a. Inverted surcharge 10.50 10.50
b. Double surcharge 25.00

1906, May 1

Black Surcharge

170 D1 1c on 10c olive gray 1.00 .40
a. Inverted surcharge 10.50 10.50
b. Double surcharge 14.00 14.00
c. "OMINICANA" 20.00 20.00
d. As "c," inverted 150.00
171 D1 2c on 5c olive gray 1.00 .40
a. Inverted surcharge 10.50 10.50
b. Double surcharge 35.00

The varieties small "C" or small "A" in "REPUBLICA" are found on #169, 170, 171.

Arms Type of 1901-06

1907-10 Wmk. 116

172 A18 ½c grn & blk ('08) .75 .20
173 A18 1c carmine & blk .75 .20
174 A18 2c orange brn & blk .75 .20
175 A18 5c blue & blk .75 .25
176 A18 10c red vio & blk ('10) 8.00 1.00
Nos. 172-176 (5) 11.00 1.85

No. O6 Overprinted in Red

1911, July 11 *Perf. 13½x14, 13½x13*

177 O2 2c scarlet & black 1.25 .50
a. "HABILITAOO" 8.75 6.00
b. Inverted overprint 21.00
c. Double overprint 21.00

A23

Juan Pablo Duarte — A24

1911-13 *Perf. 14*

Center in Black

178 A23 ½c orange ('13) .25 .20
179 A23 1c green .25 .20
180 A23 2c carmine .25 .20
181 A23 5c gray blue ('13) .75 .20
182 A23 10c red violet 1.25 .45
183 A23 20c olive green 8.00 7.00
184 A23 50c yellow brn ('12) 3.25 3.25
185 A23 1p violet ('12) 5.50 3.50
Nos. 178-185 (8) 19.50 15.00

See Nos. 230-232.

1914, Apr. 13 *Perf. 13x14*

Background Red, White and Blue

186 A24 ½c orange & blk .40 .30
187 A24 1c green & blk .40 .30
188 A24 2c rose & blk .40 .30
189 A24 5c slate & blk .40 .40
190 A24 10c magenta & blk .80 .70
191 A24 20c olive grn & blk 1.75 *1.90*
192 A24 50c brown & blk 2.50 *2.75*
193 A24 1p dull lilac & blk 4.00 4.00
Nos. 186-193 (8) 10.65 10.65

Cent. of the birth of Juan Pablo Duarte (1813-1876), patriot and revolutionary.

Official Stamps of 1909-12 Surcharged in Violet or Overprinted in Red:

a

b

1915, Feb. *Perf. 13½x13, 13½x14*

194 O2 (a) ½c on 20c orange & blk .50 .35
a. Inverted surcharge 6.00 6.00
b. Double surcharge 8.75 8.75
c. "Habilitado" omitted 5.25 5.25
195 O2 (b) 1c blue grn & blk .80 .25
a. Inverted overprint 6.00 6.00
b. Double overprint 7.00
c. Overprinted "1915" only 12.50
196 O2 (b) 2c scarlet & blk .80 .25
a. Inverted overprint 5.25 5.25
b. Double overprint 7.75 7.75
c. Overprinted "1915" only 8.75
d. "1915" double
197 O2 (b) 5c dk blue & blk 1.00 .25
a. Inverted overprint 7.00 7.00
b. Double overprint 8.75 8.75
c. Double ovpt., one invtd. 27.50
d. Overprinted "1915" only 8.50
198 O2 (b) 10c yel grn & blk 2.75 2.40
a. Inverted overprint 15.00
199 O2 (b) 20c orange & blk 9.00 6.50
a. "Habilitado" omitted
Nos. 194-199 (6) 14.85 10.00

#194, 196-198 are known with both perforations. #195, 199 are only perf. 13½x13.

The variety capital "I" for "1" in "Habilitado" occurs once in each sheet in all denominations.

A25

Type of 1911-13 Redrawn Overprinted "1915" in Red

TWO CENTAVOS:
Type I — "DOS" in small letters.
Type II — "DOS" in larger letters with white dot at each end of the word.

1915 Unwmk. Litho. *Perf. 11½*

200 A25 ½c violet & blk .75 .20
a. Imperf., pair 5.75
201 A25 1c yel brn & blk .75 .20
a. Imperf., pair 6.50
b. Vert. pair, imperf. horiz. 10.50
c. Horiz. pair, imperf. vert. 10.50
202 A25 2c ol grn & blk (I) 3.75 .25
a. Imperf., pair 10.00
203 A25 2c ol grn & blk (II) 6.00 .20
a. Center omitted 87.50
b. Frame omitted 87.50
c. Imperf., pair 15.00
d. Horiz. pair, imperf. vert. 15.00
204 A25 5c magenta & blk 3.25 .25
a. Pair, one without overprint 65.00
b. Imperf., pair 6.50
205 A25 10c gray blue & blk 3.75 .50
a. Imperf., pair 7.75
b. Horiz. pair, imperf. vert. 35.00
206 A25 20c rose red & blk 6.50 1.40
a. Imperf., pair 12.50
207 A25 50c green & blk 8.50 4.00
a. Imperf., pair 25.00
208 A25 1p orange & blk 17.50 7.00
a. Imperf., pair 52.50
Nos. 200-208 (9) 50.75 14.00

Type of 1915 Overprinted "1916" in Red

1916

209 A25 ½c violet & blk 1.25 .20
a. Imperf., pair 21.00
210 A25 1c green & blk 2.00 .20
a. Imperf., pair 21.00

Type of 1915 Overprinted "1917" in Red

1917-19

213 A25 ½c red lilac & blk 2.25 .30
a. Horiz. pair, imperf. btwn. 47.50 47.50
214 A25 1c yellow grn & blk 1.50 .20
a. Vert. pair, imperf. btwn. 50.00
215 A25 2c olive grn & blk 1.40 .20
a. Imperf., pair 35.00
216 A25 5c magenta & blk 16.00 .70
Nos. 213-216 (4) 21.15 1.40

Type of 1915 Overprinted "1919" in Red

1919

219 A25 2c olive grn & blk 10.00 .20

Type of 1915 Overprinted "1920" in Red

1920-27

220 A25 ½c lilac rose & blk .50 .25
a. Horiz. pair, imperf. btwn. 25.00 25.00
b. Inverted overprint
c. Double overprint
d. Double overprint, one invtd.
221 A25 1c yellow grn & blk .75 .20
a. Overprint omitted 70.00
b. Horiz. pair, imperf. btwn. 40.00
222 A25 2c olive grn & blk .75 .20
a. Vertical pair, imperf. between 27.50
223 A25 5c dp rose & blk 9.00 .50
224 A25 10c blue & black 5.00 .25
225 A25 20c rose red & blk ('27) 7.00 .50
226 A25 50c green & blk ('27) 52.50 17.50
Nos. 220-226 (7) 75.50 19.40

Type of 1915 Overprinted "1921" in Red

1921

227 A25 1c yellow grn & blk 3.00 .30
a. Horiz. pair, imperf. btwn. 45.00 45.00
b. Imperf., pair 45.00 45.00
228 A25 2c olive grn & blk 5.00 .30
a. Vert. pair, imperf. btwn. 45.00

Redrawn Design of 1915 without Overprint

1922

230 A25 1c green 2.25 .20
231 A25 2c carmine (II) 2.50 .20
232 A25 5c blue 4.00 .25
Nos. 230-232 (3) 8.75 .65

Exist imperf.

A26 A27

Second Redrawing

TEN CENTAVOS:

Type I — Numerals 2mm high. "DIEZ" in thick letters with large white dot at each end.

Type II — Numerals 3mm high. "DIEZ" in thin letters with white dot with colored center at each end.

1924-27

233 A26 1c green .90 .20
a. Vert. pair, imperf. btwn. 35.00 35.00
234 A26 2c red .70 .20
235 A26 5c blue 1.10 .20
236 A26 10c pale bl & blk (I) ('26) 12.00 3.00
236A A26 10c pale bl & blk (II) 22.50 1.10
236B A26 50c gray grn & blk ('26) 45.00 27.50
237 A26 1p orange & blk ('27) 16.00 10.50
Nos. 233-237 (7) 98.20 42.70

In the second redrawing the shield has a flat top and the design differs in many details from the stamps of 1911-13 and 1915-22.

1927

238 A27 ½c lilac rose & blk .30 .20

Exhibition Pavilion — A28

1927 **Unwmk.** ***Perf. 12***

239 A28 2c carmine .80 .50
240 A28 5c ultra 1.75 .50

Natl. and West Indian Exhib. at Santiago de los Caballeros.

Ruins of Columbus' Fortress A29

1928

241 A29 ½c lilac rose .60 .35
242 A29 1c deep green .50 .20
a. Horiz. pair, imperf. btwn. 25.00
243 A29 2c red .50 .20
244 A29 5c dark blue 1.50 .35
245 A29 10c light blue 1.75 .30
246 A29 20c rose 3.00 .40
247 A29 50c yellow green 10.50 6.50
248 A29 1p orange yellow 27.50 20.00
Nos. 241-248 (8) 45.85 28.30

Reprints exist of 1c, 2c and 10c.

Issued: 1c, 2c, 10c, Oct. 1; others, Dec.

Horacio Vasquez — A30

Convent of San Ignacio de Loyola — A31

1929, May-June

249 A30 ½c dull rose .50 .30
250 A30 1c gray green .50 .20
251 A30 2c red .60 .20
252 A30 5c dark ultra 1.25 .35
253 A30 10c pale blue 1.75 .50
Nos. 249-253 (5) 4.60 1.55

Signing of the "Frontier" treaty with Haiti.

Issue dates: 2c, May; others, June.

Imperf., Pairs

249a A30 ½c 12.50
250a A30 1c 12.50
251a A30 2c 12.50
252a A30 5c 14.00

1930, May 1 ***Perf. 11½***

254 A31 ½c red brown .65 .45
a. Imperf., pair 55.00 55.00
255 A31 1c deep green .50 .20
256 A31 2c vermilion .50 .20
a. Imperf., pair 60.00
257 A31 5c deep blue 1.25 .35
258 A31 10c light blue 3.00 1.00
Nos. 254-258 (5) 5.90 2.20

Cathedral of Santo Domingo, First Church in America A32

1931 ***Perf. 12***

260 A32 1c deep green .65 .20
a. Imperf., pair 50.00
261 A32 2c scarlet .45 .20
a. Imperf., pair 50.00
262 A32 3c violet .65 .20
263 A32 7c dark blue 2.00 .25
264 A32 8c bister 2.75 .85
265 A32 10c light blue 4.50 1.00
a. Imperf., pair 35.00
Nos. 260-265 (6) 11.00 2.70

Issued: 3c-7c, Aug. 1; others, July 11.

For overprint see No. RAC8.

A33

Overprinted or Surcharged in Black

1932, Dec. 20 ***Perf. 12***

Cross in Red

265B A33 1c yellow green .50 .45
265C A33 3c on 2c violet .70 .55
265D A33 5c blue 4.00 4.25
265E A33 7c on 10c turq bl 5.50 5.75
Nos. 265B-265E (4) 10.70 11.00

Proceeds of sale given to Red Cross. Valid Dec. 20 to Jan. 5, 1933.

Inverted and pairs, one without surcharge or overprint, exist on Nos. 265B-265D, as well as missing letters.

Fernando Arturo de Merino (1833-1906) as President — A35

Cathedral of Santo Domingo A36

Designs: ½c, 5c, 8c, Tomb of Merino. 1c, 3c, 10c, as Archbishop.

1933, Feb. 27 **Engr.** ***Perf. 14***

266 A35 ½c lt violet .35 .35
267 A35 1c yellow green .45 .25
268 A35 2c lt red .80 .75
269 A35 3c deep violet .55 .30
270 A35 5c dark blue .60 .35
271 A35 7c ultra 1.10 .50
272 A35 8c dark green 1.40 .75
273 A35 10c orange yel 1.25 .50
274 A35 20c carmine rose 2.25 1.25
275 A36 50c lemon 8.75 6.00
276 A36 1p dark brown 22.50 14.00
Nos. 266-276 (11) 40.00 25.00

For surcharges see Nos. G1-G7.

Tower of Homage, Ozama Fortress — A37

1932 **Litho.** ***Perf. 12***

278 A37 1c green 1.25 .20
279 A37 3c violet .80 .20

Issue dates: 1c, July 2; 3c, June 22.

"CORREOS" added at left

1933, May 28

283 A37 1c dark green .40 .20

President Rafael L. Trujillo
A38 A39

1933, Aug. 16 **Engr.** ***Perf. 14***

286 A38 1c yellow grn & blk .55 .35
287 A39 3c dp violet & blk .70 .35
288 A38 7c ultra & blk 1.75 .75
Nos. 286-288 (3) 3.00 1.45

42nd birthday of President Rafael Leonidas Trujillo Molina.

San Rafael Bridge — A40

1934 **Litho.** ***Perf. 12***

289 A40 ½c dull violet .70 .35
290 A40 1c dark green .90 .20
291 A40 3c violet 1.40 .20
Nos. 289-291 (3) 3.00 .75

Opening of San Rafael Bridge.

Issue dates: ½c, 3c, Mar. 3; 1c, Feb. 17.

Trujillo Bridge A41

1934

292 A41 ½c red brown .50 .25
293 A41 1c green .75 .20
294 A41 3c purple 1.10 .20
Nos. 292-294 (3) 2.35 .65

Opening of the General Trujillo Bridge near Ciudad Trujillo.

Issue dates: 1c, Aug. 24. Others, Sept. 7.

Ramfis Bridge A42

1935, Apr. 6

295 A42 1c green .45 .20
296 A42 3c yellow brown .50 .20
297 A42 5c brown violet 1.60 1.00
298 A42 10c rose 3.25 1.40
Nos. 295-298 (4) 5.80 2.80

Issued in commemoration of the opening of the Ramfis Bridge over the Higuamo River.

President Trujillo — A43

A44

A45

1935 ***Perf. 11***

299 A43 3c yellow & brown .25 .20
300 A44 5c org red, bl, red & bis .35 .20
301 A45 7c ultra, bl, red & brn .50 .20
302 A44 10c red vio, bl, red & bis .75 .20
Nos. 299-302 (4) 1.85 .80

Ratification of a treaty setting the frontier between Dominican Republic and Haiti.

Issued: 3c, 10/29; 5c, 10c, 11/25; 7c, 11/8.

National Palace A46

1935, Apr. 1 ***Perf. 11½***

303 A46 25c yellow orange 2.75 .30

Obligatory for all mail addressed to the president and cabinet ministers.

Post Office, Santiago A47

1936

304 A47 ½c bright violet .30 .35
305 A47 1c green .30 .20

Issue dates: ½c, Jan. 14; 1c, Jan. 4.

George Washington Ave., Ciudad Trujillo — A48

1936, Feb. 22

306 A48 ½c brn & vio brn .40 .45
a. Imperf., pair 52.50
307 A48 2c carmine & brn .40 .30
308 A48 3c yellow org & red brn .65 .20
309 A48 7c ultra, blue & brn 1.25 1.25
a. Imperf., pair 52.50
Nos. 306-309 (4) 2.70 2.20

Dedication of George Washington Avenue, Ciudad Trujillo.

José Nuñez de Cáceres — A49

Felix M. del Monte — A55

Proposed National Library — A56

1c, Gen. Gregorio Luperon. 2c, Emiliano Tejera. 3c, Pres. Trujillo. 5c, Jose Reyes. 7c, Gen. Antonio Duverge. 25c, Francisco J. Peynado. 30c, Salome Urena. 50c, Gen. Jose M. Cabral. 1p, Manuel de Jesus Galvan. 2p, Gaston F. Deligne.

1936 Unwmk. Engr. ***Perf. 13½, 14***

310 A49 ½c dull violet .30 .20
311 A49 1c dark green .25 .20
312 A49 2c carmine .30 .20
313 A49 3c violet .30 .20
314 A49 5c deep ultra .55 .30
315 A49 7c slate blue 1.00 .55
316 A55 10c orange 1.00 .30
317 A56 20c olive green 3.75 2.75
318 A55 25c gray violet 6.00 *8.00*
319 A55 30c scarlet 7.50 *10.00*
320 A55 50c black brown 8.00 5.50
321 A55 1p black 27.50 *32.50*
322 A55 2p yellow brown 65.00 *80.00*
Nos. 310-322 (13) 121.45 *140.70*

The funds derived from the sale of these stamps were returned to the National Treasury Fund for the erection of a building for the National Library and Archives.

Issued: 3c, 7c, Mar. 18; others, May 22.

President Trujillo and Obelisk — A62

1937, Jan. 11 Litho. ***Perf. 11½***

323 A62 1c green .20 .20
324 A62 3c violet .40 .20
325 A62 7c blue & turq blue 1.00 1.00
Nos. 323-325 (3) 1.60 1.40

1st anniv. of naming Ciudad Trujillo.

Discus Thrower and Flag — A63

1937, Aug. 14

Flag in Red and Blue

326 A63 1c dark green *8.00* .75
327 A63 3c violet *10.50* .75
328 A63 7c dark blue *19.00* 3.75
Nos. 326-328 (3) 37.50 5.25

1st Natl. Olympic Games, Aug. 16, 1937.

Symbolical of Peace, Labor and Progress — A64

1937, Sept. 18 ***Perf. 12***

329 A64 3c purple .35 .20

"8th Year of the Benefactor."

Monument to Father Francisco Xavier Billini (1837-90) — A65

1937, Dec. 29

330 A65 ½c deep orange .20 .20
331 A65 5c purple .45 .20

Globe and Torch of Liberty — A66

1938, Feb. 22 ***Perf. 11½***

332 A66 1c green .40 .20
333 A66 3c purple .50 .20
334 A66 10c orange 1.00 .20
Nos. 332-334 (3) 1.90 .60

150th anniv. of the Constitution of the US.

Pledge of Trinitarians, City Gate and National Flag — A67

1938, July 16 ***Perf. 12***

335 A67 1c green, red & dk bl .40 .20
336 A67 3c purple, red & bl .45 .20
337 A67 10c orange, red & bl .90 .40
Nos. 335-337 (3) 1.75 .80

Trinitarians and patriots, Francisco Del Rosario Sanchez, Ramon Matias Mella and Juan Pablo Duarte, who helped free their country from foreign domination.

Seal of the University of Santo Domingo — A68

1938, Oct. 28

338 A68 ½c orange .30 .25
339 A68 1c dp green & lt green .30 .20
340 A68 3c purple & pale vio .40 .20
341 A68 7c dp blue & lt blue .75 .35
Nos. 338-341 (4) 1.75 1.00

Founding of the University of Santo Domingo, on Oct. 28, 1538.

Trylon and Perisphere, Flag and Proposed Columbus Lighthouse — A69

1939, Apr. 30 Litho. ***Perf. 12***

Flag in Blue and Red

342 A69 ½c red org & org .35 .20
343 A69 1c green & lt green .40 .20
344 A69 3c purple & pale vio .40 .20
345 A69 10c orange & yellow 1.25 .65
Nos. 342-345,C33 (5) 3.80 1.85

New York World's Fair.

A70

A71

1939, Sept. ***Typo.***

346 A70 ½c black & pale gray .30 .20
347 A70 1c black & yel grn .40 .20
348 A70 3c black & yel brn .40 .20
349 A70 7c black & dp ultra 1.00 .90
350 A70 10c black & brt red vio 1.50 .40
Nos. 346-350 (5) 3.60 1.90

José Trujillo Valdez (1863-1935), father of President Trujillo Molina.

1940, Apr. 14 Litho. ***Perf. 11½***

Map of the Americas and flags of 21 American republics.

Flags in National Colors

351 A71 1c deep green .20 .20
352 A71 2c carmine .30 .20
353 A71 3c red violet .45 .20
354 A71 10c orange .90 .20
355 A71 1p chestnut 13.00 9.50
Nos. 351-355 (5) 14.85 10.30

Pan American Union, 50th anniv.

Sir Rowland Hill — A72

1940, May 6 ***Perf. 12***

356 A72 3c brt red vio & rose lil 2.50 .40
357 A72 7c dk blue & lt blue 5.50 1.40

Centenary of first postage stamp.

Julia Molina Trujillo A73

1940, May 26

358 A73 1c grn, lt grn & dk grn .35 .20
359 A73 2c brt red, buff & dp rose .35 .25
360 A73 3c org, dl org & brn org .50 .20
361 A73 7c bl, pale bl & dk bl 1.00 .35
Nos. 358-361 (4) 2.20 1.00

Issued in commemoration of Mother's Day.

Map of Caribbean A74

1940, June 6 ***Perf. 11½***

362 A74 3c brt car & pale rose .40 .20
363 A74 7c dk blue & lt blue .75 .20
364 A74 1p yel grn & pale grn 7.50 6.50
Nos. 362-364 (3) 8.65 6.90

2nd Inter-American Caribbean Conf. held at Ciudad Trujillo, May 31 to June 6.

Marion Military Hospital — A75

1940, Dec. 24

365 A75 ½c chestnut & fawn .25 .20

Fortress, Ciudad Trujillo A76

Statue of Columbus, Ciudad Trujillo — A77

1941

366 A76 1c dk green & lt green .20 .20
367 A77 2c brt red & rose .20 .20
368 A77 10c orange brn & buff .55 .25
Nos. 366-368 (3) .95 .65

Issue dates: 1c, Mar. 27; others, Apr. 7.

Sánchez, Duarte, Mella and Trujillo — A78

1941, May 16

369 A78 3c brt red lil & red vio .25 .20
370 A78 4c brt red, crim & pale rose .40 .20
371 A78 13c dk blue & lt blue .60 .35
372 A78 15c orange brn & buff 2.00 1.50
373 A78 17c lt bl, bl & pale bl 2.00 1.50
374 A78 1p org, yel brn & pale org 7.75 7.00
375 A78 2p lt gray & pale gray 17.00 7.25
Nos. 369-375 (7) 30.00 18.00

Trujillo-Hull Treaty signed Sept. 24, 1940 and effective Apr. 1, 1941.

Bastion of February 27 — A79

1941, Oct. 20

376 A79 5c brt blue & lt blue .50 .20

School, Torch of Knowledge, Pres. Trujillo — A80

1941

377 A80 ½c chestnut & fawn .20 .20
378 A80 1c dk green & lt green .25 .20

Education campaign.
Issue dates: ½c, Dec. 12, 1c, Dec. 2.

Reserve Bank of Dominican Republic A81

1942 **Unwmk.**

379 A81 5c lt brown & buff .40 .20
380 A81 17c dp blue & lt blue .70 .45

Founding of the Reserve Bank, 10/24/41.

Representation of Transportation A82

Virgin of Altagracia A83

1942, Aug. 15

381 A82 3c dk brn, grn yel & lt bl *3.00 .50*
382 A82 15c pur, grn, yel & lt bl *8.25 3.50*

Day of Posts and Telegraph, 8th anniv.

1942, Aug. 15

383 A83 ½c gray & pale gray .75 .20
384 A83 1c dp grn & lt grn 1.50 .20
385 A83 3c brt red lil & lil 9.50 .20
386 A83 5c dk vio brn & vio brn 2.00 .20
387 A83 10c rose pink & pink 6.75 .25
388 A83 15c dp blue & lt blue 7.50 .30
Nos. 383-388 (6) 28.00 1.35

20th anniv. of the coronation of Our Lady of Altagracia.

Bananas — A84

Cows — A85

1942-43

389 A84 3c dk brn & grn ('43) .50 .20
390 A84 4c vermilion & blk ('43) .50 .30
391 A85 5c dp blue & cop brn .50 .20
392 A85 15c dk pur & blue grn .75 .40
Nos. 389-392 (4) 2.25 1.10

Issue date: 5c, 15c, Aug. 18.

Emblems of Dominican and Trujillista Parties A86

1943, Jan. 15

393 A86 3c orange .40 .20
394 A86 4c dark red .50 .20
395 A86 13c brt red lilac 1.10 .20
396 A86 1p lt blue 5.00 1.60
Nos. 393-396 (4) 7.00 2.20

Re-election of President Rafael Trujillo Molina, May 16, 1942.

Model Market, Ciudad Trujillo A87

1944

397 A87 2c dk brown & buff .20 .20

Bastion of Feb. 27 and National Flag — A88

1944, Feb. 27 **Unwmk.**

Flag in Dark Blue and Carmine

398 A88 ½c ocher .20 .20
399 A88 1c yellow green .20 .20
400 A88 2c scarlet .20 .20
401 A88 3c brt red vio .20 .20
402 A88 5c yellow orange .20 .20
403 A88 7c brt blue .25 .25
404 A88 10c orange brown .40 .30
405 A88 20c olive green .65 .60
406 A88 50c lt blue 1.90 1.75
Nos. 398-406,C46-C48 (12) 7.00 5.80

Souvenir Sheet

Imperf

407 A88 Sheet of 12 110.00 110.00
a.-l. Single stamp 3.00 3.00

Centenary of Independence.

#407 contains 1 each of #398-406, C46-C48 with simulated perforations. Size: 141x205mm.

Battlefield and Nurse with Child A90

1944, Aug. 1

408 A90 1c dk bl grn, buff & car .20 .20
a. Vertical pair, imperf. btwn. 15.00
b. Horiz. pair, imperf. vert. 15.00
409 A90 2c dk brn, buff & car .30 .20
410 A90 3c brt bl, buff & car .30 .20
411 A90 10c rose car, buff & car .60 .20
Nos. 408-411 (4) 1.40 .80

80th anniv. of the Intl. Red Cross.

Municipal Building, San Cristóbal A91

Emblem of Communications A92

Unwmk.

1945, Jan. 10 **Litho.** ***Perf. 12***

412 A91 ½c blue & lt blue .20 .20
413 A91 1c dk green & green .20 .20
414 A91 2c red org & org .20 .20
415 A91 3c dk brown & brown .20 .20
416 A91 10c ultra & gray blue .60 .20
Nos. 412-416 (5) 1.40 1.00

Centenary of the constitution.

1945, Sept. 1

Center in Dark Blue and Carmine

417 A92 3c orange .20 .20
418 A92 20c yellow green .75 .20
419 A92 50c light blue 1.50 .55
Nos. 417-419,C53-C56 (7) 4.35 1.80

Palace of Justice, Ciudad Trujillo A93

1946 ***Perf. 11½***

420 A93 3c dk red brown & buff .20 .20

Map of Hispaniola — A94

1946, Aug. 4 ***Perf. 12***

421 A94 10c multicolored .40 .20
Nos. 421,C62-C63 (3) 1.35 .60

450th anniv. of the founding of Santo Domingo.

Waterfall of Jimenoa — A95

1946-47

Center Multicolored

422 A95 1c yellow grn ('47) .20 .20
423 A95 2c carmine ('47) .20 .20
424 A95 3c deep blue .20 .20
425 A95 13c red violet ('47) .35 .25
426 A95 20c chocolate ('47) .70 .25
427 A95 50c orange ('47) 1.40 1.00
Nos. 422-427,C64-C67 (10) 6.35 4.50

Nos. 422-423, 425-427 issued Mar. 18.
For surcharge see No. 540.

Executive Palace A96

1948, Feb. 27

428 A96 1c yellow green .20 .20
429 A96 3c deep blue .20 .20
Nos. 428-429,C68-C69 (4) 3.80 2.65

Church of San Francisco Ruins — A97

1949, Apr. 13 ***Perf. 11½***

430 A97 1c dk grn & pale grn .20 .20
431 A97 3c dp bl & pale bl .20 .20
Nos. 430-431,C70-C73 (6) 2.25 1.50

Gen. Pedro Santana — A98

Pigeon and Globe — A99

1949, Aug. 10

432 A98 3c deep blue & blue .20 .20

Battle of Las Carreras, cent. See #C74.

1950, Mar. 23

Center and Inscriptions in Brown

433 A99 1c green & pale green .20 .20
434 A99 2c yel grn & yel .20 .20
435 A99 5c blue & pale blue .20 .20
436 A99 7c dk vio bl & pale bl .40 .20
Nos. 433-436 (4) 1.00 .80

75th anniv. of the UPU.

Catalogue values for unused stamps in this section, from this point to the end of the section, are for Never Hinged items.

Hotel Jimani A100

Hotels: 1c, 2c, Hamaca. 5c, Montana. 15c, San Cristobal. 20c, Maguana.

1950-52

437 A100 ½c org brn & buff .20 .20
438 A100 1c dp grn & grn ('51) .20 .20
439 A100 2c red org & sal ('52) .20 .20
440 A100 5c blue & lt blue .30 .20
441 A100 15c dp orange & yel .55 .20
442 A100 20c lilac & rose lilac 1.00 .20
443 A100 1p chocolate & yel 4.00 1.60
Nos. 437-443,C75-C76 (9) 9.95 5.00

Issue dates: 1c, Dec. 1, 1951; 2c, Jan. 11, 1952; others, Sept. 8, 1950.

The ½c, 15c and 20c exist imperf.

Ruins of Church and Hospital of San Nicolas de Bari A101

School of Medicine — A102

Queen Isabella I — A103

1950, Oct. 2

444 A101 2c dk green & rose brn .20 .20
445 A102 5c vio blue & org brn .30 .20
Nos. 444-445,C77 (3) 1.10 .60

13th Pan-American Health Conference. Exist imperf.

1951, Oct. 12

446 A103 5c dk blue & red brn .50 .20

500th anniversary of the birth of Queen Isabella I of Spain. Exists imperf.

Dr. Salvador B. Gautier Hospital A104

1952, Aug.

447 A104 1c dark green .20 .20
448 A104 2c red .20 .20
449 A104 5c violet blue .40 .20
Nos. 447-449,C78-C79 (5) 3.90 2.95

Columbus Lighthouse and Flags of 21 Republics A105

1953, Jan. 6 **Engr.** ***Perf. 13***

450 A105 2c dark green .25 .20
451 A105 5c deep blue .35 .20
452 A105 10c deep carmine .60 .25
Nos. 450-452,C80-C86 (10) 5.35 3.65

Treasury Building, Ciudad Trujillo A106

Sugar Industry, "Central Rio Haina" A107

1953 **Litho.** ***Perf. 11½***

453 A106 ½c brown .20 .20
454 A106 2c dark blue .20 .20
455 A107 5c blue & vio brn .20 .20
456 A106 15c orange .75 .25
Nos. 453-456 (4) 1.35 .85

For surcharge see No. 539.

José Marti — A108

Airport A114

Monument to the Peace of Trujillo — A109

1954 ***Perf. 12½***

457 A108 10c dp blue & dk brown .45 .20

Centenary of the birth of Jose Marti (1853-1895), Cuban patriot.

1954, May 25

458 A109 2c green .20 .20
459 A109 7c blue .25 .20
460 A109 20c orange .75 .20
Nos. 458-460 (3) 1.20 .60

See No. 493.

Rotary Emblem A110

1955, Feb. 23 ***Perf. 12***

461 A110 7c deep blue .60 .20

50th anniv., Rotary Intl. See No. C90.

Gen. Rafael L. Trujillo — A111

4c, Trujillo in civilian clothes. 7c, Trujillo statue. 10c, Symbols of culture & prosperity.

1955, May 16 **Engr.** ***Perf. 13½x13***

462 A111 2c red .30 .20
463 A111 4c lt olive green .30 .20
464 A111 7c indigo .35 .20
465 A111 10c brown .85 .20
Nos. 462-465,C91-C93 (7) 4.50 1.80

25th anniversary of the Trujillo era.

General Rafael L. Trujillo — A112

Angelita Trujillo — A113

1955, Dec. 20 **Unwmk.** ***Perf. 13***

466 A112 7c deep claret .35 .20
467 A112 10c dark blue .50 .20
Nos. 466-467,C94 (3) 1.20 .60

1955, Dec. 20 **Litho.** ***Perf. 12½***

468 A113 10c blue & ultra .45 .20

Nos. 466-468 were issued to publicize the International Fair of Peace and Brotherhood in Ciudad Trujillo, Dec. 1955.

Cedar — A115

1956, Apr. 6 ***Perf. 12½***

469 A114 1c brown .20 .20
470 A114 2c red orange .20 .20
Nos. 469-470,C95 (3) .80 .60

3rd Caribbean conf. of the ICAO.

1956, Dec. 8 ***Perf. 11½x12***

471 A115 5c car rose & grn 1.10 .20
472 A115 6c red vio & grn 1.40 .20
Nos. 471-472,C96 (3) 4.10 .60

Reforestation program.

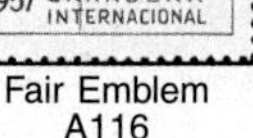

Fair Emblem A116

Fanny Blankers-Koen, Netherlands A117

1957, Jan. 10 ***Perf. 12½***

473 A116 7c blue, lt brn & ver .35 .20

2nd International Livestock Show, Ciudad Trujillo, Jan. 10-20, 1957. Exists imperf.

Engraved & Lithographed

1957, Jan. 24 ***Perf. 11½, Imperf.***

Olympic Winners and Flags: 2c, Jesse Owens, US. 3c, Kee Chung Sohn, Japan. 5c, Lord Burghley, England. 7c, Bob Mathias, US.

Flags in National Colors

474 A117 1c brn, lt bl, vio & mar .20 .20
475 A117 2c dk brn, lt bl & vio .20 .20
476 A117 3c red lilac & red .20 .20
477 A117 5c red org & vio .20 .20
478 A117 7c green & violet .20 .20
Nos. 474-478,C97-C99 (8) 1.65 1.65

16th Olympic Games, Melbourne, Nov. 22-Dec. 8, 1956.

Miniature sheets of 5 exist, perf. and imperf., containing Nos. 474-478. Value, 2 sheets, perf. and imperf., $15.

For surcharges see Nos. B1-B5, B26-B30, CB1-CB3, CB16-CB18.

Lars Hall, Sweden, Pentathlon — A118

Olympic Winners and Flags: 2c, Betty Cuthbert, Australia, 100 & 200 meter dash. 3c, Egil Danielsen, Norway, javelin. 5c, Alain Mimoun, France, marathon. 7c, Norman Read, New Zealand, 50 km. walk.

Perf. 13½, Imperf.

1957, July 18 **Photo.** **Unwmk.**

Flags in National Colors

479 A118 1c brn & brt bl .20 .20
480 A118 2c org ver & dk bl .20 .20
481 A118 3c dark blue .20 .20
482 A118 5c ol & dk bl .20 .20
483 A118 7c rose brn & dk bl .20 .20
Nos. 479-483,C100-C102 (8) 1.65 1.65

1956 Olympic winners.

Miniature sheets of 8 exist, perf. and imperf., containing Nos. 479-483 and C100-C102. The center label in these sheets is printed in two forms: Olympic gold medal or Olympic flag. Sheets measure 140x140mm. Value, 4 sheets, perf. and imperf., medal and flag, $18.

A third set of similar miniature sheets (perf. and imperf.) with center label showing an incorrect version of the Dominican Republic flag (colors transposed) was printed. These sheets are said to have been briefly sold on the first day, then withdrawn as the misprint was discovered. Value, 2 sheets, perf. & imperf., $150.

For surcharges see #B6-B10, CB4-CB6.

Gerald Ouellette, Canada, Small Bore Rifle, Prone — A119

Ron Delaney, Ireland, 1,500 Meter Run — A120

Olympic Winners and Flags: 3c, Tenley Albright, US, figure skating. 5c, Joaquin Capilla, Mexico, platform diving. 7c, Ercole Baldini, Italy, individual road race (cycling).

Engraved and Lithographed

1957, Nov. 12 ***Perf. 13½, Imperf.***

Flags in National Colors

484 A119 1c red brown .20 .20
485 A120 2c gray brown .20 .20
486 A119 3c violet .20 .20
487 A120 5c red orange .20 .20
488 A119 7c Prus green .20 .20
Nos. 484-488,C103-C105 (8) 1.65 1.65

1956 Olympic winners.

Miniature sheets of 5 exist, perf. and imperf., containing Nos. 484-488. Value, 2 sheets, perf. and imperf., $5.50.

For surcharges see Nos. B11-B20, CB7-CB12.

Mahogany Flower — A121

Cervantes, Globe, Book — A122

1957-58 **Litho.** ***Perf. 12½***

489 A121 2c green & maroon .20 .20

Perf. 12

490 A121 4c lilac & rose ('58) .20 .20
491 A121 7c ultra & gray grn .35 .20
492 A121 25c brown & org ('58) .90 .30
Nos. 489-492 (4) 1.65 .90

Sizes: No. 489, 25x29¼mm; Nos. 490-492, 24x28¾mm. In 1959, the 2c was reissued in size 24¼x28½mm with slightly different tones of green and maroon.

Issued: 2c, 10/24; 7c, 11/6; 4c, 25c, 4/7/58.

For surcharges see Nos. 537-538.

Type of 1954, Redrawn

Perf. 12x11½

1957, June 12 **Unwmk.**

493 A109 7c bright blue .50 .20

On No. 493 the cent symbol is smaller, the shading of the sky and steps stronger and the letters in "Correos" shorter and bolder.

1958, Apr. 23 **Litho.** ***Perf. 12½***

494 A122 4c yellow green .20 .20
495 A122 7c red lilac .20 .20
496 A122 10c lt olive brown .30 .20
Nos. 494-496 (3) .70 .60

4th Book Fair, Apr. 23-28. Exist imperf.

Gen. Rafael L. Trujillo — A123

1958, Aug. 16 *Perf. 12*

497 A123 2c red lilac & yel .20 .20
498 A123 4c green & yel .20 .20
499 A123 7c brown & yel .20 .20
a. Souv. sheet of 3, #497-499, imperf. .75 .60
Nos. 497-499 (3) .60 .60

25th anniv. of Gen. Trujillo's designation as "Benefactor of his country."

S. S. Rhadames A124

1958, Oct. 27 *Perf. 12½*

500 A124 7c bright blue .90 .25

Day of the Dominican Merchant Marine. Exists imperf.

Shozo Sasahara, Japan, Featherweight Wrestling — A125

Olympic Winners and Flags: 1c, Gillian Sheen, England, fencing, vert. 2c, Milton Campbell, US, decathlon, vert. 5c, Madeleine Berthod, Switzerland, downhill skiing. 7c, Murray Rose, Australia, 400 & 1,500 meter freestyle.

Perf. 13½, Imperf.

1958, Oct. 30 **Photo.**

Flags in National Colors

501 A125 1c rose, ind & ultra .20 .20
502 A125 2c brown & blue .20 .20
503 A125 3c gray, vio, blk & buff .20 .20
504 A125 5c rose, dk bl, brn & red .20 .20
505 A125 7c lt brn, dk bl & red .20 .20
Nos. 501-505,C106-C108 (8) 1.75 1.75

1956 Olympic winners.
Miniature sheets of 5 exist, perf. and imperf. containing Nos. 501-505. Value, 2 sheets, perf. and imperf., $5.
For surcharges see #B21-B25, CB13-CB15.

Globe and Symbolic Fire — A126

1958, Nov. 3 **Litho.** *Perf. 11½*

506 A126 7c blue & dp carmine .30 .20

UNESCO Headquarters in Paris opening, Nov. 3.

Dominican Republic Pavilion, Brussels Fair — A127

1958, Dec. 9 **Unwmk.** *Perf. 12½*

507 A127 7c blue green .25 .20
Nos. 507,C109-C110 (3) 1.10 .75

Universal & Intl. Exposition at Brussels.

Gen. Trujillo Placing Wreath on Altar of the Nation — A128

1959, July 10 *Perf. 12*

508 A128 9c brn, grn, red & gold .25 .20
a. Souv. sheet of 1, imperf. .50 .50

29th anniversary of the Trujillo regime.

Lt. Leonidas Rhadames Trujillo, Team Captain — A129

Jamaican Polo Team A130

Design: 10c, Lt. Trujillo on polo pony.

1959, May 15

509 A129 2c violet .20 .20
510 A130 7c yellow brown .35 .25
511 A130 10c green .45 .25
Nos. 509-511,C111 (4) 1.35 1.00

Jamaica-Dominican Republic polo match at Ciudad Trujillo.

Symbolical of Census A131

1959, Aug. 15 **Litho.** *Perf. 12½*

Flag in Ultramarine and Red

512 A131 1c blue & black .20 .20
513 A131 9c green & black .25 .20
514 A131 13c orange & black .50 .25
Nos. 512-514 (3) .95 .65

Issued to publicize the 1960 census.

Trujillo Stadium — A132

1959, Aug. 27

515 A132 9c green & gray .40 .25

Issued to publicize the 3rd Pan American Games, Chicago, Aug. 27-Sept. 7.

Charles V A133

Rhadames Bridge — A134

1959, Oct. 12 **Unwmk.** *Perf. 12*

516 A133 5c bright pink .20 .20
517 A133 9c violet blue .25 .20

400th anniv. of the death of Charles V (1500-1558), Holy Roman Emperor.

1959-60 **Litho.** *Perf. 12*

1c and No. 520, Different view of bridge.

518 A134 1c green & gray ('60) .30 .20
519 A134 2c ultra & gray .30 .20
520 A134 2c red & gray ('60) .30 .20
521 A134 5c brn & dull red brn .30 .20
Nos. 518-521 (4) 1.20 .80

Issued: #519, 10/22; 5c, 11/30; 1c, #520, 2/6.
For surcharge see No. 536.

Sosua Refugee Settlement and WRY Emblem — A135

1960, Apr. 7 *Perf. 12½*

Center in Gray

522 A135 5c red brn & yel grn .20 .20
523 A135 9c carmine & lt blue .20 .20
524 A135 13c orange & green .40 .20
Nos. 522-524,C113-C114 (5) 2.20 1.20

World Refugee Year, 7/1/59-6/30/60.
For surcharges see Nos. B31-B33.

Sholam Takhti, Iran, Lightweight Wrestling — A136

Olympic Winners: 2c, Masaru Furukawa, Japan, 200 meter breast stroke. 3c, Mildred McDaniel, US, high jump. 5c, Terence Spinks, England, featherweight boxing. 7c, Carlo Pavesi, Italy, fencing.

Perf. 13½, Imperf.

1960, Sept. 14 **Photo.**

Flags in National Colors

525 A136 1c red, yel grn & blk .20 .20
526 A136 2c org, grnsh bl & brn .20 .20
527 A136 3c henna brn & bl .20 .20
528 A136 5c brown & ultra .20 .20
529 A136 7c grn, bl & rose brn .20 .20
Nos. 525-529,C115-C117 (8) 1.70 1.70

17th Olympic Games, Rome, 8/25-9/11.
Miniature sheets of 5 exist, perf. and imperf., containing Nos. 525-529. Value, 2 sheets, perf. & imperf., $5.
For surcharges see #B34-B38, CB21-CB23.

Post Office, Ciudad Trujillo A137

1960, Aug. 26 **Litho.** *Perf. 11½x12*

530 A137 2c ultra & gray .20 .20

Exists imperf.

Cattle A138

1960, Aug. 30

531 A138 9c carmine & gray .25 .20

Issued to publicize the Agricultural and Industrial Fair, San Juan de la Maguana.

Nos. 518, 490-491, 453, 427 Surcharged in Red, Black or Blue

1960-61 *Perf. 12*

536 A134 2c on 1c grn & gray (R) .20 .20
537 A121 9c on 4c lilac & rose .50 .20
a. Inverted surcharge 21.00
538 A121 9c on 7c ultra & gray grn (R) .50 .20
539 A106 36c on ½c brown 1.40 1.25
a. Inverted surcharge 18.00
540 A95 1p on 50c multi (Bl) 3.25 2.40
Nos. 536-540 (5) 5.85 4.25

Issue dates: No. 536, Dec. 30, 1960; No. 537, Dec. 20, 1960; others, Feb. 4, 1961.

Trujillo Memorial A139

Coffee, Cacao A140

1961 **Unwmk.** *Perf. 11½*

548 A139 1c brown .20 .20
549 A139 2c green .20 .20
550 A139 4c rose lilac .35 *.30*
551 A139 5c light blue .35 .20
552 A139 9c red orange .35 .20
Nos. 548-552 (5) 1.45 1.10

Gen. Rafael L. Trujillo (1891-1961).
Issued: 2c, 8/7; 4c, 10/24; others 8/30.

1961, Dec. 30 **Litho.** *Perf. 12½*

553 A140 1c blue green .20 .20
554 A140 2c orange brown .20 .20
555 A140 4c violet .20 .20
556 A140 5c blue .20 .20
557 A140 9c gray .35 .20
Nos. 553-557,C118-C119 (7) 1.90 1.75

Exist imperf.

Dagger Pointing at Mosquito — A141

1962, Apr. 29 Photo. *Perf. 12*

558 A141 10c brt pink & red lilac .30 .20
559 A141 20c pale brn & brn .45 .25
560 A141 25c pale grn & yel grn .60 .30
Nos. 558-560,B39-B40,C120-C121,CB24-CB25 (9) 4.10 2.80

WHO drive to eradicate malaria.

Broken Fetters and Laurel A142

"Justice," Map of Dominican Republic — A143

Farm, Factory and Flag — A144

Design: 20c, Flag, torch and inscription.

1962, May 30 Litho. *Perf. 12½*

561 A142 1c grn, yel, ultra & red .20 .20
562 A143 9c bister ultra & red .30 .20
563 A142 20c lt blue, ultra & red .60 .25
a. Souvenir sheet of 3, #561-563 1.25 1.25
564 A143 1p lilac, ultra & red 3.00 1.40
Nos. 561-564,C122-C123 (6) 5.50 3.05

1st anniv. of end of Trujillo era. Exist imperf.

1962, May 22

565 A144 1c ultra, red & green .20 .20
566 A144 2c ultra & red .20 .20
567 A144 3c ultra, red & brown .20 .20
568 A144 5c ultra, red & blue .20 .20
569 A144 15c ultra, red & orange .30 .30
Nos. 565-569 (5) 1.10 1.10

Map and Laurel A145

1962, June 14 Litho.

570 A145 1c black .30 .20

Honoring the martyrs of June 1959 revolution.

Western Hemisphere and Carrier Pigeon — A146

Archbishop Adolfo Alejandro Nouel — A147

1962, Oct. 23 Unwmk. *Perf. 12½*

571 A146 2c rose red .20 .20
572 A146 9c orange .20 .20
573 A146 14c blue green .25 .20
Nos. 571-573,C124-C125 (5) 1.30 1.20

50th anniv. of the founding of the Postal Union of the Americas and Spain, UPAE.

1962, Dec. 18

574 A147 2c bl grn & dull bl .20 .20
575 A147 9c orange & red brn .25 .20
576 A147 13c maroon & vio brn .30 .20
Nos. 574-576,C126-C127 (5) 1.60 1.30

Cent. of the birth of Archbishop Adolfo Alejandro Nouel, President of Dominican Republic in 1911.

Globe, Banner and Emblems A148

1963, Apr. 15 Unwmk. *Perf. 11½*
Banner in Dark Blue & Red

577 A148 2c green .20 .20
578 A148 5c brt rose lilac .20 .20
579 A148 9c orange .30 .20
Nos. 577-579,B41-B43 (6) 1.40 1.30

FAO "Freedom from Hunger" campaign.

Juan Pablo Duarte — A149

1963, July 7 Litho. *Perf. 12x11½*

580 A149 2c shown .20 .20
581 A149 7c Francisco Sanchez .20 .20
582 A149 9c Ramon Mella .20 .20
Nos. 580-582 (3) .60 .60

120th anniv. of separation from Haiti. See #C128.

Ulises F. Espaillat, Benigno F. de Rojas and Pedro F. Bono — A150

Designs: 4c, Generals Santiago Rodriguez, Jose Cabrera and Benito Moncion. 5c, Capotillo monument. 9c, Generals Gaspar Polanco, Gregorio Luperon and Jose A. Salcedo.

1963, Aug. 16 Unwmk. *Perf. 11½*

583 A150 2c green .20 .20
584 A150 4c red orange .20 .20
585 A150 5c brown .20 .20
586 A150 9c bright blue .20 .20
a. Souvenir sheet of 4 1.00 1.00
Nos. 583-586 (4) .80 .80

Cent. of the Restoration. #586a contains 4 imperf. stamps similar to #583-586.

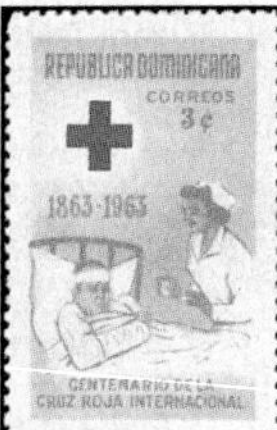

Patient and Nurse — A151

Scales, Globe, UNESCO Emblem A152

1963, Oct. 25 Unwmk. *Perf. 12½*

587 A151 3c gray & carmine .20 .20
588 A151 6c emerald & red .20 .20
Nos. 587-C588,C129 (3) .70 .65

Centenary of International Red Cross. Exist imperf. See No. C129.

1963, Dec. 10 Litho.

589 A152 6c pink & deep pink .20 .20
590 A152 50c lt green & green .65 .65
Nos. 589-590,C130-C131 (4) 1.30 1.25

Universal Declaration of Human Rights, 15th anniv. Exist imperf.

Ramses II Battling the Hittites (from Abu Simbel) — A153

Design: 6c, Two heads of Ramses II.

1964, Mar. 8 Unwmk. *Perf. 12½*

591 A153 3c pale pink & ver .20 .20
592 A153 6c pale blue & ultra .20 .20
593 A153 9c pale rose & red brn .20 .20
Nos. 591-593,C132-C133 (5) 1.10 1.00

UNESCO world campaign to save historic monuments in Nubia.

For surcharges see Nos. B44-B46.

Maximo Gomez — A154

Palm Chat — A155

1964, Apr. 30 Litho.

594 A154 2c lt blue & blue .25 .20
595 A154 6c dull pink & dull claret .25 .20

Bicent. of the founding of the town of Bani.

1964, June 8 Unwmk. *Perf. 12½*

Design: 6c, Hispaniolan parrot.

Size: 27x37½mm

596 A155 3c ultra, brn & yel *1.90* .20
597 A155 6c gray & multi *2.40* .20
Nos. 596-597,C134 (3) 8.55 .60

See Nos. 602-604.

Rocket Leaving Earth A156

Designs: 1c, Launching of rocket, vert. 3c, Space capsule orbiting earth. 6c, As 2c.

1964, July 28 Litho.

598 A156 1c sky blue .20 .20
599 A156 2c emerald .20 .20
600 A156 3c blue .20 .20
601 A156 6c sky blue .25 .20
Nos. 598-601,C135-C136 (6) 1.40 1.25

Conquest of space.

Bird Type of 1964

Designs: 1c, Narrow-billed tody. 2c, Hispaniolan emerald hummingbird. 6c, Hispaniolan trogon.

1964, Nov. 7 *Perf. 11½*

Size: 26x37mm

Birds in Natural Colors

602 A155 1c bright pink *1.90* .20
603 A155 2c dark brown *1.90* .20
604 A155 6c blue *3.00* .20
Nos. 602-604 (3) 6.80 .60

Universal Postal Union and United Nations Emblems A157

1964, Dec. 5 Litho. *Perf. 12½*

605 A157 1c red .20 .20
606 A157 4c green .20 .20
607 A157 5c orange .20 .20
Nos. 605-607,C138 (4) .85 .80

15th UPU Cong., Vienna, May-June 1964.

International Cooperation Year Emblem A158

1965, Feb. 16 Unwmk. *Perf. 12½*

608 A158 2c lt blue & ultra .20 .20
609 A158 3c emerald & dk grn .20 .20
610 A158 6c salmon pink & red .20 .20
Nos. 608-610,C139 (4) .90 .85

UN Intl. Cooperation Year.

Virgin of Altagracia A159

Flags of 21 American Nations — A160

Design: 2c, Hands holding lily.

1965, Mar. 18 Unwmk. *Perf. 12½*

611 A159 2c grn, emer & dp rose .20 .20
612 A159 6c multicolored .30 .25
Nos. 611-612,C140 (3) .80 .70

4th Mariological Cong. and 11th Intl. Marian Cong. #612 exists imperf.

1965, Apr. 14 Litho. *Perf. 11½*

613 A160 2c brown, yel & multi .20 .20
614 A160 6c red lilac & multi .30 .20

Organization of American States.

Stamp of 1865 (No. 1) — A161

1965, Dec. 28 Litho. *Perf. 12½*

615 A161 1c pink, buff & blk .20 .20
616 A161 2c blue, buff & blk .20 .20
617 A161 6c emerald, buff & blk .20 .20
a. Souvenir sheet of 2 .75 .75
Nos. 615-617,C142-C143 (5) 1.10 1.00

Cent. of 1st Dominican postage stamps. #617a shows replicas of #1-2. Sold for 50c.

WHO Headquarters, Geneva — A162

1966, May 21 Litho. *Perf. 12½*

618 A162 6c blue .20 .20
619 A162 10c red lilac .25 .20

New WHO Headquarters, Geneva.

Man Holding Map of Republic — A163

1966, May 23

620 A163 2c black & brt green	.20	.20
621 A163 6c black & dp orange	.25	.20

General elections, June 1, 1966.

Ascia Monuste — A164

Natl. Altar — A165

1966 Litho. *Perf. 12½*

Various Butterflies in Natural Colors

Size: 31x21mm

622 A164 1c blue & vio bl	.40	.20
623 A164 2c lt grn & brt grn	.40	.20
624 A164 3c lt gray & gray	.40	.20
625 A164 6c pink & magenta	.50	.25
626 A164 8c buff & brown	.85	.40
Nos. 622-626,C146-C148 (8)	19.05	3.50

Issued: 1c, 9/7; 3c, 9/11; others, 11/8.
For surcharges see #B47-B51, CB28-CB30.

1967, Jan. 18 Litho. *Perf. 11½*

627 A165 1c bright blue	.20	.20
628 A165 2c carmine rose	.20	.20
629 A165 3c emerald	.20	.20
630 A165 4c gray	.20	.20
631 A165 5c orange yellow	.20	.20
632 A165 6c orange	.20	.20
Nos. 627-632,C149-C151 (9)	1.90	1.85

Map of Republic and Emblem A166

1967, Mar. 30 Litho. *Perf. 12½*

633 A166 2c yellow, blue & blk	.20	.20
634 A166 6c orange, blue & blk	.20	.20
635 A166 10c emerald, blue & blk	.50	.40
Nos. 633-635 (3)	.90	.80

Development Year, 1967.

Rook and Knight A167

1967, June 23 Litho. *Perf. 12½*

636 A167 25c multicolored	*2.25*	.40

5th Central American Chess Championships, Santo Domingo. See Nos. C152-C152a.

Alliance for Progress A168

Institute Emblem A169

1967, Sept. 16 Litho. *Perf. 12½*

637 A168 1c bright green	.20	.20
Nos. 637,C153-C154 (3)	.85	.70

6th anniv. of the Alliance for Progress.

1967, Oct. 7

638 A169 3c bright green	.20	.20
639 A169 6c salmon pink	.20	.20
Nos. 638-639,C155 (3)	.85	.65

25th anniversary of the Inter-American Agriculture Institute.

Globe and Satellite A170

1968, June 15 Typo. *Perf. 12*

640 A170 6c black & multi	.25	.20
Nos. 640,C156-C157 (3)	.85	.70

World Meteorological Day, Mar. 23.

Boxers A171

1968, June 29

641 A171 6c rose red & dp claret	.25	.20
Nos. 641,C158-C159 (3)	.80	.60

Fight between Carlos Ortiz, Puerto Rico, and Teo Cruz, Dominican Republic, for the World Lightweight Boxing Championship.

Lions Emblem — A172

1968, Aug. 9 Litho. *Perf. 11½*

642 A172 6c brown & multi	.25	.20

Lions Intl., 50th anniv. (in 1967). See #C160.

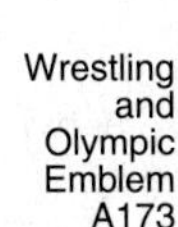

Wrestling and Olympic Emblem A173

1968, Nov. 12 Litho. *Perf. 11½*

643 A173 1c shown	.20	.20
644 A173 6c Running	.25	.20
645 A173 25c Boxing	.75	.40
Nos. 643-645,C161-C162 (5)	2.20	1.65

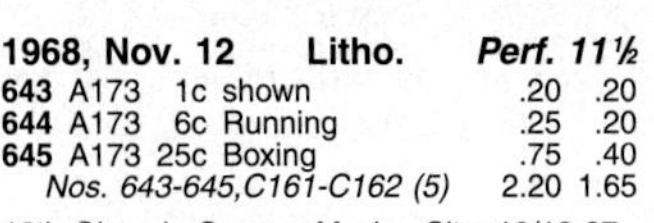
19th Olympic Games, Mexico City, 10/12-27.

Map of Americas and House — A174

Stool in Human Form A175

1969, Jan. 25 Litho. *Perf. 12½*

646 A174 6c brt bl, lt bl & grn	.20	.20

7th Inter-American Conference for Savings and Loans, Santo Domingo, Jan. 25-31. See No. C163.

1969, Jan. 31 Litho. *Perf. 12½*

Taino Art: 2c, Wood carved mother figure, vert. 3c, Face carved on 3-cornered stone. 4c, Stone hatchet, vert. 5c, Clay pot.

647 A175 1c yellow, org & blk	.20	.20
648 A175 2c lt grn, grn & blk	.20	.20
649 A175 3c citron, ol & brt grn	.20	.20
650 A175 4c lt lil, lil & brt grn	.20	.20
651 A175 5c yellow, org & brn	.20	.20
Nos. 647-651,C164-C166 (8)	1.75	1.70

Taino art flourished in the West Indies at the time of Columbus.

Community Day Emblem — A176

COTAL Emblem — A177

Headquarters Building and COTAL Emblem — A178

1969, Mar. 25 Litho. *Perf. 12½*

652 A176 6c dull green & gold	.25	.20

Community Development Day, Mar. 22.

1969, May 25 Litho. *Perf. 12½*

Design: 2c, Boy and COTAL emblem.

653 A177 1c lt & dk blue & red	.20	.20
654 A177 2c emerald & dk grn	.20	.20
655 A178 6c vermilion & pink	.20	.20
Nos. 653-655,C167 (4)	.85	.80

12th Congress of the Confederation of Latin American Tourist Organizations (COTAL), Santo Domingo, May 25-29.

ILO Emblem — A179

Sliding into Base — A180

1969, June 27 Litho. *Perf. 12½*

656 A179 6c lt grnsh bl, grnsh bl & blk	.25	.20

50th anniv. of the ILO. See No. C168.

1969, Aug. 15 Litho. *Perf. 12½*

Designs: 1c, Catching a fly ball. 2c, View of Cibao Stadium, horiz.

Size: 21x31mm (1c, 3c); 43x30mm (2c)

657 A180 1c green & gray	.20	.20
658 A180 2c green & lt green	.20	.20
659 A180 3c purple & red brown	.20	.20
Nos. 657-659,C169-C171 (6)	4.95	3.50

17th World Amateur Baseball Championships, Santo Domingo.

Las Damas Dam A181

Tavera Dam — A182

Designs: 2c, Las Damas hydroelectric station, vert. 6c, Arroyo Hondo substation.

1969 Litho. *Perf. 12*

660 A181 2c green & multi	.20	.20
661 A181 3c dk blue & multi	.20	.20
662 A181 6c brt rose lilac	.20	.20
663 A182 6c multicolored	.25	.20
Nos. 660-663,C172-C173 (6)	1.50	1.20

National electrification plan.
Issued: #660-662, Sept. 15; #663, Oct. 15.

Juan Pablo Duarte — A183

Map of Republic, People, Census Emblem A184

1970, Jan. 26 Litho. *Perf. 12*

664 A183 1c emerald & dk grn	.20	.20
665 A183 2c sal pink & dp car	.20	.20
666 A183 3c brt pink & plum	.20	.20
667 A183 6c blue & violet blue	.20	.20
Nos. 664-667,C174 (5)	1.25	1.05

Issued for Duarte Day in memory of Juan Pablo Duarte (1813-1876), liberator.

1970, Feb. 6 *Perf. 11*

Design: 6c, Census emblem and inscription.

668 A184 5c emerald & blk	.20	.20
669 A184 6c ultra & blue	.20	.20
Nos. 668-669,C175 (3)	.85	.65

Census of 1970.

Abelardo Rodriguez Urdaneta — A185

"One of Many" A186

1970, Feb. 20 Litho. *Perf. 12½*

670 A185 3c ultramarine .20 .20
671 A186 6c green & yel grn .20 .20
Nos. 670-671,C176 (3) .70 .60

Issued to honor Abelardo Rodriguez Urdaneta, sculptor.

Masonic Symbols — A187

1970, Mar. 2

672 A187 6c green .20 .20

8th Inter-American Masonic Conference, Santo Domingo, Mar. 1-7. See No. C177.

Communications Satellite — A188

1970, May 25 Litho. *Perf. 12½*

673 A188 20c olive & gray .50 .30

World Telecommunications Day. See #C178.

UPU Headquarters, Bern — A189

1970, June 5 *Perf. 11*

674 A189 6c gray & brown .20 .20

Inauguration of the new UPU headquarters in Bern. See No. C179.

Education Year Emblem — A190

Pedro Alejandrino Pina — A191

1970, June 26 Litho. *Perf. 12½*

675 A190 4c rose lilac .20 .20

Issued for International Education Year, 1970. See No. C180.

1970, Aug. 24 Litho. *Perf. 12½*

676 A191 6c lt red brn & blk .20 .20

Pedro Alejandrino Pina (1820-70), author.

Children Reading A192

1970, Oct. 12 Litho. *Perf. 12½*

677 A192 5c dull green .20 .20
Nos. 677,C181-C182 (3) .75 .60

1st World Exhibition of Books and Culture Festival, Santo Domingo, Oct. 11-Dec. 11.

Virgin of Altagracia — A193

Rodriguez Objio — A194

1971, Jan. 20 Litho. *Perf. 12½*

678 A193 3c multicolored .25 .20

Inauguration of the Basilica of Our Lady of Altagracia. See No. C184.

1971, June 18 Litho. *Perf. 11*

679 A194 6c light blue .20 .20

Manuel Rodriguez Objio (1838-1871), poet.

Boxing and Canoeing — A195

1971, Sept. 10

680 A195 2c shown .20 .20
681 A195 5c Basketball .20 .20
Nos. 680-681,C186 (3) .65 .60

2nd National Games.

Goat and Fruit A196

Designs: 2c, Cow and goose. 3c, Cacao and horse. 6c, Bananas, coffee and pig.

1971, Sept. 29 *Perf. 12½*

682 A196 1c brown & multi .25 .20
683 A196 2c plum & multi .25 .20
684 A196 3c green & multi .25 .20
685 A196 6c blue & multi .25 .20
Nos. 682-685,C187 (5) 1.50 1.10

6th Natl. agriculture and livestock census.

José Nuñez de Cáceres — A197

Shepherds and Star — A198

1971, Dec. 1 *Perf. 11*

686 A197 6c lt bl, lil & dk bl .20 .20

Sesquicentennial of first national independence. See No. C188.

1971, Dec. 10 *Perf. 12½*

687 A198 6c blue, brown & yel .20 .20

Christmas 1971. See No. C189.

UNICEF Emblem, Child on Beach — A199

1971, Dec. 14 Litho. *Perf. 11*

688 A199 6c gray blue & multi .20 .20

UNICEF, 25th anniv. See No. C190.

Book Year Emblem A200

Taino Mask — A201

1972, Jan. 25 *Perf. 12½*

689 A200 1c green, ultra & red .20 .20
690 A200 2c brown, ultra & red .20 .20
Nos. 689-690,C191 (3) .70 .65

Intl. Book Year 1972.

1972, May 10 Litho. *Perf. 11*

4c, Ladle and amulet. 6c, Human figure.

691 A201 2c pink & multi .20 .20
692 A201 4c black, bl & ocher .20 .20
693 A201 6c gray & multi .20 .20
Nos. 691-693,C194-C196 (6) 1.85 1.45

Taino art. See note after No. 651.

Globe A202

1972, May 17 *Perf. 12½*

694 A202 6c blue & multi .20 .20

4th World Telecommunications Day. See No. C197.

"1972," Stamps and Map of Dominican Republic A203

1972, June 3

695 A203 2c green & multi .20 .20

First National Philatelic Exhibition, Santo Domingo, June 3-17. See No. C198.

Basketball — A204

1972, Aug. 25 Litho. *Perf. 12½*

696 A204 2c blue & multi .25 .20

20th Olympic Games, Munich, Aug. 26-Sept. 11. See No. C199.

Club Emblem A205

1972, Sept. 29 Litho. *Perf. 10½*

697 A205 1c lt green & multi .20 .20

50th anniversary of the Club Activo 20-30 International. See No. C200.

Emilio A. Morel A206

1972, Oct. 20 *Perf. 12½*

698 A206 6c brt pink & multi .20 .20

Emilio A. Morel (1884-1958), poet and journalist. See No. C201.

Central Bank Building A207

1972, Oct. 23

699	A207 1c shown	.20	.20
700	A207 5c 1-peso note	.20	.20
	Nos. 699-700,C202 (3)	1.05	.85

25th anniv. of Central Bank.

Holy Family — A208

Poinsettia A209

1972, Nov. 21

701	A208 2c rose lil, pur & gold	.25	.20
702	A209 6c red & multi	.25	.20
	Nos. 701-702,C203 (3)	.95	.60

Christmas 1972.

Mail Box and Student A210

1972, Dec. 15

703	A210 2c rose red	.20	.20
704	A210 6c blue	.20	.20
705	A210 10c emerald	.30	.20
	Nos. 703-705 (3)	.70	.60

Publicity for correspondence schools.

Tavera Dam A211

1973, Feb. 26 Litho. *Perf. 12½*

706	A211 10c multicolored	.30	.20

Inauguration of the Tavera Dam.

Various Sports — A212

Designs: a, UL. b, UR. c, LL. d, LR.

1973, Mar. 30 *Perf. 13½x13*

707	A212 Block of 4	.40	*.50*
a.-d.	2c, any single	.20	.20
708	A212 Block of 4	3.75	*3.75*
a.-d.	25c, any single	.75	.25
	Nos. 707-708,C204-C205 (4)	7.50	*7.60*

12th Central American and Caribbean Games, Santo Domingo, Summer 1974.

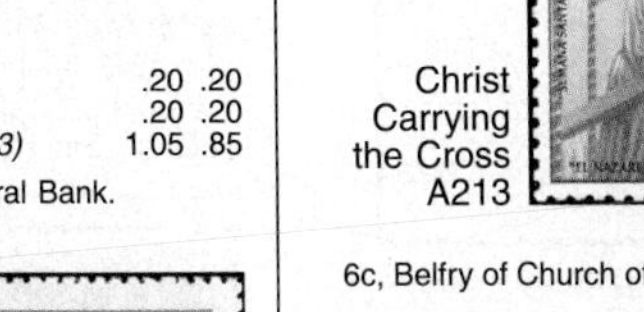

Christ Carrying the Cross A213

6c, Belfry of Church of Our Lady of Carmen.

1973, Apr. 18 Litho. *Perf. 10½*

709	A213 2c multicolored	.20	.20
710	A213 6c multicolored, vert.	.20	.20
	Nos. 709-710,C206 (3)	.80	.60

Holy Week, 1973.

WMO Emblem, Weather Satellite, "Weather" A214

Mask, Cibao — A215

1973, Aug. 10 Litho. *Perf. 13½x13*

711	A214 6c magenta & multi	.20	.20

Centenary of international meteorological cooperation. See No. C208.

1973, Oct. 12 Litho. *Perf. 10½*

712	A215 1c Maguey drum, horiz	.20	.20
713	A215 2c Carved amber, horiz	.20	.20
714	A215 4c shown	.20	.20
715	A215 6c Pottery	.20	.20
	Nos. 712-715,C210-C211 (6)	1.30	1.20

Opening of Museum of Mankind in Santo Domingo.

Nativity A216

Christmas: 6c, Stained glass window, vert.

Perf. 13½x13, 13x13½

1973, Nov. 26

716	A216 2c black, bl & yel	.20	.20
717	A216 6c rose & multi	.20	.20
	Nos. 716-717,C212 (3)	.65	.60

No. 717 exists imperf.

Dominican Scout Emblem A217

Design: 5c, Scouts and flag.

1973, Dec. 7 Litho. *Perf. 12*

Size: 35x35mm

718	A217 1c ultra & multi	.20	.20

Size: 26x36mm

719	A217 5c black & multi	.20	.20
	Nos. 718-719,C213 (3)	1.05	.95

Dominican Republic Boy Scouts, 50th anniv.

Sports Palace, Basketball Players A218

Design: 6c, Bicyclist and race track.

1974, Feb. 25 Litho. *Perf. 13½*

720	A218 2c red brown & multi	.20	.20
721	A218 6c yellow & multi	.20	.20
	Nos. 720-721,C214-C215 (4)	1.00	.80

12th Central American and Caribbean Games, Santo Domingo, 1974.

Bell Tower, Cathedral of Santo Domingo — A219

Mater Dolorosa — A220

1974, June 27 Litho. *Perf. 13½*

722	A219 2c multicolored	.20	.20
723	A220 6c multicolored	.25	.20
	Nos. 722-723,C216 (3)	.75	.60

Holy Week 1974.

Francisco del Rosario Sanchez Bridge — A221

1974, July 12 *Perf. 12*

724	A221 6c multicolored	.20	.20

See No. C217.

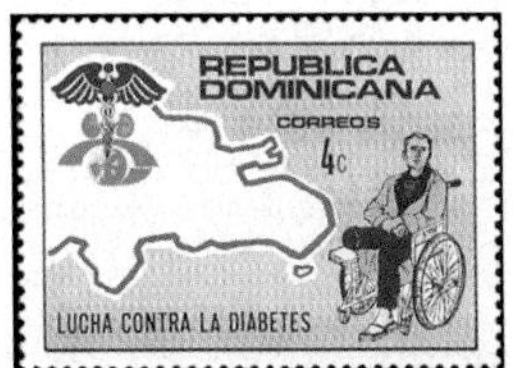

Map, Emblem and Patient — A222

Design: 5c, Map of Dominican Republic, diabetics' emblem and pancreas.

1974, Aug. 22 Litho. *Perf. 13*

725	A222 4c blue & multi	.20	.20
726	A222 5c yellow grn & multi	.20	.20
	Nos. 725-726,C218-C219 (4)	1.90	1.40

Fight against diabetes.

Train and UPU Emblem A223

Design: 6c, Mail coach and UPU emblem.

1974, Oct. 9 Litho. *Perf. 13½*

727	A223 2c blue & multi	.60	.60
728	A223 6c brown & multi	.25	.20
	Nos. 727-728,C220-C221 (4)	2.85	1.55

Cent. of UPU.

Golfers — A224

Design: 2c, Championship emblem and badge of Dominican Golf Association, horiz.

1974, Oct. 24 *Perf. 13x13½, 13½x13*

729	A224 2c yellow & blk	.20	.20
730	A224 6c blue & multi	.25	.20
	Nos. 729-730,C222-C223 (4)	1.60	1.00

World Amateur Golf Championships.

Christmas Decorations A225

Virgin and Child — A226

1974, Dec. 3 Litho. *Perf. 12*

731	A225 2c multicolored	.20	.20
732	A226 6c multicolored	.20	.20
	Nos. 731-732,C224 (3)	.70	.60

Christmas 1974.

Tomatoes, FAO Emblem — A227

1974, Dec. 5

733	A227 2c shown	.70	.20
734	A227 3c Avocados	.70	.20
735	A227 5c Coconuts	.70	.20
	Nos. 733-735,C225 (4)	3.20	.80

World Food Program, 10th anniv.

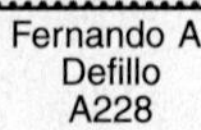

Fernando A. Defillo A228

Tower, Our Lady of the Rosary Convent A229

1975, Feb. 14 Litho. *Perf. 13½x13*

736 A228 1c dull brown .20 .20
737 A228 6c dull green .20 .20

Dr. Defillo (1874-1949), physician.

1975, Mar. 26 Litho. *Perf. 13½*

Design: 2c, Jesus saying "I am the Resurrection and the Life."

738 A229 2c brown & multi .20 .20
739 A229 6c multicolored .20 .20
Nos. 738-739,C226 (3) .70 .60

Holy Week 1975.

Hands (Steel Beams) with Symbols of Agriculture, Industry A230

1975, May 19 Litho. *Perf. 10½x10*

740 A230 6c dull blue & multi .20 .20

16th Assembly of the Governors of the International Development Bank, Santo Domingo, May 1975. See No. C228.

Satellite Tracking Station — A231

1975, June 21 Litho. *Perf. 13½*

741 A231 5c multicolored .20 .20

Opening of first earth satellite tracking station in Dominican Republic. See No. C229.

Apollo A232

1975, July 24

Size: 35x25mm

742 A232 1c shown .25 .20
743 A232 4c Soyuz .25 .20
Nos. 742-743,C230 (3) 5.75 3.65

Apollo Soyuz space test project (Russo-American cooperation), launching July 15; link-up, July 17.

Father Rafael C. Castellanos A233

1975, Aug. 6 Litho. *Perf. 12*

744 A233 6c brown & buff .20 .20

Castellanos (1875-1934), 1st Apostolic Administrator in Dominican Republic.

Women and Men Around IWY Emblem — A234

1975, Aug. 6 *Perf. 13*

745 A234 3c orange & multi .20 .20

International Women's Year 1975.

Guacanagarix A235

Basketball A236

Indian Chiefs: 2c, Guarionex. 3c, Caonabo. 4c, Bohechio. 5c, Cayacoa. 6c, Anacona (woman). 9c, Hatuey.

1975, Sept. 27 Litho. *Perf. 12*

746 A235 1c yellow & multi .25 .20
747 A235 2c salmon & multi .25 .20
748 A235 3c violet bl & multi .25 .20
749 A235 4c green & multi .25 .20
750 A235 5c blue & multi .25 .20
751 A235 6c violet & multi .25 .20
752 A235 9c rose & multi .30 .25
Nos. 746-752,C231-C233 (10) 2.65 2.20

1975, Oct. 24 Litho. *Perf. 12*

Design: 6c, Baseball and Games' emblem.

753 A236 2c pink & multi .20 .20
754 A236 6c orange & multi .20 .20
Nos. 753-754,C234-C235 (4) 1.00 .85

7th Pan-American Games, Mexico City, Oct. 13-26.

Carolers — A237

6c, Dominican nativity with farmers & shepherds.

1975, Dec. 12 Litho. *Perf. 13x13½*

755 A237 2c yellow & multi .20 .20
756 A237 6c blue & multi .25 .20
Nos. 755-756,C236 (3) .70 .60

Christmas 1975.

Abudefdul Marginatus — A238

1976, Jan. 23 Litho. *Perf. 13*

757 A238 10c shown .45 .25
758 A238 10c Doncella .45 .25
759 A238 10c Carajuelo .45 .25
760 A238 10c Reina de los Angeles .45 .25
761 A238 10c Pargo Colorado .45 .25
a. Strip of 5, #757-761 5.75 5.75

Ascension, by J. Priego — A239

"Separacion Dominicana" and Adm. Cambiaso A240

2c, Mary Magdalene, by Enrique Godoy.

1976, Apr. 14 Litho. *Perf. 13½*

762 A239 2c blue & multi .20 .20
763 A239 6c yellow & multi .25 .20
Nos. 762-763,C238 (3) .75 .65

Holy Week 1976.

1976, Apr. 15 *Perf. 13½x13*

764 A240 20c multicolored .85 .45

Naval Battle off Tortuga, Apr. 15, 1844.

Maps of US and Dominican Republic — A241

Design: 9c, Maps within cogwheels.

1976, May 29 Litho. *Perf. 13½*

765 A241 6c violet bl & multi .20 .20
766 A241 9c violet bl & multi .20 .20
Nos. 765-766,C239-C240 (4) 1.85 1.70

American Bicentennial.

Flags of Dominican Republic and Spain A242

1976, May 31

767 A242 6c multicolored .35 .20

Visit of King Juan Carlos I and Queen Sofia of Spain. See No. C241.

Various Telephones A243

1976, July 15 *Perf. 12x12½*

768 A243 6c multicolored .20 .20

Cent. of 1st telephone call by Alexander Graham Bell, Mar. 10, 1876. See No. C242.

Vision of Duarte, by Luis Desangles — A244

Juan Pablo Duarte, by Rhadames Mejia — A245

1976, July 20 Litho. *Perf. 13x13½*

769 A244 2c multicolored .20 .20

Perf. 13½

770 A245 6c multicolored .20 .20
Nos. 769-770,C243-C244 (4) 1.80 1.35

Juan Pablo Duarte, liberation hero, death centenary.

Fire Hydrant — A246

Design: 6c, Firemen's emblem.

1976, Sept. 13 Litho. *Perf. 12*

771 A246 4c multicolored .20 .20
772 A246 6c multicolored .25 .20
Nos. 771-772,C245 (3) .75 .60

Honoring firemen. Nos. 771-772 inscribed "Corrreos."

Radio and Atom Symbols A247

1976, Oct. 8 Litho. *Perf. 13½*

773 A247 6c red & black .20 .20

Dominican Radio Club, 50th anniv. See #C246.

Spain, Central and South America, Galleon A248

1976, Oct. 22 Litho. *Perf. 13½*

774 A248 6c multicolored .25 .20

Spanish heritage. See No. C247.

Boxing and Montreal Emblem A249

Design: 3c, Weight lifting.

1976, Oct. 22 *Perf. 12*

775 A249 2c blue & multi .20 .20
776 A249 3c multicolored .20 .20
Nos. 775-776,C248-C249 (4) 1.55 1.10

21st Olympic Games, Montreal, Canada, July 17-Aug. 1.

Virgin and Child — A250

Three Kings — A251

1976, Dec. 8 Litho. *Perf. 13½*

777 A250 2c multicolored .20 .20
778 A251 6c multicolored .20 .20
Nos. 777-778,C250 (3) .70 .65

Christmas 1976.

Cable Car and Beach Scenes A252

1977, Jan. 7

779 A252 6c multicolored .20 .20
Nos. 779,C251-C253 (4) 1.20 .90

Tourist publicity.

Championship Emblem — A253

1977, Mar. 4 Litho. *Perf. 13½*

780 A253 3c rose & multi .20 .20
781 A253 5c yellow & multi .20 .20
Nos. 780-781,C254-C255 (4) 1.55 1.10

10th Central American and Caribbean Children's and Young People's Swimming Championships, Santo Domingo.

Christ Carrying Cross — A254

Design: 6c, Head with crown of thorns.

1977, Apr. 18 Litho. *Perf. 13½x13*

782 A254 2c multicolored .20 .20
783 A254 6c black & rose .25 .20
Nos. 782-783,C256 (3) .75 .60

Holy Week 1977.

Doves, Lions Emblem A255

1977, May 6 *Perf. 13½x13*

784 A255 2c lt blue & multi .20 .20
785 A255 6c salmon & multi .20 .20
Nos. 784-785,C257 (3) .65 .60

12th annual Dominican Republic Lions Convention.

Battle Scene A256

1977, June 15 Litho. *Perf. 13x13½*

786 A256 20c multicolored .85 .35

Dominican Navy.

Water Lily — A257

National Botanical Garden: 4c, "Flor de Mayo" (orchid). 6c, Sebesten.

1977, Aug. 19 Litho. *Perf. 12*

787 A257 2c multicolored .25 .20
788 A257 4c multicolored .25 .20
789 A257 6c multicolored .25 .20
Nos. 787-789,C259-C260 (5) 2.15 1.60

Chart and Computers — A258

1977, Nov. 30 Litho. *Perf. 13*

790 A258 6c multicolored .20 .20

7th Interamerican Statistics Conf. See #C261.

Solenodon Paradoxus — A259

Design: 20c, Iguana and Congress emblem.

1977, Dec. 29 Litho. *Perf. 13*

791 A259 6c multicolored *1.40* .20
792 A259 20c multicolored *2.75* .30
Nos. 791-792,C262-C263 (4) 9.15 1.15

8th Pan-American Veterinary and Zoo-technical Congress.

Main Gate, Casa del Cordon, 1503 — A260

Crown of Thorns, Tools at the Cross — A261

1978, Jan. 19 *Perf. 13x13½*
Size: 26x36mm

793 A260 6c multicolored .20 .20

Spanish heritage. See No. C264.

1978, Mar. 21 Litho. *Perf. 12*

6c, Head of Jesus with crown of thorns.

Size: 22x33mm

794 A261 2c multicolored .20 .20
795 A261 6c slate .30 .20
Nos. 794-795,C265-C266 (4) 1.15 .90

Holy Week 1978.

Cardinal Octavio A. Beras Rojas — A262

Pres. Manuel de Troncoso — A263

1978, May 5 Litho. *Perf. 13*

796 A262 6c multicolored .20 .20

First Cardinal from Dominican Republic, consecrated May 24, 1976. See No. C268.

1978, June 12 Litho. *Perf. 13½*

797 A263 2c black, rose & brn .20 .20
798 A263 6c black, gray & brn .30 .25

Manuel de Jesus Troncoso de la Concha (1878-1955), pres. of Dominican Republic, 1940-42.

Father Juan N. Zegri y Moreno — A264

1978, July 11 Litho. *Perf. 13x13½*

799 A264 6c multicolored .20 .20

Congregation of the Merciful Sisters of Charity, centenary. See No. C273.

Boxing and Games' Emblem A265

1978, July 21 *Perf. 12*

800 A265 2c shown .25 .20
801 A265 6c Weight lifting .25 .20
Nos. 800-801,C274-C275 (4) 1.05 .80

13th Central American & Caribbean Games, Medellin, Colombia.

Sun over Landscape A266

Ships of Columbus, Map of Dominican Republic — A267

Design: 6c, Sun over beach and boat.

1978, Sept. 12 Litho. *Perf. 12*

802 A266 2c multicolored .30 .20
803 A266 6c multicolored .30 .20
Nos. 802-803,C280-C281 (4) 1.25 .80

Tourist publicity.

1978, Oct. 12 Litho. *Perf. 13½*

804 A267 2c multicolored .20 .20

Spanish heritage. See No. C282.

Dove, Lamp, Poinsettia A268

Design: 6c, Dominican family and star, vert.

1978, Dec. 5 Litho. *Perf. 12*

805 A268 2c multicolored .20 .20
806 A268 6c multicolored .25 .20
Nos. 805-806,C284 (3) .75 .65

Christmas 1978.

Starving Child, IYC Emblem — A269

Crucifixion A270

1979, Feb. 26 Litho. *Perf. 12*
807 A269 2c orange & black .20 .20
Nos. 807,C287-C289 (4) 1.80 1.35

Intl. Year of the Child.

1979, Apr. 9 Litho. *Perf. 13½*

Design: 3c, Jesus carrying cross, horiz.

808 A270 2c multicolored .25 .20
809 A270 3c multicolored .30 .20
Nos. 808-809,C290 (3) 1.80 1.30

Holy Week.

Stigmaphyllon Periplocifolium — A271

1979, May 17 Litho. *Perf. 12*
810 A271 50c multicolored 1.00 .50
Nos. 810,C293-C295 (4) 2.25 1.50

Dr. Rafael M. Moscoso National Botanical Garden.

Heart, Diseased Blood Vessel A272

Design: 1p, Cardiology Institute and heart.

1979, June 2 Litho. *Perf. 13½*
811 A272 3c multicolored .20 .20
812 A272 1p multicolored 1.75 .75
Nos. 811-812,C296 (3) 2.20 1.15

Dominican Cardiology Institute.

Baseball, Games' Emblem A273

3c, Bicycling and Games' emblem, vert.

1979, June 20
813 A273 2c multicolored .20 .20
814 A273 3c multicolored .20 .20
Nos. 813-814,C297 (3) .70 .65

8th Pan American Games, Puerto Rico, June 30-July 15.

Soccer — A274

Thomas A. Edison — A275

Design: 25c, Swimming, horiz.

1979, Aug. 9 Litho. *Perf. 12*
815 A274 2c multicolored .20 .20
816 A274 25c multicolored .35 .25
Nos. 815-816,C298 (3) .85 .70

Third National Games.

1979, Aug. 27 *Perf. 13½*
817 A275 25c multicolored .60 .45

Cent. of invention of electric light. See #C300.

Hand Holding Electric Plug A276

Design: 6c, Filling automobile gas tank.

1979, Aug. 30
818 A276 2c multicolored .20 .20
819 A276 6c multicolored .25 .25

Energy conservation.

Parrot A277

Birds: 6c, Temnotrogon roseigaster.

1979, Sept. 12 Litho. *Perf. 12*
820 A277 2c multicolored *1.50* .20
821 A277 6c multicolored *1.50* .20
Nos. 820-821,C301-C303 (5) 14.40 1.80

A278

A279

Lions Emblem, Map of Dominican Republic.

1979, Nov. 13 Litho. *Perf. 12*
822 A278 20c multicolored .45 .35

Lions International Club of Dominican Republic, 10th anniversary. See No. C304.

1979, Dec. 18 Litho. *Perf. 12*
823 A279 2c Holy Family .20 .20

Christmas 1979. See No. C305.

A280

A281

Design: Jesus Carrying Cross.

1980, Mar. 27 Litho. *Perf. 12*
824 A280 3c multicolored .20 .20
Nos. 824,C306-C307 (3) .70 .65

Holy Week.

1980, May 15 Litho. *Perf. 13½*
825 A281 1c shown .30 .20
826 A281 2c Coffee .30 .20
827 A281 3c Plantain .30 .20
828 A281 4c Sugar cane .30 .20
829 A281 5c Corn .30 .20
Nos. 825-829 (5) 1.50 1.00

Cacao Harvest (Agriculture Year)

Cotuf Gold Mine, Pueblo Viejo, Flag of Dominican Republic A282

1980, July 8 Litho. *Perf. 13½*
830 A282 6c multicolored .25 .20
Nos. 830,C310-C311 (3) 1.55 1.10

Nationalization of gold mining.

Blind Man's Buff A283

1980, July 21 *Perf. 12*
831 A283 3c shown .20 .20
832 A283 4c Marbles .20 .20
833 A283 5c Drawing in sand .25 .25
834 A283 6c Hopscotch .25 .25
Nos. 831-834 (4) .90 .90

Iguana A284

1980, Aug. 30 Litho. *Perf. 12*
835 A284 20c multicolored *2.00* .45
Nos. 835,C314-C317 (5) 11.10 2.25

Dance, by Jaime Colson A285

Perf. 13x13½, 13½x13
1980, Sept. 23 Litho.
836 A285 3c *shown* .25 .20
837 A285 50c *Woman, by Gilberto Hernandez Ortega*, vert. .90 .60
Nos. 836-837,C318-C319 (4) 1.95 1.40

Three Kings — A286

Salcedo Province Cent. — A287

1980, Dec. 5 Litho. *Perf. 13½*
838 A286 3c shown .20 .20
839 A286 6c Carolers .25 .20
Nos. 838-839,C327 (3) .75 .65

Christmas 1980.

1981, Jan. 14 Litho. *Perf. 13½*
840 A287 6c multicolored .20 .20

See No. C328.

Juan Pablo Duarte, Liberation Hero, 105th Anniv. of Death — A288

1981, Feb. 6 Litho. *Perf. 12*
841 A288 2c sepia & deep bister .20 .20

Gymnast — A289

Mother Mazzarello A290

1981, Mar. 31 Litho. *Perf. 13½*

842 A289 1c shown .25 .20
843 A289 2c Running .25 .20
844 A289 3c Pole vault .25 .20
845 A289 6c Boxing .30 .20
Nos. 842-845,C331 (5) 1.40 1.05

5th National Games.

1981, Apr. 14 *Perf. 12*

846 A290 6c multicolored .20 .20

Mother Maria Mazzarello (1837-1881), founder of Daughters of Mary.

A291

A292

1981, May 18 Litho. *Perf. 13½*

847 A291 6c gray vio & lt gray .20 .20

Pedro Henriquez Urena, Historian (1884-1946)

1981, June 30 Litho. *Perf. 12*

848 A292 2c shown .20 .20
849 A292 6c River, forest .25 .20

Forest conservation.

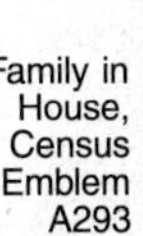

Family in House, Census Emblem A293

1981, Aug. 14 Litho. *Perf. 12*

850 A293 3c shown .20 .20
851 A293 6c Farmer .25 .20

1981 natl. population and housing census.

A294

A295

1981, Dec. 23 Litho. *Perf. 13½*

852 A294 2c Bells .20 .20
853 A294 3c Poinsettia .20 .20
Nos. 852-853,C353 (3) .90 .70

Christmas.

1982, Jan. 29 Litho. *Perf. 13½*

854 A295 2c Juan Pablo Duarte .20 .20

National Elections A296

Designs: Voters casting votes. 3c, 6c vert.

1982, Mar. 30 Litho. *Perf. 13½*

855 A296 2c multicolored .20 .20
856 A296 3c multicolored .20 .20
857 A296 6c multicolored .25 .25
Nos. 855-857 (3) .65 .65

A297

A298

Energy Conservation: Various forms of energy.

1982, May 10 Litho. *Perf. 12*

858 A297 1c multicolored .20 .20
859 A297 2c multicolored .20 .20
860 A297 3c multicolored .20 .20
861 A297 4c multicolored .25 .25
862 A297 5c multicolored .25 .25
863 A297 6c multicolored .25 .25
Nos. 858-863 (6) 1.35 1.35

1982, Aug. 2 *Perf. 12x12½*

864 A298 6c multicolored .25 .20

Emilio Prud'Homme (1856-1932), composer.

Pres. Antonio Guzman Fernandez (1911-1982) A299

1982, Aug. 4 *Perf. 13x13½*

865 A299 6c multicolored .25 .20

14th Central American and Caribbean Games A300

1982, Aug. 13 *Perf. 12, Imperf.*

866 A300 3c Baseball .50 .20

See Nos. C368-C370.

San Pedro de Macoris Province Centenary — A301

1982, Aug. 26 *Perf. 13*

867 A301 1c Wagon .20 .20
868 A301 2c Stained-glass window .20 .20
869 A301 5c Views .30 .25
Nos. 867-869,C375 (4) 1.10 .95

Size of 2c, 25x35mm.

St. Teresa of Jesus of Avila (1515-1582) A302

1982, Nov. 17 Litho. *Perf. 13½*

870 A302 6c multicolored .25 .20

Christmas 1982 — A303

Environmental Protection A304

Various Christmas balls.

1982, Dec. 8

871 A303 6c multicolored .25 .20

See No. C380.

1982, Dec. 15 *Perf. 12*

872 A304 2c Bird .20 .20
873 A304 3c Water .20 .20
874 A304 6c Forest .20 .20
875 A304 20c Fish .50 .35
Nos. 872-875 (4) 1.10 .95

Natl. Literacy Campaign A305

1983, Mar. 9 Litho. *Perf. 13½*

876 A305 2c Vowels on blackboard .20 .20
877 A305 3c Writing, reading .20 .20
878 A305 6c Children, pencil .25 .20
Nos. 876-878 (3) .65 .60

A306

A307

5c, similar arms, incorporating stylized centenary monument.

1983, Apr. 4 *Perf. 12*

879 A306 1c multicolored .20 .20
880 A306 5c multicolored .25 .20

Mao City centenary.

1983, Apr. 25 Litho. *Perf. 12*

Dominican Historians: 2c, Antonio del Monte y Tejada (1780-1861). 3c, Manuel Ubaldo Gomez (1857-1941). 5c, Emiliano Tejera (1841-1923). 6c, Bernardo Pichardo (1877-1924). 7c, Americo Lugo (1870-1952). 10c, José Gabriel Garcia (1834-1910). 7c, 10c airmail.

881 A307 2c multicolored .20 .20
882 A307 3c multicolored .20 .20
883 A307 5c multicolored .20 .20
884 A307 6c multicolored .25 .20
885 A307 7c multicolored .25 .25
886 A307 10c multicolored .30 .30
Nos. 881-886 (6) 1.40 1.35

National Anthem, 100th Anniv. A308

Emilio Prud'Homme, & Jose Reyes, composer.

1983, Sept. 13 Litho. *Perf. 13½*

887 A308 6c copper red & blk .20 .20

Free Masons, 125th Anniv. — A309

Church of Our Lady of Regla, 300th Anniv. — A310

1983, Oct. 24 Litho. *Perf. 12*

888 A309 4c Emblem .20 .20

1983, Nov. 5 *Perf. 13½*

889 A310 3c Church .20 .20
890 A310 6c Statue .25 .20

450th Anniv. of Monte Cristi Province — A311

6th Natl. Games — A312

1983, Nov. 25 *Perf. 12*

891 A311 1c Tower .20 .20
892 A311 2c Arms .20 .20
893 A311 5c Cuban independence site, horiz. .25 .20
894 A311 7c Workers, horiz. .25 .20
Nos. 891-894 (4) .90 .80

1983, Dec. 9

895 A312 6c Bicycling, boxing, baseball .20 .20
896 A312 10c Gymnast, weight lifting, swimming .25 .20

10c airmail.

Restoration of the Republic, 120th Anniv. A313

1983, Dec. 30 Litho. *Perf. 13½*

897 A313 1c Capotillo Heroes Monument .20 .20

140th Anniv. of Independence — A314

Designs: 6c, Matia Ramon Mella (Patriot), flag. 25c, Mella's Blunderbuss rifle, Gate of Deliverance (independence declaration site).

1984, Feb. 24 Litho. *Perf. 13½*

898 A314 6c multicolored .20 .20
899 A314 25c multicolored .60 .35

Heriberto Pieter (1884-1972), Physician, First Negro Graduate — A315

1984, Mar. 16

900 A315 3c multicolored .25 .20

Battle of Barranquita, 67th Anniv. — A316

1983, Dec. 30 *Perf. 12*

901 A316 5c multicolored .20 .20

Battle of Santiago, 140th Anniv. A317

1984, Mar. 29 *Perf. 13½*

902 A317 7c multicolored .25 .25

Coast Guard Ship DC-1, 1934 A318

1984, Apr. 13 Litho.

903 A318 10c multicolored .30 .20

Navy Day and 140th anniv. of Battle of Tortuguero.

Birth Centenary of Pedro Henriquez Urena — A319

1984, June 29 Litho. *Perf. 12*

904 A319 7c Salome Urena .20 .20
905 A319 10c Text .25 .25
906 A319 22c Urena .30 .25
Nos. 904-906 (3) .75 .70

Monument to Heroes of June 1959 A320

1984, June 20 *Perf. 13½*

907 A320 6c silver & blue .25 .25

The feat of Constanza Maimon and Estero Hondo, 25th anniv.

1984 Summer Olympics A321

1984, Aug. 1

908 A321 1p Hurdles 1.60 1.60
909 A321 1p Weightlifting 1.60 1.60
910 A321 1p Boxing 1.60 1.60
911 A321 1p Baseball 1.60 1.60
a. Block of 4, #908-911 12.00 12.00
Nos. 908-911 (4) 6.40 6.40

Protection of Fauna — A322

1984, Oct. 3 Litho. *Perf. 12*

912 A322 10c Owl *2.25* .25
913 A322 15c Flamingo *3.00* .30
914 A322 25c Wild Pig *3.75* .35
915 A322 35c Solenodon *5.25* .55
Nos. 912-915 (4) 14.25 1.45

500th Anniv. of Discovery of America A323

1984, Oct. 10 Litho. *Perf. 13½x13*

916 A323 10c Landing on Hispaniola .20 .20
917 A323 35c Destruction of Ft. Navidad .50 .30
918 A323 65c First Mass in America .85 .60
919 A323 1p Battle of Santo Cerro 1.25 .80
Nos. 916-919 (4) 2.80 1.90

Visit of Pope John Paul II — A324

1984, Oct. 11 Litho. *Perf. 13x13½*

920 Block of 4 7.50 7.50
a. A324 75c shown 1.50 1.50
b. A324 75c Pope, map of Caribbean 1.50 1.50
c. A324 75c Pope, globe 1.50 1.50
d. A324 75c Bishop's crozier 1.50 1.50

150th Anniv. of Birth of Maximo Gomez (1986) A325

1984, Dec. 6 Litho. *Perf. 13½*

921 A325 10c Gomez on horseback .20 .20
922 A325 20c Maximo Gomez .25 .20

Christmas 1984 A326

Perf. 13½x13, 13x13½

1984, Dec. 14 Litho.

923 A326 5c multicolored .20 .20
924 A326 10c multicolored, vert. .25 .25

Sacrifice of the Child, by Eligio Pichardo A327

Paintings and sculpture: 10c, The Pumpkin Sellers, by Gaspar Mario Cruz; 25c, The Market, by Celeste Woss y Gil; 50c, Horses in the Rain, by Dario Suro.

1984, Dec. 19 Litho. *Perf. 13½*

925 A327 5c multi .40 .20
926 A327 10c multi, vert. .40 .20
927 A327 25c multi .45 .25
928 A327 50c multi 1.10 .35
Nos. 925-928 (4) 2.35 1.00

Day of Our Lady of Altagracia A328

1985, Jan. 21

929 A328 5c Old church at Higuey, 1572 .25 .20
930 A328 10c Our Lady of Altagracia 1514, vert. .25 .20
931 A328 25c Basilica of the Protector, Higuey 1971, vert. .50 .30
Nos. 929-931 (3) 1.00 .70

Independence, 141st Anniv. — A329

Painting: The Fathers of Our Country (Duarte, Sanchez and Mella).

1985, Mar. 8 *Perf. 12½*

932 A329 5c multicolored .20 .20
933 A329 10c multicolored .25 .20
934 A329 25c multicolored .45 .25
Nos. 932-934 (3) .90 .65

Battle of Azua, 141st Anniv. A330

1985, Apr. 8 Litho. *Perf. 13½*

935 A330 10c Gen. Antonio Duverge, Statue .35 .20

A331

A332

1985, Apr. 15 Litho.

936 A331 25c Santo Domingo Lighthouse, 1853 .40 .25

Battle of Tortuguero, 141st anniv.

1985, Apr. 15 Litho. *Perf. 12*

937 A332 35c multicolored .85 .30

American Airforces Cooperation System, 25th anniv.

A333

A334

1985, May 24 Litho. *Perf. 13½*

938	A333 10c Don Carlos M. Rojas, 1st gov.	.30	.30

Espaillat Province cent.

1985, July 5 Litho. *Perf. 12*

939	A334 5c Table tennis	.25	.20
940	A334 10c Walking race	.30	.30

MOCA '85, 7th Natl. Games.

Intl. Youth Year A335

1985, July 29 *Perf. 13½*

941	A335 5c Youth	.30	.20
942	A335 25c The Haitises	.85	.30
943	A335 35c Mt. Duarte summit	.90	.30
944	A335 2p Mt. Duarte	5.75	2.25
	Nos. 941-944 (4)	7.80	3.05

Interamerican Development Bank, 25th Anniv. — A336

10c, Haina Harbor. 25c, Map of development sites. 1p, Tavera-Bao-Lopez Hydroelectric Complex.

1985, Aug. 23

945	A336 10c multicolored	.25	.20
946	A336 25c multicolored	.50	.35
947	A336 1p multicolored	2.25	1.50
	Nos. 945-947 (3)	3.00	2.05

Intl. Decade for Women — A337

15th Central American and Caribbean Games, Santiago — A338

Design: Evangelina Rodriguez (1879-1947), first Dominican woman doctor.

1985, Sept. 26

948	A337 10c multicolored	.30	.20

1985, Oct. 9 *Perf. 12*

949	A338 5c multicolored	.40	.25
950	A338 25c multicolored	1.10	.35

4th Adm. Christopher Columbus Regatta, Casa de Espana A339

Designs: 50c, Founding of Santo Domingo, 1496. 65c, Chapel of Our Lady of the Rosary, 1496, Santo Domingo. 1p, Columbus, American Indian and old Spanish coat of arms.

1985, Oct. 10 *Perf. 13½*

951	A339 35c multicolored	1.10	.60
952	A339 50c multicolored	1.40	.90
953	A339 65c multicolored	1.90	1.10
954	A339 1p multicolored	3.50	1.90
	Nos. 951-954 (4)	7.90	4.50

Discovery of America, 500th anniv. (in 1992).

Cacique Enriquillo — A340

Archbishop Fernando Arturo de Merino — A341

Designs: 5c, Enriquillo in the Bahuroco Mountains, mural detail.

1985, Oct. 31

955	A340 5c multicolored	.20	.20
956	A340 10c multicolored	.45	.25

Enriquillo (d. 1536), leader of revolution against Spain. Size of No. 955: 47x33mm.

1985, Dec. 3 *Perf. 12*

957	A341 25c multicolored	.50	.35

Cent. of holy orders granted to Merino (1833-1906), pres. of the republic 1880-82.

Mirabal Sisters, Political Martyrs 1960 A342

1985, Dec. 18 *Perf. 13½*

958	A342 10c multicolored	.30	.20

Christmas A343

1985, Dec. 18

959	A343 10c multicolored	.30	.20
960	A343 25c multicolored	.70	.35

Day of Independence, Feb. 27 — A344

Design: Mausoleum of founding fathers Duarte, Sanchez and Mella.

1986, Feb. 26 Litho. *Perf. 13½*

961	A344 5c multicolored	.25	.20
962	A344 10c multicolored	.25	.25

Holy Week A345

Colonial churches.

1986, Apr. 10

963	A345 5c San Miguel	.40	.25
964	A345 5c San Andres	.40	.25
965	A345 10c Santa Barbara	.40	.25
966	A345 10c San Lazaro	.40	.25
967	A345 10c San Carlos	.40	.25
	Nos. 963-967 (5)	2.00	1.25

Navy Day A346

Design: Juan Bautista Cambiaso, Juan Bautista Maggiolo and Juan Alejandro Acosta, 1884 independence battle heroes.

1986, Apr. 15

968	A346 10c multicolored	.30	.20

Natl. Elections — A347

Natl. Postal Institute Inauguration A348

1986, Apr. 29

969	A347 5c Voters, map	.25	.20
970	A347 10c Ballot box	.30	.25

1986, June 10

971	A348 10c gold, blue & red	.30	.20
972	A348 25c silver, blue & red	.70	.30
973	A348 50c black, blue & red	1.40	.50
	Nos. 971-973 (3)	2.40	1.00

Central America and Caribbean Games, Santiago — A349

1986, July 17 Litho. *Perf. 13½*

974	A349 10c Weight lifting	.30	.20
975	A349 25c Gymnastics	.60	.30
976	A349 35c Diving	.90	.35
977	A349 50c Equestrian	1.10	.55
	Nos. 974-977 (4)	2.90	1.40

Historians A350

Designs: 5c, Ercilia Pepin (b. 1886), vert. 10c, Ramon Emilio Jimenez (b. 1886) and Victor Garrido (1886-1972).

1986, Aug. 1 Litho. *Perf. 13½*

978	A350 5c silver & dull brn	.25	.20
979	A350 10c silver & dull brn	.25	.20

A351

A352

Discovery of America, 500th Anniv. (in 1992) — A353

Designs: 25c, Yachts racing, 5th Adm. Christopher Columbus Regatta, Casa de Espana. 50c, Columbus founding La Isabela City. 65c, Exploration of the hidalgos. 1p, Columbus returning to the Court of Ferdinand and Isabella. 1.50p, Emblems.

1986, Oct. 10 Litho. *Perf. 13½*

980	A351 25c multicolored	.55	.30
981	A352 50c multicolored	1.25	.45
982	A352 65c multicolored	1.50	.75
983	A352 1p multicolored	2.25	1.00

Textured Paper

Size: 86x58mm

Imperf

984	A353 1.50p multicolored	5.00	5.00
	Nos. 980-984 (5)	10.55	7.50

1986 World Cup Soccer Championships, Mexico — A354

Medicinal Plants — A355

Various soccer plays.

1986, Oct. 21 *Perf. 13½*

985	A354 50c multicolored	1.10	.50
986	A354 75c multicolored	2.25	.85

1986, Dec. 5

987	A355 5c Zea mays	.20	.20
988	A355 10c Bixa orellana	.20	.20
989	A355 25c Momordica charantia	.50	.20
990	A355 50c Annona muricata	1.00	.40
	Nos. 987-990 (4)	1.90	1.00

Second Caribbean Pharmacopeia Seminar.

Christmas A356

1986, Dec. 19

991	A356 5c Urban scene	.40	.25
992	A356 25c Rural scene	1.00	.30

A357

A358

1986, Dec. 31 Litho. *Perf. 13½*

993	A357 10c shown	.30	.20
994	A357 25c Portrait, c. 1900	.60	.30

Maximo Gomez (1836-1905), revolutionary, statesman.

1987, Mar. 30 Litho. *Perf. 13½*

995	A358 50c brt blue, blk & red	1.10	.55

16th Pan American Ophthalmological Conf., Apr. 5-10.

A359

A360

Stained-glass window, San Juan Bosco church, Santo Domingo: Ascension of Christ to Heaven.

1987, May 28

996	A359 35c multicolored	1.10	.40

1987, Aug. 21

Edible plants.

997	A360 5c Sorghum bicolor	.20	.20
998	A360 25c Martanta arundinacea	.40	.25
999	A360 65c Calathaea allouia	1.50	.75
1000	A360 1p Voandzeia subterranea	2.25	1.10
	Nos. 997-1000 (4)	4.35	2.30

Activo 20-30 Intl., 25th Anniv. A361

1987, Aug. 26

1001	A361 35c multicolored	1.00	.35

Adm. Christopher Columbus Regatta A362

A363

Columbus Memorial, Santo Domingo — A364

1987, Oct. 14

1002	A362 50c shown	1.25	.45
1003	A363 75c shown	1.75	.65
1004	A363 1p Building Ft. Santiago	2.40	.90
1005	A363 1.50p Columbus imprisoned by Bombadilla	3.75	1.40

Size: 82x70mm

Imperf

1006	A364 2.50p shown	8.00	5.00
	Nos. 1002-1006 (5)	17.15	8.40

Discovery of America, 500th anniv. in 1992.

A365

A366

1987, Sept. 28

1007	A365 40c multicolored	.85	.40

Junior Olympics, La Vega, 50th anniv.

1987, Nov. 10 Litho. *Perf. 13½*

Historians and authors: 10c, Jose Antonio Hungria. 25c, Joaquin Sergio Inchaustegui.

1008	A366 10c buff & brown	.25	.20
1009	A366 25c pale grn & grn	.60	.25

SAN CRISTOBAL '87, 8th Natl. Games — A367

1987, Nov. 19

1010	A367 5c Baseball	.50	.20
1011	A367 10c Boxing	.25	.20
1012	A367 50c Judo	1.10	.55
	Nos. 1010-1012 (3)	1.85	.95

Christmas 1987 A368

1987, Dec. 9 Litho. *Perf. 13½*

1013	A368 10c Roasting pig	.40	.20
1014	A368 50c Arriving at airport	1.10	.45

Fr. Xavier Billini (b. 1837) — A369

1987, Dec. 18 Litho. *Perf. 13½*

1015	A369 10c Statue	.25	.20
1016	A369 25c Portrait	.55	.30
1017	A369 75c Ana Hernandez de Billini, his mother	1.60	.90
	Nos. 1015-1017 (3)	2.40	1.40

Frank Feliz, Sr., and Aircraft A370

1987, Dec. 22

1018	A370 25c shown	.45	.25

Size: 86x106mm

Imperf

1019	A370 2p No. C30, map	6.50	6.00

Pan-American goodwill flight to South American countries by the planes Colon, Pinta, Nina and Santa Maria, 50th anniv.

Flora A371

1988, Feb. 3 Litho. *Perf. 13½*

1020	A371 50c Bromelia pinguin	1.40	.55
1021	A371 50c Tillandsia fasciculata	1.40	.55
1022	A371 50c Tillandsia hotteana, vert.	1.40	.55
1023	A371 50c Tillandsia compacta, vert.	1.40	.55
	Nos. 1020-1023 (4)	5.60	2.20

St. John Bosco (1815-1888) A372

1988, Feb. 23 Litho. *Perf. 13½*

1024	A372 10c shown	.25	.20
1025	A372 70c Stained-glass window	1.10	.75

Dominican Rehabilitation Assoc., 25th Anniv. — A373

1988, Mar. 1

1026	A373 20c multicolored	.45	.25

A374

A375

1988, Apr. 6 Litho. *Perf. 13½*
1027 A374 20c dk red brn & lt fawn .45 .25

Dr. Manuel Emilio Perdomo (b.1886).

1988, Apr. 29 Litho. *Perf. 13½*
1028 A375 20c multicolored .45 .25

Dominican College of Engineers, Architects and Surveyors (CODIA), 25th Anniv.

Independence Day, Mexico — A376

Flags and: No. 1029, Fr. Miguel Hidalgo y Costilla (1753-1811), Mexican revolutionary. No. 1030, Juan Pablo Duarte (1813-1876), father of Dominican independence.

1988, Sept. 12 Litho. *Perf. 13½*
1029 A376 50c multicolored 1.10 .50
1030 A376 50c multicolored 1.10 .50

1988 Summer Olympics, Seoul A377

1988, Sept. 21 Litho. *Perf. 13½*

1031	A377	50c Running, vert.	.95	.20
1032	A377	70c Table tennis, vert.	1.50	.35
1033	A377	1p Judo, vert.	2.40	.40
1034	A377	1.50p Mural by Tete Marella	3.50	.75
		Nos. 1031-1034 (4)	8.35	1.70

A378

Discovery of America, 500th Anniv. (in 1992) — A379

Designs: 50c, 7th Adm. Christopher Columbus Regatta, Casa de Espana, 1988. 70c, La Concepcion Fortress, La Vega Real, 1494. 1.50p, Ft. Bonao. 2p, Nicolas de Ovando (c. 1451-1511), governor of Spanish possessions in America from 1502 to 1509. 3p, Mausoleum of Christopher Columbus, Santo Domingo Cathedral.

1988, Oct. 14 *Perf. 13½*

1035	A378	50c multicolored	.95	.50
1036	A378	70c multicolored	1.60	.75
1037	A378	1.50p multicolored	3.25	1.50
1038	A378	2p multicolored	4.75	1.90

Size: 78x109mm

Imperf

1039	A379	3p multicolored	5.00	5.00
		Nos. 1035-1039 (5)	15.55	9.65

Discovery of America, 500th anniv. (in 1992). No. 1038 inscribed "1501-1509."

Duverge Parish, Cent. — A380

1988, July 13 Litho. *Perf. 13½*
1040 A380 50c multicolored 1.25 .40

A381

Trinitarians, 150th Anniv. — A382

1988, Nov. 11

1041	A381	10c shown	.40	.20
1042	A382	1p Trinitarian Plaza	1.90	.40
1043	A382	5p Independence Plaza	11.50	3.00
		Nos. 1041-1043 (3)	13.80	3.60

See footnote after No. 337.

Pharmacology and Biochemistry A383

The Holy Family, 1504, by Miguel Angel — A384

1988, Nov. 28 Litho. *Perf. 13½*
1044 A383 1p multicolored 1.50 1.25

13th Pan American and 16th Central American Congresses.

1988, Dec. 12

1045	A384	10c shown	.25	.20
1046	A384	20c Stained-glass window	.45	.30

Christmas.

Municipal Technical Advisory Organization (LIGA), 50th Anniv. — A385

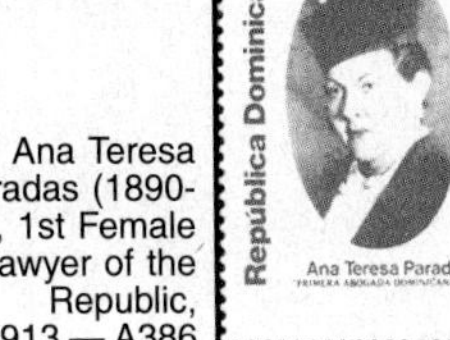

Ana Teresa Paradas (1890-1960), 1st Female Lawyer of the Republic, 1913 — A386

1988, Dec. 23
1047 A385 20c multicolored .45 .30

1988, Dec. 26
1048 A386 20c deep claret .45 .30

French Revolution Bicent. A387

1989, Mar. 10 Litho. *Perf. 13½*
1049 A387 3p red & violet blue 2.25 2.25

Battle of Tortuga, Apr. 15, 1844 A388

1989, Apr. 14 Litho. *Perf. 13½*
1050 A388 40c multicolored .70 .45

Natl. Anti-drug Campaign A389

1989, May 15

1051	A389	10c multicolored	.30	.20
1052	A389	20c multicolored	.35	.20
1053	A389	50c multicolored	.60	.20
1054	A389	70c multicolored	.85	.30
1055	A389	1p multicolored	1.25	.30
1056	A389	1.50p multicolored	1.75	.40
1057	A389	2p multicolored	2.40	.60
1058	A389	5p multicolored	6.00	1.25
1059	A389	10p multicolored	11.50	3.00
		Nos. 1051-1059 (9)	25.00	6.45

Mother's Day A390

1989, May 30 Litho. *Perf. 13½*
1060 A390 20c multicolored .25 .20

Eugenio Maria de Hostos (b. 1839) — A391

Gen. Gregorio Luperon (b. 1839) — A392

1989, Aug. 22 Litho. *Perf. 13½*
1061 A391 20c multicolored .35 .20

1989, Aug. 28
1062 A392 20c multicolored .35 .20

Little League Baseball, 50th Anniv. A393

1989, Sept. 29
1063 A393 1p multicolored 1.50 .75

Diabetes '89, 7th Latin American Congress A394

1989, Oct. 9 Litho. *Perf. 13½*
1064 A394 1p multicolored 1.50 .60

America Issue A395

UPAE emblem, pre-Columbian artifacts and customs: 20c, Cohoba silver statue and ritual dance. 1p, Taina mortar, pestle and family preparing cazabe.

1989, Oct. 12

1065	A395	20c multicolored	.40	.20
1066	A395	1p multicolored	2.25	1.25

8th Adm. Christopher Columbus Regatta, Casa de Espana — A396

European Colonization of the Americas — A397

Designs: 70c, Fr. Pedro de Cordoba converting the Indians to Catholicism. 1p, Christopher Columbus trading with the Indians. 3p, Sermon of Pedro de Cordoba.

1989, Oct. 13

1067 A396 50c shown .45 .25
1068 A397 70c shown .60 .40
1069 A397 1p multicolored .80 .55
1070 A397 3p multicolored 2.75 1.60
Nos. 1067-1070 (4) 4.60 2.80

Discovery of America, 500th anniv. (in 1992).

Natl. Afforestation A398

1989, Oct. 30 Litho. *Perf. 13½*

1071 A398 10c shown .20 .20
1072 A398 20c Tree .25 .20
1073 A398 50c Forest .70 .45
1074 A398 1p Sapling, mature trees 1.60 .90
Nos. 1071-1074 (4) 2.75 1.75

9th Natl. Games, La Vega — A399

Holy Week (Easter) — A400

1990, Mar. 20 Litho. *Perf. 13½*

1075 A399 10c Cycling .20 .20
1076 A399 20c Running .30 .25
1077 A399 50c Basketball .85 .60
Nos. 1075-1077 (3) 1.35 1.05

1990, Apr. 5

1078 A400 20c shown .30 .25
1079 A400 50c Jesus carrying cross .85 .60

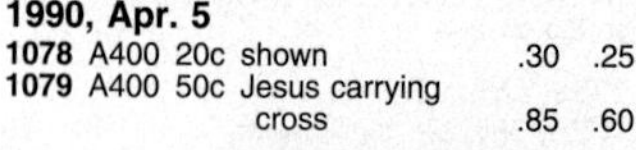

Labor Day, Cent. A401

1990, Apr. 30 Litho. *Perf. 13½*

1080 A401 1p multicolored 1.50 .65

Urban Renewal A402

1990, May 10

1081 A402 10c shown .20 .20
1082 A402 20c Highway underpass .20 .20
1083 A402 50c Library .70 .25
1084 A402 1p City street 1.60 .65
Nos. 1081-1084 (4) 2.70 1.30

No. 1084 inscribed $100 instead of $1.00.

Penny Black, 150th Anniv. — A403

1990, May 29

1085 A403 1p multicolored 1.50 1.10

Size: 62x80mm

Imperf

1086 A403 3p Sir Rowland Hill, Penny Black 4.50 4.50

Organization of American States, Cent. — A404

1990, Oct. 5 Litho. *Perf. 13½*

1087 A404 2p Flags 3.50 2.25

Children's Drawings A405

1990, Aug. 7

1088 A405 50c House of Tostado .85 .55
1089 A405 50c Ruins of St. Nicolas of Bari .85 .55

Discovery of America, 500th Anniv. (in 1992) A406

Designs: 1p, Fight at the Gulf of Arrows. 2p, Columbus talking with Guacanagari Indians. 5p, Columbus and Caonabo Indian prisoner.

1990, Oct. 12

1090 A406 1p multicolored 1.75 1.10
1091 A406 2p multicolored 3.50 2.25
1092 A406 5p multicolored 8.75 5.75
Nos. 1090-1092 (3) 14.00 9.10

9th Adm. Christopher Columbus Regatta — A407

1990, Oct. 12

1093 A407 50c multicolored .75 .55

America Issue A408

UPAE emblem and: 50c, Men in canoe. 3p, Man on hammock.

1990, Nov. 7 Litho. *Perf. 13½*

1094 A408 50c multicolored .85 .60
1095 A408 3p multicolored 5.00 3.75

A409

A410

Discovery of Hispaniola: 50c, 1st official mass in Americas. 1p, Arms of 1st religious order in Americas. 3p, Map of island, horiz. 4p, Christopher Columbus, 1st viceroy and governor in Americas.

1991, July 17 Litho. *Perf. 13½*

1096 A409 50c multicolored .75 .40
1097 A409 1p multicolored 1.50 .85
1098 A409 3p multicolored 3.00 1.50
1099 A409 4p multicolored 7.50 4.25
Nos. 1096-1099 (4) 12.75 7.00

1991

1100 A410 30c Boxing .40 .20
1101 A410 50c Cycling 1.25 .50
1102 A410 1p Bowling 2.50 1.00
Nos. 1100-1102 (3) 4.15 1.70

11th Pan American Games, Havana.

Dr. Tomas Eudoro Perez Rancier, Birth Cent. — A411

1991, July 3

1103 A411 2p yellow & black 4.25 1.50

10th Columbus Regatta, Casa de Espana — A412

Discovery of America, 500th Anniv. (in 1992) A413

Designs: 50c, Encounter of three cultures. 3p, Columbus and Dr. Alvarez Chanca caring for sick. 4p, Rebellion of Enriquillo.

1991, Oct. 15 Litho. *Perf. 13½*

1104 A412 30c multicolored .60 .20
1105 A413 50c multicolored .75 .30
1106 A413 3p multicolored 4.50 1.75
1107 A413 4p multicolored 6.00 2.50
Nos. 1104-1107 (4) 11.85 4.75

See No. 1116.

A414

A415

1991, Nov. 18

1108 A414 3p black & red 4.25 1.75

Cornea Bank.

1991 Litho. *Perf. 13½*

1109 A415 1p Santa Maria 1.00 .50
1110 A415 3p Christopher Columbus 3.00 2.10

America issue.

33rd Meeting of Inter-American Development Bank Governors, Santo Domingo — A416

1992 Litho. *Perf. 13½*

1111 A416 1p multicolored 1.50 .75

A417

A418

1992 Litho. *Perf. 13½*
1112 A417 3p multicolored 4.50 1.75

Espanola '92 Philatelic Exposition.

1992 Litho. *Perf. 13½*

Valentin Salinero, Order of the Apostles founder.

1113 A418 1p blue & brown 1.50 .75

Order of the Apostles, cent.

Ruins of Monastery of San Francisco A419

Designs: 3p, Ruins of San Nicolas hospital, first in the Americas.

1992, July 28
1114 A419 50c multicolored .60 .35
1115 A419 3p multicolored 4.75 2.50

Type of 1991 and

A420

Designs: 50c, Racing yacht. 1p, Native women, Columbus. 2p, Natives offering Columbus tobacco. 3p, Native woman, Columbus, corn.

1992, Oct. 6 Litho. *Perf. 13½*
1116 A412 50c multicolored .70 .35
1117 A420 1p multicolored 1.60 .75
1118 A420 2p multicolored 3.25 1.50
1119 A420 3p multicolored 4.25 1.75
Nos. 1116-1119 (4) 9.80 4.35

11th Columbus Regatta (#1116), Discovery of America, 500th anniv. (#1117-1119).

23rd Convention of the Alliance of Panamerican Round Tables, Santo Domingo — A421

1992, Oct. 14
1120 A421 1p multicolored 1.50 .60

Visit by Pope John Paul II A422

Cathedrals: 50c, Vega. 3p, Santo Domingo.

1992, Oct. 1 Photo.
1121 A422 50c multicolored 1.40 .60
1122 A422 3p multicolored 4.00 1.75

Columbus Lighthouse A423

1992, Oct. 12 Litho.
1123 A423 30c multicolored .85 .35
1124 A423 1p multicolored 1.75 .60

Size: 70x133mm
Imperf
1125 A423 3p Lighthouse at night 5.00 5.00

America Issue A424

Designs: 50c, First royal residence in America, Santo Domingo. 3p, First viceregal residence in America, Royal Palace, Colon.

1992, Nov. 13 Litho. *Perf. 13½*
1126 A424 50c multicolored .50 .35
1127 A424 3p multicolored 2.75 1.75

A425

Natl. Census — A426

1992, Dec. 2 Litho. *Perf. 13½*
1128 A425 30c Torch bearer .40 .20
1129 A425 1p Emblems 1.25 .50
1130 A425 4p Judo 6.50 2.50
Nos. 1128-1130 (3) 8.15 3.20

1992 Natl. Sports Games, San Juan. Secretary of Sports, Education, Exercise and Recreation (#1129).

1992-93 Litho. *Perf. 13½*
1131 A426 50c black, buff & blue .70 .25
1132 A426 1p blk, brn & blue 1.40 .50
1133 A426 3p blk, gray & bl 4.75 1.75
1134 A426 4p blk, yel grn & bl 6.00 2.00
Nos. 1131-1134 (4) 12.85 4.50

Issued: 50c, 1p, 5/12/92; 3p, 4p, 9/9/93.

A427

A428

1993, May 30
1135 A427 30c multicolored .45 .20
1136 A427 50c multicolored .75 .30
1137 A427 1p multicolored 1.60 .60
Nos. 1135-1137 (3) 2.80 1.10

Ema Balaguer, humanitarian.

1993, Oct. 7 Litho. *Perf. 13½*
1138 A428 30c shown .50 .25
1139 A428 1p Emblem, flags 1.50 .60

Rotary Club of Santo Domingo, 50th anniv.

17th Central American & Caribbean Games, Ponce A429

1993, Dec. 21 Litho. *Perf. 13½*
1140 A429 50c Tennis .60 .20
1141 A429 4p Swimming 6.25 1.50

Natl. Education Plan — A430

Spanish America — A431

1993, Dec. 8
1142 A430 1.50p multicolored 2.25 .75

1993, Dec. 28
1143 A431 50c First university lecturn .70 .25
1144 A431 3p First city coat of arms 4.75 1.25

America Issue A432

1993, Dec. 30
1145 A432 1p Aratinga chloroptera 1.25 .50
1146 A432 3p Cyclura cornuta 4.75 2.00

Opening of New Natl. Post Office A433

1993, Nov. 12
Color of Inscription
1147 A433 1p olive .75 .50
1148 A433 3p red 2.25 1.40
1149 A433 4p blue 3.00 1.75
1150 A433 5p green 3.75 2.00
1151 A433 10p black 7.50 4.00

Size: 105x96mm
Imperf
1152 A433 5p black 8.75 8.75
Nos. 1147-1152 (6) 26.00 18.40

First Mass in America, 500th Anniv. — A434

1994, Feb. 3 Litho. *Perf. 13½*
1153 A434 2p multicolored 3.00 1.00

5th Natl. Philatelic Exhibition A435

1994, Feb. 25
1154 A435 3p multicolored 4.50 1.40

Natl. Independence, 150th Anniv. — A436

No. 1155: a, Men with document, left side of table. b, Document on right side of table, men. c, Flag. d, Couple at window. e, Child holding material, mother making flag.

No. 1156: a, Men looking upward, shooting muskets. b, Men with guns, swords looking backwards. c, Natl. coat of arms. d, Men with guns, swords, one pointing upward. e, Men with weapons, one with flag.

10p, Three men, angel carrying musket, flag.

1994, Feb. 26
Strips of 5
1155 A436 2p #a.-e. 8.25 4.00
1156 A436 3p #a.-e. 12.50 6.00

Size: 161x104mm
Imperf
1157 A436 10p multicolored 9.75 9.75
Nos. 1155-1157 (3) 30.50 19.75

#1155a-1155b, 1155d-1155e, 1156a-1156b, 1156d-1156e have a continuous design.

Solenodon Paradoxus A437

Designs: a, Crawling on rock. b, Walking in leaves. c, Looking up. d, With food in mouth.

1994, Mar. 15 Litho. *Perf. 13½*
1158 A437 1p Block of 4, #a.-d. 6.00 2.00

World Wildlife Fund.

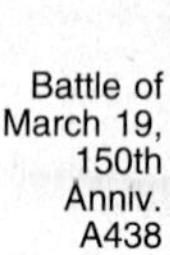

Battle of March 19, 150th Anniv. A438

#1160, Soldiers advancing uphill toward fort.

1994

1159 A438 2p multicolored 3.00 1.00
1160 A438 2p multicolored 3.00 1.00

Issued: #1159, Mar. 18; #1160, Mar. 29.

Virgin of Amparo — A439

Natl. Elections, May 16 — A440

1994, Apr. 15 Litho. *Perf. 13½*

1161 A439 3p multicolored 4.50 1.40

Battle of Puerto Tortuguero, 150th anniv.

1994, Apr. 4

1162 A440 2p multicolored 3.00 1.00

1994 World Cup Soccer Championships, US — A441

1994, June 24 Litho. *Perf. 13½*

1163 A441 4p multicolored 4.75 1.50
1164 A441 6p multicolored 6.75 2.00

Ema Balaguer City of Children A442

1994, July 20 Litho. *Perf. 13½*

1165 A442 1p magenta & brown 2.75 .40

Stamp Day A443

1994, Oct. 18 Litho. *Perf. 13½*

1166 A443 5p Type A3 7.25 2.00

America Issue — A444

1994, Oct. 28

1167 A444 2p Pony Express 2.75 1.00
1168 A444 6p Sailing ship 9.00 3.00

Province of LaVega, 500th Anniv. A445

3p, Ruins of San Francisco Monastery.

1994, Nov. 24 Litho. *Perf. 13½*

1169 A445 3p multicolored 6.75 1.40

First Church the New World, 500th Anniv. — A446

a, "La Isabela," cradle of evangelization. b, "Temple of the Americas," first mission.

1994, Dec. 5 *Perf. 11½*

1170 A446 3p Pair, #a.-b. 9.00 2.50

A447

A448

1994, Nov. 6 *Perf. 13½*

1171 A447 3p multicolored 4.50 1.40

Constitution, 150th anniv.

1994, Nov. 18

Christmas: 2p, Holy family's flight into Egypt. 3p, Modern family of three standing at river's edge.

1172 A448 2p multicolored 3.25 1.00
1173 A448 3p multicolored 4.25 1.40

Intl. Year of the Family.

Firsts in America — A449

1994, Dec. 21 Litho. *Perf. 13½*

1174 A449 2p Circulating coins 3.00 .75
1175 A449 5p Sermon for Justice 7.00 2.00

Snakes A450

#1176, Hypsirhynchus ferox. #1177, Antillophis parvifrons. #1178, Uromacer catesbyi. #1179, Epicrates striatus.

1994, Dec. 26

1176 A450 2p multicolored 3.00 .75
1177 A450 2p multicolored 3.00 .75
a. Pair, #1176-1177 6.00 5.50
1178 A450 2p multicolored 3.00 .75
1179 A450 2p multicolored 3.00 .75
a. Pair, #1178-1179 6.00 5.50

Nos. 1177a, 1179a are continuous designs.

Pan American Games, Mar Del Plata, Argentina A451

1995, Apr. 20 *Perf. 13½*

1180 A451 4p Tae kwon do 4.50 1.50
1181 A451 13p Tennis 13.50 4.50

FAO, 50th Anniv. — A452

1995, Apr. 21 Litho. *Perf. 11½*

1182 A452 4p multicolored 4.50 1.50

A453

A454

Designs: 2p, Jose Marti, Maximo Gomez. 3p, Marti. 4p, Marti seated at desk, Gomez.

1995, May 19 Litho. *Perf. 13½*

1183 A453 2p multicolored 1.40 .20
1184 A453 3p multicolored 1.90 .30
1185 A453 4p multicolored 2.75 .40
Nos. 1183-1185 (3) 6.05 .90

Jose Marti (1853-95), Montecristi Manifesto, cent.

1995, May 22

1186 A454 3p multicolored 1.90 .30

Basketball, cent.

Medicinal Plants — A455

1995, May 26

1187 A455 2p Pimenta ozua 1.40 .20
1188 A455 2p Melocactus communis 1.40 .20
1189 A455 3p Smilax 1.90 .30
1190 A455 3p Zamia 1.90 .30
Nos. 1187-1190 (4) 6.60 1.00

Tourism A456

4p, San Souci Port. 5p, Barahona Airport. 6p, G. Luperon Airport. 13p, Airport of the Americas.

1995, June 21

1191 A456 4p multicolored 2.50 .40
1192 A456 5p multicolored 3.25 .60
1193 A456 6p multicolored 4.00 .70
1194 A456 13p multicolored 8.25 1.50
Nos. 1191-1194 (4) 18.00 3.20

Santiago de Los Caballeros, 500th Anniv. A457

1995, July 29 Litho. *Perf. 13½*

1195 A457 3p Jacagua ruins 4.50 .70

Whales A458

Designs: No. 1196, Physeter macrocephalus. No. 1197, Balaenoptera borealis. No. 1198, Ziphius cavirostris. No. 1199, Megaptera novaeangliae.

1995, Aug. 14

1196 A458 3p multicolored 1.75 .30
1197 A458 3p multicolored 1.75 .30
1198 A458 3p multicolored 1.75 .30
1199 A458 3p multicolored 1.75 .30
Nos. 1196-1199 (4) 7.00 1.20

Stamp Day A459

1995, Oct. 18 Litho. *Perf. 13½*
1200 A459 4p No. 37 3.00 .40

Popular Singers — A460

1995, Oct. 8
1201 A460 2p Rafael Colon 1.50 .20
1202 A460 3p Casandra Damiron 2.00 .30

Cathedral of Santiago, Cent. A461

1995, Dec. 28 Litho. *Perf. 13½*
1203 A461 3p multicolored 2.25 .30

4th World Conference of Women, Beijing — A462

1995, Nov. 23
1204 A462 2p multicolored 5.25 .20

Volleyball, Cent. — A463

Norceca '95 — A464

Singers — A465

1995, Oct. 19 *Imperf.*
1205 A463 5p multicolored 3.75 .60

Perf. 13½
1206 A464 6p multicolored 4.25 .70

1995, Dec. 27 *Perf. 13½*
1207 A465 2p Antonio Mesa 1.60 .20
1208 A465 2p Julieta Otero 1.60 .20
1209 A465 2p Susano Polanco 1.60 .20
Nos. 1207-1209 (3) 4.80 .60

Columbus Lighthouse A466

1995, Dec. 5
1210 A466 10p dk bl, bl & gray 7.25 1.10

See Nos. 1241, 1265, 1299, 1337, 1371.

A467

UN, 50th Anniv. A468

1995, Oct. 24
1211 A467 2p multicolored 1.50 .20

Perf. 11½
1212 A468 6p multicolored 4.50 .70

Environmental Protection — A469

America issue: 2p, Flamingos, sea gull. 6p, Manglar.

1995, Dec. 19 Litho. *Perf. 13½*
1213 A469 2p multicolored 1.40 .25
1214 A469 6p multicolored 4.50 .75

Dominican Republic Air Force, 50th Anniv. A470

Aircraft: a, O2U-35D Corsair. b, PT-17 Stearman. c, AT-6 Texan. d, PBY-5A Catalina. e, TF-10 Beaufighter. f, FB-6 Mosquito. g, P-38 Lightning. h, P-51D Mustang. i, B-17G Flying Fortress. j, P-47D Thunderbolt. k, FB-5 Vampire. l, C-46 Commander. m, B-26 Invader. n, C-47 Skytrain. o, T-28D Trojan. p, T-33A Silverstar. q, Cessna T-41D. r, T-34 Mentor. s, Cessna O-2A. t, A-37B Dragonfly.

1995, Dec. 30
1215 A470 2p Sheet of 20, #a-t 11.00 5.50

See No. 1228.

UNICEF, 50th Anniv. — A471

1996, Feb. 23
1216 A471 2p shown 1.25 .25
1217 A471 4p Mirror image of #1216 2.25 .50

Intl. Sailing Competition A472

1996, Mar. 8
1218 A472 5p multicolored 3.00 .70

Eduardo Brito, Singer, 50th Death Anniv. — A473

1996, Jan. 15
1219 A473 1p shown .45 .20
1220 A473 2p With maracas .95 .25
1221 A473 3p Portrait 1.50 .40
Nos. 1219-1221 (3) 2.90 .85

No. 1220 is 54x35mm.

Natl. Journalist Day — A474

Design: Arturo J. Pellerano Alfau, Dr. Freddy Gaton Arce, Rafael Herrera Cabral.

1996, Apr. 17 Litho. *Perf. 13½*
1222 A474 5p multicolored 3.50 .70

ESPAMER '96, Seville — A475

1996, June 7 Litho. *Perf. 13½*
1223 A475 15p multicolored 9.00 1.50

1996 Summer Olympic Games, Atlanta — A476

1996, July 5
1224 A476 5p Judo 2.75 .50
1225 A476 15p Torch 8.75 1.50

Modern Olympic Games, Cent. — A477

1996, July 5
1226 A477 6p Greece No. 118 3.50 .70
1227 A477 15p No. 328 8.50 1.50

Dominican Republic Air Force, 50th Anniv. Type of 1995

Helicoptors: a, Sikorsky S-55. b, Alouette II. c, Alouette III. d, OH-6A Cayuse. e, Bell 205 A-1. f, Dauphin II SA.365C.

1996, July 31 Litho. *Perf. 13½*
1228 A470 3p Sheet of 6, #a.-f. 5.75 2.50

World Day Against Illegal Drugs — A478

1996, Sept. 23 Litho. *Perf. 13½*
1229 A478 15p multicolored 8.50 1.50

Mail Delivery A479

#1230, World delivery, putting mail in letter box, mailman receiving mail on motorcycle. #1231, Woman giving mail to man on horseback, vert. #1232, Child holding letter beside mailbox.

1996, July 17 Litho. *Perf. 13½*
1230 A479 3p multicolored 1.75 .40
1231 A479 3p multicolored 1.75 .40
1232 A479 3p multicolored 1.75 .40
Nos. 1230-1232 (3) 5.25 1.20

America Issue — A480

1996, Oct. 15 Litho. *Perf. 13½*
1233 A480 2p Men's costume 1.25 .25
1234 A480 6p Women's costume 3.50 .75

Stamp Day A481

1996, Oct. 18

1235 A481 5p No. 142 3.00 .70

26th Intl. Sunfish Championships — A482

6p, Sun, natl. flag, sailboat, vert. 10p, Man sailing boat.

1996, Oct. 16

1236 A482 6p multicolored 3.50 .90
1237 A482 10p multicolored 5.75 1.40

A483

A484

1996, Nov. 25 Litho. *Perf. 13½*

1238 A483 5p green & multi 3.00 .65
1239 A483 10p pink & multi 5.75 1.25

Intl. Day to End Violence Against Women.

1996, Nov. 11

Birds: a, Buteo ridgwayi. b, Aratinga chloroptera. c, Amazona ventralis. d, Hyetornis rufigularis. e, Saurothera longirostris. f, Siphonorhis brewsteri. g, Chlorostilbon swainsonii. h, Todus angustirostris. i, Todus subulatus. j, Temnotrogon roseigaster. k, Nesoctites micromegas. l, Melanerpes striatus. n, Turdus swalesi. n, Carduelis dominicensis. o, Dulus dominicus. p, Microligea palustris. q, Vireo nanus. r, Xenoligea montanta. s, Turdus swalesi dodae. t, Calyptophilus frugivorus tertius. u, Corvus leucognaphalus. v, Calyptophilus frugivorus neibae.

1240 A484 2p Sheet of 22, #a-v 25.00 20.00

Lighthouse Type of 1995

1996, Dec. 27 Litho. *Perf. 13½*

1241 A466 10p grn, sil & gray 5.75 1.25

Turtles A485

a, Dermochelys coriacea. b, Caretta caretta. c, Chelonia mydas. d, Eretmochelys imbricata.

1996, Dec. 30

1242 A485 5p Block of 4, #a.-d. 9.00 7.50

Natl. Youth Day — A486

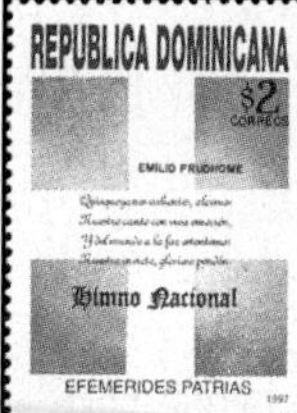

National Anthem — A487

1997, Jan. 31

1243 A486 3p multicolored 1.75 .45

1997, Feb. 26

Designs: 2p, Lyrics, by Emilio Prudhome. 3p, Music, by Jose Reyes.

1244 A487 2p multicolored 1.25 .25
1245 A487 3p multicolored 1.75 .40

Salomé Urena (1850-97), Poet — A488

Comet Hale-Bopp A489

1997, Mar. 6 *Perf. 13½*

1246 A488 3p multicolored 1.75 .40

1997, Apr. 1

1247 A489 5p multicolored 4.25 .65

Size: 72x47mm

Imperf

1248 A489 10p multicolored 8.75 8.75

A490

11th Natl. Sports Games, Mao '97 — A491

2p, Mascot running with torch. 3p, Mascot in batting stance, vert. 5p, Runner breaking finish line.

1997, Apr. 3

1249 A490 2p multicolored 1.75 .25
1250 A491 3p multicolored 2.75 .40
1251 A491 5p multicolored 4.25 .65
Nos. 1249-1251 (3) 8.75 1.30

A492

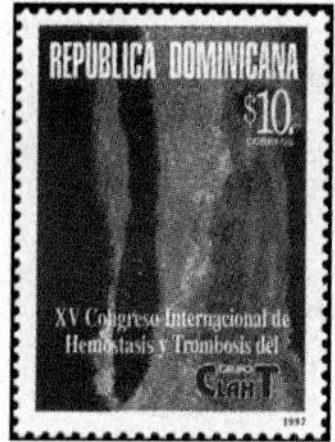

A493

Design: 10p, 5p, Heinrich von Stephan (1831-97), founder of UPU.

1997, Apr. 8 Litho. *Perf. 13½*

1252 A492 10p multicolored 5.75 1.25

Souvenir Sheet

Imperf

1253 A492 5p like #1252 3.00 .65

No. 1253 has simulated perforations.

1997, Apr. 29 *Perf. 13½*

1254 A493 10p multicolored 8.75 1.25

25th Intl. Congress of CLAHT (Caracas and Latin American Group of Hemostasis and Thrombosis).

Gregorio Luperón (1839-1897), Politician — A494

House of Spain, 80th Anniv. — A495

1997, May 21

1255 A494 3p multicolored 1.75 .40

1997, July 4

1256 A495 5p multicolored 3.00 .65

First Peso Coin, Cent. A496

1997, Aug. 6 Litho. *Perf. 13½*

1257 A496 2p multicolored 1.25 .20

A497

Coronation of the Image of Our Lady of Alta Gracia, 75th Anniv. — A498

1997, Aug. 12

1258 A497 3p multicolored 1.75 .20
1259 A498 5p multicolored 3.00 .35

America Issue A499

Life of a postman: 2p, Dog grabbing pants leg of postman on motorcycle. 6p, Dog tearing pants leg of postman with letter.

1997, Oct. 9 Litho. *Perf. 13½*

1260 A499 2p multicolored 1.10 .25

Size: 35½x35½mm

1261 A499 6p multicolored 3.00 .65

Mother Teresa (1910-97) A500

1997, Oct. 17

1262 A500 5p multicolored 2.50 .55

Stamp Day — A501

1997, Oct. 18

1263 A501 5p Nos. 108, 322 2.50 .55

Central Bank of the Dominican Republic, 50th Anniv. — A502

1997, Oct. 30 *Perf. 11½*

1264 A502 10p multicolored 5.00 1.10

Lighthouse Type of 1995

1997, Dec. 15 Litho. *Perf. 13½*

1265 A466 10p bright rose & gray 5.75 1.50

Bats
A503

a, Erophylius bombifrons. b, Brachyphylla nana. c, Molossus molossus. d, Lasiurus borealis.

1997, Nov. 11
1266 A503 5p Block of 4, #a.-d. 8.50 8.50

Dominican Air Force, 50th Anniv.
A504

Insignias: a, Air Force, red, white, and blue target. b, Northern Air Command, "shark plane." c, Air Command, eagle's wings over target. d, Rescue Force, eagle. e, Maintenance Command. f, Combat Force, dragon, target.

1997, Dec. 19
1267 A504 3p Sheet of 6, #a.-f. 10.50 10.50

Construction of the National Palace, 50th Anniv. — A505

1997, Dec. 30 Litho. *Perf. 13½*
1268 A505 10p multicolored 5.75 1.50

First Regional Symposium on Pre-Columbian Culture and Caribbean Contemporary Art — A506

1998, Jan. 28
1269 A506 6p multicolored 3.50 .85

A507

A508

1998, Apr. 2 Litho. *Perf. 13½*
1270 A507 10p multicolored 5.75 .65

American Chamber of Commerce of the Dominican Republic, 75th anniv.

1998, Apr. 26

Book Fair: 3p, Natl. Book Fair, 25th anniv. 5p, Intl. Book Fair, Santo Domingo '98.

1271 A508 3p black, blue & red 1.75 .20

Size: 35x33mm

1272 A508 5p black, blue & red 3.00 .35

Organization of American States, 50th Anniv. — A509

1998, Apr. 30
1273 A509 5p blue & multi 3.00 .35
1274 A509 5p pink & multi 3.00 .35

Establishment of the State of Israel, 50th Anniv. — A510

1998, Apr. 30
1275 A510 10p multicolored 5.75 .65

Dominican Air Force, 50th Anniv. — A511

a, Gen. Frank Felix Miranda, portrait at left. b, Early aircraft. c, Col. Ernesto Tejeda, portrait at right. d, As "c," portrait at left. e, As "a," portrait at right.

1998, June 26

Sheet of 6

1276 A511 3p #a, c-e, 2 b 10.00 10.00

City of Santo Domingo, 500th Anniv. A512

2p, Sun clock. 3p, St. Lazaro Church & Hospital. 4p, First Cathedral in America. 5p, Royal Palace. 6p, Tower of Honor. 10p, St. Nicolas of Bari Church & Hospital.

1998, Aug. 6 Litho. *Perf. 13½*
1277 A512 2p multi, vert. 1.10 .20
1278 A512 3p multi 1.75 .20
1279 A512 4p multi 2.25 .25
1280 A512 5p multi 3.00 .35
1281 A512 6p multi 3.50 .40
1282 A512 10p multi, vert. 5.75 .60
Nos. 1277-1282 (6) 17.35 2.00

National Theater, 25th Anniv. — A513

1998, Aug. 14 *Perf. 13x13½*
1283 A513 10p multicolored 5.75 .65

Latin Union, 44th Anniv. A514

1998, Aug. 26 *Perf. 13½*
1284 A514 10p multicolored 5.75 .65

ICCO (Intl. Cocoa Organization of America & Europe), 25th Anniv. — A515

1998, Sept. 3
1285 A515 10p multicolored 5.75 .65

Nino Ferrua (1909-79), Stamp Designer A516

1998, Oct. 18 Litho. *Perf. 13½x13*
1286 A516 5p multicolored 3.00 .35

Stamp Day.

Pontificate of John Paul II, 20th Anniv. A517

1998, Oct. 22 *Perf. 13½*
1287 A517 5p shown 3.00 .35
1288 A517 10p Portrait, diff. 5.75 .65

Medicinal Plants — A518

a, Pimenta racemosa. b, Pimenta haitiensis. c, Cymbopogon citratus. d, Citrus aurantium.

1998, Nov. 2
1289 A518 3p Block of 4, #a.-d. 6.50 .75

Famous Women A519

America Issue: 2p, Juana Saltitopa standing with cannon. 6p, Anacaona, Indian maiden, group of Indians.

1998, Nov. 5
1290 A519 2p multicolored 1.25 .20
1291 A519 6p multicolored 3.50 .40

A520

A521

1998, Nov. 20
1292 A520 5p multicolored 1.60 .35

Intl. Year of the Ocean.

1998, Nov. 23
1293 A521 5p multicolored 1.60 .35

Expofila '98, Santo Domingo. Santo Domingo, 500th anniv.

National Military Heroes — A522

Designs: a, Fernando Valerio. b, Benito Moncion. c, Jose Maria Cabral. d, Antonio Duverge. e, Gregorio Luperon. f, Jose A. Salcedo. g, Fco. A. Salcedo. h, Gaspar Polanco. i, Santiago Rodriguez. j, Juan Bta. Cambiaso. k, Jose J. Puello. l, Jose Ma. Imbert. m, Juan A. Acosta. n, Marcos Adon. o, Matias R. Mella. p, Francisco R. Sanchez. q, Juan Pablo Duarte. r, Olegario Tenares. s, Pedro Santana. t, Juan Sanchez Ramirez.

1998, Nov. 29
1294 A522 3p Sheet of 20, #a.-t. 19.00 17.50

1st Natl. Paper Money, 150th Anniv. — A523

1998, Nov. 30 *Perf. 11½*
1295 A523 10p multicolored 3.25 .65

Christmas A524

1998, Dec. 7 *Perf. 13½*
1296 A524 2p Roasting hog .65 .20
1297 A524 5p Magi 1.75 .35

Universal Declaration of Human Rights, 50th Anniv. A525

1998, Dec. 10
1298 A525 10p multicolored 3.25 .65

Columbus Lighthouse Type of 1995

1998, Dec. 11
1299 A466 10p orange & black 3.25 .65

Shells A526

Designs: a, Lyria vegai. b, Strombus gigas. c, Cittarium pica. d, Nerita peloronta.

1998, Dec. 16
1300 A526 5p Block of 4, #a.-d. 6.50 1.25

Gaspar Hernández (1798-1858), Priest — A527

1998, Dec. 18
1301 A527 3p multicolored 1.00 .20

Dominican Society of Endocrinology and Nutrition, 25th Anniv. — A528

1999, Feb. 24 **Litho.** *Perf. 13¼*
1302 A528 10p multicolored 3.25 .65

Office of Comptroller General — A529

1999, May 4 **Litho.** *Perf. 13¼*
1303 A529 2p multicolored .65 .20

Export Industries A530

Perf. 13½x13¼, 13¼x13½

1999, Apr. 30 **Litho.**
1304 A530 6p Tobacco 2.00 .40
1305 A530 10p Textiles, vert. 3.25 .65

Pan American Games, Winnipeg - A530a

1999, July 29 **Litho.** *Perf. 13¼x13½*
1306 A530a 5p Baseball 1.50 .35
1307 A530a 6p Weight lifting 2.00 .40

Native Plants — A531

Designs: a, Pseudophoenix ekmanii. b, Murtigia calabura. c, Pouteria dominguensis. d, Rubus dominguensis focke.

1999, July 13
1308 A531 5p Block of 4, #a.-d. 6.50 6.50

Presidents of the Dominican Republic A532

Designs: a, Tomas Bobadilla y Briones. b, Pedro Santana. c, Manuel Jimenez. d, Buenaventura Baez. e, Manuel de Regla Mota. f, José Desiderio Valverde. g, José A. Salcedo. h, Gaspar Polanco.

1999, Aug. 31 *Perf. 13½x13¼*
1309 A532 3p Sheet of 8, #a.-h. + label 5.00 5.00

A533

Sovereign Military Order of Malta A534

Perf. 13¼x13½

1999, Sept. 20 **Litho.**
1310 A533 2p multicolored .65 .20

Perf. 13½

1311 A534 10p multicolored 3.25 .60

Paintings by José Vela Zanetti (1913-99) — A535

Various paintings.

Perf. 13½x13¼, 13¼x 13½

1999, Sept. 8
1312 A535 2p multi, vert. .40 .20
1313 A535 3p multi, vert. .65 .20
1314 A535 5p multi 1.00 .30
1315 A535 6p multi, vert. 1.25 .40
1316 A535 10p multi, vert. 2.00 .60
Nos. 1312-1316 (5) 5.30 1.70

Insects A536

Designs: a, Strataegus quadrifoveatus. b, Anetia jaegeri. c, Polyancistroydes tettigonidae. d, Aploppus phasmidae.

1999, Sept. 10 *Perf. 13½x13¼*
1317 A536 5p Block of 4, #a.-d. 4.00 4.00

SOS Children's Villages, 50th Anniv. — A537

Intl. Year of the Elderly — A538

1999, Sept. 29 *Perf. 13¼x13½*
1318 A537 10p multicolored 1.50 .60

1999, Oct. 1
1319 A538 2p Man .25 .20
1320 A538 5p Woman .60 .30

A539

A540

1999, Oct. 5
1321 A539 5p multicolored .60 .30

World Education Day.

1999, Oct. 18

Designs: 2p, Skull and crossbones, land mines, shattered gun. 6p, Mushroom cloud.

1322 A540 2p multicolored .25 .20
1323 A540 6p multicolored .75 .40

America Issue, a new millennium without arms.

Stamp Day — A541

1999, Oct. 22
1324 A541 5p Luis F. Thomen .60 .30

Account of Gen. Juan Pablo Duarte A542

1999, July 16 *Perf. 13½*
1325 A542 3p multicolored .40 .20

A543

Contemporary Writers — A544

Perf. 13¼x13½, 13½x13¼

1999, June 23

1326	A543	2p multicolored	.25	.20
1327	A544	10p multicolored	1.25	.60

Dermatological Society, 50th Anniv. — A545

1999, Sept. 15 Litho. *Perf. 13¼*

1328	A545	3p multi	.40	.20

Millennium — A546

3p, Earth, trees. 5p, Scientific achievements.

Perf. 13¼x13½

1999, Nov. 10 Litho.

1329	A546	3p multi	.35	.20
1330	A546	5p multi	.60	.30

2nd Summit of African, Caribbean and Pacific Heads of State — A547

Emblem and: 5p, Map of Caribbean area, whale. 6p, Map of Pacific area, Easter Island statues. 10p, Map of Africa, lion.

1999, Nov. 23

1331	A547	5p multi	.60	.30
1332	A547	6p multi	.75	.35
1333	A547	10p multi	1.25	.60
		Nos. 1331-1333 (3)	2.60	1.25

UPU, 125th Anniv. A548

6p, Globe, envelope, computer, electronic circuits. 10p, Envelope, electronic circuits.

1999, Nov. 29

1334	A548	6p multi	.75	.35

Size: 50x75mm

Imperf

1335	A548	10p multi	1.25	.60

Union of Latin American Universities, 50th Anniv. — A549

1999, Dec. 3 *Perf. 13½x13¼*

1336	A549	6p multi	.75	.35

Lighthouse Type of 1995

1999, Dec. 14 *Perf. 13¼x13½*

1337	A466	10p brown & silver	1.25	.60

Classical Musicians A550

#1338, José de Jésus Ravelo (1876-1951), clarinet. #1339, Juan Francisco Garcia (1892-1974), cornet. #1340, Manuel Simo (1916-88), saxophone.

1999, Dec. 17

1338	A550	5p multi	.60	.30
1339	A550	5p multi	.60	.30
1340	A550	5p multi	.60	.30
		Nos. 1338-1340 (3)	1.80	.90

Municipal Notes, Cent. — A551

Notes and background colors - No. 1341: a, Santo Domingo, San Pedro de Macorís, deep purple. b, Puerto Plata, Moca, purple.

No. 1342, vert.: a, Santiago, Cotui, blue green. b, San Francisco de Macorís, La Vega, golden brown. c, San Cristobal, Samana, peacock blue.

No. 1343: a, As No. 1342a, green background. b, As No. 1342b, brown background. c, As No. 1342c, Prussian blue background.

1999, Dec. 30 *Perf. 13¼*

1341	A551	2p Pair, #a.-b.	.50	.25
1342	A551	2p Strip of 3, #a.-c.	.75	.35

Souvenir Sheet

Imperf

1343	A551	2p Sheet of 5, #1341a-1341b, 1343a-1343c	1.25	.60

Chamber of Spanish Commerce and Industry, 75th Anniv. — A552

1999, Dec. 30 *Perf. 13¼x13½*

1344	A552	10p multi	1.25	.60

Fight Against Drugs A553

2000, Feb. 17 Litho. *Perf. 13½*

1345	A553	5p multi	.65	.30

Hogar Crea Dominicana Inc., 25th anniv.

Duarte Institute — A554

2000, Feb. 25 *Perf. 13¼*

1346	A554	2p multi	.25	.20

Prevention of Child Abuse — A555

2000, Mar. 31

1347	A555	2p multi	.25	.20

National Police A556

2000, Apr. 6 *Perf. 13½*

1348	A556	2p shown	.25	.20

Size: 37x28mm

Perf. 13½x13¼

1349	A556	5p Crest	.65	.30

Dominican Institute of Industrial Technology, 25th Anniv. A557

2000, Apr. 11 *Perf. 13½*

1350	A557	2p multi	.25	.20

Independencia Province, 50th Anniv. — A558

2000, Apr. 15

1351	A558	3p multi	.40	.20

A559

12th Natl. Games, La Romana A560

2000, Apr. 27 *Perf. 13½x13¼*

1352	A559	2p Baseball	.25	.20
1353	A559	3p Boxing	.40	.20

Perf. 13½

1354	A560	5p Emblem	.65	.30
		Nos. 1352-1354 (3)	1.30	.70

Paintings A561

Designs: 5p, The Violinist, by Darío Suro. 10p, Self-portrait, by Théodore Chassériau.

2000, May 5 *Perf. 13¼*

1355	A561	5p multi	.65	.30
1356	A561	10p multi	1.25	.65

Presidential Elections A562

2000, May 12

1357	A562	2p multi	.25	.20

Classical Musicians A563

#1358, Julio Alberto Hernandez Camejo (1900-99), pianist. #1359, Ramon Diaz (1901-76), bassoonist. #1360, Enrique de Marchena Dujarric (1908-88), pianist.

2000, May 31 ***Perf. 13½***

1358 A563 5p multi .65 .30
1359 A563 5p multi .65 .30
1360 A563 5p multi .65 .30
Nos. 1358-1360 (3) 1.95 .90

Expo 2000, Hanover A564

2000, June 1

1361 A564 5p shown .65 .30
1362 A564 10p Emblem, diff. 1.25 .65

Art by Jaime Colson — A565

Designs: 2p, Woman on horseback. 3p, Abstract. 5p, Musicians and dancers, horiz. 6p, Nudes. 10p, Colson.

2000 **Litho.** ***Perf. 13¼***

1363-1367 A565 Set of 5 3.50 1.75

Holy Year 2000 A566

Churches: 2p, Santo Cristo de los Milagros de Bayaguana Sanctuary. 5p, Santa Maria la Menor Cathedral, first in the Americas, vert. 10p, Nuestra Señora de la Altagracia Basilica, vert.

2000 ***Perf. 13½x13¼, 13¼x13½***

1368-1370 A566 Set of 3 2.25 1.10

Lighthouse Type of 1995

2000 ***Perf. 13¼x13½***

1371 A466 10p buff, brn & sil 1.25 .65

Dominican Republic — Republic of China Diplomatic Relations A566a

Flags of Dominican Republic and Republic of China and: 5p, Illustration of dragon. 10p, Carved dragon.

Serpentine Die Cut 11¼

2000, Dec. 15 **Litho.**

Self-Adhesive

1371A-1371B A566a Set of 2 2.00 1.00

America Issue — Campaign Against AIDS — A566b

Designs: 2p, Child. 6p, AIDS patient (38x38mm).

2000, Dec. 21 **Self-Adhesive**

1371C-1371D A566b Set of 2 1.10 .55

UN High Commissioner for Refugees, 50th Anniv. — A566c

2000, Dec. 29 **Self-Adhesive**

1371E A566c 10p multi 1.40 .70

Environmental Protection — A567

Designs: 2p, Lizard on leaf, vert. $3, House. $5, River rapids, vert.

Serpentine Die Cut 11¼

2000 **Litho.**

Self-Adhesive

1372-1374 A567 Set of 3 1.25 .65

Lighthouse Type of 1995

2001 **Litho.** ***Perf. 13¼x13½***

1375 A466 15p lt bl, dk bl & sil 2.00 1.00

Concepcion Bona, Seamstress of First Dominican Republic Flag, Cent. of Death — A568

2001 ***Perf. 13½x13¼***

1376 A568 10p multi 1.40 .70

Stamp Day — A569

2001

1377 A569 5p multi .70 .35

Year of Dialogue Among Civilizations A570

2001 ***Perf. 13¼x13½***

1378 A570 12p multi 1.50 .75

America Issue - UNESCO World Heritage A571

Designs: 4p, San Felipe Fort. 15p, Ruins of San Nicolas de Bari Hospital (27x37mm).

2001 ***Perf. 13½, 13¼x13½ (15p)***

1379-1380 A571 Set of 2 2.50 1.25

Mushrooms — A572

No. 1383: a, Pycnoporus sanguineus. b, Morchella elata. c, Mycena epipterygia. d, Coriolopsis polyzona.

Perf. 13¼x13½

2001, Sept. 13 **Litho.**

1383 A572 6p Block of 4, #a-d 4.00 2.00

Presidents of the Dominican Republic — A574

No. 1385: a, Gen. José María Cabral. b, Gen. Gregório Luperón. c, Gen. Ignacio María González. d, Ulises Espaillat. e, Pedro A. Pimentel. f, Federico de Jesús García. g, Frenando Arturo de Mariño. h, Gen. Ulises Heureaux.

2001, Sept. 27 **Litho.** ***Perf. 13¼***

1385 A574 6p Sheet of 8, #a-h, + label 8.00 4.00

Blessed Josemaría Escrivá de Balaguer (1902-75), Founder of Opus Dei — A575

2002, Aug. 29 ***Perf. 13½x13¼***

1386 A575 10p multi 1.75 .85

Loyola Polytechnic Institute, 50th Anniv. — A576

2002, Oct. 24 ***Perf. 13¼x13½***

1387 A576 6p multi 1.00 .50

12th Iberoamerican Heads of State Summit — A577

Designs: 12p, Flags below map. 15p, Flags above map.

Perf. 13¾x13½

2002, Nov. 14 **Litho.**

1388-1389 A577 Set of 2 4.75 2.40

America Issue — Youth Education and Literacy — A578

Designs: 4p, Teacher helping child write. 15p, Child writing on blackboard.

2002, Dec. 20 ***Perf. 13¼x13½***

1390-1391 A578 Set of 2 3.50 1.75

Coccothrinax Spissa — A579

Perf. 13¼x13½

2002, Dec. 20 **Litho.**

1392 A579 10p multi 1.75 .85

2003 Pan American Games, Santo Domingo — A580

Color of "2003" in design: 4p, Light green blue. 6p, Blue. 12p, Red.

2003, Feb. 25
1393-1395 A580 Set of 3 2.75 1.40

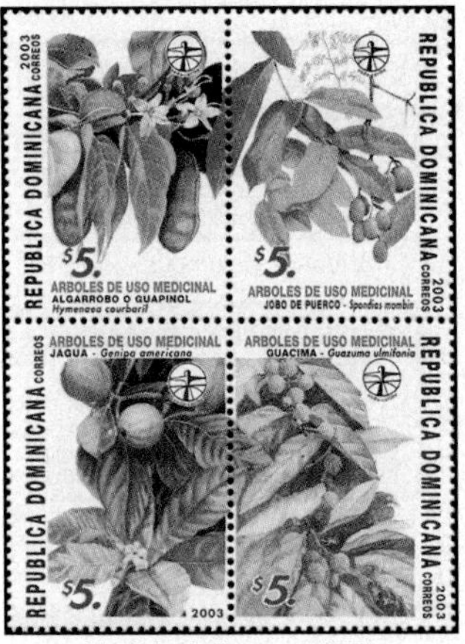

Medicinal Plants — A581

No. 1396: a, Hymenaea courbaril. b, Spondias mombin. c, Genipa americana. d, Guazuma ulmifonia.

2003
1396 A581 5p Block of 4, #a-d 2.60 1.25

Dr. José Francisco Peña Gomez (1937-98), Politician A582

2003 Litho. & Engr. *Perf. 11½*
1397 A582 10p multi 1.40 .70

José Marti (1853-95), Cuban Patriot — A583

2003 Litho. *Perf. 13x13¼*
1398 A583 15p multi 2.00 1.00

America Issue — Flora and Fauna — A584

Designs: 5p, Aristelliger lar. 15p, Corpernicia berteroana, vert.

2003 *Perf. 13½x13¼, 13¼x13½*
1399-1400 A584 Set of 2 2.75 1.40

Election of Pope John Paul II, 25th Anniv. — A585

Pope John Paul II: 10p, With hand touching face. 15p, Blessing crowd, horiz.
25p, Vignettes of 10p and 15p stamps.

2003 *Perf. 13¼x13½, 13½x13¼*
1401-1402 A585 Set of 2 3.25 1.60

Size: 57x85mm

Imperf

1403 A585 25p multi 3.25 1.60

National Council for Children A586

2004 *Perf. 13½x13¼*
1404 A586 7p multi .95 .45

SEMI-POSTAL STAMPS

Catalogue values for unused stamps in this section are for Never Hinged items.

Nos. 474-478 Surcharged in Red

Engraved and Lithographed
1957, Feb. 8 Unwmk. *Perf. 11½*
Flags in National Colors

B1	A117	1c + 2c brn, lt bl, vio & mar	.20	.20
B2	A117	2c + 2c dk brn, lt bl & vio	.20	.20
B3	A117	3c + 2c red lilac & red	.20	.20
B4	A117	5c + 2c red orange & vio	.20	.20
B5	A117	7c + 2c green & violet	.30	.30
		Nos. B1-B5,CB1-CB3 (8)	2.20	2.20

The surtax was to aid Hungarian refugees.
A similar 25c surcharge was applied to the miniature sheets described in the footnote following No. 478. Value, 2 sheets, perf. and imperf., $32.50

Nos. 479-483 Surcharged in Red Orange

1957, Sept. 9 Photo. *Perf. 13½*
Flags in National Colors

B6	A118	1c + 2c brown & brt bl	.20	.20
B7	A118	2c + 2c org ver & dk bl	.30	.30
B8	A118	3c + 2c dark blue	.35	.35
B9	A118	5c + 2c olive & dk bl	.45	.45
B10	A118	7c + 2c rose brn & dk bl	.50	.50
		Nos. B6-B10,CB4-CB6 (8)	3.55	3.50

Cent. of the birth of Lord Baden Powell and the 50th anniv. of the Scout Movement. The surtax was for the Dominican Republic Boy Scouts.
A similar 5c surcharge was applied to the miniature sheets described in the footnote following No. 483. Value 4 sheets, perf. and imperf., medal and flag, $60.

Types of Olympic Regular Issue, 1957, Surcharged in Carmine

a

b

1958, May 26 Engr. & Litho.
Flags in National Colors
Pink Paper

B11	A119(a)	1c + 2c red brown	.20	.20
B12	A119(b)	1c + 2c red brown	.20	.20
B13	A120(a)	2c + 2c gray brown	.25	.25
B14	A120(b)	2c + 2c gray brown	.25	.25
B15	A119(a)	3c + 2c violet	.25	.25
B16	A119(b)	3c + 2c violet	.25	.25
B17	A120(a)	5c + 2c red orange	.35	.35
B18	A120(b)	5c + 2c red orange	.35	.35
B19	A119(a)	7c + 2c Prus green	.40	.40
B20	A119(b)	7c + 2c Prus green	.40	.40
		Nos. B11-B20,CB7-CB12 (16)	5.00	5.00

Surtax for the UN Relief and Works Agency for Palestine Refugees.
A similar 5c surcharge, plus marginal United Nations emblem and "UNRWA," was applied to the miniature sheets described in the footnote following No. 488. Value, 4 sheets, perf. and imperf., $20.

Nos. 501-505 Surcharged

Perf. 13½
1959, Apr. 13 Photo. Unwmk.
Flags in National Colors

B21	A125	1c + 2c rose, indigo & ultra	.30	.30
B22	A125	1c + 2c brown & blue	.35	.35
B23	A125	3c + 2c gray, vio, blk & buff	.40	.40
B24	A125	5c + 2c rose, dk bl, brn & red	.50	.50
B25	A125	7c + 2c lt brn, dk bl & red	.55	.55
		Nos. B21-B25,CB13-CB15 (8)	4.30	4.30

International Geophysical Year, 1957-58.
A similar 5c surcharge was applied to the miniature sheets described in the footnote following No. 505. Value, 2 sheets, perf. and imperf., $40.

Type of 1957 Surcharged in Red

Engraved and Lithographed
1959, Sept. 10 Unwmk. *Imperf.*
Flags in National Colors

B26	A117	1c + 2c brn, lt bl, vio & mar	.30	.30
B27	A117	2c + 2c dk brn, lt bl & vio	.30	.30
B28	A117	3c + 2c red lilac & red	.35	.35
B29	A117	5c + 2c red org & vio	.35	.35
B30	A117	7c + 2c green & violet	.45	.45
		Nos. B26-B30,CB16-CB18 (8)	3.25	3.25

3rd Pan American Games, Chicago, Aug. 27-Sept. 7, 1959.

Nos. 522-524 Surcharged in Red

1960, Apr. 7 Litho. *Perf. 12½*
Center in Gray

B31	A135	5c + 5c red brn & yel grn	.30	.30
B32	A135	9c + 5c car & lt bl	.30	.30
B33	A135	13c + 5c org & grn	.65	.65
		Nos. B31-B33,CB19-CB20 (5)	2.00	2.00

World Refugee Year, July 1, 1959-June 30, 1960. The surtax was for aid to refugees.
Souvenir sheets exist perf. and imperf., containing one each of Nos. B31-B33 and CB19-CB20. Value, 2 sheets, perf. and imperf., $12.50

Nos. 525-529 Surcharged: "XV ANIVERSARIO DE LA UNESCO +2c"

1962, Jan. 8 Photo. *Perf. 13½*
Flags in National Colors

B34	A136	1c + 2c red, yel grn & blk	.25	.25
B35	A136	2c + 2c org, grnsh bl & brn	.25	.25
B36	A136	3c + 2c henna brn & bl	.25	.25
B37	A136	5c + 2c brown & ultra	.25	.25
B38	A136	7c + 2c grn, bl & rose brn	.25	.25
		Nos. B34-B38,CB21-CB23 (8)	2.10	2.10

15th anniv. (in 1961) of UNESCO.
A similar 5c surcharge was applied to the miniature sheets described in the footnote following No. 529. Value, 2 sheets, perf. and imperf., $16.

Anti-Malaria Type of 1962
1962, Apr. 29 Litho. *Perf. 12*

B39	A141	10c + 2c brt pink & red lil	.30	.30
B40	A141	20c + 2c pale brn & brn	.45	.45

Freedom from Hunger Type of 1963

1963, Apr. 15 Unwmk. *Perf. 11½*

Banner in Dark Blue & Red

B41 A148 2c + 1c green .20 .20
B42 A148 5c + 2c brt rose lil .25 .25
B43 A148 9c + 2c orange .25 .25
Nos. B41-B43 (3) .70 .70

A souvenir sheet contains three imperf. stamps similar to #B41-B43. Value, $1.50.

Nos. 591-593 Surcharged

1964, Mar. 8 *Perf. 12½*

B44 A153 3c + 2c pale pink & ver .20 .20
B45 A153 6c + 2c pale bl & ultra .20 .20
B46 A153 9c + 2c pale rose & red brn .25 .25
Nos. B44-B46,CB26-CB27 (5) 1.05 1.05

UNESCO world campaign to save historic monuments in Nubia.

Nos. 622-626 Surcharged

1966, Dec. 9 Litho. *Perf. 12½*

Size: 31x21mm

B47 A164 1c + 2c multi .85 .25
B48 A164 2c + 2c multi .65 .20
B49 A164 3c + 2c multi .65 .20
B50 A164 6c + 4c multi .85 .45
B51 A164 8c + 4c multi 1.25 .55
Nos. B47-B51,CB28-CB30 (8) 11.85 7.10

Surtax for victims of Hurricane Inez.

AIR POST STAMPS

Map of Hispaniola — AP1

Perf. 11½

1928, May 31 Litho. Unwmk.

C1 AP1 10c deep ultra 4.50 2.00

1930

C2 AP1 10c ocher 3.00 2.00
a. Vert. pair, imperf. btwn. *600.00*
C3 AP1 15c scarlet 6.00 3.00
C4 AP1 20c dull green 2.75 .50
C5 AP1 30c violet 6.00 3.25
Nos. C2-C5 (4) 17.75 8.75

#C2-C5 have only "CENTAVOS" in lower panel. Issued: 10c, 20c, 1/24; 15c, 30c, 2/14.

1930

C6 AP1 10c light blue 1.50 .60
C7 AP1 15c blue green 3.00 .90
C8 AP1 20c yellow brown 3.25 .45
a. Horiz. pair, imperf. vert. 450.00 450.00
C9 AP1 30c chocolate 5.50 1.50
Nos. C6-C9 (4) 13.25 3.45

Issue dates: 10c, 15c, 20c, Sept.; 30c, Oct.

Batwing Sundial Erected in 1753 — AP2

1931-33 *Perf. 12*

C10 AP2 10c carmine 3.25 .50
C11 AP2 10c light blue 1.40 .50
C12 AP2 10c dark green 5.50 2.50
C13 AP2 15c rose lilac 2.50 .50
C14 AP2 20c dark blue 5.50 2.10
a. Numerals reading up at left and down at right 5.00 2.50
b. Imperf., pair 250.00
C15 AP2 30c green 2.25 .25
C16 AP2 50c red brown 5.50 .50
C17 AP2 1p deep orange 7.50 2.50
Nos. C10-C17 (8) 33.40 9.35

Issued: #C11, 7/2/32; #C12, 5/28/33; others 8/16.

Airplane and Ozama Fortress AP3

1933, Nov. 20

C18 AP3 10c dark blue 3.00 .50

Airplane and Trujillo Bridge AP4

1934, Sept. 20

C19 AP4 10c dark blue 3.00 .50

Symbolic of Flight AP5

1935, Apr. 29

C20 AP5 10c lt blue & dk blue 1.40 .40

AP6

1936, Feb. 11 *Perf. 11½*

C21 AP6 10c dk bl & turq bl 2.25 .40

Allegory of Flight AP7

1936, Oct. 17

C22 AP7 10c dk bl, bl & turq bl 2.00 .30

Macoris Airport AP8

1937, Oct. 22

C23 AP8 10c green .90 .20

Fleet of Columbus AP9

Air Fleet AP10

Proposed Columbus Lighthouse — AP11

1937, Nov. 9 *Perf. 12*

C24 AP9 10c rose red 1.50 1.25
C25 AP10 15c purple 1.25 .85
C26 AP11 20c dk bl & lt bl 1.25 .90
C27 AP10 25c red violet 1.75 1.00
C28 AP11 30c yellow green 1.50 1.00
C29 AP10 50c brown 3.25 1.25
C30 AP11 75c dk olive grn 9.00 9.00
C31 AP9 1p orange 5.50 1.75
Nos. C24-C31 (8) 25.00 17.00

Goodwill flight to all American countries by the planes "Colon," "Pinta," "Nina" and "Santa Maria."

#C30 was reproduced imperf. on #1019.

Pan American Clipper AP12

1938, July 30

C32 AP12 10c green 1.00 .20

Trylon and Perisphere, Plane and Proposed Columbus Lighthouse — AP13

1939, Apr. 30

C33 AP13 10c green & lt green 1.40 .60

New York World's Fair.

Airplane AP14

1939, Oct. 18

C34 AP14 10c green & dp green 1.40 .20
a. Pair, imperf. btwn. *450.00*

Proposed Columbus Lighthouse, Plane and Caravels — AP15

Christopher Columbus and Proposed Lighthouse — AP16

Proposed Lighthouse — AP17

Christopher Columbus — AP18

Caravel — AP19

1940, Oct. 12

C35 AP15 10c sapphire & lt bl .85 .45
C36 AP16 15c org brn & brn 1.10 .75
C37 AP17 20c rose red & red 1.10 .75
C38 AP18 25c brt red lil & red vio 1.10 .35
C39 AP19 50c green & lt green 2.25 1.25
Nos. C35-C39 (5) 6.40 3.55

Discovery of America by Columbus and proposed Columbus memorial lighthouse in Dominican Republic.

Posts and Telegraph Building, San Cristobal AP20

1941, Feb. 21

C40 AP20 10c brt red lil & pale lil rose .40 .20

Globe, Wing and Letter AP21

1942, Feb. 13

C41 AP21 10c dark violet brn .50 .25
C42 AP21 75c deep orange 2.75 1.75

Plane AP22

1943, Sept. 1

C43 AP22 10c brt red lilac .30 .20
C44 AP22 20c dp blue & blue .35 .20
C45 AP22 25c yellow olive 5.00 2.40
Nos. C43-C45 (3) 5.65 2.80

Plane, Flag, Coat of Arms and Torch of Liberty — AP23

1944, Feb. 27 ***Perf. 11½***

Flag in Gray, Dark Blue, Carmine

C46 AP23 10c multicolored .35 .20
C47 AP23 20c multicolored .45 .20
C48 AP23 1p multicolored 2.00 1.50
Nos. C46-C48 (3) 2.80 1.90

Centenary of Independence. See No. 407 for souvenir sheet listing.

Communications Building, Ciudad Trujillo — AP24

1944, Nov. 12 Litho. ***Perf. 12***

C49 AP24 9c yel grn & blue .20 .20
C50 AP24 13c dull brn & rose car .25 .20
C51 AP24 25c org & dull red .35 .20
b. Vert. pair, imperf. btwn. 45.00
C52 AP24 30c black & ultra .75 .65
Nos. C49-C52 (4) 1.55 1.25

Twenty booklets of 100 (25 panes of 4) of the 25c were issued. All booklets are still intact.

Communications Type

1945, Sept. 1

Center in Dark Blue and Carmine

C53 A92 7c deep yellow green .30 .25
C54 A92 12c red orange .35 .20
C55 A92 13c deep blue .45 .20
C56 A92 25c orange brown .80 .20
Nos. C53-C56 (4) 1.90 .85

AP26

Flags and National Anthem AP27

Unwmk.

1946, Feb. 27 Litho. ***Perf. 12***

Center in Dark Blue, Deep Carmine and Black

C57 AP26 10c carmine .40 .30
C58 AP26 15c blue .90 .75
C59 AP26 20c chocolate 1.10 .75
C60 AP26 35c orange 1.25 .85
C61 AP27 1p grn, yel grn & cit 12.00 8.75
Nos. C57-C61 (5) 15.65 11.40

Nos. C57-C61 exist imperf.

Map Type of Regular Issue

1946, Aug. 4

C62 A94 10c multicolored .35 .20
C63 A94 13c multicolored .60 .20

Waterfall Type of Regular Issue

1947, Mar. 18 Litho.

Center Multicolored

C64 A95 18c light blue .45 .35
C65 A95 23c carmine .70 .55
C66 A95 50c red violet .90 .50
C67 A95 75c chocolate 1.25 1.00
Nos. C64-C67 (4) 3.30 2.40

Palace Type of Regular Issue

1948, Feb. 27

C68 A96 37c orange brown .90 .75
C69 A96 1p orange yellow 2.50 1.50

Ruins Type of Regular Issue

1949 Unwmk. ***Perf. 11½***

C70 A97 7c ol grn & pale ol grn .25 .20
C71 A97 10c orange brn & buff .25 .20
C72 A97 15c brt rose & pale pink .55 .25
C73 A97 20c green & pale green .80 .45
Nos. C70-C73 (4) 1.85 1.10

Issue dates: 10c, Apr. 4; others, Apr. 13.

Las Carreras Monument — AP32

1949, Aug. 10

C74 AP32 10c red & pink .25 .20

Cent. of the Battle of Las Carreras.

Catalogue values for unused stamps in this section, from this point to the end of the section, are for Never Hinged items.

Hotel Type of Regular Issue

Hotels: 12c, Montana. 37c, San Cristobal.

1950, Sept. 8

C75 A100 12c dk blue & blue .50 .20
C76 A100 37c carmine & pink 3.00 2.00

Map, Plane and Caduceus AP34

1950, Oct. 2

C77 AP34 12c orange brn & yel .60 .20

13th Pan-American Health Conf. Exists imperf.

Hospital Type of Regular Issue

1952, Aug.

C78 A104 23c deep blue .85 .85
C79 A104 29c carmine 2.25 1.50

Columbus Lighthouse and Plane AP36

Ano Mariano Initials in Monogram AP37

1953, Jan. 6 Engr. ***Perf. 13***

C80 AP36 12c ocher .30 .20
C81 AP36 14c dark blue .20 .20
C82 AP36 20c black brown .60 .45
C83 AP36 23c deep plum .35 .30
C84 AP36 25c dark blue .70 .55
C85 AP36 29c deep green .60 .50
C86 AP36 1p red brown 1.40 .80
a. Miniature sheet of 10 15.00 15.00
Nos. C80-C86 (7) 4.15 3.00

No. C86a is lithographed and contains Nos. 450-452 and C80-C86, in slightly different shades. Sheet measures 190x130mm and is imperf. with simulated perforations.

A miniature sheet similar to No. C86a, but measuring 200x163mm and in folder, exists. Value $100.

1954, Aug. 5 Litho. ***Perf. 11½***

C87 AP37 8c claret .20 .20
C88 AP37 11c blue .20 .20
C89 AP37 33c brown orange .80 .50
Nos. C87-C89 (3) 1.20 .90

Marian Year. Nos. C87-C89 exist imperf.

Rotary Type of Regular Issue

1955, Feb. 23 ***Perf. 12***

C90 A110 11c rose red .35 .20

Flags — AP39

Portraits of General Hector B. Trujillo: 25c, In civilian clothes. 33c, In uniform.

1955, May 16 Engr. ***Perf. 13½x13***

C91 AP39 11c blue, yel & car .55 .20
C92 AP39 25c rose violet .90 .30
C93 AP39 33c orange brown 1.25 .50
Nos. C91-C93 (3) 2.70 1.00

The center of No. C91 is litho. 25th anniv. of the inauguration of the Trujillo era.

Fair Type of Regular Issue

1955, Dec. 20 Unwmk. ***Perf. 13***

C94 A112 11c vermilion .35 .20

ICAO Type of Regular Issue

1956, Apr. 6 Litho. ***Perf. 12½***

C95 A114 11c ultra .40 .20

Tree Type of Regular Issue

Design: 13c, Mahogany tree.

1956, Dec. 8 Litho. ***Perf. 11½x12***

C96 A115 13c orange & green *1.60* .20

Type of Regular Issue, 1957

Olympic Winners and Flags: 11c, Paavo Nurmi, Finland. 16c, Ugo Frigerio, Italy. 17c, Mildred Didrikson ("Didrickson" on stamp), US.

Engraved and Lithographed
Perf. 11½, Imperf.

1957, Jan. 24 Unwmk.

Flags in National Colors

C97 A117 11c ultra & red org .20 .20
C98 A117 16c carmine & lt grn .20 .20
C99 A117 17c black, vio & red .25 .25
Nos. C97-C99 (3) .65 .65

16th Olympic Games, Melbourne, Nov. 22-Dec. 8, 1956.

Souvenir sheets of 3 exist, perf. and imperf., containing Nos. C97-C99.

Value, 2 sheets, perf. & imperf., $15.

For surcharges see Nos. CB1-CB3, CB16-CB18.

Type of Regular Issue

Olympic Winners and Flags: 11c, Robert Morrow, US, 100 & 200 meter dash. 16c, Chris Brasher, England, steeplechase. 17c, A. Ferreira Da Silva, Brazil, hop, step and jump.

Perf. 13½, Imperf.

1957, July 18 Photo.

Flags in National Colors

C100 A118 11c yellow grn & dk bl .20 .20
C101 A118 16c lilac & dk blue .20 .20
C102 A118 17c brown & blue grn .25 .25
Nos. C100-C102 (3) .65 .65

1956 Olympic winners.

See note on miniature sheets following No. 483.

For surcharges see Nos. CB4-CB6.

Types of Regular Issue

Olympic Winners and Flags: 11c, Hans Winkler, Germany, individual jumping. 16c, Alfred Oerter, US, discus throw. 17c, Shirley Strickland, Australia, 800 meter hurdles.

Engraved and Lithographed
Perf. 13½, Imperf.

1957, Nov. 12 Unwmk.

Flags in National Colors

C103 A119 11c ultra .20 .20
C104 A120 16c rose carmine .20 .20
C105 A119 17c claret .25 .25
Nos. C103-C105 (3) .65 .65

1956 Olympic winners.

Miniature sheets of 3 exist, perf. and imperf., containing Nos. C103-C105. Value, 2 sheets, perf. and imperf., $5.50.

For surcharges see Nos. CB7-CB12.

Type of Regular Issue

Olympic Winners and Flags: 11c, Charles Jenkins, 400 & 800 meter run, and Thomas Courtney, 1,600 meter relay, US. 16c, Field hockey team, India. 17c, Yachting team, Sweden.

Perf. 13½, Imperf.

1958, Oct. 30 Unwmk. Photo.

Flags in National Colors

C106 A125 11c blue, olive & brn .25 .25
C107 A125 16c lt grn, org & dk bl .25 .25
C108 A125 17c ver, blue & yel .25 .25
Nos. C106-C108 (3) .75 .75

1956 Olympic winners.

Miniature sheets of 3 exist, perf. and imperf., containing Nos. C106-C108. Value, 2 sheets, perf. and imperf., $3.

For surcharges see Nos. CB13-CB15.

Fair Type of Regular Issue

1958, Dec. 9 Litho. ***Perf. 12½***

C109 A127 9c gray .25 .20
C110 A127 25c lt violet .60 .35
a. Souv. sheet of 3, #C109-C110, 507, imperf. 1.75 1.75

Polo Type of Regular Issue

1959, May 15 ***Perf. 12***

C111 A130 11c Dominican polo team .35 .30

"San Cristobal" Plane — AP42

Perf. 11½

1960, Feb. 25 Unwmk. Litho.

C112 AP42 13c org, bl, grn & gray .30 .20

Dominican Civil Aviation.

Children and WRY Emblem AP43

1960, Apr. 7 ***Perf. 12½***

C113 AP43 10c plum, gray & grn .60 .30
C114 AP43 13c gray & green .80 .30

World Refugee Year, 7/1/59-6/30/60.

For surcharges see Nos. CB19-CB20.

Olympic Type of Regular Issue

Olympic Winners: 11c, Pat McCormick, US, diving. 16c, Mithat Bayrack, Turkey, welter-weight wrestling. 17c, Ursula Happe, Germany, 200 meter breast stroke.

Perf. 13½, Imperf.

1960, Sept. 14 Photo.

Flags in National Colors

C115 A136 11c blue, gray & brn .20 .20
C116 A136 16c red, brown & ol .25 .25
C117 A136 17c black, blue & ocher .25 .25
Nos. C115-C117 (3) .70 .70

17th Olympic Games, Rome, 8/25-9/11.

Miniature sheets of 3 exist, perf. and imperf., containing Nos. C115-C117. Value, 2 sheets, perf. and imperf., $3.75.

For surcharges see Nos. CB21-CB23.

Coffee-Cacao Type of Regular Issue

1961, Dec. 30 Litho. ***Perf. 12½***

C118 A140 13c orange ver .25 .25
C119 A140 33c brt yellow .50 .50

Exist imperf.

Anti-Malaria Type of Regular Issue

1962, Apr. 29 Unwmk. *Perf. 12*

C120 A141 13c pink & red .40 .20
C121 A141 33c org & dp org .70 .45

See Nos. CB24-CB25.

Type of Regular Issue

Designs: 13c, Broken fetters and laurel. 50c, Flag, torch and inscription.

1962, May 30 *Perf. 12½*

C122 A142 13c brn, yel, ol, ultra & red .30 .25
C123 A142 50c rose lilac, ultra & red 1.10 .75

No. C122 exists imperf.

UPAE Type of Regular Issue

1962, Oct. 23 *Perf. 12½*

C124 A146 13c bright blue .25 .20
C125 A146 22c dull red brown .40 .40

Exist imperf.

Nouel Type of Regular Issue

Design: Frame altered with rosary and cross surrounding portrait.

1962, Dec. 18

C126 A147 13c blue & pale blue .35 .20
C127 A147 25c vio & pale vio .50 .50
a. Souv. sheet, #C126-C127, imperf .90 .90

Exist imperf.

Sanchez, Duarte, Mella — AP44

1963, July 7 Litho. *Perf. 11½x12*

C128 AP44 15c orange .30 .25

120th anniv. of separation from Haiti.

World Map — AP45

1963, Oct. 25 Unwmk. *Perf. 12½*

C129 AP45 10c gray & carmine .30 .25

Cent. of Intl. Red Cross. Exists imperf.

Human Rights Type

1963, Dec. 10 Litho.

C130 A152 7c fawn & red brn .20 .20
C131 A152 10c lt blue & blue .25 .20

Exist imperf.

Ramses II Battling the Hittites (from Abu Simbel) — AP46

1964, Mar. 8 *Perf. 12½*

C132 AP46 10c brt violet .25 .20
C133 AP46 13c yellow .25 .20

UNESCO world campaign to save historic monuments in Nubia. Exist imperf.

For surcharges see Nos. CB26-CB27.

Striated Woodpecker — AP47

1964, June 8 Litho.

C134 AP47 10c multicolored *4.25* .20

Type of Space Issue

Designs: 7c, Rocket leaving earth. 10c, Space capsule orbiting earth.

1964, July 28 Unwmk. *Perf. 12½*

C135 A156 7c brt green .25 .20
C136 A156 10c violet blue .30 .25
a. Souvenir sheet 3.00 3.00

No. C136a contains 7c and 10c stamps similar to Nos. C135-C136 with simulated perforation.

Pres. John F. Kennedy — AP48

1964, Nov. 22 *Perf. 11½*

C137 AP48 10c buff & dk brown .45 .25

President John F. Kennedy (1917-63). Sheets of 10 (5x2) and sheets of 50.

UPU Type of Regular Issue

1964, Dec. 5 Litho. *Perf. 12½*

C138 A157 7c blue .25 .20

ICY Type of Regular Issue

1965, Feb. 16 Unwmk. *Perf. 12½*

C139 A158 10c lilac & violet .30 .25

Basilica of Our Lady of Altagracia — AP49

1965, Mar. 18 Unwmk. *Perf. 12½*

C140 AP49 10c multicolored .30 .25

Fourth Mariological Congress and the Eleventh International Marian Congress.

Abraham Lincoln — AP50

1965, Apr. 15 Litho. *Perf. 12½*

C141 AP50 17c bright blue .45 .35

Cent. of the death of Abraham Lincoln.

Stamp Centenary Type of 1965

Design: Stamp of 1865, (No. 2).

1965, Dec. 28 Litho. *Perf. 12½*

C142 A161 7c violet, lt grn & blk .25 .20
C143 A161 10c yellow, lt grn & blk .25 .20

ITU Emblem, Old and New Communication Equipment — AP51

1966, Apr. 6 Litho. *Perf. 12½*

C144 AP51 28c pink & carmine .60 .60
C145 AP51 45c brt grn & grn .90 .90

Cent. (in 1965) of the ITU.

Butterfly Type of Regular Issue

1966, Nov. 8 Litho. *Perf. 12½*

Various Butterflies in Natural Colors

Size: 35x24mm

C146 A164 10c lt violet & violet 5.25 .25
C147 A164 50c org & dp org 5.50 .90
C148 A164 75c pink & rose red 5.75 1.10
Nos. C146-C148 (3) 16.50 2.25

For surcharges see Nos. CB28-CB30.

Altar Type of Regular Issue

1967, Jan. 18 Litho. *Perf. 11½*

C149 A165 7c lt olive green .20 .20
C150 A165 10c lilac .20 .20
C151 A165 20c yellow brown .30 .25
Nos. C149-C151 (3) .70 .65

Chess Type of Regular Issue

Design: 10c, Pawn and Bishop.

1967, June 23 Litho. *Perf. 12½*

C152 A167 10c ol, lt ol & blk *1.10* .25
a. Souvenir sheet *9.00* 2.00

No. C152a contains 2 imperf. stamps similar to Nos. 636 and C152.

Alliance for Progress Type

1967, Sept. 16 Litho. *Perf. 12½*

C153 A168 8c gray .30 .25
C154 A168 10c blue .35 .25

Cornucopia and Emblem — AP52

Latin American Flags — AP53

1967, Oct. 7

C155 AP52 12c multicolored .45 .25

25th anniversary of the Inter-American Agriculture Institute.

Satellite Type of Regular Issue

1968, June 15 Typo. *Perf. 12*

C156 A170 10c dp blue & multi .25 .20
C157 A170 15c purple & multi .35 .30

Boxing Type of Regular Issue

Designs: Two views of boxing match.

1968, June 29

C158 A171 7c orange yel & grn .25 .20
C159 A171 10c gray & blue .30 .20

See note after No. 641.

Lions Type of Regular Issue

1968, Aug. 9 Litho. *Perf. 11½*

C160 A172 10c ultra & multi .25 .20

Olympic Type of Regular Issue

Designs (Olympic Emblem and): 10c, Weight lifting. 33c, Pistol shooting.

1968, Nov. 12 Litho. *Perf. 11½*

C161 A173 10c buff & multi .25 .25
C162 A173 33c pink & multi .75 .60

1969, Jan. 25 Litho. *Perf. 12½*

C163 AP53 10c pink & multi .25 .20

7th Inter-American Savings and Loan Conference, Santo Domingo, Jan. 25-31.

Taino Art Type of Regular Issue

7c, Various vomiting spoons with human heads, vert. 10c, Female torso forming drinking vessel. 20c, Vase with human head, vert.

1969, Jan. 31 Litho. *Perf. 12½*

C164 A175 7c lt bl, bl & lem .20 .20
C165 A175 10c pink, ver & brn .25 .20
C166 A175 20c yellow, org & brn .30 .30
Nos. C164-C166 (3) .75 .70

COTAL Type of Regular Issue

10c, Airport of the Americas and COTAL emblem.

1969, May 25 Litho. *Perf. 12½*

C167 A178 10c brown & pale fawn .25 .20

ILO Type of Regular Issue

1969, June 27 Litho. *Perf. 12½*

C168 A179 10c rose, red & black .20 .20

Baseball Type of Regular Issue

Designs: 7c, Bleachers, Tetelo Vargas Stadium, horiz. 10c, Batter, catcher and umpire. 1p, Quisqueya Stadium, horiz.

1969, Aug. 15 Litho. *Perf. 12½*

Size: 43x30mm (7c, 1p); 21x31mm (10c)

C169 A180 7c magenta & org .40 .25
C170 A180 10c mar & rose red .45 .25
C171 A180 1p violet blue & brn 3.50 2.40
Nos. C169-C171 (3) 4.35 2.90

Electrification Types of Regular Issue

Design: No. C172, Rio Haina steam plant. No. C173, Valdesa Dam.

1969 Litho. *Perf. 12*

C172 A181 10c orange ver .30 .20
C173 A182 10c multicolored .35 .20

Issued: #C172, Sept. 15; #C173, Oct. 15.

Duarte Type of Regular Issue

1970, Jan. 26 Litho. *Perf. 12*

C174 A183 10c brown & dk brown .45 .25

Census Type of Regular Issue

Design: 10c, Buildings and census emblem.

1970, Feb. 6 *Perf. 11*

C175 A184 10c lt blue & multi .45 .25

Sculpture Type of Regular Issue

Design: 10c, The Prisoner, by Abelardo Rodriguez Urdaneta, vert.

1970, Feb. 20 Litho. *Perf. 12½*

C176 A186 10c bluish gray .30 .20

Masonic Type of Regular Issue

1970, Mar. 2

C177 A187 10c brown .20 .20

Satellite Type of Regular Issue

1970, May 25 Litho. *Perf. 12½*

C178 A188 7c blue & gray .25 .20

UPU Type of Regular Issue

1970, June 5 *Perf. 11*

C179 A189 10c yellow & brown .25 .20

Education Year Type of Regular Issue

1970, June 26 Litho. *Perf. 12½*

C180 A190 15c bright pink .45 .25

Dancers — AP54

Album, Globe and Emblem — AP55

Design: 10c, UN emblem and wheel.

1970, Oct. 12 Litho. *Perf. 12½*

C181 AP54 7c blue & multi .25 .20
C182 AP54 10c pink & multi .30 .20

1st World Exhib. of Books and Culture Festival, Santo Domingo, Oct. 11-Dec. 11.

1970, Oct. 26 Litho. *Perf. 11*

C183 AP55 10c multicolored .30 .25

EXFILCA 70, 2nd Interamerican Philatelic Exhibition, Caracas, Venezuela, 11/27-12/6.

Basilica of Our Lady of Altagracia — AP56

1971, Jan. 20 Litho. *Perf. 12½*

C184 AP56 17c multicolored .65 .35

Inauguration of the Basilica of Our Lady of Altagracia.

Map of Dominican Republic, CARE Package AP57

1971, May 28 Litho. *Perf. 12½*

C185 AP57 10c blue & green .25 .20

25th anniversary of CARE, a US-Canadian Cooperative for American Relief Everywhere.

Sports Type of Regular Issue

1971, Sept. 10 *Perf. 11*

C186 A195 7c Volleyball .25 .20

Animal Type of Regular Issue

Design: 25c, Cock and grain.

1971, Sept. 29 *Perf. 12½*

C187 A196 25c black & multi .50 .30

Independence Type

10c, Dominican-Colombian flag of 1821.

1971, Dec. 1 *Perf. 11*

C188 A197 10c vio bl, yel & red .25 .20

Christmas Type of Regular Issue

1971, Dec. 10 *Perf. 12½*

C189 A198 10c Bell, 1493 .20 .20

UNICEF Type of Regular Issue

Design: UNICEF emblem & child on beach.

1971, Dec. 14 *Perf. 11*

C190 A199 15c multicolored .45 .30

Book Year Type of Regular Issue

1972, Jan. 25 Litho. *Perf. 12½*

C191 A200 12c lilac, dk bl & red .30 .25

Magnifying Glass over Peru on Map of Americas — AP58

"Your Heart is your Health" — AP59

1972, Mar. 7 Litho. *Perf. 12*

C192 AP58 10c blue & multi .30 .25

EXFILIMA '71, 3rd Inter-American Philatelic Exposition, Lima, Peru, Nov. 6-14, 1971.

1972, Apr. 27 Litho. *Perf. 11*

C193 AP59 7c red & multi .25 .20

World Health Day.

Taino Art Type of 1972

Taino Art: 8c, Ritual vessel showing human figures. 10c, Trumpet (shell). 25c, Carved vomiting spoons. All horiz.

1972, May 10 Litho. *Perf. 11*

C194 A201 8c multicolored .20 .20
C195 A201 10c lt blue & multi .30 .20
C196 A201 25c multicolored .75 .45
Nos. C194-C196 (3) 1.25 .85

Telecommunications Type of Regular Issue

1972, May 17 *Perf. 12½*

C197 A202 21c yellow & multi .60 .30

Exhibition Type of Regular Issue

1972, June 3

C198 A203 33c orange & multi .60 .40

Olympic Type of Regular Issue

1972, Aug. 25 Litho. *Perf. 12½*

C199 A204 33c Running .75 .50

Club Type of Regular Issue

1972, Sept. 29 Litho. *Perf. 10½*

C200 A205 20c blue & multi .40 .25

Morel Type of Regular Issue

1972, Oct. 20 Litho. *Perf. 12½*

C201 A206 10c multicolored .25 .20

Bank Type of Regular Issue

25c, 1947 silver coin, entrance to the Mint.

1972, Oct. 23

C202 A207 25c ocher & multi .65 .45

"La Navidad" Fortress, 1492 AP60

1972, Nov. 21 Litho. *Perf. 12½*

C203 AP60 10c multicolored .45 .20

Christmas 1972.

Sports Type of Regular Issue

Various sports; a, UL. b, UR. c, LL. d, LR.

1973, Mar. 30 Litho. *Perf. 13½x13*

C204 A212 Block of 4 1.25 1.25
a.-d. 8c, any single .25 .25
C205 A212 Block of 4 2.10 2.10
a.-d. 10c, any single .50 .30

Easter Type 1973

10c, Belfry of Church of Our Lady of Help.

1973, Apr. 18 Litho. *Perf. 10½*

C206 A213 10c multicolored .40 .20

North and South America on Globe — AP61

1973, May 29 Litho. *Perf. 12*

C207 AP61 7c multicolored .25 .20

Pan-American Health Organization, 70th anniversary (in 1972).

WMO Type of Regular Issue

1973, Aug. 10 Litho. *Perf. 13½x13*

C208 A214 7c green & multi .25 .20

INTERPOL Emblem Police Scientist AP62

1973, Sept. 28 Litho. *Perf. 10½*

C209 AP62 10c vio bl, bl & emer .30 .20

50th anniversary of International Criminal Police Organization.

Handicraft Type of Regular Issue

1973, Oct. 12

C210 A215 7c Sailing ship, mosaic .20 .20
C211 A215 10c Maracas rattles, horiz. .30 .20

Christmas Type of Regular Issue

Design: 10c, Angels adoring Christ Child.

1973, Nov. 26 Litho. *Perf. 13½x13*

C212 A216 10c multicolored .25 .20

Scout Type of Regular Issue

21c, Scouts cooking, Lord Baden-Powell.

1973, Dec. 7 Litho. *Perf. 12*

C213 A217 21c red & multi .65 .55

Sport Type of Regular Issue

10c, Olympic swimming pool and diver. 25c, Olympic Stadium, soccer and discus.

1974, Feb. 25 Litho. *Perf. 13½*

C214 A218 10c blue & multi .20 .20
C215 A218 25c multicolored .40 .20

The Last Supper AP63

1974, June 27 Litho. *Perf. 13½*

C216 AP63 10c multicolored .30 .20

Holy Week 1974.

Bridge Type

Design: 10c, Higuamo Bridge.

1974, July 12 *Perf. 12*

C217 A221 10c multicolored .30 .20

Diabetes Type

Map of Dominican Republic, Diabetics' Emblem and: 7c, Kidney. 33c, Eye & heart.

1974, Aug. 22 Litho. *Perf. 13*

C218 A222 7c yellow & multi .25 .25
C219 A222 33c lt blue & multi 1.25 .75

UPU Type

1974, Oct. 9 Litho. *Perf. 13½*

C220 A223 7c Ships .50 .25
C221 A223 33c Jet 1.50 .50
a. Souvenir sheet of 4 4.25 4.25

No. C221a contains Nos. 727-728, C220-C221 forming continuous design.

Golfers and Championship Emblem — AP64

20c, Golfer and Golf Association emblem.

1974, Oct. 24 Litho. *Perf. 13x13½*

C222 AP64 10c green & multi .40 .20
C223 AP64 20c green & multi .75 .40

World Amateur Golf Championships.

Hand Holding Dove AP65

1974, Dec. 3 Litho. *Perf. 12*

C224 AP65 10c multicolored .30 .20

Christmas 1974.

FAO Type

10c, Bee, beehive and barrel of honey.

1974, Dec. 5

C225 A227 10c multicolored 1.10 .20

Chrismon, Lamb, Candle and Palm — AP66

Spain No. 1, España 75 Emblem — AP67

1975, Mar. 26 Litho. *Perf. 13½*

C226 AP66 10c gold & multi .30 .20

Holy Week 1975.

1975, Apr. 10

C227 AP67 12c red, yel & blk .40 .25

Espana 75, International Philatelic Exhibition, Madrid, Apr. 4-13.

Development Bank Type

1975, May 19 Litho. *Perf. 10½x10*

C228 A230 10c rose car & multi .30 .20

Three Satellites and Globe AP68

1975, June 21 Litho. *Perf. 13½*

C229 AP68 15c multicolored .45 .35

Opening of first earth satellite tracking station in Dominican Republic.

Apollo Type

Design: 2p, Apollo-Soyuz link-up over earth.

1975, July 24 *Perf. 13*

Size: 42x28mm

C230 A232 2p multicolored 5.25 3.25

Indian Chief Type

7c, Mayobanex. 8c, Cotubanama & Juan de Esquivel. 10c, Enriquillo & Mencia.

1975, Sept. 27 Litho. *Perf. 12*
C231 A235 7c lt green & multi .25 .25
C232 A235 8c orange & multi .30 .25
C233 A235 10c gray & multi .30 .25
Nos. C231-C233 (3) .85 .75

Volleyball AP69

10c, Weight lifting and Games' emblem.

1975, Oct. 24 Litho. *Perf. 12*
C234 AP69 7c blue & multi .25 .20
C235 AP69 10c multicolored .35 .25

7th Pan-American Games, Mexico City, Oct. 13-26.

Christmas Type

Design: 10c, Dove and peace message.

1975, Dec. 12 Litho. *Perf. 13x13½*
C236 A237 10c yellow & multi .25 .20

Valdesia Dam — AP70

1976, Jan. 26 Litho. *Perf. 13*
C237 AP70 10c multicolored .30 .20

Holy Week Type 1976

Design: 10c, Crucifixion, by Eliezer Castillo.

1976, Apr. 14 Litho. *Perf. 13½*
C238 A239 10c multicolored .30 .25

Bicentennial Type and

George Washington, Independence Hall — AP71

Design: 10c, Hands holding maps of US and Dominican Republic.

1976, May 29 Litho. *Perf. 13½*
C239 A241 10c vio bl, grn & blk .35 .20
C240 AP71 75c black & orange 1.10 1.10

American Bicentennial; No. C240 also for Interphil 76 International Philatelic Exhibition, Philadelphia, Pa., May 29-June 6.

King Juan Carlos I and Queen Sofia — AP72

1976, May 31
C241 AP72 21c multicolored .60 .60

Visit of King Juan Carlos I and Queen Sofia of Spain.

Telephone Type

Design: 10c, Alexander Graham Bell and telephones, 1876 and 1976.

1976, July 15
C242 A243 10c multicolored .30 .20

Duarte Types

10c, Scroll with Duarte letter and Dominican flag. 33c, Duarte return from Exile, by E. Godoy.

1976, July 20 Litho. *Perf. 13½*
C243 A245 10c blue & multi .30 .20
Perf. 13x13½
C244 A244 33c brown & multi 1.10 .75

Fire Engine AP73

1976, Sept. 13 Litho. *Perf. 12*
C245 AP73 10c multicolored .30 .20

Honoring firemen.

Radio Club Type

1976, Oct. 8 Litho. *Perf. 13½*
C246 A247 10c blue & black .30 .20

Various People — AP74

1976, Oct. 22 Litho. *Perf. 13½*
C247 AP74 21c multicolored .35 .35

Spanish heritage.

Olympic Games Type

1976, Oct. 22 *Perf. 12*
C248 A249 10c Running .30 .20
C249 A249 25c Basketball .85 .50

Christmas Type

Design: 10c, Angel with bells.

1976, Dec. 8 Litho. *Perf. 13½*
C250 A251 10c multicolored .30 .25

Tourist Activities AP75

Tourist publicity: 12c, Angling and hotel. 25c, Horseback riding and waterfall, vert.

1977, Jan. 7
Size: 36x36mm
C251 AP75 10c multicolored .25 .20
Size: 34x25½mm, 25½x34mm
C252 AP75 12c multicolored .25 .20
C253 AP75 25c multicolored .50 .30
Nos. C251-C253 (3) 1.00 .70

Championship Type

1977, Mar. 4 Litho. *Perf. 13½*
C254 A253 10c yel grn & multi .30 .20
C255 A253 25c lt brown & multi .85 .50

Holy Week Type 1977

Design: 10c, Belfry and open book.

1977, Apr. 18 Litho. *Perf. 13½x13*
C256 A254 10c multicolored .30 .20

Lions Type

1977, May 6 *Perf. 13½x13*
C257 A255 7c lt green & multi .25 .20

Caravel under Sail — AP76

Melon Cactus — AP77

1977, July 16 Litho. *Perf. 13*
C258 AP76 10c multicolored .30 .20

Miss Universe Contest, held in Dominican Republic.

1977, Aug. 19 Litho. *Perf. 12*

Design: 33c, Coccothrinax (tree).

C259 AP77 7c multicolored .30 .25
C260 AP77 33c multicolored 1.10 .75

National Botanical Garden.

Chart and Factories — AP78

1977, Nov. 30 Litho. *Perf. 13x13½*
C261 AP78 28c multicolored .50 .50

7th Interamerican Statistics Conference.

Animal Type

Congress Emblem and: 10c, "Dorado," red Roman stud bull. 25c, Flamingo, vert.

1977, Dec. 29 Litho. *Perf. 13*
C262 A259 10c multicolored *1.75* .25
C263 A259 25c multicolored *3.25* .40

Spanish Heritage Type

21c, Window, Casa del Tostado, 16th cent.

1978, Jan. 19 *Perf. 13x13½*
Size: 28x41mm
C264 A260 21c multicolored .40 .35

Holy Week Type, 1978

7c, Facade, Santo Domingo Cathedral. 10c, Facade of Dominican Convent.

1978, Mar. 21 Litho. *Perf. 12*
Size: 27x36mm
C265 A261 7c multicolored .25 .25
C266 A261 10c multicolored .40 .25

Schooner Duarte AP79

1978, Apr. 15 Litho. *Perf. 13½*
C267 AP79 7c multicolored .35 .20

Dominican naval forces training ship.

Cardinal Type

1978, May 5 Litho. *Perf. 13*
C268 A262 10c multicolored .30 .20

Antenna AP80

1978, May 17 Litho. *Perf. 13½*
C269 AP80 25c silver & multi .55 .35

10th World Telecommunications Day.

No. C1 and Map AP81

1978, June 6
C270 AP81 10c multicolored .30 .20

1st Dominican Rep. airmail stamp, 50th anniv.

Globe, Soccer Ball, Emblem — AP82

Crown, Cross and Rosary Emblem — AP83

33c, Soccer field, Argentina '78 emblem, globe.

1978, June 29
C271 AP82 12c multicolored .40 .30
C272 AP82 33c multicolored .85 .85

11th World Cup Soccer Championship, Argentina, June 1-25.

1978, July 11 *Perf. 13x13½*
C273 AP83 21c multicolored .65 .65

Congregation of the Merciful Sisters of Charity, centenary.

Sports Type

1978, July 21 Litho. *Perf. 13½*
C274 A265 7c Baseball, vert. .25 .20
C275 A265 10c Basketball, vert. .30 .20

REPUBLICA DOMINICANA

10c CORREO AEREO

Wright Brothers and Glider, 1902 AP84

Designs: 7c, Diagrams of Flyer I and jet, vert. 13c, Diagram of air flow over wing. 45c, Flyer I over world map.

1978, Aug. 8 *Perf. 12*
C276 AP84 7c multicolored .25 .20
C277 AP84 10c multicolored .35 .20
C278 AP84 13c multicolored .55 .25
C279 AP84 45c multicolored 1.50 .95
Nos. C276-C279 (4) 2.65 1.60

75th anniversary of first powered flight.

Tourist Type

Designs: 7c, Sun and musical instruments. 10c, Sun and plane over Santo Domingo.

1978, Sept. 12 Litho. *Perf. 12*

C280 A266 7c multicolored .30 .20
C281 A266 10c multicolored .35 .20

People and Globe AP85

1978, Oct. 12 Litho. *Perf. 13½*

C282 AP85 21c multicolored .45 .45

Spanish heritage.

Dominican Republic and UN Flags AP86

1978, Oct. 23 *Perf. 12*

C283 AP86 33c multicolored .60 .60

33rd anniversary of the United Nations.

Statue of the Virgin — AP87

Pope John Paul II — AP88

1978, Dec. 5 Litho. *Perf. 12*

C284 AP87 10c multicolored .30 .25

Christmas 1978.

1979, Jan. 25 Litho. *Perf. 13½*

C285 AP88 10c multicolored 3.00 3.00

Visit of Pope John Paul II to the Dominican Republic, Jan. 25-26.

Map of Beata Island AP89

1979, Jan. 25 *Perf. 12*

C286 AP89 10c multicolored .30 .20

1st expedition of radio amateurs to Beata Is.

Year of the Child Type, 1979

Designs (ICY Emblem and): 7c, Children reading book. 10c, Symbolic head and protective hands. 33c, Hands and jars.

1979, Feb. 26

C287 A269 7c multicolored .20 .20
C288 A269 10c multicolored .30 .20
C289 A269 33c multicolored 1.10 .75
Nos. C287-C289 (3) 1.60 1.15

Pope John Paul II Giving Benediction AP90

Adm. Juan Bautista Cambiaso AP91

1979, Apr. 9 Litho. *Perf. 13½*

C290 AP90 10c multicolored 1.25 .90

Holy Week.

1979, Apr. 14 *Perf. 12*

C291 AP91 10c multicolored .30 .20

135th anniv. of the Battle of Tortuguero.

Map of Dominican Rep., Album, Magnifier AP92

1979, Apr. 18

C292 AP92 33c multicolored .60 .60

EXFILNA, 3rd National Philatelic Exhibition, Apr. 18-22.

Flower Type

Designs: 7c, Passionflower. 10c, Isidorea pungens. 13c, Calotropis procera.

1979, May 17 Litho. *Perf. 12*

C293 A271 7c multicolored .30 .30
C294 A271 10c multicolored .40 .25
C295 A271 13c multicolored .55 .45
Nos. C293-C295 (3) 1.25 1.00

Cardiology Type, 1979

10c, Figure of man showing blood circulation.

1979, June 2 Litho. *Perf. 13½*

C296 A272 10c multicolored, vert. .25 .20

Sports Type

7c, Runner and Games' emblem, vert.

1979, June 20

C297 A273 7c multicolored .30 .25

Soccer Type

1979, Aug. 9 Litho. *Perf. 12*

C298 A273 10c Tennis, vert. .30 .25

Rowland Hill, Dominican Republic No. 1 — AP93

1979, Aug. 21 *Perf. 13½*

C299 AP93 2p multicolored 3.00 2.50

Sir Rowland Hill (1795-1879), originator of penny postage.

Electric Light Type

Design: 10c, "100" and light bulb, horiz.

1979, Aug. 27 *Perf. 13½*

C300 A275 10c multicolored .30 .25

Bird Type

Birds: 7c, Phaenicophilus palmarum. 10c, Calyptophilus frugivorus tertius. 45c, Icterus dominicensis.

1979, Sept. 12 Litho. *Perf. 12*

C301 A277 7c multicolored *1.90* .25
C302 A277 10c multicolored *2.75* .25
C303 A277 45c multicolored *6.75* .90
Nos. C301-C303 (3) 11.40 1.40

Lions Type

10c, Melvin Jones, organization founder.

1979, Nov. 13 Litho. *Perf. 12*

C304 A278 10c multicolored .30 .20

Christmas Type

Christmas: 10c, Three Kings riding camels.

1979, Dec. 18 Litho. *Perf. 12*

C305 A279 10c multicolored .25 .25

Holy Week Type

1980, Mar. 27 Litho. *Perf. 12*

C306 A280 7c Crucifixion .20 .20
C307 A280 10c Resurrection .30 .25

Navy Day — AP94

1980, Apr. 15 Litho. *Perf. 13½*

C308 AP94 21c multicolored .45 .40

Dominican Philatelic Society, 25th Anniversary AP95

1980, Apr. 18

C309 AP95 10c multicolored .30 .25

Gold Type

1980, July 8 Litho. *Perf. 13½*

C310 A282 10c Drag line mining .45 .35
C311 A282 33c Mine .85 .55

Tourism Secretariat Emblem — AP96

1980, Aug. 26 Litho. *Perf. 13½*

C312 AP96 10c shown .30 .25
C313 AP96 33c Conf. emblem 1.10 .75

World Tourism Conf., Manila, Sept. 27.

Iguana Type

1980, Aug. 30 *Perf. 12*

C314 A284 7c American crocodile *1.50* .25
C315 A284 10c Cuban rat *1.60* .30
C316 A284 25c Manatee *2.50* .50
C317 A284 45c Turtle *3.50* .75
Nos. C314-C317 (4) 9.10 1.80

Painting Type

1980, Sept. 23 Litho. *Perf. 13½x13*

C318 A285 10c Abstract, by Paul Guidicelli, vert. .30 .25
C319 A285 17c Farmer, by Yoryi Morel, vert. .50 .35

Visit of Radio Amateurs to Catalina Island AP97

1980, Oct. 3

C320 AP97 7c multicolored .25 .25

Rotary International, 75th Anniversary — AP98

1980, Oct. 23 Litho. *Perf. 12*

C321 AP98 10c Globe, emblem, vert. .40 .30
C322 AP98 33c shown .75 .75

Carrier Pigeons, UPU Emblem AP99

1980, Oct. 31 *Perf. 13½*

C323 AP99 33c shown .30 .25
C324 AP99 45c Pigeons, diff. .45 .30
C325 AP99 50c Pigeon, stamp .90 .45
Nos. C323-C325 (3) 1.65 1.00

Souvenir Sheet

Imperf

C326 AP99 1.10p UPU emblem 1.25 1.25

UPU cent. No. C326 contains one 48½x31mm stamp.

Christmas Type

1980, Dec. 5 Litho. *Perf. 13½*

C327 A286 10c Holy Family .30 .25

Christmas 1980.

Salcedo Type

Design: Map and arms of Salcedo.

1981, Jan. 14 Litho. *Perf. 13½*

C328 A287 10c multicolored .25 .25

AP100

AP101

Industrial Symbols, Seminar Emblem.

1981, Feb. 18 Litho. *Perf. 13½*

C329 AP100 10c shown .30 .25
C330 AP100 33c Seminar emblem .55 .25

CODIA Chemical Engineering Seminar.

National Games Type

1981, Mar. 31 Litho. *Perf. 13½*

C331 A289 10c Baseball .35 .25

1981, Apr. 15

Design: Admiral Juan Alejandro Acosta.

C332 AP101 10c multicolored .25 .20

Battle of Tortuguero anniversary.

13th World Telecommunications Day — AP102

1981, May 16 Litho. *Perf. 12*
C333 AP102 10c multicolored .25 .20

Heinrich von Stephan AP103

Worker in Wheelchair AP104

1981, July 15 Litho. *Perf. 13½*
C334 AP103 33c tan & lt red brn .75 .75

Birth sesquicentennial of UPU founder.

1981, July 24
C335 AP104 7c Stylized people .30 .30
C336 AP104 33c shown .75 .75

Intl. Year of the Disabled.

EXPURIDOM '81 Intl. Stamp Show, Santo Domingo, July 31-Aug. 2 — AP105

1981, July 31
C337 AP105 7c multicolored .25 .20

Bullet Holes in Target, Competition Emblem AP106

1981, Aug. 12
C338 AP106 10c shown .20 .20
C339 AP106 15c Riflemen .30 .25
C340 AP106 25c Pistol shooting .50 .40
Nos. C338-C340 (3) 1.00 .85

2nd World Sharpshooting Championship.

Exports — AP107

World Food Day — AP108

1981, Oct. 16 Litho. *Perf. 12*
C341 AP107 7c Jewelry .35 .25
C342 AP107 10c Handicrafts .45 .25
C343 AP107 11c Fruit .35 .30
C344 AP107 17c Vegetables .60 .40
Nos. C341-C344 (4) 1.75 1.20

1981, Oct. 16 Litho. *Perf. 13½*
C345 AP108 10c Fruits .45 .25
C346 AP108 50c Vegetables 1.10 1.00

5th Natl. Games AP109

1981, Dec. 5 Litho. *Perf. 13½*
C347 AP109 10c Javelin, vert. .30 .25
C348 AP109 50c Cycling 1.50 1.50

Orchids AP110

1981, Dec. 14
C349 AP110 7c Encyclia cochleata .45 .20
C350 AP110 10c Broughtonia domingensis .60 .25
C351 AP110 25c Encyclia truncata .90 .55
C352 AP110 75c Elleanthus capitatus 2.25 1.50
Nos. C349-C352 (4) 4.20 2.50

Christmas Type

1981, Dec. 23
C353 A294 10c Dove, sun .50 .30

Battle of Tortuguero Anniv. AP111

1982, Apr. 15 Litho. *Perf. 13½*
C354 AP111 10c Naval Academy, cadets .30 .25

1982 World Cup Soccer — AP112

American Air Forces Cooperation System — AP113

Designs: Various soccer players.

1982, Apr. 19
C355 AP112 10c multicolored .40 .30
C356 AP112 21c multicolored .40 .25
C357 AP112 33c multicolored .75 .75
Nos. C355-C357 (3) 1.55 1.30

1982, Apr. 12 *Perf. 12*
C358 AP113 10c multicolored .30 .25

Scouting Year AP114

1982, Apr. 30 Litho. *Perf. 13½*
C359 AP114 10c Baden-Powell, vert. .20 .20
C360 AP114 15c Globe .30 .25
C361 AP114 25c Baden-Powell, scout, vert. .45 .30
Nos. C359-C361 (3) .95 .75

Dancers — AP115

Espamer '82 Emblem — AP116

1982, June 1 Litho. *Perf. 13½*
C362 AP115 7c Emblem .20 .20
C363 AP115 10c Cathedral, Casa del Tostado, Santo Domingo .25 .20
C364 AP115 33c shown .85 .85
Nos. C362-C364 (3) 1.30 1.25

Tourist Org. of the Americas, 25th Congress (COTAL '82), Santo Domingo.

1982, July 5

Espamer '82 Intl. Stamp Exhibition, San Juan, Oct. 12-17: Symbolic stamps.

C365 AP116 7c multi .20 .20
C366 AP116 13c multi, horiz. .30 .25
C367 AP116 50c multi, horiz. 1.40 1.10
Nos. C365-C367 (3) 1.90 1.55

Sports Type

1982, Aug. 13 *Perf. 12, Imperf.*
C368 A300 10c Basketball .25 .20
C369 A300 13c Boxing .45 .25
C370 A300 25c Gymnast .55 .30
Nos. C368-C370 (3) 1.25 .75

Harbor, by Alejandro Bonilla — AP117

Paintings: 10c, Portrait of a Woman, by Leopoldo Navarro. 45c, Amelia Francasci, by Luis Desangles. 2p, Portrait, by Abelardo Rodriguez Urdaneta. 10c, 45c, 2p vert.

1982, Aug. 20 *Perf. 13, Imperf.*
C371 AP117 7c multicolored .25 .20
C372 AP117 10c multicolored .30 .25
C373 AP117 45c multicolored 1.50 1.00
C374 AP117 2p multicolored 6.75 4.00
Nos. C371-C374 (4) 8.80 5.45

San Pedro de Macoris Type

1982, Aug. 26
Size: 42x29mm
C375 A301 7c Lake .40 .30

35th Anniv. of Central Bank AP118

1982, Oct. 22 Litho. *Perf. 13½x13*
C376 AP118 10c multicolored .30 .25

490th Anniv. of Discovery of America AP119

1982, Oct. 7 Litho. *Perf. 13½*
C377 AP119 7c Map *1.00* .80
C378 AP119 10c Santa Maria, vert. *1.25* .90
C379 AP119 21c Columbus, vert. *1.50* .90
Nos. C377-C379 (3) *3.75* 2.60

Christmas Type

1982, Dec. 8
C380 A303 10c multicolored .40 .20

French Alliance Centenary AP120

1983, Mar. 31 Litho. *Perf. 13½*
C381 AP120 33c multicolored .50 .45

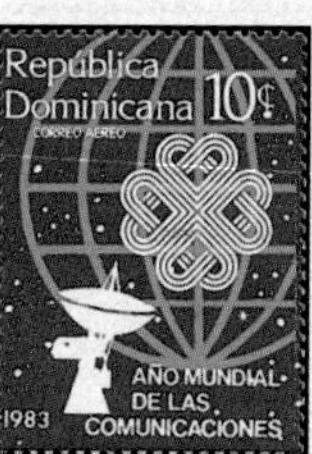

Battle of Tortuguero Anniv. AP121

1983, Apr. 15 Litho. *Perf. 13½*
C382 AP121 15c Frigate Mella-451 .60 .25

World Communications Year — AP122

1983, May 6 Litho. *Perf. 13½*
C383 AP122 10c dk blue & blue .30 .25

AP123

AP124

1983, July 5 Litho. *Perf. 13½*

C384 AP123 9c multicolored .25 .20

Simon Bolivar (1783-1830).

1983, Aug. 22 Litho. *Perf. 12*

C385 AP124 7c Gymnast, basketball .35 .20
C386 AP124 10c Highjump, boxing .45 .20
C387 AP124 15c Baseball, weight lifting, bicycling .55 .25
Nos. C385-C387 (3) 1.35 .65

9th Pan American Games, Caracas, Aug. 13-28.

491st Anniv. of Discovery of America AP125

1983, Oct. 11 Litho. *Perf. 13½*

C388 AP125 10c Columbus' ships, map *1.00* .35
C389 AP125 21c Santa Maria (trophy) *1.50* .55
C390 AP125 33c Yacht Sotavento, vert. *1.60* .60
Nos. C388-C390 (3) *4.10* 1.50

Size: 103x103mm

Imperf

C391 AP125 50c Ship models 15.00 *15.00*

10th Anniv. of Latin American Civil Aviation Commission — AP126

1983, Dec. 7

C392 AP126 10c dark blue .25 .20

Funeral Procession, by Juan Bautista Gomez — AP127

Designs: 15c, Meeting of Maximo Gomez and Jose Marti in Guayubin, by Enrique Garcia Godoy. 21c, St. Francis, by Angel Perdomo, vert. 33c, Portrait of a Girl, by Adriana Billini, vert.

1983, Dec. 26 *Perf. 13½*

C393 AP127 10c multicolored .35 .20
C394 AP127 15c multicolored .35 .20
C395 AP127 21c multicolored .40 .25
C396 AP127 33c multicolored .60 .25
Nos. C393-C396 (4) 1.70 .90

Christmas 1983 — AP128

1983, Dec. 13 Litho. *Perf. 13½*

C397 AP128 10c Bells, ornaments .30 .20

AIR POST SEMI-POSTAL STAMPS

Catalogue values for unused stamps in this section are for Never Hinged items.

Nos. C97-C99 Surcharged in Red like Nos. B1-B5

Engraved and Lithographed

1957, Feb. 8 Unwmk. *Perf. 11½*

Flags in National Colors

CB1 A117 11c + 2c ultra & red org .30 .30
CB2 A117 16c + 2c car & lt grn .40 .40
CB3 A117 17c + 2c blk, vio & red .40 .40
Nos. CB1-CB3 (3) 1.10 1.10

The surtax was to aid Hungarian refugees. A similar 25c surcharge was applied to the souvenir sheets described in the footnote following No. C99. Value, 2 sheets, perf. and imperf., $17.50.

Nos. C100-C102 Surcharged in Red Orange like Nos. B6-B10

1957, Sept. 9 Photo. *Perf. 13½*

Flags in National Colors

CB4 A118 11c + 2c yel grn & dk bl .50 .45
CB5 A118 16c + 2c lilac & dk bl .60 .60
CB6 A118 17c + 2c brn & bl grn .65 .65
Nos. CB4-CB6 (3) 1.75 1.70

See note after No. B10.

A similar 5c surcharge was applied to the miniature sheets described in the footnote following No. 483. Value, 4 sheets, perf. & imperf., medal and flag, $40.

Types of Olympic Air Post Stamps, 1957, Surcharged in Carmine like Nos. B11-B20

1958, May 26 Engr. & Litho.

Flags in National Colors

Pink Paper

CB7 A119(a) 11c + 2c ultra .30 .30
CB8 A119(b) 11c + 2c ultra .30 .30
CB9 A120(a) 16c + 2c rose car .35 .35
CB10 A120(b) 16c + 2c rose car .35 .35
CB11 A119(a) 17c + 2c claret .40 .40
CB12 A119(b) 17c + 2c claret .40 .40
Nos. CB7-CB12 (6) 2.10 2.10

A similar 5c surcharge, plus marginal UN emblem and "UNRWA," was applied to the miniature sheets described in the footnote following No. C105. Value, 4 sheets, perf. and imperf., $20.

Nos. C106-C108 Surcharged like Nos. B21-B25

1959, Apr. 13 Photo. *Perf. 13½*

Flags in National Colors

CB13 A125 11c + 2c blue, ol & brn .50 .50
CB14 A125 16c + 2c lt grn, org & dk bl .70 .70
CB15 A125 17c + 2c ver bl & yel 1.00 1.00
Nos. CB13-CB15 (3) 2.20 2.20

A similar 5c surcharge was applied to the miniature sheets described in the footnote following No. C108. Value, 2 sheets, perf. and imperf., $25.

Type of Regular Issue 1957 Surcharged in Red like Nos. B26-B30

Engraved and Lithographed

1959, Sept. 10 *Imperf.*

Flags in National Colors

CB16 A117 11c + 2c ultra & red org .45 .45
CB17 A117 16c + 2c carmine & lt grn .50 .50
CB18 A117 17c + 2c black, vio & red .55 .55
Nos. CB16-CB18 (3) 1.50 1.50

Nos. C113-C114 Surcharged in Red like Nos. B31-B33

1960, Apr. 7 Litho. *Perf. 12½*

CB19 AP43 10c + 5c plum, gray & grn .30 .30
CB20 AP43 13c + 5c gray & green .45 .45

World Refugee Year.
For souvenir sheets see note after No. B33.

Nos. C115-C117 Surcharged: "XV ANIVERSARIO DE LA UNESCO + 2c"

Perf. 13½

1962, Jan. 8 Unwmk. Photo.

Flags in National Colors

CB21 A136 11c + 2c blue, gray & brn .25 .25
CB22 A136 16c + 2c red, brn & ol .30 .30
CB23 A136 17c + 2c blk, bl & ocher .30 .30
Nos. CB21-CB23 (3) .85 .85

See note after No. B38.

A similar 5c surcharge was applied to the miniature sheets described in the footnote following No. C117. Value, 2 sheets, perf. and imperf., $7.50.

Anti-Malaria Type of 1962

1962, Apr. 29 Litho. *Perf. 12*

CB24 A141 13c + 2c pink & red .30 .25
CB25 A141 33c + 2c org & dp org .60 .40

Souvenir sheets exist, perf. and imperf. containing one each of Nos. B39-B40, CB24-CB25 and a 25c+2c pale grn and yel grn.

Nos. C132-C133 Surcharged like Nos. B44-B46

1964, Mar. 8

CB26 AP46 10c + 2c brt violet .20 .20
CB27 AP46 13c + 2c yellow .20 .20

Nos. C146-C148 Surcharged like Nos. B47-B51

1966, Dec. 9 Litho. *Perf. 12½*

Size: 35x24mm

CB28 A164 10c + 5c multi 1.60 .60
CB29 A164 50c + 10c multi 2.50 2.10
CB30 A164 75c + 10c multi 3.50 2.75
Nos. CB28-CB30 (3) 7.60 5.45

AIR POST OFFICIAL STAMPS

Nos. O13-O14 Overprinted in Blue

Unwmk.

1930, Dec. 3 Typo. *Perf. 12*

CO1 O3 10c light blue 11.50 *12.00*
a. Pair, one without ovpt. *900.00*
CO2 O3 20c orange 11.50 *12.00*

SPECIAL DELIVERY STAMPS

Biplane SD1

Perf. 11½

1920, Apr. Unwmk. Litho.

E1 SD1 10c deep ultra 5.50 1.25
a. Imperf., pair

Special Delivery Messenger — SD2

1925

E2 SD2 10c dark blue 16.00 4.50

SD3

1927

E3 SD3 10c red brown 5.00 1.25
a. "E EXPRESO" at top 55.00 55.00

Type of 1927

1941 Redrawn

E4 SD3 10c yellow green 2.75 *3.00*
E5 SD3 10c dark blue green 2.40 .60

The redrawn design differs slightly from SD3. Issue dates: #E4, Mar. 27; #E5, Aug. 7.

Emblem of Communications — SD4

1945, Sept. 1 *Perf. 12*

E6 SD4 10c rose car, car & dk bl .90 .20

Catalogue values for unused stamps in this section, from this point to the end of the section, are for Never Hinged items.

SD5

1950 Litho. Unwmk.

E7 SD5 10c multicolored .50 .20

Exists imperf.

Modern Communications System — SD6

1956, Aug. 18 *Perf. 11½*

E8 SD6 25c green 1.00 .30

Carrier Pigeon SD7

1967 Litho. *Perf. 11½*

E9 SD7 25c light blue .55 .25

Carrier Pigeon, Globe — SD8

Messenger, Plane — SD9

1978, Aug. 2 Litho. *Perf. 13½*

E10 SD8 25c multicolored .75 .30

1979, Nov. 30 *Perf. 13½*

E11 SD9 25c multicolored .45 .25

Motorcycling — SD10

1989, May Litho. *Perf. 13½*

E12 SD10 1p multicolored 1.60 .75

Postman SD11

1999 Litho. *Perf. 13½x13¼*

E13 SD11 8p multicolored 2.75 2.75

INSURED LETTER STAMPS

Merino Issue of 1933 Surcharged in Red or Black

1935, Feb. 1 Unwmk. *Perf. 14*

G1 A35 8c on 7c ultra .60 .20
 a. Inverted surcharge 18.00
G2 A35 15c on 10c org yel .65 .20
 a. Inverted surcharge 18.00
G3 A35 30c on 8c dk green 1.75 .90
G4 A35 45c on 20c car rose (Bk) 3.00 1.00
G5 A36 70c on 50c lemon 6.00 1.25
 Nos. G1-G5 (5) 12.00 3.55

Merino Issue of 1933 Surcharged in Red

1940

G6 A35 8c on ½c lt vio 2.00 2.00
G7 A35 8c on 7c ultra 3.25 3.25

Coat of Arms — IL1

1940-45 Litho. *Perf. 11½*
Arms in Black

G8 IL1 8c brown red .60 .25
 a. 8c dk red, no shading on inner frame 1.00 .20
G9 IL1 15c dp orange ('45) 1.25 .20
G10 IL1 30c dk green ('41) 1.50 .20
 a. 30c yellow green 1.50 .20
G11 IL1 45c ultra ('44) 1.50 .30
G12 IL1 70c olive brn ('44) 1.75 .30
 Nos. G8-G12 (5) 6.60 1.25

See Nos. G13-G16, G24-G27.

Catalogue values for unused stamps in this section, from this point to the end of the section, are for Never Hinged items.

Redrawn Type of 1940-45

1952-53
Arms in Black

G13 IL1 8c car lake ('53) 2.40 .50
G14 IL1 15c red orange ('53) 1.75 .75
G15 IL1 70c dp brown car 5.25 1.50
 Nos. G13-G15 (3) 9.40 2.75

Larger and bolder numerals on 8c and 15c. Smaller and bolder "70." There are many other minor differences in the design.

Type of 1940-45

1954
Arms in Black, 15x16mm

G16 IL1 10c carmine .75 .25

Coat of Arms — IL2

1955-69 Unwmk. Litho. *Perf. 11½*
Arms in Black, 13½x11½mm

G17 IL2 10c carmine rose .35 .20
G18 IL2 15c red orange ('56) 3.75 1.50
G19 IL2 20c red orange ('58) .90 .30
 a. 20c orange ('69) .90 .30
 b. 20c orange, retouched ('69) 3.50 1.25
G20 IL2 30c dark green ('55) 1.40 .30
G21 IL2 40c dark green ('58) 1.50 .90
 a. 40c lt yellow grn ('62) 1.50 .45
G22 IL2 45c ultra ('56) 4.00 3.75
G23 IL2 70c dp brn car ('56) 5.00 2.00
 Nos. G17-G23 (7) 16.90 8.95

On No. G19b the horizontal shading lines of shield are omitted.

See Nos. G28-G37.

Type of 1940-45
Second Redrawing

1963 *Perf. 12½*
Arms in Black, 17x16mm

G24 IL1 10c red orange 1.25 .30
G25 IL1 20c orange 1.50 .50

Third Redrawing

1966 Litho. *Perf. 12½*
Arms in Black, 14x14mm

G26 IL1 10c violet .40 .20
G27 IL1 40c orange 1.50 1.00

Type of 1955-62

1968 Litho. *Perf. 11½*
Arms in Black, 13½x11½mm

G28 IL2 20c red 2.00 .75
G29 IL2 60c yellow 1.50 1.50

1973-76 Litho. *Perf. 12½*
Arms in Black, 11x11mm

G30 IL2 10c car rose ('76) .50 .35
G31 IL2 20c yellow 1.40 .90
G32 IL2 20c orange ('76) 1.75 .50
G33 IL2 40c yel grn 1.60 1.00
 a. 40c green ('76) 3.00 3.00
G34 IL2 70c blue 1.75 1.90
 Nos. G30-G34 (5) 7.00 4.65

1973 *Perf. 11½*
Arms in Black, 13½x11½mm

G35 IL2 10c dark violet .90 .30

1978, Aug. 9 *Perf. 10½*
Arms in Black, 11x11mm

G36 IL2 10c rose magenta .35 .20
G37 IL2 40c bright green 1.50 1.50

IL3

1982-83 Litho. *Perf. 10½*
Arms in Black

G38 IL3 10c deep magenta .20 .20
G39 IL3 20c deep orange .35 .30
G40 IL3 40c bluish green .75 .50
 Nos. G38-G40 (3) 1.30 1.00

IL4

1986 Litho. *Perf. 10½*
Arms in Black

G41 IL4 20c brt rose lilac .30 .25
G42 IL4 60c orange 1.00 .70
G43 IL4 1p light blue 1.60 1.10
G44 IL4 1.25p pink 2.10 1.40
G45 IL4 1.50p vermilion 2.50 1.50
G46 IL4 3p light green 5.00 3.25
G47 IL4 3.50p olive bister 6.00 3.75
G48 IL4 4p yellow 6.75 4.50
G49 IL4 4.50p lt blue grn 7.50 5.00
G50 IL4 5p brown olive 8.25 5.50
G51 IL4 6p gray 9.75 6.75
G52 IL4 6.50p lt ultra 11.00 7.50
 Nos. G41-G52 (12) 61.75 41.20

Issue dates: #G42-G43, G45, July 16. #G46-G52, Sept. 2. #G41, G44, Nov. 6.

Coat of Arms — IL5

1989-90 Litho. *Perf. 13½*
Arms in Black

G53 IL5 20c brt lilac rose .25 .20
G54 IL5 60c orange ('90) .75 .45
G55 IL5 1p sky blue 1.25 .75
G56 IL5 1.25p lt salmon pink 1.50 .90
G57 IL5 1.50p dark red 1.90 1.10
 Nos. G53-G57 (5) 5.65 3.40

"RD$" in lower left square on #G55-G57.

IL6

1994, Oct. Litho. *Perf. 13½*
Arms in Black

G58 IL6 50c lilac rose .20 .20
G59 IL6 1p sky blue .25 .25
G60 IL6 1.50p red .30 .30
G61 IL6 2p pink .50 .50
G62 IL6 3p violet blue .60 .60
G63 IL6 5p yellow .90 .90
G64 IL6 6p apple green 1.25 1.25
G65 IL6 8p green 1.40 1.40
G66 IL6 10p silver gray 1.90 1.90
 Nos. G58-G66 (9) 7.30 7.30

POSTAGE DUE STAMPS

D1

1901 Unwmk. Typo. *Perf. 14*

J1 D1 2c olive gray .70 .20
J2 D1 4c olive gray .90 .20
J3 D1 5c olive gray 1.50 .30
J4 D1 10c olive gray 2.75 .75
 Nos. J1-J4 (4) 5.85 1.45

For surcharges and overprint see Nos. 162-165, 169-171.

1909 Wmk. 116

J5 D1 2c olive gray 1.50 .50
J6 D1 4c olive gray 1.50 .50
J7 D1 6c olive gray 2.00 .75
J8 D1 10c olive gray 4.00 2.50
 Nos. J5-J8 (4) 9.00 4.25

1913

J9 D1 2c olive green .45 .20
J10 D1 4c olive green .50 .20
J11 D1 6c olive green .80 .35
J12 D1 10c olive green .90 .40
 Nos. J9-J12 (4) 2.65 1.15

1922 Unwmk. Litho. *Perf. 11½*

J13 D1 1c olive green .55 .55

Catalogue values for unused stamps in this section, from this point to the end of the section, are for Never Hinged items.

D2

D3

1942

J14 D2 1c dk red & pale pink .25 .20
J15 D2 2c dk bl & pale bl .25 .20
J16 D2 4c dk grn & pale grn .25 .25
J17 D2 6c green & buff .30 .25
J18 D2 8c yel org & pale yel .30 .30
J19 D2 10c mag & pale pink .40 .40
 Nos. J14-J19 (6) 1.75 1.60

1955
Size: 20½x25mm

J20 D2 2c dark blue 1.40 1.00

1959 Litho. *Perf. 11½*
Size: 21x25½mm

J21 D3 1c dark car rose 1.25 1.25
J22 D3 2c dark blue 1.25 1.25
J23 D3 4c green 3.00 3.00
 Nos. J21-J23 (3) 5.50 5.50

OFFICIAL STAMPS

Bastion of February 27 O1

Unwmk.

1902, Feb. 25 Litho. *Perf. 12*

O1 O1 2c scarlet & blk .50 .30
O2 O1 5c dk blue & blk .65 .25
O3 O1 10c yel grn & blk .75 .45
O4 O1 20c yellow & blk 1.00 .40
 a. Imperf., pair 10.00
 Nos. O1-O4 (4) 2.90 1.40

For overprints and surcharge see #157-161.

Bastion of Feb. 27
O2

Columbus Lighthouse
O3

Perf. 13½x13, 13½x14

1909-12 Wmk. 116 Typo.

O5 O2 1c blue grn & blk .30 .20
O6 O2 2c scarlet & blk .35 .20
O7 O2 5c dk blue & blk .75 .30
O8 O2 10c yel grn & blk ('12) 1.10 .70
O9 O2 20c orange & blk ('12) 2.00 1.60
Nos. O5-O9 (5) 4.50 3.00

The 2c, 5c are found in both perforations; 1c, 20c perf. 13½x13; 10c perf. 13½x14.

For overprints and surcharge see #177, 194-199.

1928 Unwmk. *Perf. 12*

O10 O3 1c green .20 .20
O11 O3 2c red .20 .20
O12 O3 5c ultramarine .25 .25
O13 O3 10c light blue .30 .30
O14 O3 20c orange .45 .45
Nos. O10-O14 (5) 1.40 1.40

For overprints see Nos. CO1-CO2.

Proposed Columbus Lighthouse
O4

1937 Litho. *Perf. 11½*

O15 O4 3c dark purple .85 .20
O16 O4 7c indigo & blue .90 .30
O17 O4 10c orange yellow 1.00 .45
Nos. O15-O17 (3) 2.75 .95

Proposed Columbus Lighthouse
O5

1939-41

O18 O5 1c dp grn & lt grn .35 .20
O19 O5 2c crim & pale pink .35 .20
O20 O5 3c purple & lt vio .35 .20
O21 O5 5c dk bl & lt bl ('40) .60 .30
O21A O5 5c lt blue ('41) 1.50 1.00
O22 O5 7c brt bl & lt bl ('41) 1.10 .20
O23 O5 10c yel org & pale org ('41) 1.10 .35
O24 O5 20c brn org & buff ('41) 3.00 .50
O25 O5 50c brt red lil & pale lil ('41) 3.50 1.50
Nos. O18-O25 (9) 11.85 4.45

Catalogue values for unused stamps in this section, from this point to the end of the section, are for Never Hinged items.

Type of 1939

1950 Redrawn

O26 O5 50c dp car & rose 6.25 1.25

The numerals "50" measure 3mm, and are close to left and right frames; numerals measure 4mm on No. O25. There are other minor differences.

Denominations in "Centavos Oro"

1950

O27 O5 5c light blue .55 .20
O28 O5 10c yel & pale yel .65 .30
O29 O5 20c dl org brn & buff .70 .50
Nos. O27-O29 (3) 1.90 1.00

Letters of top inscription are 1½mm high.

Type of 1939-41
Second Redrawing
Denominations in "Centavos Oro"

1956 Unwmk. *Perf. 11½*

O30 O5 7c blue & lt blue .50 .50
O31 O5 20c yellow brn & buff 1.25 1.25
O32 O5 50c red lil & brt pink 3.25 3.25
Nos. O30-O32 (3) 5.00 5.00

The letters of top inscription are 2mm high, the trees at base of monument have been redrawn, etc. On No. O32 the numerals are similar to No. O26.

POSTAL TAX STAMPS

Santo Domingo after Hurricane
PT1

Hurricane's Effect on Capital
PT2

1930, Dec. Unwmk. Litho. *Perf. 12*

RA1 PT1 1c green & rose .20 .20
RA2 PT1 2c red rose .20 .20
RA3 PT2 5c ultra & rose .30 .20
RA4 PT2 10c yellow & rose .35 .30

Imperf

RA5 PT1 1c green & rose .40 .30
RA6 PT1 2c red & rose .50 .30
RA7 PT2 5c ultra & rose .60 .50
RA8 PT2 10c yellow & rose .90 .75
Nos. RA1-RA8 (8) 3.45 2.75

For surcharges see Nos. RAC1-RAC7.

Tête bêche Pairs

RA1a PT1 1c green & rose 1.75 1.75
RA2a PT1 2c red rose 1.75 1.50
RA3a PT1 5c ultra & rose 1.75 2.10
RA4a PT1 10c yellow & rose 2.10 2.10
RA5a PT1 1c green & rose 1.75 1.75
RA6a PT1 2c red & rose 1.75 1.75
RA7a PT1 5c ultra & rose 2.10 2.10
RA8a PT1 10c yellow & rose 2.10 2.10
Nos. RA1a-RA8a (8) 15.05 15.15

Dr. Martos Sanatorium — PT3

Nurse and Child — PT4

1944, Apr. 1 Litho. *Perf. 11½*

RA9 PT3 1c dp bl, sl bl & red .30 .25

1947, Apr. 1 Unwmk.

RA10 PT4 1c dp bl, pale bl & car .45 .25

Sanatorium of the Holy Help — PT5

1949, Apr. 1

RA11 PT5 1c dp bl, pale bl & car .35 .25

Youth Holding Banner
PT6

"Suffer Little Children to Come Unto Me"
PT7

1950, Apr. 1 *Perf. 11½*

RA12 PT6 1c dp bl, pale bl & car .25 .25

1950, Dec. 1 *Perf. 12*

Size: 22½x32mm

RA13 PT7 1c lt bl & pale bl .60 .25
b. Perf. 12½ ('52) 3.00 .25

Vertical line centering side borders merges into dots toward the bottom. See Nos. RA13A, RA17, RA19, RA26, RA32, RA35.

The tax was for child welfare.

1951, Dec. 1 Redrawn

RA13A PT7 1c lt blue & pale blue 3.00 .25

In the redrawn stamp, the standing child, a blonde in No. RA13, is changed to a brunette; more foliage has been added above child's head and to branches showing in upper right corner. Vertical dashes in side borders.

Tuberculosis Sanatorium, Santiago — PT8

1952, Apr. 1 Litho. *Perf. 11½*

RA14 PT8 1c lt blue & car .25 .25

Sword, Serpent and Crab — PT9

1953, Feb. 1 Unwmk. *Perf. 12.*

RA15 PT9 1c carmine .35 .25

The tax was for the Dominican League Against Cancer. See Nos. RA18, RA21, RA43, RA46, RA51, RA56, RA61, RA67, RA72, RA76, RA82, RA88, RA93, RA96.

Tuberculosis Dispensary for Children — PT10

1953, Apr. 1 Litho. *Perf. 12½*

RA16 PT10 1c dp bl, pale bl & red .25 .25

See No. RA22.

Jesus Type of 1950
Second Redrawing

1953, Dec. 1 *Perf. 11½*

Size: 22x31mm

RA17 PT7 1c blue .35 .20

Solid shading in sky reduced to a few scattered dots. Girl's left arm indicated. Rough white dots in side borders.

Cancer Type of 1952

1954, Oct. 1 Redrawn *Perf. 12½*

RA18 PT9 1c rose carmine .25 .20
a. 1c red orange ('58) .30 .20
b. 1c carmine ('70) 1.25 .20

Upper right serif of numeral "1" eliminated; diagonal line added through "C" and period removed; sword extended, placing top on a line with top of "1." Dots of background screen arranged diagonally. Many other differences.

The tax was for the Dominican League Against Cancer. No. RA18a exists imperf.

On No. RA18b background screen eliminates white outline of crab.

Jesus Type of 1950

1954, Dec. 1 Third Redrawing

Size: 23x32¾mm

RA19 PT7 1c bright blue .25 .20
a. 1c pale blue ('59) .20 .20

Center completely screened. Tiny white horizontal rectangles in side borders.

Catalogue values for unused stamps in this section, from this point to the end of the section, are for Never Hinged items.

Lorraine Cross as Bell Clapper — PT11

1955, Apr. 1 Litho. *Perf. 11½x12*

RA20 PT11 1c black, yel & red .30 .25

Cancer Type of 1952
Second Redrawing

1956, Oct. 1 *Perf. 12½*

RA21 PT9 1c carmine .35 .20
a. 1c red orange ('64) 1.00 .50

Similar to No. RA18, but dots of background screen arranged in vertical and horizontal rows. Outlines of central device, lettering and frame clearly delineated. "C" of cent-sign smaller. Upper claw in solid color.

TB Dispensary Type of 1953
Redrawn

1954, Apr. 1

RA22 PT10 1c blue & red .70 .25
a. Red (cross) omitted 55.00

No. RA22 has third color omitted; clouds added; bolder letters and numerals.

Angelita Trujillo
PT12

Lorraine Cross
PT13

1955, Dec. 1 Unwmk. *Perf. 12½*

RA23 PT12 1c violet .60 .25

The tax was for child welfare.

1956, Apr. 1 Litho. *Perf. 11½*

RA24 PT13 1c blk, grn, lem & red .30 .25

The tax was for the Anti-Tuberculosis League. Inscribed: B.C.G. (Bacillus Calmette-Guerin).

PT14

PT15

1957, Apr. 1

RA25 PT14 1c red, blk, yel, grn & bl .30 .25

Jesus Type of 1950
Fourth Redrawing

1956, Dec. 1 Unwmk. *Perf. 12*
Size: 21¾x31¼mm

RA26 PT7 1c blue .30 .20

Thin white lines around numeral boxes. Girl's bouquet touches Jesus' sleeve. Tiny white squares or rectangles in side borders. Foliage at either side of "Era de Trujillo" panel.

1958, Apr. 1 Litho. *Perf. 12½*
RA27 PT15 1c brown car & red .25 .20

Inscribed "1959"

1959, Apr. 1
RA28 PT15 1c brown car & red .25 .20

PT16

PT17

1960, Apr. 1 Litho. *Perf. 12*
RA29 PT16 1c bl, pale yel & red .30 .25

1961, Apr. 1 Unwmk. *Perf. 11½*
RA30 PT17 1c blue & red .25 .20

Nos. RA29-RA30: tax was for the Anti-Tuberculosis League.
See No. RA33.

Maria de los Angeles M. de Trujillo and Housing Project
PT18

1961, Aug. 1 Litho. *Perf. 12*
RA31 PT18 1c carmine rose .30 .25

The tax was for aid to the needy.
Nos. RA31-RA33 exist imperf.

Jesus Type of 1950
Fifth Redrawing

1961, Dec. 1 Unwmk. *Perf. 12½*
RA32 PT7 1c blue .30 .25

No. RA32 is similar to No. RA19, but "Era de Trujillo" has been replaced by a solid color panel.

Type of 1961 Dated "1962"

1962, Apr. 2 *Perf. 12½*
RA33 PT17 1c blue & red .60 .25

Tax for the Anti-Tuberculosis League.

Man's Chest
PT19

Hibiscus
PT20

1963, Apr. 1 *Perf. 12x11½*
RA34 PT19 1c ultra & red .30 .25

Jesus Type of 1950
Sixth Redrawing

1963, Dec. 1 *Perf. 11½*
Size: 21¾x32mm

RA35 PT7 1c blue .30 .25
a. 1c deep blue ('64) .30 .25

No. RA35 is similar to No. RA26, but "Era de Trujillo" panel has been omitted.

1966, Apr. 1 Litho. *Perf. 11½*
RA36 PT20 1c emerald & car .25 .20

Tax for the Anti-Tuberculosis League.

Domingoa Nodosa — PT21

Civil Defense Emblem — PT22

1967, Apr. 1 Litho. *Perf. 12½*
RA37 PT21 1c lilac & red .75 .25

Tax for the Anti-Tuberculosis League.

1967, July 1 Litho. *Rouletted 13*
RA38 PT22 1c multicolored .25 .20

Tax for the Civil Defense Organization.

Boy, School and Yule Bells — PT23

Hand Holding Invalid — PT24

1967, Dec. 1 Litho. *Perf. 12½*
RA39 PT23 1c rose red & pink .35 .25

1968 *Perf. 11*
RA40 PT23 1c vermilion .30 .20

No. RA40 has screened background; No. RA39, smooth background.
The tax was for child welfare.
See Nos. RA49A, RA52, RA57, RA62, RA68, RA73, RA77, RA81.

1968, Mar. 19 Litho. *Perf. 12½*
RA41 PT24 1c green & yellow .25 .20
a. 1c olive green & deep yellow, perf. 11½x12 ('69) .25 .20

The tax was for the rehabilitation of the handicapped. See Nos. RA47, RA50, RA54.

Dogbane
PT25

Schoolyard, Torch
PT26

1968, Apr. 25 Litho. *Perf. 12½*
RA42 PT25 1c emerald, yel & red .25 .20

The tax was for the Anti-Tuberculosis League. See Nos. RA45, RA49.

Redrawn Cancer Type of 1955

1968, Oct. 1 Litho. *Perf. 12*
RA43 PT9 1c emerald .25 .20

The tax was for the Dominican League against Cancer.

1969, Feb. 1 Litho. *Perf. 12½*
RA44 PT26 1c light blue .30 .25

Issued for Education Year 1969.

Flower Type of 1968

Design: No. RA45, Violets.

1969, Apr. 25 Litho. *Perf. 12½*
RA45 PT25 1c emerald, lil & red .45 .25

Tax for the Anti-Tuberculosis League.

Redrawn Cancer Type of 1955

1969, Oct. 1 Litho. *Perf. 11*
RA46 PT9 1c brt rose lilac .25 .20

Tax for Dominican League against Cancer.

Invalid Type of 1968

1970, Mar. 2 *Perf. 12½*
RA47 PT24 1c blue .25 .20

The tax was for the rehabilitation of the handicapped.

Book, Sun and Education Year Emblem
PT27

Communications Emblem
PT28

1970, Feb. 6 *Perf. 11*
RA48 PT27 1c bright pink .25 .20

International Education Year.

Flower Type of 1968

Design: 1c, Eleanthus capitatus; cross in upper left corner, denomination in lower right.

1970, Apr. 30 *Perf. 11*
RA49 PT25 1c emerald, red & yel .75 .25

Tax for Anti-Tuberculosis League.

Boy Type of 1967

1970, Dec. 1 *Perf. 12½*
RA49A PT23 1c orange .30 .25

1971, Jan. 2 Litho. *Perf. 11*
Size: 17½x20½mm

RA49B PT28 1c vio bl & red (white frame) .30 .25

Tax was for Postal and Telegraph Communications School.
See #RA53, RA58, RA63, RA69, RA78, RA91.

Invalid Type of 1968

1971, Mar. 1 Litho. *Perf. 11*
RA50 PT24 1c brt rose lilac .30 .25

Tax for rehabilitation of the handicapped.

Cancer Type of 1952
Third Redrawing

1971, Oct. 1 *Perf. 11½*
RA51 PT9 1c dp yellow green .30 .25

Background of No. RA51 appears white and design stands out. No. RA43 has greenish background and design appears faint. Numeral "1" on No. RA51 is 3½mm high, on No. RA43 it is 3mm.

Boy Type of 1967

1971, Dec. 1 Litho. *Perf. 11*
RA52 PT23 1c green .30 .25

Communications Type of 1971

1972, Jan. 3 Litho. *Perf. 12½*
Size: 19x22mm

RA53 PT28 1c dk bl & red (bl frame) .25 .20

Tax was for the Postal and Telegraph Communications School.

Invalid Type of 1968

1972, Mar. 1 Litho. *Perf. 11½*
RA54 PT24 1c brown .60 .25

Orchid — PT29

1972, Apr. 2 *Perf. 11*
RA55 PT29 1c lt grn, red & yel 1.10 .30

Tax was for the Anti-Tuberculosis League.

Redrawn Cancer Type of 1954-58

1972, Oct. 2 *Perf. 12½*
RA56 PT9 1c orange .25 .20

Tax for Dominican League against Cancer.

Boy Type of 1967

1972, Dec. 1 *Perf. 12*
RA57 PT23 1c violet .25 .20

Tax was for child welfare.

Communications Type of 1971

1973, Jan. 2 *Perf. 10½*
Size: 19x22mm

RA58 PT28 1c dk bl & red (red frame) .25 .20

Tax was for Postal and Telegraph Communications School.

Invalid
PT30

Hibiscus
PT31

1973, Mar. 1 Litho. *Perf. 12½*
Size: 21x25mm

RA59 PT30 1c olive .25 .20

Tax was for the Dominican Rehabilitation Association. See Nos. RA66, RA70, RA74, RA79, RA86.

1973, Apr. 17 Litho. *Perf. 10½*
RA60 PT31 1c multicolored .75 .25

Tax was for Anti-Tuberculosis League. Exists imperf.

Cancer Type of 1952 Redrawn and "1973" Added

1973, Oct. 1 *Perf. 13½*
RA61 PT9 1c olive green .30 .25

Tax was for Dominican League Against Cancer.

Boy Type of 1967

1973, Dec. 1 Litho. *Perf. 13x13½*
RA62 PT23 1c blue .60 .25

Communications Type of 1971

1973, Nov. 3 *Perf. 10½*
Size: 19x22mm

RA63 PT28 1c bl & red (lt grn frame) .25 .20

Tax was for Postal and Telegraph Communications School. Exists imperf.

Invalid Type of 1973

1974, Mar. 1 Litho. *Perf. 10½*
Size: 22x27½mm

RA66 PT30 1c light ultra .30 .25

See note after No. RA59.

Cancer Type of 1952 Redrawn and "1974" Added

1974, Oct. 1 *Perf. 12*
RA67 PT9 1c orange .30 .25

Tax for Dominican League Against Cancer.

Boy Type of 1967

1974, Dec. 2 Litho. *Perf. 11½*
RA68 PT23 1c dk brown & buff .25 .20

Communications Type of 1971

1974, Nov. 13 *Perf. 10½*
RA69 PT28 1c blue & red (yel frame) .25 .20

Invalid Type of 1973 Dated "1975"

1975, Mar. 1 *Perf. 13½x13*
Size: 21x32mm
RA70 PT30 1c olive brown .30 .25

See note after No. RA59.

Catteeyopsis Rosea
PT32

Oncidium Colochilum
PT33

1975, Apr. 1 *Perf. 12*
RA71 PT32 1c blue & multi .95 .70

Tax was for Anti-Tuberculosis League.

Cancer Type of 1952 Redrawn and "1975" Added

1975, Oct. 1 Litho. *Perf. 12*
RA72 PT9 1c violet blue .30 .25

Tax was for Dominican League Against Cancer. Exists imperf.

Boy Type of 1967

1975, Dec. 1 Litho. *Perf. 12*
RA73 PT23 1c red orange .25 .20

Tax was for child welfare.

Invalid Type of 1973 Dated "1976"

1976, Mar. 1 Litho. *Perf. 12*
Size: 21x31mm
RA74 PT30 1c ultra .30 .25

See note after No. RA59.

1976, Apr. 6 *Perf. 13x13½*
RA75 PT33 1c green & multi .60 .25

Tax was for Anti-Tuberculosis League. See No. RA80, RA84.

Cancer Type of 1952 Redrawn and "1976" Added

1976, Oct. 1 Litho. *Perf. 13½*
RA76 PT9 1c green .30 .25

Tax was for Dominican League Against Cancer.

Boy Type of 1967

1976, Dec. 1 Litho. *Perf. 13½*
RA77 PT23 1c purple .30 .25

Tax was for child welfare.

Communications Type of 1971

1977, Jan. 7 Litho. *Perf. 10½*
Size: 19x22mm
RA78 PT28 1c blue & red (lil frame) .25 .20

Tax was for Postal and Telegraph Communications School.

Invalid Type of 1973 Dated "1977"

1977, Mar. 11 *Perf. 12*
Size: 21x31mm
RA79 PT30 1c ultra .30 .25

See note after No. RA59.

Orchid Type of 1976 Dated "1977"

Orchid: Oncidium variegatum.

1977, Apr. 22 Litho. *Perf. 13½*
RA80 PT33 1c multicolored .75 .25

Tax was for Anti-Tuberculosis League.

Boy Type of 1967

1977, Dec. 27 Litho. *Perf. 12*
RA81 PT23 1c emerald .25 .20

Tax was for child welfare.

Cancer Type of 1952 Redrawn and "1977" Added

1978, Oct. 2 Litho. *Perf. 13½*
RA82 PT9 1c lilac rose .30 .25

Tax for Dominican League Against Cancer.

Mother, Child, Holly — PT34

University Seal — PT35

1978, Dec. 1 Litho. *Perf. 13½*
RA83 PT34 1c green .25 .20

Tax was for child welfare. See Nos. RA89, RA92, RA97.

Orchid Type of 1973 Dated "1978"

Flower: Yellow alder.

1979, Apr. Litho. *Perf. 13½*
RA84 PT33 1c lt blue & multi .75 .25

Tax was for Anti-Tuberculosis League.

1979, Feb. 10 Litho. *Perf. 13½*
RA85 PT35 2c ultra & gray .25 .20

450th anniv. of University of Santo Domingo.

Invalid Type of 1973 Dated "1978"

1979, Mar. 1 Litho. *Perf. 12*
RA86 PT30 1c emerald .25 .20

See note after No. RA59.

Invalid
PT36

Turnera Ulmifolia (Marilope)
PT37

1980, Mar. 28 Litho. *Perf. 13½*
RA87 PT36 1c olive & citron .60 .25

Cancer Type of 1952 Redrawn and "1980" Added

1980, Oct. 1
RA88 PT9 1c violet & dk pur .25 .20

Mother and Child Type of 1978

1980, Dec. 1 Litho. *Perf. 13½*
RA89 PT34 1c bright blue .25 .20

1981, Apr. 27 Litho. *Perf. 12*
RA90 PT37 1c multicolored .25 .20

Tax was for Anti-Tuberculosis League. See Nos. RA98-RA99.

Communications Type of 1971

1981, Feb. Litho. *Perf. 10½*
RA91 PT28 1c blue & red (lt bl frame) .60 .25

Mother and Child Type of 1978

1982, Dec. 1 Litho. *Perf. 12x12½*
RA92 PT34 1c lt bluish green .25 .20

Inscribed 1981.

Cancer Type of 1952 Redrawn and "1981" Added

1982 Litho. *Perf. 13½*
RA93 PT9 1c blue & dp blue .60 .25

PT38

Disabled — PT39

1983, Apr. 29 Litho. *Perf. 12*
RA94 PT38 1c multicolored .25 .20

Tax was for Red Cross.

1984 Litho. *Perf. 13½*
RA95 PT39 1c sky blue .25 .20

Cancer Type of 1952 Redrawn and "1983" Added

1983, Oct. 1 Litho. *Perf. 13½*
RA96 PT9 1c lt bluish grn & dk grn .25 .20

Mother and Child Type of 1978

1983, Dec. 1 Litho. *Perf. 12*
RA97 PT34 1c light green .25 .20

Inscribed 1983.

Flower Type of 1981 Dated "1983" or "1984"

1983-85 Litho. *Perf. 12x12½*
RA98 PT37 1c 1983 .25 .20
RA99 PT37 1c 1984 .25 .20

Issued: #RA98, 4/19/83; #RA99, 4/1/85.

POSTAL TAX AIR POST STAMPS

Postal Tax Stamps Surcharged in Red or Gold

1930, Dec. 3 Unwmk. *Perf. 12*
RAC1 PT2 5c + 5c blk & rose (R) 25.00 25.00
  a. Tête bêche pair 125.00
  b. "Habilitado Para" missing 52.50
RAC2 PT2 10c + 10c blk & rose (R) 25.00 25.00
  a. Tête bêche pair 125.00
  b. "Habilitado Para" missing 52.50
  c. Gold surcharge 95.00 95.00
  d. As "c," tête bêche pair 450.00
  e. As "c" and "b" 250.00

Nos. RAC1-RAC2 were on sale one day.

RAC4 PT2 5c + 5c ultra & rose (R) 6.00 6.00
  a. Tête bêche pair 45.00
  b. Inverted surcharge 42.50
  c. Tête bêche pair, inverted surcharge 600.00
  d. Pair, one without surcharge 190.00
  e. "Habilitado Para" missing 15.00
RAC5 PT2 10c + 10c yel & rose (G) 4.50 4.50
  a. Tête bêche pair 42.50
  b. "Habilitado Para" missing 18.00

Imperf

RAC6 PT2 5c + 5c ultra & rose (R) 6.00 6.00
  a. Tête bêche pair 52.50
  b. "Habilitado Para" missing 18.00
RAC7 PT2 10c + 10c yel & rose (G) 6.00 6.00
  a. Tête bêche pair 52.50
  b. "Habilitado Para" missing 18.00
  Nos. RAC1-RAC7 (6) 72.50 72.50

It was obligatory to use Nos. RA1-RA8 and RAC1-RAC7 on all postal matter, in amounts equal to the ordinary postage.

This surtax was for the aid of sufferers from the hurricane of Sept. 3, 1930.

No. 261 Overprinted in Green

1933, Oct. 11
RAC8 A32 2c scarlet .35 .30
  a. Double overprint 9.00
  b. Pair, one without overprint 375.00

By official decree a copy of this stamp, in addition to the regular postage, had to be used on every letter, etc., sent by the internal air post service.

DUBAI

dü-ˈbī

LOCATION — Oman Peninsula, Arabia, on Persian Gulf
GOVT. — Sheikdom under British protection
AREA — 1,500 sq. mi.
POP. — 60,000
CAPITAL — Dubai

Dubai is one of six Persian Gulf sheikdoms to join the United Arab Emirates which proclaimed its independence Dec. 2, 1971. See United Arab Emirates.

100 Naye Paise = 1 Rupee
100 Dirhams = 1 Riyal (1966)

Imperforate
Many issues were accompanied by smaller quantities of imperforate stamps.

Catalogue values for all unused stamps in this country are for Never Hinged items.

Hermit Crab — A1

Sheik Rashid bin Said al Maktum — A2

2np, 20np, Cuttlefish. 3np, 25np, Snail. 4np, 30np, Crab. 5np, 35np, Sea urchin. 10np, 50np, Sea shell. 1r, Fortress wall. 2r, View of Dubai. 3r, Fortress wall. 5r, View of Dubai.

Perf. 12x11½

1963, June 15 Litho. Unwmk.

No.	Type	Description	Unused	Used
1	A1	1np dl bl & car rose	.30	.20
2	A1	2np lt bl & bis brn	.35	.20
3	A1	3np green & sepia	.35	.20
4	A1	4np pink & orange	.35	.20
5	A1	5np violet & blk	.35	.20
6	A1	10np brn org & blk	.35	.25
7	A1	15np gray ol & dp car	.70	.25
8	A1	20np rose red & org brn	.75	.40
9	A1	25np ap grn & red brn	.90	.40
10	A1	30np gray & red	1.00	.40
11	A1	35np dl lil & dl vio	1.00	.40
12	A1	50np org & sepia	1.60	.75
13	A1	1r brt bl & red org	3.50	1.25
14	A1	2r dull yel & brn	7.00	3.00
15	A1	3r rose car & blk	10.50	4.50
16	A1	5r grn & dl red brn	17.00	7.50

Perf. 12

No.	Type	Description	Unused	Used
17	A2	10r rose lake, grnsh bl & blk	35.00	15.00
		Nos. 1-17 (17)	81.00	35.10

Dhows A3

Designs: 2np, First-aid tent. 3np, Camel caravan. 4np, Butterfly.

1963, Sept. 1 Unwmk. *Perf. 12*

No.	Type	Description	Unused	Used
18	A3	1np ultra, yel & red	.45	.25
19	A3	2np brn, yel & red	.45	.25
20	A3	3np red brn, org & red	.45	.25
21	A3	4np brn, brt grn & red	.45	.25
		Nos. 18-21,C9-C12 (8)	8.90	3.70

Intl. Red Cross, cent. Exist perf. 10½.
Four imperf. souvenir sheets exist in the denominations and designs of Nos. C9-C12, with "Air-Mail" omitted and colors changed. Size: 119x99mm. Value $50.
For overprints see Nos. C52-C54.

A4

A5

Anopheles Mosquito: 2np, Mosquito and entwined snakes. 3np, Mosquitoes over swamp.

1963, Dec. 20 Unwmk. *Perf. 12*

No.	Type	Description	Unused	Used
22	A4	1np emer & red brn	.20	.20
23	A4	1np red & dark brn	.20	.20
24	A4	1np blue & carmine	.20	.20
25	A4	2np brn & orange	.20	.20
26	A4	2np carmine & blue	.20	.20
27	A4	3np org brn & blue	.20	.20
		Nos. 22-27,C13-C15 (9)	3.20	2.00

WHO drive to eradicate malaria.

1964 Unwmk.

Designs: 1np, Scouts forming pyramid. 2np, Bugler. 3np, Cub Scouts. 4np, Scouts and bugler. 5np, Scouts presenting flag.

No.	Type	Description	Unused	Used
28	A5	1np dk brn & ocher	.20	.20
29	A5	2np car rose & sep	.20	.20
30	A5	3np blue & red org	.20	.20
31	A5	4np carmine & blue	.20	.20
32	A5	5np ind & bluish grn	.35	.20
		Nos. 28-32,C20-C24 (10)	6.30	2.90

11th Boy Scout Jamboree, Marathon, Greece, Aug., 1963.
For overprints see Nos. C47-C51.

Unisphere, New York Skyline and Dubai Harbor — A6

2np, 4np, 10np, Views of NYC and Dubai.

1964, Apr. 22 Litho. *Perf. 12*

No.	Type	Description	Unused	Used
33	A6	1np dk bl & rose red	.20	.20
34	A6	2np dl red, lil rose & bl	.20	.20
35	A6	3np brown & green	.20	.20
36	A6	4np emer, brt grn & red	.20	.20
37	A6	5np ol, sl grn & lil	.20	.20
38	A6	10np brn org, red org & blk	.70	.50
		Nos. 33-38,C36-C38 (9)	5.95	3.80

New York World's Fair, 1964-65.

Gymnast — A8

Designs: 2np, 5np, 20np, 40np, Various exercises on bar. 3np, 30np, Various exercises on vaulting horse. 4np, 10np, 1r, Various exercises on rings.

1964 Photo. *Perf. 14*

No.	Type	Description	Unused	Used
43	A8	1np org brn & yel grn	.20	.20
44	A8	2np dk brn & grnsh bl	.20	.20
45	A8	3np ultra & org brn	.20	.20
46	A8	4np dk pur & yel	.25	.20
47	A8	5np ocher & dk bl	.25	.20
48	A8	10np brt bl & ocher	.25	.20
49	A8	20np ol & lil rose	.30	.20
50	A8	30np dk bl & yel	.60	.25
51	A8	40np Prus grn & dl org	1.10	.50
52	A8	1r rose vio & grnsh bl	2.75	1.25
		Nos. 43-52 (10)	6.10	3.40

18th Olympic Games, Tokyo, Oct. 10-25, 1964. An imperf. miniature sheet contains a 67x67mm stamp similar to No. 52. Value $8.

Palace — A9

Sheik Rashid bin Said — A10

Designs: 20np, 25np, View of new Dubai. 35np, 40np, Bridge and dhow. 60np, 1r, Bridge. 1.25r, Minaret. 1.50r, 3r, Old Dubai.

1966, May 30 Photo. *Perf. 14x14½*
Size: 23x18mm

No.	Type	Description	Unused	Used
53	A9	5np brown & indigo	.20	.20
54	A9	10np black & orange	.20	.20
55	A9	15np ultra & brown	.35	.25

Perf. 13
Size: 27½x20½mm

No.	Type	Description	Unused	Used
56	A9	20np blue & red brn	.45	.30
57	A9	25np org ver & ultra	.45	.40
58	A9	35np violet & emer	.70	.50
59	A9	40np grnsh bl & bl	1.00	.50

Perf. 14½
Size: 31½x24mm

No.	Type	Description	Unused	Used
60	A9	60np yel grn & org ver	1.50	1.00
61	A9	1r ultra & blue	2.25	1.50
62	A9	1.25r brn org & blk	3.00	2.00
63	A9	1.50r rose lil & yel grn	5.25	2.10
64	A9	3r dk ol bis & vio	9.25	4.00

Engr.
Perf. 14

No.	Type	Description	Unused	Used
65	A10	5r rose carmine	16.00	7.50
66	A10	10r dark blue	35.00	16.00
		Nos. 53-66 (14)	75.60	36.45

Nos. 53-62, 64-66 Overprinted with New Currency Names and Bars

1967

No.	Type	Description	Unused	Used
67	A9	5d on 5np	.25	.20
68	A9	10d on 10np	.25	.20
69	A9	15d on 15np	.45	.20
70	A9	20d on 20np	.70	.25
71	A9	25d on 25np	.80	.25
72	A9	35d on 35np	.90	.25
73	A9	40d on 40np	1.25	.30
74	A9	60d on 60np	2.25	.35
75	A9	1r on 1r	3.00	.50
76	A9	1.25r on 1.25r	5.50	1.00
77	A9	3r on 3r	9.50	3.00
78	A10	5r on 5r	17.00	6.00
79	A10	10r on 10r	27.50	11.50
		Nos. 67-79 (13)	69.35	24.00

Sheik and Falcon — A11

Dhow — A12

Litho. & Engr.
1967, Aug. 21 *Perf. 13½*

No.	Type	Description	Unused	Used
80	A11	5d dp car & org	1.00	.30
81	A11	10d sepia & green	1.00	.20
82	A11	20d dp cl & bl gray	1.25	.30
83	A11	35d slate & car	1.75	.30
84	A11	60d vio bl & emer	3.25	.50
85	A11	1r green & lilac	4.75	.50
86	A12	1.25r lt bl & claret	4.75	.65
87	A12	3r dull vio & claret	8.25	1.75
88	A12	5r brt grn & vio	18.00	3.75
89	A12	10r lil rose & grn	26.00	6.75
		Nos. 80-89 (10)	70.00	15.00

S. S. Bamora, 1914 — A13

35d, De Havilland 66 plane, 1930. 60d, S. S. Sirdhana, 1947. 1r, Armstrong Whitworth 15 "Atlanta," 1938. 1.25r, S. S. Chandpara, 1949. 3r, BOAC Sunderland amphibian plane, 1943. No. 96, Freighter Bombala, 1961, and BOAC Super VC10, 1967.

1969, Feb. 12 Litho. *Perf. 14x13½*

No.	Type	Description	Unused	Used
90	A13	25d lt grn, bl & blk	.25	*.20*
91	A13	35d multicolored	.25	*.20*
92	A13	60d multicolored	.80	*.20*
93	A13	1r lil, blk & dl yel	1.00	*.20*
94	A13	1.25r gray, blk & dp org	1.25	*.20*
95	A13	3r pink, blk & bl grn	2.10	*.35*
		Nos. 90-95 (6)	5.65	*1.35*

Miniature Sheet
Imperf

No.	Type	Description	Unused	Used
96	A13	1.25r pink, blk & bl grn	7.00	7.00

60 years of postal service.

Mother and Children, by Rubens A14

Arab Mother's Day: 60d, Madonna and Child, by Murillo. 1r, Mother and Child, by Francesco Mazzuoli. 3r, Madonna and Child, by Correggio.

1969, Mar. 21 Litho. *Perf. 13½*

No.	Type	Description	Unused	Used
97	A14	60d silver & multi	.65	*.20*
98	A14	1r silver & multi	1.25	*.20*
99	A14	1.25r silver & multi	1.50	*.20*
100	A14	3r silver & multi	3.25	*.40*
		Nos. 97-100 (4)	6.65	*1.00*

Porkfish — A15

1969, May 26 Litho. *Perf. 11*

101	A15 60d	shown	1.75	*.35*
102	A15 60d	Spotted grouper	1.75	*.35*
103	A15 60d	Moonfish	1.75	*.35*
104	A15 60d	Sweetlips	1.75	*.35*
105	A15 60d	Blue angel	1.75	*.35*
106	A15 60d	Texas skate	1.75	*.35*
107	A15 60d	Striped butterflyfish	1.75	*.35*
108	A15 60d	Imperial angelfish	1.75	*.35*
	Nos. 101-108 (8)		14.00	*2.80*

Nos. 101-108 printed in same sheet of 16 (4x4).

Explorers and Map of Arabia — A16

1969, July 21 Litho. *Perf. 13½x13*

109	A16 35d	brown & green	.95	*.20*
110	A16 60d	vio & sepia	1.40	*.20*
111	A16 1r	green & dl bl	4.25	*.20*
112	A16 1.25r	gray & rose car	5.25	*.20*
	Nos. 109-112 (4)		11.85	*.80*

European explorers of Arabia: Sir Richard Francis Burton (1821-1890), Charles Montagu Doughty (1843-1926), Johann Ludwig Burckhardt (1784-1817) and Wilfred Patrick Thesiger (1910-).

Construction of World's First Underwater Oil Storage Tank — A17

Designs: 20d, Launching of oil storage tank. 35d, Oil storage tank in place on ocean ground. 60d, Sheik Rashid bin Said, offshore drilling platform and monument commemorating first oil export. 1r, Offshore production platform and helicopter port.

1969, Oct. 13 Litho. *Perf. 11*

113	A17 5d	blue & multi	.25	*.20*
114	A17 20d	blue & multi	.85	*.20*
115	A17 35d	blue & multi	1.60	*.20*
116	A17 60d	blue & multi	2.50	*.20*
117	A17 1r	blue & multi	3.50	*.20*
	Nos. 113-117 (5)		8.70	*1.00*

Astronauts Collecting Moon Rocks — A18

Designs: 1r, Astronaut at foot of ladder. 1.25r, Astronauts planting American flag.

1969, Dec. 15 Litho. *Perf. 14½*

118		Strip of 3	4.50	*.30*
a.	A18	60d multicolored	.45	*.20*
b.	A18	1r multicolored	.90	*.20*
c.	A18	1.25r multicolored (airmail)	1.90	*.20*

The 1.25r is inscribed "AIRMAIL."

Sizes: 60d and 1r, 28½x41mm; 1.25r, 60½x41mm.

See note after US No. C76.

Ocean Weather Ship Launching Radio Sonde, and Hastings Plane — A19

WMO Emblem and: 1r, Kew-type radio sonde, weather balloon and radar antenna. 1.25r, Tiros satellite and weather sounding rocket. 3r, Ariel satellite and rocket launching.

1970, Mar. 23 Litho. *Perf. 11*

121	A19 60d	dl grn, brn & blk	.45	*.20*
122	A19 1r	brown & multi	.85	*.20*
123	A19 1.25r	dk blue & multi	.95	*.20*
124	A19 3r	multicolored	2.25	*.30*
	Nos. 121-124 (4)		4.50	*.90*

10th World Meteorological Day.

UPU Headquarters and Monument, Bern — A20

60d, UPU monument, Bern, telecommunications satellite and London PO tower.

1970, May 20 Litho. *Perf. 13½x14*

125	A20 5d	lt green & multi	.65	*.20*
126	A20 60d	dp blue & multi	1.60	*.20*

UPU Headquarters opening, May 20.

Charles Dickens, London Skyline — A21

60d, Dickens' portrait, vert. 1.25r, Dickens & "Old Curiosity Shop." 3r, Bound volumes.

1970, July 23 Litho. *Perf. 13½*

127	A21 60d	olive & multi	.70	*.20*
128	A21 1r	multicolored	.85	*.20*
129	A21 1.25r	buff & multi	1.00	*.20*
130	A21 3r	multicolored	3.25	*.50*
	Nos. 127-130 (4)		5.80	*1.10*

Dickens (1812-70), English novelist.

The Graham Children, by William Hogarth — A22

Paintings: 60d, Caroline Murat and her Children, by François Pascal Gerard, vert. 1r, Napoleon with the Children on the Terrace in St. Cloud, by Louis Ducis.

1970, Oct. 1 Litho. *Perf. 13½*

131	A22 35d	multicolored	.75	.20
132	A22 60d	multicolored	1.25	.20
133	A22 1r	multicolored	2.00	.20
	Nos. 131-133 (3)		4.00	.60

Issued for Children's Day.

National Bank of Dubai A24

Sheik Rashid bin Said — A23

Television Station — A25

Designs: 10d, Boat building. 20d, Al Maktum Bascule Bridge. 35d, Great Mosque, Dubai, vert. 1r, Dubai International Airport, horiz. 1.25r, Port Rashid harbor project, horiz. 3r, Rashid Hospital, horiz. 5r, Dubai Trade School, horiz.

Perf. 14x14½, 14½x14

1970-71 Litho.

134	A23 5d	multi ('71)	.30	.20
135	A24 10d	multi ('71)	.30	.20
136	A24 20d	multi ('71)	.50	.20
137	A24 35d	multi ('71)	.65	.20
138	A24 60d	multicolored	1.00	.20

Perf. 14

139	A25 1r	multicolored	1.50	.20
140	A25 1.25r	multicolored	1.50	.20
141	A25 3r	multicolored	4.50	.25
142	A25 5r	multicolored	7.25	.40
143	A25 10r	multi ('71)	17.50	.85
	Nos. 134-143 (10)		35.00	2.90

Dubai Airport A26

Designs: 1.25r, Airport entrance.

1971, May 15 Litho. *Perf. 13½x14*

144	A26 1r	multicolored	3.25	.20
145	A26 1.25r	multicolored	4.00	.20

Opening of Dubai International Airport.

Map With Tracking Stations, Satellites A27

1971, June 21 Litho. *Perf. 14½*

146	A27 60d	multicolored	.60	.30

Outer Space Telecommunications Cong., Paris, Mar. 29-Apr. 2. See Nos. C55-C56.

Fan, Scout Emblem, Map of Japan — A28

Designs: 1r, Boy Scouts in kayaks. 1.25r, Mountaineering. 3r, Campfire, horiz.

Perf. 14x13½, 13½x14

1971, Aug. 30 Litho.

147	A28 60d	multicolored	.50	*.20*
148	A28 1r	multicolored	1.00	*.20*
149	A28 1.25r	multicolored	1.25	*.20*
150	A28 3r	multicolored	2.75	*.30*
	Nos. 147-150 (4)		5.50	*.90*

13th Boy Scout World Jamboree, Asagiri Plain, Japan, Aug. 2-10.

Albrecht Dürer, Self-portrait — A29

1971, Oct. 18 *Perf. 14x13½*

151	A29 60d	gold & multi	.75	*.20*

See Nos. C57-C59.

Boy in Meadow A30

5r, Boys playing and UNICEF emblem.

1971, Dec. 11 *Perf. 13½*

152	A30 60d	multi	.45	*.20*
153	A30 5r	multi, horiz.	2.00	*.25*

25th anniv. of UNICEF. See No. C60.

Ludwig van Beethoven A31

Portrait: 10d, Leonardo da Vinci.

1972, Feb. 7

154	A31 10d	lt tan & multi	.30	*.20*
155	A31 35d	lt tan & multi	.45	*.20*

See Nos. C61-C62.

Olympic Emblems, Gymnast on Rings — A32

1972, July 31 Litho. *Perf. 13½*

156	A32 35d	shown	.55	*.20*
157	A32 40d	Fencing	.65	*.20*
158	A32 65d	Hockey	.80	*.20*
	Nos. 156-158,C65-C67 (6)		7.50	1.20

20th Olympic Games, Munich, 8/26-9/11.

Stamps of Dubai were replaced in 1972 by those of United Arab Emirates.

AIR POST STAMPS

Type of Regular Issue and

Peregrine Falcon — AP1 Wheat — AP2

Design: A1, Falcon over bridge.

Perf. 12x11½, 11½x12

1963, June 15 Litho. Unwmk.

C1	A1	20np dk red brn & lt blue	1.75	.25
C2	AP1	25np ol & blk brn	1.90	.30
C3	A1	30np red org & blk	2.25	.35
C4	AP1	40np grayish brn & dk violet	2.40	.40
C5	A1	50np emer & rose cl	3.00	.55
C6	AP1	60np brn org & blk	3.50	.55
C7	A1	75np vio & dp grn	5.50	.60
C8	AP1	1r org & red brn	6.50	.75
		Nos. C1-C8 (8)	26.80	3.75

Red Cross Type

Designs: 20np, Dhows. 30np, First-aid tent. 40np, Camel caravan. 50np, Butterfly.

1963, Sept. 1 Unwmk. Perf. 12

C9	A3	20np brown, yel & red	1.25	.50
C10	A3	30np dk bl, buff & red	1.25	.50
C11	A3	40np black, yel & red	1.60	.60
C12	A3	50np vio, lt bl & red	3.00	1.10
		Nos. C9-C12 (4)	7.10	2.70

Malaria Type

Designs: 30np, Anopheles mosquito. 40np, Mosquito and coiled arrows. 70np, Mosquitoes over swamp.

1963, Dec. 20 Unwmk. Perf. 12

C13	A4	30np purple & emer	.50	.20
C14	A4	40np red & dull grn	.60	.25
C15	A4	70np slate & citron	.90	.35
		Nos. C13-C15 (3)	2.00	.80

Three imperf. souv. sheets exist containing 4 stamps each in changed colors similar to #C13-C15. Value $30.

1963, Dec. 30 Litho.

40np, Wheat and palm tree. 70np, Hands holding wheat. 1r, Woman carrying basket.

C16	AP2	30np vio bl & ocher	.55	.30
C17	AP2	40np red & olive	.80	.45
C18	AP2	70np green & orange	1.25	.65
C19	AP2	1r org brn & Prus bl	1.90	1.00
		Nos. C16-C19 (4)	4.50	2.40

Boy Scout Type

Designs: 20np, Human pyramid. 30np, Bugler. 40np, Cub Scouts. 70np, Scouts and bugler. 1r, Scouts presenting flag.

1964, Jan. 20

C20	A5	20np green & dk brn	.30	.20
C21	A5	30np lilac & ocher	.65	.25
C22	A5	40np vio bl & yel grn	.80	.30
C23	A5	70np dk grn & gray	1.40	.45
C24	A5	1r vio bl & red org	2.00	.70
		Nos. C20-C24 (5)	5.15	1.90

Five imperf. souv. sheets exist containing 4 stamps each in changed colors similar to #C20-C24. Value $60.

For overprints see Nos. C47-C51.

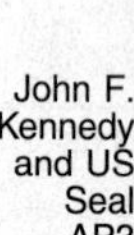

John F. Kennedy and US Seal AP3

1964, Jan. 15 Litho.

C25	AP3	75np grn & blk, *lt grn*	.90	.55
C26	AP3	1r ocher & blk, *tan*	1.25	.60
C27	AP3	1.25r mag & blk, *gray*	1.60	.85
		Nos. C25-C27 (3)	3.75	2.00

Pres. John F. Kennedy (1917-1963). A souvenir sheet contains one imperf. 1.25r in buff and black with simulated perforations. Value $6.

For overprints see Nos. C52-C54.

Spacecraft — AP4

Designs: 1np, 5np, Ascending rocket, vert. 2np, 1r, Mercury capsule, vert. 4np, 2r, Twin spacecraft.

1964, Jan. 25 Unwmk. Perf. 12

C28	AP4	1np emerald & org	.20	.20
C29	AP4	2np multicolored	.20	.20
C30	AP4	3np multicolored	.25	.20
C31	AP4	4np multicolored	.25	.20
C32	AP4	5np blue & orange	.25	.20
C33	AP4	1r vio bl, dp car & buff	.90	.70
C34	AP4	1.50r vio bl, dp car & buff	1.60	1.25
C35	AP4	2r blue, yel & red	2.00	1.50
		Nos. C28-C35 (8)	5.65	4.45

Issued to honor the astronauts. An imperf. souvenir sheet contains one stamp similar to No. C35. Value $7.

New York World's Fair Type

Statue of Liberty and ships in Dubai harbor.

1964, Apr. 22 Litho.

C36	A6	75np gray bl, ultra & blk	.85	.40
C37	A6	2r gray grn, dk brn & bis	1.40	.80
C38	A6	3r dl grn, gray ol & dp org	2.00	1.10
		Nos. C36-C38 (3)	4.25	2.30

An imperf. souvenir sheet contains 2 stamps in Statue of Liberty design: 2r dark brown and rose carmine, and 3r ultramarine and gold. Value $10.

Scales and Flame AP5

1964, Apr. 30 Litho. Perf. 12

C39	AP5	35np bl, brn & scar	.60	.30
C40	AP5	50np lt bl, dk grn & scar	.75	.35
C41	AP5	1r grnsh bl, blk & scar	1.40	.60
C42	AP5	3r lt ultra, ultra, & scar	4.00	2.00
		Nos. C39-C42 (4)	6.75	3.25

15th anniv. of the Universal Declaration of Human Rights. An imperf. souvenir sheet contains one 3r light green, ultramarine and scarlet stamp. Value $7.50.

Nos. C20-C24 Overprinted in Red and Black (Shield in Red)

1964, June 20

C47	A5	20np green & dk brn	.90	.40
C48	A5	30np lilac & ocher	1.10	.50
C49	A5	40np vio bl & yel grn	1.75	.75
C50	A5	70np dk grn & gray	3.00	1.25
C51	A5	1r vio bl & red org	4.25	1.75
		Nos. C47-C51 (5)	11.00	4.65

9th Winter Olympic Games, Innsbruck, Austria, Jan. 29-Feb. 9, 1964.

A similar but unauthorized overprint, with shield in black, exists on Nos. 28-32, C20-C24, and the five souvenir sheets mentioned below No. C24. The Dubai G.P.O. calls this black-shield overprint "bogus."

Nos. C25-C27 Overprinted in Brown or Green

1964, Sept. 15

C52	AP3	75np (Br)	2.00	2.00
C53	AP3	1r (G)	2.40	2.40
C54	AP3	1.25r (G)	3.00	3.00
		Nos. C52-C54 (3)	7.40	7.40

Pres. John F. Kennedy 48th birth anniv. The same overprint in black was applied to the souv. sheet noted after No. C27.

Communications Type

Designs: 1r, Intelsat 4, tracking station on globe and rocket. 5r, Eiffel Tower, Syncom 3 and Goonhilly radar station.

1971, June 21 Litho. Perf. 14½

C55	A27	1r lt brown & multi	.60	*.20*
C56	A27	5r multicolored	3.00	*.45*

Portrait Type

1r, Newton. 1.25r, Avicenna. 3r, Voltaire.

1971, Oct. 18 Litho. Perf. 14x13½

C57	A29	1r gold & multi	1.00	*.20*
C58	A29	1.25r gold & multi	1.25	*.20*
C59	A29	3r gold & multi	3.75	*.45*
		Nos. C57-C59 (3)	6.00	*.85*

UNICEF Type

1r, Mother, children, UNICEF emblem.

1971, Dec. 11 Perf. 13½

C60	A30	1r gold & multi	1.00	*.20*

Portrait Type

75d, Khalil Gibran. 5r, Charles de Gaulle.

1972, Feb. 7 Litho. Perf. 13½

C61	A31	75d lt tan & multi	.75	*.20*
C62	A31	5r lt tan & multi	5.25	*.35*

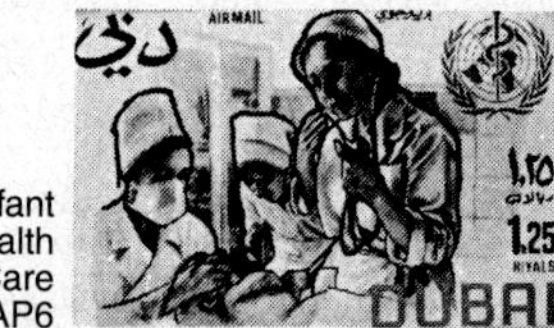

Infant Health Care AP6

Design: 75d, Nurse supervising children at meal, and WHO emblem, vert.

1972, Apr. 7 Litho. Perf. 14x13½

C63	AP6	75d multicolored	1.60	*.20*
C64	AP6	1.25r multicolored	2.40	*.25*

World Health Day.

Olympic Type

1972, July 31 Litho. Perf. 13½

C65	A32	75d Water polo	1.50	*.20*
C66	A32	1r Steeplechase	1.75	*.20*
C67	A32	1.25r Running	2.25	*.20*
		Nos. C65-C67 (3)	5.50	*.60*

POSTAGE DUE STAMPS

Type of Regular Issue

Designs: 1np, 4np, 15np, Clam. 2np, 5np, 25np, Mussel. 3np, 10np, 35np, Oyster.

Perf. 12x11½

1963, June 15 Litho. Unwmk.

J1	A1	1np gray grn & ver	.60	.25
J2	A1	2np lemon & brt bl	.75	.35
J3	A1	3np dl rose & green	1.25	.50
J4	A1	4np light grn & mag	1.60	.75
J5	A1	5np vermilion & blk	1.90	.90
J6	A1	10np citron & violet	2.40	1.25
J7	A1	15np brt ultra & ver	3.25	1.50
J8	A1	25np buff & olive grn	3.75	1.60
J9	A1	35np turq bl & dp org	4.50	1.90
		Nos. J1-J9 (9)	20.00	9.00

Sheik Rashid bin Said — D1

1972, May 22 Litho. Perf. 14x14½

J10	D1	5d blk & gray grn	1.00	.40
J11	D1	10d vio bl, blk & bis	1.00	.40
J12	D1	20d sl grn, blk & brick red	1.50	.60
J13	D1	30d grnsh gray, blk & lil	4.00	1.60
J14	D1	50d lilac, brn & bis	7.50	3.00
		Nos. J10-J14 (5)	15.00	6.00

EAST AFRICA AND UGANDA PROTECTORATES

'ēst 'a-fri-kə and ü-'gan-də prə-'tek-t̡ə-ˌrəts

LOCATION — Central East Africa, bordering on the Indian Ocean
GOVT. — British Protectorate
AREA — 350,000 sq. mi. (approx.)
POP. — 6,503,507 (approx.)
CAPITAL — Mombasa

This territory, formerly administered by the British East Africa Colony, was divided between Kenya Colony and the Uganda Protectorate. See Kenya, Uganda and Tanzania.

16 Annas = 1 Rupee
100 Cents = 1 Rupee (1907)

Altered high value stamps of East Africa and Uganda are plentiful. Expertization by competent authorities is recommended.

A1 A2

King Edward VII

1903 Typo. Wmk. 2 Perf. 14

1	A1	½a gray green	4.50	*14.00*
2	A1	1a car & black	2.00	1.10
3	A1	2a vio & dull vio	9.75	3.00
4	A1	2½a ultramarine	14.00	*55.00*
5	A1	3a gray grn & brn	19.00	*62.50*
6	A1	4a blk & gray grn	12.50	*25.00*
7	A1	5a org brn & blk	21.00	*55.00*
8	A1	8a pale blue & blk	24.00	*45.00*

Wmk. 1

9	A2	1r gray green	18.00	*62.50*
10	A2	2r vio & dull vio	80.00	92.50
11	A2	3r blk & gray grn	100.00	*190.00*
12	A2	4r lt green & blk	110.00	*175.00*
13	A2	5r car & black	110.00	*190.00*
14	A2	10r ultra & black	210.00	375.00
15	A2	20r ol gray & blk	625.00	*1,250.*
16	A2	50r org brn & blk	1,600.	*2,900.*
		Nos. 1-14 (14)	734.75	*1,345.*

Nos. 9 and 14 are on both ordinary and chalky paper. Values are for examples on ordinary paper. Values are for the least expensive varieties. See "Scott Classic Specialized Catalogue of Stamps & Covers" for detailed listings.

1904-07 Wmk. 3 Chalky Paper

17	A1	½a gray green	8.50	3.75
18a	A1	1a car & black	4.25	.90
19	A1	2a vio & dull vio	3.00	3.00
20	A1	2½a blue	9.25	*35.00*
a.		2½a blue & ultramarine	8.50	*19.00*
21	A1	3a gray grn & brn	4.25	*32.50*
22	A1	4a blk & gray grn	8.50	*21.00*
23	A1	5a org brn & blk	7.50	*32.50*
24a	A1	8a pale blue & blk	8.00	*9.75*
25	A2	1r gray green	30.00	*70.00*
26	A2	2r vio & dl vio	42.50	*62.50*
27	A2	3r blk & gray grn	62.50	*110.00*
28	A2	4r lt green & blk	85.00	*160.00*
29	A2	5r car & black	95.00	*125.00*

29A	A2	10r ultra & black	190.00	210.00
30	A2	20r ol gray & blk	625.00	*1,100.*
30A	A2	50r org brn & blk	1,750.	*3,100.*
		Nos. 17-29 (13)	368.25	*665.90*

Nos. 17-19, 21-24 are on both ordinary and chalky paper. No. 20 is on ordinary paper. Values are for the least expensive varieties. See "Scott Classic Specialized Catalogue of Stamps & Covers" for detailed listings.

1907-08

31	A1	1c brown ('08)	2.90	.20
32	A1	3c gray green	14.00	.80
33	A1	6c carmine, ptd from two plates ('07)	3.00	.20
34	A1	10c citron & violet	10.50	9.75
35	A1	12c red vio & dl vio	11.50	3.00
36	A1	15c ultramarine	22.50	9.75
37	A1	25c blk & blue green	9.75	*8.00*
38	A1	50c org brn & green	14.00	14.00
39	A1	75c pale bl & gray blk ('08)	5.00	*35.00*
		Nos. 31-39 (9)	93.15	*80.70*

Nos. 31-33, 36 are on ordinary paper.

There are two dies of the 6c differing very slightly in many details.

A3

King George V — A4

1912-18 Ordinary Paper Wmk. 3

40	A3	1c black	.35	*2.00*
41	A3	3c green	2.25	.70
a.		Booklet pane of 6		
42	A3	6c carmine	.80	.70
a.		Booklet pane of 6		
43	A3	10c orange	2.25	.55
44	A3	12c gray	3.00	.55
45	A3	15c ultramarine	3.00	.90

Chalky Paper

46	A3	25c scar & blk, *yel*	.55	*1.40*
47	A3	50c violet & black	1.75	1.40
48	A3	75c black, *green*	1.75	*19.00*
a.		75c black, *emerald*	12.50	*57.50*
b.		75c blk, *bl grn,* olive back	7.00	8.50
c.		75c blk, *emer,* olive back	47.50	*175.00*
49	A4	1r black, *green*	2.00	*4.75*
a.		1r black, *emerald*	5.75	*57.50*
50	A4	2r blk & red, *bl*	22.50	*42.50*
51	A4	3r gray grn & vio	22.50	*95.00*
52	A4	4r grn & red, *yel*	50.00	*110.00*
53	A4	5r dl vio & ultra	55.00	*160.00*
54	A4	10r grn & red, *grn*	125.00	*210.00*
55	A4	20r vio & blk, *red*	350.00	350.00
56	A4	20r bl & violet, *blue* ('18)	400.00	*450.00*
57	A4	50r gray grn & rose red	625.00	*700.00*
58	A4	100r blk & vio, *red*	4,900.	*2,600.*
59	A4	500r red & grn, *grn*	18,500.	
		Nos. 40-54 (15)	292.70	*649.45*

1914 Surface-colored Paper

60	A3	25c scarlet & blk, *yel*	.60	*5.00*
61	A3	75c black, *green*	1.10	*18.00*

Stamps of types A3 and A4 with watermark 4 are listed under Kenya, Uganda and Tanzania.

The 1r through 50r with revenue cancellations sell for minimal prices. The 100r and 500r were available for postage but were nearly always used fiscally.

For surcharge see No. 62.

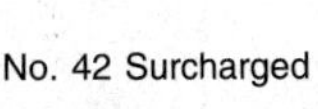

No. 42 Surcharged

1919

62	A3	4c on 6c carmine	1.40	.20
a.		Double surcharge	140.00	*225.00*
b.		Without squares over old value	45.00	*80.00*
c.		Pair, one without surcharge	1,500.	*1,700.*
d.		Inverted surcharge	300.00	*425.00*

For later issues see Kenya, Uganda and Tanzania.

For stamps of East Africa and Uganda overprinted "G. E. A." see German East Africa.

EASTERN RUMELIA

'ē-stərn rü-'mēl-yə

(South Bulgaria)

LOCATION — In southern Bulgaria
GOVT. — An autonomous unit of the Turkish Empire.
CAPITAL — Philippopolis (Plovdiv)

In 1885 the province of Eastern Rumelia revolted against Turkish rule and united with Bulgaria, adopting the new name of South Bulgaria. This union was assured by the Treaty of Bucharest in 1886, following the war between Serbia and Bulgaria.

40 Paras = 1 Piaster

Counterfeits of all overprints are plentiful.

No. 1

A2

A3

Stamps of Turkey, 1876-84, Overprinted in Blue

1880 Unwmk. *Perf. 13½*

1	A5	½pi on 20pa yel grn	32.50	30.00
3	A2	10pa blk & rose	*37.50*	
4	A2	20pa vio & grn	35.00	32.50
6	A2	2pi blk & buff	65.00	62.50
7	A2	5pi red & bl	210.00	240.00
8	A3	10pa blk & red lil	20.00	

Nos. 3 & 8 were not placed in use.

Inverted and double overprints of all values exist.

Same, with Extra Overprint "R. O."

9	A3	10pa blk & red lil	37.50	37.50

Crescent and Turkish Inscriptions of Value — A4

1881 Typo. *Perf. 13½*

10	A4	5pa blk & olive	2.40	.60
11	A4	10pa blk & green	7.25	.60
12	A4	20pa blk & rose	.60	.60
13	A4	1pi blk & blue	2.75	2.25
14	A4	5pi rose & blue	24.00	*35.00*

Tête bêche pairs, imperforates and all perf. 11½ copies of Nos. 10-14 were not placed in use, and were found only in the remainder stock. This is true also of a 10pa cliché in the 20pa plate, and of a cliché of Turkey No. 63 in the 1pi plate. See the *Scott Classic Catalogue.*

1884 *Perf. 11½*

15	A4	5pa lil & pale lil	.30	.30
16	A4	10pa grn & pale grn	.20	.30
17	A4	20pa car & pale rose	.30	
18	A4	1pi bl & pale bl	.60	
19	A4	5pi brn & pale brn	*160.00*	

Nos. 17-19 were not placed in use.

Nos. 15-19 imperf. are from remainders.

See the *Scott Classic Catalogue for perf 13½ listings.*

For overprints see Turkey Nos. 542-545.

South Bulgaria

Counterfeits of all overprints are plentiful.

Nos. 10-14 Overprinted in Two Types:

a

b

Type a - Four toes on each foot.
Type b - Three toes on each foot.

1885 Unwmk. *Perf. 13½*

Blue Overprint

20	A4 (a)	5pa blk & olive	*100.00*	*110.00*
21	A4 (a)	10pa blk & grn	*350.00*	*350.00*
22	A4 (a)	20pa blk & rose	100.00	110.00
23	A4 (a)	1pi blk & bl	19.00	*24.00*
24	A4 (b)	5pi rose & bl	*275.00*	*290.00*

See the *Scott Classic Catalogue* for #22-23, type b, #24, type a, and #22, perf 11½, types a and b.

Black Overprint

24B	A4 (a)	20pa blk & rose	175.00	—
25	A4 (a)	1pi blk & bl	15.00	*18.00*
26	A4 (b)	5pi rose & bl	*350.00*	*350.00*

See the *Scott Classic Catalogue* for #25 type b.

Same Overprint on Nos. 15-17

Perf. 11½, 13½ (#30)

Blue Overprint

27	A4 (b)	5pa lil & pale lil	9.50	*15.00*
28	A4 (b)	10pa grn & pale grn	12.00	*24.00*
29	A4 (a)	20pa car & pale rose	12.00	*18.00*

Black Overprint

30	A4 (b)	5pa lil & pale lil	16.00	*21.00*
31	A4 (a)	10pa grn & pale grn	16.00	*21.00*
32	A4 (b)	20pa car & pale rose	13.00	*18.00*

See the *Scott Classic Catalogue* for #27-28, 30, 32, type a, #29, 31, type b; #27, perf 13½, types a and b, #30, perf 11½ type b, and #31, perf 13½, type a.

Nos. 10-17 Handstamped in Black in Two Types:

a

b

Type a — First letter at top circular.
Type b — First letter at top oval.

1885 *Perf. 13½*

33	A4 (b)	5pa blk & olive	*275.00*	
34	A4 (b)	10pa blk & grn	*275.00*	
35	A4 (b)	20pa blk & rose	35.00	*47.50*
36	A4 (a)	1pi blk & bl	35.00	*42.50*
37	A4 (a)	5pi rose & bl	*275.00*	*325.00*

See the *Scott Classic Catalogue* for #33-35 type a and #36 type b.

Perf. 13½

38	A4 (a)	5pa lil & pale lil	10.00	10.00

Perf. 11½

39	A4 (a)	10pa grn & pale grn	9.00	*9.50*
40	A4 (a)	20pa car & pale rose	9.00	*13.00*

See the *Scott Classic Catalogue* for #38-40, type b, and #38, perf 11½, types a and b.

Nos. 20-40 exist with inverted and double handstamps. Overprints in unlisted colors are proofs.

The stamps of South Bulgaria were superseded in 1886 by those of Bulgaria.

EASTERN SILESIA

'ē-stərn sī-'lē-zh̦ē-ˌə

LOCATION — In central Europe
GOVT. — Austrian crownland
AREA — 1,987 sq. mi.
POP. — 680,422 (estimated 1920)
CAPITAL — Troppau

After World War I, this territory was occupied by Czechoslovakia and eventually was divided between Poland and Czechoslovakia, the dividing line running through Teschen.

100 Heller = 1 Krone
100 Fennigi = 1 Marka

Plebiscite Issues

Stamps of Czechoslovakia 1918-20, Overprinted in Black, Blue, Violet or Red

1920 Unwmk. *Imperf.*

1	A2	1h dark brown	.20	.30
2	A1	3h red violet	.20	.20
3	A2	5h blue green	22.50	22.50
4	A2	15h red	11.00	11.00
5	A1	20h blue green	.20	.20
6	A2	25h dull violet	.75	.75
7	A1	30h bister (R)	.20	.20
8	A1	40h red orange	.30	.30
9	A2	50h dull violet	.60	.45
10	A2	50h dark blue	2.50	1.50
11	A2	60h orange (Bl)	.75	.75
12	A2	75h slate (R)	.50	.75
13	A2	80h olive grn (R)	.50	.75
14	A1	100h brown	1.10	1.10
15	A2	120h gray blk (R)	1.50	2.25
16	A1	200h ultra (R)	1.50	2.00
17	A2	300h green (R)	6.00	7.50
18	A1	400h purple (R)	2.00	3.00
20	A2	500h red brn (Bl)	5.00	6.00
a.		Black overprint	6.00	9.00
21	A2	1000h violet (Bl)	12.50	13.50
a.		Black overprint	60.00	75.00
		Nos. 1-21 (20)	69.80	75.00

Perf. 11½, 13¾

22	A2	1h dark brown	.20	.20
23	A2	5h blue green	.30	.25
24	A2	10h yellow green	.30	.25
a.		Imperf.	*250.00*	*200.00*
25	A2	15h red	.50	.20
26	A2	20h rose	.50	.35
a.		Imperf.	*300.00*	*250.00*
27	A2	25h dull violet	.50	.35
28	A2	30h red violet (Bl)	.35	.35
29	A2	60h orange (Bl)	.50	.50
30	A1	200h ultra (R)	3.00	3.00
		Nos. 22-30 (9)	6.15	5.45

The letters "S. O." are the initials of "Silésie Orientale."

Forged cancellations are found on #1-30.

Overprinted in Carmine or Violet

31	A4	500h sl, *grysh* (C)	37.50	
32	A4	1000h blk brn, *brnsh*	37.50	

Excellent counterfeits of this overprint exist.

Stamps of Poland, 1919, Overprinted

1920 *Perf. 11½*

41	A10	5f green	.20	.20
42	A10	10f red brown	.20	.20
43	A10	15f light red	.20	.20
44	A11	25f olive green	.20	.20
45	A11	50f blue green	.20	.20

Overprinted

46	A12	1k deep green	.20	.20
47	A12	1.50k brown	.20	.20
48	A12	2k dark blue	.20	.20
49	A13	2.50k dull violet	.20	.20
50	A14	5k slate blue	.20	.20
		Nos. 41-50 (10)	2.00	2.00

SPECIAL DELIVERY STAMPS

Czechoslovakia Special Delivery Stamps Overprinted in Blue

1920 Unwmk. *Imperf.*

E1	SD1	2h red violet, *yel*	.20	.20
a.		Black overprint	4.50	.80
E2	SD1	5h yellow green, *yel*	.20	.20
a.		Black overprint	7.00	5.00

Nos. E1-E2a exist on white paper.

POSTAGE DUE STAMPS

Czechoslovakia Postage Due Stamps Overprinted In Blue or Red

1920 Unwmk. *Imperf.*

J1	D1	5h deep bis (Bl)	.25	.20
a.		Black overprint	70.00	60.00
J2	D1	10h deep bister	.25	.20
J3	D1	15h deep bister	.25	.20
J4	D1	20h deep bister	.25	.20
J5	D1	25h deep bister	.25	.20
J6	D1	30h deep bister	.25	.20
J7	D1	40h deep bister	.50	.25
J8	D1	50h deep bister	2.50	3.00
J9	D1	100h blk brn (R)	2.50	3.00
J10	D1	500h gray grn (R)	5.50	4.50
J11	D1	1000h purple (R)	8.00	11.50
		Nos. J1-J11 (11)	20.50	23.45

Forged cancellations exist.

NEWSPAPER STAMPS

Czechoslovakia Newspaper Stamps Overprinted in Black like Nos. 1-30

1920 Unwmk. *Imperf.*

P1	N1	2h gray green	.30	.30
P2	N1	6h red	.20	.20
P3	N1	10h dull violet	.20	.20
P4	N1	20h blue	.30	.25
P5	N1	30h gray brown	.30	.25
		Nos. P1-P5 (5)	1.30	1.20

ECUADOR

'e-kwə-,dor

LOCATION — Northwest coast of South America, bordering on the Pacific Ocean
GOVT. — Republic
AREA — 116,270 (?) sq. mi.
POP. — 12,562,496 (1999 est.)
CAPITAL — Quito

The Republic of Ecuador was so constituted on May 11, 1830, after the Civil War which separated the original members of the Republic of Colombia, founded by Simon Bolivar by uniting the Presidency of Quito with the Viceroyalty of New Grenada and the Captaincy of Venezuela. The Presidency of Quito became the Republic of Ecuador.

8 Reales = 1 Peso
100 Centavos = 1 Sucre (1881)

Catalogue values for unused stamps in this country are for Never Hinged items, beginning with Scott 453 in the regular postage section, Scott C147 in the airpost section, Scott CO19 in the airpost officials section, Scott O201 in the officials section, Scott RA60 in the postal tax section, and all entries in the Galapagos section.

Watermarks

Wmk. 117 — Liberty Cap

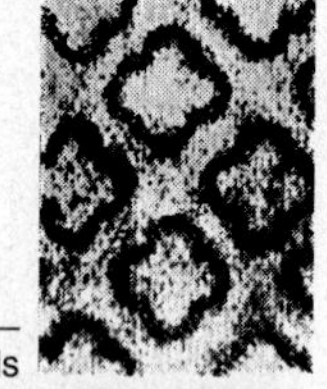

Wmk. 127 — Quatrefoils

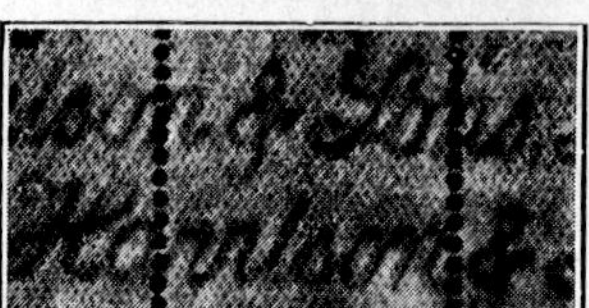

Wmk. 233 — "Harrison & Sons, London" in Script Letters

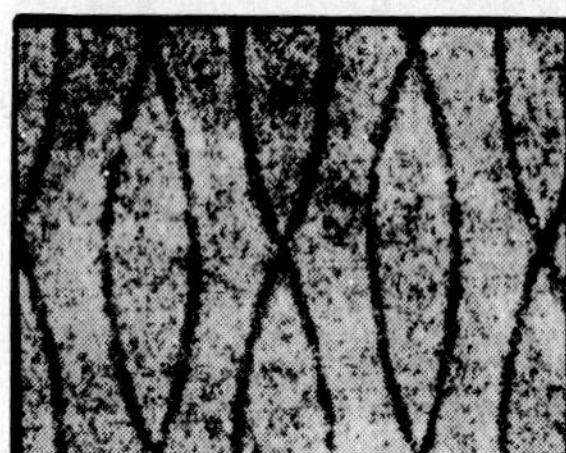

Wmk. 340 — Alternating Interlaced Wavy Lines

Wmk. 367 — Liberty Cap, Emblem, Inscription

Wmk. 395 — Emblem, Inscription

Coat of Arms
A1 A2

1865-72 Unwmk. Typo. *Imperf.*

Quadrille Paper

1	A1	1r yellow ('72)	29.00	25.00

Wove Paper

2	A1	½r ultra	17.00	8.75
a.		½r gray blue ('67)	17.00	8.75
b.		Batonne paper ('70)	25.00	15.00
c.		Blue paper ('72)	125.00	82.50
3	A1	1r buff	22.50	11.00
a.		1r orange buff	27.50	13.00
4	A1	1r yellow	13.00	9.25
a.		1r olive yellow ('66)	19.00	15.00
b.		Laid paper	125.00	82.50
c.		Half used as ½r on cover		900.00
d.		Batonne paper	25.00	19.00
5	A1	1r green	190.00	22.50
a.		Half used as ½r on cover		900.00
6	A2	4r red ('66)	250.00	100.00
a.		4r red brown ('66)	350.00	100.00
b.		Arms in circle	250.00	150.00
c.		Printed on both sides	550.00	—
d.		Half used as 2r on cover		1,600.
		Nos. 1-6 (6)	521.50	176.50

Letter paper embossed with arms of Ecuador was used in printing a number of sheets of Nos. 2, 4-6.

Papermakers' watermarks are known on No. 2 ("Bath" and crown) and No. 4 ("Rolland Freres").

On the 4r the oval holding the coat of arms is usually 13½-14mm wide, but on about one-fifth of the stamps in the sheet it is 15-15½mm wide, almost a circle.

The 2r, 8r and 12r, type A1, are bogus.

Proofs of the ½r, type A1, are known in black and green.

An essay of type A2 shows the condor's head facing right.

1871-72

Blue-surface Paper

7	A1	½r ultra	22.50	14.00
8	A1	1r yellow	125.00	45.00

Unofficial reprints of types A1-A2 differ in color, have a different sheet makeup and lack gum. Type A1 reprints usually have a double frameline at left. All stamps on blue paper with horiz. blue lines are reprints.

A3

A4

1872 White Paper Litho. *Perf. 11*

9	A3	½r blue	13.00	3.00
10	A4	1r yellow	15.00	4.50
11	A3	1p rose	3.00	*10.00*
		Nos. 9-11 (3)	31.00	*17.50*

The 1r surcharged 4c is fraudulent.

A5

A6

A7

A8

A9

A10

1881, Nov. 1 Engr. *Perf. 12*

12	A5	1c yellow brn	.20	.20
13	A6	2c lake	.20	.20
14	A7	5c blue	2.60	.40
15	A8	10c orange	.20	.20
16	A9	20c gray violet	.20	.20
17	A10	50c blue green	.80	*2.00*
		Nos. 12-17 (6)	4.20	*3.20*

The 1c surcharged 3c, and 20c surcharged 5c are fraudulent.

For overprints see Nos. O1-O6.

No. 17 Surcharged in Black

DIEZ
CENTAVOS

1883, Apr.

18	A10	10c on 50c blue grn	19.00	15.00
a.		Double surcharge		

Dangerous forgeries exist.

A12

A13

A14

A15

1887

19	A12	1c blue green	.20	.20
20	A13	2c vermilion	.35	.20
21	A14	5c blue	1.10	.25
22	A15	80c olive green	2.00	*5.50*
		Nos. 19-22 (4)	3.65	*6.15*

For overprints see Nos. O7-O10.

President Juan Flores — A16

1892

23	A16	1c orange	.20	.20
24	A16	2c dk brown	.20	.20
25	A16	5c vermilion	.20	.20
26	A16	10c green	.20	.20
27	A16	20c red brown	.20	.20
28	A16	50c maroon	.20	*.30*
29	A16	1s blue	.20	*.70*
30	A16	5s purple	.50	*1.00*
		Nos. 23-30 (8)	1.90	*3.00*

The issues of 1892, 1894, 1895 and 1896 were printed by the Hamilton Bank Note Co., New York, to the order of N. F. Seebeck, who held a contract for stamps with the government of Ecuador.

No. 30 in green is said to be an essay or color trial.

For surcharges and overprints see Nos. 31-37, O11-O17.

Nos. 29 and 30 Surcharged in Black

1893

Surcharge Measures 25½x2½mm

31	A16	5c on 1s blue	2.00	2.00
32	A16	5c on 5s purple	4.75	3.50
a.		Double surcharge		

Surcharge Measures 24x2¼mm

33	A16	5c on 1s blue	1.25	1.00
a.		Double surcharge, one inverted		
34	A16	5c on 5s purple	5.00	4.00
a.		Double surcharge, one invtd.		

Nos. 28-30 Surcharged in Black

No.	Type	Description	Unused	Used
35	A16	5c on 50c maroon	.50	.45
a.		Inverted surcharge	1.75	
36	A16	5c on 1s blue	.85	.70
37	A16	5c on 5s purple	4.00	3.50
		Nos. 31-37 (7)	18.35	15.15

Pres. Juan Flores
A19

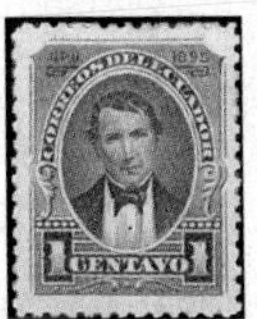

Pres. Vicente Rocafuerte
A20

No.	Type	Description	Unused	Used
38	A19	5c on 5s lake	1.00	1.00

It is stated that No. 38 was used exclusively as a postage stamp and not for telegrams.

1894 Dated 1894 *Perf. 12*

Various Frames

No.	Type	Description	Unused	Used
39	A20	1c blue	.20	.20
40	A20	2c yellow brn	.20	.20
41	A20	5c green	.20	.20
b.		Perf. 14	2.90	1.00
42	A20	10c vermilion	.35	.30
43	A20	20c black	.55	.35
44	A20	50c orange	2.90	1.00
45	A20	1s carmine	4.75	2.00
46	A20	5s dark blue	6.00	3.00
		Nos. 39-46 (8)	15.15	7.25

1895

Same, Dated "1895"

No.	Type	Description	Unused	Used
47	A20	1c blue	.45	.35
48	A20	2c yellow brn	.45	.35
49	A20	5c green	.35	.25
50	A20	10c vermilion	.35	.20
51	A20	20c black	.50	.50
52	A20	50c orange	1.75	1.10
53	A20	1s carmine	10.50	4.00
54	A20	5s dark blue	4.25	2.00
		Nos. 47-54 (8)	18.60	8.75

Reprints of the 2c, 10c, 50c, 1s and 5s of the 1894-95 issues are generally on thick paper. Original issues are on thin to medium thick paper. To distinguish reprints from originals, a comparison of paper thickness, paper color, gum, printing clarity and direction of paper weave is necessary. Value 20 cents each.

For overprints see #77-112, O20-O33, O50-O91.

A21

A22

A23

A24

A25

A26

A27

A28

1896 Wmk. 117

No.	Type	Description	Unused	Used
55	A21	1c dk green	.35	.30
56	A22	2c red	.35	.20
57	A23	5c blue	.35	.20
58	A24	10c bister brn	.30	*.45*
59	A25	20c orange	.70	*1.00*
60	A26	50c dark blue	1.00	*1.50*
61	A27	1s yellow brn	2.00	*2.00*
62	A28	5s violet	*7.00*	2.75
		Nos. 55-62 (8)	12.05	*8.40*

Unwmk.

No.	Type	Description	Unused	Used
62A	A21	1c dk green	.50	.20
62B	A22	2c red	.55	.20
62C	A23	5c blue	.55	.35
62D	A24	10c bister brn	.35	*.70*
62E	A25	20c orange	3.00	*2.75*
62F	A26	50c dark blue	1.00	*1.40*
62G	A27	1s yellow brn	3.00	*4.00*
62H	A28	5s violet	*7.50*	*3.00*
		Nos. 62A-62H (8)	*16.45*	*12.60*

Reprints of Nos. 55-62H are on very thick paper, with paper weave direction vertical. Value 20 cents each.

For surcharges and overprints see Nos. 74, 76, 113-114, O34-O49.

Vicente Roca, Diego Noboa and José Olmedo — A28a

General Juan Francisco Elizalde — A28b

Perf. 11½

1896, Oct. 9 Unwmk. Litho.

No.	Type	Description	Unused	Used
63	A28a	1c rose	.35	*.40*
64	A28b	2c blue	.35	*.45*
65	A28a	5c green	.50	*.50*
66	A28b	10c ocher	.50	*.50*
67	A28a	20c red	.70	*2.00*
68	A28b	50c violet	1.10	*3.25*
69	A28a	1s orange	2.00	*5.50*
		Nos. 63-69 (7)	5.50	*12.60*

Success of the Liberal Party in 1845 & 1895. For overprints see Nos. 115-125.

A29

Black Surcharge

1896, Nov. *Perf. 12*

No.	Type	Description	Unused	Used
70	A29	1c on 1c ver, "1893-1894"	.50	.30
a.		Inverted surcharge	1.25	1.00
b.		Double surcharge	4.00	3.50
71	A29	2c on 2c bl, "1893-1894"	1.00	.85
a.		Inverted surcharge	2.00	1.75
72	A29	5c on 10c org, "1887-1888"	1.00	.30
a.		Inverted surcharge	2.00	.85
b.		Double surcharge	3.50	2.00
c.		Surcharged "2cts"	.50	.40
d.		"1893-1894"	3.00	2.50
73	A29	10c on 4c brn, "1887-1888"	1.00	.55
a.		Inverted surcharge	2.00	.85
b.		Double surcharge	3.00	1.75
c.		Double surcharge, one inverted		
d.		Surcharged "1 cto"	1.00	*1.40*
e.		"1891-1892"	8.50	6.75
		Nos. 70-73 (4)	3.50	2.00

Similar surcharges of type A29 include: Dated "1887-1888"- 1c on 1c blue green, 1c on 2c red, 1c on 4c brown, 1c on 10c yellow; 2c on 2c red, 2c on 10c yellow; 10c on 1c green.

Dated "1891-1892"- 1c on 1c blue green, 1c on 4c brown.

Dated "1893-1894"- 2c on 10c yellow; 10c on 1c vermilion, 10c on 10s black.

For overprints see Nos. O18-O19.

Nos. 59-60 Surcharged in Black or Red

1896, Oct. Wmk. 117

No.	Type	Description	Unused	Used
74	A25	5c on 20c orange	17.50	17.50
76	A26	10c on 50c dk bl (R)	17.50	17.50
a.		Double surcharge		

The surcharge is diag., horiz. or vert.

Overprinted

On Issue of 1894

1897 Unwmk.

No.	Type	Description	Unused	Used
77	A20	1c blue	1.10	1.10
78	A20	2c yellow brn	.95	.65
79	A20	5c green	.45	.45
80	A20	10c vermilion	1.40	1.10
81	A20	20c black	1.50	1.40
82	A20	50c orange	3.25	1.60
83	A20	1s carmine	9.50	3.25
84	A20	5s dark blue	55.00	45.00
		Nos. 77-84 (8)	73.15	54.55

On Issue of 1895

No.	Type	Description	Unused	Used
85	A20	1c blue	3.00	2.75
86	A20	2c yellow brn	1.10	1.10
87	A20	5c green	.95	.80
88	A20	10c vermilion	3.50	3.00
89	A20	20c black	.95	.85
90	A20	50c orange	16.00	6.50
91	A20	1s carmine	7.25	3.75
92	A20	5s dark blue	7.25	7.25
		Nos. 85-92 (8)	40.00	26.00

Overprinted

On Issue of 1894

No.	Type	Description	Unused	Used
93	A20	1c blue	.70	.45
94	A20	2c yellow brn	.60	.35
95	A20	5c green	.30	.25
96	A20	10c vermilion	1.75	.85
97	A20	20c black	1.90	1.25
98	A20	50c orange	3.50	1.40
99	A20	1s carmine	6.50	4.25
100	A20	5s dark blue	57.50	42.50
		Nos. 93-100 (8)	72.75	51.30

On Issue of 1895

No.	Type	Description	Unused	Used
101	A20	1c blue	1.60	.80
102	A20	2c yellow brn	.80	.80
103	A20	5c green	.85	.50
104	A20	10c vermilion	2.75	2.25
105	A20	20c black	2.50	.60
106	A20	50c orange	.90	.90
107	A20	1s carmine	4.00	3.50
108	A20	5s dark blue	4.75	4.75
		Nos. 101-108 (8)	18.15	14.10

Overprints on Nos. 77-108 are to be found reading upward from left to right and downward from left to right, as well as inverted.

Overprinted **1897 Y 1898**

On Issue of 1894

1897

No.	Type	Description	Unused	Used
109	A20	10c vermilion	65.00	57.50

On Issue of 1895

No.	Type	Description	Unused	Used
110	A20	2c yellow brn	50.00	45.00
111	A20	1s carmine	65.00	57.50
112	A20	5s dark blue	65.00	50.00
		Nos. 109-112 (4)	245.00	210.00

Nos. 56, 59 Overprinted like Nos. 93-108

1897, June Wmk. 117

No.	Type	Description	Unused	Used
113	A22	2c red	50.00	40.00
114	A25	20c orange	55.00	47.50

Many forged overprints on Nos. 77-114 exist, made on original stamps and reprints.

Stamps or Types of 1896 Overprinted like Nos. 93-108

1897 Unwmk. *Perf. 11½*

No.	Type	Description	Unused	Used
115	A28a	1c rose	1.25	1.25
116	A28b	2c blue	1.00	1.00
117	A28b	10c ocher	1.00	1.00
118	A28a	1s yellow	5.00	5.00
		Nos. 115-118 (4)	8.25	8.25

No. 63 Overprinted like Nos. 77-92

1897

No.	Type	Description	Unused	Used
119	A28a	1c rose	.60	.50

Nos. 63-66 Overprinted in Black

1897

No.	Type	Description	Unused	Used
122	A28a	1c rose	2.25	2.00
123	A28b	2c blue	2.25	2.00
124	A28a	5c green	2.25	2.00
125	A28b	10c ocher	2.25	2.00
a.		Double overprint	5.25	4.75
		Nos. 122-125 (4)	9.00	8.00

The 20c, 50c and 1s with this overprint in black and all values of the issue overprinted in blue are reprints.

Overprint Inverted

No.	Type	Description	Unused	Used
122a	A28a	1c	3.00	2.75
123a	A28b	2c	3.00	2.75
124a	A28a	5c	3.00	2.75
125b	A28b	10c	2.75	2.75

Coat of Arms — A33

1897, June 23 Engr. *Perf. 14-16*

No.	Type	Description	Unused	Used
127	A33	1c dk yellow grn	.20	.20
128	A33	2c orange red	.20	.20
129	A33	5c lake	.20	.20
130	A33	10c dk brown	.20	.20
131	A33	20c yellow	.30	*.40*
132	A33	50c dull blue	.30	*.65*
133	A33	1s gray	.55	*.80*
134	A33	5s dark lilac	.75	*1.10*
		Nos. 127-134 (8)	2.70	*3.75*

No. 135

No. 136

1899, May

No.	Type	Description	Unused	Used
135	A33	1c on 2c orange red	1.50	.80
136	A33	5c on 10c brown	1.25	.50
a.		Double surcharge		

Luis Vargas Torres
A36

Abdón Calderón
A37

Juan Montalvo
A38

José Mejia
A39

Santa Cruz y Espejo — A40

Pedro Carbo — A41

José Joaquin Olmedo A42

Pedro Moncayo A43

1899 *Perf. 12½-16*

No.	Type	Description	Unused	Used
137	A36	1c gray blue & blk	.20	.20
a.		Horiz. pair, imperf. vert.		
138	A37	2c brown lil & blk	.20	.20
139	A38	5c lake & blk	.35	.20
140	A39	10c violet & blk	.35	.20
141	A40	20c green & blk	.35	.20
142	A41	50c lil rose & blk	.85	.55
143	A42	1s ocher & blk	4.00	1.75
144	A43	5s lilac & blk	7.25	5.00
		Nos. 137-144 (8)	13.55	8.30

1901

No.	Type	Description	Unused	Used
145	A36	1c scarlet & blk	.30	.20
146	A37	2c green & blk	.30	.20
147	A38	5c gray lil & blk	.30	.20
148	A39	10c dp blue & blk	.35	.25
149	A40	20c gray & blk	.35	.25
150	A41	50c lt blue & blk	1.10	.65
151	A42	1s brown & blk	4.00	1.75
152	A43	5s gray blk & blk	6.00	4.00
		Nos. 145-152 (8)	12.70	7.50

In July, 1902, following the theft of a quantity of stamps during a fire at Guayaquil, the Government authorized the governors of the provinces to handstamp their stocks. Many varieties of these handstamps exist.

Other control marks were used in 1907.

For overprints see Nos. O103-O106, O167.

A44

Surcharged on Revenue Stamp Dated 1901-1902

1903-06 *Perf. 14, 15*

No.	Type	Description	Unused	Used
153	A44	1c on 5c gray lil ('06)	.25	.20
154	A44	1c on 20c gray ('06)	3.25	2.25
155	A44	1c on 25c yellow	.50	.20
a.		Double surcharge		
156	A44	1c on 1s bl ('06)	26.00	25.00
157	A44	3c on 5c gray lil ('06)	3.25	2.00
158	A44	3c on 20c gray ('06)	8.50	7.50
159	A44	3c on 25c yel ('06)	8.00	7.50
159A	A44	3c on 1s blue ('06)	1.25	1.10
		Nos. 153-159A (8)	51.00	45.75

Counterfeits are plentiful.

See #191-197.

Capt. Abdón Calderón
A45 A46

1904, July 31 *Perf. 12*

No.	Type	Description	Unused	Used
160	A45	1c red & blk	.35	.25
161	A45	2c blue & blk	.40	.25
162	A46	5c yellow & blk	1.25	.75
163	A45	10c red & blk	2.50	.75
164	A45	20c blue & blk	6.50	2.00
165	A46	50c yellow & blk	55.00	30.00
		Nos. 160-165 (6)	66.00	34.00

Centenary of the birth of Calderón.

Presidents

Vicente Roca — A47

Diego Noboa — A48

Francisco Robles — A49

José M. Urvina — A50

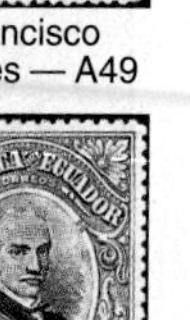

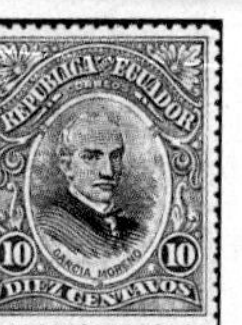

García Moreno A51

Jerónimo Carrión A52

Javier Espinoza A53

Antonio Borrero A54

1907, July *Perf. 14, 15*

No.	Type	Description	Unused	Used
166	A47	1c red & blk	.25	.20
167	A48	2c pale blue & blk	.50	.20
168	A49	3c orange & blk	.75	.20
169	A50	5c lilac rose & blk	1.00	.20
170	A51	10c dp blue & blk	2.00	.20
171	A52	20c yellow grn & blk	3.00	.25
172	A53	50c violet & blk	6.00	.55
173	A54	1s green & blk	8.00	1.40
		Nos. 166-173 (8)	21.50	3.20

The stamps of the 1907 issue frequently have control marks similar to those found on the 1899 and 1901 issues. These marks were applied to distinguish the stamps issued in the various provinces and to serve as a check on local officials.

Locomotive — A55

García Moreno — A56

Gen. Eloy Alfaro — A57

Abelardo Moncayo — A58

Archer Harman — A59

James Sivewright — A60

Mt. Chimborazo A61

1908, June 25

No.	Type	Description	Unused	Used
174	A55	1c red brown	.70	*1.40*
175	A56	2c blue & blk	.90	*1.50*
176	A57	5c claret & blk	1.75	*3.50*
177	A58	10c ocher & blk	1.25	*1.90*
178	A59	20c green & blk	1.25	*2.50*
179	A60	50c gray & blk	1.25	*2.50*
180	A61	1s black	2.50	*5.25*
		Nos. 174-180 (7)	9.60	18.55

Opening of the Guayaquil-Quito Railway.

José Mejía Vallejo — A62

Principal Exposition Building — A70

Designs: 2c, Francisco J. E. Santa Cruz y Espejo. 3c, Francisco Ascásubi. 5c, Juan Salinas. 10c, Juan Pio de Montúfar. 20c, Carlos de Montúfar. 40c, Juan de Dios Morales. 1s, Manuel R. de Quiroga.

1909, Aug. 10 *Perf. 12*

No.	Type	Description	Unused	Used
181	A62	1c green	.25	*.45*
182	A62	2c blue	.25	*.45*
183	A62	3c orange	.25	*.50*
184	A62	5c claret	.25	*.50*
185	A62	10c yellow brn	.30	*.50*
186	A62	20c gray	.30	*.70*
187	A62	50c vermilion	.30	*.70*
188	A62	1s olive grn	.35	*.95*
189	A70	5s violet	.75	*1.90*
		Nos. 181-189 (9)	3.00	*6.65*

National Exposition of 1909.

Surcharged

1909

No.	Type	Description	Unused	Used
190	A68	5c on 50c vermilion	.55	.50

Revenue Stamps Surcharged as in 1903

1910 *Perf. 14, 15*

Stamps Dated 1905-1906

No.	Type	Description	Unused	Used
191	A44	1c on 5c green	1.00	.70
192	A44	5c on 20c blue	4.00	.85
193	A44	5c on 25c violet	7.50	1.50

Stamps Dated 1907-1908

No.	Type	Description	Unused	Used
194	A44	1c on 5c green	.20	.20
195	A44	5c on 20c blue	6.00	4.00
196	A44	5c on 25c violet	.50	.20

Stamp Dated 1909-1910

No.	Type	Description	Unused	Used
197	A44	5c on 20c blue	*32.50*	*25.00*
		Nos. 191-197 (7)	*51.70*	*32.45*

Presidents

Roca — A71

Noboa — A72

Robles — A73

Urvina — A74

Moreno A75

Borrero A76

1911-28 *Perf. 12*

No.	Type	Description	Unused	Used
198	A71	1c scarlet & blk	.35	.20
199	A71	1c orange ('16)	.35	.20
200	A71	1c lt blue ('25)	.20	.20
201	A72	2c blue & blk	.45	.20
202	A72	2c green ('16)	.45	.20
203	A72	2c dk violet ('25)	.45	.20
204	A73	3c orange & blk ('13)	1.00	.25
205	A73	3c black ('15)	.60	.20
206	A74	5c scarlet & blk	.80	.20
207	A74	5c violet ('15)	.80	.20
208	A74	5c rose ('25)	.30	.20
209	A74	5c dk brown ('28)	.30	.20
210	A75	10c dp blue & blk	1.00	.20
211	A75	10c dp blue ('15)	1.00	.20
212	A75	10c yellow grn ('25)	.30	.20
213	A75	10c black ('28)	.75	.20
214	A76	1s green & blk	5.00	1.00
215	A76	1s orange & blk ('27)	3.50	.20
		Nos. 198-215 (18)	17.60	4.45

For overprints see Nos. 260-262, 264-265, O107-O122, O124-O134, O156-O157, O160-O162, O164-O166, O168-O173, O175-O178, O183-O184, O189, RA1.

A77

1912 *Perf. 14, 15*

No.	Type	Description	Unused	Used
216	A77	1c on 1s green	.45	.45
217	A77	2c on 2s carmine	1.00	.70
218	A77	2c on 5s dull blue	.70	.70
219	A77	2c on 10s yellow	2.00	2.00
a.		Inverted surcharge	8.00	6.00
		Nos. 216-219 (4)	4.15	3.85

No. 216 exists with narrow "V" and small "U" in "UN" and Nos. 217, 218 and 219 with "D" with serifs or small "O" in "DOS."

Enrique Váldez — A78

Jerónimo Carrión — A79

Javier Espinoza — A80

1915-17 *Perf. 12*

220 A78 4c red & blk	.20	.20
221 A79 20c green & blk ('17)	1.40	.20
222 A80 50c dp violet & blk	2.25	.35
Nos. 220-222 (3)	3.85	.75

For overprints see #O123, O135, O163, O174.

Olmedo — A86

Monument to "Fathers of the Country" — A95

Laurel Wreath and Star — A104

Designs: 2c, Rafael Ximena. 3c, Roca. 4c, Luis F. Vivero. 5c, Luis Febres Cordero. 6c, Francisco Lavayen. 7c, Jorge Antonio de Elizalde. 8c, Baltazar Garcia. 9c, Jose de Antepara. 15c, Luis Urdaneta. 20c, Jose M. Villamil. 30c, Miguel Letamendi. 40c, Gregorio Escobedo. 50c, Gen. Antonio Jose de Sucre. 60c, Juan Illingworth. 70c, Roca. 80c, Rocafuerte. 1s, Simon Bolivar.

1920

223 A86 1c yellow grn	.20	.20
224 A86 2c carmine	.20	.20
225 A86 3c yellow brn	.20	.20
226 A86 4c myrtle green	.30	.20
227 A86 5c pale blue	.30	.20
228 A86 6c red orange	.55	.30
229 A86 7c brown	1.25	.50
230 A86 8c apple green	.75	.35
231 A86 9c lake	2.25	1.00
232 A95 10c lt blue	1.00	.20
233 A86 15c dk gray	1.25	.35
234 A86 20c dk violet	1.25	.20
235 A86 30c brt violet	2.25	.90
236 A86 40c dk brown	4.00	1.40
237 A86 50c dk green	2.75	.35
238 A86 60c dk blue	5.00	1.50
239 A86 70c gray	8.00	3.25
240 A86 80c orange yel	8.50	3.25
241 A104 90c green	9.00	3.25
242 A86 1s pale blue	12.50	5.50
Nos. 223-242 (20)	61.50	23.30

Cent. of the independence of Guayaquil.
For overprints and surcharges see Nos. 263, 274-292, O136-O155, O179-O182, O185-O188.

Postal Tax Stamp of 1924 Overprinted

1925

259 PT6 20c bister brown	1.25	.50

Stamps of 1915-25 Overprinted in Black or Red Upright (1c, 3c, 5c) or Inverted (2c, 4c, 10c)

1926

260 A71 1c lt blue	4.50	4.00
261 A72 2c dk violet	4.50	4.00
262 A73 3c black (R)	4.50	4.00
263 A86 4c myrtle green	4.50	4.00
264 A74 5c rose	6.75	4.00
265 A75 10c yellow grn	6.75	4.00
Nos. 260-265 (6)	31.50	24.00

Quito-Esmeraldas railway opening.
Upright overprints on 2c, 4c, 10c and inverted overprints on 1c, 3c, 5c sell for more.

Postal Tax Stamps of 1920-24 Overprinted

1927

266 PT6 1c olive green	.20	.20
a. "POSTAI"	1.40	.85
b. Double overprint	2.00	.85
c. Inverted overprint	2.00	.85
267 PT6 2c deep green	.20	.20
a. "POSTAI"	1.40	.85
b. Double overprint	2.00	.85
268 PT6 20c bister brown	.70	.20
a. "POSTAI"	8.50	5.00
Nos. 266-268 (3)	1.10	.60

Quito Post Office — A109

1927, June

269 A109 5c orange	.25	.20
270 A109 10c dark green	.35	.20
271 A109 20c violet	.40	.20
Nos. 269-271 (3)	1.00	.60

Opening of new Quito P.O.
For overprint see No. O190.

Postal Tax Stamp of 1924 Overprinted in Dark Blue

POSTAL

1928

273 PT6 20c bister brown	.25	.20
a. Double overprint, one inverted	2.00	.70

See No. 339 for 10c with same overprint.

Nos. 235, 239-240 Overprinted in Red Brown and Surcharged in Dark Blue

1928, July 8

274 A86 10c on 30c violet	4.00	4.00
275 A86 50c on 70c gray	5.00	5.00
276 A86 1s on 80c org yel	6.00	6.00
Nos. 274-276 (3)	15.00	15.00

Quito-Cayambe railway opening.

Stamps of 1920 Surcharged

1928, Oct. 9

277 A86 1c on 1c yel grn	8.50	8.50
278 A86 1c on 2c car	.20	.20
279 A86 2c on 3c yel brn	1.25	1.25
a. Dbl. surch., one reading up	20.00	20.00
280 A86 2c on 4c myr grn	.85	.85
281 A86 2c on 5c lt blue	.35	.30
a. Dbl. surch., one reading up	20.00	20.00
282 A86 2c on 7c brown	42.50	42.50
283 A86 5c on 6c red org	.25	.20
a. "5 ctvos." omitted	25.00	25.00
284 A86 10c on 7c brown	.70	.70
285 A86 20c on 8c apple grn	.25	.20
a. Double surcharge		
286 A95 40c on 10c blue	2.25	2.25
287 A86 40c on 15c dk gray	.70	.70
288 A86 50c on 20c dk vio	8.00	8.00
289 A86 1s on 40c dk brown	2.50	2.50
290 A86 5s on 50c dk green	2.90	2.90
291 A86 10s on 60c dk blue	11.00	11.00

With Additional Surcharge in Red

292 A86 10c on 2c on 7c brn	.35	.35
a. Red surcharge double	20.00	20.00
Nos. 277-292 (16)	82.55	82.40

National Assembly of 1928.
Counterfeit overprints exist of #277-291.

A111

A112

Surcharged in Various Colors

1928, Oct. 31 *Perf. 14*

293 A111 5c on 20c gray lil (Bk)	.85	.70
294 A111 10c on 20c gray lil (R)	.85	.70
295 A111 20c on 1s grn (O)	.85	.70
296 A111 50c on 1s grn (Bl)	.95	.55
297 A111 1s on 1s grn (V)	1.25	.70
298 A111 5s on 2s red (G)	3.75	3.50
299 A111 10s on 2s red (Br)	4.75	4.75
a. Black surcharge	5.00	5.00
Nos. 293-299 (7)	13.25	11.60

Quito-Otavalo railway opening.
See Nos. 586-587.

Postal Tax Stamp of 1924 Overprinted in Red

1929 *Perf. 12*

302 PT6 2c deep green	.20	.20

There are two types of overprint on No. 302 differing slightly.

1929

Red Overprint

303 A112 1c dark blue	.20	.20
a. Overprint reading down	.20	.20

See Nos. 586-587.

Plowing — A113

Cultivating Cacao — A114

Cacao Pod — A115

Loading Sugar Cane — A119

Growing Tobacco — A116

Exportation of Fruits — A117

Landscape — A118

Scene in Quito A120

Scene in Quito A121

Olmedo — A122

Monument to Simón Bolívar — A125

Designs: 2s, Sucre. 5s, Bolivar.

1930, Aug. 1 *Perf. 12½*

304 A113 1c yellow & car	.20	.20
305 A114 2c yellow & grn	.20	.20
306 A115 5c dp grn & vio brn	.25	.20
307 A116 6c yellow & red	.30	.20
308 A117 10c orange & ol grn	.30	.20
309 A118 16c red & yel grn	.35	.25
310 A119 20c ultra & yel	.55	.20
311 A120 40c orange & sepia	.65	.20

312 A121 50c orange & sepia .65 .35
313 A122 1s dp green & blk 2.25 .40
314 A122 2s dk blue & blk 3.50 .65
315 A122 5s dk violet & blk 6.50 1.25
316 A125 10s car rose & blk 23.00 4.25
Nos. 304-316 (13) 38.70 8.55

Centenary of founding of republic.
For surcharges and overprints see Nos. 319-320, 331-338, RA25, RA33, RA40.

A126

A127

Red Overprint

1933 ***Perf. 15***
317 A126 10c olive brown .50 .20

Blue Overprint

318 A127 10c olive brown .30 .20
a. Inverted overprint 5.00 5.00

For overprint see No. 339.

Nos. 307, 309 Surcharged in Black

1933 ***Perf. 12½***
319 A116 5c on 6c yellow & red .25 .20
320 A118 10c on 16c red & yel grn .40 .20
a. Inverted overprint 4.00 4.00

Landscape
A128

Mt. Chimborazo
A129

1934-45 ***Perf. 12***
321 A128 5c violet .70 .35
322 A128 5c blue .70 .35
323 A128 5c dark brown .70 .35
323A A128 5c slate blk ('45) .70 .35
324 A128 10c rose .70 .35
325 A128 10c dark green .70 .35
326 A128 10c brown .70 .35
327 A128 10c orange .70 .35
328 A128 10c olive green .70 .35
329 A128 10c gray blk ('35) .70 .35
329A A128 10c red lilac ('44) .70 .35

Perf. 14

330 A129 1s carmine rose 1.00 .40
Nos. 321-330 (12) 8.70 4.25

Stamps of 1930 Surcharged or Ovptd. in various colors similar to:

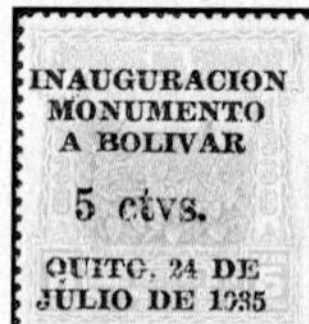

1935 ***Perf. 12½***
331 A116 5c on 6c (Bl) .35 .25
332 A116 10c on 6c (G) .50 .25
333 A119 20c (R) .70 .25
334 A120 40c (G) .95 .25
335 A121 50c (G) 1.10 .30
336 A122 1s on 5s (Gold) 2.50 .80
337 A122 2s on 5s (Gold) 3.50 1.25
338 A125 5s on 10s (Bl) 6.00 3.25
Nos. 331-338,C35-C38 (12) 42.60 23.60

Unveiling of a monument to Bolivar at Quito, July 24, 1935.

The 5-stamp Sociedad Colombista Panamericana series of 1935 and 5 airmail stamps of a similar design are not recognized by this Catalogue as having been issued primarily for postal purposes. Value for 10-value set, unused $3.25, used $6.50.

Telegraph Stamp Overprinted Diagonally in Red like No. 273

1935 ***Perf. 14½***
339 A126 10c olive brown .25 .25

Map of Galápagos Islands
A130

Galapagos Land Iguana
A131

Galápagos Tortoise — A132

Charles R. Darwin — A133

Columbus
A134

Island Scene
A135

1936 ***Perf. 14***
340 A130 2c black .75 .25
341 A131 5c olive grn 1.00 .25
342 A132 10c brown 2.00 .25
343 A133 20c dk violet 2.25 .30
344 A134 1s dk carmine 3.50 .55
345 A135 2s dark blue 5.50 .95
Nos. 340-345 (6) 15.00 2.55

Cent. of the visit of Charles Darwin to the Galápagos Islands, Sept. 17, 1835.
For overprints see Nos. O191-O195.

Tobacco Stamp Overprinted in Black

1936 ***Rouletted 7***
346 PT7 1c rose red .25 .25
a. Horiz. pair, imperf. vert.
b. Double surcharge

No. 346 is similar to type PT7 but does not include "CASA CORREOS."

Louis Godin, Charles M. de la Condamine and Pierre Bouguer
A136

Portraits: 5c, 20c, Antonio Ulloa, La Condamine and Jorge Juan.

1936 **Engr.** ***Perf. 12½***
347 A136 2c deep blue .30 .25
348 A136 5c dark green .30 .25
349 A136 10c deep orange .30 .25
350 A136 20c violet .45 .25
351 A136 50c dark red .70 .25
Nos. 347-351,C39-C42 (9) 3.80 2.15

Bicentenary of Geodesical Mission to Quito.

Independence Monument — A137

1936 ***Perf. 13½x14***
352 A137 2c green 1.40 .85
353 A137 5c dark violet 1.40 .85
354 A137 10c carmine rose 1.40 .85
355 A137 20c black 1.40 .85
356 A137 50c blue 2.10 1.40
357 A137 1s dark red 2.90 2.50
Nos. 352-357,C43-C50 (14) 32.60 29.30

1st Intl. Philatelic Exhibition at Quito.

Coat of Arms — A138

Overprint in Black or Red

1937 ***Perf. 12½***
359 A138 5c olive green 1.10 .25
360 A138 10c dark blue (R) 1.10 .20

For overprint see No. 562.

Andean Landscape
A139

Atahualpa, the Last Inca
A140

Hat Weavers — A141

Coast Landscape
A142

Gold Washing
A143

1937, Aug. 19 ***Perf. 11½***
361 A139 2c green .25 .25
362 A140 5c deep rose .25 .25
363 A141 10c blue .25 .25
364 A142 20c deep rose .60 .25
365 A143 1s olive green .80 .30
Nos. 361-365 (5) 2.15 1.30

For overprints see Nos. O196-O200.

"Liberty" Carrying Flag of Ecuador — A144

Engraved and Lithographed

1938, Feb. 22 ***Perf. 12***

Center Multicolored

366 A144 2c blue .20 .20
367 A144 5c violet .25 .20
368 A144 10c black .35 .20
369 A144 20c brown .45 .20
370 A144 50c black .70 .20
371 A144 1s olive blk 1.10 .25
372 A144 2s dk brn 2.10 .35
Nos. 366-372,C57-C63 (14) 10.80 3.50

US Constitution, 150th anniversary.
For overprints and surcharges see Nos. 413-415, 444-446, RA46, RA52.

A145

A146

A147

A148

Designs: 10c, Winged figure holding globe. 50c, Cactus, winged wheel. 1s, "Communications." 2s, "Construction."

Perf. 13, 13x13½
1938, Oct. 30 **Engr.**
373 A145 10c bright ultra .20 .20
374 A146 50c deep red violet .20 .20
375 A147 1s copper red .35 .20
376 A148 2s dark green .55 .20
Nos. 373-376 (4) 1.30 .80

Progress of Ecuador Exhibition.
For overprints see Nos. C105-C113.

Parade of Athletes — A149

Runner — A150

Basketball — A151

Wrestlers
A152

Diver
A153

1939, Mar. ***Perf. 12***
377 A149 5c carmine rose 1.90 .35
378 A150 10c deep blue 2.25 .45
379 A151 50c gray olive 3.25 .60

380 A152 1s dull violet 5.00 .60
381 A153 2s dull olive green 6.75 .75
Nos. 377-381,C65-C69 (10) 36.00 4.55

First Bolivarian Games (1938), Bogota.

Dolores Mission
A154

Trylon and Perisphere
A155

1939, June 16 ***Perf. 12½x13***
382 A154 2c blue green .25 .25
383 A154 5c rose red .25 .25
384 A154 10c ultra .25 .25
385 A154 50c yellow brown .50 .25
386 A154 1s black .80 .25
387 A154 2s purple 1.10 .30
Nos. 382-387,C73-C79 (13) 5.25 2.95

Golden Gate International Exposition.
For surcharges see Nos. 429, 436.

1939, June 30
388 A155 2c lt olive green .25 .25
389 A155 5c red orange .25 .25
390 A155 10c ultra .25 .25
391 A155 50c slate gray .40 .25
392 A155 1s rose carmine .70 .25
393 A155 2s black brown .85 .30
Nos. 388-393,C80-C86 (13) 4.75 2.95

New York World's Fair.
For surcharge see No. 437.

Flags of the 21 American Republics — A156

1940 ***Perf. 12***
394 A156 5c dp rose & blk .20 .20
395 A156 10c dk blue & blk .20 .20
396 A156 50c Prus green & blk .30 .20
397 A156 1s dp violet & blk .45 .25
Nos. 394-397,C87-C90 (8) 3.10 2.10

Pan American Union, 50th anniversary.

Francisco J. E. Santa Cruz y Espejo — A157

1941, Dec. 15
398 A157 30c blue .35 .20
399 A157 1s red orange .60 .25
Nos. 398-399,C91-C92 (4) 5.35 1.10

Exposition of Journalism held under the auspices of the Natl. Newspaper Men's Union.

Francisco de Orellana
A158

Gonzalo Pizarro
A159

View of Guayaquil
A160

View of Quito — A161

1942, Jan. 30
400 A158 10c sepia .35 .25
401 A159 40c deep rose .95 .25
402 A160 1s violet 1.40 .25
403 A161 2s dark blue 1.90 .35
Nos. 400-403,C93-C96 (8) 9.35 2.20

400th anniv. of the discovery and exploration of the Amazon River by Orellana.

Remigio Crespo Toral
A162

Alfredo Baquerizo Moreno
A163

1942 ***Perf. 13½***
404 A162 10c green .20 .20
405 A162 50c brown .35 .20
Nos. 404-405,C97 (3) .90 .60

1942
406 A163 10c green .25 .25

Mt. Chimborazo
A164

1942-47 ***Perf. 12***
407 A164 30c red brown .30 .25
407A A164 30c lt blue ('43) .30 .25
407B A164 30c red orange ('44) .30 .25
407C A164 30c green ('47) .30 .25
Nos. 407-407C (4) 1.20 1.00

View of Guayaquil
A165

1942-44
408 A165 20c red .35 .20
408A A165 20c deep blue ('44) .35 .20

Gen. Eloy Alfaro — A166

Devil's Nose — A167

President Alfaro (1842-1912): 30c, Military College. 1s, Montecristi, Alfaro's birthplace.

1942
409 A166 10c dk rose & blk .20 .20
410 A167 20c ol blk & red brn .20 .20
411 A167 30c ol gray & grn .25 .20
412 A167 1s slate & salmon .60 .25
Nos. 409-412,C98-C101 (8) 5.60 3.10

Nos. 370-372 Overprinted in Red Brown

1943, Apr. 15 ***Perf. 11½***
413 A144 50c multicolored .35 .35
414 A144 1s multicolored .70 .70
415 A144 2s multicolored 1.10 1.10
Nos. 413-415,C102-C104 (6) 6.10 5.00

Visit of US Vice-Pres. Henry A. Wallace.

"30 Centavos" — A170

Black Surcharge

1943 ***Perf. 12½***
416 A170 30c on 50c red brn .35 .25
 a. Without bars .35 .25

Map Showing US and Ecuador — A171

1943, Oct. 9 ***Perf. 12***
417 A171 10c dull violet .25 .25
418 A171 20c red brown .25 .25
419 A171 30c orange .25 .25
420 A171 50c olive green .30 .30
421 A171 1s deep violet .35 .35
422 A171 10s olive bister 3.50 3.25
Nos. 417-422,C114-C118 (11) 12.55 8.65

Good will tour of Pres. Arroyo del Rio in 1942.

1944, Feb. 7
423 A171 10c yellow green .25 .25
424 A171 20c rose pink .25 .25
425 A171 30c dark gray brown .25 .25
426 A171 50c deep red lilac .25 .25
427 A171 1s olive gray .35 .35
428 A171 10s red orange 4.00 3.25
Nos. 423-428,C119-C123 (11) 9.50 7.20

For surcharges see Nos. B1-B6.

No. 385 Surcharged in Black

1944 **Unwmk.** ***Perf. 12½x13***
429 A154 30c on 50c yel brn .25 .20

Archbishop Federico González Suárez, Birth Cent. — A172

1944 ***Perf. 12***
430 A172 10c deep blue .20 .20
431 A172 20c green .20 .20
432 A172 30c dk violet brn .25 .20
433 A172 1s dull violet .45 .25
Nos. 430-433,C124-C127 (8) 4.60 3.10

Air Post Stamps Nos. C76 and C83 Surcharged in Black

1944 ***Perf. 12½x13***
434 AP15 30c on 50c rose vio .20 .20
435 AP16 30c on 50c sl grn .20 .20

Nos. 382 and 388 Surcharged in Black

1944-45
436 A154 5c on 2c bl grn .25 .20
 a. Double surcharge 4.00
437 A155 5c on 2c lt ol grn ('45) .25 .20

Government Palace, Quito — A173

1944 **Engr.** ***Perf. 11***
438 A173 10c dark green .20 .20
439 A173 30c blue .20 .20

For surcharges see Nos. 452, RAC1-RAC2.

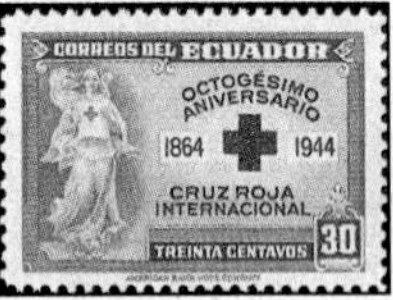

Symbol of the Red Cross
A174

1945, Apr. 25 ***Perf. 12***
Cross in Rose
440 A174 30c bister brown .50 .25
441 A174 1s red brown .60 .35
442 A174 5s turq green 1.10 .90
443 A174 10s scarlet 3.00 2.50
Nos. 440-443,C131-C134 (8) 12.10 9.10

International Red Cross, 80th anniversary.

Nos. 370 to 372 Overprinted in Dark Blue and Gold

1945, Oct. 2 ***Perf. 11½***
Center Multicolored
444 A144 50c black .30 .25
 a. Double overprint
445 A144 1s olive black .45 .45
446 A144 2s dark brown .95 .85
Nos. 444-446,C139-C141 (6) 3.30 3.05

Visit of Pres. Juan Antonio Rios of Chile.

General Antonio José de Sucre, 150th Birth Anniv. — A175

1945, Nov. 14 **Engr.** ***Perf. 12***

447 A175 10c olive .25 .25
448 A175 20c red brown .25 .20
449 A175 40c olive gray .25 .20
450 A175 1s dark green .50 .25
451 A175 2s sepia .75 .50
Nos. 447-451,C142-C146 (10) 4.95 4.30

No. 438 Surcharged in Blue

1945 ***Perf. 11***

452 A173 20c on 10c dark green .20 .20
a. Fancy bar omitted

Catalogue values for unused stamps in this section, from this point to the end of the section, are for Never Hinged items.

Map of Pan-American Highway and Arms of Loja — A176

1946, Apr. 22 **Engr.** ***Perf. 12***

453 A176 20c red brown .25 .25
454 A176 30c bright green .25 .25
455 A176 1s bright ultra .25 .25
456 A176 5s deep red lilac .70 .70
457 A176 10s scarlet 1.60 1.10
Nos. 453-457,C147-C151 (10) 6.05 4.10

Torch of Democracy — A177

Popular Suffrage A178

Flag of Ecuador — A179

Pres. José M. Velasco Ibarra — A180

1946, Aug. 9 **Unwmk.** ***Perf. 12½***

458 A177 5c dark blue .20 .20
459 A178 10c Prus green .20 .20
460 A179 20c carmine .25 .20
461 A180 30c chocolate .45 .20
Nos. 458-461,C152-C155 (8) 3.00 1.85

Revolution of May 28, 1944, 2nd anniv.

"30 Ctvs." — A181

Black Surcharge

1946

462 A181 30c on 50c red brown .35 .20

For overprint see No. 484.

Nos. CO13-CO14 With Additional Overprint in Black

1946 ***Perf. 11½***

463 AP7 10c chestnut .20 .20
464 AP7 20c olive black .20 .20

Instructor and Student — A182

1946, Sept. 16 ***Perf. 12½***

465 A182 10c deep blue .20 .20
466 A182 20c chocolate .20 .20
467 A182 30c dark green .20 .20
468 A182 50c bluish blk .25 .25
469 A182 1s dark red .35 .30
470 A182 10s dark violet 2.50 .65
Nos. 465-470,C156-C160 (11) 8.20 3.40

Campaign for adult education.

Mariana de Jesus Paredes y Flores — A183

Urn — A184

1946, Nov. 28

471 A183 10c black brown .25 .25
472 A183 20c green .25 .25
473 A183 30c purple .25 .25
474 A184 1s rose brown .35 .25
Nos. 471-474,C161-C164 (8) 3.45 2.65

300th anniv. of the death of the Blessed Mariana de Jesus Paredes y Flores.

Pres. Vicente Rocafuerte A185

Jesuits' Church Quito A186

45c, 50c, 80c, F.J.E. de Santa Cruz y Espejo.

1947, Nov. 27 ***Perf. 12***

475 A185 5c redsh brown .20 .20
476 A185 10c sepia .20 .20
477 A185 15c gray black .20 .20
478 A186 20c redsh brown .20 .20
479 A186 30c red violet .25 .20
480 A186 40c brt ultra .30 .20
481 A185 45c dk slate grn .35 .20
482 A185 50c olive black .35 .20
483 A185 80c orange red .55 .20
Nos. 475-483,C165-C171 (16) 4.60 3.20

For overprints and surcharges see Nos. 489, 496, 525-527.

Type of 1946, Overprinted "POSTAL" in Black but Without Additional Surcharge

1948 **Engr.**

484 A181 10c orange .45 .25

Andrés Bello A188

Flagship of Columbus A189

1948, Apr. 21 ***Perf. 13***

485 A188 20c lt blue .25 .25
486 A188 30c rose carmine .25 .25
487 A188 40c blue green .25 .25
488 A188 1s black brown .35 .25
Nos. 485-488,C172-C174 (7) 1.95 1.65

83rd anniversary of the death of Andrés Bello (1781-1865), educator.

No. 480 Overprinted in Black

1948, May 24 ***Perf. 12***

489 A186 40c bright ultra .30 .30

See No. C175.

1948 ***Perf. 14***

490 A189 10c dark blue green .20 .20
491 A189 20c brown .20 .20
492 A189 30c dark purple .40 .20
493 A189 50c deep claret .50 .20
494 A189 1s ultra 1.10 .40
495 A189 5s carmine 2.00 .45
Nos. 490-495,C176-C180 (11) 8.65 4.00

Issued to publicize the proposed Columbus Memorial Lighthouse near Ciudad Trujillo, Dominican Republic.

No. 483 Overprinted in Blue

1948 ***Perf. 12***

"MANANA" Reading Down

496 A185 80c orange red .25 .25

Issued to publicize the National Fair of Today and Tomorrow, 1948. See No. C181.

Telegrafo I in Flight — A190

Book and Pen — A191

1948 **Engr.** ***Perf. 12½***

497 A190 30c red orange .25 .25
498 A190 40c rose lilac .25 .25
499 A190 60c violet blue .25 .25
500 A190 1s brown red .25 .25
501 A190 3s brown .80 .35
502 A190 5s gray black .90 .35
Nos. 497-502,C182-C187 (12) 5.50 3.45

25th anniversary (in 1945) of the first postal flight in Ecuador.

1948, Oct. 12 **Unwmk.** ***Perf. 14***

503 A191 10c deep claret .20 .20
504 A191 20c brown .20 .20
505 A191 30c dark green .25 .20
506 A191 50c red .25 .20
507 A191 1s purple .30 .25
508 A191 10s dull blue 3.00 .60
Nos. 503-508,C188-C192 (11) 8.40 3.75

Campaign for adult education.

A192

Franklin D. Roosevelt and Two of "Four Freedoms" — A193

1948, Oct. 24 ***Perf. 12½***

509 A192 10c rose brn & gray .25 .25
510 A192 20c brn ol & bl .25 .25
511 A193 30c ol bis & car rose .25 .25
512 A193 40c red vio & sep .30 .25
513 A193 1s org brn & car .35 .30
Nos. 509-513,C193-C197 (10) 3.25 2.30

Maldonado and Map — A194

Riobamba Aqueduct A195

Maldonado on Bank of Riobamba A196

Pedro V. Maldonado A197

1948, Nov. 17 **Engr.** **Unwmk.**

514 A194 5c gray blk & ver .25 .20
515 A195 10c car & gray blk .30 .20
516 A196 30c bis brn & ultra .35 .20
517 A195 40c sage grn & vio .45 .20
518 A194 50c grn & car .50 .25
519 A197 1s brn & slate bl .65 .30
Nos. 514-519,C198-C201 (10) 4.10 2.15

Bicentenary of the death of Pedro Vicente Maldonado, geographer.

For overprints and surcharges see Nos. 537-540.

A198

Miguel de Cervantes Saavedra
A199

1949, May 2 *Perf. 12½x12*

520 A198 30c dk car rose & dp ultra	.40	.20
521 A199 60c bis & brn vio	.60	.30
522 A198 1s grn & rose car	1.00	.20
523 A199 2s gray blk & red brn	2.00	.30
524 A198 5s choc & aqua	3.50	1.00
Nos. 520-524,C202-C206 (10)	13.95	4.90

400th anniv. of the birth of Miguel de Cervantes Saavedra, novelist, playwright and poet.

No. 480 Surcharged in Carmine

1949, June 15 *Perf. 12*

525 A186 10c on 40c brt ultra	.25	.20
526 A186 20c on 40c brt ultra	.35	.20
a. Double surcharge		
527 A186 30c on 40c brt ultra	.35	.20
Nos. 525-527,C207-C209 (6)	1.65	1.20

2nd Natl. Eucharistic Cong., Quito, 6/49. No. 526 exists se-tenant with No. 527.

Monument on Equator — A200

1949, June **Engr.** *Perf. 12½x12*

528 A200 10c deep plum .25 .20

For overprint see No. 536.

No. 542 Surcharged in Black and Carmine

1949 *Perf. 12x12½*

529 A203 10c on 50c green	.25	.25
530 A203 20c on 50c green	.25	.25
531 A203 30c on 50c green	.30	.25
Nos. 529-531,C210-C213 (7)	2.95	1.85

Universal Postal Union, 75th anniversary.

Consular Service Stamps Surcharged in Black

Arms of Ecuador — R1

1949 *Perf. 12*

532 R1 20c on 25c red brown	.20	.20
533 R1 30c on 50c gray	.25	.20

For other overprints and surcharges on type R1 see Nos. 544-549, 566-570, C245, C249-C252, RA60-RA62, RA72.

Nos. RA49A and RA55 Overprinted in Black

a

1950 **Unwmk.** *Perf. 12*

534 PT18 5c green	.20	.20
535 PT21 5c blue	.20	.20

Overprint 15mm on No. 534.

Nos. 528 and 517 to 519 Overprinted or Surcharged in Black or Carmine

1950, Feb. 10 *Perf. 12½x12*

536 A200 10c dp plum .25 .25

Perf. 12½

537 A195 20c on 40c sage grn & vio	.45	.45
538 A195 30c on 40c sage grn & vio	.50	.50
539 A194 50c grn & car	.75	.75
540 A197 1s brn & slate bl (C)	1.00	1.00

No. C220 Overprinted Type "a" in Carmine

Perf. 11

Overprint 15mm long

541 A173 10s violet	2.50	1.25
Nos. 536-541,C216-C220 (11)	8.70	6.25

Nos. 536-541 publicize adult education.

San Pablo Lake — A203

Perf. 12x12½

1950, May **Engr.** **Unwmk.**

542 A203 50c green .25 .20

For surcharges see Nos. 529-531.

Consular Service Stamp Surcharged "CORREOS" and New Value Vertically in Black

1950 *Perf. 12*

544 R1 30c on 50c gray .30 .25

Consular Service Stamps Overprinted or Surcharged in Black

b

c

d

e

f

g

1951 **Unwmk.** *Perf. 12*

545 R1 (b) 5c on 10c car rose	.25	.25
546 R1 (c) 10c car rose	.25	.25
547 R1 (d) 10c car rose	.25	.25
548 R1 (e) 20c on 25c red brn	.25	.25
549 R1 (e) 30c on 50c gray	.25	.25
550 R2 (f) 40c on 25c blue	.30	.25
551 R2 (g) 50c on 25c blue	.35	.25
Nos. 545-551 (7)	1.90	1.75

See #552-554, C233-C234, C246-C248, RA67.

Consular Service Stamps Surcharged in Black

1951

552 R2 20c on 25c blue	.35	.20
553 R2 30c on 25c blue	.35	.20

Adult education. See Nos. C225-C226.

Consular Service Stamp Surcharged in Black

1951

554 R2 $0.30 on 50c car rose .25 .25

Reliquary of St. Mariana and Vatican — A204

Perf. 12½x12

1952, Feb. **Engr.** **Unwmk.**

555 A204 10c emer & red brn	.35	.25
556 A204 20c dp bl & pur	.35	.25
557 A204 30c car & bl grn	.35	.25
Nos. 555-557,C227-C230 (7)	3.10	1.55

Issued to publicize the canonization of Mariana de Jesus Paredes y Flores.

Presidents Galo Plaza and Harry Truman — A205

2s, Pres. Plaza addressing US Congress.

1952, Mar. 26 *Perf. 12*

558 A205 1s rose car & gray blk	.30	.25
559 A205 2s dl bl & sepia	.70	.40
Nos. 558-559,C231-C232 (4)	2.30	1.80

1951 visit of Pres. Galo Plaza y Lasso to the US.

R3

Fiscal Stamps Surcharged or Overprinted Type "c" Horizontally in Carmine or Black

1952 **Unwmk.** **Engr.** *Perf. 12*

560 R3 20c on 30c dp bl (C)	.30	.25
561 R3 30c deep blue	.25	.20

Diagonal Overprint

562 A138 50c purple	.25	.20
Nos. 560-562 (3)	.80	.65

For overprints and surcharge see Nos. RA68-RA69, RA71.

Pres. José M. Urvina, Slave and "Liberty" A206

Hyphen-hole Perf. 7x6½

1952 **Litho.**

563 A206 20c red & green	.20	.20
564 A206 30c red & vio bl	.25	.20
565 A206 50c blue & car	.40	.20
Nos. 563-565,C236-C239 (7)	6.45	2.05

Centenary of abolition of slavery in Ecuador. Counterfeits exist.

Consular Service Stamps Surcharged in Black — f

1952-53 **Unwmk.** *Perf. 12*

566 R1 10c on 20s blue ('53)	.25	.20
567 R1 20c on 10s gray ('53)	.25	.20
568 R1 20c on 20s blue	.25	.20

569 R1 30c on 10s gray ('53) .25 .20
570 R1 30c on 20s blue .25 .20
Nos. 566-570 (5) 1.25 1.00

Similar surcharges of 60c and 90c on the 20s blue are said to be bogus.

Teacher and Students — A207

New Citizens Voting — A208

Designs: 10c, Instructor with student. 30c, Teaching the alphabet.

1953, Apr. 13 **Engr.**
571 A207 5c lt bl .20 .20
572 A207 10c dk car rose .25 .20
573 A208 20c brt brn org .30 .20
574 A208 30c dp red lil .40 .20
Nos. 571-574,C240-C241 (6) 2.80 1.20

1952 adult education campaign.

A209

Cuicocha Lagoon — A210

Black Surcharge

1953
575 A209 40c on 50c purple .30 .25

1953 **Engr.** ***Perf. 13x12½***

Designs: 10c, Equatorial Line monument. 20c, Quininde countryside. 30c, Tomebamba river. 40c, La Chilintosa rock. 50c, Iliniza Mountains.

Frames in Black
576 A210 5c brt bl .20 .20
577 A210 10c brt grn .20 .20
578 A210 20c purple .20 .20
579 A210 30c brown .20 .20
580 A210 40c orange .20 .20
581 A210 50c dp car .30 .20
Nos. 576-581 (6) 1.30 1.20

A211

A212

Carlos Maria Cardinal de la Torre and arches.

1954, Jan. **Photo.** ***Perf. 8½***
582 A211 30c blk & ver .20 .20
583 A211 50c blk & rose lil .20 .20
Nos. 582-583,C253-C255 (5) 1.50 1.00

1st anniv. of the elevation of Archbishop de la Torre to Cardinal.

1954, Apr. 22
584 A212 30c blk & gray .35 .35
585 A212 50c blk brn & yel .35 .35
Nos. 584-585,C256-C260 (7) 2.25 2.00

Queen Isabella I (1451-1504) of Spain, 500th birth anniv.

Type of 1929; "POSTAL" Overprint Larger, No Letterspacing

1954-55 **Unwmk.** ***Perf. 12***
586 A112 5c ol grn ('55) .30 .20
587 A112 10c orange .30 .20

The normal overprint on Nos. 586-587 reads up. It also exists reading down.

Indian Messenger A213

Products of Ecuador A214

1954, Aug. 2 **Litho.** ***Perf. 11***
588 A213 30c dk brn .30 .20

Day of the Postal Employee. See No. C263.

1954, Sept. 24 **Photo.**
589 A214 10c orange .20 .20
590 A214 20c vermilion .20 .20
591 A214 30c rose pink .20 .20
592 A214 40c dk gray grn .30 .20
593 A214 50c yel brn .40 .20
Nos. 589-593 (5) 1.30 1.00

José Abel Castillo — A215

Babahoyo River Los Rios — A216

Perf. 11½x11
1955, Oct. 19 **Engr.** **Unwmk.**
594 A215 30c olive bister .20 .20
595 A215 50c dk gray .20 .20
Nos. 594-595,C282-C286 (7) 4.05 1.75

30th anniv. of the 1st flight of the "Telegrafo I" and to honor Castillo, aviation pioneer.

1955-56 **Photo.** ***Perf. 13***

Designs: 5c, Palms, Esmeraldas. 10c, Fishermen, Manabi. 30c, Guayaquil, Guayas. 50c, Pital River, El Oro. 70c, Cactus, Galapagos Isls. 80c, Orchids, Napo-Pastaza. 1s, Aguacate Mission, Zamora-Chinchipe. 2s, Jibaro Indian, Morona-Santiago.

596 A216 5c yel grn ('56) .50 .25
597 A216 10c blue ('56) .50 .25
598 A216 20c brown .50 .25
599 A216 30c dk gray .50 .25
600 A216 50c bl grn .50 .25
601 A216 70c ol ('56) .50 .25
602 A216 80c dp vio ('56) 1.25 .25
603 A216 1s org ('56) .65 .25
604 A216 2s rose red ('56) 1.25 .25
Nos. 596-604 (9) 6.15 2.25

See #620-630, 670, C288-C297, C310-C311.

Brother Juan Adam Schwarz, S. J. — A217

1956, Aug. 27 **Engr.** ***Perf. 13½***
605 A217 5c yel grn .20 .20
606 A217 10c org red .20 .20
607 A217 20c lt vio .20 .20
608 A217 30c dk grn .20 .20
609 A217 40c blue .20 .20
610 A217 50c dp ultra .20 .20
611 A217 70c orange .20 .20
Nos. 605-611,C302-C305 (11) 2.40 2.20

Bicentennial of printing in Ecuador and honoring Brother Juan Adam Schwarz, S.J.

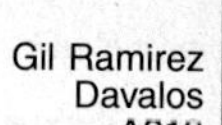

Andres Hurtado de Mendoza — A218

Gil Ramirez Davalos A219

Designs: 20c, Brother Vincent Solano.

1957, Apr. 7 **Unwmk.** ***Perf. 12***
612 A218 5c dk bl, *pink* .20 .20
613 A219 10c grn, *grnsh* .20 .20
614 A218 20c choc, *buff* .20 .20
a. Souvenir sheet of 4, imperf. .40 .40
Nos. 612-614,C312-C314 (6) 1.35 1.20

4th cent. of the founding of Cuenca.

#614a contains 2 5c gray & 2 20c brown red stamps in designs similar to #612, 614. It was printed on white ungummed paper.

Francisco Marcos, Gen. Pedro Alcantara Herran and Santos Michelena A220

1957, Sept. 5 **Engr.** ***Perf. 14½x14***
615 A220 40c yellow .20 .20
616 A220 50c ultra .20 .20
617 A220 2s dk red .50 .20
Nos. 615-617 (3) .90 .60

7th Postal Congress of the Americas and Spain (in 1955).

Souvenir Sheets

Various Railroad Scenes — A221

1957 **Litho.** ***Perf. 10½x11***
618 A221 20c Sheet of 5 6.00 2.75
619 A221 30c Sheet of 5 6.00 2.75

Issued to commemorate the opening of the Quito-Ibarra-San Lorenzo railroad.

Nos. 618-619 contain 2 orange yellow, 1 ultramarine and 2 carmine stamps, each in a different design.

Scenic Type of 1955-56.

Designs as before, except: 40c, as 70c. 90c, as 80c. No. 629, San Pablo, Imbabura.

1957-58 **Photo.** ***Perf. 13***
620 A216 5c light blue .50 .20
621 A216 10c brown .50 .20
622 A216 20c crimson rose .50 .20
623 A216 20c yel green .50 .20
624 A216 30c rose red .50 .20
625 A216 40c chalky blue .70 .20
626 A216 50c lt vio .50 .20
627 A216 90c brt ultra .65 .20
628 A216 1s dark brown .50 .20
629 A216 1s gray blk ('58) .50 .20
630 A216 2s brown .80 .20
Nos. 620-630 (11) 6.15 2.20

Blue and Yellow Macaw — A222

Birds: 20c, Red-breasted toucan. 30c, Condor. 40c, Black-tailed and sword-tailed hummingbirds.

Perf. 13½x13
1958, Jan. 7 **Litho.** **Unwmk.**
Birds in Natural Colors
634 A222 10c red brn .70 .20
635 A222 20c dk gray .70 .20
636 A222 30c brt yel grn 1.75 .20
637 A222 40c red org 1.75 .20
Nos. 634-637 (4) 4.90 .80

Carlos Sanz de Santamaria A223

Richard M. Nixon and Flags — A224

#640, Dr. Ramon Villeda Morales, flags. 2.20s, José Carlos de Macedo Soares, horizontal flags.

1958 ***Perf. 12***
Flags in Red, Blue, Yellow & Green
638 A223 1.80s dl vio .40 .20
639 A224 2s dk grn .40 .20
640 A224 2s dk brn .40 .20
641 A223 2.20s blk brn .40 .20
Nos. 638-641 (4) 1.60 .80

Visits: Colombia's Foreign Minister Dr. Carlos Sanz de Santamaria; US Vice Pres. Nixon, May 9-10; Pres. Ramon Villeda Morales of Honduras; Brazil's Foreign Minister José Carlos de Macedo Soares. See Nos. C419-C421. For overprints and surcharges see Nos. 775-775C, C419-C421, C460.

Locomotive of 1908 A225

Garcia Moreno, Jose Caamano, L. Plaza and Eloy Alfaro — A226

Design: 50c, Diesel locomotive.

Perf. 13½x14, 14
1958, Aug. 9 **Photo.** **Unwmk.**
642 A225 30c brn blk .20 .20
643 A225 50c dk car .30 .20
644 A226 5s dk brn 1.10 .70
Nos. 642-644 (3) 1.60 1.10

Guayaquil-Quito railroad, 50th anniv.

Cardinal — A227

Birds: 30c, Andean cock-of-the-rock. 50c, Glossy cowbird. 60c, Red-fronted Amazon.

1958 Litho. *Perf. 13½x13*
Birds in Natural Colors

645 A227 20c bluish grn, blk & red .80 .20
646 A227 30c buff, blk & brt bl .85 .20
647 A227 50c org, blk & grn 1.25 .35
648 A227 60c pale rose, blk & bluish grn 2.10 .35
Nos. 645-648 (4) 5.00 1.10

UNESCO Building and Eiffel Tower, Paris — A228

1958, Nov. 3 Engr. *Perf. 12½*

649 A228 80c brown .35 .20

UNESCO Headquarters in Paris opening, Nov. 3.

Globe and Satellites — A229

Virgin of Quito — A230

1958, Dec. 20 Photo. *Perf. 14x13½*

650 A229 1.80s dark blue .85 .35

International Geophysical Year, 1957-58.
For overprints see Nos. 718, C422.

1959, Sept. 8 Unwmk. *Perf. 13*

651 A230 5c ol grn .25 .20
652 A230 10c yel brn .25 .20
653 A230 20c purple .25 .20
654 A230 30c ultra .25 .20
655 A230 80c dk car rose .25 .20
Nos. 651-655 (5) 1.25 1.00

See No. C290. For surcharges and overprint see Nos. 695-699.

Uprooted Oak Emblem — A231

1960, Apr. 7 Litho. *Perf. 14x13*

656 A231 80c rose car & grn .25 .20

World Refugee Year, 7/1/59-6/30/60.
For overprints see Nos. 709, 719, O205.

Great Anteater and Arms — A232

Animals: 40c, Tapir and map. 80c, Spectacled bear and arms. 1s, Puma and map.

1960, May 14 Photo. *Perf. 13*

657 A232 20c org, grn & blk .35 .20
658 A232 40c yel grn, bl grn & brn .55 .20
659 A232 80c bl, blk & red brn .95 .20
660 A232 1s Prus bl, plum & ocher 1.60 .30
Nos. 657-660 (4) 3.45 .90

Founding of the city of Baeza, 4th cent.
See Nos. 676-679.

Hotel Quito A233

#662, Dormitory, Catholic University. #663, Dormitory, Central University. #664, Airport, Quito. #665, Overpass on Highway to Quito. #666, Security Bank. #667, Ministry of Foreign Affairs. #668, Government Palace. #669, Legislative Palace.

Perf. 11x11½
1960, Aug. 8 Engr. Unwmk.

661 A233 1s dk pur & redsh brn .20 .20
662 A233 1s dk bl & brn .20 .20
663 A233 1s blk & red .20 .20
664 A233 1s dk bl & ultra .20 .20
665 A233 1s dk pur & dk car rose .20 .20
666 A233 1s blk & ol bis .20 .20
667 A233 1s dk pur & turq .20 .20
668 A233 1s dk bl & grn .20 .20
669 A233 1s blk & vio .20 .20
Nos. 661-669 (9) 1.80 1.80

11th Inter-American Conference, Quito.
For surcharges see Nos. 700-708.

Type of Regular Issue, 1955-56
Souvenir Sheet

Design: Orchids, Napo-Pastaza.

1960 Photo. *Perf. 13*
Yellow Paper

670 Sheet of 2 2.25 2.25
a. A216 80c deep violet .85 .40
b. A216 90c deep green .85 .40

25th anniv. of Asociacion Filatelica Ecuatoriana. Marginal inscription in silver. Exists with silver inscription omitted.

"Freedom of Expression" — A234

Manabi Bridge A235

10c, "Freedom to vote." 20c, "Freedom to work." 30c, Coins, "Monetary stability."

1960, Aug. 29 Litho. *Perf. 13*

671 A234 5c dk bl .25 .20
672 A234 10c lt vio .25 .20
673 A234 20c orange .25 .20
674 A234 30c bluish grn .25 .20
675 A235 40c brn & bluish grn .25 .20
Nos. 671-675 (5) 1.25 1.00

Achievements of President Camilo Ponce Enriquez. See Nos. C370-C374.

Animal Type of 1960.

Animals: 10c, Collared peccary. 20c, Kinkajou. 80c, Jaguar. 1s, Mountain coati.

Unwmk.
1961, July 13 Photo. *Perf. 13*

676 A232 10c grn, rose red & blk .40 .20
677 A232 20c vio, grnsh bl & brn .70 .20
678 A232 80c red org, dl yel & blk 1.25 .30
679 A232 1s brn, brt grn & org 1.90 .40
Nos. 676-679 (4) 4.25 1.10

Founding of the city of Tena, 400th anniv.

Graphium Pausianus A236

Butterflies: 30c, Papilio torquatus leptalea. 50c, Graphium molops molops. 80c, Battus lycidas.

1961, July 13 Litho. *Perf. 13½*

680 A236 20c pink & multi .35 .20
681 A236 30c lt ultra & multi .70 .20
682 A236 50c org & multi .70 .20
683 A236 80c bl grn & multi 1.40 .20
Nos. 680-683 (4) 3.15 .80

See Nos. 711-713.

Galapagos Islands Nos. L1-L3 Overprinted in Black or Red

1961, Oct. 31 Photo. *Perf. 12*

684 A1 20c dk brn .25 .20
685 A2 50c violet .25 .20
686 A1 1s dk ol grn (R) .55 .30
Nos. 684-686,C389-C391 (6) 2.75 1.75

Establishment of maritime biological stations on Galapagos Islands by UNESCO. Overprint arranged differently on 20c, 1s.
See Nos. C389-C391.

Daniel Enrique Proano School A237

Designs: 60c, Loja-Zamora highway, vert. 80c, Aguirre Abad College, Guayaquil. 1s, Army quarters, Quito.

Perf. 11x11½, 11½x11
1962, Jan. 10 Engr. Unwmk.

687 A237 50c dl bl & blk .35 .20
688 A237 60c ol grn & blk .35 .20
689 A237 80c org red & blk .35 .20
690 A237 1s rose lake & blk .35 .20
Nos. 687-690 (4) 1.40 .80

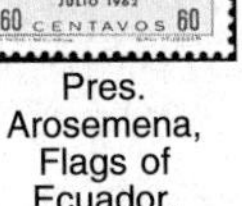

Pres. Arosemena, Flags of Ecuador, US — A238

Protection for The Family — A239

Designs (Arosemena and): 10c, Flags of Ecuador. 20c, Flags of Ecuador and Panama.

1963, July 1 Litho. *Perf. 14*

691 A238 10c buff & multi .20 .20
692 A238 20c multi .25 .20
693 A238 60c multi .25 .20
Nos. 691-693,C409-C411 (6) 2.10 1.35

Issued to commemorate Pres. Carlos J. Arosemena's friendship trip, July 1962.
Imperfs exist. Value $9.

1963, July 9 Unwmk. *Perf. 14*

694 A239 10c ultra, red, gray & blk .25 .20

Social Insurance, 25th anniv. See #C413.

No. 655 Overprinted or Surcharged in Black or Blue

1963 Photo. *Perf. 13*

695 A230 10c on 80c dk car rose .25 .20
696 A230 20c on 80c dk car rose .25 .20
697 A230 50c on 80c dk car rose .25 .20
698 A230 60c on 80c dk car rose (Bl) .25 .20
699 A230 80c dk car rose .25 .20
Nos. 695-699 (5) 1.25 1.00

Nos. 661-669 Surcharged

1964, Apr. 20 Engr. *Perf. 11x11½*

700 A233 10c on 1s dk pur & redsh brn .25 .20
701 A233 10c on 1s dk pur & turq .25 .20
702 A233 20c on 1s dk bl & brn .25 .20
703 A233 20c on 1s dk bl & grn .25 .20
704 A233 30c on 1s dk pur & dk car rose .25 .20
705 A233 40c on 1s blk & ol bis .25 .20
706 A233 60c on 1s blk & red .25 .20
707 A233 80c on 1s dk bl & ultra .25 .20
708 A233 80c on 1s blk & vio .25 .20
Nos. 700-708 (9) 2.25 1.80

No. 656 Overprinted in Black or Light Ultramarine

1964 Litho. *Perf. 14x13*

709 A231 80c rose car & grn 1.40 1.00

Butterfly Type of 1961

Butterflies: Same as on Nos. 680, 682-683.

1964, June Litho. *Perf. 13½*

711 A236 20c brt grn & multi .55 .20
712 A236 50c sal pink & multi .95 .20
713 A236 80c lt red brn & multi 1.50 .20
Nos. 711-713 (3) 3.00 .60

Alliance for Progress Emblem, Agriculture and Industry A240

Designs: 50c, Emblem, gear wheels, mountain and seashore. 80c, Emblem, banana worker, fish, factory and ship.

1964, Aug. 26 Unwmk. *Perf. 12*

715 A240 40c bis brn & vio .20 .20
716 A240 50c red org & blk .25 .20
717 A240 80c bl & dk brn .35 .20
Nos. 715-717 (3) .80 .60

Issued to publicize the Alliance for Progress which aims to stimulate economic growth and raise living standards in Latin America.

No. 650 Overprinted in Red

1964 Photo. *Perf. 14x13½*
718 A229 1.80s dark blue 2.10 1.75

No. 656 Overprinted

Illustration reduced.

1964, July Litho. *Perf. 14x13*
719 A231 80c block of 4 2.90 2.90

Organization of American States.

World Map and Banana Tree — A241

1964, Oct. 26 *Perf. 12½x12*
720 A241 50c dk brn, gray & gray ol .25 .20
721 A241 80c blk, org & gray ol .25 .20

Issued to publicize the Banana Conference, Oct.-Nov. 1964. See Nos. C427-C428a.

King Philip II of Spain and Map of Upper Amazon River A242

Designs (Map and): 20c, Juan de Salinas de Loyola. 30c, Hernando de Santillan.

1964, Dec. 6 Litho. *Perf. 13½*
722 A242 10c rose, blk & buff .25 .25
723 A242 20c bl grn, blk & buff .25 .25
724 A242 30c bl, blk & buff .25 .25
Nos. 722-724 (3) .75 .75

4th centenary of the establishment of the Royal High Court in Quito.

Pole Vaulting A243

1964, Dec. 16 *Perf. 14x13½*
725 A243 80c vio bl, yel grn & brn .25 .20

18th Olympic Games, Tokyo, Oct. 10-25. See Nos. C432-C434.

Peter Fleming and Two-toed Sloth — A244

Designs: 20c, James Elliot and armadillo. 30c, T. Edward McCully, Jr., and squirrel. 40c, Roger Youderian and deer. 60c, Nathaniel (Nate) Saint and plane over Napo River.

1965 Unwmk. *Perf. 13½*
726 A244 20c emerald & multi .70 .25
727 A244 30c yellow & multi .70 .25
728 A244 40c lilac & multi .70 .25
729 A244 60c multi .70 .25
730 A244 80c multi .70 .25
Nos. 726-730 (5) 3.50 1.25

Issued in memory of five American Protestant missionaries, killed by the Auca Indians, 1/8/56.
Issue dates: 80c, May 11; others, July 8.

Juan B. Vázquez and Benigno Malo College — A245

1965, June 6 Litho. *Perf. 14*
731 A245 20c blk, yel & vio bl .20 .20
732 A245 60c blk, red, yel & vio bl .20 .20
733 A245 80c blk, emer, yel & vio bl .20 .20
Nos. 731-733 (3) .60 .60

Centenary (in 1964) of the founding of Benigno Malo National College.

National Anthem, Juan Leon Mera and Antonio Neumane A246

1965, Aug. 10 Litho. *Perf. 13½*
734 A246 50c pink & blk .20 .20
735 A246 80c lt grn & blk .25 .20
736 A246 5s bis & blk .55 .35
737 A246 10s lt ultra & blk 1.00 .75
Nos. 734-737 (4) 2.00 1.50

Cent. of the national anthem. The name of the poet Juan Leon Mera is misspelled on the stamps.
For surcharges see Nos. 766C, 766H.

Torch and Athletes (Shot Put, Discus, Javelin and Hammer Throw) — A247

50c, 1s, Runners. 60c, 1.50s, Soccer.

1965, Nov. 20 *Perf. 12x12½*
738 A247 40c org, gold, & blk .20 .20
739 A247 50c org ver, gold & blk .20 .20
740 A247 60c bl, gold & blk .20 .20
741 A247 80c brt yel grn, gold & blk .30 .20
742 A247 1s lt vio, gold & blk .30 .20
743 A247 1.50s brt pink, gold & blk .50 .35
Nos. 738-743,C435-C440 (12) 4.30 2.85

Issued to publicize the 5th Bolivarian Games, held at Guayaquil and Quito.
For surcharges see #766B, 766D, C449.

Stamps of 1865 A248

1965, Dec. 30 Litho. *Perf. 13½*
Stamps of 1865 in Yellow, Ultramarine & Green
744 A248 80c rose red .20 .20
745 A248 1.30s rose lilac .30 .20
746 A248 2s chocolate .45 .20
747 A248 4s black .65 .20
a. Souv. sheet, #744-747, imperf. 2.50 2.50
Nos. 744-747 (4) 1.60 .80

Cent. of Ecuadorian postage stamps.

The postal validity of some of the following sets has been questioned.

ITU Centenary — A248a

1966, Jan. 27 Litho. *Perf. 12x12½*
748 A248a 10c Telstar .20 .20
748A A248a 10c Syncom .20 .20
748B A248a 80c Relay .20 .20
748C A248a 1.50s Luna 3 .35 .30
748D A248a 3s Echo II 1.75 1.10
f. Souv. sheet of 3, #748, 748B, 748D, perf. 14x12½ 14.00
748E A248a 4s E. Branly, Marconi, Bell, E. Belin 1.90 1.40
g. Souv. sheet of 3, #748A, 748C, 748E, perf. 14x12½ 14.00
Nos. 748-748E (6) 4.60 3.40

1.50s, 3s, 4s are airmail.
Nos. 748Df, 748Eg are printed on surface colored paper. Exist imperf.

Space Exploration — A248b

10c, Edward White's space walk, June 8, 1965. 1s, Gemini 5, Aug. 21, 1965. 1.30s, Solar system. 2s, Charles Conrad, L. Gordon Cooper, Gemini 5, Aug. 21-29, 1965. 2.50s, Gemini 6. 3.50s, Alexei L. Leonov's space walk, Mar. 18, 1965.

1966, Jan. 27 *Perf. 12x12½*
749 A248b 10c multicolored .20 .20
749A A248b 1s multicolored .30 .20
749B A248b 1.30s multicolored .30 .20
749C A248b 2s multicolored 1.10 .65
749D A248b 2.50s multicolored 1.10 .65
749E A248b 3.50s multicolored 2.50 2.50
f. Souv. sheet of 3, #749, 749B, 749E, perf. 14x12½ 12.00 7.00
Nos. 749-749E (6) 5.50 4.40

1.30s, 2s, 2.50s, 3.50s are airmail.
No. 749Ef is printed on surface colored paper. Exists imperf.

Dante's Dream by Rossetti — A248c

Designs: 80c, Dante and Beatrix by Holliday. 2s, Galileo Galilei, 400th birth cent., vert. 3s, Dante, 700th birth cent., vert.

1966, June *Perf. 13½x14, 14x13½*
750 A248c 10c multicolored .20 .20
750A A248c 80c multicolored .20 .20
750B A248c 2s multicolored 2.10 1.40
750C A248c 3s multicolored 2.25 2.25
d. Souv. sheet of 3, #750, 750A, 750C, perf. 12x12½ 15.00 15.00
Nos. 750-750C (4) 4.75 4.05

Nos. 750A-750B are airmail. No. 750Cd exists imperf. Value $15.

Pavonine Quetzal — A249

Birds: 50c, Blue-crowned motmot. 60c, Paradise tanager. 80c, Wire-tailed manakin.

1966, June 17 Litho. *Perf. 13½*
Birds in Natural Colors
751 A249 40c dl rose & blk 1.00 .20
751A A249 50c sal & blk 1.00 .20
751B A249 60c lt ocher & blk 1.00 .20
751C A249 80c lt bl & blk 1.00 .20
Nos. 751-751C,C441-C448 (12) 21.55 4.30

For surcharges see Nos. 766E-766F, C450, C455-C457.

Pope Paul VI — A249a

Pope Paul VI and: 1.30s, Nativity. 3.50s, Virgin of Merced.

1966, June 24 *Perf. 12½x12*
752 A249a 10c multicolored .25 .20
752A A249a 1.30s multicolored .70 .50
752B A249a 3.50s multicolored 2.10 2.10
c. Souv. sheet of 3, #752, perf. 14x13½, 752A-752B, perf. 12½x12 15.00 15.00
Nos. 752-752B (3) 3.05 2.80

Nos. 752A-752B are airmail.
No. 752Bc is printed on surface colored paper. Exists imperf. Value $15.

Sir Winston Churchill, (1874-1965) — A249b

Famous Men: 10c, Dag Hammarskjold, vert. 1.50s, Albert Schweitzer, vert. 2.50s, John F. Kennedy, vert. 4s, Churchill, Kennedy.

Perf. 14x13½, 13½x14

1966, June 24

753 A249b 10c vio bl, brn & blk .20 .20
753A A249b 1s ver, bl & blk .30 .20
753B A249b 1.50s brn, lil rose & blk .70 .35
753C A249b 2.50s ver, bl & blk 1.75 1.00
753D A249b 4s bl, blk & brn 2.10 1.60
e. Souv. sheet of 3, #753, 753B, 753D 40.00 40.00
Nos. 753-753D (5) 5.05 3.35

Nos. 753C-753D are airmail.

No. 753De is printed on surface colored paper. 10c stamp is perf. 14x13½, 1.50s is perf. 14x13½x14x12, 4s is perf. 12x12½x13x12½. Exists imperf. Value $40.

History of Summer Olympics — A249c

1966, June 27 ***Perf. 12x12½***

754 A249c 10c Long jump .20 .20
754A A249c 10c Wrestling .20 .20
754B A249c 80c Discus, javelin .45 .20
754C A249c 1.30s Chariot racing 1.10 .35
754D A249c 3s High jump 1.75 .85
f. Souv. sheet of 3, #754, 754B, 754D 11.00 7.00
754E A249c 3.50s Discus 2.90 1.10
g. Souv. sheet of 3, #754A, 754C, 754E 11.00 7.00
Nos. 754-754E (6) 6.60 2.90

Nos. 754C-754D are airmail.

Nos. 754Df, 754Eg are printed on surface colored paper.

Nos. 754Df and 754Eg exist imperf.

1968 Winter Olympics, Grenoble — A249d

1966, June 27 ***Perf. 14***

755 A249d 10c Speedskating .20 .20
755A A249d 1s Ice hockey .35 .20
755B A249d 1.50s Ski jumping .55 .30
755C A249d 2s Cross country skiing 1.10 .45
755D A249d 2.50s Downhill skiing 1.40 1.40
755E A249d 4s Figure skating 1.75 1.75
f. Souv. sheet of 3, #755, 755B, 755E, perf. 14x13½ 7.00 5.25
Nos. 755-755E (6) 5.35 4.30

Nos. 755B-755E are airmail.

No. 755f is printed on surface colored paper. Exists imperf.

French-American Cooperation in Space — A249e

Designs: 1.50s, French satellite D-1, Mt. Gros observatory, vert. 4s, John F. Kennedy, satellites.

1966 ***Perf. 13½x14, 14x13½***

756 A249e 10c multicolored .30 .25
756A A249e 1.50s multicolored 1.60 1.10
756B A249e 4s multicolored 3.50 2.10
c. Sheet of 3, #756-756B 14.00 10.00
Nos. 756-756B (3) 5.40 3.45

Nos. 756A-756B are airmail.

Moon Exploration A249f

1966 ***Perf. 14***

758 A249f 10c Surveyor .20 .20
758A A249f 80c Luna 10 .20 .20
758B A249f 1s Luna 9 .20 .20
758C A249f 2s Astronaut flight trainer .70 .45
758D A249f 2.50s Ranger 7 .85 .70
758E A249f 3s Lunar Orbiter 1 1.10 1.10
f. Sheet of 3, #758, 758A, 758E 10.00 10.00
Nos. 758-758E (6) 3.25 2.85

Nos. 758C-758E are airmail. Stamps in No. 758f have colored pattern in border. No. 758f exists imperf. Value $10.

1968 Summer Olympics, Mexico City — A249g

Paintings by Mexican artists: 10c, Wanderer by Diego Rivera. 1s, Workers by Jose Orozco. 1.30s, Pres. Juarez by Orozco. 2s, Mother and Child by David Siqueiros. 2.50s, Two Women by Rivera. 3.50s, New Democracy by Siqueiros.

1967, Mar. 13 ***Perf. 14***

759 A249g 10c multicolored .20 .20
759A A249g 1s multicolored .50 .20
759B A249g 1.30s multicolored .70 .30
759C A249g 2s multicolored .85 .50
759D A249g 2.50s multicolored 1.10 1.10
759E A249g 3.50s multicolored 2.00 1.75
f. Sheet of 3, #759, 759B, 759E 14.00
Nos. 759-759E (6) 5.35 4.05

Nos. 759B-759E are airmail.

No. 759f is printed on surface colored paper that differs slightly from Nos. 759-759E. Exists imperf.

1968 Summer Olympics, Mexico City — A249h

1967, Mar. 13

760 A249h 10c Soccer .20 .20
760A A249h 10c Hurdles .20 .20
760B A249h 80c Track .20 .20
760C A249h 1.50s Fencing .65 .30
760D A249h 3s High jump 1.40 1.10
f. Souv. sheet of 3, #760A, 760B, 760D 14.00 7.00
760E A249h 4s Swimming 2.90 1.40
g. Souv. sheet of 3, #760, 760C, 760E 11.00 7.00
Nos. 760-760E (6) 5.55 3.40

Nos. 760C-760E are airmail.

Nos. 760f-760g are printed on surface colored paper. Exist imperf.

4th Natl. Eucharistic Congress A249i

Paintings: 10c, Madonna and Child by unknown artist. 60c, Holy Family by Rodriguez. 80c, Madonna and Child by Samaniego. 1s, Good Shepherd by Samaniego. 1.50s, Assumption of the Virgin by Vargas. 2s, Man in Prayer by Santiago.

1967, May 10

761 A249i 10c multicolored .20 .20
761A A249i 60c multicolored .50 .30
761B A249i 80c multicolored .75 .30
761C A249i 1s multicolored .95 .50
761D A249i 1.50s multicolored 1.40 .70
761E A249i 2s multicolored 2.25 .70
Nos. 761-761E (6) 6.05 2.70

Nos. 761D-761E are airmail. Frames and inscriptions vary greatly.

Madonna and Child Enthroned by Guido Reni A249j

Paintings of the Madonna and Child by: 40c, van Hemesen. 50c, Memling. 1.30s, Durer. 2.50s, Raphael. 3s, Murillo.

1967, May 25 ***Perf. 14x13½***

762 A249j 10c multicolored .20 .20
762A A249j 40c multicolored .20 .20
762B A249j 50c multicolored .20 .20
762C A249j 1.30s multicolored .65 .30
762D A249j 2.50s multicolored 1.60 .85
762E A249j 3s multicolored 2.50 1.10
Nos. 762-762E (6) 5.35 2.85

Nos. 762C-762E are airmail.

Portrait of a Young Woman by Rogier van der Weyden A249k

Designs: 1s, Helene Fourment by Rubens. 1.50s, Venetian Woman by Durer. 2s, Lady Sheffield by Gainsborough. 2.50s, Suzon by Manet. 4s, Lady with a Unicorn by Raphael.

1967, Sept. 9 ***Perf. 14x13½***

763 A249k 10c multicolored .20 .20
763A A249k 1s multicolored .50 .30
763B A249k 1.50s multicolored 1.10 .40
763C A249k 2s multicolored 1.40 .55
763D A249k 2.50s multicolored 2.10 .70
763E A249k 4s multicolored 2.50 1.10
f. Sheet of 3, #763, 763B, 763E, perf. 14 11.00 7.00
Nos. 763-763E (6) 7.80 3.25

Nos. 763B-763E are airmail.

Stamps in No. 763f have colored pattern in border. Exists imperf.

John F. Kennedy, 50th Birth Anniv. A249l

JFK and: No. 764A, Dag Hammarskjold. 80c, Pope Paul VI. 1.30s, Konrad Adenauer. 3s, Charles de Gaulle. 3.50s, Winston Churchill.

Perf. 14x13½, 13½x14

1967, Sept. 11

764 A249l 10c lil, brn & bl .20 .20
764A A249l 10c yel, brn & sky bl .20 .20
764B A249l 80c yel, brn & sal .20 .20
764C A249l 1.30s yel, brn & pink 1.75 .70
764D A249l 3s yel, brn & yel grn 2.50 1.25
764E A249l 3.50s yel, brn & bl 3.50 1.60
Nos. 764-764E (6) 8.35 4.15

Souvenir Sheets

764F Sheet of 3 15.00 7.00
h. like #764, 35x27mm
i. like #764B, 35x27mm
j. like #764D, 35x27mm
764G Sheet of 3 15.00 7.00
k. like #764A, 35x27mm
l. like #764C, 35x27mm
m. like #764E, 35x27mm

Nos. 764C-764E are airmail. Nos. 764A-764E horiz. Stamps in Nos. 764F-764G have colored pattern in border.

Nos. 764F and 764G exist imperf.

Christmas — A249m

Designs: No. 765A, Children's procession. 40c, Candlelight procession. 50c, Children singing. 60c, Processional. 2.50s, Christmas celebration.

1967, Dec. 29 ***Perf. 13x14***

765 A249m 10c multicolored .35 .20
765A A249m 10c multicolored .35 .20
765B A249m 40c multicolored .35 .20
765C A249m 50c multicolored .35 .20
765D A249m 60c multicolored .35 .20
765E A249m 2.50s multicolored 11.00 9.00
Nos. 765-765E (6) 12.75 10.00

No. 765E is airmail. See Nos. 768-768F.

Various Surcharges on Issues of 1956-66

1967-68

766 AP72 30c on 1.10s (C337) .30 .20
766A AP66 40c on 1.70s (C292) .30 .20
766B A247 40c on 3.50s (C438) .30 .20
766C A246 50c on 5s (736) ('68) .30 .20
766D A247 80c on 1.50s (743) .35 .20
766E A249 80c on 2.50s (C445) .35 .20
766F A249 1s on 4s (C447) .45 .20

766G AP66 1.30s on 1.90s (C293) .55 .45
766H A246 2s on 10s (737) ('68) .70 .20
Nos. 766-766H,C449-C450 (11) 4.30 2.50

The surcharge on Nos. 766B-766C, 766E and 766G-766H includes "Resello." The obliteration of old denomination and arrangement of surcharges differ on each stamp.

Bust of Peñaherrera, Central University, Quito — A250

50c, Law books. 80c, Open book, laurel, horiz.

Perf. 12x12½, 12½x12

1967, Dec. 29 **Litho.**

767 A250 50c brt grn & blk .20 .20
767A A250 60c rose & blk .20 .20
767B A250 80c rose lil & blk .20 .20
Nos. 767-767B,C451-C452 (5) 1.10 1.00

Cent. (in 1964) of the birth of Dr. Victor Manuel Peñaherrera (1864-1932), author of the civil and criminal codes of Ecuador.

Christmas Type of 1967

Native Christian Art: 10c, Mourning of the Death of Christ, by Manuel Chili. 80c, Ascension of the Holy Virgin, vert. 1s, The Holy Virgin. 1.30s, Coronation of the Holy Virgin, by Bernardo Rodriguez, vert. 1.50s, Madonna and Child with the Heavenly Host, vert. 2s, Madonna and Child, by Manuel Samaniego, vert. 3s, Immaculate Conception, by Bernardo de Legranda, vert. 3.50s, Passion of Christ, by Chili, vert. 4s, The Holy Virgin of Quito, by de Legranda, vert.

1968 Jan. 19 ***Perf. 13½x14, 14x13½***

768 A249m 10c multicolored .25 .25
768A A249m 80c multicolored .25 .25
768B A249m 1s multicolored .25 .25
768C A249m 1.30s multicolored .25 .25
768D A249m 1.50s multicolored .55 .30
768E A249m 2s multicolored .70 .70
Nos. 768-768E (6) 2.25 2.00

Souvenir Sheet

Perf. 14

768F Sheet of 3 18.00 11.00
g. A249m 3s multicolored
h. A249m 3.50s multicolored
i. A249m 4s multicolored

Nos. 768C-768F are airmail. No. 768F exists imperf. Value same.

Tourism Year — A250a

20c, Woman from Otavalo. 30c, Colorado Indian. 40c, Petroglyph of a cat. 50c, Petroglyph of a mythological predator. 60c, Woman in a bazaar. 80c, 1s, 1.30s, Petroglyphs, diff. 1.50s, Colonial street, Quito. 2s, Amulet.

1968, Apr. 1 ***Perf. 13½x14***

769 A250a 20c multicolored .20 .20
769A A250a 30c multicolored .20 .20
769B A250a 40c multicolored .20 .20
769C A250a 50c multicolored .20 .20
769D A250a 60c multicolored .20 .20
769E A250a 80c multicolored .20 .20
769F A250a 1s multicolored .30 .20
769G A250a 1.30s multicolored .20 .20
769H A250a 1.50s multicolored .30 .20
769I A250a 2s multicolored .35 .20
Nos. 769-769I (10) 2.35 2.00

Ninth Congress of the Confederation of Latin American Tourist Organizations (COTAL). Nos. 769G-769I are airmail.

Otto Arosemena Gomez — A251

Lions Emblem — A252

Design: 1s, Page from the Constitution.

1968, May 9 **Litho.** ***Perf. 13½x14***

770 A251 80c lil & multi .20 .20
770A A251 1s multi .20 .20
Nos. 770-770A,C453-C454 (4) .90 .80

First anniversary of the administration of Pres. Otto Arosemena Gomez.

1968, May 24 **Litho.** ***Perf. 13½x14***

771 A252 80c multi .20 .20
771A A252 1.30s multi .25 .20
771B A252 2s pink & multi .30 .20
c. Souvenir sheet of 1 4.25 4.25
Nos. 771-771B (3) .75 .60

50th anniv. (in 1967) of Lions Intl.
No. 771c contains one 5s 39x49mm stamp. Exists imperf.

Pope Paul VI, Visit to Latin America — A252a

39th Intl. Eucharistic Congress, Bogota, Colombia A252b

60c, Pope Paul VI, vert. 1s, Madonna by Botticelli. 1.30s, Pope Paul VI with flags of South American nations. 2s, Madonna and Child by Durer.

1969 ***Perf. 13½x14, 14x13½***

772 A252a 40c multicolored .20 .20
772A A252a 60c multicolored .30 .20
772B A252b 1s multicolored .95 .30
772C A252a 1.30s multicolored .70 .35
e. Souv. sheet of 3, #772, 772A, 772C, imperf. 4.00 2.25
772D A252b 2s multicolored
f. Souv. sheet of 2, #772B, 772D, imperf. 4.00 2.25
Nos. 772-772D (4) 2.15 1.05

Nos. 772C-772D are airmail. Nos. 772-772f overprinted in silver with the national coat of arms.

Madonna with the Angel by Rogier van der Weyden A252c

Paintings by various artists showing the life of the Virgin Mary.

1969 ***Perf. 14x13½, 13½x14***

773 A252c 40c shown .20 .20
773A A252c 60c Van der Weyden, diff. .20 .20
773B A252c 1s Raphael .30 .20
773C A252c 1.30s Veronese 1.10 .55
e. Souv. sheet of 2, #773B-773C, imperf. 5.50 2.25
773D A252c 2s Van der Weyden, horiz.
f. Souv. sheet of 3, #773-773A, 773D, imperf. 5.50 2.25
Nos. 773-773D (4) 1.80 1.15

Nos. 773-773Df overprinted in silver with the national coat of arms. Nos. 773C-773D are airmail.

Nos. C331 and C326 Surcharged in Violet and Dark Blue

a

b

1969, Jan. 10 ***Perf. 11½, 14x13½***

774 AP79 (a) 40c on 1.30s (V) .50 .25
774A AP76 (b) 50c on 1.30s (DBl) .50 .25

Type of 1958 Surcharged and Overprinted in Plum and Black

Design: Ignacio Luis Arcaya, Foreign Minister of Venezuela.

1969, Mar. **Litho.** ***Perf. 12***

Flags in Red, Blue and Yellow

775 A223 50c on 2s sepia .20 .20
775A A223 80c on 2s sepia .20 .20
775B A223 1s on 2s sepia .20 .20
775C A223 2s sepia .20 .20
Nos. 775-775C,C455-C457 (7) 2.30 1.55

Nos. 775-775C were not issued without overprint. The obliteration of old denomination on No. 775A is a small square around a star. Overprint is plum, except for the black small coat of arms on right flag.

Map of Ecuador and Oriental Region — A253

Surcharge typographed in Dark Blue, Red Brown, Black or Lilac

1969 **Litho.** ***Perf. 14***

776 A253 20c on 30c (DBl) .50 .30
776A A253 40c on 30c (RBr) .50 .30
777 A253 50c on 30c (DBl) .50 .30
778 A253 60c on 30c (DBl) .50 .30
778A A253 60c on 30c (Bk) .65 .65
778B A253 80c on 30c (DBl) — 25.00
779 A253 80c on 30c (Bk) .50 .30
780 A253 1s on 30c (L) .50 .30
780A A253 1s on 30c (DBl) 2.00 1.25
781 A253 1.30s on 30c (Bk) .90 .40
782 A253 1.50s on 30c (Bk) .90 .40
783 A253 2s on 30c (DBl) 1.00 .40
784 A253 3s on 30c (DBl) 1.25 .45
784A A253 4s on 30c (DBl) 3.25 3.25
785 A253 4s on 30c (Bk) 1.25 .40
786 A253 5s on 30c (Bk) 1.60 .55
Nos. 776-786 (16) 15.80 34.55

Not issued without surcharge.

M. L. King, John and Robert Kennedy — A254

Thecla Coronata — A255

1969-70 **Typo.** ***Perf. 12½***

787 A254 4s blk, bl, grn & buff .45 .20

Perf. 13½

788 A254 4s blk, lt bl & grn ('70) .45 .20

In memory of John F. Kennedy, Robert F. Kennedy and Martin Luther King, Jr.

1970 **Litho.** ***Perf. 12½***

Butterflies: 20c, Papilio zabreus. 30c, Heliconius chestertoni. 40c, Papilio pausanias. 50c, Pereute leucodrosime. 60c, Metamorpha dido. 80c, Morpho cypris. 1s, Catagramma astarte.

789 A255 10c buff & multi 1.40 .30
790 A255 20c lt grn & multi 1.40 .30
791 A255 30c pink & multi 1.40 .30
792 A255 40c lt bl & multi 1.40 .20
793 A255 50c gold & multi 1.40 .20
794 A255 60c salmon & multi 1.40 .20
795 A255 80c silver & multi 1.40 .20
796 A255 1s lt grn & multi 1.40 .20

Same, White Background

Perf. 13½

797 A255 10c multi 1.40 .30
798 A255 20c multi 1.40 .30
799 A255 30c multi 1.40 .30
800 A255 40c multi 1.40 .20
801 A255 50c multi 1.40 .20
802 A255 60c multi 1.40 .20
803 A255 80c multi 1.40 .20
804 A255 1s multi 1.40 .20
Nos. 789-804,C461-C464 (20) 28.00 4.60

Surcharged Revenue Stamps
A256 A257

1970, June 16 **Litho.** ***Perf. 14***

Red Surcharge

805 A256 1s on 1s light blue .20 .20
806 A256 1.30s on 1s light blue .20 .20
807 A256 1.50s on 1s light blue .25 .25
808 A256 2s on 1s light blue .30 .20
809 A256 5s on 1s light blue .60 .30
810 A256 10s on 1s light blue 1.25 .50
Nos. 805-810 (6) 2.80 1.65

1970 **Typo.** ***Perf. 12***

Black Surcharge

811 A257 60c on 1s violet .20 .20
812 A257 80c on 1s violet .20 .20
813 A257 1s on 1s violet .20 .20
814 A257 1.10s on 1s violet .20 .20

815 A257 1.30s on 1s violet .20 .20
816 A257 1.50s on 1s violet .30 .20
817 A257 2s on 1s violet .30 .20
818 A257 2.20s on 1s violet .35 .20
819 A257 3s on 1s violet .45 .20
Nos. 811-819 (9) 2.40 1.80

1970

820 A257 1.10s on 2s green .20 .20
821 A257 1.30s on 2s green .20 .20
822 A257 1.50s on 2s green .30 .20
823 A257 2s on 2s green .30 .20
824 A257 3.40s on 2s green .45 .20
825 A257 5s on 2s green .65 .20
826 A257 10s on 2s green 1.10 .20
827 A257 20s on 2s green 2.00 .65
828 A257 50s on 2s green 4.25 2.10
Nos. 820-828 (9) 9.45 4.15

1970

829 A257 3s on 5s blue .45 .20
830 A257 5s on 5s blue .55 .30
831 A257 10s on 40s orange 1.10 .55
Nos. 829-831 (3) 2.10 1.05

Arms of Zamora Chinchipe — A258 Flags of Ecuador and Chile — A259

Design: 1s, Arms and flag of Esmeraldas.

1971 Litho. *Perf. 10½*

832 A258 50c pale yel & multi .20 .20
833 A258 1s sal & multi .20 .20
Nos. 832-833,C465-C469 (7) 3.10 1.70

1971, Sept. *Perf. 12½*

840 A259 1.30s blk & multi .20 .20
Nos. 840,C481-C482 (3) .70 .60

Visit of Pres. Salvador Allende of Chile, Aug. 24.

Ismael Pérez Pazmiño — A260

1971, Sept. 16 *Perf. 12x11½*

841 A260 1s grn & multi .20 .20
Nos. 841,C485-C486 (3) .70 .60

"El Universo," newspaper founded by Ismael Pérez Pazmiño, 50th anniv.

CARE Package — A261 Flags of Ecuador and Argentina — A262

1971-72 *Perf. 12½*

842 A261 30c lilac ('72) .20 .20
843 A261 40c emerald ('72) .20 .20
844 A261 50c blue .20 .20
845 A261 60c carmine .20 .20
846 A261 80c lt brn ('72) .20 .20
Nos. 842-846 (5) 1.00 1.00

25th anniversary of CARE, a US-Canadian Cooperative for American Relief Everywhere.

1972 *Perf. 11½*

847 A262 1s blk & multi .20 .20
Nos. 847,C491-C492 (3) .90 .70

Visit of Lt. Gen. Alejandro Agustin Lanusse, president of Argentina, Jan. 25.

Jesus Giving Keys to St. Peter, by Miguel de Santiago A263

Ecuadorian Paintings: 1.10s, Virgin of Mercy, Quito School. 2s, Virgin Mary, by Manuel Samaniego.

1972, Apr. 24 Litho. *Perf. 14x13½*

848 A263 50c black & multi .20 .20
849 A263 1.10s black & multi .30 .30
850 A263 2s black & multi .50 .50
a. Souvenir sheet of 3 1.60 1.60
Nos. 848-850,C494-C495 (5) 2.30 1.80

No. 850a contains 3 imperf. stamps similar to Nos. 848-850.

1972, May 4

Ecuadorian Statues: 50c, Our Lady of Sorrow, by Caspicara. 1.10s, Nativity, Quito School, horiz. 2s, Virgin of Quito, anonymous.

851 A263 50c blk & multi .20 .20
852 A263 1.10s blk & multi .30 .30
853 A263 2s blk & multi .45 .45
a. Souv. sheet of 3 2.50 2.10
Nos. 851-853,C496-C497 (5) 2.20 1.75

Letters of "Ecuador" 3mm high on Nos. 851-853, 7mm high on Nos. 848-850. No. 853a contains 3 imperf. stamps similar to Nos. 851-853.

A264

A265

Designs: 30c, Gen. Juan Ignacio Pareja. 40c, Juan José Flores. 50c, Leon de Febres Cordero. 60c, Ignacio Torres. 70c, Francisco de Paula Santander. 1s, José M. Cordova.

1972, May 24 *Perf. 12½*

854 A264 30c blue & multi .20 .20
855 A264 40c blue & multi .20 .20
856 A264 50c blue & multi .20 .20
857 A264 60c blue & multi .20 .20
858 A264 70c blue & multi .20 .20
859 A264 1s blue & multi .20 .20
Nos. 854-859,C498-C503 (12) 5.10 3.50

Sesquicentennial of the Battle of Pichincha and the liberation of Quito.

1972, July Photo. *Perf. 13*

Designs: 2s, Woman Wearing Poncho. 3s, Striped poncho. 5s, Embroidered poncho. 10s, Metal vase.

860 A265 2s multicolored .20 .20
861 A265 3s multicolored .45 .30
862 A265 5s multicolored .55 .50
863 A265 10s dp blue & multi 1.25 1.00
a. Souvenir sheet of 4 3.50 3.50
Nos. 860-863,C504-C507 (8) 5.10 3.60

Handicraft of Ecuador. No. 863a contains 4 imperf. stamps similar to Nos. 860-863.

Sucre Statue, Santo Domingo — A266 Radar Station — A267

1.80s, San Agustin Convent. 2.30s, Plaza de la Independencia. 2.50s, Bolivar statue, La Alameda. 4.75s, Chapel door.

1972, Dec. 6 Litho. *Perf. 11½*

864 A266 1.20s yel & multi .20 .20
865 A266 1.80s yel & multi .20 .20
866 A266 2.30s yel & multi .20 .20
867 A266 2.50s yel & multi .35 .20
868 A266 4.75s yel & multi .50 .25
Nos. 864-868,C518-C524 (12) 5.20 3.05

Sesquicentennial of the Battle of Pichincha.

1973, Apr. 5 Wmk. 367

869 A267 1s multicolored .25 .20

Inauguration of earth telecommunications station, Oct. 19, 1972.

Blue-footed Boobies A268

Wmk. 367, Unwmkd. (#872)

1973 Litho. *Perf. 11½x12*

870 A268 30c shown .35 .20
871 A268 40c Blue-faced booby .35 .20
872 A268 50c Oyster-catcher .35 .20
873 A268 60c California sea lions .70 .25
874 A268 70c Galapagos giant tortoise .85 .25
875 A268 1s California sea lion 1.25 .25
Nos. 870-875,C527-C528 (8) 7.35 1.75

Elevation of Galapagos Islands to a province of Ecuador.

Issue dates: 50c, Oct. 3; others Aug. 16.

Black-chinned Mountain Tanager — A269

Birds of Ecuador: 2s, Moriche oriole. 3s, Toucan barbet, vert. 5s, Masked crimson tanager, vert. 10s, Blue-necked tanager, vert.

Perf. 11x11½, 11½x11

1973, Dec. 6 Litho. Unwmk.

876 A269 1s brick red & multi .45 .20
877 A269 2s lt blue & multi .80 .20
878 A269 3s lt green & multi .80 .20
879 A269 5s pale lilac & multi 1.60 .45
880 A269 10s pale yel grn & multi 3.50 .95
Nos. 876-880 (5) 7.15 2.00

Two souvenir sheets exist: one contains 2 imperf. stamps similar to Nos. 876-877 with yellow margin and black inscription; the other 3 stamps similar to Nos. 878-880; gray margin and black inscription including "Aereo." Both sheets dated "1972." Size: 143x84mm.

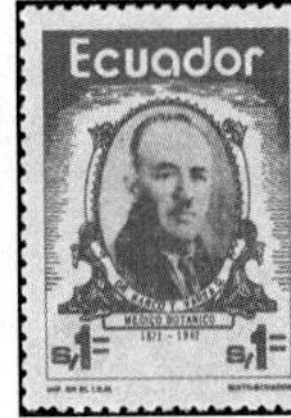

Marco T. Varea, Botanist — A270

Portraits: 60c, Pio Jaramillo Alvarado, writer. 70c, Prof. Luciano Andrade M. No. 883, Marco T. Varea, botanist. No. 884, Dr. Juan Modesto Carbo Noboa, medical researcher. No. 885, Alfredo J. Valenzuela. No. 886, Capt. Edmundo Chiriboga G. 1.20s, Francisco Campos R., scientist. 1.80s, Luis Vernaza Lazarte, philanthropist.

1974 Unwmk. *Perf. 12x11½*

881 A270 60c crimson rose .20 .20
882 A270 70c lilac .20 .20
883 A270 1s ultra .20 .20
884 A270 1s orange .20 .20
885 A270 1s emerald .20 .20
886 A270 1s brown .20 .20
887 A270 1.20s apple green .30 .20
889 A270 1.80s lt blue .40 .25
Nos. 881-889 (8) 1.90 1.65

Arcade A271

Designs: 30c, Monastery, entrance. 40c, Church. 50c, View of Church through gate, vert. 60c, Chapel, vert. 70c, Church and cemetery, vert.

Perf. 11½x12, 12x11½

1975, Feb. 4 Litho.

896 A271 20c yellow & multi .25 .20
897 A271 30c yellow & multi .25 .20
898 A271 40c yellow & multi .25 .20
899 A271 50c yellow & multi .25 .20
900 A271 60c yellow & multi .25 .20
901 A271 70c yellow & multi .25 .20
Nos. 896-901 (6) 1.50 1.20

Colonial Monastery, Tilipulo, Cotopaxi Province.

Angel Polibio Chaves, Founder of Bolivar Province — A272

Portrait: No. 903, Emilio Estrada Ycaza (1916-1961), archeologist.

1975 Litho. *Perf. 12x11½*

902 A272 80c violet bl & lt bl .20 .20
903 A272 80c vermilion & pink .20 .20

Issue dates: #902, Feb. 21; #903, Mar. 25.

R. Rodriguez Palacios and A. Duran Quintero — A273 "Woman of Action" — A274

1975, Apr. 1 Litho. *Perf. 12x11½*

910 A273 1s multicolored .20 .20
Nos. 910,C547-C548 (3) .70 .60

Meeting of the Ministers for Public Works of Ecuador and Colombia, July 27, 1973.

1975, June

Design: No. 912, "Woman of Peace."

911 A274 1s yellow & multi .20 .20
912 A274 1s blue & multi .20 .20

International Women's Year 1975.

Planes, Soldier and Ship — A275

1975, July 9 *Perf. 11½x12*
913 A275 2s multicolored .30 .25

3 years of Natl. Revolutionary Government.

Hurdling — A276

Designs: Modern sports drawn Inca style.

1975, Sept. 11 Litho. *Perf. 11½*
914 A276 20c shown .35 .25
915 A276 20c Chess .35 .25
916 A276 30c Basketball .35 .25
917 A276 30c Boxing .35 .25
918 A276 40c Bicycling .35 .25
919 A276 40c Steeplechase .35 .25
920 A276 50c Soccer .35 .25
921 A276 50c Fencing .35 .25
922 A276 60c Golf .35 .25
923 A276 60c Vaulting .35 .25
924 A276 70c Judo (standing) .35 .25
925 A276 70c Wrestling .35 .25
926 A276 80c Swimming .35 .25
927 A276 80c Weight lifting .35 .25
928 A276 1s Table Tennis .35 .25
929 A276 1s Paddle ball .35 .25
Nos. 914-929,C554-C558 (21) 7.90 5.00

3rd Ecuadorian Games.

Genciana A277

Designs: Ecuadorian plants.

Perf. 12x11½, 11½x12
1975, Nov. 18 Litho.
930 A277 20c Orchid, vert .20 .20
931 A277 30c shown .20 .20
932 A277 40c Bromeliaceae cactaceae, vert .25 .20
933 A277 50c Orchid .25 .20
934 A277 60c Orchid .30 .20
935 A277 80c Flowering cactus .30 .20
936 A277 1s Orchid .50 .20
Nos. 930-936,C559-C563 (12) 4.85 2.95

Venus, Chorrera Culture — A278

Female Mask, Tolita Culture — A279

Designs: 30c, Venus, Valdivia Culture. 40c, Seated man, Chorrera Culture. 50c, Man with poncho, Panzaleo Culture (late). 60c, Mythical head, Cashaloma Culture. 80c, Musician, Tolita Culture. No. 943, Chief Priest, Mantefia Culture. No. 945, Ornament, Tolita Culture. No. 946, Angry mask, Tolita Culture.

1976, Feb. 12 Litho. *Perf. 11½*
937 A278 20c multicolored .30 .20
938 A278 30c multicolored .30 .20
939 A278 40c multicolored .30 .20
940 A278 50c multicolored .30 .20
941 A278 60c multicolored .30 .20
942 A278 80c multicolored .30 .20
943 A278 1s multicolored .30 .20
944 A279 1s multicolored .30 .20
945 A279 1s multicolored .30 .20
946 A279 1s multicolored .30 .20
Nos. 937-946,C568-C572 (15) 5.45 3.30

Archaeological artifacts.

Strawberries A280

Carlos Amable Ortiz (1859-1937) A281

1976, Mar. 30
947 A280 1s blue & multi .25 .20
Nos. 947,C573-C574 (3) 1.00 .60

25th Flower and Fruit Festival, Ambato.

1976, Mar. 15 Litho. *Perf. 11½*

No. 949, Sixto Maria Duran (1875-1947). No. 950, Segundo Cueva Celi (1901-1969). No. 951, Cristobal Ojeda Davila (1910-1952). No. 952, Luis Alberto Valencia (1918-1970).

948 A281 1s ver & multi .25 .20
949 A281 1s orange & multi .25 .20
950 A281 1s lt green & multi .25 .20
951 A281 1s blue & multi .25 .20
952 A281 1s lt brn & multi .25 .20
Nos. 948-952 (5) 1.25 1.00

Ecuadorian composers and musicians.

Institute Emblem A282

1977, Aug. 15 Litho. *Perf. 11½x12*
953 A282 2s multicolored .25 .20

11th General Assembly of Pan-American Institute of Geography and History, Quito, Aug. 15-30. See Nos. C597-C597a.

Hands Holding Rotary Emblem A283

José Peralta — A284

1977, Aug. 31 Litho. *Perf. 12*
954 A283 1s multicolored .20 .20
955 A283 2s multicolored .30 .20

Souvenir Sheets

Imperf
956 A283 5s multicolored 1.10 1.10
957 A283 10s multicolored 1.40 1.40

Rotary Club of Guayaquil, 50th anniv.

1977 Litho. *Perf. 11½*

Design: 2.40s, Peralta statue.

958 A284 1.80s multi .20 .20
959 A284 2.40s multi .25 .20
Nos. 958-959,C609 (3) .80 .65

José Peralta (1855-1937), writer.

Blue-faced Booby A285

Galapagos Birds: 1.80s, Red-footed booby. 2.40s, Blue-footed boobies. 3.40s, Gull. 4.40s, Galapagos hawk. 5.40s, Map of Galapagos Islands and boobies, vert.

Perf. 11½x12, 12x11½
1977, Nov. 29 Litho.
960 A285 1.20s multi .35 .20
961 A285 1.80s multi .50 .20
962 A285 2.40s multi .85 .20
963 A285 3.40s multi 1.25 .20
964 A285 4.40s multi 1.75 .25
965 A285 5.40s multi 2.25 .25
Nos. 960-965 (6) 6.95 1.30

Dr. Corral Moscoso Hospital, Cuenca A286

1978, Apr. 12 Litho. *Perf. 11½x12*
966 A286 3s multicolored .25 .20
Nos. 966,C613-C614 (3) 1.75 1.00

Inauguration (in 1977) of Dr. Vicente Corral Moscoso Regional Hospital, Cuenca.

Surveyor Plane over Ecuador — A287

Latin-American Lions Emblem — A288

1978, Apr. 12 Litho. *Perf. 11½*
967 A287 6s multicolored .55 .30
Nos. 967,C619-C620 (3) 2.85 2.20

Military Geographical Institute, 50th anniv.

1978
968 A288 3s multi .55 .20
969 A288 4.20s multi .80 .20
Nos. 968-969,C621-C623 (5) 3.75 2.00

7th meeting of Latin American Lions, Jan. 25-29.

70th Anniversary Emblem — A289

1978, Sept. Litho. *Perf. 11½*
970 A289 4.20s gray & multi .35 .20

70th anniversary of Filanbanco (Philanthropic Bank). See No. C626.

Goalmouth and Net — A290

Designs: 1.80s, "Gauchito" and Games emblem, vert. 4.40s, "Gauchito," vert.

1978, Nov. 1 Litho. *Perf. 12*
971 A290 1.20s multi .20 .20
972 A290 1.80s multi .20 .20
973 A290 4.40s multi .45 .20
Nos. 971-973,C627-C629 (6) 2.75 1.70

11th World Cup Soccer Championship, Argentina, June 1-25.

Symbols for Male and Female — A291

1979, Feb. 15 Litho. *Perf. 12x11½*
974 A291 3.40s multi .35 .20

Inter-American Women's Commission, 50th anniversary.

Emblem A292

1979, June 21 Litho. *Perf. 11½x12*
975 A292 4.40s multi .30 .20
976 A292 5.40s multi .45 .25

Ecuadorian Mortgage Bank, 16th anniv.

Street Scene, Quito — A293

Perf. 12x11½
1979, Aug. 3 Litho. Unwmk.
977 A293 3.40s multi .25 .20
Nos. 977,C651-C653 (4) 4.35 2.25

Natl. heritage: Quito & Galapagos Islands.

Jose Joaquin de Olmedo (1780-1847), Physician — A294

Chief Enriquillo, Dominican Republic — A295

1980, Apr. 29 Litho. *Perf. 12x11½*
978 A294 3s multi .20 .20
979 A294 5s multi .35 .30
Nos. 978-979,C662 (3) 1.35 1.00

First Pres. of Free State of Guayaquil, 1820.

Wmk. 367, Unwmkd. (#981-983)
1980, May 12

Indo-American Tribal Chiefs: 3.40s, Guaycaypuro, Venezuela. No. 982, Abayuba, Uruguay. No. 983, Atlacatl, Salvador.

980 A295 3s multi .35 .20
981 A295 3.40s multi .65 .30
982 A295 5s multi 1.25 .45
983 A295 5s multi 1.25 .45
Nos. 980-983,C663-C678 (20) 33.25 8.40

King Juan Carlos and Queen Sofia, Visit to Ecuador A296

Perf. 11½x12

1980, May 18 **Unwmk.**
984 A296 3.40s multi .35 .20

See No. C679.

Cofan Indian, Napo Province — A297

1980, June 10 Litho. *Perf. 12x11½*
985 A297 3s shown .35 .20
986 A297 3.40s Zuleta woman, Imbabura .35 .20
987 A297 5s Chota woman, Imbabura .55 .20
Nos. 985-987,C681-C684 (7) 5.75 3.95

Basilica, Our Lady of Mercy Church, Quito A298

1980, July 7 Litho. *Perf. 11½*
988 A298 3.40s shown .35 .20
989 A298 3.40s Balcony .35 .20
989A A298 3.40s Dome and cupolas .35 .20

Sizes: 91x116mm, 116x91mm

Imperf

990 A298 5s multi 1.40 1.40
990A A298 5s multi, horiz. 1.40 1.40
990B A298 5s multi 1.40 1.40
Nos. 988-990B,C685-C691 (13) 12.30 8.80

Virgin of Mercy, patron saint of Ecuadorian armed forces. No. 990 contains designs of Nos. C686, C685, 989. No. 990A contains designs of Nos. C688, C691, C690. No. 990B contains designs of Nos. C689, C687, 989A, 988.

Olympic Torch and Rings — A299

Coronation of Virgin of Cisne, 50th Anniv. — A300

Perf. 12x11½

1980, July 19 **Wmk. 395>**
991 A299 5s multi .70 .20
992 A299 7.60s multi 1.25 .30
Nos. 991-992,C695-C696 (4) 3.65 1.70

Souvenir Sheet

Imperf

993 A299 30s multi 5.00 5.00

22nd Summer Olympic Games, Moscow, July 19-Aug. 3.

No. 993 contains vignettes in designs of Nos. 991 and C695.

1980 Litho. *Perf. 11½*
994 A300 1.20s shown .20 .20
995 A300 3.40s Different statue .30 .20

J.J. Olmeda, Father de Velasco, Flags of Ecuador and Riobamba, Constitution A301

1980, Sept. 20 Litho. *Perf. 11½*
996 A301 3.40s multi .20 .20
997 A301 5s multi .55 .35
Nos. 996-997,C700-C701 (4) 2.05 1.20

Souvenir Sheet

Imperf

998 A301 30s multi 2.50 2.50

Constitutional Assembly of Riobamba sesquicentennial. #998 contains vignettes in designs of #996-997.

Young Indian Girl — A302

Perf. 12x11½

1980, Oct. 9 Litho. Wmk. 395
999 A302 1.20s multi .20 .20
1000 A302 3.40s multi .45 .20
Nos. 999-1000,C703-C704 (4) 2.40 1.35

Democratic government, 1st anniversary.

OPEC Emblem A303

1980, Nov. 8 *Perf. 11½x12*
1001 A303 3.40s multi .45 .20

20th anniversary of OPEC. See No. C706.

Decorative Hedges, Capitol Gardens, Carchi A304

1980, Nov. 21 *Perf. 13*
1002 A304 3s multi .35 .20
Nos. 1002,C707-C708 (3) 2.85 1.45

Carchi province centennial.

Cattleya Maxima A305

Designs: Orchids.

1980, Nov. 22 *Perf. 11½x12*
1003 A305 1.20s *shown* .55 .20
1004 A305 3s *Comparattia speciosa* .80 .30
1005 A305 3.40s *Cattleya ir-icolor* .95 .35
Nos. 1003-1005,C709-C712 (7) 17.80 5.10

Souvenir Sheet

Imperf

1006 A305 20s multi 4.50 3.25

No. 1006 contains vignettes in designs of Nos. 1003-1005.

Pope John Paul II and Children — A306

1980, Dec. 27 *Perf. 12*
1007 A306 3.40s multi .50 .20
Nos. 1007,C715-C716 (3) 2.25 1.20

Christmas and visit of Pope John Paul II.

Carlos and Jorge Mantilla Ortega, Editors of El Comercio — A307

El Comercio Newspaper, 75th Anniv.: 3.40s, Editors Cesar & Carlos Mantilla Jacome.

1981, Jan. 6
1008 A307 2s multi .20 .20
1009 A307 3.40s multi .35 .20

Soldier on Map of Ecuador A308

1981, Mar. 10 Litho. *Perf. 13*
1010 A308 3.40s shown .20 .20
1011 A308 3.40s Pres. Roldos .20 .20

National defense.

Theodore E. Gildred and Ecuador I A309

1981, Mar. 31 Litho. *Perf. 13*
1012 A309 2s lt bl & blk .20 .20

Ecuador-US flight, 50th anniv.

A310

A311

1981, Apr. 10
1013 A310 2s multi .30 .20

Octavio Cordero Palacios (1870-1930), humanist.

1981 Litho. *Perf. 13*
1014 A311 2s multi .20 .20
Nos. 1014,C721-C722 (3) 2.10 1.20

Radio station HCJB, 50th anniv.

Virgin of Dolorosa A312

1981, Apr. 30 Litho. *Perf. 12*
1015 A312 2s shown .20 .20
1016 A312 2s San Gabriel College Church .20 .20

Miracle of the painting of the Virgin of Dolorosa at San Gabriel College, 75th anniv.

Dr. Rafael Mendoza Aviles Bridge Inauguration A313

1981, July 25 *Perf. 13*
1017 A313 2s multi .30 .20

Pablo Picasso (1881-1973), Painter — A313a

1981, Oct. 26 Litho. *Imperf.*
1017A A313a 20s multi 2.00 2.00
Nos. 1017A,C728-C731 (5) 6.60 5.55

No. 1017A contains design of No. C728, additional portrait.

World Food Day — A314

1981, Dec. 31 Litho. *Perf. 13½x13*
1018 A314 5s multi .45 .20

See No. C732

Transnave Shipping Co. 10th Anniv. — A315

Intl. Year of the Disabled — A316

1982, Jan. 21 Litho. *Perf. 13*
1019 A315 3.50s Freighter Isla Salango .45 .20

1982, Feb. 25
1020 A316 3.40s Man in wheel-chair .30 .20
Nos. 1020,C733-C734 (3) 1.55 .85

Arch — A317

Juan Montalvo Birth Sesqui. — A318

1982, May **Litho.** ***Perf. 13***
1021 A317 2s shown .20 .20
1022 A317 3s Houses .35 .20

Miniature Sheet
Perf. 12½ on 2 Sides

1023 Sheet of 4, 18th cent. map of Quito 4.50 4.50
a.-d. A317 6s multi 1.10 .50

QUITEX '82, 4th Natl. Stamp Exhib., Quito, Apr. 16-22. #1023 contains 4 48x31mm stamps.

1982 ***Perf. 13***
1024 A318 2s Portrait .20 .20
1025 A318 3s Mausoleum .20 .20
Nos. 1024-1025,C735 (3) 1.20 .85

American Air Forces Cooperation System — A319

4th World Swimming Champ., Guayaquil A320

1982
1026 A319 5s Emblem .30 .20

1982, July 30
1027 A320 1.80s Stadium .20 .20
1028 A320 3.40s Water polo .30 .20
Nos. 1027-1028,C736-C737 (4) 2.15 1.20

A321

A322

1982, Dec. **Litho.** ***Perf. 13***
1029 A321 5.40s shown .20 .20
1030 A321 6s Statue .30 .20

Juan L. Mera (1832-?), Writer, by Victor Mideros.

1983, Mar. 28 **Litho.** ***Perf. 13***
1031 A322 2s multi .30 .20

St. Teresa of Jesus of Avila (1515-82).

Sea Lions A323

Flamingoes A324

1983, June 17 **Litho.** ***Perf. 13***
1032 A323 3s multi .70 .20
1033 A324 5s multi 1.10 .20

Ecuadorian rule over Galapagos Islds., sesqui. (3s); Charles Darwin (1809-1882).

Pres. Rocafuerte A325

Simon Bolivar A326

Perf. 13x13½
1983, Aug. 26 **Litho.** **Wmk. 395**
1034 A325 5s Statue .25 .20
1035 A325 20s Portrait .70 .30
1036 A326 20s Portrait .70 .30
Nos. 1034-1036 (3) 1.65 .80

Vicente Rocafuerte Bejarano, president, 1833-39 (Nos. 1034-1035).

A327

A328

1983, Sept. 3
1037 A327 5s River .30 .20
1038 A327 10s Dam .55 .45

Size: 110x89mm
Imperf

1039 A327 20s Dam, river 2.10 2.10
Nos. 1037-1039 (3) 2.95 2.75

Paute hydroelectric plant opening. No. 1039 is airmail.

Wmk. 395
1983, Nov. 10 **Litho.** ***Perf. 13***
1040 A328 2s multi .30 .20

World Communication Year.

A329

A330

1983, Sept. **Litho.** ***Perf. 13***
1041 A329 3s multi .30 .20

Cent. of Bolivar and El Oro Provinces (1984).

1984, Mar. **Litho.** ***Perf. 13***
1042 A330 15s Engraving .35 .20

Atahualpa (1497-1529), last Incan ruler.

A331

Christmas 1983 — A331a

Creche figures.

Perf. 13½x13, 13x13½
1984, July 7 **Litho.**
1043 A331 5s Jesus & the teachers .25 .20
1044 A331 5s Three kings .25 .20
1045 A331 5s Holy Family .25 .20
1046 A331a 6s Priest .25 .20
Nos. 1043-1046 (4) 1.00 .80

Foreign Policy of Pres. Hurtado A332

State visits.

1984, July 10 ***Perf. 13½x13***
1047 A332 8s Brazil .30 .20
1048 A332 9s PRC .35 .20
1049 A332 24s UN 1.00 .70
1050 A332 28s US 1.25 .75
1051 A332 29s Venezuela 1.25 .85
1052 A332 37s Latin American Economic Conf., Quito 1.60 1.10
Nos. 1047-1052 (6) 5.75 3.80

Miguel Diaz Cueva (1884-1942), Lawyer A333

1984, Aug. 8 **Litho.** ***Perf. 13½x13***
1053 A333 10s multicolored .55 .20

1984 Winter Olympics A334

Manned Flight Bicentenary A335

Perf. 13x13½, 12x11½ (6s)
1984, Aug. 15
1054 A334 2s Emblem .20 .20
1055 A334 4s Ice skating .20 .20
1056 A334 6s Skating, diff. .20 .20
1057 A334 10s Skiing .45 .20
Nos. 1054-1057 (4) 1.05 .80

1984, Aug. 15 ***Perf. 13x13½***
1058 A335 3s Montgolfier .20 .20
1059 A335 6s Charlier's balloon, Paris, 1789 .35 .20

Souvenir Sheet

1060 A335 20s Graf Zeppelin, Montgolfier 1.40 .85

No. 1060 is airmail and contains one imperf. stamp (50x37mm).

SAN MATEO '83, Esmeraldas A336

1984 **Litho.** ***Perf. 13***
1061 A336 8s La Marimba folk dance 1.40 .20

Size: 89x110mm
Imperf

1061A A336 15s La Marimba, diff. .85 .85

No. 1061A is airmail.

Jose Maria de Jesus Yerovi (b. 1824), 4th Archbishop of Quito — A337

1984
1062 A337 5s multi .30 .20

Canonization of Brother Miguel A338

1984 **Litho.** ***Perf. 13***
1063 A338 9s Academy of Languages .30 .20
1064 A338 24s Vatican City, vert. .85 .55

Imperf
Size: 110x90mm

1065 A338 28s Home of Brother Miguel 2.50 1.40
Nos. 1063-1065 (3) 3.65 2.15

No. 1065, airmail, has black control number.

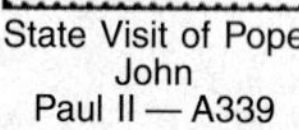
State Visit of Pope John Paul II — A339

Beatification of Mercedes de Jesus Molina — A340

1985, Jan. 23 **Litho.** ***Perf. 13x13½***
1066 A339 1.60s Papal arms .70 .20
1067 A339 5s Blessing crowd .70 .20
1068 A339 9s World map, itinerary .70 .20
1069 A339 28s Pope waving 1.90 .35
1070 A339 29s Portrait 2.10 .45

Size: 90x109mm
Imperf

1071 A339 30s Pope holding crosier 5.25 5.25
Nos. 1066-1071 (6) 11.35 6.65

1985, Jan. 23

Paintings, sculpture.

1072 A340 1.60s Portrait .20 .20
1073 A340 5s Czestochowa Madonna .20 .20
1074 A340 9s Alborada Madonna .35 .20

Size: 90x110mm
Imperf

1075 A340 20s Mercedes de Jesus, children 2.10 2.10
Nos. 1072-1075 (4) 2.85 2.70

Visit of Pope John Paul II, birth bimillennium of the Virgin Mary.

Samuel Valarezo Delgado, Naturalist, Politician — A341

1985, Feb.

1076 A341 2s Bird .20 .20
1077 A341 3s Swordfish, tuna .20 .20
1078 A341 6s Portrait .30 .20
Nos. 1076-1078 (3) .70 .60

ESPANA '84, Madrid A342

1985, Apr. 25 ***Perf. 13½x13***

1079 A342 6s Emblem .20 .20
1080 A342 10s Spanish royal family .35 .20

Size: 110x90mm

Imperf

1081 A342 15s Retiro Park, exhibition site 1.50 1.50

Dr. Pio Jaramillo Alvarado (1884-1968), Historian A343

1985, May 17

1082 A343 6s multi .25 .20

Ingenio Valdez Sugar Refinery — A344

Designs: 50s, Sugar cane, emblem. 100s, Rafael Valdez Cervantes, founder.

1985, June **Litho.** ***Perf. 13***

1082A A344 50s multi .95 .50
1082B A344 100s multi 2.00 .95

Size: 110x90mm

Imperf

1083 A344 30s multi 1.60 1.60
Nos. 1082A-1083 (3) 4.55 3.05

Chamber of Commerce, 10th Anniv. A345

50s, Natl. and American Statues of Liberty.

1985, Aug. 15 ***Perf. 13½x13***

1084 A345 24s multicolored .65 .30
1085 A345 28s multicolored .80 .45

Size: 110x90mm

Imperf

1086 A345 50s multicolored 2.00 2.00
Nos. 1084-1086 (3) 3.45 2.75

Natl. Philatelic Assoc., AFE, 50th Anniv. — A346

1985, Aug. 25 ***Perf. 12***

1087 A346 25s AFE emblem .50 .30
1088 A346 30s No. 357, horiz. .80 .45

Guayaquil Fire Dept., 150th Anniv. A347

1985, Oct. 10 ***Perf. 13½x13***

1089 A347 6s Steam fire pump, 1882 .20 .20
1090 A347 10s Fire Wagon, 1899 .35 .20
1091 A347 20s Anniv. emblem, natl. flag .70 .50
Nos. 1089-1091 (3) 1.25 .90

Natl. Infant Survival Campaign A348

1st Natl. Phil. Cong., Quito, Nov. 25-28 A349

1985, Oct. ***Perf. 13x13½***

1092 A348 10s Boy, girl, tree .35 .20

1985, Nov. ***Perf. 13x13½, 13½x13***

20th cent. illustrations, natl. cultural collection: 5s, Supreme Court, Quito, by J. M. Roura. 10s, Riobamba Cathedral, by O. Munaz. 15s, House of 100 Windows, by J. M. Roura, horiz. 20s, Rural cottage near Cuenca, by J. M. Roura.

No. 1097: a, Stampless cover, 1779, Riobamba. b, Hand press, 1864, Quito. c, Postrider, 1880, Cuenca. d, Monoplane, 1st airmail flight, 1919, Guayaquil.

1093 A349 5s multi .20 .20
1094 A349 10s multi .35 .20
1095 A349 15s multi .50 .35
1096 A349 20s multi .70 .50
Nos. 1093-1096 (4) 1.75 1.25

Souvenir Sheet

1097 Sheet of 4 1.00 1.00
a.-d. A349 5s, any single .20 .20

AFE, 50th anniv. #1097 contains 53x42mm stamps, perf. 13x12½ on 2 sides.

10th Bolivarian Games, Cuenca A350

1985, Nov. ***Perf. 13½x13***

1098 A350 10s Boxing .45 .20
1099 A350 25s Women's gymnastics .55 .30
1100 A350 30s Discus .70 .35
Nos. 1098-1100 (3) 1.70 .85

BAE Calderon, Navy Cent. — A351

Military anniv.: #1102, Fighter plane, Air Force 65th anniv. #1103, Army & paratroops emblems, Special Forces 30th anniv.

1985, Dec. ***Perf. 13x13½***

1101 A351 10s multi .35 .20
1102 A351 10s multi .35 .20
1103 A351 10s multi .35 .20
Nos. 1101-1103 (3) 1.05 .60

UN, 40th Anniv. A352

1985, Oct. **Litho.** ***Perf. 13***

1104 A352 10s UN flag .35 .20
1105 A352 20s Natl. flag .35 .20

Size: 110x90mm

Imperf

1106 A352 50s UN Building 1.00 1.00
Nos. 1104-1106 (3) 1.70 1.40

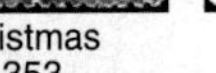

Christmas A353

Indigenous Flowers A354

1985, Nov.

1107 A353 5s Child riding donkey .20 .20
1108 A353 10s Baked goods .35 .20
1109 A353 15s Riding donkey, diff. .50 .45

Size: 90x110mm

Imperf

1110 A353 30s like 5s 1.25 1.25
Nos. 1107-1110 (4) 2.30 2.10

1986, Feb.

1111 A354 24s Embotrium grandiforum .85 .30
1112 A354 28s Topobea sp. 1.40 .30
1113 A354 29s Befaria resinosa mutis 1.75 .35

Size: 110x90mm

Imperf

1114 A354 15s multi 5.50 3.25
Nos. 1111-1114 (4) 9.50 4.20

No. 1114 contains designs of Nos. 1111, 1113, 1112; black control number.

Discovery of the Galapagos Islds., 450th Anniv. A355

Map of the Islands — A356

1986, Feb. 12

1115 A355 10s Land iguana .35 .20
1116 A355 20s Sea lion .70 .45
1117 A355 30s Frigate birds 1.10 .70
1118 A355 40s Penguins 1.40 1.00
1119 A355 50s Sea turtle 1.75 1.10
1120 A355 100s Charles Darwin 3.50 2.50
1121 A355 200s Bishop Tomas de Berlenga, discoverer 7.00 4.50

Perf. 12½ on 2 Sides

1122 A356 Sheet of 4 8.50 8.50
a.-d. 50s, any single 1.50 1.50
Nos. 1115-1122 (8) 24.30 18.95

No. 1122 contains 53x42mm stamps.

Inter-American Development Bank, 25th Anniv. — A357

5s, Antonio Ortiz Mena, pres. 1971-88. 10s, Felipe Herrera, pres. 1960-71. 50s, Emblem.

1986, Mar. 6

1123 A357 5s multi .30 .20
1124 A357 10s multi .45 .20
1125 A357 50s multi .85 .65
Nos. 1123-1125 (3) 1.60 1.05

Guayaquil Tennis Club, 75th Anniv. A358

1986, Mar. 7

1126 A358 10s Emblem .35 .20
1127 A358 10s Francisco Segura Cano, vert. .35 .20
1128 A358 10s Andres Gomez Santos, vert. .35 .20
Nos. 1126-1128 (3) 1.05 .60

1986 World Cup Soccer Championships, Mexico — A359

1986, May 5

1129 A359 5s Shot .20 .20
1130 A359 10s Block .45 .20

An imperf. stamp exists picturing flags, player and emblem. Value $8.50.

Meeting of Presidents Cordero and Betancourt of Colombia, Feb. 1985 A360

1986 Litho. *Perf. 13½x13*
1131 A360 20s Presidents .35 .20
1132 A360 20s Embracing .35 .20

Exports A361

35s, #1137c, Shrimp. 40s, #1137b, Tuna. 45s, #1137a, Sardines. #1137d, MICIP emblem.

1986, Apr. 12
1133 A361 35s ultra & ver .80 .35
1134 A361 40s red & yel grn .80 .35
1135 A361 45s car & dk yel .95 .55

Perf. 12½ on 2 Sides
1137 Sheet of 4 1.75 1.75
a.-d. A361 10s, any single .40 .40
Nos. 1133-1137 (4) 4.30 3.00

No. 1137 contains 4 53x42mm stamps.

A362

La Condamine's First Geodesic Mission, 250th Anniv. — A363

#1141a, Triangulation map for determining equatorial meridian, 1736. #1141b, Partial map of the Maranon & Amazon Rivers, by Samuel Fritz, 1743-1744. #1141c, Base of measurement, Yaruqui plains. #1141d, Caraburo & Dyambaru Pyramids near Quito. #1141 has a continuous design.

1986, July 10 Litho. *Perf. 13½x13*
1138 A362 10s La Condamine .30 .20
1139 A362 15s Maldonado .35 .20
1140 A362 20s Middle of the World, Quito .45 .20
Nos. 1138-1140 (3) 1.10 .60

Souvenir Sheet

Perf. 12½ on 2 Sides
1141 A363 Sheet of 4 2.10 2.10
a.-d. 10s any single .40 .40

Chambers of Commerce A364

1986 Litho. *Perf. 13½x13*
1142 A364 10s Pichincha .25 .20
1143 A364 10s Cuenca .25 .20
1144 A364 10s Guayaquil .25 .20
Nos. 1142-1144 (3) .75 .60

Civil Service and Communications Ministry, 57th Anniv. — A365

Organization emblems.

1986, Dec. Litho. *Perf. 13x13½*
1145 A365 5s State railway .20 .20
1146 A365 10s Post office .20 .20
1147 A365 15s Communications .45 .20
1148 A365 20s Ministry of Public Works .50 .35
Nos. 1145-1148 (4) 1.35 .95

A366

A367

1987, Feb. 16 Litho. *Perf. 13x13½*
1149 A366 5s multi .30 .20

Chamber of Agriculture of the 1st Zone, 50th anniv.

Litho. & Typo.

1988, Jan. 6 *Perf. 13*

Col. Luis Vargas Torres (d. 1887): 50s, Portrait. #1151, Combat unit, c. 1885. #1152a, Torres & his mother, Delfina. #1152b, Letter to Delfina written by Torres during imprisonment, 1882. #1152c, Arms of Ecuador & combat unit.

1150 A367 50s yel grn, blk & gold .85 .45
1151 A367 100s ver, gold & ultra 1.75 .85

Size: 95x140mm

Perf. 12 on One or Two Sides
1152 Block of 3 5.25 5.25
a.-c. A367 100s any single 1.50 1.50
Nos. 1150-1152 (3) 7.85 6.55

Sizes: #1152a, 1152c, 95x28mm, #1152b, 95x83mm.

Founding of Guayaquil, 450th Anniv. A368

15s, Street in Las Penas. 30s, Rafael Mendoza Aviles Bridge. 40s, Francisco de Orellana (c. 1490-1546), Spanish explorer, founder, & reenactment of landing, 1538.

1988, Feb. 19 Litho. *Perf. 13*
1153 A368 15s multi, vert. .20 .20
1154 A368 30s multi .35 .20
1155 A368 40s multi .45 .20
Nos. 1153-1155 (3) 1.00 .60

Social Security Foundation (IESS), 60th Anniv. A369

1988, Mar. 11
1156 A369 50s shown .70 .35
1157 A369 100s multi, diff. 1.25 .70

Dr. Pedro Moncayo y Esparza (1807-1888), Author, Politician A370

1988, Apr. 28 Litho. *Perf. 14x13½*
1158 A370 10s Yaguarcocha Lake .20 .20
1159 A370 15s shown .20 .20
1160 A370 20s Residence .20 .20

Size: 89x110mm

Imperf
1161 A370 100s Full-length portrait 1.10 1.10
Nos. 1158-1161 (4) 1.70 1.70

A371

Avianca Airlines, 60th Anniv. — A372

1988, May 12 Litho. *Perf. 14x13½*
1162 A371 10s Junkers F-13 .20 .20
1163 A371 20s Dornier Wal seaplane .20 .20
1164 A371 30s Ford 5AT trimotor .30 .20
1165 A371 40s Boeing 247-D .35 .20
1166 A371 50s Boeing 720-059B .45 .30
1167 A371 100s Douglas DC-3 1.00 .45
1168 A371 200s Boeing 727-200 1.90 1.00
1169 A371 300s Sikorsky S-38 3.00 1.40

Perf. 13½x14
1170 A372 500s shown 5.00 2.50
Nos. 1162-1170 (9) 12.40 6.45

San Gabriel College, 125th Anniv. A373

1988, July 25 Litho. *Perf. 14x13½*
1171 A373 15s Contemporary facility .20 .20
1172 A373 35s College entrance, 19th cent. .50 .30

A374

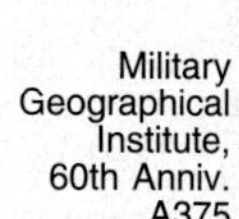

Military Geographical Institute, 60th Anniv. A375

1988, July 25 *Perf. 12½ on 2 Sides*

Size of No. 1173: 110x90mm
1173 A374 Block of 4 1.40 1.40
a.-d. 5s any single .30 .30

Perf. 13½
1174 A375 25s Planetarium .35 .20
1175 A375 50s Zeiss projector .70 .20
1176 A375 60s Anniv. emblem .80 .30
1177 A375 500s Creation, mural by E. Kingman 5.00 2.50
Nos. 1173-1177 (5) 8.25 4.60

In 1996 Nos. 1174, 1183, 1265 were surcharged 800s, 2600s 400s respectively. Only a few sets were sold to the public. The balance were sold by postal employees at greatly inflated prices.

Salesian Brothers in Ecuador, Cent. A376

Designs: 10s, St. John Bosco (1815-88), vert. 50s, 1st Salesian Cong. in Ecuador. 100s, Bosco, Salesian Brothers monument and Andes Mountains.

1988, July 29 Litho. *Perf. 13½*
1178 A376 10s multi .20 .20
1179 A376 50s multi .65 .30

Size: 89x110mm

Imperf
1180 A376 100s multi 1.75 1.10
Nos. 1178-1180 (3) 2.60 1.60

Francisco Coello, Founder — A377

Social Services Council, Guayaquil, Cent. — A378

Flag: a, Emblem (upper left portion). b, Emblem (upper right portion). c, Emblem (lower left portion) and "100 ANOS." d, Emblem (lower right portion) and "DE TRADICION DE FE, AMPARO Y ESPERANZA."

1988, Nov. 24 Litho. *Perf. 13½x14*
1181 A377 15s shown .20 .20
1182 A377 20s Eduardo Arosemena, 1st Director .20 .20
1183 A377 45s Emblem .45 .20

Size: 110x90mm

Perf. 12½ on 2 Sides
1184 A378 Block of 4 1.10 1.10
a.-d. 10s any single .20 .20
Nos. 1181-1184 (4) 1.95 1.70

For surcharge see note following No. 1177.

A379

Azuay Bank, 75th Anniv. — A380

Perf. 14x13½, 13½x14

1989, Mar. 1 Litho.

1185 A379 20s shown .20 .20
1186 A379 40s multi, vert. .30 .20

Size: 90x110mm

Imperf

1187 A380 500s shown 7.00 1.75
Nos. 1185-1187 (3) 7.50 2.15

1988 Summer Olympics, Seoul — A381

Character trademark demonstrating sports.

1989, Mar. 20 ***Perf. 13½x14***

1188 A381 10s Running .20 .20
1189 A381 20s Boxing .20 .20
1190 A381 30s Cycling .30 .20
1191 A381 40s Shooting .30 .20
1192 A381 100s Diving .70 .45
1193 A381 200s Weight lifting 1.40 .95
1194 A381 300s Tae kwon do 2.10 1.40

Size: 90x110mm

Imperf

1195 A381 200s Emblems 2.10 2.10
Nos. 1188-1195 (8) 7.30 5.70

RUMINAHUI '88 — A382

Designs: 50s, *Bird*, by Joaquin Tinta, vert. 70s, Matriz Church, Sangolqui. 300s, Monument to Ruminahui in Sangolqui, Pichincha.

Perf. 14x13½, 13½x14

1989, May 2 Litho. Wmk. 395

1196 A382 50s multi .55 .20
1197 A382 70s multi .85 .20

Size: 90x111mm

Imperf

1198 A382 300s multi 4.50 .85
Nos. 1196-1198 (3) 5.90 1.25

Cantonization, 50th anniv.

Benjamin Carrion Mora, Educator A383

Perf. 13½x14, 14x13½

1989, May 10 Litho.

1199 A383 50s Portrait, vert. .30 .20
1200 A383 70s Loja landscape .45 .20
1201 A383 1000s University 6.75 3.50

Size: 110x90mm

Imperf

1202 A383 200s Portrait, diff. 1.50 1.50
Nos. 1199-1202 (4) 9.00 5.40

2nd Intl. Art Biennial A384

Prize-winning art: 40s, *The Gilded Frame*, by Myrna Baez. 70s, *Paraguay III*, by Carlos Colorabino, vert. 100s, Ordinance establishing the art exhibition. 180s, *Modulation 892*, by Julio Le Parc, vert.

Perf. 14x13½, 13½x14, Imperf. (100s)

1989, June 2 Litho.

Size of No. 1205: 110x90mm

1203 A384 40s multi .35 .20
1204 A384 70s multi .70 .20
1205 A384 100s multi 1.40 .65
1206 A384 180s multi 1.10 .70
Nos. 1203-1206 (4) 3.55 1.75

Guayaquil Chamber of Commerce, Cent. A385

Perf. 13½x14, 14x13½, Imperf. (No. 1208)

1989, June 20 Litho.

Size of No. 1208: 110x91mm

1207 A385 50s Founder Ignacio Molestina, vert. .30 .20
1208 A385 200s Flags 1.90 1.10
1209 A385 300s Headquarters 1.25 1.25
1210 A385 500s Flags, diff. 2.90 1.75
Nos. 1207-1210 (4) 6.35 4.30

French Revolution, Bicent. A386

20s, French natl. colors, anniv. emblem. 50s, Cathedral fresco. 100s, Rooster. 200s, Symbols of the revolution. 600s, Story board showing events of the revolution.

1989, July 11 ***Perf. 13½x14, 14x13½***

1211 A386 20s multi, vert. .20 .20
1212 A386 50s multi .35 .20
1213 A386 100s multi, vert. .55 .35

Size: 90x110mm

Imperf

1214 A386 200s multi, vert. 1.25 1.25
1215 A386 600s multi, vert. 5.00 5.00
Nos. 1211-1215 (5) 7.35 7.00

A387

Ministry of Public Works and Communications A388

#1216a, MOP emblem, 2-lane roadway. #1216b, State railway emblem, train. #1216c, Postal service emblem, airmail cover. #1216d, Telecommunications (IETEL) emblem, wall telephone. #1217, MOP, IETEL, postal service & state railway emblems. 100s, IETEL emblem. 200s, MOP emblem.

1989, July 7 ***Perf. 12½ on 2 Sides***

1216 A387 Block of 4 2.00 2.00
a.-d. 50s any single .40 .40

Perf. 13½x14

1217 A388 50s shown .30 .20
1218 A388 100s multi .55 .35
1219 A388 200s multi 1.25 .70
Nos. 1216-1219 (4) 4.10 3.25

MOP, 60th anniv.; national communications, 105th anniv. (No. 1216d, 100s).

Natl. Red Cross, Intl. Red Cross and Red Crescent Societies, 125th Annivs. A389

1989, Sept. 14 Litho. ***Perf. 13½***

1220 A389 10s Medical volunteer, vert. .20 .20
1221 A389 30s shown .20 .20
1222 A389 200s Two volunteers 1.40 .85
Nos. 1220-1222 (3) 1.80 1.25

Juan Montalvo (1832-1889), Writer A390

1989, Nov. 11 Litho. ***Perf. 14x13½***

1223 A390 50s Mausoleum, Ambato .30 .20
1224 A390 100s Portrait (detail) .70 .45
1225 A390 200s Monument, Ambato 1.25 .95

Size: 90x110mm

Imperf

1226 A390 200s Portrait 1.10 1.10
Nos. 1223-1226 (4) 3.35 2.70

America Issue A391

UPAE emblem and pre-Columbian pottery.

1990, Mar. 6 Litho. ***Perf. 13½***

1227 A391 200s La Tolita incensory, vert. 1.25 .85
1228 A391 300s Warrior (plate) 2.00 1.25

Dated 1989.

Dr. Luis Carlos Jaramillo Leon, Founder A392

#1233a, Dr. Leon. #1230, 1233b, Federico Malo Andrade, honorary president. 130s, #1233c, Roberto Crespo Toral, 1st president. 200s, Alfonso Jaramillo Leon, founder.

1990, Jan. 17 Litho. ***Perf. 13½***

1229 A392 100s shown .65 .45
1230 A392 100s multicolored .65 .45
1231 A392 130s multicolored .85 .55
1232 A392 200s multicolored 1.25 .85

Size: 91x38mm

Perf. 12½ Horiz. on 1 or 2 sides

1233 Block of 3 2.10 2.10
a.-c. A392 100s any single .50 .50
Nos. 1229-1233 (5) 5.50 4.40

Chamber of Commerce, 70th anniversary.

World Cup Soccer, Italy — A393

1990, July 12 Litho. ***Perf. 13½***

1234 A393 100s shown .45 .20
1235 A393 200s Soccer player .85 .45
1236 A393 300s Map of Italy, trophy 1.40 .65

Imperf

Size: 110x90mm

1237 A393 200s Player, flags 1.25 1.25

Size: 60x90mm

1238 A393 300s World Cup Trophy 1.75 1.75
Nos. 1234-1238 (5) 5.70 4.30

Nos. 1235-1236, 1238 vert.

A394

A396

A395

1990, June 12 ***Perf. 13½***

1239 A394 100s multi .45 .20
1240 A394 200s Church tower, book .85 .45

College of St. Mariana, cent.

1990, Sept. 7 Litho. ***Perf. 13½***

Tourism: No. 100s, No. 1244c, Iguana. 200s, No. 1244b, La Compania Church, Quito. 300s, No. 1244a, Old man from Vilcabamba. No. 1244d, Locomotive.

1241 A395 100s multi .50 .20
1242 A395 200s multi, vert. 1.10 .35
1243 A395 300s multi 1.60 .50

Size: 111x90mm

Perf. 12½ on 2 sides

1244 Block of 4 5.25 1.75
a.-d. A395 100s any single .35 .20
Nos. 1241-1244 (4) 8.45 2.80

1990, Sept. 1 ***Perf. 13½***

National Census: 100s, No. 1248a, People and house. 200s, No. 1248b, Map. 300s, No. 1248c, Census breakdown, pencil.

1245 A396 100s multicolored .35 .20
1246 A396 200s multicolored, horiz. .80 .35
1247 A396 300s multicolored 1.10 .50

Size: 109x88mm

Perf. 12½ on 2 sides

1248 Block of 3 1.25 1.25
a.-c. A396 100s any single .30 .30
Nos. 1245-1248 (4) 3.50 2.30

A397

A398

1990, Nov. 2 Litho. ***Perf. 14***

1249 A397 200s Flags .80 .35
1250 A397 300s shown 1.10 .50

Organization of Petroleum Exporting Countries (OPEC), 30th anniv.

1990, Oct. 31 ***Perf. 13½x14***
1251 A398 200s Emblem .80 .35
1252 A398 300s Wooden parrots 1.10 .50

Size: 92x110mm

Imperf

1253 A398 200s Wooden parrots, diff. 1.25 1.25
Nos. 1251-1253 (3) 3.15 2.10

Artisans' Organization, 25th anniv.

Flowers — A399

Wmk. 395

1990, Nov. 12 **Litho.** ***Perf. 13½***
1254 A399 100s Sobralia .70 .20
1255 A399 100s Blakea, vert. .70 .20
1256 A399 100s Cattleya, vert. .70 .20
1257 A399 100s Loasa, vert. .70 .20
Nos. 1254-1257 (4) 2.80 .80

Discovery of America, 500th Anniv. (in 1992) A400

1990, Dec. 31 **Litho.** ***Perf. 13½***
1258 A400 100s Ancient dwelling .45 .20
1259 A400 200s Mangrove swamp 1.00 .35

Natl. Union of Journalists, 50th Anniv. A401

1991, Feb. 28
1260 A401 200s shown .80 .50
1261 A401 300s Eugenio Espejo, writer 1.25 .55
1262 A401 400s Union emblem 1.40 .80
Nos. 1260-1262 (3) 3.45 1.85

Radio Quito, 50th Anniv. A402

Designs: 200s, Man with microphone, vert. 500s, Family listening to radio.

1991, Apr. 10
1263 A402 200s multicolored .50 .30
1264 A402 500s multicolored 1.40 .65

Dr. Pablo A. Suarez, Birth Cent. — A403

1991, Sept. 16 **Wmk. 395**
1265 A403 70s multicolored .30 .20

Dated 1990.
For surcharge see note following No. 1177.

America Issue A404

UPAEP emblem and: 200s, Columbus' ships. 500s, Columbus, landing in America.

1991, Oct. 18 **Litho.** ***Perf. 13½x13***
1266 A404 200s multicolored .70 .35
1267 A404 500s multicolored 1.60 .80

A405

A406

Designs: Cultural artifacts.

Wmk. 395

1991, Nov. 14 **Litho.** ***Perf. 13½***
1268 A405 100s Cat censer .45 .20
1269 A405 200s Statue of old man's head .85 .30
1270 A405 300s Zoomorphic statue 1.40 .50
Nos. 1268-1270 (3) 2.70 1.00

Dated 1990. See No. 1291.

1991 ***Perf. 13***

Design: 500s, Woman in profile.

1271 A406 300s shown .85 .45
1272 A406 500s multicolored 1.40 .70

Day of Non-violence Toward Women.

Jacinto Jijon y Caamano, Archaeologist, Birth Cent. — A407

1991, Dec. 11 ***Perf. 13½***
1273 A407 200s Portrait, vert. .55 .30
1274 A407 300s shown .85 .45

Pres. Rodrigo Borja, Ecuador and Pres. Jaime Paz Zamora, Bolivia — A408

1991, Dec. 10 ***Perf. 14x13½***
1275 A408 500s multicolored 1.40 .70

Pres. Rodrigo Borja's Visit to the UN — A409

Wmk. 395

1992, Jan. 24 **Litho.** ***Perf. 14***
1276 A409 100s multicolored .25 .20
1277 A409 1000s Flags, world map 2.50 1.25

Battle of Jambeli, 50th Anniv. — A410

#1278, Gunboat Calderon and Capt. Raphael Moran Valverde. #1279, Dispatch boat Atahualpa and Ens. Victor Naranjo Fiallo. #1280, Valverde, Fiallo and ships.

1992, Apr. 7
1278 A410 300s multicolored .50 .35
1279 A410 500s multicolored 1.00 .65

Size: 110x90mm

Imperf

1280 A410 500s multicolored 2.10 1.75
Nos. 1278-1280 (3) 3.60 2.75

Galapagos Islands Wildlife — A411

Designs: No. 1281, Giant tortoise. No. 1282, Galapagos penguin, vert. No. 1283, Zalophus californianus, vert. No. 1284, Swallow-tailed gull. No. 1285, Fregata minor. No. 1286, Land iguana.

1992, Apr. 10 **Litho.** ***Perf. 13½***
1281 A411 100s multicolored .55 .35
1282 A411 100s multicolored .55 .35
1283 A411 100s multicolored .55 .35
1284 A411 100s multicolored .55 .35
1285 A411 100s multicolored .55 .35
1286 A411 100s multicolored .55 .35
Nos. 1281-1286 (6) 3.30 2.10

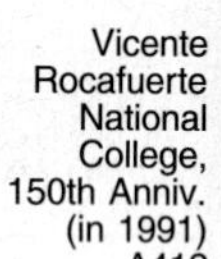

Vicente Rocafuerte National College, 150th Anniv. (in 1991) A412

Perf. 14x13½

1992, Apr. 29 **Litho.** **Wmk. 395**
1287 A412 200s shown .50 .30
1288 A412 400s Vicente Rocafuerte .95 .45

Eloy Alfaro (1842-1912), President — A413

Designs: 300s, Portrait, vert.

Perf. 13½x14, 14x13½

1992, Aug. 26 **Litho.** **Wmk. 395**
1289 A413 300s multicolored .55 .35
1290 A413 700s multicolored 1.25 .65

Cultural Artifacts Type of 1991

1992, Sept. 6 **Litho.** ***Perf. 13½***
1291 A405 400s Ceremonial mask 1.10 .45

Dated 1990.

Discovery of America, 500th Anniv. A414

Wmk. 395

1992, Oct. 15 **Litho.** ***Perf. 13½***
1292 A414 200s Sailing ship .55 .30
1293 A414 400s Columbus, map, vert. 1.10 .55

Andres F. Cordova (b. 1892) A415

1992, Nov. 17 **Litho.** ***Perf. 13½***
1294 A415 300s multicolored .70 .35

Beatification of Narcisa of Jesus — A416

1992, Nov. 30 ***Perf. 13½***
1295 A416 100s multicolored .30 .20

A417

A418

Christmas: 300s, Infant Jesus of Saqueo, 18th cent. 600s, Stable scene, Infant Jesus asleep on hay.

1992, Dec. 14 ***Perf. 13½***
1296 A417 300s multicolored .70 .35
1297 A417 600s multicolored 1.40 .70

1992, Dec. 29
1298 A418 200s multicolored .55 .30

Father Juan de Velasco, Death Bicent.

Frogs — A419

A420

Perf. 13½x14

1993, Jan. 28 **Litho.** **Wmk. 395**
1299 A419 300s Agalychnis spurelli .50 .35
1300 A419 300s Atelopus bomolochos .50 .35
1301 A419 600s Gastrotheca plumbea 1.10 .70
1302 A419 600s Hyla picturata 1.10 .70
1303 A419 900s Dendrobates sp. 1.60 1.10
1304 A419 900s Sphaenorhyncus lacteus 1.60 1.10
Nos. 1299-1304 (6) 6.40 4.30

1993, Feb. 16 **Litho.** ***Perf. 13x13½***
1305 A420 300s blue .65 .20

J. Roberto Paez, (1893-1983), co-founder of social security.

1397 A470 1200s multicolored 1.40 .70
1398 A470 2000s multicolored 2.50 1.10
Nos. 1392-1398 (7) 7.80 3.55

Size: 120x100mm

1399 A470 2000s multicolored 3.00 3.00

Nos. 1392-1396 were printed in strips of 2 each.

Civil Aviation, 50th Anniv. A471

1996, Aug. 8
1400 A471 2000s multicolored 2.50 1.10

1996 Summer Olympic Games, Atlanta A472

Atlanta Games emblem and: 1000s, Mascot carrying torch. No. 1402, Emblem of Olympic Committee of Ecuador. 3000s, Jefferson Perez, vert.

No. 1404, Perez, gold medalist, 20-kilometer walk, walking.

1996
1401 A472 1000s multicolored 1.25 .55
1402 A472 2000s multicolored 2.25 1.10
a. Pair, #1401-1402 3.50 3.50
1403 A472 3000s multicolored 3.25 1.75
Nos. 1401-1403 (3) 6.75 3.40

Size: 100x120mm

Imperf

1404 A472 2000s multicolored 3.00 3.00

Fight Against Drug Abuse — A473

Dr. Eduardo Salazar Gomez, Birth Cent. — A474

1996 Litho. Wmk. 395 *Perf. 13*
1408 A473 2000s multicolored 3.00 1.50

1996
1409 A474 1000s multicolored 1.60 .75

Catholic University, Quito, 50th Anniv. A475

Junior League Organization A476

Designs: 400s, Outside view of building, horiz. 800s, Entrance.

1996
1410 A475 400s multicolored .65 .35
1411 A475 800s multicolored 1.25 .65

1996
1412 A476 2000s Children's faces, horiz. 3.25 1.50
1413 A476 2600s shown 4.00 2.00

Catholic University, Quito, 50th Anniv. A477

1996, Nov.
1414 A477 2000s multicolored 3.00 1.50

The Universe Daily Newspaper, 75th Anniv. — A478

1996, Dec.
1415 A478 2000s multicolored 3.00 1.50

Private Technical University, Loja — A479

1996, Dec. 9
1416 A479 4700s multicolored 7.00 3.25

UNICEF, 50th Anniv. A480

1996, Dec. 11
1417 A480 2000s multicolored 3.00 1.50

Christmas A481

Children's paintings: 600s, Merry Chrismas All Over the World. 800s, World of Peace and Love. 2000s, Christmas.

1996, Dec. 19
1418 A481 600s multicolored .95 .50
1419 A481 800s multicolored 1.25 .65

Size: 51x31mm

Perf. 13½

1420 A481 2000s multicolored 3.00 1.50
Nos. 1418-1420 (3) 5.20 2.65

Preserving the Ecological System A482

America '95: 1000s, Voltur grypus. 1500s, Harpia harpyja, vert.

1996, Dec. 30 *Perf. 13*
1421 A482 1000s multicolored 1.50 .80
1422 A482 1500s multicolored 2.25 1.10

Typical Children's Costumes — A483

America '96: No. 1423, "Bordando" girl, Zuleta. No. 1424, Girl from Otavalo.

1996, Dec. 30
1423 A483 2600s multicolored 4.25 1.25
1424 A483 2600s multicolored 4.25 3.75
a. Pair, #1423-1424 8.50 8.50

Mejia Natl. Institute, Cent. A484

Design: Jose Mejia Lequerica, building.

1997, Jan. 10
1425 A484 1000s multicolored 1.50 .75

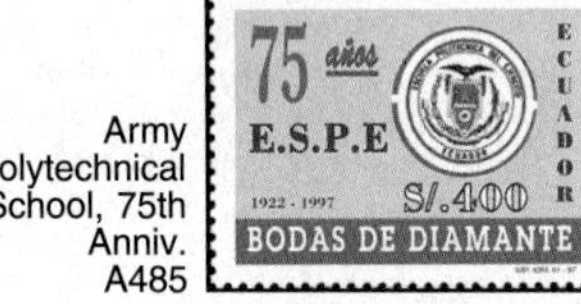

Army Polytechnical School, 75th Anniv. A485

Wmk. 395

1997, June 16 Typo. *Perf. 13*
1426 A485 400s multicolored .70 .30

Natl. Experimental College, Ambato, 50th Anniv. A486

1997, June 20
1427 A486 600s multicolored .90 .50

Vicente Rocafuerte (1783-1847), First Constitutional President of Ecuador — A487

1997, July 1
1428 A487 400s multicolored .70 .30

49th Intl. Congress of the Americanists A488

1997, July 3
1429 A488 2000s multicolored 3.00 1.40

Butterflies A489

Designs: 400s, Actinote equatoria. 600s, Dismorphia amphione. 800s, Marpesia corinna. 2000s, Marpesia berania. 2600s, Morpho helenor.

1997, July 21
1430 A489 400s multicolored .70 .30
1431 A489 600s multicolored .95 .35
1432 A489 800s multicolored 1.25 .50
1433 A489 2000s multicolored 3.00 1.25
1434 A489 2600s multicolored 4.25 1.60
Nos. 1430-1434 (5) 10.15 4.00

Air Club of Ecuador, 66th Anniv. A490

1997, July 23
1435 A490 2600s multicolored 4.25 1.60

Orchids — A491

400s, Epidendrum secundum. 600s, Epidendrum. 800s, Oncidium cultratrum. 2000s, Oncidium sp mariposa. 2600s, Pleurothalis corrulensis.

1997, Aug. 14 Litho. *Perf. 13*
1436 A491 400s multicolored .70 .30
1437 A491 600s multicolored .95 .40
1438 A491 800s multicolored 1.25 .50
1439 A491 2000s multicolored 3.00 1.25
1440 A491 2600s multicolored 4.25 1.60
Nos. 1436-1440 (5) 10.15 4.05

Rocks and Minerals — A492

1997, Oct. 6 Litho. *Perf. 13*
1441 A492 400s Quartz .70 .30
1442 A492 600s Chalcopyrite .95 .40
1443 A492 800s Gold 1.25 .50
1444 A492 2000s Petrified wood 3.00 1.25
1445 A492 2600s Pyrite 4.25 1.60
Nos. 1441-1445 (5) 10.15 4.05

A493

A494

Christmas (Children's designs): 400s, Santa as postman delivering letters over world. 2600s, Star on Christmas tree reaching for letters, airplane under tree. 3000s, Child dreaming of angels carrying letters.

1997, Dec. 22 Litho. *Perf. 13*
1446 A493 400s multicolored .70 .30
1447 A493 2600s multicolored 4.25 1.60
1448 A493 3000s multicolored 5.00 2.00
Nos. 1446-1448 (3) 9.95 3.90

1997, Dec. 29
1449 A494 800s Life of a Postman 1.25 .55
1450 A494 2000s On bicycle 3.00 1.25

America issue.

A495

A496

Matilde Hidalgo de Procel (1889-1974), physician, social reformer.

1998, Mar. 6 Litho. *Perf. 13*
1451 A495 2000s multicolored 2.00 1.25

Intl. Women's Day.

Wmk. 395

1998, Apr. 22 Litho. *Perf. 13*
1452 A496 2000s multicolored 3.50 2.25

Dr. Misael Acosta Solis, botanist.

Organization of American States (OAS), 50th Anniv. A497

1998, Apr. 30
1453 A497 2600s multicolored 2.50 1.60

1998 World Cup Soccer Championships, France — A498

Designs: 2600s, Trophy, mascot, vert. 3000s, Two players, trophy.

1998, May
1454 A498 2000s multicolored 2.00 1.25
1455 A498 2600s multicolored 2.50 1.60
1456 A498 3000s multicolored 3.00 1.90
Nos. 1454-1456 (3) 7.50 4.75

Flowers — A499 Galapagos Flora — A500

600s, Gypsophila paniculata. 800s, Banana flowers. 2000s, Roses. 2600s, Asters.

1998, June
1457 A499 600s multicolored .60 .35
1458 A499 800s multicolored .80 .50
1459 A499 2000s multicolored 2.00 1.25
1460 A499 2600s multicolored 2.50 1.50
Nos. 1457-1460 (4) 5.90 3.60

1998, July

Designs: 600s, Jasminocereus thouarsii. 1000s, Cordia lutea lamarck. 2600s, Momordica charantia.

1461 A500 600s multicolored .60 .35
1462 A500 1000s multicolored 1.00 .60
1463 A500 2600s multicolored 2.50 1.60
Nos. 1461-1463 (3) 4.10 2.55

Tourism A501

600s, St. Augustine Church, Quito. 800s, Monument to the Heroes of the Independence, Guayaquil. 2000s, Equator Monument, Quito. 2600s, Mojanda Lake.

1998, July
1464 A501 600s multi, vert. .60 .35
1465 A501 800s multi, vert. .80 .50
1466 A501 2000s multi 2.00 1.25
1467 A501 2600s multi 2.50 1.60
Nos. 1464-1467 (4) 5.90 3.70

Emiliano Ortega Espinosa (1898-1974), Educator A502

Perf. 13¼x13, 13x13¼

1998 Litho. Wmk. 395
1468 A502 400s shown .50 .30
1469 A502 4700s Portrait, vert. 5.25 3.50

A503 A504

Carlos Cueva Tamariz (1898-1991), educator.

Perf. 13x13¼

1998, Nov. Litho. Wmk. 395
1470 A503 2600s multicolored 2.50 1.60

Wmk. 395

1998, Nov. 20 Litho. *Perf. 13*
1471 A504 600s multicolored .60 .40

Radio Club of Guayaquil, 75th anniv.

6th South American Games — A505

Designs: 400s, Mascot. 1000s, Games poster, tennis rackets, hurdles, sailing, hammer throw, bowling, boxing. 2600s, Mascot, parallel bars, wrestling, judo, fencing, running, swimming, shooting, cycling.

1998
1472 A505 400s multicolored .50 .30
1473 A505 1000s multicolored 1.00 .60
1474 A505 2600s multicolored 2.50 1.60
Nos. 1472-1474 (3) 4.00 2.50

Paintings by Eduardo Kingman (1913-85) A506

Designs: 600s, Ecuadoran Woman, vert. 800s, World Without Answers.

1998, Dec. 10
1475 A506 600s multicolored .60 .35
1476 A506 800s multicolored .80 .50

Manuela Sáenz (1797-1856), Mistress of Simon Bolívar — A507

1999, Jan. 19
1477 A507 1000s multicolored .90 .55

America issue. Exists imperf.

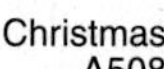

Christmas A508

Children's drawings: 1000s, Santa posting letters on tree. 2600s, People holding up giant letter, vert. 3000s, Santas parachuting with letters, nativity scene, tree, vert.

1998, Dec. 22
1478 A508 1000s multicolored .90 .55
1479 A508 2600s multicolored 2.25 1.40
1480 A508 3000s multicolored 2.50 1.60
Nos. 1478-1480 (3) 5.65 3.55

Los Tayos Caves A509

1999, Feb. 25 Litho. *Perf. 13*
1481 A509 1000s Man in cave, vert. .80 .50
1482 A509 2600s shown 2.25 1.40

Napal, the Age of Wrath, by Oswaldo Guayasamin (1919-99) — A510

Wmk. 395

1999, May 12 Litho. *Perf. 13*
1483 A510 2000s multicolored 1.75 .55

Iberoamerica art exhibition.

Universal Day of Human Rights A511

1999, May 28
1484 A511 4000s multicolored 3.50 2.25

Eloy Alfaro Superior Military College, Cent. A512

5200s, Cannon, monument, flags, buildings. 9400s, Honor Guard, modern building.

1999, June 4
1485 A512 5200s multicolored 4.50 2.50
1486 A512 9400s multicolored 7.50 4.75

Puyo, 100th Anniv. — A513

Designs: a, Bromeliad. b, Ara chloroptera.

1999, June 2
1487 A513 4000s Pair, #a.-b. 7.00 5.00

Dr. Rafael Barahona Andrade (1827-98) A514

Perf. 13¼x13

1999, June 17 Litho. Wmk. 395
1488 A514 5200s multi 4.50 2.50

Generals — A515

Designs: 2000s, Manuel Antonio de Luzarraga y Echezurria (1776-1859). 4000s, Tomas Carlos Wright (1799-1868).

1999, Aug. 11 *Perf. 13x13¼*
1489-1490 A515 Set of 2 5.25 3.25

Galapagos Islands Flora and Fauna A516

No. 1491, vert.: a, Phoenicopterus ruber. b, Buteo galapagoensis. c, Amblyrhynchus cristatus. d, Conolophus subcristatus. e, Opuntia galapageia. f, Pyrocephalus rubinus. g, Sula nebouxii. h, Sula dactylatra. i, Scalesia villosa. j, G. elephantopus abingdoni.

No. 1492: a, Brachycereus nesioticus. b, Dendroica petechia. c, Nannopterum harrisi. d, Tursiops truncatus. e, Pentaceraster cumingi. f, G. elephantopus porteri. g, Microlophus albemarlensis. h, Arctocephalus galapagoensis. i, Spheniscus mendiculus. j, Geospiza scandens.

Perf. 13x13¼, 13¼x13

1999, Sept. 3 Litho. Wmk. 395
1491 Strip of 10 *37.50 24.00*
a.-j. A516 7000s Any single *3.50 1.25*
1492 Strip of 10 *80.00 50.00*
a.-j. A516 15,000s Any single *7.00 4.50*

Intl. Year of Older Persons A517

Designs: No. 1493, 1000s, Hands of child and old person. No. 1494, 1000s, Emblem.

Perf. 13¼x13

1999, Sept. 22 Litho. Wmk. 395
1493-1494 A517 Set of 2 1.50 1.00

SOS Children's Villages, 50th Anniv. — A518

a, 2000s, Two children. b, 2000s, One child. Illustration reduced.

1999, Sept. 30
1495 A518 Pair, #a-b 2.25 1.40

America Issue, A World Without Arms — A519

No. 1496: a, World map. b, Tree, bird, Earth. Illustration reduced.

Perf. 13¼x13

1999, Dec. 11 Litho. Wmk. 395

1496 A519 4000s Pair, #a-b *5.00 3.00*

UPU, 125th Anniv. A520

Design: 8000s, UPU emblem. 1000s, Ecuadorian Postal Service mascot, vert. 4000s, Dove with letter, vert.

Perf. 13¼x12¾

1999, Dec. 11 Litho. Wmk. 395

1497	A520 1000s multi		.45	.25
1498	A520 4000s multi		1.75	1.00
1499	A520 8000s multi		3.50	2.25
	Nos. 1497-1499 (3)		5.70	3.50

Ecuador as Secretary General of Permanent South Pacific Commission A521

Perf. 13x13¼

1999, Dec. 21 Litho. Wmk. 395

1500 A521 7000s multi *3.75 2.40*

Machala Tourism A522

Designs: No. 1501, Banana flower and city. No. 1502, vert.: a, Monument to banana plantation workers. b, City Hall.

1999, Dec. 28 ***Perf. 13¼x13, 13x13¼***

1501 A522 3000s multi *1.60 .95*

1502 A522 3000s Pair, #a-b *3.25 1.90*

EMELEC Soccer Team — A523

#1503: a, Jorge Bolanos. b, Carlos Raffo. No. 1504, EMELEC team photo, 1957. No. 1505, Player, vert.

Perf. 13x13¼, 13¼x13

2000, Jan. 7 Litho.

1503	A523 1000s Pair, #a-b	*.40*	*.40*
1504	A523 2000s multi	*.40*	*.25*
1505	A523 2000s multi	*.40*	*.25*

Guayas Philanthropic Society, 150th Anniv. A524

Designs: 1000s, Building. 2000s, Founder Juan Maria Martinez Coello. 4000s, Emblem.

Perf. 13¼x13

2000, Jan. 19 Litho. Wmk. 395

1506-1508 A524 Set of 3 *1.50 .80*

Dual Nationality Day — A525

2000, Jan. 24 ***Perf. 13x13¼***

1509 A525 7000s multi *1.25 .75*

Cuenca, World Heritage Site — A526

No. 1510: a, Buildings. b, Puente Roto and Tomebamba River. c, Church bell gable, Concepcion Monastery. d, Cathedral and city skyline. e, San José Church.

2000, Mar. 24 ***Perf. 13¼x13***

1510 Horiz. strip of 5 *3.50 3.50*

a.-e. A526 4000s Any single *.65 .35*

Nicolas Lapentti, Tennis Player — A527

2000, Mar. 26 ***Perf. 13x13¼***

1511 A527 8000s multi *1.60 .95*

Birds — A528

No. 1512: a, Diglossa cyanea. b, Oreotrochilus chimborazo. c, Trogon personatus. d, Colibri coruscans. e, Atlapetes rufinucha.

2000, Apr. 7

1512 Horiz. strip of 5 *8.00 8.00*

a.-e. A528 8000s Any single *1.40 .95*

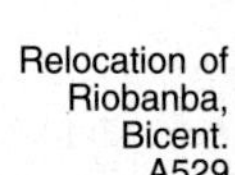

Relocation of Riobanba, Bicent. A529

Designs: No. 1513, Mt. Chimborazo. No. 1514: a, Riobamba Cathedral. b, Statue of Pedro Vicente Maldonado.

2000, Apr. 13 ***Perf. 13¼x13, 13x13¼***

1513 A529 8000s multi *1.60 .95*

1514 A529 8000s Pair, #a-b 3.25 3.25

Gen. Eloy Alfaro, Founder of Natl. Music Conservatory A530

2000, Apr. 19 ***Perf. 13x13¼***

1515 A530 10,000s multi *1.75 .95*

Natl. Music Conservatory, cent.

Climbing of Mt. Everest by Ivan Vallejo Ricaurte A531

2000, May 23 ***Perf. 13¼x13***

1516 A531 8000s multi *1.25 .70*

100 Cents=1 Dollar

Dolores Sucre Fiscal College, 50th Anniv. — A532

Perf. 13x13¼

2000 Litho. Wmk. 395

1517 A532 32c multi .65 .30

Training Ship Guayas — A533

2000, July 5 ***Perf. 13x13¼***

1518 A533 68c multi 1.40 .70

Imperf

Size: 90x110mm

1519 A533 $1 multi 2.00 1.00

Battle of Jambeli, 59th Anniv., Navy Day — A534

2000 ***Perf. 13¼x13***

1520 A534 16c multi .35 .20

Guayaquil Civic Renovation A535

2000, July ***Perf. 13x13¼***

1521 A535 84c multi 1.75 .85

Megaptera Novaeangliae — A536

2000, Aug. 3 ***Perf. 13¼x13***

1522 A536 84c multi 1.75 .85

Imperf

Size: 90x110mm

1523 A536 $1 Two whales 2.00 1.00

American and Caribbean Dog Show, Quito A537

2000, Aug. ***Perf. 13¼x13***

1524 A537 68c multi 1.40 .70

Guayaquil Tennis Club, 90th Anniv. A538

2000, Aug. Wmk. 395

1525 A538 84c multi 1.75 .85

Alberto Spencer, Soccer Player — A539

2000 ***Perf. 13x13¼***

1526 A539 68c multi 1.40 .70

Imperf

Size: 69x99mm

1527 A539 $1 Spencer, crowd 2.00 1.00

2000 Summer Olympics, Sydney — A540

Ecuadoran team emblem, Games emblem and: 32c Mascots. 68c, Runner Jefferson Perez Marchista. 84c, Weight lifter Boris Burov, Olympic flag, horiz.

2000, Sept. ***Perf. 13x13¼, 13¼x13***

1528-1530 A540 Set of 3 3.75 1.90

Salinas Yacht Club, 60th Anniv. A541

Designs: No. 1531a, Lighthouse, vert. Nos. 1531b, 1533, Sailboat, vert. 68c, Sailboats, fisherman, waterskier, scuba diver.

2000, Oct. ***Perf. 13x13¼***

1531 A541 32c Horiz. pair, #a-b 1.25 .65

Perf. 13¼x13

1532 A541 68c multi 1.40 .70

Imperf

Size: 69x100mm

1533 A541 $1 multi 2.00 1.00

Inter-American Development Bank, 40th Anniv. — A542

Designs: No. 1534a, 68c, No. 1536a, 25c, Salsipuedes Bridge, Felipe Herrera. No. 1534b, 68c, No. 1536b, 25c, Daule-Peripa Dam, Antonio Ortiz Mena. No. 1535a, 84c, No. 1536c, 25c, Enrique Iglesias, Ucubamba Water Treatment Plant. No. 1535b, 84c, No. 1536d, 25c, Bank emblem, History Museum, Quito.

Illustration reduced.

2000, Oct. 27 ***Perf. 13¼x13***

Horiz. Pairs, #a-b

1534-1535 A542 Set of 2 6.00 3.00

Rouletted 14 on 2 sides

1536 A542 25c Sheet of 4, #a-d 2.00 1.00

Size of Nos. 1536a-1536b, 75x48mm; Nos. 1536c-1536d, 75x42mm.

National Union of Journalists A543

2000, Nov. 1 ***Perf. 13¼x13***

1537 A543 16c multi .35 .20

Civil Registry, Cent. — A544

No. 1538: a, People, flag, computer. b, Fingerprint, family.

2000, Oct. 27 ***Perf. 13x13¼***

1538 A544 68c Horiz. pair, #a-b 2.75 1.40

Mama Negra Festival, Latacunga — A545

No. 1539: a, Mama Negra with doll. b, Man in Moor King costume.

2000, Nov. ***Perf. 13x13¼***

1539 A545 32c Horiz. pair, #a-b 1.25 .65

Imperf

Size: 100x68mm

1540 A545 $1 Mama Negra, doll, diff. 2.00 1.00

Ministry of Labor, 75th Anniv. — A546

2000, Nov. 15 ***Perf. 13x13¼***

1541 A546 68c multi 1.40 .70

Intl. Fruits and Flowers Festival, Ambato, 50th Anniv. A547

No. 1542, horiz.: a, Tungurahua Volcano. b, Aerial view of Ambato.

No. 1544, horiz.: a, Flower. b. Fruit.

2000, Nov. ***Perf. 13¾***

1542 A547 32c Vert. pair, #a-b 1.25 .65
1543 A547 84c shown 1.75 .85
1544 A547 84c Vert. pair, #a-b 3.50 1.75
Nos. 1542-1544 (3) 6.50 3.25

Imperf

Size: 68x100mm

1545 A547 $1 Ambato 2.00 1.00

Christmas — A548

Children's art by — No. 1546, 68c: a, Giannina Rhor Isaias. b, Josue Remache Romero. No. 1547, 84c: a, Maria Cedeño Bazurtto. b, Juan Alban Salazar.

$1, Walther Carvache.

Illustration reduced.

2000, Dec. 15 ***Perf. 13¼x13***

Horiz. Pairs, #a-b

1546-1547 A548 Set of 2 6.00 3.00

Imperf

Size: 100x69mm

1548 A548 $1 multi 2.00 1.00

Expoflores Flower Producer and Exporter Association A549

2000 ***Perf. 13x13¼***

1549 A549 68c multi 1.40 .70

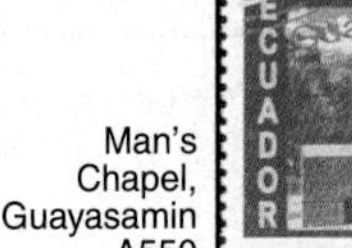

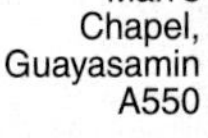

Man's Chapel, Guayasamin A550

2000 ***Perf. 13¼x13***

1550 A550 16c multi .35 .20

Spanish Chamber of Commerce in Ecuador, 80th Anniv. — A551

2000, Dec. ***Perf. 13x13¼***

1551 A551 16c multi .35 .20

Intl. Volunteers Year — A552

2000 **Wmk. 395**

1552 A552 16c multi .35 .20

Restoration of Bolivar Theater, Quito — A553

Designs: 16c, Piano, banquet room. 32c, Stage, orchestra, horiz.

2000, Dec. ***Perf. 13x13¼, 13¼x13***

1553-1554 A553 Set of 2 .95 .50

Spondylus Princeps A554

2000, Dec. 16 ***Perf. 13¾***

1555 A554 84c multi 1.75 .85

Imperf

Size: 69x99mm

1556 A554 $1 multi 2.00 1.00

America Issue, Fight Against AIDS — A555

No. 1557: a, Strands. b, Earth.

2000 ***Perf. 13x13¼***

1557 A555 84c Horiz. pair, #a-b 3.50 1.75

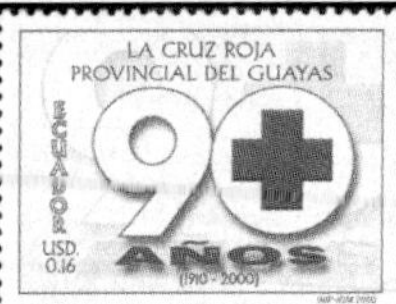

Guayas Province Red Cross, 90th Anniv. A556

2000 ***Perf. 13¼x13***

1558 A556 16c multi .35 .20

Guayas Sports Federation, 78th Anniv. — A557

2000, Dec. ***Perf. 13x13¼***

1559 A557 16c multi .35 .20

Landscapes A557a

Designs: No. 1559A, 16c, Andean region. No. 1559B, 16c, Pacific coast. 32c, Tourism emblem. 68c, Amazonia. 84c, Galápagos Islands.

Perf. 13¼x12¾

2001, Jan. 24 **Litho.** **Wmk. 395**

1559A A557a 16c multi .40 .20
1559B A557a 16c multi .40 .20
1559C A557a 32c multi .70 .35
1559D A557a 68c multi 1.50 .75
1559E A557a 68c multi 1.50 .75
Nos. 1559A-1559E (5) 4.50 2.25

Guayas Soccer Team, 50th Anniv. A558

2001, Mar. 8 ***Perf. 13¼x13***

1560 A558 68c multi 1.40 .70

Census — A558a

Census — A558b

Perf. 12¾x13¼

2001, Mar. 12 **Litho.** **Wmk. 395**

1560A A558a 68c multi — —
1560B A558b 68c multi — —
c. Horiz. pair, #1560A-1560B — —

Dr. Raúl Clemente Huerta A559

2001, Apr. 4 ***Perf. 13¼x13***

1561 A559 68c multi 1.40 .70

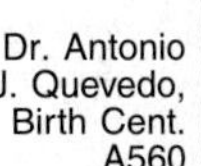

Dr. Antonio J. Quevedo, Birth Cent.
A560

2001, Apr. 5 **Litho.**
1562 A560 84c multi 1.75 .85

Military Geographic Institute
A560a

No. 1562A: b, Soldier, building. c, Computer, printing press.

Perf. 13¼x12¾

2001, Apr. 11 **Litho.** **Wmk. 395**
1562A A560a 68c Vert. pair, #b-c 2.75 1.40

Automobile Club of Ecuador, 50th Anniv.
A561

2001, May 15 **Wmk. 395**
1563 A561 84c multi 1.75 .85

San Francisco de Peleusí Church, Azogues — A561a

Perf. 12¾x13¼

2001, May **Litho.** **Wmk. 395**
1563A A561a 84c multi 1.75 .85

Women's Training Institute — A562

2001, Apr. 10 ***Perf. 13x13¼***
1564 A562 84c multi 1.75 .85

Intl. Women's Day
A563

No. 1565: a, Woman, child, corn. b, Woman, emblem.

2001, Apr. 2 ***Perf. 13¼x13***
1565 A563 84c Vert. pair, #a-b 3.50 1.75

Secular Education at Manuela Cañizares University, Cent.
A564

2001, Mar. 29 **Wmk. 395**
1566 A564 84c multi 1.75 .85

Ecuador Merchant Marines, Cent. — A565

2001, Jan. 2001 ***Perf. 13x13¼***
1567 A565 16c multi .35 .20

Ambato Technical University, 32nd Anniv.
A566

No. 1568: a, Building. b, Painting.

2001 ***Perf. 13¼x13***
1568 A566 32c Vert. pair, #a-b 1.25 .65

Galapagos Islands Scenes — A567

No. 1569: a, Española Island (shown). b, San Cristobal Island. c, Bartolome Island. d, Española Island, diff. e, Bartolome and Santiago Islands.
$1, Bird on rock, Española Island.

2001, Feb. 17 ***Perf. 13¾***
1569 Horiz. strip of 5 1.75 .80
a.-e. A567 16c Any single .35 .20

Imperf

Size: 100x70mm

1570 A567 $1 multi 2.00 1.00

Alexander von Humboldt (1769-1859), Naturalist — A568

Perf. 13x13¼

2001, June 14 **Litho.** **Wmk. 395**
1571 A568 84c multi 1.75 .85

Ecuadorian Atomic Energy Commission
A568a

2001, Aug. 3 **Litho.** ***Perf. 12¾x13¼***
1571A A568a 70c multi 1.40 .70

Lebanese Union, 80th Anniv. — A569

No. 1572: a, Building and emblem. b, Emblem.
Illustration reduced.

2001, Aug. 30 ***Perf. 13¼x13***
1572 A569 16c Horiz. pair, #a-b .65 .35

Manta Port Authority — A570

No. 1573: a, Emblem. b, Ships in port.
Illustration reduced.

2001, Sept. 28
1573 A570 68c Horiz. pair, #a-b 2.75 1.40

Esmereldas Province Tourism — A571

No. 1574: a, Beach. b, Musicians and dancers on beach.
Illustration reduced.

2001
1574 A571 86c Horiz. pair, #a-b 3.50 1.75

Latin American Writers — A572

No. 1575: a, Claudia Lars (1899-1974), Salvadoran poet. b, Federico Proaño (1848-94), Ecuadoran journalist.

2001, Aug. 28 ***Perf. 13x13¼***
1575 A572 86c Horiz. pair, #a-b 3.50 1.75

Andean Condor Preservation — A573

No. 1576: a, Condor and chick. b, Condor heads, FRAPZOO emblem.
$1, Condor in flight, FRAPZOO emblem.

2001, July 23 ***Perf. 13x13¼***
1576 A573 86c Horiz. pair, #a-b 3.50 1.75

Imperf

Size: 68x99mm

1577 A573 $1 multi 2.00 1.00

Ecuador — Peru Peace Accords
A574

No. 1578: a, Map of Ecuador and Peru. b, Soldier. c, Flags of military obeservers. d, Amazon River. e, Men in field.

2001, May 22 ***Perf. 13¼x13***
1578 Horiz. strip of 5 7.00 3.50
a.-e. A574 68c Any single 1.40 .70

Archidona Canton — A575

No. 1579: a, Phragmipedium orchid. b, Saimiri sciureus. c, B. macrophylla. d, Church. e, Kichwa Indian family.

2001, Apr. 28 ***Perf. 13x13¼***
1579 Vert. strip of 5 8.50 4.25
a.-e. A575 84c Any single 1.70 .85

Ecotourism in Baños
A576

No. 1580: a, Orchid. b, Basilica, Baños. c, Tungurahua Volcano. d, Pailon del Diablo Waterfall. e, Statue of Virgin of Rosario de Agua Santa.
$1, Pailon del Diablo Waterfall, orchid.

2001 ***Perf. 13¼x13***
1580 Horiz. strip of 5 8.75 4.50
a.-e. A576 86c Any single 1.75 .90

Imperf

Size: 68x99mm

1581 A576 $1 multi 2.00 1.00

Guayas Educational Journalists Association, 30th Anniv.
A577

Perf. 13¼x13

2001, Oct. 15 **Litho.** **Wmk. 395**
1582 A577 16c multi .35 .20

Foundation for Development of Cattle Ranching, 15th Anniv. — A578

2001, Aug. 15 ***Perf. 13x13¼***
1583 A578 16c multi .35 .20

City Gates, Loja — A579

2001 ***Perf. 13¼x13***
1584 A579 32c multi .65 .30

Quito Municipal District Directorate of Security A580

2001, Nov. 26
1585 A580 68c multi 1.40 .70

Salvador Bustamante Celi (1876-1935), Musician A581

2001
1586 A581 68c multi 1.40 .70

Marcel Laniado de Wind (1927-98), First Pres. of Natl. Modernization Council — A582

2001, Aug. 6 ***Perf. 13x13¼***
1587 A582 70c multi 1.40 .70

Bernardino Cardinal Echeverria (1912-2000) A583

2001, Nov. 14
1588 A583 84c multi 1.75 .85

José Joaquin Olmedo (1780-1847), Statesman and Poet — A584

2001, Nov. 8
1589 A584 84c multi 1.75 .85

El Angel Ecological Reserve — A585

No. 1590: a, Paja de Paramo. b, Frailejón. Illustration reduced.

2001 ***Perf. 13¼x13***
1590 A585 16c Horiz. pair, #a-b .65 .30

Yahuarcocha Race Track — A586

No. 1591: a, Race track and lake. b, Lake. Illustration reduced.

2001, Nov. 30
1591 A586 68c Horiz. pair, #a-b 2.75 1.40

World Food Day — A587

No. 1592: a, Wheat ears. b, Food baskets. Illustration reduced.

2001, Nov. 5
1592 A587 84c Horiz. pair, #a-b 3.50 1.75

Art of Voroshilov Bazante A588

No. 1593: a, Spatial composition. b, Abstract, artists name at LR. c, Urban landscape. d, Abstract, diff., "Abstracto" at UL, denomination at LL. e, Abstract, denomination at LR.

2001, Nov.
1593 Horiz. strip of 5 8.75 4.25
a.-e. A588 84c Any single 1.75 .85

Wilson Popenoe Private Foundation A589

2001, Nov. 19 Litho. ***Perf. 13¼x13***
1594 A589 16c multi .35 .20

FAO Food Program A590

2001, Aug. 15
1595 A590 84c multi 1.75 .85

Rotary District 4400, 75th Anniv. — A591

2001, Nov. 30 ***Perf. 13x13¼***
1596 A591 84c multi 1.75 .85

Pres. Camilo Ponce Enriquez (1912-76) A592

Pedro Vicente Maldonado (1702-48), Geographer A593

2001
1597 A592 84c multi 1.75 .85

2001, Dec. 12
1598 A593 84c multi 1.75 .85

Otonga Foundation — A595

No. 1599: a, Frog on branch. b, Mustela frenata.

2001, Oct. 31
1599 A595 16c Horiz. pair, #a-b .65 .35

Tourism in Zaruma — A596

No. 1600: a, Virgen del Carmen. b, Orchid. Illustration reduced.

2001, Dec. 12 ***Perf. 13¼x13***
1600 A596 68c Horiz. pair, #a-b 2.75 1.40

Radio HCJB, 70th Anniv. — A597

No. 1601: a, Microphone. b, Announcer. Illustration reduced.

2001, Dec. 21
1601 A597 68c Horiz. pair, #a-b 2.75 1.40

Tennis A598

No. 1602: a, Davis Cup. b, K. Lapentti, G. Lapentti, L.A. Morejón, A. Intriago and R. Viver. c, Francisco Guzman and Miguel Olvera. d, Pancho Segura. e, Andres Gomez.

2001, Nov. 1
1602 Horiz. strip of 5 7.00 3.50
a.-e. A598 68c Any single 1.40 .70

Church Paintings of Wilfrido Martínez — A599

No. 1603: a, San Francisco (artist's name is vert.). b, Guapulo. c, San Francisco (artist's name is horiz.). d, La Compania. e, El Rosario.

2002, Apr. 9 ***Perf. 13¾***
1603 Horiz. strip of 5 9.00 4.50
a.-e. A599 90c Any single 1.80 .90

First Judicial Summit of the Americas, Quito A600

Perf. 13¼x13
2002, Jan. 8 Litho. Wmk. 395
1604 A600 68c multi 1.40 .70

Union Club, Guayaquil — A601

2002, Apr. 25 ***Perf. 13x13¼***
1605 A601 90c multi 1.90 .95

South American Soccer Confederation A602

Designs: 25c, Confederation Pres. Nicolás Leoz. 40c, Confederation emblem, soccer players. 70c, Emblem of Emelec team.

2002, Jan. 29
1606-1608 A602 Set of 3 2.75 1.40

World Conservation Union — A603

Designs: 70c, Fish, man's head. 85c, Leopard, man, horiz.
$1, Bird, animals, women and children, horiz.

2002, Feb. 21 ***Perf. 13x13¼, 13¼x13***
1609-1610 A603 Set of 2 3.25 1.60

Imperf

Size: 100x70mm

1611 A603 $1 multi 2.00 1.00

UN High Commissioner for Refugees — A604

Designs: 70c, Emblem. 85c, Child.
$1, Refugees carrying belongings, horiz.

2002, Feb. 28 ***Perf. 13x13¼***
1612-1613 A604 Set of 2 3.25 1.60

Imperf

Size: 100x70mm

1614 A604 $1 multi 2.00 1.00

Ecuadorian Educational Credit and Scholarship Institute — A605

No. 1615: a, Student using microscope. b, Emblem.

2002, Apr. 30 *Perf. 13x13¼*
1615 A605 25c Horiz. pair, #a-b 1.00 .50

Cuenca Soccer Team — A606

No. 1616: a, Team photo. b, Emblem, player dribbling.
Illustration reduced.

2002, Apr. 19 *Perf. 13¼x13*
1616 A606 25c Horiz. pair, #a-b 1.00 .50

Imbabura Province History — A607

No. 1617: a, Building. b, Statue.

2002, Mar. 27 *Perf. 13x13¼*
1617 A607 40c Horiz. pair, #a-b 1.60 .80

Crucita — A608

No. 1618: a, Parachutist with sun on horizon. b, Prachutist above beach.
Illustration reduced.

2002, Mar. 28 *Perf. 13¼x13*
1618 A608 40c Horiz. pair, #a-b 1.60 .80

Mountains A609

No. 1619: a, Mt. Altar (trees in foreground). b, Mt. Chimborazo. c, Mt. Carihuayrazo. d, Mt. Altar (lake in foreground). e, Mt. Cubillin.

2002, Apr. 19
1619 Horiz. strip of 5 9.00 4.50
a.-e. A609 90c Any single 1.80 .90

Endangered Frogs A610

No. 1620: a, Atelopus bomolochos. b, Atelopus longirostris. c, Atelopus pachydermus. d, Atelopus arthuri. e, Atelopus sp.
$1, Atelopus ignescens.

2002, Mar. 25 *Perf. 13¼x13*
1620 Horiz. strip of 5 10.50 5.25
a.-e. A610 $1.05 Any single 2.10 1.00

Imperf

Size: 100x70mm

1621 A610 $1 multi 2.00 1.00

National Anti-narcotics Police — A611

No. 1622: a, Policeman and dog. b, Emblem.

Perf. 13x13¼

2002, Apr. 23 Litho. Wmk. 395
1622 A611 40c Horiz. pair, #a-b 1.60 .80

2002 World Cup Soccer Championships, Japan and Korea — A612

Designs: 90c, Ecuadorian Soccer Federation emblem, vert. $1.05, $2, Emblem, team photo, players in action.

2002, Apr. 28 *Perf. 13x13¼, 13¼x13*
1623-1624 A612 Set of 2 4.00 2.00

Imperf

Size: 100x70mm

1625 A612 $2 multi 4.00 2.00

Dr. Servio Aguirre Villamagua, Forest Conservationist — A613

No. 1626: a, Aguirre. b, Plant.
Illustration reduced.

2002, May 22 *Perf. 13¼x13*
1626 A613 40c Horiz. pair, #a-b 1.60 .80

Food and Agriculture Organization in Ecuador, 50th Anniv. A614

2002, May 30
1627 A614 $1.05 multi 2.10 1.10

Galapagos Islands Fauna A615

No. 1628: a, Grapsus grapsus. b, Conolophus subcristatus.
No. 1629, vert.: a, Sula sula websteri. b, Phoenicopterus ruber.
No. 1630, Amblyrhynchus cristatus.
No. 1631, vert.: a, Pair of Zalophus californianus wollebacki. b, One Zalophus californianus wollebacki.
No. 1632, Sula nebouxxi excisa, vert.
No. 1633, vert.: a, Sula dactylatra granti. b, Emblem of Iberoamerican Summit on Tourism and Environment.
$2, Bird, tourists, tourist ship.

2002, May 31 *Perf. 13¼x13, 13x13¼*
1628 A615 25c Horiz. pair, #a-b 1.00 .50
1629 A615 40c Horiz. pair, #a-b 1.60 .80
1630 A615 90c multi 1.90 .95
1631 A615 90c Horiz. pair, #a-b 3.75 1.90
1632 A615 $1.05 multi 2.10 1.10
1633 A615 $1.05 Horiz. pair, #a-b 4.25 2.10
Nos. 1628-1633 (6) 14.60 7.35

Imperf

Size: 100x68mm

1634 A615 $2 multi 4.00 2.00

Ministry of Foreign Relations — A616

2002, June 5 *Perf. 13x13¼*
1635 A616 90c multi 1.90 .95

Army Polytechnic School, 80th Anniv. A617

2002, June 13 *Perf. 13¼x13*
1636 A617 25c multi .50 .25

Military Engineers, Cent. A618

Designs: No. 1637, 40c, Castle of Engineering. No. 1638, 40c, Castle of Engineering, Military engineers in action, vert.
$2, Castle of Engineering, engineers in action, emblems of military groups.

Perf. 13¼x13, 13x13¼

2002, June 19
1637-1638 A618 Set of 2 1.60 .80

Imperf

Size: 100x68mm

1639 A618 $2 multi 4.00 2.00

Dr. Alfredo Pérez Guerrero (1901-66), Academic — A619

2002, July 4 *Perf. 13x13¼*
1640 A619 25c multi .50 .25

20th Anniv. of Ecuador's Second Place Finish In World Taekwondo Championships — A620

2002, July 18 *Perf. 13¼x13*
1641 A620 40c multi .80 .40

Orellana Province — A621

No. 1642: a, Three native men. b, Man in tree.
Illustration reduced.

2002, July 30 **Wmk. 395**
1642 A621 25c Horiz. pair, #a-b 1.00 .50

CARE in Ecuador, 40th Anniv. — A622

No. 1643: a, Two children. b, Boy.

2002, July 30 *Perf. 13x13¼*
1643 A622 90c Horiz. pair, #a-b 3.75 1.90

Macará Region A623

2002, Aug. 10 *Perf. 13¼x13*
1644 A623 40c multi .80 .40

Intl. Organization for Migration, 50th Anniv. — A624

Quito Philharmonic Society, 50th Anniv. — A625

2002, Aug. 18 *Perf. 13x13¼*
1645 A624 $1.05 multi 2.10 1.10

2002, Aug. 29
1646 A625 25c multi .50 .25

Comptroller General, 75th Anniv. — A625a

Perf. 13x13¼

2002, Sept. 26 Litho. Wmk. 395
1646A A625a 40c multi .80 .40

Second World Meeting of Mountain People — A626

No. 1647 — Emblem of World Meeting and: a, Mountain. b, Group of people. c, Houses in valley. d, Town. e, Other emblems.

2002, Sept. 18
1647 Horiz. strip of 5 9.50 4.75
a.-e. A626 90c Any single 1.90 .95

Pujili Dancer — A627

Perf. 13x13¼
2002, Oct. 14 Litho. Wmk. 395
1648 A627 $1.05 multi 2.10 1.10

Paintings of Leonardo Hidalgo A629

No. 1650: a, La Dolorosa. b, El Hombre Cargando su Fruto. c, Frida Kahlo. d, El Hombre Fuerte del Mar. e, Jesus.

Wmk. 395
2002, Oct. 3 Litho. *Perf. 13¾*
1650 Horiz. strip of 5 9.00 4.50
a.-e. A629 90c Any single 1.80 .90

Pan-American Health Organization, Cent. — A630

2002, Dec. 2 *Perf. 13¼x12¾*
1651 A630 $1.05 multi 2.10 1.10

Lo Nuestro Art Exhibition — A631

No. 1652: a, Wall with six works of art. b, Walls with 16 works of art.
Illustration reduced.

2002, Dec. 15
1652 A631 25c Horiz. pair, #a-b 1.00 .50

Catholic University, 40th Anniv. A632

2002, Dec. 18
1653 A632 40c multi .80 .40

America Issue — UNESCO World Heritage Sites — A633

No. 1654: a, Cupola of San Blas Church, Cuenca. b, Society of Jesus Church, Quito.

2002, Dec. 18 *Perf. 12¾x13¼*
1654 A633 25c Horiz. pair, #a-b 1.00 .50

Dated 2001.

America Issue — Youth, Education and Literacy — A634

No. 1655: a, Students and blackboard. b, Toddler and books.
Illustration reduced.

2002, Dec. 18 *Perf. 13¼x12¾*
1655 A634 25c Horiz. pair, #a-b 1.00 .50

Second Meeting of South American Presidents, Guayaquil — A635

No. 1656: a, Meeting emblem. b, Emblem, presidents and flags.
Illustration reduced.

2003, Jan. 13
1656 A635 $1.05 Horiz. pair, #a-b 4.25 2.10

Papal Benediction for Ecuadorian Emigrants — A636

2003, Jan. 24 *Perf. 12¾x13¼*
1657 A636 $1.05 multi 2.10 1.10

Size: 68x100mm
Imperf
1658 A636 $2 multi 4.00 2.00

World Vison — A637

2003, Feb. 6 *Perf. 12¾x13¼*
1659 A637 40c multi .80 .40

Intl. Women's Day — A638

2003, Mar. 8 Wmk. 395
1660 A638 $1.05 multi 2.10 1.10

Agustin Cueva Vallejo (1820-73), Physician — A639

2003, Mar. 13 Litho.
1661 A639 40c multi .80 .40

Blasco Moscoso Cuesta, Founder of Pichincha Sports Writers Association — A640

2003, Mar. 14
1662 A640 25c multi .50 .25

Cuenca Artisan Products A641

No. 1663: a, Azuay University domes. b, Tinware. c, Jewelry. d, Fireworks. e, Saddles.
No. 1664: a, Engraving. b, Metallurgy. c, Baskets. d, Embroidery. e, Ceramics.
$2, Assorted products.

2003, Mar. 27 *Perf. 13¼x12¾*
1663 Horiz. strip of 5 2.50 1.25
a.-e. A641 25c Any single .50 .25
1664 Horiz. strip of 5 10.50 5.25
a.-e. A641 $1.05 Any single 2.10 1.00

Size: 100x68mm
Imperf
1665 A641 $2 multi 4.00 2.00

Flora and Fauna A642

No. 1666: a, Curculionidae. b, Lycidae. c, Acridoidea. d, Aracnidae. e, Liliacea.

2003, Apr. 4 *Perf. 13¼x12¾*
1666 Horiz. strip of 5 10.50 5.25
a.-e. A642 $1.05 Any single 2.10 1.00

Military Geographic Institute, 75th Anniv. A643

Designs: No. 1667, 40c, No. 1669, $2, Painting by Eduardo Kingman. No. 1668, 40c, Institute emblem, vert.

Perf. 13¼x12¾, 12¾x13¼
2003, Apr. 11
1667-1668 A643 Set of 2 1.60 .80

Size: 100x68mm
Imperf
1669 A643 $2 multi 4.00 2.00

Galápagos Marine Reserve — A644

Designs: 40c, Stylized butterfly.
No. 1671, $1.05, horiz.: a, Sphyrna lewini. b, Chelonia mydas agassisi.
No. 1672, $1.05, horiz.: a, Xanthichthys mento. b, Zanclus cornutus.
$2, Tubastrea coccinea, horiz.

Perf. 12¾x13¼, 13¼x12¾
2003, May 9
1670 A644 40c multi .80 .40

Horiz. Pairs, #a-b
1671-1672 A644 Set of 2 8.50 4.25

Size: 100x68mm
Imperf
1673 A644 $2 multi 4.00 2.00

Intl. Tourism Trade Fair of Ecuador A645

No. 1674: a, Monkey in tree. b, Birds. c, Embroidery. d, Mountain. e, Hat seller on beach.

2003, May 14 *Perf. 13¼x12¾*
1674 Vert. strip of 5 2.50 1.25
a.-e. A645 25c Any single .50 .25

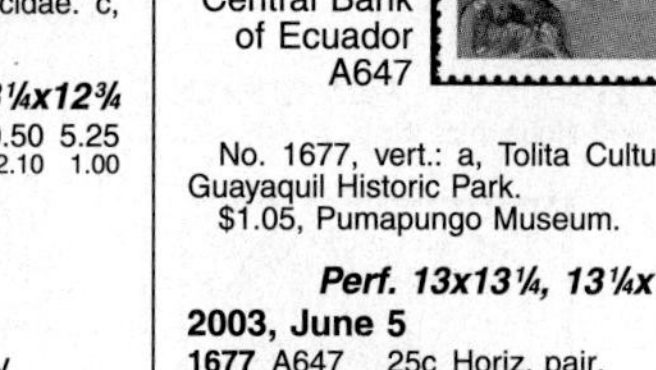
Artifacts of Pre-Columbian Cultures — A646

No. 1675, 25c: a, Gold bell with monkey. b, Amphora.
No. 1676, 25c: a, Sculpture of a man. b, Three-footed pot.

Perf. 13x13¼
2003, May 16 Litho. Wmk. 395
Horiz. pairs, #a-b
1675-1676 A646 Set of 2 2.00 1.00

Central Bank of Ecuador A647

No. 1677, vert.: a, Tolita Culture mask. b, Guayaquil Historic Park.
$1.05, Pumapungo Museum.

Perf. 13x13¼, 13¼x13
2003, June 5 Litho.
1677 A647 25c Horiz. pair, #a-b 1.00 .50
1678 A647 $1.05 multi 2.10 1.10

Philately and Guayaquil A648

No. 1679, horiz.: a, British consular cover to Veracruz with British stamp and cancel. b, Stampless cover.
No. 1680, horiz.: a, SCADTA first flight cover. b, French consular cover to Lima with French stamps and cancels.
$1.05, Philatelic magazines.
$2, Guayaquil Philatelic Club emblem, Ecuadoran stamps, horiz.

2003, July 22 ***Perf. 13¾***

1679	A648	40c Vert. pair, #a-b	1.60	.80
1680	A648	40c Vert. pair, #a-b	1.60	.80
1681	A648	$1.05 multi	2.10	1.10
		Nos. 1679-1681 (3)	5.30	2.70

Size: 100x69mm

Imperf

1682	A648	$2 multi	4.00	2.00

Guayaquil Urban Renewal A649

No. 1683: a, Punta Cerro Santa Ana. b, Plaza Colón. c, Malecón Gardens. d, Crystal Palace. e, Plaza de San Francisco.

2003, July 26 ***Perf. 13¼x13***

1683	Horiz. strip of 5	9.00	4.50
a.-e.	A649 90c Any single	1.80	.90

World Bird Festival A650

Designs: No. 1684, $1.05, Geranoaetus melanoleucus. No. 1685, $1.05, Harpia harpyja, vert.

2003, Sept. 2 ***Perf. 13¼x13, 13x13¼***

1684-1685	A650	Set of 2	4.25	2.10

Zamora-Chinchipe Province, 50th Anniv. — A651

No. 1686: a, Shown. b, Eira barbara. c, Boa constrictor. d, Tapirus terrestris. e, Psophia crepitans.

2003, Nov. 7 ***Perf. 13¼x13***

1686	Vert. strip of 5	2.50	1.25
a.-e.	A651 25c Any single	.50	.25

America Issue — Flora and Fauna — A652

No. 1687: a, Semnornis ramphastinus. b, Bomarea glaucescens.

Perf. 13x13¼

2003, Nov. 1 Litho. Wmk. 395

1687	A652	$1.05 Horiz. pair, #a-b	4.25	2.10

Selection of Quito as World Heritage Site, 25th Anniv. A653

Churches: 40c, El Sagrario. No. 1689a, La Compañia de Jesus. No. 1689b, Santa Barbara. $1.05, San Francisco, vert.

2003, Nov. 1 ***Perf. 13¼x13, 13x13¼***

1688	A653	40c multi	.80	.40
1689	A653	90c Horiz. pair, #a-b	3.75	1.90
1690	A653	$1.05 multi	2.10	1.10
		Nos. 1688-1690 (3)	6.65	3.40

Christmas A654

Children's art by: No. 1691a, Stephanie Pacheco. No. 1691b, Sebastián Tejada. 40c, María Claudia Iturralde, vert. 90c, Luis Antonio Ortega. $1.05, Angel Andrés Castro, vert.

2003, Nov. 1

1691	A654	25c Horiz. pair, #a-b	1.00	.50
1692	A654	40c multi	.80	.40
1693	A654	90c multi	1.90	.90
1694	A654	$1.05 multi	2.10	1.10
		Nos. 1691-1694 (4)	5.80	2.90

Treasures of Guayaquil Municipal Museum A655

No. 1695: a, Santiago de Guayaquil Act of Independence. b, Punaes ceremonial stone. c, Proclamation of Mariano Donoso. d, Tzantzas. e, Manteño-Huancavilca totem.

2003, Dec. 1 ***Perf. 13¼x13***

1695	Horiz. strip of 5	4.00	2.00
a.-e.	A655 40c Any single	.80	.40

Selection of Galapagos Islands as World Heritage Site, 25th Anniv. — A656

No. 1696: a, Zalophus californianus wollebacki. b, Fregata minor palmerstoni. c, Sula nebouxxi excisa. d, Isla Bartolomé. e, Two Sula nebouxxi excisa shaped as "25."

2003, Nov. 26 ***Perf. 13x13¼***

1696	Horiz. strip of 5	4.00	2.00
a.-e.	A656 40c Any single	.80	.40

Army Aviation Instruction, 50th Anniv. — A657

No. 1697, 40c: a, Mountain, airplanes, emblem. b, Airplane in flight, men on ground.
No. 1698, 40c, horiz.: a, Helicopter and soldiers. b, Airplanes, mountain, people.

2004, Jan. 21 ***Perf. 13x13¼, 13¼x13***
Horiz. pairs, #a-b

1697-1698	A657	Set of 2	3.25	1.60

Military Geographical Institute's Role in National Development — A658

2004, Apr. 14 ***Perf. 13¼x13***

1699	A658	$1.05 multi	2.10	1.10

Commander Rafael Morán Valverde, Military Hero — A659

2004, Apr. 5 ***Perf. 13x13¼***

1700	A659	$1.05 multi	2.10	1.10

Intl. Philately Day — A660

No. 1701: a, Ecuador #2, Greece #1. b, Cover with six stamps.
$2, Various stamps, tongs, magnifying glass, stamp catalogues.
Illustration reduced.

2004, May 6 ***Perf. 13¼x13***

1701	A660	75c Horiz. pair, #a-b	3.00	1.50

Imperf

Size: 100x68mm

1702	A660	$2 multi	4.00	2.00

Ecuadorian Volleyball Federation A661

Perf. 13x13¼

2004, May 27 Litho. Wmk. 395

1703	A661	75c multi	1.50	.75

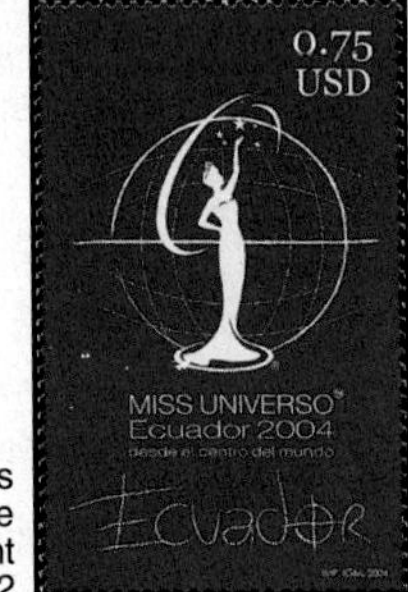

2004 Miss Universe Pageant A662

2004, May 29 ***Perf. 13¾***

1704	A662	75c multi	1.50	.75

Sculpture by Mario Tapia A663

No. 1705: a, Adolescencia. b, Beato Chaminade. c, Delfin de Galapagos. d, Pelicano. e, Homenaje a Carlo Vidano.
$2, Similar to No. 1705b.

2004, June 1 ***Perf. 13¼x13***

1705	Horiz. strip of 5	9.00	4.50
a.-e.	A663 90c Any single	1.80	.90

Imperf

Size: 100x69mm

1706	A663	$2 multi	4.00	2.00

Pedro Vicente Maldonado (1704-48), Cartographer A664

2004, June 25 ***Perf. 13x13¼***

1707	A664	90c multi	1.90	.95

Dr. Agustín Cueva Tamariz (1903-79) — A665

2004, June 30 **Litho.**

1708	A665	90c multi	1.90	.95

34th General Assembly of the Organization of American States — A666

2004, July 4 **Wmk. 395**

1709	A666	75c multi	1.50	.75

Dr. Angl Felicísmo Rojas (b. 1909), Writer — A667

2004, July 11

1710	A667	50c multi	1.00	.50

Ecuadoran and Spanish Postal Money Orders A668

2004, Aug. 3 ***Perf. 13¼x13***

1711	A668	$1.05 multi	2.10	1.10

2004 Summer Olympics, Athens — A669

No. 1712 — 2004 Summer Olympics emblem, Ecuadoran Olympic Committee emblem and: a, 2004 Olympics mascots. b, Alexandra Escobar Guerrero.

2004, Aug. 3 ***Perf. 13x13¼***

1712	A669	$1.05 Horiz. pair, #a-b	4.25	2.25

Ecuador Orchid Association, 30th Anniv. — A670

Designs: 25c, Cattleya maxima. $1.05, Epidendrum bracteolatum.

2004, Sept. 30
1713-1714 A670 Set of 2 2.60 1.30

SEMI-POSTAL STAMPS

Nos. 423-428 Surcharged in Carmine or Blue:

1944, May 9 Unwmk. *Perf. 12*
B1 A171 10c + 10c yel grn (C) .30 .30
B2 A171 20c + 20c rose pink .30 .30
B3 A171 30c + 20c dk gray brn .30 .30
B4 A171 50c + 20c dp red lil .60 .60
B5 A171 1s + 50c ol gray (C) 1.00 1.00
B6 A171 10s + 2s red orange 3.50 3.50
Nos. B1-B6 (6) 6.00 6.00

The surtax aided Mendez Hospital.

AIR POST STAMPS

In 1928-30, the internal airmail service of Ecuador was handled by the Sociedad Colombo-Alemana de Transportes Aereos ("SCADTA") under government sanction. During this period SCADTA issued stamps which were the only legal franking for airmail service except that handled under contract with Pan American-Grace Airways. SCADTA issues are Nos. C1-C6, C16-C25, CF1-CF2.

Colombia Air Post Stamps of 1923 Surcharged in Carmine

"Provisional" at 45 degree Angle
Perf. 14x14½

1928, Aug. 28 Wmk. 116
C1 AP6 50c on 10c green 110.00 70.00
C2 AP6 75c on 15c car 210.00 160.00
C3 AP6 1s on 20c gray 70.00 42.50
C4 AP6 1½s on 30c blue 45.00 35.00
C5 AP6 3s on 60c brown 85.00 52.50
Nos. C1-C5 (5) 520.00 360.00

"Provisional" at 41 degree Angle

1929, Mar. 20
C1a AP6 50c on 10c green 125.00 110.00
C2a AP6 75c on 15c carmine 225.00 175.00
C3a AP6 1s on 20c gray 225.00 175.00
Nos. C1a-C3a (3) 575.00 460.00

Same with "Cts." Between Surcharged Numerals

C6 AP6 50c on 10c green *700.00 1,700.*

A 75c on 15c carmine with "Cts." between the surcharged numerals exists. There is no evidence that it was regularly issued or used.
For overprints see Nos. CF3-CF3a.

Plane over River Guayas — AP1

Unwmk.
1929, May 5 Engr. *Perf. 12*
C8 AP1 2c black .20 .20
C9 AP1 5c carmine rose .20 .20
C10 AP1 10c deep brown .20 .20
C11 AP1 20c dark violet .45 .20
C12 AP1 50c deep green .80 .45
C13 AP1 1s dark blue 2.50 2.10
C14 AP1 5s orange yellow 10.00 8.50
C15 AP1 10s orange red 52.50 45.00
Nos. C8-C15 (8) 66.85 56.85

Establishment of commercial air service in Ecuador. The stamps were available for all forms of postal service and were largely used for franking ordinary letters.
Nos. C13-C15 show numerals in color on white background. Counterfeits of No. C15 exist.
See #C26-C31. For overprints and surcharge see #C32-C38, C287, CO1-CO12.

Jesuit Church La Compania AP2

Mount Chimborazo AP3

Wmk. 127
1929, Apr. 1 Litho. *Perf. 14*
C16 AP2 50c red brown 2.25 2.25
C17 AP2 75c green 2.25 2.25
C18 AP2 1s rose 3.50 2.25
C19 AP2 1½s gray blue 3.50 2.25
C20 AP2 2s violet 5.75 4.50
C21 AP2 3s brown 5.75 4.50
C22 AP3 5s lt blue 20.00 14.00
C23 AP3 10s lt red 42.50 30.00
C24 AP3 15s violet 70.00 60.00
C25 AP3 25s olive green 92.50 70.00
Nos. C16-C25 (10) 248.00 192.00

For overprint see No. CF2.

Plane Type of 1929

1930-44 Unwmk. Engr. *Perf. 12*
C26 AP1 1s carmine lake 2.75 .45
C27 AP1 1s green ('44) .35 .20
C28 AP1 5s olive green 4.25 3.25
C29 AP1 5s purple ('44) .80 .20
C30 AP1 10s black 12.00 4.25
C31 AP1 10s brt ultra ('44) 1.75 .25
Nos. C26-C31 (6) 21.90 8.60

Nos. C26-C31 show numerals in color on white background.
For surcharge see No. C287.

Type of 1929 Overprinted in Various Colors

AP4

1930, June 4
C32 AP4 1s car lake (Bk) 17.50 17.50
a. Double ovpt. (R Br + Bk) 75.00
C33 AP4 5s olive grn (Bl) 17.50 17.50
C34 AP4 10s black (R Br) 17.50 17.50
Nos. C32-C34 (3) 52.50 52.50

Flight of Capt. Benjamin Mendez from Bogota to Quito, bearing a crown of flowers for the tomb of Grand Marshal Sucre.

Air Post Official Stamps of 1929-30 Overprinted in Various Colors or Surcharged Similarly in Upper & Lower Case

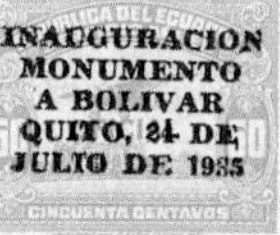

1935, July 24
C35 AP1 50c deep green (Bl) 6.75 4.25
C36 AP1 50c olive brn (R) 6.75 4.25
C37 AP1 1s on 5s ol grn (Bk) 6.75 4.25
a. Double surcharge 95.00
C38 AP1 2s on 10s black (R) 6.75 4.25
Nos. C35-C38 (4) 27.00 17.00

Unveiling of a monument to Bolívar at Quito, July 24th, 1935.

Geodesical Mission Issue

Nos. 349-351 Overprinted in Blue or Black and Type of Regular issue

1936, July 3 *Perf. 12½*
C39 A136 10c deep orange (Bl) .35 .20
C40 A136 20c violet (Bk) .35 .20
C41 A136 50c dark red (Bl) .35 .20
C42 A136 70c black .70 .30
Nos. C39-C42 (4) 1.75 .90

For surcharge see No. RA42.

Philatelic Exhibition Issue

Type of Regular Issue Overprinted "AEREA"

1936, Oct. 20 *Perf. 13½x14*
C43 A137 2c rose 3.50 3.50
C44 A137 5c brown orange 3.50 3.50
C45 A137 10c brown 3.50 3.50
C46 A137 20c ultra 3.50 3.50
C47 A137 50c red violet 3.50 3.50
C48 A137 1s green 3.50 3.50
Nos. C43-C48 (6) 21.00 21.00

Condor and Plane — AP6

Perf. 13½
C49 AP6 70c orange brown .50 .50
C50 AP6 1s dull violet .50 .50

Nos. C43-C50 were issued for the 1st Intl. Phil. Exhib. at Quito.

Condor over "El Altar" — AP7

1937-46 *Perf. 11½, 12*
C51 AP7 10c chestnut 2.00 .20
C52 AP7 20c olive black 2.50 .20
C53 AP7 40c rose car ('46) 2.50 .20
C54 AP7 70c black brown 3.50 .20
C55 AP7 1s gray black 5.50 .20
C56 AP7 2s dark violet 11.00 .50
Nos. C51-C56 (6) 27.00 1.50

Issue dates: 40c, Oct. 7; others, Aug. 19.
For overprints see #463-464, CO13-CO17.

Portrait of Washington, American Eagle and Flags — AP8

and 1938, Feb. 9 Engr. Litho. *Perf. 12*
Center Multicolored
C57 AP8 2c brown .20 .20
C58 AP8 5c black .20 .20
C59 AP8 10c brown .20 .20
C60 AP8 20c dark blue .35 .20
C61 AP8 50c violet .70 .20
C62 AP8 1s black 1.25 .20
C63 AP8 2s violet 2.75 .70
Nos. C57-C63 (7) 5.65 1.90

150th anniv. of the US Constitution.
In 1947, Nos. C61-C63 were overprinted in dark blue: "Primero la Patria!" and plane. These revolutionary propaganda stamps were later renounced by decree.
For overprints see #C102-C104, C139-C141.

No. RA35 Surcharged in Red

1938, Nov. 16 *Perf. 13½*
C64 PT12 65c on 3c ultra .20 .20

A national airmail concession was given to the Sociedad Ecuatoriano de Transportes Aereos (SEDTA) in July, 1938. No. RA35 was surcharged for SEDTA postal requirements. SEDTA operated through 1940.

Army Horseman — AP9

Woman Runner — AP10

Tennis — AP11

Boxing — AP12

Olympic Fire — AP13

1939, Mar. Engr. *Perf. 12*
C65 AP9 5c lt green .55 .20
C66 AP10 10c salmon .80 .20
C67 AP11 50c redsh brown 4.00 .20
C68 AP12 1s black brown 5.00 .35
C69 AP13 2s rose carmine 6.50 .85
Nos. C65-C69 (5) 16.85 1.80

First Bolivarian Games (1938).

Plane over Chimborazo AP14

1939, May 1 *Perf. 13x12½*
C70 AP14 1s yellow brown .20 .20
C71 AP14 2s rose violet .35 .20
C72 AP14 5s black .95 .20
Nos. C70-C72 (3) 1.50 .60

Golden Gate Bridge and Mountain Peak — AP15

Empire State Building and Mountain Peak — AP16

1939 *Perf. 12½x13*
C73 AP15 2c black .20 .20
C74 AP15 5c rose red .20 .20
C75 AP15 10c indigo .20 .20
C76 AP15 50c rose violet .20 .20
C77 AP15 1s chocolate .30 .20
C78 AP15 2s yellow brown .35 .20
C79 AP15 5s emerald .65 .20
Nos. C73-C79 (7) 2.10 1.40

Golden Gate International Exposition.
For surcharge & overprint see #434, CO18.

1939
C80 AP16 2c brown orange .20 .20
C81 AP16 5c dark carmine .20 .20
C82 AP16 10c indigo .20 .20
C83 AP16 50c slate green .20 .20
C84 AP16 1s deep orange .25 .20
C85 AP16 2s dk red violet .30 .20
C86 AP16 5s dark gray .70 .20
Nos. C80-C86 (7) 2.05 1.40

New York World's Fair.
For surcharge see No. 435.

Map of the Americas and Airplane — AP17

1940, July 9
C87 AP17 10c red org & blue .20 .20
C88 AP17 70c sepia & blue .20 .20
C89 AP17 1s copper brn & blue .30 .20
C90 AP17 10s black & blue 1.25 .65
Nos. C87-C90 (4) 1.95 1.25

Pan American Union, 50th anniversary.

Journalism Type

1941, Dec. 15
C91 A157 3s rose carmine 1.40 .20
C92 A157 10s yellow orange 3.00 .45

See note after No. 399.

Old Map of South America Showing Amazon River — AP19

Panoramic View of Amazon River — AP20

Designs: 70c, Gonzalo de Pineda. 5s, Painting of the expedition.

1942, Jan. 30
C93 AP19 40c black & buff .80 .20
C94 AP19 70c olive 1.10 .20
C95 AP20 2s dark green 1.25 .20
C96 AP19 5s rose 1.60 .50
Nos. C93-C96 (4) 4.75 1.10

See note after No. 403.

Remigio Crespo Toral Type

1942, Sept. 1 *Perf. 13½*
C97 A162 10c dull violet .35 .20

Alfaro Types

70c, Gen. Eloy Alfaro. 1s, Devils's Nose. 3s, Military College. 5s, Montecristi, Alfaro's birthplace.

1943, Feb. 16 *Perf. 12*
C98 A166 70c dk rose & blk .50 .20
C99 A167 1s ol blk & red brn .85 .50
C100 A167 3s ol gray & grn 1.25 .70
C101 A167 5s slate & salmon 1.75 .85
Nos. C98-C101 (4) 4.35 2.25

Nos. C61-C63 Overprinted in Red Brown

1943, Apr. 15 *Perf. 11½*
Center Multicolored
C102 AP8 50c violet 1.10 .70
C103 AP8 1s black 1.25 .75
C104 AP8 2s violet 1.60 1.40
Nos. C102-C104 (3) 3.95 2.85

Visit of US Vice-Pres. Henry A. Wallace.

Nos. 374-376 Overprinted "AEREO LOOR A BOLIVIA JUNIO 11-1943" (like Nos. C111-C113)

1943, June 11 *Perf. 13*
C105 A146 50c dp red violet .20 .20
C106 A147 1s copper red .30 .20
C107 A148 2s dark green .35 .20
Nos. C105-C107 (3) .85 .60

Visit of Pres. Eurique Penaranda of Bolivia. Vertical overprints on Nos. C105-C106.

Nos. 374-376 Overprinted "AEREO LOOR A PARAGUAY JULIO 5-1943" (like Nos. C111-C113)

1943, July 5
C108 A146 50c dp red violet .20 .20
a. Double overprint 40.00
C109 A147 1s copper red .50 .50
C110 A148 2s dark green .70 .70
Nos. C108-C110 (3) 1.40 1.40

Visit of Pres. Higinio Morinlgo of Paraguay. Vertical overprints on Nos. C108-C109.

Nos. 374-376 Overprinted in Black

A E R E O

LOOR A VENEZUELA

JULIO 23 — 1943

1943, July 23
C111 A146 50c dp red violet .20 .20
C112 A147 1s copper red .30 .20
C113 A148 2s dark green .35 .20
Nos. C111-C113 (3) .85 .60

Issued to commemorate the visit of President Isaias Medina Angarita of Venezuela.
Vertical overprint on Nos. C111-C112.
See Nos. C105-C110.

President Arroyo del Rio Addressing US Congress — AP26

1943, Oct. 9 *Perf. 12*
C114 AP26 50c dark brown .35 .30
C115 AP26 70c brt rose .50 .30
C116 AP26 3s dark blue .55 .35
C117 AP26 5s dark green 1.25 .65
C118 AP26 10s olive black 5.00 2.40
Nos. C114-C118 (5) 7.65 4.00

Good will tour of Pres. Arroyo del Rio in 1942.
For surcharges see Nos. CB1-CB5.

1944, Feb. 7
C119 AP26 50c dp red lilac .35 .35
C120 AP26 70c red brown .65 .35
C121 AP26 3s turq green .65 .35
C122 AP26 5s brt ultra 1.10 .70
C123 AP26 10s scarlet 1.40 .85
Nos. C119-C123 (5) 4.15 2.60
Nos. C114-C123 (10) 11.80 6.60

Church of San Francisco, Quito — AP27

1944, Feb. 13
C124 AP27 70c turq green .50 .35
C125 AP27 1s olive .50 .35
C126 AP27 3s red orange 1.10 .70
C127 AP27 5s carmine rose 1.40 .85
Nos. C124-C127 (4) 3.50 2.25

See note after No. 433.

Palace Type

1944 **Engr.** *Perf. 11*
C128 A173 3s orange .35 .20
C129 A173 5s dark brown .65 .20
C130 A173 10s dark red 1.25 .20
Nos. C128-C130 (3) 2.25 .60

See No. C221. For overprints and surcharges see Nos. 541, C136-C138, C210-C213, C218-C220, C223-C224, C277-C279.

Red Cross Type

1945, Apr. 25 **Unwmk.** *Perf. 12*
Cross in Rose
C131 A174 2s deep blue .75 .55
C132 A174 3s green .90 .65
C133 A174 5s dark violet 1.25 .90
C134 A174 10s carmine rose 4.00 3.00
Nos. C131-C134 (4) 6.90 5.10

No. RA55 Surcharged in Black

1945, June 8
C135 PT21 40c on 5c blue .20 .20
a. Double surcharge 10.00

Counterfeits exist.

Nos. C128-C130 Overprinted in Green

1945, Sept. 6 *Perf. 11*
C136 A173 3s orange .50 .50
a. Inverted overprint 25.00
b. Double overprint 25.00
C137 A173 5s dark brown .65 .65
C138 A173 10s dark red 1.60 1.25
Nos. C136-C138 (3) 2.75 2.40

Nos. C61-C63 Overprinted in Dark Blue and Gold like Nos. 444-446

1945, Oct. 2 *Perf. 12*
Center Multicolored
C139 AP8 50c violet .40 .35
C140 AP8 1s black .50 .50
C141 AP8 2s violet .70 .65
Nos. C139-C141 (3) 1.60 1.50

Visit of Pres. Juan Antonio Rios of Chile.

Monument to Liberty — AP30

1945, Nov. 14 **Engr.**
C142 AP30 30c blue .20 .20
C143 AP30 40c rose carmine .20 .20
C144 AP30 1s dull violet .40 .35
C145 AP30 3s gray black .90 .90
C146 AP30 5s purple brown 1.25 1.25
Nos. C142-C146 (5) 2.95 2.90

Gen. Antonio Jose de Sucre, 150th birth anniv.

Catalogue values for unused stamps in this section, from this point to the end of the section, are for Never Hinged items.

Highway Type

1946, Apr. 22 **Unwmk.**
C147 A176 1s carmine rose .30 .20
C148 A176 2s violet .35 .30
C149 A176 3s turq green .55 .30
C150 A176 5s red orange .70 .40
C151 A176 10s dark blue 1.10 .35
Nos. C147-C151 (5) 3.00 1.55

Revolution Types

1946, Aug. 9 *Perf. 12½*
C152 A177 40c deep claret .20 .20
C153 A178 1s sepia .20 .20
C154 A179 2s indigo .55 .20
C155 A180 3s olive green .95 .45
Nos. C152-C155 (4) 1.90 1.05

National Union of Periodicals, Initials and Quill Pen — AP36

1946, Sept. 16
C156 AP36 50c dull purple .30 .20
C157 AP36 70c dark green .35 .20
C158 AP36 3s red .60 .30
C159 AP36 5s indigo .75 .35
C160 AP36 10s chocolate 2.50 .55
Nos. C156-C160 (5) 4.50 1.60

Campaign for adult education.

The Blessed Mariana Teaching Children — AP37

"Lily of Quito" — AP38

1946, Nov. 28 **Unwmk.**
C161 AP37 40c chocolate .20 .20
C162 AP37 60c deep blue .30 .30
C163 AP38 3s orange yellow .60 .50
C164 AP38 5s green 1.25 .65
Nos. C161-C164 (4) 2.35 1.65

300th anniv. of the death of the Blessed Mariana de Jesus Paredes y Flores.

Rocafuerte Type

60c-1.10s, Jual de Velasco. 1.30s-2s, Riobamba Irrigation Canal.

1947, Nov. 27 *Perf. 12*
C165 A185 60c dark green .20 .20
C166 A185 70c purple .20 .20
C167 A185 1s black brown .20 .20
C168 A185 1.10s car rose .20 .20
C169 A185 1.30s deep blue .20 .20
C170 A185 1.90s olive bister .50 .20
C171 A185 2s olive green .50 .20
Nos. C165-C171 (7) 2.00 1.40

For overprints & surcharges see #C175, C181, C207-C209, C215, C216-C217, C222, C235.

Bello Type

1948, Apr. 21 *Perf. 13*
C172 A188 60c magenta .20 .20
C173 A188 1.30s dk blue grn .35 .20
C174 A188 1.90s dk rose car .30 .25
Nos. C172-C174 (3) .85 .65

No. C166 Overprinted in Black

1948, May 24 *Perf. 12*
C175 A185 70c purple .50 .35

Columbus — AP42

1948, May 26 *Perf. 14*
C176 AP42 50c olive green .20 .20
C177 AP42 70c rose carmine .20 .20
C178 AP42 3c ultra .60 .50
C179 AP42 5s brown .75 .65
C180 AP42 10s deep violet 2.50 .80
Nos. C176-C180 (5) 4.25 2.35

See note after No. 495.

No. C169 Overprinted in Carmine like No. 496 (MANANA reads up)

1948, Aug. 26 **Unwmk.** *Perf. 12*
C181 A185 1.30s deep blue .40 .25

National Fair of Today and Tomorrow, 1948.

Elia Liut and Telegrafo I AP43

Teacher and Pupils AP44

1948, Sept. 10 *Perf. 12½*
C182 AP43 60c rose red .35 .20
C183 AP43 1s green .35 .25
C184 AP43 1.30s deep claret .35 .25
C185 AP43 1.90s deep violet .35 .25
C186 AP43 2s dark brown .50 .30
C187 AP43 5s blue .90 .50
Nos. C182-C187 (6) 2.80 1.75

25th anniv. (in 1945) of the 1st postal flight in Ecuador.

1948, Oct. 12 *Perf. 14*
C188 AP44 50c violet .35 .20
C189 AP44 70c deep blue .35 .20
C190 AP44 3s dark green .65 .45
C191 AP44 5s red .95 .55
C192 AP44 10s brown 1.90 .70
Nos. C188-C192 (5) 4.20 2.10

Campaign for adult education.

AP45

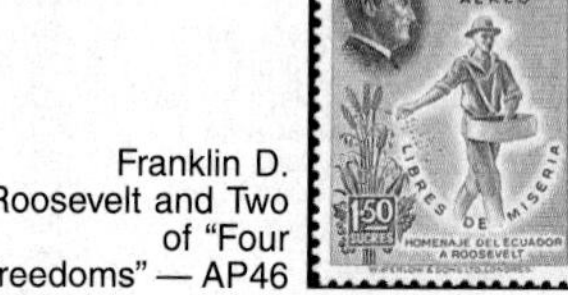

Franklin D. Roosevelt and Two of "Four Freedoms" — AP46

1948, Oct. 24 *Perf. 12½*
C193 AP45 60c emer & org brn .20 .20
C194 AP45 1s car rose & slate .20 .20
C195 AP46 1.50s grn & red brn .20 .20
C196 AP46 2s red & black .45 .20
C197 AP46 5s ultra & blk .80 .20
Nos. C193-C197 (5) 1.85 1.00

Maldonado Types

1948, Nov. 17
C198 A196 60c dp org & rose car .35 .20
C199 A197 90c red & gray blk .35 .20
C200 A196 1.30s pur & dp org .45 .20
C201 A197 2s dp bl & dull grn .45 .20
Nos. C198-C201 (4) 1.60 .80

See note after No. 519.

Juan Montalvo and Cervantes AP47

Don Quixote — AP48

1949, May 2 **Engr.** *Perf. 12½x12*
C202 AP47 1.30s ol brn & ultra 2.00 2.00
C203 AP48 1.90s grn & rose car .50 .25
C204 AP47 3s vio & org brn .70 .25
C205 AP48 5s red & gray blk 1.25 .20
C206 AP47 10s red lil & aqua 2.00 .20
Nos. C202-C206 (5) 6.45 2.90

400th anniv. of the birth of Miguel de Cervantes Saavedra, novelist, playwright and poet, and the 60th anniv. of the death of Juan Montalvo (1832-89), Ecuadorean writer.
For surcharges see Nos. C225-C226.

No. C168 Surcharged in Blue

1949, June 15 *Perf. 12*
C207 A185 50c on 1.10s car rose .20 .20
C208 A185 60c on 1.10s car rose .20 .20
C209 A185 90c on 1.10s car rose .30 .20
Nos. C207-C209 (3) .70 .60

2nd Eucharistic Cong., Quito, June 1949.

No. C128 Surcharged in Black

1949, Oct. 11 *Perf. 11*
C210 A173 60c on 3s orange .35 .30
a. Double surcharge 15.00
C211 A173 90c on 3s orange .35 .20
C212 A173 1s on 3s orange .45 .30
C213 A173 2s on 3s orange 1.00 .30
Nos. C210-C213 (4) 2.15 1.10

"SUCRE(S)" in capitals on Nos. C212-C213.
75th anniv. of the UPU.

AP49

Black Surcharge

1950 **Unwmk.** *Perf. 12*
C214 AP49 60c on 50c gray .25 .20
a. Double surcharge 15.00

No. C170 Surcharged with New Value in Black

C215 A185 90c on 1.90s ol bis .30 .20

Nos. C168, C128-C129 and Type of 1944 Surcharged or Overprinted in Black or Carmine

1950, Feb. 10 *Perf. 12*
C216 A185 50c on 1.10s .30 .30
C217 A185 70c on 1.10s .35 .30

Perf. 11
C218 A173 3s orange .55 .50
C219 A173 5s dark brown (C) .80 .45
C220 A173 10s violet (C) 1.25 .50
Nos. C216-C220 (5) 3.25 2.05

Issued to publicize adult education.
For overprint see No. 541.

Govt. Palace Type of 1944

1950, May 15 **Engr.** *Perf. 11*
C221 A173 10s violet 1.10 .20

For surcharges see Nos. C277-C279.

No. C169 Surcharged with New Value in Black

1950 *Perf. 12*
C222 A185 90c on 1.30s dp blue .20 .20

See No. C235.

Nos. C128-C129 Overprinted in Black

1951, July 28 **Unwmk.** *Perf. 11*
C223 A173 3s orange .85 .85
C224 A173 5s dark brown 1.40 1.25

20,000th crossing of the equator by Pan American-Grace Airways planes.

Nos. C202-C203 Surcharged in Black

1951 **Unwmk.** *Perf. 12½x12*
C225 AP47 60c on 1.30s .25 .20
C226 AP48 1s on 1.90s .25 .20
a. Inverted surcharge 12.00

Issued to publicize adult education.

St. Mariana de Jesus — AP50

1952, Feb. 15 **Engr.**
C227 AP50 60c plum & aqua .45 .20
C228 AP50 90c dk grn & lt ultra .50 .20
C229 AP50 1s car & dk grn .55 .20
C230 AP50 2s indigo & rose lil .55 .20
Nos. C227-C230 (4) 2.06 .80

Canonization of Mariana de Jesus Paredes y Flores.

Plaza Visit to US Issue

3s, as No. 558. 5s, as No. 559.

1952, Mar. 26 *Perf. 12*
C231 A205 3s lilac & bl grn .45 .30
C232 A205 5s red brn & ol gray .85 .85
a. Souv. sheet of 2, #C231-C232 2.25 4.50

Consular Service Stamps Surcharged "AEREO" and New Value in Black

1952 **Unwmk.** *Perf. 12*
C233 R2 60c on 1s green .25 .20
C234 R2 1s on 1s green .25 .20

Type R2 illustrated above No. 545.

No. C169 Surcharged with New Value in Carmine

C235 A185 90c on 1.30s dp bl .20 .20
Nos. C233-C235 (3) .70 .60

See No. C222.

Pres. José M. Urvina and Allegory of Freedom AP52

Torch of Knowledge AP53

Hyphen-hole Perf. 7x6½

1952, Nov. 18 **Litho.**
C236 AP52 60c rose red & blue 1.40 .45
C237 AP52 90c lilac & red 1.40 .50
C238 AP52 1s orange & green 1.40 .20
C239 AP52 2s red brn & blue 1.40 .30
Nos. C236-C239 (4) 5.60 1.45

Centenary of abolition of slavery in Ecuador. Counterfeits exist.

Unwmk.

1953, Apr. 13 **Engr.** *Perf. 12*

Design: 2s, Aged couple studying alphabet.

C240 AP53 1s dark blue .70 .20
C241 AP53 2s red orange .95 .20

1952 adult education campaign.

Globe Showing Part of Western Hemisphere AP54

1953, June 5 *Perf. 12½x12*
C242 AP54 60c orange yellow .20 .20
C243 AP54 90c dark blue .35 .35
C244 AP54 3s carmine .55 .45
Nos. C242-C244 (3) 1.10 1.00

Issued to publicize the crossing of the equator by the Pan-American highway.

Consular Service Stamps Surcharged in Black

a

b

1953-54 ***Perf. 12***

No.	Type	Description	Unused	Used
C245	R1 (a)	60c on 2s brown	.25	.20
C246	R2 (a)	60c on 5s sep ('54)	.25	.20
C247	R2 (a)	70c on 5s sep ('54)	.25	.20
C248	R2 (a)	90c on 50c car rose ('54)	.25	.20
C249	R1 (b)	1s on 2s brown	.25	.20
C250	R1 (a)	1s on 2s brn ('54)	.25	.20
C251	R1 (a)	2s on 2s brn ('54)	.45	.20
C252	R1 (a)	3s on 5s vio ('54)	.60	.20
		Nos. C245-C252 (8)	2.55	1.60

Surcharge is horizontal on Nos. C245, C247 and C248.

Carlos Maria Cardinal de la Torre — AP55

Queen Isabella I — AP56

1954, Jan. 13 **Photo.** ***Perf. 8½***

Center in Black

No.	Type	Description	Unused	Used
C253	AP55	60c rose lilac	.25	.20
C254	AP55	90c green	.35	.20
C255	AP55	3s orange	.50	.20
		Nos. C253-C255 (3)	1.10	.60

1st anniv. of the elevation of Archbishop de la Torre to Cardinal.

1954, Apr. 22

No.	Type	Description	Unused	Used
C256	AP56	60c dk grn & grn	.20	*.30*
C257	AP56	90c lil rose	.20	.30
C258	AP56	1s blk & pale lil	.20	*.30*
C259	AP56	2s blk brn & pale bl	.25	.20
C260	AP56	5s blk brn & buff	.70	.20
		Nos. C256-C260 (5)	1.55	1.30

See note with No. 585.

Post Office, Guayaquil AP57

1954, May 19 **Engr.** ***Perf. 12½x12***

Black Surcharge

No.	Type	Description	Unused	Used
C261	AP57	80c on 20c red	.25	.20
C262	AP57	1s on 20c red	.25	.20

25th anniversary of Pan American-Grace Airways' operation in Ecuador.

Plane, Gateway and Wheel — AP58

Unwmk.

1954, Aug. 2 **Litho.** ***Perf. 11***

No.	Type	Description	Unused	Used
C263	AP58	80c blue	.30	.20

Day of the Postal Employee.

San Pablo Lagoon AP59

1954, Sept. 24 **Photo.**

No.	Type	Description	Unused	Used
C264	AP59	60c orange	.25	.20
C265	AP59	70c rose pink	.25	.20
C266	AP59	90c dp grn	.25	.20
C267	AP59	1s dk gray grn	.25	.20
C268	AP59	2s blue	.30	.20
C269	AP59	3s yel brn	.50	.20
		Nos. C264-C269 (6)	1.80	1.20

Glorification of Abdon Calderon Garaicoa AP60

Capt. Calderon — AP61

1954, Oct. 1

No.	Type	Description	Unused	Used
C270	AP60	80c rose pink	.30	.20
C271	AP61	90c blue	.30	.20

150th anniversary of the birth of Capt. Abdon Calderon Garaicoa.

El Cebollar College AP62

Brother Miguel Instructing Boys — AP63

Designs: 90c, Francisco Febres Cordero (Brother Miguel). 2.50s, Tomb of Brother Miguel. 3s, Monument to Brother Miguel.

1954, Dec. 3 **Unwmk.** ***Perf. 11***

No.	Type	Description	Unused	Used
C272	AP62	70c dk grn	.20	.20
C273	AP63	80c dk brn	.20	.20
C274	AP63	90c dk gray bl	.20	.20
C275	AP63	2.50s indigo	.35	.20
C276	AP62	3s lil rose	.50	.35
		Nos. C272-C276 (5)	1.45	1.15

Centenary of the birth of Francisco Febres Cordero (Brother Miguel).

No. C221 Surcharged in Various Colors

1955, May 25

No.	Type	Description	Unused	Used
C277	A173	1s on 10s vio (Bk)	.20	.20
C278	A173	1.70s on 10s vio (C)	.30	.20
C279	A173	4.20s on 10s vio (Br)	.50	.35
		Nos. C277-C279 (3)	1.00	.75

Denomination in larger type on No. C279. National Exhibition of Daily Periodicals.

"La Rotonda," Guayaquil, and Rotary Emblem AP64

Design: 90c, Eugenio Espejo hospital, Quito, and Rotary emblem.

1955, July 9 **Engr.** ***Perf. 12½***

No.	Type	Description	Unused	Used
C280	AP64	80c dark brown	.25	.25
C281	AP64	90c dark grown	.35	.35

50th anniv. of the founding of Rotary Intl.

José Abel Castillo AP65

2s, 5s, José Abel Castillo, Map of Ecuador.

1955, Oct. 19 ***Perf. 11x11½***

No.	Type	Description	Unused	Used
C282	AP65	60c chocolate	.50	.20
C283	AP65	90c light olive green	.50	.20
C284	AP65	1s lilac	.55	.20
C285	AP65	2s vermilion	.70	.20
C286	AP65	5s ultra	1.40	.55
		Nos. C282-C286 (5)	3.65	1.35

See note after No. 595.

No. C29 Surcharged in Black

1955, Oct. 24 ***Perf. 12***

No.	Type	Description	Unused	Used
C287	AP1	1s on 5s purple	.30	.20

A similar surcharge on No. C29, set in two lines with letters 5mm high and no X's or black-out line of squares, was privately applied.

San Pablo, Imbabura — AP66

50s, Rumichaca Caves. 1.30s, Virgin of Quito. 1.50s, Cotopaxi Volcano. 1.70s, Tungurahua Volcano, Tungurahua. 1.90s, Guanacos. 2.40s, Mat market. 2.50s, Ruins at Incapirca. 4.20s, El Carmen, Cuenca, Azuay. 4.80s, Santo Domingo Church.

1956, Jan. 2 **Photo.** ***Perf. 13***

No.	Type	Description	Unused	Used
C288	AP66	50c slate blue	1.10	.20
C289	AP66	1s ultra	1.10	.20
C290	AP66	1.30s crimson	1.75	.20
C291	AP66	1.50s dp grn	1.10	.20
C292	AP66	1.70s yel brn	.75	.20
C293	AP66	1.90s olive	1.40	.20
C294	AP66	2.40s red org	1.50	.20
C295	AP66	2.50s violet	1.50	.20
C296	AP66	4.20s black	1.90	.20
C297	AP66	4.80s yel org	3.00	.30
		Nos. C288-C297 (10)	15.10	2.10

See Nos. C310-C311. For surcharges see Nos. 766A, 766G.

Honorato Vazquez — AP67

Title Page of First Book — AP68

1956, May 28 **Engr.**

Various Portraits

No.	Type	Description	Unused	Used
C298	AP67	1s yellow green	.25	.20
C299	AP67	1.50s red	.25	.20
C300	AP67	1.70s bright blue	.25	.20
C301	AP67	1.90s slate blue	.25	.20
		Nos. C298-C301 (4)	1.00	.80

Birth centenary (in 1955) of Honorato Vazquez, statesman.

1956, Aug. 27 **Unwmk.** ***Perf. 13½***

No.	Type	Description	Unused	Used
C302	AP68	1s black	.25	.20
C303	AP68	1.70s slate bl	.25	.20
C304	AP68	2s blk brn	.25	.20
C305	AP68	3s redsh brn	.25	.20
		Nos. C302-C305 (4)	1.00	.80

Bicentenary of printing in Ecuador.

Hands Reaching for UN Emblem AP69

1956, Oct. 24 ***Perf. 14***

No.	Type	Description	Unused	Used
C307	AP69	1.70s red org	.35	.20

10th anniv. of the UN (in 1955). See No. C319. For overprint see No. C426.

Coat of Arms and Basketball Player — AP70

Designs: 1.70s, Map of South America with flags and girl basketball players.

1956, Dec. 28 **Photo.** ***Perf. 14½x14***

No.	Type	Description	Unused	Used
C308	AP70	1s red lilac	.45	.20
C309	AP70	1.70s deep green	.65	.20

6th South American Women's Basketball Championship, Aug. 1956.

Scenic Type of 1956

1957, Jan. 2 ***Perf. 13***

No.	Type	Description	Unused	Used
C310	AP66	50c bl grn	.65	.20
C311	AP66	1s orange	.65	.20

Type of Regular Issue, 1957

Designs: 50c, Map of Cuenca, 16th century. 80c, Cathedral of Cuenca. 1s, Modern City Hall.

Unwmk.

1957, Apr. 7 **Photo.** ***Perf. 12***

No.	Type	Description	Unused	Used
C312	A219	50c brn, *cr*	.20	.20
a.		Souvenir sheet of 4	1.00	1.00
C313	A219	80c red, *bluish*	.25	.20
C314	A219	1s pur, *yel*	.30	.20
a.		Souvenir sheet of 3	2.00	2.00
		Nos. C312-C314 (3)	.75	.60

No. C312a contains 4 imperf. 50c stamps similar to No. 613, but inscribed "AEREO" and printed in green. The sheet is printed on white ungummed paper.

No. C314a contains 3 imperf. stamps in designs similar to Nos. C312-C314, but with colors changed to orange (50c), brown (80c), violet (1s). The sheet is printed on white ungummed paper.

Gabriela Mistral — AP71

Arms of Espejo, Carchi — AP72

Unwmk.

1957, Sept. 18 **Litho.** ***Perf. 14***

No.	Type	Description	Unused	Used
C315	AP71	2s lt bl, blk & red	.35	.20

Issued to honor Gabriela Mistral (1889-1957), Chilean poet and educator.

See Nos. C406-C407.

1957, Nov. 16 ***Perf. 14½x13½***

Arms of Cantons: 2s, Montufar. 4.20s, Tulcan.

Coat of Arms Multicolored

No.	Type	Description	Unused	Used
C316	AP72	1s carmine	.35	.20
C317	AP72	2s black	.35	.20
C318	AP72	4.20s ultra	.70	.20
		Nos. C316-C318 (3)	1.40	.60

Province of Carchi.

See Nos. C334-C337, C355-C364, C392-C395. For surcharge see No. 766.

Redrawn UN Type of 1956

1957, Dec. 10 Engr. *Perf. 14*

C319	AP69	2s greenish blue	.35	.25

Honoring the UN. Dates, as on No. C307, are omitted; inscribed: "Homenaje a las Naciones Unidas."

Mater Dolorosa, San Gabriel College — AP73

Rafael Maria Arizaga — AP74

#C321, 1s, Door of San Gabriel College, Quito.

1958, Apr. 27 Engr. *Perf. 14*

C320	AP73	30c rose cl, *dp rose*	.25	.20
C321	AP73	30c rose cl, *dp rose*	.25	.20
a.		Pair, #C320-C321	.60	.60
C322	AP73	1s dk bl, *lt bl*	.25	.20
C323	AP73	1.70s dk bl, *lt bl*	.25	.20
a.		Pair, #C322-C323	.60	.60

Miracle of San Gabriel College, Quito, 50th anniv.

1958, July 21 Litho.

C324	AP74	1s multi	.30	.20

Rafael Maria Arizaga (1858-1933), writer.
See Nos. C343, C350, C412.

Daule River Bridge AP75

1958, July 25 Engr. *Perf. 13½x14*

C325	AP75	1.30s green	.35	.20

Issued to commemorate the opening of the River Daule bridge in Guayas province.
See Nos. C367-C369.

Basketball Player — AP76

Symbolical of the Eucharist — AP77

1958, Sept. 1 Photo. *Perf. 14x13½*

C326	AP76	1.30s dk grn & lt brn	.35	.30

South American basketball championships.
For surcharge see No. 774A.

1958, Sept. 25 Litho. Unwmk.

Design: 60c, Cathedral of Guayaquil.

C327	AP77	10c vio & buff	.35	.20
C328	AP77	60c org & vio brn	.35	.20
C329	AP77	1s brn & lt bl	.35	.20
		Nos. C327-C329 (3)	1.05	.60

Souvenir Sheet

Symbolical of the Eucharist — AP78

Perf. 13½x14

C330	AP78	Sheet of 4	1.75	1.50
a.-d.		40c dark blue, any single	.20	.20

3rd National Eucharistic Congress.

Stamps of 1865 and 1920 — AP79

Designs: 2s, Stamps of 1920 and 1948. 4.20s, Municipal museum and library.

1958, Oct. 8 Photo. *Perf. 11½*
Granite Paper

C331	AP79	1.30s grn & brn red	.20	.20
C332	AP79	2s bl & vio	.50	.30
C333	AP79	4.20s dk brn	.60	.40
		Nos. C331-C333 (3)	1.30	.90

National Philatelic Exposition (EXFIGUA), Guayaquil, Oct. 4-14.
For surcharge see No. 774.

Coat of Arms Type of 1957

Province of Imbabura

Arms of Cantons: 50c, Cotacachi. 60c, Antonio Ante. 80c, Otalvo. 1.10s, Ibarra.

1958, Nov. 9 Litho. *Perf. 14½x13½*
Coats of Arms Multicolored

C334	AP72	50c blk & red	.35	.20
C335	AP72	60c blk, bl & red	.35	.20
C336	AP72	80c blk & yel	.35	.20
C337	AP72	1.10s blk & red	.35	.20
		Nos. C334-C337 (4)	1.40	.80

Charles V — AP80

Paul Rivet — AP81

Engr. & Photo.
1958, Dec. 12 *Perf. 14x13½*

C338	AP80	2s brn red & dk brn	.30	.20
C339	AP80	4.20s dk gray & red brn	.40	.30

400th anniv. of the death of Charles V, Holy Roman Emperor.

1958, Dec. 29 Photo. *Perf. 11½*
Granite Paper

C340	AP81	1s brown	.30	.20

Issued in honor of Paul Rivet (1876-1958), French anthropologist.

1959, May 6

Portrait: 2s, Alexander von Humboldt.

C341	AP81	2s slate	.25	.20

Cent. of the death of Alexander von Humboldt, German naturalist and geographer.

Front Page of "El Telegrafo" — AP82

1959, Feb. Litho. *Perf. 13½*

C342	AP82	1.30s bl grn & blk	.25	.20

75th anniv. of Ecuador's oldest newspaper.

Portrait Type of 1958

José Luis Tamayo (1858-1947), lawyer.

1959, June 26 Unwmk. *Perf. 14*
Portrait Multicolored

C343	AP74	1.30s lt grn, bl & sal	.30	.20

El Sagrario & House of Manuela Canizares AP83

Condor — AP84

Designs: 80c, Hall at San Agustin. 1s, First words of the constitutional act. 2s, Entrance to Cuartel Real. 4.20s, Allegory of Liberty.

Unwmk.
1959, Aug. 28 Photo. *Perf. 14*

C344	AP83	20c ultra & lt brn	.25	.20
C345	AP83	80c brt bl & dp org	.25	.20
C346	AP83	1s dk red & dk ol	.25	.20
C347	AP84	1.30s brt bl & org	.25	.20
C348	AP84	2s ultra & org brn	.25	.20
C349	AP84	4.20s scar & brt bl	.40	.30
		Nos. C344-C349 (6)	1.65	1.30

Sesquicentennial of the revolution.

Portrait Type of 1958

1s, Alfredo Baquerizo Moreno (1859-1951), statesman.

1959, Sept. 26 Litho. *Perf. 14*

C350	AP74	1s gray, red & salmon	.30	.20

Pope Pius XII — AP85

1959, Oct. 9 Unwmk. *Perf. 14½*

C351	AP85	1.30s multi	.35	.20

Issued in memory of Pope Plus XII.

Flags of Argentina, Bolivia, Brazil, Guatemala, Haiti, Mexico and Peru — AP86

Flags of: 80c, Chile, Costa Rica, Cuba, Dominican Republic, Panama, Paraguay, United States. 1.30s, Colombia, Ecuador, Honduras, Nicaragua, Salvador, Uruguay, Venezuela.

1959, Oct. 12 *Perf. 13½*

C352	AP86	50c multi	.20	.20
C353	AP86	80c yel, red & bl	.20	.20
C354	AP86	1.30s multi	.35	.20
		Nos. C352-C354 (3)	.75	.60

Organization of American States.
For overprints see #C423-C425, CO19-CO21.

Arms of the Cantons Type of 1957

Province of Pichincha

10c, Rumiñahui. 40c, Pedro Moncayo. 1s, Mejia. 1.30s, Cayambe. 4.20s, Quito.

Perf. 14½x13½
1959-60 Unwmk. Litho.
Coat of Arms Multicolored

C355	AP72	10c blk & dk red ('60)	.35	.20
C356	AP72	40c blk & yel	.35	.20
C357	AP72	1s blk & brn ('60)	.35	.20
C358	AP72	1.30s blk & grn ('60)	.35	.20
C359	AP72	4.20s blk & org	.35	.20
		Nos. C355-C359 (5)	1.75	1.00

Province of Cotopaxi

40c, Pangua. 60c, Pujili. 70c, Saquisili. 1s, Salcedo. 1.30s, Latacunga.

1960
Coat of Arms Multicolored

C360	AP72	40c blk & car	.25	.20
C361	AP72	60c blk & bl	.25	.20
C362	AP72	70c blk & turq	.25	.20
C363	AP72	1s blk & red org	.25	.20
C364	AP72	1.30s blk & org	.30	.20
		Nos. C360-C364 (5)	1.30	1.00

Flags of American Nations — AP87

1960, Feb. 23 *Perf. 13x12½*

C365	AP87	1.30s multi	.20	.20
C366	AP87	2s multi	.25	.20

11th Inter-American Conference, Feb. 1960.

Bridge Type of 1958.

Bridges: No. C367, Juntas. No. C368, Saracay. 2s, Railroad bridge, Ambato.

1960 Litho. *Perf. 13½*

C367	AP75	1.30s chocolate	.25	.20

Photo. *Perf. 12½*

C368	AP75	1.30s emerald	.25	.20
C369	AP75	2s brown	.35	.20
		Nos. C367-C369 (3)	.85	.60

Building of three new bridges.

Bahia-Chone Road — AP88

Pres. Camilo Ponce Enriquez AP89

Designs: 4.20s, Public Works Building, Cuenca. 5s, El Coca airport. 10s, New Harbor, Guayaquil.

1960, Aug. Litho. *Perf. 14*

C370	AP88	1.30s blk & dl yel	.20	.20
C371	AP88	4.20s rose car & lt grn	.30	.30
C372	AP88	5s dk brn & yel	.45	.35
C373	AP88	10s dk bl & bl	1.00	.35

Perf. 11x11½

C374 AP89 2s org brn & blk 1.40 .25
Nos. C370-C374 (5) 3.35 1.45

Nos. C370-C374 publicize the achievements of Pres. Camilo Ponce Enriquez (1956-1960).
Issued: #C370-C373, 8/24; #C374, 8/31.

Red Cross Building, Quito and Henri Dunant AP90

1960, Oct. 5 Unwmk. *Perf. 13x14*
C375 AP90 2s rose vio & car .45 .20

Centenary (in 1959) of Red Cross idea.
For overprint see No. C408.

El Belen Church, Quito — AP91

1961, Jan. 14 *Perf. 12½*
C376 AP91 3s multi .40 .20

Ecuador's participation in the 1960 Barcelona Philatelic Congress.

Map of Ecuador and Amazon River System AP92

1961, Feb. 27 Litho. *Perf. 10½*
C377 AP92 80c salmpn, claret & grn .25 .20
C378 AP92 1.30s gray, slate & grn .35 .20
C379 AP92 2s beige, red & grn .50 .20
Nos. C377-C379 (3) 1.10 .60

Amazon Week, and the 132nd anniversary of the Battle of Tarqui against Peru.

Juan Montalvo, Juan Leon Mera, Juan Benigno Vela — AP93

Hugo Ortiz G. — AP94

1961, Apr. 13 Unwmk. *Perf. 13*
C380 AP93 1.30s salmon & blk .35 .20

Centenary of Tungurahua province.

1961, May 25 *Perf. 14x14½*

Design: No. C382, Ortiz monument.

C381 AP94 1.30s grnsh bl, blk & yel .25 .20
C382 AP94 1.30s grnsh bl, pur, ol & brn .25 .20

Lt. Hugo Ortiz G., killed in battle 8/2/41.

Condor and Airplane Stamp of 1936 AP95

1.30s, Map of South America and stamp of 1865. 2s, Bolivar monument stamp of 1930.

Perf. 10½

1961, May 25 Litho. Unwmk.

Size: 41x28mm

C383 AP95 80c org & vio .20 .20

Size: 41x34mm

C384 AP95 1.30s bl, yel, ol & car .30 .25

Size: 40½x37mm

C385 AP95 2s car rose & blk .45 .25
Nos. C383-C385 (3) .95 .70

Third National Philatelic Exhibition, Quito, May 25-June 3, 1961.

Arms of Los Rios and Egret — AP96

1961, May 27 *Perf. 14½x13½*

Coat of Arms Multicolored

C386 AP96 2s bl & blk .35 .30

Centenary (in 1960) of Los Rios province.

Gabriel Garcia Moreno — AP97

Remigio Crespo Toral — AP98

1961, Sept. 24 Unwmk. *Perf. 12*
C387 AP97 1s bl, brn & buff .30 .20

Centenary of the restoration of national integrity.

1961, Nov. 3 Unwmk. *Perf. 14*
C388 AP98 50c multi .30 .20

Centenary of the birth of Remigio Crespo Toral, poet laureate of Ecuador.

Galapagos Islands Nos. LC1-LC3 Overprinted in Black or Red: "Estacion de Biologia Maritima de Galapagos" and "UNESCO 1961" (Similar to #684-686)

1961, Oct. 31 Photo. *Perf. 12*
C389 A1 1s dp bl .35 .20
a. "de Galapagos" on top line 2.00 2.00
C390 A1 1.80s rose vio .60 .30
a. UNESCO emblem omitted 1.25 1.25
C391 A1 4.20s blk (R) .75 .55
Nos. C389-C391 (3) 1.70 1.05

Establishment of maritime biological stations on Galapagos Islands by UNESCO.

Arms of the Cantons Type of 1957

Province of Tungurahua

50c, Pillaro. 1s, Pelileo. 1.30s, Baños. 2s, Ambato.

Perf. 14½x13½

1962, Mar. 30 Litho. Unwmk.

Coats of Arms Multicolored

C392 AP72 50c black .20 .20
C393 AP72 1s black .20 .20
C394 AP72 1.30s black .25 .20
C395 AP72 2s black .45 .20
Nos. C392-C395 (4) 1.10 .80

Pres. Arosemena and Prince Philip, Arms of Ecuador and Great Britain and Equator Monument AP99

Perf. 14x13½

1962, Feb. 17 Wmk. 340
C396 AP99 1.30s bl, sepia, red & yel .20 .20
C397 AP99 2s multi .35 .20

Visit of Prince Philip, Duke of Edinburgh, to Ecuador, Feb. 17-20, 1962.

Mountain Farming — AP100

Perf. 12½

1963, Mar. 21 Unwmk. Litho.
C398 AP100 30c emer, yel & blk .20 .20
C399 AP100 3s dl red, grn & org .50 .20
C400 AP100 4.20s bl, blk & yel .70 .45
Nos. C398-C400 (3) 1.40 .85

FAO "Freedom from Hunger" campaign. Exist imperf. Value $32.50.

Mosquito and Malaria Eradication Emblem AP101

1963, Apr. 17 Unwmk. *Perf. 12½*
C401 AP101 50c multi .20 .20
C402 AP101 80c multi .20 .20
C403 AP101 2s multi .30 .20
Nos. C401-C403 (3) .70 .60

WHO drive to eradicate malaria.

Stagecoach and Jet Plane AP102

1963, May 7 Litho.
C404 AP102 2s org & car rose .30 .20
C405 AP102 4.20s claret & ultra .50 .35

1st Intl. Postal Conference, Paris, 1863.

Type of 1957 Inscribed "Islas Galapagos," Surcharged with New Value and Overprinted "Ecuador" in Black or Red

1963, June 19 Unwmk. *Perf. 14*
C406 AP71 5s on 2s gray, dk bl & red .80 .60
C407 AP71 10s on 2s gray, dk bl & red (R) 1.40 1.40

The basic 2s exists without surcharge and overprint. No. C407 exists with "ECUADOR" omitted, and with both "ECUADOR" and "10 SUCRES" double.

No. C375 Overprinted: "1863-1963/Centenario/de la Fundación/ de la Cruz Roja/Internacional"

1963, June 21 Photo. *Perf. 13x14*
C408 AP90 2s rose vio & car .30 .20

Intl. Red Cross, centenary.

Type of Regular Issue, 1963

Arosemena and: 70c, Flags of Ecuador. 2s, Flags of Ecuador, Panama. 4s, Flags of Ecuador, US.

1963, July 1 Litho. *Perf. 14*
C409 A238 70c pale bl & multi .20 .20
C410 A238 2s pink & multi .35 .20
C411 A238 4s lt bl & multi .85 .35
Nos. C409-C411 (3) 1.40 .75

Imperfs exist. Value $15.

Portrait Type of 1958

Portrait: 2s, Dr. Mariano Cueva (1812-82).

Unwmk.

1963, July 4 Litho. *Perf. 14*
C412 AP74 2s lt grn & multi .35 .20

Social Insurance Symbol — AP103

Mother and Child — AP104

1963, July 9 Litho.
C413 AP103 10s brn, bl, gray & ocher .90 .70

25th anniversary of Social Insurance. Exists imperf. Value $9.

1963, July 28 *Perf. 12½*
C414 AP104 1.30s org, dk bl & blk .20 .20
C415 AP104 5s gray, red & brn .45 .45

7th Pan-American and South American Pediatrics Congresses, Quito.

Simon Bolivar Airport, Guayaquil AP105

1963, July 25 *Perf. 14*
C416 AP105 60c gray .20 .20
C417 AP105 70c dl grn .20 .20
C418 AP105 5s brn vio .50 .35
Nos. C416-C418 (3) .90 .75

Opening of Simon Bolivar Airport, Guayaquil, July 15, 1962.
Exist imperf. Value $4.50.

Nos. 638, 640-641 Overprinted "AEREO"

1964 *Perf. 12*

Flags in National Colors

C419 A223 1.80s dl vio .50 .35
C420 A224 2s dk brn .50 .35
C421 A223 2.20s blk brn .50 .35
Nos. C419-C421 (3) 1.50 1.05

On 1.80s and 2.20s, "AEREO" is vertical, reading down.

No. 650 Overprinted in Gold: "FARO DE COLON / AEREO"

1964 Photo. *Perf. 14x13½*
C422 A229 1.80s dk bl 2.50 1.50

Nos. C352-C354 Overprinted

Illustration reduced.

1964 Litho. *Perf. 13½*
C423 AP86 50c bl & multi .65 .45
C424 AP86 80c yel & multi .65 .45
C425 AP86 1.30s pale grn & multi .65 .45
Nos. C423-C425 (3) 1.95 1.35

No. C307 Overprinted: "DECLARACION / DERECHOS HUMANOS / 1964 / XV-ANIV"

Unwmk.

1964, Sept. 29 Engr. *Perf. 14*

C426 AP69 1.70s red org .35 .20

15th anniversary (in 1963) of the Universal Declaration of Human Rights.

Banana Type

1964, Oct. 26 Litho. *Perf. 12½x12*

C427 A241 4.20s blk, bis & gray ol .30 .20
C428 A241 10s blk, scar & gray ol .50 .40
a. Souv. sheet of 4 2.10 2.10

No. C428a contains imperf. stamps similar to Nos. 720-721 and C427-C428.

John F. Kennedy, Flag-draped Coffin and John Jr. — AP106

1964, Nov. 22 Litho. *Perf. 14*

C429 AP106 4.20s multi .85 .65
C430 AP106 5s multi 1.10 .80
C431 AP106 10s multi 2.00 1.10
a. Souv. sheet of 3 7.00 7.00
Nos. C429-C431 (3) 3.95 2.55

President John F. Kennedy (1917-63).
No. C431a contains stamps similar to Nos. C429-C431, imperf.

Olympic Type

1.30s, Gymnast, vert. 1.80s, Hurdler. 2s, Basketball.

Perf. 13½x14, 14x13½

1964, Dec. 16 Unwmk.

C432 A243 1.30s vio bl, ver & brn .25 .20
C433 A243 1.80s vio bl & multi .25 .20
C434 A243 2s red & multi .25 .20
a. Souv. sheet of 4 2.90 2.90
Nos. C432-C434 (3) .75 .60

No. C434a contains stamps similar to Nos. 725 and C432-C434, imperf.

Sports Type

Torch and Athletes: 2s, 3s, Diver, gymnast, wrestlers and weight lifter. 2.50s, 4s, Bicyclists. 3.50s, 5s, Jumpers.

1965, Nov. 20 Litho. *Perf. 12x12½*

C435 A247 2s bl, gold & blk .40 .20
C436 A247 2.50s org, gold & blk .40 .20
C437 A247 3s brt pink, gold & blk .40 .20
C438 A247 3.50s lt vio, gold & bl .45 .45
C439 A247 4s brt yel grn, gold & blk .45 .20
C440 A247 5s red org, gold & blk .50 .25
a. Souv. sheet of 12 8.00 8.00
Nos. C435-C440 (6) 2.60 1.50

No. C440a contains 12 imperf. stamps similar to Nos. 738-743 and C435-C440.
For surcharges see Nos. 766B, C449.

Bird Type

Birds: 1s, Yellow grosbeak. 1.30s, Black-headed parrot. 1.50s, Scarlet tanager. 2s, Sapphire quail-dove. 2.50s, Violet-tailed sylph. 3s, Lemon-throated barbet. 4s, Yellow-tailed oriole. 10s, Collared puffbird.

1966, June 17 Litho. *Perf. 13½*

Birds in Natural Colors

C441 A249 1s lt red brn & blk 1.10 .20
C442 A249 1.30s pink & blk 1.10 .20
C443 A249 1.50s pale grn & blk 1.10 .20
C444 A249 2s sal & blk 1.75 .30
C445 A249 2.50s lt yel grn & blk 1.75 .30
C446 A249 3s sal & blk 2.50 .35
C447 A249 4s gray & blk 3.25 .55
C448 A249 10s beige & blk 5.00 1.40
Nos. C441-C448 (8) 17.55 3.50

For surcharges see Nos. 766E-766F, C450, C455-C457.

Nos. C436 and C443 Surcharged

1967

C449 A247 80c on 2.50s multi .35 .25
C450 A249 80c on 1.50s multi .35 .20

Old denomination on No. C449 is obliterated with heavy bar; the surcharge on No. C450 includes "Resello" and an ornament over old denomination.

Peñaherrera Monument, Quito — AP107

Design: 2s, Peñaherrera statue.

1967, Dec. 29 Litho. *Perf. 12x12½*

C451 AP107 1.30s blk & org .25 .20
C452 AP107 2s blk & lt ultra .25 .20

See note after No. 763.

Arosemena Type

1.30s, Inauguration. 2s, Pres. Arosemena speaking in Punta del Este.

1968, May 9 Litho. *Perf. 13½x14*

C453 A251 1.30s multi .25 .20
C454 A251 2s multi .25 .20

No. C448 Surcharged in Plum, Dark Blue or Green

1969, Jan. 9 Litho. *Perf. 13½*

Bird in Natural Colors

C455 A249 80c on 10s beige (P) .50 .25
C456 A249 1s on 10s beige (DBl) .50 .25
C457 A249 2s on 10s beige (G) .50 .25
Nos. C455-C457 (3) 1.50 .75

"Operation Friendship" AP108

1969-70 Typo. *Perf. 13½*

C458 AP108 2s yel, blk, red & lt bl .25 .20
a. Perf. 12½ .25 .20
C459 AP108 2s bl, blk, car & yel ('70) .25 .20

Friendship campaign. Medallion background on Nos. C458 and C458a is blue; on No. C459, yellow.
No. C459 exists imperf. Value $5.

No. 639 Surcharged in Gold "S/. 5 AEREO" and Bar

1969, Nov. 25 Litho. *Perf. 12*

C460 A224 5s on 2s multi 1.60 .50

Butterfly Type

Butterflies: 1.30s, Morpho peleides. 1.50s, Anartia amathea.

1970 Litho. *Perf. 12½*

C461 A255 1.30s multi 1.40 .20
C462 A255 1.50s pink & multi 1.40 .20

Same, White Background

1970 *Perf. 13½*

C463 A255 1.30s multi 1.40 .20
C464 A255 1.50s multi 1.40 .20

Arms Type

Provincial Arms and Flags: 1.30s, El Oro. 2s, Loja. 3s, Manabi. 5s, Pichincha. 10s, Guayas.

1971 Litho. *Perf. 10½*

C465 A258 1.30s pink & multi .25 .20
C466 A258 2s multi .30 .20
C467 A258 3s multi .45 .25
C468 A258 5s multi .60 .30
C469 A258 10s multi 1.10 .35
Nos. C465-C469 (5) 2.70 1.30

Presentation of the Virgin — AP109

Pres. Allende and Chilean Flag AP110

Art of Quito: 1.50s, Blessed Anne at Prayer. 2s, St. Theresa de Jesus. 2.50s, Altar of Carmen, horiz. 3s, Descent from the Cross. 4s, Christ of St. Mariana de Jesus. 5s, Shrine of St. Anthony. 10s, Cross of San Diego.

1971 *Perf. 11½*

Inscriptions in Black

C473 AP109 1.30s multi .20 .20
C474 AP109 1.50s multi .25 .20
C475 AP109 2s multi .25 .20
C476 AP109 2.50s multi .35 .20
C477 AP109 3s multi .45 .20
C478 AP109 4s multi .55 .20
C479 AP109 5s multi .55 .30
C480 AP109 10s multi 1.25 .55
Nos. C473-C480 (8) 3.85 2.05

1971, Aug. 24 *Perf. 12½*

2.10s, Pres. José M. Velasco Ibarra of Ecuador, Pres. Salvador Allende of Chile, national flags.

C481 AP110 2s multi .25 .20
C482 AP110 2.10s multi .25 .20

Visit of Pres. Salvador Allende of Chile, Aug. 24.

Globe and Emblem AP111

1971

C483 AP111 5s black .70 .35
C484 AP111 5.50s dl pur & blk .70 .35

Opening of Postal Museum, Aug. 24, 1971.
Exist imperf. Value $7.50.

Pazmiño Type

1971, Sept. 16 *Perf. 12x11½*

C485 A260 1.50s grn & multi .20 .20
C486 A260 2.50s grn & multi .30 .20

AP112

AP113

Designs: 5s, Map of Americas. 10s, Converging roads and map. 20s, Map of Americas and Equator. 50s, Mountain road and monument on Equator.

1971 *Perf. 11½*

C487 AP112 5s org & multi .70 .40
C488 AP112 10s org & blk 1.10 .85
C489 AP112 20s blk, bl & brt rose 1.75 1.40
C490 AP112 50s bl, blk & gray 2.90 2.10
Nos. C487-C490 (4) 6.45 4.75

11th Pan-American Road Congress.
Issued: 5s, 10s, 50s, 11/15; 20s, 11/22.
No. C488 exists imperf. Value $8.

1972

Design: 3s, Arms of Ecuador and Argentina. 5s, Presidents José M. Velasco Ibarra and Alejandro Agustin Lanusse.

C491 AP113 3s blk & multi .25 .20
C492 AP113 5s blk & multi .45 .30

Visit of Lt. Gen. Alejandro Agustin Lanusse, president of Argentina, Jan. 25.

Flame, Scales, Map of Americas AP114

1972, Apr. 24 Litho. *Perf. 12½*

C493 AP114 1.30s bl & red .30 .20

17th Conference of the Interamerican Federation of Lawyers, Quito, Apr. 24.

Religious Paintings Type of Regular Issue

Ecuadorian Paintings: 3s, Virgin of the Flowers, by Miguel de Santiago. 10s, Virgin of the Rosary, by Quito School.

1972, Apr. 24 *Perf. 14x13½*

C494 A263 3s blk & multi .30 .30
C495 A263 10s blk & multi 1.00 .50
a. Souv. sheet of 2, #C494-C495 1.50 1.50

1972, May 4

Ecuadorian Statues: 3s, St. Dominic, Quito School. 10s, St. Rosa of Lima, by Bernardo de Legarda.

C496 A263 3s blk & multi .30 .30
C497 A263 10s blk & multi .95 .50
a. Souv. sheet of 2, #C496-C497 2.50 2.10

Letters of "Ecuador" 3mm high on #C496-C497, 7mm high on #C494-C495.

Portrait Type

Designs (Generals, from Paintings): 1.30s, José Maria Saenz. 3s, Tomás Wright. 4s, Antonio Farfan. 5s, Antonio José de Sucre. 10s, Simon Bolivar. 20s, Arms of Ecuador.

1972, May 24

C498 A264 1.30s bl & multi .20 .20
C499 A264 3s bl & multi .25 .20
C500 A264 4s bl & multi .30 .20
C501 A264 5s bl & multi .50 .30
C502 A264 10s bl & multi .90 .50
C503 A264 20s bl & multi 1.75 .90
Nos. C498-C503 (6) 3.90 2.30

Artisan Type

Handicraft of Ecuador: 2s, Woman wearing flowered poncho. 3s, Striped poncho. 5s, Poncho with roses. 10s, Gold sunburst sculpture.

1972, July Photo. *Perf. 13*

C504 A265 2s multi .25 .20
C505 A265 3s multi .45 .25
C506 A265 5s multi .70 .35
C507 A265 10s org red & multi 1.25 .80
a. Souv. sheet of 4, #C504-C507 3.50 3.50
Nos. C504-C507 (4) 2.65 1.60

Epidendrum Orchid — AP115

1972 Photo. Perf. 12½

C508 AP115 4s shown	1.40	1.25
C509 AP115 6s Canna	1.75	1.50
C510 AP115 10s Jimson weed	3.25	3.00
a. Souv. sheet of 3, #C508-C510	7.50	6.25
Nos. C508-C510 (3)	6.40	5.75

Exists imperf.

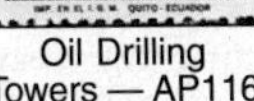

Oil Drilling Towers — AP116

Coat of Arms — AP117

1972, Oct. 17 Litho. Perf. 11½

C511 AP116 1.30s bl & multi	.25	.20

Ecuadorian oil industry.

1972, Nov. 18 Litho. Perf. 11½

Arms Multicolored

C512 AP117 2s black	.25	.20
C513 AP117 3s black	.25	.20
C514 AP117 4s black	.30	.20
C515 AP117 4.50s black	.30	.20
C516 AP117 6.30s black	.65	.30
C517 AP117 6.90s black	.65	.30
Nos. C512-C517 (6)	2.40	1.40

Pichincha Type

Designs: 2.40s, Corridor, San Agustin. 4.50s, La Merced Convent. 5.50s, Column base. 6.30s, Chapter Hall, San Agustin. 6.90s, Interior, San Agustin. 7.40s, Crucifixion, Cantuña Chapel. 7.90s, Decorated ceiling, San Agustin.

1972, Dec. 6 Wmk. 367

C518 A266 2.40s yel & multi	.25	.20
C519 A266 4.50s yel & multi	.40	.20
C520 A266 5.50s yel & multi	.50	.20
C521 A266 6.30s yel & multi	.55	.35
C522 A266 6.90s yel & multi	.60	.35
C523 A266 7.40s yel & multi	.70	.35
C524 A266 7.90s yel & multi	.75	.35
Nos. C518-C524 (7)	3.75	2.00

UN Emblem — AP118

OAS Emblem — AP119

1973, Mar. 23 Unwmk.

C525 AP118 1.30s lt bl & blk	.25	.20

25th anniversary of the Economic Committee for Latin America (CEPAL).

1973, Apr. 14 Wmk. 367

C526 AP119 1.50s multi	.30	.20
a. Unwatermarked	.30	.20

Day of the Americas and "Philately for Peace."

Bird Type

1973 Unwmk. Perf. 11½x11

C527 A268 1.30s Blue-footed booby	1.75	.20
C528 A268 3s Brown pelican	1.75	.20

Presidents Lara and Caldera AP120

1973, June 15 Wmk. 367

C529 AP120 3s multi	.35	.20

Visit of Venezuela Pres. Rafael Caldera, Feb. 5-7.

Silver Coin, 1934 — AP121

Globe, OPEC Emblem, Oil Derrick — AP122

Ecuadorian Coins: 10s, Silver coin, obverse. 50s, Gold coin, 1928.

Unwmk.

1973, Dec. 14 Photo. Perf. 14

C530 AP121 5s multi	.50	.35
C531 AP121 10s multi	.85	.55
C532 AP121 50s multi	4.00	2.25
a. Souvenir sheet of 3	6.00	6.00
Nos. C530-C532 (3)	5.35	3.15

No. C532a contains one each of Nos. C530-C532; Dated "1972." Exists imperf. Value, same.

A gold marginal overprint was applied in 1974 to No. C532a (perf. and imperf.): "X Campeonato Mundial de Football / Munich - 1974." Value, each $60.

A carmine overprint was applied in 1974 to No. C532a (perf. and imperf.): "Seminario de Telecommunicaciones Rurales, / Septiembre-1974 / Quito-Ecuador" and ITU emblem. Value, each $8.50.

1974, June 15 Litho. Perf. 11½

C533 AP122 2s multi	.30	.20

Meeting of Organization of Oil Exporting Countries, Quito, June 15-24.

Ecuadorian Flag, UPU Emblem — AP123

1974, July 15 Litho. Perf. 11½

C534 AP123 1.30s multi	.25	.20

Centenary of Universal Postal Union.

Two 25s souvenir sheets exist. These were sold on a restricted basis. Value, each $40.

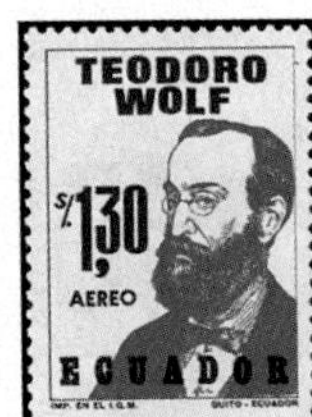

Teodoro Wolf AP124

Capt. Edmundo Chiriboga AP125

1974 Litho. Perf. 12x11½

C535 AP124 1.30s blk & ultra	.20	.20
C536 AP125 1.50s gray	.25	.20

Teodoro Wolf, geographer; Edmundo Chiriboga, national hero.

Issued: #C535, Nov. 29; #C536, Dec. 4.

Congress Emblem AP126

1974, Dec. 8 Litho. Perf. 11½x12

C537 AP126 5s bl & multi	.35	.20

8th Inter-American Postmasters' Cong., Quito.

Map of Americas and Coat of Arms AP127

Manuel J. Calle, Journalist AP128

1975, Feb. 1 Perf. 12x11½

C538 AP127 3s bl & multi	.35	.20

EXFIGUA Stamp Exhibition and 5th General Assembly of Federation Inter-Americana de Filatelia, Guayaquil, Nov. 1973.

1975 Perf. 12x11½

#C540, Leopoldo Benites V., president of UN General Assembly, 1973-74; #C541, Adofo H. Simmonds G. (1892-1969), journalists; #C542, Juan de Dios Martinez Mera, President of Ecuador, birth centenary.

C539 AP128 5s lilac rose	.45	.20
C540 AP128 5s gray	.45	.20
C541 AP128 5s violet	.45	.30
C542 AP128 5s blk & rose red	.45	.20
Nos. C539-C542 (4)	1.80	.90

Pres. Guillermo Rodriguez Lara — AP129

1975 Unwmk. Perf. 12

C546 AP129 5s vermilion & blk	.50	.30

State visit of Pres. Guillermo Rodriguez Lara to Algeria, Romania and Venezuela.

Meeting Type of 1975

1.50s, Rafael Rodriguez Palacio & Argelino Duran Quintero meeting at border in Ruichacha. 2s, Signing border agreement.

1975, Apr. 1 Litho. Perf. 12x11½

C547 A273 1.50s multi	.25	.20
C548 A273 2s multi	.25	.20

Sacred Heart (Painting) AP130

Quito Cathedral AP131

Design: 2s, Monstrance.

1975, Apr. 28 Litho. Perf. 12x11½

C549 AP130 1.30s yel & multi	.20	.20
C550 AP130 2s bl & multi	.20	.20
C551 AP131 3s multi	.30	.20
Nos. C549-C551 (3)	.70	.60

3rd Bolivarian Eucharistic Congress, Quito, June 9-16, 1974.

J. Delgado Panchana with Trophy — AP132

J. Delgado Panchana Swimming AP133

Perf. 12x11½, 11½x12

1975, June 12 Unwmk.

C552 AP132 1.30s bl & multi	.20	.20
C553 AP133 3s blk & multi	.30	.20

Jorge Delgado Panchana, South American swimming champion, 1971 and 1974.

Sports Type of 1975

1975, Sept. 11 Litho. Perf. 11½

C554 A276 1.30s Tennis	.35	.20
C555 A276 2s Target shooting	.35	.20
C556 A276 2.80s Volleyball	.45	.20
C557 A276 3s Raft with sails	.45	.20
C558 A276 5s Mask	.70	.20
Nos. C554-C558 (5)	2.30	1.00

Flower Type of 1975

1975, Nov. 18 Litho. Perf. 11½x12

C559 A277 1.30s Pitcairnia pungens	.20	.20
C560 A277 2s Scarlet sage	.35	.20
C561 A277 3s Amaryllis	.50	.30
C562 A277 4s Opuntia quitense	.70	.35
C563 A277 5s Amaryllis	1.10	.50
Nos. C559-C563 (5)	2.85	1.55

Tail Assemblies and Emblem — AP134

Planes over Map of Ecuador — AP135

1975, Dec. 17 Litho. Perf. 11½

C564 AP134 1.30s bl & multi	.30	.20
C565 AP135 3s multi	.35	.20

TAME, Military Transport Airline, 13th anniv.

Benalcázar Statue — AP136

1976, Feb. 6 Litho. Perf. 11½

C566 AP136 2s multi	.25	.20
C567 AP136 3s multi	.25	.20

Sebastián de Benalcázar (1495-1550), Spanish conquistador, founder of Quito.

Archaeology Type of 1975

1.30s, Seated man, Carchi Culture. 2s, Funerary urn, Tuncahuan Culture. 3s, Priest, Bahia de Caraquez Culture. 4s, Snail's shell, Cuasmal Culture. 5s, Bowl supported by figurines, Guangala Culture.

1976, Feb. 12 Litho. Perf. 11½

C568 A278 1.30s multi	.20	.20
C569 A278 2s multi	.30	.20
C570 A278 3s multi	.45	.30
C571 A278 4s multi	.65	.30
C572 A278 5s multi	.85	.30
Nos. C568-C572 (5)	2.45	1.30

Fruit Type of 1976

1976, Mar. 30

C573 A280 2s Apples .00 .20
C574 A280 5s Rose .45 .20

Lufthansa Jet — AP137

1976, June 25 Litho. *Perf. 12*

C575 AP137 10s bl & multi 1.50 .35

Lufthansa, 50th anniversary.

An imperf. 20s miniature sheet exists, similar to No. C575 enlarged, with overprinted black bar covering line below "Lufthansa." Size: 90x115mm.

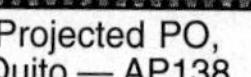
Projected PO, Quito — AP138

Fruit Peddler — AP139

1976, Aug. 10 Litho. *Perf. 12*

C576 AP138 5s blk & multi .30 .20

Design for new General Post Office, Quito.

1976, July 25

#C578, Longshoreman. #C579, Cerros del Carmen & Santa Ana, hills of Guayaquil, horiz. #C580, Sebastián de Belalcázar. #C581, Francisco de Orellana. #C582, Chief Guayas & his wife Quila.

C577 AP139 1.30s red & multi .20 .20
C578 AP139 1.30s red & multi .20 .20
C579 AP139 1.30s red & multi .20 .20
C580 AP139 2s red & multi .20 .20
C581 AP139 2s red & multi .20 .20
C582 AP139 2s red & multi .20 .20
Nos. C577-C582 (6) 1.20 1.20

Founding of Quayaquil, 441st anniversary.

Emblem and Laurel AP140

1976, Aug. 9

C583 AP140 1.30s yel & multi .25 .20

Bolivarian Soc. of Ecuador, 50th anniv.

Western Hemisphere and Equator Monument AP141

Congress Emblem AP142

1976, Sept. 6

C584 AP141 2s multi .25 .20

Souvenir Sheet
Imperf

C585 AP141 5s multi 2.75 2.75

3rd Conf. of Pan-American Transport Ministers, Quito, Sept. 6-11. No. C585 contains design similar to No. C584 with black denomination and red control number in margin.

1976, Sept. 27 Litho. *Perf. 11½*

C586 AP142 1.30s bl & multi .30 .20
C587 AP142 3s bl & multi .40 .30

Souvenir Sheet
Imperf

C588 AP142 10s bl & multi 1.50 1.00

10th Inter-American Congress of the Construction Industry, Quito, Sept. 27-30.

George Washington AP143

American Bicentennial: 5s, Naval battle, Sept. 23, 1779, in which the Bonhomme Richard, commanded by John Paul Jones, defeated and captured the Serapis, British man-of-war, off Yorkshire coast, horiz.

1976, Oct. 18 Litho. *Perf. 12*

C589 AP143 3s blk & multi .60 .30
C590 AP143 5s red brn & yel .90 .45

Dr. Hideyo Noguchi — AP144

Luis Cordero — AP145

1976 Litho. *Perf. 11½*

C591 AP144 3s yel & multi .35 .20

Dr. Hideyo Noguchi (1876-1928), bacteriologist (at Rockefeller Institute). A 10s imperf. miniature sheet in same design exists without "Aereo." Size: 95x114mm.

1976, Dec. Litho. *Perf. 11½*

C592 AP145 2s multi .25 .20

Luis Cordero (1833-1912), president of Ecuador.

Mariuxi Febres Cordero — AP146

1976, Dec. *Perf. 11½*

C593 AP146 3s multi .25 .20

Mariuxi Febres Cordero, South American swimming champion.

Flags and Monument AP147

1976, Nov. 9 *Perf. 12*

C594 AP147 3s multi .25 .20

Miniature Sheet
Imperf

C595 AP147 5s multi 1.60 .50

2nd Meeting of the Agriculture Ministers of the Andean Countries, Quito, Nov. 8-10.

Sister Catalina — AP148

Congress Hall, Quito — AP149

1977, June 17 Litho. *Perf. 12x11½*

C596 AP148 1.30s blk & pale salmon .30 .20

Sister Catalina de Jesus Herrera (1717-1795), writer.

1977, Aug. 15 Litho. *Perf. 12x11½*

C597 AP149 5s multi .45 .20
a. 10s souvenir sheet 1.50 1.50

11th General Assembly of Pan-American Institute of Geography and History, Quito, Aug. 15-30. No. C597a contains the designs of types A282 and AP149 without denominations and with simulated perforations.

Pres. Alfonso López Michelsen, Flag of Colombia — AP150

Designs: 5s, Pres. López M. of Colombia, Pres. Alfredo Povedo B. of Ecuador and aide. 7s, as 5s, vert. 9s, 10s, Presidents with aides.

1977 *Perf. 12*

C598 AP150 2.60s multi .45 .20
C599 AP150 5s multi .65 .25
C600 AP150 7s multi .70 .35
C601 AP150 9s multi 1.10 .55

Imperf

C602 AP150 10s multi .85 .70
Nos. C598-C602 (5) 3.75 2.05

Meeting of the Presidents of Ecuador and Colombia and Declaration of Putumayo, Feb. 25, 1977. Nos. C598-C602 are overprinted in multiple fluorescent, colorless rows: INSTITUTO GEOGRAFICO MILITAR GOBIERNO DEL ECUADOR.

Ceramic Figure, Tolita Culture AP151

9s, Divine Shepherdess, sculpture by Bernardo de Legarda. 11s, The Fruit Seller, sculpture by Legarda. 20s, Sun God, pre-Columbian gold mask.

1977, Aug. 24 *Perf. 12*

C603 AP151 7s gold & multi 1.00 .30
C604 AP151 9s gold & multi 1.25 .35
C605 AP151 11s gold & multi 1.60 .75
Nos. C603-C605 (3) 3.85 1.40

Souvenir Sheet
Gold Embossed
Imperf

C606 AP151 20s vio, bl, blk & gold 6.25 3.25

Central Bank of Ecuador, 50th anniversary. Nos. C603-C605 overprinted like Nos. C598-C602.

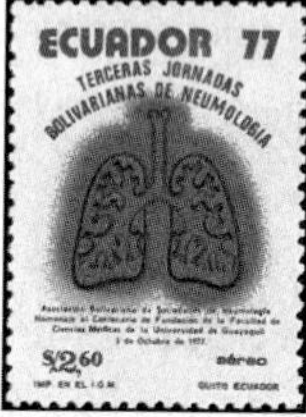
Lungs — AP152

Brother Miguel, St. Peter's, Rome — AP153

1977, Oct. 5 Litho. *Perf. 12x11½*

C607 AP152 2.60s multi .30 .25

3rd Cong. of the Bolivarian Pneumonic Soc. and cent. of the founding of the medical faculty of the University of Guayaquil.

1977

C608 AP153 2.60s multi .25 .20

Beatification of Brother Miguel.

Peralta Type

2.60s, Titles of works by Peralta & his bookmark.

1977 *Perf. 11½*

C609 A284 2.60s multi .35 .25

Broadcast Tower — AP154

Remigio Romero y Cordero — AP155

1977, Dec. 2 Litho. *Perf. 12x11½*

C610 AP154 5s multi .35 .35

9th World Telecommunications Day.

1978, Mar. 2 Litho. *Perf. 12½x11½*

C611 AP155 3s multi .30 .20
C612 AP155 10.60s multi .45 .25

Imperf

C612A AP155 10s multi 1.10 1.10
Nos. C611-C612A (3) 1.85 1.55

Remigio Romero y Cordero (1895-1967), poet.

No. C612A contains a vignette similar to Nos. C611-C612.

Dr. Vicente Corral Moscoso AP156

Faces AP157

5s, Hospital emblem with Caduceus.

1978, Apr. 12 Litho. *Imperf.*
C613 AP156 5s multi .55 .30

Perf. 12x11½
C614 AP156 7.60s multi .95 .50

Inauguration (in 1977) of Dr. Vicente Corral Moscoso Regional Hospital, Cuenca.

1978, Mar. 17

Designs: 9s, Emblems and flags of Ecuador. 10s, 11s, Hands reaching for light.

C615 AP157 7s multicolored .60 .20
C616 AP157 9s multicolored .85 .20
C617 AP157 11s multicolored 1.00 .20

Imperf
C618 AP157 10s multicolored 1.00 1.00
Nos. C615-C618 (4) 3.45 1.60

Ecuadorian Social Security Institute, 50th anniv.

Geographical Institute Type

7.60s, Plane over map of Ecuador with mountains.

1978, Apr. 12 Litho. *Perf. 11½*
C619 A287 7.60s multi .90 .50

Imperf
C620 A287 10s multi 1.40 1.40

No. C620 contains 2 vignettes with simulated perforations in designs of Nos. 967 and C619.

Lions Type

1978 *Perf. 11½*
C621 A288 5s multi .50 .20
C622 A288 6.20s multi .80 .30

Imperf
C623 A288 10s multi 1.10 1.10
Nos. C621-C623 (3) 2.40 1.60

No. C623 contains a vignette similar to Nos. C621-C622.

San Martin — AP158

1978, Apr. 13 Litho. *Perf. 12*
C624 AP158 10.60s multi 1.40 .50

Imperf
C625 AP158 10s multi 1.40 1.40

Gen. José de San Martin (1778-1850), soldier and statesman. No. C625 contains a vignette similar to No. C624.

Bank Type

Design: 5s, Bank emblem.

1978, Sept. Litho. *Perf. 11½*
C626 A289 5s gray & multi .30 .20

Soccer Type

Designs: 2.60s, "Gauchito" and Games' emblem. 5s, "Gauchito." 7s, Soccer ball. 9s, Games' emblem, vert. 10s, Games' emblem.

1978, Nov. 1 *Perf. 12*
C627 A290 2.60s multi .25 .20
C628 A290 7s multi .70 .35
C629 A290 9s multi .95 .55

Imperf
C630 A290 5s blk & bl 5.25 5.25
C631 A290 10s blk & bl 5.25 5.25
Nos. C627-C631 (5) 12.40 11.60

Bernardo O'Higgins AP159

Old Men of Vilcabamba AP160

1978, Nov. 11 Litho. *Perf. 12x11½*
C632 AP159 10.60s multi .70 .30

Imperf
C633 AP159 10s multi 1.25 .75

Gen. Bernardo O'Higgins (1778-1842), Chilean soldier and statesman. No. C633 contains a vignette similar to No. C632.

1978, Nov. 11 *Perf. 12x11½*
C634 AP160 5s multi .40 .25

Vilcabamba, valley of longevity.

Humphrey AP161

Virgin and Child AP162

1978, Nov. 27 Litho. *Perf. 12x11½*
C635 AP61 5s multi .40 .25

Hubert H. Humphrey (1911-1978), Vice President of the US.

1978

Children's Drawings: 4.60s, Holy Family. 6.20s, Candle and children.

C636 AP162 2.20s multi .20 .20
C637 AP162 4.60s multi .45 .25
C638 AP162 6.20s multi .75 .35
Nos. C636-C638 (3) 1.40 .80

Christmas 1978.

Village, by Anibal Villacis AP163

Ecuadorian Painters: No. C640, Mountain Village, by Gilberto Almeida. No. C641, Bay, by Roura Oxandaberro. No. C642, Abstract, by Luis Molinari. No. C643, Statue, by Oswaldo Viteri. No. C644, Tools, by Enrique Tabara.

1978, Dec. 9 *Perf. 12*
C639 AP163 5s multi .50 .25
C640 AP163 5s multi .50 .25
C641 AP163 5s multi .50 .25
C642 AP163 5s multi .50 .25
C643 AP163 5s multi .50 .25
C644 AP163 5s multi .50 .25
Nos. C639-C644 (6) 3.00 1.50

House and Monument AP164

Design: 3.40s, Monument, vert.

1979, Feb. 27 Litho. *Perf. 12*
C645 AP164 2.40s multi .30 .20
C646 AP164 3.40s multi .30 .20

Imperf
C647 AP164 10s multi 1.00 1.00
Nos. C645-C647 (3) 1.60 1.40

Sesquicentennial of Battle of Portete and Tarqui. #C647 contains vignettes similar to #C645-C646.

Fish and Ship — AP165

Flags of Ecuador and U.S. — AP166

7s, Map of Ecuador & Galapagos showing territorial waters. 9s, Map of South America with west-coast territorial waters.

Perf. 12x11½, 11½x12
1979, July 23 Litho. Wmk. 367
C648 AP165 5s multi .75 .25
C649 AP165 7s multi, horiz. 1.00 .35
C650 AP165 9s multi 1.40 .50
Nos. C648-C650 (3) 3.15 1.10

Declaration of 200-mile territorial limit, 25th anniversary.

1979, Aug. 3 *Perf. 12x11½*

Designs: 10.60s, Bells in Quito clock tower, horiz. 13.60s, Aerial view of Galapagos coast.

C651 A293 10.60s multi 1.00 .50
C652 A293 13.60s multi 1.10 .65

Size: 115x91mm

Imperf

Unwmk.
C653 A293 10s multi 2.00 .90
Nos. C651-C653 (3) 4.10 2.05

National heritage: Quito and Galapagos Islands. No. C653 contains vignettes similar to Nos. 977, C651-C652.

1979, Aug. Wmk. 367 *Perf. 11½x12*
C654 AP166 7.60s multi .40 .40
C655 AP166 10.60s multi .60 .60

Size: 115x91mm

Imperf

Unwmk.
C656 AP166 10s multi 1.00 .65
Nos. C654-C656 (3) 2.00 1.65

5th anniv. of Ecuador-US Chamber of Commerce. No. C656 contains vignettes similar to Nos. C654-C655.

Smiling Girl, IYC Emblem — AP167

Perf. 12x11½
1979, Sept. 7 Litho. Wmk. 367
C657 AP167 10s multi .70 .40

International Year of the Child.

Citizens and Flag of Ecuador AP168

Design: 10.60s, Pres. Jaime Roldas Aguilera, flag of Ecuador, vert.

Perf. 11½
1979, Sept. 27 Litho. Unwmk.
C658 AP168 7.60s multi .85 .35

Wmk. 367
C659 AP168 10.60s multi 1.00 .30

Restoration of democracy to Ecuador.

Ecuador Coat of Arms, Olympic Rings and Eagle — AP169

Perf. 12x11½
1979, Nov. 23 Unwmk.
C660 AP169 28s multi 1.60 1.00

5th National Games, Cuenca.

CIESPAL Building, Quito AP170

Perf. 11½x12½
1979, Dec. 26 Wmk. 367
C661 AP170 10.60s multi .70 .40

Opening of Ecuadorian Institute of Engineers building.

Olmedo Type

Perf. 12x11½
1980, Apr. 29 Litho. Unwmk.
C662 A294 10s multi .80 .50

Tribal Chief Type

Indo-American Tribal Chiefs: #C663, Cuauhtemoc, Mexico. #C664, Lempira, Honduras. #C665, Nicaragua. #C666, Lambaré, Paraguay. #C667, Urraca, Panama. #C668, Anacaona, Haiti. #C669, Caupolican, Chile. #C670, Tacun-Uman, Guatemala. #C671, Calarca, Colombia. #C672, Garabito, Costa Rica. #C673, Hatuey, Cuba. #C674, Cmarao, Brazil. #C675, Tehuelche, Argentina. #C676, Tupaj Katri, Bolivia. 17.80s, Sequoyah, US. 22.80s, Ruminahui, Ecuador.

Wmk. 367 (#C663, C667), Unwmkd.
1980, May 12
C663 A295 7.60s multi 1.25 .30
C664 A295 7.60s multi 1.25 .30
C665 A295 7.60s multi 1.25 .30
C666 A295 10s multi 1.60 .35
C667 A295 10s multi 1.60 .35
C668 A295 10.60s multi 1.60 .35
C669 A295 10.60s multi 1.60 .35
C670 A295 10.60s multi 1.60 .35
C671 A295 12.80s multi 2.10 .45
C672 A295 12.80s multi 2.10 .45
C673 A295 12.80s multi 2.10 .45
C674 A295 13.60s multi 2.10 .45
C675 A295 13.60s multi 2.10 .45
C676 A295 13.60s multi 2.10 .45
C677 A295 17.80s multi 2.50 .55
C678 A295 22.80s multi 2.90 1.10
Nos. C663-C678 (16) 29.75 7.00

Royal Visit Type

Perf. 11½x12
1980, May 18 Unwmk.
C679 A296 10.60s multi .65 .40

Pichincha Provincial Development Council Building — AP171

1980, June 1 *Perf. 12x11½*
C680 AP171 10.60s multi 1.10 .50

Progress in Pichincha Province.

Indian Type

1980, June 10 Litho. *Perf. 12x11½*

C681 A297 7.60s Salasaca boy, Tungurahua .85 .65
C682 A297 10s Amula woman, Chimborazo 1.00 .75
C683 A297 10.60s Canar woman, Canar 1.25 .85
C684 A297 13.60s Colorado Indian, Pichincha 1.40 1.10
Nos. C681-C684 (4) 4.50 3.35

Virgin of Mercy Type

1980, July 7 Litho. *Perf. 11½*

C685 A298 7.60s Cupola, cloisters .75 .50
C686 A298 7.60s Gold screen .75 .50
C687 A298 7.60s Quito from basilica tower .75 .50
C688 A298 10.60s Retable 1.00 .50
C689 A298 10.60s Pulpit 1.00 .50
C690 A298 13.60s Cupola 1.40 .75
C691 A298 13.60s Statue of Virgin 1.40 .75
Nos. C685-C691 (7) 7.05 4.00

UPU Monument AP172

Marshal Sucre, by Marco Sales AP173

Design: 17.80s, Mail box, 1880.

1980, July 7 *Perf. 12*

C692 AP172 10.60s multi 1.00 .50
C693 AP172 17.80s multi 1.75 .75

Souvenir Sheet

C694 AP172 25s multi 3.00 2.50

UPU membership cent. No. C694 contains designs of C692 and C693, horiz., perf. 11½.

Olympic Type.

Design: 10.60s, 13.60s, Moscow '80 emblem, Olympic rings.

Perf. 12x11½

1980, July 19 **Wmk. 395**

C695 A299 10.60s multi .70 .50
C696 A299 13.60s multi 1.00 .70

Souvenir Sheet

C697 A299 30s multi 5.00 5.00

No. C697 contains vignettes in designs of Nos. 991 and C695.

1980

C698 AP173 10.60s multi .70 .50

Marshal Antonio Jose de Sucre, death sesquicentennial.

Rotary International, 75th Anniversary AP174

1980, Aug. 4 *Perf. 11½*

C699 AP174 10s multi 1.10 .50

Riobamba Type

Design: 7.60s, 10.60s, Monstrance, Riobamba Cathedral, vert.

1980, Sept. 20 Litho. *Perf. 11½*

C700 A301 7.60s multi .55 .30
C701 A301 10.60s multi .75 .35

Souvenir Sheet

Imperf

C702 A301 30s multi 1.90 1.90

No. C702 contains vignettes in designs of Nos. 996-997.

Democracy Type

7.60s, 10.60s, Pres. Aguilera and voter.

Perf. 12x11½

1980, Oct. 9 Litho. Wmk. 395

C703 A302 7.60s multi .75 .45
C704 A302 10.60s multi 1.00 .50

Souvenir Sheet

Imperf

C705 A302 15s multi 1.10 1.10

No. C705 contains vignettes in designs of Nos. 999 and C703.

OPEC Type

20th Anniversary of OPEC: 7.60s, Men holding OPEC emblem, vert.

1980, Nov. 8 *Perf. 11½x12*

C706 A303 7.60s multi .55 .45

Carchi Province Type

10.60s, Governor's Palace, vert. 17.80s, Victory Museum, Central Square, vert.

1980, Nov. 21 *Perf. 13*

C707 A304 10.60c multi 1.00 .50
C708 A304 17.80s multi 1.50 .75

Orchid Type

Perf. 12x11½, 11½x12

1980, Nov. 22

C709 A305 7.60s *Anguloa uniflora* 2.25 .55
C710 A305 10.60s *Scuticaria salesiana* 2.75 .35
C711 A305 50s *Helcia sanguinolenta*, vert. 4.50 1.10
C712 A305 100s *Anguloa virginalis* 6.00 2.25
Nos. C709-C712 (4) 15.50 4.25

Souvenir Sheets

Imperf

C713 A305 20s multi 4.50 3.25
C714 A305 20s multi 4.50 3.25

Nos. C713-C714 contain vignettes in designs of Nos. C709, C711 and C710, C712 respectively.

Christmas Type

7.60s, Pope blessing crowd. 10.60s, Portrait.

1980, Dec. 27 *Perf. 12*

C715 A306 7.60s multi, vert. .75 .45
C716 A306 10.60s multi, vert. 1.00 .55

Isidro Cueva — AP175

Simon Bolivar, by Marco Salas — AP176

1980, Nov. 20 *Perf. 13*

C717 AP175 18.20s multi 1.90 .95

Dr. Isidro Ayora Cueva, former president, birth centenary.

1980, Dec. 17 *Perf. 11½*

C718 AP176 13.60s multi 1.40 .70

Simon Bolivar death sesquicentennial.

Turtle, Galapagos Islands AP177

100s, Oldest Ecuadorian mail box, 1793.

1981, Feb. 12 Litho. *Perf. 13*

C719 AP177 50s multi 5.00 3.25
C720 AP177 100s multi, vert. 6.25 4.25

HCJB Type

1981 Litho. *Perf. 13*

C721 A311 7.60s Emblem, horiz. .80 .45
C722 A311 10.60s Emblem, diff 1.10 .55

Soccer Players — AP178

1981, July 8

C723 AP178 7.60s Emblem .80 .45
C724 AP178 10.60s shown 1.00 .45
C725 AP178 13.60s World Cup 1.25 .70
Nos. C723-C725 (3) 3.05 1.60

Souvenir Sheets

C726 AP178 20s multi 3.25 3.25
C727 AP178 20s multi 3.25 3.25

1982 World Cup Soccer Championship. Nos. C726-C727 contain vignettes in designs of Nos. C723 and C724 respectively.

Picasso Type

1981, Oct. 26 Litho. *Perf. 13*

C728 A313a 7.60s Still-life .70 .35
C729 A313a 10.60s First Communion, vert. .85 .45
C730 A313a 13.60s Las Meninas, vert. .95 .65

Size: 110x90mm

Imperf

C731 A313a 20s multi 2.10 2.10
Nos. C728-C731 (4) 4.60 3.55

No. C731 contains designs of Nos. C730, C729.

World Food Day Type

1981, Dec. 31 Litho. *Perf. 13x13½*

C732 A314 10.60s Farming, vert. 1.00 .50

IYD Type

1982, Feb. 25 Litho. *Perf. 13*

C733 A316 7.60s Emblem .55 .30
C734 A316 10.60s Man with crutch .70 .35

Montalvo Type

1982 Litho. *Perf. 13*

C735 A318 5s Home, horiz. .80 .45

Swimming Type

1982, July 30

C736 A320 10.20s Emblem, vert. .70 .35
C737 A320 14.20s Diving, vert. .95 .45

Pres. Jaime Roldos, (1940-81), Mrs. Martha Roldos, Independence Monument, Quito — AP179

1983, May 25 Litho. *Perf. 12*

C738 AP179 13.60s multi .55 .40

Souvenir Sheet

Imperf

C739 AP179 20s multi .85 .85

AIR POST SEMI-POSTAL STAMPS

Nos. C119-C123 Surcharged in Blue or Rod:

1944, May 9 Unwmk. *Perf. 12*

CB1 AP26 50c + 50c 3.25 3.25
CB2 AP26 70c + 30c 3.25 3.25
CB3 AP26 3s + 50c (R) 3.25 3.25
CB4 AP26 5s + 1s (R) 3.25 3.25
CB5 AP26 10s + 2s 3.25 3.25
Nos. CB1-CB5 (5) 16.25 16.25

The surtax aided Mendez Hospital.

AIR POST REGISTRATION STAMPS

Issued by Sociedad Colombo-Alemana de Transportes Aereos (SCADTA)

Nos. C3 and C3a Overprinted "R" in Carmine

1928-29 Wmk. 116 *Perf. 14x14½*

CF1 AP6 1s on 20c (#C3) 140.00 110.00
a. 1s on 20c (#C3a) ('29) 175.00 140.00

No. C18 Overprinted "R" in Black

1929, Apr. 1 Wmk. 127 *Perf. 14*

CF2 AP2 1s rose 75.00 60.00

AIR POST OFFICIAL STAMPS

Nos. C8-C15 Overprinted in Red or Black

1929, May Unwmk. *Perf. 12*

CO1 AP1 2c black (R) .50 .50
CO2 AP1 5c carmine rose .50 .50
CO3 AP1 10c deep brown .50 .50
CO4 AP1 20c dark violet .50 .50
CO5 AP1 50c deep green 1.60 1.60
CO6 AP1 1s dark blue 1.60 1.60
a. Inverted overprint 240.00
CO7 AP1 5s orange yellow 7.00 6.00
CO8 AP1 10s orange red 85.00 60.00
Nos. CO1-CO8 (8) 97.20 71.20

Establishment of commercial air service in Ecuador.

Counterfeits of No. CO8 exist.

See Nos. CO9-CO12. For overprints and surcharges see Nos. C35-C38.

1930, Jan. 9

CO9 AP1 50c olive brown 1.40 1.40
CO10 AP1 1s carmine lake 1.75 1.75
CO11 AP1 5s olive green 4.25 4.25
CO12 AP1 10s black 8.50 8.50
Nos. CO9-CO12 (4) 15.90 15.90

For surcharges & overprint see #C36-C38.

Air Post Stamps of 1937 Overprinted in Black

1937, Aug. 19

CO13 AP7 10c chestnut .25 .20
CO14 AP7 20c olive black .25 .20
CO15 AP7 70c black brown .30 .25
CO16 AP7 1s gray black .35 .25
CO17 AP7 2s dark violet .35 .35
Nos. CO13-CO17 (5) 1.50 1.25

For overprints see Nos. 463-464.

No. C79 Overprinted in Black

1940, Aug. 1 *Perf. 12½x13*
CO18 AP15 5s emerald .85 .65

Catalogue values for unused stamps in this section, from this point to the end of the section, are for Never Hinged items.

Nos. C352-C354 Overprinted: "1961 oficial"

1964 *Perf. 13½*
CO19 AP86 50c multi .85 .85
CO20 AP86 80c multi .85 .85
CO21 AP86 1.30s multi .85 .85
Nos. CO19-CO21 (3) 2.55 2.55

SPECIAL DELIVERY STAMPS

SD1

1928 **Unwmk.** *Perf. 12*
E1 SD1 2c on 2c blue 4.00 *4.50*
E2 SD1 5c on 2c blue 3.50 *4.50*
E3 SD1 10c on 2c blue 3.50 *3.00*
a. "10 CTVOS" inverted 10.50 *13.00*
E4 SD1 20c on 2c blue 5.00 *4.50*
E5 SD1 50c on 2c blue 6.00 *4.50*
Nos. E1-E5 (5) 22.00 *21.00*

No. RA49A Surcharged in Red

1945
E6 PT18 20c on 5c green .30 .20

LATE FEE STAMP

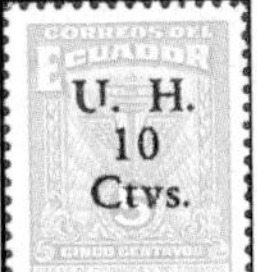

No. RA49A Surcharged in Black

1945 **Unwmk.** *Perf. 12*
I1 PT18 10c on 5c green .20 .20

POSTAGE DUE STAMPS

Numeral — D1

Coat of Arms — D2

1896 **Engr.** **Wmk. 117** *Perf. 12*
J1 D1 1c blue green 2.90 *3.25*
J2 D1 2c blue green 2.90 *3.25*
J3 D1 5c blue green 2.90 *3.25*
J4 D1 10c blue green 2.90 *3.25*
J5 D1 20c blue green 2.90 *4.25*
J6 D1 50c blue green 2.90 *6.50*
J7 D1 100c blue green 2.90 *8.50*
Nos. J1-J7 (7) 20.30 *32.25*

Reprints are on very thick paper with distinct watermark and vertical paper-weave direction. Value 20c each.

Unwmk.
J8 D1 1c blue green *2.50 3.00*
J9 D1 2c blue green *2.50 3.00*
J10 D1 5c blue green *2.50 3.00*
J11 D1 10c blue green *2.50 3.00*
J12 D1 20c blue green *2.50 3.75*
J13 D1 50c blue green *2.50 5.25*
J14 D1 100c blue green *2.50 7.50*
Nos. J8-J14 (7) 17.50 *28.50*

1929
J15 D2 5c deep blue .20 .20
J16 D2 10c orange yellow .20 .20
J17 D2 20c red .30 .30
Nos. J15-J17 (3) .70 .70

Numeral — D3

Perf. 13½
1958, Nov. **Unwmk.** **Litho.**
J18 D3 10c bright lilac .25 .20
J19 D3 50c emerald .25 .20
J20 D3 1s maroon .30 .20
J21 D3 2s red .35 .20
Nos. J18-J21 (4) 1.15 .80

OFFICIAL STAMPS

Regular Issues of 1881 and 1887 Handstamped in Black

1886 **Unwmk.** *Perf. 12*
O1 A5 1c yellow brown .85 .85
O2 A6 2c lake 1.00 1.00
O3 A7 5c blue 2.25 *2.90*
O4 A8 10c orange 1.75 1.10
O5 A9 20c gray violet 1.75 1.75
O6 A10 50c blue green 5.00 3.75
Nos. O1-O6 (6) 12.60 11.35

1887
O7 A12 1c green 1.10 .85
O8 A13 2c vermilion 1.10 1.10
O9 A14 5c blue 1.75 .85
O10 A15 80c olive green 5.75 3.25
Nos. O7-O10 (4) 9.70 6.05

Nos. O1-O10 are known with red handstamp but these are believed to be speculative.
The overprint on the 1886-87 issues is handstamped and is found in various positions.

Flores — O1

Arms — O1a

1892
Carmine Overprint
O11 O1 1c ultramarine .20 .20
O12 O1 2c ultramarine .20 .20
O13 O1 5c ultramarine .20 .20
O14 O1 10c ultramarine .20 *.30*
O15 O1 20c ultramarine .20 *.30*
O16 O1 50c ultramarine .20 *.45*
O17 O1 1s ultramarine .35 *.50*
Nos. O11-O17 (7) 1.55 2.15

1894
O18 O1a 1c slate green (R) 8.50
O19 O1a 2c lake (Bk) 8.50

Nos. O18 and O19 were not placed in use.

Rocafuerte — O2

Dated 1894

1894
Carmine Overprint
O20 O2 1c gray black .20 *.35*
O21 O2 2c gray black .20 .20
O22 O2 5c gray black .20 .20
O23 O2 10c gray black .25 *.35*
O24 O2 20c gray black .35 .35
O25 O2 50c gray black 1.25 1.25
O26 O2 1s gray black 2.00 1.90
Nos. O20-O26 (7) 4.45 4.60

Dated 1895

1895
Carmine Overprint
O27 O2 1c gray black 1.75 1.75
O28 O2 2c gray black 2.50 2.50
O29 O2 5c gray black .50 .50
O30 O2 10c gray black 2.50 2.50
O31 O2 20c gray black 3.75 3.50
O32 O2 50c gray black *25.00 25.00*
O33 O2 1s gray black 1.25 1.25
Nos. O27-O33 (7) *37.25 37.00*

Reprints of 1894-95 issues are on very thick paper with paper weave found both horizontal and vertical for all denominations. Values: Nos. O20-O26, 35c each; O27-O33, 20c each. Generally they are blacker than originals.
For overprints see Nos. O50-O91.

Types of 1896 Overprinted in Carmine

1896 **Wmk. 117**
O34 A21 1c olive bister .35 .35
O35 A22 2c olive bister .35 .35
O36 A23 5c olive bister .35 .35
O37 A24 10c olive bister .35 .35
O38 A25 20c olive bister .35 .35
O39 A26 50c olive bister .35 .35
O40 A27 1s olive bister 1.00 1.00
O41 A28 5s olive bister 2.00 2.00
Nos. O34-O41 (8) 5.10 5.10

Reprints of Nos. O34-O41 are on thick paper with vertical paper weave direction. Value 20 cents each.

Unwmk.
O42 A21 1c olive bister 1.00 1.00
O43 A22 2c olive bister 1.00 1.00
O44 A23 5c olive bister 1.00 1.00
O45 A24 10c olive bister 1.00 1.00
O46 A25 20c olive bister 1.00 1.00
O47 A26 50c olive bister 1.00 1.00
O48 A27 1s olive bister 2.50 *2.50*
O49 A28 5s olive bister 3.50 3.50
Nos. O42-O49 (8) 12.00 12.00

Reprints of Nos. O42-O49 all have overprint in black. Value 20 cents each.

#O20-O26 Overprinted

1897-98
O50 O2 1c gray black *4.00 4.00*
O51 O2 2c gray black *5.00 5.00*
O52 O2 5c gray black *45.00 45.00*
O53 O2 10c gray black *4.25 4.25*
O54 O2 20c gray black *2.00 1.25*
O55 O2 50c gray black *10.00 10.00*
O56 O2 1s gray black *16.00 16.00*
Nos. O50-O56 (7) *86.25 85.50*

#O20-O26 Overprinted

O57 O2 1c gray black *1.25 1.25*
O58 O2 2c gray black *3.00 1.00*
O59 O2 5c gray black *35.00 35.00*
O60 O2 10c gray black *45.00 45.00*
O61 O2 20c gray black *1.25 1.25*
O62 O2 50c gray black *4.75 3.75*
O63 O2 1s gray black *60.00 60.00*
Nos. O57-O63 (7) *150.25 147.25*

#O20-O26 Overprinted **1897 y 1898**

O64 O2 1c gray black *8.50 8.50*
O65 O2 2c gray black *8.50 8.50*
O66 O2 5c gray black *8.50 8.50*
O67 O2 10c gray black *8.50 8.50*
O68 O2 20c gray black *8.50 8.50*
O69 O2 50c gray black *8.50 8.50*
O70 O2 1s gray black *8.50 8.50*
Nos. O64-O70 (7) *59.50 59.50*

#O27-O33 Overprinted in Black like Nos. O50-O56
O71 O2 1c gray black *2.00 2.00*
O72 O2 2c gray black *1.50 1.50*
O73 O2 5c gray black *2.00 2.00*
O74 O2 10c gray black *2.00 2.00*
O75 O2 20c gray black *4.00 4.00*
O76 O2 50c gray black *140.00* 140.00
O77 O2 1s gray black *40.00 40.00*
Nos. O71-O77 (7) 191.50 191.50

#O27-O33 Overprinted like #O57-O63
O78 O2 1c gray black *.90 .90*
O79 O2 2c gray black *.70 .70*
O80 O2 5c gray black *1.75 1.75*
O81 O2 10c gray black *.70 .70*
O82 O2 20c gray black *.70 .45*
O83 O2 50c gray black *1.40 .55*
O84 O2 1s gray black *6.00 6.00*

#O27-O33 Overprinted like #O64-O70
O85 O2 1c gray black *40.00 40.00*
O86 O2 2c gray black *1.10 1.10*
O87 O2 5c gray black *.70 .70*
O88 O2 10c gray black *35.00 35.00*
O89 O2 20c gray black *60.00 60.00*
O90 O2 50c gray black *13.00 13.00*
O91 O2 1s gray black *80.00 80.00*
Nos. O85-O91 (7) *229.80 229.80*

Many forged overprints of Nos. O50-O91 exist, made on the original stamps and reprints.

O3

Black Surcharge

1898-99 *Perf. 15, 16*
O92 O3 5c on 50c lilac .25 .25
a. Inverted surcharge 2.00 2.00
O93 O3 10c on 20s org .50 .50
a. Double surcharge 2.75 1.50
O94 O3 10c on 50c lilac *70.00 70.00*
O95 O3 20c on 50c lilac 1.90 1.90
O96 O3 20c on 50s green 1.90 1.90
Nos. O92-O96 (5) *74.55 74.55*

Green Surcharge
O97 O3 5c on 50c lilac 1.00 1.00
a. Double surcharge 2.50
b. Double surcharge, blk and grn 6.00
c. As "b," blk surch. invtd. 2.50

Red Surcharge

1899
O98 O3 5c on 50c lilac 1.10 1.10
a. Double surcharge 2.50
b. Dbl. surch., blk and red 3.00
O99 O3 20c on 50s green 1.90 1.90
a. Inverted surcharge 5.00
b. Dbl. surch., red and blk 8.00

Similar Surcharge in Black Value in Words in Two Lines
O100 O3 1c on 5c blue *325.00*

Red Surcharge
O101 O3 2c on 5c blue *575.00*
O102 O3 4c on 20c blue *400.00*

Types of Regular Issue of 1899 Overprinted in Black

1899 *Perf. 14, 15*
O103 A37 2c orange & blk .35 *.80*
O104 A39 10c orange & blk .35 *.80*
O105 A40 20c orange & blk .25 *1.25*
O106 A41 50c orange & blk .25 *1.60*
Nos. O103-O106 (4) 1.20 *4.45*

For overprint see No. O167.

The above overprint was applied to remainders of the postage stamps of 1904 with the idea of increasing their salability. They were never regularly in use as official stamps.

Regular Issue of 1911-13 Overprinted in Black

1913 *Perf. 12*

O107 A71 1c scarlet & blk 1.75 1.75
O108 A72 2c blue & blk 1.75 1.75
O109 A73 3c orange & blk 1.10 1.10
O110 A74 5c scarlet & blk 2.25 2.25
O111 A75 10c blue & blk 2.25 2.25
Nos. O107-O111 (5) 9.10 9.10

Regular Issue of 1911-13 Overprinted

Overprint 22x3½mm

1916-17

O112 A72 2c blue & blk 12.50 9.00
O113 A74 5c scarlet & blk 12.50 9.00
O114 A75 10c blue & blk 7.50 6.00
Nos. O112-O114 (3) 32.50 24.00

Overprint 25x4mm

O115 A71 1c scarlet & blk .55 .55
O116 A72 2c blue & blk .80 .80
a. Inverted overprint 2.50 2.50
O117 A73 3c orange & blk .50 .50
O118 A74 5c scarlet & blk .80 .80
O119 A75 10c blue & blk .80 .80
Nos. O115-O119 (5) 3.45 3.45

Same Overprint On Regular Issue of 1915-17

O120 A71 1c orange .70 .70
O121 A72 2c green .70 .70
O122 A73 3c black 1.10 1.10
O123 A78 4c red & blk 1.10 1.10
a. Inverted overprint 7.50
O124 A74 5c violet .70 .70
O125 A75 10c blue 1.40 1.40
O126 A79 20c green & blk 7.50 7.50
Nos. O120-O126 (7) 13.20 13.20

Regular Issues of 1911-17 Overprinted in Black or Red

O127 A71 1c orange .45 .45
O128 A72 2c green .35 .35
O129 A73 3c black (Bk) .45 .45
O130 A73 3c black (R) .45 .35
a. Inverted overprint
O131 A78 4c red & blk .45 .45
O132 A74 5c violet .85 .35
O133 A75 10c blue & blk 2.25 .85
O134 A75 10c blue .45 .45
O135 A79 20c green & blk 2.25 .85
Nos. O127-O135 (9) 7.95 4.55

Regular Issue of 1920 Overprinted

1920

O136 A86 1c green .55 .55
a. Inverted overprint 8.50 —
O137 A86 2c carmine .45 .45
O138 A86 3c yellow brn .55 .55
O139 A86 4c dark green .85 .85
a. Inverted overprint 8.50 —
O140 A86 5c blue .85 .85
O141 A86 6c orange .55 .55
O142 A86 7c brown .85 .85
O143 A86 8c yellow green 1.10 1.10
O144 A86 9c red 1.40 1.40
O145 A95 10c blue .85 .85
O146 A86 15c gray 4.50 4.50
O147 A86 20c deep violet 6.00 6.00
O148 A86 30c violet 7.00 7.00
O149 A86 40c dark brown 8.50 8.50
O150 A86 50c dark green 6.00 6.00
O151 A86 60c dark blue 7.00 7.00
O152 A86 70c gray 7.00 7.00
O153 A86 80c yellow 8.50 8.50
O154 A104 90c green 8.50 8.50
O155 A86 1s blue 18.00 18.00
Nos. O136-O155 (20) 89.00 89.00

Cent. of the independence of Guayaquil.

Stamps of 1911 Overprinted

1922

O156 A71 1c scarlet & blk 3.50 3.50
O157 A72 2c blue & blk 1.90 1.90

Revenue Stamps of 1919-1920 Overprinted like Nos. O156 and O157

1924

O158 PT3 1c dark blue .85 .85
O159 PT3 2c green 5.00 5.00

Regular Issues of 1911-17 Overprinted

OFICIAL

1924

O160 A71 1c orange 2.90 2.90
a. Inverted overprint 7.50

Overprinted in Black or Red

O161 A72 2c green .25 .25
O162 A73 3c black (R) .35 .35
O163 A78 4c red & blk .55 .55
O164 A74 5c violet .55 .55
O165 A75 10c deep blue .55 .55
O166 A76 1s green & blk 2.90 2.90
Nos. O160-O166 (7) 8.05 8.05

No. O106 with Additional Overprint

1924 *Perf. 14, 15*

O167 A41 50c orange & blk 1.10 1.10

#O160-O167 exist with inverted overprint.

No. 199 Overprinted

1924 *Perf. 12*

O168 A71 1c orange 2.25 2.25

Regular Issues of 1911-25 Overprinted

1925

O169 A71 1c scarlet & blk 4.50 1.75
a. Inverted overprint 7.50
O170 A71 1c orange .25 .25
a. Inverted overprint 2.00
O171 A72 2c green .25 .25
a. Inverted overprint 2.00
O172 A73 3c black (Bk) .25 .25
O173 A73 3c black (R) .45 .45
O174 A78 4c red & blk .25 .25
O175 A74 5c violet .35 .35
O176 A74 5c rose .35 .35
O177 A75 10c deep blue .25 .25
Nos. O169-O177 (9) 6.90 4.15

Regular Issues of 1916-25 Overprinted Vertically Up or Down

1927, Oct.

O178 A71 1c orange .85 .85
O179 A86 2c carmine .85 .85
O180 A86 3c yellow brown .85 .85
O181 A86 4c myrtle green .85 .85
O182 A86 5c pale blue .85 .85
O183 A75 10c yellow green .85 .85
Nos. O178-O183 (6) 5.10 5.10

Regular Issues of 1920-27 Overprinted

1928

O184 A71 1c lt blue .45 .45
O185 A86 2c carmine .45 .45
O186 A86 3c yellow brown .45 .45
a. Inverted overprint 2.50
O187 A86 4c myrtle green .45 .45
O188 A86 5c lt blue .45 .45
O189 A75 10c yellow green .45 .45
O190 A109 20c violet 4.50 1.10
a. Overprint reading up 1.75 1.10
Nos. O184-O190 (7) 7.20 3.80

The overprint is placed vertically reading down on No. O190.

Regular Issue of 1936 Overprinted in Black

1936 *Perf. 14*

O191 A131 5c olive green .25 .25
O192 A132 10c brown .25 .25
O193 A133 20c dark violet .35 .35
O194 A134 1s dark carmine .55 .55
O195 A135 2s dark blue .85 .85
Nos. O191-O195 (5) 2.25 2.25

Regular Postage Stamps of 1937 Overprinted in Black

1937 *Perf. 11½*

O196 A139 2c green .20 .20
O197 A140 5c deep rose .20 .20
O198 A141 10c blue .20 .20
O199 A142 20c deep rose .20 .20
O200 A143 1s olive green .20 .20
Nos. O196-O200 (5) 1.00 1.00

Catalogue values for unused stamps in this section, from this point to the end of the section, are for Never Hinged items.

Tobacco Stamp, Overprinted in Black

CORRESPONDENCIA OFICIAL

1946 **Unwmk.** ***Rouletted***

O201 PT7 1c rose red .85 .85

Communications Building, Quito — O4

1947 **Unwmk.** **Litho.** ***Perf. 11***

O202 O4 30c brown .30 .20
O203 O4 30c greenish blue .30 .20
a. Imperf., pair
O204 O4 30c purple .30 .20
Nos. O202-O204 (3) .90 .60

Nos. O202 to O204 overprinted "Primero la Patria!" and plane in dark blue are said to be essays.

No. 719 with Additional Diagonal Overprint

Illustration reduced.

1964 ***Perf. 14x13***

O205 A231 80c block of 4 2.90 2.90

The "OEA" overprint covers four stamps, the "oficial" overprint is applied to every stamp.

A set of 20 imperforate items in the above Roosevelt design, some overprinted with the initials of various government ministries, was released in 1949. Later that year a set of 8 miniature sheets, bearing the same design plus a marginal inscription, "Presidencia (or Vicepresidencia) de la Republica," and a frame-line were released. In the editors' opinion, information justifying the listing of these issues has not been received.

POSTAL TAX STAMPS

Roca — PT1

1920 Unwmk. ***Perf. 12***

RA1 PT1 1c orange .30 .30

PT2 PT3

RA2 PT2 1c red & blue .55 .20
- *a.* "de" inverted 5.25 5.25
- *b.* Double overprint 5.00 .60
- *c.* Inverted overprint 5.00 .60

RA3 PT3 1c deep blue .65 .20
- *a.* Inverted overprint 3.00 1.00
- *b.* Double overprint 3.00 1.00

For overprints see Nos. O158-O159.

PT4 PT5

Red or Black Surcharge or Overprint

Stamp Dated 1911-1912

RA4 PT4 20c deep blue 27.50 15.00

Stamp Dated 1913-1914

RA5 PT4 20c deep blue (R) 1.10 .35

Stamp Dated 1917-1918

RA6 PT4 20c olive green (R) 3.25 .55
- *a.* Dated 1919-20 *12.50*

RA7 PT5 1c on 2c green .45 .20

Stamp Dated 1911-1912

RA8 PT5 1c on 5c green .45 .20
- *a.* Double surcharge

Stamp Dated 1913-1914

RA9 PT5 1c on 5c green 4.00 .55
- *a.* Double surcharge 6.00 4.00

On Nos. RA7, RA8 and RA9 the surcharge is found reading upward or downward.

For surcharges see Nos. RA15-RA16.

Post Office — PT6

1920-24 Engr.

RA10 PT6 1c olive green .20 .20
RA11 PT6 2c deep green .20 .20
RA12 PT6 20c bister brn ('24) .70 .20
RA13 PT6 2s violet 4.50 3.25
RA14 PT6 5s blue 7.75 5.75
Nos. RA10-RA14 (5) 13.35 9.60

For overprints and surcharge see Nos. 259, 266-268, 273, 302, RA17.

Revenue Stamps of 1917-18 Surcharged Vertically in Red reading up or down

1921-22

RA15 PT5 20c on 1c dk blue 27.50 3.25
RA16 PT5 20c on 2c green 27.50 3.25

No. RA12 Surcharged in Green

1924

RA17 PT6 2c on 20c bis brn .30 .20
- *a.* Inverted surcharge 6.00 5.00
- *b.* Double surcharge 2.00 2.00

PT7

1924 ***Rouletted 7***

RA18 PT7 1c rose red .45 .20
- *a.* Inverted overprint 1.75

Similar Design, Eagle at left

Perf. 12

RA19 PT7 2c blue .45 .20
- *a.* Inverted overprint 1.75 1.75

For overprints & surcharges see #346, O201, RA32, RA34, RA37, RA44-RA45, RA47.

PT8

Inscribed "Timbre Fiscal"

1924

RA20 PT8 1c yellow 2.25 .85
RA21 PT8 2c dark blue .70 .35

Inscribed "Region Oriental"

RA22 PT8 1c yellow .35 .30
RA23 PT8 2c dark blue .70 .35
Nos. RA20-RA23 (4) 4.00 1.85

Overprint on No. RA22 reads down or up.

Revenue Stamp Overprinted in Blue

1934

RA24 2c green .20 .20
- *a.* Blue overprint inverted 1.75 1.75
- *b.* Blue ovpt. dbl., one invtd. 2.00 1.25

No. 310 Overprinted in Red

Perf. 12½

RA25 A119 20c ultra & yel .25 .20

Telegraph Stamp Overprinted in Red, like No. RA24, and Surcharged diagonally in Black

1934 ***Perf. 14***

RA26 2c on 10c olive brn .35 .20
- *a.* Double surcharge 2.75

Overprint Blue, Surcharge Red

RA27 2c on 10c olive brn .35 .20

PT9 PT10

Symbols of Post and Telegraph Service PT11

1934-36 ***Perf. 12***

RA28 PT9 2c green .30 .20
- *a.* Both overprints in red ('36) .30 .20

Postal Tax stamp of 1920-24, overprinted in red "POSTAL" has been again overprinted "CASA de Correos y Teleg. de Guayaquil" in black.

Perf. 14½x14

1934 Photo. Wmk. 233

RA29 PT10 2c yellow green .20 .20

For the rebuilding of the GPO at Guayaquil.

For surcharge see No. RA31.

1935

RA30 PT11 20c claret .25 .20

For the rebuilding of the GPO at Guayaquil.

No. RA29 Surcharged in Red and Overprinted in Black

1935

RA31 PT10 3c on 2c yel grn .20 .20
- *a.* Double surcharge

Social and Rural Workers' Insurance Fund.

Tobacco Stamp Surcharged in Black

1936 Unwmk. ***Rouletted 7***

RA32 PT7 3c on 1c rose red .30 .20
- *a.* Lines of words reversed 1.00 .20
- *b.* Horiz. pair, imperf. vert.

Issued for the Social and Rural Workers' Insurance Fund.

No. 310 Overprinted in Black

1936 ***Perf. 12½***

RA33 A119 20c ultra & yel .30 .20
- *a.* Double overprint

Tobacco Stamp Surcharged in Black

1936 ***Rouletted 7***

RA34 PT7 3c on 1c rose red .30 .20

Social and Rural Workers' Insurance Fund.

Worker — PT12

1936 Engr. ***Perf. 13½***

RA35 PT12 3c ultra .20 .20

Social and Rural Workers' Insurance Fund.

For surcharges see Nos. C64, RA36, RA53-RA54.

Surcharged in Black

1936

RA36 PT13 5c on 3c ultra .30 .20

This combines the 2c for the rebuilding of the post office with the 3c for the Social and Rural Workers' Insurance Fund.

National Defense Issue

Tobacco Stamp, Surcharged in Black

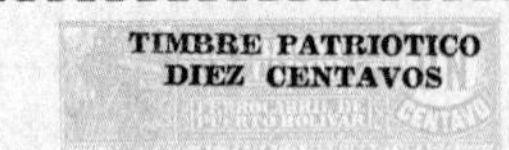

1936 ***Rouletted 7***

RA37 PT7 10c on 1c rose .45 .20
- *a.* Double surcharge

Symbolical of Defense — PT14

1937-42 ***Perf. 12½***

RA38 PT14 10c deep blue .45 .20

A 1s violet and 2s green exist in type PT14.

For surcharge see No. RA40.

PT15

Overprinted or Surcharged in Black

Perf. 13½, 11½

1937 Engr. & Typo.

RA39 PT15 5c lt brn & red 1.00 .25
- *d.* Inverted overprint 10.00

1942 ***Perf. 12, 11½***

RA39A PT15 20c on 5c rose pink & red 32.50 7.00
RA39B PT15 20c on 1s yel brn & red 32.50 7.00
RA39C PT15 20c on 2s grn & red 32.50 7.00
Nos. RA39A-RA39C (3) 97.50 21.00

A 50c dark blue and red exists.

No. RA38 Surcharged in Red

1937 **Engr.** ***Perf. 12½***
RA40 PT14 5c on 10c dp blue .55 .20

Map of Ecuador — PT16

1938 ***Perf. 14x13½***
RA41 PT16 5c carmine rose .35 .20

Social and Rural Workers' Insurance Fund.

No. C42 Surcharged in Red

1938 ***Perf. 12½***
RA42 AP5 20c on 70c black .55 .20

No. 307 Surcharged in Red

1938
RA43 A116 5c on 6c yel & red .20 .20

This stamp was obligatory on all mail from Nov. 23rd to 30th, 1938. The tax was for the Intl. Union for the Control of Cancer.

Tobacco Stamp, Surcharged in Black

POSTAL ADICIONAL
CINCO CENTAVOS

1939 ***Rouletted***
RA44 PT7 5c on 1c rose .35 .20
a. Double surcharge
b. Triple surcharge

Tobacco Stamp, Surcharged in Blue

CASAS DE CORREOS
Y TELEGRAFOS
CINCO CENTAVOS

1940
RA45 PT7 5c on 1c rose red .50 .20
a. Double surcharge 3.50 3.50

No. 370 Surcharged in Carmine

1940 ***Perf. 11½***
RA46 A144 20c on 50c blk & multi .25 .20
a. Double surcharge, one inverted

Tobacco Stamp, Surcharged in Black

TIMBRE PATRIOTICO
VEINTE CENTAVOS

1940 ***Rouletted***
RA47 PT7 20c on 1c rose red 3.00 .50

Farmer Plowing PT17

Communication Symbols PT18

1940 ***Perf. 13x13½***
RA48 PT17 5c carmine rose .35 .20

1940-43 ***Perf. 12***
RA49 PT18 5c copper brown .35 .20
RA49A PT18 5c green ('43) .35 .20

For overprint & surcharges see #534, E6, I1.

Pursuit Planes PT19

Warrior Shielding Women PT20

1941 ***Perf. 11½x13***
RA50 PT19 20c ultra .55 .20

The tax was used for national defense.

1942-46 **Engr.** ***Perf. 12***
RA51 PT20 20c dark blue .55 .20
RA51A PT20 40c black brown ('46) .55 .20

The tax was used for national defense.
A 20c carmine, 20c brown and 30c gray exist lithographed in type PT20.

No. 370 Surcharged in Carmine

1942 ***Perf. 11½***
RA52 A144 20c on 50c multi .55 .20
a. Double surcharge 5.00

No. RA35 Surcharged in Red

ADICIONAL
CINCO
CENTAVOS

1943 ***Perf. 13½***
RA53 PT12 5c on 3c ultra .30 .20

No. RA53 with Additional Surcharge in Black

1943
RA54 PT12 5c on 5c on 3c ultra .55 .20

Peons — PT21

Coat of Arms — PT22

1943 ***Perf. 12***
RA55 PT21 5c blue .45 .20

The tax was for farm workers.
For overprint & surcharge see #535, C135.

Revenue Stamp (as No. RA64) Overprinted or Surcharged in Black

TIMBRE
PATRIOTICO

No. RA56

No. RA57

1943 ***Perf. 12½***
RA56 20c red orange *35.00* 1.50

1943 ***Perf. 12***
RA57 20c on 10c orange 1.10 .25
a. Double surcharge

1943 ***Perf. 12½***
RA58 PT22 20c orange red .35 .20

The tax was for national defense.

No. RA58 Surcharged in Black

1944
RA59 PT22 30c on 20c org red .35 .20
a. Double surcharge

Catalogue values for unused stamps in this section, from this point to the end of the section, are for Never Hinged items.

Consular Service Stamps Surcharged in Black

1951 **Unwmk.** ***Perf. 12***
RA60 R1 20c on 1s red .30 .20
RA61 R1 20c on 2s brown .30 .20
RA62 R1 20c on 5s violet .30 .20
Nos. RA60-RA62 (3) .90 .60

Teacher and Pupils in Schoolyard — PT23

PT24

1952 **Engr.** ***Perf. 13***
RA63 PT23 20c blue green .30 .20

Revenue Stamp Overprinted "PATRIOTICO / SANITARIO"

1952 ***Perf. 12***
RA64 PT24 40(c) olive green .55 .20

For overprints & surcharges see #RA56-RA57

Woman Holding Flag — PT25

PT26

1953 ***Perf. 12½***
RA65 PT25 40c ultra .65 .20

Telegraph Stamp Surcharged "ESCOLAR 20 Centavos" in Black

1954 **Unwmk.** ***Perf. 13***
RA66 PT26 20c on 30c red brn .50 .20

Revenue Stamps Surcharged or Overprinted Horizontally in Black "PRO TURISMO 1954"

1954 **Unwmk.** ***Perf. 12***
RA67 R2 10c on 25c blue .65 .20
RA68 R3 10c on 50c org red .65 .20
RA69 R3 10c carmine .65 .20
Nos. RA67-RA69 (3) 1.95 .60

PT27

Telegraph Stamp Surcharged "Pro-Turismo 1954 10 ctvs. 10"

1954 ***Perf. 13***
RA70 PT27 10c on 30c red brn 1.10 .20

Revenue Stamp Overprinted in Black

1954 ***Perf. 12***
RA71 R3 20c olive black .85 .20

Consular Service Stamp Surcharged in Black

1954
RA72 R1 20c on 10s gray .85 .20

Young Student at Desk
PT28

Globe, Ship, Plane
PT29

Imprint: "Heraclio Fournier.-Vitoria"

1954 **Photo.** ***Perf. 11***
RA73 PT28 20c rose pink .55 .20

See No. RA76.

1954 **Engr.** ***Perf. 12***
RA74 PT29 10c dp magenta .80 .20

Soldier Kissing Flag — PT30

1955 **Photo.** ***Perf. 11***
RA75 PT30 40c blue 1.10 .20

See No. RA77.

Types of 1954-55 Redrawn.
Imprint: "Thomas de la Rue & Co. Ltd."

1957 **Unwmk.** ***Perf. 13***
RA76 PT28 20c rose pink .55 .20

Perf. 14x14½
RA77 PT30 40c blue 1.10 .20

No. RA77 is inscribed "Republica del Ecuador."

AIR POST POSTAL TAX STAMPS

No. 438 Surcharged in Black or Carmine

1945 **Unwmk.** ***Perf. 11***
RAC1 A173 20c on 10c dk grn .35 .20
a. Pair, one without surcharge 45.00
RAC2 A173 20c on 10c dk grn (C) .35 .20

Obligatory on letters and parcel post carried on planes in the domestic service.

Liberty, Mercury and Planes
PTAP1

1946 **Engr.** ***Perf. 12***
RAC3 PTAP1 20c orange brown .35 .20

GALAPAGOS ISLANDS

Issued for use in the Galapagos Islands (Columbus Archipelago), a province of Ecuador, but were commonly used throughout the country.

Catalogue values for unused stamps in this section are for Never Hinged items.

Sea Lions — A1

Map — A2

Design: 1s, Marine iguana.

Unwmk.

1957, July 15 **Photo.** ***Perf. 12***
L1 A1 20c dark brown 1.00 .20
L2 A2 50c violet .65 .20
L3 A1 1s dull olive green 3.25 .55
Nos. L1-L3 (3) 4.90 .95
Nos. L1-L3,LC1-LC3 (6) 12.75 2.45

125th anniv. of Ecuador's possession of the Galapagos Islands, and publicizing the islands.

See Nos. LC1-LC3. For overprints see Nos. 684-686, C389-C391.

GALAPAGOS AIR POST STAMPS

Type of Regular Issue

1s, Santa Cruz Island. 1.80s, Map of Galapagos archipelago. 4.20s, Galapagos giant tortoise.

Unwmk.

1957, July 19 **Photo.** ***Perf. 12***
LC1 A1 1s deep blue .85 .20
LC2 A1 1.80s rose violet 1.75 .45
LC3 A1 4.20s black 5.25 .85
Nos. LC1-LC3 (3) 7.85 1.50

For overprints see Nos. C389-C391.

Redrawn Type of Ecuador, 1956

1959, Jan. 3 **Engr.** ***Perf. 14***
LC4 AP69 2s lt olive green .85 .50

Issued to honor the United Nations. See note after No. C407.

EGYPT

'ē-jəpt

LOCATION — Northern Africa, bordering on the Mediterranean and the Red Sea
GOVT. — Republic
AREA — 386,900 sq. mi.
POP. — 61,404,000 (1997 est.)
CAPITAL — Cairo

Modern Egypt was a part of Turkey until 1914 when a British protectorate was declared over the country and the Khedive was deposed in favor of Hussein Kamil under the title of sultan. In 1922 the protectorate ended and the reigning sultan was declared king of the new monarchy. Egypt became a republic on June 18, 1953. Egypt merged with Syria in 1958 to form the United Arab Republic. Syria left this union in 1961. In 1971 Egypt took the name of Arab Republic of Egypt.

40 Paras = 1 Piaster
1000 Milliemes = 100 Piasters = 1 Pound (1888)
1000 Milliemes = 1 Pound (1953)
1000 Milliemes = 100 Piasters = 1 Pound (1982)

Catalogue values for unused stamps in this country are for Never Hinged items, beginning with Scott 241 in the regular postage section, Scott B1 in the semi-postal section, Scott C38 in the airpost section, Scott CB1 in the airpost semi-postal section, Scott E5 in the special delivery section, Scott J40 in the postage due section, Scott M16 in the military stamps section, Scott O60 in the officials section, Scott N1 in the occupation section, Scott NC1 in the occupation airpost section, Scott NE1 in the occupation special delivery section, and Scott NJ1 in the occupation postage due section.

Watermarks

Wmk. 118 — Pyramid and Star

Wmk. 119 — Crescent and Star

Wmk. 120 — Triple Crescent and Star

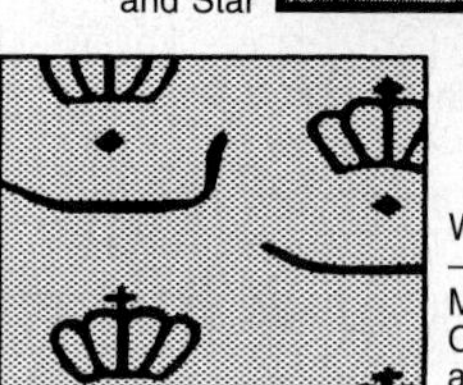

Wmk. 195 — Multiple Crown and Arabic F

"F" in watermark stands for Fuad.

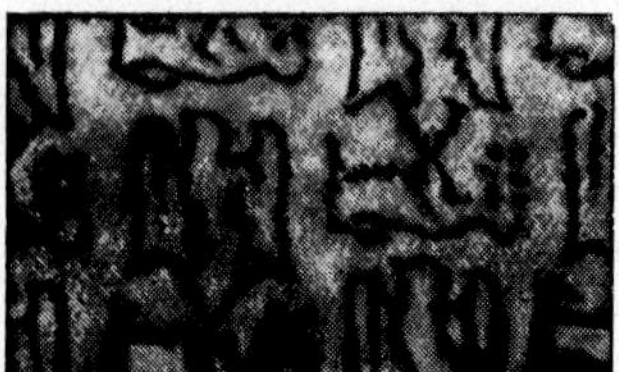

Wmk. 315 — Multiple Eagle

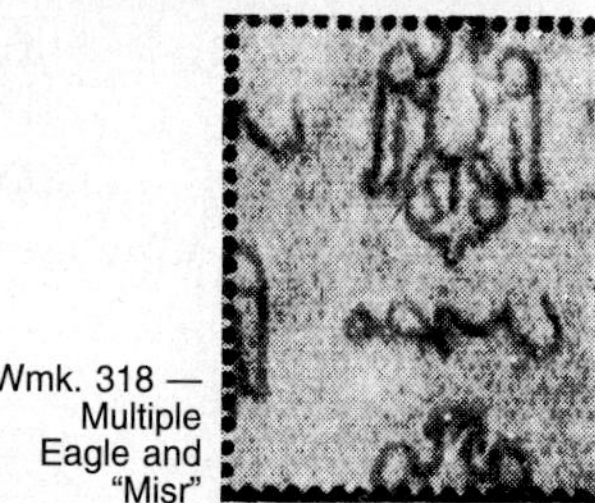

Wmk. 318 — Multiple Eagle and "Misr"

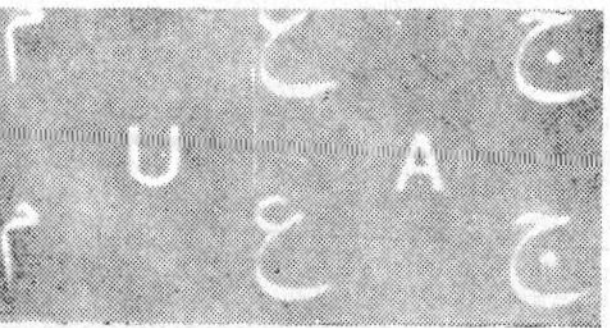

Wmk. 328 — U A R

Wmk. 342 — Coat of Arms, Multiple

Values for unused stamps are for examples with original gum as defined in the catalogue introduction. Very fine examples of Nos. 1-15 will have perforations that are clear of the framelines but with the design noticeably off center. Well centered stamps are extremely scarce and will command substantial premiums.

Turkish Suzerainty

A1

A2

A3

A4

A5

A6

A7

Surcharged in Black

Wmk. 118

1866, Jan. 1 Litho. ***Perf. 12½***

1	A1 5pa greenish gray	47.50	30.00
a.	Imperf., pair	225.00	
b.	Pair, imperf. between	350.00	
c.	Perf. 12½x13	57.50	55.00
d.	Perf. 13	300.00	*350.00*
2	A2 10pa brown	62.50	32.50
a.	Imperf., pair	190.00	
b.	Pair, imperf. between	400.00	
c.	Perf. 13	200.00	*210.00*
d.	Perf. 12½x15	300.00	*325.00*
e.	Perf. 12½x13	92.50	55.00
3	A3 20pa blue	80.00	35.00
a.	Imperf., pair	275.00	
b.	Pair, imperf. between	450.00	
c.	Perf. 12½x13	110.00	95.00
d.	Perf. 13	475.00	275.00
4	A4 2pi yellow	100.00	47.50
a.	Imperf.	*125.00*	*125.00*
b.	Imperf. vert. or horiz., pair	400.00	400.00
c.	Perf. 12½x15	150.00	
d.	Diagonal half used as 1pi on cover		*2,600.*
e.	Perf. 12½x13, 13x12½	140.00	55.00
5	A5 5pi rose	275.00	200.00
a.	Imperf.	375.00	375.00
b.	Imperf. vert. or horiz., pair	*1,150.*	
d.	Inscription of 10pi, imperf.	575.00	
e.	Perf. 12½x13, 13x12½	325.00	200.00
f.	As "d," perf. 12½x15	1,000.	850.00
6	A6 10pi slate bl	325.00	*275.00*
a.	Imperf.	*375.00*	375.00
b.	Pair, imperf. between	*2,250.*	
c.	Perf. 12½x13, 13x12½	475.00	475.00
d.	Perf. 13	*1,850.*	

Unwmk.

Typo.

7	A7 1pi rose lilac	67.50	5.50
a.	Imperf.	110.00	
b.	Horiz. pair, imperf vert.	450.00	
c.	Perf. 12½x13, 13x12½	100.00	25.00
d.	Perf. 13	350.00	210.00
	Nos. 1-7 (7)	957.50	625.50

Single imperforates of types A1-A10 are sometimes simulated by trimming wide-margined copies of perforated stamps.

No. 4d must be dated between July 16 and July 31, 1867.

Proofs of #1-7 are on smooth white paper, unwatermarked and imperforate. Proofs of #7 are on thinner paper than No. 7a.

Sphinx and Pyramid — A8

Perf. 15x12½

1867-69 Litho. Wmk. 119

8	A8 5pa orange	22.50	11.00
a.	Imperf.	—	—
b.	Horiz. pair, imperf between	175.00	
c.	Vert. pair, imperf between	—	
9	A8 10pa lilac ('69)	60.00	11.00
a.	10pa violet	82.50	14.00
b.	Half used as 5pa on newspaper piece		850.00
11	A8 20pa yel grn ('69)	110.00	11.00
a.	20pa blue green	125.00	17.00
13	A8 1pi rose red	11.00	1.10
a.	Imperf, pair	110.00	
b.	Pair, imperf. between	175.00	
d.	Rouletted	60.00	
e.	1pi lake red	125.00	32.50
14	A8 2pi blue	125.00	17.00
a.	Imperf.	—	
b.	Horiz. pair, imperf. vert.	500.00	
d.	Perf. 12½	250.00	
15	A8 5pi brown	325.00	190.00
	Nos. 8-15 (6)	653.50	241.10

There are 4 types of each value, so placed that any block of 4 contains all types.

A9

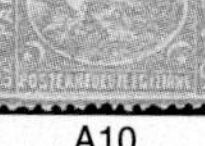

A10

Clear Impressions
Thick Opaque Paper

Typographed by the Government at Boulac

Perf. 12½x13½ Clean-cut

1872 Wmk. 119

19	A9 5pa brown	7.50	5.00
20	A9 10pa lilac	6.25	3.25
21	A9 20pa blue	50.00	3.75
22	A9 1pi rose red	57.50	2.25
h.	Half used as 20pa on cover		675.00
23	A9 2pi dull yellow	97.50	4.50
j.	Half used as 1p on cover		750.00
24	A9 2½pi dull violet	82.50	11.00
25	A9 5pi green	300.00	35.00
i.	Tête bêche pair		
	Nos. 19-25 (7)	601.25	64.75

Perf. 13½ Clean-cut

19a	A9 5pa brown	27.50	9.25
20a	A9 10pa dull lilac	6.25	3.25
21a	A9 20pa blue	90.00	20.00
22a	A9 1pi rose red	82.50	3.50
23a	A9 2pi dull yellow	55.00	4.25
24a	A9 2½pi dull violet	800.00	210.00
25a	A9 5pi green	325.00	62.50

Litho.

21m	A9 20pa blue, perf. 12½x13½	140.00	50.00
21n	A9 20pa blue, perf. 13½	225.00	57.50
21p	A9 20pa blue, imperf.	—	
22m	A9 1pi rose red, perf. 12½x13½	550.00	11.00
22n	A9 1pi rose red, perf. 13½	875.00	25.00

Typographed
Blurred Impressions
Thinner Paper
Perf. 12½ Rough

1874-75 **Wmk. 119**
26 A10 5pa brown ('75) 7.25 3.50
e. Imperf. — —
f. Vert. pair, imperf. horiz. 110.00 *125.00*
g. Tête bêche pair 40.00 40.00
20b A9 10pa gray lilac 8.50 3.00
g. Tête bêche pair 150.00 150.00
21b A9 20pa gray blue 90.00 3.25
k. Half used as 10pa on cover —
22b A9 1pi vermilion 5.50 .70
f. Imperf. — —
g. Tête bêche pair 100.00 100.00
23b A9 2pi yellow 75.00 3.25
i. Tête bêche pair 475.00 475.00
24b A9 2½pi deep violet 9.25 5.50
e. Imperf. — —
f. Tête bêche pair 400.00 —
25b A9 5pi yellow green 60.00 22.50
e. Imperf. —

No. 26f normally occurs tête-bêche.

Perf. 13½x12½ Rough

26c A10 5pa brown 6.25 3.50
i. Tête bêche pair 62.50 62.50
20c A9 10pa gray lilac 12.00 3.25
i. Tête bêche pair 150.00 175.00
21c A9 20pa gray blue 8.50 2.75
h. Pair, imperf. between 350.00
22c A9 1pi vermilion 55.00 1.40
i. Tête bêche pair 400.00 375.00
23c A9 2pi yellow 6.00 5.75
g. Tête bêche pair 450.00 450.00
k. Half used as 1pi on cover *2,800.*

Perf. 12½x13½ Rough

23d A9 2pi yellow ('75) 62.50 10.00
h. Tête bêche pair *1,000.*
24d A9 2½pi dp violet ('75) 45.00 22.50
i. Tête bêche pair *1,150.* *1,000.*
25d A9 5pi yel green ('75) 350.00 325.00

Nos. 24b, 24d Surcharged in Black

1879, Jan. 1 ***Perf. 12½ Rough***
27 A9 5pa on 2½pi dull vio 6.50 6.50
a. Imperf. — —
b. Tête bêche pair *4,000.*
c. Inverted surcharge 75.00 75.00
d. Perf. 12½x13½ rough 7.25 *8.75*
e. As "d," tête bêche pair
f. As "d," inverted surcharge 140.00 140.00
28 A9 10pa on 2½pi dull vio 11.00 11.00
a. Imperf.
b. Tête bêche pair *1,750.*
c. Inverted surcharge 82.50 82.50
d. Perf. 12½x13½ rough 17.00 17.00
e. As "d," tête bêche pair 1,750.
f. As "d," inverted surcharge 125.00 125.00

A11 A12

A13 A14

A15 A16

1879-93 **Typo.** ***Perf. 14x13½***
29 A11 5pa brown 1.10 .25
30 A12 10pa violet 45.00 2.75
31 A12 10pa lil rose ('81) 60.00 5.75
32 A12 10pa gray ('82) 13.25 1.60
33 A12 10pa green ('84) .80 .65
34 A13 20pa ultra 62.50 1.50
35 A13 20pa rose ('84) 17.00 .50
36 A14 1pi rose 13.00 .20
37 A14 1pi ultra ('84) 2.50 .20
38 A15 2pi orange yel 17.00 .95
39 A15 2pi orange brn 12.0 .95
40 A16 5pi green 70.00 8.75
41 A16 5pi gray ('84) 12.00 .50
Nos. 29-41 (13) 326.15 24.55

#29-31, 35-41 imperf, are proofs.

Nos. 37, 39, 41, exist on both ordinary and chalky paper. See *Scott Classic Specialized Catalogue of Stamps & Covers* for detailed listings.

For overprints see Nos. 42, O6-O7.

A17

1884, Feb. 1
42 A17 20pa on 5pi green 13.00 1.40
a. Inverted surcharge 70.00 62.50

A18

A19

A20

A21

A22 A23

1888-1906
43a A18 1m brown .55 .20
44a A19 2m green .55 .20
45 A20 3m maroon ('92) 2.50 1.10
46a A20 3m orange ('93) 1.65 .20
47 A21 4m brown red ('06) 1.40 .20
48 A22 5m carmine rose 1.40 .20
49 A23 10p purple ('89) 16.50 .85
Nos. 43a-49 (7) 24.55 2.95

#43-44, 47-48 imperf, are proofs.

Nos. 43-44, 46, 48-49 exist on both ordinary and chalky paper, No. 47 only on chalky-surfaced paper. See *Scott Classic Specialized Catalogue of Stamps & Covers* for detailed listings.

For overprints, see O2-O5, O8-O10, O14-O15.

Boats on Nile A24

Cleopatra A25

Ras-el-Tin Palace A26

Giza Pyramids A27

Sphinx A28

Colossi of Thebes A29

Pylon of Karnak and Temple of Khonsu — A30

Citadel at Cairo — A31

Rock Temple of Abu Simbel — A32

Aswan Dam — A33

Perf. 13½x14

1914, Jan. 8 **Wmk. 119**
Chalk-surfaced Paper
50 A24 1m olive brown .35 .35
51 A25 2m dp green .25 .20
52 A26 3m orange .50 .35
53 A27 4m red 1.00 .55
54 A28 5m lake .65 .20
a. Booklet pane of 6
55 A29 10m dk blue 1.25 .20

Perf. 14

56 A30 20m olive grn 2.75 .20
57 A31 50m red violet 5.00 .65
58 A32 100m black 22.50 .55
59 A33 200m plum 24.00 2.75
Nos. 50-59 (10) 58.25 6.00

All values of this issue exist imperforate on both watermarked and unwatermarked paper but are not known to have been issued in that condition.

See Nos. 61-69, 72-74. For overprints and surcharge see Nos. 60, 78-91, O11-O13, O16-O27, O30.

British Protectorate

No. 52 Surcharged

1915, Oct. 15
60 A26 2m on 3m orange .90 .75
a. Inverted surcharge 150.00 150.00

Scenic Types of 1914 and

Statue of Ramses II
A34 A35

1921-22 **Wmk. 120** ***Perf. 13½x14***
Chalk-surfaced Paper
61 A24 1m olive brown .35 *.55*
62 A25 2m dp green 1.75 1.75
63 A25 2m red ('22) 2.25 .60
64 A26 3m orange 1.00 .70
65 A27 4m green ('22) 2.50 *3.25*
66 A28 5m lake 1.00 .20
67 A28 5m pink 1.90 .20
68 A29 10m dp blue 1.75 .20
69 A29 10m lake ('22) 1.50 .25
70 A34 15m indigo ('22) 3.00 .20
71 A35 15m indigo ('22) 16.00 2.50

Perf. 14

72 A30 20m olive green 3.75 .20
73 A31 50m maroon 6.25 .35
74 A32 100m black 40.00 3.25
Nos. 61-74 (14) 83.00 14.20

For overprints see Nos. O28-O29.

Independent Kingdom

Stamps of 1921-22 Overprinted

1922, Oct. 10
78 A24 1m olive brown .80 .50
a. Inverted overprint 45.00 45.00
b. Double overprint 55.00 55.00
79 A25 2m red .60 .35
a. Double overprint 45.00 45.00
80 A26 3m orange .80 .50
81 A27 4m green .45 .45
b. Inverted overprint
82 A28 5m pink 1.50 .20
83 A29 10m lake 1.50 .20
84 A34 15m indigo 3.00 .50
85 A35 15m indigo 2.50 .50

Perf. 14

86 A30 20m olive green 3.00 .35
a. Inverted overprint 150.00 150.00
b. Double overprint 90.00 90.00
87 A31 50m maroon 3.75 .50
a. Inverted overprint 325.00 275.00
88 A32 100m black 15.00 .65
a. Inverted overprint 160.00 160.00
b. Double overprint 160.00 160.00
Nos. 78-88 (11) 32.90 4.70

Same Overprint on Nos. 58-59
Wmk. Crescent and Star (119)
90 A32 100m black 62.50 22.50
91 A33 200m plum 11.00 1.10

Proclamation of the Egyptian monarchy.

The overprint signifies "The Egyptian Kingdom, March 15, 1922." It exists in four types, one lithographed and three typographed on #78-87, but lithographed only on #88-91.

King Fuad
A36 A37

Wmk. 120
1923-24 **Photo.** ***Perf. 13½***
Size 18x22½mm
92 A36 1m orange .20 .20
93 A36 2m black .50 .20
94 A36 3m brown .45 .25
a. Imperf., pair 160.00
95 A36 4m yellow grn .35 .20
96 A36 5m orange brn .20 .20
a. Imperf., pair 22.00
97 A36 10m rose .95 .20
98 A36 15m ultra 2.25 .20

Perf. 14
Size: 22x28mm
99 A36 20m dk green 2.50 .20
100 A36 50m myrtle grn 4.75 .20
101 A36 100m red violet 11.00 .25
102 A36 200m violet ('24) 22.50 1.00
a. Imperf., pair 275.00

103 A37 £1 ultra & dk vio ('24) 125.00 13.00
a. Imperf., pair 050.00
Nos. 92-103 (12) 170.65 16.10

For overprints & surcharge see #167, O31-O38.

Thoth Carving Name of King Fuad — A38

1925, Apr. Litho. *Perf. 11*
105 A38 5m brown 5.50 3.25
106 A38 10m rose 7.75 5.00
107 A38 15m ultra 10.00 7.25
Nos. 105-107 (3) 23.25 15.50

International Geographical Congress, Cairo.
Nos. 106-107 exist with both white and yellowish gum.

Oxen Plowing A39

1926 Wmk. 195 *Perf. 13x13½*
108 A39 5m lt brown 2.25 .40
109 A39 10m brt rose 2.25 .40
110 A39 15m dp blue 2.25 .40
111 A39 50m Prus green 7.75 2.25
112 A39 100m brown vio 13.00 3.75
113 A39 200m brt violet 17.50 7.00
Nos. 108-113 (6) 45.00 14.20

12th Agricultural and Industrial Exhibition at Gezira.
For surcharges see Nos. 115-117.

King Fuad — A40

Perf. 14x14½
1926, Apr. 2 Photo. Wmk. 120
114 A40 50p brn vio & red vio 82.50 7.00

58th birthday of King Fuad.
For overprint and surcharge see #124, 166.

Nos. 111-113 Surcharged

Perf. 13x13½
1926, Aug. 24 Wmk. 195
115 A39 5m on 50m Prus grn 1.40 1.40
116 A39 10m on 100m brn vio 1.40 1.40
117 A39 15m on 200m brt vio 1.40 1.40
a. Double surcharge 175.00
Nos. 115-117 (3) 4.20 4.20

Ship of Hatshepsut — A41

1926, Dec. 9 Litho. *Perf. 13x13½*
118 A41 5m brown & blk 1.60 .70
119 A41 10m dp red & blk 1.90 .95
120 A41 15m dp blue & blk 1.90 .95
Nos. 118-120 (3) 5.40 2.60

International Navigation Congress, Cairo.
For overprints see Nos. 121-123.

Nos. 118-120, 114 Overprinted

1926, Dec. 21
121 A41 (a) 5m 150.00 110.00
122 A41 (a) 10m 150.00 110.00
123 A41 (a) 15m 150.00 110.00

Perf. 14x14½
Wmk. 120
124 A40 (b) 50p 1,200. 800.00

Inauguration of Port Fuad opposite Port Said.
Nos. 121-123 have a block over "Le Caire" at lower left.
Forgeries of Nos. 121-124 exist.

Branch of Cotton A42

Perf. 13x13½
1927, Jan. 25 Wmk. 195
125 A42 5m dk brown & sl grn .70 .55
126 A42 10m dp red & slate grn 1.75 .80
127 A42 15m dp blue & slate grn 1.75 .80
Nos. 125-127 (3) 4.20 2.15

International Cotton Congress, Cairo.

King Fuad
A43 A44

A45

A46

Perf. 13x13½
1927-37 Wmk. 195 Photo.
128 A43 1m orange .20 .20
129 A43 2m black .20 .20
130 A43 3m olive brn .20 .20
131 A43 3m dp green ('30) .20 .20
132 A43 4m yellow grn .35 .20
133 A43 4m brown ('30) .40 .20
134 A43 4m dp green ('34) .70 .20
135 A43 5m dk red brn ('29) .20 .20
b. 5m chestnut .20 .20
136 A43 10m dk red ('29) .45 .20
a. 10m orange red .70 .20
137 A43 10m purple ('34) 1.40 .20
138 A43 13m car rose ('32) .40 .20
139 A43 15m ultra .75 .20
140 A43 15m dk violet ('34) 1.60 .20
141 A43 20m ultra ('34) 2.75 .20

Early printings of Nos. 128, 129, 130, 132, 135, 136 and 139 were from plates with screen of vertical dots in the vignette; later printings show screen of diagonal dots.

Perf. 13½x14
142 A44 20m olive grn .75 .20
143 A44 20m ultra ('32) 1.90 .20
144 A44 40m olive brn ('32) .95 .20
145 A44 50m Prus green .75 .20
a. 50m greenish blue 1.25 .20
146 A44 100m brown vio 3.00 .20
a. 100m claret 3.00 .20
147 A44 200m deep violet 4.50 .20

Printings of Nos. 142, 145 and 146, made in 1929 and later, were from new plates with stronger impressions and darker colors.

Lithographed; Center Photogravure
Perf. 13x13½
148 A45 500m choc & Prus bl ('32) 72.50 2.75
a. Entirely photogravure 55.00 6.25
149 A46 £1 dk grn & org brn ('37) 55.00 2.25
a. Entirely photogravure 55.00 3.75
Nos. 128-149 (22) 149.15 9.00

Statue of Amenhotep, Son of Hapu — A47

1927, Dec. 29 Photo. *Perf. 13½x13*
150 A47 5m orange brown .45 .25
151 A47 10m copper red .75 .40
152 A47 15m deep blue 1.60 .45
Nos. 150-152 (3) 2.80 1.10

Statistical Congress, Cairo.

Imhotep — A48 Mohammed Ali Pasha — A49

1928, Dec. 15
153 A48 5m orange brown .75 .35
154 A49 10m copper red .75 .35

Intl. Congress of Medicine at Cairo and the cent. of the Faculty of Medicine at Cairo.

Prince Farouk — A50

1929, Feb. 11 Litho.
155 A50 5m choc & gray 1.40 1.40
156 A50 10m dull red & gray 1.40 1.40
157 A50 15m ultra & gray 1.40 1.40
158 A50 20m Prus blue & gray 1.40 1.40
Nos. 155-158 (4) 5.60 5.60

Ninth birthday of Prince Farouk.
Nos. 155-158 with black or brown centers are trial color proofs. They were sent to the UPU, but were never placed on sale to the public, although some are known used.

Tomb Fresco at El-Bersheh — A51

1931, Feb. 15 *Perf. 13x13½*
163 A51 5m brown .75 .35
164 A51 10m copper red 1.50 .35
165 A51 15m dark blue 2.00 .45
Nos. 163-165 (3) 4.25 1.15

14th Agricultural & Industrial Exhib., Cairo.

Nos. 114 and 103 Surcharged with Bars and

1932 Wmk. 120 *Perf. 14x14½*
166 A40 50m on 50p 8.00 .90
Perf. 14
167 A37 100m on £1 140.00 140.00

Locomotive of 1852 — A52

Perf. 13x13½
1933, Jan. 19 Litho. Wmk. 195
168 A52 5m shown 9.00 4.00
169 A52 13m 1859 15.00 7.50
170 A52 15m 1862 15.00 7.50
171 A52 2m 1932 15.00 7.50
Nos. 168-171 (4) 54.00 26.50

International Railroad Congress, Heliopolis.

Commercial Passenger Airplane — A56

Dornier Do-X
A57

Graf Zeppelin
A58

1933, Dec. 20 **Photo.**

172	A56	5m brown	3.00	1.60
173	A56	10m brt violet	9.00	6.00
174	A57	13m brown car	11.00	8.50
175	A57	15m violet	11.00	7.75
176	A58	20m blue	13.00	9.00
		Nos. 172-176 (5)	47.00	32.85

International Aviation Congress, Cairo.

A59

Khedive Ismail Pasha — A60

1934, Feb. 1 ***Perf. 13½***

177	A59	1m dp orange	.40	.20
178	A59	2m black	.40	.20
179	A59	3m brown	.50	.25
180	A59	4m blue green	.75	.20
181	A59	5m red brown	.75	.20
182	A59	10m violet	1.50	.20
183	A59	13m copper red	2.00	1.00
184	A59	15m dull violet	2.00	.80
185	A59	20m ultra	1.50	.20
186	A59	50m Prus blue	4.50	.35
187	A59	100m olive grn	9.00	.65
188	A59	200m dp violet	32.50	3.00

Perf. 13½x13

189	A60	50p brown	125.00	50.00
190	A60	£1 Prus blue	190.00	80.00
		Nos. 177-190 (14)	370.80	137.25

10th Congress of UPU, Cairo.

King Fuad — A61

1936-37 ***Perf. 13½***

191	A61	1m dull orange	.40	.20
192	A61	2m black	.40	.20
193	A61	4m dk green	.40	.20
194	A61	5m chestnut	.40	.20
195	A61	10m purple ('37)	1.75	.20
196	A61	15m brown violet	1.75	.20
197	A61	20m sapphire	2.00	.20
		Nos. 191-197 (7)	7.10	1.40

Entrance to Agricultural Building — A62

Agricultural Building — A63

Design: 15m, 20m, Industrial Building.

1936, Feb. 15 ***Perf. 13½x13***

198	A62	5m brown	.50	.40

Perf. 13x13½

199	A63	10m violet	1.00	.55
200	A63	13m copper red	1.50	.90
201	A63	15m dark violet	1.10	.60
202	A63	20m blue	2.00	1.50
		Nos. 198-202 (5)	6.10	3.95

15th Agricultural & Industrial Exhib., Cairo.

Signing of Treaty — A65

1936, Dec. 22 ***Perf. 11***

203	A65	5m brown	.65	.25
204	A65	15m dk violet	.75	.40
205	A65	20m sapphire	2.00	.45
		Nos. 203-205 (3)	3.40	1.10

Signing of Anglo-Egyptian Treaty, 8/26/36.

King Farouk — A66

Medal for Montreux Conf. — A67

1937-44 **Wmk. 195** ***Perf. 13x13½***

206	A66	1m brown org	.30	.20
207	A66	2m vermilion	.30	.20
208	A66	3m brown	.30	.20
209	A66	4m green	.30	.20
210	A66	5m red brown	.30	.20
211	A66	6m lt yel grn ('40)	.30	.20
212	A66	10m purple	.30	.20
213	A66	13m rose car	.30	.20
214	A66	15m dk vio brn	.30	.20
215	A66	20m blue	.30	.20
216	A66	20m lil gray ('44)	.35	.20
		Nos. 206-216 (11)	3.35	2.20

For overprints see Nos. 301, 303, 345, 348, 360E, N3, N6, N8, N22, N25, N27.

1937, Oct. 15 ***Perf. 13½x13***

217	A67	5m red brown	.50	.20
218	A67	15m dk violet	.75	.35
219	A67	20m sapphire	.80	.40
		Nos. 217-219 (3)	2.05	.95

Intl. Treaty signed at Montreux, Switzerland, under which foreign privileges in Egypt were to end in 1949.

Eye of Ré — A68

1937, Dec. 8 ***Perf. 13x13½***

220	A68	5m brown	.60	.45
221	A68	15m dk violet	.90	.45
222	A68	20m sapphire	1.10	.45
		Nos. 220-222 (3)	2.60	1.35

15th Ophthalmological Congress, Cairo, December, 1937.

King Farouk, Queen Farida — A69

1938, Jan. 20 ***Perf. 11***

223	A69	5m red brown	5.00	1.40

Royal wedding of King Farouk and Farida Zulficar.

Inscribed: "11 Fevrier 1938"

1938, Feb. 11

224	A69	£1 green & sepia	150.00	100.00

King Farouk's 18th birthday.

Cotton Picker — A70

1938, Jan. 26 ***Perf. 13½x13***

225	A70	5m red brown	.50	.40
226	A70	15m dk violet	2.00	.75
227	A70	20m sapphire	1.50	.65
		Nos. 225-227 (3)	4.00	1.80

18th International Cotton Congress at Cairo.

Pyramids of Giza and Colossus of Thebes
A71

1938, Feb. 1 ***Perf. 13x13½***

228	A71	5m red brown	1.00	.55
229	A71	15m dk violet	1.50	.70
230	A71	20m sapphire	1.75	.70
		Nos. 228-230 (3)	4.25	1.95

Intl. Telecommunication Conf., Cairo.

Branch of Hydnocarpus — A72

1938, Mar. 21 ***Perf. 13x13½***

231	A72	5m red brown	1.00	.40
232	A72	15m dk violet	1.60	.50
233	A72	20m sapphire	1.60	.50
		Nos. 231-233 (3)	4.20	1.40

International Leprosy Congress, Cairo.

King Farouk and Pyramids — A73

King Farouk
A74 A75

Backgrounds: 40m, Hussan Mosque. 50m, Cairo Citadel. 100m, Aswan Dam. 200m, Cairo University.

1939-46 **Photo.** ***Perf. 14x13½***

234	A73	30m gray	.50	.20
a.		30m slate gray	.50	.20
234B	A73	30m ol grn ('46)	.55	.20
235	A73	40m dk brown	.60	.20
236	A73	50m Prus green	.70	.20
237	A73	100m brown vio	.80	.20
238	A73	200m dk violet	2.00	.20

Perf. 13½x13

239	A74	50p green & sep	4.50	.35
240	A75	£1 dp bl & dk brn	11.00	.40
		Nos. 234-240 (8)	20.65	1.95

For £1 with A77 portrait, see No. 269D. See Nos. 267-269D. For overprints see Nos. 310-314, 316, 355-358, 360, 363-364, N13-N19, N32-N38.

Catalogue values for unused stamps in this section, from this point to the end of the section, are for Never Hinged items.

King Fuad
A76

King Farouk
A77

1944, Apr. 28 ***Perf. 13½x13***

241	A76	10m dk violet	.35	.20

8th anniv. of the death of King Fuad.

1944-50 **Wmk. 195** ***Perf. 13x13½***

242	A77	1m yellow brn ('45)	.35	.20
243	A77	2m red org ('45)	.35	.20
244	A77	3m sepia ('46)	.75	.75
245	A77	4m dp green ('45)	.35	.20
246	A77	5m red brown ('46)	.35	.20
247	A77	10m dp violet	.35	.20
247A	A77	13m rose red ('50)	5.00	5.00
248	A77	15m dk violet ('45)	.35	.20
249	A77	17m olive grn	.35	.20
250	A77	20m dk gray ('45)	.35	.20
251	A77	22m dp blue ('45)	.40	.20
		Nos. 242-251 (11)	8.95	7.55

For overprints see Nos. 299-300, 302, 304-309, 343-344, 346-347, 349-354, 360B, 361-362, N1-N2, N4-N5, N7, N9-N12, N20-N21, N23-N24, N26, N28-N31.

King Farouk — A78

Khedive Ismail Pasha — A79

1945, Feb. 10 ***Perf. 13½x13***

252	A78	10m deep violet	.35	.20

25th birthday of King Farouk.

1945, Mar. 2 **Photo.**

253	A79	10m dark olive	.35	.20

50th anniv. of death of Khedive Ismail Pasha.

Flags of Arab Nations — A80

1945, July 29

254 A80 10m violet .35 .20
255 A80 22m dp yellow grn .40 .20

League of Arab Nations Conference, Cairo, Mar. 22, 1945.

Flags of Egypt and Saudi Arabia A81

Perf. 13x13½

1946, Jan. 10 Wmk. 195

256 A81 10m dp yellow grn .35 .20

Visit of King Ibn Saud, Jan. 1946.

Citadel, Cairo A82

1946, Aug. 9

257 A82 10m yel brn & dp yel grn .35 .20

Withdrawal of British troops from Cairo Citadel, Aug. 9, 1946.

King Farouk and Inchas Palace, Cairo A83

2m, Prince Abdullah, Yemen. 3m, Pres. Bechara el-Khoury, Lebanon. 4m, King Abdul Aziz ibn Saud, Saudi Arabia. 5m, King Faisal II, Iraq. 10m, Amir Abdullah ibn Hussein, Jordan. 15m, Pres. Shukri el Kouatly, Syria.

1946, Nov. 9

258 A83 1m dp yellow grn .60 .20
259 A83 2m sepia .60 .20
260 A83 3m deep blue .60 .20
261 A83 4m brown orange .60 .20
262 A83 5m brown red .60 .20
263 A83 10m dark gray .75 .20
264 A83 15m deep violet .75 .20
Nos. 258-264 (7) 4.50 1.40

Arab League Cong. at Cairo, May 28, 1946.

Parliament Building, Cairo — A84

1947, Apr. 7 Photo.

265 A84 10m green .35 .20

36th conf. of the Interparliamentary Union, Apr. 1947.

Raising Egyptian Flag over Kasr-el-Nil Barracks — A85

King Farouk — A85a

1947, May 6 *Perf. 13½x13*

266 A85 10m dp plum & yel grn .35 .20

Withdrawal of British troops from the Nile Delta.

Farouk Types 1939 Redrawn

1947-51 Wmk. 195 *Perf. 14x13½*

267 A73 30m olive green .40 .20
268 A73 40m dk brown .50 .20
269 A73 50m Prus grn ('48) .75 .20
269A A73 100m dk brn vio ('49) 1.75 .20
269B A73 200m dk violet ('49) 4.50 .20

Perf. 13½x13

269C A85a 50p green & sep ('51) 15.00 1.90
269D A75 £1 dp bl & dk brn ('50) 30.00 1.10
Nos. 267-269D (7) 52.90 4.00

The king faces slightly to the left and clouds have been added in the sky on Nos. 267-269B. Backgrounds as in 1939-46 issue. Portrait on £1 as on type A77.

For overprints see Nos. 315, 359.

Field and Branch of Cotton — A86

Map and Infantry Column — A87

Perf. 13½x13

1948, Apr. 1 Wmk. 195

270 A86 10m olive green .35 .20

Intl. Cotton Cong. held at Cairo in Apr. 1948.

1948, June 15 *Perf. 11½x11*

271 A87 10m green .35 .20

Arrival of Egyptian troops at Gaza, 5/15/48.

Ibrahim Pasha (1789-1848) — A88

1948, Nov. 10 *Perf. 13x13½*

272 A88 10m brn red & dp grn .35 .20

Statue, "The Nile" A89

Protection of Industry and Agriculture — A90

Perf. 13x13½

1949, Mar. 1 Photo. Wmk. 195

273 A89 1m dk green .35 .20
274 A89 10m purple .35 .20
275 A89 17m crimson .35 .20
276 A89 22m deep blue .40 .40

Perf. 11½x11

277 A90 30m dk brown .50 .50
Nos. 273-277 (5) 1.95 1.50

Souvenir Sheets
Photo. & Litho.
Imperf

278 Sheet of 4 2.00 2.00
a. A89 1m red brown .40 .40
b. A89 10m dark brown .40 .40
c. A89 17m brown orange .40 .40
d. A89 22m dark Prussian green .40 .40
279 Sheet of 2 2.25 2.25
a. A90 10m violet gray 1.00 1.00
b. A90 30m red orange 1.00 1.00

16th Agricultural & Industrial Expo., Cairo.

Mohammed Ali and Map — A93

Globe — A94

Perf. 11½x11

1949, Aug. 2 Photo. Wmk. 195

280 A93 10m orange brn & grn .40 .20

Centenary of death of Mohammed Ali.

1949, Oct. 9 *Perf. 13½x13*

281 A94 10m rose brown .35 .20
282 A94 22m violet .75 .25
283 A94 30m dull blue 1.00 .40
Nos. 281-283 (3) 2.10 .85

75th anniv. of the UPU.

Scales of Justice A95

1949, Oct. 14 *Perf. 13x13½*

284 A95 10m deep olive green .35 .20

End of the Mixed Judiciary System, 10/14/49.

Desert Scene A96

1950, Dec. 27

285 A96 10m violet & red brn .40 .20

Opening of the Fuad I Institute of the Desert.

Fuad I University A97

1950, Dec. 27

286 A97 22m dp green & claret .50 .25

Founding of Fuad I University, 25th anniv.

Globe and Khedive Ismail Pasha A98

1950, Dec. 27

287 A98 30m claret & dp grn .50 .25

75th anniv. of Royal Geographic Society of Egypt.

Picking Cotton — A99

1951, Feb. 24

290 A99 10m olive green .35 .20

International Cotton Congress, 1951.

King Farouk and Queen Narriman — A100

1951, May 6 Photo. *Perf. 11x11½*

291 A100 10m green & red brn 1.50 1.50
a. Souvenir sheet 2.25 1.60

Marriage of King Farouk and Narriman Sadek, May 6, 1951.

Stadium Entrance A101

Arms of Alexandria and Olympic Emblem — A102

King Farouk A103

1951, Oct. 5 *Perf. 13x13½, 13½x13*

292 A101 10m brown .50 .25
293 A102 22m dp green .75 .45
294 A103 30m blue & dp grn .85 .55
a. Souvenir sheet of 3, #292-294 5.50 5.00
Nos. 292-294 (3) 2.10 1.25

Issued to publicize the first Mediterranean Games, Alexandria, Oct. 5-20, 1951.

Winged Figure and Map — A105

Designs: 22m, King Farouk and Map. 30m, King Farouk and Flag.

Dated "16 Oct. 1951"

1952, Feb. 11 *Perf. 13½x13*

296 A105 10m dp green .50 .25
297 A105 22m plum & dp grn .75 .45
298 A105 30m green & brown 1.00 .55
a. Souvenir sheet of 3, #296-298 4.50 3.75
Nos. 296-298 (3) 2.25 1.25

Abrogation of the Anglo-Egyptian treaty.

Stamps of 1937-51 Overprinted in Various Colors

Perf. 13x13½

1952, Jan. 17 **Wmk. 195**

299 A77 1m yellow brown .35 .20
300 A77 2m red org (Bl) .35 .20
301 A66 3m brown (Bl) .35 .20
302 A77 4m dp green (RV) .35 .20
303 A66 6m lt yel grn (RV) .75 .20
304 A77 10m dp vio (C) .35 .20
305 A77 13m rose red (Bl) 1.75 .20
306 A77 15m dk violet (C) .75 .20
307 A77 17m olive grn (C) 1.75 .20
308 A77 20m dk gray (RV) 1.25 .20
309 A77 22m dp blue (C) 1.75 .50

No. 244, the 3m sepia, exists with this overprint but was not regularly issued or used.

Same Overprint, 24½mm Wide, on Nos. 267 to 269B

Perf. 14x13½

310 A73 30m olive grn (DkBl) .50 .20
a. Black overprint .85 .20
311 A73 40m dk brown (G) .75 .20
312 A73 50m Prus grn (C) .85 .20
313 A73 100m dk brn vio (C) 1.25 .20
314 A73 200m dk violet (C) 3.00 .20

Same Overprint, 19mm Wide, on Nos. 269C-269D

Perf. 13½x13

315 A85a 50p grn & sep (C) 15.00 2.25
316 A75 £1 dp bl & dk brn (Bl) 25.00 2.50
Nos. 299-316 (18) 56.10 8.25

The overprint translates: King of Egypt and the Sudan, Oct. 16, 1951.

Overprints in colors other than as listed are color trials.

Egyptian Flag — A106

Perf. 13½x13

1952, May 6 **Photo.** **Wmk. 195**

317 A106 10m org yel, dp bl & dp grn .35 .20
a. Souvenir sheet of 1 2.75 2.25

Issued to commemorate the birth of Crown Prince Ahmed Fuad, Jan. 16, 1952.

"Dawn of New Era" A107

Symbolical of Egypt Freed — A108

Designs: 10m, "Egypt" with raised sword. 22m, Citizens marching with flag.

Perf. 13x13½, 13½x13

1952, Nov. 23

Dated: "23 Juillet 1952"

318 A107 4m dp green & org .35 .20
319 A107 10m dp grn & cop brn .35 .20
320 A108 17m brn org & dp grn .40 .20
321 A108 22m choc & dp grn .60 .25
Nos. 318-321 (4) 1.70 .85

Change of government, July 23, 1952.

Republic

Farmer A109

Soldier A110

Mosque of Sultan Hassan — A111

Queen Nefertiti — A112

1953-56 *Perf. 13x13½*

322 A109 1m red brown .35 .20
323 A109 2m dk lilac .35 .20
324 A109 3m brt blue .35 .20
325 A109 4m dk green .35 .20
326 A110 10m dk brown *("Defence")* .35 .20
327 A110 10m dk brown *("Defense")* .35 .20
328 A110 15m gray .35 .20
329 A110 17m dk grnsh blue .35 .20
330 A110 20m purple .35 .20

Perf. 13½

331 A111 30m dull green .35 .20
332 A111 32m brt blue .35 .20
333 A111 35m violet ('55) .60 .20
334 A111 37m gldn brn ('56) 1.75 .20
335 A111 40m red brown .40 .20
336 A111 50m violet brn .50 .20
337 A112 100m henna brn 1.00 .20
338 A112 200m dk grnsh blue 2.50 .20
339 A112 500m purple 5.50 .65
340 A112 £1 dk grn, blk & red 15.00 .70
Nos. 322-340 (19) 31.10 4.75

Nos. 327-330 are inscribed "Defense."
See No. 490. For overprints and surcharges see Nos. 460, 500, N44-N56, N72.

Stamps of 1939-51 Overprinted in Black with Three Bars to Obliterate Portrait

1953 *Perf. 13x13½, 13½x13*

343 A77 1m yellow brn .35 .20
344 A77 2m red orange .35 .20
345 A66 3m brown 1.00 1.00
346 A77 3m sepia .35 .20
347 A77 4m dp green .35 .20
348 A66 6m lt yellow grn .35 .20
349 A77 10m dp violet .35 .20
350 A77 13m rose red .50 .20
351 A77 15m dk violet .35 .20
352 A77 17m olive grn .35 .20
353 A77 20m dk gray .50 .20
354 A77 22m deep blue .55 .20
355 A73 30m ol grn (#267) .55 .20
356 A73 50m Prus grn (#269) .75 .20
357 A73 100m dk brn vio (#269A) .85 .20
358 A73 200m dk violet (#269B) 3.50 .70
359 A85a 50p grn & sepia 7.00 1.50
360 A75 £1 dp bl & dk brn (#269D) 17.50 3.75
Nos. 343-360 (18) 35.50 9.75

No. 206 with this overprint is a forgery.

Same Overprint on Nos. 300, 303-305, 311 and 314

360B A77 2m red orange .40 .20
360E A66 6m lt yel grn *3.00*
361 A77 10m dp violet 1.50 .90
362 A77 13m rose red .75 .25
363 A73 40m dk brown .85 .25
364 A73 200m dk violet 3.75 .50
Nos. 360B,361-364 (5) 7.25 2.10

Practically all values of Nos. 343-364 exist with double overprint. Other values of the 1952 overprinted issue are known with counterfeit bars.

Symbols of Electronic Progress A113

1953, Nov. 23 **Photo.** *Perf. 13x13½*

365 A113 10m brt blue .35 .20

Electronics Exposition, Cairo, Nov. 23.

Crowd Acclaiming the Republic A114

Farmer A115

Design: 30m, Crowd, flag and eagle.

Perf. 13½x13

1954, June 18 **Wmk. 195**

366 A114 10m brown .35 .20
367 A114 30m deep blue .50 .20

Proclamation of the republic, 1st anniv.

1954-55 *Perf. 13x13½*

368 A115 1m red brown .35 .20
369 A115 2m dark lilac .35 .20
370 A115 3m brt blue .35 .20
371 A115 4m dk green ('55) .35 .20
372 A115 5m dp car ('55) .35 .20
Nos. 368-372 (5) 1.75 1.00

For overprints see Nos. N39-N43.

Egyptian Flag, Map — A116

Globe — A117

Design: 35m, Bugler, soldier and map.

1954, Nov. 4 *Perf. 13½x13*

373 A116 10m rose vio & grn .35 .20
374 A116 35m ver, blk & bl grn .40 .25

Agreement of Oct. 19, 1954, with Great Britain for the evacuation of the Suez Canal zone by British troops.

Arab Postal Union Issue

1955, Jan. 1

375 A117 5m yellow brn .20 .20
376 A117 10m green .20 .20
377 A117 37m violet .45 .25
Nos. 375-377 (3) .85 .65

Founding of the Arab Postal Union, 7/1/54.
For overprints see Nos. 381-383.

Paul P. Harris and Rotary Emblem — A118

35m, Globe, wings and Rotary emblem.

Perf. 13½x13

1955, Feb. 23 **Wmk. 195**

378 A118 10m claret .25 .20
379 A118 35m blue .65 .20

50th anniv. of the founding of Rotary Intl.

Nos. 375-377 Overprinted

1955, Nov. 1

381 A117 5m yellow brown .20 .20
382 A117 10m green .20 .20
383 A117 37m violet .50 .40
Nos. 381-383 (3) .90 .80

Arab Postal Union Congress held at Cairo, Mar. 15, 1955.

Map of Africa and Asia, Olive Branch and Rings A119

Globe, Torch, Dove and Olive Branch — A120

1956, July 29 ***Perf. 13x13½, 13½x13***
384 A119 10m chestnut & green .20 .20
385 A120 35m org yel & dull pur .35 .35

Afro-Asian Festival, Cairo, July, 1956.

Map of Suez Canal and Ship — A121

Queen Nefertiti — A122

Perf. 11½x11
1956, Sept. 26 **Wmk. 195**
386 A121 10m blue & buff .55 .55

Nationalization of the Suez Canal, July 26, 1956. See No. 393.

1956, Oct. 15 ***Perf. 13½x13***
387 A122 10m dark green .55 .45

Intl. Museum Week (UNESCO), Oct. 8-14.

Egyptians Defending Port Said — A123

1956, Dec. 20 **Litho.** ***Perf. 11x11½***
388 A123 10m brown violet .25 .20

Honoring the defenders of Port Said.

No. 388 Overprinted in Carmine Rose

1957, Jan. 14
389 A123 10m brown violet .25 .20

Evacuation of Port Said by British and French troops, Dec. 22, 1956.

Old and New Trains A124

1957, Jan. 30 **Photo.** ***Perf. 13x13½***
390 A124 10m red violet & gray .20 .20

100th anniv. of the Egyptian Railway System (in 1956).

Mother and Children A125

1957, Mar. 21
391 A125 10m crimson .20 .20

Mother's Day, 1957.

Battle Scene A126

Perf. 13x13½
1957, Mar. 28 **Wmk. 195**
392 A126 10m bright blue .20 .20

Victory over the British at Rosetta, , 150th anniv.

Type of 1956; New Inscriptions in English

1957, Apr. 15 ***Perf. 11½x11***
393 A121 100m blue & yel grn .70 .55

Reopening of the Suez Canal.

No. 393 is inscribed: "Nationalisation of Suez Canal Co. Guarantees Freedom of Navigation" and "Reopening 1957."

Map of Gaza Strip — A127

Perf. 13½x13
1957, May 4 **Photo.** **Wmk. 195**
394 A127 10m Prus blue .40 .20

"Gaza Part of Arab Nation."

For overprint see No. N57.

Al Azhar University A128

1957, Apr. 27 ***Perf. 13x13½***
New Arabic Date in Red
395 A128 10m brt violet .20 .20
396 A128 15m violet brown .25 .20
397 A128 20m dark gray .40 .25
Nos. 395-397 (3) .85 .65

Millenary of Al Azhar University, Cairo.

Shepheard's Hotel, Cairo — A129

Gate, Palace and Eagle — A130

Perf. 13½x13
1957, July 20 **Wmk. 195**
398 A129 10m brt violet .20 .20

Reopening of Shepheard's Hotel, Cairo.

Perf. 11½x11
1957, July 22 **Wmk. 315**
399 A130 10m yellow & brown .20 .20

First meeting of New National Assembly.

Amasis I in Battle of Avaris, 1580 B.C. A131

Designs: No. 401, Sultan Saladin, Hitteen, 1187 A. D. No. 402, Louis IX of France in chains, Mansourah, 1250, vert. No. 403, Map of Middle East, Ein Galout, 1260. No. 404, Port Said, 1956.

Inscribed:
"Egypt Tomb of Aggressors 1957"

1957, July 26 ***Perf. 13x13½, 13½x13***
400 A131 10m carmine rose .20 .20
401 A131 10m dk olive grn .20 .20
402 A131 10m brown violet .20 .20
403 A131 10m grnsh blue .20 .20
404 A131 10m yellow brown .20 .20
Nos. 400-404 (5) 1.00 1.00

No. 400 exists with Wmk. 195.

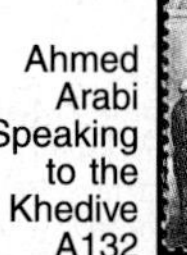

Ahmed Arabi Speaking to the Khedive A132

Perf. 13x13½
1957, Sept. 16 **Wmk. 315**
405 A132 10m deep violet .20 .20

75th anniversary of Arabi Revolution.

Hafez Ibrahim — A133

Portrait: No. 407, Ahmed Shawky.

1957, Oct. 14 ***Perf. 13½x13***
406 A133 10m dull red brn .20 .20
407 A133 10m olive green .20 .20
a. Pair, #406-407 .35 .20

25th anniv. of the deaths of Hafez Ibrahim and Ahmed Shawky, poets.

MiG and Ilyushin Planes A134

Design: No. 409, Viscount plane.

1957, Dec. 19 ***Perf. 13x13½***
408 A134 10m ultra .20 .20
409 A134 10m green .20 .20
a. Pair, #408-409 .25 .20

25th anniv. of the Egyptian Air Force and of Misrair, the Egyptian airline.

Pyramids, Dove and Globe A135

1957, Dec. 26 **Photo.** **Wmk. 315**
410 A135 5m brown orange .20 .20
411 A135 10m green .20 .20
412 A135 15m brt violet .20 .20
Nos. 410-412 (3) .60 .60

Afro-Asian Peoples Conf., Cairo, 12/26-1/2.

Farmer's Wife A136

Ramses II A137

"Industry" — A138

1957-58 **Wmk. 315** ***Perf. 13½***
413 A136 1m blue green ('58) .20 .20
414 A137 10m violet .20 .20

1958 **Wmk. 318**
415 A136 1m lt blue green .20 .20
416 A138 5m brown .20 .20
417 A137 10m violet .20 .20
Nos. 413-417 (5) 1.00 1.00

See #438-444, 474-488, 535. For overprints see #N58-N63, N66-N68, N75, N77-N78.

Cyclists — A139

Mustafa Kamel — A140

Perf. 13½x13
1958, Jan. 12 **Wmk. 315**
418 A139 10m lt red brown .20 .20

5th Intl. Bicycle Race, Egypt, Jan. 12-26.

1958, Feb. 10 **Photo.** **Wmk. 318**
419 A140 10m blue gray .25 .20

50th anniversary of the death of Mustafa Kamel, orator and politician.

United Arab Republic

Linked Maps of Egypt and Syria — A141

Cotton — A142

Perf. 11½x11

1958, Mar. 22 **Wmk. 318**

436	A141	10m yellow & green	.20	.20

Birth of United Arab Republic. See #C90. See also Syria-UAR Nos. 1 and C1.

1958, Apr. 5 ***Perf. 13½x13***

437	A142	10m Prussian blue	.20	.20

Intl. Fair for Egyptian Cotton, Apr., 1958.

Types of 1957-58 Inscribed "U.A.R. EGYPT" and

Princess Nofret — A143

Designs: 1m, Farmer's wife. 2m, Ibn-Tulun's Mosque. 4m, 14th century glass lamp (design lacks "1963" of A217). 5m, "Industry" (factories and cogwheel). 10m, Ramses II. 35m, "Commerce" (eagle, ship and cargo).

1958 ***Perf. 13½x14***

438	A136	1m crimson	.20	.20
439	A138	2m blue	.20	.20
440	A143	3m dk red brown	.20	.20
441	A217	4m green	.20	.20
442	A138	5m brown	.20	.20
443	A137	10m violet	.20	.20
444	A138	35m lt ultra	.65	.20
		Nos. 438-444 (7)	1.85	1.40

See Nos. 474-488, 532-533, N62-N68, N75-N78.

Qasim Amin — A144

Doves, Broken Chain and Globe — A145

1958, Apr. 23 ***Perf. 13½x13***

445	A144	10m deep blue	.20	.20

50th anniversary of the death of Qasim Amin, author of "Emancipation of Women."

1958, June 18

446	A145	10m violet	.20	.20

5th anniv. of the republic and to publicize the struggle of peoples and individuals for freedom.

For overprint see No. N69.

Cement Industry — A146

UAR Flag — A147

Industries: No. 448, Textile. No. 449, Iron & steel. No. 450, Petroleum (Oil). No. 451, Electricity and fertilizers.

Perf. 13½x13

1958, July 23 **Photo.** **Wmk. 318**

447	A146	10m red brown	.20	.20
448	A146	10m blue green	.20	.20
449	A146	10m bright red	.20	.20
450	A146	10m olive green	.20	.20
451	A146	10m dark blue	.20	.20
a.		Strip of 5, #447-451	.75	.50

Souvenir Sheet

Imperf

452	A147	50m grn, dp car & blk	7.50	6.00

Revolution of July 23, 1952, 6th anniv.

Sayed Darwich A148

Hand Holding Torch, Broken Chain and Flag A149

1958, Sept. 15 ***Perf. 13½x13***

453	A148	10m violet brown	.20	.20

35th anniv. of the death of Sayed Darwich, Arab composer.

1958, Oct. 14 **Photo.** **Wmk. 318**

454	A149	10m carmine rose	.20	.20

Establishment of the Republic of Iraq. See Syria-UAR No. 13.

Maps and Cogwheels — A150

1958, Dec. 8 ***Perf. 13x13½***

455	A150	10m blue	.20	.20

Issued to publicize the Economic Conference of Afro-Asian Countries, Cairo, Dec. 8.

Overprinted in Red in English and Arabic in 3 Lines: "Industrial and Agricultural Production Fair"

1958, Dec. 9

456	A150	10m lt red brown	.20	.20

Issued to publicize the Industrial and Agricultural Production Fair, Cairo, Dec. 9.

Dr. Mahmoud Azmy and UN Emblem A151

1958, Dec. 10

457	A151	10m dull violet	.20	.20
458	A151	35m green	.30	.20

10th anniv. of the signing of the Universal Declaration of Human Rights.

For overprints see Nos. N70-N71.

University Building, Sphinx, "Education" and God Thoth — A152

1958, Dec. 21 **Photo.** **Wmk. 318**

459	A152	10m grnsh black	.20	.20

50th anniversary of Cairo University.

No. 337 Surcharged

1959, Jan. 20 **Wmk. 195** ***Perf. 13½***

460	A112	55m on 100m henna brn	.40	.25

For overprint see No. N72.

Emblem A153

1959, Feb. 2 ***Perf. 13x13½***

461	A153	10m lt olive green	.20	.20

Afro-Asian Youth Conf., Cairo, Feb. 2.

See Syria UAR issues for stamps of designs A141, A149, A154, A156, A157, A162, A170, A172, A173, A179 with denominations in piasters (p).

Arms of UAR — A154

Perf. 13½x13

1959, Feb. 22 **Photo.** **Wmk. 318**

462	A154	10m green, blk & red	.20	.20

First anniversary, United Arab Republic. See Syria UAR No. 17.

Nile Hilton Hotel A155

1959, Feb. 22 ***Perf. 13x13½***

463	A155	10m dark gray	.20	.20

Opening of the Nile Hilton Hotel, Cairo.

Globe, Radio and Telegraph A156

1959, Mar. 1

464	A156	10m violet	.20	.20

Arab Union of Telecommunications. See Syria-UAR Nos. C20-C21.

United Arab States Issue

Flags of UAR and Yemen A157

1959, Mar. 8

465	A157	10m sl grn, car & blk	.20	.20

First anniversary of United Arab States. See Syria-UAR No. 16.

Oil Derrick and Pipe Line — A158

Perf. 13½x13

1959, Apr. 16 **Litho.** **Wmk. 318**

466	A158	10m lt bl & dk bl	.20	.20

First Arab Petroleum Congress, Cairo.

Railroad A159

Designs: No. 468, Bus on highway. No. 469, River barge. No. 470, Ocean liner. No. 471, Telecommunications on map. No. 472, Stamp printing building, Heliopolis. No. 472A, Ship, train, plane and motorcycle mail carrier.

1959, July 23 **Photo.** ***Perf. 13x13½***

Frame in Gray

467	A159	10m maroon	.60	.20
468	A159	10m green	.60	.20
469	A159	10m violet	.60	.20
470	A159	10m dark blue	.60	.20
471	A159	10m dull purple	.60	.20
472	A159	10m scarlet	.60	.20
		Nos. 467-472 (6)	3.60	1.20

Souvenir Sheet

Imperf

472A	A159	50m green & red	*6.00*	*5.00*

No. 472A for the 7th anniv. of the Egyptian revolution of 1952 and was sold only with 5 sets of Nos. 467-472.

Globe, Swallows and Map — A160

1959, Aug. 8 ***Perf. 13½x13***

473	A160	10m maroon	.20	.20

Convention of the Assoc. of Arab Emigrants in the US.

Types of 1953-58 without "Egypt" and

St. Simon's Gate, Bosra, Syria — A161

Designs: 1m, Farmer's wife. 2m, Ibn-Tulun's Mosque. 3m, Princess Nofret. 4m, 14th century glass lamp (design lacks "1963" of A217). 5m, "Industry" (factories and cogwheel). 10m, Ramses II. 15m, Omayyad Mosque, Damascus. 20m, Lotus vase, Tutankhamen treasure.

35m, Eagle, ship and cargo. 40m, Scribe statue. 45m, Saladin's citadel, Aleppo. 55m, Eagle, cotton and wheat. 60m, Dam and factory. 100m, Eagle, hand, cotton and grain. 200m, Palmyra ruins, Syria. 500m, Queen Nefertiti, inscribed "UAR" (no ovpt.).

Perf. 13½x14, 14x13½

1959-60	**Wmk. 328**		**Photo.**	
474 A136	1m vermilion		.20	.20
475 A138	2m dp blue ('60)		.20	.20
476 A143	3m maroon		.20	.20
477 A217	4m green ('60)		.20	.20
478 A138	5m black ('60)		.20	.20
479 A137	10m dk ol grn		.20	.20
480 A138	15m deep claret		.20	.20
481 A138	20m crimson ('60)		.20	.20
482 A161	30m brown vio		.30	.20
483 A138	35m lt vio bl ('60)		.30	.20
484 A143	40m sepia		.55	.20
485 A161	45m lil gray ('60)		.90	.20
486 A138	55m brt blue grn		.90	.20
487 A138	60m dp purple ('60)		.55	.20
488 A138	100m org & sl grn ('60)		2.00	.20
489 A161	200m lt blue & mar		3.00	.20
490 A112	500m dk gray & red ('60)		5.75	.20
	Nos. 474-490 (17)		15.85	3.40

See Nos. 532-535.

Shield and Cogwheel — A162

Perf. 13½x13

1959, Oct. 20 Photo. Wmk. 328

491 A162 10m brt car rose .20 .20

Issued for Army Day, 1959.
See Syria-UAR No. 32.

Cairo Museum A163

1959, Nov. 18 ***Perf. 13x13½***

492 A163 10m olive gray .20 .20

Centenary of Cairo museum.

Abu Simbel Temple of Ramses II — A164

1959, Dec. 22 ***Perf. 11x11½***

493 A164 10m lt red brn, *pnksh* .20 .20

Issued as propaganda to save historic monuments in Nubia threatened by the construction of Aswan High Dam.

Postrider, 12th Century A165

1960, Jan. 2 ***Perf. 13x13½***

494 A165 10m dark blue .20 .20

Issued for Post Day, Jan. 2.

Hydroelectric Power Station, Aswan Dam — A166

1960, Jan. 9

495 A166 10m violet blk .20 .20

Inauguration of the Aswan Dam hydroelectric power station, Jan. 9.

A167

10m, Arabic and English Description of Aswan High Dam. 35m, Architect's Drawing of Aswan High Dam.

1960, Jan. 9 ***Perf. 11x11½***

496	10m claret	.40	.20
497	35m claret	.60	.20
a.	A167 Pair, #496-497	1.00	.20

Start of work on the Aswan High Dam.

Symbols of Agriculture and Industry — A169

Arms and Flag — A170

1960, Jan. 16 ***Perf. 13½x13***

498 A169 10m gray grn & sl grn .20 .20

Industrial and Agricultural Fair, Cairo.

1960, Feb. 22 Photo. Wmk. 328

499 A170 10m green, blk & red .20 .20

2nd anniversary of the proclamation of the United Arab Republic.
See Syria-UAR No. 38.

No. 340 Overprinted "UAR" in English and Arabic in Red

Perf. 13½ **Wmk. 195**

1960

500 A112 £1 dk grn, blk & red 11.00 2.00

"Art" — A171

Perf. 13½x13

1960, Mar. 1 Wmk. 328

501 A171 10m brown .20 .20

Issued to publicize the 3rd Biennial Exhibition of Fine Arts in Alexandria.

Arab League Center, Cairo A172

1960, Mar. 22 Photo. ***Perf. 13x13½***

502 A172 10m dull grn & blk .20 .20

Opening of Arab League Center and Arab Postal Museum, Cairo.
See Syria-UAR No. 40.

Refugees Pointing to Map of Palestine A173

1960, Apr. 7

503 A173 10m orange ver .40 .20
504 A173 35m Prus blue .60 .20

World Refugee Year, 7/1/59-6/30/60.

See Nos. N73-N74. See also Syria-UAR Nos. 43-44.

Weight Lifter — A174

Stadium, Cairo — A175

Sports: No. 506, Basketball. No. 507, Soccer. No. 508, Fencing. No. 509, Rowing. 30m, Steeplechase, horiz. 35m, Swimming, horiz.

Perf. 13½x13

1960, July 23	**Photo.**	**Wmk. 328**	
505 A174	5m gray	.40	.20
506 A174	5m brown	.40	.20
507 A174	5m dp claret	.40	.20
508 A174	10m brt carmine	.40	.20
509 A174	10m gray green	.40	.20
a.	Vert. or horiz. strip, #505-509	2.00	
510 A174	30m purple	.50	.20
511 A174	35m dark blue	.60	.20
	Nos. 505-511 (7)	3.10	1.40

Souvenir Sheet

Imperf

512 A175 100m car & brown 1.75 1.00

Nos. 505-511 for the 17th Olympic Games, Rome, Aug. 25-Sept. 11.

Dove and UN Emblem — A176

35m, Lights surrounding UN emblem, horiz.

Perf. 13½x13

1960, Oct. 24 Wmk. 328

513 A176 10m purple .20 .20
514 A176 35m brt rose .25 .20

15th anniversary of United Nations.

Abu Simbel Temple of Queen Nefertari — A177

Perf. 11x11½

1960, Nov. 14 Photo. Wmk. 328

515 A177 10m ocher, *buff* .20 .20

Issued as propaganda to save historic monuments in Nubia and in connection with the UNESCO meeting, Paris, Nov. 14.

Model Post Office A178

1961, Jan. 2 ***Perf. 13x13½***

516 A178 10m brt car rose .20 .20

Issued for Post Day, Jan. 2.

Eagle, Fasces and Victory Wreath — A179

Wheat and Globe Surrounded by Flags — A180

1961, Feb. 22 ***Perf. 13½x13***

517 A179 10m dull violet .20 .20

3rd anniversary of United Arab Republic.
See Syria-UAR No. 50.

1961, Mar. 21 Wmk. 328

518 A180 10m vermilion .20 .20

Intl. Agricultural Exhib., Cairo, 3/21-4/20.

Patrice Lumumba and Map A181

Reading Braille and WHO Emblem A182

1961, Mar. 30 ***Perf. 13½x13***
519 A181 10m black .20 .20

Africa Day, Apr. 15 and 3rd Conf. of Independent African States, Cairo, Mar. 25-31.

1961, Apr. 6 **Photo.**
520 A182 10m red brown .20 .20

WHO Day. See Nos. B21, N80.

Tower of Cairo — A183

Arab Woman and Son, Palestine Map — A184

1961, Apr. 11 ***Perf. 13½x13***
521 A183 10m grnsh blue .20 .20

Opening of the 600-foot Tower of Cairo, on island of Gizireh. See No. C95.

1961, May 15 **Wmk. 328**
522 A184 10m brt green .30 .20

Issued for Palestine Day. See No. N79.

Symbols of Industry and Electricity A185

Chart and Workers — A186

#524, New buildings and family. #525, Ship, train, bus and radio. #526, Dam, cotton and field. #527, Hand holding candle and family.

1961, July 23 **Photo.** ***Perf. 13x13½***
523 A185 10m dp carmine .40 .20
524 A185 10m brt blue .40 .20
525 A185 10m dk vio brown .40 .20
526 A185 35m dk green .50 .20
527 A185 35m brt purple .50 .20
Nos. 523-527 (5) 2.20 1.00

Souvenir Sheet

Imperf

528 A186 100m red brown 2.50 .75

9th anniv. of the revolution.

Map of Suez Canal and Ships — A187

Perf. 11½x11

1961, July 26 **Unwmk.**
529 A187 10m olive .20 .20

Suez Canal Co. nationalization, 5th anniv.

Various Enterprises of Misr Bank — A188

Perf. 13x13½

1961, Aug. 22 **Wmk. 328**
530 A188 10m red brn, *pnksh* .20 .20

The 41st anniversary of Misr Bank.

Flag, Ship's Wheel and Battleship — A189

1961, Aug. 29 **Photo.** ***Perf. 13½x13***
531 A189 10m deep blue .20 .20

Issued for Navy Day.

Type A136 Redrawn, Type A138, Type A217 and:

Eagle of Saladin over Cairo — A190

Designs: 1m, Farmer's wife. 4m, 14th cent. glass lamp. 35m, "Commerce."

1961, Aug. 31 **Unwmk.** ***Perf. 11½***
532 A136 1m blue .20 .20
533 A217 4m olive .20 .20
534 A190 10m purple .20 .20
535 A138 35m slate blue .25 .20
Nos. 532-535 (4) .85 .80

Smaller of two Arabic inscriptions in new positions: 1m, at right above Egyptian numeral; 4m, upward to spot beside waist of lamp; 35m, upper left corner below "UAR." On 4m, "UAR" is 2mm deep instead of 1mm. "Egypt" omitted as in 1959-60.

UN Emblem, Book, Cogwheel, Corn — A191

Perf. 13½x13

1961, Oct. 24 **Photo.** **Wmk. 328**

Design: 35m, Globe and cogwheel, horiz.

536 A191 10m black & ocher .20 .20
537 A191 35m blue grn & brn .20 .20

UN Technical Assistance Program and 16th anniv. of the UN.
See Nos. N81-N82.

Trajan's Kiosk, Philae — A192

1961, Nov. 4 **Unwmk.** ***Perf. 11½***
Size: 60x27mm
538 A192 10m dp vio blue .30 .20

15th anniv. of UNESCO, and to publicize UNESCO's help in safeguarding the monuments of Nubia.

Palette, Brushes, Map of Mediterranean A193

Atom and Educational Symbols A194

1961, Dec. 14 **Wmk. 328** ***Perf. 13½***
539 A193 10m dk red brown .20 .20

Issued to publicize the 4th Biennial Exhibition of Fine Arts in Alexandria.

1961, Dec. 18
540 A194 10m dull purple .20 .20

Issued to publicize Education Day.
See No. N83.

Arms of UAR A195

1961, Dec. 23 **Unwmk.** ***Perf. 11½***
541 A195 10m brt pink, brt grn & blk .20 .20

Victory Day. See No. N84.

Sphinx at Giza — A196

1961, Dec. 27 ***Perf. 11x11½***
542 A196 10m black .20 .20

Issued to publicize the "Sound and Light" Project, the installation of floodlights and sound equipment at the site of the Pyramids and Sphinx.

Post Office Printing Plant, Nasser City A197

1962, Jan. 2 **Photo.** ***Perf. 11½x11***
543 A197 10m dk brown .20 .20

Issued for Post Day, Jan. 2.

Map of Africa, King Mohammed V of Morocco and Flags — A198

1962, Jan. 4 ***Perf. 11x11½***
544 A198 10m indigo .20 .20

African Charter, Casablanca, 1st anniv.

Girl Scout Saluting and Emblem A199

Perf. 13x13½

1962, Feb. 22 **Wmk. 328**
545 A199 10m bright blue .25 .20

Egyptian Girl Scouts' 25th anniversary.

Arab Refugees, Flag and Map — A200

Mother and Child — A201

1962, Mar. 7 ***Perf. 13½x13***
546 A200 10m dark slate green .20 .20

5th anniv. of the liberation of the Gaza Strip.
See No. N85.

1962, Mar. 21 **Photo.**
547 A201 10m dk violet brn .20 .20

Issued for Arab Mother's Day, Mar. 21.

Map of Africa and Post Horn — A202

1962, Apr. 23 **Wmk. 328**
548 A202 10m crimson & ocher .30 .20
549 A202 50m dp blue & ocher .60 .20

Establishment of African Postal Union.

Cadets on Parade and Academy Emblem A203

1962, June 18 *Perf. 13x13½*

550 A203 10m green .20 .20

Egyptian Military Academy, 150th anniv.

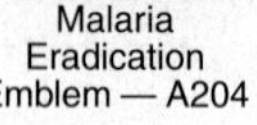

Malaria Eradication Emblem — A204

Theodor Bilharz — A205

1962, June 20 *Perf. 13½x13*

551 A204 10m dk brown & red .20 .20
552 A204 35m dk green & blue .25 .20

WHO drive to eradicate malaria.
See Nos. N87-N88.

1962, June 24 *Perf. 11x11½*

553 A205 10m brown orange .20 .20

Dr. Theodor Bilharz (1825-1862), German physician who first described bilharziasis, an endemic disease in Egypt.

Patrice Lumumba and Map of Africa — A206

Hand on Charter — A207

1962, July 1 **Photo.** **Wmk. 342**

554 A206 10m rose & red .20 .20

Issued in memory of Patrice Lumumba (1925-61), Premier of Congo.

1962, July 10 *Perf. 11x11½*

555 A207 10m brt blue & dk brn .20 .20

Proclamation of the National Charter.

"Birth of the Revolution" A208

Symbolic Designs: #557, Proclamation (Scroll and book). #558, Agricultural Reform (Farm and crescent). #559, Bandung Conference (Dove, globe and olive branch). #560, Birth of UAR (Eagle and flag). #561, Industrialization (cogwheel, factory, ship and bus). #562, Aswan High Dam. #563, Social Revolution (Modern buildings and emblem). 100m, Arms of UAR, emblems of Afro-Asian and African countries and UN.

1962, July 23 *Perf. 11½*

556 A208 10m brn, dk red brn & pink .20 .20
557 A208 10m dk blue & sepia .20 .20
558 A208 10m sepia & brt bl .20 .20
559 A208 10m olive & dk ultra .20 .20
560 A208 10m grn, blk & red .20 .20
561 A208 10m brn org & indigo .20 .20
562 A208 10m brn org & vio blk .20 .20
563 A208 10m orange & blk .20 .20
Nos. 556-563 (8) 1.60 1.60

Souvenir Sheets

Perf. 11½

564 A208 100m grn, pink, red & blk 1.10 .75

10th anniv. of the revolution.
#564 exists imperf. Same value.

Mahmoud Moukhtar, Museum and Sculpture A209

1962, July 24 *Perf. 11½x11*

565 A209 10m lt vio bl & olive .30 .20

Opening of the Moukhtar Museum, Island of Gezireh. The sculpture is "La Vestale de Secrets" by Moukhtar.

Flag of Algeria and Map of Africa Showing Algeria — A210

1962, Aug. 15 *Perf. 11x11½*

566 A210 10m multicolored .20 .20

Algeria's independence, July 1, 1962.

Rocket, Arms of UAR and Atom Symbol — A211

1962, Sept. 1 **Photo.** **Wmk. 342**

567 A211 10m brt grn, red & blk .20 .20

Launching of UAR rockets.

Rifle and Target — A212

Map of Africa, Table Tennis Paddle, Net and Ball — A213

1962, Sept. 18 *Perf. 11½*

568 A212 5m green, blk & red .40 .20
569 A213 5m green, blk & red .40 .20
a. Pair, #568-569 .80 .20
570 A212 10m bister, bl & dk grn .50 .20
571 A213 10m bister, bl & dk grn .50 .20
a. Pair, #570-571 1.00 .25
572 A212 35m dp ultra, red & blk 1.00 .20
573 A213 35m dp ultra, red & blk 1.00 .20
a. Pair, #572-573 2.00 .45
Nos. 568-573 (6) 3.80 1.20

38th World Shooting Championships and the 1st African Table Tennis Tournament. Types A212 and A213 are printed se-tenant at the base.

Dag Hammarskjold and UN Emblem — A214

Perf. 11½x11

1962, Oct. 24 **Photo.** **Wmk. 342**

Portrait in Slate Blue

574 A214 5m deep lilac .40 .20
575 A214 10m olive .50 .20
576 A214 35m deep ultra .65 .20
Nos. 574-576 (3) 1.55 .60

Dag Hammarskjold, Secretary General of the UN, 1953-61, and 17th anniv. of the UN.
See Nos. N89-N91.

Queen Nefertari Crowned by Isis and Hathor — A215

1962, Oct. 31 *Perf. 11½*

577 A215 10m blue & ocher .20 .20

Issued to publicize the UNESCO campaign to safeguard the monuments of Nubia.

Jet Trainer, Hawker Hart Biplane and College Emblem A216

1962, Nov. 2 *Perf. 11½x11*

578 A216 10m bl, dk bl & crim .20 .20

25th anniversary of Air Force College.

14th Century Glass Lamp and "1963" — A217

Yemen Flag and Hand with Torch — A218

1963, Feb. 20 *Perf. 11x11½*

579 A217 4m dk brn, grn & car .20 .20

Issued for use on greeting cards.
See Nos. 441, 477, 533, N76, N92. For overprint see No. N65.

1963, Mar. 14 **Photo.** **Wmk. 342**

580 A218 10m olive & brt car .20 .20

Establishment of Yemen Arab Republic.

Tennis Player, Pyramids and Globe A219

Perf. 11½x11

1963, Mar. 20 **Unwmk.**

581 A219 10m gray, blk & brn .20 .20

Intl. Lawn Tennis Championships, Cairo.

Cow, UN and FAO Emblems A220

Designs: 10m, Corn, wheat and emblems, vert. 35m, Wheat, corn and emblems.

Perf. 11½x11, 11x11½

1963, Mar. 21 **Wmk. 342**

582 A220 5m violet & dp org .20 .20
583 A220 10m ultra & yel .20 .20
584 A220 35m blue, yel & blk .25 .20
Nos. 582-584 (3) .65 .60

FAO "Freedom from Hunger" campaign.
See Nos. N93-N95.

Centenary Emblem — A221

Design: 35m, Globe and emblem.

1963, May 8 **Unwmk.** *Perf. 11x11½*

585 A221 10m lt blue, red & mar .20 .20
586 A221 35m lt blue & red .25 .20

Centenary of the Red Cross.
See Nos. N96-N97.

Arab Socialist Union Emblem A222

50m, Tools, torch & symbol of National Charter.

Wmk. 342

1963, July 23 **Photo.** *Perf. 11½*

587 A222 10m slate & rose pink .20 .20

Souvenir Sheets

Perf. 11½

588 A222 50m vio bl & org yel .90 .75

11th anniv. of the revolution and to publicize the Arab Socialist Union.
#588 exists imperf. Same value.

Television Station, Cairo, and Screen A223

1963, Aug. 1 *Perf. 11½x11*

589 A223 10m dk blue & yel .20 .20

2nd Intl. Television Festival, Alexandria, 9/1-10.

Queen Nefertari A224

Swimmer and Map of Suez Canal A225

Designs: 10m, Great Hypostyle Hall, Abu Simbel. 35m, Ramses in moonlight.

Wmk. 342

1963, Oct. 1 Photo. *Perf. 11*
Size: 25x42mm (5m, 35m); 28x61mm (10m)

590 A224 5m brt vio blue & yel .20 .20
591 A224 10m gray, blk & red org .20 .20
592 A224 35m org yel & blk .45 .20
Nos. 590-592 (3) .85 .60

UNESCO world campaign to save historic monuments in Nubia.
See Nos. N98-N100.

1963, Oct. 15

593 A225 10m blue & sal rose .20 .20

Intl. Suez Canal Swimming Championship.

Ministry of Agriculture — A226

Perf. 11½x11

1963, Nov. 20 Wmk. 342

594 A226 10m multicolored .20 .20

50th anniv. of the Ministry of Agriculture.

Modern Building and Map of Africa and Asia A227

1963, Dec. 7

595 A227 10m multicolored .20 .20

Afro-Asian Housing Congress, Dec. 7-12.

Scales, Globe, UN Emblem A228

1963, Dec. 10

596 A228 5m dk green & yel .20 .20
597 A228 10m blue, gray & blk .20 .20
598 A228 35m rose red, pink & red .25 .20
Nos. 596-598 (3) .65 .60

15th anniv. of the Universal Declaration of Human Rights.
See Nos. N101-N103.

Sculpture, Arms of Alexandria and Palette with Flags — A229

1963, Dec. 12 *Perf. 11x11½*

599 A229 10m pale bl, dk bl & brn .20 .20

Issued to publicize the 5th Biennial Exhibition of Fine Arts in Alexandria.

Lion and Nile Hilton Hotel — A230

Vase, 13th Century — A231

Pharaoh Userkaf (5th Dynasty) A232

Designs: 1m, Vase, 14th century. 2m, Ivory headrest. 3m, Pharaonic calcite boat. 4m, Minaret and gate. 5m, Nile and Aswan High Dam. 10m, Eagle of Saladin over pyramids. 15m, Window, Ibn Tulun's mosque. No. 608, Mitwalli Gate, Cairo. 35m, Nefertari. 40m, Tower Hotel. 55m, Sultan Hassan's Mosque. 60m, Courtyard, Al Azhar University. 200m, Head of Ramses II. 500m, Funerary mask of Tutankhamen.

1964-67 Unwmk. Photo. *Perf. 11*
Size: Nos. 608, 612, 19x24mm; others, 24x29mm

600 A231 1m citron & ultra .20 .20
601 A230 2m magenta & bis .20 .20
602 A230 3m sal, org & bl .20 .20
603 A235 4m och, blk & ultra .30 .20
604 A230 5m brn & brt blue .20 .20
a. 5m brown & dark blue .45 .20
605 A231 10m green, dk brn & lt brn .20 .20
606 A230 15m ultra & yel .20 .20
607 A230 20m brn org & blk .25 .20
608 A231 20m lt olive grn ('67) .25 .20
609 A231 30m yellow & brown .30 .20
610 A231 35m sal, och & ultra .30 .20
611 A231 40m ultra & yellow .40 .20
612 A231 55m brt red lil ('67) .65 .20
613 A231 60m grnsh bl & yel brn .55 .20

Wmk. 342

614 A232 100m dk vio brn & sl 1.40 .20
615 A232 200m bluish blk & yel brn 3.00 .40
616 A232 500m ultra & dp org 5.25 .80
Nos. 600-616 (17) 13.85 4.20

Nos. 603 & N107 lack the vertically arranged dates which appear at lower right on #619.
See Nos. N104-N116.

HSN Commission Emblem — A233

Perf. 11x11½

1964, Jan. 10 Wmk. 342

617 A233 10m dull bl, dk bl & yel .20 .20

1st conf. of the Commission of Health, Sanitation and Nutrition.

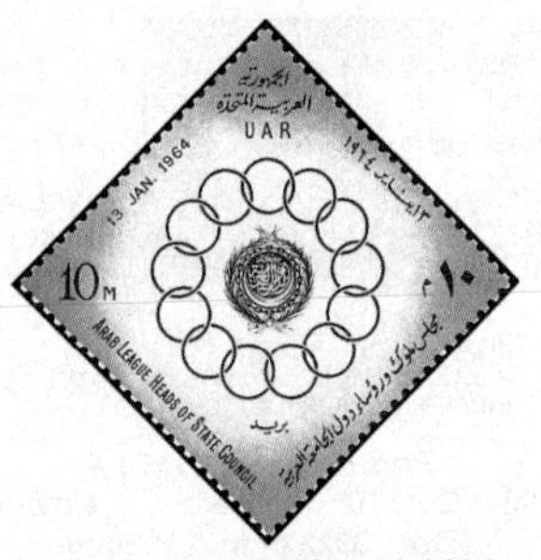

Arab League Emblem — A234

1964, Jan. 13 *Perf. 11*

618 A234 10m brt green & blk .20 .20

1st meeting of the Heads of State of the Arab League, Cairo, January.
See No. N117.

Minaret at Night — A235

1964 Unwmk. *Perf. 11*

619 A235 4m emerald, blk & red .20 .20

Issued for use on greeting cards.
See Nos. 603, N107, N118.

Old and New Dwellings and Map of Nubia A236

Perf. 11½x11

1964, Feb. 27 Photo. Wmk. 342

620 A236 10m dull vio & yel .20 .20

Resettlement of Nubian population.

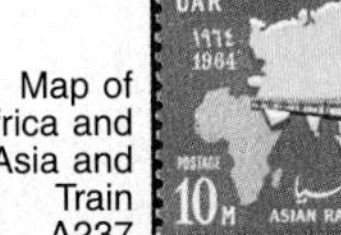

Map of Africa and Asia and Train A237

1964, Mar. 21

621 A237 10m dull bl, dk bl & yel .20 .20

Asian Railway Conference, Cairo, Mar. 21.

Ikhnaton and Nefertiti with Children — A238

1964, Mar. 21 *Perf. 11x11½*

622 A238 10m dk brown & ultra .20 .20

Issued for Arab Mother's Day, Mar. 21.

APU Emblem — A239

WHO Emblem — A240

1964, Apr. 1 Photo. Wmk. 342

623 A239 10m org brn & bl, *sal* .20 .20

Permanent Office of the APU, 10th anniv.
See No. N119.

1964, Apr. 7

624 A240 10m dk blue & red .20 .20

World Health Day (Anti-Tuberculosis).
See No. N120.

Statue of Liberty, World's Fair Pavilion and Pyramids A241

1964, Apr. 22 *Perf. 11½x11*

625 A241 10m brt green & ol, *grysh* .25 .20

New York World's Fair, 1964-65.

Nile and Aswan High Dam A242

1964, May 15 Unwmk. *Perf. 11½*

626 A242 10m black & blue .20 .20

The diversion of the Nile.

"Land Reclamation" — A243

Design: No. 628, "Electricity," Aswan High Dam hydroelectric station.

1964, July 23 *Perf. 11½*

627 A243 10m yellow & emer .20 .20
628 A243 10m green & blk .20 .20

Land reclamation and hydroelectric power due to the Aswan High Dam.
An imperf. souvenir sheet, issued July 23, contains two 50m black and blue stamps showing Aswan High Dam before and after diversion of the Nile. Value $2.

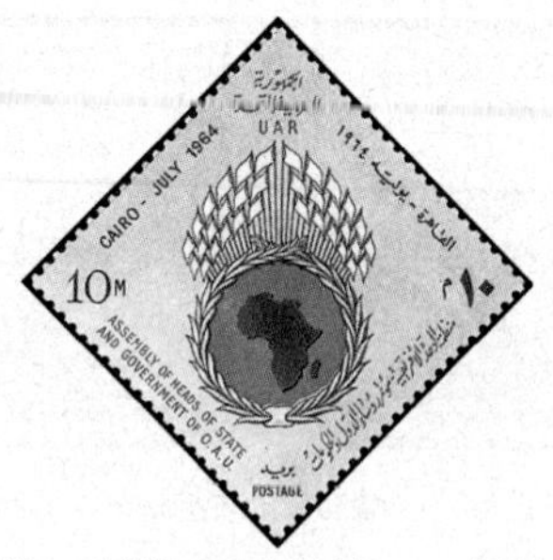

Map of Africa and 34 Flags — A244

1964, July 17 **Photo.**
629 A244 10m brn, brt bl & blk .20 .20

Assembly of Heads of State and Government of the Organization for African Unity at Cairo in July.

Jamboree Emblem — A245

Design: No. 631, Emblem of Air Scouts.

1964, Aug. 28 **Unwmk.** ***Perf. 11½***
630 A245 10m red, grn & blk .25 .20
631 A245 10m green & red .25 .20
a. Pair, #630-631 .45 .20

The 6th Pan Arab Jamboree, Alexandria.

Flag of Algeria A246

1964, Sept. 5 ***Perf. 11½x11***

Flags in Original Colors

632 A246 10m Algeria .25 .20
633 A246 10m Iraq .25 .20
634 A246 10m Jordan .25 .20
635 A246 10m Kuwait .25 .20
636 A246 10m Lebanon .25 .20
637 A246 10m Libya .25 .20
638 A246 10m Morocco .25 .20
639 A246 10m Saudi Arabia .25 .20
640 A246 10m Sudan .25 .20
641 A246 10m Syria .25 .20
642 A246 10m Tunisia .25 .20
643 A246 10m UAR .25 .20
644 A246 10m Yemen .25 .20
Nos. 632-644 (13) 3.25 2.60

2nd meeting of the Heads of State of the Arab League, Alexandria, Sept. 1964.

World Map, Dove, Olive Branches and Pyramids — A247

1964, Oct. 5 ***Perf. 11½***
645 A247 10m slate blue & yel .20 .20

Conference of Heads of State of Non-Aligned Countries, Cairo, Oct. 1964.

Pharaonic Athletes A248

Designs from ancient decorations: 10m, Four athletes, vert. 35m, Wrestlers, vert. 50m, Pharaoh in chariot hunting.

Perf. 11½x11, 11x11½

1964, Oct. 10 **Photo.** **Unwmk.**

Sizes: 39x22mm, 22x39mm

646 A248 5m lt green & org .25 .20
647 A248 10m slate bl & lt brn .25 .20
648 A248 35m dull vio & lt brn .50 .20

Size: 58x24mm

649 A248 50m ultra & brn org .90 .25
Nos. 646-649 (4) 1.90 .85

18th Olympic Games Tokyo, Oct. 10-25.

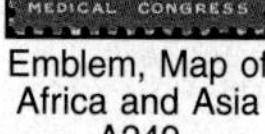

Emblem, Map of Africa and Asia A249

Map of Africa, Communication Symbols A250

1964, Oct. 10 ***Perf. 11x11½***
650 A249 10m violet & yellow .20 .20

First Afro-Asian Medical Congress.

1964, Oct. 24
651 A250 10m green & blk .20 .20

Pan-African and Malagasy Posts and Telecommunications Cong., Cairo, Oct. 24-Nov. 6.

Horus and Facade of Nefertari Temple, Abu Simbel A251

Ramses II — A252

Designs: 35m, A god holding rope of life, Abu Simbel. 50m, Isis of Kalabsha, horiz.

1964, Oct. 24 ***Perf. 11½, 11x11½***
652 A251 5m grnsh bl & yel brn .25 .20
653 A252 10m sepia & brt yel .40 .20
654 A251 35m brown org & indigo 1.00 .30
Nos. 652-654 (3) 1.65 .70

Souvenir Sheet

Imperf

655 A252 50m olive & vio blk 1.40 .70

"Save the Monuments of Nubia" campaign. No. 655 contains one horiz. stamp.

Emblems of Cooperation, Rural Handicraft and Women's Work — A253

Perf. 11½x11

1964, Dec. 8 **Photo.** **Unwmk.**
656 A253 10m yellow & dk blue .20 .20

25th anniv. of the Ministry of Social Affairs.

UN, UNESCO Emblems, Pyramids A254

Minaret, Mardani Mosque A255

1964, Dec. 24 ***Perf. 11x11½***
657 A254 10m ultra & yellow .20 .20

Issued for UNESCO Day.

1965, Jan. 20 **Photo.** ***Perf. 11***
658 A255 4m blue & dk brown .20 .20

Issued for use on greeting cards.
See No. N121.

Police Emblem over City A256

Oil Derrick and Emblem A257

Perf. 11x11½

1965, Jan. 25 **Wmk. 342**
659 A256 10m black & yellow .45 .20

Issued for Police Day.

1965, Mar. 16 **Photo.**
660 A257 10m dk brown & yellow .35 .20

5th Arab Petroleum Congress and the 2nd Arab Petroleum Exhibition.

Flags and Emblem of the Arab League — A258

Red Crescent and WHO Emblem — A259

Design: 20m, Arab League emblem, horiz.

1965, Mar. 22 **Wmk. 342**
661 A258 10m green, red & blk .40 .25
662 A258 20m ultra & brown .60 .30

20th anniversary of the Arab League.

See Nos. N122-N123.

1965, Apr. 7 **Photo.**
663 A259 10m blue & crimson .30 .20

World Health Day (Smallpox: Constant Alert).
See No. N124.

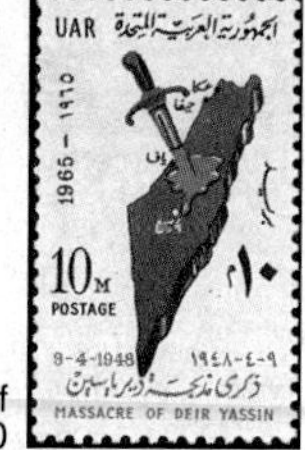

Dagger in Map of Palestine — A260

1965, Apr. 9 ***Perf. 11x11½***
664 A260 10m black & red .75 .20

Deir Yassin massacre, Apr. 9, 1948.
See No. N125.

ITU Emblem, Old and New Communication Equipment — A261

1965, May 17 ***Perf. 11½x11***
665 A261 5m violet blk & yel .20 .20
666 A261 10m red & yellow .25 .20
667 A261 35m dk blue, ultra & yel .75 .50
Nos. 665-667 (3) 1.20 .90

Cent. of the ITU. See #N126-N128.

Library Aflame and Lamp A262

1965, June 7 **Photo.** **Wmk. 342**
668 A262 10m black, grn & red .25 .20

Burning of the Library of Algiers, 6/7/62.

Sheik Mohammed Abdo (1850-1905), Mufti of Egypt — A263

1965, July 11 ***Perf. 11x11½***
669 A263 10m Prus blue & bis brn .20 .20

Pouring Ladle (Heavy Industry) A264

President Gamal Abdel Nasser and Emblems of Arab League, African Unity Organization, Afro-Asian Countries and UN — A265

#670, Search for off-shore oil. #672, Housing, construction in Nasser City (diamond shaped).

1965, July 23 *Perf. 11½*

670 A264 10m indigo & lt blue .20 .20
671 A264 10m brown & yellow .20 .20
672 A264 10m yel brn & blk .20 .20
673 A265 100m lt green & blk 2.25 1.40
Nos. 670-673 (4) 2.85 2.00

13th anniversary of the revolution.

The 100m was printed in sheets of six, consisting of two singles and two vertical pairs. Margins and gutters contain multiple UAR coat of arms in light green. Size: 240x330mm.

4th Pan Arab Games Emblem A266

Map and Emblems of Previous Games — A267

#675, Swimmers Zeitun & Abd el Gelil, arms of Alexandria. 35m, Race horse "Saadoon."

Perf. 11½x11; 11½ (#676)

1965, Sept. 2 Photo. Wmk. 342

674 A266 5m blue & red .20 .20
675 A266 10m dp blue & dk brn .25 .20
676 A267 10m org brn & dp bl .30 .20
677 A266 35m green & brown .50 .30
Nos. 674-677 (4) 1.25 .90

4th Pan Arab Games, Cairo, Sept. 2-11. #675 for the long-distance swimming competition at Alexandria, a part of the Games.

Map of Arab Countries, Emblem of Arab League and Broken Chain A268

1965, Sept. 13 Photo. *Perf. 11½*

678 A268 10m brown & yellow .20 .20

3rd Arab Summit Conf., Casablanca, 9/13.

Land Forces Emblem and Sun — A269

Perf. 11x11½

1965, Oct. 20 Wmk. 342

679 A269 10m bister brn & blk .25 .20

Issued for Land Forces Day.

Map of Africa, Torch and Olive Branches — A270

1965, Oct. 21 *Perf. 11½*

680 A270 10m dull pur & car rose .20 .20

Assembly of Heads of State of the Organization for African Unity.

Ramses II, Abu Simbel, and ICY Emblem A271

Pillars, Philae, and UN Emblem — A272

Designs: 35m, Two Ramses II statues, Abu Simbel and UNESCO emblem. 50m, Cartouche of Ramses II and ICY emblem, horiz.

Wmk. 342

1965, Oct. 24 Photo. *Perf. 11½*

681 A271 5m yellow & slate grn .30 .20
682 A272 10m blue & black .60 .20
683 A271 35m dk violet & yel 1.10 .75
Nos. 681-683 (3) 2.00 1.15

Souvenir Sheet

Imperf

684 A272 50m brt ultra & dk brn 1.90 1.90

Intl. cooperation in saving the Nubian monuments. No. 684 also for the 20th anniv. of the UN. No. 684 contains one 42x25mm stamp.

Al-Maqrizi, Buildings and Books A273

Perf. 11½x11

1965, Nov. 20 Photo. Wmk. 342

685 A273 10m olive & dk slate grn .20 .20

Ahmed Al-Maqrizi (1365-1442), historian.

Flag of UAR, Arms of Alexandria and Art Symbols — A274

1965, Dec. 16 *Perf. 11x11½*

686 A274 10m multicolored .20 .20

6th Biennial Exhibition of Fine Arts in Alexandria, Dec. 16, 1965-Mar. 31, 1966.

Parchment Letter, Carrier Pigeon and Postrider A275

1966, Jan. 2 Wmk. 342 *Perf. 11½*

687 A275 10m multicolored .35 .20
Nos. 687,CB1-CB2 (3) 3.75 3.60

Post Day, Jan. 2.

Lamp and Arch — A276

Exhibition Poster — A277

1966, Jan. 10 Unwmk. *Perf. 11*

688 A276 4m violet & dp org .20 .20

Issued for use on greeting cards.

Perf. 11x11½

1966, Jan. 27 Wmk. 342

689 A277 10m lt blue & blk .20 .20

Industrial Exhibition, Jan. 29-Feb.

Arab League Emblem — A278

Printed Page and Torch — A279

1966, Mar. 22 Photo. Wmk. 342

690 A278 10m brt yellow & pur .20 .20

Arab Publicity Week, Mar. 22-28.

1966, Mar. 25 *Perf. 11x11½*

691 A279 10m dp orange & sl blue .20 .20

Centenary of the national press.

Traffic Signal at Night — A280

Hands Holding Torch, Flags of UAR & Iraq — A281

1966, May 4 Photo. Wmk. 342

692 A280 10m green & red .35 .20

Issued for Traffic Day.

1966, May 26 *Perf. 11x11½*

693 A281 10m dp claret, rose red & brt grn .20 .20

Friendship between UAR and Iraq.

Workers and UN Emblem A282

Perf. 11½x11

1966, June 1 Photo. Wmk. 342

694 A282 5m blue grn & blk .20 .20
695 A282 10m brt rose lil & grn .20 .20
696 A282 35m orange & black .40 .30
Nos. 694-696 (3) .80 .70

50th session of the ILO.

Mobilization Dept. Emblem, People and City — A283

1966, June 30 *Perf. 11x11½*

697 A283 10m dull pur & brn .20 .20

Population sample, May 31-June 16.

"Salah el Din," Crane and Cogwheel A284

Present-day Basket Dance and Pharaonic Dance — A285

#699, Transfer of first stones of Abu Simbel. #700, Development of Sinai (map of Red Sea area and Sinai Peninsula). #701, El Maadi Hospital and nurse with patient.

Wmk. 342

1966, July 23 Photo. *Perf. 11½*

698 A284 10m orange & multi .25 .20
699 A284 10m brt green & multi .25 .20
700 A284 10m yellow & multi .25 .20
701 A284 10m lt blue & multi .25 .20
Nos. 698-701 (4) 1.00 .80

Souvenir Sheet

Imperf

702 A285 100m multicolored 2.00 2.00

14th anniv. of the revolution.

Suez Canal Headquarters, Ships and Map of Canal — A286

1966, July 26 ***Perf. 11½***

703 A286 10m blue & crimson .35 .20

Suez Canal nationalization, 10th anniv.

Cotton, Farmers with Plow and Tractor A287

Perf. 11½x11

1966, Sept. 9 Photo. Wmk. 342

704 A287 5m shown .20 .20
705 A287 10m Rice .20 .20
706 A287 35m Onions .35 .25
Nos. 704-706 (3) .75 .65

Issued for Farmer's Day.

WHO Headquarters, Geneva — A288

Designs: 10m, UN refugee emblem. 35m, UNICEF emblem.

Perf. 11½x11

1966, Oct. 24 Wmk. 342

707 A288 5m olive & brt pur .20 .20
708 A288 10m orange & brt pur .20 .20
709 A288 35m lt blue & brt pur .45 .20
Nos. 707-709 (3) .85 .60

21st anniversary of the United Nations.
See Nos. N129-N131.

World Map and Festival Emblem A289

1966, Nov. 8 Photo.

710 A289 10m brt purple & yellow .20 .20

5th Intl. Television Festival, Nov. 1-10.

Arms of UAR, Rocket and Pylon A290

1966, Dec. 23 Wmk. 342 ***Perf. 11½***

711 A290 10m brt grn & car rose .20 .20

Issued for Victory Day.
See No. N132.

Jackal A291

35m, Alabaster head from Tutankhamen treasure.

1967, Jan. 2 Photo.

712 A291 10m slate, yel & brn .50 .20
713 A291 35m bl, dk vio & ocher 1.00 .30

Issued for Post Day, Jan. 2.

Carnations A292

Workers Planting Tree A293

1967, Jan. 10 Unwmk. ***Perf. 11***

714 A292 4m citron & purple .20 .20

Issued for use on greeting cards.

Perf. 11x11½

1967, Mar. 15 Wmk. 342

715 A293 10m brt green & blk vio .20 .20

Issued to publicize the Tree Festival.

Gamal el-Dine el-Afaghani and Arab League Emblem — A294

1967, Mar. 22 Photo. Wmk. 342

716 A294 10m dp green & dk brn .20 .20

Arab Publicity Week, Mar. 22-28.
See No. N133.

Census Emblem, Man, Woman and Factory A295

1967, Apr. 23 ***Perf. 11½x11***

717 A295 10m black & dp org .20 .20

First industrial census.

Brickmaking Fresco, Tomb of Rekhmire, Thebes, 1504-1450 B.C. — A296

1967, May 1 Photo. Wmk. 342

718 A296 10m olive & orange .20 .20

Issued for Labor Day, 1967.
See No. N134.

Ramses II and Queen Nefertari — A297

Design: 35m, Shooting geese, frieze from tomb of Atet at Meidum, c. 2724 B. C.

Perf. 11½x11

1967, June 7 Photo. Wmk. 342

719 A297 10m multicolored .50 .20
720 A297 35m dk green & org 1.50 .75
Nos. 719-720,C113-C115 (5) 5.00 2.40

Issued for International Tourist Year, 1967.

President Nasser, Crowd and Map of Palestine A298

1967, June 22 ***Perf. 11½***

721 A298 10m dp org, yel & ol 2.00 .75

Issued to publicize Arab solidarity for "the defense of Palestine."

Souvenir Sheet

National Products — A299

1967, July 23 Wmk. 342 ***Imperf.***

722 A299 100m multicolored 2.00 1.25

15th anniv. of the revolution.

Salama Higazi — A300

Perf. 11x11½

1967, Oct. 14 Photo. Wmk. 342

723 A300 20m brown & dk blue .80 .20

50th anniversary of the death of Salama Higazi, pioneer of Egyptian lyric stage.

Stag on Ceramic Disk A301

Design: 55m, Apse showing Christ in Glory, Madonna and Saints, Coptic Museum, and UNESCO Emblem.

1967, Oct. 24 ***Perf. 11½***

724 A301 20m dull rose & dk bl .40 .20
725 A301 55m dk slate grn & yel .85 .25
Nos. 724-725,C117 (3) 2.25 .95

22nd anniv. of the UN.

Savings Bank and Postal Authority Emblems A302

1967, Oct. 31 ***Perf. 11½x11***

726 A302 20m sal pink & dk blue .20 .20

International Savings Day.

Rose — A303

Unwmk.

1967, Dec. 15 Photo. ***Perf. 11***

727 A303 5m green & rose lilac .20 .20

Issued for use on greeting cards.

Pharaonic Dress — A304

Aswan High Dam and Power Lines — A305

Designs: Various pharaonic dresses from temple decorations.

Perf. 11x11½

1968, Jan. 2 Wmk. 342

728 A304 20m brown, grn & buff .75 .20
729 A304 55m lt grn, yel & sepia 1.25 .30
730 A304 80m dk brn, bl & brt rose 2.00 .60
Nos. 728-730 (3) 4.00 1.10

Issued for Post Day, Jan. 2.
See Nos. 752-755.

1968, Jan. 9

731 A305 20m yel, bl & dk brn .20 .20

1st electricity generated by the Aswan Hydroelectric Station.

Alabaster Vessel, Tutankhamen Treasure A306

Girl, Moon and Paint Brushes A308

Capital of Coptic Limestone Pillar A307

Perf. 11x11½, 11½

1968, Jan. 20 Photo. Wmk. 342

732 A306 20m dk ultra, yel & brn .35 .20
733 A307 80m lt grn, dk pur & ol grn .65 .30

2nd International Festival of Museums.

1968, Feb. 15 ***Perf. 11x11½***

734 A308 20m brt blue & black .20 .20

7th Biennial Exhibition of Fine Arts, Alexandria, Feb. 15.

Cattle and Veterinarian — A309

Perf. 11½x11

1968, May 4 Photo. Wmk. 342

735 A309 20m brown, yel & grn .35 .20

8th Arab Veterinary Congress, Cairo.

Human Rights Flame — A310

Perf. 11x11½

1968, July 1 Photo. Wmk. 342

736 A310 20m citron, crim & grn .20 .20
737 A310 60m sky blue, crim & grn .40 .40

International Human Rights Year, 1968.

Open Book with Symbols of Science, Victory Election Result A311

Workers, Cogwheel with Coat of Arms and Open Book — A312

1968, July 23 ***Perf. 11½***

738 A311 20m rose red & sl grn .20 .20

Souvenir Sheet

Imperf

739 A312 100m lt grn, org & pur .90 .80

16th anniversary of the revolution.

Imhotep and WHO Emblem A313

No. 741, Avicenna and WHO emblem.

Perf. 11½x11

1968, Sept. 1 Photo. Wmk. 342

740 A313 20m blue, yel & brn .30 .20
741 A313 20m yellow, bl & brn .30 .20
a. Pair, #740-741 .60 .30

20th anniv. of the WHO. Nos. 740-741 printed in checkerboard sheets of 50 (5x10).

Table Tennis — A314

Perf. 11x11½

1968, Sept. 20 Photo. Wmk. 342

742 A314 20m lt green & dk brn .40 .20

First Mediterranean Table Tennis Tournament, Alexandria, Sept. 20-27.

Factories and Fair Emblem A315

1968, Oct. 20 Wmk. 342 ***Perf. 11½***

743 A315 20m bl gray, red & sl bl .20 .20

Cairo International Industrial Fair.

Temples of Philae — A316

Refugees, Map of Palestine, Refugee Year Emblem A317

55m, Temple at Philae & UNESCO emblem.

1968, Oct. 24 Photo.

744 A316 20m multicolored .50 .20
745 A317 30m multicolored .75 .50
746 A317 55m lt blue, yel & blk 1.25 .75
Nos. 744-746 (3) 2.50 1.45

Issued for United Nations Day, Oct. 24.

Egyptian Boy Scout Emblem — A318

1968, Nov. 1

747 A318 10m dull org & vio bl .30 .20

50th anniversary of Egyptian Boy Scouts.

Pharaonic Sports A319

Design: 30m, Pharaonic sports, diff.

1968, Nov. 1

748 A319 20m pale ol, pale sal & blk .40 .20
749 A319 30m pale blue, buff & pur .60 .20

19th Olympic Games, Mexico City, 10/12-27.

Aly Moubarak A320

Lotus A321

1968, Nov. 9 ***Perf. 11½***

750 A320 20m green, brn & bister .25 .20

Aly Moubarak (1823-93), founder of the modern educational system in Egypt.

1968, Dec. 11 Photo. Wmk. 342

751 A321 5m brt blue, grn & yel .30 .20

Issued for use on greeting cards.

Son of Ramses III — A322

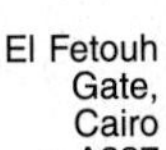

Hefni Nassef — A323

Pharaonic Dress: No. 753, Ramses III. No. 754, Girl carrying basket on her head. 55m, Queen of the New Empire in transparent dress.

1969, Jan. 2 Photo. ***Perf. 11½***

752 A322 5m blue & multi .45 .20
753 A322 20m blue & multi .75 .30
754 A322 20m blue & multi .90 .35
755 A322 55m blue & multi 2.25 .65
Nos. 752-755 (4) 4.35 1.50

Issued for Post Day, Jan. 2.

Perf. 11x11½

1969, Mar. 2 Photo. Wmk. 342

Portrait: No. 757, Mohammed Farid.

756 A323 20m purple & brown .30 .20
757 A323 20m emerald & brown .30 .20
a. Pair, #756-757 .60 .30

50th anniv. of the death of Hefni Nassef (1860-1919) writer and government worker, and Mohammed Farid (1867-1919), lawyer and Speaker of the Nationalist Party.

Teacher and Children A324

ILO Emblem and Factory Chimneys A325

1969, Mar. 2 ***Perf. 11x11½***

758 A324 20m multicolored .20 .20

Arab Teacher's Day.

1969, Apr. 11 Photo. Wmk. 342

759 A325 20m brown, ultra & car .20 .20

50th anniv. of the ILO.

Flag of Algeria, Africa Day and Tourist Year Emblems A326

Perf. 11½x11

1969, May 25 Litho. Wmk. 342

760 A326 10m Algeria .50 .25
761 A326 10m Botswana .50 .25
762 A326 10m Burundi .50 .25
763 A326 10m Cameroun .50 .25
764 A326 10m Cent. Afr. Rep. .50 .25
765 A326 10m Chad .50 .25
766 A326 10m Congo, ex-Belgian .50 .25
767 A326 10m Congo, ex-French .50 .25
768 A326 10m Dahomey .50 .25
769 A326 10m Equatorial Guinea .50 .25
770 A326 10m Ethiopia .50 .25
771 A326 10m Gabon .50 .25
772 A326 10m Gambia .50 .25
773 A326 10m Ghana .50 .25
774 A326 10m Guinea .50 .25
775 A326 10m Ivory Coast .50 .25
776 A326 10m Kenya .50 .25
777 A326 10m Lesotho .50 .25
778 A326 10m Liberia .50 .25
779 A326 10m Libya .50 .25
780 A326 10m Malagasy .50 .25
781 A326 10m Malawi .50 .25
782 A326 10m Mali .50 .25
783 A326 10m Mauritania .50 .25
784 A326 10m Mauritius .50 .25
785 A326 10m Morocco .50 .25
786 A326 10m Niger .50 .25
787 A326 10m Nigeria .50 .25
788 A326 10m Rwanda .50 .25
789 A326 10m Senegal .50 .25
790 A326 10m Sierra Leone .50 .25
791 A326 10m Somalia .50 .25
792 A326 10m Sudan .50 .25
793 A326 10m Swaziland .50 .25
794 A326 10m Tanzania .50 .25
795 A326 10m Togo .50 .25
796 A326 10m Tunisia .50 .25
797 A326 10m Uganda .50 .25
798 A326 10m UAR .50 .25
799 A326 10m Upper Volta .50 .25
800 A326 10m Zambia .50 .25
Nos. 760-800 (41) 20.50 10.25

El Fetouh Gate, Cairo A327

Sculptures from the Egyptian Museum, Cairo — A328

Millenary of Cairo — A329

#802, Al Azhar University. #803, The Citadel. #805, Sculptures, Coptic Museum. #806, Glass plate and vase, Fatimid dynasty, Islamic Museum. #807a, Islamic coin. #807b, Fatimist era jewelry. #807c, Copper vase. #807d, Coins and plaque.

Perf. 11½x11

1969, July 23 Photo. Wmk. 342

801 A327 10m dk brown & multi .20 .20
802 A327 10m green & multi .20 .20
803 A327 10m blue & multi .20 .20

Perf. 11½

804 A328 20m yellow grn & multi .40 .20
805 A328 20m dp ultra & multi .40 .20
806 A328 20m brown & multi .40 .20
Nos. 801-806 (6) 1.80 1.20

Souvenir Sheet

807 A329 Sheet of 4 5.00 5.00
a. 20m dark blue & multi 1.25 .90
b. 20m lilac & multi 1.25 .90
c. 20m yellow & multi 1.25 .90
d. 20m dark green & multi 1.25 .90

Millenium of the founding of Cairo.

African Development Bank Emblem — A330

Perf. 11x11½

1969, Sept. 10 Photo. Wmk. 342

808 A330 20m emerald, yel & vio .20 .20

African Development Bank, 5th anniv.

Pharaonic Boat and UN Emblem A331

Temple of Philae Inundated and UNESCO Emblem A332

Design: 5m, King and Queen from Abu Simbel Temple and UNESCO Emblem (size: 21x38mm).

Perf. 11x11½, 11½x11

1969, Oct. 24 Photo. Wmk. 342

809 A332 5m brown & multi .20 .20
810 A331 20m yellow & ultra .35 .20

Perf. 11½

811 A332 55m yellow & multi .75 .30
Nos. 809-811 (3) 1.30 .70

Issued for United Nations Day.

Ships of 1869 and 1967 and Maps of Africa and Suez Canal — A333

1969, Nov. 15 ***Perf. 11½x11***

812 A333 20m lt blue & multi .50 .20

Centenary of the Suez Canal.

Cairo Opera House and Performance of Aida — A334

1969, Nov. 15

813 A334 20m multicolored .50 .20

Centenary of the Cairo Opera House.

Crowd with Egyptian and Revolutionary Flags — A335

1969, Nov. 15 ***Perf. 11½x11***

814 A335 20m brt grn, dull lil & red .50 .20

Revolution of 1919.

Ancient Arithmetic and Computer Cards A336

Perf. 11½x11

1969, Dec. 17 Photo. Wmk. 342

815 A336 20m multicolored .30 .20

Intl. Congress for Scientific Accounting, Cairo, Dec. 17-19.

Poinsettia A337

Sakkara Step Pyramid A338

El Fetouh Gate, Cairo — A339

Fountain, Sultan Hassan Mosque, Cairo — A340

King Khafre (Ruled c. 2850 B.C.) A341

1969, Dec. 24 Unwmk. ***Perf. 11***

816 A337 5m yellow, grn & car .20 .20

Issued for use on greeting cards.

Wmk. 342 (20m, £1), Unwmkd.
Photo.; Engr. (20m, 55m)

1969-70 ***Perf. 11***

Designs: 5m, Al Azhar Mosque. 10m, Luxor Temple. 50m, Qaitbay Fort, Alexandria.

817 A338 1m multi ('70) .20 .20
818 A338 5m multi ('70) .20 .20
819 A338 10m multi ('70) .25 .20
820 A339 20m dark brown .45 .20
821 A338 50m multi ('70) .70 .20
822 A340 55m slate green .90 .20

Perf. 11½

Photo. & Engr.

823 A341 £1 org & sl grn ('70) 20.00 3.25
Nos. 817-823 (7) 22.70 4.45

See #889-891, 893-897, 899, 901-902, 904.

Veiled Women, by Mahmoud Said — A342

Perf. 11x11½

1970, Jan. 2 Photo. Wmk. 342

824 A342 100m blue & multi 1.75 1.00

Post Day. Sheet of 8 with 2 panes of 4.

Parliament, Scales, Globe and Laurel — A343

1970, Feb. 2 ***Perf. 11½x11***

825 A343 20m blue, vio bl & ocher .35 .20

Intl. Conf. of Parliamentarians on the Middle East Crisis, Cairo, Feb. 2-5.

Map of Arab League Countries, Flag and Emblem A344

Perf. 11½x11

1970, Mar. 22 Photo. Wmk. 342

826 A344 30m brn org, grn & dk pur .35 .20

Arab League, 25th anniv. See No. B42.

Mena House and Sheraton Hotel — A345

1970, Mar. 23

827 A345 20m olive, org & bl .40 .20

Centenary of Mena House and the inauguration of the Cairo Sheraton Hotel.

Manufacture of Medicine — A346

1970, Apr. 20

828 A346 20m brown, yel & bl .60 .20

Production of medicines in Egypt, 30th anniv.

Mermaid — A347

1970, Apr. 20 ***Perf. 11x11½***

829 A347 20m orange, blk & ultra .30 .20

8th Biennial Exhibition of Fine Arts, Alexandria, March 12.

Misr Bank and Talaat Harb — A348

ITU Emblem — A349

1970, May 7 Photo. Wmk. 342

830 A348 20m multicolored .25 .20

50th anniversary of Misr Bank.

1970, May 17 ***Perf. 11x11½***

831 A349 20m dk brn, yel & dull bl .25 .20

World Telecommunications Day.

UPU Headquarters, Bern — A350

1970, May 20 ***Perf. 11½x11***

832 A350 20m multicolored .25 .20

Inauguration of the UPU Headquarters in Bern. See No. C128.

Basketball Player and Map of Africa — A351

UPU, UN and U.P.A.F. Emblems A352

#834, Soccer player, map of Africa & cup, horiz.

Perf. 11x11½, 11½x11

1970, May 25 Photo. Wmk. 342

833 A351 20m lt blue, yel & brn .45 .20
834 A351 20m yellow & multi .40 .20
835 A352 20m ocher, grn & blk .30 .20
Nos. 833-835 (3) 1.15 .60

Africa Day. #833 also for the 5th African basketball championship for men; #834 the annual African Soccer championship; #835 publicizes the African Postal Union seminar.

Fist and Freed Bird — A353

1970, July 23 Photo. *Perf. 11*

836 A353 20m lt green, org & blk .50 .20

Souvenir Sheet

Imperf

837 A353 100m lt blue, dp org & blk 1.75 1.25

18th anniv. of the revolution.

Al Aqsa Mosque on Fire — A354

1970, Aug. 21 Wmk. 342 *Perf. 11*

838 A354 20m multicolored .75 .20
839 A354 60m brt blue & multi 1.75 .75

1st anniv. of the burning of Al Aqsa Mosque, Jerusalem.

Standardization Emblems — A355

1970, Oct. 14 Wmk. 342 *Perf. 11*

840 A355 20m yellow, ultra & grn .30 .20

World Standards Day and 25th anniv. of the Intl. Standardization Organization, ISO.

UN Emblem, Scales and Dove — A356

Temple at Philae A357

Child, Education Year and UN Emblems A358

Designs: 10m, UN emblem. No. 845, 2nd Temple at Philae (denomination at left).

Perf. 11 (5m), 11½ (others)

1970, Oct. 24 Photo. Wmk. 342

841 A356 5m lt bl, rose lil & sl .20 .20
842 A357 10m yel, brn & lt bl .20 .20
843 A358 20m slate & multi .35 .20
844 A357 55m brn, bl & ocher .50 .30
845 A357 55m brn, bl & ocher .50 .25
a. Strip of 3, #842, 844-845 1.60 .70
Nos. 841-845,B43 (6) 2.50 1.75

25th anniv. of the UN. #843 also for Intl. Education Year; #842, 844-845, the work of UNESCO in saving the Temples of Philae. #845a printed in sheets of 35 (15 #842, 10 each #844-845). #844-845 show continuous picture of the Temples at Philae.

Gamal Abdel Nasser — A359

1970, Nov. 6 Wmk. 342 *Perf. 11*

846 A359 5m sky blue & blk .20 .20
847 A359 20m gray green & blk .40 .20
Nos. 846-847,C129-C130 (4) 3.10 1.00

Gamal Abdel Nasser (1918-70), Pres. of Egypt.

Medical Association Building — A360

#849, Old & new National Library. #850, Egyptian Credo (Nasser quotation). #851, Engineering Society, old & new buildings. #852, Government Printing Offices, old & new buildings.

1970, Dec. 20 Photo. *Perf. 11*

848 A360 20m yel, grn & brn .30 .20
849 A360 20m green & multi .30 .20
850 A360 20m lt blue & brn .30 .20
851 A360 20m blue, yel & brn .30 .20
852 A360 20m blue, yel & brn .30 .20
a. Strip of 5, #848-852 1.50 .50

50th anniv. of Egyptian Medical Assoc. (#848); cent. of Natl. Library (#849); Egyptian Engineering Assoc. (#851); sesqui. of Government Printing Offices (#852).

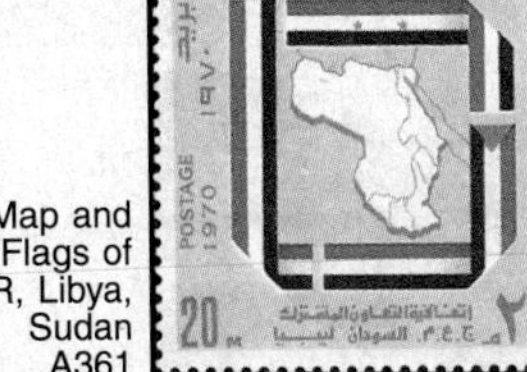

Map and Flags of UAR, Libya, Sudan A361

1970, Dec. 27 *Perf. 11½*

853 A361 20m lt grn, car & blk .30 .20

Signing of the Charter of Tripoli affirming the unity of UAR, Libya & the Sudan, 12/27/70.

Qalawun Minaret — A362

Designs (Minarets): 10m, As Saleh. 20m, Isna. 55m, Al Hakim.

1971, Jan. 2 Wmk. 342 *Perf. 11*

854 A362 5m green & multi .30 .20
855 A362 10m green & multi .70 .25
856 A362 20m green & multi 1.25 .55
857 A362 55m green & multi 2.25 1.00
a. Strip of 4, #854-857 + label 7.50 2.50

Post Day, 1971.
See Nos. 905-908, 932-935.

Gamal Abdel Nasser A363

Photogravure and Engraved

1971 Wmk. 342 *Perf. 11½*

858 A363 200m brn vio & dk bl 3.00 .75
859 A363 500m blue & black 6.00 2.00

Souvenir Sheet

Design: Portrait facing right.

Imperf

860 Sheet of 2 6.00 5.00
a. A363 100m light green & black 2.00 1.50
b. A363 200m blue & black 3.00 2.50

No. 860 commemorates inauguration of the Aswan High Dam, which is shown in margin.
Issued: #860, 1/15; #858-859, 2/1.
See No. 903.

Cotton and Globe A364

1971, Mar. 6 Photo. *Perf. 11½x11*

861 A364 20m lt green, blue & brn .40 .20

Egyptian cotton.

Arab Countries, and Arab Postal Union Emblem A365

1971, Mar. 6 Wmk. 342

862 A365 20m lt bl, org & sl grn .40 .20

9th Arab Postal Cong., Cairo, 3/6-25. See #C131.

Cairo Fair Emblem — A366

1971, Mar. 6 *Perf. 11x11½*

863 A366 20m plum, blk & org .25 .20

Cairo International Fair, March 2-23.

Nesy Ra, Apers Papyrus and WHO Emblem A367

Perf. 11½x11

1971, Apr. 30 Photo. Wmk. 342

864 A367 20m yellow bis & pur .45 .20

World Health Organization Day.

Gamal Abdel Nasser — A368

1971, May 1 *Perf. 11*

865 A368 20m purple & bl gray .35 .20
866 A368 55m blue & purple 1.25 .40

Map of Africa, Telecommunications Symbols — A369

1971, May 17 *Perf. 11½x11*

867 A369 20m blue & multi .35 .20

Pan-African telecommunications system.

Wheelwright A370

Hand Holding Wheat and Laurel A371

Candle Lighting Africa — A372

Perf. 11x11½

1971, July 23 Photo. Wmk. 342

868 A370 20m yellow & multi .30 .20
869 A371 20m tan, grn & ocher .30 .20

Souvenir Sheet

Imperf

870 A372 100m blue & multi 1.50 1.50

19th anniv. of the July Revolution. No. 870 contains one stamp with simulated perforations in gold.

Arab Postal Union Emblem A373

1971, Aug. 3 *Perf. 11½*

871 A373 20m black, yel & grn .30 .20

25th anniv. of the Conf. of Sofar, Lebanon, establishing the APU. See No. C135.

Arab Republic of Egypt

Three Links A374

Perf. 11½x11

1971, Sept. 28 Photo. Wmk. 342

872 A374 20m gray, org brn & blk .50 .25

Confederation of Arab Republics (Egypt, Syria and Libya). See No. C136.

Gamal Abdel Nasser A375

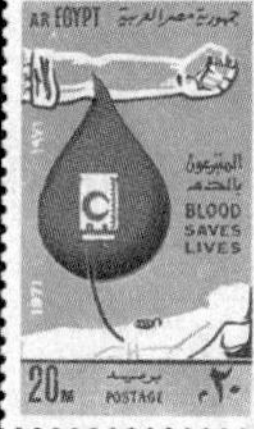

Blood Donation A376

1971, Sept. 28 *Perf. 11x11½*

873 A375 5m slate grn & vio brn .20 .20
874 A375 20m violet brn & ultra .40 .20
875 A375 30m ultra & brown .60 .20
876 A375 55m brown & emerald .80 .20
Nos. 873-876 (4) 2.00 .80

Death of Pres. Gamal Abdel Nasser, 1st anniv.

1971, Oct. 24

877 A376 20m green & carmine .50 .20

"Blood Saves Lives."

Princess Nursing Child, UNICEF Emblem A377

Submerged Pillar, Philae, UNESCO Emblem A379

Equality Year Emblem A378

Perf. 11x11½, 11½x11

1971, Oct. 24 Photo. Wmk. 342

878 A377 5m buff, blk & org brn .20 .20
879 A378 20m red brn, grn, yel & blk .40 .20
880 A379 55m black, lt bl, yel & brn .90 .20
Nos. 878-880,C137 (4) 2.25 .85

UN Day. No. 878 honors UN Intl. Children's Fund; No. 879 for Intl. Year Against Racial Discrimination; No. 880 honors UNESCO.

Postal Traffic Center, Alexandria A380

1971, Oct. 31 *Perf. 11½x11*

881 A380 20m blue & bister .35 .20

Opening of Postal Traffic Center in Alexandria.

Sunflower A381

Abdalla El Nadim A382

1971, Nov. 13 *Perf. 11*

882 A381 5m lt blue & multi .20 .20

For use on greeting cards.

1971, Nov. 14 *Perf. 11x11½*

883 A382 20m green & brown .35 .20

Abdalla El Nadim (1845-1896), journalist, publisher, connected with Orabi Revolution.

Section of Earth's Crust, Map of Africa on Globe A383

1971, Nov. 27 *Perf. 11½x11*

884 A383 20m ultra, yel & brn .50 .20

75th anniv. of Egyptian Geological Survey and Intl. Conference, Nov. 27-Dec. 1.

Postal Union Emblem, Letter and Dove A384

55m, African Postal Union emblem and letter.

1971, Dec. 2

885 A384 5m multicolored .20 .20
886 A384 20m olive, blk & org .20 .20
887 A384 55m red, blk & blue .35 .20
Nos. 885-887,C138 (4) 1.25 .80

10th anniversary of African Postal Union.

Money and Safe Deposit Box A385

1971, Dec. 23 *Perf. 11½*

888 A385 20m rose, brn & grn .45 .20

70th anniversary of Postal Savings Bank.

Types of 1969-70, 1971

Inscribed "A. R. Egypt" and

Ramses II — A385a

Designs as before and: No. 894, King Citi I. No. 897, View of Alexandria. No. 898, Queen Nefertari. No. 900, Sphinx and Middle Pyramid. 100m, Cairo Mosque. 200m, Head of Pharaoh Userkaf.

Wmk. 342 (#892A, 901-904)

1972-76 Photo. Unwmk. *Perf. 11*

889	A338	1m multi	.20	.20
890	A338	1m dk brn ('73)	.20	.20
891	A338	5m multi	.20	.20
892	A385a	5m olive ('73)	.20	.20
892A	A385a	5m bister ('76)	.20	.20
893	A338	10m multi	.20	.20
894	A338	10m lt brn ('73)	.20	.20
895	A339	20m olive	.35	.20
896	A339	20m purple ('73)	.20	.20
897	A338	50m multi	.30	.20
898	A385a	50m dull bl ('73)	.25	.20
899	A340	55m red lilac	.30	.20
900	A340	55m green ('74)	.65	.30
901	A339	100m lt blue, dp org & blk	.45	.30

Perf. 11½

Photo. & Engr.

902	A341	200m yel grn & brn	1.10	.45
903	A363	500m bl & choc	6.50	4.00
904	A341	£1 orange & sl grn	18.00	6.00
		Nos. 889-904 (17)	29.50	13.45

Minaret Type of 1971

5m, West Minaret, Nasser Mosque. 20m, East Minaret, Nasser Mosque. 30m, Minaret, Al Gawli Mosque. 55m, Minaret, Ibn Tulun Mosque.

Wmk. 342

1972, Jan. 2 Photo. *Perf. 11*

905 A362 5m dk green & multi .25 .20
906 A362 20m dk green & multi .75 .20
907 A362 30m dk green & multi 1.60 .25
908 A362 55m dk green & multi 2.40 .50
a. Strip of 4, #905-908 + label 7.50 1.25

Post Day, 1972.

Police Emblem and Activities — A386

1972, Jan. 25 *Perf. 11½*

909 A386 20m dull blue, brn & yel .90 .20

Police Day 1972.

UNESCO, UN and Book Year Emblems — A387

1972, Jan. 25 *Perf. 11x11½*

910 A387 20m lt yel grn, vio bl & yel .35 .20

International Book Year 1972.

Alexandria Biennale A388

1972, Feb. 15 Wmk. 342 *Perf. 11½*

911 A388 20m black, brt rose & yel .45 .20

9th Biennial Exhibition of Fine Arts, Alexandria, Mar., 1972.

Fair Emblem A389

Abdel Moniem Riad A390

1972, Mar. 5 *Perf. 11x11½*

912 A389 20m blue, org & yel grn .35 .20

International Cairo Fair.

1972, Mar. 21 Photo. Wmk. 342

913 A390 20m blue & brown .75 .20

In memory of Brig. Gen. Abdel Moniem Riad (1919-1969), military hero.

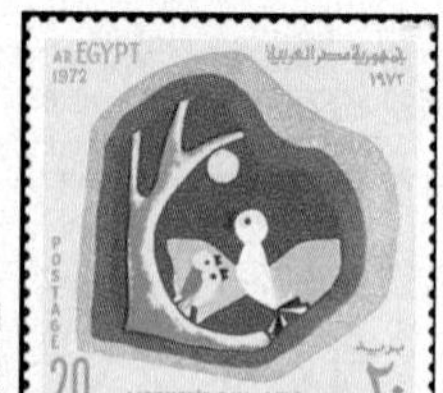

Bird Feeding Young A391

1972, Mar. 21 *Perf. 11½*

914 A391 20m yellow & multi .45 .20

Mother's Day.

Tutankhamen — A392

Design: 55m, Back of chair with king's name and symbols of eternity.

1972, May 22 **Unwmk.**

915 A392 20m gray, blk & ocher 1.00 .25
916 A392 55m purple & yellow 3.00 .75
Nos. 915-916,C142-C143 (4) 10.00 5.00

Discovery of the tomb of Tutankhamen by Howard Carter & Lord Carnarvon, 50th anniv. See No. C144.

Queen Nefertiti A393

Wmk. 342

1972, May 22 Photo. ***Perf. 11½***

917 A393 20m red, blk & gold .30 .20

Soc. of the Friends of Art, 50th anniv.

Map of Africa — A394

1972, May 25 ***Perf. 11x11½***

918 A394 20m purple, bl & brn .30 .20

Africa Day.

Atom Symbol, "Faith and Science" A395

Design: No. 920, Egyptian coat of arms.

1972, July 23 ***Perf. 11½***

919 A395 20m blue, claret & blk .40 .20
920 A395 20m ol grn, gold & blk .40 .20

20th anniversary of the revolution.

Boxing, Olympic and Motion Emblems — A396

Designs (Olympic and Motion Emblems and): 10m, Wrestling. 20m, Basketball.

1972, Aug. 17 ***Perf. 11½x11***

921 A396 5m blue & multi .20 .20
922 A396 10m yellow & multi .20 .20
923 A396 20m ver & multi .35 .20
Nos. 921-923,C149-C152 (7) 3.00 1.85

20th Olympic Games, Munich, 8/26-9/11.

Flag of Confederation of Arab Republics — A397

1972, Sept. 1 Wmk. 342 ***Perf. 11½***

924 A397 20m carmine, bis & blk .40 .20

Confederation of Arab Republics, 1st anniv.

Red Crescent, TB and UN Emblems — A398

Heart and WHO Emblem A399

Refugees, UNRWA Emblem, Map of Palestine — A400

Design: 55m, Inundated Temple of Philae, UNESCO emblem.

Perf. 11x11½ (#925), 11½ (#926, 928), 11 (#927)

1972, Oct. 24 **Photo.**

925 A398 10m brn org, red & bl .25 .20
926 A399 20m green, yel & blk .40 .20
927 A400 30m lt bl, pur & lt brn .75 .35
928 A399 55m brn, gold & bluish gray 1.60 .50
Nos. 925-927 (3) 1.40 .75

UN Day. #925 is for the 14th Regional Tuberculosis Conf., Cairo, 1972; #926 World Health Month; #927 publicizes aid to refugees & #928 the UN campaign to save the Temples at Philae.

Morning Glory — A401

1972, Oct. 24 ***Perf. 11***

929 A401 10m yel, lilac & grn .30 .20

For use on greeting cards.

"Seeing Eye" A402

1972, Nov. 30 ***Perf. 11½***

930 A402 20m multicolored .50 .20

Social Work Day.

Sculling Race, View of Luxor — A403

1972, Dec. 17 Wmk. 342 ***Perf. 11***

931 A403 20m blue & brown .55 .20

3rd Nile Intl. Rowing Festival, Dec. 1972.

Minaret Type of 1971

10m, Al Maridani, 1338. 20m, Bashtak, 1337. 30m, Qusun, 1330. 55m, Al Gashankir, 1306.

1973, Jan. 2

Frame in Bright Yellow Green

932 A362 10m multicolored .40 .20
933 A362 20m multicolored .75 .25
934 A362 30m multicolored 1.60 .40
935 A362 55m multicolored 2.25 1.00
a. Strip of 4, #932-935 + Label 8.00 1.50

Post Day, 1973.

Cairo Fair Emblem A404

Perf. 11½x11

1973, Mar. 21 Photo. Wmk. 342

936 A404 20m gray & multi .30 .20

International Cairo Fair.

Family — A405

1973, Mar. 21 ***Perf. 11x11½***

937 A405 20m multicolored .35 .20

Family planning.

Sania Girls' School and Hoda Sharawi A406

Perf. 11½x11

1973, July 15 Photo. Wmk. 342

938 A406 20m ultra & green .30 .20

Centenary of education for girls and 50th anniversary of the Egyptian Women's Union, founded by Hoda Sharawi.

Rifaa el Tahtawi — A407

1973, July 15 ***Perf. 11x11½***

939 A407 20m brt green, ol & brn .40 .20

Centenary of the death of Rifaa el Tahtawi, champion of democracy and principal of language school.

Omar Makram A408

Abdel Rahman al Gabarti, Historian A409

"Reconstruction and Battle" — A410

No. 941, Mohamed Korayem, martyr.

1973, July 23

940 A408 20m yel grn, bl & brn .40 .20
941 A408 20m lt grn, bl & brn .40 .20
942 A409 20m ocher & brown .40 .20
Nos. 940-942 (3) 1.20 .60

Souvenir Sheet

Imperf

943 A410 110m gold, bl & blk 1.60 1.60

Revolution establishing the republic, 21st anniv.

Grain, Cow, FAO Emblem A411

Perf. 11½x11

1973, Oct. 24 **Wmk. 342**

944 A411 10m brn, dk bl & yel grn .30 .20

10th anniv. of the World Food Org.

Inundated Temples at Philae A412

1973, Oct. 24 ***Perf. 11½***
945 A412 55m blue, pur & org 1.75 .75

UNESCO campaign to save the temples at Philae.

Bank Building A413

1973, Oct. 24
946 A413 20m brn org, grn & blk .35 .20

75th anniv. of the National Bank of Egypt.

Rose — A414

1973, Oct. 24 ***Perf. 11***
947 A414 10m blue & multi .20 .20

For use on greeting cards.

Human Rights Flame A415

Taha Hussein A416

Perf. 11x11½

1973, Dec. 8 Photo. Wmk. 342
948 A415 20m yel grn, dk bl & car .30 .20

25th anniversary of the Universal Declaration of Human Rights.

1973, Dec. 10
949 A416 20m dk blue, brn & emer .30 .20

Dr. Taha Hussein (1893-1973), "Father of Education" in Egypt, writer, philosopher.

Pres. Sadat, Flag and Battle of Oct. 6 — A417

1973, Dec. 23 ***Perf. 11x11½***
950 A417 20m yellow, blk & red .75 .35

October War against Israel (crossing of Suez Canal by Egyptian forces, Oct. 6, 1973). See No. 959.

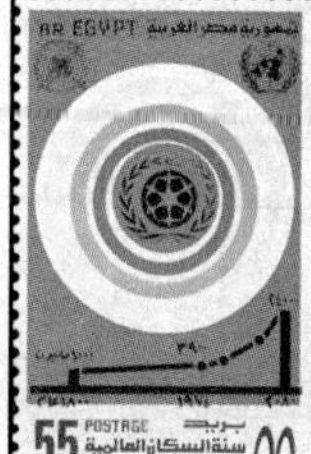
WPY Emblem and Chart — A418

Cairo Fair Emblem — A419

1974, Mar. 21 Wmk. 342 ***Perf. 11***
951 A418 55m org, grn & dk bl .60 .30

World Population Year.

1974, Mar. 21 **Photo.**
952 A419 20m blue & multi .30 .20

Cairo International Fair.

Nurse and Medal of Angels of Ramadan 10 — A420

1974, May 15 ***Perf. 11½***
953 A420 55m multicolored .60 .20

Nurses' and World Hospital Day.

Workers, Relief Carving from Queen Tee's Tomb, Sakhara — A421

1974, May 15 ***Perf. 11***
954 A421 20m yellow, blue & brn .40 .20

Workers' Day.

Pres. Sadat, Troops Crossing Suez Canal — A422

"Reconstruction," Map of Suez Canal and New Building — A423

Sheet of Aluminum A424

Design: 110m, Pres. Sadat's "October Working Paper," symbols of science and development.

1974, July 20 Photo. ***Perf. 11x11½***
955 A422 20m multicolored .50 .25
956 A423 20m blue, gold & blk .50 .25

Perf. 11½

957 A424 20m plum & silver .50 .25
Nos. 955-957 (3) 1.50 .75

Souvenir Sheet

Imperf

958 A424 110m green & multi 1.75 1.75

22nd anniv. of the revolution establishing the republic and for the end of the October War. No. 958 contains one 52x59mm stamp.

Pres. Sadat and Flag — A425

Perf. 11x11½

1974, Oct. 6 Wmk. 342
959 A425 20m yellow, blk & red .75 .25

1st anniv. of Battle. See No. 950.

Palette and Brushes A426

1974, Oct. 6 ***Perf. 11½***
960 A426 30m purple, yel & blk .50 .20

6th Exhibition of Plastic Art.

Teachers and Pupils — A427

1974, Oct. 6 ***Perf. 11x11½***
961 A427 20m multicolored .35 .20

Teachers' Day.

Souvenir Sheet

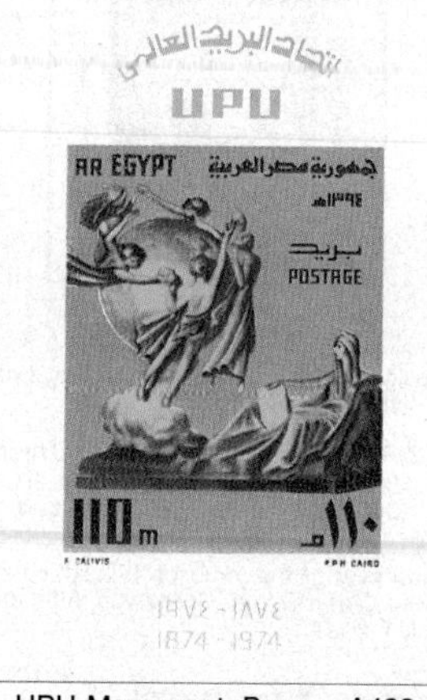
UPU Monument, Bern — A428

1974, Oct. 6 ***Imperf.***
962 A428 110m gold & multi 3.00 2.25

Cent. of the UPU.

Emblems, Cogwheel and Calipers — A429

Refugee Camp under Attack and UN Refugee Organization Emblem — A430

Child and UNICEF Emblem A431

Temple of Philae — A432

1974, Oct. 24 ***Perf. 11½, 11x11½***
963 A429 10m black, bl & yel .30 .20
964 A430 20m dp org, bl & blk .50 .20
965 A431 30m green, bl & brn .70 .30
966 A432 55m black, bl & yel 1.50 .50
Nos. 963-966 (4) 3.00 1.20

UN Day. World Standards Day (10m); Palestinian refugee repatriation (20m); Family Planning (30m); Campaign to save Temple of Philae (55m).

Calla Lily — A433

1974, Nov. 7 *Perf. 11*
967 A433 10m ultra & multi .30 .20

For use on greeting cards.

10m-coins, Smokestacks and Grain — A434

1974, Nov. 7 *Perf. 11½x11*
968 A434 20m yel grn, dk bl & sil .35 .20

International Savings Day.

Organization Emblem and Medical Services — A435

1974, Nov. 7 *Perf. 11½*
969 A435 30m vio, red & gold .50 .20

Health Insurance Organization, 10th anniv.

Mustafa Lutfy El Manfalouty A436

Abbas Mahmoud El Akkad A437

Perf. 11x11½

1974, Dec. 8 Photo. Wmk. 342
970 A436 20m blue blk & brn .30 .20
971 A437 20m brown & bl blk .30 .20
a. Pair, #970-971 .60 .20

Arab writers; El Manfalouty (1876-1924) and El Akkad (1889-1964).

Goddess Maat Facing God Thoth — A438

Fish-shaped Vase — A439

Pharaonic Golden Vase — A440

Sign of Life, Mirror — A441

Wmk. 342

1975, Jan. 2 Photo. *Perf. 11½*
972 A438 20m silver & multi .25 .20
973 A439 30m multicolored .30 .20
974 A440 55m multicolored .70 .35
975 A441 110m blue & multi 1.50 .60
Nos. 972-975 (4) 2.75 1.35

Post Day 1975. Egyptian art works from 12th-5th centuries B.C.

Om Kolthoum — A442

Perf. 11½

1975, Mar. 3 Photo. Unwmk.
976 A442 20m brown .50 .20

In memory of Om Kolthoum, singer.

Crescent, Globe, Al Aqsa and Kaaba — A443

Cairo Fair Emblem — A444

1975, Mar. 25
977 A443 20m multicolored .50 .20

Mohammed's Birthday.

Perf. 11x11½

1975, Mar. 25 Wmk. 342
978 A444 20m multicolored .25 .20

International Cairo Fair.

Kasr El Ainy Hospital WHO Emblem A445

Perf. 11½x11

1975, May 7 Photo. Wmk. 342
979 A445 20m dk brown & blue .50 .20

World Health Organization Day.

Children Reading Book — A446

Children and Line Graph — A447

1975, May 7 *Perf. 11x11½*
980 A446 20m multicolored .40 .20
981 A447 20m multicolored .40 .20

Science Day.

Suez Canal, Globe, Ships, Pres. Sadat — A448

1975, June 5 *Perf. 11½*
982 A448 20m blue, brn & blk 1.00 .30
Nos. 982,C166-C167 (3) 2.95 1.30

Reopening of the Suez Canal, June 5.

Belmabgoknis Flowers — A449

1975, July 30 Photo. Wmk. 342
983 A449 10m green & blue .30 .20

For use on greeting cards.

Sphinx and Pyramids Illuminated — A450

Rural Electrification — A451

Map of Egypt with Tourist Sites — A452

Illustration A452 is reduced.

1975, July 23
984 A450 20m black, org & grn .40 .20
985 A451 20m dk blue & brown .40 .20

Perf. 11

986 A452 110m multicolored 3.50 2.00
Nos. 984-986 (3) 4.30 2.40

23rd anniversary of the revolution establishing the republic. No. 986 printed in sheets of 6 (2x3). Size: 71x80mm.

Volleyball — A453

1975, Aug. 2 Photo. *Perf. 11x11½*
987 A453 20m shown .60 .20
988 A453 20m Running .60 .20
989 A453 20m Torch and flag bearers .60 .20
990 A453 20m Basketball .60 .20
991 A453 20m Soccer .60 .20
a. Strip of 5, #987-991 3.00 .50

6th Arab School Tournament.

Egyptian Flag and Tanks A454

1975 Photo. Unwmk. *Perf. 11½*
992 A454 20m multicolored .75 .25

Two-line Arabic Inscription in Bottom Panel, "M" over "20"

992A A454 20m multicolored .75 .25

No. 992 for 2nd anniv. of October War against Israel, "The Spark;" No. 992A, the Intl. Symposium on October War against Israel 1973, Cairo University, Oct. 27-31.

Issue dates: #992, Oct. 6; #992A, Oct. 24.

Arrows Pointing to Fluke, and Emblems A455

Submerged Wall and Sculpture, UNESCO Emblem A456

Perf. 11x11½

1975, Oct. 24 **Wmk. 342**

993 A455 20m multicolored .50 .20
994 A456 55m multicolored 1.50 .30

UN Day. 20m for Intl. Conf. on Schistosomiasis (Bilharziasis); 55m for UNESCO help in saving temples at Philae. See #C169-C170.

Pharaonic Gate, University Emblem — A457

Al Biruni — A458

1975, Nov. 15 **Photo.** **Wmk. 342**

995 A457 20m multicolored .20 .20

Ain Shams University, 25th anniversary.

1975, Dec. 23 **Photo.** ***Perf. 11x11½***

Arab Philosophers: No. 997, Al Farabi and lute. No. 998, Al Kanady, book and compass.

996 A458 20m blue, brn & grn .50 .20
997 A458 20m blue, brn & grn .50 .20
998 A458 20m blue, brn & grn .50 .20
Nos. 996-998 (3) 1.50 .60

Ibex (Prow) — A459

Post Day (from Tutankhamen's Tomb): 30m, Lioness. 55m, Cow's head (Goddess Hawthor). 110m, Hippopotamus' head (God Horus).

1976, Jan. 2 **Unwmk.** ***Perf. 11½***

999 A459 20m multicolored .75 .30

Wmk. 342

1000 A459 30m brown, gold & ultra 1.25 .35
1001 A459 55m multicolored 2.25 1.10
1002 A459 110m multicolored 3.25 2.25
Nos. 999-1002 (4) 7.50 4.00

Lake, Aswan Dam, Industry and Agriculture — A460

Perf. 11½x11

1976, Jan. 27 **Photo.** **Wmk. 342**

1003 A460 20m multicolored .50 .20

Filling of lake formed by Aswan High Dam.

Fair Emblem — A461

Commemorative Medal — A462

1976, Mar. 15 ***Perf. 11x11½***

1004 A461 20m orange & purple .20 .20

9th International Cairo Fair, Mar. 8-27.

1976, Mar. 15 **Wmk. 342**

1005 A462 20m olive, yel & blk .20 .20

11th Biennial Exhibition of Fine Arts, Alexandria.

Hands Shielding Invalid A463

1976, Apr. 7 **Photo.** ***Perf. 11½***

1006 A463 20m dk grn, lt grn & yel .35 .20

Founding of Faithfulness and Hope Society.

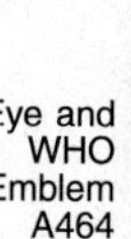

Eye and WHO Emblem A464

1976, Apr. 7

1007 A464 20m dk brn, yel & grn .50 .20

World Health Day: "Foresight prevents blindness."

Pres. Sadat, Legal Department Emblem — A465

Perf. 11½x11

1976, May 15 **Photo.** **Wmk. 342**

1008 A465 20m olive & multi .25 .20

Centenary of State Legal Department.

Scales of Justice — A466

1976, May 15 ***Perf. 11x11½***

1009 A466 20m carmine, blk & grn .25 .20

5th anniversary of Rectification Movement.

Al Ahram Front Page, First Issue A467

Perf. 11½x11

1976, June 25 **Photo.** **Wmk. 342**

1010 A467 20m bister & multi .40 .20

Centenary of Al-Ahram newspaper.

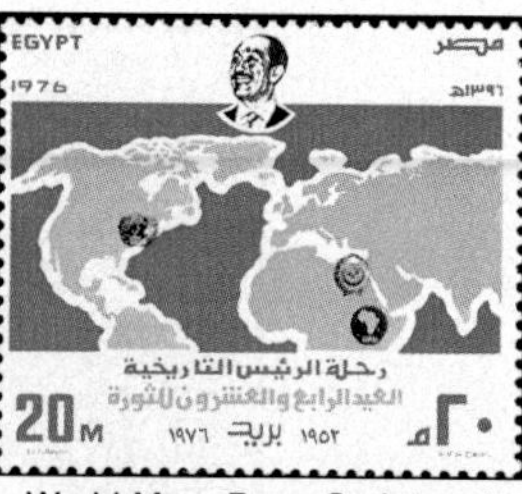

World Map, Pres. Sadat and Emblems — A468

1976, July 23 ***Perf. 11x11½***

1011 A468 20m bl, blk & yel .40 .20

Size: 240x216mm

Imperf

1012 A468 110m bl, brn & yel 2.00 1.00

24th anniv. of the revolution. No. 1012 design is similar to No. 1011.

Scarborough Lily — A469

1976, Sept. 10 **Photo.** ***Perf. 11***

1013 A469 10m multicolored .20 .20

For use on greeting cards.

Reconstruction of Sinai by Irrigation — A470

Abu Redice Oil Wells and Refinery — A471

Unknown Soldier, Memorial Pyramid for October War — A472

1976, Oct. 6 ***Perf. 11x11½***

1014 A470 20m multicolored .40 .20
1015 A471 20m multicolored .40 .20

Size: 65x77mm

1016 A472 110m grn, bl & blk 2.50 2.50

October War against Israel, 3rd anniv.

Papyrus with Children's Animal Story — A473

Al Aqsa Mosque, Palestinian Refugees — A474

55m, Isis, from Philae Temple, UNESCO emblem, vert. 110m, UNESCO emblem & "30."

Perf. 11½, 11½x11

1976, Oct. 24 **Photo.** **Wmk. 342**

1017 A473 20m dk bl, bis & brn .30 .20
1018 A474 30m brn, grn & blk .45 .20
1019 A473 55m dk blue & bister .85 .30
1020 A474 110m lt grn, vio bl & red 1.40 .50
Nos. 1017-1020 (4) 3.00 1.20

30th anniversary of UNESCO.

Census Chart A475

1976, Nov. 22 **Photo.** ***Perf. 11½x11***

1021 A475 20m multicolored .35 .20

10th General Population and Housing Census.

A476

A477

Design: Nile and commemorative medal.

1976, Nov. 22 ***Perf. 11x11½***

1022 A476 20m green & brown .35 .20

Geographical Soc. of Egypt, cent. (in 1975).

1977, Jan. 2 Photo. *Perf. 11x11½*

Post Day: 20m, Ikhnaton. 30m, Ikhnaton's daughter. 55m, Nefertiti, Ikhnaton's wife. 110m, Ikhnaton, front view.

1023	A477	20m multicolored	.30	.20
1024	A477	30m multicolored	.30	.20
1025	A477	55m multicolored	.65	.25
1026	A477	110m multicolored	2.75	.60
		Nos. 1023-1026 (4)	4.00	1.25

Policeman, Emblem and Emergency Car — A478

Perf. 11½x11

1977, Feb. 25 Photo. Wmk. 342

1027 A478 20m multicolored .60 .20

Police Day.

Map of Africa, Arab League Emblem — A479

1977, Mar 7 *Perf. 11x11½*

1028 A479 55m multicolored .50 .20

First Afro-Arab Summit Conference, Cairo.

Fair Emblem, Pharaonic Ship A480

1977, Mar. 7 *Perf. 11½x11*

1029 A480 20m green, blk & red .25 .20

10th International Cairo Fair.

King Faisal — A481

Healthy and Crippled Children — A482

1977, Mar. 22 Photo. *Perf. 11x11½*

1030 A481 20m indigo & brown .35 .20

King Faisal Ben Abdel-Aziz Al Saud of Saudi Arabia (1906-1975).

1977, Apr. 12 Wmk. 342

1031 A482 20m multicolored .50 .20

National campaign to fight poliomyelitis.

APU Emblem, Members' Flags A483

1977, Apr. 12 *Perf. 11½*

1032	A483	20m blue & multi	.25	.20
1033	A483	30m gray & multi	.25	.20

25th anniv. of Arab Postal Union (APU).

Children's Village A484

Perf. 11½x11

1977, May 7 Photo. Wmk. 342

1034	A484	20m multicolored	.25	.20
1035	A484	55m multicolored	.75	.40

Inauguration of Children's Village, Cairo.

Loom, Spindle and Factory A485

1977, May 7

1036 A485 20m multicolored .35 .20

Egyptian Spinning and Weaving Company, El Mehalla el Kobra, 50th anniv.

Satellite, Globe, ITU Emblem — A486

1977, May 17 *Perf. 11x11½*

1037 A486 110m dk blue & multi 1.25 .50

World Telecommunications Day.

Flag and "25" A487

Egyptian Flag and Eagle — A488

Perf. 11½x11

1977, July 23 Photo. Wmk. 342

1038 A487 20m silver, car & blk .30 .20

Perf. 11x11½

1039 A488 110m multicolored 1.50 1.00

25th anniversary of July 23rd Revolution. No. 1039 printed in sheets of six. Size: 75x83mm.

Saad Zaghloul A489

Archbishop Capucci, Map of Palestine A490

Perf. 11x11½

1977, Aug. 23 Photo. Wmk. 342

1040 A489 20m dk green & dk brn .20 .20

Saad Zaghloul, leader of 1919 Revolution, 50th death anniversary.

1977, Sept. 1

1041 A490 45m emerald & blue .75 .25

Palestinian Archbishop Hilarion Capucci, jailed by Israel in 1974.

Bird-of-Paradise Flower — A491

1977, Sept. 3

1042 A491 10m multicolored .20 .20

For use on greeting cards.

Proclamation Greening the Land — A492

Perf. 11x11½

1977, Sept. 25 Photo. Wmk. 342

1043 A492 20m multicolored .20 .20

Agrarian Reform Law, 25th anniversary.

Soldier, Tanks, Medal of Oct. 6 A493

Anwar Sadat — A494

1977, Oct. 6 *Perf. 11½x11*

1044 A493 20m multicolored .30 .20

Unwmk.

Perf. 11

1045 A494 140m dk brn, gold & red 3.50 3.50

October War against Israel, 4th anniv. No. 1045 printed in sheets of 16.

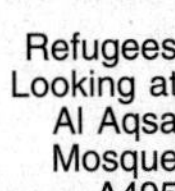

Refugees Looking at Al Aqsa Mosque A495

Goddess Taueret and Spirit of Flight (Horus) A496

Mural Relief, Temple of Philae — A497

Wmk. 342

1977, Oct. 24 Photo. *Perf. 11*

1046	A495	45m green, red & blk	.40	.20
1047	A496	55m dp blue & yellow	.60	.25
1048	A497	140m ol bis & dk brn	1.50	.80
		Nos. 1046-1048 (3)	2.50	1.25

United Nations Day.

Electric Trains, First Egyptian Locomotive — A498

1977, Oct. 22

1049 A498 20m multicolored 1.00 .20

125th anniversary of Egyptian railroads.

Film and Eye A499

1977, Nov. 16 *Perf. 11½x11*

1050 A499 20m gray, blk & gold .35 .20

50th anniversary of Egyptian cinema.

Natural Gas Well and Refinery — A500

1977, Nov. 17 Photo.

1051 A500 20m multicolored .40 .20

National Oil Festival, celebrating the acquisition of Sinai oil wells.

Pres. Sadat and Dome of the Rock A501

Perf. 11½x11

1977, Dec. 31 Photo. Wmk. 342

1052	A501	20m green, brn & blk	.60	.20
1053	A501	140m green, blk & brn	2.25	.80

Pres. Sadat's peace mission to Israel.

Ramses II — A502

Post Day: 45m, Queen Nefertari, bas-relief.

1978, Jan. 2 *Perf. 11½*

1054	A502	20m green, blk & gold	.50	.20
1055	A502	45m orange, blk & ol	1.00	.60

Post Day 1978.

Water Wheels, Fayum — A503

Flying Duck, from Floor in Ikhnaton's Palace A504

5m, Birdhouse, 10m, Statue of Horus. 20m, Al Rifa'i Mosque, Cairo. 50m, Monastery, Wadi al-Natrun. 55m, Ruins of Edfu Temple. 70m, 80m, Bridge of Oct. 6. 85m, Medum pyramid. 100m, Facade, El Morsi Mosque, Alexandria. 200m, Column, Alexandria, Sphinx. 500m, Arabian stallion.

Wmk. 342, Unwmkd. (30m, 70m, 80m)

1978-85 *Perf. 11½*

1056	A503	1m slate blue	.20	.20
a.		Unwmkd. ('79)	.20	.20
b.		1m gray ('83)	.20	.20
c.		1m gray, unwmkd. ('83)	.20	.20
1057	A503	5m bister brn	.20	.20
a.		5m dull brn, unwmkd. (79)	.20	.20
1058	A503	10m brt green	.20	.20
a.		Unwmkd. ('79)	.20	.20
1059	A503	20m dk brown	.20	.20
b.		Unwmkd. ('79)	.20	.20
1059A	A503	30m sepia	.20	.20
1060	A503	50m Prus blue	.25	.20
a.		Unwmkd. ('79)	.25	.20
b.		Unwmkd., brt blue ('87)	.25	.20
1061	A503	55m olive	.25	.20
1062	A503	70m olive ('79)	.30	.20
1062A	A503	80m olive ('82)	.35	.20
1063	A503	85m dp purple	.40	.20
a.		Unwmkd. ('85)	.40	.20
1064	A503	100m brown	.45	.20
a.		Unwmkd. ('85)	.65	.25
1065	A503	200m bl & indigo	.90	.40
1066	A504	500m multicolored	2.25	.65
1067	A504	£1 multicolored	4.50	1.25
		Nos. 1056-1067 (14)	10.65	4.50

Issued: 500m, £1, 2/27/78; 70m, 8/22/79; others, 7/23/78.

Fair Emblem and Wheat A505

1978, Mar. 15 *Perf. 11½*

1072	A505	20m multicolored	.20	.20

11th Cairo International Fair, Mar. 11-25.

Emblem, Kasr El Ainy School A506

1978, Mar. 18 *Perf. 11½x11*

1073	A506	20m lt blue, blk & gold	.20	.20

Kasr El Ainy School of Medicine, 150th anniv.

A507

#1074, Soldiers and Emblem. #1075, Youssef El Sebai.

1978, Mar. 30 *Perf. 11x11½*

1074	20m multicolored	.30	.20
1075	20m bister brown	.30	.20
a.	A507 Pair, #1074-1075	.60	.20

Youssef El Sebai, newspaper editor, assassinated on Cyprus and in memory of the commandos killed in raid on Cyprus.

Biennale Medal, Statue for Entrance to Port Said A509

1978, Apr. 1 *Perf. 11½*

1076	A509	20m blue, grn & blk	.25	.25

12th Biennial Exhibition of Fine Arts, Alexandria.

Child with Smallpox, UN Emblem A510

1978, Apr. 7 Photo. *Perf. 11½*

1077	A510	20m multicolored	.20	.20

Eradication of smallpox.

Heart & Arrow, UN Emblem — A511

Anwar Sadat — A512

1978, Apr. 7 Wmk. 342

1078	A511	20m multicolored	.20	.20

Fight against hypertension.

1978, May 15 Photo. *Perf. 11½x11*

1079	A512	20m green, brn & gold	.35	.20

7th anniversary of Rectification Movement.

Social Security Emblem — A513

1978, May 16 *Perf. 11*

1080	A513	20m lt green & dk brn	.20	.20

General Organization of Insurance and Pensions (Social Security), 25th anniversary.

New Cities on Map of Egypt — A514

Map of Egypt and Sudan, Wheat — A515

Wmk. 342

1978, July 23 Photo. *Perf. 11½*

1081	A514	20m multicolored	.50	.20
1082	A515	45m multicolored	1.00	.20

26th anniversary of July 23rd revolution.

Symbols of Egyptian Ministries — A516

1978, Aug. 28 Photo. *Perf. 11½x11*

1083	A516	20m multicolored	.35	.20

Centenary of Egyptian Ministerial System.

Pres. Sadat and "Spirit of Egypt" Showing Way — A517

1978, Oct. 6 Photo. *Perf. 11x11½*

1084	A517	20m multicolored	.50	.20

October War against Israel, 5th anniv.

Human Rights Emblem — A518

Dove and Human Rights Emblem — A520

Kobet al Sakra Mosque, Refugee Camp A519

UN Day: 55m, Temple at Biga and UNESCO emblem, horiz.

Perf. 11, 11½ (45m)

1978, Oct. 24 Photo. Wmk. 342

1085	A518	20m multicolored	.20	.20
1086	A519	45m multicolored	.75	.20
1087	A518	55m multicolored	.30	.20
1088	A520	140m multicolored	1.75	.25
		Nos. 1085-1088 (4)	3.00	.85

Pilgrims, Mt. Arafat and Holy Kaaba — A521

1978, Nov. 7 Photo. *Perf. 11*
1089 A521 45m multicolored .50 .20

Pilgrimage to Mecca.

Tahtib Horse Dance — A522

1978, Nov. 7
1090 A522 10m multicolored .30 .20
1091 A522 20m multicolored .30 .20

UN Emblem, Globe and Grain A523

1978, Nov. 11 Photo. *Perf. 11½*
1092 A523 20m green, dk bl & yel .20 .20

Technical Cooperation Among Developing Countries Conf., Buenos Aires, Sept. 1978.

Pipes, Map and Emblem of Sumed Pipeline A524

1978, Nov. 11
1093 A524 20m brown, bl & yel .30 .20

Inauguration of Sumed pipeline from Suez to Alexandria, 1st anniversary.

Mastheads A525

Abu el Walid A526

1978, Dec. 24 *Perf. 11x11½*
1094 A525 20m brown & black .30 .20

El Wakea el Masriya newspaper, 150th anniv.

1978, Dec. 24
1095 A526 45m brt green & indigo .50 .20

800th death anniv. of Abu el Walid ibn Rashid.

Helwan Observatory and Sky — A527

1978, Dec. 30 Wmk. 342
1096 A527 20m multicolored .40 .20

Helwan Observatory, 75th anniversary.

Second Daughter of Ramses II A528

Ramses Statues, Abu Simbel, and Cartouches — A529

1979, Jan. 2 Photo. *Perf. 11*
1097 A528 20m brown & yellow .25 .20

Perf. 11½x11
1098 A529 140m multicolored 1.50 .25

Post Day 1979.

Book, Reader and Globe A530

Perf. 11½x11
1979, Feb. 1 Photo. Wmk. 342
1099 A530 20m yellow grn & brown .20 .20

Cairo 11th International Book Fair.

Wheat, Globe, Fair Emblem — A531

Perf. 11x11½
1979, Mar. 17 Photo. Unwmk.
1100 A531 20m blue, org & blk .20 .20

12th Cairo International Fair, Mar.-Apr.

Skull, Poppy, Agency Emblem — A532

1979, Mar. 20 *Perf. 11*
1101 A532 70m multicolored .90 .20

Anti-Narcotics General Administration, 50th anniv.

Isis Holding Horus — A533

1979, Mar. 21
1102 A533 140m multicolored 1.50 .35

Mother's Day.

World Map and Book — A534

Perf. 11x11½
1979, Mar. 22 Wmk. 342
1103 A534 45m yellow, bl & brn .20 .20

Cultural achievements of the Arabs.

Pres. Sadat's Signature, Peace Doves A535

Wmk. 342
1979, Mar. 31 Photo. *Perf. 11½*
1104 A535 70m brt green & red .75 .20
1105 A535 140m yellow grn & red 1.25 .35

Signing of Peace Treaty between Egypt and Israel, Mar. 26.

1979, May 26 Photo. *Perf. 11½*
1106 A535 20m yellow & dk brn .30 .20

Return of Al Arish to Egypt.

Honeycomb with Food Symbols A536

1979, May 15
1107 A536 20m multicolored .20 .20

8th anniversary of movement to establish food security.

Coins, 1959, 1979 A537

Perf. 11½x11
1979, June 1 Wmk. 342 Photo.
1108 A537 20m yellow & gray .20 .20

25th anniversary of the Egyptian Mint.

Egypt No. 1104 under Magnifying Glass — A538

1979, June 1 *Perf. 11*
1109 A538 20m green, blk & brn .25 .20

Philatelic Society of Egypt, 50th anniversary.

Book, Atom Symbol, Rising Sun — A539

"23 July," "Revolution" and "Peace" — A540

Perf. 11½x11
1979, July 23 Wmk. 342
1110 A539 20m multicolored .20 .20

Miniature Sheet
Imperf
1111 A540 140m multicolored 2.00 1.00

27th anniversary of July 23rd revolution.

Musicians — A541

1979, Aug. 22 *Perf. 11½*
1112 A541 10m multicolored .20 .20

For use on greeting cards.

Dove over Map of Suez Canal A542

Wmk. 342

1979, Oct. 6 Photo. *Perf. 11½*
1113 A542 20m blue & brown .40 .20

October War against Israel, 6th anniv.

Prehistoric Mammal Skeleton, Map of Africa — A543

Perf. 11½x11
1979, Oct. 9 Photo. Wmk. 342
1114 A543 20m multicolored 1.00 .20

Egyptian Geological Museum, 75th anniv.

T Square on Drawing Board — A544

1979, Oct. 11 *Perf. 11*
1115 A544 20m multicolored .40 .20

Engineers Day.

Human Rights Emblem Over Globe — A545

Boy Balancing IYC Emblem — A546

Perf. 11½
1979, Oct. 24 Photo. Unwmk.
1116 A545 45m multicolored .25 .25
1117 A546 140m multicolored 1.00 .50

UN Day and Intl. Year of the Child.

International Savings Day — A547

1979, Oct. 31
1118 A547 70m multicolored .60 .25

A548

A549

Design: Shooting championship emblem.

1979, Nov. 16
1119 A548 20m multicolored .35 .20

20th International Military Shooting Championship, Cairo.

1979, Nov. 29 *Perf. 11x11½*
1120 A549 45m multicolored .50 .20

International Palestinian Solidarity Day.

Dove Holding Grain, Rotary Emblem, Globe A550

1979, Dec. 3 Photo. *Perf. 11½*
1121 A550 140m multicolored 1.00 .50

Rotary Intl., 75th anniv,; Cairo Rotary Club, 50th anniv.

Arms Factories, 25th Anniversary — A551

Perf. 11½x11
1979, Dec. 23 Photo. Wmk. 342
1122 A551 20m lt olive grn & brn .20 .20

Aly El Garem (1881-1949) A552

Pharaonic Capital A553

Poets: No. 1124, Mahmoud Samy El Baroudy (1839-1904).

1979, Dec. 25 *Perf. 11x11½*
1123 A552 20m dk brn & yel brn .30 .20
1124 A552 20m brown & dk brown .30 .20
a. Pair, #1123-1124 .60 .60

1980, Jan. 2 Unwmk. *Perf. 11½*

Post Day: Various Pharaonic capitals.

1125	A553	20m multicolored	.25	.20
1126	A553	45m multicolored	.35	.20
1127	A553	70m multicolored	.60	.20
1128	A553	140m multicolored	1.75	.35
a.		Strip of 4, #1125-1128	4.00	2.00

Golden Goddess of Writing, Fair Emblem — A554

Exhibition Catalogue and Medal — A555

1980, Feb. 2 Photo. *Perf. 11½*
1129 A554 20m multicolored .50 .20

12th Cairo Intl. Book Fair, Jan. 24-Feb. 4.

1980, Feb. 2
1130 A555 20m multicolored .30 .20

13th Biennial Exhibition of Fine Arts, Alexandria.

13th Cairo International Fair — A556

1980, Mar. 8 Photo. *Perf. 11x11½*
1131 A556 20m multicolored .30 .20

Kiosk of Trajan — A557

a, Kiosk of Tratan. b, Temple of Korasy, entry at right. c, Temple of Ksalabsha, carvings on frame. d, Temple of Philae, 5 columns..

1980, Mar. 10 *Perf. 11½*
1132 Strip of 4 + label 3.50 3.50
a.-d. A557 70m, any single .70 .40

UNESCO campaign to save Nubian monuments, 20th anniversary. Shown on stamps are Temples of Philae, Kalabsha, Korasy.

Physicians' Day — A558

1980, Mar. 18 *Perf. 11x11½*
1133 A558 20m multicolored .30 .20

Rectification Movement, 9th Anniversary — A559

Perf. 11½x11
1980, May 15 Photo. Wmk. 342
1134 A559 20m multicolored .30 .20

Re-opening of Suez Canal, 5th Anniversary — A560

1980, June 5 *Perf. 11½*
1135 A560 140m multicolored 1.00 .35

Prevention of Cruelty to Animals Week A561

1980, June 5
1136 A561 20m lt yel grn & gray .35 .20

Industry Day A562

Perf. 11½x11
1980, July 12 Photo. Wmk. 342
1137 A562 20m multicolored .20 .20

Leaf with Text A563

Family Protection Emblem — A564

1980, July 23 *Perf. 11½*
1138 A563 20m multicolored .30 .20

Souvenir Sheet
Imperf

1139 A564 140m multicolored 2.00 .40

July 23rd Revolution, 28th anniv.; Social Security Year.

Erksous Seller and Nakrazan Player — A565

Perf. 11½
1980, Aug. 8 Unwmk. Photo.
1140 A565 10m multicolored .20 .20

For use on greeting cards.

October War Against Israel, 7th Anniv. — A566

1980, Oct. 6 **Litho.**
1141 A566 20m multicolored .25 .20

Islamic and Coptic Columns A567

International Telecommunications Union Emblem — A568

Wmk. 342
1980, Oct. 24 Photo. *Perf. 11½*
1142 A567 70m multicolored .50 .40
1143 A568 140m multicolored 1.00 .60

UN Day. Campaign to save Egyptian monuments (70m), Intl. Telecommunications Day (140m).

Hegira (Pilgrimage Year) A569

1980, Nov. 9 Litho. *Perf. 11x11½*
1144 A569 45m multicolored .40 .20

Opening of Suez Canal Third Branch A570

Perf. 11½x11
1980, Dec. 16 Photo. Wmk. 342
1145 A570 70m multicolored .50 .20

Mustafa Sadek El-Rafai (1880-1927), Writer — A571

#1147, Ali Mustafa Mousharafa (1898-1950), mathematician (with glasses). #1148, Ali Ibrahim (1880-1947), surgeon.

1980, Dec. 23 *Perf. 11x11½*
1146 A571 20m green & brown .25 .20
1147 A571 20m green & brown .25 .20
1148 A571 20m green & brown .25 .20
a. Strip of 3, #1146-1148 1.25 .50

See Nos. 1178-1179.

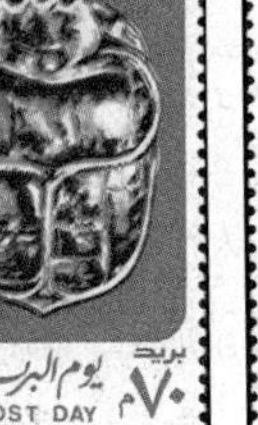
Ladybug Scarab Emblem — A572

von Stephan, UPU — A573

Perf. 11½
1981, Jan. 2 Photo. Unwmk.
1149 A572 70m shown .70 .20
1150 A572 70m Scarab, reverse .70 .20

Post Day.

Perf. 11x11½
1981, Jan. 7 Wmk. 342
1151 A573 140m grnsh bl & dk brn 1.25 .50

Heinrich von Stephan (1831-97), founder of UPU.

13th Cairo International Book Fair — A574

1981, Feb. 1 *Perf. 11½x11*
1152 A574 20m multicolored .30 .20

14th Cairo International Fair, Mar. 14-28 — A575

Perf. 11x11½
1981, Mar. 14 Photo. Wmk. 342
1153 A575 20m multicolored .30 .20

Rural Electrification Authority, 10th Anniversary — A576

1981, Mar. 18
1154 A576 20m multicolored .25 .20

Veterans' Day — A577

Intl. Dentistry Conf., Cairo — A578

1981, Mar. 26
1155 A577 20m multicolored .30 .20

Perf. 11x11½
1981, Apr. 14 Photo. Wmk. 342
1156 A578 20m red & olive .30 .20

Trade Union Emblem — A579

Nurses' Day — A580

Perf. 11x11½
1981, May 1 Photo. Wmk. 342
1157 A579 20m brt blue & dk brn .20 .20

International Confederation of Arab Trade Unions, 25th anniv.

1981, May 12
1158 A580 20m multicolored .20 .20

Irrigation Equipment (Electrification Movement) — A581

1981, May 15 *Perf. 11½*
1159 A581 20m multicolored .20 .20

Air Force Day — A582

Perf. 11x11½
1981, June 30 Photo. Wmk. 342
1160 A582 20m multicolored .25 .20

Flag Surrounding Map of Suez Canal — A583

Wmk. 342
1981, July 23 Photo. *Perf. 11½*
1161 A583 20m multicolored .25 .20
1162 A583 20m Emblems .25 .20

July 23rd Revolution, 29th anniv.; Social Defense Year.

1981 Feasts — A584

Wmk. 342
1981, July 29 Photo. *Perf. 11*
1163 A584 10m multicolored .20 .20

A585

A586

1981, Aug. 10 *Perf. 11x11½*
1164 A585 140m Kemal Ataturk 1.25 .50

Perf. 11x11½
1981, Sept. 9 Photo. Wmk. 342
1165 A586 20m Arabi Pasha, Leader of Egyptian Force .20 .20

Orabi Revolution centenary.

A587

A588

1981, Sept. 14

1166 A587 45m Athlete, Pyramids, Sphinx .50 .20

World Muscular Athletics Championships, Cairo.

Perf. 11x11½

1981, Sept. 26 Photo. Wmk. 342

1167 A588 45m multicolored .30 .20

Ministry of Industry and Mineral Resources, 25th anniv.

20th Intl. Occupational Health Congress, Cairo — A589

1981, Sept. 28 *Perf. 11½x11*

1168 A589 20m multicolored .25 .20

October War Against Israel, 8th Anniv. A590

1981, Oct. 6

1169 A590 20m multicolored .25 .20

World Food Day A591

13th World Telecommunications Day — A592

Intl. Year of the Disabled — A593

Fight Against Apartheid A594

Perf. 11½x11, 11x11½

1981, Oct. 24 Photo. Wmk. 342

1170 A591 10m multicolored .20 .20
1171 A592 20m multicolored .20 .20
1172 A593 45m multicolored .25 .20
1173 A594 230m multicolored 1.90 .70
Nos. 1170-1173 (4) 2.55 1.30

United Nations Day.

Pres. Anwar Sadat (1917-81) — A595

Perf. 11x11½

1981, Nov. 14 Unwmk.

1174 A595 30m multicolored 1.00 .50
1175 A595 230m multicolored 2.75 2.00

Establishment of Shura Family Council — A596

Perf. 11½x11

1981, Dec. 12 Photo. Wmk. 342

1176 A596 45m purple & yellow .25 .20

Agricultural Credit and Development Bank, 50th Anniv. — A597

1981, Dec. 15 *Perf. 11x11½*

1177 A597 20m multicolored .20 .20

Famous Men Type of 1980

30m, Ali el-Ghayati (1885-1956), journalist. 60m, Omar Ebn sl-Fared (1181-1234), Sufi poet.

Perf. 11x11½

1981, Dec. 21 Photo. Wmk. 342

1178 A571 30m green & brown .20 .20
1179 A571 60m green & brown .30 .20
a. Pair, #1178-1179 .50 .25

20th Anniv. of African Postal Union A598

1981, Dec. 21 *Perf. 11½x11*

1180 A598 60m multicolored .50 .20

14th Cairo Intl. Book Fair — A599

Arab Trade Union of Egypt, 25th Anniv. — A600

1982, Jan. 28

1181 A599 3p brown & yellow .30 .20

1982, Jan. 30

1182 A600 3p multicolored .20 .20

Khartoum Branch of Cairo University, 25th Anniv. A601

Perf. 11½x11

1982, Mar. 4 Wmk. 342

1183 A601 6p blue & green .40 .20

15th Cairo Intl. Fair — A602

1982, Mar. 13 *Perf. 11x11½*

1184 A602 3p multicolored .20 .20

50th Anniv. of Al-Ghardaka Marine Biological Station — A603

Fish of the Red Sea.

1982, Apr. 24 Litho. *Perf. 11½x11*

1185 10m Lined butterfly fish .45 .30
1186 30m Blue-banded sea perch .65 .35
1187 60m Batfish .75 .50
1188 230m Blue-spotted boxfish 1.90 1.00
a. A603 Block of 4, #1185-1188 3.00 1.00

Liberation of the Sinai — A604

1982, Apr. 25 Photo. *Perf. 11x11½*

1189 A604 3p multicolored .30 .20

50th Anniv. of Egypt Air A605

1982, May 7 Photo. *Perf. 11½x11*

1190 A605 23p multicolored 1.75 1.00

Minaret — A606

Al Azhar Mosque — A607

a, shown. b, Two terraces. c, Three terraces. d, Two turrets at top.

Perf. 11x11½

1982, June 28 Photo. Wmk. 342

1191 Strip of 4 + label 2.50 2.50
a.-d. A606 6p any single, multi .40 .25

Souvenir Sheet

Unwmk. *Imperf.*

1192 A607 23p multicolored 3.00 1.50

Al Azhar Mosque millennium. No. 1192 airmail.

Dove — A608

Flower in Natl. Colors — A609

Perf. 11x11½

1982, July 23 Photo. Wmk. 342

1193 A608 3p multicolored .20 .20

Souvenir Sheet

Imperf

1194 A609 23p multicolored 2.00 1.00

30th anniv. of July 23rd Revolution.

World Tourism Day A610

Design: Sphinx, pyramid of Cheops, St. Catherine's Tower.

Perf. 11½x11

1982, Sept. 27 Photo. Wmk. 342

1195 A610 23p multicolored 2.00 1.00

October War Against Israel, 9th Anniv. A611

1982, Oct. 6

1196 A611 3p Memorial, map .30 .20

Biennale of Alexandria Art Exhibition — A612

1982, Oct. 17 ***Perf. 11x11½***

1197 A612 3p multicolored .20 .20

10th Anniv. of UN Conference on Human Environment — A613

2nd UN Conference on Peaceful Uses of Outer Space, Vienna, Aug. 9-21 — A614

Scouting Year A615

TB Bacillus Centenary A616

Perf. 11½x11, 11½ (A615)

1982, Oct. 24

1198 A613 3p multicolored .30 .20
1199 A614 6p multicolored .60 .20
1200 A615 6p multicolored .60 .20
1201 A616 8p multicolored .70 .20
Nos. 1198-1201 (4) 2.20 .80

United Nations Day.

50th Anniv. of Air Force A617

1982, Nov. 2 ***Perf. 11½x11***

1202 A617 3p Jet, plane .35 .20

Ahmed Chawki (1868-1932) and Hafez Ibrahim (1871-1932), Poets — A618

Perf. 11½x11

1982, Nov. 25 Photo. Wmk. 342

1203 A618 6p multicolored .40 .20

Natl. Research Center, 25th Anniv. — A619

1982, Dec. 12 Photo. ***Perf. 11x11½***

1204 A619 3p red & blue .50 .20

50th Anniv. of Arab Language Society A620

1982, Dec. 25 ***Perf. 11½x11***

1205 A620 6p multicolored .50 .20

Year of the Aged — A621

Post Day A622

1982, Dec. 25 ***Perf. 11x11½***

1206 A621 23p multicolored 1.75 1.00

1983, Jan. 2 ***Perf. 11½***

1207 A622 3p multicolored .25 .20

15th Cairo Intl. Book Fair — A623

Perf. 11x11½

1983, Jan. 25 Photo. Wmk. 342

1208 A623 3p blue & red .40 .20

Police Day A624

1983, Jan. 25 ***Perf. 11½x11***

1209 A624 3p multicolored .30 .20

16th Cairo Intl. Fair — A625

5th UN African Map Conf., Cairo — A626

Perf. 11x11½

1983, Mar. 2 Photo. Wmk. 342

1210 A625 3p multicolored .20 .20

1983, Mar. 2

1211 A626 3p lt green & blue .40 .20

African Ministers of Transport, Communications and Planning, 3rd Conference — A627

1983, Mar. 8 ***Perf. 11½x11***

1212 A627 23p green & blue 1.00 .60

A628

A629

1983, Mar. 20 ***Perf. 11x11½***

1213 A628 3p Heading .25 .20
1214 A628 3p Kick .25 .20
a. Pair, #1213-1214 .50 .50

Victory in African Soccer Cup.

Perf. 11x11½

1983, Apr. 2 Photo. Wmk. 342

1215 A629 3p olive & red .35 .20

World Health Day and Natl. Blood Donation Campaign.

Org. of African Trade Union Unity A630

Perf. 11½x11

1983, Apr. 21 Photo. Wmk. 342

1216 A630 3p multicolored .35 .20

1st Anniv. of Sinai Liberation A631

75th Anniv. of Entomology Society A632

1983, Apr. 25 ***Perf. 11x11½***

1217 A631 3p multicolored .35 .20

1983, May 23

1218 A632 3p Emblem (Holy Scarab) .35 .20

Flowers — A633

1983, June 11 Photo. ***Perf. 11½x11***

1219 A633 20m green & org red .20 .20

5th African Handball Championship, Cairo — A634

Perf. 11½x11

1983, July 22 Photo. Wmk. 342

1220 A634 6p brown & dk grn .30 .20

31st Anniv. of Revolution A635

Simon Bolivar (1783-1830) A636

1983, July 23 ***Perf. 11½***

1221 A635 3p multicolored .20 .20

1983, Aug. ***Perf. 11x11½***

1222 A636 23p brown & dull grn .85 .60

Centenary of Arrival of Natl. Hero Orabi in Ceylon A637

Perf. 11½x11

1983, Aug. 25 Photo. Wmk. 342

1223 A637 3p Map, Orabi, El-Zahra School .20 .20

Islamic Vase, Museum Building A638

1983, Sept. 14 Photo. ***Perf. 11½x11***

1224 A638 3p yel brn & dk brn .50 .20

Reopening of Islamic Museum.

October War Against Israel, 10th Anniv. — A639

2nd Pharaonic Race — A640

1983, Oct. 6 ***Perf. 11½***

1225 A639 3p multicolored .35 .20

1983, Oct. 17 ***Perf. 11½***

1226 A640 23p multicolored 1.00 .60

United Nations Day — A641

1983, Oct. 24 Photo. ***Perf. 11***

1227 A641 3p IMO, ships, horiz. .20 .20
1228 A641 6p ITU, UPU .20 .20
1229 A641 6p FAO, UN, grain .20 .20
1230 A641 23p UN, ocean 2.00 .60
Nos. 1227-1230 (4) 2.60 1.20

4th World Karate Championship, Cairo — A642

1983, Nov. Photo. ***Perf. 13***

1231 A642 3p multicolored .30 .20

Intl. Palestinian Cooperation Day — A643

1983, Nov. 29 Photo. ***Perf. 13x13½***

1232 A643 6p Dome of the Rock .60 .20

75th Anniv. of Faculty of Fine Arts, Cairo A644

1983, Nov. 30 ***Perf. 13***

1233 A644 3p multicolored .20 .20

75th Anniv. of Cairo University — A645

1983, Nov. 30 ***Perf. 11x11½***

1234 A645 3p multicolored .20 .20

Intl. Egyptian Society of Mother and Child Care A646

1983, Nov. 30 ***Perf. 11½x11***

1235 A646 3p multicolored .20 .20

Org. of African Unity, 20th Anniv. — A647

World Heritage Convention, 10th Anniv. — A648

Perf. 11x11½

1983, Dec. 20 Photo. Wmk. 342

1236 A647 3p multicolored .20 .20

1983, Dec. 24

1237 Strip of 3 1.00 1.00
a. A648 3p Wood carving, Islamic .30 .25
b. A648 3p Coptic tapestry .30 .25
c. A648 3p Ramses II Thebes .30 .25

Post Day A649

Restored Forts: 6p, Quatbay. 23p, Mosque, Salah El-Din.

1984, Jan. 2 ***Perf. 13***

1238 A649 6p multicolored .25 .20
1239 A649 23p multicolored 1.00 .60

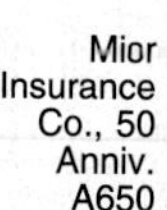

Mior Insurance Co., 50 Anniv. A650

1984, Jan. 14 ***Perf. 11½x11***

1240 A650 3p multicolored .30 .20

16th Cairo Intl. Book Fair — A651

Perf. 13½x13

1984, Jan. 26 Photo. Wmk. 342

1241 A651 3p multicolored .30 .20

17th Cairo Intl. Fair A652

Perf. 11½x11

1984, Mar. 10 Photo. Wmk. 342

1242 A652 3p multicolored .25 .20

25th Anniv. of Asyut University A653

75th Anniv. of Cooperative Unions A654

1984, Mar. 10 ***Perf. 11x11½***

1243 A653 3p multicolored .20 .20

1984, Mar. 17

1244 A654 3p multicolored .20 .20

World Theater Day — A655

Mahmoud Mokhtar (1891-1934), Sculptor — A656

Perf. 11x11½, 11½x11

1984, Mar. 27 Photo. Unwmk.

1245 A655 3p Masks .20 .20
1246 A656 3p Pride of the Nile .20 .20

World Health Day and Fight Against Polio — A657

Perf. 11½x11

1984, Apr. 7 Photo. Wmk. 342

1247 A657 3p Polio vaccine .30 .20

2nd Anniv. of Sinai Liberation — A658

1984, Apr. 25

1248 A658 3p Doves, map .20 .20

Africa Day A659

Perf. 12½x13½

1984, May 25 Photo. Wmk. 342

1249 A659 3p Map, UN emblem .20 .20

Satellite, Waves — A660

Flower — A661

1984, May 31 ***Perf. 11x11½***

1250 A660 3p multicolored .20 .20

Radio broadcasting in Egypt, 50th anniv.

1984, June 1

1251 A661 2p red & green .30 .20

Intl. Cairo Arab Arts Biennale — A662

1984, June 1 ***Perf. 13½x12½***

1252 A662 3p multicolored .20 .20

July Revolution, 32nd Anniv. — A663

Wmk. 342

1984, July 23 Photo. ***Perf. 11***

1253 A663 3p Atomic energy, agriculture .20 .20

A664

A665

1984 Summer Olympics: a, Boxing. b, Basketball. c, Volleyball. d, Soccer.

1984, July 28

1254 Strip of 4 + label 3.00 3.00
a.-d. A664 3p any single .20 .20

Size: 130x80mm

Imperf

1255 A664 30p like #1254 2.25 2.25

Wmk. 342

1984, Aug. 13 Photo. *Perf. 11*

1256 A665 3p bl & multi .20 .20
1257 A665 23p grn & multi 1.25 .60

2nd Genl. Conference of Egyptians Abroad, Aug. 11-15, Cairo.

Youth Hostels, 30th Anniv. — A666

Egypt Tour Co., 50th Anniv. — A667

Perf. 11x11½

1984, Sept. 22 Photo. Wmk. 342

1258 A666 3p Youths, emblem .20 .20

1984, Sept. 27

1259 A667 3p Emblem, sphinx .30 .20

October War Against Israel, 11th Anniv. — A668

Egypt-Sudan Unity — A669

1984, Oct. 6

1260 A668 3p Map, eagle .20 .20

1984, Oct. 12

1261 A669 3p Map of Nile, arms .25 .20

UN Day — A670

Tanks, Emblem — A671

Perf. 13½x12½

1984, Oct. 24 Photo. Wmk. 342

1262 A670 3p UNICEF Emblem, child .20 .20

UN campaign for infant survival.

1984, Nov. 10

1263 A671 3p multicolored .20 .20

Military Equipment Exhibition, Cairo, Nov. 10-14.

Tolon Mosque, Egypt A672

1984, Dec. 23 Photo. *Perf. 11½x11*

1264 A672 3p multicolored .25 .20

Ahmed Ebn Tolon (A.D. 835-884), Gov. of Egypt, founder of Kataea City.

A673

A674

1984, Dec. 23 *Perf. 11x11½*

1265 A673 3p multicolored .20 .20

Kamel el-Kilany (1897-1959), author.

Perf. 11x11½

1984, Dec. 26 Photo. Wmk. 342

Globe and congress emblem.

1266 A674 3p lt blue, ver & blk .20 .20

29th Intl. Congress on the History of Medicine, Dec. 27, 1984-Jan. 1, 1985, Cairo.

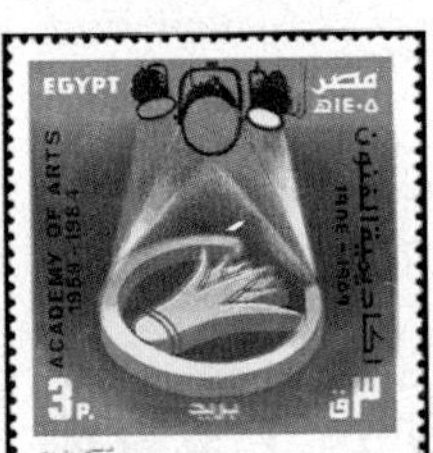
Academy of the Arts, 25th Anniv. A675

1984, Dec. 31 *Perf. 13*

1267 A675 3p Emblem in spotlights .20 .20

Pharaoh Receiving Message, Natl. Postal Museum, Cairo A676

1985, Jan. 2 *Perf. 11½x11*

1268 A676 3p brown, lt bl & ver .20 .20

Postal Museum, 50th anniv.

Intl. Union of Architects, 15th Conference, Jan. 14-Feb. 15 — A677

1985, Jan. 20

1269 A677 3p multicolored .20 .20

Seated Pharaonic Scribe — A678

Wheat, Cogwheels, Fair Emblem — A679

1985, Jan. 22 *Perf. 11x11½*

1270 A678 3p brt org & dk blue grn .20 .20

17th Intl. Book Fair, Jan. 22-Feb. 3, Cairo.

1985, Mar. 9 *Perf. 13½x13*

1271 A679 3p multicolored .20 .20

18th Intl. Fair, Mar. 9-22, Cairo.

Return of Sinai to Egypt, 3rd Anniv. — A680

1985, Apr. 25 Wmk. 342 Litho.

1272 A680 5p multicolored .20 .20

Ancient Artifacts — A681

A681a

Designs: 1p, God Mout, limestone sculpture, 360-340 B.C. 2p, No. 1281, Five wading birds, bas-relief. 3p, No. 1276, Seated statue, Ramses II, Temple of Luxor. No. 1276A, Vase. 8p, 15p, Slave bearing votive fruit offering, mural. 10p, Double-handled flask. 11p, Sculpted head of woman. No. 1282, Pitcher. 30p, 50p, Decanter. 35p, Temple of Karnak carved capitals. £1, Mosque.

1985-90 Photo. Unwmk. *Perf. 11½*

1273	A681	1p brown olive	.20	.20
1274	A681	2p brt grnsh bl	.20	.20
1275	A681	3p yellow brown	.20	.20
1276	A681	5p dk violet	.20	.20
1276A	A681	5p lemon	.20	.20
1277	A681	8p pale ol grn, sep & brn	.25	.20
1278	A681	10p dk vio & bl	.30	.20
1279	A681	11p dk violet	.30	.30
1280	A681	15p pale yel, sep & brn	.30	.30
1281	A681	20p yellow green	.30	.30
1282	A681	20p dk grn & yel	.30	.30
1283	A681	30p ol bis & buff	.35	.35
1284	A681	35p sep & pale yel	.45	.45
1285	A681	50p purple & buff	.60	.60
1285A	A681a	£1 brown & buff	1.50	1.50
1286	A681a	£2 sepia & yel	2.50	2.50
		Nos. 1273-1286 (16)	8.15	8.00

Issued: 1p, 2p, 3p, #1276, 8p, 11p, 15p, 5/1/85; 35p, 7/7/85; #1281, 4/1/86; 10p, 10/1/89; £2, 12/1/89; #1282, 2/1/90; 30p, 50p, 2/5/90; £1, 2/8/90; #1276A, 12/15/90.
Nos. 1276A, 1278 are 18x23mm.
No. 1278 exists dated "1990."
See Nos. 1467, 1470, 1472.

Helwan University School of Music, 50th Anniv. A682

1985, May 15

1287 A682 5p multicolored .20 .20

El-Moulid Bride, Folk Doll — A683

1985

1288 A683 2p orange & multi .20 .20
1289 A683 5p red & multi .20 .20

Festivals 1985. Issued: 2p, 6/11; 5p, 8/10.

A684

A685

Winning teams: a, b, Cairo Sports Stadium. c, El-Mokawiloon Club, white uniform, 1983. d, Natl. Club, red uniform, 1984. e, El-Zamalek Club, orange uniform, 1984.

1985, June 17 *Perf. 13½x13*

1290 Strip of 5 .80 .65
a.-e. A684 5p any single .20 .20

1985 Africa Cup Soccer Championships. Cairo Sports Stadium, 25th anniv. Nos. 1290a-1290b have continuous design.

1985, July 23 *Perf. 11½x11*

1291 A685 5p blue, brn & yel .20 .20

Egyptian Television, 25th anniv. Egyptian Revolution, 33rd anniv.

Suez Canal Reopening, 10th Anniv. — A686

Perf. 13x13½

1985, July 23 Litho. Wmk. 342

1292 A686 5p multicolored .20 .20

Egyptian Revolution, 33rd anniv.

Ahmed Hamdi Memorial Underwater Tunnel — A687

1985, July 23 ***Perf. 13½x13***
1293 A687 5p blue, vio & org .20 .20

Egyptian Revolution, 33rd anniv.

Souvenir Sheet

Aswan High Dam, 25th Anniv. — A688

Wmk. 342
1985, July 23 Photo. ***Imperf.***
1294 A688 30p multicolored 1.00 .75

Heart, Map, Olive Laurel, Conference Emblem — A689

1985, Aug. 10 Litho. ***Perf. 13½x13***
1295 A689 15p multicolored .60 .40

Egyptian Emigrants, 3rd general conference, Aug. 10-14, Cairo.

Natl. Tourism Ministry, 50th Anniv. — A690

1985, Sept. 10 ***Perf. 13x13½***
1296 A690 5p multicolored .20 .20

October War Against Israel, 12th Anniv. — A691

1985, Oct. 6
1297 A691 5p multicolored .20 .20

Air Scouts Assoc., 30th Anniv. — A692

1985, Oct. 15 Photo. ***Perf. 11½***
1298 A692 5p Emblem .20 .20

A693

UN, 40th Anniv. — A694

1985, Oct. 24
1299 A693 5p UN emblem, weather map .20 .20

UN Day, Meteorology Day.

1985, Oct. 24
1300 A694 15p multicolored .60 .40

Intl. Youth Year — A695

A696

1985, Oct. 24
1301 A695 5p multicolored .20 .20

1985, Oct. 24
1302 A696 15p blue & int blue .60 .40

Intl. Communications Development Program.

A697

A698

Emblem, hieroglyphics of Hassi Raa, 1st known dentist.

1985, Oct. 29 ***Perf. 11x11½***
1303 A697 5p beige & pale bl vio .20 .20

2nd Intl. Dentistry Conference.

1985, Nov. 18 Photo. ***Perf. 11½***
1304 A698 5p Emblem, squash player .20 .20

1985 World Squash Championships, Nov. 18-Dec. 4.

A699

A700

1985, Nov. 2 Litho. ***Perf. 13½x13***
1305 A699 5p multicolored .20 .20

4th Intl. Conference on the Biography and Sunna of Mohammed.

1985, Dec. 1 Photo. ***Perf. 11x11½***
1306 A700 5p multicolored .20 .20

1st Conference on the Development of Vocational Training.

Natl. Olympic Committee, 75th Anniv. — A701

18th Intl. Book Fair, Cairo — A702

1985, Dec. 28 Photo. ***Perf. 13x13½***
1307 A701 5p multicolored .20 .20

1986, Jan. 21 ***Perf. 11x11½***
1308 A702 5p Pharaonic scribe .20 .20

CODATU III — A703

1986, Jan. 26 ***Perf. 11½***
1309 A703 5p lt ol grn, ver & grnsh bl .20 .20

3rd Intl. Conference on Urban Transportation in Developing Countries, Cairo.

Central Bank, 25th Anniv. — A704

1986, Jan. 30 ***Perf. 13x13½***
1310 A704 5p multicolored .20 .20

Cairo Postal Traffic Center Inauguration — A705

1986, Jan. 30 ***Perf. 11½x11***
1311 A705 5p blue & dk brown .20 .20

Pharaonic Mural, Btah Hotteb's Tomb at Saqqara A706

1986, Feb. 27 Photo. ***Perf. 11½x11***
1312 A706 5p yel, gldn brn & brn .20 .20

Faculty of Commerce, Cairo Univ., 75th anniv.

Cairo Intl. Fair, Mar. 8-21 — A707

1986, Mar. 8 Litho. ***Perf. 13½x13***
1313 A707 5p multicolored .20 .20

Queen Nefertiti, Sinai — A708

Perf. 13x13½
1986, Apr. 25 Litho. Wmk. 342
1314 A708 5p multicolored .20 .20

Return of the Sinai to Egypt, 4th anniv.

Ministry of Health, 50th Anniv. — A709

1986, Apr. 10 *Perf. 13½x13*
1315 A709 5p multicolored .20 .20

1986 Census — A710

1986, May 26 **Photo.** *Perf. 11½*
1316 A710 15p brn, grnsh bl & yel bis .60 .60

Egypt, Winner of African Soccer Cup — A711

Festivals, Roses — A712

1986, May 31 *Perf. 13½x13*
1317 A711 5p English inscription below cup .20 .20
1318 A711 5p Arabic .20 .20
a. Pair, #1317-1318 .40 .40

1986, June 2 *Perf. 11½*
1319 A712 5p multicolored .20 .20

World Environment Day — A713

1986, June 5 *Perf. 13½x13*
1320 A713 15p Emblem, smoke-stacks .60 .60

July 23rd Revolution, 34th Anniv. A714

1986, July 23 **Litho.** *Perf. 13*
1321 A714 5p gray grn, scar & yel bis .20 .20

6th African Roads Conference, Cairo, Sept. 22-26 — A715

Perf. 13½x13
1986, Sept. 21 **Litho.** **Wmk. 342**
1322 A715 15p multicolored .60 .60

October War Against Israel, 13th Anniv. A716

1986, Oct. 6 **Litho.** *Perf. 13*
1323 A716 5p multicolored .20 .20

Engineers' Syndicate, 40th Anniv. A717

1986, Oct. 11 **Photo.** *Perf. 11½*
1324 A717 5p lt blue, brn & pale grn .20 .20

Workers' Cultural Education Assoc., 25th Anniv. — A718

Intl. Peace Year — A719

1986, Oct. 11 *Perf. 11x11½*
1325 A718 5p orange & rose vio .20 .20

1986, Oct. 24
1326 A719 5p blue, grn & pale sal .20 .20

First Oil Well in Egypt, Cent. — A720

1986, Nov. 7 **Photo.** *Perf. 11½*
1327 A720 5p dull grn, blk & pale yel .20 .20

UN Child Survival Campaign A721

1986, Nov. 20 **Litho.** *Perf. 13*
1328 A721 5p multicolored .20 .20

Ahmed Amin, Philosopher A722

National Theater, 50th Anniv. — A723

1986, Dec. 20 *Perf. 11½*
1329 A722 5p pale grn, pale yel & brn .20 .20

1986, Dec. 20 *Perf. 13½x13*
1330 A723 5p multicolored .20 .20

Post Day A724

Step Pyramid, Saqqara, King Zoser.

Perf. 13x13½
1987, Jan. 2 **Litho.** **Wmk. 342**
1331 A724 5p multicolored .20 .20

19th Intl. Book Fair, Cairo A725

1987, Jan. 25 **Litho.** *Perf. 13*
1332 A725 5p multicolored .20 .20

5th World Conference on Islamic Education A726

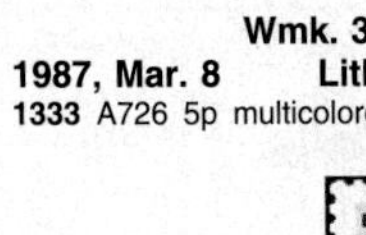

Wmk. 342
1987, Mar. 8 **Litho.** *Perf. 13*
1333 A726 5p multicolored .20 .20

20th Intl. Fair, Cairo — A727

1987, Mar. 21 **Photo.** *Perf. 11½*
1334 A727 5p Good workers medal .20 .20

Veteran's Day A728

1987, Mar. 26
1335 A728 5p multicolored .20 .20

Intl. Gardens Inauguration, Nasser City — A729

1987, Mar. 30 **Litho.** *Perf. 13*
1336 A729 15p multicolored .60 .60

World Health Day A730

1987, Apr. 7 **Photo.** *Perf. 11½*
1337 A730 5p Mother feeding child .20 .20

Litho.
Perf. 13
1338 A730 5p Oral rehydration therapy .20 .20

A731

Natl. Team Victory at 1986 Intl. Soccer Championships — A732

Trophies: No. 1339a, Al Ahly Cup. No. 1339b, National Cup. No. 1339c, Al Zamalek Cup. No. 1340, Natl. flag, Cairo Stadium and trophies pictured on No. 1339.

1987, Apr. 19 Litho. *Perf. 13½x13*
1339 Strip of 3 .60 .60
a.-c. A731 5p any single .20 .20

Size: 115x85mm

Imperf

1340 A732 30p multicolored 1.25 1.25

A733

A734

Salah El Din Citadel, Pharoah's Is., Sinai.

1987, Apr. 25
1341 A733 5p sky blue & lt brown .20 .20

Return of the Sinai to Egypt, 5th anniv.

1987, May 21 Photo. *Perf. 11½*

Festivals.

1342 A734 5p Dahlia .20 .20

Cultural Heritage Exhibition — A735

1987, June 17 Litho. *Perf. 13x13½*
1343 A735 15p multicolored .60 .60

Tourism Year — A736

a, Column and Sphinx, Alexandria. b, St. Catherine's Monastery, Mt. Sinai. c, Colossi of Thebes. d, Temple of Theban Triad, Luxor.

1987, June 18
1344 Block of 4 2.25 2.25
a.-d. A736 15p any single .55 .55

See No. C187.

National Day A737

1987, June 26 *Perf. 13*
1345 A737 5p multicolored .20 .20

Industry-Agriculture Exhibition — A738

1987, July 23 Photo. *Perf. 11½*
1346 A738 5p grn, dull org & blk .20 .20

Intl. Year of Shelter for the Homeless A739

1987, Sept. 2 Litho. *Perf. 13*
1347 A739 5p multicolored .20 .20

World Architects' Day.

Aida, Performed at Al Ahram Pyramid, Giza A740

Radamis and troops returning from Ethiopia.

1987, Sept. 21
1348 A740 15p multicolored .60 .60

Size: 70x70mm

Imperf

1349 A740 30p multicolored 1.25 1.25

Greater Cairo Subway Inauguration — A741

1987, Sept. 27 *Perf. 13x13½*
1350 A741 5p multicolored .20 .20

Industry Day A742

1987, Oct. 1 *Perf. 13*
1351 A742 5p multicolored .20 .20

Battle of Hettin, 700th Anniv. — A743

1987, Oct. 6 Photo. *Perf. 11x11½*
1352 A743 5p multicolored .20 .20

UPU Emblem A744

Perf. 11½

1987, Oct. 24 Unwmk. Photo.
1353 A744 5p multicolored .20 .20

UN Executive Council, 40th anniv.; UPU Consultative Council, 30th anniv.

16th Art Biennial of Alexandria A745

1987, Nov. 7 Litho. *Perf. 13½x13*
1354 A745 5p multicolored .20 .20

Second Intl. Defense Equipment Exhibition, Cairo, Nov. 9-13 — A746

Perf. 13x13½

1987, Nov. 9 Litho. Unwmk.
1355 A746 5p multicolored .20 .20

2nd Pan-Arab Congress on Anaesthesia and Intensive Care — A747

Unwmk.

1987, Dec. 1 Litho. *Perf. 13*
1356 A747 5p multicolored .20 .20

Intl. Orthopedic and Traumatology Conference A748

1987, Dec. 1 *Perf. 13½x13*
1357 A748 5p gray, red brn & bl .20 .20

Selim Hassan (1887-1961), Egyptologist, and Hieroglyphs A749

Abdel Hamid Badawi (1887-1965), Jurist, and Scales of Justice — A750

Perf. 13½x13

1987, Dec. 30 Litho. Unwmk.
1358 A749 5p multicolored .20 .20
1359 A750 5p multicolored .20 .20

Stamp Day 1988 — A751

Pyramids of the Pharaohs and: a, Cheops. b, Chefren. c, Mycerinus. No. 1360 has a continuous design.

1988, Jan. 2
1360 A751 Strip of 3 1.50 1.50
a.-c. 15p, any single .45 .45

Afro-Asian Peoples Solidarity Organization, 30th Anniv. — A752

1988, Jan. 10 ***Perf. 13x13½***
1361 A752 15p multicolored .50 .50

20th Intl. Book Fair, Cairo — A753

1988, Jan. 26 ***Perf. 13½x13***
1362 A753 5p multicolored .20 .20

Martrans (Natl. Shipping Line), 25th Anniv. A754

Unwmk.
1988, Mar. 3 **Litho.** ***Perf. 13***
1363 A754 5p multicolored .20 .20

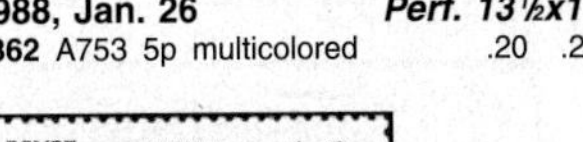

Cairo Intl. Fair A755

1988, Mar. 12 **Photo.** ***Perf. 11½x11***
1364 A755 5p multicolored .20 .20

World Health Day 1988: Diabetes A756

1988 Festivals A757

Perf. 11x11½
1988, Apr. 7 **Photo.** **Unwmk.**
1365 A756 5p multicolored .20 .20

1988, Apr. 17 ***Perf. 11½***
1366 A757 5p grn, brn org & brn .20 .20

African Postal Union, 25th Anniv. — A758

1988, Apr. 23 **Litho.** ***Perf. 13x13½***
1367 A758 15p brt blue .60 .60

Oppose Racial Discrimination — A759

1988, May 25 **Photo.** ***Perf. 11½***
1368 A759 5p multicolored .20 .20

Taw Fek-Hakem (1902-1987), Playwright, Novelist — A760

1988, Aug. 5 **Photo.** ***Perf. 11½***
1369 A760 5p brt grn bl & org brn .20 .20

See Nos. 1383-1384, 1479-1480, 1486, 1500-1502, 1543-1546.

Faculty of Art Education, 50th Anniv. A761

Perf. 11½
1988, Sept. 10 **Photo.** **Unwmk.**
1370 A761 5p multicolored .20 .20

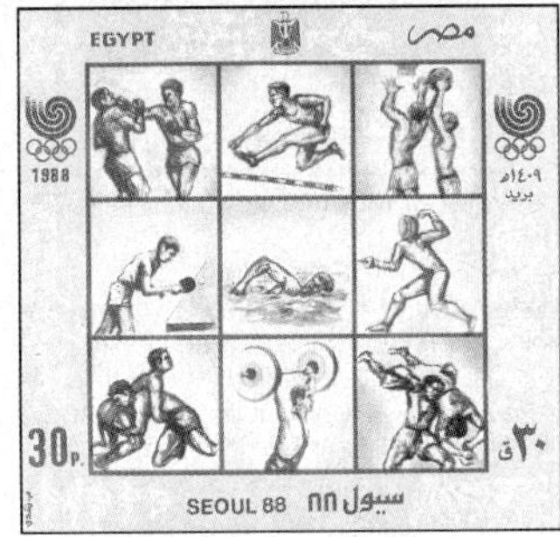
A762

1988 Summer Olympics, Seoul — A763

1988, Sept. 17 **Litho.** ***Perf. 13***
1371 A762 15p multicolored .60 .60

Size: 96x91mm
Imperf.
1372 A763 30p multicolored 1.00 1.00

No. 1371 is airmail.

October War Against Israel, 15th Anniv. — A764

Perf. 13x13½
1988, Oct. 6 **Litho.** **Unwmk.**
1373 A764 5p multicolored .20 .20

A765

Opening of the Opera House — A766

1988, Oct. 10 ***Perf. 11½***
1374 A765 5p multicolored .20 .20

Size: 112x75mm
Imperf
1375 A766 50p multicolored 1.50 1.50

Intl. Red Cross and Red Crescent Organizations, 125th Annivs. — A767

Perf. 11½
1988, Oct. 24 **Photo.** **Unwmk.**
1376 A767 5p green, blk & red .20 .20

WHO, 40th Anniv. — A768

1988, Oct. 24 ***Perf. 11x11½***
1377 A768 20p multicolored .80 .80

Naguib Mahfouz, 1988 Nobel Prize Winner for Literature — A769

1988, Nov. 7 **Litho.** ***Perf. 13x13½***
1378 A769 5p multicolored .20 .20

See No. C190.

Arab Scouting Organization, 75th Anniv. — A770

1988, Nov. 10
1379 A770 25p multicolored .80 .80

Return of Taba to Egypt — A771

1988, Nov. 15
1380 A771 5p multicolored .20 .20

Intl. Conference on Orthopedic Surgery, Cairo, Nov. 15-18 — A772

1988, Nov. 15 **Photo.** ***Perf. 11½x11***
1381 A772 5p buff, brt yel grn & brn .20 .20

A773

1988, Dec. 3 ***Perf. 11½***
1382 A773 5p multicolored .20 .20

Ministry of Agriculture, 75th anniv.

A774

Perf. 13½x13

1988, Dec. 29 Litho. Unwmk.

Famous Men: No. 1383, Mohamed Hussein Hekal (1888-1956), author, politician. No. 1384, Ahmed Lotfi El Sayed (1872-1963), educator, politician.

1383 A774 5p green & red brn .20 .20
1384 A774 5p green & red brn .20 .20
a. Pair, #1383-1384 .40 .40

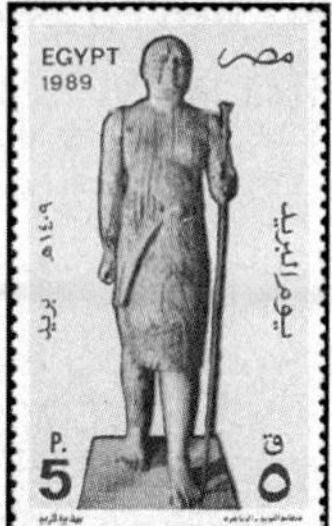

A775

A776

Statues: 5p, Statue of K. Abr, a priest, 5th cent. No. 1386, Queen Nefert, 4th Dynasty. No. 1387, King Ra Hoteb, 4th Dynasty.

1989, Jan. 2

1385 A775 5p multicolored .20 .20
1386 A775 25p multicolored .80 .80
1387 A775 25p multicolored .80 .80
a. Pair, #1386-1387 2.00 2.00
Nos. 1385-1387 (3) 1.80 1.80

Stamp Day.

1989, Jan. 10

1388 A776 5p dull green .20 .20

Jawaharlal Nehru (1889-1964), 1st Prime Minister of independent India.

Nile Hilton Hotel, 30th Anniv. — A777

1989, Feb. 22 Litho. *Perf. 13x13½*

1389 A777 5p multicolored .20 .20

Return of Taba to Egypt A778

Unwmk.

1989, Mar. 15 Litho. *Perf. 13*

1390 A778 5p multicolored .20 .20

2nd Stage of Cairo Subway A779

1989, Apr. 12 Litho. *Perf. 13*

1391 A779 5p multicolored .20 .20

Festivals — A780

1989, May 4 Photo. *Perf. 11½*

1392 A780 5p multicolored .20 .20

1st Arab Olympic Day A781

1989, May 24

1393 A781 5p tan, blk & dull grn .20 .20

Interparliamentary Union, Cent. — A782

Pyramids and the Parliament Building, Cairo.

1989, June 29 Litho. *Perf. 13x13½*

1394 A782 25p shown 1.00 1.00

Size: 87x76mm

Imperf

1395 A782 25p multi, diff. 1.00 1.00

French Revolution, Bicent. — A783

1989, July 14 Photo. *Perf. 11½*

1396 A783 25p multicolored 1.00 1.00

African Development Bank, 25th Anniv. — A784

Perf. 11½

1989, Oct. 1 Photo. Unwmk.

1397 A784 10p multicolored .20 .20

A785

October War Against Israel, 16th Anniv. — A786

1989, Oct. 6 *Perf. 13*

1398 Strip of 3 .45 .45
a. A785 10p shown .20 .20
b. A786 10p shown .20 .20
c. A785 10p Battle scene .20 .20

See No. 1424.

Aga Khan Award for Architecture A788

Perf. 11½

1989, Oct. 15 Photo. Unwmk.

1400 A788 35p multicolored .50 .50

Natl. Health Insurance Plan, 25th Anniv. A789

1989, Oct. 24

1401 A789 10p blk, gray & ver .20 .20

World Post Day — A790

1989, Oct. 24 *Perf. 11x11½*

1402 A790 35p blue, blk & brt yel .50 .50

Statues of Memnon, Thebes — A791

Perf. 11½

1989, Nov. 12 Photo. Unwmk.

1403 A791 10p lt vio, blk & brt yel grn .20 .20

Intl. Cong. & Convention Assoc. (ICCA) annual convention, Nov. 11-18, Cairo.

Cairo University School of Agriculture, Cent. — A792

1989, Nov. 15

1404 A792 10p pale grn, blk & brt yel .20 .20

Cairo Intl. Conference Center — A793

1989, Nov. 20 *Perf. 11½x11*

1405 A793 5p multicolored .20 .20

Road Safety Soc., 20th Anniv. — A794

1989, Nov. 20 *Perf. 11½*

1406 A794 10p multicolored .20 .20

Alexandria University, 50th Anniv. — A795

1989, Nov. 30 *Perf. 11x11½*

1407 A795 10p pale blue & tan .20 .20

Portrait of Pasha, Monument in Opera Square, Cairo A796

Perf. 11½x11

1989, Dec. 31 Photo. Unwmk.

1408 A796 10p multicolored .20 .20

Ibrahim Pasha (d. 1838), army commander from 1825 to 1828.

Famous Men

A797 A798

1989, Dec. 31 *Perf. 11x11½*

1409 A797 10p grn & dk ol grn .20 .20
1410 A798 10p golden brown .20 .20

Abd El-Rahman El-Rafei (b. 1889), historian (No. 1409); Abdel Kader El Mazni (b. 1889), man of letters (No. 1410).

See Nos. 1431-1432.

Statue of Priest Ranofr — A799

Relief Sculpture of Betah Hoteb — A800

1990, Jan. 2 ***Perf. 13½x13***

1411	A799 30p multicolored		.45	.45
1412	A800 30p multicolored		.45	.45
a.	Pair, #1411-1412		.90	.90

Stamp Day.

Arab Cooperation Council, 1st Anniv. — A801

Perf. 13x13½

1990, Feb. 16 Photo. Unwmk.

1413	A801 10p multicolored	.20	.20
1414	A801 35p multicolored	.50	.50

Emblem, Conference Center A802

Road Safety Emblems A803

Perf. 13½x13

1990, Mar. 10 Litho. Unwmk.

1415	A802 10p brt yel grn, red & blk	.20	.20

Size: 80x59mm

Imperf

1416	A802 30p multicolored	.45	.45

African Parliamentary Union 13th general conference, Mar. 10-15.

1990, Mar. 19 Photo. ***Perf. 11x11½***

1417	A803 10p multicolored	.20	.20

Intl. Conference on Road Safety & Accidents in Developing Countries, Mar. 19-22.

Festivals 1990 — A804

1990, Apr. 24 ***Perf. 11½***

1418	A804 10p multicolored	.20	.20

Sinai Liberation, 8th Anniv. A805

1990, Apr. 25

1419	A805 10p blue, blk & yel grn	.20	.20

World Cup Soccer Championships, Italy — A806

1990, May 26 Litho. ***Perf. 13½x13***

1420	A806 10p multicolored	.20	.20

Souvenir Sheet

Imperf

1421	A806 50p Flags, trophy	.75	.75

World Basketball Championships, Argentina — A807

1990, Aug. 8 ***Perf. 13x13½***

1422	A807 10p multicolored	.20	.20

Natl. Population Council, 5th Anniv. — A808

1990, Sept. 15 ***Perf. 13½x13***

1423	A808 10p brown & yel grn	.20	.20

October War Against Israel Type

1990, Oct. 6 Litho. ***Perf. 13x13½***

1424	Strip of 3	.45	.45
a.	A785 10p Bunker, tank	.20	.20
b.	A786 10p like #1398b	.20	.20
c.	A785 10p Troops with flag, flame thrower	.20	.20

Egyptian Postal Service, 125th Anniv. — A809

1990, Oct. 9

1425	A809 10p lt blue, blk & red	.20	.20

Dar El Eloum Faculty, Cent. A810

1990, Oct. 13 Litho. ***Perf. 13***

1426	A810 10p multicolored	.20	.20

UN Development Program, 40th Anniv. — A811

ITU, 125th Anniv. — A812

1990, Oct. 24 ***Perf. 11½***

1427	A811 30p yel, bl grn & yel grn	.45	.45

Perf. 13

1428	A812 30p multicolored	.45	.45

UN Day.

Ras Mohammed Natl. Park — A813

Various tropical fish and coral reefs.

1990, Dec. 22 Litho. ***Perf. 13***

1429	A813 Block of 4	.90	.90
a.-b.	10p any single	.20	.20
c.-d.	20p any single	.30	.30

Day of the Disabled — A814

1990. Dec. 15 Photo. ***Perf. 11***

1430	A814 10p multicolored	.20	.20

Mohamed Fahmy Abdel Meguid Bey, Medical Reformer A815

Nabaweya Moussa (1890-1951), Educator A816

Perf. 11x11½

1990, Dec. 30 Unwmk.

1431	A815 10p Prus bl, brn & org	.20	.20
1432	A816 10p grn, org brn & blk	.20	.20

Stamp Day — A817

1991, Jan. 1 Litho. ***Perf. 13½x13***

1433	A817 5p No. 1	.20	.20
1434	A817 10p No. 2	.20	.20
1435	A817 20p No. 3	.30	.30
a.	Strip of 3, #1433-1435	.55	.55

See Nos. 1443-1446, 1459-1460.

Veterinary Surgeon Syndicate, 50th Anniv. — A818

1991, Feb. 28 Photo. ***Perf. 11½***

1436	A818 10p multicolored	.20	.20

Syndicate of Journalists, 50th Anniv. — A819

1991, Apr. Photo. ***Perf. 11½***

1437	A819 10p multicolored	.20	.20

Festivals — A820

1991, Apr. 13
1438 A820 10p multicolored .20 .20

Giza Zoo, Cent. — A821

1991, June 15 Litho. *Imperf.*
Size: 80x63mm
1439 A821 50p multicolored .75 .75

Mahmoud Mokhtar (1891-1934), Sculptor — A822

Mohamed Nagi (1888-1956), Painter — A823

Perf. 13x13½, 13½x13
1991, June 11 Litho.
1440 A822 10p multicolored .20 .20
1441 A823 10p multicolored .20 .20

Faculty of Engineering — A824

1991, June 30 *Perf. 13x13½*
1442 A824 10p multicolored .20 .20

Stamp Day Type

Designs: No. 1443, #5. No. 1444, #4. No. 1445, #7. No. 1446, Sphinx, pyramid, #6.

1991, July 23 *Perf. 13*
1443 A817 10p orange & blk .20 .20
1444 A817 10p yellow & blk .20 .20
1445 A817 10p lilac & blk .20 .20
a. Strip of 3, #1443-1445 .45 .45

Size: 80x60mm
Imperf
1446 A817 50p multicolored .75 .75
Nos. 1443-1446 (4) 1.35 1.35

Mohamed Abdel el Wahab, Musician A825

1991, Aug. 28 *Perf. 13*
1447 A825 10p multicolored .20 .20

5th Africa Games, Cairo — A826

#1448, Karate, judo. #1449, Table tennis, field hockey, tennis. #1450, Running, gymnastics, swimming. #1451, Soccer, basketball, shooting. #1452, Boxing, wrestling, weightlifting. #1453, Handball, cycling, volleyball. #1454, Games mascot, vert. #1455, Mascot, emblem, torch.

Perf. 13x13½
1991, Sept. Litho. Unwmk.
1448 A826 10p multicolored .20 .20
1449 A826 10p multicolored .20 .20
a. Pair, #1448-1449 .30 .30
1450 A826 10p multicolored .20 .20
1451 A826 10p multicolored .20 .20
a. Pair, #1450-1451 .30 .30
1452 A826 10p multicolored .20 .20
1453 A826 10p multicolored .20 .20
a. Pair, #1452-1453 .30 .30

Perf. 13½x13
1454 A826 10p multicolored .20 .20

Size: 80x60mm
Imperf
1455 A826 50p multicolored .75 .75
Nos. 1448-1455 (8) 2.15 2.15

Intl. Statistics Institute, 48th Session A827

1991, Sept. 9
1456 A827 10p multicolored .20 .20

Opening of Dar Al Eftaa Religious Center — A828

1991, Oct. 1 Litho. *Perf. 13*
1457 A828 10p multicolored .20 .20

October War Against Israel, 18th Anniv. — A829

1991, Oct. 6 *Perf. 13x13½*
1458 A829 10p multicolored .20 .20

Stamp Day Type

Designs: 10p, #6. £1, Stamp exhibition emblem, hieroglyphics, pyramids, sphinx.

1991, Oct. 7 *Perf. 13*
1459 A817 10p blue & black .20 .20

Size: 90x60mm
Imperf
1460 A817 £1 multicolored *3.00 3.00*

Natl. Philatelic Exhibition, Cairo, 10/7-12 (#1460). No. 1460 sold with £1 at exhibition.

Ancient Artifacts Type of 1985
Perf. 11½x11
1990-92 Unwmk. Photo.
Size: 18x23mm
1467 A681 10p like #1278 .20 .20
1470 A681 30p like #1283 .45 .45
1472 A681 50p like #1285 .50 .50
Nos. 1467-1472 (3) 1.15 1.15

Issued: 10p, 1/20/90; 30p, 9/1/91; 50p, 7/11/92.

United Nations Day — A830

#1477, Brick hands housing people. #1478, Woman learning to write, fingerprint, vert.

Perf. 13x13½, 13½x13
1991, Oct. 24 Litho.
1476 A830 10p shown .20 .20
1477 A830 10p multicolored .20 .20
1478 A830 10p multicolored .20 .20
Nos. 1476-1478 (3) .60 .60

Famous Men Type of 1988
Inscribed "1991"

Designs: No. 1479, Dr. Zaki Mubarak (1891-1952), writer and poet. No. 1480, Abd El Kader Hamza (1879-1941), journalist.

1991, Dec. 23 Photo. *Perf. 13½x13*
1479 A760 10p olive brown .20 .20
1480 A760 10p gray .20 .20

A831

Post Day — A832

1992, Jan. 2 Litho. *Perf. 13*
1481 A831 10p shown .20 .20
1482 A831 45p Bird mosaic .70 .70

Perf. 14
1483 A832 70p shown 1.10 1.10
Nos. 1481-1483 (3) 2.00 2.00

Nos. 1482-1483 are airmail.

Police Day — A833

1992, Jan. 25 *Perf. 14*
1484 A833 10p multicolored .20 .20

25th Cairo Intl. Fair A834

1992, Feb. 15 Litho. *Perf. 14*
1485 A834 10p multicolored .20 .20

Famous Men Type of 1988
Inscribed "1992"

10p, Sayed Darwish (1882-1923), musician.

1992, Mar. 17 Photo. *Perf. 14x13½*
1486 A760 10p dull org & olive .20 .20

Festivals — A835

1992, Mar. 18 *Perf. 11½*
1487 A835 10p Egyptian hoopoe .20 .20

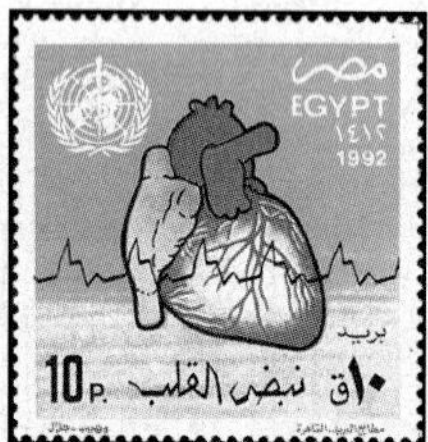
World Health Day A836

1992, Apr. 20 Litho. *Perf. 13*
1488 A836 10p multicolored .20 .20

Aswan Dam, 90th Anniv. A837

1992, July Litho. *Perf. 13*
1489 A837 10p No. 487 .20 .20

20th Arab Scout Jamboree — A838

1992, July 10 *Perf. 13x13½*
1490 A838 10p multicolored .20 .20

A839

A840

1992, July 20 ***Perf. 13½x13***
1491 A839 10p multicolored .20 .20

Size: 80x60mm

Imperf

1492 A839 70p Summer Games' emblem .75 .75

1992 Summer Olympics, Barcelona.

1992, Sept. 14 Litho. ***Perf. 13½x13***
1493 A840 10p multicolored .20 .20

El Helal Magazine, cent.

Alexandria World Festival — A841

1992, Sept. 27 ***Perf. 13x13½***
1494 A841 70p multicolored .75 .75

Congress of Federation of World and American Travel Companies, Cairo — A842

1992, Sept. 20
1495 A842 70p multicolored .75 .75

World Post Day A843

1992, Oct. 9 Litho. ***Perf. 13***
1496 A843 10p dk bl, lt bl & blk .20 .20

Children's Day — A844

1992, Oct. 24 Litho. ***Perf. 13½x13***
1497 A844 10p multicolored .20 .20

Intl. Conference on Food, Agriculture and World Health A845

1992, Oct. 24 ***Perf. 13***
1498 A845 70p multicolored .75 .75

A846

A847

1992, Nov. 21 ***Perf. 13½x13***
1499 A846 10p multicolored .20 .20

20th Arab Scout Conference, Cairo.

Famous Men Type of 1988
Inscribed "1992"

#1500, Talaat Harb, economist. #1501, Mohamed Taymour, writer. #1502, Dr. Ahmed Zaki Abu Shadi (with glasses), physician & poet.

1992, Dec. 23 Photo. ***Perf. 13½x13***
1500 A760 10p blue & brown .20 .20
1501 A760 10p citron & blue gray .20 .20
1502 A760 10p citron & blue gray .20 .20
a. Pair, #1501-1502 .20 .20
Nos. 1500-1502 (3) .60 .60

1993, Jan. 2 Litho. ***Perf. 13½x13***

Pharaohs: 10p, Sesostris I. 45p, Amenemhet III. 70p, Hur I.

1503 A847 10p brown & yellow .20 .20
1504 A847 45p brown & yellow .45 .45
1505 A847 70p brown & yellow .70 .70
a. Strip of 3, #1503-1505 1.35 1.35

Post Day.

Intl. Book Fair, Cairo — A848

1993, Jan. 26 Litho. ***Perf. 13½x13***
1506 A848 15p multicolored .20 .20

A849

A849a

A849b

A849c

A849d

A849f

A849g

A849e

A849h

Artifacts: A849, Bust. A849a, Sphinx. A849b, Bust of princess. A849c, Ramses II. A849d, Queen Ti. A849e, Horemheb. A849f, As A849b. A849g, Amenhotep III. £1, Head of a woman. £2, Woman wearing headdress. £5, Pharaonic capital.

Photo., Litho. (#1511)

1993-99 Unwmk. ***Perf. 11½x11,***

1507 A849 5p multi .20 .20
1508 A849a 15p brn & bis .20 .20
1509 A849a 15p brn & bis .20 .20
1510 A849b 25p brn & org brn .25 .25
1511 A849c 55p blk & bl .60 .60

Size: 21x25mm

Perf. 11¼

1512 A849 5p dp cl & brick red .20 .20
1513 A849d 5p brown .20 .20
a. Wmk. 342 .20 .20
1514 A849a 15p brn & bis .20 .20
1515 A849e 20p blk & gray .20 .20
a. Wmk. 342 .20 .20
1516 A849f 25p brn & org brn .30 .30
1517 A849f 25p black brown .20 .20
1518 A849c 55p blk & lt bl .55 .55
1519 A849g 75p blk & brn .70 .70

Perf. 11½

1520 A849h £1 slate & blk 1.25 1.25
1521 A849h £2 brn & grn 2.40 2.40
1521A A849h £5 brn & gold 5.00 5.00
Nos. 1507-1521A (16) 12.65 12.65

Warning: Avoid using watermark fluid on Nos. 1513-1513a and 1515-1515a. Images will be adversely affected.

Body of Sphinx on Nos. 1509, 1514 stops above value, and extends through value on No. 1508.

Issued: #1507-1508, 2/1; #1509, 3/10; £1, £2, 4/1; #1511, 7/1/93; £5, 8/1/93; #1512, 1514, 1518, 10/30/94; #1516, 6/25/94; 20p, 2/1/97; 75p, 3/25/97; #1517, 1998; #1513a, 1515a, 1999.

See Nos. C205-C206A.

Architects' Association, 75th Anniv. — A850

1993, Feb. 28 Litho. ***Perf. 13x13½***
1522 A850 15p multicolored .20 .20

New Building for Ministry of Foreign Affairs A851

1993, Mar. 15 ***Perf. 13***
1523 A851 15p multicolored .20 .20
1524 A851 80p multicolored 1.00 1.00

Diplomacy Day (#1523). No. 1524 is airmail.

Feasts — A852

1993, Mar. 20 Litho. ***Perf. 13x13½***
1525 A852 15p Opuntia .20 .20

Newspaper, Le Progres Egyptien, Cent. — A853

1993, Apr. 15 Litho. ***Perf. 13x13½***
1526 A853 15p multicolored .20 .20

A854

A855

1993, May 15 Litho. ***Perf. 13½x13***

1527 A854 15p multicolored .20 .20

World Telecommunications Day.

1993, June 15 Litho. ***Perf. 13½x13***

1528 A855 15p multicolored .20 .20

UN Conference on Human Rights, Vienna.

Organization of African Unity — A856

1993, June 26 ***Perf. 13***

1529 A856 15p yel grn & multi .20 .20
1530 A856 80p red violet & multi .85 .85

No. 1530 is airmail.

World PTT Conference, Cairo — A857

1993, Sept. 4 Litho. ***Perf. 13***

1531 A857 15p multicolored .20 .20

Salah El-Din El Ayubi (1137-1193), Dome of the Rock — A858

1993, Sept. 4

1532 A858 55p multicolored .60 .60

A859

A860

1993, Oct. 6

1533 A859 15p multicolored .20 .20

October War Against Israel, 20th Anniv.

1993, Oct. 12 ***Perf. 13½x13***

1534 A860 15p cream & multi .20 .20
1535 A860 55p silver & multi .60 .60
1536 A860 80p gold & multi .90 .90

Imperf

Size: 90x70mm

1537 A860 80p multicolored .90 .90
Nos. 1534-1537 (4) 2.60 2.60

Pres. Mohamed Hosni Mubarak, Third Term.

Reduction of Natural Disasters A861

1993, Oct. 24 Litho. ***Perf. 13***

1538 A861 80p multicolored .90 .90

Electricity in Egypt, Cent. — A862

1993, Oct. 24 ***Perf. 13½x13***

1539 A862 15p multicolored .20 .20

Intl. Conference on Big Dams, Cairo — A863

1993, Nov. 19 Litho. ***Perf. 13***

1540 A863 15p multicolored .20 .20

35th Military Intl. Soccer Championship — A864

1993, Dec. 1 Litho. ***Perf. 13x13½***

1541 A864 15p orange & multi .20 .20
1542 A864 15p Trophy, emblem .20 .20

9th Men's Junior World Handball Championship (#1542).

Famous Men Type of 1988
Inscribed "1993"

#1543, A. Al. Bishry. #1544, M.F. Abu Hadeed. #1545, M.B. Al. Tunisy. #1546, Ali Moubarak.

1993, Dec. 25 ***Perf. 13½x13***

1543 A760 15p blue .20 .20
1544 A760 15p blue black .20 .20
1545 A760 15p light violet .20 .20
1546 A760 15p green .20 .20
Nos. 1543-1546 (4) .80 .80

Post Day — A865

1994, Jan. 2

1547 A865 15p Amenhotep III .20 .20
1548 A865 55p Queen Hatshepsut .60 .60
1549 A865 80p Thutmose III .90 .90
Nos. 1547-1549 (3) 1.70 1.70

Congress of Egyptian Sedimentary Geology Society — A866

1994, Jan. 4 Litho. ***Perf. 13x13½***

1550 A866 15p multicolored .20 .20

Birds A867

1994, Mar. 3 Litho. ***Perf. 13***

1551 A867 Block of 4, #a.-d. .75 .75
a. 15p Egyptian swallow .20 .20
b. 15p Fire crest .20 .20
c. 15p Rose-ringed parrot .20 .20
d. 15p Goldfinch .20 .20

Festivals 1994.

A868

A869

1994, Mar. 25 ***Perf. 13½x13***

1552 A868 15p multicolored .20 .20

Arab Scouting, 40th anniv.

1994, Apr. 9 Litho. ***Perf. 13½x13***

1553 A869 15p multicolored .20 .20

27th Cairo Intl. Fair.

A870

A871

1994, Apr. 15 Litho. ***Perf. 13***

1554 A870 15p green & brown .20 .20

1994 African Telecommunications Exhibition, Cairo.

1994, Apr. 30 Litho. ***Perf. 13***

1555 A871 15p grn, blk & blue .20 .20

Natl. Afforestation Campaign.

5th Arab Energy Conference, Cairo. — A872

Litho.
Perf. 13

1994, July 5

1556 A872 15p multicolored .20 .20

Signing of Washington Accord for Palestinian Self-Rule in Gaza and Jericho — A873

1994, May 4 Litho. *Perf. 13*
1557 A873 15p multicolored .20 .20

18th Biennial Art Exhibition, Alexandria — A874

1994, May 21
1558 A874 15p yel, blk & gray .20 .20

Organization of African Unity — A875

1994, May 25
1559 A875 15p multicolored .20 .20

Natl. Reading Festival — A876

1994, June 15
1560 A876 15p multicolored .20 .20

ILO, 75th Anniv. — A877

1994, June 28 Litho. *Perf. 13½x13*
1561 A877 15p multicolored .20 .20

Intl. Conference on Population and Development, Cairo — A878

15p, Conference, UN emblems. 80p, Drawings, hieroglyphics, conference emblem.

1994, Sept. 5 Litho. *Perf. 13*
1562 A878 15p multi .20 .20
1563 A878 80p multi, vert. .50 .50

No. 1563 is airmail.

World Junior Squash Championships — A879

1994, Sept. 14 Litho. *Perf. 13*
1564 A879 15p multicolored .20 .20

World Post Day A880

1994, Oct. 9 Litho. *Perf. 13*
1565 A880 15p multicolored .20 .20

Intl. Red Cross & Red Crescent Societies, 75th Anniv. — A881

1994, Oct. 24
1566 A881 80p multicolored .50 .50

Akhbar El-Yom Newpaper, 50th Anniv. — A882

1994, Nov. 11
1567 A882 15p multicolored .20 .20

African Field Hockey Club Championships — A883

1994, Nov. 14 Litho. *Perf. 13*
1568 A883 15p multicolored .20 .20

A884

Opera Aida, by Verdi — A885

1994, Nov. 26
1569 A884 15p multicolored .20 .20

Imperf

Size: 58x69mm

1570 A885 80p multicolored .90 .90

No. 1570 is airmail.

Intl. Olympic Committee, Cent. — A886

Egyptian Youth Hostels Assoc., 40th Anniv. — A887

1994, Dec. 10 *Perf. 13*
1571 A886 15p multicolored .20 .20

1994, Dec. 24
1572 A887 15p multicolored .20 .20

Intl. Speed Ball Federation, 10th Anniv. — A888

1994, Dec. 25
1573 A888 15p multicolored .20 .20

African Development Bank, 30th Anniv. — A889

1994, Dec. 26
1574 A889 15p multicolored .20 .20

Opening of Suez Canal, 125th Anniv. — A890

Design: 80p, Map, inaugural ceremony.

1994, Dec. 27
1575 A890 15p multicolored .20 .20
1576 A890 80p multicolored .90 .90

No. 1576 is airmail.

Famous Men — A891

Post Day — A892

1994, Dec. 29
1577 A891 15p Hassan Fathy, engineer .20 .20
1578 A891 15p Mahmoud Taimour, writer .20 .20

1995, Jan. 2 Litho. *Perf. 13½x13*

15p, Statue of Akhenaton. 55p, Golden mask of King Tutankhamen. 80p, Statue of Nefertiti.

1579 A892 15p multicolored .20 .20
1580 A892 55p multicolored .60 .60
1581 A892 80p multicolored .90 .90
Nos. 1579-1581 (3) 1.70 1.70

World Tourism Organization, 20th Anniv. — A893

1995, Jan. 2 *Perf. 13x13½*
1582 A893 15p multicolored .20 .20

Festivals — A894

1995, Feb. 25 Litho. *Perf. 13x13½*
1583 A894 15p multicolored .20 .20

Egyptian Women's Day — A895

1995, Mar. 16 Litho. *Perf. 13x13½*
1584 A895 15p multicolored .20 .20

Arab League, 50th Anniv. — A896

1995, Mar. 22 *Perf. 13½x13*
1585 A896 15p blue & multi .20 .20
1586 A896 55p green & multi .60 .60

Sheraton Hotel, Cairo, 25th Anniv. — A897

1995, Mar. 28 *Perf. 13x13½*
1587 A897 15p multicolored .20 .20

Misr Bank, 75th Anniv. — A898

1995, May 7 Litho. *Perf. 13½x13*
1588 A898 15p multicolored .20 .20

World Telecommunications Day — A899

1995, May 31 *Perf. 13x13½*
1589 A899 80p multicolored .50 .50

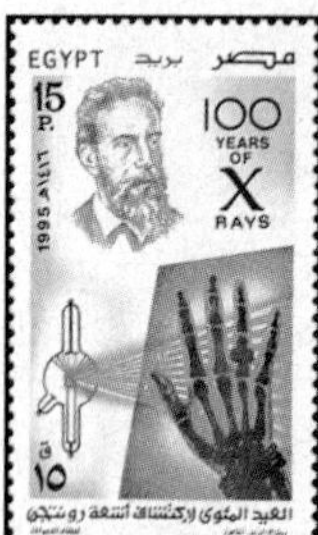

Wilhelm Roentgen (1845-1923), Discovery of the X-Ray, Cent. — A900

1995, May Litho. *Perf. 13½x13*
1590 A900 15p multicolored .20 .20

Membership in World Heritage Committee, 20th Anniv. (in 1994) — A901

Artifacts from the Shaft of Luxor: No. 1591, Goddess Hathor. No. 1592, God Atoum. 80p, God Amon and Horemheb.

1995, July 23 Litho. *Perf. 13½x13*
1591 15p multicolored .20 .20
1592 15p multicolored .20 .20
a. A901 Pair, #1591-1592 .20 .20
1593 A901 80p multicolored .50 .50
Nos. 1591-1593 (3) .90 .90

#1592a is a continuous design. #1593 is airmail.

21st Intl. Conference on Pediatrics, Cairo A902

1995, Sept. 10 Litho. *Perf. 13*
1594 A902 15p multicolored .20 .20

Intl. Ozone Day — A903

1995, Sept. 16 Litho. *Perf. 13x12½*
1595 A903 15p green & multi .20 .20
1596 A903 55p brown & multi .60 .60
1597 A903 80p blue & multi .85 .85
Nos. 1595-1597 (3) 1.65 1.65

See Nos. 1622-1623.

World Tourism Day A904

1995, Sept. 25 *Perf. 12½x13*
1598 A904 15p multicolored .20 .20

Government Printing House, 175th Anniv. — A905

1995, Sept. 27
1599 A905 15p multicolored .20 .20

Sun Verticality on Abu Simbel Temple A906

1995, Oct. 22 Litho. *Perf. 12½x13*
1600 A906 15p multicolored .20 .20

Opening of New Esna Dam — A907

1995, Nov. 25 *Perf. 12½*
1601 A907 15p multicolored .20 .20

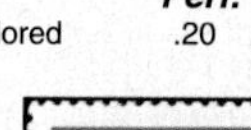

Egyptian Engineers Assoc., 75th Anniv. A908

1995, Dec. 20 *Perf. 13*
1602 A908 15p multicolored .20 .20

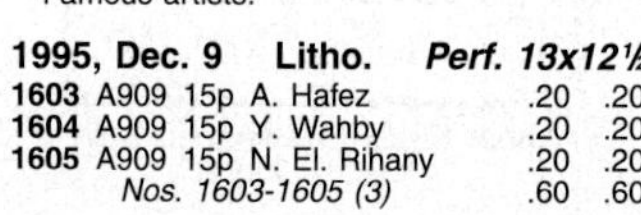

A909 A910

Famous artists.

1995, Dec. 9 Litho. *Perf. 13x12½*
1603 A909 15p A. Hafez .20 .20
1604 A909 15p Y. Wahby .20 .20
1605 A909 15p N. El. Rihany .20 .20
Nos. 1603-1605 (3) .60 .60

1995, Dec. 23 Litho. *Perf. 13x12½*
1606 A910 15p multicolored .20 .20

Motion Pictures, cent.

Post Day A911

Ancient paintings: 55p, Man facing right. 80p, Man facing left. 100p, Playing flute, dancers.

1996, Jan. 2 Litho. *Perf. 13½x13*
1607 55p multicolored .30 .30
1608 80p multicolored .45 .45
a. A911 Pair, Nos. 1607-1608 .75 .75

Imperf
Size: 88x72mm
1609 A911 100p multicolored .60 .60

Nos. 1607-1608 are airmail.

Feasts — A912

1996, Feb. 15 *Perf. 12½*
1610 A912 15p blue flowers .20 .20
1611 A912 15p red flowers .20 .20
a. Pair, No. 1610-1611 .20 .20

A913 A914

1996, Mar. 13 Litho. *Perf. 13x12½*
1612 A913 15p pink & multi .20 .20
1613 A913 80p brown & multi .45 .45

Summit of Peace Makers, Sharm al-Sheikh. No. 1613 is airmail.

1996, Mar. 16
1614 A914 15p multicolored .20 .20

29th Intl. Fair, Cairo.

Egyptian Geological Survey, Cent. A915

1996, Mar. 18 *Perf. 12½x13*
1615 A915 15p multicolored .20 .20

A916 A917

1996, Apr. 11 Litho. *Perf. 13x12½*
1616 A916 15p blue & multi .20 .20
1617 A916 80p pink & multi .45 .45

Signing of African Nuclear Weapon-Free Zone Treaty.

1996, Apr. 20 Litho. *Perf. 13x12½*
1618 A917 15p multicolored .20 .20

Egyptian Society of Accountants and Auditors, 50th anniv.

A918 A919

1996, May 4
1619 A918 15p multicolored .20 .20

General census.

1996, July 15 Litho. *Perf. 13x12½*

1996 Summer Olympics, Atlanta: 15p, Atlanta 1996 emblem. £1, Emblem surrounded by sports pictograms.

1620 A919 15p lilac & multi .20 .20

Size: 63x103mm

Imperf

1621 A919 £1 black & multi .75 .75

No. 1621 is airmail.

Intl. Ozone Day Type of 1995

1996, Sept. 16 Litho. *Perf. 13x12½*

1622 A903 15p pink & multi .20 .20
1623 A903 80p gray & multi .50 .50

No. 1623 is airmail.

A920

A921

1996, Sept. 19

1624 A920 80p multicolored .50 .50

2nd Alexandriate World Festival.

1996, Sept. 21

1625 A921 15p grn, blk & bl .20 .20

Scientific Research and Technology Academy, 25th anniv.

Opening of 2nd Line of Greater Cairo Subway System A922

1996, Oct. 7 *Perf. 12½x13*

1626 A922 15p multicolored .20 .20

Rowing Festival A923

1996

1627 A923 15p multicolored .20 .20

Courts of the State Council, 50th Anniv. A924

1996, Nov. 2 Litho. *Perf. 12½x13*

1628 A924 15p blue & claret .20 .20

A925

A926

1996, Nov. 4 *Perf. 13x12½*

1629 A925 15p yel, blk & blue .20 .20

Intl. Federation Training Development Organization World Conf.

1996, Nov. 12 Litho. *Perf. 13x12½*

Cairo Economic Summit (MENA): £1, Graph, earth, gear, olive branch, wheat.

1630 A926 15p shown .20 .20

Size: 65x45mm

Imperf

1631 A926 £1 multicolored .60 .60

No. 1631 is airmail.

A927

A928

1996, Nov. 13 *Perf. 13x12½*

1632 A927 15p multicolored .20 .20

1996 World Food Summit, Rome.

1996, Nov. 16

National Day of El-Gharbia Governorate: Al Sayd Ahmed El-Badawy mosque, Tanta.

1633 A928 15p multicolored .20 .20

A929

A930

Famous artists.

1996, Dec. 28 Litho. *Perf. 13x12½*

1634 A929 20p Ali El-Kassar .20 .20
1635 A929 20p George Abyad .20 .20
1636 A929 20p Mohamed Kareem .20 .20
1637 A929 20p Fatma Roshdi .20 .20
Nos. 1634-1637 (4) .80 .80

See Nos. 1666-1669.

1997, Jan. 2

1638 A930 20p multicolored .20 .20

Size: 61x80mm

Imperf

1639 A930 £1 multicolored .60 .60

Discovery of Tutankhamen's tomb, 75th anniv.

No. 1639 is airmail.

Police Day A931

1997, Jan. 25 Litho. *Perf. 13x13½*

1640 A931 20p multicolored .20 .20

Feasts — A932

1997, Feb. 1 *Perf. 13*

1641 A932 20p pink flowers .20 .20
1642 A932 20p white fowers .20 .20
a. Pair, #1641-1642 .20 .20

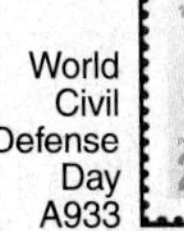

World Civil Defense Day A933

1997, Mar. 10 Litho. *Perf. 13x13½*

1643 A933 20p multicolored .20 .20

30th Cairo Intl. Fair — A934

1997, Mar. 19 *Perf. 13½x13*

1644 A934 20p multicolored .20 .20

Mahmoud Said, Photographer, Artist, Birth Cent. — A935

The City, By Mahmoud Said — A936

Illustration reduced (A936).

1997, Apr. 12 Litho. *Perf. 12½*

1645 A935 20p multicolored .20 .20

Size: 80x60mm

Imperf

1646 A936 £1 multicolored .60 .60

No. 1646 is airmail.

Institute of African Research and Studies, 50th Anniv. — A937

1997, May 27 Litho. *Perf. 13*

1647 A937 75p multicolored .45 .45

New Headquarters of State Information Service — A938

1997, Aug. 16 Litho. *Perf. 12½*

1648 A938 20p multicolored .20 .20

A939

A940

£1, Mascot, soccer ball, playing field, emblems.

1997, Sept. 4 *Perf. 13x12½*

1649 A939 20p multicolored .20 .20
1650 AP81 75p multicolored .45 .45

Size: 75x55mm

Imperf

1651 A939 £1 multicolored .60 .60

Nos. 1650-1651 are airmail. Under 17 FIFA World Soccer Championships, Egypt.

1997, Sept. 16 *Perf. 13*

1652 A940 20p lt bl grn & multi .20 .20
1653 A940 £1 pink & multi .60 .60

Montreal Protocol on Substances that Deplete the Ozone Layer, 10th anniv. No. 1653 is airmail.

Completion of Second Stage of Metro Line No. 2 — A941

1997, Sept. 27 *Perf. 12½x13*

1654 A941 20p multicolored .20 .20

Premiere in Egypt of Opera Aida, by Verdi, 125th Anniv. A942

1997, Oct. 12 *Perf. 13*

1655 A942 20p multicolored .20 .20

Size: 80x75mm

Imperf

1656 A942 £1 like #1655 .60 .60

No. 1656 is airmail.

Queen Nefertari — A943

1997, Oct. 25 Litho. *Perf. 13*

1657 A943 £1 multicolored .60 .60

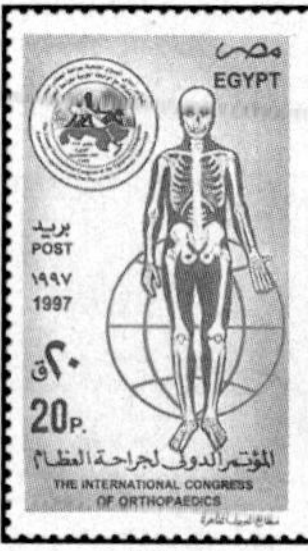
A944

A945

1997, Nov. 17 Litho. *Perf. 13*
1658 A944 20p multicolored .20 .20

Intl. Congress of Orthopedics, Cairo.

1997, Nov. 22 *Perf. 13x12½*

Designs: 20p, Goddess Selket. £1, Scarab, baboon pendant.

1659 A945 20p black & gold .20 .20

Size: 73x62mm

Imperf

1660 A945 £1 multicolored .60 .60

No. 1660 is airmail. Discovery of King Tutanhkamen's tomb, 75th anniv.

Inauguration of Nubia Monument Museum — A946

1997, Nov. 23 *Perf. 13*
1661 A946 20p multicolored .20 .20

Arab Land Bank, 50th Anniv. — A947

1997, Dec. 10 *Perf. 12½*
1662 A947 20p multicolored .20 .20

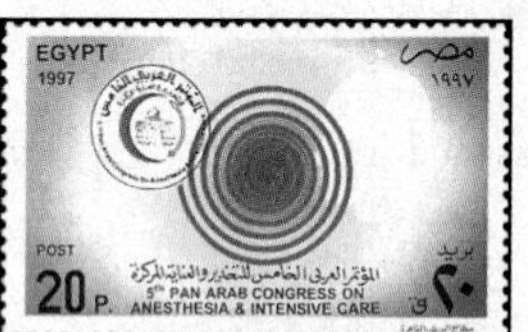
5th Pan Arab Congress on Anesthesia and Intensive Care — A948

1997, Dec. 9 Litho. *Perf. 13*
1663 A948 20p multicolored .20 .20

El Salaam Canal — A949

1997, Dec. 28
1664 A949 20p multicolored .20 .20

Liberation of Sinai, 15th anniv.

A950

A951

Famous Artists Type of 1996 and A950

1997, Dec. 23 Litho. *Perf. 13x12½*
1665 A950 20p blue .20 .20
1666 A929 20p Zaky Tolaimat .20 .20
1667 A929 20p Ismael Yassen .20 .20
1668 A929 20p Zaky Roustom .20 .20
1669 A929 20p Soliman Naguib .20 .20
a. Strip of 5, #1665-1669 .70 .70

1998, Jan. 2 *Perf. 13*

Stamp Day: 20p, King Tutankhamen's guard. 75p, King Ramses III. £1, Cover of King Tutankhamen's coffin.

1670 A951 20p multicolored .20 .20
1671 A951 75p multicolored .55 .55

Size: 26x43mm

1672 A951 £1 multicolored .70 .70

Nos. 1671-1672 are airmail.

Feasts — A952

1998, Jan. 20
1673 20p multicolored .20 .20
1674 20p multicolored .20 .20
a. A952 Pair, #1673-1674 .30 .30

Intl. Cairo Fair — A954

Natl. Bank of Egypt, Cent. — A955

1998, Mar. 11 Litho. *Perf. 13*
1675 A954 20p multicolored .20 .20

1998, Mar. 12
1676 A955 20p multicolored .20 .20

Tutankhamen A956

Thutmose IV A957

1998 Litho. *Perf. 13¼x12½*
1677 A956 £2 multicolored 1.40 1.40
1678 A957 £5 purple & black 3.50 3.50

Issued: £2, 4/23; £5, 3/23.

A958

A959

1998, Apr. 14 *Perf. 13*
1679 A958 20p green & multi .20 .20
1680 A958 75p blue & multi .55 .55

Size: 70x52mm

Imperf

1681 A958 £1 Natl. flags, map, trophy .70 .70

Egypt, winners of 21st African Cup of Nations soccer competition.
Nos. 1680-1681 are airmail.

1998, May 30 Litho. *Perf. 13*
1682 A959 20p Egyptian Satellite "Nile Sat" .20 .20

World Environment Day — A960

1998, June 5
1683 A960 20p shown .20 .20

Size: 43x62mm

Imperf

1684 A960 £1 Fauna, emblems .70 .70

No. 1684 is airmail.

A961

A962

1998, June 14
1685 A961 20p blue & black .20 .20
1686 A961 £1 yellow, green & black .70 .70

Dr. Ahmed Zewail, winner of Franklin Institute award.
No. 1686 is airmail.

1998, July 15

Imam Sheikh Mohamed Metwalli Al-Shaarawi.

1687 A962 20p buff & multi .20 .20
1688 A962 £1 green & multi .70 .70

No. 1688 is airmail.

A963

A964

1998, Sept. 12 Litho. *Perf. 13*
1689 A963 20p multicolored .20 .20

Day of the Nile Flood.

1998, Sept. 30 Litho. *Perf. 13*
1690 A964 20p multicolored .20 .20

Chemistry Administration, cent.

October War Against Israel, 25th Anniv. — A965

1998, Oct. 6 Litho. *Perf. 13*
1691 A965 20p multicolored .20 .20

Size: 50x70mm

Imperf

1692 A965 £2 like #1691 1.40 1.40

No. 1692 is airmail.

Egyptian Survey Authority, Cent. — A966

1998, Oct. 15 *Perf. 13*
1693 A966 20p multicolored .20 .20

Cairo University, 90th Anniv. — A967

1998, Dec. 7 Litho. *Perf. 13*
1694 A967 20p multicolored .20 .20

A968

A970

1998, Dec. 17 Litho. *Perf. 13*
1695 A968 20p multicolored .20 .20

Egyptian trade unions, cent.

1999, Jan. 2 Litho. *Perf. 13*

Post Day (19th Dynasty): 20p, Queen Nefertari, Goddess Isis. 125p, God Osiris, Goddess Isis.

1696 A970 20p multicolored .20 .20

Size: 41x61mm

Imperf

1697 A970 125p multicolored .75 .75

No. 1697 is airmail.

Feasts — A971

1999, Jan. 5 *Perf. 13*
1698 20p multicolored .20 .20
1699 20p multicolored .20 .20
a. A971 Pair, #1698-1699 .20 .20

Intl. Women's Day — A973

1999, Mar. 7 Litho. *Perf. 13*
1700 A973 20p multicolored .20 .20

Cairo Intl. Fair — A974

1999, Mar. 9
1701 A974 20p multicolored .20 .20

Opening of Metro Line Beneath Nile River — A975

1999, Apr. Litho. *Perf. 13*
1702 A975 20p multicolored .20 .20

A976

UPU, 125th Anniv. — A977

1999, Apr. 21
1703 A976 20p shown .20 .20
1704 A976 £1 multi .60 .60
1705 A977 125p shown .75 .75

Size: 50x70mm

Imperf

1706 A977 125p multi .75 .75
Nos. 1703-1706 (4) 2.30 2.30

Nos. 1704-1706 are airmail.

A978

A980

1999, May 8 *Perf. 13*
1707 A978 20p green & multi .20 .20
1708 A978 125p buff, red & multi .75 .75

Geneva Conventions, 50th anniv. No. 1708 is airmail.

1999, May 20 Litho. *Perf. 13x12¾*
1710 A980 20p green & multi .20 .20
1711 A980 £1 buff & multi .60 .60

African Development Bank, 35th Meeting, Cairo. No. 1711 is airmail.

16th Men's Handball World Championship — A981

20p, Stylized player with ball, pyramids. 1£, Mascot with ball, Sphinx, pyramids, globe. 125p, Mascot with ball, goalie, pyramids.

1999, June 1 *Perf. 13*
1712 A981 20p multicolored .20 .20
1713 A981 £1 multicolored .60 .60
1714 A981 125p multicolored .75 .75
Nos. 1712-1714 (3) 1.55 1.55

Nos. 1713-1714 are airmail.

Goddess Selket — A982

1999, June 23 Litho. *Perf. 13*
1715 A982 25p multicolored .20 .20

See Nos. 1750, 1754.

SOS Children's Village, 50th Anniv. — A983

1999, June 23 *Perf. 12¾x13¼*
1716 A983 20p grn, blk & blue .20 .20
1717 A983 125p buff, blk & bl .75 .75

No. 1717 is airmail.

A984

A985

#1718, Sameera Moussa (1917-52), Physicist. #1719, Aisha Abdul Rahman (1913-98), writer. #1720, Ahmed Eldemerdash Touny (1907-97), member of Intl. Olympic Committee.

1999 Litho. *Perf. 13x12¾*
1718 A984 20p multicolored .20 .20
1719 A984 20p multicolored .20 .20
1720 A984 20p multicolored .20 .20
Nos. 1718-1720 (3) .60 .60

Issued: #1718-1719, 7/23; #1720, 8/13.
See Nos. 1730-1733.

1999, Oct. 5 Litho. *Perf. 13x12¾*
1721 A985 20p org & multi .20 .20
1722 A985 £1 silver & multi .60 .60
1723 A985 125p gold & multi .75 .75

Imperf

1724 A985 125p multicolored .75 .75
Nos. 1721-1724 (4) 2.30 2.30

Pres. Hosni Mubarak, 4th term.
Nos. 1722-1724 are airmail.

A986

A987

1999, Nov. 15 Litho. *Perf. 13¼x13*

Background Color

1725 A986 20p green .20 .20
1726 A986 £1 red vio .60 .60
1727 A986 125p purple .75 .75
Nos. 1725-1727 (3) 1.55 1.55

Intl. Year of the Elderly. Nos. 1726-1727 are airmail.

1999, Nov. 20
1728 A987 20p multi .20 .20

Children's Day.

Famous People Type of 1999

#1730, Farid El Attrash (1913-76), singer, movie star. #1731, Laila Mourad (1918-95), singer, movie star. #1732, Anwar Wagdi (1911-55), actor, director. #1733, Asia Dagher (1901-86), actor, producer.

1999, Dec. 30 Litho. ***Perf. 13x12¾***

1730 A984 20p lt bl & blk .20 .20
1731 A984 20p lt bl & blk .20 .20
1732 A984 20p lt bl & blk .20 .20
1733 A984 20p lt bl & blk .20 .20
Nos. 1730-1733 (4) .80 .80

Millennium
A989

20p, "1999" & "2000." 125p, Countdown of years. £2, Holy Family, Virgin Tree.

2000, Jan. 1 ***Perf. 13x12¾***

1734 A989 20p multi .20 .20
1735 A989 125p multi .75 .75

Size: 70x50mm

Imperf

1736 A989 £2 multi, horiz. 1.25 1.25
Nos. 1734-1736 (3) 2.20 2.20

Nos. 1735-1736 are airmail.

A990

Post Day — A991

2000, Jan. 2 ***Perf. 13¼x12¾***

1737 A990 20p multi .20 .20
1738 A991 20p multi .20 .20
a. Pair, #1737-1738 .40 .40

Size: 70x50mm

Imperf

1739 A991 125p Chariot, horiz. .75 .75
Nos. 1737-1739 (3) 1.15 1.15

Ain Shams University, 50th Anniv. — A992

2000, Jan. 3 ***Perf. 13¼x13***

1740 A992 20p multi .20 .20

Feasts
A993 A994

2000, Jan. 5 ***Perf. 13x13¼***

1741 A993 20p multi .20 .20
1742 A994 20p multi .20 .20
a. Pair, #1741-1742 .40 .40

A995

A996

2000, Jan. 20 ***Perf. 13¼x13***

1743 A995 20p multi .20 .20

Islamic Development Bank, 25th anniv.

2000, Feb. 28 ***Perf. 13¼x12¾***

1744 A996 125p multi .75 .75

Common Market for Eastern and Southern Africa Economic Conference.

Death of Om Kolthoum, 25th Anniv. — A997

Europe-Africa Summit, Cairo — A999

8th Intl. Congress of Egyptologists — A998

2000, Mar. 11 ***Perf. 13¼x13***

1745 A997 20p multi .20 .20

2000, Mar. 28 ***Perf. 13x13¼***

1746 A998 20p multi .20 .20

2000, Apr. 3 ***Perf. 13¼x13***

1747 A999 125p multi .75 .75

Group of 15 Developing Nations, 10th Summit, Cairo — A1000

Perf. 12¾x13¼

2000, June 19 Litho.

1748 A1000 125p multi .75 .75

Goddess Selket Type of 1999 and

Scene from 20th Dynasty
A1003

Nofret, Wife of Rahotep
A1004

King Seostris
A1005

Princess Merit Aton
A1006

20th Dynasty — A1007

Pyramid at Snefru
A1008

Wife of Sheikh-el-Balad
A1009

King Psusennes I
A1010

King Tutankhamen
A1011

Obelisk of Ramses II
A1011a

Temple of Karnak
A1012

Perf. 12¾x13¼, 11¼ (#1752-1755, 1757), 11x11½ (#1758-1760), 13¼x12¾ (#1756, 1761, 1763)

Photo., Litho. (#1751, 1761, 1763)

2000-2002

1750 A982 10p multi .20 .20
1751 A1003 10p multi .20 .20
1752 A1004 20p multi .20 .20
1753 A1005 25p multi .20 .20
1754 A982 30p multi .30 .20
1755 A1006 30p multi .20 .20
1756 A1007 50p multi .20 .20
1757 A1008 £1 multi .45 .45
1758 A1009 110p multi .50 .50
1759 A1010 125p multi .55 .55
1760 A1011 150p multi .65 .65
1761 A1011a 225p multi 1.00 1.00
1763 A1012 £5 multi 2.25 2.25
Nos. 1750-1763 (13) 6.90 6.80

Issued: 20p, 6/25; 10p, 3/25/01; 30p, 6/11/01. Nos. 1751, 1755, 225p, 5/25/02; 110p, 6/4/02; 125p, 6/20/02; 150p, 6/15/02; £5, 6/1/02. 30p, 50p, #1, 6/30/02.

Intl. Day Against Drug Abuse — A1013

Perf. 12¾x13¼

2000, June 26 Litho.

1764 A1013 20p multi .20 .20

See No. 1796.

Natl. Insurance Company, Cent. — A1014

Perf. 13¼x12¾

2000, Aug. 20 Litho.

1765 A1014 20p shown .20 .20

Imperf

Size: 96x75mm

1766 A1014 125p Emblem, building, horiz. .75 .75

2000 Summer Olympics, Sydney A1015

Background colors: 20p, Light blue. 125p, Pink.

2000, Sept. 9 ***Perf. 13¼x12¾***
1767-1768 A1015 Set of 2 .80 .80

No. 1768 is airmail.

Productive Cooperative Union, 25th Anniv. — A1016

2000, Sept. 15 ***Perf. 12¾x13¼***
1769 A1016 20p multi .20 .20

Opening of Fourth Stage of Second Cairo Subway Line — A1017

2000, Oct. 7
1770 A1017 20p multi .20 .20

World Post Day — A1018

2000, Oct. 9
1771 A1018 125p multi .75 .75

Solidarity with Palestinians — A1019

Palestinian Authority flag and: 20p, Dome of the Rock, Jerusalem, vert. No. 1773, 125p, shown. No. 1774, 125p, Dome of the Rock, father and boy, vert.

Perf. 13¼x12¾, 12¾x13¼
2000, Nov. 29
1772-1774 A1019 Set of 3 1.50 1.50

No. 1774 is airmail.

Opening of El-Ferdan Railway Bridge — A1020

2000, Dec. 2 ***Perf. 12¾x13¼***
1775 A1020 20p multi .20 .20

Disabled Person's Day — A1021

2000, Dec. 9 ***Perf. 13¼x12¾***
1776 A1021 20p multi .20 .20

Opening of Al-Azhar Professional Building — A1022

2000, Dec. 10 ***Perf. 12¾x13¼***
1777 A1022 20p multi .20 .20

Famous Egyptians A1023

No. 1778: a, Karem Mahmoud, artist (yellow background). b, Mahmoud El-Miligi, artist (green background). c, Mohamed Fawzi, musician (pink background). d, Hussein Riyad, artist (lilac background). e, Abdel Wares Asser, artist (light blue background).

2000, Dec. 24 ***Perf. 13¼x12¾***
1778 Horiz. strip of 5 1.00 1.00
a.-e. A1023 20p Any single .20 .20

Feasts — A1024

a, Red and yellow flowers. b, Purple flowers.

Perf. 12¾x13¼
2000, Dec. 23 **Litho.**
1779 A1024 20p Pair, #a-b .40 .40

Jerusalem, City of Peace — A1025

Illustration reduced.

2001, Jan. 1 ***Imperf.***
1780 A1025 £2 multi 1.00 1.00

Post Day — A1026

Ancient Egyptian art: 20p, 8 standing figures. #1782, 125p, 3 large standing figures.

2001, Jan. 2 ***Perf. 12¾x13¼***
1781-1782 A1026 Set of 2 .75 .75

Imperf

Size: 80x60mm

1783 A1026 125p Chariot .75 .75

No. 1782 is airmail.

Arab Labor Organization, 36th Anniv. — A1027

Perf. 13¼x12¾
2001, Feb. 10 **Litho.**
1784 A1027 20p multi .20 .20

Postal Savings Bank, Cent. — A1028

2001, Mar. 1
1785 A1028 20p multi .20 .20

Natl. Council for Women, 1st Anniv. — A1029

Background colors: 30p, Pink. 125p, Blue.

2001, Mar. 16 ***Perf. 12¾x13¼***
1786-1787 A1029 Set of 2 1.00 .80

No. 1787 is airmail.

Cairo Intl. Fair — A1030

2001, Mar. 21 ***Perf. 13¼x12¾***
1788 A1030 30p multi .20 .20

Helwan University, 25th Anniv. — A1031

2001, May 4 ***Perf. 12¾x13¼***
1789 A1031 30p multi .20 .20

Inauguration of Alexandria Library — A1032

2001, May 20
1790 A1032 125p multi .75 .75

African Conference on the Future of Children A1033

Background color: 30p, Blue. 125p, Red.

2001, May 28 ***Perf. 13¼x12¾***
1791-1792 A1033 Set of 2 1.00 .80

No. 1792 is airmail.

World Environment Day — A1034

2001, June 5 **Litho.** ***Perf. 13¼x12¾***
1793 A1034 125p multi .75 .75

World Military Soccer Championships A1035

Designs: 30p, Emblem. 125p, Emblem and map.

Perf. 13¼x12¾

2001, June 21 **Litho.**
1794-1795 A1035 Set of 2 1.00 .80

Intl. Day Against Drug Abuse Type of 2000

2001, June 26 ***Perf. 12¾x13¼***
1796 A1013 30p multi .20 .20

Egypt's Victory in World Military Soccer Championships — A1036

Illustration reduced.

2001, July 6 **Litho.** ***Imperf.***
1797 A1036 125p multi .75 .75

Egyptian Railways, 150th Anniv. — A1037

2001, July 12 ***Perf. 12¾x13¼***
1798 A1037 30p multi .20 .20

Poets — A1038

No. 1799: a, Aziz Abaza Pasha (1898-73), blue background. b, Ahmed Rami (1892-1981), pink background.

2001, July 28 ***Perf. 13¼x12¾***
1799 A1038 30p Horiz. pair, #a-b .30 .30

Intl. Volunteers Year — A1039

2001, Aug. 18
1800 A1039 125p multi .75 .75

Ismailia Folklore Festival — A1040

2001, Aug. 20
1801 A1040 30p multi .20 .20

Satellite Telecommunications Ground Stations, 25th Anniv. — A1041

2001, Sept. 8 ***Perf. 12¾x13¼***
1802 A1041 30p multi .20 .20

Year of Dialogue Among Civilizations A1042

Designs: No. 1803, 125p, Emblem. No. 1804, 125p, UN emblem, globe, symbols of various civilizations, horiz.

Perf. 13¼x12¾, 12¾x13¼

2001, Oct. 9
1803-1804 A1042 Set of 2 1.50 1.25

Opening of Suez Canal Bridge — A1043

No. 1805: a, 30p, Bridge, ship. b, 125p, Bridge, road.

No. 1806, Bridge, ship and flags of Egypt and Japan.

Illustration reduced.

2001, Oct. 10 ***Perf. 12¾x13¼***
1805 A1043 Horiz. pair, #a-b .75 .75

Imperf

Size: 81x60mm

1806 A1043 125p multi .75 .75

Ancient Gold Masks — A1044

Designs: No. 1807, 30p, Mask of San Xing Dui, China, green background. No. 1808, 30p, Funerary mask of King Tutankhamun, brown background.

2001, Oct. 12 ***Perf. 12¾x13¼***
1807-1808 A1044 Set of 2 .30 .30

See People's Republic of China 3141-3142.

Opening of Azhar Tunnels, Cairo — A1045

2001, Oct. 28 ***Perf. 13¼x12¾***
1809 A1045 30p multi .20 .20

El-Menoufia University, 25th Anniv. — A1046

2001, Nov. 25
1810 A1046 30p multi .20 .20

Feasts — A1047

No.1811: a, Black and white bird on branch. b, Sea gulls. c, Parrot. d, Blue bird on branch.

2001, Dec. 5
1811 A1047 30p Block of 4, #a-d 1.00 .55

Musicians — A1048

No. 1812: a, Zakaria Ahmed (1896-1961) with scarf around neck (4). b, Riyadh El-Sonbati (1908-81) with glasses with rectangular lenses (3). c, Mahmoud El-Sherif (1912-90) (2). d, Mohamed El-Kasabgi (1898-1966) with glasses with round lenses (1). Stamp numbers, shown in parentheses, are found at the bottom center in Arabian script. Illustration reduced.

2001, Dec.
1812 A1048 30p Horiz. strip of 4 1.00 .55

Painting From Tomb of Anhur Khawi — A1049

Painting from Tomb of Irinefer — A1050

Illustration A1050 reduced.

2002, Jan. 2 **Litho.** ***Perf. 12¾x13¼***
1813 A1049 30p multi .20 .20

Imperf

Size: 79x60mm

1814 A1050 125p multi .75 .75

Stamp Day.

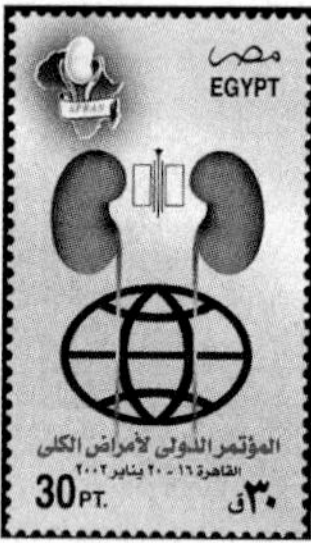

Intl. Nephrology Congress A1051

2002, Jan. 16 **Litho.** ***Perf. 13¼x12¾***
1815 A1051 30p multi .20 .20

Police Day, 50th Anniv. A1052

2002, Jan. 25 ***Perf. 12¾x13¼***
1816 A1052 30p multi .20 .20

Imperf

Size: 79x50mm

1817 A1052 30p multi .20 .20

Return of Sinai to Egypt, 20th Anniv. — A1053

2002, Apr. 25 ***Perf. 13¼x12¾***
1818 A1053 30p multi .20 .20

Cairo Bank, 50th Anniv. — A1054

2002, May 15
1819 A1054 30p multi .20 .20

Weight Lifters — A1055

No. 1820: a, Ibrahim Shams, 1948 (weights over head). b, Khidre el Touney, 1936 (weights at knees).

2002, June 1
1820 A1055 30p Horiz. pair, #a-b .25 .25

Al Akhbar Newspaper, 50th Anniv. — A1056

2002, June 15 ***Perf. 12¾x13¼***
1821 A1056 30p multi .20 .20

Nos. 318-322 and Egyptian Arms — A1057

Illustration reduced.

2002, July 23 **Litho.** ***Imperf.***
1822 A1057 125p multi .55 .55
July 23rd Revolution, 50th anniv.

Aswan Dam, Cent. — A1058

No. 1823: a, Dam. b, Dam and buildings.
Illustration reduced.

2002, Aug. 15 ***Perf. 12¾x13¼***
1823 A1058 30p horiz. pair, #a-b .30 .30

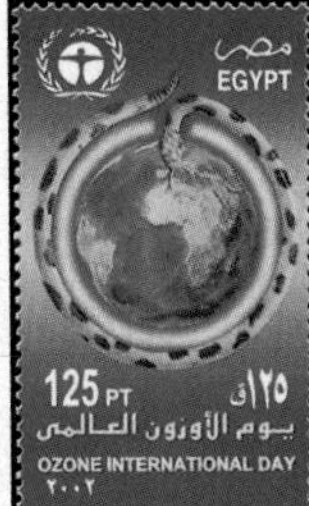
Intl. Day for Preservation of the Ozone Layer — A1059

2002, Sept. 16 ***Perf. 13¼x12¾***
1824 A1059 125p multi .55 .55

18th Intl. Conference on Road Safety, Cairo — A1060

2002, Sept. 22
1825 A1060 30p multi .20 .20

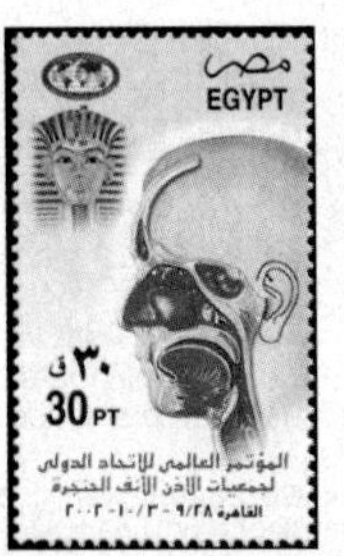
17th Congress of Intl. Federation of Otorhinolaryngological Societies, Cairo — A1061

2002, Sept. 28
1826 A1061 30p multi .20 .20

World Post Day — A1062

2002, Oct. 9
1827 A1062 125p multi .55 .55

Opening of Alexandria Library — A1063

Ancient Alexandria Library — A1064

Designs: 30p, Library exterior. 125p, Pillar, sun on horizon, vert.

Perf. 12¾x13¼, 13¼x12¾
2002, Oct. 16
1828-1829 A1063 Set of 2 .70 .70

Size: 60x80mm
Imperf
1830 A1064 125p multi .55 .55

Hassan Faek, Actor — A1065

Aziza Amir, Actress — A1066

Farid Shawki, Actor — A1067

Mary Mounib, Actress — A1068

2002, Nov. 23 ***Perf. 13¼x12¾***
1831 Horiz. strip of 4 .50 .50
a. A1065 30p tan & black .20 .20
b. A1066 30p tan & black .20 .20
c. A1067 30p tan & black .20 .20
d. A1068 30p tan & black .20 .20

A1069

A1070

A1071

Birds — A1072

2002, Dec. 3 ***Perf. 13¼x12¾***
1832 Block of 4 .50 .50
a. A1069 30p multi .20 .20
b. A1070 30p multi .20 .20
c. A1071 30p multi .20 .20
d. A1072 30p multi .20 .20

Egyptian Museum, Cent. — A1073

2002, Dec. 11 ***Perf. 12¾x13¼***
1833 A1073 30p shown .20 .20

Size: 80x60mm
Imperf
1834 A1073 125p Entrance, statue of Cheops .55 .55

Opening of Aswan Suspension Bridge — A1074

No. 1835: a, Bridge and support cables. b, Bridge towers.
Illustration reduced.

2002, Dec. 17 ***Perf. 12¾x13¼***
1835 A1074 30p Horiz. pair, #a-b .30 .30

Suez Canal University, 25th Anniv. — A1075

2002, Dec. 29 ***Perf. 13¼x12¾***
1836 A1075 30p multi .20 .20

Toshka Land Reclamation Project — A1076

2002, Dec. 31 ***Perf. 12¾x13¼***
1837 A1076 30p multi .20 .20

A1077

A1078

Post Day — A1079

2003, Jan. 2
1838 A1077 30p multi .20 .20
1839 A1078 30p multi .20 .20
1840 A1079 125p multi .55 .55
Nos. 1838-1840 (3) .95 .95

Cairo Intl. Communications and Information Technology Fair — A1080

2003, Jan. 12 Litho. ***Perf. 13¼x12¾***
1841 A1080 30p multi .20 .20

Intl. Nile Children's Song Festival — A1081

Background color: 30p, Brown. 125p, Green.

2003, Jan. 28 ***Perf. 12¾x13¼***
1842-1843 A1081 Set of 2 .60 .60

Intl. Table Tennis Championships — A1082

Background color: 30p, Blue. 125p, Orange.

2003, Feb. 3
1844-1845 A1082 Set of 2 .60 .60

Tenth Intl. Building and Construction Conference A1083

Background color: 30p, Orange. 125p, Blue.

2003, Apr. 1 ***Perf. 13¼x12¾***
1846-1847 A1083 Set of 2 .55 .55

Arab Lawyer's Union, 60th Anniv. — A1084

Background color: 30p, Blue. 125p, Lilac.

2003, Apr. 25 ***Perf. 12¾x13¼***
1848-1849 A1084 Set of 2 .55 .55

Inauguration of First Phase of Smart Village Project — A1085

Denomination color: 30p, White. 125p, Yellow. £1, White.

2003, July 1 ***Perf. 12¾x13¼***
1850-1851 A1085 Set of 2 .55 .55

Size: 79x59mm

Imperf

1852 A1085 £1 multi .35 .35

Writers — A1086

No. 1853: a, Ihsan Abdul Qudous (1919-90) (wearing checked tie). b, Youssef Idris (1927-91) (wearing solid tie).

2003, July 28 ***Perf. 13¼x12¾***
1853 A1086 30p Horiz. pair, #a-b .20 .20

African Men's Basketball Championships A1087

Background color: 30p, Black. 125p, Blue.

2003, Aug. 12
1854-1855 A1087 Set of 2 .50 .50

Natl. Institute of Astronomical and Geophysical Research, Cent. — A1088

2003, Sept. 7 ***Perf. 12¾x13¼***
1856 A1088 30p multi .20 .20

World Tourism Day — A1089

Denomination color: 30p, White. 125p, Red.

Perf. 12¾x13¼

2003, Sept. 27 **Litho.**
1857-1858 A1089 Set of 2 .50 .50

Egypt's Bid for Hosting 2010 World Cup Soccer Championships — A1090

Designs: 30p, Emblem, vert. 125p, Emblem, funerary mask of King Tutankhamen.

Perf. 13¼x12¾, 12¾x13¼

2003, Sept. 27
1859-1860 A1090 Set of 2 .50 .50

October War Against Israel, 30th Anniv. — A1091

2003, Oct. 6 ***Perf. 13¼x12¾***
1861 A1091 30p multi .20 .20

World Post Day — A1092

2003, Oct. 9
1862 A1092 125p multi .40 .40

National Bar Association, 91st Anniv. — A1093

2003, Oct. 30
1863 A1093 30p multi .20 .20

Festivals — A1094

No. 1864: a, Pink orchids. b, White rose. c, Red rose. d, Sunflower.

2003, Nov. 23 ***Perf. 14***
1864 A1094 30p Block of 4, #a-d .40 .40

Film Directors — A1095

No. 1865: a, Salah Abou Seif (balding man with open collar). b, Kamal Selim (round eyeglasses) c, Henri Barakat (square eyeglasses). d, Hassan El Emam.
Illustration reduced.

2003, Dec. 1 ***Perf. 13¼x12¾***
1865 A1095 30p Horiz. strip of 4, #a-d .40 .40

El Gomhoreya Newspaper, 50th Anniv. — A1096

2003, Dec. 7
1866 A1096 30p multi .20 .20

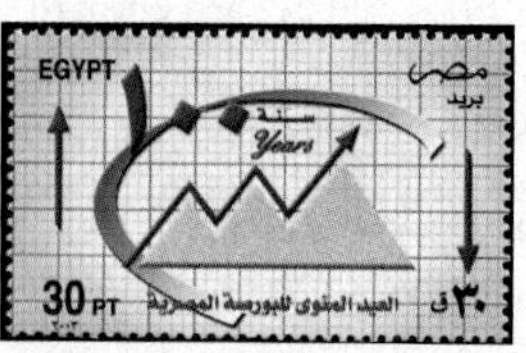

Cairo Bourse, Cent. — A1097

2003, Dec. 7 ***Perf. 12¾x13¼***
1867 A1097 30p multi .20 .20

Mrs. Suzanne Mubarak, Emblems of Fifth E-9 Ministerial Review Meeting and UNESCO — A1098

Background color: 30p, Blue. 125p, Orange. £2, Blue.

Perf. 12¾x13¼

2003, Dec. 18 **Litho.**

1868-1869 A1098 Set of 2 .50 .50

Imperf

Size: 79x60mm

1870 A1098 £2 multi .65 .65

Delta International Bank, 25th Anniv. — A1099

Background color: 30p, Green. 125p, Blue. £2, Green and blue, horiz.

2004, Jan. 1 ***Perf. 12¾x13¼***

1871-1872 A1099 Set of 2 .50 .50

Imperf

Size: 80x60mm

1873 A1099 £2 multi .65 .65

Post Day A1100

Denominations: 30p, 125p.

2004, Jan. 2 ***Perf. 12¾x13¼***

1874-1875 A1100 Set of 2 .50 .50

Eighth Intl. Telecommunications Conference — A1101

2004, Jan. 17

1876 A1101 30p multi .20 .20

Treasures of Egypt A1102

No. 1877: a, Sinai. b, Pyramids at dusk. c, Egyptian Bedouin. d, Red Sea corals. e, Suez Canal, Ferdinand-Marie de Lesseps, Khedive Ismail. f, Ramadan lanterns. g, Nile felucca. h, White Western Desert. i, Maydum Pyramid.

No. 1878: a, St. Catherine Monastery, Sinai. b, Icon of Sts. Paul and Anthony. c, Mosque of Muhammad Ali. d, Lamp, Old Cairo. e, Emblem of Sultan Qaytbay. f, Minaret, Cairo. g, Mosque of al-Azhar. h, Coptic priest and icon, Cairo. i, Ben Ezra Synagogue.

No. 1879: a, Ankh. b, Rosetta Stone. c, Sarcophagus of Ahmes Meritamun. d, Stela of Amenmhat. e, Sphinx. f, Udjat. g, Canopic jars of Tutankhamun. h, Cartouche of Tutankhamun. i, Egyptian scribe.

No. 1880: a, Sphinx, diff. b, Queen Nefertiti. c, Tutankhamun.

2004, Jan. 22 **Litho.** ***Perf. 13x13¼***

1877	Booklet pane of 9	*1.25*	—
a.-i.	A1102 30p Any single	.20	.20
1878	Booklet pane of 9	*5.50*	—
a.-i.	A1102 125p Any single	.60	.60

Litho. & Embossed, Litho. & Embossed With Foil Application (£10)

1879	Booklet pane of 9	*8.75*	—
a.-i.	A1102 £2 Any single	.95	.95

Perf. 13¼

1880	Booklet pane of 3	*9.50*	—
a.-b.	A1102 £5 Either single, 38x51mm	2.25	2.25
c.	A1102 £10 gold & multi, 38x51mm	4.50	4.50
	Complete booklet, #1877-1880	*25.00*	

Complete booklet sold for €10.

Morkos Hanna — A1103

Ahmed Lotfi — A1104

Mahmoud Abu el Nasr — A1105

Abd el Aziz Fahmy — A1106

Ibrahim el Helbawi — A1107

Makram Ebeid — A1108

Mohammad Naguib el Gharabli — A1109

Mohammad Bassiouni A1110

Mohammad Hafez Ramadan A1111

Mohammad Abu Shadi — A1112

Mahmoud Fahmi Goundia — A1113

Kamel Youssof Saleh — A1114

Abd el Hamid Abd el Hakk — A1115

Mohammad Ali Allouba — A1116

Kamel Sedki Beck — A1117

Bar Association Emblem — A1118

Abd el Rahman el Rafei — A1119

Abd el Fattah el Shalkany A1120

Mohammad Sabri Abu Alam — A1121

Omar Omar — A1122

Sameh Ashour — A1123

Ahmed el Khawaga A1124

Abd el Aziz el Shorgabi A1125

Mostafa el Baradei — A1126

2004, Feb. Litho. *Perf. 13¼x12¾*

1881	Block of 25	2.50	2.50
a.	A1103 30p bright blue & black	.20	.20
b.	A1104 30p bright blue & black	.20	.20
c.	A1105 30p bright blue & black	.20	.20
d.	A1106 30p bright blue & black	.20	.20
e.	A1107 30p bright blue & black	.20	.20
f.	A1108 30p pink & black	.20	.20
g.	A1109 30p pink & black	.20	.20
h.	A1110 30p pink & black	.20	.20
i.	A1111 30p pink & black	.20	.20
j.	A1112 30p pink & black	.20	.20
k.	A1113 30p orange & black	.20	.20
l.	A1114 30p orange & black	.20	.20
m.	A1115 30p orange & black	.20	.20
n.	A1116 30p orange & black	.20	.20
o.	A1117 30p orange & black	.20	.20
p.	A1118 30p green & multi	.20	.20
q.	A1119 30p green & black	.20	.20
r.	A1120 30p green & black	.20	.20
s.	A1121 30p green & black	.20	.20
t.	A1122 30p green & black	.20	.20
u.	A1118 30p dark blue & multi	.20	.20
v.	A1123 30p dark blue & black	.20	.20
w.	A1124 30p dark blue & black	.20	.20
x.	A1125 30p dark blue & black	.20	.20
y.	A1126 30p dark blue & black	.20	.20

National Bar Association, 92nd anniv.

IBM Corporation in Egypt, 50th Anniv. — A1127

2004, Feb. 24
1882 A1127 30p multi .20 .20

Cairo Rotary Club, 75th Anniv. — A1128

2004, Mar. 11
1883 A1128 30p multi .20 .20

Egyptian Victory in Regional Computer Programming and Information Technology Competition A1129

2004, Mar. 15
1884 A1129 30p multi .20 .20

National Women's Day — A1130

Background colors: 30p, Blue. 125p, Red orange.

2004, Mar. 16 Litho.
1885-1886 A1130 Set of 2 .50 .50

Anti-Narcotics General Administration, 75th Anniv. — A1131

2004, Mar. 20 *Perf. 12¾x13¼*
1887 A1131 30p multi .20 .20

Imperf

Size: 80x60mm

1888 A1131 125p multi .40 .40

Orphan's Day — A1132

2004, Apr. 2 *Perf. 13¼x12¾*
1889 A1132 30p multi .20 .20

Telecom Africa Fair and Conference, Cairo — A1133

2004, May 4 *Perf. 12¾x13¼*
1890 A1133 30p multi .20 .20

Egyptian Philatelic Society, 75th Anniv. — A1134

Designs: 30p, Emblem. 125p, Emblem, stamp, magnifying glass, tongs.

2004, May 20 *Perf. 13¼x12¾*
1891 A1134 30p multi .20 .20

Imperf

Size: 80x60mm

1892 A1134 125p multi .40 .40

State Information Service, 50th Anniv. — A1135

2004, May 30 *Perf. 12¾x13¼*
1893 A1135 30p multi .20 .20

Tenth Radio and Television Festival, Cairo — A1136

Designs: 30p, Festival emblem, green background. £1, Fesitval emblem, brown background. 125p, Sphinx, festival emblem, film, horiz.
£2, Like 125p, horiz.

Perf. 13¼x12¾, 12¾x13¼

2004, June 1
1894-1896 A1136 Set of 3 .85 .85

Imperf

Size: 80x60mm

1897 A1136 £2 multi .65 .65

Pres. Hosni Mubarak, "Education for All" Arab Regional Conference Emblem — A1137

Stylized Children, Emblems A1138

Perf. 12¾x13¼, 13¼x12¾

2004, June 1

1898	A1137 30p yel & multi	.20	.20
1899	A1137 125p red org & multi	.40	.40
1900	A1138 125p multi	.40	.40
	Nos. 1898-1900 (3)	1.00	1.00

Imperf

Size: 80x60mm

1901 A1137 £2 blue & multi .65 .65

Construction and Housing Bank, 25th Anniv. — A1139

2004, June 24 ***Perf. 13¼x12¾***
1902 A1139 30p multi .20 .20

2004 Summer Olympics, Athens — A1140

Background color: 30p, Gray. 150p, Orange yellow.

Perf. 13¼x12¾
2004, Aug. 13 **Litho.**
1903-1904 A1140 Set of 2 .60 .60

Scouting in Egypt, 90th Anniv. — A1141

2004, Aug. 15 ***Perf. 12¾x13¼***
1905 A1141 30p multi .20 .20

14th Intl. Folklore Festival, Ismailia — A1142

2004, Aug. 24 ***Perf. 13¼x12¾***
1906 A1142 30p multi .20 .20

Administrative Attorneys, 50th Anniv. — A1143

2004, Sept. 16 ***Perf. 13¼x12¾***
1907 A1143 30p multi .20 .20

Imperf
Size: 60x80mm
1908 A1143 £1 multi .35 .35

Egyptian National Archives, 50th Anniv. — A1144

2004, Sept. 20 ***Perf. 12¾x13¼***
1909 A1144 30p multi .20 .20

Light and Hope Society, 50th Anniv. — A1145

2004, Sept. 26
1910 A1145 30p multi .20 .20

General Arab Journalists Union, 10th Conference A1146

2004, Oct. 2 ***Perf. 13¼x12¾***
1911 A1146 125p multi .40 .40

Military Production Day, 50th Anniv. — A1147

2004, Oct. 6 ***Perf. 12¾x13¼***
1912 A1147 30p multi .20 .20

World Post Day — A1148

2004, Oct. 9
1913 A1148 150p multi .50 .50

Egyptian Youth Hostels Association, 50th Anniv. — A1149

2004, Oct. 20 ***Perf. 13¼x12¾***
1914 A1149 30p multi .20 .20

SEMI-POSTAL STAMPS

Catalogue values for unused stamps in this section are for Never Hinged items.

Princess Ferial — SP1

Perf. 13½x14
1940, May 17 **Photo.** **Wmk. 195**
B1 SP1 5m + 5m copper brown .55 .45

No. B1 Overprinted in Green

1943, Nov. 17
B2 SP1 5m + 5m 4.50 3.75
a. Arabic date "1493" 175.00 150.00

The surtax on Nos. B1 and B2 was for the children's fund.

First Postage Stamp of Egypt SP2

Khedive Ismail Pasha SP3

#B5, King Fuad. #B6, King Farouk.

Perf. 13x13½
1946, Feb. 28 **Wmk. 195**

B3	SP2	1m + 1m gray	.20	.20
B4	SP3	10m + 10m violet	.20	.20
B5	SP3	17m + 17m brown	.20	.20
B6	SP3	22m + 22m yel grn	.20	.20
a.		Souv. sheet, #B3-B6, perf. 8½	32.50	32.50
b.		As "a," imperf.	32.50	32.50
		Nos. B3-B6 (4)	.80	.80

80th anniv. of Egypt's 1st postage stamp. Nos. B6a, B6b measure 129x171mm.

Goddess Hathor, King Men-kau-Re (Mycerinus) and Jackalheaded Goddess — SP7

Ramesseum, Thebes — SP8

Queen Nefertiti SP9

Funerary Mask of King Tutankhamen SP10

Perf. 13½x13
1947, Mar. 9 **Wmk. 195**

B9	SP7	5m + 5m slate	.20	.20
B10	SP8	15m + 15m dp blue	.40	.25
B11	SP9	30m + 30m henna brn	.50	.45
B12	SP10	50m + 50m brown	.70	.65
		Nos. B9-B12 (4)	1.80	1.55

Intl. Exposition of Contemporary Art, Cairo.

Boy Scout Emblem — SP11

Scout Emblems: 20m+10m, Sea Scouts. 35m+15m, Air Explorers.

1956, July 25 **Photo.** ***Perf. 13½x13***

B13	SP11	10m + 10m green	.30	.20
B14	SP11	20m + 10m ultra	.40	.25
B15	SP11	35m + 15m blue	.55	.25
		Nos. B13-B15 (3)	1.25	.70

2nd Arab Scout Jamboree, Alexandria-Aboukir, 1956.

Souvenir sheets, perf. and imperf., contain one each of Nos. B13-B15. Size: 118x158mm. Value $750 each.

Ambulance — SP12

1957, May 13 ***Perf. 13x13½***
B16 SP12 10m + 5m rose red .20 .20

50th anniv. of the Public Aid Society.

United Arab Republic

Eye and Map of Africa, Europe and Asia SP13

Postal Emblem SP14

Perf. 13½x13
1958, Mar. 1 **Photo.** **Wmk. 318**
B17 SP13 10m + 5m orange .30 .25

1st Afro-Asian Cong. of Ophthalmology, Cairo.

The surtax was for centers to aid the blind.

1959, Jan. 2
B18 SP14 10m + 5m bl grn, red & blk .30 .20

Post Day. The surtax went to the social fund for postal employees.

See Syria UAR issues No. B1 for similar stamp with denominations in piasters (p).

Children and UN Emblem SP15

Arab League Building, Cairo, and Emblem SP16

1959, Oct. 24 Wmk. 328
B19 SP15 10m + 5m brown lake .30 .20
B20 SP15 35m + 10m dk blue .50 .20

Issued for International Children's Day and to honor UNICEF.

Braille Type of Regular Issue, 1961

1961, Apr. 6 ***Perf. 13½x13***
B21 A182 35m + 15m yel & brn .35 .20

1962, Mar. 22 Photo. Wmk. 328
B22 SP16 10m + 5m gray .20 .20

Arab Publicity Week, Mar. 22-28.
See No. N86.

Postal Emblem — SP17

Stamp of 1866 — SP18

1963, Jan. 2 Wmk. 342 ***Perf. 11½***
B23 SP17 20m +10m brt grn, red & blk .35 .25
B24 SP18 40m +20m blk & brn org .50 .40
B25 SP18 40m +20m brn org & blk .50 .40
a. Pair, #B24-B25 1.10 1.10
Nos. B23-B25 (3) 1.35 1.05

Post Day, Jan. 2 and 1966 exhibition of the FIP.

Arms of UAR and Pyramids SP19

1964, Jan. 2 Wmk. 342 ***Perf. 11***
B26 SP19 10m + 5m org yel & grn .65 .40
B27 SP19 80m + 40m grnsh bl & blk 1.40 .75
B28 SP19 115m + 55m org brn & blk 1.60 1.00
Nos. B26-B28 (3) 3.65 2.15

Issued for Post Day. Jan. 2.

Type of 1963 and

SP20

Postal Emblem — SP20a

#B30, Emblem of Postal Secondary School. 80m+40m, Postal emblem, gearwheel, laurel wreath.

Perf. 11½

1965, Jan. 2 Unwmk. Photo.
B29 SP20 10m + 5m lt grn & car .20 .20
B30 SP20 10m + 5m ultra, car & blk .20 .20
a. Pair, #B29-B30 .40 .40
B31 SP20a 80m + 40m rose, brt grn & blk .60 .50
Nos. B29-B31 (3) 1.00 .90

Issued for Post Day, Jan. 2. No. B31 also publicizes the Stamp Centenary Exhibition.

Souvenir Sheet

Stamps of Egypt, 1866 — SP21

1966, Jan. 2 Wmk. 342 ***Imperf.***
B32 SP21 140m + 60m blk, sl bl & rose 2.00 2.00

Post Day, 1966, and cent. of the 1st Egyptian postage stamps.

Pharaonic "Mediator" — SP22

Design: 115m+40m, Pharaonic guard.

1967, Jan. 2 Wmk. 342 ***Perf. 11½***
B33 SP22 80m + 20m multi 1.50 .65
B34 SP22 115m + 40m multi 2.50 1.75

Issued for Post Day, Jan. 2.

Grand Canal, Doges' Palace, Venice, and Santa Maria del Fiore, Florence — SP23

115m+30m, Piazetta and Campanile, Venice, and Palazzo Vecchio, Florence.

Perf. 11½x11

1967, Dec. 9 Photo. Wmk. 342
B35 SP23 80m + 20m grn, yel & brn .65 .30
B36 SP23 115m + 30m ol, yel & sl bl 1.00 .50

The surtax was to help save the cultural monuments of Venice and Florence, damaged in the 1966 floods.

Boy and Girl — SP24

Emblem and Flags of Arab League — SP25

Design: No. B38, Five children and arch.

Wmk. 342

1968, Dec. 11 Photo. ***Perf. 11***
B37 SP24 20m + 10m car, bl & lt brn .25 .20
B38 SP24 20m + 10m vio bl, sep & lt grn .25 .20

Children's Day & 22nd anniv. of UNICEF.

1969, Mar. 22 ***Perf. 11x11½***
B39 SP25 20m + 10m multi .25 .20

Arab Publicity Week, Mar. 22-28.

Refugee Family SP26

1969, Oct. 24 Photo. ***Perf. 11½***
B40 SP26 30m + 10m multi .65 .25

Issued for United Nations Day.

Men of Three Races, Human Rights Emblem SP27

1970, Mar. 21 ***Perf. 11½x11***
B41 SP27 20m + 10m multi .25 .20

Issued to publicize the International Day for the Elimination of Racial Discrimination.

Arab League Type

1970, Mar. 22 Wmk. 342
B42 A344 20m + 10m bl, grn & brn .65 .25

Map of Palestine and Refugees SP28

Perf. 11½x11

1970, Oct. 24 Photo. Wmk. 342
B43 SP28 20m + 10m multi .75 .60

25th anniv. of the UN and to draw attention to the plight of the Palestinian refugees.

Arab Republic of Egypt

Blind Girl, WHO and Society Emblems — SP29

1973, Oct. 24 Photo. ***Perf. 11x11½***
B44 SP29 20m + 10m blue & gold .25 .20

25th anniv. of WHO and for the Light and Hope Soc., which educates and helps blind girls.

Map of Africa, OAU Emblem SP30

Social Work Day Emblem SP31

Perf. 11x11½

1973, Dec. 8 Photo. Wmk. 342
B45 SP30 55m + 20m multi 1.40 .75

Organization for African Unity, 10th anniv.

1973, Dec. 8
B46 SP31 20m + 10m multi .25 .20

Social Work Day.

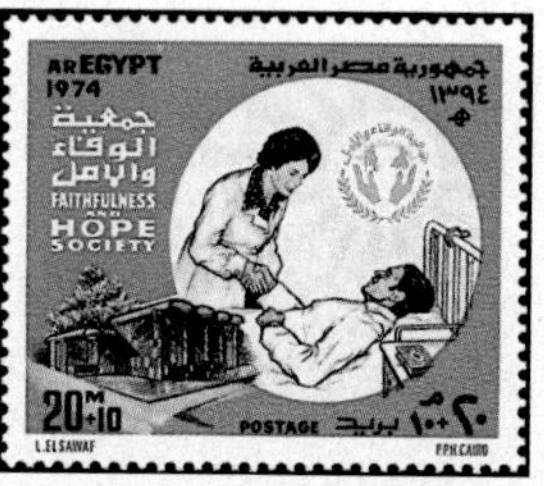

Jihan al Sadat Consoling Wounded Man — SP32

1974, Mar. 21 Wmk. 342 ***Perf. 11***
B47 SP32 20m + 10m multi .55 .20

Faithfulness and Hope Society.

Afghan Solidarity SP33

Wmk. 342

1981, July 15 Photo. ***Perf. 11½***
B48 SP33 20m + 10m multi .20 .20

Size: 30x25mm

1981 Photo. ***Perf. 11½***
B49 SP33 20m + 10m multi 1.00 .25

Map of Sudan, Dunes, Dead Tree — SP34

1986, Mar. 25 Photo. *Perf. 13x13½*
B50 SP34 15p + 5p multi .50 .40

Fight against drought and desertification of the Sudan. Surtax for drought relief.

Organization of African Unity, 25th Anniv. — SP35

1988, May 25 Litho. *Perf. 13*
B51 SP35 15p +10p multi .80 .80

AIR POST STAMPS

Mail Plane in Flight AP1

Perf. 13x13½

1926, Mar. 10 Wmk. 195 Photo.
C1 AP1 27m deep violet 11.00 3.50

1929, July 17
C2 AP1 27m orange brown 4.50 2.25

Zeppelin Issue

No. C2 Surcharged in Blue or Violet

1931, Apr. 6
C3 AP1 50m on 27m (Bl) 27.50 20.00
a. "1951" instead of "1931" 32.50 32.50
C4 AP1 100m on 27m (V) 27.50 20.00

Airplane over Giza Pyramids AP2

1933-38 Litho. *Perf. 13x13½*
C5 AP2 1m orange & blk .30 .20
C6 AP2 2m gray & blk .60 .35
C7 AP2 2m org red & blk ('38) .60 .45
C8 AP2 3m ol brn & blk .30 .20
C9 AP2 4m green & blk .40 .30
C10 AP2 5m dp brown & blk .30 .20
C11 AP2 6m dk green & blk .50 .45
C12 AP2 7m dk blue & blk .40 .25
C13 AP2 8m violet & blk .30 .20
C14 AP2 9m dp red & blk .60 .50
C15 AP2 10m violet & brn .40 .20
C16 AP2 20m dk green & brn .30 .20
C17 AP2 30m dull blue & brn .40 .20
C18 AP2 40m dp red & brn 7.00 .20
C19 AP2 50m orange & brn 5.00 .20
C20 AP2 60m gray & brn 2.00 .20
C21 AP2 70m dk blue & bl grn 1.50 .20
C22 AP2 80m ol brn & bl grn 1.50 .20
C23 AP2 90m org & bl grn 1.75 .20
C24 AP2 100m vio & bl grn 2.00 .20
C25 AP2 200m dp red & bl grn 8.00 .35
Nos. C5-C25 (21) 34.15 5.45

See #C34-C37. For overprint see #C38.

Type of 1933

1941-43 Photo.
C34 AP2 5m copper brn ('43) .20 .20
C35 AP2 10m violet .25 .20
C36 AP2 25m dk vio brn ('43) .25 .20
C37 AP2 30m green .30 .20
Nos. C34-C37 (4) 1.00 .80

Catalogue values for unused stamps in this section, from this point to the end of the section, are for Never Hinged items.

No. C37 Overprinted in Black

1946, Oct. 1
C38 AP2 30m green .30 .20
a. Double overprint 90.00 62.50
b. Inverted overprint 125.00 100.00

Middle East Intl. Air Navigation Congress, Cairo, Oct. 1946.

King Farouk, Delta Dam and DC-3 Plane AP3

Perf. 13x13½

1947, Feb. 19 Photo. Wmk. 195
C39 AP3 2m red orange .20 .20
C40 AP3 3m dk brown .20 .20
C41 AP3 5m red brown .20 .20
C42 AP3 7m dp yellow org .20 .20
C43 AP3 8m green .20 .20
C44 AP3 10m violet .20 .20
C45 AP3 20m brt blue .20 .20
C46 AP3 30m brown violet .30 .20
C47 AP3 40m carmine rose .40 .20
C48 AP3 50m Prus green .45 .20
C49 AP3 100m olive green 1.25 .35
C50 AP3 200m dark gray 2.00 .65
Nos. C39-C50 (12) 5.80 3.00

For overprints see Nos. C51-C64, C67-C89, NC1-NC30.

Nos. C49 and C50 Surcharged in Black

1948, Aug. 23
C51 AP3 13m on 100m .45 .25
C52 AP3 22m on 200m .55 .30
a. Date omitted

Inaugural flights of "Services Aeriens Internationaux d'Egypte" from Cairo to Athens and Rome, Aug. 23, 1948.

Nos. C39 to C50 Overprinted in Various Colors

Overprint 27mm Wide

1952, Jan. Wmk. 195 *Perf. 13x13½*
C53 AP3 2m red orange (Bl) .20 .20
C54 AP3 3m dark brown (RV) .20 .20
C55 AP3 5m red brown .20 .20
C56 AP3 7m dp yel org (Bl) .20 .20
C57 AP3 8m green (RV) .20 .20
C58 AP3 10m violet (G) .40 .25
C59 AP3 20m brt blue (RV) .90 .50
C60 AP3 30m brown vio (G) .40 .20
C61 AP3 40m carmine rose 1.90 .40
C62 AP3 50m Prus green (RV) 1.10 .75
C63 AP3 100m olive green 2.25 1.25
C64 AP3 200m dark gray (RV) 3.25 2.00
Nos. C53-C64 (12) 11.20 6.35

See notes after No. 316.

Delta Dam and Douglas DC-3 AP4

1953 Photo.
C65 AP4 5m red brown .20 .20
C66 AP4 15m olive green .45 .20

For overprints see Nos. NC31-NC32.

Nos. C39-C49 Overprinted in Black with Three Bars to Obliterate Portrait

1953
C67 AP3 2m red orange .20 .20
C68 AP3 3m dk brown .30 .20
C69 AP3 5m red brown .20 .20
C70 AP3 7m dp yellow org .40 .20
C71 AP3 8m green .20 .20
C72 AP3 10m violet *15.00*
C73 AP3 20m brt blue .20 .20
C74 AP3 30m brown violet .30 .20
C75 AP3 40m carmine rose .35 .25
C76 AP3 50m Prus green 2.00 .30
C77 AP3 100m olive green 2.00 .75
C77A AP3 200m gray *30.00*

Nos. C72 and C77A are in question. They are not known postally used.

Nos. C53-C64 Overprinted in Black with Three Bars to Obliterate Portrait

1953
C78 AP3 2m red orange .20 .20
C79 AP3 3m dark brown .20 .20
C80 AP3 5m red brown .20 .20
C82 AP3 8m green .25 .20
C83 AP3 10m violet .20 .20
C85 AP3 30m brown violet .25 .20
C87 AP3 50m Prus green .40 .25
C88 AP3 100m olive green .55 .40
C89 AP3 200m dark gray 5.75 1.75
Nos. C78-C89 (9) 8.00 3.60

Practically all values of Nos. C67-C89 exist with double overprint. The 7m, 20m and 40m with this overprint are forgeries.

United Arab Republic
Type of Regular Issue

Perf. 11½x11

1958, Mar. 22 Photo. Wmk. 318
C90 A141 15m ultra & red brn .25 .20

Pyramids at Giza AP5

Al Azhar University AP6

Designs: 15m, Colossi of Memnon, Thebes. 90m, St. Catherine Monastery, Mt. Sinai.

1959-60 Wmk. 328 *Perf. 13x13½*
C91 AP5 5m bright red .20 .20
C92 AP5 15m dk dull violet .20 .20
C93 AP6 60m dk green .40 .25
C94 AP5 90m brown car ('60) .80 .20
Nos. C91-C94 (4) 1.60 .85

Nos. C91-C93 exist imperf. See Nos. C101, C105, NC33.

Tower of Cairo Type, Redrawn

1961, May 1 *Perf. 13½x13*
C95 A183 50m bright blue .40 .20

Top inscription has been replaced by two airplanes.

Weather Vane, Anemometer and UN World Meteorological Organization Emblem — AP7

Perf. 11½x11

1962, Mar. 23 Photo. Unwmk.
C96 AP7 60m yellow & dp blue .45 .25

2nd World Meteorological Day, Mar. 23.

Patrice Lumumba and Map of Africa — AP8

Perf. 13½x13

1962, July 1 Wmk. 328
C97 AP8 35m multicolored .30 .20

Patrice Lumumba (1925-61), Premier of Congo.

Maritime Station, Alexandria — AP9

Designs: 30m, International Airport, Cairo. 40m, Railroad Station, Luxor.

1963, Mar. 18 *Perf. 13x13½*
C98 AP9 20m dark brown .20 .20
C99 AP9 30m carmine rose .20 .20
C100 AP9 40m black .30 .20
Nos. C98-C100 (3) .70 .60

Type of 1959-60 and

Temple of Queen Nefertari, Abu Simbel AP10

Arch and Tower of Cairo — AP11

Designs: 80m, Al Azhar University seen through arch. 140m, Ramses II, Abu Simbel.

Perf. 11½x11, 11x11½

1963-65 Photo. Wmk. 342

C101 AP6 80m vio blk & brt bl 2.25 .35
C102 AP10 115m brown & yel .70 .45
C103 AP10 140m pale vio, blk & org red .85 .60

Unwmk.

C104 AP11 50m yel brn & brt bl .30 .20
C105 AP6 80m vio bl & lt bl 1.90 .25
Nos. C101-C105 (5) 6.00 1.85

Issued: 50m, 11/2/64; #C105, 2/13/65; others, 10/24/63.
See Nos. NC34-NC36.

Weather Vane, Anemometer and WMO Emblem — AP12

Perf. 11½x11

1965, Mar. 23 Wmk. 342

C106 AP12 80m dk blue & rose lil .40 .25

Fifth World Meteorological Day.
See No. NC37.

Game Board from Tomb of Tutankhamen — AP13

1965, July 1 Photo. Unwmk.

C107 AP13 10m yellow & dk blue .35 .20

See No. NC38.

Temples at Abu Simbel — AP14

1966, Apr. 28 Wmk. 342 *Perf. 11½*

C108 AP14 20m multicolored .20 .20
C109 AP14 80m multicolored .40 .20

Issued to commemorate the transfer of the temples of Abu Simbel to a hilltop, 1963-66.

Scout Camp and Jamboree Emblem AP15

1966, Aug. 10 *Perf. 11½x11*

C110 AP15 20m olive & rose .25 .20

7th Pan-Arab Boy Scout Jamboree, Good Daim, Libya, Aug. 12.

St. Catherine Monastery, Mt. Sinai — AP16

1966, Nov. 30 Photo. Wmk. 342

C111 AP16 80m multicolored .60 .20

St. Catherine Monastery, Sinai, 1400th anniv.

Cairo Airport AP17

1967, Apr. 26 *Perf. 11½x11*

C112 AP17 20m sky bl, sl grn & lt brn .20 .20

Hotel El Alamein and Map of Nile Delta AP18

Intl. Tourist Year: 80m, The Virgin's Tree, Virgin Mary and Child. 115m, Fishing in the Red Sea.

1967, June 7 Wmk. 342 *Perf. 11½*

C113 AP18 20m dull pur, sl grn & dl org .25 .20
C114 AP18 80m blue & multi 1.00 .50
C115 AP18 115m brown, org & bl 1.75 .75
Nos. C113-C115 (3) 3.00 1.45

Oil Derricks, Map of Egypt AP19

1967, July 23 Photo.

C116 AP19 50m org & bluish blk .40 .20

15th anniversary of the revolution.

Type of Regular Issue, 1967

Design: 80m, Back of Tutankhamen's throne and UNESCO emblem.

1967, Oct. 24 Wmk. 342 *Perf. 11½*

C117 A301 80m blue & yellow 1.00 .50

Koran — AP20

1968, Mar. 25 Wmk. 342 *Perf. 11½*

C118 AP20 30m lilac, bl & yel .75 .25
C119 AP20 80m lilac, bl & yel 1.50 .50
a. Pair, #C118-C119 + label 2.25 1.00

1400th anniv. of the Koran. Nos. C118-C119 are printed in miniature sheets of 4 containing 2 each of Nos. C118-C119.

St. Mark and St. Mark's Cathedral — AP21

1968, June 25 Wmk. 342 *Perf. 11½*

C120 AP21 80m brt grn, dk brn & dp car .60 .20

Martyrdom of St. Mark, 1900th anniv. and the consecration of St. Mark's Cathedral, Cairo.

Map of United Arab Airlines and Boeing 707 AP22

Design: No. C122, Ilyushin 18 and routes of United Arab Airlines.

1968-69 Photo. *Perf. 11½x11*

C121 AP22 55m blue, ocher & car .35 .20
C122 AP22 55m bl, yel & vio blk ('69) .35 .20

1st flights of a Boeing 707 and an Ilyushin 18 for United Arab Airlines.

Mahatma Gandhi, Arms of India and UAR AP23

Imam El Boukhary AP24

1969, Sept. 10 *Perf. 11x11½*

C123 AP23 80m lt blue, ocher & brn 2.00 .20

Mohandas K. Gandhi (1869-1948), leader in India's fight for independence.

1969, Dec. 27 Photo. Wmk. 342

C124 AP24 30m lt olive & dk brown .20 .20

1100th anniv. of the death of the Imam El Boukhary (824-870), philosopher and writer.

Azzahir Beybars Mosque AP25

1969, Dec. 27 Engr. *Perf. 11½x11*

C125 AP25 30m red lilac .20 .20

700th anniv. of the founding of the Azzahir Beybars Mosque, Cairo.

Lenin (1870-1924) — AP26

Perf. 11x11½

1970, Apr. 22 Photo. Wmk. 342

C126 AP26 80m lt green & brown .45 .20

Phantom Fighters and Destroyed Factory AP27

1970, May 1 *Perf. 11½x11*

C127 AP27 80m yel, grn & dk vio brn .60 .20

Issued to commemorate the destruction of the Abu-Zaabal factory by Israeli planes.

UPU Type of Regular Issue

1970, May 20 Photo. Wmk. 342

C128 A350 80m multicolored .40 .20

Nasser and Burial Mosque — AP28

1970, Nov. 6 Wmk. 342 *Perf. 11*

C129 AP28 30m olive & blk .75 .20
C130 AP28 80m brown & blk 1.75 .40

Gamal Abdel Nasser (1918-70), Pres. of Egypt.

Postal Congress Type

Perf. 11½x11

1971, Mar. 6 Photo. Wmk. 342

C131 A365 30m lt ol, org & sl grn .40 .20

Nasser, El Rifaei and Sultan Hussein Mosques AP29

Designs: 85m, Nasser and Ramses Square, Cairo. 110m, Nasser, Sphinx and pyramids.

Perf. 11½x11

1971, July 1 Photo. Wmk. 342

C132 AP29 30m multicolored 1.00 .20
C133 AP29 85m multicolored 2.00 .25
C134 AP29 110m multicolored 3.00 .35
Nos. C132-C134 (3) 6.00 .80

APU Type of Regular Issue

1971, Aug. 3 Wmk. 342 *Perf. 11½*

C135 A373 30m brown, yel & bl .20 .20

Arab Republic of Egypt Confederation Type

Perf. 11½x11

1971, Sept. 28 Photo. Wmk. 342

C136 A374 30m gray, sl grn & dk pur .20 .20

Al Aqsa Mosque and Woman AP30

Wmk. 342

1971, Oct. 24 Photo. *Perf. 11½*

C137 AP30 30m bl, yel, brn & grn .75 .25

25th anniv. of the UN (in 1970) and return of Palestinian refugees.

Postal Union Type

30m, African Postal Union emblem & letter.

1971, Dec. 2 *Perf. 11½x11*

C138 A384 30m green, blk & bl .50 .20

Aida, Triumphal March AP31

1971, Dec. 23 Wmk. 342 *Perf. 11½*

C139 AP31 110m dk brn, yel & sl grn 1.00 .20

Centenary of the first performance of the opera Aida, by Giuseppe Verdi.

Globe, Glider, Rocket Club Emblem
AP32

St. Catherine's Monastery on Fire
AP33

1972, Feb. 11 ***Perf. 11x11½***
C140 AP32 30m blue, ocher & yel .20 .20

International Aerospace Education Conference, Cairo, Jan. 11-13.

Perf. 11½x11
1972, Feb. 15 **Unwmk.**
C141 AP33 110m dp car, org & blk 1.00 .20

The burning of St. Catherine's Monastery in Sinai Desert, Nov. 30, 1971.

Tutankhamen in Garden — AP34

Tutankhamen, from 2nd Sarcophagus — AP35

Design: No. C143, Ankhesenamun.

1972, May 22 **Photo.** ***Perf. 11½***
C142 AP34 110m brn org, bl & grn 3.00 2.00
C143 AP34 110m brn org, bl & grn 3.00 2.00
a. Pair, #C142-C143 6.00 4.00

Souvenir Sheet

Imperf

C144 AP35 200m gold & multi 15.00 12.50

50th anniv. of the discovery of the tomb of Tutankhamen. No. C143a has continuous design.

Souvenir Sheet

Flag of Confederation of Arab Republics — AP36

1972, July 23 **Photo.** ***Imperf.***
C145 AP36 110m gold, dp car & blk 3.00 .75

20th anniversary of the revolution.

Temples at Abu Simbel
AP37

Designs: 30m, Al Azhar Mosque and St. George's Church. 110m, Pyramids at Giza.

1972 **Wmk. 342** ***Perf. 11½x11***
C146 AP37 30m blue, brn & buff .40 .20
C147 AP37 85m bl, brn & ocher 1.25 .20
C148 AP37 110m multicolored 1.60 .20
Nos. C146-C148 (3) 3.25 .60

Issued: #C146, C148, 11/22; #C147, 8/1.

Olympic Type of Regular Issue

Olympic and Motion Emblems and: #C149, Handball. #C150, Weight lifting. 50m, Swimming. 55m, Gymnastics. All vertical.

1972, Aug. 17 ***Perf. 11x11½***
C149 A396 30m multicolored .30 .20
C150 A396 30m yellow & multi .30 .20
C151 A396 50m blue & multi .75 .35
C152 A396 55m multicolored .90 .50
Nos. C149-C152 (4) 2.25 1.25

Champollion, Rosetta Stone, Hieroglyphics — AP38

1972, Oct. 16
C153 AP38 110m gold, grn & blk 4.00 .25

Sesquicentennial of the deciphering of Egyptian hieroglyphics by Jean-François Champollion.

World Map, Telephone, Radar, ITU Emblem — AP39

1973, Mar. 21 **Photo.** ***Perf. 11***
C154 AP39 30m lt bl, dk bl & blk .20 .20

5th World Telecommunications Day.

Karnak Temple, Luxor — AP40

Hand Dripping Blood and Falling Plane — AP41

1973, Mar. 21
C155 AP40 110m dp ultra, blk & rose 1.00 .45

Sound and light at Karnak.

1973, May 1 ***Perf. 11x11½***
C156 AP41 110m multicolored 6.00 .50

Israeli attack on Libyan civilian plane, Feb. 1973.

WMO Emblem, Weather Vane — AP42

1973, Oct. 24 ***Perf. 11x11½***
C157 AP42 110m blue, gold & pur 2.00 .25

Cent. of intl. meteorological cooperation.

Refugees, Map of Palestine
AP43

1973, Oct. 24 ***Perf. 11½***
C158 AP43 30m dk brn, yel & bl 2.00 .20

Plight of Palestinian refugees.

INTERPOL Emblem
AP44

Postal and UPU Emblems
AP45

Perf. 11x11½
1973, Dec. 8 **Photo.** **Wmk. 342**
C159 AP44 110m black & multi 1.00 .20

Intl. Criminal Police Organization, 50th anniv.

1974, Jan. 2 **Unwmk.** ***Perf. 11***

Post Day (UPU Emblems and): 30m, APU emblem. 55m, African Postal Union emblem. 110m, UPU emblem.

Size: 26x46½mm

C160 AP45 20m gray, red & blk .30 .20
C161 AP45 30m sal, blk & pur .40 .20
C162 AP45 55m emerald, blk & brt mag .90 .20

Size: 37x37½mm

Perf. 11½

C163 AP45 110m lt bl, blk & gold 1.25 .25
Nos. C160-C163 (4) 2.85 .85

Solar Bark of Khufu (Cheops) — AP46

Wmk. 342

1974, Mar. 21 **Photo.** ***Perf. 11½***
C164 AP46 110m blue, gold & brn 2.00 .25

Solar Bark Museum.

Hotel Meridien
AP47

1974, Oct. 6 ***Perf. 11½x11***
C165 AP47 110m multicolored .75 .25

Opening of Hotel Meridien, Cairo.

Suez Canal Type of 1975

1975, June 5 ***Perf. 11½***
C166 A448 30m bl, yel grn & ind .55 .25
C167 A448 110m indigo & blue 1.40 .75

Irrigation Commission Emblem — AP48

1975, July 20
C168 AP48 110m orange & dk grn .90 .25

9th Intl. Congress on Irrigation and Drainage, Moscow, and 25th anniv. of the Intl. Commission on Irrigation and Drainage.

Refugees and UNWRA Emblem — AP49

Woman and IWY Emblem — AP50

Perf. 11x11½
1975, Oct. 24 **Photo.** **Wmk. 342**
C169 AP49 30m multicolored 1.00 .25

Unwmk.

C170 AP50 110m olive, org & blk 2.00 .35

UN Day. 30m publicizes UN help for refugees; 110m is for Intl. Women's Year 1975.

Step Pyramid, Sakhara, and Entrance Gate AP51

Designs: 45m, 60m, Plane over Giza Pyramids. 140m, Plane over boats on Nile.

Perf. 11½x11

1978-82 Photo. Wmk. 342

C171	AP51	45m yel & brown	.20	.20
C171A	AP51	60m olive	.25	.20
C172	AP51	115m blue & brown	.50	.20
C173	AP51	140m blue & purple	.55	.25
C173A	AP51	185m bl, sep & gray brn	.80	.50
		Nos. C171-C173A (5)	2.30	1.35

Issued: 60m, 1/15/82; 185m, 1982; others, 1/1/78.

Flyer and UN ICAO Emblem — AP52

Perf. 11x11½

1978, Dec. 30 Photo. Wmk. 342

C174 AP52 140m blue, blk & brn .60 .30

75th anniversary of 1st powered flight.

Seeing Eye Medallion AP53

Perf. 11½x11

1981, Oct. 1 Photo. Wmk. 342

C175 AP53 230m multicolored .95 .30

Hilton Ramses Hotel Opening — AP54

Perf. 11x11½

1982, Mar. 15 Photo. Wmk. 342

C176 AP54 18½p multi .75 .25

Temple of Horus, Edfu AP55

Designs: 15p, like 6p. 18½p, 25p, Statue of Akhnaton, Thebes, hieroglyphics, vert. 23p, 30p, Giza pyramids.

1985 Photo. *Perf. 11½x11, 11x11½*

C177	AP55	6p lt blue & dk bl grn	.20	.20
C178	AP55	15p grnsh bl & brn	.45	.30
C179	AP55	18½p grn, sep & dp yel	.50	.35
C180	AP55	23p grnsh bl, sep & yel bis	.65	.40
C181	AP55	25p lt bl, sep & yel bis	.70	.40
a.		Unwmkd. ('87)	.85	.45
C182	AP55	30p grnsh bl, sep & org yel	1.00	.55
a.		Unwmkd. ('87)	1.00	.55
		Nos. C177-C182 (6)	3.50	2.20

Issued: 6p, 18½p, 23p, 3/1; 15p, 25p, 30p, 5/1.

See No. C236.

Post Day — AP56

Narmer Board, oldest known hieroglyphic inscriptions: No. C183a, Tablet obverse. No. C183b, Reverse.

1986, Jan. 2 Photo. *Perf. 13½x13*

C183	AP56	Pair	1.25	1.25
a.-b.		15p any single	.60	.60

Map, Jet, AFRAA Emblem AP57

1986, Apr. 7 Photo. *Perf. 11½*

C184 AP57 15p blue, yel & blk .40 .40

African Airlines Assoc., 18th General Assembly, Cairo, Apr. 7-10.

World Food Day AP58

UNESCO, 40th Anniv. — AP59

Perf. 13½x13, 13x13½

1986, Oct. 24 Litho.

C185	AP58	15p multicolored	.70	.70
C186	AP59	15p multicolored	.70	.70

UN Day.

Tourism Year — AP60

Design: Column and Sphinx in Alexandria, St. Catherine's Monastery in Mt. Sinai, Colossi of Thebes and Temple of Theban Triad in Luxor.

Unwmk.

1987, Sept. 30 Litho. *Imperf.*

Size: 140x90mm

C187 AP60 30p multicolored 1.40 1.40

Palestinian Uprising — AP61

1988, Sept. 28 Litho. *Perf. 12x13½*

C188 AP61 25p multicolored .80 .80

UN Day AP62

1988, Oct. 20 Litho. *Perf. 13x13½*

C189 AP62 25p multicolored .80 .80

Nobel Prize Type of 1988

1988, Nov. 7

C190 A769 25p multicolored .80 .80

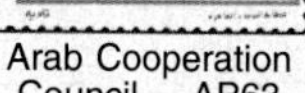
Arab Cooperation Council — AP63

Architecture and Art — AP64

1989, May 10 Litho. *Perf. 13½x13*

C191 AP63 25p Flags .80 .80

Size: 89x80mm

Imperf

C192 AP63 50p Flags, seal 2.00 2.00

1989-91 Photo. *Perf. 11x11½*

C193	AP64	20p Balcony	.30	.30
C194	AP64	25p Brazier	.40	.40
C195	AP64	35p shown	.50	.50
C196	AP64	45p Tapestry	.70	.70
C197	AP64	45p like #C195	.70	.70
C198	AP64	50p Stag (dish)	.75	.75
C199	AP64	55p 4 animals (plate)	.80	.80
C200	AP64	60p like #C198	.90	.90
C201	AP64	65p like #C197	1.00	1.00
C202	AP64	70p like #C193	1.10	1.10
C203	AP64	85p like #C198	1.25	1.25
		Nos. C193-C203 (11)	8.40	8.40

Issued: 35p, 60p, 10/1/89; 55p, 1/1/90; #C197, C202, 1/25/91; 65p, 85p, 7/20/91; others, 4/1/89.

AP65

Funerary Mask of King Tutankhamen — AP66

King Tutankhamen AP66a

1993-99 Litho. *Perf. 11½*

C204	AP65	55p multicolored	1.00	.55
C205	AP66	80p multicolored	2.00	.80

Photo.

Perf. 11x11¼

C206	AP66a	£1 black & brown	.65	.65
b.		Wmk. 342	.65	.65
		Nos. C204-C206 (3)	3.65	2.00

Issued: 55p, 80p, 3/1/93; £1, 1997; #C206b, 1999.

See No. C231.

ICAO, 50th Anniv. — AP67

1994, Sept. 16 Litho. *Perf. 13*

C207 AP67 80p multicolored .50 .50

Intl. Year of the Family — AP68

1994, Oct. 24 Litho. *Perf. 13*

C208 AP68 80p multicolored .50 .50

Arab League for Education, Culture, & Science Organization — AP69

1995, July 25 Litho. *Perf. 13x13½*

C209 AP69 55p multicolored .35 .35

UN Organizations, 50th Anniv. — AP70

Perf. 12½x13, 13x12½

1995, Oct. 24 Litho.

C210	AP70	80p UN	.85	.85
C211	AP70	80p FAO	.85	.85
C212	AP70	80p UNESCO, vert.	.85	.85
		Nos. C210-C212 (3)	2.55	2.55

Arab Summit, Cairo — AP71

1996, June 21 Litho. *Perf. 13x12½*
C213 AP71 55p multicolored .30 .30

16th Intl. Conference on Irrigation and Drainage, Cairo — AP72

1996, Sept. 15 Litho. *Perf. 12½x13*
C214 AP72 80p multicolored .60 .60

Intl. Tourism Day — AP73

1996, Sept. 27 *Perf. 13*
C215 AP73 80p multicolored .45 .45

Arabian Horse Day — AP74

World Post Day — AP75

1996 *Perf. 13x12½*
C216 AP74 55p grn, blk & gray .30 .30

1996, Oct. 9 Litho. *Perf. 13x12½*
C217 AP75 80p multicolored .50 .50

AP76

AP77

1996, Oct. 24
C218 AP76 55p multicolored .30 .30

Cairo, Arab cultural capital of 1996.

1996, Oct. 24
C219 AP77 80p multicolored .50 .50

UNICEF, 50th anniv.

World Meteorological Day — AP78

Thutmose III — AP79

1997, Mar. 23 Litho. *Perf. 13x12½*
C220 AP78 £1 multicolored .90 .90

1997, Mar. 25 Photo. *Perf. 11x11½*
C221 AP79 75p blk, bl & gray .70 .70

Heinrich von Stephan (1831-97) — AP80

1997, Apr. 15 Litho. *Perf. 13*
C222 AP80 £1 multicolored .60 .60

AP81

1997, Sept. 11
C223 AP81 £1 multicolored .60 .60

98th Intl. Parliamentary Conference, Cairo.

AP82

AP83

1997, Sept. 10 Litho. *Perf. 13*
C224 AP82 75p multicolored .45 .45

1997 Egyptian Team, top medal winners of 8th Pan Arab Games, Beirut, Lebanon.

1997, Sept. 27 *Perf. 13x12½*
C225 AP83 £1 multicolored .60 .60

Sarabas (180-211), mumified Egyptian.

World Book and Copyright Day AP84

1997, Oct. 24 Litho. *Perf. 12½x13*
C226 AP84 £1 multicolored .60 .60

African Ministries of Transport and Communications, 11th Conference — AP85

1997, Nov. 22 Litho. *Perf. 13x12½*
C227 AP85 75p multicolored .45 .45

Arab Scout Movement, 85th Anniv. — AP86

1997, Nov. 24 *Perf. 12½x13*
C228 AP86 75p multicolored .45 .45

8th G-15 Summit Meeting — AP87

Lighthouse of Alexandria AP88

1998, May 11 Litho. *Perf. 13*
C229 AP87 £1 multicolored .70 .70

1998, May 20 Litho. *Perf. 13*
C230 AP88 £1 multicolored .60 .60

King Tut Type of 1997

1998, July 25 Litho. *Perf. 11x11¼*
C231 AP66a 125p Tutankhamen .75 .75
a. Wmk. 342 ('99) .75 .75

AP90

AP91

1998, Aug. 3 *Perf. 13*
C232 AP90 £1 multicolored .60 .60

Arab Post Day.

1998, Oct. 9 Litho. *Perf. 13*
C233 AP91 125p multicolored .85 .85

World Post Day.

AP92

AP93

1998, Oct. 22
C234 AP92 125p multicolored .85 .85

67th Interpol Meeting, Cairo.

1998, Oct. 24
C235 AP93 125p multicolored .85 .85

Universal Declaration of Human Rights, 50th anniv.

Statue of Akhnaton Type of 1985

1998 Litho. *Perf. 13*
C236 AP55 25p lt bl, brn & tan .20 .20

AP94

AP95

1999, Oct. 12 Litho. ***Perf. 13x12¾***
C237 AP94 125p multicolored .85 .85

Performance of opera "Aida" at the Pyramids.

1999, Oct. 16
C238 AP95 125p multicolored .85 .85

Discovery of the Rosetta Stone, bicent.

World Tourism Day — AP96

Perf. 13¼x12¾
2000, Sept. 27 Litho.
C239 AP96 125p multi .85 .85

Awarding of Nobel Prize for Chemistry to Dr. Ahmed Zewail — AP97

Illustration reduced.

1999, Dec. 10 ***Imperf.***
C240 AP97 125p multi .75 .75

UN High Commissioner for Refugees, 50th Anniv. — AP98

2000, Dec. 13
C241 AP98 125p multi .85 .85

AIR POST SEMI-POSTAL STAMPS

Catalogue values for unused stamps in this section are for Never Hinged items.

United Arab Republic

Pharaonic Mail Carriers and Papyrus Plants SPAP1

Design: 115m+55m, Jet plane, world map and stamp of Egypt, 1926 (No. C1).

Wmk. 342
1966, Jan. 2 Photo. ***Perf. 11½***
CB1 SPAP1 80m + 40m multi 1.50 1.50
CB2 SPAP1 115m + 55m multi 1.90 1.90
a. Pair, #CB1-CB2 3.50 3.50

Post Day, Jan. 2.

SPECIAL DELIVERY STAMPS

Motorcycle Postman — SD1

Perf. 13x13½
1926, Nov. 28 Photo. Wmk. 195
E1 SD1 20m dark green 17.00 2.75

1929, Sept.
E2 SD1 20m brown red & black .55 .20

Inscribed "Postes Expres"

1943-44 Litho.
E3 SD1 26m brn red & gray blk .65 .45
E4 SD1 40m dl brn & pale gray ('44) .50 .20

For overprints see Nos. E5, NE1.

Catalogue values for unused stamps in this section, from this point to the end of the section, are for Never Hinged items.

No. E4 Overprinted in Black

Overprint 27mm Wide

1952, Jan.
E5 SD1 40m dl brn & pale gray .80 .25

See notes after No. 316.

POSTAGE DUE STAMPS

D1

D2

Wmk. Crescent and Star (119)
1884, Jan. 1 Litho. ***Perf. 10½***
J1 D1 10pa red 40.00 9.00
a. Horiz. pair, imperf. vert. 125.00
J2 D1 20pa red 110.00 22.50
J3 D1 1pi red 125.00 40.00
J4 D1 2pi red 225.00 11.00
J5 D1 5pi red 17.00 *35.00*

1886, Aug. 1 Unwmk.
J6 D1 10pa red 52.50 7.00
a. Horiz. pair, imperf. vert. 125.00
J7 D1 20pa red 225.00 30.00
J8 D1 1pi red 26.00 5.00
a. Pair, imperf. between 135.00
J9 D1 2pi red 26.00 5.00
a. Pair, imperf. between 135.00

1888, Jan. 1 ***Perf. 11½***
J10 D2 2m green 8.25 *12.00*
a. Horiz. pair, imperf. between 190.00
J11 D2 5m rose red 27.50 12.00
J12 D2 1pi blue 140.00 40.00
a. Pair, imperf. between 225.00
J13 D2 2pi yellow 150.00 12.00
J14 D2 5pi gray 210.00 190.00
a. Period after "PIASTRES" 275.00 250.00

Excellent counterfeits of #J1-J14 are plentiful.

There are 4 types of each of Nos. J1-J14, so placed that any block of 4 contains all types.

D3

Perf. 14x13½
1889 Wmk. 119 Typo.
J15 D3 2m green 7.00 .55
a. Half used as 1m on cover 275.00
J16 D3 4m maroon 2.50 .55
J17 D3 1pi ultra 5.75 .55
J18 D3 2pi orange 6.00 .80
a. Half used as 1p on cover —

Nos. J15-J18 exist on both ordinary and chalky paper. Imperf. examples of Nos. J15-J17 are proofs.

Black Surcharge

D4

1898
J19 D4 3m on 2pi orange .65 *2.75*
a. Inverted surcharge 65.00 *82.50*
c. Pair, one without surcharge —
f. Double surcharge 225.00 —

There are two types of this surcharge. In type I, the spacing between the last two Arabic characters at the right is 2mm. In type II, this spacing is 3mm, and there is an added sign on top of the second character from the right. See *Scott Classic Specialized Catalogue of Stamps & Covers* for detailed listing.

D5

D6

1921 Wmk. 120 ***Perf. 14x13½***
J20 D5 2m green .25 .25
J21 D5 4m vermilion 1.10 .45
J22 D6 10m deep blue 1.10 .55
Nos. J20-J22 (3) 2.45 1.25

1921-22
J23 D5 2m vermilion .25 .20
J24 D5 4m green .25 .20
J25 D6 10m lake ('22) .40 .20

Nos. J18, J23-J25 Overprinted

1922, Oct. 10 Wmk. 119
J26 D3 2pi orange 2.75 .55
a. Overprint right side up 6.00 2.75

Wmk. 120
J27 D5 2m vermilion .40 .20
J28 D5 4m green .55 .25
J29 D6 10m lake .90 .35

Overprint on Nos. J26-J29 is inverted.

Arabic Numeral — D7

Perf. 13x13½
1927-56 Litho. Wmk. 195
Size: 18x22½mm
J30 D7 2m slate .40 .20
J31 D7 2m orange ('30) .20 .20
J32 D7 4m green .25 .20
J33 D7 4m ol brn ('32) 1.10 .20
J34 D7 5m brown .70 .20
J35 D7 6m gray grn ('41) .40 .20
J36 D7 8m brn vio .40 .20
J37 D7 10m brick red ('29) .45 .20
a. 10m deep red .55 .20
J38 D7 12m rose lake ('41) .65 .20
J38A D7 20m dk red ('56) 1.10 .45

Perf. 14
Size: 22x28mm
J39 D7 30m purple 2.25 .75

See Nos. J47-J59. For overprints see Nos. J40-J46, NJ1-NJ7.

Catalogue values for unused stamps in this section, from this point to the end of the section, are for Never Hinged items.

Postage Due Stamps and Type of 1927 Overprinted in Various Colors

1952, Jan. 16 ***Perf. 13x13½***
J40 D7 2m orange (Bl) .20 .20
J41 D7 4m green .20 .20
J42 D7 6m gray grn (RV) .30 .20
J43 D7 8m brn vio (Bl) .25 .20
J44 D7 10m dl rose (Bl) .65 .20
a. 10m brown red (Bk) .40 .20
J45 D7 12m rose lake (Bl) .35 .20

Perf. 14
J46 D7 30m purple (C) 1.00 .30

See notes after No. 316.

United Arab Republic

1960 Wmk. 318 ***Perf. 13x13½***
Size: 18x22½mm
J47 D7 2m orange .30 .20
J48 D7 4m light green .40 .20
J49 D7 6m green .50 .20
J50 D7 8m brown vio .40 .20
J51 D7 12m rose brown .65 .25
J52 D7 20m dull rose brn 1.00 .25

Perf. 14
Size: 22x28mm
J53 D7 30m violet 3.50 .50

1962 Wmk. 328 ***Perf. 13x13½***
Size: 18x22½mm
J54 D7 2m salmon .25 .20
J55 D7 4m light green .45 .20
J56 D7 10m red brown .65 .25
J57 D7 12m rose brown 1.25 .40
J58 D7 20m dull rose brn 1.60 .75

Perf. 14
Size: 22x28mm
J59 D7 30m light violet 2.00 1.10

D8

1965 Unwmk. Photo. ***Perf. 11***
J60 D8 2m org & vio blk .20 .20
J61 D8 8m lt bl & dk bl .20 .20
J62 D8 10m yel & emer .20 .20
J63 D8 20m lt bl & vio blk .25 .20
J64 D8 40m org & emer .50 .20

MILITARY STAMPS

The "British Forces" and "Army post" stamps were special issues provided at a reduced rate for the purchase and use by the British military forces in Egypt and their families for ordinary letters sent to Great Britain and Ireland by a concessionary arrangement made with the Egyptian government. From Nov. 1, 1932 to Feb. 29, 1936, in order to take advantage of the concessionary rate, it was mandatory to use #M1-M11 by affixing them to the backs of envelopes. An "Egypt Postage Prepaid" handstamp was applied to the face of the envelopes. Envelopes bearing these stamps were to be posted only at British military post boxes. Envelopes bearing the 1936-39 "Army Post" stamps (#M12-M15, issued by the Egyptian Postal Administration), also were sold at the concessionary rate and also were to be posted only at British military post boxes. The "Army Post" stamps were withdrawn in 1941, but the concession continued without the use of special stamps. The concession was finally canceled in 1951.

Imperf examples of Nos. M1-M4, M6, M9 (without overprint) and M10 are proofs.

M1

Unwmk.

1932, Nov. 1 Perf. 11
M1 M1 1pi red & deep blue 77.50 4.25

For similar design see #M3.

M2

1932, Nov. 26 Typo. Perf. 11½
M2 M2 3m blk, *sage grn* 55.00 *77.50*

See #M4, M6, M10.

M3

1933, Aug. Typo. Perf. 11
M3 M3 1pi red & deep blue 26.00 1.10

Camel Type of 1932

1933, Nov. 13 Typo. Perf. 11½
M4 M2 3m brown lake 8.75 *52.50*

M4

1934, June 1 Photo. Perf. 14½x14
M5 M4 1pi bright carmine 42.50 1.10

See #M7-M8. For overprint and surcharge see #M9, M11.

Camel Type of 1932

1934, Nov. 17 Typo. Perf. 11½
M6 M2 3m deep blue 8.25 *27.50*

Type of 1934

1934, Dec. 5 Photo. Perf. 14½x14
M7 M4 1pi green 4.50 4.50

Type of 1934

1935, Apr. 24 Perf. 13½x14
M8 M4 1pi bright carmine 2.50 *2.75*

Type of 1934 Overprinted in Red

1935, May 6 Perf. 14
M9 M4 1pi ultramarine 210.00 190.00

Camel Type of 1932

1935, Nov. 23 Typo. Perf. 11½
M10 M2 3m vermilion 2.25 *30.00*

No. M8 Surcharged

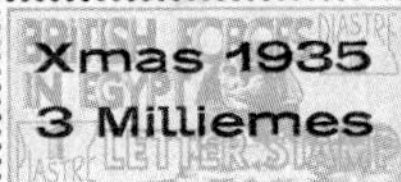

1935, Dec. 16 Photo. Perf. 13½x14
M11 M4 3m on 1pi brt car 19.00 *82.50*

Fuad Type of 1927
Inscribed "Army Post"

M5

1936, Mar. 1 Wmk. 195
M12 M5 3m green 1.10 1.10
M13 M5 10m carmine 2.50 .20

King Farouk — M6

1939, Dec. 16 Perf. 13x13½
M14 M6 3m green 1.90 *3.50*
M15 M6 10m carmine rose 2.50 .20

Catalogue values for unused stamps in this section, from this point to the end of the section, are for Never Hinged items.

United Arab Republic

Arms of UAR and Military Emblems — M7

Perf. 11x11½
1971, Apr. 15 Photo. Wmk. 342
M16 M7 10m purple .20 .20

OFFICIAL STAMPS

O1

Wmk. Crescent and Star (119)

1893, Jan. 1 Typo. Perf. 14x13½
O1 O1 orange brown 1.25 .20

No. O1 exists on ordinary and chalky paper. Imperf. examples of No. O1 are proofs.

Regular Issues of 1884-93 Overprinted

1907
O2 A18 1m brown .80 .20
O3 A19 2m green .80 .20
O4 A20 3m orange .80 .20
O5 A22 5m car rose 1.10 .20
O6 A14 1pi ultra 1.60 .20
O7 A16 5pi gray 5.50 .20
Nos. O2-O7 (6) 10.60 1.20

Nos. O2-O3, O5-O7 imperf. are proofs.

Overprinted

1913
O8 A22 5m carmine rose 1.60 .20
a. Inverted overprint 27.50
b. No period after "S" 4.75 1.90

Regular Issues Overprinted

1914-15

On Issues of 1888-1906

O9 A19 2m green .25 .20
a. Inverted overprint 15.00 11.00
b. Double overprint 175.00
c. No period after "S" 4.50 3.25
O10 A21 4m brown red 1.10 .20
a. Inverted overprint 100.00 60.00

On Issue of 1914

O11 A24 1m olive brown .20 .20
a. No period after "S" 1.75 1.40
O12 A26 3m orange .20 .20
a. No period after "S" 3.75 2.75
O13 A28 5m lake .45 .20
a. No period after "S" 2.75 2.25
b. Two periods after "S" 2.75 2.25
Nos. O9-O13 (5) 2.20 1.00

Regular Issues Overprinted

1915, Oct.

On Issues of 1888-1906

O14 A19 2m green .55 .20
a. Inverted overprint 7.25 5.50
b. Double overprint 11.00
O15 A21 4m brown red .70 .20

On Issue of 1914

O16 A28 5m lake .45 .20
a. Pair, one without overprint 150.00
Nos. O14-O16 (3) 1.70 .60

Regular Issues Overprinted

1922 Wmk. 120

On Issue of 1921-22

O17 A24 1m olive brown 3.75 1.10
O18 A25 2m red 3.75 1.10
O19 A26 3m orange 65.00 65.00
O20 A28 5m pink 3.75 1.60
Nos. O17-O20 (4) 76.25 68.80

Regular Issues of 1921-22 Overprinted

1922
O21 A24 1m olive brn .25 .25
O22 A25 2m red .25 .20
O23 A26 3m orange 1.25 .90
O24 A27 4m green 1.75 1.25
a. Two periods after "H" none after "S" 72.50 72.50
O25 A28 5m pink .45 .20
a. Two periods after "H" none after "S" 37.50 37.50
O26 A29 10m deep blue 1.25 .70
O27 A29 10m lake ('23) 2.25 .70
a. Two periods after "H" none after "S" 55.00 42.50
O28 A34 15m indigo 1.50 .90
O29 A35 15m indigo 100.00 90.00
a. Two periods after "H" none after "S" 225.00 225.00
O30 A31 50m maroon 7.25 2.75

Regular Issue of 1923 Overprinted in Black or Red

1924 Perf. 13½x14
O31 A36 1m orange .45 .25
O32 A36 2m gray (R) .55 .35
O33 A36 3m brown 1.50 .60
O34 A36 4m yellow green 1.75 .70
O35 A36 5m orange brown .55 .20
O36 A36 10m rose 1.60 .25
O37 A36 15m ultra 1.75 .50

Perf. 14

O38 A36 50m myrtle green 4.50 1.40
Nos. O31-O38 (8) 12.65 4.25

O2

O3

Perf. 13x13½

1926-35 Litho. Wmk. 195

Size: 18½x22mm

O39 O2 1m lt orange .20 .20
O40 O2 2m black .20 .20
O41 O2 3m olive brn .20 .20
O42 O2 4m lt green .20 .20
O43 O2 5m brown .20 .20
O44 O2 10m dull red .45 .20
O45 O2 10m brt vio ('34) .20 .20
O46 O2 15m dp blue .65 .20
O47 O2 15m brown vio ('34) .25 .20
O48 O2 20m dp blue ('35) .35 .20

Perf. 13½

Size: 22½x27½mm

O49 O2 20m olive green 1.60 .20
O50 O2 50m myrtle green 1.25 .20
Nos. O39-O50 (12) 5.75 2.40

1938, Dec.

Size: 22½x19mm

O51 O3 1m orange .20 .20
O52 O3 2m red .20 .20
O53 O3 3m olive brown .20 .20
O54 O3 4m yel green .20 .20
O55 O3 5m brown .20 .20
O56 O3 10m brt violet .20 .20
O57 O3 15m rose violet .20 .20
O58 O3 20m blue .20 .20

Perf. 14x13½

Size: 26½x22mm

O59 O3 50m myrtle green .45 .20
Nos. O51-O59 (9) 2.05 1.80

Catalogue values for unused stamps in this section, from this point to the end of the section, are for Never Hinged items.

Nos. O51 to O59 Overprinted in Various Colors

Overprint 19mm Wide

1952, Jan. Perf. 13x13½
O60 O3 1m orange (Br) .20 .20
O61 O3 2m red (Br) .20 .20
O62 O3 3m olive brn (Bl) .20 .20
O63 O3 4m yel green (Bl) .20 .20
O64 O3 5m brown (Bl) .20 .20
O65 O3 10m brt violet (Bl) .20 .20
O66 O3 15m rose violet (Bl) .20 .20
O67 O3 20m blue .25 .20

Overprint 24½mm Wide

Perf. 14x13½

O68 O3 50m myrtle grn (RV) .80 .45
Nos. O60-O68 (9) 2.45 2.05

See notes after No. 316.

United Arab Republic

O4

Arms of UAR — O5

Perf. 13x13½

1959 Litho. Wmk. 318

O69 O4 10m brown violet .40 .20
O70 O4 35m chalky blue .80 .20

1962-63 Wmk. 328

O71 O4 1m orange ('63) .20 .20
O72 O4 4m yel grn ('63) .20 .20
O73 O4 5m brown .20 .20
O74 O4 10m dk brown .20 .20
O75 O4 35m dark blue .25 .25
O76 O4 50m green .40 .40
O77 O4 100m violet ('63) .75 .40
O78 O4 200m rose red ('63) 1.60 .75
O79 O4 500m gray ('63) 4.00 2.25
Nos. O71-O79 (9) 7.80 4.85

Perf. 11½x11

1966-68 Unwmk. Photo.

O80 O5 1m ultra .20 .20
O81 O5 4m brown .20 .20
O82 O5 5m olive .20 .20
O83 O5 10m brown blk .20 .20
O84 O5 20m magenta .20 .20
O85 O5 35m dk purple .25 .20
O86 O5 50m orange .30 .20
O87 O5 55m dk purple .30 .20

Wmk. 342

O88 O5 100m brt grn & brick red .80 .40
O89 O5 200m blue & brick red 1.50 .50
O90 O5 500m olive & brick red 3.00 1.25
Nos. O80-O90 (11) 7.15 3.75

1969 Wmk. 342

O91 O5 10m magenta .20 .20

Arab Republic of Egypt

Arms of Egypt

O6 O7

Wmk. 342

1972, June 30 Photo. *Perf. 11*

O92 O6 1m black & vio blue .20 .20
a. 1m black & light blue ('75) .20 .20
O93 O6 10m black & car .20 .20
a. 10m black & rose red ('76) .20 .20
O94 O6 20m black & olive .20 .20
O95 O6 50m black & orange .25 .20
O96 O6 55m black & purple .30 .20

1973

O97 O6 20m lilac & sepia .20 .20
a. 20m purple & light brown ('76) .20 .20
O98 O6 70m black & grn ('79) .50 .25

1982 Photo. Unwmk. *Perf. 11*

O99 O6 30m purple & brown .20 .20
O100 O6 60m black & orange .25 .20
O101 O6 80m black & green .30 .20
Nos. O92-O101 (10) 2.60 2.05

Issued: 30m, 2/12; 60m, 2/24; 80m, 2/18.

1985-89 Photo. *Perf. 11½*

Size: 21x25mm

O102 O7 1p vermilion .20 .20
O103 O7 2p brown .20 .20
O104 O7 3p sepia .20 .20
O105 O7 5p orange yel .20 .20
O106 O7 8p green .25 .20
O107 O7 10p brown olive .20 .20
O108 O7 15p dull violet .50 .35
O109 O7 20p blue .65 .50
O110 O7 25p red .40 .35
O111 O7 30p dull violet .45 .45
O112 O7 50p green 1.60 1.25
O113 O7 60p myrtle green .90 .90
Nos. O102-O113 (12) 5.75 5.00

Issued: 1p, 3p, 5p, 8p, 15p, 5/1/85; 20p, 50p, 4/88; 10p, 30p, 60p, 12/1/89; 2p, 25p, 1989.

1991-99 Wmk. 342 *Perf. 11½x11*

Size: 18x22mm

O114 O7 5p orange yellow .20 .20
O115 O7 10p brown violet .20 .20
O116 O7 15p brown .20 .20
O117 O7 20p blue .20 .20
O118 O7 20p violet .20 .20
O119 O7 25p purple .25 .25
O120 O7 30p dk violet .45 .45
O121 O7 50p green .75 .75
O122 O7 55p red .60 .60
O123 O7 75p brown .45 .45
O124 O7 £1 green blue 1.25 1.25
O125 O7 £2 green 2.40 2.40
Nos. O114-O125 (12) 7.15 7.15

Issued: 10p, 30p, 7/1/91; 50p, 12/1/91; 55p, 4/1/93; £1, £2, 3/22/94; #O123, 75p, 2/1/97; #O118, 4/11/99.

Arms Type of 1985-89

Perf. 11½x11

2001, Mar. 25 Photo. Unwmk.

Size: 18x22mm

O127 O7 10p brown .20 .20

Issued: 10p, 3/25.

Arms Type of 1985-89

Perf. 11½x11

2002 ? Photo. Unwmk.

O131 O7 30p violet .20 .20

OCCUPATION STAMPS

Catalogue values for unused stamps in this section are for Never Hinged items.

For Use in Palestine

Stamps of 1939-46 Overprinted in Red, Green or Black — a

Perf. 13x13½, 13½x13

1948, May 15 Wmk. 195

N1 A77 1m yellow brn (G) .20 .20
N2 A77 2m red org (G) .20 .20
N3 A66 3m brown (G) .20 .20
N4 A77 4m dp green .20 .20
N5 A77 5m red brown (Bk) .20 .20
N6 A66 6m lt yel grn (Bk) .20 .20
N7 A77 10m dp violet .20 .20
N8 A66 13m rose car (G) .20 .20
N9 A77 15m dk violet .20 .20
N10 A77 17m olive green .20 .20
N11 A77 20m dk gray .20 .20
N12 A77 22m deep blue .25 .25
N13 A74 50pi green & sep 4.75 4.75
N14 A75 £1 dp bl & dk brn 9.25 5.75

The two lines of the overprint are more widely separated on Nos. N13 and N14.

Nos. 267-269, 237 and 238 Overprinted in Red

b

Perf. 14x13½

N15 A73 30m olive green .60 .60
N16 A73 40m dark brown .75 .75
N17 A73 50m Prus green 1.10 1.10
N18 A73 100m brown violet 1.40 1.40
N19 A73 200m dark violet 4.00 4.00
Nos. N1-N19 (19) 24.30 20.80

Overprint arranged to fit size of stamps.

Nos. N1-N19 Overprinted in Black with Three Bars to Obliterate Portrait

Perf. 13x13½, 13½x13, 14x13½

1953 Wmk. 195

N20 A77 1m yellow brown .20 .20
N21 A77 2m red orange .20 .20
N22 A66 3m brown .20 .20
N23 A77 4m deep green .20 .20
N24 A77 5m red brown .20 .20
N25 A66 6m lt yel grn .20 .20
N26 A77 10m deep violet .25 .25
N27 A66 13m rose carmine .30 .30
N28 A77 15m dark violet .30 .30
N29 A77 17m olive green .30 .30
N30 A77 20m dark gray .30 .30
N31 A77 22m deep blue .50 .50
N32 A73 30m olive green .55 .55
N33 A73 40m dark brown .90 .90
N34 A73 50m Prus green 1.40 1.40
N35 A73 100m brown violet 2.75 2.75
N36 A73 200m dark violet 6.25 6.25
N37 A74 50pi green & sepia 17.50 17.50
N38 A75 £1 dp bl & dk brn 27.50 27.50
Nos. N20-N38 (19) 60.00 60.00

Regular Issue of 1953-55 Overprinted Type "a" in Blue or Red

1954-56 *Perf. 13x13½*

N39 A115 1m red brown .20 .20
N40 A115 2m dark lilac .20 .20
N41 A115 3m brt blue (R) .20 .20
N42 A115 4m dark green (R) .20 .20
N43 A115 5m deep carmine .20 .20
N44 A110 10m dark brown .20 .20
N45 A110 15m gray (R) .20 .20
N46 A110 17m dk grnsh bl (R) .20 .20
N47 A110 20m purple (R) ('54) .20 .20

Nos. 331-333 and 335-340 Overprinted in Blue or Red — c

Perf. 13½

N48 A111 30m dull green (R) .25 .25
N49 A111 32m brt blue (R) .30 .30
N50 A111 35m violet (R) .35 .35
N51 A111 40m red brown .55 .55
N52 A111 50m violet brown .60 .60
N53 A112 100m henna brown 1.40 1.40
N54 A112 200m dk grnsh bl (R) 2.75 2.75
N55 A112 500m purple (R) 12.00 12.00
N56 A112 £1 dk grn, blk & red (R) ('56) 20.00 20.00
Nos. N39-N56 (18) 40.00 40.00

Type of 1957 Overprinted in Red — d

1957 Wmk. 195 *Perf. 13½x13*

N57 A127 10m blue green 1.10 1.10

Nos. 414-417 Overprinted Type "d" in Red

1957-58 Wmk. 315 *Perf. 13½*

N58 A137 10m violet .20 .20

Wmk. 318

N59 A136 1m lt bl grn ('58) .20 .20
N60 A138 5m brown ('58) .20 .20
N61 A137 10m violet ('58) .20 .20
Nos. N58-N61 (4) .80 .80

United Arab Republic

Nos. 438-444 Overprinted Type "d" in Red or Green

Perf. 13½x14

1958 Wmk. 318 Photo.

N62 A136 1m crimson .20 .20
N63 A138 2m blue .20 .20
N64 A143 3m dk red brn (G) .20 .20
N65 A217 4m green .20 .20
N66 A138 5m brown .20 .20
N67 A137 10m violet .20 .20
N68 A138 35m lt ultra .25 .25
Nos. N62-N68 (7) 1.45 1.45

Same Overprint in Red on Freedom Struggle Type of 1958

1958 *Perf. 13½x13*

N69 A145 10m dark brown .65 .65

Same Overprint in Green on Declaration of Human Rights Type

1958 *Perf. 13x13½*

N70 A151 10m rose violet .65 .65
N71 A151 35m red brown 1.00 1.00

No. 460 Overprinted Type "d" in Green

1959 Wmk. 195 *Perf. 13½*

N72 A112 55m on 100m henna brn .50 .50

World Refugee Year Type

"PALESTINE" Added in English and Arabic to Stamps of Egypt

OS1

***Perf.* 13x13½ Wmk. 328**

1960

N73 OS1 10m orange brown .20 .20
N74 OS1 35m dk blue gray .30 .30

Type of Regular Issue 1959-60

1960 *Perf. 13½x14*

N75 A136 1m brown orange .20 .20
N76 A217 4m olive gray .20 .20
N77 A138 5m dk dull pur .20 .20
N78 A137 10m dk olive grn .20 .20
Nos. N75-N78 (4) .80 .80

Palestine Day Type

1961, May 15 *Perf. 13½x13*

N79 A184 10m purple .20 .20

WHO Day Type

1961 Wmk. 328 *Perf. 13½x13*

N80 A182 10m blue .20 .20

U.N.T.A.P. Type

1961, Oct. 24

N81 A191 10m dk blue & org .20 .20
N82 A191 35m vermilion & blk .20 .20

Education Day Type

1961, Dec. 18 Photo. *Perf. 13½*

N83 A194 10m red brown .20 .20

Victory Day Type

1961, Dec. 23 Unwmk. *Perf. 11½*

N84 A195 10m brn org & brn .20 .20

Gaza Strip Type

Perf. 13½x13

1962, Mar. 7 Wmk. 328

N85 A200 10m red brown .20 .20

Arab Publicity Week Type

1962, Mar. 22 *Perf. 13½x13*

N86 SP16 10m dark purple .20 .20

Anti-Malaria Type

1962, June 20 Photo.

N87 A204 10m brn & dk car rose .20 .20
N88 A204 35m black & yellow .25 .25

Hammarskjold Type

Perf. 11½x11

1962, Oct. 24 Wmk. 342

Portrait in Slate Blue

N89 A214 5m bright rose .20 .20
N90 A214 10m brown .20 .20
N91 A214 35m blue .25 .25
Nos. N89-N91 (3) .65 .65

Lamp Type of Regular Issue

Perf. 11x11½

1963, Feb. 20 Unwmk.

N92 A217 4m dk brn, org & ultra .20 .20

"Freedom from Hunger" Type

Perf. 11½x11, 11x11½

1963, Mar. 21 Wmk. 342

N93 A220 5m lt grn & dp org .20 .20
N94 A220 10m olive & yellow .20 .20
N95 A220 35m dull pur, yel & blk .25 .25
Nos. N93-N95 (3) .65 .65

Red Cross Centenary Type

Designs: 10m, Centenary emblem, bottom panel added. 35m, Globe and emblem, top and bottom panels added.

1963, May 8 Unwmk. *Perf. 11x11½*
N96 A221 10m dk blue & crim .20 .20
N97 A221 35m crim & dk blue .25 .25

"Save Abu Simbel" Type, 1963

1963, Oct. 15 Wmk. 342 *Perf. 11*
N98 A224 5m black & yellow .20 .20
N99 A224 10m gray, blk & yellow .20 .20
N100 A224 35m org yel & violet .25 .25
Nos. N98-N100 (3) .65 .65

Human Rights Type

1963, Dec. 10 Photo. *Perf. 11½x11*
N101 A228 5m dk brown & yellow .20 .20
N102 A228 10m dp claret, gray & blk .20 .20
N103 A228 35m lt grn, pale grn & blk .25 .25
Nos. N101-N103 (3) .65 .65

Types of Regular Issue

1964 Unwmk. *Perf. 11*
N104 A231 1m citron & lt vio .20 .20
N105 A230 2m orange & slate .20 .20
N106 A230 3m blue & ocher .20 .20
N107 A235 4m ol gray, ol, brn & rose .20 .20
N108 A230 5m rose & brt blue .20 .20
a. 5m rose & dark blue 1.00 1.00
N109 A231 10m ol, rose & brn .20 .20
N110 A230 15m lilac & yellow .30 .30
N111 A230 20m brown blk & ol .20 .20
N112 A231 30m dp org & ind .30 .30
N113 A231 35m buff, ocher & emer .40 .40
N114 A231 40m ultra & emer .40 .40
N115 A231 60m grnsh bl & brn org .80 .80

Wmk. 342

N116 A232 100m bluish blk & yel brn .80 .80
Nos. N104-N116 (13) 4.40 4.40

Arab League Council Type

1964, Jan. 13 Photo.
N117 A234 10m olive & black .20 .20

Minaret Type

1964 Unwmk. *Perf. 11*
N118 A235 4m ol, red brn & red .20 .20

Arab Postal Union Type

1964, Apr. 1 Wmk. 342 *Perf. 11*
N119 A239 10m emer & ultra, *lt grn* .20 .20

WHO Type

1964, Apr. 7
N120 A240 10m violet blk & red .20 .20

Minaret Type

1965, Jan. 20 Unwmk. *Perf. 11*
N121 A255 4m green & dk brn .20 .20

Arab League Type

1965, Mar. 22 Wmk. 342 *Perf. 11*
N122 A258 10m green, red & blk .20 .20
N123 A258 20m green & brown .20 .20

World Health Day Type

1965, Apr. 7 Wmk. 342 *Perf. 11*
N124 A259 10m brt green & crim .20 .20

Massacre Type

1965, Apr. 9 Photo.
N125 A260 10m slate blue & red .20 .20

ITU Type

1965, May 17 Wmk. 342 *Perf. 11*
N126 A261 5m sl grn, sl bl & yel .20 .20
N127 A261 10m car, rose red & gray .20 .20
N128 A261 35m vio bl, ultra & yel .20 .20
Nos. N126-N128 (3) .60 .60

United Nations Type

5m, WHO Headquarters Building, Geneva. 10m, UN Refugee emblem. 35m, UNICEF emblem.

1966, Oct. 24 Wmk. 342 *Perf. 11*
N129 A288 5m rose & brt pur .20 .20
N130 A288 10m yel brn & brt pur .20 .20
N131 A288 35m brt green & brt pur .20 .20
Nos. N129-N131 (3) .60 .60

Victory Day Type
Wmk. 342

1966, Dec. 23 Photo. *Perf. 11½*
N132 A290 10m olive & car rose .20 .20

Arab Publicity Week Type
Perf. 11x11½

1967, Mar. 22 Photo. Wmk. 342
N133 A294 10m vio blue & brn .20 .20

Labor Day Type
Perf. 11½x11

1967, May 1 Photo. Wmk. 342
N134 A296 10m olive & sepia .20 .20

OCCUPATION AIR POST STAMPS

Catalogue values for unused stamps in this section are for Never Hinged items.

Nos. C39-C50 Overprinted Type "b" in Black, Carmine or Red

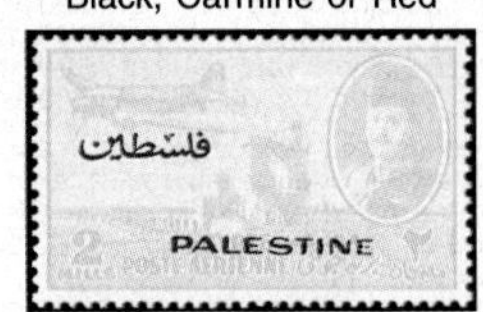

Perf. 13x13½

1948, May 15 Wmk. 195
NC1 AP3 2m red org (Bk) .20 .20
NC2 AP3 3m dk brn (C) .20 .20
NC3 AP3 5m red brn (Bk) .20 .20
NC4 AP3 7m dp yel org (Bk) .20 .20
NC5 AP3 8m green (C) .20 .20
NC6 AP3 10m violet .20 .20
NC7 AP3 20m brt bl .25 .25
NC8 AP3 30m brn vio (Bk) .40 .40
NC9 AP3 40m car rose (Bk) .50 .50
NC10 AP3 50m Prus grn .75 .75
NC11 AP3 100m olive grn 1.25 1.25
NC12 AP3 200m dark gray 4.00 4.00
Nos. NC1-NC12 (12) 8.35 8.35

Nos. NC1-NC12 Overprinted in Black with Three Bars to Obliterate Portrait

1953
NC13 AP3 2m red org .70 .70
NC14 AP3 3m dk brn .20 .20
NC15 AP3 5m red brn 2.75 2.75
NC16 AP3 7m dp yel org .40 .40
NC17 AP3 8m green .60 .60
NC18 AP3 10m violet .20 .20
NC19 AP3 20m brt bl .50 .50
NC20 AP3 30m brn vio .60 .60
NC21 AP3 40m car rose .60 .60
NC22 AP3 50m Prus grn 3.00 3.00
NC23 AP3 100m olive grn 17.00 17.00
NC24 AP3 200m dk gray 8.00 8.00
Nos. NC13-NC24 (12) 34.55 34.55

Nos. NC1-NC3, NC6, NC10, NC11 with Additional Overprint in Various Colors

Overprinted in Black with Three Bars to Obliterate Portrait

1953
NC25 AP3 2m red org (Bk + Bl) .20 .20
NC26 AP3 3m dk brn (Bk + RV) 2.10 2.10
NC27 AP3 5m red brn (Bk) .20 .20
NC28 AP3 10m vio (R + G) 4.25 4.25
NC29 AP3 50m Prus grn (R + RV) 2.75 2.75
NC30 AP3 100m ol grn (R + Bk) 12.50 12.50
Nos. NC25-NC30 (6) 22.00 22.00

Nos. C65-C66 Overprinted Type "b" in Black or Red

1955 Wmk. 195 *Perf. 13x13½*
NC31 AP4 5m red brn .75 .75
NC32 AP4 15m ol grn (R) 1.00 1.00

United Arab Republic Type of 1963

"PALESTINE" Added in Arabic and English to Air Post Stamps

OAP1

Perf. 11½x11

1963, Oct. 24 Photo. Wmk. 342
NC33 AP6 80m blk & brt bl 1.10 1.10
NC34 AP10 115m blk & yel 1.60 1.60
NC35 AP10 140m bl, ultra & org red 2.00 2.00
Nos. NC33-N (3) 4.70 4.70

Cairo Tower Type, 1964

1964, Nov. 2 Unwmk. *Perf. 11x11½*
NC36 AP11 50m dl vio & lt bl .45 .45

World Meteorological Day Type

1965, Mar. 23 Wmk. 342 *Perf. 11*
NC37 AP12 80m dk bl & org .80 .80

Tutankhamen Type of 1965

1965, July 1 Photo. *Perf. 11*
NC38 AP13 10m brn org & brt grn .40 .40

OCCUPATION SPECIAL DELIVERY STAMP

Catalogue values for unused stamps in this section are for Never Hinged items.

No. E4 Overprinted Type "b" in Carmine

1948 Wmk. 195 *Perf. 13x13½*
NE1 SD1 40m dl brn & pale gray 1.00 1.00

OCCUPATION POSTAGE DUE STAMPS

Catalogue values for unused stamps in this section are for Never Hinged items.

Postage Due Stamps of Egypt, 1927-41, Overprinted Type "a" in Black or Rose

1948 Wmk. 195 *Perf. 13x13½*
NJ1 D7 2m orange .20 .20
NJ2 D7 4m green (R) .20 .20
NJ3 D7 6m gray green .20 .20
NJ4 D7 8m brown violet .25 .25
NJ5 D7 10m brick red .25 .25
NJ6 D7 12m rose lake .40 .40

Overprinted Type "b" in Red
Perf. 14
Size: 22x28mm

NJ7 D7 30m purple .90 .90
Nos. NJ1-NJ7 (7) 2.40 2.40

ELOBEY, ANNOBON AND CORISCO

,el-ə-'bā, ,an-ə-'bän and kə-'ris-,kō

LOCATION — A group of islands near the Guinea Coast of western Africa
GOVT. — Spanish colonial possessions administered as part of the Continental Guinea District. A second district under the same governor-general included Fernando Po.
AREA — 13¾ sq. mi.
POP. — 2,950 (estimated 1910)
CAPITAL — Santa Isabel

100 Centimos = 1 Peseta

King Alfonso XIII — A1

1903 Unwmk. Typo. *Perf. 14*

Control Numbers on Back

No.	Type	Value	Color	Unused	Used
1	A1	¼c	carmine	.55	.30
2	A1	½c	dk violet	.55	.30
3	A1	1c	black	.55	.30
4	A1	2c	red	.55	.30
5	A1	3c	dk green	.45	.30
6	A1	4c	dk blue grn	.55	.30
7	A1	5c	violet	.55	.30
8	A1	10c	rose lake	1.10	1.25
9	A1	15c	orange buff	3.25	1.40
10	A1	25c	dark blue	5.25	4.50
11	A1	50c	red brown	7.00	7.75
12	A1	75c	black brn	7.00	10.50
13	A1	1p	orange red	11.00	15.00
14	A1	2p	chocolate	29.00	45.00
15	A1	3p	dp olive grn	45.00	55.00
16	A1	4p	claret	100.00	75.00
17	A1	5p	blue green	110.00	77.50
18	A1	10p	dull blue	225.00	125.00
			Nos. 1-18 (18)	547.35	420.00
			Set, never hinged	850.00	

Dated "1905"

1905

Control Numbers on Back

No.	Type	Value	Color	Unused	Used
19	A1	1c	carmine	.80	.50
20	A1	2c	dp violet	3.50	.50
21	A1	3c	black	.80	.50
22	A1	4c	dull red	.80	.50
23	A1	5c	dp green	.80	.50
24	A1	10c	blue grn	2.75	.65
25	A1	15c	violet	3.50	3.00
26	A1	25c	rose lake	3.50	3.00
27	A1	50c	orange buff	6.25	4.50
28	A1	75c	dark blue	6.25	4.50
29	A1	1p	red brown	12.50	9.75
30	A1	2p	black brn	13.50	14.50
31	A1	3p	orange red	13.50	15.00
32	A1	4p	dk brown	100.00	55.00
33	A1	5p	bronze grn	110.00	57.50
34	A1	10p	claret	275.00	175.00
			Nos. 19-34 (16)	553.45	344.90
			Set, never hinged	975.00	

Nos. 19-22 Surcharged in Black or Red

1906

No.	Description	Unused	Used
35	A1 10c on 1c rose (Bk)	9.00	5.50
a.	Inverted surcharge	9.00	5.50
b.	Value omitted	27.50	14.50
c.	Frame omitted	14.50	6.50
d.	Double surcharge	9.00	5.50
e.	Surcharged "15 cents"	27.50	14.50
f.	Surcharged "25 cents"	47.50	21.00
g.	Surcharged "50 cents"	35.00	21.00
h.	"1906" omitted	16.00	6.50
36	A1 15c on 2c dp vio (R)	9.00	5.50
a.	Frame omitted	11.00	5.00
b.	Surcharged "25 cents"	15.00	8.00
c.	Inverted surcharge	9.00	5.50
d.	Double surcharge	9.00	5.50
37	A1 25c on 3c blk (R)	9.00	5.50
a.	Inverted surcharge	9.00	5.50
b.	Double surcharge	9.00	5.50
c.	Surcharged "15 cents"	15.00	8.00
d.	Surcharged "50 cents"	22.50	10.00
38	A1 50c on 4c red (Bk)	9.00	5.50
a.	Inverted surcharge	9.00	5.50
b.	Value omitted	32.50	16.00
c.	Frame omitted	16.00	7.25
e.	Double surcharge	9.00	5.50
f.	"1906" omitted	16.00	7.25
g.	Surcharged "10 cents"	30.00	14.50
h.	Surcharged "25 cents"	30.00	14.50
	Nos. 35-38 (4)	36.00	22.00

Eight other surcharges were prepared but not issued: 10c on 50c, 75c, 1p, 2p and 3p; 15c on 50c and 5p; 50c on 5c.

Exist with surcharges in different colors; #35 in blue, red or violet, #36 in black or violet, #37 in black or violet, #38 in blue, violet or red. Value, set of 10, $135.

King Alfonso XIII — A2

1907

Control Numbers on Back

No.	Type	Value	Color	Unused	Used
39	A2	1c	dk violet	.45	.30
40	A2	2c	black	.45	.30
41	A2	3c	red orange	.45	.30
42	A2	4c	dk green	.45	.30
43	A2	5c	blue green	.45	.30
44	A2	10c	violet	3.75	3.50
45	A2	15c	carmine	1.25	1.25
46	A2	25c	orange	1.25	1.25
47	A2	50c	blue	1.25	1.25
48	A2	75c	brown	3.75	1.60
49	A2	1p	black brn	6.25	3.75
50	A2	2p	orange red	9.50	4.25
51	A2	3p	dk brown	8.75	4.25
52	A2	4p	bronze grn	9.50	4.25
53	A2	5p	claret	12.50	4.75
54	A2	10p	rose	30.00	15.00
			Nos. 39-54 (16)	90.00	46.60
			Set, never hinged	160.00	

Stamps of 1907 Surcharged

1908-09

Black Surcharge

No.	Description	Unused	Used
55	A2 5c on 3c red org ('09)	2.50	1.25
56	A2 5c on 4c dk grn ('09)	2.50	1.25
57	A2 5c on 10c violet	5.25	5.00
58	A2 25c on 10c violet	27.50	15.00
	Nos. 55-58 (4)	37.75	22.50

1910

Red Surcharge

No.	Description	Unused	Used
59	A2 5c on 1c dark violet	2.00	1.00
60	A2 5c on 2c black	2.00	1.00

Nos. 55-60 exist with surcharge inverted (value set, $100 unused or used); with double surcharge, one black, one red (value set, $300 unused or used); with "PARA" omitted (value set, $150.00 unused or used)

The same 5c surcharge was also applied to Nos. 45-54, but these were not issued (value set, $250).

In 1909, stamps of Spanish Guinea replaced those of Elobey, Annobon and Corisco.

1909 **CORREOS**
10 cen de peseta

Revenue stamps surcharged as above were unauthorized although some were postally used.

EPIRUS

i-'pī-rəs

LOCATION — Southeastern Europe comprising parts of Greece and Albania.

This territory formerly belonged to Turkey but is now divided between Greece and Albania. The northern part of the Greek section, now a part of Albania, set up a provisional government during 1912-13 and issued postage stamps but it collapsed in 1916, following Greek occupation. The name "Epirus" is taken from the Greek word meaning "Mainland."

100 Lepta = 1 Drachma

Chimarra Issue

Double-headed Eagle, Skull and Crossbones — A1

Handstamped

1914 (Feb.) Unwmk. *Imperf.*

Control Mark in Blue

Without Gum

No.	Type	Value	Color	Unused	Used
1	A1	1 l	black & blue	175.00	125.00
2	A1	5 l	blue & red	175.00	125.00
3	A1	10 l	red & blk	175.00	125.00
4	A1	25 l	blue & red	175.00	125.00
			Nos. 1-4 (4)	850.00	600.00

All values exist without control mark. This mark is a solid blue oval, about 12x8mm, containing the colorless Greek letters "SP," the first two letters of Spiromilios, the Chimarra commander.

All four exist with value inverted and the 1, 5 and 10 l with value double.

Some experts question the official character of this issue. Counterfeits are plentiful.

Provisional Government Issues

Infantryman with Rifle
A2 A3

Serrate Roulette 13½

1914 (Mar.) Litho.

No.	Type	Value	Color	Unused	Used
5	A2	1 l	orange	.35	.35
6	A2	5 l	green	.35	.35
7	A3	10 l	carmine	.35	.35
8	A3	25 l	deep blue	.35	.35
9	A2	50 l	brown	.75	.75
10	A2	1d	violet	1.50	1.50
11	A2	2d	blue	9.00	9.00
12	A2	5d	gray green	11.00	11.00
			Nos. 5-12 (8)	23.65	23.65

15 values, 5 l to 5d, of Turkish stamps surcharged "Epirus Autonomous" and new values in Greek were on sale for a few days in Argyrokastron (Gjirokaster).

Flag of Epirus — A5

1914 (Aug.)

No.	Type	Value	Color	Unused	Used
15	A5	1 l	brown & blue	.40	*.50*
16	A5	5 l	green & blue	.40	*.50*
17	A5	10 l	rose red & blue	.45	*.60*
18	A5	25 l	dk blue & blue	.70	*.80*
19	A5	50 l	violet & blue	.70	*.85*
20	A5	1d	carmine & blue	3.50	*5.00*
21	A5	2d	orange & blue	1.25	*1.75*
22	A5	5d	dk green & blue	4.00	*5.00*
			Nos. 15-22 (8)	11.40	*15.00*

Koritsa Issue

A7

1914

No.	Type	Value	Color	Unused	Used
26	A7	25 l	dk blue & blue	4.00	4.50
27	A7	50 l	violet & blue	5.00	5.00

Chimarra Issue

1911-23 Issues of Greece Overprinted

1914 (Aug.)

No.	Type	Value	Color	Unused	Used
34	A24	1 l	green	*17.50*	*17.50*
35	A25	2 l	carmine	*16.00*	*16.00*
36	A24	3 l	vermilion	*16.00*	*16.00*
37	A26	5 l	green	*17.50*	*17.50*
38	A24	10 l	carmine	*18.00*	*18.00*
39	A25	20 l	slate	*25.00*	*25.00*
40	A25	25 l	blue	*65.00*	*65.00*
41	A26	50 l	violet brn	*85.00*	*85.00*
			Nos. 34-41 (8)	*260.00*	*260.00*

The 2 l and 3 l are engraved stamps of the 1911-21 issue, the others are lithographed stamps of the 1912-23 issue.

Overprint reads: "Greek Chimarra 1914."

Stamps of this issue are with or without a black monogram (S.S., for S. Spiromilios) in manuscript. Counterfeits are plentiful.

Stamps of the following designs were not regularly issued for postal purposes in the opinion of the editors.

From 1914: 1st design, 3 varieties. 2nd design, 6 varieties. 3rd design, 7 varieties. 4th and 5th designs, 15 varieties.

From 1920: 6th design, 4 varieties.

OCCUPATION STAMPS

Issued under Greek Occupation

Greek Occupation Stamps of 1913 Overprinted Horizontally

Serrate Roulette 13½

1914-15	Black Overprint	Unwmk.	
N1 O1	1 l brown	.25	.25
N2 O2	2 l red	.30	.30
b.	2 l rose	.80	.80
N4 O2	3 l orange	.70	.70
N5 O1	5 l green	2.25	1.00
N6 O1	10 l rose red	2.50	1.00
N7 O1	20 l violet	7.50	2.50
N8 O2	25 l pale blue	2.50	1.10
N9 O1	30 l gray green	11.00	4.50
N10 O2	40 l indigo	15.00	9.00
N11 O1	50 l dark blue	16.00	10.00
N12 O2	1d violet brown	45.00	45.00
	Nos. N1-N12 (11)	103.00	75.35

The overprint exists double on 6 denominations (1 l, 2 l both, 3 l, 5 l, 10 l and 1d); inverted on all but 25 l, 40 l; double, one inverted, 5 l. Values, $15 and up.

Red Overprint

N1a O1	1 l brown	3.50	
N2a O2	2 l red	3.50	
N4a O2	3 l orange	3.50	
N5a O1	5 l green	3.50	

Nos. N1a-N5a were not issued. Exist canceled.

Regular Issues of Greece, 1911-23, Overprinted

On Issue of 1911-21

1916		Engr.	
N17 A24	3 l vermilion	6.50	5.00
N18 A26	30 l carmine rose	62.50	60.00
N19 A27	1d ultra	50.00	50.00
N20 A27	2d vermilion	62.50	60.00
N21 A27	3d carmine rose	75.00	75.00
N22 A27	5d ultra	350.00	350.00
a.	Double overprint	450.00	450.00
	Nos. N17-N22 (6)	606.50	600.00

Overprints on Nos. N18-N21 read up, on No. N22 reads down. Overprint on No. N17 exists reading down but most read up.

On Issue of 1912-23

1916		Litho.	
N23 A24	1 l green	.50	.50
N24 A25	2 l carmine	.50	.50
N25 A24	3 l vermilion	.80	.80
N26 A26	5 l green	.80	.80
N27 A24	10 l carmine	.90	.90
N28 A25	20 l slate	1.25	1.25
N29 A25	25 l blue	2.25	2.25
N30 A26	30 l rose	4.00	4.00
N31 A25	40 l indigo	4.00	4.00
N32 A26	50 l violet brown	5.00	5.00
	Nos. N23-N32 (10)	20.00	20.00

Overprints on Nos. N28-N29, N31-N32 read up. Nos. N23-N27 N30 exist reading down but most read up.

In each sheet there are two varieties in the overprint: the "I" in "Epirus" omitted and an inverted "L" in place of the first letter of the word.

Counterfeits exist of Nos. N1-N32.

Postage stamps issued in 1940-41, during Greek occupation, are listed under Greece.

EQUATORIAL GUINEA

ˌē-kwə-ˈtō-ē-əl ˈgi-nē

LOCATION — Gulf of Guinea, West Africa
GOVT. — Republic
AREA — 10,832 sq. mi.
POP. — 465,746 (1999 est.)
CAPITAL — Malabo

The Spanish provinces Fernando Po and Rio Muni united and became independent as the Republic of Equatorial Guinea, Oct. 12, 1968.

100 Centimos = 1 Peseta
100 centimos = 1 ekuele, bipkwele is plural (1973)
100 centimes = 1 CFA franc (1985)

Catalogue values for all unused stamps in this country are for Never Hinged items.

Clasped Hands and Laurel — A1

Pres. Francisco Macias Nguema — A2

Unwmk.

1968, Oct. 12	Photo.	*Perf. 13*	
1 A1	1p dp bl, gold & sep	.30	.30
2 A1	1.50p dk grn, gold & brn	.30	.30
3 A1	6p cop red, gold & brn	.30	.30
	Nos. 1-3 (3)	.90	.90

Attainment of independence, Oct. 12, 1968.

1970, Jan. 27		*Perf. 13x12½*	
4 A2	50c dl org, brn & crim	.20	.20
5 A2	1p pink, grn & lil	.20	.20
6 A2	1.50p pale ol, brn & bl grn	.25	.20
7 A2	2p buff, grn & ol	.25	.20
8 A2	2.50p pale grn, dk grn & dk bl	.30	.20
9 A2	10p bis, Prus bl & vio brn	1.00	.20
10 A2	25p gray, blk & brn	2.10	.20
	Nos. 4-10 (7)	4.30	1.40

Pres. Macias Nguema and Cock — A3

1971, Apr.	Photo.	*Perf. 13*	
11 A3	3p lt bl & multi	.25	.20
12 A3	5p buff & multi	.30	.20
13 A3	10p pale lilac & multi	.70	.20
14 A3	25p pale grn & multi	1.25	.20
	Nos. 11-14 (4)	2.50	.80

2nd anniv. of independence, Oct. 12, 1970.

Torch, Bow and Arrows — A4

1972	Photo.	*Perf. 11½*	
15 A4	50p ocher & multi	1.10	.40

"3rd Triumphal Year."

Apollo 15, set of seven, 1p, 3p, 5p, 8p, 10p, airmail 15p, 25p, plus two airmail semi-postal gold foil perf. 200p+25p, imperf. 250p+50p, and two souv. sheets, perf. 25p+200p, imperf. 50p+250p, issued Jan. 28. Nos. 7201-7211.

1972 Winter Olympics, Sapporo, set of seven, 1p, 2p, 3p, 5p, 8p, airmail 15p, 50p, plus two airmail semi-postal gold foil perf., imperf., 200p+25p, 250p+50p, and two souv. sheets, perf. 200p+25p, imperf. 250p+50p, issued Feb. 3, 1972. Nos. 7212-7222.

Christmas, paintings, set of seven, 1p, 3p, 5p, 8p, 10p, airmail 15p, 25p, plus two airmail semi-postal gold foil perf. 200p+25p, imperf. 250p+50p, and two souv. sheets, perf. 25p+200p, imperf. 50p+250p (Virgin and Child by da Vinci, Murillo, Raphael, Mabuse, van der Weyden, Durer), issued Feb. 20. Nos. 7223-7233.

Easter, set of seven, 1p, 3p, 5p, 8p, 10p, airmail 15p, 25p, plus two airmail semi-postal gold foil perf., imperf., 200p+25p, 250p+50p (designs by Velazquez and El Greco), two souv. sheets, perf. (25p, 200p), and imperf. 250p+50p, issued Apr. 28. Nos. 7234-7244.

1972 Summer Olympics, Munich, set of seven, 1p, 2p, 3p, 5p, 8p, airmail 15p, 50p, plus two airmail semi-postal souv. sheets, perf. 200p+25p, imperf. 250p+50p, and presentation folder with two gold foil, perf. 200p+25p, imperf. 250p+50p, issued May 5, 1972. Nos. 7245-7255.

Gold Medal Winners, Sapporo, set of seven, 1p, 2p, 3p, 5p, 8p, airmail 15p, 50p, plus 12 airmail semi-postal gold foil perf. 200p+25p (6), imperf. 250p+50p (6), imperf. souv. sheet 250p+50p, and perf. souv. sheet of two (25p, 200p), issued May 25. Nos. 7256-7276.

Black Gold Medal Winners, Munich, set of seven, 1p, 2p, 3p, 5p, 8p, airmail 15p, 50p, plus 18 gold foil airmail semi-postal perf. 200p+25p (9), imperf. 250p+50p (9), and two souv. sheets, perf. 200p+25p, imperf. 250p+50p, issued June 26. Nos. 7277-72103.

Olympic Games, Regatta in Kiel and Oberschleissheim, set of seven, 1p, 2p, 3p, 5p, 8p, airmail 15p, 50p, plus four airmail semi-postal gold foil, perf. 200p+25p (2), imperf. 250p+50p (2), and two souv. sheets, perf. 200p+25p, imperf. 250p+50p, issued July 25. Nos. 72104-72116.

1972 Summer Olympics, Munich, set of seven, 1p, 2p, 3p, 5p, 8p, airmail 15p, 50p, plus two airmail semi-postal souv. sheets, perf. 200p+25p, imperf, 250p+50p, issued Aug. 10, 1972; and 20 gold foil, perf. 200p+25p (10), imperf. 250+50p (10), issued Aug. 17. Nos. 72117-72145.

Olympic Equestrian Events, set of seven, 1p, 2p, 3p, 5p, 8p, airmail 15p, 50p, plus two airmail semi-postal souv. sheets, perf. 200p+25p, imperf. 250p+50p, two gold foil, perf. 200p+25p, imperf. 250p+50p, four gold foil souv. sheets of two, 200p+25p (2 perf., 2 imperf.), and 16 souv. sheets, perf. 200p+25p (8), imperf. 250p+50p (8), issued Aug. 24. Nos. 72146-72176.

Japanese Railroad Cent. (locomotives), set of seven, 1p, 3p, 5p, 8p, 10p, airmail 15p, 25p, plus 2 airmail semi-postal souv. sheets, perf. 200p+25p, imperf. 250p+50p, 11 gold foil souv. sheets of 1, perf. 200p+25p (9), imperf. 200p+25p (2), and 2 souv. sheets of 2, perf., imperf., 200p+25p, issued Sept. 21. Nos. 72177-72198.

Gold Medal Winners, Munich, set of seven, 1p, 2p, 3p, 5p, 8p, airmail 15p, 50p, plus two airmail semi-postal souv. sheets, perf. 200p+25p, imperf. 250p+50p, and four gold foil souv. sheets, perf. 200p+25p (2), imperf. 250p+50p (2), issued Oct. 30. Nos. 72199-72211.

Christmas and 500th Birth Anniv. of Lucas Cranach, Madonnas and Christmas seals, set of seven, 1p, 3p, 5p, 8p, 10p, airmail 15p, 25p (Giotto, Schongauer, Fouquet, de Morales, Fini, David, Sassetta), plus two airmail semi-postal souv. sheets, perf. 200p+25p, imperf. 250p+50p, 12 gold foil souv. sheets, perf. 200p+25p (6), imperf. 250p+50p (6), two souv. sheets of two, perf., imperf., 200p+25p, and ovptd. 200p+25p stamp, issued Nov. 22. Nos. 72212-72234.

American and Russian Astronaut Memorial, set of seven, 1p, 3p, 5p, 8p, 10p, airmail 15p, 25p, plus two airmail semi-postal souv. sheets, perf. 200p+25p, imperf. 250p+50p, and four gold foil ovptd. "Apollo 16 and 17" perf. 200p+25p (2), imperf. 250p+50p (2), issued Dec. 14. Nos. 72235-72247.

United Natl. Workers' Party Emblem — A5

1973	Litho.	*Perf. 13½x13*	
16 A5	1p multi	.25	.25
17 A5	1.50p multi	.25	.25
18 A5	2p multi	.25	.25
19 A5	4p multi	.25	.25
20 A5	5p multi	.25	.25
	Nos. 16-20 (5)	1.25	1.25

Natl. Independence, 4th Anniv. — A6

Pres. Macias Nguema and: 1.50p, Agriculture. 2p, 4p, Education. 3p, 5p, Natl. defense.

1973		*Perf. 13½*	
21 A6	1.50p multi	.25	.25
22 A6	2p multi	.25	.25
23 A6	3p multi	.25	.25
24 A6	4p multi	.25	.25
25 A6	5p multi	.25	.25
	Nos. 21-25 (5)	1.25	1.25

1973

Transatlantic Yacht Race, set of seven, 1p, 2p, 3p, 5p, 8p, airmail 15p, 50p, and two airmail semi-postal souv. sheets, perf. 200p+25p, imperf. 250p+50p, issued Jan. 22. Nos. 7301-7309.

Renoir paintings, set of seven, 1p, 2p, 3p, 5p, 8p, airmail 15p, 50p, plus two airmail semi-postal gold foil, perf. 200p+25p, imperf. 250p+50p, and two souv. sheets, perf. 200p+25p, imperf. 250p+50p, issued Feb. 22. Nos. 7310-7320.

Conquest of Venus (spacecraft), set of seven, 1p, 3p, 5p, 8p, 10p, airmail 5p, 25p, and two airmail semi-postal souv. sheets, perf. 200p+25p, imperf. 250p+50p, issued Mar. 22. Nos. 7321-7329.

Apollo 11-17 Flights, gold foil airmail semi-postal souv. sheets, perf. 200p+25p (7), 250p+50p (7), and four souv. sheets of two, perf. 200p+25p (2), imperf. 250p+50p (2), issued Mar. 22. Nos. 7330-7347.

Easter, paintings, set of seven, 1p, 3p, 5p, 8p, 10p, airmail 15p, 25p (Verrocchio, Perugino, Tintoretto, Witz,

Pontormo), plus two airmail semi-postal souv. sheets, perf. 200p+25p, imperf. 250p+50p, and four gold foil issue of 1972 souv. sheets ovptd., perf. 200p+25p (2), imperf. 250p+50p (2), issued Apr. 25. Nos. 7348-7360.

Copernicus, 500th birth anniv. (US and USSR space explorations), four gold foil airmail semi-postal souv. sheets, perf. 200p+25p (2), imperf. 250p+50p (2), issued May 15. Nos. 7361-7364.

Tour de France bicycle race, set of seven, 1p, 2p, 3p, 5p, 8p, airmail 15p, 50p, and two airmail semi-postal souv. sheets, perf. 200p+25p, imperf. 250p+50p, issued May 22. Nos. 7365-7373.

Paintings, set of seven, 1p, 2p, 3p, 5p, 8p, airmail 15p, 50p, and two airmail semi-postal souv. sheets, 200p+25p, imperf. 250p+50p, issued June 29. Nos. 7374-7382.

1974 World Cup Soccer Championships, Munich, set of nine, 5c, 10c, 15c, 20c, 25c, 55c, 60c, airmail 5p, 70p, and two airmail souv. sheets, perf. 130p, imperf. 200p, issued Aug. 30. Nos. 7383-7393.

Rubens paintings, set of seven, 1p, 2p, 3p, 5p, 8p, airmail 15p, 50p, and two airmail semi-postal souv. sheets, perf. (25p, 200p), imperf. (50p, 250p), issued Sept. 23. Nos. 7394-73102.

1974 World Cup Soccer Championships, Munich, four gold foil airmail souv. sheets, perf. 130e (2), imperf. 200e (2), and two souv. sheets of two, perf. 130e, imperf. 200e, issued Oct. 24. Nos. 73103-73108.

Christmas, paintings, set of seven, 1p, 3p, 5p, 8p, 10p, airmail 15p, 25p, and two airmail semi-postal souv. sheets, perf. 200p+25p, imperf. 250p+50p (Nativity, by van der Weyden, Bosco, de Carvajal, Mabuse, Lucas Jordan, P. Goecke, Maino, Fabriano, Lochner), issued Oct. 30. Nos. 73109-73117.

Apollo Program and J.F. Kennedy, two gold foil airmail semi-postals, perf. 200p+25p, imperf. 250p+50p, and two souv. sheets, perf. 200p+25p, imperf. 250p+50p, issued Nov. 10. Nos. 73118-73121.

World Cup Soccer (famous players), set of nine, 30c, 35c, 40c, 45c, 50c, 65c, 70c, airmail 8p, 60p, and two airmail souv. sheets, perf. 130p, imperf. 200p, issued Nov. 20. Nos. 73122-73132.

Princess Anne's Wedding, six gold foil airmail souv. sheets, perf., imperf., two sheets of one, each 250e, one sheet of two 250e, issued Dec. 17. Nos. 73133-73141.

Pablo Picasso Memorial (Blue Period paintings), set of seven, 30c, 35c, 40c, 45c, 50c, airmail 8e, 60e, and two airmail souv. sheets, perf. 130e, imperf. 200e, issued Dec. 20. Nos. 73142-73150.

1974

Copernicus, 500th birth anniv., set of seven, 5c, 10c, 15c, 20c, 4e, airmail 10e, 70e, two airmail souv. sheets, perf. 130e, imperf. 200e, issued Feb. 8, 1974; eight gold foil airmail souv. sheets, perf. 130e (3), 250e, imperf. 200e (3), 300e, and four souv. sheets of two, perf. 250e (2), imperf. 250e (2), issued Apr. 10. Nos. 7401-7421.

World Cup Soccer Championships (final games), set of nine, 75c, 80c, 85c, 90c, 95c, 1e, 1.25e, airmail 10e, 50e, and two airmail souv. sheets, perf. 130e, imperf. 200e, issued Feb. 28. Nos. 7422-7432.

Easter, paintings, set of seven, 1p, 3p, 5p, 8p, 10p, airmail 15p, 25p (Fra Angelico, Castagno, Allori, Multscher, della Francesca, Pleydenwurff, Correggio), and two airmail semi-postal souv. sheets, perf. 200p+25p, imperf. 250p+50p, issued Mar. 27. Nos. 7433-7441.

Holy Year 1975 (famous churches), set of seven, 5c, 10c, 15c, 20c, 3.50e, airmail 10e, 70e, and two airmail souv. sheets, perf. 130e, imperf. 200e, issued Apr. 11. Nos. 7442-7450.

World Cup Soccer (contemporary players), set of nine, 1.50, 1.75, 2, 2.25, 2.50, 3, 3.50e, airmail 10, 60e, and 2 airmail souv. sheets of 2, perf. (2x65e), imperf. (2x100e), issued Apr. 30. Nos. 7451-7461.

UPU Cent. (transportation from messenger to rocket), set of seven, 60c, 70c, 80c, 1e, 1.50e, airmail 30e, 50e, and two airmail souv. sheets, perf. 225e, imperf. (150e, 150e), issued May 30; three airmail deluxe souv. sheets, 130e, and 2x130e, issued June 8. Nos. 7462-7472A.

Picasso Memorial (Pink Period paintings), set of seven, 55c, 60c, 65c, 70c, 75c, airmail 10e, 50e, and two airmail souv. sheets, perf. 130e, imperf. 200e, issued June 28. Nos. 7473-7481.

World Cup Soccer Championships, gold foil airmail souv. sheets, four sheets of one, 130e (2), 250e (2), two sheets of two (2x130e; 2x250e), issued July 8. Nos. 7482-7487.

Aleksander Solzhenitsyn, two gold foil airmail souv. sheets, perf. 250e, imperf. 300e, issued July 25. Nos. 7488-7489.

Opening of American West, set of seven, 30c, 35c, 40c, 45c, 50c, airmail 8p, 60p, and two souv. sheets, perf. 130p, imperf. 200p, issued July 30. Nos. 7490-7498.

Flowers, set of 14, 5c, 10c, 15c, 20c, 25c, 1p, 3p, 5p, 8p, 10p, airmail 5p, 15p, 25p, 70p, and 4 airmail souv. sheets, perf. 130p, 25p+200p, imperf. 200p, 50p+250p, issued Aug. 20. Nos. 7499-74116.

Christmas, set of seven, 60c, 70c, 80c, 1e, 1.50e, airmail 30e, 50e, and two souv. sheets, perf. 225e, imperf. 300e, issued Sept. 16. Nos. 74117-74125.

Barcelona Soccer Team, 75th anniv., set of seven, 1e, 3e, 5e, 8e, 10e, airmail 15e, 60e, miniature sheet of seven plus label, two airmail souv. sheets, perf. 200e, imperf. 300e, and two gold foil airmail souv. sheets, perf., imperf., 200e each, issued Sept. 25. Nos. 74126-74137.

UPU Cent. and ESPANA 75, set of seven, 1.25e, 1.50e, 1.75e, 2e, 2.25e, airmail 35e, 60e, and 2 airmail souv. sheets, perf. 225e, imperf. 300e, issued Oct. 9; 6 gold foil sheets, perf. 250e, 250e, 2x250e, imperf. 300e, 300e, 2x300e, issued Oct. 14. Nos. 74138-74152.

Nature Protection

Australian Animals, set of seven, 80c, 85c, 90c, 95c, 1e, airmail 15e, 40e, and two airmail souv. sheets, perf. 130e, imperf. 200e, issued Oct. 25. Nos. 74153-74161.

African Animals, set of seven, 55c, 60c, 65c, 70c, 75c, airmail 10e, 70e, and two airmail souv. sheets, perf. 130e, imperf. 200e, issued Nov. 6. Nos. 74162-74170.

Australian and South American Birds, set of 14, 1.25p, 1.50p, 1.75p, 2p, 2.25p, 2.50p, 2.75p, 3p, 3.50p, 4p, airmail 20p, 25p, 30p, 35p, and four souv. sheets, perf. 130p (2), imperf. 200p (2), issued Nov. 26. Nos. 74171-74188.

Endangered Species, set of 15, 10c, 15c, 20c, 25c, 30c, 35c, 40c, 45c, 50c, 55c, 60c, 1e, 2e, airmail 10e, 70e, se-tenant in sheet of 15, issued Dec. 17. Nos. 74189-74203.

Monkeys, various species, set of 16, 5c, 10c, 15c, 20c, 25c, 30c, 35c, 40c, 45c, 50c, 55c, 60c, 1e, 2e, airmail 10e, 70e, se-tenant in sheet of 16, issued Dec. 27. Nos. 74204-74219.

Cats, various species, set of 16, 5c, 10c, 15c, 20c, 25c, 30c, 35c, 40c, 45c, 50c, 55c, 60c, 1e, 2e, airmail 10e, 70e, se-tenant in sheet of 16, issued Dec. 27. Nos. 74220-74235.

Fish, various species, set of 16, 5c, 10c, 15c, 20c, 25c, 30c, 35c, 40c, 45c, 50c, 55c, 60c, 1e, 2e, airmail 10e, 70e, se-tenant in sheet of 16, issued Dec. 27. Nos. 74236-74251.

Butterflies, various species, set of 16, 5c, 10c, 15c, 20c, 25c, 30c, 35c, 40c, 45c, 50c, 55c, 60c, 1e, 2e, airmail 10e, 70e, se-tenant in sheet of 16, issued Dec. 27. Nos. 74252-74267.

1975

Picasso Memorial (paintings from last period), set of seven, 5c, 10c, 15c, 20c, 25c, airmail 5e, 70e, and two souv. sheets, perf. 130e, imperf. 200e, issued Jan. 27. Nos. 7501-7509.

ARPHILA 75 Phil. Exhib., Paris, 8 gold foil airmail souv. sheets: perf. 3 sheets of 1 250e, 1 sheet of 2 250e, imperf. 3 sheets of 1 300e, 1 sheet of 2 300e, issued Jan. 27. Nos. 7510-7517.

Easter and Holy Year 1975, set of seven, 60c, 70c, 80c, 1e, 1.50e, airmail 30e, 50e, and two airmail souv. sheets, perf. 225e, imperf. 300e, issued Feb. 15. Nos. 7518-7526.

1976 Winter Olympics, Innsbruck, set of 11, 5c, 10c, 15c, 20c, 25c, 30c, 35c, 40c, 45c, 25e, 70e, two airmail souv. sheets, perf. 130e, imperf. 200e, and two gold foil airmail souv. sheets, 1 sheet of 1 250e, 1 sheet of 2 250e, issued Mar. 10. Nos. 7527-7541.

Don Quixote, set of seven, 30c, 35c, 40c, 45c, 50c, airmail 25e, 60e, and two airmail souv. sheets, perf. 130e, imperf. 200e, issued Apr. 4. Nos. 7542-7550.

American Bicent. (1st issue), set of nine, 5c, 20c, 40c, 75c, 2e, 5e, 8e, airmail 25e, 30e, and two airmail souv. sheets, perf. 130e, imperf. 200e, issued Apr. 30. Nos. 7551-7561.

American Bicent. (2nd issue), set of nine, 10c, 30c, 50c, 1e, 3e, 6e, 10e, airmail 12e, 40e, and two airmail souv. sheets, perf. 130e, imperf. 200e, issued Apr. 30. Nos. 7562-7572.

American Bicent. (Presidents), set of 18, 5c, 10c, 20c, 30c, 40c, 50c, 75c, 1e, 2e, 3e, 5e, 6e, 8e, 10e, airmail 12e, 25e, 30e, 40e, four airmail souv. sheets, perf. 225e (2), imperf. 300e (2), and six embossed gold foil airmail souv. sheets, perf. 200e, 200e, 2x200e, imperf. 300e, 300e, 2x300e, issued July 4. Nos. 7573-75100.

Bull Fight, set of seven, 80c, 85c, 90c, 95c, 8e, airmail 35e, 40e, and two airmail souv. sheets, perf. 130e, imperf. 200e, issued May 26. Nos. 75101-75109.

Apollo-Soyuz Space Project, set of 11, 1e, 2e, 3e, 5e, 5.50e, 7e, 7.50e, 9e, 15e, airmail 20e, 30e, and two airmail souv. sheets, perf. 225e, imperf. 300e, issued June 20, 1975; airmail souv. sheet, perf. 250e, issued July 17. Nos. 75110-75123.

Famous Painters, Nudes, set of 16, 5c, 10c, 15c, 20c, 25c, 30c, 35c, 40c, 45c, 50c, 55c, 60c, 1e, 2e, airmail 10e, 70e (Egyptian Greek, Roman, Indian art, Goes, Durer, Liss, Beniort, Renoir, Gauguin, Stenlen, Picasso, Modigliani, Matisse, Padua), se-tenant in sheet of 16, and 20 airmail embossed gold foil souv. sheetlets, perf. 200p+25p (10), imperf. 250p+50p (10), issued Aug. 10. Nos. 75124-75159.

Conquerors of the Sea, set of 14, 30c, 35c, 40c, 45c, 50c, 55c, 60c, 65c, 70c, 75c, airmail 8p, 10p, 50p, 60p, and four airmail souv. sheets, perf. 130p (2), imperf. 200p (2), issued Sept. 5. Nos. 75160-75177.

Christmas and Holy Year, 1975, set of seven, 60c, 70c, 80c, 1e, 1.50e, airmail 30e, 50e (Jordan, Barocci, Vereycke, Rubens, Mengo, Del Castillo, Cavedone), two airmail souv. sheets, perf. 225e, imperf. 300e, plus four embossed gold foil souv. sheets, perf. 200e (2), imperf. 300e (2), and two gold foil miniature sheets of two, perf. 200e+200e, imperf. 300e+300e, issued Oct. Nos. 75178-75192.

President Macias, IWY, set of eight, 1.50e, 3e, 3.50e, 5e, 7e, 10e, airmail 100e, 300e, and two imperf. airmail souv. sheets (world events), 100e (US 2c Yorktown), 300e, issued Dec. 25. Nos. 75193-75202.

1976

Cavalry Uniforms, set of seven, 5c, 10c, 15c, 20c, 25c, airmail 5p, 70p, and two airmail souv. sheets, perf. 130p, imperf. 200p, issued Feb. 2. Nos. 7601-7609.

1976 Winter Olympics, Innsbruck, set of 11, 50c, 55c, 60c, 65c, 70c, 75c, 80c, 85c, 90c, airmail 35e, 60e, and two airmail souv. sheets, perf. 130e, imperf. 200e, issued Feb. Nos. 7610-7622.

1976 Summer Olympics, Montreal, Ancient to Modern Games, set of seven, 50c, 60c, 70c, 80c, 90c, airmail 35e, 60e, and two airmail souv. sheets, perf. 225e, imperf. 300e, issued Feb. Nos. 7623-7631.

1976 Summer Olympics, Montreal, set of seven, 50c, 60c, 70c, 80c, 90c, airmail 30e, 60e, plus two airmail souv. sheets, perf. 225e, imperf. 300e, four embossed gold foil airmail souv. sheets, per. 250e (2), imperf. 300e (2), and two imperf. miniature sheets of two, perf. 2x250e, imperf. 2x300e, issued Mar. 5. Nos. 7632-7646.

El Greco, paintings, set of seven, 1e, 3e, 5e, 8e, 10e, airmail 15e, 25e, and two airmail semi-postal souv. sheets, perf. 200e+25e, imperf. 250e+50e, issued Apr. 5. Nos. 7647-7655.

1976 Summer Olympics, modern games, set of 11, 50c, 55c, 60c, 65c, 70c, 75c, 80c, 85c, 90c, airmail 35e, 60e, plus two airmail souv. sheets, perf. 225e, imperf. 300e, four embossed gold foil airmail souv. sheets, perf. 250e (2), imperf. 300e (2), and two miniature sheets of two, perf. 2x250e, imperf. 2x300e, issued May 7. Nos. 7656-7674.

UN 30th Anniv., airmail souv. sheet, 250e, issued June. No. 7675.

Contemporary Automobiles, set of seven, 1p, 3p, 5p, 8p, 10p, airmail 15p, 25p, and two airmail semi-postal souv. sheets, perf. 200p+24p, imperf. 250p+50p, issued June 10. Nos. 7675-7684.

Nature Protection

European Animals, set of seven, 5c, 10c, 15c, 20c, 25c, airmail 5p, 70p, and two airmail souv. sheets, perf. 130p, imperf. 200p, issued July 1. Nos. 7685-7693.

Asian Animals, set of seven, 30c, 35c, 40c, 45c, 8p, airmail 50c, 60p, and two airmail souv. sheets, perf. 130p, imperf. 200p, issued Sept. 20. Nos. 7694-74102.

Asian Birds, set of seven, 55c, 60c, 65c, 70c, 75c, airmail 10p, 50p, and two airmail souv. sheets, perf. 130p, imperf. 200p, issued Sept. 20. Nos. 76103-76111.

European Birds, set of seven, 5c, 10c, 15c, 20c, 25c, airmail 5p, 70p, and two airmail souv. sheets, perf. 130p, imperf. 200p, issued Sept. 20. Nos. 76112-76120.

North American Birds, set of seven, 80c, 85c, 90c, 95c, 1p, airmail 15p, 40p, and two airmail souv. sheets, perf. 130p, imperf. 200p, issued Sept. 20. Nos. 76121-76129.

Motorcycle Aces, set of 16, two each 1e, 2e, 3e, 4e, 5e, 10e, 30e, 40e, in se-tenant blocks of eight diff. values, issued July 22. Nos. 76130-76145.

1976 Summer Olympics, Montreal, set of five, 10e, 25e se-tenant strip of 3, airmail 200e, and imperf. airmail souv. sheet, 300e, issued Aug. 7. Nos. 76146-76151.

South American Flowers, set of seven, 30c, 35c, 40c, 45c, 50c, airmail 8p, 60p, and two airmail souv. sheets, perf. 130p, imperf. 200p, issued Aug. 16. Nos. 76152-76160.

Oceania, set of seven, 80c, 85c, 90c, 95c, 1p, airmail 15p, 40p, and two airmail souv. sheets, perf. 130p, imperf. 200p, issued 1976. Nos. 76161-76169.

1977

Butterflies, set of seven, 80c, 85c, 90c, 95c, 8e, airmail 35e, 40e, and two airmail souv. sheets, perf. 130e, imperf. 200e, issued Jan. Nos. 7701-7709.

Madrid Real, 75th Anniv., set of nine, 2e, 4e, 5e, 8e, 10e, 15e, airmail 20e, 35e, 150e, issued Jan. Nos. 7710-7718.

Ancient Carriages, set of 16, 5c, 10c, 15c, 20c, 25c, 30c, 35c, 40c, 45c, 50c, 55c, 60c, 1e, 2e, airmail 10e, 70e, issued Feb. Nos. 7719-7734.

Chinese Art, set of seven, 60c, 70c, 80c, 1e, 1.50e, airmail 30e, 50e, and two airmail souv. sheets, perf. 130e, imperf. 200e, issued Feb. Nos. 7735-7743.

African Masks, set of seven, 5c, 10c, 15c, 20c, 25c, airmail 5e, 70e, and two airmail souv. sheets, perf. 130e, imperf. 200e, issued Mar. Nos. 7744-7752.

North American Animals, set of seven, 1.25e, 1.50e, 1.75e, 2e, 2.25e, airmail 20e, 50e, and two airmail souv. sheets, perf. 130e, imperf. 200e, issued 1977. Nos. 7753-7761.

World Cup Soccer Championships, Argentina '78 (famous players), set of eight, 2e, 4e, 5e, 8e, 10e, 15e, airmail 20e, 35e, and two airmail souv. sheets, perf. 150e, imperf. 250e, issued July 25. Nos. 7762-7771.

World Cup Soccer (famous teams), se-tenant set of eight, 2e, 4e, 5e, 8e, 10e, 15e, airmail 20e, 35e, and two gold foil embossed souv. sheets, 500e (AMPHILEX '77, Cutty Sark, Concorde), airmail 500e (World Cup), issued Aug. 25.Nos. 7772-7781.

Napoleon, Life and Battle Scenes, se-tenant sheet of 16, 5c, 10c, 15c, 20c, 25c, 30c, 35c, 40c, 45c, 50c, 55c, 60c, 1e, 2e, airmail 10e, 70e, issued Aug. 20. Nos. 7782-7797.

Napoleon, Military Uniforms, se-tenant sheet of 16, 5c, 10c, 15c, 20c, 25c, 30c, 35c, 40c, 45c, 50c, 55c, 60c, 1e, 2e, airmail 10e, 70e, issued Aug. 20. Nos. 7798-77113.

South American Animals, set of seven, 2.50e, 2.75e, 3e, 3.50e, 4e, airmail 25e, 35e, and two airmail souv. sheets, perf. 130e, imperf. 200e, issued Aug. Nos. 77114-77122.

USSR Space Program, 20th Anniv., set of eight, 2e, 4e, 5e, 8e, 10e, 15e, airmail 20e, 35e, and two airmail souv. sheets, imperf. 150e, perf. 250e, issued Dec. 15. Nos. 77123-77132.

1978

Ancient Sailing Ships, set of 12, 5c, 10c, 15c, 20c, 25c, airmail 5e, 70e, also 5e, 10e, 20e, 25e, 70e, plus four airmail souv. sheets, perf. 150e, 225e, imperf. 250e, 300e, and two embossed gold foil airmail souv. sheets, perf., imperf., 500e, issued Jan. 6. Nos. 7801-7818.

1980 Winter Olympics, Lake Placid, set of five, 5e, 10e, 20e, 25e, airmail 70e, two airmail souv. sheets, perf. 150e, imperf. 250e, and two embossed gold foil airmail souv. sheets, perf., imperf., 500e, issued Jan. 17. Nos. 7819-7827.

1980 Summer Olympics, Moscow, set of eight, 2e, 3e, 5e, 8e, 10e, 15e, airmail 30e, 50e, two airmail souv. sheets, perf. 150e, imperf. 250e, and two embossed gold foil airmail souv. sheets, perf., imperf., 500e, issued Jan. 17. Nos. 7828-7839.

1980 Summer Olympic Water Games, Tallinn, set of five, 5e, 10e, 20e, 25e, airmail 70e, two airmail souv. sheets, perf. 150e, imperf. 250e, and two embossed gold foil airmail souv. sheets, perf., imperf., 500e, issued Jan. 17. Nos. 7840-7848.

Eliz. II Coronation, 25th Anniv., set of eight, 2e, 5e, 8e, 10e, 12e, 15e, airmail 30e, 50e, and two airmail souv. sheets, perf. 150e, imperf. 250e, issued Apr. 25. Nos. 7849-7858.

English Knights of 1200-1350 A.D., set of seven, 5e, 10e, 15e, 20e, 25e, airmail 15e, 70e, and two airmail souv. sheets, perf. 130e, imperf. 250e, issued Apr. 25. Nos. 7859-7867.

Old Locomotives, set of seven, 1e, 2e, 3e, 5e, 10e, airmail 25e, 70e, and two airmail souv. sheets, perf. 150e, imperf. 250e, issued Aug. Nos. 7868-7876.

Prehistoric Animals, set of seven, 30e, 35e, 40e, 45e, 50e, airmail 25e, 60e, and airmail souv. sheet, 130e, issued Aug. Nos. 7877-7884.

Francisco Goya, "Maja Vestida," airmail souv. sheet, 150e, issued Aug. No. 7885.

Peter Paul Rubens - UNICEF, airmail souv. sheet, 250e, issued Aug. No. 7886.

Europa - CEPT - Europhila '78, airmail souv. sheet, 250e, issued Aug. No. 7887.

30th Intl. Stamp Fair, Riccione, airmail souv. sheet, 150e, issued Aug. Nos. 7888.

Eliz. II Coronation, 25th anniv., airmail souv. sheet of three, 150e, issued

CEPT, airmail souv. sheet, 250e, issued Aug. Nos. 7890.

World Cup Soccer Championships, Argentina '78 and Spain '82, airmail souv. sheet, 150e, issued Aug. Nos. 7891.

Christmas, Titian painting, "The Virgin," airmail souv. sheet, 150e, issued Aug. Nos. 7892.

Natl. Independence, 5th Anniv. (in 1973) — A7

1979 *Perf. 13x13½*

26 A7 1e Ekuele coin 1.10 .25

Natl. Independence, 5th Anniv. (in 1973) — A8

1979

27	A8	1e	Port Bata	.20	.20
28	A8	1.50e	State Palace	.25	.25
29	A8	2b	Central Bank, Bata	.30	.30
30	A8	2.50b	Nguema Biyogo Bridge	.35	.35
31	A8	3b	Port, palace, bank, bridge	.60	.60
			Nos. 27-31 (5)	1.70	1.70

Pres. Nguema — A9

Independence Martyrs — A10

1979 *Perf. 13½x13*

32 A9 1.50e multi .50 .35

United Natl. Workers's Party (PUNT), 3rd Congress.

1979

33	A10	1e	Enrique Nvo	.20	.20
34	A10	1.50e	Salvador Ndongo Ekang	.30	.30
35	A10	2b	Acacio Mane	.40	.40
			Nos. 33-35 (3)	.90	.90

Agricultural Experiment Year A11

1979 *Perf. 13x13½*

36 A11 1e multi .65 .25

37 A11 1.50e multi, diff. .95 .35

Independence Martyrs — A12 Natl. Coat of Arms — A13

1981, Mar. **Photo.** *Perf. 13½x12½*

38	A12	5b	Obiang Esono Nguema	.55	.20
39	A12	15b	Fermando Nvara Engonga	.55	.20
40	A12	25b	Ela Edjodjomo Mangue	.55	.20
41	A12	35b	Obiang Nguema Moasogo, president	.75	.20
42	A12	50b	Hipolito Micha Eworo	1.10	.20
43	A13	100b	multi	2.25	.35
			Nos. 38-43 (6)	5.75	1.35

Dated 1980.

Christmas 1980 A14

1981, Mar. 30 *Perf. 13½*

44 A14 8b Cathedral, infant .25 .20

45 A14 25b Bells, youth .30 .20

Dated 1980.

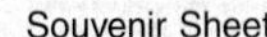

Souvenir Sheet

Pres. Obiang Nguema Mbasogo — A15

1981, Aug. 30 **Litho.** *Imperf.*

46 A15 400b multi 7.75 2.25

State Visit of King Juan Carlos of Spain — A16

Perf. 13x13½, 13½x13

1981, Nov. 30

47	A16	50b	Government reception	.95	.20
48	A16	100b	Arrival at airport	1.75	.35
49	A16	150b	King, Pres. Mbasogo, vert.	2.75	.60
			Nos. 47-49 (3)	5.45	1.15

State Visit of Pope John Paul II — A17

1982, Feb. 18

50	A17	100b	Papal and natl. arms	1.90	.70
51	A17	200b	Pres. Mbasogo greeting Pope	3.50	1.40
52	A17	300b	Pope, vert.	5.25	2.10
			Nos. 50-52 (3)	10.65	4.20

Christmas 1981 A18

1982, Feb. 25 **Photo.**

53 A18 100b Carolers, vert. 1.25 .35

54 A18 150b Magi, African youth 1.90 .60

Dated 1981.

1982 World Cup Soccer Championships, Spain — A19

1982, June 13 *Perf. 13½*

55	A19	40b	Emblem	.55	.25
56	A19	60b	Naranjito character trademark	.80	.35
57	A19	100b	World Cup trophy	1.40	.60
58	A19	200b	Players, palm tree, emblem	2.75	1.10
			Nos. 55-58 (4)	5.50	2.30

Fauna
A20

1983, Feb. 4 **Litho.**

59 A20 40b Gorilla .65 .20
60 A20 60b Hippopotamus 1.10 .25
61 A20 80b Atherurus africanus 1.50 .35
62 A20 120b Felis pardus 2.25 .50
Nos. 59-62 (4) 5.50 1.30

Dated 1982.

Christmas
1982
A21

1983, Feb. 25 **Photo.**

63 A21 100b Stars .95 .35
64 A21 200b King offering frankincense 2.25 .75

Dated 1982.

World Communications Year — A22

1983, July 18 **Litho.**

65 A22 150b Postal runner 1.00 .45
66 A22 200b Microwave station, drimmer 2.40 1.00

Banana
Trees
A23

1983, Oct. 8

67 A23 300b shown 3.25 1.00
68 A23 400b Forest, vert. 4.50 1.40

Christmas
1983
A24

1984

69 A24 80b Folk dancer, musical instruments .90 .30
70 A24 100b Holy Family 1.10 .50

Dated 1983.

Turtle Hunting, Rio Muni — A26

World Food Day — A27

1984, May 1

73 A26 125b Hunting Whales, horiz. 1.25 .50
74 A26 150b shown 1.50 .60

1984, Sept.

75 A27 60b Papaya 1.00 .40
76 A27 80b Malanga 1.25 .50

Abstract Wood-Carved Figurines and Art — A28

Designs: 25b, *Black Gazelle* and *Anxiety.* 30b, *Black Gazelle,* diff., and *Woman.* 60b, *Man and woman,* vert. 75b, *Poster,* vert. 100b, *Mother and Child,* vert. 150b, *Man and Woman,* diff., and *Bust of a Woman.*

1984, Nov. 15

77 A28 25b multi .25 .20
78 A28 30b multi .35 .20
79 A28 60b multi .65 .25
80 A28 75b multi .85 .30
81 A28 100b multi 1.10 .40
82 A28 150b multi 1.60 .60
Nos. 77-82 (6) 4.80 1.95

Christmas
A29

1984, Dec. 24

83 A29 60b Mother and child, vert. .70 .25
84 A29 100b Musical instruments 1.00 .40

Immaculate Conception Missions, Cent. — A30

50fr, Emblem, vert. 60fr, Map, nun and youths, vert. 80fr, First Guinean nuns. 125fr, Missionaries landing at Bata Beach, 1885.

1985, Apr. ***Perf. 14***

85 A30 50fr multi .45 .20
86 A30 60fr multi .50 .20
87 A30 80fr multi .60 .20
88 A30 125fr multi 1.10 .40
Nos. 85-88 (4) 2.65 1.00

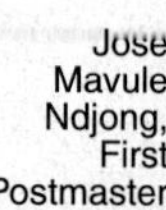

Jose
Mavule
Ndjong,
First
Postmaster
A31

1985, July ***Perf. 13½***

89 A31 50fr Postal emblem, vert. .85 .20
90 A31 80fr shown 1.50 .35

Equatorial Guinea Postal Service.

Christmas
A32

1985, Dec.

91 A32 40fr Nativity .55 .20
92 A32 70fr Folk band, dancers, mother and child .90 .35

Nature Conservation — A33

1985

93 A33 15fr Crab, snail .75 .20
94 A33 35fr Butterflies, bees, birds 1.40 .25
95 A33 45fr Flowering plants 2.10 .35
96 A33 65fr Spraying and harvesting cacao 3.25 .50
Nos. 93-96 (4) 7.50 1.30

Folklore — A34

A35

1986, Apr. 15

97 A34 10fr Ndowe dance, Mekuyo, horiz. .25 .20
98 A34 50fr Fang dance, Mokom .50 .20
99 A34 65fr Cacha Bubi, Bisila .65 .25
100 A34 80fr Fang dance, Ndong-Mba .80 .35
Nos. 97-100 (4) 2.20 1.00

1986, June 25

1986 World Cup Soccer Championships, Mexico: Various soccer plays.

101 A35 50fr multi, horiz. .25 .20
102 A35 100fr multi, horiz. .75 .25
103 A35 150fr multi 1.10 .40
104 A35 200fr multi 1.40 .55
Nos. 101-104 (4) 3.50 1.40

Christmas — A36

Conf. of the Union of Central African States — A37

1986, Dec. 12

105 A36 100fr Musical instruments, horiz. .85 .35
106 A36 150fr Holy Family, lamb 1.40 .50

1986, Dec. 29

107 A37 80fr Flags, map .80 .35
108 A37 100fr Emblem, map, horiz. 1.00 .40

Campaign
Against
Hunger
A38

1987, June 5

109 A38 60fr Chicken .65 .25
110 A38 80fr Fish .95 .35
111 A38 100fr Wheat 1.10 .40
Nos. 109-111 (3) 2.70 1.00

Intl. Peace
Year
A39

1987, July 15 **Litho.** ***Perf. 13½***

112 A39 100fr shown .75 .40
113 A39 200fr Hands holding dove 1.60 .80

Stamp Day
1987
A40

1987, Oct. 5 **Litho.** ***Perf. 13½***

114 A40 150fr shown 1.25 .50
115 A40 300fr Posting envelope 2.75 .85

Christmas
1987 — A41

Mother and child (wood carvings).

1987, Dec. 22 **Litho.** ***Perf. 13½***

116 A41 80fr multi .95 .35
117 A41 100fr multi, diff. 1.40 .50

Climbing Palm Tree — A42

Democratic Party — A43

1988, May 4 Litho. *Perf. 13½*

118	A42	50fr shown	.50	.20
119	A42	75fr Woman carrying fish	.60	.30
120	A42	150fr Chopping down trees	1.25	.60
		Nos. 118-120 (3)	2.35	1.10

1988, Nov. 16

121	A43	40fr Crest	.35	.20
122	A43	75fr Torch, motto, horiz.	.60	.30
123	A43	100fr Torch, flag, weaving, horiz.	.85	.40
		Nos. 121-123 (3)	1.80	.90

Cultural Revolution Day — A44

Geometric shapes.

1988, June 4

124	A44	35fr shown	.25	.20
125	A44	50fr Squares, sphere	.35	.20
126	A44	100fr Bird	.75	.50
		Nos. 124-126 (3)	1.35	.90

Christmas — A45

1988, Dec. 22

127	A45	50fr shown	.40	.20
128	A45	100fr Mother and child	.95	.40

Natl. Independence, 20th Anniv. — A46

Designs: 10fr, Lumber on truck. 35fr, Folk dancers. 45fr, Officials on dais.

1989, Apr. 14 Litho. *Perf. 14*

129	A46	10fr multicolored	.25	.20
130	A46	35fr multicolored	.30	.20
131	A46	45fr multicolored	.35	.20
		Nos. 129-131 (3)	.90	.60

Youths Bathing, Ilachi Falls — A47

25fr, Waterfall in the jungle. 60fr, Boy drinking from fruit, boys swimming at Luba Beach.

1989, July 7 *Perf. 13½*

132	A47	15fr shown	.20	.20
133	A47	25fr multicolored	.25	.20
134	A47	60fr multicolored	.45	.25
		Nos. 132-134 (3)	.90	.65

1st Congress of the Democratic Party of Equatorial Guinea A48

1989, Oct. 23 Litho. *Perf. 13½*

135	A48	25fr shown	.30	.20
136	A48	35fr Torch, vert.	.50	.20
137	A48	40fr Pres. Nguema, vert.	.60	.20
		Nos. 135-137 (3)	1.40	.60

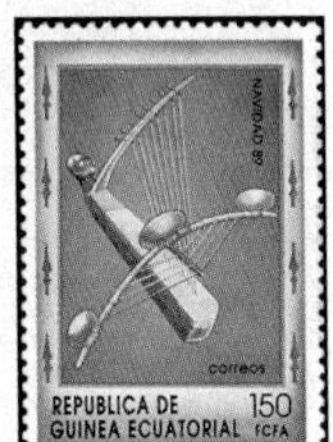

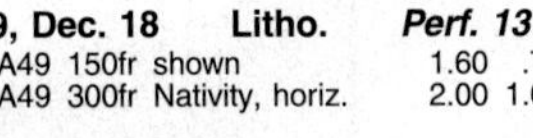

Christmas — A49

1989, Dec. 18 Litho. *Perf. 13½*

138	A49	150fr shown	1.60	.75
139	A49	300fr Nativity, horiz.	2.00	1.00

Boy Scouts A50

1990, Mar. 23 Litho. *Perf. 13*

140	A50	100fr Lord Baden-Powell	1.75	.50
141	A50	250fr Salute	4.00	1.10
142	A50	350fr Bugler	5.25	1.50
		Nos. 140-142 (3)	11.00	3.10

World Cup Soccer Championships, Italy — A51

1990, June 8 Litho. *Perf. 13*

143	A51	100fr Soccer player, map	.75	.35
144	A51	250fr Goalkeeper	1.50	.65
145	A51	350fr Trophy	2.25	1.00
		Nos. 143-145 (3)	4.50	2.00

Musical Instruments of the Ndowe People — A52

Instruments of the: 250fr, Fang. 350fr, Bubi.

1990, June 19

146	A52	100fr multicolored	.50	.20
147	A52	250fr multicolored	1.10	.50
148	A52	350fr multicolored	1.50	.75
		Nos. 146-148 (3)	3.10	1.45

Discovery of America, 500th Anniv. (in 1992) A53

1990, Oct. 10

149	A53	170fr Arrival in New World	1.00	.35
150	A53	300fr Columbus' fleet	1.75	.55

Christmas — A54

1990, Dec. 23 Litho. *Perf. 13½*

151	A54	170fr shown	1.00	.45
152	A54	300fr Bubi tribesman	1.75	.75

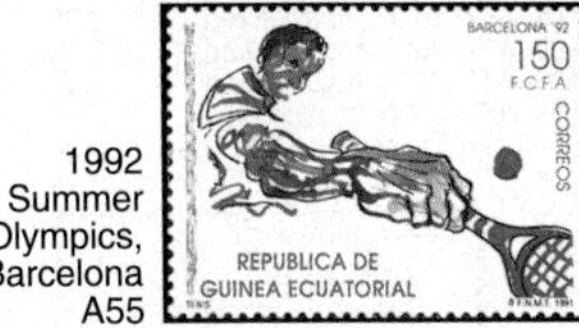

1992 Summer Olympics, Barcelona A55

1991, Apr. 22 Litho. *Perf. 13½x14*

153	A55	150fr Tennis	2.10	.75
154	A55	250fr Cycling	3.25	1.10

Souvenir Sheet

155	A55	500fr Equestrian	14.50	6.00

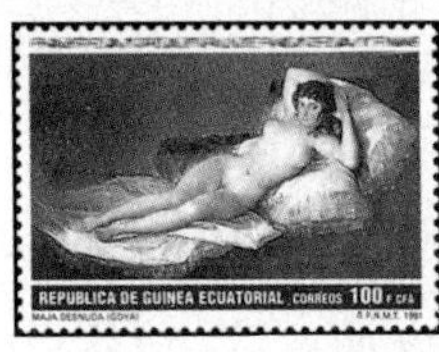

La Maja Desnuda by Goya A56

Designs: 250fr, Eve by Durer, vert. 350fr, The Three Graces by Rubens, vert.

1991, May 6 Litho. *Perf. 14*

156	A56	100fr shown	1.75	.50
157	A56	250fr multicolored	3.75	1.10
158	A56	350fr multicolored	5.00	1.50
		Nos. 156-158 (3)	10.50	3.10

Madrillus Sphinx — A57

1991, July 1 Litho. *Perf. 13½x14*

159	A57	25fr shown	1.75	.50
160	A57	25fr Face	1.75	.50
161	A57	25fr Seated	1.75	.50
162	A57	25fr Walking, horiz.	1.75	.50
		Nos. 159-162 (4)	7.00	2.00

World Wildlife Fund.

Discovery of America, 500th Anniv. A58

Captains, ships: 150fr, Vicente Yanez Pinzon, Nina. 260fr, Martin Alonso Pinzon, Pinta. 350fr, Christopher Columbus, Santa Maria.

1991 Litho. *Perf. 13½x14*

163	A58	150fr multicolored	1.10	.40
164	A58	250fr multicolored	2.00	.75
165	A58	350fr multicolored	2.75	1.25
		Nos. 163-165 (3)	5.85	2.40

Locomotives — A59

150fr, Electric, Japan, 1932. 250fr, Steam, US, 1873. 500fr, Steam, Germany, 1841.

1991, Sept. 10

166	A59	150fr multicolored	1.25	.50
167	A59	250fr multicolored	2.00	.75

Souvenir Sheet

168	A59	500fr multicolored	12.50	6.00

1992 Summer Olympics, Barcelona A60

1992, Feb. 12 Litho. *Perf. 13½x14*

169	A60	200fr Basketball	1.75	.75
170	A60	300fr Swimming	2.50	1.10

Souvenir Sheet

171	A60	400fr Baseball	20.00	8.50

Souvenir Sheet

Discovery of America, 500th Anniv. — A61

Columbus: a, 300fr, Departing from Palos, Spain. b, 500fr, Landing in New World.

1992, Apr. 8

172	A61	Sheet of 2, #a.-b.	20.00	9.50

Motion Pictures, Cent. A61a

Scenes from movies: 100fr, Humphrey Bogart, Ingrid Bergman, Dooley Wilson in "Casablanca," 1942. 250fr, "Viridiana," 1961. 350fr, Laurel and Hardy in "Sons of the Desert," 1933.

1992, Sept. Litho. *Perf. 14*

172C	A61a	100fr multicolored	.90	.20
172D	A61a	250fr multicolored	1.75	.45
172E	A61a	350fr multicolored	2.75	.60
		Nos. 172C-172E (3)	5.40	1.25

A62

A62a

Mushrooms: 75fr, Termitomyces globulus. 125fr, Termitomyces le testui. 150fr, Termitomyces robustus.

1992, Nov. Litho. *Perf. 14x13½*

173 A62 75fr multicolored .60 .20
174 A62 125fr multicolored 1.00 .35
175 A62 150fr multicolored 1.25 .45
Nos. 173-175 (3) 2.85 1.00

1992 Litho. *Perf. 14x13½*

Wildlife Protection: 150fr, Halcyon malimbicus. 250fr, Corythaeola cristata. 500fr, Mariposa nymphalidae, horiz.

175A A62a 150fr multicolored 1.75 .50
175B A62a 250fr multicolored 3.25 1.00

Souvenir Sheet

Perf. 13½x14

175C A62a 500fr multicolored 14.50 6.50

Virgin and Child with Virtuous Saints, by Claudio Coello (c. 1635-1693) — A63

Paintings, by Jacob Jordaens (1593-1678): 300fr, Apollo Conquering Marsias. 400fr, Meleager and Atalanta.

1993, Mar. Litho. *Perf. 13½x14*

176 A63 200fr multicolored 2.50 .75
177 A63 300fr multicolored 3.50 1.25

Souvenir Sheet

178 A63 400fr multicolored 17.00 8.00

1992 Olympic Gold Medalists A64

Designs: 100fr, Quincy Watts, 400-meter dash, US. 250fr, Martin Lopez Zubero, swimming, Spain. 350fr, Petra Kronberger, women's slalom, Austria. 400fr, Flying Dutchman class yachting, Spain.

1993 Litho. *Perf. 13½x14*

179 A64 100fr multicolored .90 .35
180 A64 250fr multicolored 1.90 .75
181 A64 350fr multicolored 2.50 1.00
182 A64 400fr multicolored 3.00 1.25
Nos. 179-182 (4) 8.30 3.35

Scene from Romeo and Juliet, by Tchaikovsky — A65

Design: 200fr, Scene from Faust, by Charles-Francois Gounod (1818-93).

1993, June Litho. *Perf. 13½x14*

183 A65 100fr multicolored .85 .40
184 A65 200fr multicolored 1.50 .75

First Ford Gasoline Engine, Cent. A66

1993 *Perf. 13½x14, 14x13½*

185 A66 200fr First Ford vehicle 3.50 1.00
186 A66 300fr Ford Model T 5.50 1.50
187 A66 400fr Henry Ford, vert. 7.75 2.10
Nos. 185-187 (3) 16.75 4.60

25th Anniv. of Independence — A67

Designs: 150fr, Pres. Obiang Nguema Mbasogo, vert. 250fr, Cargo ship, map, communications . 300fr, Hydroelectric plant, Riaba. 350fr, Bridge.

Perf. 14x13½, 13½x14

1993, Oct. 12 Litho.

188 A67 150fr multicolored 1.25 .50
189 A67 250fr multicolored 2.00 .75
190 A67 300fr multicolored 2.50 1.00
191 A67 350fr multicolored 2.75 1.10
Nos. 188-191 (4) 8.50 3.35

1994 World Cup Soccer Championships, US — A68

Designs: 200fr, German team, 1990 champions. 300fr, Rose Bowl Stadium, Pasadena, Calif. 500fr, Player kicking ball, vert.

1994 Litho. *Perf. 13½x14, 14x13½*

192 A68 200fr multicolored 1.25 .45
193 A68 300fr multicolored 1.75 .65
194 A68 500fr multicolored 3.25 1.10
Nos. 192-194 (3) 6.25 2.20

First Manned Moon Landing, 25th Anniv. A69

Designs: 500fr, Lunar module, Eagle. 700fr, "Buzz" Aldrin, Michael Collins, Neil Armstrong. 900fr, Footprint on moon, astronaut.

1994 *Perf. 13½x14*

195 A69 500fr multicolored 2.75 .70
196 A69 700fr multicolored 4.25 1.00
197 A69 900fr multicolored 6.50 1.75
Nos. 195-197 (3) 13.50 3.45

Dinosaurs A70

Designs: 300fr, Chasmosaurus. 500fr, Tyrannosaurus rex. 700fr, Triceratops. 800fr, Styracosaurus, deinonychus.

1994

198 A70 300fr multicolored 1.50 .65
199 A70 500fr multicolored 2.75 1.10
200 A70 700fr multicolored 3.75 1.60
Nos. 198-200 (3) 8.00 3.35

Souvenir Sheet

201 A70 800fr multicolored 16.00 16.00

Famous Men A71

Designs: 300fr, Jean Renoir (1894-1979), French film director. 500fr, Ferdinand de Lesseps (1805-94), French diplomat, promoter of Suez Canal. 600fr, Antoine de Saint Exupery (1900-44), French aviator, writer. 700fr, Walter Gropius (1883-1969), architect.

1994 Litho. *Perf. 13½x14*

202 A71 300fr multicolored 2.00 .75
203 A71 500fr multicolored 3.25 1.25
204 A71 600fr multicolored 3.75 1.50
205 A71 700fr multicolored 4.50 1.75
Nos. 202-205 (4) 13.50 5.25

Establishment of The Bauhaus, 75th anniv. (#205).

Minerals A72

1994 Litho. *Perf. 13½x14*

206 A72 300fr Aurichalcite 2.00 1.00
207 A72 400fr Pyromorphite 2.50 1.40
208 A72 600fr Fluorite 3.25 1.90
209 A72 700fr Halite 4.25 2.25
Nos. 206-209 (4) 12.00 6.55

Domestic Animals A73

Designs: a, Cat. b, Dog. c, Pig.

1995 Litho. *Perf. 13½x14*

210 Strip of 3, #a.-c. 8.50 8.50
a.-c. A73 500fr Any single 1.50 1.50

Butterflies & Orchids A74

a, Hypolimnas salmacis. b, Myrina silenus. c, Palla ussheri. d, Pseudacraea boisduvali.

1995

211 Strip of 4, #a.-d. 8.50 8.50
a.-d. A74 400fr Any single 1.50 1.50

Anniversaries — A75

Designs: a, 350fr, End of World War II, 50th Anniv. b, 450fr, UN, 50th anniv. c, 600fr, Sir Rowland Hill, birth bicent.

1995 Litho. *Perf. 13½x14*

212 Strip of 3, #a.-c. 8.50 8.50
a. A75 350fr multi 1.25 1.25
b. A75 450fr multi 1.50 1.50
c. A75 600fr multi 2.25 2.25

Trains A76

Designs: No. 213a, English steam engine. b, German diesel engine. c, Japanese Shinkansen train.

800fr, Swiss electric locomotive.

1995

213 Strip of 3, #a.-c. 12.50 12.50
a.-c. A76 500fr Any single 2.00 2.00

Souvenir Sheet

214 A76 800fr multicolored 9.00 9.00

Formula 1 Driving Champions A77

Designs: a, Juan Manuel Fangio. b, Ayrton Senna. c, Jim Clark. d, Jochen Rindt.

1995 Litho. *Perf. 14*

215 Strip of 4, #a.-d. 10.00 10.00
a.-d. A77 400fr Any single 1.50 1.50

Motion Pictures, Cent. A78

Designs: a, Marilyn Monroe. b, Elvis Presley. c, James Dean. d, Vittorio de Sica.

1996 Litho. *Perf. 14*

216 Strip of 4, #a.-d. 9.00 9.00
a.-d. A78 350fr Any single 1.50 1.50

Famous People A79

Designs: a, Alfred Nobel (1833-96), inventor, philanthropist. b, Anton Bruckner (1824-96), composer. c, Abraham and Three Angels, by Giovanni B. Tiepolo (1696-1770).

800fr, Family of Charles IV, by Francisco de Goya, (1746-1828).

1996

217 Strip of 3, #a.-c. 12.50 12.50
a.-c. A79 500fr Any single 2.00 2.00

Souvenir Sheet

218 A79 800fr multicolored 7.75 7.75

Chess A80

Designs: a, World Chess Festival for youth and children, Minorca, Spain. b, Women's World Chess Championship, Jaén, Spain. c, Men's World Chess Championship, Karpov versus Kamsky, Elista, Kalmyk. d, Chess Olympiad, Yerevan, Armenia.

1996 Litho. *Perf. 14*

219 Strip of 4, #a.-d. 10.00 10.00
a.-d. A80 400fr Any single 1.50 1.50

1996 Summer Olympic Games, Atlanta A81

Designs: a, Olympic Stadium, Athens, 1896. b, Cycling. c, Tennis. d, Equestrian show jumping.

1996 Litho. *Perf. 14*

220 Strip of 4, #a.-d. 10.00 10.00
a.-d. A81 400fr Any single 1.50 1.50

Ships A82

Designs: a, Paddle steamer with sails, 19th cent. b, Bark "Galatea," 1896. c, Modern ferry.

1996

221 Strip of 3, #a.-c. 11.00 11.00
a.-c. A82 500fr Any single 2.00 2.00

Franz Schubert (1797-1828), Composer — A83

Miguel de Cervantes (1547-1616), Novelist — A84

Designs: a, shown. b, Chinese Lunar New Year, 1997, (Year of the Ox). c, Johannes Brahms (1833-97), composer.
Illustration A84 reduced.

1997, Apr. 23 Litho. *Perf. 14*

222 Strip of 3, #a.-c. 9.00 9.00
a.-c. A83 500fr Any single 2.00 2.00

Souvenir Sheet

223 A84 800fr multicolored 5.50 5.50

Mushrooms — A85

a, Sparassis laminosa. b, Amanita pantherina. c, Morchella esculenta. d, Aleuria aurantia.

1997

224 Strip of 4, #a.-d. 11.00 11.00
a.-d. A85 400fr Any single 1.75 1.75

1998 World Cup Soccer Championships, France — A86

Designs: a, Players with ball on field. b, Stadium. c, Kicking ball.

1997 Litho. *Perf. 14*

225 Strip of 3, #a.-c. 6.00 6.00
a.-c. A86 300fr Any single 1.10 1.10

Fauna A88

a, Snake. b, Snail. c, Turtle. d, Monitor lizard.

1998 Litho. *Perf. 14*

230 Strip of 4, #a.-d. 10.00 10.00
a.-d. A88 400fr Any single 1.50 1.50

A89 A90

Military Uniforms: a, Alsace Regiment, French Infantry, 18th cent. b, English Marine, 18th cent. c, Georgian Hussars Regiment, Russian Calvary, 18th cent. d, Prussian Artillery, 19th cent.

1998

231 Strip of 4, #a.-d. 10.00 10.00
a.-d. A89 400fr Any single 1.50 1.50

1999 Litho. *Perf. 14*

Easter (Museum paintings): a, Crucifixion of Christ, by Velázquez. b, Adoration of the Magi, by Rubens. c, Holy Family, by Michelangelo.

232 Strip of 3, #a.-c. 10.00 10.00
a.-c. A90 500fr Any single 2.00 2.00

Orchids — A91

Designs: a, Angraecum eburneum. b, Paphiopedilum insigne. c, Ansellia africana. d, Cattleya leopoldii.

1999

233 Strip of 4, #a.-d. 10.00 10.00
a.-d. A91 400fr Any single 1.50 1.50

Birth and Death Anniversaries A92

No. 234: a, 750fr, Portrait of Frederic Chopin (1810-49), by Eugene Delacroix. b, 100fr, Christ Crowned With Thorns, by Anthony Van Dyck (1599-1641). c, 250fr, Portrait of Johann Wolfgang von Goethe (1749-1832), by Joseph Carl Stieler. d, 500fr, Jacques-Etienne Montgolfiere (1745-1799) and balloon.

1999 Litho. *Perf. 14x13¾*

234 Horiz. strip of 4, #a-d 10.00 10.00
a. A92 750fr multi 3.00 3.00
b. A92 100fr multi .35 .35
c. A92 250fr multi 1.10 1.10
d. A92 500fr multi 2.00 2.00

Parrots — A93

No. 235: a, Aratinga guarouba. b, Ara ambigua. c, Anodorhynchus hyacinthinus.
800fr, Alisterus amboinensis.

1999

235 Vert. strip of 3, #a-c 9.00 9.00
a.-c. A93 500fr any single 2.00 2.00

Souvenir Sheet

236 A93 800fr multi 5.50 5.50

Locomotives — A94

No. 237: a, Swiss. b, German. c, Japanese.

2000 Litho. *Perf. 13¾x14*

237 Horiz. strip of 3 7.00 7.00
a.-c. A94 500fr Any single 2.25 2.25

Souvenir Sheet

238 A94 800fr AVE Train 3.50 3.50

Butterflies A95

a, Fabriciana niobe. b, Palaeochrysophanus hippothoe. c, Inachis io. d, Apatura iris.

2000

239 Horiz. strip of 4 7.50 7.50
a.-d. A95 400fr Any single 1.75 1.75

UPU, 125th Anniv. (in 1999) A96

2000 Litho. *Perf. 13¾*

240 A96 400fr multi 1.75 1.75

Mushrooms A97

No. 241: a, Gyroporus cyanescens. b, Terfezia arenaria. c, Battarrea stevenii. d, Amanita muscaria.

2001 Litho. *Perf. 13¾*

241 Horiz. strip of 4 4.50 4.50
a.-d. A97 400fr Any single 1.10 1.10

Fire Trucks A98

No. 242: a, Truck, 1915. b, Tanker, 1943. c, Ladder truck, 1966. d, Merryweather pumper, 1888.

2001

242 Horiz. strip of 4 4.50 4.50
a.-d. A98 400fr Any single 1.10 1.10

Soldiers — A99

No. 243: a, Infantry officer, 1700. b, Harquebusier, 1534. c, Musketeer, 17th cent. d, Fusilier, 1815.

2001 Litho. *Perf. 14x13¾*

243 Horiz. strip of 4 4.50 4.50
a.-d. A99 400fr Any single 1.10 1.10

Prehistoric Animals A100

No. 244: a, Carnotaurus sastrei. b, Iberomesornis romerali. c, Troodon.
800fr, Diplodocus carnegiei.

2001 *Perf. 13¾x14*

244 Horiz. strip of 3 4.25 4.25
a.-c. A100 500fr Any single 1.40 1.40

Souvenir Sheet

245 A100 800fr multi 2.25 2.25

Millennium A101

Designs: No. 246, 200fr, Intl. Conference Center. No. 247, 200fr, Offshore petroleum exploration. No. 248, 200fr, Women's Plaza, Malabo.
400fr, Statue at Intl. Conference Center, vert.

2001 Litho. *Perf. 13¾x14*

246-248 A101 Set of 3 1.60 1.60

Souvenir Sheet

Perf. 14x13¾

249 A101 400fr multi 1.10 1.10

Flora — A102

No. 250: a, Alstonia congensis. b, Harongana madagascariensis. c, Caloncoba glauca. d, Cassia occidentalis.

2002 *Perf. 14x13¾*

250 Horiz. strip of 4 5.25 5.25
a.-d. A102 400fr Any single 1.25 1.25

Automobiles — A103

No. 251: a, 1924 Rochet Schneider 20,000. b, 1930 Bugatti T49. c, 1931 Ford Model A. d, 1925 Alfa Romeo RLSS.

2002 ***Perf. 13¾x14***

251	Vert. strip of 4	5.25	5.25
a.-d.	A103 400fr Any single	1.25	1.25

Butterflies A104

No. 252: a, Papilio menestheus canui. b, Papilio policenes. c, Papilio tynderaeus. d, Papilio zalmoxis.

2002

252	Strip of 4	5.25	5.25
a.-d.	A104 400fr Any single	1.25	1.25

Famous Men A105

No. 253: a, Victor Hugo (1802-85), writer. b, Santiago Ramón y Cajal (1852-1934), histologist. c, Emile Zola (1840-1902), writer.

2002

253	Horiz. strip of 3	3.75	3.75
a.-c.	A105 400fr Any single	1.25	1.25

2002 World Cup Soccer Championships, Japan and Korea — A106

No. 254: a, Player with yellow shirt with knee on ground. b, Stadium. c, Player with yellow shirt on ground.

2002

254	Horiz. strip of 3	4.75	4.75
a.-c.	A106 500fr Any single	1.50	1.50

Souvenir Sheet

2002 Chess Olympiad, Bled, Slovenia — A107

2002

255	A107 800fr multi	2.60	2.60

Anniversaries and Events — A108

No. 256: a, Painting by Henri de Toulouse-Lautrec (1864-1901). b, Year of Dialoguo Among Civilizations. c, Giuseppe Verdi (1813-1901), composer.

2004 ? **Litho.** ***Perf. 14x13¾***

256	Vert. strip of 3	4.50	4.50
a.-c.	A108 400fr Any single	1.50	1.50

Dated 2001. Stamps did not appear in philatelic market until 2004.

Anniversaries and Events — A109

No. 257: a, Tour de France bicycle race, cent. b, Painting by Vincent van Gogh (1853-90). c, Wright Brothers and Wright Flyer.

2004 ? ***Perf. 13¾x14***

257	Horiz. strip of 3	5.50	5.50
a.	A109 400fr multi	1.50	1.50
b.	A109 500fr multi	1.75	1.75
c.	A109 600fr multi	2.25	2.25

Dated 2003. Stamps did not appear in philatelic market until 2004.

Minerals A110

2004 ?

258	Vert. strip of 4	7.50	7.50
a.	A110 400fr Realgar	1.50	1.50
b.	A110 450fr Gypsum	1.75	1.75
c.	A110 550fr Red quartz	2.00	2.00
d.	A110 600fr Chrysoberyl	2.25	2.25

Dated 2003. Stamps did not appear in philatelic market until 2004.

Lighthouses A111

Designs: a, Marina Lighthouse, Luba, Equatorial Guinea. b, La Plata Lighthouse, Spain. c, Prodecao Lighthouse, Luba. d, Torre de Hércules, Spain.

2004 ? ***Perf. 14x13¾***

259	Horiz. strip of 4	7.50	7.50
a.	A111 400fr multi	1.50	1.50
b.	A111 450fr multi	1.75	1.75
c.	A111 550fr multi	2.00	2.00
d.	A111 600fr multi	2.25	2.25

Dated 2003. Stamps did not appear in philatelic market until 2004.

Space Shuttle Columbia Accident — A112

No. 260: a, Rocket lift-off. b, Rocket on launch pad. c, Flight crew patch.
1000fr, View of earth from outer space.

2004 ?

260	Vert. strip of 3	6.75	6.75
a.	A112 500fr multi	1.90	1.90
b.	A112 600fr multi	2.25	2.25
c.	A112 700fr multi	2.60	2.60

Souvenir Sheet

261	A112 1000fr multi	3.75	3.75

Dated 2003. Stamps did not appear in philatelic market until 2004.

Motorcycles — A113

No. 262: a, 1944-47 Soriano Tigre. b, 1970 Derbi 50 Grand Prix. c, 1938 DKW 250 with sidecar.
1000fr, Harley-Davidson VRSCA V-Rod.

2004 ?

262	Horiz. strip of 3	5.50	5.50
a.	A113 450fr multi	1.60	1.60
b.	A113 500fr multi	1.90	1.90
c.	A113 550fr multi	2.00	2.00

Souvenir Sheet

263	A113 1000fr multi	3.75	3.75

Dated 2003. Stamps did not appear in philatelic market until 2004.

SPECIAL DELIVERY STAMPS

Archer with Crossbow — SD1

1971, Oct. 12 **Photo.** ***Perf. 12½x13***

E1	SD1	4p blue & multi	.75	.20
E2	SD1	8p rose & multi	1.25	.20

3rd anniversary of independence.

ERITREA

ˌer-ə-ˈtrē-ə

LOCATION — In northeast Africa, bordering on the Red Sea, Sudan, Ethiopia and Djibouti.
GOVT. — Independent state
AREA — 45,300 (?) sq. mi.
POP. — 3,984,723 (1999 est.)
CAPITAL — Asmara

Formerly an Italian colony, Eritrea was incorporated as a State of Italian East Africa in 1936.

Under British occupation (1941-52) until it became part of Ethiopia as its northernmost region. Eritrea became independent May 24, 1993.

100 Centesimi = 1 Lira
100 cents = 1 birr (1991)
100 cents = 1 nakfa (1997)

Catalogue values for unused stamps in this country are for Never Hinged items, beginning with Scott 200 in the regular postage section.

All used values to about 1916 are for postally used stamps. From 1916-1934, used values in italics are for postally used stamps. CTO's, for stamps valued postally used, sell for about the same as unused, hinged stamps.

Watermark

Wmk. 140 — Crown

Stamps of Italy Overprinted

a

b

1892 **Wmk. 140** ***Perf. 14***

Overprinted Type "a" in Black

1	A6	1c bronze grn	5.00	2.75
a.		Inverted overprint	350.00	325.00
b.		Double overprint	1,050.	
		Never hinged	1,350.	
c.		Vert. pair, one without overprint	*2,000.*	
		Never hinged	—	
2	A7	2c orange brn	2.10	1.40
a.		Inverted overprint	325.00	275.00
b.		Double overprint	1,050.	
		Never hinged	1,350.	
3	A33	5c green	55.00	3.50
a.		Inverted overprint	*3,900.*	*2,300.*
		Never hinged	—	

Overprinted Type "b" in Black

4	A17	10c claret	62.50	3.50
5	A17	20c orange	140.00	2.75
6	A17	25c blue	500.00	17.50
7	A25	40c brown	5.75	*8.50*
8	A26	45c slate green	5.75	*13.00*
9	A27	60c violet	5.75	*25.00*
10	A28	1 l brown & yel	17.50	*25.00*
11	A38	5 l blue & rose	350.00	210.00
		Nos. 1-11 (11)	1,149.	*312.90*
		Set, never hinged	2,700.	

1895-99

Overprinted type "a" in Black

12	A39	1c brown ('99)	7.50	4.50
13	A40	2c org brn ('99)	.90	.90
14	A41	5c green	.90	.90
a.		Inverted overprint	350.00	*1,950.*

Overprinted type "b" in Black

15	A34	10c claret ('98)	.90	.90
16	A35	20c orange	1.25	1.25
17	A36	25c blue	1.50	1.90
18	A37	45c olive grn	11.00	*11.00*
		Nos. 12-18 (7)	23.95	*21.35*
		Set, never hinged	60.00	

1903-28

Overprinted type "a" in Black

19	A42	1c brown	.20	*1.00*
a.		Inverted overprint	110.00	110.00
20	A43	2c orange brn	.20	*.60*
21	A44	5c blue green	29.00	.60
22	A45	10c claret	37.50	.60
23	A45	20c orange	2.40	1.00
24	A45	25c blue	210.00	10.50
a.		Double overprint	425.00	—
25	A45	40c brown	275.00	17.00
26	A45	45c olive grn	3.50	*7.00*
27	A45	50c violet	90.00	19.00
28	A46	75c dk red & rose ('28)	45.00	9.50
29	A46	1 l brown & grn	3.50	.75

30 A46 1.25 l bl & ultra ('28) 29.00 9.50
31 A46 2 l dk grn & org ('25) 57.50 57.50
32 A46 2.50 l dk grn & org ('28) 90.00 27.00
33 A46 5 l blue & rose 17.50 17.00
Nos. 19-33 (15) 890.30 178.55
Set, never hinged 1,800.

Surcharged in Black

1905

34 A45 15c on 20c orange 22.50 4.50
Never hinged 45.00

1908-28

Overprinted type "a" in Black

35 A48 5c green 1.10 .90
36 A48 10c claret ('09) 1.10 .90
37 A48 15c slate ('20) 15.00 7.25
38 A49 20c green ('25) 11.50 8.75
39 A49 20c lilac brn ('28) 3.75 3.25
40 A49 25c blue ('09) 4.25 1.90
41 A49 30c gray ('25) 11.50 11.50
42 A49 40c brown ('16) 29.00 *26.00*
43 A49 50c violet ('16) 9.50 1.90
44 A49 60c brn car ('18) 16.00 16.00
a. Printed on both sides *700.00*
45 A49 60c brn org ('28) 82.50 *90.00*
46 A51 10 l gray grn & red ('16) 275.00 *375.00*
Nos. 35-46 (12) 460.20 *543.35*
Set, never hinged 900.00

See No. 53.

A1

Government Building at Massaua — A2

1910-29 Unwmk. Engr. *Perf. 13½*

47 A1 15c slate 225.00 10.50
a. Perf. 11 ('29) 42.50 35.00
Never hinged 82.50
48 A2 25c dark blue 5.75 *11.50*
a. Perf. 12 375.00 375.00

For surcharges see Nos. 51-52.

A3

Farmer Plowing — A4

1914-28

49 A3 5c green .90 *2.25*
a. Perf. 11 ('28) 125.00 35.00
Never hinged 275.00
50 A4 10c carmine 3.50 3.00
a. Perf. 11 ('28) 19.00 *30.00*
Never hinged 37.50
b. Perf. 13½x14 67.50 67.50

No. 47 Surcharged in Red or Black

1916

51 A1 5c on 15c slate (R) 6.00 *10.50*
52 A1 20c on 15c slate 3.00 2.75
a. "CEN" for "CENT" 35.00 35.00
b. "CENT" omitted 190.00 *160.00*
c. "ENT" 18.00 *26.00*
Set, never hinged 18.00

Italy No. 113 Overprinted in Black — f

1921 Wmk. 140 *Perf. 14*

53 A50 20c brown orange 3.75 *10.00*
Never hinged 8.00

Victory Issue

Italian Victory Stamps of 1921 Overprinted type "f" 13mm long

1922

54 A64 5c olive green 1.50 *6.00*
55 A64 10c red 1.50 *6.00*
56 A64 15c slate green 1.50 *8.25*
57 A64 25c ultra 1.50 *8.25*
Nos. 54-57 (4) 6.00 *28.50*
Set, never hinged 11.50

Somalia Nos. 10-16 Overprinted In Black and Bars over Original Values

g

1922 Wmk. 140

58 A1 2c on 1b brn 5.25 *11.50*
59 A1 5c on 2b bl grn 5.25 *6.75*
60 A2 10c on 1a claret 5.25 2.25
61 A2 15c on 2a brn org 5.25 2.25
62 A2 25c on 2½a blue 5.25 2.25
63 A2 50c on 5a yellow 13.00 7.75
a. "ERITREA" double 700.00
64 A2 1 l on 10a lilac 13.00 14.00
a. "ERITREA" double 700.00 700.00
Nos. 58-64 (7) 52.25 *46.75*
Set, never hinged 110.00

See Nos. 81-87.

Propagation of the Faith Issue

Italy Nos. 143-146 Overprinted

1923

65 A68 20c ol grn & brn org 6.50 *22.50*
66 A68 30c claret & brn org 6.50 *22.50*
67 A68 50c vio & brn org 4.25 *25.00*
68 A68 1 l bl & brn org 4.25 *32.50*
Nos. 65-68 (4) 21.50 *102.50*
Set, never hinged 37.50

Fascisti Issue

Italy Nos. 159-164 Overprinted in Red or Black — j

1923 Unwmk. *Perf. 14*

69 A69 10c dk green (R) 3.75 *9.00*
70 A69 30c dk violet (R) 3.75 *9.00*
71 A69 50c brown carmine 3.75 *9.00*

Wmk. 140

72 A70 1 l blue 3.75 *24.00*
73 A70 2 l brown 3.75 *30.00*
74 A71 5 l black & blue (R) 3.75 *37.50*
Nos. 69-74 (6) 22.50 *118.50*
Set, never hinged 45.00

Manzoni Issue

Italy Nos. 165-170 Overprinted in Red

1924 *Perf. 14*

75 A72 10c brn red & blk 5.75 *24.00*
76 A72 15c blue grn & blk 5.75 *24.00*
77 A72 30c black & slate 5.75 *24.00*
78 A72 50c org brn & blk 5.75 *24.00*
79 A72 1 l blue & blk 45.00 *190.00*
80 A72 5 l violet & blk 425.00 *1,500.*
Nos. 75-79 (5) 68.00 *286.00*

On Nos. 79 and 80 the overprint is placed vertically at the left side.

Somalia Nos. 10-16 Overprinted type "g" in Blue or Red

1924

Bars over Original Values

81 A1 2c on 1b brn 16.00 *19.00*
82 A1 5c on 2b bl grn (R) 12.50 *12.50*
83 A2 10c on 1a rose red 5.75 *10.00*
84 A2 15c on 2a brn org 3.75 *6.75*
a. Pair, one without "ERITREA" 800.00
Never hinged 1,000.
85 A2 25c on 2½a bl (R) 5.75 *6.75*
a. Double surcharge 575.00
86 A2 50c on 5a yellow 5.75 *12.50*
87 A2 1 l on 10a lil (R) 5.75 *17.00*
Nos. 81-87 (7) 55.25 *84.50*
Set, never hinged 110.00

Stamps of Italy, 1901-08 Overprinted type "j" in Black

1924

88 A42 1c brown 5.50 *7.75*
a. Inverted overprint 210.00
89 A43 2c orange brown 3.50 *6.25*
90 A48 5c green 7.50 *6.25*
Nos. 88-90 (3) 16.50 *20.25*
Set, never hinged 37.50

Victor Emmanuel Issue

Italy Nos. 175-177 Overprinted — k

1925-26 Unwmk. *Perf. 11*

91 A78 60c brown car .50 *3.50*
a. Perf. 13½ 4.50 *12.50*
92 A78 1 l dark blue .70 *5.50*
a. Perf. 13½ *12,750.* *2,850.*
Never hinged *16,000.*

Perf. 13½

93 A78 1.25 l dk blue ('26) 3.50 *18.00*
a. Perf. 11 1.10 *13.50*
Nos. 91-93 (3) 4.70 *27.00*
Set, never hinged 9.00

Saint Francis of Assisi Issue

Italian Stamps of 1926 Overprinted

1926 Wmk. 140 *Perf. 14*

94 A79 20c gray green 1.90 *9.00*
95 A80 40c dark violet 1.90 *9.00*
96 A81 60c red violet 1.90 *16.00*

Overprinted in Red

Unwmk. *Perf. 11*

97 A82 1.25 l dark blue 1.90 *22.50*

Perf. 14

98 A83 5 l + 2.50 l ol grn 4.25 *45.00*
Nos. 94-98 (5) 11.85 *101.50*
Set, never hinged 22.50

Italian Stamps of 1926 Overprinted type "f" in Black

1926 Wmk. 140 *Perf. 14*

99 A46 75c dk red & rose 42.50 8.00
a. Double overprint 275.00
100 A46 1.25 l blue & ultra 26.00 8.00
101 A46 2.50 l dk grn & org 67.50 18.00
Nos. 99-101 (3) 136.00 34.00
Set, never hinged 275.00

Volta Issue

Type of Italy, 1927, Overprinted — o

1927

102 A84 20c purple 4.50 *24.00*
103 A84 50c deep orange 8.00 *16.00*
a. Double overprint 190.00
104 A84 1.25 l brt blue 10.00 *32.50*
Nos. 102-104 (3) 22.50 *72.50*
Set, never hinged 45.00

Italian Stamps of 1925-28 Overprinted type "a" in Black

1928-29

105 A86 7½c lt brown ('29) 11.50 *37.50*
106 A86 50c brt violet 42.50 24.00
Set, never hinged 110.00

Italian Stamps of 1927-28 Overprinted type "f"

1928-29

107 A86 50c brt violet 29.00 *24.00*
Never hinged 57.50

Unwmk. *Perf. 11*

107A A85 1.75 l deep brown 50.00 15.00
Never hinged 100.00

Italy No. 192 Overprinted type "o"

1928 Wmk. 140 *Perf. 14*

108 A85 50c brown & slate 11.50 3.25
Never hinged 22.50

Monte Cassino Issue

Types of 1929 Issue of Italy Overprinted in Red or Blue

1929 *Perf. 14*

109 A96 20c dk green (R) 4.25 *10.00*
110 A96 25c red orange (Bl) 4.25 *10.00*
111 A98 50c + 10c crim (Bl) 4.25 *12.50*
112 A98 75c + 15c ol brn (R) 4.25 *12.50*
113 A96 1.25 l + 25c dl vio (R) 8.25 *20.00*
114 A98 5 l + 1 l saph (R) 8.25 *24.00*

Overprinted in Red

Unwmk.

115 A100 10 l + 2 l gray brn 8.25 *32.50*
Nos. 109-115 (7) 41.75 *121.50*
Set, never hinged 80.00

Royal Wedding Issue

Type of Italian Stamps of 1930 Overprinted

1930			Wmk. 140	
116	A101	20c yellow green	.90	*4.25*
117	A101	50c + 10c dp org	.70	*5.75*
118	A101	1.25 l + 25c rose red	.70	*13.00*
		Nos. 116-118 (3)	2.30	*23.00*
		Set, never hinged	4.50	

Lancer — A5

Scene in Massaua A6

2c, 35c, Lancer. 5c, 10c, Postman. 15c, Lineman. 25c, Askari (infantryman). 2 l, Railroad viaduct. 5 l, Asmara Deghe Selam. 10 l, Camels.

1930	Wmk. 140	Litho.	*Perf. 14*	
119	A5	2c brt bl & blk	.90	*6.00*
120	A5	5c dk vio & blk	1.40	.90
121	A5	10c yel brn & blk	1.40	.45
122	A5	15c dk grn & blk	1.40	.70
123	A5	25c gray grn & blk	1.40	.45
124	A5	35c red brn & blk	4.50	*10.00*
125	A6	1 l dk bl & blk	1.40	.45
126	A6	2 l choc & blk	4.50	*10.00*
127	A6	5 l ol grn & blk	8.00	*18.00*
128	A6	10 l dl bl & blk	11.50	*32.50*
		Nos. 119-128 (10)	36.40	*79.45*
		Set, never hinged	72.50	

Ferrucci Issue

Types of Italian Stamps of 1930 Overprinted type "f" in Red or Blue

1930				
129	A102	20c violet (R)	1.40	*2.25*
130	A103	25c dk green (R)	1.40	*2.25*
131	A103	50c black (R)	1.40	*4.50*
132	A103	1.25 l dp blue (R)	1.40	*6.75*
133	A104	5 l + 2 l dp car (Bl)	3.75	*16.00*
		Nos. 129-133 (5)	9.35	*31.75*
		Set, never hinged	18.00	

Virgil Issue

Types of Italian Stamps of 1930 Overprinted in Red or Blue

1930			Photo.	
134	A106	15c violet black	.70	*5.00*
135	A106	20c orange brown	.70	*2.40*
136	A106	25c dark green	.70	*1.90*
137	A106	30c lt brown	.70	*2.40*
138	A106	50c dull violet	.70	*1.90*
139	A106	75c rose red	.70	*3.75*
140	A106	1.25 l gray blue	.70	*5.00*

Unwmk.			Engr.	
141	A106	5 l + 1.50 l dk vio	3.25	*26.00*
142	A106	10 l + 2.50 l ol brn	3.25	*42.50*
		Nos. 134-142 (9)	11.40	*90.85*
		Set, never hinged	22.50	

Saint Anthony of Padua Issue

Types of Italian Stamps of 1931 Overprinted type "f" in Blue, Red or Black

1931		Photo.	Wmk. 140	
143	A116	20c brown (Bl)	1.25	*9.00*
144	A116	25c green (R)	1.25	*4.50*
145	A118	30c gray brn (Bl)	1.25	*4.50*
146	A118	50c dl violet (Bl)	1.25	*4.50*
147	A120	1.25 l slate bl (R)	1.25	*4.50*

Unwmk.			Engr.	
148	A121	75c black (R)	1.25	*20.00*
149	A122	5 l + 2.50 l dk brn (Bk)	3.75	*50.00*
		Nos. 143-149 (7)	11.25	*97.00*
		Set, never hinged	22.50	

Victor Emmanuel III — A13

1931		Photo.	Wmk. 140	
150	A13	7½c olive brown	.50	*1.40*
151	A13	20c slate bl & car	.45	.20
152	A13	30c ol grn & brn vio	.50	.20
153	A13	40c bl & yel grn	.65	.20
154	A13	50c bis brn & ol	.20	.20
155	A13	75c carmine rose	1.90	.20
156	A13	1.25 l violet & indigo	2.75	1.10
157	A13	2.50 l dull green	3.25	3.25
		Nos. 150-157 (8)	10.20	6.75
		Set, never hinged	20.00	

Camel A14

Temple Ruins — A18

Designs: 2c, 10c, Camel. 5c, 15c, Shark fishery. 25c, Baobab tree. 35c, Pastoral scene. 2 l, African elephant. 5 l, Eritrean man. 10 l, Eritrean woman.

1934		Photo.	Wmk. 140	
158	A14	2c deep blue	.45	*2.25*
159	A14	5c black	.50	.25
160	A14	10c brown	1.10	.20
161	A14	15c orange brn	1.40	*1.50*
162	A14	25c gray green	.75	.20
163	A14	35c purple	2.75	*3.75*
164	A18	1 l dk blue gray	.20	.20
165	A14	2 l olive black	11.50	1.50
166	A18	5 l carmine rose	6.00	3.50
167	A18	10 l red orange	9.00	*11.50*
		Nos. 158-167 (10)	33.65	*24.85*
		Set, never hinged	67.50	

Abruzzi Issue

Types of 1934 Issue Overprinted in Black or Red

1934				
168	A14	10c dull blue (R)	6.75	*13.50*
169	A14	15c blue	6.75	*13.50*
170	A14	35c green (R)	4.50	*13.50*
171	A18	1 l copper red	4.50	*13.50*
172	A14	2 l rose red	11.50	*13.50*
173	A18	5 l purple (R)	5.75	*20.00*
174	A18	10 l olive grn (R)	5.75	*24.00*
		Nos. 168-174 (7)	45.50	*111.50*
		Set, never hinged	90.00	

Grant's Gazelle A22

1934			Photo.	
175	A22	5c ol grn & brn	3.50	*11.50*
176	A22	10c yel brn & blk	3.50	*11.50*
177	A22	20c scar & indigo	3.50	*9.00*
178	A22	50c dk vio & brn	3.50	*9.00*
179	A22	60c org brn & ind	3.50	*12.50*
180	A22	1.25 l dk bl & grn	3.50	*19.00*
		Nos. 175-180 (6)	21.00	*72.50*
		Set, never hinged	42.50	

Second Colonial Arts Exhibition, Naples. See Nos. C1-C6.

Between 1981 and 1986 unofficial labels appeared showing such non-Eritrean subjects as the British royal weddings, Queen Mother, Queen's birthday, and the Duke & Duchess of York. These labels are not listed.

In 1978, two sets of stamps were issued for use within liberated areas of Eritrea and to publicize the liberation effort. A May 26 set of 5c, 10c, 80c and 1b commemorated the 8th anniv. of the Eritrean People's Liberation Front (EPLF). An August 1 set of 80c, 1b, 1.50b featured the Future of Eritrea theme. A September 1, 1991 set of 5c, 15c and 20c was issued with a Freedom Fighter design in orange and black almost identical to design A24. Although the 80c from the 1st 1978 issue was available at the Asmara post office in late 1992 and early 1993, there is no evidence that any of these stamps were available at the time of independence. Thus these stamps are more properly considered locals and provisionals.

Freedom Fighter with EPLF Flags
A23 A24

1991, Jan. 16	Typo.	*Perf. 11 rough*		
192	A23	5c lt bl, blk & org	—	
193	A23	15c pale green, blk & org	—	
194	A23	20c pale yel, blk & org	—	
195	A23	3b silver, blk & org	—	—
195	A23	5b gold, blk & org	—	—

See footnotes following #199.

1993, Feb. 1	Litho.	*Perf. 10*		
197	A24	5c lt bl, blk & org	4.50	
198	A24	15c pale grn, blk & org	4.50	—
199	A24	20c pale yel, blk & org	4.50	—

Nos. 192-199 commemorate 30 years of the war for national liberation.

Nos. 192-199 were issued for local use, and became valid for international mail on Sept. 13, 1993.

Catalogue values for unused stamps in this section, from this point to the end of the section, are for Never Hinged items.

Referendum for Independence A25

Designs: 15c, Placing ballot in box. 60c, Group of arrows pointing right, one pointing left. 75c, Signs indicating "yes" & "no." 1b, Candle burning. 2b, Peace dove, horn over country map.

Perf. 14x15

1993, Apr. 22		Litho.	Wmk. 373	
200	A25	15c multicolored	*.50*	*.50*
201	A25	60c multicolored	*1.75*	*1.75*
202	A25	75c multicolored	*2.00*	*2.00*
203	A25	1b multicolored	*2.25*	*2.25*
204	A25	2b multicolored	*3.50*	*3.50*
		Nos. 200-204 (5)	10.00	10.00

Natl. Flag — A26

1993	Litho.	*Perf. 11 rough*		
		Blue Border		
205	A26	5c multicolored	—	
206	A26	20c multicolored	—	
207	A26	35c multicolored	—	—
208	A26	50c multicolored	—	
209	A26	70c multicolored	—	
210	A26	80c multicolored	—	

The border of the 40c, No. 215, is similar to that of this issue but it was issued with next set. And the type face of the "0.40" matches that set.

1994	Litho.	*Perf. 11 rough*		
		Color of Border		
211	A26	5c brown	*.20*	*.20*
212	A26	15c red	*.20*	*.20*
213	A26	20c gold	—	
214	A26	25c lt blue	*.20*	*.20*
215	A26	40c blue	—	—
216	A26	60c yellow	*.30*	*.30*
217	A26	70c purple	*.35*	*.35*
218	A26	3b light green	2.50	2.50
219	A26	5b silver	*2.50*	*2.50*

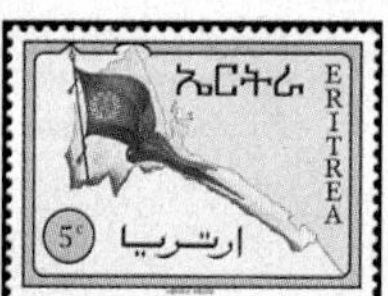

Flag & Map — A27

1994, Sept. 2	Litho.	*Perf. 13½x14*		
		Color of Border		
220	A27	5c deep yellow	*.20*	*.20*
221	A27	10c yellow green	*.20*	*.20*
222	A27	20c salmon	*.20*	*.20*
223	A27	25c red	*.20*	*.20*
224	A27	40c lilac rose	*.25*	*.25*
225	A27	60c blue green	*.35*	*.35*
226	A27	70c dark green	*.40*	*.40*
227	A27	1b yellow	*.55*	*.55*
228	A27	2b orange	*1.00*	*1.00*
229	A27	3b blue violet	*1.40*	*1.40*
230	A27	5b red lilac	*2.00*	*2.00*
231	A27	10b pale violet	*3.25*	*3.25*
		Nos. 220-231 (12)	10.00	10.00

World Tourism Organization, 20th Anniv. — A29

Perf. 14x13½, 13½x14

1995, Jan. 2 Litho.

232	A29	10c Fishing from boat	.25	.20
233	A29	35c Monument, vert.	.25	.20
234	A29	85c Winding road	.50	.25
235	A29	2b Stone dwelling, vert.	1.00	.55
		Nos. 232-235 (4)	2.00	1.20

Fish — A30

Designs: 30c, Horned butterflyfish. 55c, Gonochaetodon larvatus. 70c, Shrimp lobster. 1b, Bluestripe snapper.

1995, Apr. 1 *Perf. 14x13½*

236	A30	30c multicolored	.30	.30
237	A30	55c multicolored	.50	.50
238	A30	70c multicolored	.65	.65
239	A30	1b multicolored	.90	.90
		Nos. 236-239 (4)	2.35	2.35

Independence Day — A31

Designs: 25c, Breaking chains, mountain, buildings, animals. 40c, Raising natl. flag, vert. 70c, Three men, holding natl. flag, sword, vert. 3b, Natl. flag, fireworks, vert.

Perf. 14x13½, 13½x14

1995, May 23 Litho.

240	A31	25c multicolored	.30	.30
241	A31	40c multicolored	.30	.30
242	A31	70c multicolored	.30	.30
243	A31	3b multicolored	1.25	1.25
		Nos. 240-243 (4)	2.15	2.15

Future Development Plan — A32

1995, Aug. 28 Litho. *Perf. 13*

244	A32	60c Building bridge	.40	.40
245	A32	80c Trees	.55	.55
246	A32	90c Rural village	.65	.65
247	A32	1b Camels	.70	.70
		Nos. 244-247 (4)	2.30	2.30

A33

A34

1995, Oct. 23 *Perf. 13½x14*

248	A33	40c shown	.25	.25
249	A33	60c Tree, emblem	.35	.35
250	A33	70c Dove, "50," emblem	.40	.40
251	A33	2b like No. 248	1.50	1.50
		Nos. 248-251 (4)	2.50	2.50

UN, 50th anniv.

1995, Oct. 2 *Perf. 13½x14, 14x13½*

COMESA, Committee for Economic Growth and Development in Southern Africa: 40c, Map of African member countries. 50c, Tree with country names on branches. 60c, Emblem, 3b, Emblem surrounded by country flags, horiz.

252	A34	40c multicolored	.25	.25
253	A34	50c multicolored	.45	.45
254	A34	60c multicolored	.45	.45
255	A34	3b multicolored	1.75	1.75
		Nos. 252-255 (4)	2.90	2.90

FAO, 50th Anniv. — A35

5c, Food bowl with world map on it, spoon. 25c, Men with tractor. 80c, Mother bird feeding chicks. 3b, Vegetables in horn of plenty.

1995, Dec. 18 Litho. *Perf. 13x14*

256	A35	5c multicolored	.25	.25
257	A35	25c multicolored	.25	.25
258	A35	80c multicolored	.50	.50
259	A35	3b multicolored	2.00	2.00
		Nos. 256-259 (4)	3.00	3.00

Endangered Fauna — A36

No. 260: a, Green monkey. b, Aardwolf. c, Dugong. d, Maned rat.

Beisa oryx: No. 261: a, With young. b, One facing left. c, Two with heads together. d, One facing right.

White-eyed gull: No. 262: a, Preening. b, In flight. c, Two standing. d, One facing right.

1996, July 15 Litho. *Perf. 14*

260-262	A36	3b Strip of 4, #a.-d., each	6.25	6.25

Nos. 260-262 were issued in sheets of 12 stamps. No. 261 for World Wildlife Fund.

Martyrs Day — A37

1996, June 17 Litho. *Perf. 13½x14*

263	A37	40c People, flag	.25	.25
264	A37	60c At grave	.30	.30
265	A37	70c Mother, child	.40	.40
266	A37	80c Planting crops	.45	.45
		Nos. 263-266 (4)	1.40	1.40

1996 Summer Olympic Games, Atlanta A38

No. 267, Cycling. No. 268, Basketball, vert. No. 269, Volleyball, vert. No. 270, Soccer.

No. 271, vert: a, Volleyball. b, Laurel wreath. c, Basketball. d, Torch. e, Cycling, yellow shirt. f, Torch, diff. g, Cycling, green shirt. h, Gold medal. i, Soccer.

#272, Soccer, vert. #273, Cycling, vert.

1996, Nov. 20 Litho. *Perf. 14*

267-270	A38	3b Set of 4	6.00	6.00
271	A38	2b Sheet of 9, #a.-i.	9.00	9.00

Souvenir Sheets

272-273	A38	10b each	5.00	5.00

UNICEF, 50th Anniv. A39

UNICEF emblem and: 40c, Mother with child. 55c, Nurse helping child. 60c, Weighing baby. 95c, Boy with one leg walking with crutch.

1996 Litho. *Perf. 14x13½*

274	A39	40c multicolored	.25	.25
275	A39	55c multicolored	.25	.25
276	A39	60c multicolored	.25	.25
277	A39	95c multicolored	.40	.40
		Nos. 274-277 (4)	1.15	1.15

Revival of Eritrea Railway A40

Designs: 40c, Repairing track. 55c, Steam train arriving at station. 60c, Train shuttle transporting people. 95c, Train tunnel.

1996

278	A40	40c multicolored	.30	.30
279	A40	55c multicolored	.30	.30
280	A40	60c multicolored	.30	.30
281	A40	95c multicolored	.70	.70
		Nos. 278-281 (4)	1.60	1.60

National Service A41

40c, Service members, speaker's platform, flags, vert. 55c, People looking over mountainside, vert. 60c, People digging ditches. 95c, Man standing on mountain top, overlooking valley, lake.

1996 *Perf. 13½x14, 14x13½*

282	A41	40c multicolored	.25	.25
283	A41	55c multicolored	.25	.25
284	A41	60c multicolored	.25	.25
285	A41	95c multicolored	.45	.45
		Nos. 282-285 (4)	1.20	1.20

Butterflies and Moths A42

1b, Pieris napi. 2b, Heliconius melpomerie. 4b, Ornithoptera goliath. 8b, Heliconius astraea.

No. 290, vert: a, Psaphis eusehemoides. b, Papilio brookiana. c, Parnassius charitonius. d, Morpho cypris. e, Dariaus plexippus. f, Precis octavia. g, Teinopalpus imperialis. h, Samia gloreri. i, Automeris nyctimene.

No. 291: a, Papilio polymnestar. b, Ornithoptera paradiseo. c, Graphium marcellus. d, Panaxia quadripunctaria. e, Cardui japonica. f, Papilio childrence. g, Philosamea cynthis. h, Actias luna. i, Heticopis acit.

No. 292, Papilio glaucus. No. 293, Parnassius phoebus.

1997, June 16 Litho. *Perf. 14*

286-289	A42	Set of 4	5.50	5.50

Sheets of 9

290-291	A42	3b #a.-i., each	11.00	11.00

Souvenir Sheets

292-293	A42	10b each	4.50	4.50

Environmental Protection — A43

1997 Litho. *Perf. 14x13½*

294	A43	60c Irrigation	.25	.25
295	A43	90c Reforestation	.40	.40
296	A43	95c Preventing erosion	.50	.50
		Nos. 294-296 (3)	1.15	1.15

Marine Life A44

No. 297: a, Sergeant major, white tipped reef shark. b, Hawksbill turtle, devil ray (e). c, Surgeonfish. d, Red sea houndfish, humpback whale (a, g). e, Devil ray (b, f, h). f, Devil ray (e, c), two-banded clownfish. g, Long-nosed butterflyfish. h, Red sea houndfish (g), yellow sweetlips (i). i, White moray eel.

No. 298: a, Masked butterflyfish. b, Suckerfish (a), whale shark (a). c, Sunrise dottyback, bluefin trevally. d, Moon wrasse (a), purple moon angel (a), two-banded anemonefish. e, Lionfish (b, f). f, White tipped shark, sand diver fish. g, Golden jacks (d), lunar tailed grouper. h, Batfish (e, i). i, Black triggerfish.

No. 299, Powder-blue surgeonfish. No. 300, Twin-spot wrasse.

1997, Dec. 29 Litho. *Perf. 14*

Sheets of 9

297-298	A44	3n #a.-i., each	10.00	10.00

Souvenir Sheets

299-300	A44	10n each	4.00	4.00

A45

A46

Natl. Constitution: 10c, Speaker, crowd seated beneath tree. 40c, Dove, scales of justice. 85c, Hands holding constitution.

1997 Litho. *Perf. 13½x14*

301-303	A45	Set of 3	.65	.65

1998, Mar. 16 Litho. *Perf. 14*

Birds — No. 304: a, African darter (b, d, e). b, White-headed vulture (e). c, Egyptian vulture (f). d, Yellow-billed hornbill (g). e, Helmeted guineafowl (d, f). f, Secretary bird (d, e, i). g, Martial eagle (h). h, Bateleur eagle (i). i, Red-billed queleas.

No. 305: a, Black-headed weaver. b, Abyssinian roller (c, f). c, Abyssinian ground hornbill (b, e, f). d, Lichtenstein's sandgrouse. e, Erckel's francolin (d, g, h). f, Arabian bustard (e, i). g, Chestnut-backed finch-lark. h, Desert lark. i, Bifasciated lark.

#306, Peregrine falcon. #307, Hoopoe.

Sheets of 9

304-305	A46	3n #a.-i., each	11.00	11.00

Souvenir Sheets

306-307	A46	10n each	4.00	4.00

Dwellings — A47

Traditional Hair Styles — A48

1998, July 1 Litho. *Perf. 13½x14*

308	A47	50c Highlanders	.30	.30
309	A47	60c Lowlanders	.30	.30
310	A47	85c Danakils (Afars)	.60	.60
		Nos. 308-310 (3)	1.20	1.20

1998 Litho. *Perf. 13½x14*

311	A48	10c Cunama	.30	.30
312	A48	50c Tignnys	.30	.30
313	A48	85c Bilen	.55	.55
314	A48	95c Tigre	.55	.55
		Nos. 311-314 (4)	1.70	1.70

Dated 1997.

A49

A50

Traditional Musical Instruments: 15c, Chirawata. 60c, Imbilta, malaket, shambeko. 75c, Kobero. 85c, K'rar.

1998, Dec. 28 Litho. *Perf. 13½x14*

315	A49	15c multicolored	.35	.35
316	A49	60c multicolored	.35	.35
317	A49	75c multicolored	.50	.50
318	A49	85c multicolored	.65	.65
		Nos. 315-318 (4)	1.85	1.85

1999 Litho. *Perf. 13¼x14*

319	A50	60c green & multi	.45	.45
320	A50	1n red & multi	.70	.70
321	A50	3n blue & multi	2.10	2.10
		Nos. 319-321 (3)	3.25	3.25

Independence, 8th Anniv.

1997 Introduction of Nakfa Currency — A51

Bank notes: 10c, 1 Nakfa. 60c, 5 Nakfa. 80c, 10 Nakfa. 1n, 20 Nakfa. 2n, 50 Nakfa. 3n, 100 Nakfa.

1999, Nov. 8 Litho. *Perf. 13¼*

322	A51	10c multicolored	.45	.45
323	A51	60c multicolored	.45	.45
324	A51	80c multicolored	.45	.45
325	A51	1n multicolored	.70	.70
326	A51	2n multicolored	1.40	1.40
327	A51	3n multicolored	2.00	2.00
		Nos. 322-327 (6)	5.45	5.45

Natl. Union of Eritrean Women, 20th Anniv. A52

Designs: 5c, Woman and child, vert. 10c, Three women. 25c, Women and flag. 1n, Woman with binoculars.

1999 *Perf. 13¼x14, 14x13¼*

328	A52	5c multicolored	.25	.25
329	A52	10c multicolored	.25	.25
330	A52	25c multicolored	.25	.25
331	A52	1n multicolored	.40	.40
		Nos. 328-331 (4)	1.15	1.15

A53

Marine Life A54

No. 332: a, Coachwhip ray. b, Sulfur damselfish. c, "Gray moray." d, Sabre squirrelfish. e, Rusty parrotfish. f, "Striped eel catfish."

No. 333: a, Spangled emperor. b, Devil scorpionfish. c, Crown squirrelfish. d, Vanikoro sweeper. e, Sergeant major. f, Giant manta.

No. 334: a, Chilomycterus spilostylus. b, Dascyllus marginatus. c, Balistapus undulatus. d, Pomacanthus semicirculatus. e, Rhinecanthus assasi. f, Millepora.

No. 335: a, Epinephalus fasciata. b, Pygoplites diacanthus. c, Cephalopholis miniata. d, Centropyge eibli. e, Ostracion cubicus. f, Heniochus acuminatus.

No. 336, Centropyge flavissimus. No. 337, Larabicus quadrilineatus. No. 338, Anthias squamipinnis. 15n, Pomacanthus maculosus.

2000, Apr. 17 Litho. *Perf. 14*

Sheets of 6, #a.-f.

332-333	A53	3n each	6.75	6.75
334-335	A54	3n each	6.75	6.75

Souvenir Sheets

336-338	A54	10n each	3.50	3.50
339	A54	15n multi	4.50	4.50

Illustrations on Nos. 332c and 332f were switched.

A55

Flag and: 5c, Man with sword. 10c, Ship Denden Assab. 25c, Independence Day festivities. 60c, Soldiers and barracks. 1n, Finger, heart and map. 2n, People under tree. 3n, Ballot box. 5n, Eritrean seal, military plane, tank, ship. 7n, Seal. 10n, Ten-nakfa note.

Perf. 13¾x13¼

2000, Mar. 17 Litho.

340-349	A55	Set of 10	11.00	11.00

Worldwide Fund for Nature (WWF) — A56

Proteles cristatus: a, Laying down. b. Pair in den. c, Walking. d, Close up.
Illustration reduced.

2001, Oct. 1 Litho. *Perf. 14*

350	A56	3n Block of 4, #a-d	2.60	2.60

Wild Animals — A57

No. 351, 3n: a, Salt's dik-dik. b, Klipspringer. c, Greater kudu. d, Soemmering's gazelle. e, Dorcas gazelle. f, Somali wild ass.

No. 352, 3n: a, Aardvark. b, Black-backed jackal. c, Striped hyena. d, Spotted hyena. e, East African leopard. f, African elephant.

2001, Oct. 29

Sheets of 6, #a-f

351-352	A57	Set of 2	7.75	7.75

Struggle for Independence, 10th Anniv. — A58

Designs: 20c, Women, flag, jewelry. 60c, Doves, stylized flag, vert. 1n, Bees, honeycomb, flag, vert. 3n, Men with sticks, vert.

Perf. 13x13¼, 13¼x13

2001, May 23 Litho.

353-356	A58	Set of 4	1.75	1.75

Liberation of Nakfa, 25th Anniv. A59

Designs: 50c, Denden. 1n, Town of Nakfa, 1977 (77x27mm). 3n, First Organizational Congress of the Eritrean People's Liberation Front (77x27mm).

2002, Mar. 23 Litho. *Perf. 14x13¼*

357-359	A59	Set of 3	1.10	1.10

Martyr's Day — A60

Designs: 1n, People and map. 2n, Hand, map of Badma area, and flag. 3n, Map and ship. 5n, Dove, map and dead man (49x29mm, triangular).

Perf. 14x13¼, 13½ (5n)

2002, June 20

360-363	A60	Set of 4	2.75	2.75

Dr. Fred C. Hollows (1929-93), Ophthalmologist A61

Designs: 50c, Portrait. 1n, Hollows wearing ophthalmological equipment. 2n, Hollows with man.

2003, Feb. 10 *Perf. 13¼x14*

364-366	A61	Set of 3	.75	.75

Eritrea — People's Republic of China Diplomatic Relations, 10th Anniv. A62

2003, May 24 *Perf. 12*

367	A62	4.50n multi	.95	.95

Eritrean postal authorities have declared "illegal" the following items:

Sheetlet of nine 5n stamps depicting Trains;

Sheetlets of nine 3n stamps depicting Marilyn Monroe (two different), Dogs, The Beatles "Yellow Submarine," September 11 firefighters, Brigitte Bardot, Grace Kelly, Sophia Loren, Golf etiquette, Sexy actresses, Sexy models, Boris Vallejo nudes, Dorian Cleavenger, Michael Möbius, Olivia, Ricky Carralero, Concorde;

Sheetlets of six stamps with various denominations depicting Lighthouses (with Rotary emblem) (two different), Hopper paintings (two different), Vettriano paintings (two different), Marilyn Monroe (two different), Elvgren pin-ups (two different), Teddy bears (two different);

Sheetlets of six 3n stamps depicting Van Gogh paintings, Paintings of nudes;

Sheetlets of five 3n stamps depicting Corot paintings, Pisarro paintings, Renoir paintings, Elvis Presley, Marilyn Monroe;

Sheetlets of four stamps with various denominations depicting Pandas (with Scouting emblem), Crocodiles (with Scouting emblem), Buffalos (with Rotary emblem), Elephants (with Rotary emblem), Monkeys (with Scouting emblem), Lizards (with Scouting emblem), Snakes (with Scouting Emblem), Turtles (with Rotary emblem), Wild cats (with Scouting emblem), Birds of prey (with Rotary emblem), Fowl (with Rotary emblem), Parrots (with Scouting emblem), Penguins (with Rotary emblem), Fish (with Rotary emblem), Marine life (with Scouting emblem), Mushrooms (with Rotary emblem), Butterflies (with Scouting emblem), Bees (with Scouting emblem), Spiders (with Scouting emblem);

Sheetlets of four 3n stamps depicting Dinosaurs (with Scouting emblem), Dinosaurs (with Rotary emblem) Elephants (with Scouting emblem), Elephants (with Rotary emblem), Horses (with Scouting emblem), Horses (with Rotary emblem), Birds (with Scouting emblem), Birds (with Rotary emblem), Penguins (with Scouting emblem), Penguins (with Rotary emblem), Orchids (with Scouting emblem), Orchids (with Rotary emblem), Butterflies (with Scouting emblem), Butterflies (with Rotary emblem), Cars (with Scouting emblem), Cars (with Rotary emblem), Motorcycles (with Scouting emblem), Motorcycles (with Rotary emblem), Trains (with Scouting emblem), Trains (with Rotary emblem);

Sheetlets of three 5n stamps depicting Dinosaurs (with Rotary emblem) (two different), Pandas;

Strips of three 5n stamps depicting Steam trains (four different);

Souvenir sheet with one 8n stamp depicting Steam Trains (with Rotary emblem) (two different), Dinosaurs (with Rotary emblem), Pandas (with Scouting emblem), Elephants (with Scouting emblem), Tigers (with Scouting emblem), Birds of prey (with Scouting emblem);

Sourvenir sheets with one 5n stamp depicting Marilyn Monroe (six different), Lighthouses (with Rotary emblem) (four different), Teddy bears (four different), Hopper paintings (two different), Vettriano paintings (two different).

Eritrean Railway A63

2003 Litho. *Perf. 14x13¼*

Denomination Color

No.	Type	Description	Unused	Used
368	A63	5c Prussian blue	.20	.20
369	A63	10c greenish blk	.20	.20
370	A63	15c lilac	.20	.20
371	A63	35c violet	.20	.20
372	A63	50c orange	.20	.20
373	A63	90c olive green	.20	.20
374	A63	1n red	.20	.20
375	A63	2n blue violet	.40	.40
376	A63	10n red	2.10	2.10
		Nos. 368-376 (9)	3.90	3.90

Liberation of Massawa, 14th Anniv. A64

Designs: 40c, Tanks as fountains. 50c, Boat with soldiers.

No. 379: a, 3n, Crashed airplane, people, soldiers in shallow water. b, 3n, Tank, soldier, flag, boat. c, 4n, People, buildings at shore.

2004

No.	Type	Description	Unused	Used
377-378	A64	Set of 2	.20	.20

Miniature Sheet

No.	Type	Description	Unused	Used
379	A64	Sheet of 3, #a-c	1.50	1.50

SEMI-POSTAL STAMPS

Many issues of Italy and Italian Colonies include one or more semipostal denominations. To avoid splitting sets, these issues are generally listed as regular postage, airmail, etc., unless all values carry a surtax.

Italy Nos. B1-B3 Overprinted type "f"

1915-16 Wmk. 140 *Perf. 14*

No.	Type	Description	Unused	Used
B1	SP1	10c + 5c rose	1.90	*10.00*
a.		"EPITREA"	22.50	*32.50*
b.		Inverted overprint	275.00	275.00
B2	SP2	15c + 5c slate	10.00	*19.00*
B3	SP2	20c + 5c orange	3.50	*21.00*
a.		"EPITREA"	25.00	*35.00*
b.		Inverted overprint	325.00	325.00
c.		Pair, one without ovpt.	—	*1,750.*
		Nos. B1-B3 (3)	15.40	*50.00*
		Set, never hinged	30.00	

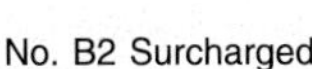

No. B2 Surcharged

1916

No.	Type	Description	Unused	Used
B4	SP2	20c on 15c+5c slate	11.50	*21.00*
		Never hinged	27.50	
a.		"EPITREA"	42.50	*65.00*
b.		Pair, one without overprint	850.00	
		Never hinged	1,050.	

Counterfeits exist of the minor varieties of Nos. B1, B3-B4.

Holy Year Issue

Italy Nos. B20-B25 Overprinted in Black or Red

1925 *Perf. 12*

No.	Type	Description	Unused	Used
B5	SP4	20c + 10c dk grn & brn	2.25	*13.50*
B6	SP4	30c + 15c dk brn & brn	2.25	*17.00*
a.		Double overprint		
B7	SP4	50c + 25c vio & brn	2.25	*13.50*
B8	SP4	60c + 30c dp rose & brn	2.25	*19.00*
a.		Inverted overprint		
B9	SP8	1 l + 50c dp bl & vio (R)	2.25	*25.00*
B10	SP8	5 l + 2.50 l org brn & vio (R)	2.25	*35.00*
		Nos. B5-B10 (6)	13.50	*123.00*
		Set, never hinged	26.00	

The existence of Nos. B6a, B8a has been questioned.

Colonial Institute Issue

"Peace" Substituting Spade for Sword — SP1

1926 Typo. *Perf. 14*

No.	Type	Description	Unused	Used
B11	SP1	5c + 5c brown	.50	*5.00*
B12	SP1	10c + 5c olive grn	.50	*5.00*
B13	SP1	20c + 5c blue grn	.50	*5.00*
B14	SP1	40c + 5c brown red	.50	*5.00*
B15	SP1	60c + 5c orange	.50	*5.00*
B16	SP1	1 l + 5c blue	.50	*8.00*
		Nos. B11-B16 (6)	3.00	*33.00*
		Set, never hinged	6.75	

The surtax of 5c on each stamp was for the Italian Colonial Institute.

Types of Italian Semi-Postal Stamps of 1926 Overprinted type "k"

1927 Unwmk. *Perf. 11½*

No.	Type	Description	Unused	Used
B17	SP10	40c + 20c dk brn & blk	2.10	*19.00*
B18	SP10	60c + 30c brn red & ol brn	2.10	*19.00*
B19	SP10	1.25 l + 60c dp bl & blk	2.10	*35.00*
B20	SP10	5 l + 2.50 l dk grn & blk	3.00	*50.00*
		Nos. B17-B20 (4)	9.30	*123.00*

The surtax on these stamps was for the charitable work of the Voluntary Militia for Italian National Defense.

Fascism and Victory SP2

Agriculture SP3

1928 Wmk. 140 Typo. *Perf. 14*

No.	Type	Description	Unused	Used
B21	SP2	20c + 5c blue grn	1.60	*6.75*
B22	SP2	30c + 5c red	1.60	*6.75*
B23	SP2	50c + 10c purple	1.60	*10.00*
B24	SP2	1.25 l + 20c dk blue	1.60	*12.50*
		Nos. B21-B24 (4)	6.40	*36.00*
		Set, never hinged	13.50	

The surtax was for the Society Africana d'Italia, whose 46th anniv. was commemorated by the issue.

Types of Italian Semi-Postal Stamps of 1928 Overprinted type "f"

1929 Unwmk. *Perf. 11*

No.	Type	Description	Unused	Used
B25	SP10	30c + 10c red & blk	2.75	*14.50*
B26	SP10	50c + 20c vio & blk	2.75	*17.00*
B27	SP10	1.25 l + 50c brn & bl	3.75	*24.00*
B28	SP10	5 l + 2 l olive grn & blk	3.75	*45.00*
		Nos. B25-B28 (4)	13.00	*100.50*
		Set, never hinged	27.50	

Surtax for the charitable work of the Voluntary Militia for Italian Natl. Defense.

Types of Italian Semi-Postal Stamps of 1929 Overprinted type "f" in Black or Red

1930 *Perf. 14*

No.	Type	Description	Unused	Used
B29	SP10	30c + 10c dk grn & bl grn (Bk)	11.50	*20.00*
B30	SP10	50c + 10c dk grn & vio	11.50	*24.00*
B31	SP10	1.25 l + 30c ol brn & red brn	11.50	*35.00*
B32	SP10	5 l + 1.50 l ind & grn	45.00	*77.50*
		Nos. B29-B32 (4)	79.50	*156.50*
		Set, never hinged	150.00	

Surtax for the charitable work of the Voluntary Militia for Italian Natl. Defense.

1930 Photo. Wmk. 140

No.	Type	Description	Unused	Used
B33	SP3	50c + 20c ol brn	2.25	*12.50*
B34	SP3	1.25 l + 20c dp bl	2.25	*12.50*
B35	SP3	1.75 l + 20c green	2.25	*16.00*
B36	SP3	2.55 l + 50c purple	2.25	*24.00*
B37	SP3	5 l + 1 l dp car	3.50	*37.50*
		Nos. B33-37 (5)	12.50	*102.50*
		Set, never hinged	27.00	

Italian Colonial Agricultural Institute, 25th anniv. The surtax aided that institution.

AIR POST STAMPS

Desert Scene AP1

Design: 80c, 1 l, 2 l, Plane and globe.

Wmk. Crowns (140)

1934 Photo. *Perf. 14*

No.	Type	Description	Unused	Used
C1	AP1	25c sl bl & org red	3.50	*11.50*
C2	AP1	50c grn & indigo	3.50	*9.00*
C3	AP1	75c brn & org red	3.50	*9.00*
C4	AP1	80c org brn & ol grn	3.50	*11.50*
C5	AP1	1 l scar & ol grn	3.50	*12.50*
C6	AP1	2 l dk bl & brn	3.50	*19.00*
		Nos. C1-C6 (6)	21.00	*72.50*
		Set, never hinged	42.50	

Second Colonial Arts Exhibition, Naples.

Plowing AP3

Plane and Cacti AP6

25c, 1.50 l, Plowing. 50c, 2 l, Plane over mountain pass. 60c, 5 l, Plane and trees. 75c, 10 l, Plane and cacti. 1 l, 3 l, Bridge.

1936 Photo.

No.	Type	Description	Unused	Used
C7	AP3	25c deep green	.90	*2.25*
C8	AP3	50c dark brown	.70	.20
C9	AP3	60c brown orange	1.50	*5.75*
C10	AP6	75c orange brown	1.40	.90
C11	AP3	1 l deep blue	.20	.20
C12	AP3	1.50 l purple	.90	.45
C13	AP3	2 l gray blue	1.10	*2.10*
C14	AP3	3 l copper red	12.50	8.00
C15	AP3	5 l green	5.75	4.25
C16	AP6	10 l rose red	16.00	8.00
		Nos. C7-C16 (10)	40.95	32.10
		Set, never hinged	80.00	

AIR POST SEMI-POSTAL STAMPS

King Victor Emmanuel III — SPAP1

1934 Wmk. 140 Photo. *Perf. 14*

No.	Type	Description	Unused	Used
CB1	SPAP1	25c + 10c	3.25	*5.25*
CB2	SPAP1	50c + 10c	3.25	*5.25*
CB3	SPAP1	75c + 15c	3.25	*5.25*
CB4	SPAP1	80c + 15c	3.25	*5.25*
CB5	SPAP1	1 l + 20c	3.25	*5.25*
CB6	SPAP1	2 l + 20c	3.25	*5.25*
CB7	SPAP1	3 l + 25c	22.50	*52.50*
CB8	SPAP1	5 l + 25c	22.50	*52.50*
CB9	SPAP1	10 l + 30c	22.50	*52.50*
CB10	SPAP1	25 l + 2 l	22.50	*52.50*
		Nos. CB1-CB10 (10)	109.50	*241.50*
		Set, never hinged	210.00	

65th birthday of King Victor Emmanuel III and the nonstop flight from Rome to Mogadiscio. Used values are for stamps canceled to order.

AIR POST SEMI-POSTAL OFFICIAL STAMP

Type of Air Post Semi-Postal Stamps, 1934, Overprinted Crown and "SERVIZIO DI STATO" in Black

1934 Wmk. 140 *Perf. 14*

No.	Type	Description	Unused	Used
CBO1	SPAP1	25 l + 2 l cop red	*1,800.*	
		Never hinged	*2,300.*	

SPECIAL DELIVERY STAMPS

Special Delivery Stamps of Italy, Overprinted type "a"

1907 Wmk. 140 *Perf. 14*

No.	Type	Description	Unused	Used
E1	SD1	25c rose red	20.00	16.00
		Never hinged	40.00	
a.		Double overprint		

1909

No.	Type	Description	Unused	Used
E2	SD2	30c blue & rose	100.00	*125.00*
		Never hinged	210.00	

1920

No.	Type	Description	Unused	Used
E3	SD1	50c dull red	2.75	*18.00*
		Never hinged	5.25	

"Italia" SD1

1924 Engr. Unwmk.

No.	Type	Description	Unused	Used
E4	SD1	60c dk red & brn	5.75	*18.00*
a.		Perf. 13½	14.50	*37.50*
E5	SD1	2 l dk blue & red	14.50	*22.50*
		Set, never hinged	42.50	

For surcharges see Nos. E6-E8.

Nos. E4 and E5 Surcharged in Dark Blue or Red:

v

w

1926

E6 SD1 70c on 60c (Bl) 5.75 *11.50*
E7 SD1 2.50 l on 2 l (R) 14.50 *22.50*
Set, never hinged 40.00

Type of 1924 Surcharged in Blue or Black:

1927-35 ***Perf. 11***

E8 SD1 1.25 l on 60c dk red & brn (Bl) 10.00 2.75
Never hinged 25.00
a. Perf. 14 (Bl) ('37) 55.00 10.50
Never hinged 140.00
b. Perf. 11 (Bk) ('35) *6,000.* 425.00
Never hinged *7,500.*
c. Perf. 14 (Bk) ('35) 160.00 25.00
Never hinged 325.00

AUTHORIZED DELIVERY STAMP

Authorized Delivery Stamp of Italy, No. EY2, Overprinted Type "f" in Black

1939-41 **Wmk. 140** ***Perf. 14***

EY1 AD2 10c dk brown ('41) .50
a. 10c reddish brown 17.00 *20.00*
Never hinged 35.00

On No. EY1a, which was used in Italian East Africa, the overprint hits the figures "10." On No. EY1, which was sold in Rome, the overprint falls above the 10's.

POSTAGE DUE STAMPS

Postage Due Stamps of Italy Overprinted type "a" at Top

1903 **Wmk. 140** ***Perf. 14***

J1 D3 5c buff & mag 9.00 *22.50*
a. Double overprint 275.00
J2 D3 10c buff & mag 8.00 *22.50*
J3 D3 20c buff & mag 8.00 *12.50*
J4 D3 30c buff & mag 11.50 *17.00*
J5 D3 40c buff & mag 29.00 *37.50*
J6 D3 50c buff & mag 50.00 37.50
J7 D3 60c buff & mag 11.50 *32.50*
J8 D3 1 l blue & mag 9.00 *18.00*
J9 D3 2 l blue & mag 90.00 75.00
J10 D3 5 l blue & mag 190.00 140.00
J11 D3 10 l blue & mag 1,700. 275.00
Never hinged 2,500.
Set #J1-J10, never hinged 400.00

Same with Overprint at Bottom

1920-22

J1b D3 5c buff & magenta .90 *5.75*
c. Numeral and ovpt. invtd. 275.00
J2a D3 10c buff & magenta 1.40 *5.75*
J3a D3 20c buff & magenta 450.00 190.00
J4a D3 30c buff & magenta 37.50 18.00
J5a D3 40c buff & magenta 27.50 20.00
J6a D3 50c buff & magenta 11.50 *37.50*
J7a D3 60c buff & magenta 11.50 *37.50*
J8a D3 1 l blue & magenta 22.50 16.00
J9a D3 2 l blue & magenta 1,000. 500.00
J10a D3 5 l blue & magenta 225.00 190.00
J11a D3 10 l blue & magenta 24.00 *35.00*
Set, never hinged 2,500.

1903 **Wmk. 140**

J12 D4 50 l yellow 425.00 140.00
J13 D4 100 l blue 275.00 70.00
Set, never hinged 1,050.

1927

J14 D3 60c buff & brown 65.00 *72.50*
Never hinged 95.00

Postage Due Stamps of Italy, 1934, Overprinted type "j" in Black

1934

J15 D6 5c brown .20 *4.50*
J16 D6 10c blue .20 *1.10*
J17 D6 20c rose red 2.40 *2.25*
a. Inverted overprint 65.00
J18 D6 25c green 2.40 *5.00*
J19 D6 30c red orange 2.40 *5.00*
J20 D6 40c black brown 2.40 *5.00*
J21 D6 50c violet 2.40 .90
J22 D6 60c black 5.00 *8.00*
J23 D7 1 l red orange 2.40 1.10
J24 D7 2 l green 20.00 *22.50*
J25 D7 5 l violet 24.00 *26.00*
J26 D7 10 l blue 26.00 *32.50*
J27 D7 20 l carmine rose 32.50 *37.50*
Nos. J15-J27 (13) 122.30 *151.35*
Set, never hinged 240.00

The existence of No. J17a has been questioned.

PARCEL POST STAMPS

These stamps were used by affixing them to the way bill so that one half remained on it following the parcel, the other half staying on the receipt given the sender. Most used halves are right halves. Complete stamps were obtainable canceled, probably to order. Both unused and used values are for complete stamps.

Parcel Post Stamps of Italy, 1914-17, Overprinted type "j" in Black on Each Half

1916 **Wmk. 140** ***Perf. 13½***

Q1 PP2 5c brown 72.50 *80.00*
Q2 PP2 10c deep blue *1,550.* *2,100.*
Never hinged *2,350.*
Q3 PP2 25c red 150.00 *110.00*
Q4 PP2 50c orange 29.00 *80.00*
Q5 PP2 1 l violet 67.50 *80.00*
Q6 PP2 2 l green 45.00 *80.00*
Q7 PP2 3 l bister 500.00 *67.50*
Q8 PP2 4 l slate 500.00 *140.00*
Set #Q1, Q3-Q8, never hinged 2,000.

Halves Used

Q1, Q7-Q8 1.90
Q2 45.00
Q3 1.00
Q4 .20
Q5-Q6 .20

Overprinted type "f" on Each Half

1917-24

Q9 PP2 5c brown 2.25 *4.50*
Q10 PP2 10c deep blue 2.25 *4.50*
Q11 PP2 20c black 2.25 *4.50*
Q12 PP2 25c red 2.25 *4.50*
Q13 PP2 50c orange 4.50 *6.75*
Q14 PP2 1 l violet 4.50 *6.75*
Q15 PP2 2 l green 4.50 *6.75*
Q16 PP2 3 l bister 4.50 *6.75*
Q17 PP2 4 l slate 4.50 *6.75*
Q18 PP2 10 l rose lil ('24) 50.00 *65.00*
Q19 PP2 12 l red brn ('24) 110.00 *150.00*
Q20 PP2 15 l olive grn ('24) 110.00 *150.00*
Q21 PP2 20 l brn vio ('24) 110.00 *150.00*
Nos. Q9-Q21 (13) 411.50 *566.75*
Set, never hinged 600.00

Halves Used

Q9-Q16 .20
Q17 .20
Q18 .25
Q19 .75
Q20 .20
Q21 1.90

Parcel Post Stamps of Italy, 1927-39, Overprinted type "f" on Each Half

1927-37

Q21A PP3 10c dp bl ('37) *3,900.* 375.00
Never hinged *4,850.*
Q22 PP3 25c red ('37) 225.00 20.00
Q23 PP3 30c ultra ('29) .90 *9.00*
Q24 PP3 50c orange ('36) 225.00 11.50
Q25 PP3 60c red ('29) .90 *9.00*
Q26 PP3 1 l brn vio ('36) 190.00 13.50
a. 1 l lilac 210.00 13.50
Q27 PP3 2 l green ('36) 150.00 13.50
Q28 PP3 3 l bister 3.75 *18.00*
Q29 PP3 4 l gray 3.75 *18.00*
Q30 PP3 10 l rose lil ('36) 325.00 325.00
Q31 PP3 20 l lil brn ('36) 325.00 325.00
Nos. Q22-Q31 (10) 1,449.
Set, never hinged 2,100.
Nos. Q21A-Q31 (11) 1,137.

Halves Used

Q21A 10.00
Q22-Q25, Q27-Q28 .20
Q26, Q26a, Q29 .20
Q30 .75
Q31 1.50

ESTONIA

e-ˈstō-nē-ə

LOCATION — Northern Europe, bordering on the Baltic Sea and the Gulf of Finland
GOVT. — Independent republic
AREA — 17,462 sq. mi.
POP. — 1,408,523 (1999 est.)
CAPITAL — Tallinn

Formerly a part of the Russia empire, Estonia declared its independence in 1918. In 1940 it was incorporated in the Union of Soviet Socialist Republics.

Estonia declared its independence from the USSR on Aug. 20, 1991. Estonian independence was recognized by the Soviet Union on Sept. 6, 1991.

100 Kopecks = 1 Ruble (1918, 1991)
100 Penni = 1 Mark (1919)
100 Sents = 1 Kroon (1928, 1992)

Catalogue values for unused stamps in this country are for Never Hinged items, beginning with Scott 200 in the regular postage section, Scott B60 in the semi-postal section, and Scott F1 in the registration section.

Watermark

Wmk. 207 — Arms of Finland in the Sheet

Illustration reduced. Watermark covers a large part of sheet.

A1 A2

1918-19 **Unwmk.** **Litho.** ***Imperf.***

1 A1 5k pale red .50 *.50*
2 A1 15k bright blue .50 *.60*
3 A2 35p brown ('19) 1.00 .90
a. Printed on both sides *90.00*
b. 35p olive 30.00 30.00
4 A2 70p olive grn ('19) 1.50 1.25
Nos. 1-4 (4) 3.50 *3.25*

Nos. 1-4 exist privately perforated.

Russian Stamps of 1909-17 Handstamped in Violet or Black

1919, May 7 ***Perf. 14, 14½x15, 13½***

8 A14 1k orange *1,750.* *1,750.*
9 A14 2k green 25.00 *25.00*
10 A14 3k red 30.00 *26.00*
11 A14 5k claret 25.00 *22.50*
12 A15 10k dk bl (Bk) 45.00 *42.50*
13 A15 10k dk bl 150.00 *150.00*
14 A14 10k on 7k lt bl *400.00* *400.00*
15 A11 15k red brn & bl 35.00 *35.00*
16 A11 25k grn & vio 40.00 *37.50*
17 A11 35k red brn & grn *1,500.* *1,500.*
18 A8 50k vio & grn 87.50 87.50
19 A9 1r pale brn, brn & org 150.00 150.00
20 A13 10r scar, yel & gray *3,250.* *3,250.*

Imperf

21 A14 1k orange 22.50 *22.50*
22 A14 2k green *325.00* *325.00*
23 A14 3k red 42.50 42.50
24 A9 1r pale brn, brn & red org *210.00* *210.00*
25 A12 3½r maroon & grn *400.00* *400.00*
26 A13 5r dk bl, grn & pale bl *500.00* *500.00*

Provisionally issued at Tallinn. This overprint has been extensively counterfeited. Values are for genuine examples competently expertized. No. 20 is always creased.

Gulls — A3

1919, May 13 ***Imperf.***

27 A3 5p yellow 2.25 2.25

A4 A5 A6

A7 Viking Ship — A8

1919-20 ***Perf. 11½***

28 A4 10p green .25 .25

Imperf

29 A4 5p orange .20 .20
30 A4 10p green .20 .20
31 A5 15p rose .20 .20
32 A6 35p blue .25 .20
33 A7 70p dl vio ('20) .25 .20
34 A8 1m bl & blk brn .55 .25
a. Gray granite paper ('20) .35 .20
35 A8 5m yel & blk 1.25 .50
a. Gray granite paper ('20) .75 .25
36 A8 15m yel grn & vio ('20) 2.50 .50
37 A8 25m ultra & blk brn ('20) 3.50 1.60
Nos. 28-37 (10) 9.15 4.10
Set, never hinged 15.00

The 5m exists with inverted center. Not a postal item.

See #76-77. For surcharges see #55, 57.

Skyline of Tallinn — A9

1920-24 ***Imperf.***

Pelure Paper

39 A9 25p green .25 .25
40 A9 25p yellow ('24) .25 *.30*
41 A9 35p rose .25 .25
42 A9 50p green ('21) .25 .25
43 A9 1m vermilion .65 .25
44 A9 2m blue .55 .25
45 A9 2m ultramarine .45 .25
46 A9 2.50m blue .65 .25
Nos. 39-46 (8) 3.30 2.05
Set, never hinged 9.00

Nos. 39-46 with sewing machine perforation are unofficial.

For surcharge see No. 56.

Stamps of 1919-20 Surcharged

1920 ***Imperf.***

No.	Type	Description	Unused	Used
55	A5	1m on 15p rose	.30	.30
56	A9	1m on 35p rose	.45	.45
57	A7	2m on 70p dl vio	.50	.50
		Nos. 55-57 (3)	1.25	1.25
		Set, never hinged	3.00	

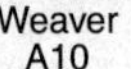

Weaver A10

Blacksmith A11

1922-23 **Typo.** ***Imperf.***

No.	Type	Description	Unused	Used
58	A10	½m orange ('23)	2.00	*3.00*
59	A10	1m brown ('23)	2.75	2.25
60	A10	2m yellow green	2.00	2.00
61	A10	2½m claret	5.00	3.00
62	A11	5m rose	5.00	3.00
63	A11	9m red ('23)	8.00	6.00
64	A11	10m deep blue	6.00	5.00
		Nos. 58-64 (7)	30.75	24.25
		Set, never hinged	60.00	

1922-25 ***Perf. 14***

No.	Type	Description	Unused	Used
65	A10	½m orange ('23)	.65	.20
66	A10	1m brown ('23)	.80	.20
67	A10	2m yellow green	1.40	.20
68	A10	2½m claret	1.40	.20
69	A10	3m blue green ('24)	1.50	.20
70	A11	5m rose	5.00	.20
71	A11	9m red ('23)	3.00	1.00
72	A11	10m deep blue	4.00	.20
73	A11	12m red ('25)	4.00	.90
74	A11	15m plum ('25)	4.00	.25
75	A11	20m ultra ('25)	15.00	.20
		Nos. 65-75 (11)	40.75	3.75
		Set, never hinged	75.00	

See No. 89. For surcharges see Nos. 84-88.

Viking Ship Type of 1920

1922, June 8 ***Perf. 14x13½***

No.	Type	Description	Unused	Used
76	A8	15m yel grn & vio	5.00	.60
77	A8	25m ultra & blk brn	9.00	2.00
		Set, never hinged	22.50	

Map of Estonia — A13

1923-24

Paper with Lilac Network

No.	Type	Description	Unused	Used
78	A13	100m ol grn & bl	20.00	2.75

Paper with Buff Network

No.	Type	Description	Unused	Used
79	A13	300m brn & bl ('24)	50.00	12.50
		Set, never hinged	110.00	

For surcharges see Nos. 106-107.

National Theater, Tallinn — A14

1924, Dec. 9 ***Perf. 14x13½***

Paper with Blue Network

No.	Type	Description	Unused	Used
81	A14	30m violet & blk	10.00	2.75

Paper with Rose Network

No.	Type	Description	Unused	Used
82	A14	70m car rose & blk	15.00	5.00
		Set, never hinged	25.00	

For surcharge see No. 105.

Vanemuine Theater, Tartu — A15

1927, Oct. 25

Paper with Lilac Network

No.	Type	Description	Unused	Used
83	A15	40m dp bl & ol brn	10.00	2.75
		Never hinged	15.00	

Stamps of 1922-25 Surcharged in New Currency in Red or Black

1928 ***Perf. 14***

No.	Type	Description	Unused	Used
84	A10	2s yellow green	1.50	.20
85	A11	5s rose red (B)	1.50	.20
86	A11	10s deep blue	2.00	.20
a.		Imperf., pair	*750.00*	—
87	A11	15s plum (B)	6.50	.25
88	A11	20s ultra	4.50	.30
		Nos. 84-88 (5)	16.00	1.15
		Set, never hinged	26.00	

10th anniversary of independence.

3rd Philatelic Exhibition Issue

Blacksmith Type of 1922-23

1928, July 6

No.	Type	Description	Unused	Used
89	A11	10m gray	5.00	*6.00*
		Never hinged	9.00	

Sold only at Tallinn Philatelic Exhibition. Exists imperf.

Arms — A16

Paper with Network in Parenthesis

1928-40 ***Perf. 14, 14½x14***

No.	Type	Description	Unused	Used
90	A16	1s dk gray (bl)	.30	.20
a.		Thick gray-toned laid paper ('40)	7.50	4.50
91	A16	2s yel grn (org)	.40	.20
92	A16	4s grn (brn) ('29)	.50	.20
93	A16	5s red (grn)	3.00	.20
a.		5 feet on lowest lion	30.00	20.00
94	A16	8s vio (buff) ('29)	1.60	.20
95	A16	10s lt bl (lilac)	2.00	.20
96	A16	12s crimson (grn)	1.50	.20
97	A16	15s yel (blue)	1.75	.20
98	A16	15s car (gray) ('35)	6.00	.45
99	A16	20s slate bl (red)	2.75	.20
100	A16	25s red vio (grn) ('29)	6.00	.20
101	A16	25s bl (brn) ('35)	6.00	.40
102	A16	40s red org (bl) ('29)	7.00	.30
103	A16	60s gray (brn) ('29)	10.00	.50
104	A16	80s brn (bl) ('29)	10.00	1.00
		Nos. 90-104 (15)	58.80	4.65
		Set, never hinged	85.00	

Types of 1924 Issues Surcharged:

1930, Sept. 1 ***Perf. 14x13½***

Paper with Green Network

No.	Type	Description	Unused	Used
105	A14	1k on 70m car & blk	7.00	3.00

Paper with Rose Network

No.	Type	Description	Unused	Used
106	A13	2k on 300m brn & bl	14.50	7.50

Paper with Blue Network

No.	Type	Description	Unused	Used
107	A13	3k on 300m brn & bl	35.00	18.00
		Nos. 105-107 (3)	56.50	28.50
		Set, never hinged	125.00	

University Observatory A17

University of Tartu A18

Paper with Network as in Parenthesis

1932, June 1 ***Perf. 14***

No.	Type	Description	Unused	Used
108	A17	5s red (yellow)	5.50	.60
109	A18	10s light bl (lilac)	1.50	.60
110	A17	12s car (blue)	8.00	2.75
111	A18	20s dk bl (green)	6.00	1.10
		Nos. 108-111 (4)	21.00	5.05
		Set, never hinged	35.00	

University of Tartu tercentenary.

Narva Falls — A19

Ancient Bard Playing Harp — A20

1933, Apr. 1 **Photo.** ***Perf. 14x13½***

No.	Type	Description	Unused	Used
112	A19	1k gray black	7.00	.65
		Never hinged	15.00	

See No. 149.

Paper with Network as in Parenthesis

1933, May 29 **Typo.** ***Perf. 14***

No.	Type	Description	Unused	Used
113	A20	2s green (orange)	1.50	.20
114	A20	5s red (green)	2.00	.20
115	A20	10s blue (lilac)	2.50	.20
		Nos. 113-115 (3)	6.00	.60
		Set, never hinged	12.50	

Tenth National Song Festival.
Nos. 113-115 exist imperf. Value $100.

Woman Harvester A21

Pres. Konstantin Päts A22

1935, Mar. 1 **Engr.** ***Perf. 13½***

No.	Type	Description	Unused	Used
116	A21	3k black brown	.50	*1.00*
		Never hinged	.65	

1936-40 **Typo.** ***Perf. 14***

No.	Type	Description	Unused	Used
117	A22	1s chocolate	.40	.25
118	A22	2s yellow green	.40	.25
119	A22	3s dp org ('40)	10.00	7.50
120	A22	4s rose vio	.75	.25
121	A22	5s lt blue grn	.75	.30
122	A22	6s rose lake	.90	.25
123	A22	6s dp green ('40)	25.00	25.00
124	A22	10s greenish blue	.80	.25
125	A22	15s crim rose ('37)	1.25	.25
126	A22	15s dp bl ('40)	4.00	2.25
127	A22	18s dp car ('39)	25.00	9.00
128	A22	20s brt vio	1.25	.35
129	A22	25s dk bl ('38)	6.00	.35
130	A22	30s bister ('38)	4.25	.35
131	A22	30s ultra ('39)	20.00	5.00
132	A22	50s org brn	7.00	.85
133	A22	60s brt pink	12.50	4.50
		Nos. 117-133 (17)	120.25	56.95
		Set, never hinged	175.00	

St. Brigitta Convent Entrance A23

Ruins of Convent, Pirita River A24

Front View of Convent — A25

Seal of Convent — A26

Paper with Network as in Parenthesis

1936, June 10 ***Perf. 13½***

No.	Type	Description	Unused	Used
134	A23	5s green (buff)	.35	.20
135	A24	10s blue (lil)	.55	.20
136	A25	15s red (org)	.85	1.25
137	A26	25s ultra (brn)	1.25	*1.75*
		Nos. 134-137 (4)	3.00	*3.40*
		Set, never hinged	6.00	

St. Brigitta Convent, 500th anniversary.

Harbor at Tallinn — A27

1938, Apr. 11 **Engr.** ***Perf. 14***

No.	Type	Description	Unused	Used
138	A27	2k blue	.75	*1.25*
		Never hinged	.90	

Friedrich R. Faehlmann A28

Friedrich R. Kreutzwald A29

1938, June 15 **Typo.** ***Perf. 13½***

No.	Type	Description	Unused	Used
139	A28	5s dark green	.70	.50
140	A29	10s deep brown	.70	.50
141	A29	15s dark carmine	1.00	.90
142	A28	25s ultra	1.60	1.40
a.		Sheet of 4, #139-142	10.00	*12.00*
		Nos. 139-142 (4)	4.00	3.30
		Set, never hinged	7.75	

Society of Estonian Scholars centenary.

Hospital at Pärnu — A30

Beach Hotel — A31

1939, June 20 **Typo.** ***Perf. 14x13½***

No.	Type	Description	Unused	Used
144	A30	5s dark green	.70	.35
145	A31	10s deep red violet	.50	.40
146	A30	18s dark carmine	1.50	1.50
147	A31	30s deep blue	1.75	1.75
a.		Sheet of 4, #144-147	12.00	*20.00*
		Nos. 144-147 (4)	4.45	4.00
		Set, never hinged	10.00	

Cent. of health resort and baths at Pärnu.

Narva Falls Type of 1933

1940, Apr. 15 **Engr.**
149 A19 1k slate green .70 1.25
Never hinged .85

The sky consists of heavy horizontal lines and the background consists of horizontal and vertical lines.

Carrier Pigeon and Plane — A32

1940, July 30 **Typo.**
150 A32 3s red orange .20 .20
151 A32 10s purple .20 .20
152 A32 15s rose brown .20 .20
153 A32 30s dark blue 1.00 .75
Nos. 150-153 (4) 1.60 1.35
Set, never hinged 2.50

Centenary of the first postage stamp.
The 15s exists imperf. Value $5.

Catalogue values for unused stamps in this section, from this point to the end of the section, are for Never Hinged items.

Natl. Arms — A40

A41

1991, Oct. 1 **Litho.** ***Perf. 13x12½***
200 A40 5k salmon & red .20 .20
201 A40 10k lt grn & dk bl grn .20 .20
202 A40 15k lt bl & dk bl .20 .20
203 A40 30k vio & gray .20 .20
204 A40 50k org & brn .25 .25
205 A40 70k pink & purple .25 .25
206 A40 90k pur & rose lilac .30 .30

Size: 20½x27mm
Engr.
Perf. 12½ Horiz.
207 A40 1r dark brown .35 .35
208 A40 2r lt bl & dk bl .70 .70
Nos. 200-208 (9) 2.65 2.65

See Nos. 211-213, 299-301, 314-314A, 317, 333-334, 339-340.

Perf. 13½x14, 14x13½
1991, Nov. 1 **Litho.**
209 A41 1.50r Flag, vert. .90 .90
210 A41 2.50r shown 1.25 1.25

National Arms — A42

1992, Mar. 16 **Litho.** ***Perf. 13x12½***
211 A42 E (1r) lemon .20 .20
212 A42 I (20r) blue green .75 .75
213 A42 A (40r) blue 1.90 1.90
Nos. 211-213 (3) 2.85 2.85

No. 211 was valid for postage within Estonia. No. 212 was valid for postage within Europe. No. 213 was valid for overseas mail.

No. 202 Surcharged and Arms Types of 1991-1992

And

Natl. Arms — A42a

Perf. 14, 13x12½ (#214, 217, 219-220)

1992-96
214 A42 E (10s) orange .20 .20
215 A40 10s blue & gray .20 .20
216 A40 50s gray & brt bl .20 .20
217 A40 60s on 15k #202 .20 .20
218 A40 60s lilac & olive .20 .20
219 A42 I (1k) emerald .60 .60
220 A42 A (2k) violet blue 1.25 1.25
221 A42a 5k bis & red vio 1.00 1.00
a. 5k yel orange & red violet 1.00 1.00
222 A42a 10k blue & olive 1.90 1.90
223 A42a 20k pale lilac & slate grn 3.75 3.75
Nos. 214-223 (10) 9.50 9.50

Coil Stamps
Engr.
Size: 20½x27mm
Perf. 12½ Horiz.
224 A42 X (10s) brown .20 .20
225 A42 X (10s) olive .20 .20
226 A42 X (10s) black .20 .20
227 A42 Z (30s) red lilac .20 .20
228 A42 Z (30s) red .20 .20
229 A42 Z (30s) dark blue .20 .20

Litho.
230 A42 60s lilac brown .20 .20
Nos. 224-230 (7) 1.40 1.40

Issued: #214, 219-220, 6/22; #224, 8/29; #225, 9/25; #226, 10/31; #227, 11/16; #228, 12/1; #229, 12/22; #230, 1/8/93; #217, 3/5/93; 10s, 50s, 3/23 1993; 10k, 5/25/93; 5k, 7/7/93; #218, 8/5/93; 20k, 9/8/93; #221a, 9/19/96.

See note after No. 213. Nos. 224-229 were valid for postage within Estonia.
See No. F1.

A44

A45

Birds of the Baltic shores.

1992, Oct. 3 **Litho. & Engr.** ***Perf. 13***
Booklet Stamps
231 A44 1k Pandion haliaetus .20 .20
232 A44 1k Limosa limosa .20 .20
233 A44 1k Mergus merganser .20 .20
234 A44 1k Tadorna todorna .20 .20
a. Booklet pane of 4, #231-234 1.25

See Latvia Nos. 332-335a, Lithuania Nos. 427-430a and Sweden Nos. 1975-1978a.

1992, Dec, 15 **Litho.** ***Perf. 14***
235 A45 30s gray & multi .20 .20
236 A45 2k light brown & multi .40 .40

Christmas.
Exist on ordinary and fluorescent paper. Values are for former.

Friendship A46

1993, Feb. 8 **Litho.** ***Perf. 14***
237 A46 1k multicolored .20 .20
a. Booklet pane of 6 1.25

See Finland No. 906.

A47

A48

1993, Feb. 16 ***Perf. 13x13½***
238 A47 60s black & multi .20 .20
239 A47 1k violet & multi .25 .25
240 A47 2k blue & multi .35 .35
Nos. 238-240 (3) .80 .80

First Republic, 75th anniv.

1993, June 9 **Litho.** ***Perf. 13½x14***
241 A48 60s Wrestling .20 .20
242 A48 1k +25s Viking ship, map .25 .25
243 A48 2k Shot put with rock .40 .40
Nos. 241-243 (3) .85 .85

First Baltic sea games.

Tallinn Castle — A49

Designs: 1k, Toolse Castle. #245, Paide Castle, vert. #245A, Purtse Castle. 2.70k, Narva Fortress. 2.90k, Haapsalu Cathedral. 3k, Monks' Tower, Kiiu. 3.20k, Rakvere Castle. 4k, Kuressaare Castle. 4.80k, Viljandi Castle.

1993-97 **Litho.** ***Perf. 14***
243A A49 1k gray & black .20 .20
244 A49 2k tan & brown .35 .35
245 A49 2.50k lt vio & dk vio .45 .45
245A A49 2.50k gray .45 .45
246 A49 2.70k lt blue & dk blue .45 .45
247 A49 2.90k lt grn & dk grn .50 .50
248 A49 3k rose & brown .50 .50
249 A49 3.20k lt grn & dk grn .75 .75
250 A49 4k lt gray vio & gray vio .75 .75
251 A49 4.80k dull org & brn .80 .80
Nos. 243A-251 (10) 5.20 5.20

Issued: 1k, 2/22/94; 2k, 10/12/93; 2.70k, 12/10/93; 2.90k, 12/23/93; 3k, 3/31/94; 3.20, 12/28/94; 4k, 9/20/94; #245, 1/25/96; 245A, 7/25/96; 4.80k, 1/21/97.

This is an expanding set. Numbers may change.

First Estonian Postage Stamp, 75th Anniv. — A50

1993, Nov. 13 **Litho.** ***Perf. 14***
259 A50 1k multicolored .20 .20

Souvenir Sheet
Imperf
260 A50 4k multicolored 2.75 2.75
a. Ovptd. in sheet margin 15.00 15.00

No. 260 sold for 5k. Overprint on No. 260a reads "FILATEELIANAITUS / MARE BALTICUM '93 / 24.-28. NOVEMBER 1993".

Christmas A51

80s, Haapsalu Cathedral. 2k, Tallinn Church.

1993, Nov. **Litho.** ***Perf. 14***
261 A51 80s red .20 .20
262 A51 2k blue, vert. .35 .35

See Nos. 279-280.

Lydia Koidula — A52

1993, Dec. 14 **Litho.** ***Perf. 14***
263 A52 1k multicolored .25 .25

A53

A54

1994, Jan. 26
264 A53 1k +25s Ski jumping .25 .25
265 A53 2k Speed skating .35 .35

1994 Winter Olympics, Lillehammer.

1994, May 31 **Litho.** ***Perf. 13½x14***

Festival badges: 1k+25s, Tartu, 1869. 2k, Tallinn, 1923. 3k, Tallinn, 1969.
15k, Anniversary badge.

266 A54 1k +25s olive & multi .20 .20
267 A54 2k blue & brown .35 .35
268 A54 3k brown, buff & bister .50 .50
Nos. 266-268 (3) 1.05 1.05

Souvenir Sheet
269 A54 15k multicolored 2.50 2.50

All Estonian Song Festival, 125th anniv.

Flying Squirrel — A55

A56

1994, June 27 **Litho.** ***Perf. 13½x14***
270 A55 1k shown .25 .25
271 A55 2k On leafy branch .35 .35
272 A55 3k In fir tree .50 .50
273 A55 4k With young .70 .70
Nos. 270-273 (4) 1.80 1.80

World Wildlife Fund.

1994, July 19

Europa (Estonian Inventions): 1k, Rotating horizontal millstones, by Aleksander Mikiver. 2.70k, First mini-camera, by Walter Zapp.

274 A56 1k multicolored .25 .25
275 A56 2.70k multicolored .45 .45

A57

A58

Folk Costumes.

1994, Aug. 23 Litho. *Perf. 14*

276 A57 1k Jamaja .25 .25
277 A57 1k Mustjala .25 .25

See Nos. 286-287, 303-304, 325-326, 347-348, 369-370.

1994, Sept. 27 Litho. *Perf. 13½*

278 A58 1.70k multicolored .30 .30

Estonian Art Museum, 75th anniv.

Christmas Type of 1993

Designs: 1.20k, Ruhnu Church, vert. 2.50k, Urvaste Church.

1994, Nov. 15 Litho. *Perf. 14*

279 A51 1.20k brown .25 .25
280 A51 2.50k green .50 .50

For surcharge see No. B63.

A59

A60

1994, Oct. 18

281 A59 1.70k multicolored .35 .35

Intl. Year of the Family.

1994, Dec. 9

Gustavus II Adolphus (1594-1632), King of Sweden.

282 A60 2.50k lilac .60 .60

A61

A62

1995, Jan. 26 Litho. *Perf. 14*

283 A61 1.70k Branta leucopsis .30 .30
284 A61 3.20k Anser anser .55 .55

Matsalu Nature Reserve.

1995, Feb. 28 Litho. *Perf. 14*

Farm Laborer's Family at Table, by Efraim Allsalu.

285 A62 2.70k multicolored .50 .50

FAO, 50th anniv.

Folk Costumes Type of 1994

1995, Mar. 30 Litho. *Perf. 14*

286 A57 1.70k Muhu couple .35 .35
287 A57 1.70k Three Muhu girls .35 .35

A63

A64

Via Baltica Highway Project: #288, 289a, Beach Hotel, Parnu. #289b, Castle, Bauska, Latvia. #289c, Kaunas, Lithuania.

1995, Apr. 20 Litho. *Perf. 14*

288 A63 1.70k multicolored .35 .35

Souvenir Sheet

289 A63 3.20k Sheet of 3, #a.-c. 1.75 1.75

See Latvia Nos. 394-395, Lithuania Nos. 508-509.

1995, Apr. 20 Litho. *Perf. 14*

290 A64 2.70k multicolored .45 .45

Europa. Liberation of Nazi Concentration Camps, 50th anniv.

UN, 50th Anniv. — A65

1995, June 1 Litho. *Perf. 14*

291 A65 4k multicolored .70 .70

Pakri Lighthouse A66

1995, July 5 Litho. *Perf. 14*

292 A66 1.70k multicolored .30 .30

See Nos. 309, 318, 338, 356, 388-389, 408.

Vanemuine Theater, 125th Anniv. — A67

1995, Aug. 14 Litho. *Perf. 14*

293 A67 1.70k multicolored .30 .30

Louis Pasteur (1822-95) A68

1995, Sept. 20 Litho. *Perf. 14*

294 A68 2.70k multicolored .45 .45

Finno-Ugric Peoples A69

Aleksander Kunileid (1845-75), Composer A70

Ethnographic object, languages: a, 2.50k, Drawing on shaman's drum, Saami. b, 3.50k, Duck-shaped brooch, Mordva, Mari. c, 4.50k, Duck-feet necklace pendant, Udmurdi, Komi. d, 2.50k, Khanty band ornament, Ungari, Mansi, Handi. e, 3.50k, Bronze amulet, Neenetsi, Eenetsi, Nganassaani, Solkupi, Kamassi. f, 4.50k, Karelian writing on birchbark, Eesti, Vadia, Soome, Liivi, Isuri, Karjala, Vespa.

1995, Oct. 17 Litho. *Perf. 14*

Miniature Sheet

295 A69 Sheet of 6, #a.-f. 3.25 3.25

1995, Nov. 1 Engr. *Perf. 12½ Horiz.*

296 A70 2k dark blue black .35 .35

Christmas — A71

Churches: 2k, St. Martin's, Türi. 3.50k, Charles' Church of the Toompea Congregation, Tallinn.

1995, Nov. 15 Litho. *Perf. 14*

297 A71 2k yellow orange .35 .35
298 A71 3.50k dull carmine .60 .60

See Nos. 315-316, 331.

Natl. Arms Type of 1991

1995, Oct. 26 Litho. *Perf. 14*

299 A40 20s blue green & black .20 .20
300 A40 30s gray & magenta .20 .20
301 A40 80s lilac & blue black .25 .25
a. Perf. 13 .25 .25
Nos. 299-301 (3) .65 .65

No. 301a issued in 1996.

Submarine *Lembit* — A72

1996, Feb. 29 Litho. *Perf. 14*

302 A72 2.50k multicolored .45 .45

See No. 308, 328.

Folk Costume Type of 1994

1996, Mar. 26 Litho. *Perf. 14*

303 A57 2.50k Emmaste .45 .45
304 A57 2.50k Reigi .45 .45

A73

A74

Designs: a, 2.50k, First gold medal, 1896. b, 3.50k, Alfred Neuland, weight lifter, first to win gold medal for Estonia, 1920. c, 4k, Cyclist.

1996, Apr. 25 Litho. *Perf. 14*

305 A73 Sheet of 3, #a.-c. 1.75 1.75

Modern Olympic Games, Cent. & 1996 Summer Olympics, Atlanta.

1996, May 10

Europa: Marie Under (1883-1980), poet.

306 A74 2.50k multicolored .45 .45

Radio, Cent. — A75

1996, June 27 Litho. *Perf. 14*

307 A75 3.50k Guglielmo Marconi .60 .60

Ship Type of 1996

Design: Icebreaker, Suur Toll.

1996, Aug. 30 Litho. *Perf. 14*

308 A72 2.50k multicolored .45 .45

Lighthouse Type of 1995

1996, Sept. 25 Litho. *Perf. 14*

309 A66 2.50k Vaindloo .45 .45

Estonian Narrow Gauge Railway, Cent. — A76

Designs: 3.20k, Class Gk steam locomotive. 3.50k, DeM 1 diesel motor wagon. 4.50k, Class Sk steam locomotive.

1996, Oct. 17 Litho. *Perf. 14*

310 A76 3.20k multicolored .55 .55
311 A76 3.50k multicolored .60 .60
312 A76 4.50k multicolored .75 .75
Nos. 310-312 (3) 1.90 1.90

See No. 397.

Christmas A77

1996, Nov. 27 Litho. *Perf. 14*

313 A77 2.50k multicolored .45 .45

Natl. Arms Type of 1991

1996-97 *Perf. 14*

314 A40 3.30k lilac and claret .55 .55

Perf. 13x13¼

314A A40 3.30k blue & lt claret .60 .60

Issued: #314, 12/2; #314A, 12/10/97.

Church Type of 1995

Christmas: 3.30k, Harju-Madise Church. 4.50k, Holy Spirit Church, Tallinn.

1996, Dec. 12

315 A71 3.30k blue .55 .55
316 A71 4.50k pink .75 .75

Natl. Arms Type of 1991

1996, Oct. 24 Litho. *Perf. 13½*

317 A40 2.50k grn & dark grn .45 .45

Lighthouse Type of 1995

1997, Feb. 11 Litho. *Perf. 14*

318 A66 3.30k Ruhnu .55 .55

Tallinn Zoo — A78

a, Haliaeetus pelagicus. b, Mustela lutreola. c, Aegypius monachus. d, Panthera pardus orientalis. e, Diceros bicornis. f, Capra cylindricornis.

1997, Mar. 26 Litho. *Perf. 14*

319 A78 3.30k Sheet of 6, #a.-f. 3.50 3.50

Heinrich von Stephan (1831-97), Founder of UPU — A79

1997, Apr. 8 Litho. *Perf. 14*
320 A79 7k black & bister 1.25 1.25

A80

A81

1997, May 5 Litho. *Perf. 14*
321 A80 4.80k Goldspinners Fairy Tale 1.00 1.00

Europa.

1997, May 10

No. 323: a, like #322. b, Linijkugis, 17th cent. c, Kurenas, 16th cent.

322 A81 3.30k multicolored *.55 .55*

Perf. 14x14½

323 A81 4.50k Sheet of 3, #a.-c. 2.25 2.25

Maasilinn ship, 16th cent.

See Latvia Nos. 443-444, Lithuania Nos. 571-572.

Folk Costume Type of 1994

1997, June 10 Litho. *Perf. 14*
325 A57 3.30k Ruhnu .60 .60
326 A57 3.30k Vormsi .60 .60

One Kroon Coin — A82

1997, June 12 Litho. *Perf. 14*
327 A82 50k bl grn, blk & gray 8.50 8.50

See Nos. 345, 363, 391.

Ship Type of 1996

Design: Four-masted barkentine, Tormilind.

1997, July 2
328 A72 5.50k multicolored .95 .95

Stone Bridge, Tartu — A83

1997, Sept. 16 Litho. *Perf. 14*
329 A83 3.30k multicolored .55 .55

Wastne Testament, Estonian Bible Translation, 1686 — A84

1997, Oct. 14 Litho. *Perf. 14*
330 A84 3.50k multicolored .60 .60

Church Type of 1995

Christmas: St. Anne's, Halliste.

1997, Nov. 27 Litho. *Perf. 14*
331 A71 3.30k brown .55 .55

Christmas A85

1997, Dec. 3
332 A85 2.90k Elves .50 .50

Natl. Arms Type of 1991

1998, Jan. 19 Litho. *Perf. 13x13½*
333 A40 3.10k lt violet & rose .55 .55
334 A40 3.60k lt blue & ultra .60 .60
a. 3.60k gray & vio bl .60 .60

Issued: #334a, 8/4/98.

1998 Winter Olympic Games, Nagano — A86

1998, Jan. 28 Litho. *Perf. 14*
335 A86 3.60k multicolored .60 .60

Republic of Estonia, 80th Anniv. — A87

Illustration reduced.

1998, Feb. 6 Litho. *Imperf.*
336 A87 7k Proclamation, arms 1.25 1.25

Eduard Viiralt (1898-1954), Print Artist — A88

Various sections of print, "Hell," showing faces: a, 3.60k, shown. b, 3.60k, Explosion coming from center figure. c, 5.50k, Cat on top of one figure's head. d, 5.50k, Faces within faces.

1998, Feb. 18 *Perf. 14*
337 A88 Sheet of 4, #a.-d. 3.00 3.00

Lighthouse Type of 1995

1998, Mar. 12 Litho. *Perf. 14*
338 A66 3.60k Kunda .60 .60

Natl. Arms Type of 1991

1998, Mar. 16 *Perf. 13*
339 A40 10s grn bl & brn blk .20 .20
340 A40 4.50k pale orange & brick red .75 .75

Issued: 10s, 3/25/97; 4.50k, 3/16/98.

A88a A89

1998, Apr. 16 Litho. *Perf. 14*
341 A88a 7k multicolored 1.25 1.25

1998 World Cup Soccer Championship, France.

1998, May 5 Litho. *Perf. 14*
342 A89 5.20k St. John's Day .90 .90

Europa.

Use of Lübeck Charter in Tallinn, 750th Anniv. — A90

1998, June 1
343 A90 4.80k multicolored .80 .80

Beautiful Homes Year — A91

1998, June 16 Litho. *Perf. 14*
344 A91 3.60k multicolored .60 .60

One Kroon Coin Type of 1997

1998, June 18
345 A82 25k green, gray & black 4.25 4.25

A92 A93

1998, Aug. 4 Litho. *Perf. 14*
346 A92 5.50k multicolored .95 .95

470 Class World Yachting Championships.

Folk Costume Type of 1994

1998, Aug. 21 Litho. *Perf. 14*
347 A57 3.60k Kihnu couple .60 .60
348 A57 3.60k Kihnu family .60 .60

1998, Sept. 3
349 A93 3.60k yel, blue & blk .60 .60

Juhan Jaik (1899-1948), author.

Tallinn Zoo — A94

Design: Panthera tigris altaica.

1998, Sept. 17
350 A94 3.60k multicolored .60 .60

See No. 357.

Estonian Post, 80th Anniv. — A95

1998, Oct. 22 Litho. *Perf. 14*
351 A95 3.60k multicolored .60 .60

Military Aid from Finland, 90th Anniv. — A96

1998, Nov. 5 Litho. *Perf. 14*
352 A96 4.50k Freedom Cross .75 .75

Christmas A97

1998, Nov. 26 Litho. *Perf. 14*
353 A97 3.10k Santa, child, vert. .55 .55
354 A97 5k shown .85 .85

Friedrich Robert Faehlmann, Founder of Learned Estonian Society, Birth Bicent. — A98

1998, Dec. 2
355 A98 3.60k multicolored .60 .60

Lighthouse Type of 1995

1999, Jan. 20 Litho. *Perf. 14*
356 A66 3.60k Vilsandi .60 .60

Tallinn Zoo Type of 1998

1999, Feb. 18 Litho. *Perf. 14*
357 A94 3.60k Uncia uncia .60 .60

Council of Europe, 50th Anniv. — A99

1999, Mar. 24 Litho. *Perf. 14*
358 A99 5.50k multicolored .95 .95

Estonian Pres. Lennart Meri, 70th Birthday A100

1999, Mar. 29
359 A100 3.60k multicolored .60 .60

Tolkuse Bog — A101

1999, Apr. 27 Litho. *Perf. 14*
360 A101 5.50k multicolored .95 .95

Europa.

Bank of Estonia, 80th Anniv. — A102

1999, May 3 Litho. *Perf. 14*
361 A102 5k multicolored .85 .85

Olustvere Manor — A103

1999, June 1
362 A103 3.60k multicolored .60 .60

See No. 395.

One Kroon Coin Type of 1997

1999, June 18 Litho. *Perf. 14*
363 A82 100k bl, bister & blk 17.00 17.00

Estonian Natl. Anthem — A104

1999, June 30 Litho. *Perf. 14*
364 A104 3.60k multicolored .60 .60

No. 364 is printed se-tenant with label.

Tower on Suur Munamägi, Highest Point in Baltic Countries A105

1999, July 17
365 A105 5.20k multicolored .90 .90

A106

A107

Families holding hands and: 3.60k, Estonian flag.

No. 367: a, like #366. b, Latvian flag. c, Lithuanian flag.

1999, Aug. 23 Litho. *Perf. 14*
366 A106 3.60k multicolored .60 .60

Souvenir Sheet

367 A106 5.50k Sheet of 3, #a.-c. 2.75 2.75

Baltic Chain, 10th Anniv.
See Latvia #493-494, Lithuania #639-640.

1999, Sept. 23 Litho. *Perf. 14x13¾*
368 A107 7k multicolored 1.25 1.25

UPU, 125th Anniv.

Folk Costumes Type of 1994

1999, Oct. 12 Litho. *Perf. 13¾x14*
369 A57 3.60k Setu couple .60 .60
370 A57 5k Setu man, boy .85 .85

Three Lions — A108

Perf. 13x13¼, 13¾x14 (#371, 373, 374, 378-382)

1999-2002 Litho.

No.	Type	Value	Description	Unused	Used
371	A108	10s	brn & dk brn	.20	.20
372	A108	30s	lt bl & dk bl	.20	.20
a.			Perf. 13¾x14	.20	.20
373	A108	30s	blue & slate blue, dated 2003	.20	.20
374	A108	50s	olive & dk grn	.20	.20
375	A108	1k	brown & fawn	.20	.20
376	A108	2k	gray	.35	.35
377	A108	3.60k	sky bl & dk bl	.60	.60
a.			Bright blue green ('00)	.60	.60
378	A108	4.40k	grn & bl grn	.75	.65
379	A108	4.40k	bl grn & brt bl grn, wide 2001 date	.75	.25
380	A108	4.40k	Prus bl & lt bl, narrow 2001 date	.75	.25
381	A108	4.40k	green & lt grn, dated 2002	.75	.25
382	A108	4.40k	grn & apple grn, dated 2002	.75	.25
382A	A108	4.40k	ol grn & apple grn, dated 2003	.75	.30
382B	A108	5k	grn & lt grn	.85	.85
382C	A108	6k	bis & yel	1.00	1.00
382D	A108	6.50k	bis & org	1.10	1.10
382E	A108	8k	lake & pink	1.40	1.40
			Nos. 371-382E (17)	10.80	8.25

Issued: 30s, 2k, 11/4; 3.60k (378), 10/22; #377a, 3/31/00; No. 378, 8/21/00; 6k, 10/12/00; 6.50k, 10/5/00; 8k, 10/19/00; No. 372a: 4/17/01; 1k, 5k, 8/28/01; 10s, 2/2/02. 50s, 1/7/03; No. 373, 3/11/03; No. 379, 4/17/01; No. 380, 9/24/01; No. 381, 2/2/02; No. 382, 11/14/02; No. 382A, 3/11/03.

No. 378 exists dated 2001 and 2002. No. 382B exists dated 2002.

The background color of No. 379 is bolder than that on No. 380.

Christmas A109

1999, Nov. 25 Litho. *Perf. 14x13¾*
383 A109 3.10k multicolored .55 .55

A110

A111

1999, Nov. 25 *Perf. 13¾x14*
384 A110 7k multicolored 1.25 1.25

1st public Christmas tree in Tallinn, 1441.

Christmas Lottery A110a

1999, Dec. 1 Litho. *Perf. 14x13¾*
384A A110a 3.10k + 1.90k multi .65 .65

1999, Dec. 14 Litho. *Perf. 13¾x14*
385 A111 5.50k Millennium .95 .95

2000 Census — A112

2000, Jan. 5
386 A112 3.60k multicolored .60 .60

Tartu Peace Treaty, 80th Anniv. — A113

2000, Feb. 2 Litho. *Perf. 14x13¾*
387 A113 3.60k multi .60 .60

Lighthouse Type of 1995

2000, Feb. 25
388 A66 3.60k Ristna .60 .60
389 A66 3.60k Kopu .60 .60
a. Pair, #388-389 1.25 1.25

Congress, 10th Anniv. — A114

2000, Mar. 9 *Perf. 13¾x14*
390 A114 3.60k multi .60 .60

One Kroon Coin Type of 1997

2000, Mar. 14 *Perf. 14x13¾*
391 A82 10k red, sil & blk 1.75 1.75

Cornflower (Natl. Flower) — A115

2000, Apr. 7
392 A115 4.80k multi .80 .80

Natl. Book Year — A116

2000, Apr. 22 *Perf. 13¾x14*
393 A116 3.60k multi .60 .60

First book printed in Estonian language, 475th anniv.

Europa, 2000
Common Design Type

2000, May 9
394 CD17 4.80k multi .80 .80

Manor Type of 1999

2000, May 23 Litho. *Perf. 14x13¾*
395 A103 3.60k Palmse Hall .60 .60

Tallinn Zoo — A117

2000, June 13 Litho. *Perf. 14x13¾*
396 A117 3.60k Naemorhedus caudatus .60 .60

Railway Type of 1996

4.50k, Viljandi-Tallinn Railway, cent.

2000, June 30
397 A76 4.50k multi .80 .80

9th Intl. Finno-Ugric Congress A118

2000, Aug. 1
398 A118 5k multi .85 .85

2000 Summer Olympics, Sydney — A119

2000, Sept. 5 Litho. *Perf. 13¾x14*
399 A119 8k multi 1.40 1.40

Folk Costume Type of 1994

Designs: 4.40k, Hargla. 8k, Polva.

2000, Sept. 12
400-401 A57 Set of 2 2.10 2.10

August Mälk (1900-87), Writer — A120

2000, Sept. 20 *Perf. 14x13¾*
402 A120 4.40k multi .75 .75

Lake Peipus Fish — A121

No. 403: a, Osmerus eperlanus spirinchus. b, Stizostedion lucioperka.

2000, Oct. 25

403 Horiz. pair + central label 2.25 2.25
a.-b. A121 6.50k Any single 1.00 1.00

See Russia No. 6607.

Souvenir Sheet

Estonian Bookplates, Cent. — A122

Various bookplates. Denominiations in: a, LR. b, UR.
Illustration reduced.

2000, Nov. 11 ***Perf. 13¾x14***
404 A122 6k Sheet of 2, #a-b 2.10 2.10

Christmas A123

3.60k, Horn and bow. 6k, Ornament.

2000, Nov. 29 ***Perf. 14x13¾***
405-406 A123 Set of 2 1.60 1.60

Erki Nool, Olympic Decathlon Champion A124

2001, Jan. 10 Litho. ***Perf. 14x13¾***
407 A124 4.40k multi 1.00 1.00

Lighthouse Type of 1995

2001, Jan. 24
408 A66 4.40k Mohni .75 .75

Valentine's Day — A125

2001, Feb. 6 Litho. ***Perf. 13¾x14***
409 A125 4.40k multi .75 .75

Stenbock House, Seat of Government A126

2001, Feb. 20 ***Perf. 14x13¾***
410 A126 6.50k multi 1.10 1.10

Souvenir Sheet

Paintings of Johann Köler (1826-99) — A127

No. 411: a, Girl on the Spring, 1858-62. b, Eve of the Pomegranate, 1879-80.

2001, Feb. 27
411 A127 4.40k Sheet of 2, #a-b 1.50 1.50

European Year of Languages A128

2001, Mar. 6
412 A128 4.40k multi .75 .75

Vanellus Vanellus A129

2001, Apr. 4 ***Perf. 12¾x13***
413 A129 4.40k multi .75 .75

Manor Type of 1999

2001, Apr. 17 ***Perf. 14x13¾***
414 A103 4.40k Laupa Hall .75 .75

Europa — A130

2001, May 9 ***Perf. 13¾x14***
415 A130 6.50k multi 1.10 1.10

Kalev Sports Association, Cent. — A131

2001, May 24
416 A131 6.50k multi 1.10 1.10

Pärnu, 750th Anniv. — A132

2001, June 5 Litho. ***Perf. 14x13¾***
417 A132 4.40k multi .75 .75

Illustrations from Pokuland, by Edgar Valter — A133

Characters and — No. 418: a, Lake. b, Owl. c, Crane. d, Bird in nest.
No. 419: a, Fence. b, Flowers. c, Dog. d, Moon.

2001, June 19

418 Booklet pane of 4 2.25
a.-d. A133 3.60k Any single .60 .60
419 Booklet pane of 4 3.00
a.-d. A133 4.40k Any single .75 .75
Booklet, #418-419 6.00

Entire booklet sold for 35k, 3k of which went to the Pokuland Project of the Estonian Nature Fund.

Restoration of Independence, 10th Anniv. — A134

2001, Aug. 7 ***Perf. 13¾x14***
420 A134 4.40k multi .75 .75

Establishment of St. Mary's Land, 800th Anniv. — A135

2001, Aug. 15 ***Perf. 14x13¾***
421 A135 6.50k multi 1.10 1.10

Resumption of Issuing Stamps, 10th Anniv. — A136

2001, Sept. 4 ***Perf. 13¾x14***
422 A136 4.40k #200 .75 .75

Baltic Coast Landscapes A137

Designs: 4.40k, No. 424a, Lahemaa. No. 424b, Vidzeme. No. 424c, Palanga.

2001, Sept. 15 ***Perf. 14x13¾***
423 A137 4.40k multi .75 .75

Souvenir Sheet

Perf. 13¼x13½

424 Sheet of 3 3.00 3.00
a.-c. A137 6k Any single 1.00 1.00

No. 424 contains three 35x29mm stamps. See Lithuania Nos.
See Latvia Nos. 534-535, Lithuania Nos. 698-699.

Tallinn Zoo — A138

2001, Oct. 4 ***Perf. 14x13¾***
425 A138 4.40k Alligator sinensis .75 .75

Estonia 26/9 Racing Car — A139

2001, Oct. 23
426 A139 6k multi 1.00 1.00

Folk Costume Type of 1994

Designs: 4.40k, Paistu woman. 7.50k, Tarvastu man.

2001, Nov. 7 Litho. ***Perf. 13¾x14***
427-428 A57 Set of 2 2.00 2.00

A140

Christmas A141

Perf. 13¾x14, 14x13¾

2001, Nov. 22
429 A140 3.60k multi .60 .60
430 A141 6.50k multi 1.10 1.10

Radio Broadcasting in Estonia, 75th Anniv. — A142

2001, Dec. 4 ***Perf. 14x13¾***
431 A142 4.40k multi 1.25 1.25

2002 Winter Olympics, Salt Lake City — A143

2002, Jan. 10 Litho. ***Perf. 14x13¾***
432 A143 8k multi 1.40 1.40

Manor Type of 1999

2002, Jan. 22
433 A103 4.40k Sangaste Hall .75 .75

Lighthouse Type of 1995

2002, Feb. 20
434 A66 4.40k Laidunina .75 .75

Bird Type of 2001

Design: Passer domesticus and Passer montanus.

2002, Mar. 7 ***Perf. 12¾x13***
435 A129 4.40k multi .75 .75

Spring Flowers — A144

2002, Mar. 20 ***Perf. 14x13¾***
436 A144 4.40k multi .75 .75

Estonian Puppet Theater, 50th Anniv. — A145

2002, Mar. 27 ***Perf. 13¾x14***
437 A145 4.40k multi + label .75 .75

PTO-4 Training Airplane — A146

2002, Apr. 10 ***Perf. 14x13¾***
438 A146 6k multi 1.00 1.00

Andrus Veerpalu, Gold Medalist at 2002 Winter Olympics A147

2002, Apr. 12
439 A147 4.40k multi .75 .75

Tartu University Anniversaries — A148

No. 440: a, Main building, 1806-09, founding act of 1632. b, University Library, 1982, text from Biblia Latina.

2002, Apr. 24
440 A148 4.40k Horiz. pair, #a-b, + central label 1.50 1.50

Europa A149

2002, May 9 ***Perf. 12¾x13***
441 A149 6.50k multi 1.10 1.10

Re-adoption of Constitution, 10th Anniv. — A150

2002, May 23 ***Perf. 13¾x14***
442 A150 4.40k multi .75 .75

Adoption of Lübeck Charter by Town of Rakvere, 700th Anniv. — A151

2002, June 5
443 A151 4.40k multi .75 .75

Souvenir Sheet

Re-introduction of the Kroon, 10th Anniv. — A152

No. 444 — Portraits from bank notes: a, Lydia Koidula, poet. b, Carl Rober Jakobson, journalist.

2002, June 10 ***Perf. 14x13¾***
444 A152 4.40k Sheet of 2, #a-b 1.50 1.50

Souvenir Sheet

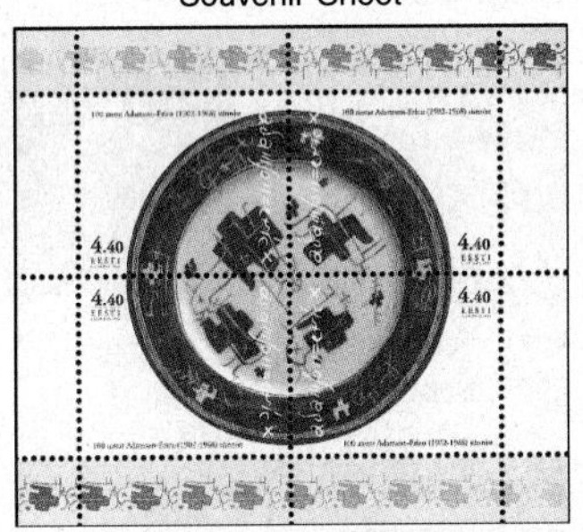
Adamson-Eric (1902-68), Painter — A153

Denomination at: a, LL. b, LR. c, UL. d, UR.

2002, Aug. 8 **Litho.** ***Perf. 14x13¾***
445 A153 4.40k Sheet of 4, #a-d 3.00 3.00

Sus Scrofa A154

2002, Aug. 21 ***Perf. 12¾x13***
446 A154 4.40k multi .75 .75

Limestone, Estonia's National Stone A155

2002, Sept. 18
447 A155 4.40k multi .75 .75

Folk Costume Type of 1994

Designs: 4.40k, Kolga-Jaani women. 5.50k, Suure-Jaani boy and girl.

2002, Oct. 1 ***Perf. 13¾x14***
448-449 A57 Set of 2 1.50 1.50

A156

Christmas — A157

Perf. 14x13¾, 13¾x14
2002, Nov. 20 **Litho.**
450 A156 3.60k Reindeer .60 .60
451 A157 6.50k Christmas tree 1.10 1.10

Lighthouse Type of 1995

2003, Jan. 15 ***Perf. 14x13¾***
452 A66 4.40k Keri .75 .75

Anton Hansen Tammsaare (1878-1940), Novelist — A158

2003, Jan. 30 **Litho.** ***Perf. 14x13¾***
453 A158 4.40k multi .75 .40

Pica Pica A159

2003, Feb. 13 ***Perf. 12¾x13***
454 A159 4.40k multi .75 .40

Spring Flowers — A160

No. 455: a, Tulips. b, Helleborus purpurascens. c, Narcissus poeticus. d, Crocus vernus.

2003, Mar. 20 ***Perf. 13¾x14***
455 A160 4.40k Sheet of 4, #a-d 3.00 1.50
e. Booklet pane, like #455, without date in margin 3.00 —
Complete booklet, #455e 3.00

Manor Type of 1999

2003, Apr. 9 ***Perf. 14x13¾***
456 A103 4.40k Alatskivi Hall .75 .40

Pres. Arnold Rüütel, 75th Birthday — A161

2003, Apr. 24
457 A161 4.40k multi + label .75 .40

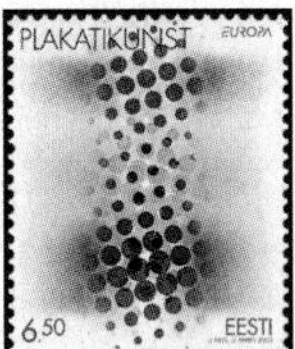
Europa — A162

2003, May 8 ***Perf. 13¾x14***
458 A162 6.50k multi 1.10 .55

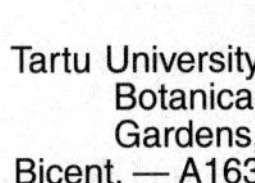

Tartu University Botanical Gardens, Bicent. — A163

2003, June 11 **Litho.** ***Perf. 14x13¾***
459 A163 4.40k multi .75 .40

14th Junior World Orienteering Championships A164

2003, June 27
460 A164 7.50k multi 1.25 .65

Circumnavigation of Adam Johann von Krusenstern (1770-1846) — A165

2003, Aug. 6 ***Perf. 12½***
461 A165 8k multi 1.40 .70

Phoca Hispida A166

2003, Aug. 27 ***Perf. 12¾x13***
462 A166 4.40k multi .75 .40

Adm. Fabian Gottlieb von Bellingshausen (1778-1852) — A167

2003, Sept. 10
463 A167 8k multi 1.40 .70

Ancient Trade Routes — A168

Map and: No. 464, 6.50k, Silver coin of Prince Volodymyr Sviatoslavovych, Slavic warship with sail. No. 465, 6.50k, Arrival of Scandinavian Seamen, coin of Danish King Svend Estridsen.

2003, Sept. 10 ***Perf. 11½***
464-465 A168 Set of 2 2.25 1.10

See Ukraine No. 524.

Three Lions Type of 1999-2002

2003-04 Litho. ***Perf. 13¾x14***
467 A108 20s blk & gray .20 .20
472 A108 4.40k ol grn & apple grn .75 .40
473 A108 5k dk grn & apple grn, dated 2004 .80 .80
474 A108 5.50k dk grn & yel grn .85 .85

Issued: 20s, 4.40k, 8/22; 5k, 1/20/04; 5.50k, 3/25/04.

Folk Costume Type of 1994

Designs: 4.40k, Aksi woman and girl. 6.50k, Otepää man, woman and girl.

2003, Oct. 9 Litho. ***Perf. 13¾x14***
476-477 A57 Set of 2 1.90 .95

A169

Christmas A170

2003, Nov. 26 ***Perf. 14x13¾***
478 A169 3.60k multi .60 .30
479 A170 6k multi 1.00 .50

Souvenir Sheet

Friedrich Reinhold Kreutzwald (1803-82), Writer — A171

No. 480: a, 4.40k, Illustration by Kristjan Raud of "Voyage to the End of the World," from "Kalevipoeg," by Kreutzwald. b, 6.50k, Portrait of Kreutzwald.

2003, Dec. 4 ***Perf. 13x12¾***
480 A171 Sheet of 2, #a-b 1.90 1.90

Lighthouse Type of 1995

2004, Jan. 7 Litho. ***Perf. 14x13¾***
481 A66 4.40k Sorgu .75 .75

Canis Lupus A172

2004, Feb. 3 ***Perf. 12¾x13***
482 A172 4.40k multi .75 .75

Voyage Around Cape Horn of the Hioma, 150th Anniv. — A173

2004, Feb. 18 ***Perf. 13¾x14***
483 A173 8k multi 1.25 1.25

Spring Flowers Type of 2003

No. 484: a, Viola riviniana. b, Anemone nemorosa. c, Hepatica nobilis. d, Trollius europaeus.

2004, Mar. 17
484 A160 4.40k Sheet of 4, #a-d 2.75 2.75
e. Booklet pane, like #484 without date in margin 2.75 —
Complete booklet, #484e 2.75

Bird Type of 2003

2004, Apr. 6 ***Perf. 12¾x13***
485 A159 4.40k Ciconia ciconia .70 .70

Admission to European Union A174

2004, May 1 ***Perf. 13¼x13***
486 A174 6.50k multi 1.00 1.00

Europa — A175

Illustration reduced.

2004, May 4 ***Perf. 13***
487 A175 6.50k multi 1.00 1.00

Tallinn Town Hall, 600th Anniv. A176

2004, May 13 Litho. ***Perf. 12¾x13***
488 A176 4.40k multi .70 .70

Consecration of Estonian Flag, 120th Anniv. — A177

2004, June 4 ***Perf. 13¾x14***
489 A177 4.40k multi .70 .70

Manor Type of 1999

2004, June 15 ***Perf. 14x13¾***
490 A103 4.40k Vasalemma Hall .70 .70

Admission to NATO — A178

2004, June 28 ***Perf. 13¾x14***
491 A178 6k multi .95 .95

2004 Summer Olympics, Athens — A179

2004, July 15 Litho. ***Perf. 13¾x14***
492 A179 8k multi 1.25 1.25

Dragon Class Yachting European Championships — A180

2004, Aug. 17 ***Perf. 14x13¾***
493 A180 6k multi .95 .95

Taraxacum Officinale — A181

Serpentine Die Cut 12½
2004, Sept. 14
Self-Adhesive
494 A181 30s multi .20 .20

County Arms — A182

2004, Sept. 28 **Self-Adhesive**
495 A182 4.40k Harjumaa .70 .70
496 A182 4.40k Hiiumaa .70 .70

Folk Costumes Type of 1994

Designs: 4.40k, Viru-Jaagupi boy and girl. 7.50k, Jõhvi woman and girl.

2004, Oct. 5 Litho. ***Perf. 13¾x14***
497-498 A57 Set of 2 1.90 1.90

A183

Christmas A184

2004, Nov. 23 ***Perf. 13¾x14***
499 A183 4.40k multi .80 .80
Perf. 14x13¾
500 A184 6.50k multi 1.10 1.10

SEMI-POSTAL STAMPS

Assisting Wounded Soldier — SP1

Offering Aid to Wounded Hero — SP2

1920, June Unwmk. Litho. ***Imperf.***
B1 SP1 35p + 10p red & ol grn .25 *.35*
B2 SP2 70p + 15p dp bl & brn .25 *.35*

Surcharged

1920
B3 SP1 1m on No. B1 .30 .25
B4 SP2 2m on No. B2 .30 .25

Nurse and Wounded Soldier — SP3

1921, Aug. 1 ***Imperf.***
B5 SP3 2½ (3½)m org, brn & car .90 *1.00*
B6 SP3 5 (7)m ultra, brn & car .90 *1.00*

1922, Apr. 26 ***Perf. 13½x14***
B7 SP3 2½ (3½)m org, brn & car .90 *1.00*
a. Vert. pair, imperf. horiz. 20.00 20.00
B8 SP3 5 (7)m ultra, brn & car .90 *1.00*
a. Vert. pair, imperf. horiz. 20.00 20.00

Nos. B5-B8 Overprinted

1923, Oct. 8 ***Imperf.***
B9 SP3 2½ (3½)m 20.00 *22.50*
B10 SP3 5 (7)m 30.00 *27.50*
Perf. 13½x14
B11 SP3 2½ (3½)m 35.00 *35.00*
a. Vert. pair, imperf. horiz. 90.00 *150.00*
B12 SP3 5 (7)m 35.00 35.00
a. Vert. pair, imperf. horiz. 90.00 *150.00*
Nos. B9-B12 (4) 120.00 *120.00*

Excellent forgeries are plentiful.

Nos. B7 and B8 Surcharged

1926, June 15

B13 SP3	5 (6)m on #B7	3.50	3.50
a.	Vert. pair, imperf. horiz.	10.00	10.00
B14 SP3	10 (12)m on #B8	4.00	4.00
a.	Vert. pair, imperf. horiz.	10.00	10.00

Nos. B5-B14 had the franking value of the lower figure. They were sold for the higher figure, the excess going to the Red Cross Society.

Kuressaare Castle SP4

Tartu Cathedral SP5

Tallinn Castle SP6

Narva Fortress SP7

View of Tallinn — SP8

Laid Paper

Perf. 14½x14

1927, Nov. 19 Typo. Wmk. 207

B15 SP4	5m + 5m bl grn & ol, *grysh*	.90	*1.00*
B16 SP5	10m + 10m dp bl & brn, *cream*	.90	*1.00*
B17 SP6	12m + 12m rose red & ol grn, *bluish*	.90	*2.00*

Perf. 14x13½

B18 SP7	20m + 20m bl & choc, *gray*	1.75	*2.00*
B19 SP8	40m + 40m org brn & slate, *buff*	1.75	*3.00*
	Nos. B15-B19 (5)	6.20	9.00

The money derived from the surtax was donated to the Committee for the commemoration of War for Liberation.

Red Cross Issue

Symbolical of Succor to Injured — SP9

Symbolical of "Light of Hope" — SP10

1931, Aug. 1 Unwmk. *Perf. 13½*

B20 SP9	2s + 3s grn & car	6.00	5.00
B21 SP10	5s + 3s red & car	6.00	5.00
B22 SP10	10s + 3s lt bl & car	6.00	5.00
B23 SP9	20s + 3s dk bl & car	7.50	7.50
	Nos. B20-B23 (4)	25.50	*22.50*
	Set, never hinged	35.00	

Nurse and Child SP11

Taagepera Sanatorium SP12

Lorraine Cross and Flower — SP13

Paper with Network as in Parenthesis

1933, Oct. 1 *Perf. 14, 14½*

B24 SP11	5s + 3s ver (grn)	4.25	5.00
B25 SP12	10s + 3s lt bl & red (vio)	4.25	5.00
B26 SP13	12s + 3s rose & red (grn)	4.75	5.00
B27 SP12	20s + 3s dk bl & red (org)	7.50	7.50
	Nos. B24-B27 (4)	20.75	22.50
	Set, never hinged	40.00	

The surtax was for a fund to combat tuberculosis.

Coats of Arms

Narva — SP14

Pärnu — SP15

Tartu — SP16

Tallinn — SP17

Paper with Network as in Parenthesis

1936, Feb. 1 *Perf. 13½*

B28 SP14	10s + 10s grn & ultra (gray)	3.50	*5.00*
B29 SP15	15s + 15s car & bl (gray)	3.50	*5.00*
B30 SP16	25s + 25s gray bl & red (brn)	4.50	*7.00*
B31 SP17	50s + 50s blk & dl org (ol)	10.00	*18.00*
	Nos. B28-B31 (4)	21.50	*35.00*
	Set, never hinged	35.00	

Paide SP18

Rakvere SP19

Valga SP20

Viljandi SP21

Paper with Network as in Parenthesis

1937, Jan. 2 *Perf. 13½x14*

B32 SP18	10s + 10s grn (gray)	3.00	*5.00*
B33 SP19	15s + 15s red brn (gray)	3.00	*5.00*
B34 SP20	25s + 25s dk bl (lil)	5.00	*6.00*
B35 SP21	50s + 50s dk vio (gray)	9.00	*10.00*
	Nos. B32-B35 (4)	20.00	26.00
	Set, never hinged	40.00	

Baltiski — SP22

Võru — SP23

Haapsalu SP24

Kuressaare SP25

Designs are the armorial bearings of various cities

1938, Jan. 21

Paper with Gray Network

B36 SP22	10s + 10s dk brn	3.00	*3.25*
B37 SP23	15s + 15s car & grn	3.50	*3.50*
B38 SP24	25s + 25s dk bl & car	5.00	*5.00*
B39 SP25	50s + 50s blk & org yel	7.00	*8.75*
a.	Sheet of 4, #B36-B39	35.00	30.00
	Nos. B36-B39 (4)	18.50	*20.50*
	Set, never hinged	40.00	

Annual charity ball, Tallinn, Jan. 2, 1938.

Viljandimaa SP27

Pärnumaa SP28

Tartumaa SP29

Harjumaa SP30

Designs are the armorial bearings of various districts

1939, Jan. 10 *Perf. 13½*

Paper with Gray Network

B41 SP27	10s + 10s dk bl grn	3.50	*4.50*
B42 SP28	15s + 15s carmine	4.00	*5.00*
B43 SP29	25s + 25s dk blue	5.50	*7.25*
B44 SP30	50s + 50s brn lake	8.50	*15.00*
a.	Sheet of 4, #B41-B44	30.00	*40.00*
	Nos. B41-B44 (4)	21.50	*31.75*
	Set, never hinged	40.00	

Võrumaa SP32

Järvamaa SP33

Läänemaa SP34

Saaremaa SP35

Designs are the armorial bearings of various districts

1940, Jan. 2 Typo. *Perf. 13½*

Paper with Gray Network

B46 SP32	10s + 10s dp grn & ultra	2.50	*3.00*
B47 SP33	15s + 15s dk car & ultra	2.50	*3.00*
B48 SP34	25s + 25s dk bl & scar	3.00	*5.00*
B49 SP35	50s + 50s ocher & ultra	4.00	*8.00*
	Nos. B46-B49 (4)	12.00	19.00
	Set, never hinged	25.00	

Catalogue values for unused stamps in this section, from this point to the end of the section, are for Never Hinged items.

1992 Summer Olympics, Barcelona — SP40

1992, June 22 Litho. *Perf. 14*

B60 SP40	1r +50k red	.25	.25
B61 SP40	3r +1.50r green	1.00	1.00
B62 SP40	5r +2.50r blue & blk	.50	.50
	Nos. B60-B62 (3)	1.75	1.75

While face values are shown in kopecks and rubles, the stamps were sold in the new currency at the rate of 1 ruble = 10 sents.

No. 280 Surcharged

1994, Nov. 18 Litho. *Perf. 14*

B63 A51	2.50k +20k green	5.00	4.00

Surtax for benefit of survivors of sinking of ferry "Estonia."

Haliaeetus Albicilla — SP41

1995, Aug. 29 Litho. *Perf. 14*

B64 SP41	2k +25k black & blue	.45	.45

Surtax for Keep the Estonian Sea Clean Assoc.

AIR POST STAMPS

Airplane AP1

Unwmk.

1920, Mar. 13 Typo. *Imperf.*

C1 AP1	5m yel, blk & lt grn	3.00	*4.00*

No. C1 Overprinted "1923" in Red

1923, Oct. 1

C2 AP1	5m multicolored	6.50	*8.50*

No. C1 Surcharged in Red

1923, Oct. 1

C3 AP1	15m on 5m multi	9.00	*12.00*

Pairs of No. C1 Surcharged in Black or Red

1923, Oct.

C4	AP1	10m on 5m+5m (B)	7.00	*10.00*
C5	AP1	20m on 5m+5m	17.50	*22.50*
C6	AP1	45m on 5m+5m	75.00	*100.00*

Rough Perf. 11½

C7	AP1	10m on 5m+5m (B)	*425.00*	*450.00*
C8	AP1	20m on 5m+5m	*175.00*	*225.00*
		Nos. C4-C8 (5)	*699.50*	*807.50*

The pairs comprising Nos. C7 and C8 are imperforate between. Forged surcharges and perforations abound. Authentication is required.

Monoplane in Flight — AP2

Designs: Various views of planes in flight.

1924, Feb. 12 ***Imperf.***

C9	AP2	5m yellow & blk	2.00	*4.00*
C10	AP2	10m blue & blk	2.00	*4.00*
C11	AP2	15m red & blk	2.00	*4.00*
C12	AP2	20m green & blk	2.00	*3.00*
C13	AP2	45m violet & blk	1.75	*6.00*
		Nos. C9-C13 (5)	9.75	*21.00*

The paper is covered with a faint network in pale shades of the frame colors. There are four varieties of the frames and five of the pictures.

1925, July 15 ***Perf. 13½***

C14	AP2	5m yellow & blk	1.50	*2.00*
C15	AP2	10m blue & blk	1.50	*2.00*
C16	AP2	15m red & blk	1.50	*3.00*
C17	AP2	20m green & blk	1.50	*2.50*
C18	AP2	45m violet & blk	1.50	*3.00*
		Nos. C14-C18 (5)	7.50	*12.50*

Counterfeits of Nos. C1-C18 are plentiful.

REGISTRATION STAMP

Catalogue values for unused stamps in this section are for Never Hinged items.

Arms Type of 1992

1992, Mar. 16 Litho. ***Perf. 13x12½***

F1	A42	R (10r) pink & red	*.50*	*.50*

OCCUPATION STAMPS

Issued under German Occupation

For Use in Tartu (Dorpat)

Russian Stamps of 1909-12 Surcharged

1918 Unwmk. ***Perf. 14x14½***

N1	A15	20pf on 10k dk bl	35.00	*50.00*
N2	A8	40pf on 20k bl & car	35.00	*50.00*
		Set, never hinged	77.50	

Forged overprints exist.

Estonian Arms and Swastika — OS1

Perf. 11½

1941, Aug. Typo. Unwmk.

N3	OS1	15k brown	10.00	10.00
N4	OS1	20k green	10.00	10.00
N5	OS1	30k dark blue	10.00	10.00
		Nos. N3-N5 (3)	30.00	30.00
		Set, never hinged	50.00	

Exist imperf. Value, set, $100.

Nos. N3-N5 were issued on both ordinary paper with colorless gum and thick chalky paper with yellow gum. Same values.

OCCUPATION SEMI-POSTAL STAMPS

Castle Tower, Tallinn — OSP1

Designs: 20k+20k, Stone Bridge, Tartu, horiz. 30k+30k, Narva Castle, horiz. 50k+50k, Tallinn view, horiz. 60k+60k, Tartu University. 100k+100k, Narva Castle, close view.

Paper with Gray Network

Perf. 11½

1941, Sept. 29 Photo. Unwmk.

NB1	OSP1	15k + 15k dk brn	.60	*1.00*
NB2	OSP1	20k + 20k red lil	.60	*1.00*
NB3	OSP1	30k + 30k dk bl	.60	*1.00*
NB4	OSP1	50k + 50k bluish grn	.70	*2.50*
NB5	OSP1	60k + 60k car	1.00	*2.50*
NB6	OSP1	100k + 100k gray	1.50	*3.00*
		Nos. NB1-NB6 (6)	5.00	*11.00*
		Set, never hinged	12.00	

Nos. NB1-NB6 exist imperf. Value, set unused $20, used $40.

A miniature sheet containing one each of Nos. NB1-NB6, imperf., exists in various colors. Value, mint $40, used $60. It was not postally valid. Reproductions are common.

ETHIOPIA

ˌē-thē-ˈō-pē-ə

(Abyssinia)

LOCATION — Northeastern Africa
GOVT. — Republic (1988)
AREA — 426,260 sq. mi.
POP. — 59,680,383 (1999 est.)
CAPITAL — Addis Ababa

During the Italian occupation (1936-1941) Nos. N1-N7 were used, also stamps of Italian East Africa, Eritrea and Somalia.

During the British administration (1941-42) stamps of Great Britain and Kenya were used when available.

16 Guerche = 1 Menelik Dollar or 1 Maria Theresa Dollar
100 Centimes = 1 Franc (1905)
40 Paras = 1 Piaster (1908)
16 Mehalek = 1 Thaler or Talari (1928)
100 Centimes = 1 Thaler (1936)
100 Cents = 1 Ethiopian Dollar (1946)
100 Cents = 1 Birr (1978)

Catalogue values for unused stamps in this country are for Never Hinged items, beginning with Scott 247 in the regular postage section, Scott B6 in the semi-postal section, Scott C18 in the airpost section, Scott E1 in the special delivery section, and Scott J57 in the postage due section.

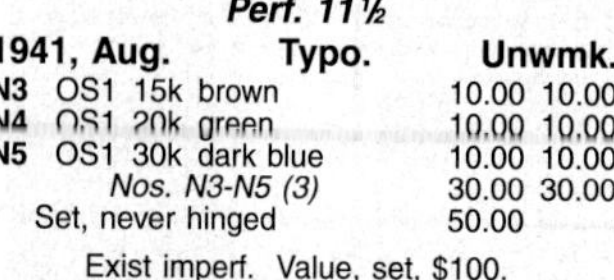

Watermarks

Wmk. 140 — Crown

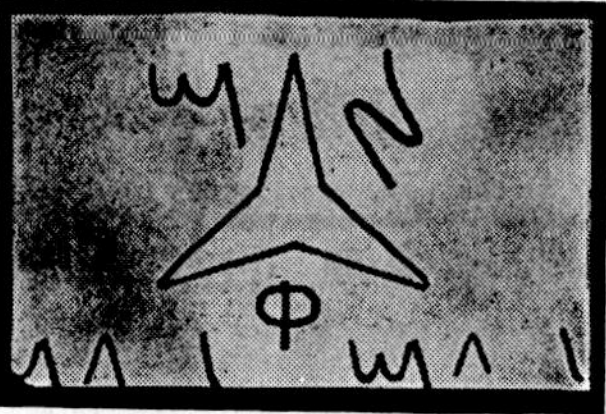

Wmk. 282 — Ethiopian Star and Amharic Characters, Multiple

Excellent forgeries of Nos. 1-86 exist.

Very Fine examples of Nos. 1-86 and J1-J42 will have perforations touching the design on one or more sides due to the narrow spacing of the stamps on the plates and imperfect perforating methods. Stamps with margins clear on all sides are scarce and command high premiums.

On March 9, 1894 Menelik II awarded Alfred Ilg a concession to develop a railway, including postal service. Ilg's stamps, Nos. 1-79, were valid locally and to Djibouti. Mail to other countries had to bear stamps of Obock, Somali Coast, etc.

Ethiopia joined the UPU Nov. 1, 1908.

Menelik II
A1

Lion of Judah
A2

Anharic numeral "8"

Perf. 14x13½

1895, Jan. Unwmk. Typo.

1	A1	¼g green	2.00	2.00
2	A1	½g red	2.00	2.00
3	A1	1g blue	2.00	2.00
4	A1	2g dark brown	2.00	2.00
5	A2	4g lilac brown	2.00	2.00
6	A2	8g violet	2.00	2.00
7	A2	16g black	2.00	2.00
		Nos. 1-7 (7)	14.00	14.00

For 4g, 8g and 16g stamps of type A1, see Nos. J3a, J4a and J7a.

Earliest reported use is Jan. 29, 1895.

Forged cancellations are plentiful.

For overprints see #8-86, J8-J28, J36-J42. For surcharges see #94-100, J29-J35.

Nos. 1-7 Handstamped in Violet or Blue

Overprint 9¼x2½mm, Serifs on "E"

1901, July 18

8	A1	¼g green	17.00	17.00
9	A1	½g red	17.00	17.00
10	A1	1g blue	17.00	17.00
11	A1	2g dark brown	17.00	17.00
12	A2	4g lilac brown	21.00	21.00
13	A2	8g violet	35.00	35.00
14	A2	16g black	42.50	42.50
		Nos. 8-14 (7)	166.50	166.50

Violet overprints were issued July 18, 1901, for postal use, while the blue overprints were issued in Jan. 1902 for philatelic purposes. The blue overprints were not used in the mails. Values for unused stamps are for examples with blue overprints. Unused stamps with violet overprints are worth much more.

Overprints 8¼mm wide are unofficial reproductions.

Nos. 1-7 Handstamped in Violet, Blue or Black

Overprint 11x3mm, Low Colons

1902, Apr. 1

15	A1	¼g green	6.00	6.00
16	A1	½g red	9.00	7.00
17	A1	1g blue	9.50	9.50
18	A1	2g dark brown	12.00	11.00
19	A2	4g lilac brown	19.00	15.00
20	A2	8g violet	26.00	26.00
21	A2	16g black	40.00	40.00
		Nos. 15-21 (7)	121.50	114.50

The handstamp reads "Bosta" (Post).

Overprints 10¾mm and 11mm wide with raised colons are unofficial reproductions.

Nos. 1-7 Handstamped in Violet, Blue or Black

Overprint 16x3¾mm

1903, Apr. 15

22	A1	¼g green	6.75	6.75
23	A1	½g red	10.00	10.00
24	A1	1g blue	12.00	12.00
25	A1	2g dark brown	14.00	14.00
26	A2	4g lilac brown	21.00	21.00
27	A2	8g violet	29.00	29.00
28	A2	16g black	42.50	42.50
		Nos. 22-28 (7)	135.25	135.25

The handstamp reads "Malekt." (Also "Melekt," message).

Original stamps have blurred colons. Unofficial reproductions have clean colons.

Nos. 22-23 have black overprints only. All other colors are fakes.

Nos. 1-7 Handstamped in Violet or Blue

Overprint 18¼mm Wide

1904, Dec.

36	A1	¼g green	12.00
37	A1	½g red	12.00
38	A1	1g blue	15.00
39	A1	2g dark brown	17.50
40	A2	4g lilac brown	22.50
41	A2	8g violet	45.00
42	A2	16g black	52.50
		Nos. 36-42 (7)	176.50

The handstamp reads "Malekathe" (message). This set was never issued.

Preceding Issues Surcharged with New Values in French Currency in Blue, Violet, Rose or Black:

a

b

Overprint 3mm High

1905, Jan. 1

On Nos. 1-7

43	A1 (a)	5c on ¼g	7.50	7.50
44	A1 (a)	10c on ½g	7.50	7.50
45	A1 (a)	20c on 1g	7.50	7.50
46	A1 (a)	40c on 2g	7.50	7.50
47	A2 (a)	80c on 4g	14.00	14.00

No.	Type	Description	Unused	Used
48	A2 (b)	1.60fr on 8g	17.50	21.00
49	A2 (b)	3.20fr on 16g	25.00	25.00
		Nos. 43-49 (7)	86.50	90.00

Nos. 48-49 exist with period or comma.

On No. 8, "Ethiopie" in Blue

No.	Type	Description	Unused	Used
50	A1 (a)	5c on ¼g	100.00	100.00

On No. 15, "Bosta" in Black

No.	Type	Description	Unused	Used
51	A1 (a)	5c on ¼g	30.00	30.00

On No. 22, "Malekt" in Black

No.	Type	Description	Unused	Used
52	A1 (a)	5c on ¼g	60.00	60.00

Unofficial reproductions exist of Nos. 50, 51, 52. The 5c on #36, 10c, 20c, 40c, 80c, and 1.60fr surcharges exist as unofficial reproductions only.

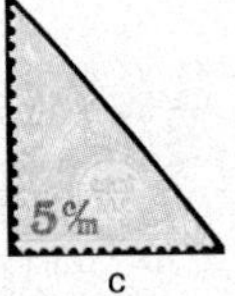
c

d

1905

On No. 2

No.	Type	Description	Unused	Used
54	A1 (c)	5c on half of ½g	5.00	5.00

On No. 21, "Bosta" in Black

No.	Type	Description	Unused	Used
55	A2 (d)	5c on 16g blk	200.00	100.00

On #55, "Bosta" is in black.

On No. 28, "Malekt" in Black

No.	Type	Description	Unused	Used
56	A2 (d)	5c on 16g blk	250.00	250.00
		Nos. 54-56 (3)	455.00	355.00

Nos. 55-56 issued Mar. 30.

The overprints and surcharges on Nos. 8 to 56 inclusive were handstamped, the work being very roughly done.

As is usual with handstamped overprints and surcharges there are many inverted and double, but most of them are fakes or unofficial reproductions.

Surcharged with New Values in Various Colors

and in Violet:

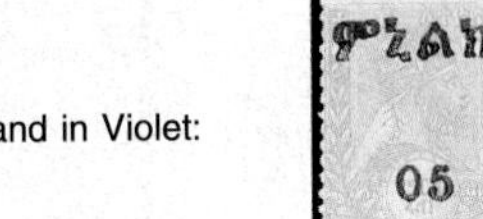

Overprint 14¾x3½mm

1906, Jan. 1

No.	Type	Description	Unused	Used
57	A1	5c on ¼g green	5.50	5.50
58	A1	10c on ½g red	8.50	8.50
59	A1	20c on 1g blue	8.50	8.50
60	A1	40c on 2g dk brn	8.50	8.50
61	A2	80c on 4g lilac brn	10.00	10.00
62	A2	1.60fr on 8g violet	15.00	15.00
63	A2	3.20fr on 16g black	32.50	32.50
		Nos. 57-63 (7)	88.50	88.50

Two types of the 4-character overprint ("Menelik"): 14x¾x3½mm and 16x4mm.

Surcharged with New Values

and in Violet Brown:

Overprint 16x4¼mm

1906, July 1

No.	Type	Description	Unused	Used
64	A1	5c on ¼g grn	7.25	7.25
a.		Surcharged "20"	50.00	50.00
65	A1	10c on ½g red	8.50	8.50
66	A1	20c on 1g blue	12.00	12.00
67	A1	40c on 2g dk brn	12.00	12.00
68	A2	80c on 4g lil brn	17.50	17.50
69	A2	1.60fr on 8g vio	17.50	17.50
70	A2	3.20fr on 16g blk	32.50	32.50
		Nos. 64-70 (7)	107.25	107.25

The control overprint reads "Menelik."

Surcharged in Violet:

e f

1907, July 1

No.	Type	Description	Unused	Used
71	A1 (e)	¼ on ¼g grn	7.00	7.00
72	A1 (e)	½ on ½g red	7.00	7.00
73	A1 (f)	1 on 1g blue	8.25	8.25
74	A1 (f)	2 on 2g dk brn	9.00	9.00
a.		Surcharged "40"	50.00	
75	A2 (f)	4 on 4g lil brn	9.75	9.75
a.		Surcharged "80"	47.50	
76	A2 (f)	8 on 8g vio	21.00	21.00
77	A2 (f)	16 on 16g blk	27.50	27.50
		Nos. 71-77 (7)	89.50	89.50

Nos. 71-72 are also found with stars farther away from figures.

The control overprint reads "Dagmawi" ("Second"), meaning Emperor Menelik II.

Nos. 2, 23 Surcharged in Bluish Green

1908, Aug. (?)

No.	Type	Description	Unused	Used
78	A1	1pi on ½g red (#2)	8.00	8.00
79	A1	1pi on ½g red (#23)	850.00	—

Official reproductions exist. Value, set $25.

Forgeries exist.

The surcharges on Nos. 57-78 are handstamped and are found double, inverted, etc.

Surcharged in Black

1908, Nov. 1

No.	Type	Description	Unused	Used
80	A1	¼p on ¼g grn	1.25	1.25
81	A1	½p on ½g red	1.25	1.25
82	A1	1p on 1g blue	1.75	1.75
83	A1	2p on 2g dk brn	3.00	3.00
84	A2	4p on 4g lil brn	4.25	4.25
85	A2	8p on 8g vio	10.00	10.00
86	A2	16p on 16g blk	15.00	15.00
		Nos. 80-86 (7)	36.50	36.50

Surcharges on Nos. 80-85 are found double, inverted, etc. Forgeries exist.

These are the 1st stamps valid for international mail.

King Solomon's Throne — A3

Menelik in Native Costume — A4

Menelik in Royal Dress — A5

1909, Jan. *Perf. 11½*

No.	Type	Description	Unused	Used
87	A3	¼g blue green	.60	.50
88	A3	½g rose	.65	.50
89	A3	1g green & org	3.50	1.25
90	A4	2g blue	2.50	1.50
91	A4	4g green & car	3.75	3.25
92	A5	8g ver & dp grn	9.00	5.75
93	A5	16g ver & car	12.50	9.00
		Nos. 87-93 (7)	32.50	21.75

For overprints see Nos. 101-115, J43-J49, J55-J56. For surcharges see Nos. 116-119.

Nos. 1-7 Handstamped and Surcharged in ms.

1911, Oct. 1 *Perf. 14x13½*

No.	Type	Description	Unused	Used
94	A1	¼g on ¼g grn	40.00	
95	A1	½g on ½g red	40.00	
96	A1	1g on 1g blue	40.00	
97	A1	2g on 2g dk brn	40.00	
98	A2	4g on 4g lil brn	40.00	
99	A2	8g on 8g violet	40.00	
100	A2	16g on 16g black	40.00	
		Nos. 94-100 (7)	280.00	

Nos. 94-100 are provisionals used at Dire-Dawa for 5 days. The overprint is abbreviated from "Affranchissement Exceptionnel Faute Timbres" (Special Franking Lacking Stamps). The overprints and surcharges were applied to stamps on cover and then canceled.

Nos. 94-100 without surcharges are forgeries.

Stamps of 1909 Handstamped in Violet or Black:

Nos. 101-102

Nos. 104-107

1917, Mar. 30 *Perf. 11½*

No.	Type	Description	Unused	Used
101	A3	¼g blue grn (V)	4.00	4.00
102	A3	½g rose (V)	4.00	4.00
104	A4	2g blue (Bk)	5.00	5.00
105	A4	4g grn & car (Bk)	10.00	10.00
106	A5	8g ver & dp grn (Bk)	15.00	15.00
107	A5	16g ver & car (Bk)	30.00	30.00
		Nos. 101-107 (6)	68.00	68.00

Coronation of Empress Zauditu and appointment of Prince Tafari as Regent and Heir to the throne.

Exist with overprint inverted and double.

Stamps of 1909 Overprinted in Blue, Black or Red:

Nos. 108-111

Nos. 112-115

1917, Oct. 1

No.	Type	Description	Unused	Used
108	A3	¼g blue grn (Bl)	1.00	1.00
109	A3	½g rose (Bl)	1.00	1.00
110	A3	1g grn & org (Bl)	2.00	2.00
111	A4	2g blue (R)	75.00	85.00
112	A4	2g blue (Bk)	1.00	1.00
113	A4	4g grn & car (Bl)	1.00	1.00
a.		Black overprint	10.00	10.00
114	A5	8g ver & dp grn (Bl)	1.00	1.00
115	A5	16g ver & car (Bl)	2.00	2.00
		Nos. 108-115 (8)	84.00	94.00

Coronation of Empress Zauditu.

Nos. 108-115 all exist with double overprint, inverted overprint, double overprint, one inverted, and various combinations.

Nos. 114-115 with Additional Surcharge

k

l

m n

1917, May 28

No.	Type	Description	Unused	Used
116	A5 (k)	¼g on 8g	2.50	2.50
117	A5 (l)	½g on 8g	2.50	2.50
118	A5 (m)	1g on 16g	6.50	6.50
119	A5 (n)	2g on 16g	7.00	7.00
		Nos. 116-119 (4)	18.50	18.50

Nos. 116-119 all exist with the numerals double and inverted and No. 116 with the Amharic surcharge missing.

Sommering's Gazelle — A6

Prince Tafari — A9

Cathedral of St. George A12

Empress Waizeri Zauditu — A18

¼g, Giraffes. ½g, Leopard. 2g, Prince Tafari, diff. 4g, Prince Tafari, diff. 8g, White rhinoceros. 12g, Somali ostriches. 1t, African elephant. 2t, Water buffalo. 3t, Lions. 5t, 10t, Empress Zauditu.

1919, July 16 Typo. *Perf. 11½*

120	A6	⅛g violet & brn	.20	.20
121	A6	¼g bl grn & drab	.20	.20
122	A6	½g scar & ol grn	.20	.20
123	A9	1g rose lil & gray grn	.20	.20
124	A9	2g dp ultra & fawn	.20	.20
125	A9	4g turq bl & org	.20	*2.50*
126	A12	6g lt blue & org	.25	.20
127	A12	8g ol grn & blk brn	.35	.20
128	A12	12g red vio & gray	.50	.30
129	A12	1t rose & gray blk	.90	.40
130	A12	2t black & brown	2.50	
131	A12	3t grn & dp org	2.50	1.90
132	A18	4t brn & lil rose	3.00	2.50
133	A18	5t carmine & gray	4.00	4.00
134	A18	10t gray grn & bis	8.00	5.25
		Nos. 120-134 (15)	23.20	
		Nos. 120-129,131-134 (14)		18.25

No. 130 was not issued.

For overprints see Nos. J50-J54. For surcharges see Nos. 135-154.

Reprints have brownish gum that is cracked diagonally. Originals have smooth, white gum. Reprints exist imperf. and some values with inverted centers. Value for set, unused or canceled, $5.

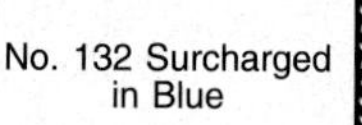

No. 132 Surcharged in Blue

1919, Oct.

135 A18 4g on 4t brn & lil rose 3.00 3.00

Nos. 135-154

The Amharic surcharge indicates the new value and, therefore, varies on Nos. 135-154. There are numerous defective letters and figures, several types of the "2" of "½," the errors "guerhce," "gnerche," etc.

Many varieties of surcharge, such as double, inverted, lines transposed or omitted, and inverted "2" in "½," exist.

There are many irregularly produced settings in imitation of Nos. 136-154 which differ slightly from the originals. These may be essays or proofs.

Stamps of 1919 Surcharged

1921-22

136	A6	½g on ⅛g vio & brn ('22)	1.00	1.00
137	A6	1g on ¼g grn & db	2.50	1.00
138	A9	2g on 1g lil brn & gray grn ('22)	1.00	1.50
139	A18	2g on 4t brn & lil rose ('22)	35.00	15.00
140	A6	2½g on ½g scar & ol grn	1.00	*1.50*
141	A9	4g on 2g ultra & fawn ('22)	1.00	*1.25*
		Nos. 136-141 (6)	41.50	21.25

No. 139 has been forged.

Stamps and Type of 1919 Surcharged

1925-28

142	A12	½g on 1t rose & gray blk ('26)	1.00	1.00
a.		Without colon ('28)	12.50	12.50
143	A18	½g on 5t car & gray ('26)	2.00	1.00
144	A12	1g on 6g bl & org	1.00	1.00
145	A12	1g on 12g lil & gray	400.00	400.00
146	A12	1g on 3t grn & org ('26)	22.50	16.00
147	A18	1g on 10t gray grn & bis ('26)	1.00	*1.00*
		Nos. 142-147 (6)	427.50	420.00

On #142 the surcharge is at the left side of the stamp, reading upward. On #142a it is at the right, reading downward. The two surcharges are from different, though similar, settings. On #146 the surcharge is at the right, reading upward. See note following #154.

Type of 1919 Surcharged

1926

147A A12 1g on 12g lil & gray 400.00

Forgeries exist.

Nos. 126-128 Surcharged

1926

148	A12	½g on 8g	3.00	1.25
149	A12	1g on 6g	80.00	50.00
150	A12	1g on 12g	350.00	
		Nos. 148-150 (3)	433.00	51.25

The Amharic line has 7 (½g) or 6 characters (1g).

Nos. 126-128, 131 Surcharged

1927

151	A12	½g on 8g	1.50	1.50
152	A12	1g on 6g	60.00	40.00
153	A12	1g on 12g	5.00	1.50
154	A12	1g on 3t	400.00	
		Nos. 151-154 (4)	466.50	43.00

The Amharic line has 7 (½g) or 4 characters (1g). No. 152 has the lines closer together than do the others.

Forgeries of No. 154 exist.

Prince Tafari — A22

Empress Zauditu — A23

1928, Sept. 5 Typo. *Perf. 13½x14*

155	A22	⅛m org & lt bl	.50	.45
156	A23	¼m ind & red org	.30	.45
157	A22	½m gray grn & blk	.50	.45
158	A23	1m dk car & blk	.30	.45
159	A22	2m dk bl & blk	.30	.45
160	A23	4m yel & olive	.30	.45
161	A22	8m vio & olive	.80	.45
162	A23	1t org brn & vio	.95	.65
163	A22	2t grn & bister	1.40	1.10
164	A23	3t choc & grn	2.25	1.25
		Nos. 155-164 (10)	7.60	6.15

For overprints and surcharges see Nos. 165-209, 217-230, C1-C10.

Preceding Issue Overprinted in Black, Violet or Red

1928, Sept. 1

165	A22	⅛m (Bk)	1.25	1.25
166	A23	¼m (V)	1.25	1.25
167	A22	½m (V)	1.25	1.25
168	A23	1m (V)	1.25	1.25
169	A22	2m (R)	1.25	1.25
170	A23	4m (Bk)	1.25	1.25
171	A22	8m (R)	1.25	1.25
172	A23	1t (Bk)	1.25	1.25
173	A22	2t (R)	1.90	1.90
174	A23	3t (R)	2.75	2.75
		Nos. 165-174 (10)	14.65	14.65

Opening of General Post Office, Addis Ababa.

Exist with overprint inverted, double, double, one inverted, etc.

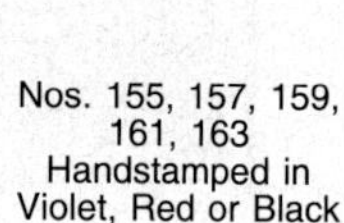

Nos. 155, 157, 159, 161, 163 Handstamped in Violet, Red or Black

1928, Oct. 7

175	A22	⅛m (V)	1.40	1.40
176	A22	½m (R)	1.40	1.40
177	A22	2m (R)	1.40	1.40
178	A22	8m (Bk)	1.40	1.40
179	A22	2t (V)	1.40	1.40
		Nos. 175-179 (5)	7.00	7.00

Crowning of Prince Tafari as king (Negus) on Oct. 7, 1928.

Nos. 175-177 exist with overprint vertical, inverted, double, etc.

Forgeries exist.

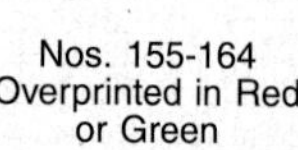

Nos. 155-164 Overprinted in Red or Green

1930, Apr. 3

180	A22	⅛m org & lt bl (R)	.25	.35
181	A23	¼m ind & red org (G)	.35	.35
182	A22	½m gray grn & blk (R)	.25	.35
183	A23	1m dk car & blk (G)	.35	.35
184	A22	2m dk bl & blk (R)	.35	.35
185	A23	4m yel & ol (R)	.50	.50
186	A22	8m vio & ol (R)	1.00	1.00
187	A23	1t org brn & vio (R)	2.25	2.25
188	A22	2t grn & bis (R)	3.00	3.00
189	A23	3t choc & grn (R)	4.00	4.00
		Nos. 180-189 (10)	12.30	12.50

Proclamation of King Tafari as King of Kings of Abyssinia under the name "Haile Selassie."

A similar overprint, set in four vertical lines, was printed on all denominations of the 1928 issue. It was not considered satisfactory and was rejected. The trial impressions were not placed on sale to the public, but some copies reached private hands and have been passed through the post.

Nos. 155-164 Overprinted in Red or Olive Brown

1930, Apr. 3

190	A22	⅛m orange & lt bl	.35	.35
191	A23	¼m ind & red org (OB)	.35	.35
192	A22	½m gray grn & blk	.75	.75
193	A23	1m dk car & blk (OB)	.35	.35
194	A22	2m dk blue & blk	.35	.35
195	A23	4m yellow & ol	.60	.60
196	A22	8m violet & ol	1.00	1.00
197	A23	1t org brn & vio	2.25	2.25
198	A22	2t green & bister	3.00	3.00
199	A23	3t chocolate & grn	3.75	3.75
		Nos. 190-199 (10)	12.75	12.75

Proclamation of King Tafari as Emperor Haile Selassie.

All stamps of this series exist with "H" of "HAILE" omitted and with many other varieties.

Nos. 155-164 Handstamped in Violet or Red

1930, Nov. 2

200	A22	⅛m (V)	.40	.40
201	A23	¼m (V)	.40	.40
202	A22	½m (R)	.40	.40
203	A23	1m (V)	.40	.40
204	A22	2m (R)	.40	.40
205	A23	4m (V)	.40	.40
206	A22	8m (V or R)	.90	.90
207	A23	1t (V)	1.25	1.25
208	A22	2t (V or R)	2.00	2.00
209	A23	3t (V or R)	3.00	3.00
		Nos. 200-209 (10)	9.55	9.55

Coronation of Emperor Haile Selassie, Nov. 2, 1930.

Haile Selassie Coronation Monument, Symbols of Empire — A24

1930 Engr. *Perf. 12½*

210	A24	1g orange	.40	.40
211	A24	2g ultra	.40	.40
212	A24	4g violet	.40	.40
213	A24	8g dull green	.70	.65
214	A24	1t brown	1.00	1.00
215	A24	3t green	1.50	1.50
216	A24	5t red brown	1.50	1.50
		Nos. 210-216 (7)	5.90	5.85

Coronation of Emperor Haile Selassie. Issued: 4g, 11/2; others, 11/23.

Reprints of Nos. 210 to 216 exist. Colors are more yellow and the ink is thicker and slightly glossy. Ink on the originals is dull and granular. Value 35c each.

Nos. 158-160, 164 Surcharged in Green, Red or Blue

Type I Type II

1931 *Perf. 13½x14*

No.	Type	Description	Unused	Used
217	A23	⅛m on 1m	.35	.35
218	A22	⅛m on 2m (R)	.35	.35
219	A23	⅛m on 4m	.35	.35
220	A23	¼m on 1m (Bl)	.35	.35
221	A22	¼m on 2m (R)	1.00	1.00
222	A23	¼m on 4m	1.00	1.00
225	A23	½m on 1m (Bl)	1.00	1.00
226	A22	½m on 2m (R)	1.00	1.00
227	A23	½m on 4m, type II	1.00	1.00
a.		½m on 4m, type I	9.00	9.00
228	A23	½m on 3t (R)	7.50	7.50
230	A22	1m on 2m (R)	1.25	1.25
		Nos. 217-230 (11)	15.15	15.15

The ½m on ⅛m orange & light blue and ½m on ¼m indigo & red orange were clandestinely printed and never sold at the post office.

No. 230 with double surcharge in red and blue is a color trial.

Many varieties exist.

Issued: 1m, Apr.; others, 4/20.

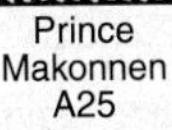

Prince Makonnen A25

Empress Menen A27

View of Hawash River and Railroad Bridge A26

Designs: 2g, 8g, Haile Selassie (profile). 4g, 1t, Statue of Menelik II. 3t, Empress Menen (full face). 5t, Haile Selassie (full face).

Perf. 12½, 12x12½, 12½x12

1931, June 27 **Engr.**

No.	Type	Description	Unused	Used
232	A25	⅛g red	.40	.20
233	A26	¼g olive green	.40	.20
234	A25	½g dark violet	.40	.20
235	A27	1g red orange	.50	.25
236	A27	2g ultra	.50	.25
237	A25	4g violet	.90	.40
238	A27	8g blue green	2.00	2.00
239	A25	1t chocolate	24.00	10.00
240	A27	3t yellow green	7.00	3.00
241	A27	5t red brown	12.00	5.50
		Nos. 232-241 (10)	48.10	22.00

For overprints see Nos. B1-B5. For surcharges see Nos. 242-246.

Reprints of Nos. 232-236, 238-240 are on thinner and whiter paper than the originals. On originals the ink is dull and granular. On reprints, heavy, caked and shiny. Value 20c each.

Nos. 232-236 Surcharged in Blue or Carmine similar to cut

1936, Jan. 29 *Perf. 12x12½, 12½x12*

No.	Type	Description	Unused	Used
242	A25	1c on ⅛g red	1.40	1.00
243	A26	2c on ¼g ol grn (C)	1.40	1.00
244	A25	3c on ½g dk vio	1.40	1.10
245	A27	5c on 1g red org	2.50	1.50
246	A27	10c on 2g ultra (C)	3.25	1.90
		Nos. 242-246 (5)	9.95	6.50

Catalogue values for unused stamps in this section, from this point to the end of the section, are for Never Hinged items.

Haile Selassie I

A32 A33

1942, Mar. 23 **Litho.** *Perf. 14x13½*

No.	Type	Description	Unused	Used
247	A32	4c lt bl grn, ind & blk	.50	.25
248	A32	10c rose, indigo & blk	1.50	.45
249	A32	20c dp ultra, ind & blk	3.00	.80
		Nos. 247-249 (3)	5.00	1.50

1942-43 **Unwmk.**

No.	Type	Description	Unused	Used
250	A33	4c lt bl grn & indigo	.50	.20
251	A33	8c yel org & indigo	.60	.20
252	A33	10c rose & indigo	.85	.20
253	A33	12c dull vio & indigo	.85	.25
254	A33	20c dp ultra & indigo	1.10	.40
255	A33	25c dull grn & indigo	1.60	.60
256	A33	50c dull brn & indigo	2.75	1.00
257	A33	60c lilac & indigo	3.75	1.25
		Nos. 250-257 (8)	12.00	4.10

Issued: 25c, 50c, 60c, 4/1/43; others, 6/22/42.

For surcharges see #258-262, 284, C18-C20.

Nos. 250-254 Surcharged in Black or Brown

1943, Nov. 3

No.	Type	Description	Unused	Used
258	A33	5c on 4c	45.00	45.00
259	A33	10c on 8c	45.00	45.00
260	A33	15c on 10c	45.00	45.00
261	A33	20c on 12c (Br)	45.00	45.00
262	A33	30c on 20c (Br)	45.00	45.00
		Nos. 258-262 (5)	225.00	225.00

Restoration of the Obelisk in Myazzia Place, Addis Ababa, and the 14th anniv. of the coronation of Emperor Haile Selassie.

On No. 262, "3" is surcharged on "2" of "20" to make "30."

A small number of sets exist with a somewhat different handstamped surcharge.

Palace of Menelik II A34

Menelik II — A35

Statue — A36

50c, Mausoleum. 65c, Menelik II (with scepter).

1944, Dec. 31 **Litho.** *Perf. 10½*

No.	Type	Description	Unused	Used
263	A34	5c green	1.25	.65
264	A35	10c red lilac	1.75	.85
265	A36	20c deep blue	3.00	1.75
266	A34	50c dull purple	3.50	1.75
267	A35	65c bister brown	6.50	2.75
		Nos. 263-267 (5)	16.00	7.75

Cent. of the birth of Menelik II, 8/18/44. Printed on gum-impregnated paper.

Unissued Semi-Postal Stamps Overprinted in Carmine:

Nurse & Baby — A39

Various Designs Inscribed "Croix Rouge"

1945, Aug. 7 **Photo.** *Perf. 11½*

No.	Type	Description	Unused	Used
268	A39	5c brt green	.95	.45
269	A39	10c brt red	.95	.45
270	A39	25c brt blue	.95	.45
271	A39	50c dk yellow brn	5.00	2.00
272	A39	1t brt violet	7.75	2.75
		Nos. 268-272 (5)	15.60	6.10

Nos. 268-272 without overprint were ordered printed in Switzerland before Ethiopia fell to the invading Italians, so were not delivered to Addis Ababa. After that country's liberation, the set was overprinted "V" and issued for ordinary postage. These stamps exist without overprint, but were not so issued. Value $1.25.

Some values exist inverted or double.

Forged overprints exist.

For surcharges see #B11-B15, B36-B40.

Lion of Judah — A44

Menelik II — A45

Mail Transport, Old and New A46

Designs: 50c, Old Post Office, Addis Ababa. 70c, Menelik II and Haile Selassie.

1947, Apr. 18 **Engr.** *Perf. 13*

No.	Type	Description	Unused	Used
273	A44	10c yellow org	2.50	.50
274	A45	20c deep blue	3.75	.75
275	A46	30c orange brn	5.75	1.25
276	A46	50c dk slate grn	13.00	2.50
277	A46	70c red violet	25.00	5.00
		Nos. 273-277 (5)	50.00	10.00

50th anniv. of Ethiopia's postal system.

Haile Selassie and Franklin D. Roosevelt — A49

Design: 65c, Roosevelt and US Flags.

Engraved and Photogravure

1947, May 23 **Unwmk.** *Perf. 12½*

No.	Type	Description	Unused	Used
278	A49	12c car lake & bl grn	.80	1.00
279	A49	25c dk blue & rose	.80	1.00
280	A49	65c blk, red & dp bl	1.60	2.00
		Nos. 278-280,C21-C22 (5)	15.20	15.00

King Sahle Selassie Reclining A50

King Sahle Selassie — A52

Design: 30c, View of Ankober.

1947, May 1 **Engr.** *Perf. 13*

No.	Type	Description	Unused	Used
281	A50	20c deep blue	1.75	.75
282	A50	30c dark purple	2.75	1.00
283	A52	$1 deep green	6.50	3.00
		Nos. 281-283 (3)	11.00	4.75

150th anniversary of Selassie dynasty.

No. 255 Surcharged in Orange

1947, July 14 *Perf. 14x13½*

No.	Type	Description	Unused	Used
284	A33	12c on 25c	60.00	60.00

Amba Alaguie A53

Designs: 2c, Trinity Church. 4c, Debra Sina. 5c, Mecan, near Achanguie. 8c, Lake Tana. 12c, 15c, Parliament Building, Addis Ababa. 20c, Aiba, near Mai Cheo. 30c, Bahr Bridge over Blue Nile. 60c, 70c, Canoe on Lake Tana. $1, Omo Falls. $3, Mt. Alamata. $5, Ras Dashan Mountains.

Perf. 13x13½

1947-53 **Engr.** **Wmk. 282**

No.	Type	Description	Unused	Used
285	A53	1c rose violet	.20	.20
286	A53	2c blue violet	.20	.20
a.		Unwatermarked ('51)	37.50	15.00
287	A53	4c green	.25	.20
288	A53	5c dark green	.25	.20
289	A53	8c deep orange	.45	.20
290	A53	12c red	.55	.20
290A	A53	15c dk ol brn ('53)	.50	.20
291	A53	20c blue	.80	.30
292	A53	30c orange brown	1.40	.40
292A	A53	60c red ('51)	1.60	.70
293	A53	70c rose lilac	2.25	.50
294	A53	$1 dk carmine rose	3.75	.50

295 A53 $3 bright blue 10.00 2.00
296 A53 $5 olive 16.00 4.00
Nos. 285-296 (14) 38.20 9.80

Issue dates: 15c, May 25, 1953; 60c, Feb. 10, 1951; others, Aug. 23, 1947.

Shades exist.

For overprints see Nos. 355-356. For surcharges see Nos. B6-B10, B16-B20.

Empress Waizero Menen and Emperor Haile Selassie A54

1949, May 5 Wmk. 282 *Perf. 13*
297 A54 20c blue 1.50 .70
298 A54 30c yellow org 1.50 .90
299 A54 50c purple 3.00 1.60
300 A54 80c green 3.50 2.00
301 A54 $1 red 6.25 3.00
Nos. 297-301 (5) 15.75 8.20

Central ornaments differ on each denomination.

8th anniv. of Ethiopia's liberation from Italian occupation.

Dejach Balcha Hospital A55

Abuna Petros — A56

Designs: 20c, Haile Selassie raising flag. 30c, Lion of Judah statue. 50c, Empress Waizero Menen, Haile Selassie and building.

Perf. 13x13½, 13½x13
1950, Nov. 2 Engr. Wmk. 282
302 A55 5c purple .95 .30
303 A56 10c deep plum 2.50 .60
304 A56 20c deep carmine 3.50 .75
305 A56 30c green 5.75 1.50
306 A55 50c deep blue 10.00 3.00
Nos. 302-306 (5) 22.70 6.15

20th anniv. of the coronation of Emperor Haile Selassie and Empress Menen.

Abbaye Bridge — A57

1951, Jan. 1 Unwmk. *Perf. 14*
308 A57 5c dk green & dk brn 3.50 .50
309 A57 10c dp orange & blk 5.00 .50
310 A57 15c dp blue & org brn 7.00 .50
311 A57 30c olive & lil rose 12.50 .80
312 A57 60c brown & dp bl 17.50 2.00
313 A57 80c purple & green 25.00 3.00
Nos. 308-313 (6) 70.50 7.30

Opening of the Abbaye Bridge over the Blue Nile.

Tomb of Prince Makonnen A58

1951, Mar. 2
Center in Black
314 A58 5c dark green 2.50 .60
315 A58 10c deep ultra 2.50 .05
316 A58 15c blue 4.50 .35
317 A58 30c claret 9.25 1.35
318 A58 80c rose carmine 12.50 2.00
319 A58 $1 orange brown 16.00 2.00
Nos. 314-319 (6) 47.25 6.65

55th anniversary of the Battle of Adwa.

Emperor Haile Selassie — A59

1952, July 23 *Perf. 13½*
320 A59 5c dark green .40 .20
321 A59 10c red orange .70 .25
322 A59 15c black 1.00 .35
323 A59 25c ultra 1.40 .35
324 A59 30c violet 1.75 .60
325 A59 50c rose red 2.50 .85
326 A59 65c chocolate 4.25 1.50
Nos. 320-326 (7) 12.00 4.10

60th birthday of Haile Selassie.

Open Road to Sea A60

Designs: 25c, 50c, Road and broken chain. 65c, Map. 80c, Allegory: Reunion. $1, Haile Selassie raising flag. $2, Ethiopian flag and seascape. $3, Haile Selassie addressing League of Nations.

Wmk. 282
1952, Sept. 11 Engr. *Perf. 13*
327 A60 15c brown carmine .85 .20
328 A60 25c red brown 1.10 .40
329 A60 30c yellow brown 2.00 .60
330 A60 50c purple 2.25 .75
331 A60 65c gray 3.50 .90
332 A60 80c blue green 4.00 .60
333 A60 $1 rose carmine 8.00 1.25
334 A60 $2 deep blue 14.00 2.00
335 A60 $3 magenta 30.00 3.50
Nos. 327-335 (9) 65.70 10.20

Issued to celebrate Ethiopia's federation with Eritrea, effected Sept. 11, 1952.

Haile Selassie and New Ethiopian Port A61

15c, 30c, Haile Selassie on deck of ship.

1953, Oct. 4
337 A61 10c red & dk brn 2.75 1.00
338 A61 15c blue & dk grn 3.00 1.00
339 A61 25c orange & dk brn 5.25 2.00
340 A61 30c red brn & dk grn 9.50 3.00
341 A61 50c purple & dk brn 17.00 4.00
Nos. 337-341 (5) 37.50 11.00

Federation of Ethiopia and Eritrea, 1st anniv.

Princess Tsahai at a Sickbed A62

Perf. 13x13½
1955, July 8 Engr. Wmk. 282
Cross Typo. in Red
342 A62 15c choc & ultra 1.00 .50
343 A62 20c green & orange 1.50 .60
344 A62 30c ultra & green 2.50 .75
Nos. 342-344 (3) 5.00 1.85

Ethiopian Red Cross, 20th anniv.
For surcharges see Nos. B33-B35.

Promulgating the Constitution — A63

Bishops' Consecration by Archbishop — A64

25c, Kagnew Battalion. 35c, Reunion with the Motherland. 50c, "Progress." 65c, Empress Waizero Menen & Emperor Haile Selassie.

Perf. 12½
1955, Nov. 3 Unwmk. Engr.
345 A63 5c green & choc .50 .25
346 A64 20c carmine & brn 1.10 .40
347 A64 25c magenta & gray 1.50 .60
348 A63 35c brown & red org 2.00 .75
349 A64 50c dk brn & ultra 3.00 1.10
350 A64 65c violet & car 4.25 1.75
Nos. 345-350 (6) 12.35 4.85

Silver jubilee of the coronation of Emperor Haile Selassie and Empress Waizero Menen.

Emperor Haile Selassie and Fair Emblem — A65

1955, Nov. 5 Wmk. 282
351 A65 5c green & ol grn .60 .20
352 A65 10c car & dp ultra .90 .25
353 A65 15c vio blk & grn 1.25 .35
354 A65 50c mag & red brn 1.75 .90
Nos. 351-354 (4) 4.50 1.70

Silver Jubilee Fair, Addis Ababa.

Nos. 291 and 292A Overprinted

1960, Apr. 7 *Perf. 13x13½*
355 A53 20c blue 1.50 1.00
356 A53 60c red 2.50 2.00

WRY, July 1, 1959-June 30, 1960.
The 60c without serifs is a trial printing.

Map of Africa, "Liberty" and Haile Selassie — A66

Emperor Haile Selassie — A67

Perf. 13½
1960, June 14 Engr. Unwmk.
357 A66 20c orange & green .60 .60
358 A66 80c orange & violet 1.50 .60
359 A66 $1 orange & maroon 1.75 .80
Nos. 357-359 (3) 3.85 2.00

2nd Conf. of Independent African States at Tunis. Issued in sheets of 10.

1960, Nov. 2 Wmk. 282 *Perf. 14*
360 A67 10c brown & blue .40 .20
361 A67 25c violet & emerald .85 .30
362 A67 50c dk bl & org yel 1.50 1.00
363 A67 65c slate grn & sal pink 2.00 1.00
364 A67 $1 indigo & rose vio 3.25 1.50
Nos. 360-364 (5) 8.00 4.00

30th anniv. of the coronation of Emperor Haile Selassie.

Africa Hall, UN Economic Commission for Africa — A68

1961, Apr. 15 Wmk. 282 *Perf. 14*
365 A68 80c ultra 1.00 .50

Africa Freedom Day, Apr. 15. Sheets of 10.

Map of Ethiopia, Olive Branch A69

1961, May 5 *Perf. 13x13½*
366 A69 20c green .25 .20
367 A69 30c violet blue .35 .20
368 A69 $1 brown 1.40 .60
Nos. 366-368 (3) 2.00 1.00

20th anniv. of Ethiopia's liberation from Italian occupation.

African Wild Ass A70

1961, June 16 Wmk. 282 *Perf. 14*
369 A70 5c shown .20 .20
370 A70 15c Eland .25 .20
371 A70 25c Elephant .35 .20
372 A70 35c Giraffe .50 .20
373 A70 50c Beisa .60 .35
374 A70 $1 Lion 1.90 .85
Nos. 369-374 (6) 3.80 2.00

Issued in sheets of 10. Used values are for CTO's.

Emperor Haile Selassie and Empress Waizero Menen — A71

1961, July 27 Unwmk. *Perf. 11*
375 A71 10c green .50 .25
376 A71 50c violet blue .90 .45
377 A71 $1 carmine rose 1.60 .90
Nos. 375-377 (3) 3.00 1.60

Golden wedding anniv. of the Emperor and Empress.

Warlike Horsemanship (Guks) — A72

15c, Hockey. 20c, Bicycling. 30c, Soccer. 50c, 1960 Olympic marathon winner, Abebe Bikila.

Photogravure and Engraved

1962, Jan. 14 *Perf. 12x11½*

378 A72 10c yel grn & car .20 .20
379 A72 15c pink & dk brn .20 .20
380 A72 20c red & black .25 .20
381 A72 30c ultra & dl pur .45 .20
382 A72 50c yellow & green .90 .20
Nos. 378-382 (5) 2.00 1.00

Third Africa Football (soccer) Cup, Addis Ababa, Jan. 14-22.

Malaria Eradication Emblem, World Map and Mosquito — A73

Wmk. 282

1962, Apr. 7 **Engr.** *Perf. 13½*

383 A73 15c black .20 .20
384 A73 30c purple .40 .25
385 A73 60c red brown 1.00 .55
Nos. 383-385 (3) 1.60 1.00

WHO drive to eradicate malaria.

Abyssinian Ground Hornbill A74

Birds: 15c, Abyssinian roller. 30c, Bataleur, vert. 50c, Double-toothed barbet, vert. $1, Didric cuckoo.

Perf. 11½

1962, May 5 **Unwmk.** **Photo.**

Granite Paper

386 A74 5c multicolored .25 .20
387 A74 15c emer, brn & ultra .45 .20
388 A74 30c lt brn, blk & red .85 .25
389 A74 50c multicolored 1.60 .60
390 A74 $1 multicolored 3.50 1.25
Nos. 386-390 (5) 6.65 2.50

See Nos. C77-C81, C97-C101, C107-C111.

Assab Hospital A75

15c, School at Assab. 20c, Church at Massawa. 50c, Mosque at Massawa. 60c, Assab port.

Wmk. 282

1962, Sept. 11 **Engr.** *Perf. 13½*

391 A75 3c purple .20 .20
392 A75 15c dark blue .20 .20
393 A75 20c green .25 .20
394 A75 50c brown .50 .25
395 A75 60c carmine rose .75 .35
Nos. 391-395 (5) 1.90 1.20

Federation of Ethiopia and Eritrea, 10th anniv.

King Bazen, Madonna and Stars over Bethlehem — A76

15c, Ezana, obelisks &temple. 20c, Kaleb & sailing fleet. 50c, Lalibela, rock-church and frescoes, vert. 60c, King Yekuno Amlak & Abuna Tekle Haimanot preaching in Ankober. 75c, King Zara Yacob & Maskal celebration. $1, King Lebna Dengel & battle against Mohammed Gragn.

Perf. 14½

1962, Nov. 2 **Unwmk.** **Photo.**

396 A76 10c multicolored .20 .20
397 A76 15c multicolored .25 .20
398 A76 20c multicolored .30 .20
399 A76 50c multicolored .50 .20
400 A76 60c multicolored .60 .30
401 A76 75c multicolored .90 .50
402 A76 $1 multicolored 1.25 .75
Nos. 396-402 (7) 4.00 2.35

32nd anniv. of the coronation of Emperor Haile Selassie and to commemorate ancient kings and saints.

Map of Ethiopian Telephone Network — A77

Wheat Emblem — A78

Designs: 50c, Radio mast and waves. 60c, Telegraph pole and rising sun.

Perf. 13½x14

1963, Jan. 1 **Engr.** **Wmk. 282**

403 A77 10c dark red .40 .20
404 A77 50c ultra 1.00 .40
405 A77 60c brown 1.25 .50
Nos. 403-405 (3) 2.65 1.10

10th anniv. of the Imperial Board of Telecommunications.

1963, Mar. 21 **Unwmk.** *Perf. 13½*

406 A78 5c deep rose .20 .20
407 A78 10c rose carmine .20 .20
408 A78 15c violet blue .20 .20
409 A78 30c emerald .30 .20
Nos. 406-409 (4) .90 .80

FAO "Freedom from Hunger" campaign.

Abuna Salama — A79

Queen of Sheba — A80

Spiritual Leaders: 15c, Abuna Aregawi. 30c, Abuna Tekle Haimanot. 40c. Yared. 60c, Zara Yacob.

1964, Jan. 3 **Unwmk.** *Perf. 13½*

410 A79 10c blue .45 .20
411 A79 15c dark green .75 .20
412 A79 30c brown red 1.10 .45
413 A79 40c dark blue 2.00 .75
414 A79 60c brown 2.75 1.40
Nos. 410-414 (5) 7.05 3.00

1964, Mar. 2 **Photo.** *Perf. 11½*

Ethiopian Empresses: 15c, Helen. 50c, Seble Wongel. 60c, Mentiwab. 80c, Taitu, consort of Menelik II.

Granite Paper

415 A80 10c multicolored .50 .20
416 A80 15c multicolored .60 .20
417 A80 50c multicolored 1.25 .50
418 A80 60c multicolored 2.25 .85
419 A80 80c multicolored 2.75 1.25
Nos. 415-419 (5) 7.35 3.00

Priest Teaching Alphabet to Children — A81

Eleanor Roosevelt (1884-1962) — A82

10c, Classroom. 15c, Woman learning to read. 40c, Students in chemistry laboratory. 60c, Graduation procession.

1964, June 1 **Unwmk.** *Perf. 11½*

Granite Paper

420 A81 5c brown .20 .20
421 A81 10c emerald .20 .20
422 A81 15c rose vio, vert. .20 .20
423 A81 40c vio blue, vert. .60 .25
424 A81 60c dark pur, vert. 1.00 .50
Nos. 420-424 (5) 2.20 1.35

Issued to publicize education.

1964, Oct. 11 **Photo.**

Granite Paper

Portrait in Slate Blue

425 A82 10c yellow bister .20 .20
426 A82 60c orange brown .80 .50
427 A82 80c green & gold 1.00 .70
Nos. 425-427 (3) 2.00 1.40

King Serse Dengel and View of Gondar, 1563 A83

Ethiopian Leaders: 10c, King Fasiladas and Gondar in 1632. 20c, King Yassu the Great and Gondar in 1682. 25c, Emperor Theodore II and map of Ethiopia. 60c, Emperor John IV and Battle of Gura, 1876. 80c, Emperor Menelik II and Battle of Adwa, 1896.

1964, Dec. 12 **Photo.** *Perf. 14½x14*

428 A83 5c multicolored .20 .20
429 A83 10c multicolored .20 .20
430 A83 20c multicolored .30 .20
431 A83 25c multicolored .50 .20
432 A83 60c multicolored .95 .50
433 A83 80c multicolored 1.10 .70
Nos. 428-433 (6) 3.25 2.00

Ethiopian Rose — A84

Flowers: 10c, Kosso tree. 25c, St.-John's-wort. 35c, Parrot's-beak. 60c, Maskal daisy.

1965, Mar. 30 *Perf. 12x13½*

434 A84 5c multicolored .20 .20
435 A84 10c multicolored .20 .20
436 A84 25c multicolored .45 .20
437 A84 35c multicolored .85 .25
438 A84 60c green, yel & org 1.10 .40
Nos. 434-438 (5) 2.80 1.25

ITU Emblem, Old and New Communication Symbols — A85

Perf. 13½x14½

1965, May 17 **Litho.** **Unwmk.**

439 A85 5c blue, indigo & yel .20 .20
440 A85 10c blue, indigo & org .25 .20
441 A85 60c blue, indigo & lil rose .90 .50
Nos. 439-441 (3) 1.35 .90

Cent. of the ITU.

Laboratory A86

Designs: 5c, Textile spinning mill. 10c, Sugar factory. 20c, Mountain road. 25c, Autobus. 30c, Diesel locomotive and bridge. 35c, Railroad station, Addis Ababa.

1965, July 19 **Photo.** *Perf. 11½*

Granite Paper

Portrait in Black

442 A86 3c sepia .20 .20
443 A86 5c dull pur & buff .20 .20
444 A86 10c black & gray .20 .20
445 A86 20c green & pale yel .25 .20
446 A86 25c dk brown & yel .35 .20
447 A86 30c maroon & gray .55 .25
448 A86 35c dk blue & gray .65 .35
Nos. 442-448 (7) 2.40 1.60

For overprints see Nos. 609-612.

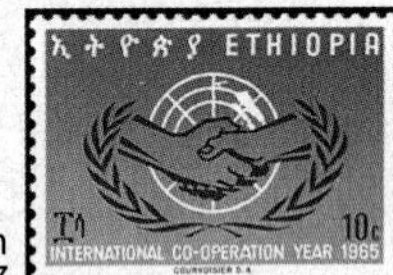

ICY Emblem A87

1965, Oct. 24 **Unwmk.** *Perf. 11½*

Granite Paper

449 A87 10c blue & red brn .25 .20
450 A87 50c dp blue & red brn .75 .40
451 A87 80c vio blue & red brn 1.00 .60
Nos. 449-451 (3) 2.00 1.20

International Cooperation Year, 1965.

National Bank Emblem A88

Designs: 10c, Commercial Bank emblem. 60c, Natl. and Commercial Bank buildings.

1965, Nov. 2 **Photo.** *Perf. 13*

452 A88 10c dp car, blk & indigo .35 .20
453 A88 30c ultra, blk & indigo .65 .30
454 A88 60c black, yel & indigo 1.00 .50
Nos. 452-454 (3) 2.00 1.00

Natl. and Commercial Banks of Ethiopia.

"Light and Peace" Press Building A89

1966, Apr. 5 **Engr.** *Perf. 13*

455 A89 5c pink & black .20 .20
456 A89 15c lt yel grn & blk .35 .20
457 A89 30c orange yel & blk .60 .30
Nos. 455-457 (3) 1.15 .70

Opening of the "Light and Peace" Printing Press building.

Kabaro Drum — A90

Musical Instruments: 10c, Bagana harp. 35c, Messenko guitar. 50c, Krar lyre. 60c, Wachent flutes.

1966, Sept. 9 Photo. *Perf. 13½*

458 A90 5c brt green & blk .20 .20
459 A90 10c dull blue & blk .20 .20
460 A90 35c orange & blk .60 .25
461 A90 50c yellow & blk .90 .35
462 A90 60c rose car & blk 1.10 .60
Nos. 458-462 (5) 3.00 1.60

Emperor Haile Selassie — A91

1966, Nov. 1 Unwmk. *Perf. 12*

463 A91 10c black, gold & grn .20 .20
464 A91 15c black, gold & dp car .35 .20
465 A91 40c black & gold 1.00 .60
Nos. 463-465 (3) 1.55 1.00

50 years of leadership of Emperor Haile Selassie.

UNESCO Emblem and Map of Africa A92

Wmk. 282

1966, Nov. 30 Litho. *Perf. 13½*

466 A92 15c blue car & blk .35 .20
467 A92 60c olive, brn & dk bl .90 .45

20th anniv. of UNESCO.

WHO Headquarters, Geneva — A93

1966, Nov. 30

468 A93 5c olive, ultra & brn .80 .20
469 A93 40c brown, pur & emer 2.50 .35

Opening of WHO Headquarters, Geneva.

Expo '67 Ethiopian Pavilion and Columns of Axum (Replica) — A94

Perf. 12x13½

1967, May 2 Photo. Unwmk.

470 A94 30c brt blue & multi .50 .25
471 A94 45c multicolored .65 .30
472 A94 80c gray & multi 1.25 .45
Nos. 470-472 (3) 2.40 1.00

EXPO '67, Intl. Exhibition, Montreal, Apr. 28-Oct. 27, 1967.

Diesel Train and Map — A95

1967, June 7 Photo. *Perf. 12*

473 A95 15c multicolored .60 .30
474 A95 30c multicolored 1.40 .75
475 A95 50c multicolored 2.00 .95
Nos. 473-475 (3) 4.00 2.00

Djibouti-Addis Ababa railroad, 50th anniv.

Papilionidae Aethiops — A96

Various Butterflies.

Perf. 13½x13

1967, June 30 Photo. Unwmk.

476 A96 5c buff & multi .35 .20
477 A96 10c lilac & multi .75 .20
478 A96 20c multicolored 1.25 .45
479 A96 35c blue & multi 2.50 .90
480 A96 40c multicolored 4.00 1.25
Nos. 476-480 (5) 8.85 3.00

Emperor Haile Selassie and Lion of Judah A97

1967, July 21 *Perf. 11½*

Granite Paper

481 A97 10c dk brn, emer & gold .25 .20
482 A97 15c dk brn, yel & gold .40 .20
483 A97 $1 dk brn, red & gold 1.75 .75
Nos. 481-483 (3) 2.40 1.15

Souvenir Sheet

484 A97 $1 dk brn, pur & gold 7.00 7.00

75th birthday of Emperor Haile Selassie.

Microscope and Ethiopian Flag — A98

1967, Nov. 6 Litho. *Perf. 13*

Flag in Grn, Yel, Red & Blk

485 A98 5c blue .20 .20
486 A98 30c ocher .50 .25
487 A98 $1 violet 1.75 .80
Nos. 485-487 (3) 2.45 1.25

2nd Intl. Conf. on the Global Impact of Applied Microbiology, Addis Ababa, 11/6-12.

Wall Painting from Debre Berhan Selassie Church, Gondar, 17th Century — A99

ITY Emblem and: 25c, Votive throne from Atsbe Dera, 4th Cent. B.C., vert. 35c, Prehistoric cave painting, Harar Province. 50c, Prehistoric stone tools, Melke Kontoure, vert.

1967, Nov. 20 Photo. *Perf. 14½*

488 A99 15c multicolored 2.00 1.00
489 A99 25c yel grn, buff & blk 2.00 1.00
490 A99 35c green, brn & blk 2.00 1.00
491 A99 50c yellow & blk 3.00 2.00
Nos. 488-491 (4) 9.00 5.00

International Tourist Year, 1967.

A100

A101

Crosses of Lalibela: 5c, Processional Bronze Cross, Biet-Maryam Church. 10c, Processional copper cross. 15c, Copper cross, Biet-Maryam church. 20c, Lalibela-style cross. 50c, Chiseled copper cross, Madhani Alem church.

1967, Dec. 7 Photo. *Perf. 14½*

Crosses in Silver

492 A100 5c yellow & blk .20 .20
493 A100 10c red orange & blk .20 .20
494 A100 15c violet & blk .30 .20
495 A100 20c brt rose & blk .45 .20
496 A100 50c orange yel & blk 1.40 .50
Nos. 492-496 (5) 2.55 1.30

Perf. 14x13½

1968, Apr. 18 Litho. Unwmk.

Designs: 10c, Emperor Theodore (1818?-1868). 20c, Emperor Theodore and lions, horiz. 50c, Imperial crown.

497 A101 10c lt vio, ocher & brn .30 .20
498 A101 20c lilac, brn & dk vio .50 .20
499 A101 50c dk grn, org & rose cl 1.00 .40
Nos. 497-499 (3) 1.80 .80

Human Rights Flame A102

1968, May 31 Unwmk. *Perf. 14½*

500 A102 15c pink, red & blk .30 .30
501 A102 $1 lt bl, brt bl & blk 1.50 1.50

International Human Rights Year, 1968.

Shah Riza Pahlavi, Emperor and Flags A103

1968, June 3 Litho. *Perf. 13½*

502 A103 5c multicolored .20 .20
503 A103 15c multicolored .25 .25
504 A103 30c multicolored .85 .85
Nos. 502-504 (3) 1.30 1.30

Visit of Shah Mohammed Riza Pahlavi of Iran.

Emperor Haile Selassie Appealing to League of Nations, 1935 — A104

35c, African Unity Building and map of Africa. $1, World map, symbolizing intl. relations.

1968, July 22 Photo. *Perf. 14x13½*

505 A104 15c bl, red, blk & gold .25 .20
506 A104 35c blk, emer, red & gold .50 .50
507 A104 $1 dk bl, lil, blk & gold 1.50 2.00
Nos. 505-507 (3) 2.25 2.70

Ethiopia's struggle for peace. Issued with tabs on bottom row.

WHO Emblem A105

Perf. 14x13½

1968, Aug. 30 Litho. Unwmk.

508 A105 15c brt green & blk .25 .25
509 A105 60c red lilac & blk .90 .90

20th anniv. of the WHO.

Abebe Bikila, Marathon Runner A106

1968, Oct. 12 *Perf. 11½*

510 A106 10c shown .20 .20
511 A106 15c Soccer .25 .25
512 A106 20c Boxing .30 .30
513 A106 40c Basketball .60 .60
514 A106 50c Bicycling .90 .90
Nos. 510-514 (5) 2.25 2.25

19th Olympic Games, Mexico City, 10/12-27.

Arrussi Woman — A107

Regional Costumes: 15c, Man from Gemu Gefa. 20c, Gojam man. 30c, Kefa man. 35c, Harar woman. 50c, Ilubabor grass coat. 60c, Woman from Eritrea.

Perf. 13½x13

1968, Dec. 10 Photo. Unwmk.

515 A107 5c silver & multi .25 .20
516 A107 15c silver & multi .25 .20
517 A107 20c silver & multi .25 .20
518 A107 30c silver & multi .35 .30
519 A107 35c silver & multi .40 .35
520 A107 50c silver & multi .80 .60
521 A107 60c silver & multi 1.10 .85
Nos. 515-521 (7) 3.40 2.70

See Nos. 575-581.

Message Stick and Amharic Postal Emblem A108

1969, Mar. 10 Litho. *Perf. 14*

522 A108 10c emerald, blk & brn .50 .50
523 A108 15c yellow, blk & brn .50 .50
524 A108 35c multicolored .75 .75
Nos. 522-524 (3) 1.75 1.75

Ethiopian postal service, 75th anniv.

ILO Emblem A109

1969, Apr. 11 Litho. *Perf. 14½*
525 A109 15c orange & blk .30 .30
526 A109 60c emerald & blk 1.25 1.25

50th anniv. of the ILO.

Dove, Red Cross, Crescent, Lion and Sun Emblems A110

1969, May 8 Wmk. 282 *Perf. 13*
527 A110 5c lt ultra, blk & red .20 .20
528 A110 15c lt ultra, grn & red .30 .30
529 A110 30c lt ultra, vio bl & red .60 .60
Nos. 527-529 (3) 1.10 1.10

League of Red Cross Societies, 50th anniv.

Endybis Silver Coin, 3rd Century — A111

Ancient Ethiopian Coins: 10c, Gold of Ezana, 4th cent. 15c, Gold of Kaleb, 6th cent. 30c, Bronze of Armah, 7th cent. 40c, Bronze of Wazena, 7th cent. 50c, Silver of Gersem, 8th cent.

1969, June 19 Photo. *Perf. 14½*
530 A111 5c ultra, blk & sil .20 .20
531 A111 10c brt red, blk & gold .25 .25
532 A111 15c brown, blk & gold .35 .35
533 A111 30c dp car, blk & brnz .65 .65
534 A111 40c dk green, blk & brnz .80 .80
535 A111 50c dp violet, blk & sil 1.25 1.25
Nos. 530-535 (6) 3.50 3.50

Zebras and Tourist Year Emblem A112

Designs: 10c, Camping. 15c, Fishing. 20c, Water skiing. 25c, Mountaineering, vert.

Perf. 13x13½, 13½x13
1969, Aug. 29 Litho. Unwmk.
536 A112 5c multicolored .20 .20
537 A112 10c multicolored .20 .20
538 A112 15c multicolored .25 .30
539 A112 20c multicolored .40 .50
540 A112 25c multicolored .50 .80
Nos. 536-540 (5) 1.55 2.00

International Year of African Tourism.

Stylized Bird and UN Emblem A113

UN 25th anniv.: 30c, Stylized flowers, UN and peace emblems, vert. 60c, Stylized bird, UN emblem and plane.

1969, Oct. 24 Unwmk. *Perf. 11½*
541 A113 10c lt blue & multi .20 .20
542 A113 30c lt blue & multi .45 .45
543 A113 60c lt blue & multi 1.00 1.00
Nos. 541-543 (3) 1.65 1.65

Ancient Cross and Holy Family A114

Designs: Various ancient crosses.

Perf. 14½x13½
1969, Dec. 10 Photo.
544 A114 5c black, yel & dk bl .20 .20
545 A114 10c black & yellow .20 .30
546 A114 25c black, yel & grn .50 .75
547 A114 60c black & ocher 1.25 1.50
Nos. 544-547 (4) 2.15 2.75

Ancient Figurines — A115

Ancient Ethiopian Pottery: 20c, Vases, Yeha period, 4th-3rd centuries B.C. 25c, Vases and jugs, Axum, 4th-6th centuries A.D. 35c, Bird-shaped jug and jugs, Matara, 4th-6th centuries A.D. 60c, Decorated pottery, Adulis, 6th-7th centuries A.D.

1970, Feb. 6 Photo. *Perf. 14½*
548 A115 10c black & multi .50 .50
549 A115 20c black & multi .50 .50
550 A115 25c black & multi .50 .50
551 A115 35c black & multi 1.00 1.00
552 A115 60c black & multi 2.00 2.00
Nos. 548-552 (5) 4.50 4.50

Medhane Alem Church — A116

Rock Churches of Lalibela, 12th-13th Centuries: 10c, Bieta Emmanuel. 15c, The four Rock Churches of Lalibela. 20c, Bieta Mariam. 50c, Bieta Giorgis.

1970, Apr. 15 Unwmk. *Perf. 13*
553 A116 5c brown & multi .20 .20
554 A116 10c brown & multi .20 .20
555 A116 15c brown & multi .30 .30
556 A116 20c brown & multi .50 .50
557 A116 50c brown & multi 1.15 1.15
Nos. 553-557 (5) 2.35 2.35

Sailfish Tang A117

Tropical Fish: 10c, Undulate triggerfish. 15c, Orange butterflyfish. 25c, Butterflyfish. 50c, Imperial Angelfish.

1970, June 19 Photo. *Perf. 12½*
558 A117 5c multicolored .20 .20
559 A117 10c multicolored .20 .20
560 A117 15c multicolored .30 .30
561 A117 25c multicolored .70 .70
562 A117 50c multicolored 1.40 1.40
Nos. 558-562 (5) 2.80 2.80

Education Year Emblem — A118

1970, Aug. 14 Unwmk. *Perf. 13½*
563 A118 10c multicolored .20 .20
564 A118 20c gold, ultra & emer .35 .35
565 A118 50c gold, emer & org .85 .85
Nos. 563-565 (3) 1.40 1.40

Issued for International Education Year.

Map of Africa — A119

30c, Flag of Organization of African Unity. 40c, OAU Headquarters, Addis Ababa.

1970, Sept. 21 Photo. *Perf. 13½*
566 A119 20c multicolored .25 .25
567 A119 30c multicolored .40 .40
568 A119 40c green & multi .75 .75
Nos. 566-568 (3) 1.40 1.40

Africa Unity Day and Organization of African Unity.

Emperor Haile Selassie — A120

1970, Oct. 30 Unwmk. *Perf. 14½*
569 A120 15c Prus bl & multi .20 .20
570 A120 50c multicolored .65 .65
571 A120 60c multicolored 1.50 1.25
Nos. 569-571 (3) 2.35 2.10

Coronation, 40th anniv.

Buildings — A121

1970, Dec. 30 Litho. *Perf. 13½*
572 A121 10c ver & multi .20 .20
573 A121 50c brown & multi 1.00 1.00
574 A121 80c multicolored 1.25 1.25
Nos. 572-574 (3) 2.45 2.45

Opening of new Posts, Telecommunications and General Post Office buildings.

Costume Type of 1968

Regional Costumes: 5c, Warrior from Begemdir and Semien. 10c, Woman from Bale. 15c, Warrior from Welega. 20c,Woman from Shoa. 25c, Man from Sidamo. 40c, Woman from Tigre. 50c, Man from Welo.

1971, Feb. 17 Photo. *Perf. 11½*
Granite Paper
575 A107 5c gold & multi .20 .20
576 A107 10c gold & multi .20 .20
577 A107 15c gold & multi .25 .25
578 A107 20c gold & multi .30 .30
579 A107 25c gold & multi .40 .40
580 A107 40c gold & multi .55 .55
581 A107 50c gold & multi 1.10 1.10
Nos. 575-581 (7) 3.00 3.00

Plane's Tail with Emblem — A122

Designs: 10c, Ethiopian scenes. 20c, Nose of Boeing 707. 60c, Pilots in cockpit, and engine. 80c, Globe with routes shown.

1971, Apr. 8 *Perf. 14½x14*
582 A122 5c multicolored .20 .20
583 A122 10c multicolored .20 .20
584 A122 20c multicolored .30 .30
585 A122 60c multicolored 1.00 1.00
586 A122 80c multicolored 1.40 1.40
Nos. 582-586 (5) 3.10 3.10

Ethiopian Airlines, 25th anniversary. Issued with tabs on bottom row.

Fountain of Life, 15th Century Gospel Book — A123

Ethiopian Paintings: 10c, King David, 15th cent. manuscript. 25c, St. George, 17th cent. painting on canvas. 50c, King Lalibela, 18th cent. painting on wood. 60c, Yared singing before King Kaleb. Mural in Axum Cathedral.

1971, June 15 Photo. *Perf. 11½*
Granite Paper
587 A123 5c tan & multi .20 .20
588 A123 10c pale sal & multi .20 .20
589 A123 25c lemon & multi .30 .30
590 A123 50c yellow & multi .80 .80
591 A123 60c gray & multi 1.25 1.25
Nos. 587-591 (5) 2.75 2.75

Black and White Heads, Globes A124

Designs: 60c, Black and white hand holding globe. 80c, Four races, globes.

1971, Aug. 31 Unwmk.
592 A124 10c org, red brn & blk .20 .20
593 A124 60c green, bl & blk .75 .75
594 A124 80c bl, org, yel & blk 1.25 1.25
Nos. 592-594 (3) 2.20 2.20

Intl. Year Against Racial Discrimination.

Emperor Menelik II and Reading of Treaty of Ucciali A125

Contemporary Paintings: 30c, Menelik II on horseback gathering the tribes. 50c, Ethiopians and Italians in Battle of Adwa. 60c, Menelik II and Taitu at head of their armies.

1971, Oct. 20 Litho. *Perf. 13½*

595 A125 10c multicolored .20 .20
596 A125 30c multicolored .50 .50
597 A125 50c multicolored .75 .75
598 A125 60c multicolored 1.25 1.25
Nos. 595-598 (4) 2.70 2.70

75th anniversary of victory of Adwa over the Italians, March 1, 1896.

Two telephones, 1897, Menelik II and Prince Makonnen — A126

Designs: 10c, Haile Selassie Broadcasting and Map of Ethiopia. 30c, Ethiopians around television set. 40c, Telephone microwave circuits. 60c, Map of Africa on globe and telephone dial.

1971, Nov. 2

599 A126 5c brown & multi .20 .20
600 A126 10c yellow & multi .20 .20
601 A126 30c vio bl & multi .40 .40
602 A126 40c black & multi .55 .55
603 A126 60c vio bl & multi 1.10 1.10
Nos. 599-603 (5) 2.45 2.45

Telecommunications in Ethiopia, 75th anniv.

UNICEF Emblem, Mother and Child — A127

UNICEF Emblem and: 10c, Children drinking milk. 15c, Man holding sick child. 30c, Kindergarten class. 50c, Father and son.

1971, Dec. 15 Unwmk.

604 A127 5c yellow & multi .20 .20
605 A127 10c pale brn & multi .20 .20
606 A127 15c rose & multi .20 .20
607 A127 30c violet & multi .45 .45
608 A127 50c green & multi .75 .75
Nos. 604-608 (5) 1.80 1.80

25th anniv. of UNICEF.

Nos. 445-448 Overprinted

1972, Jan. 28 Photo. *Perf. 11*

Portrait in Black

609 A86 20c grn & pale yel .30 .30
610 A86 25c dk brn & yel .45 .45
611 A86 30c maroon & gray .65 .65
612 A86 35c dk blue & gray .80 .80
Nos. 609-612 (4) 2.20 2.20

1st meeting of UN Security Council in Africa.

River Boat on Lake Haik — A128

1972, Feb. 7 Litho. *Perf. 11½*

Granite Paper

613 A128 10c shown .25 .20
614 A128 20c Boats on Lake Abaya .40 .30
615 A128 30c on Lake Tana .75 .60
616 A128 60c on Baro River 1.60 1.25
Nos. 613-616 (4) 3.00 2.35

Proclamation of Cyrus the Great — A129

1972, Mar. 28 Photo. *Perf. 14x14½*

617 A129 10c red & multi .20 .20
618 A129 60c emerald & multi .90 .90
619 A129 80c gray & multi 1.25 1.25
Nos. 617-619 (3) 2.35 2.35

2500th anniversary of the founding of the Persian empire by Cyrus the Great.

Houses, Sidamo Province A130

Ethiopian Architecture: 10c, Tigre Province. 20c, Eritrea Province. 40c, Addis Ababa. 80c, Shoa Province.

1972, Apr. 11 Litho. *Perf. 13½*

620 A130 5c black & multi .20 .20
621 A130 10c black, gray & brn .20 .20
622 A130 20c black & multi .30 .30
623 A130 40c black, bl grn & brn .60 .60
624 A130 80c black, brn & red brn 1.40 1.40
Nos. 620-624 (5) 2.70 2.70

Hands Holding Map of Ethiopia — A131

10c, Hands shielding Ethiopians. 25c, Map of Africa, hands reaching for African Unity emblem. 50c, Brown & white hands clasped, UN emblem. 60c, Hands protecting dove. Each denomination shows different portrait of the Emperor.

Perf. 14½x14

1972, July 21 Litho. Unwmk.

625 A131 5c scarlet & multi .20 .20
626 A131 10c ultra & multi .20 .20
627 A131 25c vio bl & multi .30 .30
628 A131 50c lt blue & multi .65 .65
629 A131 60c brown & multi .80 .80
Nos. 625-629 (5) 2.15 2.15

80th birthday of Emperor Haile Selassie.

Running, Flags of Mexico, Japan, Italy — A132

1972, Aug. 25 *Perf. 13½x13*

630 A132 10c shown .20 .20
631 A132 30c Soccer .40 .40
632 A132 50c Bicycling .80 .80
633 A132 60c Boxing 1.10 1.10
Nos. 630-633 (4) 2.50 2.50

20th Olympic Games, Munich, Germany, Aug. 26-Sept. 11.

Open Bible, Cross and Orbit A133

Designs: 50c, First and 1972 headquarters of the British and Foreign Bible Society, vert. 80c, First Amharic Bible.

1972, Sept. 25 Photo. *Perf. 13½*

634 A133 20c deep red & multi .30 .30
635 A133 50c deep red & multi .65 .65
636 A133 80c deep red & multi 1.25 1.25
Nos. 634-636 (3) 2.20 2.20

United Bible Societies World Assembly, Addis Ababa, Sept. 1972.

Security Council Meeting A134

Designs: 60c, Building where Security Council met. 80c, Map of Africa with flags of participating members.

1972, Nov. 1 Litho. *Perf. 13½*

637 A134 10c lt bl & vio bl .20 .20
638 A134 60c multicolored .75 .75
639 A134 80c multicolored 1.50 1.50
Nos. 637-639 (3) 2.45 2.45

First United Nations Security Council meeting, Addis Ababa, Jan. 28-Feb. 4, 1972.

Fish in Polluted Sea A135

Designs: 30c, Fisherman, beacon, family. 80c, Polluted seashore.

1973, Feb. 23 Photo. *Perf. 13½*

640 A135 20c gold & multi .30 .30
641 A135 30c gold & multi .45 .45
642 A135 80c gold & multi 1.25 1.25
Nos. 640-642 (3) 2.00 2.00

World message from the sea, Ethiopian anti-pollution campaign.

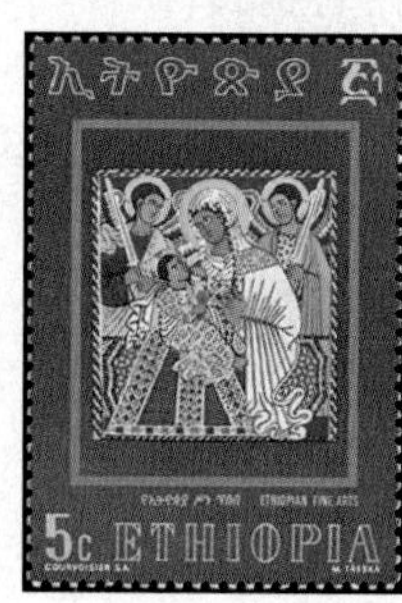

INTERPOL and Ethiopian Police Emblems — A136

50c, INTERPOL emblem & General Secretariat, Paris. 60c, INTERPOL emblem.

1973, Mar. 20 Photo. *Perf. 13½*

643 A136 40c dull orange & blk .65 .65
644 A136 50c blue, blk & yel .85 .85
645 A136 60c dk carmine & blk 1.00 1.00
Nos. 643-645 (3) 2.50 2.50

50th anniversary of International Criminal Police Organization (INTERPOL).

Virgin of Emperor Zara Yaqob A137

Ethiopian Art: 15c, Crucifixion, Zara Yaqob period. 30c, Virgin and Child, from Entoto Mariam Church. 40c, Christ, contemporary mosaic. 80c, The Evangelists, contemporary bas-relief.

1973, May 15 Photo. *Perf. 11½*

Granite Paper

646 A137 5c brown & multi .20 .20
647 A137 15c dp blue & multi .20 .20
648 A137 30c gray grn & multi .50 .50
649 A137 40c multicolored .60 .60
650 A137 80c slate & multi 1.50 1.50
Nos. 646-650 (5) 3.00 3.00

Free African States in 1963 and 1973 A138

Designs (Map of Africa and): 10c, Flags of OAU members. 20c, Symbols of progress. 40c, Dove and people. 80c, Emblems of various UN agencies.

1973 May 25 *Perf. 14½x14*

651 A138 5c red & multi .20 .20
652 A138 10c ol gray & multi .20 .20
653 A138 20c green & multi .35 .35
654 A138 40c sepia & multi .70 .70
655 A138 80c lt blue & multi 1.75 1.75
Nos. 651-655 (5) 3.20 3.20

OAU, 10th anniv.

Scouts Saluting Ethiopian and Scout Flags — A139

Designs: 15c, Road and road sign. 30c, Girl Scout reading to old man. 40c, Scout and disabled people. 60c, Ethiopian Boy Scout.

1973, July 10 Photo. *Perf. 11½*

Granite Paper

656 A139 5c blue & multi .20 .20
657 A139 15c lt green & multi .25 .25
658 A139 30c yellow & multi .50 .50
659 A139 40c crimson & multi .65 .65
660 A139 60c violet & multi 1.25 1.25
Nos. 656-660 (5) 2.85 2.85

24th Boy Scout World Conference, Nairobi, Kenya, July 16-21.

WMO Emblem A140

50c, WMO emblem, anemometer. 60c, Weather satellite over earth, WMO emblem.

1973, Sept. 4 Photo. *Perf. 13½*

661 A140 40c black, bl & dl bl .55 .55
662 A140 50c dull blue & blk .65 .65
663 A140 60c dull blue & multi 1.00 1.00
Nos. 661-663 (3) 2.20 2.20

Cent. of intl. meteorological cooperation. Printed with tabs at top of sheet inscribed in Amharic and tabs at bottom with "ETHIOPIA."

Prince Makonnen, Duke of Harar — A141

Human Rights Flame — A142

5c, Old wall of Harar. 20c, Operating room. 40c, Boy Scouts learning 1st aid & hospital. 80c, Prince Makonnen & hospital.

1973, Nov. 1 Unwmk. *Perf. 14½*

No.	Type	Value	Description	Unused	Used
664	A141	5c	gray & multi	.20	.20
665	A141	10c	red brn & multi	.20	.20
666	A141	20c	green & multi	.30	.30
667	A141	40c	brown red & multi	.80	.65
668	A141	80c	ultra & multi	1.50	1.40
			Nos. 664-668 (5)	3.00	2.75

Opening of Prince Makonnen Memorial Hospital.

Perf. 11½

1973, Nov. 16 Photo. Unwmk.

Granite Paper

No.	Type	Value	Description	Unused	Used
669	A142	40c	yel, gold & dk grn	.60	.60
670	A142	50c	lt grn, gold & dk grn	.75	.75
671	A142	60c	org, gold & dk grn	1.00	1.00
			Nos. 669-671 (3)	2.35	2.35

25th anniversary of the Universal Declaration of Human Rights.

Emperor Haile Selassie — A143

1973, Nov. 5 Photo. *Perf. 11½*

No.	Type	Value	Description	Unused	Used
672	A143	5c	yellow & multi	.20	.20
673	A143	10c	brt blue & multi	.20	.20
674	A143	15c	green & multi	.25	.20
675	A143	20c	dull yel & multi	.35	.20
676	A143	25c	multicolored	.40	.20
677	A143	30c	multicolored	.45	.20
678	A143	35c	multicolored	.50	.20
679	A143	40c	ultra & multi	.55	.20
680	A143	45c	multicolored	.65	.25
681	A143	50c	orange & multi	.70	.25
682	A143	55c	magenta & multi	.95	.50
683	A143	60c	multicolored	1.10	.65
684	A143	70c	red org & multi	1.25	.70
685	A143	90c	brt vio & multi	1.60	.85
686	A143	$1	multicolored	2.00	1.10
687	A143	$2	orange & multi	3.75	2.00
688	A143	$3	multicolored	5.75	3.00
689	A143	$5	multicolored	9.50	5.00
			Nos. 672-689 (18)	30.15	15.90

Wicker Furniture A144

Designs: Various wicker baskets, wall hangings, dinnerware.

1974, Jan. 31 Photo. *Perf. 11½*

Granite Paper

No.	Type	Value	Description	Unused	Used
690	A144	5c	violet bl & multi	.20	.20
691	A144	10c	violet bl & multi	.20	.20
692	A144	30c	violet bl & multi	.35	.35
693	A144	50c	violet bl & multi	.65	.65
694	A144	60c	violet bl & multi	.80	.80
			Nos. 690-694 (5)	2.20	2.20

Cow, Calf, Syringe — A145

Designs: 15c, Inoculation of cattle. 20c, Bullock and syringe. 50c, Laboratory technician, cow's head, syringe. 60c, Map of Ethiopia, cattle, syringe.

1974, Feb. 20 Litho. *Perf. 13½x13*

No.	Type	Value	Description	Unused	Used
695	A145	5c	sepia & multi	.20	.20
696	A145	15c	ultra & multi	.20	.20
697	A145	20c	ultra & multi	.20	.20
698	A145	50c	orange & multi	.80	.80
699	A145	60c	gold & multi	1.10	1.10
			Nos. 695-699 (5)	2.50	2.50

Campaign against cattle plague.

Umbrella Makers A146

Designs: 30c, Weaving. 50c, Child care. 60c, Foundation headquarters.

1974, Apr. 17 Photo. *Perf. 14½*

No.	Type	Value	Description	Unused	Used
700	A146	10c	lt lilac & multi	.20	.20
701	A146	30c	multicolored	.30	.30
702	A146	50c	multicolored	.60	.60
703	A146	60c	blue & multi	.75	.75
			Nos. 700-703 (4)	1.85	1.85

20th anniv. of Haile Selassie Foundation.

Ceremonial Robe — A147

Designs: Ceremonial robes.

1974, June 26 Litho. *Perf. 13*

No.	Type	Value	Description	Unused	Used
704	A147	15c	multicolored	.30	.30
705	A147	25c	ocher & multi	.50	.50
706	A147	35c	green & multi	.95	.95
707	A147	40c	lt brown & multi	1.10	1.10
708	A147	60c	gray & multi	1.60	1.60
			Nos. 704-708 (5)	4.45	4.45

World Population Statistics — A148

Designs: 50c, "Larger families-lower living standard." 60c, Rising population graph.

1974, Aug. 19 Photo. *Perf. 14½*

No.	Type	Value	Description	Unused	Used
709	A148	40c	yellow & multi	1.00	1.00
710	A148	50c	violet & multi	1.25	1.25
711	A148	60c	green & multi	1.60	1.60
			Nos. 709-711 (3)	3.85	3.85

World Population Year 1974.

UPU Emblem, Letter Carrier's Staff — A149

Celebration Around "Damara" Pillar — A150

UPU Emblem and: 50c, Letters and flags. 60c, Globe. 70c, Headquarters, Bern.

1974, Oct. 9 Photo. *Perf. 11½*

Granite Paper

No.	Type	Value	Description	Unused	Used
712	A149	15c	yellow & multi	.40	.30
713	A149	50c	multicolored	1.10	.85
714	A149	60c	ultra & multi	1.40	1.10
715	A149	70c	multicolored	1.60	1.25
			Nos. 712-715 (4)	4.50	3.50

Centenary of Universal Postal Union.

1974, Dec. 17 Photo. *Perf. 14x14½*

5c, Site of Gishen Mariam Monastery. 20c, Cross and festivities. 80c, Torch (Chibos) Parade.

No.	Type	Value	Description	Unused	Used
716	A150	5c	yellow & multi	.25	.20
717	A150	10c	yellow & multi	.30	.25
718	A150	20c	yellow & multi	.55	.45
719	A150	80c	yellow & multi	2.00	1.60
			Nos. 716-719 (4)	3.10	2.50

Meskel Festival, Sept. 26-27, commemorating the finding in the 4th century of the True Cross, of which a fragment is kept at Gishen Mariam Monastery in Welo Province.

Precis Clelia — A151

Adoration of the Kings — A152

Butterflies: 25c, Charaxes achaemenes. 45c, Papilio dardanus. 50c, Charaxes druceanus. 60c, Papilio demodocus.

1975, Feb. 18 Photo. *Perf. 12x12½*

No.	Type	Value	Description	Unused	Used
720	A151	10c	silver & multi	.35	.30
721	A151	25c	gold & multi	.80	.70
722	A151	45c	purple & multi	1.75	1.50
723	A151	50c	green & multi	2.40	2.00
724	A151	60c	brt blue & multi	3.00	2.50
			Nos. 720-724 (5)	8.30	7.00

1975, Apr. 23 Photo. *Perf. 11½*

10c, Baptism of Jesus. 15c, Jesus teaching in the Temple. 30c, Jesus giving sight to the blind. 40c, Crucifixion. 80c, Resurrection.

Granite Paper

No.	Type	Value	Description	Unused	Used
725	A152	5c	brown & multi	.20	.20
726	A152	10c	black & multi	.25	.20
727	A152	15c	dk brown & multi	.35	.30
728	A152	30c	dk brown & multi	.55	.55
729	A152	40c	black & multi	1.10	1.00
730	A152	80c	slate & multi	1.90	1.75
			Nos. 725-730 (6)	4.35	4.00

Murals from Ethiopian churches.

Wild Animals A153

1975, May 27 Photo. *Perf. 11½*

Granite Paper

No.	Type	Value	Description	Unused	Used
731	A153	5c	Warthog	.40	.35
732	A153	10c	Aardvark	.40	.35
733	A153	20c	Semien wolf	.65	.55
734	A153	40c	Gelada baboon	1.60	1.40
735	A153	80c	Civet	3.50	3.00
			Nos. 731-735 (5)	6.55	5.65

"Peace," Dove, Globe, IWY Emblem — A154

50c, Symbols of development. 90c, Equality between men and women.

1975, June 30 Litho. *Perf. 14x14½*

No.	Type	Value	Description	Unused	Used
736	A154	40c	blue & black	.65	.50
737	A154	50c	salmon & multi	.85	.70
738	A154	90c	multicolored	1.50	1.25
			Nos. 736-738 (3)	3.00	2.45

International Women's Year 1975.

Postal Museum A155

Various interior views of Postal Museum.

1975, Aug. 19 Photo. *Perf. 13x12½*

No.	Type	Value	Description	Unused	Used
739	A155	10c	ocher & multi	.35	.30
740	A155	30c	pink & multi	.60	.50
741	A155	60c	multicolored	1.40	1.10
742	A155	70c	lt green & multi	1.50	1.25
			Nos. 739-742 (4)	3.85	3.15

Ethiopian Natl. Postal Museum, opening.

Map of Ethiopia and Sun — A156

1975, Sept. 11 Photo. *Perf. 11½*

Granite Paper

No.	Type	Value	Description	Unused	Used
743	A156	5c	lilac & multi	.20	.20
744	A156	10c	ultra & multi	.20	.20
745	A156	25c	brown & multi	.25	.25
746	A156	50c	yellow & multi	.75	.60
747	A156	90c	brt green & multi	1.60	1.25
			Nos. 743-747 (5)	3.00	2.50

1st anniv. of Ethiopian revolution.

UN Emblem A157

1975, Oct. 24 Photo. *Perf. 11½*

No.	Type	Value	Description	Unused	Used
748	A157	40c	lilac & multi	.80	.65
749	A157	50c	multicolored	.90	.75
750	A157	90c	blue & multi	1.75	1.40
			Nos. 748-750 (3)	3.45	2.80

United Nations, 30th anniversary.

Regional Hair Styles — A158

Delphinium Wellbyi — A159

1975, Dec. 15 Photo. *Perf. 11½*

No.	Type	Value	Description	Unused	Used
751	A158	5c	Ilubabor	.30	.25
752	A158	15c	Arusi	.35	.30
753	A158	20c	Eritrea	.50	.40
754	A158	30c	Bale	.65	.55
755	A158	35c	Kefa	.90	.75
756	A158	50c	Begemir	1.10	.90
757	A158	60c	Shoa	1.40	1.10
			Nos. 751-757 (7)	5.20	4.25

See Nos. 832-838.

1976, Jan. 15 Photo. *Perf. 11½*

Flowers: 10c, Plectocephalus varians. 20c, Brachystelma asmarensis, horiz. 40c, Ceropegia inflata. 80c, Erythrina brucei.

No.	Type	Value	Description	Unused	Used
758	A159	5c	multicolored	.20	.20
759	A159	10c	multicolored	.30	.25
760	A159	20c	multicolored	.35	.30
761	A159	40c	multicolored	.90	.75
762	A159	80c	multicolored	1.60	1.25
			Nos. 758-762 (5)	3.35	2.75

Goalkeeper, Map of Africa, Games' Emblem
A160

Designs: Various scenes from soccer, map of Africa and ball.

1976, Feb. 27 Photo. *Perf. 14½*

763 A160 5c orange & multi .20 .20
764 A160 10c yellow & multi .30 .25
765 A160 25c lilac & multi .40 .35
766 A160 50c green & multi .85 .70
767 A160 90c brt grn & multi 1.60 1.25
Nos. 763-767 (5) 3.35 2.75

10th African Cup of Nations, Addis Ababa and Dire Dawa, Feb. 29-Mar. 14.

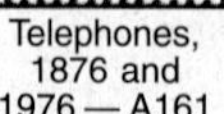

Telephones, 1876 and 1976 — A161

Ethiopian Jewelry — A162

Designs: 60c, Alexander Graham Bell. 90c, Transmission tower.

1976, Mar. 10 Litho. *Perf. 12x13½*

768 A161 30c lt ocher & multi .70 .50
769 A161 60c emerald & multi 1.40 1.10
770 A161 90c ver, blk & buff 1.90 1.50
Nos. 768-770 (3) 4.00 3.10

Centenary of first telephone call by Alexander Graham Bell, Mar. 10, 1876.

1976, May 14 Photo. *Perf. 11½*

Designs: Women wearing various kinds of Ethiopian jewelry.

Granite Paper

771 A162 5c blue & multi .20 .20
772 A162 10c plum & multi .25 .20
773 A162 20c gray & multi .50 .35
774 A162 40c green & multi .80 .65
775 A162 80c orange & multi 1.75 1.40
Nos. 771-775 (5) 3.50 2.80

Boxing — A163

Hands Holding Map of Ethiopia — A164

Designs (Montreal Olympic Emblem and): 80c, Runner and maple leaf. 90c, Bicycling.

1976, July 15 Litho. *Perf. 12½x12*

776 A163 10c multicolored .35 .30
777 A163 80c brt red, blk & grn 1.75 1.40
778 A163 90c brt red & multi 1.90 1.50
Nos. 776-778 (3) 4.00 3.20

21st Olympic Games, Montreal, Canada, July 17-Aug. 1.

1976, Aug. 5 Photo. *Perf. 14½*

779 A164 5c rose & multi .20 .20
780 A164 10c olive & multi .25 .20
781 A164 25c orange & multi .35 .25
782 A164 50c multicolored .75 .60
783 A164 90c dk blue & multi 1.25 1.00
Nos. 779-783 (5) 2.80 2.25

Development through cooperation.

Revolution Emblem: Eye and Map
A165

1976, Sept. 9 Photo. *Perf. 13½*

784 A165 5c multicolored .20 .20
785 A165 10c multicolored .25 .20
786 A165 25c multicolored .35 .25
787 A165 50c yellow & multi .75 .60
788 A165 90c green & multi 1.25 1.00
Nos. 784-788 (5) 2.80 2.25

2nd anniversary of the revolution.

Sunburst Around Crest — A166

Plane Over Man with Donkey — A167

1976, Sept. 13 Photo. *Perf. 11½*

789 A166 5c green, gold & blk .20 .20
790 A166 10c org, gold & blk .25 .20
791 A166 15c grnsh bl, gold & blk .35 .20
792 A166 20c lilac, gold & blk .40 .20
793 A166 25c brt grn, gold & blk .50 .20
794 A166 30c car, gold & blk .60 .20
795 A166 35c yel, gold & blk .70 .20
796 A166 40c ol, gold & blk .80 .30
797 A166 45c brt grn, gold & blk .90 .35
798 A166 50c car rose, gold & blk 1.10 .40
799 A166 55c ultra, gold & blk 1.10 .45
800 A166 60c fawn, gold & blk 1.25 .45
801 A166 70c rose, gold & blk 1.50 .50
802 A166 90c blue, gold & blk 1.75 .65
803 A166 $1 dull grn, gold & blk 2.25 .75
804 A166 $2 gray, gold & blk 4.50 1.50
805 A166 $3 brn vio, gold & blk 6.25 2.25
806 A166 $5 slate bl, gold & blk 10.50 3.75
Nos. 789-806 (18) 34.90 12.75

Denomination Expressed as "BIRR"

1983, June 16

806A A166 1b dull grn, gold & blk 2.25
806B A166 2b gray, gold & blk 4.50
806C A166 3b brn vio, gold & blk 6.25

1976, Oct. 28 Litho. *Perf. 12x12½*

10c, Globe showing routes. 25c, Crew and passengers forming star. 50c, Propeller and jet engine. 90c, Airplanes surrounding map of Ethiopia.

807 A167 5c dull bl & multi .30 .25
808 A167 10c lilac & multi .40 .30
809 A167 25c multicolored .50 .40
810 A167 50c orange & multi 1.10 .85
811 A167 90c olive & multi 1.90 1.50
Nos. 807-811 (5) 4.20 3.30

Ethiopian Airlines, 30th anniversary.

Tortoises
A168

Hand Holding Makeshift Hammer
A169

Reptiles: 20c, Chameleon. 30c, Python. 40c, Monitor lizard. 80c, Nile crocodiles.

1976, Dec. 15 Photo. *Perf. 14½*

812 A168 10c multicolored .35 .30
813 A168 20c multicolored .45 .40
814 A168 30c multicolored .70 .60
815 A168 40c multicolored .95 .80
816 A168 80c multicolored 2.00 1.75
Nos. 812-816 (5) 4.45 3.85

1977, Jan. 20 Litho. *Perf. 12½*

Designs: 5c, Hands holding bowl and plane dropping food. 45c, Infant with empty bowl, and bank note. 60c, Map of affected area, footprints and tire tracks. 80c, Film strip, camera and Ethiopian sitting between eggshells.

817 A169 5c multicolored .20 .20
818 A169 10c multicolored .40 .30
819 A169 45c multicolored .85 .65
820 A169 60c multicolored 1.10 .90
821 A169 80c multicolored 1.40 1.10
Nos. 817-821 (5) 3.95 3.15

Ethiopian Relief and Rehabilitation Commission for drought and disaster areas.

Elephant and Ruins, Axum, 7th Century
A170

Designs: 10c, Ibex and temple, 5th century, B.C., Yeha. 25c, Megalithic dolmen and pottery, Sourre Kabanawa. 50c, Awash Valley, stone axe, Acheulean period. 80c, Omo Valley, hominid jawbone.

1977, Mar. 15 Photo. *Perf. 13½*

822 A170 5c gold & multi .25 .20
823 A170 10c gold & multi .35 .30
824 A170 25c gold & multi .55 .45
825 A170 50c gold & multi .85 .70
826 A170 80c gold & multi 1.40 1.10
Nos. 822-826 (5) 3.40 2.75

Archaeological sites and finds in Ethiopia.

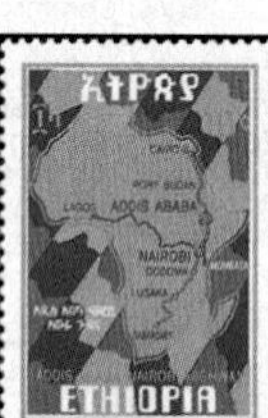

Map of Africa with Trans-East Highway — A171

1977, Mar. 30 *Perf. 14*

827 A171 10c gold & multi .25 .20
828 A171 20c gold & multi .35 .30
829 A171 40c gold & multi .75 .60
830 A171 50c gold & multi .85 .70
831 A171 60c gold & multi 1.00 .85
Nos. 827-831 (5) 3.20 2.65

Addis Ababa to Nairobi Highway and projected highways to Cairo, Egypt, and Gaborone, Botswana.

Hairstyle Type of 1975

1977, Apr. 28 Photo. *Perf. 11½*

832 A158 5c Welega .20 .20
833 A158 10c Gojam .25 .20
834 A158 15c Tigre .35 .30
835 A158 20c Harar .45 .40
836 A158 25c Gemu Gefa .65 .55
837 A158 40c Sidamo .95 .80
838 A158 50c Welo 1.10 1.00
Nos. 832-838 (7) 3.95 3.45

Addis Ababa
A172

Towns of Ethiopia: 10c, Asmara. 25c, Harar. 50c, Jima. 90c, Dese.

1977, June 20 Photo. *Perf. 14½*

839 A172 5c silver & multi .20 .20
840 A172 10c silver & multi .35 .30
841 A172 25c silver & multi .40 .35
842 A172 50c silver & multi .80 .70
843 A172 90c silver & multi 1.40 1.25
Nos. 839-843 (5) 3.15 2.80

Terebratula Abyssinica — A173

Fractured Imperial Crown — A174

Fossil Shells: 10c, Terebratula subalata. 25c, Cuculloea lefeburiaua. 50c, Ostrea plicatissima. 90c, Trigonia cousobrina.

1977, Aug. 15 Photo. *Perf. 14x13½*

844 A173 5c multicolored .25 .20
845 A173 10c multicolored .40 .35
846 A173 25c multicolored .50 .40
847 A173 50c multicolored 1.00 .85
848 A173 90c multicolored 1.75 1.40
Nos. 844-848 (5) 3.90 3.20

1977, Sept. 9 Litho. *Perf. 15*

Designs: 10c, Symbol of the Revolution (spade, axe, torch). 25c, Warriors, hammer and sickle, map of Ethiopia. 60c, Soldier, farmer and map. 80c, Map and emblem of revolutionary government.

849 A174 5c multicolored .20 .20
850 A174 10c multicolored .35 .30
851 A174 25c multicolored .40 .35
852 A174 60c multicolored .95 .80
853 A174 80c multicolored 1.25 1.10
Nos. 849-853 (5) 3.15 2.75

Third anniversary of the revolution.

Cicindela Petitii — A175

Lenin, Globe, Map of Ethiopia and Emblem — A176

Insects: 10c, Heliocopris dillonii. 25c, Poekilocerus vignaudii. 50c, Pepsis heros. 90c, Pepsis dedjaz.

1977, Sept. 30 Photo. *Perf. 14x13½*

854 A175 5c multicolored .55 .50
855 A175 10c multicolored .55 .50
856 A175 25c multicolored 1.00 .90
857 A175 50c multicolored 1.90 1.75
858 A175 90c multicolored 3.50 3.25
Nos. 854-858 (5) 7.50 6.90

1977, Nov. 15 Litho. *Perf. 12*

859 A176 5c orange & multi .25 .20
860 A176 10c multicolored .35 .25
861 A176 25c salmon & multi .45 .35
862 A176 50c lt blue & multi .95 .70
863 A176 90c yellow & multi 1.50 1.10
Nos. 859-863 (5) 3.50 2.60

60th anniv. of Russian October Revolution.

Chondrostoma Dilloni — A177

Salt-water Fish: 10c, Ostracion cubicus. 25c, Serranus summana. 50c, Serranus luti. 90c, Tetraodon maculatus.

1978, Jan. 20 Litho. *Perf. 15½*

864 A177 5c multicolored .45 .35
865 A177 10c multicolored .50 .40
866 A177 25c multicolored .80 .65
867 A177 50c multicolored 1.50 1.25
868 A177 90c multicolored 2.75 2.25
Nos. 864-868 (5) 6.00 4.90

Domestic Animals — A178

1978, Mar. 27 Litho. *Perf. 13½x14*

869 A178 5c Cattle .20 .20
870 A178 10c Mules .30 .25
871 A178 25c Goats .50 .40
872 A178 50c Dromedaries 1.00 .80
873 A178 90c Horses 1.90 1.50
Nos. 869-873 (5) 3.90 3.15

Weapons and Shield, Map of Ethiopia — A179

Bronze Ibex, 5th Century B.C. — A180

"Call of the Motherland." (Map of Ethiopia and): 10c, Civilian fighters. 25c, Map of Africa. 60c, Soldiers. 80c, Red Cross nurse and wounded man.

1978, May Litho. *Perf. 15½*

874 A179 5c multicolored .20 .20
875 A179 10c multicolored .25 .20
876 A179 25c multicolored .45 .35
877 A179 60c multicolored 1.10 .80
878 A179 80c multicolored 1.50 1.10
Nos. 874-878 (5) 3.50 2.65

1978, June 21 Litho. *Perf. 15½*

Ancient Bronzes: 10c, Lion, Yeha, 5th cent. B.C., horiz. 25c, Lamp with ibex attacked by dog, Matara, 1st cent. B.C. 50c, Goat, Axum, 3rd cent. A.D., horiz. 90c, Ax, chisel and sickle, Yeha, 5th-4th centuries B.C.

879 A180 5c multicolored .20 .20
880 A180 10c multicolored .30 .25
881 A180 25c multicolored .50 .40
882 A180 50c multicolored 1.00 .80
883 A180 90c multicolored 1.90 1.50
Nos. 879-883 (5) 3.90 3.15

See Nos. 1024-1027.

Globe and Argentina '78 Emblem A181

20c, Soccer player kicking ball. 30c, Two players embracing, net and ball. 55c, World map and ball. 70c, Soccer field, vert.

Perf. 14x13½, 13½x14

1978, July 19 Litho.

884 A181 5c multicolored .20 .20
885 A181 20c multicolored .45 .35
886 A181 30c multicolored .60 .50
887 A181 55c multicolored 1.25 .95
888 A181 70c multicolored 1.60 1.25
Nos. 884-888 (5) 4.10 3.25

11th World Cup Soccer Championship, Argentina, June 1-25.

Map of Africa, Oppressed African — A182

Namibia Day: 10c, Policeman pointing gun. 25c, Sniper with gun. 60c, African caught in net. 80c, Head of free man.

1978, Aug. 25 *Perf. 12½x13½*

889 A182 5c multicolored .20 .20
890 A182 10c multicolored .25 .20
891 A182 25c multicolored .45 .35
892 A182 60c multicolored 1.10 .80
893 A182 80c multicolored 1.50 1.10
Nos. 889-893 (5) 3.50 2.65

Soldiers, Guerrilla and Jets A183

Design: 1b, People looking toward sun, crushing snake, flags.

1978, Sept. 8 Photo. *Perf. 14*

894 A183 80c multicolored 1.25 .90
895 A183 1b multicolored 1.75 1.25

4th anniversary of revolution.

Hand and Globe with Tools — A184

Designs: 15c, Symbols of energy, communications, education, medicine, agriculture and industry. 25c, Cogwheels and world map. 60c, Globe and hands passing wrench. 70c, Flying geese and turtle over globe.

1978, Nov. 14 Litho. *Perf. 12x12½*

896 A184 10c multicolored .20 .20
897 A184 15c multicolored .25 .20
898 A184 25c multicolored .45 .35
899 A184 60c multicolored 1.10 .80
900 A184 70c multicolored 1.25 .90
Nos. 896-900 (5) 3.25 2.45

Technical Cooperation Among Developing Countries Conference, Buenos Aires, Argentina, Sept. 1978.

Human Rights Emblem — A185

1978, Dec. 7 Photo. *Perf. 12½x13½*

901 A185 5c multicolored .25 .20
902 A185 15c multicolored .25 .20
903 A185 25c multicolored .35 .30
904 A185 35c multicolored .50 .40
905 A185 1b multicolored 1.75 1.40
Nos. 901-905 (5) 3.10 2.50

Declaration of Human Rights, 30th anniv.

Broken Chain, Anti-Apartheid Emblem — A186

Stele from Osole — A187

1978, Dec. 28 Litho. *Perf. 12½x12*

906 A186 5c multicolored .20 .20
907 A186 20c multicolored .30 .25
908 A186 30c multicolored .40 .35
909 A186 55c multicolored .85 .70
910 A186 70c multicolored 1.25 1.00
Nos. 906-910 (5) 3.00 2.50

Anti-Apartheid Year.

1979, Jan. 25 *Perf. 14*

Ancient Carved Stones, Soddo Region: 10c, Anthropomorphous stele, Gorashino. 25c, Leaning stone, Wado. 60c, Round stones, Ambeut. 80c, Bas-relief, Tiya.

911 A187 5c multicolored .20 .20
912 A187 10c multicolored .30 .25
913 A187 25c multicolored .50 .40
914 A187 60c multicolored 1.00 .85
915 A187 80c multicolored 1.40 1.10
Nos. 911-915 (5) 3.40 2.80

Cotton Plantation A188

Shemma Industry: 10c, Women spinning cotton yarn. 20c, Man reeling cotton. 65c, Weaver. 80c, Shemma (Natl. dress).

1979, Mar. 15 Litho. *Perf. 15½*

916 A188 5c multicolored .20 .20
917 A188 10c multicolored .35 .30
918 A188 20c multicolored .40 .35
919 A188 65c multicolored 1.40 1.10
920 A188 80c multicolored 1.75 1.40
Nos. 916-920 (5) 4.10 3.35

Ethiopian Trees — A189

1979, Apr. 26 Photo. *Perf. 13½x14*

921 A189 5c Grar .20 .20
922 A189 10c Weira .25 .20
923 A189 25c Tidh .40 .30
924 A189 50c Shola .95 .70
925 A189 90c Zigba 1.75 1.25
Nos. 921-925 (5) 3.55 2.65

Agricultural Development A190

Revolutionary Development Campaign: 15c, Industry. 25c, Transportation and communication. 60c, Education and health. 70c, Commerce.

1979, July 3 Litho. *Perf. 12x12½*

926 A190 10c multicolored .20 .20
927 A190 15c multicolored .30 .20
928 A190 25c multicolored .45 .30
929 A190 60c multicolored 1.10 .75
930 A190 70c multicolored 1.50 1.00
Nos. 926-930 (5) 3.55 2.45

IYC Emblem — A191

Intl. Year of the Child: 15c, Adults leading children. 25c, Adult helping child. 60c, IYC emblem surrounded by children. 70c, Adult and children embracing.

1979, Aug. 16 Litho. *Perf. 12x12½*

931 A191 10c multicolored .20 .20
932 A191 15c multicolored .35 .30
933 A191 25c multicolored .55 .45
934 A191 60c multicolored 1.25 1.10
935 A191 70c multicolored 1.50 1.25
Nos. 931-935 (5) 3.85 3.30

Guerrilla Fighters — A192

15c, Soldiers. 25c, Map of Africa within cogwheel, star. 60c, Students with book, torch. 70c, Family, hammer & sickle emblem.

1979, Sept. 11 Photo. *Perf. 14*

936 A192 10c multicolored .25 .20
937 A192 15c multicolored .40 .30
938 A192 25c multicolored .55 .45
939 A192 60c multicolored 1.40 1.10
940 A192 70c multicolored 1.60 1.25
Nos. 936-940 (5) 4.20 3.30

Fifth anniversary of revolution.

Telephone Receiver A193

Incense Container A194

Telecom Emblem and: 5c, Symbolic waves. 35c, Satellite beaming to earth. 45c, Dish antenna. 65c, Television cameraman.

1979, Sept. Photo. *Perf. 11½*

941 A193 5c multicolored .30 .25
942 A193 30c multicolored .60 .40
943 A193 35c multicolored .75 .50
944 A193 45c multicolored .95 .65
945 A193 65c multicolored 1.40 .95
Nos. 941-945 (5) 4.00 2.75

3rd World Telecommunications Exhibition, Geneva, Sept. 20-26.

1979, Nov. 15 Litho. *Perf. 15*

946 A194 5c shown .25 .20
947 A194 10c Vase .40 .30
948 A194 25c Earthenware cover .60 .45
949 A194 60c Milk container 1.40 1.10
950 A194 80c Storage container 1.75 1.40
Nos. 946-950 (5) 4.40 3.45

Wooden Grain Bowl — A195

Lappet-faced Vulture — A196

1980, Jan. Litho. *Perf. 13½x13*

951 A195 5c shown .40 .30
952 A195 30c Chair, stool .70 .55
953 A195 35c Mortar, pestle .75 .60
954 A195 45c Buckets 1.10 .85
955 A195 65c Storage jars 1.60 1.25
Nos. 951-955 (5) 4.55 3.55

1980, Feb. 12 *Perf. 13½x14*

Birds of Prey: 15c, Long-crested hawk eagle. 25c, Secretary bird. 60c, Abyssinian long-eared owl. 70c, Lanner falcon.

956 A196 10c multicolored .55 .45
957 A196 15c multicolored .75 .60
958 A196 25c multicolored 1.25 .95
959 A196 60c multicolored 2.50 2.25
960 A196 70c multicolored 4.00 3.50
Nos. 956-960 (5) 9.05 7.75

Fight Against Cigarette Smoking — A197

1980, Apr. 7 Photo. *Perf. 13x13½*

961 A197 20c shown .45 .35
962 A197 60c Cigarette 1.40 1.10
963 A197 1b Respiratory system 2.20 1.75
Nos. 961-963 (3) 4.05 3.20

"110" and Lenin House Museum A198

Lenin, 110th "Birthday" (Paintings): 15c, In hiding. 20c, As a young man. 40c, Returning to Russia. 1b, Speaking on the Goelro Plan.

1980, Apr. 22 Litho. *Perf. 12x12½*

964 A198 5c multicolored .25 .20
965 A198 15c multicolored .30 .25
966 A198 20c multicolored .45 .35
967 A198 40c multicolored .85 .70
968 A198 1b multicolored 2.10 1.75
Nos. 964-968 (5) 3.95 3.25

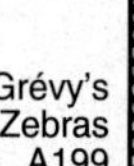

Grévy's Zebras A199

1980, June 10 Litho. *Perf. 12½x12*

969 A199 10c shown .35 .30
970 A199 15c Gazelles .50 .40
971 A199 25c Wild hunting dogs .85 .70
972 A199 60c Swayne's hartebeests 1.90 1.60
973 A199 70c Cheetahs 2.25 1.90
Nos. 969-973 (5) 5.85 4.90

Runner, Moscow '80 Emblem — A200

1980, July 19 Photo. *Perf. 11½x12*

974 A200 30c shown .70 .55
975 A200 70c Gymnast 1.60 1.25
976 A200 80c Boxing 1.75 1.40
Nos. 974-976 (3) 4.05 3.20

22nd Summer Olympic Games, Moscow, July 19-Aug. 3.

Removing Blindfold — A201

Bamboo Folk Craft — A202

1980, Sept. 11 Photo. *Perf. 14x13½*

977 A201 30c shown .65 .40
978 A201 40c Revolutionary .80 .50
979 A201 50c Woman breaking chain 1.10 .65
980 A201 70c Russian & Ethiopian flags 1.50 .90
Nos. 977-980 (4) 4.05 2.45

6th anniversary of revolution.

1980, Oct. 23 Litho. *Perf. 14*

981 A202 5c Bamboo food basket .25 .20
982 A202 15c Lamp shade .30 .25
983 A202 25c Stool .50 .40
984 A202 35c Fruit basket .60 .50
985 A202 1b Lamp shade 1.75 1.40
Nos. 981-985 (5) 3.40 2.75

Mekotkocha (Used in Weeding) A203

Traditional Harvesting Tools: 15c, Layda (grain separator). 40c, Mensh (fork). 45c, Mededekia (soil turner). 70c, Mofer & Kenber (plow and yoke).

1980, Dec. 18 Litho. *Perf. 12½x12*

986 A203 10c multicolored .25 .20
987 A203 15c multicolored .30 .25
988 A203 40c multicolored .75 .60
989 A203 45c multicolored .85 .70
990 A203 70c multicolored 1.25 1.00
Nos. 986-990 (5) 3.40 2.75

Baro River Bridge Opening A204

1981, Feb. 28 Photo. *Perf. 13½x13*

991 A204 15c Canoes and ferry .35 .30
992 A204 65c Bridge construction 1.40 1.10
993 A204 1b shown 2.25 1.75
Nos. 991-993 (3) 4.00 3.15

Semien National Park — A205

World Heritage Year: 5c, Wawel Castle, Poland. 15c, Quito Cathedral, Ecuador. 20c, Old Slave Quarters, Goree Island, Senegal. 30c, Mesa Verde Indian Village, US. 1b, L'Anse aux Meadows excavation, Canada.

Perf. 11x11½, 11½x11

1981, Mar. 10 Photo.

994 A205 5c multicolored .25 .20
995 A205 15c multicolored .40 .30
996 A205 20c multicolored .50 .40
997 A205 30c multicolored .70 .55
998 A205 80c multicolored 1.75 1.40
999 A205 1b multicolored 2.25 1.75
Nos. 994-999 (6) 5.85 4.60

1981, June 16 Photo.

10c, Biet Medhanialem Church, Ethiopia. 15c, Nahanni Natl. Park, Canada. 20c, Yellowstone River Lower Falls, U.S. 30c, Aachen Cathedral, Germany. 80c, Kicker Rock, San Cristobal Island, Ecuador. 1b, The Lizak corridor, Holy Cross Chapel, Cracow, Poland.

1000 A205 10c multi .25 .20
1001 A205 15c multi .35 .30
1002 A205 20c multi .60 .50
1003 A205 30c multi .85 .70
1004 A205 80c multi 2.25 1.90
1005 A205 1b multi, vert. 2.75 2.25
Nos. 1000-1005 (6) 7.05 5.85

Ancient Drinking Vessel A206

1981, May 5 Litho. *Perf. 12½x12*

1006 A206 20c shown .40 .30
1007 A206 25c Spice container .50 .40
1008 A206 35c Jug .60 .50

1009 A206 40c Cooking pot holder .80 .65
1010 A206 60c Animal figurine 1.25 .95
Nos. 1006-1010 (5) 3.55 2.80

Intl. Year of the Disabled — A207

7th Anniv. of Revolution A208

1981, July 16 Photo. *Perf. 11½x12*

1011 A207 5c Prostheses .30 .20
1012 A207 15c Boys writing .35 .25
1013 A207 20c Activities .40 .30
1014 A207 40c Knitting .85 .60
1015 A207 1b Weaving 2.10 1.50
Nos. 1011-1015 (5) 4.00 2.85

1981, Sept. 10 *Perf. 14*

1016 A208 20c Children's Center .40 .25
1017 A208 60c Heroes' Center 1.00 .75
1018 A208 1b Serto Ader (state newspaper) 1.60 1.25
Nos. 1016-1018 (3) 3.00 2.25

World Food Day — A209

1981, Oct. 15 Litho. *Perf. 13½x12½*

1019 A209 5c Wheat airlift .20 .20
1020 A209 15c Plowing .25 .20
1021 A209 20c Malnutrition .30 .25
1022 A209 40c Agriculture education .75 .60
1023 A209 1b Cattle, corn 1.75 1.40
Nos. 1019-1023 (5) 3.25 2.65

Ancient Bronze Type of 1978

1981, Dec. 15 Litho. *Perf. 14x13½*

1024 A180 15c Pitcher .25 .20
1025 A180 45c Tsenatsil (musical instrument) .75 .60
1026 A180 50c Pitcher, diff. .85 .70
1027 A180 70c Pot 1.20 .95
Nos. 1024-1027 (4) 3.05 2.45

Horn Artifacts — A210

1982, Feb. 18 Photo. *Perf. 12x12½*

1028 A210 10c Tobacco containers .20 .20
1029 A210 15c Cup .25 .20
1030 A210 40c Container, diff. .75 .60
1031 A210 45c Goblet .80 .65
1032 A210 70c Spoons 1.25 1.00
Nos. 1028-1032 (5) 3.25 2.65

Coffee Cultivation A211

1982, May, 6 Photo. *Perf. 13½*

1033 A211 5c Plants .20 .20
1034 A211 15c Bushes .25 .20
1035 A211 25c Mature bushes .50 .40
1036 A211 35c Picking beans .65 .50
1037 A211 1b Drinking coffee 1.90 1.50
Nos. 1033-1037 (5) 3.50 2.80

1982 World Cup — A212

Various soccer plays.

Perf. 13½x12½

1982, June 10 Litho.

1038 A212 5c multicolored .25 .20
1039 A212 15c multicolored .30 .25
1040 A212 20c multicolored .40 .30
1041 A212 40c multicolored .75 .60
1042 A212 1b multicolored 1.75 1.40
Nos. 1038-1042 (5) 3.45 2.75

TB Bacillus Centenary A213

1982, July 12 Litho. *Perf. 13½x12½*

1043 A213 15c Cow .30 .25
1044 A213 20c Magnifying glass .45 .35
1045 A213 30c Koch, microscope .65 .50
1046 A213 35c Koch .80 .60
1047 A213 80c Man coughing 1.75 1.40
Nos. 1043-1047 (5) 3.95 3.10

8th Anniv. of Revolution — A214

Designs: Symbols of justice.

1982, Sept. 10 *Perf. 12½x13½*

1048 A214 80c multicolored 1.40 1.00
1049 A214 1b multicolored 1.60 1.25

World Standards Day — A215

1982, Oct. 14 Litho. *Perf. 13½x12½*

1050 A215 5c Hand, foot, square .20 .20
1051 A215 15c Scales .25 .20
1052 A215 20c Rulers .30 .25
1053 A215 40c Weights .75 .60
1054 A215 1b Emblem 1.75 1.40
Nos. 1050-1054 (5) 3.25 2.65

10th Anniv. of UN Conference on Human Environment A216

1982, Dec. 13 Litho. *Perf. 12*

1055 A216 5c Wildlife conservation .20 .20
1056 A216 15c Environmental health and settlement .25 .20
1057 A216 20c Forest protection .35 .30
1058 A216 40c Natl. literacy campaign .70 .60
1059 A216 1b Soil and water conservation 1.75 1.50
Nos. 1055-1059 (5) 3.25 2.80

Cave of Sof Omar A217

Various views.

1983, Feb. 10 Photo. *Perf. 13½*

1060 A217 5c multicolored .20 .20
1061 A217 10c multicolored .20 .20
1062 A217 15c multicolored .25 .20
1063 A217 70c multicolored 1.00 .85
1064 A217 80c multicolored 1.25 1.00
Nos. 1060-1064 (5) 2.90 2.45

A218

A219

1983, Apr. 29 Photo. *Perf. 14*

1065 A218 80c multicolored 1.25 1.10
1066 A218 1b multicolored 1.75 1.40

25th Anniv. of Economic Commission for Africa.

Perf. 12½x11½

1983, June 3 Photo.

1067 A219 85c Emblem 1.40 1.25
1068 A219 1b Lighthouse, ship 1.90 1.60

25th Anniv. of Intl. Maritime Org.

WCY A220

9th Anniv. of Revolution A221

1983, July 22 Litho.

1069 A220 25c UPU emblem .50 .45
1070 A220 55c Dish antenna, emblems 1.25 1.00
1071 A220 1b Bridge, tunnel 2.25 1.90
Nos. 1069-1071 (3) 4.00 3.35

1983, Sept. 10 Litho. *Perf. 14½*

1072 A221 25c Dove .40 .30
1073 A221 55c Star 1.00 .75
1074 A221 1b Emblems 1.90 1.40
Nos. 1072-1074 (3) 3.30 2.45

Musical Instruments — A222

Charaxes Galawadiwosi A223

1983, Oct. 17 Litho. *Perf. 12½x13½*

1075 A222 5c Hura .25 .20
1076 A222 15c Dinke .35 .30
1077 A222 20c Meleket .40 .35
1078 A222 40c Embilta .85 .70
1079 A222 1b Tom 2.10 1.75
Nos. 1075-1079 (5) 3.95 3.30

1983, Dec. 13 Photo. *Perf. 14*

1080 A223 10c shown .60 .40
1081 A223 15c Epiphora elianae .90 .60
1082 A223 55c Batuana rougeoti 2.75 2.25
1083 A223 1b Achaea saboeareginae 4.75 4.00
Nos. 1080-1083 (4) 9.00 7.25

Intl. Anti-Apartheid Year (1983) — A224

Perf. 13½x12½

1984, Feb. 10 Litho.

1084 A224 5c multicolored .20 .20
1085 A224 15c multicolored .25 .20
1086 A224 20c multicolored .40 .30
1087 A224 40c multicolored .80 .60
1088 A224 1b multicolored 1.90 1.40
Nos. 1084-1088 (5) 3.55 2.70

Local Flowers — A225

Traditional Houses — A226

1984, Apr. 13 Litho. *Perf. 13½*

1089 A225 5c Protea gaguedi .25 .20
1090 A225 25c Sedum epidendrum .70 .60
1091 A225 50c Echinops amplexicaulis 1.50 1.25
1092 A225 1b Canarina eminii 3.00 2.50
Nos. 1089-1092 (4) 5.45 4.55

1984, Aug. 3 Photo.

1093 A226 15c Konso .30 .25
1094 A226 65c Dorze 1.25 1.00
1095 A226 1b Harer 2.00 1.60
Nos. 1093-1095 (3) 3.55 2.85

10th Anniv. of the Revolution A227

1984, Sept. 10 Photo. *Perf. 11½*

1096 A227 5c Sept. 12, 1974 .20 .20
1097 A227 10c Mar. 4, 1975 .30 .20
1098 A227 15c Apr. 20, 1976 .40 .30
1099 A227 20c Feb. 11, 1977 .55 .40
1100 A227 25c Mar. 1978 .65 .45
1101 A227 40c July 8, 1980 1.00 .70
1102 A227 45c Dec. 17, 1980 1.25 .85
1103 A227 50c Sept. 15, 1980 1.40 .95
1104 A227 70c Sept. 18, 1981 1.75 1.25
1105 A227 1b June 6, 1983 2.50 1.90
Nos. 1096-1105 (10) 10.00 7.20

Traditional Sports A228

1984, Dec. 7 Photo. *Perf. 14*

1106 A228 5c Gugs .25 .20
1107 A228 25c Tigil .50 .40
1108 A228 50c Genna .85 .70
1109 A228 1b Gebeta 1.75 1.50
Nos. 1106-1109 (4) 3.35 2.80

Birds — A229

1985, Jan. 4 Photo. *Perf. 14½*

1110 A229 5c Francolinus harwoodi .25 .20
1111 A229 15c Rallus rougetti .55 .45
1112 A229 80c Merops pusillus 2.75 2.25
1113 A229 85c Malimbus rubriceps 3.00 2.40
Nos. 1110-1113 (4) 6.55 5.30

Indigenous Fauna A230

1985, Feb. 4 Litho. *Perf. 12½x12*

1114 A230 20c Hippopotamus amphibius .60 .50
1115 A230 25c Litocranius walleri .80 .65
1116 A230 40c Sylvicapra grimmia 1.25 1.00
1117 A230 1b Rhynchotragus guentheri 3.00 2.40
Nos. 1114-1117 (4) 5.65 4.55

Freshwater Fish — A231

1985, Apr. 3 *Perf. 13½*

1118 A231 10c Barbus degeni .40 .35
1119 A231 20c Labeo cylindricus .45 .40
1120 A231 55c Protopterus annectens 1.25 1.10
1121 A231 1b Alestes dentex 2.40 2.00
Nos. 1118-1121 (4) 4.50 3.85

Medicinal Plants A232

1985, May 23 *Perf. 11½x12½*

1122 A232 10c Securidaca longepedunculata .35 .25
1123 A232 20c Plumbago zeylanicum .45 .35
1124 A232 55c Brucea antidysenteric 1.10 .85
1125 A232 1b Dorstenia barminiana 2.10 1.75
Nos. 1122-1125 (4) 4.00 3.20

Ethiopian Red Cross Soc., 50th Anniv. — A233

1985, Aug. 6 Litho. *Perf. 13½x13*

1126 A233 35c multicolored .75 .60
1127 A233 55c multicolored 1.25 .95
1128 A233 1b multicolored 2.00 1.60
Nos. 1126-1128 (3) 4.00 3.15

Ethiopian Revolution, 11th Anniv. — A234

10c, Kombolcha Mills, Welo Region. 80c, Muger Cement Factory, Mokoda, Shoa. 1b, Relocating famine and drought victims.

1985, Sept. 10 Litho. *Perf. 13½*

1129 A234 10c multicolored .25 .20
1130 A234 80c multicolored 1.75 1.40
1131 A234 1b multicolored 2.00 1.60
Nos. 1129-1131 (3) 4.00 3.20

UN 40th Anniv. — A235

1985, Nov. 22 Litho. *Perf. 13½x14*

1132 A235 25c multicolored .50 .45
1133 A235 55c multicolored 1.25 .95
1134 A235 1b multicolored 2.25 1.90
Nos. 1132-1134 (3) 4.00 3.30

Anti-Polio Campaign A236

1986, Jan. 10 Litho. *Perf. 11½x12½*

1135 A236 5c Boy, prosthesis .25 .20
1136 A236 10c Boy on crutches .30 .25
1137 A236 20c Nurse, boy .45 .35
1138 A236 55c Man, sewing machine 1.10 .90
1139 A236 1b Nurse, mother, child 1.90 1.50
Nos. 1135-1139 (5) 4.00 3.20

Indigenous Trees A237

1986, Feb. 10 *Perf. 13½x14½*

1140 A237 10c Millettia ferruginea .35 .30
1141 A237 30c Syzygium guineense .55 .50
1142 A237 50c Cordia africana 1.10 .90
1143 A237 1b Hagenia abyssinica 2.00 1.60
Nos. 1140-1143 (4) 4.00 3.30

Spices — A238

1986, Mar. 10 *Perf. 13½*

1144 A238 10c Zingiber officinale rosc .25 .25
1145 A238 15c Ocimum bacilicum .40 .30
1146 A238 55c Sinapsis alba 1.10 .90
1147 A238 1b Cuminum cyminum 2.25 1.75
Nos. 1144-1147 (4) 4.00 3.20

Current Coins, Obverse and Reverse A239

1986, May 9 Litho. *Perf. 13½x14*

1148	A239	5c	1-cent	.20	.20
1149	A239	10c	25-cent	.35	.30
1150	A239	35c	5-cent	.70	.65
1151	A239	50c	50-cent	1.00	.90
1152	A239	1b	10-cent	2.10	1.90
			Nos. 1148-1152 (5)	4.35	3.95

Discovery of 3.5 Million Year-old Hominid Skeleton, "Lucy" — A240

1986, July 4 *Perf. 13½*

1153	A240	2b	multicolored	4.75	4.25

Ethiopian Revolution, 12th Anniv. — A241

Designs: 20c, Military service. 30c, Tiglachin monument. 55c, Delachin Exhibition emblem. 85c, Food processing plant, Merti.

1986, Sept. 10 Litho. *Perf. 14*

1154	A241	20c	multicolored	.40	.35
1155	A241	30c	multicolored	.60	.50
1156	A241	55c	multicolored	1.25	.90
1157	A241	85c	multicolored	1.75	1.40
			Nos. 1154-1157 (4)	4.00	3.15

Ethiopian Airlines, 40th Anniv. — A242

Intl. Peace Year — A243

1986, Oct. 14

1158	A242	10c	DC-7	.20	.20
1159	A242	20c	DC-3	.30	.30
1160	A242	30c	Personnel, jet tail	.60	.50
1161	A242	40c	Engine	.80	.70
1162	A242	1b	DC-7, map	2.10	1.75
			Nos. 1158-1162 (5)	4.00	3.45

1986, Nov. 13 *Perf. 13½*

1163	A243	10c	multicolored	.40	.30
1164	A243	80c	multicolored	1.60	1.40
1165	A243	1b	multicolored	2.00	1.75
			Nos. 1163-1165 (3)	4.00	3.45

UN Child Survival Campaign — A244

1986, Dec. 11 *Perf. 12½*

1166	A244	10c	Breast feeding	.35	.30
1167	A244	35c	Immunization	.65	.60
1168	A244	50c	Hygiene	1.00	.80
1169	A244	1b	Growth monitoring	2.00	1.60
			Nos. 1166-1169 (4)	4.00	3.30

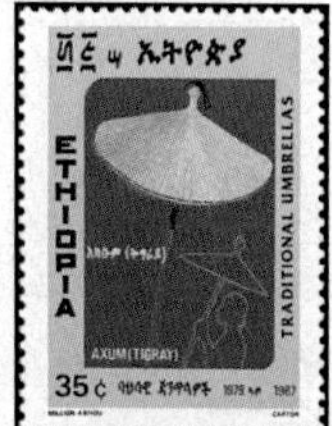

Umbrellas A245

1987, Feb. 10 *Perf. 13½*

1170	A245	35c	Axum	.75	.60
1171	A245	55c	Negele-Borena	1.25	.95
1172	A245	1b	Jimma	2.00	1.60
			Nos. 1170-1172 (3)	4.00	3.15

Artwork by Afewerk Tekle (b. 1932) A246

Designs: 50c, Defender of His Country - Afar, stained glass window. 2b, Defender of His Country - Adwa, painting.

1987, Mar. 19 Litho. *Perf. 13½*

1173	A246	50c	multicolored	1.00	.85
1174	A246	2b	multicolored	3.75	3.50

Stained Glass Windows by Afewerk Tekle — A247

1987, June 16 Photo. *Perf. 11½x12*

Granite Paper

1175	A247	50c	multicolored	*5.75*	*4.00*

Size: 26x38mm

1176	A247	80c	multicolored	*7.75*	*5.50*
1177	A247	1b	multicolored	*11.50*	*8.00*
			Nos. 1175-1177 (3)	*25.00*	*17.50*

Struggle of the African People.
Sold out in Addis Ababa on date of issue.

Simien Fox A248

1987, June 29 Litho. *Perf. 13½*

1178	A248	5c	multicolored	.20	.20
1179	A248	10c	multicolored	.25	.20
1180	A248	15c	multicolored	.35	.30
1181	A248	20c	multicolored	.55	.35
1182	A248	25c	multicolored	.65	.45
1183	A248	45c	multicolored	.90	.75
1184	A248	55c	multicolored	1.10	.90
			Nos. 1178-1184 (7)	4.00	3.15

For overprints see Nos. 1234-1237. For similar design see A294a.

Ethiopian Revolution, 13th Anniv. A249

1987, Sept. 10 *Perf. 12½*

1185	A249	5c	Constitution, free-dom of press	.30	.20
1186	A249	10c	Popular elections	.40	.30
1187	A249	80c	Referendum	1.40	1.25
1188	A249	1b	Bahir Dar Airport, map	1.90	1.60
			Nos. 1185-1188 (4)	4.00	3.35

Addis Ababa, Cent. A251

"100" and views: 5c, Emperor Menelik II, Empress Taitu and city. 10c, Traditional buildings. 80c, Central Addis Ababa. 1b, Aerial view of city.

1987, Sept. 7 *Perf. 13½*

1193	A251	5c	multicolored	.30	.20
1194	A251	10c	multicolored	.40	.30
1195	A251	80c	multicolored	1.40	1.25
1196	A251	1b	multicolored	1.90	1.60
			Nos. 1193-1196 (4)	4.00	3.35

Wooden Spoons A252

1987, Nov. 30

1197	A252	85c	Hurso, Harerge	1.25	1.10
1198	A252	1b	Borena, Sidamo	1.75	1.40

Intl. Year of Shelter for the Homeless A253

1988, Jan. Litho. *Perf. 13*

1199	A253	10c	Village revitaliza-tion program	.30	.25
1200	A253	35c	Resettlement pro-gram	.60	.50
1201	A253	50c	Urban improve-ment	.90	.75
1202	A253	1b	Cooperative and government housing	1.75	1.40
			Nos. 1199-1202 (4)	3.55	2.90

October Revolution, Russia, 70th Anniv. (in 1987) — A254

Painting: 1b, Lenin receiving Workers' Council delegates in the Smolny Institute.

1988, Feb. 17 *Perf. 12½x12*

1203	A254	1b	multicolored	1.75	1.40

Traditional Hunting Methods and Prey — A255

1988, Mar. 30 Litho. *Perf. 13½*

1204	A255	85c	Bow and arrow	1.50	1.50
1205	A255	1b	Double-pronged spear	2.00	2.00

A256

A257

1988, May 6

1206	A256	85c	multicolored	1.40	1.25
1207	A256	1b	multicolored	1.60	1.40

Intl. Red Cross and Red Crescent Organizations, 125th annivs.

1988, June 7 Photo. *Perf. 11½x12*

1208	A257	2b	multicolored	2.50	2.00

Organizaton of African Unity, 25th anniv.

Ethiopian Revolution, 14th Anniv. A258

Design: Various details of *The Victory of Ethiopia,* six-panel mural by Afewerk Tekle (b. 1932) in the museum of the Heroes Center, Debre Zeit.

1988, June 28 Litho. *Perf. 13½x13*

1209	A258	10c	Jet over farm, vert.	.20	.20
1210	A258	20c	Farm workers on road, vert.	.25	.20
1211	A258	35c	Allegory of unity, vert.	.45	.40
1212	A258	55c	Jet over industry	.70	.60
1213	A258	80c	Steel works	1.00	.85
1214	A258	1b	Weaving	1.40	1.25
			Nos. 1209-1214 (6)	4.00	3.50

Nos. 1209-1211 vert.

Women, Bracelets and Maps A259

1988, July 27 Litho. *Perf. 13x13½*

1215	A259	15c	Sidamo	.25	.20
1216	A259	85c	Arsi	1.25	1.00
1217	A259	1b	Harerge	1.50	1.25
			Nos. 1215-1217 (3)	3.00	2.45

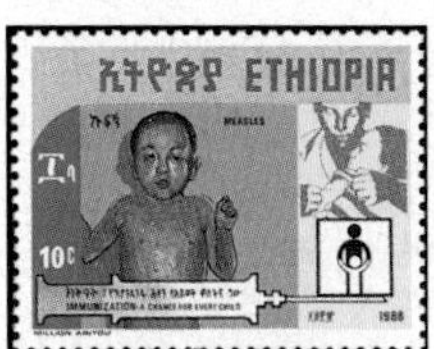
Immunize Every Child A260

1988, June 14 Litho. *Perf. 13x13½*
1218 A260 10c Measles .25 .20
1219 A260 35c Tetanus .50 .45
1220 A260 50c Whooping cough .75 .60
1221 A260 1b Diphtheria 1.50 1.25
Nos. 1218-1221 (4) 3.00 2.50

Intl. Fund for Agricultural Development (IFAD), 10th Anniv. — A261

1988, Aug. 16 *Perf. 13½*
1222 A261 15c Monetary aid .25 .25
1223 A261 85c Farming activities 1.10 1.10
1224 A261 1b Harvest 1.25 1.25
Nos. 1222-1224 (3) 2.60 2.60

People's Democratic Republic of Ethiopia, 1st Anniv. — A262

5c, 1st Session of the natl. Shengo (congress). 10c, Mengistu Haile-Mariam, 1st president of the republic. 80c, Natl. crest, flag & crowd. 1b, State assembly building.

1988, Sept. 9 *Perf. 14*
1225 A262 5c multicolored .20 .20
1226 A262 10c multicolored .20 .20
1227 A262 80c multicolored 1.25 1.00
1228 A262 1b multicolored 1.60 1.40
Nos. 1225-1228 (4) 3.25 2.80

Bank Notes A263

1988, Nov. 10 Photo. *Perf. 13*
1229 A263 5c 1-Birr .20 .20
1230 A263 10c 5-Birr .25 .25
1231 A263 20c 10-Birr .30 .30
1232 A263 75c 50-Birr 1.00 1.00
1233 A263 85c 100-Birr 1.25 1.25
Nos. 1229-1233 (5) 3.00 3.00

Nos. 1181-1184 Overprinted "WORLD AIDS DAY" in Two Languages

1988, Dec. 1 Litho. *Perf. 13½*
1234 A248 20c multicolored *4.50 4.25*
1235 A248 25c multicolored *6.00 5.25*
1236 A248 45c multicolored *12.00 10.00*
1237 A248 55c multicolored *12.50 10.50*
Nos. 1234-1237 (4) *35.00 30.00*

Intl. Day for the Fight Against AIDS.

WHO, 40th Anniv. A264

1988, Dec. 30 Litho. *Perf. 14*
1238 A264 50c multicolored .80 .55
1239 A264 65c multicolored 1.10 .80
1240 A264 85c multicolored 1.60 1.10
Nos. 1238-1240 (3) 3.50 2.45

Traditional Musical Instruments A265

1989, Feb. 9 *Perf. 13x13½*
1241 A265 30c Gere .40 .35
1242 A265 40c Fanfa .60 .50
1243 A265 50c Chancha .75 .60
1244 A265 85c Negareet 1.25 1.00
Nos. 1241-1244 (4) 3.00 2.45

Ethiopian Shipping Lines, 25th Anniv. A266

1989, Mar. 27 Litho. *Perf. 14*
1245 A266 15c *Abyot* .30 .25
1246 A266 30c *Wolwol* .55 .45
1247 A266 55c *Queen of Sheba* .95 .80
1248 A266 1b *Abbay Wonz* 1.75 1.10
Nos. 1245-1248 (4) 3.55 2.60

Birds — A267

1989, May 18 Litho. *Perf. 13½x13*
1249 A267 10c Yellow-fronted parrot .30 .25
1250 A267 35c White-winged cliff chat .70 .60
1251 A267 50c Yellow-throated seed eater 1.00 .85
1252 A267 1b Black-headed forest oriole 2.00 1.75
Nos. 1249-1252 (4) 4.00 3.45

Production of Early Manuscripts — A268

1989, June 16 Litho. *Perf. 13½*
1253 A268 5c Preparing vellum .20 .20
1254 A268 10c Ink horns, pens .25 .20
1255 A268 20c Scribe .35 .30
1256 A268 75c Book binding 1.25 1.00
1257 A268 85c Illuminated manuscript 1.50 1.10
Nos. 1253-1257 (5) 3.55 2.80

Indigenous Wildlife — A269

1989, July 18
1258 A269 30c Greater kudu .55 .50
1259 A269 40c Lesser kudu .70 .60
1260 A269 50c Roan antelope 1.00 .90
1261 A269 85c Nile lechwe 1.75 1.50
Nos. 1258-1261 (4) 4.00 3.50

People's Democratic Republic of Ethiopia, 2nd Anniv. A270

Designs: 15c, Melka Wakana Hydroelectric Power Station. 75c, Adea Berga Dairy Farm. 1b, Pawe Hospital.

1989, Sept. 8
1262 A270 15c multicolored .25 .20
1263 A270 75c multicolored 1.40 1.00
1264 A270 1b multicolored 1.90 1.40
Nos. 1262-1264 (3) 3.55 2.60

African Development Bank, 25th Anniv. — A271

1989, Nov. 10 Litho. *Perf. 13½x13*
1265 A271 20c multicolored .25 .25
1266 A271 80c multicolored 1.25 1.00
1267 A271 1b multicolored 1.50 1.25
Nos. 1265-1267 (3) 3.00 2.50

Pan-African Postal Union, 10th Anniv. — A272

1990, Jan. 18 Litho. *Perf. 13½*
1268 A272 50c multicolored .80 .70
1269 A272 70c multicolored 1.10 1.00
1270 A272 80c multicolored 1.25 1.10
Nos. 1268-1270 (3) 3.15 2.80

UNESCO World Literacy Year — A273

15c, Illiterate man holding newspaper upside down. 85c, Adults learning alphabet in school. 1b, Literate man holding newspaper upright.

1990, Mar. 13
1271 A273 15c multicolored .25 .20
1272 A273 85c multicolored 1.50 1.25
1273 A273 1b multicolored 1.75 1.40
Nos. 1271-1273 (3) 3.50 2.85

Abebe Bikila, Marathon Runner A274

1990, Apr. 17
1274 A274 5c Race .20 .20
1275 A274 10c Flag bearer, Olympic team .25 .20
1276 A274 20c Race, Rome Olympics .30 .25
1277 A274 75c Race, Tokyo Olympics 1.25 1.00
1278 A274 85c Bikila, trophies, vert. 1.50 1.25
Nos. 1274-1278 (5) 3.50 2.90

Flag — A275

1990, Apr. 30 Litho. *Perf. 13½x13*
1279 A275 5c multicolored .20 .20
1280 A275 10c multicolored .20 .20
1281 A275 15c multicolored .25 .20
1282 A275 20c multicolored .35 .30
1283 A275 25c multicolored .40 .35
1284 A275 30c multicolored .45 .40
1285 A275 35c multicolored .50 .45
1286 A275 40c multicolored .55 .50
1287 A275 45c multicolored .75 .65
1288 A275 50c multicolored .75 .65
1289 A275 55c multicolored .80 .70
1290 A275 60c multicolored .90 .80
1291 A275 70c multicolored 1.00 .90
1292 A275 80c multicolored 1.10 1.00
1293 A275 85c multicolored 1.25 1.10
1294 A275 90c multicolored 1.40 1.25
1295 A275 1b multicolored 1.40 1.25
1296 A275 2b multicolored 3.00 2.75
1297 A275 3b multicolored 4.50 4.00
Nos. 1279-1297 (19) 19.75 17.65

Dated 1989.

Sowing of Teff A276

1990, May 18 Litho. *Perf. 13½*
1298 A276 5c shown .20 .20
1299 A276 10c Harvesting .25 .20
1300 A276 20c Threshing .35 .30
1301 A276 75c Storage, preparation 1.25 1.00
1302 A276 85c Consumption 1.40 1.10
Nos. 1298-1302 (5) 3.45 2.80

Walia Ibex — A277

1990, June 18 *Perf. 14x13½*
1303 A277 5c multi .25 .20
1304 A277 15c multi .80 .70
1305 A277 20c multi 1.10 .95
1306 A277 1b multi, horiz. 5.75 5.25
Nos. 1303-1306 (4) 7.90 7.10

World AIDS Day A278

1991, Jan. 31 Litho. *Perf. 14*
1307 A278 15c Stages of disease .25 .20
1308 A278 85c Education 1.50 1.25
1309 A278 1b Causes, preventatives 1.75 1.40
Nos. 1307-1309 (3) 3.50 2.85

Intl. Decade for Natural Disaster Reduction A279

Map of disaster-prone African areas and: 5c, Volcano. 10c, Earthquake. 15c, Drought. 30c, Flood. 50c, Red Cross health education. 1b, Red Cross assisting fire victims.

1991, Apr. 9 Litho. *Perf. 14*

1310 A279 5c multicolored .20 .20
1311 A279 10c multicolored .20 .20
1312 A279 15c multicolored .25 .20
1313 A279 30c multicolored .45 .35
1314 A279 50c multicolored .95 .65
1315 A279 1b multicolored 1.90 1.40
Nos. 1310-1315 (6) 3.95 3.00

The Cannon of Tewodros A280

Designs: 15c, Villagers receiving cannon 85c, Warriors leaving with cannon. 1b, Hauling cannon up mountainside.

1991, June 18 Litho. *Perf. 13½*

1316 A280 15c multicolored .25 .20
1317 A280 85c multicolored 1.25 1.10
1318 A280 1b multicolored 1.50 1.25
Nos. 1316-1318 (3) 3.00 2.55

Fish A281

1991, Sept. 6 Litho. *Perf. 13½*

1319 A281 5c Lacepede .20 .20
1320 A281 15c Black-finned butterflyfish .30 .20
1321 A281 80c Regal angelfish 1.10 1.00
1322 A281 1b Bleeker 1.50 1.25
Nos. 1319-1322 (4) 3.10 2.65

A282

A283

Traditional Ceremonial Robes: Various robes.

1992, Jan. 1 Litho. *Perf. 13½x14*

1323 A282 5c yellow & multi .20 .20
1324 A282 15c orange & multi .30 .20
1325 A282 80c yel green & multi 1.10 1.00
1326 A282 1b blue & multi 1.50 1.25
Nos. 1323-1326 (4) 3.10 2.65

1992, Mar. 5 Litho. *Perf. 13½x14*

Flowers: 5c, Cissus quadrangularis. 15c, Delphinium dasycaulon. 80c, Epilobium hirsutum. 1b, Kniphofia foliosa.

1327 A283 5c multicolored .20 .20
1328 A283 15c multicolored .30 .20
1329 A283 80c multicolored 1.10 1.00
1330 A283 1b multicolored 1.50 1.25
Nos. 1327-1330 (4) 3.10 2.65

Traditional Homes A284

1992, May 14 Litho. *Perf. 12½x12*

1331 A284 15c Afar .20 .20
1332 A284 35c Anuak .45 .40
1333 A284 50c Gimira .75 .65
1334 A284 1b Oromo 1.60 1.25
Nos. 1331-1334 (4) 3.00 2.50

A285

A286

Pottery.

1992, May Litho. *Perf. 13x13½*

1335 A285 15c Cover .25 .20
1336 A285 85c Jug 1.25 1.10
1337 A285 1b Tall jar 1.50 1.25
Nos. 1335-1337 (3) 3.00 2.55

1992, Sept. 29 *Perf. 14x13½*

1338 A286 20c multicolored .25 .25
1339 A286 80c multicolored 1.25 1.00
1340 A286 1b multicolored 1.50 1.25
Nos. 1338-1340 (3) 3.00 2.50

Pan-African Rinderpest campaign.

A287

Birds — A288

Musical instruments.

1993, Feb. 16 Litho. *Perf. 14x13½*

1341 A287 15c Catchel .25 .20
1342 A287 35c Huldudwa .50 .40
1343 A287 50c Dita .75 .55
1344 A287 1b Atamo 1.50 1.10
Nos. 1341-1344 (4) 3.00 2.25

1993, Apr. 22 Litho. *Perf. 14x13½*

1345 A288 15c Banded barbet .45 .45
1346 A288 35c Ruppell's chat .50 .50
1347 A288 50c Abyssinian catbird .65 .60
1348 A288 1b White-billed starling 1.40 1.25
Nos. 1345-1348 (4) 3.00 2.80

Animals A289

1993, May 14 *Perf. 13½x14*

1349 A289 15c Honey badger .20 .20
1350 A289 35c Spotted necked otter .30 .20
1351 A289 50c Rock hyrax .35 .25
1352 A289 1b White-tailed mongoose .65 .50
Nos. 1349-1352 (4) 1.50 1.15

Herbs — A290

1993, June 10 *Perf. 14x13½*

1353 A290 5c Caraway seed .25 .20
1354 A290 15c Garlic .50 .35
1355 A290 80c Turmeric 1.00 .70
1356 A290 1b Capsicum peppers 1.25 .85
Nos. 1353-1356 (4) 3.00 2.10

Butterflies A291

Insects — A292

1993, July 9 Litho. *Perf. 14x13½*

1357 A291 20c Papilio echerioides .45 .45
1358 A291 30c Papilio rex .50 .50
1359 A291 50c Graphium policenes .65 .60
1360 A291 1b Graphium leonidas 1.40 1.25
Nos. 1357-1360 (4) 3.00 2.80

1993, Aug. 10

1361 A292 15c C. Variabilis .20 .20
1362 A292 35c Lycus trabeatus .30 .20
1363 A292 50c Malachius bifasciatus .35 .25
1364 A292 1b Homoeogryllus xanthographus .65 .50
Nos. 1361-1364 (4) 1.50 1.15

Trees A293

1993, Oct. 12 Litho. *Perf. 13½x14*

1365 A293 15c Euphorbia ampliphylla .25 .20
1366 A293 35c Erythrina brucei .30 .25
1367 A293 50c Draceana steudneri .45 .35
1368 A293 1b Allophylus abyssinicus .70 .60
Nos. 1365-1368 (4) 1.70 1.40

Lakes A294

1993, Dec. 14

1369 A294 15c Wonchi .20 .20
1370 A294 35c Zuquala .30 .25
1371 A294 50c Ashengi .40 .35
1372 A294 1b Tana .70 .60
Nos. 1369-1372 (4) 1.60 1.40

Simien Fox — A294a

Rough Perf. 13½

1994, Jan. 18 Litho.

Color of Border

1372A A294a 5c violet
1372B A294a 10c brown
1372C A294a 15c lemon
1372D A294a 20c salmon
1372E A294a 40c pale rose
1372F A294a 55c dull green
1372G A294a 60c dark blue
1372H A294a 80c bright blue
1372I A294a 85c gray green
1372J A294a 1b bright green
Nos. 1372A-1372J (10) 22.00

Nos. 1372A-1372J have rough perforations and a poor quality printing impression. Dated "1991."

See Nos. 1393A-1393T. For overprints see Nos. 1393U-1393X, 1396A-1396D.

A295

A296

Transitional government: 15c, First anniversary of EPRDF's control of Addis Ababa. 35c, Transition Conference. 50c, National, regional elections. 1b, Coat of arms of Transitional Government.

1994, Mar. 31 Litho. *Perf. 14*

1373 A295 15c multicolored .20 .20
1374 A295 35c multicolored .30 .20
1375 A295 50c multicolored .35 .25
1376 A295 1b multicolored .65 .45
Nos. 1373-1376 (4) 1.50 1.10

1994, May 17 *Perf. 13½*

1377 A296 15c blue & multi .30 .20
1378 A296 85c green & multi .50 .35
1379 A296 1b violet & multi .70 .45
Nos. 1377-1379 (3) 1.50 1.00

Intl. Year of the Family.

Ethiopian Postal Service, Cent. A297

Designs: 60c, Early, modern postal workers, Scott Type A1. 75c, Early letter carriers. 80c, Older building, methods of transportation. 85c, People, mail buses. 1b, Modern methods of transportation, modern high-rise building.

1994, July 4 Litho. *Perf. 13½*

1380 A297 60c multicolored .45 .30
1381 A297 75c multicolored .50 .35
1382 A297 80c multicolored .55 .40
1383 A297 85c multicolored .60 .40
1384 A297 1b multicolored .90 .65
a. Souvenir sheet, #1380-1384 + label 2.25 2.25
Nos. 1380-1384 (5) 3.00 2.10

Enset Plant — A298

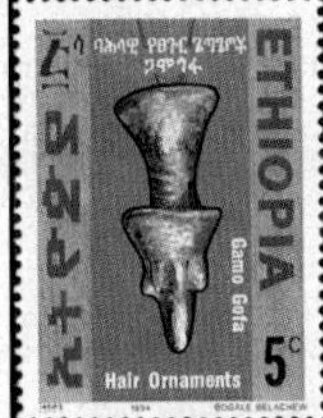
Hair Ornaments A299

1994, Aug. 3

1385 A298 10c shown .20 .20
1386 A298 15c Young plants, hut .25 .20
1387 A298 25c Root, women processing leaves .25 .20
1388 A298 50c Mature plants .30 .25
1389 A298 1b Uses as food .60 .45
Nos. 1385-1389 (5) 1.60 1.30

1994, Sept. 2

1390 A299 5c Gamo gofa .20 .20
1391 A299 15c Sidamo .25 .20
1392 A299 80c Gamo gofa, diff. .40 .30
1393 A299 1b Wello .55 .45
Nos. 1390-1393 (4) 1.40 1.15

Simien Fox Type of 1994

1994, Oct. 18 Litho. *Perf. 14*

Size: 39x25mm

Color of Border

1393A A294a 5c dull lilac
1393B A294a 10c brown
1393C A294a 15c lemon
1393D A294a 20c salmon
1393E A294a 25c lemon
1393F A294a 30c yellow brown
1393G A294a 35c orange
1393H A294a 40c pale rose
1393I A294a 45c pale red org
1393J A294a 50c rose lilac
1393K A294a 55c pale green
1393L A294a 60c dark blue
1393M A294a 65c pale lilac
1393N A294a 70c bright green
1393O A294a 75c pale bl grn
1393P A294a 80c bright blue
1393Q A294a 85c dark green-ish blue
1393R A294a 90c pale brown
1393S A294a 1b greenish blue
1393T A294a 2b yellow brown
Nos. 1393A-1393T (20) 40.00

Nos. 1393A-1393T have sharp impressions, Questa imprint, clean perforations. Dated "1993."

Nos. 1393L, 1393P-1393Q, 1393S Ovptd. in Blue

1994, Oct. 20 Litho. *Perf. 14*

1393U A294a 60c on #1393L 20.00 3.00
1393V A294a 80c on #1393P 25.00 4.00
1393W A294a 85c on #1393Q 50.00 7.50
1393X A294a 1b on #1393S 55.00 8.00
Nos. 1393U-1393X (4) 150.00 22.50

UNFPA, 50th anniv.

ICAO, 50th Anniv. A300

1994, Dec. 7 Litho. *Perf. 13½*

1394 A300 20c mag, lt bl & yel .30 .20
1395 A300 80c yel & lt bl .50 .35
1396 A300 1b dk bl, lt bl & yel .60 .45
Nos. 1394-1396 (3) 1.40 1.00

Nos. 1393M-1393O, 1393R Ovptd.

1994, Dec. 20 Litho. *Perf. 14*

1396A A294a 65c on #1393M 20.00 3.00
1396B A294a 70c on #1393N 25.00 4.00
1396C A294a 75c on #1393O 50.00 7.50
1396D A294a 90c on #1393R 55.00 8.00
Nos. 1396A-1396D (4) 150.00 22.50

African Development Bank, 30th anniv.

Baskets for Serving Food A301

1995, June 7 Litho. *Perf. 13½*

1397 A301 30c Erbo .25 .20
1398 A301 70c Sedieka .40 .35
1399 A301 1b Tirar .65 .55
Nos. 1397-1399 (3) 1.30 1.10

Traditional Hair Styles — A302

1995, July 5 Litho. *Perf. 13½*

1400 A302 25c Kuncho .20 .20
1401 A302 75c Gamme .50 .40
1402 A302 1b Sadulla .60 .50
Nos. 1400-1402 (3) 1.30 1.10

FAO, 50th Anniv. A303

1995, Aug. 29 Litho. *Perf. 13½*

1403 A303 20c green & multi .20 .20
1404 A303 80c blue & multi .50 .40
1405 A303 1b brown & multi .60 .50
Nos. 1403-1405 (3) 1.30 1.10

Cultivating Tools A304

1995, Sept. 7

1406 A304 15c Dangora .20 .20
1407 A304 35c Gheso .25 .20
1408 A304 50c Akafa .30 .25
1409 A304 1b Ankasse .55 .45
Nos. 1406-1409 (4) 1.30 1.10

UN, 50th Anniv. — A305

1995, Oct. 18 Litho. *Perf. 13½*

Color of UN Emblem

1410 A305 20c black .30 .30
1411 A305 80c bister .40 .45
1412 A305 1b blue .60 .65
Nos. 1410-1412 (3) 1.30 1.40

Intergovernmental Authority on Drought and Development (IGADD), 10th Anniv. — A306

Flags of member nations and: 15c, Seedling being planted in arid region. 35c, People carrying supplies through desert. 50c, Person picking fruit. 1b, Map of member nations.

1995, Dec. 27 Litho. *Perf. 13½*

1413 A306 15c multicolored .20 .20
1414 A306 35c multicolored .25 .20
1415 A306 50c multicolored .35 .30
1416 A306 1b multicolored .50 .40
Nos. 1413-1416 (4) 1.30 1.10

Victory at Battle of Adwa, Cent. — A307

Designs: 40c, Battle sites. 50c, Map of Africa focused at Ethiopia. 60c, Troops, ship. 70c, Warriors, soldiers in two battle scenes. 80c, Italians surrendering, Ethiopian troops, cannons. 1b, Emperor Menelik II, constitution, Empress Taitu.

1996, Mar. 2 Litho. *Perf. 13½x14½*

1417 A307 40c multicolored .20 .20
1418 A307 50c multicolored .25 .25
1419 A307 60c multicolored .35 .30
1420 A307 70c multicolored .40 .35
1421 A307 80c multicolored .55 .45
1422 A307 1b multicolored .75 .60
a. Souvenir sheet, #1417-1422 3.00 3.00
Nos. 1417-1422 (6) 2.50 2.15

UN Volunteers, 25th Anniv. A308

Designs: 20c, People, temporary housing huts. 30c, Planting seedlings. 50c, Instructing students. 1b, Caring for infant.

1996, June 6 Litho. *Perf. 13½*

1423 A308 20c multicolored .20 .20
1424 A309 30c multicolored .25 .20
1425 A309 50c multicolored .30 .25
1426 A309 1b multicolored .55 .45
Nos. 1423-1426 (4) 1.30 1.10

1996 Summer Olympic Games, Atlanta A310

1996, Aug. 1 Litho. *Perf. 12½x12*

Overprint in Black

1427 A310 15c Boxing .20 .20
1428 A310 20c Swimming .25 .20
1429 A310 40c Cycling .30 .25
1430 A310 85c Athletics .45 .35
1431 A310 1b Soccer .50 .40
Nos. 1427-1431 (5) 1.70 1.40

Nos. 1427-1431 were originally prepared for the 1984 Summer Olympic Games in Los Angeles, but were not released due to the Soviet-led boycott.

A311

A312

UNICEF, 50th Anniv.: 10c, Emblems. 15c, Mother, child receiving vaccination. 25c, Woman carrying water, boy drinking from faucet. 50c, Children studying. 1b, Mother breastfeeding infant.

1996, Sept. 10 Litho. *Perf. 13½*

1432 A311 10c multicolored .20 .20
1433 A311 15c multicolored .25 .20
1434 A311 25c multicolored .30 .25
1435 A311 50c multicolored .40 .30
1436 A311 1b multicolored .55 .50
Nos. 1432-1436 (5) 1.70 1.45

1996, Dec. 26 Litho. *Perf. 13½*

Creation of Federal Democratic Republic of Ethiopia: 10c, People discussing new Constitution, approved Dec. 8, 1994. 20c, Ballot boxes, hand placing ballot in box. 30c, Marking ballot, placing into box, tower building, items from country's environment. 40c, Building, ballot, assembly hall. 1b, Natl. flag, transition of power.

1437 A312 10c multicolored .20 .20
1438 A312 20c multicolored .20 .20
1439 A312 30c multicolored .20 .20
1440 A312 40c multicolored .25 .20
1441 A312 1b multicolored .45 .35
Nos. 1437-1441 (5) 1.30 1.15

Traditional Baskets — A313

1997, Feb. 20 Litho. *Perf. 13½*

1442 A313 5c Jimma .20 .20
1443 A313 15c Wello .25 .20
1444 A313 80c Welega .35 .30
1445 A313 1b Shewa .50 .40
Nos. 1442-1445 (4) 1.30 1.10

Traditional Baskets A314

1997, May 22 Litho. *Perf. 13½*
1446 A314 35c Arssi .30 .25
1447 A314 65c Gojam .45 .35
1448 A314 1b Harer .65 .50
Nos. 1446-1448 (3) 1.40 1.10

See Nos. 1464-1466.

UN Decade Against Drug Abuse & Illicit Trafficking A315

1997, Sept. 9 Litho. *Perf. 14*
1449 A315 20c green & multi .30 .25
1450 A315 80c brown & multi .45 .35
1451 A315 1b blue & multi .65 .50
Nos. 1449-1451 (3) 1.40 1.10

Historic Buildings, Addis Ababa A316

45c, Bitweded Haile Giorgis' house. 55c, Alfred Ilg's house, vert. 3b, Menelik's Elfign.

Perf. 14½x14, 14x14½
1997, Dec. 23 Litho.
1452 A316 45c multicolored .25 .20
1453 A316 55c multicolored .40 .30
1454 A316 3b multicolored 1.10 .90
Nos. 1452-1454 (3) 1.75 1.40

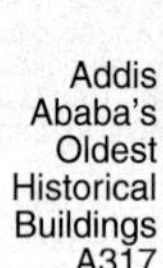

Addis Ababa's Oldest Historical Buildings A317

Designs: 60c, Ras Biru W/Gabriel's house. 75c, Sheh Hojele Alhassen's house. 80c, Fitawrari H/Giorgis Dinegde's house. 85c, Etege Taitu Hotel. 1b, Dejazmach Wube Atnafseged's house.

1997, Dec. 30 Litho. *Perf. 14½x14*
1455 A317 60c multicolored .30 .25
1456 A317 75c multicolored .35 .30
1457 A317 80c multicolored .35 .30
1458 A317 85c multicolored .40 .35
1459 A317 1b multicolored .50 .40
Nos. 1455-1459 (5) 1.90 1.60

Pan African Postal Union, 18th Anniv. A318

Union's emblem and wildlife: 45c, Deculla bushback. 55c, Soemmering's gazelle. 1b, Defassa waterbuck. 2b, Black buffalo.

1998, Mar. 25 Litho. *Perf. 14½x14*
1460 A318 45c multicolored .25 .20
1461 A318 55c multicolored .30 .25
1462 A318 1b multicolored .50 .40
1463 A318 2b multicolored .85 .75
Nos. 1460-1463 (4) 1.90 1.60

Traditional Basket Type of 1997

1998, May 21 Litho. *Perf. 13½*
1464 A314 45c Gonder .20 .20
1465 A314 55c Harere .30 .30
1466 A314 3b Tigray 1.40 1.10
Nos. 1464-1466 (3) 1.90 1.60

Golden-Backed Woodpecker A319

1998, Jan. 12 Photo. *Perf. 11½*
Granite Paper
Panel Color
1467 A319 5c green blue .20 .20
1468 A319 10c yellow .20 .20
1469 A319 15c blue .20 .20
1470 A319 20c light brown .20 .20
1471 A319 25c violet .20 .20
1472 A319 30c light blue .20 .20
1473 A319 35c salmon rose .20 .20
1474 A319 40c lilac .20 .20
1475 A319 45c green .20 .20
1476 A319 50c salmon .25 .20
1477 A319 55c blue .25 .20
1478 A319 60c brick red .30 .25
1479 A319 65c light gray .40 .30
1480 A319 70c bright yellow .45 .35
1481 A319 75c pale violet .45 .35
1482 A319 80c apple green .45 .35
1483 A319 85c gray .45 .35
1484 A319 90c orange .50 .40
1485 A319 1b yellow green .50 .40
1486 A319 2b pale rose 1.10 .90
1487 A319 3b lilac rose 1.60 1.25
1488 A319 5b bister 2.75 2.10
1489 A319 10b orange yellow 5.75 4.50
Nos. 1467-1489 (23) 17.00 13.70

Agreement for Return of Axum Obelisk from Italy — A320

45c, Map of Italy, pieces of obelisk. 55c, Obelisk in Rome. 3b, Map of E. Africa, obelisk, ruins of Axum.

1998, Sept. 3 Litho. *Perf. 13½*
1490 A320 45c multicolored .20 .20
1491 A320 55c multicolored .40 .40
1492 A320 3b multicolored 1.40 1.10
Nos. 1490-1492 (3) 2.00 1.70

Ethiopia-Djibouti Railway, Cent. — A321

Designs: 45c, Men carrying rails during construction. 55c, Early steam train, CFE 404. 1b, Terminal building. 2b, Modern train, BB 1212.

1998, Nov. 24 Litho. *Perf. 11½*
Granite Paper
1493 A321 45c multicolored .35 .30
1494 A321 55c multicolored .35 .30
1495 A321 1b multicolored .55 .45
1496 A321 2b multicolored .85 .75
Nos. 1493-1496 (4) 2.10 1.80

Universal Declaration of Human Rights, 50th Anniv. A322

1998, Dec. 23 Litho. *Perf. 13x13½*
1497 A322 45c red & multi .35 .25
1498 A322 55c yellow & multi .35 .25
1499 A322 1b green & multi .55 .40
1500 A322 2b blue & multi .85 .80
Nos. 1497-1500 (4) 2.10 1.70

Mother Teresa (1910-97) — A323

Various portraits.

1999, Mar. 9 Litho. *Perf. 13½x13*
1501 A323 45c brown & multi .25 .20
1502 A323 55c green & multi .30 .25
1503 A323 1b yel org & multi .40 .35
1504 A323 2b blue & multi .85 .70
Nos. 1501-1504 (4) 1.80 1.50

Intl. Year of the Ocean A324

1999, May 6 Litho. *Perf. 13½x13¼*
1505 A324 45c black & multi .20 .20
1506 A324 55c red & multi .25 .20
1507 A324 1b blue & multi .50 .40
1508 A324 2b green & multi .85 .70
Nos. 1505-1508 (4) 1.80 1.50

World Environment Day — A325

1999, June 17 Litho. *Perf. 13½*
1509 A325 45c pink & multi .20 .20
1510 A325 55c vio & multi .25 .20
1511 A325 1b yel org & multi .50 .40
1512 A325 2b grn & multi .85 .70
Nos. 1509-1512 (4) 1.80 1.50

National Parks — A326

45c, Abijata, Shalla Lakes. 70c, Nechisar. 85c, Bale Mountains. 2b, Awash.

Perf. 13¾x13¼, 13¼x13¾
1999, Sept. 8 Litho.
1513 A326 45c multi, vert. .35 .30
1514 A326 70c multi, vert. .45 .40
1515 A326 85c multi, vert. .50 .40
1516 A326 2b multi 1.25 1.00

See Nos. 1521-1524.

Nos. 1513-1516 (4) 2.55 2.10

UPU, 125th Anniv. — A327

1999, Oct. 28 *Perf. 13¼x13*
1517 A327 20c multicolored .25 .20
1518 A327 80c multicolored .35 .30
1519 A327 1b multicolored .60 .50
1520 A327 2b multicolored .90 .75
Nos. 1517-1520 (4) 2.10 1.75

National Parks Type of 1999

Designs: 50c, Omo, vert. 70c, Mago, vert. 80c, Yangudi-Rassa, vert. 2b, Gambella.

1999, Nov. 30 Litho. *Perf. 13¼*
1521-1524 A326 Set of 4 2.00 1.00

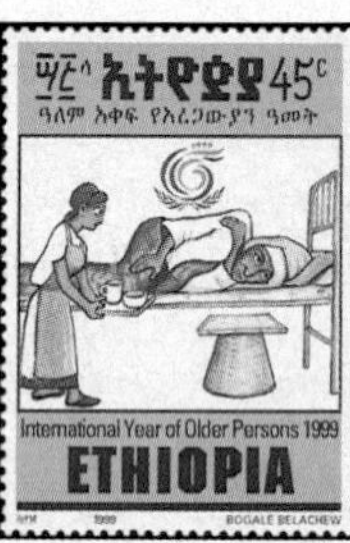

Intl. Year of Older Persons A328

45c, Woman attending to sick man. 70c, Older people gardening. 85c, Four men, bench. 2b, Older man, two young people.

1999, Dec. 30 *Perf. 13¾x13¼*
1525-1528 A328 Set of 4 2.10 1.75

Alexander Pushkin, Writer, Birth Bicent. (in 1999) — A329

Various portraits: 45c, 70c, 85c, 2b.

2000, Mar. 9 Litho. *Perf. 13¾x13¼*
1529-1532 A329 Set of 4 2.10 1.75

Worldwide Fund for Nature (WWF) — A330

Grevy's zebra: a, Grazing. b, Running. c, Resting. d, Head.

2000, Jan. 30 Litho. *Perf. 13¼x13¾*
1533 Strip of 4 *7.50 5.00*
a. A330 45c multi *.60 .45*
b. A330 55c multi *.75 .55*
c. A330 1b multi *1.40 1.00*
d. A330 3b multi *4.25 3.00*

Operation Sunset — A331

Designs: 45c, Lecturer, students. 55c, Soldiers, flag ceremony. 1b, People, house. 2b, Agriculture, construction.

2000, June 27 ***Perf. 13¾***
1534-1537 A331 Set of 4 2.10 1.75

Flags A332

Designs: 25c, Harar Region. 30c, Oromia Region. 50c, Amhara Region. 60c, Tigre Region. 70c, Benishangi Region. 80c, Somalia Region. 90c, Peoples of the South Region. 95c, Gambella Region. 1b, Afar Region. 2b, Ethiopia.

2000, Oct. 26 ***Perf. 13¼x13¾***
1538-1547 A332 Set of 10 4.25 3.50

Afro Ayigeba, Cross of St. Lalibela A333

2000, Apr. 27 ***Perf. 13¾x13¼***
1548 A333 4b multi 2.40 1.90

Menelik's Bushbuck A334

Perf. 13¾x13¼
2000, June 19 **Litho.**

Frame Color

1548A A334 5c dk Prus blue
1549 A334 10c lilac
1549A A334 15c blue
1549B A334 20c yellow bister
1549C A334 25c purple
1549D A334 30c lt Prus blue
1549E A334 35c brt red
1549F A334 40c lilac
1549G A334 45c emerald
1549H A334 50c red
1549I A334 55c blue
1549J A334 60c yellow orange
1549K A334 65c deep blue
1549L A334 70c dull blue
1549M A334 75c orange yellow
1549N A334 80c carmine
1549O A334 85c light blue
1550 A334 90c ocher
1551 A334 1b green
1552 A334 2b red violet
1553 A334 3b purple
1554 A334 5b dark carmine
1555 A334 10b light carmine

Haile Gebreselassie, Runner — A335

Design: #1157, 50c, Gebrselassie running. #1157A, 60c, Gebreselassie running, diff. #1157B, 90c, Gebreselassie running, diff.

2000, Nov. 9 **Litho.** ***Perf. 13½***
1557-1558 A335 Set of 4 2.10 1.60

World Meteorological Organization, 50th Anniv. — A336

Color of inscriptions: 40c, Gray. 75c, Green. 85c, Brown. 2b, Blue.

2000, Oct. 10 **Litho.** ***Perf. 13½***
1559-1562 A336 Set of 4 2.10 1.60

Addis Ababa University, 50th Anniv. — A337

2000, Nov. 30 ***Perf. 13½x14¼***
1563 A337 4b multi 2.10 1.60

UN High Commissioner for Refugees, 50th Anniv. — A338

Frame color: 40c, Brown. 75c, Green. 85c, Brown. 2b, Gold.

2000 Dec. 14 ***Perf. 13½x14***
1564-1567 A338 Set of 4 2.10 1.60

Freshwater Fish — A340

Designs: 45c, Catfish. 55c, Tilapia. 3b, Nile perch.

2001, July 26 **Litho.** ***Perf. 14¼***
1572-1574 A340 Set of 3 2.10 1.60

Traditional Means of Transportation — A341

Designs: 40c, Man on horseback, horse-drawn cart. 60c, Camel caravan. 1b, Man on horseback, horse carrying load. 2b, Man on donkey, donkeys carrying goods.

2001, Aug. 30 ***Perf. 13¼x13½***
1575-1578 A341 Set of 4 2.10 1.60

Year of Dialogue Among Civilizations A342

Color of country name: 25c, Light blue. 75c, White. 1b, Light yellow. 2b, Pink.

2001, Oct. 9 ***Perf. 14***
1579-1582 A342 Set of 4 2.10 1.60

Birds — A343

Designs: 50c, White-tailed swallow. 60c, Spot-breasted plover. 90c, Abyssinian longclaw. 2b, Prince Ruspoli's turaco.

2001, Nov. 29 ***Perf. 14¼***
1583-1586 A343 Set of 4 2.10 1.60

Traditional Beehives A344

Various beehives: 40c, 70c, 90c, 2b.

2002, Jan. 24 **Litho.** ***Perf. 14***
1587-1590 A344 Set of 4 2.10 1.60

Traditional Grain Storage — A345

Designs: 30c, Gota. 70c, Bekollo Gotera. 1b, Gotera. 2b, Gotera, diff.

2002, Mar. 28 ***Perf. 13½x14***
1591-1594 A345 Set of 4 2.10 1.60

Lions Club Intl. — A346

Lions Club Intl. emblem and: 45c, Quality emblem. 55c, Woman at pump. 1b, Eye doctor treating patient. 2b, Man in wheelchair.

2002, Apr. 26 **Litho.** ***Perf. 13x13¼***
1595-1598 A346 Set of 4 2.10 1.60

Trees A347

Designs: 50c, Acacia abyssinica. 60c, Boswellia papyrifera, vert. 90c, Aningeria adolfi-freiderici, vert. 2b, Prunus africana, vert.

Perf. 13½x13¼, 13¼x13½
2002, June 27
1599-1602 A347 Set of 4 2.00 1.60

Traditional Beehives A348

Various beehives with panel colors of: 45c, Pink. 55c, Yellow. 1b, Light blue. 2b, Light green.

2002, Sept. 19 **Litho.** ***Perf. 13¼x13***
1603-1606 A348 Set of 4 1.25 1.00

Granite — A349

Designs: 45c, Sidamo. 55c, Harrar. 1b, Tigray. 2b, Wollega.

2002, Oct. 24 ***Perf. 13x13¼***
1607-1610 A349 Set of 4 1.25 1.00

Konso Waka A350

Various wooden sculptures with background colors of: 40c, Green. 60c, Blue. 1b, Yellow. 2b, Red.

2002, Nov. 28 ***Perf. 14***
1611-1614 A350 Set of 4 1.25 1.00

Menelik's Bushbuck — A351

2002, Dec. 12 ***Perf. 13½x13¾***

Frame Color

1615 A351 5c brt grn blue .20 .20
1616 A351 10c lilac .20 .20
1617 A351 15c bright blue .20 .20
1618 A351 20c brn orange .20 .20

1619 A351 25c purple .20 .20
1620 A351 30c bright blue .20 .20
1621 A351 35c carmine .20 .20
1622 A351 40c purple .20 .20
1623 A351 45c emerald .20 .20
1624 A351 50c red .20 .20
1625 A351 55c blue .20 .20
1626 A351 60c bright yel .20 .20
1627 A351 65c red .20 .20
1628 A351 70c light blue .20 .20
1629 A351 75c bright yel .20 .20
1630 A351 80c carmine .20 .20
1631 A351 85c bright blue .20 .20
1632 A351 90c orange brn .20 .20
1633 A351 95c green .25 .25
1634 A351 1b red violet .25 .25
1635 A351 2b purple .45 .45
1636 A351 3b blue .70 .70
1637 A351 5b dull red 1.25 1.25
1638 A351 10b light green 2.40 2.40
1639 A351 20b rose pink 4.75 4.75
Nos. 1615-1639 (25) 13.65 13.65

Oil Crops A352

Designs: 40c, Abyssinian mustard. 60c, Linseed. 3b, Niger seed.

2002, Dec. 31 Litho. *Perf. 13¼x13*
1640-1642 A352 Set of 3 1.00 1.00

Pan-African Postal Union, 23rd Anniv. — A353

Background color: 20c, Green. 80c, Blue green. 1b, Orange brown. 2b, Purple.

2003, Feb. 18 *Perf. 13x13¼*
1643-1646 A353 Set of 4 .95 .95

Opals — A354

Designs: 45c, Milk opal. 60c, Brown precious opal. 95c, Fire opal. 2b, Yellow precious opal.

2003, May 8 *Perf. 14*
1647-1650 A354 Set of 4 .95 .95

Emperor Tewodros's Amulet — A355

Various views with frame color of: 40c, Green. 60c, Yellow orange. 3b, Red.

2003, Sept. 4 Litho. *Perf. 13x13¼*
1651-1653 A355 Set of 3 .95 .95

Flowers — A356

Designs: 45c, Kniphofia isoetfolia. 55c, Kniphofia insignis. 1b, Crinum bambusetum. 2b, Crinum abyssinicum, horiz.

2003, Nov. 27 Litho. *Perf. 13x13¼*
1654-1657 A356 Set of 4 .95 .95

Konso Terracing System A357

Designs: 40c, Village, crops. 60c, Man and woman, ears of grains. 1b, Terraces, tool. 2b, Farmers working on terraces, crops.

2003, Dec. 30 *Perf. 13¼x13¾*
1658-1661 A357 Set of 4 .95 .95

Amaranths A358

Designs: 20c, Seeds. 80c, White amaranth. 1b, Red amaranth. 2b, Amaranth bread.

2004, Mar. 11 Litho. *Perf. 13¼x14*
1662-1665 A358 Set of 4 .95 .95

Marble A359

Designs: 25c, Sabian multicolored marble. 75c, Eshet blue marble. 1b, Sabian rose green marble. 2b, Sabian purple marble.

2004, July 27 *Perf. 14*
1666-1669 A359 Set of 4 .95 .95

SEMI-POSTAL STAMPS

Types of 1931, Overprinted in Red at Upper Left

Perf. 12x12½, 12½x12
1936, Feb. 24 Unwmk.
B1 A27 1g light green .45 .45
B2 A27 2g rose .45 .45
B3 A25 4g blue .45 .45
B4 A27 8g brown .65 .65
B5 A25 1t purple .65 .65
Nos. B1-B5 (5) 2.65 2.65

Nos. B1-B5 were sold at twice face value, the surtax going to the Red Cross.

Catalogue values for unused stamps in this section, from this point to the end of the section, are for Never Hinged items.

Nos. 289, 290, 292-294 Surcharged in Blue

Perf. 13x13½
1949, June 13 Wmk. 282
B6 A53 8c + 8c deep org 2.00 2.00
B7 A53 12c + 5c red 2.00 2.00
B8 A53 30c + 15c org brn 3.00 3.00
B9 A53 70c + 70c rose lilac 18.00 18.00
B10 A53 $1 + 80c dk car rose 24.00 24.00
Nos. B6-B10 (5) 49.00 49.00

No. B10 exists with "80+" error.
See Nos. B16-B20.

Type A39 Surcharged in Red or Carmine

Perf. 11½
1950, May 8 Unwmk. Photo.
Various Designs
Inscribed "Croix Rouge"
B11 A39 5c + 10c brt grn .85 1.25
B12 A39 10c + 10c brt red 1.25 1.50
B13 A39 25c + 10c brt bl 2.00 2.75
B14 A39 50c + 10c dk yel brn 5.75 4.50
B15 A39 1t + 10c brt vio 9.00 10.00
Nos. B11-B15 (5) 18.85 20.00

The surtax was for the Red Cross.

The surcharge includes two dots which invalidate the original surtax. The original surcharge with uneven cross was red, a 1951 printing with even cross was carmine. Forgeries exist.

Nos. B6-B10 Overprinted in Black

Perf. 13x13½
1951, Nov. 17 Wmk. 282
B16 A53 8c + 8c dp org .70 .70
B17 A53 12c + 5c red .70 .70
B18 A53 30c + 15c org brn 1.10 1.10
B19 A53 70c + 70c rose lilac 9.50 9.50
B20 A53 $1 + 80c dk car rose 14.00 14.00
Nos. B16-B20 (5) 26.00 26.00

Tree, Staff and Snake — SP1

Wmk. 282
1951, Nov. 25 Engr. *Perf. 13*
Lower Panel in Red
B21 SP1 5c + 2c dp bl grn .35 .20
B22 SP1 10c + 3c orange .50 .25
B23 SP1 15c + 3c dp bl .65 .40
B24 SP1 30c + 5c red 1.50 1.00
B25 SP1 50c + 7c red brn 3.25 2.00
B26 SP1 $1 + 10c purple 5.75 3.00
Nos. B21-B26 (6) 12.00 6.85

The surtax was for anti-tuberculosis work.

1958, Dec. 1
Lower Panel in Red
B27 SP1 20c + 3c dl pur .40 .30
B28 SP1 25c + 4c emerald .50 .35
B29 SP1 35c + 5c rose vio .75 .40
B30 SP1 60c + 7c vio bl 1.50 .80
B31 SP1 65c + 7c violet 3.00 1.75
B32 SP1 80c + 9c car rose 5.00 3.00
Nos. B27-B32 (6) 11.15 6.60
Nos. B21-B32 (12) 23.15 13.45

The surtax was for anti-tuberculosis work.

Nos. B21-B32 were the only stamps on sale from Dec. 1-25, 1958.

Type of Regular Issue, 1955, Overprinted and Surcharged

Engr.; Cross Typo. in Red
1959, May 30 Wmk. 282
B33 A62 15c + 2c olive bister & rose red .60 .60
B34 A62 20c + 3c vio & emer .75 .75
B35 A62 30c + 5c rose car & grnsh bl 1.25 1.25
Nos. B33-B35 (3) 2.60 2.60

Cent. of the Intl. Red Cross idea. Surtax for the Red Cross.

The overprint includes the cross, "RED CROSS CENTENARY" and date in two languages. The surcharge includes the date in Amharic and the new surtax. The surcharge was applied locally.

Design A39 Surcharged

Perf. 11½
1960, May 7 Photo. Unwmk.
B36 A39 5c + 1c brt green .50 .50
B37 A39 10c + 2c brt red .75 .60
B38 A39 25c + 3c brt blue 1.10 .75
B39 A39 50c + 4c dk yel brn 1.75 1.50
B40 A39 1t + 5c brt vio 3.00 2.75
Nos. B36-B40 (5) 7.10 6.10

25th anniversary of Ethiopian Red Cross. Forgeries exist.

Crippled Boy on Crutches — SP2

Wmk. 282

1963, July 23 Engr. *Perf. 13½*

B41	SP2 10c + 2c ultra	.25	.25
B42	SP2 15c + 3c red	.35	.30
B43	SP2 50c + 5c brt green	1.10	1.00
B44	SP2 60c + 5c red lilac	1.75	1.25
	Nos. B41-B44 (4)	3.45	2.80

The surtax was to aid the disabled.

AIR POST STAMPS

Regular Issue of 1928 Handstamped in Violet, Red, Black or Green

Perf. 13½x14

1929, Aug. 17 Unwmk.

C1	A22	⅛m orange & lt bl	.90	*1.00*
C2	A23	¼m ind & red org	.90	*1.00*
C3	A22	½m gray grn & blk	.90	*1.00*
C4	A23	1m dk car & blk	.90	*1.00*
C5	A22	2m dk blue & blk	1.00	*1.25*
C6	A23	4m yellow & olive	1.00	*1.25*
C7	A22	8m violet & olive	1.00	*1.25*
C8	A23	1t org brn & vio	1.25	*1.25*
C9	A22	2t green & bister	1.60	*2.00*
C10	A23	3t choc & grn	1.75	*2.00*
		Nos. C1-C10 (10)	11.20	*13.00*

The overprint signifies "17 August 1929-Airplane of the Ethiopian Government." The stamps commemorate the arrival at Addis Ababa of the 1st airplane of the Ethiopian Government.

There are 3 types of the overprint: (I) 19½mm high; "colon" at right of bottom word. (II) 20mm high; same "colon." (III) 19½mm high; no "colon." Many errors exist.

Symbols of Empire, Airplane and Map — AP1

1931, June 17 Engr. *Perf. 12½*

C11	AP1 1g orange red	.20	*.25*
C12	AP1 2g ultra	.20	*.30*
C13	AP1 4g violet	.20	*.40*
C14	AP1 8g blue green	.50	*.80*
C15	AP1 1t olive brown	1.25	*1.00*
C16	AP1 2t carmine	2.25	*3.75*
C17	AP1 3t yellow green	3.25	*5.00*
	Nos. C11-C17 (7)	7.85	*11.50*

Nos. C11 to C17 exist imperforate.

Reprints of C11 to C17 exist. Paper is thinner and gum whiter than the originals and the ink is heavy and shiny. Originals have ink that is dull and granular. Reprints usually sell at about one-tenth of above values.

Catalogue values for unused stamps in this section, from this point to the end of the section, are for Never Hinged items.

Nos. 250, 255 and 257 Surcharged in Black

a

b

Perf. 14x13½

1947, Mar. 20 Unwmk.

C18	A33 (a) 12c on 4c	50.00	50.00
C19	A33 (b) 50c on 25c	45.00	45.00
a.	"26-12-46"	225.00	
C20	A33 (b) $2 on 60c	75.00	75.00
a.	"26-12-46"	300.00	
	Nos. C18-C20 (3)	170.00	170.00
	Set, hinged	110.00	

Resumption of airmail service, 12/29/46.

Franklin D. Roosevelt AP2

Design: $2, Haile Selassie.

Engraved and Photogravure

1947, May 23 *Perf. 12½*

C21	AP2 $1 dk purple & sepia	5.00	4.00
C22	AP2 $2 carmine & dp blue	7.00	7.00

Farmer Plowing AP3

Designs: 10c, 25c, Zoquala, extinct volcano. 30c, 35c, Tesissat Falls, Abai River. 65c, 70c, Amba Alaguie. $1, Sacala, source of Nile. $3, Gorgora and Dembia, Lake Tana. $5, Magdala, former capital. $10, Ras Dashan, mountain peak.

Perf. 13x13½

1947-55 Wmk. 282 Engr.

C23	AP3 8c purple brown	.20	.20
C24	AP3 10c bright green	.20	.20
C25	AP3 25c dull pur ('52)	.35	.20
C26	AP3 30c orange yellow	.50	.20
C27	AP3 35c blue ('55)	.50	.25
C28	AP3 65c purple ('51)	.60	.40
C29	AP3 70c red	.90	.40
C30	AP3 $1 deep blue	1.00	.50
C31	AP3 $3 rose lilac	4.00	2.50
C32	AP3 $5 red brown	7.50	3.50
C33	AP3 $10 rose violet	15.00	9.00
	Nos. C23-C33 (11)	30.75	17.35

For overprints see Nos. C64-C70.

UPU Monument, Bern — AP4

1950, Apr. 3 Unwmk. *Perf. 12½*

C34	AP4 5c green & red	.20	.20
C35	AP4 15c dk sl grn & car	.25	.25
C36	AP4 25c org yel & grn	.30	.25
C37	AP4 50c carmine & ultra	.75	.60
	Nos. C34-C37 (4)	1.50	1.30

75th anniv. of the UPU.

Convair Plane over Mountains AP5

Engraved and Lithographed

1955, Dec. 30 Unwmk. *Perf. 12½*

Center Multicolored

C38	AP5 10c gray green	.40	.20
C39	AP5 15c carmine	.50	.25
C40	AP5 20c violet	.75	.40
	Nos. C38-C40 (3)	1.65	.85

10th anniversary of Ethiopian Airlines.

Promulgating the Constitution — AP6

Perf. 14x13½

1956, July 16 Engr. Wmk. 282

C41	AP6 10c redsh brn & ultra	.25	.30
C42	AP6 15c dk car rose & ol grn	.40	.45
C43	AP6 20c blue & org red	.60	.45
C44	AP6 25c purple & green	.75	.70
C45	AP6 30c dk grn & red brn	1.00	1.10
	Nos. C41-C45 (5)	3.00	3.00

25th anniversary of the constitution.

Aksum AP7

Ancient Capitals: 10c, Lalibela. 15c, Gondar. 20c, Mekele. 25c, Ankober.

1957, Feb. 7 *Perf. 14*

Centers in Green

C46	AP7 5c red brown	.50	.25
C47	AP7 10c rose carmine	.50	.25
C48	AP7 15c red orange	.60	.30
C49	AP7 20c ultramarine	.85	.45
C50	AP7 25c claret	1.25	.65
	Nos. C46-C50 (5)	3.70	1.90

Amharic "A" — AP8

Designs: Various Amharic characters and views of Addis Ababa. The characters, arranged by values, spell Addis Ababa.

1957, Feb. 14 Engr.

Amharic Letters in Scarlet

C51	AP8 5c ultra, *sal pink*	.20	.20
C52	AP8 10c ol grn, *pink*	.25	.20
C53	AP8 15c dl pur, *yel*	.40	.20
C54	AP8 20c grn, *buff*	.50	.25
C55	AP8 25c plum, *pale bl*	.75	.30
C56	AP8 30c red, *pale grn*	.90	.35
	Nos. C51-C56 (6)	3.00	1.50

70th anniversary of Addis Ababa.

Map, Rock Church at Lalibela and Obelisk AP9

1958, Apr. 15 Wmk. 282 *Perf. 13½*

C57	AP9 10c green	.20	.20
C58	AP9 20c rose red	.30	.20
C59	AP9 30c bright blue	.50	.25
	Nos. C57-C59 (3)	1.00	.65

Conf. of Independent African States, Accra, Apr. 15-22.

Map of Africa and UN Emblem AP10

1958, Dec. 29 *Perf. 13*

C60	AP10 5c emerald	.20	.20
C61	AP10 20c carmine rose	.25	.20
C62	AP10 25c ultramarine	.30	.25
C63	AP10 50c pale purple	.60	.35
	Nos. C60-C63 (4)	1.35	1.00

1st session of the UN Economic Conf. for Africa, opened in Addis Ababa Dec. 29.

Nos. C23-C29 Overprinted

Perf. 13x13½

1959, Aug. 16 Engr. Wmk. 282

C64	AP3 8c purple brown	.30	.25
C65	AP3 10c brt green	.40	.30
C66	AP3 25c dull purple	.60	.35
C67	AP3 30c orange yellow	.65	.50
C68	AP3 35c blue	.85	.55
C69	AP3 65c purple	1.25	.85
C70	AP3 70c red	1.60	1.10
	Nos. C64-C70 (7)	5.65	3.90

30th anniv. of Ethiopian airmail service.

Ethiopian Soldier and Map of Congo — AP11

Globe with Map of Africa — AP12

Perf. 11½

1962, July 23 Unwmk. Photo.

Granite Paper

C71	AP11 15c org, bl, brn & grn	.20	.20
C72	AP11 50c pur, bl, brn & grn	.40	.30
C73	AP11 60c red, bl, brn & grn	.70	.35
	Nos. C71-C73 (3)	1.30	.85

2nd anniv. of the Ethiopian contingent of the UN forces in the Congo and in honor of the 70th birthday of Emperor Haile Selassie.

1963, May 22

Granite Paper

C74	AP12 10c magenta & blk	.20	.20
C75	AP12 40c emerald & blk	.40	.25
C76	AP12 60c blue & blk	.70	.35
	Nos. C74-C76 (3)	1.30	.80

Conf. of African heads of state for African Unity, Addis Ababa.

Bird Type of Regular Issue

Birds: 10c, Black-headed forest oriole. 15c, Broad-tailed paradise whydah, vert. 20c, Lammergeier, vert. 50c, White-checked touraco. 80c, Purple indigo bird.

1963, Sept. 12 ***Perf. 11½***

Granite Paper

C77 A74 10c multicolored .25 .20
C78 A74 15c multicolored .30 .20
C79 A74 20c blue, blk & ocher .60 .25
C80 A74 50c lemon & multi .95 .45
C81 A74 80c ultra, blk & brn 1.90 .75
Nos. C77-C81 (5) 4.00 1.85

Swimming AP13

Sport: 10c, Basketball, vert. 15c, Javelin. 80c, Soccer game in stadium.

Perf. 14x13½

1964, Sept. 15 **Litho.** **Unwmk.**

C82 AP13 5c multicolored .20 .20
C83 AP13 10c multicolored .20 .20
C84 AP13 15c multicolored .35 .30
C85 AP13 80c multicolored 1.25 .60
Nos. C82-C85 (4) 2.00 1.30

18th Olympic Games, Tokyo, Oct. 10-25.

Queen Elizabeth II and Emperor Haile Selassie — AP14

1965, Feb. 1 **Photo.** ***Perf. 11½***

Granite Paper

C86 AP14 5c multicolored .20 .20
C87 AP14 35c multicolored .50 .30
C88 AP14 60c multicolored .85 .50
Nos. C86-C88 (3) 1.55 1.00

Visit of Queen Elizabeth II, Feb. 1-8.

Koka Dam and Power Plant — AP15

Designs: 15c, Sugar cane field. 50c, Blue Nile bridge. 60c, Gondar castles. 80c, Coffee tree. $1, Cattle at water hole. $3, Camels at well. $5, Ethiopian Air Lines jet plane.

1965, July 19 **Unwmk.** ***Perf. 11½***

Granite Paper

Portrait in Black

C89 AP15 15c vio brn & buff .20 .20
C90 AP15 40c vio bl & lt bl .45 .30
C91 AP15 50c grn & lt bl .60 .35
C92 AP15 60c claret & yel .75 .45
C93 AP15 80c grn, yel & red .90 .50
C94 AP15 $1 brn & lt bl 1.10 .60
C95 AP15 $3 claret & pink 3.50 1.60
C96 AP15 $5 ultra & lt bl 7.50 3.00
Nos. C89-C96 (8) 15.00 7.00

Bird Type of Regular Issue

Birds: 10c, White-collared kingfisher. 15c, Blue-breasted bee-eater. 25c, African paradise flycatcher. 40c, Village weaver. 60c, White-collared pigeon.

1966, Feb. 15 **Photo.** ***Perf. 11½***

Granite Paper

C97 A74 10c dull yel & multi .25 .20
C98 A74 15c lt blue & multi .35 .20
C99 A74 25c gray & multi .70 .35
C100 A74 40c pink & multi 1.40 .50
C101 A74 60c multicolored 1.60 .75
Nos. C97-C101 (5) 4.30 2.00

Black Rhinoceros — AP16

Animals: 10c, Leopard. 20c, Black-and-white colobus (monkey). 30c, Mountain nyala. 60c, Nubian ibex.

1966, June 20 **Litho.** ***Perf. 13***

C102 AP16 5c dp grn, blk & gray .20 .20
C103 AP16 10c grn, blk & ocher .25 .20
C104 AP16 20c cit, blk & grn .50 .20
C105 AP16 30c yel grn, blk & ocher .75 .20
C106 AP16 60c yel grn, blk & dk brn 1.50 .30
Nos. C102-C106 (5) 3.20 1.10

Bird Type of Regular Issue

Birds: 10c, Blue-winged goose, vert. 15c, Yellow-billed duck. 20c, Wattled ibis. 25c, Striped swallow. 40c, Black-winged lovebird, vert.

1967, Sept. 29 **Photo.** ***Perf. 11½***

Granite Paper

C107 A74 10c lt ultra & multi .20 .20
C108 A74 15c green & multi .35 .20
C109 A74 20c yellow & multi .40 .20
C110 A74 25c salmon & multi .65 .20
C111 A74 40c pink & multi 1.40 .50
Nos. C107-C111 (5) 3.00 1.30

SPECIAL DELIVERY STAMPS

Catalogue values for unused stamps in this section are for Never Hinged items.

Motorcycle Messenger — SD1

Addis Ababa Post Office SD2

Unwmk.

1947, Apr. 24 **Engr.** ***Perf. 13***

E1 SD1 30c orange brown 3.00 .75
E2 SD2 50c blue 5.00 2.00

1954-62 **Wmk. 282**

E3 SD1 30c org brown ('62) 3.00 2.00
E4 SD2 50c blue 2.00 .75

POSTAGE DUE STAMPS

Very Fine examples of Nos. J1-J42 will have perforations touching the design on one or more sides.

Nos. 1-4 and unissued values Overprinted

1895 **Unwmk.** ***Perf. 14x13½***

Black Overprint

J1 A1 ¼g green 1.25
J2 A1 ½g red 1.25
J3 A1 4g lilac brown .90
a. Without overprint .90
J4 A1 8g violet .90
a. Without overprint .90

Red Overprint

J5 A1 1g blue 1.25
J6 A1 2g dark brown 1.25
J7 A1 16g black .90
a. Without overprint .90
Nos. J1-J7 (7) 7.70

Nos. J1-J7 were not issued.

Nos. 1-7 Handstamped in Various Colors:

a

b

1905, Apr.

J8 A1 (a) ¼g green 42.50 42.50
J9 A1 (a) ½g red 42.50 42.50
J10 A1 (a) 1g blue 42.50 42.50
J11 A1 (a) 2g dk brown 42.50 42.50
J12 A2 (a) 4g lilac brown 42.50 42.50
J13 A2 (a) 8g violet 42.50 42.50
J14 A2 (a) 16g black 42.50 42.50
Nos. J7-J14 (8) 298.40 297.50

1905, June 1

J15 A1 (b) ¼g green 42.50 42.50
J16 A1 (b) ½g red 42.50 42.50
J17 A1 (b) 1g blue 42.50 42.50
J18 A1 (b) 2g dark brown 42.50 42.50
J19 A2 (b) 4g lilac brown 42.50 42.50
J20 A2 (b) 8g violet 42.50 42.50
J21 A2 (b) 16g black 42.50 42.50
Nos. J15-J21 (7) 297.50 297.50

Excellent forgeries of Nos. J8-J42 exist.

Nos. 1-7 Handstamped in Blue or Violet

1905, Dec.

J22 A1 ¼g green 10.00 10.00
J23 A1 ½g red 10.00 10.00
J24 A1 1g blue 10.00 10.00
J25 A1 2g dark brown 10.00 10.00
J26 A2 4g lilac brown 10.00 10.00
J27 A2 8g violet 15.00 15.00
J28 A2 16g black 21.00 21.00
Nos. J22-J28 (7) 86.00 86.00

Nos. J22-J27 exist with inverted overprint, also No. J22 with double overprint.
Forgeries exist.

With Additional Surcharge of Value Handstamped as on Nos. 71-77

1907, July 1

J29 A1 (e) ¼ on ¼g grn 14.00 14.00
J30 A1 (e) ½ on ½g red 14.00 14.00
J31 A1 (f) 1 on 1g blue 14.00 14.00
J32 A1 (f) 2 on 2g dk brown 14.00 14.00
J33 A2 (f) 4 on 4g lilac brn 14.00 14.00
J34 A2 (f) 8 on 8g violet 14.00 14.00
J35 A2 (f) 16 on 16g blk 22.50 22.50
Nos. J29-J35 (7) 106.50 106.50

Many errors exist, most of them are unofficial reproductions.

Nos. 1-7 Handstamped in Black

1908, Dec. 1

J36 A1 ¼g green 1.00 .90
J37 A1 ½g red 1.00 .90
J38 A1 1g blue 1.00 .90
J39 A1 2g dark brown 1.25 1.10
J40 A2 4g lilac brown 1.75 1.75
J41 A2 8g violet 4.00 4.50
J42 A2 16g black 12.50 14.00
Nos. J36-J42 (7) 22.50 24.05

Nos. J36 to J42 exist with inverted overprint and Nos. J36, J37, J38 and J40 with double overprint.
Forgeries of Nos. J36-J56 exist.

Same Handstamp on Nos. 87-93

1912, Dec. 1 ***Perf. 11½***

J43 A3 ¼g blue green 1.25 .85
J44 A3 ½g rose 1.25 1.10

1913, July 1

J45 A3 1g green & org 4.25 3.00
J46 A4 2g blue 5.00 4.25
J47 A4 4g green & car 7.50 5.00
J48 A5 8g ver & dp grn 10.00 8.00
J49 A5 16g ver & car 25.00 19.00
Nos. J43-J49 (7) 54.25 41.20

Nos. J43-J49, all exist with inverted, double and double, one inverted overprint.

Same Handstamp on Nos. 120-124 in Blue Black

1925-27 ***Perf. 11½***

J50 A6 ⅛g violet & brn *18.00 18.00*
J51 A6 ¼g bl grn & db *18.00 18.00*
J52 A6 ½g scar & ol grn *20.00 20.00*
J53 A9 1g rose lil & gray grn *20.00 20.00*
J54 A9 2g dp ultra & fawn *20.00 20.00*
Nos. J50-J54 (5) *96.00 96.00*

Same Handstamp on Nos. 110, 112

1930 (?)

J55 A3 1g green & orange *30.00 30.00*
J56 A4 2g blue *30.00 30.00*

The status of Nos. J55-J56 is questioned.

Catalogue values for unused stamps in this section, from this point to the end of the section, are for Never Hinged items.

D2

Perf. 11½

1951, Apr. 2 **Unwmk.** **Litho.**

J57 D2 1c emerald .35 .20
J58 D2 5c rose red .55 .20
J59 D2 10c violet .75 .30
J60 D2 20c ocher 1.10 .65
J61 D2 50c bright ultra 2.00 1.50
J62 D2 $1 rose lilac 4.25 2.00
Nos. J57-J62 (6) 9.00 4.85

OCCUPATION STAMPS

Issued under Italian Occupation

100 Centesimi = 1 Lira

OS1

Emperor Victor Emmanuel III — OS2

1936 **Wmk. 140** ***Perf. 14***

N1 OS1 10c orange brown 8.25 5.50
N2 OS1 20c purple 7.75 1.75
N3 OS2 25c dark green 3.75 .35
N4 OS2 30c dark brown 3.75 .85
N5 OS2 50c rose carmine 1.00 .20
N6 OS1 75c deep orange 15.00 4.00
N7 OS1 1.25 l deep blue 16.00 6.25
Nos. N1-N7 (7) 55.50 18.90
Set, never hinged 110.00

Issued: #N3-N5, May 22; others Dec. 5.
For later issues see Italian East Africa.

FALKLAND ISLANDS

'fol-klənd 'ī-ləndz

LOCATION — A group of islands about 300 miles east of the Straits of Magellan at the southern limit of South America
GOVT. — British Crown Colony
AREA — 4,700 sq. mi.
POP. — 2,607 (1996)
CAPITAL — Stanley

Dependencies of the Falklands are South Georgia and South Sandwich. In March 1962, three other dependencies — South Shetland Islands, South Orkneys and Graham Land—became the new separate colony of British Antarctic Territory. In 1985 South Georgia and the South Sandwich Islands became a separate colony.

12 Pence = 1 Shilling
20 Shillings = 1 Pound
100 Pence = 1 Pound (1971)

Catalogue values for unused stamps in this country are for Never Hinged items, beginning with Scott 97 in the regular postage section, Scott B1 in the semi-postal section, Scott J1 in the postage due section, Scott 1L1 in Falkland Island Dependencies regular issues, Scott 1LB1 in Falkland Island Dependencies semi-postals, and Scott 2L1, 3L1, 4L1, 5L1 in the Issues for Separate Islands.

Values for unused stamps are for examples with original gum as defined in the catalogue introduction.

Nos. 1-4, 7-8, and some printings of Nos. 5-6, exist with straight edges on one or two sides, being the imperforate margins of the sheets. This occurs in 24 out of 60 stamps. Catalogue values are for stamps with perforations on all sides.

Queen Victoria — A1

1878-79 Unwmk. Engr. *Perf. 14*

1 A1 1p claret 775.00 *500.00*
2 A1 4p dark gray ('79) 1,300. 200.00
3 A1 6p green 90.00 75.00
4 A1 1sh bister brown 72.50 75.00

1883-95 Wmk. 2

5 A1 1p brt claret ('94) 120.00 95.00
a. 1p claret 400.00 175.00
b. Horiz. pair, imperf. vert. *52,500.*
c. 1p red brown ('91) 220.00 90.00
d. Diag. half of #5c used as ½p on cover *3,000.*
6 A1 4p olive gray ('95) 12.00 27.50
a. 4p gray black 425.00 95.00
b. 4p olive gray black ('89) 150.00 57.50
c. 4p brownish black ('94) 850.00 375.00

No. 6c has watermark reversed.
For surcharge see No. 19E.

1886 Wmk. 2 Sideways

7 A1 1p claret 75.00 57.50
a. 1p brownish claret 110.00 55.00
b. Diagonal half of #7a used as ½p on cover *2,600.*
8 A1 4p olive gray 450.00 50.00
a. 4p pale gray black 725.00 72.50

For surcharge see No. 19.

1891-1902 Wmk. 2

9 A1 ½p green ('92) 19.00 *18.00*
a. ½p blue green 25.00 *30.00*
10 A1 ½p yel green ('99) 2.25 *3.50*
11 A1 1p orange brown 80.00 67.50
a. Diagonal half used as ½p on cover *2,250.*
11B A1 1p pale red 6.50 5.00
12 A1 1p org red ('02) 13.00 4.75
a. 1p Venetian red ('95) 23.00 20.00
13 A1 2p magenta ('96) 6.00 12.50
14 A1 2½p deep blue ('94) 275.00 160.00
15 A1 2½p ultra ('94) 30.00 12.50
a. 2½p pale ultra ('98) 35.00 16.00
b. 2½p dull blue 175.00 27.50
c. 2½p deep ultra ('01) 40.00 40.00
d. 2½p pale chalky ultra 160.00 50.00
16 A1 6p yellow ('96) 35.00 50.00
a. 6p orange ('92) 65.00 50.00
17 A1 9p ver ('96) 42.50 *65.00*
a. 9p salmon 50.00 *65.00*
18 A1 1sh gray brn ('95) 60.00 *65.00*
a. 1sh bister brown ('96) 55.00 55.00
Nos. 9-18 (11) 569.25 463.75

Nos. 7 and 5a Surcharged in Black

1891 Wmk. 2 Sideways

19 A1 ½p on half of 1p, #7 650. 360.
d. Unsevered pair 3,000. 1,350.

Wmk. 2

19E A1 ½p on half of 1p, #5a 775. 325.
f. Unsevered pair 3,850. 1,700.

Genuine used bisects should be canceled with a segmented circular cork cancel. Any other cancel must be linked by date to known mail ship departures. This surcharge exists on "souvenir" bisects, including copies of No. 11, and can be found inverted, double and sideways.

A3

A4

1898 Wmk. 1

20 A3 2sh6p dark blue 275.00 300.00
21 A4 5sh brown red 225.00 275.00

King Edward VII
A5 A6

1904-07 Wmk. 3 *Perf. 14*

22 A5 ½p yellow green 5.25 1.80
23 A5 1p red, wmk. sideways ('07) 1.20 *2.50*
a. Wmk. upright ('04) 13.50 *1.80*
24 A5 2p dull vio ('05) 20.00 *32.50*
25 A5 2½p ultramarine 35.00 10.00
a. 2½p deep blue 300.00 200.00
26 A5 6p orange ('05) 45.00 *57.50*
27 A5 1sh bis brn ('05) 47.50 40.00
28 A6 3sh gray green 160.00 150.00
29 A6 5sh dull red ('05) 230.00 180.00
Nos. 22-29 (8) 543.95 474.30

King George V
A7 A8

1912-14

30 A7 ½p yellow green 3.00 3.25
31 A7 1p red 4.50 2.50
32 A7 2p brown violet 8.50 19.00
33 A7 2½p deep ultra 9.50 *19.00*
34 A7 6p orange 17.50 *22.50*
35 A7 1sh bister brown 40.00 *37.50*
36 A8 3sh dark green 100.00 *95.00*
37 A8 5sh brown red 95.00 *120.00*
38 A8 5sh plum ('14) 220.00 *220.00*
39 A8 10sh red, *green* 200.00 *300.00*
40 A8 £1 black, *red* 525.00 *600.00*
Nos. 30-40 (11) 1,223. *1,438.*

For overprints see Nos. MR1-MR3.

1921-29 Wmk. 4

41 A7 ½p yellow green 3.50 *4.50*
42 A7 1p red ('24) 6.00 1.50
43 A7 2p brown vio ('23) 9.50 8.50
44 A7 2½p dark blue 8.00 *20.00*
a. 2½p Prussian blue ('29) 375.00 *550.00*
45 A7 2½p vio, *yel* ('23) 6.00 *42.50*
46 A7 6p orange ('25) 9.50 *45.00*
47 A7 1sh bister brown 20.00 *57.50*
48 A8 3sh dk green ('23) 95.00 *190.00*
Nos. 41-48 (8) 157.50 *369.50*

No. 43 Surcharged

1928

52 A7 2½p on 2p brn vio *1,000.* *1,000.*
a. Double surcharge *39,000.*

Beware of forged surcharges.

King George V — A9

1929-31 *Perf. 14*

54 A9 ½p green 1.25 *3.00*
55 A9 1p scarlet 4.00 .80
56 A9 2p gray 3.25 3.00
57 A9 2½p blue 3.25 *2.25*
58 A9 4p deep orange 20.00 *14.00*
59 A9 6p brown violet 20.00 *14.00*
60 A9 1sh black, *green* 25.00 *35.00*
a. 1sh black, *emerald* 26.00 *30.00*
61 A9 2sh6p red, *blue* 52.50 52.50
62 A9 5sh green, *yel* 85.00 *100.00*
63 A9 10sh red, *green* 160.00 *200.00*

Wmk. 3

64 A9 £1 black, *red* 350.00 425.00
Nos. 54-64 (11) 724.25 849.55

Issue dates: 4p, 1931, others, Sept. 2.

Romney Marsh Ram — A10

Iceberg A11

Whaling Ship — A12

Port Louis A13

Map of the Islands A14

South Georgia
A15

Blue Whale
A16

Government House
A17

Battle Memorial — A18

King Penguin — A19

Coat of Arms — A20

King George V — A21

1933, Jan. 2 Wmk. 4 *Perf. 12*

65	A10	½p green & blk	2.00	6.00
66	A11	1p dl red & blk	4.00	2.00
67	A12	1½p lt bl & blk	16.00	*20.00*
68	A13	2p ol brn & blk	12.50	*25.00*
69	A14	3p dl vio & blk	17.50	*20.00*
70	A15	4p orange & blk	20.00	*20.00*
71	A16	6p gray & black	57.50	*65.00*
72	A17	1sh ol grn & blk	50.00	*75.00*
73	A18	2sh6p dp vio & blk	200.00	200.00
74	A19	5sh yellow & blk	625.00	*850.00*
a.		5sh yellow orange & black	1,750.	*1,950.*
75	A20	10sh lt brn & blk	700.00	*975.00*
76	A21	£1 rose & black	1,850.	*2,250.*
		Nos. 65-76 (12)	3,554.	*4,508.*

Cent. of the permanent occupation of the islands as a British colony.

Common Design Types pictured following the introduction.

Silver Jubilee Issue
Common Design Type

1935, May 7 *Perf. 11x12*

77	CD301	1p carmine & blue	1.25	.50
78	CD301	2½p ultra & brown	2.50	2.10
79	CD301	4p indigo & grn	5.00	5.50
80	CD301	1sh brn vio & ind	11.00	4.75
		Nos. 77-80 (4)	19.75	12.85
		Set, never hinged	37.50	

Coronation Issue
Common Design Type

1937, May 12 *Perf. 11x11½*

81	CD302	½p deep green	.20	.20
82	CD302	1p dark carmine	.35	*.50*
83	CD302	2½p deep ultra	.60	*.80*
		Nos. 81-83 (3)	1.15	1.50
		Set, never hinged	2.00	

Whale Jawbones (Centennial Monument) — A22

#85, 86A, Black-necked swan. #85B, 86, Battle memorial. 2½p, 3p, Flock of sheep. 4p, Upland goose. 6p, R.R.S. "Discovery II." 9p, R.R.S. "William Scoresby." 1sh, Mt. Sugar Top. 1sh3p, Turkey vultures. 2sh6p, Gentoo penguins. 5sh, Sea lions. 10sh, Deception Island. £1, Arms of Colony.

1938-46 *Perf. 12*

84	A22	½p green & blk	.20	.20
85	A22	1p red & black	2.50	2.50
a.		1p rose carmine & black	16.00	1.75
85B	A22	1p dk vio & blk	.20	.20
86	A22	2p dk vio & blk	1.75	1.75
86A	A22	2p rose car & black	.25	.25
87	A22	2½p ultra & blk	1.50	1.25
87A	A22	3p dp bl & blk	.75	.75
88	A22	4p rose vio & blk	1.75	1.75
89	A22	6p brown & blk	5.00	4.25
90	A22	9p sl bl & blk	1.75	1.50
91	A22	1sh dull blue	7.75	3.00
92	A22	1sh3p car & blk	1.75	*3.00*
93	A22	2sh6p gray black	37.50	21.00
94	A22	5sh org brown & ultra	55.00	42.50
a.		5sh yel brown & indigo	625.00	300.00
95	A22	10sh org & blk	60.00	42.50
96	A22	£1 dk vio & blk	125.00	85.00
		Nos. 84-96 (16)	302.65	211.40
		Set, never hinged	460.00	

Issued: #85B, 86A, 3p, 7/14/41; 1sh3p, 12/10/46; No. 94a, 1942; others, 1/3/38.

See Nos. 101-102. For overprints see Nos. 2L1-2L8, 3L1-3L8, 4L1-4L8, 5L1-5L8.

Catalogue values for unused stamps in this section, from this point to the end of the section, are for Never Hinged items.

Peace Issue
Common Design Type
Perf. 13½x14

1946, Oct. 7 Engr. Wmk. 4

97	CD303	1p purple	.35	.25
98	CD303	3p deep blue	.55	.25

Silver Wedding Issue
Common Design Types

1948, Nov. 1 Photo. *Perf. 14x14½*

99	CD304	2½p bright ultra	1.25	.60

Engr.; Name Typo.
Perf. 11½x11

100	CD305	£1 purple	110.00	75.00

Types of 1938-46

2½p, Upland geese. 6p, R.R.S. "Discovery II."

Perf. 12

1949, June 15 Engr. Wmk. 4

101	A22	2½p dp blue & black	5.50	*7.25*
102	A22	6p gray black	4.75	3.50

UPU Issue
Common Design Types
Engr.; Name Typo. on 3p, 1sh3p

1949, Oct. 10 *Perf. 13½, 11x11½*

103	CD306	1p violet	.60	.60
104	CD307	3p indigo	1.50	1.50
105	CD308	1sh3p green	5.00	4.50
106	CD309	2sh blue	11.00	9.50
		Nos. 103-106 (4)	18.10	16.10

Sheep
A35

Arms of the Colony — A36

Designs: 1p, R.M.S. Fitzroy. 2p Upland goose. 2½p, Map. 4p, Auster plane. 6p, M.S.S. John Biscoe. 9p, "Two Sisters" peaks. 1sh, Gentoo penguins. 1sh 3p, Kelp goose and gander. 2sh 6p, Sheep shearing. 5sh, Battle memorial. 10sh, Sea lion and clapmatch. £1, Hulk of "Great Britain."

Perf. 13½x13, 13x13½

1952, Jan. 2 Engr. Wmk. 4

107	A35	½p green	.70	*1.40*
108	A35	1p red	1.50	.70
109	A35	2p violet	3.50	*4.50*
110	A35	2½p ultra & blk	.95	.95
111	A36	3p deep ultra	1.00	*1.75*
112	A35	4p claret	7.25	2.75
113	A35	6p yellow brn	12.00	1.75
114	A35	9p orange yel	9.00	3.50
115	A36	1sh black	21.00	1.50
116	A35	1sh3p red orange	13.00	*9.25*
117	A36	2sh6p olive	16.00	*20.00*
118	A36	5sh red violet	10.00	*15.00*
119	A35	10sh gray	22.50	*25.00*
120	A35	£1 black	25.00	*32.50*
		Nos. 107-120 (14)	143.40	*120.55*

Coronation Issue
Common Design Type

1953, June 4 *Perf. 13½x13*

121	CD312	1p car & black	.95	1.25

Types of 1952 with Portrait of Queen Elizabeth II

1955-57 *Perf. 13½x13, 13x13½*

122	A35	½p green ('57)	.75	*1.50*
123	A35	1p red ('57)	1.25	1.25
124	A35	2p violet ('56)	3.25	*6.25*
125	A35	6p light brown	8.00	.70
126	A35	9p ocher ('57)	12.50	*21.00*
127	A36	1sh black	7.00	1.40
		Nos. 122-127 (6)	32.75	*32.10*

Marsh Starling
A37

Birds: ½p, Falkland Islands Thrush. 1p, Dominican gull. 2p, Gentoo penguins. 3p, Upland geese. 4p, Steamer ducks. 5½p, Rock-hopper penguin. 6p, black-browed albatross. 9p, Silver grebe. 1sh, Pied oystercatchers. 1sh3p, Yellow-billed teal. 2sh, Kelp geese, 5sh, King shag. 10sh, Guadelupe caracara. £1, Black-necked swan.

Perf. 13½x13

1960, Feb. 10 Engr. Wmk. 314

Center in Black

128	A37	½p green	3.50	.40
a.		Wmk. sideways ('66)	.45	.30
129	A37	1p rose red	1.40	.65
130	A37	2p blue	3.50	.85
131	A37	2½p bister brn	1.25	.25
132	A37	3p olive	.70	.25
133	A37	4p rose car	1.00	.85
134	A37	5½p violet	1.75	*1.90*
135	A37	6p sepia	2.00	.25
136	A37	9p orange	1.75	1.00
137	A37	1sh dull purple	.65	.25
138	A37	1sh3p ultra	9.00	*11.00*
139	A37	2sh brown car	25.00	2.10
140	A37	5sh grnsh blue	25.00	9.25
141	A37	10sh rose lilac	42.50	11.00
142	A37	£1 yellow org	45.00	25.00
		Nos. 128-142 (15)	164.00	65.00

Morse Key — A38

1962, Oct. 5 Photo. *Perf. 11½x11*

143	A38	6p dp org & dk red	1.00	.60
144	A38	1sh brt ol grn & dp green	1.10	1.00
145	A38	2sh brt ultra & violet	1.90	1.90
		Nos. 143-145 (3)	4.00	3.50

Falkland Islands radio station, 50th anniv.

Freedom from Hunger Issue
Common Design Type

1963, June 4 *Perf. 14x14½*

146	CD314	1sh ultramarine	13.50	5.00

Red Cross Centenary Issue
Common Design Type
Wmk. 314

1963, Sept.2 Litho. *Perf. 13*

147	CD315	1p black & red	2.25	1.00
148	CD315	1sh ultra & red	19.00	6.00

Shakespeare Issue
Common Design Type

1964, Apr. 23 Photo. *Perf. 14x14½*

149	CD316	6p black	1.40	.50

H.M.S. Glasgow
A39

6p, H.M.S. Kent. 1sh, H.M.S. Invincible. 2sh, Falkland Islands Battle Memorial, vert.

1964, Dec. 8 Engr. *Perf. 13*

150	A39	2½p ver & black	9.75	3.75
151	A39	6p blue & black	.45	.30
a.		"Glasgow" vignette	*17,000.*	
152	A39	1sh carmine & blk	.45	*1.10*

Perf. 13x14

153	A39	2sh dk blue & blk	.35	.85
		Nos. 150-153 (4)	11.00	6.00

Battle of the Falkland Islands between the British and German navies, 50th anniv.

ITU Issue
Common Design Type
Perf. 11x11½

1965, May 26 Litho. Wmk. 314

154	CD317	1p blue & dl dk bl	.65	.40
155	CD317	2sh lilac & dl yel	9.50	3.25

Intl. Cooperation Year Issue
Common Design Type

1965, Oct. 25 *Perf. 14½*

156	CD318	1p blue grn & claret	1.00	.25
157	CD318	1sh lt violet & grn	7.50	1.75

Churchill Memorial Issue
Common Design Type

1966, Jan. 24 Photo. *Perf. 14*

Design in Black, Gold and Carmine Rose

158	CD319	½p bright blue	.25	.20
159	CD319	1p green	1.25	.30
160	CD319	1sh brown	3.25	1.75
161	CD319	2sh violet	7.25	4.25
		Nos. 158-161 (4)	12.00	6.50

Human Rights Flame and Globe
A40

Perf. 14x14½

1968, July 4 Photo. Wmk. 314

162	A40	2p brt rose & multi	.20	.20
163	A40	6p brt green & multi	.40	.40
164	A40	1sh orange & multi	.65	.65
165	A40	2sh ultra & multi	1.25	1.25
		Nos. 162-165 (4)	2.50	2.50

International Human Rights Year.

Dusty Miller — A41

Falkland Islands flora: 1½p, Pig vine, horiz. 2p, Pale maiden. 3p, Dog orchard. 3½p, Sea cabbage, horiz. 4½p, Vanilla daisy. 5½p, Arrowleaf marigold, horiz. 6p, Diddle-dee, horiz. 1sh, Scurvy grass, horiz. 1sh6p, Prickly burr. 2sh, Fachine. 3sh, Lavender. 5sh, Felton's flower, horiz. £1, Yellow orchid.

1968, Oct. 9 Photo. *Perf. 14*

166 A41 ½p multicolored .20 .20
167 A41 1½p multicolored .35 .20
168 A41 2p multicolored .50 .20
169 A41 3p multicolored 5.00 .30
170 A41 3½p multicolored .25 *.40*
171 A41 4½p multicolored 1.40 .55
172 A41 5½p multicolored 1.40 .70
173 A41 6p multicolored .70 *.85*
174 A41 1sh multicolored .70 *1.75*
175 A41 1sh6p multicolored 4.00 *8.00*
176 A41 2sh multicolored 5.00 4.00
177 A41 3sh multicolored 7.00 5.75
178 A41 5sh multicolored 25.00 11.00
179 A41 £1 multicolored 11.00 6.25
Nos. 166-179 (14) 62.50 40.15

See #210-222. For surcharges see #197-209.

Beaver DHC 2 Seaplane A42

Designs: 6p, Norseman seaplane. 1sh, Auster plane. 2sh, Falkland Islands arms.

1969, Apr. 8 Litho. *Perf. 14*

180 A42 2p multicolored .20 .20
181 A42 6p multicolored .35 .35
182 A42 1sh multicolored .70 .70
183 A42 2sh multicolored 1.75 1.25
Nos. 180-183 (4) 3.00 2.50

21st anniv. of Government Air Service.

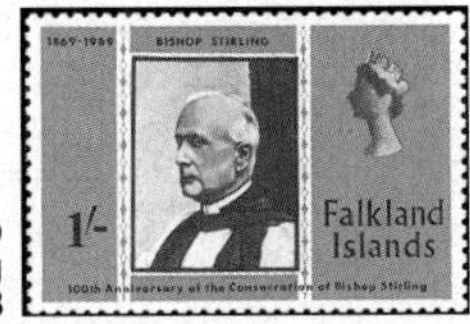

Bishop Stirling A43

2p, Holy Trinity Church, 1869. 6p, Christ Church Cathedral, 1969. 2sh, Bishop's miter.

1969, Oct. 30 *Perf. 14*

184 A43 2p emerald & black .60 .60
185 A43 6p red orange & black .60 .60
186 A43 1sh lilac & black .60 .60
187 A43 2sh yellow & multi .70 .70
Nos. 184-187 (4) 2.50 2.50

Consecration of Waite Hocking Stirling (1829-1923), as first Bishop of the Bishopric of the Falkland Islands, cent.

Gun Emplacement — A44

2p, Volunteer on horseback, vert. 1sh, Volunteer in dress uniform, vert. 2sh, Defense Force badge.

Perf. 13½x13, 13x13½

1970, Apr. 30 Litho. Wmk. 314

188 A44 2p ultra & multi .65 .30
189 A44 6p multicolored 1.25 .75
190 A44 1sh buff & multi 2.50 1.25
191 A44 2sh yellow & multi 5.25 2.50
Nos. 188-191 (4) 9.65 4.80

Falkland Islands Defense Force, 50th anniv.

The Great Britain, 1843 A45

The Great Britain in: 4p, 1845. 9p, 1876. 1sh, 1886. 2sh, 1970.

1970, Oct. 30 Litho. *Perf. 14½*

192 A45 2p lemon & multi .35 .20
193 A45 4p lilac & multi .70 .50
194 A45 9p bister & multi 1.40 1.10
195 A45 1sh org brn & multi 2.25 1.75
196 A45 2sh multicolored 4.75 3.75
Nos. 192-196 (5) 9.45 7.30

Nos. 166-178 Surcharged with New Value (Decimal Currency) and Bar

1971, Feb. 15 Photo. *Perf. 14*

197 A41 ½p on ½p multi .95 .95
198 A41 1p on 1½p multi .20 .20
199 A41 1½p on 2p multi .35 .35
200 A41 2p on 3p multi .40 .40
201 A41 2½p on 3½p multi .60 .60
202 A41 3p on 4½p multi .65 .65
203 A41 4p on 5½p multi .85 .85
204 A41 5p on 6p multi 1.10 1.10
205 A41 6p on 1sh multi 1.75 1.50
206 A41 7½p on 1sh6p multi 2.10 1.90
207 A41 10p on 2sh multi 3.25 2.75
208 A41 15p on 3sh multi 6.00 4.75
209 A41 25p on 5sh multi 12.00 9.50
Nos. 197-209 (13) 30.20 25.50

Flower Type of 1968
"p" instead of "d"

Designs as before. 1p, 2½p, 4p, 5p, 6p, 25p, horizontal.

Wmk. 314, Sideways on Vert. Stamps

1972, June 1 *Perf. 14*

210 A41 ½p Dusty miller 1.10 .90
a. Wmk. upright ('74) *12.50 22.50*
b. Wmk. 373 ('75) 3.25 *3.50*
211 A41 1p Pig vine .35 .25
212 A41 1½p Pale maiden .50 .35
213 A41 2p Dog orchid 3.25 2.50
a. Wmk. upright ('74) 27.50 3.50
214 A41 2½p Sea cabbage .85 .60
215 A41 3p Vanilla daisy .85 .70
216 A41 4p Arrowleaf marigold 1.10 .85
217 A41 5p Diddle-dee 1.25 1.00
218 A41 6p Scurvy grass 15.00 10.50
a. Wmk. sideways ('74) 1.90 *2.25*
219 A41 7½p Prickly burr 3.25 2.50
220 A41 10p Fachine 6.50 5.50
221 A41 15p Lavender 5.75 4.50
222 A41 25p Felton's flower 10.25 9.50
Nos. 210-222 (13) 50.00 39.65

No. 213 has watermark sideways.

Silver Wedding Issue, 1972
Common Design Type

Design: Queen Elizabeth II, Prince Philip, Romney Marsh sheep and giant sea lions.

1972, Nov 20 Photo. *Perf. 14x14½*

223 CD324 1p sl grn & multi .30 .30
224 CD324 10p ultra & multi 1.00 1.00

Princess Anne's Wedding Issue
Common Design Type

1973, Nov. 14 Litho. *Perf. 14*

225 CD325 5p lilac & multi .20 .20
226 CD325 15p citron & multi .70 .70

Fur Seals A46

Tourist Publicity: 4p, Trout fishing. 5p, Rockhopper penguins. 15p, Military starling.

1974, Mar. 6 Litho. Wmk. 314

227 A46 2p lt ultra & multi 2.40 .95
228 A46 4p brt blue & multi 3.25 1.40
229 A46 5p yellow & multi 10.50 1.40
230 A46 15p lt ultra & multi 12.50 3.00
Nos. 227-230 (4) 28.65 6.75

Early 19th Cent. Mail Coach, UPU Emblem — A47

UPU Cent.: 5p, Packet, 1841. 8p, First British mail planes, 1911. 16p, Catapult mail, 1920's.

1974, July 31 *Perf. 14*

231 A47 2p multicolored .25 .25
232 A47 5p multicolored .40 .40
233 A47 8p multicolored .45 .45
234 A47 16p multicolored .65 .65
Nos. 231-234 (4) 1.75 1.75

Churchill, Parliament and Big Ben A48

Design: 20p, Churchill and warships.

1974, Nov. 30 *Perf. 13x13½*

235 A48 16p multicolored 1.50 1.50
236 A48 20p multicolored 2.00 2.00
a. Souvenir sheet of 2, #235-236 8.50 8.50

Sir Winston Churchill (1874-1965).

HMS Exeter A49

Battleships: 6p, HMNZS Achilles. 8p, Admiral Graf Spee. 16p, HMS Ajax.

1974, Dec. 13 *Perf. 14*

237 A49 2p multicolored 2.25 .85
238 A49 6p multicolored 3.75 2.00
239 A49 8p multicolored 4.75 3.00
240 A49 16p multicolored 12.00 8.00
Nos. 237-240 (4) 22.75 13.85

35th anniv. of the Battle of the River Plate between British ships and the German battleship Graf Spee.

Seal and Flag Badge — A50

7½p, Coat of arms, 1925. 10p, Arms, 1948. 16p, Arms (Falkland Islands Dependencies), 1952.

1975, Oct. 28 Litho. Wmk. 373

241 A50 2p multicolored 1.00 1.00
242 A50 7½p multicolored 1.90 1.90
243 A50 10p multicolored 2.10 2.10
244 A50 16p multicolored 3.00 3.00
Nos. 241-244 (4) 8.00 8.00

Falkland Islands heraldic arms, 50th anniv.

½p-Coin and Trout A51

New Coinage: 5½p, 1p-coin and gentoo penguins, 8p, 2p-coin and upland geese. 10p, 5p-coin and black-browed albatross. 16p, 10p-coin and sea lions.

1975, Dec. 31 Litho. Wmk. 373

245 A51 2p copper & multi .20 .20
246 A51 5½p copper & multi .55 .55
247 A51 8p copper & multi 1.10 1.10
248 A51 10p silver & multi 1.75 1.75
249 A51 16p silver & multi 5.00 5.00
Nos. 245-249 (5) 8.60 8.60

Gathering Sheep — A52

Sheep Farming: 7½p, Shearing. 10p, Dipping sheep. 20p, Motor Vessel Monsunen collecting wool.

1976, Apr. 28 Litho. *Perf. 13½*

250 A52 2p multicolored .50 .25
251 A52 7½p multicolored 1.00 .50
252 A52 10p multicolored 1.50 .75
253 A52 20p multicolored 3.50 1.90
Nos. 250-253 (4) 6.50 3.40

Prince Philip, 1957 Visit A53

11p, Queen, ampulla and spoon. 33p, Queen awaiting anointment, and Knights of the Garter.

1977, Feb. 7 *Perf. 13½x14*

254 A53 6p multicolored .35 .35
a. Booklet pane of 4, wmk. 314 2.25
255 A53 11p multicolored .60 .60
a. Booklet pane of 4 3.50
256 A53 33p multicolored 1.50 1.50
a. Booklet pane of 4 8.00
Nos. 254-256 (3) 2.45 2.45

25th anniv. of the reign of Elizabeth II.

Map of West and East Falkland with Communications Centers — A54

Telecommunications: 11p, Ship to shore communications at Fox Bay. 40p, Globe with Telex tape and telephone.

1977, Oct. 24 Litho. *Perf. 14½x14*

257 A54 3p yel brown & multi .40 .25
258 A54 11p lt ultra & multi 1.00 .60
259 A54 40p rose & multi 4.25 3.00
Nos. 257-259 (3) 5.65 3.85

A.E.S., 1957-1974 — A55

Designs: Mail ships.

1978, Jan. 25 Wmk. 373 *Perf. 14*

260 A55 1p shown .25 .25
261 A55 2p Darwin, 1957-75 .25 .25
262 A55 3p Merak-N 1951-53 .25 .25
263 A55 4p Fitzroy, 1936-57 .25 .25
264 A55 5p Lafonia 1936-41 .30 .40
265 A55 6p Fleurus, 1924-33 .35 .50
266 A55 7p S.S. Falkland, 1914-34 .50 .70
267 A55 8p Oravia, 1900-12 .55 .75
268 A55 9p Memphis, 1890-97 .60 .85
269 A55 10p Black Hawk, 1873-80 .75 1.00
270 A55 20p Foam, 1963-72 .95 1.40
271 A55 25p Fairy, 1857-61 1.25 1.75
272 A55 50p Amelia, 1852-54 2.00 2.75
273 A55 £1 Nautilus, 1846-48 4.25 6.00
274 A55 £3 Hebe, 1842-46 12.00 14.00
Nos. 260-274 (15) 24.50 31.10

The 1p, 3p, 5p, 6p and 10p were also issued in booklet panes of 4.
Nos. 260-274 also issued inscribed 1982.
For overprints see Nos. 352-353.

Elizabeth II Coronation Anniversary Issue

Souvenir Sheet
Common Design Type

1978, June 2 Unwmk. *Perf. 15*

275 Sheet of 6 4.00 4.00
a. CD326 25p Red Dragon of Wales .60 .60
b. CD327 25p Elizabeth II .60 .60
c. CD328 25p Hornless ram .60 .60

No. 275 contains 2 se-tenant strips of Nos. 275a-275c, separated by horizontal gutter with commemorative and descriptive inscriptions.

Short Sunderland Mark III — A56

Design: 33p, Pane in flight and route Southampton to Stanley.

1978, Apr. 28 Wmk. 373 *Perf. 14*

276 A56 11p multicolored 2.25 1.90
277 A56 33p multicolored 4.00 3.25

First direct flight Southampton, England to Stanley, Falkland Islands, 26th anniv.

First Fox Bay PO and No. 1 — A57

Macrocystis Pyrifera — A58

Designs: 11p, Second Stanley Post Office and #2. 15p, New Island Post Office and #3. 22p, 1st Stanley Post Office and #4.

1978, Aug. 8 Litho. *Perf. 13½x13*

278 A57 3p multicolored .20 .20
279 A57 11p multicolored .40 .40
280 A57 15p multicolored .55 .55
281 A57 22p multicolored .85 .85
Nos. 278-281 (4) 2.00 2.00

Falkland Islands postage stamps, cent.

1979, Feb. 19 Litho. *Perf. 14*

Kelp: 7p, Durvillea. 11p, Lessoniae, horiz. 15p, Callophyllis, horiz. 25p, Iridea.

282 A58 3p multicolored .20 .20
283 A58 7p multicolored .40 .40
284 A58 11p multicolored .60 .60
285 A58 15p multicolored .75 .75
286 A58 25p multicolored 1.25 1.25
Nos. 282-286 (5) 3.20 3.20

Britten-Norman Islander over Map — A59

Opening of Stanley Airport: 11p, Fokker F27 over map. 15p, Fokker F28 over Stanley. 25p, Cessna 172 Skyhawk, Islander and Fokkers F27, F28 over runway.

1979, May 1 Litho. *Perf. 13½*

287 A59 3p multicolored .20 .20
288 A59 11p multicolored .75 .75
289 A59 15p multicolored 1.00 1.00
290 A59 25p multicolored 1.75 1.75
Nos. 287-290 (4) 3.70 3.70

Rowland Hill and No. 121 — A60

Sir Rowland Hill (1795-1879), originator of penny postage, and: 11p, Falkland Islands No. 1, vert. 25p, Penny Black. 33p, Falkland Islands No. 37, vert.

1979, Aug. 27 *Perf. 14*

291 A60 3p multicolored .20 .20
292 A60 11p multicolored .45 .45
293 A60 25p multicolored .90 .90
Nos. 291-293 (3) 1.55 1.55

Souvenir Sheet

294 A60 33p multicolored 1.40 1.40

Mail Delivery by Air, UPU Emblem — A61

UPU Membership Cent. (Modes of Mail Delivery): 11p, Horseback. 25p, Schooner Gwendolin.

1979, Nov. 26

295 A61 3p multicolored .20 .20
296 A61 11p multicolored .45 .45
297 A61 25p multicolored .95 .95
Nos. 295-297 (3) 1.60 1.60

Commerson's Dolphin — A62

1980, Feb. 25 Wmk. 373 *Perf. 14*

298 A62 3p Peale's porpoise, vert. .20 .20
299 A62 6p shown .25 .25
300 A62 7p Hour-glass dolphin .35 .35
301 A62 11p Spectacled porpose, vert. .50 .50
302 A62 15p Dusky dolphin .75 .75
303 A62 25p Killer whale 1.50 1.50
Nos. 298-303 (6) 3.55 3.55

Miniature Sheet

Falkland Islands Cancel, 1878 — A63

Designs: b, New Islds., 1915. c, Falklands Islds., 1901. d, Port Stanley, 1935. e, Port Stanley airmail, 1952. f, Fox Bay, 1934.

1980, May 6 Litho. *Perf. 14*

304 Sheet of 6 2.25 2.25
a.-f. A63 11p any single .35 .35

London 1980 Intl. Stamp Exhib., May 6-14.

Queen Mother Elizabeth Birthday

Common Design Type

1980, Aug. 4 Litho. *Perf. 14*

305 CD330 11p multicolored .50 .50

Striated Caracara — A64

1980, Aug. 11 Wmk. 373 *Perf. 13½*

306 A64 3p shown .35 .20
307 A64 11p Red-backed buzzard .70 .60
308 A64 15p Crested caracara .85 .70
309 A64 25p Cassin's falcon 1.60 1.40
Nos. 306-309 (4) 3.50 2.90

Port Egmont, Early Settlement — A65

1980, Dec. 22 Litho. *Perf. 14*

310 A65 3p Stanley .20 .20
311 A65 11p shown .45 .45
312 A65 25p Port Louis .95 .50
313 A65 33p Mission House, Keppel Island 1.10 .95
Nos. 310-313 (4) 2.70 2.10

Polwarth Sheep — A66

1981, Jan. 19 Litho. *Perf. 14*

314 A66 3p shown .20 .20
315 A66 11p Frisian cow and calf .40 .40
316 A66 25p Horse .85 .85
317 A66 33p Welsh collies 1.10 1.10
Nos. 314-317 (4) 2.55 2.55

Map of Falkland Islands, Bowles and Carver, 1779 — A67

1981, May 22 Litho. *Perf. 14*

318 A67 3p shown .20 .20
319 A67 10p Hawkin's Mainland, 1773 .30 .25
320 A67 13p New Isles, 1747 .40 .35
321 A67 15p French & British Islands .50 .40
322 A67 25p Falklands, 1771 .75 .60
323 A67 26p Falklands, 1764 .85 .65
Nos. 318-323 (6) 3.00 2.45

Royal Wedding Issue

Common Design Type

1981, July 22 Litho. *Perf. 13½x13*

324 CD331 10p Bouquet .25 .25
325 CD331 13p Charles .35 .35
326 CD331 52p Couple 1.10 1.10
Nos. 324-326 (3) 1.70 1.70

Duke of Edinburgh's Awards, 25th Anniv. — A68

1981, Sept. 28 Litho. *Perf. 14*

327 A68 10p Spinning .30 .30
328 A68 13p Camping .35 .35
329 A68 15p Kayaking .45 .45
330 A68 26p Duke of Edinburgh .80 .80
Nos. 327-330 (4) 1.90 1.90

The Holy Virgin, by Guido Reni (1575-1642) — A69

Rock Cod — A70

Christmas: 3p, Adoration of the Holy Child, 16th cent. Dutch. 13p, Holy Family in an Italian Landscape, 17th cent. Italian.

1981, Nov. 2 Litho. *Perf. 14*

331 A69 3p multicolored .20 .20
332 A69 13p multicolored .45 .45
333 A69 26p multicolored .80 .80
Nos. 331-333 (3) 1.45 1.45

1981, Dec. 7

Designs: Shelf fish. 5p, 15p, 25p horiz.

334 A70 5p Falkland herring .20 .20
335 A70 13p shown .40 .40
336 A70 15p Patagonian hake .50 .50
337 A70 25p Southern blue whiting .80 .80
338 A70 26p Gray-tailed skate .80 .80
Nos. 334-338 (5) 2.70 2.70

Shipwrecks — A71

1982, Feb. 15 Wmk. 373 *Perf. 14½*

339 A71 5p Lady Elizabeth, 1913 .20 .20
340 A71 13p Capricorn, 1882 .45 .45
341 A71 15p Jhelum, 1870 .55 .55
342 A71 25p Snowsquall, 1864 .75 .75
343 A71 26p St. Mary, 1890 .75 .75
Nos. 339-343 (5) 2.70 2.70

Sesquicentennial of Charles Darwin's Visit — A72

1982, Apr. 19 Litho. *Perf. 14*

344	A72 5p Darwin	.20	.20
345	A72 17p Microscope	.65	.65
346	A72 25p Warrah	1.00	1.00
347	A72 34p Beagle	1.25	1.25
	Nos. 344-347 (4)	3.10	3.10

Princess Diana Issue
Common Design Type

1982, July 5 Wmk. 373 *Perf. 13*

348	CD333 5p Arms	.40	.20
349	CD333 17p Diana	1.40	.50
350	CD333 37p Wedding	2.75	1.00
351	CD333 50p Portrait	3.75	1.40
	Nos. 348-351 (4)	8.30	3.10

Nos. 264, 271 Overprinted: "1st PARTICIPATION / COMMONWEALTH GAMES 1982"

1982, Oct. 7 Litho. *Perf. 14*

352	A55 5p multicolored	.20	.20
353	A55 25p multicolored	.65	.65

12th Commonwealth Games, Brisbane, Australia, Sept. 30-Oct. 9.

Tussock Bird — A73

1982, Dec. 6 *Perf. 15x14½*

354	A73 5p shown	.20	.20
355	A73 10p Black-chinned siskin	.25	.25
356	A73 13p Grass wren	.45	.45
357	A73 17p Black-throated finch	.60	.60
358	A73 25p Falkland-correndera pipit	1.00	1.00
359	A73 34p Dark-faced ground-tyrant	1.10	1.10
	Nos. 354-359 (6)	3.60	3.60

British Occupation Sesquicentennial — A74

1p, Raising the Standard, Port Louis, 1833. 2p, Chelsea pensioners & barracks, 1849. 5p, Wool trade, 1874. 10p, Ship repairing trade, 1850-90. 15p, Government House, early 20th cent. 20p, Battle of the Falkland Islands, 1914. 25p, Whalebone Arch centenary, 1933. 40p, Contribution to World War II effort, 1939-45. 50p, Visit of Duke of Edinburgh, 1957. £1, Royal Marines, 1933, 1983, vert. £2, Queen Elizabeth II.

1983, Jan. 1 Litho. *Perf. 14*

360	A74 1p multi, vert.	.25	.25
361	A74 2p multi	.25	.25
362	A74 5p multi, vert.	.25	.25
363	A74 10p multi	.25	.25
364	A74 15p multi	.30	.30
365	A74 20p multi, vert.	.45	.45
366	A74 25p multi	.60	.55
367	A74 40p multi, vert.	.90	.90
368	A74 50p multi	1.10	1.10
369	A74 £1 multi	1.75	2.25
370	A74 £2 multi, vert.	4.00	5.00
	Nos. 360-370 (11)	10.10	11.55

For surcharges see Nos. 402-403.

A75

1983, Mar. 14

371	A75 5p No. 69	.25	.25
372	A75 17p No. 65	.50	.50
373	A75 34p No. 75, vert.	.75	1.00
374	A75 50p No. 370, vert.	.90	1.00
	Nos. 371-374 (4)	2.40	2.75

Commonwealth Day.

First Anniv. of Liberation A76

1983, June 14 Wmk. 373 *Perf. 14*

375	A76 5p Army	.20	.20
376	A76 13p Merchant Navy	.30	.30
377	A76 17p Royal Air Force	.45	.45
378	A76 50p Royal Navy	1.25	1.25
a.	Souvenir sheet of 4, #375-378	3.25	3.25
	Nos. 375-378 (4)	2.20	2.20

Local Fruit A77

1983, Oct. 10 Litho. *Perf. 14*

379	A77 5p Diddle dee	.20	.20
380	A77 17p Tea berries	.40	.40
381	A77 25p Mountain berries	.60	.60
382	A77 34p Native strawberries	.80	.80
	Nos. 379-382 (4)	2.00	2.00

Britten-Norman Islander — A78

1983, Nov. 14 Litho. *Perf. 14*

383	A78 5p shown	.25	.20
384	A78 13p DHC-2 Beaver	.40	.25
385	A78 17p Noorduyn Norse-man	.50	.30
386	A78 50p Auster	1.25	.85
	Nos. 383-386 (4)	2.40	1.60

Green Spider A79

Insects and Spiders.

1984, Jan. 1 Litho. *Perf. 14*

387	A79 1p shown	.20	.20
388	A79 2p Ichneumon-Fly	.20	.20
389	A79 3p Brocade Moth	.20	.20
390	A79 4p Black Beetle	.20	.20
391	A79 5p Fritillary	.20	.20
392	A79 6p Green Spider, diff.	.25	.25
393	A79 7p Ichneumon-Fly, diff.	.25	.25
394	A79 8p Ochre Shoulder	.25	.25
395	A79 9p Clocker Weevil	.30	.35
396	A79 10p Hover Fly	.30	.35
397	A79 20p Weevil	.60	.75
398	A79 25p Metallic Beetle	.80	1.00
399	A79 50p Camel Cricket	1.50	1.90
400	A79 £1 Beauchene Spi-der	3.25	4.25
401	A79 £3 Southern Painted Lady	9.75	12.00
	Nos. 387-401 (15)	18.25	22.35

No. 388 exists inscribed "1986."

Nos. 364, 366 Surcharged

1984, Jan. 3 Litho. *Perf. 14*

402	A74 17p on 15p multi	.45	.45
403	A74 22p on 25p multi	.55	.55

Lloyd's List Issue
Common Design Type

1984, May 7 Wmk. 373 *Perf. 14½*

404	CD335 6p Wavertree	.25	.25
405	CD335 17p Port Stanley, 1910	.65	.65
406	CD335 22p Oravia	.80	.80
407	CD335 52p Cunard Count-ess	2.00	2.00
	Nos. 404-407 (4)	3.70	3.70

Great Grebe — A80

1984, Aug. 6 *Perf. 14½x14*

408	A80 17p shown	1.10	1.10
409	A80 22p Silver grebe	1.40	1.40
410	A80 52p Rolland's grebe	4.00	4.00
	Nos. 408-410 (3)	6.50	6.50

See Nos. 450-453.

1984 UPU Congress A81

1984, June 22 Litho. *Perf. 14*

411	A81 22p Emblem, jet, ship	.60	.60

Wildlife Conservation A82

1984, Nov. 5 Litho. *Perf. 14½*

412	A82 6p Birds	.60	.40
413	A82 17p Plants	1.25	.90
414	A82 22p Mammals	1.40	1.00
415	A82 52p Marine Life	3.00	2.25
a.	Souvenir sheet of 4, #412-415	8.50	6.00
	Nos. 412-415 (4)	6.25	4.55

Camber Railway, 1915-1927 A83

1985, Feb. 18 Litho. *Perf. 14*

416	A83 7p multicolored	.35	.30
417	A83 22p multicolored	.85	.75
418	A83 27p multicolored	.90	1.00

Size: 77x26mm

419	A83 54p multicolored	1.90	1.90
	Nos. 416-419 (4)	4.00	3.95

Queen Mother 85th Birthday
Common Design Type

Designs: 7p, Commonwealth Visitor's Reception. 22p, With Prince Charles, Mark Phillips, Princess Anne. 27p, 80th birthday celebration. 54p, Holding Prince Henry. £1, In coach with Princess Diana.

Perf. 14½x14

1985, June 7 Litho. Wmk. 384

420	CD336 7p multicolored	.20	.20
421	CD336 22p multicolored	.85	.85
422	CD336 27p multicolored	1.10	1.10
423	CD336 54p multicolored	2.10	2.10
	Nos. 420-423 (4)	4.25	4.25

Souvenir Sheet

424	CD336 £1 multicolored	4.50	4.50

Mount Pleasant Airport Opening A84

1985, May 12 Litho. *Perf. 14½*

425	A84 7p Pioneer camp, docked ship	.40	.40
426	A84 22p Construction site	1.25	1.25
427	A84 27p Runway layout	1.60	1.60
428	A84 54p Aircraft landing	3.00	3.00
	Nos. 425-428 (4)	6.25	6.25

Captain J. McBride, HMS Jason, 1765 — A85

18th-19th century naval explorers: 22p, Commodore J. Byron, HMS Dolphin and Tamar, 1765. 27p, Vice-Adm. R. Fitzroy, HMS Beagle, 1831. 54p, Adm. Sir B.J. Sulivan, HMS Philomel, 1842.

1985, Sept. 23

429	A85 7p multicolored	.50	.50
430	A85 22p multicolored	1.40	1.40
431	A85 27p multicolored	1.50	1.50
432	A85 54p multicolored	3.25	3.25
	Nos. 429-432 (4)	6.65	6.65

Philibert Commerson (1727-1773), Commerson's Dolphin — A86

Naturalists, endangered species: 22p, Rene Primevere Lesson (1794-1849), kelp. 27p, Joseph Paul Gaimard (1796-1858), diving petrel. 54p, Charles Darwin (1803-1882), Calceolaria darwinii.

1985, Nov. 4 *Perf. 14½*

433	A86 7p multicolored	.50	.35
434	A86 22p multicolored	1.50	1.10
435	A86 27p multicolored	1.75	1.25
436	A86 54p multicolored	3.50	2.50
	Nos. 433-436 (4)	7.25	5.20

Seashells A87

1986, Feb. 10 Wmk. 384 *Perf. 14½*

437	A87 7p Painted keyhole lim-pet	.40	.40
438	A87 22p Magellanic volute	1.50	1.50
439	A87 27p Falkland scallop	2.00	2.00
440	A87 54p Rough thorn drupe	4.00	4.00
	Nos. 437-440 (4)	7.90	7.90

Queen Elizabeth II 60th Birthday
Common Design Type

Designs: 10p, With Princess Margaret at St. Paul's, Waldenbury, 1932. 24p, Christmas broadcast from Sandringham, 1958. 29p, Order of the Thistle, St. Giles Cathedral, Edinburgh, 1962. 45p, Royal reception on the Britannia, US visit, 1976. 58p, Visiting Crown Agents' offices, 1983.

1986, Apr. 21 Litho. *Perf. 14x14½*

441	CD337 10p scar, blk & sil	.30	.30
442	CD337 24p ultra, blk & sil	.65	.65
443	CD337 29p green & multi	.85	.85
444	CD337 45p violet & multi	1.40	1.40
445	CD337 58p rose vio & multi	1.75	1.75
	Nos. 441-445 (5)	4.95	4.95

AMERIPEX '86 — A88

SS Great Britain's arrival in the Falkland Isls., Cent.: 10p, Maiden voyage, crossing the Atlantic, 1845. 24p, Wreck in Sparrow Cove, 1937. 29p, Refloating wreck, 1970. 58p, Restored vessel, Bristol, 1986.

1986, May 22

446 A88 10p multicolored .25 .25
447 A88 24p multicolored .75 .75
448 A88 29p multicolored 1.00 1.00
449 A88 58p multicolored 2.00 2.00
a. Souvenir sheet of 4, #446-449 4.00 4.00
Nos. 446-449 (4) 4.00 4.00

Bird Type of 1984

Rockhopper Penguins.

1986, Aug. 25 Wmk. 373 *Perf. 14½*

450 A80 10p Adult .65 .50
451 A80 24p Adults swimming 1.50 1.25
452 A80 29p Adults, diff. 2.00 1.75
453 A80 58p Adult and young 4.00 3.50
Nos. 450-453 (4) 8.15 7.00

Wedding of Prince Andrew and Sarah Ferguson — A90

Various photographs: 17p, Presenting Queen's Polo Cup, Windsor, 1986. 22p, Open carriage, wedding. 29p, Andrew wearing military fatigues.

1986, Nov. 10 Wmk. 384 *Perf. 14½*

454 A90 17p multicolored .55 .55
455 A90 22p multicolored .70 .70
456 A90 29p multicolored .90 .90
Nos. 454-456 (3) 2.15 2.15

Royal Engineers, 200th Anniv. A91

1987, Feb. 9 Litho. *Perf. 14½*

457 A91 10p Surveying Sapper Hill .55 .55
458 A91 24p Explosives disposal 1.90 1.90
459 A91 29p Boxer Bridge, Pt. Stanley 2.25 2.25
460 A91 58p Postal services, Stanley Airport 5.00 5.00
Nos. 457-460 (4) 9.70 9.70

Seals A92

1987, Apr. 27

461 A92 10p Southern sea lion .80 .80
462 A92 24p Falkland fur seal 2.25 2.25
463 A92 29p Southern elephant seal 2.40 2.40
464 A92 58p Leopard seal 4.25 4.25
Nos. 461-464 (4) 9.70 9.70

Hospitals A93

Designs: 10p, Victorian Cottage Home, c. 1912. 24p, King Edward VII Memorial Hospital, c. 1914. 29p, Churchill Wing, 1953. 58p, Prince Andrew Wing, 1987.

1987, Dec. 8 *Perf. 14*

465 A93 10p multicolored .40 .40
466 A93 24p multicolored .95 .95
467 A93 29p multicolored 1.10 1.10
468 A93 58p multicolored 2.00 2.00
Nos. 465-468 (4) 4.45 4.45

Fungi — A94

1987, Sept. 14 Litho. *Perf. 14½*

469 A94 10p Suillus luteus 1.50 1.50
470 A94 24p Mycena 2.75 2.75
471 A94 29p Camarophyllus adonis 3.75 3.75
472 A94 58p Gerronema schusteri 8.00 8.00
Nos. 469-472 (4) 16.00 16.00

1940 Morris Truck, Fitzroy A95

Classic automobiles: 24p, 1929 Citroen Kegresse, San Carlos. 29p, 1933 Ford 1-Ton Truck, Port Stanley. 58p, 1935 Ford Model T Saloon, Darwin.

1988, Apr. 11 Litho. *Perf. 14*

473 A95 10p multicolored .35 .35
474 A95 24p multicolored .85 .85
475 A95 29p multicolored 1.10 1.10
476 A95 58p multicolored 2.00 2.00
Nos. 473-476 (4) 4.30 4.30

Geese A96

1988, July 25

477 A96 10p Kelp 1.50 .35
478 A96 24p Upland 3.00 .85
479 A96 29p Ruddy-headed 3.75 1.00
480 A96 58p Ashy-headed 7.75 2.25
Nos. 477-480 (4) 16.00 4.45

Lloyds of London, 300th Anniv.

Common Design Type

Designs: 10p, Lloyd's Nelson Collection silver service. 24p, Hydroponic Gardens, horiz. 29p, Supply ship A.E.S., horiz. 58p, Wreck of the Charles Cooper near the Falklands, 1866.

1988, Nov. 14 Litho. Wmk. 373

481 CD341 10p multicolored .50 .50
482 CD341 24p multicolored 1.00 1.00
483 CD341 29p multicolored 1.25 1.25
484 CD341 58p multicolored 2.50 2.50
Nos. 481-484 (4) 5.25 5.25

Ships of Cape Horn A97

1989, Feb. 28 *Perf. 373*

485 A97 1p Padua .45 .25
486 A97 2p Priwall, vert. .45 .25
a. Wmk. 384 .60 .45
487 A97 3p Passat .45 .25
a. Wmk. 384 .60 .45
488 A97 4p Archibald Russell, vert. .45 .25
489 A97 5p Pamir, vert. .45 .25
490 A97 6p Mozart .45 .25
a. Wmk. 384 .60 .45
491 A97 7p Pommern .45 .25
492 A97 8p Preussen .60 .45
493 A97 9p Fennia .65 .50
a. Wmk. 384 1.00 .75
494 A97 10p Cassard .75 .60
495 A97 20p Lawhill 1.60 1.25
496 A97 25p Garthpool 1.90 1.40
497 A97 50p Grace Harwar 3.75 2.75
498 A97 £1 Criccieth Castle 7.00 5.50
a. Wmk. 384 7.75 6.00
499 A97 £3 Cutty Sark, vert. 22.50 18.00
500 A97 £5 Flying Cloud 30.00 22.50
Nos. 485-500 (16) 71.90 54.70

Nos. 486a, 487a, 490a, 493a, 498a are dated "1991."

Whales — A98

1989, May 15 Wmk. 384 *Perf. 14*

501 A98 10p Southern right .90 .90
502 A98 24p Minke 1.90 1.90
503 A98 29p Humpback 2.25 2.25
504 A98 58p Blue 4.75 4.75
Nos. 501-504 (4) 9.80 9.80

Sports Assoc. Activities A99

Children's drawings.

1989, Sept. 16

505 A99 5p Gymkhana .20 .20
506 A99 10p Steer Riding .25 .25
507 A99 17p Sheep shearing .55 .55
508 A99 24p Dog trial .70 .70
509 A99 29p Horse racing .95 .95
510 A99 45p Sack race 1.50 1.50
Nos. 505-510 (6) 4.15 4.15

Battles — A100

Commanders, ships and ship crests: 10p, Vice-Adm. Sturdee, HMS *Invincible.* 24p, Vice-Adm. Von Spee, SMS *Scharnhorst.* 29p, Commodore Harwood, HMS *Ajax.* 58p, Capt. Langsdorff, *Admiral Graff Spee.*

1989, Dec. 8 *Perf. 14x13½*

511 A100 10p multicolored .40 .40
512 A100 24p multicolored 1.10 1.10
513 A100 29p multicolored 1.40 1.40
514 A100 58p multicolored 2.75 2.75
Nos. 511-514 (4) 5.65 5.65

Battle of the Falklands, 75th anniv. (10p, 24p); Battle of the River Plate, 50th anniv. (29p, 58p).

Emblems and Presentation Spitfires, 1940 — A101

1990, May 3 Wmk. 373 *Perf. 14*

515 A101 12p No. 92 Squadron .60 .60
516 A101 26p No. 611 Squadron 1.40 1.40
517 A101 31p No. 92 Squadron, diff. 1.75 1.75
518 A101 62p Spitfires scramble 3.25 3.25
Nos. 515-518 (4) 7.00 7.00

Souvenir Sheet

519 A101 £1 Battle of Britain 7.50 7.50

Stamp World London '90.

For souvenir sheet similar to #519, see #530.

A102

A103

1990, Apr. 1 Wmk. 384 *Perf. 14½*

520 A102 12p Kidney Is. .50 .50
521 A102 26p Beauchene Is. 1.25 1.25
522 A102 31p Bird Is. 1.50 1.50
523 A102 62p Elephant Jason Is. 3.00 3.00
Nos. 520-523 (4) 6.25 6.25

Nature reserves and bird sanctuaries.

Queen Mother, 90th Birthday

Common Design Types

1990, Aug. 4 Wmk. 384 *Perf. 14x15*

524 CD343 26p Queen Mother in Dover 1.00 1.00

Perf. 14½

525 CD344 £1 Steering the "Queen Elizabeth," 1946 4.25 4.25

Wmk. 384

1990, Oct. 3 Litho. *Perf. 14*

526 A103 12p Black browed albatross .75 .75
527 A103 26p Adult bird 1.75 1.75
528 A103 31p Adult, chick 2.25 2.25
529 A103 62p Bird in flight 4.50 4.50
Nos. 526-529 (4) 9.25 9.25

Battle of Britain Type of 1990 inscribed "SECOND VISIT OF / HRH THE DUKE OF EDINBURGH"

Souvenir Sheet

1991, Mar. 7

530 A101 £1 multicolored 9.75 9.75

Orchids — A104

King Penguin — A105

1991, Mar. 18 Wmk. 373

531 A104 12p Gavilea australis .60 .60
532 A104 26p Codonorchis lessonii 1.40 1.40
533 A104 31p Chlorea gaudichaudii 1.75 1.75
534 A104 62p Gavilea littoralis 3.50 3.50
Nos. 531-534 (4) 7.25 7.25

1991, Aug. 26 Wmk. 384

535 A105 2p Two adults crossing bills .45 .45
536 A105 6p Two adults, one brooding .55 .55

537 A105 12p Adult with two young .95 .95
538 A105 20p Adult swimming 1.75 1.75
539 A105 31p Adult feeding young 2.50 2.50
540 A105 62p Two adults, diff. 5.50 5.50
Nos. 535-540 (6) 11.70 11.70

World Wildlife Fund.

Falkland Islands Bisects, Cent. A106

1991, Sept. 10 Wmk. 384 ***Perf. 14½***
541 A106 12p #9, #15 .65 .65
542 A106 26p On cover 1.50 1.50
543 A106 31p Unsevered pair 1.60 1.60
544 A106 62p S.S. Isis 3.25 3.25
Nos. 541-544 (4) 7.00 7.00

Discovery of America, 500th Anniv. (in 1992) — A107

Sailing ships: 14p, STV Eye of the Wind. 29p, STV Soren Larsen. 34p, Nina, Santa Maria, Pinta. 68p, Columbus and Santa Maria.

1991, Dec. 12 Wmk. 373 ***Perf. 14***
545 A107 14p multicolored .85 .85
546 A107 29p multicolored 1.75 1.75
547 A107 34p multicolored 2.25 2.25
548 A107 68p multicolored 4.25 4.25
Nos. 545-548 (4) 9.10 9.10

World Columbian Stamp Expo '92, Chicago and Genoa '92 Intl. Philatelic Exhibitions.

Queen Elizabeth II's Accession to the Throne, 40th Anniv.

Common Design Type

1992, Feb. 6
549 CD349 7p multicolored .40 .40
550 CD349 14p multicolored .65 .65
551 CD349 29p multicolored 1.25 1.25
552 CD349 34p multicolored 1.50 1.50
553 CD349 68p multicolored 3.00 3.00
Nos. 549-553 (5) 6.80 6.80

Christ Church Cathedral, Cent. — A108

1992, Feb. 21 Wmk. 384 ***Perf. 14½***
554 A108 14p Laying foundation stone .55 .55
555 A108 29p Interior, 1920 1.25 1.25
556 A108 34p Bishop's chair 1.50 1.50
557 A108 68p Without tower c. 1900, horiz. 3.00 3.00
Nos. 554-557 (4) 6.30 6.30

First Sighting of Falkland Islands by Capt. John Davis, 400th Anniv. A109

Designs: 22p, Capt. John Davis using backstaff. 29p, Capt. Davis working on chart. 34p, Queen Elizabeth I, Queen Elizabeth II. 68p, The Desire sights Falkland Islands.

1992, Aug. 14 Wmk. 373
558 A109 22p multicolored 1.25 1.25
559 A109 29p multicolored 1.50 1.50
560 A109 34p multicolored 1.75 1.75
561 A109 68p multicolored 3.50 3.50
Nos. 558-561 (4) 8.00 8.00

Falkland Islands Defense Force and West Yorkshire Regiment — A110

7p, Private, Falkland Islands Volunteers, 1892. 14p, Officer, Falkland Islands Defense Corps, 1914. 22p, Officer, Falkland Islands Defense Force, 1920. 29p, Private, Falkland Islands Defense Force, 1939-45. 34p, Officer, West Yorkshire Regiment, 1942. 68p, Private, West Yorkshire Regiment, 1942.

1992, Oct. 1 ***Perf. 14***
562 A110 7p multicolored .35 .35
563 A110 14p multicolored .70 .70
564 A110 22p multicolored 1.10 1.10
565 A110 29p multicolored 1.50 1.50
566 A110 34p multicolored 1.60 1.60
567 A110 68p multicolored 3.25 3.25
Nos. 562-567 (6) 8.50 8.50

Gulls and Terns A111

Perf. 14x14½
1993, Jan. 2 Litho. Wmk. 384
568 A111 15p South American tern .85 .85
569 A111 31p Pink breasted gull 1.75 1.75
570 A111 36p Dolphin gull 2.00 2.00
571 A111 72p Dominican gull 4.00 4.00
Nos. 568-571 (4) 8.60 8.60

Souvenir Sheet

Visit of Liner QE II to Falkland Islands — A112

Wmk. 373
1993, Jan. 22 Litho. ***Perf. 14***
572 A112 £2 multicolored 9.00 9.00

Royal Air Force, 75th Anniv.

Common Designs Type

Designs: No. 573, Lockheed Tristar. No. 574, Lockheed Hercules. No. 575, Boeing Vertol Chinook. No. 576, Avro Vulcan.
No. 577a, Hawker Siddeley Andover. b, Westland Wessex. c, Panavia Tornado F3. d, McDonnell Douglas Phantom.

Wmk. 373
1993, Apr. 3 Litho. ***Perf. 14***
573 CD350 15p multicolored .95 .95
574 CD350 15p multicolored .95 .95
575 CD350 15p multicolored .95 .95
576 CD350 15p multicolored .95 .95
Nos. 573-576 (4) 3.80 3.80

Souvenir Sheet of 4
577 CD350 36p #a.-d. 6.25 6.25

Fisheries A113

Designs: 15p, Short-finned squid. 31p, Stern haul of whiptailed hake. 36p, Fishery Patrol Vessel Falkalnds Protector. 72p, Aerial surveillance by Britten-Norman Islander.

Wmk. 384
1993, July 1 Litho. ***Perf. 14***
578 A113 15p multicolored .70 .70
579 A113 31p multicolored 1.40 1.40
580 A113 36p multicolored 1.75 1.75
581 A113 72p multicolored 3.25 3.25
Nos. 578-581 (4) 7.10 7.10

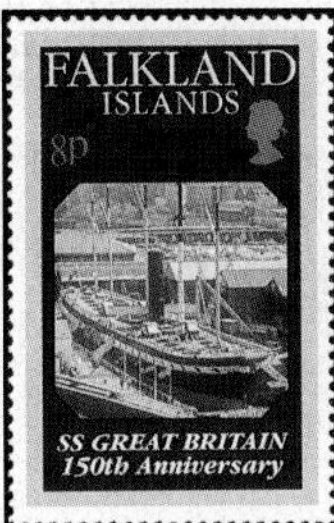

Launch of SS Great Britain, 150th Anniv. — A114

Perf. 14x13½
1993, July 19 Litho. Wmk. 384
582 A114 8p In drydock, Bristol .25 .25
583 A114 £1 At sea 4.25 4.25

Cruise Ships and Penguins A115

Wmk. 373
1993, Oct. 1 Litho. ***Perf. 14***
584 A115 16p Explorer .75 .75
585 A115 34p Rockhopper penguins 1.60 1.60
586 A115 39p World Discoverer 1.75 1.75
587 A115 78p Columbus Caravelle 3.75 3.75
Nos. 584-587 (4) 7.85 7.85

Pets — A116

Perf. 14x14½
1993, Dec. 1 Litho. Wmk. 384
588 A116 8p Pony .50 .35
589 A116 16p Lamb .90 .65
590 A116 34p Puppy, kitten 2.10 1.50

Perf. 14½x14
591 A116 39p Kitten, vert. 2.50 1.75
592 A116 78p Collie, vert. 5.00 3.50
Nos. 588-592 (5) 11.00 7.75

Ovptd. with Hong Kong '94 Emblem

1994, Feb. 18
593 A116 8p on #588 .50 .50
594 A116 16p on #589 .90 .90
595 A116 34p on #590 1.90 1.90
596 A116 39p on #591 2.10 2.10
597 A116 78p on #592 4.25 4.25
Nos. 593-597 (5) 9.65 9.65

Inshore Marine Life A117

Wmk. 384
1994, Apr. 4 Litho. ***Perf. 14***
598 A117 1p Goose barnacles, vert. .25 .25
599 A117 2p Painted shrimp .25 .25
600 A117 8p Common limpet .25 .25
601 A117 9p Mullet .30 .30
602 A117 10p Sea anemones .35 .35
603 A117 20p Rock eel .70 .70
604 A117 25p Spider crab .90 .90
605 A117 50p Lobster krill, vert. 2.00 2.00
606 A117 80p Falkland skate 3.00 3.00
607 A117 £1 Centollon crab 3.50 3.50
a. Souv. sheet of 1, wmk. 373 4.00 4.00
608 A117 £3 Rock cod 10.50 10.50
609 A117 £5 Octopus, vert. 18.00 18.00
Nos. 598-609 (12) 40.00 40.00

No. 607a for return of Hong Kong to China. Issued 7/1/97.
See No. 671.

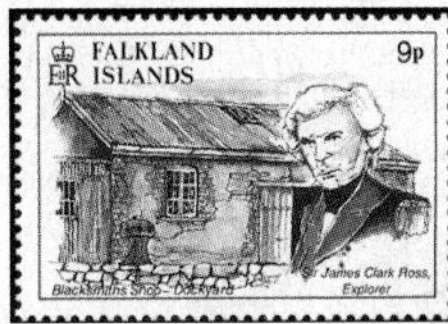

Founding of Stanley, 150th Anniv. A118

9p, Blacksmith's shop, dockyard, Sir James Clark Ross, explorer. 17p, James Leith Mody, 1st colonial chaplain, home at 21 Fitzroy Road. 30p, Stanley cottage, Dr. Henry J. Hamblin, 1st colonial surgeon. 35p, Pioneer row, Sergeant Major Henry Felton. 40p, Government House, Governor R. C. Moody R.E. 65p, View of Stanley, Edward Stanley, 14th Earl of Derby, Secretary of State for Colonies.

Wmk. 373
1994, July 1 Litho. ***Perf. 14***
610 A118 9p multicolored .40 .40
611 A118 17p multicolored .75 .75
612 A118 30p multicolored 1.40 1.40
613 A118 35p multicolored 1.50 1.50
614 A118 40p multicolored 1.75 1.75
615 A118 65p multicolored 2.75 2.75
Nos. 610-615 (6) 8.55 8.55

Methods of Transportation — A119

17p, Tristar over Gypsy Cove. 35p, Cruise ship, Sea Lion Island. 40p, FIGAS Islander, Pebble Island Beach. 65p, Land Rover, Volunteer Beach.

Wmk. 384
1994, Oct. 24 Litho. ***Perf. 14***
616 A119 17p multicolored .95 .55
617 A119 35p multicolored 2.00 1.10
618 A119 40p multicolored 2.40 1.25
619 A119 65p multicolored 3.25 2.00
Nos. 616-619 (4) 8.60 4.90

South American Missionary Society, 150th Anniv. — A120

Designs: 5p, Mission House, Keppel Island. 17p, Thomas Bridges, compiler of Yahgan dictionary. 40p, Fuegian Indians. 65p, Schooner Allen Gardiner, Capt. Allen Gardiner.

1994, Dec. 1
620 A120 5p multicolored .25 .25
621 A120 17p multicolored .75 .75
622 A120 40p multicolored 1.75 1.75
623 A120 65p multicolored 2.75 2.75
Nos. 620-623 (4) 5.50 5.50

Flowering Shrubs — A121

Designs: 9p, Lupinus arboreus. 17p, Boxwood. 30p, Fuchsia magellanica. 35p, Berberis ilicifolia. 40p, Gorse. 65p, Veronica.

Perf. 14½x14

1995, Jan. 3 Litho. Wmk. 384

624 A121 9p multicolored .35 .35
625 A121 17p multicolored .70 .70
626 A121 30p multicolored 1.40 1.40
627 A121 35p multicolored 1.75 1.75
628 A121 40p multicolored 1.90 1.90
629 A121 65p multicolored 3.25 3.25
Nos. 624-629 (6) 9.35 9.35

Shore Birds A122

Designs: 17p, Magellanic oystercatcher. 35p, Rufous chested dotterel. 40p, Black oystercatcher. 65p, Two banded plover.

Wmk. 373

1995, Mar. 1 Litho. *Perf. 13½*

630 A122 17p multicolored 1.00 1.00
631 A122 35p multicolored 2.25 2.25
632 A122 40p multicolored 2.50 2.50
633 A122 65p multicolored 4.00 4.00
Nos. 630-633 (4) 9.75 9.75

End of World War II, 50th Anniv.

Common Design Types

17p, Falkland Islands Victory Parade contingent. 35p, Governor Sir Alan Wolsey Cardinall on Bren gun carrier. 40p, HMAS Esperance Bay, 1942. 65p, HMS Exeter, 1939.
£1, Reverse of War Medal 1939-45.

Wmk. 373

1995, May 8 Litho. *Perf. 14*

634 CD351 17p multicolored 1.10 1.10
635 CD351 35p multicolored 2.25 2.25
636 CD351 40p multicolored 2.50 2.50
637 CD351 65p multicolored 4.00 4.00
Nos. 634-637 (4) 9.85 9.85

Souvenir Sheet

638 CD352 £1 multicolored 5.00 5.00

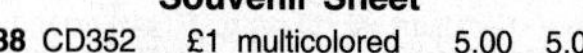

Transporting Peat — A123

Wmk. 384

1995, Aug. 1 Litho. *Perf. 14*

639 A123 17p Ox, cart .70 .70
640 A123 35p Horse, cart 1.75 1.75
641 A123 40p Tractor, sledge 1.75 1.75
642 A123 65p Truck, peat bank 3.00 3.00
Nos. 639-642 (4) 7.20 7.20

Miniature Sheet of 6

Wildlife — A124

Designs: a, Kelp geese. b, Albatross. c, Cormorants. d, Magellanic penguins. e, Fur seals. f, Rockhopper penguins.

1995, Sept. 11

643 A124 35p #a.-f. 10.00 10.00

No. 643 is a continuous design.

Wild Animals A125

1995, Nov. 6 Wmk. 373

644 A125 9p Rabbit .55 .55
645 A125 17p Hare 1.00 1.00
646 A125 35p Guanaco 2.10 2.10
647 A125 40p Fox 2.50 2.50
648 A125 65p Otter 4.00 4.00
Nos. 644-648 (5) 10.15 10.15

Visit by Princess Anne A126

Princess Anne and: 9p, Government House. 19p, San Carlos Cemetery. 30p, Christ Church Cathedral. 73p, Goose Green.

1996, Jan. 30 *Perf. 14½*

649 A126 9p multicolored .45 .45
650 A126 19p multicolored 1.00 1.00
651 A126 30p multicolored 1.75 1.75
652 A126 73p multicolored 4.00 4.00
Nos. 649-652 (4) 7.20 7.20

Queen Elizabeth II, 70th Birthday

Common Design Type

Various portraits of Queen, scenes from Falkland Islands: 17p, Steeple Jason. 40p, Ship, KV Tamar. 45p, New Island with shipwreck on beach. 65p, Community School.
£1, Queen in formal dress at Sandringham Ball.

1996, Apr. 21 *Perf. 13½*

653 CD354 17p multicolored .65 .65
654 CD354 40p multicolored 1.60 1.60
655 CD354 45p multicolored 1.75 1.75
656 CD354 65p multicolored 2.50 2.50
Nos. 653-656 (4) 6.50 6.50

Souvenir Sheet

657 CD354 £1 multicolored 4.25 4.25

CAPEX '96 A127

Mail delivery: 9p, Horseback, 1890. 40p, Norseman floatplane. 45p, Inter-island ship. 76p, Beaver floatplane.
£1, LMS Jubilee Class 4-6-0 locomotive.

1996, June 8 Wmk. 384 *Perf. 14*

658 A127 9p multicolored .50 .50
659 A127 40p multicolored 1.75 1.75
660 A127 45p multicolored 2.00 2.00
661 A127 76p multicolored 3.75 3.75
Nos. 658-661 (4) 8.00 8.00

Souvenir Sheet

662 A127 £1 multicolored 4.00 4.00

No. 662 contains one 48x32mm stamp.

Beaked Whales — A128

Designs: 9p, Southern bottlenose whale. 30p, Cuvier's beaked whale. 35p, Straptoothed beaked whale. 75p, Gray's beaked whale.

Wmk. 373

1996, Sept. 2 Litho. *Perf. 14*

663 A128 9p multicolored .50 .50
664 A128 30p multicolored 1.75 1.75
665 A128 35p multicolored 1.75 1.75
666 A128 75p multicolored 4.25 4.25
Nos. 663-666 (4) 8.25 8.25

Magellanic Penguins — A129

Designs: 17p, Two adults. 35p, Young in nest. 40p, Chick, adult. 65p, Swimming.

Wmk. 373

1997, Jan. 2 Litho. *Perf. 14*

667 A129 17p multicolored .90 .90
668 A129 35p multicolored 2.10 2.10
669 A129 40p multicolored 2.25 2.25
670 A129 65p multicolored 3.75 3.75
Nos. 667-670 (4) 9.00 9.00

Fish Type of 1994
Souvenir Sheet

Wmk. 373

1997, Feb. 3 Litho. *Perf. 14*

671 A117 £1 Smelt 5.00 5.00

Hong Kong '97.

Ferns — A130

Perf. 14½x14

1997, Mar. 3 Litho. Wmk. 373

672 A130 17p Coral .75 .75
673 A130 35p Adder's tongue 1.75 1.75
674 A130 40p Fuegian tall 2.00 2.00
675 A130 65p Small fern 3.25 3.25
Nos. 672-675 (4) 7.75 7.75

Lighthouses — A131

Wmk. 373

1997, July 1 Litho. *Perf. 14*

676 A131 9p Bull Point .65 .65
677 A131 30p Cape Pembroke 1.60 1.60
678 A131 £1 Cape Meredith 5.50 5.50
Nos. 676-678 (3) 7.75 7.75

Queen Elizabeth II and Prince Philip, 50th Wedding Anniv. — A132

#679, Queen holding flowers. #680, Prince with horse. #681, Queen riding in open carriage. #682, Prince in uniform. #683, Queen in red coat & hat, Prince. #684, Princes William and Harry on horseback.
£1.50, Queen, Prince riding in open carriage.

1997 Wmk. 384 *Perf. 14½x14*

679 9p multicolored .75 .75
680 9p multicolored .75 .75
a. A132 Pair, #679-680 1.50 1.50
681 17p multicolored 1.50 1.50
682 17p multicolored 1.50 1.50
a. A132 Pair, #681-682 3.00 3.00
683 40p multicolored 3.25 3.25
684 40p multicolored 3.25 3.25
a. A132 Pair, #683-684 6.50 6.50
Nos. 679-684 (6) 11.00 11.00

Souvenir Sheet

685 A132 £2.50 multicolored 8.00 8.00

Endangered Species — A133

Designs: 17p, Phalcoboenus australis. 19p, Otaria flavescens. 40p, Calandrinia feltonii. 73p, Aplochiton zebra.

Wmk. 373

1997, Oct. 16 Litho. *Perf. 14½*

686 A133 17p multicolored 1.25 1.25
687 A133 19p multicolored 1.40 1.40
688 A133 40p multicolored 2.50 2.50
689 A133 73p multicolored 4.75 4.75
Nos. 686-689 (4) 9.90 9.90

Fire Service in Falkland Islands, Cent. — A134

Equipment, manufacturer: 9p, Greenwich Gem, Merryweather & Son. 17p, Hatfield trailer pump, Merryweather & Son. 40p, Godiva trailer pump, Coventry Climax. 65p, Water tender type B, Carmichael Bedford.

Wmk. 384

1998, Feb. 26 Litho. *Perf. 14½*

690 A134 9p multicolored .60 .60
691 A134 17p multicolored 1.10 1.10
692 A134 40p multicolored 3.00 3.00
693 A134 65p multicolored 5.00 5.00
Nos. 690-693 (4) 9.70 9.70

Diana, Princess of Wales (1961-97)

Common Design Type

Portraits: a, Looking left. b, In red dress. c, Hand on cheek. d, Investigating land mines.

Perf. 14½x14

1998, Mar. 31 Wmk. 373

694 CD355 30p Sheet of 4, #a-d 6.00 6.00

No. 694 sold for £1.20 + 20p, with surtax from international sales being donated to the Princess Diana Memorial Fund and surtax from national sales being donated to designated local charity.

Birds A135

1p, Tawny-throated dotterel. 2p, Hudsonian godwit. 5p, Eared dove. #698, Great grebe. #699, Roseate spoonbill. 10p, Southern lapwing. 16p, Buff-necked ibis. 17p, Astral parakeet. 30p, Ashy-headed goose. 35p, American kestrel. 65p, Red-legged shag. 88p, Red shoveler. £1, Red-fronted coot. £3, Chilean flamingo. £5, Fork-tailed flycatcher.

Wmk. 373

1998, July 14 Litho. *Perf. 14*

695 A135 1p multicolored .20 .20
696 A135 2p multicolored .20 .20
697 A135 5p multicolored .20 .20
698 A135 9p multicolored .30 .30
699 A135 9p multicolored .30 .30
700 A135 10p multicolored .35 .35
701 A135 16p multicolored .50 .50

702 A135 17p multicolored .55 .55
a. Booklet pane, 2 #699, 8 #702 + 2 labels 5.00
Complete booklet, #702a 5.00
703 A135 30p multicolored 1.00 1.00
704 A135 35p multicolored 1.10 1.10
Complete booklet, 6 #704 6.75
705 A135 65p multicolored 2.00 2.00
706 A135 88p multicolored 2.75 2.75
707 A135 £1 multicolored 3.25 3.25
708 A135 £3 multicolored 10.00 10.00
709 A135 £5 multicolored 16.00 16.00
Nos. 695-709 (15) 38.70 38.70

Boats — A136

Boat, country flag, year: 17p, Penelope, Germany, 1926. 35p, Ilen, Italy, 1926. 40p, Weddell, Chile, 1940. 65p, Lively, Scotland, 1940.

Wmk. 373

1998, Sept. 30 Litho. *Perf. 14*
710 A136 17p multicolored 1.00 1.00
711 A136 35p multicolored 2.10 2.10
712 A136 40p multicolored 2.25 2.25

Size: 29x18mm

713 A136 65p multicolored 3.75 3.75
Nos. 710-713 (4) 9.10 9.10

FIGAS (First Medivac Air Ambulance Service), 50th Anniv. — A137

17p, Man carrying patient, airplane. £1, Airplane, map of Islands, float plane.

Wmk. 373

1998, Dec. 1 Litho. *Perf. 14*
714 A137 17p multicolored 1.00 1.00
715 A137 £1 multicolored 6.75 6.75

Military Uniforms — A138

Uniform, background location: 17p, Marine Private, 1776, The Block House at Port Egmont, Saunders Island. 30p, Marine Officer, 1833, Port Louis, East Falkland. 35p, Royal Marine Corporal, 1914, HMS Kent. 65p, Royal Marine Bugler, 1976, Government House.

Wmk. 373

1998, Dec. 8 Litho. *Perf. 14½*
716 A138 17p multicolored 1.10 1.10
717 A138 30p multicolored 2.10 2.10
718 A138 35p multicolored 2.25 2.25
719 A138 65p multicolored 4.50 4.50
Nos. 716-719 (4) 9.95 9.95

St. Mary's Church, Cent. A139

Wmk. 373

1999, Feb. 12 Litho. *Perf. 14*
720 A139 17p Inside view 1.00 1.00
721 A139 40p Outside view 2.40 2.40
722 A139 75p Laying corner-stone, 1899 4.50 4.50
Nos. 720-722 (3) 7.90 7.90

Australia '99, World Stamp Expo A140

25p, HMS Beagle. 35p, HMAS Australia. 40p, SS Canberra. #726, SS Great Britain. #727, All-England Eleven visit Australia, 1861-62.

1999, Mar. 5 Wmk. 384
723 A140 25p multicolored 1.75 1.75
724 A140 35p multicolored 2.50 2.50
725 A140 40p multicolored 2.75 2.75
726 A140 50p multicolored 3.50 3.50
727 A140 50p multicolored 3.50 3.50
a. Pair, #726-727 3.25 3.25
Nos. 723-727 (5) 14.00 14.00

1999 Visit of HRH Prince of Wales — A141

Perf. 14x13½

1999, Mar. 13 Litho. Wmk. 384
728 A141 £2 multicolored 11.00 11.00

Wedding of Prince Edward and Sophie Rhys-Jones
Common Design Type

Perf. 13¾x14

1999, June 15 Litho. Wmk. 384
729 CD356 80p Separate portraits 3.75 3.75
730 CD356 £1.20 Couple 6.00 6.00

PhilexFrance '99, World Philatelic Exhibition — A142

Designs: 35p, French cruiser, Jeanne d'Arc, Port Stanley, 1931. 40p, CAMS 37/11 Flying Boat's first flight.
£1, CAMS 37 Flying Boat over Port Stanley, 1931.

1999, June 21 Wmk. 373 *Perf. 14*
731 A142 35p multicolored 2.00 2.00
732 A142 40p multicolored 2.25 2.25

Souvenir Sheet

733 A142 £1 multicolored 6.25 6.25

No. 733 contains one 48x31mm stamp.

Queen Mother's Century
Common Design Type

Queen Mother: 9p, With King George VI at Port of London. 20p, With Queen Elizabeth at Women's Institute, Sandringham. 30p, With Princes Charles, William and Harry at Clarence House, 95th birthday. 67p, As Colonel-in-Chief of the Queen's Royal Hussars.
£1.40, With Ernest Shackleton, Robert F. Scott and Edward A. Wilson.

Wmk. 384

1999, Aug. 18 Litho. *Perf. 13½*
734 CD358 9p multicolored .60 .60
735 CD358 20p multicolored 1.25 1.25
736 CD358 30p multicolored 1.90 1.90
737 CD358 67p multicolored 4.25 4.25
Nos. 734-737 (4) 8.00 8.00

Souvenir Sheet

738 CD358 £1.40 multicolored 9.00 9.00

For overprint see #767.

Waterfowl A143

Perf. 14¼x14½

1999, Sept. 9 Litho. Wmk. 384
739 A143 9p Chiloe wigeon .70 .70
740 A143 17p Crested duck 1.25 1.25
741 A143 30p Brown pintail 2.25 2.25
742 A143 35p Silver teal 2.50 2.50
743 A143 40p Yellow billed teal 3.25 3.25
744 A143 65p Flightless steamer duck 4.75 4.75
Nos. 739-744 (6) 14.70 14.70

California Gold Rush A144

Designs: 9p, Vicar of Bray, 1999. 35p, Gold panning, 1849. 40p, Gold rocking cradle, 1849. 80p, Vicar of Bray, 1849.
£1, Vicar of Bray in San Francisco Harbor, 1849.

Wmk. 373

1999, Nov. 3 Litho. *Perf. 14*
745 A144 9p multicolored .60 .60
746 A144 35p multicolored 2.25 2.25
747 A144 40p multicolored 2.50 2.50
748 A144 80p multicolored 5.50 5.50
Nos. 745-748 (4) 10.85 10.85

Souvenir Sheet

Perf. 13¾

749 A144 £1 multicolored 6.25 6.25

No. 749 contains one 48x31mm stamp.

Millennium A145

Designs: No. 750, Kelp gull. No. 751, Upland goose. No. 752, Christchurch Cathedral. No. 753, Night heron. No. 754, King penguin. No. 755, Christmas at home.

1999, Dec. 6 *Perf. 14x14½*
750 A145 9p multicolored .60 .60
751 A145 9p multicolored .60 .60
752 A145 9p multicolored .60 .60
753 A145 30p multicolored 2.00 2.00
754 A145 30p multicolored 2.00 2.00
755 A145 30p multicolored 2.00 2.00
Nos. 750-755 (6) 7.80 7.80

Visit of Princess Alexandra A146

Designs: 9p, Princess in blue dress, trees. £1, Princess in patterned dress, trees.

Perf. 13¼x13¾

2000, Feb. 1 Litho. Wmk. 373
756 A146 9p multi .50 .50
757 A146 £1 multi 5.50 5.50

Sir Ernest Shackleton (1874-1922), Polar Explorer — A147

17p, Ship Endurance, discovery of the Caird Coast. 45p, Endurance trapped in pack ice. 75p, Shackleton, Chilean tugboat Yelcho.

2000, Feb. 10 Wmk. 373 *Perf. 14*
758 A147 17p multi 1.00 1.00
759 A147 45p multi 2.50 2.50
760 A147 75p multi 4.50 4.50
Nos. 758-760 (3) 8.00 8.00

See British Antarctic Territory Nos. 285-287, South Georgia and South Sandwich Islands Nos. 254-256.

British Monarchs — A148

a, Elizabeth I. b, James II. c, George I. d, William IV. e, Edward VIII. f, Elizabeth II.

2000, Feb. 29 Wmk. 373 *Perf. 14*
761 A148 40p Sheet of 6, #a.-f. 7.75 7.75

The Stamp Show 2000, London.

Prince William, 18th Birthday
Common Design Type

William: 10p, As toddler with fireman's helmet, vert. 20p, In checked suit and in navy suit, vert. 37p, With blue shirt. 43p, In gray suit and in navy suit holding flowers. 50p, As child with dog.

Perf. 13¾x14¼, 14¼x13¾

2000, June 21 Litho. Wmk. 373

Stamps with White Border

762 CD359 10p multi .50 .50
763 CD359 20p multi 1.00 1.00
764 CD359 37p multi 1.75 1.75
765 CD359 43p multi 2.00 2.00
Nos. 762-765 (4) 5.25 5.25

Souvenir Sheet

Stamps Without White Border

Perf. 14¼

766 Sheet of 5 7.00 7.00
a. CD359 10p multi .45 .45
b. CD359 20p multi .90 .90
c. CD359 37p multi 1.60 1.60
d. CD359 43p multi 1.75 1.75
e. CD359 50p multi 2.25 2.25

No. 738 Ovptd. in Gold

Wmk. 384

2000, Aug. 4 Litho. *Perf. 13½*
767 CD358 £1.40 multi 6.25 6.25

Gold overprint in sheet margin reads "100TH BIRTHDAY OF HM QUEEN / ELIZABETH THE QUEEN MOTHER."

Bridges A149

Bridges over: 20p, Malo River. 37p, Bodie Creek. 43p, Fitzroy River.

2000, Oct. 16 *Perf. 14¼x14½*
768-770 A149 Set of 3 5.00 5.00

Christmas — A150

Designs: 10p, Shepherd, sheep. 20p, Shepherds, sheep, angel. 33p, Holy family, shepherds, Magus, donkey, sheep. 43p, Angel, two Magi. 78p, Camel.

2000, Nov. 1 **Wmk. 373**
771-775 A150 Set of 5 8.00 8.00
775a Souvenir sheet, #771-775 8.00 8.00

Sunrises and Sunsets A151

Various photos: 10p, 20p, 37p, 43p.

2001, Jan. 10 ***Perf. 14½x14¼***
776-779 A151 Set of 4 4.25 4.25

Souvenir Sheet

New Year 2001 (Year of the Snake) — A152

Birds: a, Striated caracara. b, Mountain hawk eagle.

Perf. 14½x14¼
2001, Feb. 1 **Litho.** **Wmk. 373**
780 A152 37p Sheet of 2, #a-b 4.00 4.00

Hong Kong 2001 Stamp Exhibition.

Age of Victoria — A153

Designs: 3p, Falkland Islands #1. 10p, S.S. Great Britain, horiz. 20p, Stanley Harbor, 1888, horiz. 43p, Cape Pembroke Lighthouse, telephones, 1897. 93p, Royal Marines, 1900. £1.50, Queen Victoria, by Franz Xavier Winterhalter, 1859.

£1, Funeral procession for Queen Victoria.

2001, May 24 ***Perf. 14***
781-786 A153 Set of 6 12.00 12.00

Souvenir Sheet

787 A153 £1 multi 5.00 5.00

Royal Navy Connections to Falkland Islands — A154

Designs: 10p, Welfare, ship that made first recorded landing, 1690. 17p, HMS Invincible, ship in Battle of the Falklands, 1914. 20p, HMS Exeter, ship in Battle of the River Plate, 1939. 37p, SN.R6 Hovercraft, 1967. 43p, Antarctic patrol ship HMS Protector and Wasp helicopter, 1955. 68p, Desire, ship that made first sighting, 1592.

2001, July 24
788-793 A154 Set of 6 8.75 8.75

Carcass Island and its Flora and Fauna — A155

No. 794, 37p: a, Yellow violet. b, Tussac bird.

No. 795, 43p: a, Carcass Island settlement. b, Black-crowned night heron.

Wmk. 373
2001, Sept. 28 **Litho.** ***Perf. 13¾***
Pairs, #a-b
794-795 A155 Set of 2 6.50 6.50

Gentoo Penguins — A156

Designs: 10p, Birds flapping wings. 33p, Feeding young. 37p, Bird with beak open. 43p, Four birds walking.

2001, Oct. 26 ***Perf. 14½x14¼***
796-799 A156 Set of 4 5.00 5.00

Falkland Islands Company, 150th Anniv. A157

Designs: 10p, Company coat of arms, and gathering of cattle. 20p, Company flag, and ship Amelia. 43p, Manager F. E. Cobb, and company buildings. £1, Sheep farmer William Wickham Bertrand, sheep dip.

Wmk. 373
2002, Jan. 10 **Litho.** ***Perf. 14***
800-803 A157 Set of 4 6.75 6.75

Reign Of Queen Elizabeth II, 50th Anniv. Issue

Common Design Type

Designs: Nos. 804, 808a, 20p, Princess Elizabeth reading, 1945. Nos. 805, 808b, 37p, In 1977. Nos. 806, 808c, 43p, Holding Prince Charles, 1949. Nos. 807, 808d, 50p, At Garter ceremony, 1994. No. 808e, 50p, 1955 portrait by Annigoni (38x50mm).

Perf. 14¼x14½, 13¾ (#808e)
2002, Feb. 6 **Litho.** **Wmk. 373**
With Gold Frames
804-807 CD360 Set of 4 6.00 6.00

Souvenir Sheet
Without Gold Frames
808 CD360 Sheet of 5, #a-e 8.00 8.00

Falkland Islands War, 20th Anniv. — A158

No. 809, 22p: a, HMS Hermes, 1982. b, Fishery patrol vessel, 2002.

No. 810, 40p: a, Troops landing, 1982. b, Mine clearing, 2002.

No. 811, 45p: a, RAF Harrier on HMS Hermes, 1982. b, RAF Tristar, 2002.

Illustration reduced.

Wmk. 373
2002, June 14 **Litho.** ***Perf. 14***
Horiz. pairs, #a-b
809-811 A158 Set of 3 8.75 8.75

Queen Mother Elizabeth (1900-2002)

Common Design Type

Designs: 22p, Wearing hat and scarf (black and white photograph). 25p, Wearing blue hat with polka dots. Nos. 814, 816a, 95p, Wearing feathered hat (black and white photograph). Nos. 815, 816b, £1.20, Wearing blue hat.

Wmk. 373
2002, Aug. 5 **Litho.** ***Perf. 14¼***
With Purple Frames
812-815 CD361 Set of 4 10.50 10.50

Souvenir Sheet
Without Purple Frames
Perf. 14½x14¼
816 CD361 Sheet of 2, #a-b 8.75 8.75

Worldwide Fund for Nature (WWF) — A159

Penguins: 36p, Rockhopper. 40p, Magellanic. 45p, Gentoo. 70p, Macaroni.

Wmk. 373
2002, Aug. 30 **Litho.** ***Perf. 14¼***
817-820 A159 Set of 4 6.00 6.00
a. Horiz. strip of 4, #817-820 6.00 6.00

West Point Island and its Flora and Fauna — A160

No. 821, 40p: a, Felton's flower. b, Black-browed albatross.

No. 822, 45p: a, Rockhopper penguin. b, Island settlement.

Illustration reduced.

Perf. 14¼x14½
2002, Oct. 31 **Litho.** **Wmk. 373**
Horiz. Pairs, #a-b
821-822 A160 Set of 2 6.75 6.75

Visit of Prince Andrew — A161

No. 823: a, 22p, In uniform. b, £1.52, In suit and tie.

2002, Nov. 11 ***Perf. 13¼x13½***
823 A161 Horiz. pair, #a-b 7.00 7.00

Shepherds' Houses — A162

Designs: 10p, Gun Hill shanty, Little Chartres. 22p, Paragon House, Lafonia. 45p, Dos Lomas, Lafonia. £1, Old House, Shallow Bay Farm.

Wmk. 373
2003, Mar. 31 **Litho.** ***Perf. 14***
824-827 A162 Set of 4 5.75 5.75

Head of Queen Elizabeth II

Common Design Type

Wmk. 373
2003, June 2 **Litho.** ***Perf. 13¾***
828 CD362 £2 multi 8.00 8.00

Prince William, 21st Birthday

Common Design Type

Color photographs: a, In suit at right. b, With Prince Harry at left.

Wmk. 373
2003, June 21 **Litho.** ***Perf. 14¼***
829 Horiz. pair 7.75 7.75
a.-b. CD364 95p Either single 3.75 3.75

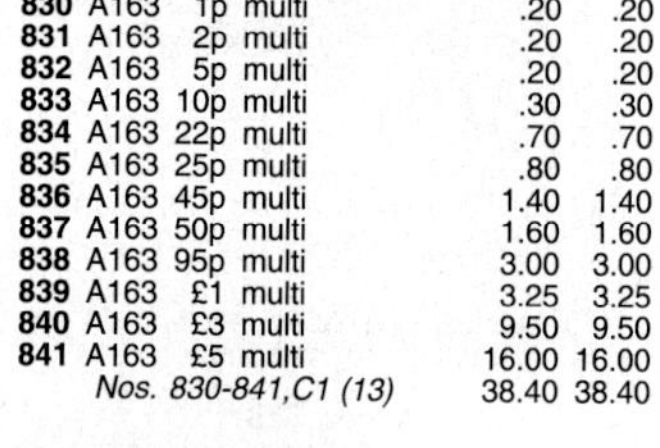

Birds — A163

Designs: 1p, Chiloe widgeon. 2p, Dolphin gull, vert. 5p, Falkland flightless steamer duck. 10p, Black-throated finch, vert. 22p, White-tufted grebe. 25p, Rufous-chested dotterel, vert. 45p, Upland goose. 50p, Dark-faced ground-tyrant, vert. 95p, Black-crowned night heron. £1, Red-backed hawk, vert. £3, Black-necked swan. £5, Short-eared owl, vert.

Perf. 13x13¼, 13¼x13
2003, July 21 **Litho.** **Wmk. 373**

830	A163	1p multi	.20	.20
831	A163	2p multi	.20	.20
832	A163	5p multi	.20	.20
833	A163	10p multi	.30	.30
834	A163	22p multi	.70	.70
835	A163	25p multi	.80	.80
836	A163	45p multi	1.40	1.40
837	A163	50p multi	1.60	1.60
838	A163	95p multi	3.00	3.00
839	A163	£1 multi	3.25	3.25
840	A163	£3 multi	9.50	9.50
841	A163	£5 multi	16.00	16.00
		Nos. 830-841,C1 (13)	38.40	38.40

Bird Life International A164

Black-browed albatross: No. 842, Adult on nest, facing right. No. 843, Chick. 40p, Heads of two adults, vert. £1, Adult on nest, facing left, vert.

16p, In flight.

Perf. 14¼x13¾, 13¾x14¼
2003, Sept. 26

842	A164	22p multi	.75	.75
a.		Perf. 14¼x14½	.75	.75
843	A164	22p multi	.75	.75
a.		Perf. 14¼x14½	.75	.75
844	A164	40p multi	1.25	1.25
a.		Perf. 14½x14¼	1.25	1.25
845	A164	£1 multi	3.25	3.25
a.		Perf. 14½x14¼	3.25	3.25
		Nos. 842-845 (4)	6.00	6.00

Souvenir Sheet

846 Sheet, #842a-846a 6.50 6.50
a. A164 16p multi, perf. 14¼x14½ .50 .50

New Island and its Flora and Fauna A165

No. 847, 40p: a, Striated caracara. b, Lady's slipper.

No. 848, 45p: a, Stone Cottage. b, King penguin.

Wmk. 373

2003, Oct. 24 Litho. *Perf. 13¾*

Pairs, #a-b

847-848	A165	Set of 2	5.75 5.75

Christmas — A166

Various depictions of Pale maiden flower: 16p, 30p, 40p, 95p.

2003, Nov. 3 *Perf. 14x14¼*

849-852	A166	Set of 4	6.25 6.25

Sheep Farming A167

Designs: 19p, Traditional hand shearing. 22p, Driving the sheep. 45p, Big House, Hill Cove. 70p, The early years. £1, Wool collection, SS Fitzroy.

Unwmk.

2004, Apr. 30 Litho. *Perf. 14*

853-857	A167	Set of 5	9.25 9.25

Wildlife Conservation in Falkland Islands, 25th Anniv. — A168

Designs: 20p, Man planting tussac grass. 24p, People cleaning beach. 50p, Satellite tracking of rockhopper penguins. £1, Weighing of albatross chick.

2004, June 17 Litho. *Perf. 14*

858-861	A168	Set of 4	7.25 7.25

Sir Rowland Hill (1795-1879) and Falkland Islands Postage Stamps — A169

Hill and: 24p, #20. 50p, #74. 75p, #94. £1, #151a.

2004, Aug. 31 Litho. *Perf. 13¼*

862-865	A169	Set of 4	9.00 9.00

Sea Lion Island and its Flora and Fauna — A170

No. 866, 42p: a, King cormorant. b, Dog orchid.
No. 867, 50p: a, Magellanic penguin. b, Sea Lion Lodge.
Illustration reduced.

2004, Sept. 15 *Perf. 13¾*

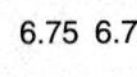

Pairs, #a-b

866-867	A170	Set of 2	6.75 6.75

Owls — A171

Designs: 18p, Head of short-eared owl. 45p, Short-eared owl. 50p, Barn owl in flight. £1.50, Barn owl.
£2, Barn owl in flight, horiz.

2004, Oct. 25

868-871	A171	Set of 4	9.75 9.75

Souvenir Sheet

872	A171	£2 multi	7.50 7.50

SEMI-POSTAL STAMPS

Catalogue values for unused stamps in this section are for Never Hinged items.

Rebuilding after Conflict with Argentina — SP1

Wmk. 373

1982, Sept. 13 Litho. *Perf. 11*

B1	SP1	£1 + £1 Battle sites	3.00 3.00

Liberation of Falkland Islands, 10th Anniv. — SP2

Designs: 14p+6p, San Carlos Cemetery. 29p+11p, 1982 War Memorial, Port Stanley. 34p+16p, South Atlantic Medal. 68p+32p, Government House, Port Stanley.

Wmk. 373

1992, June 14 Litho. *Perf. 14*

B2	SP2	14p + 6p multicolored	.60	.60
B3	SP2	29p + 11p multicolored	1.25	1.25
B4	SP2	34p + 16p multicolored	1.75	1.75
B5	SP2	68p + 32p multicolored	3.25	3.25
a.		Souvenir sheet of 4, #B2-B5	8.00	8.00
		Nos. B2-B5 (4)	6.85	6.85

Surtax for Soldiers', Sailors' and Airmen's Families Association.

AIR POST STAMPS

Bird Type of 2003

Design: Rockhopper penguins, vert.

Serpentine Die Cut 6x6½

Syncopated

2003, Sept. 19 Litho.

Booklet Stamp

Self-Adhesive

C1	A163	(40p) multi	1.25 1.25
a.		Booklet pane of 8	10.00

POSTAGE DUE STAMPS

Catalogue values for unused stamps in this section are for never hinged items.

Penguin — D1

Perf. 14½x14

1991, Jan. 7 Litho. Wmk. 373

J1	D1	1p lilac rose & lake	.20	.20
J2	D1	2p buff & brown org	.20	.20
J3	D1	3p yel & orange yel	.20	.20
J4	D1	4p lt bl grn & dk bl grn	.25	.20
J5	D1	5p sky blue & Prus bl	.25	.20
J6	D1	10p lt blue & dk blue	.35	.25
J7	D1	20p lt violet & dk vio	.90	.55
J8	D1	50p brt yel grn & dk yel green	2.00	1.25
		Nos. J1-J8 (8)	4.35	3.05

WAR TAX STAMPS

Regular Issue of 1912-14 Overprinted

1918, Oct. 7 Wmk. 3 *Perf. 14*

MR1	A7	½p yellow green	.55	*7.25*
MR2	A7	1p red	.55	*4.00*
a.		Double overprint	*2,500.*	
MR3	A7	1sh bister brown	6.50	*52.50*
a.		Pair, one without overprint	8,000.	
		Nos. MR1-MR3 (3)	7.60	*63.75*

No. MR3a probably is caused by a foldover and is not constant.

FALKLAND ISLANDS DEPENDENCIES

Catalogue values for unused stamps in this section are for Never Hinged items.

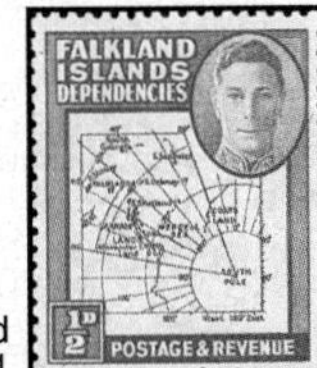

Map of Falkland Islands — A1

Engr., Center Litho. in Black

1946, Feb. 1 Wmk. 4 *Perf. 12*

1L1	A1	½p yellow green	.95	*1.50*
1L2	A1	1p blue violet	.95	*1.90*
1L3	A1	2p deep carmine	.95	*1.90*
1L4	A1	3p ultramarine	1.90	*1.90*
1L5	A1	4p deep plum	1.90	*3.00*
1L6	A1	6p orange yellow	3.00	*3.50*
1L7	A1	9p brown	3.00	*3.50*
1L8	A1	1sh rose violet	5.75	*7.50*
		Nos. 1L1-1L8 (8)	18.40	*24.70*

Nos. 1-8 were reissued in 1948, printed on more opaque paper with the lines of the map finer and clearer. Value for set, unused or used $120.

See No. 1L13.

Common Design Types pictured following the introduction.

Peace Issue

Common Design Type

1946, Oct. 4 *Perf. 13½x14*

1L9	CD303	1p purple	.60	.20
1L10	CD303	3p deep blue	1.10	.20

Silver Wedding Issue

Common Design Types

1948, Dec. 6 Photo. *Perf. 14x14½*

1L11	CD304	2½p brt ultra	1.25	1.25

Perf. 11½x11

Engr.

1L12	CD305	1sh blue violet	5.75	5.75

Type of 1946

1949, Mar. 6 *Perf. 12*

Center Litho. in Black

1L13	A1	2½p deep blue	12.50	12.00

UPU Issue

Common Design Types

Engr.; Name Typo. on 2p, 3p

1949, Oct. 10 *Perf. 13½, 11x11½*

1L14	CD306	1p violet	1.60	1.90
1L15	CD307	2p deep carmine	4.25	1.90
1L16	CD308	3p indigo	6.50	4.25
1L17	CD309	6p red orange	11.00	8.50
		Nos. 1L14-1L17 (4)	23.35	16.55

Coronation Issue

Common Design Type

1953, June 4 *Perf. 13½x13*

1L18	CD312	1p purple & black	1.50	1.50

John Biscoe — A2

Trepassey — A3

Ships: 1½p, Wyatt Earp. 2p, Eagle. 2½p, Penola. 3p, Discovery II. 4p, William Scoresby. 6p, Discovery. 9p, Endurance. 1sh, Deutschland. 2sh, Pourquoi-pas? 2sh6p, Français. 5sh, Scotia. 10sh, Antarctic. £1, Belgica.

1954, Feb. 1 Engr. *Perf. 12½*

Center in Black

1L19	A2	½p blue green	.20	*2.00*
1L20	A3	1p sepia	1.75	1.50
1L21	A3	1½p olive	2.00	1.75
1L22	A3	2p rose red	1.25	.20
1L23	A3	2½p yellow	1.25	.20
1L24	A3	3p ultra	1.25	.20
1L25	A3	4p red violet	3.00	.45
1L26	A2	6p rose violet	3.50	.45
1L27	A2	9p black	3.50	1.25
1L28	A3	1sh org brown	3.50	1.00
1L29	A3	2sh lilac rose	18.00	10.00
1L30	A2	2sh6p blue gray	19.00	6.25
1L31	A2	5sh violet	40.00	6.75
1L32	A3	10sh brt blue	55.00	18.00
1L33	A2	£1 black	87.50	50.00
		Nos. 1L19-1L33 (15)	240.70	100.00

Nos. 20, 23-24, 26 Overprinted in Black

1956, Jan 30 Center in Black

1L34	A3	1p sepia	.20	.20
1L35	A3	2½p yellow	.50	.50
1L36	A3	3p ultramarine	.60	.60
1L37	A2	6p rose violet	.70	.70
		Nos. 1L34-1L37 (4)	2.00	2.00

Trans-Antarctic Expedition, 1955-1958.

A4

Wmk. 373

1980, May 5 Litho. *Perf. 13½*

1L38 A4 1p Map of Dependencies .20 .25
1L39 A4 2p Shag Rocks .20 .25
1L40 A4 3p Bird and Willis Islds. .20 .25
1L41 A4 4p Gulbrandsen Lake .20 .25
1L42 A4 5p King Edward Point .20 .25
1L43 A4 6p Shackleton's Memorial Cross .20 .25
1L44 A4 7p Shackleton's grave .20 .25
1L45 A4 8p Grytviken Church .20 .25
1L46 A4 9p Coaling Hulk "Louise" .25 .30
1L47 A4 10p Clerke Rocks .25 .30
1L48 A4 20p Candlemas Island .45 .55
1L49 A4 25p Twitcher Rock, Cook Island .60 .70
1L50 A4 50p "John Biscoe" 1.10 1.25
1L51 A4 £1 "Bransfield" 2.25 2.75
1L52 A4 £3 "Endurance" 7.50 9.00
Nos. 1L38-1L52 (15) 14.00 16.85

Nos. 38-50 exist dated 1984; same values. Issued May 3, 1984.

1985, Nov. 18 Wmk. 384

1L48a A4 20p .75 1.10
1L49a A4 25p 1.00 1.25
1L50a A4 50p 2.75 3.50
1L51a A4 £1 4.00 5.00
1L52a A4 £3 12.50 16.00
Nos. 1L48a-1L52a (5) 21.00 26.85

Magellanic Clubmoss — A5

1981, Feb. 5 Litho. *Perf. 14*

1L53 A5 3p shown .25 .25
1L54 A5 6p Alpine cat's-tail .25 .25
1L55 A5 7p Greater burnet .25 .25
1L56 A5 11p Antarctic bedstraw .35 .35
1L57 A5 15p Brown rush .50 .50
a. Brown missing —
1L58 A5 25p Antarctic hair grass .75 .75
Nos. 1L53-1L58 (6) 2.35 2.35

Royal Wedding Issue
Common Design Type

1981, July 22 Litho. *Perf. 14*

1L59 CD331 10p Bouquet .25 .25
1L60 CD331 13p Charles .35 .35
1L61 CD331 52p Couple .85 .85
Nos. 1L59-1L61 (3) 1.45 1.45

Reindeer in Spring — A6

1982, Jan. 29 Litho. *Perf. 14*

1L62 A6 5p shown .20 .20
1L63 A6 13p Autumn .45 .45
1L64 A6 25p Winter .80 .80
1L65 A6 26p Late winter .85 .85
Nos. 1L62-1L65 (4) 2.30 2.30

Gamasellus Racovitzai — A7

1982, Mar. 16 Litho. *Perf. 14*

1L66 A7 5p shown .20 .20
1L67 A7 10p Alaskozetes antarcticus .25 .25
1L68 A7 13p Cryptopygus antarcticus .30 .30
1L69 A7 15p Notiomaso australis .40 .40
1L70 A7 25p Hydromedion sparsutum .60 .60
1L71 A7 26p Parochlus steinenii .65 .65
Nos. 1L66-1L71 (6) 2.40 2.40

Princess Diana Issue
Common Design Type

1982, July 1 Litho. *Perf. 14x14½*

1L72 CD333 5p Arms .45 .20
1L73 CD333 17p Diana 1.40 .60
a. Perf. 14 9.00 9.00
1L74 CD333 37p Wedding 3.25 1.40
1L75 CD333 50p Portrait 4.25 1.75
Nos. 1L72-1L75 (4) 9.35 3.95

Crustacea — A8

Perf. 14½x14

1984, Mar. 23 Wmk. 373

1L76 A8 5p Euphausia superba .20 .20
1L77 A8 17p Glyptonotus antarcticus .65 .65
1L78 A8 25p Epimeria monodon 1.00 1.00
1L79 A8 34p Serolis pagenstecheri 1.40 1.40
Nos. 1L76-1L79 (4) 3.25 3.25

Manned Flight Bicentenary — A9

1983, Dec. 23 Litho. *Perf. 14*

1L80 A9 5p Westland Whirlwind .20 .20
1L81 A9 13p Westland Wasp .45 .45
1L82 A9 17p Saunders-Roe Walrus .65 .65
1L83 A9 50p Auster 2.00 2.00
Nos. 1L80-1L83 (4) 3.30 3.30

South Sandwich Islds. Volcanoes — A10

1984, Nov. 8 Wmk. 373 *Perf. 14½*

1L84 A10 6p Zavodovski Isld. .60 .60
1L85 A10 17p Mt. Michael, Saunders Isld. 1.40 1.40
1L86 A10 22p Bellingshausen Isld. 2.00 2.00
1L87 A10 52p Bristol Isld. 4.75 4.75
Nos. 1L84-1L87 (4) 8.75 8.75

Albatrosses — A11

1985, May 5 Wmk. 384 *Perf. 14½*

1L88 A11 7p Diomedea chrysostoma .80 .80
1L89 A11 22p Diomedea melanophris 2.50 2.50
1L90 A11 27p Diomedea exulans 2.75 2.75
1L91 A11 54p Phoebetria palpebrata 5.75 5.75
Nos. 1L88-1L91 (4) 11.80 11.80

Queen Mother 85th Birthday
Common Design Type

Designs: 7p, 14th birthday celebration. 22p, With Princess Anne, Lady Sarah Armstrong-Jones, Prince Edward. 27p, Queen Mother. 54p, Holding Prince Henry. £1, On the Britannia.

1985, June 23 *Perf. 14½x14*

1L92 CD336 7p multicolored .25 .25
1L93 CD336 22p multicolored .75 .75
1L94 CD336 27p multicolored 1.00 1.00
1L95 CD336 54p multicolored 2.00 2.00
Nos. 1L92-1L95 (4) 4.00 4.00

Souvenir Sheet

1L96 CD336 £1 multicolored 3.75 3.75

Falkland Islands Naturalists Type of 1985

Naturalists, endangered species: 7p, Dumont d'Urville (1790-1842), kelp. 22p, Johann Reinhold Forster (1729-1798), king penguin. 27p, Johann Georg Adam Forster (1754-1794), tussock grass. 54p, Sir Joseph Banks (1743-1820), dove prion.

1985, Nov. 4 *Perf. 13½x14*

1L97 A86 7p multicolored .65 .65
1L98 A86 22p multicolored 1.60 1.60
1L99 A86 27p multicolored 2.40 2.40
1L100 A86 54p multicolored 4.75 4.75
Nos. 1L97-1L100 (4) 9.40 9.40

SEMI-POSTAL STAMP

Catalogue values for unused stamps from No. 1LB1 through 5L1 are for Never Hinged items.

Rebuilding Type of Falkland Islands

Wmk. 373

1982, Sept. 13 Litho. *Perf. 11*

1LB1 SP1 £1 Map of So. Georgia 3.00 3.00

ISSUES FOR THE SEPARATE ISLANDS

Graham Land

Nos. 84, 85B, 86A, 87A, 88-91 Overprinted in Red

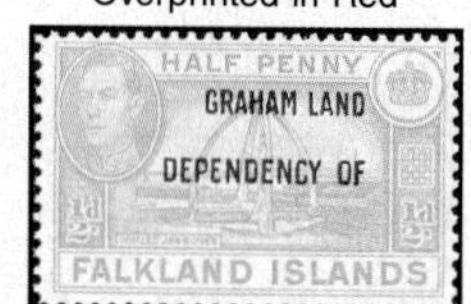

1944, Feb. 12 Wmk. 4 *Perf. 12*

2L1 A22 ½p green & black .55 .50
2L2 A22 1p dk vio & black .60 .60
2L3 A22 2p rose car & blk .90 .85
2L4 A22 3p deep bl & blk 1.25 1.10
2L5 A22 4p rose vio & blk 1.50 1.50
2L6 A22 6p brown & black 4.00 3.50
2L7 A22 9p slate bl & blk 3.00 3.00
2L8 A22 1sh dull blue 3.00 2.75
Nos. 2L1-2L8 (8) 14.80 13.80

South Georgia

1944, Apr. 3 Wmk. 4 *Perf. 12*

3L1 A22 ½p green & black .60 .50
3L2 A22 1p dark vio & blk .65 .60
3L3 A22 2p rose car & blk 1.00 .85
3L4 A22 3p deep bl & blk 1.40 1.10
3L5 A22 4p rose vio & blk 1.60 1.50
3L6 A22 6p brown & black 4.25 4.00
3L7 A22 9p slate bl & blk 3.25 3.00
3L8 A22 1sh dull blue 3.25 3.00
Nos. 3L1-3L8 (8) 16.00 14.55

South Orkneys

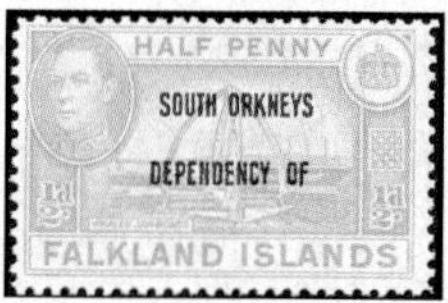

1944, Feb. 21 Wmk. 4 *Perf. 12*

4L1 A22 ½p green & black .55 .50
4L2 A22 1p dark vio & blk .60 .60
4L3 A22 2p rose car & blk .90 .85
4L4 A22 3p deep bl & blk 1.25 1.10
4L5 A22 4p rose vio & blk 1.50 1.50
4L6 A22 6p brown & black 4.00 3.50
4L7 A22 9p slate bl & blk 3.00 3.00
4L8 A22 1sh dull blue 3.00 2.75
Nos. 4L1-4L8 (8) 14.80 13.80

South Shetlands

1944 Wmk. 4 *Perf. 12*

5L1 A22 ½p green & black .50 .50
5L2 A22 1p dark vio & blk .60 .60
5L3 A22 2p rose car & blk .90 .85
5L4 A22 3p deep bl & blk 1.25 1.10
5L5 A22 4p rose vio & blk 1.50 1.50
5L6 A22 6p brown & black 4.00 3.50
5L7 A22 9p slate bl & blk 3.00 3.00
5L8 A22 1sh dull blue 3.00 2.75
Nos. 5L1-5L8 (8) 14.75 13.80

FAR EASTERN REPUBLIC

'fär 'ē-stərn ri-'pə-blik

LOCATION — In Siberia east of Lake Baikal
GOVT. — Republic
AREA — 900,745 sq. mi.
POP. — 1,560,000 (approx. 1920)
CAPITAL — Chita

A short-lived independent government was established here in 1920.

100 Kopecks = 1 Ruble

Watermark

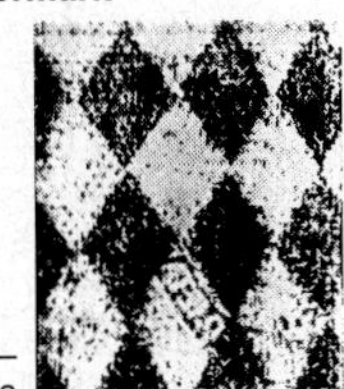

Wmk. 171 — Diamonds

Vladivostok Issue

Russian Stamps Surcharged or Overprinted:

a

b

c

On Stamps of 1909-17
Perf. 14, 14½x15, 13½

1920 Unwmk.

No.	Type	Description	Unused	Used
2	A14(a)	2k green	8.00	*10.00*
3	A14(a)	3k red	8.00	*10.00*
4	A11(b)	3k on 35k red brn & grn	20.00	20.00
5	A15(a)	4k carmine	10.10	*12.00*
6	A11(b)	4k on 70k brn & org	6.00	*8.00*
8	A11(b)	7k on 15k red brn & bl	2.00	2.00
a.		Inverted surcharge	50.00	
b.		Pair, one ovptd. "DBP" only		
9	A15(a)	10k dark blue	50.00	*55.00*
a.		Overprint on back	75.00	
10	A12(c)	10k on 3½r mar & lt grn	15.00	*20.00*
11	A11(a)	14k blue & rose	30.00	30.00
12	A11(a)	15k red brn & bl	12.00	12.00
13	A8(a)	20k blue & car	65.00	65.00
14	A11(b)	20k on 14k bl & rose	6.00	*8.00*
a.		Surcharge on back	30.00	
15	A11(a)	25k green & vio	12.50	12.00
16	A11(a)	35k red brn & grn	30.00	30.00
17	A8(a)	50k brn vio & grn	10.00	*11.50*
18	A9(a)	1r pale brn, dk brn & org	*500.00*	*500.00*

On Stamps of 1917
Imperf

No.	Type	Description	Unused	Used
21	A14(a)	1k orange	8.00	*8.50*
22	A14(a)	2k gray grn	3.00	2.50
23	A14(a)	3k red	8.00	*10.00*
25	A11(b)	7k on 15k red brn & dp bl	2.00	*5.00*
a.		Pair, one without surcharge		
b.		Pair, one ovptd. "DBP" only		
26	A12(c)	10k on 3½r mar & lt grn	10.00	*15.00*
27	A9(a)	1r pale brn, brn & red org	15.00	*20.00*

On Stamps of Siberia 1919
Perf. 14, 14½x15

No.	Type	Description	Unused	Used
30	A14(a)	35k on 2k green	5.00	*8.00*
a.		"DBP" on back	25.00	*50.00*

Imperf

No.	Type	Description	Unused	Used
31	A14(a)	35k on 2k green	15.00	15.00
32	A14(a)	70k on 1k orange	7.00	*10.00*

Counterfeit surcharges and overprints abound, including difital forgeries.

Postal Savings Stamps Surcharged for Postal Use

A1

Perf. 14½x15
Wmk. 171

No.	Type	Description	Unused	Used
35	A1(b)	1k on 5k green, *buff*	15.00	15.00
36	A1(b)	2k on 10k brown, *buff*	35.00	35.00

The letters on these stamps resembling "DBP," are the Russian initials of "Dalne Vostochnaya Respublika" (Far Eastern Republic).

Chita Issue

A2

A2a

1921 Unwmk. Typo. *Imperf.*

No.	Type	Description	Unused	Used
38	A2	2k gray green	1.50	1.50
39	A2a	4k rose	3.00	3.00
40	A2	5k claret	3.00	3.00
41	A2a	10k blue	2.25	2.25
		Nos. 38-41 (4)	9.75	9.75

For overprints see Nos. 62-65.

Blagoveshchensk Issue

A3

1921 Litho. *Imperf.*

No.	Type	Description	Unused	Used
42	A3	2r red	2.75	2.00
43	A3	3r dark green	2.75	2.00
44	A3	5r dark blue	2.75	2.00
a.		Tête bêche pair	30.00	*50.00*
45	A3	15r dark brown	2.75	2.00
46	A3	30r dark violet	2.75	2.00
a.		Tête bêche pair	30.00	*50.00*
		Nos. 42-46 (5)	13.75	10.00

Remainders of Nos. 42-46 were canceled in colored crayon or by typographed bars. These sell for half of foregoing values.

Chita Issue

A4

A5

1922 Litho. *Imperf.*

No.	Type	Description	Unused	Used
49	A4	1k orange	.45	*.75*
50	A4	3k dull red	.25	*.45*
51	A5	4k dp rose & buff	.25	*.45*
52	A4	5k orange brown	.65	.45
53	A4	7k light blue	.65	*1.25*
a.		Perf. 11½	1.00	2.00
b.		Rouletted 9	2.00	2.00
c.		Perf. 11½x roulette	4.00	3.00
54	A5	10k dk blue & red	.30	*.65*
55	A4	15k dull rose	.45	*.75*
56	A5	20k blue & red	.45	*.75*
57	A5	30k green & red org	.55	*1.00*
58	A5	50k black & red org	1.00	*1.50*
		Nos. 49-58 (10)	5.00	*8.00*

The 4k exists with "4" omitted. Value $100.

Vladivostok Issue

Stamps of 1921 Overprinted in Red

1917
7-XI
1922

1922 *Imperf.*

No.	Type	Description	Unused	Used
62	A2	2k gray green	20.00	20.00
a.		Inverted overprint	100.00	
63	A2a	4k rose	20.00	20.00
a.		Inverted overprint	100.00	
b.		Double overprint	150.00	
64	A2	5k claret	15.00	15.00
a.		Inverted overprint	100.00	
b.		Double overprint	300.00	
65	A2a	10k blue	20.00	20.00
a.		Inverted overprint	100.00	
		Nos. 62-65 (4)	75.00	75.00

Russian revolution of Nov. 1917, 5th anniv.

Once in the setting the figures "22" of 1922 have the bottom stroke curved instead of straight. Value, each $40.

Vladivostok Issue

Russian Stamps of 1922-23 Surcharged in Black or Red

Д. В.
коп. 1 коп.
золотом

1923 *Imperf.*

No.	Type	Description	Unused	Used
66	A50	1k on 100r red	.40	*.75*
a.		Inverted surcharge	45.00	
67	A50	2k on 70r violet	.40	*.75*
68	A49	5k on 10r blue (R)	.40	*.75*
69	A50	10k on 50r brown	.90	*1.25*
a.		Inverted surcharge	45.00	

Perf. 14½x15

No.	Type	Description	Unused	Used
70	A50	1k on 100r red	.90	*1.25*
		Nos. 66-70 (5)	3.00	*4.75*

OCCUPATION STAMPS

Issued under Occupation of General Semenov

Chita Issue

Russian Stamps of 1909-12 Surcharged:

р. 1 р.
a

2р.50к.
b

Р. 5 Р.
c

1920 Unwmk. *Perf. 14, 14x15½*

No.	Type	Description	Unused	Used
N1	A15 (a)	1r on 4k car	50.00	*50.00*
N2	A8 (b)	2r50k on 20k bl & car	20.00	*35.00*
N3	A14 (c)	5r on 5k claret	20.00	*45.00*
a.		Double surcharge	60.00	
N4	A11 (a)	10r on 70k brn & org	20.00	*35.00*
		Nos. N1-N4 (4)	110.00	*165.00*

FAROE ISLANDS

'far-ₒ,ü 'ī-lənds

(The Faroes)

LOCATION — North Atlantic Ocean
GOVT. — Self-governing part of Kingdom of Denmark
AREA — 540 sq. mi.
POP. — 41,059 (1999 est.)
CAPITAL — Thorshavn

100 Ore = 1 Krone

Catalogue values for unused stamps in this country are for Never Hinged items, beginning with Scott 7.

Denmark No. 97 Handstamp Surcharged

1919, Jan. Typo. *Perf. 14x14½*

No.	Type	Description	Unused	Used
1	A16	2o on 5o green	1,100.	350.00

Counterfeits of surcharge exist.

Denmark No. 88a, the bisect, was used with Denmark No. 97 in Faroe Islands Jan. 3-23, 1919.

Denmark Nos. 220, 224, 238A, 224C Surcharged in Blue or Black

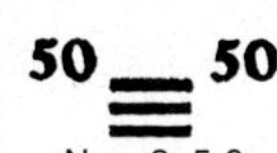

Nos. 2, 5-6

No. 3

No. 4

1940-41 Engr. *Perf. 13*

No.	Type	Description	Unused	Used
2	A32	20o on 1o ('41)	45.00	85.00
3	A32	20o on 5o ('41)	40.00	30.00
4	A30	20o on 15o (Bk)	47.50	20.00
5	A32	50o on 5o (Bk)	250.00	75.00
6	A32	60o on 6o (Bk)	100.00	175.00
		Nos. 2-6 (5)	482.50	385.00
		Set, never hinged	675.00	

Issued during British administration.

Catalogue values for unused stamps in this section, from this point to the end of the section, are for Never Hinged items.

Map of Islands, 1673 — A1

Map of North Atlantic, 1573 — A2

West Coast, Sandoy — A3

Vidoy and Svinoy, by Eyvindur Mohr — A4

Designs: 200o, like 70o. 250o, 300o, View of Streymoy and Vagar. 450o, Houses, Nes, by Ruth Smith. 500o, View of Hvitanes and Skalafjordur, by S. Joensen-Mikines.

Unwmk.

1975, Jan. 30 Engr. *Perf. 13*

No.	Type	Description	Unused	Used
7	A1	5o sepia	.20	.20
8	A2	10o emer & dark blue	.20	.20
9	A1	50o graysh green	.20	.20
10	A2	60o brown & dark blue	.95	.75
11	A3	70o vio bl & slate grn	.95	.75
12	A2	80o ocher & dark blue	.40	.40
13	A1	90o red brown	.95	.75
14	A2	120o brt bl & dark bl	.40	.35
15	A3	200o vio bl & slate grn	.40	.40
16	A3	250o multicolored	.35	.35
17	A3	300o multicolored	3.75	1.50

Photo.

Perf. 12½x13

18 A4 350o multicolored .60 .60
19 A4 450o multicolored .70 .60
20 A4 500o multicolored .80 .70
Nos. 7-20 (14) 10.85 7.75

Faroe Boat — A5

Faroe Flag — A6

Faroe Mailman — A7

Perf. 12½x13, 12 (A6)

1976, Apr. 1 Engr.; Litho. (A6)

21 A5 125o copper red 1.75 1.10
22 A6 160o multicolored .35 .25
23 A7 800o olive 1.40 .95
Nos. 21-23 (3) 3.50 2.30

Faroe Islands independent postal service, Apr. 1, 1976.

Motor Fishing Boat — A8

Faroese Fishing Vessels and Map of Islands: 125o, Inland fishing cutter. 160o, Modern seine fishing vessel. 600o, Deep-sea fishing trawler.

1977, Apr. 28 Photo. *Perf. 14½x14*

24 A8 100o green & black 5.50 5.00
25 A8 125o carmine & black 1.50 1.50
26 A8 160o blue & black .50 .50
27 A8 600o brown & black .75 .75
Nos. 24-27 (4) 8.25 7.75

Common Snipe A9

Photogravure & Engraved

1977, Sept. 29 *Perf. 14½x14*

28 A9 70o shown .20 .20
29 A9 180o Oystercatcher .40 .40
30 A9 250o Whimbrel .70 .65
Nos. 28-30 (3) 1.30 1.25

North Coast, Puffins — A10

Mykines Village — A11

Mykines Island: 140o, Tilled fields and coast. 150o, Aerial view. 180o, Map.

Perf. 13x13½, 13½x13

1978, Jan. 26 Photo.

Size: 21x28mm, 28x21mm

31 A10 100o multicolored .20 .20
32 A11 130o multicolored .25 .25
33 A11 140o multicolored .40 .40
34 A10 150o multicolored .30 .30

Size: 37x26mm

Perf. 14½x14

35 A11 180o multicolored .30 .30
Nos. 31-35 (5) 1.45 1.45

Sea Birds — A12

Old Library — A13

Lithographed and Engraved

1978, Apr. 13 *Perf. 12x12½*

36 A12 140o Gannets .70 .70
37 A12 180o Puffins .90 .90
38 A12 400o Guillemots .70 .70
Nos. 36-38 (3) 2.30 2.30

1978, Dec. 7 *Perf. 13*

39 A13 140o shown .45 .45
40 A13 180o New library .45 *.55*

Completion of New Library Building.

Girl Guide, Tent and Fire — A14

Ram — A15

1978, Dec. 7 Photo. *Perf. 13½*

41 A14 140o multicolored .50 .50

Faroese Girl Guides, 50th anniversary.

Lithographed and Engraved

1979, Mar. 19 *Perf. 12*

42 A15 25k multicolored 5.75 5.25

Denmark No. 88a — A16

Europa: 180o, Faroe Islands No. 1.

1979, May 7 *Perf. 12½*

43 A16 140o yellow & blue .50 .50
44 A16 180o rose, grn & blk .50 .50

Girl Wearing Festive Costume — A17

Children's Drawings and IYC Emblem: 150o, Fisherman. 200o, Two friends.

1979, Oct. 1 *Perf. 12*

45 A17 110o multicolored .20 .20
46 A17 150o multicolored .30 .30
47 A17 200o multicolored .35 .35
Nos. 45-47 (3) .85 .85

International Year of the Child.

Sea Plantain — A18

1980, Mar. 17 Photo. *Perf. 12x11½*

48 A18 90o *shown* .20 .20
49 A18 110o *Glacier buttercup* .20 .20
50 A18 150o *Purple saxifrage* .30 .30
51 A18 200o *Starry saxifrage* .40 .40
52 A18 400o *Lady's mantle* .70 .70
Nos. 48-52 (5) 1.80 1.80

Jakob Jakobsen (1864-1918), Linguist — A19

Coat of Arms, Virgin and Child, Gothic Pew Gable — A20

Europa: 200o, Vensel Ulrich Hammershaimb (1819-1909), theologian, linguist and folklorist.

1980, Oct. 6 Engr. *Perf. 11½*

53 A19 150o dull green .35 .35
54 A19 200o dull red brown .55 .55

Photo. & Engr.

1980, Oct. 6 *Perf. 13½*

Kirkjubour Pew Gables, 15th Century: 140o, Norwegian coat of arms, John the Baptist. 150o, Christ's head, St. Peter. 200o, Hand in halo, Apostle Paul.

55 A20 110o multicolored .25 .25
56 A20 140o multicolored .40 .40
57 A20 150o multicolored .40 .40
58 A20 200o multicolored .50 .50
Nos. 55-58 (4) 1.55 1.55

See Nos. 102-105.

A21

Sketches of Old Torshavn by Ingalzur Reyni.

1981, Mar. 2 Engr.

59 A21 110o dark green .25 .25
60 A21 140o black .40 .40
61 A21 150o dark brown .40 .40
62 A21 200o dark blue .45 .45
Nos. 59-62 (4) 1.50 1.50

The Ring Dance A22

Europa: 200o, The garter dance.

1981, June 1 Engr. *Perf. 13x14*

63 A22 150o pale rose & grn .35 .35
64 A22 200o pale yel grn & dk brn .50 .50

Rune Stones, 800-1000 AD — A23

Historic Writings: 1k, Folksong, 1846. 3k, Sheep Letter excerpt, 1298. 6k, Seal and text, 1533. 10k, Titlepage from Faeroae et Faeroa, by Lucas Jacobson Debes, library.

Photo. & Engr.

1981, Oct. 19 *Perf. 11½*

65 A23 10o multicolored .20 .20
66 A23 1k multicolored .25 .25
67 A23 3k multicolored .65 .60
68 A23 6k multicolored 1.25 1.00
69 A23 10k multicolored 2.00 2.00
Nos. 65-69 (5) 4.35 4.05

Nos. 70-80 not assigned.

Europa 1982 — A24

1982, Mar. 15 Engr. *Perf. 13½*

81 A24 1.50k Viking North Atlantic routes .35 .35
82 A24 2k Viking house foundation .50 .50

View of Gjogv, by Ingalvur av Reyni A25

1982, June 7 Litho. *Perf. 12½x13*

83 A25 180o shown .30 .30
84 A25 220o Hvalvik 1.25 1.00
85 A25 250o Kvivik .45 .45
Nos. 83-85 (3) 2.00 1.75

Ballad of Harra Paetur and Elinborg — A26

Scenes from the medieval ballad of chivalry.

1982, Sept. 27 Litho.

86 A26 220o multicolored .50 .50
87 A26 250o multicolored .60 .60
88 A26 350o multicolored .80 .80
89 A26 450o multicolored 1.10 1.10
Nos. 86-89 (4) 3.00 3.00

Cargo Ships A27

1983, Feb. 21 Litho. *Perf. 14x14½*

90 A27 220o Arcturus, 1856 .60 .60
91 A27 250o Laura, 1882 .65 .65
92 A27 700o Thyra, 1866 1.75 1.75
Nos. 90-92 (3) 3.00 3.00

Chessmen, by Pol i Buo (1791-1857) — A28

1983, May 2 Engr. *Perf. 13 Vert.*
Booklet Stamps

93 250o King 1.40 1.40
94 250o Queen 1.40 1.40
a. Bklt. pane of 6, 3 each #93-94 15.00
b. A28 Pair, #93-94 2.80 2.80

Europa 1983 — A29

Nobel Prizewinners in Medicine: 250o, Niels R. Finsen (1860-1903), ultraviolet radiation pioneer. 400o, Alexander Fleming (1881-1955), discoverer of penicillin.

1983, June 6 Engr. *Perf. 12x11½*

95 A29 250o dark blue .60 .60
96 A29 400o red brown 1.00 1.00

A30

1983, Sept. 19 Litho. *Perf. 12½x13*

97 A30 250o Tusk .75 .75
98 A30 280o Haddock 1.00 1.00
99 A30 500o Halibut 1.25 1.25
100 A30 900o Catfish 2.40 2.40
Nos. 97-100 (4) 5.40 5.40

Souvenir Sheet

Traditional Costumes — A31

Various national costumes.

1983, Nov. 4 Litho. *Perf. 12*

101 A31 Sheet of 3 7.50 7.50
a.-c. 250o multicolored 2.00 2.00

Nordic House Cultural Center opening. Margin shows Scandinavian flags.

Pew Gables Type of 1980

Designs: 250o, John, shield with three crowns. 300o, St. Jacob, shield with crossed keys. 350o, Thomas, shield with crossbeam. 400o, Judas Taddeus, Toulouse cross halo.

Photo. & Engr.

1984, Jan. 30 *Perf. 14x13½*

102 A20 250o lil, pur & dk brn .60 .60
103 A20 300o red brn, dk buff & dk brn .70 .70
104 A20 350o blk, lt gray & dk brn .80 .80
105 A20 400o ol grn, pale yel & dk brn .90 .90
Nos. 102-105 (4) 3.00 3.00

Europa (1959-84) A33

1984, Apr. 2 Engr. *Perf. 13½*

106 A33 250o red .55 .55
107 A33 500o dark blue 1.25 1.25

Sverri Patursson (1871-1960), Writer — A34

Poets: 2.50k, Joannes Patursson (1866-1946). 3k, J. H. O. Djurhuus (1881-1948). 4.50k, H.A. Djurhuus (1883-1951).

1984, May 28 Engr. *Perf. 13½*

108 A34 2k olive green .45 .45
109 A34 2.50k red .55 .55
110 A34 3k dark blue .70 .70
111 A34 4.50k violet 1.00 1.00
Nos. 108-111 (4) 2.70 2.70

Faroese Smack (Fishing Boat) — A35

Perf. 12½x13, 13x12½

1984, Sept. 10 Engr.

112 A35 280o shown .65 .65
113 A35 300o Fishermen, vert. .70 .70
114 A35 12k Helmsman, vert. 2.75 2.75
Nos. 112-114 (3) 4.10 4.10

Fairytale Illustrations by Elinborg Lutzen — A36

1984, Oct. 29 Litho. *Perf. 13 Vert.*
Booklet Stamps

115 A36 140o Beauty of the Veils 3.25 3.25
116 A36 280o Veils, diff. 3.25 3.25
117 A36 280o Girl Shy Prince 3.25 3.25
118 A36 280o The Glass Sword 3.25 3.25
119 A36 280o Little Elin 3.25 3.25
120 A36 280o The Boy and the Ox 3.25 3.25
a. Booklet pane of 6, #115-120 20.00

View of Torshavn and the Forts, by Edward Dayes A37

Dayes' Landscapes, 1789: 280o, Skaeling. 550o, View Towards the North Seen from the Hills Near Torshavn in Stremoy, Faroes. 800o, The Moving Stones in Eysturoy, Faroes.

Litho. & Engr.

1985, Feb. 4 *Perf. 13*

121 A37 250o multicolored .60 .60
122 A37 280o multicolored .70 .60
123 A37 550o multicolored 1.60 1.50
124 A37 800o multicolored 2.10 2.10
Nos. 121-124 (4) 5.00 4.80

Europa 1985 — A38

Children taking music lessons.

1985, Apr. 1 Litho. *Perf. 13½x14½*

125 A38 280o multicolored 1.00 .90
126 A38 550o multicolored 2.00 1.75

Paintings, Faroese Museum of Art A39

Designs: 550o, Winter's Day in Nolsoy, 1959, by Steffan Danielsen (1922-76). 450o, Self-Portrait, 1952, by Ruth Smith (1913-58), vert. 280o, The Garden, Hoyvik, 1973, by Thomas Arge (1942-78).

Litho. & Engr.

1985, June 3 *Perf. 12½*

127 A39 280o multicolored 1.00 1.00
128 A39 450o multicolored 1.50 1.50
129 A39 550o multicolored 2.00 1.75
Nos. 127-129 (3) 4.50 4.25

Lighthouses — A40

1985, Sept. 23 Litho. *Perf. 13½x14*

130 A40 270o Nolsoy, 1893 1.00 .90
131 A40 320o Thorshavn, 1909 1.40 1.25
132 A40 350o Mykines, 1909 1.50 1.40
133 A40 470o Map of locations 1.90 1.75
Nos. 130-133 (4) 5.80 5.30

Passenger Aviation in the Faroes, 22nd Anniv. A41

Perf. 13½ Horiz.

1985, Oct. 28 Photo.
Booklet Stamps

134 A41 300o Douglas DC-3 2.00 2.00
135 A41 300o Fokker Friendship 2.00 2.00
136 A41 300o Boeing 737 2.00 2.00
137 A41 300o Interisland LM-IKB 2.00 2.00
138 A41 300o Helicopter Snipan 2.00 2.00
a. Booklet pane of 5, #134-138 10.50 10.50

Skrimsla, Ancient Folk Ballad — A42

1986, Feb. 3 Litho. *Perf. 12½x13*

139 A42 300o Peasant in woods .90 .90
140 A42 420o Meets Giant 1.25 1.25
141 A42 550o Giant loses game 1.60 1.60
142 A42 650o Giant grants Peasant's wish 1.75 1.60
Nos. 139-142 (4) 5.50 5.35

Europa 1986 — A43

Amnesty Intl., 25th Anniv. — A44

1986, Apr. 7 Litho. *Perf. 13½*

143 A43 3k shown 1.50 1.25
144 A43 5.50k Sea pollution 2.50 2.25

1986, June 2 *Perf. 14x13½*

Winning design competition artwork.

145 A44 3k Olivur vid Neyst .85 .75
146 A44 4.70k Eli Smith 1.40 1.25
147 A44 5.50k Ranna Kunoy 1.75 1.60
Nos. 145-147 (3) 4.00 3.60

Nos. 145-146 horiz.

Souvenir Sheet

HAFNIA '87, Copenhagen — A45

Design: East Bay of Torshavn, watercolor, 1782, by Christian Rosenmeyer (1728-1802).

1986, Aug. 29 Litho. *Perf. 13x13½*

148 A45 Sheet of 3 9.00 9.00
a. 3k multicolored 3.00 3.00
b. 4.70k multicolored 3.00 3.00
c. 6.50k multicolored 3.00 3.00

Sold for 20k.

Old Stone Bridges A46

2.70k, Glyvrar on Eysturoy. 3k, Leypanagjogv on Vagar, vert. 13k, Skaelinger on Streymoy.

Perf. 13½x14½, 14½x13½

1986, Oct. 13 Engr.

149 A46 2.70k dp brown vio 1.75 1.60
150 A46 3k bluish blk 1.50 1.40
151 A46 13k gray green 3.25 3.00
Nos. 149-151 (3) 6.50 6.00

Farmhouses — A47

Traditional architecture: 300o, Depil on Borooy, 1814. 420o, Depil, diff. 470o, Frammi vio Gjonna on Streymoy, c. 1814. 650o, Frammi, diff.

1987, Feb. 9 Engr. *Perf. 13x14½*

152 A47 300o pale blue & blue .90 .90
153 A47 420o buff & brown 1.40 1.40
154 A47 470o pale grn & dp grn 1.75 1.60
155 A47 650o pale gray & black 2.25 2.25
Nos. 152-155 (4) 6.30 6.15

Europa 1987 — A48

Nordic House.

1987, Apr. 6 *Perf. 13x14*

156 A48 300o Exterior 1.00 1.00
157 A48 550o Interior 2.25 2.00

Fishing Trawlers A49

1987, June 1 Litho. *Perf. 14x13½*

158 A49 3k Joannes Patursson .90 .80
159 A49 5.50k Magnus Heinason 1.90 1.75
160 A49 8k Sjurdarberg 3.50 3.25
Nos. 158-160 (3) 6.30 5.80

Hestur (Horse) Island A50

Litho. & Engr.

1987, Sept. 7 *Perf. 13*

161 A50 270o Map .80 .75
162 A50 300o Seaport .60 .50
163 A50 420o Bird cliff 1.40 1.25
164 A50 470o Pasture, sheep 1.60 1.50
165 A50 550o Seashore 1.60 1.50
Nos. 161-165 (5) 6.00 5.50

Nos. 161, 163 and 165 vert.

Collages by Zacharias Heinesen A51

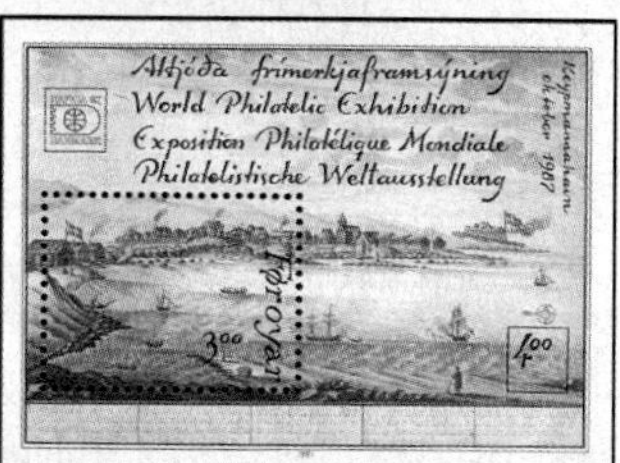
West Bay of Torshavn, Watercolor by Rosenmeyer — A52

1987, Oct. 16 Litho. *Perf. 13½x14*

166 A51 4.70k Eystaravag 1.75 1.60
167 A51 6.50k Vestaravag 2.25 2.00

Souvenir Sheet

Perf. 13½x13

168 A52 3k multicolored 3.00 3.00

HAFNIA '87. Sold for 4k.

Flowers — A53

Europa — A54

1988, Feb. 8 Litho. *Perf. 11½*

Granite Paper

169 A53 2.70k Bellis perennis 1.10 1.10
170 A53 3k Dactylorchis maculata .60 .60
171 A53 4.70k Potentilla erecta 1.60 1.60
172 A53 9k Pinguicula vulgaris 2.25 2.25
Nos. 169-172 (4) 5.55 5.55

1988, Apr. 11 Photo. *Perf. 11½*

Communication and transport.

173 A54 3k Satellite dish, satellite 1.00 1.00
174 A54 5.50k Fork lift, crane, ship 1.60 1.60

A55

A56

Writers: 270o, Jorgen-Frantz Jacobsen (1900-38). 300o, Christian Matras (b. 1900). 470o, William Heinesen (b. 1900). 650o, Hedin Bru (1901-87).

1988, June 6 Engr. *Perf. 13½*

175 A55 270o myrtle green 1.25 1.25
176 A55 300o rose lake 1.10 1.10
177 A55 470o dark blue 1.75 1.75
178 A55 650o brown black 1.90 1.90
Nos. 175-178 (4) 6.00 6.00

1988, Sept. 5 Photo. *Perf. 12*

Text, illustrations and cameo portraits of organizers: 3k, Announcement and Djoni Geil, Enok Baerentsen and H.H. Jacobsen. 3.20k, Meeting, Rasmus Effersoe, C.L. Johannesen and Samal Krakusteini. 12k, Oystercatcher and lyrics of *Now the Hour Has Come,* by poet Sverri Patursson (1871-1960), Just A. Husum, Joannes Patursson and Jens Olsen.

Granite Paper

179 A56 3k multicolored 1.00 1.00
180 A56 3.20k multicolored 1.00 1.00
181 A56 12k multicolored 4.00 4.00
Nos. 179-181 (3) 6.00 6.00

1888 Christmas meeting to preserve cultural traditions and the natl. language, cent.

Kirkjubour Cathedral Ruins A57

270o, Exterior. 300o, Arch. 470o, Crucifixion, bas-relief. 550o, Interior.

1988, Oct. 17 Engr. *Perf. 13*

182 A57 270o dark green 1.25 1.25
183 A57 300o dark bl, vert. .95 .95
184 A57 470o dark brn, vert. 1.40 1.40
185 A57 550o dark violet 1.50 1.50
Nos. 182-185 (4) 5.10 5.10

Havnar Church, Torshavn, 200th Anniv. A58

Designs: 350o, Church exterior. 500o, Crypt, vert. 15k, Bell, vert.

1989, Feb. 6 Engr. *Perf. 13*

186 A58 350o dark green 1.00 1.00
187 A58 500o dark brown 1.75 1.75
188 A58 15k deep blue 3.25 3.25
Nos. 186-188 (3) 6.00 6.00

Folk Costumes — A59

Photo. & Engr.

1989, Apr. 10 *Perf. 13½*

189 A59 350o Man 1.10 1.10
190 A59 600o Woman 2.00 2.00

Europa 1989 — A60

Wooden children's toys.

1989, Apr. 10 Photo. *Perf. 12x11½*

Granite Paper

191 A60 3.50k Boat 1.10 1.10
192 A60 6k Horse 2.00 2.00

Island Games, July 5-13 — A61

1989, June 5 Photo. *Perf. 12½*

Granite Paper

193 A61 200o Rowing .60 .60
194 A61 350o Handball 1.25 1.25
195 A61 600o Soccer 1.75 1.75
196 A61 700o Swimming 2.00 2.00
Nos. 193-196 (4) 5.60 5.60

A62

A63

Bird cliffs of Suduroy.

1989, Oct. 2 Engr. *Perf. 14x13½*

197 A62 320o Tvoran 1.00 1.00
198 A62 350o Skuvanes 1.25 1.25
199 A62 500o Beinisvord 1.60 1.60
200 A62 600o Asmundarstakkur 1.75 1.75
Nos. 197-200 (4) 5.60 5.60

1990, Feb. 5 Litho. *Perf. 14x13½*

Modern fish factory (filleting station).

201 A63 3.50k Unloading fish .75 .75
202 A63 3.70k Cleaning and sorting 1.10 1.10
203 A63 5k Filleting 1.25 1.25
204 A63 7k Packaged frozen fish 1.50 1.50
Nos. 201-204 (4) 4.60 4.60

Europa 1990 — A64

Post offices.

1990, Apr. 9 Litho. *Perf. 13½x14*

205 A64 3.50k Gjogv 1.10 1.10
206 A64 6k Klaksvik 1.90 1.90

Souvenir Sheet

Recognition of the Merkid, Flag of the Faroes, by the British, 50th Anniv. — A65

Designs: a, Flag. b, Fishing trawler *Nyggjaberg*, disappeared, 1942. c, Sloop *Saana,* sunk by the Germans, 1942.

1990, Apr. 9 Photo. *Perf. 12*

Granite Paper

207 A65 Sheet of 3 4.50 4.50
a.-c. 3.50k any single 1.50 1.50

Whales A66

1990, June 6 Photo. *Perf. 11½*

Granite Paper

208 A66 320o *Mesoplodon bidens* 1.10 1.10
209 A66 350o *Balaena mysticetus* 1.50 1.50
210 A66 600o *Eubalaena glacialis* 1.90 1.90
211 A66 700o *Hyperoodon ampullatus* 2.40 2.40
Nos. 208-211 (4) 6.90 6.90

Nolsoy Island by Steffan Danielsen A67

1990, Oct. 8 Photo. *Perf. 11½*

Granite Paper

212 A67 50o shown .20 .20
213 A67 350o Coastline .95 .95
214 A67 500o Town 1.25 1.25
215 A67 1000o Coastline, cliffs 2.60 2.60
Nos. 212-215 (4) 5.00 5.00

Flora and Fauna — A68

Europa — A69

1991, Feb. 4 Litho. *Perf. 13*

216 A68 3.70k Plantago lanceolata .95 .95
217 A68 4k Rumex longifolius .95 .95
218 A68 4.50k Amara aulica 1.10 1.10
219 A68 6.50k Lumbricus terrestris 1.75 1.75
Nos. 216-219 (4) 4.75 4.75

1991, Apr. 4 Litho. *Perf. 13*

Designs: 3.70k, Weather satellite. 6.50k, Celestial navigation.

220 A69 3.70k multicolored 1.25 1.25
221 A69 6.50k multicolored 2.25 2.25

Town of Torshavn, 125th Anniv. — A70

1991, Apr. 4 *Perf. 14x13½*

222 A70 3.70k Town Hall .90 .90
223 A70 3.70k View of town 1.10 1.10

Birds — A71

1991, June 3 Litho. *Perf. 13½*

224 A71 3.70k Rissa tridactyla 1.00 1.00
225 A71 3.70k Sterna paradisaea 1.00 1.00
a. Bklt. pane, 3 each #224-225 7.50

Village of Saksun A72

1991, June 3

226 A72 370o shown 1.00 1.00
227 A72 650o Cliffs of Vestmanna 1.75 1.75

Samal Joensen-Mikines (1906-1979), Painter — A73

1991, Oct. 7 Litho. *Perf. 13½*

228 A73 340o Funeral Procession .85 .85
229 A73 370o The Farewell .95 .95
230 A73 550o Handanagarthur 1.40 1.40
231 A73 1300o Winter morning 3.25 3.25
Nos. 228-231 (4) 6.45 6.45

Mail Boats A74

1992, Feb. 10 Litho. *Perf. 13½x14*

232 A74 200o Ruth .55 .55
233 A74 370o Ritan .95 .95
234 A74 550o Sigmundur 1.40 1.40
235 A74 800o Masin 2.10 2.10
Nos. 232-235 (4) 5.00 5.00

Europa A75

Designs: 3.70k, Map of North Atlantic, Viking ship. 6.50k, Map of Central Atlantic region, one of Columbus' ships.

1992, Apr. 6 Litho. *Perf. 13½x14*

236 A75 3.70k multicolored .90 .90
237 A75 6.50k multicolored 1.60 1.60

Souvenir Sheet

238 A75 Sheet of 2, #236-237 5.00 4.00

First landing in the Americas by Leif Erikson (#236). Discovery of America by Christopher Columbus, 500th anniv. (#237).

Seals A76

1992, June 9 Litho. *Perf. 14x13½*

239 A76 3.70k Halichoerus grypus 1.25 1.25
240 A76 3.70k Phoca vitulina 1.25 1.25
a. Bklt. pane, 3 #239, 3 #240 *16.00*

Minerals — A77

1992, June 9 Photo. *Perf. 12*

Granite Paper

241 A77 370o Stilbite 1.25 1.25
242 A77 650o Mesolite 1.75 1.75

Traditional Houses A78

1992, Oct. 5 Litho. *Perf. 13½*

243 A78 3.40k Hja Glyvra Hanusi 1.00 1.00
244 A78 3.70k I Nordragotu 1.50 1.50
245 A78 6.50k Blasastova 1.75 1.75
246 A78 8k Jakupsstova 2.00 2.00
Nos. 243-246 (4) 6.25 6.25

Nordic House Entertainers — A79

1993, Feb. 8 Litho. *Perf. 13½*

247 A79 400o Dancers 1.10 1.10
248 A79 400o Pianist 1.10 1.10
249 A79 400o Trio 1.10 1.10
a. Souv. sheet, #247-249, perf 12½ 3.50 3.50
Nos. 247-249 (3) 3.30 3.30

Village of Gjogv A80

1993, Apr. 5

250 A80 4k View toward sea 1.10 1.10
251 A80 4k Ravine, village 1.10 1.10
a. Booklet pane, 3 each #250-251 7.50

Europa — A81

Horses — A82

Sculptures by Hans Pauli Olsen: 4k, Movement. 7k, Reflection.

1993, Apr. 5

252 A81 4k multicolored 1.00 1.00
253 A81 7k multicolored 2.00 2.00

Perf. 13½x13, 13x13½

1993, June 7 Engr.

254 A82 400o shown 1.10 1.10
255 A82 20k Mare, foal, horiz. 5.25 5.25

Butterflies A83

1993, Oct. 4 Litho. *Perf. 14½*

256 A83 350o Apamea zeta 1.10 1.10
257 A83 400o Hepialus humuli 1.10 1.10
258 A83 700o Vanessa atalanta 1.75 1.75
259 A83 900o Perizoma albulata 2.25 2.25
Nos. 256-259 (4) 6.20 6.20

Fish — A84

1994, Feb. 7 Litho. *Perf. 14½*

260 A84 10o Gasterosteus aculeatus .20 .20
261 A84 4k Neocyttus helgae 1.25 1.25
262 A84 7k Salmo trutta fario 1.60 1.60
263 A84 10k Hoplostethus atlanticus 2.50 2.50
Nos. 260-263 (4) 5.55 5.55

Voyages of St. Brendan (484-577) A85

Europa: 4k, St. Brendan on island with sheep, Irish monks in boat. 7k, St. Brendan, monks sailing past volcano.

1994, Apr. 18 Litho. *Perf. 14½x14*

264 A85 4k multicolored 1.00 1.00
265 A85 7k multicolored 2.00 1.75
a. Miniature sheet of 2, #264-265 3.00 3.00

Nos. 264-265 have designers name below the design. Stamps in No. 265a do not.

See Iceland Nos. 780-781; Ireland Nos. 923-924.

Sheepdogs — A86

School of Navigation A87

Design: No. 267, Dog watching over sheep.

1994, June 6 Litho. *Perf. 13½*

266 A86 4k multicolored 1.10 1.10

Size: 39x25mm

267 A86 4k multicolored 1.10 1.10
a. Booklet pane, 3 each #266-267 6.50
Complete booklet, #267a 6.50

1994, June 6

Designs: 3.50k, Man using sextant, schooner. 7k, Ship, man at computer.

268 A87 3.50k multicolored 1.00 1.00
269 A87 7k multicolored 2.00 2.00

Brusajokil's Lay — A88

Scenes, verses of the ballad: 1k, Ship at sea. 4k, Asbjorn entering Brasajokil's cave. 6k, Ormar with cat, trolls. 7k, Ormar pulling Brusajokil's beard.

1994, Sept. 19 Litho. *Perf. 14*

270 A88 1k multicolored .20 .20
271 A88 4k multicolored 1.20 1.20
272 A88 6k multicolored 1.60 1.60
273 A88 7k multicolored 2.00 2.00
Nos. 270-273 (4) 5.00 5.00

Twelve Days of Christmas A89

#274, Goats, men, deer, hides. #275, Ducks, cattle, sheep, horses, banners, barrels.

1994, Oct. 31 Litho. *Perf. 14x13*

274 A89 4k multicolored 1.10 1.10
275 A89 4k multicolored 1.10 1.10
a. Bklt. pane, 3 each #274-275 6.50
Complete booklet, #275a 6.50

Leafhoppers — A90

Designs: 50o, Ulopa reticulata. 4k, Streptanus sordidus. 5k, Anoscopus flavostriatus. 13k, Macrosteles alpinus.

1995, Feb. 6 Litho. *Perf. 14*

276 A90 50o multicolored .20 .20
277 A90 4k multicolored 1.25 1.25
278 A90 5k multicolored 1.25 1.25
279 A90 13k multicolored 3.75 3.75
Nos. 276-279 (4) 6.45 6.45

Tourism A91

1995, Apr. 10 Litho. *Perf. 13½x14*

280 A91 4k Village of Famjin 1.25 1.25
281 A91 4k Vatnsdalur valley 1.25 1.25

Peace & Freedom A92

Europa: 4k, Island couple, "Vidar, vali og baldur." 7k, Couple looking toward sun, "Liv og livtrasir."

1995, Apr. 10 *Perf. 13x14*

282 A92 4k multicolored 1.25 1.25
283 A92 7k multicolored 2.10 2.10

Nordic Art — A93

Designs: 2k, Museum of Art, Torshavn. 4k, Woman, by Frimod Joensen, vert. 5.50k, Self-portrait, by Joensen, vert.

Perf. 13½x14, 14x13½

1995, June 12 Litho.

284 A93 2k multicolored .75 .75
285 A93 4k multicolored 1.50 1.50
286 A93 5.50k multicolored 2.00 2.00
Nos. 284-286 (3) 4.25 4.25

Corvus Corax A94

1995, June 12 ***Perf. 13½x14***

287 A94 4k Black raven 1.50 1.50
288 A94 4k White-speckled raven 1.50 1.50
a. Booklet pane, 5 each #287-288 15.00
Complete booklet, #288a 15.00

Saint Olaf (955?-1030), Patron Saint of Faroe Islands — A95

Litho. & Engr.

1995, Sept. 12 ***Perf. 13½x13***

289 A95 4k multicolored 1.50 1.50

See Aland Islands No. 119.

Early Folk Life — A95a

4k, Dairy maids carrying buckets. 6k, Peasants fleecing sheep. 15k, Schooners, saltfish being brought ashore, vert.

1995, Sept. 12 **Engr.** ***Perf. 12½***

290 A95a 4k dark green 1.50 1.50
291 A95a 6k dark brn, vert. 2.25 2.25
292 A95a 15k dark blue 5.50 5.50
Nos. 290-292 (3) 9.25 9.25

Church of Mary Catholic Church — A96

Designs: No. 293, Stained glass window. No. 294, Exterior view of church.

1995, Nov. 9 **Litho.** ***Perf. 13½***

293 A96 4k multicolored 1.50 1.50
294 A96 4k multicolored 1.50 1.50
a. Booklet pane, 5 ea #293-294 15.00
Complete booklet, #294a 15.00

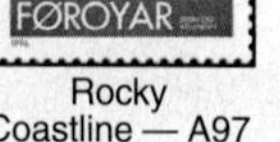

Rocky Coastline — A97 Seaweed — A98

1996, Jan. 1 **Litho.** ***Perf. 14***

295 A97 4.50k multicolored 1.50 1.50

1996, Feb. 12 ***Perf. 15***

4k, Ptilota plumosa. 5.50k, Fucus spiralis. 6k, Ascophyllum nodosum. 9k, Laminaria hyperborea.

296 A98 4k multicolored 1.40 1.40
297 A98 5.50k multicolored 2.00 2.00
298 A98 6k multicolored 2.00 2.00
299 A98 9k multicolored 3.25 3.25
Nos. 296-299 (4) 8.65 8.65

Birds — A99

A100

1996, Apr. 15 **Litho.** ***Perf. 14x15***

300 A99 4.50k Laxia curvirostra 1.50 1.50
301 A99 4.50k Bombycilla garrulus 1.50 1.50
a. Booklet pane, 5 each #300-301 16.00
Complete booklet, #301a 16.00

See Nos. 313-314.

1996, Apr. 15 ***Perf. 15x14½, 14½x15***

Europa (Wives of Faroese Seamen): 4.50k, Woman standing beside sea coast. 7.50k, Portrait of a woman, vert.

302 A100 4.50k multicolored 1.50 1.50
303 A100 7.50k multicolored 2.60 2.60

A101

Nordatlantex '96 (Children's drawings): a, Boy playing with hoop, stick, by Bugvi. b, Two girls on steet, road sign, by Gudrid. c, Girl on bicycle, car on street, by Herborg.

1996, June 7 **Litho.** ***Perf. 14½***
Souvenir Sheet of 3

304 A101 4.50k #a.-c. 4.50 4.50

A102

Litho. & Engr.

1996, June 7 ***Perf. 13***

Sea bed off the Faroes.

305 A102 10k violet & multi 3.50 3.50
306 A102 16k green & multi 5.50 5.50

See Nos. 319-320, 343, 377-378.

James Kamban (b. 1913), Sculptor, Graphic Artist A103

Works of art: 4.50k, Flock of Sheep. 6.50k, Fisherman on the Way Home. 7.50k, View from Tórshavn's Old Quarter.

1996, Sept. 16 **Litho.** ***Perf. 14***

307 A103 4.50k multicolored 1.50 1.50
308 A103 6.50k multicolored 2.25 2.25
309 A103 7.50k multicolored 2.50 2.50
Nos. 307-309 (3) 6.25 6.25

A104

Christianschurch, Klaksvík — A105

1996, Nov. 4 **Litho.** ***Perf. 14x15***

310 A104 4.50k Exterior 1.50 1.50
311 A105 4.50k Interior, altar fresco 1.50 1.50
a. Booklet pane, 6 #310, 4 #311 15.00
Complete booklet, #311a 15.00

Christmas.

Souvenir Sheet

Reign of Queen Margaret II, 25th Anniv. — A106

Illustration reduced.

1997, Jan. 14 **Litho.** ***Perf. 14½***

312 A106 4.50k multicolored 1.50 1.50

Bird Type of 1996

1997, Feb. 27 **Litho.** ***Perf. 14x15***

313 A99 4.50k Pyrrhula pyrrhula 1.50 1.50
314 A99 4.50k Carduelis flammea 1.50 1.50
a. Booklet pane, 5 each #313-314 15.00 —
Complete booklet, #314a 15.00

Mushrooms — A107

Designs: 4.50k, Hygrocybe helobia. 6k, Hygrocybe chlorophana. 6.50k, Hygrocybe virginea. 7.50k, Hygrocybe psittacina.

1997, Feb. 17 ***Perf. 14½***

315 A107 4.50k multicolored 1.50 1.50
316 A107 6k multicolored 2.00 2.00
317 A107 6.50k multicolored 2.25 2.25
318 A107 7.50k multicolored 2.50 2.50
Nos. 315-318 (4) 8.25 8.25

Map Type of 1996
Litho. & Engr.

1997, May 20 ***Perf. 13***

319 A102 11k red & multi 3.75 3.75
320 A102 18k claret & multi 6.00 6.00

Europa — A108 Kalmar Union, 600th Anniv. — A109

Legends illustrated by William Heinesen: 4.50k, The Temptations of Saint Anthony. 7.50k, The Merman sitting at bottom of sea eating fish bait.

1997, May 20 **Litho.** ***Perf. 14½***

321 A108 4.50k multicolored 1.50 1.50
322 A108 7.50k multicolored 2.50 2.50

1997, May 20 **Engr.** ***Perf. 12½***

323 A109 4.50k deep blue violet 1.50 1.50

A110

A111

Barbara, Film Shot in Faroe Islands (Scenes from film): 4.50k, Danish theologian Poul Aggerso arriving at Faroe Islands. 6.50k, Barbara and Poul. 7.50k, Barbara with men on boat. 9k, Barbara in row boat, sailing ship.

1997, Sept. 15 **Litho.** ***Perf. 14***

324 A110 4.50k multicolored 1.50 1.50
325 A110 6.50k multicolored 2.25 2.25
326 A110 7.50k multicolored 2.50 2.50
327 A110 9k multicolored 3.00 3.00
Nos. 324-327 (4) 9.25 9.25

1997, Sept. 15

Hvalvik church.

328 A111 4.50k Interior 1.30 1.30
329 A111 4.50k Exterior 1.30 1.30
a. Booklet pane, 5 each #328-329 13.00 —
Complete booklet, #329a 13.00

Birds — A112 A113

1998, Feb. 23 **Litho.** ***Perf. 14x14½***

330 A112 4.50k Sturnus vulgaris 1.50 1.50
331 A112 4.50k Turdus merula 1.50 1.50
a. Bklt. pane, 5 each #330-331 15.00
Complete booklet, #331a 15.00

1998, Feb. 23 ***Perf. 14***

Scenes from the Sigurd poem "Brynhild's Ballad": 4.50k, King Buole, daughter Brynhild. 6.50k, Sigurd riding through wall of fire on horseback. 7.50k, Sigurd, Brynhild together. 10k, Guthrun alone leading horse.

332 A113 4.50k multicolored 1.50 1.50
333 A113 6.50k multicolored 2.25 2.25
334 A113 7.50k multicolored 2.50 2.50
335 A113 10k multicolored 3.50 3.50
Nos. 332-335 (4) 9.75 9.75

Europa — A114 A115

1998, May 18 **Litho.** ***Perf. 14***

336 A114 4.50k Parade 1.50 1.50
337 A114 7.50k Processional 2.50 2.50

Olavsoka, Natl. Festival of Faroe Islands.

1998, May 18 ***Perf. 14½***

338 A115 7.50k multicolored 2.50 2.50

UN Declaration of Human Rights, 50th anniv.

Intl. Year of the Ocean A116

Toothed whales: 4k, Lagenorhynchus acutus. 4.50k, Orcinus orca. 7k, Tursiops truncatus. 9k, Delphinapterus leucas.

1998, May 18 *Perf. 14½x14*
339 A116 4k multicolored 1.40 1.40
340 A116 4.50k multicolored 1.50 1.50
341 A116 7k multicolored 2.40 2.40
342 A116 9k multicolored 3.00 3.00
Nos. 339-342 (4) 8.30 8.30

Map Type of 1996
Litho. & Engr.

1998, Sept. 14 *Perf. 13*
343 A102 14k multicolored 4.50 4.50

Frederickschurch A117

1998, Sept. 14 Litho. *Perf. 14*
344 A117 4.50k Exterior, coast-line 1.50 1.50
345 A117 4.50k Interior 1.50 1.50
a. Bklt. pane, 5 each #344-345 15.00
Complete booklet, #345a 15.00

A118 A119

Paintings by Hans Hansen (1920-70): 4.50k, Fell-field, 1966. 5.50k, Village Interior, 1965. 6.50k, Portrait of Farmer Ólavur í Utistovu from Mikladalur, 1968. 8k, Self-portrait, 1968.

Perf. 13½x14, 14x13½

1998, Sept. 14
346 A118 4.50k multi 1.50 1.50
347 A118 5.50k multi 1.90 1.90
348 A118 6.50k multi, vert. 2.25 2.25
349 A118 8k multi, vert. 2.75 2.75
Nos. 346-349 (4) 8.40 8.40

1999, Feb. 22 Litho. *Perf. 13½*

Birds.

350 A119 4.50k Passer domesticus 1.50 1.50
351 A119 4.50k Troglodytes troglodytes 1.50 1.50
a. Bklt. pane, 5 each #350-351 15.00
Complete booklet, #351a 15.00

Ships Named "Smyril" A120

1999, Feb. 22 *Perf. 14½x14*
352 A120 4.50k 1895 1.50 1.50
353 A120 5k 1932 1.75 1.75
354 A120 8k 1967 2.75 2.75
355 A120 13k 1975 4.50 4.50
Nos. 352-355 (4) 10.50 10.50

Northern Islands A121

1999, May 25 Litho. *Perf. 13½*
356 A121 50o Kalsoy .20 .20
357 A121 100o Vithoy .35 .35
358 A121 400o Svinoy 1.40 1.40
359 A121 450o Fugloy 1.50 1.50
360 A121 600o Kunoy 2.00 2.00
361 A121 800o Borthoy 2.75 2.75
Nos. 356-361 (6) 8.20 8.20

See Nos. 383-386.

Waterfalls — A122

Europa: 6k, Svartifossur. 8k, Foldarafossur.

1999, May 25 *Perf. 14x14½*
362 A122 6k multicolored 2.00 2.00
363 A122 8k multicolored 2.75 2.75

Abstract Paintings of Ingálvur av Reyni — A123

1999, Sept. 27 Litho. *Perf. 12½*
364 A123 4.50k Bygd 1.50 1.50
365 A123 6k Húsavik 2.00 2.00
366 A123 8k Reytt regn 2.75 2.75
367 A123 20k Genta 6.75 6.75
Nos. 364-367 (4) 13.00 13.00

Bible Stories — A124

1999, Sept. 27 *Perf. 14½x14*
368 A124 450o John 1:1-5 1.50 1.50
a. Booklet pane of 6 9.00
Complete booklet, #368a 9.00
369 A124 600o Luke 1:26-28 2.00 2.00
a. Booklet pane of 6 12.00
Complete booklet, #369a 12.00

See Nos. 387-388.

A125 A126

Christianity in the Faroes, 1000th Anniv.: 4.50k, Man on rocks in ocean. 5.50k, Monk with cross, man with sword. 8k, People, flags. 16k, Cross in sky.

Perf. 13½x13¼

2000, Feb. 21 Litho.
370 A125 4.50k multi 1.50 1.50
371 A125 5.50k multi 1.90 1.90
372 A125 8k multi 2.75 2.75
373 A125 16k multi 5.50 5.50
Nos. 370-373 (4) 11.65 11.65

2000, Feb. 21

School and: No. 374, Sanna av Skarthi, Anna Suffia Rasmussen, wives of founders. No. 375, Rasmus Rasmussen (1871-1962), Símun av Skarthi (1872-1942), school founders.

374 A126 4.50k multi 1.50 1.50
375 A126 4.50k multi 1.50 1.50
a. Bklt. pane, 4 ea #374-375 12.00
Complete booklet, #375a 12.00

Faroese Folk High School, cent.

Europa, 2000
Common Design Type

2000, May 9 Litho. *Perf. 13¼x13*
376 CD17 8k multi 2.75 2.75

Map Type of 1996
Litho. & Engr.

2000, May 22 *Perf. 13¼x13*
377 A102 15k multi 5.00 5.00
378 A102 22k multi 7.50 7.50

Stampin' The Future Children's Stamp Design Contest Winners A127

Art by: 4k, Katrin Mortensen. 4.50k, Sigga Andreassen. 6k, Steingrímur Joensen. 8k, Dion Dam Frandsen.

2000, May 22 Litho. *Perf. 13x13¼*
379 A127 4k multi 1.40 1.40
380 A127 4.50k multi 1.50 1.50
381 A127 6k multi 2.00 2.00
382 A127 8k multi 2.75 2.75
Nos. 379-382 (4) 7.65 7.65

Island Type of 1999

2000, Sept. 18 Litho. *Perf. 13½*
383 A121 200o Skúvoy .70 .70
384 A121 650o Hestoy 2.25 2.25
385 A121 750o Koltur 2.50 2.50
386 A121 1000o Nólsoy 3.50 3.50
Nos. 383-386 (4) 8.95 8.95

Bible Story Type of 1999

2000, Sept. 18 Litho. *Perf. 13x13¼*
387 A124 4.50k Micah 5:1 1.50 1.50
a. Booklet pane of 6 9.00
Booklet, #387a 9.00
388 A124 6k John 1:14 2.00 2.00
a. Booklet pane of 6 12.00
Booklet, #388a 12.00

Pew Gables Type of 1980

Kirkjubour pew gables: 430o, St. Andrew with cross. 650o, St. Bartholomew. 800o, Unknown apostle. 18k, Unknown apostle, diff.

Photo. & Engr.

2001, Feb. 12 *Perf. 12¾x12½*
389 A20 450o multi 1.50 1.50
390 A20 650o multi 2.25 2.25
391 A20 800o multi 2.75 2.75
392 A20 18k multi 6.00 6.00
Nos. 389-392 (4) 12.50 12.50

Faroese Red Cross, 75th Anniv. A128

Designs: 4.50k, Old person. 6k, Relief worker.

2001, Feb. 12 Litho. *Perf. 14½x14*
393 A128 4.50k multi 1.50 1.50
a. Booklet pane of 6 9.00
Booklet, #393a 9.00
394 A128 6k multi 2.00 2.00
a. Booklet pane of 6 12.00
Booklet, #394a 12.00

Souvenir Sheet

Faroe Islands Postal Service, 25th Anniv. — A129

No. 395: a, Boat for interisland mail transport, 19th cent. b, Tórshavn post office, 1906. c, Simon Pauli Poulsen (Morkabóndin), mail carrier.

Photo. & Engr.

2001, Apr. 1 *Perf. 13x13¼*
395 A129 4.50k Sheet of 3, #a-c 4.50 4.50

Nordic Myths and Legends About Light and Darkness — A130

No. 396: a, The Death of Hogni. b, The Tree of the Year. c, The Harp. d, Gram and Grane. e, The Ballad of Nornagest. f, Gudrun's Evil Magic.

Litho. with Foil Application

2001, Apr. 1 *Perf. 13½x13¼*
396 A130 6k Sheet of 6, #a-f 12.00 12.00

Hafnia 2001 Philatelic Exhibition, Copenhagen.

Paintings by Zacharias Heinesen A131

Designs: 4k, The Artist's Mother, 1992. 4.50k, Úti á Reyni, 1974. 10k, Ur Vágunum, 2000. 15k, Sunrise, 1975.

2001, June 11 Litho. *Perf. 13¼x13*
397 A131 4k multi 1.40 1.40
398 A131 4.50k multi 1.50 1.50
399 A131 10k multi 3.50 3.50
400 A131 15k multi 5.00 5.00
Nos. 397-400 (4) 11.40 11.40

Europa A132

Hydroelectric power stations: 6k, Fossáverkith. 8k, Eithisverkith.

2001, June 11 *Perf. 13x13½*

401 A132 6k multi 2.00 2.00
402 A132 8k multi 2.75 2.75

Whales — A133

Designs: 4.50k, Physeter macrocephalus. 6.50k, Balaenoptera physalus. 9k, Balaenoptera musculus. 20k, Balaenoptera borealis.

Perf. 13¾x13¼

2001, Sept. 17 **Litho.**

403 A133 4.50k multi 1.50 1.50
404 A133 6.50k multi 2.25 2.25
405 A133 9k multi 3.00 3.00
406 A133 20k multi 6.75 6.75
Nos. 403-406 (4) 13.50 13.50

Bible Stories Type of 1999

2001, Sept. 17 *Perf. 13*

407 A124 5k Luke 2:34-35 1.75 1.75
408 A124 6.50k Matthew 2:18 2.25 2.25

Mollusks — A134

Designs: 5k, Sepiola atlantica. 7k, Modiolus modiolus. 7.50k, Polycera faeroensis. 18k, Buccinum undatum.

2002, Feb. 11 **Litho.** *Perf. 13*

409 A134 5k multi 1.75 1.75
410 A134 7k multi 2.40 2.40
411 A134 7.50k multi 2.50 2.50
412 A134 18k multi 6.00 6.00
Nos. 409-412 (4) 12.65 12.65

Portions of the designs were applied by a thermographic process producing a shiny, raised effect.

Souvenir Sheet

Viking Voyages — A135

No. 413: a, Navigation tool. b, Viking sailor on boat. c, Viking boat.

Litho. & Engr.

2002, Feb. 11 *Perf. 13*

413 A135 6.50k Sheet of 3, #a-c 6.75 6.75

Europa A136

Designs: 6.50k, Clowns. 8k, Various circus performers.

2002, Apr. 8 **Litho.** *Perf. 13¼x13½*

414 A136 6.50k multi 2.25 2.25
415 A136 8k multi 2.75 2.75

Art by Tróndur Patursson A137

Designs: 5k, Bládypi. 6.50k, Kosmiska Rúmith.

2002, Apr. 8

416 A137 5k multi 1.75 1.75
417 A137 6.50k multi 2.25 2.25
a. Booklet pane of 8, 4 each #416-417 16.00 —
Booklet, #417a 16.00

Eggs and Chicks — A138

Designs: 5k, Numenius phaeopus. 7.50k, Gallinago gallinago. 12k, Haematopus ostralegus. 20k, Pluvialis apricaria.

2002, June 17 *Perf. 14x14½*

418 A138 5k multi 1.75 1.75
419 A138 7.50k multi 2.50 2.50
420 A138 12k multi 4.00 4.00
421 A138 20k multi 6.75 6.75
Nos. 418-421 (4) 15.00 15.00

Souvenir Sheet

Faroese Representative Council, 150th Anniv. — A139

Designs: 5k, Royal book and seal. 6.50k, Royal book, Protocol of 1852.

2002, June 17 *Perf. 14*

422 A139 Sheet of 2, #a-b 4.00 4.00

Falco Columbarius Subaesalon — A140

Litho. & Embossed

2002, Sept. 23 *Perf. 13¼*

423 A140 30k multi 10.00 10.00

Gota Church — A141

2002, Sept. 23 **Litho.** *Perf. 12½*

424 A141 5k Exterior 1.75 1.75
425 A141 6.50k Interior 2.25 2.25
a. Booklet pane, 5 each #424-425 20.00 —
Booklet, #425a 20.00

Souvenir Sheet

Intl. Council for the Exploration of the Sea, Cent. — A142

No. 426: a, Micromesistius poutassou and island. b, Exploration ship Magnus Heinason and fish.

Litho. & Engr.

2002, Sept. 23 *Perf. 13*

426 A142 8k Sheet of 2, #a-b 5.50 5.50

See Denmark Nos. 1237-1238, Greenland Nos. 401-402.

Opening of Vagár-Streymoy Tunnel, Nov. 2002 — A143

Designs: No. 427, Wheeled tunneling machine at right. No. 428, Workers in red uniforms at left.

2003, Feb. 24 **Litho.** *Perf. 13¼x13*

427 A143 5k multi 1.50 1.50
428 A143 5k multi 1.50 1.50
a. Booklet pane, 5 each #427-428 15.00 —
Complete booklet, #428a 15.00

Voluspá, Ancient Norse Poem — A144

No. 429: a, Seeress Heid holding staff. b, Heid sees animal and man in vision. c, Nude man and woman. d, Scribe and horseman. e, Battle between group with swords and man with hammer. f, Horseman and warriors. g, Men, large sword. h, Longboat. i, Attack on man holding spear, fire. j, Two figures with staffs, winged serpent.

2003, Feb. 24 *Perf. 14*

429 A144 Sheet of 10 19.00 19.00
a.-j. 6.50k Any single 1.90 1.90

Europa — A145

Poster art for Nordic House: 6.50k, Fish Tree, by Astrid Andreasen, 1991. 8k, Ceramics by Guthrith Poulsen, 1997.

2003, Apr. 14 *Perf. 13½x13¼*

430 A145 6.50k multi 1.90 1.90
431 A145 8k multi 2.25 2.25

Children's Songs — A146

No. 432: a, Woman playing hopscotch (26x44mm). b, Boy on rocks, moon (26x44mm). c, Girl with missing teeth (26x26mm). d, Boy with toy sailboat (26x26mm). e, Oat, horse and girl (26x26mm). f, Butterfly and fly (26x26mm). g, Girl in bed, boy with stars (44x26mm). h, Cat on stairs, mouse (26x36mm). i, Man playing drums (26x26mm). j, King and queen in longboat (44x26mm).

Perf. 13¼, 13¼x13¼x13¼x14 (#432g, 432j), 13¼x14 (#432h)

2003, Apr. 14

432 A146 Sheet of 10 14.00 14.00
a.-j. 5k Any single 1.40 1.40

Small Towns A147

2003, June 10 **Litho.** *Perf. 13x13¼*

433 A147 5k Bour 1.60 1.60
434 A147 5k Gásadalur 1.60 1.60

Communities With Post Offices 100 Years Old — A148

No. 435: a, Fuglafjorthur. b, Strendur. c, Sandur. d, Eithi. e, Vestmanna. f, Vágur. g, Mithvágur. h, Hvalba.

2003, June 10 *Perf. 13¼x13*

435 A148 Sheet of 8 13.00 13.00
a.-h. 5k Any single 1.60 1.60

Theologians — A149

Designs: 5k, Jesper Rasmussen Brochmand (1585-1652). 6.50k, Thomas Kingo (1634-1703).

2003, Sept. 22 *Perf. 13x13¼*

436 A149 5k multi 1.50 1.50
437 A149 6.50k multi 2.00 2.00
a. Booklet pane, 5 each #436-437 17.50 —
Complete booklet, #437a 17.50

Souvenir Sheet

Dancing in the Inn's Smoking Room, by Emil Krause — A150

Litho. & Engr.

2003, Sept. 22 *Perf. 12¼*

438 A150 25k multi 8.00 8.00

100th Faroese stamp engraved by Czeslaw Slania.

Islands Type of 1999

2004, Jan. 26 Litho. *Perf. 13½*

439 A121 550o Stóra Dímun 1.90 1.90
440 A121 700o Lítla Dímun 2.40 2.40

Suthuroy Island — A151

No. 441: a, Sigmundargjogv, Sandvik. b, Fiskieithi, Hvalba. c, A Hamri, Frothba. d, Tjaldavíkshólmur, Oravík. e, Fossurin Stóri, Fámjin. f, Hovsfjorthur, Hov. g, I Eystrum, Porkeri. h, A Okrum. i, I Horg, Sumba. j, I Akrabergi.

2004, Jan. 26 *Perf. 13x13¼*

441 A151 5k Sheet of 10, #a-j 17.00 17.00

1854 Cruise of Yacht "Maria" — A152

No. 442: a, Gáshólmur and Tindhólmur. b, Framvith "Diamantunum." c, Hús av tí betra slagnum. d, Mylingur sunnanífrá. e, Mylingur northanífrá. f, Kalsoyggin northanífrá. g, Raetha teir infoddu. h, Sunnari endi av Kunoynni.

2004, Mar. 26 Litho. *Perf. 13*

442 A152 6.50k Sheet of 8 17.00 17.00

Souvenir Sheet

Norse Gods — A153

No. 443: a, Thor, in boat, fighting Midgard serpent. b, Ran in fishing net.

2004, Mar. 26

443 A153 6.50k multi 4.25 4.25

Souvenir Sheet

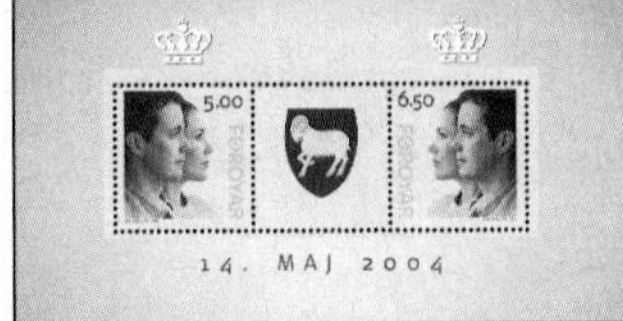

Wedding of Crown Prince Frederik and Mary Donaldson — A154

Litho. & Photo.

2004, May 14 *Perf. 13¼*

444 A154 Sheet of 2 + central label 3.75 3.75
a. 5k Couple facing right 1.60 1.60
b. 6.50k Couple facing left 2.10 2.10

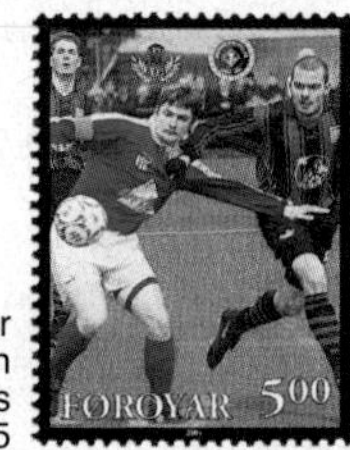

Soccer Organization Centenaries A155

Soccer players and emblems of: 5k, Klaksvík and Tórshavn teams. 6.50k, FIFA (Fédération Internationale de Football Association).

2004, May 24 Litho. *Perf. 13¼x13*

445 A155 5k multi 1.60 1.60
446 A155 6.50k multi 2.10 2.10
a. Booklet pane, 4 each #445-446 15.00 —
Complete booklet, #446a 15.00

Europa A156

Designs: 6.50k, Tourists in gorge, Hestur. 8k, Tourists at shore, Stóra Dímun.

2004, May 24 *Perf. 13x13¼*

447 A156 6.50k multi 2.10 2.10
448 A156 8k multi 2.60 2.60

Churches A157

2004, Sept. 20 Litho. *Perf. 13¼x13*

449 A157 5.50k Vágur 1.90 1.90
450 A157 7.50k Tvoroyri 2.50 2.50
a. Booklet pane, 4 each #449-450 18.00 —
Complete booklet, #450a 18.00

Poems by Janus Djurhuus (1881-1948) — A158

No. 451: a, Atlantis. b, Grímur Kamban. c, Gandkvaethi Tróndar. d, Til Foroya I-III. e, Mín sorg. f, Loki. g, I búri og Slatur. h, Heimferth Nólsoyar Páls. i, Móses á Sinai fjalli. j, Cello.

2004, Sept. 20 *Perf. 13*

451 A158 Sheet of 10 25.00 25.00
a.-j. 7.50k Any single 2.50 2.50

FERNANDO PO

fər-ˈnan-ˌdō ˈpō

LOCATION — An island in the Gulf of Guinea off west Africa.
GOVT. — Province of Spain
AREA — 800 sq. mi.
POP. — 62,612 (1960)
CAPITAL — Santa Isabel

Together with the islands of Elobey, Annobon and Corisco, Fernando Po came under the administration of Spanish Guinea. Postage stamps of Spanish Guinea were used until 1960.

The provinces of Fernando Po and Rio Muni united Oct. 12, 1968, to form the Republic of Equatorial Guinea.

100 Centimos = 1 Escudo = 2.50 Pesetas
100 Centimos = 1 Peseta
1000 Milesimas = 100 Centavos = 1 Peso (1882)

Catalogue values for unused stamps in this country are for Never Hinged items, beginning with Scott 181 in the regular postage section and Scott B1 in the semi-postal section.

Isabella II — A1

Alfonso XII — A2

1868 Unwmk. Typo. *Perf. 14*

1 A1 20c brown 425.00 125.00
a. 20c red brown 450.00 125.00

No. 1 is valued in the grade of fine, as illustrated. Examples with very fine centering are uncommon and sell for more.

Forgeries exist.

1879

Centimos de Peseta

2 A2 5c green 45.00 10.50
3 A2 10c rose 22.50 10.50
4 A2 50c blue 90.00 10.50
Nos. 2-4 (3) 157.50 31.50

1882-89

Centavos de Peso

5 A2 1c green 8.75 3.75
6 A2 2c rose 13.00 6.50
7 A2 5c gray blue 42.50 9.00
8 A2 10c dk brown ('89) 60.00 4.50
Nos. 5-8 (4) 124.25 23.75

Nos. 5-7 Handstamp Surcharged Type "a" in Blue, Black or Violet

a

1884-95

9 A2 50c on 1c green ('95) 90.00 19.00
11 A2 50c on 2c rose 27.50 6.00
12 A2 50c on 5c blue ('87) 100.00 25.00
Nos. 9-12 (3) 217.50 50.00

Inverted and double surcharges exist. No. 12 exists overprinted in carmine. Value $80.

King Alfonso XIII — A4

1894-97 *Perf. 14*

13 A4 ⅛c slate ('96) 18.00 2.50
14 A4 2c rose ('96) 13.00 2.00
15 A4 5c blue grn ('97) 13.50 2.00
16 A4 6c dk violet ('96) 11.00 2.50
17 A4 10c blk vio ('94) 300.00 65.00
18 A4 10c lake ('95) 40.00 7.50
19 A4 10c org brn ('96) 8.75 2.00
20 A4 12½c dk brown ('96) 9.50 2.50
21 A4 20c slate bl ('96) 9.50 2.50
22 A4 25c claret ('96) 19.00 2.50
Nos. 13-22 (10) 442.25 91.00

Stamps of 1894-97 Handstamped in Blue, Black or Red

b

c

Type "b" Surcharge

1896-98

23 A4 5c on 2c rose (Bl) 29.00 4.50
24 A4 5c on 10c brn vio (Bl) 92.50 12.00
25 A4 5c on 12½c brn (Bl) 20.00 3.50
a. Black surcharge 20.00 3.50
Nos. 23-25 (3) 141.50 20.00

Type "c" Surcharge

26 A4 5c on ⅛c slate (Bk) 18.00 5.25
27 A4 5c on 2c rose (Bl) 18.00 5.25
a. Black surcharge 18.00 5.25
28 A4 5c on 5c green (R) 92.50 16.50
29 A4 5c on 6c dk vio (R) 13.00 10.00
a. Violet surcharge 15.00 11.00
30 A4 5c on 10c org brn (Bk) 100.00 20.00
31 A4 5c on 12½c brn (R) 40.00 8.00
32 A4 5c on 20c sl bl (R) 22.50 7.50
33 A4 5c on 25c claret (Bk) 22.50 8.00
a. Blue surcharge 25.00 10.00
Nos. 26-33 (8) 326.50 80.50

Exist surcharged in other colors.

Type "a" Surch. in Blue or Black

1898-99

34 A4 50c on 2c rose 57.50 6.75
35 A4 50c on 10c brn vio 125.00 20.00
36 A4 50c on 10c lake 140.00 20.00
37 A4 50c on 10c org brn 125.00 20.00
38 A4 50c on 12½c brn (Bk) 110.00 12.50

The "a" surch. also exists on ⅛c, 5c & 25c.

Arms

A5 A6

Revenue Stamps Handstamped in Blue

1897-98 *Imperf.*

39 A5 5c on 10c rose 32.50 15.00
40 A6 10c rose 27.50 13.00

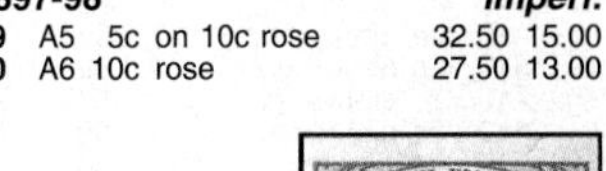

A7

A8

A9

Arms — A9a

Revenue Stamps Handstamped in Black or Red

1899 *Imperf.*

41 A7 15c on 10c green 40.00 21.00
a. Blue surcharge, vertical 35.00 19.00
42 A8 10c on 25c green 110.00 60.00
43 A9 15c on 25c green 175.00 110.00
43A A9a 15c on 25c green (R) *1,600. 1,000.*
b. Black surcharge *1,600. 1,000.*

Surcharge on No. 41 is either horizontal, inverted or vertical.

On No. 42 "CORREOS" is ovptd. in red.

King Alfonso XIII — A10

Double-lined shaded letters at sides.

1899 *Perf. 14*

44 A10 1m orange brn 1.90 .40
45 A10 2m orange brn 1.90 .40
46 A10 3m orange brn 1.90 .40
47 A10 4m orange brn 1.90 .40
48 A10 5m orange brn 1.90 .40
49 A10 1c black vio 1.90 .40
50 A10 2c dk blue grn 1.90 .40
51 A10 3c dk brown 1.90 .40
52 A10 4c orange 11.50 1.00
53 A10 5c carmine rose 1.90 .40
54 A10 6c dark blue 1.90 .40
55 A10 8c gray brn 7.00 .40
56 A10 10c vermilion 4.50 .40
57 A10 15c slate grn 4.50 .40
58 A10 20c maroon 12.00 1.00
59 A10 40c violet 82.50 17.50
60 A10 60c black 82.50 17.50
61 A10 80c red brown 82.50 17.50
62 A10 1p yellow grn 300.00 85.00
63 A10 2p slate blue 300.00 87.50
Nos. 44-63 (20) 906.00 232.20

Nos. 44-63 exist imperf. Value for set, $1,275.

See Nos. 66-85. For surcharges see Nos. 64-65, 88-88B.

1900

Surcharged type "a"

64 A10 50c on 20c maroon 15.00 2.25
a. Blue surcharge 30.00 4.50

Surcharged type "b"

64B A10 5c on 20c maroon 200.00 10.00

Surcharged type "c"

65 A10 5c on 20c maroon 8.50 2.25
Nos. 64-65 (3) 223.50 14.50

Dated "1900"

Solid letters at sides.

1900

66 A10 1m black 2.50 .45
67 A10 2m black 2.50 .45
68 A10 3m black 2.50 .45
69 A10 4m black 2.50 .45
70 A10 5m black 2.50 .45
71 A10 1c green 2.50 .45
72 A10 2c violet 2.50 .45
73 A10 3c rose 2.50 .45
74 A10 4c black brn 2.50 .45
75 A10 5c blue 2.50 .45
76 A10 6c orange 2.50 .45
77 A10 8c bronze grn 2.50 .45
78 A10 10c claret 2.50 .45
79 A10 15c dk violet 2.50 .45
80 A10 20c olive brn 2.50 .45
81 A10 40c brown 6.25 1.90
82 A10 60c green 13.50 2.10
83 A10 80c dark blue 14.00 3.25
84 A10 1p red brown 77.50 25.00
85 A10 2p orange 140.00 55.00
Nos. 66-85 (20) 288.75 94.00
Set, never hinged 400.00

Nos. 66-85 exist imperf. Value, set $1,200.

A11 A12

Revenue Stamps Overprinted or Surcharged with Handstamp in Red or Black

1900 *Imperf.*

86 A11 10c blue (R) 35.00 16.00
87 A12 5c on 10c blue 90.00 37.50
Set, never hinged 165.00

Nos. 52 and 80 Surcharged type "a" in Violet or Black

1900

88 A10 50c on 4c orange (V) 14.00 4.00
a. Green surcharge 22.50 12.00
88B A10 50c on 20c ol brn 14.00 3.50
Set, never hinged 37.50

A13 A14

1901 *Perf. 14*

89 A13 1c black 1.90 .55
90 A13 2c orange brn 1.90 .55
91 A13 3c dk violet 1.90 .55
92 A13 4c lt violet 1.90 .55
93 A13 5c orange red 1.25 .55
94 A13 10c violet brn 1.25 .55
95 A13 25c dp blue 1.25 .55
96 A13 50c claret 1.90 .55
97 A13 75c dk brown 1.50 .55
98 A13 1p blue grn 42.50 4.50
99 A13 2p red brown 25.00 7.00
100 A13 3p olive grn 25.00 9.25
101 A13 4p dull red 27.50 9.25
102 A13 5p dk green 32.50 9.25
103 A13 10p buff 72.50 27.50
Nos. 89-103 (15) 239.75 71.70
Set, never hinged 400.00

Dated "1902"

1902

Control Numbers on Back

104 A13 5c dk green 1.60 .35
105 A13 10c slate 1.75 .40
106 A13 25c claret 4.50 .65
107 A13 50c violet brn 10.50 2.25
108 A13 75c lt violet 10.50 2.25
109 A13 1p car rose 13.50 2.75
110 A13 2p olive grn 27.50 6.75
111 A13 5p orange red 37.50 15.00
Nos. 104-111 (8) 107.35 30.40
Set, never hinged 140.00

Exist imperf. Value for set, $500.

1903 *Perf. 14*

Control Numbers on Back

112 A14 ¼c dk violet .30 .20
113 A14 ½c black .30 .20
114 A14 1c scarlet .30 .20
115 A14 2c dk green .30 .20
116 A14 3c blue grn .30 .20
117 A14 4c violet .30 .20
118 A14 5c rose lake .35 .20
119 A14 10c orange buff .45 .20
120 A14 15c blue green 1.60 .65
121 A14 25c red brown 2.00 .90
122 A14 50c black brn 3.25 1.50
123 A14 75c carmine 11.00 2.75
124 A14 1p dk brown 16.00 4.50
125 A14 2p dk olive grn 21.00 5.75
126 A14 3p claret 21.00 5.75
127 A14 4p dark blue 27.50 9.00
128 A14 5p dp dull blue 40.00 12.00
129 A14 10p dull red 77.50 17.50
Nos. 112-129 (18) 220.45 61.90
Set, never hinged 325.00

Dated "1905"

1905

Control Numbers on Back

136 A14 1c dp violet .20 .20
137 A14 2c black .20 .20
138 A14 3c vermilion .20 .20
139 A14 4c dp green .20 .20
140 A14 5c blue grn .25 .20
141 A14 10c violet 1.10 .40
142 A14 15c car lake 1.10 .40
143 A14 25c orange buff 8.75 1.25
144 A14 50c green 6.00 1.90
145 A14 75c red brown 7.75 5.50
146 A14 1p dp gray brn 8.75 5.50
147 A14 2p carmine 16.00 8.25
148 A14 3p deep brown 24.00 9.50
149 A14 4p bronze grn 30.00 12.50
150 A14 5p claret 47.50 19.00
151 A14 10p deep blue 70.00 27.50
Nos. 136-151 (16) 222.00 92.70
Set, never hinged 400.00

King Alfonso XIII — A15

1907

Control Numbers on Back

152 A15 1c blue black .20 .20
153 A15 2c car rose .20 .20
154 A15 3c dp violet .20 .20
155 A15 4c black .20 .20
156 A15 5c orange buff .20 .20
157 A15 10c maroon .95 .30
158 A15 15c bronze grn .35 .20
159 A15 25c dk brown 15.00 5.50
160 A15 50c blue green .20 .20
161 A15 75c vermilion .25 .20
162 A15 1p dull blue 1.40 .35
163 A15 2p brown 6.00 2.25
164 A15 3p lake 6.00 2.25
165 A15 4p violet 6.00 2.25
166 A15 5p black brn 6.00 2.25
167 A15 10p orange brn 6.00 2.25
Nos. 152-167 (16) 49.15 19.00
Set, never hinged 92.50

No. 157 Handstamp Surcharged in Black or Blue

1908

168 A15 5c on 10c mar (Bk) 2.75 2.00
169 A15 5c on 10c mar (Bl) 9.00 5.50
Set, never hinged 15.00

The surcharge on Nos. 168-169 exist inverted, double, etc. The surcharge also exists on other stamps. A 25c on 10c also exists.

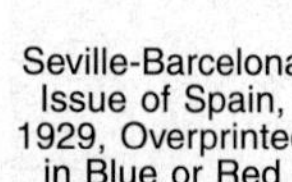

Seville-Barcelona Issue of Spain, 1929, Overprinted in Blue or Red

1929 *Perf. 11*

170 A52 5c rose lake .20 .20
171 A53 10c green (R) .20 .20
a. Perf. 14 .60 .60
172 A50 15c Prus bl (R) .20 .20
173 A51 20c purple (R) .20 .20
174 A50 25c brt rose .20 .20
175 A52 30c black brn .20 .20
176 A53 40c dk blue (R) .45 .45
177 A51 50c dp orange 1.00 1.00
178 A52 1p blue blk (R) 3.75 3.75
179 A53 4p deep rose 20.00 20.00
180 A53 10p brown 24.00 24.00
Nos. 170-180 (11) 50.40 50.40
Set, never hinged 87.50

Catalogue values for unused stamps in this section, from this point to the end of the section, are for Never Hinged items.

Virgin Mary — A16

1960 Unwmk. Photo. *Perf. 13x12½*

181 A16 25c dull gray vio .20 .20
182 A16 50c brown olive .20 .20
183 A16 75c violet brn .20 .20
184 A16 1p orange ver .20 .20
185 A16 1.50p lt blue grn .20 .20
186 A16 2p red lilac .20 .20
187 A16 3p dark blue 2.75 .70
188 A16 5p lt red brn .20 .20
189 A16 10p lt olive grn .40 .20
Nos. 181-189 (9) 4.55 2.30

Tricorn and Windmill from "The Three-Cornered Hat" by Falla — A17

Manuel de Falla A18

1960 *Perf. 13x12½, 12½x13*

190 A17 35c slate green .20 .20
191 A18 80c Prus green .20 .20

Issued to honor Manuel de Falla (1876-1946), Spanish composer.

See Nos. B1-B2.

Map of Fernando Po — A19

General Franco A20

Designs: 70c, Santa Isabel Cathedral.

Perf. 13x12½, 12½x13

1961, Oct. 1 Photo. Unwmk.

192 A19 25c gray violet .20 .20
193 A20 50c olive brown .20 .20
194 A19 70c brt green .20 .20
195 A20 1p red orange .20 .20
Nos. 192-195 (4) .80 .80

25th anniv. of the nomination of Gen. Francisco Franco as Chief of State.

Ocean Liner A21

Design: 50c, S.S. San Francisco.

1962, July 10 ***Perf. 12½x13***

196	A21	25c dull violet	.20	.20
197	A21	50c gray olive	.20	.20
198	A21	1p orange brn	.20	.20
		Nos. 196-198 (3)	.60	.60

Mailman — A22

Mail Transport Symbols A23

Perf. 13x12½, 12½x13

1962, Nov. 23 **Unwmk.**

199	A22	15c dark green	.20	.20
200	A23	35c lilac rose	.20	.20
201	A22	1p brown	.20	.20
		Nos. 199-201 (3)	.60	.60

Issued for Stamp Day.

Fetish — A24

1963, Jan. 29 ***Perf. 13x12½***

202	A24	50c olive gray	.20	.20
203	A24	1p deep magenta	.20	.20

Issued to help victims of the Seville flood.

Nuns A25

Design: 50c, Nun and child, vert.

Perf. 12½x13, 13x12½

1963, July 6 **Photo.** **Unwmk.**

204	A25	25c bright lilac	.20	.20
205	A25	50c dull green	.20	.20
206	A25	1p red orange	.20	.20
		Nos. 204-206 (3)	.60	.60

Issued for child welfare.

Child and Arms A26

1963, July 12 ***Perf. 12½x13***

207	A26	50c brown olive	.20	.20
208	A26	1p carmine rose	.20	.20

Issued for Barcelona flood relief.

Governor Chacon A27

Orange Blossoms A28

Men in Dugout Canoe A29

1964, Mar. 6 ***Perf. 12½x13, 13x12½***

209	A27	25c violet black	.20	.20
210	A28	50c dark olive	.20	.20
211	A27	1p brown red	.20	.20
		Nos. 209-211 (3)	.60	.60

Issued for Stamp Day 1963.

1964, June 1 **Photo.** ***Perf. 13x12½***

Design: 50c, Pineapple.

212	A29	25c purple	.20	.20
213	A28	50c dull olive	.20	.20
214	A29	1p deep claret	.20	.20
		Nos. 212-214 (3)	.60	.60

Issued for child welfare.

Ring-necked Francolin — A30

Designs: 15c, 70c, 3p, Ring-necked francolin. 25c, 1p, 5p, Two mallards. 50c, 1.50p, 10p, Head of great blue touraco.

1964, July 1

215	A30	15c chestnut	.20	.20
216	A30	25c dull violet	.20	.20
217	A30	50c dk olive grn	.20	.20
218	A30	70c green	.20	.20
219	A30	1p brown orange	.20	.20
220	A30	1.50p grnsh blue	.20	.20
221	A30	3p violet blue	.65	.20
222	A30	5p dull purple	1.40	.20
223	A30	10p bright green	1.90	.65
		Nos. 215-223 (9)	5.15	2.25

The Three Kings A31

Designs: 50c, 1.50p, Caspar, vert.

Perf. 13x12½, 12½x13

1964, Nov. 23 **Unwmk.**

224	A31	50c green	.20	.20
225	A31	1p orange ver	.20	.20
226	A31	1.50p deep green	.20	.20
227	A31	3p ultra	1.50	.70
		Nos. 224-227 (4)	2.10	1.30

Issued for Stamp Day, 1964.

Boy — A32

Woman Fruit Picker — A33

1.50p, Girl learning to write, and church.

1964, Mar. 1 **Photo.** ***Perf. 13x12½***

228	A32	50c indigo	.20	.20
229	A33	1p dark red	.20	.20
230	A33	1.50p grnsh blue	.20	.20
		Nos. 228-230 (3)	.60	.60

Issued to commemorate 25 years of peace.

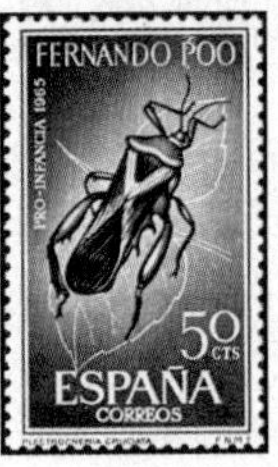

Plectrocnemia Cruciata — A34

Design: 1p, Metopodontus savagei, horiz.

Perf. 13x12½, 12½x13

1965, June 1 **Photo.** **Unwmk.**

231	A34	50c slate green	.20	.20
232	A34	1p rose red	.20	.20
233	A34	1.50p Prus blue	.20	.20
		Nos. 231-233 (3)	.60	.60

Issued for child welfare.

Pole Vault A35

Arms of Fernando Po — A36

Perf. 12½x13, 13x12½

1965, Nov. 23 **Photo.** **Unwmk.**

234	A35	50c yellow green	.20	.20
235	A36	1p brt org brn	.20	.20
236	A35	1.50p brt blue	.20	.20
		Nos. 234-236 (3)	.60	.60

Issued for Stamp Day, 1965.

Children Reading A37

1.50p, St. Elizabeth of Hungary, vert.

Perf. 12½x13, 13x12½

1966, June 1 **Photo.** **Unwmk.**

237	A37	50c dark green	.20	.20
238	A37	1p brown red	.20	.20
239	A37	1.50p dark blue	.20	.20
		Nos. 237-239 (3)	.60	.60

Issued for child welfare.

White-nosed Monkey — A38

Stamp Day: 40c, 4p, Head of moustached monkey, vert.

1966, Nov. 23 **Photo.** ***Perf. 13***

240	A38	10c dk blue & yel	.20	.20
241	A38	40c lt brn, bl & blk	.20	.20
242	A38	1.50p ol bis, brn org & blk	.20	.20
243	A38	4p sl grn, brn org & blk	.20	.20
		Nos. 240-243 (4)	.80	.80

Flowers — A39

Designs: 40c, 4p, Six flowers.

1967, June 1 **Photo.** ***Perf. 13***

244	A39	10c brt car & pale grn	.20	.20
245	A39	40c red brn & org	.20	.20
246	A39	1.50p red lil & lt red brn	.20	.20
247	A39	4p dk blue & lt grn	.20	.20
		Nos. 244-247 (4)	.80	.80

Issued for child welfare.

Linsang — A40

Stamp Day: 1.50p, Needle-clawed galago, vert. 3.50p, Fraser's scaly-tailed flying squirrel.

1967, Nov. 23 **Photo.** ***Perf. 13***

248	A40	1p black & bister	.20	.20
249	A40	1.50p brown & olive	.20	.20
250	A40	3.50p rose lake & dl grn	.25	.20
		Nos. 248-250 (3)	.65	.60

Stamp of 1868, No. 1, and Arms of San Carlos A41

Fernando Po No. 1 and: 1.50p, Arms of Santa Isabel. 2.50p, Arms of Fernando Po.

1968, Feb. 4 **Photo.** ***Perf. 13***

251	A41	1p brt plum & brn org	.20	.20
252	A41	1.50p dp blue & brn org	.20	.20
253	A41	2.50p brn & brn org	.20	.20
		Nos. 251-253 (3)	.60	.60

Centenary of the first postage stamp.

Signs of the Zodiac — A42

1968, Apr. 25 **Photo.** ***Perf. 13***

254	A42	1p Libra	.20	.20
255	A42	1.50p Leo	.20	.20
256	A42	2.50p Aquarius	.20	.20
		Nos. 254-256 (3)	.60	.60

Issued for child welfare.

SEMI-POSTAL STAMPS

Catalogue values for unused stamps in this section are for Never Hinged items.

Types of Regular Issue, 1960

Designs: 10c+5c, Manuel de Falla. 15c+5c, Dancers from "Love, the Magician."

Perf. 12½x13, 13x12½

1960 Photo. Unwmk.

No.	Type	Description	Unused	Used
B1	A18	10c + 5c maroon	.20	.20
B2	A17	15c + 5c dk brn & bister	.20	.20

The surtax was for child welfare.

Whale SP1

Design: Nos. B4, B6, Harpooning whale.

1961 *Perf. 12½x13*

No.	Type	Description	Unused	Used
B3	SP1	10c + 5c rose brown	.20	.20
B4	SP1	20c + 5c dk slate grn	.20	.20
B5	SP1	30c + 10c olive brn	.20	.20
B6	SP1	50c + 20c dark brn	.20	.20
		Nos. B3-B6 (4)	.80	.80

Issued for Stamp Day, 1960.

Hand Blessing Woman — SP2

Design: 25c+10c, Boy making sign of the cross, and crucifix.

1961, June 21 *Perf. 13x12½*

No.	Type	Description	Unused	Used
B7	SP2	10c + 5c rose brn	.20	.20
B8	SP2	25c + 10c gray vio	.20	.20
B9	SP2	80c + 20c dk grn	.20	.20
		Nos. B7-B9 (3)	.60	.60

The surtax was for child welfare.

Ethiopian Tortoise SP3

Stamp Day: 25c+10c, 1p+10c, Native carriers, palms and shore.

1961, Nov. 23 *Perf. 12½x13*

No.	Type	Description	Unused	Used
B10	SP3	10c + 5c rose red	.20	.20
B11	SP3	25c + 10c dk pur	.20	.20
B12	SP3	30c + 10c vio brn	.20	.20
B13	SP3	1p + 10c red org	.20	.20
		Nos. B10-B13 (4)	.80	.80

FIJI

'fē-ₑjē

LOCATION — Group of 332 islands (106 inhabited) in the South Pacific Ocean east of Vanuatu
GOVT. — Independent nation in British Commonwealth
AREA — 7,078 sq. mi.
POP. — 812,918 (1999 est.)
CAPITAL — Suva

A British colony since 1874, Fiji became fully independent in 1970.

12 Pence = 1 Shilling
20 Shillings = 1 Pound
100 Cents = 1 Dollar (1872-74, 1969)

Syncopated Perforations

Type A (1st stamp #873): On shorter sides, the seventh hole from the larger side is an oval hole equal in width to three holes.

Catalogue values for unused stamps in this country are for Never Hinged items, beginning with Scott 137 in the regular postage section and Scott B1 in the semi-postal section.

Values for unused stamps are for examples with original gum as defined in the catalogue introduction except for Nos. 1-10 which are valued without gum. Additionally, Nos. 1-10 are valued with roulettes showing on two or more sides, but expect small faults which do not detract from the appearance of the stamps. Very few examples of Nos. 1-10 will be found free of faults and these will command substantial premiums.

Watermark

Wmk. 17 — FIJI POSTAGE Across Center Row of Sheet

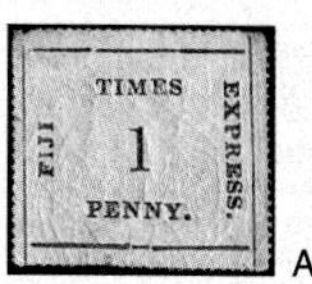

A1

1870 Unwmk. Typeset ***Rouletted***
Quadrille Paper

No.	Type	Description	Unused	Used
1	A1	1p black, *pink*	3,750.	*4,000.*
2	A1	3p black, *pink*	4,000.	4,000.
3	A1	6p black, *pink*	2,350.	*2,750.*
5	A1	1sh black, *pink*	1,750.	*2,250.*

1871 Laid Batonne Paper

No.	Type	Description	Unused	Used
6	A1	1p black, *pink*	1,000.	*2,000.*
7	A1	3p black, *pink*	1,750.	*3,250.*
8	A1	6p black, *pink*	1,300.	*2,000.*
9	A1	9p black, *pink*	2,200.	*3,500.*
10	A1	1sh black, *pink*	1,500.	1,600.

This service was established by the *Fiji Times*, a weekly newspaper, for the delivery of the newspaper. Since there was no postal service to the other islands, delivery of letters to agents of the newspaper on the islands was offered to the public.

Nos. 1-5 were printed in the same sheet, one horizontal row of 6 of each (6p, 1sh, 1p, 3p). Nos. 6-10 were printed from the same plate with three 9p replacing three 3p.

Most used examples have pen cancels.

Up to three sets of imitations exist. One on pink laid paper, pin-perforated, measuring 22½x16mm. Originals measure 22½x18½mm. A later printing was made on pink wove paper.

Forgeries also exist plus fake cancellations.

Crown and "CR" (Cakobau Rex)

A2 A3

A4

1871 Typo. Wmk. 17 ***Perf. 12½***
Wove Paper

No.	Type	Description	Unused	Used
15	A2	1p blue	62.50	*140.00*
16	A3	3p green	125.00	*400.00*
17	A4	6p rose	150.00	*325.00*
		Nos. 15-17 (3)	337.50	*865.00*

Sheets of 50 (10x5).

For overprints and surcharges see #18-39.

Stamps of 1871 Surcharged in Black

1872, Jan. 13

No.	Type	Description	Unused	Used
18	A2	2c on 1p blue	37.50	*57.50*
19	A3	6c on 3p green	75.00	75.00
20	A4	12c on 6p rose	100.00	85.00
		Nos. 18-20 (3)	212.50	217.50

Nos. 18-20 with Additional Overprint in Black:

b

V.R.
c

1874, Oct. 10

No.	Type	Description	Unused	Used
21	A2(b)	2c on 1p blue	1,150.	325.00
22	A2(c)	2c on 1p blue	1,000.	300.00
a.		Invtd. "A" instead of "V"	2,600.	1,500.
b.		Period after "R" is a Maltese Cross	2,600.	1,500.
23	A3(b)	6c on 3p green	2,100.	1,000.
24	A3(c)	6c on 3p green	1,650.	775.00
a.		Inverted "A"	4,250.	1,850.
b.		Period after "R" is a Maltese Cross	4,250.	1,850.
25	A4(b)	12c on 6p rose	900.00	250.00
a.		"V.R." inverted	5,750.	
26	A4(c)	12c on 6p rose	725.00	275.00
a.		Inverted "A"	2,250.	1,350.
b.		Period after "R" is a Maltese Cross	2,250.	1,350.
c.		"V.R." inverted	—	5,000.

Types "b" and "c" were in the same sheet.

Nos. 23-26 with Additional Surcharge in Black or Red 2d.

1875

No.	Type	Description	Unused	Used
27	A3(b)	2p on 6c on 3p	1,950.	750.00
a.		Period btwn. "2" and "d"	3,500.	1,400.
b.		"V.R." double	4,000.	3,750.
28	A3(b)	2p on 6c on 3p (R)	750.00	325.00
a.		Period btwn. "2" and "d"	1,750.	750.00
29	A3(c)	2p on 6c on 3p	1,650.	525.00
a.		Inverted "A"	3,750.	1,400.
b.		Period after "R" is a Maltese Cross	3,750.	1,400.
c.		No period after "2d"	3,750.	1,400.
30	A3(c)	2p on 6c on 3p (R)	600.00	225.00
a.		Inverted "A"	1,750.	750.00
b.		Period after "R" is a Maltese Cross	1,750.	750.00
c.		No period after "2d"	1,850.	750.00
31	A4(b)	2p on 12c on 6p	2,250.	950.00
a.		Period btwn. "2" and "d"		
b.		No period after "2d"		
c.		"2d, VR" double		4,250.
32	A4(c)	2p on 12c on 6p	2,100.	900.00
a.		Inverted "A"	2,750.	1,250.
b.		No period after "2d"		
c.		"2d, VR" double		4,250.

Types of 1871 Overprinted or Surcharged in Black:

e

f

1876, Jan. 31 Unwmk.
Wove Paper

No.	Type	Description	Unused	Used
33	A2(e)	1p ultramarine	57.50	57.50
a.		Inverted surcharge		
b.		Dbl. impression of stamp	1,000.	
c.		Horiz. pair, imperf vert.	1,000.	
34	A3(e+f)	2p on 3p dk grn	52.50	*60.00*
a.		Dbl. surch. "Two Pence"		
35	A4(e)	6p rose	70.00	65.00
b.		Surcharge inverted		
c.		Dbl. impression of stamp	2,850.	
		Nos. 33-35 (3)	180.00	182.50

1877 Laid Paper

No.	Type	Description	Unused	Used
36	A2(e)	1p ultramarine	20.00	*32.50*
a.		Horiz. pair, imperf. vert.	1,100.	
37	A3(e+f)	2p on 3p dk grn	65.00	*75.00*
38	A3(e+f)	4p on 3p lilac	95.00	30.00
a.		Horiz. pair, imperf. vert.	1,000.	
39	A4(e)	6p rose	55.00	32.50
a.		Horiz. pair, imperf. vert.	800.00	
		Nos. 36-39 (4)	235.00	*170.00*

Many of the preceding stamps are known imperforate. They are printer's waste and were never issued.

A12

A13

Queen Victoria
A14 A15

Perf. 10-13½ & Compound

1878-90 Wove Paper Typo.

No.	Type	Description	Unused	Used
40	A12	1p ultra ('79)	10.00	7.50
a.		1p blue	60.00	3.75
41	A12	2p green	15.00	1.10
b.		2p ultramarine (error)	*28,500.*	
42	A12	4p brt vio ('90)	8.50	7.00
a.		4p mauve	11.50	8.50
43	A13	6p brt rose ('80)	7.50	4.25
a.		Printed on both sides	1,150.	975.00
44	A14	1sh yel brn ('99)	40.00	10.00
a.		1sh deep brown ('81)	95.00	22.50

Litho.

No.	Type	Description	Unused	Used
45	A15	5sh blk & red brn ('82)	62.50	37.50
		Nos. 40-45 (6)	143.50	67.35

Official facsimiles of the 5sh were officially made in 1900, differing in shades and detail of design from No. 45. They exist imperf., perf. 10 and 12; are all canceled "SUVA" and usually dated "15 Dec., 00."

No. 41b was not put on sale. All copies were supposed to be destroyed.

For surcharges see Nos. 46-52.

Surcharged type "f" in Black

1878-90 Typo.

No.	Type	Description	Unused	Used
46	A12	2p on 3p green	6.50	*22.50*
47	A12	4p on 1p vio ('90)	47.50	30.00
48	A12	4p on 2p lilac ('83)	85.00	12.50
		Nos. 46-48 (3)	139.00	65.00

Nos. 40-43 Surcharged in Black:

g h i j

1891-92 ***Perf. 10***

No.	Type	Description	Unused	Used
49	A12(g)	½p on 1p ('92)	50.00	*75.00*
50	A12(h)	2½p on 2p	50.00	*57.50*
a.		Wider space (2mm) between "2" and "½"	150.00	*160.00*
51	A12(i)	5p on 4p ('92)	57.50	*75.00*
52	A13(j)	5p on 6p ('92)	62.50	*80.00*
a.		"FIVE" and "PENCE" 3mm apart	75.00	*80.00*
		Nos. 49-52 (4)	220.00	*287.50*

A18

Fijian Canoe — A19

A20

1891-96 *Perf. 10-12 & Compound*
53 A18 ½p grnsh blk ('92) 1.40 *3.00*
a. ½p gray 3.50 *6.00*
54 A19 1p black ('93) 5.00 *5.50*
55 A19 1p lilac rose ('96) 5.00 1.00
56 A19 2p green ('93) 6.50 1.10
a. Perf. 10x12 ('94) 700.00 425.00
57 A20 2½ red brown 5.75 5.75
58 A19 5p ultra ('93) 15.00 8.50
Nos. 53-58 (6) 38.65 24.85

Edward VII
A22

George V
A23

1903, Feb. 1 Wmk. 2 *Perf. 14*
59 A22 ½p pale green & gray green 2.60 2.25
60 A22 1p black & violet, *red* 15.00 .65
61 A22 2p orange & violet 4.50 1.40
62 A22 2½p ultramarine & violet, *blue* 16.00 4.00
63 A22 3p red violet & violet 1.75 *4.50*
64 A22 4p black & violet 1.75 *2.75*
65 A22 5p green & violet 1.75 *3.00*
66 A22 6p carmine rose & violet 1.75 *3.00*
67 A22 1sh carmine rose & green 12.50 *70.00*
68 A22 5sh black & green 62.50 *150.00*
69 A22 £1 ultramarine & gray 400.00 *550.00*
Revenue cancel 70.00
Nos. 59-68 (10) 120.10 *241.55*

Numerals of 2p, 4p, 6p and 5sh of type A22 are in color on plain tablet.

1904-12 Wmk. 3

Ordinary Paper
70 A22 ½p pale green & green ('04) 15.00 3.50
70A A22 ½p green ('08) 12.50 3.50
71 A22 1p black & violet, *red* ('04) 30.00 .20
72 A22 1p carmine ('06) 11.00 .20
73 A22 2½p ultramarine ('10) 7.50 *8.50*

Chalky Paper
74 A22 6p violet ('10) 15.00 *30.00*
75 A22 1sh carmine rose & green ('09) 30.00 *45.00*
76 A22 1sh black, *green* ('11) 5.00 *11.00*
77 A22 5sh scarlet & green, *yellow* ('11) 65.00 *75.00*
78 A22 £1 black & violet, *red* ('12) 375.00 *325.00*
Nos. 70-77 (9) 191.00 *176.90*

Die I

For description of Dies I and II see back of this section of the Catalogue.

1912-23

Ordinary Paper
79 A23 ¼p brown ('16) 1.50 .45
80 A23 ½p green 1.40 .55
81 A23 1p scarlet 2.25 .75
a. 1p carmine ('16) 2.25 .25
82 A23 2p gray ('14) 2.00 .20
83 A23 2½p ultramarine ('14) 3.50 4.00
84 A23 3p violet, *yellow* 2.25 *4.00*
a. Die II ('21) 2.75 *25.00*
85 A23 4p red & black, *yellow* ('14) 3.75 *15.00*
a. Die II ('23) 3.75 *27.50*

Chalky Paper
86 A23 5p ol green & dl violet ('14) 5.50 *12.50*
87 A23 6p red violet & dl violet ('14) 2.40 *6.00*
88 A23 1sh black, *green* 1.10 *14.00*
a. 1sh blk, *blue green*, olive back 4.50 *11.00*
b. 1sh black, *emerald* ('21) 6.25 *45.00*
c. Die II ('22) 3.25 *27.50*
89 A23 2sh 6p red & black, *blue* 37.50 *35.00*
90 A23 5sh scarlet & green, *yellow* 37.50 *45.00*

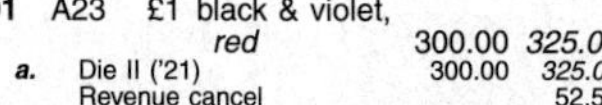
91 A23 £1 black & violet, *red* 300.00 *325.00*
a. Die II ('21) 300.00 *325.00*
Revenue cancel 52.50

Surface-colored Paper
92 A23 1sh black, *green* 1.25 *12.50*
Nos. 79-90,92 (13) 101.90 *149.95*

Numerals of ¼p, 1½p, 2p, 4p, 6p, 2sh, 2sh6p and 5sh of type A23 are in color on plain tablet.

For overprints see Nos. MR1-MR2.

Die II

1922-27 Wmk. 4

Ordinary Paper
93 A23 ¼p dark brown 3.00 *27.50*
94 A23 ½p green .85 *2.40*
95 A23 1p rose red 2.75 *1.25*
96 A23 1p violet ('27) 1.40 .20
97 A23 1½p rose red ('27) 4.50 2.00
98 A23 2p gray 1.40 .20
99 A23 3p ultramarine ('23) 3.00 1.20
100 A23 4p red & black, *yellow* 5.75 *7.50*
101 A23 5p ol green & dl violet 1.75 *2.25*
102 A23 6p red violet & dull violet 2.40 1.50

Chalky Paper
103 A23 1sh black, *emerald* 5.50 *6.75*
104 A23 2sh ultra & violet, *blue* ('27) 30.00 *67.50*
105 A23 2sh6p red & black, *blue* 12.50 *35.00*
106 A23 5sh scarlet & green, *yellow* 37.50 *75.00*
Nos. 93-106 (14) 112.30 *230.25*

Common Design Types pictured following the introduction.

Silver Jubilee Issue
Common Design Type

1935, May 6 *Perf. 13½x14*
110 CD301 1½p carmine & blue .85 *5.75*
111 CD301 2p gray blk & ultra 1.40 *.25*
112 CD301 3p blue & brown 2.50 *2.75*
113 CD301 1sh brt vio & indigo 4.25 *5.00*
Nos. 110-113 (4) 9.00 *13.75*
Set, never hinged 16.00

Coronation Issue
Common Design Type

1937, May 12 *Perf. 11x11½*
114 CD302 1p dark violet .45 .25
115 CD302 2p gray black .45 *.85*
116 CD302 3p indigo .45 *.85*
Nos. 114-116 (3) 1.35 1.95
Set, never hinged 1.75

Outrigger Canoe — A24

Fijian Village — A25

Outrigger Canoe A26

Map of Fiji Islands A27

Canoe and Arms of Fiji — A28

Sugar Cane — A29

Spear Fishing at Night — A30

Arms of Fiji — A31

Suva Harbor — A32

River Scene — A33

Fijian House — A34

Papaya Tree — A35

Bugler — A36

Designs: No. 121, Government buildings. 8p, 1sh5p, 1sh6p, Arms of Fiji.

Perf. 13½, 12½ (1p)

1938-55 Engr. Wmk. 4
117 A24 ½p green .25 1.00
c. Perf. 14 ('41) 16.00 4.50
d. Perf. 12 ('48) .80 *4.00*
118 A25 1p blue & brn .40 .25
119 A26 1½p rose car (empty canoe) 12.00 2.00
120 A27 2p grn & org brn (no "180 degree") 30.00 .50
121 A27 2p mag & grn .45 .80
a. Perf. 12 ('46) .45 .90

Perf. 12½, 13x12 (6p), 14 (8p)
122 A28 3p dp ultra .80 .40
123 A29 5p rose red & bl 32.50 13.00
124 A29 5p rose red & yel grn .25 *.40*
125 A27 6p blk (no "180 degree") 50.00 16.00
126 A31 8p rose car .80 3.00
a. Perf. 13 ('50) .55 *3.50*
127 A30 1sh black & yel .60 *.90*

Perf. 14
128 A31 1sh5p car & black .20 .20
128A A31 1sh6p ultra 2.75 3.50
b. Perf. 13 ('55) 1.10 *20.00*

Perf. 12½
129 A32 2sh vio & org 2.00 .55
130 A33 2sh6p brn & grn 2.25 2.00
131 A34 5sh dk vio & grn 2.25 2.25
131A A35 10sh emer & brn org 27.50 *52.50*
131B A36 £1 car & ultra 37.50 *65.00*
Nos. 117-131B (18) 202.50 *164.25*

Issued: 1sh5p, 6/13/40; 5p, 10/1/40; #121, 5/19/42; 8p, 11/15/48; 10sh, £1, 3/13/50; 1sh6p, 8/1/50; others, 4/5/38.

Types of 1938-40
Redrawn

Perf. 13½ (1½p, 2p, 6p), 14 (2½p)

1940-49 Wmk. 4
132 A26 1½p rose car (man in canoe) 1.00 *1.00*
a. Perf. 12 ('49) .80 *1.60*
b. Perf. 14 ('42) 14.50 *25.00*
133 A27 2p grn & org brn ("180 degree") 12.50 *21.00*
134 A27 2½p grn & org brn .50 *1.25*
a. Perf. 12 ('48) .80 .60
b. Perf. 13½ ('42) .55 *1.00*
135 A27 6p blk ("180 degree") 2.50 3.00
a. Perf. 12 ('47) 1.40 2.00
Nos. 132-135 (4) 16.50 *26.25*

No. 132, type A26, has a man sitting in the canoe.

Nos. 133-135, type A27, have 180 degree added to the lower right hand corner of the design.

Issued: 2½p, 1/6/42; others 10/1/40.

No. 133 Surcharged in Black

1941, Feb. 10 *Perf. 13½*
136 A27 2½p on 2p grn & org brn 1.50 —
Never hinged 2.50

Catalogue values for unused stamps in this section, from this point to the end of the section, are for Never Hinged items.

Peace Issue
Common Design Type

1946, Aug. 17 *Perf. 13½*
137 CD303 2½p bright green .20 *.60*
138 CD303 3p deep blue .20 .20

Silver Wedding Issue
Common Design Types

1948, Dec. 17 Photo. *Perf. 14x14½*
139 CD304 2½p dark green .70 *1.00*

Engr.; Name Typo.
Perf. 11½x11
140 CD305 5sh blue violet 22.50 16.00

UPU Issue
Common Design Types

Engr.; Name Typo. on 3p, 8p
Perf. 13½, 11x11½

1949, Oct. 10 Wmk. 4
141 CD306 2p red violet .65 .50
142 CD307 3p indigo 4.00 2.50
143 CD308 8p dp carmine .65 *2.50*
144 CD309 1sh6p blue .70 *1.10*
Nos. 141-144 (4) 6.00 6.60

Coronation Issue
Common Design Type

1953, June 2 *Perf. 13½x13*
145 CD312 2½p dk green & blk 1.00 .60

Type of 1938-40 with Portrait of Queen Elizabeth II Inscribed: "Royal Visit 1953"

1953, Dec. 16 *Perf. 13*
146 A31 8p carmine lake .65 .35

Visit of Queen Elizabeth II and the Duke of Edinburgh, 1953.

Types of 1938-50 with Portrait of Queen Elizabeth II, and:

A39

Loading Copra A40

Designs: 1sh6p, Sugar cane train. 2sh, Bananas for export. 5sh, Gold industry.

Perf. 11½, 11½x11, 12, 12½, 13

1954-56 **Engr.**

147 A24 ½p green .20 *1.25*
148 A39 1p grnsh blue 2.00 .20
149 A39 1½p brown 1.10 .65
150 A27 2p mag & green 1.40 .40
151 A39 2½p blue vio 2.75 .20
152 A40 3p purple & brn 3.00 .20
154 A27 6p black 3.00 .85
155 A31 8p carmine lake 4.25 1.25
156 A30 1sh black & yel 2.75 .20
157 A40 1sh6p grn & dp ultra 21.00 1.00
158 A40 2sh brt car & black 6.25 .50
159 A33 2sh6p brn & bl grn 1.40 .20
160 A40 5sh dp ultra & yel 17.00 1.25
161 A35 10sh emer & brn org 8.00 *20.00*
162 A36 £1 car & ultra 42.50 19.00
Nos. 147-162 (15) 116.60 47.15

Issued: 2p, 1sh, 2sh6p, 2/1/54; ½p, 6p, 8p, 10sh, £1, 7/1/54; 1p, 6/1/56; 1½p, 2½p, 3p, 1sh6p, 2sh, 5sh, 10/1/56.

Types of 1954-56 and:

Nautilus Shells — A41

Hibiscus — A42

Kandavu Parrot A43

½p, 2p, 2½p, Queen Elizabeth II (A39). 1p, Queen, turtles in bottom panels. 6p, Fijian beating drum (lali). 10p, Yaqona ceremony. 1sh, South Pacific map. 2sh6p, Nadi Airport. 10sh, Cutting sugar cane. £1, Arms of Fiji.

Perf. 11½ (A39, A41); 11½x11 (A40); 14½x14 (A42); 14x14½ (A43)

Engr. (A39, A40, A41); others Photo.

1959-63 **Wmk. 4**

163 A39 ½p green ('61) .25 *2.75*
164 A41 1p dk blue ('62) 4.00 2.75
165 A41 1½p dk brown ('62) 3.25 2.00
166 A39 2p crim rose ('61) .90 .20
167 A39 2½p brown org ('62) 2.75 4.25
168 A40 6p blk & car rose ('61) 2.25 .20
169 A42 8p gray, red, yel & grn ('61) .90 .40
170 A40 10p car & brn ('63) 1.10 .80
171 A40 1sh dk bl & bl ('61) 2.75 .75
172 A40 2sh6p pur & blk ('61) 4.50 1.40
173 A43 4sh dk grn, red, bl & emer 3.25 2.40
174 A40 10sh sep & emer ('61) 8.00 8.00
175 A40 £1 org & blk ('61) 24.00 10.00
Nos. 163-175 (13) 57.90 35.90

Issued: 4sh, 7/13; 8p, 8/1; ½p, 2p, 6p, 1sh, 2sh6p, 10sh, £1, 11/14; 1p, 1½p, 2½p, 12/3; 10p, 4/1.

For type overprinted see No. 205.

Types of 1954-63 and:

Elizabeth II — A44

1sh6p, 180th meridian and Intl. Date Line. 2sh, White orchids. 5sh, Orange dove.

Perf. 11½ (A41); 12½ (A44); 11½x11 (A40); 14x14½ (A43)

Engr. (A40, A41); others Photo.

1962-67 **Wmk. 314**

176 A41 1p dark blue ('64) .75 *4.25*
177 A39 2p crim rose ('65) .95 .20
178 A44 3p rose cl & multi .20 .20
179 A40 6p blk & car rose ('64) 1.10 .20
180 A42 9p ultra, red, yel & grn ('63) 1.10 1.00
181 A40 10p car & brn ('64) 1.10 .85
182 A40 1sh dk bl & bl ('66) 1.90 .75
183 A43 1sh6p dk bl & multi 2.25 1.60
184 A42 2sh gold, yel grn & grn 11.00 5.75
185 A40 2sh6p pur & blk ('65) 2.25 1.25
186 A43 4sh grn & multi, wmk. sideways ('67) 4.75 3.25
a. As #186, wmk. upright ('64) 3.50 6.50
b. 4sh dark green & multi ('66) 4.00 5.25
187 A43 5sh dk gray, yel & red 8.00 1.00
188 A40 10sh sep & emer ('64) 5.50 5.75
189 A40 £1 org & blk ('64) 21.00 15.00
Nos. 176-189 (14) 61.85 41.05

Issued: 3p, 1sh6p, 2sh, 5sh, 12/3; 9p, #186a, 4/1; 1p, 10p, 10sh, 1/14; 6p, £1, 6/9; 2p, 2sh6p, 8/3; #186b, 3/1; #186, 2/16.

Nos. 178 and 171 Overprinted: "ROYAL VISIT 1963"

1963, Feb. 1

196 A44 3p multicolored .50 .35
197 A40 1sh dark blue & blue .50 .35

Visit of Elizabeth II & Prince Philip, Feb. 3.

Freedom from Hunger Issue

Common Design Type

1963, June 4 Photo. *Perf. 14x14½*

198 CD314 2sh ultramarine 8.25 4.50

Running A45

9p, Throwing the discus, vert. 1sh, Field hockey, vert. 2sh6p, Women's high jump.

Perf. 14½x14, 14x14½

1963, Aug. 6 **Wmk. 314**

199 A45 3p yel, blk & brn .75 .20
200 A45 9p violet, blk & brn .75 1.50
201 A45 1sh green, blk & brn .75 .25
202 A45 2sh6p blue, blk & brn 1.75 1.75
Nos. 199-202 (4) 4.00 3.70

1st So. Pacific Games, Suva, 8/29-9/7.

Red Cross Centenary Issue

Common Design Type

1963, Sept. 2 Litho. *Perf. 13*

203 CD315 2p black & red 1.50 .30
204 CD315 2sh ultra & red 4.50 4.50

Type of 1959-63 Overprinted

1963, Dec. 2 Engr. *Perf. 11½x11*

205 A40 1sh dark blue & blue 1.00 .35

Opening of the Commonwealth Pacific (telephone) Cable service, COMPAC.

Fiji Scout Badge — A46

Scouts of India, Fiji and Europe Tying Knot — A47

1964, Aug. 3 Photo. *Perf. 12½*

206 A46 3p multicolored .65 .50
207 A47 1sh ocher & purple 1.00 .75

50th anniv. of the founding of the Fiji Boy Scouts.

Amphibian "Aotearoa," 1939 — A48

Map of Fiji and Tonga Islands and Plane A49

Design: 6p, Heron plane.

1964, Oct. 24 *Perf. 12½, 14½*

208 A48 3p brt red & black .65 .35
209 A48 6p ultra & red 1.10 1.10
210 A49 1sh grnsh blue & black 1.10 1.10
Nos. 208-210 (3) 2.85 2.55

Fiji-Tonga airmail service, 25th anniv.

ITU Issue

Common Design Type

Perf. 11x11½

1965, May 17 Litho. Wmk. 314

211 CD317 3p blue & rose red .50 .30
212 CD317 2sh yel & bister 3.50 3.50

Intl. Cooperation Year Issue

Common Design Type

1965, Oct. 25 *Perf. 14½*

213 CD318 2p blue grn & claret .40 .40
214 CD318 2sh6p lt vio & grn 2.60 2.10

Churchill Memorial Issue

Common Design Type

1966, Jan. 24 Photo. *Perf. 14*

Design in Black, Gold and Carmine Rose

215 CD319 3p brt blue 1.25 .35
216 CD319 9p green 1.75 1.75
217 CD319 1sh brown 1.75 .35
218 CD319 2sh6p violet 2.00 2.00
Nos. 215-218 (4) 6.75 4.45

World Cup Soccer Issue

Common Design Type

1966, July 1 Litho. *Perf. 14*

219 CD321 2p multicolored .60 .30
220 CD321 2sh multicolored 1.75 .90

H.M.S. Pandora and Split Island, Rotuma A50

Designs: 10p, Rotuma chiefs, Pandora, and Rotuma's position in Pacific. 1sh6p, Rotuma islanders welcoming Pandora.

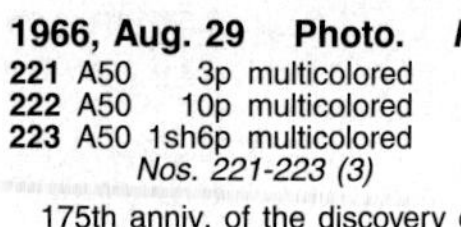

1966, Aug. 29 Photo. *Perf. 14x13*

221 A50 3p multicolored .60 .25
222 A50 10p multicolored .75 .40
223 A50 1sh6p multicolored 1.00 1.00
Nos. 221-223 (3) 2.35 1.65

175th anniv. of the discovery of Hotuma, a group of eight islands forming part of the colony of Fiji.

WHO Headquarters Issue

Common Design Type

1966, Sept. 20 Litho. *Perf. 14*

224 CD322 6p multicolored 2.10 .50
225 CD322 2sh6p multicolored 4.50 4.00

Woman Runner A51

Designs: 9p, Shot put, vert. 1sh, Diver.

1966, Dec. 8 Photo. *Perf. 14x14½*

226 A51 3p ol, black & lt brn .40 .40
227 A51 9p brt blue, blk & brn .65 .65
228 A51 1sh blue green & multi .65 .65
Nos. 226-228 (3) 1.70 1.70

2nd South Pacific Games, Noumea, New Caledonia, Dec. 8-18.

Military Band A52

Intl. Tourist Year: 9p, Reef diving. 1sh, Beqa fire walkers. 2sh, Liner Oriana and Mt. Rama volcano.

1967, Oct. 20 *Perf. 14x13*

229 A52 3p multi & gold .90 .20
230 A52 9p multi & silver .35 .25
231 A52 1sh multi & gold .35 .35
232 A52 2sh multi & silver .90 .60
Nos. 229-232 (4) 2.50 1.40

Admiral Bligh, H.M.S. Providence and Old Map of "Feejee" A53

Designs: 1sh, Bligh's longboat being chased by double canoe and map of Fiji Islands. 2sh6p, Bligh's tomb, St. Mary's Cemetery, Lambeth, London.

Perf. 15x14, 12½x13 (1sh)

1967, Dec. 7 Photo. Wmk. 314

Size: 35x21mm

233 A53 4p emer, blk & yel .30 .30

Size: 54x20mm

234 A53 1sh brt bl, brn org & blk .45 .45

Size: 35x21mm

235 A53 2sh6p sepia & multi 1.25 1.25
Nos. 233-235 (3) 2.00 2.00

150th anniv. of the death of Adm. William Bligh (1754-1817), captain of the Bounty and principal discoverer of the Fiji Islands.

Simmonds "Spartan" Seaplane — A54

Designs: 6p, Fiji Airways Hawker-Siddeley H748 and emblems of various airlines. 1sh, Fokker "Southern Cross," Capt. Charles Kingsford-Smith, his crew and Southern Cross constellation. 2sh, Lockheed Altair "Lady Southern Cross."

Perf. 14x14½

1968, June 5 Wmk. 314

236 A54 2p green & black .30 .30
237 A54 6p brt blue, car & blk .30 .30
238 A54 1sh dp violet & green .50 .50
239 A54 2sh orange brn & dk blue .90 .90
Nos. 236-239 (4) 2.00 2.00

40th anniv. of the first Trans-Pacific Flight through Fiji under Capt. Charles Kingsford-Smith.

Fijian Bures — A55

Eastern Reef Heron — A56

1p, Passion fruit flowers. 2p, Nautilus pompilius shell. 4p, Hawk moth. 6p, Reef butterflyfish. 9p, Bamboo raft (bilibili). 10p, Tiger moth. 1sh, Black marlin. 1sh6p, Orange-breasted honey eaters. 2sh, Ringed sea snake, horiz. 2sh6p, Outrigger canoes (takia), horiz. 3sh, Golden cowrie shell. 4sh, Emperor gold mine and gold ore. 5sh, Bamboo orchids, horiz. 10sh, Tabua (ceremonial whale's tooth). £1, Coat of Arms and Queen Elizabeth II, horiz.

Perf. 13½ (A55), 14 (A56)

1968, July 15 Photo. Wmk. 314

240 A55 ½p multicolored .20 .20
241 A55 1p multicolored .20 .20
242 A55 2p multicolored .20 .20
243 A56 3p multicolored .30 .20
244 A55 4p multicolored .65 .20
245 A55 6p multicolored .25 .30
246 A55 9p multicolored .20 .45
247 A55 10p multicolored 1.00 .60
248 A56 1sh multicolored 1.25 .65
249 A56 1sh6p multicolored 2.75 .75
250 A56 2sh multicolored 1.50 1.50
251 A56 2sh6p multicolored 1.50 1.50
252 A55 3sh multicolored 3.00 2.00
253 A56 4sh multicolored 5.25 1.75
254 A56 5sh multicolored 2.60 2.25
255 A56 10sh multicolored 4.00 3.50
256 A56 £1 red & multi 5.00 4.00
Nos. 240-256 (17) 29.85 20.25

See Nos. 260-276.

WHO Emblem, Map of Fiji and Nurses — A57

WHO Emblem and: 9p, Medical team loading patient on stretcher on dinghy and medical ship "Vuniwai." 3sh, People playing on beach.

1968, Dec. 9 Litho. *Perf. 14*

257 A57 3p blue green & multi .20 .20
258 A57 9p brt blue & multi .30 .30
259 A57 3sh dk blue & multi .90 .90
Nos. 257-259 (3) 1.40 1.40

WHO, 20th anniv.

Types of 1968
Values in Cents and Dollars

Designs: 1c, Passion fruit flowers. 2c, Nautilus pompilius shell. 3c, Reef heron. 4c, Hawk moth. 5c, Reef butterflyfish. 6c, Fijian bures. 8c, Bamboo raft. 9c, Tiger moth. 10c, Black marlin. 15c, Orange-breasted honey-eater. 20c, Ringed sea snake, horiz. 25c, Outrigger canoes (takia), horiz. 30c, Golden cowrie shell. 40c Emperor gold mine and gold ore. 50c, Bamboo orchids, horiz. $1, Tabua (ceremonial whale's tooth). $2, Coat of Arms and Queen Elizabeth II, horiz.

Perf. 13½ (A55), 14 (A56)

1969, Jan. 13 Photo. Wmk. 314

260 A55 1c multicolored .20 .20
261 A55 2c multicolored .20 .20
262 A56 3c multicolored .50 .35
263 A55 4c multicolored 1.25 .35
264 A55 5c multicolored .20 .20
265 A55 6c multicolored .20 .20
266 A55 8c multicolored .20 .20
267 A55 9c multicolored 1.25 *1.60*
268 A56 10c multicolored .20 .20
269 A56 15c multicolored 7.25 3.50
270 A56 20c multicolored .90 .65
271 A56 25c multicolored .90 .25
272 A55 30c multicolored 5.25 1.40
273 A56 40c multicolored 6.00 3.25
274 A56 50c multicolored 3.50 .25
275 A56 $1 multicolored 5.00 2.00
276 A56 $2 red & multi 6.00 5.00
Nos. 260-276 (17) 39.00 19.80

For overprints & surcharges see #286-288, B5-B6.

Fiji Soldiers and Map of Solomon Islands A58

Designs: 10c, Flags of Fiji Military Force, soldiers in full and battle dress. 25c, Cpl. Sefanaia Sukanaivalu and Victoria Cross.

1969, June 23 Wmk. 314 *Perf. 14*

277 A58 3c emerald & multi .80 .80
278 A58 10c red & multi .95 .95
279 A58 25c black & multi 1.25 1.25
Nos. 277-279 (3) 3.00 3.00

25th anniv. of the Fiji Military Forces campaign in the Solomon Islands and of the posthumous award of the Victoria Cross to Cpl. Sefanaia Sukanaivalu.

Yachting — A59

Designs: 4c, Javelin. 20c, Winners and South Pacific Games medal.

1969, Aug. 18 Photo. *Perf. 14½x14*

280 A59 4c red, brown & blk .45 .45
281 A59 8c blue & black .60 .60
282 A59 20c olive grn, blk & ocher 1.25 1.25
Nos. 280-282 (3) 2.30 2.30

3rd South Pacific Games, Port Moresby, Papua New Guinea, Aug. 13-23.

Students in Laboratory — A60

2c, Map of South Pacific and mortarboard. 8c, Site of University at Royal New Zealand Air Force Seaplane Station, Laucala Bay, RNZAF badge and Sunderland flying boat.

1969, Nov. 10 *Perf. 14x14½*

283 A60 2c multicolored .30 .30
284 A60 8c red & multi .50 .50
285 A60 25c dk green & multi 1.40 1.40
Nos. 283-285 (3) 2.20 2.20

Inauguration of the University of the South Pacific, Laucala Bay, Suva.

Nos. 261, 268 and 271 Overprinted: "ROYAL VISIT / 1970"

1970, Mar. 4 *Perf. 13½, 14*

286 A55 2c multicolored .30 .30
287 A56 10c multicolored .40 .40
288 A55 25c multicolored 1.75 1.75
Nos. 286-288 (3) 2.45 2.45

Visit of Queen Elizabeth II, Prince Philip and Princess Anne, Mar. 4-5.

Nuns Sitting under Chaulmoogra Tree, and Chaulmoogra Fruit — A61

Designs: 10c, Paintings by Semisi Maya (former patient). No. 290, Cascade, vert. No. 291, Sea urchins, vert. 30c, Aerial view of Makogai Hospital.

Perf. 14x14½, 14½x14

1970, May 25 Photo. Wmk. 314

289 A61 2c brt pink & multi .50 .50
290 A61 10c gray green & blk .75 .75
291 A61 10c blue, car & blk .75 .75
a. Pair, #290-291 1.50 1.50
292 A61 30c orange & multi 2.00 2.00
Nos. 289-292 (4) 4.00 4.00

Closing of the Leprosy Hospital on Makogai Island in 1969.

Abel Tasman and Ship's Log, 1643 — A62

3c, Capt. James Cook & "Endeavour." 8c, Capt. William Bligh & longboat, 1789. 25c, Man of Fiji & Fijian ocean-going canoe.

1970, Aug. 18 Litho. *Perf. 13x12½*

293 A62 2c blue green & multi 1.00 1.00
294 A62 3c gray green & multi 1.25 1.25
295 A62 8c multicolored 1.50 1.50
296 A62 25c dull lilac & multi 2.25 2.25
Nos. 293-296 (4) 6.00 6.00

Discoverers and explorers of Fiji Islands.

King Cakobau and Cession Stone at Lavuka A63

Designs: 3c, Chinese, Fijian, Indian and European children. 10c, Prime Minister Ratu Sir Kamisese Mara and flag of Fiji. 25c, Fijian male dancer and Indian female dancer.

1970, Oct. 10 Wmk. 314 *Perf. 14*

297 A63 2c multicolored .25 .25
298 A63 3c multicolored .35 .35
299 A63 10c multicolored .55 .55
300 A63 25c multicolored 1.60 1.60
Nos. 297-300 (4) 2.75 2.75

Fijian independence.

Fiji Nos. 1 and 3 — A64

15c, Fiji #15, 44, 59, 81, 127, 166. 20c, Fiji Times Office, Levuka, & G. P. O., Suva.

1970, Nov. 2 Photo. *Perf. 14½x14*

Size: 35x21mm

301 A64 4c multicolored .40 .40

Size: 60x21½mm

302 A64 15c multicolored 1.10 1.10

Size: 35x21mm

303 A64 20c multicolored 1.50 1.50
Nos. 301-303 (3) 3.00 3.00

Centenary of first postage stamps of Fiji.

Gray- backed White Eyes — A65

Yellow- breasted Musk Parrots — A66

Designs: 1c, Cirrhopetalum umbellatum. 2c, Cardinal honey eaters. 3c, Calanthe furcata.4c, Bulbophyllum. 6c, Phaius tancarvilliae. 8c,Blue-crested broadbills. 10c, Acanthephippiumvitiense. 15c, Dendrobium tokai. 20c, Slaty flycatchers. 25c, Kandavu honey eaters. 30c, Dendrobium gordonii. 50c, White-throated pigeon. $1, Collared lories (kula). $2, Dendrobium platygastrium. (Orchids shown on 1c, 3c, 4c, 6c, 10c, 15c, 30c, $2.)

Wmk. 314 Upright

1971-72 Litho. *Perf. 13½x14*

305 A65 1c blk & multi ('72) .20 .20
306 A65 2c carmine & multi .20 .20
307 A65 3c multi ('72) .85 .20
308 A65 4c blk & multi ('72) .75 1.50
309 A65 5c brown & multi 2.75 .25
310 A65 6c lt bl & multi ('72) .45 .30
311 A65 8c black & multi .50 .35
312 A65 10c multi ('72) .55 .40
313 A65 15c multi ('72) 2.50 .55
314 A65 20c gray & multi 1.50 .60

Perf. 14

315 A66 25c sepia & multi 1.50 .95
316 A66 30c grn & multi ('72) 3.00 1.10
317 A66 40c blue & multi 3.50 1.50
318 A66 50c gray & multi 4.00 1.90
319 A66 $1 red & multi 6.25 3.75
320 A66 $2 multi ('72) 12.50 7.25
Nos. 305-320 (16) 41.00 21.00

Issued: 5c, 20c, 40c, 50c, 8/6; 2c, 8c, 25c, $1, 11/22; 1c, 10c, 30c, $2, 1/4; 3c, 4c, 6c, 15c, 6/23.

1972-74 Wmk. 314 Sideways

306c A65 2c ('73) .70 *11.00*
307a A65 3c ('73) 2.00 .60
308a A65 4c ('73) 6.50 .90
309a A65 5c ('73) 6.50 4.25
310a A65 6c ('73) 8.75 1.60
311a A65 8c ('73) 4.25 1.00
313a A65 15c ('73) 3.75 2.75
314a A65 20c 14.00 2.50
315a A66 25c ('73) 2.00 1.10
317a A66 40c ('74) 3.25 *8.75*
318a A66 50c ('74) 3.25 *4.25*
319a A66 $1 3.25 *6.50*
320a A66 $2 4.25 *7.00*
Nos. 306c-320a (13) 62.45 52.20

Issued: 20c, $1, $2, 11/17; 3c, 5c, 3/8; 4c, 6c, 8c, 15c, 25c, 4/11; 2c, 12/12; 40c, 50c, 3/15.

1975-77 Wmk. 373

305b A65 1c 1.00 *4.75*
306d A65 2c 1.00 *4.75*
307b A65 3c .50 *4.75*
308b A65 4c ('76) 4.50 .20
309b A65 5c 1.60 *4.75*
310b A65 6c ('76) 3.75 .20
311b A65 8c ('76) .45 .20
312b A65 10c .50 *2.25*
313b A65 15c ('76) 3.25 .50
314b A65 20c ('77) 4.75 .65
316b A66 30c ('76) 6.75 1.10
317b A66 40c ('76) 3.75 .70
318b A66 50c ('76) 3.75 .80
319b A66 $1 ('76) 3.75 1.75
320b A66 $2 ('76) 1.90 1.75
Nos. 305b-320b (15) 41.20 29.10

Issued: 1c, 2c, 3c, 5c, 10c, 4/9; 20c, 7/15; others, 9/3.

Women's Basketball — A67

Community Education — A68

1971, Sept. 6 Wmk. 314 *Perf. 14*

321 A67 8c shown .50 .50
322 A67 10c Running .75 .75
323 A67 25c Weight lifting 1.50 1.50
Nos. 321-323 (3) 2.75 2.75

4th South Pacific Games, Papeete, French Polynesia, Sept. 8-19.

1972, Feb. 7

Designs: 4c, Public health. 50c, Economic growth (farm scenes).

324 A68 2c bright rose & multi .20 .20
325 A68 4c gray & multi .30 .30
326 A68 50c bright blue & multi 2.00 2.00
Nos. 324-326 (3) 2.50 2.50

South Pacific Commission, 25th anniv.

Arts Festival Emblem — A69

Rugby — A70

1972, Apr. 10

327 A69 10c blue, org & black .50 .50

South Pacific Festival of Arts, May 6-20.

Silver Wedding Issue, 1972
Common Design Type

Queen Elizabeth II, Prince Philip, flowers, shells.

1972, Nov. 20 Photo. *Perf. 14x14½*

328 CD324 10c slate grn & multi .40 .40
329 CD324 25c red lilac & multi .60 .60

1973, Mar. 9 Litho. *Perf. 14*

330 A70 2c shown .40 .40
331 A70 8c Tackle .80 .80
332 A70 25c Kicking ball 1.25 1.25
Nos. 330-332 (3) 2.45 2.45

60th anniversary of Fiji Rugby Union.

Forestry Development — A71

Development projects: 8c, Irrigation of rice field. 10c, Low income housing. 25c, Highway construction.

1973, July 23 *Perf. 14*

333 A71 5c multicolored .30 .30
334 A71 8c multicolored .40 .40
335 A71 10c multicolored .45 .45
336 A71 25c multicolored 1.25 1.25
Nos. 333-336 (4) 2.40 2.40

Holy Family — A72

Runners — A73

Festivals: 10c, Diwali (Candles; Indian New Year). 20c, Id-Ul-Fitar (Friendly greeting and mosque; Moslem, Ramadan). 25c, Chinese New Year (dragon dance).

1973, Oct. 26 *Perf. 14x14½*

337 A72 3c blue & multi .45 .45
338 A72 10c purple & multi .45 .45
339 A72 20c emerald & multi .75 .75
340 A72 25c red & multi .75 .75
Nos. 337-340 (4) 2.40 2.40

Festivals celebrated by various groups in Fiji.

1974, Jan. 7

341 A73 3c shown .60 .35
342 A73 8c Boxing .60 .35
343 A73 50c Lawn bowling 2.25 2.25
Nos. 341-343 (3) 3.45 2.95

10th British Commonwealth Games, Christchurch, N.Z., Jan. 24-Feb. 2.

Centenary of Cricket in Fiji — A74

Designs: 3c, Bowler. 25c, Batsman and wicketkeeper. 40c, Fielder, horiz.

Perf. 14x14½, 14½x14

1974, Feb. 21 Litho.

344 A74 3c multicolored 1.00 1.00
345 A74 25c multicolored 1.40 1.40
346 A74 40c multicolored 1.60 1.60
Nos. 344-346 (3) 4.00 4.00

Mailman and UPU Emblem A75

UPU Emblem and: 8c, Loading mail on ship. 30c, Post office and truck. 50c, Jet.

1974, May 22 Wmk. 314 *Perf. 14*

347 A75 3c orange & multi .40 .40
348 A75 8c multicolored .45 .45
349 A75 30c lt blue & multi .75 .75
350 A75 50c multicolored 1.40 1.40
Nos. 347-350 (4) 3.00 3.00

Centenary of the Universal Postal Union.

Cub Scouts A76

Designs: 10c, Boy Scouts reading map. 40c, Scouts and Fiji flag, vert.

1974, Aug. 30

351 A76 3c multicolored .25 .25
352 A76 10c multicolored .75 .75
353 A76 40c multicolored 2.00 2.00
Nos. 351-353 (3) 3.00 3.00

First National Boy Scout Jamboree, Lautoka, Viti Levu Island.

Cakobau Club and Flag — A77

King Cakobau, Queen Victoria A78

Design: 50c, Signing ceremony at Levuka.

1974, Oct. 9 Litho. *Perf. 13½x13*

354 A77 3c multicolored .20 .20
355 A78 8c multicolored .40 .40
356 A78 50c multicolored 1.10 1.10
Nos. 354-356 (3) 1.70 1.70

Deed of Cession, cent. and 4th anniv. of independence.

Diwali, Hindu Festival of Lights — A79

Designs: 15c, Id-Ul-Fitar (women exchanging greetings under moon). 25c, Chinese New Year (girl twirling streamer, and fireworks). 30c, Christmas (man and woman singing hymns, and star).

1975, Oct. 31 Wmk. 373 *Perf. 14*

357 A79 3c black & multi .20 .20
358 A79 15c black & multi .45 .45
359 A79 25c black & multi .90 .90
360 A79 30c black & multi 1.10 1.10
a. Souvenir sheet of 4, #357-360 7.00 7.00
Nos. 357-360 (4) 2.65 2.65

Festivals celebrated by various groups in Fiji.

Steam Locomotive No. 21 — A80

Sugar mill trains: 15c, Diesel locomotive No. 8. 20c, Diesel locomotive No. 1. 30c, Free passenger train.

1976, Jan. 26 Litho. *Perf. 14½*

361 A80 4c yellow & multi .45 .45
362 A80 15c salmon & multi 1.10 1.10
363 A80 20c multicolored 1.50 1.50
364 A80 30c blue & multi 2.25 2.25
Nos. 361-364 (4) 5.30 5.30

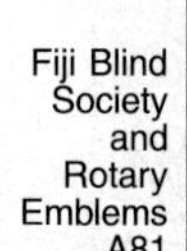

Fiji Blind Society and Rotary Emblems A81

Rotary Intl. of Fiji, 40th Anniv.: 25c, Ambulance and Rotary emblems.

Perf. 13x13½

1976, Mar. 26 Wmk. 373

365 A81 10c lt green, brn, ultra .40 .40
366 A81 25c multicolored 1.00 1.00

De Havilland Drover — A82

Planes: 15c, BAC One-Eleven. 25c, Hawker-Siddeley 748. 30c, Britten Norman Trislander.

1976, Sept. 1 Litho. *Perf. 14*

367 A82 4c multicolored .20 .20
368 A82 15c multicolored .80 .80
369 A82 25c multicolored 2.00 2.00
370 A82 30c multicolored 2.25 2.25
Nos. 367-370 (4) 5.25 5.25

Fiji air service, 25th anniversary.

Queen's Visit, 1970 — A83

Designs: 25c, King Edward's Chair. 30c, Queen wearing cloth-of-gold supertunica.

1977, Feb. 7 Litho. *Perf. 14x13½*

371 A83 10c silver & multi .25 .25
372 A83 25c silver & multi .75 .75
373 A83 30c silver & multi .90 .90
Nos. 371-373 (3) 1.90 1.90

25th anniv. of reign of Elizabeth II.

World Map, Sinusoidal Projection — A84

Design: 30c, Map showing Fiji Islands.

Wmk. 373

1977, Apr. 12 Litho. *Perf. 14½*

374 A84 4c multicolored .20 .20
375 A84 30c multicolored 1.10 1.10

First Joint Council of Ministers Conference of the European Economic Community (EEC) and of African, Caribbean and Pacific States (ACP).

Hibiscus A85

1977, Aug. 27 Wmk. 373 *Perf. 14*

376 A85 4c red .20 .20
377 A85 15c orange .40 .35
378 A85 30c pink .90 .70
379 A85 35c yellow 1.10 .90
Nos. 376-379 (4) 2.60 2.15

Fiji Hibiscus Festival, 21st anniversary.

Drua, Double Canoe A86

Canoes: 15c, Tabilai. 25c, Takia, dugout outrigger canoe. 40c, Camakau.

1977, Nov. 7 Litho. *Perf. 14½*

380 A86 4c multicolored .20 .20
381 A86 15c multicolored .40 .30
382 A86 25c multicolored .70 .60
383 A86 40c multicolored .90 *.90*
Nos. 380-383 (4) 2.20 2.00

Elizabeth II Coronation Anniversary Issue

Common Design Types
Souvenir Sheet
Unwmk.

1978, Apr. 21 Litho. *Perf. 15*

384	Sheet of 6	3.25	3.25
a.	CD326 25c White hart of Richard II	.60	.60
b.	CD327 25c Elizabeth II	.60	.60
c.	CD328 25c Banded iguana	.60	.60

No. 384 contains 2 se-tenant strips of Nos. 348a-348c, separated by horizontal gutter.

Southern Cross on Naselai Beach — A87

4c, Fiji Defence Force surrounding Southern Cross. 25c, Wright Flyer. 30c, Bristol F2B.

1978, June 26 Wmk. 373 *Perf. 14½*

385	A87	4c multicolored	.20	.20
386	A87	15c multicolored	.40	.30
387	A87	25c multicolored	.75	.60
388	A87	30c multicolored	1.10	.75
		Nos. 385-388 (4)	2.45	1.85

50th anniv. of Kingsford-Smith's Trans-Pacific flight, May 31-June 10, 1928 (4c, 15c); 75th anniv. of Wright brothers' first powered flight, Dec. 17, 1903 (25c); 60th anniv. of Royal Air Force, Apr. 1, 1918 (30c).

Necklace of Sperm Whale Teeth A88

Fiji artifacts: 4c, Wooden oil dish in shape of man, vert. 25c, Twin water bottles. 30c, Carved throwing club (Ula), vert.

1978, Aug. 14 Litho. *Perf. 14*

389	A88	4c multicolored	.30	.30
390	A88	15c multicolored	.35	.35
391	A88	25c multicolored	.60	.60
392	A88	30c multicolored	.75	.75
		Nos. 389-392 (4)	2.00	2.00

Christmas Wreath and Candles A89

Festivals: 15c, Diwali (oil lamps). 25c, Id-Ul-Fitr (fruit, coffeepot and cups). 40c, Chinese New Year (paper dragon).

1978, Oct. 30 *Perf. 14*

393	A89	4c multicolored	.25	.25
394	A89	15c multicolored	.35	.35
395	A89	25c multicolored	.55	.55
396	A89	40c multicolored	.85	.85
		Nos. 393-396 (4)	2.00	2.00

Banded Iguana A90

Endangered species and Wildlife Fund emblem: 15c, Tree frog. 25c, Long-legged warbler. 30c, Pink-billed parrot finch.

1979, Mar. 19 Litho. Wmk. 373

397	A90	4c multicolored	*2.00*	*2.00*
398	A90	15c multicolored	*5.00*	*5.00*
399	A90	25c multicolored	*8.00*	*8.00*
400	A90	30c multicolored	*10.00*	*10.00*
		Nos. 397-400 (4)	*25.00*	*25.00*

Indian Women Making Music A91

15c, Indian men sitting around kava bowl. 30c, Indian sugar cane, houses. 40c, Sailing ship Leonidas, map of South Pacific.

1979, May 11 Wmk. 373 *Perf. 14*

401	A91	4c multicolored	.20	.20
402	A91	15c multicolored	.25	.25
403	A91	30c multicolored	.45	.45
404	A91	40c multicolored	.65	.65
		Nos. 401-404 (4)	1.55	1.55

Arrival of Indians as indentured laborers, cent.

Soccer A92

Games Emblem and: 15c, Rugby. 30c, Tennis. 40c, Weight lifting.

1979, July 2 Litho. *Perf. 14*

405	A92	4c multicolored	.30	.30
406	A92	15c multicolored	.45	.45
407	A92	30c multicolored	.90	.90
408	A92	40c multicolored	1.25	1.25
		Nos. 405-408 (4)	2.90	2.90

6th South Pacific Games.

Old Town Hall, Suva A93

2c, Dudley Church, Suva. 3c, Telecommunications building, Suva. 4c, 5c, Lautoka Mosque. 6c, GPO, Suva. 8c, 12c, Levuka Public School. 10c, Visitors' Bureau, Suva. 15c, Colonial War Memorial Hospital Suva. 18c, Labasa Sugar Mill. 20c, Rewa Bridge, Nausori. 30c Sacred Heart Cathedral, Suva. 35c Grand Pacific Hotel, Suva. 45c, Shiva Temple, Suva. 50c Serua Island Village. $1, Solo Lighthouse. $2, Baker memorial Hall, Nausori. $5, Government House.

1979-91 Wmk. 373 *Perf. 14*

409	A93	1c multi	.20	.20
410	A93	2c multi	.20	.20
411	A93	3c multi	.20	.20
411B	A93	4c multi	.20	.20
412	A93	5c multi	.20	.20
413	A93	6c multi	.20	.20
414	A93	10c multi	.20	.20
415	A93	12c multi	.20	.20
416	A93	15c multi	.20	.20
417	A93	18c multi	.25	.25
418	A93	20c multi	.30	.30
419	A93	30c multi, vert.	.35	.35
420	A93	35c multi	.40	.40
421	A93	45c multi	.45	.45
422	A93	50c multi	.60	.60

Perf. 14x13½, 13½x14

Size: 29x45mm, 45x29mm

423	A93	$1 multi, vert.	1.10	1.10
424	A93	$2 multi	2.25	2.25

Size: 48x31mm

425	A93	$5 multi	5.50	5.50
		Nos. 409-425 (18)	13.00	13.00

All denominations except 4c issued without inscribed dates. 4c inscribed 1991. Reissues include: 1c inscribed 1994; 2c inscribed 1983, 1986, 1991, 1993 and 1994; 3c inscribed 1993; 4c inscribed 1993 and 1994; 10c inscribed 1991; 12c inscribed 1993 and 1994; 15c inscribed 1991; 20c inscribed 1993 and 1994; 50c inscribed 1994.

Issued: 5c, 6c, 12c, 18c, 35c-$2, 12/22/80; #411B, 11/1991; others, 11/11/79.

1986-91 Wmk. 384

409a	A93	1c	.50	.50
410a	A93	2c	.50	.50
411a	A93	3c	.50	.50
411c	A93	4c	.55	.55
413A	A93	8c	.55	.55
414a	A93	10c	.55	.55
416a	A93	15c	.55	.55
418a	A93	20c	.90	1.10
420a	A93	35c	1.10	1.40
422a	A93	50c	1.75	2.00
423a	A93	$1	3.25	4.00
		Nos. 409a-423a (11)	10.70	12.20

1c inscribed 1991, reissued inscribed 1992; 2c inscribed 1986, reissued inscribed 1988 and 1991; 3c inscribed 1988, reissued inscribed 1991 and 1992; 4c inscribed 1988, reissued inscribed 1991 and 1992; 8c inscribed 1986; 10c inscribed 1990, reissued inscribed 1991; 15c inscribed 1991, reissued inscribed 1992; 20c inscribed 1988, reissued inscribed 1990 and 1992; 35c, 50c and $1 each inscribed 1991, each reissued inscribed 1992.

Issued: 2c, 4/86; 8c, 12/1/86; 3c, 4c, 20c, 6/1/88; 10c, 3/1/90; 1c, 15c, 35c, 50c, $1, 3/11/90.

Southern Cross, 1873, London 1980 Emblem A94

1980, Apr. 28 Wmk. 373 *Perf. 13½*

426	A94	6c shown	.25	.25
427	A94	20c Levuka, 1910	.30	.30
428	A94	45c Matua, 1936	.70	.70
429	A94	50c Oronsay, 1951	.75	.75
		Nos. 426-429 (4)	2.00	2.00

London 80 Intl. Stamp Exhib., May 6-14.

Sovi Bay A95

1980, Aug. 18 *Perf. 13½x14*

430	A95	6c shown	.20	.20
431	A95	20c Yanuca Island, evening scene	.25	.25
432	A95	45c Dravuni Beach	.55	.55
433	A95	50c Wakaya Island	.65	.65
		Nos. 430-433 (4)	1.65	1.65

Opening of Parliament, 1979 — A96

1980, Oct. 6 Litho. *Perf. 13*

434	A96	6c shown	.20	.20
435	A96	20c Coat of arms, vert.	.25	.25
436	A96	45c Fiji flag	.50	.50
437	A96	50c Elizabeth II, vert.	.60	.60
		Nos. 434-437 (4)	1.55	1.55

Independence, 10th anniversary.

Coastal Scene, by Semisi Maya A97

Intl. Year of the Disabled: Paintings and portrait of disabled artist Semisi Maya.

1981, Apr. 21 Wmk. 373 *Perf. 14*

438	A97	6c shown	.20	.20
439	A97	35c Underwater Scene	.45	.45
440	A97	50c Maya Painting, vert.	.60	.60
441	A97	60c Peacock, vert.	.75	.75
		Nos. 438-441 (4)	2.00	2.00

Royal Wedding Issue

Common Design Type

1981, July 22 Wmk. 373 *Perf. 14*

442	CD331	6c Bouquet	.20	.20
443	CD331	45c Charles	.50	.50
444	CD331	$1 Couple	1.10	1.10
		Nos. 442-444 (3)	1.80	1.80

Operator Assistance Center — A98

1981, Aug. 7 Litho. *Perf. 14*

445	A98	6c shown	.25	.20
446	A98	35c Microwave station, map	.60	.55
447	A98	50c Satellite earth station	1.00	.75
448	A98	60c Cableship Retriever	1.10	.90
		Nos. 445-448 (4)	2.95	*2.40*

World Food Day — A99

1981, Sept. 21 Litho. *Perf. 14½x14*

449	A99	20c multicolored	.50	.50

Ratu Sir Lala Sukuna, First Legislative Council Speaker — A100

1981, Oct. 19 Litho. *Perf. 14*

450	A100	6c shown	.20	.20
451	A100	35c Mace, flag	.55	.55
452	A100	50c Suva Civic Center	.75	.75
		Nos. 450-452 (3)	1.50	1.50

Souvenir Sheet

453	A100	60c Emblem, participants' flags	.90	.90

27th Commonwealth Parliamentary Assoc. Conf., Suva.

World War II Aircraft A101

1981, Dec. 7 Litho. *Perf. 14*

454	A101	6c Bell P-39 Aircobra	1.10	.20
455	A101	18c Consolidated PBY-5 Catalina	2.40	.30
456	A101	35c Curtiss P-40 Warhawk	4.00	.65
457	A101	60c Short Singapore	4.50	1.00
		Nos. 454-457 (4)	12.00	2.15

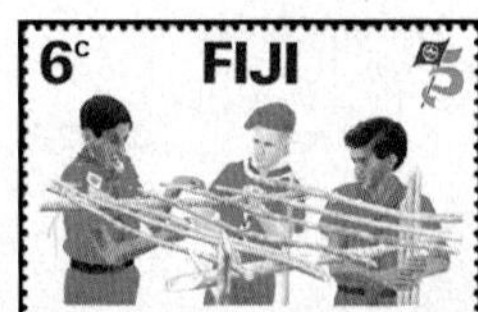

Scouting Year A102

1982, Feb. 22 Litho. *Perf. 14½*

458	A102	6c Building	.25	.25
459	A102	20c Sailing, vert.	.40	.40
460	A102	45c Campfire	.85	.85
461	A102	60c Baden-Powell, vert.	1.10	1.10
		Nos. 458-461 (4)	2.60	2.60

Disciplined Forces — A103

1982, May 10 Wmk. 373 *Perf. 14*

462 A103 12c UN checkpoint .50 .20
463 A103 30c Construction project 1.25 .50
464 A103 40c Police, car 2.00 .65
465 A103 70c Navy ship 2.25 *1.25*
Nos. 462-465 (4) 6.00 2.60

1982 World Cup A104

1982, June 15 Litho. *Perf. 14*

466 A104 6c Fiji Soccer Assoc. emblem .20 .20
467 A104 18c Flag, ball .30 .30
468 A104 50c Stadium .80 .80
469 A104 90c Emblem 1.50 1.50
Nos. 466-469 (4) 2.80 2.80

Princess Diana Issue
Common Design Type

1982, July 1 *Perf. 14½x14*

470 CD333 20c Arms .60 .60
471 CD333 35c Diana 1.00 1.00
472 CD333 45c Wedding 1.50 1.50
473 CD333 $1 Portrait 3.25 3.25
Nos. 470-473 (4) 6.35 6.35

October Royal Visit — A105

1982, Nov. 1 Litho. *Perf. 14*

474 A105 6c Duke of Edinburgh .20 .20
475 A105 45c Elizabeth II .80 .80

Souvenir Sheet

476 Sheet of 3 3.75 3.75
c. A105 $1 Britannia 1.60 1.60

No. 476 contains Nos. 474-475 and 476c.

Christmas A106

1982, Nov. 22 *Perf. 14x14½*

477 A106 6c Holy Family .20 .20
478 A106 20c Adoration of the Kings .40 .40
479 A106 35c Carolers .75 .75
Nos. 477-479 (3) 1.35 1.35

Souvenir Sheet

480 A106 $1 Faith, from The Three Virtues, by Raphael 2.00 2.00

Red-throated Lory — A107

Parrots.

1983, Feb. 14 Litho. *Perf. 14*

481 A107 20c shown 1.50 1.50
482 A107 40c Blue-crowned lory 2.25 2.25
483 A107 55c Sulphur-breasted musk parrot 3.50 3.50
484 A107 70c Red-breasted musk parrot 4.25 4.25
Nos. 481-484 (4) 11.50 11.50

A108

1983, Mar. 14

485 A108 8c Traditional house .20 .20
486 A108 25c Barefoot firewalkers .35 .35
487 A108 50c Sugar cane crop .70 .70
488 A108 80c Kava Yagona ceremony 1.10 1.10
Nos. 485-488 (4) 2.35 2.35

Commonwealth Day.

Manned Flight Bicentenary — A109

1983, July 18 Wmk. 373 *Perf. 14*

489 A109 8c Montgolfiere, 1783 .45 .20
490 A109 20c Wright Flyer .55 .35
491 A109 25c DC-3 .65 .40
492 A109 40c DeHavilland Comet 1.00 .70
493 A109 50c Boeing 747 1.25 .85
494 A109 58c Columbia space shuttle 1.60 1.00
Nos. 489-494 (6) 5.50 3.50

Cordia Subcordata A110

Earth Satellite Station, Fijian Playing Lali A111

Flowers.

1983, Sept. 26 Litho. *Perf. 14*

495 A110 8c shown .20 .20
496 A110 25c Gmelina vitiensis .35 .35
497 A110 40c Carruthersia scandens .60 .60
498 A110 $1 Amylotheca insularum 1.50 1.50
Nos. 495-498 (4) 2.65 2.65

See Nos. 505-508.

Perf. 14x13½

1983, Nov. 7 Wmk. 373

499 A111 50c multicolored .85 .85

Dacryopinax Spathularia A112

Various fungi.

1984, Jan. 9 *Perf. 14x13½, 13½x14*

500 A112 8c shown .65 .20
501 A112 15c Podoscypha involuta 1.10 .45
502 A112 40c Lentinus squarrosulus 2.25 1.10
503 A112 50c Scleroderma flavidum 3.50 1.50
504 A112 $1 Phillipsia domingensis 6.50 2.75
Nos. 500-504 (5) 14.00 6.00

Flower Type of 1983

1984 Litho. *Perf. 14x14½*

505 A110 15c Pseuderanthemum laxiflorum .25 .25
506 A110 20c Storkiella vitiensis .30 .30
507 A110 50c Paphia vitiensis .80 .80
508 A110 70c Elaeocarpus storkii 1.10 1.10
Nos. 505-508 (4) 2.45 2.45

Lloyd's List Issue
Common Design Type
Perf. 14½x14

1984, May 7 Wmk. 373

509 CD335 8c Tui Lau on reef .40 .40
510 CD335 40c Tofua 1.50 1.50
511 CD335 55c Canberra 2.00 2.00
512 CD335 60c Suva Wharf 2.25 2.25
Nos. 509-512 (4) 6.15 6.15

Souvenir Sheet

1984 UPU Congress — A113

1984, June 14 Litho. *Perf. 14½*

513 A113 25c Map 2.25 2.25

Ausipex '84 — A114

1984, Sept. 17 Wmk. 373 *Perf. 14*

514 A114 8c Yalavou cattle .20 .20
515 A114 25c Wailoa Power Station, vert. .50 .50
516 A114 40c Boeing 737 .80 .80
517 A114 $1 Cargo ship Fua Kavenga 2.10 2.10
Nos. 514-517 (4) 3.60 3.60

Christmas A115

1984, Nov. 5 Litho. *Perf. 14*

518 A115 8c Church on hill .20 .20
519 A115 20c Sailing .35 .35
520 A115 25c Santa, children, tree .40 .40
521 A115 40c Going to church .65 .65
522 A115 $1 Family, tree, vert. 1.75 1.75
Nos. 518-522 (5) 3.35 3.35

Butterflies A116

1985, Feb. 4 *Perf. 14*

523 A116 8c Monarch 1.00 .25
524 A116 25c Common eggfly 2.50 .80
525 A116 40c Long-tailed blue, vert. 3.75 1.25
526 A116 $1 Meadow argus, vert. 9.50 3.25
Nos. 523-526 (4) 16.75 5.55

EXPO '85, Tsukuba, Japan — A117

1985, Mar. 18 Litho. *Perf. 14*

527 A117 20c Outrigger canoe, Toberua Isl. .50 .45
528 A117 25c Wainivula Falls .55 .50
529 A117 50c Mana Island 1.25 1.10
530 A117 $1 Sawa-I-Lau Caves 2.50 2.25
Nos. 527-530 (4) 4.80 4.30

Queen Mother 85th Birthday Issue
Common Design Type
Perf. 14½x14

1985, June 7 Wmk. 384

531 CD336 8c Holding Prince Andrew .20 .20
532 CD336 25c With Prince Charles .50 .50
533 CD336 40c On Oaks Day, Epsom Races .80 .80
534 CD336 50c Holding Prince Henry 1.00 1.00
Nos. 531-534 (4) 2.50 2.50

Souvenir Sheet

535 CD336 $1 In Royal Wedding Cavalcade, 1981 2.75 2.75

Shallow Water Fish A118

1985, Sept. 23 *Perf. 14½*

536 A118 40c Horned squirrel fish 1.40 1.00
537 A118 50c Yellow-banded goatfish 2.00 1.25
538 A118 55c Fairy cod 2.10 1.40
539 A118 $1 Peacock rock cod 3.75 2.50
Nos. 536-539 (4) 9.25 6.15

Sea Birds — A119

1985, Nov. 4 *Perf. 14*

540 A119 15c Collared petrel 1.10 .40
541 A119 20c Lesser frigate bird 2.10 .65
542 A119 50c Brown booby 5.50 1.50
543 A119 $1 Crested tern 10.00 3.75
Nos. 540-543 (4) 18.70 6.30

Queen Elizabeth II 60th Birthday Issue
Common Design Type

20c, With the Duke of York at the Royal Tournament, 1936. 25c, On Buckingham Palace balcony, wedding of Princess Margaret and Anthony Armstrong-Jones, 1960. 40c, Inspecting the Guard of Honor, Suva, 1982. 50c, State visit to Luxembourg, 1976. $1, Visiting Crown Agents' offices, 1983.

Perf. 14x14½

1986, Apr. 21 Wmk. 384

544 CD337 20c scar, blk & sil .40 .40
545 CD337 25c ultra & multi .45 .45
546 CD337 40c green & multi .75 .75
547 CD337 50c violet & multi .95 .95
548 CD337 $1 rose vio & multi 1.90 1.90
Nos. 544-548 (5) 4.45 4.45

Intl. Peace Year — A120

Halley's Comet — A121

1986, June 23 Wmk. 373 *Perf. 14½*

No.	Type	Value	Description	Unused	Used
549	A120	8c	shown	.20	.20
550	A120	40c	Dove	.75	.75

1986, July 7 *Perf. 13½*

No.	Type	Value	Description	Unused	Used
551	A121	25c	Newton's reflector telescope	.60	.45
552	A121	40c	Comet over Lomaiviti	.90	.75
553	A121	$1	Comet nucleus, Giotto probe	4.50	1.90
			Nos. 551-553 (3)	6.00	3.10

Reptiles and Amphibians — A122

1986, Aug. 1 *Perf. 14½*

No.	Type	Value	Description	Unused	Used
554	A122	8c	Ground frog	.30	.20
555	A122	20c	Burrowing snake	.50	*.55*
556	A122	25c	Spotted gecko	.55	*.70*
557	A122	40c	Crested iguana	.90	*1.00*
558	A122	50c	Blotched skink	2.25	1.25
559	A122	$1	Speckled skink	4.50	2.75
			Nos. 554-559 (6)	9.00	6.45

Ancient War Clubs — A123

Cone Shells — A124

1986, Nov. 10 Wmk. 384 *Perf. 14*

No.	Type	Value	Description	Unused	Used
560	A123	25c	Gatawaka	.75	.65
561	A123	40c	Siriti	1.00	.85
562	A123	50c	Bulibuli	1.25	1.10
563	A123	$1	Culacula	2.75	2.40
			Nos. 560-563 (4)	5.75	5.00

1987, Feb. 26 Litho. *Perf. 14x14½*

No.	Type	Value	Description	Unused	Used
564	A124	15c	Weasel	.60	.35
565	A124	20c	Pertusus	.65	.45
566	A124	25c	Admiral	1.10	.60
567	A124	40c	Leaden	1.40	.95
568	A124	50c	Imperial	2.75	1.25
569	A124	$1	Geography	5.50	2.50
			Nos. 564-569 (6)	12.00	6.10

Souvenir Sheet

Tagimoucia Flower — A125

1987, Apr. 23 Wmk. 373 *Perf. 14½*

No.	Type	Value	Description	Unused	Used
570	A125	$1	multicolored	4.00	2.75

No. 570 Overprinted with CAPEX '87 Emblem

1987, June 13

No.	Type	Value	Description	Unused	Used
571	A125	$1	multicolored	20.00	20.00

Intl. Year of Shelter for the Homeless A126

1987, July 20 *Perf. 14*

No.	Type	Value	Description	Unused	Used
572	A126	55c	Hut	.70	.70
573	A126	70c	Government housing	.95	.95

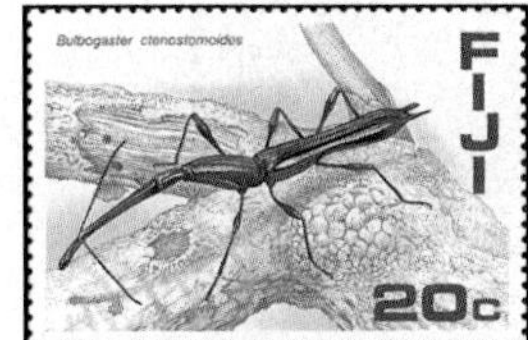

Beetles — A127

1987, Sept. 7 Wmk. 384

No.	Type	Value	Description	Unused	Used
574	A127	20c	Bulbogaster ctenostomoides	1.00	.45
575	A127	25c	Paracupta flaviventris	1.60	.60
576	A127	40c	Cerambyrhynchus schoenherri	2.00	.90
577	A127	50c	Rhinoscapha lagopyga	3.50	1.10
578	A127	$1	Xixuthrus heros	7.50	2.25
			Nos. 574-578 (5)	15.60	5.30

Christmas — A128

1987, Nov. 19

No.	Type	Value	Description	Unused	Used
579	A128	8c	Holy Family, vert.	.25	.20
580	A128	40c	Shepherds see star	1.00	.65
581	A128	50c	Three Kings follow star	2.75	.75
582	A128	$1	Adoration of the Magi	5.75	1.50
			Nos. 579-582 (4)	9.75	3.10

World Expo '88, Apr. 30-Oct. 30, Brisbane, Australia A129

1988, Apr. 27 Litho. *Perf. 14*

No.	Type	Value	Description	Unused	Used
583	A129	30c	Windsurfing	1.75	1.75

Intl. Council of Women, Cent. A130

1988, June 14

No.	Type	Value	Description	Unused	Used
584	A130	45c	Fiji Nouna	.80	.80

Pottery A131

Wmk. 384, 373 (69c)

1988, Aug. 29 Litho. *Perf. 13½*

No.	Type	Value	Description	Unused	Used
585	A131	9c	Lapita (bowl)	.20	.20
586	A131	23c	Kuro (cooking pot)	.30	.30
587	A131	58c	Saqa (ritual drinking vessel)	.70	.70
588	A131	63c	Saqa, diff.	.75	.75
589	A131	69c	Ramarama (oil lamp)	.80	.80
590	A131	75c	Kuro, diff., vert.	.90	.90
			Nos. 585-590 (6)	3.65	3.65

Fiji Tree Frog — A132

Indigenous Flowering Plants — A133

1988, Oct. 3 Wmk. 384 *Perf. 14*

No.	Type	Value	Description	Unused	Used
591	A132	18c	multi	4.50	4.50
592	A132	23c	multi, diff.	5.25	5.25
593	A132	30c	multi, diff.	6.50	6.50
594	A132	45c	multi, diff.	11.00	11.00
			Nos. 591-594 (4)	27.25	27.25

World Wildlife Fund.

1988, Nov. 21 Wmk. 373

No.	Type	Value	Description	Unused	Used
595	A133	9c	Dendrobium mohlianum	.20	.20
596	A133	30c	Dendrobium cattilare	.60	.55
597	A133	45c	Degeneria vitiensis	.85	.75
598	A133	$1	Degeneria roseiflora	2.25	1.75
			Nos. 595-598 (4)	3.90	3.25

Intl. Red Cross and Red Crescent Orgs., 125th Anniv. — A134

1989, Feb. 6 Wmk. 384

No.	Type	Value	Description	Unused	Used
599	A134	58c	Battle of Solferino, 1859	1.25	.80
600	A134	63c	Jean-Henri Dunant, vert.	1.50	.85
601	A134	69c	Medicine	1.60	.95
602	A134	$1	Anniv. emblem, vert.	3.50	1.40
			Nos. 599-602 (4)	7.85	4.00

Epic Voyage of William Bligh A135

Designs: 45c, Plans (line drawing) of the Bounty's launch. 58c, Diary and inscription on artifacts "The cup I eat my miserable allowance out of." 80c, Silhouette, lightning, quote "O Almighty God, relieve us. . ." $1, Map of Bligh's Islands, launch and compass rose.

1989, Apr. 28 *Perf. 14½*

No.	Type	Value	Description	Unused	Used
603	A135	45c	multicolored	1.90	.65
604	A135	58c	multicolored	2.40	.85
605	A135	80c	multicolored	4.00	1.10
606	A135	$1	multicolored	5.50	1.40
			Nos. 603-606 (4)	13.80	4.00

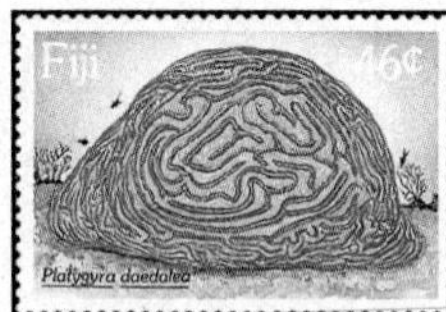

Coral A136

1989, Aug. 21 Wmk. 373 *Perf. 14*

No.	Type	Value	Description	Unused	Used
607	A136	46c	Platygyra daedalea	2.40	2.40
608	A136	60c	Caulastrea furcata	3.00	3.00
609	A136	75c	Acropora echinata	3.75	3.75
610	A136	90c	Acropora humilis	4.75	4.75
			Nos. 607-610 (4)	13.90	13.90

Nos. 609-610 vert.

1990 World Cup Soccer Championships, Italy — A137

Various Fijian soccer players.

1989, Sept. 25 Wmk. 384 *Perf. 14½*

No.	Type	Value	Description	Unused	Used
611	A137	35c	shown	1.60	1.60
612	A137	63c	multi, diff.	2.50	2.50
613	A137	70c	multi, diff.	3.00	3.00
614	A137	85c	multi, diff.	3.50	3.50
			Nos. 611-614 (4)	10.60	10.60

Christmas A138

1989, Nov. 1 Wmk. 373

No.	Type	Value	Description	Unused	Used
615	A138	9c	Church service	.35	.35
616	A138	45c	*Delonix regia* tree	1.10	1.10
617	A138	$1	Holy family	2.10	2.10
618	A138	$1.40	Tree, Fijian children	3.00	3.00
			Nos. 615-618 (4)	6.55	6.55

Fish A139

1990, Apr. 23 Litho. Wmk. 384

No.	Type	Value	Description	Unused	Used
619	A139	50c	Mangrove jack	2.75	2.75
620	A139	70c	Orange-spotted therapon perch	4.00	4.00
621	A139	85c	Spotted scat	4.50	4.50
622	A139	$1	Flagtail	5.50	5.50
			Nos. 619-622 (4)	16.75	16.75

Souvenir Sheet

Stamp World London '90 — A140

1990, May 1

No.	Type	Value	Description	Unused	Used
623	A140		Sheet of 2	11.00	5.00
a.			$1 No. 243	3.50	1.50
b.			$2 No. 249	7.00	3.50

Soil Conservation — A141

50c, Vertiver grass contours. 70c, Mulching. 90c, Contour cultivation. $1, Proper land use.

1990, July 23 Litho. Wmk. 373

625 A141 50c multi 1.10 1.10
626 A141 70c multi 1.60 1.60
627 A141 90c multi 2.10 2.10
628 A141 $1 multi, vert. 2.25 2.25
Nos. 625-628 (4) 7.05 7.05

Trees — A142

1990, Oct. 2

629 A142 25c Dacrydium nidulum .90 .90
630 A142 35c Decusso-carpus vitiensis 1.10 1.10
631 A142 $1 Agathis vitiensis 3.50 3.50
632 A142 $1.55 Santalum yasi 5.00 5.00
Nos. 629-632 (4) 10.50 10.50

Christmas — A143

Christmas carols: 10c, Hark! The Herald Angels Sing. 35c, Silent Night. 65c, Joy to the World! $1, The Race that Long in Darkness Pined.

1990, Nov. 26 Wmk. 373 *Perf. 14*

633 A143 10c multicolored .40 .40
634 A143 35c multicolored 1.10 1.10
635 A143 65c multicolored 2.00 2.00
636 A143 $1 multicolored 3.00 3.00
Nos. 633-636 (4) 6.50 6.50

Scenic Views — A144

1991, Feb. 25 Wmk. 384

637 A144 35c Sigatoka sand dunes 1.50 1.50
638 A144 50c Monu, Monuriki Islands 2.50 2.50
639 A144 65c Ravilevu Nature Reserve 3.00 3.00
640 A144 $1 Colo-I-Suva Forest Park 5.00 5.00
Nos. 637-640 (4) 12.00 12.00

Discovery of Rotuma Island, Bicent. A145

1991, Aug. 8 Wmk. 373 *Perf. 14*

641 A145 54c HMS Pandora 2.75 2.75
642 A145 70c Map of Rotuma Island 3.50 3.50
643 A145 75c Natives 3.75 3.75
644 A145 $1 Mt. Solroroa, Uea Island 5.00 5.00
Nos. 641-644 (4) 15.00 15.00

Crabs A146

Designs: 38c, Scylla serrata. 54c, Metopograpsus messor. 96c, Parasesarma erythrodactyla. $1.65, Cardisoma carnifex.

1991, Sept. 26 *Perf. 14½x14*

645 A146 38c multicolored 1.10 1.10
646 A146 54c multicolored 1.75 1.75
647 A146 96c multicolored 2.75 2.75
648 A146 $1.65 multicolored 5.50 5.50
Nos. 645-648 (4) 11.10 11.10

Christmas A147

Designs: 11c, Mary, Joseph travelling to Bethlehem. 75c, Manger scene. 96c, Jesus being blessed at temple in Jerusalem. $1, Baby Jesus.

1991, Oct. 31 Wmk. 384 *Perf. 14*

649 A147 11c multicolored .45 .45
650 A147 75c multicolroed 2.10 2.10
651 A147 96c multicolored 2.50 2.50
652 A147 $1 multicolored 2.50 2.50
Nos. 649-652 (4) 7.55 7.55

Air Pacific, 40th Anniv. A148

Airplanes: 54c, Dragon Rapide, Harold Gatty, founder. 75c, Douglas DC3. 96c, ATR 42. $1.40, Boeing 767.

1991, Nov. 18 *Perf. 14½*

653 A148 54c multicolored 2.50 2.50
654 A148 75c multicolored 3.00 3.00
655 A148 96c multicolored 3.75 3.75
656 A148 $1.40 multicolored 5.75 5.75
Nos. 653-656 (4) 15.00 15.00

Expo '92, Seville A149

Designs: 27c, Traditional dance and costumes. 75c, Faces of people. 96c, Train and gold bars. $1.40, Cruise ship in port.

Perf. 14½x14

1992, Mar. 23 Litho. Wmk. 373

657 A149 27c multicolored 1.25 1.25
658 A149 75c multicolored 3.25 3.25
659 A149 96c multicolored 4.75 4.75
660 A149 $1.40 multicolored 6.25 6.25
Nos. 657-660 (4) 15.50 15.50

Inter-Islands Shipping — A150

1992, June 22 *Perf. 14*

661 A150 38c Tabusoro 1.60 1.60
662 A150 54c Degei II 2.25 2.25
663 A150 $1.40 Dausoko 5.50 5.50
664 A150 $1.65 Nivanga 6.25 6.25
Nos. 661-664 (4) 15.60 15.60

1992 Summer Olympics, Barcelona — A151

1992, July 30 *Perf. 13½*

665 A151 20c Running .65 .65
666 A151 86c Yachting 2.75 2.75
667 A151 $1.34 Swimming 4.00 4.00
668 A151 $1.50 Judo 5.00 5.00
Nos. 665-668 (4) 12.40 12.40

Levuka A152

30c, European War Memorial. 42c, Map. 59c, Beach Street. 77c, Sacred Heart Church, vert. $2, Deed of Cession Site, vert.

1992, Sept. 21 *Perf. 14½*

669 A152 30c multicolored .45 .45
670 A152 42c multicolored .60 .60
671 A152 59c multicolored .90 .90
672 A152 77c multicolored 1.10 1.10
673 A152 $2 multicolored 3.25 3.25
Nos. 669-673 (5) 6.30 6.30

Intl. Planned Parenthood Federation, 40th Anniv. — A153

1992, Nov. 2 *Perf. 15x14½*

674 A153 77c Globe 1.50 1.50
675 A153 $2 Family 3.75 3.75

Christmas — A154

Bible interpretations: 12c, "God so loved the world..." 77c, "We love because God first loved us." 83c, "It is more blessed to give..." $2, "Every good gift..."

1992, Nov. 17

676 A154 12c multicolored .35 .35
677 A154 77c multicolored 1.90 1.90
678 A154 83c multicolored 2.25 2.25
679 A154 $2 multicolored 5.50 5.50
Nos. 676-679 (4) 10.00 10.00

Peace Corps in Fiji, 25th Anniv. A155

Designs: 59c, Voluntary service. 77c, Fiji/US friendship. $1, Education. $2, Income generating business through volunteer help.

Wmk. 373

1993, Feb. 22 Litho. *Perf. 14½*

680 A155 59c multicolored 1.25 1.25
681 A155 77c multicolored 1.60 1.60
682 A155 $1 multicolored 2.00 2.00
683 A155 $2 multicolored 4.25 4.25
Nos. 680-683 (4) 9.10 9.10

Hong Kong Rugby Sevens — A156

Designs: 77c, Players performing traditional Cibi Dance. $1.06, Two players, map of Fiji, Hong Kong, and Australia. $2, Stadium, players in scrum.

Perf. 14x15

1993, Mar. 26 Litho. Wmk. 384

684 A156 77c multicolored 1.75 1.75
685 A156 $1.06 multicolored 2.50 2.50
686 A156 $2 multicolored 4.50 4.50
Nos. 684-686 (3) 8.75 8.75

Royal Air Force, 75th Anniv.

Common Design Type

Designs: 59c, Gloster Gauntlet. 77c, Armstrong Whitworth Whitley. 83c, Bristol F2b. $2, Hawker Tempest.

No. 691: a, Vickers Vildebeest. b, Handley Page Hampden. c, Vickers Vimy. d, British Aerospace Hawk.

1993, Apr. 1 *Perf. 14*

687 CD350 59c multicolored 1.25 1.25
688 CD350 77c multicolored 1.60 1.60
689 CD350 83c multicolored 1.60 1.60
690 CD350 $2 multicolored 4.50 4.50
Nos. 687-690 (4) 8.95 8.95

Souvenir Sheet of 4

691 CD350 $1 #a.-d. 10.00 10.00
a. Overprinted in sheet margin 9.00 9.00

Overprint on No. 691a is exhibition emblem for Hong Kong '94.

Nudibranchs A157

Wmk. 373

1993, July 27 Litho. *Perf. 14*

692 A157 12c Chromodoris fidelis .50 .50
693 A157 42c Halgerda carlsoni 1.25 1.25
694 A157 53c Chromodoris lochi 1.75 1.75
695 A157 83c Glaucus atlanticus 2.75 2.75
696 A157 $1 Phyllidia bourguini 3.25 3.25
697 A157 $2 Hexabranchus sanguineus 6.50 6.50
Nos. 692-697 (6) 16.00 16.00

Tropical Fruit — A158

Wmk. 373

1993, Oct. 25 Litho. *Perf. 13½*

698 A158 30c Mango 1.10 1.10
699 A158 42c Guava 1.90 1.90
700 A158 $1 Lemon 4.00 4.00
701 A158 $2 Soursop 8.00 8.00
Nos. 698-701 (4) 15.00 15.00

Souvenir Sheet

Hong Kong '94 — A159

Butterflies: a, Caper white. b, Blue branded king crow. c, Vagrant. d, Glasswing.

Perf. 14½x13

1994, Feb. 18 Litho. Wmk. 373

702 A159 $1 Sheet of 4, #a.-d. 9.00 9.00

Easter A160

59c, The Last Supper. 77c, The Crucifixion. $1, The Resurrection. $2, Jesus showing his wounds to his disciples.

Perf. 14x15, 15x14

1994, Mar. 31 Litho. Wmk. 373

703 A160 59c multi 1.25 1.25
704 A160 77c multi, vert. 1.75 1.75
705 A160 $1 multi 2.00 2.00
706 A160 $2 multi, vert. 4.25 4.25
Nos. 703-706 (4) 9.25 9.25

Edible Seaweeds A161

42c, Codium bulbopilum. 83c, Coulerpa racemosa. $1, Hypnea pannosa. $2, Gracilaria.

Wmk. 384

1994, June 6 Litho. *Perf. 14*

707 A161 42c multicolored 1.25 .95
708 A161 83c multicolored 2.25 1.90
709 A161 $1 multicolored 2.75 2.40
710 A161 $2 multicolored 5.75 4.75
Nos. 707-710 (4) 12.00 10.00

Souvenir Sheet

White-Collared Kingfisher — A162

Designs: a, On branch. b, In flight.

Wmk. 373

1994, Aug. Litho. *Perf. 13½*

711 A162 $1.50 Sheet of 2, #a.-b. 12.50 12.50
c. Overprinted in sheet margin 12.00 12.00

Overprint on No. 711c consists of exhibition emblem and "JAKARTA '95."

Issued: #711, 8/16; #711c, 8/19.

Souvenir Sheet

Singpex '94 — A163

Neoveitchia storckii: a, Complete tree. b. Fruits, inflorescence.

1994, Aug. 31 Wmk. 384 *Perf. 14*

712 A163 $1.50 Sheet of 2, #a.-b. 11.00 11.00

First Catholic Missionaries in Fiji, 150th Anniv. — A164

Wmk. 373

1994, Dec. 16 Litho. *Perf. 14*

713 A164 23c Father Ioane Batita .60 .60
714 A164 31c Local catechist .70 .70
715 A164 44c Sacred Heart Cathedral .95 .95
716 A164 63c Lomary Church 1.25 1.25
717 A164 81c Pope Gregory XVI 1.75 1.75
718 A164 $2 Pope John Paul II 4.00 4.00
Nos. 713-718 (6) 9.25 9.25

Souvenir Sheet

Ecotourism in Fiji — A165

Designs: a, Waterfalls, banded iguana. b, Mountain trekking, Fiji tree frog. c, Bilibili River trip, kingfisher. d, Historic sites, flying fox.

Wmk. 373

1995, Mar. 27 Litho. *Perf. 14*

719 A165 81c Sheet of 4, #a.-d. 8.00 8.00

End of World War II, 50th Anniv.

Common Design Types

Designs: 13c, Fijian regiment guarding crashed Japanese Zero Fighter. 63c, Kameli Airstrip, Solomon Islands, built by Fijian regiment. 87c, Corp. Sukanaivalu VC, Victoria Cross. $1.12, HMS Fiji.

$2, Reverse side of War Medal 1939-45.

Wmk. 373

1995, May 8 Litho. *Perf. 13½*

720 CD351 13c multicolored .50 .50
721 CD351 63c multicolored 2.75 2.75
722 CD351 87c multicolored 3.75 3.75
723 CD351 $1.12 multicolored 5.00 5.00
Nos. 720-723 (4) 12.00 12.00

Souvenir Sheet

Perf. 14

724 CD352 $2 multicolored 5.00 5.00

Birds — A166

1995 Litho. Wmk. 373 *Perf. 13*

725 A166 1c Red-headed parrotfinch .20 .20
726 A166 2c Golden whistler .20 .20
727 A166 3c Ogea flycatcher .20 .20
728 A166 4c Peale's pigeon .20 .20
729 A166 6c Blue-crested broadbill .20 .20
730 A166 13c Island thrush .20 .20
731 A166 23c Many-colored fruit dove .35 .35
732 A166 31c Mangrove heron .45 .45
733 A166 44c Purple swamphen .75 .75
734 A166 63c Fiji goshawk 1.00 1.00
735 A166 81c Kadavu fantail 1.40 1.40
736 A166 87c Collared lory 1.50 1.50
737 A166 $1 Scarlet robin 1.60 1.60
738 A166 $2 Peregrine falcon 3.25 3.25
739 A166 $3 Barn owl 4.75 4.75
739A A166 $5 Yellow-breasted musk parrot 8.75 8.75
Nos. 725-739A (16) 25.00 25.00

Issued: 13c, 23c, 31c, 44c, 63c, 81c, $2, $3, 7/25; 1c, 2c, 3c, 4c, 6c, 87c, $1, $5, 11/7.

See No. 1011.

Souvenir Sheet

Singapore '95 — A167

Orchids: a, Arundina graminifolia. b, Phaius tankervilliae.

Wmk. 373

1995, Sept. 1 Litho. *Perf. 14*

740 A167 $1 Sheet of 2, #a.-b. 9.00 9.00

Independence, 25th Anniv. — A168

Designs: 81c, Pres. Kamisese Mara, Parliament Building. 87c, Fijian youth. $1.06, Playing rugby. $2, Air Pacific Boeing 747.

Wmk. 373

1995, Oct. 4 Litho. *Perf. 14*

741 A168 81c multicolored 1.60 1.60
742 A168 87c multicolored 1.90 1.90
743 A168 $1.06 multicolored 2.25 2.25
744 A168 $2 multicolored 4.25 4.25
Nos. 741-744 (4) 10.00 10.00

Christmas — A169

Paintings: 10c, Praying Madonna with the Crown of Stars, from Correggio Workshop. 63c, Madonna and Child with Crowns on porcelain. 87c, The Holy Virgin with the Holy Child and St. John, after Titian. $2, The Holy Family and St. John, from Rubens Workshop.

Wmk. 373

1995, Nov. 22 Litho. *Perf. 13*

745 A169 10c multicolored .25 .25
746 A169 63c multicolored 1.25 1.25
747 A169 87c multicolored 1.75 1.75
748 A169 $2 multicolored 4.00 4.00
Nos. 745-748 (4) 7.25 7.25

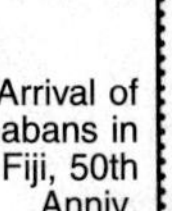

Arrival of Banabans in Fiji, 50th Anniv. A170

Perf. 14x14½, 14½x14

1996, Jan. 24 Litho. Wmk. 373

749 A170 81c Trolling lure 2.25 2.25
750 A170 87c Canoes 2.50 2.50
751 A170 $1.12 Warrior, vert. 2.75 2.75
752 A170 $2 Frigate bird, vert. 5.25 5.25
Nos. 749-752 (4) 12.75 12.75

A171

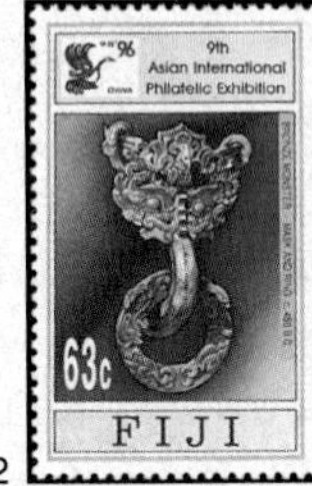

A172

Radio, Cent.: 44c, L2B portable tape recorder. 63c, Fiji Broadcasting Center. 81c, Communications satellite in orbit. $3, Marconi.

Wmk. 373

1996, Mar. 11 Litho. *Perf. 14½*

753 A171 44c multicolored .90 .90
754 A171 63c multicolored 1.25 1.25
755 A171 81c multicolored 1.60 1.60
756 A171 $3 multicolored 6.25 6.25
Nos. 753-756 (4) 10.00 10.00

Wmk. 384

1996, Apr. 25 Litho. *Perf. 13½*

Ancient Chinese artifacts: 63c, Bronze monster mask and ring, c. 450 BC. 81c, Archer, 210 BC. $1, Plate, Hsuan Te Period, 1426-35. $2, Central Asian horseman, dated 706.

30c, Yan Deng Mountain.

757 A172 63c multicolored 1.25 1.25
758 A172 81c multicolored 1.50 1.50
759 A172 $1 multicolored 2.00 2.00
760 A172 $2 multicolored 4.25 4.25
Nos. 757-760 (4) 9.00 9.00

Souvenir Sheet

Perf. 13½x13

761 A172 30c multicolored 2.00 2.00

No. 761 contains one 48x76mm stamp.

CHINA '96, 9th Asian Intl. Philatelic Exhibition.

A173

A174

Wmk. 373

1996, June 18 Litho. *Perf. 14*

762 A173 31c Hurdling .65 .65
763 A173 63c Judo 1.50 1.50
764 A173 87c Sailboarding 2.10 2.10
765 A173 $1.12 Swimming 2.50 2.50
Nos. 762-765 (4) 6.75 6.75

Souvenir Sheet

766 A173 $2 Athlete, 1896 4.00 4.00

Modern Olympic Games, cent.

1996, July 1

31c, Computerized telephone exchange, horiz. 44c, Mail being unloaded, horiz. 81c, Manual switchboard operator. $1, Mail delivery.

No. 771: a, #117. b, #527.

767 A174 31c multicolored .60 .60
768 A174 44c multicolored .80 .80
769 A174 81c multicolored 1.40 1.40
770 A174 $1 multicolored 1.90 1.90
Nos. 767-770 (4) 4.70 4.70

Souvenir Sheet of 2

771 A174 $1.50 #a.-b. 5.00 5.00

Creation of independent Postal, Telecommunications Companies.

UNICEF, 50th Anniv. A175

Designs: 81c, "Our children, our future." 87c, Village scene. $1, "Living in harmony the world over." $2, "Their future."

Wmk. 384

1996, Aug. 13 Litho. *Perf. 14*

772 A175 81c multicolored 2.00 2.00
773 A175 87c multicolored 2.00 2.00
774 A175 $1 multicolored 2.25 2.25
775 A175 $2 multicolored 4.50 4.50
Nos. 772-775 (4) 10.75 10.75

Nadi Intl. Airport, 50th Anniv. A176

Designs: 31c, First airplane in Fiji, 1921. 44c, Nadi Airport commences Commercial Operations, 1946. 63c, First jet in Fiji, 1959. 87c, Airport entrance. $1, Control tower, 1996. $2, Global positioning system, first commercial use, 1994.

Wmk. 373

1996, Oct. 1 Litho. *Perf. 14*

776 A176 31c multicolored .75 .75
777 A176 44c multicolored 1.00 1.00
778 A176 63c multicolored 1.50 1.50
779 A176 87c multicolored 2.00 2.00
780 A176 $1 multicolored 2.25 2.25
781 A176 $2 multicolored 4.50 4.50
Nos. 776-781 (6) 12.00 12.00

Christmas — A177

Scene from the Christmas story and native story or scene: 13c, Angel Gabriel & Mary, beating of Lali. 81c, Shepherds with sheep, Fijian canoe. $1, Wise men on camels, multiracial Fiji. $3, Mary, Christ Child in stable, blowing of conch shell.

1996, Nov. 20 Wmk. 373

782 A177 13c multicolored .30 .30
783 A177 81c multicolored 2.00 2.00
784 A177 $1 multicolored 2.40 2.40
785 A177 $3 multicolored 7.25 7.25
Nos. 782-785 (4) 11.95 11.95

Hong Kong '97 A178

Cattle: a, Brahman. b, Freisian (Holstein). c, Hereford. d, Fiji draught bullock.

1997, Feb. 12

786 A178 $1 Sheet of 4, #a.-d. 9.00 9.00

Souvenir Sheet

Black-Faced Shrikebill — A179

Illustration reduced.

1997, Feb. 21 *Perf. 14x15*

787 A179 $2 multicolored 3.75 3.75

Singpex '97.

Orchids — A180

Designs: 81c, Dendrobium biflorum. 87c, Dendrobium dactylodes. $1.06, Spathoglottis pacifica. $2, Dendrobium macropus.

Wmk. 384

1997, Apr. 22 Litho. *Perf. 14*

788 A180 81c multicolored 1.75 1.75
789 A180 87c multicolored 1.75 1.75

Wmk. 373

790 A180 $1.06 multicolored 2.25 2.25
791 A180 $2 multicolored 4.00 4.00
Nos. 788-791 (4) 9.75 9.75

Souvenir Sheet

Hawksbill Turtle A181

Designs: a, 63c, Female laying eggs. b, 81c, Baby turtles emerging from nest. c, $1.06 Young turtles in water. d, $2, One adult in water, coral.

1997, May 26 Wmk. 373

792 A181 Sheet of 4, #a.-d. 11.00 11.00

Coral A182

Designs: 63c, Branching hard coral 87c, Massive hard coral. $1, Soft coral, sinularia. $3, Soft coral, dendronephthya.

Wmk. 373

1997, July 16 Litho. *Perf. 14*

793 A182 63c multicolored 1.40 1.40
794 A182 87c multicolored 1.90 1.90
795 A182 $1 multicolored 2.25 2.25
796 A182 $3 multicolored 6.75 6.75
Nos. 793-796 (4) 12.30 12.30

Fijian Monkey-faced Bat — A183

63c, With nose pointed downward. 81c, Hanging below flower. $2, Between leaves on tree branch.

Perf. 13½

1997, Oct. 15 Litho. Unwmk.

797 A183 44c multicolored .90 .90
798 A183 63c multicolored 1.25 1.25
799 A183 81c multicolored 1.75 1.75
800 A183 $2 multicolored 4.00 4.00
a. Sheet, 2 each #797-800 16.00 16.00
Nos. 797-800 (4) 7.90 7.90

World Wildlife Fund.

Christmas A184

Designs: 13c, Angel, shepherd. 31c, Birth of Jesus. 87c, Magi. $3, Madonna and Child.

Perf. 14x14½

1997, Nov. 18 Wmk. 373

801 A184 13c multicolored .20 .20
802 A184 31c multicolored .60 .60
803 A184 87c multicolored 1.60 1.60
804 A184 $3 multicolored 5.50 5.50
Nos. 801-804 (4) 7.90 7.90

A185 A186

1997 Rugby World Cup Sevens Champions: a, 50c, Waisale Serevi, captain, highest point scorer. b, 50c, Taniela Qauqau. c, 50c, Jope Tuikabe. d, 50c, Leveni Duvuduvukula. e, 50c, Inoke Maraiwai. f, 50c, Aminiasi Naituyaga. g, 50c, Lemeki Koroi. h, 50c, Marika Vunibaka, highest try scorer. i, 50c, Luke Erenavula. j, 50c, Manasa Bari. k, $1, Entire team.

Wmk. 373

1997, Oct. 30 Litho. *Perf. 14*

805 A185 Sheet of 11, #a.-k. 11.00 11.00

No. 805k is 53x39mm.

Wmk. 373

1998, Jan. 20 Litho. *Perf. 14*

Chief's Traditional Costumes: 81c, War dress. 87c, Formal dress. $1.12, Presentation dress. $2, Highland war dress.

806 A186 81c multicolored 1.25 1.25
807 A186 87c multicolored 1.25 1.25
808 A186 $1.12 multicolored 1.75 1.75
809 A186 $2 multicolored 3.00 3.00
Nos. 806-809 (4) 7.25 7.25

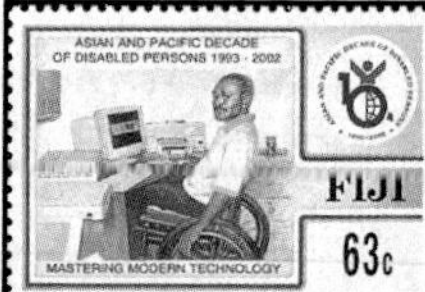

Asian and Pacific Decade of Disabled Persons, 1993-2000 A187

63c, Mastering modern technology. 87c, Assisting the will to overcome. $1, Using natural born skills. $2, Competing to win.

Wmk. 373

1998, Mar. 18 Litho. *Perf. 13*

810 A187 63c multicolored 1.00 1.00
811 A187 87c multicolored 1.40 1.40
812 A187 $1 multicolored 1.50 1.50
813 A187 $2 multicolored 3.00 3.00
Nos. 810-813 (4) 6.90 6.90

Royal Air Force, 80th Anniv.

Common Design Type of 1993 Re-Inscribed

Designs: 44c, R34 Airship. 63c, Handley Page Heyford. 87c, Supermarine Swift FR.5. $2, Westland Whirlwind.

No. 818: a, Sopwith Dolphin. b, Avro 504K. c, Vickers Warwick V. d, Shorts Belfast.

1998, Apr. 1 *Perf. 13½x14*

814 CD350 44c multicolored 1.00 1.00
815 CD350 63c multicolored 1.25 1.25
816 CD350 87c multicolored 1.75 1.75
817 CD350 $2 multicolored 4.00 4.00
Nos. 814-817 (4) 8.00 8.00

Souvenir Sheet of 4

818 CD350 $1 #a.-d. 6.50 6.50

Diana, Princess of Wales (1961-97)

Common Design Type

Design: No. 819, Wearing plaid jacket.

No. 820: a, Wearing blue jacket. b, In high-collared blouse. c, Holding flowers.

1998, Mar. 31 Litho. *Perf. 14x14½*

819 CD355 81c multicolored .75 .75
820 CD355 81c Sheet of 4, #819, a.-c. 5.25 5.25

No. 820 sold for $3.24 + 50c, with surtax from international sales being donated to the Princess Diana Memorial Fund and surtax from national sales being donated to designated local charity.

Sperm Whale A188

Wmk. 373

1998, June 22 Litho. *Perf. 14*

821 A188 63c shown 1.25 1.25
822 A188 81c Adult, calf 1.75 1.75
823 A188 87c Breaching 1.75 1.75
824 A188 $2 Sperm whale tooth 4.00 4.00
a. Souvenir sheet 6.00 6.00
Nos. 821-824 (4) 8.75 8.75

16th Commonwealth Games, Kuala Lumpur, Malaysia — A189

Wmk. 384

1998, Sept. 11 Litho. *Perf. 14*

825 A189 44c Athletics .70 .70
826 A189 63c Lawn bowls 1.00 1.00
827 A189 81c Javelin 1.40 1.40
828 A189 $1.12 Weight lifting 1.90 1.90
Nos. 825-828 (4) 5.00 5.00

Souvenir Sheet

829 A189 $2 Waisale Serevi, rugby sevens 4.00 4.00

Maritime Heritage A190

Designs: 13c, Takia, hollowed-out log with outrigger. 44c, Camakau, sailing canoe. 87c, Drua, twin-hulled sailing canoe. $3, MV Pioneer motor yacht.
$1.50, Camakau, map of Fiji.

Wmk. 384

1998, Oct. 26 Litho. *Perf. 13½*

830 A190 13c multicolored .30 .30
831 A190 44c multicolored .85 .85
832 A190 87c multicolored 1.60 1.60
833 A190 $3 multicolored 5.25 5.25
Nos. 830-833 (4) 8.00 8.00

Souvenir Sheet

834 A190 $1.50 multicolored 3.75 3.75

Australia '99, World Stamp Expo (#834).
See Nos. 843-847.

Christmas A191

Children's drawings: 13c, "Jesus in a Manger." 50c, "A Time for Family and Friends." $1, "What Christmas Means to Me," vert. $2, "The Joy of Christmas," vert.

1998, Nov. 23 Wmk. 373

835 A191 13c multicolored .25 .25
836 A191 50c multicolored .80 .80
837 A191 $1 multicolored 1.60 1.60
838 A191 $2 multicolored 3.25 3.25
Nos. 835-838 (4) 5.90 5.90

Traditional Dances — A192

Designs: 13c, Vakamalolo (women's sitting dance). 81c, Mekeiwau (club dance). 87c, Seasea (women's fan dance). $3, Meke ni yaqona (Kava serving dance).

Wmk. 373

1999, Jan. 20 Litho. *Perf. 14½*

839 A192 13c multicolored .25 .25
840 A192 81c multicolored 1.25 1.25
841 A192 87c multicolored 1.50 1.50
842 A192 $3 multicolored 4.75 4.75
Nos. 839-842 (4) 7.75 7.75

Maritime Heritage Type of 1998

Designs: 63c, SS Toufua, 1920-30's. 81c, MF Adi Beti, 1920-30's. $1, SS Niagara, 1920-30's. $2, MV Royal Viking Sun, 1990's.
$1.50, SS. Makatea, 1920's.

1999, Mar. 19 Wmk. 384 *Perf. 13½*

843 A190 63c multicolored 1.10 1.10
844 A190 81c multicolored 1.40 1.40
845 A190 $1 multicolored 1.75 1.75
846 A190 $2 multicolored 3.50 3.50
Nos. 843-846 (4) 7.75 7.75

Souvenir Sheet

847 A190 $1.50 multicolored 3.75 3.75

Australia '99, World Stamp Exhibition (#847).

Souvenir Sheet

Ducks — A193

a, Wandering whistling. b, Pacific black.

1999, Apr. 27 Wmk. 373

848 A193 $2 Sheet of 2, #a.-b. 5.75 5.75

IBRA '99, Intl. Philatelic Exhibition, Nuremberg.

Orchids — A194

Designs: 44c, Calanthe ventilabrum. 63c, Dendrobium prasinum. 81c, Dendrobium macrophyllum. $3, Dendrobium tokai.

1999, June 28

849 A194 44c multicolored .75 .75
850 A194 63c multicolored 1.00 1.00
851 A194 81c multicolored 1.25 1.25
852 A194 $3 multicolored 5.00 5.00
Nos. 849-852 (4) 8.00 8.00

1st Manned Moon Landing, 30th Anniv.

Common Design Type

13c, Astronaut waves goodbye. 87c, Stage 3 fires towards moon. $1, Aldrin walks on lunar surface. $2, Command module fires towards earth.
$2, Looking at earth from moon.

Perf. 14x13¾

1999, July 20 Wmk. 384

853 CD357 13c multicolored .25 .25
854 CD357 87c multicolored 1.50 1.50
855 CD357 $1 multicolored 1.75 1.75
856 CD357 $2 multicolored 3.50 3.50
Nos. 853-856 (4) 7.00 7.00

Souvenir Sheet

Perf. 14

857 CD357 $2 multicolored 4.00 4.00

No. 857 contains one circular stamp 40mm in diameter.

Queen Mother's Century

Common Design Type

Queen Mother: 13c, Visiting Hull to see bomb damage. 63c, With Prince Charles. 81c, As Colonel-in-Chief of Light Infantry. $3, With Prince Charles at Clarence House.
$2, With crowd on Armistice Day.

Wmk. 384

1999, Aug. 18 Litho. *Perf. 13½*

858 CD358 13c multicolored .25 .25
859 CD358 63c multicolored 1.10 1.10
860 CD358 81c multicolored 1.50 1.50
861 CD358 $3 multicolored 5.00 5.00
Nos. 858-861 (4) 7.85 7.85

Souvenir Sheet

862 CD358 $2 multicolored 5.00 5.00

UPU, 125th Anniv. A195

Sugar Mills rolling stock: 50c, Diesel locomotive. 87c, Steam locomotive. $1, Diesel locomotive, diff. $2, Free passenger train.

Wmk. 373

1999, Oct. 26 Litho. *Perf. 13¾*

863 A195 50c multicolored .60 .60
864 A195 87c multicolored 1.25 1.25
865 A195 $1 multicolored 1.40 1.40
866 A195 $2 multicolored 2.75 2.75
Nos. 863-866 (4) 6.00 6.00

Christmas — A196

Designs: 13c, Giving gifts. 31c, Angels and star. 63c, Bible, Magi, Holy family. 87c, Joseph, mary, donkey, vert. $1, Mary, Jesus, animals, vert. $2, Children, Santa, vert.

Perf. 13¼x13

1999, Nov. 29 Litho. Wmk. 373

867 A196 13c multicolored .20 .20
868 A196 31c multicolored .45 .45
869 A196 63c multicolored .90 .90
870 A196 87c multicolored 1.25 1.25
871 A196 $1 multicolored 1.40 1.40
872 A196 $2 multicolored 2.75 2.75
Nos. 867-872 (6) 6.95 6.95

Millennium A197

Designs: No. 873, Outstretched hands, islands (arch at top). No. 874, Map, flag (arch at right). No. 875, Globe, warrior beating lali, temple (arch at bottom). No. 876, Globe, drua, red line (arch at left).
No. 877: a, Fiji petrel (arch at top). b, Crested iguana, islands (arch at top). c, Red prawns (arch at bottom). d, Tagimaucia (arch at bottom).

Perf. 13¼ Syncopated Type A

Litho. with Foil Application

2000, Jan. 1 Unwmk.

873 A197 $5 gold & multi 6.00 6.00
874 A197 $5 gold & multi 6.00 6.00
875 A197 $5 gold & multi 6.00 6.00
876 A197 $5 gold & multi 6.00 6.00
Nos. 873-876 (4) 24.00 24.00

Souvenir Sheet

877 A197 $10 Sheet of 4, #a-d 45.00 45.00

Beetles — A198

Designs: 15c, Paracupta sulcata. 87c, Agrilus sp. $1.06, Cyphogastra abdominalis. $2, Paracupta sp.

Perf. 13¾x14

2000, Mar. 14 Litho. Wmk. 373

878 A198 15c multi .25 .25
879 A198 87c multi 1.25 1.25
880 A198 $1.06 multi 1.50 1.50
881 A198 $2 multi 2.75 2.75
Nos. 878-881 (4) 5.75 5.75

Sesame Street — A199

No. 882: a, Big Bird. b, Oscar the Grouch. c, Cookie Monster. d, Grover. e, Elmo. f, Ernie. g, Zoe. h, The Count. i, Bert.
No. 883, Big Bird, Elmo and Ernie, horiz. No. 884, Cookie Monster, Bert and Ernie, horiz.
Illustration reduced.

Perf. 14½x14¾

2000, Apr. 20 Litho. Wmk. 373

882 A199 50c Sheet of 9, #a-i 5.75 5.75

Souvenir Sheets

Perf. 14¾x14½

883 A199 $2 multi 3.00 3.00
884 A199 $2 multi 3.00 3.00

The Stamp Show 2000, London (#882).

Pres. Ratu Sir Kamisese Mara, 80th Birthday — A200

President with: 15c, Lumberjack, timber truck. 81c, Women. $1, Workers in cane field. $3, Ships.

2000, May 13 *Perf. 14x13¾*

885 A200 15c multi .25 .25
886 A200 81c multi 1.00 1.00
887 A200 $1 multi 1.25 1.25
888 A200 $3 multi 4.25 4.25
Nos. 885-888 (4) 6.75 6.75

Prince William, 18th Birthday

Common Design Type

William: Nos. 889, 893a, As child, wearing fireman's helmet, vert. Nos. 890, 893b, Wearing navy suit, vert. Nos. 891, 893c, Wearing scarf. Nos. 892, 893d, Wearing suit and wearing blue shirt. No. 893e, As child, wearing camouflage and beret.

Perf. 13¾x14¼, 14¼x13¾

2000, June 21 Wmk. 373

Stamps With White Border

889 CD359 $1 multi 1.50 1.50
890 CD359 $1 multi 1.50 1.50
891 CD359 $1 multi 1.50 1.50
892 CD359 $1 multi 1.50 1.50
Nos. 889-892 (4) 6.00 6.00

Souvenir Sheet

Stamps Without White Border

Perf. 14¼

893 CD359 $1 Sheet of 5, #a-e 7.00 7.00

2000 Summer Olympics, Sydney — A201

Wmk. 373

2000, Aug. 8 Litho. *Perf. 13¾*

894 A201 44c Swimming, vert. .50 .50
895 A201 87c Judo, vert. 1.25 1.25
896 A201 $1 Running 1.50 1.50
897 A201 $2 Windsurfing 2.75 2.75
Nos. 894-897 (4) 6.00 6.00

Souvenir Sheet

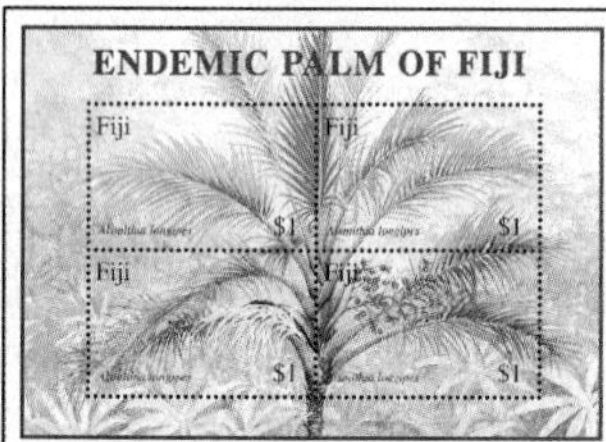

Alsmithia Longipes — A202

No. 898: a, Red frond at R. b, Red frond at L. c, Yellow frond. d, Fruit.
Illustration reduced.

Wmk. 373

2000, Sept. 12 Litho. *Perf. 13½*

898 A202 $1 Sheet of 4, #a-d 6.00 6.00

Lapita Pottery Shards and Discovery Sites — A203

44c, Yanuca Island. 63c, Mago Island. $1, Ugaga Island. $2, Sigatoka sand dunes.

2000, Oct. 24 *Perf. 13¾*

899-902 A203 Set of 4 5.75 5.75

Christmas A204

Designs: 15c, Jungle. 81c, Cliffside trail. 87c, Coastal village. $3, Outrigger canoe.

2000, Nov. 21

903-906 A204 Set of 4 6.25 6.25

Souvenir Sheet

Taveuni Rain Forest — A205

Designs: a, Orange dove. b, Xixuthrus heyrovskyi.

Perf. 13¾x13½

2001, Feb. 1 Litho. Unwmk.

907 A205 $2 Sheet of 2, #a-b 5.00 5.00

Moths A206

Designs: 17c, Macroglossum hirundo vitiensis. 48c, Hippotion celerio. 69c, Gnathothlibus erotus eras. 89c, Theretra pinastrina intersecta. $1.17, Deilephila placida torenia. $2, Psilogramma jordana.

2001, Mar. 20 *Perf. 13¼x13*

908-913 A206 Set of 6 6.50 6.50

Souvenir Sheet

Gallus Gallus — A207

Designs: a, Hen. b, Rooster.

2001, May 22 *Perf. 13¾x14*

914 A207 $2 Sheet of 2, #a-b 5.00 5.00

Society for Prevention of Cruelty — A208

Designs: 34c, Girl, cat. 96c, Boy, dogs. $1.23, Girl, cat, diff. $2, Boy, dog.

Perf. 14x13¾

2001, June 26 Litho. Unwmk.

915-918 A208 Set of 4 5.00 5.00

Pigeons — A209

Designs: 69c, White-throated. 89c, Pacific, vert. $1.23, Peal's, vert. $2, Rock.

2001, July 20 *Perf. 14x14¾, 14¾x14*

919-922 A209 Set of 4 5.00 5.00

Westpac Pacific Bank, 100th Anniv. in Fiji — A210

Bank office in: 48c, 1901. 96c, 1916. $1, 1934. $2, 2001.

2001, Aug. 10 *Perf. 13¼x13¾*

923-926 A210 Set of 4 5.00 5.00

Fish A211

Designs: 50c, Yellowfin tuna. 96c, Wahoo. $1.17, Dolphin fish. $2, Pacific blue marlin.

2001, Aug. 23

927-930 A211 Set of 4 5.00 5.00

Christmas A212

Designs: 17c, Angel appears to Mary. 34c Nativity. 48c, Adoration of the shepherds. 69c, Adoration of the Magi. 89c, Flight to Egypt. $2, Fijian Chirst child.

2001, Oct. 29 Litho. *Perf. 13¾x13¼*

931-936 A212 Set of 6 5.00 5.00

Colonial Financial Services Group, 125th Anniv. in Fiji — A213

Designs: 17c, Bank office. 48c, Women using automatic teller machine. $1, Suva Private Hospital. $3, Hoisting of British flag.

2001, Nov. 16 Litho. *Perf. 13¼*

937-940 A213 Set of 4 5.00 5.00

Air Pacific, 50th Anniv. — A214

No. 941: a, De Havilland Drover. b, Hawker Siddley HS-748. c, Douglas DC-10-30. d, Boeing 747-200.

2001, Nov. 30 Litho. *Perf. 13*

941 Horiz. strip of 4 5.00 5.00
a. A214 89c multi .85 .85
b. A214 96c multi 1.00 1.00
c. A214 $1 multi 1.10 1.10
d. A214 $2 multi 2.00 2.00

Spices — A215

Designs: 69c, Pepper. 89c, Nutmeg. $1, Vanilla. $2, Cinnamon.

2002, Mar. 12 Litho. *Perf. 13¼*

942-945 A215 Set of 4 5.00 5.00

Souvenir Sheet

Balaka Palm — A216

Palm and: a, Bird, butterfly, beetle. b, Lizard, butterfly

2002, Apr. 29

946 A216 $2 Sheet of 2, #a-b 5.00 5.00

Freshwater Fish — A217

Designs: 48c, Redigobius sp. 96c, Spotted flagtail. $1.23, Silverstripe mudskipper. $2, Snakehead gudgeon.

2002, May 13

947-950 A217 Set of 4 5.00 5.00

Fruit — A218

Designs: 25c, Breadfruit. 34c, Wi. $1, Jakfruit. $3, Avocado.

2002, July 25 Litho. *Perf. 13¾x13¼*

951-954 A218 Set of 4 5.00 5.00

Murex Shells — A219

Designs: 69c, Saul's murex. 96c, Caltrop murex. $1, Purple Pacific drupe. $2, Ramose murex.

2002, Aug. 20 *Perf. 13¾*

955-958 A219 Set of 4 4.50 4.50

Fiji Goshawk — A220

Designs: 48c, Goshawk and eggs. 89c, Chicks in nest. $1, Juvenile on branch. $3, Adult.

2002, Sept. 10
959-962 A220 Set of 4 5.00 5.00

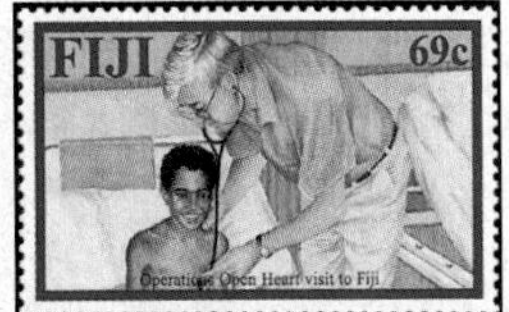

2002 Operation Open Heart Visit to Fiji — A221

Designs: 34c, Doctors performing operation, vert. 69c, Doctor listening to patient's heart with stethoscope. $1.17, Technician administering echocardiogram. $2, Administration of anesthesia to patient, vert.

2002, Oct. 30 ***Perf. 13¼***
963-966 A221 Set of 4 5.00 5.00

Fiji Natural Artesian Water — A222

Designs: 25c, Bottle of water, flowers, vert. 48c, Bottling plant. $1, Delivery truck. $3, Children with bottled water, vert.

2002, Nov. 5
967-970 A222 Set of 4 6.00 6.00

Christmas — A223

Designs: 17c, Christian church. 89c, Mosque. $1, Hindu temple. $3, Christian church, diff.

2002, Nov. 20
971-974 A223 Set of 4 6.00 6.00

Post Fiji, Ltd. Improvements — A224

Designs: 48c, General Post Office. 96c, Post Fiji Mail Center. $1, Post Fiji Logistics Center. $2, Smart Mail.

2003, Mar. 19 Litho. ***Perf. 13¼***
975-978 A224 Set of 4 5.25 5.25

Souvenir Sheet

Intl. Year of Fresh Water — A225

No. 979: a, Top of waterfall, flowers. b, Base of waterfall, butterfly.

2003, Apr. 22
979 A225 $2 Sheet of 2, #a-b 5.25 5.25

2003 South Pacific Games, Suva — A226

Designs: 10c, Track athlete with arms raised. 14c, Baseball. 20c, Netball. No. 983, $5, Shot put.

No. 984, $5, Flags of participating nations, venues, volleyball players.

2003 ***Perf. 13¼***
980-983 A226 Set of 4 6.00 6.00

Size: 120x85mm

Imperf

984 A226 $5 multi 5.50 5.50

Issued: Nos. 980-983, 5/26; No. 984, 6/28.

Fish A227

Siganus uspi: 58c, Fish, crab and coral. 83c, Two fish and coral. $1.15, Two fish, coral, and other fish species. $3, Fish and coral.

2003, Aug. 12 ***Perf. 13¼***
985-988 A227 Set of 4 6.00 6.00

Bird Life International A228

Designs: 41c, Long-legged warbler. 60c, Silktail. $1.07, Red-throated lorikeet. $3, Pink-billed parrot finch.

2003, Sept. 16
989-992 A228 Set of 4 5.50 5.50

Geckos A229

Designs: 83c, Pacific slender-toed gecko. $1.07, Indopacific tree gecko. $1.15, Mann's gecko. $2, Voracious gecko.

2003, Oct. 21 Litho. ***Perf. 13¼***
993-996 A229 Set of 4 5.75 5.75

Christmas — A230

Children's art: 18c, Children, Christmas tree. 41c, Children, flag of Fiji. 58c, Children, Santa Claus, reindeer pulling sleighs, vert. 83c, Santa Claus on chimney, gifts, children, Christmas tree, vert. $1.07, Children with candles, Christmas tree, vert. $1.15, Santa Claus, children, bell, rainbow, vert.

$1.41, Handshake.

2003, Nov. 26 Litho. ***Perf. 13¼***
997-1002 A230 Set of 6 5.00 5.00

Souvenir Sheet

1003 A230 $1.41 multi 1.60 1.60

Tagimoucia — A231

2003, Dec. 1 Litho. ***Perf. 14½x14***
1004 A231 50c multi + label 1.75 1.75

Sold in sheets of 10 stamps + 10 labels that could be personalized for $15 per sheet.

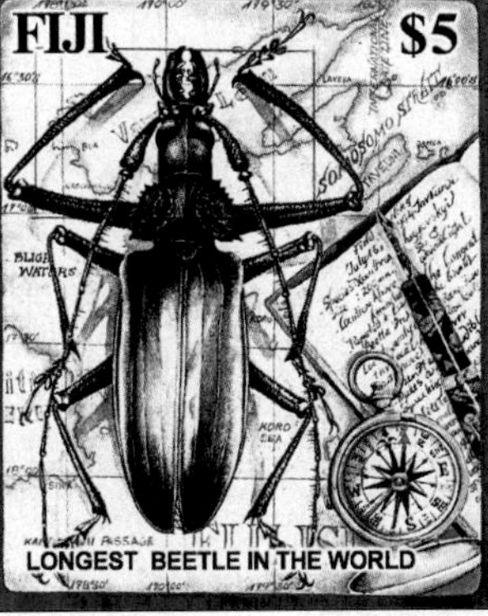

Xixuthrus Heyrovskyi, Longest Beetle in the World — A232

Illustration reduced.

2003, Feb. 27 ***Imperf.***
1005 A232 $5 multi 6.00 6.00

Miniature Sheet

Worldwide Fund for Nature (WWF) — A233

No. 1006: a, 58c, Skipjack tuna. b, 83c, Albacore tuna. c, $1.07, Yellowfin tuna. d, $3, Bigeye tuna.

2004, Apr. 7 ***Perf. 13¼***
1006 A233 Sheet of 4, #a-d 6.50 6.50
e. Like #1006, with artist's name at LL of each stamp 6.50 6.50

Land Snails A234

Designs: 18c, Malleated placostyle. 41c, Kandavu placostyle. $1.15, Fragile orpiella. $3, Thin Fijian placostyle.

2004, May 28
1007-1010 A234 Set of 4 5.50 5.50

Bird Type of 1995

Perf. 13¼x13

2004, June 26 **Unwmk.**
1011 A166 18c Island thrush .20 .20

Coral Reef Shrimp — A235

Designs: 58c, Boxer shrimp. 83c, Bumblebee shrimp. $1.07, Mantis shrimp. $3, Anemone shrimp.

2004, June 30 ***Perf. 13¼***
1012-1015 A235 Set of 4 6.50 6.50

Birds A236

Designs: 41c, Wandering tattler. 58c, Whimbrel. $1.15, Pacific golden plover. $3, Bristle-thighed curlew.

2004, July 28
1016-1019 A236 Set of 4 5.75 5.75

2004 Summer Olympics, Athens A237

Designs: 41c, Swimming. 58c, Judo, vert. $1.40, Weight lifting, vert. $2, Makelesi Bulikiobo, runner.

2004, Aug. 12
1020-1023 A237 Set of 4 5.00 5.00

Musket Cove to Port Vila Yacht Race, 25th Anniv. — A238

Various yachts: 83c, $1.07, $1.15, $2. $1.07 and $2 are vert.

2004, Sept. 18 *Perf. 14¼*

1024-1027	A238	Set of 4	6.00	6.00
1027a		Souvenir sheet of 1	2.40	2.40

See Vanuatu Nos. 858-861.

Souvenir Sheet

Coconut Crab — A239

2004, Oct. 20 **Litho.** *Perf. 14*

1028	A239 $5 multi		6.00	6.00

Papilio Schmeltzii — A240

Designs: 58c, Newly-emerged adult, vert. 83c, Larva. $1.41, Adult. $3, Pupa, vert.

Perf. 14x14½, 14½x14

2004, Nov. 10

1029-1032	A240	Set of 4	7.00	7.00

SEMI-POSTAL STAMPS

Catalogue values for unused stamps in this section are for Never Hinged items.

Children at Play — SP1

Rugby Player — SP2

Perf. 13x13½

1951, Sept. 17 **Engr.** **Wmk. 4**

B1	SP1 1p + 1p brown		.25	.25
B2	SP2 2p + 1p deep green		.30	.30

Bamboo River Raft — SP3

Design: 2½p+½p, Cross of Lorraine.

1954, Apr. 1 *Perf. 11x11½*

B3	SP3 1½p + ½p green & brn		.25	.25
B4	SP3 2½p + ½p black & org		.30	.30

Nos. 269 and 272 Surcharged

1972, Dec. 4 **Photo.** *Perf. 14, 13½*

B5	A56 15c + 5c multi		.50	.50
B6	A55 30c + 10c multi		1.10	1.10

Indian Boy, Map of Fiji SP4

Map of Fiji and: 15c+2c, European girl. 30c+3c, Chinese girl. 40c+4c, Fijian boy.

Wmk. 373

1979, Sept. 17 **Litho.** *Perf. 14½*

B7	SP4 4c + 1c multicolored		.20	.20
B8	SP4 15c + 2c multicolored		.25	.25
B9	SP4 30c + 3c multicolored		.50	.50
B10	SP4 40c + 4c multicolored		.70	.70
	Nos. B7-B10 (4)		1.65	1.65

The surtax was for IYC fund.

POSTAGE DUE STAMPS

D1

D2

POSTAGE DUE 1d. FIJI

D3

1917 **Unwmk.** **Typeset** *Perf. 11*

Laid Papers; Without Gum

J1	D1 ½p black		850.00	425.00
J2	D2 ½p black		550.00	300.00
J3	D3 1p black		375.00	92.50
J4	D3 2p black		325.00	75.00
J5	D3 3p black		400.00	92.50
J6	D3 4p black		850.00	425.00
	Nos. J1-J6 (6)		3,350.	1,410.

There were 2 printings of No. J3. In the 1st the stamps were 25mm wide including the margins. In the 2nd the clichés were set a little closer, and the stamps were 23mm wide.

D4

D5

Perf. 14

1918, June 1 **Typo.** **Wmk. 3**

J7	D4 ½p black		4.25	*20.00*
J8	D4 1p black		4.25	*15.00*
J9	D4 2p black		5.50	*22.50*
J10	D4 3p black		7.00	*27.50*
J11	D4 4p black		8.25	*40.00*
	Nos. J7-J11 (5)		29.25	*125.00*

1940 **Wmk. 4** *Perf. 12½*

J12	D5	1p bright green	4.75	*62.50*
J13	D5	2p bright green	8.50	*62.50*
J14	D5	3p bright green	11.00	*77.50*
J15	D5	4p bright green	12.00	*82.50*
J16	D5	5p bright green	15.00	*82.50*
J17	D5	6p bright green	8.00	*87.50*
J18	D5	1sh dk carmine	20.00	*140.00*
J19	D5	1sh6p dk carmine	20.00	*200.00*
		Nos. J12-J19 (8)	99.25	*795.00*
		Set, never hinged	140.00	

WAR TAX STAMPS

Regular Issue of 1912-16 Overprinted

Die I

1916 **Wmk. 3** *Perf. 14*

MR1	A23 ½p green		.85	*3.00*
a.	Inverted overprint		700.00	
b.	Double overprint			
MR2	A23 1p scarlet		2.00	.75
a.	1p carmine		30.00	26.00
b.	Pair, one without ovpt.		*9,000.*	
c.	Inverted overprint		800.00	

#MR2b may exist only in horiz. strips of 12.

FINLAND

'fin-lənd

(Suomi)

LOCATION — Northern Europe bordering on the Gulfs of Bothnia and Finland
GOVT. — Republic
AREA — 130,119 sq. mi.
POP. — 5,147,349 (1997)
CAPITAL — Helsinki

Finland was a Grand Duchy of the Russian Empire from 1809 until December 1917, when it declared its independence.

100 Kopecks = 1 Ruble
100 Pennia = 1 Markka (1866)
100 Cents = 1 Euro (2002)

Catalogue values for unused stamps in this country are for Never Hinged items, beginning with Scott 220 in the regular postage section, Scott B39 in the semi-postal section, Scott C2 in the air-post section, Scott M1 in the military stamp section, and Scott Q6 in the parcel post section.

Unused stamps are valued with original gum as defined in the catalogue introduction except for Nos. 1-3B which are valued without gum. Used values for Nos. 1-3B are for pen-canceled copies. Very fine examples of the serpentine rouletted issues, Nos. 4-13c, will have roulettes cutting the design slightly on one or more sides and will have all "teeth" complete and intact. Stamps with roulettes clear of the design on all four sides are extremely scarce and sell for substantial premiums.

Watermarks

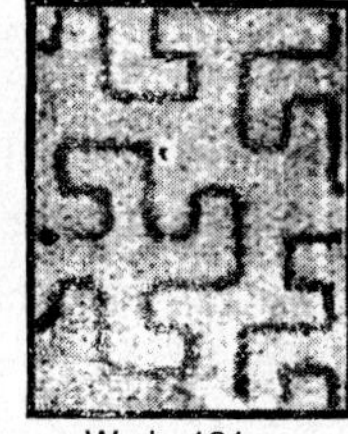

Wmk. 121 — Multiple Swastika

Wmk. 208 — Post Horn

Wmk. 168 — Wavy Lines and Letters

Wmk. 273 — Roses

Wmk. 363 — Tree Stump

Syncopated Perforations

Type A (1st stamp #1065): On one longer side, groups of five holes are separated by an oval hole equal in width to eight holes.

Type B (1st stamp, #1142): On the top groups of 3 holes at left and right and a middle group of 4 holes separated by rectangular perforations equal in width to 4 holes.

Issues under Russian Empire

Coat of Arms — A1

1856 **Unwmk.** **Typo.** *Imperf.*

Small Pearls in Post Horns

Wove Paper

1	A1 5k blue	*6,000.*	1,400.
	Cut to shape		125.
	Pen and town cancellation		1,750.
	Cut to shape		150.
	Town cancellation		2,750.
	Cut to shape		175.
a.	Tête bêche pair	*62,500.*	*57,500.*
	Pen and town cancellation		*62,500.*
2	A1 10k rose	7,750.	360.00
	Cut to shape		45.
	Pen and town cancellation		525.00
	Cut to shape		70.
	Town cancellation		850.00
	Cut to shape		80.
a.	Tête bêche pair	*62,500.*	*52,500.*
	Pen and town cancellation		*57,500.*

1858

Wide Vertically Laid Paper

2C	A1 10k rose	—	1,250.
	Cut to shape		190.
	Pen and town cancellation		1,650.
	Cut to shape		250.
	Town cancellation		2,100.
	Cut to shape		325.
d.	Tête bêche pair		—

The wide vertically laid paper has 13-14 distinct lines per 2cm. The 10k rose also exists on a narrow laid paper with lines sometimes indistinct. Value, about 45 per cent of that for a wide laid paper example.

A 5k blue with small pearls exists on narrow vertically laid paper. It is rare.

Stamps on diagonally laid paper are envelope cut squares.

Large Pearls in Post Horns

Wove Paper

3	A1 5k blue	*7,750.*	1,250.
	Cut to shape		95.
	Pen and town cancellation		1,450.
	Cut to shape		125.
	Town cancellation		2,250.
	Cut to shape		160.
a.	Tête bêche pair		*46,000.*
	Pen and town cancellation		*51,500.*

1859 Wide Vertically Laid Paper

3B A1 5k blue — 15,500.
Cut to shape 2,000.
Pen and town cancellation 21,000.
Cut to shape 3,000.

Reprints of Nos. 2 and 3, made in 1862, are on brownish paper, on vertically laid paper, and in tête bêche pairs on normal and vertically laid paper. Reprints of 1871, 1881 and 1893 are on yellowish or white paper. Value for least costly of each, $85.

In 1956, Nos. 2 and 3 were reprinted for the Centenary with post horn watermark and gum. Value, $85 each.

Coat of Arms — A2

1860 *Serpentine Roulette 7½, 8*

Four types of indentation are noted:

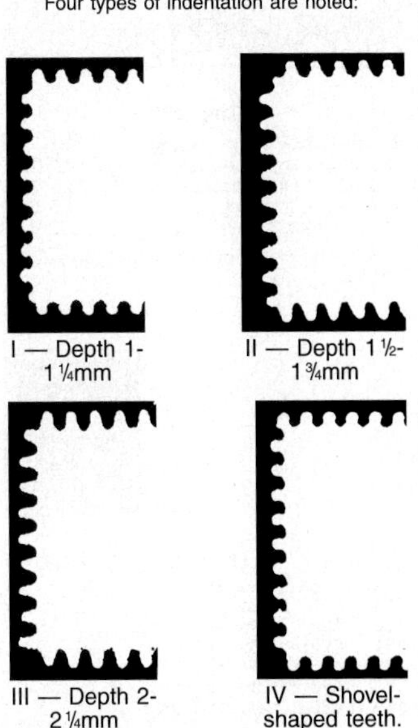

I — Depth 1-1¼mm
II — Depth 1½-1¾mm
III — Depth 2-2¼mm
IV — Shovel-shaped teeth. Depth 1¼-1½mm

Wove Paper

4 A2 5k blue, *bluish*, I 625.00 160.00
a. Roulette II 750.00 210.00
b. Perf. vert.
5 A2 10k rose, *pale rose*, I 525.00 52.50
a. Roulette II 1,050. 150.00

A3

A4

1866-74 *Serpentine Roulette*

6 A3 5p pur brn, *lil*, I ('73) 350.00 160.00
a. Roulette II 3,750.
b. 5p red brn, *lil*, III ('71) 300.00 160.00
7 A3 8p blk, *grn*, III ('67) 250.00 160.00
a. Ribbed paper, III ('72) 1,050. 825.00
b. Roulette II ('74) 325.00 250.00
c. As "b," ribbed paper ('74) 310.00 210.00
d. Roulette I ('73) 475.00 300.00
e. As "d," ribbed paper 1,050. 425.00
f. Serpentine roulette 10½ ('67) 12,500.
8 A3 10p blk, *yel*, III ('70) 625.00 325.00
a. 10p blk, *buff*, II 725.00 400.00
b. 10p blk, *buff*, I ('73) 675.00 340.00
9 A3 20p bl, *bl*, III 525.00 52.50
a. Roulette II 525.00 82.50
b. Roulette I ('73) 625.00 110.00
c. Roulette IV ('74) — 1,050.
d. Perf. horiz. —
e. Printed on both sides (40p blue on back) —
10 A3 40p rose, *lil rose*, III 460.00 62.50
a. Ribbed paper, III ('73) 625.00 190.00
b. Roulette II 475.00 77.50
c. As "b," ribbed paper ('73) 625.00 160.00
d. Roulette I 675.00 160.00
e. As "d," ribbed paper 625.00 110.00
f. Roulette IV — 2,100.
g. As "f," ribbed paper — —
h. Serpentine roulette 10½ —
11 A4 1m yel brn, III ('67) 2,100. 800.00
a. Roulette II 2,600. 1,550.

Nos. 7f and 10h are private roulettes and are also known in compound serpentine roulette 10½ and 7½.

Nos. 4-11 were reprinted in 1893 on thick wove paper. Colors differ from originals. Roulette type IV. Value for Nos. 4-5, each $40, Nos. 6-10, each $50. Value for No. 11, $55.

Thin or Thick Laid Paper

12 A3 5p red brn, *lil*, III 260.00 140.00
a. Roulette II 275.00 275.00
b. Roulette I 260.00 275.00
d. 5p blk, *buff*, roul. III (error) 20,000.
e. Tête bêche pair —
13 A3 10p black, *buff*, III 625.00 260.00
a. 10p black, *yel*, II 775.00 260.00
b. 10p black, *yel*, I 1,050. 675.00
c. 10p red brown, *lil*, III (error) 7,250. 6,500.

Forgeries of No. 13c exist.

A5

1875 *Perf. 14x13½*

16 A5 32p lake 2,050. 425.00

1875-81 *Perf. 11*

17 A5 2p gray 45.00 52.50
18 A5 5p orange 125.00 11.00
a. 5p yellow 125.00 11.00
19 A5 8p blue green 200.00 52.50
a. 8p yellow green 200.00 77.50
20 A5 10p brown ('81) 525.00 55.00
21 A5 20p ultra 140.00 3.00
a. 20p blue 150.00 5.25
b. 20p Prussian blue 310.00 35.00
c. Tête bêche pair 3,100.
22 A5 25p carmine ('79) 260.00 13.50
a. 25p rose 360.00 52.50
23 A5 32p carmine 410.00 57.50
a. 32p rose 500.00 160.00
24 A5 1m violet ('77) 725.00 160.00
Nos. 17-24 (8) 2,430. 405.00

A souvenir card issued in 1974 for NORDIA 1975 reproduced a block of four of the unissued "1 MARKKAA" design.

Nos. 19, 23 were reprinted in 1893, perf. 12½. Value $17.50 each.

1881-83 *Perf. 12½*

25 A5 2p gray 11.00 12.50
a. Imperf., pair 500.00
26 A5 5p orange 47.50 6.00
a. Tête bêche pair 6,250. 4,100.
b. Imperf. vert., pair —
c. Imperf. horiz., pair —
27 A5 10p brown 90.00 17.00
28 A5 20p ultra 50.00 1.50
a. 20p blue 50.00 1.50
b. Tête bêche pair 2,600. 2,100.
c. Imperf., pair —
29 A5 25p rose 40.00 9.25
a. 25p carmine 57.50 16.00
b. Tête bêche pair — —
30 A5 1m violet ('82) 360.00 40.00
Nos. 25-30 (6) 598.50 86.25

Nos. 27-29 were reprinted in 1893 in deeper shades, perf. 12½. Value $35 each.

Most copies of No. 28c are from printer's waste.

1881 *Perf. 11x12½*

26d A5 5p orange 410.00 82.50
27a A5 10p brown 850.00 225.00
28d A5 20p ultra 525.00 40.00
28e A5 20p blue 525.00 40.00
29c A5 25p rose 625.00 160.00
29d A5 25p carmine 525.00 110.00
30a A5 1m violet 1,350.

1881 *Perf. 12½x11*

26e A5 5p orange 410.00 82.50
27b A5 10p brown — 300.00
28f A5 20p ultra 525.00 40.00
28g A5 20p blue 525.00 40.00
29e A5 25p rose — 260.00
29f A5 25p carmine 525.00 100.00

1885 *Perf. 12½*

31 A5 5p emerald 16.00 .55
a. 5p yellow green 18.00 1.00
b. Tête bêche pair — 8,250.
32 A5 10p carmine 24.00 2.50
a. 10p rose 24.00 2.50
33 A5 20p orange 30.00 .45
a. 20p yellow 35.00 1.60
b. Tête bêche pair — 3,250.
34 A5 25p ultra 57.50 3.25
a. 25p blue 52.50 2.75
35 A5 1m gray & rose 30.00 18.00
36 A5 5m green & rose 400.00 300.00
37 A5 10m brown & rose 500.00 500.00

A6

1889-92 *Perf. 12½*

38 A6 2p slate ('90) .50 .75
39 A6 5p green ('90) 27.50 .20
40 A6 10p carmine ('90) 52.50 .50
a. 10p rose ('90) 67.50 .55
b. Imperf. 90.00 90.00
41 A6 20p orange ('92) 62.50 .30
a. 20p yellow ('90) 67.50 1.00
42 A6 25p ultra ('91) 62.50 .75
a. 25p blue 67.50 1.00
43 A6 1m slate & rose ('92) 4.00 3.25
a. 1m brnsh gray & rose ('90) 22.50 3.50
44 A6 5m green & rose ('90) 22.50 62.50
45 A6 10m brown & rose ('90) 32.50 82.50
Nos. 38-45 (8) 264.50 150.75

The 2p slate, perf. 14x13, is believed to be an essay.

See Nos. 60-63.

See Russia for types similar to A7-A18.

Finnish stamps have "dot in circle" devices or are inscribed "Markka," "Markkaa," "Pen." or "Pennia."

Imperial Arms of Russia
A7 A8 A9

A10

A11

Laid Paper

1891-92 Wmk. 168 *Perf. 14½x15*

46 A7 1k orange yel 4.50 9.50
47 A7 2k green 5.50 8.00
48 A7 3k carmine 10.50 14.50
49 A8 4k rose 12.50 12.50
50 A7 7k dark blue 5.50 2.25
51 A8 10k dark blue 12.50 13.50
52 A9 14k blue & rose 18.00 24.00
53 A8 20k blue & car 16.00 15.00
54 A9 35k violet & grn 22.50 47.50
55 A8 50k violet & grn 27.50 30.00

Perf. 13½

56 A10 1r brown & org 77.50 77.50
57 A11 3½r black & gray 275.00 400.00
a. 3½r black & yellow (error) 11,500. 14,000.
58 A11 7r black & yellow 200.00 260.00
Nos. 46-58 (13) 687.50 914.25

Forgeries of Nos. 57, 57a, 58 exist.

Type of 1889-90

Wove Paper

1895-96 Unwmk. *Perf. 14x13*

60 A6 5p green .50 .35
61 A6 10p rose .60 .45
62 A6 20p orange .50 .20
a. Imperf. 125.00 —
63 A6 25p ultra .80 .60
a. 25p blue 1.60 .65
b. Imperf. 100.00 —
Nos. 60-63 (4) 2.40 1.60

A12

A13

A14

A15

1901 Litho. *Perf. 14½x15*

Chalky Paper

64 A12 2p yellow 4.00 4.00
65 A12 5p green 8.00 .65
66 A13 10p carmine 22.50 1.00
67 A12 20p dark blue 52.50 .55
68 A14 1m violet & grn 260.00 8.00

Perf. 13½

69 A15 10m black & gray 250.00 250.00
Nos. 64-69 (6) 597.00 264.20

Imperf sheets of 10p and 20p, stolen during production, were privately perforated 11½ to defraud the P.O. Uncanceled imperfs. of Nos. 65-68 are believed to be proofs.

See Nos. 70-75, 82.

Types of 1901 Redrawn

No. 64

No. 70

2p. On No. 64, the "2" below "II" is shifted slightly leftward. On No. 70, the "2" is centered below "II."

No. 65 No. 71

5p. On No. 65, the frame lines are very close. On No. 71, a clear white space separates them.

Nos. 66, 67 Nos. 72, 73

10p, 20p. On Nos. 66-67, the horizontal central background lines are faint and broken. On Nos. 72-73, they are clear and solid, though still thin.

20p. On No. 67, "H" close to "2" with period midway. On No. 73 they are slightly separated with period close to "H."

No. 68 Nos. 74, 74a

1m. On No. 68, the "1" following "MARKKA" lacks serif at base. On Nos. 74-74a, this "1" has serif.

No. 69 No. 75

10m. On No. 69, the serifs of "M" and "A" in top and bottom panels do not touch. On No. 75, the serifs join.

1901-14 Typo. *Perf. 14, 14½x15*

Ordinary Paper

70 A12 2p orange .50 .70
71 A12 5p green 1.60 .20
72 A13 10p carmine 8.25 .20
b. Background inverted 13.50 2.00
73 A12 20p dark blue 4.00 .20
74 A14 1m lil & grn, perf. 14 ('14) .75 .40
a. 1m violet & blue green, perf. 14½x15 ('02) 8.00 .90
Nos. 70-74 (5) 15.10 1.70

Perf. 13½

75 A15 10m blk & drab ('03) 125.00 42.50

Imperf.

70a A12 2p 290.00 410.00
71b A12 5p 77.50 160.00
72a A13 10p 90.00 160.00
73a A12 20p 160.00 160.00
74b A14 1m 150.00 160.00
Nos. 70a-74b (5) 767.50 1,050.

A16 A17 A18

1911-16 *Perf. 14, 14½x15*

77 A16 2p orange .20 .20
78 A16 5p green .25 .20
a. Imperf. 410.00
b. Perf. 14½x15 360.00 62.50
79 A17 10p rose .20 .20
a. Imperf. 77.50 160.00
b. Perf. 14½x15 60.00 2.00
80 A16 20p deep blue .20 .20
a. Imperf. 150.00 1.10
81 A18 40p violet & blue .20 .20
a. Perf. 14½x15 3,100. 3,100.
Nos. 77-81 (5) 1.05 1.00

There are three minor types of No. 79.

Perf. 14½

82 A15 10m blk & grnsh gray ('16) 110.00 160.00
a. Horiz. pair, imperf. vert. 2,900.

Republic
Helsinki Issue

Arms of the Republic
A19 A20

Two types of the 40p.
Type I — Thin figures of value.
Type II — Thick figures of value.

1917-29 Unwmk. *Perf. 14, 14½x15*

83 A19 5p green .20 .20
84 A19 5p gray ('19) .20 .20
85 A19 10p rose .25 .20
a. Imperf., pair 200.00 250.00
86 A19 10p green ('19) 2.00 .40
a. Perf. 14½x15 1,600.
87 A19 10p lt blue ('21) .25 .20
88 A19 20p buff .25 .20
89 A19 20p rose ('20) .50 .20
90 A19 20p brown ('24) .50 .40
91 A19 25p blue .20 .20
92 A19 25p lt brown ('19) .20 .20
93 A19 30p green ('23) .25 .20
94 A19 40p violet (I) .20 .20
a. Perf. 14½x15 200.00 10.00
95 A19 40p bl grn (II) ('29) .20 .50
a. Type I ('24) 8.00 2.50
96 A19 50p orange brn .20 .20
97 A19 50p dp blue ('19) 2.50 .20
a. Perf. 14½x15 600.00
98 A19 50p green ('21) 3.00 .20
a. Perf. 14½x15 .30 2.50
99 A19 60p red vio ('21) .30 .20
a. Imperf., pair 75.00 100.00
100 A19 75p yellow ('21) .20 .30
101 A19 1m dull rose & blk 9.00 .20
102 A19 1m red org ('25) 4.50 12.50
103 A19 1½m bl grn & red vio ('29) .20 .20
a. Perf. 14½x15 .20 .30
104 A19 2m grn & blk ('21) 2.25 .50
105 A19 2m dk blue & ind ('22) 1.50 .20
a. Perf. 14½x15 .50 1.00
106 A19 3m bl & blk ('21) 60.00 .20
107 A19 5m red vio & blk 14.00 .20
108 A19 10m brn & gray blk, perf. 14 .60 1.00
a. 10m light brown & black, perf. 14½x15 ('29) 2.50 300.00
110 A19 25m dull red & yel ('21) .75 18.00
Nos. 83-108,110 (27) 104.20 37.40

Copies of a 2½p gray of this type exist. They are proofs from the original die which were distributed through the UPU. No plate was made for this denomination.

See Nos. 127-140, 143-152. For surcharge and overprints see Nos. 119-126, 153-154.

Vasa Issue

1918 Litho. *Perf. 11½*

111 A20 5p green .20 .60
112 A20 10p red .20 .40
113 A20 30p slate .20 .95
114 A20 40p brown vio .20 .75
115 A20 50p orange brn .20 .95
116 A20 70p gray brown 1.50 10.00
117 A20 1m red & gray .30 .95
118 A20 5m red violet & gray 30.00 50.00
Nos. 111-118 (8) 32.80 64.60

Nos. 111-118 exist imperforate but were not regularly issued in that condition.

Sheet margin copies, perf. on 3 sides, imperf. on margin side, were sold by post office.

Stamps and Type of 1917-29 Surcharged

1919 *Perf. 14*

119 A19 10p on 5p green .30 .35
120 A19 20p on 10p rose .30 .35
121 A19 50p on 25p blue .60 .35
122 A19 75p on 20p orange .30 .30
Nos. 119-122 (4) 1.50 1.35

Stamps and Type of 1917-29 Surcharged:

Nos. 123-125 No. 126

1921

123 A19 30p on 10p grn .55 .75
124 A19 60p on 40p red violet 2.50 .50
125 A19 90p on 20p rose .35 .20
126 A19 1½m on 50p blue 1.25 .35
a. Thin "2" in "½" 9.00 4.75
b. Imperf., pair 225.00 300.00
Nos. 123-126 (4) 4.65 1.80

Arms Type of 1917-29
Perf. 14, 14½x15

1925-29 Wmk. 121

127 A19 10p ultra ('27) .45 .75
128 A19 20p brown .45 .65
129 A19 25p brn org ('29) .65 40.00
130 A19 30p yel green .20 .20
131 A19 40p blue grn (I) 1.50 .35
a. Type II 2.25 .35
132 A19 50p gray grn ('27) .35 .35
133 A19 60p red violet .20 .20
134 A19 1m dp orange 3.25 .20
135 A19 1½m blue grn & red vio 3.50 .20
136 A19 2m dk bl & ind .30 .20
137 A19 3m chlky blue & blk .90 .20
138 A19 5m red vio & blk .25 .20
139 A19 10m lt brn & blk ('27) 3.00 12.00
140 A19 25m dp org & yel ('27) 17.50 200.00
Nos. 127-140 (14) 32.50 255.50

A21

Wmk. 208

1927, Dec. 6 Typo. *Perf. 14*

141 A21 1½m deep violet .20 .30
142 A21 2m deep blue .25 1.00

10th anniv. of Finnish independence.

Arms Type of 1917-29

1927-29 Wmk. 208 *Perf. 14½x15*

143 A19 20p lt brown ('29) 1.00 8.50
144 A19 40p bl grn (II) ('28) .20 .20
145 A19 50p gray grn ('28) .20 .20
146 A19 1m dp orange .20 .20
a. Imperf., pair 125.00 140.00
b. Perf. 14 1.00 1.00
147 A19 1½m bl grn & red vio ('28) 1.50 .20
a. Perf. 14 700.00 9.00
148 A19 2m dk bl & ind ('28) .35 .30
149 A19 3m chlky bl & blk .35 .30
a. Perf. 14 1.50 1.50
150 A19 5m red vio & blk ('28) .60 .60
151 A19 10m lt brown & blk 1.00 29.00
152 A19 25m brown org & yel 1.10 110.00
Nos. 143-152 (10) 6.50 149.50

Nos. 146-147 Overprinted

1928, Nov. 10 Litho. Wmk. 208

153 A19 1m deep orange 6.50 12.50
154 A19 1½m bl grn & red vio 6.50 12.50

Nos. 153 and 154 were sold exclusively at the Helsinki Philatelic Exhibition, Nov. 10-18, 1928, and were valid only during that period.

S. S. "Bore" Leaving Turku — A23

Turku Cathedral — A24

Turku Castle — A25

Wmk. 208

1929, May 22 Typo. *Perf. 14*

155 A23 1m olive green 1.40 2.75
156 A24 1½m chocolate 2.25 2.75
157 A25 2m dark gray .85 3.00
Nos. 155-157 (3) 4.50 8.50

Founding of the city of Turku (Abo), 700th anniv.

A26

1930-46 Unwmk. *Perf. 14*

158 A26 5p chocolate .20 .20
159 A26 10p dull violet .20 .20
160 A26 20p yel grn .30 .35
161 A26 25p yel brn .20 .20
162 A26 40p bl grn 1.75 .35
163 A26 50p yellow .45 .35
164 A26 50p blue grn ('32) .20 .20
b. Imperf., pair 125.00 125.00
165 A26 60p dark gray .35 .45
165A A26 75p dp org ('42) .20 .20
166 A26 1m red org .45 .20
166B A26 1m yel grn ('42) .20 .20
167 A26 1.20m crimson .35 .50
168 A26 1.25m yel ('32) .20 .20
169 A26 1½m red vio 2.00 .20
170 A26 1½m car ('32) .20 .20
170A A26 1½m sl ('40) .20 .20
170B A26 1.75m org yel ('40) .55 .20
171 A26 2m indigo .30 .20
172 A26 2m dp vio ('32) 6.00 .20
173 A26 2m car ('36) .20 .20
Complete booklet, panes of 4 #161, 164, 166, 168, 173 5.00
173B A26 2m yel org ('42) .30 .20
173C A26 2m blue grn ('45) .20 .20
174 A26 2½m brt bl ('32) 2.00 .20
174A A26 2½m car ('42) .20 .20
174B A26 2.75m rose vio ('40) .20 .20
175 A26 3m olive blk 22.50 .20
175B A26 3m car ('45) .20 .20
175C A26 3m yel ('45) .35 .45
176 A26 3½m brt bl ('36) 5.50 .20
176A A26 3½m olive ('42) .20 .20
176B A26 4m olive ('45) .35 .20
176C A26 4½m saph ('42) .20 .20
176D A26 5m saph ('45) .35 .20
176E A26 5m pur ('45) .35 .20
j. Imperf., pair 125.00 125.00
176F A26 5m yel ('46) .70 .20
k. Imperf., pair 110.00 125.00
176G A26 6m car ('45) .35 .20
m. Imperf., pair 125.00 125.00
176H A26 8m pur ('46) .20 .20
176I A26 10m saph ('45) .70 .20
Nos. 158-176I (38) 49.35 8.85

See #257-262, 270-274, 291-296, 302-304. For surcharges & overprints see #195-196, 212, 221-222, 243, 250, 275, M2-M3.

Stamps of types A26-A29 overprinted "ITA KARJALA" are listed under Karelia, Nos. N1-N15.

Castle in Savonlinna A27

Lake Saima — A28

Woodchopper A29

1930 **Engr.**

177	A27	5m blue	.20	.20
178	A28	10m gray lilac	50.00	2.50
179	A29	25m black brown	.95	.20
		Nos. 177-179 (3)	51.15	2.90

See #205, 305. For overprint see #C1.

Elias Lönnrot — A30

Seal of Finnish Literary Society — A31

1931, Jan. 1 **Typo.**

180	A30	1m olive brown	2.75	*3.50*
181	A31	1½m dull blue	14.00	3.50

Centenary of Finnish Literary Society.

A32

1931, Feb. 28

182	A32	1½m red	2.75	*6.00*
183	A32	2m blue	2.75	*7.00*

1st use of postage stamps in Finland, 75th anniv.

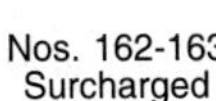
Nos. 162-163 Surcharged

1931, Dec.

195	A26	50p on 40p blue grn	1.40	.60
196	A26	1.25m on 50p yellow	4.00	1.50

Svinhufvud A33

Alexis Kivi A34

1931, Dec. 15

197	A33	2m gray blue & blk	1.50	*2.00*

Pres. Pehr Eyvind Svinhufvud, 70th birthday.

Lake Saima Type of 1930

1932-43 **Re-engraved**

205	A28	10m red violet ('43)	.35	.20
a.		10m dark violet	17.50	.50

On Nos. 205 and 205a the lines of the islands, the clouds and the foliage are much deeper and stronger than on No. 178.

1934, Oct. 10 **Typo.**

206	A34	2m red violet	2.25	2.25
		Never hinged	3.25	

Alexis Kivi, Finnish poet (1834-1872).

Bards Reciting the "Kalevala" A35

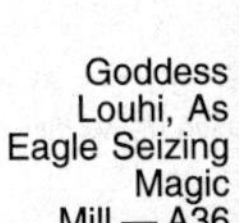
Goddess Louhi, As Eagle Seizing Magic Mill — A36

Kullervo — A37

1935, Feb. 28 **Engr.**

207	A35	1¼m brown lake	1.25	1.25
208	A36	2m black	3.00	.70
209	A37	2½m blue	3.00	1.75
		Nos. 207-209 (3)	7.25	3.70
		Set, never hinged	12.00	

Cent. of the publication of the "Kalevala" (Finnish National Epic).

No. 170 Surcharged in Black

1937, Feb.

212	A26	2m on 1½m car	3.25	.90
		Never hinged	7.00	

Gustaf Mannerheim — A38

Swede-Finn Co-operation in Colonization A39

1937, June 4 **Photo.** ***Perf. 14***

213	A38	2m ultra	.50	*.75*
		Never hinged	1.50	

70th birthday of Field Marshal Baron Carl Gustaf Mannerheim, June 4th, 1937.

1938, June 1

214	A39	3½m dark brown	1.25	*3.00*
		Never hinged	2.50	

Tercentenary of the colonization of Delaware by Swedes and Finns.

Early Post Office — A40

Designs: 1¼m, Mail delivery in 1700. 2m, Modern mail plane. 3½m, Helsinki post office.

1938, Sept. 6 **Photo.** ***Perf. 14***

215	A40	50p green	.35	.75
216	A40	1¼m dk blue	1.25	*2.25*
217	A40	2m scarlet	1.25	.90
218	A40	3½m slate black	3.50	*3.50*
		Nos. 215-218 (4)	6.35	7.40
		Set, never hinged	10.00	

300th anniv. of the Finnish Postal System.

Margin strips of each denomination (3 of #215, 2 each of #216, 217, 218) were pasted on to advertising sheets and stapled into a booklet. Value, $100.

Post Office, Helsinki — A44

1939-42 **Photo.**

219	A44	4m brown black	.20	.20

Engr.

219A	A44	7m black brn ('42)	.30	.20
219B	A44	9m rose lake ('42)	.30	.20
		Nos. 219-219B (3)	.80	.60
		Set, never hinged	2.25	

See No. 248.

Catalogue values for unused stamps in this section, from this point to the end of the section, are for Never Hinged items.

University of Helsinki — A45

1940, May 1 **Photo.**

220	A45	2m dp blue & blue	.50	*.90*

300th anniv. of the founding of the University of Helsinki.

Nos. 168 and 173 Surcharged in Black

1940, June 16 **Typo.**

221	A26	1.75m on 1.25m yel	1.50	1.50
222	A26	2.75m on 2m carmine	4.50	.60

President Kallio Reviewing Military Band — A46

1941, May 24 **Engr.**

223	A46	2.75m black	.50	*.60*

Pres. Kyösti Kallio (1873-1940).

Castle at Viborg — A47

1941, Aug. 30 **Typo.**

224	A47	1.75m yellow orange	.60	.50
225	A47	2.75m rose violet	.60	.75
226	A47	3.50m blue	.90	1.10

Field Marshal Mannerheim A48

Pres. Risto Ryti A49

1941, Dec. 31 **Engr.** **Wmk. 273**

227	A48	50p dull green	.90	1.25
228	A48	1.75m deep brown	.90	*1.25*
229	A48	2m dark red	.90	1.25
230	A48	2.75m dull vio brn	.90	*1.25*
231	A48	3.50m deep blue	.90	*1.25*
232	A48	5m slate blue	.90	*1.25*
		Nos. 227-232 (6)	5.40	*7.50*
233	A49	50p dull green	.75	1.25
234	A49	1.75m deep brown	.75	*1.25*
235	A49	2m dark red	.75	1.25
236	A49	2.75m dull vio brn	.75	*1.25*
237	A49	3.50m deep blue	.75	*1.25*
238	A49	5m slate blue	.75	*1.25*
		Nos. 233-238 (6)	4.50	*7.50*

Types A48-A49 overprinted "ITA KARJALA" are listed under Karelia, Nos. N16-N27.

Häme Bridge, Tampere A50

South Harbor, Helsinki — A51

1942 **Unwmk.**

239 A50	50m dull brown vio	2.00	.20
240 A51	100m indigo	3.00	.20

See No. 350.

Altar and Open Bible — A52

17th Century Printer — A53

1942, Oct. 10

241 A52	2.75m dk brown	.40	*.80*
242 A53	3.50m violet blue	.80	*1.25*

300th anniv. of the printing of the 1st Bible in Finnish.

No. 174B Surcharged in Black

1943, Feb. 1

243 A26	3.50m on 2.75m rose vio	.25	.40

Minna Canth (1844-96), Author and Playwright — A54

1944, Mar. 20

244 A54	3.50m dk olive grn	.60	*1.00*

Pres. P. E. Svinhufvud A55

K. J. Stahlberg A56

1944, Aug. 1

245 A55	3.50m black	.40	*.80*

Death of President Svinhufvud (1861-1944).

1945, May 16 **Engr.** ***Perf. 14***

246 A56	3.50m brown vio	.25	*.40*

80th birthday of Dr. K. J. Stahlberg.

Castle in Savonlinna A57

Jean Sibelius — A58

1945, Sept. 4

247 A57	15m lilac rose	1.75	.20
248 A44	20m sepia	1.75	.20

For a 35m of type A57, see No. 280.

1945, Dec. 8

249 A58	5m dk slate green	.40	.40

Jean Sibelius (1865-1957), composer.

No. 176E Surcharged with New Value and Bars in Black

1946, Mar. 16

250 A26	8(m) on 5m purple	.35	.20

Victorious Athletes — A59

Lighthouse at Uto — A60

1946, June 1 **Engr.** ***Perf. 13½***

251 A59	8m brown violet	.25	*.40*

3rd Sports Festival, Helsinki, June 27-30, 1946.

1946, Sept. 19

252 A60	8m deep violet	.25	*.40*

250th anniv. of the Finnish Department of Pilots and Lighthouses.

Post Bus — A61

1946-47 **Unwmk.** ***Perf. 14***

253 A61	16m gray black	.75	.75
253A A61	30m gray black ('47)	1.75	.20

Issue dates: 16m, Oct. 16, 30m, Feb. 10.

Old Town Hall, Porvoo — A62

Cathedral, Porvoo — A63

1946, Dec. 3

254 A62	5m gray black	.25	*.50*
255 A63	8m deep claret	.30	*.50*

600th anniv. of the founding of the city of Porvoo (Borga).

Waterfront, Tammisaari A64

1946, Dec. 14

256 A64	8m grnsh black	.25	*.50*

400th anniv. of the founding of the town of Tammisaari (Ekenas).

Lion Type of 1930

1947 **Typo.** ***Perf. 14***

257 A26	2½m dark green	.25	.20
258 A26	3m slate gray	.25	.20
259 A26	6m deep orange	1.25	.30
260 A26	7m carmine	.75	.20
261 A26	10m purple	2.10	.20
262 A26	12m deep blue	1.75	.20
	Nos. 257-262 (6)	6.35	1.30

Issued: 3m, 6/9; 7m, 12m, 2/10; others, 1/20.

Pres. Juho K. Paasikivi — A65

Postal Savings Emblem — A66

1947, Mar. 15 **Engr.**

263 A65	10m gray black	.35	*.40*

1947, Apr. 1

264 A66	10m brown violet	.30	*.40*

60th anniv. of the foundation of the Finnish Postal Savings Bank.

Ilmarinen, the Plowman A67

Girl and Boy Athletes A68

1947, June 2

265 A67	10m gray black	.30	*.40*

2nd year of peace following WW II.

1947, June 2

266 A68	10m bright blue	.30	*.40*

Finnish Athletic Festival, Helsinki, June 29-July 3, 1947.

Wheat and Savings Bank Assoc. Emblem — A69

Sower — A70

1947, Aug. 21

267 A69	10m red brown	.30	*.40*

Finnish Savings Bank Assoc., 125th anniv.

1947, Nov. 1

268 A70	10m gray black	.30	*.40*

150th anniv. of Finnish Agricultural Societies.

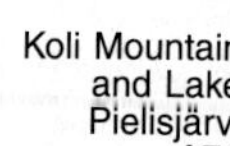

Koli Mountain and Lake Pielisjärvi A71

Statue of Michael Agricola — A72

1947, Nov. 1

269 A71	10m indigo	.30	*.40*

60th anniv. of the Finnish Touring Assoc.

Lion Type of 1930

1948 **Typo.** ***Perf. 14***

270 A26	3m dark green	2.00	.20
271 A26	6m yellow green	.90	.30
272 A26	9m carmine	.85	.20
273 A26	15m dark blue	3.25	.20
274 A26	24m brown lake	1.00	.20
	Nos. 270-274 (5)	8.00	1.10

Issued: 3m, 2/9; 24m, 4/26; others, 9/13.

No. 261 Surcharged with New Value and Bars in Black

1948, Feb. 9

275 A26	12(m) on 10m purple	.80	.20

1948, Oct. 2 **Engr.** ***Perf. 14***

12m, Agricola translating New Testament.

276 A72	7m rose violet	.85	*1.10*
277 A72	12m gray blue	.85	*1.10*

400th anniv. of publication of the Finnish translation of the New Testament, by Michael Agricola.

Sveaborg Fortress A73

Post Rider — A74

1948, Oct. 15

278 A73	12m deep green	1.10	*1.40*

200th anniv. of the construction of Sveaborg Fortress on the Gulf of Finland.

1948, Oct. 27

279 A74	12m green	7.00	*12.00*

Helsinki Philatelic Exhibition. Sold only at exhibition for 62m, of which 50m was entrance fee.

Castle Type of 1945

1949

280 A57	35m violet	5.00	.20

Sawmill and Cellulose Plant — A75

Pine Tree and Globe — A76

Woman with Torch — A77

1949, June 15

281 A75 9m brown 1.60 *2.00*
282 A76 15m dull green 1.60 *2.00*

Issued to publicize the Third World Forestry Congress, Helsinki, July 10-20, 1949.

1949, July 16 Engr. *Perf. 14*

283 A77 5m dull green 3.00 *6.50*
284 A77 15m red *(Worker)* 3.00 *6.50*

50th anniv. of the Finnish labor movement.

Harbor of Lappeenranta (Willmanstrand) — A78

Raahe (Brahestad) — A79

1949

285 A78 5m dk blue grn .65 .60
286 A79 9m brown carmine .85 .85
287 A78 15m brt blue *(Kristiinan-kaupunki)* 1.50 *2.25*
Nos. 285-287 (3) 3.00 3.70

300th anniv. of the founding of Willmanstrand, Brahestad and Kristinestad (Kristiinan-kaupunki).
Issued: 5m, 8/6; 9m, 8/13; 15m, 7/30.

Technical High School Badge — A80

Hannes Gebhard — A81

1949, Sept. 13

288 A80 15m ultra .75 *.80*

Founding of the technical school, cent.

1949, Oct. 2

289 A81 15m dull green .75 *.80*

Establishment of Finnish cooperatives, 50th anniv.

Finnish Lake Country — A82

1949, Oct. 8

290 A82 15m blue 1.00 .85

75th anniv. of the UPU.

Lion Type of 1930

1950, Jan. 9 Typo. *Perf. 14*

291 A26 8m brt green 1.75 1.75
292 A26 9m red orange 1.25 .30
293 A26 10m violet brown 4.25 .20
294 A26 12m scarlet .85 .20
295 A26 15m plum 10.00 .20
296 A26 20m deep blue 5.00 .20
Nos. 291-296 (6) 23.10 2.85

Forsell's Map of Old Helsinki — A83

J. A. Ehrenstrom and C. L. Engel — A84

City Hall — A85

1950, June 11 Engr.

297 A83 5m emerald .35 *.55*
298 A84 9m brown .60 *.85*
299 A85 15m deep blue .45 *.60*
Nos. 297-299 (3) 1.40 2.00

400th anniv. of the founding of Helsinki.

J. K. Paasikivi — A86

View of Kajaani — A87

1950, Nov. 27

300 A86 20m deep ultra .50 .30

80th birthday of Pres. J. K. Paasikivi.

1951, July 7 Unwmk. *Perf. 14*

301 A87 20m red brown .60 .50

Tercentenary of Kajaani.

Lion and Chopper Types of 1930

1952, Jan. 18 Typo.

302 A26 10m emerald 2.75 .20
303 A26 15m red 3.00 .20
304 A26 25m blue 3.00 .20

Engr.

305 A29 40m black brown 3.00 .20
Nos. 302-305 (4) 11.75 .80

Arms of Pietarsaari A88

Rooftops of Vaasa A89

1952, June 19 Unwmk. *Perf. 14*

306 A88 25m blue .80 .80

300th anniv. of the founding of Pietarsaari (Jacobstad).

1952, Aug. 3

307 A89 25m brown .80 .80

Centenary of the burning of Vaasa.

Chess Symbols — A90

Torch Bearers — A91

1952, Aug. 10

308 A90 25m gray 1.60 *1.75*

10th Chess Olympics, Helsinki, 8/10-31/52.

1953, Jan. 27

309 A91 25m blue 1.00 .90

Temperance movement in Finland, cent.

Air View of Hamina (Fredrikshamn) A92

Ivar Wilskman — A93

1953, June 20

310 A92 25m dk gray green .85 .75

Tercentenary of Hamina.

1954, Feb. 26

311 A93 25m blue .75 .75

Centenary of the birth of Prof. Ivar Wilskman, "father of gymnastics in Finland."

Arms of Finland A94

"In the Outer Archipelago" A95

1954-59 *Perf. 11½*

312 A94 1m red brown ('55) .45 .20
313 A94 2m green ('55) .45 .20
314 A94 3m deep orange .45 .20
314A A94 4m gray ('58) .40 .20
315 A94 5m violet blue .75 .20
316 A94 10m blue green 1.10 .20
a. Bklt. pane of 5 (vert. strip) 20.00 20.00
Complete booklet, #316a 22.50
317 A94 15m rose red 2.25 .20
318 A94 15m yellow org ('57) 5.00 .20
319 A94 20m rose lilac 9.00 .20
320 A94 20m rose red ('56) 1.75 .20
321 A94 25m deep blue 2.75 .20
322 A94 25m rose lilac ('59) 10.00 .20
323 A94 30m lt ultra ('56) 2.25 .20
Nos. 312-323 (13) 36.60 2.60

See Nos. 398, 400-405A, 457-459, 461A-462, 464-464B.

1954, July 21 *Perf. 14*

324 A95 25m black .65 .50

Cent. of the birth of Albert Edelfelt, painter.

J. J. Nervander A96

1955, Feb. 23

325 A96 25m blue .80 .60

150th anniv. of the birth of J. J. Nervander, astronomer and poet.

Composite of Finnish Public Buildings A97

Bishop Henrik with Foot on Lalli, his Murderer A98

1955, Mar. 30 Engr. *Perf. 14*

326 A97 25m gray 12.50 *15.00*

Sold for 125m, which included the price of admission to the Natl. Postage Stamp Exhibition, Helsinki, Mar. 30-Apr. 3, 1955.

1955, May 19

25m, Arrival of Bishop Henrik and monks.

327 A98 15m rose brown .80 .65
328 A98 25m green .80 .65

Adoption of Christianity in Finland, 800th anniv.

Conference Hall, Helsinki — A99

1955, Aug. 25

329 A99 25m bluish green 1.10 *1.25*

44th conf. of the Interparliamentarian Union, Helsinki, Aug. 25-31, 1955.

Sailing Vessel and Merchant A100

1955, Sept. 2

330 A100 25m sepia 1.25 1.25

350th anniv. of founding of Oulu.

Town Hall, Lahti — A101

Radio Sender, Map of Finland — A102

1955, Nov. 1 *Perf. 14x13½*

331 A101 25m violet blue 1.10 1.10

50th anniversary of founding of Lahti.

1955, Dec. 10 *Perf. 14*

Designs: 15m, Otto Nyberg. 25m, Telegraph wires and pines under snow.

Inscribed: Lennatin 1855-1955 Telegrafen

332 A102 10m green 1.50 1.50
333 A102 15m dull violet 1.50 1.50
334 A102 25m lt ultra 1.50 1.50
Nos. 332-334 (3) 4.50 4.50

Cent. of the telegraph in Finland.

A103

A104

1956, Jan. 26 Unwmk. *Perf. 14*

335 A103 25m Lighthouse, Porkkala Peninsula .70 .50

Return of the Porkkala Region to Finland by Russia, Jan. 1956.

1956-57 *Perf. 11½*

30m, 50m, Church at Lammi. 40m, House of Parliament. 60m, Fortress of Olavinlinna (Olofsborg).

336	A104	30m gray olive	1.00	.20
337	A104	40m dull purple	2.50	.20
338	A104	50m gray ol ('57)	5.75	.20
338A	A104	60m pale pur ('57)	11.00	.20
		Nos. 336-338A (4)	20.25	.80

Issued: 30m, 3/4; 40m, 3/11; 50m, 3/3; 60m, 4/7. See Nos. 406-408A.

Johan V. Snellman A105

Gymnast and Athletes A106

1956, May 12 Engr. *Perf. 14*

339 A105 25m dk violet brn .65 .50

Johan V. Snellman (1806-81), statesman.

1956, June 28

340 A106 30m violet blue .90 .60

Finnish Gymnastic and Sports Games, Helsinki, June 28-July 1, 1956.

A107

Wmk. 208

1956, July 7 Typo. *Rouletted*

341 A107 30m deep ultra 3.50 *5.00*

a. Tête bêche pair 7.25 *10.50*

b. Pane of 10 37.50 *55.00*

Issued to publicize the FINLANDIA Philatelic Exhibition, Helsinki, July 7-15, 1956.

Printed in sheets containing four 2x5 panes, with white margins around each group. The stamps in each double row are printed tete-beche, making the position of the watermark differ in the vertical row of each pane of ten.

Sold for 155m, price including entrance ticket to exhibition.

Town Hall at Vasa — A108

Unwmk.

1956, Oct. 2 Engr. *Perf. 14*

342 A108 30m bright blue .75 .50

350th anniversary of Vasa.

Northern Countries Issue

Whooper Swans — A108a

1956, Oct. 30 *Perf. 12½*

343 A108a 20m rose red 2.75 1.25

344 A108a 30m ultra 10.00 1.10

See footnote after Denmark No. 362.

University Clinic, Helsinki A109

Scout Sign, Emblem and Globe — A110

1956, Dec. 17 *Perf. 11½*

345 A109 30m dull green 2.25 .75

Public health service in Finland, bicent.

1957, Feb. 22 *Perf. 14*

346 A110 30m ultra 1.50 .70

50th anniversary of Boy Scouts.

Arms Holding Hammers and Laurel — A111

"Lex" from Seal of Parliament — A112

Design: 20m, Factories and cogwheel.

1957 Engr. *Perf. 13½*

347 A111 20m dark blue .75 .45

348 A111 30m carmine .75 .60

50th anniv.: Central Fed. of Finnish Employers (20m, issued 9/27); Finnish Trade Union Movement (30m, issued 4/15).

1957, May 23 *Perf. 14*

349 A112 30m olive gray 1.00 .60

50th anniv. of the Finnish parliament.

Harbor Type of 1942

1957 Unwmk. *Perf. 14*

350 A51 100m grnsh blue 7.00 .20

Ida Aalberg — A114

Arms of Finland A115

1957, Dec. 4 *Perf. 14*

351 A114 30m vio gray & mar .70 .55

Birth cent. of Ida Aalberg, Finnish actress.

1957, Dec. 6 *Perf. 11½*

352 A115 30m blue .75 .55

40th anniv. of Finland's independence.

Jean Sibelius — A116

Ski Jump — A117

1957, Dec. 8 *Perf. 14*

353 A116 30m black 1.25 .55

Jean Sibelius (1865-1957), composer.

1958, Feb. 1 Engr. *Perf. 11½*

Design: 30m, Skier, vert.

354 A117 20m slate green .65 *.85*

355 A117 30m blue .75 .45

Nordic championships of the Intl. Ski Federation, Lahti.

"March of the Bjorneborgienses," by Edelfelt — A118

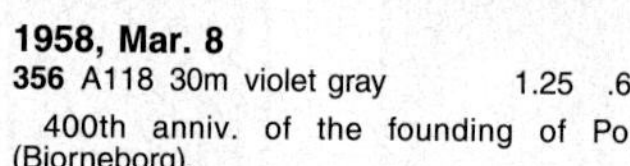

1958, Mar. 8

356 A118 30m violet gray 1.25 .65

400th anniv. of the founding of Pori (Bjorneborg).

South Harbor, Helsinki A119

1958, June 2 Unwmk. *Perf. 11½*

357 A119 100m bluish green 20.00 .20

See No. 410.

Seal of Jyväskylä Lyceum A120

1958, Oct. 1 *Perf. 11½*

358 A120 30m rose carmine 1.25 .70

Cent. of the founding of the 1st Finnish secondary school.

Chrismon and Globe — A121

Diet at Porvoo, 1809 — A122

1959, Jan. 19

359 A121 30m dull violet .85 .60

Finnish Missionary Society, cent.

1959, Mar. 22 *Perf. 11½*

360 A122 30m dk blue gray .80 .60

150th anniv. of the inauguration of the Diet at Porvoo.

Saw Cutting Log — A123

Pyhakoski Power Station — A124

1959, May 13 Engr.

361 A123 10m shown .45 .45

362 A123 30m Forest .70 *.70*

No. 361 for the cent. of the establishment of the 1st steam saw-mill in Finland; No. 362, the cent. of the Dept. of Forestry.

1959, May 24

363 A124 75m gray 4.00 .20

See No. 409.

Oil Lamp — A125

Woman Gymnast A126

1959, Dec. 19

364 A125 30m blue .75 .40

Cent. of the liberation of the country trade.

1959, Nov. 14 Unwmk.

365 A126 30m rose lilac .75 .40

Finnish women's gymnastics and the cent. of the birth of Elin Oihonna Kallio, pioneer of Finnish women's physical education.

Arms of Six New Towns — A127

1960, Jan. 2 *Perf. 14*

366 A127 30m light violet .75 .40

Issued to commemorate the founding of new towns in Finland: Hyvinkaa, Kouvola, Riihimaki, Rovaniemi, Salo and Seinajoki.

Type of 1860 Issue A128

1960, Mar. 25 Typo. *Rouletted 4½*
367 A128 30m blue & gray 6.00 7.50

Cent. of Finland's serpentine roulette stamps, and in connection with HELSINKI 1960, 40th anniv. exhib. of the Federation of Philatelic Societies of Finland, Mar. 25-31. Sold only at the exhibition for 150m including entrance ticket.

Mother and Child, Waiting Crowd and Uprooted Oak Emblem A129

1960, Apr. 7 Engr. *Perf. 11½*
368 A129 30m rose claret .55 .45
369 A129 40m dark blue .55 .45

World Refugee Year, 7/1/59-6/30/60.

Johan Gadolin A130

Hj. Nortamo A131

1960, June 4 *Perf. 11½*
370 A130 30m dark brown .60 .60

Bicent. of the birth of Gadolin, chemist.

1960, June 13 Unwmk.
371 A131 30m gray green .70 .40

Cent. of the birth of Hj. Nortamo (Hjalmar Nordberg), writer.

Symbolic Tree and Cuckoo A132

1960, June 18
372 A132 30m vermilion .75 .40

Karelian Natl. Festival, Helsinki, June 18-19.

Geodetic Instrument A133

Urho Kekkonen — A134

Design: 30m, Aurora borealis and globe.

1960, July 26 Unwmk. *Perf. 13½*
373 A133 10m blue & pale brn .40 .30
374 A133 30m ver & rose car .75 .40

12th General Assembly of the Intl. Union of Geodesy and Geophysics, Helsinki.

1960, Sept. 3 Engr. *Perf. 11½*
375 A134 30m violet blue .80 .40

Issued to honor President Urho Kekkonen on his 60th birthday.

Common Design Types pictured following the introduction.

Europa Issue, 1960
Common Design Type

1960, Sept. 19 *Perf. 13½*
Size: 30½x21mm.
376 CD3 30m dk bl & Prus bl .60 .60
377 CD3 40m dk brn & plum .60 .60

A 30m gray similar to No. 376 was printed with simulated perforations in a non-valid souvenir sheet privately released in London for STAMPEX 1961.

Uno Cygnaeus A135

"Pommern" and Arms of Mariehamn A136

1960, Oct. 13 *Perf. 11½*
378 A135 30m dull violet .90 .40

150th anniv. of the birth of Pastor Uno Cygnaeus, founder of elementary schools.

1961, Feb. 21 *Perf. 11½*
379 A136 30m grnsh blue 3.00 1.25

Centenary of the founding of Mariehamn.

Lake and Rowboat A137

Turku Castle — A138

1961 Engr. Unwmk.
380 A137 5m green .30 .20
381 A138 125m slate green 18.00 .30

See Nos. 399, 411.

Postal Savings Bank Emblem — A139

Symbol of Standardization — A140

1961, May 24
382 A139 30m Prus green .75 .40

75th anniv. of Finland's Postal Savings Bank.

1961, June 5 Litho. *Perf. 14x13½*
383 A140 30m dk sl grn & org .75 .40

Meeting of the Intl. Organization for Standardization (ISO), Helsinki, June 5.

Juhani Aho A141

Various Buildings A142

Perf. 11½
1961, Sept. 11 Unwmk. Engr.
384 A141 30m red brown .75 .40

Juhani Aho (1861-1921), writer.

1961, Oct. 16 *Perf. 11½*
385 A142 30m slate .75 .40

150 years of the Central Board of Buildings.

Arvid Jarnefelt A143

1961, Nov. 16
386 A143 30m deep claret .75 .40

Cent. of the birth of Arvid Jarnefelt, writer.

Bank of Finland — A144

First Finnish Locomotive — A145

1961, Dec. 12 Engr. *Perf. 11½*
387 A144 30m brown violet .75 .40

150th anniversary of Bank of Finland.

1962, Jan. 31 Unwmk. *Perf. 11½*

30m, Steam locomotive & timber car. 40m, Diesel locomotive & passenger train.

388 A145 10m gray green 1.00 .45
389 A145 30m violet blue 1.50 .45
390 A145 40m dull red brown 3.50 .60
Nos. 388-390 (3) 6.00 1.50

Centenary of the Finnish State Railways.

Mora Stone — A146

1962, Feb. 15
391 A146 30m gray brown .75 .40

Issued to commemorate 600 years of political rights of the Finnish people.

Senate Place, Helsinki A147

1962, Apr. 8 Unwmk. *Perf. 11½*
392 A147 30m violet brown .75 .40

Sesquicentennial of the proclamation of Helsinki as capital of Finland.

Customs Emblem A148

Staff of Mercury — A149

1962, Apr. 11
393 A148 30m red .75 .40

Finnish Board of Customs, sesquicentennial.

1962, May 21 Engr.
394 A149 30m bluish green .75 .40

Cent. of the 1st commercial bank in Finland.

Santeri Alkio — A150

Finnish Labor Emblem and Conveyor Belt — A151

1962, June 17 Unwmk. *Perf. 11½*
395 A150 30m brown carmine .75 .40

Cent. of the birth of Santeri Alkio, writer and pioneer of the young people's societies in Finland.

1962, Oct. 19
396 A151 30m chocolate .75 .40

National production progress.

Survey Plane and Compass — A152

1962, Nov. 14
397 A152 30m yellow green .75 .40

Finnish Land Survey Board, 150th anniv.

Types of 1954-61 and

House of Parliament — A152a

Church at Lammi — A152b

Fortress of Olavinlinna — A152c

Log Floating A153

Parainen Bridge — A154

Farm on Lake Shore — A155

Aerial View of Punkaharju — A155a

Ristikallio in Kuusamo A156

1963-67 Engr. *Perf. 11½*

398 A94 5p violet blue .35 .20
a. Booklet pane of 2 (vert. pair) 22.50 20.00
b. Bklt. pane of 2 (horiz. pair) 12.00 10.00
399 A137 5p green .25 .20
400 A94 10p blue green .40 .20
a. Booklet pane of 2 (vert. pair) 22.50 20.00
401 A94 15p yellow org 1.00 .20
402 A94 20p rose red .60 .20
a. Booklet pane of 2 (vert. pair) 22.50
Complete booklet, #398a, 400a, 402a 70.00
b. Bklt. pane, 2 #400, 1 #402 + label; horiz. strip 40.00 30.00
Complete booklet, #398b, 402b 90.00
c. Bklt. pane, 2 #398, 2 #400, 1 #402; horiz. strip 3.00 3.00
Complete booklet, #402c 4.00
403 A94 25p rose lilac 1.00 .20
404 A94 30p lt ultra 5.50 .20
404A A94 30p blue gray ('65) .60 .20
405 A94 35p blue 1.00 .20
405A A94 40p ultra ('67) 1.40 .20
406 A152a 40p dull purple 3.00 .20
407 A152b 50p gray olive 4.50 .20
408 A152c 60p pale purple 7.50 .20
408A A152c 65p pale pur ('67) 1.00 .20
409 A124 75p gray 1.60 .20
410 A119 1m bluish grn .45 .20
411 A138 1.25m slate grn 1.50 .20
412 A153 1.50m dk grnsh gray 1.50 .20
413 A154 1.75m blue 1.40 .20
414 A155 2m green ('64) 13.00 .20
414A A155a 2.50m ultra & yel ('67) 6.00 .20
415 A156 5m dk slate grn ('64) 16.00 .30
Nos. 398-415 (22) 69.55 4.50

Pennia denominations expressed: "0.05," "0.10," etc.

Four stamps of type A94 (5p, 10p, 20p, 25p) come in two types: I. Four vertical lines in "O" of SUOMI. II. Three lines in "O."

For similar designs see #457-470A.

Mother and Child — A157

1963, Mar. 21 Unwmk. *Perf. 11½*
416 A157 40p red brown .60 .40

FAO "Freedom from Hunger" campaign.

"Christ Today" — A158

Design: 10p, Crown of thorns and medieval cross of consecration.

1963, July 30 Engr. *Perf. 11½*
417 A158 10p maroon .30 *.45*
418 A158 30p dark green .55 .45

4th assembly of the Lutheran World Federation, Helsinki, July 30-Aug. 8.

Europa Issue, 1963
Common Design Type

1963, Sept. 16
Size: 30x20mm
419 CD6 40p red lilac 1.75 .60

Assembly Building, Helsinki A159

1963, Sept. 18
420 A159 30p violet blue .70 .40

Representative Assembly of Finland, cent.

Convair Metropolitan A160

M. A. Castrén A161

Design: 40p, Caravelle jetliner.

1963, Nov. 1
421 A160 35p slate green .85 .35
422 A160 40p brt ultra .85 .35

40th anniversary of Finnish air traffic.

1963, Dec. 2 Unwmk.
423 A161 35p violet blue .90 .40

Matthias Alexander Castrén (1813-52), ethnologist and philologist.

Stone Elk's Head, 2000 B.C. — A162

Emil Nestor Setälä — A163

1964, Feb. 5 Litho. *Perf. 11½*
424 A162 35p ocher & slate grn .90 .40

Cent. of the Finnish Artists' Association. The soapstone sculpture was found at Huittinen.

1964, Feb. 27 Engr.
425 A163 35p dk red brown .90 .40

Emil Nestor Setälä (1864-1946), philologist, minister of education and foreign affairs and chancellor of Abo University.

Staff of Aesculapius A164

1964, June 13 Unwmk. *Perf. 11½*
426 A164 40p slate green 1.10 .40

18th General Assembly of the World Medical Association, Helsinki, June 13-19, 1964.

Ice Hockey — A165

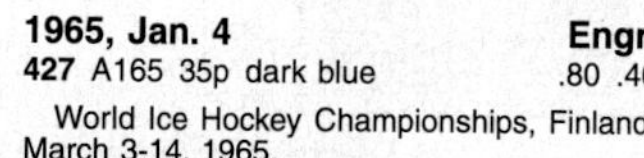

1965, Jan. 4 Engr.
427 A165 35p dark blue .80 .40

World Ice Hockey Championships, Finland, March 3-14, 1965.

Design from Centenary Medal — A166

1965, Feb. 6 Unwmk. *Perf. 11½*
428 A166 35p olive gray .80 .40

Centenary of communal self-government in Finland.

K. J. Stahlberg and "Lex" by W. Runeberg A167

1965, Mar. 22 Engr.
429 A167 35p brown .80 .40

Kaarlo Juho Stahlberg (1865-1952), 1st Pres. of Finland.

International Cooperation Year Emblem A168

1965, Apr. 2 Litho. *Perf. 14*
430 A168 40p bis, dull red, blk & grn .80 .40

UN International Cooperation Year.

"Fratricide" by Gallen-Kallela A169

Sibelius, Piano and Score — A170

35p, Girl's Head by Akseli Gallen-Kallela.

1965, Apr. 26 *Perf. 13½x14*
431 A169 25p multicolored 1.25 .45
432 A169 35p multicolored 1.25 .45

Centenary of the birth of the painter Aksell Gallen-Kallela.

1965, May 15 Engr. *Perf. 11½*

Design: 35p, Musical score and bird.

433 A170 25p violet .70 .40
434 A170 35p dull green .70 .40

Jean Sibelius (1865-1957), composer.

Antenna for Satellite Telecommunication — A171

"Winter Day" by Pekka Halonen — A172

1965, May 17
435 A171 35p blue .80 .40

Cent. of the ITU.

Perf. 14x13½
1965, Sept. 23 Litho. Unwmk.
436 A172 35p gold & multi 1.60 .55

Centenary of the birth of the painter Pekka Halonen.

Europa Issue, 1965
Common Design Type
Engraved and Lithographed

1965, Sept. 27 *Perf. 13½x14*
437 CD8 40p bister, red brn, dk bl & grn 1.10 .40

"Growth" — A173

Old Post Office — A174

1966, May 11 Litho. *Perf. 14*
438 A173 35p vio blue & blue .70 .30

Centenary of the promulgation of the Elementary School Decree.

1966, June 11 Litho. *Perf. 14*
439 A174 35p ocher, yel, dk bl & blk 8.50 *9.25*

Cent. of the 1st postage stamps in Finnish currency, and in connection with the NORDIA Stamp Exhibition, Helsinki, June 11-15. The stamp was sold only to buyers of a 1.25m exhibition entrance ticket.

UNESCO Emblem and World Map — A175

Finnish Police Emblem — A176

Lithographed and Engraved
1966, Oct. 9 *Perf. 14*
440 A175 40p grn, yel, blk & brn org .70 .30

20th anniv. of UNESCO.

1966, Oct. 15
441 A176 35p dp ultra, blk & sil .70 .30

Issued to honor the Finnish police.

Insurance Sesquicentennial Medal — A177

1966, Oct. 28 Engr. & Photo.
442 A177 35p maroon, olive & blk .70 .30

150th anniv. of the Finnish insurance system.

UNICEF Emblem A178

1966, Nov. 14
443 A178 15p lt ultra, pur & grn .40 .30

Activities of UNICEF.

"FINEFTA," Finnish Flag and Circle — A179

1967, Feb. 15 Engr. *Perf. 14*
444 A179 40p ultra 1.00 .30

European Free Trade Association, EFTA. See note after Denmark No. 431.

Windmill and Arms of Uusikaupunki A180

Mannerheim Monument by Aimo Tukiainen A181

Lithographed and Engraved
1967, Apr. 19 *Perf. 14*
445 A180 40p multicolored .70 .30

350th anniv. of Uusikaupunki (Nystad).

1967, June 4 *Perf. 14*
446 A181 40p violet & multi .65 .30

Cent. of the birth of Field Marshal Carl Gustav Emil Mannerheim.

Double Mortise Corner — A182

Watermark of Thomasböle Paper Mill — A183

1967, June 16 Litho. & Photo.
447 A182 40p multicolored .65 .30

Issued to honor Finnish settlers in Sweden.

1967, Sept. 6 *Perf. 14*
448 A183 40p olive & black .65 .30

300th anniv. of the Finnish paper industry.

Martin Luther, by Lucas Cranach A184

Photogravure and Engraved
1967, Nov. 4 *Perf. 14*
449 A184 40p bister & brown .65 .30

450th anniversary of the Reformation.

"Wood and Water" Globe and Flag — A185

Designs (Globe, Flag and): 25p, Flying swan. 40p, Ear of wheat.

1967, Dec. 5 *Perf. 11½*
450 A185 20p green & blue .70 .30
451 A185 25p ultra & blue .70 .30
452 A185 40p magenta & bl .70 .30
Nos. 450-452 (3) 2.10 .90

50th anniv. of Finland's independence.

Zachris Topelius and Blue Bird — A186

1968, Jan. 14 Litho. *Perf. 14*
453 A186 25p blue & multi .65 .30

Topelius (1818-98), writer and educator.

Skiers and Ski Lift — A187

1968, Feb. 19 Photo. *Perf. 14*
454 A187 25p multicolored .65 .30

Winter Tourism in Finland.

Paper Making, by Hannes Autere — A188

1968, Mar. 12 Litho. Wmk. 363
455 A188 45p dk red, brn & org .65 .30

Finnish paper industry and 150th anniv. of the oldest Finnish paper mill, Tervakoski, whose own watermark was used for this stamp.

World Health Organization Emblem A189

Lithographed and Photogravure
1968, Apr. 6 Unwmk. *Perf. 14*
456 A189 40p red org, dk blue & gold .65 .30

To honor World Health Organization.

Lion Type of 1954-58 and

Market Place and Mermaid Fountain, Helsinki A190

Keuru Wooden Church, 1758 — A191

Häme Bridge, Tampere A192

Finnish Arms from Grave of King Gustav Vasa, 1581 — A194

25p, Post bus. 30p, Aquarium-Planetarium, Tampere. No. 463, P.O., Tampere. #465, National Museum, Helsinki, vert. #467A, like 70p. 1.30m, Helsinki railroad station.

Engr. (type A94, except #459A);
Litho. (#459A, 465 & type A190);
Engr. & Litho. (others)
Perf. 11½; 12½ (type A190); 14 (#465, 470A); 13½ (#470)

1968-78
457 A94 1p lt red brn .40 .20
458 A94 2p gray green .40 .20
459 A94 4p gray .40 .20
459A A94 5p violet blue .40 .20
460 A192 25p multi ('71) .40 .20
461 A191 30p multi ('71) 1.00 .20
461A A94 35p dull org ('74) .40 .20
b. Bklt. pane of 4, #459A, 461A, 400, 464A + label 2.50 2.50
Complete booklet, #461b 3.00
462 A94 40p orange ('73) .60 .20
a. Bklt. pane of 3, #462, 2 #404A + 2 labels 5.00 5.00
Complete booklet, #462a 6.50
463 A192 40p multi ('73) 1.00 .20
464 A94 50p lt ultra ('70) 1.00 .20
c. Bklt. pane of 5, #401, 403, 464, 2 #459A + 5 labels 9.50 9.00
Complete booklet, #464c 10.00
464A A94 50p rose lake ('74) .80 .20
d. Bklt. pane of 4, #400, 464A, 2 #402 + label 1.75 1.75
Complete booklet, #464Ad 2.00
464B A94 60p blue ('73) .60 .20
465 A191 60p multi ('73) .45 .20
466 A190 70p multi ('73) .80 .20
467 A191 80p multi ('70) 5.00 .20
467A A190 80p multi ('76) .45 .20
468 A192 90p multicolored 2.00 .20
469 A191 1.30m multi ('71) 1.00 .20
470 A194 10m multi ('74) 4.25 .40
470A A194 20m multi ('78) 8.75 .75
Nos. 457-470A (20) 30.10 4.75

Issued: 5p, 6/72.

Infantry Monument, Vaasa — A195

Camping Ground A196

Designs: 25p, War Memorial (cross), Hietaniemi Cemetery. 40p, Soldier, 1968.

1968, June 4 Photo. *Perf. 14*
471 A195 20p lt violet & multi .80 .35
472 A195 25p lt blue & multi .80 .35
473 A195 40p orange & multi .80 .35
Nos. 471-473 (3) 2.40 1.05

To honor Finnish national defense.

1968, June 10 Litho.
474 A196 25p multicolored .65 .30

Issued to publicize Finland for summer vacations.

Paper, Pulp and Pine — A197

Mustola Lock, Saima Canal — A198

Lithographed and Embossed
1968, July 2 Unwmk. *Perf. 14*
475 A197 40p multicolored .65 .30

Finnish wood industry.

1968, Aug. 5 Litho. *Perf. 14*
476 A198 40p multicolored .65 .30

Opening of the Saima Canal.

Ships in Harbor and Emblem of Central Chamber of Commerce A200

Oskar Merikanto and Pipe Organ — A199

1968, Aug. 5 Unwmk.
477 A199 40p vio, silver & lt brn .65 .30

Centenary of the birth of Oskar Merikanto, composer.

Welder — A201

1968, Sept. 13 Litho. *Perf. 14*
478 A200 40p lt bl, brt bl & blk .65 .30

Publicizing economic development and for the 50th anniv. of the Central Chamber of Commerce of Finland.

1968, Oct. 11 Litho. *Perf. 14*
479 A201 40p blue & multi .65 .30

Finnish metal industry.

Lyre, Students' Emblem — A202

Five Ancient Ships — A203

Lithographed and Engraved
1968, Nov. 24 *Perf. 14*
480 A202 40p ultra, vio bl & gold .65 .30

Issued to publicize the work of the student unions in Finnish social life.

Nordic Cooperation Issue
1968, Feb. 28 Engr. *Perf. 11½*
481 A203 40p lt ultra 1.75 .30

See footnote after Denmark No. 455.

Town Hall and Arms of Kemi — A203a

1969, Mar. 5 Photo. *Perf. 14*
482 A203a 40p multicolored .65 .30

Centenary of the town of Kemi.

Europa Issue, 1969
Common Design Type
1969, Apr. 28 Photo. *Perf. 14*
Size: 30x20mm
483 CD12 40p dl rose, vio bl & dk bl *5.00* 1.00

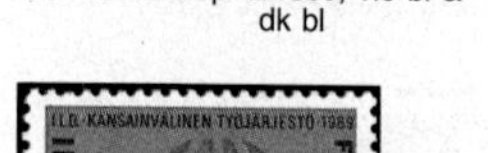

ILO Emblem A204

Armas Järnefelt — A205

Lithographed and Engraved
1969, June 2 *Perf. 11½*
484 A204 40p dp rose & vio blue .65 .30

50th anniv. of the ILO.

1969, Aug. 14 Photo. *Perf. 14*
485 A205 40p multicolored .65 .30

Järnefelt (1869-1958), composer and conductor. Portrait on stamp by Vilho Sjöström.

Emblems and Flag — A206

Johannes Linnankoski — A207

1969, Sept. 19 Photo. *Perf. 14*
486 A206 40p lt bl, blk, grn & lil .65 .30

Publicizinge the importance of National and International Fairs in Finnish economy.

1969, Oct. 18 Litho.
487 A207 40p dk brn red & multi .65 .30

Linnankoski (1869-1913), writer.

Educational Symbols A208

Lithographed and Engraved
1969, Nov. 24 *Perf. 11½*
488 A208 40p gray, vio & grn .65 .30

Centenary of the Central School Board.

DC-8-62 CF Plane and Helsinki Airport — A209

1969, Dec. 22 Photo. *Perf. 14*
489 A209 25p sky blue & multi .85 .30

Golden Eagle — A210

1970, Feb. 10 Litho. *Perf. 14*
490 A210 30p multicolored 2.75 .65

Year of Nature Conservation, 1970.

Swatches in Shape of Factories A211

1970, Mar. 9 Litho. *Perf. 14*
491 A211 50p multicolored .70 .30

Finnish textile industry.

Molecule Diagram and Factories A212

UNESCO Emblem and Lenin — A213

Atom Diagram and Laurel — A214

UN Emblem and Globe — A215

1970, Mar. 26 Photo. *Perf. 14*
492 A212 50p multicolored .70 .30

Finnish chemical industry.

1970 Litho. and Engr.
493 A213 30p gold & multi .70 .25
494 A214 30p red & multi .70 .25

Photogravure and Gold Embossed
495 A215 50p bl, vio bl & gold .70 .25
Nos. 493-495 (3) 2.10 .75

25th anniv. of the UN. No. 493 also publicizes the UNESCO-sponsored Lenin Symposium, Tampere, Apr. 6-10. No. 494 also publicizes the Nuclear Data Conf. of the Atomic Energy Commission, Otaniemi (Helsinki), June 15-19.
Issued: #493, 4/6; #494, 6/15; #495, 10/24.

Handicapped Volleyball Player — A216

Meeting of Auroraseura Society — A217

1970, June 27 Litho. *Perf. 14*
496 A216 50p orange, red & blk .75 .30

Issued to publicize the position of handicapped civilians and war veterans in society and their potential contributions to it.

1970, Aug. 15 Photo. *Perf. 14*
497 A217 50p multicolored .65 .30

200th anniv. of the Auroraseura Soc., dedicated to the study of Finnish history, geography, economy and language. The design of the stamp is after a painting by Eero Jarnefelt.

Uusikaarlepyy Arms, Church and 17th Cent. Building A218

Design: No. 499, Arms of Kokkola, harbor, Sports Palace and 17th century building.

1970 *Perf. 14*
498 A218 50p multicolored .70 .30
499 A218 50p multicolored .70 .30

Towns of Uusikaarlepyy and Kokkola, 350th anniv.
Issued: #498, Aug. 21; #499, Sept. 17.

Urho Kekkonen, Medal by Aimo Tukiainen — A219

1970, Sept. 3 Litho. & Engr.
500 A219 50p ultra, sil & blk .75 .30

70th birthday of Pres. Urho Kekkonen.

Globe, Maps of US, Finland, USSR A220

Pres. Paasikivi by Essi Renavall A221

Lithographed and Gold Embossed
1970, Nov. 2
501 A220 50p blk, bl, pink & gold .70 .30

Strategic Arms Limitation Talks (SALT) between the US & USSR, Helsinki, 11/2-12/18.

1970, Nov. 27 Photo. *Perf. 14*
502 A221 50p gold, brt bl & slate .85 .30

Centenary of the birth of Juho Kusti Paasikivi (1870-1956), President of Finland.

Cogwheels A222

1971, Jan. 28 Litho. *Perf. 14*
503 A222 50p multicolored .70 .30

Finnish industry.

Europa Issue, 1971
Common Design Type
1971, May 3 Litho. *Perf. 14*
Size: 30x20mm
504 CD14 50p dp rose, yel & blk 4.75 .60

Tornio Church — A223

Front Page, January 15, 1771 — A224

1971, May 12 Litho. *Perf. 14*
505 A223 50p multicolored .85 .30

350th anniversary of the town of Tornio.

1971, June 1 Litho. *Perf. 14*
506 A224 50p multicolored .65 .30

Bicentenary of the Finnish press.

Athletes in Helsinki Stadium A225

50p, Running & javelin in Helsinki Stadium.

1971, July 5 Litho. *Perf. 14*

507 A225 30p multicolored .90 .40
508 A225 50p multicolored 1.90 .40

European Athletic Championships.

Sailboats A226

1971, July 14

509 A226 50p multicolored 1.00 .30

International Lightning Class Championships, Helsinki, July 14-Aug. 1.

Silver Tea Pot, Guild's Emblem, Tools — A227

1971, Aug. 6

510 A227 50p lilac & multi .70 .30

600th anniv. of Finnish goldsmiths' art.

"Plastic Buttons and Houses" A228

Photogravure and Embossed

1971, Oct. 20 *Perf. 14*

511 A228 50p multicolored .75 .30

Finnish plastics industry.

Europa Issue 1972
Common Design Type

1972, May 2 Litho. *Perf. 14*
Size: 20x30mm

512 CD15 30p dk red & multi 3.00 .60
513 CD15 50p lt brn & multi 4.00 .60

Finnish National Theater A229

1972, May 22. Litho. *Perf. 14*

514 A229 50p lt violet & multi .75 .30

Centenary of the Finnish National Theater, founded by Kaarlo and Emilie Bergbom.

Globe, US and USSR Flags — A230

1972, June 2

515 A230 50p multicolored 1.40 .35

Strategic Arms Limitation Talks (SALT), final meeting, Helsinki, Mar. 28-May 26; treaty signed, Moscow, May 26.

Map and Arms of Aland — A231

Training Ship Suomen Joutsen — A232

1972, June 9

516 A231 50p multicolored 4.00 .75

1st Provincial Meeting of Aland, 50th anniv.

1972, June 19

517 A232 50p orange & multi 1.10 .35

Tall Ships' Race 1972, Helsinki, Aug. 20.

Costume from Perni, 12th Cent. — A233

Circle Surrounding Map of Europe — A234

1972, Nov. 19 Litho. *Perf. 13*

518 A233 50p shown 2.00 .50
519 A233 50p Couple, Tenhola, 18th cent. 2.00 .50
520 A233 50p Girl, Nastola, 19th cent. 2.00 .50
521 A233 50p Man, Voyni, 19th cent. 2.00 .50
522 A233 50p Lapps, Inari, 19th cent. 2.00 .50
a. Strip of 5, #518-522 10.00 12.00
Complete booklet, 2 each #518-522 30.00

Regional costumes.
See Nos. 533-537.

1972, Dec. 11 *Perf. 14x13½*

523 A234 50p multicolored 2.00 .40

Preparatory Conference on European Security and Cooperation.

Book, Finnish and Soviet Colors — A235

Litho.; Gold Embossed

1973, Apr. 6 *Perf. 14*

524 A235 60p gold & multi .50 .30

Soviet-Finnish Treaty of Friendship, 25th anniv.

Kyösti Kallio (1873-1940), Pres. of Finland — A236

1973, Apr. 10 Litho. *Perf. 13*

525 A236 60p multicolored .50 .30

Europa Issue 1973
Common Design Type

1973, Apr. 30 Photo. *Perf. 14*
Size: 31x21mm

526 CD16 60p bl, brt bl & emer 1.50 .40

Nordic Cooperation Issue

Nordic House, Reykjavik A236a

1973, June 26 Engr. *Perf. 12½*

527 A236a 60p multicolored .90 .30
528 A236a 70p multicolored .90 .30

A century of postal cooperation among Denmark, Finland, Iceland, Norway and Sweden, and in connection with the Nordic Postal Conference, Reykjavik.

Map of Europe, "EUROPA" as a Maze — A237

Litho. & Embossed

1973, July 3 *Perf. 13*

529 A237 70p multicolored .70 .30

Conference for European Security and Cooperation, Helsinki, July 1973.

Paddling A238

Radiosonde, WMO Emblem — A239

1973, July 18 Litho. *Perf. 14*

530 A238 60p multicolored .65 .30

Canoeing World Championships, Tampere, July 26-29.

1973, Aug. 6 Litho. *Perf. 14*

531 A239 60p multicolored .50 .30

Cent. of intl. meteorological cooperation.

Eliel Saarinen and Design for Parliament, Helsinki A240

1973, Aug. 20 *Perf. 12½x13*

532 A240 60p multicolored .50 .30

Eliel Saarinen (1873-1950), architect.

Costume Type of 1972

1973, Oct. 10 Litho. *Perf. 13*

533 A233 60p Woman, Kaukola 4.25 .50
534 A233 60p Woman, Jaaski 4.25 .50
535 A233 60p Married couple, Koivisto 4.25 .50
536 A233 60p Mother and son, Sakyla 4.25 .50
537 A233 60p Girl, Hainavesi 4.25 .50
a. Strip of 5, #533-537 22.50 12.00

Regional costumes.

DC10-30 Jet — A241

1973, Nov. 1 Litho. *Perf. 14*

538 A241 60p multicolored .70 .35

50th anniv. of regular air service, Finnair.

Santa Claus in Reindeer Sleigh — A242

1973, Nov. 15 Litho. *Perf. 14*

539 A242 30p multicolored .65 .25

Christmas 1973.

"The Barber of Seville" A243

1973, Nov. 21

540 A243 60p multicolored .70 .35

Centenary of opera in Finland.

Production of Porcelain Jug — A244

Nurmi, by Waino Aaltonen — A245

1973, Nov. 23

541 A244 60p blue & multi .70 .35

Finnish porcelain.

1973, Dec. 11

542 A245 60p multicolored .70 .35

Paavo Nurmi (1897-1973), runner, Olympic winner, 1920-1924-1928.

Arms, Map and Harbor of Hanko — A246

1974, Jan. 10 Litho. *Perf. 14*

543 A246 60p blue & multi .70 .35

Centenary of the town of Hanko.

Ice Hockey A247

1974, Mar. 5 Litho. *Perf. 14*

544 A247 60p multicolored .70 .35

European and World Ice Hockey Championships, held in Finland.

Seagulls (7 Baltic States) A248

1974, Mar. 18 ***Perf. 12½***
545 A248 60p multicolored .70 .35

Protection of marine environment of the Baltic Sea.

Goddess of Freedom, by Waino Aaltonen — A249

Ilmari Kianto and Old Pine — A250

1974, Apr. 29 **Litho.** ***Perf. 13x12½***
546 A249 70p multicolored *4.50* .40

Europa.

1974, May 7 ***Perf. 13***
547 A250 60p multicolored .65 .35

Ilmari Kianto (1874-1970), writer.

Society Emblem, Symbol A251

Lithographed and Embossed

1974, June 12 ***Perf. 13½x14***
548 A251 60p gold & multi .65 .35

Centenary of Adult Education.

Grid A252

UPU Emblem A253

1974, June 14 **Litho.** ***Perf. 14x13½***
549 A252 60p multicolored .65 .35

Rationalization Year in Finland, dedicated to economic and business improvements.

1974, Oct. 10 **Litho.** ***Perf. 13½x14***
550 A253 60p multicolored .65 .35
551 A253 70p multicolored .65 .35

Centenary of Universal Postal Union.

Elves Distributing Gifts — A254

1974, Nov. 16 **Litho.** ***Perf. 14x13½***
552 A254 35p multicolored 1.10 .35

Christmas 1974.

Concrete Bridge and Granite Bridge, Aunessilta — A255

Litho. & Engr.

1974, Dec. 17 ***Perf. 14***
553 A255 60p multicolored .65 .35

Royal Finnish Directorate of Roads and Waterways, 175th anniversary.

Coat of Arms, 1581 — A256

Chimneyless Log Sauna — A256a

Carved Wooden Distaffs A258

Kirvu Weather Vane A258a

Cheese Frames A257

1.50m, Wood-carved high drinking bowl, 1542.

1975-90 **Engr.** ***Perf. 11½; 14 (2m)***

555	A256	10p red lilac ('78)	.20	.20
a.		Bklt. pane of 4 (#555, 2 #556, #559) + label	1.75	1.75
		Complete booklet, #555a	2.00	
b.		Bklt. pane of 5 (2 #555, #557, #563, #564)	1.90	1.75
		Complete booklet, #555b	2.50	
c.		As "a," no label	.50	.50
		Complete booklet, #555c	.75	
d.		Perf. 13x12½	.20	.20
556	A256	20p olive ('77)	.20	.20
a.		20p yellow bister ('87)	.20	.20
b.		As "a," perf. 13x12½	.20	.20
557	A256	30p carmine ('77)	.20	.20
557A	A256	30p car, litho.	.20	.20
558	A256	40p orange	.20	.20
a.		Perf. 13x12½, litho. & engr.	1.00	.20
559	A256	50p green ('76)	.20	.20
a.		Perf. 13x12½	.20	.20
560	A256	60p blue	.25	.20
a.		Perf. 13x12½	.30	.20
561	A256	70p sepia	.35	.20
562	A256	80p dl red & bl grn ('76)	.40	.20
a.		Perf. 13x12½	.40	.40
563	A256	90p vio bl ('77)	.40	.20
564	A256	1.10m yellow ('79)	.50	.20
565	A256	1.20m dk blue ('79)	.50	.20
566	A258	1.50m multi ('76)	.65	.20

Litho.

567	A256a	2m multi ('77)	.90	.20

Lithographed and Engraved

568	A257	2.50m multi ('76)	1.10	.20
a.		Perf. 14	2.00	.20
569	A258	4.50m multi ('76)	2.00	.20
a.		Perf. 14	3.00	.20
570	A258a	5m multi ('77)	2.25	.20
		Nos. 555-570 (17)	10.50	3.40

Issued: #557A, 6/3/80; #560a, 7/25/88; #555d, 7/25/89; #562a, 3/1/90; #558a, 8/18/94; #568a, 12/28/88; #569a, 9/26/88; No. 556b, 4/3/98.

See Nos. 629, 631-633, 711-715, 861.

Finland No. 16 — A259

Girl Combing Hair, by Magnus Enckell — A260

Lithographed and Typographed

1975, Apr. 26 ***Perf. 13***
571 A259 70p multicolored 3.75 4.00

Nordia 75 Philatelic Exhibition, Helsinki, Apr. 26-May 1. Sold only at exhibition for 3m including entrance ticket.

1975, Apr. 28 **Litho.** ***Perf. 13x12½***

Europa: 90p, Washerwoman, by Tyko Sallinen (1879-1955).

572 A260 70p gray & multi *2.75* .40
573 A260 90p tan & multi *2.75* .40

Balance of Justice, Sword of Legality — A261

Rescue Boat and Sinking Ship — A262

1975, May 7 ***Perf. 14***
574 A261 70p vio blue & multi .60 .30

Sesquicentennial of State Economy Comptroller's Office.

1975, June 2 **Litho.** ***Perf. 14***
575 A262 70p multicolored .65 .30

12th Intl. Salvage Conf., Finland, stressing importance of coordinating sea, air and communications resources in salvage operations.

Safe and Unsafe Levels of Drugs — A263

1975, July 21 **Litho.** ***Perf. 14***
576 A263 70p multicolored .60 .30

Importance of pharmacological studies and for the 6th Intl. Pharmacology Cong., Helsinki.

Olavinlinna Castle A264

1975, July 29 ***Perf. 13***
577 A264 70p multicolored .65 .30

500th anniversary of Olavinlinna Castle.

Swallows over Finlandia Hall — A265

"Men and Women Working for Peace" — A266

1975, July 30
578 A265 90p multicolored .90 .30

European Security and Cooperation Conference, Helsinki, July 30-Aug. 1. (The swallows of the design represent freedom, mobility and continuity.) See No. 709.

1975, Oct. 24 **Litho.** ***Perf. 13x12½***
579 A266 70p multicolored .60 .30

International Women's Year 1975.

"Continuity and Growth" — A267

Boys as Three Kings and Herod — A268

1975, Oct. 29 ***Perf. 13***
580 A267 70p brown & multi .60 .30

Industrial Art and for the centenary of the Finnish Society of Industrial Art.

1975, Nov. 8 ***Perf. 14***
581 A268 40p blue & multi .65 .20

Christmas 1975.

Top Border of State Debenture A269

Lithographed and Engraved

1976, Jan. 9 ***Perf. 11½***
582 A269 80p multicolored .60 .30

Centenary of State Treasury.

Glider over Lake Region A270

1976, Jan. 13 **Litho.** ***Perf. 14***
583 A270 80p multicolored .90 .30

15th World Glider Championships, Rayskala, June 13-27.

Prof. Heikki Klemetti (1876-1953), Musician & Writer — A271

1976, Feb. 14 Litho. *Perf. 13*
584 A271 80p green & multi .65 .30

Map with Areas of Different Dialects — A272

Aino Ackté, by Albert Edelfelt — A273

1976, Mar. 10 Litho. *Perf. 13*
585 A272 80p multicolored .65 .30

Finnish Language Society, centenary.

1976, Apr. 23
586 A273 70p yellow & multi .80 .30

Aino Ackté (1876-1944), opera singer.

Europa Issue 1976

Knife from Voyri, Sheath and Belt — A274

1976, May 3 Litho. *Perf. 13*
587 A274 80p violet bl & multi 4.25 .60

Radio and Television A275

1976, Sept. 9 Litho. *Perf. 13*
588 A275 80p multicolored .60 .30

Radio broadcasting in Finland, 50th anniv.

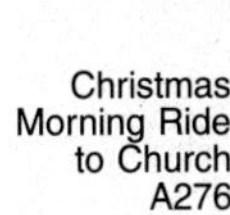

Christmas Morning Ride to Church A276

1976, Oct. 23 Litho. *Perf. 14*
589 A276 50p multicolored .60 .20

Christmas 1976.

Turku Chapter Seal (Virgin and Child) A277

1976, Nov. 1 Litho. *Perf. 12½*
590 A277 80p buff, brn & red .60 .30

Cathedral Chapter of Turku, 700th anniv.

Alvar Aalto, Finlandia Hall, Helsinki A278

1976, Nov. 4
591 A278 80p multicolored .60 .30

Hugo Alvar Henrik Aalto (1898-1976), architect.

Ice Dancers — A280 Five Water Lilies — A281

1977, Jan. 25 Litho. *Perf. 13*
592 A280 90p multicolored .60 .30

European Figure Skating Championships, Finland, Jan. 25-29.

Photogravure and Engraved

1977, Feb. 2 *Perf. 12½*
593 A281 90p brt green & multi .80 .30
594 A281 1m ultra & multi .80 .30

Nordic countries cooperation for protection of the environment and 25th Session of Nordic Council, Helsinki, Feb. 19.

Icebreaker Rescuing Merchantman A282

1977, Mar. 2 Litho. *Perf. 13*
595 A282 90p multicolored .55 .30

Winter navigation between Finland and Sweden, centenary.

Nuclear Reactor A283

1977, Mar. 3 *Perf. 12½x13*
596 A283 90p multicolored .55 .30

Opening of nuclear power station on Hästholmen Island.

Europa Issue 1977

Autumn Landscape, Northern Finland — A284

1977, May 2 Litho. *Perf. 12½x13*
597 A284 90p multicolored 3.75 .40

Tree, Birds and Nest — A285 Orthodox Church, Valamo Cloister — A286

1977, May 4 *Perf. 13x12½*
598 A285 90p multicolored .55 .30

75th anniversary of cooperative banks.

1977, May 31 Litho. *Perf. 14*
599 A286 90p multicolored .55 .30

Consecration festival of new Orthodox Church at Valamo Cloister, Heinävesi; 800th anniversary of introduction of orthodoxy in Karelia and of founding of Valamo Cloister.

Paavo Ruotsalainen (1777-1852), Lay Leader of Pietists in Finland — A287

1977, July 8 Litho. *Perf. 13*
600 A287 90p multicolored .55 .30

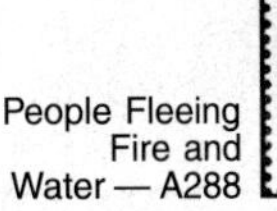

People Fleeing Fire and Water — A288

Volleyball — A289

1977, Sept. 14 Litho. *Perf. 14*
601 A288 90p multicolored .55 .30

Civil defense for security.

1977, Sept. 15
602 A289 90p multicolored .60 .30

European Women's Volleyball Championships, Finland, Sept. 29-Oct. 2.

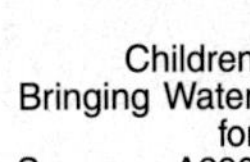

Children Bringing Water for Sauna — A290

1977, Oct. 25
603 A290 50p multicolored .50 .20

Christmas 1977.

Finnish Flag — A291

Wall Telephone, 1880, New Telephone — A292

1977, Dec. 5 Litho. *Perf. 14*
Size: 31x21mm
604 A291 80p multicolored .60 .25
Size: 37x25mm
Perf. 13
605 A291 1m multicolored .85 .25

Finland's declaration of independence, 60th anniv.

1977, Dec. 9 *Perf. 14*
606 A292 1m multicolored .60 .30

Centenary of first telephone in Finland.

Harbor, Sunila Factory, Kotka Arms — A293

1978, Jan. 2 Litho. *Perf. 14*
607 A293 1m multicolored .60 .30

Centenary of founding of Kotka.

Paimio Sanitarium by Alvar Aalto — A294

Europa: 1.20m, Hvittrask studio house, 1902, horiz.

1978, May 2 Litho. *Perf. 13*
608 A294 1m multicolored 7.50 .75
609 A294 1.20m multicolored 7.50 6.00

Rural Bus Service A295

1978, June 8 Litho. *Perf. 14*
610 A295 1m multicolored .60 .30

Eino Leino and Eagle — A296

1978, July 6 Litho. *Perf. 13*
611 A296 1m multicolored .60 .30

Eino Leino (1878-1926), poet.

Function Theory and Rhythmical Lines — A297

1978, Aug. 15 Litho. *Perf. 14*
612 A297 1m multicolored .60 .30

ICM 78, International Congress of Mathematicians, Helsinki, Aug. 15-23.

Child Feeding Birds — A298

1978, Oct. 23 Litho. *Perf. 14*
613 A298 50p multicolored .50 .20

Christmas 1978.

A299

A300

1979, Jan. 2 Litho. *Perf. 13*
614 A299 1.10m multicolored 2.75 .30

International Year of the Child.

1979, Feb. 7 Litho. *Perf. 14*
615 A300 1.10m Runner .90 .30

8th Orienteering World Championships, Finland, Sept. 1-4.

Old School, Hamina, Academy Flag — A301

1979, Mar. 20 Litho. *Perf. 14*
616 A301 1.10m multicolored .60 .30

200th anniv. of Finnish Military Academy.

A302

A303

Design: Turku Cathedral and Castle, Prinkkala house, Brahe statue.

1979, Mar. 31
617 A302 1.10m multicolored .60 .30

1979, May 2 Litho. *Perf. 14*
618 A303 1.10m Streetcar, Helsinki .60 .30

Non-polluting urban transportation.

View of Tampere, 1779 — A304

View of Tampere, 1979 — A305

1979, May 2
619 A304 90p multicolored .60 .30

1979, Oct. 1 *Perf. 13*
620 A305 1.10m multicolored .60 .30

Bicentenary of founding of Tampere.

Optical Telegraph, 1796, Map of Islands A306

Europa: 1.10m, Letter of Queen Christina to Per Brahe, 1638, establishing postal service.

1979, May 2 *Perf. 13*
621 A306 1.10m multi *2.50* .40
622 A306 1.30m multi, vert *5.00* .90

Shops and Merchants' Signs — A307

1979, Sept. 26 *Perf. 14*
623 A307 1.10m multicolored .60 .30

Business and industry regulation centenary.

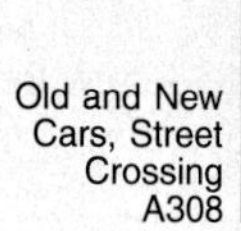
Old and New Cars, Street Crossing A308

1979, Oct. 1
624 A308 1.10m multicolored .60 .30

Road safety.

Elves Feeding Horse — A309

1979, Oct. 24
625 A309 60p multicolored .50 .20

Christmas 1979.

Korppi House, Lapinjarvi A310

Farm houses, First Row: Syrjala House, Tammela, 2 stamps in continuous design; Murtovaara House, Valtimo; Antila House, Lapua. Second row: Lofts, Pohjanmaa; Courtyard gate, Kanajarvi House, Kalvola; Main door, Havuselka House, Kauhajoki; Maki-Rasinpera House and dinner bell tower; Gable and eaves, Rasula Kuortane granary.

1979, Oct. 27 Litho. *Perf. 13*
626 Booklet pane of 10 5.00 5.00
a.-j. A310 1.10m single stamp .50 .30
Complete booklet, #626 5.00

See design A349a.

Type of 1975 and

Kauhaneva Swamp A315

Hame Castle, Hameenlinna A316

Windmill, Harrstrom A318

Multiharju Forest, Seitseminen Natl. Park — A319

Shuttle, Raanu Designs A322

Kaspaikka Towel Design — A323

Bridal Rug, Teisko, 1815 — A324

Iron-forged Door, Hollola Church — A325

Iron Fish Spear c. 1100 — A326

Design: 1.80m, Eastern Gulf natl. park.

Litho. & Engr., Litho., Engr.
1979-98 *Perf. 14, 11½ (A256, A318)*
627 A315 70p multicolored .30 .20
628 A316 90p brown red .25 .20
629 A256 1m red brown .40 .40
a. Perf. 13x12½ ('98) .40 .20
630 A318 1m bl & red brn .25 .20
631 A256 1.30m dk green .60 .20
631A A256 1.30m dk green, litho. .60 .25
b. Booklet pane, #555-556, 557A, 560, 631A 1.75 1.75
Complete booklet, #641Ab 2.00
632 A256 1.40m purple .60 .20
633 A256 1.50m grnsh blue .65 .20
634 A319 1.60m multicolored .70 .20
635 A315 1.80m multicolored 1.25 .20
636 A322 3m multicolored 1.25 .20
637 A323 6m multicolored 2.50 .20
638 A324 7m multicolored 3.00 .75
639 A325 8m multicolored 3.50 .25
640 A326 9m blk & dk bl 4.00 .30
Nos. 627-640 (15) 19.85 3.95

Coil Stamps
Perf. 11½ Vert.
641 A316 90p brown red .40 .25
Perf. 12½ Horiz.
642 A318 1m blue & red brn .50 .25

Issued: 3m, 10/27/79; 6m, 4/9/80; #629, 1/2/81; 70p, 1/12/81; 90p, 9/1/82; 1.60m, 2/8/82; 7m, 2/15/82; #631, 1/3/83; #630, 642, 1/12/83; 1.80m, 8m, 2/10/83; 1.40m, 9m, 1/2/84; 1.50m, 1/2/85; #631A, 11/1/85.

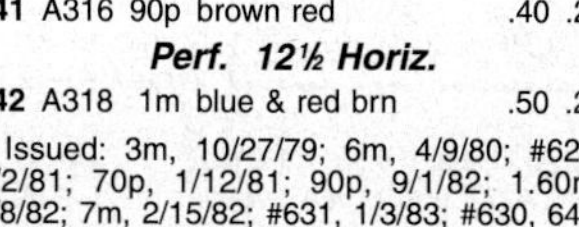

Maria Jotuni (1880-1943), Writer — A327

1980, Apr. 9 Litho.
643 A327 1.10m multicolored .60 .25

Frans Eemil Sillanpaa (1888-1964), Writer — A328

Europa: 1.30m, Artturi Ilmari Virtanen (1895-1973), chemist, vert.

1980, Apr. 28 *Perf. 13*
644 A328 1.10m multicolored *1.75* .45
645 A328 1.30m multicolored *2.00* .75

Pres. Urho Kekkonen, 80th Birthday — A329

1980, Sept. 3 Litho. *Perf. 13*
646 A329 1.10m multicolored .65 .25

Nordic Cooperation Issue

Back-piece Harness, 19th century A330

1980, Sept. 9 *Perf. 14*
647 A330 1.10m shown .60 .30
648 A330 1.30m Collar harness, vert. .60 .40

Biathlon A331

1980, Oct. 17 Litho. *Perf. 14*
649 A331 1.10m multicolored .60 .25

World Biathlon Championship, Lahti, Feb. 10-15, 1981.

Pull the Roller, Weighing out the Salt — A332

Christmas 1980 (Traditional Games): 1.10m, Putting out the shoemaker's eye.

1980, Oct. 27

650 A332 60p multicolored .25 .20
651 A332 1.10m multicolored .70 .20

Boxing Match — A333

Glass Blowing A334

1981, Feb. 28 Litho. *Perf. 14*

652 A333 1.10m multicolored .60 .25

European Boxing Championships, Tampere, May 2-10.

1981, Mar. 12

653 A334 1.10m multicolored .60 .25

Glass industry, 300th anniversary.

Mail Boat Furst Menschikoff, 1836 — A335

Litho & Engr.

1981, May 6 *Perf. 13*

654 A335 1.10m brown & tan 3.50 3.25

Nordia '81 Stamp Exhibition, Helsinki, May 6-10. Sold only at exhibition for 3m including entrance ticket.

Europa Issue 1981

Rowing to Church A336

1981, May 18 Litho. *Perf. 13*

655 A336 1.10m shown *.80* .35
656 A336 1.50m Midsummer's Eve dance *1.60* .55

Traffic Conference Emblem — A337

Boy and Girl Riding Pegasus A338

1981, May 26 Litho. *Perf. 14*

657 A337 1.10m multicolored .45 .25

European Conference of Ministers of Transport, May 25-28.

1981, June 11

658 A338 1m multicolored .45 .25

Youth associations centenary.

Intl. Year of the Disabled — A339

1981, Sept. 2 Litho. *Perf. 13*

659 A339 1.10m multicolored .60 .25

Christmas 1981 — A340

1981, Oct. 27 Litho. *Perf. 14*

660 A340 70p Children, Christmas tree .30 .20
661 A340 1.10m Decorating tree, vert. .50 .30

"Om Konsten att Ratt Behaga" First Issue (Periodicals Bicentenary) A341

1982, Jan. 15

662 A341 1.20m multicolored .60 .25

Kuopio Bicentenary A343

Score, String Instrument Neck A344

1982, Mar. 4 Litho. *Perf. 14*

664 A343 1.20m multicolored .60 .25

1982, Mar. 11 *Perf. 13*

665 A344 1.20m multicolored .60 .25

Centenaries of Sibelius Academy of Music and Helsinki Orchestra.

Electric Power Plant Centenary A345

1982, Mar. 15 *Perf. 14*

666 A345 1.20m multicolored .60 .25

Gardening A346

1982, Apr. 16 Litho. *Perf. 14*

667 A346 1.10m multicolored .50 .25

Europa — A347

1.20m, Publication of Abckiria (1st Finnish book), 1543 (Sculpture of Mikael Agricola, translator, by Oskari Jauhiainen, 1951). 1.50m, Turku Academy, 1st Finnish university (Turku Academy Inaugural Procession, 1640, after Albert Edelfelt).

1982, Apr. 29 Litho. *Perf. 13x12½*

668 A347 1.20m multicolored *1.75* .50

Size: 47x31mm

Perf. 12½

669 A347 1.50m multicolored *1.75* .50

Intl. Monetary Fund and World Bank Emblems A348

1982, May 12 *Perf. 14*

670 A348 1.60m multicolored .70 .25

IMF Interim Committee and IMF-WB Joint Development Committee Meeting, Helsinki, May 12-14.

75th Anniv. of Unicameral Parliament A349

1982, May 25

671 A349 2.40m Future, by Waino Aaltonen, Parliament 1.00 .40

Manor Houses A349a

1st Row: a, Kuitia, Parainen, 1490. b, Louhisaari, Askainen, 1655. c, Frugard, Joroinen, 1780. d, Jokioinen, 1798. e, Moisio, Elimaki, 1820.

2nd Row: f, Sjundby, Siuntio, 1560. g, Fagervik, Inkoo, 1773. h, Mustio, Karjaa, 1792. i, Fiskars, Pohja, 1818. j, Kotkaniemi, Vihti, 1836.

1982, June 14 Litho. *Perf. 13x13½*

672 Booklet pane of 10 8.00 8.00
a.-j. A349a 1.20m single stamp .80 .40
Complete booklet, #672 9.00

See design A310.

Christmas 1982 — A350

1982, Oct. 25

673 A350 90p Feeding forest animals .50 .25
674 A350 1.20m Children eating porridge .50 .25

Nordic Cooperation A351

1983, Mar. 24 Litho. *Perf. 14*

675 A351 1.20m Panning for gold .50 .25
676 A351 1.30m Kitkajoki River rapids .60 .25

World Communications Year — A352

1983, Apr. 9 Litho. *Perf. 13*

677 A352 1.30m Postal services .60 .25
678 A352 1.70m Sound waves, optical cables .75 .40

Europa 1983 A353

1983, May 2 Litho. *Perf. 12½x13*

679 A353 1.30m Flash smelting method *7.00* .50
680 A353 1.70m Temppeliaukio Church *8.00* 1.00

Pres. Lauri Kristian Relander (1883-1942) A354

Running A355

1983, May 31 Litho. *Perf. 14*

681 A354 1.30m multicolored .65 .30

1983, June 6

682 A355 1.20m Javelin, horiz. .60 .40
683 A355 1.30m shown .65 .30

First World Athletic Championships, Helsinki, Aug. 7-14.

Toivo Kuula (1883-1918), Composer — A356

1983, July 7 *Perf. 14*

684 A356 1.30m multicolored .65 .30

Christmas 1983 — A357

Childrens drawings: 1m, Santa, reindeer, sled and gifts by Eija Myllyviita. 1.30m, Two candles by Camilla Lindberg.

Engr., Litho.

1983, Nov. 4 *Perf. 12, 14*

685 A357 1m dark blue .50 .30
686 A357 1.30m multi, vert. .65 .30

A358

A360

1983, Nov. 25 **Litho.** ***Perf. 14***

687 A358 1.30m brt blue & blk .65 .30

President Mauno Henrik Koivisto, 60th birthday.

1984, Mar. 1 **Engr.** ***Perf. 12***

689 A360 1.10m Letters (2nd class rate) .50 .20

Photo. & Engr.

690 A360 1.40m Automated sorting (1st class rate), vert. .65 .20

Inauguration of Nordic postal rates.

Museum Pieces — A361

Work and Skill — A362

Designs: No. 691, Pottery, 3200 B.C.; Silver chalice, 1416; Crossbow, 16th cent. No. 692, Kaplan hydraulic turbine.

1984, Apr. 30 **Litho.** ***Perf. 13½***

691 A361 1.40m multicolored .65 .30
692 A362 1.40m multicolored .65 .30

Europa (1959-84) A363

1984, May 7 ***Perf. 12½x13***

693 A363 1.40m multicolored *5.00* .25
694 A363 2m multicolored *5.00* .90

Dentistry — A364

1984, Aug. 27 **Litho.** ***Perf. 14***

695 A364 1.40m Dentist, teeth .65 .30

Astronomy A365

1984, Sept. 12

696 A365 1.10m Observatory, planets, sun .50 .25

Aleksis Kivi (1834-72), Writer — A366

1984, Oct. 10 **Litho.** ***Perf. 14***

697 A366 1.40m Song of my Heart .65 .30

Christmas 1984 — A367

Litho. & Engr.

1984, Nov. 30 ***Perf. 12***

698 A367 1.10m Father Christmas, brownie .50 .25

Common Law of 1734 — A368

1984, Dec. 6 ***Perf. 14***

699 A368 2m Statute Book .90 .40

25th Anniv. of EFTA — A369

1985, Feb. 2 **Litho.**

700 A369 1.20m multicolored .55 .25

100th Anniv. of Society of Swedish Literature in Finland A370

1985, Feb. 5 **Litho.**

701 A370 1.50m Johan Ludvig Runeberg .70 .30

A371

A372

1985, Feb. 18 **Litho.** ***Perf. 11½x12***

702 A371 1.50m Icon .70 .30

Order of St. Sergei and St. Herman, 100th anniv.

Litho. & Engr.

1985, Feb. 28 ***Perf. 13x12½***

703 A372 1.50m Pedri Semeikka .70 .30
704 A372 2.10m Larin Paraske .95 .45

150th anniv. of Kalevala.

A373

A374

Litho. & Engr.

1985, May 15 ***Perf. 13***

705 A373 1.50m Mermaid and sea lions 5.00 *6.25*

NORDIA 1985 philatelic exhibition, May 15-19. Sold for 10m, which included admission ticket.

Photo. & Engr.

1985, May 18 ***Perf. 11½***

Finnish Banknote Cent.: banknotes of 1886, 1909, 1922, 1945 and 1955.

706 Booklet pane of 8 5.50 7.00
a.-h. A374 1.50m any single .65 .30
Complete booklet, #706 6.00

A375

A376

Europa: 1.50m, Children playing the recorder. 2.10m, Excerpt "Ramus Virens Olivarum" from the "Piae Cantiones," 1582.

1985, June 17 **Litho.** ***Perf. 13***

707 A375 1.50m multicolored *6.75* .30
708 A375 2.10m multicolored *7.50* .90

Security Conference Type of 1975

1985, June 19 **Litho.**

709 A265 2.10m multicolored .95 .45

European Security and Cooperation Conference, 10th Anniv.

1985, Sept. 5 **Litho.** ***Perf. 14***

710 A376 1.50m Provincial arms, Count's seal .70 .30

Provincial Administration Established by Count Per Brahe, 350th Anniv.

Arms Type of 1975 and

Kerimaki Church A376a

Urho Kekkonen Natl. Park — A376b

Tulip Damask Table Cloth, 18th Cent. A377

Postal Service A377a

Brown Bear — A377b

Perf. 11½, 13x12½ (2m)

1985-90 **Engr., Litho. (2m)**

711 A256 1.60m vermilion .35 .20
712 A256 1.70m black .75 .20
a. Bklt. pane, #558, 560, 2 each #555, 556a, 712 + 2 labels 6.00 6.00
Complete booklet, #712a 8.50
713 A256 1.80m olive green .80 .20
a. Bklt. pane, 2 ea #555d, 560a, 713b 2.25 2.25
Complete booklet, #713a 2.50
b. Perf. 13x12½ .75 .30
714 A256 1.90m brt orange .85 .25
715 A256 2m blue grn, bklt. stamp .90 .30
a. Bklt. pane, #562a, 2 ea #715, 555d 1.75 1.75
Complete booklet, #715a 2.00

Litho. ***Perf. 14***

716 A376a 2.20m multi .95 .25
717 A376b 2.40m multi 1.00 .25
718 A377 12m multi 5.25 .75

Litho. & Engr.
Perf. 13x12½

719 A377b 50m blk, grn & lt red brn 24.00 5.50
Nos. 711-719 (9) 34.85 7.90

No. 712a contains two labels inscribed to publicize FINLANDIA '88.

Issued: 12m, 9/13/85; 1.60m, 1/2/86; 1.70m, 1/2/87; #712a, 8/10/87; 1.80m, 1/4/88; 2.20m, 2.40m, 1/20/88; #713b, 7/25/88; 1.90m, 1/2/89; 2m, 1/19/90; 50m, 8/30/89.

Booklet Stamps

#720, Telephone, mailbox. #721, Postal truck, transport plane. #722, Transport plane, fork lift. #723, Postman delivering letter. #724, Woman accepting letter.

Perf. 12½ on 3 Sides

1988, Feb. 1 **Litho.**

720 A377a 1.80m multicolored .65 .35
721 A377a 1.80m multicolored .65 .35
722 A377a 1.80m multicolored .65 .35
723 A377a 1.80m multicolored .65 .35
724 A377a 1.80m multicolored .65 .35
a. Bklt. pane, 2 each #720-724 7.50 6.50
Complete booklet, #724a 7.50
Nos. 720-724 (5) 3.25 1.75

Nos. 721-722 and 723-724 printed se-tenant in continuous designs. No. 724c sold for 14m to households on mainland Finland. Each household entitled to buy 2 booklets at discount price from Feb. 1 to May 31, with coupon.

Miniature Sheet

Postal Map, 1698 A378

Designs: a, Postman on foot. c, Sailing vessel, diff. d, Postrider, vert.

Litho. & Engr.

1985, Oct. 16 ***Perf. 14***

728 Sheet of 4 3.50 3.50
a.-d. A378 1.50m any single .85 .85

FINLANDIA '88, 350th anniv. of Finnish Postal Service, founded in 1638 by Gov.-Gen. Per Brahe. Sheet sold for 8m.

Intl. Youth Year — A379

Christmas 1985 — A380

1985, Nov. 1 **Litho.** ***Perf. 13***

729 A379 1.50m multicolored .70 .30

1985, Nov. 29 ***Perf. 14***

730 A380 1.20m Bird, tulips .55 .30
731 A380 1.20m Cross of St. Thomas, hyacinths .55 .30

Natl. Geological Society, Cent. — A390

1986, Feb. 8 Litho. *Perf. 14*
732 A390 1.30m Orbicular granite .60 .30
733 A390 1.60m Rapaviki .75 .50
734 A390 2.10m Veined gneiss .95 .50
Nos. 732-734 (3) 2.30 1.30

Europa 1986 A391

1986, Apr. 10 *Perf. 12½x13*
735 A391 1.60m Saimaa ringed seal *5.50* .30
736 A391 2.20m Environmental conservation *6.00* .90

Conference Palace, Baghdad, 1982 — A392

Natl. Construction Year. b, Lahti Theater, 1983. c, Kuusamo Municipal Offices, 1978. d, Hamina Court Building, 1983. e, Finnish Embassy, New Delhi, 1986. f, Western Sakyla Daycare Center, 1980.

1986, Apr. 19 *Perf. 14*
737 Booklet pane of 6 4.00 3.50
a.-f. A392 1.60m, any single .65 .40
Complete booklet, #737 4.00

Nordic Cooperation Issue 1986 — A393

Sister towns.

1986, May 27 Litho. *Perf. 14*
738 A393 1.60m Joensuu .75 .40
739 A393 2.20m Jyvaskyla 1.00 .50

Souvenir Sheet

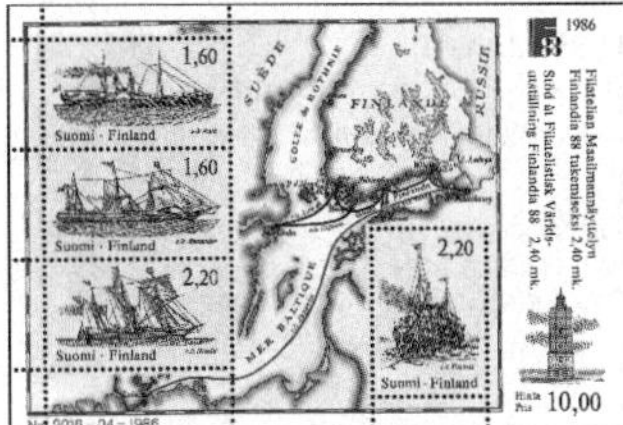

FINLANDIA '88 — A394

Postal ships: a, Iron paddle steamer Aura, Stockholm-St. Petersburg, 1858. b, Screw vessel Alexander, Helsinki-Tallinn-Lubeck, 1859. c, Steamship Nicolai, Helsinki-Tallinn-St. Petersburg, 1858. d, 1st Ice steamship Express II, Helsinki-Stockholm, 1877-98, vert.

Litho. & Engr.

1986, Aug. 29 *Perf. 13*
740 A394 Sheet of 4 4.25 *4.75*
a.-b. 1.60m, any single 1.00 *1.10*
c.-d. 2.20m, any single 1.00 *1.10*

Sold for 10k.

Pierre-Louis Moreau de Maupertuis (1698-1759) — A395

1986, Sept. 5 Litho. *Perf. 12½x13*
741 A395 1.60m multicolored .75 .30

Lapland Expedition, 250th anniv., proved Earth's poles are flattened.
See France No. 2016.

Urho Kaleva Kekkonen (1900-86), Pres. — A396

Intl. Peace Year — A397

1986, Sept. 30 Engr. *Perf. 14*
742 A396 5m black 2.25 2.00

1986, Oct. 13 Litho. *Perf. 13*
743 A397 1.60m multicolored .75 .30

A398

Christmas A399

Photo. & Engr.

1986, Oct. 31 *Perf. 12*
744 1.30m Denomination at L .60 .30
745 1.30m Denomination at R .60 .30
a. A398 Pair, #744-745 1.25 .75
746 A399 1.60m Elves .80 .40
Nos. 744-746 (3) 2.00 1.00

No. 744a has a continuous design.

Postal Savings Bank, Cent. — A400

1987, Jan. 2 Litho. *Perf. 14*
747 A400 1.70m multicolored .75 .40

Natl. Tourism, Cent. — A401

1987, Feb. 4 Litho. *Perf. 14*
748 A401 1.70m Winter .75 .40
749 A401 2.30m Summer 1.00 .50

A402

A403

1987, Feb. 4 *Perf. 14*
750 A402 1.40m multicolored .65 .30

Metric system in Finland, cent.

1987, Feb. 17 Litho. *Perf. 14*
751 A403 2.10m multicolored .90 .45

Leevi Madetoja (1887-1947), composer.

European Wrestling Championships A404

1987 World Bowling Championships A405

1987, Feb. 17
752 A404 1.70m multicolored .75 .40

1987, Apr. 13
753 A405 1.70m multicolored .75 .40

Mental Health — A406

1987, Apr. 13
754 A406 1.70m multicolored .75 .40

Souvenir Sheet

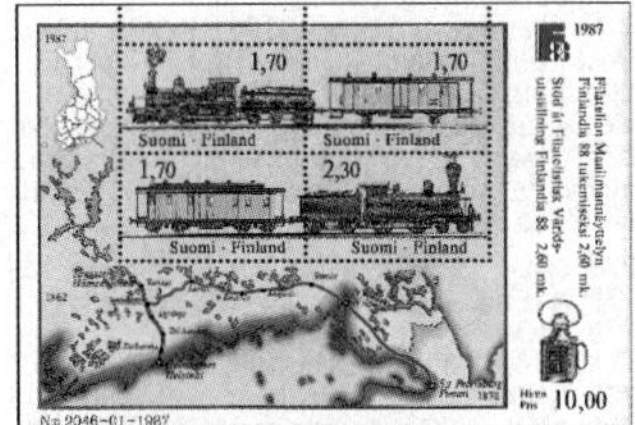

FINLANDIA '88 — A407

Locomotives and mail cars: a, Steam locomotive, 6-wheeled tender. b, 4-window mail car. c, 7-window mail car.

Litho. & Engr.

1987, May 8 *Perf. 12½x13*
755 A407 Sheet of 4 10.00 10.00
a.-c. 1.70m any single 2.50 2.50
d. 2.30m multicolored 2.50 2.50

Sold for 10m.

Europa 1987 A408

Modern architecture: 1.70m, Tampere Main Library, 1986, designed by Raili and Reima Pietila. 2.30m, Stoa Monument, Helsinki, c. 1981, by sculptor Hannu Siren.

1987, May 15 Litho. *Perf. 13*
756 A408 1.70m multicolored *5.50* .25
757 A408 2.30m multicolored *5.50* 1.00

Natl. Art Museum, Ateneum, Cent. — A409

Paintings: a, Strawberry Girl, by Nils Schillmark (1745-1804). b, Still-life on a Lady's Work Table, by Ferdinand von Wright (1822-1906). c, Old Woman with Basket, by Albert Edelfelt (1854-1906). d, Boy and Crow, by Akseli Gallen-Kallela (1865-1931). e, Late Winter, by Tyko Sallinen (1879-1955).

1987, May 15
758 Booklet pane of 5 7.00
a.-e. A409 1.70m any single 1.25 .40
Complete booklet, #758 7.00

A410

A411

1987, Aug. 12 *Perf. 14*
759 A410 1.70m multicolored .80 .25

European Physics Soc. 7th gen. conf., Helsinki, Aug. 10-14.

1987, Oct. 12
760 A411 1.70m ultra, sil & pale lt gray .75 .25

Size: 30x41mm

761 A411 10m dark ultra, lt blue & sil 4.50 1.60

Natl. independence, 70th anniv.

Ylppo, Child and Lastenlinna Children's Hospital A412

1987, Oct. 27
762 A412 1.70m multicolored .75 .25

Arvo Ylppo (b. 1887), pediatrics pioneer.

Christmas A413

Finnish News Agency (STT), Cent. A414

1987, Oct. 30
763 A413 1.40m Santa Claus, youths, horiz. .65 .20
764 A413 1.70m shown .75 .20

1987, Nov. 1
765 A414 2.30m multicolored 1.00 .65

Lauri "Tahko" Pihkala (1888-1981), Promulgator of Sports and Physical Education A415

1988, Jan. 5 Litho. *Perf. 14*
766 A415 1.80m blk, chalky blue & brt blue .80 .25

A416

1988, Mar. 14 Litho.
767 A416 1.40m multicolored .60 .20

Meteorological Institute, 150th anniv.

Settlement of New Sweden in America, 350th Anniv. — A417

Design: 17th Century European settlers negotiating with 3 American Indians, map of New Sweden, the Swedish ships Kalmar Nyckel and Fogel Grip, based on an 18th cent. illustration from a Swedish book about the American Colonies.

Litho. & Engr.

1988, Mar. 29 *Perf. 13*
768 A417 3m multicolored 1.25 .60

See US No. C117 and Sweden No. 1672.

FINLANDIA '88, June 1-12, Helsinki Fair Center — A418

Agathon Faberge (1876-1951), famed philatelist, & rarities from his collection.

Booklet Stamp

1988, May 2 **Litho.** *Perf. 13*
769 A418 5m Pane of 1+2 labels 12.50 14.00
Complete booklet, #769 12.50

350th Anniv. of the Finnish Postal Service. No. 769 sold for 30m to include the price of adult admission to the exhibition.

Achievements of Finnish Athletes at the 1988 Winter Olympics, Calgary — A419

Design: Matti Nykanen, gold medalist in all 3 ski jumping events at the '88 Games.

1988, Apr. 6 *Perf. 14*
770 A419 1.80m multicolored .80 .25

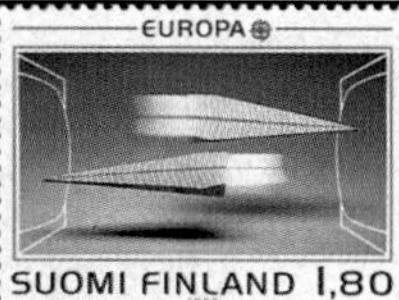

Europa 1988 A420

Communication and transport.

1988, May 23 **Litho.** *Perf. 13*
771 A420 1.80m shown *5.00* .25
772 A420 2.40m Horse-drawn tram, 1890 *5.00* 1.00

Souvenir Sheet

FINLANDIA '88 — A421

1st airmail flights: a, Finnish air force Breguet 14 biplane transporting mail from Helsinki to Tallinn, Feb. 12, 1920. b, AERO Junkers F-13 making 1st airmail night flight from Helsinki to Copenhagen, May 15, 1930. c, AERO Douglas DC-3, 1st intl. route, Helsinki-Norrkoping-Copenhagen-Amsterdam, 1947. d, Douglas DC 10-30, 1975-88, inauguration of Helsinki-Beijing route, June 2, 1988.

Litho. & Engr.

1988, June 2 *Perf. 13½*
773 Sheet of 4 10.00 *10.00*
a.-c. A421 1.80m any single 2.25 2.25
d. A421 2.40m multicolored 2.25 2.25

Sold for 11m.

Turku Fire Brigade, 150th Anniv. — A422

Design: 1902 Horse-drawn, steam-driven fire pump, preserved at the brigade.

1988, Aug. 15 **Litho.** *Perf. 14*
774 A422 2.20m multicolored .95 .55

A423 A424

Missale Aboense, the 1st printed book in Finland, 500th anniv.

1988, Aug. 17
775 A423 1.80m multicolored .80 .25

Booklet Stamps

1988, Sept. 6 **Litho.** *Perf. 13*

Finnish Postal Service, 350th Anniv.: #776, Postal tariff issued by Queen Christina of Sweden, Sept. 6, 1638. #777, Postal cart, c. 1880. #778, Leyland Sherpa 185 mail van, 1976. #779, Malmi P.O. interior. #780, Skier using mobile telephone, c. 1970. #781, Telecommunications satellite in orbit.

776 A424 1.80m multicolored .85 .45
777 A424 1.80m multicolored .85 .45
778 A424 1.80m multicolored .85 .45
779 A424 1.80m multicolored .85 .45
780 A424 1.80m multicolored .85 .45
781 A424 1.80m multicolored .85 .45
a. Booklet pane of 6, #776-781 5.25 5.50
Complete booklet, #781a 5.50

Children's Playgroups (Preschool) A425

1988, Oct. 10 *Perf. 14*
782 A425 1.80m multicolored .80 .25

Christmas A426

1988, Nov. 4 **Litho.**
783 A426 1.40m multicolored .70 .20
784 A426 1.80m multicolored .80 .20

Hameenlinna Township, 350th Anniv. — A427

Design: Market square, coat of arms and 17th century plan of the town.

1989, Jan. 19 **Litho.**
785 A427 1.90m multicolored .85 .25

1989 Nordic Ski Championships, Lahti, Feb. 17-26 — A428

1989, Jan. 25
786 A428 1.90m multicolored .85 .25

Salvation Army in Finland, Cent. — A429

Photography, 150th Anniv. — A430

1989, Feb. 6 **Litho.**
787 A429 1.90m multicolored .85 .25

1989, Feb. 6
788 A430 1.50m Photographer, box camera, c.1900 .65 .30

31st Intl. Physiology Congress, Basel, July 9-14 — A431

Design: Congress emblem, silhouettes of Robert Tigerstedt and Ragnar Granit, eye, flowmeter measuring flow of blood through heart, color-sensitive retinal cells and microelectrode.

1989, Mar. 2
789 A431 1.90m multicolored .85 .25

Sports — A432

1989, Mar. 10 **Booklet Stamps**
790 A432 1.90m Skiing .85 .30
791 A432 1.90m Jogging .85 .30
792 A432 1.90m Cycling .85 .30
793 A432 1.90m Canoeing .85 .30
a. Booklet pane of 4, #790-793 2.25 2.00
Complete booklet, #793a 3.00

Souvenir Sheet

Finnish Kennel Club, Cent. — A433

Dogs: a, Lapponian herder. b, Finnish spitz. c, Karelian bear dog. d, Finnish hound.

1989, Mar. 17 **Litho.** *Perf. 14*
794 A433 Sheet of 4 3.75 3.75
a.-d. 1.90m any single .90 .50

Europa — A434 A435

1989, Mar. 31 *Perf. 13*
795 A434 1.90m Hopscotch *2.50* .25
796 A434 2.50m Sledding *2.50* .70

1989, Apr. 20 *Perf. 14*

Nordic Cooperation Year: Folk Costumes.

797 A435 1.90m Sakyla (man) .90 .25
798 A435 2.50m Veteli (woman) 1.10 .55

Finnish Pharmacies, 300th Anniv. — A436

Foxglove, distilling apparatus, mortar, flask.

1989, June 2 **Litho.**
799 A436 1.90m multicolored .85 .25

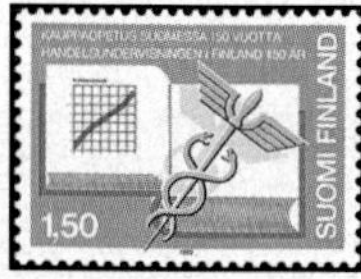

A437

A438

1989, June 2
800 A437 1.90m multicolored .85 .25

Savonlinna Municipal Charter, 350th anniv.

1989, June 12
801 A438 1.90m *Panthera uncia* .85 .25
802 A438 2.50m *Capra falconeri* 1.10 .75

Helsinki Zoo, cent.

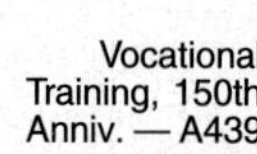

Vocational Training, 150th Anniv. — A439

Interparliamentary Union, Cent. — A440

Council of Europe, 40th Anniv. — A441

1989, Sept. 4 **Litho.** *Perf. 14*
803 A439 1.50m multicolored .65 .30
804 A440 1.90m multicolored .85 .25
805 A441 2.50m multicolored 1.10 .50
Nos. 803-805 (3) 2.60 1.05

Admission of Finland to the Council of Europe (2.50m).

A442

A443

1989, Oct. 9 **Litho.**
806 A442 1.90m multicolored .85 .25

Hannes Kolehmainen (1889-1966) winning the 5000-meter race at the Stockholm Olympics, 1912.

1989, Oct. 20
807 A443 1.90m multicolored .85 .25

Continuing Education in Finland, cent.

A444

A445

Christmas: 1.90m, Sodankyla Church, Siberian jays in snow.

1989, Nov. 3
808 A444 1.50m shown .70 .20
809 A444 1.90m multicolored .85 .20

1990, Jan. 19 **Litho.** ***Perf. 13x13½***
810 A445 1.90m multicolored .90 .90
811 A445 2.50m multicolored 1.10 1.00

Incorporation of the State Posts and Telecommunications Services.
Emblem of the corporation was produced by holography. Soaking may affect the design.

Musical Soc. of Turku and Finnish Orchestras, 200th Annivs. A446

1990, Jan. 26 ***Perf. 14***
812 A446 1.90m multicolored .90 .25

Disabled Veteran's Assoc., 50th Anniv. — A447

1990, Mar. 13 **Litho.**
813 A447 2m multicolored .90 .25

End of the Winter (Russo-Finnish) War, 50th Anniv. — A448

1990, Mar. 13
814 A448 2m blue .90 .25

University of Helsinki, 350th Anniv. — A449

University crest and: 2m, Queen Christina on horseback. 3.20m, Degree ceremony procession in front of the main university building.

1990, Mar. 26 **Litho.** ***Perf. 13***
815 A449 2m multicolored .90 .25
816 A449 3.20m multicolored 1.40 .75

Europa 1990 A450

Post Offices: 2m, Lapp man, P.O. at Nuvvus, Mt. Nuvvus Ailigas. 2.70m, Turku main P.O.

1990, Mar. 26 ***Perf. 12½x13***
817 A450 2m multicolored *6.00* .25
818 A450 2.70m multicolored *6.00* .70

Rural Postal Service and Address Reform, Cent. — A451

1990, Apr. 19 **Litho.** ***Perf. 13***
819 A451 2m multicolored .90 .25

"Ali Baba and the Forty Thieves" A452

"Story of the Great Musician" A453

"Story of the Giants, the Witches and the Daughter of the Sun" A454

"The Golden Bird, the Golden Horse and the Princess" A455

"Lamb Brother" A456

"The Snow Queen" A457

Fairy tale illustrations by Rudolf Koivu.

Booklet Stamps
Perf. 14 on 3 sides

1990, Aug. 29 **Litho.**
820 A452 2m multicolored 1.25 .30
821 A453 2m multicolored 1.25 .30
822 A454 2m multicolored 1.25 .30
823 A455 2m multicolored 1.25 .30
824 A456 2m multicolored 1.25 .30
825 A457 2m multicolored 1.25 .30
a. Booklet pane of 6, #820-825 8.00 9.00
Complete booklet, #825a 9.00

Souvenir Sheet

Horse Care — A458

a, Feeding. b, Riding. c, Watering. d, Currying.

1990, Oct. 10 **Litho.** ***Perf. 14***
826 A458 Sheet of 4 3.75 2.75
a.-d. 2m any single .90 .40

Christmas A459

1990, Nov. 2
827 A459 1.70m Santa's elves .85 .20
828 A459 2m Santa, reindeer 1.00 .20

Provincial Flowers

A460

A460a

A460b

A460c

A460d

A460e

A460f

A460g

A460h

A460i

A460j

A460k

1990-99 ***Perf. 13x12½***
829 A460 2m Wood anemone .90 .20
830 A460 2.10m Rowan .90 .20
831 A460 2.70m Heather 1.10 .30
832 A460 2.90m Sea buckthorn 1.25 .30
833 A460 3.50m Oak 1.50 .40
834 A460a 2 Globeflower .95 .30
835 A460b 1 Hepatica 1.25 .20
Nos. 829-835 (7) 7.85 1.90

Self-Adhesive
Die Cut

836 A460c 2 Iris .95 .20
a. Booklet pane of 20 17.50 15.00
837 A460 2.10m like #830 .90 .20
838 A460d 1 Rosebay willowherb 1.25 .20
839 A460e 1 Labrador tea 1.25 .20
a. Booklet pane of 10 12.50 12.50
840 A460f 1 Karelian rose 1.25 .20
841 A460g 1 Daisy 1.25 .20
842 A460h 1 Water lily 1.25 .20
843 A460i 1 Bird cherry 1.25 .20
844 A460j 1 Harebell 1.25 .20
845 A460k 1 Cowslip 1.25 .20
Nos. 836-845 (10) 11.85 2.00

Issued: 2m, 2.70m, 1/19/90; #830, 2.90m, 3.50m, 2/5/90; 2.10m, 1991; #834-835, 3/2/92; #838, 10/9/92; #836, 3/1/93; #839, 6/14/93; #840, 5/5/94; #841, 3/15/95; #842, 6/3/96; #843, 3/18/97; #844, 3/12/98; #845, 4/28/99.
#834 sold for 1.60m, #836 sold for 1.90m, #835, 838 for 2.10m, #839-840 for 2.30m, #841-844 sold for 2.80m, #845 sold for 3m at time of release.
#837-838, 840-845 issued in sheets of 10. Nos. 836a and 839a were issued as complete booklets. The peelable backing serves as a booklet cover.
The numbers on the stamps represent the class of mail for which each was intended at time of release.

A461

A462

1991, Mar. 1 ***Perf. 14***
846 A461 2.10m multicolored .90 .25

World Hockey Championships, Turku.

1991, Mar. 1
847 A462 2.10m Cooking class .90 .25

Home economics teacher education, cent.

Sauna Type of 1977 and:

Birds — A463

Perf. 13x12½, 14 (#861)
1991-99 **Litho.**
Booklet Stamps (#848-859)

848 A463 10p Great tit .40 .20
849 A463 10p Wagtail .20 .20
850 A463 10p Aegolius funereus .30 .60
850A A463 20p Phoenicurus phoenicurus 1.50 .60
851 A463 60p Chaffinches 1.50 .30
852 A463 60p Robin 1.50 .50
856 A463 2.10m Bullfinch .90 .20
a. Bklt. pane, #851, 2 each #848, 856 3.00 3.00
Complete booklet, #856a 3.25
857 A463 2.10m Waxwing .90 .25
a. Bklt. pane, #852, 2 each #849, 857 3.00 3.00
Complete booklet, #857a 3.25
859 A463 2.30m Dendrocopos leucotos 1.00 .30
a. Booklet pane of #850A, 2 each #850, #859 + 1 label 4.00 4.00
Complete booklet, #859a 4.25

Sheet Stamp

861 A256a 4.80m multicolored 2.10 .65
Nos. 848-861 (10) 10.30 3.80

Issued: #848, 851, 856, 3/20/91; #849, 852, 857, 4/22/92; #850, 850A, 859, 6/4/93. 861, 7/1/99.
"SUOMI" is in upper left on #849, 852, 857.

Fishing A464 | Tourism A465

Designs: a, Fly fisherman, trout. b, Perch, bobber. c, Crayfish, trap. d, Trawling for herring. e, Stocking powan.

1991, Mar. 20 ***Perf. 14***

863	Booklet pane of 5	4.75	5.00
a.-e.	A464 2.10m any single	.90	.30
	Complete booklet, #863	5.00	

1991, June 4 Litho. ***Perf. 14***

864	A465 2.10m Seurasaari Island	.90	.25
865	A465 2.90m Steamship, Lake Saimaa	1.25	.65

Europa A466

European map and: 2.10m, Human figures. 2.90m, Satellites, dish antennae.

1991, June 7 Litho. ***Perf. 12½x13***

866	A466 2.10m multicolored	*5.50*	.25
867	A466 2.90m multicolored	*5.50*	.75

Alfred W. Finch (1854-1930) A467

Designs: 2.10m, Iris, ceramic vase. 2.90m, Painting, The English Coast at Dover.

1991, Sept. 7 Litho. ***Perf. 13***

868	A467 2.10m multicolored	1.50	.25
869	A467 2.90m multicolored	1.50	.60

See Belgium No. 1410.

Finnish Candy Industry, Cent. — A468

1991, Sept. 17 Photo. ***Perf. 11½***

870	A468 2.10m multicolored	.90	.25

Souvenir Sheets

Children's Stamp Designs — A469

a, Sun. b, Rainbow. c, Cows grazing.

1991, Sept. 17 Litho. ***Perf. 13½***

871	A469 Sheet of 3	2.75	2.10
a.-c.	2.10m any single	.90	.50

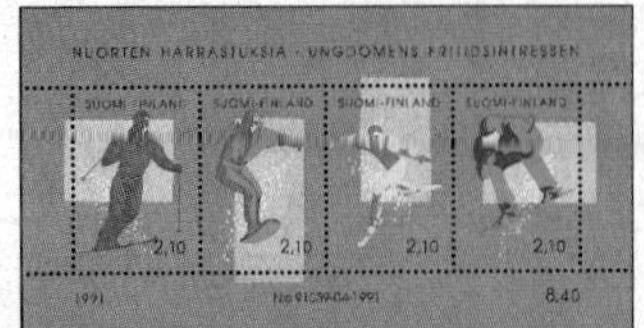

Skiing — A470

1991, Oct. 4 ***Perf. 14***

Color of skisuit: a, red. b, green. c, yellow. d, blue.

872	A470 Sheet of 4	3.75	3.00
a.-d.	2.10m any single	.90	.50

Town Status for Iisalmi, Cent. — A471

1991, Oct. 18 Litho. ***Perf. 14***

873	A471 2.10m multicolored	.90	.55

Christmas A472

1.80m, Santa, animals carrying candles. 2.10m, Reindeer pulling Santa's sleigh.

1991, Nov. 1 Litho. ***Perf. 14***

874	A472 1.80m multi	1.00	.25
875	A472 2.10m multi, vert.	1.00	.25

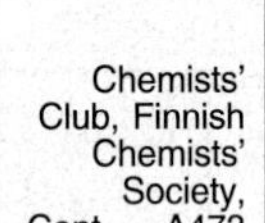

Chemists' Club, Finnish Chemists' Society, Cent. — A473

1991, Nov. 1

876	A473 2.10m multi	.90	.25
877	A473 2.10m multi, diff.	.90	.25
a.	Pair, #876-877 + label	2.25	2.25

Second and third vertical branches merge while second and third branches below almost touch in the upper left part of camphor molecular structure on No. 877. Nos. 876-877 are designed to produce a three dimensional effect when viewed together.

1992 Olympic Games A474

Designs: No. 878, Skier, Albertville. No. 879, Swimmer, Barcelona.

1992, Feb. 4 Litho. ***Perf. 14***

878	A474 2.10m multicolored	1.00	.25
879	A474 2.90m multicolored	1.25	.50

Expo '92, Seville — A475

1992, Mar. 20 Litho. ***Perf. 14***

880	A475 3.40m multicolored	1.50	.75

Conference on Security and Cooperation in Europe, Helsinki A476

1992, Mar. 20 ***Perf. 14½x15***

881	A476 16m multicolored	7.00	2.50

Town of Rauma, 550th Anniv. — A477

1992, Mar. 27 ***Perf. 14***

882	A477 2.10m multicolored	1.00	.25

Healthy Brains — A478

1992, Mar. 27

883	A478 3.50m multicolored	1.50	.90

Discovery of America, 500th Anniv. A479

1992, May 8 Litho. ***Perf. 12½x13***

884	A479 2.10m Santa Maria, map	*2.50*	.35
885	A479 2.10m Map, Columbus	*2.50*	.35
a.	Pair, #884-885	*5.00*	4.00

Europa.

Finnish Technology A480

Hologram of trees and: 2.10m, Drawing of blowing machine. 2.90m, Schematic of electronic circuits. 3.40m, Triangles and grid.

1992, May 8 ***Perf. 13x12½***

886	A480 2.10m multicolored	.90	.30
887	A480 2.90m multicolored	1.25	.55
888	A480 3.40m multicolored	1.50	.90
	Nos. 886-888 (3)	3.65	1.75

First Finnish patent granted, sesqui. (#886), Finnish chairmanship of Eureka (#887), Government Technology Research Center, 50th anniv. (#888).

Nos. 886-888 have holographic images. Soaking in water may affect the hologram.

Natl. Board of Agriculture, Cent. — A481

1992, June 4 Litho. ***Perf. 14***

889	A481 2.10m Currant harvesting	.90	.25

Finnish Women A482

#890, Aurora Karamzin (1808-1902), founder of Deaconesses' Institution of Helsinki. #891, Baroness Sophie Mannerheim (1863-1928), reformer of nursing education. #892, Laimi Leidenius (1877-1938), physician and educator. #893, Miina Sillanpaa (1866-1952), Minister for social affairs. #894, Edith Sodergran (1892-1923), poet. #895, Kreeta Haapasalo (1813-1893), folk singer.

Litho. & Engr.

1992, June 8 ***Perf. 14***

Booklet Stamps

890	A482 2.10m multicolored	.90	.40
891	A482 2.10m multicolored	.90	.40
892	A482 2.10m multicolored	.90	.40
893	A482 2.10m multicolored	.90	.40
894	A482 2.10m multicolored	.90	.40
895	A482 2.10m multicolored	.90	.40
a.	Booklet pane of 6, #890-895	5.50	5.00
	Complete booklet, #895a	5.50	

Child's Painting A483

Independence, 75th Anniv. — A484

1992, Oct. 5 Litho. ***Perf. 13***

896	A483 2.10m multicolored	.90	.25

Souvenir Sheet

Perf. 13½

897	A484 2.10m multicolored	.90	.75

Nordia '93 — A485

A486

Illustrations depicting "Moomin" characters, by Tove Jansson: No. 898, Winter scene, ice covered bridges. No. 899, Winter scene in forest. No. 900, Boats in water. No. 901, Characters on beach.

Perf. 13 on 3 Sides

1992, Oct. 9 Litho.

Booklet Stamps

898	A485 2.10m multicolored	1.75	.45
899	A485 2.10m multicolored	1.75	.45
900	A485 2.10m multicolored	1.75	.45
901	A485 2.10m multicolored	1.75	.45
a.	Booklet pane of 4, #898-901	7.50	7.50
	Complete booklet, #901a	7.75	

1992, Oct. 20 Litho. ***Perf. 13***

902	A486 2.10m multicolored	.90	.25

Printing in Finland, 350th anniv.

Christmas A487

Designs: 1.80m, Church of St. Lawrence, Vantaa. 2.10m, Stained glass window of nativity scene, Karkkila Church, vert.

1992, Oct. 30 Litho. *Perf. 14*
903 A487 1.80m multicolored 1.00 .20
904 A487 2.10m multicolored 1.00 .20

Central Chamber of Commerce, 75th Anniv. — A488

1993, Feb. 8 Litho. *Perf. 14*
905 A488 1.60m multicolored .70 .30

Friendship A489

1993, Feb. 8 Litho. *Perf. 14*
906 A489 1 multicolored 1.00 .25
a. Booklet pane of 5 + label 5.50 5.50
Complete booklet, 2 #906a 11.00

No. 906 sold for 2m at time of release. See note following No. 845.
See Estonia No. 237.

Alopex Lagopus — A490

a, Adult with winter white coat. b, Face, full view, winter white coat. c, Mother, kits, summer coat. d, Two on rock, summer coat.

1993, Mar. 19 Litho. *Perf. 12½x13*
907 A490 2.30m Block of 4, #a-d 3.75 3.75

World Wildlife Fund.

Sculptures A491

Europa: 2m, Rumba, by Martti Aiha. 2.90m, Complete Works, by Kari Caven.

1993, Apr. 26 *Perf. 13*
908 A491 2m multicolored *2.00* .25
909 A491 2.90m multicolored *1.50* .65

Organized Philately in Finland, Cent. — A492

1993, May 6 *Perf. 13x12½*
910 A492 2.30m Rosa pimpinellifolia 1.00 .40

Vyborg Castle, 700th Anniv. A493

1993, May 6 *Perf. 13½*
911 A493 2.30m multicolored 1.00 .25

Tourism A494

1993, May 7 *Perf. 13x12½*
912 A494 2.30m Naantali 1.00 .25
913 A494 2.90m Imatra 1.25 .40

550th anniv. of Naantali (#912).

A495

A496

Independent Finland Defense Forces, 75th Anniv.: 2.30m, Finnish landscape in form of soldier's silhouette. 3.40m, UN checkpoint of Finnish battalion, Middle East.

1993, June 4 Litho. *Perf. 14*
914 A495 2.30m multicolored 1.00 .25
915 A495 3.40m multicolored 1.50 .90

1993, June 14 Litho. *Perf. 12½x13*

Art by Martta Wendelin (1893-1986): #916, Boy on skis, 1936. #917, Mother, daughter knitting, 1931. #918, Children building snowman, 1931. #919, Mother, children at fence, 1935. #920, Girl with lamb, 1936.

Booklet Stamps

916 A496 2.30m multicolored 1.00 .45
917 A496 2.30m multicolored 1.00 .45
918 A496 2.30m multicolored 1.00 .45
919 A496 2.30m multicolored 1.00 .45
920 A496 2.30m multicolored 1.00 .45
a. Booklet pane of 5, #916-920 5.00 5.00
Complete booklet, #920a 5.25

Water Birds — A497

#921, Flock of gavia arctica. #922, Pair of gavia arctica. #923, Mergus merganser. #924, Anas platyrhynchos. #925, Mergus serrator.

Perf. 12½x13 on 3 or 4 Sides
1993, Sept. 20 Litho.

Booklet Stamps

921 A497 2.30m multicolored 1.00 .30
922 A497 2.30m multicolored 1.00 .30

Size: 26x40mm

923 A497 2.30m multicolored 1.00 .30
924 A497 2.30m multicolored 1.00 .30
925 A497 2.30m multicolored 1.00 .30
a. Booklet pane of 5, #921-925 4.00 4.00
Complete booklet, #925a 4.25

Physical Education in Finnish Schools, 150th Anniv. — A498

1993, Oct. 8 *Perf. 14*
926 A498 2.30m multicolored 1.00 .25

Souvenir Sheet

New Opera House, Helsinki A499

Operas and ballet: a, 2.30m, Ostrobothnians, by Leevi Madetoja. b, 2.30m, The Faun (four dancers), by Claude Debussy. c, 2.90m, Giselle, by Adolphe Adam. d, 3.40m, The Magic Flute, by Wolfgang Amadeus Mozart.

1993, Oct. 8 *Perf. 13*
927 A499 Sheet of 4, #a.-d. 4.75 4.75

Christmas A500

Pres. Mauno Koivisto, 70th Birthday A501

1993, Nov. 5 Litho. *Perf. 14*
928 A500 1.80m Christmas tree, elves .80 .25
a. Booklet pane of 10 10.00 10.00
Complete booklet, #928a 10.00
929 A500 2.30m Three angels 1.00 .25

1993, Nov. 25
930 A501 2.30m multicolored 1.00 .25

Friendship — A502

Moomin characters: No. 931, Two standing. No. 932, Seven running.

1994, Jan. 27 Litho. *Perf. 12½x13*

Booklet Stamps

931 A502 1 multicolored 1.60 .25
932 A502 1 multicolored 1.60 .25
a. Bklt. pane, 4 each #931-932 13.50 12.00
Complete booklet, #932a 13.50

Nos. 931-932 each sold for 2.30m at time of release. See note following No. 845.

Souvenir Sheet

Intl. Olympic Committee, Cent. — A503

Winter Olympics medalists from Finland: a, Marja-Liisa Kirvesniemi, Marjo Matikainen, cross-country skiing. b, Clas Thunberg, speed skating. c, Veikko Kankkonen, ski jumping. d, Veikko Hakulinen, cross-country skiing.

1994, Jan. 27 *Perf. 13*
933 A503 4.20m Sheet of 4, #a-d 5.75 5.75

See No. 939.

A504

Waino Aaltonen (1894-1966), Sculptor — A505

1994, Mar. 8
934 A504 2m "Peace" .90 .25
935 A505 2m "Muse" .90 .25
a. Pair, #934-935 1.90 1.40

Postal Service Civil Servants' Federation, Cent. — A506

1994, Mar. 11
936 A506 2.30m multicolored 1.00 .25

Finnish Technology A507

Europa: 2.30m, Paper roll, nitrogen fixation, safety lock, ice breaker MS Fennica. 4.20m, Radiosonde, fishing lure, mobile phone, wind power plant.

1994, Mar. 18
937 A507 2.30m multicolored *1.50* .25
938 A507 4.20m multicolored *2.00* 1.25

Olympic Athlete Type of 1994
Souvenir Sheet

Finnish athletes: a, Riitta Salin, Pirjo Haggman, runners. b, Lasse Viren, runner. c, Tiina Lillak, javelin thrower. d, Pentti Nikula, pole vaulter.

1994, May 5 Litho. *Perf. 13*
939 A503 4.20m Sheet of 4, #a-d 5.75 5.75

European Track & Field Championships, Finlandia '95.

Finlandia '95, Helsinki — A508

1994, May 10 *Perf. 13½x13*
940 A508 16m Coccinella septempunctata 7.50 7.50

See Nos. 962, 1009.

Miniature Sheet

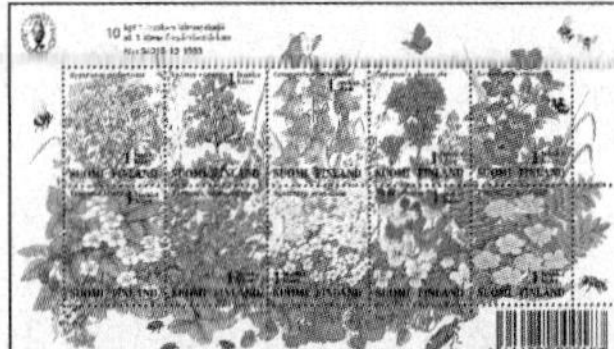

Wildflowers — A509

Designs: a, Hypericum perforatum (b). b, Lychnis viscaria. c, Campanula rotundifolia. d, Campanula glomerata. e, Geranium sanguineum (d). f, Fragaria vesca. g, Veronica chamaedrys (f, h). h, Saxifraga granulata (c, i). i, Viola tricolor (j). j, Potentilla anserina.

1994, June 1 *Perf. 12*

941 A509 1 Sheet of 10, #a.-j. 17.50 12.50

No. 941 sold for 23m at time of release. See note following No. 845.

Finland-Sweden Track and Field Meet — A510

#942, Seppo Raty, Finland, javelin. #943, Patrick Sjoberg, Sweden, high jump.

1994, Aug. 26 **Litho.** *Perf. 12½*

Booklet Stamps

942 A510 2.40m multicolored 1.00 .25
943 A510 2.40m multicolored 1.00 .25
a. Booklet pane, 2 each #942-943 4.25 3.00
Complete booklet, #943a 4.25

See Sweden Nos. 2091-2092.

Population Registers, 450th Anniv. — A511

1994, Sept. 1

944 A511 2.40m multicolored 1.00 .25

Intl. Year of the Family — A512

1994, Sept. 1

945 A512 3.40m multicolored 1.50 .65

Souvenir Sheet

Letter Writing Day — A513

Dog Hill Kids in the Post Office: a, At Post Office window. b, Standing in doorway, mail cart. c, Blowing horn, pig. d, Putting letters in mailbox.

1994, Oct. 7 **Litho.** *Perf. 14*

946 A513 2.80m Sheet of 4, #a-d 5.00 5.00

Christmas A514

2.10m, Reindeer, bullfinches on antlers. 2.80m, Elves among snow-covered trees.

1994, Nov. 4

947 A514 2.10m multi .90 .25
a. Booklet pane of 10 9.00 10.00
Complete booklet, #947a 9.00
948 A514 2.80m multi, vert. 1.25 .40

Greetings — A515

"Dog Hill Kids," sending/receiving greetings: No. 949, Delivering mail to Moon, spaceman. No. 950, Cat writing letter, clown. No. 951, Receiving mail from postman, baby. No. 952, Writing in bed, friend. No. 953, Winter scene at mailbox, characters at beach. No. 954, On bus, girl friend. No. 955, Standing at microphone with guitar, fan. No. 956, Baby in play pen, teddy bear.

Perf. 13 on 3 Sides

1995, Jan. 30 **Litho.**

Booklet Stamps

949 A515 2.80m multicolored 1.25 .50
950 A515 2.80m multicolored 1.25 .50
951 A515 2.80m multicolored 1.25 .50
952 A515 2.80m multicolored 1.25 .50
953 A515 2.80m multicolored 1.25 .50
954 A515 2.80m multicolored 1.25 .50
955 A515 2.80m multicolored 1.25 .50
956 A515 2.80m multicolored 1.25 .50
a. Booklet pane, #949-956 10.00
Complete booklet, 956a 10.00

Nos. 949-952 are printed tete beche with Nos. 953-956. Soaking in water may affect the holographic images on Nos. 949-956.

Souvenir Sheet

Team Sports — A516

a, Paivi Ikola, pesapallo. b, Jari Kurri, ice hockey. c, Jari Litmanen, soccer. d, Lea Hakala, basketball.

1995, Jan. 30 *Perf. 13*

957 A516 3.40m Sheet of 4, #a-d 4.25 4.25

See No. 961.

Membership in European Union — A517

1995, Jan. 30 *Perf. 14*

958 A517 3.50m multicolored 1.50 .75

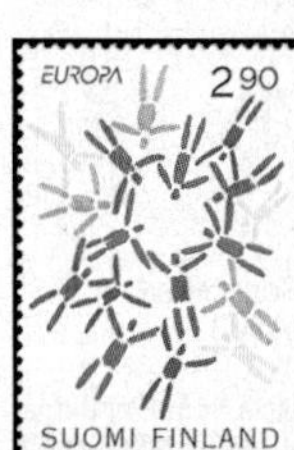

Peace & Liberty — A518

Europa: 2.90m, Stylized parachutists.

1995, Mar. 1 **Litho.** *Perf. 14*

959 A518 2.90m multicolored 1.50 .50

Endangered Species — A519

Designs: a, Felis lynx. b, Lake, forest. c, Rocks, lake. d, Pusa hispida.

1995, Mar. 1 *Perf. 13*

960 A519 2.90m Block of 4, #a-d 5.25 5.25

Nos. 960a-960b, 960c-960d are continuous designs. See Russia No. 6249.

Athlete Type of 1995

Souvenir Sheet

Motor sports drivers in cars, on motorcycles: a, Timo Makinen. b, Juha Kankkunen. c, Tommi Ahvala. d, Heikki Mikkola.

1995, May 10 **Litho.** *Perf. 13*

961 A516 3.50m Sheet of 4, #a.-d. 6.25 6.25

Insect Type of 1994

1995, May 11

962 A508 19m Geotrupes stercorarius 9.00 9.00

Tourism — A520

Designs: 2.80m, Linnanmaki amusement park, Helsinki. 2.90m, Town of Mantyharju.

1995, May 12

963 A520 2.80m multicolored 1.25 .55
964 A520 2.90m multicolored 1.25 .65

Town of Loviisa, 250th Anniv. — A521

1995, June 30 **Litho.** *Perf. 14*

965 A521 3.20m multicolored 1.40 1.10

Intl. Union of Forestry Research Organizations, 20th World Congress, Tampere — A522

Designs: No. 966, Betula pendula. No. 967, Pinus sylvestris. No. 968, Picea abies. No. 969, Research, tree grown from needle.

Perf. 14 on 2 or 3 Sides

1995, Aug. 8 **Litho.**

Booklet Stamps

966 A522 2.80m multicolored 1.25 .50
967 A522 2.80m multicolored 1.25 .50
968 A522 2.80m multicolored 1.25 .50
969 A522 2.80m multicolored 1.25 .50
a. Booklet pane of 4, #966-969 5.00 4.25
Complete booklet, #969a 5.00 4.25

Wilhelm Roentgen (1845-1923), Discovery of the X-Ray, Cent. — A523

1995, Aug. 8 *Perf. 14*

970 A523 4.30m multicolored 1.90 1.25

Cats — A525

1995, Oct. 9 **Litho.** *Perf. 13½*

972 A525 2.80m Somali 1.25 .50
973 A525 2.80m Siamese 1.25 .50
974 A525 2.80m Norwegian forest 1.25 .50
975 A525 2.80m Persian 1.25 .50

Size: 59x35mm

976 A525 2.80m European domestic female 1.25 .50
977 A525 2.80m Three kittens, frog 1.25 .50
a. Booklet pane of 6, #972-977 7.50
Complete booklet, #977a 7.50

UN, 50th Anniv. — A526

1995, Oct. 20 *Perf. 14*

978 A526 3.40m multicolored 1.50 1.00

A527

Christmas A528

1995, Nov. 3 **Litho.** *Perf. 14*

979 A527 2m Santa on skates .90 .20
980 A528 2.80m Poinsettias 1.25 .60

Letter Stamps A529

UNICEF, 50th Anniv. A530

1996, Feb 2 **Litho.** *Perf. 13½x14*

Booklet Stamps

981 A529 1m "M" .45 .30
982 A529 1m "O" .45 .30
983 A529 1m "I" .45 .30
984 A529 1m "H" .45 .30
985 A529 1m "E" .45 .30
986 A529 1m "J" .45 .30
987 A529 1m "A" .45 .30
988 A529 1m "N" .45 .30
989 A529 1m "T" .45 .30
990 A529 1m "P" .45 .30
991 A529 1m "U" .45 .30

992 A529 1m "S" .45 .30
a. Booklet pane of 12, #981-992 5.50
Complete booklet, No. 992a 5.50

1996, Feb. 2 *Perf. 14*
993 A530 2.80m multicolored 1.25 .50

Women's Gymnastics in Finland, Cent. — A531

1996, Feb. 26 **Litho.** *Perf. 13*
994 A531 2.80m multicolored 1.25 .50

Woman Suffrage, 90th Anniv. A532

Litho. & Engr.
1996, Mar. 8 *Perf. 13*
995 A532 3.20m multicolored 1.40 .85

Europa.

Cinema, Cent. — A533

Finnish films: No. 996, "Juha," 1937. No. 997, "Laveata Tieta," 1931. No. 998, "Tuntematon Sotilas," 1935. No. 999, Oldest known photo of a motion picture show, 1896. No. 1000, "Jäniksen Vuosi," 1977. No. 1001, "Valkoinen Peura," 1952. No. 1002, "Kaikki Rakastavat," 1935. No. 1003, "Varjoja Paratiisissa," 1986.

1996, Apr. 1 **Litho.** *Perf. 14x13½*
Booklet Stamps

996 A533 2.80m multicolored 1.25 .55
997 A533 2.80m multicolored 1.25 .55
998 A533 2.80m multicolored 1.25 .55
999 A533 2.80m multicolored 1.25 .55
1000 A533 2.80m multicolored 1.25 .55
1001 A533 2.80m multicolored 1.25 .55
1002 A533 2.80m multicolored 1.25 .55
1003 A533 2.80m multicolored 1.25 .55
a. Bklt. pane of 8, #996-1003 10.00
Complete booklet, #1003a 10.00

Radio, Cent. — A534

1996, Apr. 25 *Perf. 14*
1004 A534 4.30m multicolored 1.90 1.10

1996 Summer Olympic Games, Atlanta — A535

1996, June 3 **Litho.** *Perf. 12 Vert.*
Booklet Stamps

1005 A535 3.40m Kayaking 1.50 1.00
1006 A535 3.40m Sailing 1.50 1.00
1007 A535 3.40m Rowing 1.50 1.00
1008 A535 3.40m Swimming 1.50 1.00
a. Booklet pane of 4, #1005-1008 6.00
Complete booklet, #1008a 6.00

Insect Type of 1994

1996, July 1 **Litho.** *Perf. 13*
1009 A508 19m Dytiscus marginalis 8.25 9.00

Shore Birds — A536

#1010, Gallinago gallinago. #1011, Haematopus ostralegus. #1012, Scolopax rusticola. #1013, Vanellus vanellus. #1014, Numenius arquata.

Perf. 13½ on 3 Sides

1996, Sept. 6 **Litho. & Engr.**
1010 A536 2.80m multicolored 1.25 .50
1011 A536 2.80m multicolored 1.25 .50
1012 A536 2.80m multicolored 1.25 .50
1013 A536 2.80m multicolored 1.25 .50

Size: 30x52mm

1014 A536 2.80m multicolored 1.25 .50
a. Sheet of 5, #1010-1014 6.25 5.25

Finnish Comic Strips — A537

#1015, "Professor Itikainen" examining plant with magnifying glass, by Ilmari Vainio. #1016, "Pekka Puupää (Peter Blockhead)" taking letter from mailbox, by Ola Fogelberg. #1017, "Joonas" holding drawing pencil, by Veikko Savolainen. #1018, "Mämmilä" wearing helmet, by Tarmo Koivisto. #1019, "Rymy-Eetu" smoking pipe, by Erkki Tanttu. #1020, "Kieku" writing letter, by Asmo Alho. # 1021, "Pikku Risunen" with animal, by Riitta Uusitalo. # 1022, "Kiti" holding up pencil, by Kati Kovács.

1996, Oct. 9 **Litho.** *Perf. 13½*
Booklet Stamps

1015 A537 2.80m black & red 1.25 .50
1016 A537 2.80m black & red 1.25 .50
1017 A537 2.80m red & black 1.25 .50
1018 A537 2.80m black & red 1.25 .50
1019 A537 2.80m black & red 1.25 .50
1020 A537 2.80m red & black 1.25 .50
1021 A537 2.80m red & black 1.25 .50
1022 A537 2.80m red & black 1.25 .50
a. Bklt. pane of 8, #1015-1022 10.00
Complete booklet, #1022a 10.00

Christmas A538

2m, Snowman, Santa, gnome playing muscical instruments. 2.80m, Rabbit, reindeer watching northern lights. 3.20m, Santa reading letters.

1996, Nov. 1 **Litho.** *Perf. 14*
1023 A538 2m multi 1.00 .20
1024 A538 2.80m multi 1.25 .50
1025 A538 3.20m multi, vert. 1.40 .60
Nos. 1023-1025 (3) 3.65 1.30

Greetings Stamps — A539

End of 19th cent.: #1026, Two angels. #1027, Flowers in basket. #1028, Hand reaching through garland, bluebird. #1029, Boy, girl dancing. #1030, Boy, envelope, shamrocks. #1031, Clasping hands through heart-shaped garlands. #1032, Roses. #1033, Angel.

Perf. 13x12½ on 3 Sides

1997, Jan. 30 **Litho.**
Booklet Stamps

1026 A539 1 multicolored 1.60 .50
1027 A539 1 multicolored 1.60 .50
1028 A539 1 multicolored 1.60 .50
1029 A539 1 multicolored 1.60 .50
1030 A539 1 multicolored 1.60 .50
1031 A539 1 multicolored 1.60 .50
1032 A539 1 multicolored 1.60 .50
1033 A539 1 multicolored 1.60 .50
a. Bklt. pane of 8, #1026-1033 13.50
Complete booklet, #1033a 13.50

Nos. 1026-1033 sold for 2.80m on day of issue.
Number on stamp represents class of mail.

Mail Order Sales in Finland, Cent. — A540

1997, Jan. 30 *Perf. 13½x14*
1034 A540 2.80m multicolored 1.25 .25

1997 Ice Hockey World Championships, Helsinki — A541

1997, Jan. 30
1035 A541 2.80m multicolored 1.25 .25

On each stamp from the right vertical row of the sheet, No. 1035 exists without the thin, curved black line at the center right edge of the stamp.

Lepus Timidus A542

1997, Mar. 4 **Litho.** *Perf. 14*
1036 A542 2.80m multicolored 1.25 .25

Saami Folktale, "Girl Who Turned into a Golden Merganser" — A543

Europa: 3.20m, Duck, girl, prince. 3.40m, Girl falling into crevice.

1997, Mar. 4 *Perf. 13*
1037 A543 3.20m multicolored 1.40 .50
1038 A543 3.40m multicolored 1.50 .60

Paavo Nurmi (1897-1973), Winner of 9 Olympic Gold Medals — A544

1997, Mar. 18 *Perf. 14*
1039 A544 3.40m multicolored 1.50 .85

Southwest Archipelago Natl. Park — A545

Litho. & Engr.
1997, Apr. 25 *Perf. 14*
1040 A545 4.30m multicolored 1.90 1.00

Tango — A546

A547

1997, May 19 **Litho.**
1041 A546 1 multicolored 1.60 .25
Complete booklet of 5 8.25

No. 1041 sold for 2.80m on day of release.
Number on stamp represents class of mail.

1997, May 19 *Perf. 13½*

Sailing Ships: #1042, Astrid. #1043, Jacobstads Wapen. #1044, Tradewind. #1045, Merikokko. #1046, Suomen Joutsen. #1047, Sigyn.

Booklet Stamps

1042 A547 2.80m multicolored 1.25 .50
1043 A547 2.80m multicolored 1.25 .50
1044 A547 2.80m multicolored 1.25 .50
1045 A547 2.80m multicolored 1.25 .50

Size: 48x25½mm

1046 A547 2.80m multicolored 1.25 .50
1047 A547 2.80m multicolored 1.25 .50
a. Booklet pane of 6, #1042-1047 7.50
Complete booklet, #1047a 7.50

Pres. Martti Ahtisaari, 60th Birthday A548

1997, June 23 **Litho.** *Perf. 14*
1048 A548 2.80m multicolored 1.25 .25

Independence, 80th Anniv. — A549

Four seasons: No. 1049, Spring, lily-of-the-valley (natl. flower). No. 1050, Summer, white clouds. No. 1051, Fall, colorful leaves. No. 1052, Winter, snow crystals.

Perf. 13x12½ on 2 or 3 Sides

1997, June 23
Booklet Stamps

1049 A549 2.80m multicolored 1.25 .50
1050 A549 2.80m multicolored 1.25 .50
1051 A549 2.80m multicolored 1.25 .50
1052 A549 2.80m multicolored 1.25 .50
a. Booklet pane, #1049-1052 5.00
Complete booklet, #1052a 5.00

Souvenir Sheet

A550

Grus Grus (Cranes): a, With young. b, With frog. c, Performing mating dance. d, In flight.

1997, Aug. 19 **Litho.** *Perf. 14*
1053 A550 2.80m Sheet of 4, #a.-d. 5.00 5.00

A551

1997, Oct. 9 Litho. *Perf. 14¼*

Finnish Writers Assoc. (Covers from books): No. 1054, "Seven Brothers," by Aleksis Kivi. No. 1055, "Sinuhe the Egyptian," by Mika Waltari. No. 1056, "Täällä Pohjantähden alla I," by Väinö Linna. No. 1057, "Hyvästi Iijoki," by Kalle Päätalo. No. 1058, "Haukka, minum rakkaani," by Kaari Utrio. No. 1059, "Juhannustanssit," by Hannu Salama. No. 1060, "Manillaköysi," by Veijo Meri. No. 1061, "Uppo-Nalle ja Kumma," by Elina Karjalainen.

Booklet Stamps

1054 A551 2.80m multicolored 1.25 .50
1055 A551 2.80m multicolored 1.25 .50
1056 A551 2.80m multicolored 1.25 .50
1057 A551 2.80m multicolored 1.25 .50
1058 A551 2.80m multicolored 1.25 .50
1059 A551 2.80m multicolored 1.25 .50
1060 A551 2.80m multicolored 1.25 .50
1061 A551 2.80m multicolored 1.25 .50
a. Booklet pane, #1054-1061 10.00
Complete booklet, #1061a 10.00

No. 1056 has been discovered perf 14½x14¼. The other values also should exist thus. The editors would like to examine such stamps.

Christmas A552

1997, Oct. 31

1062 A552 2m Village .90 .20
1063 A552 2.80m Candelabra, vert. 1.25 .50
1064 A552 3.20m Church, vert. 1.40 .60
Nos. 1062-1064 (3) 3.55 1.30

Wildlife A553

2nd, Stizostedion lucioperca. 1st, Turdus merula.

Die Cut 10 Horiz., Syncopated Type A

1998, Jan. 15 Litho.

Self-Adhesive

Coil Stamps

1065 A553 2 multicolored 1.50 .25
1066 A553 1 multicolored 1.60 .25

Nos. 1065-1066 were valued at 2.40m and 2.80m, respectively, on date of issue. Number on stamp represents class of mail.
See Nos. 1099-1100.

A554 A555

Moomin Cartoon Characters, by Tove Jansson: No. 1067, Boy Moomin drawing with pad and pencil. No. 1068, Girl Moomin in sunshine. No. 1069, Organ grinder. No. 1070, Boy Moomin giving flower to girl Moomin.

1998, Jan. 15 *Perf. 13 (on 3 Sides)*

Booklet Stamps

1067 A554 1 multicolored 1.60 .50
1068 A554 1 multicolored 1.60 .50
1069 A554 1 multicolored 1.60 .50
1070 A554 1 multicolored 1.60 .50
a. Booklet pane, #1067-1070 6.50
Complete booklet, #1070a 6.50

Nos. 1067-1070 each sold for 2.80m on day of issue. Number on stamp represents class of mail.
See No. 1127.

1998, Feb. 3 *Perf. 14*

1071 A555 2.80m multicolored 1.25 .25

Finnish Federation of Nurses, cent.

A556 A557

Valentine's Day Surprise Stamps. (Designs beneath scratch-off heart): b, Musical notes, two dogs. c, Elephant, mouse and flowers. d, Puppy, sealed envelope. e, Kittens, kittens hugging. f, Dog with nose in air, bouquet of flowers. g, Flowers, two rodents.

1998, Feb. 3 *Perf. 12*

1072 1 Sheet of 6 10.00 6.25
a. A556 Any single, unscratched 1.60 .50
b.-g. A556 Any single, scratched heart .50

Nos. 1072b-1072g were each valued at 2.80m on day of issue. Number on stamp represents class of mail. Unused value for No. 1072a is with attached selvage. Inscriptions are shown in selvage above or below each stamp.

1998, Mar. 27 Litho. *Perf. 14*

1073 A557 2.80m Tussilago farfara 1.25 .25

National Festivals A558

Europa: 3.20m, Boy and girl, balloons, "Vappu" (May Day). 3.40m, Boy and girl in a dream floating over water, Midsummer Festival.

1998, Mar. 27 *Perf. 14x14½*

1074 A558 3.20m multicolored 1.40 .50
1075 A558 3.40m multicolored 1.50 .60

Finnish Marine Research Institute, 80th Anniv. — A559

Designs: 2.80m, Research vessel, "Aranda." 3.20m, "Vega," chart showing route of Nils Adolf Erik Nordenskjold's expedition.

Litho. & Engr.

1998, May 7 *Perf. 14x13*

1076 A559 2.80m multicolored 1.25 .50
1077 A559 3.20m multicolored 1.40 .60

First Performance of National Anthem, 150th Anniv. — A560

1998, May 7 *Perf. 13*

1078 A560 5m multicolored 2.25 .25

Puppies A561

#1079, Bernese Mountain dog. #1080, Puli. #1081, Boxer. #1082, Bichon Frisé. #1083, Finnish lapphound. #1084, Wire-haired dachshund. #1085, Scottish cairn terrier. #1086, Labrador retriever.

Perf. 13½x13 on 2 or 3 Sides

1998, June 4 Litho.

Booklet Stamps

1079 A561 1 multicolored 1.60 .50
1080 A561 1 multicolored 1.60 .50
1081 A561 1 multicolored 1.60 .50
1082 A561 1 multicolored 1.60 .50
1083 A561 1 multicolored 1.60 .50
1084 A561 1 multicolored 1.60 .50
1085 A561 1 multicolored 1.60 .50
1086 A561 1 multicolored 1.60 .50
a. Booklet pane, #1079-1086 13.50
Complete booklet, #1086a 13.50

Nos. 1079-1086 each sold for 2.80m on day of issue. Number on stamp represents class of mail.

Owls — A562 Cycling — A563

Designs: a, Bubo bubo. b, Wing of bubo bubo. c, Bubo bubo, aegolius funereus. d, Strix nebulosa. e, Nyctea scandiaca.

1998, Sept. 4 Litho. *Perf. 13½*

1087 Sheet of 5 + label 6.75 6.75
a.-e. A562 3m any single 1.25 .50

#1087b is 52x27mm; #1087c-1087d, 26x44mm; #1087e, 30x44mm.
See No. 1113.

1998, Sept. 4 *Perf. 14*

1088 A563 3m multicolored 1.25 .25

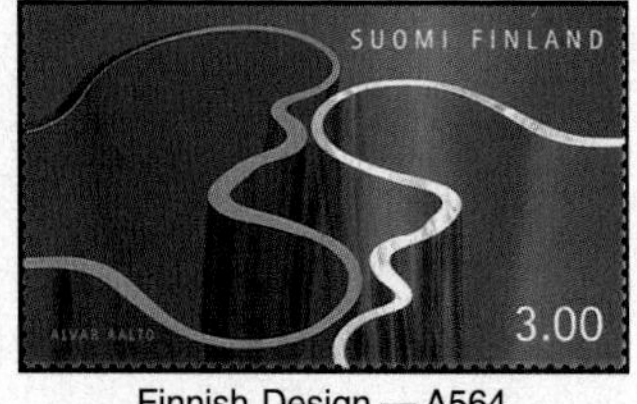

Finnish Design — A564

#1089, Savoy vases, by Alvar Aalto. #1090, Karuselli chair, by Yrjö Kukkapuro. #1091, Tasaraita knitwear, designed by Annika Rimala for Marimekko. #1092, Kilta tableware set, by Kaj Franck. #1093, Cast iron pot, by Timo Sarpaneva. #1094, Carelia cutlery set, by Bertel Gardberg.
Illustration reduced.

Perf. 13½ on 3 Sides

1998, Oct. 9 Litho.

Booklet Stamps

1089 A564 3m multicolored 1.25 .50
1090 A564 3m multicolored 1.25 .50
1091 A564 3m multicolored 1.25 .50
1092 A564 3m multicolored 1.25 .50
1093 A564 3m multicolored 1.25 .50
1094 A564 3m multicolored 1.25 .50
a. Booklet pane, #1089-1094 8.00
Complete booklet, #1094a 8.00

Nos. 1090-1091, 1093-1094 are 29x34mm.

Christmas A565

Designs: 2m, Christmas tree, children, vert. 3m, Children, dog riding sled. 3.20m, Winter scene of cottage in center of island.

1998, Oct. 30 *Perf. 14*

1095 A565 2m multicolored .90 .20
1096 A565 3m multicolored 1.25 .50
1097 A565 3.20m multicolored 1.40 .60
Nos. 1095-1097 (3) 3.55 1.30

Souvenir Sheet

Mika Häkkinen, Formula 1 Driving Champion — A566

Illustration reduced.

1999, Jan. 15 *Perf. 13½*

1098 A566 3m multicolored 1.25 1.25

Native Wildlife Type of 1998

2nd, Salmo salar. 1st, Luscinia svecica.

1999, Jan. 27 Litho. *Die Cut*

Coil Stamps

Self-Adhesive

1099 A553 2 multi 1.50 .25

Die Cut

1100 A553 1 multi, vert. 1.60 .25

Nos. 1099-1100 were valued at 2.40m and 3m, respectively, on day of issue. Number on stamp represents class of mail.

Friendship A567

Animals' tails: No. 1101, Zebra, lion. No. 1102, Dog, cat.

Serpentine Die Cut Perf. 13xDie Cut

1999, Jan. 27

Booklet Stamps

Self-Adhesive

1101 A567 3m multicolored 1.25 .50
1102 A567 3m multicolored 1.25 .50
a. Bklt. pane, 3 each #1101-1102 8.00

No. 1102a is a complete booklet.

Finnish Labor Movement, Cent. — A568

1999, Jan. 27 *Perf. 13½*

1103 A568 4.50m multicolored 2.00 1.10

Finland's Roads — A569

#1104, Snow-covered landscape, Arctic Ocean Road. #1105, Freeway interchanges, Jyväsjtkä Lakeshore Road. #1106, Raippaluoto Bridge. #1107, Wooded drive, Kitee.

1999, Feb. 15 Litho. *Perf. 14 Horiz.*

Booklet Stamps

1104 A569 3m multicolored	1.25	.50
a. Perf. 12¾ horiz.	1.50	.50
1105 A569 3m multicolored	1.25	.50
a. Perf. 12¾ horiz.	1.50	.50
1106 A569 3m multicolored	1.25	.50
a. Perf. 12¾ horiz.	1.50	.50
1107 A569 3m multicolored	1.25	.50
a. Booklet pane, #1104-1107	5.00	
Complete booklet, #1107a	6.00	
b. Perf. 12¾ horiz.	1.50	.50
c. Booklet pane, #1104a, 1105a, 1106a, 1107b		5.00

A570 A571

Women's Kalevala-style brooches: a, Horse clasp. b, Bird clasp. c, Virusmäki clasp.

1999, Feb. 15 *Perf. 13½x14*

1108 Sheet of 3	4.00	3.00
a.-c. A570 3m any single	1.25	.50

1st Publication of Legend of the Kalevala, 150th Anniv.

1999, Mar. 15 *Perf. 13x13½*

1109 A571 3m Crocus vernus	1.25	.50

Martha Organization, Cent. — A572

1999, Mar. 15 *Perf. 13½x13*

1110 A572 3m multicolored	1.25	.50

Europa A573

1999, Mar. 15 *Perf. 13½x14*

1111 A573 2.70m Esplanade Park	1.10	.50
1112 A573 3.20m Ruissalo Park	1.40	.60

Bird Type of 1998

Designs: a, Luscinia luscinia. b, Cuculus canorus. c, Botaurus stellaris. d, Caprimulgus europaeus. e, Crex crex.

1999, May 18 *Perf. 13½*

1113 Sheet of 5 + label	6.75	6.75
a.-e. A562 3m any single	1.25	.50

No. 1113b is 25x43mm. No. 1113c is 45x30mm. No. 1113d-1113e are 26x37mm.

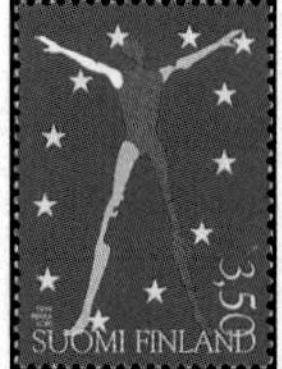

Finland's Presidency of European Union — A574

1999, July 1 Litho. *Perf. 13¾x13½*

1114 A574 3.50m multicolored	1.50	.65

Finnish Entertainers A575

a, Harmony Sisters, Vera (1914-97), Maire (1916-95) & Raija (1918-97) Valtonen. b, Olavi Virta (1915-72), singer. c, Georg Malmstén (1902-81), composer, conductor. d, Topi Kärki (1915-22), composer, and Reino (Repe) Helismaa (1913-65), lyricist. e, Tapio Rautavaara (1915-79), singer. f, Esa Parkarinen (1911-89), musician, actor.

Perf. 13¼ on 3 Sides

1999, Sept. 6 Litho.

1115 Booklet pane of 6	9.25	
a.-f. A575 3.50m any single	1.50	.65
Complete booklet, #1115	9.25	

Nos. 1115a, 1115d are each 60x34mm.

Finnish Commercial Product Design — A576

a, Fiskars cutting tools. b, Zoel/Versoul guitars. c, Ergo II/Silenta hearing protectors. d, Ponsse Cobra HS 10 tree harvester. e, Suunto compass. f, Exel Avanti QLS ski pole.
Illustration reduced.

Perf. 13¼ on 3 sides

1999, Oct 8 Litho.

1116 Booklet pane of 6	9.25	
a.-f. A576 3.50m any single	1.25	.65
Complete booklet, #1116	9.25	

Size of b, c, e, f: 30x35mm.

"The Nativity," by Giorgio di Chirico (1888-1978) A577

Rabbits, Birds — A578

1999, Nov. 5 *Perf. 14*

1117 A578 2.50m Santa Claus, vert.	1.10	.20
1118 A577 3m multicolored	1.25	.50
1119 A578 3.50m multicolored	1.50	.60
Nos. 1117-1119 (3)	3.85	1.30

Christmas. See Italy Nos. 2314-2315.

Sveaborg Fortress — A579

2000, Jan. 12 Litho. *Perf. 13¾x13½*

1120 A579 7.20m multi	3.00	.60

Helsinki, 450th Anniv. A580

Designs: No. 1121, Baltic herring market (designer's name at UL).
No. 1122: a, Museum of Contemporary Art (blue building), vert. b, Cathedral, Senate Square (green building). c, Finlandia Hall (orange building). d, Glass Palace Film and Media Center (red building), vert.
No. 1123: a, Quest for the Lost Crown, Sveaborg Fortress (children and arch), vert. b, Like No. 1121, no designer's name. c, Forces of Light City Festival. d, Cellist at outdoor concert, Kaivopuisto Park.

2000, Jan. 12 *Perf. 14*

1121 A580 3.50m multi	1.50	.65

Perf. 14½x14¾ (vert. stamps), 14¾x14½

1122 Booklet pane of 4	6.25	
a.-d. A580 3.50m Any single	1.50	.65
1123 Booklet pane of 4	6.25	
a.-d. A580 3.50m Any single	1.50	.65
Complete booklet, #1122-1123	12.50	

Valentine's Day — A581

Designs: a, Earth as backpack. b, Painters on ladder. c, Birds in balloon. d, Alien with magnet. e, Boy with heart-shaped balloon. f, Polar bear and igloo.

Perf. 13x12¾ on 3 sides

2000, Jan. 12

1124 Bklt. pane of 6 + 4 labels	6.75	
a.-f. A581 3.50m Any single	1.25	.65
Complete booklet, #1124	6.75	

Souvenir Sheet of 2

Tommi Mäkinen, 1999 Rally World Champion — A582

a, Mäkinen behind wheel. b, Race car.
Illustration reduced.

2000, Mar. 3 *Perf. 13x13¼*

1125 A582 3.50m #a.-b.	2.25	2.25

Easter — A583

2000, Mar. 15 *Perf. 13¾x13¼*

1126 A583 3.50m Caltha palustris	1.50	.65

Moomin Type of 1998

a, Rat with broom looking at Moomins. b, Moomin with uniform, figures sprouting from ground. c, Moomin with hat in forest. d, Moomin with hat, children, in front of stove.

Perf. 13x12¾ on 3 sides

2000, Mar. 15

1127 Booklet pane of 4	6.75	
a.-d. A554 1 Any single	1.60	.65
Complete booklet, #1127	6.75	
e. As #1127, perf. 13¼ on 3 sides	6.75	
f.-i. As #a-d, perf. 13¼ on 3 sides	1.60	.65
Booklet, #1127e	6.75	

Nos. 1127a-1127d sold for 3.50m on day of issue. Number on stamp represents class of mail.
Issued: No. 1127e, 7/10/00.

Jubilee Year — A584

Turku Cathedral: a, Nave. b, Woman, votive candles. c, Christ on the Mount of Transfiguration, alterpiece. d, Infant baptism.

2000, Mar. 15 Litho. *Perf. 14 Vert.*

1128 Booklet pane of 4	6.25	
a.-d. A584 3.50m Any single	1.50	.65
Complete booklet, #1128	6.25	

Europa, 2000

Common Design Type

2000, May 9 *Perf. 13¼x13*

1129 CD17 3.50m multi	1.50	.50

Provincial Flowers

Spring Anemone A585

Blue Cornflower A586

Pulsatilla Patens — A587

Die Cut Perf. 13x12½

2000-2001 Litho.

Self-Adhesive

1130 A585 1 multi	1.60	.20
1131 A586 1 multi	1.60	.20
1132 A587 1 multi	1.60	.20
a. Pane, 5 each #1131-1132	17.00	

Number on stamp represents class of mail. No. 1130 sold for 3.50m at time of release and was issued in sheets of 10. Nos. 1131-1132 each sold for 3.60m on day of issue.
Issued: No. 1130, 5/9. Nos. 1131-1132, 5/16/01.
This is an expanding set.

Souvenir Sheet

Science — A595

Designs: a, Children, molecuar model (triangular stamp). b, Man's face, DNA strand (rhomboid stamp). c, Man's face, Sierpinski triangles (square stamp).
Illustration reduced.

2000, May 30 *Perf. 14¼*

1140 A595 3.50m Sheet of 3, #a.-c.	4.75	4.75

No. 1140 has holographic image. Soaking in water may affect the hologram.

Finnish Design — A596

No. 1141: a, Rug, by Akseli Gallen-Kallela (1865-1931). b, Pearl Bird, by Birger Kaipiainen (1915-88). c, Pot, by Kylikki Salmenhaara (1915-81). d, Leaf, by Tapio Wirkkala (1915-85). e, Detail from damask, by Dora Jung (1906-80). f, Glass vase, by Valter Jung (1879-1946).
Illustration reduced.

Perf. 13¼ on 3 sides

2000, Sept. 5 Litho.

1141 Booklet pane of 6	9.25	
a.-f. A596 3.50m Any single	1.50	.65
Booklet, #1141	9.25	

Size of b, c, e, f: 30x35mm.

Coregonus Lavaretus A597

Lagopus Lagopus A598

Die Cut 10 Horiz. Sync. Type B

2000, Sept. 5

Self-Adhesive

Coil Stamps

1142 A597 2 multi 1.50 .25

Die Cut 10 Horiz. Sync. Type A

1143 A598 1 multi 1.60 .25

Nos. 1142-1143 sold for 3m and 3.50m respectively on day of sale.

On modern stamps bearing the "denominations" "1" or "2," the number represents the class of mail.

Christmas A599

2.50m, Costumed Tiernapojat carol singers. 3.50m, Bullfinch on door ornament, vert.

Serpentine Die Cut 14¼

2000, Nov. 3 **Photo.**

Self-Adhesive

1144-1145 A599 Set of 2 2.50 .80

Christmas Type of 2000

Design: No. 1146, Like #1145.

Serpentine Die Cut 13¾

2000, Nov. 3 **Litho.**

Self-Adhesive

1146 A599 3.50m multi + label 1.90 1.90

No. 1146 issued in sheets of 20 that sold for 120m, together with a separate sheet of stickers that could be affixed on the label. The labels attached to the stamps are separated by a row of interrupted serpentine die cutting. Labels could be personalized with photographs taken at some sale sites.

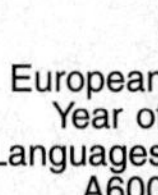

European Year of Languages A600

2001, Jan. 17 **Litho.** ***Perf. 13¼***

1147 A600 1 multi 1.60 .65

No. 1147 sold for 3.50m on day of sale.

World Ski Championships, Lahti — A601

No. 1148: a, Ski jumper Janne Ahonen (yellow helmet). b, Skier Mika Myllylä. Illustration reduced.

2001, Jan. 17

1148 A601 3.50m Horiz. pair, #a-b 2.25 2.25

Valentine's Day — A602

No. 1149: a, Oval wreath. b, Basket of flowers, letter. c, Heart-shaped wreath. d, Bouquet of flowers, letter. e, Flowers, tea set. f, Flowers, heart-shaped pastry.

Serpentine Die Cut 11½x11¾ on 3 Sides

2001, Jan. 17 **Photo.**

Self-Adhesive

1149 Booklet pane of 6 10.00
a.-f. A602 1 Any single 1.60 .65
Booklet, #1149 10.00

Nos. 1149a-1149f each sold for 3.50m on day of issue.

Souvenir Sheet

Donald Duck Comics in Finland, 50th Anniv. — A603

No. 1150: a, Mickey Mouse, Donald Duck, Santa Claus, Goofy. b, First comics, silhouette of boy. c, Tin soldier with Finnish flag, Chip and Dale (25x30mm). d, Finnish epic hero Väinämöinen, silhouette of Donald Duck. e, Helsinki Cathedral, Donald Duck.

Perf. 7¾ on 3 or 4 Sides

2001, Mar. 13 **Litho.**

1150 A603 1 Sheet of 5, #a-e 8.25 5.00

Nos. 1150a-1150e sold for 3.50m each on day of issue.

Santa Claus and Sleigh — A604

Serpentine Die Cut 14½x14

2001, Apr. 2

Self-Adhesive

1151 A604 1 multi 1.60 .65

No. 1151 sold for 3.60m on day of issue.

Europa A605

2001, Apr. 2 ***Perf. 13x13½***

1152 A605 5.40m multi 2.40 1.25

Easter — A606

No. 1153: a, Chick. b. Decorated egg. Illustration reduced.

2001, Apr. 2 ***Perf. 13¼***

1153 A606 3.60m Horiz. pair, #a-b 2.25 2.25

Souvenir Sheet

Verla Mill, UNESCO World Heritage Site — A607

Denominations in: a, UL. b, UR. c, LL. d, LR.

2001, Apr. 2

1154 A607 3.60m Sheet of 4, #a-d 6.50 6.50

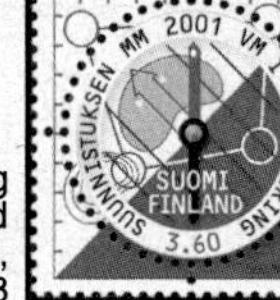
Orienteering World Championships, Tampere — A608

2001, May 16

1155 A608 3.60m multi 1.60 .65

Values are for stamps with surrounding selvage.

Souvenir Sheet

Woodpeckers — A609

No. 1156: a, Dendrocopos minor (32x36mm). b, Picoides tridactylus (29x36mm). c, Dendrocopos leucotos (32x42mm). d, Dendrocopos major (29x42mm). e, Picus canus (32x41mm). f, Dryocopus martius (29x41mm).

Perf. 14½x14¼ on 2, 3 or 4 Sides

2001, May 16

1156 A609 3.60m Sheet of 6, #a-f 6.75 6.75

Marine Life — A610

No. 1157: a, Lampetra fluviatilis. b, Aspius aspius. c, Coregonus albula.

Type C Syncopation (1st stamp, #1157): On the top, groups of 3 holes at left and right and a central group of four holes, separated by 2 oval holes equal in width to 4 holes.

Perf. 10 Horiz. Sync. Type C

2001, Sept. 6 **Photo.**

Self-Adhesive

Coil Stamps

1157 Horiz. strip of 3 4.75
a.-c. A610 2 Any single 1.50 .50

Nos. 1157a-1157c were sold in boxes of 100 stamps that sold at a discount price of 270m on day of sale. The franking value on the day of sale for each stamp was 3m.

Birds A611

No. 1158: a, Parus caeruleus. b, Motacilla alba. c, Oriolus oriolus.

Perf. 10 Horiz. Sync. Type B

2001, Sept. 6 **Photo.**

Self-Adhesive

Coil Stamps

1158 Horiz. strip of 3 5.00 3.50
a.-c. A611 1 Any single 1.60 .65

Nos. 1158a-1158c were sold in boxes of 100 stamps that sold at a discount price of 330m on day of sale. The franking value on the day of sale for each stamp was 3.60m.

History of Gulf of Finland A612

No. 1159: a, Utö Lighthouse. b, Wreck of the St. Mikael. c, Diver exploring St. Mikael. d, Opossum shrimp, isopod. e, Ship's cabin and nautical chart (32x55mm).

Perf. 13¼x13¾ on 2 or 3 Sides

2001, Sept. 6 **Litho.**

1159 Booklet pane of 5 8.25 —
a.-e. A612 1 Any single 1.60 .65
Booklet, #1159 8.25

Nos. 1159a-1159e each sold for 3.60m on day of sale.

Christmas A613

Designs: 2.50m, Elf reading Santa's book, candle. 3.60m, Elf delivering package on sled, horiz.

Serpentine Die Cut 14¼

2001, Oct. 26 **Photo.**

Self-Adhesive

1160 A613 2.50m multi 1.10 .45
1161 A613 3.60m multi 1.60 .65

Slightly larger examples of Nos. 1160-1161 serpentine die cut 14 are known on first day and other covers produced by the postal service. They were not sold unused to the public.

100 Cents = 1 Euro (€)

Flowers — A614

National Symbols A615

Heraldic Lion — A616

Type A614 — No. 1162, Myosotis scorpioides: a, Forty-one flowers. b, Four flowers, five buds. c, One flower, four buds. d, Entire plant. e, Five flowers.

No. 1163, Convallaria majallis: a, Leaf, stem with five flowers. b, Two leaves, stem with eight flowers. c, Two flowers. d, Two leaves, stem with five flowers. e, Entire plants.

Type A615: 50c, Swan, vert. 60c, Birch. 1, Flag and bird. 90c, Kymintehtaalta, by Victor Westerholm. €1.30, Granite cliff. €2.50, Spruce. €3.50, Pine.

Die Cut Perf. 15

2002, Jan. 1 **Photo.**

Self-Adhesive

1162 Vert. strip of 5 .60 .60
a.-e. A614 5c Any single .20 .20
1163 Vert. strip of 5 1.25 1.25
a.-e. A614 10c Any single .25 .20

Die Cut Perf. 14

1164 A615 50c multi 1.25 .90
1165 A615 60c multi 1.25 1.10

Die Cut Perf. 13¾

1166 A615 1 multi 1.60 1.10
a. Booklet pane of 8 13.50
Booklet, #1166a 13.50

Die Cut Perf. 14¾x15

1167 A615 90c multi 2.25 1.60

Die Cut Perf. 12 Syncopated

1168 A616 €1 blue & multi 2.50 1.75

Die Cut Perf. 14¾x15

1169 A615 €1.30 multi 3.25 2.40

Die Cut Perf. 14

1170 A615 €2.50 multi 6.25 4.50
1171 A615 €3.50 multi 8.75 6.25

Die Cut Perf. 12 Syncopated

1172 A616 €5 red & multi 12.50 9.00
Nos. 1162-1172 (11) 41.45 30.45

No. 1166 sold for 60c on day of issue.

Die cut perf 14 examples of Nos. 1162a-1162e, 1167 and 1169 exist on first day and other covers produced by the postal service. They were not sold unused to the public.

Easter — A617

Die Cut Perf. 14

2002, Mar. 6 **Photo.**

Self-Adhesive

1173 A617 60c multi 1.10 1.10

Souvenir Sheet

Elias Lönnrot (1802-84), Botanist, Linguist — A618

No. 1174: a, Plantain. b, Opening lines of "Kalevala" (denomination at UL). c, Closing lines of "Kalevala" (denomination at UR). d, Portrait.

Perf. 13¼ on 3 or 4 Sides

2002, Mar. 6 **Litho.**

1174 A618 60c Sheet of 4, #a-d 4.50 4.50

Souvenir Sheet

Old Rauma, UNESCO World Heritage Site — A619

Denominations at: a, UL. b, UR. c, LL. d, LR.

2002, Mar. 6 ***Perf. 13½***

1175 A619 60c Sheet of 4, #a-d 4.50 4.50

Europa — A620

2002, Apr. 15 ***Perf. 13***

1176 A620 60c multi 1.10 1.10

Gulf of Finland Type of 2001

No. 1177: a, Birds, fish. b, Sailboat, plankton. c, Flounder on sea bed. d, Shrimp, herring. e, Tvärminne Zoological Station, ship, isopod, oceanographic equipment, mussels (32x55mm).

Perf. 13¼x13¾ on 2 or 3 Sides

2002, Apr. 15

1177 Booklet pane of 5 8.25 —
a.-e. A612 1 Any single 1.60 1.10
Booklet, #1177 8.25

Nos. 1177a-1177e each sold for 60c on day of issue.

Sibelius Monument, Helsinki, by Eila Hiltunen A621

2002, May 3 ***Perf. 13***

1178 A621 60c multi 1.10 1.10

National Symbols Type of 2002 Without Finland Post Emblem

Designs: 60c, Juniperus communis. 1, Reindeer in Lapland.

Die Cut Perf. 14

2002, Oct. 9 **Photo.**

Self-Adhesive

1179 A615 60c multi 1.60 1.25
1180 A615 1 multi 1.60 1.25

No. 1180 sold for 60c on day of issue.

Christmas A622

Designs: 45c, Horse-drawn sleigh. 60c, Angel with trumpet, vert.

Serpentine Die Cut 14¼

2002, Nov. 1

Self-Adhesive

1181-1182 A622 Set of 2 2.10 2.10

Fish — A623

No. 1183: a, Abramis brama. b, Salmo trutta lacustris. c, Esox lucius.

Syncopated Die Cut Perf. 10 Horiz.

2003, Jan. 15

Self-Adhesive

Coil Stamps

1183 Horiz. strip of 3 4.75 3.00
a.-c. A623 2 Any single 1.50 1.00

Nos. 1183a-1183c were sold in boxes of 100 that sold at a discount price of €47 on day of issue. The franking value on the day of issue for each stamp was 50c.

Birds — A624

No. 1184: a, Cuculus canorus. b, Alauda arvensis. c, Perisoreus infaustus.

Syncopated Die Cut Perf. 10 Horiz.

2003, Jan. 15

Self-Adhesive

Coil Stamps

1184 Horiz. strip of 3 5.00 3.75
a.-c. A624 1 Any single 1.60 1.25

Nos. 1184a-1184c were sold in boxes of 100 that sold at a discount price of €57 on day of issue. The franking value on the day of issue for each stamp was 60c.

Viivi and Wagner, by Jussi Tuomola — A625

No. 1185: a, Viivi and Wagner running. b, Viivi and Wagner dancing. c, Viivi writing love letter. d, Wagner and Viivi in bed. e, Viivi and Wagner kissing. f, Wagner reading love letter.

Serpentine Die Cut 11½x11¾ on 3 Sides

2003, Jan. 15

Self-Adhesive

1185 Booklet pane of 6 10.00
a.-f. A625 1 Any single 1.60 1.25
Booklet, #1185 10.00

Nos. 1185a-1185f each sold for 60c on day of issue.

Ice Hockey World Championships — A626

2003, Mar. 3 **Litho.** ***Perf. 13¼x13¾***

1186 A626 65c multi 1.40 1.40

St. Bridget (1303-73) A627

Viola Wittrockiana A628

2003, Mar. 3 ***Perf. 13***

1187 A627 65c multi 1.40 1.40

Die Cut Perf. 13¾x14

2003, Mar. 3 **Photo.**

Self-Adhesive

1188 A628 65c multi 1.40 1.40

Fighting Wood Grouses, by Ferdinand von Wright — A629

2003, Mar. 3 ***Die Cut Perf. 13¾***

Self-Adhesive

1189 A629 90c multi 2.00 2.00

Airplanes A630

No. 1190: a, Super Caravelle. b, Airbus 320. c, Junkers Ju 52/3m. d, Douglas DC-3.

Perf. 14x14½ on 3 Sides

2003, Mar. 3

1190 Booklet pane of 4 + 4 etiquettes 5.75 —
a.-d. A630 65c Any single 1.40 1.40
Complete booklet, #1190 5.75

Finnair, 80th anniv.; Powered flight, cent.

Europa A631

No. 1191 — Posters by Lasse Hietala: a, Woman with newspaper. b, Hearts.

2003, May 7 **Litho.** ***Perf. 13¾x13¼***

1191 A631 65c Pair, #a-b 3.00 3.00

Souvenir Sheet

Flora and Fauna Seen in Summer — A632

No. 1192: a, Moth, flowers (35x29mm). b, Dragonfly, grasshopper (44x35mm). c, Grasshopper, caterpillar, thistle (35x25mm). d, Frog, flowers, butterfly, insects (44x36mm). e, Magpie, snail, flowers (35x46mm). f, Hedgehog, bee, ant, spider, flowers (44x29mm).

Perf. 14½ on 2 or 3 Sides

2003, May 7

1192 A632 65c Sheet of 6, #a-f 9.00 9.00

Moomins A633

No. 1193: a, Moomin ancestors. b, Moomins around stove. c, Moomin standing on hands in water. d, Moomin and fox. e, Moomin looking at film negative. f, Moomin with hat, flowers.

Serpentine Die Cut 11½x11¾ on 3 Sides

2003, May 7 Photo.

Self-Adhesive

1193 Booklet pane of 6 9.00
a.-f. A633 1 Any single 1.50 1.50
Complete booklet, #1193 9.00

Nos. 1193a-1193f each sold for 65c on day of issue.

Cupid A634

Serpentine Die Cut 11½ Syncopated

2003, May 14 Litho.

Self-Adhesive

1194 A634 1 multi 1.50 1.50

No. 1194 could be personalized. It sold for 65c on day of issue.

Lingonberries — A635

Serpentine Die Cut 14

2003, Sept. 10 Photo.

Self-Adhesive

1195 A635 65c multi 1.50 1.50

Philanthropists A636

No. 1196: a, Juho (1852-1913) and Maria (1858-1923) Lallukka. b, Emil Aaltonen (1869-1949), vert. c, Heikki Huhtamäki (1900-70), vert. d, Antti (1883-1962) and Jenny Wihuri. e, Alfred Kordelin (1868-1917), vert. f, Amos Anderson (1878-1961), vert.

Perf. 13¼x13¾, 13¾x13¼ on 3 Sides

2003, Sept. 10 Litho.

1196 Booklet pane of 6 9.00 —
a.-f. A636 65c Any single 1.50 1.50
Complete booklet, #1196 9.00

Lighthouses — A637

No. 1197: a, Bengtskär. b, Russarö. c, Rönnskär. d, Harmaja Grahara. e, Söderskär.

2003, Sept. 10 ***Perf. 13¼x13¾***

1197 A637 Sheet of 5 7.50 7.50
a.-e. 1 Any single 1.50 1.50

Nos. 1197a-1197e sold for 65c on day of issue. Size of No. 1197a, 28x45mm; Nos. 1197b-1197e, 21x36mm.

Christmas A638

Designs: 45c, Elf mailing letter. 65c, Elf with ginger biscuit on baking pan, vert.

Serpentine Die Cut 14x14¼, 14¼x14

2003, Oct. 31 Photo.

Self-Adhesive

1198-1199 A638 Set of 2 2.60 2.60

Slightly larger versions of No. 1198 with a serpentine die cutting of 13¼x13¾ and of No. 1199 with a serpentine die cutting of 13¾x13¼ exist only on first day and other covers produced by the postal service. They were not sold unused to the public.

Apples A639

Serpentine Die Cut 11½ Syncopated

2003, Oct. 31 Litho.

Self-Adhesive

1200 A639 1 multi 1.50 1.50

No. 1200 could be personalized. It sold for 65c on day of issue.

Pres. Tarja Halonen, 60th Birthday — A640

2003, Dec. 1 Litho. ***Perf. 13***

1201 A640 65c multi 1.60 1.60

Linnaea Borealis — A641

Die Cut Perf. 14

2004, Jan. 14 Photo.

Self-Adhesive

1202 A641 30c multi .75 .75

Souvenir Sheet

Johan Ludvig Runeberg (1804-77), Poet — A642

No. 1203: a, Title page of *Tales of Ensign Stahl.* b, Sven Dufva with gun. c, Illustration for "Our Country." d, Sculpture of Runeberg.

Perf. 13½x13¼ on 3 or 4 Sides

2004, Jan. 14 Litho.

1203 A642 65c Sheet of 4, #a-d 6.50 6.50

Jean Sibelius (1865-1957), Composer A643

No. 1204: a, Satu, and Sibelius, paintings by Akseli Gallen-Kallela. b, Hands of Sibelius on piano keyboard. c, Swans, musical score by Sibelius.

No. 1205: a, Sibelius' house, Ainola. b, Sibelius and wife, Aino. c, Score of "Voces Intimae."

Die Cut Perf. 10 Horiz., Syncopated at Top

2004, Jan. 14 Photo.

Coil Stamps

Self-Adhesive

1204 Horiz. strip of 3 4.25
a.-c. A643 2 Any single 1.40 1.40
1205 Horiz. strip of 3 5.00
a.-c. A643 1 Any single 1.60 1.60

Nos. 1204a-1204c each sold for 55c on day of issue and have two short syncopations; Nos. 1205a-1205c each sold for 65c on day of issue, and have one large syncopation.

Love — A644

Text and: a, Rose. b, Man kissing. c, Woman's eye. d, Man and woman embracing. e, Elderly woman. f, Hand pulling petal from daisy.

Serpentine Die Cut 11½x11¾ on 3 Sides

2004, Jan. 14

Self-Adhesive

1206 Booklet pane of 6 9.75
a.-f. A644 1 Any single 1.60 1.60

Nos. 1206a-1206f each sold for 65c on day of issue.

Ursus Arctos — A645

2004, Mar. 1 ***Die Cut Perf. 14***

Self-Adhesive

1207 A645 2 multi 1.40 1.40

No. 1207 sold for 55c on day of issue.

Rose — A646

2004, Mar. 1 Booklet Stamp

Self-Adhesive

1208 A646 1 multi 1.60 1.60
a. Booklet pane of 10 16.00

No. 1208 sold for 65c on day of issue. Booklet pane was sold folded.

Easter Flowers — A647

Die Cut Perf. 14

2004, Mar. 1 Litho.

Self-Adhesive

1209 A647 65c multi 1.60 1.60

Heraldic Lion Type of 2002

Die Cut Perf. 12 Syncopated

2004, Mar. 1

Self-Adhesive

1210 A616 €3 multi 7.50 7.50

Swallows A648

Orchid A649

Serpentine Die Cut 11½ Syncopated

2004, Mar. 26

Self-Adhesive

1211 A648 1 multi 1.60 1.60
1212 A649 1 multi 1.60 1.60

Nos. 1211-1212 each sold for 65c on day of issue, and they could be personalized.

Souvenir Sheet

Norse Gods — A650

No. 1213: a, Head of Luonnotar (33x30mm). b, Luonnotar with arms extended (22x42mm).

Perf. 14¼x14½ (#1213a), 14½x14 (#1213b)

2004, Mar. 26
1213 A650 65c Sheet of 2, #a-b 3.25 3.25

Forest Animals — A651

No. 1214: a, Red squirrel (40x40mm). b, Raven (40x31mm). c, Variable hare (40x34mm). d, Stoat (40x37mm). e, Lizard (40x34mm). f, Red fox (40x40mm).

Perf. 13¼x14 on 2 or 3 Sides

2004, Apr. 28
1214 A651 65c Sheet of 6, #a-f 9.25 9.25

Fragaria Vesca — A652

Die Cut Perf. 14

2004, Apr. 28 **Photo.**

Self-Adhesive

1215 A652 65c multi 1.60 1.60

Luxembourg Gardens, by Albert Edelfelt (1854-1905) A653

2004, Apr. 28 **Self-Adhesive**
1216 A653 1 multi 1.60 1.60

No. 1216 sold for 65c on day of issue.

Europa — A654

No. 1217: a, People around campfire. b, Family in rowboat.

2004, Apr. 28 **Litho.** ***Perf. 13***
1217 A654 65c Horiz. pair, #a-b 3.25 3.25

Snufkin and Moomintroll A655

Litho. & Embossed

2004, Sept. 8 ***Perf. 13***

Flocked Paper

1218 A655 1 multi 1.60 1.60

No. 1218 sold for 65c on day of issue.

Shipwreck Treasures A656

No. 1219: a, Tankard. b, Fabric seal. c, Gold watch. d, Powder keg. e, Figurehead (23x40mm).

Perf. 14¼x13 on 3 or 4 Sides

2004, Sept. 8

1219	Booklet pane of 5	8.00	—
a.-e.	A656 1 Any single	1.60	1.60
	Complete booklet, #1219	8.00	

Stamps sold for 65c each on day of issue.

Souvenir Sheet

Sammallahdenmäki, UNESCO World Heritage Site — A657

No. 1220: a, Stone wall and trees. b, Lichen-covered rocks.

2004, Sept. 8 **Litho.** ***Perf. 14¾x14¼***
1220 A657 65c Sheet of 2, #a-b 3.25 3.25

Rights of the Child — A658

No. 1221: a, Two girls. b, Boy painting. Illustration reduced

2004, Oct. 29 ***Perf. 13***
1221 A658 65c Horiz. pair, #a-b 3.50 3.50

Christmas A659

Designs: 45c, Boy writing Santa Claus. 65c, Christmas tree branch, candle, ornaments, vert.

Serpentine Die Cut 13¼x13¾, 13¾x13¼

2004, Oct. 29 **Photo.**

Self-Adhesive

1222-1223 A659 Set of 2 3.00 3.00

SEMI-POSTAL STAMPS

Arms — SP1

Unwmk.

1922, May 15 **Typo.** ***Perf. 14***

B1	SP1 1m + 50p gray & red	.75	*7.00*
	Never hinged	1.40	
a.	Perf. 13x13½	6.50	
	Never hinged	10.50	

Red Cross Standard SP2

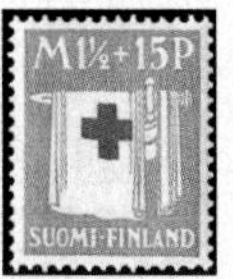

Symbolic SP3

Ship of Mercy — SP4

1930, Feb. 6

B2	SP2 1m + 10p red org & red	1.50	*7.50*
B3	SP3 1½m + 15p grysh grn & red	1.25	*7.50*
B4	SP4 2m + 20p dk bl & red	3.50	*35.00*
	Nos. B2-B4 (3)	6.25	*50.00*
	Set, never hinged	9.00	

The surtax on this and subsequent similar issues was for the benefit of the Red Cross Society of Finland.

Church in Hattula — SP5

SP8

Designs: 1½m+15p, Castle of Hameenlinna. 2m+20p, Fortress of Viipuri.

1931, Jan. 1 **Engr.**

Cross in Red

B5	SP5 1m + 10p gray grn	1.25	*9.00*
B6	SP5 1½m + 15p lil brn	6.50	11.00
B7	SP5 2m + 20p dull bl	1.10	*21.00*
	Nos. B5-B7 (3)	8.85	*41.00*
	Set, never hinged	22.50	

1931, Oct. 15 **Typo.** ***Rouletted 4, 5***

B8	SP8 1m + 4m black	15.00	*30.00*
	Never hinged	22.50	

The surtax was to assist the Postal Museum of Finland in purchasing the Richard Granberg collection of entire envelopes.

Helsinki University Library — SP9

Nikolai Church at Helsinki — SP10

2½m+25p, Parliament Building, Helsinki.

1932, Jan. 1 ***Perf. 14***

B9	SP9 1¼m + 10p ol bis & red	1.40	*9.25*
B10	SP10 2m + 20p dp vio & red	.70	*4.50*
B11	SP9 2½m + 25p lt blue & red	1.00	*15.00*
	Nos. B9-B11 (3)	3.10	*28.75*
	Set, never hinged	6.00	

Bishop Magnus Tawast SP12

Michael Agricola SP13

Design: 2½m+25p, Isacus Rothovius.

1933, Jan. 20 **Engr.**

B12	SP12 1¼m + 10p blk brn & red	2.50	*7.00*
B13	SP13 2m + 20p brn vio & red	.55	*3.00*
B14	SP13 2½m + 25p indigo & red	.75	*4.50*
	Nos. B12-B14 (3)	3.80	*14.50*
	Set, never hinged	7.50	

Evert Horn — SP15

Designs: 2m+20p, Torsten Stalhandske. 2½m+25p, Jakob (Lazy Jake) de la Gardie.

1934, Jan.

Cross in Red

B15	SP15 1¼m + 10p brown	.80	*2.25*
B16	SP15 2m + 20p gray lil	1.40	*4.00*
B17	SP15 2½m + 25p gray	.80	*2.75*
	Nos. B15-B17 (3)	3.00	*9.00*
	Set, never hinged	4.75	

Mathias Calonius SP18

Robert Henrik Rehbinder SP21

Designs: 2m+20p, Henrik C. Porthan. 2½m+25p, Anders Chydenius.

1935, Jan. 1

Cross in Red

B18	SP18 1¼m + 15p brown	.75	*2.25*
B19	SP18 2m + 20p gray lil	1.75	*4.00*
B20	SP18 2½m + 25p gray bl	.55	*2.25*
	Nos. B18-B20 (3)	3.05	*8.50*
	Set, never hinged	4.50	

1936, Jan. 1

2m+20p, Count Gustaf Mauritz Armfelt. 2½m+25p, Count Arvid Bernard Horn.

Cross in Red

B21	SP21 1¼m + 15p dk brn	.50	*2.25*
B22	SP21 2m + 20p vio brn	2.75	*6.00*
B23	SP21 2½m + 25p blue	.50	*2.25*
	Nos. B21-B23 (3)	3.75	*10.50*
	Set, never hinged	7.50	

Type "Uusimaa" SP24

Type "Turunmaa" — SP25

Design: 3½m+35p, Type "Hameenmaa."

1937, Jan. 1

Cross in Red

B24 SP24 1¼m + 15p brown .60 *2.25*
B25 SP25 2m + 20p brn lake 11.00 5.50
B26 SP24 3½m + 35p indigo .60 *2.50*
Nos. B24-B26 (3) 12.20 10.25
Set, never hinged 30.00

Aukuste Makipeska SP27

Skiing SP31

Designs: 1¼m+15p, Robert Isidor Orn. 2m+20p, Edward Bergenheim. 3½m+35p, Johan Mauritz Nordenstam.

1938, Jan. 5 **Engr.**

Cross in Red

B27 SP27 50p + 5p dk grn .45 *1.00*
B28 SP27 1¼m + 15p dk brn .90 *2.25*
B29 SP27 2m + 20p rose lake 4.50 4.50
B30 SP27 3½m + 35p dk blue .60 *2.25*
Nos. B27-B30 (4) 6.45 *10.00*
Set, never hinged 13.50

1938, Jan. 18

Designs: #B32, Skijumper. #B33, Skier.

B31 SP31 1.25m + 75p sl grn 2.50 *9.00*
B32 SP31 2m + 1m dk car 2.50 *9.00*
B33 SP31 3.50m + 1.50m dk blue 2.50 *9.00*
Nos. B31-B33 (3) 7.50 *27.00*
Set, never hinged 13.50

Ski championships held at Lahti.

Soldier — SP34

Battlefield at Solferino SP35

1938, May 16

B34 SP34 2m + ½m blue 1.25 *3.00*
Never hinged 2.50

Victory of the White Army over the Red Guards. The surtax was for the benefit of the members of the Union of the Finnish Front.

1939, Jan. 2

Cross in Scarlet

B35 SP35 50p + 5p dk grn .60 .60
B36 SP35 1¼m + 15p dk brn .60 *1.50*
B37 SP35 2m + 20p lake 9.00 9.00
B38 SP35 3½m + 35p dk bl .50 *2.00*
Nos. B35-B38 (4) 10.70 13.40
Set, never hinged 22.50

Intl. Red Cross Soc., 75th anniv.

Catalogue values for unused stamps in this section, from this point to the end of the section, are for Never Hinged items.

Soldiers with Crossbows SP36

Arms of Finland SP40

1¼m+15p, Cavalryman. 2m+20p, Soldier of Charles XII of Sweden. 3½m+35p, Officer and soldier of War with Russia, 1808-1809.

1940, Jan. 3

Cross in Red

B39 SP36 50p + 5p dk grn .70 *1.00*
B40 SP36 1¼m + 15p dk brn 1.50 *1.60*
B41 SP36 2m + 20p lake 2.00 1.60
B42 SP36 3½m + 35p dp ultra 2.00 3.00
Nos. B39-B42 (4) 6.20 7.20

The surtax aided the Finnish Red Cross.

1940, Feb. 15 **Litho.**

B43 SP40 2m +2m indigo .40 *.80*

The surtax was given to a fund for the preservation of neutrality.

Mason SP41

Soldier's Emblem SP45

1.75m+15p, Farmer plowing. 2.75m+25p, Mother and child. 3.50m+35p, Finnish flag.

1941, Jan. 2 **Engr.**

Cross in Red

B44 SP41 50p + 5p green .55 *.70*
B45 SP41 1.75m + 15p brown 1.40 *1.25*
B46 SP41 2.75m + 25p brn car 6.50 6.50
B47 SP41 3.50m + 35p dp ultra 1.40 *1.75*
Nos. B44-B47 (4) 9.85 10.20

See Nos. B65-B68.

1941, May 24 **Unwmk.**

B48 SP45 2.75m + 25p brt ultra .75 .75

The surtax was for the aid of the soldiers who fought in the Russo-Finnish War.

Aland Arms — SP46

Lapland Arms — SP51

Coats of Arms: 1.75m+15p, Nyland. 2.75m+25p, Finland's first arms. 3.50m+35p, Karelia. 4.75m+45p, Satakunta.

1942, Jan. 2 ***Perf. 14***

Cross in Red

B49 SP46 50p + 5p green .90 *1.25*
B50 SP46 1.75m + 15p brown 1.25 *1.90*
B51 SP46 2.75m + 25p dark red 1.25 *1.90*
B52 SP46 3.50m + 35p deep ultra 1.25 *1.90*
B53 SP46 4.75m + 45p dk sl grn .90 *1.90*
Nos. B49-B53 (5) 5.55 *8.85*

The surtax aided the Finnish Red Cross.

1943, Jan. 6 **Inscribed "1943"**

Coats of Arms: 2m+20p, Hame. 3.50m+35p, Eastern Bothnia. 4.50m+45p, Savo.

Cross in Red

B54 SP51 50p + 5p green .40 *1.00*
B55 SP51 2m + 20p brown .85 *1.50*
B56 SP51 3.50m + 35p dark red .85 *1.50*
B57 SP51 4.50m + 45p brt ultra 1.40 *4.00*
Nos. B54-B57 (4) 3.50 *8.00*

The surtax aided the Finnish Red Cross.

Soldier's Helmet and Sword — SP55

Mother and Children — SP56

1943, Feb. 1 ***Perf. 13***

B58 SP55 2m + 50p dk brown .40 *.70*
B59 SP56 3.50m + 1m brown red .40 *.70*

The surtax was for national welfare.

Red Cross Train — SP57

2m+50p, Ambulance. 3.50m+75p, Red Cross Hospital, Helsinki. 4.50m+1m, Hospital plane.

1944, Jan. 2 ***Perf. 14***

Cross in Red

B60 SP57 50p + 25p green .25 .25
B61 SP57 2m + 50p sepia .35 *.45*
B62 SP57 3.50m + 75p ver .35 *.45*
B63 SP57 4.50m + 1m brt ultra .70 *1.10*
Nos. B60-B63 (4) 1.65 *2.25*

The surtax aided the Finnish Red Cross.

Symbols of Peace SP61

Wrestling SP62

1944, Dec. 1

B64 SP61 3.50m + 1.50m dk red brn .40 *.65*

The surtax was for national welfare.

Type of 1941 Inscribed "1945"

1945, May 2 **Photo. & Engr.**

Cross in Red

B65 SP41 1m + 25p green .20 *.30*
B66 SP41 2m + 50p brown .20 *.45*
B67 SP41 3.50m + 75p brn car .20 *.45*
B68 SP41 4.50m + 1m dp ultra .40 *.80*
Nos. B65-B68 (4) 1.00 2.00

The surtax was for the Finnish Red Cross.

1945, Apr. 16 **Engr.** ***Perf. 13½***

2m+1m, Gymnast. 3.50m+1.75m, Runner. 4.50m+2.25m, Skier. 7m+3.50m, Javelin thrower.

B69 SP62 1m + 50p bluish grn .20 *.55*
B70 SP62 2m + 1m dp red .20 *.55*
B71 SP62 3.50m + 1.75m dull vio .20 *.55*
B72 SP62 4.50m + 2.25m ultra .30 *.70*
B73 SP62 7m + 3.50m dull brn .50 *1.10*
Nos. B69-B73 (5) 1.40 3.45

Fishing SP67

Nurse and Children SP71

Designs: 3m+75p, Churning. 5m+1.25m, Reaping. 10m+2.50m, Logging.

Engraved; Cross Typo. in Red

1946, Jan. 7

B74 SP67 1m + 25p dull grn .30 *.45*
B75 SP67 3m + 75p lilac brn .25 *.30*
B76 SP67 5m + 1.25m rose red .30 *.45*
a. Red cross omitted *450.00*
B77 SP67 10m + 2.50m ultra .40 *.60*
Nos. B74-B77 (4) 1.25 *1.80*

The surtax was for the Finnish Red Cross.

1946, Sept. 2 **Engr.**

Design: 8m+2m, Doctor examining infant.

B78 SP71 5m + 1m green .30 *.45*
B79 SP71 8m + 2m brown vio .30 *.45*

The surtax was for the prevention of tuberculosis.

Nos. B78 and B79 Surcharged with New Values in Black

1947, Apr. 1

B80 SP71 6m + 1m on 5m + 1m .30 *.55*
B81 SP71 10m + 2m on 8m + 2m .30 *.55*

The surtax was for the prevention of tuberculosis.

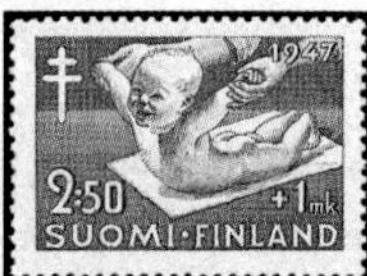

SP73

Medical Examination of Infants — SP74

Designs: 10m+2.50m, Infant held by the feet. 12m+3m, Mme. Alli Paasikivi and a child. 20m+5m, Infant standing.

1947, Sept. 15 **Engr.**

B82 SP73 2.50m + 1m green .35 *1.00*
B83 SP74 6m + 1.50m dk red .45 *1.00*
B84 SP74 10m + 2.50m red brn .55 *1.00*
B85 SP73 12m + 3m dp blue .70 *1.50*
B86 SP74 20m + 5m dk red vio .85 *2.00*
Nos. B82-B86 (5) 2.90 *6.50*

The surtax was for the prevention of tuberculosis.
For surcharges see Nos. B91-B93.

Zachris Topelius — SP78

7m+2m, Fredrik Pacius. 12m+3m, Johan L. Runeberg. 20m+5m, Fredrik Cygnaeus.

Engraved; Cross Typo. in Red

1948, May 10 Unwmk. *Perf. 14*

B87 SP78 3m + 1m green .40 *.60*
B88 SP78 7m + 2m rose red .50 *.65*
B89 SP78 12m + 3m brt blue .55 *.75*
B90 SP78 20m + 5m dk vio .65 *.90*
Nos. B87-B90 (4) 2.10 2.90

The surtax was for the Finnish Red Cross.

Nos. B83, B84 and B86 Surcharged with New Values and Bars in Black

1948, Sept. 13 Engr. *Perf. 13½*

B91 SP74 7m + 2m on #B83 1.25 *2.50*
B92 SP74 15m + 3m on #B84 1.25 *2.50*
B93 SP74 24m + 6m on #B86 1.50 *2.50*
Nos. B91-B93 (3) 4.00 7.50

The surtax was for the prevention of tuberculosis.

Tying Birch Boughs SP79

Wood Anemone SP83

9m+3m, Bathers in Sauna house. 15m+5m, Rural bath house. 30m+10m, Cold plunge in lake.

Engraved; Cross Typo. in Red

1949, May 5 *Perf. 13½x14*

B94 SP79 5m + 2m dull grn .35 *.50*
B95 SP79 9m + 3m dk car .60 *.75*
B96 SP79 15m + 5m dp blue .60 *.75*
B97 SP79 30m + 10m dk vio brn 1.10 *1.75*
Nos. B94-B97 (4) 2.65 3.75

The surtax was for the Finnish Red Cross.

1949, June 2 Engr.

Inscribed: "1949"

B98 SP83 5m + 2m shown .40 *.75*
B99 SP83 9m + 3m Wild rose .45 *.75*
B100 SP83 15m + 5m Coltsfoot .55 *1.10*
Nos. B98-B100 (3) 1.40 2.60

The surtax was for the prevention of tuberculosis.

Similar to Type of 1949

Designs: 5m+2m, Water lily. 9m+3m, Pasqueflower. 15m+5m, Bell flower cluster.

1950, Apr. 1

Inscribed: "1950"

B101 SP83 5m + 2m emer 1.60 1.60
B102 SP83 9m + 3m rose car 1.50 1.50
B103 SP83 15m + 5m blue 1.50 1.50
Nos. B101-B103 (3) 4.60 4.60

The surtax was for the prevention of tuberculosis.

Hospital Entrance, Helsinki SP84

Blood Donor's Medal SP86

Design: 12m+3m, Giving blood.

Engraved; Cross Typo. in Red

1951, Mar. 17 Unwmk. *Perf. 14*

B104 SP84 7m + 2m chocolate .80 *1.10*
B105 SP84 12m + 3m bl vio .80 *1.10*
B106 SP86 20m + 5m car 1.50 *2.00*
Nos. B104-B106 (3) 3.10 *4.20*

The surtax was for the Finnish Red Cross.

Capercaillie — SP87

Designs: 12m+3m, European cranes. 20m+5m, Caspian terns.

1951, Oct. 26 Engr.

B107 SP87 7m + 2m dk grn 1.60 *2.25*
B108 SP87 12m + 3m rose brn 1.60 *2.25*
B109 SP87 20m + 5m blue 1.60 *2.25*
Nos. B107-B109 (3) 4.80 *6.75*

The surtax was for the prevention of tuberculosis.

Diver — SP88

Soccer Players SP89

#B112, Stadum, Helsinki. #B113, Runners.

1951-52

B110 SP88 12m + 2m rose car .65 *1.10*
B111 SP89 15m + 2m grn ('52) .65 *1.10*
B112 SP88 20m + 3m deep blue .65 *1.10*
B113 SP89 25m + 4m brn ('52) .65 *1.10*
Nos. B110-B113 (4) 2.60 *4.40*

XV Olympic Games, Helsinki, 1952. The surtax was to help finance the games.

Margin blocks of four of each denomination were cut from regular or perf-through-margin sheets and pasted by the selvage, overlapping, in a printed folder to create a kind of souvenir booklet. Value $50.

Field Marshal Mannerheim SP90

Great Titmouse SP91

Engraved; Cross Typo. in Red

1952, Mar. 4

B114 SP90 10m + 2m gray 1.10 *1.50*
B115 SP90 15m + 3m rose vio 1.10 *1.50*
B116 SP90 25m + 5m blue 1.10 *1.50*
Nos. B114-B116 (3) 3.30 *4.50*

The surtax was for the Red Cross.

1952, Dec. 4 Engr.

Designs: 15m+3m, Spotted flycatchers and nest. 25m+5m, Swift.

B117 SP91 10m + 2m green 1.50 *1.90*
B118 SP91 15m + 3m plum 1.50 *1.90*
B119 SP91 25m + 5m deep blue 1.50 *1.90*
Nos. B117-B119 (3) 4.50 *5.70*

The surtax was for the prevention of tuberculosis.

European Red Squirrel SP92

#B121, Brown bear. #B122, European elk.

Unwmk.

1953, Nov. 16 Engr. *Perf. 14*

B120 SP92 10m + 2m red brown 2.00 *2.25*
B121 SP92 15m + 3m violet 2.00 *2.25*
B122 SP92 25m + 5m dark grn 2.00 *2.25*
Nos. B120-B122 (3) 6.00 *6.75*

Surtax for the prevention of tuberculosis.

Children Receiving Parcel from Welfare Worker — SP93

Designs: 15m+3m, Aged woman knitting. 25m+5m, Blind basket-maker and dog.

Engraved; Cross Typo. in Red

1954, Mar. 8 *Perf. 11½*

B123 SP93 10m + 2m dk ol grn 1.00 *1.25*
B124 SP93 15m + 3m dk blue 1.00 *1.25*
B125 SP93 25m + 5m dk brown 1.00 *1.25*
Nos. B123-B125 (3) 3.00 *3.75*

The surtax was for the Finnish Red Cross.

Bumblebees, Dandelions — SP94

European Perch — SP95

15m+3m, Butterfly. 25m+5m, Dragonfly.

Engraved; Cross Typo. in Red

1954, Dec. 7 *Perf. 14*

B126 SP94 10m + 2m brown 1.50 1.25
B127 SP94 15m + 3m carmine 1.50 1.25
B128 SP94 25m + 5m blue 1.50 1.25
Nos. B126-B128 (3) 4.50 3.75

The surtax was for the prevention of tuberculosis.

Engraved; Cross Typo. in Red

1955, Sept. 26 *Perf. 14*

Designs: 15m+3m, Northern pike. 25m+5m, Atlantic salmon.

B129 SP95 10m + 2m dl grn 1.50 1.25
B130 SP95 15m + 3m vio brn 1.50 1.25
B131 SP95 25m + 5m dk bl 1.50 1.25
Nos. B129-B131 (3) 4.50 3.75

Surtax for the Anti-Tuberculosis Society.

Gen. von Dobeln in Battle of Juthas, 1808 SP96

Waxwing SP97

Illustrations by Albert Edelfelter from J. L. Runeberg's "Tales of Ensign Stal": 15m+3m, Col. J. Z. Duncker holding flag. 25m+5m, Son of fallen Soldier.

Engraved; Cross Typo. in Red

1955, Nov. 24

B132 SP96 10m + 2m dp ultra 1.00 1.00
B133 SP96 15m + 3m dk red brn 1.00 1.00
B134 SP96 25m + 5m green 1.00 1.00
Nos. B132-B134 (3) 3.00 3.00

The surtax was for the Red Cross.

Engraved; Cross Typo. in Red

1956, Sept. 25 *Perf. 11½*

Birds: 20m+3m, Eagle owl. 30m+5m, Mute swan.

B135 SP97 10m + 2m dl red brn 1.40 1.25
B136 SP97 20m + 3m bl grn 1.60 1.40
B137 SP97 30m + 5m blue 1.60 1.50
Nos. B135-B137 (3) 4.60 4.15

Surtax for the Anti-Tuberculosis Society.

Pekka Aulin SP98

Wolverine (Glutton) SP99

Portraits: 10m+2m, Leonard von Pfaler. 20m+3m, Gustaf Johansson. 30m+5m, Viktor Magnus von Born.

Engraved; Cross Typo. in Red

1956, Nov. 26 Unwmk.

B138 SP98 5m + 1m grysh grn .80 .75
B139 SP98 10m + 2m brown 1.00 .90
B140 SP98 20m + 3m magenta 1.10 1.10
B141 SP98 30m + 5m lt ultra 1.10 1.10
Nos. B138-B141 (4) 4.00 3.85

The surtax was for the Red Cross.

Engraved; Cross Typo. in Red

1957, Sept. 5 *Perf. 11½*

20m+3m, Lynx. 30m+5m, Reindeer.

B142 SP99 10m + 2m dull purple 1.25 1.10
B143 SP99 20m + 3m sepia 1.40 1.25
B144 SP99 30m + 5m dark blue 1.50 1.25
Nos. B142-B144 (3) 4.15 3.60

The surtax was for the Anti-Tuberculosis Society. See Nos. B160-B165.

Red Cross Flag SP100

Raspberry SP101

1957, Nov. 25 Engr. *Perf. 14*

Cross in Red

B145 SP100 10m + 2m ol grn 1.60 1.40
B146 SP100 20m + 3m maroon 1.60 1.40
B147 SP100 30m + 5m dull blue 1.60 1.40
Nos. B145-B147 (3) 4.80 4.20

80th anniv. of the Finnish Red Cross.

Type of 1952

Flowers: 10m+2m, Lily of the Valley. 20m+3m, Red clover. 30m+5m, Hepatica.

Engraved; Cross Typo. in Red

1958, May 5 Unwmk. *Perf. 14*

B148 SP91 10m + 2m green 1.25 .90
B149 SP91 20m + 3m lilac rose 1.50 1.10
B150 SP91 30m + 5m ultra 1.50 1.10
Nos. B148-B150 (3) 4.25 3.10

Surtax for the Anti-Tuberculosis Society.

Engraved; Cross Typo. in Red

1958, Nov. 20 ***Perf. 11½***

20m+3m, Cowberry. 30m+5m, Blueberry.

B151 SP101 10m + 2m orange 1.00 .80
B152 SP101 20m + 3m red 1.40 1.10
B153 SP101 30m + 5m dk blue 1.40 1.10
Nos. B151-B153 (3) 3.80 3.00

The surtax was for the Red Cross.

Daisy — SP102

Reindeer SP103

20m+5m, Primrose. 30m+5m, Cornflower.

Engraved; Cross Typo. in Red

1959, Sept. 7 **Unwmk.**

B154 SP102 10m + 2m green 1.90 1.25
B155 SP102 20m + 3m lt brown 2.50 1.60
B156 SP102 30m + 5m blue 2.50 1.60
Nos. B154-B156 (3) 6.90 4.45

Surtax for the Anti-Tuberculosis Society.

Engraved; Cross Typo. in Red

1960, Nov. 24 ***Perf. 11½***

#B158, Lapp & lasso. #B159, Mountains.

B157 SP103 10m + 2m dk gray 1.00 1.00
B158 SP103 20m + 3m gray vio 1.25 1.50
B159 SP103 30m + 5m rose vio 1.25 1.50
Nos. B157-B159 (3) 3.50 4.00

The surtax was for the Red Cross.

Animal Type of 1957

Designs: 10m+2m, Muskrat. 20m+3m, Otter. 30m+5m, Seal.

Engr.; Cross at right, Typo. in Red

1961, Sept. 4

B160 SP99 10m + 2m brn car 1.00 .90
B161 SP99 20m + 3m slate bl 1.25 1.40
B162 SP99 30m + 5m bl grn 1.25 1.40
Nos. B160-B162 (3) 3.50 3.70

Surtax for the Anti-Tuberculosis Society.

Animal Type of 1957.

Designs: 10m+2m, Hare. 20m+3m, Pine marten. 30m+5m, Ermine.

Engraved; Cross Typo. in Red

1962, Oct. 1

B163 SP99 10m + 2m gray 1.40 .90
B164 SP99 20m + 3m dl red brn 1.75 1.25
B165 SP99 30m + 5m vio bl 1.75 1.25
Nos. B163-B165 (3) 4.90 3.40

The surtax was for the Anti-Tuberculosis Society.

Cross and Outstretched Hands SP104

Engraved; Cross Typo. in Red

1963, May 8 **Unwmk.** ***Perf. 11½***

B166 SP104 10p + 2p red brn .75 .75
B167 SP104 20p + 3p violet .90 .90
B168 SP104 30p + 5p green .90 .90
Nos. B166-B168 (3) 2.55 2.55

The surtax was for the Red Cross.

Attending the Wounded SP105

Red Cross Activities: 25p+4p, Hospital ship. 35p+5p, Prisoner-of-war health examination. 40p+7p, Gift parcel distribution.

Engraved; Cross Typo. in Red

1964, May 26 ***Perf. 11½***

B169 SP105 15p + 3p vio bl .65 .65
B170 SP105 25p + 4p green .90 .75
B171 SP105 35p + 5p vio brn .90 .75
B172 SP105 40p + 7p dk ol grn .90 .75
Nos. B169-B172 (4) 3.35 2.90

The surtax was for the Red Cross.

Finnish Spitz — SP106

Artificial Respiration — SP107

Designs: 25p+4p, Karelian bear dog. 35p+5p, Finnish hunting dog.

Engraved; Cross Typo. in Red

1965, May 10 ***Perf. 11½***

B173 SP106 15p + 3p org brn 1.25 .90
B174 SP106 25p + 4p black 1.40 1.10
B175 SP106 35p + 5p gray brn 1.50 1.10
Nos. B173-B175 (3) 4.15 3.10

Surtax for Anti-Tuberculosis Society.

1966, May 7 **Litho.** ***Perf. 14***

First Aid: 25p+4p, Skin diver rescuing occupants of submerged car. 35p+5p, Helicopter rescue in winter.

B176 SP107 15p + 3p multi .90 .80
B177 SP107 25p + 4p multi .90 .80
B178 SP107 35p + 5p multi .90 .80
Nos. B176-B178 (3) 2.70 2.40

The surtax was for the Red Cross.

Birch — SP108

Horse-drawn Ambulance SP109

Trees: 25p+4p, Pine. 40p+7p, Spruce.

1967, May 12 **Litho.** ***Perf. 14***

B179 SP108 20p + 3p multi .75 .75
B180 SP108 25p + 4p multi .75 .75
B181 SP108 40p + 7p multi .75 .75
Nos. B179-B181 (3) 2.25 2.25

Surtax for Anti-Tuberculosis Society.
See Nos. B185-B187.

1967, Nov. 24 **Litho.** ***Perf. 14***

25p+4p, Ambulance, 1967. 40p+7p, Red Cross.

Cross in Red

B182 SP109 20p + 3p dl yel, grn & blk .75 .75
B183 SP109 25p + 4p vio & blk .75 .75
B184 SP109 40p + 7p dk grn, blk & dk ol .75 .75
Nos. B182-B184 (3) 2.25 2.25

The surtax was for the Red Cross.

Tree Type of 1967

Trees: 20p+3p, Juniper. 25+4p, Aspen. 40p+7p, Chokecherry.

1969, May 12 **Litho.** ***Perf. 14***

B185 SP108 20p + 3p multi .75 .75
B186 SP108 25p + 4p multi .75 .75
B187 SP108 40p + 7p multi .75 .75
Nos. B185-B187 (3) 2.25 2.25

Surtax for Anti-Tuberculosis Society.

"On the Lapp's Magic Rock" SP110

Designs: 30p+6p, Juhani blowing horn on Impivaara Rock, vert. 50p+10p, The Pale Maiden. The designs are from illustrations by Askeli Gallen-Kallelas for "The Seven Brothers" by Aleksis Kivi.

1970, May 8 **Litho.** ***Perf. 14***

B188 SP110 25p + 5p multi .70 .60
B189 SP110 30p + 6p multi .70 .60
B190 SP110 50p + 10p multi .70 .60
Nos. B188-B190 (3) 2.10 1.80

The surtax was for the Red Cross.

Cutting and Loading Timber SP111

Designs: 30p+6p, Floating logs downstream. 50p+10p, Sorting logs at sawmill.

1971, Apr. 25 **Litho.** ***Perf. 14***

B191 SP111 25p + 5p multi .70 .60
B192 SP111 30p + 6p multi .70 .60
B193 SP111 50p + 10p multi .70 .60
Nos. B191-B193 (3) 2.10 1.80

Surtax for Anti-Tuberculosis Society.

Blood Donor and Nurse SP112

30p+6p, Blood research (microscope, slides), vert. 50p+10p, Blood transfusion.

1972, Oct. 23

B194 SP112 25p + 5p multi .65 .65
B195 SP112 30p + 6p multi .65 .65
B196 SP112 50p + 10p multi .65 .65
Nos. B194-B196 (3) 1.95 1.95

Surtax was for the Red Cross.

Girl with Lamb, by Hugo Simberg — SP113

Paintings: 40p+10p, Summer Evening, by Vilho Sjöström. 60p+15p, Woman at Mountain Foun ain, by Juho Rissanen.

1973, Sept. 12 **Litho.** ***Perf. 13x12½***

B197 SP113 30p + 5p multi .60 .60
B198 SP113 40p + 10p multi .90 .90
B199 SP113 60p + 15p multi .90 .90
Nos. B197-B199 (3) 2.40 2.40

Surtax for the Finnish Anti-Tuberculosis Assoc. Birth centenaries of featured artists.

Morel SP114

Mushrooms: 50p+10p, Chanterelle. 60p+15p, Boletus edulis.

1974, Sept. 24 **Litho.** ***Perf. 12½x13***

B200 SP114 35p + 5p multi 1.50 1.10
B201 SP114 50p + 10p multi 1.50 1.10
B202 SP114 60p + 15p multi 1.50 1.10
Nos. B200-B202 (3) 4.50 3.30

Finnish Red Cross.

Echo, by Ellen Thesleff (1869-1954) SP115

Paintings: 60p+15p, Hilda Wiik, by Maria Wiik (1853-1928). 70p+20p, At Home (old woman in chair), by Helene Schjerfbeck (1862-1946).

1975, Sept. 30 **Litho.** ***Perf. 13x12½***

B203 SP115 40p + 10p multi .70 .65
B204 SP115 60p + 15p multi .90 .80
B205 SP115 70p + 20p multi .90 .80
Nos. B203-B205 (3) 2.50 2.25

Finnish Red Cross. In honor of International Women's Year paintings by women artists were chosen.

Disabled Veterans' Emblem SP116

Lithographed and Photogravure

1976, Jan. 15 ***Perf. 14***

B206 SP116 70p + 30p multi 1.00 .95

The surtax was for hospitals for disabled war veterans.

Wedding Procession SP117

Designs: 70p+15p, Wedding dance, vert. 80p+20p, Bride, groom, matron and pastor at wedding dinner.

1976, Sept. 15 **Litho.** ***Perf. 13***

B207 SP117 50p + 10p multi .45 .45
B208 SP117 70p + 15p multi .60 .60
B209 SP117 80p + 20p multi .65 .65
Nos. B207-B209 (3) 1.70 1.70

Surtax for Anti-Tuberculosis Society.

Disaster Relief SP118

Designs: 80p+15p, Community work. 90p+20p, Blood transfusion service.

1977, Jan. 19 **Litho.** ***Perf. 14***

B210 SP118 50p + 10p multi .50 .50
B211 SP118 80p + 15p multi .70 .70
B212 SP118 90p + 20p multi .70 .70
Nos. B210-B212 (3) 1.90 1.90

Finnish Red Cross centenary.

Long-distance Skiing SP119

Design: 1m+50p, Ski jump.

1977, Oct. 5 Litho. *Perf. 13*
B213 SP119 80p + 40p multi 2.25 2.25
B214 SP119 1m + 50p multi 1.25 1.25

Surtax was for World Ski Championships, Lahti, Feb. 17-26, 1978.

Saffron Milkcap SP120

Edible Mushrooms: 80p+15p, Parasol, vert. 1m+20p, Gypsy.

1978, Sept. 13 Litho. *Perf. 13*
B215 SP120 50p + 10p multi 1.00 .80
B216 SP120 80p + 15p multi 1.25 1.25
B217 SP120 1m + 20p multi 1.25 1.25
Nos. B215-B217 (3) 3.50 3.30

Surtax was for Red Cross. See Nos. B221-B223.

Pehr Kalm, 1716-1779 SP121

Finnish Scientists: 90p+15p, Title page of Pehr Adrian Gadd's (1727-97) book, vert. 1.10m+20p, Petter Forsskal (1732-63).

Perf. 12½x13, 13x12½
1979, Sept. 26 Litho.
B218 SP121 60p + 10p multi .40 .40
B219 SP121 90p + 15p multi .65 .65
B220 SP121 1.10m + 20p multi .65 .65
Nos. B218-B220 (3) 1.70 1.70

Surtax for Finnish Anti-Tuberculosis Assoc.

Mushroom Type of 1978

Edible Mushrooms: 60p+10p, Woolly milk-cap. 90p+15p, Orange-cap boletus, vert. 1.10m+20p, Russula paludosa.

1980, Apr. 19 Litho. *Perf. 13*
B221 SP120 60p + 10p multi .65 .45
B222 SP120 90p + 15p multi .80 .60
B223 SP120 1.10m + 20p multi .80 .60
Nos. B221-B223 (3) 2.25 1.65

Surtax was for Red Cross.

Fuchsia — SP122

1981, Aug. 24 Litho. *Perf. 13*
B224 SP122 70p + 10p shown .45 .45
B225 SP122 1m + 15p African violet .60 .60
B226 SP122 1.10m + 20p Geranium .75 .75
Nos. B224-B226 (3) 1.80 1.80

Surtax was for Red Cross.

Garden Dormouse SP123

1982, Aug. 16 Litho. *Perf. 13*
B227 SP123 90p + 10p shown .40 .35
B228 SP123 1.10m + 15p Flying squirrels .55 .45
B229 SP123 1.20m + 20p European minks .60 .50
Nos. B227-B229 (3) 1.55 1.30

Surtax was for Red Cross. No. B228 vert.

Forest and Wetland Plants SP124

1m+20p, Chickweed wintergreen. 1.20m+25p, Marsh violet. 1.30m+30p, Marsh marigold.

1983, July 7 Litho. *Perf. 13*
B230 SP124 1m + 20p multi .50 .35
B231 SP124 1.20m + 25p multi .65 .50
B232 SP124 1.30m + 30p multi .65 .50
Nos. B230-B232 (3) 1.80 1.35

Surtax for Finnish Anti-Tuberculosis Assoc.

Globe Puzzle — SP125

Butterflies SP126

2m+40p, Symbolic world communication.

1984, May 28 Litho. *Perf. 13*
B233 SP125 1.40m + 35p multi .55 .55
B234 SP125 2m + 40p multi .75 .75

Surtax for Red Cross.

1986, May 22 Litho. *Perf. 13*

#B235, Anthocharis cardamines. #B236, Nymphalis antiopa. #B237, Parnassius apollo.

B235 SP126 1.60m + 40p multi .90 .60
B236 SP126 2.10m + 45p multi 1.25 1.00
B237 SP126 5m + 50p multi 2.50 2.50
Nos. B235-B237 (3) 4.65 4.10

Surtax for Red Cross.

Festivals SP127

1988, Mar. 14 Litho. *Perf. 13*
B238 SP127 1.40m +40p Christmas .75 .75
B239 SP127 1.80m +45p Easter 1.00 1.00
B240 SP127 2.40m +50p Midsummer 1.25 1.25
Nos. B238-B240 (3) 3.00 3.00

Surtax for the Red Cross.

Heodes virgaureae on Goldrod Plant SP128

Butterflies and plants: No. B242, *Agrodiaetus amandus* on meadow vetchling. No. B243, *Inachis io* on tufted vetch.

1990, Apr. 6 Photo. *Perf. 12x11½*
B241 SP128 1.50m +40p multi .75 .75
B242 SP128 2m +50p multi 1.00 1.00
B243 SP128 2.70m +60p multi 1.25 1.25
Nos. B241-B243 (3) 3.00 3.00

Surtax for the natl. Red Cross Soc.

Paintings by Helene Schjerfbeck — SP129

Designs: #B244a, The Little Convalescent, #B244b, Green Still-Life.

1991, Mar. 8 Litho. *Perf. 13*
B244 SP129 Pair 2.00 2.00
a.-b. 2.10m +50p any single 1.00 1.00

Surtax for philately.

Butterflies SP130

#B245, Xestia brunneopicta. #B246, Acerbia alpina. #B247, Baptria tibiale.

Litho. & Embossed
1992, Apr. 22 *Perf. 13*
B245 SP130 1.60m +40p multi .75 .75
B246 SP130 2.10m +50p multi 1.00 1.00
B247 SP130 5m +60p multi 2.00 2.00
Nos. B245-B247 (3) 3.75 3.75

Surtax for Finnish Red Cross. Embossed "Arla 100" in braille for Arla Institute, training center for the blind, cent.

Autumn Landscape of Lake Pielisjarvi, by Eero Jarnefelt SP131

a, Tree-covered hill. b, Lake shoreline.

1993, Mar. 19 Litho. *Perf. 13*
B248 SP131 2.30m + 70p Pair, #a.-b. 1.60 1.60

Surtax for philately.

Finnhorses SP132

1994, Mar. 11 Litho. *Perf. 13*
B249 SP132 2m +40p Draft horses .85 .85
B250 SP132 2.30m +50p Trotter .95 .95
B251 SP132 4.20m +60p War horses, vert. 1.60 1.60
Nos. B249-B251 (3) 3.40 3.40

Surtax for Finnish Red Cross.

Paintings, by Albert Edelfelt (1854-1905) — SP133

#B252, Playing Boys on the Shore. #B253, Queen Blanche.

1995, Mar. 1 Litho. *Perf. 13½*
B252 2.40m +60p multi 1.25 1.25

Size: 22x31mm

B253 2.40m +60p multi 1.25 1.25
a. SP133 Pair, #B252-B253 2.50 2.50

Surtax for philately.

Chickens SP134

1996, Mar. 18 Litho. *Perf. 13*
B254 SP134 2.80m +60p Chicks 1.50 1.50
B255 SP134 3.20m +70p Hens 1.75 1.75
B256 SP134 3.40m +70p Rooster, vert. 1.75 1.75
Nos. B254-B256 (3) 5.00 5.00

Surtax for Finnish Red Cross.

The Aino Myth, by Akseli Gallen-Kallela (1865-1931) SP135

Designs: No. B257, Väinämöinen proposing marriage to Aino in forest. No. B258, Aino jumping into water to escape Väinämöinen. No. B259, Aino at shore for bath.

1997, Sept. 5 Litho. *Perf. 13½x13*
Booklet Stamps
B257 SP135 2.80m +60p multi 1.40 1.40
B258 SP135 2.80m +60p multi 1.40 1.40
B259 SP135 2.80m +60p multi 1.40 1.40
a. Booklet pane, #B257-B259 4.20 4.20
Complete booklet, #B259a 4.20

No. B258 is 33x46mm.

Pigs — SP136

2.80m+60p, Sow, piglets. 3.20m+70p, Three piglets. 3.40m+70p, Pig's head.

1998, Mar. 12 Litho. *Perf. 13*
B260 SP136 2.80m +60p multi 1.25 1.25
B261 SP136 3.20m +70p multi 1.40 1.40
B262 SP136 3.40m +70p multi 1.50 1.50
Nos. B260-B262 (3) 4.15 4.15

Surtax for Finnish Red Cross.

Paintings by Hugo Simberg (1873-1917) SP137

a, Garden of Death. b, Wounded Angel.

Perf. 13¼x13¾
1999, Sept. 24 Litho.
B263 Booklet pane of 2 2.50 2.50
a.-b. SP137 3.50m +50p any single 1.25
Complete booklet, #B263 2.50

Surtax for philately.

Cow and Calf — SP138

Perf. 13¾x13¼

2000, Mar. 15 **Litho.**
D204 OP100 0.50m +70p Dull, vert. 1.40 1.40

Perf. 13¼x13¾

B265 SP138 4.80m +80p shown 1.75 1.75

Surtax for Finnish Red Cross.

AIR POST STAMPS

No. 178 Overprinted in Red

1930, Sept. 24 **Unwmk.** ***Perf. 14***
C1 A28 10m gray lilac 125.00 *200.00*
Never hinged 200.00
a. 1830 for 1930 2,000. *3,250.*

Overprinted expressly for use on mail carried in "Graf Zeppelin" on return flight from Finland to Germany on Sept. 24, 1930, after which trip the stamps ceased to be valid for postage. Forgeries are almost always on No. 205, rather than No. 178.

Catalogue values for unused stamps in this section, from this point to the end of the section, are for Never Hinged items.

Douglas DC-2 — AP1

1944 **Engr.**
C2 AP1 3.50m dark brown .35 *.65*

Air Transport Service anniv, 1923-43.

Douglas DC-6 Over Winter Landscape — AP2

1950, Feb. 13
C3 AP2 300m blue 20.00 6.25

Available also for ordinary postage.

Redrawn

1958, Jan. 20 ***Perf. 11½***
C4 AP2 300(m) blue 35.00 1.00

On No. C4 "mk" is omitted.
See Nos. C9-C9a.

Convair 440 over Lakes — AP3

1958, Oct. 31 **Unwmk.** ***Perf. 11½***
C5 AP3 34m blue 1.00 .95

No. C5 Surcharged with New Value and Bars

1959, Apr. 5
C6 AP3 45m on 34m blue 2.00 2.00

1959, Nov. 2
C7 AP3 45m blue 2.00 .50

1963, Feb. 15
C8 AP3 45p blue 1.40 .55

On No. C7 the denomination is "45." On No. C8 it is "0.45."

DC-6 Type, Comma After "3"

Type I — 16 lines in "O"
Type II — 13 lines in "O"

1963, Oct. 10
C9 AP2 3m blue, Type II ('73) 2.00 .25
a. Type I 22.50 1.00

Convair Type of 1958

1970, July 15
C10 AP3 57p ultra 1.40 *1.50*

MILITARY STAMPS

Catalogue values for unused stamps in this section are for Never Hinged items.

M1

Unwmk.

1941, Nov. 1 **Typo.** ***Imperf.***
M1 M1 (4m) blk, *dk org* .25 *.45*

#M1 has simulated roulette printed in black.

Type of 1930-46 Overprinted in Black

1943, Oct. 16 ***Perf. 14***
M2 A26 2m deep orange .30 *.35*
M3 A26 3½m greenish blue .30 *.35*

Post Horn and Sword — M2

1943 **Size: 29½x19½mm**
M4 M2 (2m) green .20 *.35*
M5 M2 (3m) rose violet .20 *.35*

1944 **Size: 20x16mm**
M6 M2 (2m) green .20 .20
M7 M2 (3m) rose violet .20 .20

Post Horns and Arms of Finland — M3

1963, Sept. 26 **Litho.** ***Perf. 14***
M8 M3 violet blue *150.00 150.00*

Used during maneuvers Sept. 30-Oct. 5, 1963. Valid from Sept. 26.

No. M8 with overprint "1983" was issued 4/20/83, and used during maneuvers Apr. 24-30. Value unused $250, used $100.

PARCEL POST STAMPS

PP1

Wmk. Rose & Triangles Multiple
Rouletted 6 on 2 or 3 Sides

1949-50 **Typo.**
Q1 PP1 1m brt grn & blk 1.25 *4.50*
Q2 PP1 5m red & blk 10.50 *14.00*
Q3 PP1 20m org & blk 20.00 *22.50*
Q4 PP1 50m bl & blk ('50) 7.25 *11.00*
Q5 PP1 100m brn & blk ('50) 8.25 *11.00*
Nos. Q1-Q5 (5) 47.25 *63.00*
Set, never hinged 67.50

Catalogue values for unused stamps in this section, from this point to the end of the section, are for Never Hinged items.

Mail Bus — PP2

1952-58 **Unwmk.** **Engr.** ***Perf. 14***
Q6 PP2 5m car rose 4.00 *5.00*
Q7 PP2 20m orange 10.00 7.00
Q8 PP2 50m blue ('54) 25.00 10.00
Q9 PP2 100m brn ('58) 30.00 15.00
Nos. Q6-Q9 (4) 69.00 37.00

Mail Bus — PP3

1963 ***Perf. 12***
Q10 PP3 5p red & blk 2.25 2.25
Q11 PP3 20p org & blk 2.00 1.10
Q12 PP3 50p blue & blk 3.75 1.40
Q13 PP3 1m brn & blk 1.10 1.10
Nos. Q10-Q13 (4) 9.10 5.85

Nos. Q1-Q13 were issued only in booklets: panes of 6 for Nos. Q1-Q5, 10 for Nos. Q6-Q9 and 5 for Nos. Q10-Q13.

Used values are for regular postal or mail-bus cancels. Pen strokes, cutting or other cancels sell for half as much.

1981 SISU Bus — PP4

Photo. & Engr.

1981, Dec. 7 ***Perf. 12 Horiz.***
Q14 PP4 50p dk bl & blk .50 *2.50*
Q15 PP4 1m dk brn & blk .75 *2.50*
Q16 PP4 5m grn & blk 3.00 *5.25*
Q17 PP4 10m red & blk 6.00 *10.50*
Nos. Q14-Q17 (4) 10.25 *20.75*

Parcel post stamps invalid after Jan. 9, 1985.

ALAND ISLANDS

LOCATION — A group of 6,554 islands at the mouth of the Gulf of Bothnia, between Finland and Sweden.
GOVT. — Province of Finland
AREA — 590 sq. mi.
POP. — 23,761
CAPITAL — Mariehamn

The province of Aland was awarded to Finland in 1921 by the League of Nations. The Swedish language is spoken and the province has a considerable amount of self-determination.

Catalogue values for unused stamps in this country are for Never Hinged items.

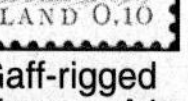

Gaff-rigged Sloop — A1

Aland Flag — A2

Midsummer Pole — A3

Landscapes — A4

Map of Scandinavia — A5

Seal of St. Olaf and Aland Province, 1326 — A6

Artifacts — A7

Sea Birds — A8

Gothic Tower, Jomala Church, 12th Cent. — A9

Mariehamn Town Hall, Designed by Architect Lars Sonck — A9a

Designs: 1.50m, Statue of Frans Petter von Knorring, vicar from 1834 to 1875, and St. Michael's Church, Finstrom, 12th cent. 1.60m, Burial site, clay hands. 1.70m, Somateria mollissima. 2.20m, Bronze Staff of Finby, apostolic decoration. 2.30m, Aythya fuligula. 5m, Outer Aland Archipelago. 8m, Farm and windmill. 12m, Melantha fusca. 20m, Ancient court site, contemporary monument.

1984-90 **Engr.** **Unwmk.** ***Perf. 12***
1 A1 10p magenta .20 .20
2 A1 20p brown olive .20 .20
3 A1 50p bright green .20 .20
4 A1 1.10m deep blue .50 .35
5 A1 1.20m black .55 .45
6 A1 1.30m dark green .60 .45

Litho.

Perf. 14, 13x14 (#8)

7 A2 1.40m multi .60 .45
8 A9 1.40m multi 1.25 1.25
9 A3 1.50m multi, I 1.10 .45
9A A3 1.50m multi, II .65 .45
10 A9 1.50m multi 1.25 1.25

Perf. 13, 14 (#13)

11	A7	1.60m multi, vert.	1.50	.50
12	A8	1.70m multi	6.00	5.00
13	A9a	1.90m multi	.85	.70
14	A4	2m multi	1.50	.60
15	A7	2.20m multi, vert.	.95	.75
16	A8	2.30m multi	2.75	2.75
17	A5	3m multi	1.25	.85
18	A4	5m multi, horiz.	2.25	1.40
19	A4	8m multi, horiz.	3.25	2.50

Litho. & Engr.

20	A6	10m multi	4.25	3.75

Litho.

21	A8	12m multi	4.00	4.00
22	A7	20m multi	8.50	8.50
		Nos. 1-22 (23)	44.15	37.00

On No. 9A (type II) "Aland" is 10½mm long, figure support is 2mm wide, pole supports are thinner, diagonal black highlighting lines in pole greenery and horizontal black line on support under the man removed.

Issued: #2-4, 7, 17, 20, 3/1/84; #1, 5, 6, 9, 1/2/85; #14, 18-19, 9/16/85; #11, 15, 22, 4/4/86; #12, 16, 21, 1/2/87; #8, 8/26/88; #13, 1/2/89; #10, 9/4/89; #9A, 5/21/90.

See Nos. 39-42, 87-92.

A10

A11

Bark Pommern and car ferries, Mariehamn West Harbor

1984, Mar. 1 Litho. *Perf. 14*

23	A10	2m multicolored	2.00	2.00

1986, Jan. 2 Litho. *Perf. 14*

24	A11	1.60m multicolored	1.50	1.25

1986 Nordic Orienteering Championships, Aug. 30-31.

Onningeby Artists' Colony, Cent. — A12

Design: Pallette, pen and ink drawing of Onningeby landscape, 1891, by Victor Westerholm (1860-1919), founder.

1986, Sept. 1 Litho.

25	A12	3.70m multicolored	1.60	1.50

Mariehamn Volunteer Fire Brigade, Cent. — A13

1987, Apr. 27 Litho. *Perf. 14*

26	A13	7m multicolored	4.00	4.00

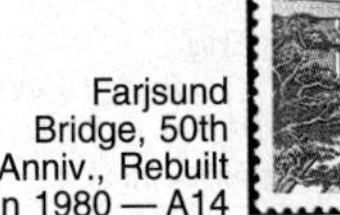

Farjsund Bridge, 50th Anniv., Rebuilt in 1980 — A14

1987, Apr. 27 Engr. *Perf. 13x13½*

27	A14	1m greenish black	.45	.45

Municipal Meeting, Finstrom, 1917 — A15

1987, Aug. 20 Litho. *Perf. 14*

28	A15	1.70m multicolored	1.10	1.10

Movement for reunification with Sweden, 70th anniv.

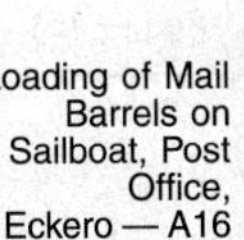

Loading of Mail Barrels on Sailboat, Post Office, Eckero — A16

1988, Jan. 4 Litho. *Perf. 14*

29	A16	1.80m multicolored	1.60	1.60

Postal Service, 350th anniv. From Feb. I to May 31, Alanders were entitled to buy 20 stamps for 28m with a discount coupon.

New Aland Farm School, Horse-Drawn Plow — A17

1988, Mar. 29 Litho. *Perf. 14*

30	A17	2.20m multicolored	1.25	1.50

Haga Farm School, cent.; Aland Farm School, 75th anniv.; 50th anniv. of experimental farming on Aland.

Sailing Ships — A18

1988, June 4 Litho. *Perf. 13*

31	A18	1.80m Albanus, 1904, vert.	1.50	1.00
32	A18	2.40m Ingrid, c. 1900	2.25	2.25
33	A18	11m Pamir, c. 1900	7.00	7.00
		Nos. 31-33 (3)	10.75	10.25

Type of 1988 and

Orchids — A19

Fish A20

Handicrafts A21

Fresco, St. Anna's Church of Kumlinge A22

Mammals A23

Geological Formations
A24 A25

Designs: 10p, Boulder field, Geta. #35, *Dactylorhiza sambucina*. #36, *Clupea harengus membras*. #37, *Erinaceus europauus*. #38, Drumlin, Finstrom. 1.70m, St. Andrew Church, Lumparland. #40, Vardo Church. #41, Hammarland Church. #42, Sottunga Church. #43, *Esox lucius*. #45, Diabase dike, Sottunga, Basskar. 2.10m, *Sciurus vulgaris*. 2.50m, *Cephalanthera longifolia*. #48, *Platichthys flesus*. #49, Pillow lava, Kumlinge, western Varpskar. #50, *Capreolus capreolus*. #51, Rouche Moutonne, Roda Kon, Lumparn. 6m, Folded gneiss, Sottunga, Gloskar. 13m, Tapestry, 1793. 14m, *Cypripedium calceolus*.

Perf. 13, 14 (#39-42, 44, 53), 15x14½ (10p, #38, 45, 49, 51-52)

1989-94 Litho.

34	A25	10p multicolored	.20	.20
35	A19	1.50m multicolored	2.00	1.75
36	A20	1.50m multicolored	1.10	.45
37	A23	1.60m multicolored	1.10	.60
38	A25	1.60m multicolored	.70	.60
39	A9	1.70m multicolored	1.10	.95
40	A9	1.80m multicolored	1.10	.95
41	A9	1.80m multicolored	1.10	.95
42	A9	1.80m multicolored	.95	.70
43	A20	2m multicolored	1.10	.45
44	A22	2m multicolored	.85	.45
45	A24	2m multicolored	.85	.70
46	A23	2.10m multicolored	1.25	.45
47	A19	2.50m multicolored	2.50	2.00
48	A20	2.70m multicolored	1.25	1.40
49	A24	2.70m multicolored	1.25	.95
50	A23	2.90m multicolored	1.40	1.75
51	A25	2.90m multicolored	1.25	1.10
52	A24	6m multicolored	2.50	2.50
53	A21	13m multicolored	5.75	5.75
54	A19	14m multicolored	8.50	8.50
		Nos. 34-54 (21)	37.80	33.15

Issued: 2.50m, 14m, #35, 4/10/89; 2.70m, #36, 43, 3/1/90; 13m, 4/19/90; 1.70m, #44, 9/10/90; 1.60m, 2.10m, #50, 3/3/91; #40, 10/9/91; #41 10/5/92; #45, 49, 52, 9/3/93; #42, 10/8/93; 10p, #38, 51, 2/1/94.

See Nos. 96, 102, 105.

Educational System of the Province, 350th Anniv. — A33

1989, May 31 Litho. *Perf. 14*

57	A33	1.90m multicolored	1.25	1.25

Souvenir Sheet

1991 Aland Island Games — A34

a, Volleyball. b, Shooting. c, Soccer. d, Running.

1991, Apr. 5 Litho. *Perf. 13x12½*

58	A34	2.10m Sheet of 4, #a.-d.	4.00	3.75

Autonomy of Aland, 70th Anniv. — A35

1991, June 4 *Perf. 13*

59	A35	16m multicolored	7.25	7.25

Kayaking A36

1991, June 4 *Perf. 14*

60	A36	2.10m shown	.95	.60
61	A36	2.90m Cycling	1.40	1.40

Rev. Frans Peter Von Knorring (1792-1875), Educator — A37

Cape Horn Congress, Mariehamn, June 8-11 — A38

1992, Mar. 2 Litho. *Perf. 13*

62 A37 2 multicolored .95 .85

Litho. & Engr.

Perf. 13½x14

63 A38 1 multicolored 1.25 1.10

No. 62 sold for 1.60m, No. 63 for 2.10m.

On stamps bearing the "denominations" "1" or "2," the number represents the class of mail.

Lighthouses A39

1992, May 8 Litho. *Perf. 13*

Booklet Stamps

64 A39 2.10m Ranno 3.00 1.40
65 A39 2.10m Salskar 3.00 1.40
66 A39 2.10m Lagskar 3.00 1.40
67 A39 2.10m Market 3.00 1.40
a. Booklet pane of 4, #64-67 12.00

First Aland Provincial Parliament, 70th Anniv. — A40

1992, June 8 Litho. *Perf. 13*

68 A40 3.40m multicolored 1.50 1.50

Joel Pettersson (1892-1937), Painter — A41

1992, June 8

69 A41 2.90m Landscape from Lemland 1.25 1.10
70 A41 16m Self-Portrait 7.00 7.00

Arms of Aland — A42

1993, Mar. 1 Litho. *Perf. 14*

71 A42 1.60m gray, sepia & blue .70 .70

Autonomy Act, Jan. 1.

Souvenir Sheet

Autonomous Postal Administration — A43

Designs: a, Inscriptions from old letter canceled in Kastelholm, vert. b, Mariehamn post office. c, Ferry, mail truck. d, New post office emblem, vert.

Perf. 12½x13, 14 (#b.-c.)

1993, Mar. 1 Litho., Engr. (#b.-c.)

72 A43 1.90m Sheet of 4, #a.-d. 2.75 2.75

Fiddler, Jan Karlsgarden Museum — A44

Folk Dresses — A45

2.30m, Boat Shed, Jan Karlsgarden Museum.

Perf. 13x12½, 12½x13

1993, May 7 Litho.

73 A44 2m multicolored .95 .70
74 A44 2.30m multi, horiz. 1.00 1.00

1993, June 1 *Perf. 12½*

Clothing from: 1.90m, Saltvik. 3.50m, Brando, Eckero, Mariehamn. 17m, Finstrom.

75 A45 1.90m multicolored .95 .70
76 A45 3.50m multicolored 1.25 1.25
77 A45 17m multicolored 7.50 7.50
Nos. 75-77 (3) 9.70 9.45

Butterflies A46

A47

Perf. 14 on 3 Sides

1994, Mar. 1 Litho.

Booklet Stamps

78 A46 2.30m Melitaea cinxia 1.00 .95
79 A46 2.30m Quercusia quercus 1.00 .95
80 A46 2.30m Parnassius mnemosyne 1.00 .95
81 A46 2.30m Hesperia comma 1.00 .95
a. Booklet pane, 2 each #78-81 8.00
Nos. 78-81 (4) 4.00 3.80

1994, May 5 Litho. *Perf. 13*

Europa, Inventions and Discoveries: 2.30m, Diagram showing transmission of von Willebrand's Disease, discovered by E. A. von Willebrand. 2.90m, Purification of heparin, by Erik Jorpes.

82 A47 2.30m multicolored 2.00 1.25
83 A47 2.90m multicolored 1.25 1.25

Types of 1989-93 and:

Ice Age Survivors — A48

Fossils — A49

Sea Birds — A50

Bronze Age — A51

Stone Age — A52

Ships — A53

Lichens — A54

Primula Veris — A55

30p, Saduria entomon, mysis relicta. 40p, Trilobita asaphus. 1.80m, Sterna paradisaea. #87, Church of Mariehamn. #88, Church of Eckerö. #89, St. Bridget's Church, Lemland. #90, Church of St. John the Baptist, Sund. #91, St. George Church, Geta. #92, Church of Brando. #93, Bronze sword, bronze dagger. #94, Ship tumulus grave. #95, Larus canus. 2.30m, Pitcher of Kallskar. #97, Pottery. #98, Myoxocephalus quadricornis. 2.60m, Larus marinus. #100, Stone tools. #101, SS Thornbury. 3.40m, Erratic boulders. 3.50m, SS Osmo. 4.30m, Phoca hispida. 7m, Potholes. 9m, Gastropoda euomophalus. 18m, Settlement. 2, Hypogmnia physodes. 1, Xanthoria parietina.

Perf. 13 (A48, A50, A52), 15x14½, 14½x15, 14½ (40p, #88-89), 14 (#87, 90),

1994-2000 Engr.

84	A48	30p	multi	.20	.20
85	A49	40p	multi	.20	.20
86	A50	1.80m	multi	.80	.80
87	A9	1.90m	multi	.85	.85
88	A9	1.90m	multi	.85	.85
89	A9	1.90m	multi	.85	.85
90	A9	2m	multi	.95	.70
91	A9	2m	multi	.90	.90
92	A9	2m	multi	.90	.90
93	A51	2m	multi	.90	.90
94	A51	2.20m	multi, vert.	.95	.95
95	A50	2.20m	multi, vert.	.95	.95
96	A24	2.30m	multi	1.00	1.00
97	A52	2.40m	multi, vert.	1.10	1.10
98	A48	2.40m	multi	1.10	1.10
99	A50	2.60m	multi	1.10	1.10
100	A52	2.80m	multi, vert.	1.25	.85
101	A53	2.80m	multi	1.25	1.25
102	A24	3.40m	multi, horiz.	1.50	1.50
103	A53	3.50m	multi	1.50	1.50
104	A48	4.30m	multi	1.90	1.90
105	A24	7m	multi, horiz.	3.00	3.00
106	A49	9m	multi	4.00	4.00
107	A52	18m	multi	8.00	8.00

Perf. 13

107A A54 2 multi .95 .95
107B A54 1 multi 1.25 1.25

Self-Adhesive

Serpentine Die Cut Perf. 10

108 A55 2.40m multi 1.10 1.10
Nos. 84-108 (27) 39.30 38.65

No. 108 was issued in sheets of 10.

Nos. 107A-107B sold for 2m and 2.40m, respectively, on day of issue.

Issued: #97, 100, 18m, 8/16/94; #90, 10/7/94; 2.30m, 3.40m, 7m, 1/2/95; #91, 9/15/95; 40p, #92, 9m, 10/9/96; 30p, #98, 4.30m, 2/3/97; #101, 103, 9/8/97; #87, 10/9/97; #88, 10/9/98; #93-94, 2/1/99; #108, 4/28/99; #107A-107B, 9/25/99; #89, 10/8/99; 1.80m, #95, 2.60m, 1/3/00.

Cargo Vessels — A58

Perf. 14 on 3 Sides

1995, Mar. 1 Litho.

Booklet Stamps

109 A58 2.30m Skuta 1.00 1.00
110 A58 2.30m Sump 1.00 1.00
111 A58 2.30m Storbat 1.00 1.00
112 A58 2.30m Jakt 1.00 1.00
a. Booklet pane, 2 each #109-112 8.00
Complete booklet, #112a 8.00
Nos. 109-112 (4) 4.00 4.00

Entry into European Union — A59

1995, Mar. 1 Litho. *Perf. 13x14*

113 A59 2.90m multicolored 1.25 1.25

Europa — A60

Tourism — A61

1995, May 5 Litho. *Perf. 13x14*

114 A60 2.80m shown 1.25 1.25
115 A60 2.90m Dove, island in sea 1.25 1.25

1995, May 12

116 A61 2 Golf .95 .70
117 A61 1 Fishing 1.25 .70

Nos. 116-117 sold for value 2m and 2.30m, respectively.

Optimist Dinghy World Championships — A62

1995, June 2 Litho. *Perf. 13½x14*

118 A62 3.40m multicolored 1.50 1.50

St. Olaf (995?-1030), Patron Saint of Aland — A63

Litho. & Engr.

1995, Sept. 15 *Perf. 13½x13*

119 A63 4.30m multicolored 1.90 1.90

See Faroe Islands No. 289

A64

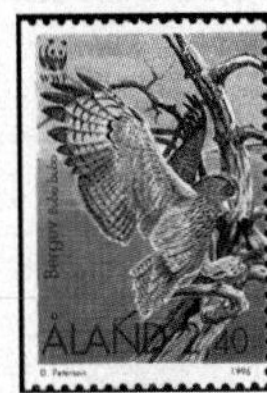
A65

Greeting Stamps (stylized designs): No. 120, Fish with natl. flag, "Hälsningar fran Aland." No. 121, Yellow bird with flower, "Grattis."

1996, Feb. 14 Litho. *Perf. 13x14*

120 A64 1 multicolored 1.25 .85
121 A64 1 multicolored 1.25 .85

Nos. 120-121 had a face value of 2.30m on day of issue.

1996, Mar. 1 *Perf. 14 on 3 Sides*

Eagle owl (bubo bubo): No. 122, Landing on tree branch over lake. No. 123, Perched on branch over lake. No. 124, Male, darker feathers. No. 125, Female, lighter feathers.

Booklet Stamps

122 A65 2.40m multicolored 1.00 1.00
123 A65 2.40m multicolored 1.00 1.00
124 A65 2.40m multicolored 1.00 1.00
125 A65 2.40m multicolored 1.00 1.00
a. Booklet pane, 2 ea #122-125 8.00
Complete booklet, No. 125a 8.00
Nos. 122-125 (4) 4.00 4.00

World Wildlife Fund.

Famous Women A66

Europa: 2.80m, Sally Salminen (1906-76), writer. 2.90m, Fanny Sundström (1883-1944), politician.

1996, May 6 Litho. *Perf. 14x13*

126 A66 2.80m multicolored 1.25 1.25
127 A66 2.90m multicolored 1.25 1.25

A67

A68

1996, June 7 Litho. *Perf. 13½x14*

128 A67 2.40m multicolored 1.10 1.10

Aland '96 Song and Music Festival.

1996, June 7 *Perf. 13*

"Haircut," by Karl Emanuel Jansson (1846-74).

129 A68 18m multicolored 8.00 8.00

Spring Flowers — A69

Designs: No. 130, Tussilago farfara. No. 131, Hepatica nobilis. No. 132, Anemone nemorosa. No. 133, Anemone ranunculoides.

1997, Feb. 3 Litho. *Perf. 14*

Booklet Stamps

130 A69 2.40m multicolored 1.10 1.10
131 A69 2.40m multicolored 1.10 1.10
132 A69 2.40m multicolored 1.10 1.10
133 A69 2.40m multicolored 1.10 1.10
a. Booklet pane, 2 each #130-133 8.75
Complete booklet, #133a 8.75

A70

A71

1997, May 3 Litho. *Perf. 14x13½*

134 A70 3.40m multicolored 1.50 1.50

1st Floorball World Championships, Aland.

1997, May 9 *Perf. 13x14*

Devil's Dance with Clergyman's Wife.

135 A71 2.90m multicolored 1.25 1.25

Europa.

Kalmar Union, 600th Anniv. — A72

Design: Kastelholm Castle, arms of Lord High Chancellor Bo Jonsson Grip.

1997, May 30 Litho. *Perf. 14x13*

136 A72 2.40m multicolored 1.10 1.10

Souvenir Sheet

Autonomy, 75th Anniv. — A73

Illustration reduced.

1997, June 9 *Perf. 13*

137 A73 20m multicolored 8.75 8.75

No. 137 contains a holographic image. Soaking in water may affect the hologram.

Horticulture A74

1998, Feb. 2 Litho. *Perf. 14½x15*

138 A74 2m Apples .90 .90
139 A74 2.40m Cucumbers 1.10 1.10

Youth Activities A75

#140, Riding moped. #141, Computer. #142, Listening to music. #143, Aerobics.

1998, Mar. 28 *Perf. 14 on 3 Sides*

Booklet Stamps

140 A75 2.40m multicolored 1.10 1.10
141 A75 2.40m multicolored 1.10 1.10
142 A75 2.40m multicolored 1.10 1.10
143 A75 2.40m multicolored 1.10 1.10
a. Booklet pane, 2 each #140-143 8.75
Complete booklet, #143a 8.75

Midsummer Celebration in Aland — A76

1998, Apr. 27 Litho. *Perf. 14*

144 A76 4.20m multicolored 1.90 1.90

Europa.

Passenger Ferry — A77

1998, May 8 *Perf. 14½*

145 A77 2.40m multicolored 1.10 1.10

Intl. Year of the Ocean — A78

1998, May 8

146 A78 6.30m multicolored 2.75 2.75

ATP Senior Tour of Champions Tennis Tournament, Mariehamn A79

Serpentine Die Cut

1998, June 25 Litho.

Self-Adhesive

147 A79 2.40m multicolored 1.10 1.10

Issued in sheets of 10.

Scouting — A80

1998, Aug. 1 *Perf. 14*

148 A80 2.80m multicolored 1.25 1.25

Foyers — A81

Homesteads: 1.60m, Seffers. 2m, Labbas. 2.90m, Abras.

1998, Sept. 11 Litho. *Perf. 14½*

149 A81 1.60m multicolored .70 .70
150 A81 2m multicolored .85 .85
151 A81 2.90m multicolored 1.25 1.25
Nos. 149-151 (3) 2.80 2.80

18th Century Furniture Ornamentation A82

Perf. 14 on 3 Sides

1999, Feb. 1 Litho.

Booklet Stamps

152 A82 2.40m Wardrobe 1.10 1.10
153 A82 2.40m Distaff 1.10 1.10
154 A82 2.40m Chest 1.10 1.10
155 A82 2.40m Spinning wheel 1.10 1.10
a. Booklet pane, 2 each #152-155 8.75
Complete booklet, #155a 8.75

Passage of Cape Horn by Grain Ships Pamir & Passat, 50th Anniv. A83

1999, Mar. 19 Litho. *Perf. 14½*

156 A83 3.40m multicolored 1.50 1.50

Beginning with No. 157, denominations are indicated on many stamps in both Markkas and Euros. The value shown is in Markkas.

Nature Reserve, Kökar — A84

1999, Apr. 28 Litho. *Perf. 13*

157 A84 2.90m multicolored 1.25 1.25

Europa.

Match Sailboat Racing — A85

1999, Aug. 5 Litho. *Perf. 14½x15*

158 A85 2.70m multicolored 1.10 1.10

UPU, 125th Anniv. A86

1999, Sept. 25

159 A86 2.90m multicolored 1.25 1.25

Finnish Cross-Country Championships, Mariehamn — A87

1999, Oct. 9 Litho. *Perf. 14¾x14½*

160 A87 3.50m multicolored 1.50 1.50

Souvenir Sheet

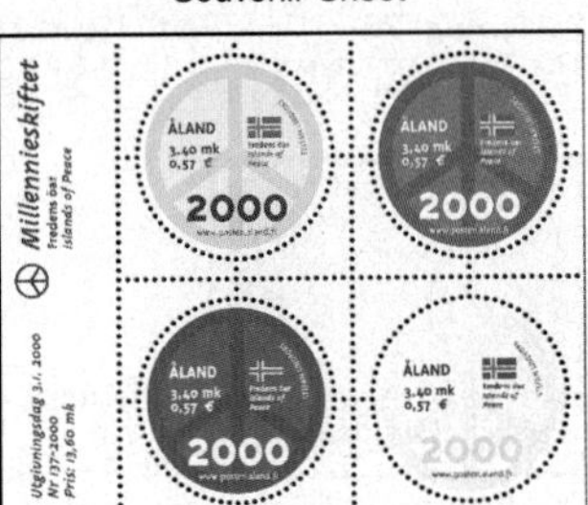
Peace Symbol, Aland Flag — A88

Background colors: a, Yellow. b, Red. c, Blue. d, White.

Litho. & Embossed

2000, Jan. 3 *Perf. 13*
161 A88 3.40m Sheet of 4, #a.-d. 6.00 6.00

Elk — A89

Elk in: No. 162, Spring. No. 163, Summer. No. 164, Autumn. No. 165, Winter.

Perf. 11¾on 3 sides
2000, Mar. 1 Litho.

Booklet Stamps

162 A89 2.60m multicolored 1.10 1.10
163 A89 2.60m multicolored 1.10 1.10
164 A89 2.60m multicolored 1.10 1.10
165 A89 2.60m multicolored 1.10 1.10
a. Block of 4, #162-165 4.50 4.50
b. Booklet pane, 2 #165a 9.00
Complete booklet, #165b 9.00

Europa, 2000
Common Design Type

2000, May 9 *Perf. 13*
166 CD17 3m multicolored 1.25 1.25

A90

A91

2000, June 9 *Die Cut Perf. 13x13¼*
Self-Adhesive
Coil Stamp
167 A90 2.60m multicolored 1.10 1.10

Gymnastics Festival, Mariehamn.

2000, July 21 Litho. *Perf. 13½x13¼*
168 A91 3.40m multicolored 1.50 1.50

Cutty Sark Tall Ships race to Mariehamn.

Vikings From Aland — A92

2000, July 28
169 A92 4.50m multicolored 2.00 2.00

Recreation of Viking market, Saltvik.

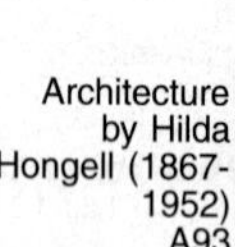

Architecture by Hilda Hongell (1867-1952) A93

2000, Aug. 25 *Perf. 13¼x13¾*
170 A93 3.80m shown 1.60 1.60
171 A93 10m House, diff. 4.50 4.50

Christianity, 2000th Anniv. — A94

2000, Oct. 9 *Perf. 13*
172 A94 3m multicolored 1.25 1.25

Church Type of 1984-90 and:

Swamp Plants — A95

Swamp plants: 1.90m, Equisetum fluviatile. 2.80m, Lycopodium annotinum. 3.50m, Polypodium vulgare.
Churches: No. 179, Föglö Church, Föglö. 2m, Kökar Church, Kökar.

Perf. 13x13¼, 13 (#178)
2000-01 Litho.
177 A95 1.90m multicolored .85 .80
178 A9 2m multicolored .90 .85
179 A9 2m multi .90 .85
180 A95 2.80m multicolored 1.25 1.25
182 A95 3.50m multicolored 1.50 1.50
Nos. 177-182 (5) 5.40 5.25

These stamps are part of an ongoing definitive set. Numbers have been reserved for additional stamps.
Issued: 2m, 10/9; 1.90m, 2.80m, 3.50m, 1/2/01; No. 179, 10/9/01.

Worldwide Fund for Nature (WWF) — A100

Polysticta stelleri: a, Pair in flight. b, Pair on rock. c, Pair in water. d, Male in water.

Perf. 13¼ on 3 sides
2001, Jan. 2 Litho.
Booklet Stamps
185 A100 Block of 4 4.50 4.50
a.-d. 2.70m any single 1.10 1.10
e. Booklet pane, 2 #185 9.00
Booklet, #185e 9.00

Valentine's Day — A101

2001, Feb. 14 *Perf. 14½x14¾*
186 A101 3.20m multicolored 1.40 1.40

Europa A102

2001, May 9 Litho. *Perf. 14½x14¾*
187 A102 3.20m multi 1.40 1.40

Windmills A103

Windmill types: 3m, Archipelago. 7m, Timbered, horiz. 20m, Nest, horiz.

Perf. 13¾x14¼, 14¼x13¾
2001, June 8
188-190 A103 Set of 3 13.00 13.00

Puppies — A104

Designs: 2, Golden retriever. 1, Wire-haired dachshund.

2001, Sept. 3 *Perf. 13¼*
191-192 A104 Set of 2 2.10 2.10

Nos. 191-192 sold for 2.30m and 2.70m respectively on day of issue.

100 Cents = 1 Euro (€)

Church Type of 1998 with Euro Denominations and

Fauna — A105

Post Terminal — A106

Mushrooms A107

Designs: 5c, Coronella austriaca. 10c, Chanterelle mushroom. 35c, Saltviks Church. 50c, King Bolete mushroom. 70c, Triturus cristatus. €2.50, Parasol mushroom.

Perf. 12½, 13 (#193, 196), 13¼ (#198), 14¾x14 (#195)
2002-03 Litho.
193 A105 5c multi .20 .20
194 A107 10c multi .25 .25
195 A9 35c multi .90 .90
196 A9 40c multi 1.00 1.00
197 A107 50c multi 1.25 1.25
198 A105 70c multi 1.75 1.75
199 A106 €1 multi 2.50 2.50
200 A107 €2.50 multi 6.50 6.50
Nos. 193-200 (8) 14.35 14.35

Issue dates: 5c, 70c, 1/2/02; €1, 2/28/02; 35c, 10/9/02; 10c, 50c, €2.50, 1/2/03. No. 196, 10/9/03.
This is an expanding set. Numbers may change.

Introduction of the Euro — A108

2002, Jan. 2 Litho. *Perf. 12½*
201 A108 60c multi 1.50 1.50

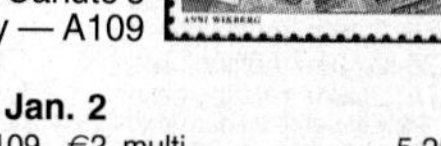
St. Canute's Day — A109

2002, Jan. 2
202 A109 €2 multi 5.25 5.25

Cuisine — A110

Flowers and: a, Gravlax, boiled potatoes. b, Fried herring, beets, mashed potatoes. c, Black bread, cheese, butter. d, Pancake with prune sauce and whipped cream, coffee.
Illustration reduced.

Perf. 13½x13¼ on 3 Sides
2002, Feb. 28 Litho.
203 A110 Block of 4 5.50 5.50
a.-d. 1 Any single 1.40 1.40
e. Booklet pane, 2 #203 11.00 —
Booklet, #203e 11.00

Nos. 203a-203d each sold for 55c on day of issue.

Europa — A111

2002, May 3 *Perf. 13¼*
204 A111 40c multi 1.00 1.00

Radar II, Sculpture by Stefan Lindfors A112

2002, May 3 *Perf. 13*
205 A112 €3 multi 7.75 7.75

"My Aland," by Lill Lindfors A113

2002, Aug. 12 Litho. *Perf. 13¼*
206 A113 90c multi 2.40 2.40

Iron Age Artifacts — A114

Designs: No. 207, 2, Buckle found in Persby. No. 208, 1, Ornamental pin found in Syllöda.

2002, Sept. 2 *Perf. 13x13¼*
207-208 A114 Set of 2 2.50 2.50

Nos. 207-208 sold for 45c and 55c respectively on day of issue.

Janne Holmén, Marathon Gold Medalist in European Track and Field Championships A115

2002, Nov. 1 ***Perf. 12½***
209 A115 1 multi 1.40 1.40

Sold for 55c on day of issue.

House Cats — A116

2003, Mar. 14 **Litho.** ***Perf. 13¼***
210 A116 2 Tovis .95 .95
211 A116 1 Randi, horiz. 1.25 1.25

Nos. 210-211 sold for 45c and 55c respectively on day of issue.

Landscape in Summer, by Elin Danielson-Gambogi (1861-1919) — A117

No. 212: a, Woman at fence. b, Tree without leaves. c, Sun. d, Boat.
Illustration reduced.

2003, Mar. 28 ***Perf. 14 Vert.***

Booklet Stamps

212 A117 Horiz. strip of 4 5.00 5.00
a.-d. 1 Any single 1.25 1.25
e. Booklet pane, 2 #212 10.00
Complete booklet, #212e 10.00

Nos. 212a-212d each sold for 55c on day of issue.

Europa — A118

2003, May 9 ***Perf. 13¼***
213 A118 45c multi 1.10 1.10

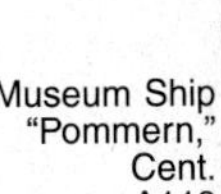

Museum Ship "Pommern," Cent. A119

2003, June 6 ***Die Cut Perf. 9¼x9½***

Booklet Stamp

Self-Adhesive

214 A119 55c multi 1.40 1.40
a. Booklet pane of 4 5.75
Complete booklet, 2 #214a 11.50

Mark and Stephen Levengood on Beach — A120

2003, June 18 ***Perf. 12½***
215 A120 55c multi 1.40 1.40

Aland Folk Music Association, 50th Anniv. — A121

2003, Aug. 1 ***Perf. 14¼***
216 A121 €1.10 buff & black 2.75 2.75

St. Lucia's Day Celebrations A122

2003, Oct. 9 **Litho.** ***Perf. 12½***
217 A122 60c multi 1.60 1.60

Mammals — A123

Designs: 20c, Mustela erminea. 60c, Vulpes vulpes. €3, Martes martes.

2004, Feb. 2 **Litho.** ***Perf. 14½x14¼***
218 A123 20c multi .50 .50
219 A123 60c multi 1.50 1.50
220 A123 €3 multi 7.75 7.75
Nos. 218-220 (3) 9.75 9.75

Souvenir Sheet

Norse Gods Fenja and Menja — A124

2004, Mar. 26 ***Perf. 14¼x14¾***
221 A124 55c multi 1.40 1.40

Aland Flag, 50th Anniv. — A125

Serpentine Die Cut 12½

2004, Apr. 23

Booklet Stamp

Self-Adhesive

222 A125 1 multi 1.50 1.50
a. Booklet pane of 4 6.00
Complete booklet, 2 #222a 12.00

Finnish Pres. Mauno Koivisto and Guests on Boat — A126

2004, Apr. 23 ***Perf. 12½***
223 A126 90c multi 2.10 2.10

Europa — A127

2004, May 10 ***Perf. 13¾x14¼***
224 A127 75c multi 1.75 1.75

Destruction of Bomarsund Fortress, 150th Anniv. — A128

No. 225: a, Fortress, six ships in harbor. b, Fortress, three ships in harbor. c, Three soldiers in foreground. d, Six soldiers in foreground.

2004, June 9 ***Perf. 13***
225 Booklet pane of 4 7.25 7.25
a.-d. A128 75c Any single 1.75 1.75
Complete booklet, 2 #225 14.50

2004 Summer Olympics, Athens A183

2004, Aug. 13 **Litho.** ***Perf. 14¼***
226 A183 80c multi 2.00 2.00

Landscapes A184

Designs: 2, Storklynkan, Brändö. 1, Prästgardsnäset Nature Reserve, Finström.

2004, Aug. 13 ***Perf. 12½***
227-228 A184 Set of 2 2.75 2.75

Nos. 227-228 sold for 50c and 60c respectively on day of issue.

Christmas A185

2004, Oct. 8 ***Perf. 14½x14¾***
229 A185 45c multi 1.10 1.10

FIUME

ˈfyü-ˌmä

LOCATION — A city and surrounding territory on the Adriatic Sea
GOVT. — Formerly a part of Italy
AREA — 8 sq. mi.
POP. — 44,956 (estimated 1924)

Formerly a port of Hungary, Fiume was claimed by Yugoslavia and Italy following World War I. During the discussion, the poet Gabriele d'Annunzio organized his legionnaires and seized Fiume, together with the islands of Arbe, Carnaro and Veglia, in the name of Italy. Yugoslavia recognized Italy's claim and the city was annexed in January, 1924.

100 Filler = 1 Korona
100 Centesimi = 1 Corona (1919)
100 Centesimi = 1 Lira

See note on FIUME-KUPA Zone, Italian Occupation, after Yugoslavia No. NJ22.

Hungarian Stamps of 1916-18 Overprinted

1918, Dec. 2 **Wmk. 137** ***Perf. 15***

On Stamps of 1916

White Numerals

1	A8	10f rose	35.00	17.50
2	A8	15f violet	17.50	10.00

Nos. 1-2 overprints are handstamped.

On Stamps of 1916-18

Colored Numerals

3	A9	2f brown orange	2.75	1.40
4	A9	3f red violet	2.75	1.40
5	A9	5f green	2.75	1.40
6	A9	6f grnsh blue	2.75	1.40
7	A9	10f rose red	40.00	15.00
8	A9	15f violet	2.75	1.40
9	A9	20f gray brown	2.75	1.40
10	A9	25f deep blue	6.00	1.75
11	A9	35f brown	4.75	2.75
12	A9	40f olive green	24.00	10.00

White Numerals

13	A10	50f red vio & lil	3.25	1.90
14	A10	75f brt bl & pale bl	7.75	2.75
15	A10	80f grn & pale grn	7.75	1.90
16	A10	1k red brn & claret	17.00	5.00
17	A10	2k ol brn & bis	3.25	1.90
18	A10	3k dk vio & ind	20.00	8.50
19	A10	5k dk brn & lt brn	47.50	12.50
20	A10	10k vio brn & vio	200.00	100.00

Inverted or double overprints exist on most of Nos. 4-15.

On Stamps of 1918

21	A11	10f scarlet	1.90	1.50
22	A11	20f dark brown	1.25	1.25
23	A12	40f olive green	14.50	4.75

The overprint on Nos. 3-23 was applied by 2 printing plates and 6 handstamps. Values are for the less costly. Values of Nos. 7, 20 and 23 are for handstamps. All genuine printed overprints on No. 7 are inverted, are extremely scarce, and sell for much more than the stated catalogue value.

Forgeries of Nos. 1-23 abound.

Postage Due Stamps of Hungary, 1915-20 Ovptd. & Surcharged in Black

1919, Jan.

24	D1	45f on 6f green & red	5.75	6.25
25	D1	45f on 20f green & red	15.00	6.25
		Set, never hinged	40.00	

Hungarian Savings Bank Stamp Surcharged in Black — A2

1919, Jan. 29

No.	Type	Description	Unused	Used
26	A2	15f on 10f dk violet	8.50	6.00
		Never hinged	17.00	

"Italy" — A3

Italian Flag on Clock-Tower in Fiume — A4

"Revolution" A5

Sailor Raising Italian Flag at Fiume (1918) A6

1919 Unwmk. Litho. *Perf. 11½*

No.	Type	Description	Unused	Used
27	A3	2c dull blue	.55	.55
28	A3	3c gray brown	.55	.55
29	A3	5c yellow green	.70	.55
30	A4	10c rose	9.00	2.10
31	A4	15c violet	.55	.55
32	A4	20c green	.90	.90
33	A5	25c dark blue	1.25	.55
34	A6	30c deep violet	.90	.55
35	A5	40c brown	1.10	1.10
36	A5	45c orange	.90	.90
37	A6	50c yellow green	.90	.55
38	A6	60c claret	1.10	.55
39	A6	1cor brown orange	1.60	.90
40	A6	2cor brt blue	1.60	1.10
41	A6	3cor orange red	2.10	1.25
42	A6	5cor deep brown	11.00	6.75
43	A6	10cor olive green	8.25	*15.00*
		Nos. 27-43 (17)	42.95	*34.40*
		Set, never hinged	90.00	

The earlier printings of Jan. and Feb. are on thin grayish paper, the Mar. printing is on semi-transparent white paper, all in sheets of 70. An Apr. printing is on white paper of medium thickness in sheets of 100. Part-perf. examples of most of this series are known.

For surcharges see Nos. 58, 60, 64, 66-69.

A7

A8

A9

A10

1919, July 28 *Perf. 11½*

No.	Type	Description	Unused	Used
46	A7	5c yellow green	.65	.55
47	A8	10c rose	.65	.55
48	A9	30c violet	3.00	1.25
49	A10	40c yellow brown	.90	*1.10*
50	A10	45c orange	3.00	1.25
51	A9	50c yellow green	3.00	1.25
52	A9	60c claret	3.00	1.25
a.		Perf. 13x12½	77.50	—
		Never hinged	110.00	
b.		Perf. 10½	190.00	
		Never hinged	290.00	
53	A9	10cor olive green	2.40	*3.50*
a.		Perf. 13x12½	30.00	*60.00*
		Never hinged	45.00	
b.		Perf. 10½	190.00	190.00
		Never hinged	290.00	
		Nos. 46-53 (8)	16.60	10.70
		Set, never hinged	32.50	

Five other denominations (25c, 1cor, 2cor, 3cor and 5cor) were not officially issued. Some copies of the 25c are known canceled.

For surcharges see Nos. 59, 61-63, 65, 70.

Stamps of 1919 Handstamp Surcharged

1919-20

No.	Type	Description	Unused	Used
58	A4	5c on 20c green ('20)	.30	.30
59	A10	5c on 25c blue	.30	.30
60	A5	10c on 45c orange	.90	.30
61	A9	15c on 30c vio ('20)	.30	.30
62	A10	15c on 45c orange	.30	.30
63	A9	15c on 60c cl ('20)	.45	.50
64	A6	25c on 50c yel grn ('20)	8.75	*11.00*
65	A9	25c on 50c yel grn ('20)	.45	*.50*
66	A6	55c on 1cor brn org	18.00	9.00
67	A6	55c on 2cor brt bl	3.00	*3.50*
68	A6	55c on 3cor org red	3.00	3.00
69	A6	55c on 5cor dp brn	3.00	3.00
70	A9	55c on 10cor ol grn	13.00	8.75
		Nos. 58-70 (13)	51.75	*40.75*
		Set, never hinged	110.00	

Semi-Postal Stamps of 1919 Surcharged:

a

b

1919-20

No.	Type	Description	Unused	Used
73	SP6(a)	5c on 5c green	.30	.20
74	SP6(a)	10c on 10c rose	.30	.20
75	SP6(a)	15c on 15c gray	.30	.20
76	SP6(a)	20c on 20c org	.30	.20
77	SP9(a)	25c on 25c bl ('20)	.30	.20
78	SP7(b)	45c on 45c ol grn	.45	.35
79	SP7(b)	60c on 60c rose	.45	.35
80	SP7(b)	80c on 80c violet	.60	.50
81	SP7(b)	1cor on 1cor sl	.45	.35
82	SP8(a)	2cor on 2cor red brn	1.00	.80
83	SP8(a)	3cor on 3cor blk brn	2.40	1.90
84	SP8(a)	5cor on 5cor yel brn	3.00	2.50
85	SP8(a)	10cor on 10cor dk vio ('20)	1.00	.80
		Nos. 73-85 (13)	10.85	8.55
		Set, never hinged	21.00	

Double or inverted surcharges, or imperf. varieties, exist on most of Nos. 73-85.

There were three settings of the surcharges on Nos. 73-85 except No. 77 which is known only with one setting.

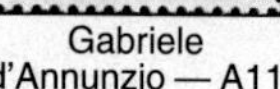

Gabriele d'Annunzio — A11

Severing the Gordian Knot — A12

1920, Sept. 12 Typo. *Perf. 11½*

Pale Buff Background

No.	Type	Description	Unused	Used
86	A11	5c green	.55	.55
87	A11	10c carmine	.55	.55
88	A11	15c dark gray	.55	.55
89	A11	20c orange	.60	.60
90	A11	25c dark blue	.90	.90
91	A11	30c red brown	.95	.95
92	A11	45c olive gray	1.50	1.50
93	A11	50c lilac	1.50	1.50
94	A11	55c bister	1.50	1.50
95	A11	1 l black	7.75	*10.00*
96	A11	2 l red violet	7.75	*11.50*
97	A11	3 l dark green	7.75	*11.50*
98	A11	5 l brown	40.00	16.00
99	A11	10 l gray violet	7.75	*11.50*
		Nos. 86-99 (14)	79.60	*69.10*
		Set, never hinged	150.00	

Counterfeits of Nos. 86 to 99 are plentiful.

For overprints see Nos. 134-148.

1920, Sept. 12

Designs: 10c, Ancient emblem of Fiume. 20c, Head of "Fiume." 25c, Hands holding daggers.

No.	Type	Description	Unused	Used
100	A12	5c green	32.50	16.00
101	A12	10c deep rose	21.00	12.00
102	A12	20c brown orange	32.50	12.00
103	A12	25c indigo	21.00	*30.00*
a.		25c blue	60.00	60.00
		Nos. 100-103 (4)	107.00	70.00
		Set, never hinged	210.00	

Anniv. of the occupation of Fiume by d'Annunzio. They were available for franking the correspondence of the legionnaires on the day of issue only, Sept. 12, 1920.

Counterfeits of Nos. 100-103 are plentiful.

For overprints and surcharges see Nos. 104-133, E4-E9.

Nos. 100-103 Overprinted or Surcharged in Black or Red and New Values

1920, Nov. 20

No.	Type	Description	Unused	Used
104	A12	1c on 5c green	1.00	.40
105	A12	2c on 25c indigo (R)	.40	.40
a.		2c on 25c blue (R)	32.50	32.50
106	A12	5c green	14.00	1.00
107	A12	10c rose	14.00	1.00
108	A12	15c on 10c rose	1.00	.55
109	A12	15c on 20c brn org	.40	*.55*
110	A12	15c on 25c ind (R)	.55	*.70*
a.		15c on 25c blue (R)	32.50	32.50
111	A12	20c brown orange	.70	.70
112	A12	25c indigo (R)	.70	.70
a.		25c blue (R)	3.50	3.50
113	A12	25c indigo (Bk)	70.00	70.00
a.		25c blue (Bk)	75.00	75.00
114	A12	25c on 10c rose	1.75	1.75
115	A12	50c on 20c brn org	4.00	1.25
116	A12	55c on 5c green	14.00	2.10
117	A12	1 l on 10c rose	24.00	10.00
118	A12	1 l on 25c ind (R)	275.00	275.00
a.		1 l on 25c blue (R)	600.00	250.00
119	A12	2 l on 5c green	22.50	13.00
120	A12	5 l on 10c rose	92.50	50.00
121	A12	10 l on 20c brn org	325.00	190.00
		Nos. 104-121 (18)	861.50	619.10
		Set, never hinged	1,750.	

The Fiume Legionnaires of d'Annunzio occupied the islands of Arbe and Veglia in the Gulf of Carnaro Nov. 13, 1920-Jan. 5, 1921.

Varieties of overprint or surcharge exist for most of Nos. 104-121.

#113, 117-121, 125, 131 have a backprint.

Nos. 106-107, 111, 113, 115-116 Overprinted or Surcharged at top

1920, Nov. 18

No.	Type	Description	Unused	Used
122	A12	5c green	3.25	3.25
123	A12	10c rose	7.75	*8.50*
124	A12	20c brown org	17.50	12.00
125	A12	25c deep blue	9.50	*12.00*
126	A12	50c on 20c brn org	19.00	12.00
127	A12	55c on 5c green	19.00	12.00
		Nos. 122-127 (6)	76.00	59.75
		Set, never hinged	190.00	

The overprint on Nos. 122-125 comes in two widths: 11mm and 14mm. Values are for the 11mm width.

Nos. 106-107, 111, 113, 115-116 Overprinted or Surcharged at top

1920, Nov. 18

No.	Type	Description	Unused	Used
128	A12	5c green	3.25	3.25
129	A12	10c rose	7.75	*8.50*
130	A12	20c brown orange	17.50	12.00
131	A12	25c deep blue	9.50	*12.00*
132	A12	50c on 20c brn org	19.00	12.00
133	A12	55c on 5c green	19.00	12.00
		Nos. 128-133 (6)	76.00	59.75
		Set, never hinged	190.00	

The overprint on Nos. 128-131 comes in two widths: 17mm and 19mm. Values are for the 17mm width.

Nos. 122-133 exist with double and inverted overprints.

Counterfeits of these overprints exist.

Nos. 86-99 Overprinted

1921, Feb. 2

Pale Buff Background

No.	Type	Description	Unused	Used
134	A11	5c green	.35	.35
135	A11	10c carmine	.35	.35
136	A11	15c dark gray	.35	*.40*
137	A11	20c orange	1.25	.85
138	A11	25c dark blue	1.25	.85
139	A11	30c red brown	1.25	.85
140	A11	45c olive gray	.70	.70
141	A11	50c lilac	1.50	1.10
142	A11	55c bister	1.25	.80
143	A11	1 l black	75.00	72.50
144	A11	2 l red violet	15.00	11.50
145	A11	3 l dark green	15.00	11.50
146	A11	5 l brown	15.00	11.50
147	A11	10 l gray violet	15.00	11.50

With Additional Surcharge

No.	Type	Description	Unused	Used
148	A11	1 l on 30c red brn	.70	.70
		Nos. 134-148 (15)	143.95	125.45
		Set, never hinged	275.00	

Most of Nos. 134-143, 148 and E10-E11 exist with inverted or double overprint.

See Nos. E10-E11.

First Constituent Assembly

Nos. B4-B15 Overprinted

1921, Apr. 24

149 SP6 5c blue green 1.40 1.40
150 SP6 10c rose 1.40 1.40
151 SP6 15c gray 1.40 1.40
152 SP6 20c orange 1.40 1.40
153 SP7 45c olive green 4.25 4.00
154 SP7 60c car rose 4.25 4.00
155 SP7 80c brt violet 5.00 5.00

With Additional Overprint "L"

156 SP7 1 l on 1cor dk sl 7.00 7.00
157 SP8 2 l on 2cor red brn 32.50 1.00
158 SP8 3 l on 3cor blk brn 32.50 32.50
159 SP8 5 l on 5cor yel brn 32.50 1.40
160 SP8 10 l on 10cor dk vio 35.00 35.00
Nos. 149-160 (12) 158.60 95.50
Set, never hinged 325.00

The overprint exists inverted on several denominations.

Second Constituent Assembly

"Constitution" Issue of 1921 With Additional Overprint "1922"

1922

161 SP6 5c blue green 1.75 .85
162 SP6 10c rose .20 *.35*
163 SP6 15c gray 7.75 2.75
164 SP6 20c orange .85 .70
165 SP7 45c olive grn 6.00 3.00
166 SP7 60c car rose .55 1.10
167 SP7 80c brt violet .55 1.10
168 SP7 1 l on 1cor dk slate .85 .70
169 SP8 2 l on 2cor red brn 7.75 4.25
170 SP8 3 l on 3cor blk brn .75 *1.10*
171 SP8 5 l on 5cor yel brn .55 *1.10*
Nos. 161-171 (11) 27.55 17.00
Set, never hinged 55.00

Nos. 161-171 have the overprint in heavier type than Nos. 149-160 and "IV" in Roman instead of sans-serif numerals.

The overprint exists inverted or double on almost all values.

Venetian Ship — A16

Roman Arch — A17

St. Vitus — A18

Rostral Column — A19

1923, Mar. 23 ***Perf. 11½***

Pale Buff Background

172 A16 5c blue green .35 .35
173 A16 10c violet .35 .35
174 A16 15c brown .35 .35
175 A17 20c orange red .35 .35
176 A17 25c dark gray .35 .35
177 A17 30c dark green .35 .35
178 A18 50c dull blue .35 .35
179 A18 60c rose .55 *1.25*
180 A18 1 l dark blue .55 *1.50*
181 A19 2 l violet brown 32.50 7.75
182 A19 3 l olive bister 24.00 14.50
183 A19 5 l yellow brown 24.00 19.00
Nos. 172-183 (12) 84.05 46.45
Set, never hinged 175.00

Nos. 172-183 Overprinted

1924, Feb. 22

Pale Buff Background

184 A16 5c blue green .35 *2.75*
185 A16 10c violet .35 *2.75*
186 A16 15c brown .60 *2.75*
187 A17 20c orange red .60 *2.75*
188 A17 25c dk gray .60 *2.75*
189 A17 30c dk green .60 *2.75*
190 A18 50c dull blue .60 *2.75*
191 A18 60c red .60 *2.75*
192 A18 1 l dark blue .60 *2.75*
193 A19 2 l violet brown 1.75 *6.00*
194 A19 3 l olive 2.75 *7.00*
195 A19 5 l yellow brown 2.75 *7.00*
Nos. 184-195 (12) 12.15 *44.75*
Set, never hinged 24.00

The overprint exists inverted on almost all values.

Nos. 172-183 Overprinted

1924, Mar. 1

Pale Buff Background

196 A16 5c blue green .35 *1.40*
197 A16 10c violet .35 *1.40*
198 A16 15c brown .35 *1.40*
199 A17 20c orange red .35 *1.40*
200 A17 25c dark gray .35 *1.40*
201 A17 30c dark green .35 *1.40*
202 A18 50c dull blue .35 *1.40*
203 A18 60c red .35 *1.40*
204 A18 1 l dark blue .35 *1.40*
205 A19 2 l violet brown .70 *2.75*
206 A19 3 l olive .70 *2.75*
207 A19 5 l yellow brown .70 *2.75*
Nos. 196-207 (12) 5.25 *20.85*
Set, never hinged 10.00

Postage stamps of Fiume were superseded by stamps of Italy.

SEMI-POSTAL STAMPS

Semi-Postal Stamps of Hungary, 1916-17 Overprinted

1918, Dec. 2 **Wmk. 137** ***Perf. 15***

B1 SP3 10f + 2f rose 2.40 1.25
a. Inverted overprint 32.50 22.50
B2 SP4 15f + 2f dl vio 2.40 1.25
a. Inverted overprint 62.50 22.50
B3 SP5 40f + 2f brn car 2.40 1.25
a. Inverted overprint 35.00 17.50
Nos. B1-B3 (3) 7.20 3.75
Set, never hinged 17.50

Examples of Nos. B1-B3 with overprint handstamped sell for higher prices.

Statue of Romulus and Remus Being Suckled by Wolf — SP6

Venetian Galley — SP7

Church of St. Mark's, Venice — SP8

Perf. 11½

1919, May 18 **Unwmk.** **Typo.**

B4 SP6 5c +5 l bl grn 7.50 4.25
B5 SP6 10c +5 l rose 7.50 4.25
B6 SP6 15c +5 l dk gray 7.50 4.25
B7 SP6 20c +5 l orange 7.50 4.25
B8 SP7 45c +5 l ol grn 7.50 4.25
B9 SP7 60c +5 l car rose 7.50 4.25
B10 SP7 80c +5 l lilac 7.50 4.25
B11 SP7 1cor +5 l dk slate 7.50 4.25
B12 SP8 2cor +5 l red brn 7.50 4.25
B13 SP8 3cor +5 l blk brn 7.50 4.25
B14 SP8 5cor +5 l yel brn 7.50 4.25
B15 SP8 10cor +5 l dk vio 7.50 4.25
Nos. B4-B15 (12) 90.00 51.00
Set, never hinged 175.00

200th day of peace. The surtax aided Fiume students in Italy. "Posta di Fiume" is printed on the back of Nos. B4-B16.

The surtax is shown on the stamps as "LIRE 5" but actually was 5cor.

For surcharges and overprints see Nos. 73-85, 149-171, J15-J26.

Dr. Antonio Grossich — SP9

1919, Sept. 20

B16 SP9 25c + 2 l blue 1.40 1.40
Never hinged 2.75

Surtax for the Dr. Grossich Foundation.

SPECIAL DELIVERY STAMPS

Special Delivery Stamp of Hungary, 1916, Overprinted like Nos. 1-23

1918, Dec. 2 **Wmk. 137** ***Perf. 15***

E1 SD1 2f gray green & red 1.75 1.40
Never hinged 3.25

Handstamped overprints sell for more.

SD3

Perf. 11½

1920, Sept. 12 **Unwmk.** **Typo.**

E2 SD3 30c slate blue 16.00 12.00
E3 SD3 50c rose 16.00 12.00
Set, never hinged 60.00

For overprints see Nos. E10-E11.

Nos. 102 and 100 Surcharged

1920, Nov.

E4 A12 30c on 20c brn org 42.50 42.50
E5 A12 50c on 5c green 70.00 35.00

Nos. E4-E5 have a backprint.

Same Surcharge as on Nos. 124, 122

E6 A12 30c on 20c brn org 75.00 47.50
E7 A12 50c on 5c green 55.00 47.50

Overprint on Nos. E6-E7 is 11mm wide.

Same Surcharge as on Nos. 130, 128

E8 A12 30c on 20c brn org 75.00 47.50
E9 A12 50c on 5c green 55.00 47.50
Nos. E4-E9 (6) 372.50 267.50
Set, never hinged 900.00

Overprint on Nos. E8-E9 is 17mm wide.

Nos. E2 and E3 Overprinted

1921, Feb. 2

E10 SD3 30c slate blue 7.00 8.75
E11 SD3 50c rose 10.50 8.75
Set, never hinged 35.00

Fiume in 16th Century SD4

1923, Mar. 23 ***Perf. 11, 11½***

E12 SD4 60c rose & buff 10.50 6.00
E13 SD4 2 l dk bl & buff 10.50 7.75
Set, never hinged 42.50

Nos. E12-E13 Overprinted

1924, Feb. 22

E14 SD4 60c car & buff .85 *4.25*
E15 SD4 2 l dk bl & buff .85 *4.25*
Set, never hinged 3.50

Nos. E12-E13 Overprinted

1924, Mar. 1

E16 SD4 60c car & buff .85 *3.50*
E17 SD4 2 l dk bl & buff .85 *3.50*
Set, never hinged 3.50

POSTAGE DUE STAMPS

Postage Due Stamps of Hungary, 1915-1916, Overprinted

1918, Dec. Wmk. 137 *Perf. 15*

J1	D1	6f green & black	90.00	24.00
J2	D1	12f green & black	75.00	24.00
J3	D1	50f green & black	27.50	12.00
		Set, never hinged	290.00	
J4	D1	1f green & red	14.00	7.00
J5	D1	2f green & red	.55	.40
J6	D1	5f green & red	3.50	2.75
J7	D1	6f green & red	.55	.40
J8	D1	10f green & red	6.25	1.75
J9	D1	12f green & red	.70	.55
J10	D1	15f green & red	12.00	10.00
J11	D1	20f green & red	.70	.55
J12	D1	30f green & red	12.00	8.75
		Nos. J4-J12 (9)	50.25	32.15
		Set, never hinged	95.00	

The overprint on Nos. J1-J12 was applied both by press and handstamp. Values are for the less costly. Inverted and double overprints exist. Excellent forgeries exist.

Eagle — D2

Perf. 11½

1919, July 28 Unwmk. Typo.

J13	D2	2c brown	1.00	.80
J14	D2	5c brown	1.25	.80
		Set, never hinged	4.25	

Semi-Postal Stamps of 1919 with Overprint "Valore Globale" Surcharged:

1921, Mar. 21

J15	SP6	2c on 15c gray	.70	.70
J16	SP6	4c on 10c rose	.60	.55
J17	SP9	5c on 25c blue	.60	.55
J18	SP6	6c on 20c orange	.60	.55
J19	SP6	10c on 20c orange	.90	.90

Surcharged:

J20	SP7	20c on 45c olive grn	1.00	*1.40*
J21	SP7	30c on 1cor dk slate	1.25	*1.10*
J22	SP7	40c on 80c violet	.80	*.70*
J23	SP7	50c on 60c carmine	.80	*.70*
J24	SP7	60c on 45c olive grn	1.00	*1.40*
J25	SP7	80c on 45c olive grn	1.00	*1.40*

Surcharged like Nos. J15-J19

J26	SP8	1 l on 2cor red brown	1.75	*1.40*
		Nos. J15-J26 (12)	11.00	*11.35*
		Set, never hinged	21.00	

See note below No. 85 regarding settings of "Valore Globale" overprint.

NEWSPAPER STAMPS

Newspaper Stamp of Hungary, 1914, Overprinted like Nos. 1-23

1918, Dec. 2 Wmk. 137 *Imperf.*

P1	N5	(2f) orange	1.75	.70
		Never hinged	3.25	

Handstamped overprints sell for more.

Eagle
N1

1919 Unwmk. *Perf. 11½*

P2	N1	2c deep buff	3.50	4.75

Re-engraved

P3	N1	2c deep buff	3.50	3.50
		Set, never hinged	14.00	

In the re-engraved stamp the top of the "2" is rounder and broader, the feet of the eagle show clearly and the diamond at bottom has six lines instead of five.

Steamer — N2

1920, Sept. 12

P4	N2	1c gray green	1.00	.70
		Never hinged	2.10	

No. P4 exists imperf.

FRANCE

'fran¸t¸s

LOCATION — Western Europe
GOVT. — Republic
AREA — 210,033 sq. mi.
POP. — 58,978,172 (1999 est.)
CAPITAL — Paris

100 Centimes = 1 Franc
100 Cents = 1 Euro (2002)

Catalogue values for unused stamps in this country are for Never Hinged items, beginning with Scott 299 in the regular postage section, Scott B42 in the semi-postal section, Scott C18 in the airpost section, Scott CB1 in the airpost semi-postal section, Scott J69 in the postage due section, Scott M10 in the military stamps section, Scott 1O1 in the section for official stamps for the Council of Europe, Scott 2O1 for the section for UNESCO, Scott S1 for franchise stamps, Scott N27 for occupation stamps, and Scott 2N1 for AMG stamps.

Ceres — A1

FORTY CENTIMES

4
Type I

4
Type II

1849-50 Typo. Unwmk. *Imperf.*

No.		Description	Unused	Used
1	A1	10c bis, *yelsh* ('50)	*1,250.*	275.00
a.		10c dark bister, *yelsh*	1,700.	325.00
b.		10c greenish bister	2,250.	350.00
e.		Tête beche pair	*62,500.*	*13,250.*
2	A1	15c green, *grnsh* ('50)	*18,500.*	725.00
a.		15c yellow green, *grnsh*	*18,500.*	800.00
c.		Tête bêche pair	—	
3	A1	20c blk, *yelsh*	300.00	40.00
a.		20c black	400.00	45.00
b.		20c black, *buff*	1,400.	225.00
c.		Tête bêche pair	*8,750.*	*5,500.*
4	A1	20c dark blue	*2,350.*	
a.		20c blue, *bluish*	*2,200.*	
b.		20c blue, *yelsh*	*2,750.*	
c.		Tête bêche pair	*62,500.*	
6	A1	25c lt bl, *bluish*	*5,500.*	30.00
a.		25c blue, *bluish* ('50)	*5,500.*	32.50
b.		25c blue, *yelsh*	*5,250.*	35.00
c.		Tête bêche pair	*140,000.*	*11,000.*
7	A1	40c org, *yelsh* (I) ('50)	*3,250.*	400.00
a.		40c org ver, *yelsh* (I)	*3,350.*	475.00
b.		40c orange, *yelsh* (II)	*22,000.*	*5,000.*
c.		Pair, types I and II	*35,000.*	*11,750.*
g.		Vertical half used as 20c on cover		*110,000.*
8	A1	1fr ver, *yelsh*	*65,000.*	*14,750.*
a.		1fr dull org red	*80,000.*	*18,500.*
b.		Tête bêche pair	*440,000.*	
c.		1fr pale ver ("Vervelle")	*20,000.*	
9	A1	1fr light carmine	*10,000.*	700.00
a.		Tête bêche pair	*155,000.*	*20,000.*
b.		1fr brown carmine	*10,000.*	800.00
c.		1fr dk car, *yelsh*	*10,000.*	750.00

No. 4, which lacks gum, was not issued due to a rate change to 25c after the stamps were prepared.

An ungummed sheet of No. 8c was found in 1895 among the effects of Anatole A. Hulot, the printer. It was sold to Ernest Vervelle, a Parisian dealer, by whose name the stamps are known.

See Nos. 329-329e, 612-613, 624.

Nos. 1, 4a, 6a, 7 and 13 are of similar designs and colors to French Colonies Nos. 9, 11, 12, 14, and 8. There are numerous shades of each. Identification by those who are not experts can be difficult, though cancellations can be used as a guide for used stamps. Because of the date of issue the Colonies stamps are similar in shades and papers to the perforated French stamps,

Nos. 23a, 54, 57-59, and are not as clearly printed. Except for No. 13, unused, the French Colonies stamps sell for much less than the values shown here for properly identified French versions.

Expertization of these stamps is recommended.

1862 Re-issue

No.		Description	Unused
1d	A1	10c bister	375.
2d	A1	15c yellow green	475.
3d	A1	20c black, *yellowish*	325.
4d	A1	20c blue	325.
6d	A1	25c blue	375.
7d	A1	40c orange (I)	475.
7e	A1	40c orange (II)	*10,000.*
h.		Pair, types I and II	*15,000.*
9d	A1	1fr pale lake	475.

The re-issues are fine impressions in lighter colors and on whiter paper than the originals. An official imitation of the essay, 25c on 20c blue, was made at the same time as the re-issues.

President Louis Napoleon — A2

Emperor Napoleon III — A3

1852

No.		Description	Unused	Used
10	A2	10c pale bister, *yelsh*	*30,000.*	475.00
a.		10c dark bister, *yelsh*	*33,000.*	675.00
11	A2	25c blue, *bluish*	*2,400.*	35.00
b.		25c dark blue, *blush*	*2,900.*	57.50

1862 Re-issue

No.		Description	Unused
10b	A2	10c bister	425.00
11a	A2	25c blue	300.00

The re-issues are in lighter colors and on whiter paper than the originals.

1853-60 *Imperf.*

Die I. The curl above the forehead directly below "R" of "EMPIRE" is made up of two lines very close together, often appearing to form a single thick line. There is no shading across the neck.

Die II. The curl is made of two distinct, more widely separated lines. There are lines of shading across the upper neck.

No.		Description	Unused	Used
12	A3	1c ol grn, *pale bl* ('60)	150.00	72.50
a.		1c bronze grn, *pale bluish*	160.00	77.50
13	A3	5c grn, *grnsh* (I) ('54)	600.00	72.50
14	A3	10c bis, *yelsh* (I)	325.00	7.00
a.		10c yellow, *yelsh* (I)	1,700.	57.50
b.		10c bister brn, *yelsh* (I)	50.00	25.00
c.		10c bis, *yelsh* (II) ('60)	450.00	25.00
15	A3	20c bl, *bluish* (I) ('54)	140.00	1.25
a.		20c dark bl, *bluish* (I)	225.00	1.50
b.		20c milky blue (I)	225.00	11.00
c.		20c blue, *lilac* (I)	3,650.	62.50
d.		20c bl, *bluish* (II) ('60)	300.00	4.00
e.		Half used as 10c on cover		*18,000.*
16	A3	20c bl, *grnsh* (II)	*3,900.*	150.00
a.		20c blue, *greenish* (I)	*4,650.*	150.00
17	A3	25c bl, *bluish* (I)	1,900.	175.00
18	A3	40c org, *yelsh* (I)	1,900.	10.00
a.		40c org ver, *yellowish*	*2,650.*	14.00
b.		Half used as 20c on cover		*62,500.*
19	A3	80c lake, *yelsh* (I) ('54)	2,500.	45.00
a.		Tête bêche pair	*350,000.*	*15,000.*
b.		Half used as 40c on cover		*28,000.*
20	A3	80c rose, *pnksh* (I) ('60)	1,800.	40.00
a.		Tete bêche pair	*50,000.*	*9,500.*
21	A3	1fr lake, *yelsh* (I)	*5,250.*	*2,500.*
a.		Tête bêche pair	*300,000.*	*100,000.*

Most values of the 1853-60 issue are known privately rouletted, pin-perf., perf. 7 and percé en scie.

1862 Re-issue

No.		Description	Unused
17c	A3	25c blue (I)	325.
19c	A3	80c lake (I)	1,500.
21c	A3	1fr lake (I)	1,150.
d.		Tête bêche pair	*30,000.*

The re-issues are in lighter colors and on whiter paper than the originals.

1862-71 *Perf. 14x13½*

No.		Description	Unused	Used
22	A3	1c ol grn, *pale bl* (II)	140.00	35.00
a.		1c bronze grn, *pale bl* (II)	140.00	35.00
23	A3	5c yel grn, *grnsh* (I)	150.00	9.50
a.		5c deep green, *grnsh* (I)	175.00	12.50
24	A3	5c grn, *pale bl* ('71) (I)	1,800.	100.00
25	A3	10c bis, *yelsh* (II)	1,300.	3.50
a.		10c yel brn, *yelsh* (II)	12.50	4.00
26	A3	20c bl, *bluish* (II)	175.00	.90
a.		Tête bêche pair (II)	3,250.	950.00
27	A3	40c org, *yelsh* (I)	11.50	7.25
28	A3	80c rose, *pnksh* (I)	1,000.	30.00
a.		80c brt rose, *pinkish* (I)	1,200.	47.50
c.		Tête bêche pair (I)	*18,500.*	*7,250.*

No. 26a imperf is from a trial printing.

A4

A5

Napoleon III — A6

1863-70 *Perf. 14x13½*

No.		Description	Unused	Used
29	A4	1c brnz grn, *pale bl* ('70)	29.00	11.00
a.		1c olive green, *pale blue*	22.50	11.50
30	A4	2c red brn, *yelsh*	87.50	22.50
b.		Half used as 1c on cover		*31,000.*
31	A4	4c gray	200.00	47.50
a.		Tete beche pair	*18,500.*	*8,000.*
d.		Half used as 2c on cover		*42,000.*
32	A5	10c bis, *yelsh* ('67)	400.00	6.50
c.		Half used as 5c on cover with other stamps		*3,100.*
33	A5	20c bl, *bluish* ('67)	160.00	1.50
c.		Half used as 10c on cover		*40,000.*
34	A5	30c brn, *yelsh* ('67)	650.00	14.50
a.		30c dk brn, *yellowish*	1,050.	30.00
35	A5	40c pale org, *yellowish*	650.00	8.75
a.		40c org, *yelsh* ('68)	675.00	11.00
c.		Half used as 20c on cover		*33,000.*
36	A5	80c rose, *pnksh* ('68)	875.00	20.00
a.		80c carmine, *yellowish*	1,050.	30.00
d.		Half used as 40c on cover		*40,000.*
e.		Quarter used as 20c on cover		*43,500.*
37	A6	5fr gray lil, *lav* ('69)	*5,000.*	775.00
a.		"5" and "F" omitted		*81,000.*
c.		5fr bluish gray, *lavender*	*5,100.*	800.00

No. 33 exists in two types, differing in the size of the dots at either side of POSTES.

On No. 37, the "5" and "F" vary in height from 3¾mm to 4½mm. The shades of the "5" and "F" may be bluer or blacker than the shade found on the rest of the stamp. All known copies of No. 37a are more or less damaged.

No. 29 was reprinted in 1887 by authority of Granet, Minister of Posts. The reprints show a yellowish shade under the ultraviolet lamp. Value $850.

For surcharge see No. 49.

Original Issue Imperfs

No.		Description	Unused
31c	A4	4c gray	240.
32b	A5	10c bister, *yellowish*	325.
33b	A5	20c blue, *bluish*	250.
36c	A5	80c rose, *pinkish*	—
37b	A6	5fr gray lilac, *lavender*	*8,100.*

Imperfs, "Rothschild" Re-issue

Paper Colors are the Same

No.		Description	Unused
29b	A4	1c olive green	950.
30a	A4	2c pale red brown	150.
31b	A4	4c pale gray	125.
32a	A5	10c pale bister	125.
33a	A5	20c pale blue	210.
34c	A5	30c pale brown	125.
35b	A5	40c pale orange	160.
36b	A5	80c rose	375.

The re-issues constitute the "Rothschild Issue." These stamps were authorized exclusively for the banker to use on his correspondence. Used copies exist.

Ceres

A7 A8

A9

A10

A11

Bordeaux Issue

On the lithographed stamps, except for type I of the 20c, the shading on the cheek and neck is in lines or dashes, not in dots. On the typographed stamps the shading is in dots. The 2c, 10c and 20c (types II and III) occur in two or more types. The most easily distinguishable are:

2c — Type A. To the left of and within the top of the left "2" are lines of shading composed of dots.

2c — Type B. These lines of dots are replaced by solid lines.

10c — Type A. The inner frame lines are of the same thickness as all other frame lines.

10c — Type B. The inner frame lines are much thicker than the others.

Three Types of the 20c.

A9 — The inscriptions in the upper and lower labels are small and there is quite a space between the upper label and the circle containing the head. There is also very little shading under the eye and in the neck.

A10 — The inscriptions in the labels are similar to those of the first type, the shading under the eye and in the neck is heavier and the upper label and circle almost touch.

A11 — The inscriptions in the labels are much larger than those of the two preceding types, and are similar to those of the other values of the same type in the set.

1870-71 Litho. *Imperf.*

38 A7 1c ol grn, *pale bl* 92.50 100.00
 a. 1c bronze grn, *pale blue* 110.00 *125.00*
39 A7 2c red brn, *yelsh* (B) 210.00 210.00
 a. 2c brick red, *yelsh* (B) 950.00 650.00
 b. 2c chestnut, *yelsh* (B) 1,300. 810.00
 c. 2c chocolate, *yelsh* (A) 700.00 700.00
40 A7 4c gray 225.00 175.00
41 A8 5c yel green, *greenish* 210.00 150.00
 a. 5c grn, *grnsh* 260.00 150.00
 b. 5c emerald, *greenish* 3,100. 1,000.
42 A8 10c bis, *yelsh* (A) 775.00 55.00
 a. 10c bister, *yellowish* (B) 775.00 77.50
43 A9 20c bl, *bluish* *17,500.* 500.00
 a. 20c dark blue, *bluish* *19,000.* 1,050.
44 A10 20c bl, *bluish* 775.00 45.00
 a. 20c dark blue, *bluish* 1,000. 85.00
 b. 20c ultra, *bluish* *19,000.* *3,300.*
45 A11 20c bl, *bluish* ('71) 900.00 18.00
 a. 20c ultra, *bluish* 2,250. 725.00
46 A8 30c brn, *yelsh* 300.00 190.00
 a. 30c blk brn, *yelsh* 1,750. 800.00
47 A8 40c org, *yelsh* 350.00 95.00
 a. 40c yel orange, *yelsh* 1,000. 175.00
 b. 40c red orange, *yelsh* 600.00 160.00
 c. 40c scarlet, *yelsh* *4,750.* *1,500.*
48 A8 80c rose, *pinkish* 400.00 240.00
 a. 80c dull rose, *pinkish* 400.00 240.00

All values of the 1870 issue are known privately rouletted, pin-perf. and perf. 14.

See Nos. 50-53.

A12

Blue Surcharge

1871 Typo. *Perf. 14x13½*

49 A12 10c on 10c bister 1,350.

#49 was never placed in use. Counterfeits exist.

A13

A14

Two types of the 40c as in the 1849-50 issue.

1870-73 Typo. *Perf. 14x13½*

50 A7 1c ol grn, *pale bl* 45.00 11.00
 a. 1c bronze grn, *pale bl* ('72) 47.50 15.00
51 A7 2c red brn, *yelsh* ('70) 80.00 15.00
52 A7 4c gray ('70) 225.00 35.00
53 A7 5c yel grn, *pale bl* ('72) 150.00 7.50
 a. 5c green 140.00 7.50
54 A13 10c bis, *yelsh* 550.00 55.00
 a. Tête beche pair *5,500.* *2,000.*
 b. Half used as 5c on cover *4,400.*
55 A13 10c bis, *rose* ('73) 300.00 11.00
 a. Tête bêche pair 4,000. 1,500.
56 A13 15c bis, *yelsh* ('71) 300.00 3.50
 a. Tête bêche pair *44,000.* *16,000.*
57 A13 20c dl bl, *bluish* 225.00 6.00
 a. 20c bright blue, *bluish* 300.00 7.50
 b. Tête bêche pair 3,600. 1,300.
 c. Half used as 10c on cover *47,500.*
 d. Quarter used as 5c on cover *45,000.*
58 A13 25c bl, *bluish* ('71) 100.00 1.50
 a. 25c dk bl, *bluish* 140.00 1.50
 b. Tête bêche pair *6,600.* *3,300.*
59 A13 40c org, *yelsh* (I) 475.00 6.50
 a. 40c orange yel, *yelsh* (I) 550.00 7.50
 b. 40c orange, *yelsh* (II) 3,250. 150.00
 c. 40c orange yel, *yelsh* (II) 3,250. 150.00
 d. Pair, types I and II *6,600.* 475.00
 f. Half used as 20c on circular *20,000.*
 g. Half used as 20c on cover *44,000.*

No. 58 exists in three main plate varieties, differing in one or another of the flower like corner ornaments.

Margins on this issue are extremely small.

Nos. 54, 57 and 58 were reprinted imperf. in 1887. See note after No. 37.

Imperf.

50b A7 1c 275.00
51a A7 2c 340.00
52a A7 4c 340.00
53b A7 5c yel grn, *pale bl* 275.00
55b A13 10c 340.00
56b A13 15c 340.00

1872-75 *Perf. 14x13½*

Larger Numerals

60 A14 10c bis, *rose* ('75) 290.00 9.50
 a. Cliché of 15c in plate of 10c *4,250.* *4,600.*
 b. Pair, #60, 60a *8,750.* *11,000.*
61 A14 15c bister ('73) 310.00 3.50
62 A14 30c brn, *yelsh* 550.00 5.75
63 A14 80c rose, *pnksh* 650.00 11.00
 Nos. 60-63 (4) 1,800. 29.75

Imperf.

62a A14 30c 450.00
63a A14 80c 600.00

Peace and Commerce ("Type Sage") — A15

Type I. The "N" of "INV" is under the "B" of "REPUBLIQUE."

Type II. The "N" of "INV" is under the "U" of "REPUBLIQUE."

1876-78 *Perf. 14x13½*

Type I

64 A15 1c grn, *grnsh* 150.00 65.00
65 A15 2c grn, *grnsh* 1,450. 200.00
66 A15 4c grn, *grnsh* 150.00 45.00
67 A15 5c grn, *grnsh* 675.00 40.00
68 A15 10c grn, *grnsh* 875.00 20.00
69 A15 15c gray lil, *grysh* 875.00 16.00
70 A15 20c red brn, *straw* 550.00 16.00
71 A15 20c bl, *bluish* *27,500.*
72 A15 25c ultra, *bluish* *8,100.* 47.50
73 A15 30c brn, *yelsh* 400.00 7.50
74 A15 40c red, *straw* ('78) 550.00 27.50
75 A15 75c car, *rose* 950.00 11.00
76 A15 1fr brnz grn, *straw* 875.00 8.75

No. 71 was never put into use.

The reprints of No. 71 are type II. They are imperforate or with forged perforation.

For overprints and surcharges see Offices in China Nos. 1-17, J7-J10, J20-J22, Offices in Egypt, Alexandria 1-15, Port Said 1-17, Offices in Turkish Empire 1-7, Cavalle 1-8, Dedeagh 1-8, Port Lagos 1-5, Vathy 1-9, Offices in Zanzibar 1-33, 50-54, Offices in Morocco 1-8, and Madagascar 14-27.

Imperf.

64a A15 1c 140.00
65a A15 2c 800.00
66a A15 4c 140.00
67a A15 5c 450.00
68a A15 10c 500.00
69a A15 15c 500.00
70a A15 20c 340.00
73a A15 30c 225.00
74a A15 40c 225.00
75a A15 75c 500.00
76a A15 1fr 340.00

Beware of French Colonies #24-29.

1876-77 *Perf. 14x13½*

Type II

77 A15 2c grn, *grnsh* 110.00 15.00
78 A15 5c grn, *grnsh* 26.00 .35
 a. Imperf. 150.00
79 A15 10c grn, *grnsh* 1,050. 200.00
80 A15 15c gray lil, *grysh* 6.50 1.50
81 A15 25c ultra, *bluish* 450.00 .75
 a. 25c blue, *bluish* 450.00 1.50
 b. Pair, types I & II *74,000.* *17,000.*
 c. Imperf. 275.00
82 A15 30c yel brn, *yelsh* 81.00 1.10
 a. 30c brown, *yellowish* 85.00 15.00
 b. Imperf. 400.00
83 A15 75c car, *rose* ('77) 1,900. 92.50
84 A15 1fr brnz grn, *straw* ('77) 125.00 6.00
 a. Imperf. 1,000.

Beware of French Colonies #31, 35.

1877-80

86 A15 1c blk, *lil bl* 5.00 .75
 a. 1c black, *gray blue* 5.00 .75
 b. Imperf. 57.50
87 A15 1c blk, *Prus bl* ('80) *11,000.* *4,000.*

Values for No. 87 are for copies with the perfs touching the design on at least one side.

88 A15 2c brn, *straw* 6.50 1.50
 a. 2c brown, *yellow* 7.50 2.25
 b. Imperf. 57.50
89 A15 3c yel, *straw* ('78) 175.00 35.00
 a. Imperf. 95.00
90 A15 4c claret, *lav* 6.50 1.50
 a. 4c vio brown, *lavender* 8.50 3.50
 b. Imperf. 57.50
91 A15 10c blk, *lavender* 32.50 .75
 a. 10c black, *rose lilac* 37.50 1.50
 b. 10c black, *lilac* 37.50 1.50
 c. Imperf. 57.50
92 A15 15c blue ('78) 24.00 .40
 a. Imperf. 81.00
 b. 15c blue, *bluish* 375.00 3.50
93 A15 25c blk, *red* ('78) 1,100. 20.00
 a. Imperf. 550.00
94 A15 35c blk, *yel* ('78) 500.00 27.50
 a. 35c blk, *yel org* 525.00 30.00
 b. Imperf. 225.00
95 A15 40c red, *straw* ('80) 95.00 1.40
 a. Imperf. 190.00
96 A15 5fr vio, *lav* 450.00 65.00
 a. 5fr red lilac, *lavender* 475.00 85.00
 b. Imperf. 600.00

Beware of French Colonies #38-40, 42, 44.

1879-90

97 A15 3c gray, *grysh* ('80) 4.50 1.40
 a. Imperf. 57.50
98 A15 20c red, *yel grn* 35.00 3.50
 a. 20c red, *deep green* ('84) 52.50 5.00
 b. Imperf. 85.00
99 A15 25c yel, *straw* 325.00 3.50
 a. Imperf. 225.00
100 A15 25c blk, *pale rose* ('86) 65.00 .75
 a. Imperf. 110.00
101 A15 50c rose, *rose* ('90) 190.00 2.25
 a. 50c carmine, *rose* 190.00 2.25
102 A15 75c dp vio, *org* ('90) 190.00 27.50
 a. 75c deep violet, *yellow* 210.00 35.00
 Nos. 97-102 (6) 809.50 38.90

Beware of French Colonies #43.

1892

Quadrille Paper

103 A15 15c blue 13.50 .30
 a. Imperf. 190.00

1898-1900

Ordinary Paper

104 A15 5c yellow green 20.00 1.50
 a. Imperf. 75.00

Type I

105 A15 5c yellow green 15.00 1.50
 a. Imperf. 450.00
106 A15 10c blk, *lavender* 22.50 2.25
 a. Imperf. 190.00
107 A15 50c car, *rose* 200.00 27.50
108 A15 2fr brn, *azure* ('00) 110.00 32.50
 b. Imperf. *2,200.*
 Nos. 104-108 (5) 367.50 65.25

See No. 226.

Reprints of A15, type II, were made in 1887 and left imperf. See note after No. 37. Value for set of 27, $3,300.

Liberty, Equality, Fraternity
A16

"The Rights of Man"
A17

Liberty and Peace
A18

1900-29 *Perf. 14x13½*

109 A16 1c gray .55 .35
110 A16 2c violet brn .75 .25
111 A16 3c orange .50 .50
 a. 3c red 17.00 5.50
112 A16 4c yellow brn 2.25 1.40
113 A16 5c green 1.75 .35
 b. Booklet pane of 10 300.00
114 A16 7½c lilac ('26) .40 .40
115 A16 10c lilac ('29) 3.40 .35
116 A17 10c carmine 22.50 1.50
 a. Numerals printed separately 20.00 8.50
117 A17 15c orange 6.75 .35
118 A17 20c brown vio 52.50 7.50
119 A17 25c blue 100.00 1.50
 a. Numerals printed separately 100.00 7.50
120 A17 30c violet 67.50 4.25
121 A18 40c red & pale bl 13.00 .60
122 A18 45c green & bl ('06) 24.00 1.60
123 A18 50c bis brn & lav 92.50 1.10
124 A18 60c vio & ultra ('20) .75 .75

125	A18	1fr claret & ol grn	25.00	.60
126	A18	2fr gray vio & yel	700.00	65.00
127	A18	2fr org & pale bl ('20)	40.00	.35
128	A18	3fr vio & bl ('25)	22.50	5.75
129	A18	3fr brt vio & rose ('27)	45.00	1.60
130	A18	5fr dk bl & buff	77.50	3.50
131	A18	10fr grn & red ('26)	100.00	12.50
132	A18	20fr mag & grn ('26)	160.00	29.00
		Nos. 109-132 (24)	1,559.	141.05

In the 10c and 25c values, the first printings show the numerals to have been impressed by a second operation, whereas, in later printings, the numerals were inserted in the plates. Two operations were used for all 20c and 30c, and one operation for the 15c.

No. 114 was issued precanceled only. Values for precanceled stamps in first column are for those which have not been through the post and have original gum. Values in the second column are for postally used, gumless stamps.

See Off. in China #34, 40-44, Off. in Crete 1-5, 10-15, Off. in Egypt, Alexandria 16-20, 26-30, 77, 84-86, Port Said 18-22, 28-32, 83, 90-92, Off. in Turkish Empire 21-26, 31-33, Cavalle 9, Dedeagh 9.

For overprints & surcharge see #197, 246, C1-C2, M1, P7. Off. in China 57, 62-65, 71, 73, 75, 83-85, J14, J27, Off. in Crete 17-20, Off. in Egypt, Alexandria 31-32, 34-35, 40-48, 57-64, 66, 71-73, Port Said 33, 35-40, 43, 46-57, 59, 65-71, 73, 78-80, Off. in Turkish Empire 35-38, 47-49, Cavalle 13-15, Dedeagh 16-18, Off. in Zanzibar 39, 45-49, 55, Off. in Morocco 11-15, 20-22, 26-29, 35-41, 49-54, 72-76, 84-85, 87-89, B6.

Imperf.

109a	A16	1c	50.00	
110a	A16	2c	50.00	55.00
111b	A16	3c	50.00	
112a	A16	4c	150.00	125.00
113a	A16	5c	67.50	
116b	A17	10c #116 or 116a	225.00	*125.00*
117a	A17	15c	160.00	*160.00*
119b	A17	25c #119 or 119a	475.00	
121a	A18	40c	175.00	140.00
122a	A18	45c	275.00	
123a	A18	50c	325.00	350.00
124a	A18	60c	550.00	
125a	A18	1fr	160.00	210.00
126a	A18	2fr	*1,200.*	
127a	A18	2fr	450.00	
128a	A18	3fr	675.00	450.00
129a	A18	3fr	425.00	
130a	A18	5fr	800.00	

Nos. 112a and 126a are valued without gum.

Flat Plate & Rotary Press

The following stamps were printed by both flat plate and rotary press: Nos. 109-113, 144-146, 163, 166, 168, 170, 177-178, 185, 192 and P7.

A19

Sower A20

1902

133	A19	10c rose red	22.50	.90
134	A19	15c pale red	8.50	.35
135	A19	20c brown violet	70.00	12.00
136	A19	25c blue	75.00	1.60
137	A19	30c lilac	200.00	12.50
		Nos. 133-137 (5)	376.00	27.35

Imperf

133a	A19	10c rose red	325.00	175.00
134a	A19	15c pale red	325.00	160.00
135a	A19	20c brown violet	400.00	
136a	A19	25c blue	600.00	
137a	A19	30c lilac	800.00	

See Off. in China #35-39, Off. in Crete 6-10, Off. in Egypt, Alexandria 21-25, 81-82, Port Said 23-27, 87-88, Off. in Turkish Empire 26-30, Cavalle 10-11, Dedeagh 10-11.

For overprints and surcharges see #M2, Off. in China 45, 58-61, 66-70, 76-82, J15-J16, J28-J30, Off. in Crete 16, Off. in Egypt, Alexandria 33, 36-39, 49-50, 52-56, 65, 67-70, B1-B4, Port Said 34, 41-42, 44-45, 57, 60-64, 77, 74-77, B1-B4, Off. in Turkish Empire 34, 39, Cavalle 12, Dedeagh 15, Off. in Zanzibar 40-44, 56-59, Off. in Morocco 16-19, 30-34, 42-48, 77-83, 86, B1-B5, B7, B9.

1903-38

138	A20	10c rose	6.50	.20
139	A20	15c slate grn	3.50	.20
b.		Booklet pane of 10	300.00	
140	A20	20c violet brn	55.00	1.40
141	A20	25c dull blue	60.00	1.10
142	A20	30c violet	140.00	4.75
143	A20	45c lt violet ('26)	5.00	1.50
144	A20	50c dull blue ('21)	22.50	.90
145	A20	50c gray grn ('26)	5.50	.90
146	A20	50c vermilion ('26)	1.10	.20
a.		Booklet pane of 10	40.00	
147	A20	50c grnsh bl ('38)	1.10	.55
148	A20	60c lt vio ('24)	5.00	1.25
149	A20	65c rose ('24)	2.25	1.10
150	A20	65c gray grn ('27)	5.75	1.60
151	A20	75c rose lil ('26)	4.50	.45
152	A20	80c ver ('25)	22.50	6.50
153	A20	85c ver ('24)	11.00	1.90
154	A20	1fr dull blue ('26)	5.00	.55
		Nos. 138-154 (17)	356.20	25.05
		Set, never hinged	900.00	

See Nos. 941, 942A. For surcharges and overprints see Nos. 229-230, 232-233, 236, 256, B25, B29, B32, B36, B40, M3-M4, M6, Offices in Turkish Empire 46, 54.

Imperf.

138a	A20	10c	150.00	
139a	A20	15c	125.00	75.00
140a	A20	20c	300.00	140.00
141a	A20	25c	275.00	
142a	A20	30c	550.00	
144a	A20	50c	100.00	
145a	A20	50c	67.50	
146b	A20	50c	45.00	
147a	A20	50c	40.00	
149a	A20	65c	175.00	
151a	A20	75c	400.00	
154a	A20	1fr	*800.00*	

No. 146b is valued without gum.

Ground A21

No Ground A22

1906, Apr. 13

With Ground Under Feet of Figure

155	A21	10c red	2.25	1.50
a.		Imperf., pair, without gum	140.00	
		As "a," with gum	225.00	

1906-37

TEN AND THIRTY-FIVE CENTIMES

Type I — Numerals and letters of the inscriptions thin.

Type II — Numerals and letters thicker.

No Ground Under the Feet

156	A22	1c olive bis ('33)	.20	.20
157	A22	2c dk green ('33)	.20	.20
158	A22	3c ver ('33)	.20	.20
159	A22	5c green ('07)	1.25	.20
a.		Imperf., pair	18.00	14.00
b.		Booklet pane of 10	75.00	
160	A22	5c orange ('21)	1.00	.20
a.		Booklet pane of 10	30.00	
161	A22	5c cerise ('34)	.25	.20
162	A22	10c red (II) ('07)	1.25	.20
a.		Imperf., pair	20.00	
b.		10c red (I) ('06)	6.50	.80
c.		Booklet pane of 10 (I)	125.00	
d.		Booklet pane of 10 (II)	75.00	
e.		Booklet pane of 6 (II)	240.00	
163	A22	10c grn (II) ('21)	.45	.20
a.		10c green (I) ('27)	29.00	29.00
b.		Booklet pane of 10 (II, "Phena")	150.00	
c.		Booklet pane of 10 (I, "Mineraline")	3,200.	
164	A22	10c ultra ('32)	1.25	.20
165	A22	15c red brn ('26)	.25	.20
a.		Booklet pane of 10	27.50	
166	A22	20c brown	2.50	.20
a.		Imperf., pair	42.50	50.00
167	A22	20c red vio ('26)	.25	.20
a.		Booklet pane of 10	7.50	
168	A22	25c blue	2.25	.20
a.		Booklet pane of 10	37.50	
b.		Imperf., pair	30.00	42.50
169	A22	25c lt brown ('27)	.25	.20
170	A22	30c orange	11.00	1.10
a.		Imperf., pair	110.00	110.00
171	A22	30c red ('21)	5.75	1.40
172	A22	30c cerise ('25)	.95	.55
a.		Booklet pane of 10	13.50	
173	A22	30c lt blue ('25)	3.25	.35
a.		Booklet pane of 10	35.00	
174	A22	30c cop red ('37)	.25	.20
a.		Booklet pane of 10	9.00	
175	A22	35c vio (II) ('26)	6.50	.75
a.		Imperf., pair	100.00	110.00
b.		35c violet (I) ('06)	100.00	4.25
c.		As "b," Imperf., pair, without gum	*450.00*	
176	A22	35c green ('37)	.45	.25
177	A22	40c olive ('25)	1.50	.35
b.		Booklet pane of 10	30.00	
178	A22	40c ver ('26)	2.25	.35
a.		Booklet pane of 10	25.00	
179	A22	40c violet ('27)	1.60	.75
180	A22	40c lt ultra ('28)	1.10	.35
181	A22	1.05fr ver ('25)	7.50	3.50
182	A22	1.10fr cerise ('27)	9.00	1.90
183	A22	1.40fr cerise ('26)	15.00	17.00
184	A22	2fr Prus grn ('31)	11.00	1.10
		Nos. 156-184 (29)	88.65	32.70
		Set, never hinged	140.00	

The 10c and 35c, type I, were slightly retouched by adding thin white outlines to the sack of grain, the underside of the right arm and the back of the skirt. It is difficult to distinguish the retouches except on clearly-printed copies. The white outlines were made stronger on the stamps of type II.

Stamps of types A16, A18, A20 and A22 were printed in 1916-20 on paper of poor quality, usually grayish and containing bits of fiber. This is called G. C. (Grande Consommation) paper.

#160, 162b, 163, 175b, 176 exist imperf.

See #241-241b. For surcharges & overprint see #227-228, 234, 238, 240, 400, B1, B24, B28, B31, B35, B37, B39, B41, M5, P8, Off. in Turkish Empire 40-45, 52, 55.

Louis Pasteur — A23

1923-26

185	A23	10c green	.55	.20
a.		Booklet pane of 10	15.00	
186	A23	15c green ('24)	1.25	.20
187	A23	20c green ('26)	2.40	.75
188	A23	30c red	.75	*1.25*
189	A23	30c green ('26)	.55	.35
190	A23	45c red ('24)	1.60	1.60
191	A23	50c blue	3.75	.35
192	A23	75c blue ('24)	3.25	.90
a.		Imperf., pair	225.00	
193	A23	90c red ('26)	9.50	2.75
194	A23	1fr blue ('25)	18.00	.35
195	A23	1.25fr blue ('26)	17.00	7.50
196	A23	1.50fr blue ('26)	4.50	.20
		Nos. 185-196 (12)	63.10	16.40
		Set, never hinged	125.00	

Nos. 185, 188 and 191 were issued to commemorate the cent. of the birth of Pasteur.

For surcharges and overprint see Nos. 231, 235, 257, B26, B30, B33, C4.

No. 125 Overprinted in Blue

1923, June 15

197	A18	1fr claret & ol grn	325.00	350.00
		Never hinged	550.00	

Allegory of Olympic Games at Paris A24

The Trophy A25

Milo of Crotona — A26

Victorious Athlete — A27

1924, Apr. 1 ***Perf. 14x13½, 13½x14***

198 A24 10c gray grn & yel grn 1.60 .80
199 A25 25c rose & dk rose 2.25 .65
200 A26 30c brn red & blk 7.50 9.50
201 A27 50c ultra & dk bl 22.50 3.50
Nos. 198-201 (4) 33.85 14.45
Set, never hinged 100.00

8th Olympic Games, Paris. Exist imperf.

Pierre de Ronsard (1524-85), Poet — A28

1924, Oct. 6 ***Perf. 14x13½***

219 A28 75c blue, *bluish* 1.60 1.25
Never hinged 2.50

"Light and Liberty" Allegory A29

Majolica Vase — A30

Potter Decorating Vase — A31

Terrace of Château A32

1924-25 ***Perf. 14x13½, 13½x14***

220 A29 10c dk grn & yel ('25) .45 .35
221 A30 15c ind & grn ('25) .45 .45
a. Imperf. 375.00
Never hinged 750.00
222 A31 25c vio brn & garnet .70 .35
223 A32 25c gray bl & vio ('25) .70 .40
a. Imperf. 425.00
Never hinged 775.00
224 A31 75c indigo & ultra 2.25 1.40
225 A29 75c dk bl & lt bl ('25) 12.50 4.25
a. Imperf. 375.00
Never hinged 600.00
Nos. 220-225 (6) 17.05 7.20
Set, never hinged 35.00

Intl. Exhibition of Decorative Modern Arts at Paris, 1925.

Philatelic Exhibition Issue
Souvenir Sheet

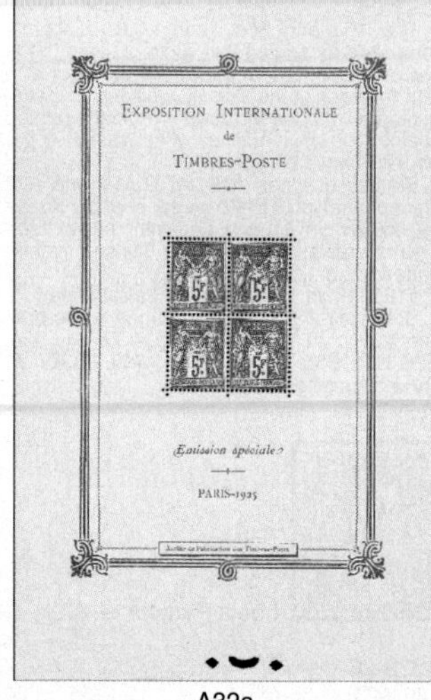
A32a

1925, May 2 ***Perf. 14x13½***

226 A32a Sheet of 4, A15 II 750.00 750.00
Never hinged 2,250.
a. Imperf. sheet *3,000.* 1,400.
Never hinged *4,750.*
b. 5fr carmine, perf. 75.00 75.00
c. 5fr carmine, imperf. 525.00
Never hinged 800.00

These were on sale only at the Intl. Phil. Exhib., Paris, May, 1925. Size: 140x220mm.

Nos. 148-149, 152-153, 173, 175, 181, 183, 192, 195 Surcharged

1926-27

227 A22 25c on 30c lt bl .20 .20
228 A22 25c on 35c violet .20 .20
a. Double surcharge 350.00
229 A20 50c on 60c lt vio ('27) .70 .75
230 A20 50c on 65c rose ('27) .35 .35
a. Inverted surcharge *1,150.* *1,125.*
231 A23 50c on 75c blue 1.10 .50
232 A20 50c on 80c ver ('27) .70 .70
233 A20 50c on 85c ver ('27) 1.40 .35
234 A22 50c on 1.05fr ver .70 .35
235 A23 50c on 1.25fr blue 1.40 .90
236 A20 55c on 60c lt vio 100.00 35.00
238 A22 90c on 1.05fr ver ('27) 1.40 1.75
240 A22 1.10fr on 1.40fr cer .70 .70
Nos. 227-240 (12) 108.85 41.75
Set, never hinged 240.00

Issue dates: Nos. 229-230, 232-234, 1927.

No. 236 is known only precanceled. See second note after No. 132.

Nos. 229, 230, 234, 238 and 240 have three bars instead of two. The 55c surcharge has thinner, larger numerals and a rounded "c." Width, including bars, is 17mm, instead of 13mm.

The 55c was used only precanceled at the Louvre in Paris, August 1926.

Strasbourg Exhibition Issue
Souvenir Sheet

A32b

1927, June 4

241 A32b Sheet of 2 650.00 600.00
Never hinged 1,450.
a. 5fr light ultra (A22) 140.00 140.00
Never hinged 275.00
b. 10fr carmine rose (A22) 140.00 140.00
Never hinged 275.00

Sold at the Strasbourg Philatelic Exhibition as souvenirs. Size: 111x140mm.

Marcelin Berthelot (1827-1907), Chemist and Statesman — A33

1927, Sept. 7

242 A33 90c dull rose 1.10 .35
Never hinged 1.75

For surcharge see No. C3.

Lafayette, Washington, S. S. Paris and Airplane "Spirit of St. Louis" — A34

1927, Sept. 15

243 A34 90c dull red 1.00 .70
a. Value omitted 1,700.
244 A34 1.50fr deep blue 3.00 1.10
a. Value omitted 1,200.
Set, never hinged 5.75

Visit of American Legionnaires to France, September, 1927. Exist imperf.

Joan of Arc — A35

1929, Mar.

245 A35 50c dull blue 1.00 .20
Never hinged 1.50
a. Booklet pane of 10 120.00
b. Imperf. 95.00

500th anniv. of the relief of Orleans by the French forces led by Joan of Arc.

No. 127 Overprinted in Blue

1929, May 18

246 A18 2fr org & pale bl *425.00 425.00*
Never hinged 725.00

Sold exclusively at the Intl. Phil. Exhib., Le Havre, May, 1929, for 7fr, which included a 5fr admission ticket.

Excellent counterfeits of No. 246 exist.

Reims Cathedral — A37

Die I, II, III

Die IV

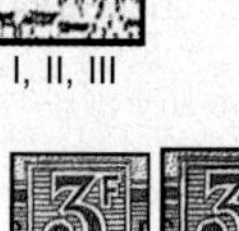
Die I Die II Die III

Die I — The window of the 1st turret on the left is made of 2 lines. The horizontal line of the frame surrounding 3F is not continuous.

Die II — Same as Die I but the line under 3F is continuous.

Die III — Same as Die II but there is a deeply cut line separating 3 and F.

Die IV — Same as Die III but the window of the first turret on the left is made of three lines.

Mont-Saint-Michel — A38

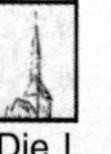
Die I

Die II

Die I — The line at the top of the spire is broken.

Die II — The line is unbroken.

Port of La Rochelle — A39

Dies I & II

Die III

Die I — The top of the "E" of "POSTES" has a serif. The oval of shading inside the "0" of "10 fr" and the outer oval are broken at their bases.

Die II — The same top has no serif. Interior and exterior of "0" broken as in Die I.

Die III — Top of "E" has no serif. Interior and exterior of "0" complete.

Pont du Gard, Nimes A40

Dies I & II

Die III

Die I — Shading of the first complete arch in the left middle tier is made of horizontal lines. Size 36x20¾mm. Perf. 13½.
Die II — Same, size 35½x21mm. Perf. 11.
Die III — Shading of same arch is made of three diagonal lines. Thin paper. Perf. 13.

1929-33 Engr. *Perf. 11, 13, 13½*

247 A37 3fr dk gray ('30) (I) 62.50 2.10
Never hinged 100.00
247A A37 3fr dk gray ('30) (II) 100.00 3.00
Never hinged 150.00
247B A37 3fr dk gray ('30) (III) 325.00 17.50
Never hinged 475.00
248 A37 3fr bluish sl ('31) (IV) 62.50 2.10
Never hinged 110.00
249 A38 5fr brn ('30) (I) 16.00 1.00
Never hinged 26.00
250 A38 5fr brn ('31) (II) 17.50 2.75
Never hinged 27.50
251 A39 10fr lt ultra (I) 75.00 10.00
Never hinged 125.00
251A A39 10fr ultra (II) 140.00 21.00
Never hinged 200.00
252 A39 10fr dk ultra ('31) (III) 70.00 4.50
Never hinged 110.00
253 A40 20fr red brown (I) 200.00 35.00
Never hinged 325.00
254 A40 20fr brt red brn ('33) (II) 700.00 225.00
Never hinged 1,050.
254A A40 20fr org brn ('31) (III) 160.00 30.00
Never hinged 275.00
Nos. 247-254A (12) 1,928. 353.95

View of Algiers A41

1929, Jan. 1 Typo.

255 A41 50c blue & rose red 1.60 .35
Never hinged 3.25

Cent. of the 1st French settlement in Algeria.

Nos. 146 and 196 Overprinted

1930, Apr. 23 *Perf. 14x13½*

256 A20 50c vermilion 1.75 1.40
257 A23 1.50fr blue 15.00 11.00
Set, never hinged 29.00

Intl. Labor Bureau, 48th Congress, Paris.

Colonial Exposition Issue

Fachi Woman — A42

French Colonials A43

1930-31 Typo. *Perf. 14x13½*

258 A42 15c gray black .80 .25
259 A42 40c dark brown 1.10 .25
260 A42 50c dark red .50 .20
a. Booklet pane of 10 12.50
261 A42 1.50fr deep blue 8.50 .35

Perf. 13½

Photo.

262 A43 1.50fr dp blue ('31) 32.50 1.40
Nos. 258-262 (5) 43.40 2.45
Set, never hinged 77.50

No. 260 has two types: type 1 shows four short downward hairlines near top of head, type 2 has no lines. Booklet stamps are type 2.

Arc de Triomphe A44

1931 Engr. *Perf. 13*

263 A44 2fr red brown 32.50 .70
Never hinged 45.00

Peace with Olive Branch — A45

1932-39 Typo. *Perf. 14x13½*

264 A45 30c dp green .70 .25
265 A45 40c brt violet .25 .20
266 A45 45c yellow brown 1.50 .75
267 A45 50c rose red .20 .20
a. Imperf., pair 140.00
b. Booklet pane of 10 5.50
268 A45 55c dull vio ('37) .50 .20
269 A45 60c ocher ('37) .20 .20
270 A45 65c violet brown .25 .20
271 A45 65c brt ultra ('37) .25 .20
a. Booklet pane of 10 7.00
272 A45 75c olive green .20 .20
273 A45 80c orange ('38) .20 .20
274 A45 90c dk red 25.00 1.40
275 A45 90c brt green ('38) .20 .20
276 A45 90c ultra ('38) .45 .20
a. Booklet pane of 10 8.50
277 A45 1fr orange 2.50 .20
278 A45 1fr rose pink ('38) 2.10 .20
279 A45 1.25fr brown ol 62.50 2.75
280 A45 1.25fr rose car ('39) 1.10 1.10
281 A45 1.40fr brt red vio ('39) 4.25 3.50
282 A45 1.50fr deep blue .20 .20
283 A45 1.75fr magenta 3.75 .35
Nos. 264-283 (20) 106.30 12.70
Set, never hinged 200.00

The 50c is found in 4 types, differing in the lines below belt and size of "c."
For surcharges and overprints see Nos. 298, 333, 401-403, 405-409, M7-M9, S1.

Le Puy-en-Velay — A46

1933 Engr. *Perf. 13*

290 A46 90c rose 2.25 .70
Never hinged 3.50

Aristide Briand A47

Paul Doumer A48

Victor Hugo — A49

1933, Dec. 11 Typo. *Perf. 14x13½*

291 A47 30c blue green 12.50 6.00
292 A48 75c red violet 25.00 .70
293 A49 1.25fr claret 4.25 1.50
Nos. 291-293 (3) 41.75 8.20
Set, never hinged 70.00

Dove and Olive Branch A50

Joseph Marie Jacquard A51

1934, Feb. 20

294 A50 1.50fr ultra 40.00 11.00
Never hinged 75.00

1934, Mar. 14 Engr. *Perf. 14x13*

295 A51 40c blue 2.00 .70
Never hinged 3.50

Jacquard (1752-1834), inventor of an improved loom for figured weaving.

Jacques Cartier A52

1934, July 18 *Perf. 13*

296 A52 75c rose lilac 25.00 1.40
297 A52 1.50fr blue 45.00 2.75
Set, never hinged 150.00

Cartier's discovery of Canada, 400th anniv.

No. 279 Surcharged

1934, Nov. *Perf. 14x13½*

298 A45 50c on 1.25fr brn ol 3.00 .35
Never hinged 5.00

Catalogue values for unused stamps in this section, from this point to the end of the section, are for Never Hinged items.

Breton River Scene A53

1935, Feb. Engr. *Perf. 13*

299 A53 2fr blue green 50.00 .70

S. S. Normandie A54

1935, Apr.

300 A54 1.50fr dark blue 17.50 1.10
a. 1.50fr blue ('36) 90.00 12.50
b. 1.50fr blue green ('36) — 12,500.
Hinged 17,500.
c. 1.50fr turquoise ('36) 300.00 32.50
Hinged 190.00

Maiden voyage of the transatlantic steamship, the "Normandie."

Benjamin Delessert A55

1935, May 20

301 A55 75c blue green 27.50 .70

Opening of the International Savings Bank Congress, May 20, 1935.

View of St. Trophime at Arles A56

Victor Hugo (1802-85) A57

1935, May 3

302 A56 3.50fr dark brown 45.00 2.75

1935, May 30 *Perf. 14x13*

303 A57 1.25fr magenta 5.00 1.40

Cardinal Richelieu — A58

Jacques Callot — A59

1935, June 12 ***Perf. 13***
304 A58 1.50fr deep rose 37.50 1.10

Tercentenary of the founding of the French Academy by Cardinal Richelieu.

1935, Nov. ***Perf. 14x13***
305 A59 75c red 13.00 .35

300th anniv. of the death of Jacques Callot, engraver.

André Marie Ampère (1775-1836), Scientist, by Louis Boilly — A60

1936, Feb. 27 ***Perf. 13***
306 A60 75c brown 27.50 1.40

Windmill at Fontvielle, Immortalized by Daudet — A61

1936, Apr. 27
307 A61 2fr ultra 4.00 .35

70th anniv. of the publication, in 1866, of Alphonse Daudet's "Lettres de mon Moulin".

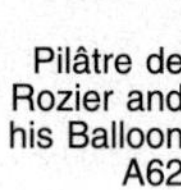

Pilâtre de Rozier and his Balloon A62

1936, June 4
308 A62 75c Prus blue 25.00 2.10

150th anniversary of the death of Jean Francois Pilâtre de Rozier, balloonist.

Rouget de Lisle — A63

"La Marseillaise" — A64

1936, June 27
309 A63 20c Prus green 3.50 1.40
310 A64 40c dark brown 7.00 2.00

Cent. of the death of Claude Joseph Rouget de Lisle, composer of "La Marseillaise."

Canadian War Memorial at Vimy Ridge A65

1936, July 26
311 A65 75c henna brown 15.00 1.40
312 A65 1.50fr dull blue 22.50 5.75

Unveiling of the Canadian War Memorial at Vimy Ridge, July 26, 1936.

A66

Jean Léon Jaurès A67

1936, July 30
313 A66 40c red brown 3.50 .70
314 A67 1.50fr ultra 20.00 2.10

Assassination of Jean Léon Jaurès (1859-1914), socialist and politician.

Herald — A68

Allegory of Exposition A69

1936, Sept. 15 **Typo.** ***Perf. 14x13½***

315	A68	20c brt violet	.35	.35
316	A68	30c Prus green	2.10	1.10
317	A68	40c ultra	1.40	.35
318	A68	50c red orange	1.40	.20
319	A69	90c carmine	16.00	5.00
320	A69	1.50fr ultra	47.50	2.50
		Nos. 315-320 (6)	68.75	9.50

Publicity for the 1937 Paris Exposition.

"Peace" A70

1936, Oct. 1 **Engr.** ***Perf. 13***
321 A70 1.50fr blue 20.00 2.75

Skiing A71

1937, Jan. 18
322 A71 1.50fr dark blue 10.00 1.40

Intl. Ski Meet at Chamonix-Mont Blanc.

Pierre Corneille, Portrait by Charles Le Brun — A72

1937, Feb. 15
323 A72 75c brown carmine 2.25 .75

300th anniv. of the publication of "Le Cid."

Paris Exposition Issue

Exposition Allegory A73

1937, Mar. 15
324 A73 1.50fr turq blue 2.50 .70

Jean Mermoz (1901-36), Aviator A74

Memorial to Mermoz — A75

1937, Apr. 22
325 A74 30c dk slate green .50 .35
326 A75 3fr dark violet 8.00 2.25
a. 3fr violet 8.75 3.00

Electric Train A76

Streamlined Locomotive A77

1937, May 31
327 A76 30c dk green .85 .75
328 A77 1.50fr dk ultra 9.50 5.00

13th International Railroad Congress.

Intl. Philatelic Exhibition Issue
Souvenir Sheet

Ceres Type A1 of 1849-50 — A77a

1937, June 18 **Typo.** ***Perf. 14x13½***

329	A77a Sheet of 4		450.00	200.00
	Hinged in margins		250.00	
a.	5c ultra & dark brown		60.00	45.00
b.	15c red & rose red		60.00	45.00
c.	30c ultra & rose red		60.00	45.00
d.	50c red & dark brown		60.00	45.00
e.	Sheet of 4, imperf		2,100.	
	Hinged in margins		1,600.	

Issued in sheets measuring 150x220mm.

The sheets were sold only at the exhibition in Paris, a ticket of admission being required for each sheet purchased.

René Descartes, by Frans Hals — A78

1937, June **Engr.** ***Perf. 13***

Inscribed "Discours sur la Méthode"

330 A78 90c copper red 2.10 .75

Inscribed "Discours de la Méthode"

331 A78 90c copper red 6.25 1.10

3rd centenary of the publication of "Discours de la Méthode" by René Descartes.

France Congratulating USA — A79

1937, Sept. 17
332 A79 1.75fr ultra 3.00 1.40

150th anniv. of the US Constitution.

No. 277 Surcharged in Red

1937, Oct. ***Perf. 14x13½***
333 A45 80c on 1fr orange .35 .20
a. Inverted surcharge 1,100.

Mountain Road at Iseran A80

1937, Oct. 4 **Engr.** ***Perf. 13***
334 A80 90c dark green 2.10 .20

Issued in commemoration of the opening of the mountain road at Iseran, Savoy.

Ceres — A81

1938-40 **Typo.** ***Perf. 14x13½***

335	A81	1.75fr dk ultra	.75	.35
336	A81	2fr car rose ('39)	.35	.20
337	A81	2.25fr ultra ('39)	10.00	.75
338	A81	2.50fr green ('39)	1.75	.35
339	A81	2.50fr vio blue ('40)	.75	.35
340	A81	3fr rose lilac ('39)	.75	.20
		Nos. 335-340 (6)	14.35	2.20

For surcharges see Nos. 397-399.

Léon Gambetta (1838-82), Lawyer and Statesman — A82

1938, Apr. 2 **Engr.** ***Perf. 13***
341 A82 55c dark violet .35 .35

Arc de Triomphe of Orange A82a

Miners A83

Keep and Gate of Vincennes A86

Palace of the Popes, Avignon A84

Medieval Walls of Carcassonne — A85

Port of St. Malo — A87

1938

342	A82a	2fr	brown black	.75	.35
343	A83	2.15fr	violet brn	5.00	.35
344	A84	3fr	car brown	16.00	2.75
345	A85	5fr	deep ultra	.80	.25
346	A86	10fr	brown, *blue*	1.40	.75
347	A87	20fr	dk blue green	55.00	11.50
	Nos. 342-347 (6)			78.95	15.95

For surcharges see Nos. 410-414.

Clément Ader, Air Pioneer A88

1938, June 16

348	A88 50fr ultra (thin paper)		100.00	55.00
	Hinged		70.00	
a.	50fr dark ultra (thick paper)		110.00	50.00
	Hinged		75.00	

Soccer Players A89

1938, June 1

349 A89 1.75fr dark ultra 18.00 9.50

World Cup Soccer Championship.

Costume of Champagne Region — A90

Jean de La Fontaine — A91

1938, June 13

350 A90 1.75fr dark ultra 4.25 2.10

Tercentenary of the birth of Dom Pierre Pérignon, discoverer of the champagne process.

1938, July 8

351 A91 55c dk blue green .75 .75

Jean de La Fontaine (1621-1695) the fabulist.

Seal of Friendship and Peace, Victoria Tower and Arc de Triomphe A92

1938, July 19

352 A92 1.75fr ultra .75 .75

Visit of King George VI and Queen Elizabeth of Great Britain to France.

Mercury A93

Self-portrait A95

1938-42 Typo. *Perf. 14x13½*

353	A93	1c	dark brown ('39)	.20	.20
354	A93	2c	slate grn ('39)	.20	.20
355	A93	5c	rose	.20	.20
356	A93	10c	ultra	.20	.20
357	A93	15c	red orange	.20	.20
358	A93	15c	orange brn ('39)	.75	.20
359	A93	20c	red violet	.20	.20
360	A93	25c	blue green	.20	.20
361	A93	30c	rose red ('39)	.20	.20
362	A93	40c	dk violet ('39)	.20	.20
363	A93	45c	lt green ('39)	.60	.35
364	A93	50c	deep blue ('39)	2.50	.35
365	A93	50c	dk green ('41)	.35	.20
366	A93	50c	grnsh blue ('42)	.20	.20
367	A93	60c	red orange ('39)	.20	.20
368	A93	70c	magenta ('39)	.20	.20
369	A93	75c	dk org brn ('39)	5.25	2.25
	Nos. 353-369 (17)			11.85	5.75

No. 366 exists imperforate. See Nos. 455-458. For overprints and surcharge see #404, 499-502.

1939, Mar. 15 Engr. *Perf. 13*

370 A95 2.25fr Prussian blue 4.50 2.10

Paul Cézanne (1839-1906), painter.

Georges Clemenceau and Battleship Clemenceau — A96

1939, Apr. 18

371 A96 90c ultra .55 .35

Laying of the keel of the warship "Clemenceau," Jan. 17, 1939.

Statue of Liberty, French Pavilion, Trylon and Perisphere A97

1939-40

372 A97 2.25fr ultra 10.00 5.00
373 A97 2.50fr ultra ('40) 12.50 6.50

New York World's Fair.

Joseph Nicéphore Niepce and Louis Jacques Mandé Daguerre A98

1939, Apr. 24

374 A98 2.25fr dark blue 12.50 5.00

Centenary of photography.

Iris — A99

Pumping Station at Marly A100

1939-44 Typo. *Perf. 14x13½*

375	A99	80c	red brown ('40)	.20	.20
376	A99	80c	yellow grn ('44)	.20	.20
377	A99	1fr	green	.80	.20
378	A99	1fr	crimson ('40)	.40	.35
a.			Booklet pane of 10	7.50	
379	A99	1fr	grnsh blue ('44)	.20	.20
380	A99	1.20fr	violet ('44)	.20	.20
381	A99	1.30fr	ultra ('40)	.20	.20
382	A99	1.50fr	red org ('41)	.20	.20
383	A99	1.50fr	henna brn ('44)	.20	.20
384	A99	2fr	violet brn ('44)	.20	.20
385	A99	2.40fr	car rose ('44)	.20	.20
386	A99	3fr	orange ('44)	.20	.20
387	A99	4fr	ultra ('44)	.20	.20
	Nos. 375-387 (13)			3.40	2.75

1939 Engr. *Perf. 13*

388 A100 2.25fr brt ultra 20.00 3.50

France's participation in the International Water Exposition at Liège.

St. Gregory of Tours — A101

1939, June 10

389 A101 90c red .55 .40

14th centenary of the birth of St. Gregory of Tours, historian and bishop.

"The Oath of the Tennis Court" by Jacques David A102

1939, June 20

390 A102 90c deep slate green 2.10 1.40

150th anniversary of French Revolution.

Cathedral of Strasbourg — A103

1939, June 23

391 A103 70c brown carmine .80 .75

500th anniv. of the completion of Strasbourg Cathedral.

Porte Chaussée, Verdun A104

1939, June 23

392 A104 90c black brown .80 .70

23rd anniv. of the Battle of Verdun.

View of Pau A105

1939, Aug. 25

393 A105 90c brt rose, *gray bl* .90 .40

Maid of Languedoc A106

Bridge at Lyons A107

1939

394 A106 70c black, *blue* .35 .35
395 A107 90c dull brown vio .55 .35

Imperforates

Nearly all French stamps issued from 1940 onward exist imperforate. Officially 20 sheets, ranging from 25 to 100 subjects, were left imperforate.

Georges Guynemer (1894-1917), World War I Ace — A108

1940, Nov. 7

396 A108 50fr ultra 9.75 7.25

Stamps of 1938-39 Surcharged in Carmine

1940-41 *Perf. 14x13½*

397 A81 1fr on 1.75fr dk ultra .20 .20
398 A81 1fr on 2.25fr ultra ('41) .20 .20
399 A81 1fr on 2.50fr grn ('41) .70 .35
Nos. 397-399 (3) 1.10 .75

Stamps of 1932-39 Surcharged in Carmine, Red (#408) or Black (#407)

1940-41 *Perf. 13, 14x13½*

400 A22 30c on 35c grn .20 .20
401 A45 50c on 55c dl vio .20 .20
a. Inverted surcharge 900.00
402 A45 50c on 65c brt ultra .20 .20
403 A45 50c on 75c ol grn .25 .20
404 A93 50c on 75c dk org brn .25 .20
405 A45 50c on 80c org .25 .20
406 A45 50c on 90c ultra .20 .20
a. Inverted surcharge 450.00
b. "05" instead of "50" *7,000.*
407 A45 1fr on 1.25fr rose car (Bk) .25 .20
408 A45 1fr on 1.40fr brt red vio (R) .25 .20
a. Double surcharge 1,100.
409 A45 1fr on 1.50fr dk bl .75 .35
410 A83 1fr on 2.15fr vio brn .20 .20
411 A85 2.50fr on 5fr dp ultra .25 .20
a. Double surcharge 325.00 125.00
412 A86 5fr on 10fr brn, *bl* 1.40 1.10
413 A87 10fr on 20fr dk bl grn 1.10 1.10
414 A88 20fr on 50fr dk ultra (#348a) 40.00 30.00
a. 20fr on 50fr ultra, thin paper (#348) 45.00 32.50
Nos. 400-414 (15) 45.75 34.75

Issued: #410, 1940; others, 1941.

Marshal Pétain A109

Frédéric Mistral A110

1941 *Perf. 13*

415 A109 40c red brown .25 .25
416 A109 80c turq blue .45 .45
417 A109 1fr red .25 .20
418 A109 2.50fr deep ultra 1.50 1.00
Nos. 415-418 (4) 2.45 1.90

1941, Feb. 20 *Perf. 14x13*

419 A110 1fr brown lake .20 .20

Issued in honor of Frédéric Mistral, poet and Nobel prize winner for literature in 1904.

Beaune Hospital A111

View of Angers A112

Ramparts of St. Louis, Aiguesmortes — A113

1941

420 A111 5fr brown black .25 .20
421 A112 10fr dark violet .45 .20
422 A113 20fr brown black .65 .45
Nos. 420-422 (3) 1.35 .85

Inscribed "Postes Francaises"

1942

Imprint: "FELTESSE" at right

423 A111 15fr brown lake .45 .30

A114

A115

Marshal Pétain — A116

A117 A118

1941-42 **Typo.** *Perf. 14x13½*

427 A114 20c lilac ('42) .20 .20
428 A114 30c rose red .20 .20
429 A114 40c ultra .20 .20
431 A115 50c dp green .20 .20
432 A115 60c violet ('42) .20 .20
433 A115 70c saph ('42) .20 .20
434 A115 70c orange ('42) .20 .20
435 A115 80c brown .20 .20
436 A115 80c emerald ('42) .20 .20
437 A115 1fr rose red .20 .20
438 A115 1.20fr red brn ('42) .20 .20
439 A116 1.50fr rose .20 .20
440 A116 1.50fr dl red brn ('42) .20 .20
a. Booklet pane of 10 2.75
441 A116 2fr blue grn ('42) .20 .20
443 A116 2.40fr rose red ('42) .20 .20
444 A116 2.50fr ultra .75 .30
445 A116 3fr orange .20 .20
446 A115 4fr ultra ('42) .20 .20
447 A115 4.50fr dk green ('42) .75 .20
Nos. 427-447 (19) 4.90 3.90

Nos. 431 to 438 measure 16½x20½mm.

No. 440 was forged by the French Underground ("Defense de la France") and used to frank clandestine journals, etc., from Feb. to June, 1944. The forgeries were ungummed, both perf. 11½ and imperf., with a back handstamp covering six stamps and including the words: "Atelier des Faux."

For surcharge see No. B134.

1942 **Engr.** *Perf. 14x13*

448 A115 4fr brt ultra .20 .20
449 A115 4.50fr dark green .20 .20
450 A117 5fr Prus green .20 .20

Perf. 13

451 A118 50fr black 3.00 1.90
Nos. 448-451 (4) 3.60 2.50

Nos. 448 and 449 measure 18x21½mm.

Jules Massenet A119

Stendhal (Marie Henri Beyle) A120

1942, June 22 *Perf. 14x13*

452 A119 4fr Prus green .20 .20

Jules Massenet (1842-1912), composer.

1942, Sept. 14 *Perf. 13*

453 A120 4fr blk brn & org red .45 .30

Stendhal (1783-1842), writer.

André Blondel — A121

Town-Hall Belfry, Arras — A122

1942, Sept. 14

454 A121 4fr dull blue .45 .30

André Eugène Blondel (1863-1938), physicist.

Mercury Type of 1938-42

Inscribed "Postes Françaises"

1942 *Perf. 14x13½*

455 A93 10c ultra .20 .20
456 A93 30c rose red .20 .20
457 A93 40c dark violet .20 .20
458 A93 50c turq blue .20 .20
Nos. 455-458 (4) .80 .80

1942, Dec. 8 **Engr.** *Perf. 13*

459 A122 10fr green .20 .20

Coats of Arms

Lyon — A123

1943 **Typo.** *Perf. 14x13½*

460 A123 5fr shown .25 .20
461 A123 10fr Brittany .40 .25
462 A123 15fr Provence 1.60 1.00
463 A123 20fr Ile de France 1.10 .75
Nos. 460-463 (4) 3.35 2.20

Antoine Lavoisier (1743-94), French Scientist — A127

1943, July 5 **Engr.** *Perf. 14x13*

464 A127 4fr ultra .25 .20

Lake Lerie and Meije Dauphiné Alps A128

1943, July 5 *Perf. 13*

465 A128 20fr dull gray grn .60 .50

Nicolas Rolin, Guigone de Salins and Hospital of Beaune A129

1943, July 21

466 A129 4fr blue .25 .20

500th anniv. of the founding of the Hospital of Beaune.

Arms of Flanders — A130

1944, Mar. 27 **Typo.** *Perf. 14x13½*

467 A130 5fr shown .20 .20
468 A130 10fr Languedoc .20 .20
469 A130 15fr Orleans .55 .30
470 A130 20fr Normandy .75 .50
Nos. 467-470 (4) 1.70 1.20

Edouard Branly — A134

Early Postal Car A135

1944, Feb. 21 **Engr.** *Perf. 14x13*

471 A134 4fr ultra .20 .20

Cent. of the birth of Edouard Branly, electrical inventor.

1944, June 10 *Perf. 13*

472 A135 1.50fr dark blue green .40 .25

Cent. of France's traveling postal service.

Chateau de Chenonceaux — A136

Claude Chappe — A137

1944, June 10

473 A136 15fr lilac brown .55 .30
a. 15fr black brown 7.50 2.50
b. 15fr black 70.00 70.00

See No. 496.

1944, Aug. 14 *Perf. 14x13*

474 A137 4fr dark ultra .20 .20

150th anniv. of the invention of an optical telegraph by Claude Chappe (1763-1805).

Gallic Cock A138

Marianne A139

1944 Litho. *Perf. 12*

No.	Type	Value	Color	Unused	Used
477	A138	10c	yellow grn	.20	.20
478	A138	30c	dk rose vio	.25	.20
479	A138	40c	blue	.20	.20
480	A138	50c	dark red	.20	.20
481	A139	60c	olive brown	.20	.20
482	A139	70c	rose lilac	.20	.20
483	A139	80c	yellow grn	.75	.75
484	A139	1fr	violet	.20	.20
485	A139	1.20fr	dp carmine	.20	.20
486	A139	1.50fr	deep blue	.20	.20
487	A138	2fr	indigo	.20	.20
488	A139	2.40fr	red orange	1.10	.90
489	A139	3fr	dp blue grn	.20	.20
490	A139	4fr	grnsh blue	.20	.20
491	A139	4.50fr	black	.20	.20
492	A139	5fr	violet blue	3.00	2.50
493	A138	10fr	violet	3.00	2.60
494	A138	15fr	olive brown	3.00	2.75
495	A138	20fr	dk slate grn	3.00	2.60
			Nos. 477-495 (19)	16.50	14.70

Nos. 477-495 were issued first in Corsica after the Allied landing, and released in Paris Nov. 15, 1944.

Chateau Type Inscribed "RF"

1944, Oct. 30 Engr. *Perf. 13*

No.	Type	Value	Color	Unused	Used
496	A136	25fr	black	.45	.35

Thomas Robert Bugeaud — A141

1944, Nov. 20

No.	Type	Value	Color	Unused	Used
497	A141	4fr	myrtle green	.20	.20

Battle of Isly, Aug. 14th, 1844.

Church of St. Denis A142

1944, Nov. 20

No.	Type	Value	Color	Unused	Used
498	A142	2.40fr	brown carmine	.20	.20

800th anniv. of the Church of St. Denis.

Type of 1938-42, Overprinted in Black

Inscribed "Postes Francaises"

1944 *Perf. 14x13½*

No.	Type	Value	Color	Unused	Used
499	A93	10c	ultra	.20	.20
500	A93	30c	rose red	.20	.20
501	A93	40c	dark violet	.20	.20
502	A93	50c	grnsh blue	.20	.20
			Nos. 499-502 (4)	.80	.80

The overprint "RF" in various forms, with or without Lorraine Cross, was also applied to stamps of the French State at Lyon and fourteen other cities.

French Forces of the Interior and Symbol of Liberation — A143

1945, Jan.

No.	Type	Value	Color	Unused	Used
503	A143	4fr	dark ultra	.30	.25

Issued to commemorate the Liberation.

Stamps of the above design, and of one incorporating "FRANCE" in the top panel, were printed by photo. in England during WW II upon order of the Free French Government. They were not issued. There are 3 values in each design; 25c green, 1fr red, 2.50fr blue. Value: set, above design, $100; set inscribed "FRANCE," $500.

Marianne — A144

Perf. 11½x12½

1944-45 Engr. Unwmk.

No.	Type	Value	Color	Unused	Used
505	A144	10c	ultra	.20	.20
506	A144	30c	bister	.20	.20
507	A144	40c	indigo	.20	.20
508	A144	50c	red orange	.20	.20
509	A144	60c	chalky blue	.20	.20
510	A144	70c	sepia	.20	.20
511	A144	80c	deep green	.20	.20
512	A144	1fr	lilac	.20	.20
513	A144	1.20fr	dk ol grn	.20	.20
514	A144	1.50fr	rose ('44)	.20	.20
515	A144	2fr	dk brown	.20	.20
516	A144	2.40fr	red	.20	.20
517	A144	3fr	brt ol grn	.20	.20
518	A144	4fr	brt ultra	.20	.20
519	A144	4.50fr	slate gray	.20	.20
520	A144	5fr	brt orange	.25	.20
521	A144	10fr	yellow grn	.30	.30
522	A144	15fr	lake	.35	.30
523	A144	20fr	brown org	1.00	.85
523A	A144	50fr	deep purple	2.10	1.75
			Nos. 505-523A (20)	7.00	6.40

The 2.40fr exists imperf. in a miniature sheet of 4 which was not issued.

Coat of Arms A145

Ceres A146

Marianne — A147

1945-47 Typo. *Perf. 14x13½*

No.	Type	Value	Color	Unused	Used
524	A145	10c	brown black	.20	.20
525	A145	30c	dk blue green	.20	.20
526	A145	40c	lilac rose	.20	.20
527	A145	50c	violet blue	.20	.20
528	A146	60c	brt ultra	.20	.20
530	A146	80c	brt green	.20	.20
531	A146	90c	dull grn ('46)	.65	.25
532	A146	1fr	rose red	.20	.20
533	A146	1.20fr	brown black	.20	.20
534	A146	1.50fr	rose lilac	.20	.20
535	A147	1.50fr	rose pink	.20	.20
536	A147	2fr	myrtle green	.20	.20
536A	A146	2fr	lt bl grn ('46)	.20	.20
537	A147	2.40fr	scarlet	.35	.25
538	A146	2.50fr	brown ('46)	.20	.20
539	A147	3fr	sepia	.20	.20
540	A147	3fr	deep rose ('46)	.20	.20
541	A147	4fr	ultra	.20	.20
541A	A147	4fr	violet ('46)	.20	.20
541B	A147	4.50fr	ultra ('47)	.20	.20
542	A147	5fr	lt green	.20	.20
542A	A147	5fr	rose pink ('47)	.20	.20
543	A147	6fr	brt ultra	.35	.25
544	A147	6fr	crim rose ('46)	1.25	.50
545	A147	10fr	red orange	.50	.30
546	A147	10fr	ultra ('46)	1.00	.40
547	A147	15fr	brt red vio	2.50	1.00
			Nos. 524-547 (27)	10.60	6.95

No. 531 is known only precanceled. See second note after No. 132.

Due to a reduction of the domestic postage rate, No. 542A was sold for 4.50fr.

See Nos. 576-580, 594-602, 614, 615, 650-654. For surcharges see Nos. 589, 610, 706, Reunion 270-276, 278, 285, 290-291, 293, 295.

1945-46 Engr. *Perf. 14x13*

No.	Type	Value	Color	Unused	Used
548	A147	4fr	dark blue	.20	.20
549	A147	10fr	dp blue ('46)	.90	.40
550	A147	15fr	brt red vio ('46)	6.50	1.25
551	A147	20fr	blue grn ('46)	.75	.40
552	A147	25fr	red ('46)	6.50	1.00
			Nos. 548-552 (5)	14.85	3.25

Marianne — A148

1945 Engr. *Perf. 13*

No.	Type	Value	Color	Unused	Used
553	A148	20fr	dark green	1.25	.60
554	A148	25fr	violet	1.65	.90
555	A148	50fr	red brown	1.75	1.40
556	A148	100fr	brt rose car	9.25	5.00
			Nos. 553-556 (4)	13.90	7.90

CFA

French stamps inscribed or surcharged "CFA" and new value are listed under Réunion at the end of the French listings.

Arms of Metz A149

Arms of Strasbourg A150

1945, Mar. 3 *Perf. 14x13*

No.	Type	Value	Color	Unused	Used
557	A149	2.40fr	dull blue	.20	.20
558	A150	4fr	black brown	.20	.20

Liberation of Metz and Strasbourg.

Costumes of Alsace and Lorraine and Cathedrals of Strasbourg and Metz A151

1945, May 16 *Perf. 13*

No.	Type	Value	Color	Unused	Used
559	A151	4fr	henna brown	.25	.20

Liberation of Alsace and Lorraine.

World Map Showing French Possessions — A152

1945, Sept. 17

No.	Type	Value	Color	Unused	Used
560	A152	2fr	Prussian blue	.20	.20

No. B193 Surcharged with New Value in Black

1946 *Perf. 14x13½*

No.	Type	Value	Color	Unused	Used
561	SP147	3fr	on 2fr+1fr red org	.20	.20

Arms of Corsica — A153

1946 Unwmk. Typo. *Perf. 14x13½*

No.	Type	Value	Description	Unused	Used
562	A153	10c	shown	.20	.20
563	A153	30c	Alsace	.20	.20
564	A153	50c	Lorraine	.20	.20
565	A153	60c	County of Nice	.20	.20
			Nos. 562-565 (4)	.80	.80

For surcharges see Reunion Nos. 268-269.

Reaching for "Peace" — A157

Holding the Dove of Peace — A158

1946, July 29 Engr. *Perf. 13*

No.	Type	Value	Color	Unused	Used
566	A157	3fr	Prussian green	.20	.20
567	A158	10fr	dark blue	.20	.20

Peace Conference of Paris, 1946.

Vézelay A159

Luxembourg Palace — A160

Rocamadour A161

Pointe du Raz, Finistère A162

1946 Unwmk. *Perf. 13*

No.	Type	Value	Color	Unused	Used
568	A159	5fr	rose violet	.20	.20
569	A160	10fr	dark blue	.20	.20
570	A161	15fr	dk violet brn	2.75	.25
571	A162	20fr	slate gray	.85	.20
			Nos. 568-571 (4)	4.00	.85

See Nos. 591-592. For surcharges see Reunion Nos. 277, 279.

Globe and Wreath — A163

1946, Nov.

No.	Type	Value	Color	Unused	Used
572	A163	10fr	dark blue	.20	.20

Gen. conf. of UNESCO, Paris, 1946.

Cannes
A164

Stanislas Square, Nancy
A165

1946-48 Engr. *Perf. 13*

573 A164 6fr rose red .75 .40
574 A165 25fr black brown 3.25 .20
575 A165 25fr dark blue ('48) 8.00 .80
Nos. 573-575 (3) 12.00 1.40

For surcharges see Reunion Nos. 280-281.

Ceres & Marianne Types of 1945

1947 Unwmk. Typo. *Perf. 14x13½*

576 A146 1.30fr dull blue .20 .20
577 A147 3fr green 1.10 .20
578 A147 3.50fr brown red .40 .20
579 A147 5fr blue .20 .20
580 A147 6fr carmine .20 .20
Nos. 576-580 (5) 2.10 1.00

Colonnade of the Louvre
A166

La Conciergerie, Paris Prison — A167

La Cité, Oldest Section of Paris
A168

Place de la Concorde
A169

1947, May 7 Engr. *Perf. 13*

581 A166 3.50fr chocolate .35 .30
582 A167 4.50fr dk slate gray .35 .30
583 A168 6fr red .75 .55
584 A169 10fr bright ultra .65 .55
Nos. 581-584 (4) 2.10 1.70

12th UPU Cong., Paris, May 7-July 7.

Auguste Pavie — A170

Francois Fénelon — A171

1947, May 30

585 A170 4.50fr sepia .20 .20

Cent. of the birth of Auguste Pavie, French pioneer in Laos.

1947, July 12

586 A171 4.50fr chocolate .20 .20

Issued to honor Francois de Salignac de la Mothe-Fénelon, prelate and writer.

Fleur-de-Lis and Double Carrick Bend — A172

1947, Aug. 2 Unwmk.

587 A172 5fr brown .20 .20

6th World Boy Scout Jamboree held at Moisson, Aug. 9th-18th, 1947.

Captured Patriot
A173

View of Conques
A174

1947, Nov. 10 Engr. *Perf. 13*

588 A173 5fr sepia .40 .35

No. 576 Surcharged in Carmine

1947, Nov. Typo. *Perf. 14x13½*

589 A146 1fr on 1.30fr dull blue .20 .20

1947, Dec. 18 Engr. *Perf. 13*

590 A174 15fr henna brown 3.25 .50

For surcharge see Reunion No. 282.

Types of 1946-47

1948 Re-engraved

591 A160 12fr rose carmine 1.50 .50
592 A160 15fr bright red .40 .40
593 A174 18fr dark blue 2.25 .25
Nos. 591-593 (3) 4.15 1.15

"FRANCE" substituted for inscriptions "RF" and "REPUBLIQUE FRANCAISE."

Marianne Type of 1945

1948-49 Typo. *Perf. 14x13½*

594 A147 2.50fr brown 2.75 1.25
595 A147 3fr lilac rose .20 .20
596 A147 4fr lt blue grn .20 .20
597 A147 4fr brown org 2.00 .50
598 A147 5fr lt blue grn .60 .20
599 A147 8fr blue .30 .20
600 A147 10fr brt violet .20 .20
601 A147 12fr ultra ('49) 2.00 .20
602 A147 15fr crim rose ('49) .55 .20
a. Booklet pane of 10 60.00
Nos. 594-602 (9) 8.80 3.15

No. 594 known only precanceled. See second note after No. 132.

François René de Chateaubriand — A175

1948, July 3 Engr. *Perf. 13*

603 A175 18fr dark blue .25 .20

Vicomte de Chateaubriand (1768-1848).

Philippe François M. de Hautecloque (Gen. Jacques Leclerc) — A176

1948, July 3

604 A176 6fr gray black .25 .20

See Nos. 692-692A.

Chaillot Palace
A177

A178

1948, Sept. 21

605 A177 12fr carmine rose .35 .30
606 A178 18fr indigo .35 .30

Meeting of the UN General Assembly, Paris, 1948.

Genissiat Dam
A179

Paul Langevin — A180

1948, Sept. 21

607 A179 12fr carmine rose .40 .30

1948, Nov. 17 *Perf. 14x13*

608 A180 5fr shown .30 .20
609 A180 8fr Jean Perrin .30 .20

Placing of the ashes of physicists Langevin (1872-1946) and Perrin (1870-1942) in the Pantheon.

No. 580 Surcharged with New Value and Bars in Black

1949, Jan. *Perf. 14x13½*

610 A147 5fr on 6fr carmine .20 .20

Arctic Scene — A181

1949, May 2 *Perf. 13*

611 A181 15fr indigo .25 .20

French polar explorations.

Types of 1849 and 1945

1949, May 9 Engr. *Imperf.*

612 A1 15fr red 3.25 3.25
613 A1 25fr deep blue 3.25 3.25

Perf. 14x13

614 A147 15fr red 3.25 3.25
615 A147 25fr deep blue 3.25 3.25
a. Strip of 4, #612-615 + label 15.00 15.00
Nos. 612-615 (4) 13.00 13.00

Cent. of the 1st French postage stamps.

Arms of Burgundy — A182

Arms: 50c, Guyenne (Aquitania). 1fr, Savoy. 2fr, Auvergne. 4fr, Anjou.

1949, May 11 Typo. *Perf. 14x13½*

616 A182 10c blue, red & yel .20 .20
617 A182 50c blue, red & yel .20 .20
618 A182 1fr brown & red .40 .20
619 A182 2fr green, yel & red .45 .20
620 A182 4fr blue, red & yel .30 .20
Nos. 616-620 (5) 1.55 1.00

See Nos. 659-663, 694-699, 733-739, 782-785. For surcharges see Reunion Nos. 283-284, 288-289, 297, 301, 305, 311.

Collegiate Church of St. Barnard and Dauphiné Arms
A183

1949, May 14 Engr. *Perf. 13*

621 A183 12fr red brown .30 .30

600th anniv. of France's acquisition of the Dauphiné region.

US and French Flags, Plane and Steamship
A184

1949, May 14

622 A184 25fr blue & carmine .55 .55

Franco-American friendship.

Cloister of St. Wandrille Abbey
A185

1949, May 18

623 A185 25fr deep ultra .25 .20

See No. 649. For surcharge see Reunion No. 287.

Type of 1849 Inscribed "1849-1949" in Lower Margin

1949, June 1

624 A1 10fr brown orange 40.00 30.00
a. Sheet of 10 400.00 350.00

Cent. of the 1st French postage stamp.

No. 624 has wide margins, 40x52mm from perforation to perforation. Sold for 110fr, which included cost of admission to the Centenary Intl. Exhib., Paris, June 1949.

Claude Chappe — A186

Jean Racine — A187

15fr, François Arago & André M. Ampère. 25fr, Emile Baudot. 50fr, Gen. Gustave A. Ferrié.

Inscribed: "C.I.T.T. PARIS 1949"

1949, June 13 Unwmk. *Perf. 13*
625 A186 10fr vermilion .85 .55
626 A186 15fr sepia .85 .55
627 A186 25fr deep claret 2.50 1.40
628 A186 50fr deep blue 4.25 1.60
Nos. 625-628 (4) 8.45 4.10

International Telegraph and Telephone Conference, Paris, May-July 1949.

1949
629 A187 12fr sepia .30 .25

Death of Jean Racine, dramatist, 250th anniv.

Abbey of St. Bertrand de Comminges A188

Meuse Valley, Ardennes A189

Mt. Gerbier de Jonc, Vivarais A190

1949 Engr.
630 A188 20fr dark red .20 .20
631 A189 40fr Prus green 12.00 .20
632 A190 50fr sepia 2.00 .20
Nos. 630-632 (3) 14.20 .60

For surcharge see Reunion No. 286.

A191

1949, Oct. 18
633 A191 15fr deep carmine .25 .25

50th anniv. of the Assembly of Presidents of Chambers of Commerce of the French Union.

UPU Allegory A192

1949, Nov. 7
634 A192 5fr dark green .25 .25
635 A192 15fr deep carmine .30 .25
636 A192 25fr deep blue 1.00 .75
Nos. 634-636 (3) 1.55 1.25

UPU, 75th anniversary.

Raymond Poincaré — A193

François Rabelais A195

Charles Péguy and Cathedral at Chartres — A194

1950, May 27 Unwmk. *Perf. 13*
637 A193 15fr indigo .30 .20

1950, June
638 A194 12fr dk brown .40 .20
639 A195 12fr red brown .40 .30

Chateau of Chateaudun — A196

1950, Nov. 25
640 A196 8fr choc & bis brn .40 .30

Madame Récamier A197

Marie de Sévigné A198

1950
641 A197 12fr dark green .40 .30
642 A198 15fr ultra .40 .30

Palace of Fontainbleau — A199

1951, Jan. 20
643 A199 12fr dark brown .35 .30

Jules Ferry — A200

Jean-Baptiste de la Salle — A202

Hands Holding Shuttle A201

1951, Mar. 17
644 A200 15fr bright red .40 .30

1951, Apr. 9
645 A201 25fr deep ultra .80 .65

Intl. Textile Exposition, Lille, April-May, 1951.

1951, Apr. 28
646 A202 15fr chocolate .45 .30

300th anniv. of the birth of Jean-Baptiste de la Salle, educator and saint.

Map and Anchor A203

1951, May 12
647 A203 15fr deep ultra .45 .40

50th anniv. of the creation of the French colonial troops.

Vincent d'Indy A204

1951, May 15
648 A204 25fr deep green 1.50 1.00

Vincent d'Indy, composer, birth cent.

Abbey Type of 1949

1951
649 A185 30fr bright blue 4.50 2.75

Marianne Type of 1945-47

1951 Typo. *Perf. 14x13½*
650 A147 5fr dull violet .25 .20
651 A147 6fr green 5.50 .40
652 A147 12fr red orange 1.10 .20
653 A147 15fr ultra .25 .20
a. Booklet pane of 10 20.00
654 A147 18fr cerise 14.00 .90
Nos. 650-654 (5) 21.10 1.90

Professors Nocard, Bouley and Chauveau; Gate at Lyons School A205

1951, June 8 Engr. *Perf. 13*
655 A205 12fr red violet .50 .40

Issued to honor Veterinary Medicine.

Gen. Picqué, Cols. Roussin and Villemin; Val de Grace Dome A206

1951, June 17 Unwmk.
656 A206 15fr red brown .60 .40

Issued to honor Military Medicine.

St. Nicholas, by Jean Didier — A207

1951, June 23
657 A207 15fr ind, dp claret & org .65 .60

Chateau Bontemps, Arbois A208

1951, June 23
658 A208 30fr indigo .60 .20

For surcharge see Reunion No. 296.

Arms Type of 1949

Arms of: 10c, Artois. 50c, Limousin. 1fr, Béarn. 2fr, Touraine. 3fr, Franche-Comté.

1951, June Typo. *Perf. 14x13½*
659 A182 10c red, vio bl & yel .20 .20
660 A182 50c green, red & blk .20 .20
661 A182 1fr blue, red & yel .25 .20
662 A182 2fr vio bl, red & yel .80 .25
663 A182 3fr red, vio bl & yel .70 .30
Nos. 659-663 (5) 2.15 1.15

Seal of Paris — A209

Maurice Noguès and Globe — A210

Unwmk.

1951, July 7 Engr. *Perf. 13*
664 A209 15fr dp bl, dk brn & red .40 .30

2,000th anniv. of the founding of Paris.

1951, Oct. 13
665 A210 12fr indigo & blue .70 .50

Maurice Nogues, aviation pioneer.

Charles Baudelaire A211

Poets: 12fr, Paul Verlaine. 15fr, Arthur Rimbaud.

1951, Oct. 27
666 A211 8fr purple .40 .40
667 A211 12fr gray .60 .60
668 A211 15fr dp green .60 .60
Nos. 666-668 (3) 1.60 1.60

Georges Clemenceau, Birth Cent. — A212

1951, Nov. 11

669 A212 15fr black brown .25 .25

Chateau du Clos, Vougeot A213

1951, Nov. 17

670 A213 30fr blk brn & brn 4.50 1.75

Chaillot Palace and Eiffel Tower A214

1951, Nov. 6

671 A214 18fr red .90 .60
672 A214 30fr deep ultra 1.60 .75

Opening of the Geneva Assembly of the United Nations, Paris, Nov. 6, 1951.

Observatory, Pic du Midi — A215

Abbaye aux Hommes, Caen — A216

1951, Dec. 22

673 A215 40fr violet 5.50 .20
674 A216 50fr black brown 4.50 .20

For surcharge see Reunion No. 294.

Marshal Jean de Lattre de Tassigny, 1890-1952 A217

1952, May 8 Unwmk. *Perf. 13*

675 A217 15fr violet brown .70 .40

See No. 717.

Gate of France, Vaucouleurs — A218

1952, May 11

676 A218 12fr brown black 1.50 .80

Flags and Monument at Narvik, Norway A219

1952, May 28

677 A219 30fr violet blue 2.50 1.25

Battle of Narvik, May 27, 1940.

Chateau de Chambord A220

1952, May 30

678 A220 20fr dark purple .45 .20

For surcharge see Reunion No. 292.

Assembly Hall, Strasbourg A221

1952, May 31

679 A221 30fr dark green 8.00 5.75

Issued to honor the Council of Europe.

Monument, Bir-Hacheim Cemetery — A222

1952, June 14

680 A222 30fr rose lake 3.00 1.25

10th anniv. of the defense of Bir-Hacheim.

Abbey of the Holy Cross, Poitiers — A223

1952, June 21

681 A223 15fr bright red .45 .30

14th cent. of the foundation of the Abbey of the Holy Cross at Poitiers.

Leonardo da Vinci, Amboise Chateau and La Signoria, Florence A224

1952, July 9

682 A224 30fr deep ultra 7.00 3.00

Leonardo da Vinci, 500th birth anniv.

Garabit Viaduct A225

1952, July 5

683 A225 15fr dark blue .65 .25

Sword and Military Medals, 1852-1952 A226

Dr. René Laennec A227

1952, July 5

684 A226 15fr choc, grn & yel .40 .35

Cent. of the creation of the Military Medal.

1952, Nov. 7

685 A227 12fr dark green .40 .35

Versailles Gate, Painted by Utrillo A228

1952, Dec. 20

686 A228 18fr violet brown 2.00 1.25

Publicity for the restoration of Versailles Palace. See No. 728.

Mannequin — A229

1953, Apr. 24 Unwmk. *Perf. 13*

687 A229 30fr blue blk & rose vio .80 .30

Dressmaking industry of France.

Gargantua of François Rabelais A230

Célimène from The Misanthrope A231

Figaro, from the Barber of Seville — A232

Hernani of Victor Hugo — A233

1953

688 A230 6fr dp plum & car .20 .20
689 A231 8fr indigo & ultra .20 .20
690 A232 12fr vio brn & dk grn .20 .20
691 A233 18fr vio brn & blk brn .30 .20
Nos. 688-691 (4) .90 .80

For surcharge see Reunion No. 298.

Type of 1948

Inscribed "Général Leclerc Maréchal de France"

1953-54

692 A176 8fr red brown .65 .35
692A A176 12fr dk grn & gray grn ('54) 2.25 1.25

Issued to honor the memory of General Jacques Leclerc.

Map and Cyclists, 1903-1953 A234

1953, July 26

693 A234 12fr red brn, ultra & blk 1.75 .75

50th anniv. of the Bicycle Tour de France.

Arms Type of 1949

50c, Picardy. 70c, Gascony. 80c, Berri. 1fr, Poitou. 2fr, Champagne. 3fr, Dauphiné.

1953 Typo. *Perf. 14x13½*

694 A182 50c blue, yel & red .20 .20
695 A182 70c red, blue & yel .20 .20
696 A182 80c blue, red & yel .20 .20
697 A182 1fr black, red & yel .25 .20
698 A182 2fr brown, bl & yel .25 .25
699 A182 3fr red, blue & yel .45 .25
Nos. 694-699 (6) 1.55 1.30

Swimming A235

1953, Nov. 28 Engr. *Perf. 13*

700 A235 20fr shown 1.90 .20
701 A235 25fr Track 9.75 .45
702 A235 30fr Fencing 1.90 .25
703 A235 40fr Canoe racing 8.75 .25
704 A235 50fr Rowing 4.75 .20
705 A235 75fr Equestrian 27.50 8.00
Nos. 700-705 (6) 54.55 9.35

For surcharges see Reunion Nos. 299-300.

No. 654 Surcharged with New Value and Bars in Black

1954 *Perf. 14x13½*

706 A147 15fr on 18fr cerise .55 .20

Farm Woman A236

Gallic Cock A237

1954 Typo.

707 A236 4fr blue .25 .20
708 A236 8fr brown red 3.75 .70
709 A237 12fr cerise 3.50 .30
710 A237 24fr blue green 13.50 3.50
Nos. 707-710 (4) 21.00 4.70

Nos. 707-710 are known only precanceled. See second note after No. 132.

See #833-834, 840-844, 910-913, 939, 952-955. For surcharges see Reunion #324, 326-327.

Tapestry and Gobelin Workshop
A238

Entrance to Exhibition Park
A239

Designs: 30fr, Book manufacture. 40fr, Porcelain and glassware. 50fr, Jewelry and metalsmith's work. 75fr, Flowers and perfumes.

1954, May 6 Engr. *Perf. 13*

711	A238	25fr red brn car & blk brn	10.50	.30
712	A238	30fr dk grn & lil gray	1.10	.20
713	A238	40fr dk brn, vio brn & org brn	3.00	.20
714	A238	50fr brt ultra, dl grn & org brn	1.00	.20
715	A238	75fr dp car & magenta	12.00	.45
		Nos. 711-715 (5)	27.60	1.35

For surcharges see Reunion Nos. 303-304.

1954, May 22

716 A239 15fr blue & dk car .35 .30

Founding of the Fair of Paris, 50th anniv.

De Lattre Type of 1952

1954, June 5

717 A217 12fr vio bl & indigo 1.75 1.10

Allied Landings
A240

1954, June 5

718 A240 15fr scarlet & ultra 1.50 .75

The 10th anniversary of the liberation.

View of Lourdes
A241

Street Corner, Quimper — A242

Views: 8fr, Seine valley, Les Andelys. 10fr, Beach at Royan. 18fr, Cheverny Chateau. 20fr, Beach, Gulf of Ajaccio.

1954

719	A241	6fr ultra, ind & dk grn	.30	.30
720	A241	8fr brt blue & dk grn	.20	.20
721	A241	10fr aqua & org brn	.20	.20
722	A242	12fr rose vio & dk vio	.30	.20
723	A241	18fr bl, dk grn & ind	2.25	.60
724	A241	20fr blk brn, bl grn & red brn	2.00	.20
		Nos. 719-724 (6)	5.25	1.70

See No. 873. For surcharges see Reunion Nos. 302, 306-310.

Abbey Ruins, Jumièges
A243

St. Philibert Abbey, Tournus
A244

1954, June 13

725 A243 12fr vio bl, ind & dk grn 1.50 .80

13th centenary of Abbey of Jumièges.

1954, June 18

726 A244 30fr indigo & blue 5.50 3.75

1st conf. of the Intl. Center of Romance Studies.

View of Stenay
A245

1954, June 26

727 A245 15fr dk brn & org brn .65 .50

Acquisition of Stenay by France, 300th anniv.

Versailles Type of 1952

1954, July 10

728 A228 18fr dp bl, ind & vio brn 8.50 4.75

Villandry Chateau
A246

1954, July 17

729 A246 18fr dk bl & dk bl grn 4.50 2.75

Napoleon Awarding Legion of Honor Decoration
A247

1954, Aug. 14

730 A247 12fr scarlet 1.25 .65

150th anniv. of the 1st Legion of Honor awards at Camp de Boulogne.

Cadets Marching Through Gateway
A248

1954, Aug. 1

731 A248 15fr vio gray, dk bl & car 1.10 .65

150th anniversary of the founding of the Military School of Saint-Cyr.

Allegory
A249

Duke de Saint-Simon
A250

1954, Oct. 4

732 A249 30fr indigo & choc 5.25 4.00

Issued to publicize the fact that the metric system was first introduced in France.

Arms Type of 1949

Arms: 50c, Maine. 70c, Navarre. 80c, Nivernais. 1fr, Bourbonnais. 2fr, Angoumois. 3fr, Aunis. 5fr, Saintonge.

1954 Typo. *Perf. 14x13½*

733	A182	50c multicolored	.20	.20
734	A182	70c green, red & yel	.25	.20
735	A182	80c blue, red & yel	.25	.20
736	A182	1fr red, blue & yel	.20	.20
737	A182	2fr black, red & yel	.20	.20
738	A182	3fr brown, red & yel	.20	.20
739	A182	5fr blue & yellow	.20	.20
		Nos. 733-739 (7)	1.50	1.40

1955, Feb. 5 Engr. *Perf. 13*

740 A250 12fr dk brn & vio brn .60 .40

Louis de Rouvroy, Duke de Saint-Simon (1675-1755).

Allegory and Rotary Emblem
A251

Marianne — A252

1955, Feb. 23

741 A251 30fr vio bl, bl & org 1.90 1.00

50th anniv. of Rotary International.

1955-59 Typo. *Perf. 14x13½*

751	A252	6fr fawn	2.75	1.75
752	A252	12fr green	2.50	1.10
a.		Bklt. pane of 10 + 2 labels	30.00	
753	A252	15fr carmine	.20	.20
a.		Booklet pane of 10	7.50	
754	A252	18fr green ('58)	.25	.20
755	A252	20fr ultra ('57)	.45	.20
756	A252	25fr rose red ('59)	1.00	.20
a.		Booklet pane of 8	10.00	
b.		Booklet pane of 10	11.00	
		Nos. 751-756 (6)	7.15	3.65

No. 751 was issued in coils of 1,000.

No. 752 was issued in panes of 10 stamps and two labels with marginal instructions for folding to form a booklet.

Nos. 754-755 are found in two types, distinguished by the numerals. On the 18fr there is no serif at left of base of the "1" on the 1st type. The 2nd type has a shorter "1" with no serifs at base. On the 20fr the 2nd type has a well formed "2" and the horiz. lines of the "F" of the denomination are longer and of equal length.

No. 756 also in two types, distinguished by border width. On the 1st type, the border is thicker than the width of the letters. On the 2nd type, the border is thinner than the width of the letters.

For surcharges see Reunion Nos. 330-331.

Philippe Lebon, Inventor of Illuminating Gas
A253

Inventors: 10fr, Barthélemy Thimonnier, sewing machine. 12fr, Nicolas Appert, canned foods. 18fr, Dr. E. H. St. Claire Deville, aluminum. 25fr, Pierre Martin, steel making. 30fr, Bernigaud de Chardonnet, rayon.

1955, Mar. 5 Engr.

757	A253	5fr dk vio bl & bl	.50	.45
758	A253	10fr dk brn & org brn	.50	.45
759	A253	12fr dk green	.65	.65
760	A253	18fr dk vio bl & ind	2.50	1.90
761	A253	25fr dk brnsh pur & vio	2.50	1.90
762	A253	30fr rose car & scar	2.50	1.90
		Nos. 757-762 (6)	9.15	7.25

St. Stephen Bridge, Limoges
A254

1955, Mar. 26 Unwmk. *Perf. 13*

763 A254 12fr yel brn & dk vio brn 1.25 .80

Gloved Model in Place de la Concorde — A255

1955, Mar. 26

764 A255 25fr blk brn, vio bl & blk .65 .20

French glove manufacturing.

Jean Pierre Claris de Florian A256

1955, Apr. 2

765 A256 12fr blue green .60 .35

200th anniv. of the birth of Jean Pierre Claris de Florian, fabulist.

Eiffel Tower and Television Antennas A257

1955, Apr. 16

766 A257 15fr indigo & ultra .80 .25

French advancement in television.

Wire Fence and Guard Tower A258

1955, Apr. 23

767 A258 12fr dk gray bl & brn blk .80 .30

10th anniv. of the liberation of concentration camps.

Electric Train A259

1955, May 11

768 A259 12fr blk brn & slate bl 2.00 1.00

Issued to publicize the electrification of the Valenciennes-Thionville railroad line.

Jacquemart of Moulins — A260

1955, May 28

769 A260 12fr black brown 1.25 .75

Jules Verne and Nautilus A261

1955, June 3

770 A261 30fr indigo 6.00 4.00

50th anniv. of the death of Jules Verne.

Auguste and Louis Lumière and Motion Picture Projector A262

1955, June 12

771 A262 30fr rose brown 4.50 3.50

Invention of motion pictures, 60th anniv.

Jacques Coeur and His Mansion at Bourges A263

1955, June 18

772 A263 12fr violet 1.90 1.25

5th centenary of the death of Jacques Coeur (1395?-1456), French merchant.

Corvette "La Capricieuse" — A264

1955, July 9

773 A264 30fr aqua & dk blue 4.50 4.25

Centenary of the voyage of La Capricieuse to Canada.

Bordeaux A265

Designs: 8fr, Marseille. 10fr, Nice. 12fr, Valentre bridge, Cahors. 18fr, Uzerche. 25fr, Fortifications, Brouage.

1955, Oct. 15

774 A265 6fr carmine lake .20 .20
775 A265 8fr indigo .45 .20
776 A265 10fr dp ultra .20 .20
777 A265 12fr violet & brn .20 .20
778 A265 18fr bluish grn & ind .60 .20
779 A265 25fr org brn & red brn .90 .20
Nos. 774-779 (6) 2.55 1.20

See Nos. 838-839. For surcharges see Reunion Nos. 312-317, 323.

Mount Pelée, Martinique A266

1955, Nov. 1

780 A266 20fr dk & lt purple 3.25 .20

Gérard de Nerval — A267

1955, Nov. 11

781 A267 12fr lake & sepia .35 .20

Centenary of the death of Gérard de Nerval (Labrunie), author.

Arms Type of 1949

Arms of: 50c, County of Foix. 70c, Marche. 80c, Roussillon. 1fr, Comtat Venaissin.

Perf. 14x13½

1955, Nov. 19 Typo. Unwmk.

782 A182 50c multicolored .20 .20
783 A182 70c red, blue & yel .20 .20
784 A182 80c brown, yel & red .20 .20
785 A182 1fr blue, red & yel .20 .20
Nos. 782-785 (4) .80 .80

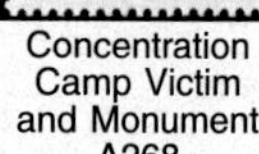

Concentration Camp Victim and Monument A268

Belfry at Douai A269

1956, Jan. 14 Engr. *Perf. 13*

786 A268 15fr brn blk & red brn .50 .35

Natl. memorial for Nazi deportation victims erected at the Natzwiller Struthof concentration camp in Alsace.

1956, Feb. 11

787 A269 15fr ultra & indigo .35 .30

Col. Emil Driant A270

1956, Feb. 21

788 A270 15fr dark blue .30 .25

40th anniv. of the death of Col. Emil Driant during the battle of Verdun.

Trench Fighting — A271

1956, Mar. 3

789 A271 30fr indigo & dk olive 1.50 .80

40th anniversary of Battle of Verdun.

Jean Henri Fabre, Entomology A272

Scientists: 15fr, Charles Tellier, Refrigeration. 18fr, Camille Flammarion, Popular Astronomy. 30fr, Paul Sabatier, Catalytic Chemistry.

1956, Apr. 7

790 A272 12fr vio brn & org brn .50 .40
791 A272 15fr vio bl & int blk .50 .40
792 A272 18fr brt ultra 1.10 1.10
793 A272 30fr Prus grn & dk grn 2.75 2.00
Nos. 790-793 (4) 4.85 3.90

Grand Trianon, Versailles A273

1956, Apr. 14

794 A273 12fr vio brn & gray grn 1.10 .75

Symbols of Latin American and French Culture A274

1956, Apr. 21

795 A274 30fr brown & red brn 1.50 1.00

Issued in recognition of the friendship between France and Latin America.

"The Smile of Reims" and Botticelli's "Spring" A275

1956, May 5

796 A275 12fr black & green .60 .40

Issued to emphasize the cultural and artistic kinship of Reims and Florence.

Leprosarium and Maltese Cross — A276

1956, May 12

797 A276 12fr sepia, red brn & red .40 .30

Issued in honor of the Knights of Malta.

St. Yves de Treguier A277

1956, May 19

798 A277 15fr bluish gray & blk .30 .20

St. Yves, patron saint of lawyers.

Marshal Franchet d'Esperey A278

Miners Monument A279

1956, May 26

799 A278 30fr deep claret 1.75 1.40

Centenary of the birth of Marshal Louis Franchet d'Esperey.

1956, June 2

800 A279 12fr violet brown .40 .35

Town Montceau-les-Mines, 100th anniv.

Basketball A280

"Rebuilding Europe" A281

Sports: 40fr, Pelota (Jai alai). 50fr, Rugby. 75fr, Mountain climbing.

1956, July 7

801 A280 30fr gray vio & blk 1.00 .20
802 A280 40fr brown & vio brn 4.00 .30
803 A280 50fr rose vio & vio 1.50 .20
804 A280 75fr indigo, grn & bl 8.50 1.50
Nos. 801-804 (4) 15.00 2.20

For surcharges see Reunion Nos. 318-321.

Europa Issue

Perf. 13½x14

1956, Sept. 15 Typo. Unwmk.

805 A281 15fr rose & rose lake *1.50* .25

Perf. 13

Engr.

806 A281 30fr lt blue & vio bl *11.00* .85

Issued to symbolize the cooperation among the six countries comprising the Coal and Steel Community.

No. 805 measures 21x35½mm, No. 806 measures 22x35½mm.

Dam at Donzère-Mondragon — A282

Cable Railway to Pic du Midi — A283

Rhine Port of Strasbourg A284

1956, Oct. 6 Engr. *Perf. 13*

807 A282 12fr gray vio & vio brn 1.25 .85
808 A283 18fr indigo 2.75 1.75
809 A284 30fr indigo & dk blue 11.00 5.00
Nos. 807-809 (3) 15.00 7.60

French technical achievements.

Antoine-Augustin Parmentier — A285

1956, Oct. 27

810 A285 12fr brown red & brown .45 .30

Parmentier, nutrition chemist, who popularized the potato in France.

Petrarch — A286

Portraits: 12fr, J. B. Lully. 15fr, J. J. Rousseau. 18fr, Benjamin Franklin. 20fr, Frederic Chopin. 30fr, Vincent van Gogh.

1956, Nov. 10

811 A286 8fr green .55 .40
812 A286 12fr claret .55 .40
813 A286 15fr dark red .90 .60
814 A286 18fr ultra 2.50 1.40
815 A286 20fr brt violet 3.00 1.10
816 A286 30fr brt grnsh blue 3.50 2.25
Nos. 811-816 (6) 11.00 6.15

Famous men who lived in France.

Pierre de Coubertin and Olympic Stadium A287

1956, Nov. 24

817 A287 30fr dk blue gray & pur 1.40 .70

Issued in honor of Baron Pierre de Coubertin, founder of the modern Olympic Games.

Homing Pigeon A288

1957, Jan. 12

818 A288 15fr dp ultra, ind & red brn .30 .25

Victor Schoelcher — A289

1957, Feb. 16 Engr.

819 A289 18fr lilac rose .35 .35

Issued in honor of Victor Schoelcher, who freed the slaves in the French Colonies.

Sèvres Porcelain A290

1957, Mar. 23 Unwmk. *Perf. 13*

820 A290 30fr ultra & vio blue .60 .35

Bicentenary of the porcelain works at Sèvres (in 1956).

Gaston Planté and Storage Battery A291

Designs: 12fr, Antoine Béclère and X-ray apparatus. 18fr, Octave Terrillon, autoclave, microscope and surgical instruments. 30fr, Etienne Oemichen and early helicopter.

1957, Apr. 13

821 A291 8fr gray blk & dp cl .20 .20
822 A291 12fr dk bl, blk & emer .40 .40
823 A291 18fr rose red & mag 1.10 1.10
824 A291 30fr green & slate grn 1.50 1.50
Nos. 821-824 (4) 3.20 3.20

Uzès Chateau A292

1957, Apr. 27

825 A292 12fr slate bl & bis brn .30 .25

Jean Moulin A293

Le Quesnoy A294

Portraits: 10fr, Honoré d'Estienne d'Orves. 12fr, Robert Keller. 18fr, Pierre Brossolette. 20fr, Jean-Baptiste Lebas.

1957, May 18

826 A293 8fr violet brown .75 .35
827 A293 10fr black & vio bl .75 .35
828 A293 12fr brown & sl grn .75 .65
829 A293 18fr purple & blk 1.40 1.10
830 A293 20fr Prus bl & dk bl 1.10 .80
Nos. 826-830 (5) 4.75 3.25

Issued in honor of the heroes of the French Underground of World War II.

See #879-882, 915-919, 959-963, 990-993.

1957, June 1

831 A294 8fr dk slate green .20 .20

See No. 837. For surcharge see Reunion No. 322.

Symbols of Justice A295

1957, June 1

832 A295 12fr sepia & ultra .20 .20

French Cour des Comptes, 150th anniv.

Farm Woman Type of 1954

1957-59 *Perf. 14x13½*

833 A236 6fr orange .20 .20
833A A236 10fr brt green ('59) .50 .20
834 A236 12fr red lilac .20 .20
Nos. 833-834 (3) .90 .60

Nos. 833-834 issued without precancellation.

Symbols of Public Works A296

1957, June 20 Engr. *Perf. 13*

835 A296 30fr sl grn, brn & ocher 1.50 .90

Brest A297

1957, July 6

836 A297 12fr gray grn & brn ol .60 .30

Scenic Types of 1955, 1957

Designs: 15fr, Le Quesnoy. 35fr, Bordeaux. 70fr, Valentre bridge, Cahors.

1957, July 19 Unwmk.

837 A294 15fr dk bl grn & sep .40 .20
838 A265 35fr dk bl grn & sl grn 2.50 .70
839 A265 70fr black & dull grn 13.50 1.40
Nos. 837-839 (3) 16.40 2.30

Gallic Cock Type of 1954

1957 Typo. *Perf. 14x13½*

840 A237 5fr olive bister .30 .20
841 A237 10fr bright blue 1.75 .30
842 A237 15fr plum 2.10 .45
843 A237 30fr bright red 6.00 .90
844 A237 45fr green 21.00 11.00
Nos. 840-844 (5) 31.15 12.85

Nos. 840-844 are known only precanceled. See second note after No. 132.

Leo Lagrange and Stadium A298

1957, Aug. 31 Engr. *Perf. 13*

845 A298 18fr lilac gray & blk .40 .30

Intl. University Games, Paris, 8/31-9/8.

"United Europe" — A299

Auguste Comte — A300

1957, Sept. 16

846 A299 20fr red brown & green *.55* .30
847 A299 35fr dk brown & blue *1.60* .65

A united Europe for peace and prosperity.

1957, Sept. 14

848 A300 35fr brown red & sepia .45 .35

Centenary of the death of Auguste Comte, mathematician and philosopher.

Roman Amphitheater, Lyon — A301

1957, Oct. 5 *Perf. 13*

849 A301 20fr brn org & brn vio .35 .30

2,000th anniv. of the founding of Lyon.

Sens River, Guadeloupe A302

Beynac-Cazenac, Dordogne A303

Nicolaus Copernicus A304

Designs: 10fr, Elysee Palace. 25fr, Chateau de Valencay, Indre. 35fr, Rouen Cathedral. 50fr, Roman Ruins, Saint-Remy. 65fr, Evian-les-Bains.

1957, Oct. 19

850	A302	8fr green & lt brn	.20	.20
851	A302	10fr dk ol bis & vio brn	.20	.20
852	A303	18fr indigo & dk brn	.20	.20
853	A302	25fr bl gray & vio brn	.55	.20
854	A303	35fr car rose & lake	.20	.20
855	A302	50fr ol grn & ol bister	.40	.20
856	A302	65fr dk blue & indigo	.60	.35
		Nos. 850-856 (7)	2.35	1.55

See #907-909. For overprint and surcharges see #1O1, Reunion 325, 328-329, 332-334.

1957, Nov. 9 **Engr.** *Perf. 13*

Portraits: 10fr, Michelangelo. 12fr, Miguel de Cervantes. 15fr, Rembrandt. 18fr, Isaac Newton. 25fr, Mozart. 35fr, Johann Wolfgang von Goethe.

857	A304	8fr dark brown	.65	.45
858	A304	10fr dark green	.65	.45
859	A304	12fr dark purple	.75	.45
860	A304	15fr brown & org brn	.95	.45
861	A304	18fr deep blue	1.25	.90
862	A304	25fr lilac & claret	1.25	.45
863	A304	35fr blue	1.50	1.10
		Nos. 857-863 (7)	7.00	4.25

Louis Jacques Thénard A305

1957, Nov. 30 **Unwmk.**

864 A305 15fr ol bis & grnsh blk .30 .30

Centenary of the death of L. J. Thenard, chemist, and the founding of the Charitable Society of the Friends of Science.

Dr. Philippe Pinel A306

Joseph Louis Lagrange A307

French Physicians: 12fr, Fernand Widal. 15fr, Charles Nicolle. 35fr, René Leriche.

1958, Jan. 25

865	A306	8fr brown olive	.75	.50
866	A306	12fr brt vio blue	.75	.50
867	A306	15fr deep blue	1.10	.60
868	A306	35fr black	1.60	1.00
		Nos. 865-868 (4)	4.20	2.60

1958, Feb. 15 *Perf. 13*

French Scientists: 12fr, Urbain Jean Joseph Leverrier. 15fr, Jean Bernard Leon Foucault. 35fr, Claude Louis Berthollet.

869	A307	8fr blue grn & vio bl	.80	.55
870	A307	12fr sepia & gray	.95	.70
871	A307	15fr slate grn & grn	1.90	.95
872	A307	35fr maroon & cop red	2.00	1.10
		Nos. 869-872 (4)	5.65	3.30

Lourdes Type of 1954

1958

873 A241 20fr grnsh bl & ol .25 .20

Le Havre A308

Maubeuge — A309

Designs: 18fr, Saint-Die. 25fr, Sete.

1958, Mar. 29 **Engr.** *Perf. 13*

874	A308	12fr ol grn & car rose	.55	.40
875	A309	15fr brt purple & brn	.55	.40
876	A309	18fr ultra & indigo	.80	.60
877	A308	25fr dk bl, bl grn & brn	1.10	.60
		Nos. 874-877 (4)	3.00	2.00

Reconstruction of war-damaged cities.

French Pavilion, Brussels A310

1958, Apr. 12

878 A310 35fr brn, dk grn & bl .30 .25

Issued for the Universal and International Exposition at Brussels.

Heroes Type of 1957

8fr, Jean Cavaillès. 12fr, Fred Scamaroni. 15fr, Simone Michel-Levy. 20fr, Jacques Bingen.

1958, Apr. 19

879	A293	8fr violet & black	.50	.30
880	A293	12fr ultra & green	.50	.30
881	A293	15fr brown & gray	1.40	.90
882	A293	20fr olive & ultra	1.10	.65
		Nos. 879-882 (4)	3.50	2.15

Issued in honor of the heroes of the French Underground in World War II.

Bowling A311

Sports: 15fr, Naval joust. 18fr, Archery, vert. 25fr, Breton wrestling, vert.

1958, Apr. 26

883	A311	12fr rose & brown	.80	.40
884	A311	15fr bl, ol gray & grn	1.10	.55
885	A311	18fr green & brown	1.90	.95
886	A311	25fr brown & indigo	2.50	1.25
		Nos. 883-886 (4)	6.30	3.15

Senlis Cathedral — A312

1958, May 17

887 A312 15fr ultra & indigo .30 .30

Bayeux Tapestry Horsemen A313

1958, June 21

888 A313 15fr blue & carmine .35 .25

Common Design Types pictured following the introduction.

Europa Issue, 1958

Common Design Type

1958, Sept. 13 **Engr.** *Perf. 13*

Size: 22x36mm

889	CD1	20fr rose red	*.55*	.20
890	CD1	35fr ultra	*1.75*	.30

Foix Chateau A314

1958, Oct. 11

891 A314 15fr ultra, grn & ol brn .25 .20

City Halls, Paris and Rome A315

1958, Oct. 11

892 A315 35fr gray, grnsh bl & rose red .30 .25

Issued to publicize the cultural ties between Rome and Paris and the need for European unity.

UNESCO Building, Paris A316

Design: 35fr, Different view of building.

1958, Nov. 1 *Perf. 13*

893	A316	20fr grnsh blue & ol bis	.20	.20
894	A316	35fr dk sl grn & red org	.20	.20

UNESCO Headquarters in Paris opening, Nov. 3.

Soldier's Grave in Wheat Field A317

Arms of Marseille A318

1958, Nov. 11

895 A317 15fr dk green & ultra .25 .20

40th anniv. of the World War I armistice.

1958-59 **Typo.** *Perf. 14x13½*

Cities: 70c, Lyon. 80c, Toulouse. 1fr, Bordeaux. 2fr, Nice. 3fr, Nantes. 5fr, Lille. 15fr, Algiers.

896	A318	50c dk blue & ultra	.20	.20
897	A318	70c multicolored	.20	.20
898	A318	80c red, blue & yel	.20	.20
899	A318	1fr dk bl, yel & red	.20	.20
900	A318	2fr dk bl, red & grn	.20	.20
901	A318	3fr multicolored	.20	.20
902	A318	5fr dk brown & red	.20	.20
903	A318	15fr multi ('59)	.20	.20
		Nos. 896-903 (8)	1.60	1.60

See Nos. 938, 940, 973, 1040-1042, 1091-1095, 1142-1144. For surcharges see Reunion Nos. 336, 345-346, 350-351, 353.

Arc de Triomphe and Flowers — A319

1959, Jan. 17 **Engr.** *Perf. 13*

904 A319 15fr brn, bl, grn, cl & red .30 .20

Paris Flower Festival.

Symbols of Learning and Medal A320

1959, Jan. 24 *Perf. 13*

905 A320 20fr lake, blk & vio .20 .20

Sesquicentennial of the Palm Leaf Medal of the French Academy.

Charles de Foucauld A321

1959, Jan. 31

906 A321 50fr dp brn, bl & mar .45 .35

Issued to honor Father Charles de Foucauld, explorer and missionary of the Sahara.

Type of 1957

Designs: 30fr, Elysee Palace. 85fr, Evian-les Bains. 100fr, Sens River, Guadeloupe.

1959, Feb. 10

907	A302	30fr dk slate green	1.90	.25
908	A302	85fr deep claret	2.75	.25
909	A302	100fr deep violet	22.50	.45
		Nos. 907-909 (3)	27.15	.95

Gallic Cock Type of 1954

1959 Typo. *Perf. 14x13½*

No.	Type	Description	Unused	Used
910	A237	8fr violet	.35	.25
911	A237	20fr yellow grn	1.75	.65
912	A237	40fr henna brn	4.00	2.25
913	A237	55fr emerald	16.00	10.00
		Nos. 910-913 (4)	22.10	13.15

Nos. 910-913 were issued with precancellation. See second note after No. 132. See Nos. 952-955.

Miners' Tools and School A322

1959, Apr. 11 Engr. *Perf. 13*

914 A322 20fr red, blk & blue .20 .20

175th anniv. of the National Mining School.

Heroes Type of 1957

Portraits: No. 915, The five martyrs of the Buffon school. No. 916, Yvonne Le Roux. No. 917, Médéric-Védy. No. 918, Louis Martin-Bret. 30fr, Gaston Moutardier.

1959, Apr. 25 Engr. *Perf. 13*

No.	Type	Description	Unused	Used
915	A293	15fr black & vio	.30	.20
916	A293	15fr mag & rose vio	.30	.30
917	A293	20fr green & grnsh bl	.30	.30
918	A293	20fr org brn & brn	.45	.40
919	A293	30fr magenta & vio	.50	.40
		Nos. 915-919 (5)	1.85	1.60

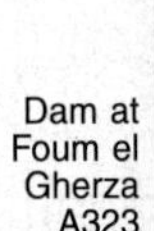

Dam at Foum el Gherza A323

Marcoule Atomic Center — A324

Designs: 30fr, Oil field at Hassi Messaoud, Sahara. 50fr, C. N. I. T. Building (Centre National des Industries et des Techniques).

1959, May 23

No.	Type	Description	Unused	Used
920	A323	15fr olive & grnsh bl	.25	.20
921	A324	20fr brt car & red brn	.45	.25
922	A324	30fr dk blue, brn & grn	.45	.40
923	A323	50fr ol grn & sl blue	.75	.40
		Nos. 920-923 (4)	1.90	1.25

French technical achievements.

Marceline Desbordes-Valmore — A325

1959, June 20

924 A325 30fr blue, brn & grn .25 .20

Centenary of the death of Marceline Desbordes-Valmore, poet.

Pilots Goujon and Rozanoff A326

1959, June 13

925 A326 20fr lt blue & org brn .40 .30

Issued in honor of Charles Goujon and Col. Constantin Rozanoff, test pilots.

Tancarville Bridge A327

1959, Aug. 1 Engr. *Perf. 13*

926 A327 30fr dk blue, brn & ol .30 .20

Marianne and Ship of State A328

Jean Jaures A329

1959, July Typo. *Perf. 14x13½*

927 A328 25fr black & red .30 .20

See No. 942. For surcharge see No. B336.

1959, Sept. 12 Engr. *Perf. 13*

928 A329 50fr chocolate .40 .25

Jean Jaures, socialist leader, birth cent.

Europa Issue, 1959

Common Design Type

1959, Sept. 19

Size: 22x36mm

929 CD2 25fr bright green *1.10* .35

930 CD2 50fr bright violet *1.75* .55

Blood Donors A330

1959, Oct. 17 Engr.

931 A330 20fr magenta & gray .25 .20

French-Spanish Handshake — A331

1959, Oct. 24 *Perf. 13*

932 A331 50fr blue, rose car & org .40 .30

300th anniv. of the signing of the Treaty of the Pyrenees.

Polio Victim Holding Crutches A332

Henri Bergson A333

1959, Oct. 31

933 A332 20fr dark blue .20 .20

Vaccination against poliomyelitis.

1959, Nov. 7

934 A333 50fr lt red brown .40 .25

Henri Bergson, philosopher, birth cent.

Avesnes-sur-Helpe — A334

Design: 30fr, Perpignan.

1959, Nov. 14

935 A334 20fr sepia & blue .25 .20

936 A334 30fr brn, dp claret & bl .25 .20

New NATO Headquarters, Paris — A335

1959, Dec. 12

937 A335 50fr green, brn & ultra .60 .40

10th anniv. of the NATO.

Types of 1958-59 and

Farm Woman A336

Sower A337

Designs: 5c, Arms of Lille. 15c, Arms of Algiers. 25c, Marianne and Ship of State.

Perf. 14x13½

1960-61 Unwmk. Typo.

No.	Type	Description	Unused	Used
938	A318	5c dk brown & red	7.25	.20
939	A336	10c brt green	.25	.20
940	A318	15c red, ultra, yel & grn	.60	.20
941	A337	20c grnsh bl & car rose	.20	.20
942	A328	25c ver & ultra	2.25	.20
b.		Booklet pane of 8	27.50	
c.		Booklet pane of 10	32.50	
942A	A337	30c gray & ultra ('61)	2.00	.30
		Nos. 938-942A (6)	12.55	1.30

See Nos. 707-708, 833-834 for the Farm Woman type (A336), but with no decimals in denominations.

For surcharges see Reunion Nos. 337-338, 341. For overprint see Algeria No. 286.

Laon Cathedral A338

Kerrata Gorge — A339

Designs: 30c, Fougères Chateau. 50c, Mosque, Tlemcen. 65c, Sioule Valley. 85c, Chaumont Viaduct. 1fr, Cilaos Church, Reunion.

1960, Jan. 16 Engr. *Perf. 13*

No.	Type	Description	Unused	Used
943	A338	15c blue & indigo	.25	.20
944	A338	30c blue, sepia & grn	3.00	.20
945	A339	45c brt vio & ol gray	.75	.20
946	A339	50c sl grn & lt cl	2.00	.20
947	A338	65c sl grn, bl & blk brn	1.10	.20
948	A338	85c blue, sep & grn	2.25	.20
949	A339	1fr vio bl, bl & grn	2.40	.20
		Nos. 943-949 (7)	11.75	1.40

For surcharges see Reunion Nos. 335, 340, 342. For overprint see Algeria Nos. 288-289.

Pierre de Nolhac A340

1960, Feb. 13

950 A340 20c black & gray .40 .30

Centenary of the birth of Pierre de Nolhac, curator of Versailles and historian.

Museum of Art and Industry, Saint-Etienne — A341

1960, Feb. 20

951 A341 30c brn, car & slate .60 .30

Gallic Cock Type of 1954

1960 Typo. *Perf. 14x13½*

No.	Type	Description	Unused	Used
952	A237	8c violet	.95	.20
953	A237	20c yellow grn	3.25	.30
954	A237	40c henna brn	7.75	2.00
955	A237	55c emerald	27.50	12.00
		Nos. 952-955 (4)	39.45	14.50

Nos. 952-955 were issued only precanceled. See second note after No. 132. See Nos. 910-913.

View of Cannes A342

1960, Mar. 5 Engr. *Perf. 13*

956 A342 50c red brn & lt grn .60 .50

Meeting of European municipal administrators, Cannes, Mar., 1960.

Woman of Savoy and Alps A343

Woman of Nice and Shore A344

1960 Unwmk. *Perf. 13*

957 A343 30c slate green .50 .35

958 A344 50c brn, yel & rose .55 .30

Cent. of the annexation of Nice and Savoy.

Heroes Type of 1957

Portraits: No. 959, Edmund Debeaumarché. No. 960, Pierre Massé. No. 961, Maurice Ripoche. No. 962, Leonce Vieljeux. 50c, Abbé René Bonpain.

1960, Mar. 26

No.	Type	Description	Unused	Used
959	A293	20c bister & blk	2.00	1.00
960	A293	20c pink & rose cl	1.60	1.00
961	A293	30c vio & brt vio	1.75	1.00
962	A293	30c sl bl & brt bl	2.25	1.50
963	A293	50c sl grn & red brn	2.50	1.90
		Nos. 959-963 (5)	10.10	6.40

Issued in honor of the heroes of the French Underground of World War II.

"Education" and Children
A345

1960, May 21 Engr. *Perf. 13*

964 A345 20c rose lilac, pur & blk .25 .20

1st secondary school in Strasbourg, 150th anniv.

Blois Chateau
A346

View of La Bourboule
A347

1960, May

965 A346 30c dk bl, sep & grn .55 .35
966 A347 50c ol brown, car & grn .55 .35

Lorraine Cross A348 Marianne A349

1960, June 18

967 A348 20c red brn, dk brn & yel grn .40 .20

20th anniv. of the French Resistance Movement in World War II.

1960, June 18 Typo. *Perf. 14x13½*

968 A349 25c lake & gray .20 .20
a. Booklet pane of 8 4.50
b. Booklet pane of 10 3.50

For surcharge see Reunion No. 339. For overprint see Algeria No. 287.

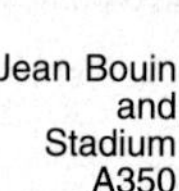

Jean Bouin and Stadium
A350

1960, July 9 Engr. *Perf. 13*

969 A350 20c blue, mag & ol gray .25 .20

17th Olympic Games, Rome, 8/25-9/11.

Europa Issue, 1960

Common Design Type

1960, Sept. 17 *Perf. 13*

Size: 36x22mm

970 CD3 25c green & bluish grn .20 .20
971 CD3 50c maroon & red lilac .30 .20

Lisieux Basilica
A351

1960, Sept. 24 *Perf. 13*

972 A351 15c blue, gray & blk .25 .20

Arms Type of 1958-59

Design: Arms of Oran.

1960, Oct. 15 Typo. *Perf. 14x13½*

973 A318 5c red, bl, yel & emer .20 .20

Madame de Stael by François Gerard — A352

1960, Oct. 22 Engr. *Perf. 13*

974 A352 30c dull claret & brn .25 .20

Madame de Stael (1766-1817), writer.

Gen. J. B. E. Estienne
A353

1960, Nov. 5

975 A353 15c lt lilac & black .20 .20

Centenary of the birth of Gen. Jean Baptiste Eugene Estienne.

Marc Sangnier and Youth Hostel at Bierville
A354

1960, Nov. 5

976 A354 20c blue, blk & lilac .20 .20

Issued to honor Marc Sangnier, founder of the French League for Youth Hostels.

Badge of Order of Liberation — A355

1960, Nov. 14 Engr. *Perf. 13*

977 A355 20c black & brt green .35 .20

Order of Liberation, 20th anniversary.

Lapwings
A356

Birds: 30c, Puffin. 45c, European teal. 50c, European bee-eaters.

1960, Nov. 12

978 A356 20c multicolored .30 .20
979 A356 30c multicolored .30 .25
980 A356 45c multicolored .95 .50
981 A356 50c multicolored .60 .25
Nos. 978-981 (4) 2.15 1.20

Issued to publicize wildlife protection.

André Honnorat
A357

1960, Nov. 19

982 A357 30c blue, blk & green .30 .25

Honnorat, statesman, fighter against tuberculosis and founder of the University City of Paris, an intl. students' community.

St. Barbara and Medieval View of School
A358

1960, Dec. 3 Engr.

983 A358 30c red, bl & ol brn .30 .30

St. Barbara School, Paris, 500th anniv.

"Mediterranean" by Aristide Maillol — A359

1961, Feb. 18 Unwmk. *Perf. 13*

984 A359 20c carmine & indigo .20 .20

Aristide Maillol, sculptor, birth cent.

Marianne by Cocteau — A360

1961, Feb. 23

985 A360 20c blue & carmine .20 .20

A second type has an extra inverted V-shaped mark (a blue flag top) at right of hair tip. Value unused $2.50, used 50 cents.

For surcharge see Reunion No. 357.

Paris Airport, Orly
A361

1961, Feb. 25

986 A361 50c blk, dk bl, & bluish grn .40 .30

Inauguration of new facilities at Orly airport.

George Méliès and Motion Picture Screen
A362

1961, Mar. 11

987 A362 50c pur, indigo & ol bis .60 .40

Cent. of the birth of George Méliès, motion picture pioneer.

Jean Baptiste Henri Lacordaire — A363

1961, Mar. 25 *Perf. 13*

988 A363 30c lt brown & black .25 .25

Cent. of the death of the Dominican monk Lacordaire, orator and liberal Catholic leader.

A364

1961, Mar. 25

989 A364 30c grn, red brn & red .30 .25

Introduction of tobacco use into France, fourth centenary. By error stamp portrays Jan Nicquet instead of Jean Nicot.

Heroes Type of 1957

Portraits: No. 990, Jacques Renouvin. No. 991, Lionel Dubray. No. 992, Paul Gateaud. No. 993, Mère Elisabeth.

1961, Apr. 22

990 A293 20c blue & lilac .70 .40
991 A293 20c gray grn & blue .70 .40
992 A293 30c brown org & blk .95 .50
993 A293 30c violet & blk 1.25 .60
Nos. 990-993 (4) 3.60 1.90

Bagnoles-de-l'Orne — A365

1961, May 6

994 A365 20c olive, ocher, bl & grn .20 .20

Dove, Olive Branch and Federation Emblem — A366

1961, May 6

995 A366 50c brt bl, grn & mar .30 .20

World Federation of Ex-Service Men.

Deauville in 19th Century
A367

1961, May 13 Engr.

996 A367 50c rose claret 1.60 .75

Centenary of Deauville.

La Champmeslé A368

Mont-Dore, Snowflake and Cable Car A369

French actors: #998, Talma. #999, Rachel. #1000, Gérard Philipe. #1001, Raimu.

1961, June 10 Unwmk. *Perf. 13*

Dark Carmine Frame

997 A368 20c choc & yel grn .60 .40
998 A368 30c brown & crimson .60 .40
999 A368 30c yel grn & sl grn .60 .40
1000 A368 50c olive & choc .95 .40
1001 A368 50c bl grn & red brn .90 .40
Nos. 997-1001 (5) 3.65 2.00

Issued to honor great French actors and in connection with the Fifth World Congress of the International Federation of Actors.

1961, July 1

1002 A369 20c orange & rose lilac .20 .20

Pierre Fauchard A370

St. Theobald's Church, Thann A371

1961, July 1

1003 A370 50c dk green & blk .45 .30

Bicentenary of the death of Pierre Fauchard, 1st surgeon dentist.

1961, July 1

1004 A371 20c sl grn, vio & brn .45 .30

800th anniversary of Thann.

Europa Issue, 1961

Common Design Type

1961, Sept. 16 *Perf. 13*

Size: 35x22mm

1005 CD4 25c vermilion .20 .20
1006 CD4 50c ultramarine .30 .30

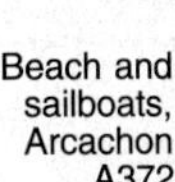
Beach and sailboats, Arcachon A372

15c, Saint-Paul, Maritime Alps. 45c, Sully-sur-Loire Chateau. 50c, View of Cognac. 65c, Rance Valley and Dinan. 85c, City hall and Rodin's Burghers, Calais. 1fr, Roman gates of Lodi, Medea, Algeria.

1961, Oct. 9 Engr. *Perf. 13*

1007 A372 15c blue & purple .20 .20
1008 A372 30c ultra, sl grn & lt brn .20 .20
1009 A372 45c vio bl, red brn & grn .20 .20
1010 A372 50c grn, Prus bl & sl .70 .20
1011 A372 65c red brn, sl grn & bl .50 .20
1012 A372 85c sl grn, sl & red brn .60 .25
1013 A372 1fr dk bl, sl & bis 3.25 .25
Nos. 1007-1013 (7) 5.65 1.50

For surcharges see Reunion Nos. 347-348. For overprint see Algeria No. 290.

Blue Nudes, by Matisse — A373

Paintings: 50c, "The Messenger," by Braque. 85c, "The Cardplayers," by Cézanne. 1fr, "The 14th July," by Roger de La Fresnaye.

1961, Nov. 10 *Perf. 13x12*

1014 A373 50c dk brn, bl, blk & gray 1.75 1.50
1015 A373 65c grn, vio, & ultra 3.50 1.75
1016 A373 85c blk, brn, red & ol 1.40 1.40
1017 A373 1fr multicolored 3.00 2.50
Nos. 1014-1017 (4) 9.65 7.15

Liner France A374

1962, Jan. 11 Engr. *Perf. 13*

1018 A374 30c dk blue, blk & car .45 .35

New French liner France.

Skier Going Downhill — A375

Maurice Bourdet — A376

1962, Jan. 27 *Perf. 13*

1019 A375 30c shown .20 .20
1020 A375 50c Slalom .30 .20

Issued to publicize the World Ski Championships, Chamonix, Feb. 1962.

1962, Feb. 17

1021 A376 30c slate .30 .20

60th anniv. of the birth of Maurice Bourdet, radio commentator and resistance hero.

Pierre-Fidele Bretonneau — A377

1962, Feb. 17

1022 A377 50c brt lilac & blue .35 .25

Centenary of the death of Pierre-Fidele Bretonneau, physician.

Chateau and Bridge, Laval, Mayenne A378

Gallic Cock A379

1962, Feb. 24

1023 A378 20c bis brn & slate grn .25 .20

1962-65 *Perf. 13*

1024 A379 25c ultra, car & brn .25 .20
a. Bklt. pane of 4 (horiz. strip) 2.50
1024B A379 30c gray grn, red & brn ('65) .85 .20
c. Booklet pane of 5 5.00
d. Booklet pane of 10 10.00

No. 1024 was also issued on experimental luminescent paper in 1963. Value $750.

Ramparts of Vannes A380

Dunkirk — A381

Paris Beach, Le Touquet A381a

1962 Engr. *Perf. 13*

1025 A380 30c dark blue .80 .40
1026 A381 95c grn, bis & red lil 1.00 .40
1027 A381a 1fr grn, red brn & bl .45 .20
Nos. 1025-1027 (3) 2.25 1.00

No. 1026 for the 300th anniv. of Dunkirk.

Stage Setting and Globe A382

1962, Mar. 24 Unwmk.

1028 A382 50c sl grn, ocher & mag .40 .25

International Day of the Theater, Mar. 27.

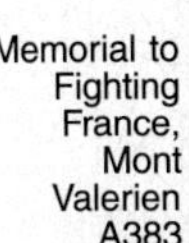
Memorial to Fighting France, Mont Valerien A383

Resistance Heroes' Monument, Vercors — A384

Design: 50c, Ile de Sein monument.

1962, Apr. 7

1029 A383 20c olive & slate grn .50 .30
1030 A384 30c bluish black .50 .30
1031 A384 50c blue & indigo .75 .40
Nos. 1029-1031 (3) 1.75 1.00

Issued to publicize memorials for the French Underground in World War II.

Malaria Eradication Emblem and Swamp — A385

Nurses with Child and Hospital — A386

1962, Apr. 14 Engr.

1032 A385 50c dk blue & dk red .30 .25

WHO drive to eradicate malaria.

1962, May 5 Unwmk. *Perf. 13*

1033 A386 30c bl grn, gray & red brn .20 .20

National Hospital Week, May 5-12.

Glider A387

20c, Planes showing development of aviation.

1962, May 12

1034 A387 15c orange red & brn .30 .20
1035 A387 20c lil rose & rose cl .35 .25

Issued to publicize sports aviation.

School Emblem — A388

1962, May 19 Engr.

1036 A388 50c mar, ocher & dk vio .35 .30

Watchmaker's School at Besançon, cent.

Louis XIV and Workers Showing Modern Gobelin A389

1962, May 26 Unwmk. *Perf. 13*

1037 A389 50c ol, sl grn & car .35 .25

Gobelin tapestry works, Paris, 300th anniv.

Blaise Pascal A390

1962, May 26

1038 A390 50c slate grn & dp org .35 .25

Blaise Pascal (1623-1662), mathematician, scientist and philosopher.

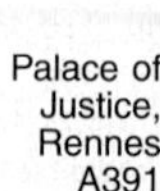

Palace of Justice, Rennes
A391

1962, June 12

1039 A391 30c blk, grysh bl & grn 1.40 .60

Arms Type of 1958-59

5c, Amiens. 10c, Troyes. 15c, Nevers.

1962-63 Typo. *Perf. 14x13½*

1040 A318 5c ver, ultra & yel .20 .20
1041 A318 10c red, ultra & yel ('63) .20 .20
1042 A318 15c ver, ultra & yel .20 .20
Nos. 1040-1042 (3) .60 .60

Phosphor Tagging

In 1970 France began to experiment with luminescence. Phosphor bands have been added to Nos. 1041, 1143, 1231, 1231C, 1292A-1294B, 1494-1498, 1560-1579B, etc.

Rose — A392

Design: 30c, Old-fashioned rose.

1962, Sept. 8 Engr. *Perf. 13*

1043 A392 20c ol, grn & brt car .40 .20
1044 A392 30c dk sl grn, ol & car .50 .30

Europa Issue, 1962

Common Design Type

1962, Sept. 15

Size: 36x22mm

1045 CD5 25c violet .20 .20
1046 CD5 50c henna brown .35 .20

Space Communications Center, Pleumeur-Bodou, France — A394

Telstar, Earth and Television Set — A395

1962, Sept. 29 Engr. *Perf. 13*

1047 A394 25c gray, yel & grn .20 .20
1048 A395 50c dk bl, grn & ultra .35 .25

1st television connection of the US and Europe through Telstar satellite, July 11-12.

For surcharges see Reunion Nos. 343-344.

"Bonjour Monsieur Courbet" by Gustave Courbet — A396

Paintings: 65c, "Madame Manet on Blue Sofa," by Edouard Manet. 1fr, "Guards officer on horseback," by Theodore Géricault, vert.

1962, Nov. 9 *Perf. 13x12, 12x13*

1049 A396 50c multicolored 2.75 1.75
1050 A396 65c multicolored 2.00 1.50
1051 A396 1fr multicolored 4.50 2.50
Nos. 1049-1051 (3) 9.25 5.75

Bathyscaph "Archimede" — A397

1963, Jan. 26 Unwmk. *Perf. 13*

1052 A397 30c dk blue & blk .25 .20

French deep-sea explorations.

Flowers and Nantes Chateau
A398

1963, Feb. 11

1053 A398 30c vio bl, car & sl grn .25 .20

Nantes flower festival.

St. Peter, Window at St. Foy de Conches
A399

50c, Jacob Wrestling with the Angel, by Delacroix.

1963, Mar. 2 *Perf. 12x13*

1054 A399 50c multicolored 3.00 1.50
1055 A399 1fr multicolored 4.00 2.50

See Nos. 1076-1077.

Hungry Woman and Wheat Emblem
A400

1963, Mar. 21 Engr. *Perf. 13*

1056 A400 50c slate grn & brn .25 .20

FAO "Freedom from Hunger" campaign.

Cemetery and Memorial, Glières — A401

Design: 50c, Memorial, Ile de la Cité, Paris.

1963, Mar. 23 Unwmk. *Perf. 13*

1057 A401 30c dk brown & olive .40 .40
1058 A401 50c indigo .40 .40

Heroes of the resistance against the Nazis.

Beethoven, Birthplace at Bonn and Rhine
A402

#1060, Emile Verhaeren, memorial at Roisin & residence. #1061, Giuseppe Mazzini, Marcus Aurelius statue & Via Appia, Rome. #1062, Emile Mayrisch, Colpach Chateau & blast furnace, Esch. #1063, Hugo de Groot, Palace of Peace, The Hague & St. Agatha Church, Delft.

1963, Apr. 27 Unwmk. *Perf. 13*

1059 A402 20c ocher, sl & brt grn .25 .25
1060 A402 20c purple, blk & mar .25 .25
1061 A402 20c maroon, sl & ol .25 .25
1062 A402 20c mar, dk brn & ocher .25 .25
1063 A402 30c dk brn, vio & ocher .25 .25
Nos. 1059-1063 (5) 1.25 1.25

Issued to honor famous men of the European Common Market countries.

Hotel des Postes and Stagecoach, 1863 — A403

1963, May 4

1064 A403 50c grayish black .25 .25

1st Intl. Postal Conference, Paris, 1863.

Lycée Louis-le-Grand, Belvédère, Panthéon and St. Etienne du Mont Church — A404

1963, May 18

1065 A404 30c slate green .25 .25

400th anniversary of the Jesuit Clermont secondary school, named after Louis XIV.

St. Peter's Church and Ramparts, Caen
A405

1963, June 1 Unwmk. *Perf. 13*

1066 A405 30c gray blue & brn .25 .25

Radio Telescope, Nançay — A406

1963, June 8 Engr.

1067 A406 50c dk bl & dk brn .35 .30

Amboise Chateau
A407

Saint-Flour — A408

Designs: 50c, Côte d'Azur Varoise. 85c, Vittel. 95c, Moissac.

1963, June 15

1068 A407 30c slate, grn & bis .25 .20
1069 A407 50c dk grn, dk bl & hn brn .40 .20
1070 A408 60c ultra, dk grn & hn brn .45 .20
1071 A407 85c dk grn, yel grn & brn 1.25 .25
1072 A408 95c dk brown & black .75 .25
Nos. 1068-1072 (5) 3.10 1.10

For surcharge see Reunion No. 355.

Water Skiing Slalom
A409

1963, Aug. 31 Unwmk. *Perf. 13*

1073 A409 30c sl grn, blk & car .25 .20

World Water Skiing Championships, Vichy.

Europa Issue, 1963

Common Design Type

1963, Sept. 14

Size: 36x22mm

1074 CD6 25c red brown .45 .25
1075 CD6 50c green .45 .25

Art Type of 1963

Designs: 85c, "The Married Couple of the Eiffel Tower," by Marc Chagall. 95c, "The Fur Merchants," window, Chartres Cathedral.

1963, Nov. 9 Engr. *Perf. 12x13*

1076 A399 85c multicolored 1.25 .90
1077 A399 95c multicolored .60 .50

Philatec Issue

Common Design Type

1963, Dec. 14 Unwmk. *Perf. 13*

1078 CD118 25c dk gray, sl grn & dk car .20 .20

For surcharge see Reunion No. 349.

Radio and Television Center, Paris
A411

1963, Dec. 15 Engr.

1079 A411 20c org brn, slate & ol .20 .20

Fire Brigade Insignia, Symbols of Fire, Water and Civilian Defense
A412

1964, Feb. 8 Engr. *Perf. 13*

1082 A412 30c blue, org & red .50 .25

Issued to honor the fire brigades and civilian defense corps.

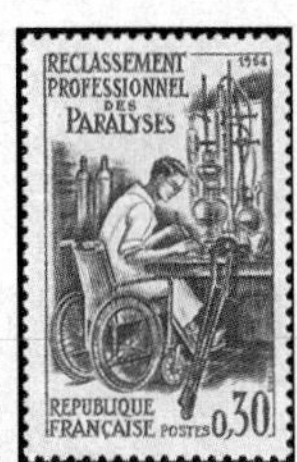

Handicapped Laboratory Technician — A413

1964, Feb. 22 Unwmk. *Perf. 13*
1083 A413 30c grn, red brn & brn .25 .20

Rehabilitation of the handicapped.

John II the Good (1319-64) by Girard d'Orleans A414

1964, Apr. 25 *Perf. 12x13*
1084 A414 1fr multicolored 1.40 1.10

Stamp of 1900 A415

Mechanized Mail Handling A416

Designs: No. 1086, Stamp of 1900, Type A17. No. 1088, Telecommunications.

1964, May 9 *Perf. 13*
1085 A415 25c bister & dk car .30 .30
1086 A415 25c bister & blue .30 .30
1087 A416 30c blk, bl & org brn .30 .30
1088 A416 30c blk, car rose & bluish grn .30 .30
a. Strip of 4, #1085-1088 + label 1.25 1.25

Printed in sheets of 20 stamps, containing five No. 1088a. The label shows the Philatec emblem in green.

Type of Semi-Postal Issue
with "25e ANNIVERSAIRE" added

1964, May 9
1089 SP208 25c multicolored .20 .20

25th anniversary, night airmail service.

Madonna and Child from Rose Window of Notre Dame A417

1964, May 23 *Perf. 12x13*
1090 A417 60c multicolored .35 .35

Notre Dame Cathedral, Paris, 800th anniv.

Arms Type of 1958-59

Arms: 1c, Niort. 2c, Guéret. 12c, Agen. 18c, Saint-Denis, Réunion. 30c, Paris.

1964-65 Typo. *Perf. 14x13½*
1091 A318 1c vio blue & yel .20 .20
1092 A318 2c emer, vio bl & yel .20 .20
1093 A318 12c black, red & yel .20 .20
1094 A318 18c multicolored .20 .20
1095 A318 30c vio bl & red ('65) .30 .20
a. Booklet pane of 10 6.50
Nos. 1091-1095 (5) 1.10 1.00

Gallic Coin — A418

Perf. 13½x14
1964-66 Typo. Unwmk.
1096 A418 10c emer & bister .75 .20
1097 A418 15c org & bister ('66) .30 .20
1098 A418 25c lilac & brn .45 .20
1099 A418 50c brt blue & brn .75 .60
Nos. 1096-1099 (4) 2.25 1.20

Nos. 1096-1099 are known only precanceled. See second note after No. 132. See Nos. 1240-1242, 1315-1318, 1421-1424.

Postrider, Rocket and Radar Equipment — A419

1964, June 5 Engr. *Perf. 13*
1100 A419 1fr brn, dk red & dk bl 17.50 17.50

Sold for 4fr, including 3fr admission to PHILATEC. Issued in sheets of 8 stamps and 8 labels (2x8 subjects with labels in horizontal rows 1, 4, 5, 8; stamps in rows 2, 3, 6, 7). Commemorative inscriptions on side margins. Value $140.

Caesar's Tower, Provins — A420

Chapel of Notre Dame du Haut, Ronchamp A421

1964-65
1101 A421 40c sl grn, dk brn & brn ('65) .20 .20
1102 A420 70c slate, grn & car .30 .20
1103 A421 1.25fr brt bl, sl grn & ol .55 .25
Nos. 1101-1103 (3) 1.05 .65

The 40c was issued in vertical coils in 1971. Every 10th coil stamp has a red control number printed twice on the back.

For surcharges see Reunion Nos. 352, 361.

Mandel — A422

Judo — A423

1964, July 4 Unwmk. *Perf. 13*
1104 A422 30c violet brown .20 .20

Georges Mandel (1885-1944), Cabinet minister, executed by the Nazis.

1964, July 4
1105 A423 50c dk blue & vio brn .25 .20

18th Olympic Games, Tokyo, 10/10-25/64.

Champlevé Enamel from Limoges, 12th Century A424

Design: No. 1107, The Lady (Claude Le Viste?) with the Unicorn, 15th cent. tapestry.

1964 *Perf. 12x13*
1106 A424 1fr multicolored 1.25 .80
1107 A424 1fr multicolored .40 .35

No. 1106 shows part of an enamel sepulchral plate portraying Geoffrey IV, Count of Anjou and Le Maine (1113-1151), who was called Geoffrey Plantagenet.

Issue dates: #1106, July 4. #1107, Oct. 31.

Paris Taxis Carrying Soldiers to Front, 1914 A425

1964, Sept. 5 Unwmk. *Perf. 13*
1108 A425 30c black, blue & red .25 .20

50th anniversary of Battle of the Marne.

Europa Issue, 1964
Common Design Type

1964, Sept. 12 Engr.
Size: 22x36mm
1109 CD7 25c dk car, dp ocher & grn .20 .20
1110 CD7 50c vio, yel grn & dk car .30 .20

Cooperation Issue
Common Design Type

1964, Nov. 6 Unwmk. *Perf. 13*
1111 CD119 25c red brn, dk brn & dk bl .20 .20

Joux Chateau — A427

1965, Feb. 6 Engr.
1112 A427 1.30fr redsh brn, brn red & dk brn .65 .20

"The English Girl from the Star" by Toulouse-Lautrec — A428

St. Paul on the Damascus Road, Window, Cathedral of Sens — A429

Leaving for the Hunt — A430

Apocalypse Tapestry, 14th Century A431

"The Red Violin" by Raoul Dufy — A432

Designs: No. 1115, "August" miniature of Book of Hours of Jean de France, Duc de Berry ("Les Très Riches Heures du Duc de Berry"), painted by Flemish brothers, Pol, Hermant and Jannequin Limbourg, 1411-16. No. 1116, Scene from oldest existing set of French tapestries, showing the Winepress of the Wrath of God (Revelations 14: 19-20).

1965 *Perf. 12x13, 13x12*
1113 A428 1fr multicolored .40 .40
1114 A429 1fr multicolored .40 .40
1115 A430 1fr multicolored .30 .30
1116 A431 1fr multicolored .30 .30
1117 A432 1fr blk, pink & car .30 .30
Nos. 1113-1117 (5) 1.70 1.70

No. 1114 issued to commemorate the 800th anniversary of the Cathedral of Sens.

Issued: #1113, 3/12; #1114, 6/5; #1115, 9/25; #1116, 10/30; #1117, 11/6.

Returning Deportees, 1945 — A433

1965, Apr. 1 Unwmk. *Perf. 13*
1118 A433 40c Prussian green .40 .30

20th anniv. of the return of people deported during World War II.

House of Youth and Culture, Troyes A434

1965, Apr. 10 Engr.
1119 A434 25c ind, brn & dk grn .25 .20

20th anniv. of the establishment of recreational cultural centers for young people.

Woman Carrying Flowers A435

Flags of France, US, USSR and Great Britain Crushing Swastika A436

1965, Apr. 24 Unwmk. *Perf. 13*
1120 A435 60c dk grn, dp org & ver .25 .20

Tourist Campaign of Welcome & Amiability.

1965, May 8
1121 A436 40c black, car & ultra .25 .20

20th anniv. of victory in World War II.

Telegraph Key, Syncom Satellite and Pleumeur-Bodou Station — A437

1965, May 17
1122 A437 60c dk blue, brn & blk .40 .30

Centenary of the ITU.

Croix de Guerre — A438

1965, May 22 Engr.
1123 A438 40c red, brn & brt grn .35 .25

50th anniv. of the Croix de Guerre medal.

Cathedral of Bourges — A439

Moustiers-Sainte-Marie — A440

Views: 30c, Road and tunnel, Mont Blanc. 60c, Aix-les-Bains, sailboat. 75c, Tarn Gorge, Lozère mountains. 95c, Vendée River, man poling boat, and windmill. 1fr, Prehistoric stone monuments, Carnac.

1965
1124 A439 30c bl, vio bl & brn vio .20 .20
1125 A439 40c gray bl & redsh brn .25 .20
1126 A440 50c grn, bl gray & bis .25 .20
1127 A439 60c blue & red brn .40 .20
1128 A440 75c brown, bl & grn .95 .60
1129 A440 95c brown, grn & bl 4.00 .80
1130 A440 1fr gray, grn & brn 1.10 .25
Nos. 1124-1130 (7) 7.15 2.45

No. 1124 for the opening of the Mont Blanc Tunnel. No. 1125 (Bourges Cathedral) was issued in connection with the French Philatelic Societies Federation Congress, held at Bourges.

Issued: 40c, June 5; 50c, June 19; 30c, 60c, July 17; others, July 10.

For surcharges see Reunion #354, 362, 365.

Europa Issue, 1965
Common Design Type

1965, Sept. 25 *Perf. 13*
Size: 36x22mm
1131 CD8 30c red .30 .30
1132 CD8 60c gray .70 .50

Planting Seedling A441

Etienne Régnault, "Le Taureau" and Coast of Reunion A442

1965, Oct. 2
1133 A441 25c slate grn, yel grn & red brn .20 .20

National reforestation campaign.

1965, Oct. 2
1134 A442 30c indigo & dk car .20 .20

Tercentenary of settlement of Reunion.

Atomic Reactor and Diagram, Symbols of Industry, Agriculture and Medicine — A443

1965, Oct. 9
1135 A443 60c brt blue & blk .35 .30

Atomic Energy Commission, 20th anniv.

Air Academy and Emblem A444

1965, Nov. 6 *Perf. 13*
1136 A444 25c dk blue & green .35 .30

Air Academy, Salon-de-Provence, 50th anniv.

French Satellite A-1 Issue
Common Design Type

Design: 60c, A-1 satellite.

1965, Nov. 30 Engr. *Perf. 13*
1137 CD121 30c Prus bl, brt bl & blk .25 .20
1138 CD121 60c blk, Prus bl & brt bl .25 .20
a. Strip of 2, #1137-1138 + label .60 .60

Launching of France's 1st satellite, 11/26/65.
For surcharges see Reunion Nos. 358-359.

Arms of Auch — A446

Cities: 20c, Saint-Lô. 25c, Mont-de-Marsan.

Typographed, Photogravure (20c)
1966 *Perf. 14x13; 14 (20c)*
1142 A446 5c blue & red .20 .20
1143 A446 20c vio bl, sil, gold & red .20 .20
1144 A446 25c red brown & ultra .45 .20
Nos. 1142-1144 (3) .85 .60

The 5c and 20c were issued in sheets and in vertical coils. In the coils, every 10th stamp has a red control number on the back.

For surcharges see Reunion Nos. 360-360A.

French Satellite D-1 Issue
Common Design Type

1966, Feb. 18 Engr. *Perf. 13*
1148 CD122 60c blue blk, grn & cl .20 .20

Horses from Bronze Vessel of Vix — A448

"The Newborn" by Georges de La Tour — A449

The Baptism of Judas (4th Century Bishop of Jerusalem) — A450

"The Moon and the Bull" Tapestry by Jean Lurçat A451

"Crispin and Scapin" by Honoré Daumier — A452

1966 *Perf. 13x12, 12x13*
1149 A448 1fr multicolored .35 .35
1150 A449 1fr multicolored .35 .35
1151 A450 1fr multicolored .35 .35
1152 A451 1fr multicolored .30 .30
1153 A452 1fr multicolored .30 .30
Nos. 1149-1153 (5) 1.65 1.65

The design of No. 1149 is a detail from a 6th century B.C. vessel, found in 1953 in a grave near Vix, Cote d'Or.

The design of No. 1151 is from a stained glass window in the 13th century Sainte-Chapelle, Paris.

No. 1150 exists in an imperf, ungummed souv. sheet with 2 progressive die proofs, issued for benefit of the Postal Museum, and not postally valid.

Issued: #1149, 3/26; #1150, 6/25; #1151, 10/22; #1152, 11/19; #1153, 12/10.

Chessboard, Knight, Emblems for King and Queen — A453

St. Michael Slaying the Dragon — A455

Rhone Bridge, Pont-Saint-Esprit — A454

1966, Apr. 2 Engr. *Perf. 13*
1154 A453 60c sepia, gray & dk vio bl .50 .40

Issued to publicize the Chess Festival.

1966, Apr. 23 Unwmk. *Perf. 13*
1155 A454 25c black & dull blue .20 .20

1966, Apr. 30 Litho. & Engr.
1156 A455 25c multicolored .20 .20

Millenium of Mont-Saint-Michel.

Stanislas Leszczynski, Lunéville Chateau — A456

1966, May 6 **Engr.**

1157 A456 25c slate, grn & brn .20 .20

200th anniv. of the reunion of Lorraine and Bar (Barrois) with France.

St. Andrew's and Sèvre River, Niort — A457

1966, May 28 **Engr.** ***Perf. 13***

1158 A457 40c brt bl, indigo & grn .25 .20

Bernard Le Bovier de Fontenelle and 1666 Meeting Room A458

1966, June 4

1159 A458 60c dk car rose & brn .25 .25

300th anniversary, Académie des Sciences.

William the Conqueror, Castle and Norman Ships — A459

1966, June 4

1160 A459 60c brown red & dp bl .40 .30

900th anniversary of Battle of Hastings.

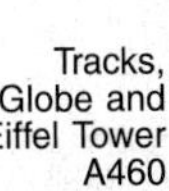

Tracks, Globe and Eiffel Tower A460

1966, June 11

1161 A460 60c dk brn, car & dull bl .65 .40

19th International Railroad Congress.

Oléron Bridge A461

1966, June 20

1162 A461 25c Prus bl, brn & bl .20 .20

Issued to commemorate the opening of Oléron Bridge, connecting Oléron Island in the Bay of Biscay with the French mainland.

Europa Issue, 1966

Common Design Type

1966, Sept. 24 **Engr.** ***Perf. 13***

Size: 22x36mm

1163 CD9 30c Prussian blue .25 .25
1164 CD9 60c red .45 .25

Vercingetorix at Gergovie, 52 B.C. — A462

Bishop Remi Baptizing King Clovis, 496 A.D. — A463

Design: 60c, Charlemagne attending school (page holding book for crowned king).

1966, Nov. 5 ***Perf. 13***

1165 A462 40c choc, grn & gray bl .25 .20
1166 A463 40c dk red brn & blk .25 .20
1167 A463 60c pur, rose car & brn .25 .20
Nos. 1165-1167 (3) .75 .60

Map of Pneumatic Post and Tube A464

1966, Nov. 11

1168 A464 1.60fr maroon & indigo .60 .30

Centenary of Paris pneumatic post system.

Val Chateau — A465

1966, Nov. 19 **Engr.** ***Perf. 13***

1169 A465 2.30fr dk bl, sl grn & brn 1.75 .30

Rance Power Station A466

1966, Dec. 3

1170 A466 60c dk bl, sl grn & brn .40 .30

Tidal power station in the estuary of the Rance River on the English Channel.

European Broadcasting Union Emblem — A467

1967, Mar. 4 **Engr.** ***Perf. 13***

1171 A467 40c dk blue & rose brn .25 .20

3rd Intl. Congress of the European Broadcasting Union, Paris, Mar. 8-22.

Father Juniet's Gig by Henri Rousseau — A468

Francois I by Jean Clouet A469

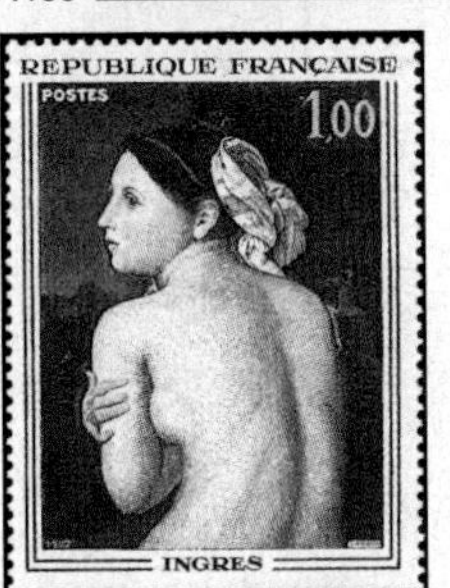

The Bather by Jean-Dominique Ingres — A470

St. Eloi, the Goldsmith, at Work — A471

1967 **Engr.** ***Perf. 13x12, 12x13***

1172 A468 1fr multicolored .40 .40
1173 A469 1fr multicolored .40 .40
1174 A470 1fr multicolored .40 .35
1175 A471 1fr multicolored .40 .35
Nos. 1172-1175 (4) 1.60 1.50

The design of No. 1175 is from a 16th century stained glass window in the Church of Sainte Madeleine, Troyes.

Issued: #1172, 4/15; #1173, 7/1; #1174, 9/9; #1175, 10/7.

Snow Crystal and Olympic Rings — A472

1967, Apr. 22 **Photo.** ***Perf. 13***

1176 A472 60c brt & lt blue & red .30 .25

Issued to publicize the 10th Winter Olympic Games, Grenoble, Feb. 6-18, 1968.

French Pavilion, EXPO '67 — A473

1967, Apr. 22 **Engr.**

1177 A473 60c dull bl & bl grn .30 .30

Intl. Exhibition EXPO '67, Montreal, Apr. 28-Oct. 27, 1967.

For surcharge see Reunion No. 363.

Europa Issue, 1967

Common Design Type

1967, Apr. 29

Size: 22x36mm

1178 CD10 30c blue & gray .30 .25
1179 CD10 60c brown & lt blue .75 .45

Great Bridge, Bordeaux A474

1967, May 8

1180 A474 25c olive, blk & brn .20 .20

Nungesser, Coli and "L'Oiseau Blanc" A475

1967, May 8

1181 A475 40c slate, dk & lt brn .40 .30

40th anniv. of the attempted transatlantic flight of Charles Nungesser and François Coil, French aviators.

Goüin House, Tours — A476

1967, May 13 **Engr.** ***Perf. 13***

1182 A476 40c vio bl, red brn & red .30 .25

Congress of the Federation of French Philatelic Societies in Tours.

Ramon and Alfort Veterinary School A477

1967, May 27

1183 A477 25c brn, dp bl & yel grn .20 .20

200th anniv. of the Alfort Veterinary School and to honor Professor Gaston Ramon (1886-1963).

Robert Esnault-Pelterie, Diamant Rocket and A-1 Satellite — A478

1967, May 27
1184 A478 60c slate & vio blue .40 .25

Issued to honor Robert Esnault-Pelterie (1881-1957), aviation and space expert.

City Hall, Saint-Quentin A479

Saint-Germain-en-Laye — A480

Views: 60c, Clock Tower, Vire. 75c, Beach, La Baule, Brittany. 95c, Harbor, Boulogne-sur-Mer. 1fr, Rodez Cathedral. 1.50fr, Morlaix; old houses, grotesque carving, viaduct.

1967
1185 A479 50c bl, sl bl & brn .30 .20
1186 A479 60c dp bl, sl bl & dk red brn .50 .25
1187 A480 70c rose car, red brn & bl .30 .20
1188 A480 75c multicolored 1.40 .50
1189 A480 95c sky bl, lil & sl grn 1.10 .60
1190 A479 1fr indigo & bl gray .50 .20
1191 A479 1.50fr brt bl, brt grn & red brn 1.10 .35
Nos. 1185-1191 (7) 5.20 2.30

Issued: 1fr, 1.50fr, June 10; 70c, June 17; 50c, 60c, 95c, July 8; 75c, July 24.

Orchids — A481

Scales of Justice, City and Harbor A483

Cross of Lorraine, Soldiers and Sailors — A482

1967, July 29 Engr. *Perf. 13*
1192 A481 40c dp car, brt pink & pur .60 .35

Orleans flower festival.

1967, Sept. 4
1193 A482 60c dk plum, dl bl & ocher .40 .30

9th Intl. Accountancy Cong., Paris, 9/6-12.

1967, Oct. 7 Engr. *Perf. 13*
1194 A483 25c brn, dp ultra & bl .20 .20

25th anniv. of the Battle of Bir Hacheim.

Marie Curie, Bowl Glowing with Radium A484

1967, Oct. 23 Engr. *Perf. 13*
1195 A484 60c dk blue & ultra .25 .25

Marie Curie (1867-1934), scientist who discovered radium and polonium, Nobel prize winner for physics and chemistry.

Lions Emblem A485

Marianne (by Cheffer) — A486

1967, Oct. 28
1196 A485 40c dk car & vio bl .75 .40

50th anniversary of Lions International. For surcharge see Reunion No. 364.

1967, Nov. 4 Engr.
1197 A486 25c dark blue .40 .20
1198 A486 30c bright lilac .45 .20
a. Booklet pane of 5 3.00
b. Booklet pane of 10 6.50

Coils (vertical) of Nos. 1197 and 1231 show a red number on the back of every 10th stamp. See Nos. 1230-1231C. For surcharges see Reunion Nos. 367-368, 389.

King Philip II (Philip Augustus) at Battle of Bouvines A487

Designs: No. 1200, Election of Hugh Capet as King, horiz. 60c, King Louis IX (St. Louis) holding audience for the poor.

1967, Nov. 13 Engr. *Perf. 13*
1199 A487 40c gray & black .25 .20
1200 A487 40c steel bl & ultra .25 .20
1201 A487 60c grn & dk red brn .40 .25
Nos. 1199-1201 (3) .90 .65

Commemorative Medal — A488

1968, Jan. 6 Engr. *Perf. 13*
1202 A488 40c dk slate grn & bis .20 .20

50th anniversary of postal checking service.

Various Road Signs — A489

1968, Feb. 24
1203 A489 25c lil, red & dk bl grn .20 .20

Issued to publicize road safety.

Prehistoric Paintings, Lascaux Cave — A490

Arearea (Merriment) by Paul Gauguin — A491

The Dance by Emile Antoine Bourdelle A492

Portrait of the Model by Auguste Renoir A493

1968 Engr. *Perf. 13x12, 12x13*
1204 A490 1fr multicolored .45 .30
1205 A491 1fr multicolored .50 .30
1206 A492 1fr car & gray olive .45 .30
1207 A493 1fr multicolored .50 .30
Nos. 1204-1207 (4) 1.90 1.20

Issue dates: #1204, Apr. 13; #1205, Sept. 21; #1206, Oct. 26; #1207, Nov. 9.

Audio-visual Institute, Royan — A494

1968, Apr. 13 *Perf. 13*
1208 A494 40c slate grn, brn & Prus bl .20 .20

5th Conference for World Cooperation with the theme of teaching living languages by audio-visual means.

Europa Issue, 1968
Common Design Type

1968, Apr. 27
Size: 36x22mm
1209 CD11 30c brt red lil & ocher *.35* .20
1210 CD11 60c brown & lake *.70* .30

Alain René Le Sage — A495

1968, May 4
1211 A495 40c blue & rose vio .20 .20

Alain René Le Sage (1668-1747), novelist and playwright.

Chateau de Langeais A496

1968, May 4
1212 A496 60c slate bl, grn & red brn .35 .30

Pierre Larousse A497

1968, May 11 Engr. *Perf. 13*
1213 A497 40c rose vio & brown .20 .20

Pierre Larousse (1817-75), grammarian, lexicographer and encyclopedist.

Gnarled Trunk and Fir Tree — A498

1968, May 18 Engr. *Perf. 13*
1214 A498 25c grnsh bl, brn & grn .20 .20

Twinning of Rambouillet Forest in France and the Black Forest in Germany.

Map of Papal Enclave, Valréas, and John XXII Receiving Homage A499

1968, May 25
1215 A499 60c brn, bis brn & pur .35 .25

Papal enclave at Valréas, 650th anniv.

Louis XIV, Arms of France and Flanders A500

1968, June 29

1216 A500 40c rose car, gray & lemon .25 .20

300th anniv. of the Treaty of Aachen which reunited Flanders with France.

Martrou Bridge, Rochefort A501

1968, July 20

1217 A501 25c sky bl, blk & dk red brn .20 .20

Letord Lorraine Bimotor Plane over Map of France A502

1968, Aug. 17 **Engr.** ***Perf. 13***

1218 A502 25c brt blue, indigo & red .40 .25

1st regularly scheduled air mail route in France from Paris to St. Nazaire, 50th anniv.

Tower de Constance, Aigues-Mortes A503

1968, Aug. 31

1219 A503 25c red brn, sky bl & olive bister .25 .20

Bicentenary of the release of Huguenot prisoners from the Tower de Constance, Aigues-Mortes.

Cathedral and Pont Vieux, Beziers A504

1968, Sept. 7 **Engr.** ***Perf. 13***

1220 A504 40c ind, bis & grn .35 .25

"Victory" over White Tower of Salonika — A505

1968, Sept. 28

1221 A505 40c red lilac & plum .20 .20

50th anniv. of the armistice on the eastern front in World War I, Sept. 29, 1918.

Louis XV, Arms of France and Corsica A506

1968, Oct. 5 ***Perf. 13***

1222 A506 25c ultra, grn & blk .20 .20

Return of Corsica to France, 200th anniv.

Relay Race A507

1968, Oct. 12

1223 A507 40c ultra, brt grn & ol brn .35 .30

19th Olympic Games, Mexico City, 10/12-27.

Polar Camp with Helicopter, Plane and Snocat Tractor — A508

1968, Oct. 19

1224 A508 40c Prus bl, lt grnsh bl & brn red .25 .20

20 years of French Polar expeditions.

For surcharge see Reunion No. 366.

Leon Bailby, Paris Opera Staircase and Hospital Beds — A509

"Victory" over Arc de Triomphe and Eternal Flame — A510

1968, Oct. 26

1225 A509 40c ocher & maroon .25 .20

50th anniv. of the "Little White Beds" children's hospital fund.

1968, Nov. 9 **Engr.** ***Perf. 13***

1226 A510 25c dk car rose & dp blue .20 .20

50th anniv. of the armistice which ended World War I.

Death of Bertrand Du Guesclin at Chateauneuf-de-Randon, 1380 — A511

#1228, King Philip IV (the Fair) and first States-General assembly, 1302, horiz. 60c, Joan of Arc leaving Vaucouleurs, 1429.

1968, Nov. 16

1227 A511 40c green, ultra & brn .30 .25

1228 A511 40c cop red, grn & gray .30 .25

1229 A511 60c vio bl, sl bl & bis .40 .25

Nos. 1227-1229 (3) 1.00 .75

See No. 1260.

Marianne Type of 1967

1969-70 **Engr.** ***Perf. 13***

1230 A486 30c green .35 .20

a. Booklet pane of 10 3.50

1231 A486 40c deep carmine .45 .20

a. Booklet pane of 5 (horiz. strip) 2.50

b. Booklet pane of 10 4.50

d. With label ('70) .50 .25

Typo. ***Perf. 14x13***

1231C A486 30c blue green .20 .20

Nos. 1230-1231C (3) 1.00 .60

No. 1231d was issued in sheets of 50 with alternating labels showing coat of arms of Perigueux, arranged checkerwise, to commemorate the inauguration of the Perigueux stamp printing plant.

The 40c coil is noted after No. 1198.

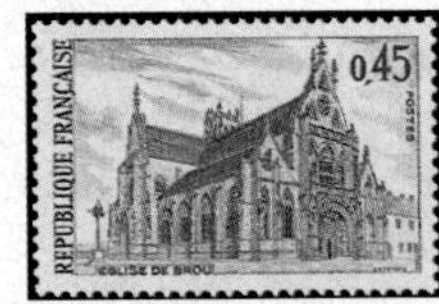

Church of Brou, Bourg-en-Bresse — A512

Views: 80c, Vouglans Dam, Jura. 85c, Chateau de Chantilly. 1.15fr, Sailboats in La Trinité-sur-Mer harbor.

1969 **Engr.** ***Perf. 13***

1232 A512 45c olive, bl & red brn .25 .20

1233 A512 80c ol bis, brn red & dk brn .45 .20

1234 A512 85c sl grn, dl bl & gray .85 .45

1235 A512 1.15fr brt bl, gray grn & brn .70 .40

Nos. 1232-1235 (4) 2.25 1.25

"February" Bas-relief from Amiens Cathedral A513

Philip the Good, by Roger van der Weyden A514

Sts. Savin and Cyprian before Ladicius, Mural, St. Savin, Vienne — A515

The Circus, by Georges Seurat A515a

1969 ***Perf. 12x13***

1236 A513 1fr dk green & brn .35 .35

1237 A514 1fr multicolored .45 .35

1238 A515 1fr multicolored .45 .35

1239 A515a 1fr multicolored .55 .45

Nos. 1236-1239 (4) 1.80 1.50

Issue dates: No. 1236, Feb. 22; No. 1237, May 3; No. 1238, June 28; No. 1239, Nov. 8.

Gallic Coin Type of 1964-66

1969 **Typo.** ***Perf. 13½x14***

1240 A418 22c brt green & vio .80 .20

1241 A418 35c red & ultra 1.65 .40

1242 A418 70c ultra & red brn 6.00 2.00

Nos. 1240-1242 (3) 8.45 2.60

Nos. 1240-1242 are known only precanceled. See note after No. 132.

Hautefort Chateau A516

1969, Apr. 5 **Engr.** ***Perf. 13***

1243 A516 70c blue, slate & bister .40 .30

Irises A517

1969, Apr. 12 **Photo.**

1244 A517 45c multicolored .35 .30

3rd Intl. Flower Show, Paris, 4/23-10/5.

Europa Issue, 1969

Common Design Type

1969, Apr. 26 **Engr.** ***Perf. 13***

Size: 36x22mm

1245 CD12 40c carmine rose .20 .20

1246 CD12 70c Prussian blue .30 .25

Albert Thomas and Thomas Memorial, Geneva A518

1969, May 10 **Engr.** ***Perf. 13***

1247 A518 70c brn, ol bis & ind .35 .30

ILO, 50th anniv., and honoring Thomas (1878-1932), director of the ILO (1920-32).

Garigliano Battle Scene, 1944 — A519

1969, May 10

1248 A519 45c black & violet .30 .20

25th anniv. of the Battle of the Garigliano against the Germans.

Chateau du Marché, Chalons-sur-Marne
A520

Parachutists over Normandy Beach
A521

1969, May 24
1249 A520 45c bis, dull bl & grn .40 .30

Federation of French Philatelic Societies, 42nd congress.

1969, May 31
1250 A521 45c dk blue & vio bl .50 .30

Landing of Special Air Service and Free French commandos in Normandy, June 6, 1944, 25th anniv.

Monument of the French Resistance, Mt. Mouchet — A522

1969, June 7
1251 A522 45c dk grn, slate & ind .50 .30

25th anniv. of the battle of Mt. Mouchet between French resistance fighters and the Germans, June 2 and 10, 1944.

French Troops Landing in Provence — A523

1969, Aug. 23 **Engr.** ***Perf. 13***
1252 A523 45c slate & blk brn .60 .30

25th anniv. of the landing of French and American forces in Provence, Aug. 15, 1944.

Russian and French Aviators — A524

1969, Oct. 18 **Engr.** ***Perf. 13***
1253 A524 45c slate, dp bl & car .55 .30

Issued to honor the French aviators of the Normandy-Neman Squadron who fought on the Russian Front, 1942-45.

Kayak on Isère River
A525

1969, Aug. 2 **Engr.** ***Perf. 13***
1254 A525 70c org brn, ol & dk bl .40 .30

Intl. Canoe and Kayak Championships, Bourg-Saint-Maurice, Savoy, July 31-Aug. 6.

Napoleon as Young Officer and his Birthplace, Ajaccio — A526

1969, Aug. 16
1255 A526 70c brt grnsh bl, ol & rose vio .45 .30

Napoleon Bonaparte (1769-1821).
For surcharge see Reunion No. 370.

Drops of Water and Diamond
A527

Mediterranean Mouflon
A528

1969, Sept. 27
1256 A527 70c blk, dp bl & brt grn .50 .30

European Water Charter.

1969, Oct. 11
1257 A528 45c ol, blk & org brn 3.00 1.00

Issued to publicize wildlife protection.

Central School of Arts and Crafts
A529

1969, Oct. 18
1258 A529 70c dk grn, yel grn & org .30 .25

Inauguration of the Central School of Arts and Crafts at Chatenay-Malabry.

Nuclear Submarine "Le Redoutable" — A530

1969, Oct. 25
1259 A530 70c dp bl, grn & sl grn .40 .30

Type of 1968 and

Henri IV and Edict of Nantes — A531

Designs: No. 1260, Pierre Terrail de Bayard wounded at Battle of Brescia (after a painting in Versailles). No. 1262, Louis XI, Charles the Bold and map of France.

1969, Nov. 8 **Engr.** ***Perf. 13***
1260 A511 80c brn, bister & blk .40 .25
1261 A531 80c blk & vio bl .50 .25
1262 A531 80c ol, dp grn & dk red brn .40 .25
Nos. 1260-1262 (3) 1.30 .75

"Firecrest" and Alain Gerbault — A532

1970, Jan. 10 **Engr.** ***Perf. 13***
1263 A532 70c ind, brt bl & gray .55 .30

Completion of Alain Gerbault's trip around the world aboard the "Firecrest," 1923-29, 40th anniv.

Gendarmery Emblem, Mountain Climber, Helicopter, Motorcyclists and Motorboat — A533

1970, Jan. 31
1264 A533 45c sl grn, dk bl & brn 1.25 .50

National Gendarmery, founded 1791.

Field Ball Player — A534

1970, Feb. 21 **Engr.** ***Perf. 13***
1265 A534 80c slate green .40 .20

7th Intl. Field Ball Games, Feb. 26-Mar. 8.

Alphonse Juin and Church of the Invalides — A535

1970, Feb. 28
1266 A535 45c gray bl & dk brn .30 .20

Issued to honor Marshal Alphonse Pierre Juin (1888-1967), military leader.

Aerotrain
A536

1970, Mar. 7
1267 A536 80c purple & gray .55 .20

Introduction of the aerotrain, which reaches a speed of 320 miles per hour.

Pierre Joseph Pelletier, Joseph Bienaimé Caventou, Quinine Formula and Cell — A537

1970, Mar. 21 **Engr.** ***Perf. 13***
1268 A537 50c slate grn, sky bl & dp car .30 .20

Discovery of quinine, 150th anniversary.

Pink Flamingos
A538

Diamant B Rocket and Radar
A539

1970, Mar. 21
1269 A538 45c olive, gray & pink .30 .20

European Nature Conservation Year, 1970.

1970, Mar. 28
1270 A539 45c bright green .45 .20

Space center in Guyana and the launching of the Diamant B rocket, Mar. 10, 1970.

Europa Issue, 1970
Common Design Type

1970, May 2 **Engr.** ***Perf. 13***
Size: 36x22mm
1271 CD13 40c deep carmine .30 .20
1272 CD13 80c sky blue .70 .20

Annunication, by Primitive Painter of Savoy, 1480 — A540

The Triumph of Flora, by Jean Baptiste Carpeaux — A541

Diana Returning from the Hunt, by François Boucher — A542

Dancer with Bouquet, by Edgar Degas A543

1970 ***Perf. 12x13, 13x12***

1273	A540 1fr multicolored		.85	.30
1274	A541 1fr red brown		.85	.30
1275	A542 1fr multicolored		.85	.40
1276	A543 1fr multicolored		.85	.40
	Nos. 1273-1276 (4)		3.40	1.40

Issue dates: #1273, May 9; #1274, July 4; #1275, Oct. 10; #1276, Nov. 14.

Arms of Lens, Miner's Lamp and Pit Head A544

1970, May 16 **Engr.** ***Perf. 13***

1277	A544 40c scarlet	.20	.20

43rd Natl. Congress of the Federation of French Philatelic Societies, Lens, May 14-21.

Diamond Rock, Martinique A545

Haute Provence Observatory and Spiral Nebula — A546

Designs: 95c, Chancelade Abbey, Dordogne. 1fr, Gosier Islet, Guadeloupe.

1970, June 20 **Engr.** ***Perf. 13***

1278	A545	50c sl grn, brt bl & plum	.35	.20
1279	A545	95c lt ol, car & brn	1.10	.40
1280	A545	1fr sl grn, brt bl & dk car rose	.60	.20
1281	A546	1.30fr dk bl, vio bl & dk grn	1.90	.60
		Nos. 1278-1281 (4)	3.95	1.40

Hand Reaching for Freedom A547

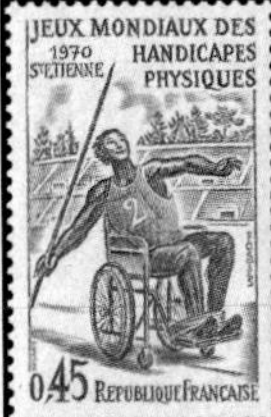

Handicapped Javelin Thrower A548

1970, June 27

1282	A547 45c vio bl, bl & bister	.40	.20

Liberation of concentration camps, 25th anniv.

1970, June 27

1283	A548 45c rose car, ultra & emer	.40	.20

Issued to publicize the International Games of the Handicapped, St. Etienne, June 1970.

Pole Vault — A549

1970, Sept. 11 **Engr.** ***Perf. 13***

1284	A549 45c car, bl & indigo	.40	.20

First European Junior Athletic Championships, Colombes, Sept. 11-13.

Royal Salt Works, Arc-et-Senans — A550

1970, Sept. 26

1285	A550 80c bl, brn & dk grn	1.50	.45

Restoration of the 18th cent. Royal Salt Works buildings, by Claude Nicolas Ledoux (1736-1806) at Arc-et-Senans, for use as a center for studies of all aspects of future human life.

Armand Jean du Plessis, Duc de Richelieu — A551

Designs: No. 1287, Battle of Fontenoy, 1745. No. 1288, Louis XIV and Versailles.

1970, Oct. 17 **Engr.** ***Perf. 13***

1286	A551 45c blk, sl & car rose	.50	.20
1287	A551 45c org, brn & indigo	.50	.20
1288	A551 45c sl grn, lem & org brn	.50	.20
	Nos. 1286-1288 (3)	1.50	.60

UN Headquarters in New York and Geneva — A552

1970, Oct. 24 **Engr.** ***Perf. 13***

1289	A552 80c ol, dp ultra & dk pur	.35	.30

25th anniversary of the United Nations.

View of Bordeaux and France No. 43 — A553

1970, Nov. 7

1290	A553 80c vio bl & gray bl	.35	.30

Centerary of the Bordeaux issue.

Col. Denfert-Rochereau and Lion of Belfort, by Frederic A. Bartholdi — A554

1970, Nov. 14

1291	A554 45c dk bl, ol & red brn	.30	.20

Centenary of the siege of Belfort during Franco-Prussian War.

Marianne (by Bequet) — A555

1971-74 **Typo.** ***Perf. 14x13***

1292	A555 45c sky blue	.30	.20
1292A	A555 60c green ('74)	.90	.20

For surcharges see Reunion #371, 397-398.

Engr. ***Perf. 13***

1293	A555 50c rose carmine	.30	.20
a.	Bklt. pane of 5 (horiz. strip)	2.25	
b.	Booklet pane of 10	3.50	
1294	A555 60c green ('74)	5.00	.20
a.	Booklet pane of 10	52.50	
1294B	A555 80c car rose ('74)	.50	.20
c.	Booklet pane of 5	3.50	
d.	Booklet pane of 10	7.25	
	Nos. 1293-1294B (3)	5.80	.60

Nos. 1294 and 1294B issued also in vertical coils with control number on back of every 10th stamp.

No. 1293 issued only in booklets and in vertical coils with red control number on back of every 10th stamp.

See Nos. 1494-1498.

St. Matthew, Sculpture from Strasbourg Cathedral A556

Winnower, by François Millet A557

The Dreamer, by Georges Rouault A558

1971 **Engr.** ***Perf. 12x13***

1295	A556 1fr dark red brown	.85	.50
1296	A557 1fr multicolored	.85	.40
1297	A558 1fr multicolored	.85	.40
	Nos. 1295-1297 (3)	2.55	1.30

Issued: #1295, 1/23; #1296, 4/3; #1297, 6/5.

Figure Skating Pair A560

1971, Feb. 20 **Engr.** ***Perf. 13***

1299	A560 80c vio bl, sl & aqua	.50	.25

World Figure Skating Championships, Lyons, Feb. 23-28.

Underwater Exploration — A561

1971, Mar. 6

1300	A561 80c blue blk & bl grn	.40	.25

International Exhibition of Ocean Exploration, Bordeaux, Mar. 9-14.

Cape Horn Clipper "Antoinette" and Solidor Castle, Saint-Malo — A562

1971, Apr. 10 **Engr.** ***Perf. 13***

1301	A562 80c blue, pur & slate	.70	.30

For surcharge see Reunion No. 372.

Pyrenean Chamois — A563

1971, Apr. 24 Engr. *Perf. 13*

1302 A563 65c bl, dk brn & brn ol .50 .20

National Park of Western Pyrenees.

Europa Issue, 1971

Common Design Type and

Santa Maria della Salute, Venice A564

1971, May 8 Engr. *Perf. 13*

1303 A564 50c blue gray & ol bis .40 .30

Size: 36x22mm

1304 CD14 80c rose lilac .60 .40

Cardinal, Nobleman and Lawyer — A565

Storming of the Bastille — A566

Design: No. 1306, Battle of Valmy.

1971

1305 A565 45c bl, rose red & pur .55 .20
1306 A565 45c bl, ol bis & brn red .55 .25
1307 A566 65c dk brn, gray bl & mag .85 .30
Nos. 1305-1307 (3) 1.95 .75

No. 1305 commemorates the opening of the Estates General, May 5, 1789; No. 1306, Battle of Valmy (Sept. 20, 1792) between French and Prussian armies; 65c, Storming of the Bastille, Paris, July 14, 1789.

Issued: #1305, 5/8; #1306, 9/18; 65c, 7/10.

Grenoble A568

1971, May 29 Engr. *Perf. 13*

1308 A568 50c ocher, lil & rose red .30 .20

44th Natl. Cong. of the Federation of French Philatelic Societies, Grenoble, May 30-31.

"Rural Family Aid" Shedding Light on Village — A569

1971, June 5

1309 A569 40c vio, bl & grn .20 .20

Aid for rural families.

For surcharge see Reunion No. 373.

Chateau and Fort de Sedan A570

Pont d'Arc, Ardèche Gorge — A571

Views: 60c, Sainte Chapelle, Riom. 65c, Fountain and tower, Dole. 90c, Tower and street, Riquewihr.

1971 Engr. *Perf. 13*

1310 A571 60c black, grn & bl .25 .20
1311 A571 65c lil, ocher & blk .35 .20
1312 A571 90c grn, vio brn & red brn .50 .20
1313 A570 1.10fr sl grn, Prus bl & brn .60 .20
1314 A571 1.40fr sl grn, bl & dk brn .75 .20
Nos. 1310-1314 (5) 2.45 1.00

Issued: 60c, 6/19; 65c, 90c, 7/3; 1.10fr, 1.40fr, 6/12.

For surcharges see Reunion Nos. 374, 381.

Gallic Coin Type of 1964-66

1971, July 1 Typo. *Perf. 13½x14*

1315 A418 26c lilac & brn .50 .20
1316 A418 30c lt brown & brn .90 .20
1317 A418 45c dull green & brn 1.75 .30
1318 A418 90c red & brown 2.25 .50
Nos. 1315-1318 (4) 5.40 1.20

Nos. 1315-1318 are known only precanceled. See second paragraph after No. 132.

Bourbon Palace A572

1971, Aug. 28 Engr. *Perf. 13*

1319 A572 90c violet blue .75 .25

59th Conf. of the Interparliamentary Union.

Embroidery and Tool Making A573

1971, Oct. 16

1320 A573 90c brn red, brt lil & cl .50 .30

40th anniv. of the first assembly of presidents of artisans' guilds.

For surcharge see Reunion No. 375.

Reunion Chameleon A574

1971, Nov. 6 Photo. *Perf. 13*

1321 A574 60c brn, yel, grn & blk 1.10 .40

Nature protection.

De Gaulle Issue

Common Design Type and

De Gaulle in Brazzaville, 1944 — A576

Designs: No. 1324, De Gaulle entering Paris, 1944. No. 1325, Pres. de Gaulle, 1970.

1971, Nov. 9 Engr.

1322 CD134 50c black 1.10 .35
1323 A576 50c ultra 1.10 .35
1324 A576 50c rose red 1.10 .35
1325 CD134 50c black 1.10 .35
a. Strip of 4, #1322-1325 + label 4.50 2.50

1st anniv. of the death of Charles de Gaulle.

See Reunion Nos. 377, 380.

Antoine Portal and first Session of Academy — A577

1971, Nov. 13

1326 A577 45c dk purple & mag .25 .20

Sesquicentennial of the founding of the National Academy of Medicine; Baron Antoine Portal was first president.

L'Etude, by Jean Honoré Fragonard A578

Women in Garden, by Claude Monet A579

St. Peter Presenting Pierre de Bourbon, by Maitre de Moulins A580

Boats, by André Derain — A581

1972 Engr. *Perf. 12x13, 13x12*

1327 A578 1fr black & multi .65 .30
1328 A579 1fr slate grn & multi .95 .30
1329 A580 2fr dk brown & multi 2.50 .80
1330 A581 2fr yellow & multi 3.50 .90
Nos. 1327-1330 (4) 7.60 2.30

Issue dates: #1327, Jan. 22; #1328, June 17; #1329, Oct. 14; #1330, Dec. 16.

Map of South Indian Ocean, Penguin and Ships — A582

1972, Jan. 29 *Perf. 13*

1331 A582 90c black, bl & ocher .65 .40

Bicentenary of discovery of the Crozet and Kerguelen Islands.

Slalom and Olympic Emblems A583

1972, Feb. 7

1332 A583 90c dk olive & dp car .50 .30

11th Winter Olympic Games, Sapporo, Japan, Feb. 3-13.

Hearts, UN Emblem, Caduceus and Pacemaker A584

1972, Apr. 8 Engr. *Perf. 13*

1333 A584 45c dk car, org & gray .30 .20

"Your heart is your health," world health month.

Red Deer, Sologne Plateau — A585

Charlieu Abbey A585a

Bazoches-du-Morvand Chateau — A586

Saint-Just Cathedral, Narbonne A587

1972 *Perf. 13*

1334 A585 1fr ocher & red brn .55 .20
1335 A585a 1.20fr sl & dull brn .50 .20
1336 A586 2fr sl grn, blk & red brn 1.00 .20
1337 A587 3.50fr bl, gray ol & car rose 1.40 .20
Nos. 1334-1337 (4) 3.45 .80

Issued: 1fr, 9/10; 1.20fr, 4/29; 2fr, 9/9; 3.50fr, 4/8.

For surcharge see Reunion No. 388.

Eagle Owl — A588

Nature protection: 60c, Salmon, horiz.

1972

1338 A588 60c grn, ind & brt bl 2.25 .60
1339 A588 65c sl, ol brn & sep 1.40 .30

Issue dates: 60c, May 27; 65c, Apr. 15.

Europa Issue 1972

Common Design Type and

Aix-la-Chapelle Cathedral — A589

1972, Apr. 22 Engr. *Perf. 13*

1340 A589 50c yel, vio brn & dk ol .30 .25

Photo.

Size: 22x36mm

1341 CD15 90c red org & multi .70 .45

Bouquet Made of Hearts and Blood Donors' Emblem A590

Newfoundlander "Côte d'Emeraude" A591

1972, May 5 Engr.

1342 A590 40c red .30 .20

20th anniv. of the Blood Donors Association of Post and Telecommunications Employees.

For surcharge see Reunion No. 383.

1972, May 6

1343 A591 90c org, vio bl & sl grn .70 .30

Cathedral, Saint-Brieuc A592

1972, May 20

1344 A592 50c lilac rose .30 .20

45th Congress of the Federation of French Philatelic Societies, Saint-Brieuc, May 21-22.

Hand Holding Symbol of Postal Code A593

1972, June 3 Typo. *Perf. 14x13*

1345 A593 30c green, blk & car .20 .20
1346 A593 50c car, blk & yel .30 .20

Introduction of postal code system.

For surcharges see Reunion Nos. 384-385.

Old and New Communications A594

1972, July 1 Engr. *Perf. 13*

1347 A594 45c slate & vio blue .30 .20

21st Intl. Congress of P.T.T. (Post, Telegraph & Telephone) Employees, Paris, 7/1-7.

Hurdler and Olympic Rings A595

1972, July 8

1348 A595 1fr deep olive .50 .20

20th Olympic Games, Munich, 8/26-9/11.

Hikers and Mt. Aigoual — A596

Bicyclist — A597

1972, July 15 Photo. *Perf. 13*

1349 A596 40c brt rose & multi 1.50 .60

Intl. Year of Tourism and 25th anniv. of the Natl. Hikers Association.

1972, July 22 Engr.

1350 A597 1fr gray, brn & lil 1.90 .60

World Bicycling Championships, Marseille, July 29-Aug. 2.

"Incroyables and Merveilleuses," 1794 — A598

French History: 60c, Bonaparte at the Arcole Bridge. 65c, Egyptian expedition (soldiers and scientists finding antiquities; pyramids in background).

1972 Engr. *Perf. 13*

1351 A598 45c ol, dk grn & car rose .55 .20
1352 A598 60c red, blk & ind .55 .25
1353 A598 65c ocher, ultra & choc .55 .30
Nos. 1351-1353 (3) 1.65 .75

. Issued: 45c, Oct. 7; 60c, 65c, Nov. 11.

Champollion, Rosetta Stone with Key Inscription — A599

1972, Oct. 14

1354 A599 90c vio bl, brn red & blk .50 .30

Sesquicentennial of the deciphering of hieroglyphs by Jean-François Champollion.

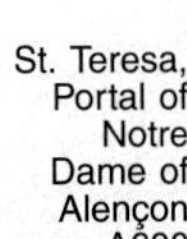

St. Teresa, Portal of Notre Dame of Alençon A600

1973, Jan. 6 Engr. *Perf. 13*

1355 A600 1fr Prus blue & indigo .60 .30

Centenary of the birth of St. Teresa of Lisieux, the Little Flower (Thérèse Martin, 1873-1897), Carmelite nun.

Anthurium (Martinique) — A601

1973, Jan. 20 Photo.

1356 A601 50c gray & multi .35 .20

Colors of France and Germany Interlaced — A602

1973, Jan. 22

1357 A602 50c multicolored .40 .20

10th anniv. of the Franco-German Cooperation Treaty. See Germany No. 1101.

Polish Immigrants — A603

1973, Feb. 3 Engr. *Perf. 13*

1358 A603 40c slate grn, dp car & brn .25 .20

50th anniversary of Polish immigration into France, 1921-1923.

Last Supper, St. Austremoine Church, Issoire — A604

Kneeling Woman, by Charles Le Brun A605

Angel, Wood, Moutier-D'Ahun — A606

Lady Playing Archlute, by Antoine Watteau A607

1973 Engr. *Perf. 12x13*

1359	A604	2fr brown & multi	1.75	.80
1360	A605	2fr dk red & yel	1.75	.80
1361	A606	2fr ol brn & vio brn	1.75	.80
1362	A607	2fr black & multi	1.75	.80
		Nos. 1359-1362 (4)	7.00	3.20

Issue dates: #1359, Feb. 10; #1360, Apr. 28; #1361, May 26; #1362, Sept. 22.

Tuileries Palace, Telephone Relays A608

Oil Tanker, Francis I Lock A609

Airbus A300-B A610

1973

1363	A608	45c ultra, sl grn & bis	.30	.20
1364	A609	90c plum, blk & bl	.55	.20
1365	A610	3fr dk brn, bl & blk	1.90	.80
		Nos. 1363-1365 (3)	2.75	1.20

French technical achievements.
Issued: 45c, 5/15; 90c, 10/27; 3fr, 4/7.

Europa Issue 1973

Common Design Type and

City Hall, Brussels, CEPT Emblem — A611

1973, Apr. 14 Engr. *Perf. 13*

1366 A611 50c brt pink & choc .50 .25

Photo.

Size: 36x22mm

1367 CD16 90c slate grn & multi 1.75 .75

Masonic Lodge Emblem A612

1973, May 12 Engr. *Perf. 13*

1368 A612 90c magenta & vio bl .55 .30

Bicentenary of the Free Masons of France.

Guadeloupe Raccoon A613

White Storks A614

1973

1369	A613	40c lilac, sepia & olive	.35	.20
1370	A614	60c blk, aqua & org red	.50	.25

Nature protection.
Issue dates: 40c, June 23; 60c, May 12.

Tourist Issue

Doubs Waterfall A615

Clos-Lucé, Amboise A617

Palace of Dukes of Burgundy, Dijon A616

Design: 90c, Gien Chateau.

1973 Engr. *Perf. 13*

1371	A615	60c multicolored	.20	.20
1372	A616	65c red & purple	.30	.20
1373	A616	90c Prus bl, ind & brn	.35	.20
1374	A617	1fr ocher, bl & sl grn	.35	.20
		Nos. 1371-1374 (4)	1.20	.80

Issued: 60c, 9/8; 65c, 5/19; 90c, 8/18; 1fr, 6/23.
For surcharge see Reunion No. 387.

Academy Emblem — A618

1973, May 26

1375 A618 1fr lil, slate grn & red .40 .25

Academy of Overseas Sciences, 50th anniv.

Racing Car and Clocks A619

1973, June 2

1376 A619 60c dk brown & blue .50 .40

24-hour automobile race at Le Mans, 50th anniv.

Five-master France II — A620

1973, June 9

1377 A620 90c ultra, Prus bl & ind .60 .25

For surcharge see Reunion No. 386.

Tower and Square, Toulouse — A621

1973, June 9

1378 A621 50c purple & red brn .25 .20

46th Congress of the Federation of French Philatelic Societies, Toulouse, June 9-12.

Dr. Armauer G. Hansen — A622

Ducretet and his Transmission Diagram — A623

1973, Sept. 29 Engr. *Perf. 13*

1379 A622 45c grn, dk ol & ocher .25 .20

Centenary of the discovery of the Hansen bacillus, the cause of leprosy.

1973, Oct. 6

1380 A623 1fr yel grn & magenta .40 .20

75th anniversary of the first transmission of radio signals from the Eiffel Tower to the Pantheon by Eugene Ducretet (1844-1915).

Molière as Sganarelle — A624

1973, Oct. 20

1381 A624 1fr dk red & olive brn .40 .20

Moliere (Jean-Baptiste Poquelin; 1622-1673), playwright and actor.

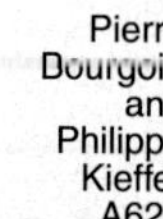

Pierre Bourgoin and Philippe Kieffer A625

1973, Oct. 27

1382 A625 1fr red, rose cl & vio bl .50 .20

Pierre Bourgoin (1907-70), and Philippe Kieffer (1899-1963), heroes of the Free French forces in World War II.

Napoleon, Jean Portalis and Palace of Justice, Paris — A626

Exhibition Halls — A627

The Coronation of Napoleon, by Jean Louis David — A628

1973 Engr. *Perf. 13*

1383	A626	45c blue, choc & gray	.30	.20
1384	A627	60c ol, sl grn & brn	.40	.20
1385	A628	1fr sl grn, ol & claret	.60	.20
		Nos. 1383-1385 (3)	1.30	.60

History of France. 45c, for the preparation of the Code Napoleon; 60c, Napoleon's encouragement of industry; 1fr, his coronation.
Issued: 45c, 11/3; 60c, 11/24; 1fr, 11/12.

Eternal Flame, Arc de Triomphe A629

Weather Vane A630

1973, Nov. 10

1386 A629 40c pur, vio bl & red .30 .20

50th anniv. of the Eternal Flame at the Arc de Triomphe, Paris.

1973, Dec. 1

1387 A630 65c ultra, blk & grn .30 .20

50th anniv. of the Dept. of Agriculture.

Human Rights Flame and Man — A631

Postal Museum — A632

1973, Dec. 8 Engr. *Perf. 13*
1388 A631 45c car, org & blk .25 .20

25th anniversary of the Universal Declaration of Human Rights.

1973, Dec. 19
1389 A632 50c maroon & bister .20 .20

Opening of new post and philately museum, Paris.

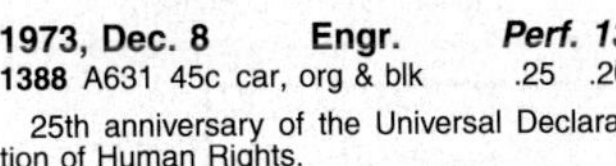
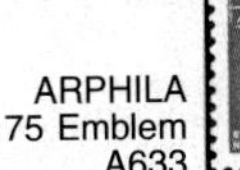

ARPHILA 75 Emblem A633

1974, Jan. 19 Engr. *Perf. 13*
1390 A633 50c brn, bl & brt lil .25 .20

ARPHILA 75 Philatelic Exhibition, Paris, June 1975.
For surcharge see Reunion No. 390.

Concorde over Charles de Gaulle Airport A634

Turbotrain T.G.V. 001 A635

Phenix Nuclear Power Station A636

1974 Engr. *Perf. 13*
1391 A634 60c pur & ol gray .40 .20
1392 A635 60c multicolored 1.10 .35
1393 A636 65c multicolored .30 .20
Nos. 1391-1393 (3) 1.80 .75

French technical achievements.
Issued: #1391, 3/18; #1392, 8/31; 65c, 9/21.

Cardinal Richelieu, by Philippe de Champaigne — A637

Painting by Joan Miró A638

Canal du Loing, by Alfred Sisley — A639

"In Honor of Nicolas Fouquet," Tapestry by Georges Mathieu A640

Engr., Photo. (#1395, 1397)
1974 *Perf. 12x13, 13x12*
1394 A637 2fr multicolored 1.25 .65
1395 A638 2fr multicolored 1.25 .65
1396 A639 2fr multicolored 1.75 .65
1397 A640 2fr multicolored 1.75 .65
Nos. 1394-1397 (4) 6.00 2.60

Nos. 1394-1397 are printed in sheets of 25 with alternating labels publicizing "ARPHILA 75," Paris, June 6-16, 1975.
Issue dates: #1394, Mar. 23; #1395, Sept. 14; #1396, Nov. 9; #1397, Nov. 16.
For surcharges see Reunion Nos. 391-394.

French Alps and Gentian A641

1974, Mar. 30 Engr. *Perf. 13*
1398 A641 65c vio blue & gray .35 .20

Centenary of the French Alpine Club.

Europa Issue 1974

"Age of Bronze," by Auguste Rodin — A642

"Air," by Aristide Maillol A643

1974, Apr. 20 *Perf. 13*
1399 A642 50c brt rose lil & blk *.40* .25
1400 A643 90c olive & brown *1.25* .50

Sea Rescue — A644

1974, Apr. 27
1401 A644 90c multicolored .40 .20

Reorganized sea rescue organization.
For surcharge see Reunion No. 395.

Council Building, View of Strasbourg and Emblem — A645

1974, May 4 Engr. *Perf. 13*
1402 A645 45c indigo, bister & bl .30 .20

25th anniversary of the Council of Europe.

Tourist Issue

View of Salers A646

Basilica of St. Nicolas de Porte — A647

Seashell over Corsica — A648

Design: 1.10fr, View of Lot Valley.

1974 Engr. *Perf. 13*
1403 A646 65c yel grn & choc .25 .20
1404 A646 1.10fr choc & sl grn .45 .20
1405 A647 2fr gray & lilac .80 .20
1406 A648 3fr multicolored 1.00 .30
Nos. 1403-1406 (4) 2.50 .90

Issued: 65c, 6/22; 1.10fr, 9/7; 2fr, 10/12; 3fr, 5/11.

Bison A649

Giant Armadillo of Guyana A650

1974
1407 A649 40c bis, choc & bl .35 .20
1408 A650 65c slate, olive & grn .35 .20

Nature protection.
Issued: #1407, May 25; #1408, Oct. 19.

Americans Landing in Normandy and Arms of Normandy — A651

General Marie-Pierre Koenig — A652

Order of the French Resistance — A653

1974
1409 A651 45c grn, rose & ind .40 .20
1410 A652 1fr multicolored .60 .20
1411 A653 1fr multicolored .50 .20
Nos. 1409-1411 (3) 1.50 .60

30th anniversary of the liberation of France from the Nazis. Design of No. 1410 includes diagram of battle of Bir-Hakeim and Free French and Bir-Hakeim memorials.
Issued: 45c, 6/8; #1410, 5/25; #1411, 11/23.
See No. B478.

Pfister House, 16th Century, Colmar — A654

1974, June 1
1412 A654 50c multicolored .20 .20

47th Congress of the Federation of French Philatelic Societies, Colmar, May 30-June 4.

Chess A655

1974, June 8
1413 A655 1fr dk brown & multi .55 .30

21st Chess Olympiad, Nice, June 6-30.

Facade with Statue of Louis XIV, and 1675 Medal — A656

1974, June 15
1414 A656 40c indigo, bl & brn .20 .20

300th anniversary of the founding of the Hotel des Invalides (Home for poor and sick officers and soldiers).

Peacocks Holding Letter, and Globe — A657

1974, Oct. 5 Engr. *Perf. 13*
1415 A657 1.20fr ultra, dp grn & dk car .50 .30

Centenary of Universal Postal Union. For surcharge see Reunion No. 396.

Copernicus and Heliocentric System — A658

1974, Oct. 12
1416 A658 1.20fr multicolored .45 .30

500th anniversary of the birth of Nicolaus Copernicus (1473-1543), Polish astronomer.

Tourist Issue

Palace of Justice, Rouen A659

Saint-Pol-de-Leon A660

Chateau de Rochechouart — A661

1975 Engr. *Perf. 13*
1417 A659 85c multicolored .35 .20
1418 A660 1.20fr bl, bis & choc .40 .20
1419 A661 1.40fr brn, ind & grn .50 .20
Nos. 1417-1419 (3) 1.25 .60

Issued: 85c, 1/25; 1.20fr, 1/18; 1.40fr, 1/11.

Snowy Egret — A662

Gallic Coin — A663

1975, Feb. 15 Engr. *Perf. 13*
1420 A662 70c brt blue & bister .40 .20

Nature protection.

1975, Feb. 16 Typo. *Perf. 13½x14*
1421 A663 42c orange & mag 1.25 .20
1422 A663 48c lt bl & red brn 1.50 .20
1423 A663 70c brt pink & red 2.50 .45
1424 A663 1.35fr lt green & brn 2.75 .65
Nos. 1421-1424 (4) 8.00 1.50

Nos. 1421-1424 are known only precanceled. See second note after No. 132. See Nos. 1460-1463, 1487-1490.

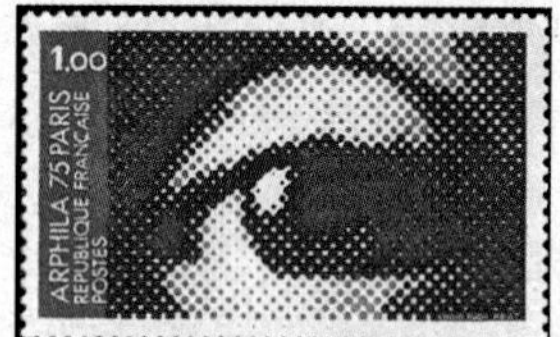
The Eye — A664

Ionic Capital — A665

Graphic Art — A666

Ceres — A667

1975 Engr. *Perf. 13*
1425 A664 1fr red, pur & org .45 .20
1426 A665 2fr grn, sl grn & mag .65 .30
1427 A666 3fr dk car & ol grn 1.00 .40
1428 A667 4fr red, sl grn & bis 1.40 .55
Nos. 1425-1428 (4) 3.50 1.45

Souvenir Sheet

1429 Sheet of 4 7.50 7.50
a. A664 2fr dp car & slate blue 1.00 1.00
b. A665 3fr brt bl, sl bl & dp car 1.40 1.40
c. A666 4fr slate blue, brt bl & plum 2.00 2.00
d. A667 6fr brt bl, sl bl & plum 2.50 2.50

ARPHILA 75, Intl. Philatelic Exhibition, Paris, 6/6-16. Issued: 1fr, 3/1; 2fr, 3/22; 3fr, 4/19; 4fr, 5/17; #1429, 4/2.

Pres. Georges Pompidou A668

Paul as Harlequin, by Picasso A669

1975, Apr. 3 Engr. *Perf. 13*
1430 A668 80c black & gray .30 .20

Georges Pompidou (1911-74), President of France, 1969-74.

1975, Apr. 26 Photo. *Perf. 13*

Europa; 1.20fr, Woman on Balcony, by Kees van Dongen

1431 A669 80c multi *.65* .35
1432 A669 1.20fr multi, horiz. *1.25* .65

Machines, Globe, Emblem A670

1975, May 3 Engr.
1433 A670 1.20fr blue, blk & red .40 .30

World Machine Tool Exhib., Paris, 6/7-26.

Senate Assembly Hall A671

1975, May 24 Engr. *Perf. 13*
1434 A671 1.20fr olive & dk car .40 .30

Centenary of the Senate of the Republic.

Meter Convention Document, Atom Diagram and Waves — A672

1975, May 31
1435 A672 1fr multicolored .35 .20

Cent. of Intl. Meter Convention, Paris, 1875.

Metro Regional Train A673

"Gazelle" Helicopter A674

1975
1436 A673 1fr indigo & brt bl .90 .20
1437 A674 1.30fr vio bl & grn .65 .35

French technical achievements. Issue dates: 1fr, June 21; 1.30fr, May 31.

Youth and Flasks, Symbols of Study and Growth — A675

1975, June 21
1438 A675 70c red pur & blk .25 .20

Student Health Foundation.

People's Theater, Bussang, and Maurice Pottecher A676

1975, Aug. 9 Engr. *Perf. 13*
1439 A676 85c multicolored .30 .20

80th anniversary of the People's Theater at Bussang, founded by Maurice Pottecher.

Regions of France

Central France A677

Aquitaine A678

Limousin A679

Picardy A680

Burgundy A681

Loire A682

Guyana A683

Auvergne A684

Poitou-Charentes
A685

Southern Pyrenees
A686

Pas-de-Calais — A687

1975-76 Engr. *Perf. 13*

1440 A677	25c blue & yel grn	.25	.20
1441 A678	60c multicolored	.25	.20
1442 A679	70c multicolored	.50	.20
1443 A680	85c bl, grn & org	.70	.20
1444 A681	1fr red, yel & mar	.70	.20
1445 A682	1.15fr bl, bis & grn	.70	.25
1446 A683	1.25fr multicolored	.55	.30
1447 A684	1.30fr dk bl & red	.55	.20
1448 A685	1.90fr sl, ol & Prus bl	.90	.20
1449 A686	2.20fr multicolored	1.00	.50
1450 A687	2.80fr car, bl & blk	1.40	.55
	Nos. 1440-1450 (11)	7.50	3.00

Issued: 85c, 11/15; 1fr, 10/25; 1.15fr, 9/6; 1.30fr, 10/4/75; 1.90fr, 12/6; 2.80fr, 12/13; 25c, 1/31/76; 2.20fr, 1/10/76; 60c, 5/22/76; 70c, 5/29/76; 1.25fr, 10/16/76.

A690 A691

French Flag, F.-H. Manhes, Jean Verneau, Pierre Kaan

1975, Sept. 27

1453 A690 1fr multicolored .35 .25

Liberation of concentration camps, 30th anniversary. F.-H. Manhes (1889-1959), Jean Verneau (1890-1944) and Pierre Kaan (1903-1945) were French resistance leaders, imprisoned in concentration camps.

1975, Oct. 11

Monument, by Joseph Riviere.

1454 A691 70c multicolored .25 .20

Land Mine Demolition Service, 30th anniversary. Monument was erected in Alsace to honor land mine victims.

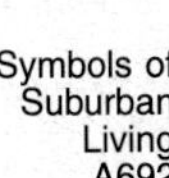

Symbols of Suburban Living
A692

1975, Oct. 18

1455 A692 1.70fr brown, bl & grn .75 .50

Creation of new towns.

Women and Rainbow — A693

1975, Nov. 8 Photo.

1456 A693 1.20fr silver & multi .45 .30

International Women's Year 1975.

Saint-Nazaire Bridge — A694

1975, Nov. 8 Engr.

1457 A694 1.40fr bl, ind & grn .60 .20

French and Russian Flags — A695

Frigate Melpomene
A696

1975, Nov. 22

1458 A695 1.20fr bl, red & ocher .50 .30

Franco-Soviet diplomatic relations, 50th anniv.

1975, Dec. 6

1459 A696 90c multicolored .80 .35

Gallic Coin Type of 1975

1976, Jan. 1 Typo. *Perf. 13½x14*

1460 A663	50c lt green & brn	1.10	.30
1461 A663	60c lilac & brn	1.75	.30
1462 A663	90c orange & brn	2.25	.65
1463 A663	1.60fr violet & brn	4.00	2.00
	Nos. 1460-1463 (4)	9.10	3.25

Nos. 1460-1463 are known only precanceled. See second note after No. 132.

Lintel, St. Genis des Fontaines Church
A697

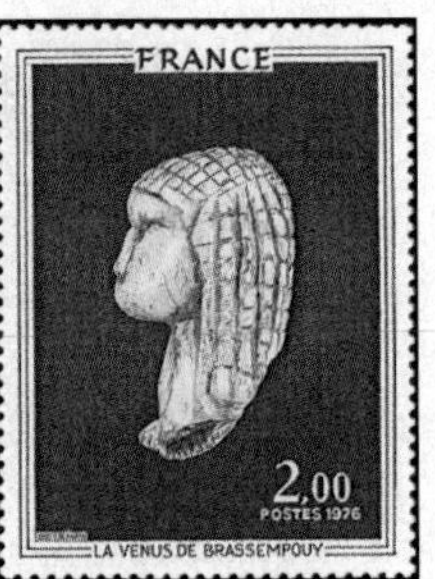

Venus of Brassempouy (Paleolithic) — A698

"The Joy of Life," by Robert Delaunay
A699

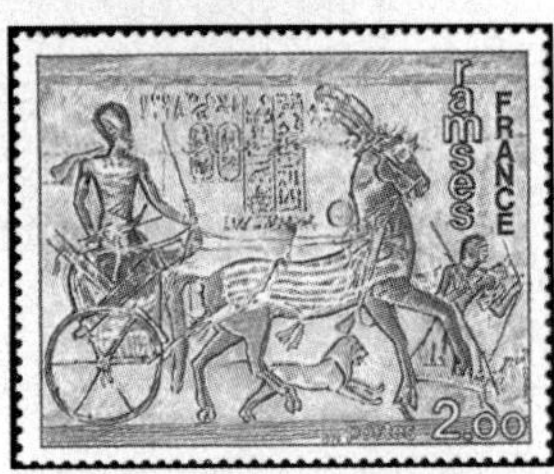

Ramses II, from Abu Simbel Temple, Egypt — A700

Still Life, by Maurice de Vlaminck — A701

1976 Engr. *Perf. 13*

1464 A697	2fr blue & slate bl	1.25	.60
1465 A698	2fr dk brn & yel	1.25	.60

Photo. *Perf. 12½x13*

1466 A699 2fr multicolored 1.25 .60

Engr. *Perf. 13x12½*

1467 A700 2fr multicolored .95 .50

Perf. 13

1468 A701	2fr multicolored	.95	.50
	Nos. 1464-1468 (5)	5.65	2.80

Issued: #1464, 1/24; #1465, 3/6; #1466, 7/24; #1467, 9/4; #1468, 12/18.

Tourist Issue

Chateau Fort de Bonaguil
A702

Lodève Cathedral — A703

Biarritz
A704

Thiers — A705 Ussel — A706

Chateau de Malmaison
A707

1976 Engr. *Perf. 13*

1469 A702	1fr multicolored	.35	.20
1470 A703	1.10fr violet blue	.40	.20
1471 A704	1.40fr multicolored	.45	.20
1472 A705	1.70fr multicolored	.55	.20
1473 A706	2fr multicolored	.85	.20
1474 A707	3fr multicolored	.95	.20
	Nos. 1469-1474 (6)	3.55	1.20

Issue dates: 1fr, 2fr, July 10; 1.10fr, Nov. 13; 1.40fr, Sept. 25; 1.70fr, Oct. 9; 3fr, Apr. 10.

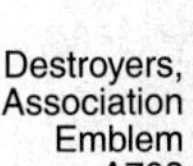

Destroyers, Association Emblem
A708

1976, Apr. 24

1475 A708 1fr vio bl, mag & lem .50 .20

Naval Reserve Officers Assoc., 50th anniv.

Gate, Rouen — A709

Young Person — A710

1976, Apr. 24

1476 A709 80c olive gray & sal .35 .20

49th Congress of the Federation of French Philatelic Societies, Rouen, Apr. 23-May 2.

1976, Apr. 27

1477 A710 60c bl grn, ind & car .35 .20

JUVAROUEN 76, International Youth Philatelic Exhibition, Rouen, Apr. 25-May 2.

Europa Issue 1976

Ceramic Pitcher, Strasbourg, 18th Century
A711

1.20fr, Sevres porcelain plate & CEPT emblem.

1976, May 8 Photo. *Perf. 13*

1478 A711	80c multicolored	.45	.30
1479 A711	1.20fr multicolored	.85	.55

Count de Vergennes and Benjamin Franklin — A712

1976, May 15 Engr. *Perf. 13*
1480 A712 1.20fr multicolored .40 .30

American Bicentennial.

— A713

A714

Battle of Verdun Memorial.

1976, June 12 Engr.
1481 A713 1fr multicolored .45 .20

Battle of Verdun, 60th anniversary.

1976, June 12 Photo.
1482 A714 1.20fr Communication .40 .20

Troncais Forest — A715

Cross of Lorraine — A716

1976, June 19 Engr.
1483 A715 70c green & multi .30 .20

Protection of the environment.

1976, June 19
1484 A716 1fr multicolored .50 .20

Association of Free French, 30th anniv.

Symphonie Communications Satellite — A717

1976, June 26 Photo.
1485 A717 1.40fr multicolored .65 .20

French technical achievements.

Gallic Coin Type of 1975

1976, July 1 Typo. *Perf. 13½x14*
1487 A663 52c ver & dk brn .65 .20
1488 A663 62c vio & dk brn 1.25 .35
1489 A663 95c tan & dk brn 1.65 .55
1490 A663 1.70fr dk bl & dk brn 3.00 1.40
Nos. 1487-1490 (4) 6.55 2.50

Nos. 1487-1490 are known only precanceled. See second note after No. 132.

Paris Summer Festival — A719

1976, July 10 Engr.
1491 A719 1fr multicolored .65 .20

Summer festival in Tuileries Gardens, Paris.

Emblem and Soldiers A720

1976, July 8
1492 A720 1fr blk, dp bl & mag .40 .20

Officers Reserve Corps, centenary.

Sailing A721

1976, July 17
1493 A721 1.20fr blue, blk & vio .45 .30

21st Olympic Games, Montreal, Canada, July 17-Aug. 1.

Marianne Type of 1971-74

1976 Typo. *Perf. 14x13*
1494 A555 80c green .40 .20

Engr. *Perf. 13*
1495 A555 80c green .45 .20
a. Booklet pane of 10 4.75
1496 A555 1fr carmine rose .45 .20
a. Booklet pane of 5 3.00
b. Booklet pane of 10 5.50
Nos. 1495-1496 (2) .90 .40

No. 1495 issued in booklets only. "POSTES" 6mm long on Nos. 1292A and 1494; 4mm on others.
#1494, 1496 were issued untagged in 1977.

Coil Stamps

1976, Aug. 1 Engr. *Perf. 13 Horiz.*
1497 A555 80c green .45 .20
1498 A555 1fr carmine rose .45 .20

Red control number on back of every 10th stamp.

Woman's Head, by Jean Carzou — A722

1976, Sept. 18 Engr. *Perf. 13x12½*
1499 A722 2fr multicolored .90 .40

Old and New Telephones A723

1976, Sept. 25 Engr. *Perf. 13*
1500 A723 1fr multicolored .40 .20

Centenary of first telephone call by Alexander Graham Bell, Mar. 10, 1876.

Festival Emblem and Trophy, Pyrenees, Hercules and Pyrène — A724

Police Emblem — A725

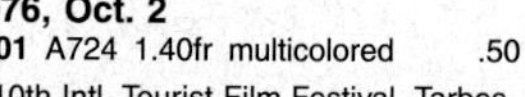

1976, Oct. 2
1501 A724 1.40fr multicolored .50 .30

10th Intl. Tourist Film Festival, Tarbes, 10/4-10.

1976, Oct. 9 Engr. *Perf. 13*
1502 A725 1.10fr ultra, red & ol .50 .20

National Police, help and protection.

Atomic Particle Accelerator, Diagram A726

1976, Oct. 22 Photo.
1503 A726 1.40fr multicolored .65 .20

European Center for Nuclear Research (CERN).

"Exhibitions" — A727

1976, Nov. 20 Engr. *Perf. 13*
1504 A727 1.50fr multicolored .75 .30

Trade Fairs and Exhibitions.

Abstract Design A728

1976, Nov. 27 Photo.
1505 A728 1.10fr multicolored .45 .20

Customs Service.

Atlantic Museum, Port Louis — A729

1976, Dec. 4 Engr.
1506 A729 1.45fr grnsh bl & olive .50 .30

Regions of France

Réunion A730

Martinique A731

Franche-Comté A732

Brittany A733

Languedoc-Roussillon — A734

Rhône-Alps A735

Champagne-Ardennes A736

Alsace A737

Photo. (1.45fr, 1.50fr, 2.50fr); Engr.

1977 *Perf. 13*
1507 A730 1.45fr grn & lil rose .50 .20
1508 A731 1.50fr multicolored .55 .25
1509 A732 2.10fr multicolored .75 .30
1510 A733 2.40fr multicolored 1.00 .20
1511 A734 2.50fr multicolored 1.00 .30
1512 A735 2.75fr Prus blue 1.25 .30
1513 A736 3.20fr multicolored 1.25 .50
1514 A737 3.90fr multicolored 1.65 .55
Nos. 1507-1514 (8) 7.95 2.60

Issued: 1.45fr, 2/5; 1.50fr, 1/29; 2.10fr, 1/8; 2.40fr, 2/19; 2.50fr, 1/15; 2.75fr, 1/22; 3.20fr, 4/16; 3.90fr, 2/26.

Pompidou Cultural Center — A738

1977, Feb. 5 Engr. *Perf. 13*
1515 A738 1fr multicolored .35 .20

Inauguration of the Georges Pompidou National Center for Art and Culture, Paris.

Dunkirk Harbor A739

1977, Feb. 12
1516 A739 50c multicolored .25 .20

Expansion of Dunkirk harbor facilities.

Bridge at Mantes, by Corot — A740

Virgin and Child, by Rubens A741

Tridimensional Design, by Victor Vasarely — A742

Head and Eagle, by Pierre-Yves Tremois A743

1977 Engr. ***Perf. 13x12½***
1517 A740 2fr multicolored 1.10 .45

Perf. 12x13
1518 A741 2fr multicolored 1.10 .45

Perf. 12½x13
1519 A742 3fr ultra & sl grn 1.50 .45

Photo.
1520 A743 3fr dark red & blk 1.90 .55
Nos. 1517-1520 (4) 5.60 1.90

Issue dates: No. 1517, Feb. 12; No. 1518, Nov. 5; No. 1519, Apr. 7; No. 1520, Sept. 17.

Hand Holding Torch and Sword — A744

Pisces — A745

1977, Mar. 5 Engr. ***Perf. 13***
1521 A744 80c ultra & multi .50 .20

"France remembers its dead."

1977-78 Engr. ***Perf. 13***

Zodiac Signs: 58c, Cancer. 61c, Sagittarius. 68c, Taurus. 73c, Aries. 78c, Libra. 1.05fr, Scorpio. 1.15fr, Capricorn. 1.25fr, Leo. 1.85fr, Aquarius. 2fr, Virgo. 2.10fr, Gemini.

1522 A745	54c	violet blue	.65	.30
1523 A745	58c	emerald	1.00	.30
1524 A745	61c	brt blue	.55	.30
1525 A745	68c	deep brown	.85	.35
1526 A745	73c	rose carmine	1.50	.55
1527 A745	78c	vermilion	.65	.35
1528 A745	1.05fr	brt lilac	1.50	.75
1529 A745	1.15fr	orange	2.25	1.10
1530 A745	1.25fr	lt olive grn	1.25	.60
1531 A745	1.85fr	slate grn	2.75	.90
1532 A745	2fr	blue green	3.00	1.75
1533 A745	2.10fr	lilac rose	1.65	1.00
		Nos. 1522-1533 (12)	17.60	8.25

Issued: 54c, 68c, 1.05fr, 1.85fr, 4/1/77; others, 1978.

Nos. 1522-1533 are known only precanceled. See second note after No. 132.

Village in Provence A746

Europa: 1.40fr, Brittany port.

1977, Apr. 23
1534 A746 1fr multicolored *.65* .25
1535 A746 1.40fr multicolored *1.25* .35

Flowers and Gardening A747

1977, Apr. 23 Engr. ***Perf. 13***
1536 A747 1.70fr multicolored .70 .30

National Horticulture Society, centenary.

Symbolic Flower A748

1977, May 7
1537 A748 1.40fr multicolored .50 .35

Intl. Flower Show, Nantes, May 12-23.

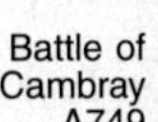

Battle of Cambray A749

1977, May 14
1538 A749 80c multicolored .35 .20

Capture of Cambray and the incorporation of Cambresis District into France, 300th anniv.

Carmes Church, School, Map of France A750

Modern Constructions A751

1977, May 14
1539 A750 1.10fr multicolored .50 .20

Catholic Institutes in France.

1977, May 21
1540 A751 1.10fr multicolored .55 .25

European Federation of the Construction Industry.

Annecy Castle A752

1977, May 28
1541 A752 1fr multicolored .60 .20

Congress of the Federation of French Philatelic Societies, Annecy, May 28-30.

Tourist Issue

Abbey, Pont-à-Mousson — A753

Abbey Tower, Saint-Amand-les-Eaux A754

Collegiate Church of Dorat A755

Fontenay Abbey A756

Bayeux Cathedral — A757

Chateau de Vitré A758

1977 Engr. ***Perf. 13***

1542 A753	1.25fr	multicolored	.40	.20
1543 A754	1.40fr	multicolored	.45	.20
1544 A755	1.45fr	multicolored	.45	.20
1545 A756	1.50fr	multicolored	.50	.20
1546 A757	1.90fr	black & yel	.60	.25
1547 A758	2.40fr	black & yel	.70	.20
		Nos. 1542-1547 (6)	3.10	1.25

Issued: 1.25fr, 10/1; 1.40fr, 9/17; 1.45fr, 7/16; 1.50fr, 6/4; 1.90fr, 7/9; 2.40fr, 9/24.

Polytechnic School and "X" — A759

1977, June 4 Engr. ***Perf. 13***
1548 A759 1.70fr multicolored .55 .20

Relocation at Palaiseau of Polytechnic School, founded 1794.

Soccer and Cup — A760

1977, June 11
1549 A760 80c multicolored .80 .20

Soccer Cup of France, 60th anniversary.

De Gaulle Memorial — A761

Stylized Map of France — A762

Photo. & Embossed

1977, June 18
1550 A761 1fr gold & multi .75 .20

5th anniversary of dedication of De Gaulle memorial at Colombey-les-Deux-Eglises.

1977, June 18 Engr. ***Perf. 13***
1551 A762 1.10fr ultra & red .55 .20

French Junior Chamber of Commerce.

Battle of Nancy A763

Arms of Burgundy A764

1977, June 25
1552 A763 1.10fr blue & slate 1.10 .40

Battle of Nancy between the Dukes of Burgundy and Lorraine, 500th anniversary.

1977, July 2
1553 A764 1.25fr ol brn & slate grn .50 .20

Annexation of Burgundy by the French Crown, 500th anniversary.

Association Emblem A765

1977, July 8
1554 A765 1.40fr ultra, olive & red .50 .25

French-speaking Parliamentary Association.

Red Cicada — A766

1977, Sept. 10 **Photo.** ***Perf. 13***
1555 A766 80c multicolored .50 .20

Nature protection.

French Handicrafts A767

1977, Oct. 1 **Engr.** ***Perf. 13***
1556 A767 1.40fr multicolored .50 .20

French craftsmen.

Industry and Agriculture — A768

1977, Oct. 22
1557 A768 80c brown & olive .30 .20

Economic & Social Council, 30th anniv.

Table Tennis A769

1977, Dec. 17 **Engr.** ***Perf. 13***
1558 A769 1.10fr multicolored 3.00 .75

French Table Tennis Federation, 50th anniv., and French team, gold medal winner, Birmingham.

Abstract, by Roger Excoffon — A770

1977, Dec. 17 ***Perf. 13x12½***
1559 A770 3fr multicolored 2.00 .50

Sabine, after David — A771

1977-78 **Engr.** ***Perf. 13***

1560	A771	1c	slate	.20	.20
1561	A771	2c	brt violet	.20	.20
1562	A771	5c	slate green	.20	.20
1563	A771	10c	red brown	.20	.20
1564	A771	15c	Prus blue	.20	.20
1565	A771	20c	brt green	.20	.20
1566	A771	30c	orange	.20	.20
1567	A771	50c	red lilac	.20	.20
1568	A771	80c	green	1.10	.20
a.			Booklet pane of 10	11.00	
1569	A771	80c	olive	.30	.20
1570	A771	1fr	red	1.25	.20
a.			Booklet pane of 5	8.50	
b.			Booklet pane of 10	15.00	
1571	A771	1fr	green	.55	.20
a.			Booklet pane of 10	5.50	
1572	A771	1.20fr	red	.55	.20
a.			Booklet pane of 5	4.25	
b.			Booklet pane of 10	7.75	
1573	A771	1.40fr	brt blue	2.00	.20
1574	A771	1.70fr	grnsh blue	.70	.20
1575	A771	2fr	emerald	.70	.20
1576	A771	2.10fr	lilac rose	.75	.20
1577	A771	3fr	dark brown	1.00	.30
			Nos. 1560-1577 (18)	10.50	3.70

Issued: #1560-1567, 1573, 1575, 1577, 4/3/78; #1568, 1570, 12/19/77; #1569, 1571, 1572, 1574, 1576, 6/5/78.

Coil Stamps

1978 ***Perf. 13 Horiz.***

1578	A771	80c	bright green	1.25	.45
1579	A771	1fr	bright green	1.00	.35
1579A	A771	1fr	bright red	1.25	.45
1579B	A771	1.20fr	bright red	1.00	.35
			Nos. 1578-1579B (4)	4.50	1.60

See Nos. 1658-1677.
For similar design inscribed "REPUBLIQUE FRANCAISE" see type A900.

Percheron, by Jacques Birr A772

Osprey — A773

1978 **Photo.** ***Perf. 13***
1580 A772 1.70fr multicolored .90 .45

Engr.

1581 A773 1.80fr multicolored .75 .25

Nature protection.
Issue dates: 1.70fr, Jan. 7; 1.80fr, Oct. 14.

Tournament, 1662, Etching — A774

Institut de France and Pont des Arts, Paris, by Bernard Buffet — A776

Horses, by Yves Brayer — A777

1978 **Engr.** ***Perf. 12x13***
1582 A774 2fr black 3.00 .95

Perf. 13x12

1584	A776	3fr multicolored	2.75	.90
1585	A777	3fr multicolored	2.00	.70
		Nos. 1582-1585 (3)	7.75	2.55

Issued: 2fr, 1/14; #1584, 2/4; #1585, 12/9.

Communications School and Tower — A778

1978, Jan. 19 **Engr.** ***Perf. 13***
1586 A778 80c Prussian blue .30 .20

Natl. Telecommunications School, cent.

Swedish and French Flags, Map of Saint Barthelemy A779

1978, Jan. 19
1587 A779 1.10fr multicolored .45 .20

Centenary of the reunion with France of Saint Barthelemy Island, West Indies.

Regions of France

Ile de France — A780

Tanker, Refinery, Flower, Upper Normandy A781

Lower Normandy A782

1978 **Photo.** ***Perf. 13***
1588 A780 1fr red, blue & blk .50 .20

Engr.

1589 A781 1.40fr multicolored .55 .20

Photo.

1590 A782 1.70fr multicolored .90 .35
Nos. 1588-1590 (3) 1.95 .75

Issued: 1fr, 3/4; 1.40fr, 1/21; 1.70fr, 3/31.

Stylized Map of France A788

Young Stamp Collector A789

1978, Feb. 11 **Engr.** ***Perf. 13***
1596 A788 1.10fr violet & green .45 .20

Program of administrative changes, 15th anniv.

1978, Feb. 25
1597 A789 80c multicolored .30 .20

JUVEXNIORT, Youth Philatelic Exhibition, Niort, Feb. 25-March 5.

Tourist Issue

Verdon Gorge — A790

Saint-Saturnin Church — A792

Pont Neuf, Paris
A791

Our Lady of Bec-Hellouin Abbey — A793

Chateau D'Esquelbecq — A794

Aubazine Abbey
A795

Fontevraud Abbey
A796

1978 Engr. *Perf. 13*

1598 A790 50c multicolored .20 .20
1599 A791 80c multicolored .35 .20
1600 A792 1fr black .35 .20
1601 A793 1.10fr multicolored .50 .20
1602 A794 1.10fr multicolored .40 .20
1603 A795 1.25fr carmine & brn .50 .20
1604 A796 1.70fr multicolored .70 .25
Nos. 1598-1604 (7) 3.00 1.45

Issued: 1.25fr, 2/18; 50c, 3/6; #1601, 3/26; 80c, 5/27; 1fr, 6/10; 1.70fr, 6/3; #1602, 6/17.

Fish and Underwater Flora — A797

1978, Apr. 15 Photo. *Perf. 13*

1605 A797 1.25fr multicolored .95 .45

Port Cros National Park, 15th anniversary.

Flowers, Butterflies and Houses — A798

1978, Apr. 22 Engr. *Perf. 13*

1606 A798 1.70fr multicolored 2.75 .35

Beautification of France campaign, 50th anniv.

Hands Shielding Source of Heat and Light
A799

1978, Apr. 22

1607 A799 1fr multicolored .60 .20

Energy conservation.

World War I Memorial near Lens — A800

Fountain of the Innocents, Paris — A801

1978, May 6

1608 A800 2fr lemon & magenta .85 .30

Colline Notre Dame de Lorette memorial of World War I.

1978, May 6

Europa: 1.40fr, Flower Park Fountain, Paris.

1609 A801 1fr multicolored *.60* .20
1610 A801 1.40fr multicolored *1.25* .50

Maurois Palace, Troyes — A802

1978, May 13

1611 A802 1fr multicolored .40 .20

51st Congress of the Federation of French Philatelic Societies, Troyes, May 13-15.

Roland Garros Tennis Court and Player — A803

1978, May 27

1612 A803 1fr multicolored 2.50 .25

Roland Garros Tennis Court, 50th anniv.

Hand and Plant — A804

Printing Office Emblem — A805

1978, Sept. 9 Engr. *Perf. 13*

1613 A804 1.30fr brown, red & grn .50 .20

Encouragement of handicrafts.

1978, Sept. 23

1614 A805 1fr multicolored .35 .20

National Printing Office, established 1538.

Fortress, Besançon, and Collegiate Church, Dole — A806

Valenciennes and Maubeuge — A807

1978

1615 A806 1.20fr multicolored .50 .20
1616 A807 1.20fr multicolored .50 .20

Reunion of Franche-Comté and Valenciennes and Maubeuge with France, 300th anniversary.

Issued: #1615, Sept. 23; #1616, Sept. 30.

Sower Type of 1906-1937 and Academy Emblem — A808

Gymnasts, Strasbourg Cathedral, Storks — A809

1978, Oct. 7

1617 A808 1fr multicolored .40 .20

Academy of Philately, 50th anniversary.

1978, Oct. 21

1618 A809 1fr multicolored .70 .20

19th World Gymnastics Championships, Strasbourg, Oct. 23-26.

Various Sports
A810

Polish Veterans' Monument
A811

1978, Oct. 21

1619 A810 1fr multicolored 1.10 .30

Sports for all.

1978, Nov. 11

1620 A811 1.70fr multicolored .60 .25

Polish veterans of World War II.

Railroad Car and Monument, Compiègne Forest, Rethondes
A812

1978, Nov. 11 Engr. *Perf. 13*

1621 A812 1.20fr indigo .75 .20

60th anniversary of World War I armistice.

Handicapped People — A813

1978, Nov. 18

1622 A813 1fr multicolored .40 .20

Rehabilitation of the handicapped.

Human Rights Emblem
A814

1978, Dec. 9 Engr. *Perf. 13*

1623 A814 1.70fr dk brown & blue .70 .30

30th anniversary of Universal Declaration of Human Rights.

Child and IYC Emblem
A815

1979, Jan. 6 Engr. *Perf. 13*

1624 A815 1.70fr multicolored 4.00 2.50

International Year of the Child.

"Music," 15th Century Miniature — A816

1979, Jan. 13 *Perf. 13x12½*

1625 A816 2fr multicolored 1.40 .70

Diana Taking a Bath, d'Ecouen Castle
A817

Church at Auvers-on-Oise, by Vincent Van Gogh — A818

Head of Marianne, by Salvador Dali
A819

Fire Dancer from The Magic Flute, by Chaplain Midy
A820

1979	**Photo.**	***Perf. 12½x13***
1626 A817 2fr multicolored	.90	.70
1627 A818 2fr multicolored	6.75	.80
1628 A819 3fr multicolored	1.25	.60
1629 A820 3fr multicolored	1.25	.60
Nos. 1626-1629 (4)	10.15	2.70

Issue dates: #1626, Sept. 22; #1627, Oct. 27; #1628, Nov. 19; #1629, Nov. 26.

Orange Agaric — A821

Mushrooms: 83c, Death trumpet. 1.30fr, Olive wood pleurotus. 2.25fr, Cauliflower claveria.

1979, Jan. 15	**Engr.**	***Perf. 13***
1630 A821 64c orange	.30	.25
1631 A821 83c brown	.50	.30
1632 A821 1.30fr yellow bister	.80	.40
1633 A821 2.25fr brown purple	1.25	.70
Nos. 1630-1633 (4)	2.85	1.65

Nos. 1630-1633 are known only precanceled. See second note after No. 132.

Victor Segalen
A822

1979, Jan. 20
1634 A822 1.50fr multicolored .50 .20

Physician, explorer and writer (1878-1919).

Hibiscus and Palms — A823

1979, Feb. 3
1635 A823 35c multicolored .20 .20

International Flower Festival, Martinique.

Buddha, Stupas, Temple of Borobudur
A824

1979, Feb. 24
1636 A824 1.80fr ol & slate grn .60 .30

Save the Temple of Borobudur, Java, campaign.

Boy, by Francisque Poulbot (1879-1946)
A825

1979, Mar. 24 **Photo.**
1637 A825 1.30fr multicolored .45 .20

Tourist Issue

Chateau de Maisons, Laffitte
A826

Bernay and St. Pierre sur Dives Abbeys — A827

View of Auray — A827a

Steenvorde Windmill — A828

Wall Painting, Niaux Cave
A829

Royal Palace, Perpignan
A830

1979	**Engr.**	***Perf. 13***
1638 A826 45c multicolored	.20	.20
1639 A827 1fr multicolored	.35	.20
1640 A827a 1fr multicolored	.35	.20
1641 A828 1.20fr multicolored	.40	.20
1642 A829 1.50fr multicolored	.45	.20
1643 A830 1.70fr multicolored	.55	.20
Nos. 1638-1643 (6)	2.30	1.20

Issued: 45c, 10/6; #1639, 6/16; #1640, 6/30; 1.20fr, 6/12; 1.50fr, 7/9; 1.70fr, 4/21.

Honey Bee
A831

1979, Mar. 31 **Engr.** ***Perf. 13***
1644 A831 1fr multicolored .50 .20

Nature protection.

St. Germain des Prés Abbey
A832

1979, Apr. 21
1645 A832 1.40fr multicolored .50 .20

Simoun Mail Monoplanes, 1935, and Map of Mail Routes — A833

Europa: 1.70fr, Floating spheres used on Seine during siege of Paris, 1870.

1979, Apr. 28
1646 A833 1.20fr multicolored *1.10* .35
1647 A833 1.70fr multicolored *1.90* .50

Ship and View of Nantes
A834

1979, May 5 **Engr.** ***Perf. 13***
1648 A834 1.20fr multicolored .40 .20

52nd National Congress of French Philatelic Societies, Nantes, May 5-7.

Royal Palace, 1789 — A835

1979, May 19
1649 A835 1fr car rose & pur .40 .20

European Elections
A836

1979, May 19 **Photo.** ***Perf. 13***
1650 A836 1.20fr multicolored .40 .20

European Parliament, 1st direct elections, June 10.

Joan of Arc Monument
A837

1979, May 24 **Engr.**
1651 A837 1.70fr brt lilac rose .70 .30

Joan of Arc, the Maid of Orleans (1412-1431).

Felix Guyon and Catheters
A840

1979, June 23
1652 A840 1.80fr sepia & blue .60 .20

Felix Guyon (1831-1920), urologist.

Lantern Tower, La Rochelle
A841

Telecom '79
A842

Towers: 88c, Chartres Cathedral. 1.40fr, Bourges Cathedral. 2.35fr, Amiens Cathedral.

1979, Aug. 13	**Engr.**	***Perf. 13***
1653 A841 68c vio brn & blk	.30	.30
1654 A841 88c ultra & blk	.40	.30
1655 A841 1.40fr gray grn & blk	.65	.50
1656 A841 2.35fr dull brn & blk	1.00	.60
Nos. 1653-1656 (4)	2.35	1.70

Nos. 1653-1656 are known only precanceled. See second note after No. 132. See Nos. 1684-1687, 1719-1722, 1814-1817.

1979, Sept. 22
1657 A842 1.10fr multicolored .40 .20

3rd World Telecommunications Exhibition.

Sabine Type of 1977-78

1979-81	**Engr.**	***Perf. 13***
1658 A771 40c brown ('81)	.20	.20
1659 A771 60c red brn ('81)	.20	.20
1660 A771 70c violet blue	.20	.20
1661 A771 90c brt lilac ('81)	.25	.20
1662 A771 1fr gray olive	.25	.20
1663 A771 1.10fr green	.70	.20
1664 A771 1.20fr green ('80)	.45	.20
1665 A771 1.30fr rose red	.70	.20
1666 A771 1.40fr rose red ('80)	.50	.20
1667 A771 1.60fr purple	1.00	.20
1668 A771 1.80fr ocher	.70	.20
1669 A771 3.50fr lt ol grn ('81)	1.00	.20
1670 A771 4fr brt car ('81)	1.10	.20
1671 A771 5fr brt grnsh bl ('81)	1.50	.20
Nos. 1658-1671 (14)	8.75	2.80

Coil Stamps

1979-80	***Perf. 13 Horiz.***	
1674 A771 1.10fr green	1.25	.20
1675 A771 1.20fr green ('80)	.55	.20
1676 A771 1.30fr rose red	1.25	.20
1677 A771 1.40fr rose red ('80)	.60	.20
Nos. 1674-1677 (4)	3.65	.80

Lorraine Region — A845

1979, Nov. 10
1678 A845 2.30fr multicolored .80 .20

Gears A847

1979, Nov. 17 ***Perf. 13***
1680 A847 1.80fr multicolored .70 .30

Central Technical School of Paris, 150th anniv.

Judo Throw A848

1979, Nov. 24 **Engr.**
1681 A848 1.60fr multicolored .50 .30

World Judo Championships, Paris, Dec.

Violins — A849

1979, Dec. 10
1682 A849 1.30fr multicolored .50 .20

Eurovision A850

1980, Jan. 12 **Engr.** ***Perf. 13x13½***
1683 A850 1.80fr multicolored 1.00 .40

Tower Type of 1979

Designs: 76c, Chateau d'Angers. 99c, Chateau de Kerjean. 1.60fr, Chateau de Pierrefonds. 2.65fr, Chateau de Tarascon.

1980, Jan. 21 **Engr.**
1684 A841 76c grnsh bl & blk .30 .30
1685 A841 99c slate grn & blk .40 .30
1686 A841 1.60fr red & blk .70 .55
1687 A841 2.65fr brn org & blk 1.10 .65
Nos. 1684-1687 (4) 2.50 1.80

Nos. 1684-1687 are known only precanceled. See second note after No. 132.

Self-portrait, by Albrecht Dürer, Philexfrance '82 Emblem — A851

Woman Holding Fan, by Ossip Zadkine A852

Abstract, by Raoul Ubak — A853

Hommage to J.S. Bach, by Jean Picart Le Doux — A854

Peasant, by Louis Le Nain A855

Woman with Blue Eyes, by Modigliani A856

Abstract, by Hans Hartung A857

Engraved, Photogravure (#1691, 1694)

1980 ***Perf. 12½x13, 13x12½***
1688 A851 2fr multicolored .85 .50
1689 A852 3fr multicolored 1.50 .70
1690 A853 3fr multicolored 1.50 .70
1691 A854 3fr multicolored 1.50 .70
1692 A855 3fr multicolored 1.50 .70
1693 A856 4fr multicolored 3.00 .85
1694 A857 4fr ultra & black 2.00 .70
Nos. 1688-1694 (7) 11.85 4.85

Issued: #1688, 6/7; #1689, 1/19; #1690, 2/2; #1691, 9/20; #1693, 10/26; #1692, 11/10; #1694, 12/20.

Giants of the North Festival — A858

French Cuisine — A859

1980, Feb. 16 ***Perf. 13***
1695 A858 1.60fr multicolored .65 .30

1980, Feb. 23
1696 A859 90c red & lt brown .75 .20

Woman Embroidering A860

Fight Against Cigarette Smoking A861

Photogravure and Engraved

1980, Mar. 29 ***Perf. 13***
1697 A860 1.10fr multicolored .40 .20

1980, Apr. 5 **Photo.** ***Perf. 13***
1698 A861 1.30fr multicolored .45 .20

Aristide Briand — A862

Europa : 1.80fr, St. Benedict.

1980, Apr. 26 **Engr.** ***Perf. 13***
1699 A862 1.30fr multicolored *.50* .25
1700 A862 1.80fr red & red brown *1.00* .50

Aristide Briand (1862-1932), prime minister, 1909-1911, 1921-1922; St. Benedict, patron saint of Europe.

Liancourt, College, Map of Northwestern France — A863

1980, May 19 **Engr.** ***Perf. 13***
1701 A863 2fr dk green & pur .65 .20

National College of Arts and Handicrafts (founded by Larochefoucauld Liancourt) bicentenary.

Cranes, Town Hall Tower, Dunkirk — A864

1980, May 24
1702 A864 1.30fr multicolored .40 .20

53rd Natl. Congress of French Federation of Philatelic Societies, Dunkirk, May 24-26.

Tourist Issue

Chateau de Maintenon A866

Cordes A865

Montauban A867

St. Peter's Abbey, Solesmes A868

Puy Cathedral A869

1980 **Engr.** ***Perf. 13***
1703 A865 1.50fr multicolored .50 .20
1704 A866 2fr multicolored .60 .20
1705 A867 2.30fr multicolored .70 .20
1706 A868 2.50fr multicolored .75 .20
1707 A869 3.20fr multicolored 1.00 .30
Nos. 1703-1707 (5) 3.55 1.10

Issued: #1703, 4/5; #1704, 6/7; #1705, 5/7; #1706, 9/20; #1707, 5/12.

Graellsia Isabellae A870

1980, May 31 **Photo.**
1708 A870 1.10fr multicolored .60 .20

Association Emblem — A871

1980, June 10 **Photo.**
1709 A871 1.30fr red & blue .45 .20

Intl. Public Relations Assoc., 25th anniv.

Marianne, French Architecture A872

1980, June 21 **Engr.**

1710 A872 1.50fr bluish & gray blk .60 .25

Heritage Year.

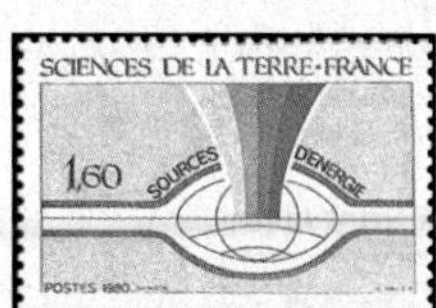

Earth Sciences A873

1980, July 5

1711 A873 1.60fr dk brown & red .55 .30

International Geological Congress.

Rochambeau's Landing — A874

1980, July 15

1712 A874 2.50fr multicolored 1.00 .35

Rochambeau's landing at Newport, R.I. (American Revolution), bicentenary.

Message of Peace, by Yaacov Agam — A875

1980, Oct. 4 **Photo.** ***Perf. 11½x13***

1713 A875 4fr multicolored 3.50 .65

French Golf Federation A876

1980, Oct. 18 **Engr.**

1714 A876 1.40fr multicolored .55 .20

Comedie Francaise, 300th Anniversary A877

1980, Oct. 18

1715 A877 2fr multicolored .65 .20

Charles de Gaulle — A878

1980, Nov. 10 **Photo.** ***Perf. 13***

1716 A878 1.40fr multicolored .75 .20

40th anniversary of De Gaulle's appeal of June 18, and 10th anniversary of his death.

Guardsman — A879

1980, Nov. 24 **Engr.** ***Perf. 13***

1717 A879 1.70fr multicolored .65 .35

Rambouillet Chateau A880

1980, Dec. 6 **Engr.** ***Perf. 13***

1718 A880 2.20fr multicolored .90 .20

Tower Type of 1979

Designs: 88c, Imperial Chapel, Ajaccio. 1.14fr, Astronomical Clock, Besancon. 1.84fr, Coucy Castle ruins. 3.05fr, Font-de-Gaume cave drawing, Les Eyzies de Tayac.

1981, Jan. 11 **Engr.** ***Perf. 13***

1719 A841 88c dp mag & blk .35 .20
1720 A841 1.14fr ultra & blk .45 .30
1721 A841 1.84fr dk green & blk .65 .45
1722 A841 3.05fr brn red & blk 1.10 .70
Nos. 1719-1722 (4) 2.55 1.65

Nos. 1719-1722 are known only precanceled. See second note after No. 132.

Microelectronics — A881

1981 **Photo.**

1723 A881 1.20fr shown .75 .20
1724 A881 1.20fr Biology .40 .20
1725 A881 1.40fr Energy .50 .25
1726 A881 1.80fr Marine exploration .65 .35
1727 A881 2fr Telemetry .80 .20
Nos. 1723-1727 (5) 3.10 1.20

Issue dates: #1723, Feb. 5; others, Mar. 28.

Abstract, by Albert Gleizes A882

1981, Feb. 28 ***Perf. 12½x13***

1728 A882 4fr multicolored 1.65 .50

The Footpath by Camille Pissaro — A883

1981, Apr. 18 **Engr.** ***Perf. 13x12½***

1729 A883 2fr multicolored 1.10 .35

Child Watering Smiling Map of France — A884

1981, Mar. 14 **Engr.** ***Perf. 13***

1730 A884 1.40fr multicolored .45 .20

Sully Chateau, Rosny-sur-Seine — A885

1981, Mar. 21

1731 A885 2.50fr multicolored .95 .20

Tourist Issue

Roman Temple, Nimes — A886

Church of St. Jean, Lyon — A887

St. Anne d'Auray Basilica — A888

Vaucelles Abbey A889

Notre Dame of Louviers A890

1981, Apr. 11 **Engr.** ***Perf. 13***

1732 A886 1.70fr multicolored .60 .20

1981

1733 A887 1.40fr dk red & dk brn .45 .20
1734 A888 2.20fr blue & black .75 .20

Issue dates: 1.40fr, May 30; 2.20fr, July 4.

1981

1735 A889 2fr red & black .60 .20
1736 A890 2.20fr red brn & dk brn .75 .30
Nos. 1732-1736 (5) 3.15 1.10

Issue dates: 2fr, Sept. 19; 2.20fr, Sept. 26.

Europa Issue 1981

Folkdances A891

1981, May 4 ***Perf. 13***

1737 A891 1.40fr Bouree *.75* .25
1738 A891 2fr Sardane *1.75* .55

Bookbinding A892

Cadets A893

1981, Apr. 4 ***Perf. 13***

1739 A892 1.50fr olive & car rose .50 .20

1981, May 16

1740 A893 2.50fr multicolored .85 .20

Military College at St. Maixent centenary.

Man Drawing Geometric Diagram — A894

1981, May 23 **Photo.**

1741 A894 2fr shown 1.75 .45
1742 A894 2fr Faces 1.75 .45
a. Pair, #1741-1742 + label 3.50 3.00

PHILEXFRANCE '82 Stamp Exhibition, Paris, June 11-21, 1982.

Theophraste Renaudot and Emile de Girardin — A895

Public Gardens, Vichy — A896

1981, May 30 **Engr.**

1743 A895 2.20fr black & red .75 .40

350th anniversary of La Gazette (founded by Renaudot), and death centenary of founder of Le Journal (de Girardin).

1981, June 6

1744 A896 1.40fr multicolored .45 .20

54th National Congress of French Federation of Philatelic Societies, Vichy.

Higher National College for Commercial Studies Centenary A897

1981, June 20 *Perf. 13*
1745 A897 1.40fr multicolored .50 .20

Sea Shore Conservation — A898

1981, June 20
1746 A898 1.60fr multicolored .60 .20

World Fencing Championship, Clermont-Ferrand, July 2-13 — A899

1981, June 27
1747 A899 1.80fr multicolored .60 .25

Sabine, after David — A900

1981, Sept. 1 **Engr.**
1755 A900 1.40fr green .85 .20
1756 A900 1.60fr red 1.00 .25
1757 A900 2.30fr blue 1.40 .40
Nos. 1755-1757 (3) 3.25 .85

Coil Stamps

1981 **Engr.** *Perf. 13 Horiz.*
1758 A900 1.40fr green .55 .20
1759 A900 1.60fr red .60 .20

Highway Safety ("Drink or Drive") A901

1981, Sept. 5 *Perf. 13*
1768 A901 1.60fr multicolored .60 .20

45th Intl. PEN Club Congress A902

Jules Ferry, Statesman A903

1981, Sept. 19 *Perf. 13*
1769 A902 2fr multicolored .75 .25

1981, Sept. 26 *Perf. 12½x13*
1770 A903 1.60fr multicolored .60 .20

Free compulsory public school centenary.

Natl. Savings Bank Centenary A904

1981, Sept. 21 **Photo.** *Perf. 13*
1771 A904 1.40fr multicolored .50 .20
1772 A904 1.60fr multicolored .55 .20

The Divers, by Edouard Pignon — A905

1981, Oct. 3 *Perf. 13x12½*
1773 A905 4fr multicolored 1.65 .30

Alleluia, by Alfred Manessier A906

1981, Dec. 19 **Photo.** *Perf. 12x13*
1774 A906 4fr multicolored 1.65 .30

Tourist Issue

Saint-Emilion — A907

Crest — A908

1981 **Engr.** *Perf. 13x12½*
1775 A907 2.60fr dk red & lt ol grn .85 .20

Perf. 13

1776 A908 2.90fr dk green 1.25 .20

Issued: #1775, Oct. 10; #1776, Nov. 28.

150th Anniv. of Naval Academy A909

1981, Oct. 17 *Perf. 13*
1777 A909 1.40fr multicolored .55 .20

A910

A911

St. Hubert Kneeling before the Stag, 15th cent. sculpture.

1981, Oct. 24
1778 A910 1.60fr multicolored .50 .20

Museum of hunting and nature.

1981, Nov. 2

V. Schoelcher, J. Jaures, J. Moulin, the Pantheon.

1779 A911 1.60fr blue & dull pur .50 .20

Intl. Year of the Disabled A912

1981, Nov. 7
1780 A912 1.60fr multicolored .50 .20

Men Leading Cattle, 2nd Cent. Roman Mosaic — A913

1981, Nov. 14 *Perf. 13x12*
1781 A913 2fr multicolored 1.10 .30

Virgil's birth bimillennium.

Martyrs of Chateaubriant A914

1981, Dec. 12 **Engr.** *Perf. 13*
1782 A914 1.40fr multicolored .50 .20

Liberty, after Delacroix — A915

1982 **Engr.** *Perf. 13*

1783	A915	5c dk green	.20	.20
1784	A915	10c dull red	.20	.20
1785	A915	15c brt rose lilac	.20	.20
1786	A915	20c brt green	.20	.20
1787	A915	30c orange	.20	.20
1788	A915	40c brown	.20	.20
a.		Bklt. pane of 5, 4 No. 1784, No. 1788 ('87)	1.00	
1789	A915	50c lilac	.20	.20
1790	A915	60c lt red brn	.20	.20
1791	A915	70c ultra	.20	.20
1792	A915	80c lt olive grn	.20	.20
1793	A915	90c brt lilac	.20	.20
1794	A915	1fr olive green	.25	.20
1795	A915	1.40fr green	.60	.20
1796	A915	1.60fr green	.45	.20
1797	A915	1.60fr red	.70	.20
1798	A915	1.80fr red	.60	.20
1799	A915	2fr brt yel grn	.60	.20
1800	A915	2.30fr blue	.60	.25
1801	A915	2.60fr blue	.70	.25
1802	A915	3fr chocolate	.70	.20
1803	A915	4fr brt carmine	1.00	.20
1804	A915	5fr gray blue	1.25	.20
		Nos. 1783-1804 (22)	9.65	4.50

Coil Stamps

Perf. 13 Horiz.

1805	A915	1.40fr green	1.00	.30
1806	A915	1.60fr red	1.25	.30
1807	A915	1.60fr green	.50	.20
1807A	A915	1.80fr red	.60	.20
		Nos. 1805-1807A (4)	3.35	1.00

Issued: 5c-50c, 1fr-1.40fr, 2fr, 2.30fr, 5fr, #1797, 1/2; 1.80fr, 2.60fr, #1796, 6/1; 60c-90c, 3fr, 4fr, 11/3.

See Nos. 1878-1897A, 2077-2080. For surcharge see No. 2115.

Tourist Issue

St. Pierre and Miquelon A916

Corsica A917

Renaissance Fountain, Aix-en Provence — A918

Collonges-la-Rouge — A919

Castle of Henry IV, Pau A920

Lille — A921

Chateau Ripaille, Haute-Savoie — A921a

1982 **Engr.** *Perf. 12½*
1808 A916 1.60fr dk blue & blk .50 .20
1809 A917 1.90fr blue & red .60 .20

Perf. 13

1810 A918 2fr multicolored .65 .20
1811 A919 3fr multicolored .90 .20
1812 A920 3fr ultra & dk bl .90 .20

Issued: 1.60fr, 1.90fr, Jan. 9; 2fr, June 21, No. 1811, July 5, No. 1812, May 15.

1982 *Perf. 13x12½*

1813 A921 1.80fr dull red & ol .55 .20
1813A A921a 2.90fr multicolored .95 .20
Nos. 1808-1813A (7) 5.05 1.40

Issue dates: 1.80fr, Oct. 16; 2.90fr, Sept. 4.

Tower Type of 1979

97c, Tanlay Castle, Yonne. 1.25fr, Salses Fort, Pyrenees-Orientales. 2.03fr, Montlhery Tower, Essonne. 3.36fr, Chateau d'If Bouches-du-Rhone.

1982, Jan. 11 **Engr.** *Perf. 13*

1814 A841 97c olive grn & blk .35 .20
1815 A841 1.25fr red & blk .40 .25
1816 A841 2.03fr sepia & blk .65 .40
1817 A841 3.36fr ultra & blk 1.10 .60
Nos. 1814-1817 (4) 2.50 1.45

Nos. 1814-1817 are known only precanceled. See second note after No. 132.

800th Birth Anniv. of St. Francis of Assisi A922

1982, Feb. 6 **Photo. & Engr.**

1818 A922 2fr black & blue .70 .20

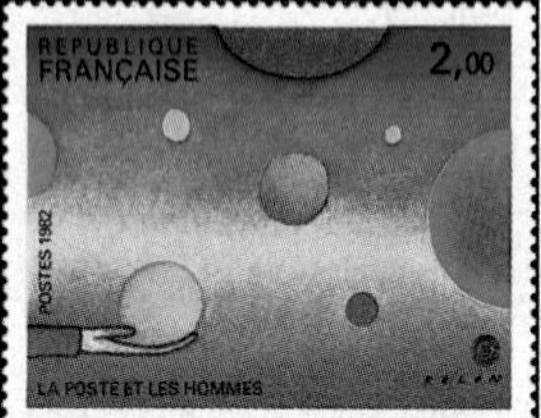

Posts and Mankind — A923

Posts and Technology — A924

Illustration reduced.

1982, Feb. 13 **Photo.**

1819 A923 2fr multicolored 4.50 1.00
1820 A924 2fr multicolored 4.50 1.00
a. Pair, #1819-1820 + label 9.00 6.50

PHILEXFRANCE '82 Stamp Exhibition, Paris, June 11-21.

Souvenir Sheet

Marianne, by Jean Cocteau — A925

1982, June 11

1821 A925 Sheet of 2 21.00 21.00
a. 4fr red & blue 9.00 9.00
b. 6fr blue & red 10.00 10.00

Sold only with 20fr show admission ticket.

Scouting Year A926

1982, Feb. 20 **Engr.**

1822 A926 2.30fr yel grn & blk .75 .30

31st Natl. Census — A927

1982, Feb. 27 **Photo.**

1823 A927 1.60fr multicolored .50 .20

Bale-Mulhouse Airport Opening — A928

1982, Mar. 15 **Engr.** *Perf. 13*

1824 A928 1.90fr multicolored .75 .20

Fight Against Racism A929

1982, Mar. 20

1825 A929 2.30fr brn & red org .85 .30

Blacksmith — A930

1982, Apr. 17

1826 A930 1.40fr multicolored .50 .20

Europa 1982 A931

1982, Apr. 24

1827 A931 1.60fr Treaty of Rome, 1957 *1.00* .35
1828 A931 2.30fr Treaty of Verdun, 843 *1.75* .60

1982 World Cup A932

1982, Apr. 28

1829 A932 1.80fr multicolored 1.00 .20

Young Greek Soldier, Hellenic Sculpture, Agude A933

1982, May 15 *Perf. 12½x13*

1830 A933 4fr multicolored 1.75 .40

Embarkation for Ostia, by Claude Gellee — A934

The Lacemaker, by Vermeer A935

Turkish Chamber, by Balthus — A936

1982 **Photo.** *Perf. 13x12½, 12½x13*

1831 A934 4fr multicolored 1.75 .50
1832 A935 4fr multicolored 1.75 .50
1833 A936 4fr multicolored 1.75 .50
Nos. 1831-1833 (3) 5.25 1.50

Issued: #1831, 6/19; #1832, 9/4; #1833, 11/6.

35th Intl. Film Festival, Cannes — A937

Natl. Space Studies Center, 20th Anniv. — A938

1982, May 15 **Photo.** *Perf. 13*

1834 A937 2.30fr multicolored .75 .35

1982, May 15 **Engr.**

1835 A938 2.60fr multicolored .95 .35

A939

A940

1982, June 4 **Photo.**

1836 A939 2.60fr multicolored .85 .30

Industrialized Countries' Summit Meeting, Versailles, June 4-6.

1982, June 4 **Engr.** *Perf. 13*

1837 A940 1.60fr ol grn & dk grn .50 .20

Jules Valles (1832-1885), writer.

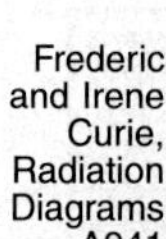

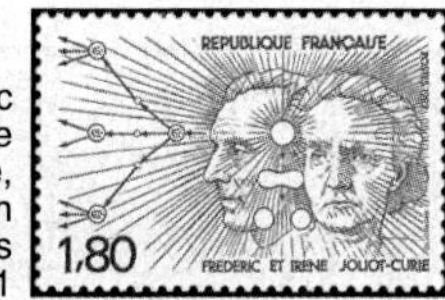

Frederic and Irene Curie, Radiation Diagrams A941

1982, June 26

1838 A941 1.80fr multicolored .70 .20

Electric Street Lighting Centenary A942

1982, July 10

1839 A942 1.80fr dk blue & vio .70 .20

The Family, by Marc Boyan A943

Photogravure and Engraved

1982, Sept. 18 *Perf. 12½x13*

1840 A943 4fr multicolored 2.00 .40

Natl. Fed. of Firemen, Cent. A944

Marionettes A945

1982, Sept. 18 **Engr.** *Perf. 13*

1841 A944 3.30fr red & sepia 1.50 .20

1982, Sept. 25

1842 A945 1.80fr multicolored .60 .20

Rugby A946

1982, Oct. 9
1843 A946 1.60fr multicolored 1.50 .20

Higher Education A947

1982, Oct. 16
1844 A947 1.80fr red & black .60 .20

TB Bacillus Centenary A948

1982, Nov. 13
1845 A948 2.60fr red & black .80 .30

St. Teresa of Avila (1515-82) A949

Leon Blum (1872-1950), Politician A950

1982, Nov. 20
1846 A949 2.10fr multicolored .65 .20

1982, Dec. 18 **Engr.** ***Perf. 13***
1847 A950 1.80fr dk brn & brn .65 .20

Cavelier de la Salle (1643-1687), Explorer — A951

1982, Dec. 18 ***Perf. 13x12½***
1848 A951 3.25fr multicolored 1.00 .20

Spring — A952

1983, Jan. 17 **Engr.** ***Perf. 13***
1849 A952 1.05fr shown .30 .20
1850 A952 1.35fr Summer .40 .20
1851 A952 2.19fr Autumn .55 .30
1852 A952 3.63fr Winter 1.00 .55
Nos. 1849-1852 (4) 2.25 1.25

Nos. 1849-1852 known only precanceled. See second note after No. 132.

Provence-Alpes-Cote d'Azur — A953

Brantome (Perigord) A954

Concarneau — A955

Noirlac Abbey A956

Jarnac A957

Charleville-Mezieres — A958

Illustration A958 reduced.

1983 **Photo.** ***Perf. 13***
1853 A953 1fr multicolored .40 .20

Engr.

Perf. 13x12½
1854 A954 1.80fr multicolored .60 .20

Perf. 13
1855 A955 3fr multicolored 1.00 .20

Perf. 13x12½
1856 A956 3.60fr multicolored 1.25 .30

Issued: 1fr, 1/8; 1.80fr, 2/5; 3fr, 6/11; 3.60fr, 7/2.

1983 ***Perf. 13x12½***
1857 A957 2fr multicolored .70 .20
1858 A958 3.10fr multicolored 1.10 .60
Nos. 1853-1858 (6) 5.05 1.70

Issued: 2fr, Oct. 8; 3.10fr, Sept. 17.

Martin Luther (1483-1546) — A959

1983, Feb. 12 **Engr.** ***Perf. 13***
1859 A959 3.30fr dk brn & tan 1.25 .25

Alliance Francaise Centenary A960

1983, Feb. 19
1860 A960 1.80fr multicolored .70 .20

Danielle Casanova (d. 1942), Resistance Leader A961

1983, Mar. 8
1861 A961 3fr blk & red brn .95 .25

World Communications Year — A962

1983, Mar. 12 **Photo.**
1862 A962 2.60fr multicolored .95 .20

Manned Flight Bicentenary — A963

1983, Mar. 19 **Photo.** ***Perf. 13***
1863 2fr Hot air balloon .80 .35
1864 3fr Hydrogen balloon 1.10 .50
a. A963 Pair, #1863-1864 + label 2.00 1.75

Female Nude, by Raphael A964

Aurora-Set, by Dewasne — A965

1983 **Engr.** ***Perf. 13***
1865 A964 4fr multicolored 1.25 .50

Photo.
1866 A965 4fr multicolored 1.25 .50

Issue dates: #1866, Mar. 19; #1865, Apr. 9.

Illustration from Perrault's Folk Tales, by Gustave Dore A966

1983, June 18 **Engr.** ***Perf. 13***
1867 A966 4fr red & black 1.25 .50

Homage to Jean Effel A967

1983, Oct. 15
1868 A967 4fr multicolored 1.50 .40

Le Lapin Agile, by Utrillo — A968

1983, Dec. 3 ***Perf. 13x12½***
1869 A968 4fr multicolored 1.50 .50

Thistle — A969

Europa 1983 — A970

1983, Apr. 23 **Engr.** ***Perf. 12½x12***
1870 A969 1fr shown .30 .20
1871 A969 2fr Martagon lily .80 .20
1872 A969 3fr Aster .90 .20
1873 A969 4fr Aconite 1.25 .35
Nos. 1870-1873 (4) 3.25 .95

1983, Apr. 29 ***Perf. 13***
1874 A970 1.80fr Symbolic shutter *3.25* .75
1875 A970 2.60fr Lens-to-screen diagram *4.25* 1.25

Centenary of Paris Convention for the Protection of Industrial Property — A971

1983, May 14 **Photo.** ***Perf. 13***
1876 A971 2fr multicolored .70 .20

French Philatelic Societies Congress, Marseille A972

1983, May 21 **Engr.** ***Perf. 13***
1877 A972 1.80fr multicolored .70 .20

Liberty Type of 1982

1983-87 **Engr.** ***Perf. 13***
1878 A915 1.70fr green .55 .20
1879 A915 1.80fr green .55 .20
1880 A915 1.90fr green .70 .20
1881 A915 2fr red .75 .20
1882 A915 2fr green .75 .20
1883 A915 2.10fr red .75 .20

1884 A915 2.20fr red .75 .20
a. Booklet pane of 10 7.50
b. Bklt. pane, #1788, 4 #1884 4.00
c. With label ('87) .75 .20
1885 A915 2.80fr blue .95 .25
1886 A915 3fr blue 1.10 .20
1887 A915 3.20fr blue 1.00 .20
1888 A915 3.40fr blue 1.25 .20
1889 A915 3.60fr blue 1.40 .20
1890 A915 10fr purple 3.00 .20
1891 A915 (1.90fr) green .70 .20
1892 A915 (2fr) green .80 .20
Nos. 1878-1892 (15) 15.00 3.05

Coil Stamps

Engr. ***Perf. 13 Horiz.***
1893 A915 1.70fr green .55 .20
1894 A915 1.80fr green .60 .20
1895 A915 1.90fr green .65 .20
1896 A915 2fr red .85 .20
1897 A915 2.10fr red 1.00 .35
1897A A915 2.20fr red .75 .20
Nos. 1893-1897A (6) 4.40 1.35

#1891 is inscribed "A," #1892 "B."

No. 1884c was issued in sheets of 50 plus 50 alternating labels picturing the PHILEX-FRANCE '89 emblem to publicize the international philatelic exhibition.

Issued: 2.80fr, 10fr, #1881, 6/1; 1.70fr, 2.10fr, 3fr, 7/1/84; 1.80fr, 2.20fr, 3.20fr, 8/1/85; 3.40fr, #1891, 8/1/86; 1.90fr, 9/13/86; #1882, 10/15/87; 3.60fr, #1892, 8/1/87.

For surcharge see No. 2115.

50th Anniv. of Air France A973

1983, June 18
1898 A973 3.45fr multicolored 1.10 .30

Treaties of Versailles and Paris Bicentenary — A974

1983, Sept. 2 ***Perf. 13x12½***
1899 A974 2.80fr multicolored 1.00 .30

Jewelry Making A975

1983, Sept. 10 **Photo.** ***Perf. 13***
1900 A975 2.20fr multicolored .70 .25

30th Anniv. of Customs Cooperation Council — A976

1983, Sept. 22 **Engr.** ***Perf. 13x12½***
1901 A976 2.30fr multicolored .70 .25

Michaux's Bicycle A977

1983, Oct. 1 **Engr.** ***Perf. 13***
1902 A977 1.60fr multicolored .60 .20

Natl. Weather Forecasting — A978

1983, Oct. 22 **Engr.** ***Perf. 12½x13***
1903 A978 1.50fr multicolored .60 .20

Berthie Albrecht (1893-1943) — A979

1983, Nov. 5
1904 A979 1.60fr dk brown & olive .60 .20
1905 A979 1.60fr Rene Levy (1906-1943) .60 .20

Resistance heroines.

A980 A981

1983, Dec. 16
1906 A980 2fr dk gray & red .60 .20

Pierre Mendes France (1907-1982), Premier.

1984, Mar. 22 ***Perf. 13***
1907 A981 3.60fr Union leader Waldeck-Rousseau 1.25 .30

Trade Union centenary.

Homage to the Cinema, by Cesar A982

1984, Feb. 4 **Engr.** ***Perf. 12½x13***
1908 A982 4fr multicolored 2.00 .60

Four Corners of the Sky, by Jean Messagier — A983

1984, Mar. 31 **Photo.** ***Perf. 13x12½***
1909 A983 4fr multicolored 1.75 .60

Dining Room Corner, at Cannet, by Pierre Bonnard — A984

Photogravure and Engraved
1984, Apr. 14 ***Perf. 12½x12***
1910 A984 4fr multicolored 1.75 .60

Pythia, by Andre Masson A985

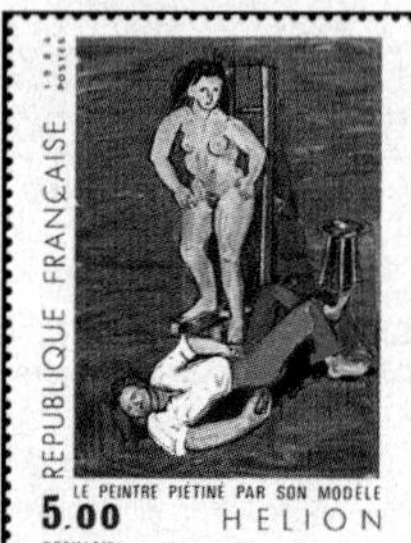

Painter at the Feet of His Model, by Helion A986

1984 **Photo.** ***Perf. 12x13***
1911 A985 5fr multicolored 1.90 .35
1912 A986 5fr multicolored 1.90 .35

Issue dates: #1911, Oct. 13; #1912, Dec. 1.

Guadeloupe — A987

1984, Feb. 25 ***Perf. 13***
1913 A987 2.30fr Map, West Indian dancers .70 .20

Vauban Citadel, Belle Ile-en-Mer A988

Cordouan Lighthouse — A989

La Grande Chartreuse Monastery, 900th Anniv. A990

Palais Ideal, Hauterives-Drome — A991

Montsegur Chateau A992

1984 **Engr.** ***Perf. 13***
1914 A988 2.50fr multicolored .85 .20
1915 A989 3.50fr multicolored 1.10 .20

Issued: #1914, 5/26; #1915, 6/23.

1984
1916 A990 1.70fr multicolored .50 .20
1917 A991 2.10fr multicolored .85 .20
1917A A992 3.70fr multicolored 1.25 .20
Nos. 1914-1917A (5) 4.55 1.00

Issued: 1.70fr, 7/7; 2.10fr, 6/30; 3.70fr, 9/15.

Flora Tristan (1803-44), Feminist A992a

1984, Mar. 8
1918 A992a 2.80fr multicolored .85 .30

Playing Card Suits — A993

1984, Apr. 11 **Engr.**
1919 A993 1.14fr Hearts .40 .20
1920 A993 1.47fr Spades .50 .25
1921 A993 2.38fr Diamonds .70 .50
1922 A993 3.95fr Clubs 1.40 .80
Nos. 1919-1922 (4) 3.00 1.75

Nos. 1919-1922 known only precanceled. See second note after No. 132.

450th Anniv. of Cartier's Landing in Quebec A994

1984, Apr. 20 **Photo. & Engr.**
1923 A994 2fr multicolored .75 .20

See Canada No. 1011.

Philex '84, Dunkirk A995

1984, Apr. 21 ***Perf. 13x12½***
1924 A995 1.60fr multicolored .50 .20

Europa (1959-84) A996

1984, Apr. 28 **Engr.** ***Perf. 13***
1925 A996 2fr red brown *1.75* .45
1926 A996 2.80fr blue *2.75* .75

2nd European Parliament Election A997

1984, Mar. 24 **Photo.** ***Perf. 13***
1927 A997 2fr multicolored .65 .20

Foreign Legion A998

1984, Apr. 30 **Engr.** ***Perf. 13x12½***
1928 A998 3.10fr multicolored .95 .30

40th Anniv. of Liberation A999

Photogravure and Engraved

1984, May 8 ***Perf. 12½x13***
1929 A999 2fr Resistance .75 .25
1930 A999 3fr Landing 1.10 .35
a. Pair, #1929-1930 + label 1.90 1.90

Olympic Events — A1000

Illustration reduced.

1984, June 1 ***Perf. 13***
1931 A1000 4fr multicolored 1.25 .55

Intl. Olympic Committee, 90th anniv. and 1984 Summer Olympics.

Engraving — A1001

1984, June 8 **Engr.**
1932 A1001 2fr multicolored .60 .20

Bordeaux A1002

1984, June 9 ***Perf. 13x12½***
1933 A1002 2fr red .60 .20

French Philatelic Societies Congress, Bordeaux.

Natl. Telecommunications College, 40th Anniv. — A1003

1984, June 16 **Photo.** ***Perf. 13***
1934 A1003 3fr Satellite, phone, keyboard .90 .25

25th Intl. Geography Congress, Paris — A1004

Illustration reduced.

1984, Aug. 25 **Engr.** ***Perf. 13x12½***
1935 A1004 3fr Alps .90 .25

Telecom I Satellite A1005

1984, Sept. 1 **Photo.** ***Perf. 13***
1936 A1005 3.20fr multicolored 1.10 .25

High-speed Train Mail Transport A1006

1984, Sept. 8
1937 A1006 2.10fr Electric train, Paris-Lyon 1.00 .20

Local Birds A1007

Marx Dormoy (1888-1941) A1008

Photogravure and Engraved

1984, Sept. 22 ***Perf. 12½x12***
1938 A1007 1fr Gypaetus barbatus .35 .20
1939 A1007 2fr Circaetus gallicus .90 .20
1940 A1007 3fr Accipiter nisus 1.00 .25
1941 A1007 5fr Peregrine falcon 1.50 .35
Nos. 1938-1941 (4) 3.75 1.00

1984, Sept. 22 **Engr.** ***Perf. 13***
1942 A1008 2.40fr multicolored .75 .20

A1009 — A1010

1984, Oct. 6 **Engr.** ***Perf. 12½x13***
1943 A1009 3fr Automobile plans 1.10 .20

100th anniv. of the automobile.

1984, Nov. 3
1944 A1010 2.10fr multicolored .65 .20

Pres. Vincent Auriol (1884-1966).

9th 5-Year Plan A1011

1984, Dec. 8 **Photo.** ***Perf. 13***
1945 A1011 2.10fr dk blue & scar .65 .20

French Language Promotion — A1012

1985, Jan. 15 **Engr.** ***Perf. 12½x13***
1946 A1012 3fr multicolored .90 .20

Tourism Issue

View of Vienne A1013

Cathedral at Montpelier A1014

St. Michel de Cuxa (Codalet) Abbey — A1015

Talmont Church, Saintonge Romane A1016

Solutre A1017

1985 ***Perf. 13x12½***
1947 A1013 1.70fr ol blk & dk grn .50 .20
1948 A1014 2.10fr sepia & org .60 .20
1949 A1015 2.20fr multicolored .60 .20
1950 A1016 3fr multicolored .80 .20
1951 A1017 3.90fr multicolored 1.00 .20
Nos. 1947-1951 (5) 3.50 1.00

Issue dates: 1.70fr, Jan. 19; 2.10fr, Mar. 30; 2.20fr, July 6; 3fr, June 15; 3.90fr, Sept. 28.

French TV, 50th Anniv. A1018

1985, Jan. 26 **Photo.** ***Perf. 13***
1952 A1018 2.50fr multicolored .75 .20

Months of the Year — A1019

1985, Feb. 11 **Engr.**
1953 A1019 1.22fr January .65 .20
1954 A1019 1.57fr February .70 .20
1955 A1019 2.55fr March 1.25 .20
1956 A1019 4.23fr April 2.25 .20

1986, Feb. 10 **Engr.** ***Perf. 13***
1957 A1019 1.28fr May .65 .20
1958 A1019 1.65fr June .70 .20
1959 A1019 2.67fr July 1.25 .20
1960 A1019 4.44fr August 2.25 .20

1987, Feb. 16 **Engr.**
1961 A1019 1.31fr September .70 .20
1962 A1019 1.69fr October .90 .20
1963 A1019 2.74fr November 1.40 .20
1964 A1019 4.56fr December 2.50 .30
Nos. 1953-1964 (12) 15.20 2.50

Nos. 1953-1964 are known only precanceled. See second note after No. 132.

St. Valentine, by Raymond Peynet A1020

1985, Feb. 14 **Photo.** ***Perf. 13x12½***
1965 A1020 2.10fr multicolored .75 .20

Pauline Kergomard (1838-1925) A1021

1985, Mar. 8 **Engr.** ***Perf. 13x12½***
1966 A1021 1.70fr int bl & cop red .50 .20

Stained Glass Window, Strasbourg Cathedral A1022

Still-life with Candle, Nicolas de Stael — A1023

1985 **Engraved** ***Perf. 12x13***
1967 A1022 5fr multicolored 4.00 .30

Photo.
Perf. 13x12
1968 A1023 5fr multicolored 3.00 .30

Issue dates: #1967, Apr. 13; #1968, June 1.

Untitled Abstract by Jean Dubuffet — A1024

Octopus Overlaid on Manuscript, by Pierre Alechinsky — A1025

Photogravure; Engraved (#1970)

1985 ***Perf. 13x12½***

1969 A1024 5fr multicolored 2.50 .20
1970 A1025 5fr multicolored 2.50 .20

Issued: #1969, Sept. 14; #1970, Oct. 12.

The Dog, Abstract by Alberto Giacometti (1901-1966) — A1026

1985, Dec. 7 Engr. ***Perf. 13x12½***

1971 A1026 5fr grnsh blk & lt lem 2.50 .25

Housing in Givors A1027

Contemporary architecture by Jean Renaude.

1985, Apr. 20 Engr. ***Perf. 13***

1972 A1027 2.40fr blk, yel org & ol grn .80 .20

Landevennec Abbey, 1500th Anniv. — A1028

1985, Apr. 20 ***Perf. 13x12½***

1973 A1028 1.70fr green & brn vio .60 .20

A1029

A1030

Europa: 2.10fr, Adam de la Halle (1240-1285), composer. 3fr, Darius Milhaud (1892-1974), composer.

1985, Apr. 27 ***Perf. 12½x13***

1974 A1029 2.10fr dr bl, blk, & brt bl *1.25* .50
1975 A1029 3fr dk bl, brt bl & blk *2.50* .75

1985, May 8 ***Perf. 13x12½***

1976 A1030 2fr Return of peace .75 .20
1977 A1030 3fr Return of liberty 1.00 .20
a. Pair, #1976-1977 + label 1.75 1.50

Liberation of France from German occupation forces, 40th anniv.

Natl. Philatelic Congress, Tours — A1031

1985, May 25 ***Perf. 12½x13***

1978 A1031 2.10fr Tours Cathedral .65 .20

Rabies Vaccine Cent. A1032

1985, June 1 ***Perf. 13x12½***

1979 A1032 1.50fr Pasteur inoculating patient .50 .20

Mystere Falcon-900 A1033

1985, June 1 ***Perf. 13***

1980 A1033 10fr blue 4.00 .45

Lake Geneva Life-Saving Society Cent. A1034

1985, June 15

1981 A1034 2.50fr blk, red & brt ultra .75 .20

UN, 40th Anniv. — A1035

Huguenot Cross — A1036

1985, June 26 ***Perf. 13x12½***

1982 A1035 3fr multicolored .90 .20

1985, Aug. 31 Engr. ***Perf. 12½x13***

1983 A1036 2.50fr dp vio, dk red brn & dk red .75 .20

King Louis XIV revoked the Edict of Nantes on Oct. 18, 1685, dispossessing French Protestants of religious and civil liberty.

A1037

A1038

Trees, leaves and fruit of the beech, elm, oak and spruce varieties.

1985, Sept. 21 Engr. ***Perf. 12½***

1984 A1037 1fr shown .35 .20
1985 A1037 2fr Ulmus montana .70 .20
1986 A1037 3fr Quercus pedunculata 1.10 .20
1987 A1037 5fr Picea abies 1.75 .25
Nos. 1984-1987 (4) 3.90 .85

1985, Nov. 2 Engr. ***Perf. 12½x13***

La France Mourning the Dead, Eternal Flame.

1988 A1038 1.80fr brn, org & lake .70 .20

Memorial Day.

A1039

A1040

1985, Nov. 9 **Engr.**

1989 A1039 3.20fr black & blue 1.00 .20

Charles Dullin, 1885-1949, impresario, theater.

1985, Nov. 16 Engr. ***Perf. 13x12½***

1990 A1040 2.20fr red & black .75 .20

National information system.

Thai Ambassadors at the Court of King Louis XIV, Painting A1041

1986, Jan. 25 Engr. ***Perf. 13***

1991 A1041 3.20fr rose lake & blk 1.00 .20

Normalization of diplomatic relations with Thailand, 300th anniv.

Leisure, by Fernand Leger A1042

1986, Feb. 1 Photo. ***Perf. 13***

1992 A1042 2.20fr multicolored .75 .20

1936 Popular Front, 50th anniv.

Venice Carnival, Paris — A1043

1986, Feb. 12 ***Perf. 12½x13***

1993 A1043 2.20fr multicolored .80 .20

La Marianne, Typograph by Raymond Gid A1044

Photogravure & Engraved

1986, Mar. 3 ***Perf. 12½x13½***

1994 A1044 5fr black & dk red 1.75 .30

Tourism Issue

Filitosa, South Corsica A1045

Loches Chateau A1046

Norman Manor, St. Germain de Livet A1047

Notre-Dame-en-Vaux Monastery, Marne — A1048

Market Square, Bastide de Monpazier, Dordogne — A1049

Illustration A1049 reduced.

1986 Engr. ***Perf. 13***

1995 A1045 1.80fr multicolored .55 .20
1996 A1046 2fr int blue & blk .65 .20
1997 A1047 2.20fr grnsh bl, brn & grn .70 .20
1998 A1048 2.50fr henna brn & sepia .80 .20

Perf. 13x12½

1999 A1049 3.90fr blk & yel org 1.25 .25
Nos. 1995-1999 (5) 3.95 1.05

Issued: 2.20fr, 3/3; 2fr, 6/14; 2.50fr, 6/9; 1.80fr, 3.90fr, 7/5.

Louise Michel (1830-1905), Anarchist — A1050

1986, Mar. 10 **Engr.**

2000 A1050 1.80fr dk red & gray blk .70 .20

City of Science and Industry, La Villette — A1051

1986, Mar. 17

2001 A1051 3.90fr multicolored 1.25 .20

Center for Modern Asia-Africa Studies A1052

1986, Apr. 12 **Photo.** ***Perf. 13***

2002 A1052 3.20fr Map 1.00 .20

Skibet, Abstract by Maurice Esteve — A1053

Virginia, Abstract by Alberto Magnelli — A1054

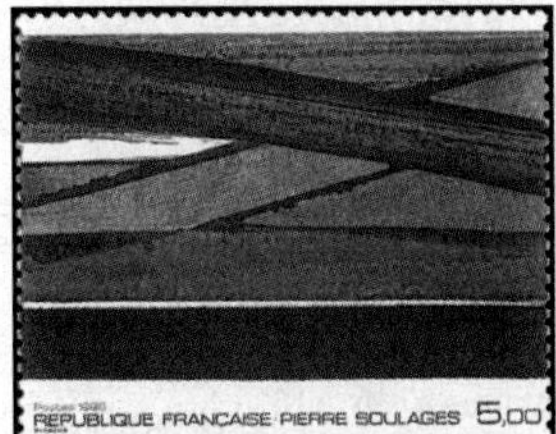

Abstract, by Pierre Soulages — A1055

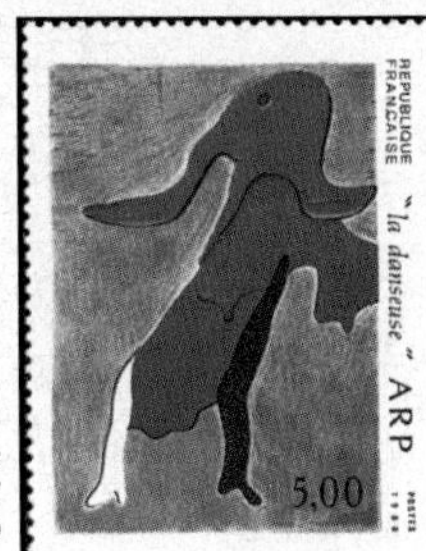

The Dancer, by Jean Arp A1056

Isabelle d'Este, by Leonardo da Vinci A1057

Perf. 12½x13, 13x12½ (#2005, 2006)

1986 **Photo., Engr. (#2005, 2007)**

2003 A1053 5fr multicolored 1.90 .20
2004 A1054 5fr multicolored 1.90 .30
2005 A1055 5fr brt vio, blk & brn gray 1.90 .30
2006 A1056 5fr multicolored 1.90 .30
2007 A1057 5fr blk, red brn & grnsh yel 1.90 .30
Nos. 2003-2007 (5) 9.50 1.40

Issued: #2003, Apr. 14; #2004, June 25; #2005, Dec. 22; #2006, 2007, Nov. 10.

Victor Basch (1863-1944), IPY Emblem — A1058

1986, Apr. 28 **Engr.** ***Perf. 13***

2008 A1058 2.50fr black & yel grn .75 .20

International Peace Year.

Europa 1986 A1059

1986, Apr. 28 ***Perf. 13x12½***

2009 A1059 2.20fr Civet cat *1.25* .40
2010 A1059 3.20fr Bat *2.50* .75

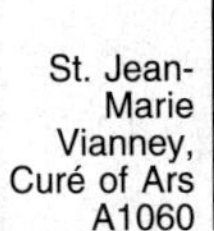

St. Jean-Marie Vianney, Curé of Ars A1060

1986, May 3 **Engr.** ***Perf. 13x12½***

2011 A1060 1.80fr sepia, brn org & brn .55 .20

Philatelic Societies Federation Congress, Nancy — A1061

1986, May 17 ***Perf. 13***

2012 A1061 2.20fr Exposition Center .70 .20

Mens World Volleyball Championship A1062

Statue of Liberty, Cent. A1063

1986, May 24 **Engr.** ***Perf. 13***

2013 A1062 2.20fr dk vio, brn vio & scar .70 .20

1986, July 4 ***Perf. 13***

2014 A1063 2.20fr scar & dk blue 1.00 .20

See US No. 2224.

1st Ascent of Mt. Blanc, 1786 A1064

1986, Aug. 8 **Engr.** ***Perf. 13x12½***

2015 A1064 2fr J. Balmat, M.G. Paccard .70 .20

Pierre-Louis Moreau de Maupertuis (1698-1759), La Condamine and Sextant — A1065

1986, Sept. 5

2016 A1065 3fr multicolored 1.00 .20

Lapland Expedition, 250th anniv., proved Earth's poles are flattened.
See Finland No. 741.

Marcassite A1066

1986, Sept. 13 ***Perf. 12½***

2017 A1066 2fr shown .60 .20
2018 A1066 3fr Quartz .90 .20
2019 A1066 4fr Calcite 1.20 .25
2020 A1066 5fr Fluorite 1.50 .30
Nos. 2017-2020 (4) 4.20 .95

Souvenir Sheet

Natl. Film Industry, 50th Anniv. A1067

Personalities and film scenes: a, Louis Feuillade, The Vampires. b, Max Linder. c, Sacha Guitry, Romance of the Trickster. d, Jean Renoir, The Grand Illusion. e, Marcel Pagnol, The Baker's Woman. f, Jean Epstein, The Three-Sided Mirror. g, Rene Clair, Women of the Night. h, Jean Gremillon, Talk of Love. i, Jacques Becker, Helmet of Gold. j, Francois Truffaut, The Young Savage.

1986, Sept. 20 **Photo.** ***Perf. 13x12½***

2021 Sheet of 10 10.00 10.00
a.-j. A1067 2.20fr any single 1.00 1.00

Scene from Le Grand Meaulnes, by Henry Alain-Fournier (b. 1886), Novelist A1068

Professional Education, Cent. A1069

1986, Oct. 4 **Engr.** ***Perf. 12½x13***

2022 A1068 2.20fr black & dk red .75 .20

1986, Oct. 4

2023 A1069 1.90fr brt vio & dp lil rose .65 .20

World Energy Conf., Cannes A1070

Mulhouse Technical Museum A1071

1986, Oct. 5 **Photo.** ***Perf. 13***

2024 A1070 3.40fr multicolored 1.10 .20

1986, Dec. 1 **Engr.**

2025 A1071 2.20fr int blue, dk red & blk .90 .20

Museum at Orsay, Opening — A1072

1986, Dec. 10 **Photo.**

2026 A1072 3.70fr bluish blk & pck bl 1.25 .25

Fulgence Bienvenue (1852-1934), and the Metro — A1073

1987, Jan. 17 **Engr.** ***Perf. 13***

2027 A1073 2.50fr vio brn, brn & dk grn .85 .20

A1074

A1075

1987, Jan. 24
2028 A1074 1.90fr grn & grnsh blk .65 .20

Raoul Follereau (1903-1977), care for lepers.

1987, Mar. 7 Engr. *Perf. 12½x13*
2029 A1075 1.90fr black & red .65 .20

Cutlery industry, Thiers.

Tourist Issue

Redon, Ille et Vilaine A1076

Azay-le-Rideau Chateau — A1077

Meuse District — A1078

De Gaulle's Home, Etretat A1079

Les Baux-de-Provence — A1080

Illustration A1078 reduced.

1987 Engr. *Perf. 13*
2030 A1076 2.20fr dp rose lil, blk & brn ol 1.10 .20
2031 A1077 2.50fr Prus blue & olive grn 1.25 .20

Perf. 12½
2032 A1078 3.70fr multicolored 1.75 .25

Photo. *Perf. 13*
2033 A1079 2.20fr multicolored .95 .20

Engr.
2034 A1080 3fr dk ol bis & dp vio 1.40 .20
Nos. 2030-2034 (5) 6.45 1.05

Issued: #2030, 3/7; #2033, 6/12; 2.50fr, 5/9; 3fr, 6/27; 3.70fr, 5/30.

Charles Edouard Jenneret (Le Corbusier) (1887-1965), Architect — A1081

1987, Apr. 11 Photo. *Perf. 13x12½*
2035 A1081 3.70fr Abstract 1.10 .25

Europa 1987 A1082

Modern architecture: 2.20fr, Metal factory at Boulogne-Billancourt, by architect Claude Vasconi. 3.40fr, Rue Mallet-Stevens housing, by Robert Mallet-Stevens.

1987, Apr. 25 Engr. *Perf. 13x12½*
2036 A1082 2.20fr dk blue & grn *2.25* .60
2037 A1082 3.40fr brn & dk grn *3.25* .85

Abstract Painting, by Bram van Velde — A1083

Woman under Parasol, by Eugene Boudin (1824-1898) — A1084

Precambrien, by Camille Bryen — A1085

World, Bronze Sculpture by Antoine Pevsner — A1086

Perf. 12½x13, 13x12½ (Nos. 2039, 2041)
Photo., Engr. (Nos. 2039, 2041)

1987
2038 A1083 5fr multicolored 1.75 .30
2039 A1084 5fr multicolored 1.75 .30
2040 A1085 5fr multicolored 1.75 .30
2041 A1086 5fr bister & blk 1.75 .25
Nos. 2038-2041 (4) 7.00 1.15

Issue dates: #2038, Apr. 25; #2039, May 23; #2040, Sept. 12; #2041, Nov. 14.

Gaspard de Montagnes, from a Manuscript Illustration — A1087

1987, May 9 Engr. *Perf. 13*
2042 A1087 1.90fr dp grn & sepia .55 .20

Henri Pourrat (1887-1959), novelist.

Natl. Philatelic Societies Congress, Lens A1088

1987, June 6 *Perf. 13x13½*
2043 A1088 2.20fr choc & red .75 .20

Involvement of U.S. Forces in WW I, 70th Anniv. A1089

Design: Stars and Stripes, troops, Gen. John J. Pershing (1860-1948), American army commander.

1987, June 13 *Perf. 13*
2044 A1089 3.40fr olive grn, saph & ver 1.10 .20

A1090

A1091

1987, June 17 Photo.
2045 A1090 2fr multicolored .65 .20

6th Intl. Cable Car Transport Congress, Grenoble.

1987, June 20 Litho.
2046 A1091 1.90fr pale chalky blue & blk .65 .20

Accession of Hugh Capet (c.938-996), 1st king of France, millenary.

A1092

A1093

1987, June 20 Engr. *Perf. 12½x13*
2047 A1092 2.20fr multicolored .75 .20

La Fleche Natl. Military School.

1987, June 27 Photo. *Perf. 13*
2048 A1093 1.90fr multicolored .65 .20

World Assembly of Expatriate Algerians, Nice.

World Wrestling Championships — A1094

1987, Aug. 21 Engr.
2049 A1094 3fr brt pur, vio gray & brt olive grn .95 .20

Mushrooms A1095

William the Conqueror (c. 1027-1087) A1096

1987, Sept. 5 *Perf. 12½*
2050 A1095 2fr Gyroporus cyanescens .60 .20
2051 A1095 3fr Gomphus clavatus .90 .20
2052 A1095 4fr Morchella conica 1.25 .30
2053 A1095 5fr Russula virescens 1.50 .40
Nos. 2050-2053 (4) 4.25 1.10

1987, Sept. 5 *Perf. 13*
2054 A1096 2fr Bayeux Tapestry detail .75 .20

Montbenoit Le Saugeais A1097

Design: Abbey of Medieval Knights, cloisters, winter scene.

1987, Sept. 19
2055 A1097 2.50fr saph, blk & scar .85 .20

Pasteur Institute, Cent. — A1098

1987, Oct. 3
2056 A1098 2.20fr dp blue & dk red .85 .20

Blaise Cendrars (1887-1961), Poet and Novelist — A1099

Treaty of Andelot, 1400th Anniv. — A1100

Pen and ink portrait by Modigliani.

1987, Nov. 6 *Perf. 12½*
2057 A1099 2fr brt grn, buff & blk .75 .20

1987, Nov. 28 *Perf. 12½x13*
2058 A1100 3.70fr multicolored 1.25 .20

Gen. Leclerc (1902-1947), Marshal of France — A1101

1987, Nov. 28 *Perf. 13x12½*
2059 A1101 2.20fr multicolored .85 .20

Liberty Type of 1982

1987-90 *Perf. 13*
2077 A915 3.70fr brt lilac rose 1.10 .20
2078 A915 (2.10fr) green ('90) .70 .20
2079 A915 (2.30fr) red ('90) .75 .20
Nos. 2077-2079 (3) 2.55 .60

Coil Stamp
Engr.
Perf. 13 Horiz.
2080 A915 2fr emerald green .70 .20

Issued: 2fr, 8/1; 3.70fr, 11/16; #2078-2079, 1/2.
Nos. 2078-2079 are inscribed "C."

Franco-German Cooperation Treaty, 25th Anniv. — A1102

1988, Jan. 15 *Perf. 13*
2086 A1102 2.20fr Adenauer, De Gaulle 1.00 .20

See Fed. Rep. of Germany No. 1546.

Marcel Dassault (1892-1986), Aircraft Designer — A1103

1988, Jan. 23 **Photo.**
2087 A1103 3.60fr brt ultra, gray blk & dk red 1.50 .30

Communications A1104

Great Synagogue, Rue Victoire, Paris A1105

Angouleme Festival prize-winning cartoons.

1988, Jan. 29 Photo. *Perf. 13½x13*
Booklet Stamps
2088 A1104 2.20fr Pellos .80 .20
2089 A1104 2.20fr Reiser .80 .20
2090 A1104 2.20fr Marijac .80 .20
2091 A1104 2.20fr Fred .80 .20
2092 A1104 2.20fr Moebius .80 .20
2093 A1104 2.20fr Gillon .80 .20
2094 A1104 2.20fr Bretecher .80 .20
2095 A1104 2.20fr Forest .80 .20
2096 A1104 2.20fr Mezieres .80 .20
2097 A1104 2.20fr Tardi .80 .20
2098 A1104 2.20fr Lob .80 .20
2099 A1104 2.20fr Bilal .80 .20
a. Bklt. pane of 12, #2088-2099 9.75

1988, Feb. 7 Litho. *Perf. 13*
2100 A1105 2fr black & gold .75 .20

The Four Elements — A1106

1988, Feb. 1 Engr. *Perf. 13*
2101 A1106 1.36fr Air .65 .20
2102 A1106 1.75fr Water .80 .20
2103 A1106 2.83fr Fire 1.25 .20
2104 A1106 4.75fr Earth 2.25 .20
Nos. 2101-2104 (4) 4.95 .80

Nos. 2101-2104 known only precanceled. See second note after No. 132.

PHILEXFRANCE '89 — A1107

1988, Mar. 4
2105 A1107 2.20fr #1885, emblem .80 .20

Postal Training College, Cent. A1108

1988, Mar. 29
2106 A1108 3.60fr multicolored 1.40 .25

Philex-Jeunes '88, Youth Stamp Show — A1109

1988, Apr. 8 *Perf. 13x12½*
2107 A1109 2fr multicolored .75 .20

Blood Donation — A1110

1988, Apr. 9 Photo. *Perf. 13½x13*
2108 A1110 2.50fr multicolored .90 .20

Europa 1988 A1111

Communication and transportation.

1988, Apr. 30 Engr. *Perf. 13*
2109 A1111 2.20fr Cables, satellites *2.00* .40
2110 A1111 3.60fr Rail cars *3.00* .65

Jean Monnet (1888-1979), Economist — A1112

1988, May 10 *Perf. 12½x13*
2111 A1112 2.20fr black & brn ol .80 .20

Philatelic Congress, Valence A1113

1988, May 21 *Perf. 13x12½*
2112 A1113 2.20fr multicolored .80 .20

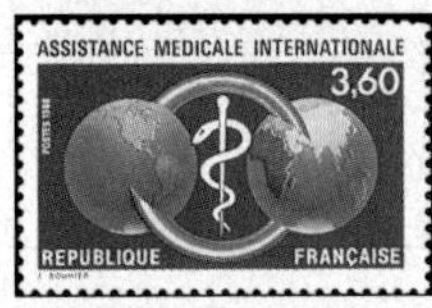
Intl. Medical Assistance A1114

1988, May 28 Photo. *Perf. 13*
2113 A1114 3.60fr multicolored 1.40 .25

Aid to the Handicapped — A1115

1988, May 28
2114 A1115 3.70fr multicolored 1.40 .30

No. 1884 Surcharged in European Currency Units

1988, Apr. 16 **Engr.**
2115 A915 2.20fr red .70 .20

Tourist Issue

Hermes Dicephalus (Roman Empire), Frejus — A1116

Ship Museum, Douarnenez — A1117

Chateau Sedieres, Correze — A1118

Cirque de Gavarnie A1119

View of Perouges, Ain A1120

1988, June 12 Engr. *Perf. 13x12½*
2116 A1116 3.70fr multicolored 1.40 .30

1988 *Perf. 13, 12½x13 (#2118)*
2117 A1117 2fr multicolored .75 .20
2118 A1118 2.20fr multicolored .80 .20
2119 A1119 3fr multicolored 1.00 .20

Issued: 2.20fr, 7/2; 2fr, 7/4; 3fr, 7/23.

1988, Sept. 10 *Perf. 13x12½*
2120 A1120 2.20fr multicolored .90 .20
Nos. 2116-2120 (5) 4.85 1.10

French Revolution, Bicent. — A1121

Designs: 3fr, Assembly of the Three Estates, Vizille. 4fr, Day of the Tiles (Barricades), Grenoble.

1988, June 18 **Engr.**
2121 A1121 3fr multicolored 1.10 .20
2122 A1121 4fr multicolored 1.50 .30
a. Pair, #2121-2122 + label 2.75 2.50

PHILEXFRANCE '89.

Buffon's Natural History — A1122

Alpine Troops, Cent. — A1123

1988, June 18 ***Perf. 12½***

2123 A1122 2fr Otters .75 .20
2124 A1122 3fr Stag 1.10 .20
2125 A1122 4fr Fox 1.50 .30
2126 A1122 5fr Badger 1.90 .40
Nos. 2123-2126 (4) 5.25 1.10

1988, June 25 ***Perf. 13***

2127 A1123 2.50fr multicolored .95 .20

Roland Garros (1888-1918), 1st Pilot to Fly Across the Mediterranean, Sept. 23, 1913 — A1124

1988, July 2 **Engr.** ***Perf. 13x12½***

2128 A1124 2fr brt grn bl & olive .75 .20

Nov. 11, 1918 Armistice Ending World War I, 70th Anniv. A1125

1988, Sept. 10 **Engr.** ***Perf. 13***

2129 A1125 2.20fr brt blue, gray & blk .75 .20

Homage to Leon Degand, Sculpture by Robert Jacobsen A1126

1988, Sept. 22 ***Perf. 12½x13***

2130 A1126 5fr blk & dp claret 1.75 .30

French-Danish cultural exchange program, 10th anniv. See Denmark No. 860.

Strasbourg, 2000th Anniv. — A1127

1988, Sept. 24 ***Perf. 13***

2131 A1127 2.20fr Municipal arms .80 .20

St. Mihiel Sepulcher, by Ligier Richier (c. 1500-1567), Sculptor — A1128

Composition, 1954, by Serge Poliakoff (1906-1969) — A1129

La Pieta de Villeneuve-les-Avignon, by Enguerrand Quarton (1444-1466) — A1130

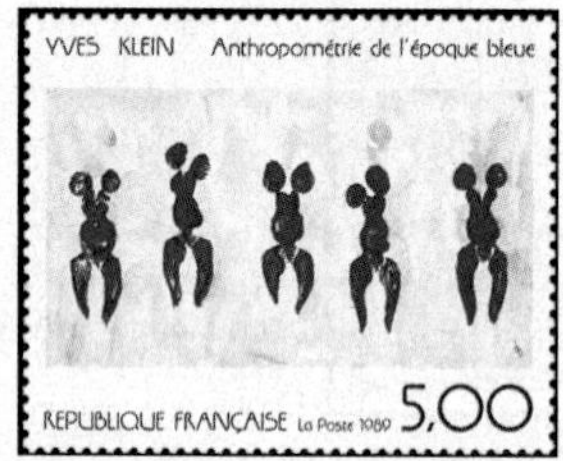

Anthropometry of the Blue Period, by Yves Klein — A1131

1988-89 **Engr.** ***Perf. 13x12½***

2132 A1128 5fr black brown 1.65 .30

Photo.

2133 A1129 5fr multicolored 1.65 .30
2134 A1130 5fr multicolored 1.90 .35
2135 A1131 5fr multi ('89) 1.90 .35
Nos. 2132-2135 (4) 7.10 1.30

Issue dates: #2132, Oct. 15; #2133, Oct. 22; #2134, Dec. 10; #2135, Jan. 21.

Thermal Springs A1132

1988, Nov. 21 **Engr.** ***Perf. 13x12½***

2136 A1132 2.20fr multicolored .75 .20

Metamecanique, by Jean Tinguely — A1133

1988, Nov. 25 **Photo.**

2137 A1133 5fr multicolored 3.00 .35

See Switzerland No. 828.

UN Declaration of Human Rights, 40th Anniv. A1134

1988, Dec. 12 **Litho.** ***Perf. 13***

2138 A1134 2.20fr dk bl & grnsh bl 1.00 .20

French Revolution, Bicent. — A1135

1989, Jan. 1 **Photo.** ***Perf. 13x12½***

2139 A1135 2.20fr red & vio blue .75 .20

Valentin Hauy (1745-1822), Founder of the School for the Blind, Paris, 1791 — A1136

Photo. & Embossed

1989, Jan. 28

2140 A1136 2.20fr multicolored .75 .20

Estienne School, Cent. — A1137

1989, Feb. 4 **Engr.** ***Perf. 12½***

2141 A1137 2.20fr gray, black & red .75 .20

European Parliament Elections A1138

1989, Mar. 4 **Litho.** ***Perf. 13***

2142 A1138 2.20fr multicolored .75 .20

A1139

1989 **Engr.** ***Perf. 12½x13***

2143 A1139 2.20fr Liberty .75 .20
2144 A1139 2.20fr Equality .75 .20
2145 A1139 2.20fr Fraternity .75 .20
a. Strip of 3, #2143-2145 + label 2.25 1.75

Bicent. of the French revolution and the Declaration of Rights of Man and the Citizen. No. 2145a contains inscribed label picturing PHILEXFRANCE '89 emblem.

Issue dates: #2143, Mar. 18; #2144, Apr. 22; #2145, May 27; #2145a, July 14.

French-Soviet Joint Space Flight — A1140

1989, Mar. 4 **Litho.** ***Perf. 13***

2146 A1140 3.60fr multicolored 1.25 .25

Historic Sights, Paris — A1141

Designs: No. 2147, Arche de la Defense. No. 2148, Eiffel Tower. No. 2149, Grand Louvre. No. 2150, Notre Dame Cathedral. No. 2151, Bastille Monument and Opera de la Bastille. #2151a has a continuous design.

1989, Apr. 21 **Engr.** ***Perf. 13x12½***

2147 A1141 2.20fr multicolored .80 .20
2148 A1141 2.20fr multicolored .80 .20
2149 A1141 2.20fr multicolored .80 .20
2150 A1141 2.20fr multicolored .80 .20
2151 A1141 2.20fr multicolored .80 .20
a. Strip of 5, #2147-2151 4.00

Europa 1989 A1142

Children's games.

1989, Apr. 29 ***Perf. 13***

2152 A1142 2.20fr Hopscotch *1.50* .35
2153 A1142 3.60fr Catch (ball) *3.50* .75

ITU Plenipotentiaries Conference, Nice — A1143

1989, May 23 **Litho.**

2154 A1143 3.70fr dk bl, dl org & red 1.25 .25

Tourist Issue

Fontainebleau Forest — A1144

Vaux le Vicomte — A1145

La Brenne — A1146

Illustrations A1145-A1146 reduced.

1989, May 20 **Engr.** ***Perf. 13***

2155 A1144 2.20fr multicolored .75 .20

Perf. 13x12½

2156 A1145 3.70fr ol bis & blk 1.25 .25
2157 A1146 4fr violet blue 1.25 .25
Nos. 2155-2157 (3) 3.25 .70

Issued: 2.20fr, 5/20; 3.70fr, 7/14; 4fr, 8/25.

World Cycling Championships, Chambery — A1147

1989, June 3 Litho. *Perf. 13*
2158 A1147 2.20fr multi .75 .20

Jehan de Malestroit, Dept. of Morbihan — A1148

1989, June 10 Engr. *Perf. 12½x13*
2159 A1148 3.70fr multicolored 1.25 .25

Preliminary Sketch (Detail) for *Oath of the Tennis Court,* by David — A1149

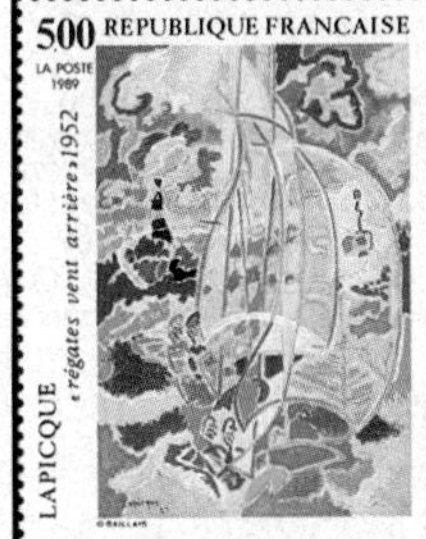

Regatta with Wind Astern, by Charles Lapicque A1150

1989, June 19 Photo. *Perf. 13x12½*
2160 A1149 5fr multicolored 1.65 .30

Perf. 12½

2161 A1150 5fr multicolored 1.50 .30

No. 2160 for French revolution bicent.
Issued: #2160, 6/19; #2161, 9/23.

Souvenir Sheet

Revolution Bicentennial — A1151

Revolutionaries: a, Madame Roland (1754-1793). b, Camille Desmoulins (1760-1794). c, Condorcet (1743-1794). d, Kellermann (1735-1820).

1989, June 26 Engr. *Perf. 13*
2162 A1151 Sheet of 4 3.00 3.00
a.-d. 2.20fr any single .75 .75

15th Summit of the Arch Meeting of Leaders from Industrial Nations, July 14-16 A1152

1989, July 14 Photo.
2163 A1152 2.20fr multicolored .75 .20

Declaration of the Rights of Man and the Citizen, Versailles, Aug. 26, 1789 — A1153

Details of an anonymous 18th-19th cent. painting in Carnavalet Museum: No. 2168a, Preamble, Article I. No. 2168b, Articles VII-XI. No. 2168c, Articles II-VI. No. 2168d, Articles XII-XVII.

Litho. & Engr.

1989, Aug. 26 *Perf. 13x11½*
2164 A1153 2.50fr Preamble, Article I .75 .20
2165 A1153 2.50fr Art. II-VI .75 .20
2166 A1153 2.50fr Art. VII-XI .75 .20
2167 A1153 2.50fr Art. XII-XVII .75 .20
a. Strip, #2164-2167 + label 3.00 .60

Souvenir Sheet

Perf. 13x12½

2168 Sheet of 4 *20.00 20.00*
a.-d. A1153 5fr any single *5.00 5.00*

No. 2168 contains 4 52x41mm stamps. Sold for 50fr, including admission fee to PHILEXFRANCE '89.

Value of No. 2168 is for examples on plain paper. Examples on fluorescent paper seem to have been distributed in North America, and may not have been distributed widely or made available in Europe. At this time the fluorescent paper examples are selling for considerably more.

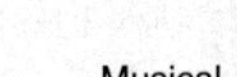

Musical Instruments — A1154

1989 Litho. *Perf. 12x12½*
2169 A1154 1.39fr Harp .50 .20
2170 A1154 1.79fr Piano .60 .20
2171 A1154 2.90fr Trumpet 1.00 .20
2172 A1154 4.84fr Violin 1.75 .20
Nos. 2169-2172 (4) 3.85 .80

Nos. 2169-2172 are known only precanceled. See second note after No. 132.
See #2233-2239, 2273-2283, 2368-2371.

TGV Atlantic A1155

1989, Sept. 23 Photo. *Perf. 13*
2173 A1155 2.50fr dk bl, sil & red 1.25 .20

Clermont-Ferrand Tramway, Cent. — A1156

1989, Oct. 28 Engr.
2174 A1156 3.70fr blk & dk ol bis 1.10 .20

Villers-Cotterets Ordinance, 450th Anniv. — A1157

1989, Oct. 28 Engr.
2175 A1157 2.20fr blk, dp cl & red .70 .20

Baron Augustin-Louis Cauchy (1789-1857), Mathematician — A1158

1989, Nov. 10 *Perf. 13x12½*
2176 A1158 3.60fr red, blk & bl grn 1.10 .20

Marshal Jean de Lattre de Tassigny (1889-1952) — A1159

1989, Nov. 18 *Perf. 13*
2177 A1159 2.20fr bl, blk & red .70 .20

Harki Soldiers of France A1160

1989, Dec. 9 Photo.
2178 A1160 2.20fr multicolored .70 .20

Marianne — A1161

1990-92 Engr. *Perf. 13*
2179 A1161 10c brn blk .20 .20
a. Bklt. pane, #2180, 4 #2179 1.00
2180 A1161 20c lt green .20 .20
2181 A1161 50c brt violet .20 .20
2182 A1161 1fr orange .35 .20
2183 A1161 2fr apple grn .70 .20
2184 A1161 2.10fr dark grn .75 .20
2185 A1161 2.20fr dark grn .75 .20
2186 A1161 2.20fr emerald .80 .20
2187 A1161 2.30fr red .75 .20
a. Bklt. pane, #2180, 4 #2187 5.00
2188 A1161 2.50fr red .85 .20
2189 A1161 3.20fr blue 1.10 .20
2190 A1161 3.40fr blue 1.10 .20
2191 A1161 3.80fr lilac rose 2.75 .20
2192 A1161 4fr lilac rose 1.40 .20
2193 A1161 4.20fr lilac rose 1.60 .20
2194 A1161 5fr greenish blue 1.80 .20
2195 A1161 10fr violet 3.75 .20
2196 A1161 (2.20fr) dk grn 1.00 .20
2197 A1161 (2.50fr) red 1.10 .20
Nos. 2179-2197 (19) 21.15 3.80

Coil Stamps

Perf. 13 Horiz.

2198 A1161 2.10fr dk grn .75 .20
2199 A1161 2.20fr dk grn .90 .20
2200 A1161 2.30fr red .80 .20
2201 A1161 2.50fr red 1.00 .20
Nos. 2198-2201 (4) 3.45 .80

Die Cut

Self-Adhesive

2202 A1161 2.30fr red .90 .20
a. Booklet pane of 10 9.00
2203 A1161 2.50fr red .95 .20
a. Booklet pane of 10 9.50
b. Booklet pane of 5 5.00
2204 A1161 (2.50fr) red 1.10 .20
a. Booklet pane of 10 11.00
Nos. 2202-2204 (3) 2.95 .60

Issued: #2187, 1/2; #2198, 1/1; 10c, 20c, 50c, 3.20fr, 3.80fr, 3/26; #2202, 1/29; #2182-2183, 2194-2195, 5/21; #2196-2197, 8/19/91; 2.20fr, 2.50fr, 3.40fr, 4fr, 9/30/91; #2179a, 2187a, 2199, 2201, 1991; 4.20fr, 9/24/92; #2203-2204, 1992; 2.10fr, 1993.

Peelable paper backing serves as booklet cover for Nos. 2202, 2203. No. 2203b has separate backing with no printing.

Nos. 2196-2197, 2204 inscribed "D."

See Nos. 2333-2348.

Lace Work A1162

1990, Feb. 3 Engr. *Perf. 13x12½*
2205 A1162 2.50fr red .80 .20

1992 Winter Olympics, Albertville — A1163

1990, Feb. 9 Photo. *Perf. 13*
2206 A1163 2.50fr multicolored .80 .20

Charles de Gaulle (1890-1970) A1164

Max Hymans (1900-1961), Planes and ACC Emblem A1165

1990, Feb. 24 Engr. *Perf. 12½x13*

2207 A1164 2.30fr brt vio, vio bl & blk .80 .20

1990, Mar. 3 *Perf. 13*

2208 A1165 2.30fr brt vio, brt bl & dk ol grn .80 .20

Profile of a Woman, by Odilon Redon A1166

Head of Christ, Wissembourg — A1167

Cambodian Dancer by Auguste Rodin — A1168

Jaune et Gris by Roger Bissiere A1169

1990 Litho. *Perf. 13½x14*

2209 A1166 5fr multicolored 2.00 .35

Perf. 12½x13

Engr.

2210 A1167 5fr multicolored 2.00 .35
2211 A1168 5fr multicolored 2.00 .35

Photo.

2212 A1169 5fr multicolored 2.00 .35
Nos. 2209-2212 (4) 8.00 1.40

Issue dates: No. 2209, Mar. 3; No. 2210, June 16; No. 2211, June 9; No. 2212, Dec. 8.

Jean Guehenno (1890-1978) A1170

Litho. & Engr.

1990, Mar. 24 *Perf. 13*

2213 A1170 3.20fr buff & red brn 1.10 .20

Tourism Series

Flaran Abbey, Gers A1171

Cluny A1172

Pont Canal de Briare A1173

Cap Canaille, Cassis A1174

1990, Apr. 21 Engr. *Perf. 13*

2214 A1171 3.80fr sepia & blk 1.40 .30

1990

2215 A1172 2.30fr multicolored .80 .20
2216 A1173 2.30fr multicolored .80 .20
2217 A1174 3.80fr multicolored 1.40 .30
Nos. 2215-2217 (3) 3.00 .70

Issued: #2215, 6/23; #2216, 7/7; 3.80fr, 7/14.

Europa 1990 A1175

Post offices.

1990, Apr. 28 Engr. *Perf. 13*

2218 A1175 2.30fr Macon *2.50* .60
2219 A1175 3.20fr Cerizay *3.50* 1.00

Arab World Institute — A1176

1990, May 5 *Perf. 12½x13*

2220 A1176 3.80fr brt bl, dk red & dp bl 1.40 .30

Labor Day, Cent. A1177

1990, May 1 Photo. *Perf. 13*

2221 A1177 2.30fr multicolored .80 .20

Villefranche-sur-Saone — A1178

1990, June 2 Engr. *Perf. 13x12½*

2222 A1178 2.30fr multicolored .80 .20

National philatelic congress.

A1179

A1181

1990, June 6 *Perf. 13x12½*

2223 A1179 2.30fr La Poste .80 .20

Whitbread trans-global yacht race.

1990, June 17 *Perf. 12½x13*

2225 A1181 2.30fr multicolored .80 .20

De Gaulle's Call for French Resistance, 50th anniv.

Franco-Brazilian House, Rio de Janeiro — A1182

1990, July 14 *Perf. 13*

2226 A1182 3.20fr multicolored 1.25 .20

See Brazil No. 2255.

A1183

A1184

Designs: Fish.

1990, Oct. 6 Engr. *Perf. 12½*

2227 A1183 2fr Rutilus rutilus .70 .20
2228 A1183 3fr Perca fluviatilis 1.00 .20
2229 A1183 4fr Salmo salar 1.40 .30
2230 A1183 5fr Esox lucius 1.75 .35
Nos. 2227-2230 (4) 4.85 1.05

1990, Sept. 29 Photo. *Perf. 12½x13*

2231 A1184 2.30fr multicolored .85 .20

Natl. Institute of Geography, 50th anniv.

Souvenir Sheet

French Revolution, Bicentennial — A1185

Designs: a, Gaspard Monge. b, Abbe Gregoire. c, Creation of the Tricolor. d, Creation of the French departments.

1990, Oct. 15 Engr. *Perf. 13*

2232 A1185 Sheet of 4 3.60 3.60
a.-d. 2.50fr any single .90 .90

Musical Instrument Type of 1989

1990, Sept. 1 Litho. *Perf. 13*

2233 A1154 1.46fr Accordion .55 .20
2234 A1154 1.89fr Breton bag-pipe .65 .20
2235 A1154 3.06fr Tambourin 1.10 .20
2236 A1154 5.10fr Hurdy-gurdy 1.90 .20
Nos. 2233-2236 (4) 4.20 .80

1990, Nov. Litho. *Perf. 13*

2237 A1154 1.93fr like #2169 .75 .20
2238 A1154 2.39fr like #2170 .90 .20
2239 A1154 2.74fr like #2172 1.10 .20
Nos. 2237-2239 (3) 2.75 .60

Nos. 2233-2239 are known only precanceled. See second note after No. 132.

Maurice Genevoix (1890-1980), Novelist — A1186

1990, Nov. 12 Engr. *Perf. 13*

2240 A1186 2.30fr lt green & blk .90 .20

Organization for Economic Cooperation and Development, 30th Anniv. — A1187

1990, Dec. 15 Litho.

2241 A1187 3.20fr dk & lt blue 1.25 .25

"The Swing" by Auguste Renoir (1841-1919) — A1188

1991, Feb. 23 Engr. *Perf. 12½x13*
2242 A1188 5fr multicolored 2.00 .40

Youth Philatelic Exhibition, Cholet
A1189

1991, Mar. 30 Litho. *Perf. 13*
2243 A1189 2.50fr multicolored 1.00 .20

Art Series

Le Noeud Noir by Georges Seurat (1859-1891) — A1190

Apres Nous La Maternite, by Max Ernst (1891-1976) — A1191

Volte Faccia by Francois Rouan
A1192

O Tableau Noir by Roberto Matta (b. 1911) — A1193

1991 Engr. *Perf. 12½x13*
2244 A1190 5fr pale yellow & blk 2.00 .40

Photo. *Perf. 13*
2245 A1191 2.50fr multicolored .85 .20

Engr. *Perf. 12½x13*
2246 A1192 5fr black 1.90 .40

Photo. *Perf. 13x12½*
2247 A1193 5fr multicolored 2.00 .40
Nos. 2244-2247 (4) 6.75 1.40

Issued: #2244, 4/13: #2245, 10/10; #2246, 11/9; #2247, 11/30.

Wolfgang Amadeus Mozart (1756-1791), Composer — A1194

1991, Apr. 9 Photo. *Perf. 13*
2248 A1194 2.50fr bl, blk & red .90 .20

National Printing Office, 350th Anniv. — A1195

1991, Apr. 13
2249 A1195 4fr multicolored 1.40 .30

Tourism Series

Chevire Bridge, Nantes — A1196

Carennac Castle
A1197

Pipe Organ, Wasquehal
A1198

Valley of Munster
A1199

1991 Engr. *Perf. 13*
2250 A1196 2.50fr multicolored .90 .20

Perf. 12x13
2251 A1197 2.50fr multicolored .90 .20

Perf. 12
2252 A1198 4fr black & buff 1.40 .30

Perf. 13x12½
2253 A1199 4fr violet 1.40 .30
Nos. 2250-2253 (4) 4.60 1.00

Issue dates: No. 2250, Apr. 27; Nos. 2251, 2253, July 6; No. 2252, June 22.

Europa
A1200

Concours Lepine, 90th Anniv.
A1201

1991, Apr. 27 *Perf. 12½x13*
2254 A1200 2.50fr Ariane launch site, French Guiana *2.25* .50
2255 A1200 3.50fr Television satellite *4.75* 1.50

Compare with No. 2483.

1991, Apr. 27 *Perf. 13*
2256 A1201 4fr multicolored 1.40 .30

French Assoc. of Small Manufacturers and Inventors.

Philatelic Society Congress, Perpignan
A1202

1991, May 18
2257 A1202 2.50fr multicolored .90 .20

French Open Tennis Championships, Cent. — A1203

1991, May 24 Engr. *Perf. 13*
2258 A1203 3.50fr multicolored 1.25 .25

Souvenir Sheet

French Revolution, Bicent. — A1204

Designs: a, Theophile Malo Corret, La Tour d'Auvergne (1743-1800). b, Liberty Tree. c, National police, bicent. d, Louis Antoine-Leon de St. Just (1767-1794).

1991, June 1 Engr. *Perf. 13*
2259 A1204 Sheet of 4 3.20 .80
a.-d. 2.50fr any single .80 .20

A1205 A1206

1991, June 13 Photo. *Perf. 13*
2260 A1205 2.50fr multicolored .90 .20

Gaston III de Foix (Febus) (1331-1391), general.

1991, Sept. 14 Engr. *Perf. 12½*

Designs: Wildlife.

2261 A1206 2fr Ursus arctos .70 .20
2262 A1206 3fr Testudo hermanni 1.10 .20
2263 A1206 4fr Castor fiber 1.40 .20
2264 A1206 5fr Alcedo atthis 1.75 .35
Nos. 2261-2264 (4) 4.95 .95

10th World Forestry Congress
A1207

1991, Sept. 22 Engr. *Perf. 13x12½*
2265 A1207 2.50fr multicolored .85 .20

School of Public Works, Cent.
A1208

1991, Oct. 5 Litho. & Engr. *Perf. 13*
2266 A1208 2.50fr multicolored .85 .20

Marcel Cerdan (1916-1949), Middleweight Boxing Champion — A1209

1991, Oct. 19 Photo. *Perf. 13*
2267 A1209 2.50fr black & red .85 .20

Amnesty International, 30th Anniv. — A1210

1991, Oct. 19
2268 A1210 3.40fr multicolored 1.10 .25

A1211 A1212

1991, Nov. 14 Engr. *Perf. 13*
2269 A1211 2.50fr Olympic flame 1.00 .20

1992 Winter Olympics, Albertville.

1991, Dec. 7 *Perf. 13*
2270 A1212 2.50fr dk & lt blue 1.00 .20

Fifth Handicapped Olympics.

Voluntary Attachment of Mayotte to France, Sesquicentennial — A1213

1991, Dec. 21 Engr.
2271 A1213 2.50fr multicolored 1.00 .20

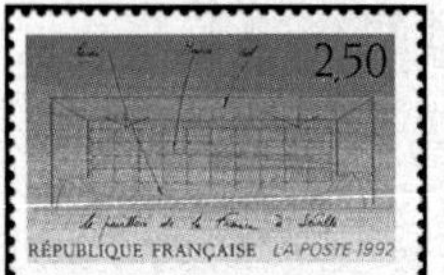

French Pavilion, Expo '92, Seville A1214

Litho. & Engr.

1992, Jan. 18 *Perf. 13*
2272 A1214 2.50fr multicolored 1.00 .20

Musical Instruments Type of 1989

Perf. 13, 12½ (1.60fr, 3.19fr)

1992, Jan. 31 Litho.

2273	A1154	1.60fr	Guitar	*32.50*	*14.00*
2274	A1154	1.98fr	like #2233	3.00	1.85
2275	A1154	2.08fr	Saxophone	1.40	1.00
2276	A1154	2.46fr	like #2234	1.40	1.00
2277	A1154	2.98fr	Banjo	1.40	1.00
2278	A1154	3.08fr	like #2235	4.25	2.40
2279	A1154	3.14fr	like #2236	1.90	1.25
2280	A1154	3.19fr	like #2169	4.25	2.10
2281	A1154	5.28fr	Xylophone	3.75	2.00
2282	A1154	5.30fr	like #2170	2.40	1.60
2283	A1154	5.32fr	like #2172	2.40	1.60
			Nos. 2273-2283 (11)	*58.65*	29.80

Nos. 2273-2283 are known only precanceled. See 2nd note after No. 132. See Nos. 2303-2306.

1992 Summer Olympics, Barcelona A1215

1992, Apr. 3 Photo. *Perf. 13*
2284 A1215 2.50fr multicolored .90 .20

See Greece No. 1730.

Marguerite d'Angouleme (1492-1549) A1216

1992, Apr. 11 Litho. *Perf. 13*
2285 A1216 3.40fr multicolored 1.25 .25

Founding of Ajaccio, 500th Anniv. A1217

Virgin and Child Beneath a Garland by Botticelli.

1992, Apr. 30 Photo. *Perf. 13*
2286 A1217 4fr multicolored 1.40 .30

A1218 A1219

Discovery of America, 500th Anniv.: 2.50fr, Map, navigation instruments. 3.40fr, Sailing ship, map.

1992, May 9 Engr. *Perf. 13x12½*
2287 A1218 2.50fr multicolored *1.75* .35
2288 A1218 3.40fr multicolored *2.75* .75

Europa.

1992, May 30 Litho. *Perf. 13*
2289 A1219 3.40fr multicolored 1.25 .25

Intl. Bread and Cereal Congress.

Tourism Series

Ourcq Canal A1220

Mt. Aiguille A1221 Biron Castle A1223

Lorient A1222

1992, May 30 Engr. *Perf. 13*
2290 A1220 4fr black, blue & grn 1.50 .30

1992, June 27 Engr. *Perf. 13*
2291 A1221 3.40fr multicolored 1.40 .30

First ascension of Mt. Aiguille, 500th anniv.

1992, July 4 Engr. *Perf. 13*
2292 A1222 4fr multicolored 1.60 .30

1992, July 4 *Perf. 12½x13*
2293 A1223 2.50fr multicolored 1.00 .20

Natl Philatelic Societies Congress, Niort A1224

1992, June 6 Photo. *Perf. 13*
2294 A1224 2.50fr multicolored .90 .20

Natl. Art Festival.

1992 Olympic Games, Albertville and Barcelona A1225

1992, June 19 *Perf. 12½x13½*
2295 A1225 2.50fr multicolored .90 .20

Tautavel Man A1226

1992, June 20 Photo. *Perf. 13*
2296 A1226 3.40fr multicolored 1.40 .30

Portrait of Jacques Callot (1592-1635), by Claude Deruet — A1227

1992, June 27 Engr. *Perf. 12x13*
2297 A1227 5fr buff & brown 1.90 .35

Flowers — A1228

2fr, Pancratium maritimum. 3fr, Drosera rotundifolia. 4fr, Orchis palustris. 5fr, Nuphar luteum.

1992, Sept. 12 Engr. *Perf. 12½*

2298	A1228	2fr	multicolored	.80	.20
2299	A1228	3fr	multicolored	1.25	.25
2300	A1228	4fr	multicolored	1.50	.30
2301	A1228	5fr	multicolored	2.00	.40
			Nos. 2298-2301 (4)	5.55	1.15

First French Republic, Bicent. A1229

1992, Sept. 26 *Perf. 13*
2302 A1229 2.50fr multicolored 1.00 .20

Musical Instruments Type of 1989

1992, Oct. Litho. *Perf. 13*

2303	A1154	1.73fr	like #2273	.70	.20
2304	A1154	2.25fr	like #2275	.90	.20
2305	A1154	3.51fr	like #2277	1.40	.30
2306	A1154	5.40fr	like #2281	2.25	.40
			Nos. 2303-2306 (4)	5.25	1.10

Nos. 2303-2306 are known only precanceled. See second note after No. 132.

Proclamation of First French Republic, Bicent. — A1230

Paintings or drawings by contemporary artists: No. 2307, Tree of Freedom, by Pierre Alechinsky. No. 2308, Portrait of a Young Man, by Martial Raysse. No. 2309, Marianne with Body and Head of Rooster, by Gerard Garouste. No. 2310, "Republique Francaise," by Jean-Charles Blais.

1992, Sept. 26 Engr. *Perf. 13*

2307	A1230	2.50fr	red	.90	.20
2308	A1230	2.50fr	red	.90	.20
2309	A1230	2.50fr	red	.90	.20
2310	A1230	2.50fr	red	.90	.20
			Nos. 2307-2310 (4)	3.60	.80

Single European Market A1231

1992, Nov. 6 Photo. *Perf. 12½x13½*
2311 A1231 2.50fr multicolored .90 .20

First Mail Flight from Nancy to Luneville, 80th Anniv. A1232

1992, Nov. 12 *Perf. 13*
2312 A1232 2.50fr multicolored .90 .20

Marcel Paul (1900-1982), Minister of Industrial Production — A1233

1992, Nov. 13 Engr.
2313 A1233 4.20fr claret & blue 1.60 .30

Contemporary Art — A1234

#2314, Le Rendezvous d'Ephese, by Paul Delvaux, Belgium. #2315, Abstract painting, by Alberto Burri, Italy. #2316, Abstract painting, by Antoni Tapies, Spain. #2317, Portrait of John Edwards, by Francis Bacon, Great Britain.

1992 Photo. *Perf. 13x12½*

2314	A1234	5fr	multicolored	1.90	.40
2315	A1234	5fr	multicolored	1.90	.40
2316	A1234	5fr	multicolored	1.90	.40
2317	A1234	5fr	multicolored	1.90	.40
			Nos. 2314-2317 (4)	7.60	1.60

Issued: #2314, 11/20; #2315-2317, 11/21.

See Nos. 2379-2390.

Gypsy Culture — A1235

1992, Dec. 5 Photo. *Perf. 13*
2318 A1235 2.50fr multicolored .95 .20

Yacht "La Poste," Entrant in Whitbread Trans-Global Race — A1236

1993, Feb. 6 Engr. *Perf. 12*
2319 A1236 2.50fr multicolored .95 .20

See No. 2375.

Water Birds — A1237

1993, Feb. 6 *Perf. 12½x12*

2320	A1237	2fr Harle piette	.75	.20
2321	A1237	3fr Fuligule nyroca	1.10	.25
2322	A1237	4fr Tadorne de belon	1.50	.30
2323	A1237	5fr Harle huppe	1.75	.35
		Nos. 2320-2323 (4)	5.10	1.10

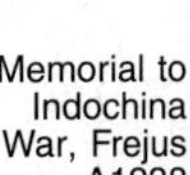

Memorial to Indochina War, Frejus A1238

Litho. & Engr.

1993, Feb. 16 *Perf. 13x13½*
2324 A1238 4fr multicolored 1.50 .30

Stamp Day — A1239

1993, Mar. 6 Photo. *Perf. 13*

2325	A1239	2.50fr red & multi	1.00	.20
2326	A1239	2.50fr +60c red & multi	1.25	.25
a.		Bklt. pane of 4 #2325, 3 #2326 + label	7.75	

Mediterranean Youth Games, Agde — A1240

1993, Mar. 13 Photo. *Perf. 13*
2327 A1240 2.50fr multicolored .90 .20

Human Rights, Intl. Mixed Masonic Order, Cent. — A1241

1993, Apr. 3 Engr. *Perf. 13*
2328 A1241 3.40fr blue & black 1.25 .25

Contemporary Art — A1242

Europa: 2.50fr, Painting, Rouge Rythme Bleu, by Olivier Debre. 3.40fr, Sculpture, Le Griffu, by Germaine Richier, vert.

Perf. 13x12½, 12½x13

1993, Apr. 17 Litho.

2329	A1242	2.50fr multicolored	.95	.30
2330	A1242	3.40fr multicolored	1.25	.70

Marianne Type of 1990

1993-96 Engr. *Perf. 13*

2333	A1161	2fr blue	.50	.20
2334	A1161	2.40fr emerald	.65	.20
2335	A1161	2.70fr emerald	.75	.25
2336	A1161	3.50fr apple green	.90	.25
2337	A1161	3.80fr blue	1.00	.35
2338	A1161	4.40fr blue	1.10	.30
2339	A1161	4.50fr mag	1.00	.30
2340	A1161	(2.50fr) red	1.00	.20
		Nos. 2333-2340 (8)	6.90	2.05

Perf. 13 Horiz.

Coil Stamps

2341	A1161	2.40fr emerald	.75	.20
2342	A1161	2.70fr emerald	.75	.20
2343	A1161	(2.80fr) red	1.10	.20

Self-Adhesive

Die Cut

2344	A1161	70c brown	1.50	.20

Serpentine Die Cut Vert.

2345	A1161	70c brown	.25	.20
2346	A1161	1fr orange	1.00	.50
a.		Booklet pane, 3 #2348, 1 #2346	4.30	
		Complete bklt., 2 #2346a	8.60	

Die Cut

2347	A1161	(2.50fr) red	1.00	.20
a.		Booklet pane of 10 (see footnote)	10.00	
b.		Bklt. pane of 4 + label	4.00	
c.		Booklet pane, #2344, 3 #2348 + label	5.00	
d.		Booklet pane of 10 (see footnote)	12.00	

Serpentine Die Cut Vert.

2348	A1161	(2.80fr) red	1.10	.20
a.		Bklt. pane of 4 + label	4.50	
b.		Booklet pane of 10 (see footnote)	11.00	
c.		Booklet pane, #2345, 3 #2347 + label	5.00	
d.		Booklet pane of 10 (see footnote)	11.00	
e.		Booklet pane of 10 (see footnote)	12.00	
f.		Booklet pane of 10 (see footnote)	11.00	

Nos. 2340, 2347 pay postage for the first class letter rate and sold for 2.50fr when first released. They have no denomination or letter inscription. Nos. 2343 and 2348 had a face value of 2.80fr when released.

No. 2347a has all stamps adjoining and has selvage covering backing paper (booklet cover), No. 2347d is comprised of two strips of 5 stamps each with yellow backing paper showing.

No. 2348b has the same format as No. 2347a. No. 2348d has a format similar to No. 2347d except there is a narrow selvage strip between the left six stamps and the right four stamps. No. 2348e is like No. 2348f but lacks the selvage strip. No. 2348f has a format similar to No. 2347a except it has a wide selvage strip between the left four stamps and the right six stamps.

Backing paper of Nos. 2347b and 2347c may have cuts along fold and were sold in a booklet for 20fr.

Issued: #2340, 2347, 4/19/93; 70c, July; 2fr, 7/31/94; #2341-2343, 4/1/94; #2345, 2348, 2/14/94; 1fr, 2.70fr, 3.80fr, 4.50fr, 3/18/96.

Tourism Series

Chinon — A1243

Illustration reduced.

Village of Minerve — A1244

Chaise-Dieu Abbey — A1245

Montbeliard — A1246

1993, Apr. 24 Engr. *Perf. 13x12½*
2355 A1243 4.20fr dk grn, ol grn & brn 1.60 .30

1993, July 17 *Perf. 13*
2356 A1244 4.20fr red brown & yel grn 1.40 .30

1993

2357	A1245	2.80fr multicolored	.95	.20
2358	A1246	4.40fr multicolored	1.50	.30
		Nos. 2355-2358 (4)	5.45	1.10

Issued: #2357, Sept. 4; #2358, Sept. 11.

Ninth European Conference on Protection of Human Rights — A1247

1993, May 8 Engr. *Perf. 12½x13*
2359 A1247 2.50fr multicolored .95 .20

Django Reinhardt (1910-1953), Musician — A1248

1993, May 14 Litho. *Perf. 13*
2360 A1248 4.20fr multicolored 1.60 .30

Louise Weiss (1893-1983), Suffragist — A1249

1993, May 15 Engr. *Perf. 13x12½*
2361 A1249 2.50fr blk, buff & red .95 .20

Philatelic Society Congress, Lille A1250

1993, May 29 Engr. *Perf. 13x12½*
2362 A1250 2.50fr bl, dk bl & lil .95 .20

Natural History Museum, Bicent. A1251

Litho. & Engr.

1993, June 5 *Perf. 13*
2363 A1251 2.50fr multicolored .95 .20

Martyrs and Heroes of the Resistance — A1252

1993, June 18 Photo. *Perf. 13*

2364		2.50fr red, black & gray	.95	.20
2365		4.20fr red, black & gray	1.60	.30
a.		A1252 Pair, #2364-2365	2.55	.50

A1254

A1255

1993, July 10 Engr. *Perf. 13x12½*
2366 A1254 2.50fr multicolored .95 .20

Claude Chappe's Semaphore Telegraph, bicent.

1993, July 10 Engr. *Perf. 12½x13*
2367 A1255 3.40fr bl, grn & red 1.15 .25

Train to Lake Artouste, Laruns, highest train ride in Europe.

Musical Instruments Type of 1989

1993, July 1 Litho. *Perf. 13*

2368	A1154	1.82fr like #2171	.60	.20
2369	A1154	2.34fr like #2235	.80	.20
2370	A1154	3.86fr like #2236	1.25	.25
2371	A1154	5.93fr like #2281	2.00	.40
		Nos. 2368-2371 (4)	4.65	1.05

Nos. 2368-2371 are known only precanceled. See note after No. 132.

Liberation of Corsica, 50th Anniv. — A1256

1993, Sept. 9 Engr. *Perf. 13*

2372 A1256 2.80fr lake, bl & blk .95 .20

Saint Thomas, by Georges de la Tour (1593-1652) — A1257

1993, Sept. 9 Photo. *Perf. 12½x13*

2373 A1257 5fr multicolored 1.75 .35

Service as Military Hospital of Val de Grace Monastery, Bicent. — A1258

1993, Sept. 25 Engr. *Perf. 13*

2374 A1258 3.70fr multicolored 1.25 .25

Whitbread Trans-Global Race Type

1993, Sept. 27 Engr. *Perf. 12*

2375 A1236 2.80fr multicolored .95 .20

The Muses, by Maurice Denis (1870-1943) — A1259

1993, Oct. 2 Photo. *Perf. 12½x13*

2376 A1259 5fr multicolored 1.75 .35

The Clowns, by Albert Gleizes (1881-1953) A1260

1993, Oct. 2 Photo. *Perf. 13½x12½*

2377 A1260 2.80fr multicolored 1.00 .20

Natl. Circus Center, Chalons-sur-Marne.

Clock Tower Bellringer Statues of Lambesc — A1261

1993, Oct. 9 Engr. *Perf. 13x12½*

2378 A1261 4.40fr multicolored 1.50 .30

European Contemporary Art Type

Designs: No. 2379, Abstract, by Takis. No. 2380, Abstract, by Maria Helena Vieira da Silva. No. 2381, Abstract Squares, by Sean Scully. No. 2382, Abstract, by Georg Baselitz, Germany.

1993-94 Photo. *Perf. 13x12½*

2379	A1234	5fr blk & ver	1.75	.35
2380	A1234	5fr multicolored	1.65	.35
2381	A1234	6.70fr multicolored	2.25	.45

Perf. 13

2382	A1234	6.70fr multicolored	2.75	.70
		Nos. 2379-2382 (4)	8.40	1.85

Issued: #2379, 10/9/93; #2380, 12/11/93; #2381, 1/29/94; #2382, 11/19/94.

Greetings A1266

Greeting, artist: #2383, Happy Birthday, Claire Wendling. #2384, Happy Birthday, Bernard Olivie. #2385, Happy Anniversary, Stephane Colman. #2386, Happy Anniversary, Guillaune Sorel. #2387, With Love, Jean-Michel Thiriet. #2388, Please Write, Etienne Davodeau. #2389, Congratulations, Johan de Moor. #2390, Good luck, "Mezzo." #2391, Best Wishes, Nicolas de Crecy. #2392, Best Wishes, Florence Magnin. #2393, Merry Christmas, Thierry Robin. #2394, Merry Christmas, Patrick Prugne.

1993, Oct. 21 Photo. *Perf. 13½x13*

Booklet Stamps

2383	A1266	2.80fr multicolored	.95	.20
2384	A1266	2.80fr multicolored	.95	.20
2385	A1266	2.80fr multicolored	.95	.20
2386	A1266	2.80fr multicolored	.95	.20
2387	A1266	2.80fr multicolored	.95	.20
2388	A1266	2.80fr multicolored	.95	.20
2389	A1266	2.80fr multicolored	.95	.20
2390	A1266	2.80fr multicolored	.95	.20
2391	A1266	2.80fr multicolored	.95	.20
2392	A1266	2.80fr multicolored	.95	.20
2393	A1266	2.80fr multicolored	.95	.20
2394	A1266	2.80fr multicolored	.95	.20
a.		Bklt. pane, #2383-2394	11.50	

Perf. 12½

2383a	A1266	2.80fr	.95	.20
2384a	A1266	2.80fr	.95	.20
2385a	A1266	2.80fr	.95	.20
2386a	A1266	2.80fr	.95	.20
2387a	A1266	2.80fr	.95	.20
2388a	A1266	2.80fr	.95	.20
2389a	A1266	2.80fr	.95	.20
2390a	A1266	2.80fr	.95	.20
2391a	A1266	2.80fr	.95	.20
2392a	A1266	2.80fr	.95	.20
2393a	A1266	2.80fr	.95	.20
2394b	A1266	2.80fr	.95	.20
c.		Booklet pane of 12, #2383a-2393a, 2394b	11.50	

Souvenir Sheet

European Stamp Exhibition, Salon du Timbre A1267

a, Rhododendrons. b, Flowers in park, Paris.

1993, Nov. 10 *Perf. 13*

2395 A1267 2.40fr #a.-b.+ 2 labels 5.00 5.00

Sold for 15fr.

Louvre Museum, Bicent. A1268

1993, Nov. 20

2396	A1268	2.80fr Louvre, 1793	1.00	.20
2397	A1268	4.40fr Louvre, 1993	1.50	.30
a.		Pair, #2396-2397	2.50	.50

Glassware, 1901 — A1269

Cast Iron, c. 1900 — A1270

Furniture, c. 1902 — A1271

Stoneware, c. 1898 — A1272

Decorative arts by: No. 2398, Emile Galle (1846-1904). No. 2399, Hector Guimard (1867-1942). No. 2400, Louis Majorelle (1859-1926). No. 2401, Pierre-Adrien Dalpayrat (1844-1910).

Perf. 13½x12½

1994. Jan. 22 Photo.

2398	A1269	2.80fr multicolored	.95	.20
2399	A1270	2.80fr multicolored	.95	.20
2400	A1271	4.40fr multicolored	1.50	.30
2401	A1272	4.40fr multicolored	1.50	.30
		Nos. 2398-2401 (4)	4.90	1.00

Stained Glass Window, St. Julian's Cathedral, Le Mans A1273

1994, Feb. 12 Engr. *Perf. 12½x13*

2402 A1273 6.70fr multicolored 2.25 .45

City of Bastia — A1274

1994, Feb. 19 *Perf. 13x12½*

2403 A1274 4.40fr blue & brown 1.50 .30

Tourism Series

Argentat A1275

1994, June 18 Engr. *Perf. 12x12½*

2404 A1275 4.40fr red brown & rose carmine 1.65 .35

European Parliamentary Elections — A1276

1994, Feb. 26 Litho. *Perf. 13*

2405 A1276 2.80fr multicolored .95 .20

Laurent Mourguet (1769-1844), Creator of Puppet, Guignol — A1277

1994, Mar. 4 Photo. *Perf. 13*

2406 A1277 2.80fr multicolored 1.00 .20

French Polytechnic Institute, Bicent. A1277a

1994, Mar. 11

2407 A1277a 2.80fr multicolored 1.00 .20

Stamp Day
A1278

1994, Mar. 12 Engr. *Perf. 13*

2408	A1278	2.80fr blue & red	*1.00*	*.20*
2409	A1278	2.80fr +60c blue & red	*1.25*	*.25*
a.		Booklet pane of 4 #2408, 3 #2409 + 1 label	*7.75*	

No. 2408 issued only in booklets.

Swedish Ballet Costume — A1279

Banquet for Gustavus III at the Trianon, 1784, by Lafrensen — A1280

French-Swedish cultural relations: No. 2411, Tuxedo costume for Swedish ballet. No. 2412, Viking ships. No. 2413, Viking ship. No. 2415, Swedish, French flags.

1994, Mar. 18 Engr. *Perf. 13*

2410	A1279	2.80fr multicolored	.95	.20
2411	A1279	2.80fr multicolored	.95	.20
2412	A1279	2.80fr multicolored	.95	.20
2413	A1279	2.80fr multicolored	.95	.20
2414	A1280	3.70fr multicolored	1.25	.25
2415	A1280	3.70fr multicolored	1.25	.25
a.		Booklet pane of #2410-2415	6.30	

See Sweden Nos. 2065-2070.

Pres. Georges Pompidou (1911-1974)
A1281

1994, Apr. 9 Engr. *Perf. 13*

2416	A1281	2.80fr olive brown	1.00	.20

Resistance of the Maquis, 50th Anniv.
A1282

1994, Apr. 9

2417	A1282	2.80fr multicolored	1.00	.20

Philexjeunes '94, Grenoble — A1283

1994, Apr. 22 Photo.

2418	A1283	2.80fr multicolored	1.00	.20

Europa
A1284

Discoveries: 2.80fr, AIDS virus, by scientists of Pasteur Institute. 3.70fr, Formula for wave properties of matter, developed by Louis de Brogile.

1994, Apr. 30 Photo. & Engr.

2419	A1284	2.80fr multicolored	1.00	.40
a.		With label	1.25	.75
2420	A1284	3.70fr multicolored	1.25	.60

No. 2419a issued Dec. 1, 1994.

Opening of Channel Tunnel — A1285

Designs: Nos. 2421, 2423, British lion, French rooster, meeting over Channel. Nos. 2422, 2424, Joined hands above speeding train.

1994, May 3 Photo. *Perf. 13*

2421	A1285	2.80fr dk blue & multi	1.00	.20
2422	A1285	2.80fr dk blue & multi	1.00	.20
a.		Pair, #2421-2422	2.00	.40
2423	A1285	4.30fr lt blue & multi	1.50	.30
2424	A1285	4.30fr multicolored	1.50	.30
a.		Pair, #2423-2424	3.00	.60
		Nos. 2421-2424 (4)	5.00	1.00

See Great Britain Nos. 1558-1561.

Asian Development Bank, Board of Governors Meeting, Nice — A1286

1994, May 3 Photo. *Perf. 13*

2425	A1286	2.80fr multicolored	1.00	.20

Federation of French Philatelic Societies, 67th Congress, Martigues
A1287

1994, May 20 Engr. *Perf. 12x12½*

2426	A1287	2.80fr multicolored	1.00	.20

Court of Cassation
A1288

Litho. & Engr.

1994, June 3 *Perf. 13*

2427	A1288	2.80fr multicolored	1.00	.20

D-Day, 50th Anniv.
A1289

No. 2429, Tank, crowd waving Allied flags.

1994, June 4 Engr.

2428	A1289	4.30fr multicolored	1.50	.30
2429	A1289	4.30fr multicolored	1.50	.30

Liberation of Paris, 50th anniv. (#2429).

Mount St. Victoire, by Paul Cezanne (1839-1906) — A1290

1994, June 18 Photo. *Perf. 13*

2430	A1290	2.80fr multicolored	1.10	.20

Intl. Olympic Committee, Cent.
A1291

1994, June 23 Litho. *Perf. 13*

2431	A1291	2.80fr multicolored	1.00	.20

Saulx River Bridge, Rupt aux Nonains
A1292

1994, July 2 Engr.

2432	A1292	2.80fr blackish blue	1.00	.20

Organ, Poitiers Cathedral — A1293

1994, July 2 *Perf. 13x12½*

2433	A1293	4.40fr multicolored	1.65	.35

Allied Landings in Provence, 50th Anniv.
A1294

1994, Aug. 13 Engr. *Perf. 13*

2434	A1294	2.80fr multicolored	1.10	.25

Moses and the Daughters of Jethro, by Nicolas Poussin (1594-1665) — A1295

Illustration reduced.

1994, Sept. 10

2435	A1295	4.40fr yel brn & blk	1.75	.35

Natl. Conservatory of Arts and Crafts, Bicent. — A1296

1994, Sept. 24 *Perf. 13x12½*

2436	A1296	2.80fr Foucault's pendulum	1.10	.25

The Great Cascade, St. Cloud Park — A1297

1994, Sept. 24 *Perf. 12½x13*

2437	A1297	3.70fr multicolored	1.50	.30

Leaves — A1298

1994 Litho. *Perf. 13*

2438	A1298	1.91fr Oak	.75	.20
2439	A1298	2.46fr Sycamore	1.00	.20
2440	A1298	4.24fr Chestnut	1.65	.30
2441	A1298	6.51fr Holly	2.50	.50
		Nos. 2438-2441 (4)	5.90	1.20

Nos. 2438-2441 are known only precanceled. See second note after No. 132.
See Nos. 2517-2520.

Ecole Normale Superieure (Teachers' School), Bicent. — A1299

1994, Oct. 8 Engr. *Perf. 13*

2442	A1299	2.80fr red & dk bl	1.10	.25

Georges Simenon (1903-89), Writer
A1300

Litho. & Engr.

1994, Oct. 15 *Perf. 13*

2443	A1300	2.80fr multicolored	1.10	.25

See Belgium No. 1567, Switzerland No. 948.

Souvenir Sheet

European Stamp Exhibition — A1301

a, Flowers in park, Paris. b, Dahlias, vert.

1994, Oct. 15 Photo. *Perf. 13*

2444	A1301	2.80fr Sheet of 2, #a.-b.	6.75	1.40

No. 2444 sold for 16fr.

Natl. Drug Addiction Prevention Day — A1302

1994, Oct. 15

2445 A1302 2.80fr multicolored 1.10 .25

Grand Lodge of France, Cent. A1303

1994, Nov. 5 **Engr.**

2446 A1303 2.80fr multicolored 1.10 .25

Alain Colas (1943-78), Sailor A1304

1994, Nov. 19

2447 A1304 3.70fr green & black 1.40 .35

French Natl. Press Federation, 50th Anniv. A1305

1994, Dec. 9 **Photo.** ***Perf. 13***

2448 A1305 2.80fr multicolored 1.10 .30

Champs Elysees — A1306

Illustration reduced.

1994, Dec. 31

2449 A1306 4.40fr multicolored 1.75 .40

No. 2449 printed with se-tenant label.

Souvenir Sheet

Motion Pictures, Cent. — A1307

Faces on screen and: a, Projector at right. b, Projector facing away from screen. c, Projector facing screen. d, Reels of film.

1995, Jan. 14 **Photo.** ***Perf. 13***

2450 A1307 Sheet of 4 4.50 4.50

a.-d. 2.80fr any single 1.10 1.10

Normandy Bridge — A1308

Illustration reduced.

1995, Jan. 20 **Engr.** ***Perf. 13***

2451 A1308 4.40fr multicolored 1.75 .40

A1309 A1310

1995, Jan. 21 ***Perf. 13x12***

2452 A1309 2.80fr multicolored 1.10 .30

European Notaries Public.

1995, Feb. 18 **Photo.** ***Perf. 13***

2453 A1310 3.70fr multicolored 1.50 .40

Louis Pasteur (1822-95).

Art Series

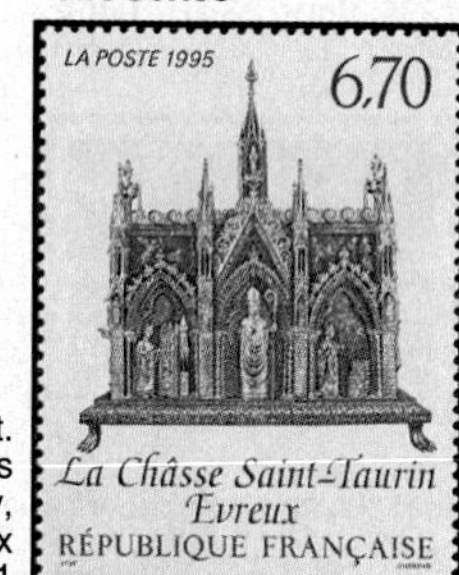

St. Taurin's Reliquary, Evreaux A1311

Study for the Dream of Happiness, by Pierre Prud'hon (1758-1823) — A1312

Abstract, by Zao Wou-ki — A1313

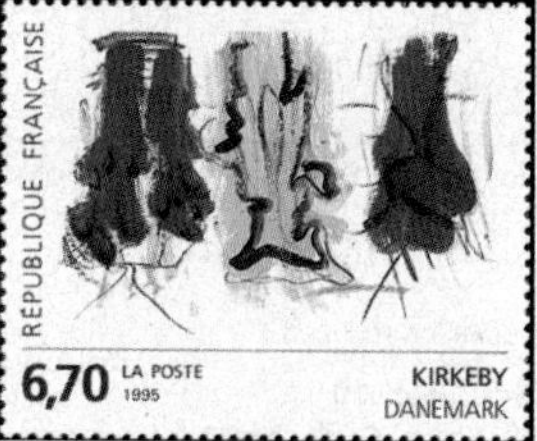

Abstract, by Per Kirkeby, Denmark — A1314

1995 **Photo. & Engr.** ***Perf. 12x13***

2454 A1311 6.70fr multicolored 2.75 1.75

Engr.

Perf. 13x12

2455 A1312 6.70fr slate & blue 2.75 .70

Litho.

Perf. 14

2456 A1313 6.70fr multicolored 2.75 .70

Photo.

Perf. 13

2457 A1314 6.70fr multicolored 2.75 .70

Nos. 2454-2457 (4) 11.00 3.85

Issued: #2454, 2/25/95; #2455, 5/12/95; #2456, 6/10/95; #2457, 9/23/95.

Tourism Series

Stenay Malt Works A1315

Remiremont, Vosges — A1316

Nyons Bridge, Drome A1317

Barbizon, Home of Landscape Artists A1318

1995, Feb. 25 **Engr.** ***Perf. 13x12½***

2458 A1315 2.80fr ol & dk grn 1.25 .30

2459 A1316 2.80fr brn, grn & bl 1.25 .30

Perf. 12½x13

2460 A1317 4.40fr multicolored 1.90 .45

Photo.

Perf. 13½

2461 A1318 4.40fr multicolored 1.75 .45

Nos. 2458-2461 (4) 6.15 1.50

Issued: #2458, 2/25/95; #2459, 5/13/95; #2460, 5/20/95; #2461, 9/30/95.

A1319

John J. Audubon (1785-1851) A1320

Designs: No. 2462, Snowy egret. No. 2463, Band-tailed pigeon. 4.30fr, Common tern. 4.40fr, Brown-colored rough-legged buzzard.

1995, Feb. 25 **Photo.** ***Perf. 12½x12***

2462 A1319 2.80fr multicolored 1.25 .30

2463 A1320 2.80fr multicolored 1.25 .30

2464 A1319 4.30fr multicolored 1.90 .50

2465 A1320 4.40fr multicolored 1.90 .50

a. Souvenir sheet of 4, #2462-2465, perf. 13 6.25 1.65

Nos. 2462-2465 (4) 6.30 1.60

Stamp Day A1321

1995, Mar. 4 **Engr.** ***Perf. 13***

2466 A1321 2.80fr multicolored 1.25 .30

2467 A1321 2.80fr +60c multi 1.40 1.40

a. Booklet pane, 4 #2466, 3 #2467+label 9.25

Complete booklet, #2467 9.25

No. 2466 issued only in booklets.

Work Councils, 50th Anniv. — A1322

1995, Mar. 7 **Engr.** ***Perf. 13***

2468 A1322 2.80fr dk bl, brn & sky bl 1.25 .30

Advanced Institute of Electricity, Cent. A1323

1995, Mar. 11 **Photo.**

2469 A1323 3.70fr multicolored 1.65 .40

Institute of Oriental Languages, Bicent. A1324

1995, Mar. 25 **Photo.** ***Perf. 13***

2470 A1324 2.80fr multicolored 1.25 .30

Jean Giono (1895-1970), Writer — A1325

1995, Mar. 25 **Engr.**

2471 A1325 3.70fr multicolored 1.65 .40

Iron and Steel Industry in Lorraine — A1326

1995, Apr. 1 ***Perf. 13x12***

2472 A1326 2.80fr multicolored 1.25 .30

End of World War II, 50th Anniv. A1327

Europa: 2.80fr, Barbed wire, laurel wreath. 3.70fr, Broken sword, emblem of European Union.

1995, Apr. 29 Photo. *Perf. 13*

2473 A1327 2.80fr multicolored 1.00 .35

2474 A1327 3.70fr multicolored 1.25 .65

Forestry Profession, Ardennes — A1328

1995, May 2 Engr. *Perf. 12½x13*

2475 A1328 4.40fr multicolored 1.90 .50

End of World War II, 50th Anniv. A1329

1995, May 8 Photo. *Perf. 13*

2476 A1329 2.80fr multicolored 1.25 .30

Natl. Assembly — A1330

1995, May 13 Photo. *Perf. 13x12½*

2477 A1330 2.80fr multicolored 1.25 .30

French's People's Relief Assoc., 50th Anniv. A1331

1995, May 20 Engr. *Perf. 12½x13*

2478 A1331 2.80fr multicolored 1.25 .30

Scenes of France — A1332

#2479, Forest, Vosges. #2480, Massif, Brittany. #2481, Wetlands, cattle, Camargue. #2482, Volcanoes, Auvergne.

1995, May 27 *Perf. 13*

2479 A1332 2.40fr green 1.00 .25

2480 A1332 2.40fr green 1.00 .25

2481 A1332 2.80fr red 1.25 .30

2482 A1332 2.80fr red 1.25 .30

Nos. 2479-2482 (4) 4.50 1.10

Ariane Rocket on Launch Pad, French Guiana — A1333

1995, June 1 Engr. *Perf. 12½x13*

2483 A1333 2.80fr bl, grn & red 1.25 .30

Compare with No. 2254.

A1334

A1335

1995, June 2 Engr. *Perf. 13*

2484 A1334 2.80fr multicolored 1.25 .30

68th Congress of French Federation of Philatelic Organizations, Orleans.

1995, June 3

2485 A1335 4.40fr Town of Correze 1.90 .45

A1336

A1337

Fables of Jean de la Fontaine (1621-95): No. 2486, The Grasshopper and The Ant. No. 2487, The Frog Who Could Make Himself Larger than an Ox. No. 2488, The Wolf and the Lamb. No. 2489, The Crow and the Fox. No. 2490, The Cat, the Weasel, and the Small Rabbit. No. 2491, The Tortoise and the Hare.

1995, June 24 Photo. *Perf. 13*

2486 A1336 2.80fr multicolored 1.25 .30

2487 A1336 2.80fr multicolored 1.25 .30

2488 A1336 2.80fr multicolored 1.25 .30

2489 A1336 2.80fr multicolored 1.25 .30

2490 A1336 2.80fr multicolored 1.25 .30

2491 A1336 2.80fr multicolored 1.25 .30

a. Strip, #2486-2491 + 2 labels 7.50 2.00

1995, July 9 Photo. *Perf. 13*

2492 A1337 2.80fr multicolored 1.25 .30

Velodrome d'Hiver raid.

André Maginot (1877-1932), Creator of Maginot Line — A1338

1995, Sept. 9 Engr. *Perf. 13*

2493 A1338 2.80fr multicolored 1.25 .30

Women's Grand Masonic Lodge of France, 50th Anniv. — A1339

1995, Sept. 16 *Perf. 13x12½*

2494 A1339 2.80fr multicolored 1.25 .30

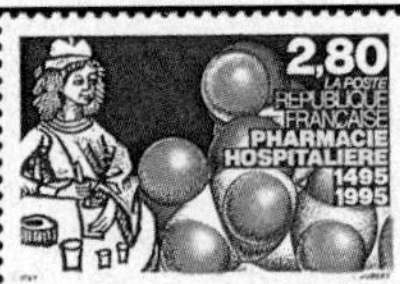

Hospital Pharmacies, 500th Anniv. — A1340

1995, Sept. 23 *Perf. 12½x13*

2495 A1340 2.80fr multicolored 1.25 .30

Natl. School of Administration, 50th Anniv. — A1341

1995, Oct. 5 Photo. *Perf. 13*

2496 A1341 2.80fr multicolored 1.25 .30

The Cradle, by Berthe Morisot (1841-95) A1342

1995, Oct. 7 Litho. *Perf. 13½x14*

2497 A1342 6.70fr multicolored 2.75 .70

The French Institute, Bicent. — A1343

1995, Oct. 14 Engr. *Perf. 12½x13*

2498 A1343 2.80fr blk, grn & red 1.25 .30

Automobile Club of France, Cent. A1344

1995, Nov. 4 Engr. *Perf. 13x12½*

2499 A1344 4.40fr blk, bl & red 1.80 .45

UN, 50th Anniv. A1345

1995, Nov. 16 Photo. *Perf. 13*

2500 A1345 4.30fr multicolored 1.75 .40

Francis Jammes (1868-1938), Poet — A1346

1995, Dec. 2 Engr. *Perf. 13*

2501 A1346 3.70fr black & blue 1.50 .40

A1347

A1348

1995, Dec. 9 Litho. & Engr.

2502 A1347 2.80fr Evry Cathedral 1.25 .30

1995, Dec. 12 Photo. *Perf. 13*

2503 A1348 2.80fr multicolored 1.25 .30

1998 World Cup Soccer Championships, France.

Art Series

Abstract, by Lucien Wercollier — A1349

Design: No. 2505, The Netherlands (Horizon), abstract photograph, by Jan Dibbets.

1996 *Perf. 13x12½*

2504 A1349 6.70fr multicolored 2.75 .70

2505 A1349 6.70fr multicolored 2.75 .70

Issued: #2504, 1/20; #2505, 2/10.

Arawak Civilization, Saint Martin — A1350

Design: 2.80fr, Dog figurine, 550 B.C.

1996, Feb. 10 Engr. *Perf. 13*

2506 A1350 2.80fr multicolored 1.25 .30

The Augustus Bridge over the Nera River, by Camille Corot (1796-1875) — A1351

1996, Mar. 2 Litho. *Perf. 13*

2507 A1351 6.70fr multicolored 2.75 .70

St. Patrick
A1352

1996, Mar. 16 **Photo.** ***Perf. 13***
2508 A1352 2.80fr multicolored 1.25 .30

The Sower, 1903 — A1353

1996, Mar. 16 **Litho. & Engr.**
2509 A1353 2.80fr multicolored 1.25 .30
2510 A1353 2.80fr +60c multi 1.40 .35
a. Booklet pane, 4 #2509, 3 #2510 + label 9.25
Complete booklet, #2510a 9.25

Stamp Day.

Jacques Rueff (1896-1978), Economist — A1354

1996, Mar. 23 **Engr.** ***Perf. 13x12½***
2511 A1354 2.80fr multicolored 1.25 .30

René Descartes (1596-1650)
A1355

1996, Mar. 30 **Engr.** ***Perf. 12½x13***
2512 A1355 4.40fr red 1.75 .40

Gas & Electric Industries, 50th Anniv.
A1356

1996, Apr. 6 **Photo.** ***Perf. 13***
2513 A1356 3fr multicolored 1.20 .30

Natl. Parks
A1357

1996, Apr. 20
2514 A1357 3fr Cévennes 1.20 .30
2515 A1357 4.40fr Vanoise 1.75 .40
2516 A1357 4.40fr Mercantour 1.75 .40
Nos. 2514-2516 (3) 4.70 1.10

See Nos. 2569-2572.

Leaf Type of 1994

1996, Mar. **Litho.** ***Perf. 13***
2517 A1298 1.87fr Ash .80 .20
2518 A1298 2.18fr Beech .90 .25
2519 A1298 4.66fr Walnut 1.90 .50
2520 A1298 7.11fr Elm 3.00 .75
Nos. 2517-2520 (4) 6.60 1.70

Nos. 2517-2520 are known only precanceled. Values for precanceled stamps in first column are for those which have not been through the post and have original gum. Values in second column are for postally used, gumless stamps.

Madame Marie de Sévigné (1626-96), Writer — A1358

1996, Apr. 27 **Photo.** ***Perf. 13***
2521 A1358 3fr multicolored 1.50 .75

Europa.

Natl. Institute of Agronomy Research, 50th Anniv.
A1359

1996, May 4 **Photo.** ***Perf. 13***
2522 A1359 3.80fr multicolored 1.60 .40

Joan of Arc's House, Domremy-La-Pucelle — A1360

1996, May 11
2523 A1360 4.50fr multicolored 1.90 .40

RAMOGE Agreement Between France, Italy, Monaco, 20th Anniv.
A1361

1996, May 14 **Photo. & Engr.**
2524 A1361 3fr multicolored 1.25 .30

See Monaco No. 1998, Italy No. 2077.

69th Congress of Federation of Philatelic Assoc., Clermont-Ferrand — A1362

1996, May 24 **Engr.** ***Perf. 13***
2525 A1362 3fr brn, red & grn 1.25 .30

Tourism Series

Bitche, Moselle
A1363

Iles Sanguinaires, Ajaccio, Southern Corsica — A1364

Thoronet Abbey, Var
A1365

Chambéry Cathedral, Savoie
A1366

1996 **Engr.** ***Perf. 12½x13***
2526 A1363 3fr multicolored 1.25 .30
2527 A1364 3fr multicolored 1.25 .30

Perf. 13x12½
2528 A1365 3.80fr brn & claret 1.60 .40

Photo.
Perf. 13
2529 A1366 4.50fr multicolored 1.90 .45

Issued: #2526, 5/25/96; #2527, 6/1/96; 3.80fr, 7/6/96; 4.50fr, 6/8/96.

1998 World Cup Soccer Championships, France — A1367

Various stylized soccer plays, name of host city in France.

1996, June 1 **Photo.** ***Perf. 13***
2530 A1367 3fr Lens 1.25 .30
2531 A1367 3fr Toulouse 1.25 .30
2532 A1367 3fr Saint-Etienne 1.25 .30
2533 A1367 3fr Montpellier 1.25 .30
Nos. 2530-2533 (4) 5.00 1.20

See Nos. 2584-2587, 2623-2624, sheet of 10, #2624a.

Art Series

Gallo-Roman Bronze Statue of Horse, Neuvy-en-Sullias, Loiret — A1368

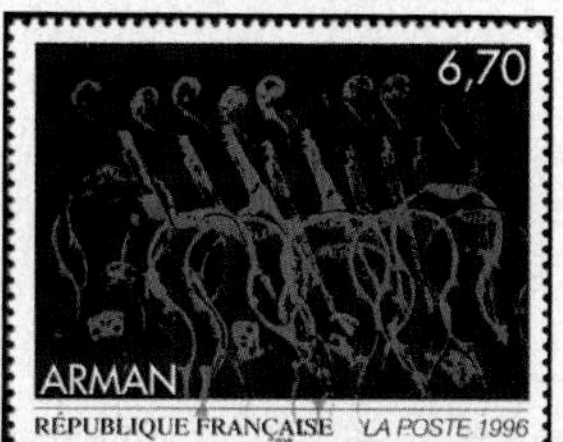

Imprints of Cello Fragments, by Arman — A1369

1996 **Engr.** ***Perf. 13***
2534 A1368 6.70fr multicolored 2.80 .70

Photo.
2535 A1369 6.70fr multicolored 2.80 .70

Issued: #2534, 6/8/96; #2535, 9/21/96.

A1371

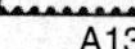

A1372

1996, June 15 **Photo.** ***Perf. 13***
2537 A1371 3fr multicolored 1.25 .30

Modern Olympic Games, cent.

1996, June 15 **Engr.** ***Perf. 12½x13***
2538 A1372 4.40fr deep purple 1.90 .45

Jacques Marette (1922-84), Member of Parliament.

A1373

A1374

1996, June 29 **Photo.** ***Perf. 13***
2539 A1373 3fr multicolored 1.25 .30

Train between Ajaccio and Vizzavona, cent.

1996, Sept. 6 **Engr.** ***Perf. 13x12½***
2540 A1374 3fr dark blue & yel 1.25 .30

Notre Dame de Fourvière Basilica, Lyon, cent.

Baptism of Clovis, 1500th Anniv.
A1375

1996, Sept. 14 ***Perf. 13***
2541 A1375 3fr multicolored 1.25 .30

Henri IV High School, Bicent. — A1376

1996, Oct. 12 **Engr.** ***Perf. 12½x13***
2542 A1376 4.50fr brown & blue 1.80 .45

UNICEF, 50th Anniv.
A1377

1996, Oct. 19 **Photo.** ***Perf. 13***
2543 A1377 4.50fr multicolored 1.80 .45

Economic and Social Council, 50th Anniv. — A1378

1996, Oct. 26 **Engr.** ***Perf. 13***
2544 A1378 3fr red, black & blue 1.20 .30

UNESCO, 50th Anniv. A1379

1996, Nov. 2 **Litho.** ***Perf. 13***
2545 A1379 3.80fr multicolored 1.50 .40

A1380 A1381

1996, Nov. 7 **Photo.** ***Perf. 13***
2546 A1380 3fr multicolored 1.20 .30

Autumn Stamp Show, 50th anniv.

1996, Nov. 16
2547 A1381 3fr multicolored 1.20 .30

Creation of French Overseas Departments, 50th anniv.

André Malraux (1901-76), Writer A1382

1996, Nov. 23 **Engr.** ***Perf. 13***
2548 A1382 3fr deep green black 1.20 .30

French School in Athens, 150th Anniv. A1383

1996, Nov. 23 **Photo.**
2549 A1383 3fr multicolored 1.20 .30

Cannes Film Festival, 50th Anniv. A1384

1996, Nov. 30
2550 A1384 3fr multicolored 1.20 .30

New National Library of France A1385

1996, Dec. 14
2551 A1385 3fr multicolored 1.20 .30

A1386 A1387

1997, Jan. 4
2552 A1386 3fr multicolored 1.20 .30

Francois Mitterrand (1916-96).

1997, Jan. 24 **Photo.** ***Perf. 13***
2553 A1387 3fr multicolored 1.20 .30

Participatory innovation.

Georges Pompidou Natl. Center of Art and Culture, 20th Anniv. A1388

1997, Jan. 31 **Engr.** ***Perf. 12½x13***
2554 A1388 3fr multicolored 1.20 .30

Happy Holiday A1389

1997, Feb. 8 **Photo.** ***Perf. 13***
2555 A1389 3fr shown 1.20 .30
2556 A1389 3fr Happy birthday 1.20 .30

Natl. School of Bridges and Highways, 250th Anniv. A1390

Photo. & Engr.

1997, Feb. 14 ***Perf. 12½x13***
2557 A1390 3fr multicolored 1.20 .30

Saint-Laurent-du-Maroni, French Guiana — A1391

Photo. & Engr.

1997, Feb. 22 ***Perf. 12½x13***
2558 A1391 3fr multicolored 1.20 .30

Art Series

Church Fresco, Tavant A1392

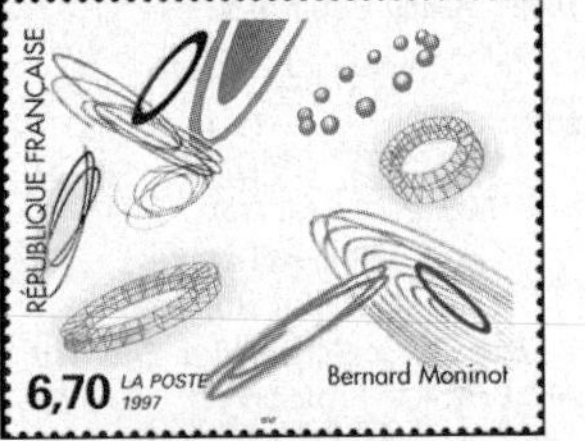

Painting by Bernard Moninot — A1393

The Thumb, Polished Bronze, by César A1394

Grapes and Pomegranates, by Jean Baptiste Chardin — A1395

1997 **Engr.** ***Perf. 13***
2559 A1392 6.70fr multicolored 2.75 .70

Photo.

2560 A1393 6.70fr multicolored 2.75 .70
2561 A1394 6.70fr multicolored 2.40 .50
2562 A1395 6.70fr multicolored 2.40 .50
Nos. 2559-2562 (4) 10.30 2.40

Issued: #2559, 3/1; #2560, 3/29; #2561, 9/13; #2562, 9/27.

Tourism Series

Millau — A1396 Guimiliau Church Close — A1398

Fresco, Saint Eutrope des Salles-Lavauguyon — A1397

Sablé-Sur-Sarthe — A1399

1997 **Engr.** ***Perf. 12½x13***
2563 A1396 3fr grn & dk bl grn 1.20 .30

Perf. 13

2564 A1397 4.50fr multicolored 1.80 .45
2565 A1398 3fr multicolored 1.20 .30

Perf. 12½x13

2566 A1399 3fr multicolored 1.10 .20
Nos. 2563-2566 (4) 5.30 1.25

Issued: #2563, 3/15; #2564, 6/14; #2565, 7/12; #2566, 9/20.

Vignette of Type A17 — A1400

Litho. & Engr.

1997, Mar. 15 ***Perf. 13½x13***
2567 A1400 3fr multicolored 1.40 .35
2568 A1400 3fr +60c multi 1.65 .40
a. Booklet pane, 4 #2567, 3 #2568 + label 10.50
Complete booklet, #2568a 10.50

Stamp Day.
No. 2567 issued only in booklets.

National Parks Type of 1996

1997, Apr. 12 **Photo.** ***Perf. 13***
2569 A1357 3fr Parc des Ecrins 1.25 .30
2570 A1357 3fr Guadeloupe Park 1.25 .30
2571 A1357 4.50fr Parc des Pyrénées 1.75 .45
2572 A1357 4.50fr Port-Cros Park 1.75 .45
Nos. 2569-2572 (4) 6.00 1.50

Puss-in-Boots A1401

1997, Apr. 26 **Engr.** ***Perf. 13***
2573 A1401 3fr blue 1.00 .60

Europa.

Philexjeunes '97, Nantes — A1402

1997, May 2 **Litho.** ***Perf. 13***
2574 A1402 3fr multicolored 1.25 .30

Cartoon Journey of a Letter A1403

"Envelope": No. 2575, Writing letter. No. 2576, Climbing ladder to go into letter box. No. 2577, On wheels. No. 2578, Following postman carrying another "Envelope." No. 2579, Held by girl. No. 2580, At feet of girl reading long letter.

1997, May 8 **Photo.** ***Perf. 13***
2575 A1403 3fr multicolored 1.25 .30
2576 A1403 3fr multicolored 1.25 .30
2577 A1403 3fr multicolored 1.25 .30
2578 A1403 3fr multicolored 1.25 .30
2579 A1403 3fr multicolored 1.25 .30
2580 A1403 3fr multicolored 1.25 .30
a. Strip of 6, #2575-2580 + label 7.50 1.80

Self-Adhesive

Serpentine Die Cut 11

2580B A1403 3fr like #2575 1.25 .30
2580C A1403 3fr like #2576 1.25 .30
2580D A1403 3fr like #2577 1.25 .30

2580E A1403 3fr like #2578 1.25 .30
2580F A1403 3fr like #2579 1.25 .30
2580G A1403 3fr like #2580 1.25 .30
h. Booklet pane, 2 each #2580B-2580G 15.00

By its nature No. 2580h is a complete booklet. The peelable paper backing serves as a booklet cover.

See Nos. 2648-2659.

Honoring French Soldiers in North Africa (1952-62) A1404

1997, May 10 Litho. *Perf. 13*
2581 A1404 3fr multicolored 1.25 .30

French Federation of Philatelic Associations, 70th Congress, Versailles — A1405

Illustration reduced.

1997, May 17 Photo. *Perf. 13*
2582 A1405 3fr multicolored 1.25 .30

Printed with se-tenant label.

Château de Plessis-Bourré, Maine and Loire Rivers — A1406

1997, May 24 Litho. & Engr.
2583 A1406 4.40fr multicolored 1.75 .45

1998 World Cup Soccer Championships Type

Stylized action scenes, name of host city in France.

1997, May 31 Photo. *Perf. 13½*
2584 A1367 3fr Lyon 1.25 .30
2585 A1367 3fr Marseilles 1.25 .30
2586 A1367 3fr Nantes 1.25 .30
2587 A1367 3fr Paris 1.25 .30
Nos. 2584-2587 (4) 5.00 1.20

Saint Martin of Tours (316-97) Apostle of the Gauls A1408

1997, July 5 Engr. *Perf. 13*
2588 A1408 4.50fr multicolored 1.80 .45

Marianne — A1409

1997, July 14 Engr. *Perf. 13*

2589	A1409	10c brown	.20	.20
2590	A1409	20c brt blue grn	.20	.20
2591	A1409	50c purple	.20	.20
2592	A1409	1fr bright org	.25	.20
2593	A1409	2fr bright blue	.50	.25
2594	A1409	2.70fr bright grn	.70	.20
2595	A1409	(3fr) red	1.10	.25
2596	A1409	3.50fr apple grn	.90	.25
2597	A1409	3.80fr blue	1.00	.25
2598	A1409	4.20fr dark org	1.10	.25
2599	A1409	4.40fr blue	1.10	.35
2600	A1409	4.50fr bright pink	1.25	.25
2601	A1409	5fr brt grn blue	1.40	.25
2602	A1409	6.70fr dark green	1.75	.30
a.		Souvenir sheet, #2594-2600, 2602	12.50	12.50
2603	A1409	10fr violet	2.75	.30
a.		Souvenir sheet, #2589-2593, 2610, 2603	7.25	7.25
		Nos. 2589-2603 (15)	14.40	3.70

Self-Adhesive Booklet Stamps

Die Cut x Serpentine Die Cut 7

2603B A1409 1fr brt org .25 .20
c. Booklet pane, #2603B, 3 #2604 2.75
Booklet, 2 #2603Bc 5.50
2604 A1409 (3fr) red 1.10 .25
a. Booklet pane of 10 11.00

Coil Stamps

Perf. 13 Horiz.

2604B A1409 2.70fr bright grn .70 .20
2605 A1409 (3fr) red 1.10 .25

Nos. 2595, 2604-2605 were valued at 3fr on day of issue.

Issued: Nos. 2602a, 2603a, 11/12/01. No. 2603B, 9/1/97.

See Nos. 2835-2835C.

1997 World Rowing Championships, Savoie — A1410

1997, Aug. 30 Engr. *Perf. 13x12½*
2606 A1410 3fr blue & magenta 1.10 .20

Basque Corsairs A1411

1997, Sept. 13 *Perf. 13*
2607 A1411 3fr multicolored 1.10 .20

Saint-Maurice Basilica, Epinal — A1412

1997, Sept. 20 *Perf. 13x12½*
2608 A1412 3fr multicolored 1.10 .20

Fresh Fish Merchants, Port of Boulogne A1413

1997, Sept. 26 *Perf. 13*
2609 A1413 3fr multicolored 1.10 .20

Japan Year — A1414

1997, Oct. 4 Engr. *Perf. 13*
2610 A1414 4.90fr multicolored 1.75 .35

1997 World Judo Championships — A1415

1997, Oct. 9 Photo. *Perf. 13*
2611 A1415 3fr multicolored 1.10 .20

Sceaux Estate, Hauts-de-Seine — A1416

1997, Oct. 11
2612 A1416 3fr multicolored 1.10 .20

Saar-Lorraine-Luxembourg Summit — A1417

1997, Oct. 16 Photo. *Perf. 13*
2613 A1417 3fr multicolored 1.10 .20

See Germany #1982, Luxembourg #972.

College of France A1418

1997, Oct. 18 Engr.
2614 A1418 4.40fr multicolored 1.50 .30

Quality — A1419

1997, Oct. 18 Photo.
2615 A1419 4.50fr multicolored 1.50 .30

A1420

Season's Greetings A1421

1997 Photo. *Perf. 13*
2616 A1420 3fr Cat & mouse 1.10 .20

Photo. & Embossed

2617 A1421 3fr Mailman 1.10 .20

Issued: No. 2616, 11/8; No. 2617, 11/22.

Protection of Abused Children — A1422

1997, Nov. 20 Photo.
2618 A1422 3fr multicolored 1.10 .20

Marshal Jacques Leclerc (Philippe de Haute Cloque) (1902-47) A1423

1997, Nov. 28 Photo. *Perf. 13*
2619 A1423 3fr multicolored 1.10 .20

Philexfrance '99, World Stamp Exposition — A1424

1997, Dec. 6 Engr.
2620 A1424 3fr red & blue 1.10 .20

Abbey of Moutier D'Ahun, Creuse A1425

1997, Dec. 13
2621 A1425 4.40fr multicolored 1.75 .35

Michel Debré (1912-96), Politician A1426

1998, Jan. 15 Photo.
2622 A1426 3fr multicolored 1.00 .20

1998 World Cup Soccer Championships Type

Stylized action scenes, name of host city in France.

1998, Jan. 24 *Perf. 13½*
2623 A1367 3fr Saint-Denis 1.10 .20
2624 A1367 3fr Bordeaux 1.10 .20
a. Sheet of 10, #2530-2533, #2584-2587, #2623-2624 + label 12.50 12.50

National Assembly, Bicent. — A1427

1998, Jan. 24 *Perf. 13*
2625 A1427 3fr multicolored 1.10 .20

Valentine's Day A1428

1998, Jan. 31

2626 A1428 3fr multicolored 1.10 .20

Office of Mediator of the Republic, 25th Anniv. A1429

1998, Feb. 5

2627 A1429 3fr multicolored 1.10 .20

A1430

1998, Feb. 28 Photo. *Perf. 12½*

2628 A1430 3fr multicolored 1.10 .25

Self-Adhesive

Serpentine Die Cut

2629 A1430 3fr like #2628 1.10 .25
 a. Booklet pane of 10 11.00
 b. Sheet of 1 + 7 labels 3.00

1998 World Cup Soccer Championships, France.

The peelable paper backing of No. 2629a serves as a booklet cover.

See No. 2665.

A1431

1998, Feb. 21 Engr. *Perf. 13½x13*

2630 A1431 3fr Detail of design A16 1.10 .25

2631 A1431 3fr +60c like #2630 1.30 .30
 a. Booklet pane, 4 #2630, 3 #2631 + label 8.30
 Complete booklet, #2631a 8.30

Stamp Day. No. 2630 issued only in booklets.

A1432

1998, Feb. 28 Engr. *Perf. 13*

2632 A1432 4.50fr blue 1.75 .35

Father Franz Stock (1904-48), prison chaplain.

Happy Birthday A1433

1998, Mar. 13 Photo. *Perf. 13x13½*

2633 A1433 3fr multicolored 1.10 .25

Union of Mulhouse with France, Bicent. A1434

1998, Mar. 14

2634 A1434 3fr multicolored 1.10 .25

Citeaux Abbey, 900th Anniv. A1435

1998, Mar. 14 Engr. *Perf. 13*

2635 A1435 3fr multicolored 1.10 .25

Sous-Préfecture Hotel, Saint-Pierre, Réunion — A1436

1998, Apr. 4 Engr. *Perf. 13*

2636 A1436 3fr multicolored 1.10 .25

Réunion's architectural heritage.

"The Return," by René Magritte — A1437

1998, Apr. 18 Photo.

2637 A1437 3fr multicolored 1.10 .25

See Belgium No. 1691.

Edict of Nantes, 400th Anniv. A1438

1998, Apr. 18 Litho.

2638 A1438 4.50fr Henry IV 1.75 .35

Art Series

Detail from "Entry of the Crusaders into Constantinople," by Delacroix (1798-1863) — A1439

Le Printemps, by Pablo Picasso (1881-1973) — A1440

Neuf Moules Malic, by Marcel Duchamp (1887-1968) — A1441

Vision After the Sermon, by Paul Gauguin (1848-1903) — A1442

1998 Engr. *Perf. 12x13*

2639 A1439 6.70fr multicolored 2.50 .50

Litho.

Perf. 13

2640 A1440 6.70fr multicolored 2.50 .50

Photo.

2641 A1441 6.70fr multicolored 2.50 .50

2642 A1442 6.70fr multicolored 2.50 .50

Issued: #2639, 4/25; #2640, 5/15; #2641, 10/17; #2642, 12/5.

Abolition of Slavery, 150th Anniv. A1443

1998, Apr. 25 Litho. *Perf. 13*

2643 A1443 3fr multicolored 1.10 .25

Tourism Series

Le Gois Causeway, Island of Noirmoutier, Vendée — A1444

Bay of Somme, Picardy — A1445

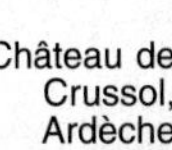

Château de Crussol, Ardèche A1446

Collegiate Church of Mantes — A1447

1998, May 2 Photo.

2644 A1444 3fr multicolored 1.10 .25

2645 A1445 3fr multicolored 1.10 .25

Engr.

2646 A1446 3fr multicolored 1.10 .25

2647 A1447 4.40fr multicolored 1.60 .35
 Nos. 2644-2647 (4) 4.90 1.10

Issued: #2644, 5/2; #2645, 6/27; #2646, 7/4; #2647, 9/19.

Journey of a Letter Type

Historic "letters:" No. 2648, Dove carrying letter, Noah's Ark. No. 2649, Egyptian writing letter on papyrus. No. 2650, Soldier running to Athens with letter to victory at Marathon. No. 2651, Knight carrying letter on horseback. No. 2652, Writing letters with quill and ink. No. 2653, Astronaut carrrying letter in space from earth to the moon.

1998, May 9 Photo. *Perf. 13x13½*

2648 A1403 3fr multicolored 1.10 .25

2649 A1403 3fr multicolored 1.10 .25

2650 A1403 3fr multicolored 1.10 .25

2651 A1403 3fr multicolored 1.10 .25

2652 A1403 3fr multicolored 1.10 .25

2653 A1403 3fr multicolored 1.10 .25
 a. Strip, #2648-2653 + label 6.75 6.75

Booklet Stamps

Self-Adhesive

Serpentine Die Cut 11

2654 A1403 3fr like #2648 1.10 .25

2655 A1403 3fr like #2649 1.10 .25

2656 A1403 3fr like #2650 1.10 .25

2657 A1403 3fr like #2651 1.10 .25

2658 A1403 3fr like #2652 1.10 .25

2659 A1403 3fr like #2653 1.10 .25
 a. Bklt. pane, 2 ea #2654-2659 13.50

By its nature No. 2659a is a complete booklet. The peelable paper backing serves as a booklet cover.

League of Human Rights, Cent. — A1448

1998, May 9 *Perf. 13*

2660 A1448 4.40fr multicolored 1.60 .35

Henri Collet (1885-1951), Composer — A1449

1998, May 15 Engr. *Perf. 12x13*

2661 A1449 4.50fr black, gray & buff 1.75 .35

French Federation of Philatelic Assoc., 71st Congress, Dunkirk — A1450

Photo. & Engr.

1998, May 29 *Perf. 13*

2662 A1450 3fr multicolored 1.10 .25

Mont-Saint-Michel — A1451

1998, June 6 Photo. *Perf. 13*

2663 A1451 3fr multicolored 1.10 .50

Natl. Music Festival — A1452

1998, June 13

2664 A1452 3fr multicolored 1.10 .25

Europa.

1998 World Cup Soccer Championships Type with Added
Inscription, "Champion du Monde"

1998, July 12 Photo. *Perf. 12½*

2665 A1430 3fr multicolored 1.10 .25

Stéphane Mallarmé (1842-98), Poet A1453

Photo. & Engr.

1998, Sept. 5 *Perf. 13*

2666 A1453 4.40fr multicolored 1.60 .35

Flowers — A1453a

1998, Sept. 9 Litho. *Perf. 13*

2666A A1453a 1.87fr Liseron .70 .20
2666B A1453a 2.18fr Coquelicot .85 .20
2666C A1453a 4.66fr Violette 1.75 .45
2666D A1453a 7.11fr Bouton d'or 2.75 .65
Nos. 2666A-2666D (4) 6.05 1.50

Nos. 2666A-2666D are known only precanceled. See second note after #132.

A1454 A1455

1998, Sept. 12 Photo.

2667 A1454 3fr multicolored 1.10 .25

Aéro Club of France, cent.

1998, Oct. 23 Photo. *Perf. 13*

"The Little Prince," by Antoine de Saint-Exupéry (1900-44): a, Standing in uniform with sword, horiz. b, Seated on wall. c, "The Little Prince on Asteroid B-612." d, Pouring water from sprinkling can. e, Walking along cliff, fox, horiz.

2668 Strip of 5 + 2 labels 5.50 5.50
a.-e. A1455 3fr any single 1.10 .25
f. Souv. sheet, #2668a-2668e 9.00 9.00

Philexfrance '99. No. 2668f was released 9/12 and sold for 25fr.

Hall of Heavenly Peace, Imperial Palace, Beijing, China A1456

1998, Sept. 12 Photo. *Perf. 13x13½*

2669 A1456 3fr shown 1.10 .25
2670 A1456 4.90fr The Louvre, France 1.90 .35

See China People's Republic #2895-2896.

Garnier Palace, Home of the Paris Opera — A1457

1998, Sept. 19 Photo. *Perf. 13*

2671 A1457 4.50fr multicolored 1.75 .35

Horses A1458

1998, Sept. 27

2672 A1458 2.70fr Camargue 1.00 .20
2673 A1458 3fr Pottok 1.10 .25
2674 A1458 3fr French trotter 1.10 .25
2675 A1458 4.50fr Ardennais 1.75 .35
Nos. 2672-2675 (4) 4.95 1.05

Paris Auto Show, Cent. A1459

1998, Oct. 1 *Perf. 12*

2676 A1459 3fr multicolored 1.10 .25

5th Republic, 40th Anniv. A1460

1998, Oct. 3 Photo. *Perf. 13*

2677 A1460 3fr blue, gray & red 1.10 .25

Saint-Dié, Capital of Vosges Mountain Region — A1461

1998, Oct. 3 Engr. *Perf. 13*

2678 A1461 3fr Tower of Liberty 1.10 .30

End of World War I, 80th Anniv. A1462

1998, Oct. 17 Photo. *Perf. 13x13½*

2679 A1462 3fr multicolored 1.10 .25

Intl. Union for the Conservation of Nature and Natural Resources, 50th Anniv. — A1463

1998, Nov. 3 Litho.

2680 A1463 3fr multicolored 1.10 .25

New Year A1464

Christmas A1465

1998, Nov. 7 Photo. *Perf. 13*

Background Colors

2681 A1464 3fr deep blue 1.10 .25
2682 A1465 3fr green 1.10 .25
2683 A1464 3fr yellow 1.10 .25
2684 A1465 3fr red 1.10 .25
2685 A1464 3fr green 1.10 .25
a. Strip of 5, #2681-2685 5.50 5.50

Issued in sheets of 10 stamps. Location of "Bonne Annee" and "Meilleurs Voeux" varies.

Doctors Without Borders A1466

1998, Nov. 21 *Perf. 13x13½*

2686 A1466 3fr multicolored 1.10 .25

European Parliament, Strasbourg A1467

1998, Dec. 5 Photo. *Perf. 13*

2687 A1467 3fr multicolored 1.10 .25

Universal Declaration of Human Rights, 50th Anniv. A1468

#2688, Faces of people of various races, globe. #2689, René Cassin (1887-1976), principal author of Declaration, Eleanor Roosevelt (1884-1962), Chaillot Palace, Paris.

1998, Dec. 10 Litho. *Perf. 13*

2688 A1468 3fr multicolored 1.10 .25
2689 A1468 3fr multicolored 1.10 .25

Discovery of Radium, Cent., ZOE Reactor, 50th Anniv. A1469

1998, Dec. 15 Photo. *Perf. 13*

2690 A1469 3fr multicolored 1.10 .25

Introduction of the Euro — A1470

1999 Engr. *Perf. 13*

2691 A1470 3fr red & blue 1.10 .25

Booklet Stamps

Self-Adhesive

Die Cut x Serpentine Die Cut 7

2691A A1470 3fr red & blue 1.10 .25
b. Booklet pane of 10 11.00

Issued: No. 2691, 1/1/99. No. 2691A, 2/15/99. Values are shown in both Francs and Euros on Nos. 2691-2691A. No. 2691Ab is a complete booklet.

Euro currency did not circulate until 2002.

French Postage Stamps, 150th Anniv. A1471

1999, Jan. 1 Photo. *Perf. 13*

Booklet Stamps

2692 A1471 3fr black & red 1.75 1.25
2693 A1471 3fr red & black 1.10 .25
a. Booklet pane, #2692, 4 #2693 + label 6.50
Complete booklet, #2693a 6.50

No. 2692 has black denomination; No. 2693 has red denomination.

Stamp Day.

Public Assistance Hospital, Paris, 150th Anniv. A1472

1999, Jan. 9
2694 A1472 3fr multicolored 1.10 .25

Diplomatic Relations with Israel, 50th Anniv. — A1473

1999, Jan. 24
2695 A1473 4.40fr multicolored 1.60 .35

Festival Stamps A1474

1999, Feb. 6 **Photo.** ***Perf. 13***
2696 A1474 3fr Stars, "Je t'aime" 1.10 .25
2697 A1474 3fr Rose 1.10 .25

Booklet Stamps
Self-Adhesive
Die Cut Perf. 10

2698 A1474 3fr like #2696 1.10 .25
2699 A1474 3fr like #2697 1.10 .25
a. Bklt. pane, 5 ea #2698-2699 11.00

No. 2699a is a complete booklet.

Art Series

St. Luke the Evangelist, Sculpture by Jean Goujon (1510-66) A1475

Painting, "Waterlillies in Moonlight," by Claude Monet (1840-1926) — A1476

Stained Glass, Cathedral of Auch, by Arnauld de Moles, 16th Cent. A1477

Charles I, King of England, by Sir Anthony Van Dyck A1478

1999 **Engr.** ***Perf. 13***
2700 A1475 6.70fr multicolored 2.50 .25

Litho.

2701 A1476 6.70fr multicolored 2.50 .50

Engr.

2702 A1477 6.70fr multicolored 2.50 .50

Photo.
Perf. 13¼x13

2703 A1478 6.70fr multicolored 2.50 .50
Nos. 2700-2703 (4) 10.00 1.75

Issued: #2700, 2/13; #2701, 5/29; #2702, 6/19; #2703, 11/11.

National Census — A1479

1999, Feb. 20 **Photo.** ***Perf. 13½***
2704 A1479 3fr multicolored 1.10 .25

Cultural Heritage of Lebanon A1480

Mosaic illustrating transformation of Zeus into bull, Natl. Museum of Beirut.

1999, Feb. 27 ***Perf. 12½***
2705 A1480 4.40fr multicolored 1.60 .35

Asterix, by Albert Uderzo and Rene Goscinny A1481

1999, Mar. 6 **Photo.** ***Perf. 13¼***
2706 A1481 3fr multicolored 1.10 .25
a. Perf. 13¼x12¾ 1.10 .25

Booklet Stamp
Perf. 13¼x12¾

2707 A1481 3fr +60c like #2706 1.25 .25
b. Booklet pane, 4 #2706a, 3 #2707 + label 8.25
Complete booklet, #2707b 8.25

Souvenir Sheet

2707A A1481 3fr +60c like #2706 1.25 1.25

Stamp Day. Stamp design in #2707A continues into the margins.

Council of Europe, 50th Anniv. A1482

1999, Mar. 19
2708 A1482 3fr multicolored 1.10 .25

A1483

Announcements — A1483a

1999, Mar. 20 ***Perf. 13***
2709 A1483 3fr Marriage (Oui) 1.10 .25
2710 A1483 3fr It's a boy (C'est un garcon) 1.10 .25
2711 A1483 3fr It's a girl(C'est une fille) 1.10 .25
2712 A1483a 3fr Thank you 1.10 .25
Nos. 2709-2712 (4) 4.40 1.00

See Nos. 2721-2722.

Souvenir Sheet

PhilexFrance '99 — A1484

Works of art: a, Venus de Milo. b, Mona Lisa, by Da Vinci. c, Liberty Guiding the People, by Delacroix.

Litho. & Engr.

1999, Mar. 26 ***Perf. 13¼***
2713 A1484 Sheet of 3 17.00 17.00
a.-b. 5fr each 5.50 5.50
c. 10fr multicolored 5.50 5.50

No. 2713 sold for 50fr, with 30fr serving as a donation to the Assoc. for the Development of Philately.

Elections to the European Parliament A1485

1999, Mar. 27 **Photo.** ***Perf. 13***
2714 A1485 3fr multicolored 1.10 .25

Richard I, the Lion-Hearted (1157-1199), King of England — A1486

1999, Apr. 10 **Engr.** ***Perf. 13x12½***
2715 A1486 3fr multicolored 1.10 .35

Tourism Series

Dieppe A1487

Haut-Koenigsbourg Castle, Bas-Rhin — A1488

Birthpalce of Champollion, Figeac — A1489

Chateau, Arnac-Pompadour — A1490

Illustration reduced (A1488).

1999 **Engr.** ***Perf. 13½***
2716 A1487 3fr multicolored 1.10 .25

Litho. & Engr.
Perf. 13

2717 A1488 3fr multicolored 1.10 .25
2718 A1489 3fr multicolored 1.10 .25

Engr.

2719 A1490 3fr multicolored 1.10 .25
Nos. 2716-2719 (4) 4.40 1.00

Issued: #2716, 4/17; #2717, 5/15; #2718, 6/26; #2719, 7/10.

The Camargue Nature Preserve A1491

1999, Apr. 24 **Photo.** ***Perf. 13x13½***
2720 A1491 3fr multicolored 1.10 .60

Europa.

Announcements Type of 1999 and

A1492

1999, May 13 **Photo.** ***Perf. 13***
2721 A1483 3fr Nice Holiday (bonnes vacances) 1.10 .25
2722 A1483 3fr Happy Birthday (joyeux anniversaire) 1.10 .25
2723 A1492 3fr Long Live Vacations (Vive les vacances) 1.10 .25
Nos. 2721-2723 (3) 3.30 .75

Saint Pierre, Martinique A1493

1999, May 15

2724 A1493 3fr multicolored 1.10 .25

Detail of "Noctuelles" Dish, by Emile Gallé, School of Nancy Museum A1494

1999, May 22

2725 A1494 3fr multicolored 1.10 .25

Souvenir Sheet

World Old Roses Competition, Lyon — A1495

a, 4.50fr, Mme. Caroline Testout. b, 3fr, Mme. Alfred Carrière. c, 4.50fr, La France.

1999, May 28 ***Perf. 13½x13***

2726 A1495 Sheet of 3, #a.-c. 4.75 4.75

Court of Saint-Emilion, 800th Anniv. — A1496

1999, May 29 Engr. ***Perf. 13¼x13***

2727 A1496 3.80fr multicolored 1.50 .25

Hotel de la Monnaie, French Mint Headquarters — A1497

1999, June 5 Engr. ***Perf. 13***

2728 A1497 4.50fr brn org & bl 1.75 .35

A1498 A1499

1999, June 12 Photo. ***Perf. 13¼***

2729 A1498 3fr multicolored 1.10 .25

Countess of Segur (1799-1874), children's storyteller.

1999, June 19 ***Perf. 13***

2730 A1499 3fr Welcome 1.10 .25

René Caillié (1799-1838), Explorer of Africa — A1500

1999, June 26 Engr. ***Perf. 13¼***

2731 A1500 4.50fr multicolored 1.75 .35

1st French Postage Stamps, 150th Anniv. A1501

1999, July 2 Photo. ***Perf. 11¾x13***

2732 A1501 6.70fr multicolored 2.50 2.50

PhilexFrance '99, World Philatelic Exhibition.

No. 2732 was printed with a se-tenant label and contains a holographic image. Soaking in water may affect the hologram.

Celebrating the Year 2000 A1502

1999, July 5 Photo. ***Perf. 13***

2733 A1502 3fr multicolored 1.10 .25

Year 2000 Stamp Design Contest Winner — A1503

1999, July 6

2734 A1503 3fr multicolored 1.10 .25

Total Solar Eclipse, Aug. 11, 1999 A1504

1999, July 8 ***Perf. 12x12¼***

2735 A1504 3fr multicolored 1.10 .25

Gathering of Tall Ships, Rouen, July 9-18 A1505

Sailing ships: a, Simón Bolivar. b, Iskra. c, Statsraad Lehmkuhl. d, Asgard II. e, Belle Poule. f, Belem. g, Amerigo Vespucci. h, Sagres. i, Europa. j, Cuauhtemoc.

1999, July 10 Photo. ***Perf. 13***

2736 1fr Sheet of 10 4.00 4.00

a.-j. A1505 any single .40 .35

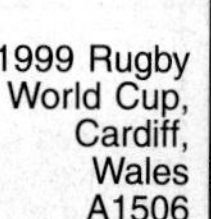

1999 Rugby World Cup, Cardiff, Wales A1506

1999, Sept. 11 Photo. ***Perf. 13¼***

2737 A1506 3fr multicolored 1.10 .25

a. Miniature sheet of 10 11.00

Value is for copy with surrounding selvage.

Frédéric Ozanam (1813-53), Historian — A1507

1999, Sept. 11 Engr. ***Perf. 13***

2738 A1507 4.50fr multicolored 1.75 .35

Emmaus Movement, 50th Anniv. A1508

1999, Sept. 26 Photo. ***Perf. 13***

2739 A1508 3fr multicolored 1.10 .25

Cats and Dogs — A1509

1999, Oct. 2 Photo. ***Perf. 13¼***

2740 A1509 2.70fr Chartreux cat 1.00 .25

2741 A1509 3fr European cat 1.10 .25

2742 A1509 3fr Pyrenean Mountain dog 1.10 .25

2743 A1509 4.50fr Brittany spaniel 1.75 .35

Nos. 2740-2743 (4) 4.95 1.10

Frédéric Chopin (1810-49), Composer A1510

1999, Oct. 17 Engr. ***Perf. 13¼***

2744 A1510 3.80fr multicolored 1.50 .25

See Poland No. 3484.

A1511

Best Wishes for Year 2000 A1512

1999, Nov. 20 Photo. ***Perf. 13x13¼***

2745 A1511 3fr multi 1.10 .25

2746 A1512 3fr multi 1.10 .25

No. 2746 was printed with se-tenant label.

Paris Metro, Cent. A1513

1999, Dec. 4 Photo. ***Perf. 13***

2747 A1513 3fr multi 1.10 .25

Council of State, Bicent. — A1514

1999, Dec. 11

2748 A1514 3fr multi 1.10 .25

Reconstruction of Lighthouses — A1515

2000, Jan. 1 Photo. ***Perf. 13x12¾***

2749 A1515 3fr multi 1.10 .25

Reconstruction of San Juan de Salvamento Lighthouse, Argentina and replication of its design at La Rochelle, France.

Hearts A1516

2000, Jan. 8 Photo. ***Perf. 13***

2750 A1516 3fr Snakes 1.10 .25

2751 A1516 3fr Face 1.10 .25

a. Souvenir sheet, 3 #2750, 2 #2751 5.50 5.50

Self-Adhesive Booklet Stamps

Serpentine Die-Cut

2752 A1516 3fr Like #2750 1.10 .25

2753 A1516 3fr Like #2751 1.10 .25

a. Bklt. pane, 5 ea #2752-2753 11.00

Values for Nos. 2750-2751 are for copies with surrounding selvage. No. 2753a is a complete booklet.

Bank of France, Bicent. — A1517

Prefectorial Corps, Bicent. — A1518

2000, Jan. 15 Litho. *Perf. 13*
2754 A1517 3fr multi 1.10 .25

2000, Feb. 17 Photo. *Perf. 13x12¼*
2755 A1518 3fr multi 1.10 .25

Art Series

Venus and the Graces Offering Gifts to a Young Girl, by Sandro Botticelli (1445-1510) — A1519

The Waltz, by Camille Claudel A1520

Visage Rouge, by Gaston Chaissac A1521

Carolignian Mosaic, Germigny-des-Prés — A1522

2000 Photo. *Perf. 13¼x13*
2756 A1519 6.70fr multi 2.50 .50
2757 A1520 6.70fr multi 2.50 .45
2758 A1521 6.70fr multi 2.50 .45
2759 A1522 6.70fr multi 2.50 .45

Issued: #2756, 2/25; #2757, 4/8; #2758, 9/23; 10/21.

Tourism Series

Carcassonne — A1523

Saint-Guilhem-Le-Désert — A1524

Gérardmer A1525

Abbey Church of Ottmarsheim — A1526

Illustration A1523 reduced.

2000 Photo. *Perf. 13*
2760 A1523 3fr multi 1.10 .25

Engr.
Perf. 13¼
2761 A1524 3fr multi 1.10 .25
2762 A1525 3fr multi 1.10 .25

Perf. 12¼x13
2763 A1526 3fr multi 1.10 .25
Nos. 2760-2763 (4) 4.40 1.00

Issued: #2760, 3/3; #2761, 4/8; #2762, 4/17; #2763, 6/17.

Tintin — A1527

2000, Mar. 11 Photo. *Perf. 13¼*
2764 A1527 3fr multi 1.10 .25
a. Perf. 13½x13 1.10 .25

Perf. 13½x13
2765 A1527 3fr + 60c multi 1.40 1.40
a. Booklet pane, 4 #2764a, 3 #2765 + label 8.50
Complete booklet, #2765a 8.50
b. Souvenir sheet of 1 1.40 1.40

Stamp Day.

Bretagne Parliament Building Restoration — A1528

2000, Mar. 25 Photo. *Perf. 13¼*
2766 A1528 3fr multi 1.10 .25

Madagascar Periwinkles — A1529

2000, Mar. 25 Litho. *Perf. 13x13¼*
2767 A1529 4.50fr multi 1.75 .35

Felicitations A1530

2000, Apr. 7 Photo. *Perf. 13x13¼*
2768 A1530 3fr multi 1.10 .25

The 20th Century — A1531

No. 2769: a, France as World Cup soccer champions, 1998, vert. b, Marcel Cerdan wins middleweight boxing title, 1948. c, Charles Lindbergh flies solo across Atlantic, 1927. d, Jean-Claude Killy wins three Winter Olympics gold medals, 1968, vert. e, Carl Lewis wins four Olympic gold medals, 1984, vert.
Illustration reduced.

Perf. 13¼x13 (vert. stamps), 13x13¼
2000, Apr. 15
2769 A1531 Sheet, 2 ea #a-e 11.00 11.00
a.-e. 3fr any single 1.10 .25

Top part of No. 2769 contains Nos. 2769a-2769e and is separated from bottom part of sheet by a row of rouletting.
See No. 2787, 2804, 2837, 2881, 2915.

Automobiles — A1532

No. 2770: a, Bugatti 35. b, Citroen Traction. c, Renault 4CV. d, Simca Chambord. e, Hispano-Suiza K6. f, Volkswagen Beetle. g, 1962 Cadillac. h, Peugeot 203. i, Citroen DS19. j, Ferrari 250 GTO.
Illustration reduced.

2000, May 5 *Perf. 13¼x13*
2770 A1532 Sheet of 10, #a.-j. 5.75 5.75
a.-e. 1fr any single .40 .20
f.-j. 2fr any single .75 .25

Europa, 2000
Common Design Type

2000, May 9 Photo. *Perf. 13¼*
2771 CD17 3fr multi 1.10 .60

Henry-Louis Duhamel du Monceau (1700-82), Agronomist — A1533

2000, May 13 Engr. *Perf. 13*
2772 A1533 4.50fr multi 1.75 .35

French Federation of Philatelic Associations, 73rd Congress, Nevers — A1534

2000, May 19 Engr. *Perf. 13¼*
2773 A1534 3fr multi 1.10 .25

A1535

A1536

2000, June 1 Photo. *Perf. 13¼x13*
2774 A1535 3fr Happy Vacation 1.10 .25

2000, June 3 Engr. *Perf. 13x12¼*
2775 A1536 3fr multi 1.10 .25

First Ascent of Annapurna, 50th anniv.

Nature A1537

2.70fr, Agrias sardanapalus butterfly. #2777, Giraffe. #2778, Allosaurus. 4.50fr, Tulipa lutea.

2000, June 17 Photo. *Perf. 13¼*
2776 A1537 2.70fr multi 1.00 .25
2777 A1537 3fr multi, vert. 1.10 .25
2778 A1537 3fr multi 1.10 .25
2779 A1537 4.50fr multi, vert 1.75 .30
a. Souvenir sheet, #2776-2779 5.00 5.00
Nos. 2776-2779 (4) 4.95 1.05

Antoine de Saint-Exupéry (1900-44), Aviator, Writer — A1538

2000, June 24 Photo. ***Perf. 13¼x13***
2780 A1538 3fr multi 1.10 .25

Yellow Train of Cerdagne, Cent. A1539

2000, July 14 ***Perf. 13x13¼***
2781 A1539 3fr multi 1.10 .25

Folklore A1540

2000, Aug. 12 Photo. ***Perf. 13***
2782 A1540 4.50fr multi 1.75 .30

2000 Summer Olympics, Sydney A1541

Designs: No. 2783, Cycling, fencing, relay racer. No. 2784, Relay racer, judo, diving.

2000, Sept. 9
2783 A1541 3fr multi 1.10 .20
2784 A1541 3fr multi 1.10 .20
a. Pair, #2783-2784 2.25 .40
b. Sheet, 5 #2784a + label 11.50

Olymphilex 2000, Sydney (#2784b).

Brother Alfred Stanke (1904-75) A1542

2000, Sept. 23 **Engr.**
2785 A1542 4.40fr multi 1.60 .30

S.O.S. Amitié, 40th Anniv. A1543

2000, Sept. 30 Litho. ***Perf. 13***
2786 A1543 3fr multi 1.10 .20

20th Century Type

No. 2787: a, Man on the Moon, 1969, vert. b, Paid vacations, 1936. c, Invention of washing machine, 1901, vert. d, Woman suffrage, 1944, vert. e, Universal Declaration of Human Rights, 1948.

Perf. 13¼x13 (vert. stamps), 13x13¼
2000, Sept. 30 **Photo.**
2787 A1531 Sheet, 2 each #a-e 11.00 11.00
a.-e. 3fr Any single 1.10 .25

The top and bottom parts of No. 2787 contains Nos. 2787a-2787e and are separated by a row of rouletting.

2001, Start of New Millennium A1544

2000, Oct. 14 Litho. ***Perf. 13***
2788 A1544 3fr multi 1.10 .25

The Lovers' Kiosk, by Peynet A1545

2000, Nov. 4 Engr. ***Perf. 13¼x13***
2789 A1545 3fr multi 1.10 .25

Endangered Birds — A1546

2000, Nov. 4 Photo. ***Perf. 13¼***
2790 A1546 3fr Kiwi 1.10 .25
2791 A1546 5.20fr Falcon 2.00 .35

See New Zealand Nos. 1688, 1694.

Start of the 3rd Millennium — A1547

Illustration reduced.

2000, Nov. 9 Photo. ***Perf. 13x13¼***
2792 A1547 3fr multi + label 1.10 .25

Issued in sheets of 10 stamps + 10 labels, which could be personalized for an extra fee.

Holiday Greetings A1548

2000, Nov. 11 ***Perf. 12¼x13***
2793 A1548 3fr Meilleurs voeux 1.10 .25
Perf. 13¼
2794 A1548 3fr Bonne année 1.10 .25

Union of Metallurgical & Mining Industries, Cent. — A1549

Engr. with Foil Application
2000, Dec. 9 ***Perf. 13x13¼***
2795 A1549 4.50fr multi 1.75 .30

World Handball Championships — A1550

2001, Jan. 20 Photo. ***Perf. 13¼***
2796 A1550 3fr multi 1.10 .25

Heart A1551

2001, Jan. 27
2797 A1551 3fr multi 1.10 .25
a. Souvenir sheet of 5 5.50 5.50

Value of No. 2797 is for copy with surrounding selvage.

Art Series

The Peasant Dance, by Pieter Breughel, the Elder — A1552

Hotel des Chevaliers de Saint-Jean-de-Jérusalem — A1553

Yvette Guilbert Singing "Linger, Longer, Loo," by Henri de Toulouse-Lautrec (1864-1901) — A1554

Honfleur at Low Tide, by Johan Barthold Jongkind — A1555

Engr., Photo (#2800), Litho (#2801)
2001 ***Perf. 13x13¼, 13¼x13 (#2800)***
2798 A1552 6.70fr multi 2.50 .50
2799 A1553 6.70fr multi 2.50 .50
2800 A1554 6.70fr multi 2.50 .50
2801 A1555 6.70fr multi 2.50 .50
Nos. 2798-2801 (4) 10.00 2.00

Issued: No. 2798, 2/3; No. 2799, 4/21; No. 2800, 9/8; No. 2801, 10/27.

Gaston Lagaffe, by André Franquin A1556

2001, Feb. 24 Photo. ***Perf. 13¼***
2802 A1556 3fr multi 1.10 .25
a. Perf. 13¼x13 1.10 .25
Perf. 13¼x13
2803 A1556 3fr +60c multi 1.40 1.40
a. Souvenir sheet of 1 1.40 1.40
b. Booklet pane, 5 #2802a, 3 #2803 9.75
Booklet, #2803b 10.00

Stamp Day.

20th Century Type of 2000

No. 2804 — Communications: a, Television. b, Compact disc. c, Advertisements, vert. d, Radio, vert. e, Portable telephone, vert.

Perf. 13¼x13 (vert. stamps), 13x13¼
2001, Mar. 17 **Photo.**
2804 A1531 Sheet, 2 each #a-e 9.00 9.00
a.-e. 3fr Any single 1.10 .25

Top part of No. 2804 contains Nos. 2804a-2804e and is separated from bottom part by a row of rouletting.

Announcements — A1557

Designs: No. 2805, It's a girl. No. 2806, It's a boy. No. 2807, Thank you. 4.50fr, Yes (marriage).

2001 ***Perf. 13***
Frame Color
2805 A1557 3fr brt pink 1.10 .25
a. Litho., stamp + label 1.75 1.75
2806 A1557 3fr brt blue 1.10 .25
a. Litho., stamp + label 1.75 1.75
2807 A1557 3fr brt yel grn 1.10 .25
a. Litho., stamp + label 1.75 1.75
2808 A1557 4.50fr orange 1.75 .30
Nos. 2805-2808 (4) 5.05 1.05

Issued: Nos. 2805-2808, 3/23; Nos. 2805a-2807a, 11/8.

Nos. 2805a-2807a were issued in sheets of 10 stamps and 10 labels that sold for 60fr on day of issue. The labels could be personalized. Frames on Nos. 2805 and 2806 look splotchy, while those on Nos. 2805a and 2806a have a distinct dot structure. The frame on No. 2807 has tightly spaced small dots, while on No. 2807a, the dots are more widely spaced.

Wildlife — A1558

2001, Apr. 21 Photo. *Perf. 13¼*

2809 A1558 2.70fr Squirrel 1.00 .25
2810 A1558 3fr Roe deer 1.10 .25
2811 A1558 3fr Hedgehog, horiz. 1.10 .25
2812 A1558 4.50fr Ermine 1.75 .30
a. Souvenir sheet, #2809-2812 5.00 1.10

Tourism Issue

Nogent-le-Rotrou A1559

Besançon A1560

Calais A1561

Château de Grignan A1562

Engr., Litho & Engr. (#2813)

2001 *Perf. 13¼x13 (#2813), 13*

2813 A1559 3fr multi 1.10 .25
2814 A1560 3fr multi 1.10 .25
2815 A1561 3fr multi 1.10 .25
2816 A1562 3fr multi 1.10 .25
Nos. 2813-2816 (4) 4.40 1.00

Issued: No. 2813, 4/28; No. 2814, 5/5; No. 2815, 6/16; No. 2816, 7/7.

Europa — A1563

2001, May 8 Photo. *Perf. 13*

2817 A1563 3fr multi 1.10 .40

Gardens of Versailles — A1564

Illustration reduced.

2001, May 12

2818 A1564 4.40fr multi 1.60 .30

Singers — A1565

Designs: No. 2819, Claude François (1939-78). No. 2820, Léo Ferré (1916-93). No. 2821, Serge Gainsbourg (1928-91). No. 2822, Dalida (1933-87). No. 2823, Michel Berger (1947-92). No. 2824, Barbara (1930-97).

2001, May 19 Photo. *Perf. 13*

2819 A1565 3fr multi 1.10 .25
2820 A1565 3fr multi 1.10 .25
2821 A1565 3fr multi 1.10 .25
2822 A1565 3fr multi 1.10 .25
2823 A1565 3fr multi 1.10 .25
2824 A1565 3fr multi 1.10 .25
a. Souvenir sheet, #2819-2824 7.00 7.00
Nos. 2819-2824 (6) 6.60 1.50

No. 2824a sold for 28fr with the Red Cross receiving 10fr of that.

Old Lyon — A1566

2001, May 19 Engr. *Perf. 13¼*

2825 A1566 3fr multi 1.10 .25

French Federation of Philatelic Associations 74th Congress, Tours — A1567

2001, June 1

2826 A1567 3fr multi 1.10 .25

Jean Vilar (1912-71), Actor A1568

Litho. & Engr.

2001, June 7 *Perf. 13*

2827 A1568 3fr multi 1.10 .25

Vacation A1569

2001, June 10 Litho. *Perf. 13*

2828 A1569 3fr multi 1.10 .25

Booklet Stamp
Self-Adhesive

2829 A1569 3fr multi 1.10 .25
a. Booklet of 10 11.00

1 Euro Coin A1570

2001, June 23 Photo. *Perf. 12½*

2830 A1570 3fr multi 1.10 .25

Value is for copy with surrounding selvage.

Albert Caquot (1881-1976), Engineer — A1571

2001, June 30 Engr. *Perf. 13¼*

2831 A1571 4.50fr multi 1.75 .30

Law Guaranteeing Freedom of Association, Cent. — A1572

2001, July 1 Photo. *Perf. 13*

2832 A1572 3fr multi 1.10 .25

Trains — A1573

No. 2833: a, Eurostar. b, American 220. c, Crocodile. d, Crampton. e, Garratt 59. f, Pacific Chapelon. g, Mallard. h, Capitole. i, Autorail Panoramique. j, 230 Class P8.

2001, July 6 Photo. *Perf. 13¼*

2833 A1573 Sheet of 10 6.00 6.00
a.-j. 1.50fr Any single .60 .20

Geneva Convention on Refugees, UN High Commisioner for Refugees, 50th Anniv. — A1574

2001, July 28 *Perf. 13*

2834 A1574 4.50fr multi 1.75 .30

Marianne Type of 1997 Inscribed "RF" at Lower Left

2001 Engr. *Perf. 13*

2835 A1409 (3fr) red 1.10 .25
d. Sheet of 15 + 15 labels 22.50 —

Serpentine Die Cut 6¾ Vert.
Self-Adhesive
Booklet Stamp

2835A A1409 (3fr) red 1.10 .25
b. Booklet of 10 11.00

2001, Aug. 1 Engr. *Perf. 13 Horiz.*
Coil Stamp
Water-Activated Gum

2835C A1409 (3fr) red 1.10 .25

Issued: Nos. 2835, 2835C, 8/1; No. 2835A, 9/24.

No. 2835d sold for €10.03. Labels could be personalized for an additional price.

"La Poste" and engraver are at right.

Pierre de Fermat (1601-65), Mathematician — A1575

2001, Aug. 19 Engr. *Perf. 13¼x13*

2836 A1575 4.50fr multi 1.25 .30

20th Century Type of 2000

No. 2837 — Science: a, First man in space. b, DNA. c, Chip cards. d, Laser. e, Penicillin.

Perf. 13¼x13 (vert. stamps), 13

2001, Sept. 22 Photo.

2837 A1531 Sheet, 2 each #a-e 11.00 11.00
a.-e. 3fr Any single 1.10 .25

Top part of No. 2837 contains Nos. 2837a-2837e and is separated from bottom part of sheet by a row of rouletting.

Astrolabe Sculpture, Val-de-Reuil A1576

2001, Sept. 29 *Perf. 13*

2838 A1576 3fr multi 1.10 .25

Halloween A1577

2001, Oct. 20

2839 A1577 3fr multi 1.10 .25
a. Souvenir sheet of 5 + 4 labels 4.50 4.50

Jean Pierre-Bloch (1905-99), Human Rights Advocate — A1578

2001, Nov. 8 Engr. *Perf. 13*

2840 A1578 4.50fr multi 1.75 .30

Albert Decaris (1901-88), Artist A1579

2001, Nov. 9 Engr. *Perf. 13¼x13*

2841 A1579 3fr multi 1.10 .25

Jacques Chaban-Delmas (1915-2000), Politician — A1580

2001, Nov. 10 Engr. *Perf. 13x13¼*

2842 A1580 3fr multi 1.10 .25

Holiday Greetings A1581

Designs: Nos. 2843, 2845 Bonne Année (Happy New Year). Nos. 2844, 2846 Meilleurs Voeux (Best wishes).

2001, Nov. 9 Litho. *Perf. 13*

2843 A1581 3fr multi 1.10 .25
2844 A1581 3fr multi 1.10 .25

Serpentine Die Cut 11
Self-Adhesive
Booklet Stamps

2845 A1581 3fr multi 1.10 .25
2846 A1581 3fr multi 1.10 .25
a. Booklet, 5 each # 2845-2846 11.00

Fountains A1582

Designs: 3fr, Nejjarine Fountain, Fez, Morocco. 3.80fr, Wallace Fountain, Paris.

2001, Dec. 14 Photo. *Perf. 13¼*

2847 A1582 3fr multi 1.10 .25
2848 A1582 3.80fr multi 1.50 .30

See Morocco Nos. 914-915.

100 Cents = 1 Euro (€)

Marianne (With Euro Denominations) A1583

Orchids A1584

2002, Jan. 1 Engr. *Perf. 13*

2849 A1583 1c yellow .20 .20
2850 A1583 2c brown .20 .20
2851 A1583 5c brt bl grn .20 .20
2852 A1583 10c purple .25 .20
2853 A1583 20c brt org .50 .20
2854 A1583 41c brt green 1.00 .20
2855 A1583 50c dk blue 1.25 .25
2856 A1583 53c apple grn 1.40 .20
2857 A1583 58c blue 1.50 .25
2858 A1583 64c dark org 1.60 .25
2859 A1583 67c brt blue 1.75 .25
a. deep blue 1.75 .25
2860 A1583 69c brt pink 1.75 .25
2861 A1583 €1 Prus blue 2.50 .30
2862 A1583 €1.02 dk green 2.50 .30
a. Souvenir sheet, #2835, 2854, 2856-2858, 2859a, 2860, 2862 12.50 12.50
2863 A1583 €2 violet 5.00 .50
a. Souvenir sheet, #2849-2853, 2855, 2861, 2863 10.00 10.00
Nos. 2849-2863 (15) 21.60 3.75

Coil Stamp
Perf. 13 Horiz.

2864 A1583 41c brt green 1.00 .20

2002, Jan. 2 Litho. *Perf. 13*

Designs: 29c, Orchis insularis. 33c, Ophrys fuciflora.

2865 A1584 29c multi .75 .20
2866 A1584 33c multi .85 .20

Nos. 2865-2866 are known only precanceled. See second note after #132.

Heart of Voh, Photograph by Yann Arthurs-Bertrand — A1585

2002, Jan. 18 Photo. *Perf. 13¼*

2867 A1585 46c multi 1.10 .25
a. Souvenir sheet of 5 5.50 5.50

Value of No. 2867 is for copy with surrounding selvage.

2002 Winter Olympics, Salt Lake City — A1586

2002, Jan. 26 *Perf. 13*

2868 A1586 46c multi 1.10 .25

Art Series

Sphere Concorde, by Jesús Rafael Soto A1587

The Kiss, by Gustav Klimt A1588

The Dancers, by Fernando Botero A1589

Self-Portrait, by Elisabeth Vigée-Lebrun — A1590

2002 Photo. *Perf. 13¼x13*

2869 A1587 75c multi 1.90 .45
2870 A1588 €1.02 multi 2.50 .50
2871 A1589 €1.02 multi 2.50 .50

Engr.

2872 A1590 €1.02 multi 2.50 .50
Nos. 2869-2872 (4) 9.40 1.95

Issued: No. 2869, 11/11. No. 2870, 2/8; No. 2871, 4/27. No. 2872, 10/12.

Alain Bosquet (1919-98), Poet — A1591

2002, Feb. 16 Engr. *Perf. 13*

2873 A1591 58c multi 1.50 .30

It's A Girl A1592

It's A Boy A1593

Yes A1594

2002, Feb. 23 Photo.

2874 A1592 46c multi 1.10 .25
2875 A1593 46c multi 1.10 .25
2876 A1594 69c multi 1.75 .30
Nos. 2874-2876 (3) 3.95 .80

Europa — A1595

2002, Mar. 2 *Perf. 13¼*

2877 A1595 46c multi 1.10 .25

Boule and Bill, by Jean Roba — A1596

Designs: 46c, Boule, Bill, bird. 46c+9c, Boule, Bill, ball.

2002, Mar. 16 *Perf. 13¼*

2878 A1596 46c multi 1.10 .25
a. Perf. 13¼x13 1.10 .25

Perf. 13¼x13

2879 A1596 46c +9c multi 1.40 1.40
a. Souvenir sheet of 1 1.40 1.40
b. Booklet pane, 5 #2878a, 3 #2879 9.75 —
Booklet, #2879b 10.00

Stamp Day. Stamp on No. 2879a has continuous design.

Nimes Amphitheater — A1597

Litho. & Engr.

2002, Mar. 22 *Perf. 13*

2880 A1597 46c multi 1.10 .25

20th Century Type of 2000

No. 2881 — Transportation: a, Concorde supersonic airplane. b, TGV train. c, Ocean liner France, vert. d, Mobylette motor scooter, vert. e, Citroen 2 CV automobile, vert.

Perf. 13, 13¼x13 (vert. stamps)

2002, Mar. 23 Photo.

2881 A1531 Sheet, 2 each #a-e 11.00 11.00
a.-e. 46c Any single 1.10 .25

Top part of No. 2881 contains Nos. 2881a-2881e and is separated from bottom part of sheet by a row of rouletting.

Encounter of Matthew Flinders and Nicolas Boudin, Bicent. A1598

Map of Australia, portrait and ship of: 46c, Flinders. 79c, Boudin.

2002, Apr. 4 *Perf. 13¼*

2882 A1598 46c multi 1.10 .25
2883 A1598 79c multi 2.00 .40

See Australia Nos. 2053-2054.

Tourism Series

La Charité-sur-Loire — A1599

Collioure A1600

Locronan
A1601

Neufchateau — A1602

Engraved (#2884, 2886), Photo. (#2885)

2002			*Perf. 13¼*	
2884	A1599	46c multi	1.10	.25
2885	A1600	46c multi	1.10	.25
2886	A1601	46c multi	1.10	.25
2887	A1602	46c multi	1.10	.25
		Nos. 2884-2887 (4)	4.40	1.00

Issue dates: No. 2884, 4/6; No. 2885, 6/22; No. 2886, 7/13; No. 2887, 10/12/02.

Numbers have been reserved for additional stamps in this set.

Birthday Greetings
A1603

Invitation
A1604

2002, Apr. 6		**Photo.**	*Perf. 13*	
2888	A1603	46c multi	1.10	.25
a.		Litho., stamp + label	1.25	1.25
2889	A1604	46c multi	1.10	.25
a.		Litho., stamp + label	1.25	1.25

Issued: Nos. 2888a, 2889a, 11/7. Nos. 2888a and 2889a were issued in sheets of 10 stamps and 10 labels that sold for €6.19 on day of issue. The labels could be personalized.

No. 2888a has a duller blue in "Anniversaire" than No. 2888, but is otherwise quite similar in appearance. The gold ink on No. 2889a has a more coppery look than that on No. 2889.

100th Paris-Roubaix Bicycle Race — A1605

2002, Mar. 13				
2890	A1605	46c multi	1.10	.25

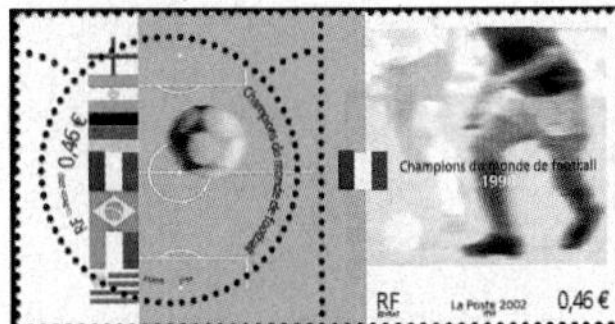

2002 World Cup Soccer Championships, Japan and Korea — A1606

No. 2891: a, Flags, soccer ball and field (32mm diameter). b, Soccer player, year of French championship.

Illustration reduced.

2002, Apr. 27			*Perf. 12¾*	
2891	A1606	Horiz. pair	2.25	2.25
a.-b.		46c Any single	1.10	.25
c.		Sheet, 5 #2891	11.50	11.50

Issued: No. 2891c, 5/18.

See Argentina No. 2184, Brazil No. 2840, Germany No. 2163, Italy No. 2526 and Uruguay No. 1946.

Marine Life
A1607

Designs: 41c, Sea turtle (tortue luth), vert. No. 2893, Killer whale (orque). No. 2894, Dolphin (grand dauphin). 69c, Seal (phoque veau marin).

2002, May 4			*Perf. 13¼*	
2892	A1607	41c multi	1.00	.25
2893	A1607	46c multi	1.10	.25
2894	A1607	46c multi	1.10	.25
2895	A1607	69c multi	1.75	.30
a.		Souvenir sheet, #2892-2895	5.00	5.00
		Nos. 2892-2895 (4)	4.95	1.05

Worldwide Fund for Nature (#2895a).

French Federation of Philatelic Associations 75th Congress, Marseilles — A1608

Illustration reduced.

2002, May 17		**Engr.**	*Perf. 13*	
2896	A1608	46c multi	1.10	.25

Legion of Honor, Bicent.
A1609

Rocamadour
A1610

2002, May 18			**Photo.**	
2897	A1609	46c multi	1.10	.25

2002, May 25			*Perf. 13¼*	
2898	A1610	46c multi	1.10	.25

Louis Delgrés (1766-1802), Soldier — A1611

2002, May 25				
2899	A1611	46c multi	1.10	.25

Vacation
A1612

2002, June 8		**Litho.**	*Perf. 13*	
2900	A1612	46c multi	1.10	.25

Self-Adhesive

Serpentine Die Cut 11

2901	A1612	46c multi	1.10	.25
a.		Booklet pane of 10	11.00	

World Disabled Athletics Championships — A1613

2002, June 15		**Photo.**	*Perf. 13¼*	
2902	A1613	46c multi	1.10	.25

Saint-Ser Chapel — A1614

2002, June 22		**Engr.**	*Perf. 13x13¼*	
2903	A1614	46c multi	1.10	.25

Metz Cathedral Stained Glass
A1615

2002, July 6		**Engr.**	*Perf. 13¼x13*	
2904	A1615	46c multi	1.10	.25

Jazz Musicians — A1616

Designs: No. 2905, Louis Armstrong (1901-71). No. 2906, Ella Fitzgerald (1918-96). No. 2907, Duke Ellington (1899-1974). No. 2908, Stéphane Grappelli (1908-97). No. 2909, Michel Petrucciani (1962-99), horiz. No. 2910, Sidney Bechet (1897-1959), horiz.

2002, July 13		**Photo.**	*Perf. 13*	
2905	A1616	46c multi	1.10	.25
2906	A1616	46c multi	1.10	.25
2907	A1616	46c multi	1.10	.25
2908	A1616	46c multi	1.10	.25
2909	A1616	46c multi	1.10	.25
2910	A1616	46c multi	1.10	.25
a.		Souvenir sheet, #2905-2910	8.50	8.50
		Nos. 2905-2910 (6)	6.60	1.50

No. 2910a sold for €4.36, with the Red Cross receiving €1.60 of that.

Pilgrimages to Notre Dame de la Salette, 150th Anniv.
A1617

2002, Aug. 15		**Engr.**	*Perf. 13¼x13*	
2911	A1617	46c multi	1.10	.25

Choreography — A1618

Illustration reduced.

2002, Sept. 13		**Photo.**	*Perf. 13x13¼*	
2912	A1618	53c multi	1.40	.30

Motorcycles — A1619

No. 2913: a, Honda 750 four. b, Terrot 500 RGST. c, Majestic. d, Norton Commando 750. e, Voxan 1000 Café Racer. f, BMW R90S. g, Harley Davidson Hydra Glide. h, Triumph Bonneville 650. i, Ducati 916. j, Yamaha 500 XT.

2002, Sept. 14			*Perf. 13¼x13*	
2913	A1619	Sheet of 10	11.50	4.50
a.-e.		16c any single	.40	.20
f.-j.		30c any single	.75	.20

Georges Perec (1936-82), Writer — A1620

2002, Sept. 21		**Engr.**	*Perf. 13¼*	
2914	A1620	46c multi	1.10	.25

20th Century Type of 2000

No. 2915 — Photographs of everyday life: a, Family on motor scooter, 1955, vert. b, Man, horse and wagon, 1947. c, Woman ironing, 1950. d, Boy at fountain, 1950, vert. e, Girl in classroom, 1965, vert.

Perf. 13¼x13 (vert. stamps), 13

2002, Sept. 28			**Photo.**	
2915	A1531	Sheet, 2 each #a-e	11.00	9.00
a.-e.		46c Any single	1.10	.25

Top part of No. 2915 contains Nos. 2915a-2915e and is separated from bottom part of sheet by a row of rouletting.

Emile Zola (1840-1902), Novelist — A1621

2002, Oct. 5			*Perf. 13*	
2916	A1621	46c multi	1.10	.25

Souvenir Sheet

European Capitals — A1622

Attractions in Rome: a, Trevi Fountain. b, Coliseum, horiz. c, Trinitá de Monti Church and Spanish Steps. d, St. Peter's Basilica, horiz.

2002, Nov. 7 ***Perf. 13¼x13, 13x13¼***
2917 A1622 Sheet of 4 4.50 4.50
a.-d. 46c Any single 1.10 .25

See No. 2985.

Globe and Microcircuits A1623

2002, Nov. 8 **Photo.** ***Perf. 13***
2918 A1623 46c multi 1.10 .25
a. Litho., stamp + label 1.25 1.25

Issued: No. 2918a, 11/7. No. 2918a was issued in sheets of 10 stamps and 10 labels that sold for €6.19 on day of issue. The labels could be personalized.

No. 2918a has a hairline at top, above "RF" that No. 2888 does not have, but is otherwise quite similar in appearance.

Holiday Greetings A1624

2002, Nov. 8 **Photo.** ***Perf. 13***
2919 A1624 46c multi 1.10 .25
a. Litho., stamp + label 1.25 1.25

Booklet Stamp

Self-Adhesive

Serpentine Die Cut 11

2920 A1624 46c multi 1.10 .25
a. Booklet pane of 10 11.00

Issued: No. 2919a, 11/7. No. 2919a was issued in sheets of 10 stamps and 10 labels that sold for €6.19 on day of issue. The labels could be personalized.

No. 2919a has a finer dot structure, which is most noticeable in the chimney smoke, than No. 2888.

Marianne Type of 1997 Inscribed "RF" at Lower Left

2002, Nov. 9 **Engr.** ***Perf. 13***
2921 A1409 (41c) bright green .85 .25

Coil Stamp

Perf. 13 Horiz.

2922 A1409 (41c) bright green .85 .25

Alexandre Dumas (Father) (1802-70), Writer A1625

2002, Nov. 30 **Photo.** ***Perf. 13***
2924 A1625 46c multi .95 .25

Léopold Sédar Senghor (1906-2001), President of Senegal, Poet — A1626

2002, Dec. 20
2925 A1626 46c multi .95 .25

Hearts A1627

2003, Jan. 11 ***Perf. 13¼***
2926 A1627 46c Four hearts 1.00 .30
a. Souvenir sheet of 5 5.00 1.25
2927 A1627 69c Roses 1.50 .35

Values for Nos. 2926-2927 are for copies with surrounding selvage.

Thank You A1628

Birth A1629

2003, Jan. 11 ***Perf. 13***
2928 A1628 46c multi 1.00 .30
2929 A1629 46c brt org & brt bl 1.00 .30

Franco-German Cooperation Treaty, 40th Anniv. — A1630

2003, Jan. 16 ***Perf. 13¼***
2930 A1630 46c multi 1.00 .30

Delegation for Land-use Planning and Regional Action, 40th Anniv. A1631

2003, Feb. 8 **Photo.** ***Perf. 13***
2931 A1631 46c multi 1.00 .30

Geneviève de Gaulle Anthonioz (1920-2002), World War II Resistance Fighter — A1632

2003, Feb. 11
2932 A1632 46c blk & ol brn 1.00 .30

Paris Chamber of Commerce and Industry, Bicent. — A1633

2003, Feb. 22 ***Perf. 13¼***
2933 A1633 46c multi 1.00 .30

Lucky Luke, by Morris (Maurice De Bevere) — A1634

Lucky Luke and Jolly Jumper: 46c, Skipping rope on ball on high wire. 46c+9c, Following dog, Rantanplan.

2003, Mar. 15 **Photo.** ***Perf. 13¼***
2934 A1634 46c multi 1.00 .30
a. Perf. 13¼x13 1.00 .30

Perf. 13¼x13

2935 A1634 46c +9c multi 1.25 1.25
a. Souvenir sheet of 1 1.25 1.25
b. Booklet pane, 5 #2934a, 3 #2935 8.75 —
Complete booklet, #2935b 8.75

Stamp Day.

Birds A1635

Designs: 41c, Colibri à tete bleue (Cyanophaia bicolor). No. 2937, Toucan ariel (Ramphastos vitellinus). No. 2938, Colibri grenat (Eulampis jugularis), vert. 69c, Terpsiphone de Bourbon (Terpsiphone bourbonnensis).

2003, Mar. 22 **Photo.** ***Perf. 13¼***
2936 A1635 41c multi .90 .25
2937 A1635 46c multi 1.00 .30
2938 A1635 46c multi 1.00 .30
2939 A1635 69c multi 1.50 .35
a. Souvenir sheet, #2936-2939 4.50 1.25
Nos. 2936-2939 (4) 4.40 1.20

Nantes A1636

2003, Apr. 4 **Engr.**
2940 A1636 46c multi 1.00 .30

Pierre Bérégovoy (1925-93), Prime Minister — A1637

2003, Apr. 30 **Engr.** ***Perf. 13x13¼***
2941 A1637 46c multi 1.10 .30

Milan Stefanik (1880-1919), Czechoslovakian General — A1638

2003, May 3 ***Perf. 13¼***
2942 A1638 50c multi 1.25 .35

See Slovakia No. 428.

Europa — A1639

2003, May 8 **Photo.**
2943 A1639 50c multi 1.25 .35

Charter of Fundamental Rights of the European Union — A1640

2003, May 8
2944 A1640 50c multi 1.25 .35

Aircraft Carrier "Charles de Gaulle" A1641

2003, May 8 **Engr.**
2945 A1641 50c multi 1.25 .30

Aspects of Life in the French Regions A1642

No. 2946: a, Beach cabins. b, Fishing net. c, Vineyards of Champagne. d, Camembert cheese, vert. e, Foie gras, vert. f, Petanque. g, Puppet show (Guignol), vert. h, Crepe, vert. i, Cassoulet. j, Limoges porcelain.

2003, May 24 **Photo.** ***Perf. 13***
2946 Sheet of 10 12.50 12.50
a.-j. A1642 50c Any single 1.25 .35

No. 2946 has three vertical rows of rouletting, separating sheet into quarters.

Nos. 2946a-2946j were also issued in large booklets containing panes of 1 of each stamp. The booklet sold for €19.

See No. 2978.

Art Series

"The Dying Slave" and "The Rebel Slave," by Michelangelo — A1643

The Red Buoy, by Paul Signac A1644

Untitled Abstract by Vassily Kandinsky A1645

Marilyn, by Andy Warhol A1646

2003 Engr. *Perf. 13¼x13*

2947 A1643	75c multi		1.75	.90

Photo.

2948 A1644	75c multi		1.75	.90

Litho.

2949 A1645	€1.11 multi		2.50	1.25
2950 A1646	€1.11 multi		2.75	1.40
	Nos. 2947-2950 (4)		8.75	4.45

Issued: No. 2947, 5/24. Nos. 2948, 2949, 7/5. No. 2950, 11/8.

Happy Birthday A1647

2003, May 31 Photo. *Perf. 13¼*

2951 A1647 50c multi		1.25	.35
a.	Souvenir sheet of 5	6.25	6.25
b.	Litho., stamp + label	1.75	1.75

Issued: No. 2951b, 2004. No. 2951b was issued in sheets of 10 stamps + 10 labels that sold for €6.67 on day of issue. The labels could be personalized. The background on No. 2951 looks splotchy while that of No. 2951b has a dot structure.

Marianne With Euro Denominations Type of 2002

2003, June 1 Engr. *Perf. 13*

2952 A1583	58c apple grn	1.40	.25
2953 A1583	70c yellow grn	1.60	.30
2954 A1583	75c bright blue	1.75	.30
2955 A1583	90c dark blue	2.10	.35
2956 A1583	€1.11 red lilac	2.60	.40
2957 A1583	€1.90 violet brown	4.50	.60
a.	Souvenir sheet, #2835, 2921, 2952-2957	17.00	17.00
	Nos. 2952-2957 (6)	13.95	2.20

No. 2957a issued 2/28/04.

Orchids Type of 2002

Designs: 30c, Platanthera chlorantha. 35c, Dactylorhiza savogiensis.

2003, June 1 Litho. *Perf. 13*

2958 A1584 30c multi		.70	.20
2959 A1584 35c multi		.85	.20

Nos. 2958-2959 are known only precanceled, See second note after #132.

French Federation of Philatelic Associations 76th Congress, Mulhouse A1648

2003, June 6 Engr. *Perf. 13¼*

2960 A1648 50c multi		1.25	.35

Vacation — A1649

Perf. 12¾x13¼

2003, June 14 Litho.

2961 A1649 50c multi		1.10	.30

Self-Adhesive

Booklet Stamp

Serpentine Die Cut 11

2962 A1649 50c multi		1.10	.30
a.	Booklet pane of 10	11.00	

Tourism Issue

Notre Dame de l'Epine Basilica — A1650

Tulle A1651

Arras — A1652

Pontarlier A1653

Perf. 13x13¼, 13 (#2965)

2003, June 21 Engr.

2963 A1650 50c multi		1.10	.30
2964 A1651 50c multi		1.10	.30
2965 A1652 50c multi		1.25	.30
2966 A1653 50c multi		1.25	.35
	Nos. 2963-2966 (4)	4.70	1.25

Issued: Nos. 2963, 2964, 6/21. No. 2965, 9/20. No. 2966, 10/11.

No. 2965, illustration reduced.

French Freemasonry, 275th Anniv. — A1654

2003, June 28 Engr. *Perf. 13¼x13*

2967 A1654 50c multi		1.10	.30

Tour de France Bicycle Race, Cent. A1655

No. 2968: a, Maurice Garin, winner of 1903 race. b, Cyclist with arms raised.

2003, June 28 Photo. *Perf. 13*

2968 A1655	Vert. pair	2.25	.60
a.-b.	50c Either single	1.10	.30

Values are for stamps with surrounding selvage.

Saint-Père Church, Yonne — A1656

2003, July 12 Engr. *Perf. 13¼*

2969 A1656 50c multi		1.10	.30

World Track and Field Championships, Paris — A1657

Illustration reduced.

2003, July 19 Photo. *Perf. 13*

2970 A1657 50c multi		1.10	.30

Characters From French Literature — A1658

Designs: No. 2971, Eugène-François Vidocq (1775-1857), convict and police official. No. 2972, Esmerelda, from *Notre-Dame de Paris,* by Victor Hugo. No. 2973, Claudine, from *Claudine* novels, by Colette. No. 2974, Nana, from *Rougon-Macquart,* by Emile Zola. No. 2975, La Comte de Monte-Cristo, from *La Comte de Monte-Cristo,* by Alexandre Dumas (pere). No. 2976, Gavroche, from *Les Miserables,* by Hugo.

2003, Aug. 30 Photo. *Perf. 13*

2971 A1658 50c multi		1.10	.30
2972 A1658 50c multi		1.10	.30
2973 A1658 50c multi		1.10	.30
2974 A1658 50c multi		1.10	.30
2975 A1658 50c multi		1.10	.30
2976 A1658 50c multi		1.10	.30
a.	Souvenir sheet, #2971-2976	10.50	10.50
	Nos. 2971-2976 (6)	6.60	1.80

No. 2976a sold for €4.60, with the Red Cross receiving €1.60 of that.

Ahmad Shah Massoud (1953-2001), Afghan Northern Alliance Leader — A1659

2003, Sept. 9

2977 A1659 50c multi		1.10	.30

Aspects of Life in French Regions Type of 2003

No. 2978: a, Chateau de Chenonceau. b, House, Alsace. c, Roof, Bourgogne. d, Genoese Tower, Corsica, vert. e, Arc de Triomphe, vert. f, Farm house, Provence. g, Pointe du Raz, vert. h, Mont Blanc, vert. i, Basque house. j, Pont du Gard.

2003, Sept. 20 Photo. *Perf. 13*

2978	Sheet of 10	12.50	12.50
a.-j.	A1642 50c Any single	1.25	.35

No. 2978 has three vertical rows of rouletting, separating sheet into quarters.

Nos. 2978a-2978j were also issued in large booklets containing panes of 1 of each stamp. The booklet sold for €19.

Gardens and Parks — A1660

No. 2979: a, Buttes-Chaumont Park. b, Jardin du Luxembourg.

2003, Sept. 27 *Perf. 13¼x13*

2979	Sheet of 2	9.00	9.00
a.-b.	A1660 €1.90 Either single	4.50	2.25

Salon du Timbre 2004. No. 2979 has four vertical rows of rouletting, separating sheet into fifths, with the two stamps in the central fifth.

Motor Vehicles — A1661

No. 2980: a, 1954 Isobloc 648 DP 102 bus (Autocar). b, 1950 SFV 302 Tractor. c, 1938 Delahaye fire truck with mechanical aerial ladder. d, Renault Kangaroo Express postal van. e, 1932 Renault TN6 Paris city bus. f, 1910 Berliet 22hp Type M delivery truck. g, 1957 Berliet T100 heavy-duty truck. h, Citroen police van. i, Citroen DS ambulance. j, 1964 Hotchkiss fire truck.

2003, Oct. 24 Photo. *Perf. 13¼*

2980 A1661 Sheet of 10 5.75 5.75
a.-e. 20c Any single .45 .20
f.-j. 30c Any single .70 .20

Philexjeunes 2003 Philatelic Exhibition, Dunkerque.

A1662

Holiday Greetings A1663

2003, Nov. 6 Photo. *Perf. 13*

2981 A1662 50c multi 1.25 .35
a. Litho., stamp + label 1.75 1.75

Litho.

2982 A1663 50c multi 1.25 .35
a. Sheet of 10 + 10 labels 17.50 17.50

Booklet Stamp
Self-Adhesive
Serpentine Die Cut 11¼

2983 A1663 50c multi 1.25 .35
a. Booklet pane of 10 12.50

Nos. 2981a, 2982a, 2004. Nos. 2981a and 2982 were issued in sheets of 10 stamps + 10 labels that sold for €6.67 each on day of issue. The labels could be personalized. The background on No. 2981 looks splotchy while that of No. 2981a has a dot structure.

A souvenir sheet containing No. 2982 was sold for €6 by mail order only. It was not available through standing order subscriptions and was not offered in the philatelic bureau's sales catalog. 50,000 copies of this sheet were printed.

Sower Type of 1903, Cent. — A1664

Serpentine Die Cut 6¾ Vert.
2003, Nov. 6 Engr.

Booklet Stamp

2984 A1664 50c red 1.25 .35
a. Booklet pane, 5 each # 2984, 2835A 12.50

European Capitals Type of 2002

No. 2985 - Attractions in Luxembourg: a, Citadelle Saint-Esprit. b, Notre Dame Cathedral, horiz. c, Adolphe Bridge, horiz. d, Grand Duke's Palace.

Perf. 13¼x13, 13x13¼
2003, Nov. 7 Photo.

2985 A1622 Sheet of 4 4.75 4.75
a.-d. 50c Any single 1.10 .30

Indian and French Artisan's Work A1665

Designs: 50c, Illumination depicting rooster, France, 15th cent. 90c, Jewelry design, India, 19th cent.

2003, Nov. 29 Engr. *Perf. 13¼x13*

2986 A1665 50c multi 1.25 .30
2987 A1665 90c multi 2.25 .40

See India No. 2040.

Launch of the Queen Mary 2 — A1666

2003, Dec. 12 Photo. *Perf. 13¼*

2988 A1666 50c multi 1.25 .30

Greetings A1667

Holes punched through dots in "i's."

2004, Jan. 9 Photo. *Perf. 13*

2989 A1667 50c shown 1.25 .35
2990 A1667 50c Un grand merci 1.25 .35

No Holes Punched Through Dots of "i's"
Stamp + Label

2991 A1667 50c Like No. 2989 1.75 1.75
2992 A1667 50c Like No. 2990 1.75 1.75

Nos. 2991-2992 were issued in sheets of 10 stamps + 10 labels that sold for €6.67 on day of issue. The labels could be personalized.

It's a Boy A1668

It's a Girl A1669

2004 Litho. *Serpentine Die Cut 11*
Stamp + Label

2993 A1668 50c multi 1.75 1.75
2994 A1669 50c multi 1.75 1.75

Booklet Stamps
Self-Adhesive

2995 A1668 50c multi 1.25 .35
a. Booklet pane of 10 12.50
2996 A1669 50c multi 1.25 .35
a. Booklet pane of 10 12.50

Nos. 2993-2994 were issued in sheets of 10 stamps + 10 labels that sold for €6.67 on day of issue. The labels could be personalized.
Nos. 2995-2996 issued 1/9/04.

Hearts A1670

Designs: 50c, Chanel No. 5 perfume bottle. 75c, Woman, Eiffel Tower.

2004, Jan. 9 Photo. *Perf. 13*

2997 A1670 50c multi 1.25 .35
a. Souvenir sheet of 5 6.25 6.25
b. Litho., stamp + label, perf. 13¼ 2.00 2.00
2998 A1670 75c multi 2.00 .40
a. Litho., stamp + label, perf. 13¼ 2.50 2.50

Nos. 2997b and 2998a were each printed in sheets of 10 stamps + 10 labels that could be personalized and sold for €6.69 and €10 respectively. On No. 2997b, there are large brown dots arranged in circles in the shading on the green rectangles, while on No. 2997 the brown dots are small and arranged in rows. On No. 2998a, the dots in the sky are larger and father apart than the tiny dots found on No. 2998.

Values are for stamps with surrounding selvage.

Tourism Issue

Lille, 2004 European Cultural Capital A1671

2004, Jan. 10 Photo. *Perf. 13*

2999 A1671 50c multi 1.25 .35

Art Series

Statue of Liberty, Sculpted by Frederic Auguste Bartholdi (1834-1904) — A1672

2004, Feb. 21 Engr. *Perf. 13¼x13*

3000 A1672 90c multi 2.25 .40

Queen Eleanor of Aquitaine (c. 1122-1204) A1673

2004, Feb. 28 *Perf. 13x13¼*

3001 A1673 50c multi 1.25 .35

Stamp Day — A1674

Characters of Walt Disney: 45c, Donald Duck. 50c, Mickey Mouse. 75c, Minnie Mouse.

2004, Mar. 6 Photo. *Perf. 13¼*

3002 A1674 50c multi 1.25 .35
a. Perf. 13¼x13 (from booklet pane) 1.25 .35

Booklet Stamps
Perf. 13¼x13

3003 A1674 45c multi 1.10 .30
3004 A1674 75c multi 1.90 .40
a. Booklet pane, 2 #3003, 4 each #3002a, 3004 15.00 —
Complete booklet, #3004a 15.00

Civil Code, Bicent. A1675

2004, Mar. 12 Engr. *Perf. 13¼x13*

3005 A1675 50c multi 1.25 .35

George Sand (1804-76), Writer A1676

2004, Mar. 20 Engr. *Perf. 13¼x13*

3006 A1676 50c multi 1.25 .35

Aspects of Life in French Regions Type of 2003

No. 3007: a, Cutlery. b, Produce of Provence, vert. c, Beaujolais grapes, vert. d, Bread. e, Woman wearing coif, vert. f, Oysters, vert. g, Quiche Lorraine. h, Bullfighting. i, Clafoutis. j, Bagpipers.

2004, Mar. 26 Photo. *Perf. 13*

3007 Sheet of 10 12.50 12.50
a.-j. A1642 50c Any single 1.25 .35

No. 3007 has three vertical rows of rouletting, separating sheet into quarters.

Clermont-Ferrand — A1677

2004, Mar. 26 Engr. *Perf. 13¼*

3008 A1677 50c multi 1.25 .35

Entente Cordiale, Cent. — A1678

Designs: 50c, Coccinelle, by Sonia Delaunay. 75c, Lace 1 (trial proof) 1968, by Sir Terry Frost.

2004, Apr. 6 Photo. *Perf. 13¼*
3009 A1678 50c multi 1.25 .35
3010 A1678 75c multi 1.90 .40

See Great Britain Nos. 2200-2201.

Road Safety — A1679

2004, Apr. 7
3011 A1679 50c multi 1.25 .35

See United Nations Offices in Geneva No. 424.

Art Series

La Méridienne d'Après Millet, by Vincent van Gogh — A1680

2004, July 2 Photo. *Perf. 13x13¼*
3012 A1680 75c multi 1.90 .95

Art Series

Un Combat de Coqs, by Jean-Léon Gérôme — A1681

Galatée aux Sphères, by Salvador Dali A1682

2004 Photo. *Perf. 13x13¼*
3013 A1681 €1.11 multi 2.75 1.40
3014 A1682 €1.11 multi 2.75 1.40

Issued: No. 3013, 4/17; No. 3014, 6/19.

Tourism Issue

Bordeaux — A1683

Vaux-sur-Mer — A1684

Notre Dame de l'Assomption Cathedral, Luçon — A1685

Illustration reduced.

2004 Litho. & Engr. *Perf. 13*
3015 A1683 50c multi 1.25 .35

Engr.
Perf. 13¼
3016 A1684 50c multi 1.25 .35
3017 A1685 50c multi 1.25 .35

Issued: No. 3015, 4/26; No. 3016, 7/17; No. 3017, 10/2.

Farm Animals A1686

2004, Apr. 26 Photo. *Perf. 13¼*
3018 A1686 45c Rabbit 1.10 .30
3019 A1686 50c Cow, vert. 1.25 .35
3020 A1686 50c Chicken 1.25 .35
3021 A1686 75c Burro, vert. 1.90 .40
a. Souvenir sheet, #3018-3021 5.50 5.50

Expansion of the European Union A1687

2004, May 1 Photo. *Perf. 13¼*
3022 A1687 50c multi 1.25 .35

Battle of Dien Bien Phu, 50th Anniv. — A1688

2004, May 7 *Perf. 13¼x13*
3023 A1688 50c multi 1.25 .35

Europa A1689

2004 Photo. *Perf. 13x13¼*
3024 A1689 50c multi 1.25 .35

Litho.
Booklet Stamp
Self-Adhesive
Serpentine Die Cut 11
3025 A1689 50c multi 1.25 .35
a. Booklet pane of 10 12.50

Issued: No. 3024, 5/9; No. 3025, 6/4.

Blake and Mortimer, Comic Book Characters by Edgar P. Jacobs A1690

Blake and Mortimer and: 50c, Brick wall, vert. €1, Blue background.

2004, May 15 Photo. *Perf. 13¼*
3026 A1690 50c multi 1.25 .35
3027 A1690 €1 multi 2.40 .70

See Belgium No. 2020.

FIFA (Fédération Internationale de Football Association), Cent. — A1691

2004, May 20 *Perf. 13¼x13*
3028 A1691 50c multi 1.25 .35

Gardens and Parks Type of 2003

No. 3029: a, Jardin des Tuileries. b, Parc Floral de Paris.

2004, June 4 *Perf. 13¼x13*
3029 Sheet of 2 9.25 9.25
a.-b. A1660 €1.90 Either single 4.50 2.25
c. Souvenir sheet, #2979a-2979b, 3029a-3029b 19.00 19.00

Salon du Timbre 2004. No. 3029 has four vertical rows of rouletting, separating sheet into fifths, with the two stamps in the central fifth.

D-Day Invasion of France, 60th Anniv. — A1692

2004, June 5 *Perf. 13*
3030 A1692 50c multi 1.25 .35

Organ Donation A1693

2004, June 22 *Perf. 13¼*
3031 A1693 50c multi 1.25 .35

Pierre Dugua de Mons, Leader of First French Settlement in Acadia, and Ship A1694

Litho. & Engr.
2004, June 26 *Perf. 13*
3032 A1694 90c multi 2.25 .65

See Canada No. 2044.

Napoleon I and the Imperial Guard — A1695

Designs: No. 3033, Light cavalry (Chasseur à cheval). No. 3034, Artilleryman and cannon (Artilleur à pied), horiz. No. 3035, Dragoon. No. 3036, Mameluke. No. 3037, Napoleon I. No. 3038, Grenadier (Grenadier à pied).

2004, June 26 Photo.
3033 A1695 50c multi 1.25 .35
3034 A1695 50c multi 1.25 .35
3035 A1695 50c multi 1.25 .35
3036 A1695 50c multi 1.25 .35
3037 A1695 50c multi 1.25 .35
3038 A1695 50c multi 1.25 .35
a. Souvenir sheet, #3033-3038 11.50 11.50
Nos. 3033-3038 (6) 7.50 2.10

No. 3038a sold for €4.60, with the Red Cross receiving €1.60 of that.

French Federation of Philatelic Associations 77th Congress, Paris — A1696

Litho. & Engr.
2004, June 27 *Perf. 13¼x13*
3039 A1696 50c multi 1.25 .35

2004 Summer Olympics, Athens — A1697

2004, June 28 Photo. *Perf. 13¼*

3040	50c Modern athletes	1.25	.35
3041	50c Ancient athletes	1.25	.35
a.	A1697 Pair, #3040-3041	2.50	.70

Printed in sheets containing five of each stamp.

A souvenir sheet containing No. 3041 was issued Aug. 2 and sold for €2.51.

Happy Birthday A1698

2004, June 30 Photo. *Perf. 13¼*

3042	A1698 50c multi	1.25	.35
a.	Souvenir sheet of 5	6.25	6.25
b.	Litho. stamp + label	2.00	2.00

No. 3042b printed in sheets of 10 stamps + 10 labels that could be personalized that sold for €8. No. 3042b has a dark green inscription at left with a distinct dot pattern. No. 3042 has a lighter green inscription.

Happy Birthday Type of 2004

2004 *Perf. 13¼*

3042b	Litho. stamp + label	2.00	2.00

No. 3042b printed in sheets of 10 stamps + 10 labels that could be personalized that sold for €8. No. 3042b has a dark green inscription at left with a distinct dot pattern. No. 3042 has a lighter green inscription.

Marianne Type of 1997 Inscribed "RF" at Lower Left and Type of 2002 With Euro Denominations

2004 Litho. *Perf. 13*

3043	Sheet of 15 + 15 labels	30.00	30.00
a.	A1583 1c orange yellow	.20	.20
b.	A1583 2c brown	.20	.20
c.	A1583 5c brt bl green	.20	.20
d.	A1583 10c purple	.25	.25
e.	A1583 20c orange	.55	.55
f.	A1583 58c apple green	1.75	1.75
g.	A1583 70c olive	2.00	2.00
h.	A1583 75c sky blue	2.25	2.25
i.	A1583 90c dark blue	2.60	2.60
j.	A1583 €1 Prussian blue	2.75	2.75
k.	A1583 €1.11 red lilac	3.25	3.25
l.	A1583 €1.90 violet brown	5.50	5.50
m.	A1583 €2 violet	5.75	5.75
n.	A1409 (45c) green	1.25	1.25
o.	A1409 (50c) red	1.50	1.50

No. 3043 sold for €10.03. Stamps have a glossy varnish.

Marianne and Emblem of World Fund to Combat AIDS, Tuberculosis and Smoking — A1699

2004, July 1 Engr. *Perf. 13*

3044	A1699 (50c) red	1.25	.35

Extreme Sports — A1700

No. 3045: a, Skateboarding. b, Parachuting. c, Sailboarding. d, Surfing. e, Luge. f, BMX bicycling. g, Paragliding. h, Jetskiing. i, Snowboarding. j, Rollerblading.

2004, July 3 Photo. *Perf. 13¼x13*

3045	A1700 Sheet of 10	6.25	6.25
a.-e.	20c Any single	.50	.50
f.-j.	30c Any single	.75	.75

Orchid Type of 2002

Design: 39c, Orchis insularis.

2004, Sept. 1 Litho. *Perf. 13*

3046	A1584 39c multi	.95	.20

No. 3046 known only precanceled. See second note after No. 132.

Aspects of Life in the French Regions Type of 2003

No. 3047: a, House, Normandy. b, Chambord Chateau. c, Gorges, Tarn, vert. d, Notre Dame Cathedral, Paris, vert. e, Windmill, vert. f, Cave dwellings. g, Creek, Cassis, vert. h, Cap-Ferret Lighthouse, vert. i, Castle ruins. j, Alpine chalet.

2004, Sept. 18 Photo. *Perf. 13*

3047	Sheet of 10	12.50	12.50
a.-j.	A1642 50c Any single	1.25	.35

No. 3047 has three vertical rows of rouletting separating sheet into quarters.

Each stamp exists in booklet pane of 1 from booklet that sold for €19.

Halloween A1701

2004, Oct. 9 Litho. *Perf. 13*

3048	A1701 50c multi	1.25	.35

Félix Eboué (1884-1944), Colonial Governor — A1702

2004, Oct. 16 Photo.

3049	A1702 50c multi	1.25	.35

Ouistreham Lighthouse A1703

2004, Oct. 30 *Perf. 13¼*

3050	A1703 50c multi	1.25	.35

block>

Marianne — A1704

Serpentine Die Cut 6¾ Vert.

2004, Nov. 10 Engr.

Booklet Stamp

Self-Adhesive

3051	A1704 50c multi	1.40	.25
a.	Booklet pane, 5 each #2835A, 3051	14.00	

European Capitals Type of 2002

No. 3052 — Attractions in Athens: a, Greek Academy. b, Parthenon. c, Odeon of Herodes Atticus. d, Church of the Holy Apostles, vert.

Perf. 13x13¼, 13¼x13

2004, Nov. 11 Photo.

3052	A1622 Sheet of 4	5.75	5.75
a.-d.	50c Any single	1.40	.40

A1705

A1706

A1707

A1708

A1709

Holiday Greetings A1710

2004, Nov. 12 Photo. *Perf. 13*

3053	A1705 50c multi	1.40	.40

Litho.

3054	A1706 50c multi + label	1.75	1.75
3055	A1707 50c multi + label	1.75	1.75
3056	A1708 50c multi + label	1.75	1.75
3057	A1709 50c multi + label	1.75	1.75
3058	A1710 50c multi + label	1.75	1.75
a.	Vert. strip of 5, #3054-3059 + 5 labels	8.75	8.75
	Miniature sheet, 2 #3058a + 10 labels	17.50	17.50

Booklet Stamps

Self-Adhesive

Serpentine Die Cut 11¼x11

3059	A1706 50c multi	1.40	.40
3060	A1707 50c multi	1.40	.40
3061	A1708 50c multi	1.40	.40
3062	A1709 50c multi	1.40	.40
3063	A1710 50c multi	1.40	.40
a.	Booklet pane, 2 each #3059-3063	14.00	
	Nos. 3053-3063 (11)	17.15	11.15

Miniature sheet containing Nos. 3054-3058 sold for €6.69. Labels could be personalized. No. 3055 exists in a souvenir sheet of 1 stamp without label that sold for €3.

Henri Wallon (1812-1904), Historian and Politician — A1711

2004, Nov. 13 Photo. *Perf. 13*

3064	A1711 50c multi	1.40	.40

Subject Index of French Commemorative Issues

FRANCE

SEMI-POSTAL STAMPS

No. 162 Surcharged in Red and:

No. B1

SP2

1914 Unwmk. Typo. ***Perf. 14x13½***

B1 A22 10c + 5c red 5.00 4.25
Never hinged 6.00
B2 SP2 10c + 5c red 27.50 3.00
Never hinged 55.00
a. Booklet pane of 10 525.00
Never hinged 700.00

Issue dates: #B1, Aug. 11; #B2, Sept. 10.
For overprint see Offices in Morocco #B8.

Widow at Grave SP3

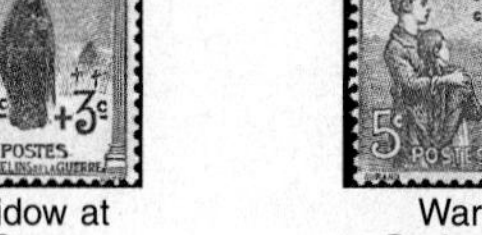

War Orphans SP4

Woman Plowing — SP5

"Trench of Bayonets" SP6

Lion of Belfort SP7

"La Marseillaise" — SP8

1917-19

B3 SP3 2c + 3c vio brn 3.50 3.00
Never hinged 6.00
B4 SP4 5c + 5c grn ('19) 18.00 6.50
Never hinged 30.00
B5 SP5 15c + 10c gray grn 25.00 16.00
Never hinged 50.00
B6 SP5 25c + 15c dp bl 75.00 40.00
Never hinged 125.00
B7 SP6 35c + 25c sl & vio 125.00 85.00
Never hinged 225.00
B8 SP7 50c + 50c pale brn & dk brn 225.00 125.00
Never hinged 450.00
B9 SP8 1fr + 1fr cl & mar 325.00 275.00
Never hinged 675.00
B10 SP8 5fr + 5fr dp bl & blk 1,300. 1,000.
Never hinged 2,700.
Nos. B3-B10 (8) 2,096. 1,550.

See #B20-B23. For surcharges see #B12-B19.

Hospital Ship and Field Hospital SP9

1918, Aug.

B11 SP9 15c + 5c sl & red 95.00 47.50
Never hinged 190.00

Semi-Postal Stamps of 1917-19 Surcharged

1922, Sept. 1

B12 SP3 2c + 1c violet brn .35 *.50*
Never hinged .70
B13 SP4 5c + 2½c green .50 *.70*
Never hinged 1.00
B14 SP5 15c + 5c gray grn 1.10 1.10
Never hinged 1.50
B15 SP5 25c + 5c deep bl 1.75 1.75
Never hinged 3.00
B16 SP6 35c + 5c sl & vio 10.00 10.00
Never hinged 16.00
B17 SP7 50c + 10c pale brn & dk brn 14.00 13.00
Never hinged 24.00
a. Pair, one without surcharge
B18 SP8 1fr + 25c cl & mar 22.50 22.50
Never hinged 40.00
B19 SP8 5fr + 1fr bl & blk 110.00 125.00
Never hinged 210.00
Nos. B12-B19 (8) 160.20 174.55
Set, never hinged 296.20

Style and arrangement of surcharge differs for each denomination.

Types of 1917-19

1926-27

B20 SP3 2c + 1c violet brn 1.00 1.00
Never hinged 1.50
B21 SP7 50c + 10c ol brn & dk brn 17.50 10.00
Never hinged 35.00
B22 SP8 1fr + 25c dp rose & red brn 40.00 30.00
Never hinged 80.00
B23 SP8 5fr + 1fr sl bl & blk 87.50 75.00
Never hinged 160.00
Nos. B20-B23 (4) 146.00 116.00

Sinking Fund Issues

Types of Regular Issues of 1903-07 Surcharged in Red or Blue

1927, Sept. 26

B24 A22 40c + 10c lt blue (R) 4.00 4.00
Never hinged 6.50
B25 A20 50c + 25c green (Bl) 6.00 6.00
Never hinged 8.50

Surcharge on #B25 differs from illustration.

Type of Regular Issue of 1923 Surcharged in Black

B26 A23 1.50fr + 50c orange 9.50 9.50
Never hinged 16.00
Nos. B24-B26 (3) 19.50 19.50

See Nos. B28-B33, B35-B37, B39-B41.

Industry and Agriculture SP10

1928, May Engr. ***Perf. 13½***

B27 SP10 1.50fr + 8.50fr dull blue 100.00 100.00
Never hinged 140.00
a. Blue green 425.00 425.00
Never hinged 600.00

Types of 1903-23 Issues Surcharged like Nos. B24-B26

1928, Oct. 1 ***Perf. 14x13½***

B28 A22 40c + 10c gray lilac (R) 8.75 8.00
Never hinged 16.00
B29 A20 50c + 25c orange brn (Bl) 22.50 20.00
Never hinged 40.00
B30 A23 1.50fr + 50c rose lilac (Bk) 35.00 27.50
Never hinged 65.00
Nos. B28-B30 (3) 66.25 55.50

Types of 1903-23 Issues Surcharged like Nos. B24-B26

1929, Oct. 1

B31 A22 40c + 10c green 15.00 12.50
Never hinged 20.00
B32 A20 50c + 25c lil rose 22.50 22.50
Never hinged 40.00
B33 A23 1.50fr + 50c chestnut 45.00 40.00
Never hinged 80.00
Nos. B31-B33 (3) 82.50 75.00

"The Smile of Reims" SP11

1930, Mar. 15 Engr. ***Perf. 13***

B34 SP11 1.50fr + 3.50fr red vio 65.00 65.00
Never hinged 90.00
a. Booklet pane of 4 250.00
Never hinged 400.00
b. Booklet pane of 8 550.00
Never hinged 800.00

Booklets containing No. B34 have two panes of 4 (#B34a) connected by a gutter, the complete piece constituting #B34b, which is stapled into the booklet through the gutter.

Types of 1903-07 Issues Surcharged like Nos. B24-B25

1930 Oct. 1 ***Perf. 14x13½***

B35 A22 40c + 10c cerise 18.00 13.00
Never hinged 32.50
B36 A20 50c + 25c gray brown 30.00 24.00
Never hinged 55.00
B37 A22 1.50fr + 50c violet 60.00 50.00
Never hinged 100.00
Nos. B35-B37 (3) 108.00 87.00

Allegory, French Provinces SP12

1931, Mar. 1 ***Perf. 13***

B38 SP12 1.50fr + 3.50fr grn 110.00 110.00
Never hinged 190.00

Types of 1903-07 Issues Surcharged like Nos. B24-B25

1931, Oct. 1 ***Perf. 14x13½***

B39 A22 40c + 10c ol grn 35.00 30.00
Never hinged 62.50
B40 A20 50c + 25c gray vio 80.00 75.00
Never hinged 150.00
B41 A22 1.50fr + 50c deep red 75.00 75.00
Never hinged 125.00
Nos. B39-B41 (3) 190.00 180.00

Catalogue values for unused stamps in this section, from this point to the end of the section, are for Never Hinged items.

"France" Giving Aid to an Intellectual SP13

Symbolic of Music SP14

1935, Dec. 9 Engr. ***Perf. 13***

B42 SP13 50c + 10c ultra 3.00 2.00
B43 SP14 50c + 2fr dull red 75.00 35.00

The surtax was for the aid of distressed and exiled intellectuals.
For surcharge see No. B47.

Statue of Liberty SP15

Children of the Unemployed SP16

1936-37

B44 SP15 50c + 25c dk blue ('37) 4.00 3.00
B45 SP15 75c + 50c violet 13.00 7.50

Surtax for the aid of political refugees.
For surcharge see No. B47.

1936, May

B46 SP16 50c + 10c copper red 4.50 3.00

The surtax was for the aid of children of the unemployed.

No. B43 Surcharged in Black

1936, Nov.

B47 SP14 20c on 50c + 2fr dull red 3.00 1.75

Jacques Callot SP17

Anatole France (Jacques Anatole Thibault) — SP18

Hector Berlioz SP19

Victor Hugo SP20

Auguste Rodin SP21

Louis Pasteur SP22

1936-37 **Engr.**

B48 SP17 20c + 10c brown car 3.00 1.50
B49 SP18 30c + 10c emer ('37) 2.50 1.50
B50 SP19 40c + 10c emer 3.00 1.75
B51 SP20 50c + 10c copper red 4.50 2.50
B52 SP21 90c + 10c rose red ('37) 8.75 5.00
B53 SP22 1.50fr + 50c deep ultra 30.00 15.00
Nos. B48-B53 (6) 51.75 27.25

The surtax was used for relief of unemployed intellectuals.

1938

B54 SP18 30c +10c brn car 2.50 1.75
B55 SP17 35c +10c dull grn 2.50 2.25
B56 SP19 55c +10c dull vio 7.50 3.00
B57 SP20 65c +10c ultra 8.00 3.00
B58 SP21 1fr +10c car lake 6.50 3.00
B59 SP22 1.75fr + 25c dp blue 26.00 12.50
Nos. B54-B59 (6) 53.00 25.50

Tug of War SP23

Foot Race SP24

Hiking — SP25

1937, June 16

B60 SP23 20c + 10c brown 2.00 1.50
B61 SP24 40c + 10c red brown 2.00 1.50
B62 SP25 50c + 10c black brn 2.00 1.50
Nos. B60-B62 (3) 6.00 4.50

The surtax was for the Recreation Fund of the employees of the Post, Telephone and Telegraph.

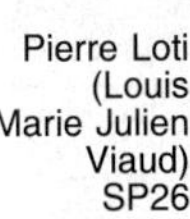

Pierre Loti (Louis Marie Julien Viaud) SP26

1937, Aug.

B63 SP26 50c + 20c rose car 4.50 2.75

The surtax was for the Pierre Loti Monument Fund.

"France" and Infant SP27

1937-39

B64 SP27 65c + 25c brown vio 3.50 1.50
B65 SP27 90c + 30c pck bl ('39) 2.50 1.75

The surtax was used for public health work.

Winged Victory of Samothrace SP28

Jean Baptiste Charcot SP29

1937, Aug.

B66 SP28 30c blue green 100.00 35.00
B67 SP28 55c red 100.00 35.00
Set, hinged 110.00

On sale at the Louvre for 2.50fr. The surtax of 1.65fr was for the benefit of the Louvre Museum.

1938-39

B68 SP29 65c + 35c dk bl grn 1.50 1.50
B69 SP29 90c + 35c brt red vio ('39) 16.00 8.75

Surtax for the benefit of French seamen.

Palace of Versailles SP30

1938, May 9

B70 SP30 1.75fr + 75c dp bl 26.00 15.00

Natl. Exposition of Painting and Sculpture at Versailles.

The surtax was for the benefit of the Versailles Concert Society.

French Soldier SP31

Monument SP32

1938, May 16

B71 SP31 55c + 70c brown vio 5.25 3.50
B72 SP31 65c + 1.10fr pck bl 5.25 3.50

The surtax was for a fund to erect a monument to the glory of the French Infantrymen.

1938, May 25

B73 SP32 55c + 45c vermilion 15.00 8.00

The surtax was for a fund to erect a monument in honor of the Army Medical Corps.

Reims Cathedral SP33

"France" Welcoming Her Sons SP34

1938, July 10

B74 SP33 65c + 35c ultra 10.00 8.75

Completion of the reconstruction of Reims Cathedral, July 10, 1938.

1938, Aug. 8

B75 SP34 65c + 60c rose car 6.00 4.00

The surtax was for the benefit of French volunteers repatriated from Spain.

Curie Issue

Common Design Type

1938, Sept. 1

B76 CD80 1.75fr + 50c dp ultra 13.00 8.75

Victory Parade Passing Arc de Triomphe SP36

1938, Oct. 8

B77 SP36 65c + 35c brown car 4.50 3.00

20th anniversary of the Armistice.

Student and Nurse — SP37

1938, Dec. 1

B78 SP37 65c + 60c pck blue 11.00 6.00

The surtax was for Student Relief.

Blind Man and Radio SP38

1938, Dec.

B79 SP38 90c + 25c brown vio 11.00 6.00

The surtax was used to help provide radios for the blind.

Civilian Facing Firing Squad — SP39

Red Cross Nurse — SP40

1939, Feb. 1

B80 SP39 90c + 35c black brn 11.00 6.00

The surtax was used to erect a monument to civilian victims of World War I.

1939, Mar. 24

B81 SP40 90c + 35c dk sl grn, turq bl & red 9.50 6.00

75th anniv. of the Intl. Red Cross Soc.

Army Engineer SP41

1939, Apr. 3

B82 SP41 70c + 50c vermilion 7.50 5.00

Army Engineering Corps. The surtax was used to erect a monument to those members who died in World War I.

Ministry of Post, Telegraph and Telephone SP42

1939, Apr. 8

B83 SP42 90c + 35c turq blue 22.50 15.00

The surtax was used to aid orphans of employees of the postal system. Opening of the new building for the Ministry of Post, Telegraph and Telephones.

Mother and Child — SP43

Eiffel Tower — SP44

1939, Apr. 24

B84 SP43 90c + 35c red 2.50 1.75

The surtax was used to aid children of the unemployed.

1939, May 5

B85 SP44 90c + 50c red violet 10.00 6.00

50th anniv. of the Eiffel Tower. The surtax was used for celebration festivities.

Puvis de Chavannes — SP45

Claude Debussy SP46

Honoré de Balzac SP47

Claude Bernard SP48

1939-40

B86 SP45 40c + 10c ver 1.10 .70
B87 SP46 70c + 10c brn vio 5.50 1.90
B87A SP46 80c + 10c brn vio ('40) 6.00 5.00
B88 SP47 90c + 10c brt red vio 5.50 1.90
B88A SP47 1fr + 10c brt red vio ('40) 6.00 5.00
B89 SP48 2.25fr + 25c brt ultra 20.00 8.00
B89A SP48 2.50fr + 25c brt ultra ('40) 6.00 5.00
Nos. B86-B89A (7) 50.10 27.50

The surtax was used to aid unemployed intellectuals.

Mothers and Children
SP49 SP50

1939, June 15

B90 SP49 70c + 80c bl, grn & vio 3.50 3.25
B91 SP50 90c + 60c dk brn, dl vio & brn 5.75 4.25

The surtax was used to aid France's repopulation campaign.

"The Letter" by Jean Honoré Fragonard
SP51

Statue of Widow and Children
SP52

1939, July 6

B92 SP51 40c + 60c brn, sep & pur 3.50 2.75

The surtax was used for the Postal Museum.

1939, July 20

B93 SP52 70c + 30c brown vio 17.50 8.50

Surtax for the benefit of French seamen.

French Soldier
SP53

Colonial Trooper
SP54

1940, Feb. 15

B94 SP53 40c + 60c sepia 2.50 1.75
B95 SP54 1fr + 50c turq blue 2.50 1.75

The surtax was used to assist the families of mobilized men.

World Map Showing French Possessions — SP55

1940, Apr. 15

B96 SP55 1fr + 25c scarlet 2.50 1.60

Marshal Joseph J. C. Joffre
SP56

Marshal Ferdinand Foch — SP57

Gen. Joseph S. Gallieni
SP58

Woman Plowing
SP59

1940, May 1

B97 SP56 80c + 45c choc 6.00 4.25
B98 SP57 1fr + 50c dk vio 5.50 3.50
B99 SP58 1.50fr + 50c brn red 5.50 3.50
B100 SP59 2.50fr + 50c indigo & dl bl 10.00 8.50
Nos. B97-B100 (4) 27.00 19.75

The surtax was used for war charities.

Doctor, Nurse, Soldier and Family
SP60

Nurse and Wounded Soldier
SP61

1940, May 12

B101 SP60 80c + 1fr dk grn & red 6.50 4.25
B102 SP61 1fr + 2fr sep & red 8.00 4.25

The surtax was used for the Red Cross.

Nurse with Injured Children — SP62

1940, Nov. 12

B103 SP62 1fr + 2fr sepia .85 .75

The surtax was used for victims of the war.

Wheat Harvest
SP63

Sowing
SP64

Picking Grapes
SP65

Grazing Cattle
SP66

1940, Dec. 2

B104 SP63 80c + 2fr brn blk 2.25 1.40
B105 SP64 1fr + 2fr chestnut 2.25 1.40
B106 SP65 1.50fr + 2fr brt vio 2.25 1.40
B107 SP66 2.50fr + 2fr dp grn 3.00 1.40
Nos. B104-B107 (4) 9.75 5.60

The surtax was for national relief.

Prisoners of War
SP67 SP68

1941, Jan. 1

B108 SP67 80c + 5fr dark grn 1.00 1.00
B109 SP68 1fr + 5fr rose brn 1.00 1.00

The surtax was for prisoners of war.

Science Fighting Cancer
SP69

1941, Feb. 20

B110 SP69 2.50fr + 50c slate blk & brn 1.25 .90

Surtax used for the control of cancer.

Type of 1941 Surcharged "+10c" in Blue

1941, Mar. 4

B111 A109 1fr + 10c crimson .20 .20

Men Hauling Coal
SP70

"France" Aiding Needy Man
SP71

1941

B112 SP70 1fr + 2fr sepia 1.75 1.40
B113 SP71 2.50fr + 7.50fr dk bl 6.00 3.00

The surtax was for Marshal Pétain's National Relief Fund.

Liner Pasteur
SP72

Red Surcharge

1941, July 17

B114 SP72 1fr + 1fr on 70c dk bl grn .20 .20

World Map, Mercator Projection
SP73

1941

B115 SP73 1fr + 1fr multi .40 .30

Fisherman — SP74

1941, Oct. 23

B116 SP74 1fr + 9fr dk blue grn .70 .70

Surtax for benefit of French seamen.

Arms of Various Cities

Nancy
SP75

Lille
SP76

Rouen
SP77

Bordeaux
SP78

Toulouse
SP79

Clermont-Ferrand
SP80

Marseille
SP81

Lyon
SP82

Rennes
SP83

Reims
SP84

Montpellier
SP85

Paris
SP86

1941 *Perf. 14x13*

B117	SP75	20c + 30c brn blk	2.25	2.25
B118	SP76	40c + 60c org brn	2.25	2.25
B119	SP77	50c + 70c grnsh blue	2.25	2.25
B120	SP78	70c + 80c rose vio	2.25	2.25
B121	SP79	80c + 1fr dp rose	2.25	2.25
B122	SP80	1fr + 1fr black	2.25	2.25
B123	SP81	1.50fr + 2fr dk bl	2.25	2.25
B124	SP82	2fr + 2fr dk vio	2.25	2.25
B125	SP83	2.50fr + 3fr brt grn	2.25	2.25
B126	SP84	3fr + 5fr org brn	2.25	2.25
B127	SP85	5fr + 6fr brt ultra	2.25	2.25
B128	SP86	10fr + 10fr dk red	2.25	2.25
		Nos. B117-B128 (12)	27.00	27.00

Count de La Pérouse SP87

1942, Mar. 23 *Perf. 13*

B129 SP87 2.50fr + 7.50fr ultra 1.10 1.00

Jean Francois de Galaup de La Pérouse, (1741-88), French navigator and explorer. The surtax was for National Relief.

Planes over Fields SP88

1942, Apr. 4

B130 SP88 1.50fr + 3.50fr lt vio 1.50 1.25

The surtax was for the benefit of French airmen and their familes.

Alexis Chabrier SP89

1942, May 18

B131 SP89 2fr + 3fr sepia .75 .75

Emmanuel Chabrier (1841-1894), composer, birth centenary. The surtax was for works of charity among musicians.

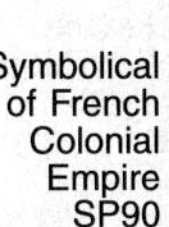

Symbolical of French Colonial Empire SP90

1942, May 18

B132 SP90 1.50fr + 8.50fr black .55 .55

The surtax was for National Relief.

Jean de Vienne SP91

1942, June 16

B133 SP91 1.50fr + 8.50fr sepia .70 .70

600th anniv. of the birth of Jean de Vienne, 1st admiral of France. The surtax was for the benefit of French seamen.

Type of Regular Issue, 1941 Surcharged in Carmine

1942, Sept. 10 *Perf. 14x13½*

B134 A116 1.50fr + 50c brt ultra .20 .20

The surtax was for national relief ("Secours National").

Arms of Various Cities

Chambéry SP92

La Rochelle SP93

Poitiers SP94

Orléans SP95

Grenoble SP96

Angers SP97

Dijon SP98

Limoges SP99

Le Havre SP100

Nantes SP101

Nice SP102

St. Etienne SP103

Perf. 14x13

1942, Oct. **Unwmk.** **Engr.**

B135	SP92	50c + 60c blk	2.75	2.75
B136	SP93	60c + 70c grnsh blue	2.75	2.75
B137	SP94	80c + 1fr rose	2.75	2.75
B138	SP95	1fr + 1.30fr dk green	2.75	2.75
B139	SP96	1.20fr + 1.50fr rose vio	2.75	2.75
B140	SP97	1.50fr + 1.80fr slate bl	2.75	2.75
B141	SP98	2fr + 2.30fr deep rose	2.75	2.75
B142	SP99	2.40fr + 2.80fr slate grn	2.75	2.75
B143	SP100	3fr + 3.50fr dp violet	2.75	2.75
B144	SP101	4fr + 5fr lt ultra	2.75	2.75
B145	SP102	4.50fr + 6fr red	2.75	2.75
B146	SP103	5fr + 7fr brt red vio	2.75	2.75
		Nos. B135-B146 (12)	33.00	33.00

The surtax was for national relief.

Tricolor Legion SP104

1942, Oct. 12 *Perf. 13*

B147	SP104	1.20 + 8.80fr dk blue	7.50	7.50
a.		Vert. pair, #B147, B148 + albino impression	16.00	16.00
B148	SP104	1.20 + 8.80fr crim	7.50	7.50

These stamps were printed in sheets of 20 stamps and 5 albino impressions arranged: 2 horizontal rows of 5 dark blue stamps, 1 row of 5 albino impressions, and 2 rows of 5 crimson stamps.

Marshal Henri Philippe Pétain SP105 SP106

1943, Feb. 8

B149	SP105	1fr + 10fr rose red	2.75	2.75
B150	SP105	1fr + 10fr blue	2.75	2.75
B151	SP106	2fr + 12fr rose red	2.75	2.75
B152	SP106	2fr + 12fr blue	2.75	2.75
a.		Strip, #B149-B152 + label	12.00	12.00

The surtax was for national relief. Printed in sheets of 20, the 10 blue stamps at left, the 10 rose red at right, separated by a vert. row of 5 white labels bearing a tri-colored battle-ax.

Marshal Pétain — SP107

"Work" — SP108

"Family" SP109

"State" SP110

Marshal Pétain — SP111

1943, June 7

B153	SP107	1.20fr + 1.40fr dull vio	13.00	12.00
B154	SP108	1.50fr + 2.50fr red	13.00	12.00
B155	SP109	2.40fr + 7fr brown	13.00	12.00
B156	SP110	4fr + 10fr dk violet	13.00	12.00
B157	SP111	5fr + 15fr red brown	13.00	12.00
a.		Strip of 5, #B153-B157	85.00	85.00

Pétain's 87th birthday.
The surtax was for national relief.

Civilians Under Air Attack — SP112

Civilians Doing Farm Work — SP113

Prisoner's Family Doing Farm Work SP114

1943, Aug. 23

B158 SP112 1.50fr + 3.50fr black .40 .40

Surtax was for bomb victims at Billancourt, Dunkirk, Lorient, Saint-Nazaire.

1943, Sept. 27

B159	SP113	1.50fr + 8.50fr sepia	.75	.75
B160	SP114	2.40fr + 7.60fr dk grn	.75	.75

The surtax was for families of war prisoners.

Michel de Montaigne SP115

Picardy Costume SP121

1.20fr+1.50fr, Francois Clouet. 1.50fr+3fr, Ambrose Paré. 2.40fr+4fr, Chevalier Pierre de Bayard. 4fr+6fr, Duke of Sully. 5fr+10fr, Henri IV.

1943, Oct. 2

B161	SP115	60c + 80c Prus green	1.75	1.75
B162	SP115	1.20fr + 1.50fr black	1.75	1.75
B163	SP115	1.50fr + 3fr deep ultra	1.75	1.75
B164	SP115	2.40fr + 4fr red	1.75	1.75
B165	SP115	4fr + 6fr dull brn red	2.00	2.00
B166	SP115	5fr + 10fr dull green	2.00	2.00
		Nos. B161-B166 (6)	11.00	11.00

The surtax was for national relief. Issued to honor famous 16th century Frenchmen.

1943, Dec. 27

Designs: 18th Century Costumes: 1.20fr+2fr, Brittany. 1.50fr+4fr, Ile de France. 2.40+5fr, Burgundy. 4fr+6fr, Auvergne. 5fr+7fr, Provence.

B167	SP121	60c + 1.30fr sepia	1.65	1.65
B168	SP121	1.20fr + 2fr lt vio	1.65	1.65
B169	SP121	1.50fr + 4fr turq blue	1.65	1.65
B170	SP121	2.40fr + 5fr rose car	1.65	1.65
B171	SP121	4fr + 6fr chlky blue	2.25	2.25
B172	SP121	5fr + 7fr red	2.25	2.25
		Nos. B167-B172 (6)	11.10	11.10

The surtax was for national relief.

Admiral Tourville SP127

Charles Gounod SP128

1944, Feb. 21

B173 SP127 4fr + 6fr dull red brn .50 .50

300th anniv. of the birth of Admiral Anne-Hilarion de Cotentin Tourville (1642-1701).

1944, Mar. 27 ***Perf. 14x13***

B174 SP128 1.50fr + 3.50fr sepia .70 .70

50th anniv. of the death of Charles Gounod, composer (1818-1893).

Marshal Pétain SP129

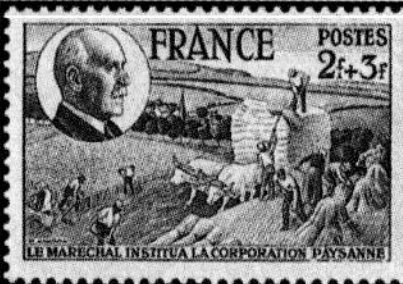
Farming SP130

Industry SP131

1944, Apr. 24 ***Perf. 13***

B175 SP129 1.50fr + 3.50fr sepia 3.00 3.00
B176 SP130 2fr + 3fr dp ultra .50 .50
B177 SP131 4fr + 6fr rose red .50 .50
Nos. B175-B177 (3) 4.00 4.00

Marshal Henri Pétain's 88th birthday.

Modern Streamliner, 19th Cent. Train SP132

Molière (Jean-Baptiste Poquelin) SP133

1944, Aug. 14

B178 SP132 4fr + 6fr black 1.75 1.75

Centenary of the Paris-Rouen, Paris-Orléans railroad.

1944, July 31

Designs: 80c+2.20fr, Jules Hardouin Mansart. 1.20fr+2.80fr, Blaise Pascal. 1.50fr+3.50fr, Louis II of Bourbon. 2fr+4fr, Jean-Baptiste Colbert. 4fr+6fr, Louis XIV.

B179 SP133 50c + 1.50fr rose car 1.50 1.50
B180 SP133 80c + 2.20fr dk green 1.25 1.25
B181 SP133 1.20fr + 2.80fr black 1.25 1.25
B182 SP133 1.50fr + 3.50fr brt ultra 1.25 1.25
B183 SP133 2fr + 4fr dull brn red 1.25 1.25
B184 SP133 4fr + 6fr red 1.25 1.25
Nos. B179-B184 (6) 7.75 7.75

Noted 17th century Frenchmen.

Angoulême SP139

Chartres SP140

Amiens SP141

Beauvais SP142

Albi — SP143

1944, Nov. 20

B185 SP139 50c + 1.50fr black .25 .25
B186 SP140 80c + 2.20fr rose vio .40 .40
B187 SP141 1.20fr + 2.80fr brn car .55 .55
B188 SP142 1.50fr + 3.50fr dp blue .55 .55
B189 SP143 4fr + 6fr orange red .55 .55
Nos. B185-B189 (5) 2.30 2.30

French Cathedrals.

Coat of Arms of Renouard de Villayer SP144

Sarah Bernhardt SP145

1944, Dec. 9 **Engr.**

B190 SP144 1.50fr + 3.50fr dp brn .20 .20

Stamp Day.

1945, May 16 **Unwmk.** ***Perf. 13***

B191 SP145 4fr + 1fr dk violet brn .30 .30

100th anniv. of the birth of Sarah Bernhardt, actress.

War Victims SP146

1945, May 16

B192 SP146 4fr + 6fr dk violet brn .20 .20

The surtax was for war victims of the P.T.T.

Tuberculosis Patient — SP147

1945, May 16 **Typo.** ***Perf. 14x13½***

B193 SP147 2fr + 1fr red orange .20 .20

Surtax for the aid of tuberculosis victims.
For surcharge see No. 561.

Boy and Girl SP148

Burning of Oradour Church SP149

1945, July 9 **Engr.** ***Perf. 13***

B194 SP148 4fr + 2fr Prus green .20 .20

The surtax was used for child welfare.

1945, Oct. 13

B195 SP149 4fr + 2fr sepia .20 .20

Destruction of Oradour, June, 1944.

Louis XI and Post Rider SP150

1945, Oct. 13

B196 SP150 2fr + 3fr deep ultra .40 .40

Stamp Day.
For overprint see French West Africa #B2.

Ruins of Dunkirk SP151

Ruins of Rouen SP152

Ruins of Caen SP153

Ruins of Saint-Malo SP154

1945, Nov. 5

B197 SP151 1.50fr + 1.50fr red brown .25 .20
B198 SP152 2fr + 2fr violet .25 .20
B199 SP153 2.40fr + 2.60fr blue .25 .20
B200 SP154 4fr + 4fr black .25 .20
Nos. B197-B200 (4) 1.00 .80

The surtax was to aid the suffering residents of Dunkirk, Rouen, Caen and Saint Malo.

Alfred Fournier SP155

Henri Becquerel SP156

1946, Feb. 4 **Engr.** ***Perf. 13***

B201 SP155 2fr + 3fr red brown .20 .20
B202 SP156 2fr + 3fr violet .20 .20

Issued to raise funds for the fight against venereal disease (#B201) and for the struggle against cancer (#B202).

No. B202 for the 50th anniv. of the discovery of radioactivity by Henri Becquerel.

See No. B221.

Church of the Invalides, Paris — SP157

1946, Mar. 11

B203 SP157 4fr + 6fr red brown .20 .20

The surtax was to aid disabled war veterans.

French Warships SP158

1946, Apr. 8

B204 SP158 2fr + 3fr gray black .30 .30

The surtax was for naval charities.

"The Letter" by Jean Siméon Chardin SP159

Fouquet de la Varane SP160

1946, May 25

B205 SP159 2fr + 3fr brown red .40 .40

The surtax was used for the Postal Museum.

1946, June 29

B206 SP160 3fr + 2fr sepia .30 .30

Stamp Day.

François Villon — SP161

Designs: 3fr+1fr, Jean Fouquet. 4fr+3fr, Philippe de Commynes. 5fr+4fr, Joan of Arc. 6fr+5fr, Jean de Gerson. 10fr+6fr, Charles VII.

1946, Oct. 28

B207 SP161 2fr + 1fr dk Prus grn 1.25 1.25
B208 SP161 3fr + 1fr dk blue vio 1.25 1.25
B209 SP161 4fr + 3fr henna brn 1.25 1.25
B210 SP161 5fr + 4fr ultra 1.25 1.25
B211 SP161 6fr + 5fr sepia 1.25 1.25
B212 SP161 10fr + 6fr red 1.25 1.25
Nos. B207-B212 (6) 7.50 7.50

Church of St. Sernin, Toulouse SP167

Notre Dame du Port, Clermont-Ferrand SP168

Cathedral of St. Front, Perigueux SP169

Cathedral of St. Julien, Le Mans SP170

Cathedral of Notre Dame, Paris SP171

François Michel le Tellier de Louvois SP172

1947 **Engr.**

B213 SP167 1fr + 1fr car rose .80 .80
B214 SP168 3fr + 2fr dk bl vio 2.25 2.25
B215 SP169 4fr + 3fr henna brn 1.10 1.10
B216 SP170 6fr + 4fr dp bl 1.10 1.10
B217 SP171 10fr + 6fr dk gray grn 2.25 2.25
Nos. B213-B217 (5) 7.50 7.50

1947, Mar. 15

B218 SP172 4.50fr + 5.50fr car rose 1.00 1.00

Stamp Day, Mar. 15, 1947.

Submarine Pens, Shipyard and Monument SP173

1947, Aug. 2

B219 SP173 6fr + 4fr bluish black .40 .40

British commando raid on the Nazi U-boat base at St. Nazaire, 1942.

Liberty Highway Marker — SP174

Louis Braille — SP175

1947, Sept. 5

B220 SP174 6fr + 4fr dk green .60 .60

The surtax was to help defray maintenance costs of the Liberty Highway.

Fournier Type of 1946

1947, Oct. 20

B221 SP155 2fr + 3fr indigo .20 .20

1948, Jan. 19

B222 SP175 6fr + 4fr purple .30 .30

Etienne Arago SP176

Alphonse de Lamartine SP177

1948, Mar. 6

B223 SP176 6fr + 4fr black brn .45 .45

Stamp Day, March 6-7, 1948.

1948, Apr. 5 **Engr.** ***Perf. 13***

Designs: 3fr+2fr, Alexandre A. Ledru-Rollin. 4fr+3fr, Louis Blanc. 5fr+4fr, Albert (Alexandre Martin). 6fr+5fr, Pierre J. Proudhon. 10fr+6fr, Louis Auguste Blanqui. 15fr+7fr, Armand Barbés. 20fr+8fr, Dennis A. Affre.

B224 SP177 1fr + 1fr dk grn 1.00 1.00
B225 SP177 3fr + 2fr henna brn 1.00 1.00
B226 SP177 4fr + 3fr vio brn 1.00 1.00
B227 SP177 5fr + 4fr lt bl grn 2.50 2.50
B228 SP177 6fr + 5fr indigo 2.00 2.00
B229 SP177 10fr + 6fr car rose 2.00 2.00
B230 SP177 15fr + 7fr sl blk 2.50 2.50
B231 SP177 20fr + 8fr purple 2.50 2.50
Nos. B224-B231 (8) 14.50 14.50

Centenary of the Revolution of 1848.

Dr. Léon Charles Albert Calmette SP178

1948, June 18

B232 SP178 6fr + 4fr dk grnsh bl .35 .35

1st Intl. Congress on the Calmette-Guerin bacillus vaccine.

Farmer — SP179

Designs: 5fr+3fr, Fisherman. 8fr+4fr, Miner. 10fr+6fr, Metal worker.

1949, Feb. 14

B233 SP179 3fr + 1fr claret .80 .35
B234 SP179 5fr + 3fr dk blue .80 .55
B235 SP179 8fr + 4fr indigo .80 .45
B236 SP179 10fr + 6fr dk red 1.00 .65
Nos. B233-B236 (4) 3.40 2.00

Etienne François de Choiseul and Post Cart SP180

Baron de la Brède et de Montesquieu SP181

1949, Mar. 26

B237 SP180 15fr + 5fr dk green 1.00 1.00

Stamp Day, Mar. 26-27, 1949.

1949, Nov. 14

Designs: 8fr+2fr, Voltaire. 10fr+3fr, Antoine Watteau. 12fr+4fr, Georges de Buffon. 15fr+5fr, Joseph F. Dupleix. 25fr+10fr, A. R. J. Turgot.

B238 SP181 5fr + 1fr dk grn 3.50 3.50
B239 SP181 8fr + 2fr indigo 3.50 3.50
B240 SP181 10fr + 3fr brn red 3.50 3.50
B241 SP181 12fr + 4fr purple 3.50 3.50
B242 SP181 15fr + 5fr rose car 4.50 4.50
B243 SP181 25fr + 10fr ultra 4.50 4.50
Nos. B238-B243 (6) 23.00 23.00

"Spring" SP182

Designs: 8fr+2fr, Summer. 12fr+3fr, Autumn. 15fr+4fr, Winter.

1949, Dec. 19

B244 SP182 5fr + 1fr green 1.75 1.75
B245 SP182 8fr + 2fr yel org 1.75 1.75
B246 SP182 12fr + 3fr purple 2.00 2.00
B247 SP182 15fr + 4fr dp blue 2.50 2.50
Nos. B244-B247 (4) 8.00 8.00

Postman — SP183

1950, Mar. 11

B248 SP183 12fr + 3fr dp bl 3.25 2.25

Stamp Day, Mar. 11-12, 1950.

André de Chénier SP184

Alexandre Brongniart, Bust by Houdon SP185

8fr+3fr, J. L. David. 10fr+4fr, Lazare Carnot. 12fr+5fr, G. J. Danton. 15fr+6fr, Maximilian Robespierre. 20fr+10fr, Louis Hoche.

1950, July 10 **Engr.** ***Perf. 13***

Frames in Indigo

B249 SP184 5fr + 2fr brn vio 8.50 8.50
B250 SP184 8fr + 3fr blk brn 8.50 8.50
B251 SP184 10fr + 4fr lake 8.50 8.50
B252 SP184 12fr + 5fr red brn 9.50 9.50
B253 SP184 15fr + 6fr dk grn 10.00 10.00
B254 SP184 20fr + 10fr dk vio bl 10.00 10.00
Nos. B249-B254 (6) 55.00 55.00

1950, Dec. 22

15fr+3fr, "L'Amour" by Etienne M. Falconet.

B255 SP185 8fr + 2fr ind & car 2.25 2.00
B256 SP185 15fr + 3fr red brn & car 2.25 2.00

The surtax was for the Red Cross.

Mail Car Interior SP186

Alfred de Musset SP187

1951, Mar. 10 **Unwmk.** ***Perf. 13***

B257 SP186 12fr + 3fr lilac gray 3.00 3.00

Stamp Day, Mar. 10-11, 1951.

1951, June 2

8fr+2fr, Eugène Delacroix. 10fr+3fr, J.-L. Gay-Lussac. 12fr+4fr, Robert Surcouf. 15fr+5fr, C. M. Talleyrand. 30fr+10fr, Napoleon I.

Frames in Dark Brown

B258 SP187 5fr + 1fr dk grn 6.75 6.75
B259 SP187 8fr + 2fr vio brn 7.25 7.25
B260 SP187 10fr + 3fr grnsh black 7.25 7.25
B261 SP187 12fr + 4fr dk vio brn 7.25 7.25
B262 SP187 15fr + 5fr brn car 7.50 7.50
B263 SP187 30fr + 10fr indigo 11.00 11.00
Nos. B258-B263 (6) 47.00 47.00

Child at Prayer by Le Maître de Moulins SP188

18th Century Child by Quentin de la Tour SP189

1951, Dec. 15

Cross in Red

B264 SP188 12fr + 3fr dk brown 3.25 2.75
B265 SP189 15fr + 5fr dp ultra 3.25 2.75

The surtax was for the Red Cross.

Stagecoach of 1844 SP190

1952, Mar. 8 *Perf. 13*

B266 SP190 12fr + 3fr dp green 4.75 4.75

Stamp Day, Mar. 8, 1952.

Gustave Flaubert — SP191

Portraits: 12fr+3fr, Edouard Manet. 15fr+4fr, Camille Saint-Saens. 18fr+5fr, Henri Poincaré. 20fr+6fr, Georges-Eugene Haussmann. 30fr+7fr, Adolphe Thiers.

1952, Oct. 18

Frames in Dark Brown

B267 SP191 8fr + 2fr indigo 5.50 5.50
B268 SP191 12fr + 3fr vio blue 5.50 5.50
B269 SP191 15fr + 4fr dk grn 5.50 5.50
B270 SP191 18fr + 5fr dk brn 7.50 7.50
B271 SP191 20fr + 6fr car 7.50 7.50
B272 SP191 30fr + 7fr purple 7.50 7.50
Nos. B267-B272 (6) 39.00 39.00

Cupid from Diana Fountain Versailles SP192

15fr+5fr, Similar detail, cupid facing left.

1952, Dec. 13

Cross in Red

B273 SP192 12fr + 3fr dk grn 4.50 4.00
B274 SP192 15fr + 5fr indigo 4.50 4.00
a. Booklet pane of 10 190.00

The surtax was for the Red Cross.

Count d'Argenson SP193

St. Bernard SP194

1953, Mar. 14

B275 SP193 12fr + 3fr dp blue 2.50 2.50

Day of the Stamp. Surtax for the Red Cross.

1953, July 9

12fr+3fr, Olivier de Serres. 15fr+4fr, Jean Philippe Rameau. 18fr+5fr, Gaspard Monge. 20fr+6fr, Jules Michelet. 30fr+7fr, Marshal Hubert Lyautey.

B276 SP194 8fr + 2fr ultra 6.00 6.00
B277 SP194 12fr + 3fr dk grn 6.00 6.00
B278 SP194 15fr + 4fr brn car 8.75 8.75
B279 SP194 18fr + 5fr dk blue 9.25 9.25
B280 SP194 20fr + 6fr dk pur 9.25 9.25
B281 SP194 30fr + 7fr brown 11.50 11.50
Nos. B276-B281 (6) 50.75 50.75

The surtax was for the Red Cross.

Madame Vigée-Lebrun and her Daughter SP195

Count Antoine de La Vallette SP196

Design: 15fr+5fr, "The Return from Baptism," by Louis Le Nain.

1953, Dec. 12

Cross in Red

B282 SP195 12fr + 3fr red brn 6.00 6.00
a. Bklt. pane, 4 each, gutter btwn. 80.00
B283 SP195 15fr + 5fr indigo 8.00 8.00

The surtax was for the Red Cross.

1954, Mar. 20 **Engr.** *Perf. 13*

B284 SP196 12fr + 3fr dp grn & choc 3.50 3.00

Stamp Day, Mar. 20, 1954.

Louis IX SP197

"The Sick Child," by Eugene Carrière SP198

Portraits: 15fr+5fr, Jacques Benigne Bossuet. 18fr+6fr, Sadi Carnot. 20fr+7fr, Antoine Bourdelle. 25fr+8fr, Dr. Emile Roux. 30fr+10fr, Paul Valéry.

1954, July 10

B285 SP197 12fr + 4fr dp bl 14.50 14.50
B286 SP197 15fr + 5fr pur 16.00 16.00
B287 SP197 18fr + 6fr dk brn 15.00 15.00
B288 SP197 20fr + 7fr crim 21.00 21.00
B289 SP197 25fr + 8fr ind 21.00 21.00
B290 SP197 30fr + 10fr dp claret 21.00 21.00
Nos. B285-B290 (6) 108.50 108.50

See Nos. B303-B308, B312-B317.

1954, Dec. 18

Design: 15fr+5fr, "Young Girl with Doves," by Jean Baptiste Greuze.

Cross in Red

B291 SP198 12fr + 3fr vio gray & indigo 7.00 7.00
a. Bklt. pane, 4 each, gutter btwn. 90.00
B292 SP198 15fr + 5fr dk brn & org brn 8.00 8.00

No. B291a for 90th anniv. of the Red Cross.
The surtax was for the Red Cross.

Balloon Post, 1870 SP199

1955, Mar. 19 **Unwmk.** *Perf. 13*

B293 SP199 12fr + 3fr multi 4.75 3.25

Stamp Day, Mar. 19-20, 1955.

King Philip II — SP200

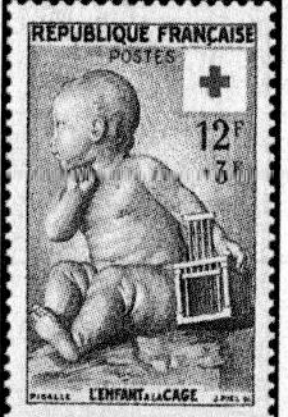
Child with Cage by Pigalle — SP201

Portraits: 15fr+6fr, Francois de Malherbé. 18fr+7fr, Sebastien de Vauban. 25fr+8fr, Charles G. de Vergennes. 30fr+9fr, Pierre S. de Laplace. 50fr+15fr, Pierre Auguste Renoir.

1955, June 11

B294 SP200 12fr + 5fr brt pur 12.50 12.50
B295 SP200 15fr + 6fr dp bl 12.50 12.50
B296 SP200 18fr + 7fr dp green 14.00 14.00
B297 SP200 25fr + 8fr gray 19.00 19.00
B298 SP200 30fr + 9fr rose brn 20.00 20.00
B299 SP200 50fr + 15fr blue grn 22.50 22.50
Nos. B294-B299 (6) 100.50 100.50

See Nos. B321-B326.

1955, Dec. 17

Design: 15fr+5fr, Child with Goose, by Boethus of Chalcedon.

Cross in Red

B300 SP201 12fr + 3fr claret 5.25 5.25
B301 SP201 15fr + 5fr dk bl 5.25 5.25
a. Booklet pane of 10 110.00

The surtax was for the Red Cross.

Francois of Taxis SP202

1956, Mar. 17 **Engr.** *Perf. 13*

B302 SP202 12fr + 3fr ultra, grn & dk brn 2.25 2.25

Stamp Day, Mar. 17-18, 1956.

Portrait Type of 1954

Portraits: No. 303, Guillaume Budé. No. B304, Jean Goujon. No. B305, Samuel de Champlain. No. B306, Jean Simeon Chardin. No. B307, Maurice Barrès. No. B308, Maurice Ravel.

1956, June 9 *Perf. 13*

B303 SP197 12fr + 3fr saph 5.25 5.25
B304 SP197 12fr + 3fr lil gray 5.25 5.25
B305 SP197 12fr + 3fr brt red 5.25 5.25
B306 SP197 15fr + 5fr green 7.75 7.75
B307 SP197 15fr + 5fr vio brn 7.75 7.75
B308 SP197 15fr + 5fr dp vio 7.75 7.75
Nos. B303-B308 (6) 39.00 39.00

Peasant Boy by Le Nain — SP203

Design: 15fr+5fr, Gilles by Watteau.

1956, Dec. 8 **Unwmk.**

Cross in Red

B309 SP203 12fr + 3fr ol gray 2.50 2.50
a. Bklt. pane, 4 ea, gutter btwn. 35.00
B310 SP203 15fr + 5fr rose lake 2.50 2.50

The surtax was for the Red Cross.

Genoese Felucca, 1750 SP204

1957, Mar. 16 *Perf. 13*

B311 SP204 12fr +3fr bluish gray & brn blk 1.50 1.40

Day of the Stamp, Mar. 16, 1957, and honoring the Maritime Postal Service.

Portrait Type of 1954

1957, June 15

Portraits: No. B312, Jean de Joinville. No. B313, Bernard Palissy. No. B314, Quentin de la Tour. No. B315, Hugues Félicité Robert de Lamennais. No. B316, George Sand. No. B317, Jules Guesde.

B312 SP197 12fr + 3fr ol gray & ol grn 2.50 2.50
B313 SP197 12fr + 3fr grnsh blk & grnsh bl 2.75 2.75
B314 SP197 15fr + 5fr cl & brt red 2.75 2.75
B315 SP197 15fr + 5fr ultra & ind 2.75 2.75
B316 SP197 18fr + 7fr grnsh blk & dk grn 3.50 3.50
B317 SP197 18fr + 7fr dk vio brn & red brn 3.50 3.50
Nos. B312-B317 (6) 17.75 17.75

Blind Man and Beggar, Engraving by Jacques Callot — SP205

Design: 20fr+8fr, Women beggars.

1957, Dec. 7 **Engr.** *Perf. 13*

B318 SP205 15fr + 7fr ultra & red 3.00 3.00
a. Bklt. pane, 4 ea, gutter btwn. 35.00
B319 SP205 20fr + 8fr dk vio brn & red 3.00 3.00

The surtax was for the Red Cross.

Motorized Mail Distribution SP206

1958, Mar. 15

B320 SP206 15fr + 5fr multi 1.40 1.10

Stamp Day, Mar. 15.

Portrait Type of 1955

Portraits: No. B321, Joachim du Bellay. No. B322, Jean Bart. No. B323, Denis Diderot. No. B324, Gustave Courbet. 20fr+8fr, J. B. Carpeaux. 35fr+15fr, Toulouse-Lautrec.

1958, June 7 **Engr.** *Perf. 13*

B321 SP200 12fr + 4fr yel grn 1.65 1.65
B322 SP200 12fr + 4fr dk blue 1.65 1.65
B323 SP200 15fr + 5fr dull cl 1.75 1.75
B324 SP200 15fr + 5fr ultra 1.75 1.75
B325 SP200 20fr + 8fr brt red 2.10 2.10
B326 SP200 35fr + 15fr green 2.10 2.10
Nos. B321-B326 (6) 11.00 11.00

St. Vincent de Paul — SP207

Portrait: 20fr+8fr, J. H. Dunant.

1958, Dec. 6 **Unwmk.**

Cross in Carmine

B327 SP207 15fr + 7fr grayish grn 1.00 1.00
a. Bklt. pane, 4 each, gutter btwn. 15.00
B328 SP207 20fr + 8fr violet 1.00 1.00

The surtax was for the Red Cross.

Plane Landing at Night SP208

1959, Mar. 21

B329 SP208 20fr + 5fr sl grn, blk & rose .45 .45

Issued for Stamp Day, Mar. 21, and to publicize night air mail service.
The surtax was for the Red Cross.
See No. 1089.

Geoffroi de Villehardouin and Ships — SP209

Designs: No. B331, André Le Nôtre and formal garden. No. B332, Jean Le Rond d'Alembert, books and wheel. No. B333, David d'Angers, statue and building. No. B334, M. F. X. Bichat and torch. No. B335, Frédéric Auguste Bartholdi, Statue of Liberty and Lion of Belfort.

1959, June 13 **Engr.** ***Perf. 13***

B330 SP209 15fr + 5fr vio blue 1.10 1.10
B331 SP209 15fr + 5fr dk sl grn 1.10 1.10
B332 SP209 20fr + 10fr olive bis 1.25 1.25
B333 SP209 20fr + 10fr dk gray 1.25 1.25
B334 SP209 30fr + 10fr dk car rose 1.65 1.65
B335 SP209 30fr + 10fr org brn 1.65 1.65
Nos. B330-B335 (6) 8.00 8.00

The surtax was for the Red Cross.

No. 927 Surcharged

1959, Dec. **Typo.** ***Perf. 14x13½***

B336 A328 25fr + 5fr black & red .30 .30

Surtax for the flood victims at Frejus.

Charles Michel de l'Epée — SP210

Design: 25fr+10fr, Valentin Hauy.

1959, Dec. 5 **Engr.** ***Perf. 13***

Cross in Carmine

B337 SP210 20fr + 10fr blk & cl 1.00 1.00
a. Bklt. pane, 4 each, gutter btwn. 15.00
B338 SP210 25fr + 10fr dk blue & blk 1.00 1.00

The surtax was for the Red Cross.

Ship Laying Underwater Cable SP211

1960, Mar. 12

B339 SP211 20c + 5c grnsh bl & dk bl .90 .90

Issued for the Day of the Stamp. The surtax went to the Red Cross.

Refugee Girl Amid Ruins — SP212

1960, Apr. 7

B340 SP212 25c + 10c grn, brn & ind .25 .20

World Refugee Year, July 1, 1959-June 30, 1960. The surtax was for aid to refugees.

Michel de L'Hospital SP213

#B342, Henri de la Tour D'Auvergne, Viscount of Turenne. #B343, Nicolas Boileau (Despreaux). #B344, Jean-Martin Charcot, M.D. #B345, Georges Bizet. 50c+15c, Edgar Degás.

1960, June 11 **Engr.** ***Perf. 13***

B341 SP213 10c + 5c pur & rose car 2.00 2.00
B342 SP213 20c + 10c ol & vio brn 3.25 3.25
B343 SP213 20c + 10c Prus grn & dp yel grn 3.25 3.25
B344 SP213 30c + 10c rose car & rose red 4.50 4.50
B345 SP213 30c + 10c dk bl & vio bl 4.50 4.50
B346 SP213 50c + 15c sl bl & gray 5.50 5.50
Nos. B341-B346 (6) 23.00 23.00

The surtax was for the Red Cross.
See Nos. B350-B355.

Staff of the Brotherhood of St. Martin — SP214

Letter Carrier, Paris 1760 — SP215

25c+10c, St. Martin, 16th cent. wood sculpture.

1960, Dec. 3 **Unwmk.** ***Perf. 13***

B347 SP214 20c + 10c rose cl & red 2.25 2.25
a. Bklt. pane, 4 each, gutter btwn. 27.50
B348 SP214 25c + 10c lt ultra & red 2.25 2.25

The surtax was for the Red Cross.

1961, Mar. 18 ***Perf. 13***

B349 SP215 20c + 5c sl grn, brn & red .75 .75

Stamp Day. Surtax for Red Cross.

Famous Men Type of 1960

Designs: 15c+5c, Bertrand Du Guesclin. B351, Pierre Puget. #B352, Charles Coulomb. 30c+10c, Antoine Drouot. 45c+10c, Honoré Daumier. 50c+15c, Guillaume Apollinaire.

1961, May 20 **Engr.**

B350 SP213 15c + 5c red brn & blk 2.00 2.00
B351 SP213 20c + 10c dk grn & lt bl 2.00 2.00
B352 SP213 20c + 10c ver & rose car 2.00 2.00
B353 SP213 30c + 10c blk & brn org 2.25 2.25
B354 SP213 45c + 10c choc & dk grn 2.25 2.25
B355 SP213 50c + 15c dk car rose & vio 2.25 2.25
Nos. B350-B355 (6) 12.75 12.75

"Love" by Rouault SP216

Medieval Royal Messenger SP217

Designs from "Miserere" by Georges Rouault: 25c+10c, "The Blind Consoles the Seeing."

1961, Dec. 2 ***Perf. 13***

B356 SP216 20c + 10c brn, blk & red 2.00 2.00
a. Bklt. pane, 4 each, gutter btwn. 25.00
B357 SP216 25c + 10c brn, blk & red 2.00 2.00

The surtax was for the Red Cross.

1962, Mar. 17

B358 SP217 20c + 5c rose red, bl & sepia .70 .70

Stamp Day. Surtax for Red Cross.

Denis Papin, Scientist SP218

Rosalie Fragonard by Fragonard SP219

Portraits: No. B360, Edme Bouchardon, sculptor. No. B361, Joseph Lakanal, educator. 30c+10c, Gustave Charpentier, composer. 45c+15c, Edouard Estaunié, writer. 50c+20c, Hyacinthe Vincent, physician and bacteriologist.

1962, June 2 **Engr.**

B359 SP218 15c + 5c bluish grn & dk gray 2.00 2.00
B360 SP218 20c + 10c cl brn 2.00 2.00
B361 SP218 20c + 10c gray & sl 2.00 2.00
B362 SP218 30c + 10c brt bl & ind 2.50 2.50
B363 SP218 45c + 15c org brn & choc 2.50 2.50
B364 SP218 50c + 20c grnsh bl & blk 3.50 3.50
Nos. B359-B364 (6) 14.50 14.50

The surtax was for the Red Cross.

1962, Dec. 8

Design: 25c+10c, Child dressed as Pierrot.

Cross in Red

B365 SP219 20c + 10c redsh brown 1.10 1.10
a. Bklt. pane, 4 ea, gutter btwn. 24.00
B366 SP219 25c + 10c dull grn 1.10 1.10

The surtax was for the Red Cross.
For surcharges see Reunion Nos. B16-B17.

Jacques Amyot, Classical Scholar SP220

30c+10c, Pierre de Marivaux, playwright. 50c+20c, Jacques Daviel, surgeon.

1963, Feb. 23 **Unwmk.** ***Perf. 13***

B367 SP220 20c + 10c mar, gray & pur 1.00 1.00
B368 SP220 30c + 10c Prus grn & mar .95 .95
B369 SP220 50c + 20c ultra, ocher & ol 1.00 1.00
Nos. B367-B369 (3) 2.95 2.95

The surtax was for the Red Cross.

Roman Chariot SP221

1963, Mar. 16 **Engr.**

B370 SP221 20c + 5c brn org & vio brn .20 .20

Stamp Day. Surtax for Red Cross.

Etienne Méhul, Composer SP222

Designs: 30c+10c, Nicolas-Louis Vauquelin, chemist. 50c+20c, Alfred de Vigny, poet.

1963, May 25 **Unwmk.** ***Perf. 13***

B371 SP222 20c + 10c dp bl, dk brn & dp org 1.10 1.10
B372 SP222 30c + 10c mag, gray ol & blk .95 .95
B373 SP222 50c + 20c sl, blk & brn 1.50 1.50
Nos. B371-B373 (3) 3.55 3.55

The surtax was for the Red Cross.

"Child with Grapes" by David d'Angers and Centenary Emblem — SP223

25c+10c, "The Fifer," by Edouard Manet.

1963, Dec. 9 **Unwmk.** ***Perf. 13***

B374 SP223 20c + 10c black & red .60 .60
a. Bklt. pane, 4 each, gutter btwn. 5.00
B375 SP223 25c + 10c sl grn & red .60 .60

Cent. of the Intl. and French Red Cross. Surtax for the Red Cross.
For surcharges see Reunion Nos. B18-B19.

Post Rider, 18th Century SP224

1964, Mar. 14 **Engr.**

B376 SP224 20c + 5c Prus green .20 .20

Issued for Stamp Day.

Resistance Memorial by Watkin, Luxembourg Gardens — SP225

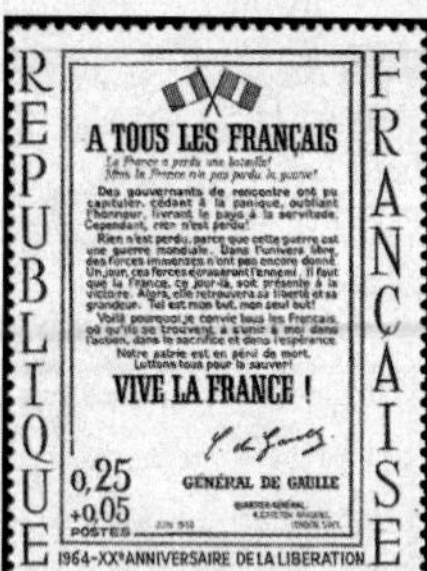

De Gaulle's 1940 Poster "A Tous les Francais" SP226

Allied Troops Landing in Normandy and Provence SP227

Designs: 20c+5c, "Deportation," concentration camp with watchtower and barbed wire. No. B380, Street fighting in Paris and Strasbourg.

1964 Engr. *Perf. 13*

B377 SP225 20c + 5c slate blk .50 .50

Perf. 12x13

B378 SP226 25c + 5c dk red, bl, red & blk .65 .65

Perf. 13

B379 SP227 30c + 5c blk, bl & org brn .50 .50
B380 SP227 30c + 5c org brn, cl & blk .60 .60
B381 SP225 50c + 5c dk grn .65 .65
Nos. B377-B381 (5) 2.90 2.90

20th anniv. of liberation from the Nazis.
Issue dates: #B377, B381, Mar. 21; #B378, June 18; #B379, June 6; #B380, Aug. 22.

President René Coty SP229

Jean Nicolas Corvisart SP230

Portraits: No. B383, John Calvin. No. B384, Pope Sylvester II (Gerbert).

1964 Unwmk. *Perf. 13*

B382 SP229 30c + 10c dp cl & blk .25 .25
B383 SP229 30c + 10c dk grn, blk & brn .25 .25
B384 SP229 30c + 10c slate & cl .25 .25
Nos. B382-B384 (3) .75 .75

The surtax was for the Red Cross.
Issued: #B382, 4/25; #B383, 5/25; #B384, 6/1.

1964, Dec. 12 Engr.

Portrait: 25c+10c, Dominique Larrey.

Cross in Carmine

B385 SP230 20c + 10c black .25 .25
a. Bklt. pane, 4 ea, gutter btwn. 3.50
B386 SP230 25c + 10c black .25 .25

Jean Nicolas Corvisart (1755-1821), physician of Napoleon I, and Dominique Larrey (1766-1842), Chief Surgeon of the Imperial Armies. The surtax was for the Red Cross.
For surcharges see Reunion Nos. B20-B21.

Paul Dukas, Composer — SP231

#B387, Duke François de La Rochefoucauld, writer. #B388, Nicolas Poussin, painter. #B389, Duke Charles of Orléans, poet.

1965, Feb. Engr. *Perf. 13*

B387 SP231 30c + 10c org brn & dk bl .40 .40
B388 SP231 30c + 10c car & dk red brn .40 .40
B389 SP231 40c + 10c dk red brn, dk red & Prus bl .50 .50
B390 SP231 40c + 10c dk brn & sl bl .50 .50
Nos. B387-B390 (4) 1.80 1.80

The surtax was for the Red Cross.
Issued: #B387, B390 2/13; #B388-B389 2/20.

Packet "La Guienne" SP232

1965, Mar. 29 Unwmk. *Perf. 13*

B391 SP232 25c + 10c multi .50 .50

Issued for Stamp Day, 1965. "La Guienne" was used for transatlantic mail service. Surtax was for the Red Cross.

Infant with Spoon by Auguste Renoir — SP233

Design: 30c+10c, Coco Writing (Renoir's daughter Claude).

1965, Dec. 11 Engr. *Perf. 13*

Cross in Carmine

B392 SP233 25c + 10c slate .20 .20
a. Bklt. pane, 4 ea, gutter btwn. 2.75
B393 SP233 30c + 10c dull red brn .25 .25

The surtax was for the Red Cross.
For surcharges see Reunion Nos. B22-B23.

Francois Mansart and Carnavalet Palace, Paris SP234

#B395, St. Pierre Fourier and Basilica of St. Pierre Fourier, Mirecourt. #B396, Marcel Proust and St. Hilaire Bridge, Illiers. #B397, Gabriel Fauré, monument and score of "Penelope." #B398, Elie Metchnikoff, microscope and Pasteur Institute. #B399, Hippolyte Taine and birthplace.

1966 Engr. *Perf. 13*

B394 SP234 30c + 10c dk red brn & grn .30 .30
B395 SP234 30c + 10c blk & gray grn .30 .30
B396 SP234 30c + 10c ind, sep & grn .30 .30
B397 SP234 30c + 10c bis brn & ind .30 .30
B398 SP234 30c + 10c blk & dl brn .30 .30
B399 SP234 30c + 10c grn & ol brn .30 .30
Nos. B394-B399 (6) 1.80 1.80

The surtax was for the Red Cross.
Issued: #B394-B396, 2/12; others, 6/25.

Engraver Cutting Die and Tools SP235

1966, Mar. 19 Engr. *Perf. 13*

B400 SP235 25c + 10c slate, dk brn & dp org .30 .30

Stamp Day. Surtax for Red Cross.

Angel of Victory, Verdun Fortress, Marching Troops — SP236

First Aid on Battlefield, 1859 — SP237

1966, May 28 *Perf. 13*

B401 SP236 30c + 5c Prus bl, ultra & dk bl .20 .20

Victory of Verdun, 50th anniversary.

1966, Dec. 10 Engr. *Perf. 13*

#B403, Nurse giving first aid to child, 1966.

Cross in Carmine

B402 SP237 25c + 10c green .30 .30
a. Bklt. pane, 4 ea, gutter btwn. 3.50
B403 SP237 30c + 10c slate .30 .30

The surtax was for the Red Cross.
For surcharges see Reunion Nos. B24-B25.

Emile Zola — SP238

Letter Carrier, 1865 — SP239

No. B405, Beaumarchais (pen name of Pierre Augustin Caron). No. B406, St. Francois de Sales (1567-1622). No. B407, Albert Camus (1913-1960).

1967 Engr. *Perf. 13*

B404 SP238 30c + 10c sl bl & bl .30 .30
B405 SP238 30c + 10c rose brn & lil .30 .30
B406 SP238 30c + 10c dl vio & pur .30 .30
B407 SP238 30c + 10c brn & dl cl .30 .30
Nos. B404-B407 (4) 1.20 1.20

The surtax was for the Red Cross.
Issued: #B404-B405, 2/4; others, 6/24.

1967, Apr. 8

B408 SP239 25c + 10c indigo, grn & red .20 .20

Issued for Stamp Day.

Ivory Flute Player — SP240

Ski Jump and Long Distance Skiing — SP241

30c+10c, Violin player, ivory carving.

1967, Dec. 16 Engr. *Perf. 13*

Cross in Carmine

B409 SP240 25c + 10c dl vio & lt brn .30 .30
a. Bklt. pane, 4 ea, gutter btwn. 3.50
B410 SP240 30c + 10c grn & lt brn .30 .30

The surtax was for the Red Cross.
For surcharges see Reunion Nos. B26-B27.

1968, Jan. 27

Designs: 40c+10c, Ice hockey. 60c+20c, Olympic flame and snowflakes. 75c+25c, Woman figure skater. 95c+35c, Slalom.

B411 SP241 30c + 10c ver, gray & brn .20 .20
B412 SP241 40c + 10c lil, lem & brt mag .25 .25
B413 SP241 60c + 20c dk grn, org & brt vio .35 .35
B414 SP241 75c + 25c brt pink, yel grn & blk .45 .45
B415 SP241 95c + 35c bl, brt pink & red brn .60 .60
Nos. B411-B415 (5) 1.85 1.85

Issued for the 10th Winter Olympic Games, Grenoble, Feb. 6-18.

Rural Mailman, 1830 — SP242

1968, Mar. 16 Engr. *Perf. 13*

B416 SP242 25c + 10c multi .20 .20

Issued for Stamp Day.

François Couperin, Composer, and Instruments SP243

Portraits: No. B418, Gen. Louis Desaix de Veygoux (1768-1800) and scene showing his death at the Battle of Marengo, Italy. No. B419, Saint-Pol-Roux (pen name of Paul-Pierre Roux, 1861-1940), Christ on the Cross and ruins of Camaret-sur-Mer. No. B420, Paul Claudel (poet and diplomat, 1868-1955) and Joan of Arc at the stake.

1968 Engr. *Perf. 13*

B417 SP243 30c + 10c pur & rose lil .20 .20
B418 SP243 30c + 10c dk grn & brn .20 .20
B419 SP243 30c + 10c cop red & ol bis .20 .20
B420 SP243 30c + 10c dk brn & lil .20 .20
Nos. B417-B420 (4) .80 .80

Issue dates: Nos. B417-B418, Mar. 23; Nos. B419-B420, July 6.

Spring, by Nicolas Mignard — SP244

Paintings by Nicolas Mignard; 30c+10c, Fall. No. B423, Summer. No. B424, Winter.

1968-69 Engr. *Perf. 13*

Cross in Carmine

B421 SP244 25c + 10c pur & sl bl .20 .20
a. Bklt. pane, 4 ea #B421-B422 with gutter btwn.) 3.00
B422 SP244 30c + 10c brn & rose car .20 .20
B423 SP244 40c + 15c dk brn & brn ('69) .30 .30
a. Bklt. pane, 4 ea #B423, B424 with gutter btwn.) 3.50

B424 SP244 40c + 15c pur & Prus bl ('69) .30 .30
Nos. B421-B424 (4) 1.00 1.00

The surtax was for the Red Cross.
For surcharges see Reunion Nos. B28-B31.

Mailmen's Omnibus, 1881
SP245

1969, Mar. 15 **Engr.** ***Perf. 13***
B425 SP245 30c + 10c brn, grn & blk .20 .20

Issued for Stamp Day.
For surcharge see Reunion No. B32.

Gen. Francois Marceau — SP246

Portraits: No. B427, Charles Augustin Sainte-Beuve (1804-1869), writer. No. B428, Albert Roussel (1869-1937), musician. No. B429, Marshal Jean Lannes (1769-1809). No. B430, Georges Cuvier (1769-1832), naturalist. No. B431, André Gide, (1869-1951), writer.

1969
B426 SP246 50c + 10c brn red .45 .45
B427 SP246 50c + 10c slate bl .45 .45
B428 SP246 50c + 10c dp vio bl .45 .45
B429 SP246 50c + 10c choc .45 .45
B430 SP246 50c + 10c dp plum .45 .45
B431 SP246 50c + 10c blue grn .45 .45
Nos. B426-B431 (6) 2.70 2.70

The surtax was for the Red Cross.
Issued: Nos. B426-B428, Mar. 24; No. B429, May 10; Nos. B430-B431, May 17.

Gen. Jacques Leclerc, La Madeleine and Battle — SP247

1969, Aug. 23 **Engr.** ***Perf. 13***
B432 SP247 45c + 10c slate & ol .60 .60

Liberation of Paris, 8/25/44, 25th anniv.

Same Inscribed "Liberation de Strasbourg"

1969, Nov. 22 **Engr.** ***Perf. 13***
B433 SP247 70c + 10c brn, choc & olive 1.40 1.40

25th anniv. of the liberation of Strasbourg.

Philibert Delorme, Architect, and Chateau d'Anet
SP248

Designs: No. B435, Louis Le Vau (1612-1670), architect, and Vaux-le-Vicomte Chateau, Paris. No. B436, Prosper Merimée (1803-1870), writer, and Carmen. No. B437, Alexandre Dumas (1802-1870), writer, and Three Musketeers. No. B438, Edouard Branly (1844-1940), physicist, electric circuit and convent of the Carmes, Paris. No. B439, Maurice de Broglie (1875-1960), physicist, and X-ray spectrograph.

1970 **Engr.** ***Perf. 13***
B434 SP248 40c + 10c slate grn .45 .45
B435 SP248 40c + 10c dk car .45 .45
B436 SP248 40c + 10c Prus blue .45 .45
B437 SP248 40c + 10c violet bl .45 .45
B438 SP248 40c + 10c dp brown .45 .45
B439 SP248 40c + 10c dk gray .45 .45
Nos. B434-B439 (6) 2.70 2.70

The surtax was for the Red Cross.
Issued: #B434-B436, 2/14; others, 4/11.

City Mailman, 1830 — SP249

"Life and Death" — SP250

1970, Mar. 14
B440 SP249 40c + 10c blk, ultra & dk car rose .30 .30

Issued for Stamp Day.
For surcharge see Reunion No. B33.

1970, Apr. 4
B441 SP250 40c + 10c brt bl, ol & car rose .25 .25

Issued to publicize the fight against cancer in connection with Health Day, Apr. 7.

Marshal de Lattre de Tassigny — SP251

1970, May 8 **Engr.** ***Perf. 13***
B442 SP251 40c + 10c slate & vio bl .50 .30

25th anniv. of the entry into Berlin of French troops under Marshal Jean de Lattre de Tassigny, May 8, 1945.

Lord and Lady, Dissay Chapel Fresco — SP252

#B444, Angel holding whips, from fresco in Dissay Castle Chapel, Vienne, c. 1500.

1970, Dec. 12 **Engr.** ***Perf. 13***
Cross in Carmine
B443 SP252 40c + 15c green .55 .45
a. Bklt. pane, 4 ea, gutter btwn. 8.00
B444 SP252 40c + 15c cop red .55 .45

The surtax was for the Red Cross.
For surcharges see Reunion Nos. B34-B35.

Daniel-Francois Auber and "Fra Diavolo" Music — SP253

#B446, Gen. Charles Diego Brosset (1898-1944), Basilica of Fourvière. #B447, Victor Grignard (1871-1935), chemist, Nobel Prize medal. #B448, Henri Farman (1874-1958), plane. #B449, Gen. Charles Georges Delestraint (1879-1945), scroll. #B450, Jean Eugène Robert-Houdin (1805-71), magician's act.

1971 **Engr.** ***Perf. 13***
B445 SP253 50c + 10c brn vio & brn .75 .60
B446 SP253 50c + 10c dk sl grn & ol gray .75 .60
B447 SP253 50c + 10c brn red & olive .75 .60
B448 SP253 50c + 10c vio bl & vio .75 .60
B449 SP253 50c + 10c pur & cl .85 .75
B450 SP253 50c + 10c sl grn & bl grn .85 .75
Nos. B445-B450 (6) 4.70 3.90

The surtax was for the Red Cross.
Issued: #B445-B446, 3/6; #B447, 5/8; #B448, 5/29; #B449-B450, 10/16.

Army Post Office, 1914-1918
SP254

1971, Mar. 27 **Engr.** ***Perf. 13***
B451 SP254 50c + 10c ol, brn & bl .35 .30

Stamp Day, 1971.
For surcharge see Reunion No. B36.

Girl with Dog, by Greuze
SP255

Aristide Bergès (1833-1904)
SP256

Design: 50c+10c, "The Dead Bird," by Jean-Baptiste Greuze (1725-1805).

1971, Dec. 11
Cross in Carmine
B452 SP255 30c + 10c violet bl .55 .55
a. Bklt. pane, 4 each, gutter btwn. 6.00
B453 SP255 50c + 10c dp car .55 .55

The surtax was for the Red Cross.
For surcharges see Reunion Nos. B37-B38.

1972 **Engr.** ***Perf. 13***

#B455, Paul de Chomedey (1612-76), founder of Montreal, and arms of Neuville-sur-Vanne. #B456, Edouard Belin (1876-1963), inventor. #B457, Louis Blériot (1872-1936), aviation pioneer. #B458, Adm. François Joseph, Count de Grasse (1722-88), hero of the American Revolution. #B459, Théophile Gautier (1811-72), writer.

B454 SP256 50c + 10c blk & grn .75 .75
B455 SP256 50c + 10c blk & bl .75 .75
B456 SP256 50c + 10c blk & lil rose .75 .75
B457 SP256 50c + 10c red & blk .75 .75
B458 SP256 50c + 10c org & blk 1.00 1.00
B459 SP256 50c + 10c blk & brn 1.00 1.00
Nos. B454-B459 (6) 5.00 5.00

The surtax was for the Red Cross.
Issued: #B454-B455, Feb. 19; #B456, June 24; #B457, July 1; #B458-B459, Sept. 9.

Rural Mailman, 1894
SP257

Nicolas Desgenettes
SP258

1972, Mar. 18 **Engr.** ***Perf. 13***
B460 SP257 50c + 10c bl, yel & ol gray .75 .35

Stamp Day 1972.
For surcharge see Reunion No. B39.

1972, Dec. 16 **Engr.** ***Perf. 13***

Designs: 30c+10c, René Nicolas Dufriche, Baron Desgenettes, M.D. (1762-1837). 50c+10c, François Joseph Broussais, M.D. (1772-1838).

B461 SP258 30c + 10c sl grn & red .65 .50
a. Bklt. pane, 4 ea, gutter btwn. 7.00
B462 SP258 50c + 10c red .65 .50

The surtax was for the Red Cross.
For surcharges see Reunion Nos. B40-B41.

Tony Garnier (1869-1948), architect — SP259

#B463, Gaspard de Coligny (1519-1572), admiral and Huguenot leader. #B464, Ernest Renan (1823-1892), philologist and historian. #B465, Alberto Santos Dumont (1873-1932), Brazilian aviator. #B466, Gabrielle-Sidonie Colette (1873-1954), writer. #B467, René Duguay-Trouin (1673-1736), naval commander. #B468, Louis Pasteur (1822-1895), chemist, bacteriologist. #B469, Tony Garnier (1869-1948), architect.

1973 **Engr.** ***Perf. 13***
B463 SP259 50c + 10c multi .85 .60
B464 SP259 50c + 10c multi .85 .60
B465 SP259 50c + 10c multi .85 .60
B466 SP259 50c + 10c multi .85 .60
B467 SP259 50c + 10c multi .85 .60
B468 SP259 50c + 10c multi .85 .65
B469 SP259 50c + 10c multi .85 .65
Nos. B463-B469 (7) 5.95 4.30

Issued: #B463, 2/17; #B464, 4/28; #B465, 5/26; #B466, 6/2; #B467, 6/9; #B468, 10/6; #B469, 11/17.

Mail Coach, 1835
SP260

1973, Mar. 24 **Engr.** ***Perf. 13***
B470 SP260 50c + 10c grnsh blue .35 .30

Stamp Day, 1973.
For surcharge see Reunion No. B42.

Mary Magdalene
SP261

St. Louis-Marie de Montfort
SP262

50c+10c, Mourning woman. Designs are from 15th cent. Tomb of Tonnerre.

1973, Dec. 1
B471 SP261 30c + 10c sl grn & red .35 .35
a. Bklt. pane, 4 each, gutter btwn. 4.50
B472 SP261 50c + 10c dk gray & red .45 .45

Surtax was for the Red Cross.
For surcharges see Reunion Nos. B43-B44.

1974, Feb. 23 **Engr.** ***Perf. 13***

Portraits: No. B474, Francis Poulenc (1899-1963), composer. No. B475, Jules Barbey d'Aurevilly (1808-1889), writer. No. B476, Jean Giraudoux (1882-1944), writer.

B473 SP262 50c + 10c multi 1.10 1.10
B474 SP262 50c + 10c multi .70 .70
B475 SP262 80c + 15c multi .80 .80
B476 SP262 80c + 15c multi .80 .80
Nos. B473-B476 (4) 3.40 3.40

Issue dates: No. B473, Mar. 9; No. B474, July 20; Nos. B475-B476, Nov. 16.

Automatically Sorted Letters — SP263

1974, Mar. 9 Engr. *Perf. 13*
B477 SP263 50c + 10c multi .25 .20

Stamp Day 1974. Automatic letter sorting center, Orleans-la-Source, opened 1/30/73.
For surcharge see Reunion No. B45.

Order of Liberation and 5 Honored Cities — SP264

1974, June 15 Engr. *Perf. 13*
B478 SP264 1fr + 10c multi .55 .30

30th anniv. of liberation from the Nazis.

"Summer" SP265 "Winter" SP266

Designs: B481, "Spring" (girl on swing). B482, "Fall" (umbrella and rabbits).

1974, Nov. 30 Engr. *Perf. 13*
B479 SP265 60c + 15c multi .50 .35
a. Bklt. pane, 4 ea, gutter btwn. 5.00
B480 SP266 80c + 15c multi .55 .45

For surcharges see Reunion Nos. B46-B46.

1975, Nov. 29
B481 SP265 60c + 15c multi .40 .30
a. Bklt. pane, 4 ea, gutter btwn. 4.75
B482 SP266 80c + 20c multi .60 .45

Surtax was for the Red Cross.

Dr. Albert Schweitzer SP267 Edmond Michelet SP268

André Siegfried and Map SP269

#B483, Albert Schweitzer (1875-1965), medical missionary. #B484, Edmond Michelet (1899-1970), Resistance hero, statesman. #B485, Robert Schuman (1886-1963), promoter of United Europe. #B486, Eugene Thomas (1903-69), minister of PTT. #B487, André Siegfried (1875-1959), political science professor, writer.

1975 Engr. *Perf. 13*
B483 SP267 80c + 20c multi .50 .50
B484 SP268 80c + 20c bl & ind .50 .50
B485 SP268 80c + 20c blk & ind .50 .50
B486 SP268 80c + 20c blk & sl .50 .50
B487 SP269 80c + 20c blk & bl .50 .50
Nos. B483-B487 (5) 2.50 2.50

Issued: #B483, 1/11; #B484, 2/22; #B485, 5/10; #B486, 6/28; #B487, 11/15.

Second Republic Mailman's Badge — SP270

1975, Mar. 8 Photo.
B488 SP270 80c + 20c multi .35 .30

Stamp Day.

"Sage" Type of 1876 SP271 Marshal A. J. de Moncey SP272

1976, Mar. 13 Engr. *Perf. 13*
B489 SP271 80c + 20c blk & lil .35 .30

Stamp Day 1976.

1976 Engr. *Perf. 13*

#B491, Max Jacob (1876-1944), Dadaist writer, by Picasso. #B492, Jean Mounet-Sully (1841-1916), actor. #B493, Gen. Pierre Daumesnil (1776-1832). #B494, Eugène Fromentin (1820-1876), painter.

B490 SP272 80c + 20c multi .45 .45
B491 SP272 80c + 20c red brn & ol .45 .45
B492 SP272 80c + 20c multi .45 .45
B493 SP272 1fr + 20c multi .45 .45
B494 SP272 1fr + 20c multi .50 .50
Nos. B490-B494 (5) 2.30 2.30

Issued: #B490, 5/22; #B491, 7/22; #B492, 8/28; #B493, 9/4; #B494, 9/25.

Anna de Noailles SP273 St. Barbara SP274

1976, Nov. 6 Engr. *Perf. 13*
B495 SP273 1fr + 20c multi .50 .50

Anna de Noailles (1876-1933), writer & poet.

1976, Nov. 20

Design: 1fr+25c, Cimmerian Sibyl. Sculptures from Brou Cathedral.

Cross in Carmine

B496 SP274 80c + 20c violet .50 .40
a. Bklt. pane, 4 ea, gutter btwn. 6.00
B497 SP274 1fr + 25c dk brown .60 .50

Surtax was for the Red Cross.

Marckolsheim Relay Station Sign — SP275

1977, Mar. 26 Engr. *Perf. 13*
B498 SP275 1fr + 20c multi .40 .40

Stamp Day.

Edouard Herriot, Statesman and Writer SP276 Christmas Figurine, Provence SP277

Designs: No. B500, Abbé Breuil (1877-1961), archaeologist. No. B501, Guillaume de Machault (1305-1377), poet and composer. No. B502, Charles Cross (1842-1888).

1977 Engr. *Perf. 13*
B499 SP276 1fr + 20c multi .60 .60
B500 SP276 1fr + 20c multi .60 .60
B501 SP276 1fr + 20c multi .60 .60
B502 SP276 1fr + 20c multi .60 .60
Nos. B499-B502 (4) 2.40 2.40

Issued: #B499, Oct. 8; #B500, Oct. 15; #B501, Nov. 12; #B502, Dec. 3.

1977, Nov. 26

1fr+25c, Christmas figurine (woman), Provence.

B503 SP277 80c + 20c red & ind .45 .45
a. Bklt. pane, 4 ea, gutter btwn. 4.50
B504 SP277 1fr + 25c red & sl grn .55 .55

Surtax was for the Red Cross.

Marie Noel, Writer — SP278 Mail Collection, 1900 — SP279

#B506, Georges Bernanos (1888-1948), writer. #B507, Leo Tolstoi (1828-1910), Russian writer. #B508, Charles Marie Leconte de Lisle (1818-1894), poet. #B509, Voltaire (1694-1778) and Jean Jacques Rousseau (1712-1778). #B510, Claude Bernard (1813-1878), physiologist.

1978 Engr. *Perf. 13*
B505 SP278 1fr + 20c multi .55 .55
B506 SP278 1fr + 20c multi .55 .55
B507 SP278 1fr + 20c multi .55 .55
B508 SP278 1fr + 20c multi .55 .55
B509 SP278 1fr + 20c multi .55 .55
B510 SP278 1fr + 20c multi .55 .55
Nos. B505-B510 (6) 3.30 3.30

Issued: #B505, 2/11; #B506, 2/18; #B507, 4/15; #B508, 3/26; #B509, 7/1; #B510, 9/16.

1978, Apr. 8 Engr. *Perf. 13*
B511 SP279 1fr + 20c multi .40 .35

Stamp Day 1978.

SP280 SP281

1fr+25c, The Hare & the Tortoise. 1.20fr+30c, The City Mouse & the Country Mouse.

1978, Dec. 2 Engr. *Perf. 13*
B512 SP280 1fr + 25c multi .55 .35
a. Bklt. pane, 4 ea, gutter btwn. 6.00
B513 SP280 1.20fr + 30c multi .70 .45

Surtax was for the Red Cross.

1979 Engr. *Perf. 13*

#B514, Ladislas Marshal de Berchény (1689-1778). #B515, Leon Jouhaux (1879-1954), labor leader. #B516, Peter Abelard (1079-1142), theologian and writer. #B517, Georges Courteline (1860-1929), humorist. #B518, Simone Weil (1909-1943), social philosopher. #B519, André Malraux (1901-1976), novelist.

B514 SP281 1.20fr + 30c multi .60 .60
B515 SP281 1.20fr + 30c multi .60 .60
B516 SP281 1.20fr + 30c multi .60 .60
B517 SP281 1.20fr + 30c multi .60 .60
B518 SP281 1.30fr + 30c multi .60 .60
B519 SP281 1.30fr + 30c multi .60 .60
Nos. B514-B519 (6) 3.60 3.60

Issued: #B514, 1/13; #B515, 5/12; #B516, 6/9; #B517, 6/25; #B518, 11/12; #B519, 11/26.

General Post Office, from 1908 Post Card SP282

1979, Mar. 10 Engr. *Perf. 13*
B520 SP282 1.20fr + 30c multi .50 .35

Stamp Day 1979.

Woman, Stained-Glass Window — SP283

Stained-glass windows, Church of St. Joan of Arc, Rouen: 1.30fr+30c, Simon the Magician.

1979, Dec. 1
B521 SP283 1.10fr + 30c multi .50 .40
a. Bklt. pane, 4 each, gutter btwn., perf. 12½x13 6.00
B522 SP283 1.30fr + 30c multi .60 .45

Surtax was for the Red Cross.

Eugene Viollet le Duc (1814-1879), Architect — SP284

Jean-Marie de Le Mennais (1780-1860), Priest and Educator — SP285

#B524, Jean Monnet (1888-1979), economist and diplomat. #B525, Viollet le Duc (1814-1879), architect and writer. #B526, Frederic Mistral (1830-1914), poet. #B527, Saint-John Perse (Alexis Leger, 1887-1975), poet and diplomat. #B528, Pierre Paul de Riquet (1604-1680), canal builder.

1980 Engr. *Perf. 13*

B523	SP284	1.30fr + 30c multi	.70	.70
B524	SP285	1.30fr + 30c multi	.70	.70
B525	SP285	1.40fr + 30c blue	.70	.70
B526	SP285	1.40fr + 30c black	.70	.70
B527	SP285	1.40fr + 30c multi	.70	.70
B528	SP284	1.40fr + 30c multi	.70	.70
		Nos. B523-B528 (6)	4.20	4.20

Issued: #B523, Feb. 16; #B524-B526, Sept. 6; #B527-B528, Oct. 11.

The Letter to Melie, by Avati, Stamp Day, 1980 — SP286

1980, Mar. 8 Photo.

B529	SP286	1.30fr + 30c multi	.60	.45

Filling the Granaries, Choir Stall Detail, Amiens Cathedral — SP287

#B531, Grapes from the Promised Land.

1980, Dec. 6 Engr. *Perf. 13*

B530	SP287	1.20fr + 30c red & dk red brn	.65	.35
B531	SP287	1.40fr + 30c red & dk red brn	.60	.45
a.		Bklt. pane, 4 each, gutter btwn., perf. 12½x13	5.00	

Sister Anne-Marie Javouhey (1779-1851), Founded Congregation of St. Joseph of Cluny — SP288

#B532, Louis Armand (1905-71), railway engineer. #B533, Louis Jouvet (1887-1951), theater director. #B534, Marc Boegner (1881-1970), peace worker. #B536, Jacques Offenbach (1819-80), composer. #B537, Pierre Teilhard de Chardin (1881-1955), philosopher. Nos. B532-B533, B537 vert.

1981 Engr. *Perf. 13*

B532	SP288	1.20 + 30c multi	.65	.65
B533	SP288	1.20 + 30c multi	.65	.65
B534	SP288	1.40 + 30c multi	.65	.60
B535	SP288	1.40 + 30c multi	.65	.60
B536	SP288	1.40 + 30c multi	.65	.60
B537	SP288	1.40 + 30c multi	.65	.60
		Nos. B532-B537 (6)	3.90	3.70

Issued: #B532, 5/23; #B533, 6/13; #B534, 11/14; #B535, 2/7; #B536, 2/14; #B537, 5/23.

The Love Letter, by Goya — SP289

1981, Mar. 7 *Perf. 13x12½*

B538	SP289	1.40 + 30c multi	1.00	.90

Stamp Day 1981.

Scourges of the Passion SP290

Guillaume Postel (1510-1581), Theologian — SP291

Stained-glass Windows, Church of the Sacred Heart, Audincourt: 1.60fr+30c, "Peace."

1981, Dec. 5 Photo. *Perf. 13*

B539	SP290	1.40 + 30c multi	.75	.65
B540	SP290	1.60 + 30c multi	.70	.45
a.		Bklt. pane, 4 ea, gutter btwn.	6.00	

1982 Engr. *Perf. 13*

#B542, Henri Mondor (1885-1962), physician. #B543, Andre Chantemesse (1851-1919), Scientist. #B544, Louis Pergaud (1882-1915), writer. #B545, Robert Debre (1882-1978), writer. #B546, Gustave Eiffel (1832-1923), engineer.

B541	SP291	1.40 + 30c multi	.60	.45
B542	SP291	1.40 + 30c dk brn & dk bl	.50	.40
B543	SP291	1.60 + 30c multi	.55	.55
B544	SP291	1.60 + 40c multi	.70	.50
B545	SP291	1.60 + 40c dk blue	.60	.50
B546	SP291	1.80 + 40c sepia	.60	.60
		Nos. B541-B546 (6)	3.55	3.00

Woman Reading, by Picasso — SP292

1982, Mar. 27 *Perf. 13x12½*

B547	SP292	1.60 + 40c multi	.80	.45

Stamp Day.

SP293

SP294

Jules Verne books: 1.60fr+30c, Five Weeks in a Balloon. 1.80fr+40c, 20,000 Leagues under the Sea.

1982, Nov. 20 *Perf. 13*

B548	SP293	1.60 + 30c multi	.60	.55
B549	SP293	1.80 + 40c multi	.60	.55
a.		Bklt. pane, 4 each, gutter btwn., perf. 12½x13	8.00	

Surtax was for Red Cross.

1983 Engr. *Perf. 12½x13*

#B550, Andre Messager (1853-1929). #B551, J.A. Gabriel (1698-1782), architect. #B552, Hector Berlioz (1803-69), composer. #B553, Max Fouchet (1913-80). #B554, Rene Cassin (1887-1976). #B555, Stendhal (Marie Henri Beyle, 1783-1842).

B550	SP294	1.60 + 30c multi	.65	.65
B551	SP294	1.60 + 30c multi	.65	.65
B552	SP294	1.80 + 40c dp lil & blk	.75	.75
B553	SP294	1.80 + 40c multi	.75	.75
B554	SP294	2fr + 40c multi	.80	.80
B555	SP294	2fr + 40c multi	.80	.80
		Nos. B550-B555 (6)	4.40	4.40

Issued: #B550, 1/15; #B551, 4/16; #B552, 1/22; #B553, 4/30; #B554, 6/25; #B555, 11/12.

Man Dictating a Letter, by Rembrandt — SP295

Photo. & Engr.

1983, Feb. 26 *Perf. 13X12½*

B556	SP295	1.80 + 40c multi	.65	.35

Stamp Day.

Virgin with Child, Baillon, 14th Cent. — SP296

Design: No. B558, Virgin with Child, Genainville, 16th Cent.

1983, Nov. 26 Engr. *Perf. 13*

B557	SP296	1.60 + 40c shown	.65	.45
B558	SP296	2fr + 40c multi	.85	.55
a.		Bklt. pane, 4 each, gutter btwn., perf. 12½x13	6.50	

Emile Littre (1801-1881), Physician — SP297

#B560, Jean Zay (1904-44). #B561, Pierre Corneille (1606-1684. #B562, Gaston Bachelard (1884-1962). #B563, Jean Paulhan (1884-1968). #B564, Evariste Galois (1811-1832).

1984 Engr. *Perf. 13*

B559	SP297	1.60fr + 40c plum & blk	.85	.85
B560	SP297	1.60fr + 40c dk grn & blk	.85	.85
B561	SP297	1.70fr + 40c dp vio & blk	.65	.65
B562	SP297	2fr + 40c gray & blk	.70	.70
B563	SP297	2.10fr + 40c dk brn & blk	.70	.70
B564	SP297	2.10fr + 40c ultra & blk	.70	.70
		Nos. B559-B564 (6)	4.45	4.45

SP298

SP299

Diderot Holding a Letter, by L.M. Van Loo.

1984, Mar. 17 Engr. *Perf. 12½x13*

B565	SP298	2fr + 40c multi	.75	.35

1984, Nov. 24 Photo. *Perf. 12½x13*

The Rose Basket, by Caly.

B566	SP299	2.10fr + 50c pnksh (basket) & multi	.65	.40
a.		Salmon (basket) & multi, perf. 13½x13	.65	.40
b.		As "a," bklt. pane of 10 + 2 labels	6.50	

Surtax was for the Red Cross.

Jules Romains (1885-1972) — SP300

Authors: No. B568, Jean-Paul Sartre (1905-1980). No. B569, Romain Rolland (1866-1944). No. B570, Roland Dorgeles (1885-1973). No. B571, Victor Hugo (1802-1885). No. B572, Francois Mauriac (1885-1970).

1985, Feb. 23 Engr. *Perf. 13*

B567	SP300	1.70fr + 40c	*3.25*	*3.25*
B568	SP300	1.70fr + 40c	*3.25*	*3.25*
B569	SP300	1.70fr + 40c	*3.25*	*3.25*
B570	SP300	2.10fr + 50c	*3.75*	*3.75*
B571	SP300	2.10fr + 50c	*3.75*	*3.75*
B572	SP300	2.10fr + 50c	*3.75*	*3.75*
a.		Bklt. pane, 1 each + 2 labels, perf. 15x14½	*40.00*	
		Nos. B567-B572 (6)	21.00	21.00

SP301

SP302

Stamp Day: Canceling apparatus invented by Eugene Daguin (1849-1888).

1985, Mar. 16 Engr. *Perf. 12½x13*

B573	SP301	2.10fr + 50c brn blk & bluish gray	.85	.85

1985, Nov. 23 Photo.

Issenheim Altarpiece retable.

B574	SP302	2.20fr + 50c multi	.85	.85
a.		As "b," bklt. pane of 10	8.50	
b.		Perf. 13½x13	.85	.85

Surtax for the Red Cross.

SP303

SP304

Famous men: No. B575, Francois Arago (1786-1853), physician, politician. No. B576, Henri Moissan (1852-1907), chemist. No. B577, Henri Fabre (1882-1984), engineer. No. B578, Marc Seguin (1786-1875), engineer. No. B579, Paul Heroult (1863-1914), chemist.

1986, Feb. 22 Engr. *Perf. 13*

B575 SP303 1.80fr + 40c multi .95 .95
B576 SP303 1.80fr + 40c multi .95 .95
B577 SP303 1.80fr + 40c multi .95 .95
B578 SP303 2.20fr + 50c multi 1.10 1.10
B579 SP303 2.20fr + 50c multi 1.10 1.10
  a. Bklt. pane of 5, #B575-B579, + 3 labels 6.00
  Nos. B575-B579 (5) 5.05 5.05

1986, Mar. 1 Engr. *Perf. 13x12½*

B580 SP304 2.20fr + 50c brn blk *6.00 6.00*

Pierre Cot (1895-1977).

Mail Britzska SP305

1986, Apr. 5 *Perf. 13*

B581 SP305 2.20fr + 60c pale tan & dk vio brn .85 .85

Booklet Stamp

B582 SP305 2.20fr + 60c buff & blk .85 .85
  a. Bklt. pane of 6 + 2 labels 7.00

Stamp Day. See Nos. B590-B591, B599-B600, B608-B609.

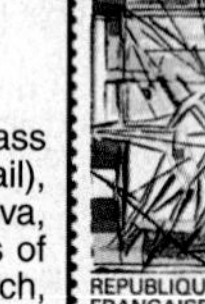

Stained Glass Window (detail), by Vieira da Silva, St. Jacques of Reims Church, Marne — SP306

1986, Nov. 24 Photo. *Perf. 12½x13*

B583 SP306 2.20fr + 60c multi .95 .95
  a. As "b," bklt. pane of 10 9.50
  b. Perf. 13½x13 .95 .95

Surtaxed to benefit the natl. Red Cross.

Physicians and Biologists SP307

#B584, Charles Richet (1850-1935). #B585, Eugene Jamot (1879-1937). #B586, Bernard Halpern (1904-1978). #B587, Alexandre Yersin (1863-1943). #B588, Jean Rostand (1894-1977). #B589, Jacques Monod (1910-1976).

1987, Feb. 21 Engr. *Perf. 13*

B584 SP307 1.90fr + 50c deep ultra .95 .95
B585 SP307 1.90fr + 50c dull lil .95 .95
B586 SP307 1.90fr + 50c grnish gray .95 .95
B587 SP307 2.20fr + 50c grnish gray 1.10 1.10
B588 SP307 2.20fr + 50c deep ultra 1.10 1.10
B589 SP307 2.20fr + 50c dull lil 1.10 1.10
  a. Bklt. pane of 6, #B584-B589
  Nos. B584-B589 (6) 6.15 6.15

Stamp Day Type of 1986

Stamp Day 1987: Berline carriage.

1987, Mar. 14 Engr.

B590 SP305 2.20fr + 60c buff & sepia .95 .95

Booklet Stamp

B591 SP305 2.20fr + 60c pale & dk bl .95 .95
  a. Bklt. pane of 6 + 2 labels 5.75

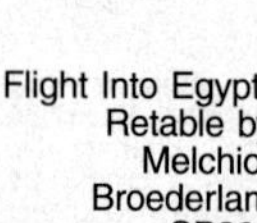

Flight Into Egypt, Retable by Melchior Broederlam SP308

1987, Nov. 21 Photo. *Perf. 12½x13*

B592 SP308 2.20fr +60c multi .95 .95
  a. As "b," bklt. pane of 10 + 2 labels 9.50
  b. Perf. 13½x13 .95 .95

Surtaxed to benefit the Red Cross.

Explorers SP309

Profiles & maps: #B593, Marquis Abraham Duquesne (1610-1688), naval commander. #B594, Pierre Andre de Suffren (1729-1788). #B595, Jean-Francois de La Perouse (1741-1788). #B596, Mahe de La Bourdonnais (1699-1753). #B597, Louis-Antoine de Bougainville (1729-1811). #B598, Jules Dumont d'Urville (1790-1842).

1988, Feb. 20 Engr. *Perf. 13*

B593 SP309 2fr + 50c multi .80 .80
B594 SP309 2fr + 50c multi .80 .80
B595 SP309 2fr + 50c multi .80 .80
B596 SP309 2.20fr + 50c multi .85 .85
B597 SP309 2.20fr + 50c multi .85 .85
B598 SP309 2.20fr + 50c multi .85 .85
  a. Bklt. pane of 6, #B593-B598 5.00

Stamp Day Type of 1986

Stamp Day 1988: Postal coach.

1988, Mar. 29 Engr.

B599 SP305 2.20fr +60c dk lilac 1.00 1.00

Booklet Stamp

B600 SP305 2.20fr +60c sepia 1.00 1.00
  a. Bklt. pane of 6 + 2 labels 6.00

Intl. Red Cross, 125th Anniv. — SP310

1988, Nov. 19 Engr. *Perf. 12½x13*

B601 SP310 2.20fr +60c multi 1.00 1.00
  a. As "b," bklt. pane of 10+2 labels 10.00
  b. Perf. 13½x13 1.00 1.00

Revolution Leaders and Heroes SP311

#B602, Emmanuel Joseph Sieyes (1748-1836). #B603, Honore Gabriel Riqueti, Comte de Mirabeau (1749-91). #B604, Louis Marie de Noailles (1756-1804). #B605, Lafayette. #B606, Antoine Pierre Joseph Marie Barnave (1761-93). #B607, Jean Baptiste Drouet (1763-1824).

1989, Feb. 25 Engr. *Perf. 13*

B602 SP311 2.20fr +50c multi .90 .90
B603 SP311 2.20fr +50c multi .90 .90
B604 SP311 2.20fr +50c multi .90 .90
B605 SP311 2.20fr +50c multi .90 .90
B606 SP311 2.20fr +50c multi .90 .90
B607 SP311 2.20fr +50c multi .90 .90
  a. Bklt. pane, 1 each + 2 labels 5.75

French Revolution, bicent.

Stamp Day Type of 1986

Design: Paris-Lyon stagecoach.

1989, Apr. 15 Engr. *Perf. 13*

B608 SP305 2.20fr +60c pale bl & dk bl .95 .95

Booklet Stamp

B609 SP305 2.20fr +60c pale lil & pur .95 .95
  a. Bklt. pane of 6 + 2 labels 5.75

Stamp Day 1989.

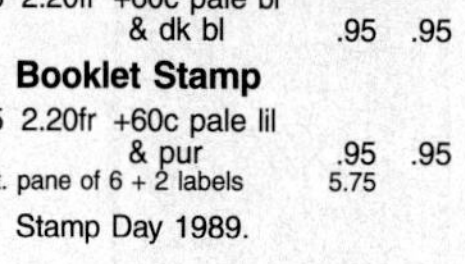

Bird From a Silk Tapestry, Lyon, 18th Cent. — SP312

1989, Nov. 18 Photo. *Perf. 12½x13*

B610 SP312 2.20fr +60c multi .90 .90
  a. As "b," bklt. pane of 10 9.00
  b. Perf. 13½x13 .90 .90

Surtax for the natl. Red Cross.

1992 Winter Olympics, Albertville SP313

1990, Feb. 9 Engr. *Perf. 13*

B611 SP313 2.30fr +20c red, bl & blk .85 .85

See Nos. B621-B627, B636-B637, B639.

Stamp Day SP314

1990, Mar. 17 Photo.

B612 SP314 2.30fr +60c ultra, bl & brt yel 1.00 1.00

Booklet Stamp

B613 SP314 2.30fr +60c ultra, grn, yel & brt grn 1.00 1.00
  a. Bklt. pane of 6 + 2 labels 6.25

SP315

SP316

Quimper or Brittany Ware Faience plate.

1990, May 5 Photo. *Perf. 12½x13*

B614 SP315 2.30fr +60c multi 1.00 1.00
  a. As "b," bklt. pane of 10+2 labels 10.00
  b. Perf. 13½x13 1.00 1.00

Surcharge benefited the Red Cross.

1990, June 16 Photo. *Perf. 13*

#B615, Aristide Bruant. #B616, Maurice Chevalier. #B617, Tino Rossi. #B618, Edith Piaf. #B619, Jacques Brel. #B620, Georges Brassens.

B615 SP316 2.30fr +50c multi 1.00 1.00
B616 SP316 2.30fr +50c multi 1.00 1.00
B617 SP316 2.30fr +50c multi 1.00 1.00
B618 SP316 2.30fr +50c multi 1.00 1.00
B619 SP316 2.30fr +50c multi 1.00 1.00
B620 SP316 2.30fr +50c multi 1.00 1.00
  a. Bklt. pane, 1 each +2 labels 6.00

Albertville Olympic Type

Designs: No. B621, Ski jumping. No. B622, Speed skiing. No. B623, Slalom skiing. No. B624, Cross-country skiing. No. B625, Ice hockey. No. B626, Luge. No. B627, Curling.

1990-91 Engr. *Perf. 13*

B621 SP313 2.30fr +20c multi .95 .95
B622 SP313 2.30fr +20c multi .95 .95
B623 SP313 2.30fr +20c multi .95 .95
B624 SP313 2.30fr +20c multi .95 .95
B625 SP313 2.30fr +20c multi .95 .95
B626 SP313 2.50fr +20c multi 1.10 1.10
B627 SP313 2.50fr +20c multi 1.10 1.10
  Nos. B621-B627 (7) 6.95 6.95

Issued: #B621, 12/22/90; #B622, 12/29/90; #B623, 1/19/91; #B624, 2/2/91; #B625, 2/9/91; #B626, 3/2/91, #B627, 4/20/91.
No. B624 inscribed "La Poste 1992."

Paul Eluard (1895-1952) — SP317

Poets: No. B629, Andre Breton (1896-1966). No. B630, Louis Aragon (1897-1982). No. B631, Francis Ponge (1899-1988). No. B632, Jacques Prevert (1900-1977). No. B633, Rene Char (1907-1988).

1991, Feb. 23 Engr. *Perf. 12½x13*

B628 SP317 2.50fr +50c multi 1.10 1.10
B629 SP317 2.50fr +50c multi 1.10 1.10
B630 SP317 2.50fr +50c multi 1.10 1.10
B631 SP317 2.50fr +50c multi 1.10 1.10
B632 SP317 2.50fr +50c multi 1.10 1.10
B633 SP317 2.50fr +50c multi 1.10 1.10
  a. Bklt. pane, 1 each +2 labels, perf. 13 6.75

Stamp Day SP318

1991, Mar. 16 Photo. *Perf. 13*

B634 SP318 2.50fr +60c blue machine 1.25 1.25
B635 SP318 2.50fr +60c purple machine 1.25 1.25
  a. Bklt. pane of 6 + 2 labels 7.50

Winter Olympics Type of 1990

#B636, Acrobatic skiing. #B637, Alpine skiing.

1991 Engr. *Perf. 13*

B636 SP313 2.50fr +20c multi .95 .95
B637 SP313 2.50fr +20c multi .95 .95

Issued: #B636, Aug. 3; #B637, Aug. 17.
Nos. B636-B637 inscribed "La Poste 1992."

The Harbor of Toulon by Francois Nardi SP319

1991, Dec. 2 Photo. *Perf. 13x12½*

B638 SP319 2.50fr +60c multi 1.10 1.10
  a. Perf. 13x13½ 1.10 1.10
  b. As "a," bklt. pane of 10 + 2 labels 11.00

Surtax for the Red Cross.

Winter Olympics Type of 1990
Miniature Sheet

a, like #B611. b, like #B621. c, like #B622. d, like #B623. e, like #B624. f, like #B625.

1992, Feb. 8 Engr. *Perf. 13*

B639 Sheet of 10 + label 12.50 12.50
  a.-f. SP313 2.50fr +20c multi 1.25 1.25

No. B639 contains one each B626-B627, B636-B637, B639a-B639f. Central label is litho.

Stamp Day SP320

1992, Mar. 7 Litho. *Perf. 13*

B640 SP320 2.50fr +60c gray people 1.10 1.10

Booklet Stamp
Photo.

B641 SP320 2.50fr +60c red people 1.10 1.10
a. Bklt. pane of 6 + 2 labels 6.60

SP321 SP322

Composers: No. B642, Cesar Franck (1822-1890). No. B643, Erik Satie (1866-1925). No. B644, Florent Schmitt (1870-1958). No. B645, Arthur Honegger (1892-1955). No. B646, Georges Auric (1899-1983). No. B647, Germaine Tailleferre (1892-1983).

1992, Apr. 11 Photo. *Perf. 13*

B642 SP321 2.50fr +50c multi 1.10 1.10
B643 SP321 2.50fr +50c multi 1.10 1.10
B644 SP321 2.50fr +50c multi 1.10 1.10
B645 SP321 2.50fr +50c multi 1.10 1.10
B646 SP321 2.50fr +50c multi 1.10 1.10
B647 SP321 2.50fr +50c multi 1.10 1.10
a. Bklt. pane of 6, #B642-B647 6.60

1992, Nov. 28 Photo. *Perf. 13½x13*

B648 SP322 2.50fr +60c multi 1.10 1.10
a. Bklt. pane of 10 + 2 labels 10.00

Mutual Aid, Strasbourg. Surtax for the Red Cross.

Writers SP323

#B649, Guy de Maupassant (1850-93). #B650, Alain (Emile Chartier) (1868-1951). #B651, Jean Cocteau (1889-1963). #B652, Marcel Pagnol (1895-1974). #B653, Andre Chamson (1900-83). #B654, Marguerite Yourcenar (1903-87).

1993, Apr. 24 Engr. *Perf. 13*

B649 SP323 2.50fr +50c multi 1.10 1.10
B650 SP323 2.50fr +50c multi 1.10 1.10
B651 SP323 2.50fr +50c multi 1.10 1.10
B652 SP323 2.50fr +50c multi 1.10 1.10
B653 SP323 2.50fr +50c multi 1.10 1.10
B654 SP323 2.50fr +50c multi 1.10 1.10
a. Bklt. pane of 6, #B649-B654 + 2 labels 6.60

When Nos. B650-B654 are normally centered, inscriptions at base of the lower panel are not parallel to the perforations at bottom. On all six stamps the lower panel is not centered between the side perforations.

SP324 SP325

St. Nicolas, Image of Metz.

1993, Nov. 27 Engr. *Perf. 12½x13*

B655 SP324 2.80fr +60c multi 1.10 1.10
a. Perf. 13½x13 1.10 1.10
b. As "a," Bklt. pane of 10 +2 labels 11.50

Surtax for Red Cross.

1994, Sept. 17 Photo. *Perf. 13*

Stage and Screen Personalities: No. B656, Yvonne Printemps (1894-1977). No. B657, Fernandel (1903-71). No. B658, Josephine Baker (1906-75). No. B659, Bourvil (1917-70). No. B660, Yves Montand (1921-91). No. B661, Coluche (1944-86).

B656 SP325 2.80fr +60c multi 1.25 1.25
B657 SP325 2.80fr +60c multi 1.25 1.25
B658 SP325 2.80fr +60c multi 1.25 1.25
B659 SP325 2.80fr +60c multi 1.25 1.25
B660 SP325 2.80fr +60c multi 1.25 1.25
B661 SP325 2.80fr +60c multi 1.25 1.25
a. Bklt. pane, #B656-B661 + 2 labels 7.50

SP326 SP327

Designs: #B662, St. Vaast, Arras Tapestry. #B663, Brussels tapestry from Reydams workshop, Horse Museum, Saumur.

1994-95 Photo. *Perf. 12½x13*

B662 SP326 2.80fr +60c multi 1.40 1.40
a. Perf. 13½x13 1.40 1.40
b. Bklt. pane, 10 #B662a + 2 labels 14.00
Complete booklet, #B662b 14.00
B663 SP326 2.80fr +60c multi 1.50 1.50
a. Perf. 13½x13 1.50 1.50
b. Bklt. pane, 10 #B663a + 2 labels 15.00
Complete booklet, #B663b 15.00

Surtax for Red Cross.
Issued: #B662, 11/26/94; #B663, 5/13/95.

1995, Nov. 25 Engr. *Perf. 13*

Provencal Nativity Figures: No. B664, The Shepherd. No. B665, The Miller. No. B666, The Simpleton and the Tambour Player. No. B667, The Fishmonger. No. B668, The Scissor Grinder. No. B669, The Elders.

B664 SP327 2.80fr +60c multi 1.40 1.40
B665 SP327 2.80fr +60c multi 1.40 1.40
B666 SP327 2.80fr +60c multi 1.40 1.40
B667 SP327 2.80fr +60c multi 1.40 1.40
B668 SP327 2.80fr +60c multi 1.40 1.40
B669 SP327 2.80fr +60c multi 1.40 1.40
a. Booklet pane, Nos. B664-B669 + 2 labels 8.50
Complete booklet, No. B669a 8.50

SP328

Famous Fictional Detectives and Criminals: #B670, Rocambole. #B671, Arsène Lupin. #B672, Joseph Rouletabille. #B673, Fantômas. #B674, Commissioner Mairgret. #B675, Nestor Burma.

1996, Oct. 5 Photo. *Perf. 13*

B670 SP328 3fr +60c multi 1.40 1.40
B671 SP328 3fr +60c multi 1.40 1.40
B672 SP328 3fr +60c multi 1.40 1.40
B673 SP328 3fr +60c multi 1.40 1.40
B674 SP328 3fr +60c multi 1.40 1.40
B675 SP328 3fr +60c multi 1.40 1.40
a. Booklet pane, #B670-B675 + 2 labels 8.40
Complete booklet, #B675a 8.40

Christmas SP329

1996, Nov. 16 Photo. *Perf. 12¾x13*

B676 SP329 3fr +60c multi 1.45 1.45

Surtax for Red Cross.

Adventure Heroes SP330

1997, Oct. 25 Photo. *Perf. 13*

B677 SP330 3fr +60c Sir Lancelot 1.25 1.25
B678 SP330 3fr +60c Pardaillan 1.25 1.25
B679 SP330 3fr +60c D'Artagnan 1.25 1.25
B680 SP330 3fr +60c Cyrano de Bergerac 1.25 1.25
B681 SP330 3fr +60c Captain Fracasse 1.25 1.25
B682 SP330 3fr +60c Le Bossu 1.25 1.25
a. Booklet pane, #B677-B682 + 2 labels 7.50
Complete booklet, #682a 7.50

Christmas, New Year — SP331

1997, Nov. 6 Photo. *Perf. 12¾x13*

B683 SP331 3fr +60c multi 1.25 1.25
a. Booklet pane of 10 12.50

Surtax for the Red Cross.

SP332

Actors of the French Cinema: #B684, Romy Schneider (1938-82). #B685, Simone Signoret (1921-85). #B686, Jean Gabin (1904-76). #B687, Louis de Funés (1914-83). #B688, Bernard Blier (1916-89). #B689, Lino Ventura (1919-87).

1998, Oct. 3 Photo. *Perf. 13*

B684 SP332 3fr +60c multi 1.40 1.40
B685 SP332 3fr +60c multi 1.40 1.40
B686 SP332 3fr +60c multi 1.40 1.40
B687 SP332 3fr +60c multi 1.40 1.40
B688 SP332 3fr +60c multi 1.40 1.40
B689 SP332 3fr +60c multi 1.40 1.40
a. Booklet pane, #B684-B689 + label 8.50
Complete booklet, #B689a 8.50

Christmas SP333

1998, Nov. 5 Photo. *Perf. 12½x13*

B690 SP333 3fr +60c multi 1.40 1.40
a. Perf. 13½x13 1.40 1.40
b. Booklet pane, 10 #B690a + 2 labels 14.00
Complete booklet, #B690b 14.00

Surtax for Red Cross.

Famous Photographers — SP334

Photographs by: #B691, Robert Doisneau (1912-94). #B692, Brassai (Gyula Halasz) (1899-1984). #B693, Jacques Lartigue (1894-1986). #B694, Henri Cartier-Bresson (b. 1908). #B695, Eugene Atget (1857-1927). #B696, Felix Nadar (1820-1910).

1999, July 10 Photo. *Perf. 13*

B691 SP334 3fr +60c multi 1.40 1.40
B692 SP334 3fr +60c multi 1.40 1.40
B693 SP334 3fr +60c multi 1.40 1.40
B694 SP334 3fr +60c multi 1.40 1.40
B695 SP334 3fr +60c multi 1.40 1.40
B696 SP334 3fr +60c multi 1.40 1.40
a. Booklet pane, #B691-B696 8.50
Complete booklet, #B696a 8.50

New Year 2000 — SP335

1999, Nov. 10 Photo. *Perf. 12¾x13*

B697 SP335 3fr +60c multi 1.40 1.40
a. Perf. 13½x13 1.40 1.40
b. Booklet pane, 10 #B697a + 2 labels 14.00
Complete booklet, #B697b 14.00

Surtax for Red Cross.

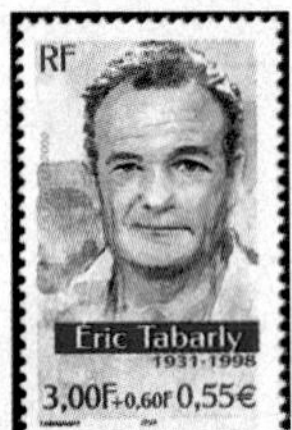

Adventurers SP336

#B698, Eric Tabarly (1931-98), sailor. #B699, Alexandra David-Néel (1868-1969), opera singer, Asian traveler. #B700, Haroun Tazieff (1914-98), vulcanologist. #B701, Paul-Emile Victor (1907-55), ethnologist, polar explorer. #B702, Jacques-Yves Cousteau (1910-97), oceanographer. #B703, Norbert Casteret (1897-1987), speleologist.

2000, Sept. 16 Photo. *Perf. 13¼x13*

B698 SP336 3fr +60c multi 1.40 1.40
B699 SP336 3fr +60c multi 1.40 1.40
B700 SP336 3fr +60c multi 1.40 1.40
B701 SP336 3fr +60c multi 1.40 1.40
B702 SP336 3fr +60c multi 1.40 1.40
B703 SP336 3fr +60c multi 1.40 1.40
a. Booklet pane, #B698-B703 8.50
Booklet, #B703a 8.50

Toy Airplane — SP337

2000, Nov. 9 Photo. *Perf. 13¼x13*

B704 SP337 3fr +60c multi 1.40 1.40
a. Booklet pane of 10 + 2 labels 14.00
Booklet, #B704a 14.00

Surtax for Red Cross.

Santa Claus and Tree Ornaments SP338

2001, Nov. 8 Photo. *Perf. 12¾x13*

B705 SP338 3fr +60c multi 1.40 1.40
a. Perf 13½x13 1.40 1.40
b. Booklet pane of 10 14.00 —
Booklet, #B705a 14.00

Surtax for Red Cross.

Infant Jesus Asleep, by Giovanni Battista Salvi — SP339

2002, Nov. 7 Photo. *Perf. 12¾x13*

B706 SP339 46c +9c multi 1.40 1.40
- *a.* Perf. 13½x13 1.40 1.40
- *b.* As "a," booklet pane of 10 14.00 —
- Booklet, #B706b 14.00

Surtax for Red Cross.

Virgin with Grapes, by Pierre Mignard — SP340

2003, Nov. 6 Photo. *Perf. 13¼x13*
Booklet Stamp

B707 SP340 50c +(16c) multi 1.50 1.50
- *a.* Booklet pane of 10 15.00 —
- Complete booklet, #B707a 15.00

Surtax for Red Cross.

Virgin With Child, Attributed to Cretan School — SP341

2004, Nov. 10 Photo. *Perf. 13¼x13*
Booklet Stamp

B708 SP341 50c +(16c) multi 1.75 1.75
- *a.* Booklet pane of 10 + 2 labels 17.50 —
- Complete booklet, #B708a 17.50

Surtax for Red Cross.

AIR POST STAMPS

Nos. 127, 130 Overprinted in Dark Blue or Black

Perf. 14x13½

1927, June 25 Unwmk.

C1 A18 2fr org & bl (DB) 200.00 225.00
- Never hinged 375.00

C2 A18 5fr dk bl & buff 200.00 225.00
- Never hinged 375.00

On sale only at the Intl. Aviation Exhib. at Marseilles, June, 1927. One set could be purchased by each holder of an admission ticket. Excellent counterfeits exist.

Nos. 242, 196 Surcharged

1928, Aug. 23

C3 A33 10fr on 90c 1,500. 1,500.
- Never hinged 2,100.
- *a.* Inverted surcharge *14,500. 15,500.*
- Never hinged *19,000.*
- *b.* Space between "10" and bars 6½mm *2,600. 3,100.*
- Never hinged *3,600.*

C4 A23 10fr on 1.50fr *7,500. 7,500.*
- Never hinged *11,000.*
- *a.* Space between "10" and bars 6½mm *9,500. 9,500.*
- Never hinged *14,000.*

Nos. C3-C4 received their surcharge in New York by order of the French consul general. They were for use in paying the 10fr fee for letters leaving the liner Ile de France on a catapulted hydroplane when the ship was one day off the coast of France on its eastward voyage.

The normal space between "10" and bars is 4½mm, but on 10 stamps in each pane of 50 the space is 6½mm. Counterfeits exist.

View of Marseille, Church of Notre Dame at Left — AP1

1930-31 Engr. *Perf. 13*

C5 AP1 1.50fr dp carmine 16.00 3.00
- Never hinged 26.00

C6 AP1 1.50fr dk bl ('31) 14.00 1.40
- Never hinged 25.00
- *a.* 1.50fr ultramarine 30.00 18.00
- Never hinged 55.00
- *b.* As "a," with perf. initials "E.I.P.A.30" 325.00 300.00
- Never hinged 500.00

No. C6a was sold at the Intl. Air Post Exhib., Paris, Nov. 6-20, 1930, at face value plus 5fr, the price of admission.

Forgeries abound of No. C6b. Certificates from recognized authorities are recommended.

Blériot's Monoplane AP2

1934, Sept. 1 *Perf. 13*

C7 AP2 2.25fr violet 15.00 4.50
- Never hinged 26.00

1st flight across the English Channel, by Louis Blériot.

Plane over Paris AP3

1936

C8 AP3 85c dp green 1.75 1.50
- Never hinged 3.00

C9 AP3 1.50fr blue 7.50 3.50
- Never hinged 13.00

C10 AP3 2.25fr violet 14.50 5.75
- Never hinged 25.00

C11 AP3 2.50fr rose 22.50 6.50
- Never hinged 32.50

C12 AP3 3fr ultra 15.00 1.10
- Never hinged 25.00

C13 AP3 3.50fr orange brn 50.00 18.00
- Never hinged 85.00

C14 AP3 50fr emerald 600.00 250.00
- Never hinged 900.00
- *a.* 50fr deep green 800.00 475.00
- Never hinged 1,250.

Nos. C8-C14 (7) 711.25 286.35

Monoplane over Paris — AP4

Paper with Red Network Overprint

1936, July 10 *Perf. 12½*

C15 AP4 50fr ultra 450.00 250.00
- Never hinged 775.00

Airplane and Galleon — AP5

Airplane and Globe AP6

1936, Aug. 17 *Perf. 13*

C16 AP5 1.50fr dk ultra 11.50 3.50
- Never hinged 22.50

C17 AP6 10fr Prus green 250.00 100.00
- Never hinged 450.00

100th air mail flight across the South Atlantic.

Catalogue values for unused stamps in this section, from this point to the end of the section, are for Never Hinged items.

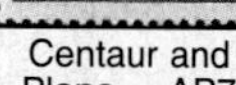

Centaur and Plane — AP7

Iris — AP8

Zeus Carrying Hebe AP9

Chariot of the Sun AP10

1946-47 Engr. Unwmk.

C18 AP7 40fr dk green .65 .20
C19 AP8 50fr rose pink .65 .20
C20 AP9 100fr dk blue ('47) 5.00 .45
C21 AP10 200fr red 4.25 .75
Nos. C18-C21 (4) 10.55 1.60

Issued: 50fr, 200fr, 5/27; 40fr, 7/1; 100fr, Jan.

For surcharges see Reunion Nos. C35-C38.

Ile de la Cité, Paris, and Gull — AP11

1947, May 7

C22 AP11 500fr dk Prus grn 42.50 42.50

UPU 12th Cong., Paris, May 7-July 7.

View of Lille AP12

Air View of Paris — AP13

200fr, Bordeaux. 300fr, Lyon. 500fr, Marseille.

1949-50 Unwmk. *Perf. 13*

C23 AP12 100fr sepia 1.40 .20
C24 AP12 200fr dk bl grn 11.00 .50
C25 AP12 300fr purple 15.00 6.50
C26 AP12 500fr brt red 52.50 3.50
C27 AP13 1000fr sep & blk, *bl* ('50) 85.00 17.00
Nos. C23-C27 (5) 164.90 27.70

For surcharges see Reunion Nos. C39-C41.

Alexander III Bridge and Petit Palais, Paris — AP14

1949, June 13

C28 AP14 100fr brown car 6.50 4.50

International Telegraph and Telephone Conference, Paris, May-July 1949.

Jet Plane, Mystère IV — AP15

Planes: 200fr, Noratlas. 500fr, Miles Magister. 1000fr, Provence.

1954, Jan. 16

C29 AP15 100fr red brn & bl 3.00 .20
C30 AP15 200fr blk brn & vio bl 11.00 .25
C31 AP15 500fr car & org 110.00 7.00
C32 AP15 1000fr vio brn, bl grn & ind 100.00 10.00
Nos. C29-C32 (4) 224.00 17.45

See No. C37. For surcharges see Reunion Nos. C42-C45, C48.

Maryse Bastié and Plane AP16

1955, June 4 Unwmk. *Perf. 13*

C33 AP16 50fr dp plum & rose pink 5.50 3.25

Issued to honor Maryse Bastié, 1898-1952.

Caravelle AP17

Designs: 300fr, Morane Saulnier 760 "Paris." 1000fr, Alouette helicopter.

1957-59 Engr. *Perf. 13*

C34 AP17 300fr sl grn, grnsh bl & sep ('59) 5.00 1.40
C35 AP17 500fr dp ultra & blk 30.00 1.60
C36 AP17 1000fr lil, ol blk & blk ('58) 50.00 13.00
Nos. C34-C36 (3) 85.00 16.00

See Nos. C38-C41. For surcharges see Reunion Nos. C46-C47, C49-C51.

Types of 1954-59

Planes: 2fr, Noratlas. 3fr, MS760, Paris. 5fr, Caravelle. 10fr, Alouette helicopter.

1960, Jan. 11

C37 AP15 2fr vio bl & ultra 1.40 .20
a. 2fr ultramarine 2.50 .20
C38 AP17 3fr sl grn, grnsh bl & sep 1.25 .20
C39 AP17 5fr dp ultra & blk 2.10 .20
C40 AP17 10fr lil, ol blk & blk 11.00 1.00
Nos. C37-C40 (4) 15.75 1.60

Type of 1957-59

Design: 2fr, Jet plane, Mystère 20.

1965, June 12 Engr. *Perf. 13*

C41 AP17 2fr slate bl & indigo .80 .20

Concorde Issue
Common Design Type

1969, Mar. 2 Engr. *Perf. 13*

C42 CD129 1fr indigo & brt bl 1.00 .35

Jean Mermoz, Antoine de Saint-Exupéry and Concorde — AP19

1970, Sept. 19 Engr. *Perf. 13*

C43 AP19 20fr blue & indigo 7.50 .40

Jean Mermoz (1901-36) and writer Antoine de Saint-Exupéry (1900-44), aviators and air mail pioneers.

Balloon, Gare d'Austerlitz, Paris — AP20

1971, Jan. 16 Engr. *Perf. 13*

C44 AP20 95c bl, vio bl, org & sl grn .90 .55

Centenary of the balloon post from besieged Paris, 1870-71.

Didier Daurat, Raymond Vanier and Plane Landing at Night — AP21

1971, Apr. 17 Engr. *Perf. 13*

C45 AP21 5fr Prus bl, blk & lt grn 1.40 .20

Didier Daurat (1891-1969) and Raymond Vanier (1895-1965), aviation pioneers.
For surcharge see Reunion No. C52.

Hélène Boucher, Maryse Hilsz and Caudron-Renault and Moth-Morane Planes — AP22

Design: 15fr, Henri Guillaumet, Paul Codos, Latécoère 521, Guillaumet's crashed plane in Andes, skyscrapers.

1972-73 Engr. *Perf. 13*

C46 AP22 10fr plum, red & sl 3.00 .20
C47 AP22 15fr dp car, gray & brn ('73) 4.50 .40

Hélène Boucher (1908-34), Maryse Hilsz (1901-46), Henri Guillaumet (1902-40) and Paul Codos (1896-1960), aviation pioneers.
Issue dates: 10fr, June 10; 15fr, Feb. 24.

Concorde AP23

1976, Jan. 10 Engr. *Perf. 13*

C48 AP23 1.70fr brt bl, red & blk .75 .35

First flight of supersonic jet Concorde from Paris to Rio de Janeiro, Jan. 21.

Planes over the Atlantic, New York-Paris — AP24

1977, June 4 Engr. *Perf. 13*

C49 AP24 1.90fr multicolored .75 .35

1st transatlantic flight by Lindbergh from NY to Paris, 50th anniv., and 1st attempted west-bound flight by French aviators Charles Nungesser and Francois Coli.

Plane over Flight Route AP25

1978, Oct. 14 Engr. *Perf. 13*

C50 AP25 1.50fr multicolored .90 .35

75th anniversary of first airmail route from Villacoublay to Pauillac, Gironde.

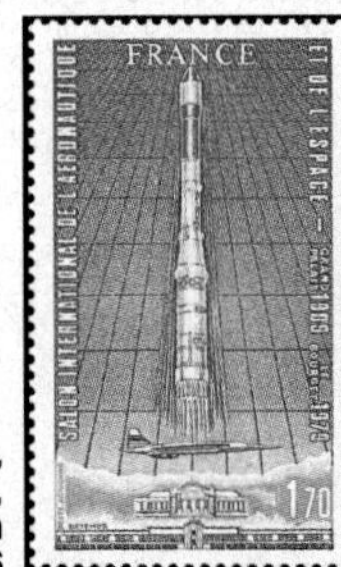

Rocket, Concorde, Exhibition Hall — AP26

1979, June 9 Engr. *Perf. 13*

C51 AP26 1.70fr ultra, org & brn 1.25 .50

33rd International Aerospace and Space Show, Le Bourget, June 11-15.

First Nonstop Transatlantic Flight, Paris-New York — AP27

1980, Aug. 30 Engr. *Perf. 13*

C52 AP27 2.50fr vio brn & ultra .75 .30

34th Intl. Space and Aeronautics Exhibition, June 5-14 AP28

1981, June 6 Engr. *Perf. 13*

C53 AP28 2fr multicolored 1.75 .35

Dieudonné Costes and Joseph Le Brix and their Breguet Bi-plane — AP29

1981, Sept. 12 Engr.

C54 AP29 10fr dk brown & red 3.00 .20

1st So. Atlantic crossing, Oct. 14-15, 1927.

Seaplane Late-300 — AP30

1982, Dec. 4 Engr.

C55 AP30 1.60fr multicolored .65 .35

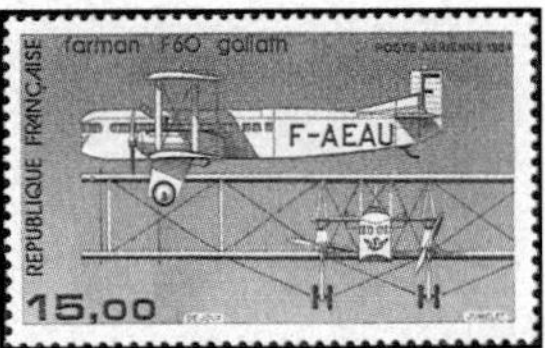

Farman F-60 Goliath — AP31

Planes: 20fr, CAMS-53 seaplane. 30fr, Wibault 283 Monoplane. 50fr, Dewoitine 338.

1984-87 Engr.

C56 AP31 15fr dark blue 4.00 .45
C57 AP31 20fr dp org ('85) 5.25 .45
C58 AP31 30fr brt vio ('86) 7.50 .90
C59 AP31 50fr green ('87) 12.50 2.75
Nos. C55-C59 (5) 29.90 4.90

Issued: 15fr, 3/3; 20fr, 3/2; 30fr, 10/11; 50fr, 4/11.

Breguet XIV — AP32

1997, Nov. 15 Photo. *Perf. 13x13¼*

C60 AP32 20fr shown 6.25 1.25
a. Perf. 13x12½ 6.25 1.25
C61 AP32 30fr Potez 25 9.00 1.50
a. Perf. 13x12½ 9.00 1.50

Issued: No. C60 11/15/97; No. C60a, 7/13/98; 30fr, 7/13/98.

Nos. C60 and C61 were issued in panes of 40 (5x8), Nos. C60a and C61a in panes of 10 (2x5).

Airbus A300-B4 — AP33

1999, Apr. 10 Photo. *Perf. 13x13¼*

C62 AP33 15fr multicolored 4.25 1.10
a. Perf. 13x12½ 4.25 1.10

No. C62 was issued in panes of 40 (5x8), No. C62a in panes of 10 (2x5).

Couzinet 70 — AP34

2000, Feb. 12 *Perf. 13¼x13¼*

C63 AP34 50fr multi 13.50 2.00
a. Perf. 13x12½ 13.50 2.00

No. C63 was issued in panes of 40 (5x8), No. C63a in panes of 10 (2x5).

First Flight of Airbus A300, 30th Anniv. — AP35

2002, Oct. 26 Photo. *Perf. 13x13¼*

C64 AP35 €3 multi 6.00 1.25

No. C64 was issued both in panes of 40 and 10, same perforation.

Jacqueline Auriol (1917-2000), Pilot, and Jet — AP36

Litho. & Engr.

2003, June 21 *Perf. 13*

C65 AP36 €4 multi 9.00 1.50
a. Miniature sheet of 10 90.00 —

Marie Marvingt (1875-1963), Pilot — AP37

Litho. & Engr.

2004, June 29 *Perf. 13¼x13*

C66 AP37 €5 multi 12.50 2.50
a. Sheet of 10 125.00 25.00

AIR POST SEMI-POSTAL STAMPS

Catalogue values for unused stamps in this section are for Never Hinged items.

Antoine de Saint-Exupéry — SPAP1

Col. Jean Dagnaux SPAP2

1948 Unwmk. Engr. *Perf. 13*
CB1 SPAP1 50fr + 30fr vio brn 1.75 1.60
CB2 SPAP2 100fr + 70fr dk blue 2.50 2.25

Modern Plane and Ader's "Eole" SPAP3

1948, Feb.
CB3 SPAP3 40fr + 10fr dk blue 1.00 .90

50th anniv. of the flight of Clément Ader's plane, the Eole, in 1897.

POSTAGE DUE STAMPS

D1

D2

1859-70 Unwmk. Litho. *Imperf.*
J1 D1 10c black *22,500.* 175.00
J2 D1 15c black ('70) 100.00 175.00

In the lithographed stamps the central bar of the "E" of "CENTIMES" is very short, and the accent on "a" slants at an angle of 30 degree, for the 10c and 17 degree for the 15c, while on the typographed the central bar of the "E" is almost as wide as the top and bottom bars and the accent on the "a" slants at an angle of 47 degree.

No. J2 is known rouletted unofficially.

1859-78 Typo.
J3 D1 10c black 21.00 14.00
J4 D1 15c black ('63) 25.00 12.00
J5 D1 20c black ('77) *2,875.*
J6 D1 25c black ('71) 110.00 42.50
J7 D1 30c black ('78) 175.00 100.00
J8 D1 40c blue ('71) 250.00 325.00
a. 40c ultramarine *5,250.* *5,000.*
b. 40c Prussian blue *1,900.*
J9 D1 60c yellow ('71) 400.00 *850.00*
J10 D1 60c blue ('78) 50.00 *110.00*
a. 60c dark blue 450.00 550.00
J10B D1 60c black *2,100.*

The 20c & 60c black were not put into use.

Nos. J3, J4, J6, J8 and J9 are known rouletted unofficially and Nos. J4, J6, J7 and J10 pin-perf. unofficially.

1882-92 *Perf. 14x13½*
J11 D2 1c black 1.50 1.50
J12 D2 2c black 18.00 21.00
J13 D2 3c black 18.00 22.50
J14 D2 4c black 35.00 35.00
J15 D2 5c black 77.50 25.00
J16 D2 10c black 70.00 1.50
J17 D2 15c black 47.50 9.75
J18 D2 20c black 250.00 110.00
J19 D2 30c black 150.00 1.40
J20 D2 40c black 95.00 52.50
J21 D2 50c blk ('92) 425.00 150.00
J22 D2 60c blk ('84) 425.00 45.00
J23 D2 1fr black 525.00 325.00
J24 D2 2fr blk ('84) 1,000. 700.00
J25 D2 5fr blk ('84) 2,250. 1,400.

Excellent counterfeits exist of Nos. J23-J25.

See Nos. J26-J45A. For overprints and surcharges see Offices in China Nos. J1-J6, J33-J40, Offices in Egypt, Alexandria J1-J5, Port Said J1-J8, Offices in Zanzibar 60-62, J1-J5, Offices in Morocco 9-10, 24-25, J1-J5, J10-J12, J17-J22, J35-J41.

1884
J26 D2 1fr brown 290.00 77.50
J27 D2 2fr brown 150.00 110.00
J28 D2 5fr brown 325.00 300.00

1893-1941
J29 D2 5c blue ('94) .25 .25
J30 D2 10c brown .25 .25
J31 D2 15c lt grn ('94) 21.00 1.00
J32 D2 20c ol grn ('06) 5.00 .45
J33 D2 25c rose ('23) 5.00 3.25
J34 D2 30c red ('94) .25 .20
J35 D2 30c org red ('94) 450.00 60.00
J36 D2 40c rose ('25) 10.50 3.50
J37 D2 45c grn ('24) 9.00 3.50
J38 D2 50c brn vio ('95) .35 .20
a. 50c lilac .35 .20
J39 D2 60c bl grn ('25) .75 .45
J40 D2 1fr rose, *straw* ('96) 475.00 275.00
J41 D2 1fr red brn, *straw* ('20) 8.50 .20
J42 D2 1fr red brn ('35) .80 .25
J43 D2 2fr red org ('10) 210.00 42.50
J44 D2 2fr brt vio ('26) .45 *.60*
J45 D2 3fr magenta ('26) .45 *.70*
J45A D2 5fr red org ('41) 1.40 1.60

D3

D4

1908-25
J46 D3 1c olive grn .75 *.85*
J47 D3 10c violet 110.00 .30
a. Imperf., pair 140.00
J48 D3 20c bister ('19) 35.00 .85
J49 D3 30c bister ('09) 14.00 .35
J50 D3 50c red ('09) 260.00 42.50
J51 D3 60c red ('25) 2.75 2.50
Nos. J46-J51 (6) 422.50 47.35

"Recouvrements" stamps were used to recover charges due on undelivered or refused mail which was returned to the sender.

For surcharges see Offices in Morocco Nos. J6-J9, J13-J16, J23-J26, J42-J45.

Nos. J49-J50 Surcharged

1917
J52 D3 20c on 30c bister 15.50 2.75
J53 D3 40c on 50c red 11.00 2.75
a. Double surcharge 335.00

In Jan. 1917 several values of the current issue of postage stamps were handstamped "T" in a triangle and used as postage due stamps.

Recouvrements Stamps of 1908-25 Surcharged

1926
J54 D3 50c on 10c lilac 3.50 2.75
J55 D3 60c on 1c ol grn 7.00 3.00
J56 D3 1fr on 60c red 14.00 7.75
J57 D3 2fr on 60c red 14.00 7.75
Nos. J54-J57 (4) 38.50 21.25

1927-31
J58 D4 1c olive grn ('28) .90 .90
J59 D4 10c rose ('31) 1.50 1.25
J60 D4 30c bister 4.25 .35
J61 D4 60c red 4.25 .35
J62 D4 1fr violet 12.00 2.75
J63 D4 1fr Prus grn ('31) 12.50 .50
J64 D4 2fr blue 70.00 32.50
J65 D4 2fr olive brn ('31) 110.00 20.00
Nos. J58-J65 (8) 215.40 58.60

Nos. J62 to J65 have the numerals of value double-lined.

Nos. J64, J62 Surcharged in Red or Black

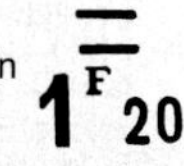

1929
J66 D4 1.20fr on 2fr blue 35.00 8.50
J67 D4 5fr on 1fr vio (Bk) 55.00 10.00
Set, never hinged 175.00

No. J61 Surcharged UN FRANC

1931
J68 D4 1fr on 60c red 25.00 2.75
Never hinged 42.50

Catalogue values for unused stamps in this section, from this point to the end of the section, are for Never Hinged items.

Sheaves of Wheat
D5 D6

Perf. 14x13½
1943-46 Unwmk. Typo.
J69 D5 10c sepia .20 .20
J70 D5 30c brt red vio .20 .20
J71 D5 50c blue grn .20 .20
J72 D5 1fr brt ultra .20 .20
J73 D5 1.50fr rose red .45 .40
J74 D5 2fr turq blue .45 .40
J75 D5 3fr brn org .45 .40
J76 D5 4fr dp vio ('45) 4.00 3.00
J77 D5 5fr brt pink .60 .40
J78 D5 10fr red org ('45) 3.50 .40
J79 D5 20fr ol bis ('46) 6.50 2.50
Nos. J69-J79 (11) 16.75 8.30

Type of 1943
Inscribed "Timbre Taxe"

1946-53
J80 D5 10c sepia ('47) 1.90 1.25
J81 D5 30c brt red vio ('47) 1.40 1.10
J82 D5 50c blue grn ('47) 11.00 5.50
J83 D5 1fr brt ultra ('47) .35 .30
J85 D5 2fr turq blue .35 .30
J86 D5 3fr brown org .35 .30
J87 D5 4fr deep violet .45 .30
J88 D5 5fr brt pink ('47) .45 .20
J89 D5 10fr red org ('47) .45 .20
J90 D5 20fr olive bis ('47) 2.00 .40
J91 D5 50fr dk green ('50) 13.00 .40
J92 D5 100fr dp green ('53) 57.50 5.75
Nos. J80-J92 (12) 89.20 16.00

For surcharges see Reunion Nos. J36-J44.

1960 Typo. *Perf. 14x13½*
J93 D6 5c bright pink 2.00 .30
J94 D6 10c red orange 3.00 .30
J95 D6 20c olive bister 3.50 .30
J96 D6 50c dark green 11.00 1.25
J97 D6 1fr deep green 37.50 3.00
Nos. J93-J97 (5) 57.00 5.15

For surcharges see Reunion Nos. J46-J48. For overprints see Algeria Nos. J49-J53.

D7

D8

Flowers: 5c, Centaury. 10c, Gentian. 15c, Corn poppy. 20c, Violets. 30c, Forget-me-not. 40c, Columbine. 50c, Clover. 1fr, Soldanel.

1964-71 Typo. *Perf. 14x13½*
J98 D7 5c car rose, red & grn ('65) .20 .20
J99 D7 10c car rose, brt bl & grn ('65) .20 .20
J100 D7 15c brn, grn & red .20 .20
J101 D7 20c dk grn, grn & vio ('71) .20 .20
J102 D7 30c brn, ultra & grn .20 .20
J103 D7 40c dk grn, scar & yel ('71) .25 .20
J104 D7 50c vio bl, car & grn ('65) .25 .20
J105 D7 1fr vio bl, lil & grn ('65) .40 .20
Nos. J98-J105 (8) 1.90 1.60

For surcharges see Reunion Nos. J49-J55.

1982-83 Engr. *Perf. 13*
J106 D8 10c Ampedus Cinnabarinus .20 .20
J107 D8 20c Dorcadion fuliginator .20 .20
J108 D8 30c Leptura cordigera .20 .20
J109 D8 40c Paederus littoralis .20 .20
J110 D8 50c Pyrochroa coccinea .20 .20
J111 D8 1fr Scarites laevigatus .30 .20
J112 D8 2fr Trichius gallicus .55 .20
J113 D8 3fr Adalia alpina .90 .20
J114 D8 4fr Apoderus coryli 1.20 .20
J115 D8 5fr Trichodes alvearius 1.50 .20
Nos. J106-J115 (10) 5.45 2.00

Issued: 30c, 40c, 3fr, 5fr, 1/3/83; others, 1/4/82.

MILITARY STAMPS

Regular Issue Overprinted in Black or Red

1901-39 Unwmk. *Perf. 14x13½*
M1 A17 15c orange ('01) 55.00 5.00
a. Inverted overprint 200.00 90.00
b. Imperf., pair 250.00
M2 A19 15c pale red ('03) 60.00 4.25
M3 A20 15c slate grn ('04) 45.00 4.00
a. No period after "M" 90.00 35.00
b. Imperf., pair 175.00
M4 A20 10c rose ('06) 27.50 5.00
a. No period after "M" 75.00 30.00
b. Imperf., pair 200.00
M5 A22 10c red ('07) .90 .60
a. Inverted overprint 72.50 42.50
b. Imperf., pair 140.00
M6 A20 50c vermilion ('29) 3.50 .60
a. No period after "M" 27.50 10.00
b. Period in front of F 27.50 10.00
M7 A45 50c rose red ('34) 2.25 .45
a. No period after "M" *20.00* *12.50*
b. Inverted overprint 100.00 77.50
M8 A45 65c brt ultra (R) ('38) .30 .30
a. No period after "M" 18.00 16.00
M9 A45 90c ultra (R) ('39) .40 .35
Nos. M1-M9 (9) 194.85 20.55

"F. M." are initials of Franchise Militaire (Military Frank). See No. S1.

Catalogue values for unused stamps in this section, from this point to the end of the section, are for Never Hinged items.

M1

Flag — M2

1946-47 Typo.
M10 M1 dark green 1.75 .65
M11 M1 rose red ('47) .30 .20

Nos. M10-M11 were valid also in the French colonies.

1964, July 20 *Perf. 13x14*
M12 M2 multicolored .30 .35

OFFICIAL STAMPS

FOR THE COUNCIL OF EUROPE

For use only on mail posted in the post office in the Council of Europe Building, Strasbourg.

Catalogue values for unused stamps in this section are for Never Hinged items.

For French stamp inscribed "Conseil de l'Europe" see No. 679.

France No. 854 Overprinted: "CONSEIL DE L'EUROPE"

Unwmk.

1958, Jan. 14 Engr. *Perf. 13*

1O1 A303 35fr car rose & lake 1.10 *2.25*

Council of Europe Flag — O1

1958-59

Flag in Ultramarine

1O2 O1 8fr red org & brn vio .20 .20
1O3 O1 20fr yel & lt brn .30 .25
1O4 O1 25fr lil rose & sl grn ('59) .60 .35
1O5 O1 35fr red .45 .45
1O6 O1 50fr lilac rose ('59) 1.10 1.00
Nos. 1O2-1O6 (5) 2.65 2.25

1963, Jan. 3

Flag in Ultramarine

1O7 O1 20c yel & lt brn 1.25 .50
1O8 O1 25c lil rose & sl grn 2.00 1.10
1O9 O1 50c lilac rose 2.00 1.65
Nos. 1O7-1O9 (3) 5.25 3.25

Centime value stamps shown the denomination as "0,20," etc.

1965-71

Flag in Ultramarine & Yellow

1O10 O1 25c ver, yel & sl grn .85 .65
1O11 O1 30c ver & yel .85 .65
1O12 O1 40c ver, yel & gray 1.25 .65
1O13 O1 50c red, yel & grn 2.50 1.25
1O14 O1 60c ver, yel & vio 1.00 .65
1O15 O1 70c ver, yel & dk brn 3.75 2.50
Nos. 1O10-1O15 (6) 10.20 6.35

Issue dates: 25c, 30c, 60c, Jan. 16, 1965; 50c, Feb. 20, 1971; others, Mar. 24, 1969.

Type of 1958 Inscribed "FRANCE"

1975-76 Engr. *Perf. 13*

Flag in Ultramarine & Yellow

1O16 O1 60c org, yel & emer 1.25 .65
1O17 O1 80c yel & mag 1.90 1.10
1O18 O1 1fr car, yel & gray ol ('76) 4.00 3.00
1O19 O1 1.20fr org, yel & bl 5.25 2.50
Nos. 1O16-1O19 (4) 12.40 7.25

Issue dates: 1fr, Oct. 16; others, Nov. 22.

New Council Headquarters, Strasbourg — O2

1977, Jan. 22 Engr. *Perf. 13*

1O20 O2 80c car & multi 1.00 .50
1O21 O2 1fr brown & multi 1.00 .50
1O22 O2 1.40fr gray & multi 2.00 1.00
Nos. 1O20-1O22 (3) 4.00 2.00

Human Rights Emblem in Upper Left Corner

1978, Oct. 14

1O23 O2 1.20fr red lilac & multi .45 .40
1O24 O2 1.70fr blue & multi .75 .55

30th anniversary of the Universal Declaration of Human Rights.

Council Headquarters Type of 1977

1980, Nov. 24 Engr. *Perf. 13*

1O25 O2 1.40fr olive .50 .45
1O26 O2 2fr blue gray .60 .55

New Council Headquarters, Strasbourg — O3

1981-84 Engr.

1O27 O3 1.40fr multicolored .50 .40
1O28 O3 1.60fr multicolored .50 .40
1O29 O3 1.70fr emerald .35 .30
1O30 O3 1.80fr multicolored .70 .55
1O31 O3 2fr multicolored .90 .60
1O32 O3 2.10fr red .35 .30
1O33 O3 2.30fr multicolored .75 .65
1O34 O3 2.60fr multicolored .90 .65
1O35 O3 2.80fr multicolored 1.00 .75
1O36 O3 3fr brt blue .52 .45
Nos. 1O27-1O36 (10) 6.47 5.05

Issued: 1.40, 1.60, 2.30fr, 11/21; 1.80, 2.60fr, 11/13/82; 2, 2.80fr, 11/21/83; 1.70, 2.10, 3fr, 11/5/84.

Youth's Leg, Sneaker, Shattered Eggshell O4

1985, Aug. 31 Engr. *Perf. 13*

1O37 O4 1.80fr brt green .55 .20
1O38 O4 2.20fr vermilion .65 .20
1O39 O4 3.20fr brt blue .90 .20
Nos. 1O37-1O39 (3) 2.10 .60

New Council Headquarters, Strasbourg — O5

1986-87 Engr. *Perf. 13*

1O40 O5 1.90fr green .55 .20
1O41 O5 2fr brt yel grn .55 .20
1O42 O5 2.20fr red .65 .20
1O43 O5 3.40fr blue 1.00 .20
1O44 O5 3.60fr brt blue .95 .20
Nos. 1O40-1O44 (5) 3.70 1.00

Issued: 1.90, 2.20, 3.40fr, 12/13; 2, 3.60fr, 10/10/87.

Council of Europe, 40th Anniv. O6

1989, Feb. 4 Litho. & Engr.

1O45 O6 2.20fr multicolored .70 .20
1O46 O6 3.60fr multicolored 1.15 .25

Denominations also inscribed in European Currency Units (ECUs).

Map of Europe O7

1990-91 Litho. *Perf. 13*

1O47 O7 2.30fr multicolored .85 .20
1O48 O7 2.50fr multicolored 1.00 .20
1O49 O7 3.20fr multicolored 1.15 .25
1O50 O7 3.40fr multicolored 1.30 .30
Nos. 1O47-1O50 (4) 4.30 .95

Issued: 2.30fr, 3.20fr, 5/26/90; 2.50fr, 3.40fr, 11/23/91.

36 Heads, by Hundertwasser O8

1994, Jan. 15 Litho. *Perf. 13*

1O51 O8 2.80fr multicolored .95 .20
1O52 O8 3.70fr multicolored 1.25 .25

Palace of Human Rights, Strasbourg O9

1996, June 1 Litho. *Perf. 13*

1O53 O9 3fr multicolored 1.25 .30
1O54 O9 3.80fr multicolored 1.60 .40

Charioteer of Delphi — O10

1999, Sept. 18 Photo. *Perf. 13*

1O55 O10 3fr shown 1.00 .25
1O56 O10 3.80fr Nike 1.25 .25

Girl, Penguin and Boy — O11

2001, Dec. 1 Litho. *Perf. 13*

1O57 O11 3fr red & multi .80 .20
1O58 O11 3.80fr grn & multi 1.00 .25

Hiker on Stars — O12

2003, Oct. 18 Litho. *Perf. 13*

1O59 O12 50c Hiker facing left 1.25 .25
1O60 O12 75c Hiker facing right 1.75 .30

FOR THE UNITED NATIONS EDUCATIONAL, SCIENTIFIC AND CULTURAL ORGANIZATION

For use only on mail posted in the post office in the UNESCO Building, Paris.

Catalogue values for unused stamps in this section are for Never Hinged items.

For French stamps inscribed "UNESCO" see Nos. 572, 893-894, 2545.

Khmer Buddha and Hermes by Praxiteles O1

1961-65 Unwmk. Engr. *Perf. 13*

2O1 O1 20c dk gray, ol bis & bl .25 .25
2O2 O1 25c blk, lake & grn .40 .30
2O3 O1 30c choc & bis brn ('65) .60 .60
2O4 O1 50c blk, red & vio bl 1.50 1.25
2O5 O1 60c grnsh bl, red brn & rose lil ('65) 1.40 1.25
Nos. 2O1-2O5 (5) 4.15 3.65

Book and Globe — O2

1966, Dec. 17

2O6 O2 25c gray .50 .50
2O7 O2 30c dark red .65 .65
2O8 O2 60c green 1.10 1.10
Nos. 2O6-2O8 (3) 2.25 2.25

20th anniversary of UNESCO.

Human Rights Flame — O3

1969-71 Engr. *Perf. 13*

2O9 O3 30c sl grn, red & dp brn .60 .40
2O10 O3 40c dk car rose, red & dp brn .95 .60
2O11 O3 50c ultra, car & brn ('71) 2.00 1.50
2O12 O3 70c pur, red & sl 3.00 2.50
Nos. 2O9-2O12 (4) 6.55 5.00

Universal Declaration of Human Rights.

Type of 1969 Inscribed "FRANCE"

1975, Nov. 15 Engr. *Perf. 13*

2O13 O3 60c grn, red & dk brn 1.10 .65
2O14 O3 80c ocher, red & red brn 1.65 1.10
2O15 O3 1.20fr ind, red & brn 4.25 3.00
Nos. 2O13-2O15 (3) 7.00 4.75

O4

1976-78 Engr. *Perf. 13*

2O16 O4 80c multi .85 .65
2O17 O4 1fr multi .85 .65
2O18 O4 1.20fr multi .50 .45
2O19 O4 1.40fr multi 2.25 1.40
2O20 O4 1.70fr multi .75 .60
Nos. 2O16-2O20 (5) 5.20 3.75

Issued: 1.20, 1.70fr, 10/14/78; others, 10/23/76.

Slave Quarters, Senegal O5

Designs: 1.40fr, Mohenjo-Daro excavations, Pakistan. 2fr, Sans-Souci Palace, Haiti.

1980, Nov. 17 Engr. *Perf. 13*

2O21 O5 1.20fr multi .45 .35
2O22 O5 1.40fr multi .50 .40
2O23 O5 2fr multi .65 .55
Nos. 2O21-2O23 (3) 1.60 1.30

Hue, Vietnam — O7

Designs: 1.40fr, Building, Fez, Morocco. 1.60fr, Seated deity, Sukhotai, Thailand. 2.30fr, Fort St. Elmo, Malta, horiz. 2.60fr, St. Michael Church ruins, Brazil.

1981-82

2O24 O7 1.40fr multi .50 .40
2O25 O7 1.60fr multi .50 .40
2O26 O7 1.80fr shown .60 .55
2O27 O7 2.30fr multi .70 .60
2O28 O7 2.60fr multi .70 .65
Nos. 2O24-2O28 (5) 3.00 2.60

Issued: 1.80fr, 2.60fr, 10/23/82; others, 12/12/81.

Mosque, Chinguetti, Mauritania O8

Architecture: 1.70fr, Church, Lalibela, Ethiopia. 1.80fr, Roman Theater and female standing sculpture, Carthage, Tunisia. 2.10fr, San'a, Yemen. 2.20fr, Old Town Square and wrought iron latticework, Havana. 2.80fr, Enclosure wall interior, Istanbul. 3fr, Church, Kotor, Yugoslavia. 3.20fr, Temple of Anuradhapura and bas-relief of two women, Sri Lanka.

1983-85 Engr.

2O29 O8 1.70fr multi .50 .30
2O30 O8 1.80fr multi .50 .20
2O31 O8 2fr multi 1.10 .65
2O32 O8 2.10fr multi .55 .30
2O33 O8 2.20fr multi .60 .20
2O34 O8 2.80fr multi 1.50 .85
2O35 O8 3fr multi .80 .45
2O36 O8 3.20fr multi .90 .20
Nos. 2O29-2O36 (8) 6.45 3.15

Issued: 2fr, 2.80fr, 10/10; 1.70fr, 2.10fr, 3fr, 10/22/84; 1.80fr, 2.20fr, 3.20fr, 10/26/85.

Tikal Temple, Guatemala — O9

1986, Dec. 6 Engr. *Perf. 13*

2O37 O9 1.90fr shown .60 .20
2O38 O9 3.40fr Bagerhat Mosque, Bangladesh 1.00 .20

The Parthenon, Athens O10

1987, Dec. 5 Engr. *Perf. 13x12½*

2O39 O10 2fr shown .65 .20
2O40 O10 3.60fr Temple of Philae, Egypt 1.10 .20

Shibam, Yemen People's Democratic Republic O11

Perf. 13x12½, 12½x13

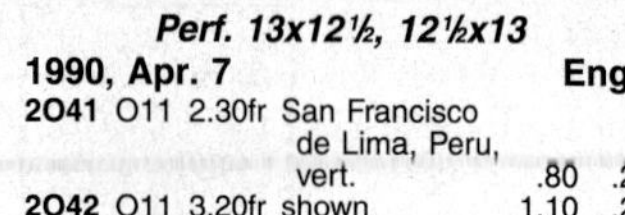

1990, Apr. 7 Engr.

2O41 O11 2.30fr San Francisco de Lima, Peru, vert. .80 .20
2O42 O11 3.20fr shown 1.10 .25

Bagdaon Temple, Nepal — O12

3.40fr, Citadel of Harat, Afghanistan, horiz.

1991, Nov. 23

2O43 O12 2.50fr choc & dk red .90 .20
2O44 O12 3.40fr grn, brn & ol 1.20 .20

Tassili N'Ajjer Natl. Park, Algeria O13

Design: 2.80fr, Angkor Wat Archaeological Park, Cambodia, vert.

1993, Oct. 23 Litho. *Perf. 13*

2O45 O13 2.80fr multicolored .95 .20
2O46 O13 3.70fr multicolored 1.25 .25

UNESCO, 50th Anniv. O14

Designs: 3fr, Uluru Natl. Park, Australia. 3.80fr, Los Glaciares Natl. Park, Argentina.

1996, June 1 Litho. *Perf. 13*

2O47 O14 3fr multicolored 1.25 .30
2O48 O14 3.80fr multicolored 1.60 .40

Detail of Dionysus Fresco, Pompeii — O15

Moai Statues, Easter Island O16

1998, Oct. 24 Litho. *Perf. 13*

2O49 O15 3fr multicolored 1.10 .25
2O50 O16 3.80fr multicolored 1.40 .30

Sphinx and Pyramids, Egypt O17

Komodo Dragon, Komodo Natl. Park, Indonesia O18

2001, Dec. 1 Litho. *Perf. 13*

2O51 O17 3fr multi .80 .25
2O52 O18 3.80fr multi 1.00 .30

Reindeer, Lapland O19

Church of the Resurrection, St. Petersburg, Russia — O20

2003, Dec. 6 Litho. *Perf. 13*

2O53 O19 50c multi 1.25 .30
2O54 O20 75c multi 1.90 .35

NEWSPAPER STAMPS

Coat of Arms — N1

1868 Unwmk. Typo. *Imperf.*

P1 N1 2c lilac 225.00 52.50
P2 N1 2c (+ 2c) blue 475.00 225.00

Perf. 12½

P3 N1 2c lilac 35.00 16.00
P4 N1 2c (+ 4c) rose 200.00 77.50
P5 N1 2c (+ 2c) blue 57.50 25.00
P6 N1 5c lilac 950.00 500.00

Nos. P2, P4, and P5 were sold for face plus an added fiscal charge indicated in parenthesis. Nos. P1, P3 and P6 were used simply as fiscals.

The 2c rose and 5c lilac imperforate and the 5c rose and 5c blue, both imperforate and perforated, were never put into use.

Nos. P1-P6 were reprinted for the 1913 Ghent Exhibition and the 1937 Paris Exhibition (PEXIP).

No. 109 Surcharged in Red

1919 *Perf. 14x13½*

P7 A16 ½c on 1c gray .20 .20
a. Inverted surcharge 950.00 875.00

No. 156 Surcharged

1933

P8 A22 ½c on 1c olive bister .20 *.30*

FRANCHISE STAMP

Catalogue values for unused stamps in this section are for Never Hinged items.

No. 276 Overprinted "F"

1939 Unwmk. *Perf. 14x13½*

S1 A45 90c ultramarine 4.00 2.75
Never hinged 6.50

No. S1 was for the use of Spanish refugees in France. "F" stands for "Franchise."

OCCUPATION STAMPS

Issued under German Occupation (Alsace and Lorraine)

OS1

1870 Typo. Unwmk. *Perf. 13½x14*

Network with Points Up

N1 OS1 1c bronze grn 70.00 70.00
a. 1c olive green 70.00 70.00
N2 OS1 2c dark brown 140.00 125.00
a. 2c red brown 140.00 125.00
N3 OS1 4c gray 150.00 85.00
N4 OS1 5c yel grn 150.00 12.00
N5 OS1 10c yel bister brn 125.00 5.00
a. 10c yel brown 125.00 5.75
b. Network lemon yellow 160.00 7.50
N6 OS1 20c ultra 140.00 12.00
N7 OS1 25c brown 175.00 85.00
a. 25c blk brown 160.00 80.00

There are three varieties of the 4c and two of the 10c, differing in the position of the figures of value, and several other setting varieties.

Network with Points Down

N8 OS1 1c olive grn 425.00 *575.00*
N9 OS1 2c red brn 210.00 *500.00*
N10 OS1 4c gray 210.00 175.00
N11 OS1 5c yel grn 4,750. 500.00
N12 OS1 10c bister 210.00 17.00
a. Network lemon yellow 225.00 50.00
N13 OS1 20c ultra 275.00 65.00
N14 OS1 25c brown 625.00 275.00

Official imitations have the network with points downward. The "P" of "Postes" is 2½mm from the border in the imitations and 3mm in the originals.

The word "Postes" measures 12¾ to 13mm on the imitations, and from 11 to 12½mm on the originals.

The imitations are perf. 13½x14½; originals, perf. 13½x14¼.

The stamps for Alsace and Lorraine were replaced by stamps of the German Empire on Jan. 1, 1872.

German Stamps of 1905-16 Surcharged:

1916 Wmk. 125 *Perf. 14, 14½*

N15 A16 3c on 3pf brown .70 .70
N16 A16 5c on 5pf green .70 .70
N17 A22 8c on 7½pf org 1.40 1.40
N18 A16 10c on 10pf car 1.40 1.40
N19 A22 15c on 15pf yel brn .70 .70
N20 A16 25c on 20pf blue .70 .70
a. 25c on 20pf ultramarine 1.40 1.40
N21 A16 40c on 30pf org & blk, *buff* 2.10 2.10
N22 A16 50c on 40pf lake & blk 2.10 2.10
N23 A16 75c on 60pf mag 9.75 9.75
N24 A16 1fr on 80pf lake & blk, *rose* 9.75 9.75

N25 A17 1fr25c on 1m car 37.50 37.50
a. Double surcharge —
N26 A21 2fr50c on 2m gray bl 37.50 37.50
a. Double surcharge —
Nos. N15-N26 (12) 104.30 104.30

These stamps were also used in parts of Belgium occupied by the German forces.

Catalogue values for unused stamps in this section, from this point to the end of the section, are for Never Hinged items.

Alsace
Issued under German Occupation

Stamps of Germany 1933-36 Overprinted in Black

1940	**Wmk. 237**		*Perf. 14*	
N27 A64	3pf olive bister		.70	.50
N28 A64	4pf dull blue		.70	.50
N29 A64	5pf brt green		.70	.50
N30 A64	6pf dark green		.70	.50
N31 A64	8pf vermilion		.70	.50
N32 A64	10pf chocolate		.70	.50
N33 A64	12pf dp carmine		.85	.50
N34 A64	15pf maroon		.90	.50
N35 A64	20pf brt blue		1.40	.65
N36 A64	25pf ultra		1.40	.65
N37 A64	30pf olive grn		1.40	.65
N38 A64	40pf red violet		2.50	.85
N39 A64	50pf dk grn & blk		6.00	2.75
N40 A64	60pf claret & blk		6.00	2.75
N41 A64	80pf dk blue & blk		14.00	6.00
N42 A64	100pf orange & blk		14.00	5.75
	Nos. N27-N42 (16)		52.65	24.05

Lorraine
Issued under German Occupation

Stamps of Germany 1933-36 Overprinted in Black

1940	**Wmk. 237**		*Perf. 14*	
N43 A64	3pf olive bister		.95	*1.00*
N44 A64	4pf dull blue		.95	*1.00*
N45 A64	5pf brt green		.95	*1.00*
N46 A64	6pf dark green		.95	.55
N47 A64	8pf vermilion		.95	*1.00*
N48 A64	10pf chocolate		1.25	.85
N49 A64	12pf deep carmine		1.25	.85
N50 A64	15pf maroon		1.25	1.00
a.	Inverted surcharge		—	
N51 A64	20pf brt blue		1.40	1.00
N52 A64	25pf ultra		1.40	1.00
N53 A64	30pf olive grn		1.90	1.00
N54 A64	40pf red violet		2.10	1.10
N55 A64	50pf dk grn & blk		5.25	3.00
N56 A64	60pf claret & blk		5.25	3.00
N57 A64	80pf dk blue & blk		15.00	6.25
N58 A64	100pf orange & blk		15.00	6.75
	Nos. N43-N58 (16)		55.80	*30.35*

Besetztes Gebiet Nordfrankreich

These three words, in a rectangular frame covering two stamps, were handstamped in black on Nos. 267, 367 and 369 and used in the Dunkerque region in July-August, 1940. The German political officer of Dunkerque authorized the overprint. The prevalence of forgeries and later favor overprints makes expertization mandatory.

ISSUED JOINTLY BY THE ALLIED MILITARY GOVERNMENT OF THE UNITED STATES AND GREAT BRITAIN, FOR CIVILIAN USE

Catalogue values for unused stamps in this section are for Never Hinged items.

Arc de Triomphe — OS2

1944	**Unwmk.**	**Litho.**	*Perf. 11*	
2N1	OS2	5c brt red violet	.35	.35
2N2	OS2	10c lt gray	.35	.35
2N3	OS2	25c brown	.35	.35
2N4	OS2	50c olive bis	.50	.50
2N5	OS2	1fr pck green	.90	.90
2N6	OS2	1.50fr rose pink	1.90	.90
2N7	OS2	2.50fr purple	.90	.90
2N8	OS2	4fr ultra	1.90	1.90
2N9	OS2	5fr black	1.90	1.90
2N10	OS2	10fr yellow org	37.50	35.00
		Nos. 2N1-2N10 (10)	46.55	43.05

1945

Denominations in Black

2N11	OS2	30c orange	.30	.30
2N12	OS2	40c pale gray	.30	.30
2N13	OS2	50c olive bis	.30	.30
2N14	OS2	60c violet	.30	.30
2N15	OS2	80c emerald	.30	.30
2N16	OS2	1.20fr brown	.30	.30
2N17	OS2	1.50fr vermilion	.30	.30
2N18	OS2	2fr yellow	.30	.30
2N19	OS2	2.40fr dark rose	.30	.30
2N20	OS2	3fr brt red violet	.30	.30
		Nos. 2N11-2N20 (10)	3.00	3.00

FRENCH OFFICES ABROAD

OFFICES IN CHINA

Prior to 1923 several of the world powers maintained their own post offices in China for the purpose of sending and receiving overseas mail. French offices were maintained in Canton, Hoi Hao (Hoihow), Kwangchowan (Kouang-tchéou-wan), Mongtseu (Mong-tseu), Packhoi (Paknoi), Tong King (Tchongking), Yunnan Fou (Yunnanfu).

100 Centimes = 1 Franc
100 Cents = 1 Piaster
100 Cents = 1 Dollar

Peace and Commerce Stamps of France Overprinted in Red or Black

1894-1900	**Unwmk.**	*Perf. 14x13½*	
1 A1	5c grn, *grnsh* (R)	2.10	1.75
2 A1	5c yel grn, I (R) ('00)	2.10	1.75
a.	Type II	35.00	21.00
3 A1	10c blk, *lav*, I (R)	6.00	1.75
a.	Type II	17.50	8.50
4 A1	15c bl (R)	7.75	2.75
5 A1	20c red, *grn*	5.00	3.25
6 A1	25c blk, *rose* (R)	6.00	1.75
a.	Double overprint	70.00	35.00
b.	Pair, one without overprint	225.00	
7 A1	30c brn, *bis*	6.00	4.00
8 A1	40c red, *straw*	6.50	5.00
9 A1	50c car, *rose*, I	17.50	10.50
a.	Red overprint	47.50	
b.	Type II (Bk)	12.00	6.00
10 A1	75c dp vio, *org* (R)	60.00	42.50
11 A1	1fr brnz grn, *straw*	11.00	4.50
a.	Double overprint	275.00	*300.00*
12 A1	2fr brn, *az* ('00)	21.00	20.00
12A A1	5fr red lil, *lav*	57.50	42.50
b.	Red overprint	450.00	
	Nos. 1-12A (13)	208.45	142.00

For surcharges and overprints see Nos. 13-17, J7-J10, J20-J23.

No. 11 Surcharged in Black **25**

13 A1	25c on 1fr brnz grn, *straw*	67.50	42.50

No. 6 Surcharged in Red — Chine 2 Cents

1901			
14 A1	2c on 25c blk, *rose*	825.00	225.00
15 A1	4c on 25c blk, *rose*	650.00	225.00
16 A1	6c on 25c blk, *rose*	825.00	300.00
17 A1	16c on 25c blk, *rose*	225.00	150.00
a.	Black surcharge		*5,500.*
	Nos. 14-17 (4)	2,525.	900.00

Stamps of Indo-China Surcharged in Black

1902-04				
18	A3	1c blk, *lil bl*	1.75	1.40
19	A3	2c brn, *buff*	2.50	2.50
20	A3	4c claret, *lav*	2.50	1.75
21	A3	5c yellow grn	3.25	1.75
22	A3	10c red	4.00	3.25
23	A3	15c gray	4.50	4.25
24	A3	20c red, *grn*	5.75	5.25
25	A3	25c blk, *rose*	7.75	7.25
26	A3	25c blue ('04)	6.50	5.25
27	A3	30c brn, *bis*	5.75	5.00
28	A3	40c red, *straw*	18.00	13.50
29	A3	50c car, *rose*	42.50	42.50
30	A3	50c brn, *az* ('04)	7.25	6.50
31	A3	75c vio, *org*	27.50	21.00
32	A3	1fr brnz grn, *straw*	32.50	29.00
33	A3	5fr red lil, *lavender*	65.00	57.50
		Nos. 18-33 (16)	237.00	207.65

The Chinese characters surcharged on Nos. 18-33 are the Chinese equivalents of the French values and therefore differ on each denomination. Another printing of these stamps was made in 1904 which differs from the first one principally in the size and shape of the letters in "CHINE," particularly the "H" which is much thinner in the second printing. Values are for the less expensive variety. Many varieties of surcharge exist.

Liberty, Equality and Fraternity
A3

"Rights of Man"
A4

A5

1902-03			**Typo.**	
34	A3	5c green	1.75	1.40
35	A4	10c rose red ('03)	1.75	1.40
36	A4	15c pale red	1.75	1.40
37	A4	20c brn vio ('03)	5.75	5.00
38	A4	25c blue ('03)	4.25	2.10
39	A4	30c lilac ('03)	6.00	5.75
40	A5	40c red & pale bl	12.50	11.00
41	A5	50c bis brn & lav	16.00	12.50
42	A5	1fr claret & ol grn	21.00	12.00
43	A5	2fr gray vio & yel	42.50	30.00
44	A5	5fr dk bl & buff	60.00	47.50
		Nos. 34-44 (11)	173.25	130.05

For surcharges and overprints see Nos. 45, 57-85, J14-J16, J27-J30.

Surcharged in Black

1903				
45	A4	5c on 15c pale red	11.00	6.50
a.		Inverted surcharge	77.50	47.50

Stamps of Indo-China, 1904-06, Surcharged as Nos. 18-33 in Black

1904-05				
46	A4	1c olive grn	1.25	1.25
47	A4	2c vio brn, *buff*	1.25	1.25
47A	A4	4c cl, *bluish*	700.00	575.00
48	A4	5c deep grn	1.25	1.25
49	A4	10c carmine	1.90	1.90
50	A4	15c org brn, *bl*	2.10	1.75
51	A4	20c red, *grn*	8.50	8.50
52	A4	25c deep blue	7.25	4.00
53	A4	40c blk, *bluish*	5.75	4.00
54	A4	1fr pale grn	275.00	225.00
55	A4	2fr brn, *org*	29.00	24.00
56	A4	10fr org brn, *grn*	110.00	100.00
		Nos. 46-56 (12)	1,143.	947.90

Many varieties of the surcharge exist.

Stamps of 1902-03 Surcharged in Black

1907			
57 A3	2c on 5c green	1.25	1.10
58 A4	4c on 10c rose red	1.25	1.10
a.	Pair, one without surcharge	—	
59 A4	6c on 15c pale red	2.00	1.60
60 A4	8c on 20c brn vio	3.50	3.50
a.	"8" inverted	42.50	42.50
61 A4	10c on 25c blue	1.10	.85
62 A5	20c on 50c bis brn & lav	3.50	2.50
a.	Double surcharge		
b.	Triple surcharge	300.00	300.00
63 A5	40c on 1fr claret & ol grn	14.00	9.00
64 A5	2pi on 5fr dk bl & buff	16.00	9.00
a.	Double surcharge	*1,750.*	*1,550.*
	Nos. 57-64 (8)	42.60	28.65

Stamps of 1902-03 Surcharged in Black

1911-22			
65 A3	2c on 5c green	1.25	1.00
66 A4	4c on 10c rose red	1.40	1.00
67 A4	6c on 15c org	3.25	1.25
68 A4	8c on 20c brn vio	1.60	1.25
69 A4	10c on 25c bl ('21)	2.50	1.10
70 A4	20c on 50c bl ('22)	40.00	32.50
71 A5	40c on 1fr cl & ol grn	4.25	2.75

No. 44 Surcharged

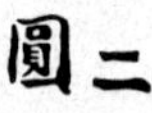

73 A5	$2 on 5fr bl & buff ('22)	125.00	92.50
	Nos. 65-73 (8)	179.25	133.35

Types of 1902-03 Surcharged like Nos. 65-71

1922			
75 A3	1c on 5c org	3.50	3.25
76 A4	2c on 10c grn	4.25	4.00
77 A4	3c on 15c org	5.75	4.50
78 A4	4c on 20c red brn	7.25	6.00
79 A4	5c on 25c dk vio	4.00	3.25
80 A4	6c on 30c red	7.75	6.50
82 A4	10c on 50c blue	9.00	6.75
83 A5	20c on 1fr claret & ol grn	25.00	22.50
84 A5	40c on 2fr org & pale bl	30.00	25.00
85 A5	$1 on 5fr dk bl & buff	110.00	110.00
	Nos. 75-85 (10)	206.50	191.75

POSTAGE DUE STAMPS

Postage Due Stamps of France Handstamped in Red or Black

1901-07	**Unwmk.**	*Perf. 14x13½*	
J1 D2	5c lt bl (R)	4.25	2.50
J2 D2	10c choc (R)	7.25	4.25
J3 D2	15c lt grn (R)	7.25	4.50
J4 D2	20c ol grn (R) ('07)	7.25	6.50
J5 D2	30c carmine	10.00	7.75
J6 D2	50c lilac	12.50	7.75
	Nos. J1-J6 (6)	48.50	33.25

Stamps of 1894-1900 Handstamped in Carmine — A PERCEVOIR

1903			
J7 A1	5c yel grn	*2,000.*	725.
a.	Purple handstamp	*2,000.*	675.
b.	5c green, *greenish*	*6,600.*	
J8 A1	10c blk, *lavender*	*6,500.*	*5,250.*
a.	Purple handstamp	*6,500.*	*5,250.*
J9 A1	15c blue	*2,000.*	675.
a.	Purple handstamp	*2,000.*	675.
J10 A1	30c brn, *bister*	*1,100.*	77.50
a.	Purple handstamp	*1,100.*	77.50

Same Handstamp on Stamps of 1902-03 in Carmine

1903			
J14 A3	5c green	*1,250.*	625.
a.	Purple handstamp	*1,300.*	625.
J15 A4	10c rose red	525.	125.
a.	Purple handstamp	525.	125.
J16 A4	15c pale red	550.	125.
a.	Purple handstamp	550.	125.

Stamps of 1894-1900 Handstamped in Carmine

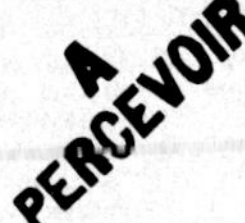

1903

No.	Type	Description	Unused	Used
J20	A1	5c yellow green	*1,700.*	250.
a.		Purple handstamp	*1,600.*	250.
b.		5c green, *greenish*	*6,600.*	
J21	A1	10c blk, *lavender*	*6,750.*	*7,000.*
a.		Purple handstamp	*6,750.*	*7,000.*
J22	A1	15c blue	825.	80.
a.		Purple handstamp	825.	80.
J23	A1	30c brn, *bister*	400.	65.
a.		Purple handstamp	400.	65.

Same Handstamp on Stamps of 1902-03 in Carmine or Purple

1903

No.	Type	Description	Unused	Used
J27	A3	5c green (C)	1,100.	550.
a.		Purple handstamp	1,100.	550.
J28	A4	10c rose red (C)	250.00	42.50
a.		Purple handstamp	250.00	42.50
J29	A4	15c pale red (C)	550.00	42.50
a.		Purple handstamp	550.00	42.50
J30	A4	30c lilac (P)	*9,000.*	*7,500.*

The handstamps on Nos. J7-J30 are found inverted, double, etc.

The cancellations on these stamps should have dates between Sept. 1, and Nov. 30, 1903, to be genuine.

Postage Due Stamps of France, 1893-1910 Surcharged like Nos. 65-71

1911

No.	Type	Description	Unused	Used
J33	D2	2c on 5c blue	1.40	1.10
a.		Double surcharge	90.00	—
J34	D2	4c on 10c choc	1.40	1.10
a.		Double surcharge	90.00	—
J35	D2	8c on 20c ol grn	1.75	1.40
a.		Double surcharge	90.00	—
J36	D2	20c on 50c lilac	1.75	1.40
		Nos. J33-J36 (4)	6.30	5.00

1922

No.	Type	Description	Unused	Used
J37	D2	1c on 5c blue	60.00	55.00
J38	D2	2c on 10c brn	82.50	72.50
J39	D2	4c on 20c ol grn	82.50	72.50
J40	D2	10c on 50c brn vio	82.50	72.50
		Nos. J37-J40 (4)	307.50	272.50

CANTON

Stamps of Indo-China, 1892-1900, Overprinted in Red

1901 Unwmk. *Perf. 14x13½*

No.	Type	Description	Unused	Used
1	A3	1c blk, *lil bl*	1.40	1.40
1A	A3	2c brn, *buff*	1.75	1.75
2	A3	4c claret, *lav*	3.25	3.25
2A	A3	5c grn, *grnsh*	450.00	450.00
3	A3	5c yel grn	2.25	2.25
4	A3	10c blk, *lavender*	5.00	5.00
5	A3	15c blue, quadrille paper	4.50	4.50
6	A3	15c gray	5.00	5.00
a.		Double overprint	16.00	
7	A3	20c red, *grn*	10.00	10.00
8	A3	25c blk, *rose*	8.50	8.50
9	A3	30c brn, *bister*	20.00	20.00
10	A3	40c red, *straw*	20.00	20.00
11	A3	50c car, *rose*	22.50	22.50
12	A3	75c dp vio, *org*	30.00	30.00
13	A3	1fr brnz grn, *straw*	30.00	30.00
14	A3	5fr red lil, *lav*	190.00	190.00
		Nos. 1-14 (16)	804.15	804.15

The Chinese characters in the overprint on Nos. 1-14 read "Canton." On Nos. 15-64, they restate the denomination of the basic stamp.

Surcharged in Black

1903-04

No.	Type	Description	Unused	Used
15	A3	1c blk, *lil bl*	2.75	2.50
16	A3	2c brn, *buff*	2.75	2.50
17	A3	4c claret, *lav*	2.75	2.50
18	A3	5c yellow green	2.75	2.50
19	A3	10c rose red	2.75	2.50
20	A3	15c gray	2.75	2.50
21	A3	20c red, *grn*	14.00	11.00
22	A3	25c blue	6.50	4.25
23	A3	25c blk, *rose* ('04)	5.00	4.25
24	A3	30c brn, *bister*	18.00	12.00
25	A3	40c red, *straw*	47.50	40.00
26	A3	50c car, *rose*	250.00	225.00
27	A3	50c brn, *az* ('04)	52.50	47.50
28	A3	75c dp vio, *org*	47.50	42.50
a.		"INDO-CHINE" inverted	*36,000.*	
29	A3	1fr brnz grn, *straw*	47.50	42.50
30	A3	5fr red lil, *lav*	50.00	47.50
		Nos. 15-30 (16)	555.00	491.50

Many varieties of the surcharge exist on #15-30.

Stamps of Indo-China, 1892-1906, Surcharged in Red or Black

A second printing of the 1906 surcharges of Canton, Hoi Hao, Kwangchowan, Mongtseu, Packhoi, Tong King and Yunnan Fou was made in 1908. The inks are grayish instead of full black and vermilion instead of carmine. Values are for the cheaper variety which usually is the second printing.

The 4c and 50c of the 1892 issue of Indo-China are known with this surcharge and similarly surcharged for other cities in China. The surcharges on these two stamps are always inverted. It is stated that they were irregularly produced and never issued.

1906

No.	Type	Description	Unused	Used
31	A4	1c ol grn (R)	1.40	1.40
32	A4	2c vio brn, *buff*	1.40	1.40
33	A4	4c cl, *bluish* (R)	1.40	1.40
34	A4	5c dp grn (R)	1.40	1.40
35	A4	10c carmine	2.10	2.10
36	A4	15c org brn, *bl*	7.25	7.25
37	A4	20c red, *grn*	3.50	3.50
38	A4	25c deep blue	3.50	3.50
39	A4	30c pale brn	4.50	4.50
40	A4	35c blk, *yel* (R)	3.25	3.25
41	A4	40c blk, *bluish* (R)	5.25	5.25
42	A4	50c bister brn	5.25	5.25
43	A3	75c dp vio, *org* (R)	40.00	40.00
44	A4	1fr pale grn	11.00	11.00
45	A4	2fr brn, *org* (R)	27.50	27.50
46	A3	5fr red lil, *lav*	62.50	62.50
47	A4	10fr org brn, *grn*	60.00	60.00
		Nos. 31-47 (17)	241.20	241.20

Surcharge exists inverted on 1c, 25c & 1fr.

Stamps of Indo-China, 1907, Surcharged "CANTON", and Chinese Characters, in Red or Blue

1908

No.	Type	Description	Unused	Used
48	A5	1c ol brn & blk	.70	.70
49	A5	2c brn & blk	.70	.70
50	A5	4c bl & blk	1.40	.95
51	A5	5c grn & blk	1.40	1.25
52	A5	10c red & blk (Bl)	1.75	1.40
53	A5	15c vio & blk	2.50	2.10
54	A6	20c vio & blk	3.25	2.75
55	A6	25c bl & blk	3.25	2.75
56	A6	30c brn & blk	5.75	5.25
57	A6	35c ol grn & blk	5.75	5.25
58	A6	40c brn & blk	7.25	5.75
59	A6	50c car & blk (Bl)	7.25	5.75
60	A7	75c ver & blk (Bl)	7.25	6.50
61	A8	1fr car & blk (Bl)	12.00	9.25
62	A9	2fr grn & blk	32.50	27.50
63	A10	5fr bl & blk	42.50	35.00
64	A11	10fr pur & blk	65.00	60.00
		Nos. 48-64 (17)	200.20	172.85

Nos. 48-64 Surcharged with New Values in Cents or Piasters in Black, Red or Blue

1919

No.	Type	Description	Unused	Used
65	A5	⅖c on 1c	.85	.80
66	A5	⅘c on 2c	.85	.80
67	A5	1⅗c on 4c (R)	.85	.80
68	A5	2c on 5c	1.10	*1.10*
69	A5	4c on 10c (Bl)	1.25	1.00
a.		Chinese "2" instead of "4"	25.00	25.00
70	A5	6c on 15c	1.60	1.25
71	A6	8c on 20c	2.75	1.25
72	A6	10c on 25c	3.50	1.25
73	A6	12c on 30c	1.40	1.40
a.		Double surcharge	92.50	92.50
74	A6	14c on 35c	1.40	1.25
a.		Closed "4"	6.75	6.75
75	A6	16c on 40c	1.40	1.25
76	A6	20c on 50c (Bl)	1.75	1.25
77	A7	30c on 75c (Bl)	1.75	1.25
78	A8	40c on 1fr (Bl)	7.25	5.00
79	A9	80c on 2fr (R)	11.00	6.75
80	A10	2pi on 5fr (R)	10.00	10.00
81	A11	4pi on 10fr (R)	11.50	11.50
		Nos. 65-81 (17)	60.20	47.90

HOI HAO

Stamps of Indo-China Overprinted in Red

1901 Unwmk. *Perf. 14x13½*

No.	Type	Description	Unused	Used
1	A3	1c blk, *lil bl*	2.50	2.50
2	A3	2c brn, *buff*	3.00	3.00
3	A3	4c claret, *lav*	3.00	3.00
4	A3	5c yel grn	3.25	3.25
5	A3	10c blk, *lavender*	5.75	5.25
6	A3	15c blue	1,450.	650.00
7	A3	15c gray	4.50	3.00
8	A3	20c red, *grn*	15.00	13.50
9	A3	25c blk, *rose*	9.00	6.75
10	A3	30c brn, *bister*	29.00	22.50
11	A3	40c red, *straw*	29.00	22.50
12	A3	50c car, *rose*	32.50	29.00
13	A3	75c dp vio, *org*	190.00	160.00
14	A3	1fr brnz grn, *straw*	650.00	550.00
15	A3	5fr red lil, *lav*	550.00	450.00
		Nos. 1-15 (15)	2,976.	1,924.

The Chinese characters in the overprint on Nos. 1-15 read "Hoi Hao." On Nos. 16-66, they restate the denomination of the basic stamp.

Surcharged in Black

1903-04

No.	Type	Description	Unused	Used
16	A3	1c blk, *lil bl*	1.25	1.25
17	A3	2c brn, *buff*	1.25	1.25
18	A3	4c claret, *lav*	2.25	2.25
19	A3	5c yel grn	2.25	2.25
20	A3	10c red	2.75	2.75
21	A3	15c gray	3.00	3.00
22	A3	20c red, *grn*	5.50	5.50
23	A3	25c blue	5.50	5.50
24	A3	25c blk, *rose* ('04)	3.50	3.50
25	A3	30c brn, *bister*	4.25	4.25
26	A3	40c red, *straw*	26.00	26.00
27	A3	50c car, *rose*	22.50	22.50
28	A3	50c brn, *az* ('04)	110.00	110.00
29	A3	75c dp vio, *org*	35.00	35.00
a.		"INDO-CHINE" inverted	*36,000.*	
30	A3	1fr brnz grn, *straw*	47.50	47.50
31	A3	5fr red lil, *lav*	150.00	150.00
		Nos. 16-31 (16)	422.50	422.50

Many varieties of the surcharge exist on #1-31.

Stamps of Indo-China, 1892-1906, Surcharged in Red or Black

1906

No.	Type	Description	Unused	Used
32	A4	1c ol grn (R)	1.75	1.75
33	A4	2c vio brn, *buff*	1.75	1.75
34	A4	4c cl, *bluish* (R)	3.00	3.00
35	A4	5c dp grn (R)	3.00	3.00
36	A4	10c carmine	3.25	3.25
37	A4	15c org brn, *bl*	6.00	6.00
38	A4	20c red, *grn*	4.75	4.75
39	A4	25c deep blue	6.50	6.50
40	A4	30c pale brn	6.50	6.50
41	A4	35c blk, *yel* (R)	11.00	11.00
42	A4	40c blk, *bluish* (R)	11.00	11.00
43	A4	50c gray brn	11.00	*11.00*
44	A3	75c dp vio, *org* (R)	27.50	27.50
45	A4	1fr pale grn	27.50	27.50
46	A4	2fr brn, *org* (R)	27.50	27.50
47	A3	5fr red lil, *lav*	90.00	90.00
48	A4	10fr org brn, *grn*	110.00	*110.00*
		Nos. 32-48 (17)	352.00	352.00

Stamps of Indo-China, 1907, Surcharged "HOI HAO" and Chinese Characters, in Red or Blue

1908

No.	Type	Description	Unused	Used
49	A5	1c ol brn & blk	.95	.95
50	A5	2c brn & blk	.95	.95
51	A5	4c bl & blk	1.10	1.10
52	A5	5c grn & blk	1.90	1.90
53	A5	10c red & blk (Bl)	1.90	1.90
54	A5	15c vio & blk	4.00	4.00
55	A6	20c vio & blk	4.75	4.75
56	A6	25c bl & blk	4.75	4.75
57	A6	30c brn & blk	4.75	4.75
58	A6	35c ol grn & blk	4.75	4.75
59	A6	40c brn & blk	5.50	5.50
61	A6	50c car & blk (Bl)	6.50	6.50
62	A7	75c ver & blk (Bl)	6.00	6.00
63	A8	1fr car & blk (Bl)	10.00	10.00
64	A9	2fr grn & blk	32.50	32.50
65	A10	5fr bl & blk	52.50	52.50
66	A11	10fr pur & blk	80.00	*80.00*
		Nos. 49-66 (17)	230.80	230.80

Nos. 49-66 Surcharged with New Values in Cents or Piasters in Black, Red or Blue

1919

No.	Type	Description	Unused	Used
67	A5	⅖c on 1c	.70	.70
68	A5	⅘c on 2c	.70	.70
69	A5	1⅗c on 4c (R)	1.10	1.10
70	A5	2c on 5c	1.40	1.40
71	A5	4c on 10c (Bl)	1.75	1.75
a.		Chinese "2" instead of "4"	7.25	7.25
72	A5	6c on 15c	1.50	1.50
73	A6	8c on 20c	2.40	2.40
a.		"S" of "CENTS" omitted	85.00	85.00
74	A6	10c on 25c	4.25	4.25
75	A6	12c on 30c	1.40	1.40
76	A6	14c on 35c	1.40	1.40
a.		Closed "4"	11.00	11.00
77	A6	16c on 40c	1.40	1.40
79	A6	20c on 50c (Bl)	1.75	1.75
80	A7	30c on 75c (Bl)	3.50	3.50
81	A8	40c on 1fr (Bl)	7.25	7.25
82	A9	80c on 2fr (R)	17.00	17.00
83	A10	2pi on 5fr (R)	47.50	47.50
a.		Triple surch. of new value	500.00	*500.00*
84	A11	4pi on 10fr (R)	140.00	*140.00*
		Nos. 67-84 (17)	235.00	235.00

KWANGCHOWAN

A Chinese Territory leased to France, 1898 to 1945.

Stamps of Indo-China, 1892-1906, Surcharged in Red or Black

1906 Unwmk. *Perf. 14x13½*

No.	Type	Description	Unused	Used
1	A4	1c ol grn (R)	1.75	1.75
2	A4	2c vio brn, *buff*	2.10	2.10
3	A4	4c cl, *bluish* (R)	2.75	2.75
4	A4	5c dp grn (R)	3.00	3.00
5	A4	10c carmine	3.00	3.00
6	A4	15c org brn, *bl*	8.00	8.00
7	A4	20c red, *grn*	3.50	3.50
8	A4	25c deep blue	3.00	3.00
9	A4	30c pale brn	3.50	3.50
10	A4	35c blk, *yel* (R)	5.75	5.75
11	A4	40c blk, *bluish* (R)	4.00	4.00
12	A4	50c bister brn	15.00	15.00
13	A3	75c dp vio, *org* (R)	21.00	21.00
14	A4	1fr pale grn	24.00	24.00
15	A4	2fr brn, *org* (R)	24.00	24.00
16	A3	5fr red lil, *lav*	160.00	160.00
17	A4	10fr org brn, *grn*	210.00	210.00
		Nos. 1-17 (17)	494.35	494.35

Various varieties of the surcharge exist on Nos. 2-10.

Stamps of Indo-China, 1907, Surcharged "KOUANG-TCHEOU" and Value in Chinese in Red or Blue

1908

No.	Type	Description	Unused	Used
18	A5	1c ol brn & blk	.95	.95
19	A5	2c brn & blk	.95	.95
20	A5	4c bl & blk	.95	.95
21	A5	5c grn & blk	1.00	1.00
22	A5	10c red & blk (Bl)	1.00	1.00
23	A5	15c vio & blk	2.40	2.40
24	A6	20c vio & blk	4.25	4.25
25	A6	25c bl & blk	4.75	4.75
26	A6	30c brn & blk	6.75	6.75
27	A6	35c ol grn & blk	9.00	9.00
28	A6	40c brn & blk	9.00	9.00
30	A6	50c car & blk (Bl)	10.00	10.00
31	A7	75c ver & blk (Bl)	10.00	10.00
32	A8	1fr car & blk (Bl)	13.00	13.00
33	A9	2fr grn & blk	22.50	22.50
34	A10	5fr bl & blk	50.00	50.00
35	A11	10fr pur & blk	70.00	70.00
a.		Double surcharge	650.00	650.00
b.		Triple surcharge	650.00	650.00
		Nos. 18-35 (17)	216.50	216.50

The Chinese characters overprinted on Nos. 1 to 35 repeat the denomination of the basic stamp.

Nos. 18-35 Surcharged with New Values in Cents or Piasters in Black, Red or Blue

1919

No.	Type	Description	Unused	Used
36	A5	⅖c on 1c	.60	.50
37	A5	⅘c on 2c	.60	.50
38	A5	1⅗c on 4c (R)	.70	.60
39	A5	2c on 5c	1.00	.60
a.		"2 CENTS" inverted	60.00	
40	A5	4c on 10c (Bl)	2.40	2.00
41	A5	6c on 15c	1.25	1.25

42	A6	8c on 20c	3.00	2.75
43	A6	10c on 25c	9.75	8.50
44	A6	12c on 30c	1.60	1.40
45	A6	14c on 35c	2.10	2.00
a.		Closed "4"	27.50	24.00
46	A6	16c on 40c	1.10	1.10
48	A6	20c on 50c (Bl)	1.25	1.25
49	A7	30c on 75c (Bl)	6.50	6.50
50	A8	40c on 1fr (Bl)	7.25	7.25
a.		"40 CENTS" inverted		
51	A9	80c on 2fr (R)	8.00	7.25
52	A10	2pi on 5fr (R)	125.00	120.00
53	A11	4pi on 10fr (R)	18.00	18.00
		Nos. 36-53 (17)	190.10	181.45

Stamps of Indo-China, 1922-23, Overprinted in Black, Red or Blue

1923

54	A12	1/10c blk & sal (Bl)	.20	.20
55	A12	1/5c dp bl & blk (R)	.20	.20
a.		Black overprint	85.00	
56	A12	2/5c ol brn & blk (R)	.20	.20
57	A12	4/5c brt rose & blk	.35	.35
58	A12	1c yel brn & blk (Bl)	.35	.35
59	A12	2c gray grn & blk (R)	.60	.60
60	A12	3c vio & blk (R)	.60	.60
61	A12	4c org & blk	.70	.70
62	A12	5c car & blk	.70	.70
63	A13	6c dl red & blk	.70	.70
64	A13	7c ol grn & blk	1.10	1.10
65	A13	8c black (R)	1.60	1.60
66	A13	9c yel & blk	1.60	1.60
67	A13	10c bl & blk	1.40	1.40
68	A13	11c vio & blk	1.40	1.40
69	A13	12c brn & blk	1.40	1.40
70	A13	15c org & blk	1.75	1.75
71	A13	20c bl & blk, *straw* (R)	1.75	1.75
72	A13	40c ver & blk, *bluish* (Bl)	2.10	2.10
73	A13	1pi bl grn & blk, *grnsh*	6.25	6.25
74	A13	2pi vio brn & blk, *pnksh* (Bl)	11.00	11.00
		Nos. 54-74 (21)	35.95	35.95

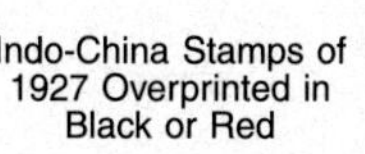

Indo-China Stamps of 1927 Overprinted in Black or Red

1927

75	A14	1/10c lt ol grn (R)	.20	.20
76	A14	1/5c yellow	.20	.20
77	A14	2/5c lt blue (R)	.35	.35
78	A14	4/5c dp brown	.35	.35
79	A14	1c orange	.50	.50
80	A14	2c blue grn (R)	.75	.75
81	A14	3c indigo (R)	.75	.75
82	A14	4c lilac rose	.75	.75
83	A14	5c deep violet	.75	.75
84	A15	6c deep red	.75	.75
85	A15	7c lt brown	.75	.75
86	A15	8c gray grn (R)	.85	.85
87	A15	9c red violet	1.00	1.00
88	A15	10c lt bl (R)	1.00	1.00
89	A15	11c orange	1.00	1.00
90	A15	12c myr grn (R)	1.00	1.00
91	A16	15c dl rose & ol brn	1.75	1.75
92	A16	20c vio & sl (R)	1.60	1.60
93	A17	25c org brn & lil rose	1.60	1.60
94	A17	30c dp bl & ol gray (R)	1.10	1.10
95	A18	40c ver & lt bl	1.10	1.10
96	A18	50c lt grn & sl (R)	1.40	1.40
97	A19	1pi dk bl, blk & yel (R)	3.00	3.00
98	A19	2pi red, dp bl & org (R)	3.50	3.50
a.		Double overprint	100.00	
		Nos. 75-98 (24)	26.00	26.00

Stamps of Indo-China, 1931-41, Overprinted in Black or Red

1937-41 ***Perf. 13, 13½***

99	A20	1/10c Prus blue	.20	.20
100	A20	1/5c lake	.20	.20
101	A20	2/5c orange red	.20	.20
102	A20	1/2c red brown	.20	.20
103	A20	4/5c dk violet	.20	.20
104	A20	1c black brown	.20	.20
105	A20	2c dk green	.20	.20
a.		Inverted overprint	100.00	
106	A21	3c dk green	.60	.60
107	A21	3c yel brn ('41)	.20	.20
108	A21	4c dk blue (R)	.70	.70
109	A21	4c dk green ('41)	.20	.20
110	A21	4c yel org ('41)	1.60	1.60
111	A21	5c dp violet	.70	.70
112	A21	5c dp green ('41)	.35	.35
113	A21	6c orange red	.50	.50
114	A21	7c black (R) ('41)	.50	.50
115	A21	8c rose lake ('41)	.50	.50
116	A21	9c blk, *yel* (R) ('41)	.60	.60
d.		Black overprint	7.25	7.25
117	A22	10c dk blue (R)	.80	.80
118	A22	10c ultra, *pink* (R) ('41)	.60	.60
119	A22	15c dk bl (R)	.60	.60
120	A22	18c bl (R) ('41)	.35	.35
121	A22	20c rose	.60	.60
122	A22	21c olive grn	.60	.60
123	A22	22c green ('41)	.35	.35
124	A22	25c dp violet	2.40	2.40
125	A22	25c dk bl (R) ('41)	.60	.60
126	A22	30c orange brn	.60	.60
127	A23	50c dk brown	.80	.80
128	A23	60c dl violet	.80	.80
129	A23	70c lt bl (R) ('41)	.60	.60
130	A23	1pi yel green	1.40	1.40
131	A23	2pi red	1.40	1.40
		Nos. 99-131 (33)	20.35	20.35

For types A20-A23 without "RF," see Nos. 137-153.

Common Design Types pictured following the introduction.

Colonial Arts Exhibition Issue

Common Design Type

Souvenir Sheet

1937 **Engr.** ***Imperf.***

132	CD79	30c green & sepia	6.50	6.50

New York World's Fair Issue

Common Design Type

1939 **Unwmk.** ***Perf. 12½x12***

133	CD82	13c carmine lake	.80	.80
134	CD82	23c ultramarine	.80	.80

Petain Issue

Indo-China Nos. 209-209A Overprinted "KOUANG TCHEOU" in Blue or Red

1941 **Engr.** ***Perf. 12½x12***

135	A27a	10c car lake (B)	.50
136	A27a	25c blue (R)	.50

Nos. 135-136 were issued by the Vichy government in France, but were not placed on sale in Kwangchowan.

For surcharges, see Nos. B9-B10.

Indo-China Types of 1937-41 without "RF" Overprinted "KOUANG TCHEOU" in Blue or Red

1942-44

137	A20	2/5c orange red	.20
138	A20	1/2c red brown	.20
139	A20	1c black brown	.20
140	A20	2c dark green	.50
141	A21	3c yellow brown	.50
142	A21	4c yellow orange	.20
143	A21	5c deep green	.35
144	A21	9c black, *yellow*	.20
145	A22	10c ultramarine, *pink* (R)	.35
146	A22	18c blue (R)	125.00
147	A22	22c green	.45
148	A22	30c orange brown	.50
149	A23	50c dark brown	.45
150	A23	60c dull violet	.45
151	A23	70c light blue (R)	.60
152	A23	1pi yellow green	.85
153	A23	2pi red	.95
		Nos. 137-153 (17)	131.95

Nos. 137-153 were issued by the Vichy government in France, but were not placed on sale in Kwangchowan.

SEMI-POSTAL STAMPS

French Revolution Issue

Common Design Type

1939 **Unwmk.** **Photo.** ***Perf. 13***

Name and Value typo. in Black

B1	CD83	6c + 2c green	5.75	5.75
B2	CD83	7c + 3c brown	5.75	5.75
B3	CD83	9c + 4c red org	5.75	5.75
B4	CD83	13c + 10c rose pink	5.75	5.75
B5	CD83	23c + 20c blue	5.75	5.75
		Nos. B1-B5 (5)	28.75	28.75

Indo-China Nos. B19A and B19C Overprinted "KOUANG-TCHEOU" in Blue or Red, and Common Design Type

1941 **Photo.** ***Perf. 13½***

B6	SP1	10c + 10c red (B)	.50
B7	CD86	15c + 30c mar & car	.50
B8	SP2	25c + 10c blue (R)	.75
		Nos. B6-B8 (3)	1.75

Nos. B6-B8 were issued by the Vichy government in France, but were not placed on sale in Kwangchowan.

Indo-China Nos. B21A-B21B Overprinted "KOUANG-TCHEOU" in Blue or Red

1944 **Engr.** ***Perf. 12½x12***

B9	A27a	5c + 15c on 25c deep blue (R)	.75
B10	A27a	+ 25c on 10c car lake	.75

Colonial Development Fund.

Nos. B9-B10 were issued by the Vichy government in France, but were not placed on sale in Kwangchowan.

AIR POST SEMI-POSTAL STAMPS

Indo-China Nos. CB2-CB4 Overprinted "KOUANG-TCHEOU" in Blue or Red

Methods and Perfs as Before

1942, June 22

CB1	SPAP1	15c + 35c green	.75
CB2	SPAP2	20c + 60c brown	.75
CB3	SPAP3	30c + 90c car red	.75
		Nos. CB1-CB3 (3)	2.25

Native children's welfare fund.

Nos. CB1-CB3 were issued by the Vichy government in France, but were not placed on sale in Kwangchowan.

Colonial Education Fund

Indo-China No. CB5 Overprinted "KOUANG-TCHEOU" in Blue or Red

Perf. 12½x13½

1942, June 22 **Engr.**

CB4	CD86a	12c + 18c blue & red	.75

No. CB4 was issued by the Vichy government in France, but was not placed on sale in Kwangchowan.

MONGTSEU (MENGTSZ)

Stamps of Indo-China Surcharged in Black

1903-04 **Unwmk.** ***Perf. 14x13½***

1	A3	1c blk, *lil bl*	6.50	6.50
2	A3	2c brn, *buff*	4.75	4.75
3	A3	4c claret, *lav*	5.75	5.75
4	A3	5c yel grn	4.25	4.25
5	A3	10c red	5.75	5.75
6	A3	15c gray	7.00	7.00
7	A3	20c red, *grn*	8.00	8.00
7C	A3	25c blk, *rose*	550.00	550.00
8	A3	25c blue	8.00	8.00
9	A3	30c brn, *bister*	6.75	6.75
10	A3	40c red, *straw*	50.00	50.00
11	A3	50c car, *rose*	325.00	325.00
12	A3	50c brn, *az* ('04)	82.50	82.50
13	A3	75c dp vio, *org*	70.00	70.00
a.		"INDO-CHINE" inverted	*50,000.*	
14	A3	1fr brnz grn, *straw*	75.00	75.00
15	A3	5fr red lil, *lav*	80.00	80.00
		Nos. 1-15 (16)	1,289.	1,289.

Many Surcharge varieties exist on #1-15.

Stamps of Indo-China, 1892-1906, Surcharged in Red or Black

1906

16	A4	1c ol grn (R)	1.25	1.25
17	A4	2c vio brn, *buff*	1.25	1.25
18	A4	4c cl, *bluish* (R)	1.25	1.25
19	A4	5c dp grn (R)	1.60	1.60
20	A4	10c carmine	1.40	1.40
21	A4	15c org brn, *bl*	3.00	3.00
22	A4	20c red, *grn*	3.00	3.00
23	A4	25c deep blue	3.50	3.50
24	A4	30c pale brn	4.00	4.00
25	A4	35c blk, *yel* (R)	3.50	3.50
26	A4	40c blk, *bluish* (R)	4.00	4.00
27	A4	50c bister brn	12.00	12.00
28	A3	75c dp vio, *org* (R)	35.00	35.00
a.		"INDO-CHINE" inverted	*50,000.*	
29	A4	1fr pale grn	16.00	16.00
30	A4	2fr brn, *org* (R)	37.50	37.50
31	A3	5fr red lil, *lav*	82.50	82.50
32	A4	10fr org brn, *grn*	110.00	110.00
a.		Chinese characters inverted	*1,350.*	*1,500.*
		Nos. 16-32 (17)	320.75	320.75

Inverted varieties of the surcharge exist on Nos. 19, 22 and 32.

Stamps of Indo-China, 1907, Surcharged "MONGTSEU" and Value in Chinese in Red or Blue

1908

33	A5	1c ol brn & blk	.70	.70
34	A5	2c brn & blk	.80	.80
35	A5	4c bl & blk	.80	.80
36	A5	5c grn & blk	.80	.80
37	A5	10c red & blk (Bl)	1.75	1.75
38	A5	15c vio & blk	1.75	1.75
39	A6	20c vio & blk	3.50	3.50
40	A6	25c bl & blk	10.00	10.00
41	A6	30c brn & blk	4.00	4.00
42	A6	35c ol grn & blk	4.75	4.75
43	A6	40c brn & blk	3.25	3.25
45	A6	50c car & blk (Bl)	4.25	4.25
46	A7	75c ver & blk (Bl)	8.50	8.50
47	A8	1fr car & blk (Bl)	8.50	8.50
48	A9	2fr grn & blk	11.50	11.50
49	A10	5fr bl & blk	67.50	67.50
50	A11	10fr pur & blk	92.50	92.50
		Nos. 33-50 (17)	224.85	224.85

The Chinese characters overprinted on Nos. 1 to 50 repeat the denomination of the basic stamp.

Nos. 33-50 Surcharged with New Values in Cents or Piasters in Black, Red or Blue

1919

51	A5	2/5c on 1c	.95	.95
52	A5	4/5c on 2c	.95	.95
53	A5	1 3/5c on 4c	1.10	1.10
54	A5	2c on 5c	.95	.95
55	A5	4c on 10c (Bl)	1.75	1.75
56	A5	6c on 15c	2.00	2.00
57	A6	8c on 20c	4.25	4.25
58	A6	10c on 25c	3.50	3.50
59	A6	12c on 30c	2.25	2.25
60	A6	14c on 35c	2.10	2.10
a.		Closed "4"	9.50	9.50
61	A6	16c on 40c	3.00	3.00
63	A6	20c on 50c (Bl)	3.25	3.25
64	A7	30c on 75c (Bl)	3.50	3.50
65	A8	40c on 1fr (Bl)	5.75	5.75
66	A9	80c on 2fr (R)	6.00	6.00
a.		Triple surch., one inverted	400.00	400.00
67	A10	2pi on 5fr (R)	100.00	100.00
a.		Triple surch., one inverted	325.00	325.00
b.		Double surcharge	525.00	525.00
68	A11	4pi on 10fr (R)	20.00	20.00
		Nos. 51-68 (17)	161.30	161.30

PAKHOI

Stamps of Indo-China Surcharged in Black

1903-04 **Unwmk.** ***Perf. 14x13½***

1	A3	1c blk, *lil bl*	4.75	4.75
2	A3	2c brn, *buff*	3.50	3.50
3	A3	4c claret, *lav*	3.50	3.50
4	A3	5c yel grn	3.00	3.00
5	A3	10c red	3.50	3.50
6	A3	15c gray	3.50	3.50
7	A3	20c red, *grn*	6.75	6.75
8	A3	25c blue	5.75	5.75
9	A3	25c blk, *rose*('04)	4.00	4.00
10	A3	30c brn, *bister*	5.75	5.75
11	A3	40c red, *straw*	35.00	35.00
12	A3	50c car, *rose*	250.00	250.00
13	A3	50c brn, *az* ('04)	35.00	35.00
14	A3	75c dp vio, *org*	45.00	45.00
a.		"INDO-CHINE" inverted	*36,000.*	
15	A3	1fr brnz grn, *straw*	45.00	45.00
16	A3	5fr red lil, *lav*	85.00	85.00
		Nos. 1-16 (16)	539.00	539.00

Many varieties of the surcharge exist.

Stamps of Indo-China 1892-1906, Surcharged in Red or Black

1906

No.	Type	Description	Unused	Used
17	A4	1c ol grn (R)	1.25	1.25
18	A4	2c vio brn, *buff*	1.25	1.25
19	A4	4c cl, *bluish* (R)	1.25	1.25
20	A4	5c dp grn (R)	1.25	1.25
21	A4	10c carmine	1.25	1.25
22	A4	15c org brn,*bl*	5.75	5.75
23	A4	20c red, *grn*	3.00	3.00
24	A4	25c deep blue	3.00	3.00
25	A4	30c pale brn	2.25	2.25
26	A4	35c blk, *yel* (R)	2.25	2.25
27	A4	40c blk, *bluish*(R)	3.00	3.00
28	A4	50c bister brn	5.75	5.75
29	A3	75c dp vio, *org* (R)	35.00	35.00
30	A4	1fr pale grn	16.00	16.00
31	A4	2fr brn, *org*(R)	29.00	29.00
32	A3	5fr red lil, *lav*	80.00	80.00
33	A4	10fr org brn, *grn*	82.50	82.50
		Nos. 17-33 (17)	273.75	273.75

Various surcharge varieties exist on #17-24.

Stamps of Indo-China, 1907, Surcharged "PAKHOI" and Value in Chinese in Red or Blue

1908

No.	Type	Description	Unused	Used
34	A5	1c ol brn & blk	.50	.50
35	A5	2c brn & blk	.50	.50
36	A5	4c bl & blk	.50	.50
37	A5	5c grn & blk	.85	.85
38	A5	10c red & blk (Bl)	.85	.85
39	A5	15c vio & blk	1.25	1.25
40	A6	20c vio & blk	1.25	1.25
41	A6	25c bl & blk	1.75	1.75
42	A6	30c brn & blk	2.25	2.25
43	A6	35c ol grn & blk	2.25	2.25
44	A6	40c brn & blk	2.25	2.25
46	A6	50c car & blk (Bl)	2.25	2.25
47	A7	75c ver & blk (Bl)	4.00	4.00
48	A8	1fr car & blk (Bl)	5.50	5.50
49	A9	2fr grn & blk	11.00	11.00
50	A10	5fr bl & blk	57.50	57.50
51	A11	10fr pur & blk	100.00	100.00
		Nos. 34-51 (17)	194.45	194.45

The Chinese characters overprinted on Nos. 1 to 51 repeat the denomination of the basic stamps.

Nos. 34-51 Surcharged with New Values in Cents or Piasters in Black, Red or Blue

1919

No.	Type	Description	Unused	Used
52	A5	⅖c on 1c	.60	.60
a.		"PAK-HOI" and Chinese double	110.00	110.00
53	A5	⅘c on 2c	.60	.60
54	A5	1⅗c on 4c (R)	.60	.60
55	A5	2c on 5c	1.40	1.40
56	A5	4c on 10c (Bl)	2.40	2.40
57	A5	6c on 15c	.95	.95
58	A6	8c on 20c	2.40	2.40
59	A6	10c on 25c	3.00	3.00
60	A6	12c on 30c	1.00	1.00
a.		"12 CENTS" double	140.00	140.00
61	A6	14c on 35c	.65	.65
a.		Closed "4"	7.25	7.25
62	A6	16c on 40c	1.75	1.75
64	A6	20c on 50c (Bl)	1.40	1.40
65	A7	30c on 75c (Bl)	3.00	3.00
66	A8	40c on 1fr (Bl)	7.25	7.25
67	A9	80c on 2fr (R)	6.00	6.00
68	A10	2pi on 5fr (R)	8.25	8.25
69	A11	4pi on 10fr (R)	20.00	20.00
		Nos. 52-69 (17)	61.25	61.25

TCHONGKING (CHUNGKING)

Stamps of Indo-China Surcharged in Black

1903-04 Unwmk. *Perf. 14x13½*

No.	Type	Description	Unused	Used
1	A3	1c blk, *lil bl*	3.00	3.00
2	A3	2c brn, *buff*	3.00	3.00
3	A3	4c claret, *lav*	3.50	3.50
4	A3	5c yel grn	3.50	3.50
5	A3	10c red	3.50	3.50
6	A3	15c gray	3.50	3.50
7	A3	20c red, *grn*	4.75	4.75
8	A3	25c blue	35.00	35.00
9	A3	25c blk, *rose* ('04)	5.75	5.75
10	A3	30c brn, *bister*	9.00	9.00
11	A3	40c red, *straw*	35.00	35.00
12	A3	50c car, *rose*	160.00	160.00
13	A3	50c brn, *az* ('04)	82.50	82.50
14	A3	75c vio, *org*	32.50	32.50
15	A3	1fr brnz grn, *straw*	40.00	40.00
16	A3	5fr red lil, *lav*	67.50	67.50
		Nos. 1-16 (16)	492.00	492.00

Many surcharge varieties exist on #1-14.

Stamps of Indo-China and French China, issued in 1902 with similar overprint, but without Chinese characters, were not officially authorized.

Stamps of Indo-China, 1892-1906, Surcharged in Red or Black

1906

No.	Type	Description	Unused	Used
17	A4	1c ol grn (R)	1.40	1.40
18	A4	2c vio brn, *buff*	1.40	1.40
19	A4	4c cl, *bluish* (R)	1.40	1.40
20	A4	5c dp grn (R)	1.75	1.75
21	A4	10c carmine	2.25	2.25
22	A4	15c org brn, *bl*	9.00	9.00
23	A4	20c red, *grn*	2.50	2.50
24	A4	25c deep blue	3.25	3.25
25	A4	30c pale brn	2.10	2.10
26	A4	35c blk, *yellow* (R)	3.25	3.25
27	A4	40c blk, *bluish* (R)	5.00	5.00
28	A4	50c bis brn	6.00	6.00
29	A3	75c dp vio, *org* (R)	35.00	35.00
30	A4	1fr pale grn	21.00	21.00
31	A4	2fr brn, *org* (R)	21.00	21.00
32	A3	5fr red lil, *lav*	72.50	72.50
33	A4	10fr org brn, *grn*	85.00	85.00
		Nos. 17-33 (17)	273.80	273.80

Variety "T" omitted in surcharge occurs once in each sheet of Nos. 17-33. Other surcharge varieties exist, such as inverted surcharge on 1c and 2c.

Stamps of Indo-China, 1907, Surcharged "TCHONGKING" and Value in Chinese in Red or Blue

1908

No.	Type	Description	Unused	Used
34	A5	1c ol brn & blk	.35	.35
35	A5	2c brn & blk	.50	.50
36	A5	4c bl & blk	.70	.70
37	A5	5c grn & blk	1.25	1.25
38	A5	10c red & blk (Bl)	1.25	1.25
39	A5	15c vio & blk	1.75	1.75
40	A6	20c vio & blk	1.90	1.90
41	A6	25c bl & blk	3.25	3.25
42	A6	30c brn & blk	2.10	2.10
43	A6	35c ol grn & blk	4.75	4.75
44	A6	40c brn & blk	9.25	9.25
45	A6	50c car & blk (Bl)	7.25	7.25
46	A7	75c ver & blk (Bl)	6.50	6.50
47	A8	1fr car & blk (Bl)	8.50	8.50
48	A9	2fr grn & blk	60.00	60.00
49	A10	5fr bl & blk	26.00	26.00
50	A11	10fr pur & blk	175.00	175.00
		Nos. 34-50 (17)	310.30	310.30

The Chinese characters overprinted on Nos. 1 to 50 repeat the denomination of the basic stamp.

Nos. 34-50 Surcharged with New Values in Cents or Piasters in Black, Red or Blue

1919

No.	Type	Description	Unused	Used
51	A5	⅖c on 1c	.80	.70
52	A5	⅘c on 2c	.80	.70
53	A5	1⅗c on 4c (R)	.80	.70
54	A5	2c on 5c	.95	.70
55	A5	4c on 10c (Bl)	.80	.70
56	A5	6c on 15c	.95	.85
57	A6	8c on 20c	2.00	.70
58	A6	10c on 25c	5.75	5.50
59	A6	12c on 30c	1.75	1.10
60	A6	14c on 35c	1.10	1.10
a.		Closed "4"	11.00	11.00
61	A6	16c on 40c	1.60	1.25
a.		"16 CENTS" double	80.00	80.00
62	A6	20c on 50c (Bl)	6.75	5.75
63	A7	30c on 75c (Bl)	1.60	1.60
64	A8	40c on 1fr (Bl)	3.50	2.10
65	A9	80c on 2fr (R)	3.25	3.00
66	A10	2pi on 5fr (R)	4.75	4.75
67	A11	4pi on 10fr (R)	9.25	9.25
		Nos. 51-67 (17)	46.40	40.45

YUNNAN FOU

(Formerly Yunnan Sen, later known as Kunming)

Stamps of Indo-China Surcharged in Black

1903-04 Unwmk. *Perf. 14x13½*

No.	Type	Description	Unused	Used
1	A3	1c blk, *lil bl*	5.00	5.00
2	A3	2c brn, *buff*	5.00	5.00
3	A3	4c claret, *lav*	5.50	5.50
4	A3	5c yel green	5.00	5.00
5	A3	10c red	5.50	5.50
6	A3	15c gray	5.50	5.50
7	A3	20c red, *grn*	7.50	7.50
8	A3	25c blue	5.00	5.00
9	A3	30c brn, *bister*	7.50	7.50
10	A3	40c red, *straw*	57.50	40.00
11	A3	50c car, *rose*	275.00	275.00
12	A3	50c brn, *az* ('04)	140.00	140.00
13	A3	75c dp vio, *org*	42.50	40.00
a.		"INDO-CHINE" inverted	*27,500.*	
14	A3	1fr brnz grn, *straw*	42.50	40.00
15	A3	5fr red lil, *lav*	85.00	85.00
		Nos. 1-15 (15)	694.00	671.50

The Chinese characters overprinted on Nos. 1 to 15 repeat the denomination of the basic stamp.

Many varieties of the surcharge exist.

Stamps of Indo-China, 1892-1906, Surcharged in Red or Black

1906 Unwmk. *Perf. 14x13½*

No.	Type	Description	Unused	Used
17	A4	1c ol grn (R)	1.75	1.75
18	A4	2c vio brn, *buff*	1.75	1.75
19	A4	4c cl, *bluish* (R)	2.25	2.25
20	A4	5c dp grn (R)	2.25	2.25
21	A4	10c carmine	3.50	3.50
22	A4	15c org brn, *bl*	8.00	8.00
23	A4	20c red, *grn*	3.50	3.50
24	A4	25c deep blue	3.50	3.50
25	A4	30c pale brn	3.50	3.50
26	A4	35c blk, *yel* (R)	5.75	5.75
27	A4	40c blk, *bluish* (R)	4.75	4.75
28	A4	50c bister brn	6.50	6.50
29	A3	75c dp vio, *org* (R)	42.50	42.50
30	A4	1fr pale grn	19.00	19.00
31	A4	2fr brn, *org* (R)	18.00	18.00
32	A3	5fr red lil, *lav*	57.50	57.50
33	A4	10fr org brn, *grn*	65.00	65.00
		Nos. 17-33 (17)	249.00	249.00

Various varieties of the surcharge exist on Nos. 18, 20, 21 and 27.

Stamps of Indo-China, 1907, Surcharged "YUNNANFOU," and Value in Chinese in Red or Blue

1908

No.	Type	Description	Unused	Used
34	A5	1c ol brn & blk	.80	.80
35	A5	2c brn & blk	.95	.95
36	A5	4c bl & blk	1.10	1.10
37	A5	5c grn & blk	1.75	1.75
38	A5	10c red & blk (Bl)	1.75	1.75
39	A5	15c vio & blk	4.25	4.25
40	A6	20c vio & blk	4.00	4.00
41	A6	25c bl & blk	5.75	5.75
42	A6	30c brn & blk	5.00	5.00
43	A6	35c ol grn & blk	5.00	5.00
44	A6	40c brn & blk	5.75	5.75
45	A6	50c car & blk (Bl)	6.50	6.50
46	A7	75c ver & blk (Bl)	6.75	6.75
47	A8	1fr car & blk (Bl)	11.00	11.00
48	A9	2fr grn & blk	19.00	19.00
a.		"YUNANNFOU"	*1,750.*	*1,750.*
49	A10	5fr bl & blk	42.50	42.50
a.		"YUNANNFOU"	*1,750.*	*1,750.*
50	A11	10fr pur & blk	82.50	82.50
a.		"YUNANNFOU"	*1,750.*	*1,750.*
		Nos. 34-50 (17)	204.35	204.35

The Chinese characters overprinted on Nos. 17-50 repeat the denomination of the basic stamp.

Nos. 34-50 Surcharged with New Values in Cents or Piasters in Black, Red or Blue

1919

No.	Type	Description	Unused	Used
51	A5	⅖c on 1c	.60	.60
a.		New value double	95.00	
52	A5	⅘c on 2c	.85	.85
53	A5	1⅗c on 4c (R)	.95	.95
54	A5	2c on 5c	1.25	1.25
a.		Triple surcharge	150.00	
55	A5	4c on 10c (Bl)	.95	.95
56	A5	6c on 15c	1.75	1.75
57	A6	8c on 20c	1.25	1.25
58	A6	10c on 25c	2.50	2.50
59	A6	12c on 30c	1.75	1.75
60	A6	14c on 35c	6.25	3.50
a.		Closed "4"	65.00	65.00
61	A6	16c on 40c	3.50	3.50
62	A6	20c on 50c (Bl)	2.00	2.00
63	A7	30c on 75c (Bl)	3.00	3.00
64	A8	40c on 1fr (Bl)	3.50	3.50
65	A9	80c on 2fr (R)	5.75	5.75
a.		Triple surch., one inverted	175.00	
66	A10	2pi on 5fr (R)	29.00	29.00
67	A11	4pi on 10fr (R)	11.00	11.00
		Nos. 51-67 (17)	75.85	73.10

CRETE

Austria, France, Italy and Great Britain maintained their own post offices in Crete during the period when that country was an autonomous state.

100 Centimes = 1 Franc

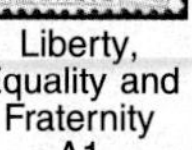

Liberty, Equality and Fraternity
A1

"Rights of Man"
A2

Liberty and Peace (Symbolized by Olive Branch)
A3

Perf. 14x13½

1902-03 Unwmk. Typo.

No.	Type	Description	Unused	Used
1	A1	1c gray	1.40	1.25
2	A1	2c violet brown	1.40	1.25
3	A1	3c red orange	1.40	1.25
4	A1	4c yellow brown	1.40	1.25
5	A1	5c green	1.40	1.25
6	A2	10c rose red	1.75	1.60
7	A2	15c pale red ('03)	2.40	1.75
8	A2	20c brown vio ('03)	3.25	2.50
9	A2	25c blue ('03)	4.25	2.50
10	A2	30c lilac ('03)	5.50	4.25
11	A3	40c red & pale bl	8.50	7.50
12	A3	50c bis brn & lav	12.00	8.50
13	A3	1fr claret & ol grn	16.00	14.00
14	A3	2fr gray vio & yel	25.00	22.50
15	A3	5fr dk blue & buff	45.00	40.00
		Nos. 1-15 (15)	130.65	111.35

A4

A5

Black Surcharge

1903

No.	Type	Description	Unused	Used
16	A4	1pi on 25c blue	35.00	29.00
17	A5	2pi on 50c bis brn & lav	57.50	42.50
18	A5	4pi on 1fr claret & ol grn	85.00	77.50
19	A5	8pi on 2fr gray vio & yel	92.50	92.50
20	A5	20pi on 5fr dk bl & buff	160.00	140.00
		Nos. 16-20 (5)	430.00	381.50

EGYPT

French post offices formerly maintained in Alexandria and Port Said.

100 Centimes = 1 Franc

ALEXANDRIA

Stamps of France Overprinted in Red, Blue or Black

1899-1900 Unwmk. *Perf. 14x13½*

No.	Type	Description	Unused	Used
1	A15	1c blk, *lil bl* (R)	1.40	1.40
a.		Double overprint	110.00	
b.		Triple overprint	125.00	

2 A15 2c brn, *buff* (Bl) 2.10 1.75
3 A15 3c gray, *grysh* (Bl) 2.10 1.75
4 A15 4c cl, *lav* (Bl) 2.50 2.10
5 A15 5c yel grn, (I) (R) 4.00 2.10
a. Type II (R) 110.00 72.50
6 A15 10c blk, *lav*, (I) (R) 5.75 5.00
a. Type II (R) 42.50 25.00
7 A15 15c blue (R) 6.00 3.25
8 A15 20c red, *grn* 10.00 5.50
a. Double overprint
9 A15 25c blk, *rose* (R) 5.00 2.75
a. Inverted overprint 57.50
b. Double ovpt., one invtd. 110.00
10 A15 30c brn, *bis* 11.00 8.50
11 A15 40c red, *straw* 9.75 9.75
12 A15 50c car, *rose* (II) 24.00 12.50
a. Type I 125.00 18.00
13 A15 1fr brnz grn, *straw* 22.50 16.00
14 A15 2fr brn, *az* ('00) 65.00 62.50
15 A15 5fr red lil, *lav* 92.50 80.00
Nos. 1-15 (15) 263.60 214.85

A2

A3

A4

1902-03
16 A2 1c gray .50 .20
17 A2 2c violet brn .50 .35
18 A2 3c red orange .50 .35
19 A2 4c yellow brn .75 .55
20 A2 5c green 1.10 .45
21 A3 10c rose red .95 .45
22 A3 15c orange 1.10 .75
a. 15c pale red ('03) 3.00 .90
23 A3 20c brn vio ('03) 2.00 1.00
24 A3 25c blue ('03) 1.00 .35
25 A3 30c violet ('03) 5.00 2.75
26 A4 40c red & pale bl 3.50 1.40
27 A4 50c bis brn & lav 6.75 2.00
28 A4 1fr cl & ol grn 6.25 2.75
29 A4 2fr gray vio & yel 16.00 7.75
30 A4 5fr dk bl & buff 19.00 11.00
Nos. 16-30 (15) 64.90 32.10

The 2c, 5c, 10c, 20c and 25c exist imperf. Value, each $32.50.

See #77-86. For surcharges see #31-73, B1-B4.

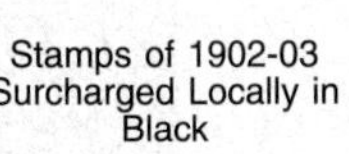
Stamps of 1902-03 Surcharged Locally in Black

1921
31 A2 2m on 5c green 5.00 2.75
32 A2 3m on 3c red org 5.00 3.75
a. Larger numeral 80.00 57.50
33 A3 4m on 10c rose 4.00 3.25
34 A2 5m on 1c dk gray 5.50 4.25
35 A2 5m on 4c yel brn 5.75 4.75
36 A3 6m on 15c orange 3.75 3.00
a. Larger numeral 65.00 65.00
37 A3 8m on 20c brn vio 5.00 3.25
a. Larger numeral 47.50 35.00
38 A3 10m on 25c blue 2.50 2.50
a. Inverted surcharge 30.00 30.00
b. Double surcharge 30.00 30.00
39 A3 12m on 30c vio 9.25 9.25
40 A2 15m on 2c vio brn 4.25 4.25

Nos. 26-30 Surcharged

41 A4 15m on 40c 12.50 11.00
42 A4 15m on 50c 7.50 7.50
43 A4 30m on 1fr 110.00 110.00
44 A4 60m on 2fr 160.00 160.00
a. Larger numeral 500.00 500.00
45 A4 150m on 5fr 250.00 250.00

Port Said Nos. 20 and 19 Surcharged like Nos. 32 and 40

45A A2 3m on 3c red org 100.00 100.00
46 A2 15m on 2c vio brn 92.50 92.50
Nos. 31-46 (17) 782.50 772.00

Alexandria No. 28 Surcharged with Two New Values

1921
46A A4 30m on 15m on 1fr 825.00 *875.00*

The surcharge "15 Mill." was made in error and is canceled by a bar.

The surcharges were lithographed on Nos. 31, 33, 38, 39 and 42 and typographed on the other stamps of the 1921 issue. Nos. 34, 36 and 37 were surcharged by both methods.

Alexandria Stamps of 1902-03 Surcharged in Paris

1921-23
47 A2 1m on 1c gray 2.25 1.60
48 A2 2m on 5c green 1.75 1.40
49 A3 4m on 10c rose 2.00 1.60
50 A3 4m on 10c green ('23) 1.40 1.40
51 A2 5m on 3c red org ('23) 4.75 3.50
52 A3 6m on 15c orange 1.40 1.10
53 A3 8m on 20c brn vio 1.40 .70
54 A3 10m on 25c blue .95 .90
55 A3 10m on 30c vio 2.75 2.25
56 A3 15m on 50c bl ('23) 3.50 2.25

Nos. 27-30 and Type of 1902 Surcharged

57 A4 15m on 50c 2.25 2.25
58 A4 30m on 1fr 2.50 1.60
59 A4 60m on 2fr *1,600.* *1,650.*
60 A4 60m on 2fr org & pale bl ('23) 7.50 7.50
61 A4 150m on 5fr 9.25 5.50
Nos. 47-58,60-61 (14) 43.65 33.55

Stamps and Types of 1902-03 Surcharged with New Values and Bars in Black

1925
62 A2 1m on 1c gray .80 .80
63 A2 2m on 5c orange .80 .80
64 A2 2m on 5c green 1.00 1.00
65 A3 4m on 10c green .80 .80
66 A2 5m on 3c red org 1.00 .80
67 A3 6m on 15c orange .95 .80
68 A3 8m on 20c brn vio 1.25 .85
69 A3 10m on 25c blue .75 .60
70 A3 15m on 50c blue 1.40 .95
71 A4 30m on 1fr cl & ol grn 2.25 1.75
72 A4 60m on 2fr org & pale bl 3.00 2.75
73 A4 150m on 5fr dk bl & buff 3.75 3.00
Nos. 62-73 (12) 17.75 14.90

Types of 1902-03 Issue

1927-28
77 A2 3m orange ('28) 1.40 1.10
81 A3 15m slate blue 1.40 1.10
82 A3 20m rose lil ('28) 4.25 3.00
84 A4 50m org & blue 7.50 5.75
85 A4 100m sl bl & buff 10.00 7.50
86 A4 250m gray grn & red 16.00 10.00
Nos. 77-86 (6) 40.55 28.45

SEMI-POSTAL STAMPS

Regular Issue of 1902-03 Surcharged in Carmine

1915 Unwmk. *Perf. 14x13½*
B1 A3 10c + 5c rose .80 .80

Sinking Fund Issue

Type of 1902-03 Issue Surcharged in Blue or Black

1927-30
B2 A3 15m + 5m deep org 3.25 3.25
B3 A3 15m + 5m red vio ('28) 3.25 3.25
a. 15m + 5m violet ('30) 7.00 7.00

Type of 1902-03 Issue Surcharged as in 1927-28

1929
B4 A3 15m + 5m fawn 5.50 5.50

POSTAGE DUE STAMPS

Postage Due Stamps of France, 1893-1920, Surcharged in Paris in Black

1922 Unwmk. *Perf. 14x13½*
J1 D2 2m on 5c blue 1.60 1.60
J2 D2 4m on 10c brown 1.60 1.60
J3 D2 10m on 30c rose red 1.90 1.90
J4 D2 15m on 50c brn vio 2.25 2.25
J5 D2 30m on 1fr red brn, *straw* 3.00 3.00
Nos. J1-J5 (5) 10.35 10.35

D3

1928 Typo.
J6 D3 1m slate 1.25 1.25
J7 D3 2m light blue .85 .85
J8 D3 4m lilac rose 1.25 1.25
J9 D3 5m gray green 1.40 1.40
J10 D3 10m light red 1.60 1.60
J11 D3 20m violet brn 1.50 1.50
J12 D3 30m green 3.25 3.25
J13 D3 40m lt violet 3.75 3.75
Nos. J6-J13 (8) 14.85 14.85

#J6-J13 were also available for use in Port Said.

PORT SAID

Stamps of France Overprinted in Red, Blue or Black

1899-1900 Unwmk. *Perf. 14x13½*
1 A15 1c blk, *lil bl* (R) 1.25 .85
2 A15 2c brn, *buff* (bl) 1.25 .95
3 A15 3c gray, *grysh* (Bl) 1.25 1.25
4 A15 4c claret, *lav* (Bl) 1.25 1.25
5 A15 5c yel grn (I) (R) 6.25 3.25
a. Type II (R) 32.50 11.00
6 A15 10c blk, *lav* (I) (R) 9.00 9.00
a. Type II (R) 47.50 35.00
7 A15 15c blue (R) 9.00 5.50
8 A15 20c red, *grn* 10.00 7.50
9 A15 25c blk, *rose* (R) 8.50 3.00
a. Double overprint 160.00
b. Inverted overprint 160.00
10 A15 30c brn, *bister* 10.00 8.50
a. Inverted overprint 175.00
11 A15 40c red, *straw* 10.00 8.50
12 A15 50c car, *rose* (II) 13.00 10.00
a. Type I 250.00 80.00
b. Double overprint (II) 275.00
13 A15 1fr brnz grn, *straw* 20.00 11.00
14 A15 2fr brn, *az* ('00) 55.00 50.00
15 A15 5fr red lil, *lav* 82.50 67.50
Nos. 1-15 (15) 238.25 188.05

Regular Issue Surcharged in Red

1899
16 A15 25c on 10c blk, *lav* 92.50 24.00
a. Inverted surcharge 200.00

With Additional Surcharge "25" in Red

17 A15 25c on 10c blk, *lav* 350.00 125.00
a. "25" inverted 1,100. 925.00
b. "25" in black *2,150.*
c. As "b," "VINGT CINQ" inverted *2,550.*
d. As "b," "25" vertical *2,550.*
e. As "c" and "d" *2,550.*

A2

A3

A4

1902-03 Typo.
18a A2 1c gray .50 .50
19 A2 2c violet brn .75 .50
20 A2 3c red orange .60 .50
21 A2 4c yellow brown .75 .60
22 A2 5c blue green .80 .60
a. 5c yellow green 3.00 2.25
23 A3 10c rose red 1.25 .75
24 A3 15c pale red ('03) 2.25 1.50
a. 15c orange 3.00 1.75
25 A3 20c brn vio ('03) 2.25 1.50
26 A3 25c blue ('03) 1.75 1.25
27 A3 30c violet ('03) 4.25 3.50
28 A4 40c red & pale bl 4.00 3.00
29 A4 50c bis brn & lav 5.75 4.75
30 A4 1fr claret & ol grn 7.00 5.75
31 A4 2fr gray vio & yel 9.75 9.75
32 A4 5fr dk bl & buff 24.00 21.00
Nos. 18a-32 (15) 65.65 55.45

See #83-92. For surcharges see #33-80, B1-B4.

Stamps of 1902-03 Surcharged Locally

1921
33 A2 2m on 5c green 5.50 5.50
a. Inverted surcharge 30.00 30.00
34 A3 4m on 10c rose 4.75 4.75
a. Inverted surcharge 30.00 30.00
35 A2 5m on 1c 7.50 7.50
a. Inverted surcharge 55.00 55.00
c. Surcharged "2 Milliemes" 37.50 37.50
36 A2 5m on 2c 10.00 10.00
a. Surcharged "2 Milliemes" 45.00 45.00
b. As "a," inverted 75.00 75.00
37 A2 5m on 3c 6.50 6.50
a. Inverted surcharge 37.50 37.50
b. On Alexandria #18 275.00 275.00
38 A2 5m on 4c 6.75 6.75
a. Inverted surcharge 57.50 57.50
39 A2 10m on 2c 10.00 10.00
40 A2 10m on 4c 13.00 13.00
a. Inverted surcharge 60.00 60.00
41 A3 10m on 25c 4.75 4.75
a. Inverted surcharge 57.50 57.50
42 A3 12m on 30c 18.00 18.00
43 A2 15m on 4c 5.75 5.75
a. Inverted surcharge 57.50 57.50
44 A3 15m on 15c pale red 37.50 37.50
a. Inverted surcharge 75.00 75.00
45 A3 15m on 20c 37.50 37.50
a. Inverted surcharge 75.00 75.00
46 A4 30m on 50c 200.00 200.00
47 A4 60m on 50c 225.00 225.00
48 A4 150m on 50c 275.00 275.00

Nos. 46, 47 and 48 have a bar between the numerals and "Millièmes," which is in capital letters.

Same Surcharge on Stamps of French Offices in Turkey, 1902-03

49 A2 2m on 2c vio brn 75.00 75.00
50 A2 5m on 1c gray 57.50 57.50
a. "5" inverted — —
Nos. 33-50 (18) 1,000. 1,000.

Nos. 28-32 Surcharged

51 A4 15m on 40c 37.50 37.50
52 A4 15m on 50c 42.50 42.50
b. Bar below 15 35.00 35.00

53 A4 30m on 1fr 175.00 175.00
54 A4 60m on 2fr 60.00 60.00
55 A4 150m on 5fr 190.00 190.00
Nos. 51-55 (5) 505.00 505.00

Overprinted "MILLtEMES"

51a A4 15m on 40c 100.00 100.00
52a A4 15m on 50c 200.00 200.00
53a A4 30m on 1fr 500.00 525.00
54a A4 60m on 2fr 200.00 225.00
55a A4 150m on 5fr 550.00 575.00
Nos. 51a-55a (5) 1,550. 1,625.

Stamps of 1902-03 Surcharged in Paris

1921-23
56 A2 1m on 1c gray .85 .85
57 A2 2m on 5c green .85 .85
58 A3 4m on 10c rose 1.75 1.75
59 A2 5m on 3c red org 5.75 5.75
60 A3 6m on 15c orange 1.75 1.75
a. 6m on 15c pale red 8.50 8.50
61 A3 8m on 20c brn vio 1.75 1.75
62 A3 10m on 25c blue 2.00 2.00
63 A3 10m on 30c violet 4.75 4.75
64 A3 15m on 50c blue 4.25 4.25

Nos. 29-32 and Type of 1902 Surcharged

65 A4 15m on 50c 4.00 4.00
66 A4 30m on 1fr 5.50 5.50
67 A4 60m on 2fr 85.00 85.00
68 A4 60m on 2fr org & pale blue 7.50 7.50
69 A4 150m on 5fr 7.50 7.50
Nos. 56-69 (14) 133.20 133.20

Stamps and Types of 1902-03 Surcharged with New Values and Bars

1925
70 A2 1m on 1c gray .60 .60
71 A2 2m on 5c green .75 .75
72 A3 4m on 10c rose red .75 .75
73 A2 5m on 3c red org .80 .80
74 A3 6m on 15c orange .80 .80
75 A3 8m on 20c brn vio .75 .75
76 A3 10m on 25c blue 1.25 1.25
77 A3 15m on 50c blue 1.25 1.25
78 A4 30m on 1fr cl & ol grn 1.75 1.75
79 A4 60m on 2fr org & pale blue 1.75 1.75
80 A4 150m on 5fr dk bl & buff 2.25 2.25
Nos. 70-80 (11) 12.70 12.70

Types of 1902-03 Issue

1927-28
83 A2 3m orange ('28) 1.25 1.25
87 A3 15m slate bl 1.50 1.50
88 A3 20m rose lil ('28) 1.60 1.60
90 A4 50m org & blue 3.00 3.00
91 A4 100m slate bl & buff 3.50 3.50
92 A4 250m gray grn & red 5.75 5.75
Nos. 83-92 (6) 16.60 16.60

SEMI-POSTAL STAMPS

Regular Issue of 1902-03 Surcharged in Carmine

1915 Unwmk. ***Perf. 14x13½***
B1 A3 10c + 5c rose .95 .95

Sinking Fund Issue

Type of 1902-03 Issue Surcharged like Alexandria Nos. B2-B3 in Blue or Black

1927-30
B2 A3 15m + 5m dp org (Bl) 1.75 1.75
B3 A3 15m + 5m red vio ('28) 1.75 1.75
a. 15m + 5m violet ('30) 3.50 3.50
B4 A3 15m + 5m fawn ('29) 2.25 2.25
Nos. B2-B4 (3) 5.75 5.75

POSTAGE DUE STAMPS

Postage Due Stamps of France, 1893-1906, Surcharged Locally in Black

15
Millièmes

1921 Unwmk. ***Perf. 14x13½***
J1 D2 12m on 10c brown 37.50 37.50
J2 D2 15m on 5c blue 40.00 40.00
J3 D2 30m on 20c ol grn 42.50 42.50
a. Inverted surcharge 575.00 575.00
J4 D2 30m on 50c red vio *2,500. 2,900.*

Same Surcharged in Red or Blue

1921
J5 D2 2m on 5c bl (R) 32.50 32.50
a. Blue surcharge 240.00 240.00
J6 D2 4m on 10c brn (Bl) 32.50 32.50
a. Surcharged "15 Milliemes" 475.00 475.00
J7 D2 10m on 30c red (Bl) 32.50 32.50
a. Inverted surcharge 100.00 100.00
J8 D2 15m on 50c brn vio (Bl) 42.50 42.50
a. Inverted surcharge 100.00 100.00
Nos. J5-J8 (4) 140.00 140.00

Nos. J5-J8 exist with second "M" in "Milliemes" inverted, also with final "S" omitted.

Alexandria Nos. J6-J13 were also available for use in Port Said.

TURKEY

Various powers maintained post offices in the Turkish Empire before World War I by authority of treaties which ended with the signing of the Treaty of Lausanne in 1923. The foreign post offices were closed Oct. 27, 1923.

100 Centimes = 1 Franc
25 Centimes = 40 Paras = 1 Piaster

A1

Stamps of France Surcharged in Black or Red

1885-1901 Unwmk. ***Perf. 14x13½***
1 A1 1pi on 25c yel, *straw* 400.00 10.00
a. Inverted surcharge *1,950. 1,850.*
2 A1 1pi on 25c blk, *rose* (R) ('86) 2.10 .70
a. Inverted surcharge 300.00 275.00
3 A1 2pi on 50c car, *rose* (II) ('90) 12.50 1.75
a. Type I ('01) 260.00 35.00
4 A1 3pi on 75c car, *rose* 18.00 9.00
5 A1 4pi on 1fr brnz grn, *straw* 18.00 9.00
6 A1 8pi on 2fr brn, *az* ('00) 26.00 16.00
7 A1 20pi on 5fr red lil, *lav* ('90) 65.00 35.00
Nos. 1-7 (7) 541.60 81.45

A2

A3

A4

A5

A6

1902-07 Typo. ***Perf. 14x13½***
21 A2 1c gray .35 .35
22 A2 2c vio brn .50 .35
23 A2 3c red org .50 .35
24 A2 4c yel brn 1.75 .75
a. Imperf., pair 57.50
25 A2 5c grn ('06) .75 .35
26 A3 10c rose red .75 .35
27 A3 15c pale red ('03) 1.75 .95
28 A3 20c brn vio ('03) 2.40 1.50
29 A3 25c blue ('07) 32.50 25.00
a. Imperf., pair 300.00
30 A3 30c lilac ('03) 3.50 1.75
31 A4 40c red & pale bl 3.50 2.00
32 A4 50c bis brn & lav ('07) 160.00 140.00
a. Imperf., pair 650.00
33 A4 1fr claret & ol grn ('07) 300.00 300.00
a. Imperf., pair 800.00

Black Surcharge

34 A5 1pi on 25c bl ('03) .80 .35
a. Second "I" omitted 7.50 6.25
b. Double surcharge 47.50 35.00
35 A6 2pi on 50c bis brn & lavender 2.50 .85
36 A6 4pi on 1fr cl & ol grn 3.00 1.00
a. Imperf., pair 550.00
37 A6 8pi on 2fr gray vio & yel 13.00 8.25
38 A6 20pi on 5fr dk bl & buff 5.75 3.00
Nos. 21-38 (18) 533.30 487.15

Nos. 29, 32-33 were used during the early part of 1907 in the French Offices at Harar and Diredawa, Ethiopia. Djibouti and Port Said stamps were also used.

No. 27 Surcharged in Green

1 Piastre
Beyrouth

1905
39 A3 1pi on 15c pale red 1,600. 250.
a. "Piastte" *4,750.* 950.

Stamps of France 1900-21 Surcharged:

On A22

On A20

On A18

1921-22
40 A22 30pa on 5c grn .60 .50
41 A22 30pa on 5c org .50 .50
42 A22 1pi20pa on 10c red .50 .50
43 A22 1pi20pa on 10c grn .75 .50
44 A22 3pi30pa on 25c bl .95 .50
45 A22 4pi20pa on 30c org 1.00 .65
a. "4" omitted 725.00
46 A20 7pi20pa on 50c bl 1.00 .65
47 A18 15pi on 1fr car & ol grn 1.60 1.25
48 A18 30pi on 2fr org & pale bl 8.25 5.75
49 A18 75pi on 5fr dk bl & buff 7.50 4.75
Nos. 40-49 (10) 22.65 15.55

Stamps of France, 1903-07, Handstamped

1923
52 A22 1pi20pa on 10c red 45.00 45.00
54 A20 3pi30pa on 15c gray grn 15.00 15.00
55 A22 7pi20pa on 35c vio 18.00 18.00
a. 1pi20pa on 35c violet 625.00 625.00
Nos. 52-55 (3) 78.00 78.00

CAVALLE (CAVALLA)

Stamps of France Overprinted or Surcharged in Red, Blue or Black

1893-1900 Unwmk. ***Perf. 14x13½***
1 A15 5c grn, *grnsh* (R) 16.00 12.50
2 A15 5c yel grn (I) ('00) (R) 16.00 12.50
3 A15 10c blk, *lav* (II) 18.00 15.00
a. 10c black, *lavender* (I) 125.00 100.00
4 A15 15c blue (R) 32.50 18.00
5 A15 1pi on 25c blk, *rose* 21.00 16.00
6 A15 2pi on 50c car, *rose* 65.00 47.50
7 A15 4pi on 1fr brnz grn, *straw* (R) 65.00 57.50
8 A15 8pi on 2fr brn, *az* ('00) (Bk) 80.00 80.00
Nos. 1-8 (8) 313.50 259.00

A3

A4

A5

A6

1902-03
9 A3 5c green 1.50 1.25
10 A4 10c rose red ('03) 1.50 1.25
11 A4 15c orange 1.75 1.25
a. 15c pale red ('03) 7.50 7.50

Surcharged in Black

12 A5 1pi on 25c bl 3.00 1.75
13 A6 2pi on 50c bis brn & lav 7.50 4.75
14 A6 4pi on 1fr cl & ol grn 9.50 7.00
15 A6 8pi on 2fr gray vio & yel 12.00 11.00
Nos. 9-15 (7) 36.75 28.25

DEDEAGH (DEDEAGATCH)

Stamps of France Overprinted or Surcharged in Red, Blue or Black

1893-1900 Unwmk. *Perf. 14x13½*

1 A15 5c grn, *grnsh* (II) (R) 10.00 9.00
2 A15 5c yel grn (I) ('00) (R) 9.50 9.00
3 A15 10c blk, *lav* (II) 16.00 13.00
a. Type I 29.00 20.00
4 A15 15c blue (R) 22.50 18.00
5 A15 1pi on 25c blk, *rose* 24.00 22.50
6 A15 2pi on 50c car, *rose* 42.50 32.50
7 A15 4pi on 1fr brnz grn, *straw* (R) 55.00 45.00
8 A15 8pi on 2fr brn, *az* ('00) (Bk) 80.00 60.00
Nos. 1-8 (8) 259.50 209.00

A3

A4

A5

A6

1902-03

9 A3 5c green 1.40 1.25
10 A4 10c rose red ('03) 1.75 1.50
11 A4 15c orange 2.25 1.40

Black Surcharge

15 A5 1pi on 25c bl ('03) 2.25 1.75
16 A6 2pi on 50c bis brn & lav 7.00 6.00
a. Double surcharge 190.00
17 A6 4pi on 1fr cl & ol grn 12.50 10.00
18 A6 8pi on 2fr gray vio & yel 18.00 16.00
Nos. 9-18 (7) 45.15 37.90

PORT LAGOS

Stamps of France Overprinted or Surcharged in Red or Blue

1893 Unwmk. *Perf. 14x13½*

1 A15 5c grn, *grnsh* (R) 18.00 18.00
2 A15 10c blk, *lav* 37.50 30.00
3 A15 15c blue (R) 57.50 47.50
4 A15 1pi on 25c blk, *rose* 47.50 40.00
5 A15 2pi on 50c car, *rose* 125.00 70.00
6 A15 4pi on 1fr brnz grn, *straw* (R) 77.50 62.50
Nos. 1-6 (6) 363.00 268.00

VATHY (SAMOS)

Stamps of France Overprinted or Surcharged in Red, Blue or Black

1894-1900 Unwmk. *Perf. 14x13½*

1 A15 5c grn, *grnsh* (R) 5.50 4.75
2 A15 5c yel grn (I) ('00) (R) 5.50 4.75
a. Type II 55.00 55.00
3 A15 10c blk, *lav* (I) 11.00 9.50
a. Type II 35.00 25.00
4 A15 15c blue (R) 9.50 9.50
5 A15 1pi on 25c blk, *rose* 12.00 6.50
6 A15 2pi on 50c car, *rose* 20.00 16.00
7 A15 4pi on 1fr brnz grn, *straw* (R) 22.50 22.50
8 A15 8pi on 2fr brn, *az* ('00) (Bk) 50.00 50.00
9 A15 20pi on 5fr lil, *lav* ('00) (Bk) 75.00 75.00
Nos. 1-9 (9) 211.00 198.50

ZANZIBAR

Until 1906 France maintained post offices in the Sultanate of Zanzibar, but in that year Great Britain assumed direct control over this protectorate and the French withdrew their postal system.

16 Annas = 1 Rupee

A1

A2

Stamps of France Surcharged in Red, Blue or Black

1894-96 Unwmk. *Perf. 14x13½*

1 A1 ½a on 5c grn, *grnsh* 5.75 3.50
2 A1 1a on 10c blk, *lav* (Bl) 10.00 8.00
3 A1 1½a on 15c bl ('96) 15.00 13.00
a. "ANNAS" 75.00 65.00
4 A1 2a on 20c red, *grn* ('96) (Bk) 12.10 10.00
a. "ANNA" 1,600. 1,600.
5 A1 2½a on 25c blk, *rose* (Bl) 7.50 5.75
a. Double surcharge 175.00
6 A1 3a on 30c brn, *bis* ('96) (Bk) 15.00 12.00
7 A1 4a on 40c red, *straw* ('96) (Bk) 17.50 17.00
8 A1 5a on 50c car, *rose* (Bl) 25.00 21.00
9 A1 7½a on 75c vio, *org* ('96) 375.00 300.00
10 A1 10a on 1fr brnz grn, *straw* 42.50 32.50
11 A1 50a on 5fr red lil, *lav* ('96) (Bk) 240.00 200.00
Nos. 1-11 (11) 765.35 622.75

1894

12 A2 ½a & 5c on 1c blk, *lil bl* (R) 150.00 *175.00*
13 A2 1a & 10c on 3c gray, *grysh* (R) 140.00 *150.00*
14 A2 2½a & 25c on 4c cl, *lav* (Bk) 180.00 *200.00*
15 A2 5a & 50c on 20c red, *grn* (Bk) 180.00 *200.00*
16 A2 10a & 1fr on 40c red, *straw* (Bk) 350.00 *375.00*
Nos. 12-16 (5) 1,000. 1,100.

There are two distinct types of the figures 5c, four of the 25c and three of each of the others of this series.

Stamps of France Surcharged in Red, Blue or Black

1896-1900

17a A15 ½a on 5c grn, *grnsh* (C) 6.50 5.00
18 A15 ½a on 5c yel grn (I) (R) 5.75 5.00
a. Type II 6.50 5.00
19 A15 1a on 10c blk, *lav* (II) (Bl) 6.50 5.00
a. Type I 15.00 12.50
20 A15 1½a on 15c bl (R) 7.50 5.75
a. Carmine surcharge 7.50 5.75
21 A15 2a on 20c red, *grn* 5.75 5.75
a. "ZANZIBAR" double 110.00
b. "ZANZIBAR" triple 140.00
22 A15 2½a on 25c blk, *rose* (Bl) 7.50 5.75
a. Inverted surcharge 175.00
23 A15 3a on 30c brn, *bis* 7.50 5.75
24 A15 4a on 40c red, *straw* 7.50 6.50
25 A15 5a on 50c rose, *rose* (II) (Bl) 30.00 20.00
a. Type I 90.00 75.00
26 A15 10a on 1fr brnz grn, *straw* (R) 18.00 13.00
27 A15 20a on 2fr brn, *az* 22.50 13.00
a. "ZANZIBAS" 500.00 *550.00*
b. "ZANZIBAR" triple *1,200.*
28 A15 50a on 5fr lil, *lav* 55.00 47.50
a. "ZANZIBAS" *3,250.*
Nos. 17a-28 (12) 180.00 138.00

For surcharges see Nos. 50-54.

A4

A5

1897

29 A4 2½a & 25c on ½a on 5c grn, *grnsh* 1,000. 140.
30 A4 2½a & 25c on 1a on 10c *lav* *3,250.* 750.
31 A4 2½a & 25c on 1½a on 15c blue *3,250.* 625.
32 A5 5a & 50c on 3a on 30c brn, *bis* *3,250.* 550.
33 A5 5a & 50c on 4a on 40c red, *straw* *3,250.* 700.

PosteFrance 2½ Annas 25c ZANZIBAR
A6

PosteFrance 5 Annas 50c ZANZIBAR
A7

Printed on the Margins of Sheets of French Stamps

Perf. 14x13½ on one or more sides

1897

34 A6 2½a & 25c grn, *grnsh* 850.
35 A6 2½a & 25c blk, *lav* *2,900.*
36 A6 2½a & 25c blue *2,250.*
37 A7 5a & 50c brn, *bis* *2,250.*
38 A7 5a & 50c red, *straw* *2,100.*

There are 5 varieties of figures in the above surcharges.

A8

A9

A10

Surcharged in Red or Black

1902-03 *Perf. 14x13½*

39 A8 ½a on 5c grn (R) 5.00 4.25
40 A9 1a on 10c rose red ('03) 5.00 5.00
41 A9 1½a on 15c pale red ('03) 11.00 9.50
42 A9 2a on 20c brn vio ('03) 12.00 10.00
43 A9 2½a on 25c bl ('03) 13.00 12.00
44 A9 3a on 30c lil ('03) 9.50 9.50
a. 5a on 30c (error) 240.00 *275.00*
45 A10 4a on 40c red & pale bl 20.00 18.00
46 A10 5a on 50c bis brn & lav 18.00 15.00
47 A10 10a on 1fr cl & ol grn 24.00 19.00
48 A10 20a on 2fr gray vio & yel 55.00 50.00
49 A10 50a on 5fr dk bl & buff 75.00 65.00
Nos. 39-49 (11) 247.50 217.25

For see Reunion Nos. 55-59.

Nos. 23-24 Surcharged in Black:

25 2½
a

50 5
b

1fr 10
c

1904

50 A15 25c & 2½a on 4a on 40c 750.
51 A15 50c & 5a on 3a on 30c 850.
52 A15 50c & 5a on 4a on 40c 850.
53 A15 1fr & 10a on 3a on 30c 1,500.
54 A15 1fr & 10a on 4a on 40c 1,500.

Nos. 39-40, 44 Surcharged in Red or Black:

2 25c
25
d

2½
e

50c
cinq
f

1fr
dix
g

55 A8 25c & 2a on ½a on 5c (R) *2,500.* 87.50
56 A9 25c & 2½a on 1a on 10c *4,500.* 90.00
a. Inverted surcharge 950.00
57 A9 25c & 2½a on 3a on 30c *1,750.*
a. Inverted surcharge *2,000.*
b. Double surch., both invtd. *2,500.*
58 A9 50c & 5a on 3a on 30c 900.00
59 A9 1fr & 10a on 3a on 30c 1,250.

No. J1-J3 With Various Surcharges Overprinted:

"Timbre" in Red

60 D1 ½a on 5c blue 350.00

Overprinted "Affrancht" in Black

61 D1 1a on 10c brown 350.00

With Red Bars Across "CHIFFRE" and "TAXE"

62 D1 1½a on 15c green 750.00

The illustrations are not exact reproductions of the new surcharges but are merely intended to show their relative positions and general styles.

POSTAGE DUE STAMPS

Postage Due Stamps of France Surcharged in Red, Blue or Black Like Nos. 17-28

1897 Unwmk. *Perf. 14x13½*

J1 D2 ½a on 5c blue (R) 16.00 8.50
J2 D2 1a on 10c brn (Bl) 16.00 8.50
a. Inverted surcharge 110.00 *125.00*
J3 D2 1½a on 15c grn (R) 21.00 10.00
J4 D2 3a on 30c car (Bk) 21.00 16.00
J5 D2 5a on 50c lil (Bl) 21.00 17.00
a. 2½a on 50c lilac (Bl) 1,000. 875.00
Nos. J1-J5 (5) 95.00 60.00

For overprints see Nos. 60-62.

REUNION

LOCATION — An island in the Indian Ocean about 400 miles east of Madagascar
GOVT. — Department of France
AREA — 970 sq. mi.
POP. — 490,000 (est. 1974)
CAPITAL — St. Denis

The colony of Réunion became an integral part of the Republic, acquiring the same status as the departments in metropolitan France, under a law effective Jan. 1, 1947.

On Jan. 1, 1975, stamps of France replaced those inscribed or overprinted "CFA."

100 Centimes = 1 Franc

Catalogue values for unused stamps in this country are for Never Hinged items, beginning with Scott 224 in the regular postage section, Scott B15 in the semi-postal section, Scott C18 in the airpost section, and Scott J26 in the postage due section.

For French stamps inscribed "Reunion" see Nos. 949, 1507.

A1

A2

1852 Unwmk. Typo. *Imperf.*
1 A1 15c black, *blue* 32,000. 17,500.
2 A2 30c black, *blue* 30,000. 17,500.

Four varieties of each value.

The reprints are printed on a more bluish paper than the originals. They have a frame of a thick and a thin line, instead of one thick and two thin lines. Value, $42.50 each.

Stamps of French Colonies Surcharged or Overprinted in Black:

a

b

1885
3 A1(a) 5c on 40c org, *yelsh* 300.00 275.00
a. Inverted surcharge 1,050. 1,050.
4 A1(a) 25c on 40c org, *yelsh* 42.50 35.00
a. Inverted surcharge 500.00 500.00
b. Double surcharge 500.00 500.00
5 A5(a) 5c on 30c brn, *yelsh* 42.50 35.00
a. "5" inverted 2,100. 2,100.
b. Double surcharge 500.00 500.00
6 A4(a) 5c on 40c org, *yelsh* (I) 35.00 29.00
a. 5c on 40c org, *yelsh* (II) 1,850. 1,850.
b. Inverted surcharge (I) 500.00 500.00
c. Double surcharge (I) 500.00 500.00
7 A8(a) 5c on 30c brn, *yelsh* 9.25 8.50
8 A8(a) 5c on 40c ver, *straw* 92.50 77.50
a. Inverted surcharge 500.00 500.00
b. Double surcharge 500.00 500.00
9 A8(a) 10c on 40c ver, *straw* 10.50 9.25
a. Inverted surcharge 500.00 500.00
b. Double surcharge 525.00 525.00
10 A8(a) 20c on 30c brn, *yelsh* 57.50 50.00

Overprint Type "b"
With or Without Accent on "E"

1891
11 A4 40c org, *yelsh* (I) 425.00 400.00
a. 40c orange, *yelsh* (II) *5,000. 5,000.*
b. Double overprint 350.00 350.00
12 A7 80c car, *pnksh* 57.50 45.00
13 A8 30c brn, *yelsh* 32.50 32.50
14 A8 40c ver, *straw* 25.00 25.00
15 A8 75c car, *rose* 325.00 325.00
16 A8 1fr brnz grn, *straw* 35.00 32.50

Perf. 14x13½
17 A9 1c blk, *lil bl* 3.50 2.75
a. Inverted overprint 25.00 25.00
b. Double overprint 42.50 42.50
18 A9 2c brn, *buff* 4.25 3.50
a. Inverted overprint 25.00 25.00
19 A9 4c claret, *lav* 7.50 5.75
a. Inverted overprint 65.00 60.00
20 A9 5c grn, *grnsh* 7.50 5.75
a. Inverted overprint 40.00 40.00
b. Double overprint 40.00 40.00
21 A9 10c blk, *lav* 27.00 5.75
a. Inverted overprint 50.00 50.00
b. Double overprint 55.00 47.50
22 A9 15c blue 42.50 5.75
a. Inverted overprint 85.00 77.50
23 A9 20c red, *grn* 30.00 22.50
a. Inverted overprint 95.00 90.00
b. Double overprint 90.00 85.00
24 A9 25c blk, *rose* 30.00 5.50
a. Inverted overprint 95.00 90.00
25 A9 35c dp vio, *yel* 25.00 18.00
b. Inverted overprint 125.00 125.00
26 A9 40c red, *straw* 60.00 47.50
a. Inverted overprint 150.00 150.00
27 A9 75c car, *rose* 600.00 500.00
a. Inverted overprint 950.00 950.00
28 A9 1fr brnz grn, *straw* 475.00 400.00
a. Inverted overprint 1,250. 1,250.
b. Double overprint 1,000. 1,000.

The varieties "RUNION," "RUENION," "REUNIONR," "ERUNION," "EUNION," "REUNIN," "REUNIOU" and "REUNOIN" are found on most stamps of this group. See *Scott Classic Specialized Catalogue of Stamps and Covers* for detailed listings. There are also many broken letters.

For surcharges see Nos. 29-33, 53-55.

No. 23 with Additional Surcharge in Black:

c

d

e

f

1891
29 A9(c) 02c on 20c red, *grn* 9.00 9.00
a. Inverted surcharge 35.00 35.00
30 A9(c) 15c on 20c red, *grn* 10.50 10.50
a. Inverted surcharge 35.00 35.00
31 A9(d) 2c on 20c red, *grn* 3.25 3.25
32 A9(e) 2c on 20c red, *grn* 2.40 2.40
33 A9(f) 2c on 20c red, *grn* 5.00 5.00
Nos. 29-33 (5) 30.15 30.15

Navigation and Commerce — A14

1892-1905 Typo. *Perf. 14x13½*
Name of Colony in Blue or Carmine
34 A14 1c blk, *lil bl* 1.25 .95
35 A14 2c brn, *buff* 1.25 .95
36 A14 4c claret, *lav* 1.90 1.60
37 A14 5c grn, *grnsh* 5.00 1.60
38 A14 5c yel grn ('00) 1.10 1.00
39 A14 10c blk, *lav* 8.00 2.00
40 A14 10c red ('00) 2.25 2.00
41 A14 15c bl, quadrille paper 21.00 2.40
42 A14 15c gray ('00) 5.25 2.00
43 A14 20c red, *grn* 13.00 6.50
44 A14 25c blk, *rose* 14.50 2.50
a. "Reunion" double 300.00 300.00
45 A14 25c blue ('00) 16.00 16.00
46 A14 30c brn, *bis* 15.00 8.50
47 A14 40c red, *straw* 21.00 16.00
48 A14 50c car, *rose* 60.00 30.00
a. "Reunion" in red and blue 350.00 350.00
49 A14 50c brn, *az* ("Reunion" in car) ('00) 42.50 35.00
50 A14 50c brn, *az* ("Reunion" in bl) ('05) 42.50 35.00
51 A14 75c dp vio, *org* 55.00 32.50
a. "Reunion" double 275.00 275.00
52 A14 1fr brnz grn, *straw* 40.00 27.50
a. "Reunion" double 300.00 300.00
Nos. 34-52 (19) 366.50 224.00

Perf. 13½x14 stamps are counterfeits.

For surcharges and overprint see Nos. 56-59, 99-106, Q1.

French Colonies No. 52 Surcharged in Black:

g

h

j

1893
53 A9(g) 2c on 20c red, *grn* 2.00 2.00
54 A9(h) 2c on 20c red, *grn* 3.25 3.25
55 A9(j) 2c on 20c red, *grn* 14.00 14.00
Nos. 53-55 (3) 19.25 19.25

Reunion Nos. 47-48, 51-52 Surcharged in Black

1901
56 A14 5c on 40c red, *straw* 3.50 3.50
a. Inverted surcharge 27.50 27.50
b. No bar 140.00 140.00
c. Thin "5"
d. "5" inverted 450.00 450.00
57 A14 5c on 50c car, *rose* 4.50 4.50
a. Inverted surcharge 27.50 27.50
b. No bar 140.00 140.00
c. Thin "5"
58 A14 15c on 75c vio, *org* 13.00 13.00
a. Inverted surcharge 35.00 35.00
b. No bar 140.00 140.00
c. Thin "5" and small "1" 25.00 25.00
d. As "c," inverted
59 A14 15c on 1fr brnz grn, *straw* 12.00 12.00
a. Inverted surcharge 35.00 35.00
b. No bar 140.00 140.00
c. Thin "5" and small "1" 25.00 25.00
d. As "c," inverted
Nos. 56-59 (4) 33.00 33.00

Map of Réunion A19

Coat of Arms and View of St. Denis A20

View of St. Pierre — A21

1907-30 Typo.
60 A19 1c vio & car rose .20 .20
61 A19 2c brn & ultra .20 .20
62 A19 4c ol grn & red .20 .20
63 A19 5c grn & red .70 .20
64 A19 5c org & vio ('22) .20 .20
65 A19 10c car & grn 1.75 .20
66 A19 10c grn ('22) .20 .20
67 A19 10c brn red & org red, *bluish* ('26) .45 .45
68 A19 15c blk & ultra .20 .20
69 A19 15c gray grn & bl grn ('26) .20 .20
70 A19 15c bl & lt red ('28) .20 .20
71 A20 20c gray grn & bl grn .20 .20
72 A20 25c dp bl & vio brn 4.25 2.00
73 A20 25c lt brn & bl ('22) .20 .20
74 A20 30c yel brn & grn .85 .50
75 A20 30c rose & pale rose ('22) .95 .95
76 A20 30c gray & car rose ('26) .35 .35
77 A20 30c dp grn & yel grn ('28) .80 .80
78 A20 35c ol grn & bl 1.10 .65
79 A20 40c gray grn & brn ('25) .45 .45
80 A20 45c vio & car rose 1.25 .65
81 A20 45c red brn & ver ('26) .55 .55
82 A20 45c vio & red org ('28) 1.90 1.75
83 A20 50c red brn & ultra 2.90 1.00
84 A20 50c bl & ultra ('22) .95 .95
85 A20 50c yel & vio ('26) .70 .70
86 A20 60c dk bl & yel brn ('26) .70 .70
87 A20 65c vio & lt bl ('28) 1.10 1.00
88 A20 75c red & car rose .55 .50
89 A20 75c ol brn & red vio ('28) 1.60 1.60
90 A20 90c brn red & brt red ('30) 5.50 5.00
91 A21 1fr ol grn & bl 1.00 .85
92 A21 1fr blue ('26) .55 .55
93 A21 1fr yel brn & lav ('28) 1.00 .50
94 A21 1.10fr org brn & rose lil ('28) .95 .70
95 A21 1.50fr dk bl & ultra ('30) 8.50 8.50
96 A21 2fr red & grn 3.25 2.10
97 A21 3fr red vio ('30) 8.50 6.25
98 A21 5fr car & vio brn 6.25 4.00
Nos. 60-98 (39) 61.35 46.40

For surcharges see #107-121, 178-180, B1-B3.

Stamps of 1892-1900 Surcharged in Black or Carmine

1912
99 A14 5c on 2c brn, *buff* .95 .95
100 A14 5c on 15c gray (C) .85 .85
a. Inverted surcharge 125.00 125.00
101 A14 5c on 20c red, *grn* 1.10 1.10
102 A14 5c on 25c blk, *rose* (C) .95 .95
103 A14 5c on 30c brn, *bis* (C) .70 .70
104 A14 10c on 40c red, *straw* .80 .80
105 A14 10c on 50c brn, *az* (C) 3.50 3.50
106 A14 10c on 75c dp vio, *org* 6.75 6.75
Nos. 99-106 (8) 15.60 15.60

Two spacings between the surcharged numerals are found on Nos. 99 to 106.

No. 62 Surcharged

1917
107 A19 1c on 4c ol grn & red 1.25 1.25
a. Inverted surcharge 40.00 40.00
b. Double surcharge 60.00 60.00

Stamps and Types of 1907-30 Surcharged in Black or Red

1922-33
108 A20 40c on 20c grn & yel .50 .50
109 A20 50c on 45c red brn & ver ('33) .80 .65
109A A20 50c on 45c vio & red org ('33) 210.00 200.00
b. Double surcharge 1,000.
110 A20 50c on 65c vio & lt bl ('33) .80 .65
111 A20 60c on 75c red & rose .55 .55
112 A19 65c on 15c blk & ultra (R) ('25) 1.25 1.25
113 A19 85c on 15c blk & ultra (R) ('25) 1.25 1.25
114 A20 85c on 75c red & cer ('25) 1.60 1.60
115 A20 90c on 75 brn red & rose red ('27) 1.60 1.60
Nos. 108-109,110-115 (8) 8.35 8.05

Stamps and Type of 1907-30 Surcharged with New Value and Bars in Black or Red

1924-27

116 A21 25c on 5fr car & brn .80 .80
a. Double surcharge 70.00
117 A21 1.25fr on 1fr bl (R) ('26) .65 .50
a. Double surcharge 80.00
118 A21 1.50fr on 1fr ind & ultra, *bluish* ('27) .95 .85
a. Double surcharge 100.00
119 A21 3fr on 5fr dl red & lt bl ('27) 2.25 2.10
120 A21 10fr on 5fr bl grn & brn red ('27) 13.00 10.50
121 A21 20fr on 5fr blk brn & rose ('27) 16.00 12.00
Nos. 116-121 (6) 33.65 26.75

Common Design Types pictured following the introduction.

Colonial Exposition Issue
Common Design Types

1931 **Engr.** ***Perf. 12½***
Name of Country Typo. in Black

122 CD70 40c dp green 3.50 3.50
123 CD71 50c violet 3.50 3.50
124 CD72 90c red orange 3.50 3.50
125 CD73 1.50fr dull blue 3.50 3.50
Nos. 122-125 (4) 14.00 14.00

Cascade of Salazie — A22

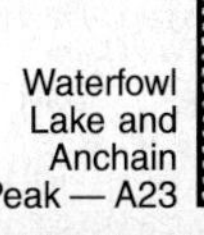

Waterfowl Lake and Anchain Peak — A23

Léon Dierx Museum, St. Denis — A24

Perf. 12, 12½ and Compound

1933-40 **Engr.**

126 A22 1c violet .20 .20
127 A22 2c dark brown .20 .20
128 A22 3c rose vio ('40) .20 .20
129 A22 4c olive green .20 .20
130 A22 5c red orange .20 .20
131 A22 10c ultramarine .20 .20
132 A22 15c black .20 .20
133 A22 20c indigo .20 .20
134 A22 25c red brown .20 .20
135 A22 30c dark green .20 .20
136 A23 35c green ('38) .35 .35
137 A23 40c ultramarine .35 .35
138 A23 40c brn blk ('40) .20 .20
139 A23 45c red violet .55 .55
140 A23 45c green ('40) .20 .20
141 A23 50c red .20 .20
142 A23 55c brn org ('38) .95 .65
143 A23 60c dull bl ('40) .20 .20
144 A23 65c olive green .70 .55
145 A23 70c ol grn ('40) .35 .35
146 A23 75c dark brown 2.90 2.75
147 A23 80c black ('38) .55 .50
148 A23 90c carmine 1.60 1.40
149 A23 90c dl rose vio ('39) .55 .55
150 A23 1fr green 1.40 .35
151 A23 1fr dk car ('38) 1.75 .35
152 A23 1fr black ('40) .45 .45
153 A24 1.25fr orange brown .50 .35
154 A24 1.25fr brt car rose ('39) .55 .55
155 A22 1.40fr pck bl ('40) .55 .55
156 A24 1.50fr ultramarine .20 .20
157 A22 1.60fr dk car rose ('40) .85 .85
158 A24 1.75fr olive green .55 .35
159 A22 1.75fr dk bl ('38) 1.10 .45
160 A24 2fr vermilion .35 .35
161 A22 2.25fr brt ultra ('39) 1.10 1.10
162 A22 2.50fr chnt ('40) .80 .80
163 A24 3fr purple .35 .35
164 A24 5fr magenta .35 .35
165 A24 10fr dark blue .70 .55
166 A24 20fr red brown 1.10 1.10
Nos. 126-166 (41) 24.30 19.85

For overprints and surcharges see Nos. 177A, 181-220, 223, C1.
60c, 1fr without "RF," see Nos. 237A-237B.

Paris International Exposition Issue
Common Design Types

1937 ***Perf. 13***

167 CD74 20c dp vio 1.60 1.60
168 CD75 30c dk grn 1.60 1.60
169 CD76 40c car rose 1.60 1.60
170 CD77 50c dk brn & blk 1.75 1.75
171 CD78 90c red 1.75 1.75
172 CD79 1.50fr ultra 1.75 1.75
Nos. 167-172 (6) 10.05 10.05

Colonial Arts Exhibition Issue
Souvenir Sheet
Common Design Type

1937 ***Imperf.***

173 CD74 3fr ultra 7.00 *8.50*

New York World's Fair Issue
Common Design Type

1939 **Engr.** ***Perf. 12½x12***

174 CD82 1.25fr car lake .95 .95
175 CD82 2.25fr ultra .95 .95

For overprints see Nos. 221-222.

St. Denis Roadstead and Marshal Pétain A25

1941 **Unwmk.** ***Perf. 11½x12***

176 A25 1fr brown .55
177 A25 2.50fr blue .55

Nos. 176-177 were issued by the Vichy government in France, but were not placed on sale in Réunion.
For surcharges, see Nos. B13-B14.

No. 144 Surcharged in Carmine

1943

177A A25a 1fr on 65c olive grn .80 .35

De Pronis Landing on Reunion — A25a

1943 ***Perf. 12½x12***

177B A25a 60c blk brn & red .35
177C A25a 80c green & blue .30
177D A25a 1.50fr dk brn red .25
177E A25a 4fr ultra & red .25
177F A25a 5fr red brn & black .35
177G A25a 10fr violet & green .35
Nos. 177B-177G,C13A-C13F (12) 3.65

300th Ann. of French settlement on Réunion.
Nos. 177B-177G were issued by the Vichy government in France, but were not placed on sale in Réunion.

Stamps of 1907 Overprinted in Blue Violet

q

1943 **Unwmk.** ***Perf. 14x13½***

178 A19(q) 4c ol gray & pale red 3.50 3.50
179 A20(q) 75c red & lil rose .95 .95
180 A21(q) 5fr car & vio brn 42.50 42.50

Stamps of 1933-40 Overprinted in Carmine, Black or Blue Violet

181 A22(r) 1c rose vio (C) .65 .65
182 A22(r) 2c blk brn (C) .65 .65
183 A22(r) 3c rose vio (C) .65 .65
184 A22(r) 4c ol yel (C) .65 .65
185 A22(r) 5c red org .65 .65
186 A22(r) 10c ultra (C) .65 .65
187 A22(r) 15c blk (C) .65 .65
188 A22(r) 20c ind (C) .65 .65
189 A22(r) 25c red brn (BlV) .85 .85
190 A22(r) 30c dk grn (C) .95 .95
191 A23(q) 35c green .55 .55
192 A23(q) 40c dl ultra (C) .55 .55
193 A23(q) 40c brn blk (C) .55 .55
194 A23(q) 45c red vio .55 .55
195 A23(q) 45c green .55 .55
196 A23(q) 50c org red .55 .55
197 A23(q) 55c brn org .55 .55
198 A23(q) 60c dl bl (C) 2.10 2.10
199 A23(q) 65c ol grn .55 .55
200 A23(q) 70c ol grn (C) 1.40 1.40
201 A23(q) 75c dk brn (C) 2.75 2.75
202 A23(q) 80c blk (C) .65 .65
203 A23(q) 90c dl rose vio .65 .65
204 A23(q) 1fr green .65 .65
205 A23(q) 1fr dk car .65 .65
206 A23(q) 1fr blk (C) 1.75 1.75
207 A24(q) 1.25fr org brn (BlV) .65 .65
208 A24(q) 1.25fr brt car rose 1.75 1.75
209 A22(r) 1.40fr pck bl (C) 1.40 1.40
210 A24(q) 1.50fr ultra (C) .65 .65
211 A22(r) 1.60fr dk car rose 1.40 1.40
212 A24(q) 1.75fr ol grn (C) 1.40 1.40
213 A22(r) 1.75fr dk bl (C) 2.75 2.75
214 A24(q) 2fr vermilion .65 .65
215 A22(r) 2.25fr brt ultra (C) 2.50 2.50
216 A22(r) 2.50fr chnt (BlV) 4.50 4.50
217 A24(q) 3fr pur (C) .65 .65
218 A24(q) 5fr brn lake (BlV) 1.40 1.40
219 A24(q) 10fr dk bl (C) 5.00 5.00
220 A24(q) 20fr red brn (BlV) 7.00 7.00

New York World's Fair Issue
Overprinted in Black or Carmine

221 CD82(q) 1.25fr car lake 2.40 2.40
222 CD82(q) 2.25fr ultra (C) 2.40 2.40
Nos. 178-222 (45) 105.45 105.45

No. 177A Overprinted Type "q"

1943 **Unwmk.** ***Perf. 12½***

223 A23 1fr on 65c ol grn .65 .65

Catalogue values for unused stamps in this section, from this point to the end of the section, are for Never Hinged items.

Produce of Réunion A26

1943 **Photo.** ***Perf. 14½x14***

224 A26 5c dull brown .20 .20
225 A26 10c dk blue .20 .20
226 A26 25c emerald .20 .20
227 A26 30c dp orange .20 .20
228 A26 40c dk slate grn .20 .20
229 A26 80c rose violet .35 .35
230 A26 1fr red brown .20 .20
231 A26 1.50fr crimson .35 .35
232 A26 2fr black .35 .35
233 A26 2.50fr ultra .50 .50
234 A26 4fr dk violet .65 .65
235 A26 5fr bister .65 .65
236 A26 10fr dark brown .95 .95
237 A26 20fr dark green 1.25 1.25
Nos. 224-237 (14) 6.25 6.25

For surcharges see Nos. 240-247.

Type of 1933-40 without "RF"

1944 **Engr.** ***Perf. 12½***

237A A23 60c dull blue .70
237B A23 1fr black & blue .70

Nos. 237A-237B were issued by the Vichy government in France, but were not placed on sale in Réunion.

Eboue Issue
Common Design Type

1945 **Engr.** ***Perf. 13***

238 CD91 2fr black .50 .50
239 CD91 25fr Prussian green .70 .70

Nos. 224, 226 and 233 Surcharged with New Values and Bars in Carmine or Black

1945 ***Perf. 14½x14***

240 A26 50c on 5c dl brn (C) .20 .20
241 A26 60c on 5c dl brn (C) .20 .20
242 A26 70c on 5c dl brn (C) .20 .20
243 A26 1.20fr on 5c dl brn (C) .35 .35
244 A26 2.40fr on 25c emer .35 .35
245 A26 3fr on 25c emer .55 .55
246 A26 4.50fr on 25c emer .55 .55
247 A26 15fr on 2.50fr ultra (C) .70 .70
Nos. 240-247 (8) 3.10 3.10

Cliff — A27

Cutting Sugar Cane — A28

Cascade A29

Banana Tree A30

Mountain Scene A31

Ship Approaching Réunion — A32

1947 **Unwmk.** **Photo.** ***Perf. 13½***

249 A27 10c org & grnsh blk .20 .20
250 A27 30c org & brt bl .20 .20
251 A27 40c org & brn .20 .20
252 A28 50c bl grn & brn .20 .20
253 A28 60c dk bl & brn .20 .20
254 A28 80c brn & ol brn .35 .35
255 A29 1fr dl bl & vio brn .35 .35
256 A29 1.20fr bl grn & gray .50 .50
257 A29 1.50fr org & vio brn .50 .50
258 A30 2fr gray bl & bl grn .50 .50
259 A30 3fr vio brn & bl grn .50 .50

260 A30 3.60fr dl red & rose red .55 .55
261 A30 4fr gray bl & buff .50 .50
262 A31 5fr rose lil & brn .70 .50
263 A31 6fr bl & brn .00 .55
264 A31 10fr org & ultra 1.75 1.10
265 A32 15fr gray bl & vio brn 2.50 2.00
266 A32 20fr bl & org 3.25 2.75
267 A32 25fr rose lil & brn 4.00 3.25
Nos. 249-267 (19) 17.75 14.90

Stamps of France, 1945-49, Surcharged in Black or Carmine

On A147

Others

1949 Unwmk. *Perf. 14x13½, 13*
268 A153 10c on 30c .20 .20
269 A153 30c on 50c .45 .20
270 A146 50c on 1fr 1.10 .70
271 A146 60c on 2fr 6.00 1.10
272 A147 1fr on 3fr 1.50 .55
273 A147 2fr on 4fr 5.75 1.25
274 A147 2.50fr on 5fr 15.00 7.75
275 A147 3fr on 6fr 1.75 1.10
276 A147 4fr on 10fr 1.60 1.25
277 A162 5fr on 20fr (C) 7.75 1.10
278 A147 6fr on 12fr 21.00 1.60
279 A160 7fr on 12fr 7.00 2.25
280 A165 8fr on 25fr (C) 29.00 2.25
281 A165 10fr on 25fr (C) 2.10 1.10
282 A174 11fr on 18fr (C) 12.00 1.60
Nos. 268-282 (15) 112.20 24.00

The letters "C. F. A." are the initials of "Colonies Francaises d'Afrique," referring to the currency which is expressed in French Africa francs.

The surcharge on Nos. 277, 279, 282 includes two bars.

1950 *Perf. 14x13½*
283 A182 10c on 50c bl, red & yel .55 .55
284 A182 1fr on 2fr grn, yel & red (#619) 7.75 2.25
285 A147 2fr on 5fr lt grn 13.50 2.75
Nos. 283-285 (3) 21.80 5.55

Surcharged Type "a" and Bars

1950-51 *Perf. 13*
286 A188 5fr on 20fr dk red 7.75 1.10
287 A185 8fr on 25fr dp ultra ('51) 7.75 1.10

Stamps of France, 1951-52, Surcharged in Black or Red

1951-52 *Perf. 14x13½, 13*
288 A182 50c on 1fr bl, red & yel .55 .55
289 A182 1fr on 2fr vio bl, red & yel (#662) .55 .55
290 A147 2fr on 5fr dl vio 3.25 1.50
291 A147 3fr on 6fr grn 6.50 1.25
292 A220 5fr on 20fr dk pur (R; '52) 2.25 1.25
293 A147 6fr on 12fr red org ('52) 7.00 1.60
294 A215 8fr on 40fr vio (R) ('52) 5.00 .55
295 A147 9fr on 18fr cerise 16.00 3.25
296 A208 15fr on 30fr ind (R) 8.50 1.75
Nos. 288-296 (9) 49.60 12.25

The surcharge on Nos. 292, 294 and 296 include two bars.

France No. 697 Surcharged Type "a" in Black

1953 *Perf. 14x13½*
297 A182 50c on 1fr blk, red & yel .20 .20

France No. 688 Surcharged in Black

Perf. 13
298 A230 3fr on 6fr dp plum & car .90 .55

France Nos. 703 and 705 Surcharged Type "a" in Red or Blue

1954
299 A235 8fr on 40fr (R) 27.50 6.50
300 A235 20fr on 75fr 62.50 27.50

France Nos. 698, 721, 713, and 715 Surcharged Type "a" in Black

Perf. 14x13½, 13
301 A182 1fr on 2fr 3.50 1.60
302 A241 4fr on 10fr 3.25 1.10
303 A238 8fr on 40fr 7.75 .55
304 A238 20fr on 75fr 10.00 1.25

The surcharge on Nos. 303 and 304 includes two bars.

France Nos. 737, 719 and 722-724 Surcharged in Black or Red
305 A182(a) 1fr on 2fr .35 .35
306 A241(a) 2fr on 6fr (R) .55 .35
307 A242(a) 6fr on 12fr 7.00 1.25
308 A241(b) 9fr on 18fr 8.25 3.75
309 A241(a) 10fr on 20fr 6.00 1.10
Nos. 299-309 (11) 136.65 45.30

The surcharge on Nos. 306-308 includes two bars; on No. 309 three bars.

France No. 720 Surcharged Type "c" in Red, Bars at Lower Left

1955 *Perf. 13*
310 A241 3fr on 8fr brt bl & dk grn 1.10 .90

France Nos. 785, 774-779 Surcharged Type "a" in Black or Red

Perf. 14x13½, 13

1955-56 Typo., Engr.
311 A182 50c on 1fr .20 .20
312 A265 2fr on 6fr ('56) .95 .55
313 A265 3fr on 8fr .80 .35
314 A265 4fr on 10fr .95 .35
315 A265 5fr on 12fr (R) .95 .35
316 A265 6fr on 18fr (R) .80 .35
317 A265 10fr on 25fr 1.10 .35
Nos. 311-317 (7) 5.75 2.50

The surcharge on Nos. 312-317 includes two bars.

France Nos. 801-804 Surcharged Type "a" or "b" in Black or Red

1956 Engr. *Perf. 13*
318 A280(a) 8fr on 30fr (R) 4.00 .90
319 A280(b) 9fr on 40fr 5.50 2.40
320 A280(a) 15fr on 50fr 7.00 1.25
321 A280(a) 20fr on 75fr (R) 6.50 1.75
Nos. 318-321 (4) 23.00 6.30

The surcharge on Nos. 318, 319 and 321 includes two bars.

France Nos. 837 and 839 Surcharged Type "a" in Red

1957 *Perf. 13*
322 A294 7fr on 15fr .90 .50
323 A265 17fr on 70fr 5.00 1.60

The surcharge on Nos. 322-323 includes two bars.

No. 322 has three types of "7" in the sheet of 50. There are 34 of the "normal" 7; 10 of a slightly thinner 7, and 6 of a slightly thicker 7.

France Nos. 755-756, 833-834, 851-855, 908, 949 Surcharged in Black or Red Type "a", "b" or

d

Typographed, Engraved

1957-60 *Perf. 14x13½, 13*
324 A236(b) 2fr on 6fr .20 .20
325 A302(b) 3fr on 10fr ('58) .35 .35
326 A236(b) 4fr on 12fr 2.75 .55
327 A236(b) 5fr on 10fr 1.60 .80
328 A303(b) 6fr on 18fr .90 .35
329 A302(a) 9fr on 25fr (R) ('58) .90 .45
330 A252(a) 10fr on 20fr (R) 1.25 .20
331 A252(a) 12fr on 25fr 5.00 .35
332 A303(a) 17fr on 35fr 2.25 1.25
333 A302(a) 20fr on 50fr 1.25 .55
334 A302(a) 25fr on 85fr 3.00 1.10
335 A339(d) 50fr on 1fr ('60) 2.25 .55
Nos. 324-335 (12) 21.70 6.70

The surcharge includes two bars on Nos. 324, 326-327, 329-331, 333 and 335.

France Nos. 973, 939 and 968 Surcharged

e

f

1961-63 Typo. *Perf. 14x13½*
336 A318(e) 2fr on 5c multi .20 .20
337 A336(e) 5fr on 10c brt grn .35 .35
338 A336(b) 5fr on 10c brt grn ('63) 1.10 .55
339 A349(f) 12fr on 25c lake & gray .20 .20
Nos. 336-339 (4) 1.85 1.30

The surcharge on No. 337 includes three bars. No. 338 has "b" surcharge and two bars.

France Nos. 943, 941 and 946 Surcharged "CFA" and New Value in Two Lines in Black or Red

Engraved, Typographed

1961 Unwmk. *Perf. 13, 14x13½*
340 A338 7fr on 15c .80 .55
341 A337 10fr on 20c .20 .20
342 A339 20fr on 50c (R) 13.00 3.25
Nos. 340-342 (3) 14.00 4.00

Surcharge on No. 342 includes 3 bars.

France Nos. 1047-1048 Surcharged with New Value, "CFA" and Two Bars

1963, Jan. 2 Engr. *Perf. 13*
343 A394 12fr on 25c .70 .70
344 A395 25fr on 50c .70 .70

1st television connection of the US and Europe through the Telstar satellite, July 11-12, 1962.

France Nos. 1040-1041, 1007 and 1009 Surcharged Similarly to Type "e"

Typographed, Engraved

1963 *Perf. 14x13½, 13*
345 A318 2fr on 5c .20 .20
346 A318 5fr on 10c .20 .20
347 A372 7fr on 15c .45 .35
348 A372 20fr on 45c .70 .55
Nos. 345-348 (4) 1.55 1.30

Two-line surcharge on No. 345; No. 347 has currency expressed in capital "F" and two heavy bars through old value; two thin bars on No. 348.

France No. 1078 Surcharged Type "e" in Two Lines in Dark Blue

1964, Feb. 8 Engr. *Perf. 13*
349 CD118 12fr on 25c .90 .80

"PHILATEC," Intl. Philatelic and Postal Techniques Exhib., Paris, June 5-21, 1964.

France Nos. 1092, 1094 and 1102 Surcharged with New Value and "CFA"

Typographed, Engraved

1964 *Perf. 14x13½, 13*
350 A318 1fr on 2c .20 .20
351 A318 6fr on 18c .20 .20
352 A420 35fr on 70c 1.10 .70
Nos. 350-352 (3) 1.50 1.10

Surcharge on No. 352 includes two bars.

France Nos. 1095, 1126, 1070 Surcharged with New Value and "CFA"

1965
353 A318 15fr on 30c .35 .20
354 A440 25fr on 50c .80 .70
355 A408 30fr on 60c 1.10 .80
Nos. 353-355 (3) 2.25 1.70

Two bars obliterate old denomination on Nos. 354-355.

Etienne Regnault, "Le Taureau" and Coast of Reunion — A33

1965, Oct. 3 Engr. *Perf. 13*
356 A33 15fr bluish blk & dk car .70 .45

Tercentenary of settlement of Reunion.

France No. 985 Surcharged with New Value, Two Bars and "CFA"

1966, Feb. 13 Engr. *Perf. 13*
357 A360 10fr on 20c bl & car 1.10 .55

French Satellite A-1 Issue

France Nos. 1137-1138 Surcharged with New Value, Two Bars and "CFA" and Red

1966, Mar. 27 Engr. *Perf. 13*
358 CD121 15fr on 30c .90 .80
359 CD121 30fr on 60c 1.00 .90
a. Strip of 2 + label 2.10 2.00

France Nos. 1142, 1143, 1101 and 1127 Surcharged with New Value, "CFA" and Two Bars

1967-69 Typo. *Perf. 14x13*
360 A446 2fr on 5c bl & red .20 .20

Photo. *Perf. 13*
360A A446 10fr on 20c multi ('69) .20 .20

Engr.
361 A421 20fr on 40c multi .90 .70
362 A439 30fr on 60c bl & red brn 1.90 1.25

EXPO '67 Issue

France No. 1177 Surcharged with New Value, "CFA" and Two Bars

1967, June 12 Engr. *Perf. 13*
363 A473 30fr on 60c dl bl & bl grn 1.90 1.25

EXPO '67, Montreal, Apr. 28-Oct. 27.

Lions Issue

France No. 1196 Surcharged in Violet Blue with New Value, "CFA" and Two Bars

1967, Oct. 29 Engr. *Perf. 13*
364 A485 20fr on 40c 2.25 1.00

50th anniversary of Lions International.

France No. 1130 Surcharged in Violet Blue with New Value, "CFA" and Two Bars

1968, Feb. 26 Engr. *Perf. 13*
365 A440 50fr on 1fr 2.00 1.25

France No. 1224 Surcharged with New Value, "CFA" and Two Bars

1968, Oct. 21 Engr. *Perf. 13*
366 A508 20fr on 40c multi 1.10 .70

20 years of French Polar expeditions.

France Nos. 1230-1231 Surcharged with New Value, "CFA" and Two Bars

1969, Apr. 13 Engr. *Perf. 13*
367 A486 15fr on 30c green .45 .35
368 A486 20fr on 40c dp car .55 .20

France No. 1255 Surcharged with New Value, "CFA" and Two Bars

1969, Aug. 18 Engr. *Perf. 13*
370 A526 35fr on 70c multi 1.10 1.00

Napoleon Bonaparte (1769-1821).

France No. 1293 Surcharged with New Value and "CFA"

1971, Jan. 16 Engr. *Perf. 13*
371 A555 25fr on 50c rose car .55 .20

France No. 1301 Surcharged with New Value and "CFA"

1971, Apr. 13 Engr. *Perf. 13*
372 A562 40fr on 80c multi 1.40 1.10

France No. 1309 Surcharged with New Value, "CFA" and 2 Bars

1971, June 5 Engr. *Perf. 13*
373 A569 15fr on 40c multi .70 .55

Aid for rural families.

France No. 1312 Surcharged with New Value and "CFA"

1971, Aug. 30 Engr. *Perf. 13*
374 A571 45fr on 90c multi .90 .70

France No. 1320 Surcharged with New Value and "CFA"

1971, Oct. 18
375 A573 45fr on 90c multi 1.10 .80

40th anniversary of the first assembly of presidents of artisans' guilds.

Réunion Chameleon A34

1971, Nov. 8 Photo. *Perf. 13*
376 A34 25fr multi 1.10 .70

Nature protection.

Common Design Type and

De Gaulle in Brazzaville, 1944 — A35

Designs: No. 377, Gen. de Gaulle, 1940. No. 379, de Gaulle entering Paris, 1944. No. 380, Pres. de Gaulle, 1970.

1971, Nov. 9 Engr.
377 CD134 25fr black 1.10 1.10
378 A35 25fr ultra 1.10 1.10
379 A35 25fr rose red 1.10 1.10
380 CD134 25fr black 1.10 1.10
a. Strip of 4 + label 6.50 6.50

Charles de Gaulle (1890-1970), president of France. Nos. 377-380 printed se-tenant in sheets of 20 containing 5 strips of 4 plus labels with Cross of Lorraine and inscription.

France No. 1313 Surcharged with New Value and "CFA"

1972, Jan. 17 Engr. *Perf. 13*
381 A570 50fr on 1.10fr multi 1.10 .90

Map of South Indian Ocean, Penguin and Ships — A36

1972, Jan. 31 Engr. *Perf. 13*
382 A36 45fr blk, bl & ocher 1.75 1.75

Bicentenary of the discovery of the Crozet and Kerguelen Islands.

France No. 1342 Surcharged with New Value, "CFA" and 2 Bars in Red

1972, May. 8 Engr. *Perf. 13*
383 A590 15fr on 40c red .70 .70

20th anniv. of Blood Donors' Assoc. of Post and Telecommunications Employees.

France Nos. 1345-1346 Surcharged with New Value, "CFA" and 2 Bars

1972, June 5 Typo. *Perf. 14x13*
384 A593 15fr on 30c multi .35 .35
385 A593 25fr on 50c multi .55 .45

Introduction of postal code system.

France No. 1377 Surcharged with New Value, "CFA" and 2 Bars in Ultramarine

1973, June 12 Engr. *Perf. 13*
386 A620 45fr on 90c multi 1.50 1.00

France Nos. 1374, 1336 Surcharged with New Value and "CFA" in Ultramarine or Red

1973 Engr. *Perf. 13*
387 A617 50fr on 1fr multi (U) .90 .70
388 A586 100fr on 2fr multi (R) 1.40 .80

On No. 388, two bars cover "2.00".
Issue dates: 50fr, June 24; 100fr, Oct. 13.

France No. 1231C Surcharged with New Value, "CFA" and 2 Bars

1973, Nov. Typo. *Perf. 14x13*
389 A486 15fr on 30c bl grn 3.75 .55

France No. 1390 Surcharged with New Value, "CFA" and 2 Bars in Red

1974, Jan. 20 Engr. *Perf. 13*
390 A633 25fr on 50c multi .55 .55

ARPHILA 75 Phil. Exhib., Paris, June 1975.

France Nos. 1394-1397 Surcharged "100 FCFA" in Black, Ultramarine or Brown

Engr. (#391, 393), Photo. (#392, 394)
1974 *Perf. 12x13, 13x12*
391 A637 100fr on 2fr (Bk) 1.90 1.10
392 A638 100fr on 2fr (U) 2.40 1.90
393 A639 100fr on 2fr (Br) 2.40 1.90
394 A640 100fr on 2fr (U) 2.40 1.90
Nos. 391-394 (4) 9.10 6.80

Nos. 391-394 printed in sheets of 25 with alternating labels publicizing "ARPHILA 75," Paris June 6-16, 1975.
Two bars obliterate original denomination on Nos. 391-393.

France No. 1401 Surcharged "45 FCFA" and 2 Bars in Red

1974, Apr. 29 Engr. *Perf. 13*
395 A644 45fr on 90c multi 1.40 1.10

Reorganized sea rescue organization.

France No. 1415 Surcharged with New Value, 2 Bars and "FCFA" in Ultramarine

1974, Oct. 6 Engr. *Perf. 13*
396 A657 60fr on 1.20fr multi 1.25 1.00

Centenary of Universal Postal Union.

France Nos. 1292A and 1294B Surcharged with New Value and "FCFA" in Ultramarine

1974, Oct. 19 Typo. *Perf. 14x13*
397 A555 30fr on 60c grn 1.25 1.25

Engr.
Perf. 13
398 A555 40fr on 80c car rose 1.50 1.25

SEMI-POSTAL STAMPS

No. 65 Surcharged in Black or Red

1915 Unwmk. *Perf. 14x13½*
B1 A19 10c + 5c (Bk) 110.00 80.00
a. Inverted surcharge 250.00 200.00
B2 A19 10c + 5c (R) 1.10 1.10
a. Inverted surcharge 55.00 55.00

No. 65 Surcharged in Red

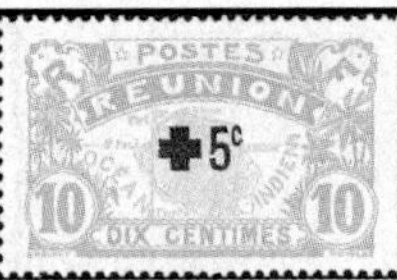

1916
B3 A19 10c + 5c 1.25 1.25

Curie Issue
Common Design Type

1938 *Perf. 13*
B4 CD80 1.75fr + 50c brt ultra 10.00 10.00

French Revolution Issue
Common Design Type

1939 Photo. Unwmk.
Name and Value Typo. in Black
B5 CD83 45c + 25c grn 9.25 9.25
B6 CD83 70c + 30c brn 9.25 9.25
B7 CD83 90c + 35c red org 9.25 9.25
B8 CD83 1.25fr + 1fr rose pink 9.25 9.25
B9 CD83 2.25fr + 2fr blue 9.25 9.25
Nos. B5-B9 (5) 46.25 46.25

Common Design Type and

Artillery Colonel — SP1

Colonial Infantry SP2

1941 Unwmk. *Perf. 13½*
B10 SP1 1fr + 1fr red 1.00
B11 CD86 1.50fr + 3fr claret 1.00
B12 SP2 2.50fr + 1fr blue 1.00
Nos. B10-B12 (3) 3.00

Nos. B10-B12 were issued by the Vichy government in France, but were not placed on sale in Reunion.

Nos. 176-177 Surcharged in Black or Red

1944 Engr. *Perf. 12½x12*
B13 50c + 1.50fr on 2.50fr deep blue (R) .55
B14 + 2.50fr on 1fr yel brn .55

Colonial Development Fund.
Nos. B13-B14 were issued by the Vichy government in France, but were not placed on sale in Réunion.

Catalogue values for unused stamps in this section, from this point to the end of the section, are for Never Hinged items.

Red Cross Issue
Common Design Type

1944 *Perf. 14½x14*
B15 CD90 5fr + 20fr black .85 .85

The surtax was for the French Red Cross and national relief.

France Nos. B365-B366 Surcharged with New Value, "CFA" and Two Bars

1962, Dec. 10 Engr. *Perf. 13*
B16 SP219 10 + 5fr on 20 + 10c 1.90 1.90
B17 SP219 12 + 5fr on 25 + 10c 2.00 2.00

The surtax was for the Red Cross.

France Nos. B374-B375 Surcharged with New Value, "CFA" and Two Bars in Red

1963, Dec. 9
B18 SP223 10 + 5fr on 20 + 10c 2.40 2.40
B19 SP223 12 + 5fr on 25 + 10c 2.40 2.40

Centenary of the Intl. Red Cross. The surtax was for the Red Cross.

France Nos. B385-B386 Surcharged with New Value, "CFA" and Two Bars in Dark Blue

1964, Dec. 13 Unwmk. *Perf. 13*
B20 SP230 10 + 5fr on 20 + 10c 1.25 1.25
B21 SP230 12 + 5fr on 25 + 10c 1.40 1.40

Jean Nicolas Corvisart (1755-1821) and Dominique Larrey (1766-1842), physicians. The surtax was for the Red Cross.

France Nos. B392-B393 Surcharged with New Value, "CFA" and Two Bars

1965, Dec. 12 Engr. *Perf. 13*
B22 SP233 12 + 5fr on 25 + 10c 1.10 1.10
B23 SP233 15 + 5fr on 30 + 10c 1.10 1.10

The surtax was for the Red Cross.

France Nos. B402-B403 Surcharged with New Value, "CFA" and Two Bars

1966, Dec. 11 Engr. *Perf. 13*
B24 SP237 12 + 5fr on 25 + 10c 1.10 1.10
B25 SP237 15 + 5fr on 30 + 10c 1.10 1.10

The surtax was for the Red Cross.

France Nos. B409-B410 Surcharged with New Value, "CFA" and Two Bars

1967, Dec. 17 Engr. *Perf. 13*
B26 SP240 12 + 5fr on 25 + 10c 2.10 2.10
B27 SP240 15 + 5fr on 30 + 10c 2.75 2.75

Surtax for the Red Cross.

France Nos. B421-B424 Surcharged with New Value, "CFA" and Two Bars

1968-69 Engr. *Perf. 13*
B28 SP244 12 + 5fr on 25 + 10c 1.25 1.10
B29 SP244 15 + 5fr on 30 + 10c 1.40 1.10
B30 SP244 20 + 7fr on 40 + 15c ('69) 1.10 1.10
B31 SP244 20 + 7fr on 40 + 15c ('69) 1.10 1.10
Nos. B28-B31 (4) 4.85 4.40

The surtax was for the Red Cross.

France No. B425 Surcharged with New Value, "CFA" and Two Bars

1969, Mar. 17 Engr. *Perf. 13*
B32 SP245 15fr + 5fr on 30c + 10c 1.10 1.10

Stamp Day.

France No. B440 Surcharged with New Value, "CFA" and Two Bars

1970, Mar. 16 Engr. *Perf. 13*
B33 SP249 20fr + 5fr on 40c + 10c .90 .80

Stamp day.

France Nos. B443-B444 Surcharged with New Value "CFA" and Two Bars

1970, Dec. 14 Engr. *Perf. 13*
B34 SP252 20 + 7fr on 40 + 15c 2.00 1.60
B35 SP252 20 + 7fr on 40 + 15c 2.00 1.90

The surtax was for the Red Cross.

France No. B451 Surcharged with New Value, "CFA" and Two Bars

1971, Mar. 29 Engr. *Perf. 13*
B36 SP254 25fr + 5fr on 50c + 10c .90 .70

Stamp Day.

France Nos. B452-B453 Surcharged with New Value, "CFA" and Two Bars

1971, Dec. 13
B37 SP255 15fr + 5fr on 30c + 10c 1.10 1.10
B38 SP255 25fr + 5fr on 50c + 10c 1.10 1.10

The surtax was for the Red Cross.

France No. B460 Surcharged with New Value and "CFA"

1972, Mar. 20 Engr. *Perf. 13*
B39 SP257 25fr + 5fr on 50c + 10c .90 .90

Stamp Day.

France Nos. B461-B462 Surcharged with New Value, "CFA" and Two Bars in Red or Green

1972, Dec. 16 Engr. *Perf. 13*
B40 SP258 15 + 5fr on 30 + 10c .90 .90
B41 SP258 25 + 5fr on 50 + 10c (G) 1.00 1.00

Surtax was for the Red Cross.

France No. B470 Surcharged with New Value, "CFA" and Two Bars in Red

1973, Mar. 26 Engr. *Perf. 13*
B42 SP260 25fr +5fr on 50c +10c 1.10 1.10

Stamp Day.

France Nos. B471-B472 Surcharged with New Value, "CFA" and Two Bars in Red

1973, Dec. 3 Engr. *Perf. 13*
B43 SP261 15 +5fr on 30c +10c 1.10 1.10
B44 SP261 25 +5fr on 50c +10c 1.10 1.10

Surtax was for the Red Cross.

France No. B477 Surcharged "25 + 5 FCFA"

1974, Mar. 11 Engr. *Perf. 13*
B45 SP263 25fr + 5fr on 50c + 10c .80 .80

Stamp Day.

France Nos. B479-B480 Surcharged with New Value, "FCFA" and Two Bars in Green or Red

1974, Nov. 30 Engr. *Perf. 13*
B46 SP265 30 + 7fr on 60 + 15c (G) 1.10 1.10
B47 SP266 40 + 7fr on 80 + 15c (R) 1.10 1.10

Surtax was for the Red Cross.

AIR POST STAMPS

No. 141 Overprinted in Blue

1937, Jan. 23 Unwmk. *Perf. 12½*
C1 A23 50c red 225.00 200.00
a. Vert. pair, one without overprint 1,300. 1,300.
b. Inverted overprint 3,500.

Flight of the "Roland Garros" from Reunion to France by aviators Laurent, Lenier and Touge in Jan.-Feb., 1937.

Airplane and Landscape — AP2

1938, Mar. 1 Engr. *Perf. 12½*
C2 AP2 3.65fr slate blue & car .70 .55
C3 AP2 6.65fr brown & org red .70 .55
C4 AP2 9.65fr car & ultra .70 .55
C5 AP2 12.65fr brown & green 1.40 1.10
Nos. C2-C5 (4) 3.50 2.75

For overprints see Nos. C14-C17.

Plane and Bridge over East River AP3

Plane and Landscape AP4

1942, Oct. 19 *Perf. 12x12½*
C6 AP3 50c olive & pur .20
C7 AP3 1fr dk bl & scar .20
C8 AP3 2fr brn & blk .35
C9 AP3 3fr rose lil & grn .65
C10 AP3 5fr red org & red brn .65

Frame Engr., Center Photo.

C11 AP4 10fr dk grn, red org & vio .65
C12 AP4 20fr dk bl, brn vio & red .65
C13 AP4 50fr brn car, Prus grn & bl .95
Nos. C6-C13 (8) 4.30

Nos. C6-C13 were issued by the Vichy government in France, but were not placed on sale in Réunion.

De Poivre — AP4a

1943 *Perf. 12½x12*
C13A AP4a 1fr sepia & red .20
C13B AP4a 2fr green & blue .20
C13C AP4a 3fr dk brown red .20
C13D AP4a 5fr ultramarine & red .35
C13E AP4a 10fr red brown & black .35
C13F AP4a 20fr violet & green .50
Nos. C13A-C13F (6) 1.80

300th Ann. of French settlement on Réunion.
Nos. C13A-C13F were issued by the Vichy government in France, but were not placed on sale in Réunion.

Nos. C2-C5 Overprinted in Black or Carmine

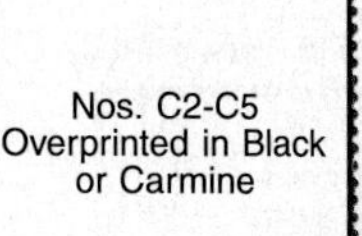

1943 Unwmk. *Perf. 12½*
C14 AP2 3.65fr sl bl & car 3.50 3.50
C15 AP2 6.65fr brn & org red 3.50 3.50
C16 AP2 9.65fr car & ultra (C) 3.50 3.50
C17 AP2 12.65fr brn & grn 3.50 3.50
Nos. C14-C17 (4) 14.00 14.00

Catalogue values for unused stamps in this section, from this point to the end of the section, are for Never Hinged items.

Common Design Type

1944 Photo. *Perf. 14½x14*
C18 CD87 1fr dk org .25 .25
C19 CD87 1.50fr brt red .25 .25
C20 CD87 5fr brn red .35 .35
C21 CD87 10fr black .55 .55
C22 CD87 25fr ultra .65 .65
C23 CD87 50fr dk grn .65 .65
C24 CD87 100fr plum .95 .95
Nos. C18-C24 (7) 3.65 3.65

Victory Issue
Common Design Type

1946, May 8 Engr. *Perf. 12½*
C25 CD92 8fr olive gray .70 .70

European victory of the Allied Nations in WWII.

Chad to Rhine Issue
Common Design Types

1946, June 6
C26 CD93 5fr orange .80 .80
C27 CD94 10fr sepia .80 .80
C28 CD95 15fr grnsh blk .80 .80
C29 CD96 20fr lilac rose 1.10 1.10
C30 CD97 25fr greenish blue 1.10 1.10
C31 CD98 50fr green 1.25 1.25
Nos. C26-C31 (6) 5.85 5.85

Shadow of Plane — AP5

Plane over Réunion — AP6

Air View of Réunion and Shadow of Plane — AP7

Perf. 13x12½
1947, Mar. 24 Photo. Unwmk.
C32 AP5 50fr ol grn & bl gray 5.75 5.75
C33 AP6 100fr dk brn & org 9.25 8.50
C34 AP7 200fr dk bl & org 10.50 9.25
Nos. C32-C34 (3) 25.50 23.50

France, Nos. C18-C21 Surcharged and Bars, in Carmine or Black

c

1949 Unwmk. *Perf. 13*
C35 AP7 20fr on 40fr (C) 2.75 1.10
C36 AP8 25fr on 50fr 3.50 1.10
C37 AP9 50fr on 100fr (C) 7.75 3.25
C38 AP10 100fr on 200fr 42.50 16.00
Nos. C35-C38 (4) 56.50 21.45

France Nos. C24, C26 and C27 Surcharged Type "c" and Bars in Black

1949-51
C39 AP12 100fr on 200fr ('51) 100.00 21.00
C40 AP12 200fr on 500fr 42.50 16.00
C41 AP13 500fr on 1000fr ('51) 250.00 175.00
Nos. C39-C41 (3) 392.50 212.00

France Nos. C29-C32 Surcharged "CFA," New Value and Bars in Blue or Red

1954, Feb. 10
C42 AP15(c) 50fr on 100fr 2.10 1.10
C43 AP15 100fr on 200fr (R) 4.25 .70
C44 AP15(c) 200fr on 500fr 32.50 11.00
C45 AP15 500fr on 1000fr 26.00 10.00
Nos. C42-C45 (4) 64.85 22.80

France Nos. C35-C36 Surcharged "CFA," New Values and Bars in Red or Black

1957-58 Engr. *Perf. 13*
C46 AP17 200fr on 500fr (R) 20.00 5.75
C47 AP17 500fr on 1000fr ('58) 20.00 10.50

France Nos. C37, C39-C40 Surcharged "CFA," New Value and Bars in Red or Black

1961-64
C48 AP15 100fr on 2fr 5.00 1.10
C49 AP17 200fr on 5fr 5.00 1.10
C50 AP17 500fr on 10fr (B;'64) 12.00 5.00
Nos. C48-C50 (3) 22.00 7.20

France No. C41 Surcharged "CFA," New Value and Two Bars in Red

1967, Jan. 27 Engr. *Perf. 13*
C51 AP17 100fr on 2fr sl bl & ind 1.60 .55

France No. C45 Surcharged in Red with "CFA," New Value and Two Bars in Red

1972, May 14 Engr. *Perf. 13*
C52 AP21 200fr on 5fr multi 4.00 1.40

AIR POST SEMI-POSTAL STAMPS

French Revolution Issue
Common Design Type

1939 Unwmk. *Perf. 13*
Name and Value Typo. in Orange
CB1 CD83 3.65fr + 4fr brn blk 17.50 17.50

Felix Guyon Hospital, St. Denis — SPAP1

Perf. 13½x12½
1942, June 22 Engr.
CB2 SPAP1 1.50fr + 3.50fr lt green .55
CB3 SPAP1 2fr + 6fr yellow brown .55

Native children's welfare fund.
Nos. CB2-CB3 were issued by the Vichy government in France, but were not placed on sale in Réunion.

Colonial Education Fund
Common Design Type

1942, June 22
CB4 CD86a 1.20fr + 1.80fr blue & red .55

No. CB4 was issued by the Vichy government in France, but was not placed on sale in Réunion.

POSTAGE DUE STAMPS

D1 D2

1889-92 Unwmk. Type-set *Imperf.*
Without Gum
J1 D1 5c black 17.50 9.00
J2 D1 10c black 21.00 9.00
J3 D1 15c black ('92) 42.50 27.50
J4 D1 20c black 32.50 16.00
J5 D1 30c black 30.00 16.00
Nos. J1-J5 (5) 143.50 77.50

Ten varieties of each value.
Nos. J1-J2, J4-J5 issued on yellowish paper in 1889; Nos. J1-J3, J5 on bluish white paper in 1892.
Nos. J1-J5 exist with double impression. Values $100-$150.

1907 **Typo.** ***Perf. 14x13½***

J6 D2 5c carmine, *yel* .50 .50
J7 D2 10c blue, *bl* .50 .50
J8 D2 15c black, *bluish* .80 .80
J9 D2 20c carmine .80 .80
J10 D2 30c green, *grnsh* 1.25 1.25
J11 D2 50c red, *green* 1.40 1.40
J12 D2 60c carmine, *bl* 1.40 1.40
J13 D2 1fr violet 1.90 1.90
Nos. J6-J13 (8) 8.55 8.55

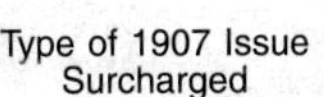

Type of 1907 Issue Surcharged

1927

J14 D2 2fr on 1fr org red 7.75 7.75
J15 D2 3fr on 1fr org brn 7.75 7.75

Arms of Réunion D3

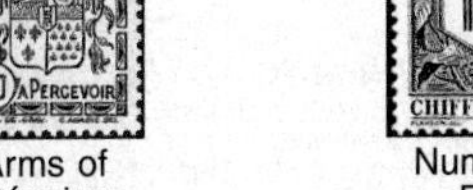

Numeral D4

1933 **Engr.** ***Perf. 13x13½***

J16 D3 5c deep violet .20 .20
J17 D3 10c dark green .20 .20
J18 D3 15c orange brown .20 .20
J19 D3 20c light red .20 .20
J20 D3 30c olive green .20 .20
J21 D3 50c ultramarine .55 .55
J22 D3 60c black brown .55 .55
J23 D3 1fr light violet .55 .55
J24 D3 2fr deep blue .55 .55
J25 D3 3fr carmine .80 .80
Nos. J16-J25 (10) 4.00 4.00

Catalogue values for unused stamps in this section, from this point to the end of the section, are for Never Hinged items.

1947 **Unwmk.** **Photo.** ***Perf. 13***

J26 D4 10c dark violet .20 .20
J27 D4 30c brown .20 .20
J28 D4 50c blue green .20 .20
J29 D4 1fr orange .30 .30
J30 D4 2fr red violet .30 .30
J31 D4 3fr red brown .45 .45
J32 D4 4fr blue .80 .80
J33 D4 5fr henna brown .95 .95
J34 D4 10fr slate green .95 .95
J35 D4 20fr violet blue .95 .60
Nos. J26-J35 (10) 5.30 4.95

France, Nos. J83-J92 Surcharged in Black

1949-53

J36 D5 10c on 1fr brt ultra .20 .20
J37 D5 50c on 2fr turq bl .35 .35
J38 D5 1fr on 3fr brn org .45 .35
J39 D5 2fr on 4fr dp vio .45 .35
J40 D5 3fr on 5fr brt pink 5.00 2.00
J41 D5 5fr on 10fr red org .80 .55
J42 D5 10fr on 20fr ol bis 1.60 1.50
J43 D5 20fr on 50fr dk grn ('50) 10.00 4.00
J44 D5 50fr on 100fr dp grn ('53) 24.00 10.00
Nos. J36-J44 (9) 42.85 19.30

Same Surcharge on France Nos. J93, J95-J96

1962-63 **Typo.** ***Perf. 14x13½***

J46 D6 1fr on 5c brt pink ('63) 2.10 .90
J47 D6 10fr on 20c ol bis ('63) 4.25 2.50
J48 D6 20fr on 50c dk grn 16.00 10.00
Nos. J46-J48 (3) 22.35 13.40

France Nos. J98-J102, J104-J105 Surcharged with New Value and "CFA"

1964-71 **Unwmk.** ***Perf. 14x13½***

J49 D7 1fr on 5c .20 .20
J50 D7 5fr on 10c .20 .20
J51 D7 7fr on 15c .35 .35
J52 D7 10fr on 20c ('71) 1.10 .45
J53 D7 15fr on 30c .45 .35
J54 D7 20fr on 50c .55 .45
J55 D7 50fr on 1fr 1.10 1.00
Nos. J49-J55 (7) 3.95 3.00

PARCEL POST STAMP

No. 40 Overprinted

1906 **Unwmk.** ***Perf. 14x13½***

Q1 A14 10c red 12.00 12.00

FRENCH COLONIES

'french 'kä-lə-nēz

From 1859 to 1906 and from 1943 to 1945 special stamps were issued for use in all French Colonies which did not have stamps of their own.

100 Centimes = 1 Franc

Catalogue values for unused stamps in this country are for Never Hinged items, beginning with Scott B1 in the semi-postal section and Scott J23 in the postage due section.

Perforations: Nos. 1-45 are known variously perforated privately.

Gum: Many of Nos. 1-45 were issued without gum. Some were gummed locally.

Reprints: Nos. 1-7, 9-12, 24, 26-42, 44 and 45 were reprinted officially in 1887. These reprints are ungummed and the colors of both design and paper are deeper or brighter than the originals. Value for Nos. 1-6, $20 each.

Eagle and Crown — A1

1859-65 **Unwmk.** **Typo.** ***Imperf.***

1 A1 1c ol grn, *pale bl* ('62) 16.00 *19.00*
2 A1 5c yel grn, *grnsh* ('62) 19.00 12.00
3 A1 10c bister, *yel* 25.00 6.50
a. Pair, one sideways 775.00 400.00
4 A1 20c bl, *bluish* ('65) 27.50 11.00
5 A1 40c org, *yelsh* 21.00 11.00
6 A1 80c car rose, *pnksh* ('65) 90.00 50.00
Nos. 1-6 (6) 198.50 109.50

For surcharges see Reunion Nos. 3-4.

Napoleon III A2 A3

Ceres A4

Napoleon III A5

1871-72 ***Imperf.***

7 A2 1c ol grn, *pale bl* ('72) 55.00 50.00
8 A3 5c yel grn, *grnsh* ('72) 825.00 350.00
9 A4 10c bis, *yelsh* 300.00 110.00
a. Tête bêche pair *35,000.* *16,500.*
10 A4 15c bis, *yelsh* ('72) 275.00 11.00
11 A4 20c blue, *bluish* 425.00 100.00
a. Tête bêche pair — *12,000.*
12 A4 25c bl, *bluish* ('72) 125.00 11.00
13 A5 30c brn, *yelsh* 125.00 40.00
14 A4 40c org, *yelsh* (I) 210.00 11.00
a. Type II *2,750.* *500.00*
b. Pair, types I & II *5,750.* *1,400.*
15 A5 80c rose, *pnksh* 825.00 92.50
Nos. 7-15 (9) 3,165. 775.50

For 40c types I-II see illustrations over France #1.

For surcharges see Reunion Nos. 5-6.

See note after France No. 9 for additional information on Nos. 8-9, 11-12, 14.

Ceres A6 A7

1872-77 ***Imperf.***

16 A6 1c ol grn, *pale bl* ('73) 11.00 *12.00*
17 A6 2c red brn, *yelsh* ('76) 400.00 650.00
18 A6 4c gray ('76) *8,900.* 450.00
19 A6 5c grn, *pale bl* 12.00 8.00
20 A7 10c bis, *rose* ('76) 190.00 11.00
21 A7 15c bister ('77) 425.00 82.50
22 A7 30c brn, *yelsh* 90.00 17.50
23 A7 80c rose, *pnksh* ('73) 500.00 125.00

No. 17 was used only in Cochin China, 1876-77. Excellent forgeries of Nos. 17 and 18 exist.

With reference to the stamps of France and French Colonies in the same designs and colors see the note after France No. 9.

Peace and Commerce A8

Commerce A9

1877-78 **Type I** ***Imperf.***

24 A8 1c grn, *grnsh* 22.00 32.50
25 A8 4c grn, *grnsh* 14.00 10.00
26 A8 30c brn, *yelsh* ('78) 32.50 32.50
27 A8 40c ver, *straw* 21.00 16.00
28 A8 75c rose, *rose* ('78) 60.00 55.00
29 A8 1fr brnz grn, *straw* 37.50 16.00
Nos. 24-29 (6) 187.00 162.00

Type II

30 A8 2c grn, *grnsh* 10.50 8.50
31 A8 5c grn, *grnsh* 14.00 4.25
32 A8 10c grn, *grnsh* 70.00 10.50
33 A8 15c gray, *grnsh* 225.00 62.50
34 A8 20c red brn, *straw* 42.50 7.00
35 A8 25c ultra *bluish* 32.50 7.50
a. 25c blue, *bluish* ('78) *3,750.* 140.00
36 A8 35c vio blk, *org* ('78) 35.00 21.00
Nos. 30-36 (7) 429.50 121.25
Nos. 24-36 (13) 616.50 283.25

1878-80

Type II

38 A8 1c blk, *lil bl* 14.00 14.00
39 A8 2c brn, *buff* 13.50 10.50
40 A8 4c claret, *lav* 19.00 19.00
41 A8 10c blk, *lav* ('79) 90.00 16.00
42 A8 15c blue ('79) 22.50 10.50
43 A8 20c red, *grn* ('79) 62.50 10.50
44 A8 25c blk, *red* ('79) 500.00 225.00
45 A8 25c yel, *straw* ('80) 600.00 21.00
Nos. 38-45 (8) 1,321. 326.50

No. 44 was used only in Mayotte, Nossi-Be and New Caledonia. Forgeries exist.

The 3c yellow, 3c gray, 15c yellow, 20c blue, 25c rose and 5fr lilac were printed together with the reprints, and were never issued.

1881-86 ***Perf. 14x13½***

46 A9 1c blk, *lil bl* 3.75 3.25
47 A9 2c brn, *buff* 3.75 3.75
48 A9 4c claret, *lav* 3.75 3.75
49 A9 5c grn, *grnsh* 4.25 2.10
50 A9 10c blk, *lavender* 8.25 3.75
51 A9 15c blue 12.00 2.10
52 A9 20c red, *yel grn* 42.50 15.00
53 A9 25c yel, *straw* 10.50 3.75
54 A9 25c blk, *rose* ('86) 10.50 2.10
55 A9 30c brn, *bis* 32.50 16.00
56 A9 35c vio blk, *yel org* 32.50 21.00
a. 35c violet black, *yellow* 82.50 42.50
57 A9 40c ver, *straw* 35.00 24.00
58 A9 75c car, *rose* 100.00 50.00
59 A9 1fr brnz grn, *straw* 60.00 32.50
Nos. 46-59 (14) 359.25 183.05

Nos. 46-59 exist imperforate. They are proofs and were not used for postage, except the 10c.

For stamps of type A9 surcharged with numerals see: Cochin China, Diego Suarez, Gabon, Malagasy (Madagascar), Nossi-Be, New Caledonia, Reunion, Senegal, Tahiti.

SEMI-POSTAL STAMPS

Catalogue values for unused stamps in this section are for Never Hinged items.

Resistance Fighters — SP1

1943 **Unwmk.** **Litho.** ***Rouletted***

B1 SP1 1.50fr + 98.50fr ind & gray 40.00 40.00
Without label 17.50 10.50

The surtax was for the benefit of patriots and the French Committee of Liberation.

No. B1 was printed in sheets of 10 (5x2) with adjoining labels showing the Lorraine cross.

Colonies Offering Aid to France SP2

1943 ***Perf. 12***

B2 SP2 9fr + 41fr red violet 2.90 2.50

Surtax for the benefit of French patriots.

Patriots and Map of France SP3

1943

B3 SP3 50c + 4.50fr yel grn 1.10 *1.40*
B4 SP3 1.50fr + 8.50fr cerise 1.10 *1.40*
B5 SP3 3fr + 12fr grnsh bl 1.10 *1.40*
B6 SP3 5fr + 15fr olive gray 1.10 *1.40*
Nos. B3-B6 (4) 4.40 5.60

Surtax for the aid of combatants and patriots.

Refugee Family SP4

1943

B7 SP4 10fr + 40fr dull blue 4.25 *5.00*

The surtax was for refugee relief work.

Woman and Child with Wing — SP5

1944
B8 SP5 10fr + 40fr grnsh blk 5.75 *5.00*

Surtax for the benefit of aviation.
Nos. B1-B8 were prepared for use in the French Colonies, but after the landing of Free French troops in Corsica they were used there and later also in Southern France. They became valid throughout France in Nov. 1944.

POSTAGE DUE STAMPS

D1

1884-85 Unwmk. Typo. *Imperf.*
J1 D1 1c black 2.75 2.75
J2 D1 2c black 2.75 2.75
J3 D1 3c black 2.75 2.75
J4 D1 4c black 3.25 2.75
J5 D1 5c black 4.25 2.10
J6 D1 10c black 6.50 4.25
J7 D1 15c black 10.50 8.25
J8 D1 20c black 10.50 8.75
J9 D1 30c black 12.00 6.50
J10 D1 40c black 16.00 6.50
J11 D1 60c black 25.00 13.50
J12 D1 1fr brown 25.00 16.00
a. 1fr black 250.00
J13 D1 2fr brown 21.00 16.00
a. 2fr black 250.00
J14 D1 5fr brown 75.00 50.00
a. 5fr black 325.00

Nos. J12a, J13a and J14a were not regularly issued.

1894-1906
J15 D1 5c pale blue .75 .75
J16 D1 10c gray brown .75 .75
J17 D1 15c pale green .90 .90
J18 D1 20c olive grn ('06) .90 .90
J19 D1 30c carmine 1.75 1.10
J20 D1 50c lilac 1.75 1.10
J21 D1 60c brown, *buff* 3.00 1.75
a. 60c dark violet, *buff* 4.00 2.10
J22 D1 1fr red, *buff* 4.25 3.25
a. 1fr rose, *buff* 17.50 15.00
Nos. J15-J22 (8) 14.05 10.50

For overprints see New Caledonia Nos. J1-J8.

Catalogue values for unused stamps in this section, from this point to the end of the section, are for Never Hinged items.

D2

1945 Litho. *Perf. 12*
J23 D2 10c slate blue .20 .20
J24 D2 15c yel green .20 .20
J25 D2 25c deep orange .20 .20
J26 D2 50c greenish blk .55 .45
J27 D2 60c copper brn .55 .45
J28 D2 1fr deep red lil .55 .35
J29 D2 2fr red .55 .45
J30 D2 4fr slate gray 2.25 2.00
J31 D2 5fr brt ultra 2.25 2.00
J32 D2 10fr purple 13.00 10.50
J33 D2 20fr dull brown 2.75 2.10
J34 D2 50fr deep green 5.00 4.25
Nos. J23-J34 (12) 28.05 23.15

FRENCH CONGO

ˈfrench ˈkäŋ-ˌgō

LOCATION — Central Africa
GOVT. — French possession

French Congo was originally a separate colony, but was joined in 1888 to Gabon and placed under one commissioner-general with a lieutenant-governor presiding in Gabon and another in French Congo. In 1894 the military holdings in Ubangi were attached to French Congo, and in 1900 the Chad military protectorate was added. Postal service was not established in Ubangi or Chad, however, at that time. In 1906 Gabon and Middle Congo were separated and French Congo ceased to exist as such. Chad and Ubangi remained attached to Middle Congo as the joint dependency of "Ubangi-Chari-Chad," and Middle Congo stamps were used there.

Issues of the Republic of the Congo are listed under Congo People's Republic (ex-French).

100 Centimes = 1 Franc

Watermarks

Wmk. 122 — Thistle Branch

Wmk. 123 — Rose Branch

Wmk. 124 — Olive Branch

Stamps of French Colonies Surcharged Horizontally in Red or Black

1891 Unwmk. *Perf. 14x13½*
1 A9 5c on 1c blk, *lil bl* (R) *5,100.* *3,500.*
2 A9 5c on 1c blk, *lil bl* 125.00 70.00
a. Double surcharge 475.00 325.00
3 A9 5c on 15c blue 225.00 100.00
a. Double surcharge 525.00 250.00
5 A9 5c on 25c blk, *rose* 80.00 32.50
a. Inverted surcharge

First "O" of "Congo" is a Capital, "Francais" with Capital "F"

1891-92
6 A9 5c on 20c red, *grn* 875.00 325.00
7 A9 5c on 25c blk, *rose* 125.00 57.50
a. Surcharge vertical 190.00 55.00
8 A9 10c on 25c blk, *rose* 175.00 42.50
a. Inverted surcharge 325.00 110.00
b. Surcharge vertical 140.00 70.00
c. First "o" of "Congo" small
d. Double surcharge 300.00 140.00
9 A9 10c on 40c red, *straw* 1,800. 300.00
10 A9 15c on 25c blk, *rose* 150.00 32.50
a. Surcharge vertical 190.00 57.50
b. Inverted surcharge
c. Double surcharge 275.00 140.00

First "O" of Congo small Surcharge Vert., Down or Up No period

11 A9 5c on 25c blk, *rose* 190.00 77.50
12 A9 10c on 25c blk, *rose*
13 A9 15c on 25c blk, *rose* 275.00 110.00

Postage Due Stamps of French Colonies Surcharged in Red or Black Reading Down or Up

1892 *Imperf.*
14 D1 5c on 5c blk (R) 120.00 100.00
15 D1 5c on 20c blk (R) 125.00 92.50
16 D1 5c on 30c blk (R) 150.00 110.00
17 D1 10c on 1fr brown 125.00 92.50
a. Double surcharge 3,250. 3,300.
b. Surcharge horiz. *1,800.*
Nos. 14-17 (4) 520.00 395.00

Excellent counterfeits of Nos. 1-17 exist.

Navigation and Commerce — A3

1892-1900 Typo. *Perf. 14x13½*
Colony Name in Blue or Carmine
18 A3 1c blk, *lil bl* 1.25 1.10
19 A3 2c brn, *buff* 2.25 1.75
a. Name double 125.00 125.00
20 A3 4c claret, *lav* 2.25 2.10
a. Name in blk and in blue 125.00 125.00
21 A3 5c grn, *grnsh* 4.25 4.25
22 A3 10c blk, *lavender* 16.00 12.50
a. Name double 625.00 450.00
23 A3 10c red ('00) 2.10 1.40
24 A3 15c blue, quadrille paper 40.00 12.50
25 A3 15c gray ('00) 6.50 4.25
26 A3 20c red, *grn* 17.50 12.00
27 A3 25c blk, *rose* 18.00 12.00
28 A3 25c blue ('00) 8.00 7.00
29 A3 30c brn, *bis* 21.00 14.00
30 A3 40c red, *straw* 40.00 22.50
31 A3 50c car, *rose* 37.50 21.00
32 A3 50c brn, *az* ('00) 8.50 7.00
a. Name double 600.00 600.00
33 A3 75c dp vio, *org* 30.00 21.00
34 A3 1fr brnz grn, *straw* 40.00 21.00
Nos. 18-34 (17) 295.10 177.35

Perf. 13½x14 stamps are counterfeits.
For surcharges see Nos. 50-51.

Leopard — A4

Bakalois Woman — A5 Coconut Grove — A6

1900 Wmk. 122 *Perf. 11*
35 A4 1c brn vio & gray lilac .55 .55
a. Background inverted 62.50 62.50
36 A4 2c brn & org .55 .55
a. 2c dark red & red 140.00 *190.00*
b. Imperf., pair 50.00 50.00
37 A4 4c scar & gray bl 1.10 .85
a. 4c dark red & red 550.00
b. Background inverted 60.00 60.00
38 A4 5c grn & gray grn 1.90 .85
a. Imperf., pair 110.00 110.00
39 A4 10c dk red & red 5.10 2.10
a. Imperf., pair 110.00 110.00
40 A4 15c dl vio & ol grn 1.90 .95
a. Imperf. pair 75.00 75.00

Wmk. 123
41 A5 20c yel grn & org 1.60 1.40
42 A5 25c bl & pale bl 2.25 1.40
43 A5 30c car rose & org 3.25 1.60
44 A5 40c org brn & brt grn 4.00 1.75
a. Imperf., pair 75.00 75.00
b. Center inverted 125.00 125.00
45 A5 50c gray vio & lil 5.25 4.50
46 A5 75c red vio & org 10.00 6.00
a. Imperf., pair 75.00 75.00

Wmk. 124
47 A6 1fr gray lil & ol 17.50 12.00
a. Center inverted 225.00 225.00
b. Imperf., pair 100.00 100.00
48 A6 2fr car & brn 30.00 18.00
a. Imperf., pair 200.00 200.00
49 A6 5fr brn org & gray 65.00 52.50
a. 5fr ocher & gray 650.00 *700.00*
b. Center inverted 325.00 325.00
c. Wmk. 123 325.00 225.00
d. Imperf., pair 350.00 350.00
Nos. 35-49 (15) 149.95 105.00

For surcharges see Nos. 52-53.

Nos. 26 and 29 Surcharged in Black

Valeur
15

1900 Unwmk. *Perf. 14x13½*
50 A3 5c on 20c red, *grn* *20,000.* *5,000.*
a. Double surcharge *13,750.*
51 A3 15c on 30c brn, *bis* *13,750.* *2,000.*
a. Double surcharge *5,000.*

Nos. 43 and 48 Surcharged in Black:

a

0,10

b

1903 Wmk. 123 *Perf. 11*
52 A5 5c on 30c 210.00 110.00
a. Inverted surcharge *2,150.*

Wmk. 124
53 A6 10c on 2fr 275.00 110.00
a. Inverted surcharge *2,200.*
b. Double surcharge *2,400.*

Counterfeits of the preceding surcharges are known.

FRENCH EQUATORIAL AFRICA

'french ˌē-kwə-'tōr-ē-əl 'a-fri-kə

LOCATION — North of Belgian Congo and south of Libya
GOVT. — French Colony
AREA — 959,256 square miles
POP. — 4,491,785
CAPITAL — Brazzaville

In 1910 Gabon and Middle Congo, with its military dependencies, were politically united as French Equatorial Africa. The component colonies were granted administrative autonomy. In 1915 Ubangi-Chari-Chad was made an autonomous civilian colony and in 1920 Chad was made a civil colony. In 1934 the four colonies were administratively united as one colony, but this federation was not completed until 1936. Each colony had its own postal administration until 1936. The postal issues of the former colonial subdivisions are listed under the names of those colonies.

In 1958, French Equatorial Africa was divided into four republics: Chad, Congo, Gabon and Central African Republic (formerly Ubangi-Chari).

Stamps other than Nos. 189-192 are inscribed with "Afrique Equatoriale Francaise" or "AEF" and the name of one of the component colonies are listed under those colonies.

100 Centimes = 1 Franc

Catalogue values for unused stamps in this country are for Never Hinged items, beginning with Scott 142 in the regular postage section, Scott B8A in the semi-postal section, Scott C17 in the airpost section, and Scott J12 in the postage due section.

Stamps of Gabon, 1932, Overprinted "Afrique Equatoriale Francaise" and Bars Similar to "a" and "b" in Black

Perf. 13x13½, 13½x13

1936 **Unwmk.**
1 A16 1c brown violet .20 .20
2 A16 2c black, *rose* .35 .35
3 A16 4c green .85 .85
4 A16 5c grnsh blue .85 .85
5 A16 10c red, *yel* .80 .80
6 A17 40c brown violet 2.25 1.75
7 A17 50c red brown 1.75 1.40
8 A17 1fr yel grn, *bl* 21.00 9.25
9 A18 1.50fr dull blue 5.75 1.60
10 A18 2fr brown red 12.00 7.00
Nos. 1-10 (10) 45.80 24.05

Stamps of Middle Congo, 1933 Overprinted in Black:

a

b

c

1936
11 A4 (b) 1c lt brown .20 .20
12 A4 (b) 2c dull blue .20 .20
13 A4 (b) 4c olive green 1.10 1.10
14 A4 (b) 5c red violet .55 .50
15 A4 (b) 10c slate 1.10 .70
16 A4 (b) 15c dk violet 1.40 1.10
17 A4 (b) 20c red, *pink* 1.40 .95
18 A4 (b) 25c orange 2.10 1.40
19 A5 (a) 40c orange brn 2.75 1.75
20 A5 (c) 50c black violet 2.75 1.75
21 A5 (c) 75c black, *pink* 3.50 2.90
22 A5 (a) 90c carmine 3.50 2.50
23 A5 (c) 1.50fr dark blue 2.10 1.40
24 A6 (a) 5fr slate blue 40.00 21.00
25 A6 (a) 10fr black 24.00 16.00
26 A6 (a) 20fr dark brown 21.00 18.00
Nos. 11-26 (16) 107.65 71.45

Common Design Types pictured following the introduction.

Paris International Exposition Issue

Common Design Types

1937, Apr. 15 **Engr.** ***Perf. 13***
27 CD74 20c dark violet 1.75 1.75
28 CD75 30c dark green 1.75 1.75
29 CD76 40c carmine rose 1.75 1.75
30 CD77 50c dk brn & bl 1.75 1.75
31 CD78 90c red 2.00 2.00
32 CD79 1.50fr ultra 2.00 2.00
Nos. 27-32 (6) 11.00 11.00

Logging on Loéme River — A1

People of Chad — A2

Pierre Savorgnan de Brazza A3

Emile Gentil — A4

Paul Crampel A5

Governor Victor Liotard A6

Two types of 25c:
Type I — Wide numerals (4mm).
Type II — Narrow numerals (3½mm).

1937-40 **Photo.** ***Perf. 13½x13***
33 A1 1c brown & yel .20 .20
34 A1 2c violet & grn .20 .20
35 A1 3c blue & yel ('40) .20 .20
36 A1 4c magenta & bl .20 .20
37 A1 5c dk & lt green .35 .20
38 A2 10c magenta & blue .20 .20
39 A2 15c blue & buff .20 .20
40 A2 20c brown & yellow .40 .55
41 A2 25c cop red & bl (I) .65 .20
a. Type II 2.10 1.40
42 A3 30c gray grn & grn .55 .35
43 A3 30c chlky bl, ind & buff ('40) .20 .20
44 A2 35c dp grn & yel ('38) .70 .50
45 A3 40c cop red & bl .20 .20
46 A3 45c dk bl & lt grn 3.50 3.00
47 A3 45c dp grn & yel grn ('40) .35 .35
48 A3 50c brown & yellow .20 .20
49 A3 55c pur & bl ('38) .55 .50
50 A3 60c mar & gray bl ('40) .45 .45
51 A4 65c dk bl & lt grn .55 .20
52 A4 70c dp vio & buff ('40) .50 .50
53 A4 75c ol blk & dl yel 4.25 3.50
54 A4 80c brn & yel ('38) .35 .35
55 A4 90c copper red & buff .35 .20
56 A4 1fr dk vio & lt grn 1.75 .80
57 A3 1fr cer & dl org ('38) 2.50 .85
58 A4 1fr bl grn & sl grn ('40) .45 .45
59 A5 1.25fr cop red & buff .95 .55
60 A5 1.40fr dk brn & pale grn ('40) .80 .80
61 A5 1.50fr dk & lt blue 1.10 .50
62 A5 1.60fr dp vio & buff ('40) .80 .80
63 A5 1.75fr brn & yel 1.40 .55
64 A4 1.75fr bl & lt bl ('38) .50 .35
65 A5 2fr dk & lt green .80 .50
66 A6 2.15fr brn, vio & yel ('38) .55 .50
67 A6 2.25fr bl & lt bl ('39) 1.25 1.25
68 A6 2.50fr rose lake & buff ('40) .85 .85
69 A6 3fr dk blue & buff .50 .20
70 A6 5fr dk & lt green 1.10 .70
71 A6 10fr dk violet & bl 2.50 1.75
72 A6 20fr ol blk & dl yel 2.90 2.10
Nos. 33-72 (40) 36.00 26.15

For overprints and surcharges see Nos. 80-127, 129-141, B2-B3, B10-B13, B22-B23.

Colonial Arts Exhibition Issue

Souvenir Sheet
Common Design Type

1937 ***Imperf.***
73 CD79 3fr red brown 8.50 *9.00*

Count Louis Edouard Bouet-Willaumez and His Ship "La Malouine" — A7

1938, Dec. 5 ***Perf. 13½***
74 A7 65c gray brown .90 .90
75 A7 1fr deep rose 1.10 1.10
76 A7 1.75fr blue 1.25 1.25
77 A7 2fr dull violet 1.50 1.50
Nos. 74-77 (4) 4.75 4.75

Centenary of Gabon.

New York World's Fair Issue

Common Design Type

1939, May 10 **Engr.** ***Perf. 12½x12***
78 CD82 1.25fr carmine lake 1.25 1.25
79 CD82 2.25fr ultra 1.25 1.25

Libreville View and Marshal Petain A7a

1941 **Engr.** ***Perf. 12½x12***
79A A7a 1fr bluish green .90
79B A7a 2.50fr blue .90

Nos. 79A-79B were issued by the Vichy government in France, but were not placed on sale in French Equatorial Africa.

For surcharges, see Nos. B36-B37.

Stamps of 1936-40, Overprinted in Carmine or Black:

Nos. 80-82, 84-88, 93

Nos. 83, 89-92, 94-125

1940-41 ***Perf. 13½x13***
80 A1 1c brn & yel (C) 1.25 1.25
81 A1 2c vio & grn (C) 1.25 1.25
82 A1 3c blue & yel (C) 1.25 1.25
83 A4 4c ol grn (No. 13) 9.25 7.75
84 A1 5c dk grn & lt grn (C) 1.25 1.25
85 A2 10c magenta & bl 1.60 1.60
86 A2 15c blue & buff (C) 1.40 1.40
87 A2 20c brn & yel (C) 1.40 1.40
88 A2 25c cop red & bl 7.00 7.00
89 A3 30c gray grn & grn (C) 13.00 8.50
90 A3 30c gray grn & grn ('41) 2.00 2.00
91 A3 30c chlky bl, ind & buff (C) ('41) 7.25 6.00
92 A3 30c chlky bl, ind & buff ('41) 8.50 7.75
93 A2 35c dp grn & yel (C) 1.60 1.60
94 A3 40c cop red & bl .95 .95
95 A3 45c dp grn & yel grn (C) .70 .50
96 A3 45c dp grn & yel grn ('41) .95 .95
97 A3 50c brn & yel (C) 5.25 4.25
98 A3 50c brn & yel ('41) 4.25 4.25
99 A3 55c pur & bl (C) .85 .80
100 A3 55c pur & bl ('41) .95 .95
101 A3 60c mar & gray bl .80 .80
102 A4 65c dk bl & lt grn .80 .80
103 A4 70c dp vio & buff .80 .80
104 A4 75c ol blk & dl yel 42.50 42.50
105 A4 80c brown & yellow .70 .70
106 A4 90c cop red & buff 1.00 1.00
107 A4 1fr bl grn & sl grn 6.75 6.50
108 A4 1fr bl grn & sl grn (C) ('41) 4.50 4.00
109 A3 1fr cer & dl org 1.75 1.75
110 A5 1.40fr dk brn & pale grn .80 .80
111 A5 1.50fr dk bl & lt bl .80 .80
112 A5 1.60fr dp vio & buff .80 .80
113 A5 1.75fr brown & yel 1.25 1.25
114 A6 2.15fr brn, vio & yel 1.25 1.25
115 A6 2.25fr bl & lt bl (C) .80 .80
116 A6 2.25fr bl & lt bl ('41) 2.40 2.40
117 A6 2.50fr rose lake & buff .85 .85
118 A6 3fr dk bl & buff (C) 1.10 1.10
119 A6 3fr dk bl & buff ('41) 2.50 2.50
120 A6 5fr dk grn & lt grn (C) 3.00 3.00
121 A6 5fr dk grn & lt grn ('41) 85.00 45.00
122 A6 10fr dk vio & bl (C) 1.90 1.90
123 A6 10fr dk vio & bl ('41) 65.00 45.00
124 A6 20fr ol blk & dl yel (C) 1.75 1.75
125 A6 20fr ol blk & dl yel ('41) 10.50 9.50
Nos. 80-125 (46) 311.20 240.20

For overprints and surcharges see Nos. 129-132, B12-B13, B22-B23.

For types of Nos. 38//61 without "RF," see Nos. 155A-155B.

Double Overprint

94a A3 40c 21.00
96a A3 45c 25.00
98a A3 50c 25.00
100a A3 55c 25.00
b. one inverted
102a A4 65c 21.00
103a A4 70c 25.00
105a A4 80c 25.00
106a A4 90c 21.00
b. one inverted 80.00
110a A5 1.40fr 25.00
111a A5 1.50fr 25.00
114a A6 2.15fr 18.00
115a A6 2.25fr 25.00
116a A6 2.25fr 25.00
117a A6 2.50fr 25.00
119a A6 3fr 25.00
123a A6 10fr
Nos. 96a-119a (14) 335.00

Nos. 48, 51 Surcharged in Black or Carmine

1940
126 A3 75c on 50c .50 .50
a. Double surcharge 25.00
127 A4 1fr on 65c (C) .50 .50
a. Double surcharge 18.00

Middle Congo No. 67 Overprinted in Carmine like No. 80

Perf. 13½

128 A4 4c olive green 42.50 35.00

Stamps of 1940 With Additional Overprint in Black

1940 ***Perf. 13½x13***

129 A4 80c brown & yel 12.00 9.25
a. Overprint without "2" 100.00
130 A4 1fr bl grn & sl grn 12.00 9.25
131 A3 1fr cer & dull org 12.00 9.25
132 A5 1.50fr dk bl & lt bl 12.00 9.25
Nos. 129-132 (4) 48.00 37.00

Arrival of General de Gaulle in Brazzaville, capital of Free France, Oct. 24, 1940.

These stamps were sold affixed to post cards and at a slight increase over face value to cover the cost of the cards.

For surcharges see #B12-B13, B22-B23.

Stamps of 1937-40 Overprinted in Black

1941

133 A1 1c brown & yel 1.25 1.25
134 A1 2c violet & grn 1.25 1.25
135 A1 3c blue & yel 1.25 1.25
136 A1 5c dk & lt green 1.25 1.25
137 A2 10c magenta & bl 1.25 1.25
138 A2 15c blue & buff 1.25 1.25
139 A2 20c brown & yel 1.25 1.25
140 A2 25c copper red & bl 4.00 4.00
141 A2 35c dp grn & yel 4.00 4.00
a. Double overprint 12.00
Nos. 133-141 (9) 16.75 16.75

There are 2 settings of the overprint on Nos. 133-141 & C10. The 1st has 1mm between lines of the overprint, the 2nd has 2mm.

Catalogue values for unused stamps in this section, from this point to the end of the section, are for Never Hinged items.

Phoenix — A8

1941 **Photo.** ***Perf. 14x14½***

142 A8 5c brown .20 .20
143 A8 10c dark blue .20 .20
144 A8 25c emerald .20 .20
145 A8 30c deep orange .20 .20
146 A8 40c dk slate grn .35 .20
147 A8 80c red brown .35 .20
148 A8 1fr deep red lilac .35 .20
149 A8 1.50fr brt red .45 .25
150 A8 2fr gray .45 .25
151 A8 2.50fr brt ultra .50 .50
152 A8 4fr dull violet .50 .50
153 A8 5fr yellow bister .50 .50
154 A8 10fr deep brown .80 .80
155 A8 20fr deep green .95 .95
Nos. 142-155 (14) 6.00 5.15

For surcharges see #158-165, B14-B21, B24-B35.

Types of 1937-40 without "RF"

1944 ***Perf. 13½***

155A A2 10c magenta & blue .50
155B A2 15c blue & buff .80
155C A3 60c maroon & gray blue .85
155D A5 1.50fr dk & lt blue 1.10
Nos. 155A-155D (4) 3.25

Nos. 155A-155D were issued by the Vichy government in France, but were not sold in French Equatorial Africa.

Eboue Issue

Common Design Type

1945 **Unwmk.** **Engr.** ***Perf. 13***

156 CD91 2fr black .30 .30
157 CD91 25fr Prussian green 1.10 1.10

Nos. 156 and 157 exist imperforate.

Nos. 142, 144 and 151 Surcharged with New Values and Bars in Red, Carmine or Black

1946 ***Perf. 14x14½***

158 A8 50c on 5c (R) .50 .50
159 A8 60c on 5c (R) .50 .50
160 A8 70c on 5c (R) .50 .50
161 A8 1.20fr on 5c (C) .50 .50
162 A8 2.40fr on 25c .80 .80
163 A8 3fr on 25c .85 .85
164 A8 4.50fr on 25c .85 .85
165 A8 15fr on 2.50fr (C) .95 .95
Nos. 158-165 (8) 5.45 5.45

Black Rhinoceros and Rock Python — A9

Jungle Scene — A10

Mountainous Shore Line — A11

Gabon Forest — A12

Niger Boatman — A13

Young Bacongo Woman — A14

1946 **Unwmk.** **Engr.** ***Perf. 12½***

166 A9 10c deep blue .20 .20
167 A9 30c violet blk .20 .20
168 A9 40c dp orange .20 .20
169 A10 50c violet bl .35 .35
170 A10 60c dk carmine .35 .35
171 A10 80c dk ol grn .35 .35
172 A11 1fr dp orange .65 .20
173 A11 1.20fr dp claret .65 .55
174 A11 1.50fr dk green .80 .70
175 A12 2fr dk vio brn .20 .20
176 A12 3fr rose carmine .50 .35
177 A12 3.60fr red brown 2.25 1.75
178 A12 4fr deep blue .35 .20
179 A13 5fr dk brown .65 .20
180 A13 6fr deep blue .65 .20
181 A13 10fr black 1.25 .35
182 A14 15fr brown 1.25 .35
183 A14 20fr dp claret 1.25 .35
184 A14 25fr black 1.50 .35
Nos. 166-184 (19) 13.60 7.40

Imperforates

Most French Equatorial Africa stamps from 1951 onward exist imperforate in issued and trial colors, and also in small presentation sheets in issued colors.

Pierre Savorgnan de Brazza — A15

1951, Nov. 5 ***Perf. 13***

185 A15 10fr indigo & dk grn .80 .20

Cent. of the birth of Pierre Savorgnan de Brazza, explorer.

Military Medal Issue

Common Design Type

Engraved and Typographed

1952, Dec. 1 ***Perf. 13***

186 CD101 15fr multicolored 4.25 4.25

Lt. Gov. Adolphe L. Cureau A16

1954, Sept. 20 **Engr.**

187 A16 15fr ol grn & red brn 1.00 .40

Savannah Monitor A17

1955, May 2 **Unwmk.**

188 A17 8fr dk grn & claret 1.50 .75

International Exhibition for Wildlife Protection, Paris, May 1955.

FIDES Issue

Boali Waterfall and Power Plant, Ubangi-Chari — A18

10fr, Cotton, Chad. 15fr, Brazzaville Hospital, Middle Congo. 20fr, Libreville Harbor, Gabon.

1956, Apr. 25 ***Perf. 13x12½***

189 A18 5fr dk brn & claret .35 .20
190 A18 10fr blk & bluish grn .35 .20
191 A18 15fr ind & gray vio .50 .30
192 A18 20fr dk red & red org .55 .45
Nos. 189-192 (4) 1.75 1.15

See note after Common Design Type CD103.

Coffee Issue

Coffee A19

1956, Oct. **Engr.** ***Perf. 13***

193 A19 10fr brn vio & vio bl .55 .20

Leprosarium at Mayumba and Maltese Cross — A20

1957, Mar. 11

194 A20 15fr grn, bl grn & red 1.10 .55

Issued in honor of the Knights of Malta.

Giant Eland A21

1957, Nov. 4

195 A21 1fr shown .35 .20
196 A21 2fr Lions .35 .20
197 A21 3fr Elephant, vert. .35 .20
198 A21 4fr Greater kudu, vert. .35 .20
Nos. 195-198 (4) 1.40 .80

WHO Building, Brazzaville A22

1958, May 19 **Engr.** ***Perf. 13***

199 A22 20fr dk green & org brn .80 .55

10th anniv. of WHO.

Flower Issue

Common Design Type

1958, July 7 **Photo.** ***Perf. 12x12½***

200 CD104 10fr Euadania .70 .35
201 CD104 25fr Spathodea .95 .55

Human Rights Issue

Common Design Type

1958, Dec. 10 **Engr.** ***Perf. 13***

202 CD105 20fr Prus grn & dk bl 1.40 .80

SEMI-POSTAL STAMPS

Common Design Type

1938, Oct. 24 **Engr.**

B1 CD80 1.75fr + 50c brt ultra 16.00 16.00

Nos. 51, 64 Surcharged in Black or Red

1938, Nov. 7 ***Perf. 13x13½***

B2 A4 65c + 35c dk bl & lt grn (R) 1.60 1.60
B3 A4 1.75fr + 50c bl & lt bl 1.60 1.60

The surtax was for welfare.

French Revolution Issue

Common Design Type

Name and Value Typo. in Black

1939, July 5 **Photo.**

B4 CD83 45c + 25c green 11.00 11.00
B5 CD83 70c + 30c brown 11.00 11.00
B6 CD83 90c + 35c red org 11.00 11.00
B7 CD83 1.25fr + 1fr rose pink 11.00 11.00
B8 CD83 2.25fr + 2fr blue 11.00 11.00
Nos. B4-B8 (5) 55.00 55.00

Surtax used for the defense of the colonies.

Catalogue values for unused stamps in this section, from this point to the end of the section, are for Never Hinged items.

Common Design Type and

Native Artilleryman SP1

Gabon Infantryman SP2

1941 Photo. *Perf. 13½*

B8A SP1 1fr + 1fr red 2.10
B8B CD86 1.50fr + 3fr maroon 2.10
B8C SP2 2.50fr + 1fr blue 2.10
Nos. 8A-8C (3) 6.30

Nos. B8A-B8C were issued by the Vichy government in France, but were not placed on sale in French Equatorial Africa.

Brazza and Stanley Pool SP3

1941 Photo. *Perf. 14½x14*

B9 SP3 1fr + 2fr dk brn & red .85 .85

The surtax was for a monument to Pierre Savorgnan de Brazza.

Nos. 67, 71 Surcharged in Red

1943, June 28 *Perf. 13½x13*

B10 A6 2.25fr + 50fr 10.50 10.50
B11 A6 10fr + 100fr 32.50 32.50

Nos. 129 and 132 with additional Surcharge in Carmine

1944

B12 A4 80c + 10fr 18.00 18.00
B13 A5 1.50fr + 15fr 18.00 18.00

Same surcharge printed Vertically on Nos. 142-146, 148, 150-151

Perf. 14x14½

B14 A8 5c + 10fr brown 5.75 5.75
B15 A8 10c + 10fr dk bl 5.75 5.75
B16 A8 25c + 10fr emer 5.75 5.75
B17 A8 30c + 10fr dp org 5.75 5.75
B18 A8 40c + 10fr dk sl grn 5.75 5.75
B19 A8 1fr + 10fr dp red lil 5.75 5.75
B20 A8 2fr + 20fr gray 5.75 5.75
B21 A8 2.50fr + 25fr brt ultra 5.50 5.50
Nos. B12-B21 (10) 81.75 81.75

Nos. 129 and 132 with additional Surcharge in Carmine

1944 *Perf. 13½x13*

B22 A4 80c + 10fr 19.00 19.00
B23 A5 1.50fr + 15fr 19.00 19.00

Same Surcharge printed Vertically on Nos. 142-146, 148, 150-155

Perf. 14x14½

B24 A8 5c + 10fr brn 5.25 5.25
B25 A8 10c + 10fr dk bl 5.25 5.25
B26 A8 25c + 10fr emer 5.75 5.75
B27 A8 30c + 10fr dp org 5.75 5.75
B28 A8 40c + 10fr dk sl grn 5.75 5.75
B29 A8 1fr + 10fr dp red lil 5.75 5.75
B30 A8 2fr + 20fr gray 5.75 5.75
B31 A8 2.50fr + 25fr brt ultra 5.75 5.75
B32 A8 4fr + 40fr dl vio 5.75 5.75
B33 A8 5fr + 50fr yel bis 5.75 5.75
B34 A8 10fr + 100fr dp brn 6.75 6.75
B35 A8 20fr + 200fr dp grn 6.75 6.75
Nos. B22-B35 (14) 108.00 108.00

Nos. B12 to B35 were issued to raise funds for the Committee to Aid the Fighting Men and Patriots of France.

Nos. 79A-79B Surcharged in Black or Red

1944 Engr. *Perf. 12½x12*

B36 50c + 1.50fr on 2.50fr deep blue (R) .80
B37 + 2.50fr on 1fr green .80

Colonial Development Fund.

Nos. B36-B37 were issued by the Vichy government in France, but were not placed on sale in French Equatorial Africa.

Red Cross Issue

Common Design Type

1944 Photo. *Perf. 14½x14*

B38 CD90 5fr + 20fr royal blue .80 .80

The surtax was for the French Red Cross and national relief.

Tropical Medicine Issue

Common Design Type

1950, May 15 Engr. *Perf. 13*

B39 CD100 10fr + 2fr dk bl grn & vio brn 4.25 4.25

The surtax was for charitable work.

AIR POST STAMPS

Hydroplane over Pointe-Noire — AP1

Trimotor over Stanley Pool — AP2

1937 Unwmk. Photo. *Perf. 13½*

C1 AP1 1.50fr ol blk & yel .20 .20
C2 AP1 2fr mag & blue .35 .35
C3 AP1 2.50fr grn & buff .35 .35
C4 AP1 3.75fr brn & lt grn .55 .55
C5 AP2 4.50fr cop red & bl .55 .55
C6 AP2 6.50fr bl & lt grn 1.10 1.10
C7 AP2 8.50fr red brn & yel 1.25 1.25
C8 AP2 10.75fr vio & lt grn 1.25 1.25
Nos. C1-C8 (8) 5.60 5.60

For overprints and surcharges see #C9-C16, CB2.

For types AP1, AP2 without "RF," see Nos. C23A-C23L.

Nos. C1, C3-C7 Overprinted in Black like Nos. 133-141

1940-41

C9 AP1 1.50fr ('41) 175.00 175.00
C10 AP1 2.50fr 1.40 1.40
C11 AP1 3.75fr ('41) 175.00 175.00
C12 AP2 4.50fr 1.75 1.75
C13 AP2 6.50fr 2.50 2.50
C14 AP2 8.50fr 1.40 1.40

No. C8 Surcharged in Carmine

C15 AP2 50fr on 10.75fr 7.50 7.50

No. C3 Surcharged in Black

C16 AP1 10fr on 2.50fr ('41) 65.00 65.00
Nos. C9-C16 (8) 429.55 429.55

Counterfeits of Nos. C9 and C11 exist.
See note following No. 141.

Catalogue values for unused stamps in this section, from this point to the end of the section, are for Never Hinged items.

Common Design Type

1941 Photo. *Perf. 14½x14*

C17 CD87 1fr dark orange .50 .35
C18 CD87 1.50fr brt red .55 .35
C19 CD87 5fr brown red .90 .55
C20 CD87 10fr black 1.00 .70
C21 CD87 25fr ultra .90 .85
C22 CD87 50fr dark green .90 .70
C23 CD87 100fr plum 1.10 .90
Nos. C17-C23 (7) 5.85 4.40

Types of 1937 without "RF" and

Sikorsky 5.43 Seaplane and Canoe — AP2a

Perf. 13½, 13 (#C23M)

1943, Oct. 18-1944 Unwmk.

C23A AP1 1.50fr ol blk & yel .20
C23B AP1 2fr mag & blue .20
C23C AP1 2.50fr grn & buff .20
C23D AP1 3.75fr brn & lt grn .35
C23E AP2 4.50fr cop red & bl .35
C23F AP2 5fr green .55
C23G AP2 6.50fr bl & lt grn .50
C23H AP2 8.50fr red brn & yel .45
C23I AP2 10fr gray & brn ('44) .50
C23J AP2 10.75fr vio & lt grn .50
C23K AP2 20fr yel & brn red ('44) .50
C23L AP2 50fr gray grn & blk ('44) .85
C23M AP2a 100fr red brown ('44) .55
Nos. C23A-C23M (13) 5.70

Issue dates: Nos. C23I, C23K-L, 4/3/44; C23M, 6/26/44.

Nos. C23A-C23M were issued by the Vichy government in France, but were not sold in French Equatorial Africa.

Victory Issue

Common Design Type

Perf. 12½

1946, May 8 Unwmk. Engr.

C24 CD92 8fr lilac rose .70 .55

Chad to Rhine Issue

Common Design Types

1946, June 6

C25 CD93 5fr dk violet .85 .85
C26 CD94 10fr slate green .85 .85
C27 CD95 15fr deep blue 1.25 1.25
C28 CD96 20fr red orange 1.25 1.25
C29 CD97 25fr sepia 1.25 1.25
C30 CD98 50fr brown carmine 1.60 1.60
Nos. C25-C30 (6) 7.05 7.05

Palms and Village — AP3

Village and Waterfront — AP4

Bearers in Jungle — AP5

1946 Engr. *Perf. 13*

C31 AP3 50fr red brn 2.00 .60
C32 AP4 100fr grnsh blk 3.25 .90
C33 AP5 200fr deep blue 6.50 1.50
Nos. C31-C33 (3) 11.75 3.00

UPU Issue

Common Design Type

1949, July 4

C34 CD99 25fr green 9.00 9.00

Brazza Holding Map — AP6

1951, Nov. 5

C35 AP6 15fr brn, indigo & red 1.10 .55

Cent. of the birth of Pierre Savorgnan de Brazza, explorer.

Archbishop Augouard and St. Anne Cathedral, Brazzaville — AP7

1952, Dec. 1

C36 AP7 15fr ol grn, dk brn & vio brn 3.50 1.75

Cent. of the birth of Archbishop Philippe-Prosper Augouard.

Anhingas — AP8

1953, Feb. 16

C37 AP8 500fr grnsh blk, blk & slate 25.00 5.50

Liberation Issue

Common Design Type

1954, June 6

C38 CD102 15fr vio & vio brn 5.75 5.75

Log Rafts — AP9

Designs: 100fr, Fishing boats and nets, Lake Chad. 200fr, Age of mechanization.

1955, Jan. 24 **Engr.**
C39 AP9 50fr ind, brn & dk grn 1.25 .55
C40 AP9 100fr aqua, dk grn & blk brn 4.50 .95
C41 AP9 200fr red & deep plum 7.00 1.75
Nos. C39-C41 (3) 12.75 3.25

Gov. Gen. Félix Eboué, View of Brazzaville and the Pantheon — AP10

1955, Apr. 30 **Unwmk.** ***Perf. 13***
C42 AP10 15fr sep, brn & slate bl 3.50 1.60

Gen. Louis Faidherbé and African Sharpshooter AP11

1957, July 20
C43 AP11 15fr sepia & org ver 2.10 1.40

Centenary of French African Troops.

AIR POST SEMI-POSTAL STAMPS

French Revolution Issue
Common Design Type
1939 **Unwmk.** **Photo.** ***Perf. 13***
Name and Value Typo. in Orange
CB1 CD83 4.50fr + 4fr brn blk 27.50 27.50

SPAP1

SPAP2

SPAP3

Unwmk.
1942, June 22 **Engr.** ***Perf. 13***
CB2 SPAP1 1.50fr + 3.50fr green 1.10
CB3 SPAP2 2fr + 6fr brown 1.10
CB4 SPAP3 3fr + 9fr carmine 1.10
Nos. CB2-CB4 (3) 3.30

Native children's welfare fund.
Nos. CB2-CB4 were issued by the Vichy government in France, but were not placed on sale in French Equatorial Africa.

Colonial Education Fund
Common Design Type
1942, June 22
CB5 CD86a 1.20fr + 1.80fr bl & red 1.10

No. CB5 was issued by the Vichy government in France, but was not placed on sale in French Equatorial Africa.

#C8 Surcharged in Red like #B10-B11
1943, June 28 ***Perf. 13½***
CB6 AP2 10.75fr + 200fr 140.00 140.00

Counterfeits exist.

POSTAGE DUE STAMPS

Numeral of Value on Equatorial Butterfly — D1

1937 **Unwmk.** **Photo.** ***Perf. 13***
J1 D1 5c redsh pur & lt bl .20 .20
J2 D1 10c cop red & buff .20 .20
J3 D1 20c dk grn & grn .20 .20
J4 D1 25c red brn & buff .20 .20
J5 D1 30c cop red & lt bl .35 .35
J6 D1 45c mag & yel grn .50 .50
J7 D1 50c dk ol grn & buff .50 .50
J8 D1 60c redsh pur & yel .65 .65
J9 D1 1fr brown & yel .80 .80
J10 D1 2fr dk bl & buff 1.00 1.00
J11 D1 3fr red brn & lt grn 1.10 1.10
Nos. J1-J11 (11) 5.70 5.70

Catalogue values for unused stamps in this section, from this point to the end of the section, are for Never Hinged items.

D2

1947 **Engr.**
J12 D2 10c red .20 .20
J13 D2 30c dp org .20 .20
J14 D2 50c greenish bl .20 .20
J15 D2 1fr carmine .20 .20
J16 D2 2fr emerald .20 .20
J17 D2 3fr dp red lil .25 .25
J18 D2 4fr dp ultra .70 .70
J19 D2 5fr red brown .70 .70
J20 D2 10fr peacock blue 1.00 1.00
J21 D2 20fr sepia 1.10 1.10
Nos. J12-J21 (10) 4.75 4.75

FRENCH GUIANA

'french gē-'a-nə

LOCATION — On the northeast coast of South America bordering on the Atlantic Ocean.
GOVT. — French colony
AREA — 34,740 sq. mi.
POP. — 28,537 (1946)
CAPITAL — Cayenne

French Guiana became an overseas department of France in 1946.

100 Centimes = 1 Franc

Catalogue values for unused stamps in this country are for Never Hinged items, beginning with Scott 171 in the regular postage section, Scott B12 in the semi-postal section, Scott C9 in the air-post section, and Scott J22 in the postage due section.

See France No. 1446 for French stamp inscribed "Guyane."

Stamps of French Colonies Surcharged in Black

Déc. 1886.
GUY. FRANÇ.
0f 05

1886, Dec. **Unwmk.** ***Imperf.***
1 A8 5c on 2c grn, *grnsh* 500.00 450.00
b. No "f" after "O" 625.00 625.00

Perf. 14x13½
2 A9 5c on 2c brn, *buff* 450.00 450.00
b. No "f" after "O" 350.00 350.00

Two types of No. 1: Surcharge 12mm high, and surcharge 10½mm high.

Avril 1887.
—
GUY FRANÇ
0f 20

"Av" of Date Line Inverted-Reversed
1887, Apr. ***Imperf.***
4 A8 20c on 35c blk, *org* 45.00 35.00

Date Line Reads "Avril 1887"
5 A8 5c on 2c grn, *grnsh* 110.00 85.00
6 A8 20c on 35c blk, *org* 250.00 210.00
7 A7 25c on 30c brn, *yelsh* 32.50 27.50

Variety "small f omitted" occurs on #5-7.

French Colonies Nos. 22 & 26 Surcharged

8 A7 5c on 30c brn, *yelsh* 110.00 110.00
a. Double surcharge 575.00 575.00
b. Inverted surcharge 775.00 850.00
c. Pair, one without surcharge 1,100.
9 A8 5c on 30c brn, *yelsh* 1,100. 1,100.

French Colonies Nos. 22 and 28 Surcharged:

1888
10 A7 5c on 30c brn, *yelsh* 110.00 90.00
b. Double surcharge
c. Inverted surcharge 375.00 400.00
11 A8 10c on 75c car, *rose* 250.00 250.00

Stamps of French Colonies Overprinted in Black

1892, Feb. 20 ***Imperf.***
12 A8 2c grn, *grnsh* 600.00 650.00
13 A7 30c brn, *yelsh* 110.00 110.00
14 A8 35c blk, *orange* *2,100.* *2,100.*
15 A8 40c red, *straw* 92.50 92.50
16 A8 75c car, *rose* 100.00 92.50
a. Inverted overprint 325.00 325.00
17 A8 1fr brnz grn, *straw* 125.00 125.00
a. Inverted overprint 525.00 500.00

1892 ***Perf. 14x13½***
18 A9 1c blk, *lil bl* 35.00 27.50
19 A9 2c brn, *buff* 32.50 30.00
20 A9 4c claret, *lav* 30.00 30.00
21 A9 5c grn, *grnsh* 32.50 27.50
a. Inverted overprint 92.50
b. Double overprint 92.50
22 A9 10c blk, *lavender* 55.00 35.00
a. Inverted overprint 125.00 125.00
23 A9 15c blue 45.00 32.50
24 A9 20c red, *grn* 40.00 32.50
25 A9 25c blk, *rose* 65.00 30.00
26 A9 30c brn, *bis* 30.00 27.50
27 A9 35c blk, *orange* 160.00 160.00
28 A9 40c red, *straw* 100.00 100.00
a. Inverted overprint 175.00 175.00
29 A9 75c car, *rose* 100.00 77.50
30 A9 1fr brnz grn, *straw* 175.00 160.00
Nos. 18-30 (13) 900.00 770.00

French Colonies No. 51 Surcharged

1892, Dec.
31 A9 5c on 15c blue 35.00 22.50

Navigation and Commerce — A12

1892-1904 **Typo.** ***Perf. 14x13½***
Name of Colony in Blue or Carmine
32 A12 1c blk, *lil bl* 1.25 1.00
33 A12 2c brn, *buff* 1.00 .90
34 A12 4c claret, *lav* 1.25 1.10
a. "GUYANE" double 175.00
35 A12 5c grn, *grnsh* 7.75 6.25
36 A12 5c yel grn ('04) 1.25 .70
37 A12 10c blk, *lavender* 8.50 5.00
38 A12 10c red ('00) 3.00 1.00
39 A12 15c blue, quadrille paper 27.50 2.50
40 A12 15c gray, *lt gray* ('00) 100.00 67.50
41 A12 20c red, *grn* 18.00 11.00
42 A12 25c blk, *rose* 16.00 3.25
43 A12 25c blue ('00) 13.00 13.00
44 A12 30c brn, *bis* 16.00 11.00
45 A12 40c red, *straw* 16.00 12.00
46 A12 50c car, *rose* 24.00 12.00
47 A12 50c brn, *az* ('00) 20.00 16.00
48 A12 75c dp vio, *org* 30.00 16.00
49 A12 1fr brn grn, *straw* 12.50 10.50
50 A12 2fr vio, *rose* ('02) 140.00 7.50
Nos. 32-50 (19) 457.00 198.20

Perf. 13½x14 stamps are counterfeits.
For surcharges see Nos. 87-93.

Great Anteater — A13

Washing Gold — A14

Palm Grove at Cayenne A15

1905-28
51 A13 1c black .20 .20
52 A13 2c blue .20 .20
53 A13 4c red brn .20 .20
54 A13 5c green .80 .60
55 A13 5c org ('22) .20 .20
56 A13 10c rose .95 .55
57 A13 10c grn ('22) .45 .30
58 A13 10c red, *bluish* ('25) .30 .30
59 A13 15c violet 1.00 .80
60 A14 20c red brn .40 .35
61 A14 25c blue 1.75 1.00
62 A14 25c vio ('22) .50 .45
63 A14 30c black 1.25 .55
64 A14 30c rose ('22) .35 .35
65 A14 30c red org ('25) .20 .20
66 A14 30c dk grn, *grnsh* ('28) .95 .95

67 A14 35c blk, *yel* ('06) .30 .20
68 A14 40c rose .55 .50
69 A14 40c black ('22) .20 .20
70 A14 45c olive ('07) .65 .50
71 A14 50c violet 2.50 2.00
72 A14 50c blue ('22) .40 .35
73 A14 50c gray ('25) .60 .35
74 A14 60c lil, *rose* ('25) .50 .45
75 A14 65c myr grn ('26) .65 .50
76 A14 75c green 1.00 .70
77 A14 85c magenta ('26) .50 .50
78 A15 1fr rose .55 .55
79 A15 1fr bl, *bluish* ('25) .65 .50
80 A15 1fr bl, *yel grn* ('28) 2.00 2.00
81 A15 1.10fr lt red ('28) 1.10 1.10
82 A15 2fr blue .70 .70
83 A15 2fr org red, *yel* ('26) 2.10 1.40
84 A15 5fr black 4.75 3.50
85 A15 10fr grn, *yel* ('24) 10.50 9.50
a. Printed on both sides 42.50 42.50
86 A15 20fr brn lake ('24) 13.50 12.00
Nos. 51-86 (36) 53.40 44.70

For surcharges see Nos. 94-108, B1-B2.

Issue of 1892 Surcharged in Black or Carmine

1912

87 A12 5c on 2c brn, *buff* .65 .65
88 A12 5c on 4c cl, *lav* (C) .65 .65
89 A12 5c on 20c red, *grn* .85 .85
90 A12 5c on 25c blk, *rose* (C) 2.50 2.50
91 A12 5c on 30c brn, *bis* (C) .80 .80
92 A12 10c on 40c red, *straw* .55 .55
93 A12 10c on 50c car, *rose* 2.50 2.50
a. Double surcharge 400.00
Nos. 87-93 (7) 8.50 8.50

Two spacings between the surcharged numerals are found on Nos. 87 to 93.

No. 59 Surcharged in Various Colors

1922

94 A13 1c on 15c vio (Bk) .35 .35
95 A13 2c on 15c vio (Bl) .35 .35
a. Inverted surcharge 65.00
96 A13 4c on 15c vio (G) .35 .35
a. Double surcharge 57.50
97 A13 5c on 15c vio (R) .35 .35
Nos. 94-97 (4) 1.40 1.40

Type of 1905-28 Surcharged in Blue

1923

98 A15 10fr on 1fr grn, *yel* 14.00 14.00
99 A15 20fr on 5fr lilac, *rose* 14.00 14.00

Stamps and Types of 1905-28 Surcharged with New Value and Bars in Black or Red

1924-27

100 A13 25c on 15c vio ('25) .40 .40
101 A15 25c on 2fr bl ('24) .55 .55
a. Double surcharge 100.00
b. Triple surcharge 110.00
102 A14 65c on 45c ol (R) ('25) 1.10 1.10
103 A14 85c on 45c ol (R) ('25) 1.10 1.10
104 A14 90c on 75c red ('27) .95 .95
105 A15 1.05fr on 2fr lt yel brn ('27) .95 .95
106 A15 1.25fr on 1fr ultra (R) ('26) 1.10 1.10
107 A15 1.50fr on 1fr lt bl ('27) 1.10 1.10
108 A15 3fr on 5fr vio ('27) 1.25 1.25
a. No period after "F" 7.75 7.75
Nos. 100-108 (9) 8.50 8.50

Carib Archer — A16

Shooting Rapids, Maroni River A17

Government Building, Cayenne — A18

1929-40 *Perf. 13½x14*

109 A16 1c gray lil & grnsh bl .20 .20
110 A16 2c dk red & bl grn .20 .20
111 A16 3c gray lil & grnsh bl ('40) .20 .20
112 A16 4c ol brn & red vio .20 .20
113 A16 5c Prus bl & red org .20 .20
114 A16 10c mag & brn .20 .20
115 A16 15c yel brn & red org .20 .20
116 A16 20c dk bl & ol grn .20 .20
117 A16 25c dk red & dk brn .35 .35

Perf. 14x13½

118 A17 30c dl & lt grn .50 .50
119 A17 30c grn & brn ('40) .30 .30
120 A17 35c Prus grn & ol grn ('38) .70 .70
121 A17 40c org brn & ol gray .20 .20
122 A17 45c grn & dk brn .70 .70
123 A17 45c ol grn & lt grn ('40) .45 .45
124 A17 50c dk bl & ol gray .30 .30
125 A17 55c vio bl & car ('38) 1.10 1.10
126 A17 60c sal & grn ('40) .45 .45
127 A17 65c sal & grn .70 .70
128 A17 70c ind & sl bl ('40) .80 .80
129 A17 75c ind & sl bl .90 .90
130 A17 80c blk & vio bl ('38) .65 .65
131 A17 90c dk red & ver .70 .70
132 A17 90c red vio & brn ('39) .80 .80
133 A17 1fr lt vio & brn .50 .50
134 A17 1fr car & lt red ('38) 1.60 1.40
135 A17 1fr blk & vio bl ('40) .50 .50
136 A18 1.05fr ver & olivine 4.50 4.00
137 A18 1.10fr ol brn & red vio 4.50 3.50
138 A18 1.25fr blk brn & bl grn ('33) .65 .65
139 A18 1.25fr rose & lt red ('39) .65 .65
140 A18 1.40fr ol brn & red vio ('40) .80 .80
141 A18 1.50fr dk bl & lt bl .30 .30
142 A18 1.60fr ol brn & bl grn ('40) .80 .80
143 A18 1.75fr brn red & blk brn ('33) 1.60 1.60
144 A18 1.75fr vio bl ('38) 1.25 .65
145 A18 2fr dk grn & rose red .45 .45
146 A18 2.25fr vio bl ('39) .80 .80
147 A18 2.50fr cop red & brn ('40) .85 .85
148 A18 3fr brn red & red vio .65 .65
149 A18 5fr dl vio & yel grn .85 .65
150 A18 10fr ol gray & dp ultra .95 .95
151 A18 20fr indigo & ver 1.50 1.50
Nos. 109-151 (43) 34.90 32.40

For types A16-A18 without "RF," see Nos. 170C-170E.

Common Design Types pictured following the introduction.

Colonial Exposition Issue
Common Design Types

1931 **Engr.** *Perf. 12½*
Name of Country in Black

152 CD70 40c dp green 3.50 3.50
153 CD71 50c violet 3.50 3.50
154 CD72 90c red orange 3.50 3.50
155 CD73 1.50fr dull blue 3.50 3.50
Nos. 152-155 (4) 14.00 14.00

Recapture of Cayenne by d'Estrées, 1676 — A19

Products of French Guiana A20

1935, Oct. 21 *Perf. 13*

156 A19 40c gray brn 3.50 3.50
157 A19 50c dull red 7.25 5.75
158 A19 1.50fr ultra 3.50 3.50
159 A20 1.75fr lilac rose 9.50 8.50
160 A20 5fr brown 7.25 7.25
161 A20 10fr blue green 7.25 7.25
Nos. 156-161 (6) 38.25 35.75

Tercentenary of the founding of French possessions in the West Indies.

Paris International Exposition Issue
Common Design Types

1937, Apr. 15

162 CD74 20c deep violet 1.00 1.00
163 CD75 30c dark green 1.00 1.00
164 CD76 40c carmine rose 1.00 1.00
165 CD77 50c dark brown 1.00 1.00
166 CD78 90c red 1.00 1.00
167 CD79 1.50fr ultra 1.00 1.00
Nos. 162-167 (6) 6.00 6.00

Colonial Arts Exhibition Issue
Souvenir Sheet
Common Design Type

1937 *Imperf.*

168 CD75 3fr violet 7.00 *8.50*

New York World's Fair Issue
Common Design Type

1939, May 10 **Engr.** *Perf. 12½x12*

169 CD82 1.25fr car lake .85 .85
170 CD82 2.25fr ultra .85 .85

View of Cayenne and Marshal Petain A21a

1941 **Engr.** *Perf. 12½x12*

170A A21a 1fr deep lilac .55 —
170B A21a 2.50fr blue .55 —

For surcharges, see Nos. B11A-B11B.

Types of 1929-40 without "RF"

1944 ***Methods and Perfs as Before***

170C A16 15c yel brn & red org .80
170D A17 1fr black & vio blue .80
170E A18 1.50fr dk blue & lt blue .95
Nos. 170C-170E (3) 2.55

Nos. 170C-170E were issued by the Vichy government in France, but were not issued in French Guiana.

Catalogue values for unused stamps in this section, from this point to the end of the section, are for Never Hinged items.

Eboue Issue
Common Design Type

1945 **Engr.** *Perf. 13*

171 CD91 2fr black .50 .50
172 CD91 25fr Prussian green .95 .95

This issue exists imperforate.

Arms of Cayenne A22

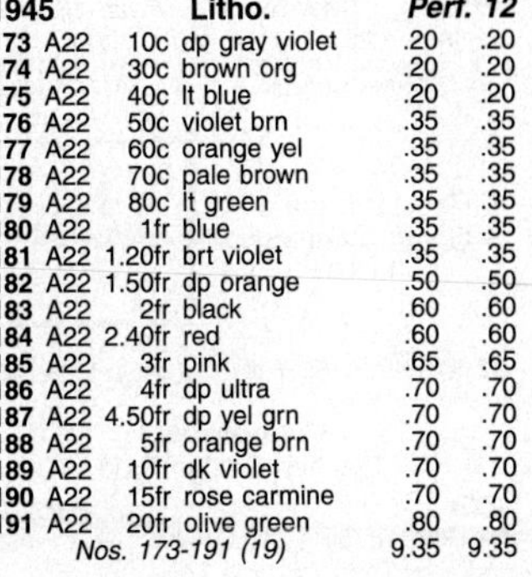

1945 **Litho.** *Perf. 12*

173 A22 10c dp gray violet .20 .20
174 A22 30c brown org .20 .20
175 A22 40c lt blue .20 .20
176 A22 50c violet brn .35 .35
177 A22 60c orange yel .35 .35
178 A22 70c pale brown .35 .35
179 A22 80c lt green .35 .35
180 A22 1fr blue .35 .35
181 A22 1.20fr brt violet .35 .35
182 A22 1.50fr dp orange .50 .50
183 A22 2fr black .60 .60
184 A22 2.40fr red .60 .60
185 A22 3fr pink .65 .65
186 A22 4fr dp ultra .70 .70
187 A22 4.50fr dp yel grn .70 .70
188 A22 5fr orange brn .70 .70
189 A22 10fr dk violet .70 .70
190 A22 15fr rose carmine .70 .70
191 A22 20fr olive green .80 .80
Nos. 173-191 (19) 9.35 9.35

Hammock A23

Guiana Girl A26

Maroni River Bank A24

Inini Scene A25

Toucans A27

Parrots A28

Perf. 13.

1947, June 2 **Unwmk.** **Engr.**

192 A23 10c dk blue grn .20 .20
193 A23 30c brt red .20 .20
194 A23 50c dk vio brn .20 .20
195 A24 60c grnsh blk .20 .20
196 A24 1fr red brn .35 .35
197 A24 1.50fr black brn .35 .35
198 A25 2fr dp yel grn .55 .50
199 A25 2.50fr dp ultra .55 .50
200 A25 3fr red brn .50 .50
201 A26 4fr black brn 1.40 .80
202 A26 5fr deep blue 1.00 .85
203 A26 6fr red brown 1.00 .85
204 A27 10fr deep ultra 4.50 3.50
205 A27 15fr black brn 4.50 4.00
206 A27 20fr red brn 6.50 4.00
207 A28 25fr brt bl grn 7.75 6.00
208 A28 40fr black brn 6.50 5.75
Nos. 192-208 (17) 36.25 28.75

SEMI-POSTAL STAMPS

Regular Issue of 1905-28 Surcharged in Red

1915 Unwmk. *Perf. 13½x14*

B1 A13 10c + 5c rose 11.00 11.00
a. Inverted surcharge 190.00 190.00
b. Double surcharge 190.00 190.00

Regular Issue of 1905-28 Surcharged in Rose

B2 A13 10c + 5c rose .85 .85

Curie Issue
Common Design Type

1938 *Perf. 13*

B3 CD80 1.75fr + 50c brt ultra 9.25 9.25

French Revolution Issue
Common Design Type

1939 Photo.

Name and Value in Black

B4 CD83 45c + 25c green 8.50 8.50
B5 CD83 70c + 30c brown 8.50 8.50
B6 CD83 90c + 35c red org 8.50 8.50
B7 CD83 1.25fr + 1fr rose pink 8.50 8.50
B8 CD83 2.25fr + 2fr blue 8.50 8.50
Nos. B4-B8 (5) 42.50 42.50

Common Design Type and

Colonial Infantryman — SP1

Colonial Policeman SP2

1941 Photo. *Perf. 13½*

B9 SP1 1fr + 1fr red .75
B10 CD86 1.50fr + 3fr maroon 1.00
B11 SP2 2.50fr + 1fr blue .75
Nos. B9-B11 (3) 2.50

Nos. B9-B11 were issued by the Vichy government in France, but were not placed on sale in French Guiana.

Nos. 170A-170B Surcharged in Black or Red

1944 Engr. *Perf. 12½x12*

B11A 50c + 1.50fr on 2.50fr deep blue (R) .55
B11B + 2.50fr on 1fr dp lilac .55

Colonial Development Fund.

Nos. B11A-B11B were issued by the Vichy government in France, but were not placed on sale in French Guiana.

Catalogue values for unused stamps in this section, from this point to the end of the section, are for Never Hinged items.

Red Cross Issue
Common Design Type

1944 *Perf. 14½x14*

B12 CD90 5fr + 20fr dk copper brn .80 .80

The surtax was for the French Red Cross and national relief.

AIR POST STAMPS

Cayenne AP1

Perf. 13½

1933, Nov. 20 Unwmk. Photo.

C1 AP1 50c orange brn .20 .20
C2 AP1 1fr yellow grn .35 .35
C3 AP1 1.50fr dk blue .50 .50
C4 AP1 2fr orange .50 .50
C5 AP1 3fr black .65 .65
C6 AP1 5fr violet .65 .65
C7 AP1 10fr olive grn .65 .65
C8 AP1 20fr scarlet .80 .80
Nos. C1-C8 (8) 4.30 4.30

For No. C1 without "RF," see No. C8A.

Catalogue values for unused stamps in this section, from this point to the end of the section, are for Never Hinged items.

Type of 1933 without "RF" and

AP1a

AP1b

Perf. 13½, 13 (#C8C)

1941-44 Photo, Engr. (#C8C)

C8A AP1 50c orange brn .50
C8B AP1a 50fr bl grn & red brown ('42) .70
C8C AP1a 100fr dk blue ('44) .70
Nos. C8A-C8C (3) 1.90

Nos. C8A-C8C were issued by the Vichy government in France, but were not placed on sale in French Guiana.

Common Design Type

1945 Photo. *Perf. 14½x14*

C9 CD87 50fr dark green .85 .85
C10 CD87 100fr plum 1.40 1.40

Victory Issue
Common Design Type

1946, May 8 Engr. *Perf. 12½*

C11 CD92 8fr black .95 .95

Chad to Rhine Issue
Common Design Types

1946, June 6

C12 CD93 5fr dk slate bl 1.00 1.00
C13 CD94 10fr lilac rose 1.00 1.00
C14 CD95 15fr dk vio brn 1.00 1.00
C15 CD96 20fr dk slate grn 1.25 1.25
C16 CD97 25fr vio brown 1.40 1.40
C17 CD98 50fr bright lilac 1.60 1.60
Nos. C12-C17 (6) 7.25 7.25

Eagles — AP2

Tapir — AP3

Toucans — AP4

1947, June 2 Engr. *Perf. 13*

C18 AP2 50fr deep green 12.00 12.00
C19 AP3 100fr red brown 9.00 9.00
C20 AP4 200fr dk gray bl 18.00 18.00
Nos. C18-C20 (3) 39.00 39.00

AIR POST SEMI-POSTAL STAMPS

French Revolution Issue
Common Design Type
Unwmk.

1939, July 5 Photo. *Perf. 13*

Name & Value Typo. in Orange

CB1 CD83 5fr + 4fr brn blk 16.00 16.00

Nurse with Mother & Child — SPAP1

Unwmk.

1942, June 22 Engr. *Perf. 13*

CB2 SPAP1 1.50fr + 50c green .70
CB3 SPAP1 2fr + 6fr brn & red .70

Native children's welfare fund.

Nos. CB2-CB3 were issued by the Vichy government in France, but were not placed on sale in French Guiana.

Colonial Education Fund
Common Design Type

1942, June 22

CB4 CD86a 1.20fr + 1.80fr blue & red .70

No. CB4 was issued by the Vichy government in France, but was not placed on sale in French Guiana.

POSTAGE DUE STAMPS

Postage Due Stamps of France, 1893-1926, Overprinted

1925-27 Unwmk. *Perf. 14x13½*

J1 D2 5c light blue .35 .35
J2 D2 10c brown .50 .50
J3 D2 20c olive green .55 .55
J4 D2 50c violet brown .80 .80
J5 D2 3fr magenta ('27) 7.00 7.00

Surcharged in Black

J6 D2 15c on 20c ol grn .50 .50
a. Blue surcharge 32.50
J7 D2 25c on 5c lt bl .80 .80
J8 D2 30c on 20c ol grn .95 .95
J9 D2 45c on 10c brn .80 .80
J10 D2 60c on 5c lt bl .80 .80
J11 D2 1fr on 20c ol grn 1.25 1.25
J12 D2 2fr on 50c vio brn 1.40 1.40
Nos. J1-J12 (12) 15.70 15.70

Royal Palms — D3

Guiana Girl — D4

1929, Oct. 14 Typo. *Perf. 13½x14*

J13 D3 5c indigo & Prus bl .30 .30
J14 D3 10c bis brn & Prus grn .30 .30
J15 D3 20c grn & rose red .30 .30
J16 D3 30c ol brn & rose red .30 .30
J17 D3 50c vio & ol brn .65 .65
J18 D3 60c brn red & ol brn .95 .95
J19 D4 1fr dp bl & org brn 1.25 1.25
J20 D4 2fr brn red & bluish grn 1.40 1.40
J21 D4 3fr violet & blk 3.25 3.25
Nos. J13-J21 (9) 8.70 8.70

Catalogue values for unused stamps in this section, from this point to the end of the section, are for Never Hinged items.

D5

1947, June 2 Engr. *Perf. 14x13*

J22 D5 10c dk car rose .20 .20
J23 D5 30c dull green .20 .20
J24 D5 50c black .20 .20
J25 D5 1fr brt ultra .35 .35
J26 D5 2fr dk brown red .35 .35
J27 D5 3fr deep violet .50 .50
J28 D5 4fr red .70 .70
J29 D5 5fr brown violet .85 .85
J30 D5 10fr blue green 1.40 1.40
J31 D5 20fr lilac rose 1.90 1.90
Nos. J22-J31 (10) 6.65 6.65

FRENCH GUINEA

'french 'gi-nē

LOCATION — On the coast of West Africa, between Portuguese Guinea and Sierra Leone.
GOVT. — French colony
AREA — 89,436 sq. mi.
POP. — 2,058,442 (est. 1941)
CAPITAL — Conakry

French Guinea stamps were replaced by those of French West Africa around 1944-45. French Guinea became the Republic of Guinea Oct. 2, 1958. See "Guinea" for issues of the republic.

100 Centimes = 1 Franc

See French West Africa No. 66 for additional stamp inscribed "Guinee" and "Afrique Occidentale Francaise."

Navigation and Commerce A1

Fulah Shepherd A2

Perf. 14x13½

1892-1900 Typo. Unwmk.

Name of Colony in Blue or Carmine

No.	Type	Description	Unused	Used
1	A1	1c black, *lilac bl*	1.00	1.00
2	A1	2c brown, *buff*	1.40	1.40
3	A1	4c claret, *lav*	1.90	1.40
4	A1	5c green, *grnsh*	6.00	3.50
5	A1	10c blk, *lavender*	5.25	3.50
6	A1	10c red ('00)	32.50	29.00
7	A1	15c blue, quadrille paper	10.00	5.00
8	A1	15c gray, *lt gray* ('00)	77.50	70.00
9	A1	20c red, *grn*	14.00	9.25
10	A1	25c black, *rose*	8.00	5.75
11	A1	25c blue ('00)	19.00	17.50
12	A1	30c brown, *bis*	29.00	24.00
13	A1	40c red, *straw*	29.00	24.00
a.		"GUINEE FRANCAISE" double	350.00	350.00
14	A1	50c car, *rose*	32.50	25.00
15	A1	50c brown, *az* ('00)	29.00	25.00
16	A1	75c dp vio, *org*	42.50	35.00
17	A1	1fr brnz grn, *straw*	35.00	29.00
		Nos. 1-17 (17)	373.55	309.30

Perf. 13½x14 stamps are counterfeits.
For surcharges see Nos. 48-54.

1904

No.	Type	Description	Unused	Used
18	A2	1c black, *yel grn*	.90	.55
19	A2	2c vio brn, *buff*	.70	.70
20	A2	4c carmine, *bl*	1.10	.95
21	A2	5c green, *grnsh*	1.25	.95
22	A2	10c carmine	2.50	1.40
23	A2	15c violet, *rose*	6.50	3.50
24	A2	20c carmine, *grn*	9.25	8.75
25	A2	25c blue	11.00	7.00
26	A2	30c brown	15.00	14.00
27	A2	40c red, *straw*	21.00	18.00
28	A2	50c brown, *az*	21.00	18.00
29	A2	75c green, *org*	26.00	20.00
30	A2	1fr brnz grn, *straw*	35.00	32.50
31	A2	2fr red, *org*	72.50	72.50
32	A2	5fr green, *yel grn*	87.50	87.50
		Nos. 18-32 (15)	311.20	286.30

For surcharges see Nos. 55-62.

Gen. Louis Faidherbé A3

Oil Palm — A4

Dr. Noel Eugène Ballay A5

1906-07

Name of Colony in Red or Blue

No.	Type	Description	Unused	Used
33	A3	1c gray	.50	.50
34	A3	2c brown	.70	.65
35	A3	4c brown, *bl*	.95	.95
36	A3	5c green	2.50	1.60
37	A3	10c carmine (B)	17.50	2.00
38	A4	20c black, *blue*	4.25	3.00
39	A4	25c blue, *pnksh*	4.25	4.25
40	A4	30c brown, *pnksh*	5.75	3.00
41	A4	35c black, *yellow*	3.25	2.00
42	A4	45c choc, *grnsh gray*	4.25	3.00
43	A4	50c dp violet	8.50	7.00
44	A4	75c blue, *org*	5.75	3.00
45	A5	1fr black, *az*	16.00	16.00
46	A5	2fr blue, *pink*	32.50	32.50
47	A5	5fr car, *straw* (B)	50.00	45.00
		Nos. 33-47 (15)	156.65	124.45

Regular Issues Surcharged in Black or Carmine

1912

On Issue of 1892-1900

No.	Type	Description	Unused	Used
48	A1	5c on 2c brown, *buff*	.80	.80
49	A1	5c on 4c cl, *lav* (C)	.80	.80
50	A1	5c on 15c blue (C)	.80	.80
51	A1	5c on 20c red, *grn*	2.90	2.90
52	A1	5c on 30c brn, *bis* (C)	3.50	3.50
53	A1	10c on 40c red, *straw*	1.40	1.40
54	A1	10c on 75c dp vio, *org*	5.75	5.75
a.		Double surcharge, inverted	210.00	

On Issue of 1904

No.	Type	Description	Unused	Used
55	A2	5c on 2c vio brn, *buff*	.70	.70
a.		Pair, one without surcharge	450.00	
56	A2	5c on 4c car, *blue*	.70	.70
57	A2	5c on 15c violet, *rose*	.80	.80
58	A2	5c on 20c car, *grn*	.80	.80
59	A2	5c on 25c blue (C)	1.00	1.00
60	A2	5c on 30c brown (C)	1.25	1.25
61	A2	10c on 40c red, *straw*	1.10	1.10
62	A2	10c on 50c brn, *az* (C)	3.25	3.25
		Nos. 48-62 (15)	25.55	25.55

Two spacings between the surcharged numerals are found on Nos. 48 to 62.

Ford at Kitim — A6

1913-33 *Perf. 13½x14*

No.	Type	Description	Unused	Used
63	A6	1c violet & bl	.20	.20
64	A6	2c brn & vio brn	.20	.20
65	A6	4c gray & black	.20	.20
66	A6	5c yel grn & bl grn	.70	.20
67	A6	5c brn vio & grn ('22)	.20	.20
68	A6	10c red org & rose	.55	.20
69	A6	10c yel grn & bl grn ('22)	.20	.20
70	A6	10c vio & ver ('25)	.45	.20
71	A6	15c vio brn & rose ('16)	.20	.20
72	A6	15c gray grn & yel grn ('25)	.20	.20
73	A6	15c red brn & rose lil ('27)	.20	.20
74	A6	20c brown & violet	.20	.20
75	A6	20c grn & bl grn ('26)	.65	.50
76	A6	20c brn red & brn ('27)	.65	.30
77	A6	25c ultra & blue	1.75	.80
78	A6	25c black & vio ('22)	.50	.50
79	A6	30c vio brn & grn	1.00	.55
80	A6	30c red org & rose ('22)	.80	.70
81	A6	30c rose red & grn ('25)	.20	.20
82	A6	30c dl grn & bl grn ('28)	1.25	.90
83	A6	35c blue & rose	.40	.20
84	A6	40c green & gray	.80	.65
85	A6	45c brown & red	.80	.65
86	A6	50c ultra & black	5.25	3.25
87	A6	50c ultra & bl ('22)	.80	.50
88	A6	50c yel brn & ol ('25)	.45	.35
89	A6	60c vio, *pnksh* ('25)	.45	.35
90	A6	65c yel brn & sl bl ('26)	1.25	1.00
91	A6	75c red & ultra	1.00	1.00
92	A6	75c indigo & dl bl ('25)	.85	.80
93	A6	75c mag & yel grn ('27)	1.25	.90
94	A6	85c ol grn & red brn ('26)	.90	.90
95	A6	90c brn red & rose ('30)	4.25	4.00
96	A6	1fr violet & black	1.00	.90
97	A6	1.10fr vio & ol brn ('28)	4.50	4.00
98	A6	1.25fr vio & yel brn ('33)	1.60	1.00
99	A6	1.50fr dk bl & lt bl ('30)	4.00	1.75
100	A6	1.75fr ol brn & vio ('33)	1.25	1.25
101	A6	2fr orange & vio brn	2.40	1.10
102	A6	3fr red violet ('30)	6.50	5.00
103	A6	5fr black & vio	9.75	9.75
104	A6	5fr dl bl & blk ('22)	2.00	1.60
		Nos. 63-104 (42)	61.75	47.75

Nos. 66 and 68 exist on both ordinary and chalky paper, No. 71 on chalky paper only.
For surcharges see Nos. 105-115, B1.

Type of 1913-33 Surcharged

1922

No.	Type	Description	Unused	Used
105	A6	60c on 75c violet, *pnksh*	.50	.50

Stamps and Type of 1913-33 Surcharged with New Value and Bars

1924-27

No.	Type	Description	Unused	Used
106	A6	25c on 2fr org & brn (R)	.35	.35
107	A6	25c on 5fr dull bl & blk	.35	.35
108	A6	65c on 75c rose & ultra ('25)	1.00	1.00
109	A6	85c on 75c rose & ultra ('25)	1.25	1.25
110	A6	90c on 75c brn red & cer ('27)	1.75	1.75
111	A6	1.25fr on 1fr dk bl & ultra ('26)	.85	.85
112	A6	1.50fr on 1fr dp bl & lt bl ('27)	1.40	1.40
113	A6	3fr on 5fr mag & sl ('27)	3.25	3.25
114	A6	10fr on 5fr bl & bl grn, *bluish* ('27)	6.50	6.50
115	A6	20fr on 5fr rose lil & brn ol, *pnksh* ('27)	13.50	13.50
		Nos. 106-115 (10)	30.20	30.20

Common Design Types pictured following the introduction.

Colonial Exposition Issue

Common Design Types

1931 Engr. *Perf. 12½*

Name of Country in Black

No.	Type	Description	Unused	Used
116	CD70	40c deep green	3.25	3.25
117	CD71	50c violet	3.25	3.25
118	CD72	90c red orange	3.25	3.25
119	CD73	1.50fr dull blue	3.25	3.25
		Nos. 116-119 (4)	13.00	13.00
		Set, never hinged	17.50	

Paris International Exposition Issue

Common Design Types

1937 *Perf. 13*

No.	Type	Description	Unused	Used
120	CD74	20c deep violet	1.25	1.25
121	CD75	30c dark green	1.25	1.25
122	CD76	40c carmine rose	1.25	1.25
123	CD77	50c dark brown	1.25	1.25
124	CD78	90c red	1.40	1.40
125	CD79	1.50fr ultra	1.40	1.40
		Nos. 120-125 (6)	7.80	7.80
		Set, never hinged	12.00	

Colonial Arts Exhibition Issue

Souvenir Sheet

Common Design Type

1937 ***Imperf.***

No.	Type	Description	Unused	Used
126	CD76	3fr Prussian green	5.75	*7.00*
		Never hinged	8.00	

Guinea Village A7

Hausa Basket Workers A8

Forest Waterfall A9

Guinea Women — A10

1938-40 *Perf. 13*

No.	Type	Description	Unused	Used
128	A7	2c vermilion	.20	.20
129	A7	3c ultra	.20	.20
130	A7	4c green	.20	.20
131	A7	5c rose car	.20	.20
132	A7	10c peacock blue	.20	.20
133	A7	15c violet brown	.20	.20
134	A8	20c dk carmine	.20	.20
135	A8	25c pck blue	.20	.20
136	A8	30c ultra	.20	.20
137	A8	35c green	.40	.40
138	A8	40c blk brn ('40)	.20	.20
139	A8	45c dk green ('40)	.20	.20
140	A8	50c red brown	.40	.40
141	A9	55c dk ultra	.80	.75
142	A9	60c dk ultra ('40)	.65	.65
143	A9	65c green	.85	.65
144	A9	70c green ('40)	1.00	1.00
145	A9	80c rose violet	.50	.45
146	A9	90c rose vio ('39)	.95	.95
147	A9	1fr orange red	2.10	1.40
148	A9	1fr brn blk ('40)	.40	.40
149	A9	1.25fr org red ('39)	1.00	1.00
150	A9	1.40fr brown ('40)	1.00	1.00
151	A9	1.50fr violet	2.00	1.40
152	A10	1.60fr org red ('40)	1.00	1.00
153	A10	1.75fr ultra	.55	.55
154	A10	2fr magenta	.80	.50
155	A10	2.25fr brt ultra ('39)	1.60	1.25
156	A10	2.50fr brn blk ('40)	1.00	1.00
157	A10	3fr peacock blue	.65	.30
158	A10	5fr rose violet	.65	.55
159	A10	10fr slate green	.95	.80
160	A10	20fr chocolate	2.00	1.40
		Nos. 128-160 (33)	23.45	20.00
		Set, never hinged	65.00	

For surcharges see Nos. B8-B11.
For types A7-A10 without "RF," see Nos. 168-174.

Caillié Issue

Common Design Type

1939 Engr. *Perf. 12½x12*

No.	Type	Description	Unused	Used
161	CD81	90c org brn & org	.70	.70
162	CD81	2fr brt violet	.80	.80
163	CD81	2.25fr ultra & dk bl	.80	.80
		Nos. 161-163 (3)	2.30	2.30

René Caillié, French explorer, death cent.

New York World's Fair Issue

Common Design Type

1939

No.	Type	Description	Unused	Used
164	CD82	1.25fr carmine lake	.85	.85
165	CD82	2.25fr ultra	.85	.85

Ford at Kitim and Marshal Petain — A11

1941 *Perf. 12x12½*

166 A11 1fr green .50 —
167 A11 2.50fr deep blue .50 —

For surcharges, see Nos. B15-B16.

Types of 1933-40 without "RF"

1943-44 *Perf. 13*

168 A7 10c peacock blue .35
169 A8 20c dk carmine .55
170 A8 30c ultramarine .55
171 A8 40c black brown .80
172 A9 60c dk ultramarine 1.00
173 A9 1.50fr violet 1.00
174 A10 2fr magenta 1.10
Nos. 168-174 (7) 5.35

Nos. 168-174 were issued by the Vichy government in France, but were not placed on sale in French Guinea.

SEMI-POSTAL STAMPS

Regular Issue of 1913 Surcharged in Red

1915 **Unwmk.** *Perf. 13½x14*

B1 A6 10c + 5c org & rose 1.10 1.00

Exists on both ordinary and chalky paper.

Curie Issue
Common Design Type

1938 **Engr.** *Perf. 13*

B2 CD80 1.75fr + 50c brt ultra 6.50 6.50

French Revolution Issue
Common Design Type

1939 **Photo.**
Name and Value Typo. in Black

B3 CD83 45c + 25c green 6.00 6.00
B4 CD83 70c + 30c brown 6.00 6.00
B5 CD83 90c + 35c red org 6.00 6.00
B6 CD83 1.25fr + 1fr rose pink 6.00 6.00
B7 CD83 2.25fr + 2fr blue 6.00 6.00
Nos. B3-B7 (5) 30.00 30.00
Set, never hinged 37.50

Stamps of 1938, Surcharged in Black

1941 **Unwmk.** *Perf. 13*

B8 A8 50c + 1fr red brn 1.75 1.75
B9 A9 80c + 2fr rose vio 4.25 4.25
B10 A9 1.50fr + 2fr brn 4.25 4.25
B11 A10 2fr + 3fr magenta 4.50 4.50
Nos. B8-B11 (4) 14.75 14.75

Common Design Type and

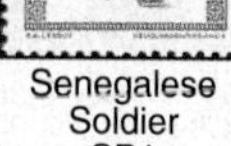

Senegalese Soldier SP1

Colonial Infantryman SP2

1941 **Unwmk.** *Perf. 13*

B12 SP1 1fr + 1fr red .95
B13 CD86 1.50fr + 3fr maroon .95
B14 SP2 2.50fr + 1fr blue .95
Nos. B12-B14 (3) 2.85

Nos. B12-B14 were issued by the Vichy government in France, but were not placed on sale in the French Guinea.

Nos. 166-167 Surcharged in Black or Red

1944 **Engr.** *Perf. 12½x12*

B15 50c + 1.50fr on 2.50fr deep blue (R) .60
B16 + 2.50fr on 1fr green .60

Colonial Development Fund.
Nos. B15-B16 were issued by the Vichy government in France, but were not placed on sale in French Guinea.

AIR POST STAMPS

Common Design Type

1940 **Unwmk.** **Engr.** *Perf. 12½x12*

C1 CD85 1.90fr ultra .45 .45
C2 CD85 2.90fr dark red .50 .50
C3 CD85 4.50fr dk gray grn .65 .65
C4 CD85 4.90fr yellow bis .65 .65
C5 CD85 6.90fr dp orange 1.00 1.00
Nos. C1-C5 (5) 3.25 3.25

Common Design Types

1942 **Engr.**

C6 CD88 50c car & blue .20
C7 CD88 1fr brown & blk .20
C8 CD88 2fr dk grn & red brn .20
C9 CD88 3fr dk bl & scar .35
C10 CD88 5fr vio & brn red .55

Frame Engraved, Center Typographed

C11 CD89 10fr multicolored .55
C12 CD89 20fr multicolored .65
C13 CD89 50fr multicolored .85 *2.50*
Nos. C6-C13 (8) 3.55

There is doubt whether Nos. C6-C12 were officially placed in use.

AIR POST SEMI-POSTAL STAMPS

Dahomey types SPAP1-SPAP3 inscribed "Guinée Frcaise" or "Guinée"

Perf. 13½x12½, 13 (#CB3)
Photo, Engr. (#CB3)

1942, June 22

CB1 SPAP1 1.50fr + 3.50fr green .55 *3.50*
CB2 SPAP2 2fr + 6fr brown .55 *3.50*
CB3 SPAP3 3fr + 9fr car red .55 *3.50*
Nos. CB1-CB3 (3) 1.65 *10.50*

Native children's welfare fund.

Colonial Education Fund
Common Design Type
Perf. 12½x13½

1942, June 22 **Engr.**

CB4 CD86a 1.20fr + 1.80fr blue & red .65 *3.50*

POSTAGE DUE STAMPS

Fulah Woman D1

Heads and Coast D2

1905 **Unwmk.** **Typo.** *Perf. 14x13½*

J1 D1 5c blue 1.40 1.40
J2 D1 10c brown 1.40 1.40
J3 D1 15c green 4.25 2.75
J4 D1 30c rose 4.25 2.75
J5 D1 50c black 7.25 7.25
J6 D1 60c dull orange 10.00 8.00
J7 D1 1fr violet 32.50 29.00
Nos. J1-J7 (7) 61.05 52.55

"Guinèe" in Red or Blue

1906-08

J8 D2 5c grn, *grnsh* ('08) 16.00 10.50
J9 D2 10c violet brn ('08) 4.25 4.25
J10 D2 15c dk blue ('08) 4.25 4.25
J11 D2 20c blk, *yellow* 4.25 3.25
J12 D2 30c red, *straw* ('08) 22.50 20.00
J13 D2 50c violet ('08) 18.00 18.00
J14 D2 60c blk, *buff* ('08) 18.00 16.00
J15 D2 1fr blk, *pnksh* ('08) 11.00 9.00
Nos. J8-J15 (8) 98.25 85.25

D3

D4

1914

J16 D3 5c green .20 .20
J17 D3 10c rose .20 .20
J18 D3 15c gray .35 .35
J19 D3 20c brown .50 .50
J20 D3 30c blue .50 .50
J21 D3 50c black .90 .70
J22 D3 60c orange 1.40 1.40
J23 D3 1fr violet 1.40 1.40
Nos. J16-J23 (8) 5.45 5.25

Type of 1914 Issue Surcharged

1927

J24 D3 2fr on 1fr lil rose 5.25 5.25
J25 D3 3fr on 1fr org brn 5.25 5.25

1938 **Engr.**

J26 D4 5c dk violet .20 .20
J27 D4 10c carmine .20 .20
J28 D4 15c green .20 .20
J29 D4 20c red brown .20 .20
J30 D4 30c rose violet .20 .20
J31 D4 50c chocolate .50 .50
J32 D4 60c peacock blue .80 .80
J33 D4 1fr vermilion .80 .80
J34 D4 2fr ultra .80 .80
J35 D4 3fr black 1.25 1.25
Nos. J26-J35 (10) 5.15 5.15

For No. J27 without "RF," see No. J36.

Type of 1938 without "RF"

1944

J36 D4 10c carmine .35

No. J36 was issued by the Vichy government in France, but was not placed on sale in French Guinea.

FRENCH INDIA

'french 'in-dē-ə

LOCATION — East coast of India bordering on Bay of Bengal.
GOVT. — French Territory
AREA — 196 sq. mi.
POP. — 323,295 (1941)
CAPITAL — Pondichéry

French India was an administrative unit comprising the five settlements of Chandernagor, Karikal, Mahé, Pondichéry and Yanaon. These united with India in 1949 and 1954.

100 Centimes = 1 Franc
24 Caches = 1 Fanon (1923)
8 Fanons = 1 Rupie

Catalogue values for unused stamps in this country are for Never Hinged items, beginning with Scott 210 in the regular postage section, Scott B14 in the semi-postal section, and Scott C7 in the airpost section.

Navigation and Commerce — A1

A2

Perf. 14x13½

1892-1907 **Typo.** **Unwmk.**
Colony Name in Blue or Carmine

1 A1 1c blk, *lil bl* .95 .70
2 A1 2c brn, *buff* 1.40 1.10
3 A1 4c claret, *lav* 1.75 1.60
4 A1 5c grn, *grnsh* 4.00 2.75
5 A1 10c blk, *lavender* 8.50 2.50
6 A1 10c red ('00) 3.25 1.75
7 A1 15c bl, quadrille paper 10.50 4.25
8 A1 15c gray, *lt gray* ('00) 25.00 22.50
9 A1 20c red, *grn* 5.25 4.00
10 A1 25c blk, *rose* 3.50 1.75
11 A1 25c blue ('00) 12.00 9.50
12 A1 30c brn, *bis* 42.50 37.50
13 A1 35c blk, *yel* ('06) 12.00 7.00
14 A1 40c red, *straw* 5.00 4.50
15 A1 45c blk, *gray grn* ('07) 4.00 3.50
16 A1 50c car, *rose* 5.00 4.50
17 A1 50c brn, *az* ('00) 11.00 11.00
18 A1 75c dp vio, *org* 7.00 7.00
19 A1 1fr brnz grn, *straw* 8.25 8.25
Nos. 1-19 (19) 170.85 135.65

Perf. 13½x14 stamps are counterfeits.

Nos. 10 and 16 Surcharged in Carmine or Black

1903

20 A1 5c on 25c blk, *rose* 250.00 160.00
21 A1 10c on 25c blk, *rose* 275.00 175.00
22 A1 15c on 25c blk, *rose* 90.00 90.00
23 A1 40c on 50c car, *rose* (Bk) 425.00 325.00
Nos. 20-23 (4) 1,040. 750.00

Counterfeits of Nos. 20-23 abound.

1903
Revenue Stamp Surcharged in Black

24 A2 5c gray blue 19.00 19.00

The bottom of the revenue stamps were cut off.

Brahma — A5

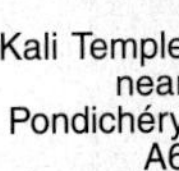

Kali Temple near Pondichéry A6

1914-22 *Perf. 13½x14, 14x13½*

No.	Type	Description	Unused	Used
25	A5	1c gray & blk	.20	.20
26	A5	2c brn vio & blk	.20	.20
27	A5	2c grn & brn vio ('22)	.20	.20
28	A5	3c brown & blk	.20	.20
29	A5	4c orange & blk	.20	.20
30	A5	5c bl grn & blk	.35	.35
31	A5	5c vio brn & blk ('22)	.20	.20
32	A5	10c dp rose & blk	.85	.85
33	A5	10c grn & blk ('22)	.50	.50
34	A5	15c vio & blk	.65	.65
35	A5	20c org red & blk	1.10	1.10
36	A5	25c blue & blk	1.10	1.10
37	A5	25c ultra & fawn ('22)	.80	.80
38	A5	30c ultra & blk	2.25	2.25
39	A5	30c rose & blk ('22)	.85	.85
40	A6	35c choc & blk	1.25	1.25
41	A6	40c org red & blk	1.25	1.25
42	A6	45c bl grn & blk	1.25	1.25
43	A6	50c dp rose & blk	1.25	1.25
44	A6	50c ultra & bl ('22)	1.40	1.40
45	A6	75c blue & blk	2.25	2.25
46	A6	1fr yellow & blk	2.25	2.25
47	A6	2fr violet & blk	4.00	4.00
48	A6	5fr ultra & blk	1.60	1.60
49	A6	5fr rose & blk ('22)	3.25	3.25
		Nos. 25-49 (25)	29.40	29.40

For surcharges see Nos. 50-79, 113-116, 156A, B1-B5.

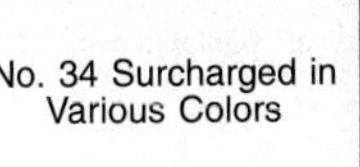

No. 34 Surcharged in Various Colors

1922

No.	Type	Description	Unused	Used
50	A5	1c on 15c (Bk)	.55	.55
51	A5	2c on 15c (Bl)	.55	.55
53	A5	5c on 15c (R)	.55	.55
		Nos. 50-53 (3)	1.65	1.65

Stamps and Types of 1914-22 Surcharged with New Values in Caches, Fanons and Rupies in Black, Red or Blue:

1923-28

No.	Type	Description	Unused	Used
54	A5	1ca on 1c gray & blk (R)	.20	.20
55	A5	2ca on 5c vio brn & blk	.20	.20
a.		Horizontal pair, imperf. between		
56	A5	3ca on 3c brn & blk	.35	.35
57	A5	4ca on 4c org & blk	.55	.55
58	A5	6ca on 10c grn & blk	.55	.55
59	A6	6ca on 45c bl grn & blk (R)	.55	.55
60	A5	10ca on 20c dp red & bl grn ('28)	1.75	1.75
61	A5	12ca on 15c vio & blk	.55	.55
62	A5	15ca on 20c org & blk	.95	.95
63	A6	16ca on 35c lt bl & yel brn ('28)	1.75	1.75
64	A5	18ca on 30c rose & blk	1.40	1.40
65	A6	20ca on 45c grn & dl red ('28)	1.25	.85
66	A5	1fa on 25c dp grn & rose red ('28)	2.25	2.25
67	A6	1fa3ca on 35c choc & blk (Bl)	.80	.80
68	A6	1fa6ca on 40c org & blk (R)	.95	.80
69	A6	1fa12ca on 50c ultra & bl (Bl)	1.10	.80
70	A6	1fa12ca on 75c bl & blk (Bl)	.95	.80
a.		Double surcharge	92.50	
71	A6	1fa16ca on 75c brn red & grn ('28)	2.25	2.00
72	A5	2fa9ca on 25c ultra & fawn (Bl)	.95	.80
73	A6	2fa12ca on 1fr vio & dk brn ('28)	2.00	2.00
74	A6	3fa3ca on 1fr yel & blk (R)	1.10	1.00
a.		Double surcharge	92.50	
75	A6	6fa6ca on 2fr vio & blk (Bl)	3.25	2.75
76	A6	1r on 1fr grn & dp bl (R) ('26)	6.50	5.00
77	A6	2r on 5fr rose & blk (R)	5.00	4.25
a.		Double surcharge	92.50	
78	A6	3r on 2fr gray & bl vio (R) ('26)	13.50	11.00
79	A6	5r on 5fr rose & blk, *grnsh* ('26)	17.50	14.50
		Nos. 54-79 (26)	68.15	58.40

Nos. 60, 63, 66 and 73 have the original value obliterated by bars.

A7

A8

1929

No.	Type	Description	Unused	Used
80	A7	1ca dk gray & blk	.20	.20
81	A7	2ca vio brn & blk	.20	.20
82	A7	3ca brn & blk	.20	.20
83	A7	4ca org & blk	.20	.20
84	A7	6ca gray grn & grn	.20	.20
85	A7	10ca brn, red & grn	.20	.20
86	A8	12ca grn & lt grn	.55	.55
87	A7	16ca brt bl & blk	.70	.70
88	A7	18ca brn red & ver	.70	.70
89	A7	20ca dk bl & grn, *bluish*	.55	.55
90	A8	1fa gray grn & rose red	.55	.50
91	A8	1fa6ca red org & blk	.55	.50
92	A8	1fa12ca dp bl & ultra	.55	.50
93	A8	1fa16ca rose red & grn	.70	.70
94	A8	2fa12ca brt vio & brn	.95	.80
95	A8	6fa6ca dl vio & blk	.95	.80
96	A8	1r gray grn & dp bl	.85	.80
97	A8	2r rose & blk	1.25	.95
98	A8	3r lt gray & gray lil	2.25	1.60
99	A8	5r rose & blk, *grnsh*	2.25	1.75
		Nos. 80-99 (20)	14.55	12.60

For overprints and surcharges see Nos. 117-134, 157-176, 184-209G.

Common Design Types pictured following the introduction.

Colonial Exposition Issue
Common Design Types

1931 **Engr.** *Perf. 12½*

No.	Type	Description	Unused	Used
100	CD70	10ca deep green	2.50	2.50
101	CD71	12ca violet	2.75	2.75
102	CD72	18ca red orange	2.75	2.75
103	CD73	1fa12ca dull blue	2.75	2.75
		Nos. 100-103 (4)	10.75	10.75

Paris International Exposition Issue
Common Design Types

1937 *Perf. 13*

No.	Type	Description	Unused	Used
104	CD74	8ca dp violet	1.10	1.10
105	CD75	12ca dk green	1.10	1.10
106	CD76	16ca car rose	1.25	1.25
107	CD77	20ca dk brown	1.25	1.25
108	CD78	1fa12ca red	1.25	1.25
109	CD79	2fa12ca ultra	1.25	1.25
		Nos. 104-109 (6)	7.20	7.20

For overprints see Nos. 135-139, 177-181.

Colonial Arts Exhibition Issue
Souvenir Sheet
Common Design Type

1937 *Imperf.*

No.	Type	Description	Unused	Used
110	CD79	5fa red violet	5.75	*7.00*

For overprint see No. 140.

New York World's Fair Issue
Common Design Type

1939 **Engr.** *Perf. 12½x12*

No.	Type	Description	Unused	Used
111	CD82	1fa12ca car lake	.95	.95
112	CD82	2fa12ca ultra	1.25	1.25

For overprints see Nos. 141-142, 182-183.

Temple near Pondichéry and Marshal Petain A9

1941 **Engr.** *Perf. 12½x12*

No.	Type	Description	Unused	Used
112A	A9	1fa16ca car & red	.50	
112B	A9	4fa4ca blue	.50	

Nos. 112A-112B were issued by the Vichy government in France, but were not placed on sale in French India.

For surcharges, see Nos. B13B-B13C.

Nos. 62, 64, 67, 72 Overprinted in Carmine or Blue (#116):

a

FRANCE LIBRE

b

1941 **Unwmk.** *Perf. 13½x14*

No.	Type	Description	Unused	Used
113	A5 (a)	15ca on 20c	57.50	57.50
114	A5 (a)	18ca on 30c	2.40	2.40
115	A6 (a)	1fa3ca on 35c	77.50	77.50
a.		Horiz. overprint	77.50	77.50
116	A5 (b)	2fa9ca on 25c	1,050.	775.00
a.		Overprint "a" (Bl)	950.00	775.00
b.		Overprint "b" (C)	*1,350.*	

Nos. 81-99 Overprinted Type "a" in Carmine or Blue

1941

No.	Type	Description	Unused	Used
117	A7	2ca (C)	8.50	8.50
118	A7	3ca (C)	2.50	2.50
119	A7	4ca (C)	6.00	6.00
120	A7	6ca (C)	1.75	1.75
121	A7	10ca (Bl)	2.75	2.75
122	A8	12ca (C)	2.00	2.00
123	A7	16ca (C)	2.10	2.10
123A	A7	18ca (Bl)	475.00	475.00
124	A7	20ca (C)	1.90	1.90
125	A8	1fa (Bl)	1.75	1.75
126	A8	1fa6ca (C)	2.50	2.50
127	A8	1fa12ca (C)	4.00	4.00
128	A8	1fa16ca (C)	1.90	1.90
129	A8	2fa12ca (C)	2.25	2.25
130	A8	6fa6ca (C)	2.25	2.25
131	A8	1r (C)	2.25	2.25
132	A8	2r (C)	2.25	2.25
133	A8	3r (C)	3.00	3.00
134	A8	5r (C)	7.00	7.00
		Nos. 117-123,124-134 (18)	56.65	56.65

Same Overprints on Paris Exposition Issue of 1937

1941 *Perf. 13*

No.	Type	Description	Unused	Used
135	CD74 (b)	8ca (C)	6.25	6.25
135A	CD74 (b)	8ca (Bl)	175.00	175.00
135B	CD74 (a)	8ca (C)	125.00	125.00
135C	CD74 (a)	8ca (Bl)	160.00	160.00
136	CD75 (a)	12ca (C)	3.50	3.50
137	CD76 (a)	16ca (Bl)	3.50	3.50
138	CD78 (a)	1fa12ca (Bl)	3.50	3.50
139	CD79 (a)	2fa12ca (C)	3.50	3.50
		Nos. 135-139 (8)	480.25	480.25

Inverted overprints exist.

Souvenir Sheet

No. 110 Overprinted "FRANCE LIBRE" Diagonally in Blue Violet

Two types of overprint:
I — Overprint 37mm. With serifs.
II — Overprint 24mm, as type "a" shown above No. 113. No serifs.

1941 **Unwmk.** *Imperf.*

No.	Type	Description	Unused	Used
140	CD79	5fa red vio (I)	575.00	450.00
a.		Type II	600.00	600.00

Overprinted on New York World's Fair Issue, 1939

Perf. 12½x12

No.	Type	Description	Unused	Used
141	CD82 (a)	1fa12ca (Bl)	2.10	2.10
142	CD82 (a)	2fa12ca (C)	2.50	2.50

Lotus Flowers — A10

1942 **Unwmk.** **Photo.** *Perf. 14x14½*

No.	Type	Description	Unused	Used
143	A10	2ca brown	.20	.20
144	A10	3ca dk blue	.20	.20
145	A10	4ca emerald	.20	.20
146	A10	6ca dk orange	.20	.20
147	A10	12ca grnsh blk	.20	.20
148	A10	16ca rose violet	.20	.20
149	A10	20ca dk red brn	.50	.50
150	A10	1fa brt red	.55	.50
151	A10	1fa18ca slate blk	.70	.65
152	A10	6fa6ca brt ultra	1.25	1.25
153	A10	1r dull violet	.95	.95
154	A10	2r bister	1.25	1.10
155	A10	3r chocolate	1.25	1.25
156	A10	5r dk green	1.60	1.60
		Nos. 143-156 (14)	9.25	9.00

Stamps of 1923-39 Overprinted in Blue or Carmine

c

d

1942-43 *Perf. 13½x14, 14x13½*

Overprinted on No. 64

No.	Type	Description	Unused	Used
156A	A5 (c)	18ca on 30c (B)	210.00	175.00

Overprinted on #81-82, 84, 86-99

No.	Type	Description	Unused	Used
157	A7 (c)	2ca (C)	1.10	1.10
a.		Black overprint	140.00	110.00
158	A7 (c)	3ca (C)	1.10	1.10
159	A7 (c)	6ca (Bl)	1.10	1.10
160	A8 (d)	12ca (Bl)	2.50	2.50
161	A7 (c)	16ca (C)	.95	.95
162	A7 (c)	18ca (Bl)	1.25	1.25
163	A7 (c)	20ca (Bl) ('43)	4.50	3.50
164	A7 (c)	20ca (C)	.95	.95
165	A8 (d)	1fa (Bl)	.95	.95

166	A8 (d)	1fa6ca (C)	1.50	1.50
167	A8 (d)	1fa12ca (C)	2.00	2.00
168	A8 (d)	1fa16ca (Bl)	1.40	1.40
169	A8 (d)	2fa12ca (Bl)	57.50	57.50
170	A8 (d)	2fa12ca (C)	2.00	2.00
171	A8 (d)	6fa6ca (C)	2.50	2.50
172	A8 (d)	1r (C)	4.50	4.50
173	A8 (d)	2r (C)	4.50	4.50
174	A8 (d)	3r (C)	4.50	4.50
175	A8 (d)	3r (Bl) ('43)	125.00	125.00
176	A8 (d)	5r (C)	4.50	4.50
		Nos. 156A-176 (21)	434.30	398.30

Same Overprints on Paris International Exposition Issue of 1937

Perf. 13

177	CD74 (c)	8ca (Bl)	5.00	4.50
178	CD75 (d)	12ca (Bl)	4.00	4.00
179	CD76 (d)	16ca (Bl)	925.00	925.00
180	CD78 (d)	1fa12ca (Bl)	1.50	1.50
181	CD79 (d)	2fa12ca (C)	2.10	2.10

Same Overprint on New York World's Fair Issue, 1939

Perf. 12½x12

182	CD82 (d)	1fa12ca (Bl)	2.50	2.50
183	CD82 (d)	2fa12ca (C)	3.50	3.50

No. 87 Surcharged in Carmine

1942-43 ***Perf. 13½x14***

184	A7	1ca on 16ca	57.50	35.00
185	A7	4ca on 16ca ('43)	57.50	35.00
186	A7	10ca on 16ca	32.50	14.00
187	A7	15ca on 16ca	30.00	14.00
188	A7	1fa3ca on 16ca ('43)	55.00	29.00
189	A7	2fa9ca on 16ca ('43)	45.00	39.00
190	A7	3fa3ca on 16ca ('43)	32.50	17.00
		Nos. 184-190 (7)	310.00	183.00

Nos. 95-99 Surcharged in Carmine

1943 ***Perf. 14x13½***

191	A8	1ca on 6fa6ca	6.75	6.75
192	A8	4ca on 6fa6ca	8.50	8.50
193	A8	10ca on 6fa6ca	2.50	2.50
194	A8	15ca on 6fa6ca	5.50	5.50
195	A8	1fa3ca on 6fa6ca	6.75	6.75
196	A8	2fa9ca on 6fa6ca	8.50	8.50
197	A8	3fa3ca on 6fa6ca	8.50	8.50
198	A8	1ca on 1r	3.50	3.50
199	A8	2ca on 1r	.95	.95
200	A8	4ca on 1r	.95	.95
201	A8	6ca on 2r	.95	.95
202	A8	10ca on 2r	1.25	1.25
203	A8	12ca on 2r	.95	.95
204	A8	15ca on 3r	.95	.95
205	A8	16ca on 3r	.85	.85
206	A8	1fa3ca on 3r	.95	.95
207	A8	1fa6ca on 5r	1.25	1.25
208	A8	1fa12ca on 5r	2.40	2.40
209	A8	1fa16ca on 5r	2.40	2.40
		Nos. 191-209 (19)	64.35	64.35

In 1943, 200 each of 27 stamps were overprinted in red or dark blue, "FRANCE TOUJOURS" and a Lorraine Cross within a circle measuring 17½mm in diameter. Overprinted were Nos. 81-99, 104-109, 111-112.

No. 95 Surcharged in Carmine with New Value and Bars

1943 Unwmk. ***Perf. 14x13½***

209A	A8	1ca on 6fa6ca	21.00	13.50
209B	A8	4ca on 6fa6ca	21.00	13.50
209C	A8	10ca on 6fa6ca	10.00	5.75
209D	A8	15ca on 6fa6ca	10.00	5.75
209E	A8	1fa3ca on 6fa6ca	15.00	13.50
209F	A8	2fa9ca on 6fa6ca	15.00	13.50
209G	A8	3fa3ca on 6fa6ca	19.00	16.00
		Nos. 209A-209G (7)	111.00	81.50

Catalogue values for unused stamps in this section, from this point to the end of the section, are for Never Hinged items.

Eboue Issue

Common Design Type

1945 Engr. ***Perf. 13***

210	CD91	3fa8ca black	.50	.50
211	CD91	5r1fa16ca Prus grn	.95	.95

Nos. 210 and 211 exist imperforate.

Apsaras — A11

Brahman Ascetic — A12

Designs: 6ca, 8ca, 10ca, Dvarabalagar. 12ca, 15ca, 1fa, Vishnu. 1fa6ca, 2fa, 2fa2ca, Dvarabalagar (foot raised). 2fa12ca, 3fa, 5fa, Temple Guardian. 7fa12ca, 1r2fa, 1r4fa12ca, Tigoupalagar.

1948 Photo. ***Perf. 13x13½***

212	A11	1ca dk ol grn	.20	.20
213	A11	2ca orange brn	.20	.20
214	A11	4ca vio, *cr*	.20	.20
215	A11	6ca yellow org	.85	.50
216	A11	8ca gray blk	.85	.85
217	A11	10ca dl yel grn, *pale grn*	.85	.85
218	A11	12ca violet brn	.55	.50
219	A11	15ca Prus grn	.55	.50
220	A11	1fa vio, *pale rose*	.85	.65
221	A11	1fa6ca brown red	.85	.65
222	A11	2fa dk green	.85	.65
223	A11	2fa2ca blue, *cr*	1.25	.85
224	A11	2fa12ca brown	1.25	.85
225	A11	3fa dp orange	1.75	.95
226	A11	5fa red vio, *rose*	1.60	.85
227	A11	7fa12ca dk brown	1.75	.85
228	A11	1r2fa brown blk	4.00	4.00
229	A11	1r4fa12ca olive grn	4.50	4.00
		Nos. 212-229 (18)	22.90	18.10

1952

230	A12	18ca rose red	1.25	1.25
231	A12	1fa15ca vio blue	1.50	1.50
232	A12	4fa olive grn	2.25	2.25
		Nos. 230-232 (3)	5.00	5.00

Military Medal Issue

Common Design Type

1952 Engr. and Typo. ***Perf. 13***

233	CD101	1fa multi	3.25	3.25

SEMI-POSTAL STAMPS

Regular Issue of 1914 Surcharged in Red

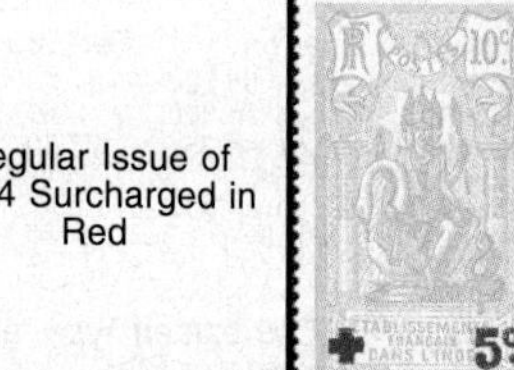

1915 Unwmk. ***Perf. 14x13½***

B1	A5	10c + 5c rose & blk	1.10	1.10
a.		Inverted surcharge	125.00	125.00

There were two printings of this surcharge; in the first it was placed at the bottom of the stamp, in the second it was near the top.

Regular Issue of 1914 Surcharged in Red

1916

B2	A5	10c + 5c rose & blk	12.00	12.00
a.		Inverted surcharge	125.00	125.00
b.		Double surcharge	125.00	125.00

Surcharged

B3	A5	10c + 5c rose & blk	2.40	2.40

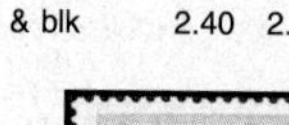

Surcharged

B4	A5	10c + 5c rose & blk	1.10	1.10

Surcharged

B5	A5	10c + 5c rose & blk	1.25	1.25

Curie Issue

Common Design Type

1938 Engr. ***Perf. 13***

B6	CD80	2fa12ca + 20ca brt ultra	7.00	7.00

French Revolution Issue

Common Design Type

1939 Photo.

Name and Value Typo. in Black

B7	CD83	18ca + 10ca grn	5.75	5.75
B8	CD83	1fa6ca + 12ca brn	5.75	5.75
B9	CD83	1fa12ca + 16ca red org	5.75	5.75
B10	CD83	1fa16ca + 1fa16ca rose pink	5.75	5.75
B11	CD83	2fa12ca + 3fa blue	5.75	5.75
		Nos. B7-B11 (5)	28.75	28.75

Common Design Type and

Non-Commissioned Officer, Native Guard — SP1

Sepoy SP2

1941 Photo. ***Perf. 13½***

B12	SP1	1fa10ca + 1fa16ca red	.90	
B13	CD86	2fa12ca + 5fa mar	.80	
B13A	SP2	4fa4ca + 1fa16ca bl	.80	
		Nos. B12-B13A (3)	2.50	

Nos. B12-B13A were issued by the Vichy government in France, but were not placed on sale in French India.

Nos. 112A-112B Surcharged in Black or Red

1944 Engr. ***Perf. 12½x12***

B13B		20ca + 2fa12ca on 4fa4ca deep blue (R)	.70	
B13C		+ 4fa4ca on 1fa16ca car & red	.70	

Colonial Development Fund.

Nos. B13B-B13C were issued by the Vichy government in France, but were not placed on sale in French India.

Catalogue values for unused stamps in this section, from this point to the end of the section, are for Never Hinged items.

Red Cross Issue

Common Design Type

1944 Photo. ***Perf. 14½x14***

B14	CD90	3fa + 1r4fa dk ol brn	.80	.80

The surtax was for the French Red Cross and national relief.

Tropical Medicine Issue

Common Design Type

1950 Engr. ***Perf. 13***

B15	CD100	1fa + 10ca ind & dp bl	2.10	2.10

The surtax was for charitable work.

AIR POST STAMPS

Common Design Type

1942 Unwmk. Photo. ***Perf. 14½x14***

C1	CD87	4fa dark orange	.70	.70
C2	CD87	1r bright red	.70	.70
C3	CD87	2r brown red	1.10	1.10
C4	CD87	5r black	1.10	1.10
C5	CD87	8r ultra	1.50	1.50
C6	CD87	10r dark green	1.50	1.50
		Nos. C1-C6 (6)	6.60	6.60

Catalogue values for unused stamps in this section, from this point to the end of the section, are for Never Hinged items.

Victory Issue

Common Design Type

1946 Engr. ***Perf. 12½***

C7	CD92	4fa dk blue green	.70	.70

Chad to Rhine Issue

Common Design Types

1946, June 6

C8	CD93	2fa12ca olive bis	.70	.70
C9	CD94	5fa dark blue	.70	.70
C10	CD95	7fa12ca dk purple	1.00	1.00
C11	CD96	1r2fa green	1.00	1.00
C12	CD97	1r4fa12ca dk car	1.25	1.25
C13	CD98	3r1fa violet brn	2.40	2.40
		Nos. C8-C13 (6)	7.05	7.05

A 3r ultramarine and red, picturing the Temple of Chindambaram, was sold at Paris June 7 to July 8, 1948, but not placed on sale in the colony. Value $5.75.

Bas-relief Figure of Goddess — AP1

Wing and Temple — AP2

Bird over Palms — AP3

Perf. 12x13, 13x12

1949 Photo. Unwmk.

C14 AP1	1r yellow & plum	4.00	2.75
C15 AP2	2r green & dk grn	4.00	3.50
C16 AP3	5r lt bl & vio brn	17.00	13.50
	Nos. C14-C16 (3)	25.00	19.75

UPU Issue

Common Design Type

1949 Engr. *Perf. 13*

C17 CD99 6fa lilac rose 6.50 6.50

Universal Postal Union, 75th anniv.

Liberation Issue

Common Design Type

1954, June 6

C18 CD102 1fa sepia & vio brn 5.75 5.75

AIR POST SEMI-POSTAL STAMPS

Girl's School SPAP1

Perf. 12½x13½

1942, June 22 Unwmk. Photo.

CB1 SPAP1	2fa12ca + 5fa20ca green	.70
CB2 SPAP1	3fa8ca + 1r2fa yel brn	.70

Native children's welfare fund.

Nos. CB1-CB2 were issued by the Vichy government in France, but were not placed on sale in French India.

Colonial Education Fund

Common Design Type

1942, June 22

CB3 CD86a 2fa + 3fa blue & red .70

No. CB3 was issued by the Vichy government in France, but was not placed on sale in French India.

POSTAGE DUE STAMPS

Postage Due Stamps of France Surcharged like Nos. 54-75 in Black, Blue or Red

1923 Unwmk. *Perf. 14x13½*

J1	D2	6ca on 10c brn	.80	.80
J2	D2	12ca on 25c rose (Bk)	.80	.80
J3	D2	15ca on 20c ol grn (R)	1.10	1.10
J4	D2	1fa6ca on 30c red	1.10	1.10
J5	D2	1fa12a on 50c brn vio	1.75	1.75
J6	D2	1fa15ca on 5c bl (Bk)	1.90	1.90
J7	D2	3fa3ca on 1fr red brn, *straw*	2.00	2.00
		Nos. J1-J7 (7)	9.45	9.45

Types of Postage Due Stamps of French Colonies, 1884-85, Surcharged with New Values as in 1923 in Red or Black Bars over Original Values

1928

J8	D1	4ca on 20c gray lil	1.10	1.10
J9	D1	1fa on 30c orange	1.50	1.50
J10	D1	1fa16ca on 5c bl blk (R)	1.50	1.50
J11	D1	3fa on 1fr lt grn	2.10	2.10
		Nos. J8-J11 (4)	6.20	6.20

D3

1929 Typo.

J12	D3	4ca deep red	.35	.35
J13	D3	6ca blue	.50	.50
J14	D3	12ca green	.50	.50
J15	D3	1fa brown	.95	.95
J16	D3	1fa12ca lilac gray	.95	.95
J17	D3	1fa16ca buff	1.25	1.25
J18	D3	3fa lilac	1.60	1.60
		Nos. J12-J18 (7)	6.10	6.10

D4

1948 Unwmk. Photo. *Perf. 13x13½*

J19	D4	1ca dk violet	.20	.20
J20	D4	2ca dk brown	.35	.35
J21	D4	6ca blue green	.35	.35
J22	D4	12ca dp orange	.50	.50
J23	D4	1fa dk car rose	.55	.55
J24	D4	1fa12ca brown	.55	.55
J25	D4	2fa dk slate bl	.95	.95
J26	D4	2fa12ca henna brn	1.25	1.25
J27	D4	5fa dk olive grn	1.75	1.75
J28	D4	1r dk blue vio	2.10	2.10
		Nos. J19-J28 (10)	8.55	8.55

FRENCH MOROCCO

'french mə-'rä-ˌkō

LOCATION — Northwest coast of Africa
GOVT. — French Protectorate
AREA — 153,870 sq. mi.
POP. — 8,340,000 (estimated 1954)
CAPITAL — Rabat

French Morocco was a French Protectorate from 1912 until 1956 when it, along with the Spanish and Tangier zones of Morocco, became the independent country, Morocco.

Stamps inscribed "Tanger" were for use in the international zone of Tangier in northern Morocco.

100 Centimos = 1 Peseta
100 Centimes = 1 franc (1917)

Catalogue values for unused stamps in this country are for Never Hinged items, beginning with Scott 177 in the regular postage section, Scott B26 in the semi-postal section, Scott C27 in the airpost section, Scott CB23A in the airpost semi-postal section, and Scott J46 in the postage due section.

French Offices in Morocco

A1

A2

Stamps of France Surcharged in Red or Black

1891-1900 Unwmk. *Perf. 14x13½*

1	A1	5c on 5c grn, *grnsh* (R)	8.50	3.50
a.		Imperf., pair	110.00	
2	A1	5c on 5c yel grn (II) (R) ('99)	24.00	21.00
a.		Type I	24.00	17.50
3	A1	10c on 10c blk, *lav* (II) (R)	24.00	2.10
a.		Type I	29.00	16.00
b.		10c on 25c black, *rose*	775.00	
4	A1	20c on 20c red, *grn*	27.50	20.00
5	A1	25c on 25c blk, *rose* (R)	21.00	2.50
a.		Double surcharge	160.00	
b.		Imperf., pair	125.00	
6	A1	50c on 50c car, *rose* (II)	70.00	29.00
a.		Type I	300.00	210.00
7	A1	1p on 1fr brnz grn, *straw*	82.50	52.50
8	A1	2p on 2fr brn, *az* (Bk) ('00)	190.00	175.00
		Nos. 1-8 (8)	447.50	305.60

No. 3b was never sent to Morocco.

France Nos. J15-J16 Overprinted in Carmine

1893

9	A2	5c black	1,900.	800.00
10	A2	10c black	1,650.	575.00

Counterfeits exist.

A3

A4

A5

Surcharged in Red or Black

1902-10

11	A3	1c on 1c gray (R) ('08)	1.40	.80
a.		Surcharge omitted		
12	A3	2c on 2c vio brn ('08)	1.40	.95
13	A3	3c on 3c red org ('08)	1.50	.95
14	A3	4c on 4c yel brn ('08)	7.75	5.25
15	A3	5c on 5c grn (R)	6.00	2.50
a.		Double surcharge		175.00
16	A4	10c on 10c rose red ('03)	4.50	1.50
a.		Surcharge omitted		
17	A4	20c on 20c brn vio ('03)	21.00	14.00
18	A4	25c on 25c bl ('03)	21.00	1.75
19	A4	35c on 35c vio ('10)	29.00	16.00
20	A5	50c on 50c bis brn & lav ('03)	40.00	9.25
21	A5	1p on 1fr cl & ol grn ('03)	82.50	55.00
22	A5	2p on 2fr gray vio & yel ('03)	110.00	67.50
		Nos. 11-22 (12)	326.05	175.45

Nos. 11-14 exist spelled CFNTIMOS or GENTIMOS.

The 25c on 25c with surcharge omitted is listed as No. 81a.

For overprints and surcharges see Nos. 26-37, 72-79, B1, B3.

Postage Due Stamps Nos. J1-J2 Handstamped

1903

24	D2	5c on 5c light blue	1,100.	925.00
25	D2	10c on 10c choc	2,100.	1,600.

Nos. 24 and 25 were used only on Oct. 10, 1903. Used copies were not canceled, the overprint serving as a cancellation.

Counterfeits exist.

Types of 1902-10 Issue Surcharged in Red or Blue

1911-17

26	A3	1c on 1c gray (R)	.55	.50
27	A3	2c on 2c vio brn	.55	.50
28	A3	3c on 3c orange	.55	.50
29	A3	5c on 5c green (R)	.80	.35
30	A4	10c on 10c rose	.65	.35
a.		Imperf., pair	200.00	
31	A4	15c on 15c org ('17)	2.25	1.60
32	A4	20c on 20c brn vio	3.50	2.50
33	A4	25c on 25c blue (R)	1.75	1.25
34	A4	35c on 35c violet (R)	6.75	2.75
35	A5	40c on 40c red & pale bl ('17)	6.00	4.00
36	A5	50c on 50c bis brn & lav (R)	17.50	9.25
37	A5	1p on 1fr cl & ol grn	13.00	5.00
		Nos. 26-37 (12)	53.85	28.55

For surcharges see Nos. B1, B3.

Six stamps of this design were issued by the Cherifien posts in 1912-13. The Administration Cherifinne des Postes, Telegraphes et Telephones was formed in 1911 under French guidance. Value set, $10 unused or used.

French Protectorate

A6

A7

A8

Issue of 1911-17 Overprinted "Protectorat Francais"

1914-21

38	A6	1c on 1c gray	.45	.30
39	A6	2c on 2c vio brn	.45	.30
40	A6	3c on 3c orange	.80	.35
41	A6	5c on 5c green	.55	.35
a.		New value omitted	210.00	210.00
42	A7	10c on 10c rose	.45	.20
a.		New value omitted	450.00	450.00
43	A7	15c on 15c org ('17)	.65	.55
a.		New value omitted	82.50	82.50

44 A7 20c on 20c brn vio 3.50 2.10
a. "Protectorat Francais" double 210.00 210.00
45 A7 25c on 25c blue 1.60 .35
a. New value omitted 250.00 250.00
46 A7 25c on 25c violet ('21) 1.00 .20
a. "Protectorat Francais" omitted 60.00 60.00
b. "Protectorat Francais" dbl. 125.00 125.00
c. "Protectorat Francais" dbl. (R + Bk) 125.00 125.00
47 A7 30c on 30c vio ('21) 12.00 6.75
48 A7 35c on 35c violet 4.00 1.25
49 A8 40c on 40c red & pale bl 12.00 6.50
a. New value omitted 240.00 240.00
50 A8 45c on 45c grn & bl ('21) 32.50 29.00
51 A8 50c on 50c bis brn & lav 1.10 .35
a. "Protectorat Francais" invtd. 110.00 110.00
b. "Protectorat Francais" dbl. *175.00 175.00*
52 A8 1p on 1fr cl & ol grn 2.40 .50
a. "Protectorat Francais" invtd. 240.00 240.00
b. New value double 140.00 140.00
c. New value dbl., one invtd. 140.00 140.00
53 A8 2p on 2fr gray vio & yel 4.00 1.10
a. New value omitted 125.00 125.00
b. "Protectorat Francais" omitted 85.00 85.00
c. New value double *125.00 125.00*
d. New value dbl., one invtd.
54 A8 5p on 5fr dk bl & buff 10.50 3.25
Nos. 38-54 (17) 87.95 53.40

For surcharges see Nos. B2, B4-B5.

Tower of Hassan, Rabat — A9

Mosque of the Andalusians, Fez — A10

City Gate Chella A11

Koutoubiah, Marrakesh A12

Bab Mansour, Meknes A13

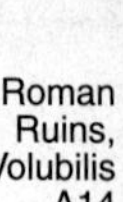

Roman Ruins, Volubilis A14

1917 Engr. *Perf. 13½x14, 14x13½*

55 A9 1c grnsh gray .35 .35
56 A9 2c brown lilac .50 .35
57 A9 3c orange brn .50 .35
a. Imperf., pair 65.00 65.00
58 A10 5c yellow grn .50 .20
59 A10 10c rose red .50 .20
60 A10 15c dark gray .50 .20
a. Imperf., pair 47.50 47.50
61 A11 20c red brown 2.50 1.75
62 A11 25c dull blue 2.90 .70
63 A11 30c gray violet 3.25 2.10
64 A12 35c orange 3.25 2.10
65 A12 40c ultra 1.10 .70
66 A12 45c gray green 21.00 8.50
67 A13 50c dk brown 4.00 2.10
a. Imperf., pair 47.50 47.50
68 A13 1fr slate 8.50 2.75
a. Imperf., pair 47.50 47.50
69 A14 2fr black brown 125.00 70.00
70 A14 5fr dk gray grn 32.50 29.00
71 A14 10fr black 32.50 29.00
Nos. 55-71 (17) 239.35 150.35

See note following #115. See #93-105. For surcharges see #120-121.

Types of the 1902-10 Issue Overprinted

1918-24 *Perf. 14x13½*

72 A3 1c gray .30 .30
73 A3 2c violet brn .35 .35
74 A3 3c red orange .55 .55
75 A3 5c green .55 .35
76 A3 5c orange ('23) 1.25 1.25
77 A4 10c rose 1.25 .95
78 A4 10c green ('24) 1.10 .95
79 A4 15c orange 1.10 .70
80 A4 20c violet brn 1.90 1.40
81 A4 25c blue 1.60 1.40
a. "TANGER" omitted 325.00 300.00
82 A4 30c red org ('24) 1.90 1.90
83 A4 35c violet 2.25 1.75
84 A5 40c red & pale bl 2.50 1.60
85 A5 50c bis brn & lav 17.50 10.50
86 A4 50c blue 12.00 8.25
87 A5 1fr claret & ol grn 9.50 4.50
88 A5 2fr org & pale bl ('24) 57.50 55.00
89 A5 5fr dk bl & buff ('24) 47.50 47.50
Nos. 72-89 (18) 160.60 139.20

Types of 1917 and

Tower of Hassan, Rabat — A15

Bab Mansour, Meknes A16

Roman Ruins, Volubilis A17

1923-27 Photo. *Perf. 13½*

90 A15 1c olive green .20 .20
91 A15 2c brown vio .20 .20
92 A15 3c yellow brn .20 .20
93 A10 5c orange .20 .20
94 A10 10c yellow grn .20 .20
95 A10 15c dk gray .20 .20
96 A11 20c red brown .20 .20
97 A11 20c red vio ('27) .35 .35
98 A11 25c ultra .20 .20
99 A11 30c deep red .20 .20
100 A11 30c turq bl ('27) .85 .50
101 A12 35c violet .80 .50
102 A12 40c orange red .20 .20
103 A12 45c deep green .20 .20
104 A16 50c dull turq .35 .20
105 A12 50c olive grn ('27) .65 .20
106 A16 60c lilac .70 .20
107 A16 75c red vio ('27) .70 .35
108 A16 1fr deep brown .50 .35
109 A16 1.05fr red brn ('27) 1.25 .55
110 A16 1.40fr dull rose ('27) .60 .50
111 A16 1.50fr turq bl ('27) 1.00 .20
112 A17 2fr olive brn 1.00 .70
113 A17 3fr dp red ('27) 1.25 .70
114 A17 5fr dk gray grn 2.75 1.60
115 A17 10fr black 7.50 3.50
Nos. 90-115 (26) 22.45 12.60

Nos. 90-110, 112-115 exist imperf. The stamps of 1917 were line engraved. Those of 1923-27 were printed by photogravure and have in the margin at lower right the imprint "Helio Vaugirard."

See #B36. For surcharges see #122-123.

No. 102 Surcharged in Black

1930

120 A12 15c on 40c orange red 1.25 1.25

Nos. 100, 106 and 110 Surcharged in Blue Similarly to No. 176

1931

121 A11 25c on 30c turq blue 1.90 1.60
a. Inverted surcharge 85.00 85.00
122 A16 50c on 60c lilac .80 .20
a. Inverted surcharge 95.00 95.00
123 A16 1fr on 1.40fr rose 2.50 1.25
a. Inverted surcharge 95.00 95.00
Nos. 121-123 (3) 5.20 3.05

Old Treasure House and Tribunal, Tangier A18

Roadstead at Agadir A19

Post Office at Casablanca A20

Moulay Idriss of the Zehroun A21

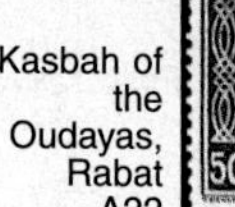

Kasbah of the Oudayas, Rabat A22

Court of the Medersa el Attarine at Fez A23

Saadiens' Tombs at Marrakesh A25

Kasbah of Si Madani el Glaoui at Ouarzazat A24

1933-34 Engr. *Perf. 13*

124 A18 1c olive blk .20 .20
125 A18 2c red violet .20 .20
126 A19 3c dark brown .20 .20
127 A19 5c brown red .20 .20
128 A20 10c blue green .20 .20
129 A20 15c black .20 .20
130 A20 20c red brown .20 .20
131 A21 25c dark blue .20 .20
132 A21 30c emerald .35 .20
133 A21 40c black brn .35 .20
134 A22 45c brown vio .55 .50
135 A22 50c dk blue grn .55 .20
a. Booklet pane of 10 12.00
b. Booklet pane of 20 25.00
136 A22 65c brown red .20 .20
a. Booklet pane of 10 12.00
b. Booklet pane of 20 25.00
137 A23 75c red violet .55 .20
138 A23 90c orange red .35 .20
139 A23 1fr deep brown .80 .35
140 A23 1.25fr black ('34) 1.10 .80
141 A24 1.50fr ultra .35 .20
142 A24 1.75fr myr grn ('34) .55 .20
143 A24 2fr yellow brn 3.25 .55
144 A24 3fr car rose 42.50 5.00
145 A25 5fr red brown 8.50 1.50
146 A25 10fr black 6.75 5.25
147 A25 20fr bluish gray 6.50 5.25
Nos. 124-147 (24) 74.80 22.40

Booklets containing Nos. 135 and 136 each have two panes of 10 (#135a, 136a) connected by a gutter, the complete piece constituting No. 135b or 136b, which is stapled into the booklet through the gutter.

For surcharges see #148, 176, B13-B20.

No. 135 Surcharged in Red

1939

148 A22 40c on 50c dk bl grn .55 .20

Mosque of Salé — A26

Sefrou — A27

Cedars — A28

Goatherd A29

Ramparts of Salé — A30

Scimitar-horned Oryxes — A31

Fez — A33

Valley of Draa A32

1939-42

No.	Type	Description	Unused	Used
149	A26	1c rose violet	.20	.20
150	A27	2c emerald	.20	.20
151	A27	3c ultra	.20	.20
152	A26	5c dk bl grn	.20	.20
153	A27	10c brt red vio	.20	.20
154	A28	15c dk green	.20	.20
155	A28	20c black grn	.20	.20
156	A29	30c deep blue	.20	.20
157	A29	40c chocolate	.20	.20
158	A29	45c Prus green	.55	.20
159	A30	50c rose red	1.50	.70
159A	A30	50c Prus grn ('40)	.20	.20
160	A30	60c turq blue	1.50	.55
160A	A30	60c choc ('40)	.20	.20
161	A31	70c dk violet	.20	.20
162	A32	75c grnsh blk	.35	.20
163	A32	80c pck bl ('40)	.20	.20
163A	A32	80c dk grn ('42)	.20	.20
164	A30	90c ultra	.20	.20
165	A28	1fr chocolate	.20	.20
165A	A32	1.20fr rose vio ('42)	.50	.20
166	A32	1.25fr henna brn	1.00	.50
167	A32	1.40fr rose violet	.35	.20
168	A30	1.50fr cop red ('40)	.20	.20
168A	A30	1.50fr rose ('42)	.20	.20
169	A33	2fr Prus green	.20	.20
170	A33	2.25fr dark blue	.50	.20
170A	A26	2.40fr red ('42)	.20	.20
171	A26	2.50fr scarlet	1.00	.50
171A	A26	2.50fr dp blue ('40)	.90	.50
172	A33	3fr black brown	.35	.20
172A	A26	4fr dp ultra ('42)	.20	.20
172B	A32	4.50fr grnsh blk ('42)	.55	.20
173	A31	5fr dark blue	.55	.35
174	A31	10fr red	.90	.55
174A	A31	15fr Prus grn ('42)	4.25	3.00
175	A31	20fr dk vio brn	1.60	1.40
		Nos. 149-175 (37)	20.55	13.65

See Nos. 197-219. For surcharges see Nos. 244, 261-262, B21-B24, B26, B28, B32.

No. 136 Surcharged in Black

1940

No.	Type	Description	Unused	Used
176	A22	35c on 65c brown red	1.40	.60
a.		Pair, one without surcharge	2.50	1.50

The surcharge was applied on alternate rows in the sheet, making No. 176a. This was done to make a pair equal 1fr, the new rate.

Catalogue values for unused stamps in this section, from this point to the end of the section, are for Never Hinged items.

One Aim Alone-Victory A34

Tower of Hassan, Rabat A35

1943 Litho. *Perf. 12*

No.	Type	Description	Unused	Used
177	A34	1.50fr deep blue	.20	.20

1943

No.	Type	Description	Unused	Used
178	A35	10c rose lilac	.20	.20
179	A35	30c blue	.20	.20
180	A35	40c lake	.20	.20
181	A35	50c blue green	.20	.20
182	A35	60c dk vio brn	.20	.20
183	A35	70c rose violet	.20	.20
184	A35	80c gray green	.20	.20
185	A35	1fr car lake	.20	.20
186	A35	1.20fr violet	.20	.20
187	A35	1.50fr red	.20	.20
188	A35	2fr lt bl grn	.20	.20
189	A35	2.40fr car rose	.20	.20
190	A35	3fr olive brn	.20	.20
191	A35	4fr dk ultra	.20	.20
192	A35	4.50fr slate blk	.20	.20
193	A35	5fr dull blue	.35	.20

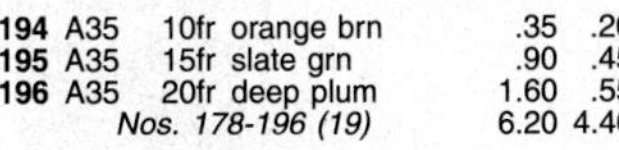

No.	Type	Description	Unused	Used
194	A35	10fr orange brn	.35	.20
195	A35	15fr slate grn	.90	.45
196	A35	20fr deep plum	1.60	.55
		Nos. 178-196 (19)	6.20	4.40

Types of 1939-42

Perf. 13½x14, 14x13½

1945-47 Typo. Unwmk.

No.	Type	Description	Unused	Used
197	A27	10c red violet	.20	.20
199	A29	40c chocolate	.20	.20
200	A30	50c Prus grn	.20	.20
203	A28	1fr choc ('46)	.20	.20
204	A32	1.20fr vio brn ('46)	.20	.20
205	A27	1.30fr blue ('47)	.35	.20
206	A30	1.50fr deep red	.20	.20
207	A33	2fr Prus grn	.20	.20
209	A33	3fr black brn	.20	.20
210	A29	3.50fr dk red ('47)	.50	.35
212	A31	4.50fr magenta ('47)	.20	.20
214	A31	5fr indigo	.55	.35
215	A32	6fr chlky bl ('46)	.30	.20
216	A31	10fr red	1.10	.55
217	A31	15fr Prus grn	1.25	.50
218	A31	20fr dk vio brn	1.40	.80
219	A31	25fr black brn	1.90	1.25
		Nos. 197-219 (17)	9.15	6.00

For surcharges see #261-263, B26, B28, B32.

The Terraces — A37

Mountain District — A39

Fortress A38

Marrakesh A40

Gardens of Fez — A41

Ouarzazat District — A42

1947-48 Engr. Unwmk. *Perf. 13*

No.	Type	Description	Unused	Used
221	A37	10c black brn	.20	.20
222	A37	30c brt red	.20	.20
223	A37	50c brt grnsh bl	.20	.20
224	A37	60c brt red vio	.20	.20
225	A38	1fr black	.20	.20
226	A38	1.50fr blue	.20	.20
227	A39	2fr brt green	.35	.20
228	A39	3fr brown red	.30	.20
229	A40	4fr dk bl vio	.20	.20
230	A41	5fr dk green	.60	.35
231	A40	6fr crimson	.20	.20
232	A41	10fr dp blue ('47)	.50	.20
233	A42	15fr dk grn ('47)	.95	.70
234	A42	20fr henna brn ('47)	.85	.35
235	A42	25fr purple ('47)	1.25	.35
		Nos. 221-235 (15)	6.40	3.95

1948-49

No.	Type	Description	Unused	Used
236	A37	30c purple	.20	.20
237	A38	2fr vio brn ('49)	.20	.20
238	A40	4fr green	.30	.20
239	A41	8fr org ('49)	.80	.50
240	A41	10fr blue	.55	.20
241	A42	10fr car rose	.35	.35
242	A38	12fr red	.55	.35
243	A42	18fr deep blue	1.10	.80
		Nos. 236-243 (8)	4.05	2.80

For surcharges see Nos. 263, 293-294.

No. 175 Surcharged with New Value and Wavy Lines in Carmine

1948

No.	Type	Description	Unused	Used
244	A31	8fr on 20fr dk vio brn	.70	.50

Fortified Oasis A43

Walled City — A44

1949

No.	Type	Description	Unused	Used
245	A43	5fr blue green	.50	.20
246	A44	15fr red	.90	.20
247	A44	25fr ultra	.90	.35
		Nos. 245-247 (3)	2.30	.75

See No. 300.

Detail, Gate of Oudayas, Rabat — A45

Nejjarine Fountain, Fez — A46

Garden, Meknes — A47

1949 *Perf. 14x13*

No.	Type	Description	Unused	Used
248	A45	10c black	.20	.20
249	A45	50c rose brn	.20	.20
250	A45	1fr blue vio	.20	.20
251	A46	2fr dk car rose	.20	.20
252	A46	3fr dark blue	.30	.20
253	A46	5fr brt green	.65	.20
254	A47	8fr dk bl grn	.85	.30
255	A47	10fr brt red	.85	.30
		Nos. 248-255 (8)	3.45	1.80

Postal Administration Building, Meknes — A48

1949, Oct. *Perf. 13*

No.	Type	Description	Unused	Used
256	A48	5fr dark green	1.40	1.40
257	A48	15fr deep carmine	1.50	1.50
258	A48	25fr deep blue	1.75	1.75
		Nos. 256-258 (3)	4.65	4.65

75th anniv. of the UPU.

Todra Valley A49

1950

No.	Type	Description	Unused	Used
259	A49	35fr red brown	.85	.20
260	A49	50fr indigo	.85	.20

See No. 270.

Nos. 204 and 205 Surcharged in Black or Blue

1950 *Perf. 14x13½, 13½x14*

No.	Type	Description	Unused	Used
261	A32	1fr on 1.20fr vio brn (Bk)	.20	.20
262	A27	1fr on 1.30fr blue (Bl)	.20	.20

The surcharge is transposed and spaced to fit the design on No. 262.

No. 231 Surcharged with New Value and Wavy Lines in Black

1951 *Perf. 13*

No.	Type	Description	Unused	Used
263	A40	5fr on 6fr crimson	.20	.20

Statue of Gen. Jacques Leclerc — A50

1951, Apr. 28 Engr.

No.	Type	Description	Unused	Used
264	A50	10fr blue green	1.40	1.40
265	A50	15fr deep carmine	1.60	1.60
266	A50	25fr indigo	1.60	1.60
		Nos. 264-266 (3)	4.60	4.60

Unveiling of a monument to Gen. Leclerc at Casablanca, Apr. 28, 1951. See No. C39.

Loustau Hospital, Oujda A51

Designs: 15fr, New Hospital, Meknes. 25fr, New Hospital, Rabat.

1951

No.	Type	Description	Unused	Used
267	A51	10fr indigo & pur	1.25	1.25
268	A51	15fr Prus grn & red brn	1.25	1.25
269	A51	25fr dk brn & ind	1.50	1.50
		Nos. 267-269 (3)	4.00	4.00

Todra Valley Type of 1950

1951

No.	Type	Description	Unused	Used
270	A49	30fr ultramarine	.85	.25

Pigeons at Fountain A52

Karaouine Mosque, Fez A53

Patio, Oudayas A54

Oudayas Point, Rabat A55

Patio of Old House — A56

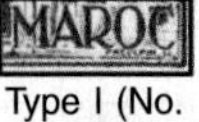

Type I (No. 275) Type II (No. 276)

Perf. 14x13, 13

1951-53 Engr. Unwmk.

No.	Type	Description	Unused	Used
271	A52	5fr magenta ('52)	.20	.20
272	A53	6fr bl grn ('52)	.20	.20
273	A52	8fr brown ('52)	.20	.20
273A	A53	10fr rose red ('53)	.20	.20
274	A53	12fr dp ultra ('52)	.35	.35
275	A54	15fr red brn (I)	1.75	.20
276	A54	15fr red brn (II)	.55	.20
277	A55	15fr pur ('52)	.55	.20
278	A55	18fr red ('52)	.95	.65
279	A56	20fr dp grnsh bl ('52)	.95	.45
		Nos. 271-279 (10)	5.90	2.85

See Nos. 297-299.

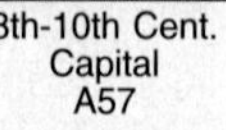

8th-10th Cent. Capital A57

Casablanca Monument A58

Capitals: 20fr, 12th Cent. 25fr, 13th-14th Cent. 50fr, 17th Cent.

1952, Apr. 5 *Perf. 13*

No.	Type	Description	Unused	Used
280	A57	15fr deep blue	1.75	1.90
281	A57	20fr red	1.75	1.90
282	A57	25fr purple	1.75	1.90
283	A57	50fr deep green	1.90	2.10
		Nos. 280-283 (4)	7.15	7.80

1952 Sept. 22 Engr. & Typo.

No.	Type	Description	Unused	Used
284	A58	15fr multicolored	2.00	1.60

Creation of the French Military Medal, cent.

Daggers of South Morocco A59

Post Rider and Public Letter-writer A60

Designs: 20fr and 25fr, Antique brooches.

1953, Mar. 27 Engr.

No.	Type	Description	Unused	Used
285	A59	15fr dk car rose	2.10	2.10
286	A59	20fr violet brn	2.10	2.10
287	A59	25fr dark blue	2.10	2.10
		Nos. 285-287 (3)	6.30	6.30

See No. C46.

1953, May 16

No.	Type	Description	Unused	Used
288	A60	15fr violet brown	1.25	1.25

Stamp Day, May 16, 1953.

Bine el Ouidane Dam — A61

1953, Nov. 3 *Perf. 13*

No.	Type	Description	Unused	Used
290	A61	15fr indigo	1.10	1.10

See No. 295.

Mogador Fortress — A62

Design: 30fr, Moorish knights.

1953, Dec. 4

No.	Type	Description	Unused	Used
291	A62	15fr green	1.40	1.25
292	A62	30fr red brown	1.40	1.25

Issued to aid Army Welfare Work.

Nos. 226 and 243 Surcharged with New Value and Wavy Lines in Black

1954

No.	Type	Description	Unused	Used
293	A38	1fr on 1.50fr blue	.20	.20
294	A42	15fr on 18fr dp bl	.50	.50

Dam Type of 1953

1954, Mar. 8

No.	Type	Description	Unused	Used
295	A61	15fr red brn & indigo	.80	.80

Station of Rural Automobile Post — A63

1954, Apr. 10

No.	Type	Description	Unused	Used
296	A63	15fr dk blue grn	.80	.65

Stamp Day, April 10, 1954.

Types of 1951-53

1954 Engr. *Perf. 14x13*

No.	Type	Description	Unused	Used
297	A52	15fr dk blue green	.50	.20

Typo.

No.	Type	Description	Unused	Used
298	A52	5fr magenta	.50	.20
299	A55	15fr rose violet	.80	.25
		Nos. 297-299 (3)	1.80	.65

Walled City Type of 1949

1954 Engr. *Perf. 13*

No.	Type	Description	Unused	Used
300	A44	25fr purple	.95	.35

Marshal Lyautey at Rabat A64

Lyautey, Builder of Cities — A65

Designs: 15fr, Marshal Lyautey at Khenifra. 50fr, Hubert Lyautey, Marshal of France.

1954, Nov. 17

No.	Type	Description	Unused	Used
301	A64	5fr indigo	1.75	1.75
302	A64	15fr dark green	1.75	1.75
303	A65	30fr rose brown	2.50	2.50
304	A65	50fr dk red brn	2.50	2.50
		Nos. 301-304 (4)	8.50	8.50

Marshal Hubert Lyautey, birth cent.

Franco-Moslem Education — A66

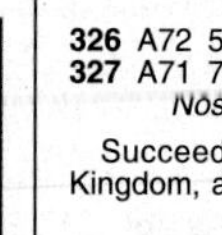

Moslem Student at Blackboard — A67

Designs: 30fr, Moslem school at Camp Boulhaut. 50fr, Moulay Idriss College at Fez.

1955, Apr. 16 Unwmk. *Perf. 13*

No.	Type	Description	Unused	Used
305	A66	5fr indigo	1.25	1.25
306	A67	15fr rose lake	1.40	1.40
307	A66	30fr chocolate	1.40	1.40
308	A67	50fr dk blue grn	1.75	1.75
		Nos. 305-308 (4)	5.80	5.80

Franco-Moslem solidarity.

Map and Rotary Emblem A68

1955, June 11

No.	Type	Description	Unused	Used
309	A68	15fr bl & org brn	1.00	.80

Rotary Intl., 59th anniv.

Post Office, Mazagan A69

1955, May 24

No.	Type	Description	Unused	Used
310	A69	15fr red	.70	.50

Stamp Day.

Bab el Chorfa, Fez A70

Mahakma (Courthouse), Casablanca A71

Fortress, Safi — A72

Designs: 50c, 1fr, 2fr, 3fr, Mrissa Gate, Salé. 10fr, 12fr, 15fr, Minaret at Rabat. 30fr, Menara Garden Marrakesh. 40fr, Tafraout Village. 50fr, Portuguese cistern, Mazagan. 75fr, Garden of Oudaya, Rabat.

1955 *Perf. 13½x13, 13x13½, 13*

No.	Type	Description	Unused	Used
311	A70	50c brn vio	.20	.20
312	A70	1fr blue	.20	.20
313	A70	2fr red lilac	.20	.20
314	A70	3fr bluish blk	.20	.20
315	A70	5fr vermilion	.80	.20
316	A70	6fr green	.35	.20
317	A70	8fr orange brn	.70	.35
318	A70	10fr violet brn	.95	.20
319	A70	12fr greenish bl	.50	.35
320	A70	15fr magenta	.80	.20
321	A71	18fr dk green	1.00	.60
322	A71	20fr brown lake	.60	.20
323	A72	25fr brt ultra	1.60	.20
324	A72	30fr green	1.40	.35
325	A72	40fr orange red	1.40	.20
326	A72	50fr black brn	4.00	.35
327	A71	75fr greenish bl	1.40	.70
		Nos. 311-327 (17)	16.30	4.90

Succeeding issues, released under the Kingdom, are listed under Morocco in Vol. 4.

SEMI-POSTAL STAMPS

French Protectorate

No. 30 Surcharged in Red

1914 Unwmk. *Perf. 14x13½*

No.	Type	Description	Unused	Used
B1	A4	10c + 5c on 10c	*18,500.*	*22,000.*

Known only with inverted red surcharge.

Same Surcharge on No. 42 with "Protectorat Francais"

No.	Type	Description	Unused	Used
B2	A7	10c + 5c on 10c rose	4.25	4.25
a.		Double surcharge	100.00	100.00
b.		Inverted surcharge	140.00	140.00
c.		"c" omitted	67.50	67.50

On Nos. B1 and B2 the cross is set up from pieces of metal (quads), the horizontal bar being made from two long pieces, the vertical bar from two short pieces. Each cross in the setting of twenty-five differs from the others.

No. 30 Handstamp Surcharged in Red

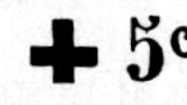

No.	Type	Description	Unused	Used
B3	A4	10c + 5c on 10c rose	*1,250.*	*900.*

No. B3 was issued at Oujda. The surcharge ink is water-soluble.

No. 42 Surcharged in Vermilion or Carmine

No.	Type	Description	Unused	Used
B4	A7	10c + 5c on 10c (V)	16.00	16.00
a.		Double surcharge	160.00	160.00
b.		Inverted surcharge	160.00	160.00
c.		Double surch., one invtd.	140.00	140.00
B5	A7	10c +5c on 10c (C)	350.00	400.00

On #B4-B5 the horizontal bar of the cross is single and not as thick as on #B1-B2.

No. B5 was sold largely at Casablanca.

SP1 SP2

Carmine Surcharge

1915

No.	Type	Description	Unused	Used
B6	SP1	5c + 5c green	2.10	1.60
a.		Inverted surcharge	210.00	210.00
B7	SP2	10c + 5c rose	3.00	3.00

No. B6 was not issued without the Red Cross surcharge. No. B7 was also used in Tangier.

SP3

SP4

France No. B2 Overprinted in Black

No.	Type	Description	Unused	Used
B8	SP3	10c + 5c red	5.25	5.25

Carmine Surcharge

1917

No.	Type	Description	Unused	Used
B9	SP4	10c + 5c on 10c rose	2.10	2.10

On No. B9 the horizontal bar of the cross is made from a single, thick piece of metal.

Marshal Hubert Lyautey — SP5

1935, May 15 Photo. *Perf. 13x13½*
B10 SP5 50c + 50c red 8.25 8.25
B11 SP5 1fr + 1fr dk grn 8.25 8.25
B12 SP5 5fr + 1fr blk brn 32.50 32.50
Nos. B10-B12 (3) 49.00 49.00

Stamps of 1933-34 Surcharged in Blue or Red

1938 *Perf. 13*
B13 A18 2c + 2c red vio 4.00 4.00
B14 A19 3c + 3c dk brn 4.00 4.00
B15 A20 20c + 20c red brn 4.00 4.00
B16 A21 40c + 40c blk brn (R) 4.00 4.00
B17 A22 65c + 65c brn red 4.00 4.00
B18 A23 1.25fr + 1.25fr blk (R) 4.00 4.00
B19 A24 2fr + 2fr yel brn 4.00 4.00
B20 A25 5fr + 5fr red brn 4.00 4.00
Nos. B13-B20 (8) 32.00 32.00

Stamps of 1939 Surcharged in Black

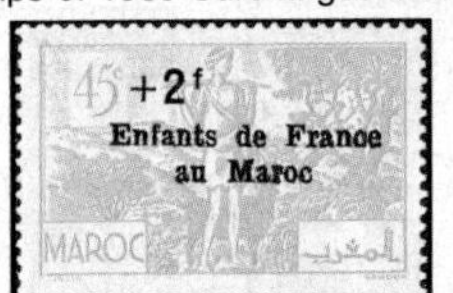

1942
B21 A29 45c + 2fr Prus grn 3.50 3.50
B22 A30 90c + 4fr ultra 3.50 3.50
B23 A32 1.25fr + 6fr henna brn 3.50 3.50
B24 A26 2.50fr + 8fr scarlet 3.50 3.50
Nos. B21-B24 (4) 14.00 14.00

The arrangement of the surcharge differs slightly on each denomination.

Catalogue values for unused stamps in this section, from this point to the end of the section, are for Never Hinged items.

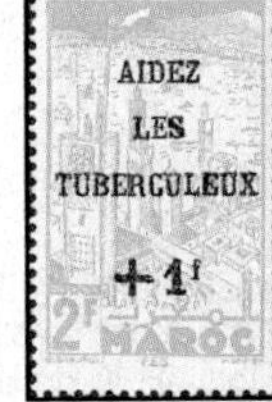

No. 207 Surcharged in Black

1945 Unwmk. *Perf. 13½x14*
B26 A33 2fr + 1fr Prus green .35 .35

For surcharge see No. B28.

Mausoleum of Marshal Lyautey — SP7

Statue of Marshal Lyautey — SP8

1945 Litho. *Perf. 11½*
B27 SP7 2fr + 3fr dark blue .35 .20

The surtax was for French works of solidarity.

No. B26 Surcharged in Red

1946 *Perf. 13½x14*
B28 A33 3fr (+ 1fr) on 2fr + 1fr .20 .20

Perf. 13½x14, 13

1946, Dec. 16 Engr.
B29 SP8 2fr + 10fr black 1.10 1.10
B30 SP8 3fr + 15fr cop red 1.10 1.10
B31 SP8 10fr + 20fr brt bl 1.75 1.75
Nos. B29-B31 (3) 3.95 3.95

The surtax was for works of solidarity.

No. 212 Surcharged in Rose Violet

1947, Mar. 15 *Perf. 13½x14*
B32 A31 4.50fr + 5.50fr magenta 1.10 1.10

Stamp Day, 1947.

Map and Symbols of Prosperity from Phosphates SP9

1947 *Perf. 13*
B33 SP9 4.50fr + 5.50fr green .95 .70

25th anniv. of the exploitations of the Cherifien Office of Phosphates.

Power — SP10 Health — SP11

1948, Feb. 9
B34 SP10 6fr + 9fr red brn 1.75 1.75
B35 SP11 10fr + 20fr dp ultra 1.75 1.75

The surtax was for combined works of Franco-Moroccan solidarity.

Type of Regular Issue of 1923, Inscribed: "Journee du Timbre 1948"

1948, Mar. 6
B36 A16 6fr + 4fr red brown .80 .70

Stamp Day, Mar. 6, 1948.

Battleship off Moroccan Coast SP12

1948, Aug.
B37 SP12 6fr + 9fr purple 1.10 1.10

The surtax was for naval charities.

Wheat Field near Meknes SP13

Designs: 2fr+5fr, Olive grove, Taroudant. 3fr+7fr, Net and coastal view. 5fr+10fr, Aguedal Gardens, Marrakesh.

1949, Apr. 12 Engr. Unwmk.
Inscribed: "SOLIDARITE 1948"
B38 SP13 1fr + 2fr orange 1.25 1.25
B39 SP13 2fr + 5fr car 1.25 1.25
B40 SP13 3fr + 7fr pck bl 1.25 1.25
B41 SP13 5fr + 10fr dk brn vio 1.25 1.25
a. Sheet of 4, #B38-B41 14.00 14.00
Nos. B38-B41,CB31-CB34 (8) 10.60 10.60

Gazelle Hunter, from 1899 Local Stamp SP14

1949, May 1
B42 SP14 10fr + 5fr choc & car rose 1.10 1.10

Stamp Day and 50th anniversary of Mazagan-Marrakesh local postage stamp.

Moroccan Soldiers, Flag SP15

Rug Weaving SP16

1949
B43 SP15 10fr + 10fr bright red 1.00 1.00

The surtax was for Army Welfare Work.

1950, Apr. 11

Designs: 2fr+5fr, Pottery making, 3fr+7fr, Bookbinding. 5fr+10fr, Copper work.

Inscribed: "SOLIDARITE 1949"
B44 SP16 1fr + 2fr dp car 1.60 1.60
B45 SP16 2fr + 5fr dk brnsh bl 1.75 1.75
B46 SP16 3fr + 7fr dk pur 1.75 1.75
B47 SP16 5fr + 10fr red brn 1.75 1.75
a. Sheet of 4, #B44-B47 14.00 14.00
Nos. B44-B47,CB36-CB39 (8) 12.45 12.45

Ruins of Sala Colonia at Chella SP17

1950, Sept. 25 Engr. *Perf. 13*
B48 SP17 10fr + 10fr dp magenta 1.25 1.25
B49 SP17 15fr + 15fr indigo 1.25 1.25

The surtax was for Army Welfare Work.

AIR POST STAMPS

French Protectorate

Biplane over Casablanca AP1

1922-27 Photo. Unwmk. *Perf. 13½*
C1 AP1 5c dp orange ('27) .35 .35
C2 AP1 25c dp ultra .85 .50
C3 AP1 50c grnsh blue .35 .35
C4 AP1 75c dp blue 62.50 9.25
C5 AP1 75c dp green .50 .20
C6 AP1 80c vio brn ('27) 1.40 .35
C7 AP1 1fr vermilion .80 .35
C8 AP1 1.40fr brn lake ('27) 2.00 .95
C9 AP1 1.90fr dp blue ('27) 2.00 1.40
C10 AP1 2fr black vio 1.90 .80
a. 2fr deep violet 1.90 1.10
C11 AP1 3fr gray blk 2.00 1.35
Nos. C1-C11 (11) 74.65 15.85

The 25c, 50c, 75c deep green and 1fr each were printed in two of three types, differing in frameline thickness, or hyphen in "Helio-Vaugirard" imprint.

Imperf., Pairs

C1a AP1 5c 42.50
C2a AP1 25c 55.00
C3a AP1 50c 42.50
C4a AP1 75c 475.00
C5a AP1 75c 60.00
C6a AP1 80c 47.50
C7a AP1 1fr 55.00
C10b AP1 2fr 175.00

Nos. C8-C9 Surcharged in Blue or Black

1931, Apr. 10
C12 AP1 1fr on 1.40fr (B) 1.40 1.40
a. Inverted surcharge 240.00 240.00
C13 AP1 1.50fr on 1.90fr (Bk) 1.40 1.40

Rabat and Tower of Hassan AP2

Casablanca AP3

1933, Jan. Engr.
C14 AP2 50c dark blue .60 .50
C15 AP2 80c orange brn .60 .45
C16 AP2 1.50fr brown red .60 .50
C17 AP3 2.50fr carmine rose 4.25 .85
C18 AP3 5fr violet 2.10 1.25
C19 AP3 10fr blue green .80 .80
Nos. C14-C19 (6) 8.95 4.35

For surcharges see Nos. CB22-CB23.

Storks and Minaret, Chella — AP4

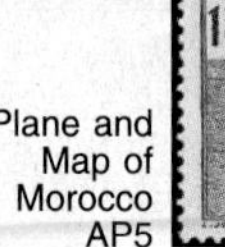

Plane and Map of Morocco AP5

1939-40 *Perf. 13*

No.	Type	Description	Unused	Used
C20	AP4	80c Prus green	.20	.20
C21	AP4	1fr dk red	.20	.20
C22	AP5	1.90fr ultra	.30	.20
C23	AP5	2fr red vio ('40)	.30	.20
C24	AP5	3fr chocolate	.30	.20
C25	AP4	5fr violet	1.10	.60
C26	AP5	10fr turq blue	1.00	.35
		Nos. C20-C26 (7)	3.40	1.95

Catalogue values for unused stamps in this section, from this point to the end of the section, are for Never Hinged items.

Plane over Oasis — AP6

1944 **Litho.** *Perf. 11½*

No.	Type	Description	Unused	Used
C27	AP6	50c Prus grn	.20	.20
C28	AP6	2fr ultra	.20	.20
C29	AP6	5fr scarlet	.20	.20
C30	AP6	10fr violet	.80	.80
C31	AP6	50fr black	1.10	1.10
C32	AP6	100fr dp bl & red	2.40	2.40
		Nos. C27-C32 (6)	4.90	4.90

For surcharge see No. CB24.

Plane AP7

1945 **Engr.** *Perf. 13*

No.	Type	Description	Unused	Used
C33	AP7	50fr sepia	.70	.70

Moulay Idriss — AP8

La Medina AP9

1947-48

No.	Type	Description	Unused	Used
C34	AP8	9fr dk rose car	.20	.20
C35	AP8	40fr dark blue	.65	.35
C36	AP8	50fr dp claret ('47)	.85	.20
C37	AP9	100fr dp grnsh bl	1.90	.80
C38	AP9	200fr henna brn	4.00	1.25
		Nos. C34-C38 (5)	7.60	2.80

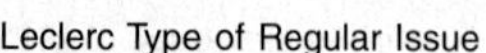

Leclerc Type of Regular Issue

1951, Apr. 28

No.	Type	Description	Unused	Used
C39	A50	50fr purple	1.75	1.75

Unveiling of a monument to Gen. Leclerc at Casablanca, Apr. 28, 1951.

Kasbah of the Oudayas, Rabat AP11

1951, May 22

No.	Type	Description	Unused	Used
C40	AP11	300fr purple	14.50	7.75

Ben Smine Sanatorium AP12

1951, June 4

No.	Type	Description	Unused	Used
C41	AP12	50fr pur & Prus grn	2.40	2.10

Fortifications, Chella — AP13

Plane Near Marrakesh AP14

Fort, Anti-Atlas Mountains AP15

View of Fez AP16

1952, Apr. 19 **Unwmk.** *Perf. 13*

No.	Type	Description	Unused	Used
C42	AP13	10fr blue green	.70	.35
C43	AP14	40fr red	1.10	.35
C44	AP15	100fr brown	2.25	.55
C45	AP16	200fr purple	6.00	4.25
		Nos. C42-C45 (4)	10.05	5.50

Antique Brooches — AP17

1953, Mar. 27

No.	Type	Description	Unused	Used
C46	AP17	50fr dark green	2.10	2.10

"City" of the Agdal, Meknes AP18

20fr, Yakoub el Mansour, Rabat. 40fr, Ainchock, Casablanca. 50fr, El Aliya, Fedala.

1954, Mar. 8

No.	Type	Description	Unused	Used
C47	AP18	10fr olive brown	1.90	1.90
C48	AP18	20fr purple	1.90	1.90
C49	AP18	40fr red brown	2.00	2.00
C50	AP18	50fr deep green	2.00	2.00
		Nos. C47-C50 (4)	7.80	7.80

Franco-Moroccan solidarity.

Naval Vessel and Sailboat AP19

Village in the Anti-Atlas AP20

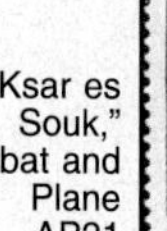

"Ksar es Souk," Rabat and Plane AP21

1954, Oct. 18

No.	Type	Description	Unused	Used
C51	AP19	15fr dk blue green	1.25	1.25
C52	AP19	30fr violet blue	1.60	1.60

1955, July 25 **Engr.** *Perf. 13*

200fr, Estuary of Bou Regreg, Rabat and Plane.

No.	Type	Description	Unused	Used
C53	AP20	100fr brt violet	1.75	.35
C54	AP20	200fr brt carmine	3.50	.80
C55	AP21	500fr grnsh blue	9.00	2.75
		Nos. C53-C55 (3)	14.25	3.90

AIR POST SEMI-POSTAL STAMPS

French Protectorate

Moorish Tribesmen SPAP1

Designs: 25c, Moor plowing with camel and burro. 50c, Caravan nearing Saffi. 75c, Walls, Marrakesh. 80c, Sheep grazing at Azrou. 1fr, Gate at Fez. 1.50fr, Aerial view of Tangier. 2fr, Aerial view of Casablanca. 3fr, Storks on old wall, Rabat. 5fr, Moorish fete.

Perf. 13½

1928, July 26 **Photo.** **Unwmk.**

No.	Type	Description	Unused	Used
CB1	SPAP1	5c dp blue	4.00	4.00
CB2	SPAP1	25c brn org	4.00	4.00
CB3	SPAP1	50c red	4.00	4.00
CB4	SPAP1	75c org brn	4.00	4.00
CB5	SPAP1	80c olive grn	4.00	4.00
CB6	SPAP1	1fr orange	4.00	4.00
CB7	SPAP1	1.50fr Prus bl	4.00	4.00
CB8	SPAP1	2fr dp brown	4.00	4.00
CB9	SPAP1	3fr dp violet	4.00	4.00
CB10	SPAP1	5fr brown blk	4.00	4.00
		Nos. CB1-CB10 (10)	40.00	40.00

These stamps were sold in sets only and at double their face value. The money received for the surtax was divided among charitable and social organizations. The stamps were not sold at post offices but solely by subscription to the Moroccan Postal Administration.

Overprinted in Red or Blue (25c, 50c, 75c, 1fr)

1929, Feb. 1

No.	Type	Description	Unused	Used
CB11	SPAP1	5c dp blue	4.00	4.00
CB12	SPAP1	25c brown org	4.00	4.00
CB13	SPAP1	50c red	4.00	4.00
CB14	SPAP1	75c org brn	4.00	4.00
CB15	SPAP1	80c olive grn	4.00	4.00
CB16	SPAP1	1fr orange	4.00	4.00
CB17	SPAP1	1.50fr Prus bl	4.00	4.00
CB18	SPAP1	2fr dp brown	4.00	4.00
CB19	SPAP1	3fr dp violet	4.00	4.00
CB20	SPAP1	5fr brown blk	4.00	4.00
		Nos. CB11-CB20 (10)	40.00	40.00

These stamps were sold at double their face values and only in Tangier. The surtax benefited various charities.

Marshal Hubert Lyautey SPAP10

1935, May 15 *Perf. 13½*

No.	Type	Description	Unused	Used
CB21	SPAP10	1.50fr + 1.50fr blue	17.00	17.00

Nos. C14, C19 Surcharged in Red

1938 *Perf. 13*

No.	Type	Description	Unused	Used
CB22	AP2	50c + 50c dk bl	4.50	4.50
CB23	AP3	10fr + 10fr bl grn	4.50	4.50

Catalogue values for unused stamps in this section, from this point to the end of the section, are for Never Hinged items.

Plane over Oasis SPAP11

Statue of Marshal Lyautey SPAP12

1944 **Litho.** *Perf. 11½*

No.	Type	Description	Unused	Used
CB23A	SPAP11	1.50fr + 98.50fr	1.40	1.25

The surtax was for charity among the liberated French.

No. C29 Surcharged in Black

1946, June 18 *Perf. 11*

No.	Type	Description	Unused	Used
CB24	AP6	5fr + 5fr scarlet	.80	.70

6th anniv. of the appeal made by Gen. Charles de Gaulle, June 18, 1940. The surtax was for the Free French Association of Morocco.

1946, Dec. **Engr.** *Perf. 13*

No.	Type	Description	Unused	Used
CB25	SPAP12	10fr +30fr dk grn	1.60	1.60

The surtax was for works of solidarity.

Replenishing Stocks of Food — SPAP13

Agriculture
SPAP14

1948, Feb. 9 **Unwmk.**

CB26 SPAP13 9fr +26fr dp grn 1.25 1.25
CB27 SPAP14 20fr +35fr brown 1.25 1.25

The surtax was for combined works of Franco-Moroccan solidarity.

Tomb of Marshal Hubert Lyautey — SPAP15

1948, May 18 ***Perf. 13***

CB28 SPAP15 10fr +25fr dk grn .95 .95

Lyautey Exposition, Paris, June, 1948.

P.T.T. Clubhouse SPAP16

1948, June 7 **Engr.**

CB29 SPAP16 6fr + 34fr dk grn 1.40 1.40
CB30 SPAP16 9fr + 51fr red brn 1.50 1.50

The surtax was used for the Moroccan P.T.T. employees vacation colony at Ifrane.

View of Agadir SPAP17

Plane over Globe SPAP18

Designs: 6fr+9fr, Fez. 9fr+16fr, Atlas Mountains. 15fr+25fr, Valley of Draa.

1949, Apr. 12 ***Perf. 13***
Inscribed: "SOLIDARITE 1948"

CB31 SPAP17 5fr +5fr dk grn 1.40 1.40
CB32 SPAP17 6fr +9fr org red 1.40 1.40
CB33 SPAP17 9fr +16fr blk brn 1.40 1.40
CB34 SPAP17 15fr +25fr ind 1.40 1.40
a. Sheet of 4, #CB31-CB34 16.00 16.00
Nos. CB31-CB34 (4) 5.60 5.60

1950, Mar. 11 **Engr. & Typo.**

CB35 SPAP18 15fr + 10fr bl grn & car .85 .85

Day of the Stamp, Mar. 11-12, 1950, and 25th anniv. of the 1st post link between Casablanca and Dakar.

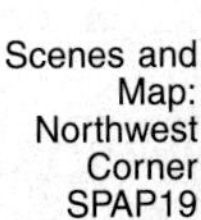

Scenes and Map: Northwest Corner SPAP19

Designs (quarters of map): 6fr+9fr, NE, 9fr+16fr, SW. 15fr+25fr, SE.

1950, Apr. 11 **Engr.**
Inscribed: "SOLIDARITE 1949"

CB36 SPAP19 5fr +5fr dp ultra 1.40 1.40
CB37 SPAP19 6fr +9fr Prus grn 1.40 1.40
CB38 SPAP19 9fr +16fr dk brn 1.40 1.40
CB39 SPAP19 15fr +25fr brn red 1.40 1.40
a. Sheet of 4, #CB36-CB39 16.00 16.00
Nos. CB36-CB39 (4) 5.60 5.60

Arch of Triumph of Caracalla at Volubilis SPAP20

1950, Sept. 25 **Unwmk.**

CB40 SPAP20 10fr + 10fr sepia 1.25 1.25
CB41 SPAP20 15fr + 15fr bl grn 1.25 1.25

The surtax was for Army Welfare Work.

Casablanca Post Office and First Air Post Stamp SPAP21

1952, Mar. 8 ***Perf. 13***

CB42 SPAP21 15fr + 5fr red brn & dp grn 3.00 3.00

Day of the Stamp, Mar. 8, 1952, and 30th anniv. of French Morocco's 1st air post stamp.

POSTAGE DUE STAMPS

French Offices in Morocco

Postage Due Stamps and Types of France Surcharged in Red or Black

1896 **Unwmk.** ***Perf. 14x13½***
On Stamps of 1891-93

J1 D2 5c on 5c lt bl (R) 5.75 3.50
J2 D2 10c on 10c choc (R) 8.50 3.50
J3 D2 30c on 30c car 21.00 16.00
a. Pair, one without surcharge
J4 D2 50c on 50c lilac 21.00 16.00
a. "S" of "CENTIMOS" omitted 240.00 175.00
J5 D2 1p on 1fr lil brn 275.00 250.00

1909-10 **On Stamps of 1908-10**

J6 D3 1c on 1c ol grn (R) 1.75 1.75
J7 D3 10c on 10c violet 26.00 22.50
J8 D3 30c on 30c bister 32.50 29.00
J9 D3 50c on 50c red 45.00 45.00
Nos. J6-J9 (4) 105.25 98.25

Postage Due Stamps of France Surcharged in Red or Blue

1911 **On Stamps of 1893-96**

J10 D2 5c on 5c blue (R) 2.90 2.90
J11 D2 10c on 10c choc (R) 11.00 11.00
a. Double surcharge 110.00 110.00
J12 D2 50c on 50c lil (Bl) 13.00 13.00

On Stamps of 1908-10

J13 D3 1c on 1c ol grn (R) 1.75 1.75
J14 D3 10c on 10c vio (R) 5.25 5.25
J15 D3 30c on 30c bis (R) 5.75 5.75
J16 D3 50c on 50c red (Bl) 11.00 11.00
Nos. J10-J16 (7) 50.65 50.65

For surcharges see Nos. JN23-J26.

French Protectorate

D4

D5

Type of 1911 Issue Overprinted "Protectorat Francais"

1915-17

J17 D4 1c on 1c black .35 .35
a. New value double 125.00
J18 D4 5c on 5c blue 1.40 1.10
J19 D4 10c on 10c choc 1.75 1.25
J20 D4 20c on 20c ol grn 1.75 1.25
J21 D4 30c on 30c rose red 4.50 4.00
J22 D4 50c on 50c vio brn 6.50 4.50
Nos. J17-J22 (6) 16.25 12.45

Nos. J13 to J16 With Additional Overprint "Protectorat Francais"

1915

J23 D3 1c on 1c ol grn .95 .95
J24 D3 10c on 10c violet 1.90 1.60
J25 D3 30c on 30c bister 2.10 1.90
J26 D3 50c on 50c red 2.10 2.00
Nos. J23-J26 (4) 7.05 6.45

1917-26 **Typo.**

J27 D5 1c black .20 .20
J28 D5 5c deep blue .20 .20
J29 D5 10c brown .45 .20
J30 D5 20c olive green 1.75 1.00
J31 D5 30c rose .20 .20
J32 D5 50c lilac brown .45 .20
J33 D5 1fr red brn, *straw* ('26) .80 .50
J34 D5 2fr violet ('26) 1.40 .85
Nos. J27-J34 (8) 5.45 3.35

See #J49-J56, Morocco #J1-J4. For surcharges see #J46-J48.

Postage Due Stamps of France, 1882-1906 Overprinted

1918

J35 D2 1c black .60 .60
J36 D2 5c blue 1.25 1.25
J37 D2 10c chocolate 1.25 1.25
J38 D2 15c green 3.00 3.00
J39 D2 20c olive green 4.00 4.00
J40 D2 30c rose red 8.50 8.50
J41 D2 50c violet brown 13.50 13.50
Nos. J35-J41 (7) 32.10 32.10

Postage Due Stamps of France, 1908-19 Overprinted

1918

J42 D3 1c olive green .60 .60
J43 D3 10c violet 1.75 1.75
J44 D3 20c bister 5.50 5.50
J45 D3 40c red 13.00 13.00
Nos. J42-J45 (4) 20.85 20.85

Catalogue values for unused stamps in this section, from this point to the end of the section, are for Never Hinged items.

Nos. J31 and J29 Surcharged

1944 **Unwmk.** ***Perf. 14x13½***

J46 D5 50c on 30c rose 1.75 1.75
J47 D5 1fr on 10c brown 3.00 3.00
J48 D5 3fr on 10c brown 7.25 7.25
Nos. J46-J48 (3) 12.00 12.00

Type of 1917-1926

1945-52 **Typo.**

J49 D5 1fr brn lake ('47) .55 .50
J50 D5 2fr rose lake ('47) .70 .55
J51 D5 3fr ultra .35 .20
J52 D5 4fr red orange .45 .20
J53 D5 5fr green .90 .35
J54 D5 10fr yellow brn 1.10 .35
J55 D5 20fr carmine ('50) 1.00 .70
J56 D5 30fr dull brn ('52) 1.60 1.10
Nos. J49-J56 (8) 6.65 3.95

PARCEL POST STAMPS

French Protectorate

PP1

1917 **Unwmk.** ***Perf. 13½x14***

Q1 PP1 5c green .70 .35
Q2 PP1 10c carmine .70 .35
Q3 PP1 20c lilac brown .70 .50
Q4 PP1 25c blue 1.25 .50
Q5 PP1 40c dark brown 1.90 .80
Q6 PP1 50c red orange 2.40 .60
Q7 PP1 75c pale slate 3.00 1.90
Q8 PP1 1fr ultra 4.00 .55
Q9 PP1 2fr gray 5.75 1.00
Q10 PP1 5fr violet 9.00 1.00
Q11 PP1 10fr black 13.00 1.00
Nos. Q1-Q11 (11) 42.40 8.55

FRENCH POLYNESIA

'french ˌpä-lə-'nē-zhə

(French Oceania)

LOCATION — South Pacific Ocean
GOVT. — French Overseas Territory
AREA — 1,522 sq. mi.
POP. — 242,073 (1999 est.)
CAPITAL — Papeete

In 1903 various French Establishments in the South Pacific were united to form a single colony. Most important of the island groups are the Society Islands, Marquesas Islands, the Tuamotu group and the Gambier, Austral, and Rapa Islands. Tahiti, largest of the Society group, ranks first in importance.

100 Centimes = 1 Franc

Catalogue values for unused stamps in this country are for Never Hinged items, beginning with Scott 136 in the regular postage section, Scott B11 in the semi-postal section, Scott C2 in the air-post section, Scott CB1 in the air-post semi-postal section, Scott J18 in the postage due section, and Scott O1 in the officials section.

Navigation and Commerce — A1

Perf. 14x13½

1892-1907 Typo. Unwmk.
Name of Colony in Blue or Carmine

1 A1 1c black, *lil bl* 1.10 1.10
2 A1 2c brown, *buff* 1.90 1.50
3 A1 4c claret, *lav* 3.00 2.25
4 A1 5c green, *grnsh* 7.75 5.75
5 A1 5c yellow grn ('06) 1.90 1.25
6 A1 10c blk, *lavender* 22.50 9.00
7 A1 10c red ('00) 1.90 1.25
8 A1 15c blue, quadrille paper 19.00 7.75
9 A1 15c gray, *lt gray* ('00) 3.75 3.00
10 A1 20c red, *grn* 15.00 6.00
11 A1 25c black, *rose* 45.00 20.00
12 A1 25c blue ('00) 15.00 10.00
13 A1 30c brown, *bis* 14.00 10.00
14 A1 35c black, *yel* ('06) 6.00 6.00
15 A1 40c red, *straw* 110.00 65.00
16 A1 45c blk, *gray grn* ('07) 5.25 *5.50*
17 A1 50c car, *rose* 8.50 7.00
18 A1 50c brown, *az* ('00) 225.00 175.00
19 A1 75c dp vio, *org* 10.00 7.75
20 A1 1fr brnz grn, *straw* 11.50 9.00
Nos. 1-20 (20) 528.05 354.10

Perf. 13½x14 stamps are counterfeits.
For overprint and surcharge see #55, B1.

Tahitian Girl — A2

Kanakas — A3

Fautaua Valley — A4

1913-30

21 A2 1c violet & brn .20 .20
22 A2 2c brown & blk .20 .20
23 A2 4c orange & bl .20 .20
24 A2 5c grn & yel grn .70 .40
25 A2 5c bl & blk ('22) .25 .25
26 A2 10c rose & org 1.25 .70
27 A2 10c bl grn & yel grn ('22) .70 .70
28 A2 10c org red & brn red, *bluish* ('26) 1.10 1.10
29 A2 15c org & blk ('15) .50 .35
a. Imperf., pair 125.00
30 A2 20c black & vio .80 .65
a. Imperf., pair 125.00
31 A2 20c grn & bl grn ('26) .70 .70
32 A2 20c brn red & dk brn ('27) 1.10 1.10
33 A3 25c ultra & blue 1.10 .80
34 A3 25c vio & rose ('22) .35 .35
35 A3 30c gray & brown 3.00 2.25
a. Imperf., pair 225.00
36 A3 30c rose & red org ('22) 1.75 1.75
37 A3 30c blk & red org ('26) .50 .50
38 A3 30c slate bl & bl grn ('27) 1.25 1.25
39 A3 35c green & rose .80 .80
40 A3 40c black & green .80 .80
41 A3 45c orange & red .80 .80
42 A3 50c dk brown & blk 11.00 8.75
43 A3 50c ultra & bl ('22) .70 .70
44 A3 50c gray & bl vio ('26) .50 .50
45 A3 60c green & blk ('26) .75 .75
46 A3 65c ol brn & red vio ('27) 2.25 2.25
47 A3 75c vio brn & vio 1.60 1.60
48 A3 90c brn red & rose ('30) 12.00 12.00
49 A4 1fr rose & black 3.00 2.25
50 A4 1.10fr vio & dk brn ('28) 1.10 1.10
51 A4 1.40fr bis brn & vio ('29) 2.90 2.90
52 A4 1.50fr ind & bl ('30) 12.00 12.00
53 A4 2fr dk brown & grn 3.00 2.25
54 A4 5fr violet & bl 7.00 7.00
Nos. 21-54 (34) 75.85 69.90

For surcharges see Nos. 56-71, B2-B4.

No. 7 Overprinted

1915

55 A1 10c red 3.50 3.50
a. Inverted overprint 125.00 125.00

For surcharge see No. B1.

No. 29 Surcharged

1916

56 A2 10c on 15c org & blk 1.75 1.75

Nos. 22, 41 and 29 Surcharged

1921

57 A2 5c on 2c brn & blk 25.00 25.00
58 A3 10c on 45c org & red 25.00 25.00
59 A2 25c on 15c org & blk 5.75 5.75
Nos. 57-59 (3) 55.75 55.75

On No. 58 the new value and date are set wide apart and without bar.

Types of 1913-30 Issue Surcharged in Black or Red

1923-27

60 A3 60c on 75c bl & brn .35 .35
61 A4 65c on 1fr dk bl & ol (R) ('25) 1.10 1.10
62 A4 85c on 1fr dk bl & ol (R) ('25) 1.10 1.10
63 A3 90c on 75c brn red & cer ('27) 1.60 1.60
Nos. 60-63 (4) 4.15 4.15

No. 26 Surcharged

1924

64 A2 45c on 10c rose & org 1.75 1.75
a. Inverted surcharge 1,800. 1,800.

Stamps and Type of 1913-30 Surcharged with New Value and Bars in Black or Red

1924-27

65 A4 25c on 2fr dk brn & grn .80 .80
66 A4 25c on 5fr vio & bl .85 .85
67 A4 1.25fr on 1fr dk bl & ultra (R) ('26) .85 .85
68 A4 1.50fr on 1fr dk bl & lt bl ('27) 2.10 2.10
69 A4 20fr on 5fr org & brt vio ('27) 24.00 18.00
Nos. 65-69 (5) 28.60 22.60

Surcharged in Black or Red

1926

70 A4 3fr on 5fr gray & blue 2.10 1.75
71 A4 10fr on 5fr grn & blk (R) 4.75 4.25

Papetoai Bay, Moorea A5

1929, Mar. 25

72 A5 3fr green & dk brn 5.75 5.75
73 A5 5fr lt blue & dk brn 10.00 10.00
74 A5 10fr lt red & dk brn 32.50 32.50
75 A5 20fr lilac & dk brn 35.00 35.00
Nos. 72-75 (4) 83.25 83.25

For overprints see Nos. 128, 130, 132, 134.

Common Design Types pictured following the introduction.

Colonial Exposition Issue

Common Design Types

1931, Apr. 13 Engr. ***Perf. 12½***
Name of Country Printed in Black

76 CD70 40c deep green 5.75 5.75
77 CD71 50c violet 5.75 5.75
78 CD72 90c red orange 5.75 5.75
79 CD73 1.50fr dull blue 5.75 5.75
Nos. 76-79 (4) 23.00 23.00

Spear Fishing A12

Tahitian Girl — A13

Idols A14

1934-39 Photo. ***Perf. 13½, 13½x13***

80 A12 1c gray black .20 .20
81 A12 2c claret .20 .20
82 A12 3c lt blue ('39) .20 .20
83 A12 4c orange .35 .35
84 A12 5c violet .55 .55
85 A12 10c dark brown .20 .20
86 A12 15c green .35 .35
87 A12 20c red .35 .35
88 A13 25c gray blue .55 .55
89 A13 30c yellow green .95 .95
90 A13 30c org brn ('39) .50 .50
91 A14 35c dp green ('38) 2.75 2.75
92 A13 40c red violet .35 .35
93 A13 45c brown orange 6.25 6.25
94 A13 45c dk green ('39) .95 .95
95 A13 50c violet .35 .35
96 A13 55c blue ('38) 5.00 5.00
97 A13 60c black ('39) .50 .50
98 A13 65c brown 2.25 2.25
99 A13 70c brt pink ('39) .80 .80
100 A13 75c olive green 6.25 6.25
101 A13 80c violet brn ('38) 1.10 1.10
102 A13 90c rose red .55 .55
103 A14 1fr red brown .55 .55
104 A14 1.25fr brown violet 5.75 5.75
105 A14 1.25fr rose red ('39) .70 .70
106 A14 1.40fr org yel ('39) .70 .70
107 A14 1.50fr blue .55 .55
108 A14 1.60fr dull vio ('39) .95 .95
109 A14 1.75fr olive 5.00 5.00
110 A14 2fr red .55 .55
111 A14 2.25fr deep blue ('39) .70 .70
112 A14 2.50fr black ('39) .80 .80
113 A14 3fr brown org ('39) 1.25 1.25
114 A14 5fr red violet ('39) .75 .75
115 A14 10fr dk grn ('39) 2.25 2.25
116 A14 20fr dk brn ('39) 2.25 2.25
Nos. 80-116 (37) 54.25 54.25

For overprints see #126-127, 129, 131, 133, 135.
For types A12-A14 without "RF," see Nos. 135A-135E.

Paris International Exposition Issue

Common Design Types

1937 Engr. ***Perf. 13***

117 CD74 20c deep violet 2.25 2.25
118 CD75 30c dark green 2.25 2.25
119 CD76 40c carmine rose 2.25 2.25
120 CD77 50c dk brn & bl 3.00 3.00
121 CD78 90c red 3.00 3.00
122 CD79 1.50fr ultra 3.75 3.75
Nos. 117-122 (6) 16.50 16.50

Colonial Arts Exhibition Issue

Souvenir Sheet
Common Design Type

1937 ***Imperf.***

123 CD78 3fr emerald 27.50 *40.00*
Never hinged 40.00

New York World's Fair Issue

Common Design Type

1939, May 10 Engr. ***Perf. 12½x12***

124 CD82 1.25fr carmine lake 1.00 1.00
125 CD82 2.25fr ultra 1.00 1.00
Set, never hinged 3.50

Fautaua Valley and Marshal Petain A15

1941 Engr. *Perf. 12½x12*
125A A15 1fr bluish green .80
125B A15 2.50fr deep blue .95
Set, never hinged 2.40

Nos. 125A-125B were issued by the Vichy government in France, but were not placed on sale in the French Polynesia.

For surcharges, see Nos. B12B-B12C.

Stamps of 1929-39 Overprinted in Black or Red

1941 *Perf. 14x13½, 13½x13*
126 A14 1fr red brown (Bk) 3.50 *3.75*
127 A14 2.50fr black 4.50 *5.00*
128 A5 3fr grn & dk brn 5.00 5.00
129 A14 3fr brn org (Bk) 5.50 5.50
130 A5 5fr lt bl & dk brn 5.00 5.00
131 A14 5fr red vio (Bk) 5.50 5.50
132 A5 10fr lt red & dk brn 14.50 14.50
133 A14 10fr dark green 50.00 —
134 A5 20fr lil & dk brn 80.00 80.00
135 A14 20fr dark brown 42.50 —
Nos. 126-135 (10) 216.00 124.25
Set, never hinged 290.00

Types of 1934-39 without "RF"

1942-44 Photo. *Perf. 13½*
135A A12 10c dark brown .50
135B A13 30c orange brown .55
135C A14 1.50fr blue .70
135D A14 10fr dark green 1.10
135E A14 20fr dark brown 1.75
Nos. 135A-135E (5) 4.60

Nos. 135A-135E were issued by the Vichy government in France, but were not placed on sale in French Polynesia.

Catalogue values for unused stamps in this section, from this point to the end of the section, are for Never Hinged items.

Ancient Double Canoe A16

1942 Photo. *Perf. 14½x14*
136 A16 5c dark brown .30 .20
137 A16 10c dk gray bl .30 .20
138 A16 25c emerald .30 .20
139 A16 30c red orange .30 .20
140 A16 40c dk slate grn .30 .20
141 A16 80c red brown .30 .20
142 A16 1fr rose violet .35 .25
143 A16 1.50fr brt red .50 .35
144 A16 2fr gray black .75 .55
145 A16 2.50fr brt ultra 1.75 1.40
146 A16 4fr dull violet 1.10 .85
147 A16 5fr bister 1.10 .85
148 A16 10fr deep brown 1.75 1.40
149 A16 20fr deep green 2.00 1.60
Nos. 136-149 (14) 11.10 8.45

For surcharges see Nos. 152-159.

Eboue Issue
Common Design Type

1945 Engr. *Perf. 13*
150 CD91 2fr black .75 .55
151 CD91 25fr Prus green 2.25 1.60

Nos. 150 and 151 exist imperforate.

Nos. 136, 138 and 145 Surcharged with New Values and Bars in Carmine or Black

1946 *Perf. 14½x14*
152 A16 50c on 5c (C) .50 .40
153 A16 60c on 5c (C) .50 .40
154 A16 70c on 5c (C) .50 .50
155 A16 1.20fr on 5c (C) .65 .50
156 A16 2.40fr on 25c (Bk) 1.25 1.00
157 A16 3fr on 25c (Bk) .80 .55
158 A16 4.50fr on 25c (Bk) 1.60 1.25
159 A16 15fr on 2.50fr (C) 1.90 1.40
Nos. 152-159 (8) 7.70 6.00

Coast of Mooréa A17

Fisherman and Catch — A18

Tahitian Girl — A20

House at Faa — A19

Island of Borabora A21

Island Women A22

1948 Unwmk. Engr. *Perf. 13*
160 A17 10c brown .35 .25
161 A17 30c blue green .35 .25
162 A17 40c deep blue .35 .25
163 A18 50c red brown .35 .25
164 A18 60c dk brown ol .55 .35
165 A18 80c brt blue .55 .35
166 A19 1fr red brown .55 .25
167 A19 1.20fr slate .55 .35
168 A19 1.50fr deep ultra .55 .35
169 A20 2fr sepia 1.10 .60
170 A20 2.40fr red brown 1.10 .75
171 A20 3fr purple 10.00 2.00
172 A20 4fr blue black 1.60 .90
173 A21 5fr sepia 2.75 1.10
174 A21 6fr steel blue 2.75 1.60
175 A21 10fr dk brown ol 3.50 1.25
176 A22 15fr vermilion 4.50 1.90
177 A22 20fr slate 5.00 2.10
178 A22 25fr sepia 7.00 3.25
Nos. 160-178 (19) 43.45 18.10

Imperforates
Most French Polynesia stamps from 1948 onward exist imperforate in issued and trial colors, and also in small presentation sheets in issued colors.

Military Medal Issue
Common Design Type

1952, Dec. 1 Engr. & Typo.
179 CD101 3fr multicolored 11.00 8.50

Girl of Borabora — A23

Girl Playing Guitar — A24

1955, Sept. 26 Engr.
180 A23 9fr dk brn, blk & red 8.50 5.50

FIDES Issue
Common Design Type

Design: 3fr, Dry dock at Papeete.

1956, Oct. 22 Engr. *Perf. 13x12½*
181 CD103 3fr grnsh blue 3.00 1.40

1958, Nov. 3 Unwmk. *Perf. 13*

Designs: 4fr, 7fr, 9fr, Man with headdress. 10fr, 20fr, Girl with shells on beach.

182 A24 10c grn & redsh brn .55 .45
183 A24 25c slate grn, cl & car .65 .50
184 A24 1fr brt bl, brn & red org .80 .55
185 A24 2fr brn, vio brn & vio .90 .55
186 A24 4fr sl grn & org yel 1.25 .90
187 A24 7fr red brn, grn & org 2.40 1.40
188 A24 9fr vio brn, grn & org 4.50 2.00
189 A24 10fr dk bl, brn & car 4.00 2.00
190 A24 20fr pur, rose red & brn 7.00 4.25
Nos. 182-190 (9) 22.05 12.60

See Nos. 304-306.

Human Rights Issue
Common Design Type

1958, Dec. 10
191 CD105 7fr dk gray & dk bl 10.00 7.00

Flower Issue
Common Design Type

1959, Jan. 3 Photo. *Perf. 12½x12*
192 CD104 4fr Breadfruit 5.00 3.00

Spear Fishing — A25

Tahitian Dancers A26

1960, May 16 Engr. *Perf. 13*
193 A25 5fr green, brn & lil 1.25 .90
194 A26 17fr ultra, brt grn & red brn 5.25 2.25

Post Office, Papeete A27

1960, Nov. 19 Unwmk. *Perf. 13*
195 A27 16fr green, bl & claret 5.00 2.90

Saraca Indica — A28

1962, July 12 Photo. *Perf. 13*
196 A28 15fr shown 14.00 11.00
197 A28 25fr Hibiscus 18.00 12.50

Map of Australia and South Pacific — A29

1962, July 18 *Perf. 13x12*
198 A29 20fr multicolored 14.00 6.25

5th South Pacific Conf., Pago Pago, July 1962.

Spined Squirrelfish A30

Fish: 10fr, One-spot butterflyfish. 30fr, Radiate lionfish. 40fr, Horned boxfish.

1962, Dec. 15 Engr. *Perf. 13*
199 A30 5fr black, mag & bis 4.50 2.00
200 A30 10fr multicolored 6.50 3.00
201 A30 30fr multicolored 13.00 8.00
202 A30 40fr multicolored 16.00 12.00
Nos. 199-202 (4) 40.00 25.00

Soccer A30a

Design: 50fr, Throwing the javelin.

1963, Aug. 29 Photo. *Perf. 12½*
203 A30a 20fr brt ultra & brn 8.00 4.50
204 A30a 50fr brt car rose & ultra 13.00 6.75

South Pacific Games, Suva, 8/29-9/7.

Red Cross Centenary Issue
Common Design Type

1963, Sept. 2 Engr. *Perf. 13*
205 CD113 15fr vio brn, gray & car 11.00 9.00

Human Rights Issue
Common Design Type

1963, Dec. 10 Unwmk. *Perf. 13*
206 CD117 7fr green & vio bl 11.00 8.00

Philatec Issue
Common Design Type

1964, Apr. 9 Unwmk. *Perf. 13*
207 CD118 25fr grn, dk sl grn & red 13.50 10.00

Tahitian Dancer A31

1964, May 14 Engr. *Perf. 13*
208 A31 1fr multicolored .35 .35
209 A31 3fr dp claret, blk & org .80 .80

Soldiers, Truck and Battle Flag — A32

1964, July 10 Photo. *Perf. 12½*
210 A32 5fr multicolored 9.00 2.75

Issued to honor the Tahitian Volunteers of the Pacific Battalion. See No. C31.

Tuamotu Scene A33

Views: 4fr, Borabora. 7fr, Papeete Harbor. 8fr, Paul Gauguin's tomb, Marquesas. 20fr, Mangareva, Gambier Islands.

1964, Dec. 1 Litho. *Perf. 12½x13*
211 A33 2fr multicolored .95 .55
212 A33 4fr multicolored 1.60 .55
213 A33 7fr multicolored 3.25 1.40
214 A33 8fr multicolored 4.25 2.00
215 A33 20fr multicolored 10.00 3.25
Nos. 211-215,C32 (6) 28.05 10.50

Painting from a School Dining Room — A34

1965, Nov. 29 Engr. *Perf. 13*
216 A34 20fr dk brn, sl grn & dk car 17.00 10.00

Publicizing the School Canteen Program. See #C38.

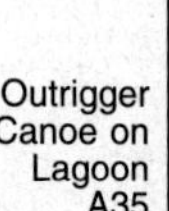

Outrigger Canoe on Lagoon A35

Ships: 11fr, Large cruising yacht, vert. 12fr, Motorboat for sport fishing. 14fr, Outrigger canoes with sails. 19fr, Schooner, vert. 22fr, Modern coaster "Oiseau des Isles II."

1966, Aug. 30 Engr. *Perf. 13*
217 A35 10fr brt ultra, emer & mar 3.00 .80
218 A35 11fr mar, dk bl & sl grn 3.00 1.40
219 A35 12fr emer, dk bl & red lil 4.00 1.60
220 A35 14fr brn, bl & slate grn 6.00 1.75
221 A35 19fr scar, sl grn & dp bl 7.00 1.90
222 A35 22fr multicolored 10.00 3.50
Nos. 217-222 (6) 33.00 10.95

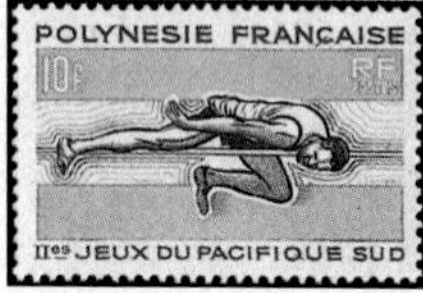

High Jump A36

Designs: 20fr, Pole vault, vert. 40fr, Women's basketball, vert. 60fr, Hurdling.

1966, Dec. 15 Engr. *Perf. 13*
223 A36 10fr dk red, lem & blk 2.00 1.25
224 A36 20fr blue, emer & blk 4.00 1.60
225 A36 40fr emer, brt pink & blk 8.00 4.00
226 A36 60fr dull yel, bl & blk 14.50 7.50
Nos. 223-226 (4) 28.50 14.35

2nd South Pacific Games, Nouméa, New Caledonia, Dec. 8-18.

Poi Pounder — A37 Javelin Throwing — A38

1967, June 15 Engr. *Perf. 13*
227 A37 50fr orange & blk 14.00 8.00

Society for Oceanic Studies, 50th anniv.

1967, July 11

5fr, Spring dance. 15fr, Horse race. 16fr, Fruit carriers' race. 21fr, Canoe race.

228 A38 5fr multi, horiz. 1.10 .75
229 A38 13fr multi 3.50 1.25
230 A38 15fr multi, horiz. 3.50 1.40
231 A38 16fr multi 3.50 2.25
232 A38 21fr multi, horiz. 7.25 4.00
Nos. 228-232 (5) 18.85 9.65

Issued to publicize the July Festival.

Earring — A39

Art of the Marquesas Islands: 10fr, Carved mother-of-pearl. 15fr, Decorated canoe paddle. 23fr, Oil vessel. 25fr, Carved stilt stirrups. 30fr, Fan handles. 35fr, Tattooed man. 50fr, Tikis.

1967-68 Engr. *Perf. 13*
233 A39 10fr dp cl, dl red & ultra 2.00 .70
234 A39 15fr black & emerald 3.00 1.50
235 A39 20fr ol gray, dk car & lt bl 4.00 1.75
236 A39 23fr dk brn, ocher & bl 5.50 3.25
237 A39 25fr dk brn, dk bl & lil 5.50 3.00
238 A39 30fr brown & red lilac 7.00 3.25
239 A39 35fr ultra & dk brn 11.00 5.00
240 A39 50fr brn, sl grn & lt bl 12.00 5.75
Nos. 233-240 (8) 50.00 24.20

Issued: 20fr, 25fr, 30fr, 50fr, 12/19/67; others 2/28/68.

WHO Anniversary Issue
Common Design Type

1968, May 4 Engr. *Perf. 13*
241 CD126 15fr bl grn, mar & dp vio 8.75 3.50
242 CD126 16fr org, lil & bl grn 8.75 5.75

Human Rights Year Issue
Common Design Type

1968, Aug. 10 Engr. *Perf. 13*
243 CD127 15fr blue, red & brn 8.75 4.75
244 CD127 16fr brn, brt pink & ultra 8.75 5.75

Tiare Apetahi A40

Flower: 17fr, Tiare Tahiti.

1969, Mar. 27 Photo. *Perf. 12½x13*
245 A40 9fr multicolored 1.60 .90
246 A40 17fr multicolored 3.50 1.60

3rd South Pacific Games, Port Moresby, Papua and New Guinea, Aug. 13-23 — A41

1969, Aug. 13 Engr. *Perf. 13*
247 A41 9fr Boxer, horiz 2.90 1.10
248 A41 17fr High jump 5.75 1.75
249 A41 18fr Runner 7.25 2.90
250 A41 22fr Long jump 9.50 5.75
Nos. 247-250 (4) 25.40 11.50

ILO Issue
Common Design Type

1969, Nov. 24 Engr. *Perf. 13*
251 CD131 17fr org, emer & ol 8.75 4.25
252 CD131 18fr org, dk brn & vio bl 8.75 5.00

Territorial Assembly A42

Buildings: 14fr, Governor's Residence. 17fr, House of Tourism. 18fr, Maeva Hotel. 24fr, Taharaa Hotel.

1969, Dec. 22 Photo. *Perf. 12½x12*
253 A42 13fr black & multi 2.50 1.10
254 A42 14fr black & multi 3.50 1.40
255 A42 17fr black & multi 5.75 2.90
256 A42 18fr black & multi 6.25 3.25
257 A42 24fr black & multi 11.00 5.75
Nos. 253-257 (5) 29.00 14.40

Stone Figure with Globe — A43

Designs: 40fr, Globe, plane, map of Polynesia and men holding "PATA" sign, horiz. 60fr, Polynesian carrying globe.

1970, Apr. 7 Engr. *Perf. 13*
258 A43 20fr deep plum, gray & bl 5.50 2.75
259 A43 40fr emer, rose lil & ultra 9.00 4.25
260 A43 60fr red brn, bl & dk brn 15.00 8.25
Nos. 258-260 (3) 29.50 15.25

Issued to publicize the 1970 Pacific Area Travel Association Congress (PATA).

UPU Headquarters Issue
Common Design Type

1970, May 20 Engr. *Perf. 13*
261 CD133 18fr maroon, pur & brn 8.00 4.00
262 CD133 20fr lilac rose, ol & ind 8.00 4.25

Night Fishing — A44

1971, May 11 Photo. *Perf. 13*
263 A44 10fr multicolored 10.00 4.25
Nos. 263,C71-C73 (4) 33.00 16.25

Flowers — A45

Designs: Various flowers. 12fr is horiz.

Perf. 12½x13, 13x12½
1971, Aug. 27
264 A45 8fr multicolored 1.60 .90
265 A45 12fr multicolored 2.75 1.40
266 A45 22fr multicolored 4.50 2.25
Nos. 264-266 (3) 8.85 4.55

Day of a Thousand Flowers.

Water-skiing Slalom — A46

Designs: 20fr, Water-skiing, jump, vert. 40fr, Figure water-skiing.

1971, Oct. 11 Engr. *Perf. 13*
267 A46 10fr grnsh bl, dk red & brn 5.00 1.75
268 A46 20fr car, emer & brn 7.25 3.25
269 A46 40fr brn, grn & lil 17.00 10.00
Nos. 267-269 (3) 29.25 15.00

World water-skiing championships, Oct. 1971.

De Gaulle Issue
Common Design Type

30fr, As general, 1940. 50fr, As president, 1970.

1971, Nov. 9 Engr. *Perf. 13*
270 CD134 30fr red lilac & blk 15.00 8.25
271 CD134 50fr red lilac & blk 21.00 12.50

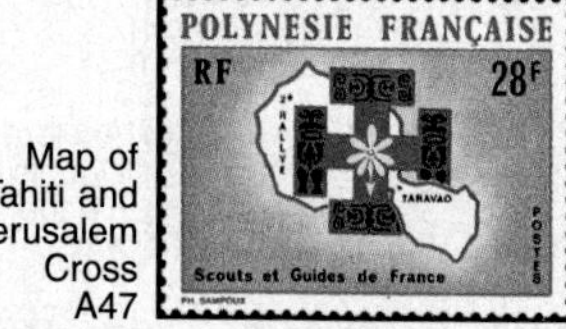

Map of Tahiti and Jerusalem Cross A47

1971, Dec. 18 Photo. *Perf. 13x12½*
272 A47 28fr lt blue & multi 11.00 6.75

2nd rally of French Boy Scouts and Guides, Taravao, French Polynesia.

"Alcoholism" A48 Mother and Child A49

1972, Mar. 24 Photo. *Perf. 13*
273 A48 20fr brown & multi 9.00 4.00

Fight against alcoholism.

1973, Sept. 26 Photo. *Perf. 12½x13*
274 A49 28fr pale yellow & multi 10.00 4.00

Day nursery.

Polynesian Golfer — A50

Design: 24fr, Atimaono Golf Course.

1974, Feb. 27 Photo. *Perf. 13*

275	A50	16fr multicolored	8.75	2.50
276	A50	24fr multicolored	11.00	4.00

Atimaono Golf Course.

Hand Throwing Life Preserver to Puppy — A51

1974, May 9 Photo. *Perf. 13*

277	A51	21fr brt blue & multi	10.50	4.50

Society for the Protection of Animals.

Around a Fire, on the Beach A52

Polynesian Views: 2fr, Lagoons and mountains. 6fr, Pebble divers. 10fr, Lonely Mountain and flowers, vert. 15fr, Sailing ship at sunset. 20fr, Lagoon and mountain.

1974, May 22

278	A52	2fr multicolored	.75	.50
279	A52	5fr multicolored	.95	.75
280	A52	6fr multicolored	1.60	.90
281	A52	10fr multicolored	1.75	1.10
282	A52	15fr multicolored	3.50	1.50
283	A52	20fr multicolored	5.75	1.75
		Nos. 278-283 (6)	14.30	6.50

Polynesian Woman and UPU Emblem — A53

Lion, Sun and Emblem — A54

1974, Oct. 9 Engr. *Perf. 13*

284	A53	65fr multicolored	10.50	6.75

Centenary of Universal Postal Union.

1975, June 17 Photo.

285	A54	26fr multicolored	12.50	4.50

15th anniv. of Lions Intl. in Tahiti.

Fish and Leaf A55

1975, July 9 Litho. *Perf. 12*

286	A55	19fr dp ultra & green	9.50	3.25

Polynesian Association for the Protection of Nature.

Georges Pompidou, Pres. of France — A55a

1976, Feb. 16 Engr. *Perf. 13*

287	A55a	49fr dk violet & black	10.50	6.00

See France No. 1430.

Alain Gerbault and Sailboat A56

1976, May 25 Photo. *Perf. 13*

288	A56	90fr multicolored	11.00	8.00

Alain Gerbault's arrival in Bora Bora, 50th anniv.

Turtle — A57

Design: 42fr, Hand protecting bird.

1976, June 24 Litho. *Perf. 12½*

289	A57	18fr multicolored	12.50	3.25
290	A57	42fr multicolored	17.00	8.00

World Ecology Day.

A. G. Bell, Telephone, Radar and Satellite — A58

1976, Sept. 15 Engr. *Perf. 13*

291	A58	37fr multicolored	9.00	4.50

Centenary of first telephone call by Alexander Graham Bell, Mar. 10, 1876.

Dugout Canoes — A59

1976, Dec. 16 Litho. *Perf. 13x12½*

292	A59	25fr Marquesas	4.00	3.00
293	A59	30fr Raiatea	5.00	4.00
294	A59	75fr Tahiti	10.00	6.00
295	A59	100fr Tuamotu	12.50	7.50
		Nos. 292-295 (4)	31.50	20.50

Sailing Ship — A60

Designs: Various sailing vessels.

1977, Dec. 22 Litho. *Perf. 13*

296	A60	20fr multicolored	5.00	1.75
297	A60	50fr multicolored	6.00	2.00
298	A60	85fr multicolored	7.00	3.25
299	A60	120fr multicolored	13.00	5.00
		Nos. 296-299 (4)	31.00	12.00

Hibiscus — A61

Girl with Shells on Beach — A62

Designs: 10fr, Vanda orchids. 16fr, Pua (fagraea berteriana). 22fr, Gardenia.

1978-79 Photo. *Perf. 12½x13*

300	A61	10fr multicolored	1.00	.45
301	A61	13fr multicolored	2.25	.90
302	A61	16fr multicolored	2.50	1.40
303	A61	22fr multicolored	1.75	.90
		Nos. 300-303 (4)	7.50	3.65

Issued: 13fr, 16fr, 8/23; 10fr, 22fr, 1/25/79.

1978, Nov. 3 Engr. *Perf. 13*

Design A24 with "1958 1978" added: 28fr, Man with headdress. 36fr, Girl playing guitar.

304	A62	20fr multicolored	3.25	.60
305	A62	28fr multicolored	4.00	1.40
306	A62	36fr multicolored	6.00	2.00
a.		Souvenir sheet of 3	30.00	30.00
		Nos. 304-306 (3)	13.25	4.00

20th anniv. of stamps inscribed: Polynesie Francaise. #306a contains #304-306 in changed colors.

Ships — A63

1978, Dec. 29 Litho. *Perf. 13x12½*

307	A63	15fr Tahiti	1.50	.75
308	A63	30fr Monowai	2.50	1.00
309	A63	75fr Tahitien	4.00	2.50
310	A63	100fr Mariposa	7.50	2.50
		Nos. 307-310 (4)	15.50	6.75

Porites Coral A64

Design: 37fr, Montipora coral.

1979, Feb. 15 *Perf. 13x12½*

311	A64	32fr multicolored	2.75	.90
312	A64	37fr multicolored	4.00	1.40

Raiatea A65

Landscapes: 1fr, Moon over Bora Bora. 2fr, Mountain peaks, Ua Pou. 3fr, Sunset over Motu Tapu. 6fr, Palm and hut, Tuamotu.

1979, Mar. 8 Photo. *Perf. 13x13½*

313	A65	1fr multicolored	.20	.20
314	A65	2fr multicolored	.20	.20
315	A65	3fr multicolored	.25	.20
316	A65	4fr multicolored	.35	.20
317	A65	5fr multicolored	.60	.30
318	A65	6fr multicolored	.75	.50
		Nos. 313-318 (6)	2.35	1.60

See Nos. 438-443 for redrawn designs.

Dance Costumes A66

1979, July 14 Litho. *Perf. 12½*

319	A66	45fr Fetia	1.60	.80
320	A66	51fr Teanuanua	2.25	.90
321	A66	74fr Temaeva	3.25	1.75
		Nos. 319-321 (3)	7.10	3.45

Hill, Great Britain No. 53, Tahiti No. 28 A67

1979, Aug. 1 Engr. *Perf. 13*
322 A67 100fr multicolored 4.00 2.75

Sir Rowland Hill (1795-1879), originator of penny postage.

Hastula Strigilata — A68

Statue Holding Rotary Emblem — A69

Shells: 28fr, Scabricola variegata. 35fr, Fusinus undatus.

1979, Aug. 22 Litho. *Perf. 12½*
323 A68 20fr multicolored 2.00 .80
324 A68 28fr multicolored 2.75 .90
325 A68 35fr multicolored 3.75 2.50
Nos. 323-325 (3) 8.50 4.20

1979, Nov. 30 Litho. *Perf. 13*
326 A69 47fr multicolored 2.75 1.60

Rotary International, 75th anniversary; Papeete Rotary Club, 20th anniversary.
For overprint see No. 330.

Myripristis Murdjan A70

Fish: 8fr, Napoleon. 12fr, Emperor.

1980, Jan. 21 Litho. *Perf. 12½*
327 A70 7fr multicolored 2.00 .45
328 A70 8fr multicolored 2.00 .60
329 A70 12fr multicolored 2.50 .75
Nos. 327-329 (3) 6.50 1.80

No. 326 Overprinted and Surcharged in Gold: "75eme / ANNIVERSAIRE / 1905-1980"

1980, Feb. 23 Litho. *Perf. 13*
330 A69 77fr on 47fr multi 5.00 2.75

Rotary International, 75th anniversary.

CNEXO Fish Hatchery A71

1980, Mar. 17 Photo. *Perf. 13x13½*
331 A71 15fr shown 1.25 .75
332 A71 22fr Crayfish 1.25 .75

Papeete Post Office Building Opening A72

1980, Apr. 30 Photo. *Perf. 13x12½*
333 A72 50fr multicolored 2.25 1.40

Tiki and Festival Emblem — A73

1980, June 30 Photo. *Perf. 13½*
334 A73 34fr shown 1.50 .75
335 A73 39fr Drum (pahu) 1.90 1.10
336 A73 49fr Ax (to'i) 2.50 1.50
a. Souv. sheet of 3, #334-336 11.00 11.00
Nos. 334-336 (3) 5.90 3.35

South Pacific Arts Festival, Port Moresby, Papua New Guinea.

Titmouse Henparrot — A74

Charles de Gaulle — A75

Perf. 13x12½, 12½x13
1980, Oct. 20 Photo.
337 A74 25fr White sea-swallow, horiz. 2.50 .75
338 A74 35fr shown 3.00 1.00
339 A74 45fr Minor frigate bird, horiz. 4.00 1.25
Nos. 337-339 (3) 9.50 3.00

1980, Nov. 9 Engr. *Perf. 12½x13*
340 A75 100fr multicolored 4.50 2.75

Naso Vlamingi (Karaua) A76

1981, Feb. 5 Litho. *Perf. 12½*
341 A76 13fr shown 2.25 .50
342 A76 16fr Lutjanus vaigensis (toau) 2.25 .60
343 A76 24fr Plectropomus leopardus (tonu) 3.00 .75
Nos. 341-343 (3) 7.50 1.85

Indoor Fish Breeding Tanks, Cnexo Hatchery A77

1981, May 14 Photo. *Perf. 13x13½*
344 A77 23fr shown 1.25 .80
345 A77 41fr Mussels 2.00 1.10

Folk Dancers A78

Perf. 13x13½, 13½x13
1981, July 10 Litho.
346 A78 26fr shown 1.10 .55
347 A78 28fr Dancer 1.10 .75
348 A78 44fr Dancers, vert. 1.90 1.10
Nos. 346-348 (3) 4.10 2.40

Sterna Bergii — A79

1981, Sept. 24 Litho. *Perf. 13*
349 A79 47fr shown 1.40 .80
350 A79 53fr Ptilinopus purpuratus, vert. 1.40 .90
351 A79 65fr Estrilda astrild, vert. 1.75 1.25
Nos. 349-351 (3) 4.55 2.95

See Nos. 370-372.

Huahine Island A80

1981, Oct. 22 Litho. *Perf. 12½*
352 A80 34fr shown 1.25 .60
353 A80 134fr Maupiti 2.75 1.60
354 A80 136fr Bora-Bora 2.75 1.60
Nos. 352-354 (3) 6.75 3.80

A81

1982, Feb. 4 Photo. *Perf. 13x13½*
355 A81 30fr Parrotfish .90 .70
356 A81 31fr Regal angel 1.25 .70
357 A81 45fr Spotted bass 1.40 1.00
Nos. 355-357 (3) 3.55 2.40

Pearl Industry A82

1982, Apr. 22 Photo. *Perf. 13x13½*
358 A82 7fr Pearl beds 1.25 .35
359 A82 8fr Extracting pearls 1.50 .35
360 A82 10fr Pearls 2.00 .50
Nos. 358-360 (3) 4.75 1.20

Tahiti "No. 1A," Emblem — A83

1982, May 12 Engr. *Perf. 13*
361 A83 150fr multicolored 5.00 3.50
a. Souvenir sheet 15.00 15.00

PHILEXFRANCE Stamp Exhibition, Paris, June 11-21. No. 361a contains No. 361 in changed colors.

King Holding Carved Scepter — A84

Designs: Coronation ceremony.

1982, July 12 Photo. *Perf. 13½x13*
362 A84 12fr shown .50 .20
363 A84 13fr King, priest .50 .20
364 A84 17fr Procession 1.00 .50
Nos. 362-364 (3) 2.00 .90

Championship Emblem — A85

1982, Aug. 13 *Perf. 13*
365 A85 90fr multicolored 2.25 1.60

4th Hobie-Cat 16 World Catamaran Sailing Championship, Tahiti, Aug. 15-21.

First Colloquium on New Energy Sources — A86

1982, Sept. 29 Litho.
366 A86 46fr multicolored 2.75 .90

Motu, Tuamotu Islet — A87

1982, Oct. 12 Litho. *Perf. 13*
367 A87 20fr shown .75 .35
368 A87 33fr Tupai Atoll 1.00 .50
369 A87 35fr Gambier Islds. 1.50 .60
Nos. 367-369 (3) 3.25 1.45

Bird Type of 1981

1982, Nov. 17 Litho. *Perf. 13*
370 A79 37fr Sacred egret 2.25 .50
371 A79 39fr Pluvialis dominica, vert. 2.25 .60

372 A79 42fr Lonchura castane-othorax 4.50 .75
Nos. 370-372 (3) 9.00 1.85

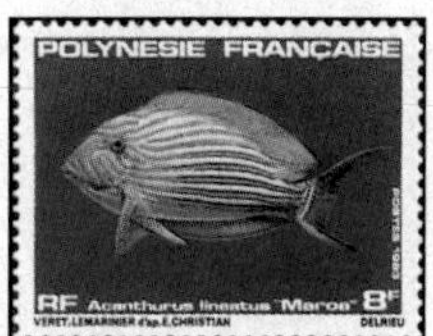

Fish — A88

1983, Feb. 9 Litho. ***Perf. 13x13½***
373 A88 8fr Acanthurus lineatus .75 .35
374 A88 10fr Caranx me-lampygus 1.00 .35
375 A88 12fr Carcharhinus mela-nopterus 1.50 .50
Nos. 373-375 (3) 3.25 1.20

The Way of the Cross, Sculpture by Damien Haturau — A89

1983, Mar. 9 Litho. ***Perf. 13***
376 A89 7fr shown 1.00 .25
377 A89 21fr Virgin and Child 1.50 .50
378 A89 23fr Christ 1.75 .35
Nos. 376-378 (3) 4.25 1.10

Traditional Hats — A90

1983, May 24 Litho. ***Perf. 13x12½***
379 A90 11fr Acacia .75 .35
380 A90 13fr Niau .75 .35
381 A90 25fr Ofe 1.00 .50
382 A90 35fr Ofe, diff. 1.25 .50
Nos. 379-382 (4) 3.75 1.70

See Nos. 393-396.

Chieftain in Traditional Costume, Sainte-Christine Isld. — A91

Traditional Costumes, Marquesas Islds.

1983, July 12 Photo. ***Perf. 13***
383 A91 15fr shown .75 .50
384 A91 17fr Man 1.00 .50
385 A91 28fr Woman 1.25 .50
Nos. 383-385 (3) 3.00 1.50

See Nos. 397-399, 419-421.

Polynesian Crowns — A92

Various flower garlands.

1983, Oct. 19 Litho. ***Perf. 13***
386 A92 41fr multicolored 1.40 .60
387 A92 44fr multicolored 1.60 .60
388 A92 45fr multicolored 2.00 .80
Nos. 386-388 (3) 5.00 2.00

See Nos. 400-402.

Martin Luther (1483-1546) A93

Tiki Carvings — A94

1983, Nov. 10 Engr. ***Perf. 13***
389 A93 90fr black, brn & lil gray 2.50 1.25

1984, Feb. 8 Litho. ***Perf. 12½x13***

Various carvings.

390 A94 14fr multicolored .80 .25
391 A94 16fr multicolored 1.00 .50
392 A94 19fr multicolored 1.25 .40
Nos. 390-392 (3) 3.05 1.15

Hat Type of 1983

1984, June 20 Litho. ***Perf. 13x12½***
393 A90 20fr Aeho ope .50 .35
394 A90 24fr Paeore .60 .35
395 A90 26fr Ofe fei .75 .50
396 A90 33fr Hua .80 .50
Nos. 393-396 (4) 2.65 1.70

Costume Type of 1983

1984, July 11 Litho. ***Perf. 13***
397 A91 34fr Tahitian playing nose flute .75 .50
398 A91 35fr Priest, Oei-eitia .90 .50
399 A91 39fr Tahitian adult and child .90 .50
Nos. 397-399 (3) 2.55 1.50

Garland Type of 1983

1984, Oct. 24 Litho. ***Perf. 13x12½***
400 A92 46fr Moto'i Lei .90 .50
401 A92 47fr Pitate Lei 1.00 .60
402 A92 53fr Bougainvillea Lei 1.25 .80
Nos. 400-402 (3) 3.15 1.90

4th Pacific Arts Festival, Noumea, New Caledonia, Dec. 8-22 — A95

1984, Nov. 20 Litho. ***Perf. 13***
403 A95 150fr Statue, head-dress 3.00 2.25

See No. C213.

Paysage D'Anaa, by Jean Masson — A96

Paintings: 50fr, Sortie Du Culte, by Jacques Boulaire. 75fr, La Fete, by Robert Tatin. 85fr, Tahitiennes Sur La Plage, by Pierre Heyman.

Perf. 12½x13, 13x12½

1984, Dec. 12 Litho.
404 A96 50fr multi, vert. 1.25 .60
405 A96 65fr multicolored 1.25 .75
406 A96 75fr multicolored 1.60 .90
407 A96 85fr multicolored 1.75 1.50
Nos. 404-407 (4) 5.85 3.75

Tiki Carvings — A97

Polynesian Faces — A98

1985, Jan. 23 Litho. ***Perf. 13½***
408 A97 30fr multicolored .60 .35
409 A97 36fr multicolored .80 .45
410 A97 40fr multicolored .90 .75
Nos. 408-410 (3) 2.30 1.55

1985, Feb. 20 Photo. ***Perf. 12½x13***
411 A98 22fr multicolored .45 .35
412 A98 39fr multicolored .80 .45
413 A98 44fr multicolored 1.00 .75
Nos. 411-413 (3) 2.25 1.55

Early Tahiti — A99

Perf. 13x12½, 12½x13

1985, Apr. 24 Litho.
414 A99 42fr Entrance to Papee-te .90 .60
415 A99 45fr Girls, vert. 1.25 .80
416 A99 48fr Papeete market 1.40 .90
Nos. 414-416 (3) 3.55 2.30

5th Intl. Congress on Coral Reefs, Tahiti A100

1985, May 28 Litho. ***Perf. 13½***
417 A100 140fr Local reef for-mation 3.00 2.00

Printed se-tenant with label picturing congress emblem.

National Flag A101

1985, June 28
418 A101 9fr Flag, natl. arms 1.50 1.00

Costume Type of 1983

18th-19th Cent. Prints, Beslu Collection.

1985, July 17 ***Perf. 13***
419 A91 38fr Tahitian dancer 1.25 .50
420 A91 55fr Man and woman from Otahiti, 1806 1.75 .75
421 A91 70fr Traditional chief 2.50 .90
Nos. 419-421 (3) 5.50 2.15

Local Foods — A103

1985-86 Litho. ***Perf. 13***
422 A103 25fr Roasted pig 1.00 .40
423 A103 35fr Pit fire 1.50 .60
423A A103 80fr Fish in coco-nut milk 2.00 1.40
423B A103 110fr Fafaru 2.50 1.75
Nos. 422-423B (4) 7.00 4.15

Issued: 25fr, 35fr, 11/14; 80fr, 110fr, 5/20/86.
See Nos. 458-459, 474-475.

Catholic Churches — A104

1985, Dec. 11 Litho. ***Perf. 13***
424 A104 90fr St. Anne's, Otepipi 1.90 1.10
425 A104 100fr St. Michael's Cathedral, Rik-itea 2.00 1.10
426 A104 120fr Cathedral, exte-rior 2.40 1.60
Nos. 424-426 (3) 6.30 3.80

Nos. 424-426 printed se-tenant with labels picturing local religious art.

Crabs A105

1986, Jan. 22 ***Perf. 13½***
427 A105 18fr Fiddler .50 .35
428 A105 29fr Hermit .75 .35
429 A105 31fr Coconut 1.00 .50
Nos. 427-429 (3) 2.25 1.20

Faces of Polynesia A106

1986, Feb. 19 ***Perf. 12½x13, 13x12½***
430 A106 43fr Boy, fish 1.00 .50
431 A106 49fr Boy, coral 1.25 .50
432 A106 51fr Boy, turtle, vert. 1.40 .60
Nos. 430-432 (3) 3.65 1.60

Old Tahiti — A107

1986, Mar. 18 *Perf. 13x12½*

433 A107 52fr Papeete 1.00 .60
434 A107 56fr Harpoon fishing 1.10 .60
435 A107 57fr Royal Palace, Papeete 1.25 .75
Nos. 433-435 (3) 3.35 1.95

Tiki Rock Carvings — A108

1986, Apr. 16

436 A108 58fr Atuona, Hiva Oa 1.75 .70
437 A108 59fr Ua Huka Hill, Hane Valley 1.75 .70

Landscapes Type Redrawn

1986-88 **Litho.** *Perf. 13½*

438 A65 1fr multi, type 2 ('88) .60 .35
a. Type 1 ('86) 2.50 1.00
b. Type 3 ('91) 8.00 4.00
439 A65 2fr multicolored .40 .20
440 A65 3fr multicolored .45 .20
441 A65 4fr multicolored ('87) .75 .30
442 A65 5fr multicolored .75 .30
443 A65 6fr multicolored .65 .30
Nos. 438-443 (6) 3.60 1.65

Nos. 438-443 printed in sharper detail, and box containing island name is taller. Nos. 439-443 margin is inscribed "CARTOR" instead of "DELRIEU."

No. 438 has three types of inscription below design: type 1, photographer's name at left, no inscription at right; type 2, photographer's name at left 9.5mm long, printer's name (Cartor) at right; type 3, photographer's name at left 12.5mm long, Cartor at right.

Traditional Crafts A109

Perf. 13x12½, 12½x13

1986, July 17 **Litho.**

444 A109 8fr Quilting, vert. .20 .20
445 A109 10fr Baskets, hats .20 .25
446 A109 12fr Grass skirts .80 .30
Nos. 444-446 (3) 1.20 .75

Building a Pirogue (Canoe) A110

1986, Oct. 21 **Litho.** *Perf. 13½*

447 A110 46fr Boat-builders 1.25 .60
448 A110 50fr Close-up 1.50 .80

Medicinal Plants — A111

Polynesians A112

1986, Nov. 19 *Perf. 13*

449 A111 40fr Phymatosorus .80 .50
450 A111 41fr Barringtonia asiatica .90 .50
451 A111 60fr Ocimum bacilicum 1.50 .90
Nos. 449-451 (3) 3.20 1.90

See Nos. 495-497.

1987, Jan. 21 **Litho.** *Perf. 13½*

452 A112 28fr Old man .60 .35
453 A112 30fr Mother and child .75 .50
454 A112 37fr Old woman 1.00 .60
Nos. 452-454 (3) 2.35 1.45

Crustaceans — A113

1987, Feb. 18 *Perf. 12½x13*

455 A113 34fr Carpilius maculatus 1.00 .50
456 A113 35fr Parribacus antarticus 1.00 .50
457 A113 39fr Justitia longimana 1.25 .50
Nos. 455-457 (3) 3.25 1.50

Local Foods Type of 1985

1987, Mar. 19 **Litho.** *Perf. 13*

458 A103 33fr Papaya poe 2.00 .60
459 A103 65fr Chicken fafa 3.00 .90

Polynesian Petroglyphs A114

1987, May 13 *Perf. 12½*

460 A114 13fr Tipaerui, Tahiti .35 .20
461 A114 21fr Turtle, Raiatea Is. .60 .35

Calling Devices and Musical Instruments, Museum of Tahiti and the Isles — A115

1987, July 1 *Perf. 13½*

462 A115 20fr Wood horn .80 .20
463 A115 26fr Triton's conch .80 .50
464 A115 33fr Nose flutes 1.00 .60
Nos. 462-464 (3) 2.60 1.30

Medicinal Plants — A116

1987, Sept. 16 *Perf. 12½x13*

465 A116 46fr Thespesia populnea 1.00 .60
466 A116 53fr Ophioglossum reticulatum 1.25 .60
467 A116 54fr Dicrocephala latifolia 1.25 .60
Nos. 465-467 (3) 3.50 1.80

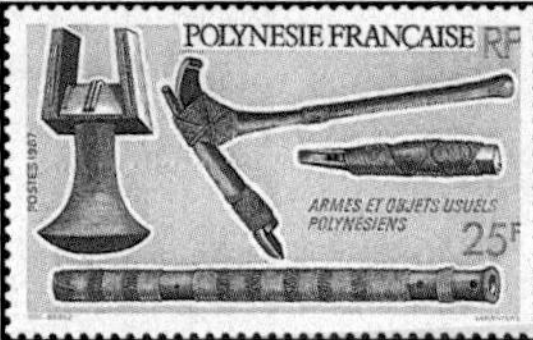

Ancient Weapons and Tools — A117

Designs: 25fr, Adze, war club, chisel, flute. 27fr, War clubs, tatooing comb, mallet. 32fr, Headdress, necklaces, nose flute.

1987, Oct. 14 **Engr.** *Perf. 13*

468 A117 25fr lt olive grn & blk .60 .40
469 A117 27fr Prus grn & int blue .75 .45
470 A117 32fr brt olive bis & brn blk .80 .55
Nos. 468-470 (3) 2.15 1.40

Catholic Missionaries — A118

Monsignors: 95fr, Rene Ildefonse Dordillon (1808-1888), bishop of the Marquesas Isls. 105fr, Tepano Jaussen (1815-1891), first bishop of Polynesia. 115fr, Paul Laurent Maze (1885-1976), archbishop of Papeete.

1987, Dec. 9 **Litho.**

471 A118 95fr multicolored 2.00 1.50
472 A118 105fr multicolored 2.25 1.75
473 A118 115fr multicolored 2.50 1.90
Nos. 471-473 (3) 6.75 5.15

Local Foods Type of 1985

1988, Jan. 12 **Litho.** *Perf. 13*

474 A103 40fr Crayfish (varo) 2.00 .60
475 A103 75fr Bananas in coconut milk 3.00 1.25

Nos. 474-475 are vert.

Authors — A119

62fr, James Norman Hall (1887-1951). 85fr, Charles Bernard Nordhoff (1887-1947).

1988, Feb. 10

476 A119 62fr multicolored 1.40 .80
477 A119 85fr multicolored 1.75 .90

Traditional Housing — A120

11fr, Taranpoo Opoa Is., Raiatea. 15fr, Tahaa Village. 17fr, Community meeting house, Tahiti.

1988, Mar. 16 **Litho.** *Perf. 13x12½*

478 A120 11fr multicolored 1.00 .30
479 A120 15fr multicolored 1.00 .30
480 A120 17fr multicolored 1.50 .30
Nos. 478-480 (3) 3.50 .90

Point Venus Lighthouse, 120th Anniv. — A121

1988, Apr. 21 **Litho.** *Perf. 13*

481 A121 400fr multicolored 8.50 6.00

Tapa-cloth Paintings by Paul Engdahl A122

1988, May 20

482 A122 52fr multicolored 1.25 .80
483 A122 54fr multicolored 1.40 .90
484 A122 64fr multicolored 1.50 1.25
Nos. 482-484 (3) 4.15 2.95

POLYSAT (Domestic Communications Network) — A123

1988, June 15 **Litho.** *Perf. 12½x12*

485 A123 300fr multicolored 6.00 4.75

Tahitian Dolls — A124

Designs: 42fr, Wearing grass skirt and headdress. 45fr, Wearing print dress and straw hat, holding guitar. 48fr, Wearing print dress and straw hat, holding straw bag.

1988, June 27 *Perf. 13x12½*

486 A124 42fr multicolored .90 .60
487 A124 45fr multicolored 1.00 .60
488 A124 48fr multicolored 1.25 .75
Nos. 486-488 (3) 3.15 1.95

Visiting a Marae at Nuku Hiva, Engraving by J. & E. Verreaux A125

1988, Aug. 1 Engr. *Perf. 13*
489 A125 68fr black brown 1.75 1.25

Size: 143x101mm

490 A125 145fr violet brn & grn 4.00 4.00

SYDPEX '88, July 30-Aug. 7, Australia. No. 490 pictures a Russian navy officer (probably Krusenstern) visiting the Marquesas Islanders; denomination LR.

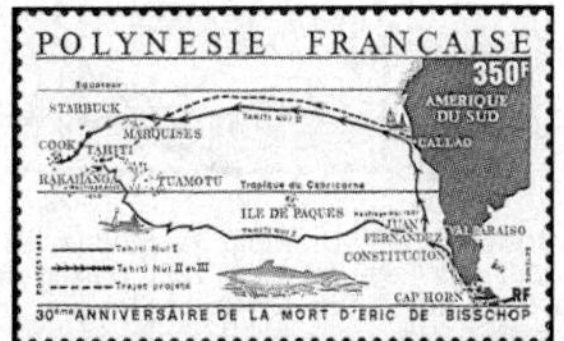

Map Linking South America and South Pacific Islands — A126

1988, Aug. 30 Engr.
491 A126 350fr multicolored 7.00 4.50

Eric de Bisschop (1890-1958), explorer who tried to prove that there was an exchange of peoples between the South Pacific islands and So. America, rather than that the island populations originated from So. America.

Seashells A127

1988, Sept. 21 Litho. *Perf. 13½*
492 A127 24fr Kermia barnardi .60 .35
493 A127 35fr Vexillum suavis 1.00 .50
494 A127 44fr Berthelinia 1.25 .75
Nos. 492-494 (3) 2.85 1.60

Medicinal Plants Type of 1986

1988, Oct. 18 Engr. *Perf. 13*
495 A111 23fr Davallia solida .60 .35
496 A111 36fr Rorippa sarmentosa 1.00 .50
497 A111 49fr Lindernia crustacea 1.25 .75
Nos. 495-497 (3) 2.85 1.60

Protestant Missionaries — A128

1988, Dec. 7 Litho.
498 A128 80fr Henry Nott (1774-1844) 1.50 .90
499 A128 90fr Papeiha (1800-40) 2.00 1.25
500 A128 100fr Samuel Raapoto (1921-76) 2.25 1.40
Nos. 498-500 (3) 5.75 3.55

Tahiti Post Office A129

1989, Jan. 12 Engr.
501 A129 30fr P.O., 1875 .75 .40
502 A129 40fr P.O., 1915 .90 .55

Center for Arts and Crafts A130

1989, Feb. 15 Litho. *Perf. 12½*
503 A130 29fr Marquesas Is. lidded bowl .75 .40
504 A130 31fr Mother-of-pearl pendant .80 .45

Copra Industry — A131

1989, Mar. 16 Litho. *Perf. 13*
505 A131 55fr Extracting copra from shell with a pa'aro, vert. *75.00 75.00*
506 A131 70fr shown *2.50 2.50*

Tapa Art — A132

43fr, Wood statue (pole), Marquesas Islands, vert. 51fr, Hand-painted bark tapestry, Society Is. 56fr, Concentric circles, Tubuai, Austral Islands.

1989, Apr. 18 Litho. *Perf. 13½*
507 A132 43fr multicolored .90 .60
508 A132 51fr shown 1.25 .75
509 A132 56fr multicolored 1.50 .90
Nos. 507-509 (3) 3.65 2.25

Polynesian Environment A133

1989, May 17 Litho. *Perf. 13x12½*
510 A133 120fr shown 3.00 1.60
511 A133 140fr Diving for seashells 3.50 1.90

Polynesian Folklore A134

Perf. 13x12½, 12½x13
1989, June 28 Litho.
512 A134 47fr Stone-lifting contest, vert. 1.25 .60
513 A134 61fr Dancer, vert. 1.50 .75
514 A134 67fr Folk singers 1.90 .80
Nos. 512-514 (3) 4.65 2.15

Bounty Castaways, from an Etching by Robert Dodd — A135

1989, July 7 Engr. *Perf. 13*
515 A135 100fr dp blue & bl grn 2.50 1.60

Souvenir Sheet

Imperf

516 A135 200fr dk ol grn & dk brn *12.50* 12.50

PHILEXFRANCE '89 and 200th annivs. of the mutiny on the *Bounty* and the French revolution.

No. 515 printed se-tenant with label picturing exhibition emblem.

Reverend-Father Patrick O'Reilly (1900-1988) A136

1989, Aug. 7 Engr. *Perf. 13x13½*
517 A136 52fr yel brn & myrtle grn 1.40 .75

Miniature Sheet

Messages A137

a, Get well soon. b, Good luck. c, Happy birthday. d, Keep in touch. e, Congratulations.

1989, Sept. 27 Litho. *Perf. 12½*
518 A137 42fr Sheet of 5, #a.-e. 7.50 7.50

Sea Shells A138

1989, Oct. 12 Litho. *Perf. 13½*
523 A138 60fr Triphoridae 1.50 .80
524 A138 69fr Muricidae favartia 1.60 .90
525 A138 73fr Muricidae morula 1.75 1.00
Nos. 523-525 (3) 4.85 2.70

Te Faaturama, c. 1892, by Gauguin A139

1989, Nov. 19 Litho. *Perf. 12½x13*
526 A139 1000fr multicolored 22.50 13.00

Legends — A140

Designs: 66fr, Maui, birth of the islands, vert. 82fr, Mt. Rotui, the pierced mountain. 88fr, Princess Hina and the eel King of Lake Vaihiria.

1989, Dec. 6 Litho. *Perf. 13*
527 A140 66fr olive brn & blk 1.25 .90
528 A140 82fr buff & blk 1.75 1.10
529 A140 88fr cream & blk 1.75 1.15
Nos. 527-529 (3) 4.75 3.15

Vanilla Orchid — A141

1990, Jan. 11 Litho.
530 A141 34fr Flower 1.40 .60
531 A141 35fr Bean pods 1.75 .60

Marine Life A142

1990, Feb. 9 Litho. *Perf. 13½*
532 A142 40fr *Kuhlia marginata* 1.40 .60
533 A142 50fr *Macrobrachium* 1.60 .75

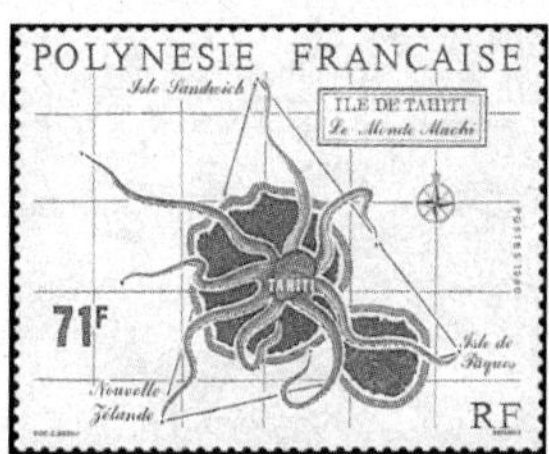

Tahiti, Center of Polynesian Triangle — A143

Maohi settlers and maps of island settlements: 58fr, Hawaiian Islands. 59fr, Easter Island. 63fr, New Zealand.

1990, Mar. 14 Engr. *Perf. 13*
534 A143 58fr black 1.75 .85
535 A143 59fr bluish gray *47.50* 22.50
536 A143 63fr olive green 2.25 .95
537 A143 71fr Prussian blue 2.50 1.10
Nos. 534-537 (4) *54.00* 25.40

See Nos. 544-545.

Papeete Village, Cent. — A144

1990, May 16 Litho.
538 A144 150fr New City Hall 3.50 2.00
539 A144 250fr Old Town Hall 5.00 3.25

A145

A146

Designs: Endangered birds.

1990, June 5 *Perf. 13½*
540 A145 13fr Porzana tabuensis .75 .20
541 A145 20fr Vini ultramarina 1.75 .35

1990, July 10 *Perf. 13*
542 A146 39fr multicolored 1.00 .60

Lions Club in Papeete, 30th anniv.

Gen. Charles de Gaulle, Birth Cent. — A147

1990, Sept. 2 **Litho.**
543 A147 200fr multi 4.00 3.00

No. 536 with Different Colors and Inscriptions

1990, Aug. 24 **Engr.** *Perf. 13*
544 A143 125fr Man, map 3.00 2.00

Souvenir Sheet

Imperf

545 A143 230fr like No. 544 6.00 6.00

New Zealand 1990.

Intl. Tourism Day — A148

1990, Sept. 27 **Litho.** *Perf. 12½*
546 A148 8f red & yellow pareo 1.00 .35
547 A148 10fr yellow pareo 1.00 .35
548 A148 12fr blue pareo 1.00 .75
Nos. 546-548 (3) 3.00 1.45

Polynesian Legends — A149

170fr, Legend of the Uru. 290fr, Pipiri-ma, vert. 375fr, Hiro, God of Thieves, vert.

1990, Nov. 7 **Litho.** *Perf. 13*
549 A149 170fr multicolored 4.00 2.50
550 A149 290fr multicolored 7.50 4.50
551 A149 375fr multicolored 11.00 5.75
Nos. 549-551 (3) 22.50 12.75

Tiare Flower — A150

Pineapple A151

Designs: 28fr, Flower crown, lei. 30fr, Flowers in bloom. 37fr, Lei.

1990, Dec. 5 *Perf. 12½*
552 A150 28fr multicolored .75 .45
553 A150 30fr multicolored 1.00 .50
554 A150 37fr multicolored 1.25 .60
Nos. 552-554 (3) 3.00 1.55

1991, Jan. 9 *Die Cut*

Self-adhesive

555 A151 42fr shown 1.10 .90
556 A151 44fr Pineapple field 1.40 1.10

#555-556 are on paper backing perf. 12½.

Marine Life A152

1991, Feb. 7 *Perf. 12½*
557 A152 7fr Nudibranch .50 .20
558 A152 9fr Galaxaura tenera .75 .20
559 A152 11fr Adusta cumingii .75 .20
Nos. 557-559 (3) 2.00 .60

Maohi Islands — A153

18th Century scenes of: 68fr, Woman of Easter Island, vert. 84fr, Twin-hulled canoe, Hawaii. 94fr, Maori village, New Zealand.

1991, Mar. 13 **Engr.** *Perf. 13*
560 A153 68fr olive 47.50 32.50
561 A153 84fr black 2.50 1.75
562 A153 94fr brown 3.00 1.75
Nos. 560-562 (3) 53.00 36.00

Basketball, Cent. — A154

1991, May 15 **Litho.** *Perf. 13*
563 A154 80fr multicolored 1.75 1.25

Birds — A155

1991, June 5 *Perf. 13½*
564 A155 17fr Halcyon gambieri .60 .25
565 A155 21fr Vini kuhlii .90 .35

Still Life with Oranges in Tahiti by Paul Gauguin — A156

1991, June 9 **Litho.** *Perf. 13*
566 A156 700fr multicolored 17.50 12.00

Sculptures of the Marquesas Islands — A157

56fr, White Tiki with Club, vert. 102fr, Warriors Carrying Tired Man, vert. 110fr, Native Canoe.

1991, July 17 **Litho.** *Perf. 13*
567 A157 56fr multicolored 1.25 .85
568 A157 102fr multicolored 2.25 1.50
569 A157 110fr multicolored 2.50 1.75
Nos. 567-569 (3) 6.00 4.10

Wolfgang Amadeus Mozart, Death Bicent. — A158

1991, Aug. 28 **Engr.** *Perf. 13x12½*
570 A158 100fr multicolored 3.50 1.75

Stone Fishing — A159

1991, Oct. 9 **Litho.** *Perf. 13*
571 A159 25fr Fishing boats, vert. .60 .40
572 A159 57fr Man hurling stone, vert. 1.25 .90
573 A159 62fr Trapped fish 1.50 1.25
Nos. 571-573 (3) 3.35 2.55

Phila Nippon '91 A160

Designs: 50fr, Drawings of marine life by Jules-Louis Lejeune, vert. 70fr, Sailing ship, La Coquille. 250fr, Contains designs from Nos. 574-575.

Perf. 12½x13, 13x12½

1991, Nov. 16 **Engr.**
574 A160 50fr multicolored 1.25 .60
575 A160 70fr multicolored 1.75 1.00

Size: 100x75mm

Imperf

576 A160 250fr multicolored 5.50 5.50
Nos. 574-576 (3) 8.50 7.10

Central Bank for Economic Co-operation, 50th Anniv. — A161

1991, Dec. 2 **Litho.** *Perf. 13x12½*
577 A161 307fr multicolored 6.50 4.50

Christmas A162

Perf. 12½x13, 13x12½

1991, Dec. 11 **Litho.**
578 A162 55fr Scuba divers 1.25 .75
579 A162 83fr Underwater scene 1.75 1.35
580 A162 86fr Nativity, vert. 1.75 1.35
Nos. 578-580 (3) 4.75 3.45

Tourism — A163

1992, Feb. 12 *Perf. 13*
581 A163 1fr shown .20 .20
582 A163 2fr Horses, beach .35 .25
583 A163 3fr Girl holding fish .50 .30
584 A163 4fr Waterfalls, vert. .60 .35
585 A163 5fr Sailing .75 .40
586 A163 6fr Waterfalls, helicopter, vert. 1.00 .45
Nos. 581-586 (6) 3.40 1.95

Views from Space — A164

1992, Mar. 18 Litho. *Perf. 13x12½*
587 A164 46fr Tahiti 1.10 .90
588 A164 72fr Mataiva 1.60 1.40
589 A164 76fr Bora Bora 1.75 1.50

Size: 130x100mm

Imperf

590 A164 230fr Satellite imaging system 5.75 5.75
Nos. 587-590 (4) 10.20 9.55

International Space Year.

World Health Day A165

1992, Apr. 7 *Perf. 13½*
591 A165 136fr multicolored 3.00 2.25

Discovery of America, 500th Anniv. — A166

1992, May 22 *Perf. 13*
592 A166 130fr multicolored 3.00 2.25

Size: 140x100mm

Imperf

593 A166 250fr multicolored 6.00 6.00

World Columbian Stamp Expo '92, Chicago.

Traditional Dances — A167

Dance from: 95fr, Tahiti. 105fr, Hawaii. 115fr, Tonga.

1992, June 17 Engr. *Perf. 13*
594 A167 95fr brown black 2.25 1.65
595 A167 105fr olive brown 2.50 1.85
596 A167 115fr red brn & olive grn 2.75 2.00
Nos. 594-596 (3) 7.50 5.50

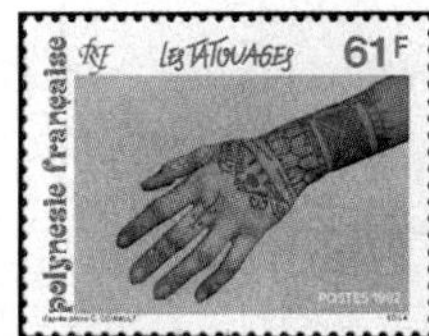

Tattoos A168

1992, July 8 Litho. *Perf. 12½*
597 A168 61fr Hand 1.75 1.00
598 A168 64fr Man, vert. 1.75 1.00

Children's Games A169

1992, Aug. 5 *Perf. 13½*
599 A169 22fr Outrigger canoe models .50 .35
600 A169 31fr String game .75 .45
601 A169 45fr Stilt game, vert. 1.25 .70
Nos. 599-601 (3) 2.50 1.50

Herman Melville, 150th Anniv. of Arrival in French Polynesia — A170

1992, Sept. 16 *Perf. 12½*
602 A170 78fr multicolored 4.50 1.25

6th Festival of Pacific Arts, Rarotonga — A171

40fr, Men on raft. 65fr, Pirogues, Tahiti.

1992, Oct. 16 Engr. *Perf. 13*
603 A171 40fr lake 1.00 .60
604 A171 65fr blue 1.75 1.00

First French Polynesian Postage Stamps, Cent. — A172

1992, Nov. 18 Photo. *Perf. 13*
605 A172 200fr multicolored 4.50 3.25

Paintings A173

55fr, Two Women Talking, by Erhard Lux. 60fr, Bouquet of Flowers, by Uschi. 75fr, Spearfisherman, by Pierre Kienlen. 85fr, Mother Nursing Child, by Octave Morillot.

1992, Dec. 9 *Perf. 12½x13*
606 A173 55fr multicolored 1.50 .75
607 A173 60fr multicolored 1.75 1.40
608 A173 75fr multicolored 1.90 1.50
609 A173 85fr multicolored 2.50 1.60
Nos. 606-609 (4) 7.65 5.25

Net Thrower A174

Bonito Fishing A175

1993, Feb. 10 Litho. *Die Cut*

Self-Adhesive

Size: 26x36mm

610 A174 46fr blue & multi 1.50 1.00

Size: 17x23mm

611 A174 46fr green & multi 1.50 1.00
a. Booklet pane of 10 15.00

1993, Mar. 10 *Perf. 13½*
612 A175 68fr Line & hook 1.60 1.25
613 A175 84fr Boat, horiz. 1.90 1.50
614 A175 86fr Drying catch 2.10 1.50
Nos. 612-614 (3) 5.60 4.25

Allied Airfield on Bora Bora, 50th Anniv. — A176

1993, Apr. 5 *Perf. 13*
615 A176 120fr multicolored 3.00 2.25

Jacques Boullaire, Artist, Birth Cent. — A177

Various scenes depicting life on: 32fr, Moorea. 36fr, Tuamotu. 39fr, Rurutu. 51fr, Nuku Hiva.

1993, May 6 Engr.
616 A177 32fr brown black .75 .60
617 A177 36fr brick red .85 .65
618 A177 39fr violet 1.00 .75
619 A177 51fr light brown 1.40 1.00
Nos. 616-619 (4) 4.00 3.00

Sports Festival — A178

1993, May 15 Litho. *Perf. 12½*
620 A178 30fr multicolored .75 .60

Australian Mathematics Competition, 15th Anniv. — A179

1993, July 1 Litho. *Perf. 13½*
621 A179 70fr multicolored 1.60 1.10

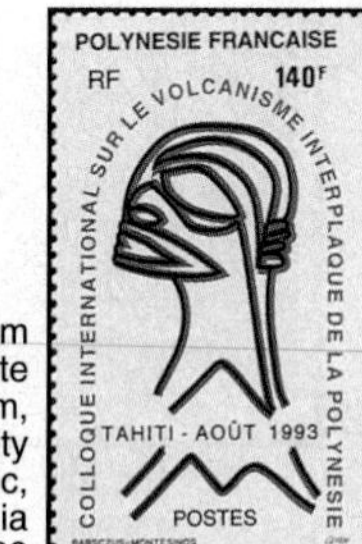

Intl. Symposium on Inter-Plate Volcanism, French University of the Pacific, Punaauia A180

1993, Aug. 2 Litho. *Perf. 13*
622 A180 140fr tan, blk & brn 3.50 2.50

Taipei '93 — A181

Tourism — A182

1993, Aug. 14 Litho. *Perf. 13½*
623 A181 46fr multicolored 2.50 .85

Exists without the Cartor imprint. Value, unused $9.75.

1993, Sept. 27

14fr, Boat tour. 20fr, Groom preparing for traditional wedding. 29fr, Beachside brunch.

624 A182 14fr multi, horiz. .60 .35
625 A182 20fr multi .65 .35
626 A182 29fr multi, horiz. .75 .45
Nos. 624-626 (3) 2.00 1.15

Exist without the Cartor imprint. Value, set unused $20.

Arrival of First French Gendarme in Tahiti, 150th Anniv. — A183

1993, Oct. 14 *Perf. 13*
627 A183 100fr multicolored 2.50 1.60

Exists without the Cartor imprint. Value, unused $15.

Alain Gerbault (1893-1941), Sailor — A184

1993, Nov. 17 Engr. *Perf. 13*
628 A184 150fr red, green & blue 4.00 2.75

Paintings — A185

Artists: 40fr, Vaea Sylvain. 70fr, A. Marere, vert. 80fr, J. Shelsher. 90fr, P.E. Victor, vert.

1993, Dec. 3 Photo. *Perf. 13*

629 A185 40fr multicolored 1.00 .70
630 A185 70fr multicolored 1.75 1.25
631 A185 80fr multicolored 1.90 1.25
632 A185 90fr multicolored 2.25 1.50
Nos. 629-632 (4) 6.90 4.70

French School of the Pacific, 30th Anniv. A186

1993, Dec. 7 Litho. *Perf. 12½*

633 A186 200fr multicolored 5.00 3.50

Whales and Dolphins A187

1994, Jan. 12 Litho. *Perf. 13½*

634 A187 25fr Whale breeching .75 .45
635 A187 68fr Dolphins 1.75 1.10
636 A187 72fr Humpback whales, vert. 2.00 1.25
Nos. 634-636 (3) 4.50 2.80

A188

A189

1994, Feb. 18 Litho. *Perf. 13½*

637 A188 51fr multicolored 2.00 .95

Hong Kong '94. New Year 1994 (Year of the Dog).

1994, Mar. 16

638 A189 180fr Sister Germaine Bruel 4.00 3.00

Arrival of Nuns from St. Joseph of Cluny, 150th anniv.

Church of Jesus Christ of Latter-day Saints in French Polynesia, 150th Anniv. A190

1994, Apr. 30 Litho. *Perf. 13½*

639 A190 154fr Tahiti temple 3.50 2.75

Conservatory of Arts and Crafts, Bicent. — A191

1994, May 25 Photo. *Perf. 13*

640 A191 316fr multicolored 7.50 5.50

Regional Associated Center of Papeete, 15th anniv.

Internal Self-Government, 10th Anniv. — A192

1994, June 29 Litho. *Perf. 13*

641 A192 500fr multicolored 12.00 7.50

Tahitian Academy, 20th Anniv. — A193

1994, July 2 Engr. *Perf. 13*

642 A193 136fr multicolored 3.00 2.00

Scenes of Old Tahiti — A194

1994, Aug. 10 Litho. *Perf. 13*

643 A194 22fr Papara .70 .40
644 A194 26fr Mataiea .80 .45
645 A194 51fr Taravao, vert. 1.50 .95
Nos. 643-645 (3) 3.00 1.80

See Nos. 673-675.

Faaturuma, by Paul Gauguin (1848-1903) A195

1994, Sept. 14 Litho. *Perf. 13*

646 A195 1000fr multicolored 22.50 15.00

Epiphyllum Oxypetalum A196

1994, Oct. 15 Litho. *Perf. 13½*

647 A196 51fr multicolored 1.75 .95

Hawaiki Nui Va'a '94 (Canoe Race) A197

Designs: a, 52fr, Yellow canoe, bow paddler. b, 76fr, Paddlers. c, 80fr, Paddlers, blue canoe. d, 94fr, Stern paddler, yellow canoe.

1994, Nov. 10 Litho. *Perf. 13½x13*

648 A197 Strip of 4, #a.-d. 8.00 4.75

No. 648 is a continuous design.

Paintings of French Polynesia — A198

62fr, Young girl, by Michelle Villemin. 78fr, Ocean tide, fish, by Michele Dallet. 102fr, Native carrying bundles of fruit, by Johel Blanchard. 110fr, View of coastline, by Pierre Lacouture.

1994, Dec. 19 Litho. *Perf. 13*

649 A198 62fr multi, vert. 1.60 .95
650 A198 78fr multi, vert. 1.90 1.25
651 A198 102fr multi, vert. 2.10 1.60
652 A198 110fr multi 2.40 1.75
Nos. 649-652 (4) 8.00 5.55

Don Domingo de Boenechea's Tautira Expedition, 220th Anniv. — A199

1995, Jan. 1

653 A199 92fr multicolored 2.75 1.40

South Pacific Tourism Year — A200

1995, Jan. 11 Litho. *Perf. 13½*

654 A200 92fr multicolored 2.25 1.40

New Year 1995 (Year of the Boar) A201

1995, Feb. 1 Litho.

655 A201 51fr multicolored 1.75 .80

Portions of the design on No. 655 were applied by a thermographic process producing a shiny, raised effect.

Exists without the Cartor imprint. Value, unused $9.

University Teacher's Training Institute of the Pacific — A202

1995, Mar. 8 Litho. *Perf. 13½*

656 A202 59fr multicolored 1.50 .95

Nature Protection A203

1995, May 4 Litho. *Perf. 13*

657 Strip of 3 + 2 labels 4.25 4.25
a. A203 22fr Head of turtle .75 .35
b. A203 29fr Turtle swimming 1.00 .50
c. A203 91fr Black coral 2.50 1.50

Louis Pasteur (1822-95) — A204

1995, May 8

658 A204 290fr dk blue & blue 7.25 5.00

Loti's Marriage, Novel by Julien Viaud (1850-1923) — A205

1995, May 19 Photo. *Perf. 13*

659 A205 66fr multicolored 1.75 1.10

A206

Birds — A207

1995, May 24 Litho. Perf. 13½
660 A206 150fr multicolored 3.50 2.25

Tahitian Monoi beauty aid.

1995, June 7
661 A207 22fr Ptilinopus huttoni .55 .35
662 A207 44fr Ducula galeata 1.10 .75

Tahitian Pearls A208

1995, June 14
663 A208 66fr shown 1.60 1.10
664 A208 84fr Eight pearls 2.10 1.40

On Nos. 663-664 portions of the design were applied by a thermographic process producing a shiny, raised effect.

Discovery of Marquesas Islands, 400th Anniv. — A209

a, Alvaro de Mendana de Neira, sailing ships. b, Pedro Fernandez de Quiros, map of islands.

1995, July 21 Litho. Perf. 13
665 Pair + label 8.00 6.00
a. A209 161fr multicolored 3.50 2.75
b. A209 195fr multicolored 4.50 3.25

A210

A211

1995, Aug. 12 Litho. Perf. 13
666 A210 83fr multicolored 2.00 1.40

10th South Pacific Games, Tahiti.

1995, Sept. 1 Perf. 13½x13

Pandanus plant: No. 667a, Entire plant. b, Flower. c, Fruit. d, Using dry leaves for weaving.

667 Strip of 4 8.50 6.00
a.-d. A211 91fr any single 2.00 1.50

Singapore '95.

UN, 50th Anniv. — A212

1995, Oct. 24 Litho. Perf. 13
668 A212 420fr multicolored 9.50 6.00

Paintings — A213

Designs: 57fr, The Paddler with the Yellow Dog, by Philippe Dubois, vert. 76fr, An Afternoon in Vaitape, by Maui Seaman, vert. 79fr, The Mama with the White Hat, by Simone Testeguide. 100fr, In Front of the Kellum House in Moorea, by Christian Deloffre.

1995, Dec. 6 Photo. Perf. 13
669 A213 57fr multicolored 1.25 .90
670 A213 76fr multicolored 1.60 1.25
671 A213 79fr multicolored 1.75 1.25
672 A213 100fr multicolored 2.25 1.60
Nos. 669-672 (4) 6.85 5.00

Scenes of Old Tahiti Type

1996, Jan. 17 Litho. Perf. 13
673 A194 18fr Fautaua .50 .30
674 A194 30fr District of Punaauia .80 .50
675 A194 35fr Tautira .95 .60
Nos. 673-675 (3) 2.25 1.40

New Year 1996 (Year of the Rat) — A214

1996, Feb. 19 Photo. Perf. 13
676 A214 51fr multicolored 1.75 .80

Portions of the design on No. 676 were applied by a thermographic process producing a shiny, raised effect.

Paul-Emile Victor (1907-95), Explorer, Writer — A215

1996, Mar. 7 Litho.
677 A215 500fr multicolored 12.00 8.00

Queen Pomare IV — A216

1996, Mar. 1 Litho. Perf. 13
678 A216 (51fr) multicolored 1.50 .80

Serpentine Die Cut 7 Vert.

Self-Adhesive

Size: 17x24mm

678A A216 (51fr) multicolored 1.75 1.15
b. Booklet pane of 5 9.00
Complete booklet, 2 #678b 18.00

Sea Shells A217

10fr, Conus pertusus. 15fr, Cypraea alisonae. 25fr, Vexillum roseotinctum.

1996, Apr. 10 Photo. Perf. 13½x13
679 A217 10fr multicolored .40 .20
680 A217 15fr multicolored .45 .25
681 A217 25fr multicolored .85 .40
Nos. 679-681 (3) 1.70 .85

Portions of the designs on Nos. 679-681 were applied by a thermographic process producing a shiny, raised effect.

Return of the Pacific Battalion, 50th Anniv. — A218

1996, May 5 Litho. Perf. 13
682 A218 100fr multicolored 2.50 1.60

CHINA '96, 9th Asian Intl. Philatelic Exhibition A219

Design: 200fr, Chinese School, Tahiti, 1940. Illustration reduced.

1996, May 18 Perf. 13x13½
683 A219 50fr multicolored 1.25 .80

Souvenir Sheet

Imperf

684 A219 200fr multicolored 4.50 3.40

Birds A220

1996, June 12 Litho. Perf. 13x13½
685 A220 66fr Sula sula 1.50 1.10
686 A220 79fr Fregata minor 1.75 1.25
687 A220 84fr Anous stolidus 1.75 1.40
Nos. 685-687 (3) 5.00 3.75

Musical Instruments A221

1996, July 10 Perf. 13x13½
688 A221 5fr Pahu, ukulele, toere .30 .20
689 A221 9fr Toere .40 .20
690 A221 14fr Pu, vivo .50 .20
Nos. 688-690 (3) 1.20 .60

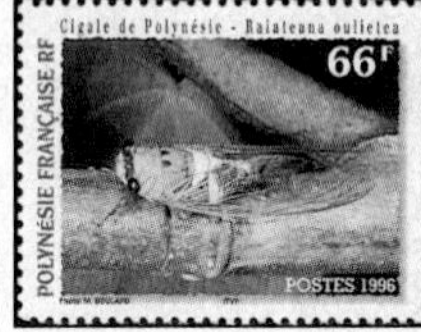
Raiateana Oulietea A222

1996, Aug. 7 Litho. Perf. 13x13½
691 A222 66fr multicolored 1.75 1.10

A223

A224

1996, Sept. 9 Litho. Perf. 13
692 A223 70fr Ruahatu, God of the Ocean 1.75 1.10

7th Pacific Arts Festival.

1996, Oct. 16 Engr. Perf. 13

Stamp Day: Young Tahitian girl (Type A2), Noho Mercier, taken from photo by Henry Lemasson (1870-1956), postal administrator.

693 A224 92fr black, red & blue 2.50 1.50

First Representative Assembly, 50th Anniv. — A225

1996, Nov. 7 Litho. *Perf. 13*
694 A225 85fr multicolored 2.25 .90

Paintings of Tahitian Women — A226

Designs: 70fr, Woman lounging on Bora Bora Beach, by Titi Bécaud. 85fr, "Woman with Crown of Auti leaves," by Maryse Noguier, vert. 92fr, "Dreamy Woman," by Christine de Dinechin, vert. 96fr, Two working women, by Andrée Lang, vert.

1996, Dec. 4 Litho. *Perf. 13*
695 A226 70fr multicolored 1.75 .75
696 A226 85fr multicolored 1.90 .90
697 A226 92fr multicolored 2.25 1.00
698 A226 96fr multicolored 2.50 1.00
Nos. 695-698 (4) 8.40 3.65

A227

A228

1997, Jan. 2 Litho. *Perf. 13*
699 A227 55fr brown 1.25 .55

Society of South Sea Studies, 80th anniv.

1997, Feb. 7 Photo. *Perf. 13½x13*
700 A228 13fr multicolored .50 .20

New Year 1997 (Year of the Ox). Portions of the design were applied by a thermographic process producing a shiny, raised effect.

Arrival of Evangelists in Tahiti, Bicent. — A229

Designs: a, Sailing ship, "Duff." b, Painting, "Transfer of the Matavai District to the L.M.S. Missionaries," by Robert Smirke.

1997, Mar. 5 Litho. *Perf. 13*
701 A229 43fr Pair, #a.-b. + label 2.10 .85

Tifaifai (Tahitian Bedspread) A230

Various leaf and floral patterns.

1997, Apr. 16
702 A230 1fr multicolored .20 .20
703 A230 5fr multicolored .20 .20
704 A230 70fr multicolored 1.60 .70
Nos. 702-704 (3) 2.00 1.10

PACIFIC 97 — A231

Sailing ships carrying mail, passengers between Tahiti and San Francisco: No. 705, Tropic Bird, 1897. No. 706, Papeete/Zélee, 1892.

1997, May 29 Litho. *Perf. 13*
705 A231 92fr multicolored 2.25 .90
706 A231 92fr multicolored 2.25 .90
a. Pair, #705-706 5.25 5.25
b. Souvenir sheet, #705-706 30.00 30.00

No. 706b sold for 400fr.

Island Scenes A232

#707, Flower. #708, Rowing canoe, sun behind mountain. #709, Throwing spears. #710. Aerial view of island. #711, Fish. #712, Women walking on beach. #713, Holding oyster shell with pearls. #714, Boat with sail down, sunset across water. #715, Snorkeling, sting ray. #716, Bananas, pineapples. #717, Palm tree, beach. #718, Women dancers in costume.

1997, June 25 Litho. *Perf. 13*
Booklet Stamps
707 A232 85fr multicolored 5.75 5.75
708 A232 85fr multicolored 5.75 5.75
709 A232 85fr multicolored 5.75 5.75
710 A232 85fr multicolored 5.75 5.75
711 A232 85fr multicolored 5.75 5.75
712 A232 85fr multicolored 5.75 5.75
a. Bklt. pane of 6, #707-712 37.50
713 A232 85fr multicolored 5.75 5.75
714 A232 85fr multicolored 5.75 5.75
715 A232 85fr multicolored 5.75 5.75
716 A232 85fr multicolored 5.75 5.75
717 A232 85fr multicolored 5.75 5.75
718 A232 85fr multicolored 5.75 5.75
a. Bklt. pane of 6, #713-718 37.50
Complete booklet, 2 each #712a, #718a 150.00

Traditional Dance Costumes A233

Designs: 4fr, Warrior's costume. 9fr, Women's costume. 11fr, Couple.

1997, July 10 Litho. *Perf. 13½x13*
719 A233 4fr multicolored .40 .20
720 A233 9fr multicolored .50 .20
721 A233 11fr multicolored .75 .20
Nos. 719-721 (3) 1.65 .60

Kon-Tiki Expedition, 50th Anniv. — A234

1997, Aug. 7 Litho. *Perf. 13*
722 A234 88fr multicolored 2.10 .80

Artists in Tahiti — A235

Designs: 85fr, Painting, "The Fruit Carrier," by Monique "Mono" Garnier-Bissol. 96fr, "Revival of Our Resources," mother of pearl painting, by Camélia Maraea. 110fr, "Tahitian Spirit," pottery, by Peter Owen, vert. 126fr, "Monoi," surrealist painting, by Elisabeth Stefanovitch.

1997, Oct. 15 Litho. *Perf. 13*
723 A235 85fr multicolored 1.90 .80
724 A235 96fr multicolored 2.00 .90
725 A235 110fr multicolored 2.50 1.00
726 A235 126fr multicolored 3.00 1.10
Nos. 723-726 (4) 9.40 3.80

Te Arii Vahine, by Paul Gauguin (1848-1903) — A236

1997, Nov. 6 Litho. *Perf. 13*
727 A236 600fr multicolored 14.00 5.75

Christmas A237

1997, Dec. 3 Litho. *Perf. 13*
728 A237 118fr multicolored 2.50 1.10

New Year 1998 (Year of the Tiger) A238

1998, Jan. 28 Photo. *Perf. 13*
729 A238 96fr multicolored 2.25 .90

Portions of the design on No. 729 were applied by a thermographic process producing a shiny, raised effect.

Domestic Airline Network — A239

Designs: a, 70fr, Grumman Widgeon, 1950. b, 85fr, DHC 6 Twin-Otter, 1968. c, 70fr, Fairchild FH 227, 1980. d, 85fr, ATR 42-500, 1998.

1998, Apr. 16 Photo. *Perf. 13*
730 A239 Strip of 4, #a.-d. + label 6.50 2.90

Orchids A240

5fr, Dendrobium "Royal King." 20fr, Oncidium "Ramsey." 50fr, Ascodenca "Laksi." 100fr, Cattleya "hybride."

1998, May 14 Photo. *Perf. 13*
731 A240 5fr multi .25 .20
732 A240 20fr multi, vert. .50 .20
733 A240 50fr multi, vert. 1.25 .45
734 A240 100fr multi 2.25 .95
Nos. 731-734 (4) 4.25 1.80

On Nos. 731-734 portions of the design were applied by a thermographic process producing a shiny, raised effect.

The Lovers, by Paul Gauguin (1848-1903) — A241

1998, June 7 Photo. *Perf. 13x12½*
735 A241 1000fr multicolored 22.50 9.00

Printed se-tenant with label.

1998 World Cup Soccer Championships, France — A242

1998, June 10
736 A242 85fr multicolored 2.00 .75

For overprint see No. 742.

Tahiti Festival of Flower and Shell Garlands — A243

Women wearing various garlands of flowers or shells.

1998, July 16 Photo. *Perf. 13½*
737 A243 55fr multicolored 1.25 .50
738 A243 65fr multicolored 1.60 .60
739 A243 70fr multicolored 1.75 .65
740 A243 80fr multicolored 2.00 .75
Nos. 737-740 (4) 6.60 2.50

Painting, "Underwater World of Polynesia," by Stanley Haumani A244

1998, Sept. 10 Photo. *Perf. 12½x13*
741 A244 200fr multicolored 4.25 2.00

No. 736 Ovptd. in Blue & Black "France / Championne / du Munde"

1998, Oct. 28 Photo. *Perf. 13½*
742 A242 85fr multicolored 1.75 .80

Autumn Philatelic Fair, Paris — A246

Watercolor paintings of Papeete Bay, by René Gillotin (1814-61): a, Beach at left, people. b, Beach at right, people.

1998, Nov. 5 *Perf. 13*
743 A246 250fr Pair, #a.-b. + label 12.00 5.00
c. Souvenir sheet, #a.-b., imperf. 12.00 5.00

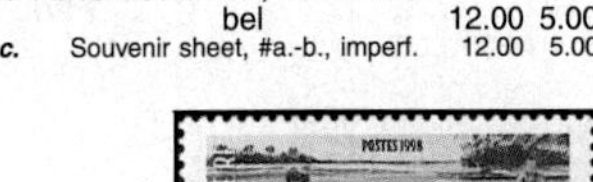

Life in Tahiti and the Islands A247

Paintings by André Deymonaz: 70fr, Return to the Market, vert. 100fr, Bonito Fish Stalls, vert. 102fr, Going Fishing. 110fr, Discussion after Church Services.

1998, Dec. 10 Photo. *Perf. 13*
744 A247 70fr multicolored 1.50 .70
745 A247 100fr multicolored 2.25 1.00
746 A247 102fr multicolored 2.25 1.00
747 A247 110fr multicolored 2.40 1.10
Nos. 744-747 (4) 8.40 3.80

St. Valentine's Day — A248

1999, Feb. 11 Litho. *Perf. 13*
748 A248 96fr multicolored 2.10 .90

New Year 1999 (Year of the Rabbit) A249

1999, Feb. 16
749 A249 118fr Rabbits, flowers 2.50 1.10

Portions of the design of No. 749 were applied by a thermographic process producing a shiny, raised effect.

Marine Life A250

Designs: 70fr, Ptérois volitans. 85fr, Hippocampus histrix. 90fr, Antennarius pictus. 120fr, Taenianotus triacanthus.

1999, Mar. 18 Photo. *Perf. 13*
750 A250 70fr multicolored 1.50 .65
751 A250 85fr multicolored 1.90 .80
752 A250 90fr multicolored 2.00 .80
753 A250 120fr multicolored 2.75 1.10
Nos. 750-753 (4) 8.15 3.35

Portions of the designs on Nos. 750-753 were applied by a thermographic process producing a shiny, raised effect.

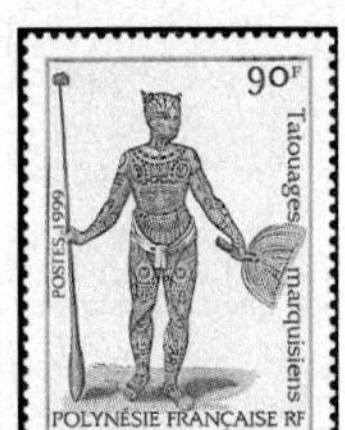

IBRA '99, World Philatelic Exhibition, Nuremberg A251

Tatooed men of Marquesas Islands, 1804: 90fr, Holding staff, fan. 120fr, Wearing blue cape.

Photo. & Engr.

1999, Apr. 27 *Perf. 13¼*
754 A251 90fr multicolored 2.00 .90
755 A251 120fr multicolored 2.75 1.25

Mother's Day A252

1999, May 27 Litho. *Perf. 13¼*
756 A252 85fr Children, vert. 1.90 .75
757 A252 120fr shown 2.75 1.00

A253

Island Fruits A254

#758, Breadfruit, vert. 120fr, Coconut.

#760: a, Papaya. b, Guava (goyave). c, Mombin. d, Rambutan. e, Star apple (pomme-etoile). f, Otaheite gooseberry (seurette). g, Rose apple. h, Star fruit (carambole). i, Spanish lime (quenette). j, Sweetsop (pomme-cannelle). k, Cashew (pomme de cajou). l, Passion fruit.

1999 Litho. *Perf. 13½x13, 13x13½*
758 A253 85fr multicolored 1.90 .75
759 A253 120fr multicolored 2.75 1.10

Souvenir Booklet

760 Complete bklt. 26.00
a.-l. A254 85fr Any single 1.90 1.40

Issued: #758, 120fr, 7/21; #760, 7/21.

No. 760 sold for 1200fr, and contains two booklet panes, containing Nos. 760a-760f, and Nos. 760g-760l.

No. 720, 1856 Letter, 1864 Postmark — A255

1999, July 2 Litho. *Perf. 13*
761 A255 180fr multicolored 4.00 2.25
a. Souvenir sheet of 1 11.00 11.00

150th anniv. of French postage stamps, PhilexFrance 99.

No. 761 issued se-tenant with label. No. 761a sold for 500fr.

Frédéric Chopin (1810-49), Composer — A256

1999, July 2 Litho. *Perf. 13*
762 A256 250fr multicolored 5.50 2.50

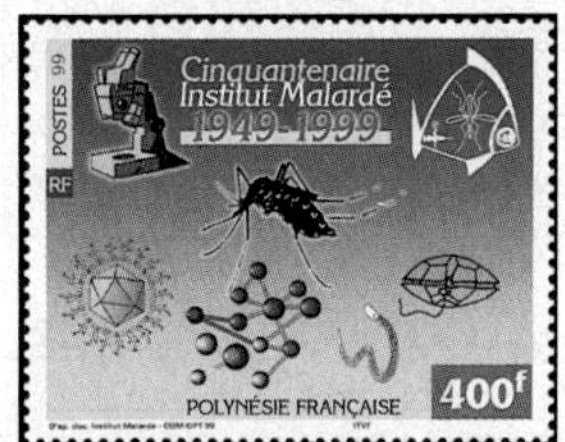

Malardé Medical Research Institute, 50th Anniv. — A257

1999, Sept. 27
763 A257 400fr multicolored 8.75 3.75

Nudes A258

Paintings by: 85fr, J. Sorgniard. 120fr, J. Dubrusk. 180fr, C. Deloffre. 250fr, J. Gandouin.

1999, Oct. 14 Litho. *Perf. 13*
764 A258 85fr multi 1.90 .75
765 A258 120fr multi 2.75 1.10
766 A258 180fr multi 4.00 1.60
767 A258 250fr multi 5.50 2.25
Nos. 764-767 (4) 14.15 5.70

Tahiti on the Eve of the Year 2000 A259

1999, Nov. 10 Litho. *Perf. 13*
768 A259 85fr multi 1.90 .75

5th Marquesas Islands Arts Festival A260

1999, Dec. 10
769 A260 90fr multi 2.00 .80

Year 2000 A261

85fr, Hands of adult and infant. 120fr, Eye.

2000, Jan. 3 *Perf. 13¼x13, 13x13¼*
770 A261 85fr multi, vert. 1.90 .75
771 A261 120fr multi 2.75 1.10

New Year 2000 (Year of the Dragon) A262

2000, Feb. 5 Litho. *Perf. 13x13¼*
772 A262 180fr multi 4.00 1.50

Portions of the design were applied by a thermographic process producing a shiny, raised effect.

Postal Service Emblem and Stamps A263

2000, Mar. 15 Litho. *Perf. 13x13¼*
773 A263 90fr multi 2.00 .75

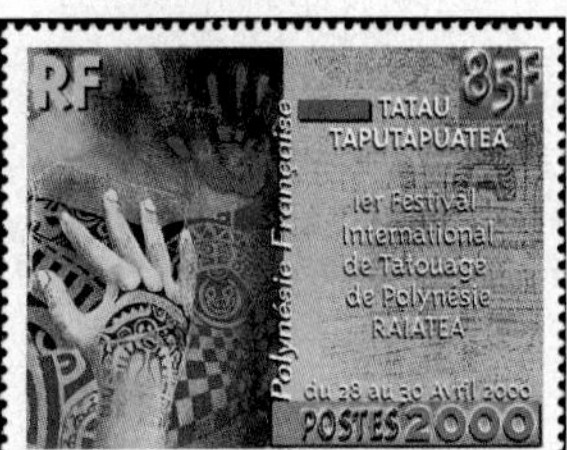

First Intl. Tattoo Festival, Raiatea — A264

Various tattoos.

2000, Apr. 28 *Perf. 13*

774	A264	85fr multi	1.90	.70
775	A264	120fr multi	2.75	.95
776	A264	130fr multi	2.90	1.00
777	A264	100fr multi	3.50	1.25
		Nos. 774-777 (4)	11.05	3.90

Beautiful Women of French Polynesia — A265

2000, May 30

778	A265	300fr multi	6.50	3.00
a.		Souvenir sheet of 1	11.00	11.00

No. 778a sold for 500fr.

Traditional Dresses — A266

Denominations: 85fr, 120fr, 160fr, 250fr.

2000, June 21 Litho. *Perf. 13¼x13*

779-782 A266 Set of 4 13.50 6.00

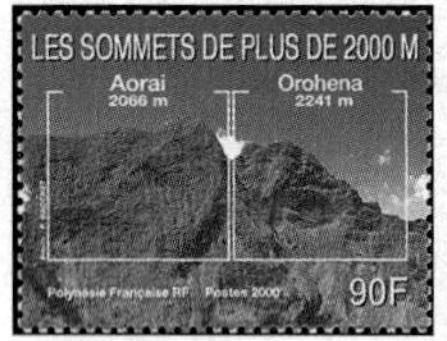

Mountains A267

Designs: 90fr, Mts. Aorai and Orohena. 180fr, Mts. Orohena and Aorai.

2000, July 10 *Perf. 13x13¼*

783-784 A267 Set of 2 6.00 2.60

Traditional Sports A268

120fr, Fruit carrying. 250fr, Stone lifting, vert.

Perf. 13x13¼, 13¼x13

2000, Sept. 15

785-786 A268 Set of 2 8.25 3.50

Native Woven Crafts A269

No. 787, Fans. No. 788, Hat.

2000, Oct. 3 Litho. *Perf. 13x13¼*

787-788 A269 85fr Set of 2 3.75 1.75

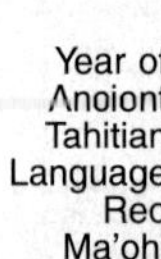

Year of Anoint Tahitian Language Reo Ma'ohi A270

2000, Nov. 9 Litho. *Perf. 13x13¼*

789 A270 120fr multi 2.75 1.20

Portions of the design were applied by a thermographic process producing a shiny, raised effect.

Advent of New Millennium — A271

2000, Dec. 28

790 A271 85fr multi 1.90 .90

Central School, Cent. — A272

Designs: No. 791, 85fr, Central School. No. 792, 85fr, Paul Gauguin High School.

2001, Jan. 16

791-792 A272 Set of 2 3.75 1.75

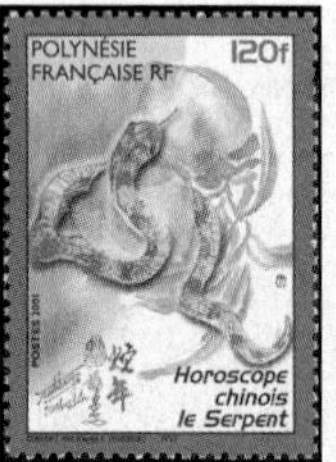

New Year 2001 (Year of the Snake) — A273

2001, Jan. 24 *Perf. 13¼x13*

793 A273 120fr multi 2.75 1.20

Portions of the design were applied by a thermographic process producing a shiny, raised effect.

Landscapes A274

Designs: 35fr, Vaiharuru Waterfall. 50fr, Vahiria Lake, horiz. 90fr, Hakaui Valley.

Perf. 13¼x13, 13x13¼

2001, Feb. 26 **Litho.**

794-796 A274 Set of 3 3.75 1.75

Year of the Polynesian Child — A275

2001, Mar. 28 Litho. *Perf. 13x13¼*

797 A275 55fr multi 1.25 .55

Polynesian Singers — A276

Designs: 85fr, Eddie Lund. 120fr, Charley Mauu. 130fr, Bimbo. 180fr, Marie Mariteragi and Emma Terangi, horiz.

2001, Apr. 12 *Perf. 13¼x13, 13x13¼*

798-801 A276 Set of 4 11.50 5.00

Volunteers of the Pacific Batallion, 60th Anniv. A277

2001, Apr. 21 *Perf. 13x13¼*

802 A277 85fr multi 1.90 .90

Surfing Waves of Teahupoo A278

2001, May 4

803 A278 120fr multi 2.75 1.20

Internal Autonomy, 17th Anniv. A279

2001, June 29 Litho. *Perf. 13*

804	A279	250fr multi	5.50	2.50
a.		Souvenir sheet of 1	11.00	11.00

No. 804a sold for 500fr.

Pirogue Racing — A280

Designs: 85fr, Male racers. 120fr, Female racers.

2001, July 12 *Perf. 13¼x13*

805-806	A280	Set of 2	4.50	2.00
a.		Souvenir sheet, #805-806, imperf.	5.50	5.50

No. 806a sold for 250fr.

Hardwood Trees A281

Designs: 90fr, Tou. 130fr, Ati. 180fr, Miro.

2001, Oct. 23 Litho. *Perf. 13x13½*

807-809 A281 Set of 3 8.75 8.00

AIDS Prevention A282

2001, Sept. 20 Litho. *Perf. 13x13¼*

810 A282 55fr multi 1.25 1.10

Year of Dialogue Among Civilizations A283

2001, Oct. 9 *Perf. 13*

811 A283 500fr multi 11.00 10.00

Perfume Flowers — A284

Designs: 35fr, Gardenia tahitensis. 50fr, Fagraea berteriana. 85fr, Gardenia jasminoides.

2001, Nov. 8 *Perf. 13¼x13*

812-814 A284 Set of 3 3.75 3.50

Portions of the designs were applied by a thermographic process producing a shiny, raised effect.

Christmas A285

2001, Dec. 6 *Perf. 13x13¼*

815 A285 120fr multi 2.75 2.40

New Year 2002 (Year of the Horse) A286

2002, Feb. 12 Litho. *Perf. 13x13¼*

816 A286 130fr multi 2.90 2.60

Portions of the design were applied by a thermographic process producing a shiny, raised effect.

Happy Holidays A287

Greetings A288

2002, Feb. 28 Background Colors

817 A287 55fr red 1.25 1.10
818 A288 55fr blue 1.25 1.10
819 A287 85fr blue 1.90 1.75
820 A288 85fr green 1.90 1.75
Nos. 817-820 (4) 6.30 5.70

10th World Outrigger Canoe Championships — A289

Canoe rowers and emblems: 120fr, 180fr.

2002, Mar. 9 Photo. *Perf. 13¼*
821-822 A289 Set of 2 6.50 6.25

Sea Urchins A290

Designs: 35fr, Echinometra sp. 50fr, Heterocentrotus trigonarius. 90fr, Echinothrix calamaris. 120fr, Toxopneustes sp.

2002, Apr. 18 Litho. *Perf. 13x13¼*
823-826 A290 Set of 4 6.50 6.25

Blood Donation — A291

2002, May 3 Litho. *Perf. 13¼x13*
827 A291 130fr multi 3.25 3.25

2002 World Cup Soccer Championships, Japan and Korea — A292

2002, May 30
828 A292 85fr multi 1.90 1.75

Traditional Sports — A293

Designs: 85fr, Coconut husking. 120fr, Fruit carrying. 250fr, Javelin throwing.

2002, June 27
829-831 A293 Set of 3 10.00 9.00

House of James Norman Hall — A294

2002, July 4 *Perf. 13x13¼*
832 A294 90fr multi 2.00 1.90

Papeete Market — A295

2002, Aug. 30 Litho. *Perf. 13*
833 A295 400fr multi 8.75 8.00
a. Souvenir sheet of 1 11.00 11.00

Amphilex 2002 Stamp Exhibition, Amsterdam (#833a). No. 833a sold for 500fr.

Pacific Oceanology Center, Vairoa A296

Designs: 55fr, Research pond, fish, shrimp, oyster, and flasks. 90fr, Aeriel view of center, fish, shrimp and oyster.

2002, Sept. 26 Photo. *Perf. 13¼*
834-835 A296 Set of 2 3.25 2.40

Taapuna Master 2002 Surfing Competition A297

2002, Oct. 21 Litho. *Perf. 13x13¼*
836 A297 120fr multi 2.75 2.00

Halophilic Flowers A298

Designs: 85fr, Hibiscus tiliaceus. 130fr, Scaveola sericea. 180fr, Guettarda speciosa.

2002, Nov. 7
837-839 A298 Set of 3 8.75 6.75

Polynesians at Festivals A299

Designs: 55fr, Dancers and bus. 120fr, Musicians, vert.

2002, Dec. 5 *Perf. 13x13¼, 13¼x13*
840-841 A299 Set of 2 3.75 3.00

New Year 2003 (Year of the Ram) — A300

2003, Feb. 1 Litho. *Perf. 13¼x13*
842 A300 120fr multi 2.75 2.25

Portions of the design was applied by a thermographic process producing a shiny, raised effect.

Polynesian Women — A301

2003, Mar. 8 Litho. *Perf. 13¼x13*
843 A301 55fr multi 1.25 1.00

Waterfalls — A302

2003, Apr. 10 *Perf. 13*
844 A302 330fr multi 7.25 6.00

Old Papeete A303

Designs: 55fr, Automobiles and buildings, vert. 85fr, Ship in harbor. 90fr, People with bicycles in front of buildings (50x28mm). 120fr, Tree-lined street (50x28mm).

Perf. 13¼x13, 13x13¼, 13
2003, May 15
845-848 A303 Set of 4 7.75 7.00
848a Souvenir sheet, #845-848 12.00 12.00

No. 848a sold for 550fr.

Fish — A304

2003, June 12 Litho. *Perf. 13*
849 A304 460fr multi 9.00 9.00

Portions of the design were applied by a thermographic process producing a shiny, raised effect.

Outrigger Canoes A305

Designs: No. 850, 85fr, shown. No. 851, 85fr, Three sailors on canoe at sea. No. 852, 85fr, Three sailors on canoe, vert. No. 853, 85fr, Sailor sitting on outrigger, vert.

Perf. 13x13¼, 13¼x13
2003, July 11 Litho.
850-853 A305 Set of 4 7.50 6.50

Firewalkers A306

Orange-banded Cowrie — A307

2003, Aug. 14 Photo. *Perf. 13¼*
854 A306 130fr multi 2.50 2.50

Perf. 13x13¼
855 A307 420fr multi 8.00 8.00

Are You Jealous? by Paul Gauguin (1848-1903) — A308

2003, Sept. 11 *Perf. 13x12¼*
856 A308 250fr multi 5.00 5.00

Office of Posts and Telecommunications Emblem — A308a

Serpentine Die Cut 6½ Vert.
2003, Oct. 1 Engr.

Booklet Stamp
Self-Adhesive

856A A308a (60fr) blue 1.25 1.25
b. Booklet pane of 10 12.50

No. 856A exists without "2003" year. See No. 869.

French Polynesian Flag A309

2003, Oct. 1 Litho. *Perf. 13x13¼*

857 A309 (60fr) multi	1.25	1.25

Tiki — A310

2003, Oct. 1 *Perf. 13¼x13*

858 A310 100fr multi	2.00	2.00

Flowers A311

Designs: 90fr, Orchid. 130fr, Rose de porcelain (torch ginger).

2003, Oct. 4 Litho. *Perf. 13x13¼*

859-860 A311 Set of 2	4.25	4.25

Portions of the designs were applied by a thermographic process producing a shiny, raised effect.

Bora Bora A312

Designs: No. 861, 60fr, Painting of Bora Bora by A. Van Der Heyde. No. 862, 60fr, Aerial photograph of Bora Bora.

2003, Nov. 6 Litho. *Perf. 13x13¼*

861-862 A312 Set of 2	2.40	2.40

Tiki — A313

2003, Dec. 6 *Perf. 13*

863 A313 190fr multi	4.00	4.00

Buildings and Palm Trees A314

2003, Dec. 19 *Perf. 13x13¼*

864 A314 90fr multi	1.90	1.90

New Year 2004 (Year of the Monkey) — A315

2004, Jan. 22 Litho. *Perf. 13¼x13*

865 A315 130fr multi	2.75	2.75

A portion of the design was applied by a thermographic process producing a shiny, raised effect.

Scenes From Everyday Life A316

Designs: 60fr, Women working with cloth. 90fr, Street scene, vert.

Perf. 13x13¼, 13¼x13

2004, Feb. 13 Litho.

866-867 A316 Set of 2	3.25	3.25

Polynesian Woman — A317

2004, Mar. 8 *Perf. 13¼x13*

868 A317 90fr multi	1.90	1.90

Post Emblem Type of 2003

Serpentine Die Cut 6½ Vert.

2004, Apr. 22 Engr.

Booklet Stamp

Self-Adhesive

869 A308a (90fr) red	1.90	1.90
a. Booklet pane of 10	19.00	

No. 869 lacks year date.

Polynesian Economic Development — A318

2004, Apr. 23 Litho. *Perf. 13x12¾*

870 A318 500fr multi	10.00	10.00

Arahurahu Marae, Paea — A319

2004, Apr. 23

871 A319 500fr multi	10.00	10.00

Vanilla — A320

2004, May 14 *Perf. 13¼x13*

872 A320 90fr multi	1.90	1.90

No. 872 is impregnated with a vanilla scent.

Mobile Snack Bars — A321

2004, May 28 *Perf. 13x12¾*

873 A321 300fr multi	6.25	6.25

Handicrafts A322

Designs: No. 874, 60fr, Artisan braiding fibers. No. 875, 60fr, Mother-of-pearl carving. No. 876, 90fr, Artisan carving statue. No. 877, 90fr, Hat.

2004, June 26 *Perf. 13x13¼*

874-877 A322 Set of 4	6.25	6.25

Portion of the designs were applied by a thermographic process producing a shiny, raised effect.

Involvement in South Pacific Area of Office of Posts and Telecommunications — A323

Designs: 100fr, Earth, Sun on horizon. 130fr, Satellite dish, building.

2004, July 23 Photo. *Perf. 13¼*

878-879 A323 Set of 2	4.75	4.75

Information Technology and Communications A324

Designs: No. 880, 190fr, Computer keyboard, "@." No. 881, 190fr, Satellite, satellite dish.

2004, Sept. 23 Litho. *Perf. 13¼x13*

880-881 A324 Set of 2	8.00	8.00

Omai, Polynesian Capt. James Cook Brought to England — A325

2004, Oct. 14 *Perf. 13*

882 A325 250fr multi	5.25	5.25

SEMI-POSTAL STAMPS

Nos. 55 and 26 Surcharged in Red

1915 Unwmk. *Perf. 14x13½*

B1 A1 10c + 5c red	22.50	22.50
a. "e" instead of "c"	57.50	57.50
b. Inverted surcharge	160.00	160.00
B2 A2 10c + 5c rose & org	7.50	7.50
a. "e" instead of "c"	40.00	40.00
b. "c" inverted	47.50	47.50
c. Inverted surcharge	225.00	225.00

Surcharged in Carmine

B3 A2 10c + 5c rose & org	3.25	3.25
a. "e" instead of "c"	25.00	25.00
b. Inverted surcharge	150.00	150.00

Surcharged in Carmine

1916
B4 A2 10c + 5c rose & org 3.25 3.25

Curie Issue
Common Design Type

1938 Engr. *Perf. 13*
B5 CD80 1.75fr + 50c brt ultra 14.00 14.00

French Revolution Issue
Common Design Type

1939 Photo.
Name and Value Typo. in Black

B6	CD83	45c + 25c grn	14.00	14.00
B7	CD83	70c + 30c brn	14.00	14.00
B8	CD83	90c + 35c red org	14.00	14.00
B9	CD83	1.25fr + 1fr rose pink	14.00	14.00
B10	CD83	2.25fr + 2fr blue	14.00	14.00
		Nos. B6-B10 (5)	70.00	70.00
		Set, never hinged	120.00	

Catalogue values for unused stamps in this section, from this point to the end of the section, are for Never Hinged items.

Common Design Type and

Marine Officer — SP1

"L'Astrolabe" — SP2

1941 Photo. *Perf. 13½*

B11	SP1	1fr + 1fr red	2.50
B12	CD86	1.50fr + 3fr maroon	2.50
B12A	SP2	2.50fr + 1fr blue	2.50
		Nos. B11-B12A (3)	7.50

Nos. B11-B12A were issued by the Vichy government in France, and were not placed on sale in French Polynesia.

Nos. 125A-125B Surcharged in Black or Red

1944 Engr. *Perf. 12½x12*

B12B	50c + 1.50fr on 2.50fr deep blue (R)	1.00
B12C	+ 2.50fr on 1fr green	1.25

Colonial Development Fund.

Nos. B12B-B12C were issued by the Vichy government in France, but were not placed on sale in French Polynesia.

Red Cross Issue
Common Design Type

1944 Photo. *Perf. 14½x14*
B13 CD90 5fr + 20fr peacock blue 1.60 1.10

The surtax was for the French Red Cross and national relief.

Tropical Medicine Issue
Common Design Type

1950, July 17 Engr. *Perf. 13*
B14 CD100 10fr + 2fr dk bl grn & dk grn 7.00 5.75

The surtax was for charitable work.

AIR POST STAMPS

Seaplane in Flight AP1

Perf. 13½

1934, Nov. 5 Unwmk. Photo.
C1 AP1 5fr green .75 .75

For overprint see No. C2.
For Type AP1 without "RF," see Nos. C1A-C1D.

Type of 1934 without "RF" and

Beach Scene — AP1a

Perf. 13½, 13 (#C1E)

1944 Photo, Engr. (#C1E)

C1A	AP1	5fr green	.60
C1B	AP1	10fr black	.90
C1C	AP1	20fr orange	.95
C1D	AP1	50fr gray blue	1.25
C1E	AP1a	100fr turquoise blue	1.25
		Nos. C1A-C1E (5)	4.95

Nos. C1A-C1E were issued by the Vichy government in France, but were not placed on sale in French Polynesia.

Catalogue values for unused stamps in this section, from this point to the end of the section, are for Never Hinged items.

No. C1 Overprinted in Red

1941
C2 AP1 5fr green 3.75 3.00

Common Design Type

1942 *Perf. 14½x14*

C3	CD87	1fr dark orange	.75	.50
C4	CD87	1.50fr bright red	.75	.60
C5	CD87	5fr brown red	1.00	.80
C6	CD87	10fr black	1.50	1.10
C7	CD87	25fr ultra	2.25	1.60
C8	CD87	50fr dark green	2.25	1.60
C9	CD87	100fr plum	2.25	1.60
		Nos. C3-C9 (7)	10.75	7.80

Victory Issue
Common Design Type

1946, May 8 Engr. *Perf. 12½*
C10 CD92 8fr dark green 2.25 1.60

Chad to Rhine Issue
Common Design Types

1946, June 6

C11	CD93	5fr red orange	1.75	1.50
C12	CD94	10fr dk olive bis	1.75	1.50
C13	CD95	15fr dk yellow grn	1.75	1.50
C14	CD96	20fr carmine	2.25	1.75
C15	CD97	25fr dk rose violet	3.00	2.50
C16	CD98	50fr black	3.50	3.00
		Nos. C11-C16 (6)	14.00	11.75

Shearwater and Moorea Landscape — AP2

Fishermen — AP3

Shearwater over Maupiti Shoreline — AP4

1948, Mar. 1 Unwmk. *Perf. 13*

C17	AP2	50fr red brown	21.00	8.75
C18	AP3	100fr purple	17.50	5.75
C19	AP4	200fr blue green	37.50	15.00
		Nos. C17-C19 (3)	76.00	29.50

UPU Issue
Common Design Type

1949
C20 CD99 10fr deep blue 14.50 11.50

Gauguin's "Nafea faaipoipo" — AP5

1953, Sept. 24
C21 AP5 14fr dk brn, dk gray grn & red 62.50 50.00

50th anniv. of the death of Paul Gauguin.

Liberation Issue
Common Design Type

1954, June 6
C22 CD102 3fr dk grnsh bl & bl grn 7.50 5.75

Bahia Peak, Borabora — AP6

1955, Sept. 26 Unwmk. *Perf. 13*
C23 AP6 13fr indigo & blue 8.00 4.00

Mother-of-Pearl Artist — AP7

Designs: 50fr, "Women of Tahiti," Gauguin, horiz. 100fr, "The White Horse," Gauguin. 200fr, Night fishing at Moorea, horiz.

1958, Nov. 3 Engr. *Perf. 13*

C24	AP7	13fr multicolored	11.50	3.75
C25	AP7	50fr multicolored	11.00	3.75
C26	AP7	100fr multicolored	17.00	5.75
C27	AP7	200fr lilac & slate	37.50	17.00
		Nos. C24-C27 (4)	77.00	30.25

Airport, Papeete — AP8

1960, Nov. 19
C28 AP8 13fr rose lil, vio, & yel grn 3.00 1.90

Telstar Issue
Common Design Type

1962, Dec. 5 *Perf. 13*
C29 CD111 50fr red lil, mar & vio bl 10.00 7.00

Tahitian Dancer — AP10

1964, May 14 Photo. *Perf. 13*
C30 AP10 15fr multicolored 4.00 2.00

Map of Tahiti and Free French Emblems — AP11

1964, July 10 Unwmk.
C31 AP11 16fr multicolored 13.50 6.75

Issued to commemorate the rallying of French Polynesia to the Free French cause.

Moorea Scene — AP12

1964, Dec. 1 Litho. *Perf. 13*
C32 AP12 23fr multicolored 8.00 2.75

ITU Issue
Common Design Type

1965, May 17 Engr. *Perf. 13*
C33 CD120 50fr vio, red brn & bl 80.00 45.00

Paul Gauguin — AP13

Design: 25fr, Gauguin Museum (stylized). 40fr, Primitive statues at Gauguin Museum.

1965 Engr. *Perf. 13*
C34 AP13 25fr olive green 7.50 3.75
C35 AP13 40fr blue green 13.50 6.75
C36 AP13 75fr brt red brown 20.00 12.50
Nos. C34-C36 (3) 41.00 23.00

Opening of Gauguin Museum, Papeete. Issued: 25fr, 75fr, 6/13. 40fr, 11/7.

Skin Diver with Spear Gun — AP14

1965, Sept. 1 Engr. *Perf. 13*
C37 AP14 50fr red brn, dl bl & dk grn 75.00 47.50

World Championships in Underwater Fishing, Tuamotu Archipelago, Sept. 1965.

Painting from a School Dining Room — AP15

Radio Tower, Globe and Palm — AP16

1965, Nov. 29
C38 AP15 80fr brn, bl, dl bl & red 20.00 14.50

School Canteen Program.

1965, Dec. 29 Engr. *Perf. 13*
C39 AP16 60fr org, grn & dk brn 17.50 12.50

50th anniversary of the first radio link between Tahiti and France.

French Satellite A-1 Issue
Common Design Type

Designs: 7fr, Diamant Rocket and launching installations. 10fr, A-1 satellite.

1966, Feb. 7
C40 CD121 7fr choc, dp grn & lil 5.00 4.25
C41 CD121 10fr lil, dp grn & dk brn 5.00 4.25
a. Pair, #C40-C41 + label 15.00 15.00

French Satellite D-1 Issue
Common Design Type

1966, May 10 Engr. *Perf. 13*
C42 CD122 20fr multicolored 6.00 4.00

Papeete Harbor — AP17

1966, June 30 Photo. *Perf. 13*
C43 AP17 50fr multicolored 14.50 9.00

"Vive Tahiti" by A. Benichou — AP18

1966, Nov. 28 Photo. *Perf. 13*
C44 AP18 13fr multicolored 11.00 5.00

Explorer's Ship and Canoe — AP19

Designs: 60fr, Polynesian costume and ship. 80fr, Louis Antoine de Bougainville, vert.

1968, Apr. 6 Engr. *Perf. 13*
C45 AP19 40fr multicolored 6.75 3.25
C46 AP19 60fr multicolored 9.00 4.50
C47 AP19 80fr multicolored 11.00 6.75
a. Souv. sheet, #C45-C47 125.00 125.00
Nos. C45-C47 (3) 26.75 14.50

200th anniv. of the discovery of Tahiti by Louis Antoine de Bougainville. Issued: 40fr, 4/6/68.

The Meal, by Paul Gauguin — AP20

1968, July 30 Photo. *Perf. 12x12½*
C48 AP20 200fr multicolored 35.00 25.00

See #C63-C67, C78-C82, C89-C93, C98.

Shot Put — AP21

PATA 1970 Poster — AP22

1968, Oct. 12 Engr. *Perf. 13*
C49 AP21 35fr dk car rose & brt grn 14.50 7.00

19th Olympic Games, Mexico City, 10/12-27.

Concorde Issue
Common Design Type

1969, Apr. 17
C50 CD129 40fr red brn & car rose 50.00 30.00

1969, July 9 Photo. *Perf. 12½x13*
C51 AP22 25fr blue & multi 17.00 6.00

Issued to publicize PATA 1970 (Pacific Area Travel Association Congress), Tahiti.

Underwater Fishing — AP23

52fr, Hand holding fish made up of flags, vert.

1969, Aug. 5 Photo. *Perf. 13*
C52 AP23 48fr blk, grnsh bl & red lil 32.50 10.50
C53 AP23 52fr bl, blk & red 37.50 17.50

Issued to publicize the World Underwater Fishing Championships.

Gen. Bonaparte as Commander of the Army in Italy, by Jean Sebastien Rouillard — AP24

1969, Oct. 15 Photo. *Perf. 12½x12*
C54 AP24 100fr car & multi 75.00 55.00

Bicentenary of the birth of Napoleon Bonaparte (1769-1821).

Eiffel Tower, Torii and EXPO Emblem — AP25

Pearl Diver Descending, and Basket — AP26

Design: 30fr, Mount Fuji, Tower of the Sun and EXPO emblem, horiz.

1970, Sept. 15 Photo. *Perf. 13*
C55 AP25 30fr multicolored 17.50 8.00
C56 AP25 50fr multicolored 25.00 11.00

EXPO '70 International Exposition, Osaka, Japan, Mar. 15-Sept. 13.

1970, Sept. 30 Engr. *Perf. 13*

Designs: 5fr, Diver collecting oysters. 18fr, Implantation into oyster, horiz. 27fr, Open oyster with pearl. 50fr, Woman with mother of pearl jewelry.

C57 AP26 2fr slate, grnsh bl & red brn 1.25 .75
C58 AP26 5fr grnsh blue, ultra & org 2.25 1.25
C59 AP26 18fr sl, mag & org 4.75 2.25
C60 AP26 27fr brt pink, brn & dl lil 8.00 4.00
C61 AP26 50fr gray, red brn & org 13.00 6.25
Nos. C57-C61 (5) 29.25 14.50

Pearl industry of French Polynesia.

The Thinker, by Auguste Rodin and Education Year Emblem — AP27

1970, Oct. 15 Engr. *Perf. 13*
C62 AP27 50fr bl, ind & fawn 16.00 8.75

International Education Year.

Painting Type of 1968

Paintings by Artists Living in Polynesia: 20fr, Woman on the Beach, by Yves de Saint-Front. 40fr, Abstract, by Frank Fay. 60fr, Woman and Shells, by Jean Guillois. 80fr, Hut under Palms, by Jean Masson. 100fr, Polynesian Girl, by Jean-Charles Bouloc, vert.

Perf. 12x12½, 12½x12
1970, Dec. 14 Photo.
C63 AP20 20fr brn & multi 9.00 4.00
C64 AP20 40fr brn & multi 13.50 7.50
C65 AP20 60fr brn & multi 18.00 11.00
C66 AP20 80fr brn & multi 22.50 16.00
C67 AP20 100fr brn & multi 30.00 22.50
Nos. C63-C67 (5) 93.00 61.00

South Pacific Games Emblem — AP28

1971, Jan. 26 *Perf. 12½*
C68 AP28 20fr ultra & multi 6.75 4.50

Publicity for 4th South Pacific Games, held in Papeete, Sept. 8-19, 1971.

Memorial Flame — AP29

1971, Mar. 19 **Photo.** ***Perf. 12½***
C69 AP29 5fr multicolored 7.50 4.00

In memory of Charles de Gaulle.

Soldier and Badge — AP30

1971, Apr. 21
C70 AP30 25fr multicolored 9.50 5.50

30th anniversary of departure of Tahitian volunteers to serve in World War II.

Water Sports Type

Designs: 15fr, Surfing, vert. 16fr, Skin diving, vert. 20fr, Water-skiing with kite.

1971, May 11 **Photo.** ***Perf. 13***

C71	A44	15fr multicolored	6.00	2.75
C72	A44	16fr multicolored	7.00	3.25
C73	A44	20fr multicolored	10.00	6.00
		Nos. C71-C73 (3)	23.00	12.00

Sailing AP31

1971, Sept. 8 ***Perf. 12½***

C74	AP31	15fr shown	5.50	3.00
C75	AP31	18fr Golf	6.75	4.00
C76	AP31	27fr Archery	11.00	6.00
C77	AP31	53fr Tennis	18.00	11.00
a.		Souv. sheet, #C74-C77	175.00	175.00
		Nos. C74-C77 (4)	41.25	24.00

4th So. Pacific Games, Papeete, Sept. 8-19.

Painting Type of 1968

Paintings by Artists Living in Polynesia: 20fr, Hut and Palms, by Isabelle Wolf. 40fr, Palms on Shore, by André Dobrowolski. 60fr, Polynesian Woman, by Françoise Séli, vert. 80fr, Holy Family, by Pierre Heymann, vert. 100fr, Crowd, by Nicolai Michoutouchkine.

1971, Dec. 15 **Photo.** ***Perf. 13***

C78	AP20	20fr multicolored	8.00	4.50
C79	AP20	40fr multicolored	12.50	7.50
C80	AP20	60fr multicolored	15.00	10.00
C81	AP20	80fr multicolored	21.00	12.50
C82	AP20	100fr multicolored	35.00	22.50
		Nos. C78-C82 (5)	91.50	57.00

Papeete Harbor — AP32

1972, Jan. 13
C83 AP32 28fr violet & multi 13.50 6.75

Free port of Papeete, 10th anniversary.

Figure Skating and Dragon AP33

1972, Jan. 25 **Engr.** ***Perf. 13***
C84 AP33 20fr ultra, lake & brt grn 10.00 7.00

11th Winter Olympic Games, Sapporo, Japan, Feb. 3-13.

South Pacific Commission Headquarters, Noumea — AP34

1972, Feb. 5 **Photo.** ***Perf. 13***
C85 AP34 21fr blue & multi 11.00 4.25

South Pacific Commission, 25th anniv.

Festival Emblem — AP35

1972, May 9 **Engr.** ***Perf. 13***
C86 AP35 36fr orange, bl & grn 6.75 4.50

So. Pacific Festival of Arts, Fiji, May 6-20.

Kon Tiki and Route, Callao to Tahiti — AP36

1972, Aug. 18 **Photo.** ***Perf. 13***
C87 AP36 16fr dk & lt bl, blk & org 10.00 5.00

25th anniversary of the arrival of the raft Kon Tiki in Tahiti.

Charles de Gaulle and Memorial — AP37

1972, Dec. 9 **Engr.** ***Perf. 13***
C88 AP37 100fr slate 55.00 35.00

Painting Type of 1968

Paintings by Artists Living in Polynesia: 20fr, Horses, by Georges Bovy. 40fr, Sailboats, by Ruy Juventin, vert. 60fr, Harbor, by André Brooke. 80fr, Farmers, by Daniel Adam, vert. 100fr, Dancers, by Aloysius Pilioko, vert.

1972, Dec. 14 **Photo.**

C89	AP20	20fr gold & multi	8.25	3.50
C90	AP20	40fr gold & multi	10.00	5.25
C91	AP20	60fr gold & multi	17.50	7.25
C92	AP20	80fr dk grn, buff & dk brn	22.50	10.00
C93	AP20	100fr gold & multi	27.50	20.00
		Nos. C89-C93 (5)	85.75	46.00

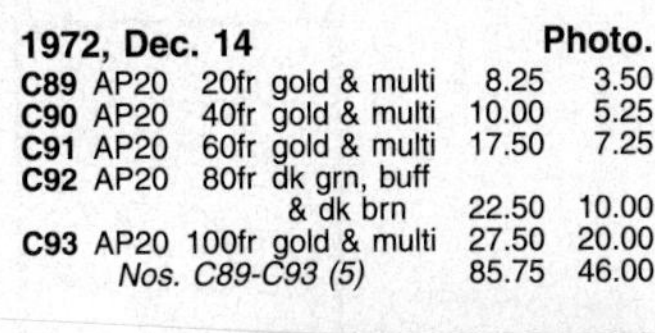

St. Teresa and Lisieux Basilica AP38

1973, Jan. 23 **Engr.** ***Perf. 13***
C94 AP38 85fr multicolored 22.50 13.50

Centenary of the birth of St. Teresa of Lisieux (1873-1897), Carmelite nun.

Nicolaus Copernicus — AP39

1973, Mar. 7 **Engr.** ***Perf. 13***
C95 AP39 100fr brn, vio bl & red lil 27.50 13.50

Copernicus (1473-1543), Polish astronomer.

Plane over Tahiti — AP40

1973, Apr. 3 **Photo.** ***Perf. 13***
C96 AP40 80fr ultra, gold & lt grn 20.00 13.50

Air France's World Tour via Tahiti.

DC-10 at Papeete Airport — AP41

1973, May 18 **Engr.** ***Perf. 13***
C97 AP41 20fr bl, ultra & sl grn 18.00 5.00

Start of DC-10 service.

Painting Type of 1968

Design: 200fr, "Ta Matete" (seated women), by Paul Gauguin.

1973, June 7 **Photo.** ***Perf. 13***
C98 AP20 200fr multicolored 25.00 17.00

Paul Gauguin (1848-1903), painter.

Pierre Loti and Characters from his Books — AP42

1973, July 4 **Engr.** ***Perf. 13***
C99 AP42 60fr multicolored 37.50 20.00

Pierre Loti (1850-1923), French naval officer and writer.

Woman with Flowers, by Eliane de Gennes AP43

Paintings by Artists Living in Polynesia: 20fr, Sun, by Jean Francois Favre. 60fr, Seascape, by Alain Sidet. 80fr, Crowded Bus, by Francois Ravello. 100fr, Stylized Boats, by Jackie Bourdin, horiz.

1973, Dec. 13 **Photo.** ***Perf. 13***

C100	AP43	20fr gold & multi	7.50	2.25
C101	AP43	40fr gold & multi	10.00	4.75
C102	AP43	60fr gold & multi	15.00	8.00
C103	AP43	80fr gold & multi	20.00	13.00
C104	AP43	100fr gold & multi	24.00	16.00
		Nos. C100-C104 (5)	76.50	44.00

Bird, Fish, Flower and Water — AP44

Catamaran under Sail — AP45

1974, June 12 **Photo.** ***Perf. 13***
C105 AP44 12fr blue & multi 7.50 3.25

Nature protection.

1974, July 22 **Engr.** ***Perf. 13***
C106 AP45 100fr multicolored 22.50 13.50

2nd Catamaran World Championships.

Still-life, by Rosine Temarui-Masson — AP46

Paintings by Artists Living in Polynesia: 40fr, Palms and House on Beach, by Marcel Chardon. 60fr, Man, by Marie-Françoise Avril. 80fr, Polynesian Woman, by Henriette Robin. 100fr, Lagoon by Moon-light, by David Farsi, horiz.

1974, Dec. 12 Photo. *Perf. 13*

C107	AP46	20fr gold & multi	16.00	7.00
C108	AP46	40fr gold & multi	21.00	8.00
C109	AP46	60fr gold & multi	25.00	10.00
C110	AP46	80fr gold & multi	35.00	13.50
C111	AP46	100fr gold & multi	50.00	22.50
		Nos. C107-C111 (5)	147.00	61.00

See Nos. C122-C126.

Polynesian Gods of Travel — AP47

Designs: 75fr, Tourville hydroplane, 1929. 100fr, Passengers leaving plane.

1975, Feb. 7 Engr. *Perf. 13*

C112	AP47	50fr sep, pur & brn	8.50	4.50
C113	AP47	75fr grn, bl & red	14.00	6.50
C114	AP47	100fr grn, sep & car	20.00	12.00
		Nos. C112-C114 (3)	42.50	23.00

Fifty years of Tahitian aviation.

French Ceres Stamp and Woman — AP48

1975, May 29 Engr. *Perf. 13*

C115	AP48	32fr ver, brn & blk	10.00	4.00

ARPHILA 75 International Philatelic Exhibition, Paris, June 6-16.

Shot Put and Games' Emblem AP50

1975, Aug. 1 Photo. *Perf. 13*

C117	AP50	25fr shown	4.00	2.25
C118	AP50	30fr Volleyball	5.75	2.75
C119	AP50	40fr Women's swimming	7.50	3.75
		Nos. C117-C119 (3)	17.25	8.75

5th South Pacific Games, Guam, Aug. 1-10.

Flowers, Athlete, View of Montreal — AP51

1975, Oct. 15 Engr. *Perf. 13*

C120	AP51	44fr brt bl, ver & blk	9.00	5.00

Pre-Olympic Year 1975.

UPU Emblem, Jet and Letters — AP52

1975, Nov. 5 Engr. *Perf. 13*

C121	AP52	100fr brn, bl & ol	19.00	10.00

World Universal Postal Union Day.

Paintings Type of 1974

Paintings by Artists Living in Polynesia: 20fr, Beach Scene, by R. Marcel Marius, horiz. 40fr, Roofs with TV antennas, by M. Anglade, horiz. 60fr, Street scene with bus, by J. Day, horiz. 80fr, Tropical waters (fish), by J. Steimetz. 100fr, Women, by A. van der Heyde.

1975, Dec. 17 Litho. *Perf. 13*

C122	AP46	20fr gold & multi	3.50	1.75
C123	AP46	40fr gold & multi	6.50	3.00
C124	AP46	60fr gold & multi	10.00	4.50
C125	AP46	80fr gold & multi	13.00	7.50
C126	AP46	100fr gold & multi	16.00	12.00
		Nos. C122-C126 (5)	49.00	28.75

Concorde — AP53

1976, Jan. 21 Engr. *Perf. 13*

C127	AP53	100fr car, bl & ind	15.00	10.00

First commercial flight of supersonic jet Concorde from Paris to Rio, Jan. 21.

Adm. Rodney, Count de la Perouse, "Barfleur" and "Triomphant" in Battle — AP54

31fr, Count de Grasse and Lord Graves, "Ville de Paris" & "Le Terible" in Chesapeake Bay Battle.

1976, Apr. 15 Engr. *Perf. 13*

C128	AP54	24fr grnsh bl, lt brn & blk	4.00	2.00
C129	AP54	31fr mag, red & lt brn	4.50	2.75

American Bicentennial.

King Pomaré I — AP55

Portraits: 21fr, King Pomaré II. 26fr, Queen Pomaré IV. 30fr, King Pomaré V.

1976, Apr. 28 Litho. *Perf. 12½*

C130	AP55	18fr olive & multi	1.50	.60
C131	AP55	21fr multicolored	1.75	.95
C132	AP55	26fr gray & multi	2.25	1.10
C133	AP55	30fr plum & multi	2.50	1.50
		Nos. C130-C133 (4)	8.00	4.15

Pomaré Dynasty. See Nos. C141-C144.

Running and Maple Leaf — AP56

Designs: 34fr, Long jump, vert. 50fr, Olympic flame and flowers.

1976, July 19 Engr. *Perf. 13*

C134	AP56	26fr ultra & multi	3.50	1.75
C135	AP56	34fr ultra & multi	5.00	2.25
C136	AP56	50fr ultra & multi	9.50	4.25
a.		Min. sheet, #C134-C136	85.00	85.00
		Nos. C134-C136 (3)	18.00	8.25

21st Olympic Games, Montreal, Canada, July 17-Aug. 1.

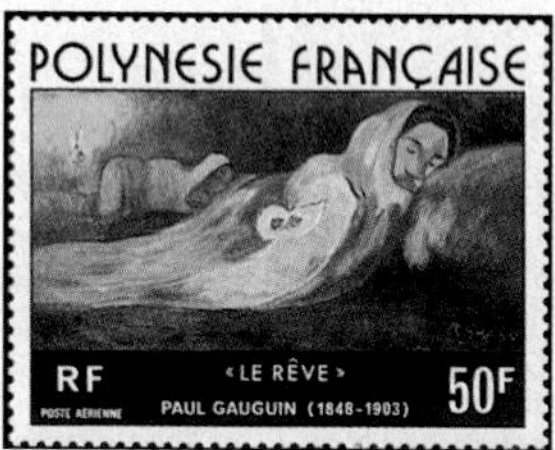

The Dream, by Paul Gauguin — AP57

1976, Oct. 17 Photo. *Perf. 13*

C137	AP57	50fr multicolored	10.00	6.00

Murex Steeriae — AP58

Pocillopora AP59

Sea Shells: 27fr, Conus Gauguini. 35fr, Conus marchionatus.

1977, Mar. 14 Photo. *Perf. 12½x13*

C138	AP58	25fr vio bl & multi	4.25	1.25
C139	AP58	27fr ultra & multi	4.25	1.50
C140	AP58	35fr blue & multi	5.00	2.00
		Nos. C138-C140 (3)	13.50	4.75

See Nos. C156-C158.

Royalty Type of 1976

19fr, King Maputeoa, Mangareva. 33fr, King Camatoa V, Raiatea. 39fr, Queen Vaekehu, Marquesas. 43fr, King Teurarii III, Rurutu.

1977, Apr. 19 Litho. *Perf. 12½*

C141	AP55	19fr dull red & multi	1.10	.80
C142	AP55	33fr dk blue & multi	1.60	1.00
C143	AP55	39fr ultra & multi	1.60	1.10
C144	AP55	43fr green & multi	2.25	1.60
		Nos. C141-C144 (4)	6.55	4.50

Polynesian rulers.

Perf. 13x12½, 12½x13

1977, May 23 Photo.

Design: 25fr, Acropora, horiz.

C145	AP59	25fr multicolored	1.75	.95
C146	AP59	33fr multicolored	2.25	1.40

3rd Symposium on Coral Reefs, Miami, Fla. See Nos. C162-C163.

De Gaulle Memorial — AP60

Tahitian Dancer — AP61

Photogravure and Embossed

1977, June 18 *Perf. 13*

C147	AP60	40fr gold & multi	4.50	3.50

5th anniversary of dedication of De Gaulle memorial at Colombey-les-Deux-Eglises.

1977, July 14 Litho. *Perf. 12½*

C148	AP61	27fr multicolored	5.00	2.50

Charles A. Lindbergh and Spirit of St. Louis — AP62

1977, Aug. 18 Litho. *Perf. 12½*

C149	AP62	28fr multicolored	7.50	3.00

Lindbergh's solo transatlantic flight from New York to Paris, 50th anniv.

Mahoe — AP63

Palms on Shore — AP64

1977, Sept. 15 Photo. *Perf. 12½x13*
C150 AP63 8fr shown 1.40 .55
C151 AP63 12fr Frangipani 1.75 .80

1977, Nov. 8 Photo. *Perf. 12½x13*
C152 AP64 32fr multicolored 10.00 3.00

Ecology, protection of trees.

Rubens' Son Albert AP65

1977, Nov. 28 Engr. *Perf. 13*
C153 AP65 100fr grnsh blk & rose cl 12.00 6.50

Peter Paul Rubens (1577-1640), painter, 400th birth anniversary.

Capt. Cook and "Discovery" — AP66

Design: 39fr, Capt. Cook and "Resolution."

1978, Jan. 20 Engr. *Perf. 13*
C154 AP66 33fr multicolored 2.50 1.60
C155 AP66 39fr multicolored 3.00 1.75

Bicentenary of Capt. James Cook's arrival in Hawaii.
For overprints see Nos. C166-C167.

Shell Type of 1977

Sea Shells: 22fr, Erosaria obvelata. 24fr, Cypraea ventriculus. 31fr, Lambis robusta.

1978, Apr. 13 Photo. *Perf. 13½x13*
C156 AP58 22fr brt blue & multi 2.50 1.25
C157 AP58 24fr brt blue & multi 2.50 1.50
C158 AP58 31fr brt blue & multi 4.00 2.50
Nos. C156-C158 (3) 9.00 5.25

Tahitian Woman and Boy, by Gauguin AP67

1978, May 7 *Perf. 13*
C159 AP67 50fr multicolored 14.00 9.00

Paul Gauguin (1848-1903).

Antenna and ITU Emblem AP68

1978, May 17 Litho. *Perf. 13*
C160 AP68 80fr gray & multi 5.00 2.75

10th World Telecommunications Day.

Soccer and Argentina '78 Emblem — AP69

1978, June 1
C161 AP69 28fr multicolored 6.00 3.00

11th World Cup Soccer Championship, Argentina, June 1-25.

Coral Type of 1977

Designs: 26fr, Fungia, horiz. 34fr, Millepora.

Perf. 13x12½, 12½x13
1978, July 13 Photo.
C162 AP59 26fr multicolored 3.00 2.00
C163 AP59 34fr multicolored 4.00 3.00

Radar Antenna, Polynesian Woman — AP70

1978, Sept. 5 Engr. *Perf. 13*
C164 AP70 50fr blue & black 3.00 1.75

Papenoo earth station.

Bird and Rainbow over Island — AP71

1978, Oct. 5 Photo.
C165 AP71 23fr multicolored 6.00 1.75

Nature protection.

Nos. C154-C155 Overprinted in Black or Violet Blue: "1779-1979 / BICENTENAIRE / DE LA / MORT DE"

1979, Feb. 14 Engr. *Perf. 13*
C166 AP66 33fr multi 4.00 2.50
C167 AP66 39fr multi (VBl) 5.00 3.50

Bicentenary of Capt. Cook's death. On No. C167 date is last line of overprint.

Children, Toys and IYC Emblem — AP72

1979, May 3 Engr. *Perf. 13*
C168 AP72 150fr multicolored 15.00 7.00

International Year of the Child.

"Do you expect a letter?" by Paul Gauguin — AP73

1979, May 20 Photo. *Perf. 13*
C169 AP73 200fr multicolored 17.50 8.00

Shell and Carved Head — AP74

1979, June 30 Engr. *Perf. 13*
C170 AP74 44fr multicolored 3.25 2.00

Museum of Tahiti and the Islands.

Conference Emblem over Island AP75

1979, Oct. 6 Photo. *Perf. 13*
C171 AP75 23fr multicolored 2.25 1.10

19th South Pacific Conf., Tahiti, Oct. 6-12.

Flying Boat "Bermuda" — AP76

Planes Used in Polynesia: 40fr, DC-4 over Papeete. 60fr, Britten-Norman "Islander." 80fr, Fairchild F-27A. 120fr, DC-8 over Tahiti.

1979, Dec. 19 Litho. *Perf. 13*
C172 AP76 24fr multicolored 1.00 .50
C173 AP76 40fr multicolored 1.75 1.00
C174 AP76 60fr multicolored 2.75 1.50
C175 AP76 80fr multicolored 3.50 2.25
C176 AP76 120fr multicolored 6.00 3.00
Nos. C172-C176 (5) 15.00 8.25

See Nos. C180-C183.

Window on Tahiti, by Henri Matisse AP77

1980, Feb. 18 Photo.
C177 AP77 150fr multicolored 8.00 5.00

Marshi Metua No Tehamana, by Gauguin AP78

1980, Aug. 24 Photo. *Perf. 13*
C178 AP78 500fr multicolored 16.00 11.00

Sydpex '80, Philatelic Exhibition, Sydney Town Hall — AP79

1980, Sept. 29 Photo. *Perf. 13*
C179 AP79 70fr multicolored 6.50 4.50

Aviation Type of 1979

1980, Dec. 15 Litho. *Perf. 13*
C180 AP76 15fr Catalina 1.25 .75
C181 AP76 26fr Twin Otter 2.50 1.00
C182 AP76 30fr CAMS 55 3.00 1.25
C183 AP76 50fr DC-6 4.50 1.75
Nos. C180-C183 (4) 11.25 4.75

And The Gold of their Bodies, by Gauguin — AP80

1981, Mar. 15 Photo. *Perf. 13*
C184 AP80 100fr multicolored 7.50 3.00

20th Anniv. of Manned Space Flight AP81

1981, June 15 Litho. *Perf. 12½*
C185 AP81 300fr multicolored 7.50 5.00

First Intl. Pirogue (6-man Canoe) Championship — AP82

1981, July 25 Litho. *Perf. 13x12½*
C186 AP82 200fr multicolored 5.00 4.00

Matavai Bay, by William Hodges — AP83

Paintings: 60fr, Poedea, by John Weber, vert. 80fr, Omai, by Joshua Reynolds, vert. 120fr, Point Venus, by George Tobin.

1981, Dec. 10 Photo. *Perf. 13*
C187 AP83 40fr multicolored 1.10 .90
C188 AP83 60fr multicolored 1.75 1.25
C189 AP83 80fr multicolored 2.75 1.75
C190 AP83 120fr multicolored 3.50 2.40
Nos. C187-C190 (4) 9.10 6.30

See Nos. C194-C197, C202-C205.

TB Bacillus Centenary — AP84

1982, Mar. 24 Engr. *Perf. 13*
C191 AP84 200fr multicolored 5.00 3.00

1982 World Cup — AP85

1982, May 18 Litho. *Perf. 13*
C192 AP85 250fr multicolored 5.75 4.00

French Overseas Possessions' Week, Sept. 18-25 — AP86

1982, Sept. 17 Engr.
C193 AP86 110fr multicolored 2.75 1.65

Painting Type of 1981

Designs: 50fr, The Tahitian, by M. Radiguet, vert. 70fr, Souvenir of Tahiti, by C. Giraud. 100fr, Beating Cloth Lengths, by Atlas JL the Younger. 160fr, Papeete Harbor, by C.F. Gordon Cumming.

1982, Dec. 15 Photo. *Perf. 13*
C194 AP83 50fr multicolored 1.75 .75
C195 AP83 70fr multicolored 2.25 1.10
C196 AP83 100fr multicolored 2.50 1.60
C197 AP83 160fr multicolored 4.50 3.25
Nos. C194-C197 (4) 11.00 6.70

Wood Cutter, by Gauguin AP87

Photo. & Engr.
1983, May 8 *Perf. 12½x13*
C198 AP87 600fr multicolored 14.00 8.00

Voyage of Capt. Bligh — AP88

1983, June 9 Litho. *Perf. 13*
C199 AP88 200fr Map, fruit 6.00 3.00

BRASILIANA '83 Intl. Stamp Exhibition, Rio de Janeiro, July 29-Aug. 7 — AP89

1983, July 29 Litho. *Perf. 13x12½*
C200 AP89 100fr multicolored 2.50 1.75
a. Souvenir sheet 6.00 6.00

1983, Aug. 4 Litho. *Perf. 13x12½*
C201 AP89 110fr Bangkok '83 3.00 2.00
a. Souvenir sheet 7.50 7.50

Painting Type of 1981

20th Cent. Paintings: 40fr, View of Moorea, by William Alister MacDonald (1861-1956). 60fr, The Fruit Carrier, by Adrian Herman Gouwe (1875-1965). 80fr, Arrival of the Destroyer Escort, by Nicolas Mordvinoff (1911-1977). 100fr, Women on a Veranda, by Charles Alfred Le Moine (1872-1918).

1983, Dec. 22 Photo. *Perf. 13*
C202 AP83 40fr multi 1.00 .75
C203 AP83 60fr multi, vert. 1.50 1.00
C204 AP83 80fr multi, vert. 1.60 1.25
C205 AP83 100fr multi 2.00 1.60
Nos. C202-C205 (4) 6.10 4.60

ESPANA '84 — AP90

Design: Maori canoers.

1984, Apr. 27 Engr. *Perf. 13*
C206 AP90 80fr brn red & dk bl 2.25 1.50

Souvenir Sheet

C207 AP90 200fr dk bl & dk red 12.00 12.00

Woman with Mango, by Gauguin AP91

Photo. & Engr.
1984, May 27 *Perf. 12½x13*
C208 AP91 400fr multicolored 9.50 6.00

Ausipex '84 — AP92

Details from Human Sacrifice of the Maori in Tahiti, 18th cent. engraving.

1984, Sept. 5 Litho. *Perf. 13x12½*
C209 AP92 120fr Worshippers 3.00 2.25
C210 AP92 120fr Preparation 3.00 2.25
a. Pair, #C209-C210 + label 7.50 7.50

Souvenir Sheet

C211 AP92 200fr Entire 9.50 9.50

Painting by Gaugin (1848-1903) — AP93

Design: Where have we come from? What are we? Where are we going?
Illustration reduced.

1985, Mar. 17 Litho. *Perf. 13½x13*
C212 AP93 550fr + label 12.00 7.50

4th Pacific Arts Festival Type

1985, July 3 Litho. *Perf. 13*
C213 A95 200fr Islander, tiki, artifacts 4.50 3.00

Intl. Youth Year — AP95

1985, Sept. 18 Litho.
C214 AP95 250fr Island youths, frigate bird 5.50 3.25

ITALIA '85 — AP96

Designs: Ship sailing into Papeete Harbor, 19th century print.

1985, Oct. 22 Engr.
C215 AP96 130fr multicolored 2.75 2.50

Souvenir Sheet

C216 AP96 240fr multicolored 7.50 7.50

1st Intl. Marlin Fishing Contest, Feb. 27-Mar. 5 — AP97

1986, Feb. 27 Litho. *Perf. 12½*
C217 AP97 300fr multicolored 6.50 4.00

Arrival of a Boat, c.1880 — AP98

1986, June 24 Engr. *Perf. 13*
C218 AP98 400fr intense blue 8.75 5.25

STOCKHOLMIA '86 — AP99

Design: Dr. Karl Solander and Anders Sparrmann, Swedish scientists who accompanied Capt. Cook, and map of Tahiti.

1986, Aug. 28 Engr. *Perf. 13*
C219 AP99 150fr multicolored 3.25 2.25

Souvenir Sheet

C220 AP99 210fr multicolored 4.75 4.75

Protestant Churches — AP100

1986, Dec. 17 Litho. *Perf. 13*
C221 AP100 80fr Tiva, 1955 1.75 .90
C222 AP100 200fr Avera, 1880 4.50 2.10
C223 AP100 300fr Papetoai, 1822 6.50 3.25
Nos. C221-C223 (3) 12.75 6.25

Broche Barracks, 120th Anniv. — AP101

1987, Apr. 21 Litho. *Perf. 12½x12*
C224 AP101 350fr multicolored 7.75 5.00

CAPEX '87 — AP102

Design: George Vancouver (1757-1798), English navigator and cartographer, chart and excerpt from ship's log.

1987, June 15 Engr. *Perf. 13*
C225 AP102 130fr + label 2.90 2.25

Imperf
Size: 143x100mm
C226 AP102 260fr multicolored 5.75 5.75

Soyez Mysterieuses, from a 5-Panel Sculpture by Paul Gauguin, Gauguin Museum — AP103

Illustration reduced.

1987, Nov. 15 *Perf. 13*
C227 AP103 600fr multicolored 14.00 9.50

AIR POST SEMI-POSTAL STAMPS

Catalogue values for unused stamps in this section are for Never Hinged items.

French Revolution Issue
Common Design Type
Unwmk.
1939, July 5 Photo. *Perf. 13*
Name and Value Typo. in Orange
CB1 CD83 5fr + 4fr brn blk 52.50 29.00

Mother & Children on Beach — SPAP1

Perf. 12½x13½
1942, June 22 Engr.
CB2 SPAP1 1.50fr + 3.50fr green 1.50
CB3 SPAP1 2fr + 6fr yellow brown 1.50

Native children's welfare fund.
Nos. CB2-CB3 were issued by the Vichy government in France, but were not placed on sale in French Polynesia.

Colonial Education Fund
Common Design Type
1942, June 22
CB4 CD86a 1.20fr + 1.80fr blue & red 1.50

No. CB4 was issued by the Vichy government in France, but was not placed on sale in French Polynesia.

POSTAGE DUE STAMPS

Postage Due Stamps of French Colonies, 1894-1906, Overprinted

1926-27 Unwmk. *Perf. 14x13½*
J1 D1 5c light blue .60 .60
J2 D1 10c brown .60 .60
J3 D1 20c olive green .95 .95
J4 D1 30c dull red 1.00 1.00
J5 D1 40c rose 2.25 2.25
J6 D1 60c blue green 2.25 2.25
J7 D1 1fr red brown, *straw* 2.25 2.25
J8 D1 3fr magenta ('27) 9.50 9.50

With Additional Surcharge of New Value
J9 D1 2fr on 1fr orange red 2.75 2.75
Nos. J1-J9 (9) 22.15 22.15

Fautaua Falls, Tahiti — D2

Tahitian Youth — D3

1929 Typo. *Perf. 13½x14*
J10 D2 5c lt blue & dk brn .50 .50
J11 D2 10c vermilion & grn .60 .60
J12 D2 30c dk brn & dk red 1.25 1.25
J13 D2 50c yel grn & dk brn 1.00 1.00
J14 D2 60c dl vio & yel grn 2.75 2.75
J15 D3 1fr Prus bl & red vio 2.25 2.25
J16 D3 2fr brn red & dk brn 1.50 1.50
J17 D3 3fr bl vio & bl grn 1.50 1.50
Nos. J10-J17 (8) 11.35 11.35

Catalogue values for unused stamps in this section, from this point to the end of the section, are for Never Hinged items.

D4

Polynesian Club — D5

1948 Engr. *Perf. 14x13*
J18 D4 10c brt blue grn .30 .20
J19 D4 30c black brown .30 .20
J20 D4 50c dk car rose .40 .25
J21 D4 1fr ultra .55 .45
J22 D4 2fr dk blue green .75 .60
J23 D4 3fr red 1.50 1.25
J24 D4 4fr violet 1.60 1.40
J25 D4 5fr lilac rose 2.40 1.90
J26 D4 10fr slate 3.25 2.25
J27 D4 20fr red brown 4.50 3.75
Nos. J18-J27 (10) 15.55 12.25

1958 Unwmk. *Perf. 14x13*
J28 D5 1fr dk brn & grn .55 .50
J29 D5 3fr bluish blk & hn brn .75 .75
J30 D5 5fr brown & ultra .90 .90
Nos. J28-J30 (3) 2.20 2.15

Tahitian Bowl — D6

1984-87 Litho. *Perf. 13*
J31 D6 1fr Mother-of-pearl fish hook, vert. .20 .20
J32 D6 3fr shown .20 .20
J33 D6 5fr Marquesan fan .20 .20
J34 D6 10fr Lamp stand, vert. .35 .35
J35 D6 20fr Wood headrest ('87) .50 .50
J36 D6 50fr Wood scoop ('87) 1.10 1.10
Nos. J31-J36 (6) 2.55 2.55

Issued: #J31-34, 3/15; #J35-J36, 8/18.

OFFICIAL STAMPS

Catalogue values for unused stamps in this section are for Never Hinged items.

Breadfruit O1

Polynesian Fruits: 2fr, 3fr, 5fr, like 1fr. 7fr, 8fr, 10fr, 15fr, "Vi Tahiti." 19fr, 20fr, 25fr, 35fr, Avocados. 50fr, 100fr, 200fr, Mangos.

1977, June 9 Litho. *Perf. 12½*
O1 O1 1fr ultra & multi .20 .20
O2 O1 2fr ultra & multi .20 .20
O3 O1 3fr ultra & multi .20 .20
O4 O1 5fr ultra & multi .20 .20
O5 O1 7fr red & multi .35 .35
O6 O1 8fr red & multi .40 .40
O7 O1 10fr red & multi .50 .50
O8 O1 15fr red & multi .75 .75
O9 O1 19fr black & multi .85 .85
O10 O1 20fr black & multi 1.00 1.00
O11 O1 25fr black & multi 1.25 1.25
O12 O1 35fr black & multi 1.60 1.60
O13 O1 50fr black & multi 1.90 1.90
O14 O1 100fr red & multi 4.00 4.00
O15 O1 200fr ultra & multi 7.50 7.50
Nos. O1-O15 (15) 20.90 20.90

1982-86 *Perf. 13*
O1a O1 1fr ultra & multi .35 .35
O2a O1 2fr ultra & multi .35 .35
O3a O1 3fr ultra & multi .50 .50
O4a O1 5fr ultra & multi 1.10 1.10
O5a O1 7fr red & multi 1.25 1.25
O6a O1 8fr red & multi 1.75 1.75
O7a O1 10fr red & multi 1.75 1.75
O8a O1 15fr red & multi ('84) 1.75 1.75
O10a O1 20fr black & multi 1.75 1.75
O11a O1 25fr black & multi ('84) 1.75 1.75
O12a O1 35fr black & multi ('84) 4.00 4.00
O13a O1 50fr black & multi ('84) 11.00 11.00
O14a O1 100fr red & multi ('86) 22.50 22.50
O15a O1 200fr ultra & multi ('86) 25.00 25.00
Nos. O1a-O15a (14) 74.80 74.80

Nos. O1-O15 have dull finish (matte) gum. Nos. O1a-O15a have shiny gum.

Stamps and Postmarks — O2

1fr, French Colonies #5. 2fr, French Colonies #27, #12. 3fr, French Colonies #29, 1884 Papeete postmark. 5fr, Newspaper franked with surcharge of Tahiti #2, 1884 Papeete postmark. 10fr, #4, 1894 octagonal postmark. 20fr, #6, #8. 46fr, #48. 51fr, #147-148, Vaitepaua-Makatea Island postmark. 70fr, Visit Tahiti postmark on postal card piece. 100fr, #181. 200fr, #C21, 1st day cancel.

1993-94 Litho. *Perf. 13½*
O16 O2 1fr multicolored .20 .20
O17 O2 2fr multicolored .20 .20
O18 O2 3fr multicolored .20 .20
O19 O2 5fr multicolored .20 .20
O20 O2 10fr multicolored .20 .20
O21 O2 20fr multicolored .50 .50
O22 O2 46fr multicolored 1.10 1.10
O22A O2 51fr multicolored 1.75 1.75
O23 O2 70fr multicolored 1.75 1.75
O24 O2 100fr multicolored 2.10 2.10
O25 O2 200fr multicolored 3.50 3.50
Nos. O16-O25 (11) 11.70 11.70

Issued: 51fr, 4/6/94; others, 1/13/93.

1997-99 Litho. *Perf. 13½x13*

Designs: 9fr, #176. 85fr, #59 with 1921 manuscript cancel, vert.

O26 O2 9fr multicolored .75 .75
O20a O2 10fr multicolored .75 .75
O21a O2 20fr multicolored .75 .75
O27 O2 85fr multicolored 1.75 1.75
O24a O2 100fr multicolored 1.75 1.75
Nos. O26-O24a (5) 5.75 5.75

Issued: #O26, O27, 4/21; #O20a, O21a, O24a, 1999.
This is an expanding set. Numbers will change.

FRENCH SOUTHERN AND ANTARCTIC TERRITORIES

'french 'sə-thərn and ˌant-ärk-tik 'ter-ə-'tōr-ēs

POP. — 130 staff

Formerly dependencies of Madagascar, these areas, comprising the Kerguelen Archipelago; St. Paul, Amsterdam and Crozet Islands and Adelle Land in Antarctica achieved territorial status on August 6, 1955.

100 Centimes = 1 Franc
100 Cents = 1 Euro (2002)

Catalogue values for all unused stamps in this country are for Never Hinged items.

Madagascar No. 289 Overprinted in Red:

Unwmk.

1955, Oct. 28 Engr. *Perf. 13*

1 A25 15f dk grn & dp ultra 14.50 *29.00*

Rockhopper Penguins, Crozet Archipelago — A1

New Amsterdam A2

Design: 10fr, 15fr, Elephant seal.

1956, Apr. 25 Engr. *Perf. 13*

2 A1	50c dk blue, sepia & yel	.45	*.75*
3 A1	1fr ultra, org & gray	.45	*.75*
4 A2	5fr blue & dp ultra	3.00	*3.25*
5 A2	8fr gray vio & dk brn	18.00	*21.00*
6 A2	10fr indigo	6.50	6.25
7 A2	15fr indigo & brn vio	8.00	7.50
	Nos. 2-7 (6)	36.40	39.50

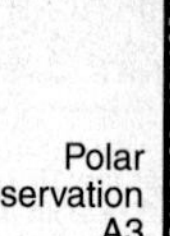

Polar Observation A3

1957, Oct. 11

8 A3	5fr black & violet	3.50	*5.00*
9 A3	10fr rose red	4.75	*5.75*
10 A3	15fr dark blue	5.75	*7.50*
	Nos. 8-10 (3)	14.00	18.25

International Geophysical Year, 1957-58.

Imperforates

Most stamps of this French possession exist imperforate in issued and trial colors, and also in small presentation sheets in issued colors.

Flower Issue

Common Design Type

Design: Pringlea, horiz.

1959 Photo. *Perf. 12½x12*

11 CD104 10fr sal, grn & yel 10.00 8.00

Common Design Types pictured following the introduction.

Light-mantled Sooty Albatross — A4

Coat of Arms — A5

Designs: 40c, Skua, horiz. 12fr, King shag.

1959, Sept. 14 Engr. *Perf. 13*

12 A4	30c blue, grn & red brn	.50	*.75*
13 A4	40c blk, dl red brn & bl	.50	*.75*
14 A4	12fr lt blue & blk	13.50	8.75
	Nos. 12-14 (3)	14.50	10.25

1959, Sept. 14 Typo. *Perf. 13x14*

15 A5 20fr ultra, lt bl & yel 21.00 11.50

Sheathbills — A6

4fr, Sea leopard, horiz. 25fr, Weddell seal at Kerguélen, horiz. 85fr, King penguin.

1960, Dec. 15 Engr. *Perf. 13*

16 A6	2fr grnsh bl, gray & choc	1.75	*2.25*
17 A6	4fr bl, dk brn & dk grn	9.50	7.50
18 A6	25fr sl grn, bis brn & blk	100.00	42.50
19 A6	85fr grnsh bl, org & blk	22.50	14.50
	Nos. 16-19 (4)	133.75	66.75

Yves-Joseph de Kerguélen-Trémarec — A7

1960, Nov. 22

20 A7 25fr red org, dk bl & brn 29.00 22.50

Yves-Joseph de Kerguélen-Trémarec, discoverer of the Kerguélen Archipelago.

Charcot, Compass Rose and "Pourquoi-pas?" — A8

1961, Dec. 26 Unwmk. *Perf. 13*

21 A8 25fr brn, grn & red 29.00 22.50

25th anniv. of the death of Commander Jean Charcot (1867-1936), Antarctic explorer.

Elephant Seals Fighting A9

1963, Feb. 11 Engr. *Perf. 13*

22 A9 8fr dk blue, blk & claret 11.00 7.50

See No. C4.

Penguins and Camp on Crozet Island A10

20fr, Research station & IQSY emblem.

1963, Dec. 16 Unwmk. *Perf. 13*

23 A10	5fr blk, red brn & Prus bl	65.00	35.00
24 A10	20fr vio, sl & red brn	80.00	55.00

Intl. Quiet Sun Year, 1964-65. See #C6.

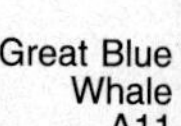

Great Blue Whale A11

Black-browed Albatross — A12

Aurora Australis, Map of Antarctica and Rocket — A13

10fr, Cape pigeons. 12fr, Phylica trees, Amsterdam Island. 15fr, Killer whale (orca).

1966-69 Engr. *Perf. 13*

25 A11	5fr brt bl & indigo	21.00	11.50
26 A12	10fr sl, ind & ol brn	32.50	25.00
27 A11	12fr brt bl, sl grn & lemon	22.50	14.00
27A A11	15fr ol, dk bl & ind	11.50	7.25
28 A12	20fr slate, ol & org	400.00	225.00
	Nos. 25-28 (5)	487.50	282.75

Issued: 5fr, 12/12; 20fr, 1/3/68; 10fr, 12fr, 1/6/69; 15fr, 12/21/69.

1967, Mar. 4 Engr. *Perf. 13*

29 A13 20fr mag, blue & blk 29.00 22.50

Launching of the 1st space rocket from Adelie Land, Jan., 1967.

Dumont d'Urville A14

1968, Jan. 20

30 A14 30fr lt ultra, dk bl & dk brn 140.00 80.00

Jules Sébastien César Dumont D'Urville (1790-1842), French naval commander and South Seas explorer.

WHO Anniversary Issue

Common Design Type

1968, May 4 Engr. *Perf. 13*

31 CD126 30fr red, yel & bl 65.00 45.00

Human Rights Year Issue

Common Design Type

1968, Aug. 10 Engr. *Perf. 13*

32 CD127 30fr grnsh bl, red & brn 60.00 45.00

Polar Camp with Helicopter, Plane and Snocat Tractor — A15

1969, Mar. 17 Engr. *Perf. 13*

33 A15 25fr Prus bl, lt grnsh bl & brn red 25.00 15.00

20 years of French Polar expeditions.

ILO Issue

Common Design Type

1970, Jan. 1 Engr. *Perf. 13*

35 CD131 20fr org, dk bl & brn 18.00 10.00

UPU Headquarters Issue

Common Design Type

1970, May 20 Engr. *Perf. 13*

36 CD133 50fr blue, plum & ol bis 42.50 27.50

Ice Fish A16

Fish: Nos. 38-43, Antarctic cods, various species. 135fr, Zanchlorhynchus spinifer.

1971 Engr. *Perf. 13*

No.	Type	Description	Unused	Used
37	A16	5fr brt grn, ind & org	1.25	.85
38	A16	10fr redsh brn & dp vio	2.00	.95
39	A16	20fr dp cl, brt grn & org	4.25	2.10
40	A16	22fr pur, brn ol & mag	4.00	3.25
41	A16	25fr grn, ind & org	6.00	2.75
42	A16	30fr sep, gray & bl vio	7.50	4.25
43	A16	35fr sl grn, dk brn & ocher	5.00	3.25
44	A16	135fr Prus bl, dp org & ol grn	10.00	5.25
		Nos. 37-44 (8)	40.00	22.65

Issued: #37-39, 41-42, 1/1; #40, 43-44, 12/22.

Map of Antarctica A17

Microzetia Mirabilis A18

1971, Dec. 22

No.	Type	Description	Unused	Used
45	A17	75fr red	26.00	24.00

Antarctic Treaty pledging peaceful uses of and scientific cooperation in Antarctica, 10th anniv.

1972

Insects: 15fr, Christiansenia dreuxi. 22f, Phtirocoris antarcticus. 30fr, Antarctophytosus atriceps. 40fr, Paractora drenxl. 140fr, Pringleophaga Kerguelenensis.

No.	Type	Description	Unused	Used
46	A18	15fr cl, org & brn	10.00	6.00
47	A18	22fr vio bl, sl grn & yel	14.00	9.00
48	A18	25fr grn, rose lil & pur	5.75	4.75
49	A18	30fr blue & multi	17.50	10.00
50	A18	40fr dk brn, ocher & blk	8.75	4.75
51	A18	140fr bl, emer & brn	12.50	8.75
		Nos. 46-51 (6)	68.50	43.25

Issued: #48, 50-51, 1/3; #46-47, 49, 12/16.

De Gaulle Issue
Common Design Type

Designs: 50fr, Gen. de Gaulle, 1940. 100fr, Pres. de Gaulle, 1970.

1972, Feb. 1 Engr. *Perf. 13*

No.	Type	Description	Unused	Used
52	CD134	50fr brt grn & blk	20.00	12.50
53	CD134	100fr brt grn & blk	25.00	20.00

Kerguelen Cabbage — A19

Designs: 61fr, Azorella selago, horiz. 87fr, Acaena ascendens, horiz.

1972-73

No.	Type	Description	Unused	Used
54	A19	45fr multicolored	10.00	5.00
55	A19	61fr multicolored	3.50	2.75
56	A19	87fr multicolored	5.75	4.00
		Nos. 54-56 (3)	19.25	11.75

Issued: 45fr, 12/18; others, 12/13/73.

Mailship Sapmer and Map of Amsterdam Island — A20

1974, Dec. 31 Engr. *Perf. 13*

No.	Type	Description	Unused	Used
57	A20	75fr bl, blk & dk brn	7.00	5.25

25th anniversary of postal service.

Antarctic Tern — A21

Designs: 50c, Antarctic petrel. 90c, Sea lioness. 1fr, Weddell seal. 1.20fr, Kerguelen cormorant, vert. 1.40fr, Gentoo penguin, vert.

1976, Jan. Engr. *Perf. 13*

No.	Type	Description	Unused	Used
58	A21	40c multicolored	4.25	2.75
59	A21	50c multicolored	4.25	2.75
60	A21	90c multicolored	7.00	4.00
61	A21	1fr multicolored	11.00	9.25
62	A21	1.20fr multicolored	14.00	11.00
63	A21	1.40fr multicolored	13.00	11.00
		Nos. 58-63 (6)	53.50	40.75

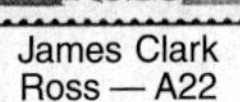

James Clark Ross — A22

James Cook — A23

Design: 30c, Climbing Mount Ross.

1976, Dec. 16 Engr. *Perf. 13*

No.	Type	Description	Unused	Used
64	A22	30c multicolored	4.50	3.00
65	A22	3fr multicolored	4.50	3.00

First climbing of Mount Ross, Kerguelen Island, Jan. 5, 1975.

1976, Dec. 16

No.	Type	Description	Unused	Used
66	A23	70c multicolored	13.50	10.00

Bicentenary of Capt. Cook's voyage past Kerguelen Island. See No. C46.

Commerson's Dolphins — A24

1977, Feb. 1 Engr. *Perf. 13*

No.	Type	Description	Unused	Used
67	A24	1.10fr Blue whale	5.50	3.25
68	A24	1.50fr shown	5.50	4.00

Macrocystis Algae — A25

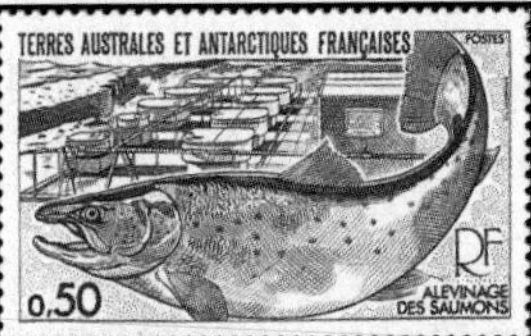

Salmon Hatchery — A26

Magga Dan — A27

Designs: 70c, Durvillea algae. 90c, Albatross. 1fr, Underwater sampling and scientists, vert. 1.40fr, Thala Dan and penguins.

1977, Dec. 20 Engr. *Perf. 13*

No.	Type	Description	Unused	Used
69	A25	40c ol brn & bis	1.10	.70
70	A26	50c dk bl & pur	1.40	1.00
71	A25	70c blk, grn & brn	1.60	1.00
72	A26	90c grn, brt bl & brn	1.60	1.00
73	A27	1fr slate	1.40	1.00
74	A27	1.20fr multi	3.25	1.60
75	A27	1.40fr multi	2.00	1.60
		Nos. 69-75 (7)	12.35	7.90

See Nos. 77-79.

A28

A29

Explorer with French and Expedition Flags.

1977, Dec. 24

No.	Type	Description	Unused	Used
76	A28	1.90fr multicolored	7.50	5.00

French Polar expeditions, 1947-48.

Types of 1977

40c, Forbin, destroyer. 50c Jeanne d'Arc, helicopter carrier. 1.40fr, Kerguelen cormorant.

1979, Jan. 1 Engr. *Perf. 13*

No.	Type	Description	Unused	Used
77	A27	40c black & blue	1.40	1.10
78	A27	50c black & blue	1.60	1.10
79	A26	1.40fr multicolored	1.60	1.10
		Nos. 77-79 (3)	4.60	3.30

1979, Jan. 1

No.	Type	Description	Unused	Used
80	A29	1.20fr citron & indigo	1.40	1.10

R. Rallier du Baty. See Nos. 97, 100, 111, 117, 129, 135, 188.

French Navigators Monument, Hobart — A30

1979, Jan. 1

No.	Type	Description	Unused	Used
81	A30	1fr multicolored	.90	.80

French navigators and explorers.

Petrel — A31

1979 Engr. *Perf. 13*

No.	Type	Description	Unused	Used
82	A31	70c Rockhopper penguins, vert.	1.00	.80
83	A31	1fr shown	1.25	.90

Commandant Bourdais — A32

1979

No.	Type	Description	Unused	Used
84	A32	1.10fr *Doudart de Lagree*, vert.	1.00	.80
85	A32	1.50fr shown	1.25	.90

Adm. Antoine d'Entrecasteaux A33

Sebastian de el Cano A34

1979

No.	Type	Description	Unused	Used
86	A33	1.20fr multicolored	1.40	1.10

1979

Discovery of Amsterdam Island, 1522: 4fr, Victoria, horiz.

No.	Type	Description	Unused	Used
87	A34	1.40fr multicolored	1.10	.80
88	A34	4fr multicolored	2.00	1.60

Adelie Penguins — A35

Adelie Penguin — A36

Sea Leopard A37

1980, Dec. 15 Engr. *Perf. 13*

No.	Type	Description	Unused	Used
89	A35	50c rose violet	1.40	1.25
90	A36	60c multicolored	1.40	.90
91	A35	1.20fr multicolored	2.00	1.10
92	A37	1.30fr multicolored	1.40	1.25
93	A37	1.80fr multicolored	1.40	1.25
		Nos. 89-93 (5)	7.60	5.75

20th Anniv. of Antarctic Treaty — A38

1981, June 23 Engr. *Perf. 13*
94 A38 1.80fr multicolored 4.50 4.50

Alouette II — A39

1981-82 Engr. *Perf. 13*
95 A39 55c brown & multi .55 .45
96 A39 65c blue & multi .55 .45

Explorer Type of 1979

1981
97 A29 1.40fr Jean Loranchet .80 .55

Landing Ship Le Gros Ventre, Kerguelen — A41

1983, Jan. 3 Engr. *Perf. 13*
98 A41 55c multicolored .90 .65

Our Lady of the Winds Statue and Church, Kerguelen — A42

1983, Jan. 3
99 A42 1.40fr multicolored .90 .90

Explorer Type of 1979

Design: Martin de Vivies, Navigator.

1983, Jan. 3
100 A29 1.60fr multicolored .90 .75

Eaton's Ducks A44

1983, Jan. 3
101 A44 1.50fr multicolored .90 .60
102 A44 1.80fr multicolored .90 .75

Trawler Austral — A45

1983, Jan. 3
103 A45 2.30fr multicolored 1.40 1.10

Freighter Lady Franklin — A46

1983, Aug. 4 Engr. *Perf. 13*
104 A46 5fr multicolored 4.00 3.00

Glaciology — A47

Design: Scientists examining glacier, base.

1984, Jan. 1 Engr. *Perf. 13*
105 A47 15c multicolored .35 .30
106 A47 1.70fr multicolored .80 .55

Crab-eating Seal — A48

Penguins — A49

1984, Jan. 1
107 A48 60c multicolored .55 .45
108 A49 70c multicolored .45 .45
109 A49 2fr multicolored 1.25 1.00
110 A48 5.90fr multicolored 2.00 1.75
Nos. 107-110 (4) 4.25 3.65

Explorer Type of 1979

1984, Jan. 1
111 A29 1.80fr Alfred Faure .90 .70

Biomass — A51

1985, Jan. 1 Engr. *Perf. 13*
112 A51 1.80fr multicolored .80 .55
113 A51 5.20fr multicolored 2.00 1.75

Emperor Penguins — A52

Snowy Petrel — A53

1985, Jan. 1 Engr. *Perf. 13*
114 A52 1.70fr multicolored 1.00 .80
115 A53 2.80fr multicolored 1.25 1.10

Port Martin — A54

1985, Jan. 1 Engr. *Perf. 13*
116 A54 2.20fr multicolored 1.25 .80

Explorer Type of 1979

1985, Jan. 1 Engr. *Perf. 13*
117 A29 2fr Andre-Frank Liotard .90 .70

Antarctic Fulmar — A56

1986, Jan. 1 Engr. *Perf. 13*
118 A56 1fr shown .55 .45
119 A56 1.70fr Giant petrels .80 .75
Nos. 118-119,C91 (3) 3.35 2.95

Echinoderms — A57

1986, Jan. 1
120 A57 1.90fr shown .90 .75

Cotula Plumosa — A58

Shipping — A59

1986, Jan. 1
121 A58 2.30fr shown .90 .75
122 A58 6.20fr Lycopodium. saururus 2.50 1.90

1986, Jan. 1
123 A59 2.10fr Var research ship .90 .85
124 A59 3fr Polarbjorn support ship 1.25 1.25

Marine Life — A60

1987, Jan. 1 Engr. *Perf. 13½x13*
125 A60 50c dk blue & org .30 .30

Flora — A61

1987, Jan. 1
126 A61 1.80fr Poa cookii .70 .50
127 A61 6.50fr Lichen, Neuropogon taylori 2.00 1.90

Marret Base, Adelie Land — A62

1987, Jan. 1
128 A62 2fr yel brn, dk ultra & lake .90 .70

Explorer Type of 1979

1987, Jan. 1
129 A29 2.20fr Adm. Mouchez 1.00 .75

Reindeer — A64

1987, Jan. 1
130 A64 2.50fr black 1.25 .80

Transport Ship Eure — A65

1987, Jan. 1
131 A65 3.20fr dk ultra, Prus grn & dk grn 1.25 1.00

Macaroni Penguins — A66

1987, Jan. 1 ***Perf. 13x12½***
132 A66 4.80fr multicolored 2.50 1.90

Elephant Grass — A67

1988, Jan. 1 **Engr.** ***Perf. 13***
133 A67 1.70fr Prus grn, emer & olive .75 .65

Rev.-Father Lejay, Explorer — A68

1988, Jan. 1
134 A68 2.20fr vio, ultra & blk .90 .80

Explorer Type of 1979

Design: Robert Gessain (1907-86).

1988, Jan. 1
135 A29 3.40fr gray, dk red & blk 1.40 1.10

Le Gros Ventre, 18th Cent. — A70

1988, Jan. 1
136 A70 3.50fr dp ultra, bl grn & brn 1.25 1.25

Mermaid and B.A.P. Jules Verne, Research Vessel — A71

1988, Jan. 1
137 A71 4.90fr gray & dk blue 2.25 1.75

La Fortune, Early 19th Cent. — A72

1988, Jan. 1
138 A72 5fr blk & dull bl grn 2.25 1.75

Wilson's Petrel — A73

1988, Jan. 1
139 A73 6.80fr blk, sepia & dl bl grn 2.75 2.25

See Nos. 143-144.

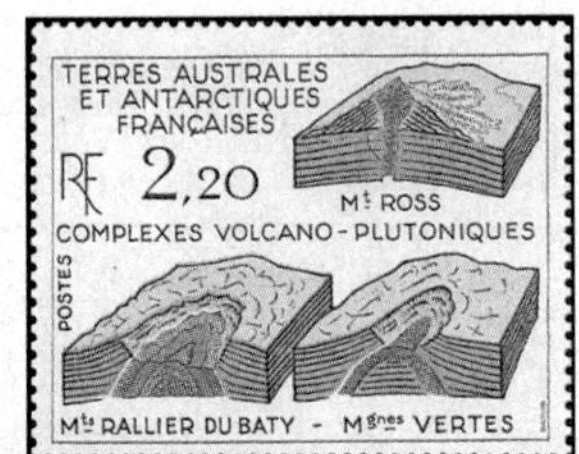
Mt. Ross Campaign (in 1987) — A74

1988, Jan. 1 ***Perf. 13x12½***
140 A74 2.20fr Volcanic rock cross-sections .75 .75
141 A74 15.10fr Kerguelen Is. 5.00 5.00
a. Pair, #140-141 + label 6.75 6.75

Darrieus System Wind Vane Electric Generator — A75

1988, Jan. 1 **Engr.** ***Perf. 13***
142 A75 1fr dark blue & blue .50 .35

Fauna Type of 1988

1989, Jan. 1 **Engr.**
143 A73 1.10fr Lithodes .40 .40
144 A73 3.60fr Blue petrel 1.40 .75

Fern A76

1989, Jan. 1
145 A76 2.80fr *Blechnum penna Marina* 1.00 .90

Minerals A77

1989, Jan. 1
146 A77 5.10fr Mesotype 1.75 1.75
147 A77 7.30fr Analcime 2.75 2.25

Henri and Rene Bossiere, Pioneers of the Kerguelen Isls. — A78

1989, Jan. 1
148 A78 2.20fr multicolored 1.10 .75

Kerguelen Is. Sheep — A79

1989, Jan. 1 ***Perf. 13½x13***
149 A79 2fr multicolored .75 .65

Scuba Diver, Adelie Coast — A80

1989, Jan. 1
150 A80 1.70fr dk olive bis, blue & dk grn .75 .60

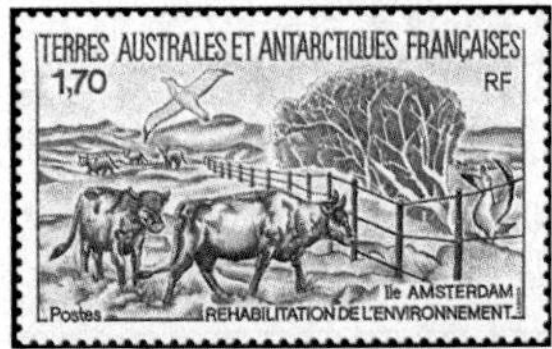
Map of Kerguelen Island, Protozoa and Copepod — A81

1990, Jan. 1 **Engr.** ***Perf. 13***
151 A81 1.10fr blk, brt blue & red brn .55 .40

Study of protista, Kerguelan Is.

Cattle on Farm, Sea Birds — A82

1990, Jan. 1
152 A82 1.70fr Prus blue, grn & brn blk .75 .60

Rehabilitation of the environment, Amsterdam Is.

Quoy and *Copendium decollata* — A83

Dumont d'Urville (1790-1842), Explorer — A84

1990, Jan. 1 ***Perf. 13½x13***
153 A83 2.20fr brt blue, blk & red brn .85 .75

Jean Rene C. Quoy (1790-1869), naturalist, navigator.

1990, Jan. 1
154 A84 3.60fr ultra & blk 1.50 1.10

Yellow-billed Albatross — A85

1990, Jan. 1 ***Perf. 13x12½***
155 A85 2.80fr multicolored 1.75 .90

Aragonite A86

1990, Jan. 1
156 A86 5.10fr deep ultra & dark yel grn 2.50 1.75

Ranunculus pseudo trullifolius — A87

1990, Jan. 1 ***Perf. 13***
157 A87 8.40fr dp bl, org & emer grn 2.90 2.75

Penguin Type of Airpost 1974

1991, Jan. 1
158 AP18 50c blue grn, bl & blk .60 .20

Postal Service at Crozet Island, 30th anniv.

Moss — A88

1991, Jan. 1 ***Perf. 13x12½***
159 A88 1.70fr gray, brn & blk .80 .65

Adm. Max Douguet (1903-1989) A89

1991, Jan. 1
160 A89 2.30fr org brn, blk & bl 1.25 .90

Lighter L'Aventure — A90

1991, Jan. 1 **Engr.** ***Perf. 13***
161 A90 3.20fr brn, grn & bl 1.50 1.25

Sea Lions — A91

1991, Jan. 1 ***Perf. 13***
162 A91 3.60fr blue & ol brn 2.25 1.40

Mordenite — A92

1991, Jan. 1
163 A92 5.20fr blk, grn bl & grn 2.50 2.00

Champsocephalus Gunnari — A93

1991, Jan. 1
164 A93 7.80fr blue & green 3.00 3.00

A94 A95

1991, Jan. 1
165 A94 9.30fr ol grn & rose red 3.75 3.50

Antarctic Treaty, 30th anniv.

1992, Jan. 1 **Engr.** ***Perf. 13***

Design: Colobanthus Kerguelensis.

166 A95 1fr bl grn, grn & brn .75 .40

Globe Challenge Yacht Race — A96

1992, Jan. 1 **Litho.**
167 A96 2.20fr multicolored 1.25 1.00

Dissostichus Eleginoides — A97

1992, Jan. 1 **Engr.**
168 A97 2.30fr blue, ol grn & red brn 1.40 1.00

Paul Tchernia A98

1992, Jan. 1 **Engr.** ***Perf. 13***
169 A98 2.50fr brown & green 1.00 1.00

Capt. Marion Dufresne (1724-1772) — A99

1992, Jan. 1 **Engr.** ***Perf. 13***
170 A99 3.70fr red, blk & bl 1.50 1.50

Supply Ship Tottan, 1951 — A100

1992, Jan. 1 **Engr.** ***Perf. 13***
171 A100 14fr blue grn, brn & bl 5.75 5.75

WOCE Program — A101

1992, Jan. 1
172 A101 25.40fr multi 11.00 10.50

Coat of Arms — A102

1992-95 **Engr.** ***Perf. 13***
173 A102 10c black .25 .20
174 A102 20c greenish blue .25 .20
175 A102 30c red .25 .20
176 A102 40c green .40 .20
177 A102 50c orange .40 .20
Nos. 173-177 (5) 1.55 1.00

Issued: 10c, 1/1/92; 20c, 30c, 1/1/93; 40c, 1/1/94; 50c, 1/2/95.

See Nos. 295-299.

Garnet A103

1993, Jan. 1 **Engr.** ***Perf. 13***
183 A103 1fr multicolored 1.25 .30

See Nos. 194, 203, 212, 222, 235, 244, 259, 279, 300.

Research Ship Marion Dufresne, 20th Anniv. — A104

Lyallia Kerguelensis A105

1993, Jan. 1
184 A104 2.20fr multicolored 1.25 .60

1993, Jan. 1
185 A105 2.30fr blue & green 1.25 .60

A106

A107

1993, Jan. 1
186 A106 2.50fr Killer whale 1.50 .70
187 A107 2.50fr Skua 1.50 .70

Explorer Type of 1979 and

Weather station, Adelie Land A108

Design: 2.50fr, Andre Prudhomme (1930-1959), Meteorologist.

1993, Jan. 1 ***Perf. 12½x13***
188 A29 2.50fr blue, blk & org 1.00 .65
189 A108 22fr org, blk & bl 8.50 6.00
a. Pair, #188-189 + label 10.00 10.00

Centriscops Obliquus — A109

1993, Jan. 1 ***Perf. 13***
190 A109 3.40fr multicolored 1.50 .90

Freighter Italo Marsano — A110

1993, Jan. 1
191 A110 3.70fr multicolored 1.60 1.00

ECOPHY Program A111

1993, Jan. 1
192 A111 14fr black, blue & brn 6.50 4.25

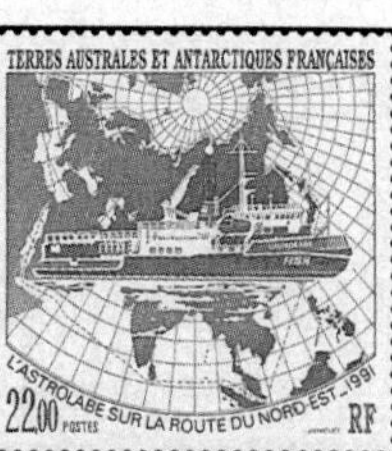

L'Astrolabe on Northeast Route, 1991 A112

1993, Jan. 1
193 A112 22fr multicolored 9.00 5.75

Mineral Type of 1993

1994, Jan. 1 **Engr.** ***Perf. 13***
194 A103 1fr Cordierite .65 .30

Felis Catus — A113

1994, Jan. 1
195 A113 2fr green & black 1.25 .50

A114

1994, Jan. 1 Engr. *Perf. 13*
196 A114 2.40fr dk brn, blk & bl 1.50 .65

A115

1994, Jan. 1
197 A115 2.80fr slate blue 1.25 .70

Robert Pommier (1919-61) A116

1994, Jan. 1
198 A116 2.80fr multicolored 1.25 .70

A117

Designs: 2.80fr, C.A. Vincendon Dumoulin (1811-58), hydrographer. 23fr, Measuring Earth's magnetic field.

1994, Jan. 1 *Perf. 12½x13*
199 2.80fr black & blue 1.25 .70
200 23fr blue & black 8.50 5.75
a. A118 Pair, #199-200 + label 10.00 10.00

Rascasse — A119

1994, Jan. 1 *Perf. 13*
201 A119 3.70fr bl grn & red brn 1.50 .95

Kerguelen of Tremarec — A120

1994, Jan. 1
202 A120 4.30fr multicolored 1.75 1.10

Mineral Type of 1993

1995, Jan. 2 Engr. *Perf. 13*
203 A103 1fr Olivine 1.00 .30

Mancoglosse Antarctique — A121

1995, Jan. 2
204 A121 2.40fr ol brn, vio & bl grn 1.25 .70

Andree (1903-90) and Edgar de la Rue (1901-91) A122

1995, Jan. 2
205 A122 2.80fr bl, red brn & mag 1.25 .85

SODAR Station — A123

1995, Jan. 2
206 A123 2.80fr vio, mag & red brn 1.25 .85

Mont D'Alsace — A124

1995, Jan. 2
207 A124 3.70fr dk bl, vio, red brn 1.75 1.10

Balaenoptera Acutorostrata — A125

1995, Jan. 2
208 A125 23fr blue, claret & ind 10.00 6.50

Sailing Ship Tamaris A126

1995, Jan. 2
209 A126 25.80fr multicolored 10.50 7.50

L'Heroine, Crozet Islands Mission, 1837 — A127

1995, Jan. 2
210 A127 27.30fr blue 11.00 7.75

Creation of the Territories, 40th Anniv. — A128

Illustration reduced.

1995, Aug. 7 Litho. *Imperf.*
Size: 143x84mm
211 A128 30fr multicolored 12.50 12.50

Mineral Type of 1993

1996, Jan. 1 Engr. *Perf. 13*
212 A103 1fr Amazonite 1.00 .30

White-chinned Petrel — A129

1996, Jan. 1
213 A129 2.40fr blue black 1.25 .70

Expedition Ship Yves de Kerguelen — A130

1996, Jan. 1
214 A130 2.80fr multicolored 1.40 .80

Benedict Point Scientific Research Station, Amsterdam Island — A131

1996, Jan. 1
215 A131 2.80fr multicolored 1.25 .80

Paul-Emile Victor (1907-1995), Polar Explorer — A132

Designs: 2.80fr, Victor crossing Greenland with sled dogs, 1936. 23fr, Victor, penguins, Dumont d'Urville Base, Adélie Land.

1996, Jan. 1
216 A132 2.80fr multicolored 1.00 .75
217 A132 23fr multicolored 10.00 6.75
a. Pair, #216-217 + label 12.00 12.00

Admiral Jacquinot (1796-1879), Antarctic Explorer — A133

1996, Jan. 1
218 A133 3.70fr dark blue & blue 1.50 1.10

Trawler Austral — A134

1996, Jan. 1 Photo. & Engr.
219 A134 4.30fr multicolored 2.25 1.40

Lycopodium Magellanicum — A135

1996, Jan. 1 Engr.
220 A135 7.70fr multicolored 3.00 2.25

Search for Micrometeorites, Cape Prudhomme — A136

1996, Jan. 1
221 A136 15fr vio, blk & grn bl 7.00 4.50

Mineral Type of 1993

1997, Jan. 1 Engr. *Perf. 13x12½*
222 A103 1fr Amethyst .75 .30

Storm Petrel — A137

1997, Jan. 1 *Perf. 13*
223 A137 2.70fr blue & indigo 1.25 .90

Rene Garcia (1915-95), Windmill A138

1997, Jan. 1
224 A138 3fr multicolored 1.25 1.00

Research Ship Marion Dufresne — A139

Illustration reduced.

Photo. & Engr.

1997, Jan. 1 *Perf. 13x12½*
225 A139 3fr multicolored 1.75 1.00

A140 A141

1997, Jan. 1 Engr. *Perf. 13*
226 A140 4fr black & brown 1.75 1.25

Jean Turquet (1867-1945).

1997, Jan. 1
227 A141 5.20fr multicolored 2.25 1.60

Church of Our Lady of Birds, Crozet Island.

A142

A143

1997, Jan. 1
228 A142 8fr multicolored 4.00 2.60

Army Health Service.

1997, Jan. 1
229 A143 29.20fr Poa Kerguelensis 12.50 9.25

French Polar Expeditions, 50th Anniv. — A144

Designs: No. 230, Greenland Expedition. No. 231, Port Martin, 1950-51, Marret Base, 1952, Adélie Land. No. 232, Dumont D'Urville, 1956, Charcot Station, Magnetic Pole, 1957.

Photo. & Engr.

1997, Feb. 28 *Perf. 13x12½*
230 A144 1fr multicolored .50 .30
231 A144 1fr multicolored .50 .30
232 A144 1fr multicolored .50 .30
a. Strip of 3, #230-232 1.50 1.50

Yves-Joseph de Kerguelen Trémarec (1734-97) — A145

3fr, Portrait. 24fr, Cook's landing at Kerguelen Island, Dec. 1776.

1997, Mar. 3 Engr. *Perf. 13*
233 3fr multicolored 1.25 .90
234 24fr multicolored 9.75 7.25
a. A145 Pair, #233-234 + label 11.00 8.25

No. 234 is 37x37mm.

Mineral Type of 1993

1998, Jan. 2 Engr. *Perf. 13*
235 A103 1fr Rock crystal .75 .25

Fisheries Management — A146

Designs: No. 236, Fishing boats. No. 237, Examining fish, performing research.

1998, Jan. 2
236 A146 2.60fr multicolored 1.40 .70
237 A146 2.60fr multicolored 1.40 .70
a. Pair, #236-237 + label 3.00 3.00

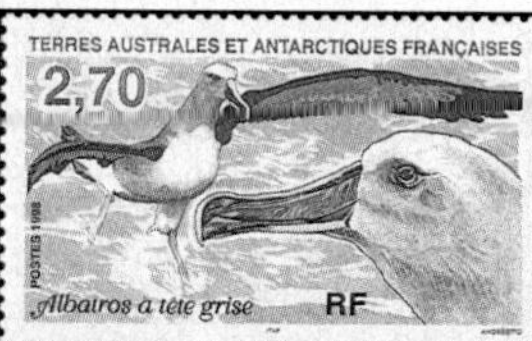

Gray-headed Albatross — A147

1998, Jan. 2
238 A147 2.70fr multicolored 1.75 .75

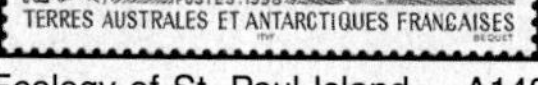

Ecology of St. Paul Island — A148

1998, Jan. 2
239 A148 3fr bl, brn & grn 1.75 .85

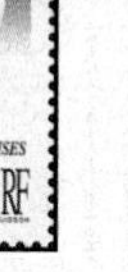

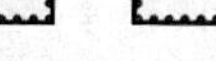

A149 A150

1998, Jan. 2 *Perf. 13x13½*
240 A149 3fr lilac, blue & black 1.60 .85

Etienne Peau, Antarctic explorer.

1998, Jan. 2
241 A150 4fr lt org, blk & red brn 1.75 1.10

Georges Laclavere (1906-94), geographer.

Mole Shark — A151

1998, Jan. 2 *Perf. 13*
242 A151 27fr multicolored 11.00 7.25

"Le Cancalais" — A152

1998, Jan. 2
243 A152 29.20fr multicolored 12.00 7.75

Mineral Type of 1993

1999, Jan. 1 Engr. *Perf. 13*
244 A103 1fr Epidote, vert. .75 .25

Chinstrap Penguin — A153

1999, Jan. 1
245 A153 2.70fr brn, blk & bl 1.10 .75

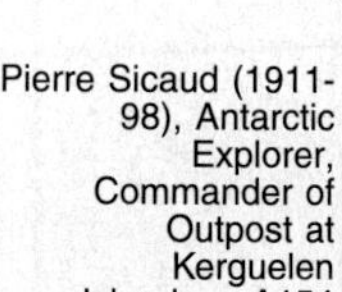

Pierre Sicaud (1911-98), Antarctic Explorer, Commander of Outpost at Kerguelen Islands — A154

1999, Jan. 1
246 A154 3fr black & green 1.25 .85

Penguins of Crozet Islands — A155

Illustration reduced.

1999, Jan. 1
247 A155 3fr multicolored 1.25 .85

Jacques-André Martin (1911-49) — A156

1999, Jan. 1
248 A156 4fr multicolored 1.60 1.10

Ray — A157

1999, Jan. 1 *Perf. 12½*
249 A157 5.20fr mag, bl & brn 2.10 1.40

F.S. Floreal — A158

1999, Jan. 1 Photo. *Perf. 13*
250 A158 5.20fr multicolored 2.10 1.40

No. 250 was printed se-tenant with label.

"Pop Cat" Program, Kerguelen Islands — A159

1999, Jan. 1 Engr.
251 A159 8fr multicolored 3.25 2.25

Study of Albatrosses on Artificial Nests
A160

1999, Jan. 1
252 A160 16fr olive, grn & blk 6.50 4.25

Amsterdam Base, Kerguelen Base, 50th Anniv. — A161

1999, Jan. 1
253 A161 3fr Amsterdam Base 1.25 .85
254 A161 24fr Kerguelen Base 9.75 6.50
a. Pair, #253-254 + label 11.00 11.00

Festuca Contracta
A162

1999, Jan. 1
255 A162 24fr dk grn, ol & bl grn 9.75 6.50

Geoleta Program — A163

1999, Jan. 1 *Perf. 13x12½*
256 A163 29.20fr blk, bl & red brn 11.75 7.75

Voyage of Marion Dufresne II — A164

a, Docked, Reunion. b, Passengers in dining salon. c, Penguins, Crozet Island. d, Postal manager of Alfred Faure, Crozet Island, vert. e, Port of France, Kerguelen Island. f, Port Couvreux, Kerguelen Island. g, Offloading stores, Port of France, Kerguelen Island. h, Port Jeanne d'arc, Kerguelen Island. i, St. Paul Island. j, Ruins of lobster cannery, St. Paul Island. k, Martin de Vivies Base, Amsterdam Island. l, Offloading cargo, Amsterdam Island.

1999, May 1 **Litho.** *Perf. 13*
257 A164 Souv. bklt., #a.-l. 65.00

Nos. 257a-257l are all non-denominated. Stamps are valid for 20 gram international letter rate. Each stamp appears on a separate booklet pane showing an enlarged design of the stamp. Booklet sold for 100fr.

Souvenir Sheet

PhilexFrance '99, World Philatelic Exhibition — A165

Antarctic postmarks on stamps: a, Malagasy Republic #280. b, Malagasy Republic #282. c, Malagasy Republic #C42. d, #21.

1999, July 2 **Litho. & Engr.** *Perf. 13*
258 A165 5.20fr Sheet of 4, #a.-d. 9.25 6.75

Nos. 258b-258c are each 40x52mm.

Mineral Type of 1993

2000, Jan. **Engr.** *Perf. 12¾x13*
259 A103 1fr Mica, *vert.* .75 .25

Puffin — A166

2000, Jan. *Perf. 13x12¾*
260 A166 2.70fr multi 1.25 .60

André Beaugé (1913-97)
A167

2000, Jan. *Perf. 12¾x13*
261 A167 3fr multi 1.25 .70

Abby Jane Morrell — A168

Sled Dog Hobbs — A170

Oceanographic Survey — A169

2000, Jan. *Perf. 13¼x13*
262 A168 4fr multi 1.60 .95

2000, Jan. *Perf. 13x12½*
263 A169 4.40fr multi 1.75 1.00

2000, Jan. *Perf. 12¾x13*
264 A170 5.20fr multi 2.10 1.25

Sleep Study — A171

Illustration reduced

2000, Jan. **Photo.** *Perf. 13x12½*
265 A171 8fr multi + label 3.25 1.90

Ship "La Perouse" — A172

2000, Jan. **Engr.** *Perf. 13x12½*
266 A172 16fr multi 6.50 3.75

Lantern Fish — A173

2000, Jan.
267 A173 24fr multi 9.75 5.50

Larose Bay — A174

2000, Jan.
268 A174 27fr multi 11.00 6.25

Explorers
A175

#269, Yves Joseph de Kerguelen-Trémarec (1734-97). #270, Jules Sébastien César Dumont D'Urville (1790-1842). #271, Raymond Rallier du Baty (1881-1978). #272, Edgar Aubert de La Rüe (1901-91). #273, Paul-Emile Victor (1907-95).

2000, Jan. *Perf. 13*

Booklet Stamps

269 A175 3fr multi 1.25 .70
270 A175 3fr multi 1.25 .70
271 A175 3fr multi 1.25 .70
272 A175 3fr multi 1.25 .70
273 A175 3fr multi 1.25 .70
a. Bklt. pane, #269-273 + 2 labels 6.50
Complete booklet, #273a 6.50

Souvenir Sheet

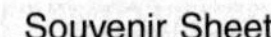

The Third Millennium — A176

No. 274: a, Penguins, Crozet Islands. b, Seals, Kerguelen Islands. c, Crustacean, Saint-Paul and Amsterdam Islands. d, Hovering vehicle, Adelie Land.

2000, Jan. **Photo.** *Perf. 13*
274 A176 3fr Sheet of 4, #a.-d. 5.00 4.25

Bird Demographic Studies — A177

Designs: 5.20fr, Bird banding. 8fr, Albatross, graph. 16fr, Emperor penguins, graph.

2000, Jan. *Perf. 13x13¼*
275 A177 5.20fr multi 2.10 1.25

Size: 50x28mm

276 A177 8fr multi 3.25 1.90
277 A177 16fr multi 6.50 3.75
a. Horiz. strip, #275-277 12.00 12.00

Relocation of Headquarters to Reunion — A178

2000, Aug. 6 **Litho.** *Perf. 13*
278 A178 27fr multi 11.00 5.50

Mineral Type of 1993

2001, Jan. 1 **Engr.** *Perf. 13x12¾*
279 A103 1fr Magnetite .75 .25

Diving Petrel — A179

2001, Jan. 1 *Perf. 13x13¼*
280 A179 2.70fr multi 1.25 .55

High Mountain Military Group A180

2001, Jan. 1 ***Perf. 13¼x13***
281 A180 3fr multi 1.25 .65

Kerguelen Arch — A181

2001, Jan. 1 ***Perf. 13***
282 A181 3fr blue gray 1.50 .65

Xavier-Charles Richert (1913-92) A182

Jean Coulomb A183

2001, Jan. 1
283 A182 3fr multi 1.25 .65

2001, Jan. 1
284 A183 4fr multi 1.60 .85

Memorial to 1874 Astronomical Observation, St. Paul Island — A184

2001, Jan. 1
285 A184 8fr brn & blk 3.25 1.75

Frigate La Fayette — A185

2001, Jan. 1 ***Perf. 13x13¼***
286 A185 16fr multi 6.50 3.50

Squid — A186

2001, Jan. 1
287 A186 24fr multi 9.75 5.00

Amateur Radio Link Between Space Station Mir and Crozet Island — A187

2001, Jan. 1 **Litho.** ***Perf. 13***
288 A187 27fr multi 11.00 5.50

Bryum Laevigatum — A188

2001, Jan. 1 **Engr.** ***Perf. 13x12½***
289 A188 29.20fr multi 11.75 6.00

Souvenir Sheet

Ships — A189

No. 290: a, Carmen. b, Austral. c, Ramuntcho. d, Samper 1.

2001, Jan. 1 ***Perf. 13x13½***
290 A189 5.20fr Sheet of 4, #a-d 8.50 4.50

Souvenir Sheet

Wildlife — A190

No. 291: a, Albatrosses. b, Emperor penguins, horiz. c, Sea lions, horiz. d, Whales.

2001, Jan. 1 **Litho.** ***Perf. 13***
291 A190 3fr Sheet of 4, #a-d 5.00 4.50

Antarctic Treaty, 40th Anniv. — A191

2001, June 23 **Engr.** ***Perf. 13x12¾***
292 A191 5.20fr dark & sky blue 2.10 1.00

Commission for the Conservation of Antarctic Marine Living Resources, 20th Anniv. — A192

2001, Oct. 22 **Litho.** ***Perf. 13***
293 A192 5.20fr multi 2.50 1.10

Voyage Booklet Type of 1999

Adélie Land: a, Boat in pack ice. b, Dumont d'Urville Base. c, Adélie penguin rookery. d, L'Astrolabe Glacier. e, Pointe Géologie Archipelago. f, Release of meteorological balloon. g, Equipment convoy. h, Helicopter transport of fresh supplies. i, Arrival of emperor penguins. j, Telecommunications center. k, Looking towards the Antarctic. l, Cape Prud'homme. m, Ship L'Astrolabe anchored. n, Dispatch of mail.

2001, Oct. 29 ***Perf. 13***
294 A164 Souvenir booklet, 2 each #a-n 65.00

Nos. 294a-294n are all non-denominated. Stamps are valid for 20 gram international letter rate. Each stamp appears ofn a separate booklet pane showing an enlarged design of the stamp and on one pane with all of the stamps and four labels found at the center of the booklet. the booklet sold for 196.78fr.

100 Cents = 1 Euro (€)

Arms Type of 1992-95 with Euro Denominations

2002, Jan. 2 **Engr.** ***Perf. 13***

295	A102	1c black	.20	.20
296	A102	2c greenish blue	.20	.20
297	A102	5c red	.20	.20
298	A102	10c green	.25	.20
299	A102	20c orange	.55	.20
		Nos. 295-299 (5)	1.40	1.00

Mineral Type of 1993 with Euro Denomination

2002, Jan. 2 **Engr.** ***Perf. 12¾x13***
300 A103 15c Nepheline, vert. .75 .20

Albatross A193

2002, Jan. 2 ***Perf. 13¼x13***
301 A193 41c multi 1.25 .50

Ship "Marion Dufresne" — A194

2002, Jan. 2 ***Perf. 13x13¼***
302 A194 46c multi 1.25 .60

1963-83 Telegraph Station, Crozet Island A195

2002, Jan. 2 **Litho.** ***Perf. 13***
303 A195 46c multi 1.25 .60

Jacques Dubois (1920-2000) A196

2002, Jan. 2 **Engr.**
304 A196 61c multi 1.60 .85

Engraved Rock, Saint Paul Island — A197

2002, Jan. 2 ***Perf. 13x13¼***
305 A197 79c multi 2.10 1.10

Kerguelen Cabbage A198

2002, Jan. 2 ***Perf. 12¼***
306 A198 €1.22 multi 3.25 1.60

Passage of the Ship "Gauss," Cent. — A199

2002, Jan. 2 ***Perf. 13x12¼***
307 A199 €2.44 multi 6.50 3.25

Crab — A200

2002, Jan. 2 ***Perf. 13x13¼***
308 A200 €3.66 multi 9.75 4.75

Pack Ice Diatoms — A201

2002, Jan. 2 Litho. ***Perf. 13***
309 A201 €4.12 multi 11.00 5.50

French Geographic Society Building, Paris — A202

2002, Jan. 2 Engr. ***Perf. 13¼x13***
310 A202 €4.45 multi + label 12.00 7.50

Cartoker Program — A203

No. 311: a, 46c, Diagram of plate tectonics. b, €3.66, Geological map of Kerguelen Island. Illustration reduced.

2002, Jan. 2 ***Perf. 13x12¼***
311 A203 Horiz. pair, #a-b, + central label 11.00 11.00

Souvenir Sheet

Olympic Games for Antarctic Animals — A204

No. 312: a, Albatrosses flying marathon. b, Langoustines diving, vert. c, Penguins riding bobsled course, vert. d, Killer whales performing synchronized swimming, vert.

2002, Jan. 2 Litho. ***Perf. 13***
312 A204 46c Sheet of 4, #a-d 5.25 5.25

Souvenir Sheet

Animals and Their Young — A205

No. 313: a, Penguins. b, Sea lions. c, Albatrosses. d, Elephant seals.

2002, Jan. 2
313 A205 79c Sheet of 4, #a-d 8.50 8.50

Introduction of the Euro A206

2002, Feb. 17
314 A206 46c blue & black 2.00 .60

Mineral Type of 1993

2003, Jan. Engr. ***Perf. 13¼***
315 A103 15c Apatite, vert. .75 .25

Lobster Processing Plant, Saint-Paul — A207

2003, Jan. ***Perf. 13x13¼***
316 A207 41c multi 1.20 .65

Luc Marie Bayle (1914-2000), Painter — A208

2003, Jan. Litho. ***Perf. 13***
317 A208 46c multi 1.25 .70

Emperor Penguins — A209

2003, Jan.
318 A209 46c multi 1.25 .70

Otice Hydroacoustic Station — A210

2003, Jan. Engr. ***Perf. 13x13¼***
319 A210 61c multi 1.60 .95

Restoration of Port Jeanne d'Arc — A211

2003, Jan. ***Perf. 13x12¼***
320 A211 79c multi 2.10 1.25

Phylica — A212

2003, Jan. ***Perf. 13x13¼***
321 A212 €1.22 multi 3.25 2.00

Ship "Bougainville" A213

2003, Jan. ***Perf. 13¼x13***
322 A213 €2.44 multi 6.50 3.75

Chub — A214

2003, Jan. Engr. ***Perf. 13x13¼***
323 A214 €3.66 multi 9.75 5.75

Ile aux Pingouins — A215

2003, Jan. ***Perf. 13x12¼***
324 A215 €3.66 black 9.75 5.75

Super Darn Antenna Array — A216

Illustration reduced.

2003, Jan. ***Perf. 13***
325 A216 €4.12 multi 11.00 6.50

Souvenir Sheet

Paintings Revised to Reflect a Less Southerly Antarctica — A217

No. 326: a, Triumph of Venus with fish and lobsters. b, King Louis XV and wife with penguins, vert. c, Jules Dumont d'Urville and wife in a grassy Adélie Land. d, Chevalier Yves de Kerguelin under umbrella, seal in pool, vert.

2003, Jan. Litho.
326 A217 46c Sheet of 4, #a-d 5.00 5.00

Protective Clothing — A218

Cold-weather outerwear from: a, 1898. b, 1912. c, 2002. d, 1980, e, 1996.

2003, Jan. Photo. ***Perf. 13¼x13***
327 Booklet pane of 5 10.50 —
a.-e. A218 79c Any single 2.10 1.25
Booklet, #327 10.50

Voyage of the Ship "Français," Cent. — A219

2003, Aug. 31 Engr. *Perf. 13x13¼*

328 Horiz. strip of 3 12.00 12.00
a. A219 79c Capt. J.-B. Charcot 2.10 1.25
b. A219 €1.22 Ship in ice, horiz. 3.25 2.00
c. A219 €2.44 Ship in harbor, horiz. 6.50 4.25

Stamp size: Nos. 328b-328c, 49x29mm.

Voyage Booklet Type of 1999

Recipes: a, Truite aux deux citrons (trout and waterfall). b, Veau d'Amsterdam à la savoyarde (cattle). c, Lapin "Volage" à la cannelle (rabbits, penguins). d, Rôti de légine de l'ile de l'est (fish). e, Civet de renne "Volcan du diable," (reindeer). f, Iles antarctiques flottantes. g, Langouste à la mode de Saint-Paul (lobster). h, Gigot de mouflon aux 5 épices et aux pommes (sheep). i, Cabot tropical (fish, ship). j, Tagine d'agneau aux épices de la Réunion (sheep). k, Moules au pastis (mussels). l, Glace à la menthe sauvage d'Amsterdam (mint plant).

2003, Nov. 6 Litho. *Perf. 13*

329 A164 Souvenir booklet, #a-l 40.00

Nos. 329a-329l are all non-denominated. Stamps are valid for 20 gram international letter rate. Each stamp appears on a separate booklet pane showing an enlarged design of the stamp. The booklet sold for €17.

Mineral Type of 1993

2004, Jan. 1 Engr. *Perf. 13¼*

330 A103 15c Chalcedony, vert. .40 .30

A220

A221

2004, Jan. 1 Engr. *Perf. 13x13¼*

331 A220 45c multi 1.10 .85

Mario Marret, director of film "Terre Adélie."

2004, Jan. 1

332 A221 50c multi 1.25 .95

Col. Robert Genty (1910-2001).

Albert Faure Base, Crozet Island, 40th Anniv. — A222

Illustration reduced.

2004, Jan. 1 Litho. & Engr.

333 A222 50c multi 1.25 .95

Péron's Dolphins — A223

2004, Jan. 1 Litho. *Perf. 13*

334 A223 75c multi 1.90 1.40

Twin Otter Flights A224

2004, Jan. 1 Photo. *Perf. 12¾*

335 A224 90c multi 2.25 1.75

Values are for stamps with surrounding selvage.

Iceberg — A225

2004, Jan. 1 Engr. *Perf. 13x13¼*

336 A225 €1.30 multi 3.25 2.40

Grave of Sailors from the Volage — A226

2004, Jan. 1 *Perf. 13¼x13*

337 A226 €2.50 multi 6.25 4.75

Krill — A227

2004, Jan. 1 *Perf. 13x13¼*

338 A227 €4 multi 10.00 7.50

Ship "Dives" — A228

2004, Jan. 1

339 A228 €4.50 multi 11.50 8.75

Souvenir Sheet

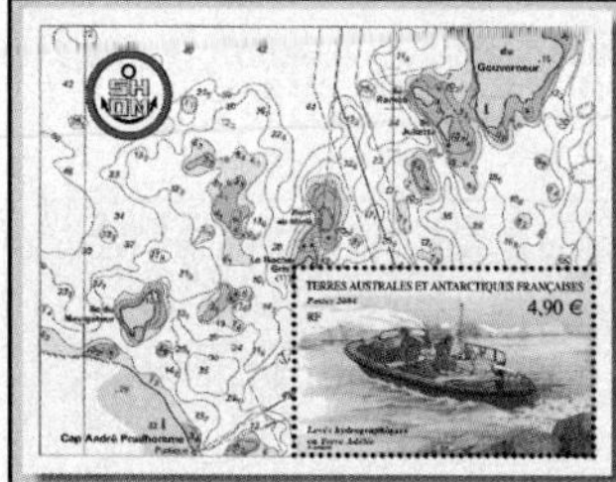

Hydrological Surveys, Adélie Land — A229

2004, Jan. 1 Litho. *Perf. 13*

340 A229 €4.90 multi 12.50 9.50

Souvenir Sheet

Imaginary "TAAFland" Theme Park — A230

No. 341: a, Whale statue, pyramidal entrance structure. b, Showgirls, seals, vert. c, Boy and girl with ice cream cones, vert. d, Woman in swimsuit, penguins.

2004, Jan. 1

341 A230 50c Sheet of 4, #a-d 5.00 3.75

Souvenir Sheet

Post Offices — A231

No. 342: a, Amsterdam Island. b, Crozet Island. c, Kerguelen Island. d, Adélie Land.

2004, Jan. 1

342 A231 90c Sheet of 4, #a-d 9.00 6.75

Penguin and Liberty Cap — A232

2004, June 26 Engr. *Perf. 13¼x13*

343 A232 €4.50 multi 11.50 11.50

AIR POST STAMPS

Emperor Penguins and Map of Antarctica — AP1

Unwmk.

1956, Apr. 25 Engr. *Perf. 13*

C1 AP1 50fr lt ol grn & dk grn 42.50 29.00
C2 AP1 100fr dl bl & indigo 35.00 25.00

Wandering Albatross — AP2

1959, Sept. 14

C3 AP2 200fr brn red, bl & blk 40.00 27.50

Adélie Penguins — AP3

1963, Feb. 11 Unwmk. *Perf. 13*

C4 AP3 50fr blk, dk bl & dp cl 42.50 32.50

Telstar Issue

Common Design Type

1963, Feb. 11

C5 CD111 50fr dp bl, ol & grn 29.00 21.00

Radio Towers, Adelie Penguins and IQSY Emblem — AP4

1963, Dec. 16 Engr.

C6 AP4 100fr bl, ver & blk 110.00 87.50

International Quiet Sun Year, 1964-65.

Discovery of Adelie Land — AP5

1965, Jan. 20 Engr. *Perf. 13*

C7 AP5 50fr blue & indigo 125.00 87.50

125th anniversary of the discovery of Adelie Land by Dumont d'Urville.

ITU Issue

Common Design Type

1965, May 17 Unwmk. *Perf. 13*

C8 CD120 30fr multi 200.00 160.00

French Satellite A-1 Issue
Common Design Type

Designs: 25fr, Diamant rocket and launching installations. 30fr, A-1 satellite.

1966, Mar. 2 Engr. *Perf. 13*
C9 CD121 25fr dk grn, choc & sl 13.50 10.00
C10 CD121 30fr choc, sl & dk grn 13.50 10.00
a. Pair, #C9-C10 + label 29.00 24.00

French Satellite D-1 Issue
Common Design Type

1966, Mar. 27
C11 CD122 50fr dk pur, lil & org 57.50 40.00

Ionospheric Research Pylon, Adelie Land — AP6

1966, Dec. 12
C12 AP6 25fr plum, bl & dk brn 32.50 17.50

Port aux Français, Emperor Penguin and Explorer — AP7

40fr, Aerial view of Saint Paul Island.

1968-69 Engr. *Perf. 13*
C13 AP7 40fr brt bl & dk gray 42.50 27.50
C14 AP7 50fr lt ultra, dk grn & blk 175.00 110.00

Issue dates: 50fr, Jan. 21; 40fr, Jan. 5, 1969.

Kerguelen Island and Rocket — AP8

Design: 30fr, Adelie Land.

1968, Apr. 22 Engr. *Perf. 13*
C15 AP8 25fr sl grn, dk brn & Prus bl 19.00 14.00
C16 AP8 30fr dk brn, sl grn & Prus bl 19.00 14.00
a. Pair, #C15-C16 + label 40.00 30.00

Space explorations with Dragon rockets, 1967-68.

Eiffel Tower, Antarctic Research Station, Ship from Paris Arms and Albatross AP9

1969, Jan. 13
C17 AP9 50fr bright blue 45.00 35.00

5th Consultative Meeting of the Antarctic Treaty Powers, Paris, Nov. 18, 1968.

Concorde Issue
Common Design Type

1969, Apr. 17
C18 CD129 85fr indigo & blue 55.00 37.50

Map of Amsterdam Island AP10

Map of Kerguelen Island — AP11

Coat of Arms AP12

Designs: 50fr, Possession Island. 200fr, Point Geology Archipelago.

1969-71 Engr. *Perf. 13*
C19 AP10 30fr brown 19.00 12.50
C20 AP11 50fr sl grn, bl & dk red 21.00 14.00
C21 AP11 100fr blue & blk 85.00 40.00
C22 AP10 200fr sl grn, brn & Prus bl 70.00 42.50
C23 AP12 500fr peacock blue 17.50 15.00
Nos. C19-C23 (5) 212.50 124.00

30fr for the 20th anniv. of the Amsterdam Island Meteorological Station.
Issued: 100fr, 500fr, 12/21; 30fr, 3/27/70; 50fr, 12/22/70; 200fr, 1/1/71.

Port-aux-Français, 1970 — AP13

Design: 40fr, Port-aux-Français, 1950.

1971, Mar. 9 Engr. *Perf. 13*
C24 AP13 40fr bl, ocher & sl grn 19.00 12.00
C25 AP13 50fr bl, grn ol & sl grn 19.00 12.00
a. Pair, #C24-C25 + label 40.00 27.50

20th anniversary of Port-aux-Français on Kerguelen Island.

Marquis de Castries Taking Possession of Crozet Island, 1772 — AP14

250fr, Fleur-de-lis flag raising on Kerguelen Is.

1972 Engr. *Perf. 13*
C26 AP14 100fr black 45.00 29.00
C27 AP14 250fr black & dk brn 100.00 45.00

Bicentenary of the discovery of the Crozet and Kerguelen Islands.
Issue dates: 100fr, Jan. 24; 250fr, Feb. 23.

M. S. Galliéni — AP15

1973, Jan. 25 Engr. *Perf. 13*
C28 AP15 100fr black & blue 25.00 17.50

Exploration voyages of the Galliéni.

"Le Mascarin," 1772 — AP16

Sailing Ships: 145fr, "L'Astrolabe," 1840. 150fr, "Le Rolland," 1774. 185fr, "La Victoire," 1522.

1973, Dec. 13 Engr. *Perf. 13*
C29 AP16 120fr brown olive 5.75 4.00
C30 AP16 145fr brt ultra 5.75 4.00
C31 AP16 150fr slate 7.00 5.00
C32 AP16 185fr ocher 9.00 6.00
Nos. C29-C32 (4) 27.50 19.00

Ships used in exploring Antarctica.
See Nos. C37-C38.

Alfred Faure Base — AP17

Design: Nos. C33-C35 show panoramic view of Alfred Faure Base.

1974, Jan. 7 Engr. *Perf. 13*
C33 AP17 75fr Prus bl, ultra & brn 8.00 5.25
C34 AP17 110fr Prus bl, ultra & brn 11.00 8.00
C35 AP17 150fr Prus bl, ultra & brn 14.00 8.00
a. Triptych, Nos. C33-C35 35.00 25.00

Alfred Faure Antarctic Base, 10th anniv.

Penguin, Map of Antarctica, Letters — AP18

1974, Oct. 9 Engr. *Perf. 13*
C36 AP18 150fr multicolored 7.00 5.50

Centenary of Universal Postal Union.

Ship Type of 1973

100fr, "Le Français." 200fr, "Pourquoi-pas?"

1974, Dec. 16 Engr. *Perf. 13*
C37 AP16 100fr brt blue 5.00 3.00
C38 AP16 200fr dk car rose 8.00 4.50

Ships used in exploring Antarctica.

Rockets over Kerguelen Islands — AP19

Design: 90fr, Northern lights over map of northern coast of Russia.

1975, Jan. 26 Engr. *Perf. 13*
C39 AP19 45fr purple & multi 7.00 4.00
C40 AP19 90fr purple & multi 9.00 5.25
a. Pair, #C39-C40 + label 19.00 13.00

Franco-Soviet magnetosphere research.

"La Curieuse" — AP20

Ships: 2.70fr, Commandant Charcot. 4fr, Marion-Dufresne.

1976, Jan. Engr. *Perf. 13*
C41 AP20 1.90fr multicolored 3.25 2.00
C42 AP20 2.70fr multicolored 5.00 3.25
C43 AP20 4fr red & multi 9.00 4.25
Nos. C41-C43 (3) 17.25 9.50

Dumont d'Urville Base, 1956 — AP21

4fr, Dumont d'Urville Base, 1976, Adelie Land.

1976, Jan.

C44 AP21 1.20fr multicolored 9.00 4.00
C45 AP21 4fr multicolored 11.00 7.25
a. Pair, #C44-C45 + label 22.50 15.00

Dumont d'Urville Antarctic Base, 20th anniv.

Capt. Cook's Ships Passing Kerguelen Island — AP22

1976, Dec. 31 Engr. *Perf. 13*

C46 AP22 3.50fr slate & blue 13.00 8.00

Bicentenary of Capt. Cook's voyage past Kerguelen Island.

Sea Lion and Cub AP23

1977-79 Engr. *Perf. 13*

C47 AP23 4fr dk blue grn ('79) 3.00 2.50
C48 AP23 10fr multicolored 10.00 9.00

Satellite Survey, Kerguelen — AP24

Designs: 70c, Geophysical laboratory. 1.90fr, Satellite and Kerguelen tracking station. 3fr, Satellites, Adelie Land.

1977-79 Engr. *Perf. 13*

C49 AP24 50c multi ('79) .90 .70
C50 AP24 70c multi ('79) .90 .70
C51 AP24 1.90fr multi ('79) 1.60 1.40
C52 AP24 2.70fr multi ('78) 2.75 2.00
C53 AP24 3fr multicolored 4.25 3.25
Nos. C49-C53 (5) 10.40 8.05

Elephant Seals — AP25

1979, Jan. 1

C54 AP25 10fr multicolored 5.50 4.50

Challenger — AP26

1979, Jan. 1

C55 AP26 2.70fr black & blue 2.00 1.75

Antarctic expeditions to Crozet and Kerguelen Islands, 1872-1876.

La Recherche and L'Esperance — AP27

1979

C56 AP27 1.90fr deep blue 1.25 1.10

Arrival of d'Entrecasteaux and Kermadec at Amsterdam Island, Mar. 28, 1792.

Lion Rock — AP28

1979

C57 AP28 90c multicolored .90 .70

Natural Arch, Kerguelen Island, 1840 — AP29

1979

C58 AP29 2.70fr multicolored 1.25 1.10

Phylica Nitida, Amsterdam Island — AP30

1979

C59 AP30 10fr multicolored 4.00 3.25

Charles de Gaulle, 10th Anniversary of Death AP31

1980, Nov. 9 Engr. *Perf. 13*

C60 AP31 5.40fr multicolored 11.00 8.00

HB-40 Castor Truck and Trailer — AP32

1980, Dec. 15

C61 AP32 2.40fr multicolored 1.25 1.00

Supply Ship Saint Marcouf — AP33

1980, Dec. 15

C62 AP33 3.50fr shown 1.60 1.10
C63 AP33 7.30fr Icebreaker Norsel 2.50 2.00

Glacial Landscape, Dumont d'Urville Sea — AP34

Chionis — AP35

Adele Dumont d'Urville (1798-1842) — AP36

Arcad III — AP37

25th Anniv. of Charcot Station — AP38

Antares — AP39

1981 Engr. *Perf. 13, 12½x13 (2fr)*

C64 AP34 1.30fr multicolored .70 .45
C65 AP35 1.50fr black .70 .50
C66 AP36 2fr black & lt brn .90 .85
C67 AP37 3.85fr multicolored 1.60 1.25
C68 AP38 5fr multicolored 1.75 1.50
C69 AP39 8.40fr multicolored 2.75 2.25
Nos. C64-C69 (6) 8.40 6.80

PHILEXFRANCE '82 Stamp Exhibition, Paris, June 11-21 — AP40

1982, June 11 Engr. *Perf. 13*

C70 AP40 8fr multicolored 5.25 5.25

French Overseas Possessions Week, Sept. 18-25 — AP41

1982, Sept. 17 Engr. *Perf. 13*

C71 AP41 5fr Commandant Charcot 1.75 1.75

Apostle Islands — AP42

1983, Jan. 3 Engr. *Perf. 13*

C72 AP42 65c multicolored .55 .35

Sputnik I, 25th Anniv. of Intl. Geophysical Year — AP43

Orange Bay Base, Cape Horn, 1883, Cent. — AP44

5.20fr, Scoresby Sound Base, Greenland, 50th anniv.

1983, Jan. 3

C73 AP43 1.50fr multicolored .60 .60
C74 AP44 3.30fr multicolored 1.75 1.75
C75 AP44 5.20fr multicolored 2.00 2.00
a. Strip of 3, #C73-C75 4.50 4.50

AP45

1983, Jan. 3

C76 AP45 4.55fr dark blue 3.75 3.00

Abstract, by G. Mathieu — AP46

Illustration reduced.

1983, Jan. 3 Photo. *Perf. 13x13½*

C77 AP46 25fr multicolored 10.00 8.00

Erebus off Antarctic Ice Cap, 1842 — AP47

Port of Joan of Arc, 1930 — AP48

1984, Jan. 1 Engr. *Perf. 13*

C78 AP47 2.60fr ultra & dk blue 1.10 1.00
C79 AP48 4.70fr multicolored 1.75 1.75

Aurora Polaris — AP49

1984, Jan. 1 Photo.

C80 AP49 3.50fr multicolored 2.00 1.25

Manned Flight Bicentenary (1983) — AP50

Various balloons and airships.

1984, Jan. 1 Engr.

C81 AP50 3.50fr multicolored 1.75 1.75
C82 AP50 7.80fr multicolored 2.75 2.75
a. Pair, #C81-C82 + label 5.00 5.00

Patrol Boat Albatros — AP51

1984, July 2 Engr. *Perf. 13*

C83 AP51 11.30fr multi 4.25 4.25

NORDPOSTA Exhibition — AP52

1984, Nov. 3 Engr. *Perf. 13*

C84 AP52 9fr Scientific Vessel Gauss 4.50 3.50

Issued se-tenant with label.

Corsican Sheep — AP53

Amsterdam Albatross AP54

1985, Jan. 1 Engr. *Perf. 13*

C85 AP53 70c Mouflons .50 .35
C86 AP54 3.90fr Diomedia amsterdamensis 1.50 1.25

La Novara, Frigate AP55

1985, Jan. 1 Engr. *Perf. 13*

C87 AP55 12.80fr La Novara at St. Paul 5.00 4.50

Explorer and Seal, by Tremois — AP56

Design: Explorer, seal, names of territories. Illustration reduced.

1985, Jan. 1 Photo. *Perf. 13x12½*

C88 AP56 30fr + label 11.00 8.50

Sailing Ships, Ropes, Flora & Fauna — AP57

1985, Aug. 6 Engr. *Perf. 13*

C89 AP57 2fr blk, brt bl & ol grn .70 .55
C90 AP57 12.80fr blk, ol grn & brt bl 3.75 3.75
a. Pair, #C89-C90 + label 5.50 5.50

French Southern & Antarctic Territories, 30th anniv. No. C90a has continuous design with center label.

Bird Type of 1986

1986, Jan. 1 Engr. *Perf. 13½x13*

C91 A56 4.60fr Sea Gulls 2.00 1.75

Antarctic Atmospheric Research, 10th Anniv. — AP58

1986, Jan. 1

C92 AP58 14fr blk, dk red & brt org 5.00 4.00

Jean Charcot (1867-1936), Explorer — AP59

1986, Jan. 1

C93 AP59 2.10fr Ship Pourquoi Pas .90 .60
C94 AP59 14fr Ship in storm 4.50 4.25
a. Pair, #C93-C94 + label 6.00 6.00

SPOT Satellite over the Antarctic — AP60

1986, May 26 Engr. *Perf. 13*

C95 AP60 8fr dp ultra, sep & dk ol grn 3.25 2.50

J.B. Charcot — AP61

1987, Jan. 1 Engr. *Perf. 13x13½*

C96 AP61 14.60fr multi 5.00 4.50

Ocean Drilling Program — AP62

1987, Jan. 1 *Perf. 13½x13*

C97 AP62 16.80fr lem, dk ultra & bluish blk 5.50 4.50

INMARSAT — AP63

1987, Mar. 2 Engr. *Perf. 13*
C98 AP63 16.80fr multi 8.00 7.50

French Polar Expeditions, 40th Anniv. — AP64

1988, Jan. 1
C99 AP64 20fr lake, ol grn & plum 8.00 6.75

Views of Penguin Is. — AP65

1988, Jan. 1
C100 AP65 3.90fr dk bl & sep 1.60 1.25
C101 AP65 15.10fr dp grn, choc brn & dk bl 5.00 5.00

See Nos. C103, C109.

Founding of Permanent Settlements in the Territories, 40th Anniv. — AP66

1989, Jan. 1 Engr. *Perf. 13½x13*
C102 AP66 15.50fr black 5.00 4.75

Island View Type

1989, Jan. 1
C103 AP65 8.40fr Apostle Islands 2.75 2.50

La Curieuse — AP68

1989, Jan. 1 *Perf. 13x12½*
C104 AP68 2.20fr multicolored .80 .70
C105 AP68 15.50fr multi, diff. 5.00 5.00
a. Pair, #C104-C105 + label 6.00 6.00

No. C105a label continues the design.

French Revolution, Bicent. — AP69

1989, July 14 Engr. *Perf. 13x12½*
C106 AP69 5fr pink, dark olive grn & dark blue 4.50 4.50

Souvenir Sheet
Perf. 13

C107 Sheet of 4 9.00 9.00
a. AP69 5fr Prus green, brt ultra & dark red 2.00 2.00

No. C107 for PHILEXFRANCE '89.

15th Antarctic Treaty Summit Conference — AP70

1989, Oct. 9 Engr. *Perf. 13*
C108 AP70 17.70fr multicolored 6.00 5.75

Island View Type

1990, Jan. 1 Engr. *Perf. 13*
C109 AP65 7.30fr Isle of Pigs, Crozet Isls. 3.00 2.40

L'Astrolabe, Expedition Team — AP72

1990, Jan. 1
C110 AP72 15.50fr dk red vio & blk 5.00 5.00

Discovery of Adelie Land by Dumont D'Urville, 150th anniv.

L'Astrolabe, Commanded by Dumont D'Urville, 1840 — AP73

1990, Jan. 1
C111 AP73 2.20fr *L'Astrolabe,* 1988 .80 .75
C112 AP73 15.50fr shown 5.00 5.00
a. Pair, #C111-C112 + label 6.50 6.50

Bird, by Folon — AP74

Illustration reduced.

1990, Jan. 1 Litho. *Perf. 12½x13*
C113 AP74 30fr multicolored 10.00 9.50

Albatross, Argos Satellite AP75

1991, Jan. 1
C114 AP75 2.10fr red brn, bl & brn 1.25 .80

Climatological Research — AP76

1991, Jan. 1 Engr. *Perf. 13*
C115 AP76 3.60fr Weather balloons, instruments 1.40 1.40
C116 AP76 20fr Research ship 7.75 7.75
a. Pair, #C115-C116 + label 10.00 10.00

Charles de Gaulle (1890-1970) — AP77

1991, Jan. 1
C117 AP77 18.80fr blk, red & bl 7.25 7.25

Cape Petrel — AP78

1992, Jan. 1 Engr. *Perf. 13*
C118 AP78 3.40fr multicolored 2.00 1.40

French Institute of Polar Research and Technology — AP79

#C120, Polar bear with man offering flowers.

1991, Dec. 16 Engr. *Perf. 13x12*
C119 AP79 15fr multicolored 5.75 5.75
C120 AP79 15fr multicolored 5.75 5.75
a. Strip, #C119-C120 + label 11.50 11.50

Christopher Columbus and Discovery of America — AP80

1992, Jan. 1 *Perf. 13*
C121 AP80 22fr multicolored 9.00 9.00

Mapping Satellite Poseidon — AP81

1992, Jan. 1 Engr. *Perf. 13*
C122 AP81 24.50fr multi 10.50 10.00

Dumont d'Urville Base, Adelie Land — AP82

Illustration reduced.

1992, Jan. 1 Litho. *Perf. 13x12½*
C123 AP82 25.70fr multi 11.50 10.50

Amateur Radio — AP83

1993, Jan. 1 Engr. *Perf. 13*
C124 AP83 2fr multicolored 1.50 .55

New Animal Biology Laboratory, Adelie Land — AP84

1993, Jan. 1
C125 AP84 25.40fr multicolored 11.00 6.75

Support Base D10 — AP85

1993, Jan. 1
C126 AP85 25.70fr ol, red & bl 11.00 7.00

Opening of Adelie Land Airfield — AP86

1993, Jan. 1
C127 AP86 30fr multicolored 11.50 8.00

Krill — AP87

1994, Jan. 1 **Engr.** ***Perf. 13***
C128 AP87 15fr black 6.00 4.00

Fishery Management — AP88

1994, Jan. 1
C129 AP88 23fr multicolored 9.00 5.75

Satellite, Ground Station — AP89

Design: 27.30fr, Lidar Station.

1994, Jan. 1
C130 AP89 26.70fr multicolored 10.00 6.50
C131 AP89 27.30fr multicolored 11.00 6.75

Arrival of Emperor Penguins — AP90

Illustration reduced.

1994, Jan. 1 ***Perf. 13x12½***
C132 AP90 28fr blue & black 10.00 7.25

Erebus Mission — AP91

1995, Jan. 2 **Engr.** ***Perf. 13***
C133 AP91 4.30fr bl, vio & slate 2.25 1.50

Moving of Winter Station, Charcot — AP92

1995, Jan. 2 **Litho.**
C134 AP92 15fr multicolored 6.25 4.25

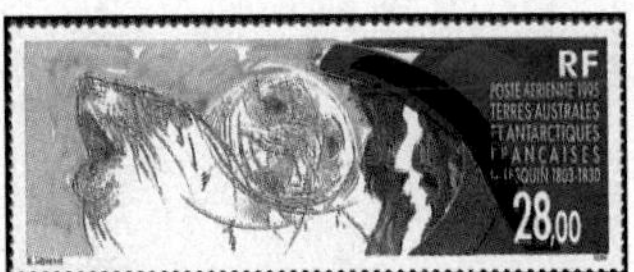

G. Lesquin (1803-30) — AP93

Illustration reduced.

1995, Jan. 2
C135 AP93 28fr multicolored 11.50 8.00

Map of East Island — AP94

1996, Jan. 1 **Engr.** ***Perf. 13***
C136 AP94 20fr multicolored 8.50 6.00

Expedition to Dome/C — AP95

1996, Jan. 1
C137 AP95 23fr dark blue 10.00 7.00

Blue Whale, Southern Whale Sanctuary — AP96

1996, Jan. 1
C138 AP96 26.70fr multicolored 12.00 8.00

Port-Couvreux — AP97

1996, Jan. 1
C139 AP97 27.30fr multicolored 11.00 8.25

Jasus Paulensis AP98

1997, Jan. 1 **Engr.** ***Perf. 12½x13***
C140 AP98 5.20fr multicolored 2.60 1.60

Racing Yacht Charentes 2 — AP99

1997, Jan. 1 **Litho.** ***Perf. 13***
C141 AP99 16fr multicolored 6.75 5.00

John Nunn, Shipwrecked 1825-29, Hope Cottage — AP100

1997, Jan. 1 **Engr.**
C142 AP100 20fr multicolored 8.50 6.25

ICOTA Program — AP101

1997, Jan. 1
C143 AP101 24fr multicolored 10.00 7.50

Harpagifer Spinosus — AP102

1997, Jan. 1
C144 AP102 27fr multicolored 11.50 8.50

EPICA Program — AP103

1998, Jan. 2 **Engr.** ***Perf. 13***
C145 AP103 5.20fr dk brn & lil 2.50 1.40

First Radio Meteorological Station, Port Aux Francais — AP104

1998, Jan. 2
C146 AP104 8fr black, blue & red 3.75 2.25

King Penguin, Argos Satellite AP105

1998, Jan. 2 ***Perf. 12½x13***
C147 AP105 16fr multicolored 6.25 4.50

Ranunculas Moseleyi AP106

1998, Jan. 2
C148 AP106 24fr multicolored 10.00 6.50

Intl. Geophysical Year, 40th Anniv. — AP107

Illustration reduced.

1998, Oct. **Engr.** ***Perf. 13x12½***
C149 AP107 5.20fr dk bl, blk & brick red 2.50 1.40

FRENCH SUDAN

'french sü-'dan

LOCATION — In northwest Africa, north of French Guinea and Ivory Coast
GOVT. — French Colony
AREA — 590,966 sq. mi.
POP. — 3,794,270 (1941)
CAPITAL — Bamako

In 1899 French Sudan was abolished as a separate colony and was divided among Dahomey, French Guinea, Ivory Coast, Senegal and Senegambia and Niger. Issues for French Sudan were resumed in 1921.

From 1906 to 1921 a part of this territory was known as Upper Senegal and Niger. A part of Upper Volta was added in 1933. See Mali.

100 Centimes = 1 Franc

See French West Africa No. 70 for stamp inscribed "Soudan Francais" and "Afrique Occidentale Francaise."

Navigation and Commerce
A1 A2

Stamps of French Colonies, Surcharged in Black

Perf. 14x13½

1894, Apr. 12 **Unwmk.**

1 A1 15c on 75c car, *rose* *3,200. 1,600.*
2 A1 25c on 1fr brnz grn, *straw* *3,500. 1,250.*

The imperforate stamp like No. 1 was made privately in Paris from a fragment of the lithographic stone which had been used in the Colony for surcharging No. 1.
Counterfeit surcharges exist.

1894-1900 **Typo.** ***Perf. 14x13½***
Name of colony in Blue or Carmine

3 A2 1c blk, *lil bl* 1.10 1.10
4 A2 2c brn, *buff* 1.75 1.75
5 A2 4c claret, *lav* 4.25 4.25
6 A2 5c grn, *grnsh* 6.75 6.75
7 A2 10c blk, *lav* 14.00 14.00
8 A2 10c red ('00) 4.50 4.50
9 A2 15c blue, quadrille paper 5.00 5.00
10 A2 15c gray, *lt gray* ('00) 5.25 5.25
11 A2 20c red, *grn* 20.00 20.00
12 A2 25c blk, *rose* 19.00 19.00
13 A2 25c blue ('00) 5.75 5.75
14 A2 30c brn, *bister* 32.50 32.50
15 A2 40c red, *straw* 25.00 25.00
16 A2 50c car, *rose* 40.00 40.00
17 A2 50c brn, *az* ('00) 9.00 9.00
18 A2 75c dp vio, *org* 35.00 35.00
19 A2 1fr brnz grn, *straw* 7.00 7.00
Nos. 3-19 (17) 235.85 235.85

Perf. 13½x14 stamps are counterfeits.
Nos. 8, 10, 13, 17 were issued in error. They were accepted for use in the other colonies.

Camel and Rider — A3

Stamps of Upper Senegal and Niger Overprinted in Black

1921-30 ***Perf. 13½x14***

21 A3 1c brn vio & vio .20 .20
22 A3 2c dk gray & dl vio .20 .20
23 A3 4c blk & blue .20 .20
24 A3 5c ol brn & dk brn .20 .20
25 A3 10c yel grn & bl grn .55 .20
26 A3 10c red vio & bl ('25) .20 .20
27 A3 15c red brn & org .20 .20
28 A3 15c yel grn & dp grn ('25) .20 .20
29 A3 15c org brn & vio ('27) 1.25 1.25
30 A3 20c brn vio & blk .20 .20
31 A3 25c blk & bl grn .70 .55
a. Booklet pane of 4
32 A3 30c red org & rose 1.10 .70
33 A3 30c bl grn & blk ('28) .45 .45
34 A3 30c dl grn & bl grn ('28) 1.40 1.40
35 A3 35c rose & vio .20 .20
36 A3 40c gray & rose .80 .65
37 A3 45c bl & ol brn .65 .55
38 A3 50c ultra & bl 1.10 .70
39 A3 50c red org & bl ('26) .85 .80
40 A3 60c vio, *pnksh* ('26) .80 .50
41 A3 65c bis & pale bl ('28) 1.25 1.25
42 A3 75c org & ol brn 1.00 .80
43 A3 90c brn red & pink ('30) 4.00 4.00
44 A3 1fr dk brn & dl vio 1.00 .95
45 A3 1.10fr gray lil & red vio ('28) 2.10 2.10
46 A3 1.50fr dp bl & bl ('30) 4.25 4.25
47 A3 2fr green & blue 1.60 1.40
48 A3 3fr red vio ('30) 8.50 8.50
a. Double overprint 125.00
49 A3 5fr violet & blk 4.50 3.75
Nos. 21-49 (29) 39.65 36.55

Type of 1921 Surcharged

1922, Sept. 28

50 A3 60c on 75c vio, *pnksh* .50 .50

Stamps and Type of 1921-30 Surcharged with New Values and Bars

1925-27

51 A3 25c on 45c .50 .50
52 A3 65c on 75c 1.40 1.10
53 A3 85c on 2fr 1.40 1.40
54 A3 85c on 5fr 1.40 1.40
55 A3 90c on 75c brn red & sal pink ('27) 1.60 1.40
56 A3 1.25fr on 1fr dp bl & lt bl (R) ('26) .95 .95
57 A3 1.50fr on 1fr dp bl & ultra ('27) .95 .95
58 A3 3fr on 5fr dl red & brn org ('27) 4.25 3.75
59 A3 10fr on 5fr brn red & bl grn ('27) 17.00 14.00
60 A3 20fr on 5fr vio & ver ('27) 21.00 19.00
Nos. 51-60 (10) 50.45 44.45

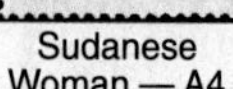

Sudanese Woman — A4

Entrance to the Residency at Djenné — A5

Sudanese Boatman — A6

1931-40 **Typo.** ***Perf. 13x14***

61 A4 1c dk red & blk .20 .20
62 A4 2c dp bl & org .20 .20
63 A4 3c dk red & blk ('40) .20 .20
64 A4 4c gray lil & rose .20 .20
65 A4 5c ind & grn .20 .20
66 A4 10c ol grn & rose .20 .20
67 A4 15c blk & brt vio .20 .20
68 A4 20c hn brn & lt bl .20 .20
69 A4 25c red vio & lt red .20 .20
70 A5 30c grn & lt grn .60 .35
71 A5 30c dk bl & red org ('40) .20 .20
72 A5 35c ol grn & grn ('38) .35 .35
73 A5 40c ol grn & pink .20 .20
74 A5 45c dk bl & red org .80 .35
75 A5 45c ol grn & grn ('40) .35 .35
76 A5 50c red & blk .20 .20
77 A5 55c ultra & car ('38) .35 .35
78 A5 60c brt bl & brn ('40) .70 .70
79 A5 65c brt vio & blk .50 .35
80 A5 70c vio bl & car rose ('40) .50 .50
81 A5 75c brt bl & ol brn 1.75 1.40
82 A5 80c car & brn ('38) .35 .35
83 A5 90c dp red & red org 1.25 .60
84 A5 90c brt vio & sl blk ('39) .50 .50
85 A5 1fr indigo & grn 5.75 1.40
86 A5 1fr rose red ('38) 3.50 1.40
87 A5 1fr car & brn ('40) .50 .50
88 A6 1.25fr vio & dl vio ('33) .50 .50
89 A6 1.25fr red ('39) .50 .50
90 A6 1.40fr brt vio & blk ('40) .60 .60
91 A6 1.50fr dk bl & ultra .50 .35
92 A6 1.60fr brn & dp bl ('40) .50 .50
93 A6 1.75fr dk brn & dp bl ('33) .60 .50
94 A6 1.75fr vio bl ('38) .60 .50
95 A6 2fr org brn & grn .60 .35
96 A6 2.25fr vio bl & ultra ('39) .65 .65
97 A6 2.50fr lt brn ('40) .95 .95
98 A6 3fr Prus grn & brn .60 .20
99 A6 5fr red & blk 1.50 .95
100 A6 10fr dl bl & grn 1.50 1.40
101 A6 20fr red vio & brn 1.90 1.75
Nos. 61-101 (41) 31.65 21.55

For surcharges see Nos. B7-B10.
For 10c and 30c, without "RF," see Nos. 120-121.

For surcharges see Nos. B7-B10.
Common Design Types pictured following the introduction.

Colonial Exposition Issue
Common Design Types

1931, Apr. 13 **Engr.** ***Perf. 12½***
Name of Country Printed in Black

102 CD70 40c deep green 2.50 2.50
103 CD71 50c violet 2.50 2.50
104 CD72 90c red orange 2.50 2.50
105 CD73 1.50fr dull blue 2.50 2.50
Nos. 102-105 (4) 10.00 10.00

Paris International Exposition Issue
Common Design Types

1937, Apr. 15 ***Perf. 13***

106 CD74 20c dp violet 1.00 1.00
107 CD75 30c dk green 1.10 1.10
108 CD76 40c carmine rose 1.10 1.10
109 CD77 50c dk brown 1.10 1.10
110 CD78 90c red 1.10 1.10
111 CD79 1.50fr ultra 1.10 1.10
Nos. 106-111 (6) 6.50 6.50

Colonial Arts Exhibition Issue
Souvenir Sheet
Common Design Type

1937 **Engr.** ***Imperf.***

112 CD77 3fr magenta & blk 5.75 *7.00*

Caillie Issue
Common Design Type

1939, Apr. 5 ***Perf. 12½x12***

113 CD81 90c org brn & org .70 .70
114 CD81 2fr brt violet .70 .70
115 CD81 2.25fr ultra & dk bl .70 .70
Nos. 113-115 (3) 2.10 2.10

New York World's Fair Issue
Common Design Type

1939, May 10

116 CD82 1.25fr carmine lake .80 .80
117 CD82 2.25fr ultra .80 .80

Entrance to the Residency at Djenné and Marshal Pétain — A7

1941 **Engr.** ***Perf. 12x12½***

118 A7 1fr green .60 *1.25*
119 A7 2.50fr blue .60 *1.25*

For surcharges, see Nos. B14-B15.

Types of 1931-40 without "RF"

1943-44 **Typo.** ***Perf. 13½x14***

120 A4 10c ol green & rose .35
121 A5 30c dk bl & red org .50

Nos. 120-121 were issued by the Vichy government in France, but were not placed on sale in French Sudan.

Stamps of French Sudan were superseded by those of French West Africa.

SEMI-POSTAL STAMPS

Curie Issue
Common Design Type
Unwmk.

1938, Oct. 24 **Engr.** ***Perf. 13***

B1 CD8075fr + 50c brt ultra 10.00 10.00

French Revolution Issue
Common Design Type

1939, July 5 **Photo.**
Name and Value Typo. in Black

B2 CD83 45c + 25c green 7.75 7.75
B3 CD83 70c + 30c brown 7.75 7.75
B4 CD83 90c + 35c red orange 7.75 7.75
B5 CD83 1.25fr + 1fr rose pink 7.75 7.75
B6 CD83 2.25fr + 2fr blue 7.75 7.75
Nos. B2-B6 (5) 38.75 38.75

Stamps of 1931-40, Surcharged in Black or Red

1941 ***Perf. 13x14***

B7 A5 50c + 1fr red & blk (R) 1.75 1.75
B8 A5 80c + 2fr car & brn 5.25 5.25
B9 A6 1.50fr + 2fr dk bl & ultra 5.25 5.25
B10 A6 2fr + 3fr org brn & grn 5.25 5.25
Nos. B7-B10 (4) 17.50 17.50

Common Design Type and

Native Officer — SP1

Aviation Officer — SP2

1941 **Photo.** ***Perf. 13½***

B11 SP1 1fr + 1fr red .85
B12 CD86 1.50fr + 3fr claret .85
B13 SP2 2.50fr + 1fr blue .85
Nos. B11-B13 (3) 2.55

Surtax for the defense of the colonies.
Issued by the Vichy government in France, but not placed on sale in French Sudan.

Petain Type of 1941
Surcharged in Black or Red

1944 **Engr.** ***Perf. 12x12½***

B14 50c + 1.50fr on 2.50fr deep blue (R) .55
B15 + 2.50fr on 1fr green .55

Colonial Development Fund.

Nos. B14-B15 were issued by the Vichy government in France, but were not placed on sale in French Sudan.

AIR POST STAMPS

Common Design Type
Perf. 12½x12

1940, Feb. 8 **Unwmk.** **Engr.**

C1 CD85 1.90fr ultra .20 .20
C2 CD85 2.90fr dark red .35 .35
C3 CD85 4.50fr dk gray green .70 .70
C4 CD85 4.90fr yellow bister .70 .70
C5 CD85 6.90fr deep orange .85 .85
Nos. C1-C5 (5) 2.80 2.80

Common Design Types

1942, Oct. 19

C6 CD88 50c carmine & bl .20 *.55*
C7 CD88 1fr brown & blk .20
C8 CD88 2fr dk grn & red brn .35
C9 CD88 3fr dk blue & scar .50
C10 CD88 5fr vio & brn red .50

Frame Engr., Center Typo.

C11 CD89 10fr ultra, ind & gray blk .80
C12 CD89 20fr rose car, mag & lt vio .95
C13 CD89 50fr yel grn, dl grn & dl bl 1.60 *2.50*
Nos. C6-C13 (8) 5.10

There is doubt whether Nos. C7-C12 were officially placed in use.

AIR POST SEMI-POSTAL STAMPS

Types of Dahomey Air Post Semi-Postal Issue
Perf. 13½x12½, 13 (#CB3)
Photo, Engr. (#CB3)

1942, June 22

CB1 SPAP1 1.50fr + 3.50fr green .50 *3.50*
CB2 SPAP2 2fr + 6fr brown .50 *3.50*
CB3 SPAP2 3fr + 9fr car red .50 *3.50*
Nos. CB1-CB3 (3) 1.50 *10.50*

Native children's welfare fund.

Colonial Education Fund
Common Design Type
Perf. 12½x13½

1942, June 22 **Engr.**

CB4 CD86a 1.20fr + 1.80fr blue & red .50 *3.50*

POSTAGE DUE STAMPS

D1

D2

Postage Due Stamps of Upper Senegal and Niger Overprinted
Perf. 14x13½

1921, Dec. **Unwmk.** **Typo.**

J1 D1 5c green .35 .35
J2 D1 10c rose .50 .50
J3 D1 15c gray .65 .65
J4 D1 20c brown .85 .85
J5 D1 30c blue .85 .85
J6 D1 50c black 1.25 1.25
J7 D1 60c orange 1.50 1.50
J8 D1 1fr violet 1.90 1.90
Nos. J1-J8 (8) 7.85 7.85

Type of 1921 Issue Surcharged

1927, Oct. 10

J9 D1 2fr on 1fr lilac rose 4.50 4.50
J10 D1 3fr on 1fr org brown 4.50 4.50

1931, Mar. 9

J11 D2 5c green .20 .20
J12 D2 10c rose .20 .20
J13 D2 15c gray .20 .20
J14 D2 20c dark brown .20 .20
J15 D2 30c dark blue .35 .35
J16 D2 50c black .35 .35
J17 D2 60c deep orange .50 .50
J18 D2 1fr violet .80 .80
J19 D2 2fr lilac rose .95 .95
J20 D2 3fr red brown 1.00 1.00
Nos. J11-J20 (10) 4.75 4.75

FRENCH WEST AFRICA

'french 'west 'a-fri-kə

LOCATION — Northwestern Africa
GOVT. — French colonial administrative unit
AREA — 1,821,768 sq. mi.
POP. — 18,777,163 (est.)
CAPITAL — Dakar

French West Africa comprised the former colonies of Senegal, French Guinea, Ivory Coast, Dahomey, French Sudan, Mauritania, Niger and Upper Volta.

In 1958, these former colonies became republics, eventually issuing their own stamps. Until the republic issues appeared, stamps of French West Africa continued in use. The Senegal and Sudanese Republics issued stamps jointly as the Federation of Mali, starting in 1959.

Catalogue values for all unused stamps in this country are for Never Hinged items.

Many stamps other than Nos. 65-72 and 77 are inscribed "Afrique Occidentale Francaise" and the name of one of the former colonies. See listings in these colonies for such stamps.

Senegal No. 156 Surcharged in Red

1943 **Unwmk.** ***Perf. 12½x12***

1 A30 1.50fr on 65c dk vio .75 .50
2 A30 5.50fr on 65c dk vio .80 .50
3 A30 50fr on 65c dk vio 2.25 1.25

Mauritania No. 91 Surcharged in Red

1943 ***Perf. 13***

4 A7 3.50fr on 65c dp grn .40 .40
5 A7 4fr on 65c dp grn .40 .40
6 A7 5fr on 65c dp grn .95 .95
7 A7 10fr on 65c dp grn .95 .95
Nos. 1-7 (7) 6.50 4.95

Senegal No. 143, 148 and 188 Surcharged with New Values in Black and Orange

1944 ***Perf. 12½x12***

8 A29 1.50fr on 15c blk (O) .40 .40
9 A29 4.50fr on 15c blk (O) .60 .60
10 A29 5.50fr on 2c brn .80 .60
11 A29 10fr on 15c blk (O) 2.00 1.25
12 CD81 20fr on 90c org brn & org 1.25 1.25
13 CD81 50fr on 90c org brn & org 2.25 1.50

Mauritania No. 109 Surcharged in Black

14 CD81 15fr on 90c org brn & org 1.25 1.25
Nos. 8-14 (7) 8.55 6.85

Common Design Types pictured following the introduction.

Eboue Issue
Common Design Type

1945 **Engr.** ***Perf. 13***

15 CD91 2fr black .50 .50
16 CD91 25fr Prussian green 1.25 1.25

Nos. 15 and 16 exist imperforate.

Colonial Soldier — A1

1945 **Litho.** ***Perf. 12½x12, 12***

17 A1 10c indigo & buff .20 .20
18 A1 30c olive & yel .20 .20
19 A1 40c blue & buff .35 .35
20 A1 50c red org & gray .35 .35
21 A1 60c ol brn & bl .35 .35
22 A1 70c mag & cit .35 .35
23 A1 80c bl grn & pale lem .35 .35
24 A1 1fr brn vio & cit .35 .35
25 A1 1.20fr gray brn & cit 2.50 1.75
26 A1 1.50fr choc & pink .45 .35
27 A1 2fr ocher and gray .50 .35
28 A1 2.40fr red & gray .70 .70
29 A1 3fr brn red & yelsh .45 .30
30 A1 4fr ultra & pink .45 .30
31 A1 4.50fr org brn & yelsh .45 .30
32 A1 5fr dk pur & yelsh .45 .30
33 A1 10fr ol grn & pink .80 .70
34 A1 15fr orange & yel 1.40 1.00
35 A1 20fr sl grn & grnsh 1.60 1.10
Nos. 17-35 (19) 12.25 9.65

Rifle Dance, Mauritania — A2

Shelling Coconuts, Togo — A6

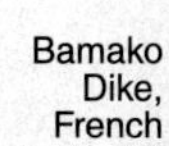

Bamako Dike, French Sudan — A3

Trading Canoe, Niger River — A4

Oasis of Bilma, Niger — A5

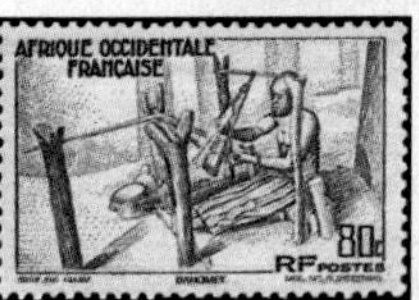

Kouandé Weaving, Dahomey A7

Donkey Caravan, Senegal A8

Crocodile and Hippopotamus, Ivory Coast — A9

Gathering Coconuts, French Guinea — A10

Peul Woman of Dienné — A12

Bamako Fountain, French Sudan A11

Bamako Market — A13

Dahomey Laborer — A14

Woman of Mauritania A15

Fula Woman, French Guinea A16

Djenné Mosque, French Sudan A17

Monorail Train, Senegal A18

Agni Woman, Ivory Coast — A19

Azwa Women at Niger River — A20

1947 Engr. Unwmk. *Perf. 12½*

36	A2	10c blue	.20	.20
37	A3	30c red brn	.20	.20
38	A4	40c gray grn	.20	.20
39	A5	50c red brn	.20	.20
40	A6	60c gray blk	.50	.35
41	A7	80c brown vio	.50	.35
42	A8	1fr maroon	.35	.20
43	A9	1.20fr dk blue grn	1.10	1.10
44	A10	1.50fr ultra	1.10	.80
45	A11	2fr red orange	.45	.20
46	A12	3fr chocolate	.50	.20
47	A13	3.60fr brown red	1.10	1.10
48	A14	4fr deep blue	.35	.20
49	A15	5fr gray green	.35	.20
50	A16	6fr dark blue	.45	.20
51	A17	10fr brn red	.80	.20
52	A18	15fr sepia	1.60	.20
53	A19	20fr chocolate	1.00	.20
54	A20	25fr grnsh blk	1.90	.35
		Nos. 36-54 (19)	12.85	6.65

Types of 1947

1948 Re-engraved

55	A6	60c brown olive	.55	.50
56	A12	3fr chocolate	.55	.35

Nos. 40 and 46 are inscribed "TOGO" in lower margin. Inscription omitted on Nos. 55 and 56.

Imperforates

Most stamps of French West Africa from 1949 onward exist imperforate in issued and trial colors, and also in small presentation sheets in issued colors.

Military Medal Issue

Common Design Type

Engraved and Typographed

1952, Dec. 1 *Perf. 13*

57 CD101 15fr multicolored 5.00 5.00

Treich Laplène and Map — A21

1952, Dec. 1 Engr.

58 A21 40fr brown lake 1.40 .25

Marcel Treich Laplène, a leading contributor to the development of Ivory Coast.

Medical Laboratory A22

1953, Nov. 18

59 A22 15fr brn, dk bl grn & blk brn .80 .20

Couple Feeding Antelopes A23

1954, Sept. 20

60 A23 25fr multicolored 1.00 .20

Gov. Noel Eugène Ballay A24

1954, Nov. 29

61 A24 8fr indigo & brown 1.10 .50

Chimpanzee — A25

Giant Pangolin A26

1955, May 2 Unwmk. *Perf. 13*

62	A25	5fr gray & dk brn	1.10	.50
63	A26	8fr brn & bl grn	1.10	.55

International Exhibition for Wildlife Protection, Paris, May 1955.

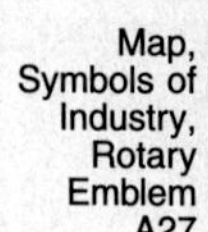

Map, Symbols of Industry, Rotary Emblem A27

1955, July 4

64 A27 15fr dark blue 1.25 .50

50th anniv. of the founding of Rotary Intl.

FIDES Issue

Mossi Railroad Upper Volta C103

1fr, Date grove, Mauritania. 2fr, Milo Bridge, French Guinea. 4fr, Cattle raising, Niger. 15fr, Farm machinery and landscape, Senegal. 17fr, Woman and Niger River, French Sudan. 20fr, Palm oil production, Dahomey. 30fr, Road construction, Ivory Coast.

1956 Engr. *Perf. 13x12½*

65	C103	1fr dk grn & dk bl grn	.55	.50
66	C103	2fr dk bl grn & bl	.95	.50
67	C103	3fr dk brn & red brn	.95	.85
68	C103	4fr dk car rose	1.25	.85
69	C103	15fr ind & ultra	1.00	.35
70	C103	17fr dk bl & ind	.95	.55
71	C103	20fr rose lake	1.10	.50
72	C103	30fr dk pur & claret	1.10	.80
		Nos. 65-72 (8)	7.85	4.90

Coffee A28a

1956, Oct. 22 *Perf. 13*

73 A28a 15fr dk blue green .55 .20

Mobile Leprosy Clinic and Maltese Cross A29

1957, Mar. 11

74 A29 15fr dk red brn, pur & red 1.25 .50

Issued in honor of the Knights of Malta.

Map of Africa — A30

1958, Feb. Unwmk. *Perf. 13*

75 A30 20fr multicolored .95 .55

6h Intl.Cong. for African Tourism at Dakar.

"Africa" and Communications Symbols — A31

1958, Mar. 15 Engr.

76 A31 15fr org, ultra & choc 1.00 .50

Stamp Day. See No. 86.

Abidjan Bridge A32

1958, Mar. 15

77 A32 20fr dk sl grn & grnsh bl 1.10 .55

Bananas A33

1958, May 19 *Perf. 13*

78 A33 20fr rose lil, dk grn & olive .95 .20

Flower Issue

Common Design Type

10fr, Gloriosa. 25fr, Adenopus. 30fr, Cyrtosperma. 40fr, Cistanche. 65fr, Crinum Moorei.

1958-59 Photo. *Perf. 12x12½*

79	CD104	10fr multicolored	.50	.20
80	CD104	25fr red, yel & grn	.95	.50
81	CD104	30fr multicolored	1.10	.80
82	CD104	40fr blk brn, grn & yel	1.60	1.10
83	CD104	65fr multicolored	1.75	.95
		Nos. 79-83 (5)	5.90	3.55

Issued: 25fr, 40fr, 1/5/59; others, 7/7/58.

Moro Naba Sagha and Map — A34

1958, Nov. 1 Engr. *Perf. 13*

84 A34 20fr ol brn, car & vio .80 .50

10th anniv. of the reestablishment of the Upper Volta territory.

Human Rights Issue

Common Design Type

1958, Dec. 10

85 CD105 20fr maroon & dk bl 1.40 1.40

Type of 1958 Redrawn

1959, Mar. 21 Engr. *Perf. 13*

86 A31 20fr red, grnsh bl & sl grn 1.75 1.75

Name of country omitted on No. 86; "RF" replaced by "CF," inscribed "Dakar-Abidjan." Stamp Day.

SEMI-POSTAL STAMPS

Red Cross Issue

Common Design Type

Perf. 14½x14

1944, Dec. Photo. Unwmk.

B1 CD90 5fr + 20fr plum 4.00 4.00

The surtax was for the French Red Cross and national relief.

Type of France, 1945, Overprinted in Black

1945, Oct. 13 Engr. *Perf. 13*

B2 SP150 2fr + 3fr orange red .60 .60

Tropical Medicine Issue

Common Design Type

1950, May 15 *Perf. 13*

B3 CD100 10fr +2fr red brn & sep 3.00 3.00

The surtax was for charitable work.

AIR POST STAMPS

Common Design Type

1945 Photo. Unwmk. *Perf. 14½x14*

C1	CD87	5.50fr ultra	1.25	.80
C2	CD87	50fr dark green	2.25	.80
C3	CD87	100fr plum	2.25	.80
		Nos. C1-C3 (3)	5.75	2.40

Victory Issue
Common Design Type

1946, May 8 Engr. *Perf. 12½*
C4 CD92 8fr violet .95 .70

Chad to Rhine Issue
Common Design Types

1946, June 6

C5	CD93	5fr brown car	1.10	1.10
C6	CD94	10fr deep blue	1.10	1.10
C7	CD95	15fr brt violet	1.25	1.25
C8	CD96	20fr dk slate grn	1.40	1.40
C9	CD97	25fr olive brn	1.75	1.75
C10	CD98	50fr brown	2.25	2.25
		Nos. C5-C10 (6)	8.85	8.85

Antoine de Saint-Exupéry, Map and Natives — AP1

Plane over Dakar — AP2

Great White Egrets in Flight — AP3

Natives and Phantom Plane — AP4

1947, Mar. 24 Engr.

C11	AP1	8fr red brown	.70	.40
C12	AP2	50fr rose violet	2.10	.70
C13	AP3	100fr ultra	8.50	3.50
C14	AP4	200fr slate gray	7.50	3.50
		Nos. C11-C14 (4)	18.80	8.10

UPU Issue
Common Design Type

1949, July 4 *Perf. 13*
C15 CD99 25fr multicolored 7.75 7.00

Vridi Canal, Abidjan — AP5

1951, Nov. 5 Unwmk. *Perf. 13*
C16 AP5 500fr red org, bl grn & dp ultra 19.00 3.50

Liberation Issue
Common Design Type

1954, June 6
C17 CD102 15fr indigo & ultra 5.75 4.25

Logging — AP6

Designs: 100fr, Radiotelephone exchange. 200fr, Baobab trees.

1954, Sept. 20

C18	AP6	50fr ol grn & org brn	2.75	.55
C19	AP6	100fr ind, dk brn & dk grn	3.50	.85
C20	AP6	200fr bl grn, grnsh blk & brn lake	11.00	2.10
		Nos. C18-C20 (3)	17.25	3.50

Gen. Louis Faidherbé and African Sharpshooter AP7

1957, July 20 Unwmk. *Perf. 13*
C21 AP7 15fr indigo & blue 1.25 1.25

Centenary of French African troops.

Gorée Island and Woman — AP8

Designs: 20fr, Map with planes and ships. 25fr, Village and modern city. 40fr, Seat of Council of French West Africa. 50fr, Worker, ship and peanut plant. 100fr, Bay of N'Gor.

1958, Mar. 15 Engr.

C22	AP8	15fr blk brn, grn & vio	.85	.65
C23	AP8	20fr blk brn, dk bl & red brn	.85	.65
C24	AP8	25fr blk vio, bis & grn	.85	.80
C25	AP8	40fr dk bl, brn & grn	1.10	.80
C26	AP8	50fr violet, brn & grn	1.75	1.10
C27	AP8	100fr brown, bl & grn	4.00	1.75
a.		Souvenir sheet of 6, #C22-C27	11.00	11.00
		Nos. C22-C27 (6)	9.40	5.75

Centenary of Dakar.

Woman Playing Native Harp — AP9

1958, Dec. 1 Unwmk. *Perf. 13*
C28 AP9 20fr red brn, blk & gray .95 .55

Inauguration of Nouakchott as capital of Mauritania.

POSTAGE DUE STAMPS

D1

1947 Engr. Unwmk. *Perf. 13*

J1	D1	10c red	.20	.20
J2	D1	30c deep orange	.20	.20
J3	D1	50c greenish blk	.20	.20
J4	D1	1fr carmine	.20	.20
J5	D1	2fr emerald	.25	.25
J6	D1	3fr red lilac	.50	.50
J7	D1	4fr deep ultra	.60	.60
J8	D1	5fr red brown	1.10	1.10
J9	D1	10fr peacock blue	1.75	1.75
J10	D1	20fr sepia	3.00	3.00
		Nos. J1-J10 (10)	8.00	8.00

OFFICIAL STAMPS

Mask — O1

Designs: Various masks.

Perf. 14x13
1958, June 2 Typo. Unwmk.

O1	O1	1fr dk brn red	.55	.45
O2	O1	3fr brt green	.35	.35
O3	O1	5fr crim rose	.35	.20
O4	O1	10fr light ultra	.50	.20
O5	O1	20fr bright red	.85	.35
O6	O1	25fr purple	.70	.35
O7	O1	30fr green	1.40	.90
O8	O1	45fr gray black	1.90	1.00
O9	O1	50fr dark red	2.25	.75
O10	O1	65fr brt ultra	2.75	.75
O11	O1	100fr olive bister	5.75	1.10
O12	O1	200fr deep green	12.50	3.00
		Nos. O1-O12 (12)	29.85	9.40

FUJEIRA

fü-'jï-rə

LOCATION — Oman Peninsula, Arabia, on Persian Gulf

GOVT. — Sheikdom under British protection

Fujeira is one of six Persian Gulf sheikdoms to join the United Arab Emirates which proclaimed independence Dec. 2, 1971. See United Arab Emirates.

100 Naye Paise = 1 Rupee

Catalogue values for all unused stamps in this country are for Never Hinged items.

Sheik Hamad bin Mohammed al Sharqi and Grebe — A1

Sheik and: 2np, 50np, Arabian oryx. 3np, 70np, Hoopoe. 4np, 1r, Wild ass. 5np, 1.50r, Herons in flight. 10np, 2r, Arabian horses. 15np, 3r, Leopard. 20np, 5r, Camels. 30np, 10r, Hawks.

Photo. & Litho.
1964 Unwmk. *Perf. 14*
Size: 36x24mm

1	A1	1np gold & multi	.20	.20
2	A1	2np gold & multi	.20	.20
3	A1	3np gold & multi	.20	.20
4	A1	4np gold & multi	.20	.20
5	A1	5np gold & multi	.20	.20
6	A1	10np gold & multi	.20	.20
7	A1	15np gold & multi	.20	.20
8	A1	20np gold & multi	.20	.20
9	A1	30np gold & multi	.20	.20
		Size: 43x28mm		
10	A1	40np gold & multi	.20	.20
11	A1	50np gold & multi	.20	.20
12	A1	70np gold & multi	.25	.20
13	A1	1r gold & multi	.30	.20
14	A1	1.50r gold & multi	.60	.20
15	A1	2r gold & multi	.80	.20
		Size: 53½x35mm		
16	A1	3r gold & multi	1.00	.25
17	A1	5r gold & multi	1.60	.35
18	A1	10r gold & multi	4.00	.50
		Nos. 1-18 (18)	10.75	4.10

Issued: 20np, 30np, 70np, 1.50r, 3r, 10r, Nov. 14; others, Sept. 22.

Sheik Hamad and Shot Put A2

1964, Dec. 6 *Perf. 14*
Size: 43x28mm

19	A2	25np shown	.20	.20
20	A2	50np Discus	.20	.20
21	A2	75np Fencing	.20	.20
22	A2	1r Boxing	.25	.20
23	A2	1.50r Relay race	.35	.20
24	A2	2r Soccer	.40	.25
		Size: 53½x35mm		
25	A2	3r Pole vaulting	.80	.40
26	A2	5r Hurdling	2.00	.50
27	A2	7.50r Equestrian	3.25	.75
		Nos. 19-27 (9)	7.65	2.90

18th Olympic Games, Tokyo, 10/10-25/64.

John F. Kennedy — A3

Kennedy: 10np, As sailor in the Pacific. 15np, As naval lieutenant. 20np, On speaker's rostrum. 25np, Sailing with family. 50np, With crowd of people. 1r, With Mrs. Kennedy, Lyndon B. Johnson. 2r, With Eisenhower on White House porch. 3r, With Mrs. Kennedy & Caroline. 5r, Portrait.

1965, Feb. 23 Photo. *Perf. 13½*
Size: 29x44mm
Black Design with Gold Inscriptions

28	A3	5np pale gray	.20	.20
29	A3	10np pale yellow	.20	.20
30	A3	15np pink	.20	.20
31	A3	20np pale greenish gray	.20	.20
32	A3	25np pale blue	.20	.20
33	A3	50np pale rose	.20	.20
		Size: 33x51mm		
34	A3	1r pale gray	.65	.20
35	A3	2r pale green	1.10	.25
36	A3	3r pale gray	1.60	.35
37	A3	5r pale yellow	2.25	.50
		Nos. 28-37 (10)	6.80	2.50

Pres. John F. Kennedy (1917-1963). A souvenir sheet contains 2 29x44mm stamps similar to Nos. 36-37 with pale blue (3r) and pale rose (5r) backgrounds.

Nos. 28-37 exist imperf.

AIR POST STAMPS

Arabian Oryx AP1

Photo. & Litho.

1965, Aug. 16 Unwmk. *Perf. 13½*

Size: 43x28mm

C1	AP1	15np Grebe	.25	.20
C2	AP1	25np shown	.25	.20
C3	AP1	35np Hoopoe	.35	.20
C4	AP1	50np Wild ass	.35	.20
C5	AP1	75np Herons in flight	.40	.20
C6	AP1	1r Arabian horses	.40	.20

Size: 53½x35mm

C7	AP1	2r Leopard	.80	.20
C8	AP1	3r Camels	1.25	.25
C9	AP1	5r Hawks	3.25	.50
		Nos. C1-C9 (9)	7.30	2.15

AIR POST OFFICIAL STAMPS

Type of Air Post Issue, 1965

Photo. & Litho.

1965, Nov. 10 Unwmk. *Perf. 13½*

Size: 43x28mm

CO1	AP1	75np Arabian horses	.40	.20

Perf. 13

Size: 53½x35mm

CO2	AP1	2r Leopard	.60	.30
CO3	AP1	3r Camels	1.40	.40
CO4	AP1	5r Hawks	2.75	.50
		Nos. CO1-CO4 (4)	5.15	1.40

OFFICIAL STAMPS

Type of Air Post Issue, 1965

Photo. & Litho.

1965, Oct. 14 Unwmk. *Perf. 13½*

Size: 43x28mm

O1	AP1	25np Grebe	.20	.20
O2	AP1	40np Arabian oryx	.20	.20
O3	AP1	50np Hoopoe	.20	.20
O4	AP1	75np Wild ass	.25	.20
O5	AP1	1r Herons in flight	.50	.20
		Nos. O1-O5 (5)	1.35	1.00

FUNCHAL

fün-'shäl

LOCATION — A city and administrative district in the Madeira island group in the Atlantic Ocean northwest of Africa

GOVT. — A part of the Republic of Portugal

POP. — 150,574 (1900)

Postage stamps of Funchal were superseded by those of Madeira. These, in turn, were displaced by the stamps of Portugal.

1000 Reis = 1 Milreis

King Carlos

A1 A2

Perf. 11½, 12½, 13½

1892-93 Typo. Unwmk.

1	A1	5r yellow	3.00	1.50
a.		Diagonal half used as 2½r on entire newspaper		5.00
b.		Perf. 11½	4.00	2.75
2	A1	10r red violet	2.50	1.50
3	A1	15r chocolate	3.25	2.50
4	A1	20r lavender	3.75	2.10
a.		Perf. 13½	8.75	6.25
5a	A1	25r dark green	4.75	1.00
6	A1	50r ultra	4.75	2.10
a.		Perf. 13½	8.75	5.50
7	A1	75r carmine	7.00	5.50
8	A1	80r yel green	14.00	9.50
a.		Perf. 13½	17.50	12.00
9	A1	100r brn, *yel* ('93)	9.00	4.00
a.		Diagonal half used as 50r on cover		100.00
10	A1	150r car, *rose* ('93)	52.50	26.00
11	A1	200r dk bl, *bl* ('93)	60.00	37.50
12	A1	300r dk bl, *sal* ('93)	60.00	47.50
		Nos. 1-12 (12)	224.50	140.70

Nos. 1-12 were printed on both enamel-surfaced and chalky papers. Values are for the most common varieties. For detailed listings, see the *Scott Classic Specialized Catalogue.*

The reprints of this issue have shiny white gum and clean-cut perforation 13½. The shades differ from those of the originals and the uncolored paper is thin.

1897-1905 *Perf. 12*

Name and Value in Black except Nos. 25 and 34

13	A2	2½r gray	.50	.35
14	A2	5r orange	.50	.35
15	A2	10r light green	.50	.35
16	A2	15r brown	5.75	4.00
17	A2	15r gray grn ('99)	3.25	2.25
18	A2	20r gray vio	1.40	.75
19	A2	25r sea green	2.75	.75
20	A2	25r car rose ('99)	1.40	.55
a.		Booklet pane of 6	—	
21	A2	50r dark blue	6.00	4.00
a.		Perf. 12½	14.50	7.25
22	A2	50r ultra ('05)	1.50	.90
23	A2	65r slate blue ('98)	1.25	.90
24	A2	75r rose	1.40	.95
25	A2	75r brn & red, *yel* ('05)	2.00	1.40
26	A2	80r violet	1.40	1.10
27	A2	100r dark blue, *blue*	1.40	1.10
a.		Diagonal half used as 50r on cover		—
28	A2	115r org brn, *pink* ('98)	2.25	1.40
29	A2	130r gray brown, *buff* ('98)	2.25	1.40
30	A2	150r lt brn, *buff*	2.75	1.25
31	A2	180r sl, *pnksh* ('98)	2.25	1.40
32	A2	200r red vio, *pale lil*	3.00	2.10
33	A2	300r blue, *rose*	3.00	2.10
34	A2	500r blk & red, *bl*	3.50	2.40
a.		Perf. 12½	11.50	7.75
		Nos. 13-34 (22)	50.00	31.75

Pronunciation Symbols

ə .... banana, collide, abut

ˈə, ˌə .... humdrum, abut

ə .... immediately preceding \l\, \n\, \m\, \ŋ\, as in battle, mitten, eaten, and sometimes open \ˈō-p^{ə}m\, lock and key \-^{ə}ŋ-\; immediately following \l\, \m\, \r\, as often in French table, prisme, titre

ər .... further, merger, bird

ˈər- / ˈə-r .... as in two different pronunciations of hurry \ˈhər-ē, ˈhə-rē\

a .... mat, map, mad, gag, snap, patch

ā .... day, fade, date, aorta, drape, cape

ä .... bother, cot, and, with most American speakers, father, cart

ȧ .... father as pronounced by speakers who do not rhyme it with *bother*; French patte

aů .... now, loud, out

b .... baby, rib

ch .... chin, nature \ˈnā-chər\

d .... did, adder

e .... bet, bed, peck

ˈē, ˌē .... beat, nosebleed, evenly, easy

ē .... easy, mealy

f .... fifty, cuff

g .... go, big, gift

h .... hat, ahead

hw .... whale as pronounced by those who do not have the same pronunciation for both *whale* and *wail*

i .... tip, banish, active

ī .... site, side, buy, tripe

j .... job, gem, edge, join, judge

k .... kin, cook, ache

k͟ .... German ich, Buch; one pronunciation of loch

l .... lily, pool

m .... murmur, dim, nymph

n .... no, own

^{n} .... indicates that a preceding vowel or diphthong is pronounced with the nasal passages open, as in French *un bon vin blanc* \œ^{n} -bō^{n} -va^{n} -blä^{n}\

ŋ .... sing \ˈsiŋ\, singer \ˈsiŋ-ər\, finger \ˈfiŋ-gər\, ink \ˈiŋk \

ō .... bone, know, beau

ȯ .... saw, all, gnaw, caught

œ .... French boeuf, German Hölle

œ̄ .... French feu, German Höhle

ȯi .... coin, destroy

p .... pepper, lip

r .... red, car, rarity

s .... source, less

sh .... as in shy, mission, machine, special (actually, this is a single sound, not two); with a hyphen between, two sounds as in *grasshopper* \ˈgras-ˌhä-pər\

t .... tie, attack, late, later, latter

th .... as in thin, ether (actually, this is a single sound, not two); with a hyphen between, two sounds as in *knighthood* \ˈnīt-ˌhu̇d\

t͟h .... then, either, this (actually, this is a single sound, not two)

ü .... rule, youth, union \ˈyün-yən\, few \ˈfyü\

u̇ .... pull, wood, book, curable \ˈkyu̇r-ə-bəl\, fury \ˈfyu̇r-ē\

ue .... German füllen, hübsch

ue̅ .... French rue, German fühlen

v .... vivid, give

w .... we, away

y .... yard, young, cue \ˈkyü\, mute \ˈmyüt\, union \ˈyün-yən\

^{y} .... indicates that during the articulation of the sound represented by the preceding character the front of the tongue has substantially the position it has for the articulation of the first sound of *yard*, as in French *digne* \dēn^{y}\

z .... zone, raise

zh .... as in vision, azure \ˈa-zhər\ (actually, this is a single sound, not two); with a hyphen between, two sounds as in *hogshead* \ˈhȯgz-ˌhed, ˈhägz-\

\ .... slant line used in pairs to mark the beginning and end of a transcription: \ˈpen\

ˈ .... mark preceding a syllable with primary (strongest) stress: \ˈpen-mən-ˌship\

ˌ .... mark preceding a syllable with secondary (medium) stress: \ˈpen-mən-ˌship\

\- .... mark of syllable division

( ) .... indicate that what is symbolized between is present in some utterances but not in others: *factory* \ˈfak-t(ə-)rē\

÷ .... indicates that many regard as unacceptable the pronunciation variant immediately following: *cupola* \ˈkyü-pə-lə, ÷-ˌlō\

Illustrated Identifier

This section pictures stamps or parts of stamp designs that will help identify postage stamps that do not have English words on them.

Many of the symbols that identify stamps of countries are shown here as well as typical examples of their stamps.

See the Index and Identifier on the previous pages for stamps with inscriptions such as "sen," "posta," "Baja Porto," "Helvetia," "K.S.A.", etc.

Linn's Stamp Identifier is now available. The 144 pages include more 2,000 inscriptions and over 500 large stamp illustrations. Available from Linn's Stamp News, P.O. Box 29, Sidney, OH 45365-0029.

1. HEADS, PICTURES AND NUMERALS

GREAT BRITAIN

Great Britain stamps never show the country name, but, except for postage dues, show a picture of the reigning monarch.

Victoria

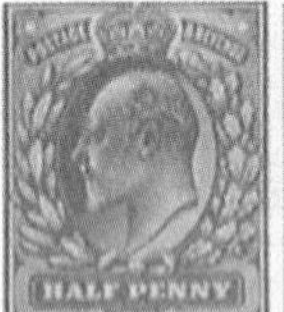

Edward VII George V Edward VIII

George VI

Elizabeth II

Some George VI and Elizabeth II stamps are surcharged in annas, new paisa or rupees. These are listed under Oman.

Silhouette (sometimes facing right, generally at the top of stamp)

The silhouette indicates this is a British stamp. It is not a U.S. stamp.

VICTORIA

Queen Victoria

INDIA

Other stamps of India show this portrait of Queen Victoria and the words "Service" and "Annas."

AUSTRIA

YUGOSLAVIA

(Also BOSNIA & HERZEGOVINA if imperf.)

BOSNIA & HERZEGOVINA

Denominations also appear in top corners instead of bottom corners.

HUNGARY

Another stamp has posthorn facing left

BRAZIL

AUSTRALIA

Kangaroo and Emu

GERMANY

Mecklenburg-Vorpommern

SWITZERLAND

PALAU

2. ORIENTAL INSCRIPTIONS

CHINA

Any stamp with this one character is from China (Imperial, Republic or People's Republic).
This character appears in a four-character overprint on stamps of Manchukuo. These stamps are local provisionals, which are unlisted. Other overprinted Manchukuo stamps show this character, but have more than four characters in the overprints. These are listed in People's Republic of China.

Some Chinese stamps show the Sun.

Most stamps of Republic of China show this series of characters.

Stamps with the China character and this character are from People's Republic of China. 人

中国人民邮政

Calligraphic form of People's Republic of China

(一)	(二)	(三)	(四)	(五)	(六)
1	2	3	4	5	6
(七)	(八)	(九)	(十)	(一十)	(二十)
7	8	9	10	11	12

Chinese stamps without China character

REPUBLIC OF CHINA

PEOPLE'S REPUBLIC OF CHINA

Mao Tse-tung

MANCHUKUO

Temple Emperor Pu-Yi

The first 3 characters are common to many Manchukuo stamps.

The last 3 characters are common to other Manchukuo stamps.

Orchid Crest

Manchukuo stamp without these elements

JAPAN

Chrysanthemum Crest Country Name

Japanese stamps without these elements

The number of characters in the center and the design of dragons on the sides will vary.

RYUKYU ISLANDS

Country Name

PHILIPPINES (Japanese Occupation)

Country Name

NORTH BORNEO (Japanese Occupation)

Indicates Japanese Occupation Country Name

MALAYA (Japanese Occupation)

Indicates Japanese Occupation Country Name

BURMA

Union of Myanmar

Union of Myanmar

(Japanese Occupation)

Indicates Japanese Occupation Country Name

Other Burma Japanese Occupation stamps without these elements

Burmese Script

KOREA

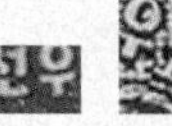

These two characters, in any order, are common to stamps from the Republic of Korea (South Korea) or of the People's Democratic Republic of Korea (North Korea).

This series of four characters can be found on the stamps of both Koreas. Most stamps of the Democratic People's Republic of Korea (North Korea) have just this inscription.

Indicates Republic of Korea (South Korea)

South Korean postage stamps issed after 1952 do not show currency expressed in Latin letters. Stamps wiith "HW," "HWAN," "WON," "WN," "W" or "W" with two lines through it, if not illustrated in listings of stamps before this date, are revenues. North Korean postage stamps do not have currency expressed in Latin letters.

Yin Yang appears on some stamps.

THAILAND

Country Name

King Chulalongkorn

King Prajadhipok and Chao P'ya Chakri

3. CENTRAL AND EASTERN ASIAN INSCRIPTIONS

INDIA - FEUDATORY STATES

Alwar

Bhor

Bundi

Similar stamps come with different designs in corners and differently drawn daggers (at center of circle).

Dhar

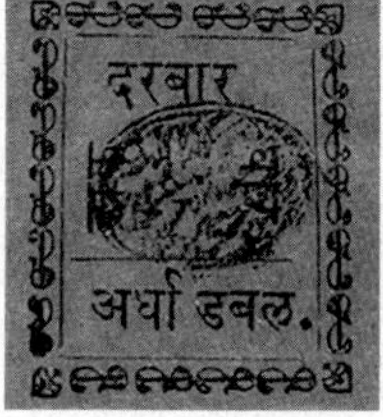

Faridkot

Hyderabad

Similar stamps exist with straight line frame around stamp, and also with different central design which is inscribed "Postage" or "Post & Receipt."

Indore

Jhalawar

A similar stamp has the central figure in an oval.

Nandgaon

Nowanuggur

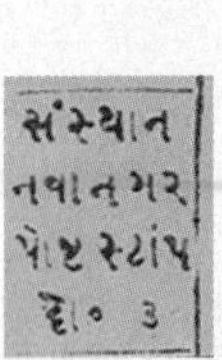

Poonch

Similar stamps exist in various sizes

Rajpeepla

Soruth

BANGLADESH

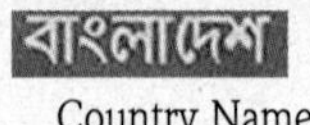

Country Name

NEPAL

Similar stamps are smaller, have squares in upper corners and have five or nine characters in central bottom panel.

TANNU TUVA

ISRAEL

GEORGIA

This inscription is found on other pictorial stamps.

Country Name

ARMENIA

The four characters are found somewhere on pictorial stamps. On some stamps only the middle two are found.

4. AFRICAN INSCRIPTIONS

ETHIOPIA

5. ARABIC INSCRIPTIONS

١ ٢ ٣ ٤ ٥
1 2 3 4 5

٦ ٧ ٨ ٩ ٠
6 7 8 9 0

AFGHANISTAN

Many early Afghanistan stamps show Tiger's head, many of these have ornaments protruding from outer ring, others show inscriptions in black.

Arabic Script

Mosque Gate & Crossed Cannons
The four characters are found somewhere on pictorial stamps. On some stamps only the middle two are found.

BAHRAIN

EGYPT

Postage

INDIA - FEUDATORY STATES

Jammu & Kashmir

Text and thickness of ovals vary. Some stamps have flower devices in corners.

India-Hyderabad

IRAN

Country Name

Royal Crown

Lion with Sword

Symbol

IRAQ

JORDAN

LEBANON

Similar types have denominations at top and slightly different design.

LIBYA

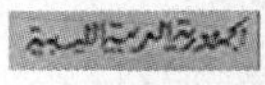

Country Name in various styles

Other Libya stamps show Eagle and Shield (head facing either direction) or Red, White and Black Shield (with or without eagle in center).

Without Country Name

SAUDI ARABIA

Tughra (Central design)

Palm Tree and Swords

SYRIA

THRACE

YEMEN

PAKISTAN

PAKISTAN - BAHAWALPUR

Country Name in top panel, star and crescent

TURKEY

Star & Crescent is a device found on many Turkish stamps, but is also found on stamps from other Arabic areas (see Pakistan-Bahawalpur)

Tughra (similar tughras can be found on stamps of Turkey in Asia, Afghanistan and Saudi Arabia)

Mohammed V

Mustafa Kemal

Plane, Star and Crescent

TURKEY IN ASIA

Other Turkey in Asia pictorials show star & crescent.
Other stamps show tughra shown under Turkey.

6. GREEK INSCRIPTIONS

GREECE

Country Name in various styles
(Some Crete stamps overprinted with the Greece country name are listed in Crete.)

Lepta

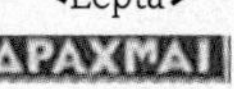

Drachma Drachmas Lepton

Abbreviated Country Name ΕΛΛ

Other forms of Country Name

No country name

CRETE

Country Name

These words are on other stamps

Grosion

Crete stamps with a surcharge that have the year "1922" are listed under Greece.

EPIRUS **IONIAN IS.**

Country Name

7. CYRILLIC INSCRIPTIONS

RUSSIA

Postage Stamp

Imperial Eagle

Postage in various styles

Abbreviation for Kopeck

Abbreviation for Ruble

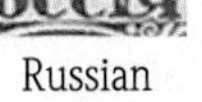

Russian

Abbreviation for Russian Soviet Federated Socialist Republic

RSFSR stamps were overprinted (see below)

Abbreviation for Union of Soviet Socialist Republics

This item is footnoted in Latvia

RUSSIA - Army of the North

"OKCA"

RUSSIA - Wenden

RUSSIAN OFFICES IN THE TURKISH EMPIRE

These letters appear on other stamps of the Russian offices.

The unoverprinted version of this stamp and a similar stamp were overprinted by various countries (see below).

ARMENIA

BELARUS

FAR EASTERN REPUBLIC

Country Name

SOUTH RUSSIA

Country Name

FINLAND

Circles and Dots on stamps similar to Imperial Russia issues

BATUM

Forms of Country Name

TRANSCAUCASIAN FEDERATED REPUBLICS

Abbreviation for Country Name

KAZAKHSTAN

ҚАЗАҚСТАН

Country Name

KYRGYZSTAN

КЫРГЫЗСТАН

Country Name

ROMANIA

TADJIKISTAN

Country Name & Abbreviation

UKRAINE

Country Name in various forms

The trident appears on many stamps, usually as an overprint.

Abbreviation for Ukrainian Soviet Socialist Republic

WESTERN UKRAINE

Abbreviation for Country Name

AZERBAIJAN

AZƏRBAYCAN

Country Name

А.С.С.Р. Abbreviation for Azerbaijan Soviet Socialist Republic

MONTENEGRO

ЦРНЕГОРЕ

ЦРНА ГОРА

Country Name in various forms

ЦР.ГОРЕ

Abbreviation for country name

No country name (A similar Montenegro stamp without country name has same vignette.)

SERBIA

СРПСКА СРБИЈА

Country Name in various forms

СРП. К.С.

Abbreviation for country name

No country name

SERBIA & MONTENEGRO

YUGOSLAVIA

Showing country name

No Country Name

MACEDONIA

МАКЕДОНИЈА

МАКЕДОНИЈА

Country Name

МАКЕДОНСКИ

Different form of Country Name

BOSNIA & HERZEGOVINA (Serb Administration)

РЕПУБЛИКА СРПСКА

Country Name

РЕПУБЛИКЕ СРПСКЕ ПТТ

Different form of Country Name

No Country Name

BULGARIA

Country Name Postage

Stotinka

Stotinki (plural) Abbreviation for Stotinki

Country Name in various forms and styles

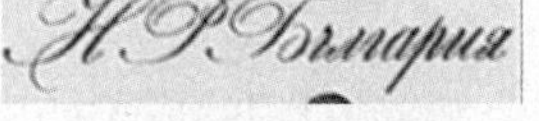

No country name

Abbreviation for Lev, leva

MONGOLIA

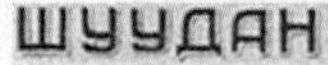

Country name in one word Tugrik in Cyrillic

Country name in two words Mung in Cyrillic

Mung in Mongolian

Tugrik in Mongolian

Arms

No Country Name

NEW COUNTRIES TO COLLECT

SCOTT ALBUM SETS

Here's an economical and easy way to get started collecting a new country. These money-saving album sets feature everything you need to get started including complete sets of pages, all the binders you need to house the collection and the handsome self-adhesive binder labels. It's an easy and simple way to get started and save a ton of money!

**Set features Universal binders.*

Item		Retail	AA*
ARGENTINA ALBUM SET			
*642SET	1858-2003	$258.99	**$161.99**
ARMENIA ALBUM SET			
642ARSET	1919-2002	$124.99	**$89.99**
AUSTRALIA ALBUM SET			
210SET	1850-2003	$329.99	**$229.99**
AUSTRALIA DEPENDENCIES ALBUM SET			
211SET	1901-2003	$359.99	**$249.99**
AUSTRIA ALBUM SET			
*300SET	1850-2003	$250.99	**$174.99**
AZERBAIJAN ALBUM SET			
642AZSET	1919-2003	$149.99	**$99.99**
BALTIC STATES ALBUM SET			
361SET	1918-2003	$199.99	**$129.99**
BANGLADESH ALBUM SET			
702SET	1919-2003	$169.99	**$99.99**
BELARUS ALBUM SET			
362BLSET	1992-2003	$139.99	**$94.99**
BELGIUM ALBUM SET			
303SET	1849-2003	$399.99	**$279.99**
BELIZE ALBUM SET			
261SET	1973-2003	$174.99	**$109.99**
BOLIVIA ALBUM SET			
643SET	1868-2002	$179.99	**$115.99**
BOSNIA & HERZEGOVINA ALBUM SET			
718SET	1879-2003	$149.99	**$99.99**
BRAZIL ALBUM SET			
644SET	1843-2003	$259.99	**$161.99**
CANADA ALBUM SET			
240SET	1851-2003	$254.99	**$189.99**
CHILE ALBUM SET			
*480SET	1878-1950	$134.99	**$99.99**
CHINA ALBUM SET			
361SET	1918-2003	$199.99	**$129.99**
COLOMBIA ALBUM SET			
646SET	1856-2003	$249.99	**$149.99**
CYPRUS ALBUM SET			
203SET	1880-2003	$149.99	**$99.99**
DENMARK ALBUM SET			
345SET	1855-2003	$179.99	**$127.99**
DOMINICA ALBUM SET			
261DMSET	1874-2003	$419.99	**$249.99**
FALKLAND ISLANDS ALBUM SET			
261FISET	1868-2002	$179.99	**$124.99**
FAROE ISLANDS ALBUM SET			
261FAISET	1919-2002	$129.99	**$99.99**
FINLAND ALBUM SET			
345FINSET	1856-2003	$189.99	**$129.99**
FRANCE ALBUM SET			
*310SET	1849-2003	$290.99	**$209.99**
GEORGIA ALBUM SET			
362GESET	1919-2003	$129.99	**$89.99**
GERMANY ALBUM SET			
*315SET	1949-2003	$449.99	**$324.99**
GIBRALTAR ALBUM SET			
203GIBSET	1918-2003	$159.99	**$114.99**
GREAT BRITAIN ALBUM SET			
*200SET	1840-2003	$274.99	**$199.99**
GREECE ALBUM SET			
320SET	1861-2003	$249.99	**$189.99**
GREENLAND ALBUM SET			
345GRNSET	1938-2003	$129.99	**$99.99**
GRENADA ALBUM SET			
261GNASET	1861-2003	$549.99	**$338.99**
GUERNSEY & ALDERNEY ALBUM SET			
202GNASET	1941-2003	$164.99	**$116.99**
HAITI ALBUM SET			
651SET	1881-2003	$199.99	**$147.99**
HONG KONG ALBUM SET			
275HKSET	1862-2003	$274.99	**$199.99**
HUNGARY ALBUM SET			
323SET	1871-2003	$449.99	**$319.99**
ICELAND ALBUM SET			
345ICESET	1873-2003	$144.99	**$104.99**
INDIA ALBUM SET			
618SET	1852-2003	$359.99	**$269.99**
IRELAND ALBUM SET			
*201SET	1941-2003	$199.99	**$142.99**
ISLE OF MAN ALBUM SET			
202IMANSET	1958-2003	$179.99	**$117.99**
ISRAEL ALBUM SET			
500SET	1948-2003	$199.99	**$149.99**
ISRAEL TABS ALBUM SET			
501SET	1948-2003	$219.99	**$159.99**
ITALY ALBUM SET			
325SET	1852-2003	$389.99	**$269.99**
JAPAN ALBUM SET			
*510SET	1871-2003	$324.99	**$239.99**
JERSEY ALBUM SET			
202JRSET	1958-2003	$179.99	**$118.99**
KAZAKHSTAN ALBUM SET			
362KAZSET	1992-2003	$324.99	**$239.99**
KUWAIT ALBUM SET			
623SET	1923-2003	$179.99	**$117.99**
KYRGYZSTAN ALBUM SET			
362KRYSET	1992-2003	$127.99	**$89.99**
LEBANON ALBUM SET			
610SET	1924-2003	$159.99	**$104.99**
MALDIVE ISLANDS ALBUM SET			
706SET	1906-2003	$434.99	**$269.99**
MALTA ALBUM SET			
203MLTSET	1860-2003	$169.99	**$109.99**
MEXICO ALBUM SET			
*430SET	1856-2003	$249.99	**$179.99**
MOLDOVA ALBUM SET			
362MVASET	1992-2003	$124.99	**$89.99**
NEPAL ALBUM SET			
621SET	1881-2003	$134.99	**$99.99**
NETHERLANDS ALBUM SET			
335SET	1852-2003	$524.99	**$374.99**
NEW ZEALAND ALBUM SET			
*220SET	1855-2003	$227.99	**$167.99**
NORWAY ALBUM SET			
345NORSET	1855-2003	$164.99	**$119.99**
OMAN ALBUM SET			
550SET	1944-2003	$139.99	**$99.99**
PAKISTAN ALBUM SET			
673SET	1947-2003	$164.99	**$104.99**
PRC ALBUM SET			
*520SET	1945-2003	$299.99	**$199.99**
PITCARIN ISLANDS ALBUM SET			
632SET	1940-2003	$139.99	**$99.99**
POLAND ALBUM SET			
338SET	1860-2003	$389.99	**$284.99**
RUSSIA ALBUM SET			
*360SET	1857-2003	$579.99	**$424.99**
SINGAPORE ALBUM SET			
275SNGSET	1948-2003	$189.99	**$129.99**
SOLOMON ISLANDS ALBUM SET			
643SET	1907-2003	$159.99	**$110.99**
SPAIN & SPANISH ANDORRA ALBUM SET			
355SET	1855-2003	$389.99	**$274.99**
ST. VINCENT ALBUM SET			
261SVSET	1861-2003	$599.99	**$389.99**
SWEDEN ALBUM SET			
345SWDSET	1855-2003	$199.99	**$137.99**
SWITZERLAND ALBUM SET			
365SET	1843-2003	$209.99	**$154.99**
TADJIKISTAN			
362TDSET	1992-2003	$124.99	**$92.99**
TAIWAN ALBUM SET			
530SET	1949-2003	$224.99	**$169.99**
TIN CAN ISLAND ALBUM SET			
716SET	1983-2002	$119.99	**$84.99**
TURKS & CAICOS ISLANDS ALBUM SET			
261TKSSET	1860-2001	$219.99	**$149.99**
TURKMENISTAN ALBUM SET			
362TKMSET	1992-2002	$19.99	**$16.99**
UZBEKISTAN ALBUM SET			
362UZSET	1992-2002	$139.99	**$95.99**
VATICAN CITY ALBUM SET			
375SET	1929-2003	$199.99	**$138.99**

Available from a stamp dealer or direct from:

Amos Hobby Publishing
P.O. Box 828, Sidney OH 45365
1-800-572-6885
www.amosadvantage.com

**AA prices apply to paid subscribers to Amos Hobby titles. Prices subject to change.*

INDEX AND IDENTIFIER

All page numbers shown are those in this Volume 2.

Postage stamps that do not have English words on them are shown in the Identifier which begins on page 1274.

D... Vol. 3

E.A.F. overprinted on stamps of Great Britain............................ Vol. 3

F. A. F. L.................................. Vol. 6

value priced **stockbooks**

Stockbooks are a classic and convenient storage alternative for many collectors. These German-made stockbooks feature heavyweight archival quality paper with 9 pockets on each page. The 8½" x 11⅝" pages are bound inside a handsome leatherette grain cover and include glassine interleaving between the pages for added protection. The Value Priced Stockbooks are available in two page styles, the white page stockbooks feature glassine pockets while the black page variety includes clear acetate pockets

WHITE PAGE STOCKBOOKS GLASSINE POCKETS

ITEM	DESCRIPTION		RETAIL
SW16BL	Blue	16 pages	$6.95
SW16GR	Green	16 pages	$6.95
SW16RD	Red	16 pages	$6.95

BLACK PAGE STOCKBOOKS ACETATE POCKETS

ITEM	COLOR	PAGES	RETAIL
ST16RD	Red	16 pages	$10.95
ST16GR	Green	16 pages	$10.95
ST16BL	Blue	16 pages	$10.95
ST16BK	Black	16 pages	$10.95
ST32RD	Red	32 pages	$16.95
ST32GR	Green	32 pages	$16.95
ST32BL	Blue	32 pages	$16.95
ST32BK	Black	32 pages	$16.95
ST64RD	Red	64 pages	$29.95
ST64GR	Green	64 pages	$29.95
ST64BL	Blue	64 pages	$29.95
ST64BK	Black	64 pages	$29.95

Scott Value Priced Stockbooks are available from your favorite dealer or direct from:

P.O. Box 828
Sidney OH 45365-0828
www.amosadvantage.com
1-800-572-6885

INDEX TO ADVERTISERS
2006 VOLUME 2

2006
VOLUME 2
DEALER DIRECTORY
YELLOW PAGE LISTINGS

This section of your Scott Catalogue contains advertisements to help you conveniently find what you need, when you need it...!

Accessories

BROOKLYN GALLERY COIN & STAMP, INC.
8725 4th Avenue
Brooklyn, NY 11209
PH: 718-745-5701
FAX: 718-745-2775
info@brooklyngallery.com
www.brooklyngallery.com

Aerophilately

HENRY GITNER PHILATELISTS, INC.
PO Box 3077-S
Middletown, NY 10940
PH: 845-343-5151
PH: 800-947-8267
FAX: 845-343-0068
hgitner@hgitner.com
www.hgitner.com

Appraisals

CONNEXUS
PO Box 819
Snow Camp, NC 27349
PH: 919-663-2267
throopbrown@stampsandstones.com

Approvals-Personalized WW & US

THE KEEPING ROOM
PO Box 257
Trumbull, CT 06611
PH: 203-372-8436

Asia

MICHAEL ROGERS, INC.
Mailing Address:
336 Grove Ave.
Winter Park, FL 32789
Walk-in Address:
Ranch Mall
325 South Orlando Ave.
Winter Park, FL 32789
PH: 407-644-2290
PH: 800-843-3751
FAX: 407-645-4434
info@michaelrogersinc.com
www.michaelrogersinc.com

Auctions

DANIEL F. KELLEHER CO., INC.
20 Walnut Street
Suite 213
Wellesley, MA 02481
PH: 781-235-0990
FAX: 781-235-0945

JACQUES C. SCHIFF, JR., INC.
195 Main Street
Ridgefield Park, NJ 07660
PH: 201-641-5566
From NYC: PH: 212-662-2777
FAX: 201-641-5705

R. MARESCH & SON LTD.
5th Floor - 6075 Yonge Street
Toronto, Ontario M2M 3W2
CANADA
PH: 416-363-7777
FAX: 416-363-6511
www.maresch.com

Auctions

THE STAMP CENTER/DUTCH COUNTRY AUCTIONS
4115 Concord Pike
Wilmington, DE 19803
PH: 302-478-8740
FAX: 302-478-8779
scdca@dol.net
www.thestampcenter.com

Auctions - Public

ALAN BLAIR STAMPS/AUCTIONS
5405 Lakeside Ave.
Suite 1
Richmond, VA 23228
PH/FAX: 800-689-5602
alanblair@prodigy.net

Austria

JOSEPH EDER
PO Box 185529
Hamden, CT 06518
PH: 203-281-0742
FAX: 203-230-2410
j.eder@worldnet.att.net
www.ederstamps.com

British Commonwealth

ARON R. HALBERSTAM PHILATELISTS, LTD.
PO Box 150168
Van Brunt Station
Brooklyn, NY 11215-0168
PH: 718-788-3978
FAX: 718-965-3099
arh@arhstamps.com
www.arhstamps.com

CENTURY STAMP CO., LTD.
Century House
1723 Lakeshore Road West
Mississauga, ON L5J 1J4
CANADA
PH: 905-822-5464
FAX: 905-822-2113
centurystamps@rogers.com
www.centurystamps.com

EMPIRE STAMP CO.
PO Box 8337
Calabasa, CA 91372-8337
PH: 800-616-7278
PH: 818-225-1181
FAX: 818-225-1182
info@empirestamps.com
www.empirestamps.com

STATESIDE STAMPS
PO Box 1036
Evart, MI 49631
PH: 231-734-9943
sreedy@netonecom.net
www.statesidestamps.com

Auctions

British Commonwealth